CD-ROM with all content from 2017 *Fundamentals*

MW01702634

2015 HVAC APPLICAT

2014 REFRIGERATION

2017 ASHRAE® HANDBOOK

FUNDAMENTALS

Inch-Pound Edition

ASHRAE, 1791 Tullie Circle, N.E., Atlanta, GA 30329
www.ashrae.org

DEDICATED TO THE ADVANCEMENT OF

THE PROFESSION AND ITS ALLIED INDUSTRIES

Volunteer members of ASHRAE Technical Committees and others compiled the information in this handbook, and it is generally reviewed and updated every four years. Comments, criticisms, and suggestions regarding the subject matter are invited. Any errors or omissions in the data should be brought to the attention of the Editor. Additions and corrections to Handbook volumes in print will be published in the Handbook published the year following their verification and, as soon as verified, on the ASHRAE Internet website.

DISCLAIMER

ASHRAE has compiled this publication with care, but ASHRAE has not investigated, and ASHRAE expressly disclaims any duty to investigate, any product, service, process, procedure, design, or the like that may be described herein. The appearance of any technical data or editorial material in this publication does not constitute endorsement, warranty, or guaranty by ASHRAE of any product, service, process, procedure, design, or the like. ASHRAE does not warrant that the information in this publication is free of errors. The entire risk of the use of any information in this publication is assumed by the user.

ISBN 978-1-939200-57-0
ISSN 1523-7222

The paper for this book is both acid- and elemental-chlorine-free and was manufactured with pulp obtained from sources using sustainable forestry practices.

CONTENTS

BUILDING ENVELOPE

MATERIALS

GENERAL

ADDITIONS AND CORRECTIONS

INDEX

Comment Pages

CONTRIBUTORS

In addition to the Technical Committees, the following individuals contributed significantly to this volume. The appropriate chapter numbers follow each contributor's name.

Kashif Nawaz (1, 4, 5)
Oak Ridge National Laboratory

Don Gatley (1)
Gatley & Associates, Inc.

Sebastian Herrmann (1)
Hochschule Zittau/Görlitz, University of Applied Sciences

Reinhard Radermacher (2)
University of Maryland

Hoseong Lee (2)
Korea University

Rick Couvillion (3, 4, 6)
University of Arkansas

Michael Ohadi (4, 6)
University of Maryland

Mirza Shah (5)

Amir H. Shooshtari (6)
University of Maryland-College Park

David Kahn (7)
RMH Group

Marcelo Acosta (7)
Armstrong Fluid Technology

Christopher F. Benson (7)
University of Utah

Steve Wise (8)
Wise Associates

Eric Sturm (8)
Ingersoll-Rand/Trane

John Elson (9)
Kansas State University

Lan Chi Nguyen Weekes (10)
InAIR Environmental, Ltd.

Elliott Horner (10)
UL Environment

Andrew Persily (10)
National Institute of Standards and Technology

Dennis Stanke (10)

Brian Krafthefer (11)
BCK Consulting

Ashish Mathur (11)
UVDI Inc.

Chang-Seo Lee (11)
Concordia University

Carolyn (Gemma) Kerr (11)

Didier Thevenard (14)
Canadian Solar

Michael Roth (14)
Klimaat Consulting & Innovation, Inc.

Christian Gueymard (14)
Solar Consulting Services

Peter Lyons (15)
Peter Lyons & Associates

Charlie Curcija (15)
Lawrence Berkeley National Laboratory

Joe Hetzel (15)
Door & Access Systems Manufacturers Association

Brian A. Rock (16)
The University of Kansas

Steven J. Emmerich (16)
National Institute of Science and Technology

Steven T. Taylor (16)
Taylor Engineering

Charles S. Barnaby (17)

Steve Bruning (18)
Newcomb & Boyd

James F. Pegues (18)
Carrier Corp.

Robert Doeffinger (18)
ZMM, Inc.

Erik Kolderup (19)
Kolderup Consulting

Timothy McDowell (19)
Thermal Energy Systems Specialists

Neal Kruis (19)
Big Ladder Software

Mitchell Paulus (19)
Texas A&M University

Malcolm Cook (19)
Loughborough University

John Pruett (19)
LEED AP ZMM Inc.

Sukjoon Oh (19)
Texas A&M University

Ron Judkoff (19)
National Renewable Energy Laboratory

Joel Neymark (19)
J. Neymark & Associates

Tianzhen Hong (19)
Lawrence Berkeley National Laboratory

Joe Huang (19)
White Box Technologies

Yuebin Yu (19)
University of Nebraska-Lincoln

Joshua New (19)
Oak Ridge National Laboratory

Ralph Muelheisen (19)
Argonne National Laboratory

Bass Abushakra (19)
U.S. Military Academy

Curtis Peters (20)
Nailor Industries

Kenneth J. Loudermilk (20)
Titus Products

Krishnan Viswanath (20)
Dynacraft Air Controls & Air Technology & Systems

Ryan Johnson (20)
Price Industries, Inc.

Chad Huggins (20)
Krueger

James Aswegan (20)
Titus Products

Herman Behls (21)
Behls & Associates

Patrick J. Brooks (21)
Eastern Sheet Metal

Scott Fisher (22)

Steve Runyan (22)
State Farm Mutual Automobile Insurance Company

Bert Blocken (24)
Eindhoven University of Technology

Ted Stathopoulos (24)
Concordia University

Yoshihide Tominaga (24)
Niigata Institute of Technology

Marcus Bianchi (25, 26)
Owens Corning

Hugo Hens (25, 26, 36)
University of Leuven

Paulo Cesar Tabares Velasco (25)
Colorado School of Mines

Diana Fisler (25)
Johns Manville

Peter Adams (25)
Morrison Hershfield, Ltd.

Laverne Dalgleish (25)
Air Barrier Association of America, Inc.

Alexander G. McGowan (26, 36)
WSP Canada, Inc.

Samuel Glass (26)
U.S. Department of Agriculture, Forest Products Laboratory

Hartwig Künzel (26, 36)
Fraunhofer Institüt für Bauphysik

Jonathan Kane (28)
UEI Test Instruments, Inc.

David Herrin (28)
University of Kentucky

Larry Brand (28)
Gas Technology Institute

Paul Sohler (28)
Crown Boiler Co.

Tom Neill (28)
Mestek Inc.

Cory Weiss (28)
Field Controls LLC

Mehdi M. Doura (28)
Lochinvar LLC

Bill Roy (28)
Timco Rubber

Jennifer Guerrero-Ferreira (28)
Bekaert Corporation

Barbara Minor (29)
Chemours Company

Van Baxter (29)
Oak Ridge National Laboratory

Mark McLinden (30)
National Institute of Standards and Technology

Kevin Connor (31)
The Dow Chemical Company

Kevin R. Brown (34, 35)
ABM

Donald M. Brundage (34)
Southern Company Services

Douglas D. Fick (34, 35)
TRC Worldwide MEP

Costas Balaras (35)
National Observatory of Athens

Lew Harriman (36)
Mason-Grant Co.

Ed Light (36)
Building Dynamics, LLC

Florian Antretter (36)
Fraunhofer Institüt für Bauphysik

Terry Beck (37)
Kansas State University

John P. Scott (37)
CanmetENERGY, Natural Resources Canada

Muhammad Tauha Ali (37)
Masdar Institute of Science and Technology

Huojun Yang (37)
North Dakota State University

Stephen Idem (37)
Tennessee Technological University

ASHRAE HANDBOOK COMMITTEE

Forrest S. Yount, Chair

2017 Fundamentals Volume Subcommittee: **David P. Yuill,** Chair

Bass Abushakra **Larry W. Akers** **Van D. Baxter** **Sheila J. Hayter** **Ramesh P. Paranjpey**

ASHRAE HANDBOOK STAFF

W. Stephen Comstock, Publisher
Director of Publications and Education

Mark S. Owen, Editor

Heather E. Kennedy, Managing Editor

Nancy F. Thysell, Typographer/Page Designer

David Soltis, Group Manager, and **Jayne E. Jackson,** Publication Traffic Administrator, Publishing Services

ASHRAE TECHNICAL COMMITTEES, TASK GROUPS, AND TECHNICAL RESOURCE GROUPS

SECTION 1.0—FUNDAMENTALS AND GENERAL

1.1 Thermodynamics and Psychrometrics
1.2 Instruments and Measurements
1.3 Heat Transfer and Fluid Flow
1.4 Control Theory and Application
1.5 Computer Applications
1.6 Terminology
1.7 Business, Management & General Legal Education
1.8 Mechanical Systems Insulation
1.9 Electrical Systems
1.10 Cogeneration Systems
1.11 Electric Motors and Motor Control
1.12 Moisture Management in Buildings
1.13 Optimization

SECTION 2.0—ENVIRONMENTAL QUALITY

2.1 Physiology and Human Environment
2.2 Plant and Animal Environment
2.3 Gaseous Air Contaminants and Gas Contaminant Removal Equipment
2.4 Particulate Air Contaminants and Particulate Contaminant Removal Equipment
2.5 Global Climate Change
2.6 Sound and Vibration
2.7 Seismic and Wind Resistant Design
2.8 Building Environmental Impacts and Sustainability
2.9 Ultraviolet Air and Surface Treatment
TG2 Heating Ventilation and Air-Conditioning Security (HVAC)

SECTION 3.0—MATERIALS AND PROCESSES

3.1 Refrigerants and Secondary Coolants
3.2 Refrigerant System Chemistry
3.3 Refrigerant Contaminant Control
3.4 Lubrication
3.6 Water Treatment
3.8 Refrigerant Containment

SECTION 4.0—LOAD CALCULATIONS AND ENERGY REQUIREMENTS

4.1 Load Calculation Data and Procedures
4.2 Climatic Information
4.3 Ventilation Requirements and Infiltration
4.4 Building Materials and Building Envelope Performance
4.5 Fenestration
4.7 Energy Calculations
4.10 Indoor Environmental Modeling
TRG4 Indoor Air Quality Procedure Development

SECTION 5.0—VENTILATION AND AIR DISTRIBUTION

5.1 Fans
5.2 Duct Design
5.3 Room Air Distribution
5.4 Industrial Process Air Cleaning (Air Pollution Control)
5.5 Air-to-Air Energy Recovery
5.6 Control of Fire and Smoke
5.7 Evaporative Cooling
5.8 Industrial Ventilation
5.9 Enclosed Vehicular Facilities
5.10 Kitchen Ventilation
5.11 Humidifying Equipment

SECTION 6.0—HEATING EQUIPMENT, HEATING AND COOLING SYSTEMS AND APPLICATIONS

6.1 Hydronic and Steam Equipment and Systems
6.2 District Energy
6.3 Central Forced Air Heating and Cooling Systems
6.5 Radiant Heating and Cooling
6.6 Service Water Heating Systems
6.7 Solar Energy Utilization
6.8 Geothermal Heat Pump and Energy Recovery Applications
6.9 Thermal Storage
6.10 Fuels and Combustion

SECTION 7.0—BUILDING PERFORMANCE

7.1 Integrated Building Design
7.2 HVAC&R Construction & Design Build Technologies
7.3 Operation and Maintenance Management
7.4 Exergy Analysis for Sustainable Buildings (EXER)
7.5 Smart Building Systems
7.6 Building Energy Performance
7.7 Testing and Balancing
7.8 Owning and Operating Costs
7.9 Building Commissioning

SECTION 8.0—AIR-CONDITIONING AND REFRIGERATION SYSTEM COMPONENTS

8.1 Positive Displacement Compressors
8.2 Centrifugal Machines
8.3 Absorption and Heat Operated Machines
8.4 Air-to-Refrigerant Heat Transfer Equipment
8.5 Liquid-to-Refrigerant Heat Exchangers
8.6 Cooling Towers and Evaporative Condensers
8.7 Variable Refrigerant Flow (VRF)
8.8 Refrigerant System Controls and Accessories
8.9 Residential Refrigerators and Food Freezers
8.10 Mechanical Dehumidification Equipment and Heat Pipes
8.11 Unitary and Room Air Conditioners and Heat Pumps
8.12 Desiccant Dehumidification Equipment and Components

SECTION 9.0—BUILDING APPLICATIONS

9.1 Large Building Air-Conditioning Systems
9.2 Industrial Air Conditioning
9.3 Transportation Air Conditioning
9.4 Justice Facilities
9.6 Healthcare Facilities
9.7 Educational Facilities
9.8 Large Building Air-Conditioning Applications
9.9 Mission Critical Facilities, Data Centers, Technology Spaces and Electronic Equipment
9.10 Laboratory Systems
9.11 Clean Spaces
9.12 Tall Buildings

SECTION 10.0—REFRIGERATION SYSTEMS

10.1 Custom Engineered Refrigeration Systems
10.2 Automatic Icemaking Plants and Skating Rinks
10.3 Refrigerant Piping, Controls, and Accessories
10.5 Refrigerated Processing and Storage
10.6 Transport Refrigeration
10.7 Commercial Food and Beverage Refrigeration Equipment
10.8 Refrigeration Load Calculations

SECTION MTG—MULTIDISCIPLINARY TASK GROUPS

MTG.ACR Air Change Rate
MTG.ASEC Avoided Sources Energy Consumption Due to Waste Heat Recovery and Heat Pump Technologies
MTG.BD Building Dampness
MTG.BIM Building Information Modeling
MTG.HCDG Hot Climate Design Guide
MTG.IAST Impact of ASHRAE Standards and Technology on Energy Savings/Performance
MTG.ISPAQE Indoor Swimming Pool Air Quality and Evaporation
MTG.LowGWP Lower Global Warming Potential Alternative Refrigerants
MTG.O&MEE Operations and Maintenance Activities That Impact Energy Efficiency
MTG.OBB Occupant Behavior in Buildings

ASHRAE Research: Improving the Quality of Life

ASHRAE is the world's foremost technical society in the fields of heating, ventilation, air conditioning, and refrigeration. Its members worldwide are individuals who share ideas, identify needs, support research, and write the industry's standards for testing and practice. The result is that engineers are better able to keep indoor environments safe and productive while protecting and preserving the outdoors for generations to come.

One of the ways that ASHRAE supports its members' and industry's need for information is through ASHRAE Research. Thousands of individuals and companies support ASHRAE Research annually, enabling ASHRAE to report new data about material properties and building physics and to promote the application of innovative technologies.

Chapters in the ASHRAE Handbook are updated through the experience of members of ASHRAE Technical Committees and through results of ASHRAE Research reported at ASHRAE conferences and published in ASHRAE special publications, *ASHRAE Transactions*, and ASHRAE's journal of archival research, *Science and Technology for the Built Environment*.

For information about ASHRAE Research or to become a member, contact ASHRAE, 1791 Tullie Circle N.E., Atlanta, GA 30329; telephone: 404-636-8400; www.ashrae.org.

Preface

The 2017 *ASHRAE Handbook—Fundamentals* covers basic principles and data used in the HVAC&R industry. The ASHRAE Technical Committees that prepare these chapters provide new information, clarify existing content, delete obsolete materials, and reorganize chapters to make the Handbook more understandable and easier to use. An accompanying CD-ROM contains all the volume's chapters in both I-P and SI units.

This edition includes a new chapter:

- Chapter 36, Moisture Management in Buildings, presents data on indoor vapor release and measured indoor/outdoor vapor pressure/concentration differences, and discusses moisture sources and sinks that can reduce materials' durability, as well as the negative effects of insufficient or excessive indoor relative humidity.

Other selected highlights include the following:

- Chapter 7, Fundamentals of Control, has new content on thermostatic valve actuators, placement of sensors, auxiliary control devices, and network architecture.
- Chapter 9, Thermal Comfort, has new content from ASHRAE research project RP-1504 on nonwestern clothing; combined chilled-ceiling, displacement ventilation, and vertical radiant temperature asymmetry effects on sedentary office work; and updates to align with ASHRAE Standard 55-2013.
- Chapter 10, Indoor Environmental Health, has updates on bioaerosols, plus new content on electronic cigarettes and on climate change.
- Chapter 11, Air Contaminants, has new content on particle sizes and settling times, particulate contaminant effects, polymerase chain reaction (PCR) measurement, volatility, mercury, e-cigarettes, and 3D printers.
- Chapter 14, Climatic Design Information, includes new data for 8118 locations worldwide—an increase of 1675 locations from the 2013 edition of the chapter—as a result of ASHRAE research project RP-1699.
- Chapter 15, Fenestration, has updated discussion on U-factor, solar-optical glazing properties, complex glazings and window coverings, tubular daylighting devices (TDDs), and spectrally selective glazing.
- Chapter 16, Ventilation and Infiltration, has been updated and revised for clarity throughout, including recent research results on envelope air leakage.
- Chapter 17, Residential Cooling and Heating Load Calculations, has updates for 2017 climate data and current standards.
- Chapter 18, Nonresidential Cooling and Heating Load Calculations, has new design data for lighting power densities, motors, kitchen equipment, LED lighting, walls and roofs, and an updated example calculation.
- Chapter 19, Energy Estimating and Modeling Methods, extensively revised, has new sections on method development history, using models, uncertainty, thermal loads and model inputs, envelope components, HVAC components, terminal components, low-energy systems, natural and hybrid ventilation, daylighting, passive heating, hybrid inverse method, and model calibration.
- Chapter 20, Space Air Diffusion, has new content on outlet types and characteristics, air curtains, thermal plumes, and air movement in occupied zones.
- Chapter 21, Duct Design, was reorganized for ease of use, and updated for data from the latest version of the *ASHRAE Duct Fitting Database*.
- Chapter 22, Pipe Design, has a new title and now incorporates the content of its sister chapter, Pipes, Tubes, and Fittings, from *HVAC Systems and Equipment*. Also added are content on PEX pipe, plus expanded applications.
- Chapter 24, Airflow Around Buildings, has new content on flow patterns around building groups and isolated buildings, environmental impacts, pollutant dispersion and exhaust reentrainment, pedestrian wind comfort and safety, and wind-driven rain.
- Chapter 30, Thermophysical Properties of Refrigerants, has new or revised data for R-1233zd(E), R-245fa, R-1234ze(E), and R-1234yf.
- Chapter 34, Energy Resources, has extensive updates for new statistics on worldwide energy use and resources.
- Chapter 35, Sustainability, has new content on the water/energy nexus, embodied energy, and climate change.

This volume is published, as a bound print volume and in electronic format on CD-ROM and online, in two editions: one using inch-pound (I-P) units of measurement, the other using the International System of Units (SI).

Corrections to the 2014, 2015, and 2016 Handbook volumes can be found on the ASHRAE website at www.ashrae.org and in the Additions and Corrections section of this volume. Corrections for this volume will be listed in subsequent volumes and on the ASHRAE website.

Reader comments are enthusiastically invited. To suggest improvements for a chapter, **please comment using the form on the ASHRAE website** or, using the cutout page(s) at the end of this volume's index, write to Handbook Editor, ASHRAE, 1791 Tullie Circle, Atlanta, GA 30329, or fax 678-539-2187, or e-mail mowen@ashrae.org.

Mark S. Owen
Editor

CHAPTER 1

PSYCHROMETRICS

PSYCHROMETRICS uses thermodynamic properties to analyze conditions and processes involving moist air. This chapter discusses perfect gas relations and their use in common heating, cooling, and humidity control problems. Formulas developed by Herrmann et al. (2009) may be used where greater precision is required.

Herrmann et al. (2009), Hyland and Wexler (1983a, 1983b), and Nelson and Sauer (2002) developed formulas for thermodynamic properties of moist air and water modeled as real gases. However, perfect gas relations can be substituted in most air-conditioning problems. Kuehn et al. (1998) showed that errors are less than 0.7% in calculating humidity ratio, enthalpy, and specific volume of saturated air at standard atmospheric pressure for a temperature range of –60 to 120°F. Furthermore, these errors decrease with decreasing pressure.

1. COMPOSITION OF DRY AND MOIST AIR

Atmospheric air contains many gaseous components as well as water vapor and miscellaneous contaminants (e.g., smoke, pollen, and gaseous pollutants not normally present in free air far from pollution sources).

Dry air is atmospheric air with all water vapor and contaminants removed. Its composition is relatively constant, but small variations in the amounts of individual components occur with time, geographic location, and altitude. Harrison (1965) lists the approximate percentage composition of dry air by volume as: nitrogen, 78.084; oxygen, 20.9476; argon, 0.934; neon, 0.001818; helium, 0.000524; methane, 0.00015; sulfur dioxide, 0 to 0.0001; hydrogen, 0.00005; and minor components such as krypton, xenon, and ozone, 0.0002. Harrison (1965) and Hyland and Wexler (1983a) used a value 0.0314 (circa 1955) for carbon dioxide. Carbon dioxide reached 0.0379 in 2005, is currently increasing by 0.00019 percent per year and is projected to reach 0.0438 in 2036 (Gatley et al. 2008; Keeling and Whorf 2005a, 2005b). Increases in carbon dioxide are offset by decreases in oxygen; consequently, the oxygen percentage in 2036 is projected to be 20.9352. Using the projected changes, the relative molecular mass for dry air for at least the first half of the 21st century is 28.966, based on the carbon-12 scale. The gas constant for dry air using the current Mohr and Taylor (2005) value for the universal gas constant is

$$R_{da} = 1545.349/28.966 = 53.350 \text{ ft}\cdot\text{lb}_f/\text{lb}_{da}\cdot{}^\circ\text{R} \quad (1)$$

Moist air is a binary (two-component) mixture of dry air and water vapor. The amount of water vapor varies from zero (dry air) to a maximum that depends on temperature and pressure. **Saturation** is a state of neutral equilibrium between moist air and the condensed water phase (liquid or solid); unless otherwise stated, it assumes a flat interface surface between moist air and the condensed phase. Saturation conditions change when the interface radius is very small (e.g., with ultrafine water droplets). The relative molecular mass of water is 18.015268 on the carbon-12 scale. The gas constant for water vapor is

$$R_w = 1545.349/18.015268 = 85.780 \text{ ft}\cdot\text{lb}_f/\text{lb}_w\cdot{}^\circ\text{R} \quad (2)$$

2. U.S. STANDARD ATMOSPHERE

The temperature and barometric pressure of atmospheric air vary considerably with altitude as well as with local geographic and weather conditions. The standard atmosphere gives a standard of reference for estimating properties at various altitudes. At sea level, standard temperature is 59°F; standard barometric pressure is 14.696 psia or 29.921 in. Hg. Temperature is assumed to decrease linearly with increasing altitude throughout the troposphere (lower atmosphere), and to be constant in the lower reaches of the stratosphere. The lower atmosphere is assumed to consist of dry air that behaves as a perfect gas. Gravity is also assumed constant at the standard value, 32.1740 ft/s². Table 1 summarizes property data for altitudes to 30,000 ft.

Pressure values in Table 1 may be calculated from

$$p = 14.696(1 - 6.8754 \times 10^{-6}Z)^{5.2559} \quad (3)$$

The equation for temperature as a function of altitude is

$$t = 59 - 0.00356620Z \quad (4)$$

where

Z = altitude, ft
p = barometric pressure, psia
t = temperature, °F

Table 1 Standard Atmospheric Data for Altitudes to 30,000 ft

Altitude, ft	Temperature, °F	Pressure, psia
–1000	62.6	15.236
–500	60.8	14.966
0	59.0	14.696
500	57.2	14.430
1,000	55.4	14.175
2,000	51.9	13.664
3,000	48.3	13.173
4,000	44.7	12.682
5,000	41.2	12.230
6,000	37.6	11.778
7,000	34.0	11.341
8,000	30.5	10.914
9,000	26.9	10.506
10,000	23.4	10.108
15,000	5.5	8.296
20,000	–12.3	6.758
30,000	–47.8	4.371

Source: Adapted from NASA (1976).

The preparation of this chapter is assigned to TC 1.1, Thermodynamics and Psychrometrics.

Equations (3) and (4) are accurate from –16,500 ft to 36,000 ft. For higher altitudes, comprehensive tables of barometric pressure and other physical properties of the standard atmosphere, in both SI and I-P units, can be found in NASA (1976).

3. THERMODYNAMIC PROPERTIES OF MOIST AIR

Table 2, developed from formulas by Herrmann et al. (2009), shows values of thermodynamic properties of moist air based on the International Temperature Scale of 1990 (ITS-90). This ideal scale differs slightly from practical temperature scales used for physical measurements. For example, the standard boiling point for water (at 14.696 psia) occurs at 211.95°F on this scale rather than at the traditional 212°F. Most measurements are currently based on ITS-90 (Preston-Thomas 1990).

The following properties are shown in Table 2:

t = Fahrenheit temperature, based on the ITS-90 and expressed relative to absolute temperature T in degrees Rankine (°R) by the following relation:

$$T = t + 459.67$$

W_s = humidity ratio at saturation; gaseous phase (moist air) exists in equilibrium with condensed phase (liquid or solid) at given temperature and pressure (standard atmospheric pressure). At given values of temperature and pressure, humidity ratio W can have any value from zero to W_s.

v_{da} = specific volume of dry air, ft^3/lb_{da}.

v_{as} = $v_s - v_{da}$, difference between specific volume of moist air at saturation and that of dry air, ft^3/lb_{da}, at same pressure and temperature.

v_s = specific volume of moist air at saturation, ft^3/lb_{da}.

h_{da} = specific enthalpy of dry air, Btu/lb_{da}. In Table 2, h_{da} is assigned a value of 0 at 0°F and standard atmospheric pressure.

h_{as} = $h_s - h_{da}$, difference between specific enthalpy of moist air at saturation and that of dry air, Btu/lb_{da}, at same pressure and temperature.

h_s = specific enthalpy of moist air at saturation, Btu/lb_{da}.

s_{da} = specific entropy of dry air, $Btu/lb_{da} \cdot °R$. In Table 2, s_{da} is assigned a value of 0 at 0°F and standard atmospheric pressure.

s_s = specific entropy of moist air at saturation $Btu/lb_{da} \cdot °R$.

Table 2 Thermodynamic Properties of Moist Air at Standard Atmospheric Pressure, 14.696 psia

Temp., °F	Humidity Ratio	Specific Volume, ft^3/lb_{da}			Specific Enthalpy, Btu/lb_{da}			Specific Entropy, $Btu/lb_{da} \cdot °F$		Temp., °F
t	W_s, lb_w/lb_{da}	v_{da}	v_{as}	v_s	h_{da}	h_{as}	h_s	s_{da}	s_s	t
–80	0.0000049	9.553	0.000	9.553	–19.218	0.005	–19.213	–0.04593	–0.04592	–80
–79	0.0000053	9.578	0.000	9.578	–18.977	0.005	–18.972	–0.04530	–0.04529	–79
–78	0.0000057	9.603	0.000	9.604	–18.737	0.006	–18.731	–0.04467	–0.04465	–78
–77	0.0000062	9.629	0.000	9.629	–18.497	0.006	–18.490	–0.04404	–0.04402	–77
–76	0.0000067	9.654	0.000	9.654	–18.256	0.007	–18.250	–0.04341	–0.04339	–76
–75	0.0000072	9.680	0.000	9.680	–18.016	0.007	–18.009	–0.04279	–0.04277	–75
–74	0.0000078	9.705	0.000	9.705	–17.776	0.008	–17.768	–0.04216	–0.04214	–74
–73	0.0000084	9.730	0.000	9.730	–17.535	0.009	–17.527	–0.04154	–0.04152	–73
–72	0.0000090	9.756	0.000	9.756	–17.295	0.009	–17.286	–0.04092	–0.04090	–72
–71	0.0000097	9.781	0.000	9.781	–17.055	0.010	–17.045	–0.04030	–0.04027	–71
–70	0.0000104	9.806	0.000	9.806	–16.814	0.011	–16.804	–0.03968	–0.03966	–70
–69	0.0000112	9.832	0.000	9.832	–16.574	0.012	–16.563	–0.03907	–0.03904	–69
–68	0.0000120	9.857	0.000	9.857	–16.334	0.012	–16.321	–0.03845	–0.03842	–68
–67	0.0000129	9.882	0.000	9.882	–16.094	0.013	–16.080	–0.03784	–0.03781	–67
–66	0.0000139	9.908	0.000	9.908	–15.853	0.014	–15.839	–0.03723	–0.03719	–66
–65	0.0000149	9.933	0.000	9.933	–15.613	0.015	–15.598	–0.03662	–0.03658	–65
–64	0.0000160	9.958	0.000	9.959	–15.373	0.017	–15.356	–0.03601	–0.03597	–64
–63	0.0000172	9.984	0.000	9.984	–15.132	0.018	–15.115	–0.03541	–0.03536	–63
–62	0.0000184	10.009	0.000	10.009	–14.892	0.019	–14.873	–0.03480	–0.03475	–62
–61	0.0000198	10.034	0.000	10.035	–14.652	0.020	–14.632	–0.03420	–0.03414	–61
–60	0.0000212	10.060	0.000	10.060	–14.412	0.022	–14.390	–0.03360	–0.03354	–60
–59	0.0000227	10.085	0.000	10.085	–14.171	0.023	–14.148	–0.03300	–0.03293	–59
–58	0.0000243	10.110	0.000	10.111	–13.931	0.025	–13.906	–0.03240	–0.03233	–58
–57	0.0000260	10.136	0.000	10.136	–13.691	0.027	–13.664	–0.03180	–0.03173	–57
–56	0.0000279	10.161	0.000	10.161	–13.451	0.029	–13.422	–0.03120	–0.03113	–56
–55	0.0000298	10.186	0.000	10.187	–13.210	0.031	–13.179	–0.03061	–0.03053	–55
–54	0.0000319	10.212	0.001	10.212	–12.970	0.033	–12.937	–0.03002	–0.02993	–54
–53	0.0000341	10.237	0.001	10.237	–12.730	0.035	–12.695	–0.02942	–0.02933	–53
–52	0.0000365	10.262	0.001	10.263	–12.490	0.038	–12.452	–0.02883	–0.02874	–52
–51	0.0000390	10.288	0.001	10.288	–12.249	0.040	–12.209	–0.02825	–0.02814	–51
–50	0.0000416	10.313	0.001	10.314	–12.009	0.043	–11.966	–0.02766	–0.02755	–50
–49	0.0000445	10.338	0.001	10.339	–11.769	0.046	–11.723	–0.02707	–0.02695	–49
–48	0.0000475	10.364	0.001	10.364	–11.529	0.049	–11.479	–0.02649	–0.02636	–48
–47	0.0000507	10.389	0.001	10.390	–11.289	0.053	–11.236	–0.02591	–0.02577	–47
–46	0.0000541	10.414	0.001	10.415	–11.048	0.056	–10.992	–0.02532	–0.02518	–46
–45	0.0000577	10.439	0.001	10.440	–10.808	0.060	–10.748	–0.02474	–0.02459	–45
–44	0.0000615	10.465	0.001	10.466	–10.568	0.064	–10.504	–0.02417	–0.02400	–44
–43	0.0000656	10.490	0.001	10.491	–10.328	0.068	–10.259	–0.02359	–0.02341	–43
–42	0.0000699	10.515	0.001	10.517	–10.087	0.073	–10.015	–0.02301	–0.02283	–42
–41	0.0000744	10.541	0.001	10.542	–9.847	0.078	–9.770	–0.02244	–0.02224	–41
–40	0.0000793	10.566	0.001	10.567	–9.607	0.083	–9.524	–0.02187	–0.02166	–40

Table 2 Thermodynamic Properties of Moist Air at Standard Atmospheric Pressure, 14.696 psia (*Continued*)

Temp., °F	Humidity Ratio	Specific Volume, ft^3/lb_{da}			Specific Enthalpy, Btu/lb_{da}			Specific Entropy, $Btu/lb_{da} \cdot °F$		Temp., °F
t	W_s, lb_w/lb_{da}	v_{da}	v_{as}	v_s	h_{da}	h_{as}	h_s	s_{da}	s_s	t
–39	0.0000844	10.591	0.001	10.593	–9.367	0.088	–9.279	–0.02129	–0.02107	–39
–38	0.0000898	10.617	0.002	10.618	–9.127	0.094	–9.033	–0.02072	–0.02049	–38
–37	0.0000956	10.642	0.002	10.644	–8.886	0.100	–8.787	–0.02015	–0.01990	–37
–36	0.0001017	10.667	0.002	10.669	–8.646	0.106	–8.540	–0.01959	–0.01932	–36
–35	0.0001081	10.693	0.002	10.695	–8.406	0.113	–8.293	–0.01902	–0.01874	–35
–34	0.0001150	10.718	0.002	10.720	–8.166	0.120	–8.046	–0.01846	–0.01816	–34
–33	0.0001222	10.743	0.002	10.745	–7.926	0.128	–7.798	–0.01789	–0.01757	–33
–32	0.0001298	10.769	0.002	10.771	–7.685	0.136	–7.550	–0.01733	–0.01699	–32
–31	0.0001379	10.794	0.002	10.796	–7.445	0.144	–7.301	–0.01677	–0.01641	–31
–30	0.0001465	10.819	0.003	10.822	–7.205	0.153	–7.052	–0.01621	–0.01583	–30
–29	0.0001555	10.845	0.003	10.847	–6.965	0.163	–6.802	–0.01565	–0.01525	–29
–28	0.0001650	10.870	0.003	10.873	–6.725	0.173	–6.552	–0.01509	–0.01467	–28
–27	0.0001751	10.895	0.003	10.898	–6.485	0.184	–6.301	–0.01454	–0.01409	–27
–26	0.0001857	10.920	0.003	10.924	–6.244	0.195	–6.050	–0.01398	–0.01351	–26
–25	0.0001970	10.946	0.003	10.949	–6.004	0.207	–5.797	–0.01343	–0.01293	–25
–24	0.0002088	10.971	0.004	10.975	–5.764	0.219	–5.545	–0.01288	–0.01234	–24
–23	0.0002213	10.996	0.004	11.000	–5.524	0.233	–5.291	–0.01233	–0.01176	–23
–22	0.0002345	11.022	0.004	11.026	–5.284	0.246	–5.037	–0.01178	–0.01118	–22
–21	0.0002485	11.047	0.004	11.051	–5.043	0.261	–4.782	–0.01123	–0.01060	–21
–20	0.0002632	11.072	0.005	11.077	–4.803	0.277	–4.527	–0.01068	–0.01002	–20
–19	0.0002786	11.098	0.005	11.103	–4.563	0.293	–4.270	–0.01014	–0.00943	–19
–18	0.0002949	11.123	0.005	11.128	–4.323	0.310	–4.013	–0.00959	–0.00885	–18
–17	0.0003121	11.148	0.006	11.154	–4.083	0.329	–3.754	–0.00905	–0.00826	–17
–16	0.0003302	11.174	0.006	11.179	–3.843	0.348	–3.495	–0.00851	–0.00768	–16
–15	0.0003493	11.199	0.006	11.205	–3.602	0.368	–3.234	–0.00797	–0.00709	–15
–14	0.0003694	11.224	0.007	11.231	–3.362	0.389	–2.973	–0.00743	–0.00650	–14
–13	0.0003905	11.249	0.007	11.257	–3.122	0.412	–2.710	–0.00689	–0.00591	–13
–12	0.0004127	11.275	0.007	11.282	–2.882	0.436	–2.446	–0.00635	–0.00532	–12
–11	0.0004361	11.300	0.008	11.308	–2.642	0.460	–2.181	–0.00582	–0.00473	–11
–10	0.0004607	11.325	0.008	11.334	–2.402	0.487	–1.915	–0.00528	–0.00414	–10
–9	0.0004866	11.351	0.009	11.360	–2.161	0.514	–1.647	–0.00475	–0.00354	–9
–8	0.0005138	11.376	0.009	11.385	–1.921	0.543	–1.378	–0.00422	–0.00294	–8
–7	0.0005425	11.401	0.010	11.411	–1.681	0.574	–1.108	–0.00369	–0.00234	–7
–6	0.0005725	11.427	0.010	11.437	–1.441	0.606	–0.835	–0.00316	–0.00174	–6
–5	0.0006041	11.452	0.011	11.463	–1.201	0.639	–0.561	–0.00263	–0.00114	–5
–4	0.0006373	11.477	0.012	11.489	–0.961	0.675	–0.286	–0.00210	–0.00053	–4
–3	0.0006721	11.502	0.012	11.515	–0.720	0.712	–0.009	–0.00157	0.00008	–3
–2	0.0007087	11.528	0.013	11.541	–0.480	0.751	0.271	–0.00105	0.00069	–2
–1	0.0007471	11.553	0.014	11.567	–0.240	0.792	0.552	–0.00052	0.00130	–1
0	0.0007875	11.578	0.015	11.593	0.000	0.835	0.835	0.00000	0.00192	0
1	0.0008298	11.604	0.015	11.619	0.240	0.880	1.121	0.00052	0.00254	1
2	0.0008741	11.629	0.016	11.645	0.480	0.928	1.408	0.00104	0.00317	2
3	0.0009207	11.654	0.017	11.671	0.720	0.978	1.698	0.00156	0.00379	3
4	0.0009695	11.680	0.018	11.698	0.961	1.030	1.991	0.00208	0.00443	4
5	0.0010207	11.705	0.019	11.724	1.201	1.085	2.286	0.00260	0.00506	5
6	0.0010743	11.730	0.020	11.750	1.441	1.142	2.583	0.00311	0.00570	6
7	0.0011306	11.755	0.021	11.777	1.681	1.203	2.884	0.00363	0.00635	7
8	0.0011895	11.781	0.022	11.803	1.921	1.266	3.187	0.00414	0.00700	8
9	0.0012512	11.806	0.024	11.830	2.161	1.332	3.493	0.00466	0.00765	9
10	0.0013158	11.831	0.025	11.856	2.402	1.401	3.803	0.00517	0.00832	10
11	0.0013835	11.857	0.026	11.883	2.642	1.474	4.116	0.00568	0.00898	11
12	0.0014544	11.882	0.028	11.910	2.882	1.550	4.432	0.00619	0.00965	12
13	0.0015286	11.907	0.029	11.936	3.122	1.630	4.752	0.00670	0.01033	13
14	0.0016062	11.933	0.031	11.963	3.362	1.714	5.076	0.00721	0.01102	14
15	0.0016874	11.958	0.032	11.990	3.603	1.801	5.403	0.00771	0.01171	15
16	0.0017724	11.983	0.034	12.017	3.843	1.892	5.735	0.00822	0.01241	16
17	0.0018613	12.008	0.036	12.044	4.083	1.988	6.071	0.00872	0.01311	17
18	0.0019543	12.034	0.038	12.071	4.323	2.088	6.411	0.00922	0.01383	18
19	0.0020515	12.059	0.040	12.099	4.563	2.193	6.756	0.00973	0.01455	19
20	0.0021531	12.084	0.042	12.126	4.803	2.303	7.106	0.01023	0.01528	20
21	0.0022593	12.110	0.044	12.153	5.044	2.417	7.461	0.01073	0.01602	21
22	0.0023703	12.135	0.046	12.181	5.284	2.537	7.821	0.01123	0.01677	22

Table 2 Thermodynamic Properties of Moist Air at Standard Atmospheric Pressure, 14.696 psia (*Continued*)

Temp., °F	Humidity Ratio	Specific Volume, ft³/lb$_{da}$			Specific Enthalpy, Btu/lb$_{da}$			Specific Entropy, Btu/lb$_{da}$·°F		Temp., °F
t	W_s, lb$_w$/lb$_{da}$	v_{da}	v_{as}	v_s	h_{da}	h_{as}	h_s	s_{da}	s_s	t
23	0.0024863	12.160	0.048	12.209	5.524	2.662	8.186	0.01173	0.01753	23
24	0.0026075	12.185	0.051	12.236	5.764	2.793	8.557	0.01222	0.01830	24
25	0.0027340	12.211	0.054	12.264	6.004	2.930	8.934	0.01272	0.01908	25
26	0.0028662	12.236	0.056	12.292	6.244	3.073	9.317	0.01321	0.01987	26
27	0.0030042	12.261	0.059	12.320	6.485	3.222	9.707	0.01371	0.02067	27
28	0.0031482	12.287	0.062	12.349	6.725	3.378	10.103	0.01420	0.02148	28
29	0.0032986	12.312	0.065	12.377	6.965	3.541	10.506	0.01469	0.02231	29
30	0.0034555	12.337	0.068	12.405	7.205	3.711	10.916	0.01518	0.02315	30
31	0.0036192	12.362	0.072	12.434	7.445	3.888	11.334	0.01567	0.02400	31
32	0.003790	12.3877	0.0753	12.4630	7.686	4.073	11.759	0.01616	0.02486	32
33	0.003947	12.4130	0.0786	12.4915	7.926	4.244	12.169	0.01665	0.02570	33
34	0.004109	12.4382	0.0820	12.5202	8.166	4.420	12.586	0.01714	0.02654	34
35	0.004278	12.4635	0.0855	12.5490	8.406	4.603	13.009	0.01762	0.02740	35
36	0.004452	12.4888	0.0892	12.5780	8.646	4.793	13.439	0.01811	0.02827	36
37	0.004633	12.5141	0.0930	12.6071	8.887	4.990	13.877	0.01859	0.02915	37
38	0.004821	12.5394	0.0969	12.6363	9.127	5.194	14.321	0.01908	0.03004	38
39	0.005015	12.5647	0.1010	12.6657	9.367	5.405	14.772	0.01956	0.03095	39
40	0.005216	12.5899	0.1053	12.6952	9.607	5.625	15.232	0.02004	0.03187	40
41	0.005425	12.6152	0.1097	12.7249	9.848	5.852	15.699	0.02052	0.03280	41
42	0.005640	12.6405	0.1143	12.7548	10.088	6.087	16.175	0.02100	0.03375	42
43	0.005864	12.6658	0.1191	12.7849	10.328	6.331	16.659	0.02148	0.03472	43
44	0.006095	12.6911	0.1240	12.8151	10.568	6.583	17.151	0.02196	0.03570	44
45	0.006335	12.7163	0.1292	12.8455	10.808	6.844	17.653	0.02243	0.03669	45
46	0.006582	12.7416	0.1345	12.8761	11.049	7.115	18.164	0.02291	0.03770	46
47	0.006839	12.7669	0.1400	12.9069	11.289	7.395	18.684	0.02338	0.03873	47
48	0.007104	12.7922	0.1457	12.9379	11.529	7.685	19.214	0.02386	0.03978	48
49	0.007379	12.8175	0.1516	12.9691	11.769	7.985	19.755	0.02433	0.04084	49
50	0.007663	12.8427	0.1578	13.0005	12.010	8.296	20.306	0.02480	0.04192	50
51	0.007956	12.8680	0.1641	13.0322	12.250	8.617	20.867	0.02527	0.04302	51
52	0.008260	12.8933	0.1707	13.0640	12.490	8.950	21.440	0.02574	0.04414	52
53	0.008574	12.9186	0.1776	13.0962	12.730	9.294	22.025	0.02621	0.04528	53
54	0.008899	12.9439	0.1847	13.1285	12.971	9.650	22.621	0.02668	0.04645	54
55	0.009235	12.9691	0.1920	13.1611	13.211	10.018	23.229	0.02715	0.04763	55
56	0.009582	12.9944	0.1996	13.1940	13.451	10.399	23.850	0.02761	0.04884	56
57	0.009940	13.0197	0.2075	13.2272	13.691	10.792	24.484	0.02808	0.05006	57
58	0.010311	13.0450	0.2156	13.2606	13.932	11.199	25.131	0.02854	0.05132	58
59	0.010694	13.0702	0.2241	13.2943	14.172	11.620	25.792	0.02901	0.05259	59
60	0.011089	13.0955	0.2328	13.3283	14.412	12.055	26.467	0.02947	0.05389	60
61	0.011498	13.1208	0.2418	13.3626	14.653	12.504	27.157	0.02993	0.05522	61
62	0.011921	13.1461	0.2512	13.3973	14.893	12.968	27.861	0.03039	0.05657	62
63	0.012357	13.1713	0.2609	13.4322	15.133	13.448	28.581	0.03085	0.05795	63
64	0.012807	13.1966	0.2709	13.4675	15.373	13.944	29.318	0.03131	0.05936	64
65	0.013272	13.2219	0.2813	13.5032	15.614	14.457	30.070	0.03177	0.06080	65
66	0.013753	13.2472	0.2920	13.5392	15.854	14.986	30.840	0.03223	0.06226	66
67	0.014249	13.2724	0.3031	13.5755	16.094	15.532	31.627	0.03268	0.06376	67
68	0.014761	13.2977	0.3146	13.6123	16.335	16.097	32.431	0.03314	0.06529	68
69	0.015289	13.3230	0.3265	13.6494	16.575	16.680	33.255	0.03360	0.06685	69
70	0.015835	13.3482	0.3388	13.6870	16.815	17.282	34.097	0.03405	0.06844	70
71	0.016398	13.3735	0.3515	13.7250	17.056	17.904	34.959	0.03450	0.07007	71
72	0.016979	13.3988	0.3646	13.7634	17.296	18.545	35.841	0.03495	0.07173	72
73	0.017578	13.4241	0.3782	13.8022	17.536	19.208	36.744	0.03541	0.07343	73
74	0.018197	13.4493	0.3922	13.8415	17.777	19.892	37.668	0.03586	0.07516	74
75	0.018835	13.4746	0.4067	13.8813	18.017	20.598	38.615	0.03631	0.07694	75
76	0.019494	13.4999	0.4217	13.9216	18.257	21.327	39.584	0.03676	0.07875	76
77	0.020173	13.5251	0.4372	13.9624	18.498	22.079	40.576	0.03720	0.08060	77
78	0.020874	13.5504	0.4533	14.0037	18.738	22.855	41.593	0.03765	0.08250	78
79	0.021597	13.5757	0.4698	14.0455	18.978	23.656	42.634	0.03810	0.08444	79
80	0.022343	13.6010	0.4869	14.0879	19.219	24.482	43.701	0.03854	0.08642	80
81	0.023112	13.6262	0.5046	14.1308	19.459	25.335	44.794	0.03899	0.08845	81
82	0.023905	13.6515	0.5229	14.1744	19.699	26.215	45.914	0.03943	0.09052	82
83	0.024723	13.6768	0.5418	14.2185	19.940	27.123	47.062	0.03988	0.09264	83
84	0.025566	13.7020	0.5613	14.2633	20.180	28.059	48.239	0.04032	0.09481	84

Table 2 Thermodynamic Properties of Moist Air at Standard Atmospheric Pressure, 14.696 psia (*Continued*)

Temp., °F	Humidity Ratio	Specific Volume, ft^3/lb_{da}			Specific Enthalpy, Btu/lb_{da}			Specific Entropy, $Btu/lb_{da} \cdot °F$		Temp., °F
t	W_s, lb_w/lb_{da}	v_{da}	v_{as}	v_s	h_{da}	h_{as}	h_s	s_{da}	s_s	t
85	0.026436	13.7273	0.5814	14.3087	20.420	29.025	49.445	0.04076	0.09703	85
86	0.027333	13.7526	0.6022	14.3548	20.661	30.021	50.682	0.04120	0.09930	86
87	0.028257	13.7778	0.6237	14.4015	20.901	31.049	51.950	0.04164	0.10163	87
88	0.029211	13.8031	0.6459	14.4490	21.142	32.109	53.251	0.04208	0.10401	88
89	0.030193	13.8284	0.6688	14.4972	21.382	33.202	54.584	0.04252	0.10645	89
90	0.031206	13.8536	0.6925	14.5462	21.622	34.330	55.952	0.04296	0.10895	90
91	0.032251	13.8789	0.7170	14.5959	21.863	35.493	57.355	0.04339	0.11150	91
92	0.033327	13.9042	0.7422	14.6464	22.103	36.692	58.795	0.04383	0.11412	92
93	0.034437	13.9294	0.7683	14.6977	22.344	37.928	60.272	0.04427	0.11681	93
94	0.035581	13.9547	0.7952	14.7499	22.584	39.204	61.788	0.04470	0.11955	94
95	0.036760	13.9800	0.8230	14.8030	22.825	40.519	63.343	0.04514	0.12237	95
96	0.037976	14.0052	0.8518	14.8570	23.065	41.875	64.940	0.04557	0.12525	96
97	0.039228	14.0305	0.8814	14.9119	23.305	43.273	66.579	0.04600	0.12821	97
98	0.040520	14.0558	0.9120	14.9678	23.546	44.715	68.261	0.04643	0.13124	98
99	0.041851	14.0810	0.9436	15.0247	23.786	46.202	69.988	0.04686	0.13434	99
100	0.043222	14.1063	0.9763	15.0826	24.027	47.735	71.762	0.04729	0.1375	100
101	0.044636	14.1316	1.0100	15.1416	24.267	49.316	73.583	0.04772	0.1408	101
102	0.046094	14.1568	1.0448	15.2016	24.508	50.946	75.453	0.04815	0.1441	102
103	0.047596	14.1821	1.0807	15.2628	24.748	52.626	77.375	0.04858	0.1476	103
104	0.049145	14.2074	1.1178	15.3252	24.989	54.360	79.348	0.04901	0.1511	104
105	0.050741	14.2326	1.1561	15.3887	25.229	56.147	81.376	0.04943	0.1547	105
106	0.052386	14.2579	1.1957	15.4535	25.470	57.990	83.459	0.04986	0.1584	106
107	0.054082	14.2831	1.2365	15.5196	25.710	59.890	85.600	0.05028	0.1622	107
108	0.055830	14.3084	1.2787	15.5871	25.951	61.850	87.801	0.05071	0.1661	108
109	0.057632	14.3337	1.3222	15.6559	26.191	63.871	90.063	0.05113	0.1701	109
110	0.059490	14.3589	1.3672	15.7261	26.432	65.956	92.387	0.05155	0.1742	110
111	0.061405	14.3842	1.4136	15.7978	26.672	68.105	94.778	0.05197	0.1784	111
112	0.063380	14.4095	1.4615	15.8710	26.913	70.323	97.236	0.05240	0.1827	112
113	0.065416	14.4347	1.5111	15.9458	27.154	72.610	99.763	0.05282	0.1872	113
114	0.067516	14.4600	1.5622	16.0222	27.394	74.969	102.363	0.05324	0.1917	114
115	0.069680	14.4852	1.6150	16.1003	27.635	77.402	105.037	0.05365	0.1964	115
116	0.071913	14.5105	1.6696	16.1801	27.875	79.913	107.788	0.05407	0.2012	116
117	0.074215	14.5358	1.7259	16.2617	28.116	82.503	110.619	0.05449	0.2062	117
118	0.076590	14.5610	1.7842	16.3452	28.356	85.176	113.532	0.05491	0.2112	118
119	0.079040	14.5863	1.8443	16.4306	28.597	87.933	116.530	0.05532	0.2164	119
120	0.081566	14.6116	1.9065	16.5180	28.838	90.779	119.617	0.05574	0.2218	120
121	0.084173	14.6368	1.9707	16.6075	29.078	93.716	122.794	0.05615	0.2273	121
122	0.086863	14.6621	2.0370	16.6991	29.319	96.747	126.066	0.05657	0.2330	122
123	0.089638	14.6873	2.1056	16.7929	29.559	99.877	129.436	0.05698	0.2388	123
124	0.092503	14.7126	2.1765	16.8891	29.800	103.107	132.907	0.05739	0.2448	124
125	0.095459	14.7379	2.2498	16.9876	30.041	106.443	136.483	0.05781	0.2510	125
126	0.098510	14.7631	2.3255	17.0886	30.281	109.887	140.168	0.05822	0.2573	126
127	0.101661	14.7884	2.4038	17.1922	30.522	113.444	143.966	0.05863	0.2638	127
128	0.104914	14.8136	2.4848	17.2985	30.763	117.118	147.881	0.05904	0.2705	128
129	0.108273	14.8389	2.5686	17.4075	31.003	120.914	151.917	0.05945	0.2775	129
130	0.111742	14.8641	2.6552	17.5194	31.244	124.836	156.080	0.05985	0.2846	130
131	0.115326	14.8894	2.7449	17.6343	31.485	128.888	160.373	0.06026	0.2919	131
132	0.119029	14.9147	2.8376	17.7523	31.725	133.077	164.802	0.06067	0.2995	132
133	0.122856	14.9399	2.9336	17.8735	31.966	137.407	169.373	0.06108	0.3072	133
134	0.126811	14.9652	3.0329	17.9981	32.207	141.884	174.090	0.06148	0.3153	134
135	0.130899	14.9904	3.1357	18.1262	32.447	146.513	178.961	0.06189	0.3235	135
136	0.135127	15.0157	3.2422	18.2579	32.688	151.302	183.990	0.06229	0.3320	136
137	0.139499	15.0410	3.3525	18.3935	32.929	156.256	189.185	0.06269	0.3408	137
138	0.144022	15.0662	3.4668	18.5330	33.170	161.382	194.552	0.06310	0.3499	138
139	0.148702	15.0915	3.5851	18.6766	33.410	166.688	200.098	0.06350	0.3593	139
140	0.153545	15.1167	3.7078	18.8245	33.651	172.181	205.832	0.06390	0.3689	140
141	0.158558	15.1420	3.8350	18.9769	33.892	177.870	211.762	0.06430	0.3789	141
142	0.163750	15.1672	3.9668	19.1340	34.133	183.762	217.895	0.06470	0.3892	142
143	0.169127	15.1925	4.1036	19.2960	34.373	189.867	224.241	0.06510	0.3998	143
144	0.174699	15.2177	4.2454	19.4632	34.614	196.195	230.809	0.06550	0.4108	144
145	0.180473	15.2430	4.3927	19.6357	34.855	202.755	237.610	0.06590	0.4222	145
146	0.186460	15.2683	4.5455	19.8138	35.096	209.558	244.654	0.06630	0.4340	146

Table 2 Thermodynamic Properties of Moist Air at Standard Atmospheric Pressure, 14.696 psia (*Continued*)

Temp., °F	Humidity Ratio	Specific Volume, ft^3/lb_{da}			Specific Enthalpy, Btu/lb_{da}			Specific Entropy, $Btu/lb_{da}\cdot°F$		Temp., °F
t	W_s, lb_w/lb_{da}	v_{da}	v_{as}	v_s	h_{da}	h_{as}	h_s	s_{da}	s_s	t
147	0.192668	15.2935	4.7042	19.9977	35.337	216.615	251.952	0.06670	0.4461	147
148	0.199109	15.3188	4.8691	20.1878	35.577	223.940	259.517	0.06709	0.4587	148
149	0.205794	15.3440	5.0404	20.3844	35.818	231.543	267.362	0.06749	0.4718	149
150	0.212734	15.3693	5.2185	20.5878	36.059	239.440	275.499	0.06788	0.4853	150
151	0.219942	15.3945	5.4037	20.7982	36.300	247.644	283.944	0.06828	0.4993	151
152	0.227432	15.4198	5.5963	21.0161	36.541	256.172	292.713	0.06867	0.5138	152
153	0.235218	15.4450	5.7969	21.2419	36.782	265.039	301.821	0.06907	0.5288	153
154	0.243316	15.4703	6.0057	21.4759	37.023	274.264	311.286	0.06946	0.5444	154
155	0.251741	15.4956	6.2232	21.7187	37.263	283.864	321.128	0.06985	0.5607	155
156	0.260512	15.5208	6.4498	21.9706	37.504	293.862	331.366	0.07024	0.5775	156
157	0.269647	15.5461	6.6862	22.2323	37.745	304.278	342.023	0.07063	0.5950	157
158	0.279167	15.5713	6.9328	22.5041	37.986	315.135	353.121	0.07103	0.6132	158
159	0.289093	15.5966	7.1902	22.7868	38.227	326.459	364.686	0.07141	0.6322	159
160	0.299450	15.6218	7.4591	23.0809	38.468	338.277	376.745	0.07180	0.6519	160
161	0.310262	15.6471	7.7401	23.3872	38.709	350.618	389.327	0.07219	0.6725	161
162	0.321556	15.6723	8.0340	23.7063	38.950	363.514	402.464	0.07258	0.6939	162
163	0.333363	15.6976	8.3415	24.0391	39.191	376.998	416.188	0.07297	0.7163	163
164	0.345715	15.7228	8.6636	24.3864	39.432	391.107	430.539	0.07335	0.7396	164
165	0.358645	15.7481	9.0010	24.7491	39.673	405.882	445.555	0.07374	0.7640	165
166	0.372193	15.7733	9.3550	25.1283	39.914	421.366	461.279	0.07413	0.7895	166
167	0.386399	15.7986	9.7265	25.5251	40.155	437.606	477.760	0.07451	0.8162	167
168	0.401307	15.8238	10.1168	25.9406	40.396	454.654	495.049	0.07490	0.8442	168
169	0.416968	15.8491	10.5272	26.3763	40.637	472.566	513.203	0.07528	0.8735	169
170	0.433435	15.8743	10.9591	26.8334	40.878	491.405	532.283	0.07566	0.9043	170
171	0.450767	15.8996	11.4141	27.3137	41.119	511.238	552.357	0.07604	0.9367	171
172	0.469029	15.9248	11.8939	27.8188	41.360	532.139	573.499	0.07643	0.9707	172
173	0.488293	15.9501	12.4006	28.3507	41.601	554.192	595.793	0.07681	1.0065	173
174	0.508636	15.9753	12.9361	28.9114	41.842	577.487	619.329	0.07719	1.0443	174
175	0.530148	16.0006	13.5029	29.5034	42.083	602.125	644.209	0.07757	1.0841	175
176	0.552926	16.0258	14.1035	30.1293	42.324	628.219	670.543	0.07795	1.1263	176
177	0.577078	16.0511	14.7408	30.7919	42.565	655.892	698.457	0.07833	1.1709	177
178	0.602726	16.0763	15.4182	31.4946	42.807	685.284	728.091	0.07871	1.2182	178
179	0.630005	16.1016	16.1393	32.2409	43.048	716.553	759.601	0.07908	1.2684	179
180	0.659068	16.1268	16.9081	33.0349	43.289	749.874	793.163	0.07946	1.3218	180
181	0.690090	16.1521	17.7293	33.8814	43.530	785.446	828.976	0.07984	1.3788	181
182	0.723265	16.1773	18.6082	34.7855	43.771	823.495	867.266	0.08021	1.4396	182
183	0.758816	16.2026	19.5506	35.7532	44.012	864.276	908.288	0.08059	1.5046	183
184	0.796999	16.2278	20.5636	36.7915	44.253	908.084	952.337	0.08096	1.5743	184
185	0.838106	16.2531	21.6549	37.9080	44.495	955.254	999.749	0.08134	1.6493	185
186	0.882474	16.2783	22.8335	39.1118	44.736	1006.177	1050.912	0.08171	1.7301	186
187	0.930497	16.3036	24.1100	40.4136	44.977	1061.301	1106.278	0.08209	1.8174	187
188	0.982632	16.3288	25.4966	41.8255	45.218	1121.155	1166.373	0.08246	1.9121	188
189	1.039415	16.3541	27.0078	43.3619	45.460	1186.355	1231.814	0.08283	2.0150	189
190	1.101481	16.3793	28.6605	45.0398	45.701	1257.632	1303.333	0.08320	2.1274	190
191	1.169588	16.4046	30.4750	46.8796	45.942	1335.856	1381.798	0.08357	2.2505	191
192	1.244642	16.4298	32.4757	48.9056	46.183	1422.072	1468.255	0.08394	2.3860	192
193	1.327743	16.4551	34.6920	51.1471	46.425	1517.543	1563.968	0.08431	2.5357	193
194	1.420236	16.4803	37.1600	53.6403	46.666	1623.817	1670.483	0.08468	2.7022	194
195	1.523781	16.5056	39.9242	56.4297	46.907	1742.805	1789.712	0.08505	2.8883	195
196	1.640457	16.5308	43.0402	59.5710	47.149	1876.896	1924.045	0.08542	3.0977	196
197	1.772899	16.5561	46.5787	63.1348	47.390	2029.122	2076.512	0.08579	3.3351	197
198	1.924494	16.5813	50.6306	67.2119	47.631	2203.380	2251.011	0.08616	3.6064	198
199	2.099679	16.6066	55.3146	71.9212	47.873	2404.772	2452.645	0.08652	3.9195	199
200	2.304372	16.6318	60.7896	77.4214	48.114	2640.109	2688.223	0.08689	4.2849	200

4. THERMODYNAMIC PROPERTIES OF WATER AT SATURATION

Table 3 shows thermodynamic properties of water at saturation for temperatures from –80 to 300°F, calculated by the formulations described by IAPWS (2007, 2009, 2011, 2014). Symbols in the table follow standard steam table nomenclature. These properties are based on ITS-90. The internal energy and entropy of saturated liquid water are both assigned the value zero at the triple point, 32.018°F. Between the triple-point and critical-point temperatures of water, both **saturated liquid** and **saturated vapor** may coexist in equilibrium; below the triple-point temperature, both **saturated ice** and **saturated vapor** may coexist in equilibrium.

Table 3 Thermodynamic Properties of Water at Saturation

Temp., °F t	Absolute Pressure p_{ws}, psia	Specific Volume, ft³/lb$_w$ Sat. Solid v_i/v_f	Evap. v_{ig}/v_{fg}	Sat. Vapor v_g	Specific Enthalpy, Btu/lb$_w$ Sat. Solid h_i/h_f	Evap. h_{ig}/h_{fg}	Sat. Vapor h_g	Specific Entropy, Btu/lb$_w$·°F Sat. Solid s_i/s_f	Evap. s_{ig}/s_{fg}	Sat. Vapor s_g	Temp., °F t
–80	0.000116	0.01732	1953807	1953807	–193.38	1219.19	1025.81	–0.4064	3.2112	2.8048	–80
–79	0.000125	0.01732	1814635	1814635	–192.98	1219.23	1026.25	–0.4054	3.2029	2.7975	–79
–78	0.000135	0.01732	1686036	1686036	–192.59	1219.28	1026.69	–0.4043	3.1946	2.7903	–78
–77	0.000145	0.01732	1567159	1567159	–192.19	1219.33	1027.13	–0.4033	3.1864	2.7831	–77
–76	0.000157	0.01732	1457224	1457224	–191.80	1219.38	1027.58	–0.4023	3.1782	2.7759	–76
–75	0.000169	0.01733	1355519	1355519	–191.40	1219.42	1028.02	–0.4012	3.1700	2.7688	–75
–74	0.000182	0.01733	1261390	1261390	–191.00	1219.46	1028.46	–0.4002	3.1619	2.7617	–74
–73	0.000196	0.01733	1174239	1174239	–190.60	1219.51	1028.90	–0.3992	3.1539	2.7547	–73
–72	0.000211	0.01733	1093518	1093518	–190.20	1219.55	1029.35	–0.3981	3.1458	2.7477	–72
–71	0.000227	0.01733	1018724	1018724	–189.80	1219.59	1029.79	–0.3971	3.1379	2.7408	–71
–70	0.000244	0.01733	949394	949394	–189.40	1219.63	1030.23	–0.3961	3.1299	2.7338	–70
–69	0.000263	0.01733	885105	885105	–189.00	1219.67	1030.67	–0.3950	3.1220	2.7270	–69
–68	0.000283	0.01733	825469	825469	–188.59	1219.71	1031.11	–0.3940	3.1141	2.7201	–68
–67	0.000304	0.01733	770128	770128	–188.19	1219.75	1031.56	–0.3930	3.1063	2.7133	–67
–66	0.000326	0.01734	718753	718753	–187.78	1219.78	1032.00	–0.3919	3.0985	2.7065	–66
–65	0.000350	0.01734	671043	671043	–187.38	1219.82	1032.44	–0.3909	3.0907	2.6998	–65
–64	0.000376	0.01734	626720	626720	–186.97	1219.85	1032.88	–0.3899	3.0830	2.6931	–64
–63	0.000404	0.01734	585529	585529	–186.56	1219.89	1033.33	–0.3888	3.0753	2.6865	–63
–62	0.000433	0.01734	547234	547234	–186.15	1219.92	1033.77	–0.3878	3.0677	2.6799	–62
–61	0.000464	0.01734	511620	511620	–185.74	1219.95	1034.21	–0.3868	3.0601	2.6733	–61
–60	0.000498	0.01734	478487	478487	–185.33	1219.98	1034.65	–0.3858	3.0525	2.6667	–60
–59	0.000533	0.01734	447651	447651	–184.92	1220.01	1035.09	–0.3847	3.0449	2.6602	–59
–58	0.000571	0.01735	418943	418943	–184.50	1220.04	1035.54	–0.3837	3.0374	2.6537	–58
–57	0.000612	0.01735	392207	392207	–184.09	1220.07	1035.98	–0.3827	3.0299	2.6473	–57
–56	0.000655	0.01735	367299	367299	–183.67	1220.09	1036.42	–0.3816	3.0225	2.6409	–56
–55	0.000701	0.01735	344086	344086	–183.26	1220.12	1036.86	–0.3806	3.0151	2.6345	–55
–54	0.000749	0.01735	322445	322445	–182.84	1220.15	1037.30	–0.3796	3.0077	2.6282	–54
–53	0.000801	0.01735	302263	302263	–182.42	1220.17	1037.75	–0.3785	3.0004	2.6219	–53
–52	0.000857	0.01735	283436	283436	–182.00	1220.19	1038.19	–0.3775	2.9931	2.6156	–52
–51	0.000916	0.01736	265866	265866	–181.58	1220.21	1038.63	–0.3765	2.9858	2.6093	–51
–50	0.000978	0.01736	249464	249464	–181.16	1220.24	1039.07	–0.3755	2.9786	2.6031	–50
–49	0.001045	0.01736	234148	234148	–180.74	1220.26	1039.52	–0.3744	2.9714	2.5970	–49
–48	0.001115	0.01736	219841	219841	–180.32	1220.28	1039.96	–0.3734	2.9642	2.5908	–48
–47	0.001191	0.01736	206472	206472	–179.89	1220.29	1040.40	–0.3724	2.9571	2.5847	–47
–46	0.001270	0.01736	193976	193976	–179.47	1220.31	1040.84	–0.3713	2.9500	2.5786	–46
–45	0.001355	0.01736	182292	182292	–179.04	1220.33	1041.28	–0.3703	2.9429	2.5726	–45
–44	0.001445	0.01736	171363	171363	–178.62	1220.34	1041.73	–0.3693	2.9359	2.5666	–44
–43	0.001540	0.01737	161139	161139	–178.19	1220.36	1042.17	–0.3683	2.9288	2.5606	–43
–42	0.001641	0.01737	151570	151570	–177.76	1220.37	1042.61	–0.3672	2.9219	2.5546	–42
–41	0.001749	0.01737	142611	142611	–177.33	1220.38	1043.05	–0.3662	2.9149	2.5487	–41
–40	0.001862	0.01737	134222	134222	–176.90	1220.39	1043.49	–0.3652	2.9080	2.5428	–40
–39	0.001983	0.01737	126363	126363	–176.47	1220.41	1043.94	–0.3642	2.9011	2.5370	–39
–38	0.002111	0.01737	118999	118999	–176.04	1220.41	1044.38	–0.3631	2.8942	2.5311	–38
–37	0.002246	0.01737	112096	112096	–175.60	1220.42	1044.82	–0.3621	2.8874	2.5253	–37
–36	0.002389	0.01738	105624	105625	–175.17	1220.43	1045.26	–0.3611	2.8806	2.5196	–36
–35	0.002541	0.01738	99555	99555	–174.73	1220.44	1045.70	–0.3600	2.8739	2.5138	–35
–34	0.002701	0.01738	93860	93860	–174.30	1220.44	1046.15	–0.3590	2.8671	2.5081	–34
–33	0.002871	0.01738	88516	88516	–173.86	1220.45	1046.59	–0.3580	2.8604	2.5024	–33
–32	0.003051	0.01738	83500	83500	–173.42	1220.45	1047.03	–0.3570	2.8537	2.4968	–32
–31	0.003241	0.01738	78790	78790	–172.98	1220.45	1047.47	–0.3559	2.8471	2.4911	–31
–30	0.003442	0.01738	74366	74366	–172.54	1220.46	1047.91	–0.3549	2.8405	2.4855	–30
–29	0.003654	0.01738	70209	70209	–172.10	1220.46	1048.36	–0.3539	2.8339	2.4800	–29
–28	0.003878	0.01739	66303	66303	–171.66	1220.46	1048.80	–0.3529	2.8273	2.4744	–28
–27	0.004115	0.01739	62631	62631	–171.22	1220.46	1049.24	–0.3518	2.8208	2.4689	–27
–26	0.004365	0.01739	59179	59179	–170.77	1220.45	1049.68	–0.3508	2.8143	2.4634	–26
–25	0.004629	0.01739	55931	55931	–170.33	1220.45	1050.12	–0.3498	2.8078	2.4580	–25
–24	0.004908	0.01739	52876	52876	–169.88	1220.45	1050.56	–0.3488	2.8013	2.4525	–24
–23	0.005202	0.01739	50000	50001	–169.43	1220.44	1051.01	–0.3477	2.7949	2.4471	–23
–22	0.005512	0.01739	47294	47294	–168.99	1220.43	1051.45	–0.3467	2.7885	2.4418	–22
–21	0.005839	0.01740	44745	44745	–168.54	1220.43	1051.89	–0.3457	2.7821	2.4364	–21
–20	0.006184	0.01740	42345	42345	–168.09	1220.42	1052.33	–0.3447	2.7758	2.4311	–20
–19	0.006548	0.01740	40084	40084	–167.64	1220.41	1052.77	–0.3436	2.7694	2.4258	–19
–18	0.006932	0.01740	37953	37953	–167.19	1220.40	1053.21	–0.3426	2.7632	2.4205	–18
–17	0.007335	0.01740	35944	35944	–166.73	1220.39	1053.65	–0.3416	2.7569	2.4153	–17
–16	0.007761	0.01740	34050	34050	–166.28	1220.38	1054.10	–0.3406	2.7506	2.4101	–16
–15	0.008209	0.01740	32264	32264	–165.82	1220.36	1054.54	–0.3396	2.7444	2.4049	–15
–14	0.008681	0.01741	30580	30580	–165.37	1220.35	1054.98	–0.3385	2.7382	2.3997	–14
–13	0.009177	0.01741	28990	28990	–164.91	1220.33	1055.42	–0.3375	2.7321	2.3946	–13

Note: Subscript i denotes values for $t \le 32$°F and subscript f denotes values for $t \ge 32$°F.

Table 3 Thermodynamic Properties of Water at Saturation (*Continued*)

Temp., °F t	Absolute Pressure p_{ws}, psia	Specific Volume, ft³/lb$_w$ Sat. Solid v_i/v_f	Evap. v_{ig}/v_{fg}	Sat. Vapor v_g	Specific Enthalpy, Btu/lb$_w$ Sat. Solid h_i/h_f	Evap. h_{ig}/h_{fg}	Sat. Vapor h_g	Specific Entropy, Btu/lb$_w$·°F Sat. Solid s_i/s_f	Evap. s_{ig}/s_{fg}	Sat. Vapor s_g	Temp., °F t
–12	0.009700	0.01741	27490	27490	–164.46	1220.32	1055.86	–0.3365	2.7259	2.3895	–12
–11	0.010249	0.01741	26073	26073	–164.00	1220.30	1056.30	–0.3355	2.7198	2.3844	–11
–10	0.010827	0.01741	24736	24736	–163.54	1220.28	1056.74	–0.3344	2.7137	2.3793	–10
–9	0.011435	0.01741	23473	23473	–163.08	1220.26	1057.18	–0.3334	2.7077	2.3743	–9
–8	0.012075	0.01741	22279	22279	–162.62	1220.24	1057.63	–0.3324	2.7016	2.3692	–8
–7	0.012747	0.01742	21151	21152	–162.15	1220.22	1058.07	–0.3314	2.6956	2.3642	–7
–6	0.013453	0.01742	20086	20086	–161.69	1220.20	1058.51	–0.3303	2.6896	2.3593	–6
–5	0.014194	0.01742	19078	19078	–161.23	1220.17	1058.95	–0.3293	2.6837	2.3543	–5
–4	0.014974	0.01742	18125	18125	–160.76	1220.15	1059.39	–0.3283	2.6777	2.3494	–4
–3	0.015792	0.01742	17223	17223	–160.29	1220.12	1059.83	–0.3273	2.6718	2.3445	–3
–2	0.016651	0.01742	16370	16370	–159.83	1220.10	1060.27	–0.3263	2.6659	2.3396	–2
–1	0.017553	0.01742	15563	15563	–159.36	1220.07	1060.71	–0.3252	2.6600	2.3348	–1
0	0.018499	0.01743	14799	14799	–158.89	1220.04	1061.15	–0.3242	2.6542	2.3300	0
1	0.019492	0.01743	14076	14076	–158.42	1220.01	1061.59	–0.3232	2.6483	2.3251	1
2	0.020533	0.01743	13391	13391	–157.95	1219.98	1062.03	–0.3222	2.6425	2.3204	2
3	0.021625	0.01743	12742	12742	–157.48	1219.95	1062.47	–0.3212	2.6368	2.3156	3
4	0.022770	0.01743	12127	12127	–157.00	1219.92	1062.91	–0.3201	2.6310	2.3109	4
5	0.023971	0.01743	11545	11545	–156.53	1219.88	1063.35	–0.3191	2.6253	2.3062	5
6	0.025229	0.01743	10992	10992	–156.05	1219.85	1063.79	–0.3181	2.6196	2.3015	6
7	0.026547	0.01744	10469	10469	–155.58	1219.81	1064.23	–0.3171	2.6139	2.2968	7
8	0.027929	0.01744	9972	9972	–155.10	1219.77	1064.67	–0.3160	2.6082	2.2921	8
9	0.029375	0.01744	9501	9501	–154.62	1219.74	1065.11	–0.3150	2.6025	2.2875	9
10	0.030890	0.01744	9055	9055	–154.15	1219.70	1065.55	–0.3140	2.5969	2.2829	10
11	0.032476	0.01744	8631	8631	–153.67	1219.66	1065.99	–0.3130	2.5913	2.2783	11
12	0.034136	0.01744	8228	8228	–153.18	1219.61	1066.43	–0.3120	2.5857	2.2738	12
13	0.035874	0.01744	7846	7846	–152.70	1219.57	1066.87	–0.3109	2.5802	2.2692	13
14	0.037692	0.01745	7484	7484	–152.22	1219.53	1067.31	–0.3099	2.5746	2.2647	14
15	0.039593	0.01745	7139	7139	–151.74	1219.48	1067.75	–0.3089	2.5691	2.2602	15
16	0.041582	0.01745	6812	6812	–151.25	1219.44	1068.19	–0.3079	2.5636	2.2557	16
17	0.043662	0.01745	6501	6501	–150.77	1219.39	1068.63	–0.3069	2.5581	2.2513	17
18	0.045837	0.01745	6205	6205	–150.28	1219.34	1069.06	–0.3058	2.5527	2.2468	18
19	0.048109	0.01745	5925	5925	–149.79	1219.29	1069.50	–0.3048	2.5473	2.2424	19
20	0.050485	0.01746	5658	5658	–149.30	1219.24	1069.94	–0.3038	2.5418	2.2380	20
21	0.052967	0.01746	5404	5404	–148.81	1219.19	1070.38	–0.3028	2.5364	2.2337	21
22	0.055560	0.01746	5162	5162	–148.32	1219.14	1070.82	–0.3018	2.5311	2.2293	22
23	0.058268	0.01746	4932	4932	–147.83	1219.09	1071.26	–0.3007	2.5257	2.2250	23
24	0.061096	0.01746	4714	4714	–147.34	1219.03	1071.69	–0.2997	2.5204	2.2207	24
25	0.064048	0.01746	4506	4506	–146.85	1218.98	1072.13	–0.2987	2.5151	2.2164	25
26	0.067130	0.01746	4308	4308	–146.35	1218.92	1072.57	–0.2977	2.5098	2.2121	26
27	0.070347	0.01747	4119	4119	–145.86	1218.86	1073.01	–0.2967	2.5045	2.2078	27
28	0.073704	0.01747	3939	3939	–145.36	1218.80	1073.44	–0.2957	2.4992	2.2036	28
29	0.077206	0.01747	3768	3768	–144.86	1218.74	1073.88	–0.2946	2.4940	2.1994	29
30	0.080858	0.01747	3605	3605	–144.36	1218.68	1074.32	–0.2936	2.4888	2.1952	30
31	0.084668	0.01747	3450	3450	–143.86	1218.62	1074.76	–0.2926	2.4836	2.1910	31
32	0.088640	0.01747	3302	3302	–143.36	1218.56	1075.19	–0.2916	2.4784	2.1868	32
Transition from saturated solid to saturated liquid											
32	0.08865	0.01602	3302.02	3302.04	–0.02	1075.21	1075.19	0.0000	2.1869	2.1868	32
33	0.09229	0.01602	3178.06	3178.08	0.99	1074.64	1075.63	0.0020	2.1813	2.1833	33
34	0.09607	0.01602	3059.30	3059.32	2.00	1074.07	1076.07	0.0041	2.1757	2.1797	34
35	0.09998	0.01602	2945.51	2945.52	3.00	1073.50	1076.51	0.0061	2.1701	2.1762	35
36	0.10403	0.01602	2836.45	2836.46	4.01	1072.93	1076.95	0.0081	2.1646	2.1727	36
37	0.10823	0.01602	2731.91	2731.92	5.02	1072.37	1077.38	0.0102	2.1591	2.1693	37
38	0.11258	0.01602	2631.68	2631.70	6.02	1071.80	1077.82	0.0122	2.1536	2.1658	38
39	0.11708	0.01602	2535.57	2535.59	7.03	1071.23	1078.26	0.0142	2.1482	2.1624	39
40	0.12173	0.01602	2443.39	2443.41	8.03	1070.67	1078.70	0.0162	2.1427	2.1590	40
41	0.12656	0.01602	2354.97	2354.98	9.04	1070.10	1079.14	0.0182	2.1373	2.1556	41
42	0.13155	0.01602	2270.13	2270.15	10.04	1069.53	1079.57	0.0202	2.1319	2.1522	42
43	0.13671	0.01602	2188.72	2188.74	11.05	1068.97	1080.01	0.0222	2.1266	2.1488	43
44	0.14205	0.01602	2110.58	2110.60	12.05	1068.40	1080.45	0.0242	2.1212	2.1454	44
45	0.14757	0.01602	2035.58	2035.59	13.05	1067.84	1080.89	0.0262	2.1159	2.1421	45
46	0.15328	0.01602	1963.56	1963.58	14.06	1067.27	1081.33	0.0282	2.1106	2.1388	46
47	0.15919	0.01602	1894.41	1894.42	15.06	1066.70	1081.76	0.0302	2.1053	2.1355	47
48	0.16530	0.01602	1827.99	1828.00	16.06	1066.14	1082.20	0.0321	2.1001	2.1322	48
49	0.17161	0.01602	1764.19	1764.20	17.06	1065.57	1082.64	0.0341	2.0948	2.1289	49
50	0.17813	0.01602	1702.88	1702.90	18.07	1065.01	1083.07	0.0361	2.0896	2.1257	50
51	0.18487	0.01602	1643.98	1643.99	19.07	1064.44	1083.51	0.0381	2.0844	2.1225	51
52	0.19184	0.01603	1587.36	1587.38	20.07	1063.88	1083.95	0.0400	2.0792	2.1192	52

*Extrapolated to represent metastable equilibrium with undercooled liquid.

Table 3 Thermodynamic Properties of Water at Saturation (*Continued*)

Temp., °F t	Absolute Pressure p_{ws}, psia	Specific Volume, ft³/lb$_w$ Sat. Liquid v_i/v_f	Evap. v_{ig}/v_{fg}	Sat. Vapor v_g	Specific Enthalpy, Btu/lb$_w$ Sat. Liquid h_i/h_f	Evap. h_{ig}/h_{fg}	Sat. Vapor h_g	Specific Entropy, Btu/lb$_w$·°F Sat. Liquid s_i/s_f	Evap. s_{ig}/s_{fg}	Sat. Vapor s_g	Temp., °F t
53	0.19903	0.01603	1532.94	1532.96	21.07	1063.31	1084.38	0.0420	2.0741	2.1160	53
54	0.20646	0.01603	1480.62	1480.64	22.07	1062.75	1084.82	0.0439	2.0689	2.1129	54
55	0.21414	0.01603	1430.31	1430.32	23.07	1062.18	1085.26	0.0459	2.0638	2.1097	55
56	0.22206	0.01603	1381.92	1381.94	24.08	1061.62	1085.69	0.0478	2.0587	2.1065	56
57	0.23024	0.01603	1335.38	1335.39	25.08	1061.05	1086.13	0.0497	2.0536	2.1034	57
58	0.23868	0.01603	1290.60	1290.61	26.08	1060.49	1086.56	0.0517	2.0486	2.1003	58
59	0.24740	0.01603	1247.51	1247.53	27.08	1059.92	1087.00	0.0536	2.0435	2.0972	59
60	0.25639	0.01603	1206.05	1206.07	28.08	1059.36	1087.44	0.0555	2.0385	2.0941	60
61	0.26567	0.01604	1166.14	1166.16	29.08	1058.79	1087.87	0.0575	2.0335	2.0910	61
62	0.27524	0.01604	1127.72	1127.74	30.08	1058.23	1088.31	0.0594	2.0285	2.0879	62
63	0.28511	0.01604	1090.73	1090.74	31.08	1057.66	1088.74	0.0613	2.0236	2.0849	63
64	0.29529	0.01604	1055.11	1055.12	32.08	1057.10	1089.18	0.0632	2.0186	2.0818	64
65	0.30579	0.01604	1020.80	1020.82	33.08	1056.53	1089.61	0.0651	2.0137	2.0788	65
66	0.31662	0.01604	987.75	987.77	34.08	1055.97	1090.05	0.0670	2.0088	2.0758	66
67	0.32777	0.01605	955.91	955.93	35.08	1055.40	1090.48	0.0689	2.0039	2.0728	67
68	0.33927	0.01605	925.23	925.25	36.08	1054.84	1090.92	0.0708	1.9990	2.0699	68
69	0.35113	0.01605	895.67	895.68	37.08	1054.27	1091.35	0.0727	1.9942	2.0669	69
70	0.36334	0.01605	867.17	867.19	38.08	1053.71	1091.78	0.0746	1.9894	2.0640	70
71	0.37592	0.01605	839.70	839.72	39.08	1053.14	1092.22	0.0765	1.9846	2.0610	71
72	0.38889	0.01606	813.21	813.23	40.08	1052.57	1092.65	0.0784	1.9798	2.0581	72
73	0.40224	0.01606	787.67	787.69	41.08	1052.01	1093.08	0.0802	1.9750	2.0552	73
74	0.41599	0.01606	763.04	763.06	42.08	1051.44	1093.52	0.0821	1.9702	2.0523	74
75	0.43015	0.01606	739.28	739.30	43.07	1050.88	1093.95	0.0840	1.9655	2.0495	75
76	0.44473	0.01606	716.36	716.38	44.07	1050.31	1094.38	0.0859	1.9607	2.0466	76
77	0.45973	0.01607	694.25	694.26	45.07	1049.74	1094.82	0.0877	1.9560	2.0438	77
78	0.47518	0.01607	672.90	672.92	46.07	1049.18	1095.25	0.0896	1.9513	2.0409	78
79	0.49108	0.01607	652.31	652.32	47.07	1048.61	1095.68	0.0914	1.9467	2.0381	79
80	0.50744	0.01607	632.43	632.44	48.07	1048.05	1096.11	0.0933	1.9420	2.0353	80
81	0.52427	0.01608	613.23	613.25	49.07	1047.48	1096.55	0.0951	1.9374	2.0325	81
82	0.54159	0.01608	594.70	594.72	50.07	1046.91	1096.98	0.0970	1.9328	2.0297	82
83	0.55940	0.01608	576.80	576.82	51.07	1046.34	1097.41	0.0988	1.9281	2.0270	83
84	0.57772	0.01608	559.52	559.54	52.06	1045.78	1097.84	0.1007	1.9236	2.0242	84
85	0.59656	0.01609	542.83	542.84	53.06	1045.21	1098.27	0.1025	1.9190	2.0215	85
86	0.61593	0.01609	526.70	526.71	54.06	1044.64	1098.70	0.1043	1.9144	2.0188	86
87	0.63585	0.01609	511.11	511.13	55.06	1044.07	1099.13	0.1062	1.9099	2.0160	87
88	0.65632	0.01609	496.05	496.07	56.06	1043.51	1099.56	0.1080	1.9054	2.0133	88
89	0.67736	0.01610	481.50	481.51	57.06	1042.94	1100.00	0.1098	1.9009	2.0107	89
90	0.69899	0.01610	467.43	467.45	58.05	1042.37	1100.43	0.1116	1.8964	2.0080	90
91	0.72122	0.01610	453.83	453.85	59.05	1041.80	1100.86	0.1134	1.8919	2.0053	91
92	0.74405	0.01611	440.68	440.70	60.05	1041.23	1101.28	0.1152	1.8874	2.0027	92
93	0.76751	0.01611	427.97	427.98	61.05	1040.67	1101.71	0.1171	1.8830	2.0000	93
94	0.79161	0.01611	415.67	415.68	62.05	1040.10	1102.14	0.1189	1.8786	1.9974	94
95	0.81636	0.01612	403.77	403.79	63.05	1039.53	1102.57	0.1207	1.8741	1.9948	95
96	0.84178	0.01612	392.27	392.28	64.04	1038.96	1103.00	0.1225	1.8697	1.9922	96
97	0.86788	0.01612	381.14	381.15	65.04	1038.39	1103.43	0.1242	1.8654	1.9896	97
98	0.89468	0.01612	370.37	370.38	66.04	1037.82	1103.86	0.1260	1.8610	1.9870	98
99	0.92220	0.01613	359.94	359.96	67.04	1037.25	1104.29	0.1278	1.8566	1.9845	99
100	0.95044	0.01613	349.85	349.87	68.04	1036.68	1104.71	0.1296	1.8523	1.9819	100
101	0.97943	0.01613	340.09	340.10	69.04	1036.11	1105.14	0.1314	1.8480	1.9794	101
102	1.00917	0.01614	330.63	330.65	70.03	1035.54	1105.57	0.1332	1.8437	1.9769	102
103	1.03970	0.01614	321.48	321.50	71.03	1034.97	1106.00	0.1350	1.8394	1.9743	103
104	1.07102	0.01614	312.62	312.63	72.03	1034.39	1106.42	0.1367	1.8351	1.9718	104
105	1.10315	0.01615	304.03	304.05	73.03	1033.82	1106.85	0.1385	1.8308	1.9693	105
106	1.13611	0.01615	295.72	295.73	74.03	1033.25	1107.28	0.1403	1.8266	1.9669	106
107	1.16992	0.01616	287.66	287.68	75.02	1032.68	1107.70	0.1420	1.8224	1.9644	107
108	1.20459	0.01616	279.86	279.88	76.02	1032.11	1108.13	0.1438	1.8181	1.9619	108
109	1.24014	0.01616	272.30	272.32	77.02	1031.53	1108.55	0.1455	1.8139	1.9595	109
110	1.27660	0.01617	264.97	264.99	78.02	1030.96	1108.98	0.1473	1.8098	1.9570	110
111	1.31397	0.01617	257.87	257.89	79.02	1030.39	1109.41	0.1490	1.8056	1.9546	111
112	1.35228	0.01617	250.99	251.01	80.02	1029.82	1109.83	0.1508	1.8014	1.9522	112
113	1.39155	0.01618	244.32	244.34	81.01	1029.24	1110.25	0.1525	1.7973	1.9498	113
114	1.43179	0.01618	237.85	237.87	82.01	1028.67	1110.68	0.1543	1.7931	1.9474	114
115	1.47304	0.01618	231.58	231.60	83.01	1028.09	1111.10	0.1560	1.7890	1.9450	115
116	1.51530	0.01619	225.50	225.51	84.01	1027.52	1111.53	0.1577	1.7849	1.9427	116
117	1.55860	0.01619	219.60	219.62	85.01	1026.94	1111.95	0.1595	1.7808	1.9403	117
118	1.60296	0.01620	213.88	213.90	86.00	1026.37	1112.37	0.1612	1.7767	1.9380	118
119	1.64839	0.01620	208.33	208.35	87.00	1025.79	1112.80	0.1629	1.7727	1.9356	119
120	1.69493	0.01620	202.95	202.96	88.00	1025.22	1113.22	0.1647	1.7686	1.9333	120

Table 3 Thermodynamic Properties of Water at Saturation (*Continued*)

Temp., °F t	Absolute Pressure p_{ws}, psia	Specific Volume, ft³/lb$_w$ Sat. Liquid v_i/v_f	Evap. v_{ig}/v_{fg}	Sat. Vapor v_g	Specific Enthalpy, Btu/lb$_w$ Sat. Liquid h_i/h_f	Evap. h_{ig}/h_{fg}	Sat. Vapor h_g	Specific Entropy, Btu/lb$_w$·°F Sat. Liquid s_i/s_f	Evap. s_{ig}/s_{fg}	Sat. Vapor s_g	Temp., °F t
121	1.74259	0.01621	197.72	197.74	89.00	1024.64	1113.64	0.1664	1.7646	1.9310	121
122	1.79140	0.01621	192.65	192.67	90.00	1024.06	1114.06	0.1681	1.7606	1.9287	122
123	1.84137	0.01622	187.73	187.75	91.00	1023.49	1114.48	0.1698	1.7565	1.9264	123
124	1.89254	0.01622	182.96	182.97	92.00	1022.91	1114.91	0.1715	1.7526	1.9241	124
125	1.94492	0.01623	178.32	178.34	92.99	1022.33	1115.33	0.1732	1.7486	1.9218	125
126	1.99853	0.01623	173.82	173.84	93.99	1021.76	1115.75	0.1749	1.7446	1.9195	126
127	2.05341	0.01623	169.45	169.47	94.99	1021.18	1116.17	0.1766	1.7406	1.9173	127
128	2.10957	0.01624	165.21	165.22	95.99	1020.60	1116.59	0.1783	1.7367	1.9150	128
129	2.16704	0.01624	161.09	161.10	96.99	1020.02	1117.01	0.1800	1.7328	1.9128	129
130	2.22584	0.01625	157.09	157.10	97.99	1019.44	1117.43	0.1817	1.7288	1.9106	130
131	2.28600	0.01625	153.20	153.22	98.99	1018.86	1117.85	0.1834	1.7249	1.9084	131
132	2.34754	0.01626	149.42	149.44	99.98	1018.28	1118.26	0.1851	1.7210	1.9061	132
133	2.41050	0.01626	145.75	145.77	100.98	1017.70	1118.68	0.1868	1.7171	1.9039	133
134	2.47489	0.01626	142.19	142.21	101.98	1017.12	1119.10	0.1885	1.7133	1.9018	134
135	2.54074	0.01627	138.73	138.74	102.98	1016.54	1119.52	0.1902	1.7094	1.8996	135
136	2.60809	0.01627	135.36	135.38	103.98	1015.96	1119.94	0.1918	1.7056	1.8974	136
137	2.67694	0.01628	132.09	132.10	104.98	1015.37	1120.35	0.1935	1.7017	1.8953	137
138	2.74735	0.01628	128.91	128.92	105.98	1014.79	1120.77	0.1952	1.6979	1.8931	138
139	2.81932	0.01629	125.81	125.83	106.98	1014.21	1121.19	0.1969	1.6941	1.8910	139
140	2.89289	0.01629	122.81	122.82	107.98	1013.62	1121.60	0.1985	1.6903	1.8888	140
141	2.96810	0.01630	119.88	119.90	108.98	1013.04	1122.02	0.2002	1.6865	1.8867	141
142	3.04496	0.01630	117.04	117.06	109.98	1012.46	1122.43	0.2019	1.6827	1.8846	142
143	3.12350	0.01631	114.28	114.29	110.98	1011.87	1122.85	0.2035	1.6790	1.8825	143
144	3.20377	0.01631	111.59	111.60	111.97	1011.29	1123.26	0.2052	1.6752	1.8804	144
145	3.28578	0.01632	108.97	108.99	112.97	1010.70	1123.68	0.2068	1.6715	1.8783	145
146	3.36957	0.01632	106.43	106.44	113.97	1010.12	1124.09	0.2085	1.6678	1.8762	146
147	3.45516	0.01633	103.95	103.97	114.97	1009.53	1124.50	0.2101	1.6640	1.8742	147
148	3.54260	0.01633	101.54	101.56	115.97	1008.94	1124.91	0.2118	1.6603	1.8721	148
149	3.63190	0.01634	99.20	99.22	116.97	1008.35	1125.33	0.2134	1.6566	1.8701	149
150	3.72311	0.01634	96.92	96.93	117.97	1007.77	1125.74	0.2151	1.6530	1.8680	150
151	3.81626	0.01635	94.70	94.71	118.97	1007.18	1126.15	0.2167	1.6493	1.8660	151
152	3.91137	0.01635	92.54	92.55	119.97	1006.59	1126.56	0.2183	1.6456	1.8640	152
153	4.00849	0.01636	90.43	90.45	120.97	1006.00	1126.97	0.2200	1.6420	1.8620	153
154	4.10764	0.01636	88.38	88.40	121.97	1005.41	1127.38	0.2216	1.6384	1.8599	154
155	4.20885	0.01637	86.39	86.40	122.97	1004.82	1127.79	0.2232	1.6347	1.8580	155
156	4.31218	0.01637	84.45	84.46	123.97	1004.23	1128.20	0.2249	1.6311	1.8560	156
157	4.41764	0.01638	82.55	82.57	124.97	1003.64	1128.61	0.2265	1.6275	1.8540	157
158	4.52527	0.01638	80.71	80.73	125.98	1003.04	1129.02	0.2281	1.6239	1.8520	158
159	4.63511	0.01639	78.92	78.93	126.98	1002.45	1129.43	0.2297	1.6203	1.8500	159
160	4.7472	0.01639	77.170	77.186	127.98	1001.86	1129.83	0.2313	1.6168	1.8481	160
161	4.8616	0.01640	75.467	75.483	128.98	1001.26	1130.24	0.2329	1.6132	1.8461	161
162	4.9783	0.01640	73.808	73.824	129.98	1000.67	1130.65	0.2346	1.6096	1.8442	162
163	5.0973	0.01641	72.191	72.207	130.98	1000.08	1131.06	0.2362	1.6061	1.8423	163
164	5.2187	0.01642	70.616	70.632	131.98	999.48	1131.46	0.2378	1.6026	1.8403	164
165	5.3426	0.01642	69.080	69.097	132.98	998.88	1131.87	0.2394	1.5991	1.8384	165
166	5.4689	0.01643	67.584	67.600	133.98	998.29	1132.27	0.2410	1.5955	1.8365	166
167	5.5978	0.01643	66.125	66.141	134.98	997.69	1132.68	0.2426	1.5920	1.8346	167
168	5.7292	0.01644	64.703	64.720	135.99	997.09	1133.08	0.2442	1.5886	1.8327	168
169	5.8632	0.01644	63.317	63.333	136.99	996.49	1133.48	0.2458	1.5851	1.8308	169
170	5.9998	0.01645	61.965	61.982	137.99	995.90	1133.89	0.2474	1.5816	1.8290	170
171	6.1390	0.01645	60.647	60.664	138.99	995.30	1134.29	0.2489	1.5782	1.8271	171
172	6.2810	0.01646	59.362	59.379	139.99	994.70	1134.69	0.2505	1.5747	1.8252	172
173	6.4258	0.01647	58.109	58.125	141.00	994.10	1135.09	0.2521	1.5713	1.8234	173
174	6.5733	0.01647	56.886	56.903	142.00	993.49	1135.49	0.2537	1.5678	1.8215	174
175	6.7237	0.01648	55.694	55.710	143.00	992.89	1135.89	0.2553	1.5644	1.8197	175
176	6.8769	0.01648	54.531	54.547	144.00	992.29	1136.29	0.2569	1.5610	1.8179	176
177	7.0331	0.01649	53.396	53.412	145.00	991.69	1136.69	0.2584	1.5576	1.8160	177
178	7.1922	0.01650	52.289	52.305	146.01	991.08	1137.09	0.2600	1.5542	1.8142	178
179	7.3544	0.01650	51.208	51.225	147.01	990.48	1137.49	0.2616	1.5508	1.8124	179
180	7.5196	0.01651	50.154	50.171	148.01	989.87	1137.89	0.2631	1.5475	1.8106	180
181	7.6879	0.01651	49.125	49.142	149.02	989.27	1138.28	0.2647	1.5441	1.8088	181
182	7.8593	0.01652	48.121	48.138	150.02	988.66	1138.68	0.2663	1.5408	1.8070	182
183	8.0339	0.01653	47.141	47.158	151.02	988.05	1139.07	0.2678	1.5374	1.8052	183
184	8.2118	0.01653	46.184	46.201	152.03	987.44	1139.47	0.2694	1.5341	1.8035	184
185	8.3930	0.01654	45.251	45.267	153.03	986.84	1139.86	0.2709	1.5308	1.8017	185
186	8.5775	0.01654	44.339	44.355	154.03	986.23	1140.26	0.2725	1.5274	1.7999	186
187	8.7653	0.01655	43.448	43.465	155.04	985.62	1140.65	0.2741	1.5241	1.7982	187
188	8.9566	0.01656	42.579	42.596	156.04	985.01	1141.05	0.2756	1.5208	1.7964	188
189	9.1514	0.01656	41.730	41.747	157.04	984.39	1141.44	0.2772	1.5175	1.7947	189

Table 3 Thermodynamic Properties of Water at Saturation (*Continued*)

Temp., °F t	Absolute Pressure p_{ws}, psia	Specific Volume, ft³/lb$_w$ Sat. Liquid v_i/v_f	Evap. v_{ig}/v_{fg}	Sat. Vapor v_g	Specific Enthalpy, Btu/lb$_w$ Sat. Liquid h_i/h_f	Evap. h_{ig}/h_{fg}	Sat. Vapor h_g	Specific Entropy, Btu/lb$_w$·°F Sat. Liquid s_i/s_f	Evap. s_{ig}/s_{fg}	Sat. Vapor s_g	Temp., °F t
190	9.3497	0.01657	40.901	40.918	158.05	983.78	1141.83	0.2787	1.5143	1.7930	190
191	9.5515	0.01658	40.092	40.108	159.05	983.17	1142.22	0.2802	1.5110	1.7912	191
192	9.7570	0.01658	39.301	39.317	160.06	982.55	1142.61	0.2818	1.5077	1.7895	192
193	9.9662	0.01659	38.528	38.545	161.06	981.94	1143.00	0.2833	1.5045	1.7878	193
194	10.1791	0.01659	37.773	37.790	162.07	981.32	1143.39	0.2849	1.5012	1.7861	194
195	10.3958	0.01660	37.036	37.053	163.07	980.71	1143.78	0.2864	1.4980	1.7844	195
196	10.6163	0.01661	36.315	36.332	164.08	980.09	1144.17	0.2879	1.4948	1.7827	196
197	10.8407	0.01661	35.611	35.628	165.08	979.47	1144.56	0.2895	1.4916	1.7810	197
198	11.0690	0.01662	34.924	34.940	166.09	978.86	1144.94	0.2910	1.4884	1.7793	198
199	11.3013	0.01663	34.251	34.268	167.09	978.24	1145.33	0.2925	1.4852	1.7777	199
200	11.5376	0.01663	33.594	33.611	168.10	977.62	1145.71	0.2940	1.4820	1.7760	200
201	11.7781	0.01664	32.952	32.968	169.10	976.99	1146.10	0.2956	1.4788	1.7743	201
202	12.0227	0.01665	32.324	32.341	170.11	976.37	1146.48	0.2971	1.4756	1.7727	202
203	12.2715	0.01665	31.710	31.727	171.12	975.75	1146.87	0.2986	1.4724	1.7710	203
204	12.5246	0.01666	31.110	31.127	172.12	975.13	1147.25	0.3001	1.4693	1.7694	204
205	12.7819	0.01667	30.524	30.540	173.13	974.50	1147.63	0.3016	1.4661	1.7678	205
206	13.0437	0.01667	29.950	29.967	174.14	973.88	1148.01	0.3031	1.4630	1.7661	206
207	13.3099	0.01668	29.389	29.406	175.14	973.25	1148.40	0.3047	1.4599	1.7645	207
208	13.5806	0.01669	28.840	28.857	176.15	972.62	1148.78	0.3062	1.4567	1.7629	208
209	13.8558	0.01669	28.304	28.321	177.16	972.00	1149.15	0.3077	1.4536	1.7613	209
210	14.1357	0.01670	27.779	27.796	178.17	971.37	1149.53	0.3092	1.4505	1.7597	210
212	14.7094	0.01671	26.764	26.781	180.18	970.11	1150.29	0.3122	1.4443	1.7565	212
214	15.3023	0.01673	25.792	25.809	182.20	968.85	1151.04	0.3152	1.4382	1.7533	214
216	15.9149	0.01674	24.862	24.879	184.21	967.58	1151.79	0.3182	1.4320	1.7502	216
218	16.5475	0.01676	23.971	23.988	186.23	966.31	1152.54	0.3211	1.4259	1.7471	218
220	17.2008	0.01677	23.118	23.135	188.25	965.03	1153.28	0.3241	1.4198	1.7440	220
222	17.8753	0.01679	22.301	22.317	190.27	963.75	1154.02	0.3271	1.4138	1.7409	222
224	18.5714	0.01680	21.517	21.534	192.29	962.47	1154.76	0.3300	1.4078	1.7378	224
226	19.2896	0.01681	20.766	20.783	194.31	961.19	1155.49	0.3330	1.4018	1.7348	226
228	20.0307	0.01683	20.046	20.063	196.33	959.89	1156.22	0.3359	1.3959	1.7318	228
230	20.7949	0.01684	19.356	19.373	198.35	958.60	1156.95	0.3388	1.3899	1.7288	230
232	21.5830	0.01686	18.693	18.710	200.37	957.30	1157.68	0.3418	1.3840	1.7258	232
234	22.3955	0.01687	18.057	18.074	202.40	956.00	1158.40	0.3447	1.3782	1.7229	234
236	23.2329	0.01689	17.447	17.464	204.42	954.69	1159.11	0.3476	1.3723	1.7199	236
238	24.0958	0.01691	16.861	16.878	206.45	953.38	1159.83	0.3505	1.3665	1.7170	238
240	24.9849	0.01692	16.299	16.316	208.47	952.06	1160.54	0.3534	1.3607	1.7141	240
242	25.9006	0.01694	15.758	15.775	210.50	950.74	1161.24	0.3563	1.3550	1.7113	242
244	26.8436	0.01695	15.239	15.256	212.53	949.42	1161.95	0.3592	1.3492	1.7084	244
246	27.8145	0.01697	14.740	14.757	214.56	948.09	1162.65	0.3620	1.3435	1.7056	246
248	28.8140	0.01698	14.260	14.277	216.59	946.75	1163.34	0.3649	1.3378	1.7028	248
250	29.8426	0.01700	13.799	13.816	218.62	945.41	1164.03	0.3678	1.3322	1.7000	250
252	30.9009	0.01702	13.356	13.373	220.65	944.07	1164.72	0.3706	1.3266	1.6972	252
254	31.9897	0.01703	12.929	12.946	222.68	942.72	1165.41	0.3735	1.3209	1.6944	254
256	33.1095	0.01705	12.518	12.535	224.72	941.37	1166.09	0.3763	1.3154	1.6917	256
258	34.2611	0.01707	12.123	12.140	226.75	940.01	1166.76	0.3792	1.3098	1.6890	258
260	35.4450	0.01708	11.743	11.760	228.79	938.65	1167.44	0.3820	1.3043	1.6862	260
262	36.6620	0.01710	11.377	11.394	230.83	937.28	1168.10	0.3848	1.2988	1.6836	262
264	37.9127	0.01712	11.024	11.041	232.87	935.90	1168.77	0.3876	1.2933	1.6809	264
266	39.1978	0.01714	10.685	10.702	234.90	934.52	1169.43	0.3904	1.2878	1.6782	266
268	40.5181	0.01715	10.357	10.374	236.94	933.14	1170.08	0.3932	1.2824	1.6756	268
270	41.8742	0.01717	10.042	10.059	238.99	931.75	1170.73	0.3960	1.2769	1.6730	270
272	43.2669	0.01719	9.738	9.755	241.03	930.35	1171.38	0.3988	1.2715	1.6704	272
274	44.6968	0.01721	9.445	9.462	243.07	928.95	1172.02	0.4016	1.2662	1.6678	274
276	46.1647	0.01722	9.162	9.180	245.12	927.54	1172.66	0.4044	1.2608	1.6652	276
278	47.6714	0.01724	8.890	8.907	247.16	926.13	1173.30	0.4071	1.2555	1.6626	278
280	49.2175	0.01726	8.627	8.644	249.21	924.71	1173.92	0.4099	1.2502	1.6601	280
282	50.8039	0.01728	8.373	8.390	251.26	923.29	1174.55	0.4127	1.2449	1.6575	282
284	52.4313	0.01730	8.128	8.146	253.31	921.86	1175.17	0.4154	1.2396	1.6550	284
286	54.1004	0.01731	7.892	7.909	255.36	920.42	1175.78	0.4182	1.2344	1.6525	286
288	55.8121	0.01733	7.664	7.681	257.41	918.98	1176.40	0.4209	1.2291	1.6500	288
290	57.5672	0.01735	7.444	7.461	259.47	917.53	1177.00	0.4236	1.2239	1.6476	290
292	59.3664	0.01737	7.231	7.248	261.52	916.08	1177.60	0.4264	1.2187	1.6451	292
294	61.2105	0.01739	7.025	7.043	263.58	914.62	1178.20	0.4291	1.2136	1.6427	294
296	63.1003	0.01741	6.827	6.844	265.64	913.15	1178.79	0.4318	1.2084	1.6402	296
298	65.0368	0.01743	6.635	6.652	267.70	911.68	1179.38	0.4345	1.2033	1.6378	298
300	67.0206	0.01745	6.449	6.467	269.76	910.20	1179.96	0.4372	1.1982	1.6354	300

The **water vapor saturation pressure** is required to determine a number of moist air properties, principally the saturation humidity ratio. Values may be obtained from Table 3 or calculated from the following formulas (Hyland and Wexler 1983b). The 1983 formulas are within 300 ppm of the latest IAPWS formulations. For higher accuracy, developers of software and others are referred to IAPWS (2007, 2011).

The saturation (sublimation) pressure over **ice** for the temperature range of –148 to 32°F is given by

$$\ln p_{ws} = C_1/T + C_2 + C_3T + C_4T^2 + C_5T^3 + C_6T^4 + C_7 \ln T \quad (5)$$

where

C_1 = –1.021 416 5 E+04
C_2 = –4.893 242 8 E+00
C_3 = –5.376 579 4 E–03
C_4 = 1.920 237 7 E–07
C_5 = 3.557 583 2 E–10
C_6 = –9.034 468 8 E–14
C_7 = 4.163 501 9 E+00

The saturation pressure over **liquid water** for the temperature range of 32 to 392°F is given by

$$\ln p_{ws} = C_8/T + C_9 + C_{10}T + C_{11}T^2 + C_{12}T^3 + C_{13} \ln T \quad (6)$$

where

C_8 = –1.044 039 7 E+04
C_9 = –1.129 465 0 E+01
C_{10} = –2.702 235 5 E–02
C_{11} = 1.289 036 0 E–05
C_{12} = –2.478 068 1 E–09
C_{13} = 6.545 967 3 E+00

In both Equations (5) and (6),

p_{ws} = saturation pressure, psia
T = absolute temperature, °R = °F + 459.67

The coefficients of Equations (5) and (6) were derived from the Hyland-Wexler equations, which are given in SI units. Because of rounding errors in the derivations and in some computers' calculating precision, results from Equations (5) and (6) may not agree precisely with Table 3 values.

The vapor pressure p_s of water in saturated moist air differs negligibly from the saturation vapor pressure p_{ws} of pure water at the same temperature. Consequently, p_s can be used in equations in place of p_{ws} with very little error:

$$p_s = x_{ws}\, p$$

where x_{ws} is the mole fraction of water vapor in saturated moist air at temperature t and pressure p, and p is the total barometric pressure of moist air.

5. HUMIDITY PARAMETERS

Basic Parameters

Humidity ratio W (or **mixing ratio**) of a given moist air sample is defined as the ratio of the mass of water vapor to the mass of dry air in the sample:

$$W = M_w/M_{da} \quad (7)$$

W equals the mole fraction ratio x_w/x_{da} multiplied by the ratio of molecular masses (18.015268/28.966 = 0.621945):

$$W = 0.621945x_w/x_{da} \quad (8)$$

Specific humidity γ is the ratio of the mass of water vapor to total mass of the moist air sample:

$$\gamma = M_w/(M_w + M_{da}) \quad (9a)$$

In terms of the humidity ratio,

$$\gamma = W/(1 + W) \quad (9b)$$

Absolute humidity (alternatively, water vapor density) d_v is the ratio of the mass of water vapor to total volume of the sample:

$$d_v = M_w/V \quad (10)$$

Density ρ of a moist air mixture is the ratio of total mass to total volume:

$$\rho = (M_{da} + M_w)/V = (1/v)(1 + W) \quad (11)$$

where v is the moist air specific volume, ft³/lb$_{da}$, as defined by Equation (24).

Humidity Parameters Involving Saturation

The following definitions of humidity parameters involve the concept of moist air saturation:

Saturation humidity ratio $W_s(t, p)$ is the humidity ratio of moist air saturated with respect to water (or ice) at the same temperature t and pressure p.

Relative humidity ϕ is the ratio of the actual water vapor partial pressure in moist air at the dew-point pressure and temperature to the reference saturation water vapor partial pressure at the dry-bulb pressure and temperature:

$$\phi = (p_{wv-enh}/p_{wvs-ref}|_{p,t}) = [f(p, t_{dp})e(t_{dp})]/[f(p, t_{db})e(t_{db})] \quad (12)$$

Note that Equations (12) and (22) have been revised so that they cover both the normal range of relative humidity where $e(t_{db}) < p$ and the extended range (e.g., atmospheric pressure drying kilns) where $e(t_{db}) \ge p$. The definitions in earlier editions applied only to the normal range.

Dew-point temperature t_d is the temperature of moist air saturated at pressure p, with the same humidity ratio W as that of the given sample of moist air. It is defined as the solution $t_d(p, W)$ of the following equation:

$$W_s(p, t_d) = W \quad (13)$$

Thermodynamic wet-bulb temperature t^* is the temperature at which water (liquid or solid), by evaporating into moist air at dry-bulb temperature t and humidity ratio W, can bring air to saturation adiabatically at the same temperature t^* while total pressure p is constant. This parameter is considered separately in the section on Thermodynamic Wet-Bulb and Dew-Point Temperature.

6. PERFECT GAS RELATIONSHIPS FOR DRY AND MOIST AIR

When moist air is considered a mixture of independent perfect gases (i.e., dry air and water vapor), each is assumed to obey the perfect gas equation of state as follows:

Dry air: $$p_{da}V = n_{da}RT \quad (14)$$

Water vapor: $$p_wV = n_wRT \quad (15)$$

where

p_{da} = partial pressure of dry air
p_w = partial pressure of water vapor
V = total mixture volume
n_{da} = number of moles of dry air
n_w = number of moles of water vapor
R = universal gas constant, 1545.349 ft·lb$_f$/lb mol·°R

T = absolute temperature, °R

The mixture also obeys the perfect gas equation:

$$pV = nRT \tag{16}$$

or

$$(p_{da} + p_w)V = (n_{da} + n_w)RT \tag{17}$$

where $p = p_{da} + p_w$ is the total mixture pressure and $n = n_{da} + n_w$ is the total number of moles in the mixture. From Equations (14) to (17), the mole fractions of dry air and water vapor are, respectively,

$$x_{da} = p_{da}/(p_{da} + p_w) = p_{da}/p \tag{18}$$

and

$$x_w = p_w/(p_{da} + p_w) = p_w/p \tag{19}$$

From Equations (8), (18), and (19), the **humidity ratio** W is

$$W = 0.621945\frac{p_w}{p - p_w} \tag{20}$$

The **saturation humidity ratio** W_s is

$$W_s = 0.621945\frac{p_{ws}}{p - p_{ws}} \tag{21}$$

The term p_{ws} represents the saturation pressure of water vapor in the absence of air at the given temperature t. This pressure p_{ws} is a function only of temperature and differs slightly from the vapor pressure of water in saturated moist air.

The **relative humidity** ϕ is defined in Equation (12). Using the second equality and eliminating the enhancement factors, which are not applicable using the perfect gas assumption, gives

$$\phi = e(t_{dp})/e(t_{db}) \tag{22}$$

Substituting Equation (21) for W_s into Equation (13),

$$\phi = \frac{\mu}{1 - (1 - \mu)(p_{ws}/p)} \tag{23}$$

Both ϕ and μ are zero for dry air and unity for saturated moist air. At intermediate states, their values differ, substantially at higher temperatures.

The **specific volume** v of a moist air mixture is expressed in terms of a unit mass of dry air:

$$v = V/M_{da} = V/(28.966n_{da}) \tag{24}$$

where V is the total volume of the mixture, M_{da} is the total mass of dry air, and n_{da} is the number of moles of dry air. By Equations (14) and (24), with the relation $p = p_{da} + p_w$,

$$v = \frac{RT}{28.966(p - p_w)} = \frac{R_{da}T}{p - p_w} \tag{25}$$

Using Equation (18),

$$v = \frac{RT(1 + 1.607858W)}{28.966p} = \frac{R_{da}T(1 + 1.607858W)}{p} \tag{26}$$

In Equations (25) and (26), v is specific volume, T is absolute temperature, p is total pressure, p_w is partial pressure of water vapor, and W is humidity ratio.

In specific units, Equation (26) may be expressed as

$$v = 0.370486(t + 459.67)(1 + 1.607858W)/p$$

where

v = specific volume, ft^3/lb_{da}
t = dry-bulb temperature, °F
W = humidity ratio, lb_w/lb_{da}
p = total pressure, psia

The **enthalpy** of a mixture of perfect gases equals the sum of the individual partial enthalpies of the components. Therefore, the specific enthalpy of moist air can be written as follows:

$$h = h_{da} + Wh_g \tag{27}$$

where h_{da} is the specific enthalpy for dry air in Btu/lb_{da} and h_g is the specific enthalpy for saturated water vapor in Btu/lb_w at the mixture's temperature. As an approximation,

$$h_{da} \approx 0.240t \tag{28}$$

$$h_g \approx 1061 + 0.444t \tag{29}$$

where t is the dry-bulb temperature in °F. The moist air specific enthalpy in Btu/lb_{da} then becomes

$$h = 0.240t + W(1061 + 0.444t) \tag{30}$$

7. THERMODYNAMIC WET-BULB AND DEW-POINT TEMPERATURE

For any state of moist air, a temperature t^* exists at which liquid (or solid) water evaporates into the air to bring it to saturation at exactly this same temperature and total pressure (Harrison 1965). During adiabatic saturation, saturated air is expelled at a temperature equal to that of the injected water. In this constant-pressure process,

- Humidity ratio increases from initial value W to W_s^*, corresponding to saturation at temperature t^*
- Enthalpy increases from initial value h to h_s^*, corresponding to saturation at temperature t^*
- Mass of water added per unit mass of dry air is $(W_s^* - W)$, which adds energy to the moist air of amount $(W_s^* - W)h_w^*$, where h_w^* denotes specific enthalpy in Btu/lb_w of water added at temperature t^*

Therefore, if the process is strictly adiabatic, conservation of enthalpy at constant total pressure requires that

$$h + (W_s^* - W)h_w^* = h_s^* \tag{31}$$

W_s^*, h_w^*, and h_s^* are functions only of temperature t^* for a fixed value of pressure. The value of t^* that satisfies Equation (31) for given values of h, W, and p is the **thermodynamic wet-bulb temperature**.

A **psychrometer** consists of two thermometers; one thermometer's bulb is covered by a wick that has been thoroughly wetted with water. When the wet bulb is placed in an airstream, water evaporates from the wick, eventually reaching an equilibrium temperature called the **wet-bulb temperature**. This process is not one of adiabatic saturation, which defines the thermodynamic wet-bulb temperature, but one of simultaneous heat and mass transfer from the wet bulb. The fundamental mechanism of this process is described by the Lewis relation [Equation (40) in Chapter 6]. Fortunately, only small corrections must be applied to wet-bulb thermometer readings to obtain the thermodynamic wet-bulb temperature.

As defined, thermodynamic wet-bulb temperature is a unique property of a given moist air sample independent of measurement techniques.

Equation (31) is exact because it defines the thermodynamic wet-bulb temperature t^*. Substituting the approximate perfect gas relation

[Equation (30)] for h, the corresponding expression for h_s^*, and the approximate relation for saturated liquid water

$$h_w^* \approx t^* - 32 \quad (32)$$

into Equation (31), and solving for the humidity ratio,

$$W = \frac{(1093 - 0.556t^*)W_s^* - 0.240(t - t^*)}{1093 + 0.444t - t^*} \quad (33)$$

where t and t^* are in °F. Below freezing, the corresponding equations are

$$h_w^* \approx -143.35 - 0.48(32 - t^*) \quad (34)$$

$$W = \frac{(1220 - 0.04t^*)W_s^* - 0.240(t - t^*)}{1220 + 0.444t - 0.48t^*} \quad (35)$$

A wet/ice-bulb thermometer is imprecise when determining moisture content at 32°F.

The **dew-point temperature t_d** of moist air with humidity ratio W and pressure p was defined as the solution $t_d(p, W)$ of $W_s(p, t_d)$. For perfect gases, this reduces to

$$p_{ws}(t_d) = p_w = (pW)/(0.621945 + W) \quad (36)$$

where p_w is the water vapor partial pressure for the moist air sample and $p_{ws}(t_d)$ is the saturation vapor pressure at temperature t_d. The saturation vapor pressure is obtained from Table 3 or by using Equation (5) or (6). Alternatively, the dew-point temperature can be calculated directly by one of the following equations (Peppers 1988):

Between dew points of 32 to 200°F,

$$t_d = C_{14} + C_{15}\alpha + C_{16}\alpha^2 + C_{17}\alpha^3 + C_{18}(p_w)^{0.1984} \quad (37)$$

Below 32°F,

$$t_d = 90.12 + 26.142\alpha + 0.8927\alpha^2 \quad (38)$$

where

t_d = dew-point temperature, °F
α = ln p_w
p_w = water vapor partial pressure, psia
C_{14} = 100.45
C_{15} = 33.193
C_{16} = 2.319
C_{17} = 0.17074
C_{18} = 1.2063

8. NUMERICAL CALCULATION OF MOIST AIR PROPERTIES

The following are outlines, citing equations and tables already presented, for calculating moist air properties using perfect gas relations. These relations are accurate enough for most engineering calculations in air-conditioning practice, and are readily adapted to either hand or computer calculating methods. For more details, refer to Tables 15 through 18 in Chapter 1 of Olivieri (1996). Graphical procedures are discussed in the section on Psychrometric Charts.

SITUATION 1.

Given: Dry-bulb temperature t, Wet-bulb temperature t^*, Pressure p

To Obtain	Use	Comments
$p_{ws}(t^*)$	Table 3 or Equation (5) or (6)	Sat. press. for temp. t^*
W_s^*	Equation (21)	Using $p_{ws}(t^*)$
W	Equation (33) or (35)	
$p_{ws}(t)$	Table 3 or Equation (5) or (6)	Sat. press. for temp. t
W_s	Equation (21)	Using $p_{ws}(t)$
ϕ	Equation (23)	Using $p_{ws}(t)$
v	Equation (26)	
h	Equation (30)	
p_w	Equation (36)	
t_d	Table 3 with Equation (36), (37), or (38)	

SITUATION 2.

Given: Dry-bulb temperature t, Dew-point temperature t_d, Pressure p

To Obtain	Use	Comments
$p_w = p_{ws}(t_d)$	Table 3 or Equation (5) or (6)	Sat. press. for temp. t_d
W	Equation (20)	
$p_{ws}(t)$	Table 3 or Equation (5) or (6)	Sat. press. for temp. t
W_s	Equation (21)	Using $p_{ws}(t)$
ϕ	Equation (23)	Using $p_{ws}(t)$
v	Equation (26)	
h	Equation (30)	
t^*	Equation (21) and (33) or (35) with Table 3 or with Equation (5) or (6)	Requires trial-and-error or numerical solution method

SITUATION 3.

Given: Dry-bulb temperature t, Relative humidity ϕ, Pressure p

To Obtain	Use	Comments
$p_{ws}(t)$	Table 3 or Equation (5) or (6)	Sat. press. for temp. t
p_w	Equation (22)	
W	Equation (20)	
W_s	Equation (21)	Using $p_{ws}(t)$
v	Equation (26)	
h	Equation (30)	
t_d	Table 3 with Equation (36), (37), or (38)	
t^*	Equation (21) and (33) or (35) with Table 3 or with Equation (5) or (6)	Requires trial-and-error or numerical solution method

Moist Air Property Tables for Standard Pressure

Table 2 shows thermodynamic properties for standard atmospheric pressure at temperatures from –80 to 200°F calculated using the ASHRAE RP-1485 (Herrmann et al. 2009) research project numerical model. Properties of intermediate moist air states can be calculated using the degree of saturation μ:

$$\text{Volume} \quad v = v_{da} + \mu v_{as} \quad (39)$$

$$\text{Enthalpy} \quad h = h_{da} + \mu h_{as} \quad (40)$$

These equations are accurate to about 662°F. At higher temperatures, errors can be significant.

9. PSYCHROMETRIC CHARTS

A psychrometric chart graphically represents the thermodynamic properties of moist air.

The choice of coordinates for a psychrometric chart is arbitrary. A chart with coordinates of enthalpy and humidity ratio provides convenient graphical solutions of many moist air problems with a minimum of thermodynamic approximations. ASHRAE developed five such psychrometric charts. Chart 1 is shown as Figure 1; the others may be obtained through ASHRAE.

Charts 1, 2, and 3 are for sea-level pressure, Chart 4 is for 5000 ft altitude (24.89 in. Hg), and Chart 5 is for 7500 ft altitude (22.65 in. Hg). All charts use oblique-angle coordinates of enthalpy and humidity ratio, and are consistent with the data of Table 2 and the properties computation methods of Hyland and Wexler (1983a) and ASHRAE research project RP-1485. Palmatier (1963) describes the geometry of chart construction applying specifically to Charts 1 and 4.

The dry-bulb temperature ranges covered by the charts are

Charts 1, 4, 5	Normal temperature	32 to 120°F
Chart 2	Low temperature	–40 to 50°F
Chart 3	High temperature	60 to 250°F

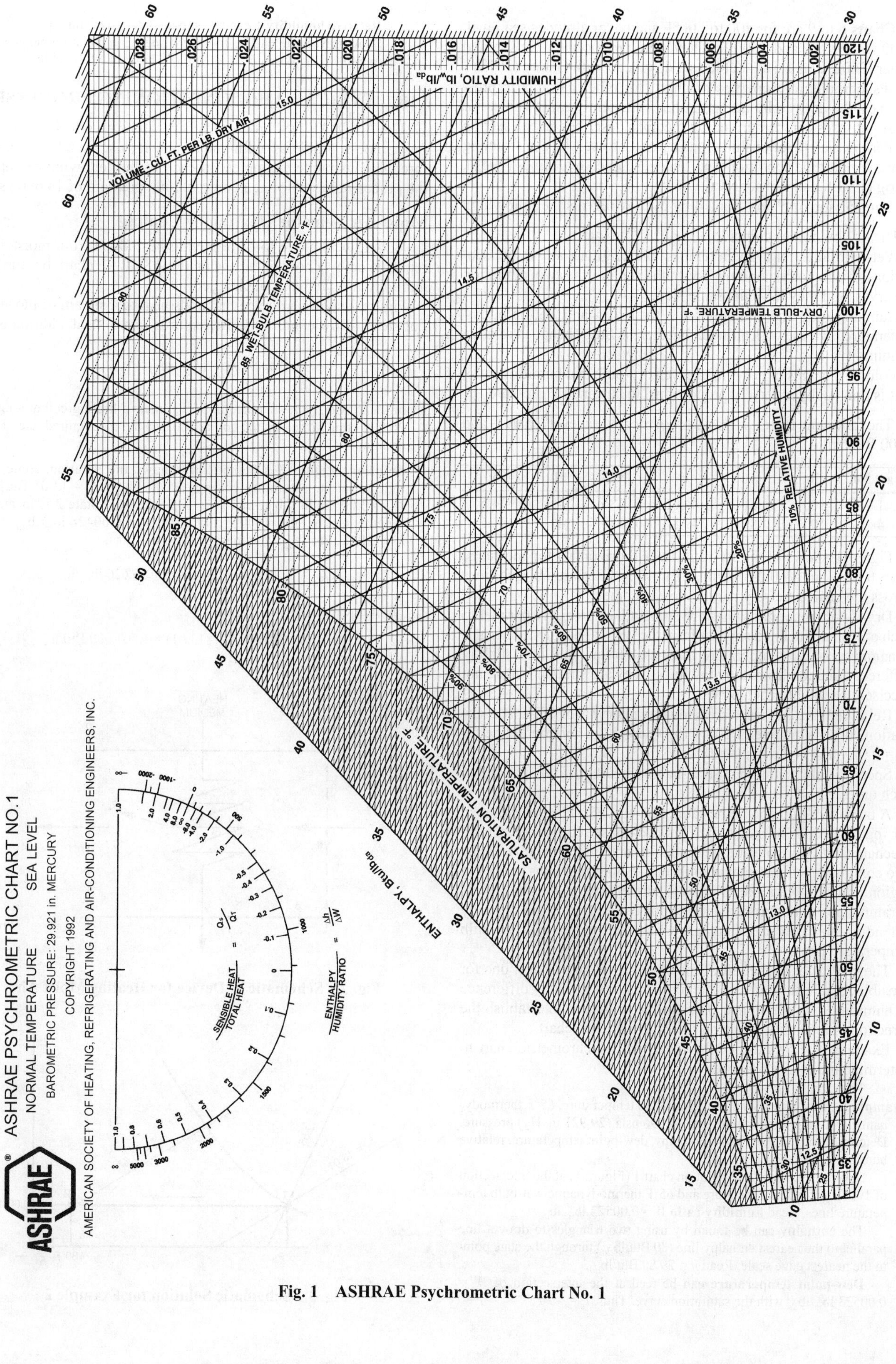

Fig. 1 ASHRAE Psychrometric Chart No. 1

Charts 6 to 9 are for 400 to 600°F and cover altitudes sea level, 2500 ft, 5000 ft, and 7500 ft. They were produced by Nelson and Sauer (2002) and are available as a download with Gatley (2013).

Psychrometric properties or charts for other barometric pressures can be derived by interpolation. Sufficiently exact values for most purposes can be derived by methods described in the section on Perfect Gas Relationships for Dry and Moist Air. Constructing charts for altitude conditions has been discussed by Haines (1961), Karig (1946), and Rohsenow (1946).

Comparison of charts 1 and 4 by overlay reveals the following:

- The dry-bulb lines coincide.
- Wet-bulb lines for a given temperature originate at the intersections of the corresponding dry-bulb line and the two saturation curves, and they have the same slope.
- Humidity ratio and enthalpy for a given dry- and wet-bulb temperature increase with altitude, but there is little change in relative humidity.
- Volume changes rapidly; for a given dry-bulb and humidity ratio, it is practically inversely proportional to barometric pressure.

The following table compares properties at sea level (chart 1) and 5000 ft (chart 4):

Chart No.	db	wb	h	W	rh	v
1	100	81	44.6	0.0186	45	14.5
4	100	81	49.8	0.0234	46	17.6

Figure 1 shows humidity ratio lines (horizontal) for the range from 0 (dry air) to 0.03 lb_w/lb_{da}. Enthalpy lines are oblique lines across the chart precisely parallel to each other.

Dry-bulb temperature lines are straight, not precisely parallel to each other, and inclined slightly from the vertical position. Thermodynamic wet-bulb temperature lines are oblique and in a slightly different direction from enthalpy lines. They are straight but are not precisely parallel to each other.

Relative humidity lines are shown in intervals of 10%. The saturation curve is the line of 100% rh, whereas the horizontal line for $W = 0$ (dry air) is the line for 0% rh.

Specific volume lines are straight but are not precisely parallel to each other.

A narrow region above the saturation curve has been developed for fog conditions of moist air. This two-phase region represents a mechanical mixture of saturated moist air and liquid water, with the two components in thermal equilibrium. Isothermal lines in the fog region coincide with extensions of thermodynamic wet-bulb temperature lines. If required, the fog region can be further expanded by extending humidity ratio, enthalpy, and thermodynamic wet-bulb temperature lines.

The protractor to the left of the chart shows two scales: one for sensible/total heat ratio, and one for the ratio of enthalpy difference to humidity ratio difference. The protractor is used to establish the direction of a condition line on the psychrometric chart.

Example 1 shows use of the ASHRAE psychrometric chart to determine moist air properties.

Example 1. Moist air exists at 100°Fdry-bulb temperature, 65°F thermodynamic wet-bulb temperature, and 14.696 psia (29.921 in. Hg) pressure. Determine the humidity ratio, enthalpy, dew-point temperature, relative humidity, and specific volume.

Solution: Locate state point on chart 1 (Figure 1) at the intersection of 100°F dry-bulb temperature and 65°F thermodynamic wet-bulb temperature lines. Read **humidity ratio** $W = 0.00523$ lb_w/lb_{da}.

The **enthalpy** can be found by using two triangles to draw a line parallel to the nearest enthalpy line (30 Btu/lb_{da}) through the state point to the nearest edge scale. Read $h = 29.80$ Btu/lb_{da}.

Dew-point temperature can be read at the intersection of $W =$ 0.00523 lb_w/lb_{da} with the saturation curve. Thus, $t_d = 40$°F.

Relative humidity ϕ can be estimated directly. Thus, $\phi = 13\%$.

Specific volume can be found by linear interpolation between the volume lines for 14.0 and 14.5 ft^3/lb_{da}. Thus, $v = 14.22$ ft^3/lb_{da}.

10. TYPICAL AIR-CONDITIONING PROCESSES

The ASHRAE psychrometric chart can be used to solve numerous process problems with moist air. Its use is best explained through illustrative examples. In each of the following examples, the process takes place at a constant total pressure of 14.696 psia.

Moist Air Sensible Heating or Cooling

Adding heat alone to or removing heat alone from moist air is represented by a horizontal line on the ASHRAE chart, because the humidity ratio remains unchanged.

Figure 2 shows a device that adds heat to a stream of moist air. For steady-flow conditions, the required rate of heat addition is

$$_1q_2 = \dot{m}_{da}(h_2 - h_1) \qquad (41)$$

Example 2. Moist air, saturated at 35°F, enters a heating coil at a rate of 20,000 cfm. Air leaves the coil at 100°F. Find the required rate of heat addition.

Solution: Figure 3 schematically shows the solution. State 1 is located on the saturation curve at 35°F. Thus, $h_1 = 13.01$ Btu/lb_{da}, $W_1 = 0.00428$ lb_w/lb_{da}, and $v_1 = 12.55$ ft^3/lb_{da}. State 2 is located at the intersection of $t = 100$°F and $W_2 = W_1 = 0.00428$ lb_w/lb_{da}. Thus, $h_2 = 28.77$ Btu/lb_{da}. The mass flow of dry air is

$$\dot{m}_{da} = (20{,}000 \times 60)/12.55 = 95{,}620\ lb_{da}/h$$

From Equation (41),

$$_1q_2 = (95{,}620)(28.77 - 13.01) = 1{,}507{,}000\ Btu/h$$

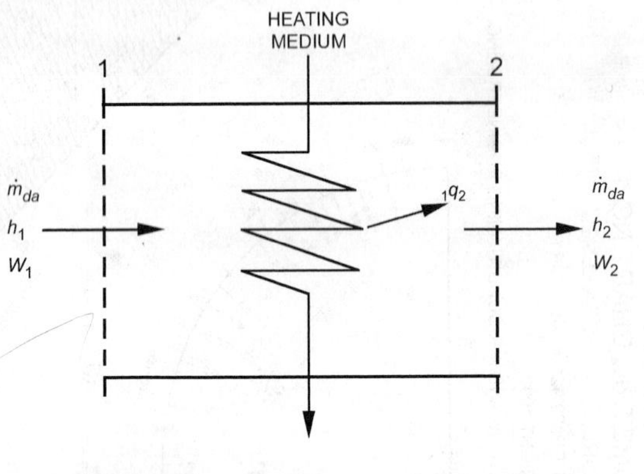

Fig. 2 Schematic of Device for Heating Moist Air

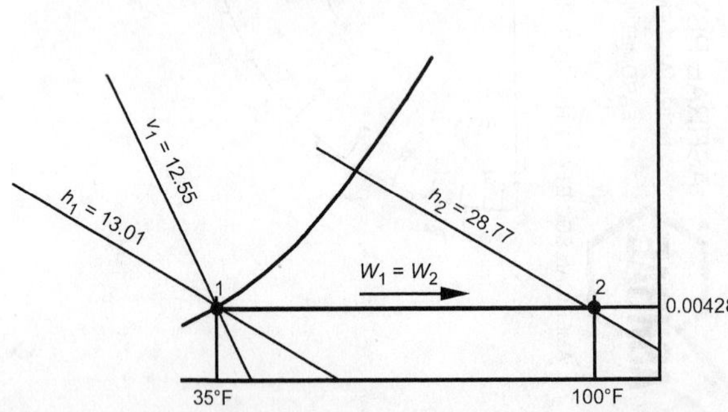

Fig. 3 Schematic Solution for Example 2

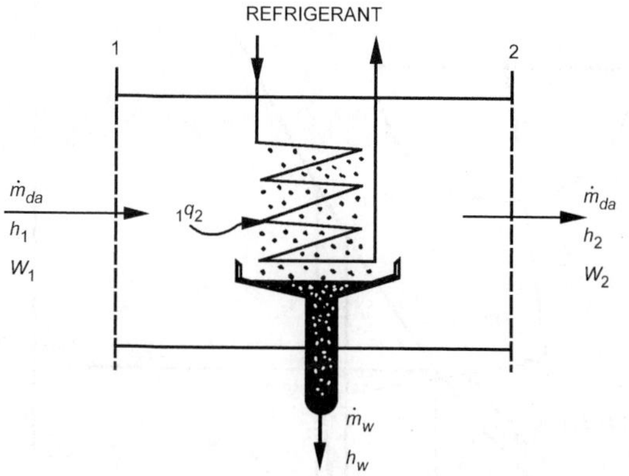

Fig. 4 Schematic of Device for Cooling Moist Air

Moist Air Cooling and Dehumidification

Moisture condensation occurs when moist air is cooled to a temperature below its initial dew point. Figure 4 shows a schematic cooling coil where moist air is assumed to be uniformly processed. Although water can be removed at various temperatures ranging from the initial dew point to the final saturation temperature, it is assumed that condensed water is cooled to the final air temperature t_2 before it drains from the system.

For the system in Figure 4, the steady-flow energy and material balance equations are

$$\dot{m}_{da}h_1 = \dot{m}_{da}h_2 + {}_1q_2 + \dot{m}_w h_{w2}$$
$$\dot{m}_{da}W_1 = \dot{m}_{da}W_2 + \dot{m}_w$$

Thus,

$$\dot{m}_w = \dot{m}_{da}(W_1 - W_2) \tag{42}$$

$$_1q_2 = \dot{m}_{da}[(h_1 - h_2) - (W_1 - W_2)h_{w2}] \tag{43}$$

Example 3. Moist air at 85°F dry-bulb temperature and 50% rh enters a cooling coil at 10,000 cfm and is processed to a final saturation condition at 50°F. Find the tons of refrigeration required.

Solution: Figure 5 shows the schematic solution. State 1 is located at the intersection of t = 85°F and ϕ = 50%. Thus, h_1 = 34.62 Btu/lb$_{da}$, W_1 = 0.01292 lb$_w$/lb$_{da}$, and v_1 = 14.01 ft³/lb$_{da}$. State 2 is located on the saturation curve at 50°F. Thus, h_2 = 20.30 Btu/lb$_{da}$ and W_2 = 0.00766 lb$_w$/lb$_{da}$. From Table 3, h_{w2} = 18.07 Btu/lb$_w$. The mass flow of dry air is

$$\dot{m}_{da} = 10{,}000/14.01 = 713.8 \text{ lb}_{da}/\text{min}$$

From Equation (43),

$$_1q_2 = 713.8[(34.62 - 20.30) - (0.01292 - 0.00788)(18.07)]$$
$$= 10{,}154 \text{ Btu/min, or } 50.77 \text{ tons of refrigeration}$$

Adiabatic Mixing of Two Moist Airstreams

A common process in air-conditioning systems is the adiabatic mixing of two moist airstreams. Figure 6 schematically shows the problem. Adiabatic mixing is governed by three equations:

$$\dot{m}_{da1}h_1 + \dot{m}_{da2}h_2 = \dot{m}_{da3}h_3$$
$$\dot{m}_{da1} + \dot{m}_{da2} = \dot{m}_{da3}$$
$$\dot{m}_{da1}W_1 + \dot{m}_{da2}W_2 = \dot{m}_{da3}W_3$$

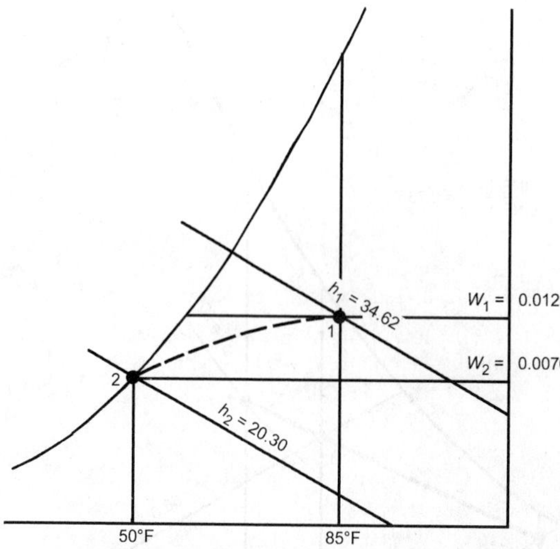

Fig. 5 Schematic Solution for Example 3

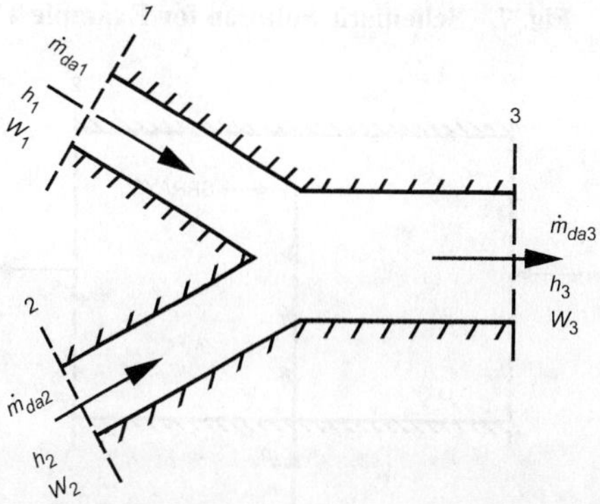

Fig. 6 Adiabatic Mixing of Two Moist Airstreams

Eliminating $\dot{m}_{da3}$ gives

$$\frac{h_2 - h_3}{h_3 - h_1} = \frac{W_2 - W_3}{W_3 - W_1} = \frac{\dot{m}_{da1}}{\dot{m}_{da2}} \tag{44}$$

according to which, on the ASHRAE chart, the state point of the resulting mixture lies on the straight line connecting the state points of the two streams being mixed, and divides the line into two segments, in the same ratio as the masses of dry air in the two streams.

Example 4. A stream of 5000 cfm of outdoor air at 40°F dry-bulb temperature and 35°F thermodynamic wet-bulb temperature is adiabatically mixed with 15,000 cfm of recirculated air at 75°F dry-bulb temperature and 50% rh. Find the dry-bulb temperature and thermodynamic wet-bulb temperature of the resulting mixture.

Solution: Figure 7 shows the schematic solution. States 1 and 2 are located on the ASHRAE chart: v_1 = 12.65 ft³/lb$_{da}$, and v_2 = 13.68 ft³/lb$_{da}$. Therefore,

$$\dot{m}_{da1} = 5000/12.65 = 395 \text{ lb}_{da}/\text{min}$$

$$\dot{m}_{da2} = 15{,}000/13.68 = 1096 \text{ lb}_{da}/\text{min}$$

According to Equation (44),

$$\frac{\text{Line 3–2}}{\text{Line 1–3}} = \frac{\dot{m}_{da1}}{\dot{m}_{da2}} \text{ or } \frac{\text{Line 1–3}}{\text{Line 1–2}} = \frac{\dot{m}_{da2}}{\dot{m}_{da3}} = \frac{1096}{1491} = 0.735$$

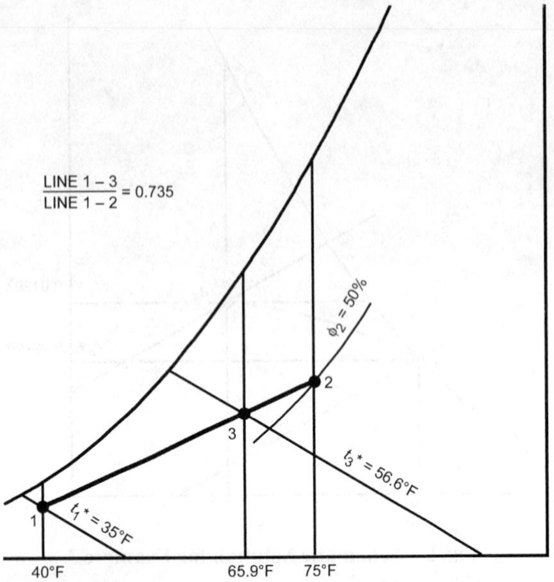

Fig. 7 Schematic Solution for Example 4

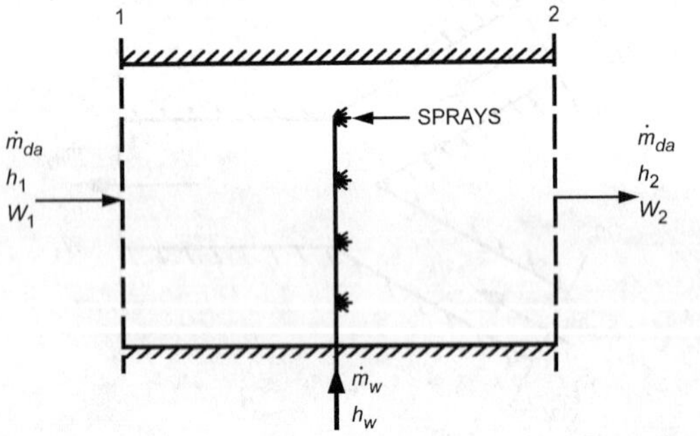

Fig. 8 Schematic Showing Injection of Water into Moist Air

Consequently, the length of line segment 1-3 is 0.735 times the length of entire line 1-2. Using a ruler, state 3 is located, and the values t_3 = 65.9°F and t_3^* = 56.6°F found.

Adiabatic Mixing of Water Injected into Moist Air

Steam or liquid water can be injected into a moist airstream to raise its humidity, as shown in Figure 8. If mixing is adiabatic, the following equations apply:

$$\dot{m}_{da} h_1 + \dot{m}_w h_w = \dot{m}_{da} h_2$$

$$\dot{m}_{da} W_1 + \dot{m}_w = \dot{m}_{da} W_2$$

Therefore,

$$\frac{h_2 - h_1}{W_2 - W_1} = \frac{\Delta h}{\Delta W} = h_w \qquad (45)$$

according to which, on the ASHRAE chart, the final state point of the moist air lies on a straight line in the direction fixed by the specific enthalpy of the injected water, drawn through the initial state point of the moist air.

Example 5. Moist air at 70°F dry-bulb and 45°F thermodynamic wet-bulb temperature is to be processed to a final dew-point temperature of 55°F by adiabatic injection of saturated steam at 230°F. The rate of dry airflow $\dot{m}_{da}$ is 200 lb_{da}/min. Find the final dry-bulb temperature of the moist air and the rate of steam flow required.

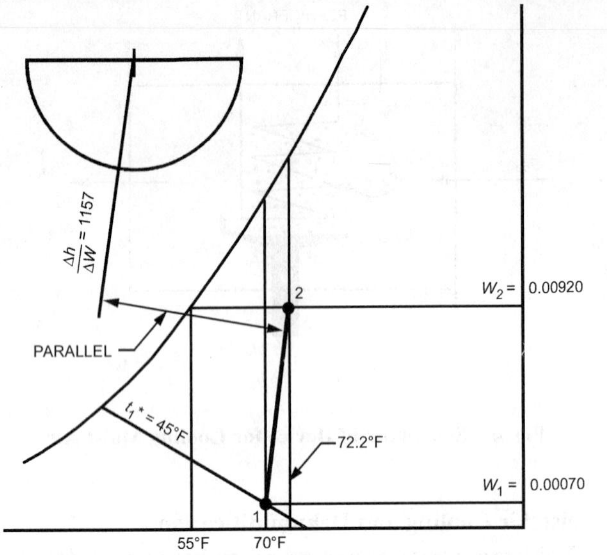

Fig. 9 Schematic Solution for Example 5

Solution: Figure 9 shows the schematic solution. By Table 3, the enthalpy of the steam h_g = 1157 Btu/lb_w. Therefore, according to Equation (45), the condition line on the ASHRAE chart connecting states 1 and 2 must have a direction:

$$\Delta h/\Delta W = 1157 \text{ Btu/lb}_w$$

The condition line can be drawn with the $\Delta h/\Delta W$ protractor. First, establish the reference line on the protractor by connecting the origin with the value $\Delta h/\Delta W$ = 1157 Btu/lb_w. Draw a second line parallel to the reference line and through the initial state point of the moist air. This second line is the condition line. State 2 is established at the intersection of the condition line with the horizontal line extended from the saturation curve at 55°F (t_{d2} = 55°F). Thus, t_2 = 72.2°F.

Values of W_2 and W_1 can be read from the chart. The required steam flow is

$$\dot{m}_w = \dot{m}_{da}(W_2 - W_1) = (200)(60)(0.00920 - 0.00070)$$
$$= 102 \text{ lb}_{steam}/\text{h}$$

Space Heat Absorption and Moist Air Moisture Gains

Air conditioning required for a space is usually determined by (1) the quantity of moist air to be supplied, and (2) the supply air condition necessary to remove given amounts of energy and water from the space at the exhaust condition specified.

Figure 10 shows a space with incident rates of energy and moisture gains. The quantity q_s denotes the net sum of all rates of heat gain in the space, arising from transfers through boundaries and from sources within the space. This heat gain involves energy addition alone and does not include energy contributions from water (or water vapor) addition. It is usually called the **sensible heat gain**. The quantity $\Sigma\dot{m}_w$ denotes the net sum of all rates of moisture gain on the space arising from transfers through boundaries and from sources within the space. Each pound of water vapor added to the space adds an amount of energy equal to its specific enthalpy.

Assuming steady-state conditions, governing equations are

$$\dot{m}_{da} h_1 + q_s + \sum(\dot{m}_w h_w) = \dot{m}_{da} h_2$$

$$\dot{m}_{da} W_1 + \sum\dot{m}_w = \dot{m}_{da} W_2$$

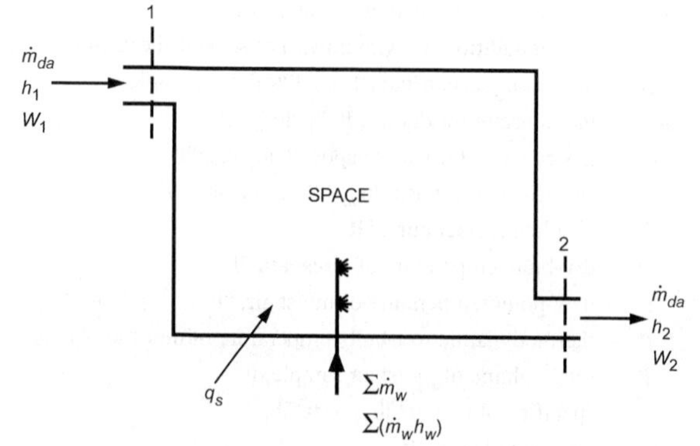

Fig. 10 Schematic of Air Conditioned Space

or

$$q_s + \sum(\dot{m}_w h_w) = \dot{m}_{da}(h_2 - h_1) \tag{46}$$

$$\sum \dot{m}_w = \dot{m}_{da}(W_2 - W_1) \tag{47}$$

The left side of Equation (46) represents the total rate of energy addition to the space from all sources. By Equations (46) and (47),

$$\frac{h_2 - h_1}{W_2 - W_1} = \frac{\Delta h}{\Delta W} = \frac{q_s + \sum(\dot{m}_w h_w)}{\sum \dot{m}_w} \tag{48}$$

according to which, on the ASHRAE chart and for a given state of withdrawn air, all possible states (conditions) for supply air must lie on a straight line drawn through the state point of withdrawn air, with its direction specified by the numerical value of $[q_s + \Sigma(\dot{m}_w h_w)]/\Sigma\dot{m}_w$. This line is the condition line for the given problem.

Example 6. Moist air is withdrawn from a room at 80°F dry-bulb temperature and 66°F thermodynamic wet-bulb temperature. The sensible rate of heat gain for the space is 30,000 Btu/h. A rate of moisture gain of 10 lb_w/h occurs from the space occupants. This moisture is assumed as saturated water vapor at 90°F. Moist air is introduced into the room at a dry-bulb temperature of 60°F. Find the required thermodynamic wet-bulb temperature and volume flow rate of the supply air.

Solution: Figure 11 shows the schematic solution. State 2 is located on the ASHRAE chart. From Table 3, the specific enthalpy of the added water vapor is h_g = 1100.43 Btu/lb_w. From Equation (48),

$$\frac{\Delta h}{\Delta W} = \frac{30{,}000 + (10)(1100.43)}{10} = 4100 \text{ Btu/lb}_w$$

With the $\Delta h/\Delta W$ protractor, establish a reference line of direction $\Delta h/\Delta W$ = 4100 Btu/lb_w. Parallel to this reference line, draw a straight line on the chart through state 2. The intersection of this line with the 60°F dry-bulb temperature line is state 1. Thus, t_1^* = 56.4°F.

An alternative (and approximately correct) procedure in establishing the condition line is to use the protractor's sensible/total heat ratio scale instead of the $\Delta h/\Delta W$ scale. The quantity $\Delta H_s/\Delta H_t$ is the ratio of rate of sensible heat gain for the space to rate of total energy gain for the space. Therefore,

$$\frac{\Delta H_s}{\Delta H_t} = \frac{q_s}{q_s + \Sigma(\dot{m}_w h_w)} = \frac{30{,}000}{30{,}000 + (10 \times 1100.43)} = 0.732$$

Note that $\Delta H_s/\Delta H_t$ = 0.732 on the protractor coincides closely with $\Delta h/\Delta W$ = 4100 Btu/lb_w.

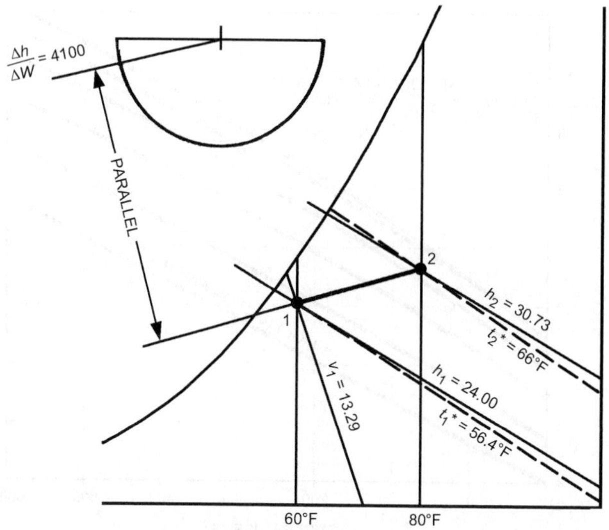

Fig. 11 Schematic Solution for Example 6

Table 4 Calculated Diffusion Coefficients for Water/Air at 14.696 psia Barometric Pressure

Temp., °F	ft²/h	Temp., °F	ft²/h	Temp., °F	ft²/h
–100	0.504	40	0.884	140	1.205
–50	0.600	50	0.915	150	1.240
–40	0.655	60	0.942	200	1.414
–30	0.682	70	0.973	250	1.600
–20	0.709	80	1.008	300	1.794
–10	0.736	90	1.042	350	1.996
0	0.767	100	1.073	400	2.205
10	0.794	110	1.104	450	2.422
20	0.825	120	1.139	500	2.647
30	0.853	130	1.170		

The flow of dry air can be calculated from either Equation (46) or (47). From Equation (46),

$$\dot{m}_{da} = \frac{q_s + \Sigma(\dot{m}_w h_w)}{h_2 - h_1} = \frac{30{,}000 + (10 \times 1100.43)}{(60)(30.73 - 24.00)}$$

$$= 101.5 \text{ lb}_{da}\text{/min}$$

At state 1, v_1 = 13.29 ft³/lb_{da}.

Therefore, supply volume = $\dot{m}_{da} v_1$ = 101.5 × 13.29 = 1349 cfm.

11. TRANSPORT PROPERTIES OF MOIST AIR

For certain scientific and experimental work, particularly in the heat transfer field, many other moist air properties are important. Generally classified as transport properties, these include diffusion coefficient, viscosity, thermal conductivity, and thermal diffusion factor. Mason and Monchick (1965) derive these properties by calculation. Table 4 and Figures 12 and 13 summarize the authors' results on the first three properties listed. Note that, within the boundaries of ASHRAE psychrometric charts 1, 2, and 3, viscosity varies little from that of dry air at normal atmospheric pressure, and thermal conductivity is essentially independent of moisture content.

12. SYMBOLS

C_1 to C_{18} = constants in Equations (5), (6), and (37)

d_v = absolute humidity of moist air, mass of water per unit volume of mixture, lb_w/ft^3

h = specific enthalpy of moist air, Btu/lb_{da}

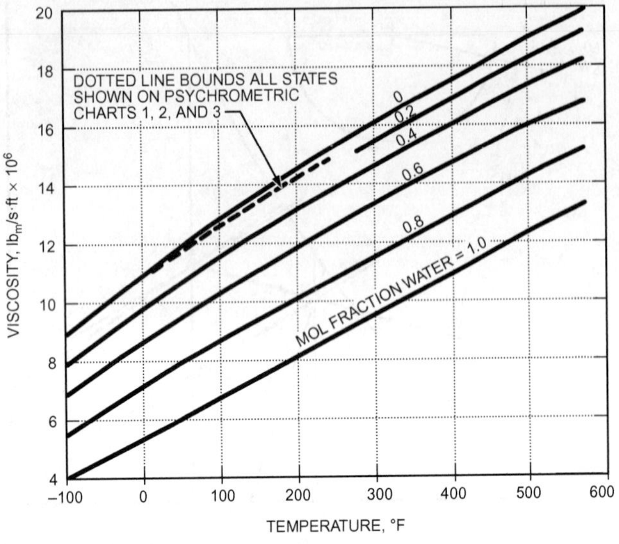

Fig. 12 Viscosity of Moist Air

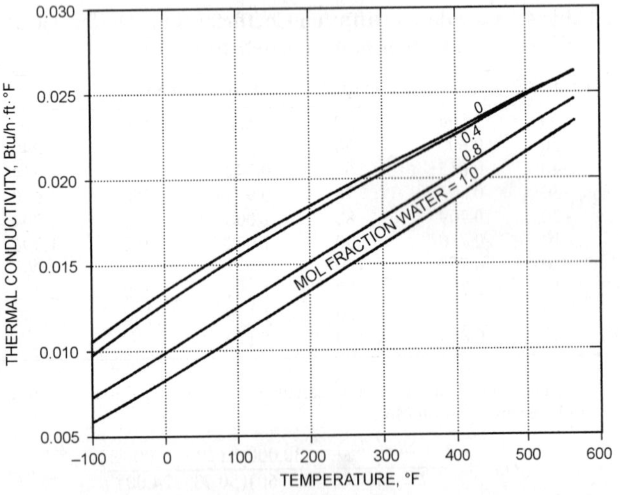

Fig. 13 Thermal Conductivity of Moist Air

H_s = rate of sensible heat gain for space, Btu/h
h_s^* = specific enthalpy of saturated moist air at thermodynamic wet-bulb temperature, Btu/lb$_{da}$
H_t = rate of total energy gain for space, Btu/h
h_w^* = specific enthalpy of condensed water (liquid or solid) at thermodynamic wet-bulb temperature and a pressure of 14.696 psia, Btu/lb$_w$
M_{da} = mass of dry air in moist air sample, lb$_{da}$
$\dot{m}_{da}$ = mass flow of dry air, per unit time, lb$_{da}$/min
M_w = mass of water vapor in moist air sample, lb$_w$
$\dot{m}_w$ = mass flow of water (any phase), per unit time, lb$_w$/min
n = $n_{da} + n_w$, total number of moles in moist air sample
n_{da} = moles of dry air
n_w = moles of water vapor
p = total pressure of moist air, psia
p_{da} = partial pressure of dry air, psia
p_s = vapor pressure of water in moist air at saturation, psia. Differs slightly from saturation pressure of pure water because of presence of air.
p_w = partial pressure of water vapor in moist air, psia
p_{ws} = pressure of saturated pure water, psia
q_s = rate of addition (or withdrawal) of sensible heat, Btu/h
R = universal gas constant, 1545.329 ft·lb$_f$/lb mole·°R
R_{da} = gas constant for dry air, ft·lb$_f$/lb$_{da}$·°R
R_w = gas constant for water vapor, ft·lb$_f$/lb$_w$·°R
s = specific entropy, Btu/lb$_{da}$·°R or Btu/lb$_w$·°R
T = absolute temperature, °R
t = dry-bulb temperature of moist air, °F
t_d = dew-point temperature of moist air, °F
t^* = thermodynamic wet-bulb temperature of moist air, °F
V = total volume of moist air sample, ft^3
v = specific volume, ft^3/lb$_{da}$ or ft^3/lb$_w$
v_T = total gas volume, ft^3
W = humidity ratio of moist air, lb$_w$/lb$_{da}$
W_s^* = humidity ratio of moist air at saturation at thermodynamic wet-bulb temperature, lb$_w$/lb$_{da}$
x_{da} = mole fraction of dry air, moles of dry air per mole of mixture
x_w = mole fraction of water, moles of water per mole of mixture
x_{ws} = mole fraction of water vapor under saturated conditions, moles of vapor per mole of saturated mixture
Z = altitude, ft

Greek

α = ln(p_w), parameter used in Equations (37) and (38)
γ = specific humidity of moist air, mass of water per unit mass of mixture
ρ = moist air density
ϕ = relative humidity, dimensionless

Subscripts

as = difference between saturated moist air and dry air
da = dry air
f = saturated liquid water
fg = difference between saturated liquid water and saturated water vapor
g = saturated water vapor
i = saturated ice
ig = difference between saturated ice and saturated water vapor
s = saturated moist air
t = total
w = water in any phase

REFERENCES

ASHRAE members can access *ASHRAE Journal* articles and ASHRAE research project final reports at technologyportal.ashrae.org. Articles and reports are also available for purchase by nonmembers in the online ASHRAE Bookstore at www.ashrae.org/bookstore.

Gatley, D.P. 2013. *Understanding psychrometrics*, 3rd ed. ASHRAE.

Gatley, D.P., S. Herrmann, and H.-J. Kretzschmar. 2008. A twenty-first century molar mass for dry air. *HVAC&R Research* (now *Science and Technology for the Built Environment*)14:655-662.

Haines, R.W. 1961. How to construct high altitude psychrometric charts. *Heating, Piping, and Air Conditioning* 33(10):144.

Harrison, L.P. 1965. Fundamental concepts and definitions relating to humidity. In *Humidity and moisture measurement and control in science and industry*, vol. 3. A. Wexler and W.A. Wildhack, eds. Reinhold, New York.

Herrmann, S., H.J. Kretzschmar, and D.P. Gatley. 2009. Thermodynamic properties of real moist air, dry air, steam, water, and ice. *HVAC&R Research* (now *Science and Technology for the Built Environment*) 15(5): 961-986.

Hyland, R.W., and A. Wexler. 1983a. Formulations for the thermodynamic properties of dry air from 173.15 K to 473.15 K, and of saturated moist air from 173.15 K to 372.15 K, at pressures to 5 MPa. *ASHRAE Transactions* 89(2A):520-535.

Hyland, R.W., and A. Wexler. 1983b. Formulations for the thermodynamic properties of the saturated phases of H_2O from 173.15 K to 473.15 K. *ASHRAE Transactions* 89(2A):500-519.

IAPWS. 2007. *Revised release on the IAPWS industrial formulation 1997 for the thermodynamic properties of water and steam.* International Association for the Properties of Water and Steam, Oakville, ON, Canada. www.iapws.org.

IAPWS. 2009. *Revised release on the equation of state 2006 for H_2O ice Ih.* International Association for the Properties of Water and Steam, Oakville, ON, Canada. www.iapws.org.

IAPWS. 2011. *Revised release on the pressure along the melting and sublimation curves of ordinary water substance.* International Association for the Properties of Water and Steam, Oakville, ON, Canada. www.iapws.org.

IAPWS. 2014. *Revised release on the IAPWS formulation 1995 for the thermodynamic properties of ordinary water substance for general and scientific use.* International Association for the Properties of Water and Steam, Oakville, ON, Canada. www.iapws.org.

Keeling, C.D., and T.P. Whorf. 2005a. *Atmospheric carbon dioxide record from Mauna Loa.* Scripps Institution of Oceanography—CO_2 Research Group. (Available at cdiac.ornl.gov/trends/co2/sio-mlo.html)

Keeling, C.D., and T.P. Whorf. 2005b. Atmospheric CO_2 records from sites in the SIO air sampling network. *Trends: A compendium of data on global change.* Carbon Dioxide Information Analysis Center, Oak Ridge National Laboratory.

Kuehn, T.H., J.W. Ramsey, and J.L. Threlkeld. 1998. *Thermal environmental engineering*, 3rd ed. Prentice-Hall, Upper Saddle River, NJ.

Mason, E.A., and L. Monchick. 1965. Survey of the equation of state and transport properties of moist gases. In *Humidity and moisture measurement and control in science and industry*, vol. 3. A. Wexler and W.A. Wildhack, eds. Reinhold, New York.

Mohr, P.J., and P.N. Taylor. 2005. CODATA recommended values of the fundamental physical constants: 2002. *Reviews of Modern Physics* 77:1-107.

NASA. 1976. U.S. Standard atmosphere, 1976. National Oceanic and Atmospheric Administration, National Aeronautics and Space Administration, and the United States Air Force. Available from National Geophysical Data Center, Boulder, CO.

Nelson, H.F., and H.J. Sauer, Jr. 2002. Formulation of high-temperature properties for moist air. *International Journal of HVAC&R Research* 8(3):311-334.

Olivieri, J. 1996. *Psychrometrics—Theory and practice.* ASHRAE.

Palmatier, E.P. 1963. Construction of the normal temperature. ASHRAE psychrometric chart. *ASHRAE Journal* 5:55.

Peppers, V.W. 1988. *A new psychrometric relation for the dewpoint temperature.* Unpublished. Available from ASHRAE.

Preston-Thomas, H. 1990. The international temperature scale of 1990 (ITS-90). *Metrologia* 27(1):3-10.

Rohsenow, W.M. 1946. Psychrometric determination of absolute humidity at elevated pressures. *Refrigerating Engineering* 51(5):423.

BIBLIOGRAPHY

Gatley, D.P. 2016. A proposed full range relative humidity definition. *ASHRAE Journal* 58(3):24-29.

Lemmon, E.W., R.T. Jacobsen, S.G. Penoncello, and D.G. Friend. 2000. Thermodynamic properties of air and mixture of nitrogen, argon, and oxygen from 60 to 2000 K at pressures to 2000 MPa. *Journal of Physical and Chemical Reference Data* 29:331-385.

NIST. 1990. Guidelines for realizing the international temperature scale of 1990 (ITS-90). NIST *Technical Note* 1265. National Institute of Technology and Standards, Gaithersburg, MD.

Wexler, A., R. Hyland, and R. Stewart. 1983. Thermodynamic properties of dry air, moist air and water and SI psychrometric charts. ASHRAE Research Projects RP-216 and RP-257, *Final Report.*

CHAPTER 2

THERMODYNAMICS AND REFRIGERATION CYCLES

THERMODYNAMICS is the study of energy, its transformations, and its relation to states of matter. This chapter covers the application of thermodynamics to refrigeration cycles. The first part reviews the first and second laws of thermodynamics and presents methods for calculating thermodynamic properties. The second and third parts address compression and absorption refrigeration cycles, two common methods of thermal energy transfer.

1. THERMODYNAMICS

A **thermodynamic system** is a region in space or a quantity of matter bounded by a closed surface. The surroundings include everything external to the system, and the system is separated from the surroundings by the system boundaries. These boundaries can be movable or fixed, real or imaginary.

Entropy and energy are important in any thermodynamic system. **Entropy** measures the molecular disorder of a system. The more mixed a system, the greater its entropy; an orderly or unmixed configuration is one of low entropy. **Energy** has the capacity for producing an effect and can be categorized into either stored or transient forms.

1.1 STORED ENERGY

Thermal (internal) energy is caused by the motion of molecules and/or intermolecular forces.

Potential energy (PE) is caused by attractive forces existing between molecules, or the elevation of the system.

$$PE = mgz \tag{1}$$

where

m = mass
g = local acceleration of gravity
z = elevation above horizontal reference plane

Kinetic energy (KE) is the energy caused by the velocity of molecules and is expressed as

$$KE = mV^2/2 \tag{2}$$

where V is the velocity of a fluid stream crossing the system boundary.

Chemical energy is caused by the arrangement of atoms composing the molecules.

Nuclear (atomic) energy derives from the cohesive forces holding protons and neutrons together as the atom's nucleus.

1.2 ENERGY IN TRANSITION

Heat Q is the mechanism that transfers energy across the boundaries of systems with differing temperatures, always toward the lower temperature. Heat is positive when energy is added to the system (see Figure 1).

Work is the mechanism that transfers energy across the boundaries of systems with differing pressures (or force of any kind), always toward the lower pressure. If the total effect produced in the system can be reduced to the raising of a weight, then nothing but work has crossed the boundary. Work is positive when energy is removed from the system (see Figure 1).

Mechanical or **shaft work W** is the energy delivered or absorbed by a mechanism, such as a turbine, air compressor, or internal combustion engine.

Flow work is energy carried into or transmitted across the system boundary because a pumping process occurs somewhere outside the system, causing fluid to enter the system. It can be more easily understood as the work done by the fluid just outside the system on the adjacent fluid entering the system to force or push it into the system. Flow work also occurs as fluid leaves the system.

$$\text{Flow work (per unit mass)} = pv \tag{3}$$

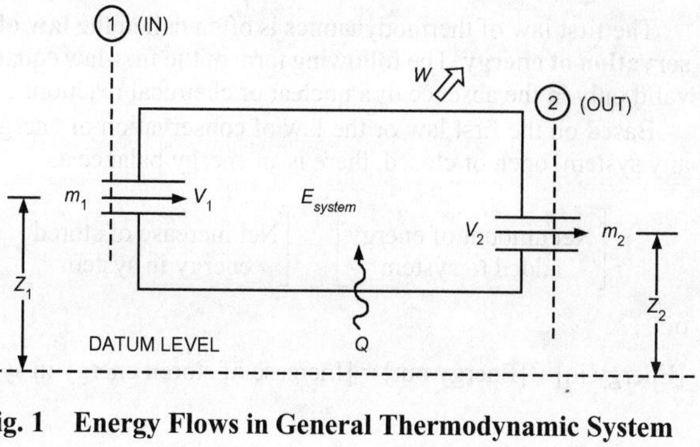

Fig. 1 Energy Flows in General Thermodynamic System

The preparation of the first and second parts of this chapter is assigned to TC 1.1, Thermodynamics and Psychrometrics. The third and fourth parts are assigned to TC 8.3, Absorption and Heat Operated Machines.

where p is pressure and v is specific volume, or the volume displaced per unit mass evaluated at the inlet or exit.

A **property** of a system is any observable characteristic of the system. The **state** of a system is defined by specifying the minimum set of independent properties. The most common thermodynamic properties are temperature T, pressure p, and specific volume v or density ρ. Additional thermodynamic properties include entropy, stored forms of energy, and enthalpy.

Frequently, thermodynamic properties combine to form other properties. **Enthalpy** h is an important property that includes internal energy and flow work and is defined as

$$h \equiv u + pv \tag{4}$$

where u is the internal energy per unit mass.

Each property in a given state has only one definite value, and any property always has the same value for a given state, regardless of how the substance arrived at that state.

A **process** is a change in state that can be defined as any change in the properties of a system. A process is described by specifying the initial and final equilibrium states, the path (if identifiable), and the interactions that take place across system boundaries during the process.

A **cycle** is a process or a series of processes wherein the initial and final states of the system are identical. Therefore, at the conclusion of a cycle, all the properties have the same value they had at the beginning. Refrigerant circulating in a closed system undergoes a cycle.

A **pure substance** has a homogeneous and invariable chemical composition. It can exist in more than one phase, but the chemical composition is the same in all phases.

If a substance is liquid at the saturation temperature and pressure, it is called a **saturated liquid**. If the temperature of the liquid is lower than the saturation temperature for the existing pressure, it is called either a **subcooled liquid** (the temperature is lower than the saturation temperature for the given pressure) or a **compressed liquid** (the pressure is greater than the saturation pressure for the given temperature).

When a substance exists as part liquid and part vapor at the saturation temperature, its **quality** is defined as the ratio of the mass of vapor to the total mass. Quality has meaning only when the substance is saturated (i.e., at saturation pressure and temperature). Pressure and temperature of saturated substances are not independent properties.

If a substance exists as a vapor at saturation temperature and pressure, it is called a **saturated vapor**. (Sometimes the term **dry saturated vapor** is used to emphasize that the quality is 100%.) When the vapor is at a temperature greater than the saturation temperature, it is a **superheated vapor**. Pressure and temperature of a superheated vapor are independent properties, because the temperature can increase while pressure remains constant. Gases such as air at room temperature and pressure are highly superheated vapors.

1.3 FIRST LAW OF THERMODYNAMICS

The first law of thermodynamics is often called the **law of conservation of energy**. The following form of the first-law equation is valid only in the absence of a nuclear or chemical reaction.

Based on the first law or the law of conservation of energy, for any system, open or closed, there is an energy balance as

$$\left[\begin{array}{c}\text{Net amount of energy}\\ \text{added to system}\end{array}\right] = \left[\begin{array}{c}\text{Net increase of stored}\\ \text{energy in system}\end{array}\right]$$

or

[Energy in] – [Energy out] = [Increase of stored energy in system]

Figure 1 illustrates energy flows into and out of a thermodynamic system. For the general case of multiple mass flows with uniform properties in and out of the system, the energy balance can be written

$$\begin{aligned}&\sum m_{in}\left(u + pv + \frac{V^2}{2} + gz\right)_{in}\\ &- \sum m_{out}\left(u + pv + \frac{V^2}{2} + gz\right)_{out} + Q - W\\ &= \left[m_f\left(u + \frac{V^2}{2} + gz\right)_f - m_i\left(u + \frac{V^2}{2} + gz\right)_i\right]_{system}\end{aligned} \tag{5}$$

where subscripts i and f refer to the initial and final states, respectively.

Nearly all important engineering processes are commonly modeled as steady-flow processes. Steady flow signifies that all quantities associated with the system do not vary with time. Consequently,

$$\sum_{\substack{\text{all streams}\\ \text{entering}}} \dot{m}\left(h + \frac{V^2}{2} + gz\right) - \sum_{\substack{\text{all streams}\\ \text{leaving}}} \dot{m}\left(h + \frac{V^2}{2} + gz\right) + \dot{Q} - \dot{W} = 0 \tag{6}$$

where $h \equiv u + pv$ as described in Equation (4).

A second common application is the closed stationary system for which the first law equation reduces to

$$Q - W = [m(u_f - u_i)]_{system} \tag{7}$$

1.4 SECOND LAW OF THERMODYNAMICS

The second law of thermodynamics differentiates and quantifies processes that only proceed in a certain direction (irreversible) from those that are reversible. The second law may be described in several ways. One method uses the concept of entropy flow in an open system and the irreversibility associated with the process. The concept of irreversibility provides added insight into the operation of cycles. For example, the larger the irreversibility in a refrigeration cycle operating with a given refrigeration load between two fixed temperature levels, the larger the amount of work required to operate the cycle. Irreversibilities include pressure drops in lines and heat exchangers, heat transfer between fluids of different temperature, and mechanical friction. Reducing total irreversibility in a cycle improves cycle performance. In the limit of no irreversibilities, a cycle attains its maximum ideal efficiency.

In an open system, the second law of thermodynamics can be described in terms of entropy as

$$dS_{system} = \frac{\delta Q}{T} + \delta m_i s_i - \delta m_e s_e + dI \tag{8}$$

where

dS_{system} = total change within system in time dt during process
$\delta m_i s_i$ = entropy increase caused by mass entering (incoming)
$\delta m_e s_e$ = entropy decrease caused by mass leaving (exiting)
$\delta Q/T$ = entropy change caused by reversible heat transfer between system and surroundings at temperature T
dI = entropy caused by irreversibilities (always positive)

Equation (8) accounts for all entropy changes in the system. Rearranged, this equation becomes

$$\delta Q = T[(\delta m_e s_e - \delta m_i s_i) + dS_{sys} - dI] \tag{9}$$

In integrated form, if inlet and outlet properties, mass flow, and interactions with the surroundings do not vary with time, the general equation for the second law is

$$(S_f - S_i)_{system} = \int_{rev} \frac{\delta Q}{T} + \sum (ms)_{in} - \sum (ms)_{out} + I \quad (10)$$

In many applications, the process can be considered to operate steadily with no change in time. The change in entropy of the system is therefore zero. The **irreversibility rate**, which is the rate of entropy production caused by irreversibilities in the process, can be determined by rearranging Equation (10):

$$\dot{I} = \sum (\dot{m}s)_{out} - \sum (\dot{m}s)_{in} - \sum \frac{\dot{Q}}{T_{surr}} \quad (11)$$

Equation (6) can be used to replace the heat transfer quantity. Note that the absolute temperature of the surroundings with which the system is exchanging heat is used in the last term. If the temperature of the surroundings is equal to the system temperature, heat is transferred reversibly and the last term in Equation (11) equals zero.

Equation (11) is commonly applied to a system with one mass flow in, the same mass flow out, no work, and negligible kinetic or potential energy flows. Combining Equations (6) and (11) yields

$$\dot{I} = \dot{m}\left[(s_{out} - s_{in}) - \frac{h_{out} - h_{in}}{T_{surr}}\right] \quad (12)$$

In a cycle, the reduction of work produced by a power cycle (or the increase in work required by a refrigeration cycle) equals the absolute ambient temperature multiplied by the sum of irreversibilities in all processes in the cycle. Thus, the difference in reversible and actual work for any refrigeration cycle, theoretical or real, operating under the same conditions, becomes

$$\dot{W}_{actual} = \dot{W}_{reversible} + T_0 \sum \dot{I} \quad (13)$$

Another second-law method to describe performance of engineering devices is the concept of **exergy** (also called the *availability, potential energy*, or *work potential*), which is the maximum useful work that could be obtained from the system at a given state in a specified environment. There is always a difference between exergy and the actual work delivered by a device; this difference represents the room for improvement. Note that exergy is a property of the system/environment combination and not of the system alone. The exergy of a system in equilibrium with its environment is zero. The state of the environment is referred to as the **dead state**, because the system cannot do any work.

Exergy transfer is in three forms (heat, work, and mass flow), and is given by

$$X_{heat} = \left(1 - \frac{T_0}{T}\right) Q$$

$$X_{work} = \begin{cases} W - W_{surr} & \text{(for boundary work)} \\ W & \text{(for other forms of work)} \end{cases}$$

$$X_{mass} = m\psi$$

where $\psi = (h - h_0) - T_0(s - s_0) + (V^2/2) + gz$ is flow exergy.

Exergy balance for any system undergoing any process can be expressed as

$$\underbrace{X_{in} - X_{out}}_{\substack{\text{Net exergy transfer by} \\ \text{heat, work, and mass}}} - \underbrace{X_{destroyed}}_{\substack{\text{Exergy} \\ \text{destruction}}} = \underbrace{\Delta X_{system}}_{\substack{\text{Change in} \\ \text{exergy}}} \quad \text{(general)}$$

$$\underbrace{\dot{X}_{in} - \dot{X}_{out}}_{\substack{\text{Rate of net exergy transfer} \\ \text{by heat, work, and mass}}} - \underbrace{\dot{X}_{destroyed}}_{\substack{\text{Rate of exergy} \\ \text{destruction}}} = \underbrace{dX_{system}/dt}_{\substack{\text{Rate of change} \\ \text{in exergy}}} \quad \text{(general, in rate form)}$$

Taking the positive direction of heat transfer as *to* the system and the positive direction of work transfer as *from* the system, the general exergy balance relations can be expressed explicitly as

$$\sum \left(1 - \frac{T_0}{T_k}\right) Q_k - [W - P_0(V_2 - V_1)] + \sum_{in} m\psi - \sum_{out} m\psi - X_{destroyed} = X_2 - X_1$$

1.5 THERMODYNAMIC ANALYSIS OF REFRIGERATION CYCLES

Refrigeration cycles transfer thermal energy from a region of low temperature T_R to one of higher temperature. Usually the higher-temperature heat sink is the ambient air or cooling water, at temperature T_0, the temperature of the surroundings.

The first and second laws of thermodynamics can be applied to individual components to determine mass and energy balances and the irreversibility of the components. This procedure is shown in later sections in this chapter.

Performance of a refrigeration cycle is usually described by a **coefficient of performance (COP)**, defined as the benefit of the cycle (amount of heat removed) divided by the required energy input to operate the cycle:

$$\text{COP} \equiv \frac{\text{Useful refrigerating effect}}{\text{Net energy supplied from external sources}} \quad (14)$$

For a mechanical vapor compression system, the net energy supplied is usually in the form of work, mechanical or electrical, and may include work to the compressor and fans or pumps. Thus,

$$\text{COP} = \frac{Q_{evap}}{W_{net}} \quad (15)$$

In an absorption refrigeration cycle, the net energy supplied is usually in the form of heat into the generator and work into the pumps and fans, or

$$\text{COP} = \frac{Q_{evap}}{Q_{gen} + W_{net}} \quad (16)$$

In many cases, work supplied to an absorption system is very small compared to the amount of heat supplied to the generator, so the work term is often neglected.

Applying the second law to an entire refrigeration cycle shows that a completely reversible cycle operating under the same conditions has the maximum possible COP. Departure of the actual cycle from an ideal reversible cycle is given by the **refrigerating efficiency**:

$$\eta_R = \frac{\text{COP}}{(\text{COP})_{rev}} \quad (17)$$

The Carnot cycle usually serves as the ideal reversible refrigeration cycle. For multistage cycles, each stage is described by a reversible cycle.

1.6 EQUATIONS OF STATE

The equation of state of a pure substance is a mathematical relation between pressure, specific volume, and temperature. When the system is in thermodynamic equilibrium,

$$f(p, v, T) = 0 \tag{18}$$

The principles of statistical mechanics are used to (1) explore the fundamental properties of matter, (2) predict an equation of state based on the statistical nature of a particular system, or (3) propose a functional form for an equation of state with unknown parameters that are determined by measuring thermodynamic properties of a substance. A fundamental equation with this basis is the **virial equation**, which is expressed as an expansion in pressure p or in reciprocal values of volume per unit mass v as

$$\frac{pv}{RT} = 1 + B'p + C'p^2 + D'p^3 + \cdots \tag{19}$$

$$\frac{pv}{RT} = 1 + (B/v) + (C/v^2) + (D/v^3) + \cdots \tag{20}$$

where coefficients B', C', D', etc., and B, C, D, etc., are the virial coefficients. B' and B are the second virial coefficients; C' and C are the third virial coefficients, etc. The virial coefficients are functions of temperature only, and values of the respective coefficients in Equations (19) and (20) are related. For example, $B' = B/RT$ and $C' = (C - B^2)/(RT)^2$.

The universal gas constant $\bar{R}$ is defined as

$$\bar{R} = \lim_{p \to 0} \frac{(p\bar{v})_T}{T} \tag{21}$$

where $(p\bar{v})_T$ is the product of the pressure and the molar specific volume along an isotherm with absolute temperature T. The current best value of $\bar{R}$ is 1545.32 ft·lb$_f$/(lb mol·°R). The gas constant R is equal to the universal gas constant $\bar{R}$ divided by the molecular weight M of the gas or gas mixture.

The quantity pv/RT is also called the **compressibility factor** Z, or

$$Z = 1 + (B/v) + (C/v^2) + (D/v^3) + \cdots \tag{22}$$

An advantage of the virial form is that statistical mechanics can be used to predict the lower-order coefficients and provide physical significance to the virial coefficients. For example, in Equation (22), the term B/v is a function of interactions between two molecules, C/v^2 between three molecules, etc. Because lower-order interactions are common, contributions of the higher-order terms are successively less. Thermodynamicists use the partition or distribution function to determine virial coefficients; however, experimental values of the second and third coefficients are preferred. For dense fluids, many higher-order terms are necessary that can neither be satisfactorily predicted from theory nor determined from experimental measurements. In general, a truncated virial expansion of four terms is valid for densities of less than one-half the value at the critical point. For higher densities, additional terms can be used and determined empirically.

Computers allow the use of very complex equations of state in calculating p-v-T values, even to high densities. The Benedict-Webb-Rubin (B-W-R) equation of state (Benedict et al. 1940) and Martin-Hou equation (1955) have had considerable use, but should generally be limited to densities less than the critical value. Strobridge (1962) suggested a modified Benedict-Webb-Rubin relation that gives excellent results at higher densities and can be used for a p-v-T surface that extends into the liquid phase.

The B-W-R equation has been used extensively for hydrocarbons (Cooper and Goldfrank 1967):

$$P = (RT/v) + (B_oRT - A_o - C_o/T^2)/v^2 + (bRT - a)/v^3 + (a\alpha)/v^6 + [c(1 + \gamma/v^2)e^{(-\gamma/v^2)}]/v^3T^2 \tag{23}$$

where the constant coefficients are A_o, B_o, C_o, a, b, c, α, and γ.

The Martin-Hou equation, developed for fluorinated hydrocarbon properties, has been used to calculate the thermodynamic property tables in Chapter 30 and in *ASHRAE Thermodynamic Properties of Refrigerants* (Stewart et al. 1986). The Martin-Hou equation is

$$p = \frac{RT}{v-b} + \frac{A_2 + B_2T + C_2e^{(-kT/T_c)}}{(v-b)^2} + \frac{A_3 + B_3T + C_3e^{(-kT/T_c)}}{(v-b)^3} + \frac{A_4 + B_4T}{(v-b)^4} + \frac{A_5 + B_5T + C_5e^{(-kT/T_c)}}{(v-b)^5} + (A_6 + B_6T)e^{av} \tag{24}$$

where the constant coefficients are A_i, B_i, C_i, k, b, and a.

Strobridge (1962) suggested an equation of state that was developed for nitrogen properties and used for most cryogenic fluids. This equation combines the B-W-R equation of state with an equation for high-density nitrogen suggested by Benedict (1937). These equations have been used successfully for liquid and vapor phases, extending in the liquid phase to the triple-point temperature and the freezing line, and in the vapor phase from 18 to 1800°R, with pressures to 150,000 psi. The Strobridge equation is accurate within the uncertainty of the measured p-v-T data:

$$p = RT\rho + \left[Rn_1T + n_2 + \frac{n_3}{T} + \frac{n_4}{T^2} + \frac{n_5}{T^4}\right]\rho^2 + (Rn_6T + n_7)\rho^3 + n_8T\rho^4 + \rho^3\left[\frac{n_9}{T^2} + \frac{n_{10}}{T^3} + \frac{n_{11}}{T^4}\right]\exp(-n_{16}\rho^2) + \rho^5\left[\frac{n_{12}}{T^2} + \frac{n_{13}}{T^3} + \frac{n_{14}}{T^4}\right]\exp(-n_{16}\rho^2) + n_{15}\rho^6 \tag{25}$$

The 15 coefficients of this equation's linear terms are determined by a least-square fit to experimental data. Hust and McCarty (1967) and Hust and Stewart (1966) give further information on methods and techniques for determining equations of state.

In the absence of experimental data, van der Waals' principle of corresponding states can predict fluid properties. This principle relates properties of similar substances by suitable reducing factors (i.e., the p-v-T surfaces of similar fluids in a given region are assumed to be of similar shape). The critical point can be used to define reducing parameters to scale the surface of one fluid to the dimensions of another. Modifications of this principle, as suggested by Kamerlingh Onnes, a Dutch cryogenic researcher, have been used to improve correspondence at low pressures. The principle of corresponding states provides useful approximations, and numerous modifications have been reported. More complex treatments for predicting properties, which recognize similarity of fluid properties, are by generalized equations of state. These equations ordinarily allow adjustment of the p-v-T surface by introducing parameters. One example (Hirschfelder et al. 1958) allows for departures from the principle of corresponding states by adding two correlating parameters.

1.7 CALCULATING THERMODYNAMIC PROPERTIES

Although equations of state provide p-v-T relations, thermodynamic analysis usually requires values for internal energy, enthalpy, and entropy. These properties have been tabulated for many substances, including refrigerants (see Chapters 1, 30, and 33), and can be extracted from such tables by interpolating manually or with a suitable computer program. This approach is appropriate for hand calculations and for relatively simple computer models; however, for many computer simulations, the overhead in memory or input and output required to use tabulated data can make this approach unacceptable. For large thermal system simulations or complex analyses, it may be more efficient to determine internal energy, enthalpy, and entropy using fundamental thermodynamic relations or curves fit to experimental data. Some of these relations are discussed in the following sections. Also, the thermodynamic relations discussed in those sections are the basis for constructing tables of thermodynamic property data. Further information on the topic may be found in references covering system modeling and thermodynamics (Howell and Buckius 1992; Stoecker 1989).

At least two intensive properties (properties independent of the quantity of substance, such as temperature, pressure, specific volume, and specific enthalpy) must be known to determine the remaining properties. If two known properties are either p, v, or T (these are relatively easy to measure and are commonly used in simulations), the third can be determined throughout the range of interest using an equation of state. Furthermore, if the specific heats at zero pressure are known, specific heat can be accurately determined from spectroscopic measurements using statistical mechanics (NASA 1971). Entropy may be considered a function of T and p, and from calculus an infinitesimal change in entropy can be written as

$$ds = \left(\frac{\partial s}{\partial T}\right)_p dT + \left(\frac{\partial s}{\partial p}\right)_T dp \tag{26}$$

Likewise, a change in enthalpy can be written as

$$dh = \left(\frac{\partial h}{\partial T}\right)_p dT + \left(\frac{\partial h}{\partial p}\right)_T dp \tag{27}$$

Using the Gibbs relation $Tds = dh - vdp$ and the definition of specific heat at constant pressure, $c_p \equiv (\partial h/\partial T)_p$, Equation (27) can be rearranged to yield

$$ds = \frac{c_p}{T}dT + \left[\left(\frac{\partial h}{\partial p}\right)_T - v\right]\frac{dp}{T} \tag{28}$$

Equations (26) and (28) combine to yield $(\partial s/\partial T)_p = c_p/T$. Then, using the Maxwell relation $(\partial s/\partial p)_T = -(\partial v/\partial T)_p$, Equation (26) may be rewritten as

$$ds = \frac{c_p}{T}dT - \left(\frac{\partial v}{\partial T}\right)_p dp \tag{29}$$

This is an expression for an exact derivative, so it follows that

$$\left(\frac{\partial c_p}{\partial p}\right)_T = -T\left(\frac{\partial^2 v}{\partial T^2}\right)_p \tag{30}$$

Integrating this expression at a fixed temperature yields

$$c_p = c_{p0} - \int_0^p T\left(\frac{\partial^2 v}{\partial T^2}\right)dp_T \tag{31}$$

where c_{p0} is the known zero-pressure specific heat, and dp_T is used to indicate that integration is performed at a fixed temperature. The second partial derivative of specific volume with respect to temperature can be determined from the equation of state. Thus, Equation (31) can be used to determine the specific heat at any pressure.

Using $Tds = dh - vdp$, Equation (29) can be written as

$$dh = c_p dT + \left[v - T\left(\frac{\partial v}{\partial T}\right)_p\right]dp \tag{32}$$

Equations (28) and (32) may be integrated at constant pressure to obtain

$$s(T_1, p_0) = s(T_0, p_0) + \int_{T_0}^{T_1}\frac{c_p}{T}dT_p \tag{33}$$

and

$$h(T_1, p_0) = h(T_0, p_0) + \int_{T_0}^{T_1}c_p\,dT \tag{34}$$

Integrating the Maxwell relation $(\partial s/\partial p)_T = -(\partial v/\partial T)_p$ gives an equation for entropy changes at a constant temperature as

$$s(T_0, p_1) = s(T_0, p_0) - \int_{p_0}^{p_1}\left(\frac{\partial v}{\partial T}\right)_p dp_T \tag{35}$$

Likewise, integrating Equation (32) along an isotherm yields the following equation for enthalpy changes at a constant temperature:

$$h(T_0, p_1) = h(T_0, p_0) + \int_{p_0}^{p_1}\left[v - T\left(\frac{\partial v}{\partial T}\right)_p\right]dp \tag{36}$$

Internal energy can be calculated from $u = h - pv$. When entropy or enthalpy are known at a reference temperature T_0 and pressure p_0, values at any temperature and pressure may be obtained by combining Equations (33) and (35) or Equations (34) and (36).

Combinations (or variations) of Equations (33) to (36) can be incorporated directly into computer subroutines to calculate properties with improved accuracy and efficiency. However, these equations are restricted to situations where the equation of state is valid and the properties vary continuously. These restrictions are violated by a change of phase such as evaporation and condensation, which are essential processes in air-conditioning and refrigerating devices. Therefore, the Clapeyron equation is of particular value; for evaporation or condensation, it gives

$$\left(\frac{dp}{dT}\right)_{sat} = \frac{s_{fg}}{v_{fg}} = \frac{h_{fg}}{Tv_{fg}} \tag{37}$$

where

s_{fg} = entropy of vaporization
h_{fg} = enthalpy of vaporization
v_{fg} = specific volume difference between vapor and liquid phases

If vapor pressure and liquid and vapor density data (all relatively easy measurements to obtain) are known at saturation, then changes in enthalpy and entropy can be calculated using Equation (37).

Phase Equilibria for Multicomponent Systems

To understand phase equilibria, consider a container full of a liquid made of two components; the more volatile component is designated i and the less volatile component j (Figure 2A). This mixture is all liquid because the temperature is low (but not so low that a solid appears). Heat added at a constant pressure raises the mixture's temperature, and a sufficient increase causes vapor to form, as shown in Figure 2B. If heat at constant pressure continues to be added, eventually the temperature becomes so high that only vapor remains in the container (Figure 2C). A temperature-concentration (T-x) diagram is useful for exploring details of this situation.

Figure 3 is a typical T-x diagram valid at a fixed pressure. The case shown in Figure 2A, a container full of liquid mixture with

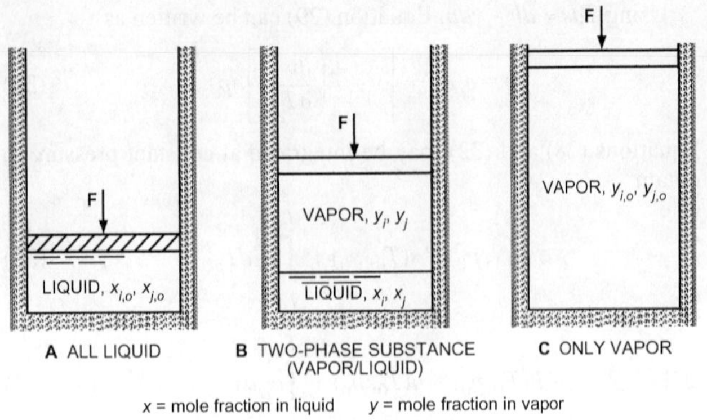

Fig. 2 Mixture of *i* and *j* Components in Constant-Pressure Container

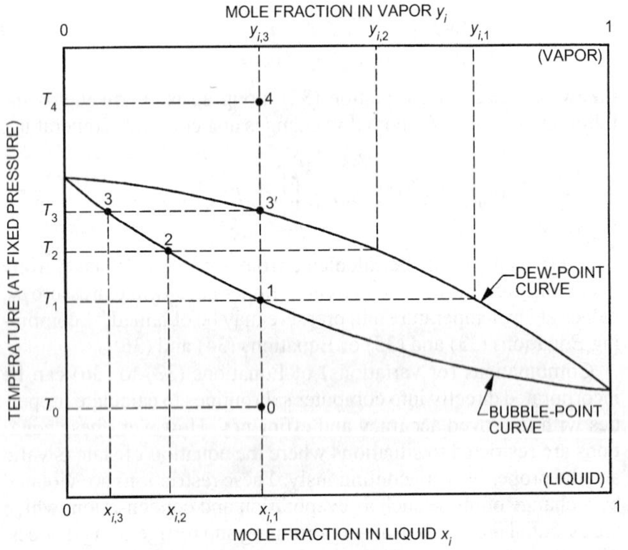

Fig. 3 Temperature-Concentration (*T-x*) Diagram for Zeotropic Mixture

mole fraction $x_{i,0}$ at temperature T_0, is point 0 on the *T-x* diagram. When heat is added, the mixture's temperature increases. The point at which vapor begins to form is the **bubble point**. Starting at point 0, the first bubble forms at temperature T_1 (point 1 on the diagram). The locus of bubble points is the **bubble-point curve**, which provides bubble points for various liquid mole fractions x_i.

When the first bubble begins to form, vapor in the bubble may not have the same mole fraction as the liquid mixture. Rather, the mole fraction of the more volatile species is higher in the vapor than in the liquid. Boiling prefers more volatile species, and the *T-x* diagram shows this behavior. At T_1, the vapor-forming bubbles have an *i* mole fraction of $y_{i,1}$. If heat continues to be added, this preferential boiling depletes the liquid of species *i* and the temperature required to continue the process increases. Again, the *T-x* diagram reflects this fact; at point 2 the *i* mole fraction in the liquid is reduced to $x_{i,2}$ and the vapor has a mole fraction of $y_{i,2}$. The temperature required to boil the mixture is increased to T_2. Position 2 on the *T-x* diagram could correspond to the physical situation shown in Figure 2B.

If constant-pressure heating continues, all the liquid eventually becomes vapor at temperature T_3. The vapor at this point is shown as position 3′ in Figure 3. At this point the *i* mole fraction in the vapor $y_{i,3}$ equals the starting mole fraction in the all-liquid mixture $x_{i,1}$. This equality is required for mass and species conservation.

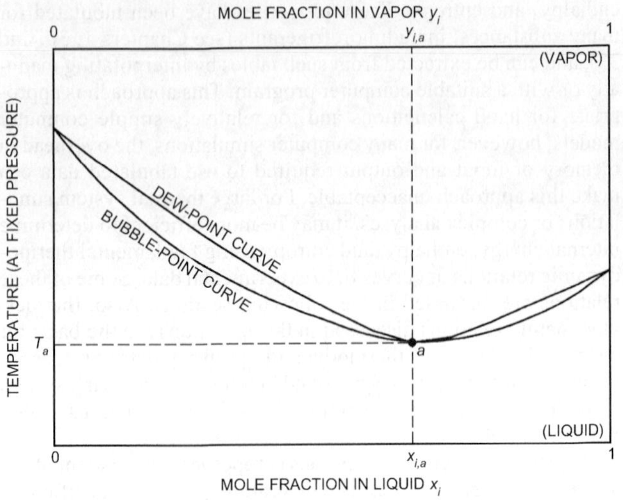

Fig. 4 Azeotropic Behavior Shown on *T-x* Diagram

Further addition of heat simply raises the vapor temperature. The final position 4 corresponds to the physical situation shown in Figure 2C.

Starting at position 4 in Figure 3, heat removal leads to initial liquid formation when position 3′ (the **dew point**) is reached. The locus of dew points is called the **dew-point curve**. Heat removal causes the liquid phase of the mixture to reverse through points 3, 2, 1, and to starting point 0. Because the composition shifts, the temperature required to boil (or condense) this mixture changes as the process proceeds. This is known as **temperature glide**. This mixture is therefore called **zeotropic**.

Most mixtures have *T-x* diagrams that behave in this fashion, but some have a markedly different feature. If the dew-point and bubble-point curves intersect at any point other than at their ends, the mixture exhibits **azeotropic** behavior at that composition. This case is shown as position *a* in the *T-x* diagram of Figure 4. If a container of liquid with a mole fraction x_a were boiled, vapor would be formed with an identical mole fraction y_a. The addition of heat at constant pressure would continue with no shift in composition and no temperature glide.

Perfect azeotropic behavior is uncommon, although near-azeotropic behavior is fairly common. The azeotropic composition is pressure dependent, so operating pressures should be considered for their effect on mixture behavior. Azeotropic and near-azeotropic refrigerant mixtures are widely used. The properties of an azeotropic mixture are such that they may be conveniently treated as pure substance properties. Phase equilibria for zeotropic mixtures, however, require special treatment, using an equation-of-state approach with appropriate mixing rules or using the fugacities with the standard state method (Tassios 1993). Refrigerant and lubricant blends are a zeotropic mixture and can be treated by these methods (Martz et al. 1996a, 1996b; Thome 1995).

2. COMPRESSION REFRIGERATION CYCLES

2.1 CARNOT CYCLE

The Carnot cycle, which is completely reversible, is a perfect model for a refrigeration cycle operating between two fixed temperatures, or between two fluids at different temperatures and each with infinite heat capacity. Reversible cycles have two important properties: (1) no refrigerating cycle may have a coefficient of performance higher than that for a reversible cycle operated between the same temperature limits, and (2) all reversible cycles, when operated between the same temperature limits, have the same coefficient of performance. Proof of both statements may be found in almost any textbook on elementary engineering thermodynamics.

Figure 5 shows the Carnot cycle on temperature-entropy coordinates. Heat is withdrawn at constant temperature T_R from the region to be refrigerated. Heat is rejected at constant ambient temperature T_0. The cycle is completed by an isentropic expansion and an isentropic compression. The energy transfers are given by

$$Q_0 = T_0(S_2 - S_3)$$

$$Q_i = T_R(S_1 - S_4) = T_R(S_2 - S_3)$$

$$W_{net} = Q_o - Q_i$$

Thus, by Equation (15),

$$\mathrm{COP} = \frac{T_R}{T_0 - T_R} \tag{38}$$

Example 1. Determine entropy change, work, and COP for the cycle shown in Figure 6. Temperature of the refrigerated space T_R is 400°R, and that of the atmosphere T_0 is 500°R. Refrigeration load is 200 Btu.

Solution:

$$\Delta S = S_1 - S_4 = Q_i/T_R = 200/400 = 0.500 \text{ Btu/°R}$$

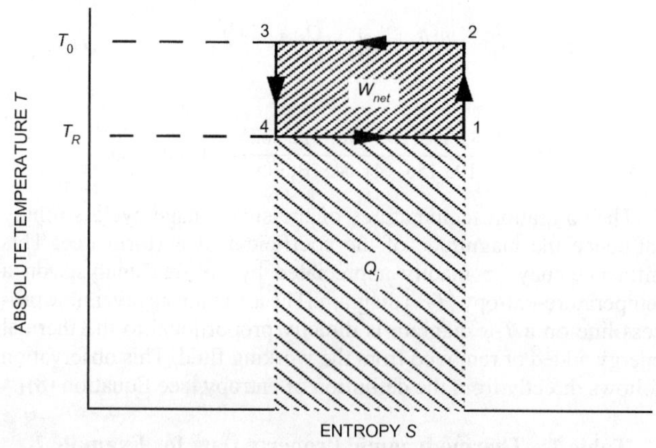

Fig. 5 Carnot Refrigeration Cycle

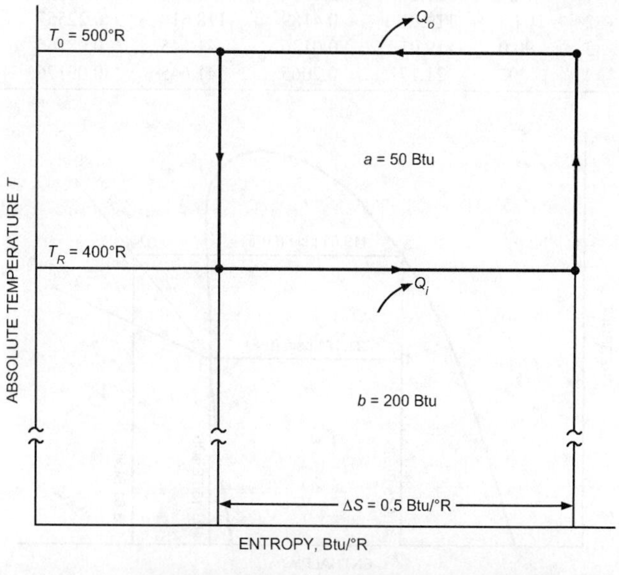

Fig. 6 Temperature-Entropy Diagram for Carnot Refrigeration Cycle of Example 1

$$W = \Delta S(T_0 - T_R) = 0.5(500 - 400) = 50 \text{ Btu}$$

$$\mathrm{COP} = Q_i/(Q_o - Q_i) = Q_i/W = 200/50 = 4$$

Flow of energy and its area representation in Figure 6 are

Energy	Btu	Area
Q_i	200	b
Q_o	250	$a + b$
W	50	a

The net change of entropy of any refrigerant in any cycle is always zero. In Example 1, the change in entropy of the refrigerated space is $\Delta S_R = -200/400 = -0.5$ Btu/°R and that of the atmosphere is $\Delta S_o = 250/500 = 0.5$ Btu/°R. The net change in entropy of the isolated system is $\Delta S_{total} = \Delta S_R + \Delta S_o = 0$.

The Carnot cycle in Figure 7 shows a process in which heat is added and rejected at constant pressure in the two-phase region of a refrigerant. Saturated liquid at state 3 expands isentropically to the low temperature and pressure of the cycle at state d. Heat is added isothermally and isobarically by evaporating the liquid-phase refrigerant from state d to state 1. The cold saturated vapor at state 1 is compressed isentropically to the high temperature in the cycle at state b. However, the pressure at state b is below the saturation pressure corresponding to the high temperature in the cycle. The compression process is completed by an isothermal compression process from state b to state c. The cycle is completed by an isothermal and isobaric heat rejection or condensing process from state c to state 3.

Applying the energy equation for a mass of refrigerant m yields (all work and heat transfer are positive)

$${}_3W_d = m(h_3 - h_d)$$

$${}_1W_b = m(h_b - h_1)$$

$${}_bW_c = T_0(S_b - S_c) - m(h_b - h_c)$$

$${}_dQ_1 = m(h_1 - h_d) = \text{Area def1d}$$

The net work for the cycle is

$$W_{net} = {}_1W_b + {}_bW_c - {}_3W_d = \text{Area d1bc3d}$$

and

$$\mathrm{COP} = \frac{{}_dQ_1}{W_{net}} = \frac{T_R}{T_0 - T_R}$$

2.2 THEORETICAL SINGLE-STAGE CYCLE USING A PURE REFRIGERANT OR AZEOTROPIC MIXTURE

A system designed to approach the ideal model shown in Figure 7 is desirable. A pure refrigerant or azeotropic mixture can be used to maintain constant temperature during phase changes by maintaining constant pressure. Because of concerns such as high initial cost and increased maintenance requirements, a practical machine

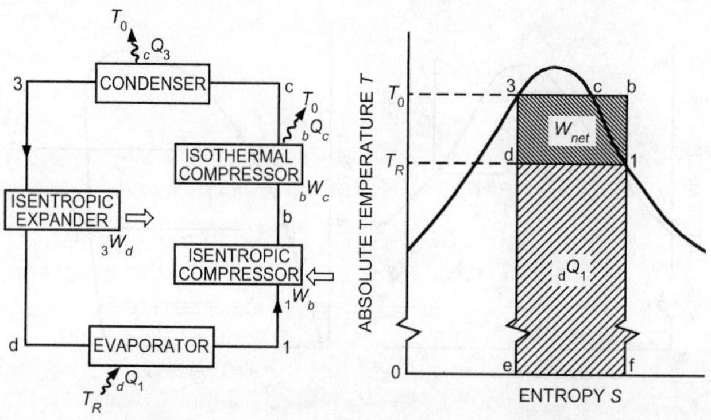

Fig. 7 Carnot Vapor Compression Cycle

has one compressor instead of two and the expander (engine or turbine) is replaced by a simple expansion valve, which throttles refrigerant from high to low pressure. Figure 8 shows the theoretical single-stage cycle used as a model for actual systems.

Applying the energy equation for a mass m of refrigerant yields

$$_4Q_1 = m(h_1 - h_4) \tag{39a}$$

$$_1W_2 = m(h_2 - h_1) \tag{39b}$$

$$_2Q_3 = m(h_2 - h_3) \tag{39c}$$

$$h_3 = h_4 \tag{39d}$$

Constant-enthalpy throttling assumes no heat transfer or change in potential or kinetic energy through the expansion valve.

The coefficient of performance is

$$\text{COP} = \frac{_4Q_1}{_1W_2} = \frac{h_1 - h_4}{h_2 - h_1} \tag{40}$$

The theoretical compressor displacement CD (at 100% volumetric efficiency) is

$$\text{CD} = \dot{m}v_1 \tag{41}$$

which is a measure of the physical size or speed of the compressor required to handle the prescribed refrigeration load.

Example 2. A theoretical single-stage cycle using R-134a as the refrigerant operates with a condensing temperature of 90°F and an evaporating temperature of 0°F. The system produces 15 tons of refrigeration. Determine the (a) thermodynamic property values at the four main state points of the cycle, (b) COP, (c) cycle refrigerating efficiency, and (d) rate of refrigerant flow.

Solution:

(a) Figure 9 shows a schematic p-h diagram for the problem with numerical property data. Saturated vapor and saturated liquid properties for states 1 and 3 are obtained from the saturation table for R-134a in Chapter 30. Properties for superheated vapor at state 2 are obtained by linear interpolation of the superheat tables for R-134a in Chapter 30. Specific volume and specific entropy values for state 4 are obtained by determining the quality of the liquid-vapor mixture from the enthalpy.

$$x_4 = \frac{h_4 - h_f}{h_g - h_f} = \frac{41.645 - 12.207}{103.156 - 12.207} = 0.3237$$

$$v_4 = v_f + x_4(v_g - v_f) = 0.01185 + 0.3237(2.1579 - 0.01185) = 0.7065 \text{ ft}^3/\text{lb}$$

$$s_4 = s_f + x_4(s_g - s_f) = 0.02771 + 0.3237(0.22557 - 0.02771) = 0.09176 \text{ Btu/lb·°R}$$

The property data are tabulated in Table 1.

(b) By Equation (40),

$$\text{COP} = \frac{103.156 - 41.645}{118.61 - 103.156} = 3.98$$

(c) By Equations (17) and (38),

$$\eta_R = \frac{\text{COP}(T_3 - T_1)}{T_1} = \frac{(3.98)(90)}{459.6} = 0.78 \text{ or } 78\%$$

(d) The mass flow of refrigerant is obtained from an energy balance on the evaporator. Thus,

$$\dot{m}(h_1 - h_4) = \dot{Q}_i = 15 \text{ tons}$$

and

$$\dot{m} = \frac{(15 \text{ tons})(200 \text{ Btu/min·ton})}{(103.156 - 41.645)\text{Btu/lb}} = 48.8 \text{ lb/min}$$

The saturation temperatures of the single-stage cycle strongly influence the magnitude of the coefficient of performance. This influence may be readily appreciated by an area analysis on a temperature-entropy (T-s) diagram. The area under a reversible process line on a T-s diagram is directly proportional to the thermal energy added or removed from the working fluid. This observation follows directly from the definition of entropy [see Equation (8)].

Table 1 Thermodynamic Property Data for Example 2

State	t, °F	p, psia	v, ft³/lb	h, Btu/lb	s, Btu/lb·°R
1	0	21.171	2.1579	103.156	0.22557
2	104.3	119.01	0.4189	118.61	0.22557
3	90.0	119.01	0.0136	41.645	0.08565
4	0	21.171	0.7065	41.645	0.09176

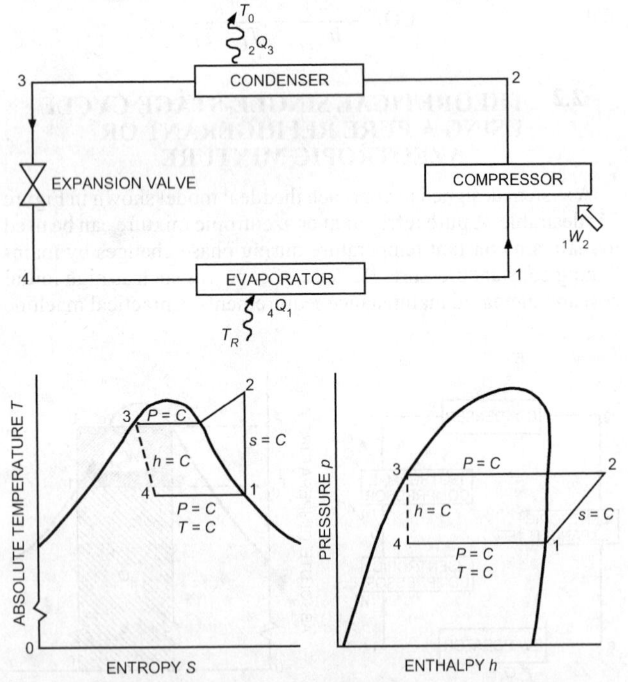

Fig. 8 Theoretical Single-Stage Vapor Compression Refrigeration Cycle

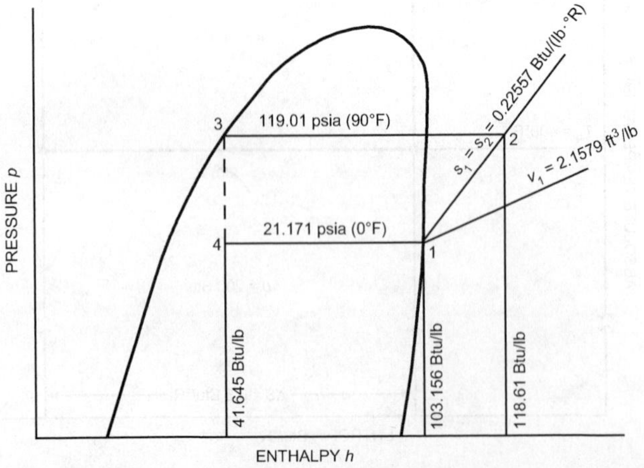

Fig. 9 Schematic p-h Diagram for Example 2

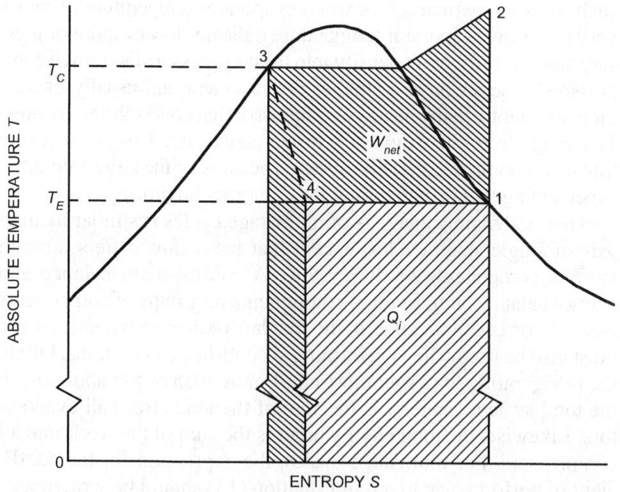

Fig. 10 Areas on *T-s* Diagram Representing Refrigerating Effect and Work Supplied for Theoretical Single-Stage Cycle

In Figure 10, the area representing Q_o is the total area under the constant-pressure curve between states 2 and 3. The area representing the refrigerating capacity Q_i is the area under the constant-pressure line connecting states 4 and 1. The net work required W_{net} equals the difference $(Q_o - Q_i)$, which is represented by the entire shaded area shown on Figure 10.

Because COP = Q_i/W_{net}, the effect on the COP of changes in evaporating temperature and condensing temperature may be observed. For example, a decrease in evaporating temperature T_E significantly increases W_{net} and slightly decreases Q_i. An increase in condensing temperature T_C produces the same results but with less effect on W_{net}. Therefore, for maximum coefficient of performance, the cycle should operate at the lowest possible condensing temperature and maximum possible evaporating temperature.

2.3 LORENZ REFRIGERATION CYCLE

The Carnot refrigeration cycle includes two assumptions that make it impractical. The heat transfer capacities of the two external fluids are assumed to be infinitely large so the external fluid temperatures remain fixed at T_0 and T_R (they become infinitely large thermal reservoirs). The Carnot cycle also has no thermal resistance between the working refrigerant and external fluids in the two heat exchange processes. As a result, the refrigerant must remain fixed at T_0 in the condenser and at T_R in the evaporator.

The Lorenz cycle eliminates the first restriction in the Carnot cycle by allowing the temperature of the two external fluids to vary during heat exchange. The second assumption of negligible thermal resistance between the working refrigerant and two external fluids remains. Therefore, the refrigerant temperature must change during the two heat exchange processes to equal the changing temperature of the external fluids. This cycle is completely reversible when operating between two fluids that each have a finite but constant heat capacity.

Figure 11 is a schematic of a Lorenz cycle. Note that this cycle does not operate between two fixed temperature limits. Heat is added to the refrigerant from state 4 to state 1. This process is assumed to be linear on *T-s* coordinates, which represents a fluid with constant heat capacity. The refrigerant temperature is increased in isentropic compression from state 1 to state 2. Process 2-3 is a heat rejection process in which the refrigerant temperature decreases linearly with heat transfer. The cycle ends with isentropic expansion between states 3 and 4.

The heat addition and heat rejection processes are parallel so the entire cycle is drawn as a parallelogram on *T-s* coordinates. A

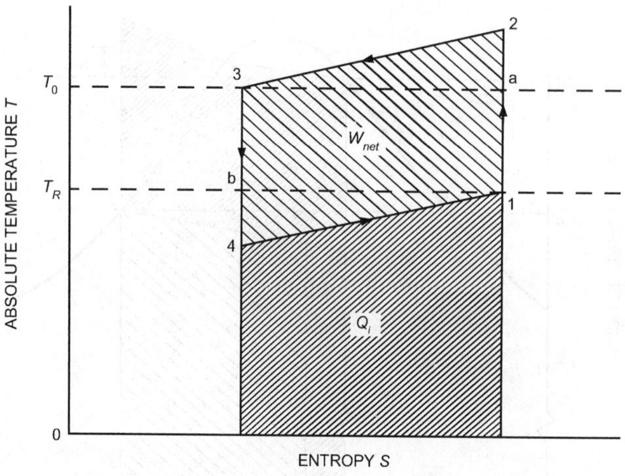

Fig. 11 Processes of Lorenz Refrigeration Cycle

Carnot refrigeration cycle operating between T_0 and T_R would lie between states 1, a, 3, and b; the Lorenz cycle has a smaller refrigerating effect and requires more work, but this cycle is a more practical reference when a refrigeration system operates between two single-phase fluids such as air or water.

The energy transfers in a Lorenz refrigeration cycle are as follows, where ΔT is the temperature change of the refrigerant during each of the two heat exchange processes.

$$Q_o = (T_0 + \Delta T/2)(S_2 - S_3)$$

$$Q_i = (T_R - \Delta T/2)(S_1 - S_4) = (T_R - \Delta T/2)(S_2 - S_3)$$

$$W_{net} = Q_o - Q_R$$

Thus by Equation (15),

$$\text{COP} = \frac{T_R - (\Delta T/2)}{T_0 - T_R + \Delta T} \tag{42}$$

Example 3. Determine the entropy change, work required, and COP for the Lorenz cycle shown in Figure 11 when the temperature of the refrigerated space is T_R = 400°R, ambient temperature is T_0 = 500°R, ΔT of the refrigerant is 10°R, and refrigeration load is 200 Btu.

Solution:

$$\Delta S = \int_4^1 \frac{\delta Q_i}{T} = \frac{Q_i}{T_R - (\Delta T/2)} = \frac{200}{395} = 0.5063 \text{ Btu/°R}$$

$$Q_o = [T_0 + (\Delta T/2)]\Delta S = (500 + 5)0.5063 = 255.68 \text{ Btu}$$

$$W_{net} = Q_o - Q_R = 255.68 - 200 = 55.68 \text{ Btu}$$

$$\text{COP} = \frac{T_R - (\Delta T/2)}{T_0 - T_R + \Delta T} = \frac{400 - (10/2)}{500 - 400 + 10} = \frac{395}{110} = 3.591$$

Note that the entropy change for the Lorenz cycle is larger than for the Carnot cycle when both operate between the same two temperature reservoirs and have the same capacity (see Example 1). That is, both the heat rejection and work requirement are larger for the Lorenz cycle. This difference is caused by the finite temperature difference between the working fluid in the cycle compared to the bounding temperature reservoirs. However, as discussed previously, the assumption of constant-temperature heat reservoirs is not necessarily a good representation of an actual refrigeration system because of the temperature changes that occur in the heat exchangers.

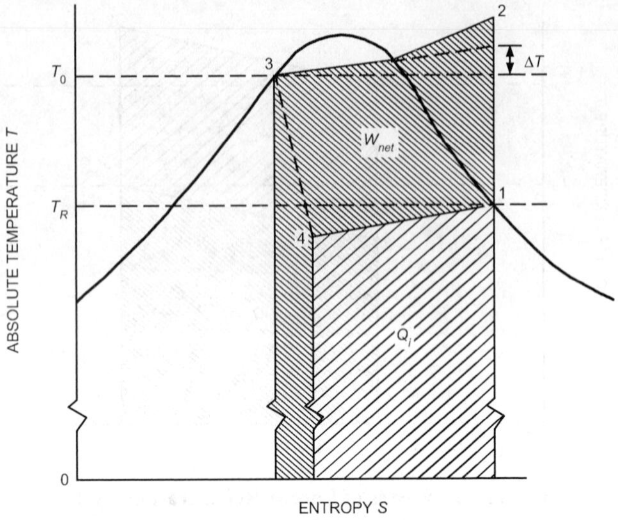

Fig. 12 Areas on *T-s* Diagram Representing Refrigerating Effect and Work Supplied for Theoretical Single-Stage Cycle Using Zeotropic Mixture as Refrigerant

2.4 THEORETICAL SINGLE-STAGE CYCLE USING ZEOTROPIC REFRIGERANT MIXTURE

A practical method to approximate the Lorenz refrigeration cycle is to use a fluid mixture as the refrigerant and the four system components shown in Figure 8. When the mixture is not azeotropic and the phase change occurs at constant pressure, the temperatures change during evaporation and condensation and the theoretical single-stage cycle can be shown on *T-s* coordinates as in Figure 12. In comparison, Figure 10 shows the system operating with a pure simple substance or an azeotropic mixture as the refrigerant. Equations (14), (15), (39), (40), and (41) apply to this cycle and to conventional cycles with constant phase change temperatures. Equation (42) should be used as the reversible cycle COP in Equation (17).

For zeotropic mixtures, the concept of constant saturation temperatures does not exist. For example, in the evaporator, the refrigerant enters at T_4 and exits at a higher temperature T_1. The temperature of saturated liquid at a given pressure is the **bubble point** and the temperature of saturated vapor at a given pressure is called the **dew point**. The temperature T_3 in Figure 12 is at the bubble point at the condensing pressure and T_1 is at the dew point at the evaporating pressure.

Areas on a *T-s* diagram representing additional work and reduced refrigerating effect from a Lorenz cycle operating between the same two temperatures T_1 and T_3 with the same value for ΔT can be analyzed. The cycle matches the Lorenz cycle most closely when counterflow heat exchangers are used for both the condenser and evaporator.

In a cycle that has heat exchangers with finite thermal resistances and finite external fluid capacity rates, Kuehn and Gronseth (1986) showed that a cycle using a refrigerant mixture has a higher coefficient of performance than one using a simple pure substance as a refrigerant. However, the improvement in COP is usually small. Mixture performance can be improved further by reducing the heat exchangers' thermal resistance and passing fluids through them in a counterflow arrangement.

2.5 MULTISTAGE VAPOR COMPRESSION REFRIGERATION CYCLES

Multistage or multipressure vapor compression refrigeration is used when several evaporators are needed at various temperatures, such as in a supermarket, or when evaporator temperature becomes very low. Low evaporator temperature indicates low evaporator pressure and low refrigerant density into the compressor. Two small compressors in series have a smaller displacement and usually operate more efficiently than one large compressor that covers the entire pressure range from the evaporator to the condenser. This is especially true in ammonia refrigeration systems because of the large amount of superheating that occurs during the compression process.

Thermodynamic analysis of multistage cycles is similar to analysis of single-stage cycles, except that mass flow differs through various components of the system. A careful mass balance and energy balance on individual components or groups of components ensures correct application of the first law of thermodynamics. Care must also be used when performing second-law calculations. Often, the refrigerating load is comprised of more than one evaporator, so the total system capacity is the sum of the loads from all evaporators. Likewise, the total energy input is the sum of the work into all compressors. For multistage cycles, the expression for the coefficient of performance given in Equation (15) should be written as

$$\text{COP} = \sum Q_i / W_{net} \tag{43}$$

When compressors are connected in series, vapor between stages should be cooled to bring the vapor to saturated conditions before proceeding to the next stage of compression. Intercooling usually minimizes displacement of the compressors, reduces the work requirement, and increases the cycle's COP. If the refrigerant temperature between stages is above ambient, a simple intercooler that removes heat from the refrigerant can be used. If the temperature is below ambient, which is the usual case, the refrigerant itself must be used to cool the vapor. This is accomplished with a flash intercooler. Figure 13 shows a cycle with a flash intercooler installed.

The superheated vapor from compressor I is bubbled through saturated liquid refrigerant at the intermediate pressure of the cycle. Some of this liquid is evaporated when heat is added from the superheated refrigerant. The result is that only saturated vapor at the intermediate pressure is fed to compressor II. A common approach is to operate the intercooler at about the geometric mean of the evaporating and condensing pressures. This operating point provides the same pressure ratio and nearly equal volumetric efficiencies for the two compressors. Example 4 illustrates the thermodynamic analysis of this cycle.

Example 4. Determine the thermodynamic properties of the eight state points shown in Figure 13, mass flows, and COP of this theoretical multistage refrigeration cycle using R-134a. The saturated evaporator temperature is 0°F, the saturated condensing temperature is 90°F, and the refrigeration load is 15 tons. The saturation temperature of the refrigerant in the intercooler is 40°F, which is nearly at the geometric mean pressure of the cycle.

Solution:

Thermodynamic property data are obtained from the saturation and superheat tables for R-134a in Chapter 30. States 1, 3, 5, and 7 are obtained directly from the saturation table. State 6 is a mixture of liquid and vapor. The quality is calculated by

$$x_6 = \frac{h_6 - h_7}{h_3 - h_7} = \frac{41.645 - 24.890}{108.856 - 24.890} = 0.19955$$

Then,

$$v_6 = v_7 + x_6(v_3 - v_7) = 0.01252 + 0.19955(0.9528 - 0.01252)$$
$$= 0.2002 \text{ ft}^3/\text{lb}$$

$$s_6 = s_7 + x_6(s_3 - s_7) = 0.05402 + 0.19955(0.22207 - 0.05402)$$
$$= 0.08755 \text{ Btu/lb}\cdot°\text{R}$$

Similarly for state 8,

$$x_8 = 0.13951, \quad v_8 = 0.3112 \text{ ft}^3/\text{lb}, \quad s_8 = 0.05531 \text{ Btu/lb}\cdot°\text{R}$$

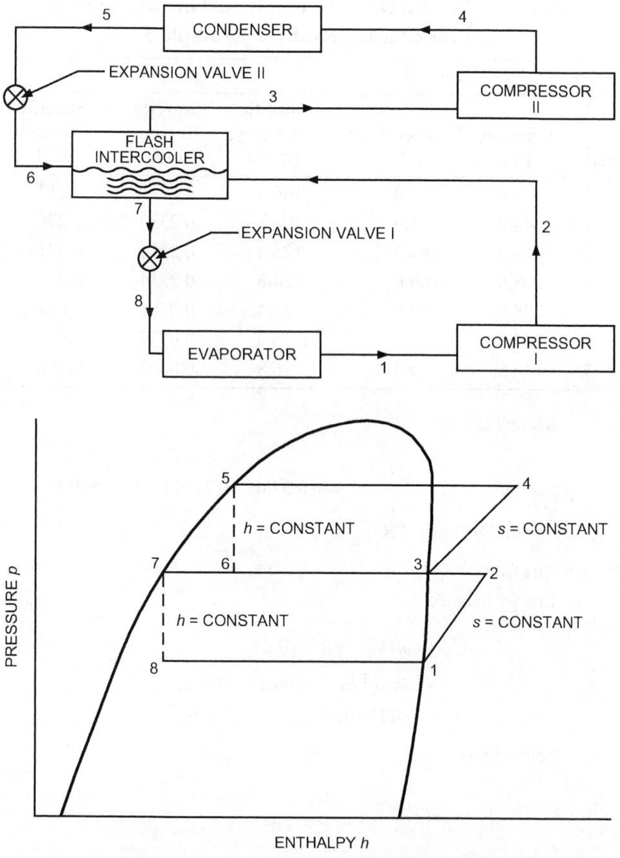

Fig. 13 Schematic and Pressure-Enthalpy Diagram for Dual-Compression, Dual-Expansion Cycle of Example 4

Table 2 Thermodynamic Property Values for Example 4

State	Temperature, °F	Pressure, psia	Specific Volume, ft³/lb	Specific Enthalpy, Btu/lb	Specific Entropy, Btu/lb·°R
1	0.00	21.171	2.1579	103.156	0.22557
2	49.03	49.741	0.9766	110.65	0.22557
3	40.00	49.741	0.9528	108.856	0.22207
4	96.39	119.01	0.4082	116.64	0.22207
5	90.00	119.01	0.01359	41.645	0.08565
6	40.00	49.741	0.2002	41.645	0.08755
7	40.00	49.741	0.01252	24.890	0.05403
8	0.00	21.171	0.3112	24.890	0.05531

States 2 and 4 are obtained from the superheat tables by linear interpolation. The thermodynamic property data are summarized in Table 2.

Mass flow through the lower circuit of the cycle is determined from an energy balance on the evaporator.

$$\dot{m}_1 = \frac{\dot{Q}_i}{h_1 - h_8} = \frac{15\ \text{tons}\ (200\ \text{Btu/min·ton})}{(103.156 - 24.890)\ \text{Btu/lb}} = 38.33\ \text{lb/min}$$

$$\dot{m}_1 = \dot{m}_2 = \dot{m}_7 = \dot{m}_8$$

For the upper circuit of the cycle,

$$\dot{m}_3 = \dot{m}_4 = \dot{m}_5 = \dot{m}_6$$

Assuming the intercooler has perfect external insulation, an energy balance on it is used to compute $\dot{m}_3$.

$$\dot{m}_6 h_6 + \dot{m}_2 h_2 = \dot{m}_7 h_7 + \dot{m}_3 h_3$$

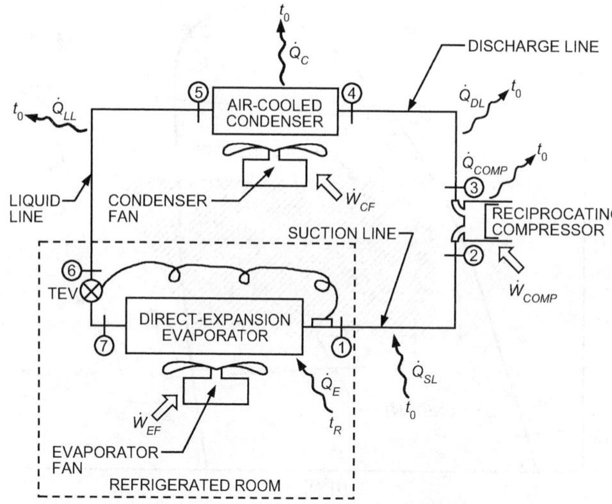

Fig. 14 Schematic of Real, Direct-Expansion, Single-Stage Mechanical Vapor-Compression Refrigeration System

Rearranging and solving for $\dot{m}_3$,

$$\dot{m}_3 = \dot{m}_2 \frac{h_7 - h_2}{h_6 - h_3} = 38.33\ \text{lb/min} \frac{24.890 - 110.65}{41.645 - 108.856} = 48.91\ \text{lb/min}$$

$$\dot{W}_{\text{I}} = \dot{m}_1(h_2 - h_1) = 38.33\ \text{lb/min}(110.65 - 103.156)\ \text{Btu/lb}$$
$$= 287.2\ \text{Btu/min}$$

$$\dot{W}_{\text{II}} = \dot{m}_3(h_4 - h_3) = 48.91\ \text{lb/min}(116.64 - 108.856)\ \text{Btu/lb}$$
$$= 380.7\ \text{Btu/min}$$

$$\text{COP} = \frac{\dot{Q}_i}{\dot{W}_{\text{I}} + \dot{W}_{\text{II}}} = \frac{15\ \text{tons}(200\ \text{Btu/min·ton})}{(287.2 + 380.7)\ \text{Btu/min}} = 4.49$$

Examples 2 and 4 have the same refrigeration load and operate with the same evaporating and condensing temperatures. The two-stage cycle in Example 4 has a higher COP and less work input than the single-stage cycle. Also, the highest refrigerant temperature leaving the compressor is about 96°F for the two-stage cycle versus about 104°F for the single-stage cycle. These differences are more pronounced for cycles operating at larger pressure ratios.

2.6 ACTUAL REFRIGERATION SYSTEMS

Actual systems operating steadily differ from the ideal cycles considered in the previous sections in many respects. Pressure drops occur everywhere in the system except in the compression process. Heat transfers between the refrigerant and its environment in all components. The actual compression process differs substantially from isentropic compression. The working fluid is not a pure substance but a mixture of refrigerant and oil. All of these deviations from a theoretical cycle cause irreversibilities in the system. Each irreversibility requires additional power into the compressor. It is useful to understand how these irreversibilities are distributed throughout a real system; this insight can be useful when design changes are contemplated or operating conditions are modified. Example 5 illustrates how the irreversibilities can be computed in a real system and how they require additional compressor power to overcome. Input data have been rounded off for ease of computation.

Example 5. An air-cooled, direct-expansion, single-stage mechanical vapor-compression refrigerator uses R-22 and operates under steady conditions. A schematic of this system is shown in Figure 14. Pressure drops occur in all piping, and heat gains or losses occur as indicated. Power input includes compressor power and the power required to operate both fans. The following performance data are obtained:

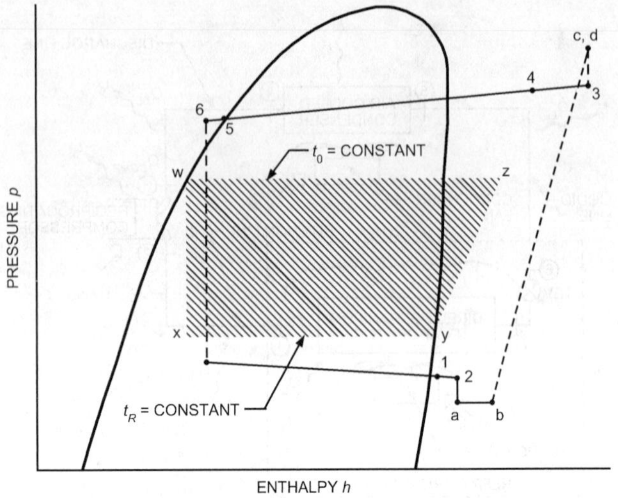

Fig. 15 Pressure-Enthalpy Diagram of Actual System and Theoretical Single-Stage System Operating Between Same Inlet Air Temperatures t_R and t_0

Ambient air temperature	t_0	=	90°F
Refrigerated space temperature	t_R	=	20°F
Refrigeration load	$\dot{Q}_{evap}$	=	2 tons
Compressor power input	$\dot{W}_{comp}$	=	3.0 hp
Condenser fan input	$\dot{W}_{CF}$	=	0.2 hp
Evaporator fan input	$\dot{W}_{EF}$	=	0.15 hp

Refrigerant pressures and temperatures are measured at the seven locations shown in Figure 14. Table 3 lists the measured and computed thermodynamic properties of the refrigerant, neglecting the dissolved oil. A pressure-enthalpy diagram of this cycle is shown in Figure 15 and is compared with a theoretical single-stage cycle operating between the air temperatures t_R and t_0.

Compute the energy transfers to the refrigerant in each component of the system and determine the second-law irreversibility rate in each component. Show that the total irreversibility rate multiplied by the absolute ambient temperature is equal to the difference between the actual power input and the power required by a Carnot cycle operating between t_R and t_0 with the same refrigerating load.

Solution: The mass flow of refrigerant is the same through all components, so it is only computed once through the evaporator. Each component in the system is analyzed sequentially, beginning with the evaporator. Equation (6) is used to perform a first-law energy balance on each component, and Equations (11) and (13) are used for the second-law analysis. Note that the temperature used in the second-law analysis is the absolute temperature.

Evaporator:

Energy balance

$$_7\dot{Q}_1 = \dot{m}(h_1 - h_7) = 24{,}000 \text{ Btu/h}$$

$$\dot{m} = \frac{24{,}000}{(106.4 - 36.8)} = 345 \text{ lb/h}$$

Second law

$$_7\dot{I}_1 = \dot{m}(s_1 - s_7) - \frac{_7\dot{Q}_1}{T_R}$$

$$= 345(0.2291 - 0.0800) - \frac{24{,}000}{479.67} = 1.405 \text{ Btu/h} \cdot \text{°R}$$

Suction Line:

Energy balance

$$_1\dot{Q}_2 = \dot{m}(h_2 - h_1) = 345(108.1 - 106.4) = 586 \text{ Btu/h}$$

Table 3 Measured and Computed Thermodynamic Properties of R-22 for Example 5

	Measured		Computed		
State	Pressure, psia	Temperature, °F	Specific Enthalpy, Btu/lb	Specific Entropy, Btu/lb·°R	Specific Volume, ft³/lb
1	45.0	15.0	106.4	0.2291	1.213
2	44.0	25.0	108.1	0.2330	1.276
3	210.0	180.0	128.8	0.2374	0.331
4	208.0	160.0	124.8	0.2314	0.318
5	205.0	94.0	37.4	0.0761	0.014
6	204.0	92.0	36.8	0.0750	0.014
7	46.5	9.0	36.8	0.0800	0.308

Second law

$$_1\dot{I}_2 = \dot{m}(s_2 - s_1) - \frac{_1\dot{Q}_2}{T_0} = 345(0.2330 - 0.2291) - 586/549.67$$

$$= 0.279 \text{ Btu/h} \cdot \text{°R}$$

Compressor:

Energy balance

$$_2\dot{Q}_3 = \dot{m}(h_3 - h_2) + {_2\dot{W}_3}$$

$$= 345(128.8 - 108.1) - 3.0(2545)$$

$$= -494 \text{ Btu/h}$$

Second law

$$_2\dot{I}_3 = \dot{m}(s_3 - s_2) - \frac{_2\dot{Q}_3}{T_0}$$

$$= 345(0.2374 - 0.2330) - (-494/549.67)$$

$$= 2.417 \text{ Btu/h} \cdot \text{°R}$$

Discharge Line:

Energy balance

$$_3\dot{Q}_4 = \dot{m}(h_4 - h_3)$$

$$= 345(124.8 - 128.8) = -1380 \text{ Btu/h}$$

Second law

$$_3\dot{I}_4 = \dot{m}(s_4 - s_3) - \frac{_3\dot{Q}_4}{T_0}$$

$$= 345(0.2314 - 0.2374) - (-1380/549.67)$$

$$= 0.441 \text{ Btu/h} \cdot \text{°R}$$

Condenser:

Energy balance

$$_4\dot{Q}_5 = \dot{m}(h_5 - h_4)$$

$$= 345(37.4 - 124.8) = -30{,}153 \text{ Btu/h}$$

Second law

$$_4\dot{I}_5 = \dot{m}(s_5 - s_4) - \frac{_4\dot{Q}_5}{T_0}$$

$$= 345(0.0761 - 0.2314) - (-30{,}153/549.67)$$

$$= 1.278 \text{ Btu/h} \cdot \text{°R}$$

Liquid Line:

Energy balance

$$_5\dot{Q}_6 = \dot{m}(h_6 - h_5)$$

$$= 345(36.8 - 37.4) = -207 \text{ Btu/h}$$

Second law

$$_5\dot{I}_6 = \dot{m}(s_6 - s_5) - \frac{_5\dot{Q}_6}{T_0}$$

$$= 345(0.0750 - 0.0761) - (-207/549.67)$$

$$= 0 \text{ Btu/h} \cdot °\text{R}$$

Expansion Device:
Energy balance

$$_6\dot{Q}_7 = \dot{m}\,(h_7 - h_6) = 0$$

Second law

$$_6\dot{I}_7 = \dot{m}(s_7 - s_6) = 345(0.0800 - 0.0750) = 1.725 \text{ Btu/h}\cdot°\text{R}$$

These results are summarized in Table 4. For the Carnot cycle,

$$\text{COP}_{Carnot} = \frac{T_R}{T_0 - T_R} = \frac{479.67}{70} = 6.852$$

The Carnot power requirement for the 2 ton load is

$$\dot{W}_{Carnot} = \frac{\dot{Q}_{evap}}{\text{COP}_{Carnot}} = \frac{24{,}000}{6.852} = 3502 \text{ Btu/h}$$

The actual power requirement for the compressor is

$$\dot{W}_{comp} = \dot{W}_{Carnot} + \dot{I}_{total}T_0$$

$$= 3502 + 7.545 \times 549.67 = 7649 \text{ Btu/h}$$

This result is within computational error of the measured power input to the compressor of 7635 Btu/h.

The analysis in Example 5 can be applied to any actual vapor compression refrigeration system. The only required information for second-law analysis is the refrigerant thermodynamic state points and mass flow rates and the temperatures in which the system is exchanging heat. In this example, the extra compressor power required to overcome the irreversibility in each component is determined. The component with the largest loss is the compressor. This loss is due to motor inefficiency, friction losses, and irreversibilities caused by pressure drops, mixing, and heat transfer between the compressor and the surroundings. Unrestrained expansion in the expansion device is the next largest (also a large loss), but could be reduced by using an expander rather than a throttling process. An expander may be economical on large machines.

All heat transfer irreversibilities on both the refrigerant side and the air side of the condenser and evaporator are included in the analysis. Refrigerant pressure drop is also included. Air-side pressure drop irreversibilities of the two heat exchangers are not included, but these are equal to the fan power requirements because all the fan power is dissipated as heat.

An overall second-law analysis, such as in Example 5, shows the designer components with the most losses, and helps determine which components should be replaced or redesigned to improve performance. However, it does not identify the nature of the losses; this requires a more detailed second-law analysis of the actual processes in terms of fluid flow and heat transfer (Liang and Kuehn 1991). A detailed analysis shows that most irreversibilities associated with heat exchangers are due to heat transfer, whereas air-side pressure drop causes a very small loss and refrigerant pressure drop causes a negligible loss. This finding indicates that promoting refrigerant heat transfer at the expense of increasing the pressure drop often improves performance. Using a thermoeconomic technique is required to determine the cost/benefits associated with reducing component irreversibilities.

Table 4 Energy Transfers and Irreversibility Rates for Refrigeration System in Example 5

Component	$\dot{Q}$, Btu/h	$\dot{W}$, Btu/h	$\dot{I}$, Btu/h·°R	$\dot{I}/\dot{I}_{total}$, %
Evaporator	24,000	0	1.405	19
Suction line	586	0	0.279	4
Compressor	–494	7635	2.417	32
Discharge line	–1380	0	0.441	6
Condenser	–30,153	0	1.278	17
Liquid line	–207	0	≈ 0	≈ 0
Expansion device	0	0	1.725	23
Totals	–7648	7635	7.545	

3. ABSORPTION REFRIGERATION CYCLES

An absorption cycle is a heat-activated thermal cycle. It exchanges only thermal energy with its surroundings; no appreciable mechanical energy is exchanged. Furthermore, no appreciable conversion of heat to work or work to heat occurs in the cycle.

Absorption cycles are used in applications where one or more of the exchanges of heat with the surroundings is the useful product (e.g., refrigeration, air conditioning, and heat pumping). The two great advantages of this type of cycle in comparison to other cycles with similar product are

- No large, rotating mechanical equipment is required
- Any source of heat can be used, including low-temperature sources (e.g., waste heat, solar heat)

3.1 IDEAL THERMAL CYCLE

All absorption cycles include at least three thermal energy exchanges with their surroundings (i.e., energy exchange at three different temperatures). The highest- and lowest-temperature heat flows are in one direction, and the mid-temperature one (or two) is in the opposite direction. In the **forward cycle**, the extreme (hottest and coldest) heat flows are into the cycle. This cycle is also called the heat amplifier, heat pump, conventional cycle, or Type I cycle. When extreme-temperature heat flows are out of the cycle, it is called a **reverse cycle**, heat transformer, temperature amplifier, temperature booster, or Type II cycle. Figure 16 illustrates both types of thermal cycles.

This fundamental constraint of heat flow into or out of the cycle at three or more different temperatures establishes the first limitation on cycle performance. By the first law of thermodynamics (at steady state),

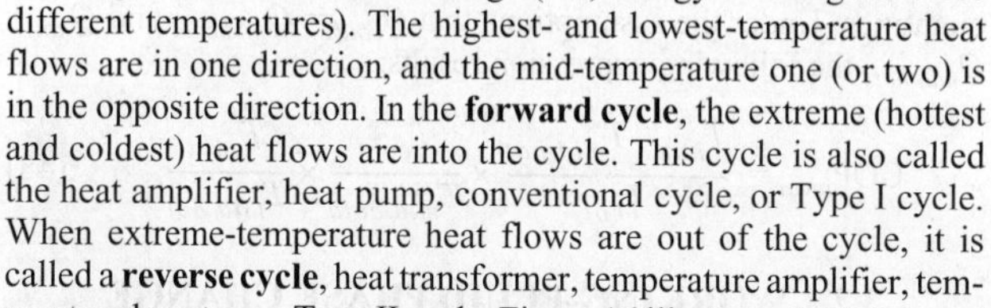

Fig. 16 Thermal Cycles

$$Q_{hot} + Q_{cold} = -Q_{mid} \tag{44}$$

(positive heat quantities are into the cycle)

The second law requires that

$$\frac{Q_{hot}}{T_{hot}} + \frac{Q_{cold}}{T_{cold}} + \frac{Q_{mid}}{T_{mid}} \geq 0 \tag{45}$$

with equality holding in the ideal case.

From these two laws alone (i.e., without invoking any further assumptions) it follows that, for the ideal forward cycle,

$$\text{COP}_{ideal} = \frac{Q_{cold}}{Q_{hot}} = \frac{T_{hot} - T_{mid}}{T_{hot}} \times \frac{T_{cold}}{T_{mid} - T_{cold}} \tag{46}$$

The heat ratio Q_{cold}/Q_{hot} is commonly called the **coefficient of performance (COP)**, which is the cooling realized divided by the driving heat supplied.

Heat rejected to ambient may be at two different temperatures, creating a **four-temperature cycle**. The ideal COP of the four-temperature cycle is also expressed by Equation (46), with T_{mid} signifying the entropic mean heat rejection temperature. In that case, T_{mid} is calculated as follows:

$$T_{mid} = \frac{Q_{mid\ hot} + Q_{mid\ cold}}{\dfrac{Q_{mid\ hot}}{T_{mid\ hot}} + \dfrac{Q_{mid\ cold}}{T_{mid\ cold}}} \tag{47}$$

This expression results from assigning all the entropy flow to the single temperature T_{mid}.

The ideal COP for the four-temperature cycle requires additional assumptions, such as the relationship between the various heat quantities. Under the assumptions that $Q_{cold} = Q_{mid\ cold}$ and $Q_{hot} = Q_{mid\ hot}$, the following expression results:

$$\text{COP}_{ideal} = \frac{T_{hot} - T_{mid\ hot}}{T_{hot}} \times \frac{T_{cold}}{T_{mid\ cold}} \times \frac{T_{cold}}{T_{mid\ hot}} \tag{48}$$

3.2 WORKING-FLUID PHASE CHANGE CONSTRAINTS

Absorption cycles require at least two working substances: a sorbent and a fluid refrigerant; these substances undergo phase changes. Given this constraint, many combinations are not achievable. The first result of invoking the phase change constraints is that the various heat flows assume known identities. As shown in Figure 17, the refrigerant phase changes occur in an evaporator and a condenser, and the sorbent phase changes in an absorber and a desorber (generator). (Note that two lines connect the evaporator to the absorber and the desorber to the condenser, with one indicating vapor flow, the second carryover of liquid. In both cases, the carryover of liquid is detrimental to system performance.) For the **forward absorption cycle**, the highest-temperature heat is always supplied to the generator,

$$Q_{hot} \equiv Q_{gen} \tag{49}$$

and the coldest heat is supplied to the evaporator:

$$Q_{cold} \equiv Q_{evap} \tag{50}$$

For the **reverse absorption cycle** (also called **heat transformer** or **type II absorption cycle**), the highest-temperature heat is rejected from the absorber, and the lowest-temperature heat is rejected from the condenser.

The second result of the phase change constraint is that, for all known refrigerants and sorbents over pressure ranges of interest,

$$Q_{evap} \approx Q_{cond} \tag{51}$$

and

$$Q_{gen} \approx Q_{abs} \tag{52}$$

These two relations are true because the latent heat of phase change (vapor ↔ condensed phase) is relatively constant when far removed from the critical point. Thus, each heat input cannot be independently adjusted.

The ideal single-effect forward-cycle COP expression is

$$\text{COP}_{ideal} \leq \frac{T_{gen} - T_{abs}}{T_{gen}} \times \frac{T_{evap}}{T_{cond} - T_{evap}} \times \frac{T_{cond}}{T_{abs}} \tag{53}$$

Equality holds only if the heat quantities at each temperature may be adjusted to specific values, which is not possible, as shown the following discussion.

The third result of invoking the phase change constraint is that only three of the four temperatures T_{evap}, T_{cond}, T_{gen}, and T_{abs} may be independently selected.

Practical liquid absorbents for absorption cycles have a significant negative deviation from behavior predicted by Raoult's law. This has the beneficial effect of reducing the required amount of absorbent recirculation, at the expense of reduced **lift** ($T_{cond} - T_{evap}$) and increased sorption duty. In practical terms, for most absorbents,

$$Q_{abs}/Q_{cond} \approx 1.2 \text{ to } 1.3 \tag{54}$$

and

$$T_{gen} - T_{abs} \approx 1.2(T_{cond} - T_{evap}) \tag{55}$$

The net result of applying these approximations and constraints to the ideal-cycle COP for the single-effect forward cycle is

$$\text{COP}_{ideal} \approx 1.2\frac{T_{evap}T_{cond}}{T_{gen}T_{abs}} \approx \frac{Q_{cond}}{Q_{abs}} \approx 0.8 \tag{56}$$

In practical terms, the temperature constraint reduces the ideal COP to about 0.9, and the heat quantity constraint further reduces it to about 0.8.

Another useful result is

$$T_{gen\ min} = T_{cond} + T_{abs} - T_{evap} \tag{57}$$

where $T_{gen\ min}$ is the minimum generator temperature necessary to achieve a given evaporator temperature.

Alternative approaches are available that lead to nearly the same upper limit on ideal-cycle COP. For example, one approach equates the exergy production from a "driving" portion of the cycle to the

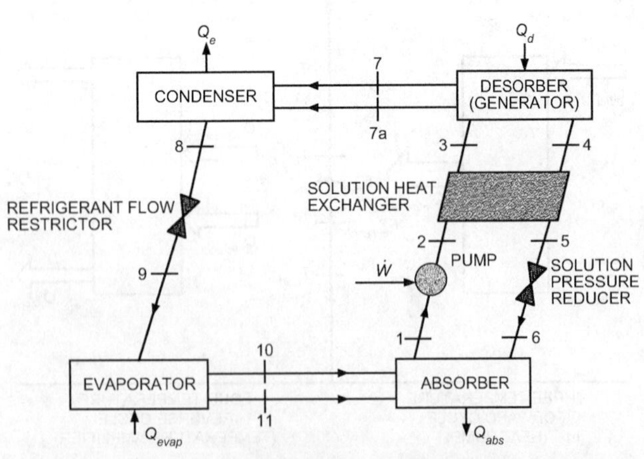

Fig. 17 Single-Effect Absorption Cycle

exergy consumption in a "cooling" portion of the cycle (Tozer and James 1997). This leads to the expression

$$COP_{ideal} \leq \frac{T_{evap}}{T_{abs}} = \frac{T_{cond}}{T_{gen}} \tag{58}$$

Another approach derives the idealized relationship between the two temperature differences that define the cycle: the cycle lift, defined previously, and **drop** ($T_{gen} - T_{abs}$).

Temperature Glide

One important limitation of simplified analysis of absorption cycle performance is that the heat quantities are assumed to be at fixed temperatures. In most actual applications, there is some temperature change (**temperature glide**) in the various fluids supplying or acquiring heat. It is most easily described by first considering situations wherein temperature glide is not present (i.e., truly isothermal heat exchanges). Examples are condensation or boiling of pure components (e.g., supplying heat by condensing steam). Any sensible heat exchange relies on temperature glide: for example, a circulating high-temperature liquid as a heat source; cooling water or air as a heat rejection medium; or circulating chilled glycol. Even latent heat exchanges can have temperature glide, as when a multicomponent mixture undergoes phase change.

When the temperature glide of one fluid stream is small compared to the cycle lift or drop, that stream can be represented by an average temperature, and the preceding analysis remains representative. However, one advantage of absorption cycles is they can maximize benefit from low-temperature, high-glide heat sources. That ability derives from the fact that the desorption process inherently embodies temperature glide, and hence can be tailored to match the heat source glide. Similarly, absorption also embodies glide, which can be made to match the glide of the heat rejection medium.

Implications of temperature glide have been analyzed for power cycles (Ibrahim and Klein 1998), but not yet for absorption cycles.

3.3 WORKING FLUIDS

Working fluids for absorption cycles fall into four categories, each requiring a different approach to cycle modeling and thermodynamic analysis. Liquid absorbents can be **nonvolatile** (i.e., vapor phase is always pure refrigerant, neglecting condensables) or **volatile** (i.e., vapor concentration varies, so cycle and component modeling must track both vapor and liquid concentration). Solid sorbents can be grouped by whether they are **physisorbents** (also known as *adsorbents*), for which, as for liquid absorbents, sorbent temperature depends on both pressure and refrigerant loading (bivariance); or **chemisorbents** (also known as **complex compounds**), for which sorbent temperature does not vary with loading, at least over small ranges.

Beyond these distinctions, various other characteristics are either necessary or desirable for suitable liquid absorbent/refrigerant pairs, as follows:

Absence of Solid Phase (Solubility Field). The refrigerant/absorbent pair should not solidify over the expected range of composition and temperature. If a solid forms, it will stop flow and shut down equipment. Controls must prevent operation beyond the acceptable solubility range.

Relative Volatility. The refrigerant should be much more volatile than the absorbent so the two can be separated easily. Otherwise, cost and heat requirements may be excessive. Many absorbents are effectively nonvolatile.

Affinity. The absorbent should have a strong affinity for the refrigerant under conditions in which absorption takes place. Affinity means a negative deviation from Raoult's law and results in an activity coefficient of less than unity for the refrigerant. Strong affinity allows less absorbent to be circulated for the same refrigeration effect, reducing sensible heat losses, and allows a smaller liquid heat exchanger to transfer heat from the absorbent to the pressurized refrigerant/absorption solution. On the other hand, as affinity increases, extra heat is required in the generators to separate refrigerant from the absorbent, and the COP suffers.

Pressure. Operating pressures, established by the refrigerant's thermodynamic properties, should be moderate. High pressure requires heavy-walled equipment, and significant electrical power may be needed to pump fluids from the low-pressure side to the high-pressure side. Vacuum requires large-volume equipment and special means of reducing pressure drop in the refrigerant vapor paths.

Stability. High chemical stability is required because fluids are subjected to severe conditions over many years of service. Instability can cause undesirable formation of gases, solids, or corrosive substances. Purity of all components charged into the system is critical for high performance and corrosion prevention.

Corrosion. Most absorption fluids corrode materials used in construction. Therefore, corrosion inhibitors are used.

Safety. Precautions as dictated by code are followed when fluids are toxic, inflammable, or at high pressure. Codes vary according to country and region.

Transport Properties. Viscosity, surface tension, thermal diffusivity, and mass diffusivity are important characteristics of the refrigerant/absorbent pair. For example, low viscosity promotes heat and mass transfer and reduces pumping power.

Latent Heat. The refrigerant latent heat should be high, so the circulation rate of the refrigerant and absorbent can be minimized.

Environmental Soundness. The two parameters of greatest concern are the global warming potential (GWP) and the ozone depletion potential (ODP). For more information on GWP and ODP, see Chapter 29.

No refrigerant/absorbent pair meets all requirements, and many requirements work at cross-purposes. For example, a greater solubility field goes hand in hand with reduced relative volatility. Thus, selecting a working pair is inherently a compromise.

Water/lithium bromide and ammonia/water offer the best compromises of thermodynamic performance and have no known detrimental environmental effect (zero ODP and zero GWP).

Ammonia/water meets most requirements, but its volatility ratio is low and it requires high operating pressures. Ammonia is also a Safety Code Group B2 fluid (ASHRAE *Standard* 34), which restricts its use indoors.

Advantages of water/lithium bromide include high (1) safety, (2) volatility ratio, (3) affinity, (4) stability, and (5) latent heat. However, this pair tends to form solids and operates at deep vacuum. Because the refrigerant turns to ice at 32°F, it cannot be used for low-temperature refrigeration. In fact, ice formation on demisters can be observed at even slightly above 32°F. Lithium bromide (LiBr) crystallizes at moderate concentrations, as would be encountered in air-cooled chillers, which ordinarily limits the pair to applications where the absorber is water cooled and the concentrations are lower. However, using a combination of salts as the absorbent can reduce this crystallization tendency enough to allow air cooling (Macriss 1968). Other disadvantages include low operating pressures and high viscosity. This is particularly detrimental to the absorption step; however, alcohols with a high relative molecular mass enhance LiBr absorption. Proper equipment design and additives can overcome these disadvantages.

Other refrigerant/absorbent pairs are listed in Table 5 (Macriss and Zawacki 1989). Several appear suitable for certain cycles and may solve some problems associated with traditional pairs. However, information on properties, stability, and corrosion is limited. Also, some of the fluids are somewhat hazardous.

Table 5 Refrigerant/Absorbent Pairs

Refrigerant	Absorbents
H_2O	Salts
	Alkali halides
	LiBr
	$LiClO_3$
	$CaCl_2$
	$ZnCl_2$
	ZnBr
	Alkali nitrates
	Alkali thiocyanates
	Bases
	Alkali hydroxides
	Acids
	H_2SO_4
	H_3PO_4
NH_3	H_2O
	Alkali thiocyanates
TFE	NMP
(Organic)	E181
	DMF
	Pyrrolidone
SO_2	Organic solvents

Alcohols such as methanol are also being considered as refrigerants. A review of working pairs is given in Macriss et al. (1988). In addition, some absorption working pairs use a conventional refrigerant, such as ammonia or water, but a solid absorbent. Examples are complex compounds in which ammonia is absorbed into solid salts that remain solid even when the salts absorb quantities of ammonia that exceed on a molar basis several times the moles of salt (Rockenfeller and Kirol 1989, 1996; Rockenfeller et al. 1992, 1993).

3.4 EFFECT OF FLUID PROPERTIES ON CYCLE PERFORMANCE

Thermodynamic observations can predict general trends of how working fluids' properties affect a cycle's performance: in all four major heat exchangers (absorber, generator, condenser, and evaporator), the amount of heat exchanged is dominated by the latent heat of the refrigerant (i.e., the component that undergoes the phase change), when any phase change of the absorbent is neglected. There are two additional contributions for the absorber and generator: heat of mixing when the condensed refrigerant is mixed with the absorbent/refrigerant solution, and heating or cooling of the refrigerant/absorbent mixture during the absorption or desorption process.

Thus, the heat requirement of the generator can be estimated as the latent heat of the refrigerant plus the heat of mixing plus the heat required to heat the remaining absorbent/refrigerant solution. Both additional terms increase the generator heat requirement and thus reduce the overall cycle efficiency. Based on this observation, the ideal absorption working fluid should have high latent heat, no heat of mixing, and a low specific heat capacity.

Furthermore, heat exchanged in the solution heat exchanger is governed by the specific heat of the fluid mixture flowing through this device. Consequently, any ineffectiveness of the heat exchanger represents a loss in absorption-cycle performance that is directly related to the specific heat capacity of the fluid mixture, reinforcing the argument that a low specific heat capacity is desirable.

Finally, losses in the expansion process of the refrigerant as it enters the evaporator are also governed by the latent heat of the refrigerant (preferably large) and its specific heat capacity (preferably small), so that as little refrigerant as possible evaporates as a result of the expansion process.

Absorption working fluids should consist of refrigerants with large latent heat and absorbents with a small heat of mixing, and both absorbent and refrigerant should have as small a specific heat capacity as possible.

Heat of mixing and latent heat are determined by functional groups within the molecule; specific heat capacity is minimized when the molecule is small and of low molecular weight. Therefore, ideal working fluids should be small molecules with as many functional groups as possible. This explains why ammonia and water are still the favored refrigerants to date for absorption cycles, and why organic fluids have not yet succeeded in commercial absorption cycle applications (because of their relatively large molecular weight).

3.5 ABSORPTION CYCLE REPRESENTATIONS

The quantities of interest to absorption cycle designers are temperature, concentration, pressure, and enthalpy. The most useful plots use linear scales and plot the key properties as straight lines. Some of the following plots are used:

- **Absorption plots** embody the vapor-liquid equilibrium of both the refrigerant and the sorbent. Plots on linear pressure-temperature coordinates have a logarithmic shape and hence are little used.
- In the **van't Hoff plot** ($\ln P$ versus $-1/T$), the constant concentration contours plot as nearly straight lines. Thus, it is more readily constructed (e.g., from sparse data) in spite of the awkward coordinates.
- The **Dühring diagram** (solution temperature versus reference temperature) retains the linearity of the van't Hoff plot but eliminates the complexity of nonlinear coordinates. Thus, it is used extensively (see Figure 20). The primary drawback is the need for a reference substance.
- The **Gibbs plot** (solution temperature versus $T \ln P$) retains most of the advantages of the Dühring plot (linear temperature coordinates, concentration contours are straight lines) but eliminates the need for a reference substance.
- The **Merkel plot** (enthalpy versus concentration) is used to assist thermodynamic calculations and to solve the distillation problems that arise with volatile absorbents. It has also been used for basic cycle analysis.
- **Temperature/entropy coordinates** are occasionally used to relate absorption cycles to their mechanical vapor compression counterparts.

3.6 CONCEPTUALIZING THE CYCLE

The basic absorption cycle shown in Figure 17 must be altered in many cases to take advantage of the available energy. Examples include the following: (1) the driving heat is much hotter than the minimum required $T_{gen\ min}$: a multistage cycle boosts the COP; and (2) the driving heat temperature is below $T_{gen\ min}$: a different multistage cycle (half-effect cycle) can reduce the $T_{gen\ min}$.

Multistage cycles have one or more of the four basic exchangers (generator, absorber, condenser, evaporator) present at two or more places in the cycle at different pressures or concentrations. A **multi-effect** cycle is a special case of multistaging, signifying the number of times the driving heat is used in the cycle. Thus, there are several types of two-stage cycles: double-effect, half-effect, and triple-effect.

Two or more single-effect absorption cycles, such as shown in Figure 17, can be combined to form a multistage cycle by coupling any of the components. **Coupling** implies either (1) sharing component(s) between the cycles to form an integrated single hermetic cycle or (2) exchanging heat between components belonging to two hermetically separate cycles that operate at (nearly) the same temperature level.

Figure 18 shows a **double-effect absorption cycle** formed by coupling the absorbers and evaporators of two single-effect cycles into an integrated, single hermetic cycle. Heat is transferred between the high-pressure condenser and intermediate-pressure generator. The heat of condensation of the refrigerant (generated in the high-temperature generator) generates additional refrigerant in the lower-temperature generator. Thus, the prime energy provided to the high-temperature generator is **cascaded** (used) twice in the cycle, making it a double-effect cycle. With the generation of additional refrigerant from a given heat input, the cycle COP increases. Commercial water/lithium bromide chillers normally use this cycle. The cycle COP can be further increased by coupling additional components and by increasing the number of cycles that are combined. This way, several different multieffect cycles can be combined by pressure-staging and/or concentration-staging. The double-effect cycle, for example, is formed by pressure staging two single-effect cycles.

Figure 19 shows twelve generic triple-effect cycles identified by Alefeld and Radermacher (1994). Cycle 5 is a pressure-staged cycle, and cycle 10 is a concentration-staged cycle. All other cycles are pressure and concentration staged. Cycle 1, which is a type of dual-loop cycle, is the only cycle consisting of two loops that does not circulate absorbent in the low-temperature portion of the cycle.

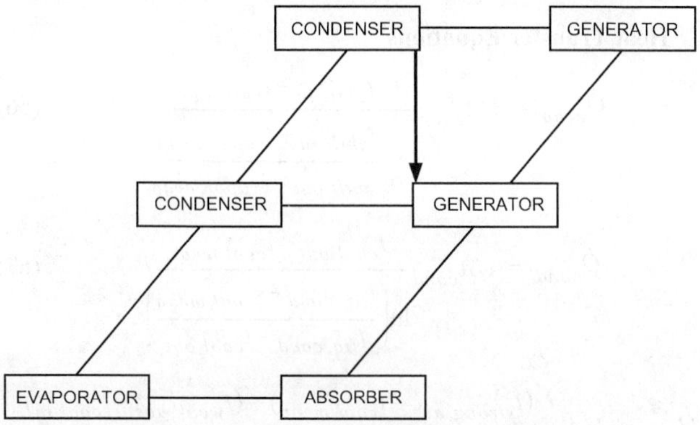

Fig. 18 Double-Effect Absorption Cycle

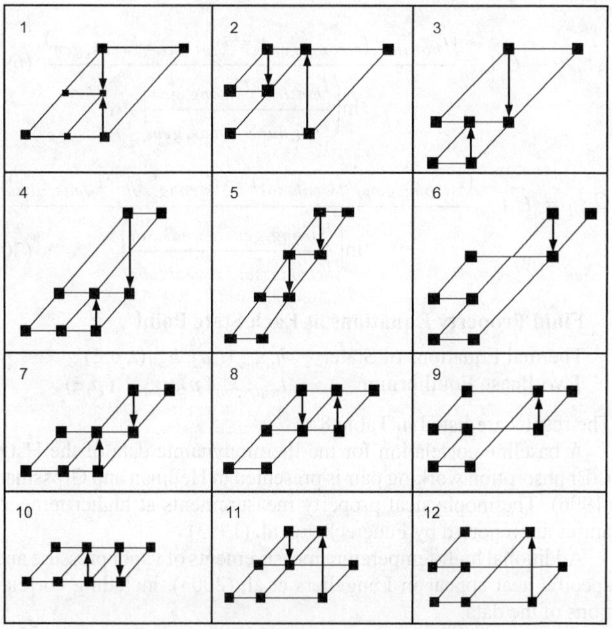

Fig. 19 Generic Triple-Effect Cycles

Each of the cycles shown in Figure 19 can be made with one, two, or sometimes three separate **hermetic loops**. Dividing a cycle into separate hermetic loops allows the use of a different working fluid in each loop. Thus, a corrosive and/or high-lift absorbent can be restricted to the loop where it is required, and a conventional additive-enhanced absorbent can be used in other loops to reduce system cost significantly. As many as 78 hermetic loop configurations can be synthesized from the twelve triple-effect cycles shown in Figure 19. For each hermetic loop configuration, further variations are possible according to the absorbent flow pattern (e.g., series or parallel), the absorption working pairs selected, and various other hardware details. Thus, literally thousands of distinct variations of the triple-effect cycle are possible.

The ideal analysis can be extended to these multistage cycles (Alefeld and Radermacher 1994). A similar range of cycle variants is possible for situations calling for the half-effect cycle, in which the available heat source temperature is below $t_{gen\ min}$.

3.7 ABSORPTION CYCLE MODELING

Analysis and Performance Simulation

A physical-mathematical model of an absorption cycle consists of four types of thermodynamic equations: mass balances, energy balances, relations describing heat and mass transfer, and equations for thermophysical properties of the working fluids.

As an example of simulation, Figure 20 shows a Dühring plot of a single-effect water/lithium bromide absorption chiller. The hot-water-driven chiller rejects waste heat from the absorber and the condenser to a stream of cooling water, and produces chilled water. A simulation of this chiller starts by specifying the assumptions (Table 6) and the design parameters and operating conditions at the design point (Table 7). Design parameters are the specified *UA* values and the flow regime (co/counter/crosscurrent, pool, or film) of all heat exchangers (evaporator, condenser, generator, absorber, solution heat exchanger) and the flow rate of weak solution through the solution pump.

One complete set of input operating parameters could be the design point values of the chilled- and cooling water temperatures $t_{chill\ in}$, $t_{chill\ out}$, $t_{cool\ in}$, $t_{cool\ out}$, hot-water flow rate $\dot{m}_{hot}$, and total cooling capacity Q_e. With this information, a cycle simulation calculates the required hot-water temperatures; cooling-water flow rate; and temperatures, pressures, and concentrations at all internal state points. Some additional assumptions are made that reduce the number of unknown parameters.

With these assumptions and the design parameters and operating conditions as specified in Table 7, the cycle simulation can be conducted by solving the following set of equations:

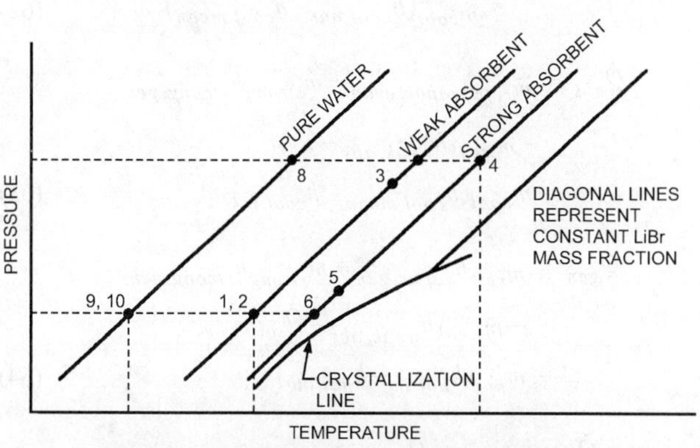

Fig. 20 Single-Effect Water/Lithium Bromide Absorption Cycle Dühring Plot

Table 6 Assumptions for Single-Effect Water/Lithium Bromide Model (Figure 20)

Assumptions
• Generator and condenser as well as evaporator and absorber are under same pressure
• Refrigerant vapor leaving evaporator is saturated pure water
• Liquid refrigerant leaving condenser is saturated
• Strong solution leaving generator is boiling
• Refrigerant vapor leaving generator has equilibrium temperature of weak solution at generator pressure
• Weak solution leaving absorber is saturated
• No liquid carryover from evaporator
• Flow restrictors are adiabatic
• Pump is isentropic
• No jacket heat losses
• LMTD (log mean temperature difference) expression adequately estimates latent changes

Table 7 Design Parameters and Operating Conditions for Single-Effect Water/Lithium Bromide Absorption Chiller

	Design Parameters	Operating Conditions
Evaporator	UA_{evap} = 605,000 Btu/h·°F, countercurrent film	$t_{chill\ in}$ = 53.6°F $t_{chill\ out}$ = 42.8°F
Condenser	UA_{cond} = 342,300 Btu/h·°F, countercurrent film	$t_{cool\ out}$ = 95°F
Absorber	UA_{abs} = 354,300 Btu/h·°F, countercurrent film-absorber	$t_{cool\ in}$ = 80.6°F
Generator	UA_{gen} = 271,800 Btu/h·°F, pool-generator	$\dot{m}_{hot}$ = 590,000 lb/h
Solution	UA_{sol} = 64,100 Btu/h·°F, countercurrent	
General	$\dot{m}_{weak}$ = 95,200 lb/h	$\dot{Q}_{evap}$ = 7.33 × 10⁶ Btu/h

Mass Balances

$$\dot{m}_{refr} + \dot{m}_{strong} = \dot{m}_{weak} \tag{59}$$

$$\dot{m}_{strong}\xi_{strong} = \dot{m}_{weak}\xi_{weak} \tag{60}$$

Energy Balances

$$\dot{Q}_{evap} = \dot{m}_{refr}(h_{vapor,\,evap} - h_{liq,\,cond}) = \dot{m}_{chill}(h_{chill\ in} - h_{chill\ out}) \tag{61}$$

$$\dot{Q}_{cond} = \dot{m}_{refr}(h_{vapor,\,gen} - h_{liq,\,cond}) = \dot{m}_{cool}(h_{cool\ out} - h_{cool\ mean}) \tag{62}$$

$$\dot{Q}_{abs} = \dot{m}_{refr}h_{vapor,\,evap} + \dot{m}_{strong}h_{strong,\,gen} - \dot{m}_{weak}h_{weak,\,abs} - \dot{Q}_{sol} = \dot{m}_{cool}(h_{cool\ mean} - h_{cool\ in}) \tag{63}$$

$$\dot{Q}_{gen} = \dot{m}_{refr}h_{vapor,\,gen} + \dot{m}_{strong}h_{strong,\,gen} - \dot{m}_{weak}h_{weak,\,abs} - \dot{Q}_{sol} = \dot{m}_{hot}(h_{hot\ in} - h_{hot\ out}) \tag{64}$$

$$\dot{Q}_{sol} = \dot{m}_{strong}(h_{strong,\,gen} - h_{strong,\,sol}) = \dot{m}_{weak}(h_{weak,\,sol} - h_{weak,\,abs}) \tag{65}$$

Table 8 Simulation Results for Single-Effect Water/Lithium Bromide Absorption Chiller

	Internal Parameters	Performance Parameters
Evaporator	$t_{vapor,evap}$ = 35.2°F $p_{sat,evap}$ = 0.1 psia	$\dot{Q}_{evap}$ = 7.33 × 10⁶ Btu/h $\dot{m}_{chill}$ = 677,000 lb/h
Condenser	$T_{liq,cond}$ = 115.2°F $p_{sat,cond}$ = 1.48 psia	$\dot{Q}_{cond}$ = 7.92 × 10⁶ Btu/h $\dot{m}_{cool}$ = 1.260 × 10⁶b/h
Absorber	ξ_{weak} = 59.6% t_{weak} = 105.3°F $t_{strong,abs}$ = 121.8°F	$\dot{Q}_{abs}$ = 10.18 × 10⁶ Btu/h $t_{cool,mean}$ = 88.7°F
Generator	ξ_{strong} = 64.6% $t_{strong,gen}$ = 218.3°F $t_{weak,gen}$ = 198.3°F $t_{weak,sol}$ = 169°F	$\dot{Q}_{gen}$ = 10.78 × 10⁶Btu/h $t_{hot\ in}$ = 257°F $t_{hot\ out}$ = 239°F
Solution	$t_{strong,sol}$ = 144.3°F $t_{weak,sol}$ = 169°F	$\dot{Q}_{sol}$ = 2.815 × 10⁶ Btu/h ε = 65.4%
General	$\dot{m}_{vapor}$ = 7380 lb/h $\dot{m}_{strong}$ = 87,800 lb/h	COP = 0.68

Heat Transfer Equations

$$\dot{Q}_{evap} = UA_{evap}\frac{t_{chill\ in} - t_{chill\ out}}{\ln\left(\frac{t_{chill\ in} - t_{vapor,\,evap}}{t_{chill\ out} - t_{vapor,\,evap}}\right)} \tag{66}$$

$$\dot{Q}_{cond} = UA_{cond}\frac{t_{cool\ out} - t_{cool\ mean}}{\ln\left(\frac{t_{liq,\,cond} - t_{cool\ mean}}{t_{liq,\,cond} - t_{cool\ out}}\right)} \tag{67}$$

$$\dot{Q}_{abs} = UA_{abs}\frac{(t_{strong,\,abs} - t_{cool\ mean}) - (t_{weak,\,abs} - t_{cool\ in})}{\ln\left(\frac{t_{strong,\,abs} - t_{cool\ mean}}{t_{weak,\,abs} - t_{cool\ in}}\right)} \tag{68}$$

$$\dot{Q}_{gen} = UA_{gen}\frac{(t_{hot\ in} - t_{strong,\,gen}) - (t_{hot\ out} - t_{weak,\,gen})}{\ln\left(\frac{t_{hot\ in} - t_{strong,\,gen}}{t_{hot\ out} - t_{weak,\,gen}}\right)} \tag{69}$$

$$\dot{Q}_{sol} = UA_{sol}\frac{(t_{strong,\,gen} - t_{weak,\,sol}) - (t_{strong,\,sol} - t_{weak,\,abs})}{\ln\left(\frac{t_{strong,\,gen} - t_{weak,\,sol}}{t_{strong,\,sol} - t_{weak,\,abs}}\right)} \tag{70}$$

Fluid Property Equations at Each State Point

Thermal Equations of State: $h_{water}(t,p)$, $h_{sol}(t,p,\xi)$
Two-Phase Equilibrium: $t_{water,\,sat}(p)$, $t_{sol,\,sat}(p,\xi)$

The results are listed in Table 8.

A baseline correlation for the thermodynamic data of the H_2O/LiBr absorption working pair is presented in Hellman and Grossman (1996). Thermophysical property measurements at higher temperatures are reported by Feuerecker et al. (1993).

Additional high-temperature measurements of vapor pressure and specific heat appear in Langeliers et al. (2003), including correlations of the data.

The *UA* values in Equations (66) to (70) account for the actual heat and mass transfer processes, which depend greatly on operating

Table 9 Inputs and Assumptions for Double-Effect Water-Lithium Bromide Model (Figure 21)

Inputs		
Capacity	$\dot{Q}_{evap}$	500 tons (refrig.)
Evaporator temperature	t_{10}	41.1°F
Desorber solution exit temperature	t_{14}	339.3°F
Condenser/absorber low temperature	t_1, t_8	108.3°F
Solution heat exchanger effectiveness	ε	0.6

Assumptions

- Steady state
- Refrigerant is pure water
- No pressure changes except through flow restrictors and pump
- State points at 1, 4, 8, 11, 14, and 18 are saturated liquid
- State point 10 is saturated vapor
- Temperature difference between high-temperature condenser and low-temperature generator is 9°F
- Parallel flow
- Both solution heat exchangers have same effectiveness
- Upper loop solution flow rate is selected such that upper condenser heat exactly matches lower generator heat requirement
- Flow restrictors are adiabatic
- Pumps are isentropic
- No jacket heat losses
- No liquid carryover from evaporator to absorber
- Vapor leaving both generators is at equilibrium temperature of entering solution stream

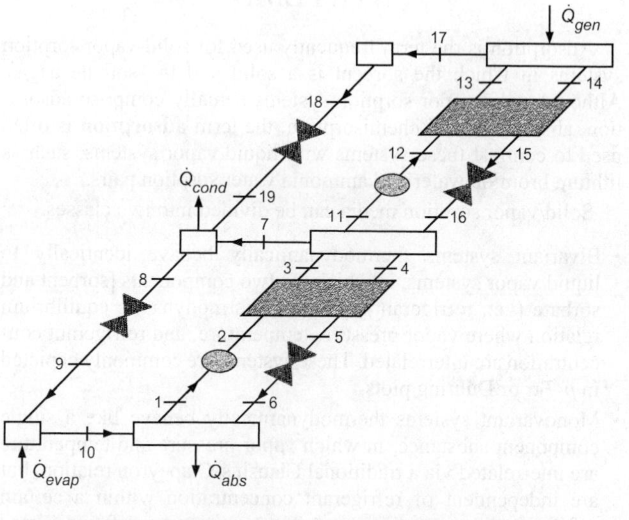

Fig. 21 Double-Effect Water/Lithium Bromide Absorption Cycle with State Points

conditions and actual heat exchanger designs. Determining these values is beyond the scope of this chapter.

Double-Effect Cycle

Double-effect cycle calculations can be performed in a manner similar to that for the single-effect cycle. Mass and energy balances of the model shown in Figure 21 were calculated using the inputs and assumptions listed in Table 9. The results are shown in Table 10. The COP is quite sensitive to several inputs and assumptions. In particular, the effectiveness of the solution heat exchangers and the driving temperature difference between the high-temperature condenser and the low-temperature generator influence the COP strongly.

Table 10 State Point Data for Double-Effect Water/Lithium Bromide Cycle (Figure 21)

Point	h, Btu/lb	$\dot{m}$, lb/min	p, psia	Q, Fraction	t, °F	x, % LiBr
1	50.6	1263.4	0.13	0.0	108.3	
2	50.6	1263.4	1.21		108.3	59.5
3	78.3	1263.4	1.21		168.1	59.5
4	106.2	1163.7	1.21	0.0	208.0	64.6
5	76.1	1163.7	1.21		137.9	64.6
6	76.1	1163.7	0.13	0.004	127.8	64.6
7	1143.2	42.3	1.21		186.2	0.0
8	76.2	99.8	1.21	0.0	108.3	0.0
9	76.2	99.8	0.13	0.063	41.1	0.0
10	1078.6	99.8	0.13	1.0	41.1	0.0
11	86.7	727.3	1.21	0.0	186.2	59.5
12	86.7	727.3	16.21		186.2	59.5
13	129.4	727.3	16.21		278.0	59.5
14	162.7	669.9	16.21	0.0	339.3	64.6
15	116.4	669.9	16.21		231.6	64.6
16	116.4	669.9	1.21	0.008	210.3	64.6
17	1197.4	57.4	16.21		312.2	0.0
18	185.0	57.4	16.21	0.0	217.0	0.0
19	185.0	57.4	1.21	0.105	108.3	0.0

$$COP = 1.195$$
$$\Delta t = 9.0°F$$
$$\varepsilon = 0.600$$
$$\dot{Q}_{abs} = 7.936 \times 10^6 \text{ Btu/h}$$
$$\dot{Q}_{gen,\ mid\text{-}pressure} = 3.488 \times 10^6 \text{ Btu/h}$$
$$\dot{Q}_{cond} = 3.085 \times 10^6 \text{ Btu/h}$$
$$\dot{Q}_{evap} = 6.000 \times 10^6 \text{ Btu/h}$$
$$\dot{Q}_{gen,\ high\text{-}pressure} = 5.019 \times 10^6 \text{ Btu/h}$$
$$\dot{Q}_{shx1} = 2.103 \times 10^6 \text{ Btu/h}$$
$$\dot{Q}_{shx2} = 1.862 \times 10^6 \text{ Btu/h}$$
$$\dot{W}_{p1} = 0.032 \text{ hp}$$
$$\dot{W}_{p2} = 0.258 \text{ hp}$$

3.8 AMMONIA/WATER ABSORPTION CYCLES

Ammonia/water absorption cycles are similar to water/lithium bromide cycles, but with some important differences because of ammonia's lower latent heat compared to water, the volatility of the absorbent, and the different pressure and solubility ranges. Ammonia's latent heat is only about half that of water, so, for the same duty, the refrigerant and absorbent mass circulation rates are roughly double that of water/lithium bromide. As a result, the sensible heat loss associated with heat exchanger approaches is greater. Accordingly, ammonia/water cycles incorporate more techniques to reclaim sensible heat, described in Hanna et al. (1995). The refrigerant heat exchanger (RHX), also known as refrigerant subcooler, which improves COP by about 8%, is the most important (Holldorff 1979). Next is the absorber heat exchanger (AHX), accompanied by a generator heat exchanger (GHX) (Phillips 1976). These either replace or supplement the traditional solution heat exchanger (SHX). These components would also benefit the water/lithium bromide cycle, except that the deep vacuum in that cycle makes them impractical there.

The volatility of the water absorbent is also key. It makes the distinction between crosscurrent, cocurrent, and countercurrent mass exchange more important in all of the latent heat exchangers (Briggs 1971). It also requires a distillation column on the high-pressure side. When improperly implemented, this column can impose both cost and COP penalties. Those penalties are avoided by refluxing the column from an internal diabatic section [e.g., solution-cooled rectifier (SCR)] rather than with an external reflux pump.

The high-pressure operating regime makes it impractical to achieve multieffect performance via pressure staging. On the other hand, the exceptionally wide solubility field facilitates concentration staging. The generator-absorber heat exchange (GAX) cycle is

Table 11 Inputs and Assumptions for Single-Effect Ammonia/Water Cycle (Figure 22)

Inputs		
Capacity	$\dot{Q}_{evap}$	500 tons (refrig.)
High-side pressure	p_{high}	211.8 psia
Low-side pressure	p_{low}	74.7 psia
Absorber exit temperature	t_1	105°F
Generator exit temperature	t_4	203°F
Rectifier vapor exit temperature	t_7	131°F
Solution heat exchanger effectiveness	ε_{shx}	0.692
Refrigerant heat exchanger effectiveness	ε_{rhx}	0.629

Assumptions

- Steady state
- No pressure changes except through flow restrictors and pump
- States at points 1, 4, 8, 11, and 14 are saturated liquid
- States at point 12 and 13 are saturated vapor
- Flow restrictors are adiabatic
- Pump is isentropic
- No jacket heat losses
- No liquid carryover from evaporator to absorber
- Vapor leaving generator is at equilibrium temperature of entering solution stream

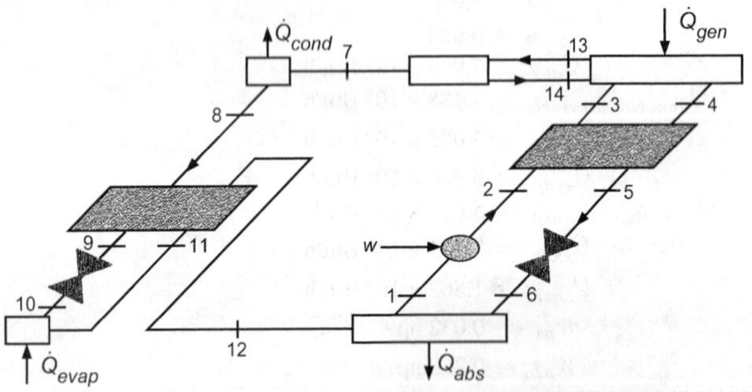

Fig. 22 Single-Effect Ammonia/Water Absorption Cycle

an especially advantageous embodiment of concentration staging (Modahl and Hayes 1988).

Ammonia/water cycles can equal the performance of water/lithium bromide cycles. The single-effect or basic GAX cycle yields the same performance as a single-effect water/lithium bromide cycle; the branched GAX cycle (Herold et al. 1991) yields the same performance as a water/lithium bromide double-effect cycle; and the VX GAX cycle (Erickson and Rane 1994) yields the same performance as a water/lithium bromide triple-effect cycle. Additional advantages of the ammonia/water cycle include refrigeration capability, air-cooling capability, all mild steel construction, extreme compactness, and capability of direct integration into industrial processes. Between heat-activated refrigerators, gas-fired residential air conditioners, and large industrial refrigeration plants, this technology has accounted for the vast majority of absorption activity over the past century.

Figure 22 shows the diagram of a typical single-effect ammonia-water absorption cycle. The inputs and assumptions in Table 11 are used to calculate a single-cycle solution, which is summarized in Table 12.

Comprehensive correlations of the thermodynamic properties of the ammonia/water absorption working pair are found in Ibrahim and Klein (1993) and Tillner-Roth and Friend (1998a, 1998b), both of which are available as commercial software. Figure 33 in Chapter 30 of this volume was prepared using the Ibrahim and Klein correlation, which is also incorporated in REFPROP (National Institute of Standards and Technology). Transport properties for ammonia/water mixtures are available in IIR (1994) and in Melinder (1998).

Table 12 State Point Data for Single-Effect Ammonia/Water Cycle (Figure 22)

Point	*h*, Btu/lb	$\dot{m}$, lb/min	*p*, psia	*Q*, Fraction	*t*, °F	*x*, Fraction NH_3
1	−24.55	1408.2	74.7	0.0	105.0	0.50094
2	−24.05	1408.2	211.8		105.5	0.50094
3	38.47	1408.2	211.8		163.0	0.50094
4	83.81	1203.0	211.8	0.0	203.0	0.41612
5	10.61	1203.0	211.8		135.6	0.41612
6	10.61	1203.0	74.7	0.006	132.0	0.41612
7	579.51	205.2	211.8	1.0	131.0	0.99809
8	76.61	205.2	211.8	0.0	100.1	0.99809
9	35.28	205.2	211.8		64.1	0.99809
10	35.28	205.2	74.7	0.049	41.1	0.99809
11	522.55	205.2	74.7	0.953	42.8	0.99809
12	563.88	205.2	74.7	1.0	87.0	0.99809
13	613.91	209.9	211.8	1.0	174.5	0.98708
14	51.72	4.6	211.8	0.0	174.5	0.50094

COP	= 0.571	$\dot{Q}_{evap}$	= 6.00×10^6 Btu/h
Δt_{rhx}	= 36.00°F	$\dot{Q}_{gen}$	= 1.051×10^7 Btu/h
Δt_{shx}	= 30.1°F	$\dot{Q}_{rhx}$	= 5.089×10^5 Btu/h
ε_{rhx}	= 0.629	$\dot{Q}_r$	= 5.805×10^5 Btu/h
ε_{shx}	= 0.692	$\dot{Q}_{shx}$	= 5.283×10^6 Btu/h
$\dot{Q}_{abs}$	= 9.784×10^6 Btu/h	$\dot{W}$	= 9.22 hp
$\dot{Q}_{cond}$	= 6.192×10^6 Btu/h		

4. ADSORPTION REFRIGERATION SYSTEMS

Adsorption is the term frequently used for solid-vapor sorption systems in which the sorbent is a solid and the sorbate a gas. Although solid-vapor sorption systems actually comprise adsorption, absorption, and chemisorption, the term **adsorption** is often used to contrast these systems with liquid/vapor systems, such as lithium bromide/water and ammonia/water sorption pairs.

Solid/vapor sorption media can be divided into two classes:

- Bivariant systems thermodynamically behave identically to liquid/vapor systems, in which the two components [sorbent and sorbate (i.e., refrigerant)] define a thermodynamic equilibrium relation where vapor pressure, temperature, and refrigerant concentration are interrelated. These systems are commonly depicted in *p-T-x* or Dühring plots.
- Monovariant systems thermodynamically behave like a single component substance, in which vapor pressure and temperature are interrelated via a traditional Clausius-Clapeyron relation, but are independent of refrigerant concentration within a certain refrigerant concentration range. These systems are often depicted in *p-T-n* or van't Hoff plots, in which each line represents a refrigerant concentration range.

Typical examples of bivariant adsorption systems are zeolites, activated carbons, and silica gels. The most common examples of monovariant systems are metal hydrides and coordinative complex compounds (including ammoniated and hydrated complex compounds).

Practical ammonia or water refrigerant uptake concentrations for bivariant materials are typically lower than observed with their liquid vapor counterparts. Monovariant metal hydrides use hydrogen as the gaseous components. Although uptake concentrations are very low (typically in the single-digit mass percentage), the heat of reaction for metal hydrides is very high, yielding an overall energy density almost comparable to other solid/vapor sorption systems. Coordinative complex compounds can have refrigerant uptake that exceeds the capability of other solid/gas systems. The concentration range within which temperature and vapor pressure are independent of the refrigerant concentration can exceed 50%; the heat of sorption is distinctively higher than for bivariant solid/gas and liquid/vapor systems, but much lower than observed with most metal hydrides. The large refrigerant concentration range of constant vapor pressure, also referred to as the **coordination sphere**, lends itself to thermal energy storage applications.

The most common coordinative complex compounds are ammoniated compounds using alkali, alkali/earth, or transition metal halides (e.g., strontium chloride, calcium chloride, calcium bromide).

Although solid/vapor systems are designed to use solid sorbents and therefore do not carry the operational risk of equipment failure caused by solidifying from a liquid (as is the case with lithium bromide), some systems, particularly complex compounds, might melt at certain temperature/pressure/concentration conditions, which can lead to irreparable equipment failure.

Refrigeration or heat pump cycles constructed with solid/vapor systems are inherently batch-type cycles in which exothermic adsorption of refrigerant is followed by typically heat-actuated endothermic desorption of refrigerant. To obtain continuous refrigeration or heating, two or more solid sorbent pressure vessels (sorbers) need to operate at the same time and out of time sequence. The advantage of such cycles compared to liquid/vapor cycles is the fact that they do not require a solution makeup circuit with a solution pump; the disadvantage is the fact that the sorbent is firmly packed or situated in heat exchange hardware, inducing a higher thermal mass and requiring more involved means for recuperation.

Advanced cycles with internal heat recovery, pressure staging, and temperature staging exist for solid/vapor systems similar to liquid/vapor system. For more information, see Alefeld and Radermacher (1994).

4.1 SYMBOLS

c_p = specific heat at constant pressure, Btu/lb·°F
COP = coefficient of performance
g = local acceleration of gravity, ft/s^2
h = enthalpy, Btu/lb
I = irreversibility, Btu/°R
$\dot{I}$ = irreversibility rate, Btu/h·°R
m = mass, lb
$\dot{m}$ = mass flow, lb/min
p = pressure, psia
Q = heat energy, Btu
$\dot{Q}$ = rate of heat flow, Btu/h
R = ideal gas constant, ft·lb/lb·°R
s = specific entropy, Btu/lb·°R
S = total entropy, Btu/°R
t = temperature, °F
T = absolute temperature, °R
u = internal energy, Btu/lb
v = specific volume, ft^3/lb
V = velocity of fluid, ft/s
W = mechanical or shaft work, Btu
$\dot{W}$ = rate of work, power, Btu/h
x = mass fraction (of either lithium bromide or ammonia)
x = vapor quality (fraction)
z = elevation above horizontal reference plane, ft
Z = compressibility factor
Δt = temperature difference, °F
ε = heat exchanger effectiveness
η = efficiency
ξ = solution concentration
ρ = density, lb/ft^3

Subscripts

abs = absorber
cg = condenser to generator
cond = condenser or cooling mode
evap = evaporator
fg = fluid to vapor
gen = generator
liq = liquid
gh = high-temperature generator
o, 0 = reference conditions, usually ambient
p = pump
R = refrigerating or evaporator conditions
r = rectifier
refr = refrigerant
rhx = refrigerant heat exchanger
sat = saturated
shx = solution heat exchanger
sol = solution

REFERENCES

Alefeld, G., and R. Radermacher. 1994. *Heat conversion systems*. CRC Press, Boca Raton.

ASHRAE. 2010. Designation and safety classification of refrigerants. ANSI/ASHRAE *Standard* 34-2010.

Benedict, M. 1937. Pressure, volume, temperature properties of nitrogen at high density, I and II. *Journal of American Chemists Society* 59(11): 2224-2233 and 2233-2242.

Benedict, M., G.B. Webb, and L.C. Rubin. 1940. An empirical equation for thermodynamic properties of light hydrocarbons and their mixtures. *Journal of Chemistry and Physics* 4:334.

Briggs, S.W. 1971. Concurrent, crosscurrent, and countercurrent absorption in ammonia-water absorption refrigeration. *ASHRAE Transactions* 77(1):171.

Cooper, H.W., and J.C. Goldfrank. 1967. B-W-R constants and new correlations. *Hydrocarbon Processing* 46(12):141.

Erickson, D.C., and M. Rane. 1994. Advanced absorption cycle: Vapor exchange GAX. *Proceedings of the International Absorption Heat Pump Conference*, Chicago.

Feuerecker, G., J. Scharfe, I. Greiter, C. Frank, and G. Alefeld. 1993. Measurement of thermophysical properties of aqueous LiBr solutions at high temperatures and concentrations. *Proceedings of the International Absorption Heat Pump Conference*, New Orleans, AES-30, pp. 493-499. American Society of Mechanical Engineers, New York.

Hanna, W.T., et al. 1995. Pinch-point analysis: An aid to understanding the GAX absorption cycle. *ASHRAE Technical Data Bulletin* 11(2).

Hellman, H.-M., and G. Grossman. 1996. Improved property data correlations of absorption fluids for computer simulation of heat pump cycles. *ASHRAE Transactions* 102(1):980-997.

Herold, K.E., et al. 1991. The branched GAX absorption heat pump cycle. *Proceedings of Absorption Heat Pump Conference*, Tokyo.

Hirschfelder, J.O., et al. 1958. Generalized equation of state for gases and liquids. *Industrial and Engineering Chemistry* 50:375.

Holldorff, G. 1979. Revisions up absorption refrigeration efficiency. *Hydrocarbon Processing* 58(7):149.

Howell, J.R., and R.O. Buckius. 1992. *Fundamentals of engineering thermodynamics*, 2nd ed. McGraw-Hill, New York.

Hust, J.G., and R.D. McCarty. 1967. Curve-fitting techniques and applications to thermodynamics. *Cryogenics* 8:200.

Hust, J.G., and R.B. Stewart. 1966. Thermodynamic property computations for system analysis. *ASHRAE Journal* 2:64.

Ibrahim, O.M., and S.A. Klein. 1993. Thermodynamic properties of ammonia-water mixtures. *ASHRAE Transactions* 99(1):1495-1502.

Ibrahim, O.M., and S.A. Klein. 1998. The maximum power cycle: A model for new cycles and new working fluids. *Proceedings of the ASME Advanced Energy Systems Division*, AES vol. 117. American Society of Mechanical Engineers. New York.

IIR. 1994. *R123—Thermodynamic and physical properties. NH_3–H_2O.* International Institute of Refrigeration, Paris.

Kuehn, T.H., and R.E. Gronseth. 1986. The effect of a nonazeotropic binary refrigerant mixture on the performance of a single stage refrigeration cycle. *Proceedings of the International Institute of Refrigeration Conference*, Purdue University, p. 119.

Langeliers, J., P. Sarkisian, and U. Rockenfeller. 2003. Vapor pressure and specific heat of Li-Br H_2O at high temperature. *ASHRAE Transactions* 109(1):423-427.

Liang, H., and T.H. Kuehn. 1991. Irreversibility analysis of a water to water mechanical compression heat pump. *Energy* 16(6):883.

Macriss, R.A. 1968. Physical properties of modified LiBr solutions. AGA Symposium on Absorption Air-Conditioning Systems, February.

Macriss, R.A., and T.S. Zawacki. 1989. Absorption fluid data survey: 1989 update. Oak Ridge National Laboratory, Oak Ridge, TN. *Report* ORNL/Sub84-47989/4.

Macriss, R.A., J.M. Gutraj, and T.S. Zawacki. 1988. *Absorption fluids data survey: Final report on worldwide data.* Institute of Gas Technology, Chicago. web.ornl.gov/info/reports/1988/3445603155476.pdf

Martin, J.J., and Y. Hou. 1955. Development of an equation of state for gases. *AIChE Journal* 1:142.

Martz, W.L., C.M. Burton, and A.M. Jacobi. 1996a. Liquid-vapor equilibria for R-22, R-134a, R-125, and R-32/125 with a polyol ester lubricant: Measurements and departure from ideality. *ASHRAE Transactions* 102(1):367-374.

Martz, W.L., C.M. Burton, and A.M. Jacobi. 1996b. Local composition modeling of the thermodynamic properties of refrigerant and oil mixtures. *International Journal of Refrigeration* 19(1):25-33.

Melinder, A. 1998. *Thermophysical properties of liquid secondary refrigerants.* Engineering Licentiate Thesis, Department of Energy Technology, The Royal Institute of Technology, Stockholm.

Modahl, R.J., and F.C. Hayes. 1988. Evaluation of commercial advanced absorption heat pump. *Proceedings of the 2nd DOE/ORNL Heat Pump Conference*, Washington, D.C.

NASA. 1971. *Computer program for calculation of complex chemical equilibrium composition, rocket performance, incident and reflected shocks and Chapman-Jouguet detonations.* SP-273. U.S. Government Printing Office, Washington, D.C.

Phillips, B. 1976. Absorption cycles for air-cooled solar air conditioning. *ASHRAE Transactions* 82(1):966.

Rockenfeller, U., and L.D. Kirol. 1989. Industrial heat pumps using complex compound working media. ASME Winter Annual Meeting, December.

Rockenfeller, U., and L.D. Kirol. 1996. Commercialization of complex-compound refrigeration modules. International Absorption Heat Pump Conference, September 1996, Montréal, Québec, Canada.

Rockenfeller, U., P. Sarkisian, and L.D. Kirol. 1992. Coordinative complex compounds for efficient storage of polar refrigerants and gases. SAE *Technical Paper* 929275. Intersociety Energy Conversion Engineering Conference, August, San Diego, CA. SAE International, Warrendale, PA. papers.sae.org/929275/.

Rockenfeller, U., L.D. Kirol, and K. Khalili. 1993. High-temperature waste heat driven cooling using sorption media. SAE *Technical Paper* 932113. 23rd International Conference on Environmental Systems, July, Colorado Springs, CO. SAE International, Warrendale, PA. papers.sae.org/932113/.

Stewart, R.B., R.T. Jacobsen, and S.G. Penoncello. 1986. *ASHRAE thermodynamic properties of refrigerants.*

Stoecker, W.F. 1989. *Design of thermal systems*, 3rd ed. McGraw-Hill, New York.

Strobridge, T.R. 1962. The thermodynamic properties of nitrogen from 64 to 300 K, between 0.1 and 200 atmospheres. National Bureau of Standards *Technical Note* 129.

Tassios, D.P. 1993. *Applied chemical engineering thermodynamics.* Springer-Verlag, New York.

Thome, J.R. 1995. Comprehensive thermodynamic approach to modeling refrigerant-lubricant oil mixtures. *International Journal of Heating, Ventilating, Air Conditioning and Refrigeration Research* (now *Science and Technology for the Built Environment*) 1(2):110.

Tillner-Roth, R., and D.G. Friend. 1998a. Survey and assessment of available measurements on thermodynamic properties of the mixture {water + ammonia}. *Journal of Physical and Chemical Reference Data* 27(1)S: 45-61.

Tillner-Roth, R., and D.G. Friend. 1998b. A Helmholtz free energy formulation of the thermodynamic properties of the mixture {water + ammonia}. *Journal of Physical and Chemical Reference Data* 27(1)S:63-96.

Tozer, R.M., and R.W. James. 1997. Fundamental thermodynamics of ideal absorption cycles. *International Journal of Refrigeration* 20(2):123-135.

BIBLIOGRAPHY

Bogart, M. 1981. *Ammonia absorption refrigeration in industrial processes.* Gulf Publishing Co., Houston.

Herold, K.E., R. Radermacher, and S.A. Klein. 1996. *Absorption chillers and heat pumps.* CRC Press, Boca Raton.

Jain, P.C., and G.K. Gable. 1971. Equilibrium property data for aqua-ammonia mixture. *ASHRAE Transactions* 77(1):149.

Moran, M.J., and H. Shapiro. 1995. Fundamentals of engineering thermodynamics, 3rd ed. John Wiley & Sons, New York.

Pátek, J., and J. Klomfar. 1995. Simple functions for fast calculations of selected thermodynamic properties of the ammonia-water system. *International Journal of Refrigeration* 18(4):228-234.

Stoecker, W.F., and J.W. Jones. 1982. *Refrigeration and air conditioning*, 2nd ed. McGraw-Hill, New York.

Van Wylen, C.J., and R.E. Sonntag. 1985. *Fundamentals of classical thermodynamics*, 3rd ed. John Wiley & Sons, New York.

Zawacki, T.S. 1999. Effect of ammonia-water mixture database on cycle calculations. *Proceedings of the International Sorption Heat Pump Conference*, Munich.

CHAPTER 3

FLUID FLOW

FLOWING fluids in HVAC&R systems can transfer heat, mass, and momentum. This chapter introduces the basics of fluid mechanics related to HVAC processes, reviews pertinent flow processes, and presents a general discussion of single-phase fluid flow analysis.

1. FLUID PROPERTIES

Solids and fluids react differently to shear stress: solids deform only a finite amount, whereas fluids deform continuously until the stress is removed. Both liquids and gases are fluids, although the natures of their molecular interactions differ strongly in both degree of compressibility and formation of a free surface (interface) in liquid. In general, liquids are considered incompressible fluids; gases may range from **compressible** to nearly **incompressible**. Liquids have unbalanced molecular cohesive forces at or near the surface (interface), so the liquid surface tends to contract and has properties similar to a stretched elastic membrane. A liquid surface, therefore, is under tension (**surface tension**).

Fluid motion can be described by several simplified models. The simplest is the **ideal-fluid** model, which assumes that the fluid has no resistance to shearing. Ideal fluid flow analysis is well developed [e.g., Schlichting (1979)], and may be valid for a wide range of applications.

Viscosity is a measure of a fluid's resistance to shear. Viscous effects are taken into account by categorizing a fluid as either Newtonian or non-Newtonian. In **Newtonian fluids**, the rate of deformation is directly proportional to the shearing stress; most fluids in the HVAC industry (e.g., water, air, most refrigerants) can be treated as Newtonian. In **non-Newtonian fluids**, the relationship between the rate of deformation and shear stress is more complicated.

Density

The density ρ of a fluid is its mass per unit volume. The densities of air and water (Fox et al. 2004) at standard indoor conditions of 68°F and 14.696 psi (sea-level atmospheric pressure) are

$$\rho_{water} = 62.4\ \text{lb}_m/\text{ft}^3$$

$$\rho_{air} = 0.0753\ \text{lb}_m/\text{ft}^3$$

Viscosity

Viscosity is the resistance of adjacent fluid layers to shear. A classic example of shear is shown in Figure 1, where a fluid is between two parallel plates, each of area A separated by distance Y. The bottom plate is fixed and the top plate is moving, which induces a shearing force in the fluid. For a Newtonian fluid, the tangential force F per unit area required to slide one plate with velocity V parallel to the other is proportional to V/Y:

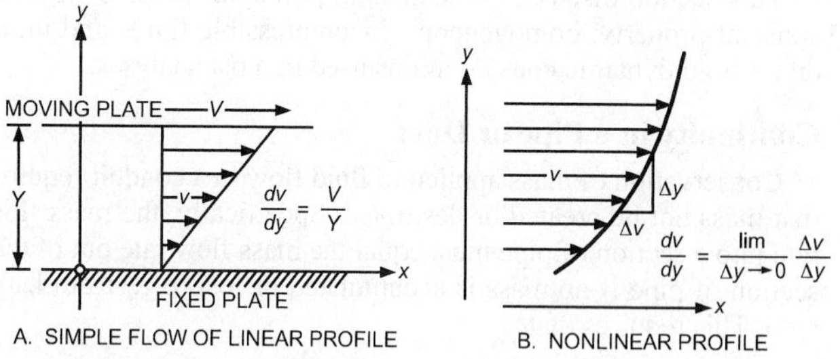

Fig. 1 Velocity Profiles and Gradients in Shear Flows

$$F/A = \mu(V/Y) \tag{1}$$

where the proportionality factor μ is the **absolute** or **dynamic viscosity** of the fluid. The ratio of F to A is the **shearing stress** τ, and V/Y is the **lateral velocity gradient** (Figure 1A). In complex flows, velocity and shear stress may vary across the flow field; this is expressed by

$$\tau = \mu \frac{dv}{dy} \tag{2}$$

The velocity gradient associated with viscous shear for a simple case involving flow velocity in the x direction but of varying magnitude in the y direction is shown in Figure 1B.

Absolute viscosity μ depends primarily on temperature. For gases (except near the critical point), viscosity increases with the square root of the absolute temperature, as predicted by the kinetic theory of gases. In contrast, a liquid's viscosity decreases as temperature increases. Absolute viscosities of various fluids are given in Chapter 33.

Absolute viscosity has dimensions of force × time/length². At standard indoor conditions, the absolute viscosities of water and dry air (Fox et al. 2004) are

$$\mu_{water} = 6.76 \times 10^{-4}\ \text{lb}_m/\text{ft}\cdot\text{s} = 2.10 \times 10^{-5}\ \text{lb}_f\cdot\text{s/ft}^2$$

$$\mu_{air} = 1.22 \times 10^{-5}\ \text{lb}_m/\text{ft}\cdot\text{s} = 3.79 \times 10^{-7}\ \text{lb}_f\cdot\text{s/ft}^2$$

Another common unit of viscosity is the **centipoise** [1 centipoise = 1 g/(s·m) = 1 mPa·s]. At standard conditions, water has a viscosity close to 1.0 centipoise.

In fluid dynamics, **kinematic viscosity** ν is sometimes used in lieu of absolute or dynamic viscosity. Kinematic viscosity is the ratio of absolute viscosity to density:

$$\nu = \mu/\rho$$

The preparation of this chapter is assigned to TC 1.3, Heat Transfer and Fluid Flow.

At standard indoor conditions, the kinematic viscosities of water and dry air (Fox et al. 2004) are

$$\nu_{water} = 1.08 \times 10^{-5}\ \text{ft}^2/\text{s}$$

$$\nu_{air} = 1.62 \times 10^{-4}\ \text{ft}^2/\text{s}$$

The **stoke** (1 cm²/s) and **centistoke** (1 mm²/s) are common units for kinematic viscosity.

Note that the inch-pound system of units often requires the conversion factor $g_c = 32.1740\ \text{lb}_m \cdot \text{ft/s}^2 \cdot \text{lb}_f$ to make some equations containing lb_f and lb_m dimensionally consistent. The conversion factor g_c is not shown in the equations, but is included as needed.

2. BASIC RELATIONS OF FLUID DYNAMICS

This section discusses fundamental principles of fluid flow for constant-property, homogeneous, incompressible fluids and introduces fluid dynamic considerations used in most analyses.

Continuity in a Pipe or Duct

Conservation of mass applied to fluid flow in a conduit requires that mass not be created or destroyed. Specifically, the mass flow rate into a section of pipe must equal the mass flow rate out of that section of pipe if no mass is accumulated or lost (e.g., from leakage). This requires that

$$\dot{m} = \int \rho v\, dA = \text{constant} \tag{3}$$

where $\dot{m}$ is mass flow rate across the area normal to flow, v is fluid velocity normal to differential area dA, and ρ is fluid density. Both ρ and v may vary over the cross section A of the conduit. When flow is effectively incompressible (ρ = constant) in a pipe or duct flow analysis, the **average velocity** is then $V = (1/A)\int v\, dA$, and the mass flow rate can be written as

$$\dot{m} = \rho V A \tag{4}$$

or

$$Q = \dot{m}/\rho = AV \tag{5}$$

where Q is **volumetric flow rate**.

Bernoulli Equation and Pressure Variation in Flow Direction

The **Bernoulli equation** is a fundamental principle of fluid flow analysis. It involves the conservation of momentum and energy along a streamline; it is not generally applicable across streamlines. Development is fairly straightforward. The first law of thermodynamics can apply to both mechanical flow energies (**kinetic** and **potential energy**) and thermal energies.

The change in energy content ΔE per unit mass of flowing fluid is a result of the work per unit mass w done on the system plus the heat per unit mass q absorbed or rejected:

$$\Delta E = w + q \tag{6}$$

Fluid energy is composed of kinetic, potential (because of elevation z), and internal (u) energies. Per unit mass of fluid, the energy change relation between two sections of the system is

$$\Delta\left(\frac{v^2}{2} + gz + u\right) = E_M - \Delta\left(\frac{p}{\rho}\right) + q \tag{7}$$

where the work terms are (1) external work E_M from a fluid machine (E_M is positive for a pump or blower) and (2) flow work p/ρ (where p = pressure), and g is the gravitational constant. Rearranging, the energy equation can be written as the **generalized Bernoulli equation**:

$$\Delta\left(\frac{v^2}{2} + gz + u + \frac{p}{\rho}\right) = E_M + q \tag{8}$$

The expression in parentheses in Equation (8) is the sum of the kinetic energy, potential energy, internal energy, and flow work per unit mass flow rate. In cases with no work interaction, no heat transfer, and no viscous frictional forces that convert mechanical energy into internal energy, this expression is constant and is known as the **Bernoulli constant** B:

$$\frac{v^2}{2} + gz + \left(\frac{p}{\rho}\right) = B \tag{9}$$

Alternative forms of this relation are obtained through multiplication by ρ or division by g:

$$p + \frac{\rho v^2}{2} + \rho gz = \rho B \tag{10}$$

$$\frac{p}{\gamma} + \frac{v^2}{2g} + z = \frac{B}{g} \tag{11}$$

where $\gamma = \rho g$ is the **weight density** (γ = weight/volume versus ρ = mass/volume). Note that Equations (9) to (11) assume no frictional losses.

The units in the first form of the Bernoulli equation [Equation (9)] are energy per unit mass; in Equation (10), energy per unit volume; in Equation (11), energy per unit weight, usually called **head**. Note that the units for head reduce to just length (i.e., $\text{ft} \cdot \text{lb}_f/\text{lb}_f$ to ft). In gas flow analysis, Equation (10) is often used, and ρgz is negligible. Equation (10) should be used when density variations occur. For liquid flows, Equation (11) is commonly used. Identical results are obtained with the three forms if the units are consistent and fluids are homogeneous.

Many systems of pipes, ducts, pumps, and blowers can be considered as one-dimensional flow along a streamline (i.e., variation in velocity across the pipe or duct is ignored, and local velocity v = average velocity V). When v varies significantly across the cross section, the kinetic energy term in the Bernoulli constant B is expressed as $\alpha V^2/2$, where the **kinetic energy factor** ($\alpha > 1$) expresses the ratio of the true kinetic energy of the velocity profile to that of the average velocity. For laminar flow in a wide rectangular channel, $\alpha = 1.54$, and in a pipe, $\alpha = 2.0$. For turbulent flow in a duct, $\alpha \approx 1$.

Heat transfer q may often be ignored. Conversion of mechanical energy to internal energy Δu may be expressed as a loss E_L. The change in the Bernoulli constant ($\Delta B = B_2 - B_1$) between stations 1 and 2 along the conduit can be expressed as

$$\left(\frac{p}{\rho} + \alpha\frac{V^2}{2} + gz\right)_1 + E_M - E_L = \left(\frac{p}{\rho} + \alpha\frac{V^2}{2} + gz\right)_2 \tag{12}$$

or, by dividing by g, in the form

$$\left(\frac{p}{\gamma} + \alpha\frac{V^2}{2g} + z\right)_1 + H_M - H_L = \left(\frac{p}{\gamma} + \alpha\frac{V^2}{2g} + z\right)_2 \tag{13}$$

Note that Equation (12) has units of energy per mass, whereas each term in Equation (13) has units of energy per weight, or head. The terms E_M and E_L are defined as positive, where $gH_M = E_M$ represents energy added to the conduit flow by pumps or blowers. A turbine or fluid motor thus has a negative H_M or E_M. *Note the*

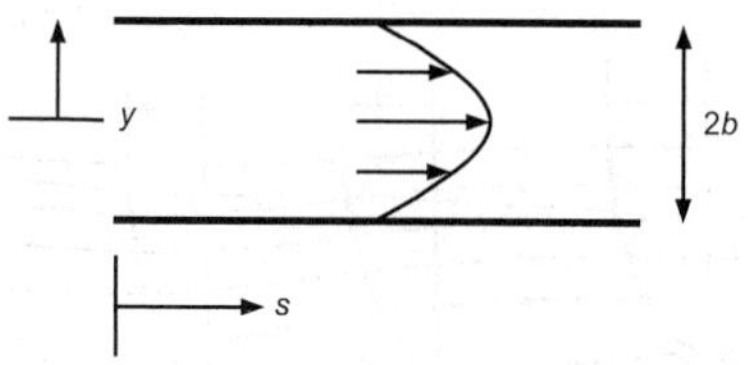

Fig. 2 Dimensions for Steady, Fully Developed Laminar Flow Equations

simplicity of Equation (13); the total head at station 1 (pressure head plus velocity head plus elevation head) plus the head added by a pump (H_M) minus the head lost through friction (H_L) is the total head at station 2.

Laminar Flow

When real-fluid effects of viscosity or turbulence are included, the continuity relation in Equation (5) is not changed, but V must be evaluated from the integral of the velocity profile, using local velocities. In fluid flow past fixed boundaries, velocity at the boundary is zero, velocity gradients exist, and shear stresses are produced. The equations of motion then become complex, and exact solutions are difficult to find except in simple cases for laminar flow between flat plates, between rotating cylinders, or within a pipe or tube.

For steady, fully developed laminar flow between two parallel plates (Figure 2), shear stress τ varies linearly with distance y from the centerline (transverse to the flow; $y = 0$ in the center of the channel). For a wide rectangular channel $2b$ tall, τ can be written as

$$\tau = \left(\frac{y}{b}\right)\tau_w = \mu\frac{dv}{dy} \tag{14}$$

where τ_w is wall shear stress $[b(dp/ds)]$, and s is flow direction. Because velocity is zero at the wall ($y = b$), Equation (14) can be integrated to yield

$$v = \left(\frac{b^2 - y^2}{2\mu}\right)\frac{dp}{ds} \tag{15}$$

The resulting parabolic velocity profile in a wide rectangular channel is commonly called **Poiseuille flow**. Maximum velocity occurs at the centerline ($y = 0$), and the average velocity V is 2/3 of the maximum velocity. From this, the longitudinal pressure drop in terms of V can be written as

$$\frac{dp}{ds} = -\left(\frac{3\mu V}{b^2}\right) \tag{16}$$

A parabolic velocity profile can also be derived for a pipe of radius R. V is 1/2 of the maximum velocity, and the pressure drop can be written as

$$\frac{dp}{ds} = -\left(\frac{8\mu V}{R^2}\right) \tag{17}$$

Turbulence

Fluid flows are generally turbulent, involving random perturbations or fluctuations of the flow (velocity and pressure), characterized by an extensive hierarchy of scales or frequencies (Robertson 1963). Flow disturbances that are not chaotic but have some degree of periodicity (e.g., the oscillating vortex trail behind bodies) have been erroneously identified as turbulence. Only flows involving random perturbations without any order or periodicity are turbulent; velocity in such a flow varies with time or locale of measurement (Figure 3).

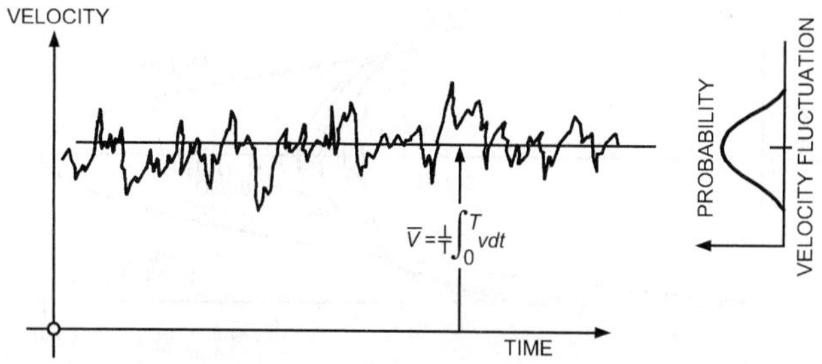

Fig. 3 Velocity Fluctuation at Point in Turbulent Flow

Turbulence can be quantified statistically. The velocity most often used is the time-averaged velocity. The strength of turbulence is characterized by the root mean square (RMS) of the instantaneous variation in velocity about this mean. Turbulence causes the fluid to transfer momentum, heat, and mass very rapidly across the flow.

Laminar and turbulent flows can be differentiated using the **Reynolds number Re**, which is a dimensionless relative ratio of inertial forces to viscous forces:

$$Re_L = VL/\nu \tag{18}$$

where L is the characteristic length scale and ν is the kinematic viscosity of the fluid. In flow through pipes, tubes, and ducts, the characteristic length scale is the **hydraulic diameter** D_h, given by

$$D_h = 4A/P_w \tag{19}$$

where A is the cross-sectional area of the pipe, duct, or tube, and P_w is the wetted perimeter.

For a round pipe, D_h equals the pipe diameter. In general, **laminar flow** in pipes or ducts exists when the Reynolds number (based on D_h) is less than 2300. Fully **turbulent flow** exists when $Re_{D_h} > 10{,}000$. For $2300 < Re_{D_h} < 10{,}000$, transitional flow exists, and predictions are unreliable.

3. BASIC FLOW PROCESSES

Wall Friction

At the boundary of real-fluid flow, the relative tangential velocity at the fluid surface is zero. Sometimes in turbulent flow studies, velocity at the wall may appear finite and nonzero, implying a **fluid slip** at the wall. However, this is not the case; the conflict results from difficulty in velocity measurements near the wall (Goldstein 1938). Zero wall velocity leads to high shear stress near the wall boundary, which slows adjacent fluid layers. Thus, a velocity profile develops near a wall, with velocity increasing from zero at the wall to an exterior value within a finite lateral distance.

Laminar and turbulent flow differ significantly in their velocity profiles. Turbulent flow profiles are flat and laminar profiles are more pointed (Figure 4). As discussed, fluid velocities of the turbulent profile near the wall must drop to zero more rapidly than those of the laminar profile, so shear stress and friction are much greater in turbulent flow. Fully developed conduit flow may be characterized by the **pipe factor**, which is the ratio of average to maximum (centerline) velocity. Viscous velocity profiles result in pipe factors of 0.667 and 0.50 for wide rectangular and axisymmetric conduits. Figure 5 indicates much higher values for rectangular and circular conduits for turbulent flow. Because of the flat velocity profiles, the kinetic energy factor α in Equations (12) and (13) ranges from 1.01 to 1.10 for fully developed turbulent pipe flow.

Boundary Layer

The boundary layer is the region close to the wall where wall friction affects flow. Boundary layer thickness (usually denoted by δ) is

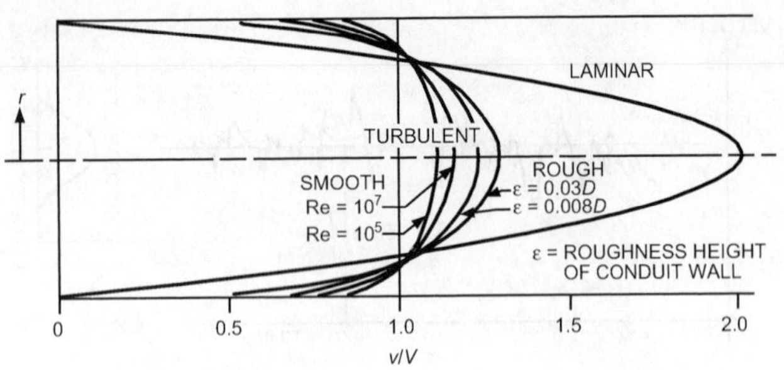

Fig. 4 Velocity Profiles of Flow in Pipes

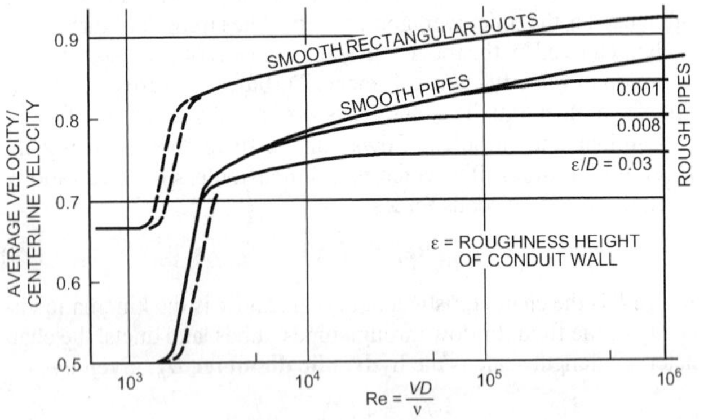

Fig. 5 Pipe Factor for Flow in Conduits

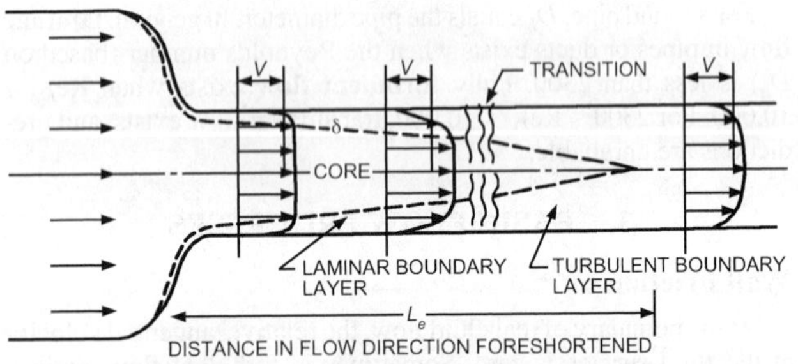

Fig. 6 Flow in Conduit Entrance Region

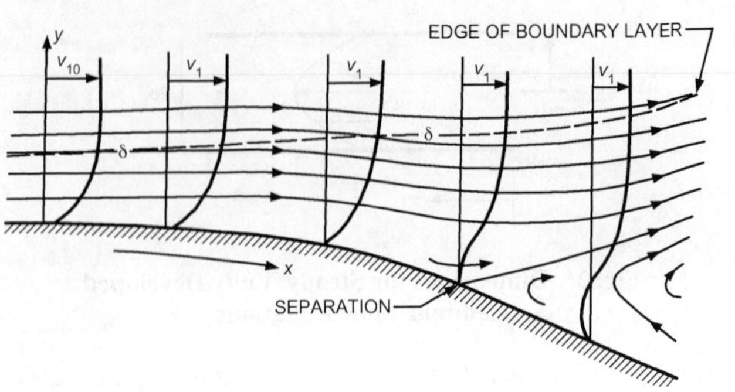

Fig. 7 Boundary Layer Flow to Separation

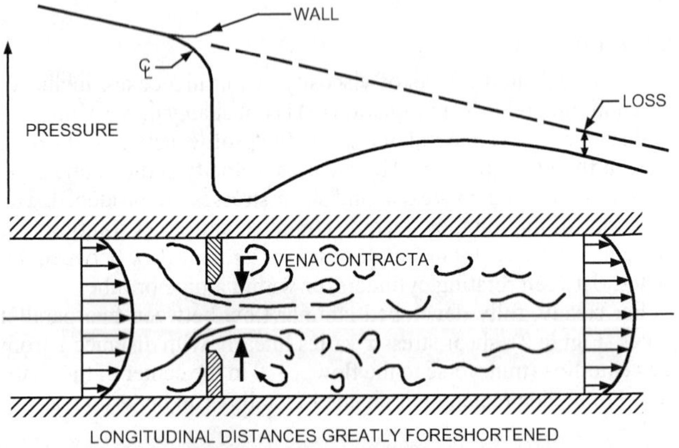

Fig. 8 Geometric Separation, Flow Development, and Loss in Flow Through Orifice

thin compared to downstream flow distance. For external flow over a body, fluid velocity varies from zero at the wall to a maximum at distance δ from the wall. Boundary layers are generally laminar near the start of their formation but may become turbulent downstream.

A significant boundary-layer occurrence exists in a pipeline or conduit following a well-rounded entrance (Figure 6). Layers grow from the walls until they meet at the center of the pipe. Near the start of the straight conduit, the layer is very thin and most likely laminar, so the uniform velocity core outside has a velocity only slightly greater than the average velocity. As the layer grows in thickness, the slower velocity near the wall requires a velocity increase in the uniform core to satisfy continuity. As flow proceeds, the wall layers grow (and centerline velocity increases) until they join, after an **entrance length L_e**. Applying the Bernoulli relation of Equation (10) to core flow indicates a decrease in pressure along the layer. Ross (1956) shows that, although the entrance length L_e is many diameters, the length in which pressure drop significantly exceeds that for fully developed flow is on the order of 10 hydraulic diameters for turbulent flow in smooth pipes.

In more general boundary-layer flows, as with wall layer development in a diffuser or for the layer developing along the surface of a strut or turning vane, pressure gradient effects can be severe and may even lead to boundary layer separation. When the outer flow velocity (v_1 in Figure 7) decreases in the flow direction, an adverse pressure gradient can cause separation, as shown in the figure. Downstream from the separation point, fluid backflows near the wall. Separation is caused by frictional velocity (thus local kinetic energy) reduction near the wall. Flow near the wall no longer has energy to move into the higher pressure imposed by the decrease in v_1 at the edge of the layer. The locale of this separation is difficult to predict, especially for the turbulent boundary layer. Analyses verify the experimental observation that a turbulent boundary layer is less subject to separation than a laminar one because of its greater kinetic energy.

Flow Patterns with Separation

In technical applications, flow with separation is common and often accepted if it is too expensive to avoid. Flow separation may be geometric or dynamic. Dynamic separation is shown in Figure 7. Geometric separation (Figures 8 and 9) results when a fluid stream passes over a very sharp corner, as with an orifice; the fluid generally leaves the corner irrespective of how much its velocity has been reduced by friction.

For geometric separation in orifice flow (Figure 8), the outer streamlines separate from the sharp corners and, because of fluid inertia, contract to a section smaller than the orifice opening. The smallest section is known as the **vena contracta** and generally has a limiting area of about six-tenths of the orifice opening. After the vena contracta, the fluid stream expands rather slowly through turbulent or laminar interaction with the fluid along its sides. Outside the jet, fluid velocity is comparatively small. Turbulence helps spread out the jet, increases losses, and brings the velocity distribution back to a more uniform profile. Finally, downstream, the velocity profile returns to the fully developed flow of Figure 4. The entrance and exit profiles can profoundly affect the vena contracta and pressure drop (Coleman 2004).

Other geometric separations (Figure 9) occur in conduits at sharp entrances, inclined plates or dampers, or sudden expansions. For these geometries, a vena contracta can be identified; for sudden expansion, its area is that of the upstream contraction. Ideal-fluid theory, using free streamlines, provides insight and predicts contraction coefficients for valves, orifices, and vanes (Robertson 1965). These geometric flow separations produce large losses. To expand a flow efficiently or to have an entrance with minimum losses, design the device with gradual contours, a diffuser, or a rounded entrance.

Flow devices with gradual contours are subject to separation that is more difficult to predict, because it involves the dynamics of boundary-layer growth under an adverse pressure gradient rather than flow over a sharp corner. A diffuser is used to reduce the loss in expansion; it is possible to expand the fluid some distance at a gentle angle without difficulty, particularly if the boundary layer is turbulent. Eventually, separation may occur (Figure 10), which is frequently asymmetrical because of irregularities. Downstream flow involves flow reversal (backflow) and excess losses. Such separation is commonly called **stall** (Kline 1959). Larger expansions may use splitters that divide the diffuser into smaller sections that are less likely to have separations (Moore and Kline 1958). Another technique for controlling separation is to bleed some low-velocity fluid near the wall (Furuya et al. 1976). Alternatively, Heskested (1970) shows that suction at the corner of a sudden expansion has a strong positive effect on geometric separation.

Drag Forces on Bodies or Struts

Bodies in moving fluid streams are subjected to appreciable fluid forces or **drag**. Conventionally, the drag force F_D on a body can be expressed in terms of a **drag coefficient** C_D:

$$F_D = C_D \rho A\left(\frac{V^2}{2}\right) \tag{20}$$

where A is the projected (normal to flow) area of the body. The drag coefficient C_D is a strong function of the body's shape and angularity,

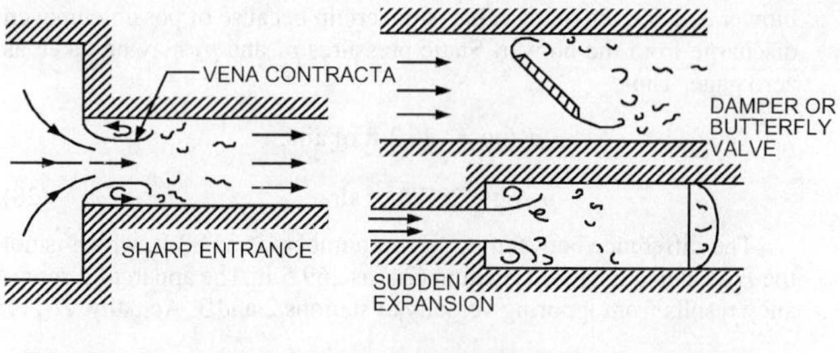

Fig. 9 Examples of Geometric Separation Encountered in Flows in Conduits

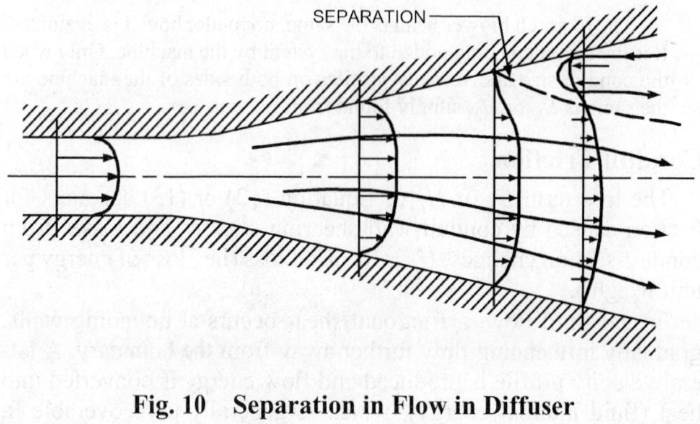

Fig. 10 Separation in Flow in Diffuser

and the Reynolds number of the relative flow in terms of the body's characteristic dimension.

For Reynolds numbers of 10^3 to 10^5, the C_D of most bodies is constant because of flow separation, but above 10^5, the C_D of rounded bodies drops suddenly as the surface boundary layer undergoes transition to turbulence. Typical C_D values are given in Table 1; Hoerner (1965) gives expanded values.

Nonisothermal Effects

When appreciable temperature variations exist, the primary fluid properties (density and viscosity) may no longer assumed to be constant, but vary across or along the flow. The Bernoulli equation [Equations (9) to (11)] must be used, because volumetric flow is not constant. With gas flows, the thermodynamic process involved must be considered. In general, this is assessed using Equation (9), written as

$$\int \frac{dp}{\rho} + \frac{V^2}{2} + gz = B \tag{21}$$

Effects of viscosity variations also appear. In nonisothermal laminar flow, the parabolic velocity profile (see Figure 4) is no longer valid. In general, for gases, viscosity increases with the square root of absolute temperature; for liquids, viscosity decreases with increasing temperature. This results in opposite effects.

For fully developed pipe flow, the linear variation in shear stress from the wall value τ_w to zero at the centerline is independent of the temperature gradient. In the section on Laminar Flow, τ is defined as $\tau = (y/b)\tau_w$, where y is the distance from the centerline and $2b$ is the wall spacing. For pipe radius $R = D/2$ and distance from the wall $y = R - r$ (Figure 11), then $\tau = \tau_w(R - y)/R$. Then, solving Equation (2) for the change in velocity yields

Table 1 Drag Coefficients

Body Shape	$10^3 < Re < 2 \times 10^5$	$Re > 3 \times 10^5$
Sphere	0.36 to 0.47	~0.1
Disk	1.12	1.12
Streamlined strut	0.1 to 0.3	< 0.1
Circular cylinder	1.0 to 1.1	0.35
Elongated rectangular strut	1.0 to 1.2	1.0 to 1.2
Square strut	~2.0	~2.0

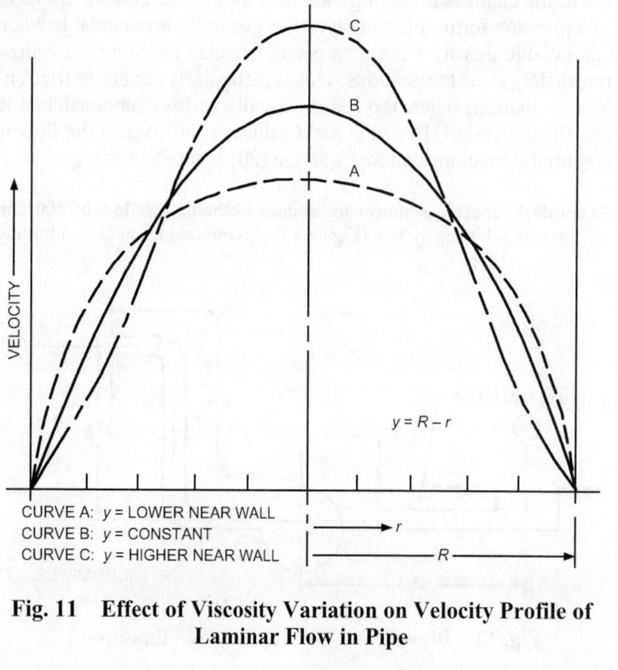

Fig. 11 Effect of Viscosity Variation on Velocity Profile of Laminar Flow in Pipe

$$dv = \left[\frac{\tau_w(R-y)}{R\mu}\right] dy = -\left(\frac{\tau_w}{R\mu}\right) r\,dr \qquad (22)$$

When fluid viscosity is lower near the wall than at the center (because of external heating of liquid or cooling of gas by heat transfer through the pipe wall), the velocity gradient is steeper near the wall and flatter near the center, so the profile is generally flattened. When liquid is cooled or gas is heated, the velocity profile is more pointed for laminar flow (Figure 11). Calculations for such flows of gases and liquid metals in pipes are in Deissler (1951). Occurrences in turbulent flow are less apparent than in laminar flow. If enough heating is applied to gaseous flows, the viscosity increase can cause reversion to laminar flow.

Buoyancy effects and the gradual approach of the fluid temperature to equilibrium with that outside the pipe can cause considerable variation in the velocity profile along the conduit. Colborne and Drobitch (1966) found the pipe factor for upward vertical flow of hot air at a Re < 2000 reduced to about 0.6 at 40 diameters from the entrance, then increased to about 0.8 at 210 diameters, and finally decreased to the isothermal value of 0.5 at the end of 320 diameters.

4. FLOW ANALYSIS

Fluid flow analysis is used to correlate pressure changes with flow rates and the nature of the conduit. For a given pipeline, either the pressure drop for a certain flow rate, or the flow rate for a certain pressure difference between the ends of the conduit, is needed. Flow analysis ultimately involves comparing a pump or blower to a conduit piping system for evaluating the expected flow rate.

Generalized Bernoulli Equation

Internal energy differences are generally small, and usually the only significant effect of heat transfer is to change the density ρ. For gas or vapor flows, use the generalized Bernoulli equation in the pressure-over-density form of Equation (12), allowing for the thermodynamic process in the pressure-density relation:

$$-\int_1^2 \frac{dp}{\rho} + \alpha_1\frac{V_1^2}{2} + E_M = \alpha_2\frac{V_2^2}{2} + E_L \qquad (23)$$

Elevation changes involving z are often negligible and are dropped. The pressure form of Equation (10) is generally unacceptable when appreciable density variations occur, because the volumetric flow rate differs at the two stations. This is particularly serious in friction-loss evaluations where the density usually varies over considerable lengths of conduit (Benedict and Carlucci 1966). When the flow is essentially incompressible, Equation (20) is satisfactory.

Example 1. Specify a blower to produce isothermal airflow of 400 cfm through a ducting system (Figure 12). Accounting for intake and fitting losses, equivalent conduit lengths are 60 and 165 ft, and flow is isothermal. Head at the inlet (station 1) and following the discharge (station 4), where velocity is zero, is the same. Frictional losses H_L are evaluated as 24.5 ft of air between stations 1 and 2, and 237 ft between stations 3 and 4.

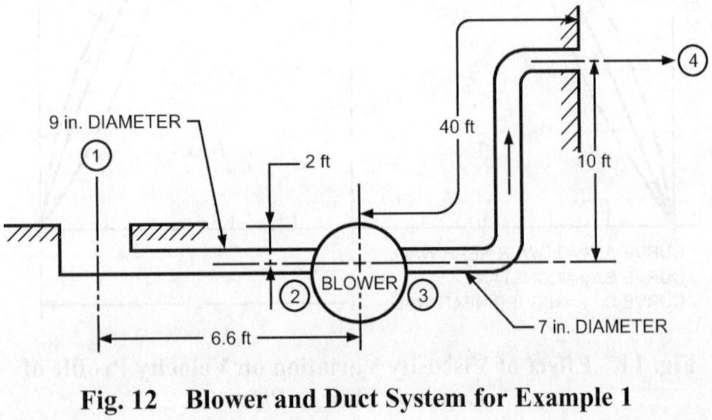

Fig. 12 Blower and Duct System for Example 1

Solution: The following form of the generalized Bernoulli relation is used in place of Equation (12), which also could be used:

$$(p_1/\rho_1 g) + \alpha_1(V_1^2/2g) + z_1 + H_M$$
$$= (p_2/\rho_2 g) + \alpha_2(V_2^2/2g) + z_2 + H_L \qquad (24)$$

The term $V_1^2/2g$ can be calculated as follows:

$$A_1 = \pi\left(\frac{D}{2}\right)^2 = \pi\left(\frac{9/12}{2}\right)^2 = 0.44 \text{ ft}^2$$

$$V_1 = Q/A_1 = \left(\frac{400 \text{ ft}^3}{\text{min}}\right)\left(\frac{1 \text{ min}}{60 \text{ s}}\right)/0.44 \text{ ft}^2 = 15.1 \text{ ft/s}$$

$$V_1^2/2g = (15.1)^2/2(32) = 3.56 \text{ ft} \qquad (25)$$

The term $V_2^2/2g$ can be calculated in a similar manner.

In Equation (24), H_M is evaluated by applying the relation between any two points on opposite sides of the blower. Because conditions at stations 1 and 4 are known, they are used, and the location-specifying subscripts on the right side of Equation (24) are changed to 4. Note that $p_1 = p_4 = p$, $\rho_1 = \rho_4 = \rho$, and $V_1 = V_4 = 0$. Thus,

$$(p/\rho g) + 0 + 2 + H_M = (p/\rho g) + 0 + 10 + (24.5 + 237) \qquad (26)$$

so H_M = 269.5 ft of air. For standard air, this corresponds to 3.89 in. of water.

The head difference measured across the blower (between stations 2 and 3) is often taken as H_M. It can be obtained by calculating the static pressure at stations 2 and 3. Applying Equation (24) successively between stations 1 and 2 and between 3 and 4 gives

$$(p_1/\rho g) + 0 + 2 + 0 = (p_2/\rho g) + (1.06 \times 3.56) + 0 + 24.5$$
$$(p_3/\rho g) + (1.03 \times 9.70) + 0 + 0 = (p_4/\rho g) + 0 + 10 + 237 \qquad (27)$$

where α just ahead of the blower is taken as 1.06, and just after the blower as 1.03; the latter value is uncertain because of possible uneven discharge from the blower. Static pressures p_1 and p_4 may be taken as zero gage. Thus,

$$p_2/\rho g = -26.2 \text{ ft of air}$$
$$p_3/\rho g = 237 \text{ ft of air} \qquad (28)$$

The difference between these two numbers is 263.2 ft, which is not the H_M calculated after Equation (24) as 269.5 ft. The apparent discrepancy results from ignoring velocity at stations 2 and 3. Actually, H_M is

$$H_M = (p_3/\rho g) + \alpha_3(V_3^2/2g) - [(p_2/\rho g) + \alpha_2(V_2^2/2g)]$$
$$= 237 + (1.03 \times 9.70) - [-26.2 + (1.06 \times 3.54)]$$
$$= 247 - (-22.5) = 269.5 \text{ ft of air} \qquad (29)$$

The required blower head is the same, no matter how it is evaluated. It is the specific energy added to the system by the machine. Only when the conduit size and velocity profiles on both sides of the machine are the same is E_M or H_M simply found from $\Delta p = p_3 - p_2$.

Conduit Friction

The loss term E_L or H_L of Equation (12) or (13) accounts for friction caused by conduit-wall shearing stresses and losses from conduit-section changes. H_L is the head loss (i.e., loss of energy per unit weight).

In real-fluid flow, a frictional shear occurs at bounding walls, gradually influencing flow further away from the boundary. A lateral velocity profile is produced and flow energy is converted into heat (fluid internal energy), which is generally unrecoverable (a

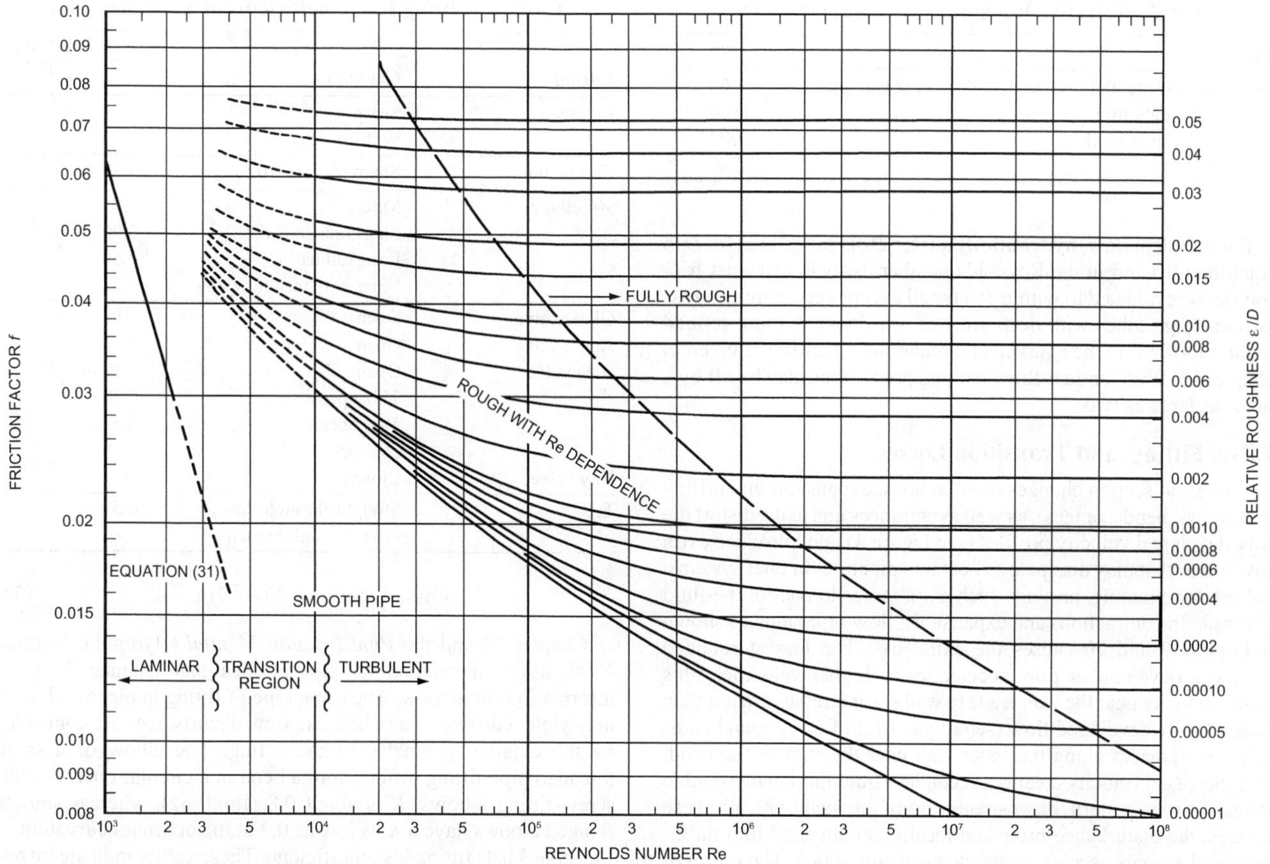

Fig. 13 Relation Between Friction Factor and Reynolds Number
(based on Moody 1944)

loss). This loss in fully developed conduit flow is evaluated using the **Darcy-Weisbach equation**:

$$H_{L_f} = f\left(\frac{L}{D}\right)\left(\frac{V^2}{2g}\right) \tag{30}$$

where L is the length of conduit of diameter D and f is the **Darcy-Weisbach friction factor**. Sometimes a numerically different relation is used with the **Fanning friction factor** (1/4 of the Darcy friction factor f). The value of f is nearly constant for turbulent flow, varying only from about 0.01 to 0.05.

For fully developed laminar-viscous flow in a pipe, loss is evaluated from Equation (17) as follows:

$$H_{L_f} = \frac{L}{\rho g}\left(\frac{8\mu V}{R^2}\right) = \frac{32 L \nu V}{D^2 g} = \frac{64}{VD/\nu}\left(\frac{L}{D}\right)\left(\frac{V^2}{2g}\right) \tag{31}$$

where $\text{Re} = VD/\nu$ and $f = 64/\text{Re}$. Thus, for laminar flow, the friction factor varies inversely with the Reynolds number. The value of 64/Re varies with channel shape. A good summary of shape factors is provided by Incropera and DeWitt (2002).

With turbulent flow, friction loss depends not only on flow conditions, as characterized by the Reynolds number, but also on the **roughness height** ε of the conduit wall surface. The variation is complex and is expressed in diagram form (Moody 1944), as shown in Figure 13. Historically, the Moody diagram has been used to determine friction factors, but empirical relations suitable for use in modeling programs have been developed. Most are applicable to limited ranges of Reynolds number and relative roughness. Churchill (1977) developed a relationship that is valid for all ranges of Reynolds numbers, and is more accurate than reading the Moody diagram:

$$f = 8\left[\left(\frac{8}{\text{Re}_{D_h}}\right)^{12} + \frac{1}{(A+B)^{1.5}}\right]^{1/12} \tag{32a}$$

$$A = \left[2.457 \ln\left(\frac{1}{\left(7/\text{Re}_{D_h}\right)^{0.9} + \left(0.27\varepsilon/D_h\right)}\right)\right]^{16} \tag{32b}$$

$$B = \left(\frac{37{,}530}{\text{Re}_{D_h}}\right)^{16} \tag{32c}$$

Inspection of the Moody diagram indicates that, for high Reynolds numbers and relative roughness, the friction factor becomes independent of the Reynolds number in a fully rough flow or fully turbulent regime. A **transition region** from laminar to turbulent flow occurs when $2000 < \text{Re} < 10{,}000$. Roughness height ε, which may increase with conduit use, fouling, or aging, is usually tabulated for different types of pipes as shown in Table 2.

Noncircular Conduits. Air ducts are often rectangular in cross section. The equivalent circular conduit corresponding to the noncircular conduit must be found before the friction factor can be determined.

Table 2 Effective Roughness of Conduit Surfaces

Material	ε, μin.
Commercially smooth brass, lead, copper, or plastic pipe	60
Steel and wrought iron	1800
Galvanized iron or steel	6000
Cast iron	10,200

For turbulent flow, **hydraulic diameter D_h** is substituted for D in Equation (30) and in the Reynolds number. Noncircular duct friction can be evaluated to within 5% for all except very extreme cross sections (e.g., tubes with deep grooves or ridges). A more refined method for finding the equivalent circular duct diameter is given in Chapter 13. With laminar flow, the loss predictions may be off by a factor as large as two.

Valve, Fitting, and Transition Losses

Valve and section changes (contractions, expansions and diffusers, elbows, bends, or tees), as well as entrances and exits, distort the fully developed velocity profiles (see Figure 4) and introduce extra flow losses that may dissipate as heat into pipelines or duct systems. Valves, for example, produce such extra losses to control the fluid flow rate. In contractions and expansions, flow separation as shown in Figures 9 and 10 causes the extra loss. The loss at rounded entrances develops as flow accelerates to higher velocities; this higher velocity near the wall leads to wall shear stresses greater than those of fully developed flow (see Figure 6). In flow around bends, velocity increases along the inner wall near the start of the bend. This increased velocity creates a secondary fluid motion in a double helical vortex pattern downstream from the bend. In all these devices, the disturbance produced locally is converted into turbulence and appears as a loss in the downstream region. The return of a disturbed flow pattern into a fully developed velocity profile may be quite slow. Ito (1962) showed that the secondary motion following a bend takes up to 100 diameters of conduit to die out but the pressure gradient settles out after 50 diameters.

In a laminar fluid flow following a rounded entrance, the **entrance length** depends on the Reynolds number:

$$L_e/D = 0.06\ \text{Re} \tag{33}$$

At Re = 2000, Equation (33) shows that a length of 120 diameters is needed to establish the parabolic velocity profile. The pressure gradient reaches the developed value of Equation (30) in fewer flow diameters. The additional loss is $1.2V^2/2g$; the change in profile from uniform to parabolic results in a loss of $1.0V^2/2g$ (because α = 2.0), and the remaining loss is caused by the excess friction. In turbulent fluid flow, only 80 to 100 diameters following the rounded entrance are needed for the velocity profile to become fully developed, but the friction loss per unit length reaches a value close to that of the fully developed flow value more quickly. After six diameters, the loss rate at a Reynolds number of 10^5 is only 14% above that of fully developed flow in the same length, whereas at 10^7, it is only 10% higher (Robertson 1963). For a sharp entrance, flow separation (see Figure 9) causes a greater disturbance, but fully developed flow is achieved in about half the length required for a rounded entrance. In a sudden expansion, the pressure change settles out in about eight times the diameter change ($D_2 - D_1$), whereas the velocity profile may take at least a 50% greater distance to return to fully developed pipe flow (Lipstein 1962).

Instead of viewing these losses as occurring over tens or hundreds of pipe diameters, it is possible to treat the entire effect of a disturbance as if it occurs at a single point in the flow direction. By treating these losses as a local phenomenon, they can be related to the velocity by the **loss coefficient K**:

Table 3 Fitting Loss Coefficients of Turbulent Flow

Fitting	Geometry	$K = \dfrac{\Delta P/\rho g}{V^2/2g}$
Entrance	Sharp	0.5
	Well-rounded	0.05
Contraction	Sharp (D_2/D_1 = 0.5)	0.38
90° elbow	Miter	1.3
	Short radius	0.90
	Long radius	0.60
	Miter with turning vanes	0.2
Globe valve	Open	10
Angle valve	Open	5
Gate valve	Open	0.19 to 0.22
	75% open	1.10
	50% open	3.6
	25% open	28.8
Any valve	Closed	∞
Tee	Straight-through flow	0.5
	Flow through branch	1.8

$$\text{Loss of section} = K(V^2/2g) \tag{34}$$

Chapter 22 and the *Pipe Friction Manual* (Hydraulic Institute 1990) have information for pipe applications. Chapter 21 gives information for airflow. The same type of fitting in pipes and ducts may yield a different loss, because flow disturbances are controlled by the detailed geometry of the fitting. The elbow of a small threaded pipe fitting differs from a bend in a circular duct. For 90° screw-fitting elbows, K is about 0.8 (Ito 1962), whereas smooth flanged elbows have a K as low as 0.2 at the optimum curvature.

Table 3 lists fitting loss coefficients.These values indicate losses, but there is considerable variance. Note that a well-rounded entrance yields a rather small K of 0.05, whereas a gate valve that is only 25% open yields a K of 28.8. Expansion flows, such as from one conduit size to another or at the exit into a room or reservoir, are not included. For such occurrences, the **Borda loss prediction** (from impulse-momentum considerations) is appropriate:

$$\text{Loss at expansion} = \frac{(V_1 - V_2)^2}{2g} = \frac{V_1^2}{2g}\left(1 - \frac{A_1}{A_2}\right)^2 \tag{35}$$

Expansion losses may be significantly reduced by avoiding or delaying separation using a gradual diffuser (see Figure 10). For a diffuser of about 7° total angle, the loss is only about one-sixth of the loss predicted by Equation (35). The diffuser loss for total angles above 45 to 60° exceeds that of the sudden expansion, but is moderately influenced by the diameter ratio of the expansion. Optimum diffuser design involves numerous factors; excellent performance can be achieved in short diffusers with splitter vanes or suction. Turning vanes in miter bends produce the least disturbance and loss for elbows; with careful design, the loss coefficient can be reduced to as low as 0.1.

For losses in smooth elbows, Ito (1962) found a Reynolds number effect (K slowly decreasing with increasing Re) and a minimum loss at a bend curvature (bend radius to diameter ratio) of 2.5. At this optimum curvature, a 45° turn had 63%, and a 180° turn approximately 120%, of the loss of a 90° bend. The loss does not vary linearly with the turning angle because secondary motion occurs.

Note that using K presumes its independence of the Reynolds number. Some investigators have documented a variation in the loss coefficient with the Reynolds number. Assuming that K varies with Re similarly to f, it is convenient to represent fitting losses as adding to the effective length of uniform conduit. The effective length of a fitting is then

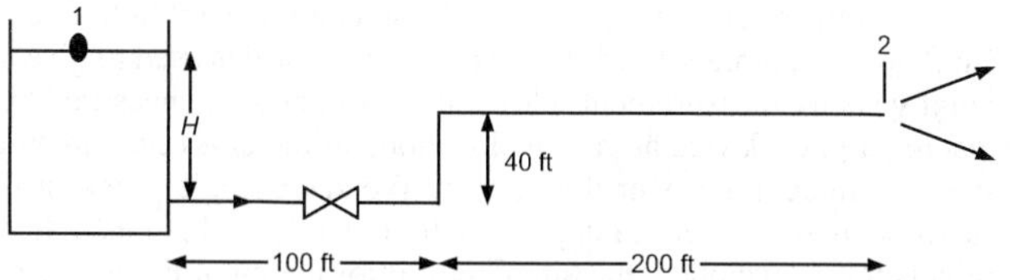

Fig. 14 Diagram for Example 2

$$L_{eff}/D = K/f_{ref} \tag{36}$$

where f_{ref} is an appropriate reference value of the friction factor. Deissler (1951) uses 0.028, and the air duct values in Chapter 21 are based on an f_{ref} of about 0.02. For rough conduits, appreciable errors can occur if the relative roughness does not correspond to that used when f_{ref} was fixed. It is unlikely that fitting losses involving separation are affected by pipe roughness. The effective length method for fitting loss evaluation is still useful.

When a conduit contains a number of section changes or fittings, the values of K are added to the fL/D friction loss, or the L_{eff}/D of the fittings are added to the conduit length L/D for evaluating the total loss H_L. This assumes that each fitting loss is fully developed and its disturbance fully smoothed out before the next section change. Such an assumption is frequently wrong, and the total loss can be overestimated. For elbow flows, the total loss of adjacent bends may be over- or underestimated. The secondary flow pattern after an elbow is such that when one follows another, perhaps in a different plane, the secondary flow of the second elbow may reinforce or partially cancel that of the first. Moving the second elbow a few diameters can reduce the total loss (from more than twice the amount) to less than the loss from one elbow. Screens or perforated plates can be used for smoothing velocity profiles (Wile 1947) and flow spreading. Their effectiveness and loss coefficients depend on their amount of open area (Baines and Peterson 1951).

Example 2. Water at 68°F flows through the piping system shown in Figure 14. Each ell has a very long radius and a loss coefficient of $K = 0.31$; the entrance at the tank is square-edged with $K = 0.5$, and the valve is a fully open globe valve with $K = 10$. The pipe roughness is 0.01 in. The density $\rho = 62.4$ lb$_m$/ft^3 and kinematic viscosity $\nu = 1.08 \times 10^{-5}$ ft^2/s.

a. If pipe diameter $D = 6$ in., what is the elevation H in the tank required to produce a flow of $Q = 2.1$ ft^3/s?

Solution: Apply Equation (13) between stations 1 and 2 in the figure. Note that $p_1 = p_2$, $V_1 \approx 0$. Assume $\alpha \approx 1$. The result is

$$z_1 - z_2 = H - 40 \text{ ft} = H_L + V_2^2/2g$$

From Equations (30) and (34), total head loss is

$$H_L = \left(\frac{fL}{D} + \sum K\right)\frac{8Q^2}{\pi^2 gD^4}$$

where $L = 340$ ft, $\sum K = 0.5 + (2 \times 0.31) + 10 = 11.1$, and $V^2/2g = V_2^2/2g = 8Q^2/(\pi^2 gD^4)$. Then, substituting into Equation (13),

$$H = 40 \text{ ft} + \left(1 + \frac{fL}{D} + \sum K\right)\frac{8Q^2}{\pi^2 gD^4}$$

To calculate the friction factor, first calculate Reynolds number and relative roughness:

$$\text{Re} = VD/\nu = 4Q/(\pi D\nu) = 495{,}150$$

$$\varepsilon/D = 0.0017$$

From the Moody diagram or Equation (32), $f = 0.023$. Then $H_L = 47.5$ ft and $H = 87.5$ ft.

b. For $H = 72$ ft and $D = 6$ in., what is the flow?

Solution: Applying Equation (13) again and inserting the expression for head loss gives

$$z_1 - z_2 = 32 \text{ ft} = \left(1 + \frac{fL}{D} + \sum K\right)\frac{8Q^2}{\pi^2 gD^4}$$

Because f depends on Q (unless flow is fully turbulent), iteration is required. The usual procedure is as follows:

1. Assume a value of f, usually the fully rough value for the given values of ε and D.
2. Use this value of f in the energy calculation and solve for Q.

$$Q = \sqrt{\frac{\pi^2 gD^4(z_1 - z_2)}{8\left(\frac{fL}{D} + \sum K + 1\right)}}$$

3. Use this value of Q to recalculate Re and get a new value of f.
4. Repeat until the new and old values of f agree to two significant figures.

Iteration	f	Q, cfs	Re	f
0	0.0223	1.706	4.02×10^5	0.0231
1	0.0231	1.690	3.98×10^5	0.0231

As shown in the table, the result after two iterations is $Q \approx 1.69$ ft^3/s.

If the resulting flow is in the fully rough zone and the fully rough value of f is used as first guess, only one iteration is required.

c. For $H = 72$ ft, what diameter pipe is needed to allow $Q = 1.9$ cfs?

Solution: The energy equation in part (b) must now be solved for D with Q known. This is difficult because the energy equation cannot be solved for D, even with an assumed value of f. If Churchill's expression for f is stored as a function in a calculator, program, or spreadsheet with an iterative equation solver, a solution can be generated. In this case, $D \approx 0.526$ ft = 6.31 in. Use the smallest available pipe size greater than 6.31 in. and adjust the valve as required to achieve the desired flow.

Alternatively, (1) guess an available pipe size, and (2) calculate Re, f, and H for $Q = 1.9$ ft^3/s. If the resulting value of H is greater than the given value of $H = 72$ ft, a larger pipe is required. If the calculated H is less than 72 ft, repeat using a smaller available pipe size.

Control Valve Characterization for Liquids

Control valves are characterized by a **discharge coefficient C_d**. As long as the Reynolds number is greater than 250, the orifice equation holds for liquids:

$$Q = C_d A_o \sqrt{2\Delta p/\rho} \tag{37}$$

where A_o is the area of the orifice opening and Δp is the pressure drop across the valve. The discharge coefficient is about 0.63 for sharp-edged configurations and 0.8 to 0.9 for chamfered or rounded configurations.

Incompressible Flow in Systems

Flow devices must be evaluated in terms of their interaction with other elements of the system [e.g., the action of valves in modifying flow rate and in matching the flow-producing device (pump or blower) with the system loss]. Analysis is by the general Bernoulli equation and the loss evaluations noted previously.

A valve regulates or stops the flow of fluid by throttling. The change in flow is not proportional to the change in area of the valve opening. Figures 15 and 16 indicate the nonlinear action of valves in controlling flow. Figure 15 shows flow in a pipe discharging water from a tank that is controlled by a gate valve. The fitting loss coefficient K values are from Table 3; the friction factor f is 0.027. The degree of control also depends on the conduit L/D ratio. For a relatively long conduit, the valve must be nearly closed before its high K

value becomes a significant portion of the loss. Figure 16 shows a control damper (essentially a butterfly valve) in a duct discharging air from a plenum held at constant pressure. With a long duct, the damper does not affect the flow rate until it is about one-quarter closed. Duct length has little effect when the damper is more than half closed. The damper closes the duct totally at the 90° position ($K = \infty$).

Flow in a system (pump or blower and conduit with fittings) involves interaction between the characteristics of the flow-producing device (pump or blower) and the loss characteristics of the pipeline or duct system. Often the devices are centrifugal, in which case the head produced decreases as flow increases, except for the lowest flow rates. System head required to overcome losses increases roughly as the square of the flow rate. The flow rate of a given system is that where the two curves of head versus flow rate intersect (point 1 in Figure 17). When a control valve (or damper) is partially closed, it increases losses and reduces flow (point 2 in Figure 17). For cases of constant head, the flow decrease caused by valving is not as great as that indicated in Figures 15 and 16.

Flow Measurement

The general principles noted (the continuity and Bernoulli equations) are basic to most fluid-metering devices. Chapter 36 has further details.

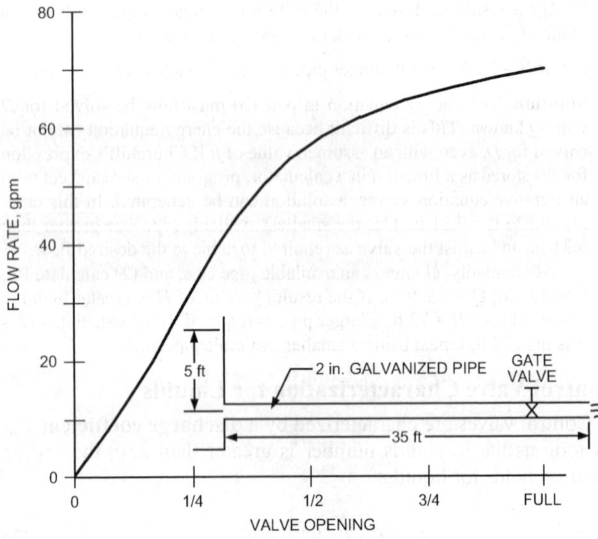

Fig. 15 Valve Action in Pipeline

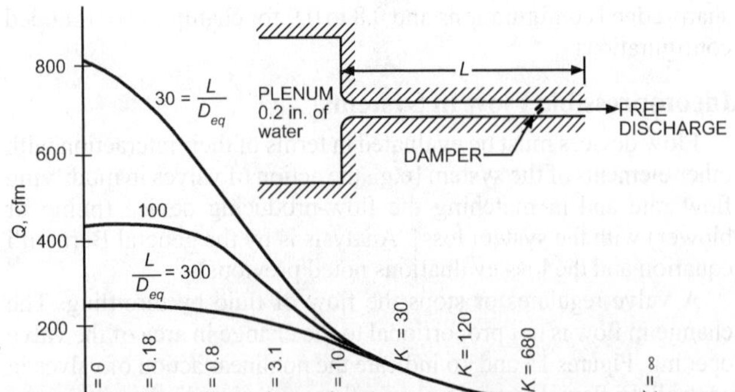

Fig. 16 Effect of Duct Length on Damper Action

The pressure difference between the stagnation point (total pressure) and the ambient fluid stream (static pressure) is used to give a point velocity measurement. Flow rate in a conduit is measured by placing a pitot device at various locations in the cross section and spatially integrating over the velocity found. A single-point measurement may be used for approximate flow rate evaluation. When flow is fully developed, the pipe-factor information of Figure 5 can be used to estimate the flow rate from a centerline measurement. Measurements can be made in one of two modes. With the pitot-static tube, the ambient (static) pressure is found from pressure taps along the side of the forward-facing portion of the tube. When this portion is not long and slender, static pressure indication will be low and velocity indication high; as a result, a tube coefficient less than unity must be used. For parallel conduit flow, wall piezometers (taps) may take the ambient pressure, and the pitot tube indicates the impact (total pressure).

The venturi meter, flow nozzle, and orifice meter are flow-rate-metering devices based on the pressure change associated with relatively sudden changes in conduit section area (Figure 18). The elbow meter (also shown in Figure 18) is another differential pressure flowmeter. The flow nozzle is similar to the venturi in action, but does not have the downstream diffuser. For all these, the flow rate is proportional to the square root of the pressure difference resulting from fluid flow. With area-change devices (venturi, flow nozzle, and orifice meter), a theoretical flow rate relation is found by applying the Bernoulli and continuity equations in Equations (12) and (3) between stations 1 and 2:

$$Q_{theoretical} = \frac{\pi d^2}{4}\sqrt{\frac{2g\Delta h}{1-\beta^4}} \tag{38}$$

where $\Delta h = h_1 - h_2 = (p_1 - p_2)/\rho g$ and $\beta = d/D$ = ratio of throat (or orifice) diameter to conduit diameter.

The actual flow rate through the device can differ because the approach flow kinetic energy factor α deviates from unity and because of small losses. More significantly, jet contraction of orifice flow is neglected in deriving Equation (38), to the extent that it can

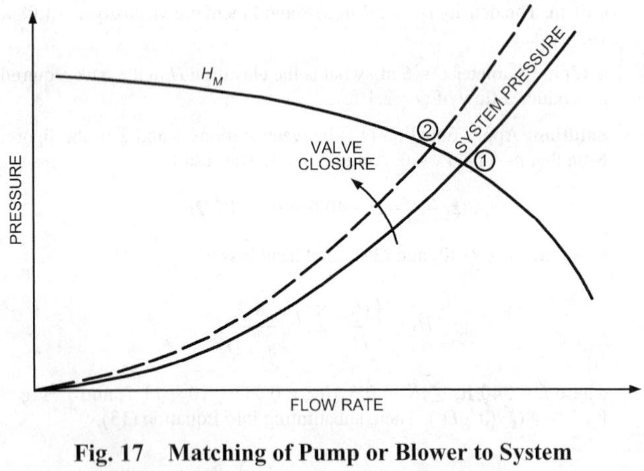

Fig. 17 Matching of Pump or Blower to System

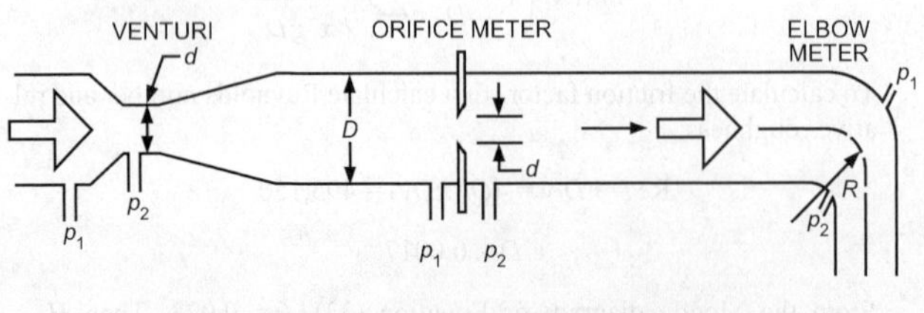

Fig. 18 Differential Pressure Flowmeters

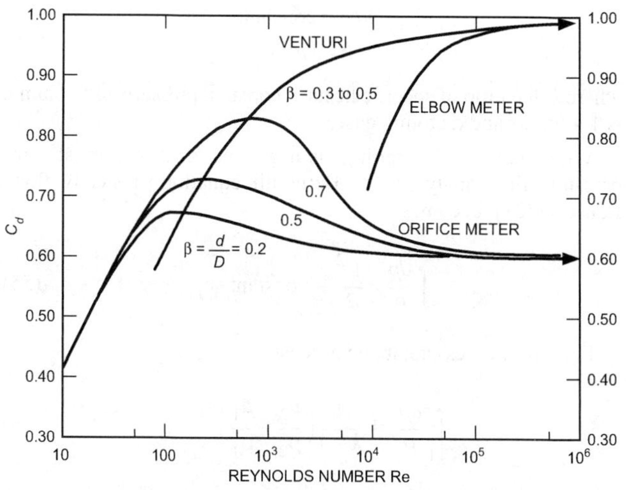

Fig. 19 Flowmeter Coefficients

reduce the effective flow area by a factor of 0.6. The effect of all these factors can be combined into the discharge coefficient C_d:

$$Q = C_d Q_{theoretical} \tag{39}$$

where Q is actual flow. In some sources, instead of being defined as in Equation (39), C_d is replaced with

$$\frac{C_d}{\sqrt{1-\beta^4}} \tag{40}$$

Take care to note the definition used by a source of C_d data.

The general mode of variation in C_d for orifices and venturis is indicated in Figure 19 as a function of Reynolds number and, to a lesser extent, diameter ratio β. For Reynolds numbers less than 10, the coefficient varies as $\sqrt{\text{Re}}$.

The elbow meter uses the pressure difference inside and outside the bend as the metering signal (Murdock et al. 1964). Momentum analysis gives the flow rate as

$$Q_{theoretical} = \frac{\pi d^2}{4}\sqrt{\frac{R}{2D}}(2g\Delta h) \tag{41}$$

where R is the radius of curvature of the bend. Again, a discharge coefficient C_d is needed; as in Figure 19, this drops off for lower Reynolds numbers (below 10^5). These devices are calibrated in pipes with fully developed velocity profiles, so they must be located far enough downstream of sections that modify the approach velocity.

Example 3. For a venturi with oil ($\rho = 50$ lb$_m$/ft^3, $\mu = 6.72\text{E-}3$ lb$_m$/ft·s), find Q for $P_1 - P_2 = 4.0$ psi = 576 lb$_f$/ft^2, $D = 12$ in. = 1 ft, $d = 6$ in. = 0.50 ft.

$$Q = C_d\frac{\pi d^2}{4}\sqrt{\frac{2(P_1-P_2)}{\rho(1-\beta^4)}}$$

where $\beta = 0.5$ ft/1.0 ft = 0.5.

Inserting numbers, being careful to ensure that the units for Q are ft^3/s, gives $Q = 5.52C_d$.

Guessing Re$_D = 10^5$ and using Figure 19 gives $C_d = 0.97$ and $Q = 0.97 \times 5.52 = 5.36$ ft^3/s.

Checking Re$_D$ using this Q gives Re = 5.0×10^4. At this Re, C_d = 0.96 and

$Q = 0.96 \times 5.52 = 5.30$ ft^3/s = 2378 gpm

Unsteady Flow

Conduit flows are not always steady. In a compressible fluid, acoustic velocity is usually high and conduit length is rather short, so the time of signal travel is negligibly small. Even in the incompressible approximation, system response is not instantaneous. If a pressure difference Δp is applied between the conduit ends, the fluid mass must be accelerated and wall friction overcome, so a finite time passes before the steady flow rate corresponding to the pressure drop is achieved.

The time it takes for an incompressible fluid in a horizontal, constant-area conduit of length L to achieve steady flow may be estimated by using the unsteady flow equation of motion with wall friction effects included. On the quasi-steady assumption, friction loss is given by Equation (30); also by continuity, V is constant along the conduit. The occurrences are characterized by the relation

$$\frac{dV}{d\theta} + \left(\frac{1}{\rho}\right)\frac{dp}{ds} + \frac{fV^2}{2D} = 0 \tag{42}$$

where θ is the time and s is the distance in flow direction. Because a certain Δp is applied over conduit length L,

$$\frac{dV}{d\theta} = \frac{\Delta p}{\rho L} - \frac{fV^2}{2D} \tag{43}$$

For laminar flow, f is given by Equation (31):

$$\frac{dV}{d\theta} = \frac{\Delta p}{\rho L} - \frac{32\mu V}{\rho D^2} = A - BV \tag{44}$$

Equation (44) can be rearranged and integrated to yield the time to reach a certain velocity:

$$\theta = \int d\theta = \int\frac{dV}{A-BV} = -\frac{1}{B}\ln(A-BV) \tag{45}$$

and

$$V = \frac{\Delta p}{L}\left(\frac{D^2}{32\mu}\right)\left[1 - \frac{\rho L}{\Delta p}\exp\left(\frac{-32\nu\theta}{D^2}\right)\right] \tag{46}$$

For long times ($\theta \to \infty$), the steady velocity is

$$V_\infty = \frac{\Delta p}{L}\left(\frac{D^2}{32\mu}\right) = \frac{\Delta p}{L}\left(\frac{R^2}{8\mu}\right) \tag{47}$$

as given by Equation (17). Then, Equation (47) becomes

$$V = V_\infty\left[1 - \frac{\rho L}{\Delta p}\exp\left(\frac{-f_\infty V_\infty \theta}{2D}\right)\right] \tag{48}$$

where

$$f_\infty = \frac{64\nu}{V_\infty D} \tag{49}$$

The general nature of velocity development for start-up flow is derived by more complex techniques; however, the temporal variation is as given here. For shutdown flow (steady flow with $\Delta p = 0$ at $\theta > 0$), flow decays exponentially as $e^{-\theta}$.

Turbulent flow analysis of Equation (42) also must be based on the quasi-steady approximation, with less justification. Daily et al. (1956) indicate that frictional resistance is slightly greater than the steady-state result for accelerating flows, but appreciably less for decelerating flows. If the friction factor is approximated as constant,

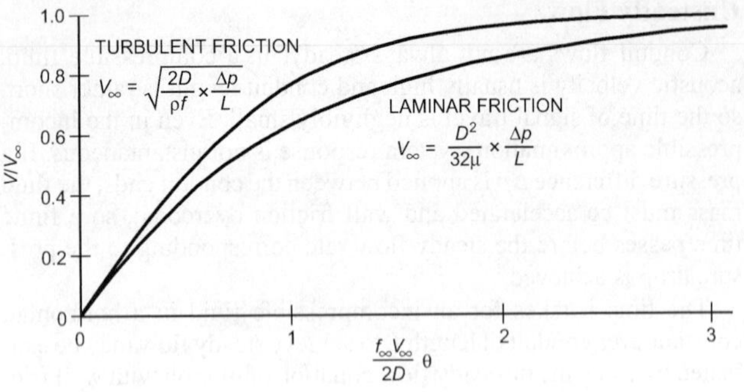

Fig. 20 Temporal Increase in Velocity Following Sudden Application of Pressure

$$\frac{dV}{d\theta} = \frac{\Delta p}{\rho L} - \frac{fV^2}{2D} = A - BV^2 \tag{50}$$

and for the accelerating flow,

$$\theta = \frac{1}{\sqrt{AB}} \tanh^{-1}\left(V\sqrt{\frac{B}{A}}\right) \tag{51}$$

or

$$V = \sqrt{A/B}\ \tanh(\theta\sqrt{AB}) \tag{52}$$

Because the hyperbolic tangent is zero when the independent variable is zero and unity when the variable is infinity, the initial ($V = 0$ at $\theta = 0$) and final conditions are verified. Thus, for long times ($\theta \rightarrow \infty$),

$$V_\infty = \sqrt{A/B} = \sqrt{\frac{\Delta p/\rho L}{f_\infty/2D}} = \sqrt{\frac{\Delta p}{\rho L}\left(\frac{2D}{f_\infty}\right)} \tag{53}$$

which is in accord with Equation (30) when f is constant (the flow regime is the fully rough one of Figure 13). The temporal velocity variation is then

$$V = V_\infty \tanh(f_\infty V_\infty \theta/2D) \tag{54}$$

In Figure 20, the turbulent velocity start-up result is compared with the laminar one, where initially the turbulent is steeper but of the same general form, increasing rapidly at the start but reaching V_∞ asymptotically.

Compressibility

All fluids are compressible to some degree; their density depends somewhat on the pressure. Steady liquid flow may ordinarily be treated as incompressible, and incompressible flow analysis is satisfactory for gases and vapors at velocities below about 4000 to 8000 fpm, except in long conduits.

For liquids in pipelines, a severe pressure surge or water hammer may be produced if flow is suddenly stopped. This pressure surge travels along the pipe at the speed of sound in the liquid, alternately compressing and decompressing the liquid. For steady gas flows in long conduits, the pressure drop along the conduit can reduce gas density enough to increase the velocity. If the conduit is long enough, the velocity may reach the speed of sound, and the Mach number (ratio of flow velocity to the speed of sound) must be considered.

Some compressible flows occur without heat gain or loss (adiabatically). If there is no friction (conversion of flow mechanical energy into internal energy), the process is reversible (isentropic) and follows the relationship

$$p/\rho^k = \text{constant}$$
$$k = c_p/c_v$$

where k, the ratio of specific heats at constant pressure and volume, is 1.4 for air and diatomic gases.

When the elevation term gz is neglected, as it is in most compressible flow analyses, the Bernoulli equation of steady flow, Equation (21), becomes

$$\int \frac{dp}{\rho} + \frac{V^2}{2} = \text{constant} \tag{55}$$

For a frictionless adiabatic process,

$$\int_1^2 \frac{dp}{\rho} = \frac{k}{k-1}\left(\frac{p_2}{\rho_2} - \frac{p_1}{\rho_1}\right) \tag{56}$$

Integrating between upstream station 1 and downstream station 2 gives

$$\frac{p_1}{\rho_1}\left(\frac{k}{k-1}\right)\left[\left(\frac{p_2}{p_1}\right)^{(k-1)/k} - 1\right] + \frac{V_2^2 - V_1^2}{2} = 0 \tag{57}$$

Equation (57) replaces the Bernoulli equation for compressible flows. If station 2 is the stagnation point at the front of a body, $V_2 = 0$, and solving Equation (57) for p_2 gives

$$p_s = p_2 = p_1\left[1 + \left(\frac{k-1}{2}\right)\frac{\rho_1 V_1^2}{kp_1}\right]^{k/(k-1)} \tag{58}$$

where p_s is the stagnation pressure.

Because the speed of sound of the gas is $a = kp/\rho$ and Mach number $M = V/a$, the stagnation pressure in Equation (58) becomes

$$p_s = p_1\left[1 + \left(\frac{k-1}{2}\right)M_1^2\right]^{k/(k-1)} \tag{59}$$

For Mach numbers less than one,

$$p_s = p_1 \frac{\rho_1 V_1^2}{2}\left[1 + \frac{M_1}{4} + \left(\frac{2-k}{24}\right)M_1^4 + \cdots\right] \tag{60}$$

When $M = 0$, Equation (60) reduces to the incompressible flow result obtained from Equation (9). When the upstream Mach number exceeds 0.2, the difference is significant. Thus, a pitot tube in air is influenced by compressibility at velocities over about 13,000 fpm.

Flow Measurement. For isentropic flow through a converging conduit such as a flow nozzle, venturi, or orifice meter, where velocity at the upstream station 1 is small, Equation (57) gives

$$V_2 = \sqrt{\frac{2k}{k-1}\left(\frac{p_1}{\rho_1}\right)\left[1 - \left(\frac{p_2}{p_1}\right)^{(k-1)/k}\right]} \tag{61}$$

The mass flow rate is

$$\dot{m} = V_2 A_2 \rho_2$$

$$= A_2 \sqrt{\frac{2k}{k-1}(p_1 \rho_1)\left[\left(\frac{p_2}{p_1}\right)^{2/k} - \left(\frac{p_2}{p_1}\right)^{(k+1)/k}\right]} \quad (62)$$

For incompressible frictionless flow, the mass flow rate is

$$\dot{m}_{in} = A_2 \rho \sqrt{2\Delta p/\rho} = A_2 \sqrt{2\rho(p_1 - p_2)} \quad (63)$$

The compressibility effect is often accounted for by the **expansion factor** ***Y***:

$$\dot{m} = Y \dot{m}_{in} = A_2 Y \sqrt{2\rho(p_1 - p_2)} \quad (64)$$

where $\rho = \rho_1$, and A_2 is the throat cross-sectional area. $Y \le 1$, with $Y = 1$ for the incompressible case. For compressible flow through orifices (ISO *Standard* 5167),

$$Y = 1 - (0.351 + 0.256\beta^4 + 0.93\beta^8)(1 - (p_2/p_1)^{1/k}) \quad (65)$$

where $\beta = D_2/D_1$. For venturis and nozzles (ISO *Standard* 5167),

$$Y = \sqrt{\frac{k}{k-1}\left(\frac{p_2}{p_1}\right)^{\frac{2}{k}} \times \frac{1-\beta^4}{1-\beta^4\left(\frac{p_2}{p_1}\right)^{\frac{2}{k}}} \times \frac{1-\left(\frac{p_2}{p_1}\right)^{\frac{k-1}{k}}}{1-\left(\frac{p_2}{p_1}\right)}} \quad (66)$$

For air ($k = 1.4$), $Y = 0.95$ for an orifice with $p_2/p_1 = 0.83$ and for a venturi at about 0.90, when these devices are of relatively small diameter ($D_2/D_1 < 0.5$).

As p_2/p_1 decreases, flow rate increases, but more slowly than for the incompressible case because of the nearly linear decrease in Y. However, if the downstream velocity reaches the local speed of sound, the mass flow rate becomes the value fixed by upstream pressure and density at the critical pressure ratio:

$$\left.\frac{p_2}{p_1}\right|_c = \left(\frac{2}{k+1}\right)^{k/(k-1)} = 0.53 \text{ for air} \quad (67)$$

At higher pressure ratios than critical, **choking** (no increase in flow with decrease in downstream pressure) occurs and is used in some flow control devices to avoid flow dependence on downstream conditions.

Using Equations (38) and (39) for the incompressible mass flow rate and adding the compressible expansion factor Y results in

$$\dot{m} = C_d Y \frac{\pi d^2}{4} \sqrt{\frac{2\rho\Delta p}{1-\beta^4}} \quad (68)$$

where d is throat diameter, and C_d is the discharge coefficient introduced in the Flow Measurement section. Note that C_d accounts for the effects of friction in the measuring device, and Y accounts for compressibility.

Example 4. For a venturi used to measure air ($k = 1.4$) flow, inlet pressure and temperature are 1 atm (absolute) and 77°F. The measured pressure at the throat is 0.8 atm (absolute). The inlet diameter is 2.5 in., and the throat diameter is 1.25 in. What is the mass flow rate? Use $C_d = 0.995$.

Solution. Using $p_2/p_1 = 0.8/1 = 0.8$ and $\beta = 1.25/2.5 = 0.5$ in Equation (66) gives $Y = 0.879$. In Equation (68), $d = 2.5$ in., $\Delta p = 0.2$ atm, and $\rho = 0.075$ lb$_m$/ft^3 at 77°F, 1 atm. The result is $\dot{m} = 0.843$ lb$_m$/s.

Compressible Conduit Flow

When friction loss is included, as it must be except for very short conduits, incompressible flow analysis applies until the pressure drop exceeds about 10% of the initial pressure. The possibility of sonic velocities at the end of relatively long conduits limits the amount of pressure reduction achieved. For an inlet Mach number of 0.2, discharge pressure can be reduced to about 0.2 of the initial pressure; for inflow at $M = 0.5$, discharge pressure cannot be less than about $0.45p_1$ (adiabatic) or about $0.6p_1$ (isothermal).

Analysis must treat density change, as evaluated from the continuity relation in Equation (3), with frictional occurrences evaluated from wall roughness and Reynolds number correlations of incompressible flow (Binder 1944). In evaluating valve and fitting losses, consider the reduction in K caused by compressibility (Benedict and Carlucci 1966). Although the analysis differs significantly, isothermal and adiabatic flows involve essentially the same pressure variation along the conduit, up to the limiting conditions.

Cavitation

Liquid flow with gas- or vapor-filled pockets can occur if the absolute pressure is reduced to vapor pressure or less. In this case, one or more cavities form, because liquids are rarely pure enough to withstand any tensile stressing or pressures less than vapor pressure for any length of time (John and Haberman 1980; Knapp et al. 1970; Robertson and Wislicenus 1969). Robertson and Wislicenus (1969) indicate significant occurrences in various technical fields, chiefly in hydraulic equipment and turbomachines.

Initial evidence of cavitation is the collapse noise of many small bubbles that appear initially as they are carried by the flow into higher-pressure regions. The noise is not deleterious and serves as a warning of the occurrence. As flow velocity further increases or pressure decreases, the severity of cavitation increases. More bubbles appear and may join to form large fixed cavities. The space they occupy becomes large enough to modify the flow pattern and alter performance of the flow device. Collapse of cavities on or near solid boundaries becomes so frequent that, in time, the cumulative impact causes cavitational erosion of the surface or excessive vibration. As a result, pumps can lose efficiency or their parts may erode locally. Control valves may be noisy or seriously damaged by cavitation.

Cavitation in orifice and valve flow is shown in Figure 21. With high upstream pressure and a low flow rate, no cavitation occurs. As pressure is reduced or flow rate increased, the minimum pressure in the flow (in the shear layer leaving the edge of the orifice) eventually approaches vapor pressure. Turbulence in this layer causes fluctuating pressures below the mean (as in vortex cores) and small bubble-like cavities. These are carried downstream into the region of pressure regain where they collapse, either in the fluid or on the wall (Figure 21A). As pressure reduces, more vapor- or gas-filled bubbles result and coalesce into larger ones. Eventually, a single large cavity results that collapses further downstream (Figure 21B).

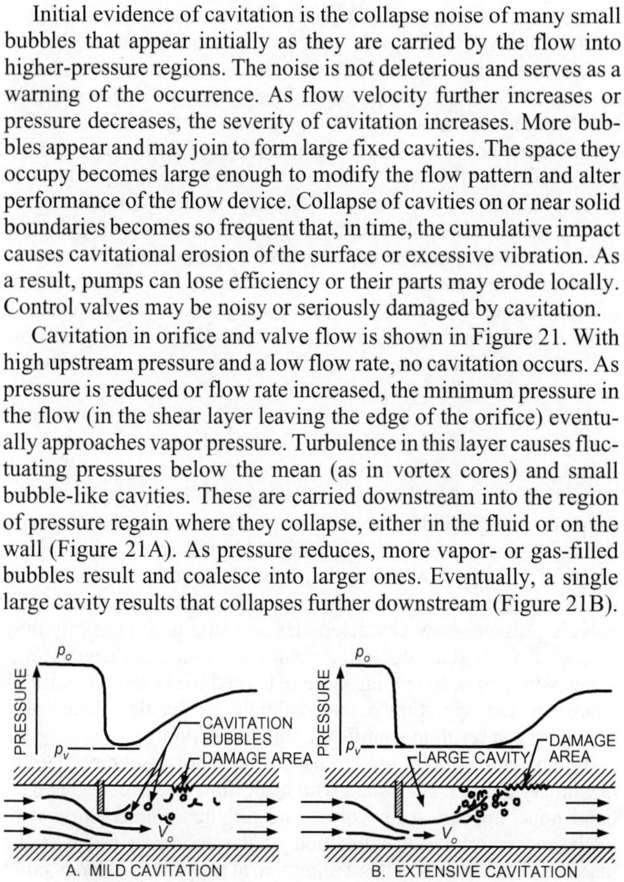

Fig. 21 Cavitation in Flows in Orifice or Valve

The region of wall damage is then as many as 20 diameters downstream from the valve or orifice plate.

Sensitivity of a device to cavitation is measured by the **cavitation index** or **cavitation number**, which is the ratio of the available pressure above vapor pressure to the dynamic pressure of the reference flow:

$$\sigma = \frac{2(p_o - p_v)}{\rho V_o^2} \tag{69}$$

where p_v is vapor pressure, and the subscript o refers to appropriate reference conditions. Valve analyses use such an index to determine when cavitation will affect the discharge coefficient (Ball 1957). With flow-metering devices such as orifices, venturis, and flow nozzles, there is little cavitation, because it occurs mostly downstream of the flow regions involved in establishing the metering action.

The detrimental effects of cavitation can be avoided by operating the liquid-flow device at high enough pressures. When this is not possible, the flow must be changed or the device must be built to withstand cavitation effects. Some materials or surface coatings are more resistant to cavitation erosion than others, but none is immune. Surface contours can be designed to delay onset of cavitation.

5. NOISE IN FLUID FLOW

Noise in flowing fluids results from unsteady flow fields and can be at discrete frequencies or broadly distributed over the audible range. With liquid flow, cavitation results in noise through the collapse of vapor bubbles. Noise in pumps or fittings (e.g., valves) can be a rattling or sharp hissing sound, which is easily eliminated by raising the system pressure. With severe cavitation, the resulting unsteady flow can produce indirect noise from induced vibration of adjacent parts. See Chapter 48 of the 2015 *ASHRAE Handbook—HVAC Applications* for more information on noise control.

Disturbed laminar flow behind cylinders can be an oscillating motion. The shedding frequency f of these vortexes is characterized by a **Strouhal number** St $= fd/V$ of about 0.21 for a circular cylinder of diameter d, over a considerable range of Reynolds numbers. This oscillating flow can be a powerful noise source, particularly when f is close to the natural frequency of the cylinder or some nearby structural member so that resonance occurs. With cylinders of another shape, such as impeller blades of a pump or blower, the characterizing Strouhal number involves the trailing-edge thickness of the member. The strength of the vortex wake, with its resulting vibrations and noise potential, can be reduced by breaking up flow with downstream splitter plates or boundary-layer trip devices (wires) on the cylinder surface.

Noises produced in pipes and ducts, especially from valves and fittings, are associated with the loss through such elements. The sound pressure of noise in water pipe flow increases linearly with head loss; broadband noise increases, but only in the lower-frequency range. Fitting-produced noise levels also increase with fitting loss (even without cavitation) and significantly exceed noise levels of the pipe flow. The relation between noise and loss is not surprising because both involve excessive flow perturbations. A valve's pressure-flow characteristics and structural elasticity may be such that for some operating point it oscillates, perhaps in resonance with part of the piping system, to produce excessive noise. A change in the operating point conditions or details of the valve geometry can result in significant noise reduction.

Pumps and blowers are strong potential noise sources. Turbomachinery noise is associated with blade-flow occurrences. Broadband noise appears from vortex and turbulence interaction with walls and is primarily a function of the operating point of the machine. For blowers, it has a minimum at the peak efficiency point (Groff et al. 1967). Narrow-band noise also appears at the blade-crossing frequency and its harmonics. Such noise can be very annoying because it stands out from the background. To reduce this noise, increase clearances between impeller and housing, and space impeller blades unevenly around the circumference.

6. SYMBOLS

A = area, ft²
A_o = area of orifice opening
B = Bernoulli constant
C_D = drag coefficient
C_d = discharge coefficient
D_h = hydraulic diameter
E_L = loss during conversion of energy from mechanical to internal
E_M = external work from fluid machine
F = tangential force per unit area required to slide one of two parallel plates
f = Darcy-Weisbach friction factor, or shedding frequency
F_D = drag force
f_{ref} = reference value of friction factor
g = gravitational acceleration, ft/s²
g_c = gravitational constant = 32.17 $lb_m \cdot ft/s^2 \cdot lb_f$
H_L = head lost through friction
H_M = head added by pump
K = loss coefficient
k = ratio of specific heats at constant pressure and volume
L = length
L_e = entrance length
L_{eff} = effective length
$\dot{m}$ = mass flow rate
p = pressure
P_w = wetted perimeter
Q = volumetric flow rate
q = heat per unit mass absorbed or rejected
R = pipe radius
Re = Reynolds number
s = flow direction
St = Strouhal number
u = internal energy
V = velocity
v = fluid velocity normal to differential area dA
w = work per unit mass
y = distance from centerline
Y = distance between two parallel plates, ft, or expansion factor
z = elevation

Greek

α = kinetic energy factor
β = d/D = ratio of throat (or orifice) diameter to conduit diameter
γ = specific weight or weight density
δ = boundary layer thickness
ΔE = change in energy content per unit mass of flowing fluid
Δp = pressure drop across valve
Δu = conversion of energy from mechanical to internal
ε = roughness height
θ = time
μ = proportionality factor for absolute or dynamic viscosity of fluid, $lb_f \cdot s/ft^2$
ν = kinematic viscosity, ft²/s
ρ = density, lb_m/ft^3
σ = cavitation index or number
τ = shear stress, lb_f/ft^2
τ_w = wall shear stress

REFERENCES

ASHRAE members can access *ASHRAE Journal* articles and ASHRAE research project final reports at technologyportal.ashrae.org. Articles and reports are also available for purchase by nonmembers in the online ASHRAE Bookstore at www.ashrae.org/bookstore.

Baines, W.D., and E.G. Peterson. 1951. An investigation of flow through screens. *ASME Transactions* 73:467.

Ball, J.W. 1957. Cavitation characteristics of gate valves and globe values used as flow regulators under heads up to about 125 ft. *ASME Transactions* 79:1275.

Benedict, R.P., and N.A. Carlucci. 1966. *Handbook of specific losses in flow systems*. Plenum Press Data Division, New York.

Binder, R.C. 1944. Limiting isothermal flow in pipes. *ASME Transactions* 66:221.

Churchill, S.W. 1977. Friction-factor equation spans all fluid flow regimes. *Chemical Engineering* 84(24):91-92.

Colborne, W.G., and A.J. Drobitch. 1966. An experimental study of non-isothermal flow in a vertical circular tube. *ASHRAE Transactions* 72(4):5.

Coleman, J.W. 2004. An experimentally validated model for two-phase sudden contraction pressure drop in microchannel tube header. *Heat Transfer Engineering* 25(3):69-77.

Daily, J.W., W.L. Hankey, R.W. Olive, and J.M. Jordan. 1956. Resistance coefficients for accelerated and decelerated flows through smooth tubes and orifices. *ASME Transactions* 78:1071-1077.

Deissler, R.G. 1951. Laminar flow in tubes with heat transfer. *National Advisory Technical Note* 2410, Committee for Aeronautics.

Fox, R.W., A.T. McDonald, and P.J. Pritchard. 2004. *Introduction to fluid mechanics*. Wiley, New York.

Furuya, Y., T. Sate, and T. Kushida. 1976. The loss of flow in the conical with suction at the entrance. *Bulletin of the Japan Society of Mechanical Engineers* 19:131.

Goldstein, S., ed. 1938. *Modern developments in fluid mechanics.* Oxford University Press, London. Reprinted by Dover Publications, New York.

Groff, G.C., J.R. Schreiner, and C.E. Bullock. 1967. Centrifugal fan sound power level prediction. *ASHRAE Transactions* 73(II):V.4.1.

Heskested, G. 1970. Further experiments with suction at a sudden enlargement. *Journal of Basic Engineering, ASME Transactions* 92D:437.

Hoerner, S.F. 1965. *Fluid dynamic drag*, 3rd ed. Hoerner Fluid Dynamics, Vancouver, WA.

Hydraulic Institute. 1990. *Engineering data book*, 2nd ed. Parsippany, NJ.

Incropera, F.P., and D.P. DeWitt. 2002. *Fundamentals of heat and mass transfer*, 5th ed. Wiley, New York.

ISO. 2003. Measurement of fluid flow by means of pressure differential devices inserted in circular cross-section conduits running full. *Standard* 5167. International Organization for Standardization, Geneva.

Ito, H. 1962. Pressure losses in smooth pipe bends. *Journal of Basic Engineering, ASME Transactions* 4(7):43.

John, J.E.A., and W.L. Haberman. 1980. *Introduction to fluid mechanics*, 2nd ed. Prentice Hall, Englewood Cliffs, NJ.

Kline, S.J. 1959. On the nature of stall. *Journal of Basic Engineering, ASME Transactions* 81D:305.

Knapp, R.T., J.W. Daily, and F.G. Hammitt. 1970. *Cavitation*. McGraw-Hill, New York.

Lipstein, N.J. 1962. Low velocity sudden expansion pipe flow. *ASHRAE Journal* 4(7):43.

Moody, L.F. 1944. Friction factors for pipe flow. *ASME Transactions* 66:672.

Moore, C.A., and S.J. Kline. 1958. Some effects of vanes and turbulence in two-dimensional wide-angle subsonic diffusers. National Advisory Committee for Aeronautics, *Technical Memo* 4080.

Murdock, J.W., C.J. Foltz, and C. Gregory. 1964. Performance characteristics of elbow flow meters. *Journal of Basic Engineering, ASME Transactions* 86D:498.

Robertson, J.M. 1963. A turbulence primer. University of Illinois–Urbana, *Engineering Experiment Station Circular* 79.

Robertson, J.M. 1965. *Hydrodynamics in theory and application*. Prentice-Hall, Englewood Cliffs, NJ.

Robertson, J.M., and G.F. Wislicenus, eds. 1969 (discussion 1970). *Cavitation state of knowledge.* American Society of Mechanical Engineers, New York.

Ross, D. 1956. Turbulent flow in the entrance region of a pipe. *ASME Transactions* 78:915.

Schlichting, H. 1979. *Boundary layer theory*, 7th ed. McGraw-Hill, New York.

Wile, D.D. 1947. Air flow measurement in the laboratory. *Refrigerating Engineering*: 515.

BIBLIOGRAPHY

Lin, C.-X., and P. Shinde. 2016. A heat transfer and friction factor correlation for low air-side Reynolds number applications of compact heat exchangers. ASHRAE Research Project RP-1535, *Final Report*.

Soumerai, H.P. 1986. Thermodynamic generalization of heat transfer and fluid-flow data. *ASHRAE Transactions* 92(1B). *Paper* SF-86-16-4.

CHAPTER 4

HEAT TRANSFER

HEAT transfer is energy transferred because of a temperature difference. Energy moves from a higher-temperature region to a lower-temperature region by one or more of three modes: **conduction**, **radiation**, and **convection**. This chapter presents elementary principles of single-phase heat transfer, with emphasis on HVAC applications. Boiling and condensation are discussed in Chapter 5. More specific information on heat transfer to or from buildings or refrigerated spaces can be found in Chapters 14 to 19, 23, and 27 of this volume and in Chapter 24 of the 2014 *ASHRAE Handbook—Refrigeration*. Physical properties of substances can be found in Chapters 26, 28, 32, and 33 of this volume and in Chapter 19 of the 2014 *ASHRAE Handbook—Refrigeration*. Heat transfer equipment, including evaporators, condensers, heating and cooling coils, furnaces, and radiators, is covered in the 2016 *ASHRAE Handbook—HVAC Systems and Equipment*. For further information on heat transfer, see the Bibliography.

1. HEAT TRANSFER PROCESSES

Conduction

Consider a wall that is 33 ft long, 10 ft tall, and 0.3 ft thick (Figure 1A). One side of the wall is maintained at t_{s1} = 77°F, and the other is kept at t_{s2} = 68°F. Heat transfer occurs at rate q through the wall from the warmer side to the cooler. The heat transfer mode is conduction (the only way energy can be transferred through a solid).

- If t_{s1} is raised from 77 to 86°F while everything else remains the same, q doubles because $t_{s1} - t_{s2}$ doubles.
- If the wall is twice as tall, thus doubling the area A_c of the wall, q doubles.
- If the wall is twice as thick, q is halved.

From these relationships,

$$q \propto \frac{(t_{s1} - t_{s2})A_c}{L}$$

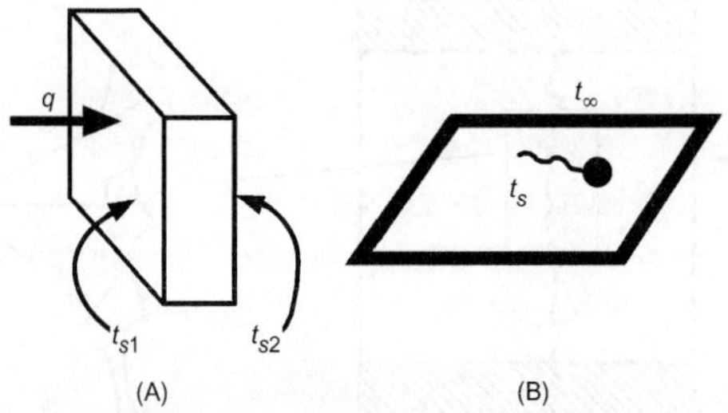

Fig. 1 (A) Conduction and (B) Convection

The preparation of this chapter is assigned to TC 1.3, Heat Transfer and Fluid Flow.

where ∝ means "proportional to" and L = wall thickness. However, this relation does not take wall material into account; if the wall were foam instead of concrete, q would clearly be less. The constant of proportionality is a material property, **thermal conductivity *k***. Thus,

$$q = k\frac{(t_{s1} - t_{s2})A_c}{L} = \frac{(t_{s1} - t_{s2})}{L/(kA_c)} \quad (1)$$

where k has units of Btu/h·ft·°F. The denominator $L/(kA_c)$ can be considered the **conduction resistance** associated with the driving potential $(t_{s1} - t_{s2})$. This is analogous to current flow through an electrical resistance, $I = (V_1 - V_2)/R$, where $(V_1 - V_2)$ is driving potential, R is electrical resistance, and current I is rate of flow of charge instead of rate of heat transfer q.

Thermal resistance has units h·°F/Btu. A wall with a resistance of 3 h·°F/Btu requires $(t_{s1} - t_{s2})$ = 3°F for heat transfer q of 1 Btu/h. The thermal/electrical resistance analogy allows tools used to solve electrical circuits to be used for heat transfer problems.

Convection

Consider a surface at temperature t_s in contact with a fluid at t_∞ (Figure 1B). **Newton's law of cooling** expresses the rate of heat transfer from the surface of area A_s as

$$q = h_c A_s(t_s - t_\infty) = \frac{(t_s - t_\infty)}{1/(h_c A_s)} \quad (2)$$

where h_c is the **heat transfer coefficient** (Table 1) and has units of Btu/h·ft²·°F. The **convection resistance** $1/(h_c A_s)$ has units of h·°F/Btu.

If $t_\infty > t_s$, heat transfers from the fluid to the surface, and q is written as just $q = h_c A_s(t_\infty - t_s)$. Resistance is the same, but the sign of the temperature difference is reversed.

For heat transfer to be considered convection, fluid in contact with the surface must be in motion; if not, the mode of heat transfer is conduction. If fluid motion is caused by an external force (e.g., fan, pump, wind), it is **forced convection**. If fluid motion results from buoyant forces caused by the surface being warmer or cooler than the fluid, it is **free** (or **natural**) **convection**.

Table 1 Heat Transfer Coefficients by Convection Type

Convection Type	h_c, Btu/h·ft²·°F
Free, gases	0.35 to 4.5
Free, liquids	1.8 to 180
Forced, gases	4.5 to 45
Forced, liquids	9 to 3500
Boiling, condensation	450 to 18,000

Radiation

Matter emits thermal radiation at its surface when its temperature is above absolute zero. This radiation is in the form of photons of varying frequency. These photons leaving the surface need no medium to transport them, unlike conduction and convection (in which heat transfer occurs through matter). The rate of thermal radiant energy emitted by a surface depends on its absolute temperature and its surface characteristics. A surface that absorbs all radiation incident upon it is called a **black surface**, and emits energy at the maximum possible rate at a given temperature. The heat emission from a black surface is given by the **Stefan-Boltzmann law:**

$$q_{emitted,\,black} = A_s W_b = A_s \sigma T_s^4$$

where $W_b = \sigma T_s^4$ is the **blackbody emissive power** in Btu/h·ft²; T_s is absolute surface temperature, °R; and $\sigma = 0.1712 \times 10^{-8}$ Btu/h·ft²·°R⁴ is the Stefan-Boltzmann constant. If a surface is not black, the emission per unit time per unit area is

$$W = \varepsilon W_b = \varepsilon \sigma T_s^4$$

where W is emissive power, and ε is emissivity, where $0 \le \varepsilon \le 1$. For a black surface, $\varepsilon = 1$.

Nonblack surfaces do not absorb all incident radiation. The absorbed radiation is

$$q_{absorbed} = \alpha A_s G$$

where **absorptivity** α is the fraction of incident radiation absorbed, and **irradiation** G is the rate of radiant energy incident on a surface per unit area of the receiving surface. For a black surface, $\alpha = 1$.

A surface's emissivity and absorptivity are often both functions of the wavelength distribution of photons emitted and absorbed, respectively, by the surface. However, in many cases, it is reasonable to assume that both α and ε are independent of wavelength. If so, $\alpha = \varepsilon$ (a **gray surface**).

Two surfaces at different temperatures that can "see" each other can exchange energy through radiation. The net exchange rate depends on the surfaces' (1) relative size, (2) relative orientation and shape, (3) temperatures, and (4) emissivity and absorptivity. However, for a small area A_s in a large enclosure at constant temperature t_{surr}, the irradiation on A_s from the surroundings is the blackbody emissive power of the surroundings $W_{b,surr}$. So, if $t_s > t_{surr}$, net heat loss from gray surface A_s in the radiation exchange with the surroundings at T_{surr} is

$$q_{net} = q_{emitted} - q_{absorbed} = \varepsilon A_s W_{bs} - \alpha A_s W_{b,surr} = \varepsilon A_s \sigma (T_s^4 - T_{surr}^4) \quad (3)$$

where $\alpha = \varepsilon$ for the gray surface. If $t_s < t_{surr}$, the expression for q_{net} is the same with the sign reversed, and q_{net} is the net gain by A_s.

Note that q_{net} can be written as

$$q_{net} = \frac{W_{bs} - W_{b,surr}}{1/(\varepsilon A_s)}$$

In this form, $E_{bs} - E_{b,surr}$ is analogous to the driving potential in an electric circuit, and $1/(\varepsilon A_s)$ is analogous to electrical resistance. This is a convenient analogy when only radiation is being considered, but if convection and radiation both occur at a surface, convection is described by a driving potential based on the difference in the first power of the temperatures, whereas radiation is described by the difference in the fourth power of the temperatures. In cases like this, it is often useful to express net radiation as

$$q_{net} = h_r A_s (t_s - t_{surr}) = (t_s - t_{surr})/(1/h_r A_s) \quad (4)$$

where $h_r = \sigma\varepsilon(T_s^2 + T_{surr}^2)(T_s + T_{surr})$ is often called a **radiation heat transfer coefficient**. The disadvantage of this form is that h_r depends on t_s, which is often the desired result of the calculation.

Combined Radiation and Convection

When $t_{surr} = t_\infty$ in Equation (4), the total heat transfer from a surface by convection and radiation combined is then

$$q = q_{rad} + q_{conv} = (t_s - t_\infty)A_s(h_r + h_c)$$

The temperature difference $t_s - t_\infty$ is in either °R or °F; the difference is the same. Either can be used; however, absolute temperatures *must* be used to calculate h_r. (Absolute temperatures are °R = °F + 459.67.) Note that h_c and h_r are always positive, and that the direction of q is determined by the sign of $(t_s - t_\infty)$.

Contact or Interface Resistance

Heat flow through two layers encounters two conduction resistances L_1/k_1A and L_2/k_2A (Figure 2). At the interface between two layers are gaps across which heat is transferred by a combination of conduction at contact points and convection and radiation across gaps. This multimode heat transfer process is usually characterized using a contact resistance coefficient R''_{cont} or contact conductance h_{cont}.

$$q = \frac{\Delta t}{R''_{cont}/A} = h_{cont} A \Delta t$$

where Δt is the temperature drop across the interface. R''_{cont} is in ft²·h·°F/Btu, and h_{cont} is in Btu/h·ft²·°F. The contact or interface resistance is $R_{cont} = R''_{cont}/A = 1/h_{cont}A$, and the resistance of the two layers combined is the sum of the resistances of the two layers and the contact resistance.

Contact resistance can be reduced by lowering surface roughnesses, increasing contact pressure, or using a conductive grease or paste to fill the gaps.

Heat Flux

The conduction heat transfer can be written as

$$q'' = \frac{q}{A_c} = \frac{k(t_{s1} - t_{s2})}{L}$$

where q'' is heat flux in Btu/h·ft². Similarly, for convection the heat flux is

$$q'' = \frac{q}{A_s} = h_c(t_s - t_\infty)$$

and net heat flux from radiation at the surface is

$$q''_{net} = \frac{q_{net}}{A_s} = \varepsilon\sigma(T_s^4 - T_{surr}^4)$$

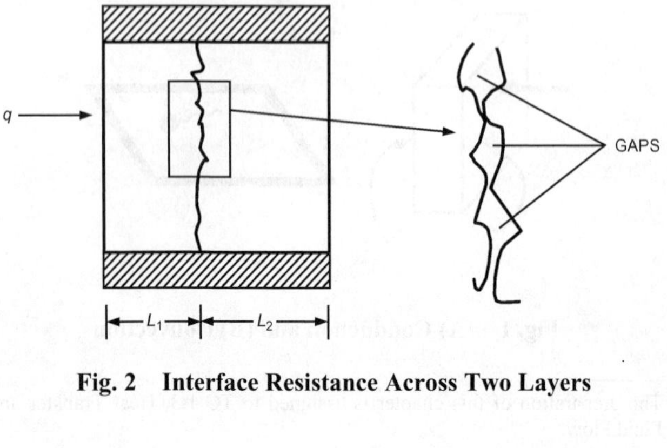

Fig. 2 Interface Resistance Across Two Layers

Overall Resistance and Heat Transfer Coefficient

In Equation (1) for conduction in a slab, Equation (4) for radiative heat transfer rate between two surfaces, and Equation (2) for convective heat transfer rate from a surface, the heat transfer rate is expressed as a temperature difference divided by a thermal resistance. Using the electrical resistance analogy, with temperature difference and heat transfer rate instead of potential difference and current, respectively, tools for solving series electrical resistance circuits can also be applied to heat transfer circuits. For example, consider the heat transfer rate from a liquid to the surrounding gas separated by a constant cross-sectional area solid, as shown in Figure 3. The heat transfer rate from the liquid to the adjacent surface is by convection, then across the solid body by conduction, and finally from the solid surface to the surroundings by both convection and radiation. A circuit using the equations for resistances in each mode is also shown. From the circuit, the heat transfer rate is

$$q = \frac{(t_{f1} - t_{f2})}{R_1 + R_2 + R_3}$$

where

$$R_1 = 1/hA \qquad R_2 = L/kA \qquad R_2 = \frac{(1/h_cA)(1/h_rA)}{(1/h_cA) + (1/h_rA)}$$

Resistance R_3 is the parallel combination of the convection and radiation resistances on the right-hand surface, $1/h_cA$ and $1/h_rA$. Equivalently, $R_3 = 1/h_{rc}A$, where h_{rc} on the air side is the sum of the convection and radiation heat transfer coefficients (i.e., $h_{rc} = h_c + h_r$).

The heat transfer rate can also be written as

$$q = UA(t_{f1} - t_{f2})$$

where U is the overall heat transfer coefficient that accounts for all the resistances involved. Note that

$$\frac{t_{f1} - t_{f2}}{q} = \frac{1}{UA} = R_1 + R_2 + R_3$$

The product UA is overall conductance, the reciprocal of overall resistance. The surface area A on which U is based is not always constant as in this example, and should always be specified when referring to U.

Heat transfer rates are equal from the warm liquid to the solid surface, through the solid, and then to the cool gas. Temperature drops across each part of the heat flow path are related to the resistances (as voltage drops are in an electric circuit), so that

$$t_{f1} - t_1 = qR_1 \qquad t_1 - t_2 = qR_2 \qquad t_2 - t_{f2} = qR_3$$

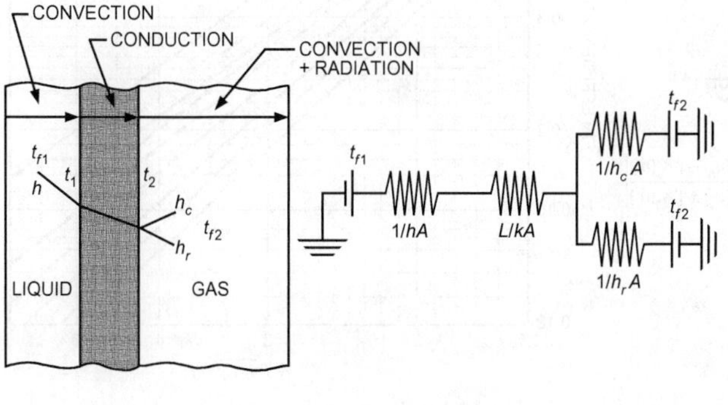

Fig. 3 Thermal Circuit

2. THERMAL CONDUCTION

One-Dimensional Steady-State Conduction

Steady-state heat transfer rates and resistances for (1) a slab of constant cross-sectional area, (2) a hollow cylinder with radial heat transfer, and (3) a hollow sphere are given in Table 2.

Example 1. Chilled water at 41°F flows in a copper pipe with a thermal conductivity k_p of 2772 Btu·in/h·ft²·°F, with internal and external diameters of ID = 4 in. and OD = 4.7 in. (Figure 4) The tube is covered with insulation 2 in. thick, with k_i = 1.4 Btu·in/h·ft²·°F. The surrounding air is at t_a = 77°F, and the heat transfer coefficient at the outer surface h_o = 1.76 Btu/h·ft²·°F. Emissivity of the outer surface is ε = 0.85. The heat transfer coefficient inside the tube is h_i = 176 Btu/h·ft²·°F. Contact resistance between the insulation and the pipe is assumed to be negligible. Find the rate of heat gain for a given length of pipe and the temperature at the pipe-insulation interface.

Solution: The outer diameter of the insulation is D_{ins} = 4.7 + 2(2) = 8.7 in. From Table 2, for L = 3.28 ft,

$$R_1 = \frac{1}{h_i \pi \mathrm{ID} L} = 1.65 \times 10^{-3}\ \mathrm{h \cdot °F/Btu}$$

$$R_2 = \frac{\ln(\mathrm{OD/ID})}{2\pi k_p L} = 3.37 \times 10^{-5}\ \mathrm{h \cdot °F/Btu}$$

$$R_3 = \frac{\ln(D_{ins}/\mathrm{OD})}{2\pi k_i L} = 0.254\ \mathrm{h \cdot °F/Btu}$$

$$R_c = \frac{1}{h_o \pi D_{ins} L} = 0.0756\ \mathrm{h \cdot °F/Btu}$$

Assuming insulation surface temperature t_s = 70°F (i.e., 530°R) and $T_{surr} = T_a$ = 537°R, $h_r = \varepsilon\sigma(T_s^2 + T_{surr}^2)(T_s + T_{surr})$ = 0.88 Btu/h·ft²·°F.

Table 2 One-Dimensional Conduction Shape Factors

	Configuration	Heat Transfer Rate	Thermal Resistance
Constant cross-sectional area slab	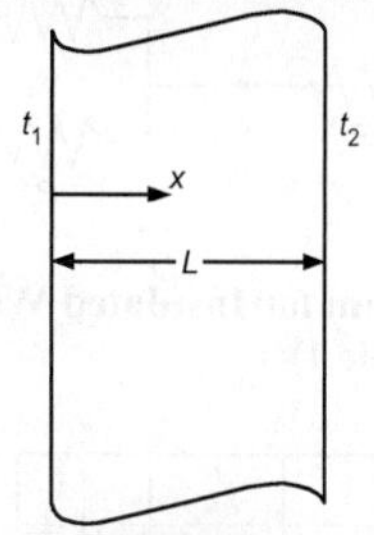	$q_x = kA_x \frac{t_1 - t_2}{L}$	$\frac{L}{kA_x}$
Hollow cylinder of length L with negligible heat transfer from end surfaces	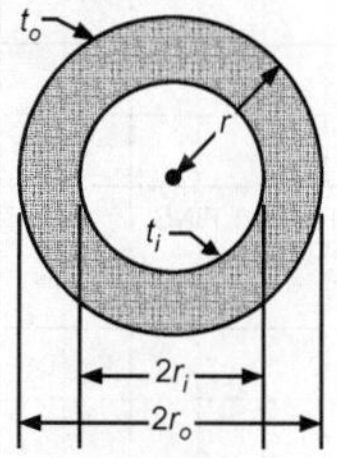	$q_r = \frac{2\pi kL(t_i - t_o)}{\ln\left(\frac{r_o}{r_i}\right)}$	$R = \frac{\ln(r_o/r_i)}{2\pi kL}$
Hollow sphere	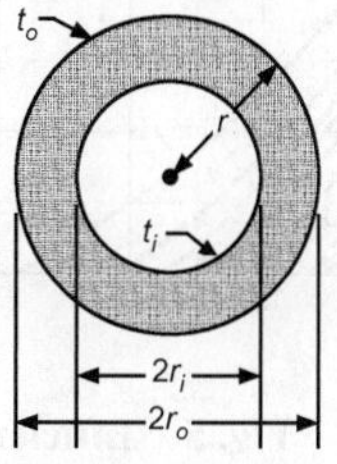	$q_r = \frac{4\pi k(t_i - t_o)}{\frac{1}{r_i} + \frac{1}{r_o}}$	$R = \frac{1/r_i - 1/r_o}{4\pi k}$

$$R_r = \frac{1}{h_r \pi D_{ins} L} = 0.151\ \text{h·°F/Btu}$$

$$R_4 = \frac{R_r R_c}{R_r + R_c} = 0.050\ \text{h·°F/Btu}$$

$$R_{tot} = R_1 + R_2 + R_3 + R_4 = 0.306\ \text{h·°F/Btu}$$

Finally, the rate of heat gain by the cold water is

$$q_{rc} = \frac{t_a - t}{R_{tot}} = 118\ \text{Btu/h}$$

Temperature at the pipe/insulation interface is

$$t_{s2} = t + q_{rc}(R_1 + R_2) = 41.2°\text{F}$$

Temperature at the insulation's surface is

$$t_{s3} = t_a - q_{rc}R_4 = 71.1°\text{F}$$

which is very close to the assumed value of 70°F.

Note the importance of the pipe/insulation interface temperature. If this temperature is below the dew point, condensation will occur that will damage the insulation. A more complete version of this kind of example is given in Chapter 6 It covers calculation of interface temperatures and the vapor pressures needed to find the corresponding dew-point temperatures at the interface, as well as methods to prevent condensation.

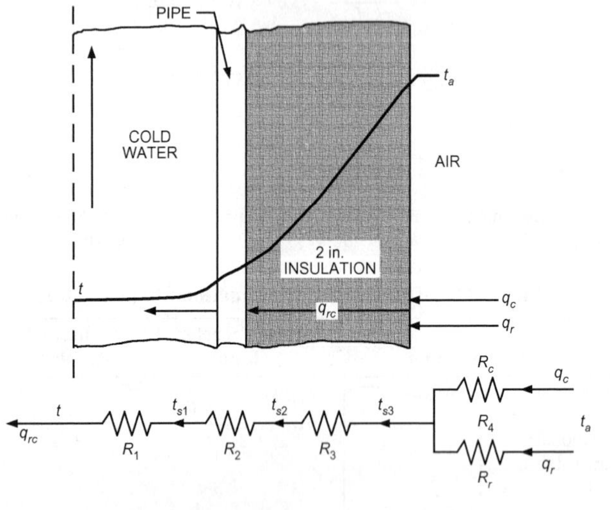

Fig. 4 Thermal Circuit Diagram for Insulated Water Pipe (Example 1)

Two- and Three-Dimensional Steady-State Conduction: Shape Factors

Mathematical solutions to a number of two and three-dimensional conduction problems are available in Carslaw and Jaeger (1959). Complex problems can also often be solved by graphical or numerical methods, as described by Adams and Rogers (1973), Croft and Lilley (1977), and Patankar (1980). There are many two- and three-dimensional steady-state cases that can be solved using conduction shape factors. Using the conduction shape factor S, the heat transfer rate is expressed as

$$q = Sk(t_1 - t_2) = (t_1 - t_2)/(1/Sk) \tag{5}$$

where k is the material's thermal conductivity, t_1 and t_2 are temperatures of two surfaces, and $1/(Sk)$ is thermal resistance. Conduction shape factors for some common configurations are given in Table 3.

Example 2. The walls and roof of a house are made of 8 in. thick concrete with $k = 5.2$ Btu·in/h·ft²·°F. The inner surface is at 68°F, and the outer surface is at 46°F. The roof is 33 × 33 ft, and the walls are 16 ft high. Find the rate of heat loss from the house through its walls and roof, including edge and corner effects.

Solution: The rate of heat transfer excluding the edges and corners is first determined:

$$A_{total} = (33 - 2 \times 8/12)(33 - 2 \times 8/12) + 4(33 - 2 \times 8/12)(16 - 8/12) = 2945\ \text{ft}^2$$

$$q_{walls+ceiling} = \frac{kA_{total}}{L}\Delta t = \frac{(5.2'me\ \text{Btu·in/h·ft}^2\text{·°F})(2945\ \text{ft}^2)}{8\ \text{in.}}$$

$$(68 - 46)°\text{F} = 42{,}114\ \text{Btu/h}$$

The shape factors for the corners and edges are in Table 2:

$$S_{corners+edges} = 4 \times S_{corner} + 4 \times S_{edge} = 4 \times 0.15(8/12)\text{ft} + 4 \times 0.54(33 - 2 \times 8/12)\text{ft} = 68.8\ \text{ft}$$

and the heat transfer rate is

$$q_{corners+edges} = S_{corners+edges}\, k\Delta t = (68.8\ \text{ft})[(5.2/12)\ \text{Btu/ft·h·°F}](68 - 46)°\text{F} = 656\ \text{Btu/h}$$

which leads to

$$q_{total} = (42{,}114 + 656)\ \text{Btu/h} = 42{,}770\ \text{Btu/h}$$

Note that the edges and corners are 1.3% of the total.

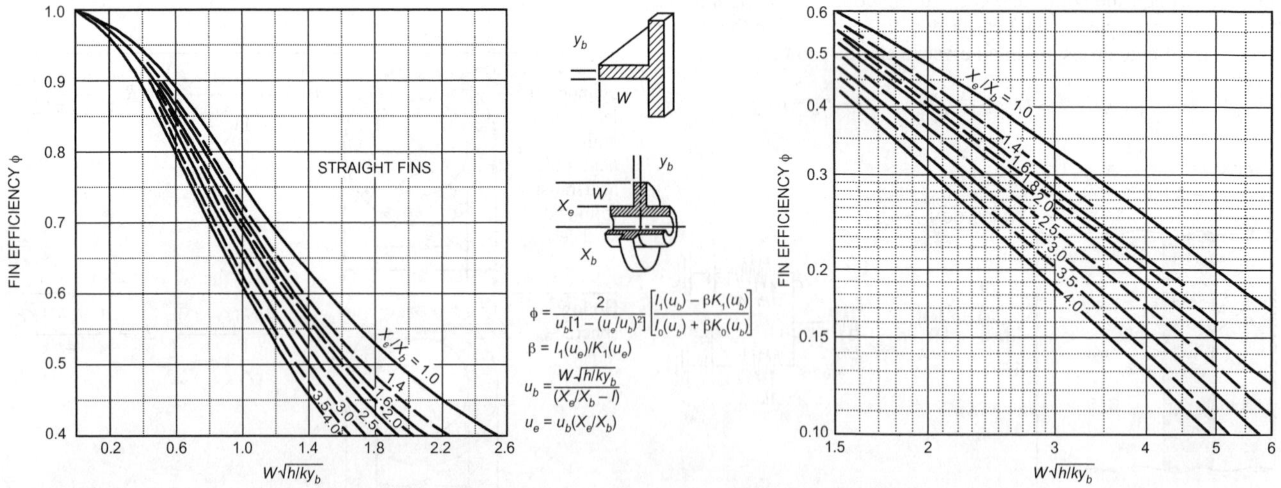

Fig. 5 Efficiency of Annular Fins of Constant Thickness

Table 3 Multidimensional Conduction Shape Factors

Configuration	Shape Factor S, ft	Restriction	
Edge of two adjoining walls	$0.54W$	$W > L/5$	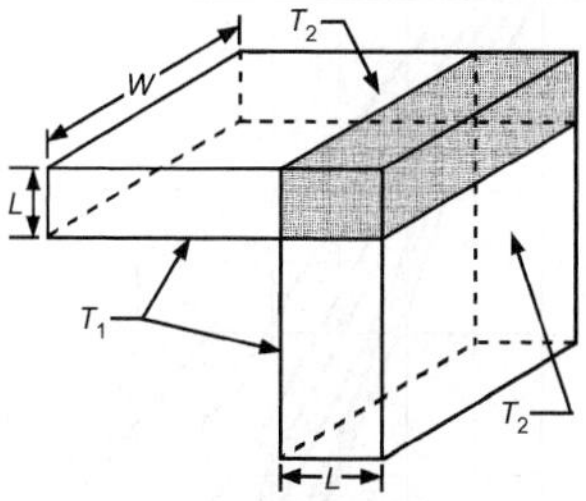
Corner of three adjoining walls (inner surface at T_1 and outer surface at T_2)	$0.15L$	$L <<$ length and width of wall	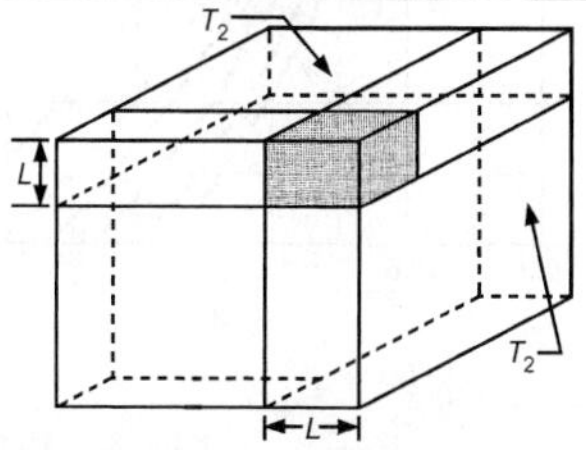
Isothermal rectangular block embedded in semi-infinite body with one face of block parallel to surface of body	$\frac{2.756L}{\left[\ln\left(1+\frac{d}{W}\right)\right]^{0.59}}\left(\frac{H}{d}\right)^{0.078}$	$L > W$ $L >> d, W, H$	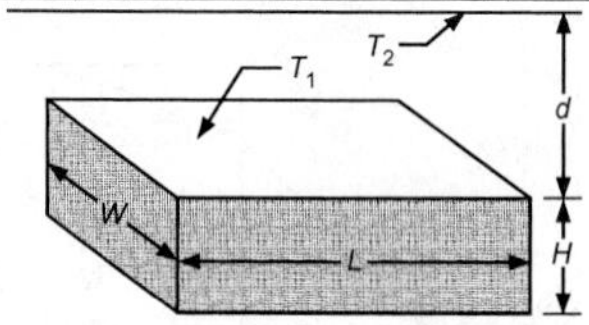
Thin isothermal rectangular plate buried in semi-infinite medium	$\frac{\pi W}{\ln(4W/L)}$	$d = 0, W > L$	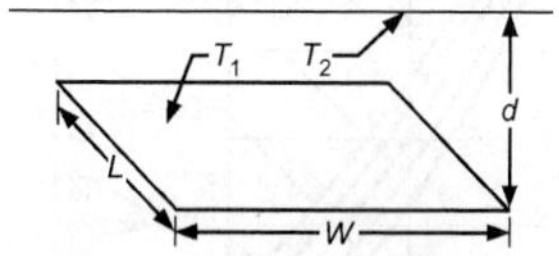
	$\frac{2\pi W}{\ln(4W/L)}$	$d >> W$ $W > L$	
	$\frac{2\pi W}{\ln(2\pi d/L)}$	$d > 2W$ $W >> L$	
Cylinder centered inside square of length L	$\frac{2\pi L}{\ln(0.54W/R)}$	$L >> W$ $W > 2R$	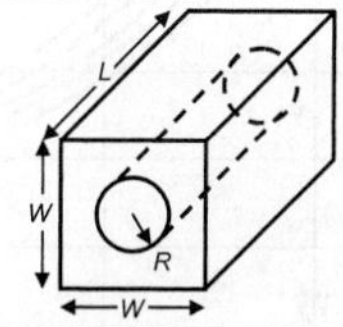
Isothermal cylinder buried in semi-infinite medium	$\frac{2\pi L}{\cosh^{-1}(d/R)}$	$L >> R$	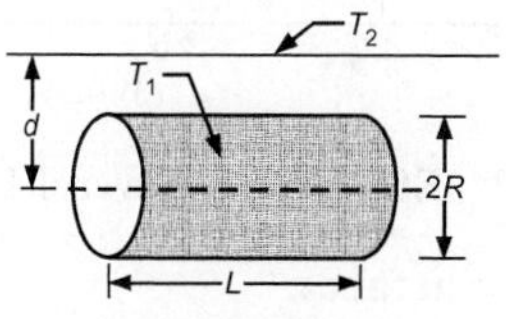
	$\frac{2\pi L}{\ln(2d/R)}$	$L >> R$ $d > 3R$	
	$\frac{2\pi L}{\ln\frac{L}{R}\left[1-\frac{\ln(L/2d)}{\ln(L/R)}\right]}$	$d >> R$ $L >> d$	
Horizontal cylinder of length L midway between two infinite, parallel, isothermal surfaces	$\frac{2\pi L}{\ln\left(\frac{4d}{R}\right)}$	$L >> d$	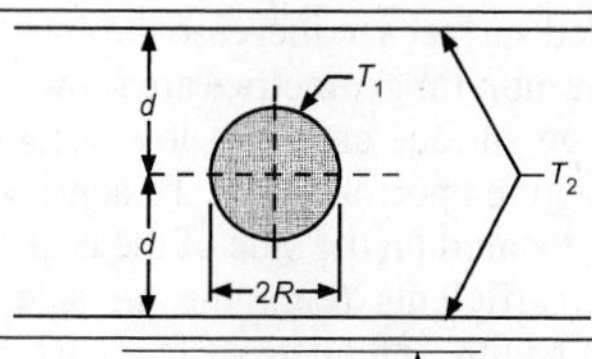
Isothermal sphere in semi-infinite medium	$\frac{4\pi R}{1-(R/2d)}$		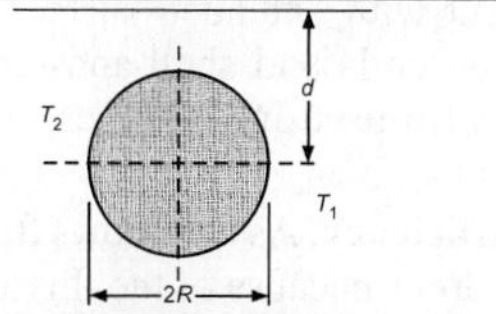
Isothermal sphere in infinite medium	$4\pi R$		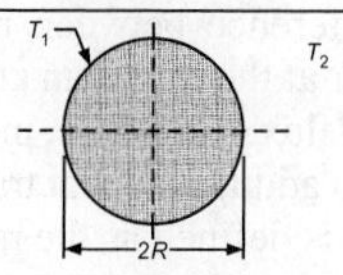

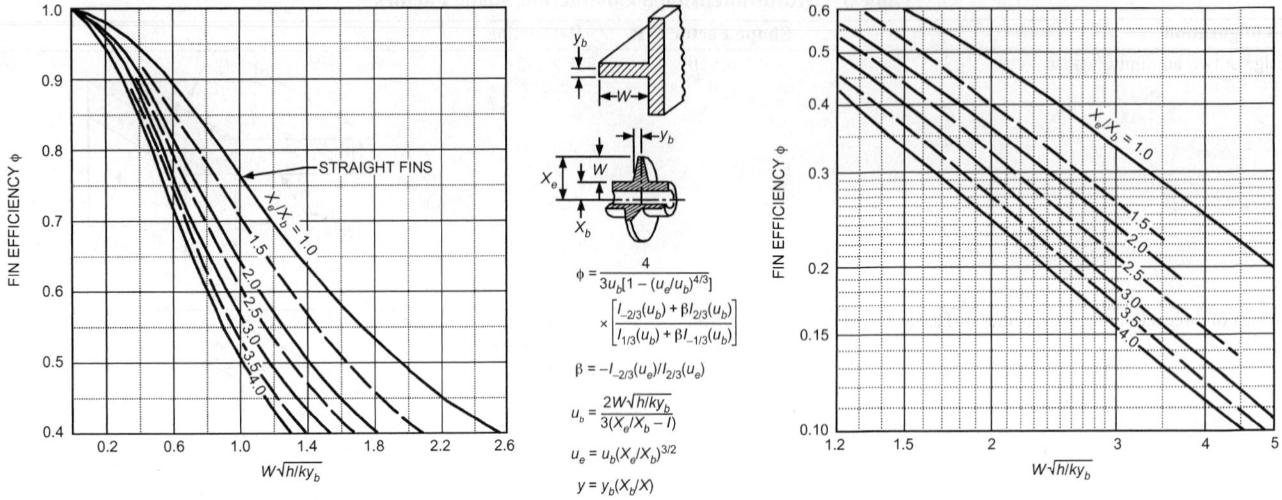

Fig. 6 Efficiency of Annular Fins with Constant Metal Area for Heat Flow

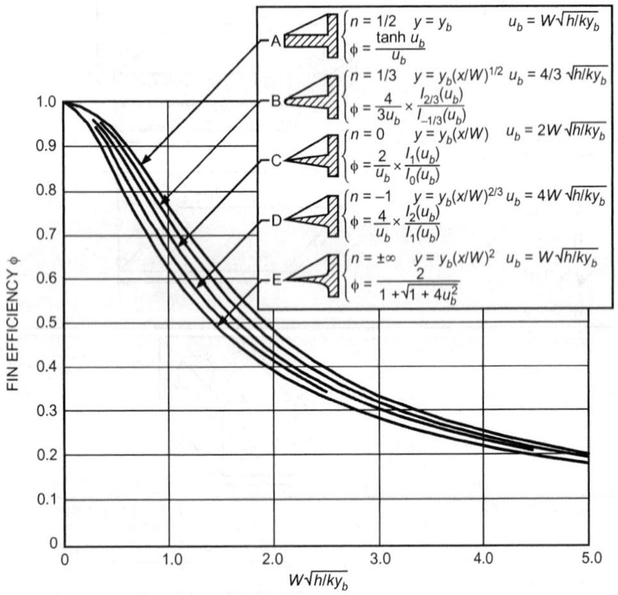

Fig. 7 Efficiency of Several Types of Straight Fins

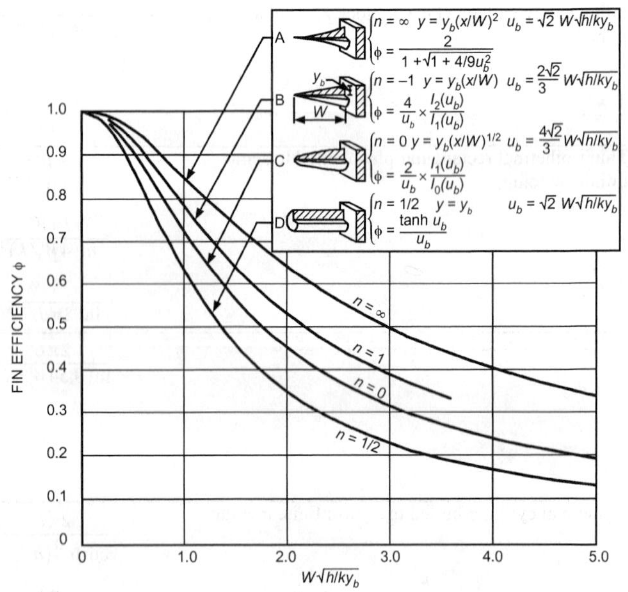

Fig. 8 Efficiency of Four Types of Spines

Extended Surfaces

Heat transfer from a surface can be increased by attaching fins or extended surfaces to increase the area available for heat transfer. A few common fin geometries are shown in Figures 5 to 8. Fins provide a large surface area in a low volume, thus lowering material costs for a given performance. To achieve optimum design, fins are generally located on the side of the heat exchanger with lower heat transfer coefficients (e.g., the air side of an air-to-water coil). Equipment with extended surfaces includes natural- and forced-convection coils and shell-and-tube evaporators and condensers. Fins are also used inside tubes in condensers and dry expansion evaporators.

Fin Efficiency. As heat flows from the root of a fin to its tip, temperature drops because of the fin material's thermal resistance. The temperature difference between the fin and surrounding fluid is therefore greater at the root than at the tip, causing a corresponding variation in heat flux. Therefore, increases in fin length result in proportionately less additional heat transfer. To account for this effect, **fin efficiency** ϕ is defined as the ratio of the actual heat transferred from the fin to the heat that would be transferred if the entire fin were at its root or base temperature:

$$\phi = \frac{q}{hA_s(t_r - t_e)} \tag{6}$$

where q is heat transfer rate into/out of the fin's root, t_e is temperature of the surrounding environment, t_r is temperature at fin root, and A_s is surface area of the fin. Fin efficiency is low for long or thin fins, or fins made of low-thermal-conductivity material. Fin efficiency decreases as the heat transfer coefficient increases because of increased heat flow. For natural convection in air-cooled condensers and evaporators, where the air-side h is low, fins can be fairly large and fabricated from low-conductivity materials such as steel instead of from copper or aluminum. For condensing and boiling, where large heat transfer coefficients are involved, fins must be very short for optimum use of material. Fin efficiencies for a few geometries are shown in Figures 5 to 8. Temperature distribution and fin efficiencies for various fin shapes are derived in most heat transfer texts.

Constant-Area Fins and Spines. For fins or spines with constant cross-sectional area [e.g., straight fins (option A in Figure 7), cylindrical spines (option D in Figure 8)], the efficiency can be calculated as

$$\phi = \frac{\tanh(mW_c)}{mW_c} \tag{7}$$

where

$m = \sqrt{hP/kA_c}$
P = fin perimeter
A_c = fin cross-sectional area
W_c = corrected fin/spine length = $W + A_c/P$
A_c/P = $d/4$ for a cylindrical spine with diameter d
= $a/4$ for an $a \times a$ square spine
= $y_b = \delta/2$ for a straight fin with thickness δ

Empirical Expressions for Fins on Tubes. Schmidt (1949) presents approximate, but reasonably accurate, analytical expressions (for computer use) for the fin efficiency of circular, rectangular, and hexagonal arrays of fins on round tubes, as shown in Figures 5, 9, and 10, respectively. Rectangular fin arrays are used for an in-line tube arrangement in finned-tube heat exchangers, and hexagonal arrays are used for staggered tubes. Schmidt's empirical solution is given by

$$\phi = \frac{\tanh(mr_bZ)}{mr_bZ} \tag{8}$$

where r_b is tube radius, $m = \sqrt{2h/k\delta}$, δ = fin thickness, and Z is given by

$$Z = [(r_e/r_b) - 1][1 + 0.35\ln(r_e/r_b)]$$

where r_e is the actual or equivalent fin tip radius. For **circular fins**, r_e/r_b is the actual ratio of fin tip radius to tube radius. For rectangular fins (Figure 9),

$$r_e/r_b = 1.28\,\Psi\sqrt{\beta - 0.2} \qquad \Psi = M/r_b \qquad \beta = L/M \ge 1$$

where M and L are defined by Figure 9 as $a/2$ or $b/2$, depending on which is greater. For hexagonal fins (Figure 10),

$$r_e/r_b = 1.27\,\Psi\sqrt{\beta - 0.3}$$

where Ψ and β are defined as previously, and M and L are defined by Figure 10 as $a/2$ or b (whichever is less) and $0.5\sqrt{(a/2)^2 + b^2}$, respectively.

For constant-thickness square fins on a round tube ($L = M$ in Figure 9), the efficiency of a constant-thickness annular fin of the same area can be used. For more accuracy, particularly with rectangular fins of large aspect ratio, divide the fin into circular sectors as described by Rich (1966).

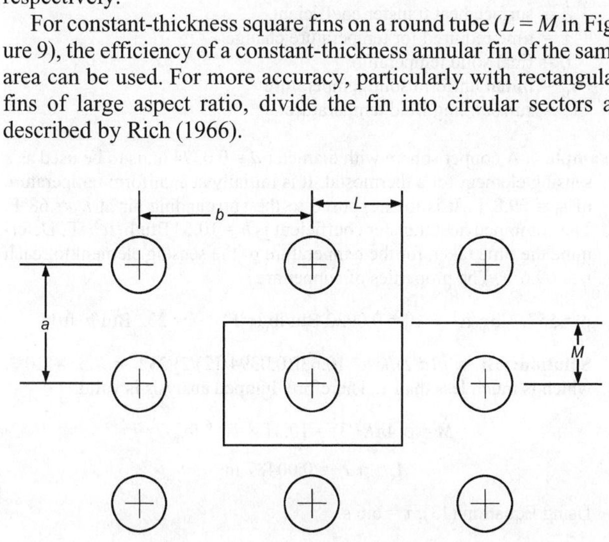

Fig. 9 Rectangular Tube Array

Other sources of information on finned surfaces are listed in the References and Bibliography.

Surface Efficiency. Heat transfer from a finned surface (e.g., a tube) that includes both fin area A_s and unfinned or prime area A_p is given by

$$q = (h_pA_p + \phi h_sA_s)(t_r - t_e) \tag{9}$$

Assuming the heat transfer coefficients for the fin and prime surfaces are equal, a **surface efficiency** ϕ_s can be derived as

$$\phi_s = \frac{A_p + \phi A_s}{A} \tag{10}$$

where $A = A_s + A_p$ is the total surface area, the sum of the fin and prime areas. The heat transfer in Equation (8) can then be written as

$$q = \phi_s hA(t_r - t_e) = \frac{t_r - t_e}{1/(\phi_s hA)} \tag{11}$$

where $1/(\phi_s hA)$ is the finned surface resistance.

Example 3. An aluminum tube with k = 1290 Btu·in/h·ft²·°F, ID = 1.8 in., and OD = 2 in. has circular aluminum fins δ = 0.04 in. thick with an outer diameter of D_{fin} = 3.9 in. There are N' = 76 fins per foot of tube length. Steam condenses inside the tube at t_i = 392°F with a large heat transfer coefficient on the inner tube surface. Air at t_∞ = 77°F is heated by the steam. The heat transfer coefficient outside the tube is 7 Btu/h·ft²·°F. Find the rate of heat transfer per foot of tube length.

Solution: From Figure 5's efficiency curve, the efficiency of these circular fins is

$$\left.\begin{aligned} &W = (D_{fin} - \text{OD})/2 = (3.9 - 2)/2 = 0.95\text{ in.} \\ &X_e/X_b = \frac{3.9/2}{2/2} = 1.95\text{ in.} \\ &W\sqrt{\frac{h}{k(\delta/2)}} = 0.95\text{ in.}\sqrt{\frac{7\text{ Btu/h}\cdot\text{ft}^2\cdot{}^\circ\text{F}}{(1290\text{ Btu}\cdot\text{in/h}\cdot\text{ft}^2\cdot{}^\circ\text{F})(0.02\text{ in.})}} = 0.49 \end{aligned}\right\}\phi = 0.89$$

The fin area for L = 1 ft is

$$A_s = N'L \times 2\pi(D_{fin}^2 - \text{OD}^2)/4 = 1338\text{ in}^2 = 9.29\text{ ft}^2$$

The unfinned area for L = 1 ft is

$$A_p = \pi \times \text{OD} \times L(1 - N'\delta) = \pi(2/12)\text{ ft} \times 1\text{ ft}(1 - 76 \times 0.04/12) = 0.39\text{ ft}^2$$

and the total area $A = A_s + A_p$ = 9.68 ft². Surface efficiency is

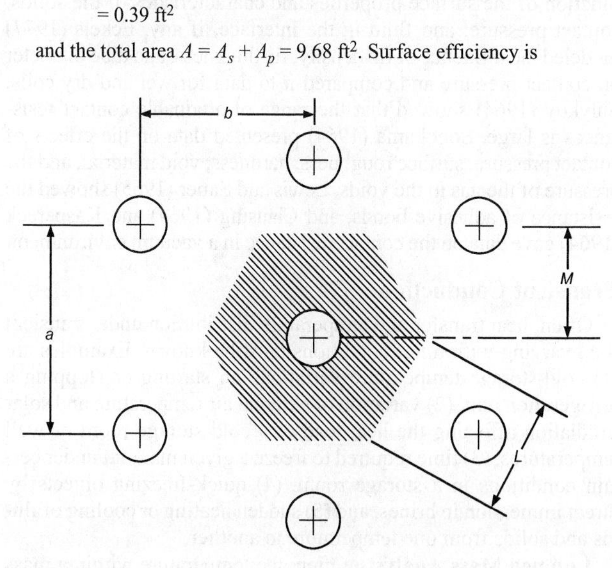

Fig. 10 Hexagonal Tube Array

$$\phi_s = \frac{\phi A_f + A_s}{A} = 0.894$$

and resistance of the finned surface is

$$R_s = \frac{1}{\phi_s hA} = 0.0165 \text{ h·°F/Btu}$$

Tube wall resistance is

$$R_{wall} = \frac{\ln(\text{OD/ID})}{2\pi L k_{tube}} = \frac{\ln(2/1.8)}{2\pi(1 \text{ ft})(1290/12) \text{ Btu·in/h·ft·°F}}$$

$$= 1.56 \times 10^{-4} \text{ h·°F/Btu}$$

The rate of heat transfer is then

$$q = \frac{t_i - t_\infty}{R_s + R_{wall}} = 18{,}912 \text{ Btu/h}$$

Had Schmidt's approach been used for fin efficiency,

$$m = \sqrt{2h/k\delta} = 6.25 \text{ ft}^{-1} \quad r_b = \text{OD}/2 = 1 \text{ in.} = 0.0833 \text{ ft}$$

$$Z = [(D_{fin}/\text{OD}) - 1][1 + 0.35 \ln(D_{fin}/\text{OD})] = 1.172$$

$$\phi = \frac{\tanh(mr_b Z)}{mr_b Z} = 0.89$$

the same ϕ as given by Figure 5.

Contact Resistance. Fins can be extruded from the prime surface (e.g., short fins on tubes in flooded evaporators or water-cooled condensers) or can be fabricated separately, sometimes of a different material, and bonded to the prime surface. Metallurgical bonds are achieved by furnace-brazing, dip-brazing, or soldering; nonmetallic bonding materials, such as epoxy resin, are also used. Mechanical bonds are obtained by tension-winding fins around tubes (spiral fins) or expanding the tubes into the fins (plate fins). Metallurgical bonding, properly done, leaves negligible thermal resistance at the joint but is not always economical. Contact resistance of a mechanical bond may or may not be negligible, depending on the application, quality of manufacture, materials, and temperatures involved. Tests of plate-fin coils with expanded tubes indicate that substantial losses in performance can occur with fins that have cracked collars, but negligible contact resistance was found in coils with continuous collars and properly expanded tubes (Dart 1959).

Contact resistance at an interface between two solids is largely a function of the surface properties and characteristics of the solids, contact pressure, and fluid in the interface, if any. Eckels (1977) modeled the influence of fin density, fin thickness, and tube diameter on contact pressure and compared it to data for wet and dry coils. Shlykov (1964) showed that the range of attainable contact resistances is large. Sonokama (1964) presented data on the effects of contact pressure, surface roughness, hardness, void material, and the pressure of the gas in the voids. Lewis and Sauer (1965) showed the resistance of adhesive bonds, and Clausing (1964) and Kaspareck (1964) gave data on the contact resistance in a vacuum environment.

Transient Conduction

Often, heat transfer and temperature distribution under transient (i.e., varying with time) conditions must be known. Examples are (1) cold-storage temperature variations on starting or stopping a refrigeration unit, (2) variation of external air temperature and solar irradiation affecting the heat load of a cold-storage room or wall temperatures, (3) time required to freeze a given material under certain conditions in a storage room, (4) quick-freezing objects by direct immersion in brines, and (5) sudden heating or cooling of fluids and solids from one temperature to another.

Lumped Mass Analysis. Often, the temperature within a mass of material can be assumed to vary with time but be uniform within the mass. Examples include a well-stirred fluid in a thin-walled container, or a thin metal plate with high thermal conductivity. In both cases, if the mass is heated or cooled at its surface, the temperature can be assumed to be a function of time only and not location within the body. Such an approximation is valid if

$$\text{Bi} = \frac{h(V/A_s)}{k} \le 0.1$$

where

- Bi = Biot number
- h = surface heat transfer coefficient
- V = material's volume
- A_s = surface area exposed to convective and/or radiative heat transfer
- k = material's thermal conductivity

The temperature is given by

$$Mc_p \frac{dt}{d\tau} = q_{net} + q_{gen} \tag{12}$$

where

- M = body mass
- c_p = specific heat
- q_{gen} = internal heat generation
- q_{net} = net heat transfer rate to substance (into substance is positive, and out of substance is negative)

Equation (12) applies to liquids and solids. If the material is a gas being heated or cooled at constant volume, replace c_p with the constant-volume specific heat c_v. The term q_{net} may include heat transfer by conduction, convection, or radiation and is the difference between the heat transfer rates into and out of the body. The term q_{gen} may include a chemical reaction (e.g., curing concrete) or heat generation from a current passing through a metal.

For a lumped mass M initially at a uniform temperature t_0 that is suddenly exposed to an environment at a different temperature t_∞, the time taken for the temperature of the mass to change to t_f is given by the solution of Equation (12) with $q_{gen} = 0$ as

$$\ln \frac{t_f - t_\infty}{t_0 - t_\infty} = -\frac{hA_s\tau}{Mc_p} \tag{13}$$

where

- M = mass of solid
- c_p = specific heat of solid
- A_s = surface area of solid
- h = surface heat transfer coefficient
- τ = time required for temperature change
- t_f = final solid temperature
- t_0 = initial uniform solid temperature
- t_∞ = surrounding fluid temperature

Example 4. A copper sphere with diameter $d = 0.0394$ in. is to be used as a sensing element for a thermostat. It is initially at a uniform temperature of $t_0 = 69.8$°F. It is then exposed to the surrounding air at $t_\infty = 68$°F. The combined heat transfer coefficient is $h = 10.63$ Btu/h·ft²·°F. Determine the time taken for the temperature of the sensing element to reach $t_f = 69.6$°F. The properties of copper are

$$\rho = 557.7 \text{ lb}_m/\text{ft}^3 \quad c_p = 0.0920 \text{ Btu/lb}_m\text{·°F} \quad k = 232 \text{ Btu/h·ft·°F}$$

Solution: Bi = $h(d/2)/k$ = 10.63[(0.0394/12)/2]/232 = 7.5×10^{-5}, which is much less than 1. Therefore, lumped analysis is valid.

$$M = \rho(4\pi R^3/3) = 10.31 \times 10^{-6} \text{ lb}_m$$

$$A_s = \pi d^2 = 0.00487 \text{ in}^2$$

Using Equation (13), $\tau = 6.6$ s.

Nonlumped Analysis. When the Biot number is greater than 0.1, variation of temperature with location within the mass is significant.

One example is the cooling time of meats in a refrigerated space: the meat's size and conductivity do not allow it to be treated as a lumped mass that cools uniformly. Nonlumped problems require solving multidimensional partial differential equations. Many common cases have been solved and presented in graphical forms (Jakob 1949, 1957; Myers 1971; Schneider 1964). In other cases, numerical methods (Croft and Lilley 1977; Patankar 1980) must be used.

Estimating Cooling Times for One-Dimensional Geometries. When a slab of thickness $2L$ or a solid cylinder or solid sphere with outer radius r_m is initially at a uniform temperature t_1, and its surface is suddenly heated or cooled by convection with a fluid at t_∞, a mathematical solution is available for the temperature t as a function of location and time τ. The solution is an infinite series. However, after a short time, the temperature is very well approximated by the first term of the series. The single-term approximations for the three cases are of the form

$$Y = Y_0 f(\mu_1 n) \tag{14}$$

where

$$Y = \frac{t - t_\infty}{t_1 - t_\infty}$$

$$Y_0 = \frac{t_0 - t_\infty}{t_1 - t_\infty} = c_1 \exp(-\mu_1^2 \mathrm{Fo})$$

t_0 = temperature at center of slab, cylinder, or sphere
Fo = $\alpha\tau/L_c^2$ = Fourier number
α = thermal diffusivity of solid = $k/\rho c_p$
L_c = L for slab, r_o for cylinder, sphere
n = x/L for slab, r/r_m for cylinder
c_1, μ_1 = coefficients that are functions of Bi
Bi = Biot number = hL_c/k
$f(\mu_1 n)$ = function of $\mu_1 n$, different for each geometry
x = distance from midplane of slab of thickness $2L$ cooled on both sides
ρ = density of solid
c_p = constant pressure specific heat of solid
k = thermal conductivity of solid

The single term solution is valid for Fo > 0.2. Values of c_1 and μ_1 are given in Table 4 for a few values of Bi, and Couvillion (2004) provides a procedure for calculating them. Expressions for c_1 for each case, along with the function $f(\mu_1 n)$, are as follows:

Slab

$$f(\mu_1 n) = \cos(\mu_1 n) \qquad c_1 = \frac{4\sin(\mu_1)}{2\mu_1 + \sin(2\mu_1)} \tag{15}$$

Long solid cylinder

$$f(\mu_1 n) = J_0(\mu_1 n) \qquad c_1 = \frac{2}{\mu_1} \times \frac{J_1(\mu_1)}{J_0^2(\mu_1) + J_1^2(\mu_1)} \tag{16}$$

Table 4 Values of c_1 and μ_1 in Equations (14) to (17)

	Slab		Solid Cylinder		Solid Sphere	
Bi	c_1	μ_1	c_1	μ_1	c_1	μ_1
0.5	1.0701	0.6533	1.1143	0.9408	1.1441	1.1656
1.0	1.1191	0.8603	1.2071	1.2558	1.2732	1.5708
2.0	1.1785	1.0769	1.3384	1.5995	1.4793	2.0288
4.0	1.2287	1.2646	1.4698	1.9081	1.7202	2.4556
6.0	1.2479	1.3496	1.5253	2.0490	1.8338	2.6537
8.0	1.2570	1.3978	1.5526	2.1286	1.8920	2.7654
10.0	1.2620	1.4289	1.5677	2.1795	1.9249	2.8363
30.0	1.2717	1.5202	1.5973	2.3261	1.9898	3.0372
50.0	1.2727	1.5400	1.6002	2.3572	1.9962	3.0788

where J_0 is the Bessel function of the first kind, order zero. It is available in math tables, spreadsheets, and software packages. $J_0(0) = 1$.

Solid sphere

$$f(\mu_1 n) = \frac{\sin(\mu_1 n)}{\mu_1 n} \qquad c_1 = \frac{4[\sin(\mu_1) - \mu_1\cos(\mu_1)]}{2\mu_1 - \sin(2\mu_1)} \tag{17}$$

These solutions are presented graphically (McAdams 1954) by Gurnie-Lurie charts (Figures 11 to 13). The charts are also valid for Fo < 0.2.

Example 5. Apples, approximated as 2.36 in. diameter solid spheres and initially at 86°F, are loaded into a chamber maintained at 32°F. If the surface heat transfer coefficient h = 2.47 Btu/h·ft²·°F, estimate the time required for the center temperature to reach t = 33.8°F.

Properties of apples are

$$\rho = 51.8\ \mathrm{lb_m/ft^3} \qquad k = 0.243\ \mathrm{Btu/h\cdot ft\cdot °F}$$

$$c_p = 0.860\ \mathrm{Btu/lb_m\cdot °F} \qquad r_m = d/2 = 1.18\ \mathrm{in.} = 0.098\ \mathrm{ft}$$

Solution: Assuming that it will take a long time for the center temperature to reach 33.8°F, use the one-term approximation Equation (14). From the values given,

$$Y = \frac{t_c - t}{t_c - t_1} = \frac{32 - 33.8}{32 - 86} = 0.0333$$

$$n = \frac{r}{r_m} = \frac{0}{0.1967} = 0 \qquad \mathrm{Bi} = \frac{hr_m}{k} = \frac{2.47 \times (0.1967/2)}{0.243} = 1$$

$$\alpha = \frac{k}{\rho c_p} = \frac{0.243}{51.8 \times 0.860} = 0.00545\ \mathrm{ft^2/h}$$

From Equations (14) and (17) with lim(sin 0/0) = 1, $Y = Y_0 = c_1 \exp(-\mu_1^2 \mathrm{Fo})$. For Bi = 1, from Table 4, c_1 = 1.2732 and μ_1 = 1.5708. Thus,

$$\mathrm{Fo} = -\frac{1}{\mu_1^2}\ln\frac{Y}{c_1} = -\frac{1}{1.5708^2}\ln 0.0333 = 1.476 = \frac{\alpha\tau}{r_m^2} = \frac{0.00545\tau}{(0.1967/2)^2}$$

$$\tau = 2.62\ \mathrm{h}$$

Note that Fo = 0.2 corresponds to an actual time of 1280 s.

Multidimensional Cooling Times. One-dimensional transient temperature solutions can be used to find the temperatures with two- and three-dimensional temperatures of solids. For example, consider a solid cylinder of length $2L$ and radius r_m exposed to a fluid at t_c on all sides with constant surface heat transfer coefficients h_1 on the end surfaces and h_2 on the cylindrical surface, as shown in Figure 14.

The two-dimensional, dimensionless temperature $Y(x_1, r_1, \tau)$ can be expressed as the product of two one-dimensional temperatures $Y_1(x_1, \tau) \times Y_2(r_1, \tau)$, where

Y_1 = dimensionless temperature of constant cross-sectional area slab at (x_1, τ), with surface heat transfer coefficient h_1 associated with two parallel surfaces
Y_2 = dimensionless temperature of solid cylinder at (r_1, τ) with surface heat transfer coefficient h_2 associated with cylindrical surface

From Figures 11 and 12 or Equations (14) to (16), determine Y_1 at $(x_1/L, \alpha\tau/L^2, h_1L/k)$ and Y_2 at $(r_1/r_m, \alpha\tau/r_m^2, h_2r_m/k)$.

Example 6. A 2.76 in. diameter by 4.92 in. high soda can, initially at t_1 = 86°F, is cooled in a chamber where the air is at t_∞ = 32°F. The heat transfer coefficient on all surfaces is h = 3.52 Btu/h·ft²·°F. Determine the maximum temperature in the can τ = 1 h after starting the cooling. Assume the properties of the soda are those of water, and that the soda inside the can behaves as a solid body.

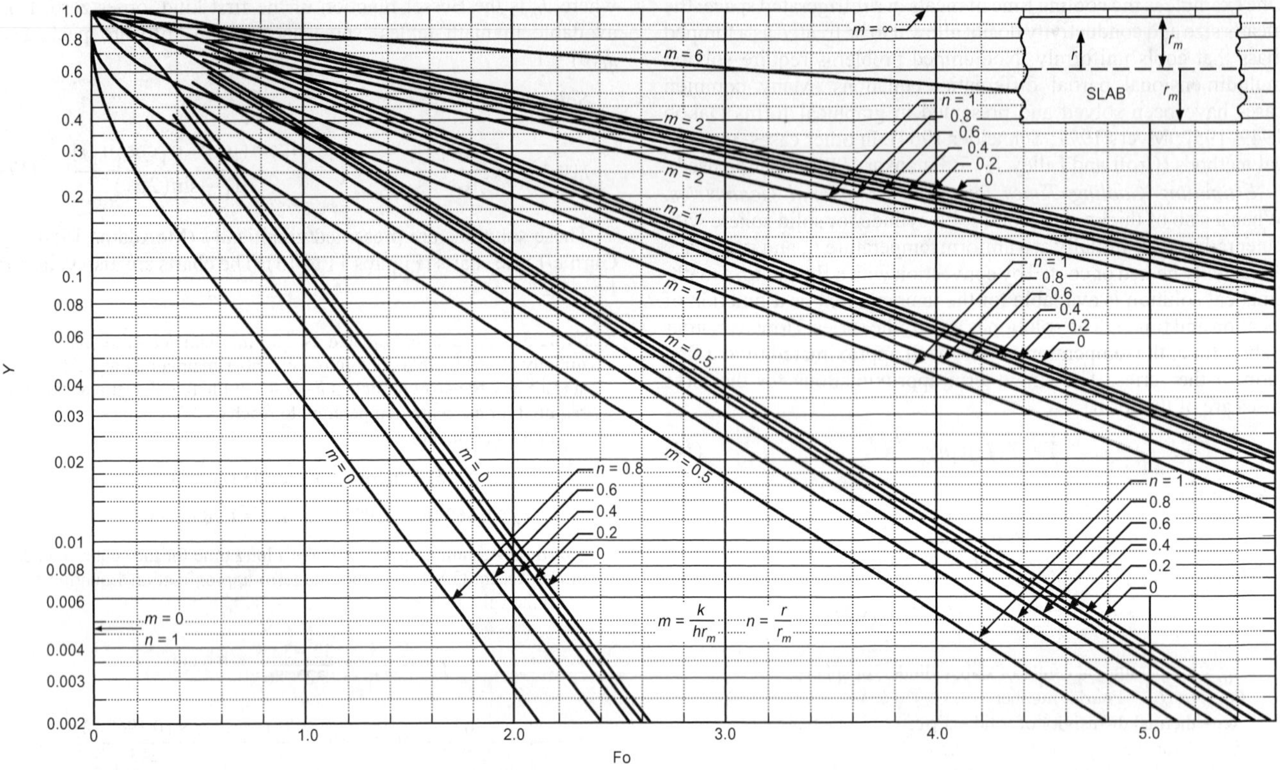

Fig. 11 Transient Temperatures for Infinite Slab, *m* = 1/Bi

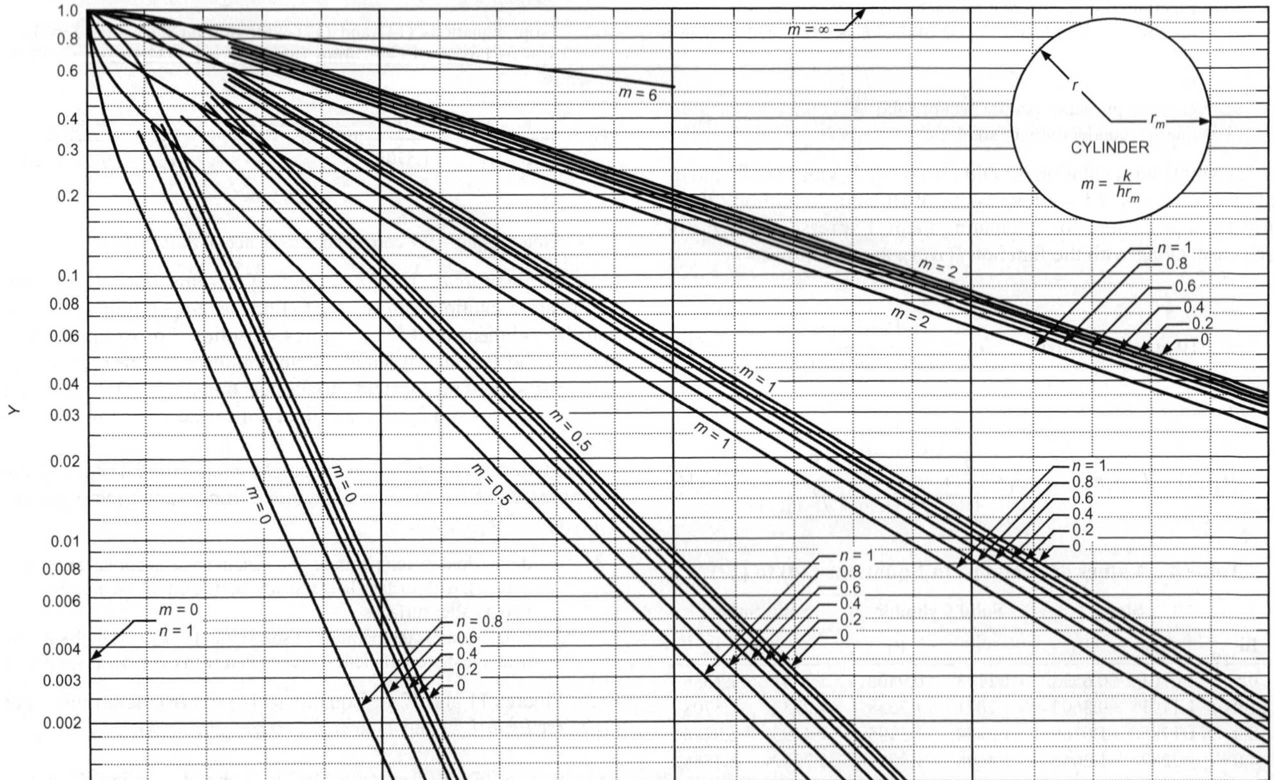

Fig. 12 Transient Temperatures for Infinite Cylinder, *m* = 1/Bi

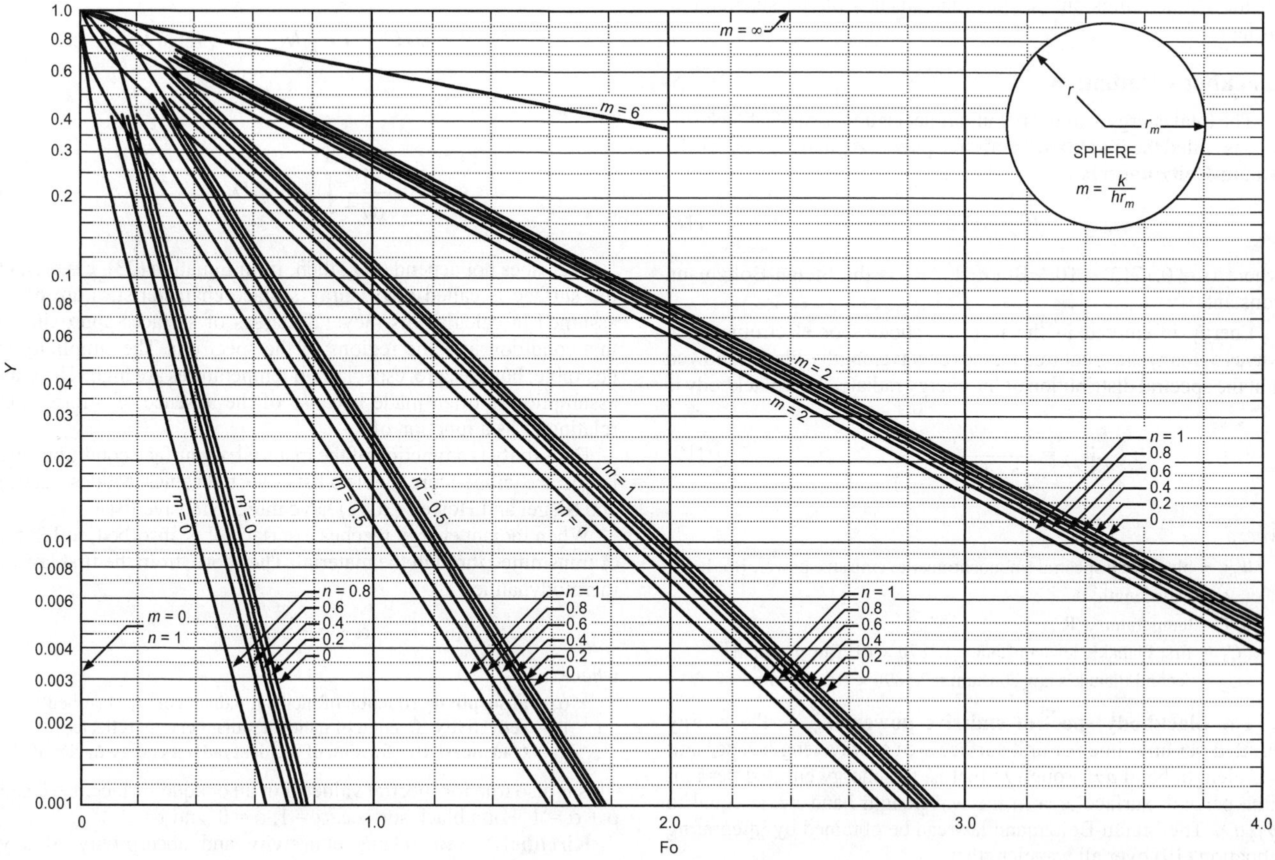

Fig. 13 Transient Temperatures for Sphere, m = 1/Bi

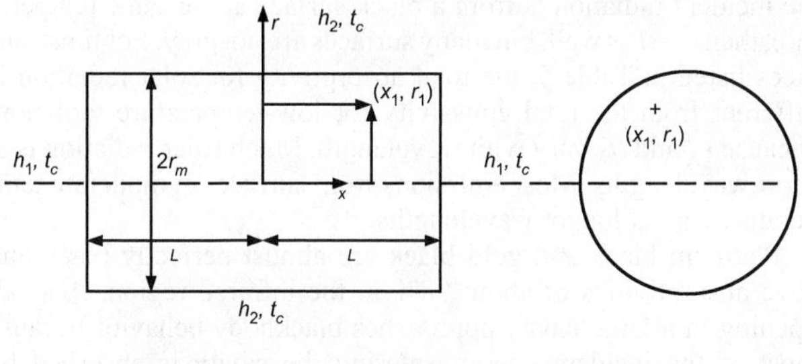

Fig. 14 Solid Cylinder Exposed to Fluid

Solution: Because the cylinder is short, the temperature of the soda is affected by the heat transfer rate from the cylindrical surface and end surfaces. The slowest change in temperature, and therefore the maximum temperature, is at the center of the cylinder. Denoting the dimensionless temperature by Y,

$$Y = Y_{cyl} \times Y_{pl}$$

where Y_{cyl} is the dimensionless temperature of an infinitely long 2.76 in. diameter cylinder, and Y_{pl} is the dimensionless temperature of a 4.92 in. thick slab. Each of them is found from the appropriate Biot and Fourier number. For evaluating the properties of water, choose a temperature of 59°F and a pressure of 1 atm. The properties of water are

$$\rho = 62.37 \text{ lb}_m/\text{ft}^3 \qquad k = 0.3406 \text{ Btu/h·ft·°F} \qquad c_p = 1.0 \text{ Btu/lb}_m\text{·°F}$$

$$\alpha = k/(\rho c_p) = 5.46 \times 10^{-3} \text{ ft}^2/\text{h} \qquad \tau = 1 \text{ h}$$

1. Determine Y_{cyl} at $n = 0$.

$$\text{Bi}_{cyl} = hr_m/k = 3.52 \times (2.76/12/2) = 1.188$$

$$\text{Fo}_{cyl} = \alpha\tau/r_m^2 = (5.46 \times 10^{-3}) \times 1/(2.76/12/2) = 0.4129$$

$\text{Fo}_{cyl} > 0.2$, so use the one-term approximation with Equations (14) and (16).

$$Y_{cyl} = c_1 \exp(-\mu^2{}_1 \text{Fo}_{cyl}) J_0(0)$$

Interpolating in Table 4 for $\text{Bi}_{cyl} = 1.188$, $\mu_{cyl} = 1.3042$, $J_0(0) = 1$, $c_{cyl} = 1.237$, $Y_{cyl} = 0.572$.

2. Determine Y_{pl} at $n = 0$.

$$\text{Bi}_{pl} = hL/k = 3.52 \times (4.92/12/2)/0.3406 = 2.119$$

$$\text{Fo}_{pl} = (5.46 \times 10^{-3}) \times 1/(4.92/12/2)^2 = 0.1299$$

$\text{Fo}_{pl} < 0.2$, so the one-term approximation is not valid. Using Figure 11, $Y_{pl} = 0.9705$. Thus,

$$Y = 0.572 \times 0.9705 = 0.5551 = (t - t_\infty)/(t_1 - t_\infty) \Rightarrow 62.0\text{°F}$$

Note: The solution may not be exact because convective motion of the soda during heat transfer has been neglected. The example illustrates the use of the technique. For well-stirred soda, with uniform temperature within the can, the lumped mass solution should be used.

3. THERMAL RADIATION

Radiation, unlike conduction and convection, does not need a solid or fluid to transport energy from a high-temperature surface to a lower-temperature one. (Radiation is in fact impeded by such a material.) The rate of radiant energy emission and its characteristics from a surface depend on the underlying material's nature, microscopic arrangement, and absolute temperature. The rate of emission from a surface is independent of the surfaces surrounding it, but the rate and characteristics of radiation incident on a surface do depend on the temperatures and spatial relationships of the surrounding surfaces.

Blackbody Radiation

The total energy emitted per unit time per unit area of a black surface is called the **blackbody emissive power W_b** and is given by the **Stefan-Boltzmann law**:

$$W_b = \sigma T^4 \tag{18}$$

where $\sigma = 0.1712 \times 10^{-8}$ Btu/h·ft²·°R⁴ is the Stefan-Boltzmann constant.

Energy is emitted in the form of photons or electromagnetic waves of many different frequencies or wavelengths. Planck showed that the spectral distribution of the energy radiated by a blackbody is

$$W_{b\lambda} = \frac{C_1}{\lambda^5 (e^{C_2/\lambda T} - 1)} \tag{19}$$

where

$W_{b\lambda}$ = blackbody spectral (monochromatic) emissive power, Btu/h·ft³
λ = wavelength, ft
T = temperature, °R
C_1 = first Planck's law constant = 1.1870×10^8 Btu·μm⁴/h·ft²
C_2 = second Planck's law constant = 2.5896×10^4 μm·°R

The **blackbody spectral emissive power $W_{b\lambda}$** is the energy emitted per unit time per unit surface area at wavelength λ per unit wavelength band $d\lambda$ around λ; that is, the energy emitted per unit time per unit surface area in the wavelength band $d\lambda$ is equal to $W_{b\lambda} d\lambda$. The Stefan-Boltzmann law can be obtained by integrating Equation (19) over all wavelengths:

$$\int_0^\infty W_{b\lambda}\, d\lambda = \sigma T^4 = W_b$$

Wien showed that the wavelength λ_{max}, at which the monochromatic emissive power is a maximum (not the maximum wavelength), is given by

$$\lambda_{max} T = 5216 \text{ μm·°R} \tag{20}$$

Equation (20) is **Wien's displacement** law; the maximum spectral emissive power shifts to shorter wavelengths as temperature increases, such that, at very high temperatures, significant emission eventually occurs over the entire visible spectrum as shorter wavelengths become more prominent. For additional details, see Incropera et al. (2007).

Actual Radiation

The blackbody emissive power W_b and blackbody spectral emissive power $W_{b\lambda}$ are the maxima at a given surface temperature. Actual surfaces emit less and are called **nonblack**. The **emissive power W** of a nonblack surface at temperature T radiating to the hemispherical region above it is given by

$$W = \varepsilon \sigma T^4 \tag{21}$$

where ε is the **total emissivity**. The **spectral emissive power W_λ** of a nonblack surface at a particular wavelength λ is given by

$$W_\lambda = \varepsilon_\lambda W_{b\lambda} \tag{22}$$

where ε_λ is the **spectral emissivity**, and $W_{b\lambda}$ is given by Equation (19). The relationship between ε and ε_λ is given by

$$W = \varepsilon\sigma T^4 = \int_0^\infty W_\lambda d\lambda = \int_0^\infty \varepsilon_\lambda W_{b\lambda} d\lambda$$

or

$$\varepsilon = \frac{1}{\sigma T^4} \int_0^\infty \varepsilon_\lambda W_{b\lambda} d\lambda \tag{23}$$

If ε_λ does not depend on λ, then, from Equation (23), $\varepsilon = \varepsilon_\lambda$, and the surface is called **gray**. Gray surface characteristics are often assumed in calculations. Several classes of surfaces approximate this condition in some regions of the spectrum. The simplicity is desirable, but use care, especially if temperatures are high. The gray assumption is often made because of the absence of information relating ε_λ as a function of λ.

Emissivity is a function of the material, its surface condition, and its surface temperature. Table 5 lists selected values; Modest (2003) and Siegel and Howell (2002) have more extensive lists.

When radiant energy reaches a surface, it is absorbed, reflected, or transmitted through the material. Therefore, from the first law of thermodynamics,

$$\alpha + \rho + \tau = 1$$

where

α = **absorptivity** (fraction of incident radiant energy absorbed)
ρ = **reflectivity** (fraction of incident radiant energy reflected)
τ = **transmissivity** (fraction of incident radiant energy transmitted)

This is also true for spectral values. For an opaque surface, $\tau = 0$ and $\rho + \alpha = 1$. For a black surface, $\alpha = 1$, $\rho = 0$, and $\tau = 0$.

Kirchhoff's law relates emissivity and absorptivity of any opaque surface from thermodynamic considerations; it states that, for any surface where incident radiation is independent of angle or where the surface emits diffusely, $\varepsilon_\lambda = \alpha_\lambda$. If the surface is gray, or the incident radiation is from a black surface at the same temperature, then $\varepsilon = \alpha$ as well, but many surfaces are not gray. For most surfaces listed in Table 5, the total absorptivity for solar radiation is different from the total emissivity for low-temperature radiation, because ε_λ and α_λ vary with wavelength. Much solar radiation is at short wavelengths. Most emissions from surfaces at moderate temperatures are at longer wavelengths.

Platinum black and gold black are almost perfectly black and have absorptivities of about 98% in the infrared region. A small opening in a large cavity approaches blackbody behavior because most of the incident energy entering the cavity is absorbed by repeated reflection within it, and very little escapes the cavity. Thus, the absorptivity and therefore the emissivity of the opening are close to unity. Some flat black paints also exhibit emissivities of 98% over a wide range of conditions. They provide a much more durable surface than gold or platinum black, and are frequently used on radiation instruments and as standard reference in emissivity or reflectance measurements.

Example 7. In outer space, the solar energy flux on a surface is 365 Btu/h·ft². Two surfaces are being considered for an absorber plate to be used on the surface of a spacecraft: one is black, and the other is specially coated for a solar absorptivity of 0.94 and emissivity of 0.1. Coolant flowing through the tubes attached to the plate maintains the plate at 612°R. The plate surface is normal to the solar flux. For each surface, determine the (1) heat transfer rate to the coolant per unit area of the plate, and (2) temperature of the surface when there is no coolant flow.

Solution: For the black surface,

$$\varepsilon = \alpha = 1, \quad \rho = 0$$

Absorbed energy flux = 365 Btu/h·ft²

Table 5 Emissivities and Absorptivities of Some Surfaces

Surface	Total Hemispherical Emissivity	Solar Absorptivity*
Aluminum		
Foil, bright dipped	0.03	0.10
Alloy: 6061	0.04	0.37
Roofing	0.24	
Asphalt	0.88	
Brass		
Oxidized	0.60	
Polished	0.04	
Brick	0.90	
Concrete, rough	0.91	0.60
Copper		
Electroplated	0.03	0.47
Black oxidized in Ebanol C	0.16	0.91
Plate, oxidized	0.76	
Glass		
Polished	0.87 to 0.92	
Pyrex	0.80	
Smooth	0.91	
Granite	0.44	
Gravel	0.30	
Ice	0.96 to 0.97	
Limestone	0.92	
Marble		
Polished or white	0.89 to 0.92	
Smooth	0.56	
Mortar, lime	0.90	
Nickel		
Electroplated	0.03	0.22
Solar absorber, electro-oxidized on copper	0.05 to 0.11	0.85
Paints		
Black		
Parsons optical, silicone high heat, epoxy	0.87 to 0.92	0.94 to 0.97
Gloss	0.90	
Enamel, heated 1000 h at 710°F	0.80	
Silver chromatone	0.24	0.20
White		
Acrylic resin	0.90	0.26
Gloss	0.85	
Epoxy	0.85	0.25
Paper, roofing or white	0.88 to 0.86	
Plaster, rough	0.89	
Refractory	0.90 to 0.94	
Sand	0.75	
Sandstone, red	0.59	
Silver, polished	0.02	
Snow, fresh	0.82	0.13
Soil	0.94	
Water	0.90	0.98
White potassium zirconium silicate	0.87	0.13

Source: Mills (1999).
*Values are for extraterrestrial conditions, except for concrete, snow, and water.

At $T_s = 612°R$, emitted energy flux = $W_b = 0.1712 \times 10^{-8} \times 612^4 = 240.2$ Btu/h·ft².

In space, there is no convection, so an energy balance on the surface gives

Heat flux to coolant = Absorbed energy flux – Emitted energy flux = 365 – 240.2 = 124.8 Btu/h·ft²

For the special surface, use solar absorptivity to determine the absorbed energy flux, and emissivity to calculate the emitted energy flux.

Absorbed energy flux = 0.94 × 365 = 343.1 Btu/h·ft²
Emitted energy flux = 0.1 × 240.2 = 24.02 Btu/h·ft²
Heat flux to coolant = 343.1 – 24.02= 319.08 Btu/h·ft²

Without coolant flow, heat flux to the coolant is zero. Therefore, absorbed energy flux = emitted energy flux. For the black surface,

$$365 = 0.1714 \times 10^{-8} \times T_s^4 \Rightarrow T_s = 679.3°R$$

For the special surface,

$$0.94 \times 365 = 0.1 \times 0.1714 \times 10^{-8} \times T_s^4 \Rightarrow T_s = 1189°R$$

Angle Factor

The foregoing discussion addressed emission from a surface and absorption of radiation leaving surrounding surfaces. Before radiation exchange among a number of surfaces can be addressed, the amount of radiation leaving one surface that is incident on another must be determined.

The fraction of all radiant energy leaving a surface i that is directly incident on surface k is the **angle factor F_{ik}** (also known as **view factor**, **shape factor**, and **configuration factor**). The angle factor from area A_k to area A_j, F_{ki}, is similarly defined, merely by interchanging the roles of i and k. The following relations assume

- All surfaces are gray or black
- Emission and reflection are diffuse (i.e., not a function of direction)
- Properties are uniform over the surfaces
- Absorptivity equals emissivity and is independent of temperature of source of incident radiation
- Material located between radiating surfaces neither emits nor absorbs radiation

These assumptions greatly simplify problems, and give good approximate results in many cases. Some of the relations for the angle factor are as follows.

Reciprocity relation.

$$F_{ik}A_i = F_{ki}A_k \tag{24a}$$

Decomposition relation. For three surfaces i, j, and k, with A_{ij} indicating one surface with two parts denoted by A_i and A_j,

$$A_kF_{k\text{-}ij} = A_kF_{k\text{-}i} + A_kF_{k\text{-}j} \tag{24b}$$

$$A_{ij}F_{ij\text{-}k} = A_iF_{i\text{-}k} + A_jF_{j\text{-}k} \tag{24c}$$

Law of corresponding corners. This law is discussed by Love (1968) and Suryanarayana (1995). Its use is shown in Example 8.

Summation rule. For an enclosure with n surfaces, some of which may be inside the enclosure,

$$\sum_{k=1}^{n} F_{ik} = 1 \tag{24d}$$

Note that a concave surface may "see itself," and $F_{ii} \neq 0$ for such a surface.

Numerical values of the angle factor for common geometries are given in Figure 15. For equations to compute angle factors for many configurations, refer to Siegel and Howell (2002).

Example 8. A picture window, 10 ft long and 6 ft high, is installed in a wall as shown in Figure 16. The bottom edge of the window is on the floor, which is 20 by 33.3 ft. Denoting the window by 1 and the floor by 234, find $F_{234\text{-}1}$.

Solution: From decomposition rule,

$$A_{234}F_{234\text{-}1} = A_2F_{2\text{-}1} + A_3F_{3\text{-}1} + A_4F_{4\text{-}1}$$

By symmetry, $A_2F_{2\text{-}1} = A_4F_{4\text{-}1}$ and $A_{234\text{-}1} = A_3F_{3\text{-}1} + 2A_2F_{2\text{-}1}$.

$$A_{23}F_{23\text{-}15} = A_2F_{2\text{-}1} + A_2F_{2\text{-}5}$$

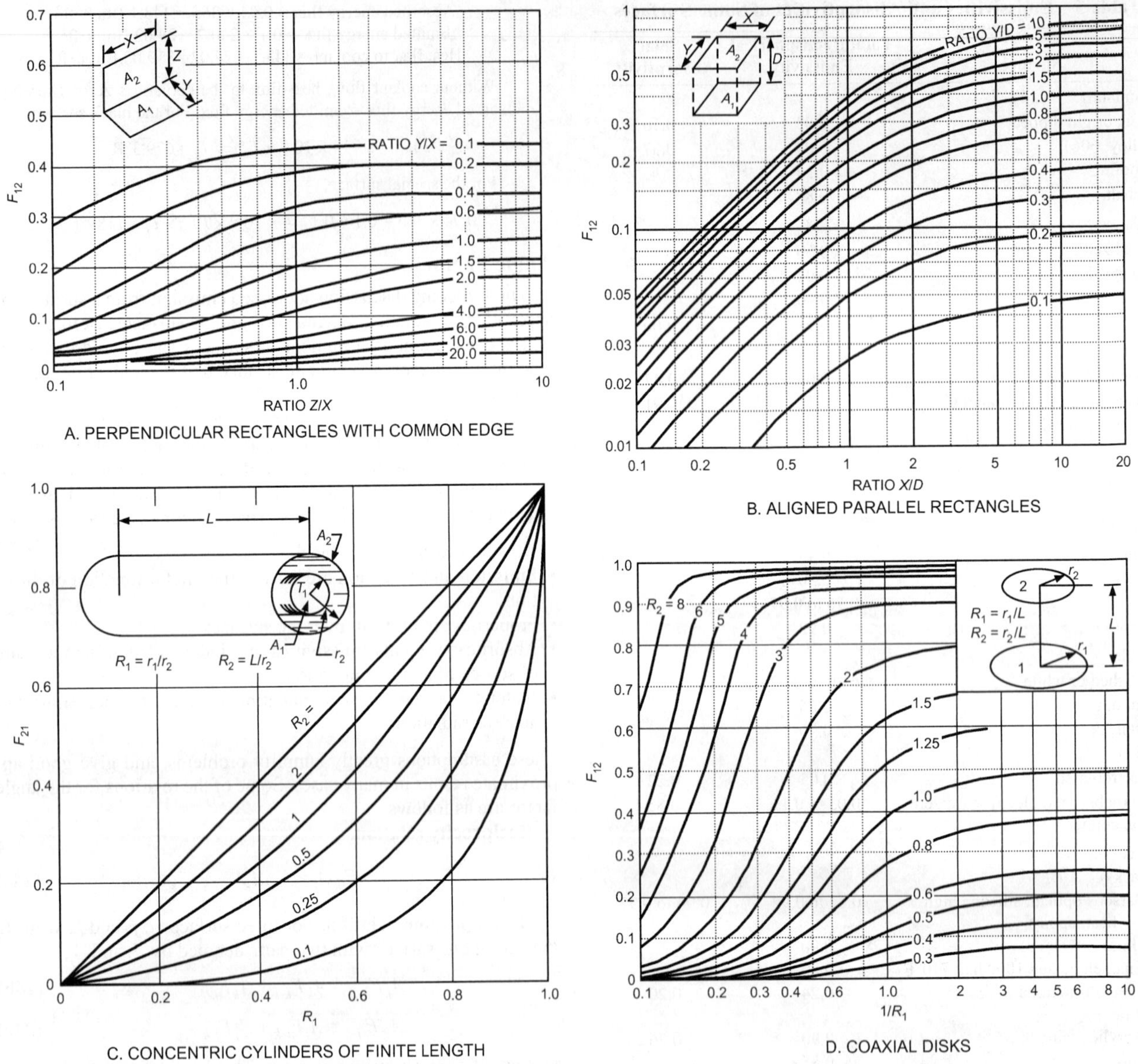

Fig. 15 Radiation Angle Factors for Various Geometries

$$+ A_3F_{3\text{-}1} + A_3F_{3\text{-}5}$$

From the law of corresponding corners, $A_2F_{2\text{-}1} = A_3F_{3\text{-}5}$; therefore $A_{23}F_{23\text{-}5} = A_2F_{2\text{-}5} + A_3F_{3\text{-}1} + 2A_2F_{2\text{-}1}$. Thus,

$$A_{234}F_{234\text{-}1} = A_3F_{3\text{-}1} + A_{23}F_{23\text{-}15} - A_2F_{2\text{-}5} - A_3F_{3\text{-}1} = A_{23}F_{23\text{-}15} - A_2F_{2\text{-}5}$$

$$A_{234} = 666 \text{ ft}^2 \qquad A_{23} = 499.5 \text{ ft}^2 \qquad A_2 = 166.5 \text{ ft}^2$$

From Figure 15A with $Y/X = 33.3/20 = 1.67$ and $Z/X = 6/15 = 0.4$, $F_{23\text{-}15} = 0.061$. With $Y/X = 33.3/5 = 6.66$ and $Z/X = 6/5 = 1.2$, $F_{25} = 0.041$. Substituting the values, $F_{234\text{-}1} = 1/666(499.5 \times 0.061 - 166.5 \times 0.041) = 0.036$.

Radiant Exchange Between Opaque Surfaces

A surface A_i radiates energy at a rate independent of its surroundings. It absorbs and reflects incident radiation from surrounding surfaces at a rate dependent on its absorptivity. The net heat transfer rate q_i is the difference between the rate radiant energy leaves the surface and the rate of incident radiant energy; it is the rate at which energy must be supplied from an external source to maintain the

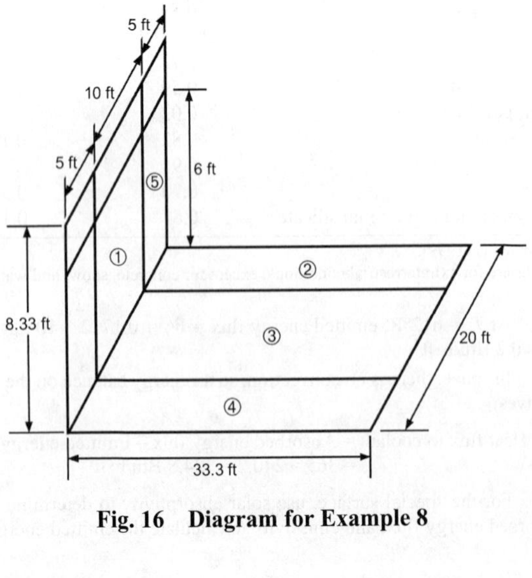

Fig. 16 Diagram for Example 8

surface at a constant temperature. The net radiant heat flux from a surface A_i is denoted by q''_i.

Several methods have been developed to solve specific radiant exchange problems. The radiosity method and thermal circuit method are presented here.

Consider the heat transfer rate from a surface of an n-surface enclosure with an intervening medium that does not participate in radiation. All surfaces are assumed gray and opaque. The **radiosity** J_i is the total rate of radiant energy leaving surface i per unit area (i.e., the sum of energy flux emitted and energy flux reflected):

$$J_i = \varepsilon_i W_b + \rho_i G_i \tag{25}$$

where G_i is the total rate of radiant energy incident on surface i per unit area. For opaque gray surfaces, the reflectivity is

$$\rho_i = 1 - \alpha_i = 1 - \varepsilon_i$$

Thus,

$$J_i = \varepsilon_i W_b + (1 - \varepsilon_i) G_i \tag{26}$$

Note that for a black surface, $\varepsilon = 1$, $\rho = 0$, and $J = W_b$.

The net radiant energy transfer q_i is the difference between the total energy leaving the surface and the total incident energy:

$$q_i = A_i (J_i - G_i) \tag{27}$$

Eliminating G_i between Equations (26) and (27),

$$q_i = \frac{W_{bi} - J_i}{(1 - \varepsilon_i)/\varepsilon_i A_i} \tag{28}$$

Radiosity Method. Consider an enclosure of n isothermal surfaces with areas of $A_1, A_2, \ldots, A_n$, and emissivities of $\varepsilon_1, \varepsilon_2, \ldots, \varepsilon_n$, respectively. Some may be at uniform but different known temperatures, and the remaining surfaces have uniform but different and known heat fluxes. The radiant energy flux incident on a surface G_i is the sum of the radiant energy reaching it from each of the n surfaces:

$$G_i A_i = \sum_{k=1}^{n} F_{ki} J_k A_k = \sum_{k=1}^{n} F_{ik} J_k A_i \quad \text{or} \quad G_i = \sum_{k=1}^{n} F_{ik} J_k \tag{29}$$

Substituting Equation (29) into Equation (26),

$$J_i = \varepsilon_i W_{bi} + (1 - \varepsilon_i) \sum_{k=1}^{n} F_{ik} J_k \tag{30}$$

Combining Equations (30) and (28),

$$J_i = \frac{q_i}{A_i} + \sum_{k=1}^{n} F_{ik} J_k \tag{31}$$

Note that in Equations (30) and (31), the summation includes surface i.

Equation (30) is for surfaces with known temperatures, and Equation (31) for those with known heat fluxes. An opening in the enclosure is treated as a black surface at the temperature of the surroundings. The resulting set of simultaneous, linear equations can be solved for the unknown J_is.

Once the radiosities (J_is) are known, the net radiant energy transfer to or from each surface or the emissive power, whichever is unknown is determined.

For surfaces where E_{bi} is known and q_i is to be determined, use Equation (28) for a nonblack surface. For a black surface, $J_i = W_{bi}$ and Equation (31) can be rearranged to give

$$\frac{q_i}{A_i} = W_{bi} - \sum_{k=1}^{n} F_{ik} J_k \tag{32}$$

At surfaces where q_i is known and E_{bi} is to be determined, rearrange Equation (28):

$$E_{bi} = J_i + q_i \left(\frac{1 - \varepsilon_i}{A_i \varepsilon_i} \right) \tag{33}$$

The temperature of the surface is then

$$T_i = \left(\frac{W_{bi}}{\sigma} \right)^{1/4} \tag{34}$$

A surface in radiant balance is one for which radiant emission is balanced by radiant absorption (i.e., heat is neither removed from nor supplied to the surface). These are called **reradiating, insulated**, or **refractory surfaces**. For these surfaces, $q_i = 0$ in Equation (31). After solving for the radiosities, W_{bi} can be found by noting that $q_i = 0$ in Equation (33) gives $W_{bi} = J_i$.

Thermal Circuit Method. Another method to determine the heat transfer rate is using thermal circuits for radiative heat transfer rates. Heat transfer rates from surface i to surface k and surface k to surface i, respectively, are given by

$$q_{i\text{-}k} = A_i F_{i\text{-}k} (J_i - J_k) \quad \text{and} \quad q_{k\text{-}i} = A_k F_{ik\text{-}i} (J_k - J_i)$$

Using the reciprocity relation $A_i F_{i\text{-}k} = A_k F_{k\text{-}i}$, the net heat transfer rate from surface i to surface k is

$$q_{ik} = q_{i\text{-}k} - q_{k\text{-}i} = A_i F_{i\text{-}k} (J_i - J_k) = \frac{J_i - J_k}{1/A_i F_{i\text{-}k}} \tag{35}$$

Equations (28) and (35) are analogous to the current in a resistance, with the numerators representing a potential difference and the denominator representing a thermal resistance. This analogy can be used to solve radiative heat transfer rates among surfaces, as illustrated in Example 9.

Using angle factors and radiation properties as defined assumes that the surfaces are diffuse radiators, which is a good assumption for most nonmetals in the infrared region, but poor for highly polished metals. Subdividing the surfaces and considering the variation of radiation properties with angle of incidence improves the approximation but increases the work required for a solution. Also note that radiation properties, such as absorptivity, have significant uncertainties, for which the final solutions should account.

Example 9. Consider a 13.1 ft wide, 16.4 ft long, 8.2 ft high room as shown in Figure 17. Heating pipes, embedded in the ceiling (1), keep its temperature at 104°F. The floor (2) is at 86°F, and the four side walls (3) are at 64°F. The emissivity of each surface is 0.8. Determine the net radiative heat transfer rate to/from each surface.

Solution: Consider the room as a three-surface enclosure. The corresponding thermal circuit is also shown. The heat transfer rates are found after finding the radiosity of each surface by solving the thermal circuit.

From Figure 15A,

$$F_{1\text{-}2} = F_{2\text{-}1} = 0.376$$

From the summation rule, $F_{1\text{-}1} + F_{1\text{-}2} + F_{1\text{-}3} = 1$. With $F_{1\text{-}1} = 0$,

$$F_{1\text{-}3} = 1 - F_{1\text{-}2} = 0.624 = F_{2\text{-}3}$$

$$R_1 = \frac{1 - \varepsilon_1}{A_1 \varepsilon_1} = \frac{1 - 0.8}{215.3 \times 0.8} = 0.00116 \text{ ft}^{-2} = R_2$$

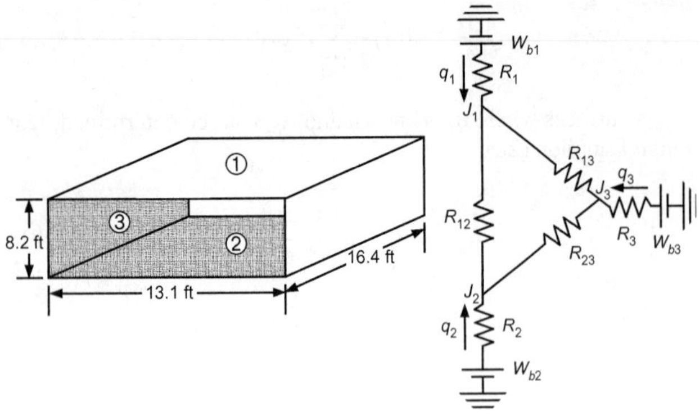

Fig. 17 Diagrams for Example 9

$$R_3 = \frac{1-\varepsilon_3}{A_3\varepsilon_3} = \frac{1-0.8}{484.4 \times 0.8} = 5.16 \times 10^{-4}\ \text{ft}^{-2}$$

$$R_{12} = \frac{1}{A_1F_{1\text{-}2}} = \frac{1}{215.3 \times 0.376} = 0.01235\ \text{ft}^{-2}$$

$$R_{13} = \frac{1}{A_1F_{1\text{-}3}} = \frac{1}{215.3 \times 0.624} = 7.44 \times 10^{-3}\ \text{ft}^{-2} = R_{23}$$

Performing a balance on each of the three J_i nodes gives

$$\text{Surface 1:}\quad \frac{W_{b1}-J_1}{R_1} + \frac{J_2-J_1}{R_{12}} + \frac{J_3-J_1}{R_{13}} = 0$$

$$\text{Surface 2:}\quad \frac{W_{b2}-J_2}{R_2} + \frac{J_1-J_2}{R_{12}} + \frac{J_3-J_2}{R_{23}} = 0$$

$$\text{Surface 3:}\quad \frac{W_{b3}-J_3}{R_3} + \frac{J_1-J_3}{R_{13}} + \frac{J_2-J_3}{R_{23}} = 0$$

$$W_{b1} = 0.1712 \times 10^{-8} \times 564^4 = 173.2\ \text{Btu/h·ft}^2$$

$$W_{b2} = 152.2\ \text{Btu/h·ft}^2 \qquad W_{b3} = 129.1\ \text{Btu/h·ft}^2$$

Substituting the values and solving for J_1, J_2, and J_3,

$$J_1 = 166.3\ \text{Btu/h·ft}^2 \quad J_2 = 150.7\ \text{Btu/h·ft}^2 \quad J_3 = 132.8\ \text{Btu/h·ft}^2$$

$$q_1 = \frac{W_{b1}-J_1}{R_1} = \frac{173.2-166.3}{0.00116} = 5948\ \text{Btu/h}$$

$$q_2 = 1293\ \text{Btu/h} \qquad q_3 = -7241\ \text{Btu/h}$$

Note that floor and ceiling must both be heated because of heat loss from the walls.

Radiation in Gases

Monatomic and diatomic gases such as oxygen, nitrogen, hydrogen, and helium are essentially transparent to thermal radiation. Their absorption and emission bands are confined mainly to the ultraviolet region of the spectrum. The gaseous vapors of most compounds, however, have absorption bands in the infrared region. Carbon monoxide, carbon dioxide, water vapor, sulfur dioxide, ammonia, acid vapors, and organic vapors absorb and emit significant amounts of energy.

Radiation exchange by opaque solids may be considered a surface phenomenon unless the material is transparent or translucent, though radiant energy does penetrate into the material. However, the penetration depths are small. Penetration into gases is very significant.

Table 6 Emissivity of CO_2 and Water Vapor in Air at 75°F

Path Length, ft	CO_2, % by Volume		Relative Humidity, %			
	0.1	0.3	1.0	10	50	100
10	0.03	0.06	0.09	0.06	0.17	0.22
100	0.09	0.12	0.16	0.22	0.39	0.47
1000	0.16	0.19	0.23	0.47	0.64	0.70

Table 7 Emissivity of Moist Air and CO_2 in Typical Room

Relative Humidity, %	ε_g
10	0.10
50	0.19
75	0.22

Beer's law states that the attenuation of radiant energy in a gas is a function of the product p_gL of the partial pressure of the gas and the path length. The monochromatic absorptivity of a body of gas of thickness L is then

$$\alpha_{\lambda L} = 1 - e^{-\alpha_\lambda L} \tag{36}$$

Because absorption occurs in discrete wavelength bands, the absorptivities of all the absorption bands must be summed over the spectral region corresponding to the temperature of the blackbody radiation passing through the gas. The monochromatic absorption coefficient α_λ is also a function of temperature and pressure of the gas; therefore, detailed treatment of gas radiation is quite complex.

Estimated emissivity for carbon dioxide and water vapor in air at 75°F is a function of concentration and path length (Table 6). Values are for an isothermal hemispherically shaped body of gas radiating at its surface. Among others, Hottel and Sarofim (1967), Modest (2003), and Siegel and Howell (2002) describe geometrical calculations in their texts on radiation heat transfer. Generally, at low values of p_gL, the mean path length L (or equivalent hemispherical radius for a gas body radiating to its surrounding surfaces) is four times the mean hydraulic radius of the enclosure. A room with a dimensional ratio of 1:1:4 has a mean path length of 0.89 times the shortest dimension when considering radiation to all walls. For a room with a dimensional ratio of 1:2:6, the mean path length for the gas radiating to all surfaces is 1.2 times the shortest dimension. The mean path length for radiation to the 2 by 6 face is 1.18 times the shortest dimension. These values are for cases where the partial pressure of the gas times the mean path length approaches zero ($p_gL \approx 0$). The factor decreases with increasing values of p_gL. For average rooms with approximately 8 ft ceilings and relative humidity ranging from 10 to 75% at 75°F, the effective path length for carbon dioxide radiation is about 85% of the ceiling height, or 6.8 ft. The effective path length for water vapor is about 93% of the ceiling height, or 7.4 ft. The effective emissivity of the water vapor and carbon dioxide radiating to the walls, ceiling, and floor of a room 16 by 48 ft with 8 ft ceilings is in Table 7.

Radiation heat transfer from the gas to the walls is then

$$q = \sigma A_w \varepsilon_g (T_g^4 - T_w^4) \tag{37}$$

The preceding discussion indicates the importance of gas radiation in environmental heat transfer problems. In large furnaces, gas radiation is the dominant mode of heat transfer, and many additional factors must be considered. Increased pressure broadens the spectral bands, and interaction of different radiating species prohibits simple summation of emissivity factors for the individual species. Nonblackbody conditions require separate calculations of emissivity and absorptivity. Hottel and Sarofim (1967) and McAdams (1954) discuss gas radiation more fully.

4. THERMAL CONVECTION

Convective heat transfer coefficients introduced previously can be estimated using correlations presented in this section.

Forced Convection

Forced-air coolers and heaters, forced-air- or water-cooled condensers and evaporators, and liquid suction heat exchangers are examples of equipment that transfer heat primarily by forced convection. Although some generalized heat transfer coefficient correlations have been mathematically derived from fundamentals, they are usually obtained from correlations of experimental data. Most correlations for forced convection are of the form

$$\mathrm{Nu} = \frac{hL_c}{k} = f(\mathrm{Re}_{Lc}, \mathrm{Pr})$$

where

Nu = Nusselt number
h = convection heat transfer coefficient
L_c = characteristic length
Re_{Lc} = $\rho V L_c/\mu = V L_c/\nu$
V = fluid velocity
Pr = Prandtl number = $c_p\mu/k$
c_p = fluid specific heat
μ = fluid dynamic viscosity
ρ = fluid density
ν = kinematic viscosity = μ/ρ
k = fluid conductivity

Fluid velocity and characteristic length depend on the geometry.

External Flow. When fluid flows over a flat plate, a **boundary layer** forms adjacent to the plate. The velocity of fluid at the plate surface is zero and increases to its maximum free-stream value at the edge of the boundary layer (Figure 18). Boundary layer formation is important because the temperature change from plate to fluid occurs across this layer. Where the boundary layer is thick, thermal resistance is great and the heat transfer coefficient is small. Flow within the boundary layer immediately downstream from the leading edge is laminar. As flow proceeds along the plate, the laminar boundary layer increases in thickness to a critical value. Then, turbulent eddies develop in the boundary layer, except in a thin laminar sublayer adjacent to the plate.

The boundary layer beyond this point is turbulent. The region between the breakdown of the laminar boundary layer and establishment of the turbulent boundary layer is the **transition region**. Because turbulent eddies greatly enhance heat transport into the main stream, the heat transfer coefficient begins to increase rapidly through the transition region. For a flat plate with a smooth leading edge, the turbulent boundary layer starts at distance x_c from the leading edge where the Reynolds number $\mathrm{Re} = Vx_c/\nu$ is in the range 300,000 to 500,000 (in some cases, higher). In a plate with a blunt front edge or other irregularities, it can start at much smaller Reynolds numbers.

Internal Flow. For tubes, channels, or ducts of small diameter at sufficiently low velocity, the laminar boundary layers on each wall grow until they meet. This happens when the Reynolds number based on tube diameter, $\mathrm{Re} = V_{avg}D/\nu$, is less than 2000 to 2300. Beyond this point, the velocity distribution does not change, and no transition to turbulent flow occurs. This is called **fully developed laminar flow**. When the Reynolds number is greater than 10,000, the boundary layers become turbulent before they meet, and fully developed turbulent flow is established (Figure 19). If flow is turbulent, three different flow regions exist. Immediately next to the wall is a **laminar sublayer**, where heat transfer occurs by thermal conduction; next is a transition region called the **buffer layer**, where both eddy mixing and conduction effects are significant; the final layer, extending to the pipe's axis, is the **turbulent region**, where the dominant mechanism of transfer is eddy mixing.

In most equipment, flow is turbulent. For low-velocity flow in small tubes, or highly viscous liquids such as glycol, the flow may be laminar.

The characteristic length for internal flow in pipes and tubes is the inside diameter. For noncircular tubes or ducts, the **hydraulic diameter D_h** is used to compute the Reynolds and Nusselt numbers. It is defined as

$$D_h = 4 \times \frac{\text{Cross-sectional area for flow}}{\text{Total wetted perimeter}} \tag{38}$$

Inserting expressions for cross-sectional area and wetted perimeter of common cross sections shows that the hydraulic diameter is equal to

- The diameter of a round pipe
- Twice the gap between two parallel plates
- The difference in diameters for an annulus
- The length of the side for square tubes or ducts

Table 8 lists various forced-convection correlations. In general, the Nusselt number is determined by the flow geometry, Reynolds number, and Prandtl number. One often useful form for turbulent internal flow is known as **Colburn's analogy**:

$$j = \frac{\mathrm{Nu}}{\mathrm{Re}\mathrm{Pr}^{1/3}} = \frac{f_F}{2}$$

where f_F is the Fanning friction factor (1/4 of the Darcy-Weisbach friction factor in Chapter 3) and j is the Colburn j-factor. It is related to the friction factor by the interrelationship of the transport of momentum and energy in turbulent flow. These factors are plotted in Figure 20.

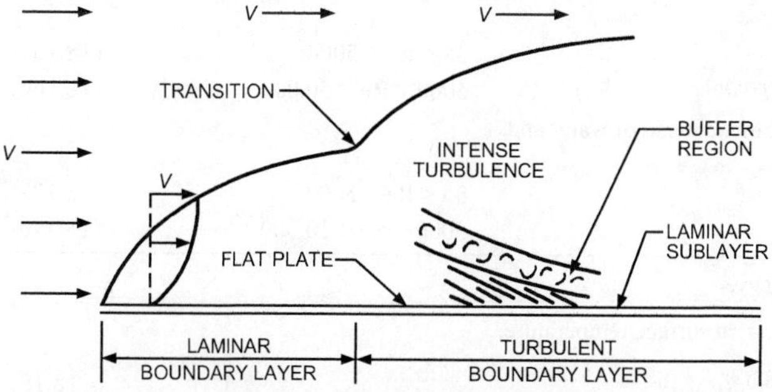

Fig. 18 External Flow Boundary Layer Build-up (Vertical Scale Magnified)

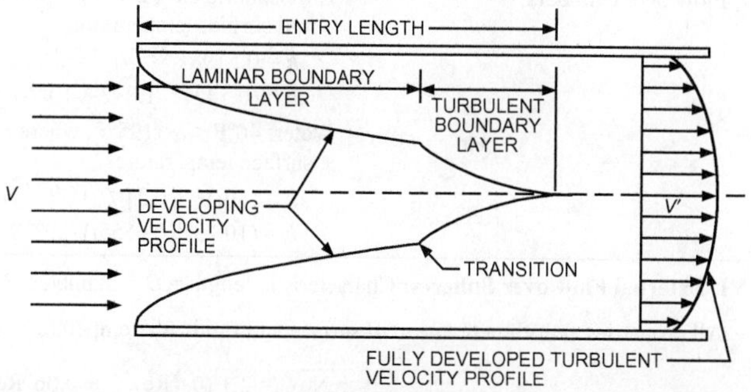

Fig. 19 Boundary Layer Build-up in Entrance Region of Tube or Channel

Table 8 Forced-Convection Correlations

I. General Correlation $Nu = f(Re, Pr)$

II. Internal Flows for Pipes and Ducts: Characteristic length = D, pipe diameter, or D_h, hydraulic diameter.

$$Re = \frac{\rho V_{avg} D_h}{\mu} = \frac{\dot{m} D_h}{A_c \mu} = \frac{Q D_h}{A_c \nu} = \frac{4\dot{m}}{\mu P_{wet}} = \frac{4Q}{\nu P_{wet}}$$

where $\dot{m}$ = mass flow rate, Q = volume flow rate, P_{wet} = wetted perimeter, A_c = cross-sectional area, and ν = kinematic viscosity (μ/ρ).

Case	Correlation	Conditions/Notes	Eq.
	$\frac{Nu}{Re\,Pr^{1/3}} = \frac{f}{2}$	Colburn's analogy (turbulent)	(T8.1)
Laminar: $Re < 2300$	$Nu = 1.86\left(\frac{Re\,Pr}{L/D}\right)^{1/3}\left(\frac{\mu}{\mu_s}\right)^{0.14}$	$\frac{L}{D} < \frac{Re\,Pr}{8}\left(\frac{\mu}{\mu_s}\right)^{0.42}$	(T8.2)[a]
Developing	$Nu = 3.66 + \frac{0.065(D/L)Re\,Pr}{1 + 0.04[(D/L)Re\,Pr]^{2/3}}$		(T8.3)
Fully developed, round	$Nu = 3.66$	Uniform surface temperature	(T8.4a)
	$Nu = 4.36$	Uniform heat flux	(T8.4b)
Turbulent:	$Nu = 0.023\,Re^{4/5}\,Pr^{0.4}$	Heating fluid $Re \geq 10{,}000$	(T8.5a)[b]
Fully developed	$Nu = 0.023\,Re^{4/5}\,Pr^{0.3}$	Cooling fluid $Re \geq 10{,}000$	(T8.5b)[b]
Evaluate properties at bulk temperature t_b except μ_s and t_s at surface temperature	$Nu = \frac{(f_s/2)(Re - 1000)Pr}{1 + 12.7(f_s/2)^{1/2}(Pr^{2/3} - 1)}\left[1 + \left(\frac{D}{L}\right)^{2/3}\right]$ For fully developed flows, set $D/L = 0$.	$f_s = \frac{1}{(1.58 \ln Re - 3.28)^2}$ Multiply Nu by $(T/T_s)^{0.45}$ for gases and by $(Pr/Pr_s)^{0.11}$ for liquids	(T8.6)[c]
	$Nu = 0.027\,Re^{4/5}\,Pr^{1/3}\left(\frac{\mu}{\mu_s}\right)^{0.14}$	For viscous fluids	(T8.7)[a]

For noncircular tubes, use hydraulic mean diameter D_h in the equations for Nu for an approximate value of h.

III. External Flows for Flat Plate: Characteristic length = L = length of plate. $Re = VL/\nu$.
All properties at arithmetic mean of surface and fluid temperatures.

Case	Correlation	Notes	Eq.
Laminar boundary layer: $Re < 5 \times 10^5$	$Nu = 0.332\,Re^{1/2}Pr^{1/3}$	Local value of h	(T8.8)
	$Nu = 0.664\,Re^{1/2}Pr^{1/3}$	Average value of h	(T8.9)
Turbulent boundary layer: $Re > 5 \times 10^5$	$Nu = 0.0296\,Re^{4/5}Pr^{1/3}$	Local value of h	(T8.10)
Turbulent boundary layer beginning at leading edge: All Re	$Nu = 0.037\,Re^{4/5}Pr^{1/3}$	Average value of h	(T8.11)
Laminar-turbulent boundary layer: $Re > 5 \times 10^5$	$Nu = (0.037\,Re^{4/5} - 871)Pr^{1/3}$	Average value $Re_c = 5 \times 10^5$	(T8.12)

IV. External Flows for Cross Flow over Cylinder: Characteristic length = D = diameter. $Re = VD/\nu$.
All properties at arithmetic mean of surface and fluid temperatures.

$$Nu = 0.3 + \frac{0.62\,Re^{1/2}Pr^{1/3}}{[1 + (0.4/Pr)^{2/3}]^{1/4}}\left[1 + \left(\frac{Re}{282{,}000}\right)^{5/8}\right]^{4/5}$$ Average value of h (T8.14)[d]

V. Simplified Approximate Equations: h is in Btu/h·ft²·°F, V is in ft/s, D is in ft, and t is in °F.

Case	Correlation	Conditions	Eq.
Flows in pipes $Re > 10{,}000$	Atmospheric air (32 to 400°F): $h = (0.3323 - 2.384 \times 10^{-4}t)V^{0.8}/D^{0.2}$		(T8.15a)[e]
	Water (5 to 400°F): $h = (67.25 + 1.146t)V^{0.8}/D^{0.2}$		(T8.15b)[e]
	Water (40 to 220°F): $h = (91.25 + 1.004t)V^{0.8}/D^{0.2}$ (McAdams 1954)		(T8.15c)[g]
Flow over cylinders	Atmospheric air: $32°F < t < 400°F$, where t = arithmetic mean of air and surface temperature.		
	$h = 0.5198V^{0.471}/D^{0.529}$	$35 < Re < 5000$	(T8.16a)
	$h = (0.5477 - 1.832 \times 10^{-4}t)V^{0.633}/D^{0.367}$	$5000 < Re < 50{,}000$	(T8.16b)
	Water: $40°F < t < 195°F$, where t = arithmetic mean of water and surface temperature.		
	$h = (80.36 + 0.2107t)V^{0.471}/D^{0.529}$	$35 < Re < 5000$	(T8.17a)
	$h = (108.9 + 0.6555t)V^{0.633}/D^{0.367}$	$5000 < Re < 50{,}000$	(T8.17b)[f]

VI. External Flow over Spheres: Characteristic length = D = diameter. $Re = VD/\nu$.

All properties at arithmetic mean of surface and fluid bulk temperature, except μ_s at surface temperature.

$$\overline{Nu}_D = 2 + (0.4Re_D^{1/2} + 0.06\,Re_D^{2/3})Pr^{0.4}(\mu/\mu_s)^{1/4}$$ (T8.18)

Sources: [a]Sieder and Tate (1936), [b]Dittus and Boelter (1930), [c]Gnielinski (1990), [d]Churchill and Bernstein (1977), [e]Based on $Nu = 0.023\,Re^{4/5}Pr^{1/3}$, [f]Based on Morgan (1975). [g]McAdams (1954).

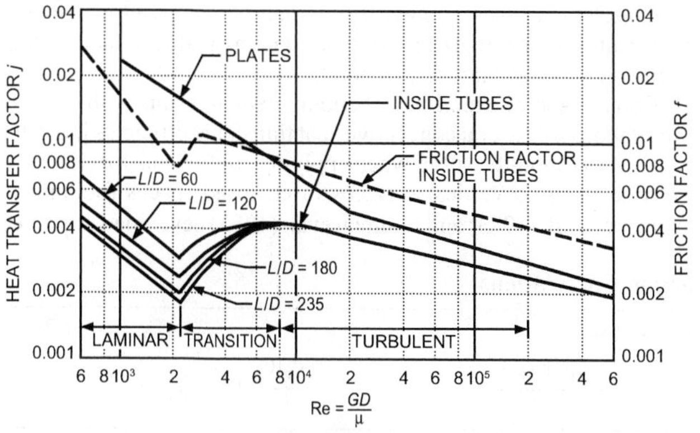

Fig. 20 Typical Dimensionless Representation of Forced-Convection Heat Transfer

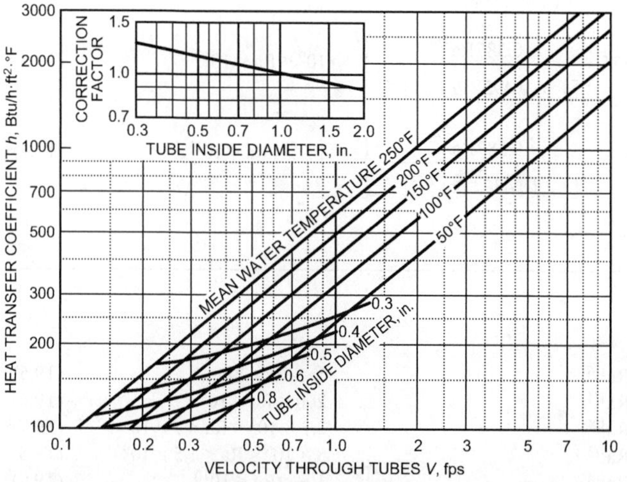

Re = 2100 at velocity where diameter curve crosses mean water temperature lines.

Fig. 21 Heat Transfer Coefficient for Turbulent Flow of Water Inside Tubes

Simplified correlations for atmospheric air are also given in Table 8. Figure 21 gives graphical solutions for water.

Example 10. An uninsulated 10 ft ID spherical tank with 0.4 in. walls is used to store iced water. Winds at $V = 15$ mph and $T_\infty = 86$°F blow over the outside of the tank. What is the rate of heat gain to the iced water? Neglect radiation, conduction resistance of tank wall, and convection resistance between ice water and tank; the outer surface temperature of the tank is 32°F.

Because the geometry is for forced convection over a sphere, use Equation (T8.18). Use the properties of air at 1 atm pressure and the freestream temperature of $T_\infty = 86$°F: $k = 0.01497$ Btu/h·ft·°F, $\nu = 1.731 \times 10^{-4}$ ft²/s, $\mu = 1.258 \times 10^{-5}$ lb$_m$/ft·s, Pr = 0.728, and $\mu_s = 1.162 \times 10^{-5}$ lb$_m$/ft·s at 32°F.

$$\text{Re} = \frac{VD}{\nu} = \frac{[(15 \times 5280/3600)\ \text{ft/s}](10\ \text{ft})}{1.731 \times 10^{-4}\ \text{ft}^2/\text{s}} = 1.271 \times 10^6$$

$$\text{Nu} = \frac{hD}{k} = 2 + \left[0.4\text{Re}^{0.5} + 0.06\text{Re}^{2/3}\right]\text{Pr}^{0.4}(\mu/\mu_s)^{1/4}$$

$$= 2 + \left[0.4(1.271 \times 10^6)^{0.5} + 0.06(1.271 \times 10^6)^{2/3}\right]$$

$$\times (0.7282)^{0.4}\left(\frac{1.258 \times 10^{-5}}{1.162 \times 10^{-5}}\right)^{1/4} = 1043$$

Note that for gases, the $(\mu/\mu_s)^{1/4}$ property correction is often negligible. For liquids, it is often significant.

$$h = \frac{k}{D}\text{Nu} = \frac{0.01497\ \text{Btu/ft·h·°F}}{10\ \text{ft}}(1043) = 1.56\ \text{Btu/h·ft}^2\text{·°F}$$

The rate of heat transfer to the iced water is

$$q = hA_s(T_s - T_\infty) = h(\pi D^2)(T_s - T_\infty)$$
$$= (1.56\ \text{Btu/h·ft}^2\text{·°F})[\pi(10\ \text{ft})^2](86 - 32)\text{°F} = 26{,}465\ \text{Btu/h}$$

With a uniform tube surface temperature and heat transfer coefficient, the exit temperature can be calculated using

$$\ln\frac{t_s - t_e}{t_s - t_i} = -\frac{hA}{\dot{m}c_p} \tag{39}$$

where t_i and t_e are the inlet and exit bulk temperatures of the fluid, t_s is the pipe/duct surface temperature, and A is the surface area inside the pipe/duct. The convective heat transfer coefficient varies in the direction of flow because of the temperature dependence of the fluid properties. In such cases, it is common to use an average value of h in Equation (39) computed either as the average of h evaluated at the inlet and exit fluid temperatures or evaluated at the average of the inlet and exit temperatures.

With uniform surface heat flux q'', the temperature of fluid t at any section can be found by applying the first law of thermodynamics:

$$\dot{m}\,c_p(t - t_i) = q''A \tag{40}$$

The surface temperature can be found using

$$q'' = h(t_s - t) \tag{41}$$

With uniform surface heat flux, surface temperature increases in the direction of flow along with the fluid.

Natural Convection. Heat transfer with fluid motion resulting solely from temperature differences (i.e., from temperature-dependent density and gravity) is natural (free) convection. Natural-convection heat transfer coefficients for gases are generally much lower than those for forced convection, and it is therefore important not to ignore radiation in calculating the total heat loss or gain. Radiant transfer may be of the same order of magnitude as natural convection, even at room temperatures; therefore, both modes must be considered when computing heat transfer rates from people, furniture, and so on in buildings (see Chapter 9).

Natural convection is important in a variety of heating and refrigeration equipment, such as (1) gravity coils used in high-humidity cold-storage rooms and in roof-mounted refrigerant condensers, (2) the evaporator and condenser of household refrigerators, (3) baseboard radiators and convectors for space heating, and (4) cooling panels for air conditioning. Natural convection is also involved in heat loss or gain to equipment casings and interconnecting ducts and pipes.

Consider heat transfer by natural convection between a cold fluid and a hot vertical surface. Fluid in immediate contact with the surface is heated by conduction, becomes lighter, and rises because of the difference in density of the adjacent fluid. The fluid's viscosity resists this motion. The heat transfer rate is influenced by fluid properties, temperature difference between the surface at t_s and environment at t_∞, and characteristic dimension L_c. Some generalized heat transfer coefficient correlations have been mathematically derived from fundamentals, but they are usually obtained from correlations of experimental data. Most correlations for natural convection are of the form

$$\text{Nu} = \frac{hL_c}{k} = f(\text{Ra}_{Lc}, \text{Pr})$$

where

Nu = Nusselt number
H = convection heat transfer coefficient

L_c = characteristic length
K = fluid thermal conductivity
Ra_{Lc} = Rayleigh number = $g\beta \Delta t L_c^3/\nu\alpha$
Δt = $|t_s - t_\infty|$
g = gravitational acceleration
β = coefficient of thermal expansion
ν = fluid kinematic viscosity = μ/ρ
α = fluid thermal diffusivity = $k/\rho c_p$
Pr = Prandtl number = ν/α

Correlations for a number of geometries are given in Table 9. Other information on natural convection is available in the Bibliography under Heat Transfer, General.

Comparison of experimental and numerical results with existing correlations for natural convective heat transfer coefficients indicates that caution should be used when applying coefficients for (isolated) vertical plates to vertical surfaces in enclosed spaces (buildings). Altmayer et al. (1983) and Bauman et al. (1983) developed improved

Table 9 Natural Convection Correlations

I. General relationships	$Nu = f(Ra, Pr)$ or $f(Ra)$		(T9.1)
Characteristic length depends on geometry	$Ra = Gr\,Pr \quad Gr = \dfrac{g\beta\rho^2\lvert\Delta t\rvert L^3}{\mu^2}$	$Pr = \dfrac{c_p\mu}{k} \quad \Delta t = \lvert t_s - t_\infty\rvert$	
II. Vertical plate			
t_s = constant	$Nu = 0.68 + \dfrac{0.67 Ra^{1/4}}{[1 + (0.492/Pr)^{9/16}]^{4/9}}$	$10^{-1} < Ra < 10^9$	(T9.2)[a]
Characteristic dimension: L = height; Properties at $(t_s + t_\infty)/2$ except β at t_∞	$Nu = \left\{0.825 + \dfrac{0.387 Ra^{1/6}}{[1 + (0.492/Pr)^{9/16}]^{8/27}}\right\}^2$	$10^9 < Ra < 10^{12}$	(T9.3)[a]
q''_s = constant; Characteristic dimension: L = height; Properties at $t_{s,\,L/2} - t_\infty$ except β at t_∞	$Nu = \left\{0.825 + \dfrac{0.387 Ra^{1/6}}{[1 + (0.437/Pr)^{9/16}]^{8/27}}\right\}^2$	$10^{-1} < Ra < 10^{12}$	(T9.4)[a]
Equations (T9.2) and (T9.3) can be used for vertical cylinders if $D/L > 35/Gr^{1/4}$ where D is diameter and L is axial length of cylinder			
III. Horizontal plate			
Characteristic dimension = $L = A/P$, where A is plate area and P is perimeter			
Properties of fluid at $(t_s + t_\infty)/2$			
Downward-facing cooled plate and upward-facing heated plate	$Nu = 0.96\, Ra^{1/6}$	$1 < Ra < 200$	(T9.5)[b]
	$Nu = 0.59\, Ra^{1/4}$	$200 < Ra < 10^4$	(T9.6)[b]
	$Nu = 0.54\, Ra^{1/4}$	$2.2 \times 10^4 < Ra < 8 \times 10^6$	(T9.7)[b]
	$Nu = 0.15\, Ra^{1/3}$	$8 \times 10^6 < Ra < 1.5 \times 10^9$	(T9.8)[b]
Downward-facing heated plate and upward-facing cooled plate	$Nu = 0.27\, Ra^{1/4}$	$10^5 < Ra < 10^{10}$	(T9.9)[b]
IV. Horizontal cylinder			
Characteristic length = d = diameter; Properties of fluid at $(t_s + t_\infty)/2$ except β at t_∞	$Nu = \left\{0.6 + \dfrac{0.387\, Ra^{1/6}}{[1 + (0.559/Pr)^{9/16}]^{8/27}}\right\}^2$	$10^9 < Ra < 10^{13}$	(T9.10)[c]
V. Sphere			
Characteristic length = D = diameter; Properties at $(t_s + t_\infty)/2$ except β at t_∞	$Nu = 2 + \dfrac{0.589\, Ra^{1/4}}{[1 + (0.469/Pr)^{9/16}]^{4/9}}$	$Ra < 10^{11}$	(T9.11)[d]
VI. Horizontal wire			
Characteristic dimension = D = diameter; Properties at $(t_s + t_\infty)/2$	$\dfrac{2}{Nu} = \ln\left(1 + \dfrac{3.3}{cRa^n}\right)$	$10^{-8} < Ra < 10^6$	(T9.12)[e]
VII. Vertical wire			
Characteristic dimension = D = diameter; L = length of wire	$Nu = c(Ra\,D/L)^{0.25} + 0.763c^{(1/6)}(Ra\,D/L)^{(1/24)}$	$c(Ra\,D/L)^{0.25} > 2 \times 10^{-3}$	(T9.13)[e]
Properties at $(t_s + t_\infty)/2$	In both Equations (T9.12) and (T9.13), $c = \dfrac{0.671}{[1 + (0.492/Pr)^{(9/16)}]^{(4/9)}}$ and $n = 0.25 + \dfrac{1}{10 + 5(Ra)^{0.175}}$		
VIII. Simplified equations with air at mean temperature of 70°F: h is in Btu/h·ft²·°F, L and D are in ft, and Δt is in °F.			
Vertical surface	$h = 0.272\left(\dfrac{\Delta t}{L}\right)^{1/4}$	$10^5 < Ra < 10^9$	(T9.14)
	$h = 0.182(\Delta t)^{1/3}$	$Ra > 10^9$	(T9.15)
Horizontal cylinder	$h = 0.213\left(\dfrac{\Delta t}{D}\right)^{1/4}$	$10^5 < Ra < 10^9$	(T9.16)
	$h = 0.178(\Delta t)^{1/3}$	$Ra > 10^9$	(T9.17)

Sources: [a]Churchill and Chu (1975a), [b]Lloyd and Moran (1974), Goldstein et al. (1973), [c]Churchill and Chu (1975b), [d]Churchill (1990), [e]Fujii et al. (1986).

correlations for calculating natural convective heat transfer from vertical surfaces in rooms under certain temperature boundary conditions.

Natural convection can affect the heat transfer coefficient in the presence of weak forced convection. As the forced-convection effect (i.e., the Reynolds number) increases, "mixed convection" (superimposed forced-on-free convection) gives way to pure forced convection. In these cases, consult other sources [e.g., Grigull et al. (1982); Metais and Eckert (1964)] describing combined free and forced convection, because the heat transfer coefficient in the mixed-convection region is often larger than that calculated based on the natural- or forced-convection calculation alone. Metais and Eckert (1964) summarize natural-, mixed-, and forced-convection regimes for vertical and horizontal tubes. Figure 22 shows the approximate limits for horizontal tubes. Other studies are described by Grigull et al. (1982).

Example 11. A horizontal electric immersion heater of 0.4 in. diameter D and 16 in. length L is rated at $q = 2500$ Btu/h. Estimate the surface temperature t_s if immersed in 68°F t_∞ water.

Solution: Because the geometry is for natural convection from a horizontal cylinder, use Equation (T9.10). If the allowable surface temperature of the heater were given, and the need were to calculate the maximum allowable power rating, this would be a straightforward sequence of calculations:

1. Calculate the film temperature $t_f = t_s + t_\infty$
2. Look up the needed water properties k, ν, Pr, α, and β at t_f.
3. Calculate Rayleigh number Ra.
4. Use Equation (T9.10) to calculate Nusselt number Nu.
5. Calculate $h = \text{Nu}k/D$.
6. $q = h\pi DL(t_s - t_\infty)$

However, in this case, given q and needing t_s, the solution is iterative. First, guess the solution t_s, execute items 1 to 5 in the preceding sequence, and use the resulting h to calculate $t_s = t_\infty + q/(h\pi DL)$. If necessary, use this value as a new guess for t_s and repeat the process.

Assume $t_s = 147$°F. Then $t_f = (147 + 68)/2 = 107.5$°F = 567°R. Use $k = 0.366$ Btu/h·ft·°F, $\nu = 6.73 \times 10^{-6}$ ft²/s, $\alpha = 1.65 \times 10^{-6}$ ft²/s, Pr = 4.08, and $\beta = 0.2224 \times 10^{-3}$/°R.

$$\text{Ra} = \frac{g\beta\Delta TD^3}{\nu\alpha} = 1.885 \times 10^6$$

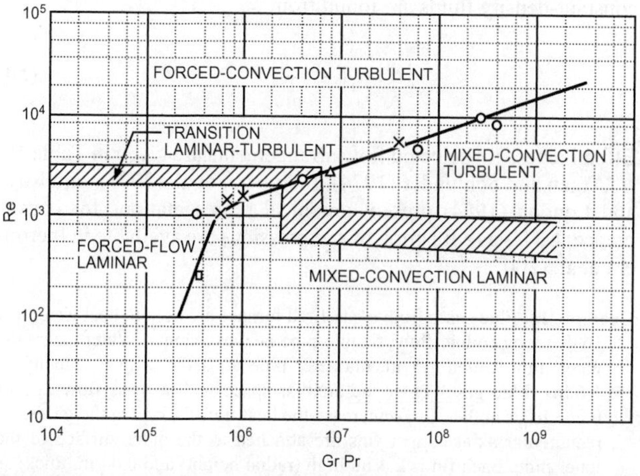

Fig. 22 Regimes of Free, Forced, and Mixed Convection—Flow in Horizontal Tubes

$$\text{Nu} = \left\{0.6 + \frac{0.387\text{Ra}^{1/6}}{\left[1 + (0.559/\text{Pr})^{9/16}\right]^{8/27}}\right\}^2 = 20.8$$

$$h = \text{Nu}k/D = 232.6 \text{ Btu/h·ft}^2\text{·°F}$$

$$t_s = t_\infty + q/(h\pi DL) = 145\text{°F}$$

The initial guess was close enough; another iteration is unnecessary.

Example 12. Chilled water at 41°F flows inside a freely suspended horizontal 0.7874 in. OD pipe at a velocity of 8.2 fps. Surrounding air is at 86°F, 70% rh. The pipe is to be insulated with cellular glass having a thermal conductivity of 0.026 Btu/h·ft·°F. Determine the radial thickness of the insulation to prevent condensation of water on the outer surface.

Solution: In Figure 23,

$t_{fi} = 41$°F $\quad t_{fo} = 86$°F $\quad d_o$ = OD of tube = 0.7874 in.

k_i = thermal conductivity of insulation material = 0.026 Btu/h·ft·°F

From the problem statement, the outer surface temperature t_o of the insulation should not be less than the dew-point temperature of air. The dew-point temperature of air at 86°F, 70% rh = 75.07°F. To determine the outer diameter of the insulation, equate the heat transfer rate per unit length of pipe (from the outer surface of the pipe to the water) to the heat transfer rate per unit length from the air to the outer surface:

$$\frac{t_o - t_{fi}}{\dfrac{1}{h_i d_i} + \dfrac{1}{2k_i}\ln\dfrac{d_o}{d_i}} = \frac{t_{fo} - t_o}{\dfrac{1}{h_{ot} d_o}} \tag{42}$$

Heat transfer from the outer surface is by natural convection to air, so the surface heat transfer coefficient h_{ot} is the sum of the convective heat transfer coefficient h_o and the radiative heat transfer coefficient h_r. With an assumed emissivity of 0.7 and using Equation (4), h_r = 0.757 Btu/h·ft²·°F. To determine the value of d_o, the values of the heat transfer coefficients associated with the inner and outer surfaces (h_i and h_o, respectively) are needed. Compute the value of h_i using Equation (T8.5a). Properties of water at an assumed temperature of 41°F are

$\rho_w = 62.43$ lb$_m$/ft³ $\quad \mu_w = 1.02 \times 10^{-3}$ lb$_m$/ft·s $\quad c_{pw} = 1.003$ Btu/lb$_m$·°F

$k_w = 0.3298$ Btu/lb$_m$·ft·°F $\quad \text{Pr}_w = 11.16$

$\text{Re}_d = \dfrac{\rho v d}{\mu} = 32{,}944 \quad \text{Nu}_d = 248.3 \quad h_i = 1248$ Btu/h·ft²·°F

To compute h_o using Equation (T9.10a), the outer diameter of the insulation material must be found. Determine it by iteration by assuming a value of d_o, computing the value of h_o, and determining the value of d_o from Equation (42). If the assumed and computed values of d_o are close to each other, the correct solution has been obtained. Otherwise, recompute h_o using the newly computed value of d_o and repeat the process.

Assume $d_o = 2$ in. Properties of air at $t_f = 81$°F and 1 atm are

$\rho = 0.0732$ lb$_m$/ft³ $\quad k = 0.01483$ Btu/h·ft·°F $\quad \mu = 1.249 \times 10^{-5}$ lb$_m$/ft·s

Pr = 0.729 $\quad \beta = 0.00183$ (at 460 + 86 = 546°R)

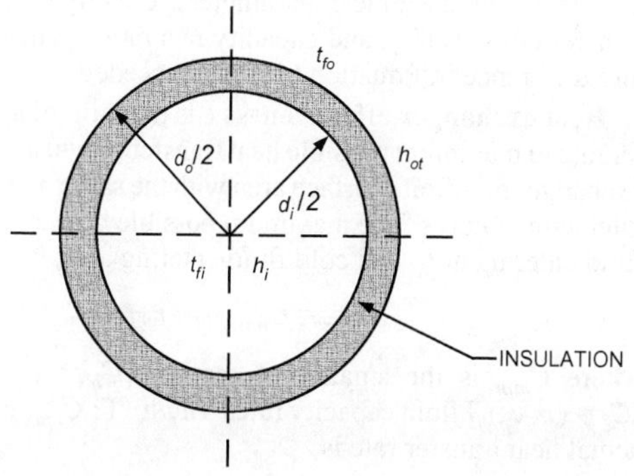

Fig. 23 Diagram for Example 12

Ra = 74,574 Nu = 7.223 h_o = 3.623 Btu/h·ft²·°F

h_{ot} = 0.643 + 0.757 = 1.400 Btu/h·ft²·°F

Solving for d_o makes the left side of Equation (42) equal to the right side, and gives d_o = 1.576 in. Now, using the new value of 1.576 in. for the outer diameter, the new values of h_o and h_{ot} are 0.680 Btu/h·ft²·°F and 1.437 Btu/h·ft²·°F, respectively. The updated value of d_o is 1.857 in. Repeating the process several times results in a final value of d_o = 1.733 in. Thus, an outer diameter of 1.7874 in. (corresponding to an insulation radial thickness of 0.5 in.) keeps the outer surface temperature at 75.4°F, higher than the dew point. [Another method is to use Equation (42) to solve for t_o for values of d_o corresponding to available insulation thicknesses and using the insulation thickness that keeps t_o above the dew-point temperature.]

5. HEAT EXCHANGERS

Mean Temperature Difference Analysis

With heat transfer from one fluid to another (separated by a solid surface) flowing through a heat exchanger, the local temperature difference Δt varies along the flow path. Heat transfer rate may be calculated using

$$q = UA\,\Delta t_m \tag{43}$$

where U is the overall uniform heat transfer coefficient, A is the area associated with the coefficient U, and Δt_m is the appropriate mean temperature difference.

For a parallel or counterflow heat exchanger, the mean temperature difference is given by

$$\Delta t_m = (\Delta t_1 - \Delta t_2)/\ln(\Delta t_1/\Delta t_2) \tag{44}$$

where Δt_1 and Δt_2 are temperature differences between the fluids at each end of the heat exchanger; Δt_m is the **logarithmic mean temperature difference (LMTD)**. For the special case of $\Delta t_1 = \Delta t_2$ (possible only with a counterflow heat exchanger with equal capacities), which leads to an indeterminate form of Equation (44), $\Delta t_m = \Delta t_1 = \Delta t_2$.

Equation (44) for Δt_m is true only if the overall coefficient and the specific heat of the fluids are constant through the heat exchanger, and no heat losses occur (often well-approximated in practice). Parker et al. (1969) give a procedure for cases with variable overall coefficient U. For heat exchangers other than parallel and counterflow, a correction factor [see Incropera et al. (2007)] is needed for Equation (44) to obtain the correct mean temperature difference.

NTU-Effectiveness (ε) Analysis

Calculations using Equations (43) and (44) for Δt_m are convenient when inlet and outlet temperatures are known for both fluids. Often, however, the temperatures of fluids leaving the exchanger are unknown. To avoid trial-and-error calculations, the **NTU-ε method** uses three dimensionless parameters: effectiveness ε, number of transfer units (NTU), and capacity rate ratio c_r; the mean temperature difference in Equation (44) is not needed.

Heat exchanger effectiveness ε is the ratio of actual heat transfer rate to maximum possible heat transfer rate in a counterflow heat exchanger of infinite surface area with the same mass flow rates and inlet temperatures. The maximum possible heat transfer rate for hot fluid entering at t_{hi} and cold fluid entering at t_{ci} is

$$q_{max} = C_{min}(t_{hi} - t_{ci}) \tag{45}$$

where C_{min} is the smaller of the hot [$C_h = (\dot{m}\,c_p)_h$] and cold [$C_c = (\dot{m}\,c_p)_h$] fluid capacity rates, Btu/h·°F; C_{max} is the larger. The actual heat transfer rate is

$$q = \varepsilon\,q_{max} \tag{46}$$

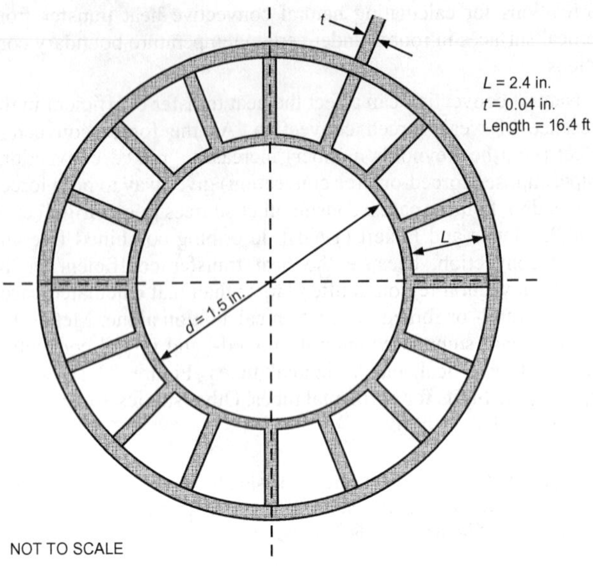

Fig. 24 Cross Section of Double-Pipe Heat Exchanger in Example 13

For a given exchanger type, heat transfer effectiveness can generally be expressed as a function of the **number of transfer units (NTU)** and the **capacity rate ratio c_r**:

$$\varepsilon = f(\text{NTU}, c_r, \text{Flow arrangement}) \tag{47}$$

where

NTU = UA/C_{min}

$c_r = C_{min}/C_{max}$

Effectiveness is independent of exchanger inlet temperatures. For any exchanger in which c_r is zero (where one fluid undergoing a phase change, as in a condenser or evaporator, has an effective $c_p = \infty$), the effectiveness is

$$\varepsilon = 1 - \exp(-\text{NTU}) \qquad c_r = 0 \tag{48}$$

The mean temperature difference in Equation (44) is then given by

$$\Delta t_m = \frac{(t_{hi} - t_{ci})\varepsilon}{\text{NTU}} \tag{49}$$

After finding the heat transfer rate q, exit temperatures for constant-density fluids are found from

$$|t_e - t_i| = \frac{q}{\dot{m}c_p} \tag{50}$$

Effectiveness for selected flow arrangements are given in Table 10.

Afgan and Schlunder (1974), Incropera, et al. (2007), and Kays and London (1984) present graphical representations for convenience. NTUs as a function of ε expressions are available in Incropera et al. (2007).

Example 13. Flue gases from a gas-fired furnace are used to heat water in a 16.4 ft long counterflow, double-pipe heat exchanger. Water enters the inner, thin-walled 1.5 in. diameter pipe at 104°F with a velocity of 1.6 fps. Flue gases enter the annular space with a mass flow rate of 0.265 lb_m/s at 392°F. To increase the heat transfer rate to the gases, 16 rectangular axial copper fins are attached to the outer surface of the inner pipe. Each fin is 2.4 in. high (radial height) and 0.04 in. thick, as shown in Figure 24. The gas-side surface heat transfer coefficient is 20 Btu/h·ft²·°F. Find the heat transfer rate and the exit temperatures of the gases and water.

Table 10 Equations for Computing Heat Exchanger Effectiveness, N = NTU

Flow Configuration	Effectiveness ε	Comments	
Parallel flow	$\dfrac{1-\exp[-N(1+c_r)]}{1+c_r}$		(T10.1)
Counterflow	$\dfrac{1-\exp[-N(1-c_r)]}{1-c_r\exp[-N(1-c_r)]}$	$c_r \neq 1$	(T10.2)
	$\dfrac{N}{1+N}$	$c_r = 1$	(T10.3)
Shell-and-tube (one-shell pass, 2, 4, etc. tube passes)	$\dfrac{2}{1+c_r+a(1+e^{-aN})/(1-e^{-aN})}$	$a = \sqrt{1+c_r^2}$	(T10.4)
Shell-and-tube (*n*-shell pass, 2*n*, 4*n*, etc. tube passes)	$\left[\left(\dfrac{1-\varepsilon_1 c_r}{1-\varepsilon_1}\right)^n - 1\right]\left[\left(\dfrac{1-\varepsilon_1 c_r}{1-\varepsilon_1}\right)^n - c_r\right]^{-1}$	ε_1 = effectiveness of one-shell pass shell-and-tube heat exchanger	(T10.5)
Cross-flow (single phase)			
Both fluids unmixed	$1-\exp\left(\dfrac{\gamma N^{0.22}}{c_r}\right)$	$\gamma = \exp(-c_r N^{0.78}) - 1$	(T10.6)
C_{max} (mixed), C_{min} (unmixed)	$\dfrac{1-\exp(-c_r\gamma)}{c_r}$	$\gamma = 1-\exp(-N)$	(T10.7)
C_{max} (unmixed), C_{min} (mixed)	$1-\exp(-\gamma/c_r)$	$\gamma = 1-\exp(-Nc_r)$	(T10.8)
Both fluids mixed	$\dfrac{N}{N/(1-e^{-N})+c_rN/(1-e^{-Nc_r})-1}$		(T10.9)
All exchangers with $c_r = 0$	$1-\exp(-N)$		(T10.10)

The heat exchanger has the following properties:

Water in the pipe $t_{ci} = 104$°F $v_c = 1.6$ ft/s

Gases $t_{hi} = 392$°F $\dot{m}_h = 0.265$ lb$_m$/s

Length of heat exchanger $L_{tube} = 16.4$ ft $d = 1.5$ in. $L = 2.4$ in.

$t = 0.04$ in. N = number of fins = 16

Solution: The heat transfer rate is computed using Equations (45) and (46), and exit temperatures from Equation (50). To find the heat transfer rates, UA and ε are needed.

$$\frac{1}{UA} = \frac{1}{(\phi_s hA)_o} + \frac{1}{(hA)_i}$$

where

h_i = convective heat transfer coefficient on water side
h_o = gas-side heat transfer coefficient
ϕ_s = surface effectiveness = $(A_{uf} + A_f\phi)/A_o$
ϕ = fin efficiency
A_{uf} = surface area of unfinned surface = $L_{tube}(\pi d - Nt) = 5.56$ ft²
A_f = fin surface area = $2LNL_{tube} = 105.0$ ft²
$A_o = A_{uf} + A_f = 110.6$ ft²
$A_i = \pi d L_{tube} = 6.44$ ft²

Step 1. Find h_i using Equation (T8.6). Properties of water at an assumed mean temperature of 113°F are

$\rho = 61.8$ lb$_m$/ft³ $c_{pc} = 0.999$ Btu/lb$_m$·°F $\mu = 4.008 \times 10^{-4}$ lb$_m$/ft·s

$k = 0.368$ Btu/h·ft·°F Pr = 3.91

$$\text{Re} = \frac{\rho v_c d}{\mu} = \frac{61.8 \times 1.6 \times (1.5/12)}{4.008 \times 10^{-4}} = 30{,}838$$

$$f_s/2 = [1.58\ln(\text{Re}) - 3.28]^{-2}/2 = (1.58\ln 30{,}838 - 3.28)^{-2}/2 = 0.00294$$

$$\text{Nu}_d = \frac{2.94 \times 10^{-3} \times (30{,}838 - 1000) \times 3.91}{1 + 12.7 \times (5.87/2 \times 10^{-3})^{1/2} \times (3.91^{2/3} - 1)} = 169.6$$

$$h_i = \frac{169.6 \times 0.368}{1.5/2} = 499 \text{ Btu/h}\cdot\text{ft}^2\cdot°\text{F}$$

Step 2. Compute fin efficiency ϕ and surface effectiveness ϕ_s. For a rectangular fin with the end of the fin not exposed,

$$\phi = \frac{\tanh(mL)}{mL}$$

For copper, $k = 232$ Btu/h·ft·°F.

$$mL = (2h_o/kt)^{1/2}L = [(2 \times 20)/(232 \times 0.04/12)]^{1/2} \times 2.4/12 = 1.44$$

$$\phi = \frac{\tanh 1.44}{1.44} = 0.62$$

$$\phi_s = (A_{uf} + \phi A_f)/A_o = (5.56 + 0.62 \times 105.0)/110.6 = 0.64$$

Step 3. Find heat exchanger effectiveness. For air at an assumed mean temperature of 347°F, $c_{ph} = 0.243$ Btu/lb$_m$·°F.

$$C_h = \dot{m}_h c_{ph} = 0.265 \times 3600 \times 0.243 = 231.8 \text{ Btu/h}\cdot°\text{F}$$

$$\dot{m}_c = \rho v_c \pi d^2/4 = [61.8 \times 1.6 \times \pi \times (1.5/12)^2] = 1.21 \text{ lb}_m/\text{s}$$

$$C_c = \dot{m}_c c_{pc} = 1.21 \times 3600 \times 0.999 = 4373 \text{ Btu/h}\cdot°\text{F}$$

$$c_r = C_{min}/C_{max} = 231.8/4373 = 0.0530$$

$$UA = [1/(0.64 \times 20 \times 110.5) + 1/(499 \times 6.44)]^{-1} = 982.1 \text{ Btu/h}\cdot°\text{F}$$

$$\text{NTU} = UA/C_{min} = 982.1/231.8 = 4.24$$

From Equation (T10.2),

$$\varepsilon = \frac{1-\exp[-N(1-c_r)]}{1-c_r\exp[-N(1-c_r)]}$$

$$= \frac{1-\exp[-4.26 \times (1-0.0530)]}{1-0.0530 \times \exp[-4.26 \times (1-0.0530)]} = 0.983$$

Step 4. Find heat transfer rate:

$$q_{max} = C_{min} \times (t_{hi} - t_{ci}) = 231.8 \times (392 - 104) = 66{,}758 \text{ Btu/h}$$

$$q = \varepsilon q_{max} = 0.983 \times 66{,}758 = 65{,}634 \text{ Btu/h}$$

Step 5. Find exit temperatures:

$$t_{he} = t_{hi} - \frac{q}{C_h} = 392 - \frac{65{,}634}{231.8} = 108.9°F$$

$$t_{ce} = t_{ci} - \frac{q}{C_c} = 104 + \frac{65{,}634}{4373} = 119°F$$

The mean temperature of water now is 111.5°F. The properties of water at this temperature are not very different from those at the assumed value of 113°F. The only property of air that needs to be updated is the specific heat, which at the updated mean temperature of 250°F is 0.242 Btu/lb$_m$·°F, which is not very different from the assumed value of 0.243 Btu/lb$_m$·°F. Therefore, no further iteration is necessary.

Plate Heat Exchangers

Plate heat exchangers (PHEs) are used regularly in HVAC&R. The three main types of plate exchangers are plate-and-frame (gasket or semiwelded), compact brazed (CBE), and shell-and-plate. The basic plate geometry is shown in Figure 25.

Plate Geometry. Different geometric parameters of a plate are defined as follows (Figure 25):

- **Chevron angle** β varies between 22 and 65°. This angle also defines the thermal hydraulic softness (low thermal efficiency and pressure drop) and hardness (high thermal efficiency and pressure drop).
- **Enlargement factor** ϕ is the ratio of developed length to protracted length.
- **Mean flow channel gap *b*** is the actual gap available for the flow: $b = p - t$.
- **Channel flow area A_x** is the actual flow area: $A_x = bw$.
- **Channel equivalent diameter d_e** is defined as $d_e = 4A_x/P$, where $P = 2(b + \phi w) = 2\phi w$, because $b << w$; therefore, $d_e = 2b/\phi$.

Heat Transfer and Pressure Drop. Table 11 (Ayub 2003) shows correlations for single-phase flow. For quick calculations with water, the correlation by Troupe et al. (1960) is recommended. For more accurate results, the other correlations shown are appropriate.

Example 14. A plate exchanger cools 5280 lb$_m$/min of 194°F beer wort by 5280 lb$_m$/min of water at 68°F. The heat exchanger dimensions are L_p = 3.28 ft, w = 1.64 ft, p = 0.394 in., t = 0.0394 in., β = 45°, and ϕ = 1.24. There are N_p = 100 plates. What is the rate of heat transfer and exit temperature of the wort? Assume the wort has the properties of water. Use k_{plate} = 28.9 Btu/h·ft·°F for the plates.

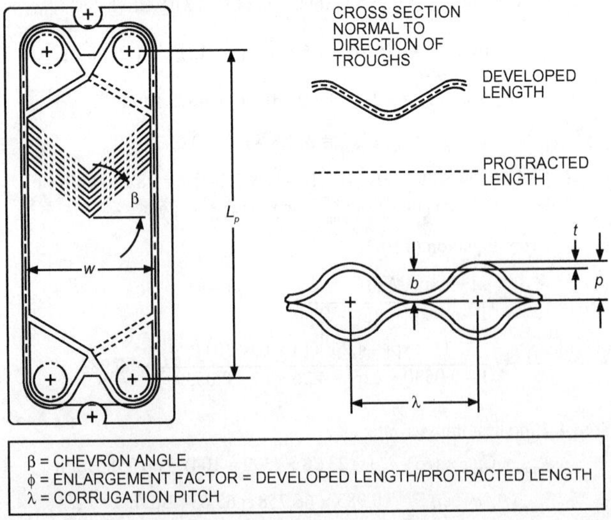

Fig. 25 Plate Parameters

Solution: The Heavner et al. (1993) correlation in Table 11 is used. It is assumed the wort is cooled to 122°F, and its average bulk temperature is 158°F. The water is assumed to be heated to 140°F, and its average bulk temperature is 104°F. The plate temperature for both fluids is assumed to be 131°F. The needed properties at these temperatures are looked up [e.g., in Wasmund (1975)] for wort at 158°F: ρ = 61.05 lb$_m$/ft³, μ = 2.715 × 10^{-4} lb$_m$/ft·s, c_p = 1.00 Btu/lb$_m$·°F, k = 0.383 Btu/h·ft·°F, and Pr = 2.56. For water at 104°F, the properties are ρ = 61.93 lb$_m$/ft³, μ = 4.388 × 10^{-4} lb$_m$/ft·s, c_p = 0.998 Btu/lb$_m$·°F, k = 0.365 Btu/h·ft·°F, and Pr = 4.34. For the wall at 131°F, μ_w = 3.387 × 10^{-4} lb$_m$/ft·s.

Values based on the heat exchanger dimensions are $b = p - t$ = 0.354 in., $A_x = bw$ = (0.354/12 ft)(1.64 ft) = 0.0484 ft², and $d_e = 2b/\phi$ = 0.5717 in. Heat transfer area $A_{HX} = N_pL_pw\phi$ = 667 ft². Flow cross section for both fluids is $A_c = (N_p/2)A_x$ = 2.422 ft². From the table for the correlation at β = 45°, C_1 = 0.195 and m = 0.692. For both fluids, $G = \dot{m}/A_c$ = 36.34 lb$_m$/ft²·s.

The heat transfer coefficient on the wort side is determined first:

$$Re_t = Gd_e/\mu = 6388$$

$$Nu = C_1\phi^{1-m}Re^m Pr^{0.5}(\mu/\mu_w)^{0.17} = 138.0$$

$$h_{wort} = Nuk/d_e = 895.2 \text{ Btu/h·ft}^2\text{·°F}$$

Similarly, the heat transfer coefficient for the water is determined:

$$Re_t = Gd_e/\mu = 3952$$

$$Nu = C_1\phi^{1-m}Re^m Pr^{0.5}(\mu/\mu_w)^{0.17} = 107.4$$

$$h_{water} = Nuk/d_e = 663.1 \text{ Btu/h·ft}^2\text{·°F}$$

If no fouling is assumed,

$$U = (1/h_{wort} + 1/h_{water} + t/k_{plate})^{-1} = 365.1 \text{ Btu/h·ft}^2\text{·°F}$$

$$UA_{HX} = 243{,}500 \text{ Btu/°F}$$

$$NTU = UA_{HX}/(\dot{m}c_p)_{min} = UA_{HX}/(\dot{m}c_p)_{water} = 0.769$$

$$c_r = (\dot{m}c_p)_{water}/(\dot{m}c_p)_{wort} = 0.998$$

For a counterflow heat exchanger, Equation (46) gives ε = 0.435. Then,

$$q = \varepsilon(\dot{m}c_p)_{min}(t_{wort,\,in} - t_{water,\,in}) = 17.37 \times 10^6 \text{ Btu/h}$$

$$t_{wort,\,out} = t_{wort,\,in} - q/(\dot{m}c_p)_{wort} = 139.3°F$$

Heat Exchanger Transients

Determining the transient behavior of heat exchangers is increasingly important in evaluating the dynamic behavior of heating and air-conditioning systems. Many studies of counterflow and parallel flow heat exchangers have been conducted; some are listed in the Bibliography.

6. HEAT TRANSFER AUGMENTATION

As discussed by Bergles (1998, 2001), techniques applied to augment (enhance) heat transfer can be classified as passive (requiring no direct application of external power) or active (requiring external power). Passive techniques include rough surfaces, extended surfaces, displaced promoters, and vortex flow devices. Active techniques include mechanical aids, surface or fluid vibration, and electrostatic fields. The effectiveness of a given augmentation technique depends largely on the mode of heat transfer or type of heat exchanger to which it is applied.

When augmentation is used, the dominant thermal resistances in the circuit should be considered. Do not invest in reducing an already low thermal resistance or increasing an already high heat transfer coefficient. Also, heat exchangers with a high NTU [number of heat exchanger transfer units; see Equation (47)] benefit little from augmentation. Finally, the increased friction factor that usually accompanies heat transfer augmentation must also be considered.

Table 11 Single-Phase Heat Transfer and Pressure Drop Correlations for Plate Exchangers

Investigator	Correlation	Comments
Troupe et al. (1960)	$\mathrm{Nu} = (0.383 - 0.505^{\,Lp/b})\,\mathrm{Re}^{0.65}\,\mathrm{Pr}^{0.4}$	$\mathrm{Re} > \mathrm{Re}_{cr}$, $10 < \mathrm{Re}_{cr} < 400$, water.
Muley and Manglik (1999)	$\mathrm{Nu} = [0.2668 - 0.006967(90-\beta) + 7.244\times10^{-5}(90-\beta)^2]$ $\times (20.78 - 50.94\phi + 41.16\phi^2 - 10.51\phi^3)$ $\times \mathrm{Re}^{0.728 - 0.0543\sin[\pi(90-\beta)/45 + 3.7]}\,\mathrm{Pr}^{1/3}(\mu/\mu_w)^{0.14}$ $f = [2.917 - 0.1277(90-\beta) + 2.016\times10^{-3}(90-\beta)^2]$ $\times (5.474 - 19.02\phi + 18.93\phi^2 - 5.341\phi^3)$ $\times \mathrm{Re}^{-\{0.2 + 0.0577\sin[\pi(90-\beta)/45] + 2.1\}}$	$\mathrm{Re} \ge 10^3$, $30 \le \beta \le 60$, $1 \le \phi \le 1.5$.
Hayes and Jokar (2009)	$\mathrm{Nu} = C\mathrm{Re}^P\,\mathrm{Pr}^{1/3}(\mu/\mu_w)^{0.14}$ $\quad f = A\,\mathrm{Re}^{-b}$	

	Water to water			Dynalene to water		
	60/60	27/60	27/27	60/60	27/60	27/27
C	0.134	0.214	0.240	0.177	0.278	0.561
P	0.712	0.698	0.724	0.744	0.745	0.726
A	1.183	1.559	3.089	0.570	21.405	3.149
b	0.095	0.079	0.060	0	0.458	0.078

Investigator	Correlation	Comments
Khan et al. (2010)	$\mathrm{Nu} = C(\beta^*)\mathrm{Re}^{P(\beta^*)}\mathrm{Pr}^{0.35}(\mu/\mu_w)^{0.14}$ $\quad f = A\,\mathrm{Re}^b$ $C(\beta^*) = 0.016\beta^* + 0.13$ $P(\beta^*) = 0.2\beta^* + 0.64$ β^* = chevron angle ratio, (β/β_{min})	$500 < \mathrm{Re} < 2500$ and $3.5 < \mathrm{Pr} < 6.0$

	Water to water		
	60°/60°	60°/30°	30°/30°
A	1.56	1.84	34.43
b	–0.24	–0.25	–0.5

Investigator	Correlation	Comments
Heavner et al. (1993)	$\mathrm{Nu} = C_1\phi^{1-m}\,\mathrm{Re}^m\,\mathrm{Pr}^{0.5}(\mu/\mu_w)^{0.17}$ $f = C_2\phi^{p+1}\,\mathrm{Re}^{-p}$ C_1, C_2, m, and p are constants and given as	$400 < \mathrm{Re} < 10{,}000$, $3.3 < \mathrm{Pr} < 5.9$, water chevron plate ($0° \le \beta \le 67°$).

β	β_{avg}	C_1	m	C_2	p
67/67	67	0.089	0.718	0.490	0.1814
67/45	56	0.118	0.720	0.545	0.1555
67/0	33.5	0.308	0.667	1.441	0.1353
45/45	45	0.195	0.692	0.687	0.1405
45/0	22.5	0.278	0.683	1.458	0.0838

Investigator	Correlation	Comments
Wanniarachchi et al. (1995)	$\mathrm{Nu} = (\mathrm{Nu}_1{}^3 + \mathrm{Nu}_t{}^3)^{1/3}\,\mathrm{Pr}^{1/3}(\mu/\mu_w)^{0.17}$ $\mathrm{Nu}_1 = 3.65\beta^{-0.455}\phi^{0.661}\,\mathrm{Re}^{0.339}$ $\mathrm{Nu}_t = 12.6\beta^{-1.142}\phi^{1-m}\,\mathrm{Re}^m$ $m = 0.646 + 0.0011\beta$ $f = (f_1{}^3 + f_t^3)^{1/3}$ $f_1 = 1774\beta^{-1.026}\phi^2\,\mathrm{Re}^{-1}$ $f_t = 46.6\beta^{-1.08}\phi^{1+p}\,\mathrm{Re}^{-p}$ $p = 0.00423\beta + 0.0000223\beta^2$	$1 \le \mathrm{Re} \le 10^4$, herringbone plates ($20° \le \beta \le 62$, $\beta > 62° = 62°$).

Source: Ayub (2003).

Passive Techniques

Finned-Tube Coils. Heat transfer coefficients for finned coils follow the basic equations of convection, condensation, and evaporation. The fin arrangement affects the values of constants and exponential powers in the equations. It is generally necessary to refer to test data for the exact coefficients.

For natural-convection finned coils (gravity coils), approximate coefficients can be obtained by considering the coil to be made of tubular and vertical fin surfaces at different temperatures and then applying the natural-convection equations to each. This is difficult because the natural-convection coefficient depends on the temperature difference, which varies at different points on the fin.

Fin efficiency should be high (80 to 90%) for optimum natural-convection heat transfer. A low fin efficiency reduces temperatures near the tip. This reduces Δt near the tip and also the coefficient h, which in natural convection depends on Δt. The coefficient of heat transfer also decreases as fin spacing decreases because of interfering convection currents from adjacent fins and reduced free-flow passage; 2 to 4 in. spacing is common. Generally, high coefficients result from large temperature differences and small flow restriction.

Edwards and Chaddock (1963) give coefficients for several circular fin-on-tube arrangements, using fin spacing δ as the characteristic length and in the form $\mathrm{Nu} = f(\mathrm{Ra}_\delta, \delta/D_o)$, where D_o is the fin diameter.

Forced-convection finned coils are used extensively in a wide variety of equipment. Fin efficiency for optimum performance is smaller than that for gravity coils because the forced-convection coefficient is almost independent of the temperature difference between surface and fluid. Very low fin efficiencies should be avoided because an inefficient surface gives a high (uneconomical) pressure drop. An efficiency of 70 to 90% is often used.

As fin spacing is decreased to obtain a large surface area for heat transfer, the coefficient generally increases because of higher air velocity between fins at the same face velocity and reduced equivalent diameter. The limit is reached when the boundary layer formed on one fin surface (see Figure 19) begins to interfere with the boundary layer formed on the adjacent fin surface, resulting in a decrease of the heat transfer coefficient, which may offset the advantage of larger surface area.

Selection of fin spacing for forced-convection finned coils usually depends on economic and practical considerations, such as fouling, frost formation, condensate drainage, cost, weight, and volume. Fins for conventional coils generally are spaced 6 to 14 per inch, except where factors such as frost formation necessitate wider spacing.

There are several ways to obtain higher coefficients with a given air velocity and surface, usually by creating air turbulence, generally with a higher pressure drop: (1) staggered tubes instead of in-line tubes for multiple-row coils; (2) artificial additional tubes, or collars or fingers made by forming the fin materials; (3) corrugated fins instead of plane fins; and (4) louvered or interrupted fins.

Figure 26 shows data for one-row coils. Thermal resistances plotted include the temperature drop through the fins, based on one square foot of total external surface area.

Internal Enhancement. Several examples of tubes with internal roughness or fins are shown in Figure 27. Rough surfaces of the spiral repeated rib variety are widely used to improve in-tube heat transfer with water, as in flooded chillers. Roughness may be produced by spirally indenting the outer wall, forming the inner wall, or inserting coils. Longitudinal or spiral internal fins in tubes can be produced by extrusion or forming and substantially increase surface area. Efficiency of extruded fins can usually be taken as unity (see the section on Fin Efficiency). Twisted strips (vortex flow devices) can be inserted as original equipment or as a retrofit (Manglik and Bergles 2002). From a practical point of view, the twisted tape width should be such that the tape can be easily inserted or removed. Ayub and Al-Fahed (1993) discuss clearance between the twisted tape and tube inside dimension.

Microfin tubes (internally finned tubes with about 60 short fins around the circumference) are widely used in refrigerant evaporation and condensers. Because gas entering the condenser in vapor-compression refrigeration is superheated, a portion of the condenser that desuperheats the flow is single phase. Some data on single-phase performance of microfin tubes, showing considerably higher heat transfer coefficients than for plain tubes, are available [e.g., Al-Fahed et al. (1993); Khanpara et al. (1986)], but the upper Reynolds numbers of about 10,000 are lower than those found in practice. ASHRAE research [e.g., Eckels (2003)] is addressing this deficiency.

The increased friction factor in microfin tubes may not require increased pumping power if the flow rate can be adjusted or the length of the heat exchanger reduced. Nelson and Bergles (1986) discuss performance evaluation criteria, especially for HVAC applications.

In chilled-water systems, fouling may, in some cases, seriously reduce the overall heat transfer coefficient U. In general, fouled enhanced tubes perform better than fouled plain tubes, as shown in studies of scaling caused by cooling tower water (Knudsen and Roy 1983) and particulate fouling (Somerscales et al. 1991). A comprehensive review of fouling with enhanced surfaces is presented by Somerscales and Bergles (1997).

Fire-tube boilers are frequently fitted with turbulators to improve the turbulent convective heat transfer coefficient (addressing the dominant thermal resistance). Also, because of high gas temperatures, radiation from the convectively heated insert to the tube wall can represent as much as 50% of the total heat transfer. (Note, however, that the magnitude of convective contribution decreases as the radiative contribution increases because of the reduced temperature difference.) Two commercial bent-strip inserts, a twisted-strip insert, and a simple bent-tab insert are depicted in Figure 28. Design equations for convection only are included in Table 12. Beckermann and Goldschmidt (1986) present procedures to include radiation, and Junkhan et al. (1985, 1988) give friction factor data and performance evaluations.

Enhanced Surfaces for Gases. Several such surfaces are depicted in Figure 29. The offset strip fin is an example of an interrupted fin that is often found in compact plate fin heat exchangers used for heat

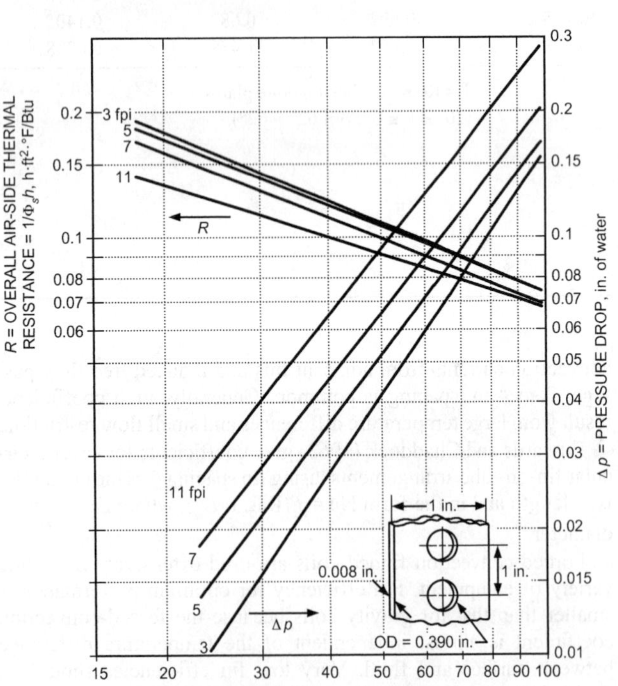

Fig. 26 Overall Air-Side Thermal Resistance and Pressure Drop for One-Row Coils
(Shepherd 1946)

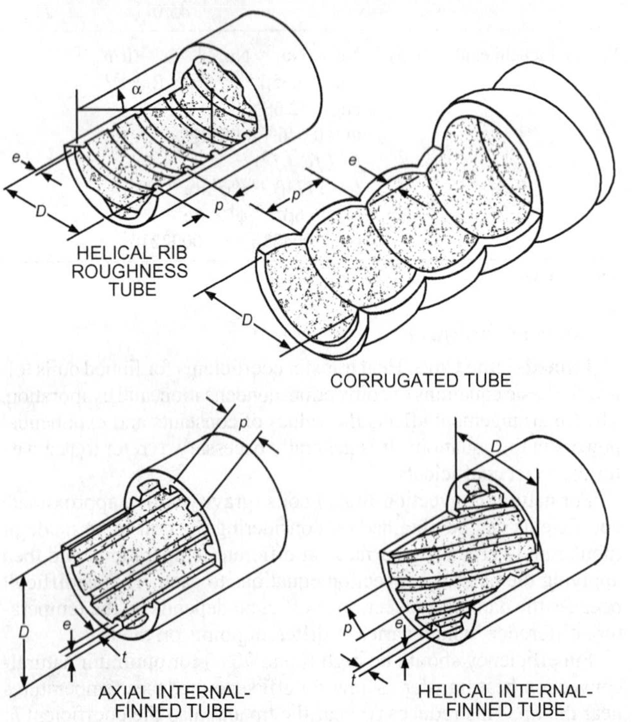

Fig. 27 Typical Tube-Side Enhancements

recovery from exhaust air. Design equations in Table 12 apply to laminar and transitional flow as well as to turbulent flow, which is a necessary feature because the small hydraulic diameter of these surfaces drives the Reynolds number down. Data for other surfaces (wavy, spine, louvered, etc.) are available in the References.

Microchannel Heat Exchangers. Microchannels for heat transfer enhancement are widely used, particularly for compact heat exchangers in automotive, aerospace, fuel cell, and high-flux electronic cooling applications. Bergles (1964) demonstrated the potential of narrow passages for heat transfer enhancement; more recent experimental and numerical work includes Adams et al. (1998), Costa et al. (1985), Kandlikar (2002), Ohadi et al. (2008), Pei et al. (2001), and Rin et al. (2006).

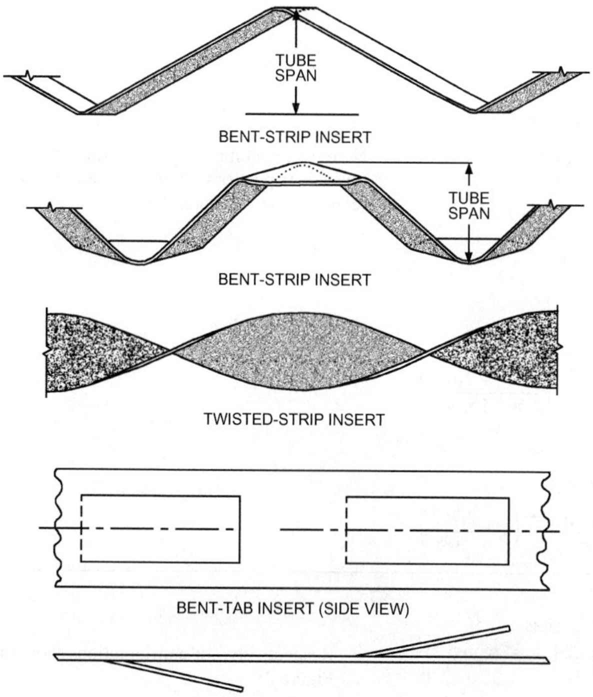

Fig. 28 Turbulators for Fire-Tube Boilers

Compared with channels of normal size, microchannels have many advantages. When properly designed, they can offer substantially higher heat transfer rates (because of their greater heat transfer surface area per unit volume and a large surface-to-volume ratio) and reduced pressure drops and pumping power requirements when compared to conventional mini- and macrochannels. Optimum flow delivery to the channels and proper heat transfer surface/channel design is critical to optimum operation of microchannels (Ohadi et al. 2012). This feature allows heat exchangers to be compact and lightweight. Despite their thin walls, microchannels can withstand high operating pressures: for example, a microchannel with a hydraulic diameter of 0.03 in. and a wall thickness of 0.012 in. can easily withstand operating pressures of up to 2030 psi. This feature makes microchannels particularly suitable for use with high-pressure refrigerants such as carbon dioxide (CO_2). For high-flux electronics (with heat flux at 1 kW/cm^2 or higher), microchannels can provide cooling with small temperature gradients (Ohadi et al. 2008). Microchannels have been used for both single-phase and phase-change heat transfer applications.

Drawbacks of microchannels include large pressure drop, high cost of manufacture, dirt clogging, and flow maldistribution, especially for two-phase flows. Most of these weaknesses, however, may be solved by optimizing design of the surface and the heat exchanger manifold and feed system.

Microchannels are fabricated by a variety of processes, depending on the dimensions and plate material (e.g., metals, plastics, silicon). Conventional machining and electrical discharge machining are two typical options; semiconductor fabrication processes are appropriate for microchannel fabrication in chip-cooling applications. Using microfabrication techniques developed by the electronics industry, three-dimensional structures as small as 0.1 μm long can be manufactured.

Fluid flow and heat transfer in microchannels may be substantially different from those encountered in the conventional tubes. Early research indicates that deviations might be particularly important for microchannels with hydraulic diameters less than 100 μm.

Recent Progress. The automotive, aerospace, and cryogenic industries have made major progress in compact evaporator development. Thermal duty and energy efficiency have substantially increased, and space constraints have become more important, encouraging greater heat transfer rates per unit volume. The hot side of the evaporators in these applications is generally air, gas, or a condensing vapor. Air-side fin geometry improvements derive from

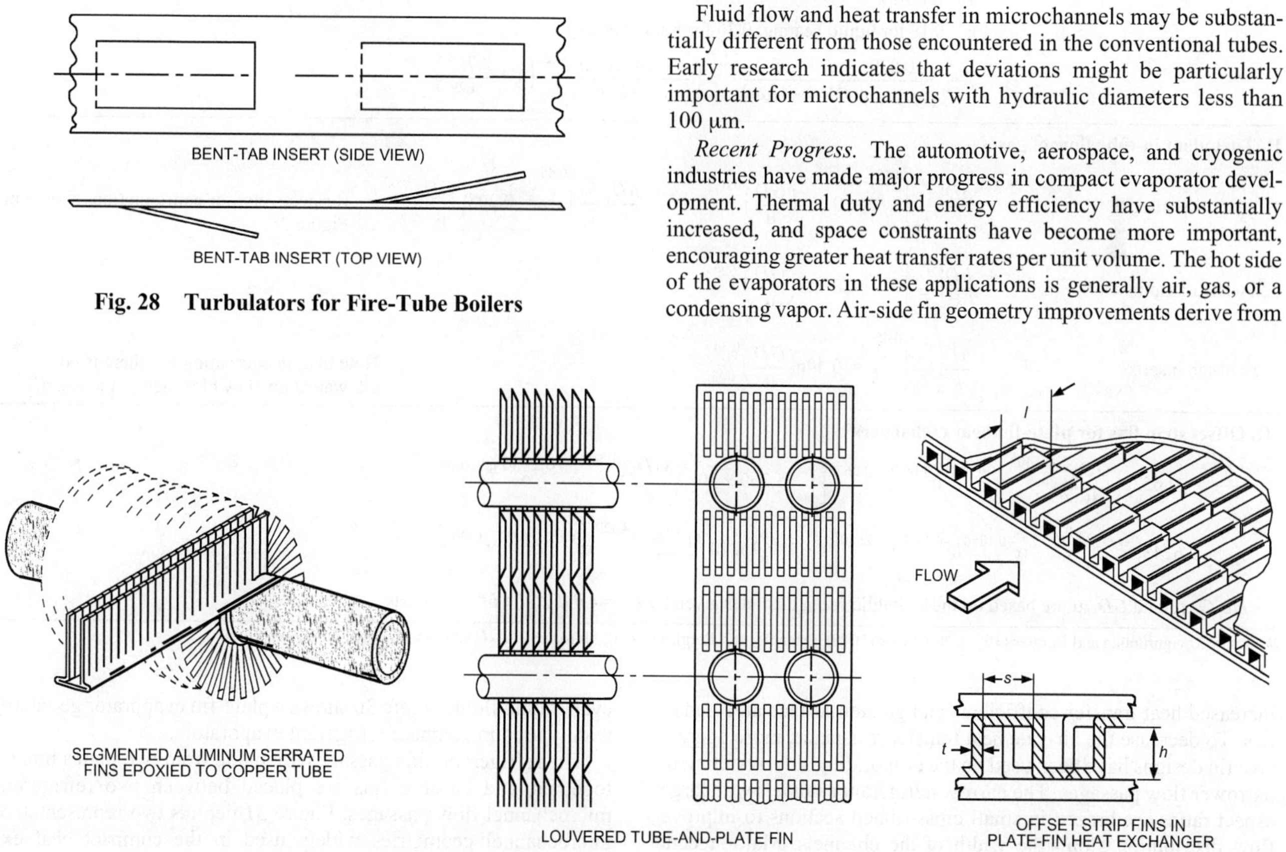

Fig. 29 Enhanced Surfaces for Gases

Table 12 Equations for Augmented Forced Convection (Single Phase)

Description	Equation	Comments
I. Turbulent in-tube flow of liquids		
Spiral repeated rib[a]	$\frac{h_a}{h_s} = \left\{\left[1 + 2.64\,\text{Re}^{0.036}\left(\frac{e}{d}\right)^{0.212}\left(\frac{p}{d}\right)^{-0.21}\left(\frac{\alpha}{90}\right)^{0.29}\text{Pr}^{-0.024}\right]^7\right\}^{1/7}$	$\text{Re} = GD/\mu$, where $G = \dot{m}/A_x$
	$\frac{f_a}{f_s} = \left\{1 + 29.1\left[\text{Re}^{w}\left(\frac{e}{d}\right)^{x}\left(\frac{p}{d}\right)^{y}\left(\frac{\alpha}{90}\right)^{z}\left(1 + \frac{2.94}{n}\right)\sin\beta\right]^{15/16}\right\}^{16/15}$	
	$w = 0.67 - 0.06(p/d) - 0.49(\alpha/90)$	
	$x = 1.37 - 0.157(p/d)$	
	$y = -1.66 \times 10^{-6}\,\text{Re} - 0.33\alpha/90$	
	$z = 4.59 + 4.11 \times 10^{-6}\,\text{Re} - 0.15(p/d)$	
	$h_s = \frac{(k/D)(f_s/2)\text{Re Pr}}{1 + 12.7(f_s/2)^{1/2}(\text{Pr}^{2/3} - 1)}$	
	$f_s = (1.58 \ln \text{Re} - 3.28)^{-2}$	
Fins[b]	$\frac{hD_h}{k} = 0.023\,\text{Pr}^{0.4}\left(\frac{GD_h}{\mu}\right)^{0.8}\left(\frac{A_F}{AF_i}\right)^{0.1}\left(\frac{A_i}{A}\right)^{0.5}(\sec\alpha)^3$	Note that, in computing Re for fins and twisted-strip inserts, there is allowance for reduced cross-sectional area.
	$f_h = 0.046\left(\frac{GD_h}{\mu}\right)^{-0.2}\left(\frac{A_F}{AF_i}\right)^{0.5}(\sec\alpha)^{0.75}$	
Twisted-strip inserts[c]	$\frac{(hd/k)}{(hd/k)_{y\to\infty}} = 1 + 0.769/y$	
	$\left(\frac{hd}{k}\right)_{y\to\infty} = 0.023\left(\frac{GD}{\mu}\right)^{0.8}\text{Pr}^{0.4}\left(\frac{\pi}{\pi - 4\delta/d}\right)^{0.8}\left(\frac{\pi + 2 - 2\delta/d}{\pi - 4\delta/d}\right)^{0.2}\phi$	
	$\phi = (\mu_b/\mu_w)^n$	
	$n = 0.18$ for liquid heating, 0.30 for liquid cooling	
	$f = \frac{0.0791}{(GD/\mu)^{0.25}}\left(\frac{\pi}{\pi - 4\delta/d}\right)^{1.75}\left(\frac{\pi + 2 - 2\delta/d}{\pi - 4\delta/d}\right)^{1.25}\left(1 + \frac{2.752}{y^{1.29}}\right)$	
II. Turbulent in-tube flow of gases		
Bent-strip inserts[d]	$\frac{hD}{k}\left(\frac{T_w}{T_b}\right)^{0.45} = 0.258\left(\frac{GD}{\mu}\right)^{0.6}$ or $\frac{hD}{k}\left(\frac{T_w}{T_b}\right)^{0.45} = 0.208\left(\frac{GD}{\mu}\right)^{0.63}$	Respectively, for configurations shown in Figure 28.
Twisted-strip inserts[d]	$\frac{hD}{k}\left(\frac{T_w}{T_b}\right)^{0.45} = 0.122\left(\frac{GD}{\mu}\right)^{0.65}$	
Bent-tab inserts[d]	$\frac{hD}{k}\left(\frac{T_w}{T_b}\right)^{0.45} = 0.406\left(\frac{GD}{\mu}\right)^{0.54}$	Note that, in computing Re, there is no allowance for flow blockage of the insert.
III. Offset strip fins for plate-fin heat exchangers[e]		
	$\frac{h}{c_pG} = 0.6522\left(\frac{GD_h}{\mu}\right)^{-0.5403}\alpha^{-0.1541}\delta^{0.1499}\gamma^{-0.0678}\left[1 + 5.269 \times 10^{-5}\left(\frac{GD_h}{\mu}\right)^{1.340}\alpha^{0.504}\delta^{0.456}\gamma^{-1.055}\right]^{0.1}$	
	$f_h = 9.6243\left(\frac{GD_h}{\mu}\right)^{-0.7422}\alpha^{-0.1856}\delta^{-0.3053}\gamma^{-0.2659}\left[1 + 7.669 \times 10^{-8}\left(\frac{GD_h}{\mu}\right)^{4.429}\alpha^{0.920}\delta^{3.767}\gamma^{0.236}\right]^{0.1}$	
	h/c_pG, f_h, and GD_h/μ are based on the hydraulic mean diameter given by $D_h = 4shl/[2(sl + hl + th) + ts]$	

Sources: [a]Ravigururajan and Bergles (1985), [b]Carnavos (1979), [c]Manglik and Bergles (1993), [d]Junkhan et al. (1985), [e]Manglik and Bergles (1990).

increased heat transfer coefficients and greater surface area densities. To decrease the air-side heat transfer resistance, more aggressive fin designs have been used on the evaporating side, resulting in narrower flow passages. The narrow refrigerant channels with large aspect ratios are brazed in small cross-ribbed sections to improve flow distribution along the width of the channels. Major recent changes in designs involve individual, small-hydraulic-diameter flow passages, arranged in multichannel configuration for the evaporating fluid. Figure 30 shows a plate-fin evaporator geometry widely used in compact refrigerant evaporators.

The refrigerant-side passages are made from two plates brazed together, and air-side fins are placed between two refrigerant microchannel flow passages. Figure 31 depicts two representative microchannel geometries widely used in the compact heat exchanger industry, with corresponding approximate nominal dimensions provided in Table 13 (Zhao et al. 2000).

Plastic heat exchangers have been suggested for HVAC applications (Pescod 1980) and are being manufactured for refrigerated sea water (RSW) applications. They can be made of materials impervious to corrosion [e.g., by acidic condensate when cooling a gaseous stream (flue gas heat recovery)], and are easily manufactured with enhanced surfaces. Several companies now offer heat exchangers in plastic, including various enhancements.

Active Techniques

Unlike passive techniques, active techniques require external power to sustain the enhancement mechanism.

Table 14 lists the more common active heat transfer augmentation techniques and the corresponding heat transfer mode believed most applicable to the particular technique. Various active techniques and their world-wide status are listed in Table 15. Except for mechanical aids, which are universally used for selected applications, most other active techniques have found limited commercial applications and are still in development. However, with increasing demand for smart and miniaturized thermal management systems, actively controlled heat transfer augmentation techniques will soon become necessary for some advanced thermal management systems. All-electric ships, airplanes, and cars use electronics for propulsion, auxiliary systems, sensors, countermeasures, and other system needs. Advances in power electronics and control systems will allow optimized and tactical allocation of total installed power among system components.

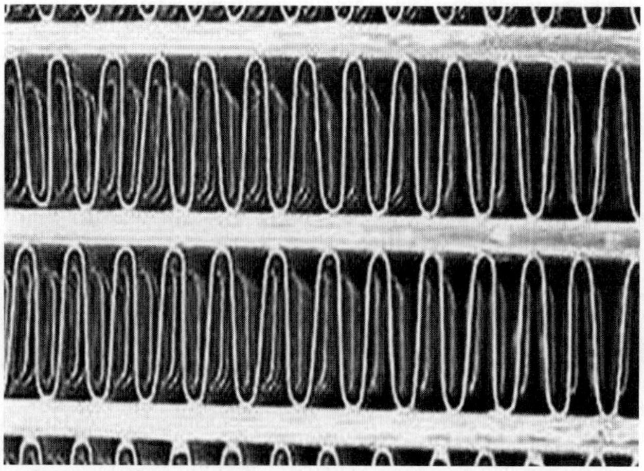

Fig. 30 Typical Refrigerant and Air-Side Flow Passages in Compact Automotive Microchannel Heat Exchanger

Table 13 Microchannel Dimensions

	Microchannel I	Microchannel II
Channel geometry	Rectangular	Triangular
Hydraulic diameter D_h, in.	0.028	0.034
Number of channels	28	25
Length L, in.	11.8	11.8
Height H, in.	0.059	0.075
Width W, in.	1.1	1.07
Wall thickness, in.	0.016	0.012

Table 14 Active Heat Transfer Augmentation Techniques and Most Relevant Heat Transfer Modes

	Heat Transfer Mode					
	Forced Convection					
Technique	(Gases)	(Liquids)	Boiling	Evaporation	Condensation	Mass Transfer
Mechanical aids	NA	**	*	*	NA	**
Surface vibration	**	**	**	**	**	***
Fluid vibration	**	**	**	**	—	**
Electrostatic/electrohydrodynamic	**	**	***	***	***	***
Suction/injection	*	**	NA	NA	**	**
Jet impingement	**	**	NA	**	NA	*
Rotation	*	*	***	***	***	***
Induced flow	**	**	NA	NA	NA	*

*** = Highly significant ** = Significant * = Somewhat significant
— = Not significant NA = Not believed to be applicable

Table 15 Worldwide Status of Active Techniques

Technique	Country or Countries
Mechanical aids	Universally used in selected applications (e.g., fluid mixers, liquid injection jets)
Surface vibration	Most recent work in United States; not significant
Fluid vibration	Sweden; mostly used for sonic cleaning
Electrostatic/electrohydrodynamic	Japan, United States, United Kingdom; successful prototypes demonstrated
Other electrical methods	United Kingdom, France, United States
Suction/injection	No recent significant developments
Jet impingement	France, United States; high-temperature units and aerospace applications
Rotation	United States (industry), United Kingdom (R&D)
Induced flow	United States; particularly combustion

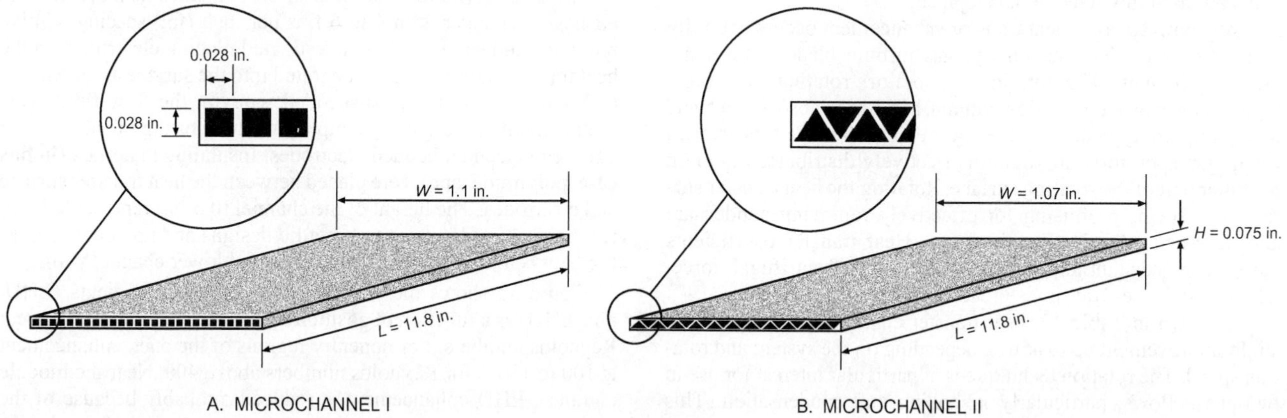

Fig. 31 Microchannel Dimensions

This in turn will require smart (online/on-demand), compact heat exchangers and thermal management systems that can communicate and respond to transient system needs. This section briefly overviews active techniques and recent progress; for additional details, see Ohadi et al. (1996).

Mechanical Aids. Augmentation by mechanical aids involves stirring the fluid mechanically. Heat exchangers that use mechanical enhancements are often called **mechanically assisted heat exchangers**. Stirrers and mixers that scrape the surface are extensively used in chemical processing of highly viscous fluids, such as blending a flow of highly viscous plastic with air. Surface scraping can also be applied to duct flow of gases. Hagge and Junkhan (1974) reported tenfold improvement in the heat transfer coefficient for laminar airflow over a flat plate. Table 16 lists selected works on mechanical aids, suction, and injection.

Injection. This method involves supplying a gas to a flowing liquid through a porous heat transfer surface or injecting a fluid of a similar type upstream of the heat transfer test section. Injected bubbles produce an agitation similar to that of nucleate boiling. Gose et al. (1957) bubbled gas through sintered or drilled heated surfaces and found that the heat transfer coefficient increased 500% in laminar flow and about 50% in turbulent flow. Tauscher et al. (1970) demonstrated up to a fivefold increase in local heat transfer coefficients by injecting a similar fluid into a turbulent tube flow, but the effect dies out at a length-to-diameter ratio of 10. Practical application of injection appears to be rather limited because of difficulty in cost-effectively supplying and removing the injection fluid.

Suction. The suction method involves removing fluid through a porous heated surface, thus reducing heat/mass transfer resistance at the surface. Kinney (1968) and Kinney and Sparrow (1970) reported that applying suction at the surface increased heat transfer coefficients for laminar film and turbulent flows, respectively. Jeng et al. (1995) conducted experiments on a vertical parallel channel with asymmetric, isothermal walls. A porous wall segment was embedded in a segment of the test section wall, and enhancement occurred as hot air was sucked from the channel. The local heat transfer coefficient increased with increasing porosity. The maximum heat transfer enhancement obtained was 140%.

Fluid or Surface Vibration. Fluid or surface vibrations occur naturally in most heat exchangers; however, naturally occurring vibration is rarely factored into thermal design. Vibration equipment is expensive, and power consumption is high. Depending on frequency and amplitude of vibration, forced convection from a wire to air is enhanced by up to 300% (Nesis et al. 1994). Using standing waves in a fluid reduced input power by 75% compared with a fan that provided the same heat transfer rate (Woods 1992). Lower frequencies are preferable because they consume less power and are less harmful to users' hearing. Vibration has not found industrial applications at this stage of development.

Rotation. Rotation heat transfer enhancement occurs naturally in rotating electrical machinery, gas turbine blades, and some other equipment. The rotating evaporator, rotating heat pipe, high-performance distillation column, and Rotex absorption cycle heat pump are typical examples of previous work in this area. In rotating evaporators, the rotation effectively distributes liquid on the outer part of the rotating surface. Rotating the heat transfer surface also seems promising for effectively removing condensate and decreasing liquid film thickness. Heat transfer coefficients have been substantially increased by using centrifugal force, which may be several times greater than the gravity force.

As shown in Table 17, heat transfer enhancement varies from slight improvement up to 450%, depending on the system and rotation speed. The rotation technique is of particular interest for use in two-phase flows, particularly in boiling and condensation. This technique is not effective in gas-to-gas heat recovery mode in laminar flow, but its application is more likely in turbulent flow. High power consumption, sealing and vibration problems, moving parts, and the expensive equipment required for rotation are some of this technique's drawbacks.

Electrohydrodynamics. Electrohydrodynamic (EHD) enhancement of single-phase heat transfer refers to coupling an electric field with the fluid field in a dielectric fluid medium. The net effect is production of secondary motions that destabilize the thermal boundary layer near the heat transfer surface, leading to heat transfer coefficients that are often an order of magnitude higher than those achievable by most conventional enhancement techniques. EHD heat transfer enhancement has applicability to both single-phase and phase-change heat transfer processes, although only enhancement of single-phase flows is discussed here.

Selected work in EHD enhancement of single-phase flow is shown in Table 18. High enhancement magnitudes have been found for single-phase air and liquid flows. However, high enhancement magnitude is not enough to warrant practical implementation. EHD electrodes must be compatible with cost-effective, mass-production technologies, and power consumption must be kept low, to minimize the required power supply cost and complexity.

The following brief overview discusses recent work on EHD enhancement of air-side heat transfer; additional details are in Ohadi et al. (2001).

EHD Air-Side Heat Transfer Augmentation. In a typical liquid-to-air heat exchanger, air-side thermal resistance is often the limiting factor to improving the overall heat transfer coefficient. Electrohydrodynamic enhancement of air-side heat transfer involves ionizing air molecules under a high-voltage, low-current electric field, leading to generation of secondary motions that are known as **corona** or **ionic wind**, generated between the charged electrode and receiving (ground) electrode. Typical wind velocities of 200 to 600 fpm have been verified experimentally. Studies of this enhancement method include Ohadi et al. (1991), who studied laminar and turbulent forced-convection heat transfer of air in tube flow, and Owsenek and Seyed-Yagoobi (1995), who investigated heat transfer augmentation of natural convection with the corona wind effect. Other studies are documented in Ohadi et al. (2001). The general finding has been that corona wind is effective for Reynolds numbers up to transitional values, 2300 or less, and becomes less effective as Re increases. At high Reynolds numbers, turbulence-induced effects overwhelm the corona wind effect.

Most studies addressed EHD air-side enhancement in classical geometries, but recent work has focused on issues of practical significance. These include (1) EHD applicability in highly compact heat exchangers, (2) electrode designs to minimize power consumptions to avoid joule heating and costly power supply requirements, and (3) cost-effective mass production of EHD-enhanced surfaces.

Lawler et al. (2002) examined air-side enhancement of an air-to-air heat exchanger with 4 to 6 fins per inch (fpi) spacing. Unlike previous studies, this study investigated placing electrodes on the heat transfer surface itself, integrated into the surface as an embedded wire, thus avoiding suspended wires in the flow field. This arrangement could greatly simplify manufacturing/fabrication for EHD-enhanced embedded electrodes. Insulating materials (in this case, polyimide tape) were placed between the heat transfer surface and electrodes. The height of the channel (0.3 in.) represented typical heights used in passive metallic designs and prevented sparking between the electrodes and upper and lower channel walls.

Figure 32 shows the ratio of heat transfer coefficients (EHD/non-EHD) as a function of position in the module for three different Reynolds numbers. For nonentry regions of the duct, enhancement is 100 to 150% for Reynolds numbers above 400. Near the module entrance, EHD enhancement is reduced, probably because of the higher heat transfer coefficient in the entry region, before viscous and thermal boundary layers have been established.

Table 16 Selected Studies on Mechanical Aids, Suction, and Injection

Source	Process	Heat Transfer Surface	Fluid	α_{max}
Valencia et al. (1996)	Natural convection	Finned tube	Air	0.5
Jeng et al. (1995)	Natural convection/ suction	Asymmetric isothermal wall	Air	1.4
Inagaki and Komori (1993)	Turbulent natural convection/suction	Vertical plate	Air	1.8
Dhir et al. (1992)	Forced convection/ injection	Tube	Air	1.45
Duignan et al. (1993)	Forced convection/film boiling	Horizontal plate	Air	2.0
Son and Dhir (1993)	Forced convection/ injection	Annuli	Air	1.85
Malhotra and Majumdar (1991)	Water to bed/stirring	Granular bed	Air	3.0
Aksan and Borak (1987)	Pool of water/stirring	Tube coils	Water	1.7
Hagge and Junkhan (1974)	Forced convection/ scraping	Cylindrical wall	Air	11.0
Hu and Shen (1996)	Turbulent natural convection	Converging ribbed tube	Air	1.0

α = Enhancement factor (ratio of enhanced to unenhanced heat transfer coefficient)

Table 17 Selected Studies on Rotation

Source	Process	Heat Transfer Surface	Fluid	Rotational Speed, rpm	α_{max}
Prakash and Zerle (1995)	Natural convection	Ribbed duct	Air	Given as a function	1.3
Mochizuki et al. (1994)	Natural convection	Serpentine duct	Air	Given as a function	3.0
Lan (1991)	Solidification	Vertical tube	Water	400	NA
McElhiney and Preckshot (1977)	External condensation	Horizontal tube	Steam	40	1.7
Nichol and Gacesa (1970)	External condensation	Vertical cylinder	Steam	2700	4.5
Astaf'ev and Baklastov (1970)	External condensation	Circular disk	Steam	2500	3.4
Tang and McDonald (1971)	Nucleate boiling	Horizontal heated circular cylinder	R-113	1400	<1.2
Marto and Gray (1971)	In-tube boiling	Vertical heated circular cylinder	Water	2660	1.6

α = Enhancement factor (ratio of enhanced to unenhanced heat transfer coefficient)

Table 18 Selected Previous Work with EHD Enhancement of Single-Phase Heat Transfer

Source	Process	Heat Transfer Surface/ Electrode	Fluid	P/Q, %	α_{max}
Poulter and Allen (1986)	Internal flow	Tube/wire	Aviation fuel-hexane	NA	20
Fernandez and Poulter (1987)	Internal flow	Tube/wire	Transformer oil	NA	23
Ohadi et al. (1995)	Internal flow	Smooth surface/rod	PAO	1.2	3.2
Ohadi et al. (1991)	Internal flow	Tube/wire	Air	15	3.2

NA = Not available
P = EHD power consumption
Q = Heat exchange rate in the heat exchanger
α = Enhancement factor (ratio of enhanced to unenhanced heat transfer coefficient)

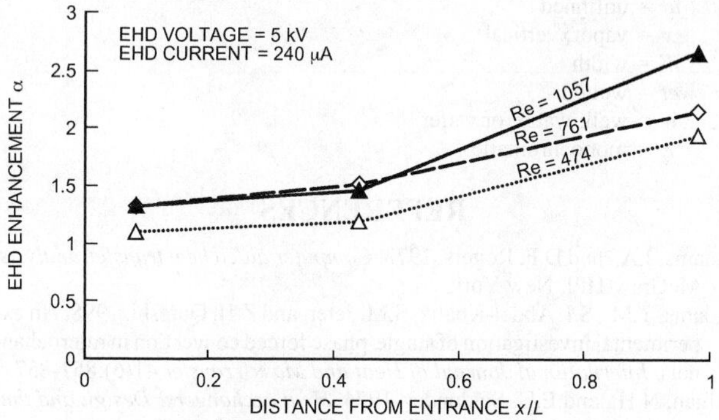

Fig. 32 Ratio of Heat Transfer Coefficient with EHD to Coefficient Without EHD as Function of Distance from Front of Module

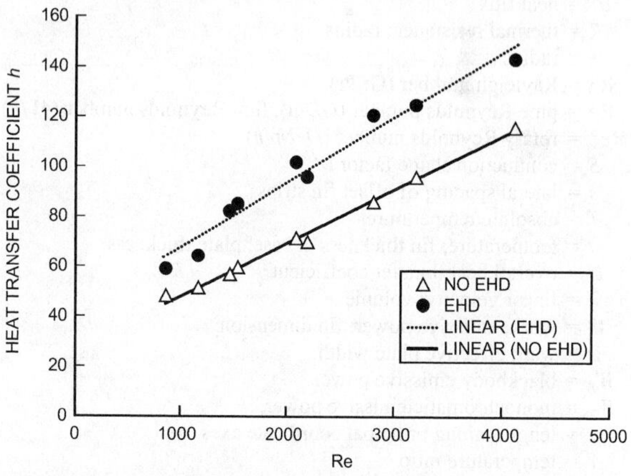

Fig. 33 Heat Transfer Coefficients (With and Without EHD) as Functions of Reynolds Number

Tests for a 6 fpi finned heat exchanger obtained comparable enhancements for Reynolds numbers up to 4000. The results are shown in Figure 33. At higher Re, the effect of EHD enhancement diminishes, as turbulence-induced enhancements predominate.

EHD can also be used for other process control applications, including frost control, enhancing liquid/vapor separation for flow maldistribution control in heat exchangers, and oil separation in heat exchanger equipment. ASHRAE has recently sponsored three EHD research projects: (1) EHD-enhanced boiling of refrigerants (Seyed-Yagoobi 1997), (2) EHD frost control in HVAC&R equipment (Ohadi 2002), and (3) EHD flow maldistribution control in heat exchangers (Seyed-Yagoobi and Feng 2005). Reports for these projects are available through ASHRAE headquarters.

7. SYMBOLS

A = surface area for heat transfer

A_F, A_x = cross-sectional flow area
b = flow channel gap
Bi = Biot number (hL/k)
C = conductance; fluid capacity rate
c = coefficient; constant
C_1, C_2 = Planck's law constants [see Equation (19)]
c_p = specific heat at constant pressure
c_r = capacity ratio
c_v = specific heat at constant volume
D = tube (inside) or rod diameter; diameter of vessel
d = diameter; prefix meaning differential
E = electric field
e = protuberance height
f = Fanning friction factor for single-phase flow; electric body force
F_{ij} = angle factor
Fo = Fourier number
G = mass velocity; irradiation; $\dot{m}/A_x$, in pipe Reynolds number (Table 12)
g = gravitational acceleration
Gr = Grashof number
Gz = Graetz number
H = height
h = heat transfer coefficient; offset strip fin height
I = modified Bessel function
J = radiosity
J_0 = Bessel function of the first kind, order zero
j = Colburn heat transfer factor
k = thermal conductivity
L = length; height of liquid film
l = length; length of one module of offset strip fins; liquid
M = mass; molecular weight
m = general exponent; inverse of Biot number
$\dot{m}$ = mass rate of flow
n = general number; ratio r/r_m (dimensionless distance); number of blades
NTU = number of exchanger heat transfer units
Nu = Nusselt number
P = perimeter
p = pressure; fin pitch; repeated rib pitch
Pr = Prandtl number
Q = volume flow rate
q = heat transfer rate
q'' = heat flux
R = thermal resistance; radius
r = radius
Ra = Rayleigh number (Gr Pr)
Re = pipe Reynolds number (GD/μ); film Reynolds number ($4\Gamma/h$)
Re* = rotary Reynolds number (D^2Np/h)
S = conduction shape factor
s = lateral spacing of offset fin strips
T = absolute temperature
t = temperature; fin thickness at base; plate thickness
U = overall heat transfer coefficient
V = linear velocity; volume
W = work; emissive power; fin dimension
w = wall; effective plate width
W_b = blackbody emissive power
W_λ = monochromatic emissive power
x, y, z = lengths along principal coordinate axes
Y = temperature ratio
y = one-half diametrical pitch of a twisted tape: length of 180° revolution/tube diameter

Greek

α = thermal diffusivity = $k/\rho c_p$; absorptivity; spiral angle for helical fins; aspect ratio of offset strip fins, s/h; enhancement factor: ratio of enhanced to unenhanced heat transfer coefficient (conditions remaining the same)
β = coefficient of thermal expansion; contact angle of rib profile; chevron angle, °
β^* = chevron angle ratio, (β/β_{min})
β_{min} = smaller of two chevron angles
Γ = mass flow of liquid per unit length
γ = ratio, t/s
δ = distance between fins; ratio t/l; thickness of twisted tape
ε = hemispherical emissivity; exchanger heat transfer effectiveness; dielectric constant
λ = wavelength; corrugation pitch
μ = absolute viscosity
ν = kinematic viscosity (μ/ρ), ft²/h
ϖ = eigenvalue
ρ = density; reflectance
σ = Stefan-Boltzmann constant, 0.1712×10^{-8} Btu/h·ft²·°R
τ = time; transmissivity
Φ = dimensionless fin resistance; Φ_{max} is maximum limiting value of Φ
ϕ = fin efficiency; angle; temperature correction factor; ratio of developed length to protracted length

Subscripts

a = augmented
b = blackbody; based on bulk fluid temperature
c = convection; critical; cold (fluid); cross section
cr = critical
e = equivalent; environment; exit
f = film; fin; final
g = gas
gen = internal generation
h = horizontal; hot (fluid); hydraulic
i = inlet; inside; particular surface (radiation); based on maximum inside (envelope) diameter
if = interface
iso = isothermal conditions
j = particular surface (radiation)
k = particular surface (radiation)
L = thickness
l = liquid
m = mean
n = counter variable
o = outside; outlet; overall; at base of fin
p = prime heat transfer surface; plate
r = radiation; root (fin); reduced
s = surface; secondary heat transfer surface; straight or plain; accounting for flow blockage of twisted tape
st = static (pressure)
t = temperature; terminal temperature; tip (fin)
uf = unfinned
v = vapor; vertical
W = width
wet = wetted
w = wall; water; or wafer
λ = monochromatic

REFERENCES

Adams, J.A., and D.F. Rogers. 1973. *Computer aided heat transfer analysis*. McGraw-Hill, New York.

Adams, T.M., S.I. Abdel-Khalik, S.M. Jeter, and Z.H. Qureshi. 1998. An experimental investigation of single-phase forced convection in microchannels. *International Journal of Heat and Mass Transfer* 41(6):851-857.

Afgan, N.H., and E.U. Schlunder. 1974. *Heat exchangers: Design and theory sourcebook*. McGraw-Hill, New York.

Aksan, D., and F. Borak. 1987. Heat transfer coefficients in coiled stirred tank systems. *Canadian Journal of Chemical Engineering* 65:1013-1014.

Al-Fahed, S.F., Z.H. Ayub, A.M. Al-Marafie, and B.M. Soliman. 1993. Heat transfer and pressure drop in a tube with internal microfins under turbulent water flow conditions. *Experimental Thermal and Fluid Science* 7:249-253.

Altmayer, E.F., A.J. Gadgil, F.S. Bauman, and R.C. Kammerud. 1983. Correlations for convective heat transfer from room surfaces. *ASHRAE Transactions* 89(2A):61-77. *Paper* DC-2764.

Astaf'ev, B.F., and A.M. Baklastov. 1970. Condensation of steam on a horizontal rotating disc. *Teploenergetika* 17:55-57.

Ayub, Z.H. 2003. Plate heat exchanger literature survey and new heat transfer and pressure drop correlations for refrigerant evaporators. *Heat Transfer Engineering* 24(5):3-16.

Ayub, Z.H., and S.F. Al-Fahed. 1993. The effect of gap width between horizontal tube and twisted tape on the pressure drop in turbulent water flow. *International Journal of Heat and Fluid Flow* 14(1):64-67.

Bauman, F., A. Gadgil, R. Kammerud, E. Altmayer, and M. Nansteel. 1983. Convective heat transfer in buildings. *ASHRAE Transactions* 89(1A): 215-233. *Paper* AC-2750.

Beckermann, C., and V. Goldschmidt. 1986. Heat transfer augmentation in the flueway of a water heater. *ASHRAE Transactions* 92(2B):485-495. *Paper* PO-86-11-1.

Bergles, A.E. 1964. Burnout in tubes of small diameter. ASME *Paper* 63-WA-182.

Bergles, A.E. 1998. Techniques to enhance heat transfer. In *Handbook of heat transfer*, 3rd ed., pp. 11.1-11.76. McGraw-Hill, New York.

Bergles, A.E. 2001. The implications and challenges of enhanced heat transfer for the chemical process industries. *Chemical Engineering Research and Design* 79:437-434.

Carnavos, T.C. 1979. Heat transfer performance of internally finned tubes in turbulent flow. In *Advances in enhanced heat transfer*, pp. 61-67. American Society of Mechanical Engineers, New York.

Carslaw, H.S., and J.C. Jaeger. 1959. *Conduction of heat in solids*. Oxford University Press, UK.

Churchill, S.W. 1990. Free convection around immersed bodies. In *Handbook of heat exchanger design*, G.F. Hewitt, ed. Hemisphere, New York.

Churchill, S.W., and M. Bernstein. 1977. A correlating equation for forced convection from gases and liquids to a circular cylinder in cross flow. *Journal of Heat Transfer* 99:300.

Churchill, S.W., and H.H.S. Chu. 1975a. Correlating equations for laminar and turbulent free convection from a vertical plate. *International Journal of Heat and Mass Transfer* 18(11):1323-1329.

Churchill, S.W., and H.H.S. Chu. 1975b. Correlating equations for laminar and turbulent free convection from a horizontal cylinder. *International Journal of Heat and Mass Transfer* 18(9):1049-1053.

Clausing, A.M. 1964. Thermal contact resistance in a vacuum environment. ASME *Paper* 64-HT-16, Seventh National Heat Transfer Conference.

Costa, R., R. Muller, and C. Tobias. 1985. Transport processes in narrow (capillary) channels. *AIChE Journal* 31:473-482.

Couvillion, R.J. 2004. Curve fits for Heisler chart eigenvalues. *Computers in Education Journal*. July-September.

Croft, D.R., and D.G. Lilley. 1977. *Heat transfer calculations using finite difference equations*. Applied Science, London.

Dart, D.M. 1959. Effect of fin bond on heat transfer. *ASHRAE Journal* 5:67.

Dhir, V.K., F. Chang, and G. Son. 1992. Enhancement of single-phase forced convection heat transfer in tubes and ducts using tangential flow injection. *Annual Report*. Contract 5087-260135. Gas Research Institute.

Dittus, F.W., and L.M.K. Boelter. 1930. Heat transfer in automobile radiators of the tubular type. *University of California Engineering Publication* 13:443.

Duignan, M., G. Greene, and T. Irvine. 1993. The effect of surface gas injection on film boiling heat transfer. *Journal of Heat Transfer* 115:986-992.

Eckels, P.W. 1977. Contact conductance of mechanically expanded plate finned tube heat exchangers. AIChE-ASME Heat Transfer Conference, Salt Lake City.

Eckels, S.J. 2003. Single-phase refrigerant heat transfer and pressure drop characterization of high Reynolds number flow for internally finned tubes including the effects of miscible oils (RP-1067). ASHRAE Research Project, *Final Report*.

Edwards, J.A., and J.B. Chaddock. 1963. An experimental investigation of the radiation and free-convection heat transfer from a cylindrical disk extended surface. *ASHRAE Transactions* 69:313.

Fernandez, J., and R. Poulter. 1987. Radial mass flow in electrohydrodynamically-enhanced forced heat transfer in tubes. *International Journal of Heat and Mass Transfer* 80:2125-2136.

Fujii, T., S. Koyama, and M. Fujii. 1986. Experimental study of free convection heat transfer from an inclined fine wire to air. *Proceedings of the VIII International Heat Transfer Conference*, San Francisco, vol. 3.

Gnielinski, V. 1990. Forced convection in ducts. In *Handbook of heat exchanger design*, G.F. Hewitt, ed. Hemisphere, New York.

Goldstein, R.J., E.M. Sparrow, and D.C. Jones. 1973. Natural convection mass transfer adjacent to horizontal plates. *International Journal of Heat and Mass Transfer* 16:1025.

Gose, E.E., E.E. Peterson, and A. Acrivos. 1957. On the rate of heat transfer in liquids with gas injection through the boundary layer. *Journal of Applied Physics* 28:1509.

Grigull, U., I. Straub, E. Hahne, and K. Stephan. 1982. Heat transfer. *Proceedings of the Seventh International Heat Transfer Conference*, Munich, vol. 3.

Hagge, J.K., and G.H. Junkhan. 1974. Experimental study of a method of mechanical augmentation of convective heat transfer in air. *Report* HTL3, ISU-ERI-Ames-74158, Nov. 1975. Iowa State University, Ames.

Hayes, N., and A. Jokar. 2009. Dynalene/water correlations to be used for condensation of CO_2 in brazed plate heat exchangers. *ASHRAE Transactions* 115(2):599-616. *Paper* LO-09-0570 (RP-1394).

Heavner, R.L., H. Kumar, and A.S. Wanniarachchi. 1993. Performance of an industrial heat exchanger: Effect of chevron angle. *AIChE Symposium Series* 295(89):262-267.

Hottel, H.C., and A.F. Sarofim. 1967. *Radiation transfer.* McGraw-Hill, New York.

Hu, Z., and J. Shen. 1996. Heat transfer enhancement in a converging passage with discrete ribs. *International Journal of Heat and Mass Transfer* 39(8):1719-1727.

Inagaki, T., and I. Komori. 1993. Experimental study of heat transfer enhancement in turbulent natural convection along a vertical flat plate, part 1: The effect of injection and suction. *Heat Transactions—Japanese Research* 22:387.

Incropera, F.P., D.P. DeWitt, T.L. Bergman, and A.S. Lavine. 2007. *Fundamentals of heat and mass transfer*, 6th ed. John Wiley & Sons, New York.

Jakob, M. 1949, 1957. *Heat transfer*, vols. I and II. John Wiley & Sons, New York.

Jeng, Y., J. Chen, and W. Aung. 1995. Heat transfer enhancement in a vertical channel with asymmetric isothermal walls by local blowing or suction. *International Journal of Heat and Fluid Flow* 16:25.

Junkhan, G.H., A.E. Bergles, V. Nirmalan, and T. Ravigururajan. 1985. Investigation of turbulators for fire tube boilers. *Journal of Heat Transfer* 107:354-360.

Junkhan, G.H., A.E. Bergles, V. Nirmalan, and W. Hanno. 1988. Performance evaluation of the effects of a group of turbulator inserts on heat transfer from gases in tubes. *ASHRAE Transactions* 94(2):1195-1212. *Paper* OT-88-05-5.

Kandlikar, S.G. 2002. Fundamental issues related to flow boiling in mini channels and microchannels. *Experimental Thermal and Fluid Science* 26:389-407.

Kaspareck, W.E. 1964. Measurement of thermal contact conductance between dissimilar metals in a vacuum. ASME *Paper* 64-HT-38, Seventh National Heat Transfer Conference.

Kays, W.M., and A.L. London. 1984. *Compact heat exchangers*, 3rd ed. McGraw-Hill, New York.

Khan, T.S., M.S. Khan, M.C. Chyu, and Z.H. Ayub. 2010. Experimental investigation of single phase convective heat transfer coefficient in a corrugated plate heat exchanger for multiple plate configurations. *Applied Thermal Engineering* 30(8-9):1058-1065.

Khanpara, J.C., A.E. Bergles, and M.B. Pate. 1986. Augmentation of R-113 in-tube condensation with micro-fin tubes. *Proceedings of the ASME Heat Transfer Division*, HTD 65, pp. 21-32.

Kinney, R.B. 1968. Fully developed frictional and heat transfer characteristics of laminar flow in porous tubes. *International Journal of Heat and Mass Transfer* 11:1393-1401.

Kinney, R.B., and E.M. Sparrow. 1970. Turbulent flow: Heat transfer and mass transfer in a tube with surface suction. *Journal of Heat Transfer* 92:117-125.

Knudsen, J.G., and B.V. Roy. 1983. Studies on scaling of cooling tower water. In *Fouling of heat enhancement surfaces*, pp. 517-530. Engineering Foundation, New York.

Lan, C.W. 1991. Effects of rotation on heat transfer fluid flow and interface in normal gravity floating zone crystal growth. *Journal of Crystal Growth* 114:517.

Lawler, J., A. Saidi, and S. Moghaddam. 2002. EHD enhanced liquid-air heat exchangers. *Final Report*, Contract M67854-00-C-0015. Advanced Thermal and Environmental Concepts, College Park, MD.

Lewis, D.M., and H.J. Sauer, Jr. 1965. The thermal resistance of adhesive bonds. *ASME Journal of Heat Transfer* 5:310.

Lloyd, J.R., and W.R. Moran. 1974. Natural convection adjacent to horizontal surfaces of various plan forms. *Journal of Heat Transfer* 96:443.

Love, T.J. 1968. *Radiative heat transfer*. Merrill, Columbus, OH.

Malhotraf, K., and A.S. Mujumdar. 1991. Wall to bed contact heat transfer rates in mechanically stirred granular beds. *International Journal of Heat and Mass Transfer* 34:427-435.

Manglik, R.M., and A.E. Bergles. 1990. The thermal-hydraulic design of the rectangular offset-strip-fin-compact heat exchanger. In *Compact heat exchangers*, pp. 123-149. Hemisphere, New York.

Manglik, R.M., and A.E. Bergles. 1993. Heat transfer and pressure drop correlation for twisted-tape insert in isothermal tubes: Part II —Transition and turbulent flows. *Journal of Heat Transfer* 115:890-896.

Manglik, R.M., and A.E. Bergles. 2002. Swirl flow heat transfer and pressure drop with twisted-tape inserts. *Advances in Heat Transfer* 36:183.

Marto, P.J., and V.H. Gray. 1971. Effects of high accelerations and heat fluxes on nucleate boiling of water in an axisymmetric rotating boiler. NASA *Technical Note* TN. D-6307. Washington, D.C.

McAdams, W.H. 1954. *Heat transmission*, 3rd ed. McGraw-Hill, New York.

McElhiney, J.E., and G.W. Preckshot. 1977. Heat transfer in the entrance length of a horizontal rotating tube. *International Journal of Heat and Mass Transfer* 20:847-854.

Metais, B., and E.R.G. Eckert. 1964. Forced, mixed and free convection regimes. *ASME Journal of Heat Transfer* 86(C2)(5):295.

Mills, A.F. 1999. *Basic heat & mass transfer*. Prentice Hall, Saddle River, NJ.

Mochizuki, S., J. Takamura, and S. Yamawaki. 1994. Heat transfer in serpentine flow passages with rotation. *Journal of Turbomachinery* 116:133.

Modest, M.F. 2003. *Radiative heat transfer*, 2nd ed. Academic Press, Oxford, U.K.

Morgan, V.T. 1975. The overall convective heat transfer from smooth circular cylinders. In *Advances in heat transfer*, vol. 11, T.F. Irvine and J.P. Hartnett, eds. Academic Press, New York.

Muley, A., and R.M. Manglik. 1999. Experimental study of turbulent flow heat transfer and pressure drop in a plate heat exchanger with chevron plates. *Journal of Heat Transfer* 121(1):110-117.

Myers, G.E. 1971. *Analytical methods in conduction heat transfer*. McGraw-Hill, New York.

Nelson, R.M., and A.E. Bergles. 1986. Performance evaluation for tubeside heat transfer enhancement of a flooded evaporative water chiller. *ASHRAE Transactions* 92(1B):739-755. *Paper* SF-86-16-2.

Nesis, E.I., A.F. Shatalov, and N.P. Karmatskii. 1994. Dependence of the heat transfer coefficient on the vibration amplitude and frequency of a vertical thin heater. *Journal of Engineering Physics and Thermophysics* 67(1-2).

Nichol, A.A., and M. Gacesa. 1970. Condensation of steam on a rotating vertical cylinder. *Journal of Heat Transfer* 144-152.

Ohadi, M.M. 2002. Control of frost accumulation in refrigeration equipment using the electrohydrodynamic (EHD) technique (RP-1100). ASHRAE Research Project, *Final Report*.

Ohadi, M.M., N. Sharaf, and D.A. Nelson. 1991. Electrohydrodynamic enhancement of heat transfer in a shell-and-tube heat exchanger. *Enhanced Heat Transfer* 4(1):19-39.

Ohadi, M.M., S. Dessiatoun, A. Singh, K. Cheung, and M. Salehi. 1995. EHD-enhancement of boiling/condensation heat transfer of alternate refrigerants. *Progress Report* 6. Presented to U.S. Department of Energy and the EHD Consortium Members, under DOE Grant DE-FG02-93CE23803.A000, Chicago, January.

Ohadi, M.M., S.V. Dessiatoun, J. Darabi, and M. Salehi. 1996. Active augmentation of single-phase and phase-change heat transfer—An overview. In *Process, enhanced, and multiphase heat transfer: A festschrift for A.E. Bergles*, pp. 277-286, R.M. Manglik and A.D. Kraus, eds. Begell House, New York.

Ohadi, M.M., J. Darabi, and B. Roget. 2001. Electrode design, fabrication, and materials science for EHD-enhanced heat and mass transfer. In *Annual review of heat transfer*, vol. 22, pp. 563-623.

Owsenek, B., and J. Seyed-Yagoobi. 1995. Experimental investigation of corona wind heat transfer enhancement with a heated horizontal flat plate. *Journal of Heat Transfer* 117:309.

Parker, J.D., J.H. Boggs, and E.F. Blick. 1969. *Introduction to fluid mechanics and heat transfer*. Addison Wesley, Reading, MA.

Patankar, S.V. 1980. *Numerical heat transfer and fluid flow*. McGraw-Hill, New York.

Pei, X.J., H.F. Ming, S.S. Guang, and P.R. Ze. 2001. Thermal–hydraulic performance of small scale micro-channel and porous-media heat-exchangers. *International Journal of Heat and Mass Transfer* 44(5): 1039-1051.

Pescod, D. 1980. An advance in plate heat exchanger geometry giving increased heat transfer. *Proceedings of the ASME Heat Transfer Division*, HTD 10, pp. 73-77.

Poulter, R., and P.H.G. Allen. 1986. Electrohydrodynamincally augmented heat and mass transfer in the shell tube heat exchanger. *Proceedings of the Eighth International Heat Transfer Conference* 6:2963-2968.

Prakash, C., and R. Zerle. 1995. Prediction of turbulent flow and heat transfer in a ribbed rectangular duct with and without rotation. *Journal of Turbomachinery* 117:255.

Ravigururajan, T.S., and A.E. Bergles. 1985. General correlations for pressure drop and heat transfer for single-phase turbulent flow in internally ribbed tubes. *Augmentation of Heat Transfer in Energy Systems*, HTD 52, pp. 9-20. American Society of Mechanical Engineers, New York.

Rich, D.G. 1966. The efficiency and thermal resistance of annular and rectangular fins. *Proceedings of the Third International Heat Transfer Conference, AIChE* 111:281-289.

Rin, Y., H.H. Jae, and K. Yongchan. 2006. Evaporative heat transfer and pressure drop of R410A in micro channels. *International Journal of Refrigeration* 29(1):92-100.

Schmidt, T.E. 1949. Heat transfer calculations for extended surfaces. *Refrigerating Engineering* 4:351-57.

Schneider, P.J. 1964. *Temperature response charts*. John Wiley & Sons, New York.

Seyed-Yagoobi, J. 1997. The applicability, design aspects, and long-term effects of EHD-enhanced heat transfer of alternate refrigerants/refrigerant mixtures for HVAC applications (RP-857). ASHRAE Research Project, *Final Report*.

Seyed-Yagoobi, J.S., and Y. Feng. 2005. Refrigerant flow mal-distribution control in evaporators using electrohydrodynamics technique (RP-1213). ASHRAE Research Project, *Final Report*.

Shepherd, D.G. 1946. Performance of one-row tube coils with thin plate fins, low velocity forced convection. *Heating, Piping, and Air Conditioning* (April).

Shlykov, Y.P. 1964. Thermal resistance of metallic contacts. *International Journal of Heat and Mass Transfer* 7(8):921.

Sieder, E.N., and C.E. Tate. 1936. Heat transfer and pressure drop of liquids in tubes. *Industrial & Engineering Chemistry Research* 28:1429.

Siegel, R., and J.R. Howell. 2002. *Thermal radiation heat transfer*, 4th ed. Taylor & Francis, New York.

Somerscales, E.F.C., and A.E. Bergles. 1997. Enhancement of heat transfer and fouling mitigation. *Advances in Heat Transfer* 30:197-253.

Somerscales, E.F.C., A.F. Pontedure, and A.E. Bergles. 1991. Particulate fouling of heat transfer tubes enhanced on their inner surface. *Fouling and enhancement interactions: Proceedings of the ASME Heat Transfer Division*, HTD 164, pp. 17-28.

Son, G., and V.K. Dhir. 1993. Enhancement of heat transfer in annulus using tangential flow injection. *Proceedings of the ASME Heat Transfer Division*, HTD 246.

Sonokama, K. 1964. Contact thermal resistance. *Journal of the Japan Society of Mechanical Engineers* 63(505):240. English translation in RSIC-215, AD-443429.

Suryanarayana, N.V. 1995. *Engineering heat transfer*. West Publishing, St. Paul, MN.

Tang, S., and T.W. McDonald. 1971. A study of boiling heat transfer from a rotating horizontal cylinder. *International Journal of Heat and Mass Transfer* 14:1643-1657.

Tauscher, W.A., E.M. Sparrow, and J.R. Lloyd. 1970. Amplification of heat transfer by local injection of fluid into a turbulent tube flow. *International Journal of Heat and Mass Transfer* 13:681-688.

Troupe, R.A., J.C. Morgan, and J. Prifiti. 1960. The plate heater versatile chemical engineering tool. *Chemical Engineering Progress* 56 (1):124-128.

Valencia, A., M. Fiebig, and V.K. Mitra. 1996. Heat transfer enhancement by longitudinal vortices in a fin tube heat exchanger. *Journal of Heat Transfer* 118:209.

Wanniarachchi, A.S., U. Ratnam, B.E. Tilton, and K. Dutta-Roy. 1995. Approximate correlations for chevron-type plate heat exchangers. *30th National Heat Transfer Conference*, ASME HTD 314, pp. 145-151.

Wasmund, R. 1976. Überarbeitete und erweiterte Reihen der mechanischen und thermischen Stoffwerte von Würze und Bier im Temperaturbereich zwischen 0 und 75°C. *Monatsschrift für Brauwissenschaft* 29:294-297.

Woods, B.G. 1992. Sonically enhanced heat transfer from a cylinder in cross flow and its impact on process power consumption. *International Journal of Heat and Mass Transfer* 35:2367-2376.

Zhao, Y., M. Molki, M.M. Ohadi, and S.V. Dessiatoun. 2000. Flow boiling of CO_2 in microchannels. *ASHRAE Transactions* 106(1):437-445. *Paper* DA-00-02-1.

BIBLIOGRAPHY

Fins

General

Gardner, K.A. 1945. Efficiency of extended surface. *ASME Transactions* 67:621.

Gunter, A.Y., and A.W. Shaw. 1945. A general correlation of friction factors for various types of surfaces in cross flow. *ASME Transactions* 11:643.

Shah, R.K., and R.L. Webb. 1981. *Compact and enhanced heat exchangers, heat exchangers, theory and practice*, pp. 425-468. J. Taborek, G.F. Hewitt, and N. Afgan, eds. Hemisphere, New York.

Webb, R.L. 1980. Air-side heat transfer in finned tube heat exchangers. *Heat Transfer Engineering* 1(3):33-49.

Smooth

Clarke, L., and R.E. Winston. 1955. Calculation of finside coefficients in longitudinal finned heat exchangers. *Chemical Engineering Progress* 3:147.

Elmahdy, A.H., and R.C. Biggs. 1979. Finned tube heat exchanger: Correlation of dry surface heat transfer data. *ASHRAE Transactions* 85:2. *Paper* DE-2544.

Ghai, M.L. 1951. Heat transfer in straight fins. General discussion on heat transfer. London Conference, September.

Gray, D.L., and R.L. Webb. 1986. Heat transfer and friction correlations for plate finned-tube heat exchangers having plain fins. *Proceedings of Eighth International Heat Transfer Conference*, San Francisco.

Wavy

Beecher, D.T., and T.J. Fagan. 1987. Effects of fin pattern on the air-side heat transfer coefficient in plate finned-tube heat exchangers. *ASHRAE Transactions* 93:2. *Paper* NT-87-21-1.

Yashu, T. 1972. Transient testing technique for heat exchanger fin. *Reito* 47(531):23-29.

Spines

Abbott, R.W., R.H. Norris, and W.A. Spofford. 1980. Compact heat exchangers for General Electric products—Sixty years of advances in design and manufacturing technologies. In *Compact heat exchangers—History, technological advancement and mechanical design problems*, ASME HTD 10, pp. 37-55. R.K. Shah, C.F. McDonald, and C.P. Howard, eds.

Moore, F.K. 1975. Analysis of large dry cooling towers with spine-fin heat exchanger elements. ASME *Paper* 75-WA/HT-46.

Rabas, T.J., and P.W. Eckels. 1975. Heat transfer and pressure drop performance of segmented surface tube bundles. ASME *Paper* 75-HT-45.

Weierman, C. 1976. Correlations ease the selection of finned tubes. *Oil and Gas Journal* 9:94-100.

Louvered

Hosoda, T., H. Uzuhashi, and N. Kobayashi. 1977. Louver fin type heat exchangers. *Heat Transfer—Japanese Research* 6(2):69-77.

Mahaymam, W., and L.P. Xu. 1983. Enhanced fins for air-cooled heat exchangers—Heat transfer and friction factor correlations. Y. Mori and W. Yang, eds. *Proceedings of the ASME-JSME Thermal Engineering Joint Conference*, Hawaii.

Senshu, T., T. Hatada, and K. Ishibane. 1979. Surface heat transfer coefficient of fins used in air-cooled heat exchangers. *Heat Transfer—Japanese Research* 8(4):16-26.

Circular

Jameson, S.L. 1945. Tube spacing in finned tube banks. *ASME Transactions* 11:633.

Katz, D.L. 1954-55. Finned tubes in heat exchangers; Cooling liquids with finned coils; Condensing vapors on finned coils; and Boiling outside finned tubes. Bulletin reprinted from *Petroleum Refiner*.

Heat Exchangers

Amooie-Foomeny, M.M. 1977. *Flow distribution in plate heat exchanger*. Ph.D. dissertation, University of Bradford, Bradford, U.K.

Buonopane, R.A., R.A. Troupe, and J.C. Morgan. 1963. Heat transfer design methods for plate heat exchangers. *Chemical Engineering Progress* 59(7):57-61.

Changal Vaie, A.A. 1975. *The performance of plate heat exchanger*. Ph.D. dissertation, University of Bradford, Bradford, U.K.

Chisholm, D., and A.S. Wanniarachchi. 1992. Maldistribution in single-pass mixed-channel plate heat exchangers. *Proceedings of the ASME Heat Transfer Division: Compact Heat Exchangers for Power and Process Industries*, HTD 201, pp. 95-99.

Clark, D.F. 1974. Plate heat exchanger design and recent developments. *The Chemical Engineer* 285:275-279.

Cooper, A. 1974. Recover more heat with plate heat exchangers. *The Chemical Engineer* 285:280-285.

Crozier, R.D., J.R. Booth, and J.E. Stewart. 1964. Heat transfer in plate and frame heat exchangers. *Chemical Engineering Progress* 60(8):43-45.

Edwards, M.F., A.A. Changal Vaie, and D.L. Parrott. 1974. Heat transfer and pressure drop characteristics of a plate heat exchanger using non-Newtonian liquids. *The Chemical Engineer* 285:286-288.

Focke, W.W., J. Zacharides, and I. Oliver. 1985. The effect of the corrugation inclination angle on the thermohydraulic performance of plate heat exchangers. *International Journal of Heat and Mass Transfer* 28(8):1469-1479.

Jackson, B.W., and R.A. Troupe. 1964. Laminar flow in a plate heat exchanger. *Chemical Engineering Progress* 60(7):65-67.

Gartner, J.R., and H.L. Harrison. 1963. Frequency response transfer functions for a tube in crossflow. *ASHRAE Transactions* 69:323.

Gartner, J.R., and H.L. Harrison. 1965. Dynamic characteristics of water-to-air crossflow heat exchangers. *ASHRAE Transactions* 71:212.

Kovalenko, L.M., and A.M. Maslov. 1970. Soviet plate heat exchangers. *Konservnaya I Ovoshchesushil Naya Promyshlennost* 7:15-17. (In Russian.)

Leuliet, J.C., J.F. Mangonnat, and M. Lalande. 1987. Etude de la perte de charge dans des echangeurs de chaleur a plaques traitant des produits non-Newtoniens. *Revue Generale de Thermique* 26 (308-309):445-450. (In French.)

Leuliet, J.C., J.F. Mangonnat, and M. Laiande. 1990. Flow and heat transfer in plate heat exchangers treating viscous Newtonian and pseudoplastic products, Part 1: Modeling the variations of the hydraulic diameter, *Canadian Journal of Chemical Engineering* 68(2):220-229.

Marriott, J. 1971. Where and how to use plate heat exchangers. *Chemical Engineering* 78:127-134.

Marriott, J. 1977. Performance of an Alfaflex plate heat exchanger. *Chemical Engineering Progress* 73(2):73-78.

Maslov, A., and L. Kovalenko. 1972. Hydraulic resistance and heat transfer in plate heat exchangers. *Molochnaya Promyshlennost* 10:20-22. (In Russian.)

McQuiston, F.C. 1981. Finned tube heat exchangers: State of the art for the air side. *ASHRAE Transactions* 87:1. *Paper* CH-81-16-2.

Moghaddam, S., K.T. Kiger, and M. Ohadi. 2006. Measurement of corona wind velocity and calculation of energy conversion efficiency for air side heat transfer enhancement in compact heat exchangers. *HVAC&R Research* (now *Science and Technology for the Built Environment*) 12(1):57-68.

Myers, G.E., J.W. Mitchell, and R. Nagaoka. 1965. A method of estimating crossflow heat exchanger transients. *ASHRAE Transactions* 71:225.

Okada, K., M. Ono, T. Tomimura, T. Okuma, H. Konno, and S. Ohtani. 1972. Design and heat transfer characteristics of a new plate heat exchanger. *Heat Transfer Japanese Research* 1(1):90-95.

Rene, F., J.C. Leuliet, and M. Lanlande. 1991. Heat transfer to Newtonian and non-Newtonian food fluids in plate heat exchangers: Experimental and numerical approaches. *Food and Bioproducts Processing: Transaction of the IChE*, Part C 69(3):115-126.

Roetzel, W., S.K. Das, and X. Luo. 1994. Measurement of the heat transfer coefficient in plate heat exchangers using a temperature oscillation technique. *International Journal of Heat and Mass Transfer* 37(1):325-331.

Rosenblad, G., and A. Kullendroff. 1975. Estimating heat transfer from mass transfer studies on plate heat exchanger surfaces, *Warme- und Stoffubertragung* 8(3):187-191.

Savostin, A.F., and A.M. Tikhonov. 1970. Investigation of the characteristics of plate type heating surfaces. *Thermal Engineering* 17:113-117.

Shooshtari, A., R. Mandel, and M.M. Ohadi. 2012. Cooling of next generation electronics for diverse applications. In *Encyclopedia of energy engineering and technology*, S. Anwar, ed. Taylor and Francis, New York.

Stermole, F.J., and M.H. Carson. 1964. Dynamics of forced flow distributed parameter heat exchangers. *AIChE Journal* 10(5):9.

Talik, A.C., L.S. Fletcher, N.K. Anand, and L.W. Swanson. 1995. Heat transfer and pressure drop characteristics of a plate heat exchanger. *Proceedings of the ASME/JSME Thermal Engineering Conference*, vol. 4, pp. 321-329.

Thomasson, R.K. 1964. Frequency response of linear counterflow heat exchangers. *Journal of Mechanical Engineering Science* 6(1):3.

Wyngaard, J.C., and F.W. Schmidt. Comparison of methods for determining transient response of shell and tube heat exchangers. ASME *Paper* 64-WA/HT-20.

Yang, W.J. Frequency response of multipass shell and tube heat exchangers to timewise variant flow perturbance. ASME *Paper* 64-HT-18.

Heat Transfer, General

Bennet, C.O., and J.E. Myers. 1984. *Momentum, heat and mass transfer*, 3rd ed. McGraw-Hill, New York.

Brown, A.I., and S.M. Marco. 1958. *Introduction to heat transfer*, 3rd ed. McGraw-Hill, New York.

Burmeister, L.C. 1983. *Convective heat transfer*. John Wiley & Sons, New York.

Chapman, A.J. 1981. *Heat transfer*, 4th ed. Macmillan, New York.

Hausen, H. 1943. Dastellung des Warmeuberganges in Rohren durch verallgemeinerte Potenzbeziehungen. *VDI Zeitung*, Supplement 4: *Verfahrenstechnik.* Quoted in R.K. Shah and M.S. Bhatti, in *Handbook of single-phase convective heat transfer*, John Wiley & Sons, New York, 1987.

Holman, J.D. 1981. *Heat transfer*, 5th ed. McGraw-Hill, New York.

Kays, W.M., and M.E. Crawford. 1993. *Convective heat and mass transfer*, 3rd ed. McGraw-Hill, New York.

Kern, D.Q., and A.D. Kraus. 1972. *Extended surface heat transfer.* McGraw-Hill, New York.

Kreith, F., and W.Z. Black. 1980. *Basic heat transfer.* Harper and Row, New York.

Lienhard, J.H. 1981. *A heat transfer textbook.* Prentice Hall, Englewood Cliffs, NJ.

McQuiston, F.C., and J.D. Parker. 1988. *Heating, ventilating and air-conditioning, analysis and design*, 4th ed. John Wiley & Sons, New York.

Rohsenow, W.M., and J.P. Hartnett, eds. 1973. *Handbook of heat transfer.* McGraw-Hill, New York.

Sissom, L.E., and D.R. Pitts. 1972. *Elements of transport phenomena.* McGraw-Hill, New York.

Smith, E.M. 1997. *Thermal design of heat exchangers*. John Wiley & Sons, Chichester, UK.

Todd, J.P., and H.B. Ellis. 1982. *Applied heat transfer*. Harper and Row, New York.

Webb, R.L., and A.E. Bergles. 1983. Heat transfer enhancement, second generation technology. *Mechanical Engineering* 6:60-67.

Welty, J.R. 1974. *Engineering heat transfer.* John Wiley & Sons, New York.

Welty, J.R., C.E. Wicks, and R.E. Wilson. 1972. *Fundamentals of momentum, heat and mass transfer.* John Wiley & Sons, New York.

Wolf, H. 1983. *Heat transfer.* Harper and Row, New York.

CHAPTER 5

TWO-PHASE FLOW

TWO-phase flow is encountered extensively in the HVAC&R industries. A combination of liquid and vapor refrigerant exists in flooded coolers, direct-expansion coolers, thermosiphon coolers, brazed and gasketed plate evaporators and condensers, and tube-in-tube evaporators and condensers, as well as in air-cooled evaporators and condensers. In heating system pipes, steam and liquid water may both be present. Because the hydrodynamic and heat transfer aspects of two-phase flow are not as well understood as those of single-phase flow, no comprehensive model has yet been created to predict pressure drops or heat transfer rates. Instead, the correlations are for specific thermal and hydrodynamic operating conditions.

This chapter introduces two-phase flow and heat transfer processes of pure substances and refrigerant mixtures. Thus, some multiphase processes that are important to HVAC&R applications are not discussed here. The 2016 *ASHRAE Handbook—HVAC Systems and Equipment* provides information on several such applications, including humidification (Chapter 22), particulate contaminants (Chapter 29), cooling towers (Chapter 40), and evaporative air cooling (Chapter 41). See Chapter 18 of the 2014 *ASHRAE Handbook—Refrigeration* for information on absorption cooling, heating, and refrigeration processes.

1. BOILING

Two-phase heat and mass transport are characterized by various flow and thermal regimes and whether vaporization occurs under natural convection or in forced flow. Unlike single-phase flow systems, the heat transfer coefficient for a two-phase mixture depends on the flow regime, thermodynamic and transport properties of both vapor and liquid, roughness of heating surface, wetting characteristics of the surface/liquid pair, orientation of the heat transfer surface, and other parameters. Therefore, it is necessary to consider each flow and boiling regime separately to determine the heat transfer coefficient.

Although much progress has been made in the past few decades, accurate data defining regime limits and determining the effects of various parameters in geometries and surfaces of practical significance are still limited to empirical correlations for select surfaces and working fluids and for specified operational ranges for which the data have been collected.

Boiling and Pool Boiling in Natural Convection Systems

Regimes of Boiling. The different regimes of pool boiling described by Farber and Scorah (1948) verified those suggested by Nukiyama (1934). These regimes are shown in Figure 1. When the temperature of the heating surface is near the fluid saturation temperature, heat is transferred by convection currents to the free surface, where evaporation occurs (region I). Transition to nucleate boiling occurs when the surface temperature exceeds saturation by a few degrees (region II).

In **nucleate boiling** (region III), a thin layer of superheated liquid forms adjacent to the heating surface. In this layer, bubbles nucleate and grow from spots on the surface. The thermal resistance of the superheated liquid film is greatly reduced by bubble-induced agitation and vaporization. Increased wall temperature increases bubble population, causing a large increase in heat flux.

As heat flux or temperature difference increases further and as more vapor forms, liquid flow toward the surface is interrupted, and

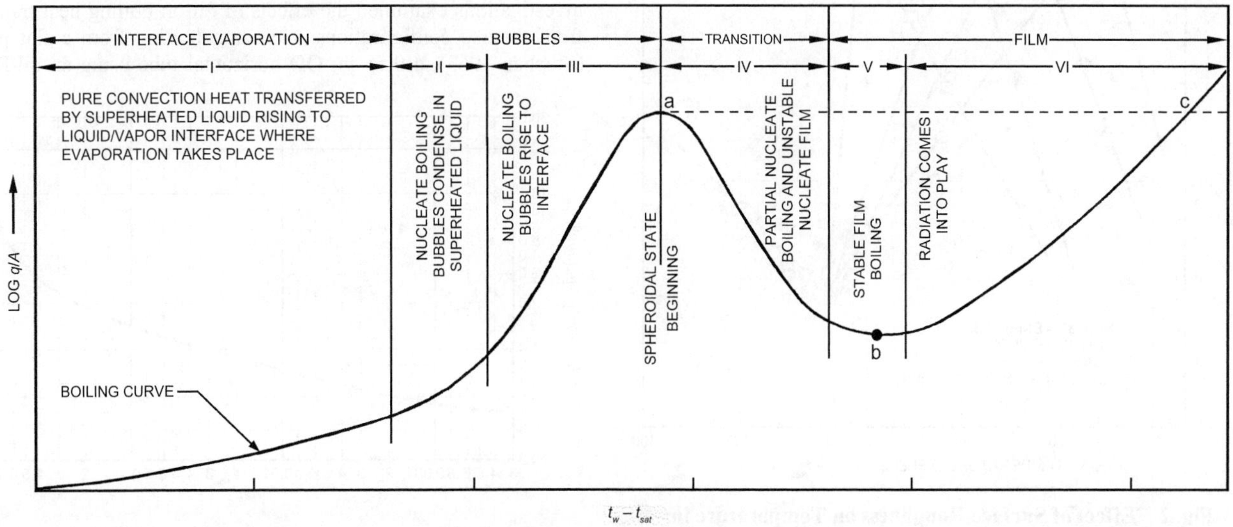

Fig. 1 Characteristic Pool Boiling Curve

The preparation of this chapter is assigned to TC 1.3, Heat Transfer and Fluid Flow.

a vapor blanket forms. This gives the **maximum heat flux**, which is at the **departure from nucleate boiling (DNB)** at point a in Figure 1. This flux is often called the **burnout heat flux** or **boiling crisis** because, for constant power-generating systems, an increase of heat flux beyond this point results in a jump of the heater temperature (to point c), often beyond the melting point of a metal heating surface.

In systems with controllable surface temperature, an increase beyond the temperature for DNB causes a decrease of heat flux density. This is the **transition boiling regime** (region IV); liquid alternately falls onto the surface and is repulsed by an explosive burst of vapor.

At sufficiently high surface temperatures, a stable vapor film forms at the heater surface; this is the **film boiling regime** (regions V and VI). Because heat transfer is by conduction (and some radiation) across the vapor film, the heater temperature is much higher than for comparable heat flux densities in the nucleate boiling regime. The **minimum film boiling (MFB)** heat flux (point b) is the lower end of the film boiling curve.

Free Surface Evaporation. In region I, where surface temperature exceeds liquid saturation temperature by less than a few degrees, no bubbles form. Evaporation occurs at the free surface by convection of superheated liquid from the heated surface. Correlations of heat transfer coefficients for this region are similar to those for fluids under ordinary natural convection [Equations (T1.1) to (T1.4)].

Nucleate Boiling. Much information is available on boiling heat transfer coefficients, but no universally reliable method is available for correlating the data. In the nucleate boiling regime, heat flux density is not a single valued function of the temperature but depends also on the nucleating characteristics of the surface, as shown by Figure 2 (Berenson 1962).

The equations proposed for correlating nucleate boiling data can be put in a form that relates heat transfer coefficient h to temperature difference $(t_s - t_{sat})$:

$$h = \text{constant}(t_s - t_{sat})^a \quad (1)$$

Exponent a is normally about 2 for a plain, smooth surface; its value depends on the thermodynamic and transport properties of the vapor and liquid. Nucleating characteristics of the surface, including the size distribution of surface cavities and wetting characteristics of the surface/liquid pair, affect the value of the multiplying constant and the value of a in Equation (1).

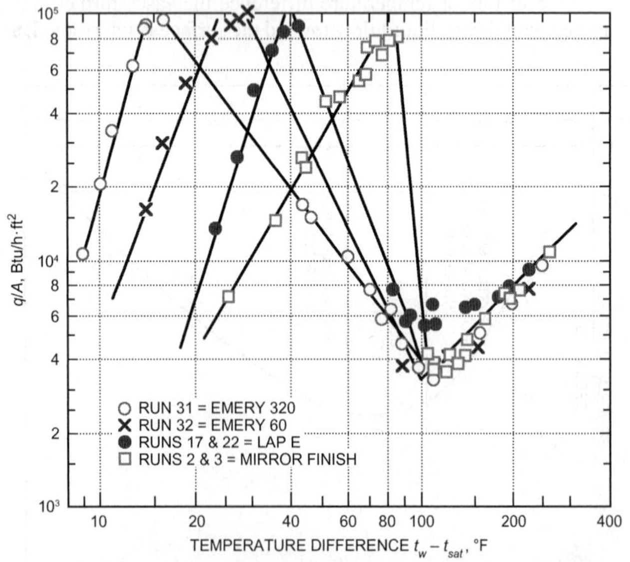

Fig. 2 Effect of Surface Roughness on Temperature in Pool Boiling of Pentane
(Berenson 1962)

In the following sections, correlations and nomographs for predicting nucleate and flow boiling of various refrigerants are given. For most cases, these correlations have been tested for refrigerants (e.g., R-11, R-12, R-113, R-114) that are now identified as environmentally harmful and are no longer used in new equipment. Thermal and fluid characteristics of alternative refrigerants/refrigerant mixtures have recently been extensively researched, and some correlations have been suggested.

Stephan and Abdelsalam (1980) developed a statistical approach for estimating heat transfer during nucleate boiling. The correlation [Equation (T1.5)] should be used with a fixed contact angle θ regardless of the fluid. Cooper (1984) proposed a dimensional correlation for nucleate boiling [Equation (T1.6)] based on analysis of a vast amount of data covering a wide range of parameters. The dimensions required are listed in Table 1. Based on inconclusive evidence, Cooper suggested a multiplier of 1.7 for copper surfaces, to be reevaluated as more data came forth. Most other researchers [e.g., Shah (2007)] have found the correlation gives better agreement without this multiplier, and thus do not recommend its use.

Gorenflo (1993) proposed a nucleate boiling correlation based on a set of reference conditions and a base heat transfer coefficient for each fluid, and provided base heat transfer coefficients for many fluids.

In addition to correlations dependent on thermodynamic and transport properties of the vapor and liquid, Borishansky et al. (1962), Lienhard and Schrock (1963), and Stephan (1992) documented a correlating method based on the law of corresponding states. The properties can be expressed in terms of fundamental molecular parameters, leading to scaling criteria based on reduced pressure $p_r = p/p_c$, where p_c is the critical thermodynamic pressure for the coolant. An example of this method of correlation is shown in Figure 3. Reference pressure p^* was chosen as $p^* = 0.029p_c$. This is a simple method for scaling the effect of pressure if data are available for one pressure level. It also is advantageous if the thermodynamic and particularly the transport properties used in several equations in Table 1 are not accurately known. In its present form, this correlation gives a value of $a = 2.33$ for the exponent in Equation (1) and consequently should apply for typical aged metal surfaces.

There are explicit heat transfer coefficient correlations based on the law of corresponding states for halogenated refrigerants (Danilova 1965), flooded evaporators (Starczewski 1965), and various other substances (Borishansky and Kosyrev 1966). Other investigations examined the effects of oil on boiling heat transfer from diverse configurations, including boiling from a flat plate (Stephan 1963), a 0.55 in. OD horizontal tube using an oil/R-12

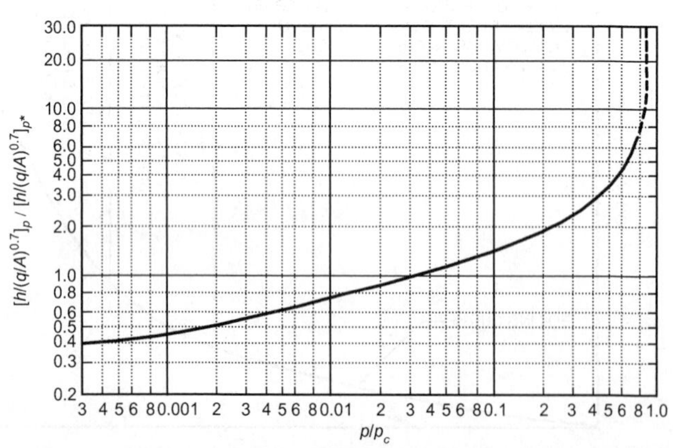

Fig. 3 Correlation of Pool Boiling Data in Terms of Reduced Pressure

Table 1 Equations for Natural Convection Boiling Heat Transfer

Description	References	Equations
Free convection	Jakob (1949, 1957)	$Nu = C(Gr)^m(Pr)^n$ (T1.1)
Free convection boiling, or boiling without bubbles for low Δt and Gr Pr < 10^8. All properties based on liquid state.		Characteristic length scale for vertical surfaces is vertical height of plate or cylinder. For horizontal surfaces, $L_c = A_s/P$, where A_s is plate surface area and P is plate perimeter, is recommended. $Gr = \frac{g\beta(t_s - t_{sat})L_c^3}{\nu^2}$
Vertical submerged surface		$Nu = 0.61(Gr)^{0.25}(Pr)^{0.25}$ (T1.2)
Horizontal submerged surface		$Nu = 0.16(Gr)^{1/3}(Pr)^{1/3}$ (T1.3)
Simplified equation for water		$h \sim 80(\Delta t)^{1/3}$, where h is in Btu/h·ft²·°F and Δt is in °F (T1.4)
Nucleate boiling	Stephan and Abdelsalam (1980)	$\frac{hD_d}{k_l} = 0.0546\left[\left(\frac{\rho_v}{\rho_l}\right)^{0.5}\left(\frac{qD_d}{Ak_lt_{sat}}\right)\right]^{0.67}\left(\frac{h_{fg}D_d^2}{\alpha_l^2}\right)^{0.248}\left(\frac{\rho_l-\rho_v}{\rho_l}\right)^{-4.33}$ (T1.5) where $D_d = 0.0208\theta\left[\frac{\sigma}{g(\rho_l-\rho_v)}\right]^{0.5}$ with $\theta = 35°$.
	Cooper (1984)	$h = 55p_r^{0.12-0.0912\ln(R_p)}(-0.4343\ln p_r)^{-0.55}M^{-0.5}\left(\frac{q}{A}\right)^{0.67}$ (T1.6) where h is in W/(m²·K), q/A is in W/m², and R_p is surface roughness in µm (if unknown, use 1 µm). Multiply h by 1.7 for copper surfaces (see text).
Critical heat flux	Kutateladze (1951)	$\frac{q/A}{\rho_v h_{fg}}\left[\frac{\rho_v^2}{\sigma g(\rho_l-\rho_v)}\right]^{0.25} = K_D$ (T1.7)
	Zuber et al. (1962)	For many liquids, K_D varies from 0.12 to 0.16; an average value of 0.13 is recommended.
Minimum heat flux in film boiling from horizontal plate	Zuber (1959)	$\frac{q}{A} = 0.09\rho_v h_{fg}\left[\frac{\sigma g(\rho_l-\rho_v)}{(\rho_l+\rho_v)^2}\right]^{1/4}$ (T1.8)
Minimum heat flux in film boiling from horizontal cylinders	Lienhard and Wong (1964)	$q/A = 0.633\left\{\left[\frac{4B^2}{1+B/2}\right]^{0.25}\right\}\left\{0.09\rho_v h_{fg}\left[\frac{g\sigma(\rho_l-\rho_v)}{(\rho_l+\rho_v)^2}\right]^{0.25}\right\}$ (T1.9) where $B = (2L_b/D)^2$ and $L_b = \left[\frac{\sigma}{g(\rho_l-\rho_v)}\right]^{0.5}$
Minimum temperature difference for film boiling from horizontal plate	Berenson (1961)	$(t_s - t_{sat}) = 0.127L_b\left(\frac{\rho_v h_{fg}}{k_v}\right)\left[\frac{g(\rho_l-\rho_v)}{\rho_l+\rho_v}\right]^{2/3}\left[\frac{\mu_v}{g(\rho_l-\rho_v)}\right]^{1/3}$ (T1.10)
Film boiling from horizontal plate	Berenson (1961)	$h = 0.425\left[\frac{k_v^3\rho_v h_{fg} g(\rho_l-\rho_v)}{\mu_v(t_s-t_{sat})L_b}\right]^{0.25}$ (T1.11)
Film boiling from horizontal cylinders	Bromley (1950)	$h = 0.62\left[\frac{k_v^3\rho_v h'_{fg} g(\rho_l-\rho_v)}{\mu_v(t_s-t_{sat})D}\right]^{0.25}$ (T1.12)
Effect of superheating	Anderson et al. (1966)	Substitute $h'_{fg} = h_{fg}\left(1 + 0.4c_{p,v}\frac{t_s-t_{sat}}{h_{fg}}\right)$ (T1.13)
Effect of radiation	Incropera and DeWitt (2002)	$h_t = h + \frac{3}{4}\frac{\varepsilon\sigma(t_s^4 - t_{sat}^4)}{t_s - t_{sat}}$
Quenching spheres	Frederking and Clark (1962)	$Nu = 0.15(Ra)^{1/3}$ for $Ra > 5 \times 10^7$ (T1.14) $Ra = \left[\frac{D^3 g(\rho_l-\rho_v)}{\nu_v^2\rho_v}Pr_v\left(\frac{h_{fg}}{c_{p,v}(t_s-t_{sat})}+0.4\right)\frac{a}{g}\right]^{1/3}$ where a = local acceleration

mixture (Tschernobyiski and Ratiani 1955), inside horizontal tubes using an oil/R-12 mixture (Breber et al. 1980; Green and Furse 1963; Worsoe-Schmidt 1959), and commercial copper tubing using R-11 and R-113 with oil content to 10% (Dougherty and Sauer 1974). Additionally, Furse (1965) examined R-11 and R-12 boiling over a flat horizontal copper surface.

Maximum Heat Flux and Film Boiling

Maximum, or critical, heat flux and the film boiling region are not as strongly affected by conditions of the heating surface as heat flux in the nucleate boiling region, making analysis of DNB and of film boiling more tractable.

Several mechanisms have been proposed for the onset of DNB [see Carey (1992) for a summary]. Each model is based on the scenario that a vapor blanket exists on portions of the heat transfer surface, greatly increasing thermal resistance. Zuber (1959) proposed that these blankets may result from Helmholtz instabilities in columns of vapor rising from the heated surface; another prominent theory supposes a macrolayer beneath the mushroom-shaped bubbles (Haramura and Katto 1983). In this case, DNB occurs when liquid beneath the bubbles is consumed before the bubbles depart and allow surrounding liquid to rewet the surface. Dhir and Liaw (1989) used a concept of bubble crowding proposed by Rohsenow and Griffith (1956) to produce a model that incorporates the effect of contact angle. Sefiane (2001) suggested that instabilities near the triple contact lines cause DNB. Fortunately, though significant disagreement remains about the mechanism of DNB, models using these differing conceptual approaches tend to lead to predictions within a factor of 2.

When DNB (point a in Figure 1) is assumed to be a hydrodynamic instability phenomenon, a simple relation [Equation (T1.7)] can be derived to predict this flux for pure, wetting liquids (Kutateladze 1951; Zuber et al. 1962). The dimensionless constant K varies from approximately 0.12 to 0.16 for a large variety of liquids. Kandlikar (2001) created a model for maximum heat flux explicitly incorporating the effects of contact angle and orientation. Equation (T1.7) compares favorably to Kandlikar's, and, because it is simpler, it is still recommended for general use. However, note that this equation is valid when the end effects are unimportant. Carey (1992) provides correlations to calculate maximum heat flux for various geometries based on this equation. Surface wettability, orientation, and roughness can affect DNB. For orientations other than upward facing, see Brusstar and Merte (1997) and Howard and Mudawar (1999). Liquid subcooling increases maximum heat flux; see Elkessabgi and Lienhard (1998) for subcooling's effects.

Van Stralen (1959) found that, for liquid mixtures, DNB is a function of concentration. As discussed by Stephan (1992), the maximum heat flux always lies between the values of the pure components. Unfortunately, the relationship of DNB to concentration is not simple, and several hypotheses [e.g., McGillis and Carey (1996); Reddy and Lienhard (1989); Van Stralen and Cole (1979)] have been put forward to explain the experimental data. For a more detailed overview of mixture boiling, refer to Thome and Shock (1984).

The minimum heat flux density (point b in Figure 1) in film boiling from a horizontal surface and a horizontal cylinder can be predicted by Equation (T1.8). The factor 0.09 was adjusted to fit experimental data; values predicted by the analysis were approximately 30% higher. The accuracy of Equation (T1.8) falls off rapidly with increasing p_r (Rohsenow et al. 1998). Berenson's (1961) Equations (T1.10) and (T1.11) predict the temperature difference at minimum heat flux and heat transfer coefficient for film boiling on a flat plate. The minimum heat flux for film boiling on a horizontal cylinder can be predicted by Equation (T1.9). As in Equation (T1.8), the factor 0.633 was adjusted to fit experimental data.

The heat transfer coefficient in film boiling from a horizontal surface can be predicted by Equation (T1.11), and from a horizontal cylinder by Equation (T1.12) (Bromley 1950).

Frederking and Clark (1962) found that, for turbulent film boiling, Equation (T1.13) agrees with data from experiments at reduced gravity (Jakob 1949, 1957; Kutateladze 1963; Rohsenow 1963; Westwater 1963).

Boiling/Evaporation in Tube Bundles

In **horizontal tube bundles**, flow may be gravity driven or pumped-assisted forced convection. In either case, subcooled liquid enters at the bottom. Sensible heat transfer and subcooled boiling occur until the liquid reaches saturation. Net vapor generation then starts, increasing velocity and thus convective heat transfer. Nucleate boiling also occurs if heat flux is high enough. Brisbane et al. (1980) proposed a computational model in which a liquid/vapor mixture moves up through the bundle, and vapor leaves at the top while liquid moves back down at the side of the bundle. Local heat transfer coefficients are calculated for each tube, considering local velocity, quality, and heat flux. To use this model, correlations for local heat transfer coefficients during subcooled and saturated boiling with flow across tubes are needed. Thome and Robinson (2004) presented a correlation that showed agreement with several data sets for saturated boiling on plain tube bundles. Shah (2005, 2007) gave general correlations for local heat transfer coefficients during subcooled boiling with cross flow, and for saturated boiling with cross flow. These are given in Table 2. Both these correlations agree with extensive databases that included all published data for single tubes and tubes inside bundles, including those correlated by Thome and Robinson (2004).

Data and design methods for bundles of finned and enhanced tubes were reviewed in Casciaro and Thome (2001), Collier and Thome (1996), and Thome (2010). Thome and Robinson (2004) carried out extensive tests on bundles of plain, finned, and enhanced tubes using three halocarbon refrigerants. The plain and finned-tube results correlated quite well with an asymptotic model combining convective and nucleate boiling (Robinson and Thome 2004a, 2004b). The results with enhanced tubes proved more difficult to explain. The correlation presented accounts for the effects of reduced pressure and local void fraction (Robinson and Thome 2004c; Thome and Robinson 2006). This data set was also used by Consolini et al. (2006) to develop models and correlations for local void fraction and pressure drop in flooded evaporator bundles.

Eckels and Gorgy (2012) and Gorgy and Eckels (2013) performed wide-ranging tests on bundles of enhanced tubes with various pitches and two refrigerants. They collected extensive data but did not attempt to test or develop any predictive method. Their data indicated that a pitch-to-diameter ratio of 1.33 was optimum.

Swain and Das (2014) performed a detailed review of literature on boiling in bundles with plain and enhanced tubes. The only well-verified correlation for plain tube bundles they identified was the Shah correlation (Table 2). For bundles of enhanced tubes, no well-verified correlation was identified. Hence, the best recourse for design is to use the data closest to the intended application.

Typical performance of vertical-tube natural circulation evaporators, based on data for water, is shown in Figure 4 (Perry 1950). Low coefficients are at low liquid levels because insufficient liquid covers the heating surface. The lower coefficient at high levels results from an adverse effect of hydrostatic head on temperature difference and circulation rate. Perry (1950) noted similar effects in horizontal shell-and-tube evaporators.

Forced-Convection Evaporation in Tubes

Flow Mechanics. When a mixture of liquid and vapor flows inside a tube, the flow pattern that develops depends on the mass fraction of liquid, fluid properties of each phase, and flow rate. In an evaporator tube, the mass fraction of liquid decreases along the circuit length, resulting in a series of changing vapor/liquid flow patterns. If the fluid enters as a subcooled liquid, the first indications of vapor generation are bubbles forming at the heated tube wall (nucleation). Subsequently, bubble, plug, churn (or semiannular), annular, spray annular, and mist flows can occur as vapor content

Table 2 Correlations for Local Heat Transfer Coefficients in Horizontal Tube Bundles

Description	References	Equations
Saturated boiling in plain tube bundles	Shah (2007)	For Bo $Fr_l^{0.3} > 0.0008$, $h_{TP} = h_{pb}$ (T2.1)
Verified range: water, pentane, halocarbons; single tubes and bundles, square in-line and triangular		For $0.00021 <$ Bo $Fr_l^{0.3} < 0.0008$, $h_{TP} = \phi_0 h_{LT}$
Pitch/D 1.17 to 1.5		For Bo $Fr_l^{0.3} > 0.00021$, $h_{TP} = 2.3h_{LT}/(Z^{0.08}\,Fr_l^{0.22})$
D = 3.2 to 25.4 mm		$h_{LT}D/k_f = 0.21(GD/\mu_f)^{0.62}\,Pr_f^{0.4}$
p_r = 0.005 to 0.19		ϕ_0 is the larger of that given by the following two equations:
G = 1.3 to 1391 kg/(m²·s)		$\phi_0 = 443\,Bo^{0.65}$
Re_l = 58 to 4,949,462		$\phi_0 = 31\,Bo^{0.33}$
Bo × 10^4 = 0.12 to 2632		h_{pb} by Cooper correlation without multiplier for copper surface, G based on narrowest gap between tubes.
Data from 18 sources		$Fr_l = G^2/(\rho_f^2 gD)$ $Z = (1/x - 1)^{0.8} p_r^{0.4}$
		All properties at saturation temperature
Subcooled boiling	Shah (2005)	Low subcooling regime, $h_{TP} = \phi_0 h_{LT}$ (T2.2)
Verified range: water and halocarbons; single tubes and tube bundles		High subcooling regime, $h_{TP} = q/\Delta t_{sat} = (\phi_0 + \Delta t_{sc}/\Delta t_{sat})h_{LT}$
D = 1.2 to 26.4 mm		ϕ_0 as for saturated boiling
p_r = 0.005 to 0.15		High subcooling regime when
Subcooling Δt_{sc} = 0 to 93 K		$q/(GC_{pf}\Delta t_{sc}) > 38(GDC_{pf}/\mu_f)$ or when Bo $< 2.56 \times 10^{-4}$
Re_l = 67 to 260,464		$\Delta t_{sat} = t_w - t_{sat}$
Bo × 10^4 = 0.6 to 1100		All properties at bulk liquid temperature
Data from 29 sources		

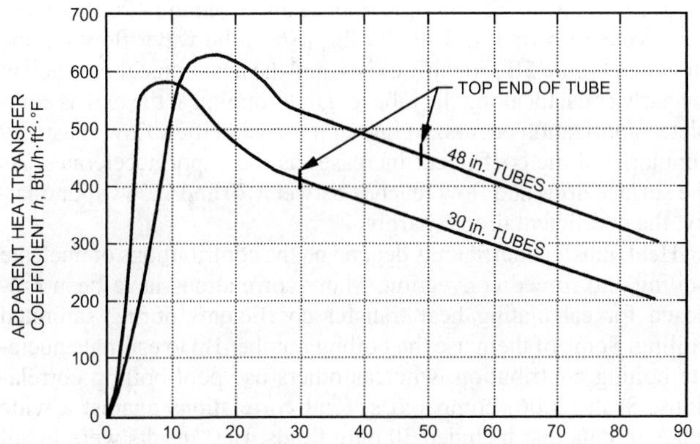

Fig. 4 Boiling Heat Transfer Coefficients for Flooded Evaporator
(Perry 1950)

increases for two-phase flows in horizontal tubes. Idealized flow patterns are shown in Figure 5A for a horizontal tube evaporator. Note that there is currently no general agreement on the names of two-phase flow patterns, and the same name may mean different patterns in vertical, horizontal, and small-tube flow. For detailed delineation of flow patterns, see Barnea and Taitel (1986) or Spedding and Spence (1993) for tubes and pipes between 0.125 and 3 in. in diameter, Coleman and Garimella (1999) for tubes less than 0.125 in. in diameter, and Thome (2001) for flow regime definitions useful in modeling heat transfer.

Increased computing power has allowed greater emphasis on flow-pattern-specific heat transfer and pressure drop models (although there is not uniform agreement among researchers and practitioners that this is always appropriate). Virtually all of the over 1000 articles on two-phase flow patterns and transitions have studied air/water or air/oil flows. Dobson and Chato (1998) found that the Mandhane et al. (1974) flow map, adjusted for the properties of refrigerants, produced satisfactory agreement with their observations in horizontal condensation. Thome (2003) summarized efforts to generate diabatic flow pattern maps in both evaporation and condensation for a number of refrigerants.

The concepts of vapor quality and void fraction are frequently used in two-phase flow models. **Vapor quality** x is the ratio of mass (or mass flow rate) of vapor to total mass (or mass flow rate) of the mixture. The usual flowing vapor quality or vapor fraction is referred to throughout this discussion. Static vapor quality is smaller because vapor in the core flows at a higher average velocity than liquid at the walls. In addition, it is very important to recognize that vapor quality as defined here is frequently not equal to the thermodynamic equilibrium quality, because of significant temperature and velocity gradients in a diabatic flowing vapor/liquid mixture. Some models use the thermodynamic equilibrium quality, and, as a result, require negative values in the subcooled boiling region and values greater than unity in the post-dryout or mist flow region. This is discussed further in Hetsroni (1986).

The **area void fraction**, or just **void fraction**, ε_v is the ratio of the tube cross section filled with vapor to the total cross-sectional area. Vapor quality and area void fraction are related by definition:

$$\frac{x}{1-x} = \frac{\rho_v}{\rho_l} \times \frac{V_v}{V_l} \times \frac{\varepsilon_v}{1-\varepsilon_v} \quad (2)$$

The ratio of velocities V_v/V_l in Equation (2) is called the **slip ratio**. Note that the static void fraction and the flowing void fraction at a given vapor quality differ by a factor equal to the slip ratio.

Because nucleation occurs at the heated surface in a thin sublayer of superheated liquid, boiling in forced convection may begin while the bulk of the liquid is subcooled. Depending on the nature of the fluid and amount of subcooling, bubbles can either collapse or continue to grow and coalesce (Figure 5A), as Gouse and Coumou (1965) observed for R-113. Bergles and Rohsenow (1964) developed a method to determine the point of incipient surface boiling.

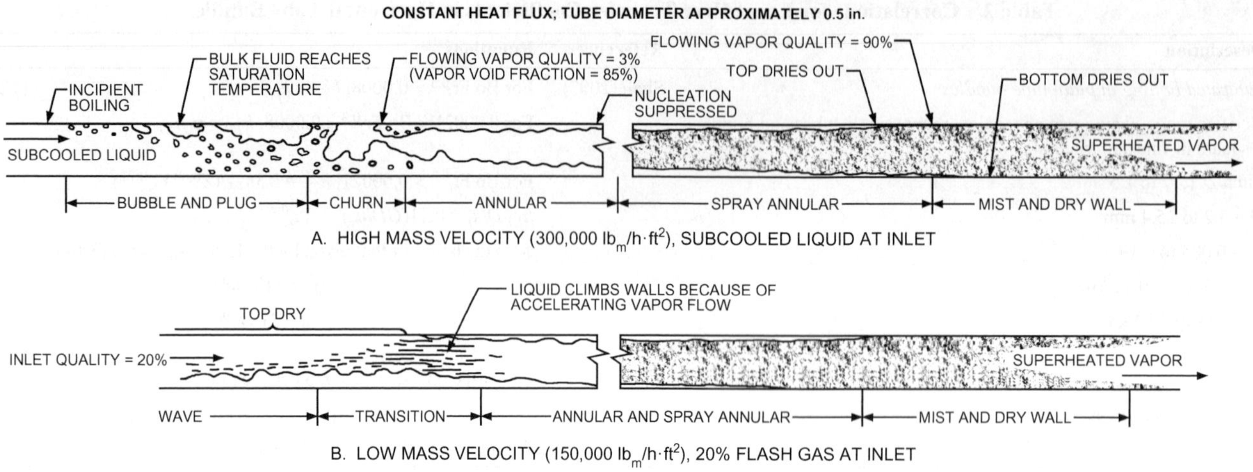

Fig. 5 Flow Regimes in Typical Smooth Horizontal Tube Evaporator

After nucleation begins, bubbles quickly agglomerate to form vapor plugs at the center of a vertical tube, or, as shown in Figure 5A, along the top surface of a horizontal tube. At the point where the bulk of the fluid reaches saturation temperature, which corresponds to local static pressure, there will be up to 1% vapor quality (and a negative thermodynamic equilibrium quality) because of the preceding surface boiling (Guerrieri and Talty 1956).

Further coalescence of vapor bubbles and plugs results in churn, or semiannular flow. If fluid velocity is high enough, a continuous vapor core surrounded by a liquid annulus at the tube wall soon forms. This occurs when the void fraction is approximately 85%; with common refrigerants, this equals a vapor quality of about 10 to 30%.

If two-phase mass velocity is high (greater than 150,000 $lb_m/h \cdot ft^2$ for a 0.5 in. tube), annular flow with small drops of entrained liquid in the vapor core (spray) can persist over a vapor quality range from about 10% to more than 90%. Refrigerant evaporators are fed from an expansion device at vapor qualities of approximately 20%, so that annular and spray annular flow predominate in most tube lengths. In a vertical tube, the liquid annulus is distributed uniformly over the periphery, but it is somewhat asymmetric in a horizontal tube (Figure 5A). As vapor quality reaches about 80% (the actual quality varies from about 70 to 90%, depending on tube diameter, mass velocity, refrigerant, and wall enhancement), portions of the surface dry out. In a horizontal tube, dryout occurs first at the top of the tube and progresses toward the bottom with increasing vapor quality (Figure 5A). Kattan et al. (1998a, 1998b) indicated a very sharp decrease in the local heat transfer coefficient as well as the pressure drop at this point.

If two-phase mass velocity is low (less than 150,000 $lb_m/h \cdot ft^2$ for a 0.5 in. horizontal tube), liquid occupies only the lower cross section of the tube. This causes a wavy type of flow at vapor qualities above about 5%. As the vapor accelerates with increasing evaporation, the interface is disturbed sufficiently to develop annular flow (Figure 5B). Liquid slugging can be superimposed on the flow configurations shown; the liquid forms a continuous, or nearly continuous, sheet over the tube cross section, and the slugs move rapidly and at irregular intervals. Kattan et al. (1998a) presented a general method for predicting flow pattern transitions (i.e., a flow pattern map) based on observations for R-134a, R-125, R-502, R-402A, R-404A, R-407C, and ammonia.

Heat Transfer. In direct-exchange (DX) evaporators, a saturated mixture of liquid and flash gas enters the evaporator. In evaporators with forced or gravity recirculation, liquid is subcooled at the entrance. Subcooled boiling usually occurs until the liquid reaches saturation. Several well-verified correlations for subcooled boiling are available [e.g., Chen (1966), Gungor and Winterton (1986), Kandlikar (1990), Li and Wu (2010a), Liu and Winterton (1991), Shah (1977, 1983)]. The last mentioned is the most verified and is given in Table 3. Note that the subcooling regime can alternatively be determined by Saha and Zuber's (1974) model, which is explicit.

For **saturated boiling**, Figure 6 gives heat transfer data for R-22 evaporating in a 0.722 in. tube (Gouse and Coumou 1965). At low mass velocities (below 150,000 $lb_m/h \cdot ft^2$), the wavy flow regime shown in Figure 5B probably exists, and the heat transfer coefficient is nearly constant along the tube length, dropping at the exit as complete vaporization occurs. At higher mass velocities, flow is usually annular, and the coefficient increases as the vapor accelerates. As the surface dries and flow reaches between 70 and 90% vapor quality, the coefficient drops sharply.

Heat transfer coefficients depend on the contributions of nucleate boiling and forced convection. Many correlations have been proposed for calculating heat transfer coefficients during saturated boiling. Some of them use the boiling number Bo to estimate nucleate boiling contribution, whereas others use pool boiling correlations. Shah (2006) compared several correlations against a wide range of data that included 30 pure fluids. Best results were found with the correlations of Shah (1982) and Gungor and Winterton (1987), the mean deviation for all data being about 17%. Both of these use the boiling number and are given in Table 3. These are applicable to all flow patterns and to horizontal and vertical tubes. Other correlations tested included Chen (1963), Kandlikar (1990), Liu and Winterton (1991), and Steiner and Taborek (1992); their performance was much inferior. Another well-validated correlation is that of Gungor and Winterton (1986), which uses a pool boiling correlation for nucleate boiling contribution. The flow-pattern-based model described by Thome (2001) includes specific models for each flow pattern type and has been tested with newer refrigerants such as R-134a and R-407C.

Recently, there has been great interest in using **carbon dioxide** as a refrigerant, and many experimental studies on its heat transfer have proposed correlations specifically for CO_2. Shah (2014a) evaluated 11 general and CO_2-specific correlations against 1052 data points from 41 data sets from 32 studies; tube diameters ranged from 0.51 to 14 mm, and pressures and flow rates varied widely. Over all tube diameters, the Liu and Winterton (1991) correlation performed best, with a mean absolute deviation of 26.1%. The Shah correlation (Table 3) also gave good agreement by using $\phi_0 = 1820\ Bo^{0.68}$, with a deviation of 26.8%. For channels with diameters

Table 3 Equations for Forced Convection Boiling in Tubes

Description	References	Equations
Horizontal and vertical tubes and annuli, saturated boiling Compiled from a database of over 3600 data points, including data for R-11, R-12, R-22, R-113, R-114, and water. Applicable to vertical flows and horizontal tubes.	Gungor and Winterton (1987)	$$h = E(h_{nb} + h_{cb}) \quad \text{(T3.1)}$$ where $$h_{cb} = 1.12\left[\frac{x}{(1-x)}\right]^{0.75}\left(\frac{\rho_f}{\rho_g}\right)^{0.41} h_f$$ $$h_{nb} = (1 + 3000\ \mathrm{Bo}^{0.86})h_f$$ $$h_f = 0.023\ \mathrm{Re}_l^{0.8}\mathrm{Pr}_l^{0.4}(k_l/D)$$ $$\mathrm{Re}_l = \frac{G(1-x)D}{\mu_l}, \quad \mathrm{Bo} = \frac{q''}{Gh_{fg}}$$ For horizontal tubes with $\mathrm{Fr}_l > 0.05$ and for vertical tubes, $E = 1$. For horizontal tube with $\mathrm{Fr}_l < 0.05$, $$E = \mathrm{Fr}_l^{(0.1-2\,\mathrm{Fr}_l)}$$ $$\mathrm{Fr}_l = \frac{G^2}{\rho_l^2 Dg}$$ For annuli, equivalent diameter based on heated perimeter.
Verified range: $D = 0.04$ to 1.1 in. $p_r = 0.0053$ to 0.78 $\mathrm{Bo} \times 10^4 = 0.22$ to 74.2 $G = 7{,}380$ to $8{,}170{,}400$ lb/h·ft² 30 fluids (water, halocarbons, cryogens, chemicals)	Shah (1982)	Boiling heat transfer coefficient h is the largest of that given by the following equations: $$h = \phi_0 h_f \quad \text{(T3.2a)}$$ where $\phi_0 = 230\ \mathrm{Bo}^{0.5}$ h_f in Equation (T3.2a) is calculated at $x = 0$. In the following equations, it is at the actual x. $$h = 1.8[\mathrm{Co}(0.38\ \mathrm{Fr}_l^{-0.3})^n]^{-0.8} h_f \quad \text{(T3.2b)}$$ $$h = F\phi_0 \exp\{2.47[\mathrm{Co}(0.38\ \mathrm{Fr}_l^{-0.3})^n]^{-0.15}\} h_f$$ $$h = F\phi_0 \exp\{2.74[\mathrm{Co}(0.38\ \mathrm{Fr}_l^{-0.3})^n]^{-0.1}\} h_f$$ where h_f and Fr_l are calculated the same way as for Gungor and Winterton correlation $$F = 0.064 \text{ if } \mathrm{Bo} > 0.0011$$ $$F = 0.067 \text{ if } \mathrm{Bo} < 0.0011$$ *Vertical*: $n = 0$ *Horizontal*: $$n = 0 \text{ if } \mathrm{Fr}_l > 0.04$$ $$n = 1 \text{ for } \mathrm{Fr}_l \le 0.04$$ $$\mathrm{Co} = \left(\frac{1-x}{x}\right)^{0.8}\left(\frac{\rho_v}{\rho_l}\right)^{0.5}$$ For annuli, equivalent diameter based on heated perimeter when gap < 4 mm and on wetted perimeter when gap > 4 mm.
Subcooled boiling in horizontal and vertical tubes and annuli Tubes: 2.4 to 27.1 dia. Annuli: gaps 1 to 6.4 mm, internal, external, and two-sided heating Fluids: water, ammonia, halocarbons, organics Tube materials: copper, SS, glass, nickel, Inconel Reduced pressure: 0.005 to 0.89 ΔT_{sc}: 0 to 153 K G: 200 to 87,000 kg/(m²·s) Re_l: 1400 to 360,000 $\mathrm{Bo} \times 10^4$: 0.1 to 54	Shah (1977, 1983)	Low-subcooling regime: $$h = q/\Delta t_{sat} = 230\ \mathrm{Bo}^{0.5} h_f \quad \text{(T3.3a)}$$ High-subcooling regime: $$h = q/\Delta t_{sat} = (230\ \mathrm{Bo}^{0.5} + \Delta t_{sc}/\Delta t_{sat})h_f \quad \text{(T3.3b)}$$ All properties at bulk fluid temperature. High-subcooling regime occurs when $$(\Delta t_{sc}/\Delta t_{sat}) > 2 \text{ or } > 0.00063\ \mathrm{Bo}^{1.25} \quad \text{(T3.3c)}$$ h_f as above with $x = 0$. For annuli, equivalent diameter based on heated perimeter when gap < 4 mm and on wetted perimeter when gap > 4 mm All properties at bulk liquid temperature except latent heat at saturation temperature.

Table 3 Equations for Forced Convection Boiling in Tubes (*Continued*)

Description	References	Equations	
Saturated boiling in round and rectangular channels	Li and Wu (2010a)	$h = 334\text{Bl}^{0.3}(\text{BoRe}_f^{0.36})^{0.4}(k_f/d_h)$	(T3.4)
		$\text{Bl} = q'_w/(Gh_{fg})$	
Compiled from a database of over 3744 data points, including data for R-123, R-236fa, ethanol, CO_2, water, and R-134a.			
D_h = 0.19 to 2.01 mm			
G: 23.4 to 1500 kg/(m²·s)		$\text{Bo} = \dfrac{g(\rho_l - \rho_g)d_h^2}{\sigma}$	
q: 3 to 715 kW/m²			
P_r (reduced pressure): 0.023-0.61			
x (mass quality): $0 < x < x_{CHF}$ (mass quality at critical heat flux)			

Note: All equations are dimensionless.

< 3 mm, the correlation of Yoon et al. (2004) was best, with a mean absolute deviation of 18.7%; the Li and Wu (2010a) correlation for minichannels had a deviation of 20.3%. Data from different studies often do not agree with one another in the same range of parameters, which suggests that some data might be erroneous.

Boiling Mixtures. Most recently developed refrigerants and those in development are mixtures of two or more fluids. Heat transfer coefficients of zeotropic mixtures are lower than those of their pure components because of mass transfer resistance, and the difference grows with increasing glide (i.e., the difference between the mixture's dew point and bubble point temperatures). Hence, the formulas presented previously may be directly used only if the glide is small (e.g., up to 1.8°F). Many calculation methods [e.g., Thome (1996)] for mixtures have been proposed in which a correction factor is applied only to the nucleate boiling terms of correlations for pure fluids. Shah (2015a) noted that mass transfer resistance also occurs during convective boiling (boiling without nucleation), so correction is also needed in this region for both nucleate boiling and convective boiling contributions. For the nucleate boiling region, the following correction factor of Thome and Shakir (1987) for pool boiling of mixtures is used:

$$F_{TS} = \left\{1 + \left(\frac{h_I}{q}\right)(t_{dew} - t_{bub})\left[1 - \exp\left(\frac{-Bq}{\rho_f h_{lg} \beta_f}\right)\right]\right\}^{-1} \quad (3)$$

where h_I is the ideal heat transfer coefficient calculated by a pool boiling correlation for pure fluids using mixture properties, B is the scaling factor (assumed to be 1: all heat transferred to bubble interface is converted to latent heat), and β_f is the liquid-phase mass transfer coefficient, which is recommended to be constant at 0.0063 fps. For the convective boiling contribution, Shah used the Bell and Ghaly (1973) correction factor for condensation heat transfer, which is given in Equation (19). For boiling, t_{dew} is replaced by the bubble point temperature t_{bub}, and h_c is replaced by the boiling heat transfer coefficient. Using this method, the Gungor and Winterton correlation in Table 3 may be written for mixtures as

$$h_{mix} = E\left[F_{TS}h_{nb} + \left(\frac{1}{h_{cb}} + \frac{Y}{h_{GS}}\right)^{-1}\right] \quad (4)$$

Other pure-fluid correlations can be similarly modified for mixtures. Shah (2015a) evaluated this method by applying it to five correlations for pure fluids and comparing them to a database for 45 mixtures of 19 fluids from 21 independent studies. The mixtures had two to six components. The data included tube diameters of 0.008 to 0.55 in., horizontal and vertical orientations, flow rates 37,000 to 686,000 lb/h·ft², reduced pressures from 0.05 to 0.63, and temperature glides up to 281°F. The Cooper correlation was used to calculate h_I in the Thome-Shakir correction factor F_{TS}. Good agreement of this method was found using the correlations of Shah (1982), Gungor and Winterton (1987), and Liu and Winterton (1991). The exception was the only data set for LNG (liquefied natural gas) which agreed with the Shah (1982) and Gungor-Winterton (1987) correlations without any correction. This is the only well-verified method available and is therefore recommended.

Mini- and Microchannels. Some correlations for conventional or macro/minichannels have been found not suitable for microchannels. Numerous definitions have been offered by the various investigators to define microchannels; most use hydraulic diameter as a criterion, though in some cases this may not be the best way to distinguish the phenomenon in microchannels from that in conventional (mini- or macro-) channels. Two widely known criteria are from

- Mehendale et al. (2000), who used hydraulic diameter to classify micro heat exchangers as follows:
  - Micro heat exchanger: 1 μm ≤ d_h ≤ 100 μm
  - Meso heat exchanger: 100 μm ≤ d_h ≤ 1 mm
  - Compact heat exchanger: 1 mm ≤ d_h ≤ 6 mm
  - Conventional heat exchanger: d_h > 6 mm
- Kandlikar and Grande (2003), who classified single- and two-phase microchannels as follows:
  - Conventional channels: d_h > 3 mm
  - Minichannels: 3 mm ≥ d_h > 200 μm
  - Microchannels: 200 μm ≥ d_h > 10 μm

Kandlikar and Grande's definition appears to be the most accepted by the technical community. Most recent experimental and modeling studies suggest that the phenomenon in channels larger than 200 μm appears to be more or less same as that in mini- and macrochannels, thus further supporting this definition for microchannels. Numerous attempts have been made to develop correlations for such channels, but most of those published were validated with only one or two data sets. Correlations from Li and Wu (2010a, 2010b) and Sun and Mishima (2009) show reasonable agreement with varied data from many sources; Li and Wu's is the most verified and has a clearly defined application range (see Table 3). Li and Wu (2010a) and Yen et al. (2003) showed that correlations by Chen (1966), Gungor and Winterton (1986), and Kandlikar (1990) over- or underpredict experimental data of microchannels. Chen's and Kandlikar's correlations underpredicted Yen et al.'s (2003) experimental data by more than an order of magnitude. In addition, Gungor and Winterton's correlation overpredicted the experimental data for channels with hydraulic diameters of 0.586 and 0.19 mm, although the correlation was well matched with data for the 2.01 mm channel. However, Li and Wu's correlation predicted the experimental data well for the range of hydraulic diameters from 0.19 mm to 2.01 mm within the ±30% band. Shah's correlation was not considered in this study, but is expected also to underpredict experimental results for microchannels, because of its fundamental similarity to Chen's correlation. Additional information about microchannels, their various classification, single-phase and phase-change heat transfer and pressure drop correlations, and their future or emerging applications can be found in Ohadi et al. (2013).

Critical Heat Flux (CHF). The preceding correlations are applicable before occurrence of dryout or critical heat flux. After that, transition boiling and film boiling occur. Hall and Mudawar (2000a, 2000b) extensively review CHF data and correlations for flow boiling in tubes.

Shah (1980a, 2016a) gave a graphical and mathematical correlation for CHF during upflow in vertical annuli. This correlation was validated with data from 58 data sets from 25 studies, including annuli with internal, external, and bilateral heating; 10 fluids, including water and refrigerants; reduced pressures from 0.016 to 0.905; flow rates from 100 to 15 759 kg/(m^2·s); tube diameters from 1.5 to 96.5 mm; annular gaps from 0.3 to 16.5 mm; ratios of length to heated equivalent diameter from 1.3 to 394; inlet qualities from –3.3 to +0.91; and critical qualities from –2.7 to +0.95. All data points were predicted with a mean absolute deviation of 16.5%. No other well-verified general correlation for annuli is available.

For upflow in vertical tubes, Shah (1979a, 1987) also gave a general graphical and mathematical correlation for CHF. Shah (2016b) further evaluated its applicability to mini/microchannels. In all, it was validated with data for single tubes and multichannels of equivalent diameters from 0.13 to 37.8 mm, reduced pressures from 0.0014 to 0.96, flow rates from 10 to 41 810 kg/(m^2·s), and qualities from –4 to +1.0. The data included 34 diverse fluids (water, liquid metals, new and old halocarbon refrigerants, hydrocarbons, and cryogens). The same data were also compared to other correlations, and the Shah correlation was found significantly more accurate. For mini/micro channels ($D \le 3$ mm), Shah's and Katto and Ohno's (1984) correlations gave mean absolute deviations of 18.9 and 33.2%, respectively.

Most evaporators used in air conditioning and refrigeration are horizontal and have nonuniform heat flux, so predicting CHF in horizontal channels is of great importance. The following correlation provides K_{hor}, the ratio of CHF in horizontal channels to CHF in vertical upflow at identical conditions (Shah 2015b):

For $x_{in} < 0$ when $L/D < 10$

$$K_{hor} = 1 \tag{5}$$

For $x_c \le 0.05$

$$K_{hor} = 0.725\,\mathrm{Fr}_l^{0.082} \le 1 \tag{6}$$

For $x_c > 0.05$

$$K_{hor} = 0.64\,\mathrm{Fr}_{TP}^{0.15} \le 1 \tag{7}$$

Thus, if K_{hor} calculated with Equation (6) or (7) is greater than 1, use $K_{hor} = 1$. According to Equation (6), $K_{hor} = 1$ at $\mathrm{Fr}_l \ge 50$. According to Equation (7), $K_{hor} = 1$ at $\mathrm{Fr}_{TP} \ge 20$.

$$K_{hor} = q_{c,hor}/q_{c,ver}$$

where $q_{c,hor}$ and $q_{c,ver}$ are the CHF in horizontal and vertical upflow, respectively.

$$\mathrm{Fr}_l = G^2/(\rho_l^2 gD) \quad \text{and} \quad \mathrm{Fr}_{TP} = x_c G/[gD\rho_g(\rho_l - \rho_g)]^{0.5}$$

where x_c is the critical quality and x_{in} is the inlet quality.

For channels with nonuniform heat flux, critical heat flux is the total heat applied over the channel surface up to CHF point divided by the surface area up to that point. For noncircular channels and for channels heated on only part of their circumference, use equivalent diameter based on heated perimeter. This correlation was compared to a database that included 10 fluids (water, refrigerants, and hydrocarbons) in single and multiple channels of diameters 0.13 to 24.3 mm, reduced pressures from 0.005 to 0.9, mass flux from 20 to 11 390 kg/(m^2·s), inlet qualities from –1.05 to 0.72, and critical qualities from –0.2 to 0.99. Data included uniform and nonuniform heat flux. With CHF for vertical channels calculated by the Shah (1987) correlation, it predicted 878 data points from 39 data sets from 18 sources, with a mean absolute deviation of 15.4%. The same data were also compared to six other correlations, but none gave good agreement.

Post-CHF Heat Transfer. After CHF, transition boiling and film boiling occur. Film boiling can be the inverted annular type or the dispersed flow type. The former occurs only for a short length, if at all. For dispersed film boiling, the most verified general correlation is by Shah (1980b) in graphical form (Figure 7), converted to equation form by Shah and Siddiqui (2000). Fr_l is same as in Table 3. It is based on the two-step physical model and validated with wide-ranging data that included cryogens, refrigerants, and organics. At the dryout point, the actual quality x_A equals equilibrium quality x_E. At larger Bo, calculate x_A from Figure 7 as follows:

1. Locate x_c on the equilibrium line.
2. If x_c is below the intersection with Fr_l curve, read x_A along this line till it intersects the Fr_l curve and then read along that curve.
3. If x_c is above the intersection with Fr_l curve, draw a tangent to the curve; x_A is then read along the tangent up to the intersection point and then along the Fr_l curve.
4. Then calculate the actual enthalpy of vapor H_g by Equation (8):

$$(x_E - x_A)/x_A h_{fg} = H_g - H_{g,sat} \tag{8}$$

For Bo < 0.0005, calculate $(x_E - x_A)$ in the same way, then multiply it by (Bo/0.0005).

$H_{g,sat}$ is the enthalpy of saturated vapor. Knowing H_g, actual vapor temperature t_g is known. Vapor-phase heat transfer coefficient is calculated by Equations (9a) and (9b) using properties at actual vapor temperature (except for water, for which film temperature is used):

For Re < 10^4

$$h_g D/k_g = 0.023(GDx_A/\mu_g\alpha)^{0.8}\,\mathrm{Pr}_g^{0.4} \tag{9a}$$

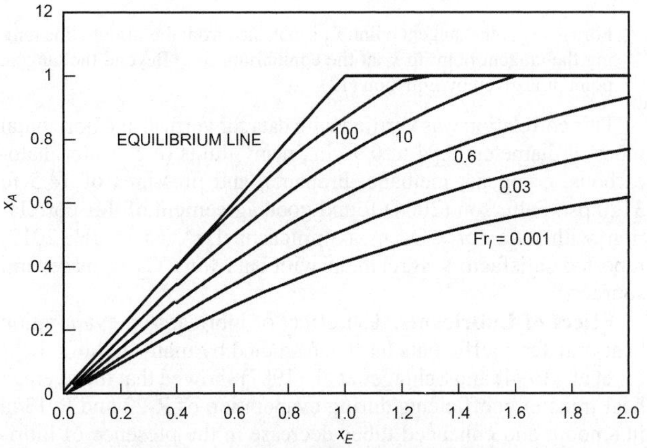

Fig. 7 Film Boiling Correlation
(Shah and Siddiqui 2000)

For Re > 10^4

$$h_g D/k_g = 0.00834(GDx_A/\mu_g\alpha)^{0.8774}\,\mathrm{Pr}_g^{\,0.6112} \tag{9b}$$

The wall temperature t_w at heat flux q is then obtained by

$$q = h_g F_{dc}(t_w - t_g) \tag{10}$$

F_{dc} is the droplet cooling factor, which is 1 except when $p_r > 0.8$ and $L/D > 30$, in which case

$$F_{dc} = 2.64p_r - 1.11 \tag{11}$$

Void fraction α is calculated by the homogeneous model, which gives

$$\alpha = \frac{x_A\rho_f}{(1 - x_A)\rho_g + \rho_f x_A} \tag{12}$$

Fr_l is defined in Table 3. The critical quality x_c is calculated by a suitable method as described in the foregoing. For horizontal tubes, wall temperatures at top and bottom are calculated as above using the x_c at that location.

Calculations for calculating x_A by equations are described now. The curves in the figure are represented by the following equations:

For $x_E \geq 0.4$,

$$x_A = (A_1 + A_2x_E + A_3x_E^2 + A_4x_E^3)\mathrm{Fr}_l^{0.064} \tag{13}$$

$$A_1 = -0.0347,\ A_2 = 0.9335,\ A_3 = -0.2875,\ A_4 = 0.035$$

x_A from Equation (13) is corrected as: If $x_A > x_E$, then $x_A = x_E$. If $x_A > 1$, then $x_A = 1$.

For $x_E < 0.4$, the correlating curves in Figure 7 are represented by lines joining x_A at $x_E = 0.4$ from Equation (13) and intersecting the equilibrium line ($x_A = x_E$) at

$$x_{A,INT} = x_{E,INT} = 0.19\ \mathrm{Fr}_l^{0.16} \tag{14}$$

Calculation is as follows:

1. For $x_c \leq x_{E,INT}$, $x_A = x_E$ for $x_E \leq x_{E,INT}$. For $x_E > x_{E,INT}$, obtain x_A from Equations (13) and (14).
2. For $x_c > x_{E,INT}$, determine the point where tangent from $x_E = x_A = x_c$ touches the curve of Equation (11). The point of tangency is at the intersection of Equations (13) and (15), obtained by simultaneous solution of the two equations.

$$x_A = x_c + (x_E - x_c)(A_2 + 2A_3x_E + 3A_4x_E^2)\ \mathrm{Fr}_l^{0.064} \tag{15}$$

For $x_E < x_E$ at the tangent point, x_A is obtained from the straight line joining the tangent point to x_c at the equilibrium line. Beyond the tangent point, it is given by Equation (12).

This correlation was verified with data for vertical and horizontal tubes of diameters 0.04 to 0.96 in., many fluids (e.g., water, halocarbons, cryogens, methane, propane), and pressures of 14.5 to 3120 psi. Petterson (2004) found good agreement of this correlation with data for CO_2 in a minichannel. Ayad et al. (2012) reported satisfactory agreement with data for CO_2 from several sources.

Effect of Lubricants. The effect of lubricant on evaporation heat transfer coefficients has been studied by many authors. Eckels et al. (1994) and Schlager et al. (1987) showed that the average heat transfer coefficients during evaporation of R-22 and R-134a in smooth and enhanced tubes decrease in the presence of lubricant (up to a 20% reduction at 5% lubricant concentration by mass). Slight enhancements at lubricant concentrations under 3% are observed with some refrigerant lubricant mixtures. Zeurcher et al. (1998) studied local heat transfer coefficients of refrigerant/lubricant mixtures in the dry-wall region of the evaporator (see Figure 5) and proposed prediction methods. The effect of lubricant concentration on local heat transfer coefficients was shown to depend on mass flux and vapor quality. At low mass fluxes (less than about 150,000 $\mathrm{lb_m/h \cdot ft^2}$), oil sharply decreased performance, whereas at higher mass fluxes (greater than 150,000 $\mathrm{lb_m/h \cdot ft^2}$), enhancements at vapor qualities in the range of 0.35 to 0.7 were seen. The foregoing information is for miscible oil/refrigerant mixtures. Shah (1975) found that miscible oil in ammonia evaporators forms thin films around the tube perimeter, drastically reducing the heat transfer coefficients. The thickness of oil film δ to account for the reduction in heat transfer during single-phase flow was given by

$$\delta/D = 0.028/\mathrm{Re}_{LT}^{0.23} \tag{16}$$

where Re_{LT} is the Reynolds number with all mass flowing in liquid form. Shah's (1976) correlation for boiling gave reasonable agreement with ammonia data when the resistance of the calculated oil film was taken into account. Chaddock and Buzzard (1986) also reported reduction of heat transfer because of oil films in an ammonia evaporator with immiscible oil. Similar results may be expected with other immiscible refrigerant/oil mixtures.

Boiling in Plate Heat Exchangers (PHEs)

For a description of plate heat exchanger geometry, see the Plate Heat Exchangers section of Chapter 4.

Little information is available on two-phase flow in plate exchangers; for brief discussions, see Hesselgreaves (1990), Jonsson (1985), Kumar (1984), Panchal (1985, 1990), Panchal and Hillis (1984), Panchal et al. (1983), Syed (1990), Thonon (1995), Thonon et al. (1995), and Young (1994).

General correlations for evaporators and condensers should be similar to those for circular and noncircular conduits, with specific constants or variables defining plate geometry. Correlations for flooded evaporators differ somewhat from those for a typical flooded shell-and-tube, where the bulk of heat transfer results mainly from pool boiling. Because of the narrow, complex passages in the PHE flooded evaporator, it is possible that most heat transfer occurs through convective boiling rather than localized nucleate boiling, which probably affects mainly the lower section of a plate in a flooded system. This aspect could be enhanced by modifying the surface structure of the lower third of the plates in contact with the refrigerant. It is also possible that the contact points (nodes) between two adjacent plates of opposite chevron enhance nucleate boiling. Each nodal contact point could create a favorable site for a reentrant cavity.

The same applies to thermosiphon and direct-expansion evaporators. The simplest approach would be to formulate a correlation of the type proposed by Pierre (1964) for varying quality, as suggested by Baskin (1991). A positive feature about a PHE evaporator is that flow is vertical, against gravity, as opposed to horizontal flow in a shell-and-tube evaporator. Therefore, the flow regime does not get too complicated and phase separation is not a severe issue, even at low mass fluxes along the flow path, which has always been a problem in ammonia shell-and-tube DX evaporators. Generally, the profile is flat, except at the end plates. For more complete analysis, correlations could be developed that involve the local bubble point temperature concept for evaluation of wall superheat and local Froude number and boiling number Bo.

Yan and Lin's (1999) experimental study of a compact brazed exchanger (CBE) with R-134a as a refrigerant reveals some interesting features about flow evaporation in plate exchangers. Heat transfer coefficients were higher compared to circular tubes, especially at high-vapor-quality convective regimes. Mass flux played a significant role, whereas heat flux had very little effect on overall performance.

Ayub (2003) presents simple correlations based on design and field data collected over a decade on ammonia and R-22 direct-expansion and flooded evaporators in North America. The goal was to formulate equations that could be readily used by a design and field engineer without referral to complicated two-phase models. The correlations take into account the effect of chevron angle of the mating plates, making it a universal correlation applied to any chevron angle plate. The correlation has a statistical error of ±8%. The expression for heat transfer coefficient is

$$h = C(k_l/d_e)(\mathrm{Re}_l^{\,2} h_{fg}/L_p)^{0.4124}(p_r)^{0.12}(65/\beta)^{0.35} \tag{17}$$

where $C = 0.1121$ for flooded and thermosiphons and $C = 0.0675$ for DX. This is a dimensional correlation where the values of k_l, d_e, h_{fg}, and L_p are in Btu/h·ft·°F, ft, Btu/lb, and ft, respectively. Chevron angle β is in degrees.

Khan et al. (2010) conducted a study to investigate the boiling of NH_3(ammonia) in brazed-plate heat exchangers. Single-phase results are presented in Table 11 of Chapter 4. Two-phase evaporation experiments were aimed to investigate the effects of heat flux, mass flux, and exit vapor quality on evaporation of ammonia in a vertical plate heat exchanger at various saturation pressures.

$$\mathrm{Nu}_{tp} = C(\beta^*)\{\mathrm{Re}_{eq}\mathrm{Bo}_{eq}\}^{m(\beta^*)}\{P^*\}^{j(\beta^*)} \tag{18}$$

$$C(\beta^*) = -173.52\beta^* + 257.12$$

$$m(\beta^*) = -0.09\beta^* + 0.0005$$

$$j(\beta^*) = 0.624\beta^* - 0.822$$

2. CONDENSING

In most applications, condensation; is initiated by removing heat at a solid/vapor interface, either through the walls of the vessel containing the saturated vapor or through the solid surface of a cooling mechanism placed in the saturated vapor. If sufficient energy is removed, the local temperature of vapor near the interface drops below its equilibrium saturation temperature. Because heat removal creates a temperature gradient, with the lowest temperature near the interface, droplets most likely form at this location. This defines one type of heterogeneous nucleation that can result in either dropwise or film condensation, depending on the physical characteristics of the solid surface and the working fluid.

Dropwise condensation occurs on the cooling solid surface when its surface free energy is relatively low compared to that of the liquid. Examples include highly polished or fatty-acid-impregnated surfaces in contact with steam. **Film condensation** occurs when a cooling surface with relatively high surface free energy contacts a fluid with lower surface free energy [see Chen (2003) and Isrealachvili (1991)]; this type of condensation occurs in most systems.

For smooth film flow, the rate of heat transport depends on the condensate film thickness, which depends on the rates of vapor condensation and condensate removal. At high reduced pressures (p_r), heat transfer coefficients for dropwise condensation are higher than those for film condensation at the same surface loading. At low reduced pressures, the reverse is true. For example, there is a reduction of 6 to 1 in the dropwise condensation coefficient of steam when saturation pressure decreases from 0.9 to 0.16 atm. One method for correlating the dropwise condensation heat transfer coefficient uses nondimensional parameters, including the effect of surface tension gradient, temperature difference, and fluid properties [see, e.g., Rose (1998)].

When condensation occurs on horizontal tubes and short vertical plates, condensate film motion is laminar. On vertical tubes and long vertical plates, film motion can become turbulent. Grober et al. (1961) suggest using a Reynolds number (Re) of 1600 as the critical point at which the flow pattern changes from laminar to turbulent. This Reynolds number is based on condensate flow rate divided by the breadth of the condensing surface. For the outside of a vertical tube, the breadth is the circumference of the tube; for the outside of a horizontal tube, the breadth is twice the length of the tube. Re = $4\Gamma/\mu_l$, where Γ is the mass flow of condensate per unit of breadth, and μ_l is the absolute (dynamic) viscosity of the condensate at film temperature t_f. In practice, condensation is usually laminar in shell-and-tube condensers with the vapor outside horizontal tubes.

Vapor velocity also affects the condensing coefficient. When this is small, condensate flows primarily by gravity and is resisted by the liquid's viscosity. When vapor velocity is high relative to the condensate film, there is appreciable drag at the vapor/liquid interface. The thickness of the condensate film, and hence the heat transfer coefficient, is affected. When vapor flow is upward, a retarding force is added to the viscous shear, increasing the film thickness. When vapor flow is downward, the film thickness decreases and the heat transfer coefficient increases. For condensation inside horizontal tubes, the force of the vapor velocity causes condensate flow. When vapor velocity is high, the transition from laminar to turbulent flow occurs at Reynolds numbers lower than 1600 (Grober et al. 1961).

When **superheated** vapor is condensed, the heat transfer coefficient depends on the surface temperature. When surface temperature is below saturation temperature, using the value of h for condensation of saturated vapor that incorporates the difference between the saturation and surface temperatures leads to insignificant error (McAdams 1954). If the surface temperature is above the saturation temperature, there is no condensation and the equations for gas convection apply.

Correlation equations for condensing heat transfer, along with their applicable geometries, fluid properties, and flow rates, are given in Table 4. The basic prediction method for laminar condensation on vertical surfaces is relatively unchanged from Nusselt's (1916). Empirical relations must be used for higher condensate flow rates, however.

For condensation on the outside surface of horizontal finned tubes, use Equation (T4.5) for liquids that drain readily from the surface (Beatty and Katz 1948). For condensing steam outside finned tubes, where liquid is retained in spaces between tubes, coefficients substantially lower than those given by this equation were reported, because of the high surface tension of water relative to other liquids. For additional data on condensation on the outside of finned tubes, please refer to Webb (1994).

Condensation on Inner Surface of Tubes

Many correlations have been proposed for heat transfer during condensation in tubes. The ones validated over the widest range of data are by Cavallini et al. (2006) and Shah (2009, 2013), the latter being an extended version of the Shah (1979b) correlation. Both these correlations note that heat transfer at high flow rate is independent of heat flux, whereas at low flow rates it is affected by heat flux. These correlations apply to all flow patterns; the Shah correlation is applicable to horizontal as well as vertical tubes (with downflow), although the Cavallini et al. correlation applies only to horizontal tubes. Other well-verified correlations for horizontal tubes are those of Dobson and Chato (1998) and Thome et al. (2003). Shah (2014b) presents a flow-pattern-based version of the Shah (2013) correlation for horizontal tubes. In this version, Regime I corresponds to stratified flow, Regime II to wavy flow, and Regime III to intermittent, annular, and mist flow. Flow patterns were determined by the El Hajal et al. (2003) map. The mean deviation of the database was comparable to that of the Shah (2013) correlation.

Table 4 Heat Transfer Coefficient/Nusselt Number Correlations for Film-Type Condensation

Description	References	Equations
Vertical surfaces, height L		
Laminar, non-wavy liquid film* $Re = 4\Gamma/\mu_l < 1800$ $\Gamma = \dot{m}_l/b$ = mass flow rate of liquid condensate per unit breadth of surface	Based on Nusselt (1916)	$h = 0.943\left[\frac{\rho_l g(\rho_l - \rho_v)h_{fg}k_l^3}{\mu_l L(t_{sat} - t_s)}\right]^{1/4}$ (T4.1)
Turbulent flow $Re = 4\Gamma/\mu_f > 1800$	McAdams (1954)	$h = 0.0077\left[\frac{k_l^3\rho_l(\rho_l - \rho_v)g}{\mu_l^2}\right]^{1/3} Re^{0.4}$ (T4.2)
Outside horizontal tubes		
Single tube* $Re = 4\Gamma/\mu_l < 3600$	Dhir and Lienhard (1971)	$h = 0.729\left[\frac{\rho_l g(\rho_l - \rho_v)h_{fg}k_l^3}{\mu_l D(t_{sat} - t_s)}\right]^{1/4}$ (T4.3)
N tubes, vertically aligned	Murase et al. (206)	$h = h_D N^{-1/n}$ (T4.4) h_D is the heat transfer coefficient for one tube calculated from Dhir and Lienhard (1971) and the value of n can vary between 4 and 6.
Finned tubes This correlation is acceptable for low-surface-tension fluids and low-fin-density tubes. It overpredicts in cases where space between tubes floods with liquid (as when either surface tension becomes relatively large or fin spacing relatively small).	Beatty and Katz (1948)	$h = 0.689\left[\frac{\rho_l^2 k_l^3 g h_{fg}}{\mu_l(t_{sat} - t_s)D_e}\right]^{1/4}$ (T4.5) $\frac{1}{D_e^{1/4}} = 1.30\frac{A_s\phi}{A_{eff}L_{mf}^{1/4}} + \frac{A_p}{A_{eff}D^{1/4}}$ $A_{eff} = A_s\phi + A_p$, $L_{mf} = \pi(D_o^2 - D_r^2)/D_o$ ϕ = fin efficiency D_o = outside tube diameter (including fins) D_r = diameter at fin root (i.e., smooth tube outer diameter) A_s = fin surface area A_p = surface area of tube between fins
Internal flow in plain channels		
Horizontal, vertical downflow in round, rectangular, triangular, semicircular, single, and multiport channels D_h = 0.0039 to 1.93 in. p_r = 0.0008 to 0.946 G = 2,952 to 1,033,200 lb/h·ft² x = 0.01 to 0.99 30 fluids, including water, hydrocarbons, new and old halocarbon refrigerants, CO_2	Shah (2009, 2013, 2016c)	Condensing heat transfer coefficient h_{TP} is given by the following equations: (T4.6) In Regime I, $h_{TP} = h_I$ In Regime II, $h_{TP} = h_I + h_{Nu}$ In Regime III, $h_{TP} = h_{Nu}$ $h_I = h_{LS}\left(1 + \frac{3.8}{Z^{0.95}}\right)\left(\frac{\mu_l}{14\mu_v}\right)^{0.0058 + 0.557p_r}$ $h_{Nu} = 1.32Re_{LS}^{-1/3}\left[\frac{\rho_l(\rho_l - \rho_v)gk_l^3}{\mu_l^2}\right]^{1/3}$ $h_{LT} = 0.023\ Re_{LS}^{0.8}\ Pr_f^{0.4}\frac{k_f}{D}$ $Re_{LT} = GD/\mu_l$ $Re_{LS} = GD(1 - x)/\mu_l$ $Re_{GS} = GDx/\mu_v$ $We_g = G^2D_h/(\rho_g\sigma)$ For horizontal tubes, Regime III if $J_g \leq 0.95(1.254 + 2.27Z^{1.249})^{-1}$ $J_g = \frac{xG}{[gD\rho_v(\rho_l - \rho_v)]^{0.5}}$ Regime I if $We_g > 100$ and $J_g \geq 0.98(Z + 0.263)^{-0.62}$ Else Regime II For vertical downflow, Regime I if $J_g \geq (2.4Z + 0.73)^{-1}$ Regime III if $J_g \leq 0.89 - 0.93\exp(-0.087Z^{-1.17})$ Else Regime II $Z = (1/x - 1)^{0.8}\ p_r^{0.4}$

Table 4 Heat Transfer Coefficient/Nusselt Number Correlations for Film-Type Condensation (*Continued*)

Description	References	Equations
		All properties at saturation temperature. For noncircular channels, equivalent diameter is based on cooled perimeter in all equations except We_g, which uses hydraulic diameter D_h.
Horizontal tubes D = 0.12 to 0.67 in. G = 29,520 to 1,653,120 lb/h·ft^2 t_s = 75 to 576°F Fluids: water, halocarbons, hydrocarbons, CO_2	Cavallini et al. (2006)	$J_{g,t} = \left\{\left[7.5/\left(4.3X_{tt}^{1.111}+1\right)\right]^{-3} + C_T^{-3}\right\}^{-1/3}$ (T4.7) C_T = 1.6 for hydrocarbons, 2.6 for all other fluids If $J_g > J_{g,t}$ $h_{TP} = h_A$ $h_A = h_{LT}[1 + 1.128x^{0.8170}(\rho_f/\rho_g)^{0.3685}B]$ $B = (\mu_f/\mu_g)^{0.2363}(1 - \mu_g/\mu_f)^{2.144}\ Pr_f^{-0.1}$ If $J_g < J_{g,t}$, $h_{TP} = [h_A(J_{g,t}/J_g)^{0.8} - h_{st}](J_g/J_{g,t}) + h_{st}$ $h_{st} = 0.725\{1 + 0.741[(1 - x)/x]^{0.3321}\}^{-1}$ $\times \{k_f^3\rho_f(\rho_f - \rho_g)gh_{fg}/[\mu_f D(t_w - t_s)]\}^{0.25}$ $+ (1 - x^{0.087})h_{LT}$
Horizontal mini/micro (D < 3 mm) round, rectangular, triangular, semicircular, single, and multiport channels D_h = 0.0039 to 0.11 in., p_r = 0.0055 to 0.942, G = 14,760 to 1,033,200 lb/h·ft^2	Shah (2016c)	Same as preceding Shah correlation except replace h_I with h_A from the Cavallini et al. correlation [Equation (T4.7)].
Inclined tubes Inclination θ = –90 to +90 degree (–90 vertical down, 0 horizontal), D = 0.05 to 0.58 in., p_r = 0.006 to 0.43.	Shah (2015d)	For θ = –30 to +90, $h_{TP,\theta} = h_{TP,0}$ For θ = –90 to –30, $h_{TP,\theta} = h_{TP,0} + (h_{TP,0} - h_{TP,-90})(\theta + 30)/60$

Note: Properties in Equation (T4.1) evaluated at $t_f = (t_{sat} + t_s)/2$; h_{fg} evaluated at t_{sat}.

*For increased accuracy, use $h'_{fg} = h_{fg} + 0.68c_{p,l}(t_{sat} - t_s)$ in place of h_{fg}.

Use caution in applying any of these correlations to carbon dioxide. Shah (2015c) compared a wide range of data for condensation of CO_2 with several well-verified general correlations. The Shah (2009, 2013) correlation gave good agreement with data for mass flux up to 300 kg/(m^2·s); its agreement with data at higher flow rates was inconsistent. None of the other correlations gave good agreement at any flow rate. Researchers have generally indicated high uncertainties in their measurements, so it is unclear which are inaccurate: data or correlations.

Some condensers have **inclined tubes** (i.e., flow direction is not horizontal or vertically down). Literature on condensation in inclined tubes was reviewed in detail by Lips and Meyer (2011) and briefly by Meyer et al. (2014). They reported that data from different sources showed different effects of inclination on heat transfer, and that no general method of prediction was available. Shah (2015d) gave a model for variation of heat transfer with inclination (Table 4). Together with the Shah correlation (2009, 2013), it gave good agreement with data from six sources (all that could be found), with mean absolute deviation of 15.7%. Note that, for upward flow, only data for cocurrent flow of condensate and vapor (i.e., flows above flooding limit) were considered.

During upward flow of vapor at low velocities (below flooding velocity), condensate flows downwards while the vapor is flowing upwards. Reflux condensers are examples. Lips and Meyer (2011) reviewed the literature on this subject; of the many experimental studies and various predictive techniques examined, none was sufficiently verified to be considered generally applicable. Palen and Yang (2001) reviewed the literature on predicting flooding velocity in reflux condensers.

Mini- and Microchannels. (See the section on Mini- and Microchannels, under Forced-Convection Evaporation in Tubes, for definitions of these channels.) Much research has been done on condensation in small channels [e.g., Awad et al. (2014)]. Many theoretical and empirical formulas have been proposed, but the only ones that have been verified with a wide range of data from many sources are by Kim and Mudawar (2013) and Shah (2016c). Kim and Mudawar (2013) presented a flow pattern based model that showed good agreement with a wide-ranging database including many fluids, horizontal and vertical channels, and hydraulic diameters from 0.424 to 6.22 mm. Shah (2016c) compared a wide range of data for horizontal channels of diameter less than 3 mm with the Shah (2013) general correlation, and found good agreement with all data except for We_g < 100, which were underpredicted. Satisfactory agreement was achieved by using Regime II instead of Regime I for such data. Thus, this modified correlation is applicable to both mini and conventional channels. Shah (2016c) also gave a new correlation in which Cavallini et al.'s (2006) heat-flux-independent regime replaced the corresponding formula in the Shah correlation. The mean absolute deviations of the Kim and Mudawar, modified Shah, and the new Shah correlations were 18.6, 17.8, and 14.6%, respectively, compared to data for single channels. Thus, the new Shah correlation is significantly more accurate than the other two and is therefore preferable.

Multicomponent Mixtures. Many refrigerants in use or in development are mixtures of pure fluids. Heat transfer in condensation of mixtures is reduced by resistance caused by mass transfer effects. The phenomena involved are complex, but Bell and Ghaly (1973) presented a simple method to estimate this resistance. It is given by the following equation:

$$\frac{1}{h_{mix}} = \frac{1}{h_c} + \frac{Y}{h_{GS}} \tag{19}$$

$$Y = xC_{pg}\frac{dt_{dew}}{dH} \tag{20}$$

where h_{mix} is the heat transfer coefficient of the mixture, h_c is the heat transfer coefficient for condensation of an equivalent pure fluid with the properties of the mixture, and H is enthalpy. The single-phase heat transfer coefficient h_{GS} is to be calculated conservatively. Shah et al. (2013) used this method together with the Shah correlation (2009), the single-phase heat transfer coefficient h_{GS} being calculated by the following equation:

$$h_{GS} = 0.023\left(\frac{GxD}{\mu_g}\right)^{0.8}\frac{\mathrm{Pr}_g^{\,0.4}k_g}{D} \tag{21}$$

It was compared to 529 test points for 36 refrigerant mixtures from 22 studies in horizontal and vertical tubes that included temperature glides up to 63.9°F. The mean absolute deviation was 18%. This method is recommended.

Plate-Type Condensers. ASHRAE-sponsored research project RP-1394 examined carbon dioxide condensation in brazed-plate heat exchangers (BPHEs) (Jokar and Hayes 2009). Three BPHEs with different interior configurations, each consisting of three channels, were tested (see Figure 25 in Chapter 4). The single-phase results of this study are presented in Table 11 of Chapter 4 and in Hayes and Jokar (2009). For the two-phase analysis, carbon dioxide was the working fluid, flowing through the middle channel, while the cooling fluid flowed through the side channels of the three different exchangers. Condensation of carbon dioxide occurred at saturation temperatures ranging from 0°F to –30°F at heat fluxes spanning 800 to 5000 Btu/h·ft² (Hayes et al. 2011, 2012). The proposed correlations are summarized as follows, where the uncertainty of the two-phase correlations was less than 8%:

$$\mathrm{Nu}_{tp} = C_1\,\mathrm{Re}_l^{\,C_2}\,\mathrm{Pr}_l^{\,C_3}\left(\frac{G^2}{\rho_l^2 c_{p,l}\Delta T}\right)^{C_4}\left(\frac{\rho_l^2 i'_{fg}}{G^2}\right)^{C_5}\left(\frac{\rho_l\sigma_l}{\mu_l G}\right)^{C_6}\left(\frac{\rho_l}{\rho_l-\rho_v}\right)^{C_7}$$

Plate	C_1	C_2	C_3	C_4	C_5	C_6	C_7
60/60	0.37	0.706	0.35	1.07	0.91	0.032	1.18
27/60	0.16	0.727	0.35	1.07	0.90	0.147	1.00
27/27	0.11	0.771	0.35	1.04	0.92	0.0105	2.00

Longo et al.'s (2014) correlation for condensation inside corrugated plate type heat exchangers was shown to agree with data from several sources for several halocarbon and hydrocarbon refrigerants, as well as CO_2.

Noncondensable Gases. Condensation heat transfer rates reduce drastically if one or more noncondensable gases are present in the condensing vapor/gas mixture. In mixtures, the condensable component is called *vapor* and the noncondensable component is called *gas*. As the mass fraction of gas increases, the heat transfer coefficient decreases in an approximately linear manner. Othmer (1929) found that the heat transfer coefficient in a steam chest with 2.89% air by volume dropped from about 2000 to about 600 Btu/h·ft²·°F.

Consider a surface cooled to temperature t_s below the saturation temperature of the vapor (Figure 8). In this system, accumulated condensate falls or is driven across the condenser surface. At a finite heat transfer rate, the temperature profile across the condensate can be estimated from Table 4; the interface of the condensate is at a temperature $t_{if} > t_s$. In the absence of gas, the interface temperature is the vapor saturation temperature at the pressure of the condenser.

The presence of noncondensable gas lowers the vapor partial pressure and hence the saturation temperature of the vapor in equilibrium with the condensate. Further, vapor movement toward the cooled surface implies similar bulk motion of the gas. At the condensing interface, vapor condenses at temperature t_{if} and is then swept out of the system as a liquid. The gas concentration rises to ultimately diffuse away from the cooled surface at the same rate as

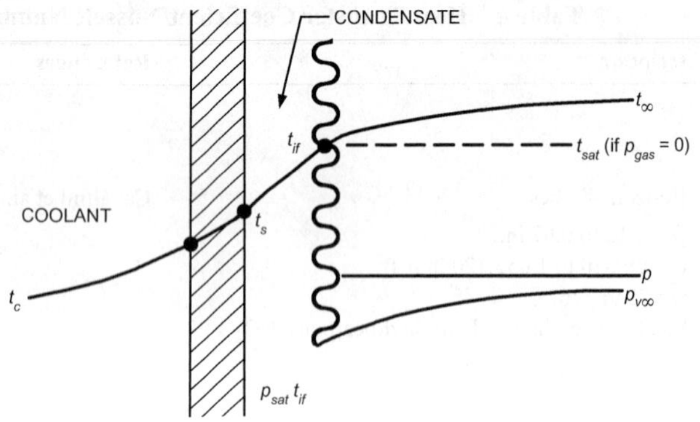

Fig. 8 Origin of Noncondensable Resistance

it is convected toward the surface (Figure 8). If the gas (mole fraction) concentration is Y_g and total pressure of the system is p, the partial pressure of the bulk gas is

$$p_{g\infty} = Y_{g\infty}p \tag{22}$$

The partial pressure of the bulk vapor is

$$p_{v\infty} = (1 - Y_{g\infty})p = Y_v p \tag{23}$$

As opposing fluxes of convection and diffusion of the gas increase, the partial pressure of gas at the condensing interface is $p_{gif} > p_{g\infty}$. By Dalton's law, assuming isobaric conditions,

$$p_{gif} + p_{vif} = p \tag{24}$$

Hence, $p_{vif} < p_{v\infty}$.

Sparrow et al. (1967) noted that thermodynamic equilibrium exists at the interface, except in the case of very low pressures or liquid metal condensation, so that

$$p_{vif} = p_{sat}(t_{if}) \tag{25}$$

where $p_{sat}(t)$ is the saturation pressure of vapor at temperature t. The available Δt for condensation across the condensate film is reduced from $(t_\infty - t_s)$ to $(t_{if} - t_s)$, where t_∞ is the bulk temperature of the condensing vapor/gas mixture, caused by the additional noncondensable resistance.

Equations in Table 4 are still valid for condensate resistance, but interface temperature t_{if} must be found. The noncondensable resistance, which accounts for the temperature difference $(t_\infty - t_{if})$, depends on heat flux (through the convecting flow to the interface) and diffusion of gas away from the interface.

For simple cases, Rose (1969), Sparrow and Lin (1964), and Sparrow et al. (1967) found solutions to the combined energy, diffusion, and momentum problem of noncondensables, but they are cumbersome.

A general method given by Colburn and Hougen (1934) can be used over a wide range if correct expressions are provided for the rate equations; add the contributions of sensible heat transport through the noncondensable gas film and latent heat transport via condensation:

$$h_g(t_\infty - t_{if}) + K_D M_v h_{fg}(p_{v\infty} - p_{vif}) = h(t_{if} - t_s) = U(t_{if} - t_c) \tag{26}$$

where h is from the appropriate equation in Table 4.

The value of the heat transfer coefficient for stagnant gas depends on the geometry and flow conditions. For flow parallel to a condenser tube, for example,

$$j = \left[\frac{h_g}{(c_p)_g G}\right]\left[\frac{(c_p)_g \mu_{gv}}{K_{Dg}}\right]^{2/3} \tag{27}$$

where j is a known function of Re = GD/μ_{gv}. The mass transfer coefficient K_D is

$$\frac{K_D}{M_m}\left[\frac{p_{g\infty} - p_{gif}}{\ln(p_{g\infty}/p_{gif})}\right]\left(\frac{\mu_{gv}}{\rho_g D}\right)^{2/3} = j \tag{28}$$

The calculation method requires substitution of Equation (28) into Equation (26). For a given flow condition, G, Re, j, M_m, $\rho_{g\infty}$, h_g, and h (or U) are known. Assume values of t_{if}; calculate $p_{sat}(t_{if}) = p_{vif}$ and hence p_{gif}. If t_s is not known, use the overall coefficient U to the coolant and t_c in place of h and t_s in Equation (26). For either case, at each location in the condenser, iterate Equation (26) until it balances, giving the condensing interface temperature and, hence, the thermal load to that point (Colburn 1951; Colburn and Hougen 1934). For more detail, refer to Chapter 10 in Collier and Thome (1996).

Other Impurities

Vapor entering the condenser often contains a small percentage of impurities such as oil. Oil forms a film on the condensing surfaces, creating additional resistance to heat transfer. Some allowance should be made for this, especially in the absence of an oil separator or when the discharge line from the compressor to the condenser is short.

3. PRESSURE DROP

Total pressure drop for two-phase flow in tubes consists of friction, change in momentum, and hydrostatic components:

$$\left(\frac{dp}{dz}\right)_{total} = \pm\left(\frac{dp}{dz}\right)_{static} + \left(\frac{dp}{dz}\right)_{mom} + \left(\frac{dp}{dz}\right)_{fric} \tag{29a}$$

where

$$\left(\frac{dp}{dz}\right)_{static} = [\varepsilon_v \rho_v + (1 - \varepsilon_v)\rho_l] g \sin\theta$$

The momentum pressure drop accounts for the acceleration of the flow, usually caused by evaporation of liquid or condensation of vapor. In this case,

$$\left(\frac{dp}{dz}\right)_{mom} = G^2\left(\frac{x^2}{\varepsilon_v \rho_v} + \frac{(1-x)^2}{(1-\varepsilon_v)\rho_l}\right) \tag{29b}$$

where G is total mass velocity. An empirical model for the void fraction with good accuracy is presented by Steiner (1993), based on the (dimensional) correlation of Rouhani and Axelsson (1970).

$$\varepsilon_v = \frac{x}{\rho_v}\left\{[1 + 0.12(1-x)]\left(\frac{x}{\rho_v} + \frac{1-x}{\rho_l}\right) + \left[\frac{1.18(1-x)[g\sigma(\rho_l - \rho_v)]^{0.25}}{G^1 \rho_l^{0.5}}\right]\right\}^{-1} \tag{29c}$$

Table 5 Constants in Equation (29d) for Different Void Fraction Correlations

Model	A_l	q_l	r_l	S_l
Homogeneous (Collier 1972)	1.0	1.0	1.0	0
Lockhart and Martinelli (1949)	0.28	0.64	0.36	0.07
Baroczy (1963)	1.0	0.74	0.65	0.13
Thome (1964)	1.0	1.0	0.89	0.18
Zivi (1964)	1.0	1.0	0.67	0
Turner and Wallis (1965)	1.0	0.72	0.40	0.08

A generalized expression for ε_v was suggested by Butterworth (1975):

$$\varepsilon_v = \left[1 + A_l\left(\frac{1-x}{x}\right)^{q_l}\left(\frac{\rho_v}{\rho_l}\right)^{r_l}\left(\frac{\mu_l}{\mu_v}\right)^{S_l}\right]^{-1} \tag{29d}$$

This generalized form represents the models of several researchers; constants and exponents needed for each model are given in Table 5. Consult Woldesemayat and Ghajar (2007) for a summary of 68 void fraction correlations for different flow patterns in horizontal and upward-inclined pipes.

The homogeneous model provides a simple method for computing the acceleration and gravitational components of pressure drop. It assumes that flow can be characterized by average fluid properties and that the velocities of liquid and vapor phases are equal (Collier and Thome 1996; Wallis 1969). The following discussion of several empirical correlations for computing frictional pressure drop in two-phase internal flow is based on Ould Didi et al. (2002).

Friedel Correlation

A common strategy in both two-phase heat transfer and pressure drop modeling is to begin with a single-phase model and determine an appropriate **two-phase multiplier** to correct for the enhanced energy and momentum transfer in two-phase flow. The Friedel (1979) correlation follows this strategy:

$$\frac{dp}{dz_{fric}} = \left(\frac{dp}{dz}\right)_{lo}\Phi_{lo}^2 \tag{30a}$$

In this case,

$$\left(\frac{dp}{dz}\right)_{lo} = 4f_l\frac{G_{tot}^2}{2\rho_l D} \tag{30b}$$

with

$$f = \frac{0.079}{\mathrm{Re}^{0.25}} \tag{30c}$$

and

$$\mathrm{Re} = \frac{G_{tot} D}{\mu} \tag{30d}$$

with $\mu = \mu_l$ used to calculate f_l for use in Equation (30b). The two-phase multiplier Φ_{lo}^2 is determined by

$$\Phi_{lo}^2 = E + \frac{3.24FH}{\mathrm{Fr}_h^{0.045}\mathrm{We}_l^{0.035}} \tag{30e}$$

where

$$\mathrm{Fr}_h = \frac{G_{tot}^2}{gD\rho_h^2} \tag{30f}$$

$$E = (1-x)^2 + x^2\left(\frac{\rho_l}{\rho_v}\right)\left(\frac{f_v}{f_l}\right) \tag{30g}$$

$$F = x^{0.78}(1-x)^{0.224} \tag{30h}$$

$$H = \left(\frac{\rho_l}{\rho_v}\right)^{0.91}\left(\frac{\mu_v}{\mu_l}\right)^{0.19}\left(1-\frac{\mu_v}{\mu_l}\right)^{0.7} \tag{30i}$$

$$\mathrm{We}_l = \frac{G_{tot}^2 D}{\sigma_t \rho_h} \tag{30j}$$

Note that friction factors in Equation (30g) are calculated from Equations (30c) and (30d) using the vapor and liquid fluid properties, respectively. The homogeneous density ρ_h is given by

$$\rho_h = \left(\frac{x}{\rho_v} + \frac{1-x}{\rho_l}\right)^{-1} \tag{30k}$$

This method is generally recommended when the viscosity ratio μ_l/μ_v is less than 1000.

Lockhart and Martinelli Correlation

One of the earliest two-phase pressure drop correlations was proposed by Martinelli and Nelson (1948) and rendered more useful by Lockhart and Martinelli (1949). A relatively straightforward implementation of this model requires that Re_l be calculated first, based on Equation (23d) and liquid properties. If $\mathrm{Re}_l > 4000$,

$$\left(\frac{dp}{dz}\right)_{fric} = \Phi_{ltt}^2\left(\frac{dp}{dz}\right)_l \tag{31a}$$

where

$$\Phi_{ltt}^2 = 1 + \frac{C}{X_{tt}} + \frac{1}{X_{tt}^2} \tag{31b}$$

and $(dp/dz)_l$ is calculated using Equation (30b).

If $\mathrm{Re}_l < 4000$,

$$\frac{dp}{dz} = \Phi_{Vtt}^2\left(\frac{dp}{dz}\right)_v \tag{31c}$$

where

$$\Phi_{Vtt}^2 = 1 + CX_{tt} + X_{tt}^2 \tag{31d}$$

In both cases,

$$X_{tt} = \left(\frac{1-x}{x}\right)^{0.9}\left(\frac{\rho_v}{\rho_l}\right)^{0.5}\left(\frac{\mu_l}{\mu_v}\right)^{0.1} \tag{31e}$$

and the subscript tt means turbulence in both liquid and vapor phases and $C = 20$ for most cases of interest in internal flow in HVAC&R systems.

Grönnerud Correlation

Much of the two-phase pressure drop modeling has been based on adiabatic air/water data. To address this, Grönnerud (1979) developed a correlation based on refrigerant flow data, also using a two-phase multiplier:

$$\left(\frac{dp}{dz}\right)_{fric} = \Phi_{lo}\left(\frac{dp}{dz}\right)_{lo} \tag{32a}$$

with

$$\Phi_{lo} = 1 + \left(\frac{dp}{dz}\right)_{\mathrm{Fr}}\left[\frac{(\rho_l/\rho_v)}{(\mu_l/\mu_v)^{0.25}} - 1\right] \tag{32b}$$

The liquid-only pressure gradient in Equation (32a) is calculated as before, using Equation (30b) with $x = 0$ and

$$\left(\frac{dp}{dz}\right)_{\mathrm{Fr}} = f_{\mathrm{Fr}}\left[x + 4\left(x^{1.8} - x^{10} f_{\mathrm{Fr}}^{0.5}\right)\right] \tag{32c}$$

The friction factor f_{Fr} in this method depends on the liquid Froude number, defined by

$$\mathrm{Fr}_l = \frac{G_{tot}^2}{gD\rho_l^2} \tag{32d}$$

If Fr_l is greater than or equal to 1, $f_{\mathrm{Fr}} = 1.0$. If $\mathrm{Fr}_l < 1$,

$$f_{\mathrm{Fr}} = \mathrm{Fr}_l^{0.3} + 0.0055\left[\ln\left(\frac{1}{\mathrm{Fr}_l}\right)\right]^2 \tag{32e}$$

Müller-Steinhagen and Heck Correlation

A simple, purely empirical correlation was proposed by Müller-Steinhagen and Heck (1986):

$$\left(\frac{dp}{dz}\right)_{fric} = \Lambda(1-x)^{1/3} + \left(\frac{dp}{dz}\right)_{vo} x^3 \tag{33a}$$

where

$$\Lambda = \left(\frac{dp}{dz}\right)_{lo} + 2\left[\left(\frac{dp}{dz}\right)_{vo} - \left(\frac{dp}{dz}\right)_{lo}\right]x \tag{33b}$$

and

$$\left(\frac{dp}{dz}\right)_{lo} = f_l\frac{2G_{tot}^2}{D\rho_l} \tag{33c}$$

$$\left(\frac{dp}{dz}\right)_{vo} = f_v\frac{2G_{tot}^2}{D\rho_v} \tag{33d}$$

where the subscript vo means vapor flow only and friction factors in Equations (33c) and (33d) are again calculated from Equations (30c) and (30d) using the liquid and vapor properties, respectively.

Wallis Correlation

The general nature of annular vapor/liquid flow in vertical pipes is indicated in Figure 9 (Wallis 1970), which plots the effective vapor friction factor versus the liquid fraction $(1 - \varepsilon_v)$, where ε_v is the vapor void fraction as defined by Equations (29c) or (29d).

The effective vapor friction factor in Figure 9 is defined as

$$f_{eff} = \left[\frac{\varepsilon_v^{2.5} D}{2\rho_v\left(\frac{4Q_v}{\pi D^2}\right)^2}\right]\left(\frac{dp}{dz}\right) \tag{34a}$$

where D is pipe diameter, ρ_v is vapor density, and Q_v is vapor volumetric flow rate. The friction factor of vapor flowing by itself in the pipe (presumed smooth) is denoted by f_v. Wallis' analysis of the flow occurrences is based on interfacial friction between the gas and liquid. The wavy film corresponds to a conduit with roughness height of about four times the liquid film thickness. Thus, the pressure drop relation for vertical flow is

$$\left(\frac{dp}{dz}\right)_{fric} = 0.01\left(\frac{\rho_v}{D^5}\right)\left(\frac{4Q_v}{\pi}\right)^2\left[\frac{1+75(1-\varepsilon_v)}{\varepsilon_v^{2.5}}\right] \quad (34b)$$

This corresponds to the Martinelli-type analysis with

$$f_{TP} = \Phi_v^2 f_v \quad (34c)$$

when

$$\Phi_v^2 = \frac{1+75(1-\varepsilon_v)}{\varepsilon_v} \quad (34d)$$

The friction factor f_v (of vapor alone) is taken as 0.02, an appropriate turbulent flow value. This calculation can be modified for more detailed consideration of factors such as Reynolds number variation in friction, gas compressibility, and entrainment (Wallis 1970).

Recommendations

Although many references recommend the Lockhart and Martinelli (1949) correlation, recent reviews of pressure drop correlations found other methods to be more accurate. Tribbe and Müller-Steinhagen (2000) found that the Müller-Steinhagen and Heck (1986) correlation worked quite well for a database of horizontal flows that included air/water, air/oil, steam, and several refrigerants. Ould Didi et al. (2002) also found that this method offered accuracies nearly as good or better than several other models; the Friedel (1979) and Grönnerud (1979) correlations also performed favorably. Note, however, that mean deviations of as much as 30% are common using these correlations; calculations for individual flow conditions can easily deviate 50% or more from measured pressure drops, so use these models as approximations only.

Evaporators and condensers often have valves, tees, bends, and other fittings that contribute to the overall pressure drop of the heat exchanger. Collier and Thome (1996) summarize methods predicting the two-phase pressure drop in these fittings.

Pressure Drop in Microchannels

Chisholm and Laird (1958) related the friction multiplier to the Lockhart-Martinelli parameter through a simple expression that depends on the coefficient C ranging from 5 to 20, depending on laminar or turbulent flow of vapor and liquid. Some researchers suggest empirical correlations for the coefficient C to determine the two-phase friction multiplier; among the most widely used are Lee and Lee's (2001) and Mishima and Hibiki's (1996). Mishima and Hibiki's correlation appears to provide a compact/simple correlation for adiabatic two-phase flow for tube diameters of 0.008 to 0.24 in., but its applicability to microchannel flows with phase change has not yet been demonstrated. It proposes

$$C = 21\left(1 - e^{-0.319 d_h}\right) \quad (35)$$

where diameter d_h is in millimetres. Cavallini et al. (2005) showed that Mishima and Hibiki's method could predict two-phase pressure drop for flow condensation of refrigerants R-134a and R-236ea in 0.055 in. minitubes. The correlation of Mishima and Hibiki (1996) evidently assumes that C depends on channel size only. Based on the observation that C depends on phase mass fluxes as well, and using experimental data from several sources as well as their own data that covered channel gaps in the 0.016 to 0.16 in. range, Lee and Lee (2001) derived the following correlation for C, for adiabatic flow in horizontal thin rectangular channels:

$$C = A\left(\frac{\mu_l^2}{\rho_l \sigma d_h}\right)^q \left(\frac{\mu_l j}{\sigma}\right)^r \mathrm{Re}_{l0}^s \quad (36)$$

where $j = G[(1-x)/\rho_l + x/\rho_g)]$ and represents the total mixture volumetric flux. The constants A, r, q, and s depend on the liquid and

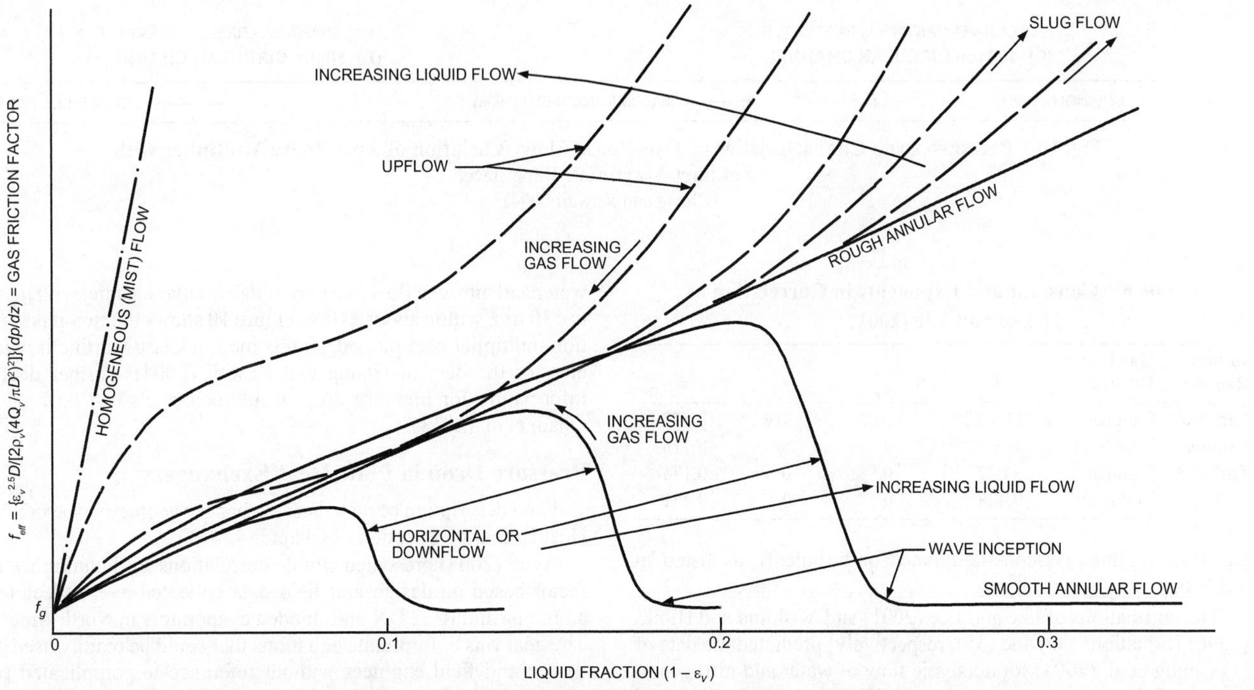

Fig. 9 Qualitative Pressure Drop Characteristics of Two-Phase Flow Regime
(Wallis 1970)

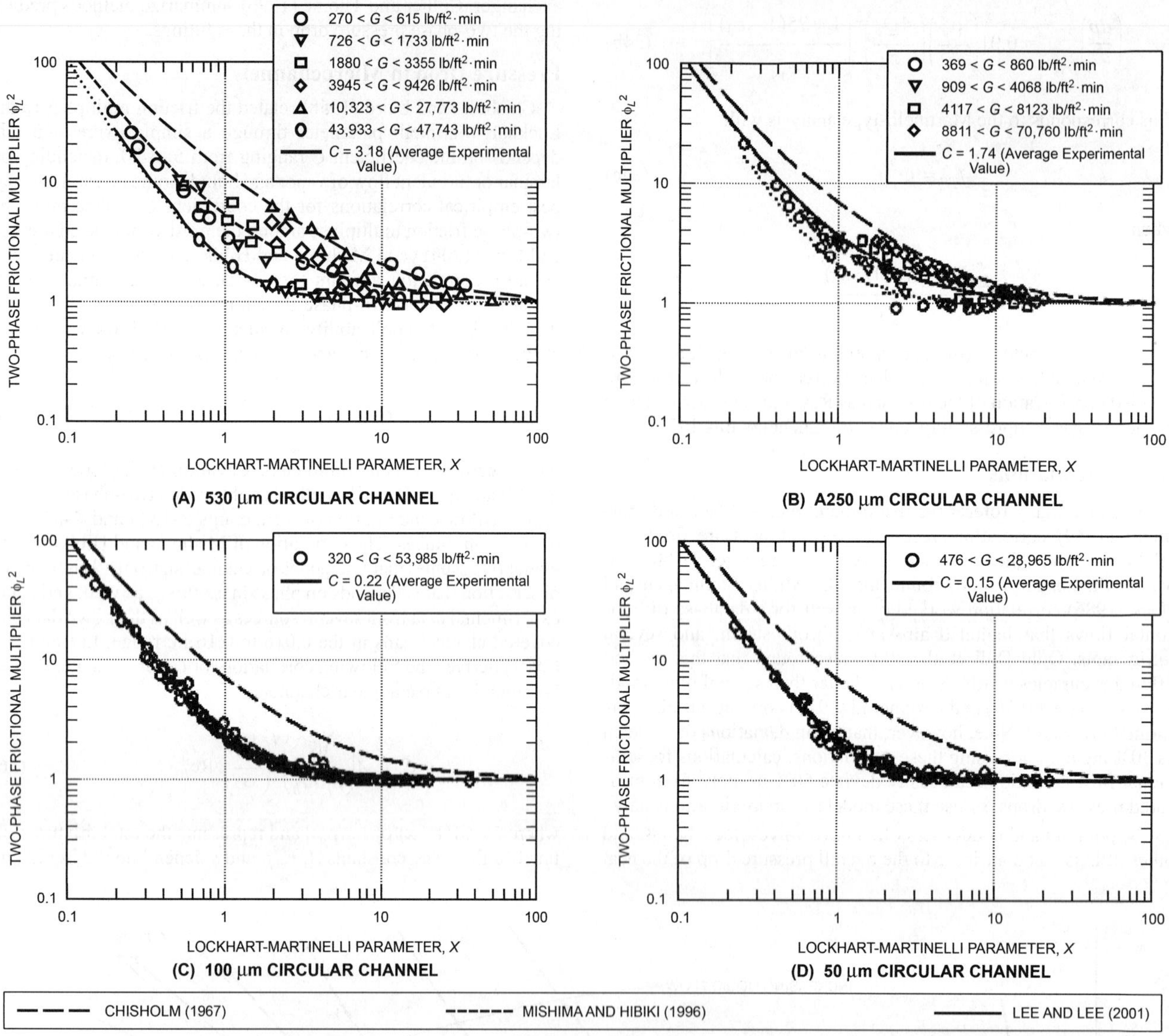

Fig. 10 Pressure Drop Characteristics of Two-Phase Flow: Variation of Two-Phase Multiplier with Lockhart-Martinelli Parameter
(Chung and Kawaji 2004)

Table 6 Constant and Exponents in Correlation of Lee and Lee (2001)

Liquid Regime	Gas Flow Regime	*A*	*q*	*r*	*s*
Laminar	Laminar	6.833×10^{-8}	−1.317	0.719	0.577
Laminar	Turbulent	6.185×10^{-2}	0	0	0.726
Turbulent	Laminar	3.627	0	0	0.174
Turbulent	Turbulent	0.408	0	0	0.451

gas flow regimes (viscous-dominated or turbulent), as listed in Table 6.

The correlations of Lee and Lee (2001) and Mishima and Hibiki (1996) [Equations (36) and (35), respectively] predicted the data of (1) Chung et al. (2004) for adiabatic flow of water and nitrogen in horizontal 96 µm square rectangular microchannels, (2) Zhao and Bi (2001) for water and airflow in a miniature triangular channel with d_h = 0.87 to 2.89 mm, and (3) Chung and Kawaji (2004) for water and nitrogen flow in a horizontal circular channel with d_h = 50 to 530 µm, within about ±10%. Figure 10 shows the two-phase friction multiplier data plotted against the Lockhart-Martinelli parameter for the data of Chung and Kawaji (2004). Further detailed information for pressure drop in microchannels can be found in Ohadi et al. (2013).

Pressure Drop in Plate Heat Exchangers

For a description of plate heat exchanger geometry, see the Plate Heat Exchangers section of Chapter 4.

Ayub (2003) presented simple correlations for Fanning friction factor based on design and field data collected over a decade on ammonia and R-22 DX and flooded evaporators in North America. The goal was to formulate equations that could be readily used by a design and field engineer without reference to complicated two-phase models. Correlations within the plates are formulated as if the entire flow were saturated vapor. The correlation is accordingly adjusted for the chevron angle, and thus generalized for application to any type of commercially available plate, with a statistical error of ±10%:

$$f = (n/\mathrm{Re}^m)(-1.89 + 6.56R - 3.69R^2) \quad (37)$$

for 30 ≤ β ≤ 65 where $R = (30/\beta)$, and β is the chevron angle in degrees. The values of m and n depend on Re.

m	*n*	Re
0.137	2.99	<4000
0.172	2.99	4000 < Re < 8000
0.161	3.15	8000 < Re < 16,000
0.195	2.99	>16,000

Pressure drop within the port holes is correlated as follows, treating the entire flow as saturated vapor:

$$\Delta p_{port} = 0.0076\rho V^2/2g \quad (38)$$

This equation accounts for pressure drop in both inlet and outlet refrigerant ports and gives the pressure drop in units of lb/in² with input for ρ in lb/ft³, V in ft/s, and g in ft/s². For evaporation of NH_3 in brazed-plate heat exchangers (BPHEs), Khan et al. (2012a, 2012b, 2014) correlated the friction factor with flow conditions.

$$f_{TP} = C(\mathrm{Re}_{eq})^m(p^*)^j \quad (39)$$

	60°/60°	60°/30°	30°/30°
C	673,336	305,590	212
m	–1.29	–1.26	–0.51
j	0.9	0.9	0.53

ASHRAE research project RP-1394 also established the following correlation for the carbon dioxide condensation in BPHEs (Jokar and Hayes 2009).

$$C_{F,TP} = C\,\mathrm{Re}^{-P} \quad (40)$$

Plate	*C*	*P*
60/60	1837.4	0.817
27/60	10.65	0
27/27	1221.3	0.815

Microengineered Surfaces for Enhanced Heat Transfer. Enhanced heat transfer surfaces are used in heat exchangers to improve performance while keeping pressure drops under control, with the net result of reduced footprint and/or weight or volume reductions and savings in capital and/or life-cycle costs. Condensing heat transfer is often enhanced with circular fins attached to the external surfaces of tubes to increase the heat transfer area. The latest generations of condensing surfaces have three-dimensional features (e.g., notches, wings) designed to promote good drainage of condensed liquid while extending the available heat transfer surface area, thus giving higher condensation heat transfer coefficients and condenser capacity. Similar enhancement methods (e.g., porous coatings, integral fins, reentrant cavities, other three-dimensional surface textures) are used to augment boiling/evaporation heat transfer on external surfaces of evaporator surfaces. Webb (1981) surveyed external boiling surfaces and compared performances of several enhanced surfaces with performance of smooth tubes. For some heat exchangers, the heat transfer coefficient for the refrigerant side is often smaller than the coefficient for the water side. Thus, enhancing the refrigerant-side surface can reduce the size of the heat exchanger and improve its performance. Most recent heat exchanger designs have augmentation on both liquid and refrigerant sides so as to avoid one side limiting the other's performance.

Internal fins and heat transfer surfaces can increase the heat transfer coefficients during evaporation or condensation in tubes. However, such enhanced features may often increase refrigerant pressure drop and reduce the heat transfer rate by decreasing the available temperature difference between hot and cold fluids, thus requiring careful design and optimization studies. For a review of internal enhancements for two-phase heat transfer, including the effects of oil, see Newell and Shah (2001). For additional information on enhancement methods in two-phase flow, see Bergles (1976, 1985), Thome (1990), and Webb (1994).

Perhaps the most effective mode of boiling heat transfer is thin-film evaporation, which maintains a thin film on the heat transfer surface at all times to avoid hot spots. The heat transfer coefficient of thin-film evaporation is directly proportional to thermal conductivity of the fluid over the film thickness; thus, the thinner the film, the higher the resulting heat transfer coefficients. Heat transfer coefficients can be several orders of magnitude larger, compared to conventional pool and convective heat transfer coefficients, whereas pressure drops can be substantially smaller than in typical convective boiling (Ohadi et al. 2013). The only limitation that has held this technology from being widely commercialized is the challenge of maintaining very thin films on the surface under wide-ranging operating conditions encountered in many systems. However, recent progress in microfabrication technologies, as well as measurement, instrumentation, and control of fluidic devices, may have substantially improved the prospect of commercially feasible thin-film evaporators. An important aspect of successful use of microchannels, for both single- and two-phase flow applications, is precise, evenly distributed liquid among the channels, which often requires careful design of liquid feed manifolds. Figure 11 depicts a schematic view of thin-film microchannels cooling over three-dimensional surfaces (Cetegen 2010).

Cetegen (2010) obtained critical heat flux in excess of 26,400 Btu/h·in², measured at average wall superheat of 101.16°F and subcooling of 15.3°F. The corresponding pressure drop was only 8.75 psi, and a resulting pumping power of only 1.1 W. The heat sink footprint area tested in this study was 0.013 × 0.013 in².

Mandel (2016) applied the force-fed microchannel heat sink (FFMHS) concept to a 0.394 × 0.394 in² heat sink directly etched into a silicon die, achieving more than 22,029 Btu/h·in² at 154.1°F, 40% thermodynamic outlet vapor quality, and subcooling of 13.79°F. The corresponding pressure drop was only 12.66 psi, and the resulting pumping power was only 0.79 W, approximately

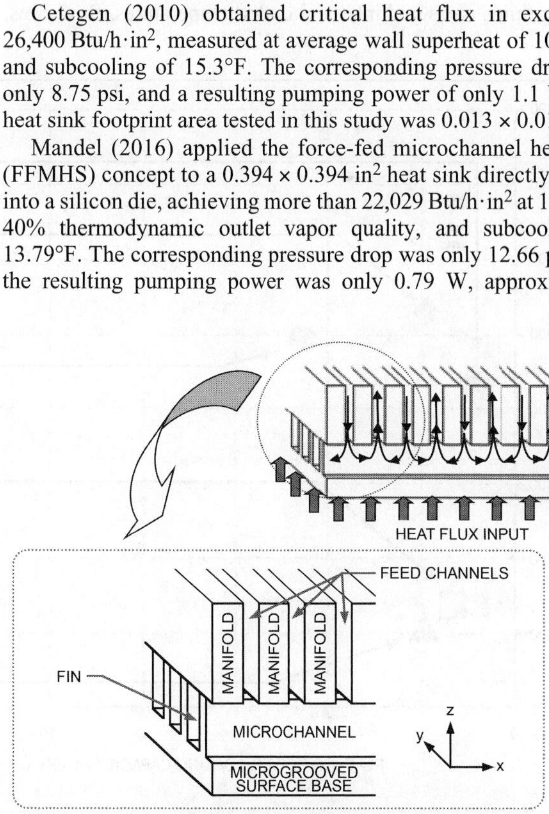

Fig. 11 Schematic Flow Representation of a Typical Force-Fed Microchannel Heat Sink (FFMHS)
(Cetegen 2010)

43.5% less than Cetegen's results despite the 64% larger heat sink area. In addition, because the substrate material was silicon, temperature dropped significantly through the substrate, and the superheat at the base of the fins was estimated to be only 75.7°F.

Comparing cooling technologies for two-phase heat transfer is more challenging than for single phase, because heat sink performance depends on many more parameters. Nevertheless, a quantitative comparison can still be made by plotting the data over the two most important parameters: here, maximum heat flux and pumping power over cooling capacity ratio. For these parameters, the performance of force-fed heat transfer was compared with other competing high-heat-flux cooling technologies by Agostini et al. (2008), Kosar and Peles (2007), Sung and Mudawar (2009), and Visaria and Mudawar (2008); the resulting graph, compiled by Cetegen (2010), is shown in Figure 12.

In addition, thin-film-enhanced evaporation in microchannels has been extended to shell-and-tube heat exchangers for enhanced evaporation heat transfer. Jha et al. (2012) found more than fourfold enhancement of the heat exchanger's overall heat transfer coefficient *U* compared to a state-of-the-art plate heat exchanger for the same operating parametric ranges. Working fluids for this study were R-245fa and water, for shell and tube sides, respectively. The pressure drops/pumping power reported in this study were substantially below those of the conventional shell-and-tube, as well as respective plate evaporators. Equally impressive results were reported with condensation heat transfer in thin-film-enhanced microchannels. Additional detailed information can be found in Ohadi et al. (2013).

Force-fed microchannel heat exchangers have also been used to enhance condensation heat transfer. Boyea et al. (2013) developed and tested a compact, lightweight manifold microgroove condenser, with 60 × 600 μm microgrooves and cooling capacity of 4 kW using different manifolds. Experiments using R-236fa and R-134a as working fluids measured inlet and outlet temperatures, flow rates, and pressure drops for the refrigerant and water sides. Overall heat transfer coefficient and pressure drop across condenser were determined, and refrigerant-side heat transfer coefficient was calculated based on water-side heat transfer coefficient. Refrigerant-side heat transfer coefficient of 60 kW/(m²·K) with pressure drop of just 7 kPa was demonstrated using R-134a. Experimental results indicate significant effect of manifold geometry on condenser performances. However, additional tests and verifications are needed to demonstrate the applicability of this technique for scaled-up, real-world condensers.

Kale and Mehendale (2015) critically assessed five microfin tube condensation correlations to determine their predictive accuracy and applicability for halogenated refrigerants and CO_2 in specific applications. This novel methodology was developed and validated against a dataset of 1163 experimental data points for CO_2, R-22, R-134a, R-410A, R-407C, R-125, and other halogenated refrigerants obtained from a large number of published works, which included diverse microfin tube geometries and condensing conditions. A similar study of the flow boiling HTC correlations was conducted by Merchant and Mehendale (2015).

Recent advancements in surface engineering offer new opportunities to enhance condensation heat transfer by drastically changing the wetting properties of the surface. Specifically, the development of superhydrophobic surfaces has been pursued to enhance dropwise condensation heat transfer, where the low droplet surface adhesion and small droplet departure sizes increase the condensation heat transfer coefficient. Figure 13 shows various microstructures of different sizes.

4. SYMBOLS

A = area, effective plate area
a = local acceleration

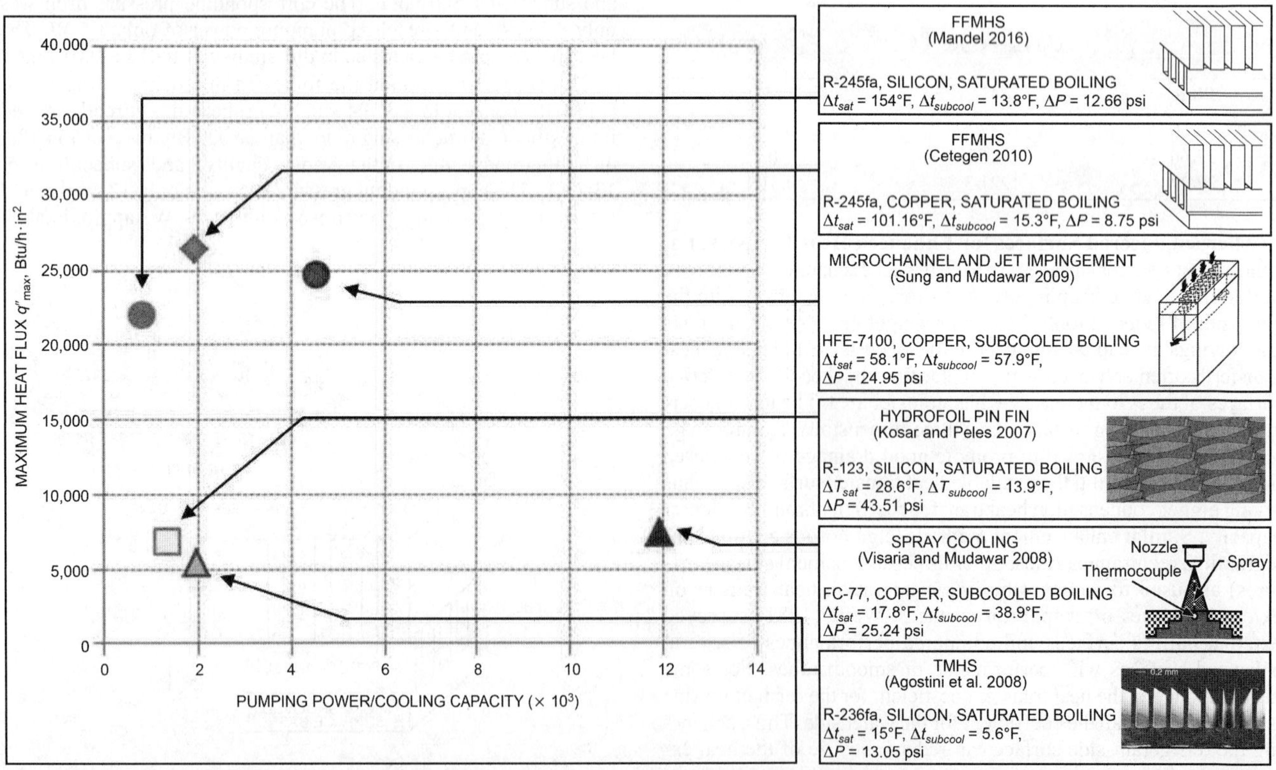

Fig. 12 Thermal Performance Comparison of Different High-Heat-Flux Cooling Technologies
(Cetegen 2010)

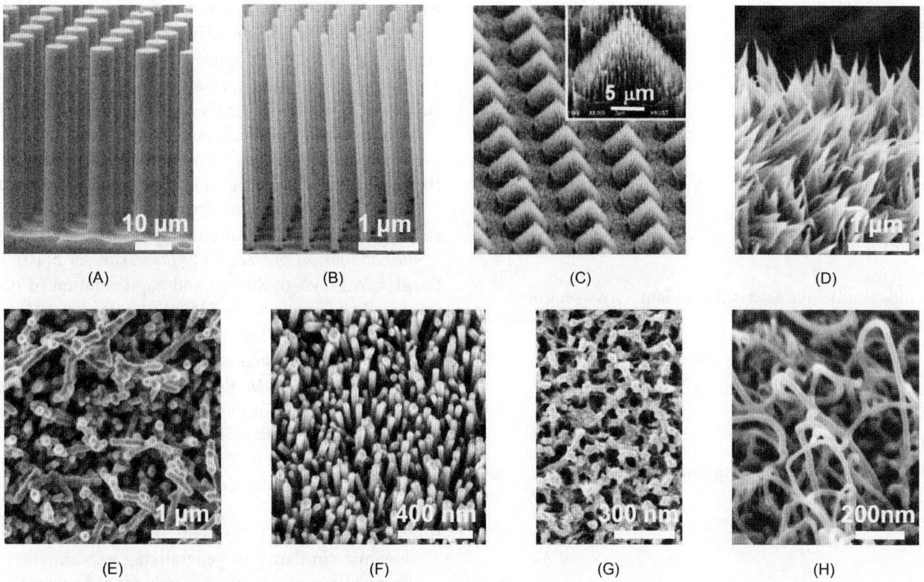

Fig. 13 Scanning Electron Microscope Images of Various Nanostructures: (A) Silicon Nanopillars (Enright et al. 2012), (B) High-Aspect-Ratio Silicon Nanopillars (Enright et al. 2012), (C) Silicon Micropost-Pyramids with Silicon Nanograss on Surface (Chen et al. 2011), (D) CuO Nanoblades (Miljkovic et al. 2013), (E) Tobacco Mosaic Virus Template Nanostructure (McCarthy et al. 2012), (F) Zinc Oxide Nanowires (Miljkovic et al. 2013), (G) Boehmitized Aluminum (Kim et al. 2013) and (H) Carbon Nanotubes (Enright et al. 2014)

b = breadth of condensing surface. For vertical tube, $b = \pi d$; for horizontal tube, $b = 2L$; flow channel gap in flat plate heat exchanger.
Bo = boiling number = $q/(Gh_{fg})$
C = coefficient or constant
C_F = Fanning friction factor
Co = Shah's convection number = $(1/x - 1)^{0.8}(\rho_g/\rho_f)^{0.5}$
c_p = specific heat at constant pressure
c_v = specific heat at constant volume
D = diameter
D_o = outside tube diameter
d = diameter; or prefix meaning differential
(dp/dz) = pressure drop
$(dp/dz)_{fric}$ = frictional pressure drop
$(dp/dz)_l$ = frictional pressure drop, assuming that liquid alone is flowing in pipe
$(dp/dz)_{mom}$ = momentum pressure drop
$(dp/dz)_v$ = frictional pressure drop, assuming that gas (or vapor) alone is flowing in pipe
Fr = Froude number
Fr_l = Froude number for total mass flow rate (vapor + liquid) = $G^2/(\rho_f^{\ 2}GD)$
f = friction factor for single-phase flow (Fanning)
G = total mass velocity (vapor + liquid); gravitational acceleration; mass flux
g_c = gravitational constant
Gr = Grashof number
h = heat transfer coefficient
h_f = single-phase liquid heat transfer coefficient
h_{fg} = latent heat of vaporization or of condensation
i'_{fg} = modified latent heat = $i_{fg}(1 + 0.68c_p\,\Delta T/i_{fg})$
j = Colburn j-factor
k = thermal conductivity
K_D = mass transfer coefficient, dimensionless coefficient (Table 1)
L = length
L_p = plate length
LT = total mass flowing as liquid
M = mass; or molecular weight
m = general exponent
$\dot{m}$ = mass flow rate
M_m = mean molecular weight of vapor/gas mixture
M_v = molecular weight of condensing vapor
N = number of tubes in vertical tier
n = general exponent
Nu = Nusselt number
P = pressure; or plate perimeter
p^* = reduced pressure (P/p_c)
p_c = critical thermodynamic pressure for coolant
p_g = partial pressure of noncondensable gas
Pr = Prandtl number
p_r = reduced pressure = p/p_c
p_v = partial pressure of vapor
Q_v = volumetric flow rate
q, q'' = heat flux
r = radius
Ra = Rayleigh number
Re = Reynolds number
R_p = surface roughness, µm
T, t = temperature
U = overall heat transfer coefficient
V = linear velocity
We = Weber number
x = quality (i.e., mass fraction of vapor); or distance in dt/dx
X_{tt} = Martinelli parameter
x, y, z = lengths along principal coordinate axes
Y_g = mole fraction of noncondensable gas
Y_v = mole fraction of vapor
Z = Shah parameter = $(1/x - 1)^{0.8}p_r^{\ 0.4}$

Greek

α = thermal diffusivity = $k/\rho c_p$
β = coefficient of thermal expansion, chevron angle
β^* = chevron angle ratio (β/β_{min})
Γ = mass rate of flow of condensate per unit of breadth (see section on Condensing)
Δ = difference between values
δ = thickness of oil film
ε = roughness of interface
ε_v = vapor void fraction
θ = contact angle, inclination angle
μ = absolute (dynamic) viscosity
μ_l = dynamic viscosity of saturated liquid

μ_v = dynamic viscosity of saturated vapor
ν = kinematic viscosity
ρ = density
ρ_l = density of saturated liquid
ρ_v = density of saturated vapor phase
σ = surface tension
Φ = two-phase multiplier
ϕ = fin efficiency

Subscripts and Superscripts

a = exponent in Equation (1)
b = bubble
c = critical, cold (fluid), characteristic, coolant, cross-sectional
dc = droplet cooling
e, eq = equivalent
eff = effective
f = film, fin, or liquid
fric = friction
g = noncondensable gas or vapor
gv = noncondensable gas and vapor mixture
h = horizontal, hot (fluid), hydraulic
i = inlet or inside
if = interface
l = liquid
m = mean
mac = convective mechanism
max = maximum
mic = nucleation mechanism
min = minimum
mom = momentum
ncb = nucleate boiling
o = outside, outlet, overall, reference
r = root (fin) or reduced pressure
s = surface or secondary heat transfer surface
sat = saturation
t = temperature or terminal temperature of tip (fin)
tot = total
TP = two-phase
tt = turbulence in both liquid and vapor phases
v = vapor or vertical
vo = vapor flow only
w = wall
∞ = bulk or far-field
* = reference

REFERENCES

ASHRAE members can access *ASHRAE Journal* articles and ASHRAE research project final reports at technologyportal.ashrae.org. Articles and reports are also available for purchase by nonmembers in the online ASHRAE Bookstore at www.ashrae.org/bookstore.

Agostini, B., J.R. Thome, M. Fabbri, and B. Michel. 2008. High heat flux two-phase cooling in silicon multimicrochannels. *IEEE Transactions on Components and Packaging Technologies* 31(3):691-701.

Anderson, W., D.G. Rich, and D.F. Geary. 1966. Evaporation of Refrigerant 22 in a horizontal 3/4-in. OD tube. *ASHRAE Transactions* 72(1):28.

Awad, M.M., A.S. Dalkilic, and S. Wongwises. 2014. A critical review on condensation heat transfer in microchannels and minichannels. *ASME Journal of Nanotechnology in Engineering and Medicine* 5(1). dx.doi.org/10.1115/1.4028092.

Ayad, F., R. Benelemir, and A. Souayed. 2012. CO_2 evaporators design for vehicle HVAC operation. *Applied Thermal Engineering* 36:330-344.

Ayub, Z.H. 2003. Plate heat exchanger literature survey and new heat transfer and pressure drop correlations for refrigerant evaporators. *Heat Transfer Engineering* 24(5):3-16.

Barnea, D., and Y. Taitel. 1986. Flow pattern transition in two-phase gas-liquid flows. In *Encyclopedia of Fluid Mechanics*, vol. 3. Gulf Publishing, Houston.

Baroczy, C.J. 1963. Correlation of liquid fraction in two-phase flow with application to liquid metals. North American Aviation *Report* SR-8171, El Segundo, CA.

Baskin, E. 1991. Applicability of plate heat exchangers in heat pumps. *ASHRAE Transactions* 97(2):305-308. *Paper* 3522.

Beatty, K.O., and D.L. Katz. 1948. Condensation of vapors on outdoor of finned tubes. *Chemical Engineering Progress* 44(1):55.

Bell, K.J., and M.A. Ghaly. 1973. An approximate generalized design method for multi-component/partial condenser. *American Institute of Chemical Engineers Symposium Series* 69:72-79.

Berenson, P.J. 1961. Film boiling heat transfer from a horizontal surface. *ASME Journal of Heat Transfer* 85:351.

Berenson, P.J. 1962. Experiments on pool boiling heat transfer. *International Journal of Heat and Mass Transfer* 5(10):985.

Bergles, A.E. 1976. Survey and augmentation of two-phase heat transfer. *ASHRAE Transactions* 82(1):891-905. *Paper* DA-76-14-1.

Bergles, A.E. 1985. Techniques to augment heat transfer. In *Handbook of heat transfer application*, 2nd ed. McGraw-Hill, New York.

Bergles, A.E., and W.M. Rohsenow. 1964. The determination of forced convection surface-boiling heat transfer. *ASME Journal of Heat Transfer*, Series C, 86(August):365.

Borishansky, W., and A. Kosyrev. 1966. Generalization of experimental data for the heat transfer coefficient in nucleate boiling. *ASHRAE Journal* (May):74.

Borishansky, V.M., I.I. Novikov, and S.S. Kutateladze. 1962. Use of thermodynamic similarity in generalizing experimental data on heat transfer. *Proceedings of the International Heat Transfer Conference.*

Boyea, D., A. Shooshtari, S.V. Dessiatoun, and M.M. Ohadi. 2013. Heat transfer and pressure drop characteristics of a liquid cooled manifold-microgroove condenser. *ASME Journal of Heat Transfer*, pp. V003T23A003. *Paper* HT2013-17781. dx.doi.org/10.1115/HT2013-17781.

Breber, G., J.W. Palen, and J. Taborek. 1980. Prediction of the horizontal tubeside condensation of pure components using flow regime criteria. *ASME Journal of Heat Transfer* 102(3):471-476.

Brisbane, T.W.C., I.D.R. Grant, and P.B.A. Whalley. 1980. Prediction method for kettle reboiler performance. *Paper* 80-HT-42. American Society of Mechanical Engineers, New York.

Bromley, L.A. 1950. Heat transfer in stable film boiling. *Chemical Engineering Progress* (46):221.

Brusstar, M.J., and H. Merte, Jr. 1997. Effects of heater surface orientation on the critical heat flux—II. A model for pool and forced convection subcooled boiling. *International Journal of Heat and Mass Transfer* 40(17):4021-4030.

Butterworth, D. 1975. A comparison of some void-fraction relationships for co-current gas-liquid flow. *International Journal of Multiphase Flow* 1:845-850.

Carey, V.P. 1992. *Liquid-vapor phase change phenomena: An introduction to the thermophysics of vaporization and condensation processes in heat transfer equipment.* Hemisphere Publishing, Washington, D.C.

Casciaro, S., and. J.R. Thome. 2001.Thermal performance of flooded evaporators, part I: Review of boiling heat transfer studies. *ASHRAE Transactions* 107(1):903-918. *Paper* AT-01-16-1.

Cavallini, A., D. Del Col, L. Doretti, M. Matkovic, L. Rossetto, and C. Zilio. 2005. Two-phase frictional pressure gradient of R236ea, R134a and R410A inside multi-port minichannels. *Experimental Thermal and Fluid Science* 29(7):861-870.

Cavallini, A., D. Del Col, L. Doretti, M. Matkovic, L. Rossetto, C. Zilio, and G. Censi. 2006. Condensation in horizontal smooth tubes: A new heat transfer model for heat exchanger design. *Heat Transfer Engineering* 27(8):31-38.

Cetegen, E. 2010. *High heat flux cooling utilizing microgrooved surfaces.* Ph.D. dissertation. School of Mechanical Engineering, University of Maryland, College Park.

Chaddock, J.B., and G.H. Buzzard. 1986. Film coefficients for in-tube evaporation of ammonia and R-502 with and without small percentages of mineral oil. *ASHRAE Transactions* 92(1A):22-40. *Paper* 2935 (RP-224).

Chen, J.C. 1963. A correlation for boiling heat transfer to saturated fluids on convective flow. ASME *Paper* 63-HT-34. American Society of Mechanical Engineers, New York.

Chen, J.C. 1966. Correlations for boiling heat transfer to saturated fluids in convective flow. *Industrial & Engineering Chemistry Research* 5:322-329.

Chen, J.C. 2003. Surface contact—Its significance for multiphase heat transfer: Diverse examples. *Journal of Heat Transfer* 125:549-566.

Chen, X.M., J. Wu, R.Y. Ma, M. Hua, N. Koratkar, S.H. Yao, and Z.K. Wang. 2011. Nanograssed micropyramidal architectures for continuous dropwise condensation. *Advanced Functional Materials* 21(24):4617-4623. dx.doi.org/10.1002/adfm.201101302.

Chisholm, D., and A.D.K. Laird. 1958. Two-phase flow in rough tubes. *ASME Transactions* 80:276-283.

Chung, P.M.-Y., and M. Kawaji. 2004. The effect of channel diameter on adiabatic two-phase flow characteristics in microchannels. *International Journal of Multiphase Flow* 30(7-8):735-761.

Chung, P.M.-Y., M. Kawaji, A. Kawahara, and Y. Shibata. 2004. Two-phase flow through square and circular microchannels—Effects of channel geometry. *Journal of Fluids Engineering* 126:546-552.

Colburn, A.P. 1951. Problems in design and research on condensers of vapours and vapour mixtures. *Proceedings of the Institute of Mechanical Engineers*, London, vol. 164, p. 448.

Colburn, A.P., and O.A. Hougen. 1934. Design of cooler condensers for mixtures of vapors with noncondensing gases. *Industrial and Engineering Chemistry* 26 (November):1178.

Coleman, J.W., and S. Garimella. 1999. Characterization of two-phase flow patterns in small-diameter round and rectangular tubes. *International Journal of Heat and Mass Transfer* 42:2869-2881.

Collier, J.G. 1972. *Convective boiling and condensation*. McGraw-Hill.

Collier, J.G., and J.R. Thome. 1996. *Convective boiling and condensation*, 3rd ed. Oxford University Press.

Consolini, L., D. Robinson, and J.R. Thome. 2006. Void fraction and two-phase pressure drops for evaporating flow over horizontal tube bundles. *Heat Transfer Engineering* 27(3):5-21.

Cooper, M.G. 1984. Heat flow rates in saturated nucleate pool boiling—A wide-ranging examination using reduced properties. *Advances in Heat Transfer* 16:157-239.

Danilova, G. 1965. Influence of pressure and temperature on heat exchange in the boiling of halogenated hydrocarbons. *Kholodilnaya Teknika* 2. English abstract, *Modern Refrigeration* (December).

Dhir, V.K., and S.P. Liaw. 1989. Framework for a unified model for nucleate and transition pool boiling. *Journal of Heat Transfer* 111:739-745.

Dhir, V.K., and J. Lienhard. 1971. Laminar film condensation on plan and axisymmetric bodies in non-uniform gravity. *Journal of Heat Transfer* 91:97-100.

Dobson, M.K., and J.C. Chato. 1998. Condensation in smooth horizontal tubes. *Journal of Heat Transfer* 120:193-213.

Dougherty, R.L., and H.J. Sauer, Jr. 1974. Nucleate pool boiling of refrigerant-oil mixtures from tubes. *ASHRAE Transactions* 80(2):175. *Paper* MO-2315.

Eckels, S., and E. Gorgy. 2012. Experimental evaluation of heat transfer impacts of tube pitch on highly enhanced surface tube bundle. ASHRAE Research Project RP-1316, *Final Report*.

Eckels, S.J., T.M. Doer, and M.B. Pate. 1994. In-tube heat transfer and pressure drop of R-134a and ester lubricant mixtures in a smooth tube and a micro-fin tube, part 1: Evaporation. *ASHRAE Transactions* 100(2):265-282. *Paper* 3810 (RP-630).

El Hajal, J., J.R. Thome, and A. Cavallini. 2003. Condensation in horizontal tubes, part I: Two-phase flow pattern map. *International Journal of Heat and Mass Transfer* 46(18):3349-3363.

Elkassabgi, Y., and J.H. Lienhard. 1988. The peak pool boiling heat fluxes from horizontal cylinders in subcooled liquids. *Journal of Heat Transfer* 110:479-492.

Enright, R., N. Miljkovic, A. Al-Obeidi, C.V. Thompson, and E.N. Wang. 2012. Condensation on superhydrophobic surfaces: The role of local energy barriers and structure length scale. *Langmuir* 40(28):14424-14432.

Enright, R., N. Miljkovic, J.L. Alvarado, K.J. Kim, and J.W. Rose. 2014. Dropwise condensation on micro- and nanostructured surfaces. *Nanoscale and Microscale Thermophysical Engineering* 18(3):223-250.

Farber, E.A., and R.L. Scorah. 1948. Heat transfer to water boiling under pressure. *ASME Transactions* (May):373.

Frederking, T.H.K., and J.A. Clark. 1962. Natural convection film boiling on a sphere. In *Advances in cryogenic engineering*, K.D. Timmerhouse, ed. Plenum Press, New York.

Friedel, L. 1979. Improved friction pressure drop correlations for horizontal and vertical two-phase pipe flow. European Two-Phase Flow Group Meeting, *Paper* E2, Ispra, Italy.

Furse, F.G. 1965. Heat transfer to Refrigerants 11 and 12 boiling over a horizontal copper surface. *ASHRAE Transactions* 71(1):231.

Gorenflo, D. 1993. *Pool boiling*. VDI-Heat Atlas. VDI-Verlag, Düsseldorf.

Gorgy, E.I., and S. Eckels. 2013. Convective boiling of R-134a and R-123 on a standard pitch enhanced tube bundle. *HVAC&R Research* (now *Science and Technology for the Built Environment*) 19(2):193-206.

Gouse, S.W., Jr., and K.G. Coumou. 1965. Heat transfer and fluid flow inside a horizontal tube evaporator, phase I. *ASHRAE Transactions* 71(2):152.

Green, G.H., and F.G. Furse. 1963. Effect of oil on heat transfer from a horizontal tube to boiling Refrigerant 12-oil mixtures. *ASHRAE Journal* (October):63.

Grober, H., S. Erk, and U. Grigull. 1961. *Fundamentals of heat transfer*. McGraw-Hill, New York.

Grönnerud, R. 1979. Investigation of liquid hold-up, flow resistance and heat transfer in circulation type evaporators, part IV: Two-phase flow resistance in boiling refrigerants. Annexe 1972-1, *Bulletin de l'Institut du Froid*.

Guerrieri, S.A., and R.D. Talty. 1956. A study of heat transfer to organic liquids in single tube boilers. *Chemical Engineering Progress Symposium Series* 52(18):69.

Gungor, K.E., and R.H.S. Winterton. 1986. A general correlation for flow boiling in tubes and annuli. *International Journal of Heat and Mass Transfer* 29:351-358.

Gungor, K.E., and R.H.S. Winterton. 1987. Simplified general correlation for saturated flow boiling and comparison of correlations with data. *Chemical Engineering Research and Design* 65:148-156.

Hall, D.D., and I. Mudawar. 2000a. Critical heat flux (CHF) for water flow in tubes—I. Compilation and assessment of world CHF data. *International Journal of Heat and Mass Transfer* 43(14):2573-2604.

Hall, D.D., and I. Mudawar. 2000b. Critical heat flux (CHF) for water flow in tubes—II: Subcooled CHF correlations. *International Journal of Heat and Mass Transfer* 43(14):2605-2640.

Haramura, Y., and Y. Katto. 1983. A new hydrodynamic model of critical heat flux, applicable widely to both pool and forced convection boiling on submerged bodies in saturated liquids. *International Journal of Heat and Mass Transfer* 26:389-399.

Hayes, N., and A. Jokar. 2009. Dynalene/water correlations to be used for condensation of CO_2 in brazed plate heat exchangers. *ASHRAE Transactions* 115(2):599-616. *Paper* LO-09-057 (RP-1394).

Hayes, N., A. Jokar, and Z. Ayub. 2011. Study of carbon dioxide condensation in chevron plate exchangers: heat transfer analysis. *International Journal of Heat and Mass Transfer* 54:1121-1131.

Hayes, N., A. Jokar, and Z. Ayub. 2012. Study of carbon dioxide condensation in chevron plate exchangers; pressure drop analysis. *International Journal of Heat and Mass Transfer* 55:2916-2925.

Hesselgreaves, J.E. 1990. The impact of compact heat exchangers on refrigeration technology and CFC replacement. *Proceedings of the 1990 USNC/IIR-Purdue Refrigeration Conference*, ASHRAE/Purdue CFC Conference, pp. 492-500.

Hetsroni, G., ed. 1986. *Handbook of multiphase systems*. Hemisphere Publishing, Washington D.C.

Howard, A.H., and I. Mudawar. 1999. Orientation effects on pool boiling critical heat flux (CHF) and modeling of CHF for near-vertical surfaces. *International Journal of Heat and Mass Transfer* 42:1665-1688.

Incropera, F.P., and D.P. DeWitt. 2002. *Fundamentals of heat and mass transfer*, 5th ed. John Wiley & Sons, New York.

Isrealachvili, J.N. 1991. *Intermolecular surface forces*. Academic Press, New York.

Jakob, M. 1949, 1957. *Heat transfer*, vols. I and II. John Wiley & Sons, New York.

Jha, V., S.V. Dessiatoun, M.M. Ohadi, and E. Al-Hajri. 2012. Experimental characterization of heat transfer and pressure drop inside a tubular evaporator utilizing advanced microgrooved surfaces. *ASME Journal of Thermal Science and Engineering Applications* 4(4).

Jokar, A., and N. Hayes. 2009. Study of carbon dioxide condensation in chevron plate exchangers. ASHRAE Research Project RP-1394, *Final Report*.

Jonsson, I. 1985. Plate heat exchangers as evaporators and condensers for refrigerants. *Australian Refrigeration, Air Conditioning and Heating* 39(9):30-31, 33-35.

Kale, K., and S.S. Mehendale. 2015. Novel application-specific methodology for the assessment of microfin tube condensation heat transfer correlations. Presented at ASME International Mechanical Engineering Congress and Exposition (IMECE), Houston.

Kandlikar, S.G. 1990. A general correlation for saturated two-phase flow boiling heat transfer inside horizontal and vertical tubes. *Journal of Heat Transfer* 112:219-228.

Kandlikar, S.G. 2001. A theoretical model to predict pool boiling CHF incorporating effects of contact angle and orientation. *Journal of Heat Transfer* 123:1071-1079.

Kandlikar, S.G., and W.J. Grande. 2003. Evolution of microchannel flow passages—Thermohydraulic performance and fabrication technology. *Heat Transfer Engineering* 24(1):3-17.

Kandlikar, S.G., S. Garimella, D. Li, S. Colin, and M.R. King, eds. 2005. *Heat transfer and fluid flow in minichannels and microchannels*. Elsevier, Amsterdam.

Kattan, N., J.R. Thome, and D. Favrat. 1998a. Flow boiling in horizontal tubes, part 1: Development of diabatic two-phase flow pattern map. *Journal of Heat Transfer* 120(1):140-147.

Kattan, N., J.R. Thome, and D. Favrat. 1998b. Flow boiling in horizontal tubes, part 3: Development of new heat transfer model based on flow patterns. *Journal of Heat Transfer* 120(1):156-165.

Katto, Y., and H. Ohno. 1984. An improved version of the generalized correlation of critical heat flux for the forced convection boiling in uniformly heated vertical tubes *International Journal of Heat and Mass Transfer* 27(9):1641-1648.

Khan, M.S. 2010. Evaporation in flooded corrugated plate heat exchangers with ammonia and ammonia/miscible oil. ASHRAE Research Project RP-1352, *Final Report*.

Khan, T.S., M.S. Khan, M-C. Chyu, and Z.H. Ayub. 2010. Experimental investigation of single phase convective heat transfer coefficient in a corrugated plate heat exchanger for multiple plate configurations. *Applied Thermal Engineering* 30(8-9):1058-1065.

Khan, M.S., T.S. Khan, M-C. Chyu, and Z.H. Ayub. 2012a. Experimental investigation of evaporation heat transfer and pressure drop of ammonia in a 30° chevron plate heat exchanger. *International Journal of Refrigeration* 35(6):1757-1765.

Khan, T.S., M.S. Khan, M-C. Chyu, and Z.H. Ayub. 2012b. Experimental investigation of evaporation heat transfer and pressure drop of ammonia in a 60° chevron plate heat exchanger. *International Journal of Refrigeration* 35(2):336-348.

Khan, M.S., T.S. Khan, M-C. Chyu, and Z.H. Ayub. 2014. Evaporation heat transfer and pressure drop of ammonia in a mixed configuration chevron plate heat exchanger. *International Journal of Refrigeration* 41:92-102.

Kim, P., M.J. Kreder, J. Alvarenga, and J. Aizenberg. 2013. Hierarchical or not? Effect of the length scale and hierarchy of the surface roughness on omniphobicity of lubricant infused substrates. *Nano Letters* 13(4):1793-1799.

Kim, S., and I. Mudawar. 2013. Universal approach to predicting heat transfer coefficient for condensing mini/micro-channel flow. *International Journal of Heat and Mass Transfer* 56(112):238-250.

Kosar, A., and Y. Peles. 2007. Boiling heat transfer in a hydrofoil-based micro pin fin heat sink. *International Journal of Heat and Mass Transfer* 50(5-6):1018-1034.

Kumar, H. 1984. The plate heat exchanger: Construction and design. *Institute of Chemical Engineering Symposium Series* 86:1275-1288.

Kutateladze, S.S. 1951. A hydrodynamic theory of changes in the boiling process under free convection. Izvestia Akademii Nauk, USSR, *Otdelenie Tekhnicheski Nauk* 4:529.

Kutateladze, S.S. 1963. *Fundamentals of heat transfer*. E. Arnold Press, London.

Lee, H.J., and S.Y. Lee. 2001. Pressure drop correlations for two-phase flow within horizontal rectangular channels with small height. *International Journal of Multiphase Flow* 27:783-796.

Li, W., and Z. Wu. 2010a. A general correlation for evaporative heat transfer in micro/mini-channels. *International Journal of Heat and Mass Transfer* 53:1778-1787.

Li, W., and Z. Wu. 2010b. A general criterion for evaporative heat transfer in micro/mini-channels. *International Journal of Heat and Mass Transfer* 53:1967-1976.

Lienhard, J.H., and V.E. Schrock. 1963. The effect of pressure, geometry and the equation of state upon peak and minimum boiling heat flux. *ASME Journal of Heat Transfer* 85:261.

Lienhard, J.H., and P.T.Y. Wong. 1964. The dominant unstable wavelength and minimum heat flux during film boiling on a horizontal cylinder. *Journal of Heat Transfer* 86:220-226.

Lips, S., and J.P. Meyer. 2011. Two-phase flow in inclined tubes with specific reference to condensation: a review. *International Journal of Multiphase Flow* 37:845-859.

Liu, Z., and R.H.S. Winterton. 1991. A general correlation for saturated and subcooled flow boiling in tubes and annuli based on a nucleate pool boiling equation. *International Journal of Heat and Mass Transfer* 34(11):2759-2766.

Lockhart, R.W., and R.C. Martinelli. 1949. Proposed correlation of data for isothermal two-phase, two-component flow in pipes. *Chemical Engineering Progress* 45(1):39-48.

Longo, G.A., G. Righetti, and C. Zilio. 2014. A new model for refrigerant condensation inside a brazed plate heat exchanger (BPHE). Presented at 15th International Heat Transfer Conference (IHTC-15), Kyoto.

Mandhane, J.M., G.A. Gregory, and K. Aziz. 1974. A flow pattern map for gas-liquid flow in horizontal pipes. *International Journal of Multiphase Flow* 1:537-553.

Martinelli, R.C., and D.B. Nelson. 1948. Prediction of pressure drops during forced circulation boiling of water. *ASME Transactions* 70:695.

McAdams, W.H. 1954. *Heat transmission*, 3rd ed. McGraw-Hill, New York.

McCarthy, M., K. Gerasopoulos, R. Enright, J.N. Culver, R. Ghodssi, and E.N. Wang. 2012. Biotemplated hierarchical surfaces and the role of dual length scales on the repellency of impacting droplets. *Applied Physics Letters* 100(26), *Paper* 263701. dx.doi.org/10.1063/1.4729935.

McGillis, W.R., and V.P. Carey. 1996. On the role of the Marangoni effects on the critical heat flux for pool boiling of binary mixture. *Journal of Heat Transfer* 118(1):103-109.

Mehendale, S.S., A.M. Jacobi, and R.K. Shah. 2000. Fluid flow and heat transfer at micro- and meso-scales with applications to heat exchanger design. *Applied Mechanics Review* 53:175-193.

Merchant, R., and S.S. Mehendale. 2015. Application-based methodology for assessment of flow boiling correlations in microfin tubes. Presented at ASME International Mechanical Engineering Congress and Exposition (IMECE), Houston.

Meyer, J.P., J. Dirker, and O.K. Adelaja. 2014. Condensation heat transfer in smooth inclined tubes for R134a at different saturation temperatures. *International Journal of Heat and Mass Transfer* 70:515-525.

Miljkovic, N., R. Enright, Y. Nam, K. Lopez, N. Dou, J. Sack, and E.N. Wang. 2013. Jumping-droplet-enhanced condensation on scalable super hydrophobic nanostructured surfaces. *Nano Letters* 13(1):179-187.

Mishima, K., and T. Hibiki. 1996. Some characteristics of air-water two-phase flow in small diameter vertical tubes. *International Journal of Multiphase Flow* 22:703-712.

Müller-Steinhagen, H., and K. Heck. 1986. A simple friction pressure drop correlation for two-phase flow in pipes. *Chemical Engineering Progress* 20:297-308.

Murase, T., H.S. Wang, and J.W. Rose. 2006. Effect of inundation for condensation of steam on smooth and enhanced condenser tubes. *International Journal of Heat and Mass Transfer* 49:3180-3189.

Nam, Y., and Y.S. Ju. 2009. Comparative study of copper oxidation schemes and their effects on surface wettability. *IMECE 2008: Heat Transfer, Fluid Flows, and Thermal Systems* 10(A-C):1833-1838.

Newell, T.A., and R.K. Shah. 2001. An assessment of refrigerant heat transfer, pressure drop, and void fraction effects in microfin tubes. *International Journal of HVAC&R Research* (now *Science and Technology for the Built Environment*) 7(2):125-153.

Nukiyama, S. 1934. The maximum and minimum values of heat transmitted from metal to boiling water under atmospheric pressure. *Journal of the Japanese Society of Mechanical Engineers* 37:367.

Nusselt, W. 1916. Die Oberflächenkondensation des Wasserdampfes. *Zeitung Verein Deutscher Ingenieure* 60:541.

Ohadi, M., K. Choo, S. Dessiatoun, and E. Cetegen. 2013. *Next generation microchannel heat exchangers*. Springer, New York.

Othmer, D.F. 1929. The condensation of steam. *Industrial and Engineering Chemistry* 21(June):576.

Ould Didi, M.B., N. Kattan and J.R. Thome. 2002. Prediction of two-phase pressure gradients of refrigerants in horizontal tubes. *International Journal of Refrigeration* 25:935-947.

Palen, J., and Z.H. Yang. 2001. Reflux condensation flooding prediction: A review of current status. *Transactions of the Institute of Chemical Engineers* 79(A):463-469.

Panchal, C.B. 1985. Condensation heat transfer in plate heat exchangers. *Two-Phase Heat Exchanger Symposium*, HTD vol. 44, pp. 45-52. American Society of Mechanical Engineers, New York.

Panchal, C.B. 1990. Experimental investigation of condensation of steam in the presence of noncondensable gases using plate heat exchangers. Argonne National Laboratory *Report* CONF-900339-1.

Panchal, C.B., and D.L. Hillis. 1984. OTEC Performance tests of the Alfa-Laval plate heat exchanger as an ammonia evaporator. Argonne National Laboratory *Report* ANL-OTEC-PS-13.

Panchal, C.B., D.L. Hillis, and A. Thomas. 1983. Convective boiling of ammonia and Freon 22 in plate heat exchangers. Argonne National Laboratory *Report* CONF-830301-13.

Perry, J.H. 1950. *Chemical engineers handbook*, 3rd ed. McGraw-Hill, New York.

Petterson, J. 2004. Flow vaporization of CO_2 in microchannel tube. *Experimental Thermal and Fluid Science* 28:111-121.

Pierre, B. 1964. Flow resistance with boiling refrigerant. *ASHRAE Journal* (September/October).

Reddy, R.P., and J.H. Lienhard. 1989. The peak heat flux in saturated ethanol-water mixtures. *Journal of Heat Transfer* 111:480-486.

Robinson, D.M., and J.R. Thome. 2004a. Local bundle boiling heat transfer coefficients on a plain tube bundle (RP-1089). *International Journal of HVAC&R Research* (now *Science and Technology for the Built Environment*) 10(1):33-51.

Robinson, D.M., and J.R. Thome. 2004b. Local bundle boiling heat transfer coefficients on an integral finned tube bundle (RP-1089). *International Journal of HVAC&R Research* (now *Science and Technology for the Built Environment*) 10(3):331-344.

Robinson, D.M., and J.R. Thome. 2004c. Local bundle boiling heat transfer coefficients on a turbo-BII HP tube bundle (RP-1089). *International Journal of HVAC&R Research* (now *Science and Technology for the Built Environment*) 10(3):331-344.

Rohsenow, W.M. 1963. Boiling heat transfer. In *Modern developments in heat transfer*, W. Ibele, ed. Academic Press, New York.

Rohsenow, W.M., and P. Griffith. 1956. Correlation of maximum heat flux data for boiling of saturated liquids. *Chemical Engineering Progress Symposium Series* 52:47-49.

Rohsenow, W.M., J.P. Hartnett, and Y.I. Cho. 1998. *Handbook of heat transfer*, 3rd ed., pp. 1570-1571. McGraw-Hill.

Rose, J.W. 1969. Condensation of a vapour in the presence of a noncondensable gas. *International Journal of Heat and Mass Transfer* 12:233.

Rose, J.W. 1998. Condensation heat transfer fundamentals. *Transactions of the Institution of Chemical Engineers* 76(A):143-152.

Rouhani, Z., and E. Axelsson. 1970. Calculation of void volume fraction in the subcooled and quality boiling regions. *International Journal of Heat and Mass Transfer* 13:383-393.

Saha, P., and N. Zuber 1974. Point of net vapor generation and vapor void fraction in subcooled boiling. *Proceedings of the 5th International Heat Transfer Conference*, vol. 4.

Schlager, L.M., M.B. Pate, and A.E. Bergles. 1987. Evaporation and condensation of refrigerant-oil mixtures in a smooth tube and micro-fin tube. *ASHRAE Transactions* 93:293-316. *Paper* 3121 (RP-469).

Sefiane, K. 2001. A new approach in the modeling of the critical heat flux and enhancement techniques. *AIChE Journal* 47(11):2402-2412.

Shah, M.M. 1975. Visual observations in ammonia evaporator. *ASHRAE Transactions* 82(1). *Paper* AC-2344.

Shah, M. M. 1976. A new correlation for heat transfer during boiling flow through pipes. *ASHRAE Transactions* 82(2):66-86. *Paper* SE-2407.

Shah, M.M. 1977. A general correlation for heat transfer during subcooled boiling in pipes. *ASHRAE Transactions* 83(1):205-217. *Paper* CH-2443.

Shah, M.M. 1979a. A generalized graphical method for predicting CHF in uniformly heated vertical tubes. *International Journal of Heat and Mass Transfer* 22:557-568.

Shah, M.M. 1979b. A general correlation for heat transfer during film condensation inside pipes. *International Journal of Heat and Mass Transfer* 22:547-556.

Shah, M.M. 1980a. A general correlation for critical heat flux in annuli. *International Journal of Heat and Mass Transfer* 23:225-234.

Shah, M.M. 1980b. A general predictive technique for heat transfer during saturated film boiling in tubes. *Heat Transfer Engineering* 2(2):51-62.

Shah, M.M. 1982. Chart correlation for saturated boiling heat transfer: Equations and further study. *ASHRAE Transactions* 88(1):185-196. *Paper* HO-2673.

Shah, M.M. 1983. Generalized prediction of heat transfer during subcooled boiling in annuli. *Heat Transfer Engineering* 4(1):24-31.

Shah, M.M. 1987. Improved general correlation for critical heat flux in uniformly heated vertical tubes. *International Journal of Heat and Fluid Flow* 8(4):326-335.

Shah, M.M. 2005. Improved general correlation for subcooled boiling heat transfer during flow across tubes and tube bundles. *International Journal of HVAC&R Research* (now *Science and Technology for the Built Environment*) 11(2):285-304.

Shah, M.M. 2006. Evaluation of general correlations for heat transfer during boiling of saturated liquids in tubes and annuli. *International Journal of HVAC&R Research* (now *Science and Technology for the Built Environment*) 12(4):1047-1064.

Shah, M.M. 2007. A general correlation for heat transfer during saturated boiling with flow across tube bundles. *HVAC&R Research* (now *Science and Technology for the Built Environment*) 13(5):749-768.

Shah, M.M. 2009. An improved general correlation for condensation for heat transfer during film condensation in plain tubes. *HVAC&R Research* (now *Science and Technology for the Built Environment*) 15(5):889-913.

Shah, M.M. 2013. General correlation for heat transfer during condensation in plain tubes: Further development and verification. *ASHRAE Transactions* 119(2).

Shah, M.M. 2014a. Evaluation of correlations for predicting heat transfer during boiling of carbon dioxide inside channels. *Proceedings of the 15th International Heat Transfer Conference* (IHTC-15), Kyoto. *Paper* 8435.

Shah, M.M., 2014b. A new flow pattern based general correlation for heat transfer during condensation in horizontal tubes. *Proceedings of the 15th International Heat Transfer Conference* (IHTC-15), Tokyo. *Paper* 8645.

Shah, M.M. 2015a. A method for predicting heat transfer during boiling of mixtures in plain tubes. *Applied Thermal Engineering*, 8:9:812-821

Shah, M.M. 2015b. A general correlation for CHF in horizontal channels. *International Journal of Refrigeration* 59:37-52.

Shah, M.M. 2015c. Prediction of heat transfer during condensation of carbon dioxide in channels. *Applied Thermal Engineering* 93:192-199. dx.doi.org/10.1016/j.applthermaleng.2015.09.016.

Shah, M. M. 2015d. Prediction of heat transfer during condensation in inclined tubes. *Applied Thermal Engineering* 94:82-89. dx.doi.org/10.1016/j.applthermaleng.2015.10.122.

Shah, M.M. 2016a. Improved general correlation for CHF in uniformly heated vertical annuli with upflow. *Heat Transfer Engineering* 37(6): 557-570. dx.doi.org/10.1080/01457632.2015.1060765.

Shah, M.M. 2016b. Applicability of general correlations for critical heat flux in conventional tubes to mini/micro channels. *Heat Transfer Engineering* 37(18). dx.doi.org/10.1080/01457632.2016.1151293.

Shah, M.M. 2016c. A correlation for heat transfer during condensation in horizontal mini/micro channels. *International Journal of Refrigeration* 64:187-202. dx.doi.org/10.1016/j.ijrefrig.2015.12.008.

Shah, M.M., and M.A. Siddiqui. 2000. A general correlation for heat transfer during dispersed flow film boiling in tubes. *Heat Transfer Engineering* 21(4):18-32.

Shah, M.M., A.M. Mahmoud, and J. Lee. 2013. An assessment of some predictive methods for in-tube condensation heat transfer of refrigerant mixtures, *ASHRAE Transactions* 119(2). *Paper* DE-13-004.

Sparrow, E.M., and S.H. Lin. 1964. Condensation in the presence of a noncondensable gas. *ASME Transactions, Journal of Heat Transfer* 86C: 430.

Sparrow, E.M., W.J. Minkowycz, and M. Saddy. 1967. Forced convection condensation in the presence of noncondensables and interfacial resistance. *International Journal of Heat and Mass Transfer* 10:1829.

Spedding, P.L., and D.R. Spence. 1993. Flow regimes in two-phase gas-liquid flow. *International Journal of Multiphase Flow* 19(2):245-280.

Starczewski, J. 1965. Generalized design of evaporation heat transfer to nucleate boiling liquids. *British Chemical Engineering* (August).

Steiner, D. 1993. *VDI-Wärmeatlas (VDI Heat Atlas)*. Verein Deutscher Ingenieure, VDI-Gesellschaft Verfahrenstechnik und Chemieingenieurwesen (GCV), Düsseldorf, Chapter Hbb.

Steiner, D., and J. Taborek. 1992. Flow boiling heat transfer in vertical tubes correlated by an asymptotic model. *Heat Transfer Engineering* 13(2): 43-69.

Stephan, K. 1963. Influence of oil on heat transfer of boiling Freon-12 and Freon-22. Eleventh International Congress of Refrigeration, IIR *Bulletin* 3.

Stephan, K. 1992. *Heat transfer in condensation and boiling*. Springer-Verlag, Berlin.

Stephan, K., and M. Abdelsalam. 1980. Heat transfer correlations for natural convection boiling. *International Journal of Heat and Mass Transfer* 23:73-87.

Sun, L., and K. Mishima 2009. An evaluation of prediction methods for saturated flow boiling heat transfer in mini-channels. *International Journal of Heat and Mass Transfer* 52:5323-5329.

Sung, M.K., and I. Mudawar. 2009. CHF determination for high-heat flux phase change cooling system incorporating both micro-channel flow and jet impingement. *International Journal of Heat and Mass Transfer* 52(3-4):610-619.

Swain, A., and M.K. Das. 2014. A review on saturated boiling of liquids on tube bundles. *Heat and Mass Transfer* 50:617. dx.doi.org/10.1007/s00231-013-1257-1.

Syed, A. 1990. The use of plate heat exchangers as evaporators and condensers in process refrigeration. Symposium on Advanced Heat Exchanger Design. Institute of Chemical Engineers, Leeds, U.K.

Thome, J.R.S. 1964. Prediction of pressure drop during forced circulation boiling water. *International Journal of Heat and Mass Transfer* 7: 709-724.

Thome, J.R. 1990. *Enhanced boiling heat transfer*. Hemisphere (Taylor and Francis), New York.

Thome, J. R. 1996. Boiling of new refrigerants: A state of the art review. *International Journal of Refrigeration* 19(7):435-457.

Thome, J.R. 2001. Flow regime based modeling of two-phase heat transfer. *Multiphase Science and Technology* 13(3-4):131-160.

Thome, J.R. 2003. Update on the Kattan-Thome-Favrat flow boiling model and flow pattern map. Fifth International Conference on Boiling Heat Transfer, Montego Bay, Jamaica.

Thome, J. R. 2010. *Engineering data book III*. Wolverine Tube, Inc. Available online at www.wlv.com.

Thome, J.R., and D. Robinson. 2004. Flooded evaporation heat transfer performance investigation for tube bundles including the effects of oil using R-410A and R-507A. ASHRAE Research Project RP-1089, *Final Report*.

Thome, J.R., and D.M. Robinson. 2006. Prediction of local bundle boiling heat transfer coefficients: Pure refrigerant boiling on plain, low fin, and turbo-BII HP tube bundles. *Heat Transfer Engineering* 27(10):20-29.

Thome, J.R. and S. Shakir. 1987. A new correlation for nucleate boiling of aqueous mixtures,. *AIChE Symposium Series* 83(257): 46-57.

Thome, J.R., and A.W. Shock. 1984. Boiling of multicomponent liquid mixtures. In *Advances in heat transfer*, vol. 16, pp. 59-156. Academic Press, New York.

Thome, J.R., J. El Hajal, and A. Cavallini. 2003. Condensation in horizontal tubes, Part 2: New heat transfer model based on flow regimes. *International Journal of Heat and Mass Transfer* 46(18):3365-3387.

Thonon, B. 1995. Design method for plate evaporators and condensers. *1st International Conference on Process Intensification for the Chemical Industry, BHR Group Conference Series Publication* 18, pp. 37-47.

Thonon, B., R. Vidil, and C. Marvillet. 1995. Recent research and developments in plate heat exchangers. *Journal of Enhanced Heat Transfer* 2(12):149-155.

Tribbe, C., and H. Müller-Steinhagen. 2000. An evaluation of the performance of phenomenological models for predicting pressure gradient during gas-liquid flow in horizontal pipelines. *International Journal of Multiphase Flow* 26:1019-1036.

Tschernobyiski, I., and G. Ratiani. 1955. *Kholodilnaya Teknika* 32.

Turner, J.M., and G.B. Wallis. 1965. The separate-cylinders model of two-phase flow. *Report* NYO-3114-6. Thayer's School of Engineering, Dartmouth College, Hanover, NH.

Van Stralen, S.J. 1959. Heat transfer to boiling binary liquid mixtures. *British Chemical Engineering* 4(January):78.

Van Stralen, S.J., and R. Cole. 1979. *Boiling phenomena*, vol. 1. Hemisphere Publishing, Washington, D.C.

Visaria, M., and I. Mudawar. 2008. Theoretical and experimental study of the effects of spray inclination on two-phases spray cooling and critical heat flux. *International Journal of Heat and Mass Transfer* 51(9-10):2398-2410.

Wallis, G.B. 1969. *One-dimensional two-phase flow*. McGraw-Hill, New York.

Wallis, G.C. 1970. Annular two-phase flow, part I: A simple theory, part II: Additional effect. *Journal of Basic Engineering* 92(1):59-72 and 73-81.

Webb, R.L. 1981. The evolution of enhanced surface geometrics for nucleate boiling. *Heat Transfer Engineering* 2(3-4):46-69.

Webb, J.R. 1994. *Enhanced boiling heat transfer*. John Wiley & Sons, New York.

Westwater, J.W. 1963. Things we don't know about boiling. In *Research in Heat Transfer*, J. Clark, ed. Pergamon Press, New York.

Woldesemayat, M.A., and A.J. Ghajar. 2007. Comparison of void fraction correlations for different flow patterns in horizontal and upward inclined pipes, *International Journal of Multiphase Flow* 33(4):347-370.

Worsoe-Schmidt, P. 1959. Some characteristics of flow-pattern and heat transfer of Freon-12 evaporating in horizontal tubes. *Ingenieren*, International edition, 3(3).

Yan, Y.-Y., and T.-F. Lin. 1999. Evaporation heat transfer and pressure drop of refrigerant R-134a in a plate heat exchanger. *Journal of Heat Transfer* 121(1):118-127.

Yen, T-H., N. Kasagi, and Y. Suzuki. 2003. Forced convective boiling heat transfer in microtubes at low mass and heat fluxes. *International Journal of Multiphase Flow* 29:1771-1792.

Yoon, S.H., E.S. Cho, Y.W. Hwang, M.S. Kim, K. Min, and Y. Kim. 2004. Characteristics of evaporative heat transfer and pressure drop of carbon dioxide and correlation development. *International Journal of Refrigeration* 27:111-119.

Young, M. 1994. Plate heat exchangers as liquid cooling evaporators in ammonia refrigeration systems. *Proceedings of the IIAR 16th Annual Meeting*, St. Louis.

Zeurcher. O., J.R. Thome, and D. Favrat. 1998. In-tube flow boiling of R-407C and R-407C/oil mixtures, part II: Plain tube results and predictions. *International Journal of HVAC&R Research* (now *Science and Technology for the Built Environment*) 4(4):373-399.

Zhao, T.S., and Q.C. Bi. 2001. Co-current air-water two-phase flow patterns in vertical triangular microchannels. *International Journal of Multiphase Flow* 27:765-782.

Zivi, S.M. 1964. Estimation of steady-state steam void-fraction by means of the principle of minimum entropy production. *Journal of Heat Transfer* 86:247-252.

Zuber, N. 1959. Hydrodynamic aspects of boiling heat transfer. U.S. Atomic Energy Commission, Technical Information Service, *Report* AECU 4439. Oak Ridge, TN.

Zuber, N., M. Tribus, and J.W. Westwater. 1962. The hydrodynamic crisis in pool boiling of saturated and subcooled liquids. *Proceedings of the International Heat Transfer Conference* 2:230, and discussion of the papers, vol. 6.

BIBLIOGRAPHY

Bar-Cohen, A., and E. Rahim. 2009. Modeling and prediction of two-phase microgap channel heat transfer characteristics. *Heat Transfer Engineering* 30(8):601-625.

Khan, T.S., M.S. Khan, M-C. Chyu, and Z.H. Ayub. 2009. Review of heat transfer and pressure drop correlations for evaporation of fluid flow in plate heat exchangers (RP-1352). *HVAC&R Research* (now *Science and Technology for the Built Environment*) 15(2):169-188.

Khan, T.S., M.S. Khan, M-C. Chyu, and Z.H. Ayub. 2015. Ammonia evaporation in a mixed configuration chevron plate heat exchanger with and without miscible oil. *International Journal of Refrigeration* 51:120-134.

Rahim, E., R. Revellin, J.R. Thome, and A. Bar-Cohen. 2011. Characterization and prediction of two phase flow regimes in miniature tubes. *International Journal of Multiphase Flow* 37(1):12-23.

Wu, Z., and W. Li. 2011. A new predictive tool for saturated critical heat flux in micro/mini-channels: Effect of heated length-to-diameter ratio. *International Journal of Heat and Mass Transfer* 54:2880-2889.

CHAPTER 6

MASS TRANSFER

MASS transfer by either molecular diffusion or convection is the transport of one component of a mixture relative to the motion of the mixture and is the result of a **concentration gradient**. Mass transfer can occur in liquids and solids as well as gases. For example, water on the wetted slats of a cooling tower evaporates into air in a cooling tower (liquid-to-gas mass transfer), and water vapor from a food product transfers to the dry air as it dries. A piece of solid CO_2 (dry ice) also gets smaller and smaller over time as the CO_2 molecules diffuse into air (solid-to-gas mass transfer). A piece of sugar added to a cup of coffee eventually dissolves and diffuses into the solution, sweetening the coffee, although the sugar molecules are much heavier than the water molecules (solid-to-liquid mass transfer). Air freshener does not just smell where sprayed, but rather the smell spreads throughout the room. The air freshener (matter) moves from an area of high concentration where sprayed to an area of low concentration far away. In an absorption chiller, low-pressure, low-temperature refrigerant vapor from the evaporator enters the thermal compressor in the absorber section, where the refrigerant vapor is absorbed by the strong absorbent (concentrated solution) and dilutes the solution.

In air conditioning, water vapor is added or removed from the air by simultaneous transfer of heat and mass (water vapor) between the airstream and a wetted surface. The wetted surface can be water droplets in an air washer, condensate on the surface of a dehumidifying coil, a spray of liquid absorbent, or wetted surfaces of an evaporative condenser. Equipment performance with these phenomena must be calculated carefully because of simultaneous heat and mass transfer.

This chapter addresses mass transfer principles and provides methods of solving a simultaneous heat and mass transfer problem involving air and water vapor, emphasizing air-conditioning processes. The formulations presented can help analyze performance of specific equipment. For discussion of performance of cooling coils, evaporative condensers, cooling towers, and air washers, see Chapters 23, 39, 40, and 41, respectively, of the 2016 *ASHRAE Handbook—HVAC Systems and Equipment*.

1. MOLECULAR DIFFUSION

Most mass transfer problems can be analyzed by considering diffusion of a gas into a second gas, a liquid, or a solid. In this chapter, the diffusing or dilute component is designated as component B, and the other component as component A. For example, when water vapor diffuses into air, the water vapor is component B and dry air is component A. Properties with subscripts *A* or *B* are local properties of that component. Properties without subscripts are local properties of the mixture.

The primary mechanism of mass diffusion at ordinary temperature and pressure conditions is **molecular diffusion**, a result of density gradient. In a binary gas mixture, the presence of a concentration gradient causes transport of matter by molecular diffusion; that is, because of random molecular motion, gas B diffuses through the mixture of gases A and B in a direction that reduces the concentration gradient.

Fick's Law

The basic equation for molecular diffusion is Fick's law. Expressing the concentration of component B of a binary mixture of components A and B in terms of the mass fraction ρ_B/ρ or mole fraction C_B/C, Fick's law is

$$J_B = -\rho D_v \frac{d(\rho_B/\rho)}{dy} = -J_A \tag{1a}$$

$$J_B^* = -CD_v \frac{d(C_B/C)}{dy} = -J_A^* \tag{1b}$$

where $\rho = \rho_A + \rho_B$ and $C = C_A + C_B$.

The minus sign indicates that the concentration gradient is negative in the direction of diffusion. The proportionality factor D_v is the **mass diffusivity** or the **diffusion coefficient**. The total mass flux $\dot{m}_B''$ and molar flux $\dot{m}_B''^*$ are due to the average velocity of the mixture plus the diffusive flux:

$$\dot{m}_B'' = \rho_B v - \rho D_v \frac{d(\rho_B/\rho)}{dy} \tag{2a}$$

$$\dot{m}_B''^* = C_B v^* - CD_v \frac{d(C_B/C)}{dy} \tag{2b}$$

where v is the mixture's mass average velocity and v^* is the molar average velocity.

Bird et al. (1960) present an analysis of Equations (1a) and (1b). Equations (1a) and (1b) are equivalent forms of Fick's law. The equation used depends on the problem and individual preference. This chapter emphasizes mass analysis rather than molar analysis. However, all results can be converted to the molar form using the relation $C_B \equiv \rho_B/M_B$.

Fick's Law for Dilute Mixtures

In many mass diffusion problems, component B is dilute, with a density much smaller than the mixture's. In this case, Equation (1a) can be written as

$$J_B = -D_v \frac{d\rho_B}{dy} \tag{3}$$

when $\rho_B << \rho$ and $\rho_A \approx \rho$.

Equation (3) can be used without significant error for water vapor diffusing through air at atmospheric pressure and a temperature less than 80°F. In this case, $\rho_B < 0.02\rho$, where ρ_B is the density of water vapor and ρ is the density of moist air (air and water vapor mixture). The error in J_B caused by replacing $\rho[d(\rho_B/\rho)/dy]$ with $d\rho_B/dy$ is less than 2%. At temperatures below 140°F where $\rho_B < 0.10\rho$, Equation (3) can still be used if errors in J_B as great as 10% are tolerable.

The preparation of this chapter is assigned to TC 1.3, Heat Transfer and Fluid Flow.

Fick's Law for Mass Diffusion Through Solids or Stagnant Fluids (Stationary Media)

Fick's law can be simplified for cases of dilute mass diffusion in solids, stagnant liquids, or stagnant gases. In these cases, $\rho_B << \rho$ and $v \approx 0$, which yields the following approximate result:

$$\dot{m}_B'' = J_B = -D_v \frac{d\rho_B}{dy} \tag{4}$$

Fick's Law for Ideal Gases with Negligible Temperature Gradient

For dilute mass diffusion, Fick's law can be written in terms of partial pressure gradient instead of concentration gradient. When gas B can be approximated as ideal,

$$p_B = \frac{\rho_B R_u T}{M_B} = C_B R_u T \tag{5}$$

and when the gradient in T is small, Equation (3) can be written as

$$J_B = -\left(\frac{M_B D_v}{R_u T}\right)\frac{dp_B}{dy} \tag{6a}$$

or

$$J_B^* = -\left(\frac{D_v}{R_u T}\right)\frac{dp_B}{dy} \tag{6b}$$

If $v \approx 0$, Equation (4) may be written as

$$\dot{m}_B'' = J_B = -\left(\frac{M_B D_v}{R_u T}\right)\frac{dp_B}{dy} \tag{7a}$$

or

$$\dot{m}_B''^* = J_B^* = -\left(\frac{D_v}{R_u T}\right)\frac{dp_B}{dy} \tag{7b}$$

The partial pressure gradient formulation for mass transfer analysis has been used extensively; this is unfortunate because the pressure formulation [Equations (6) and (7)] applies only when one component is dilute, the fluid closely approximates an ideal gas, and the temperature gradient has a negligible effect. The density (or concentration) gradient formulation expressed in Equations (1) to (4) is more general and can be applied to a wider range of mass transfer problems, including cases where neither component is dilute [Equation (1)]. The gases need not be ideal, nor the temperature gradient negligible. Consequently, this chapter emphasizes the density formulation.

Diffusion Coefficient

For a binary mixture, the diffusion coefficient D_v is a function of temperature, pressure, and composition. Experimental measurements of D_v for most binary mixtures are limited in range and accuracy. Table 1 gives a few experimental values for diffusion of some gases in air. For more detailed tables, see the Bibliography.

Table 1 Mass Diffusivities for Gases in Air*

Gas	D_v, ft²/h
Ammonia	1.08
Benzene	0.34
Carbon dioxide	0.64
Ethanol	0.46
Hydrogen	1.60
Oxygen	0.80
Water vapor	0.99

*Gases at 77°F and 14.696 psi.

In the absence of data, use equations developed from (1) theory or (2) theory with constants adjusted from limited experimental data. For binary gas mixtures at low pressure, D_v is inversely proportional to pressure, increases with increasing temperature, and is almost independent of composition for a given gas pair. Bird et al. (1960) present the following equation, developed from kinetic theory and corresponding states arguments, for estimating D_v at pressures less than $0.1p_{c\,min}$:

$$D_v = a\left(\frac{T}{\sqrt{T_{cA}T_{cB}}}\right)^b \sqrt{\frac{1}{M_A} + \frac{1}{M_B}} \times \frac{(p_{cA}p_{cB})^{1/3}(T_{cA}T_{cB})^{5/12}}{p} \tag{8}$$

where

D_v = diffusion coefficient, ft²/h
a = constant that depends on units used
b = constant, dimensionless
T = absolute temperature, °R
p = pressure, atm
M = relative molecular weight, lb_m/lb mol

Subscripts cA and cB refer to the critical states of the two gases. Analysis of experimental data gives the following values of the constants a and b:

For nonpolar gas pairs

$$a = 6.518 \times 10^{-4} \quad \text{and} \quad b = 1.823$$

For water vapor with a nonpolar gas

$$a = 8.643 \times 10^{-4} \quad \text{and} \quad b = 2.334$$

In **nonpolar gas**, intermolecular forces are independent of the relative orientation of molecules, depending only on the separation distance from each other. Air, composed almost entirely of nonpolar gases O_2 and N_2, is nonpolar.

Equation (8) is stated to agree with experimental data at atmospheric pressure to within about 8% (Bird et al. 1960).

Mass diffusivity D_v for binary mixtures at low pressure is predictable within about 10% by kinetic theory (Reid et al. 1987).

$$D_v = 2.79 \times 10^{-5} \frac{T^{1.5}}{p(\sigma_{AB})^2 \Omega_{D,AB}} \sqrt{\frac{1}{M_A} + \frac{1}{M_B}} \tag{9}$$

where

σ_{AB} = characteristic molecular diameter, nm
$\Omega_{D,AB}$ = temperature function, dimensionless

D_v is in ft²/h, p in atm, and T in °R. If the gas molecules of A and B are considered rigid spheres having diameters σ_A and σ_B [and $\sigma_{AB} = (\sigma_A/2) + (\sigma_B/2)$], all expressed in nanometres, the dimensionless function $\Omega_{D,AB}$ equals unity. More realistic models for molecules having intermolecular forces of attraction and repulsion lead to values that are functions of temperature. Bird et al. (1960) and Reid et al. (1987) present tabulations of $\Omega_{D,AB}$. These results show that D_v increases as the 2.0 power of T at low temperatures and as the 1.65 power of T at very high temperatures.

The diffusion coefficient of moist air has been calculated for Equation (8) using a simplified intermolecular potential field function for water vapor and air (Mason and Monchick 1965). The following empirical equation is for mass diffusivity of water vapor in air up to 2000°F (Sherwood and Pigford 1952):

$$D_v = \frac{1.46 \times 10^{-4}}{p}\left(\frac{T^{2.5}}{T + 441}\right) \tag{10}$$

Example 1. Evaluate the diffusion coefficient of CO_2 in air at 527.4°R and atmospheric pressure (14.696 psia) using Equation (9).

Solution: In Equation (9), D_v is in ft²/h, $\sigma_{AB} = (\sigma_A/2) + (\sigma_B/2)$, and the Lennard-Jones energy parameter $\varepsilon_{AB}/k = \sqrt{(\varepsilon_A/k)(\varepsilon_B/k)}$. Values of σ and ε for each gas are as follows:

	σ, nm	**ε/k, °R**
CO_2	0.3996	342
Air	0.3617	175

The combined values for use in Equation (9) are

$$\sigma_{AB} = 0.3996/2 + 0.3617/2 = 0.3806 \text{ nm}$$

$$\varepsilon_{AB}/k = \sqrt{(342)(175)} = 245 \text{ at } P = 1 \text{ atm and } T = 527.4°\text{R}$$

$$\frac{\varepsilon_{AB}}{kT} = \frac{245}{527.4} = 0.465 \qquad \frac{kT}{\varepsilon_{AB}} = \frac{1}{0.465} = 2.15$$

From tables for $\Omega_{D,AB}$ at $kT/\varepsilon_{AB} = 2.15$ (Bird et al. 1960; Reid et al. 1987), the collision integral $\Omega_{D,AB} = 1.047$. The molecular weights of CO_2 and air are 44 and 29, respectively. Substituting these values gives

$$D_v = 2.79 \times 10^{-5}[527.4^{1.5}/(1 \times 0.3806^2 \times 1.047)](1/44 + 1/29)^{0.5}$$
$$= 0.533 \text{ ft}^2/\text{h}$$

Diffusion of One Gas Through a Second Stagnant Gas

Figure 1 shows diffusion of one gas through a second, stagnant gas. Water vapor diffuses from the liquid surface into surrounding stationary air. It is assumed that local equilibrium exists through the gas mixture, that the gases are ideal, and that the Gibbs-Dalton law is valid, which implies that temperature gradient has a negligible effect. Water vapor diffuses because of concentration gradient, as given by Equation (6a). There is a continuous gas phase, so the mixture pressure p is constant, and the Gibbs-Dalton law yields

$$p_A + p_B = p = \text{constant} \tag{11a}$$

or

$$\frac{\rho_A}{M_A} + \frac{\rho_B}{M_B} = \frac{p}{R_u T} = \text{constant} \tag{11b}$$

The partial pressure gradient of the water vapor causes a partial pressure gradient of the air such that

$$\frac{dp_A}{dy} = -\frac{dp_B}{dy} \tag{11c}$$

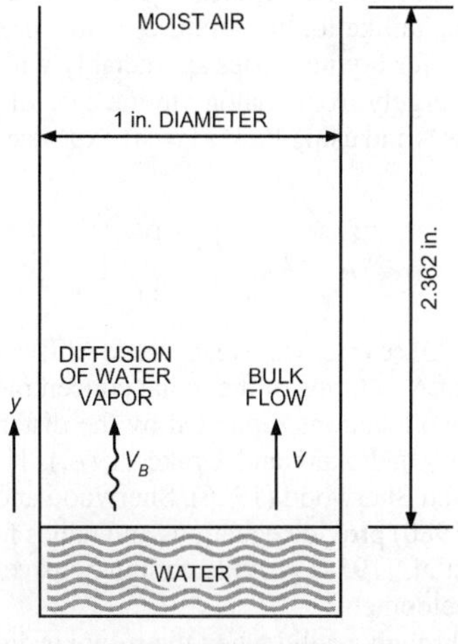

Fig. 1 Diffusion of Water Vapor Through Stagnant Air

or

$$\left(\frac{1}{M_A}\right)\frac{d\rho_A}{dy} = -\left(\frac{1}{M_B}\right)\frac{d\rho_B}{dy} \tag{12}$$

Air, then, diffuses toward the liquid water interface. Because it cannot be absorbed there, a bulk velocity v of the gas mixture is established in a direction away from the liquid surface, so that the net transport of air is zero (i.e., the air is stagnant):

$$\dot{m}''_A = -D_v\frac{d\rho_A}{dy} + \rho_A v = 0 \tag{13}$$

The bulk velocity v transports not only air but also water vapor away from the interface. Therefore, the total rate of water vapor diffusion is

$$\dot{m}''_B = -D_v\frac{d\rho_B}{dy} + \rho_B v \tag{14}$$

Substituting for the velocity v from Equation (13) and using Equations (11b) and (12) gives

$$\dot{m}''_B = \left(\frac{D_v M_B p}{\rho_A R_u T}\right)\frac{d\rho_A}{dy} \tag{15}$$

Integration yields

$$\dot{m}''_B = \frac{D_v M_B p}{R_u T}\left[\frac{\ln(\rho_{AL}/\rho_{A0})}{y_L - y_0}\right] \tag{16a}$$

or

$$\dot{m}''_B = -D_v P_{Am}\left(\frac{\rho_{BL} - \rho_{B0}}{y_L - y_0}\right) \tag{16b}$$

where

$$P_{Am} \equiv \frac{p}{p_{AL}}\rho_{AL}\left[\frac{\ln(\rho_{AL}/\rho_{A0})}{\rho_{AL} - \rho_{A0}}\right] \tag{17}$$

P_{Am} is the logarithmic mean density factor of the stagnant air. The pressure distribution for this type of diffusion is shown in Figure 2. **Stagnant** refers to the net behavior of the air; it does not move because bulk flow exactly offsets diffusion. The term P_{Am} in Equation (16b) approximately equals unity for dilute mixtures such as water vapor in air at near-atmospheric conditions. This condition makes it possible to simplify Equations (16) and implies that, for dilute mixtures, the partial pressure distribution curves in Figure 2 are straight lines.

Example 2. A vertical tube of 1 in. diameter is partially filled with water so that the distance from the water surface to the open end of the tube is 2.362 in., as shown in Figure 1. Perfectly dried air is blown over the open tube end, and the complete system is at a constant temperature of 59°F. In 200 h of steady operation, 0.00474 lb of water evaporates from the tube. The total pressure of the system is 14.696 psia (1 atm). Using these data, (1) calculate the mass diffusivity of water vapor in air, and (2) compare this experimental result with that from Equation (10).

Solution:

(1) The mass diffusion flux of water vapor from the water surface is

$$\dot{m}_B = 0.00474/200 = 0.0000237 \text{ lb/h}$$

The cross-sectional area of a 1 in. diameter tube is $\pi(0.5)^2/144 = 0.005454$ ft². Therefore, $\dot{m}''_B = 0.004345$ lb/ft²·h. The partial densities are determined from psychrometric tables.

$$\rho_{BL} = 0; \quad \rho_{B0} = 0.000801 \text{ lb/ft}^3$$

$$\rho_{AL} = 0.0765 \text{ lb/ft}^3; \quad \rho_{A0} = 0.0752 \text{ lb/ft}^3$$

Because $p = p_{AL} = 1$ atm, the logarithmic mean density factor [Equation (17)] is

$$P_{Am} = 0.0765\left[\frac{\ln(0.0765/0.0752)}{0.0765 - 0.0752}\right] = 1.009$$

The mass diffusivity is now computed from Equation (16b) as

$$D_v = \frac{-\dot{m}_B''(y_L - y_0)}{P_{Am}(\rho_{BL} - \rho_{B0})} = \frac{-(0.004345)(2.362)}{(1.009)(0 - 0.000801)(12)}$$

$$= 1.058 \text{ ft}^2/\text{h}$$

(2) By Equation (10), with $p = 14.696$ psi and $T = 59 + 460 = 519°$R,

$$D_v = \frac{0.00215}{14.696}\left(\frac{519^{2.5}}{519 + 441}\right) = 0.935 \text{ ft}^2/\text{h}$$

Neglecting the correction factor P_{Am} for this example gives a difference of less than 1% between the calculated experimental and empirically predicted values of D_v.

Equimolar Counterdiffusion

Figure 3 shows two large chambers, both containing an ideal gas mixture of two components A and B (e.g., air and water vapor) at the same total pressure p and temperature T. The two chambers are connected by a duct of length L and cross-sectional area A_{cs}. Partial pressure p_B is higher in the left chamber, and partial pressure p_A is higher in the right chamber. The partial pressure differences cause component B to migrate to the right and component A to migrate to the left.

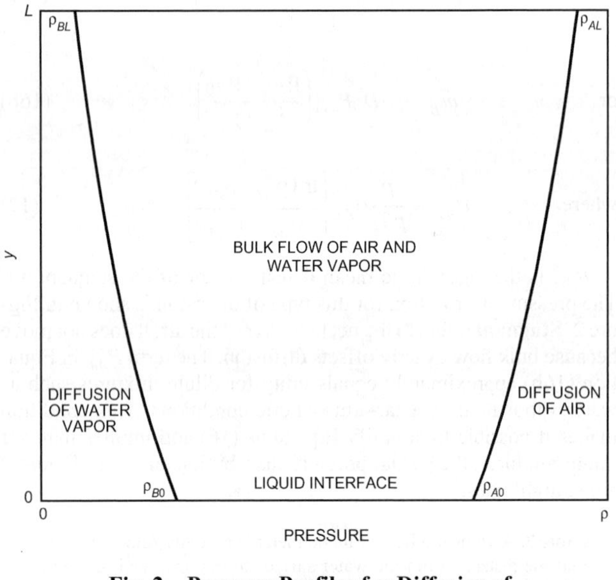

Fig. 2 Pressure Profiles for Diffusion of Water Vapor Through Stagnant Air

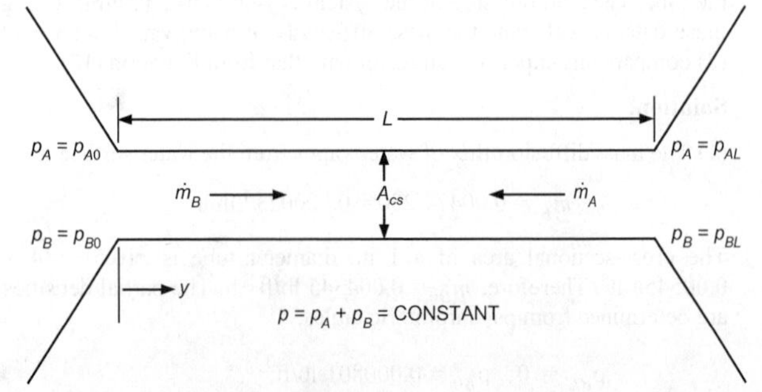

Fig. 3 Equimolar Counterdiffusion

At steady state, the molar flows of A and B must be equal but opposite:

$$\dot{m}_A''^* + \dot{m}_B''^* = 0 \tag{18}$$

because the total molar concentration C must stay the same in both chambers if p and T remain constant. Because molar fluxes are the same in both directions, the molar average velocity $v^* = 0$. Thus, Equation (7b) can be used to calculate the molar flux of B (or A):

$$\dot{m}_B''^* = \frac{-D_v}{R_u T}\frac{dp_B}{dy} \tag{19}$$

or

$$\dot{m}_B^* = \frac{A_{cs}D_v}{R_u T}\left(\frac{p_{B0} - p_{BL}}{L}\right) \tag{20}$$

or

$$\dot{m}_B = \frac{M_B A_{cs} D_v}{R_u T}\left(\frac{p_{B0} - p_{BL}}{L}\right) \tag{21}$$

Example 3. One large room is maintained at 70°F (530°R), 1 atm, 80% rh. A 60 ft long duct with cross-sectional area of 1.5 ft² connects the room to another large room at 70°F, 1 atm, 10% rh. What is the rate of water vapor diffusion between the two rooms?

Solution: Let air be component A and water vapor be component B. Equation (21) can be used to calculate the mass flow of water vapor B. Equation (10) can be used to calculate the diffusivity.

$$D_v = \frac{1.46 \times 10^{-4}}{1}\left(\frac{530^{2.5}}{530 + 441}\right) = 0.972 \text{ ft}^2/\text{h}$$

From a psychrometric table (Table 3, Chapter 1), the saturated vapor pressure at 70°F is 0.363 psi. The vapor pressure difference $p_{B0} - p_{BL}$ is

$$p_{B0} - p_{BL} = (0.8 - 0.1)0.363 \text{ psi} = 0.254 \text{ psi}$$

Then, Equation (21) gives

$$\dot{m}_b = \frac{18 \times 144 \times 1.5 \times 0.972 \times 0.254}{1545 \times 530 \times 60} = 1.90 \times 10^{-5} \text{ lb}_m/\text{h}$$

Molecular Diffusion in Liquids and Solids

Because of the greater density, diffusion is slower in liquids than in gases. No satisfactory molecular theories have been developed for calculating diffusion coefficients. The limited measured values of D_v show that, unlike for gas mixtures at low pressures, the diffusion coefficient for liquids varies appreciably with concentration.

Reasoning largely from analogy to the case of one-dimensional diffusion in gases and using Fick's law as expressed by Equation (4) gives

$$\dot{m}_B'' = D_v\left(\frac{\rho_{B1} - \rho_{B2}}{y_2 - y_1}\right) \tag{22}$$

Equation (22) expresses steady-state diffusion of solute B through solvent A in terms of the molal concentration difference of the solute at two locations separated by the distance $\Delta y = y_2 - y_1$. Bird et al. (1960), Eckert and Drake (1972), Hirschfelder et al. (1954), Reid and Sherwood (1966), Sherwood and Pigford (1952), and Treybal (1980) provide equations and tables for evaluating D_v. Hirschfelder et al. (1954) provide comprehensive treatment of the molecular developments.

Diffusion through a solid when the solute is dissolved to form a homogeneous solid solution is known as **structure-insensitive**

diffusion (Treybal 1980). This solid diffusion closely parallels diffusion through fluids, and Equation (22) can be applied to one-dimensional steady-state problems. Values of mass diffusivity are generally lower than they are for liquids and vary with temperature.

Diffusion of a gas mixture through a porous medium is common (e.g., diffusion of an air/vapor mixture through porous insulation or other vapor-permeable building materials). Vapor diffuses through the air along the tortuous narrow passages within the porous medium. Mass flux is a function of the vapor pressure gradient and diffusion coefficient, as indicated in Equation (7a). It is also a function of the structure of the pathways within the porous medium and is therefore called **structure-sensitive diffusion**. All these factors are taken into account in the following version of Equation (7a):

$$\dot{m}_B'' = -\bar{\mu}\frac{dp_B}{dy} \qquad (23)$$

where $\bar{\mu}$ is called the moisture permeability of the porous medium. For a layer of porous solid L thick, $\bar{\mu}/L$ is called the permeance, in units of the unit for which is the **perm** (= 1 grain/h·ft²·in. of mercury). Permeance is also known as **vapor flow conductance**, which is analogous to heat flow conductance in heat transfer. **Permeability** is the product of permeance and layer thickness (i.e., perm-in.), and is often given in those units.

Consider a slab $L = y_2 - y_1$ thick with cross-sectional area A_c. The vapor pressure is p_{B1} on one side of the slab and p_{B2} on the other side. If the permeability $\bar{\mu}$ is constant, integration of Equation (23) yields

$$p_B(y) = p_{B1} - \frac{y - y_1}{L}(p_{B1} - p_{B2}) \qquad (24)$$

$$\dot{m}_B'' = \frac{\dot{m}_B}{A_c} = \bar{\mu}\frac{p_{B1} - p_{B2}}{L} \quad \text{or}$$

$$\dot{m}_B = \frac{p_{B1} - p_{B2}}{L/(\bar{\mu}A_c)} \qquad (25)$$

where $\dot{m}_B$ is the vapor flow rate. In Equation (25), $p_{B1} - p_{B2}$ can be considered a driving potential, and $L/(\bar{\mu}A_c)$ a resistance. This is analogous to Equation (1) in Chapter 4, where q is the heat transfer rate, $t_{s1} - t_{s2}$ is the driving potential, and $L/(kA_c)$ is the resistance. Chapters 25 and 26 present this topic in more depth.

Example 4. A three-layer composite wall consisting of glass fiber batt insulation, a concrete block (limestone aggregate, 8 in., 36 lb, 138 lb/ft³ concrete, with two perlite-filled cores) and brick (120 lb/ft³) is shown in Figure 4. The dry-bulb temperature and indoor dew point are T_i = 72°F and $T_{i,dp}$ = 45°F, respectively. Outdoor temperature T_o = 10°F, and relative humidity rh_o = 50%. The outdoor wind speed is 15 mph.

(a) Calculate heat transfer rate through the wall (in Btu/h) per square foot of wall area.

(b) Calculate vapor flow rate through the wall (in grain/h) per square foot of wall area.

Solution

Find (1) thermal conductivity k from Table 1 in Chapter 26; (2) film resistance coefficient $1/h$, where h is convective heat transfer coefficient, from Table 10 in Chapter 26; and (3) water vapor permeability $\bar{\mu}$ from Table 6 in Chapter 26. Calculate thermal resistance $L/(kA_c)$ and diffusion resistance $L/(\bar{\mu}A_c)$, for each layer. Calculate the film thermal resistance $1/(hA_s)$ at both surfaces. $A_s = A_c$ = 1 ft² because rates per square foot of wall area are required. Determine total thermal resistance R_T and total diffusion resistance r_T. See Table 2 for values.

(a) Calculate heat transmission through the wall.

$$q = \frac{(T_i - T_o)}{R_T} = \frac{(72 - 10)°\text{F}}{16.04\ \text{h·°F/Btu}} = 3.87\ \text{Btu/h} \quad \text{or} \quad \frac{q}{A_c} = 3.87\ \text{Btu/h·ft}^2$$

(b) Calculate vapor flow rate through the wall. At T_i = 72°F and $T_{i,dp}$ = 45°F, vapor pressure p_{vi} = 0.14757 psi = 0.300456 in. of mercury. At T_o = 10°F and rh_o = 50%, p_{vo} = 0.015445 psi = 0.031446 in. of mercury. The vapor flow rate is then

$$\dot{m}_v = \frac{(p_{v,i} - p_{v,o})}{r_T} = \frac{(0.300456 - 0.031446)\ \text{in. of mercury}}{1.59\ \text{h·in. of mercury/gr}}$$

$$= 0.1692\ \text{gr/h} \quad \text{or} \quad \frac{\dot{m}_v}{A_c} = 0.1692\ \text{gr/h·ft}^2$$

2. CONVECTION OF MASS

Convection of mass involves the mass transfer mechanisms of molecular diffusion and bulk fluid motion. Fluid motion in the region adjacent to a mass transfer surface may be laminar or turbulent, depending on geometry and flow conditions.

Mass Transfer Coefficient

Convective mass transfer is analogous to convective heat transfer where geometry and boundary conditions are similar. The analogy holds for both laminar and turbulent flows and applies to both external and internal flow problems.

Mass Transfer Coefficients for External Flows. Most external convective mass transfer problems can be solved with an appropriate formulation that relates the mass transfer flux (to or from an interfacial surface) to the concentration difference across the boundary layer illustrated in Figure 5. This formulation gives rise to the convective mass transfer coefficient, defined as

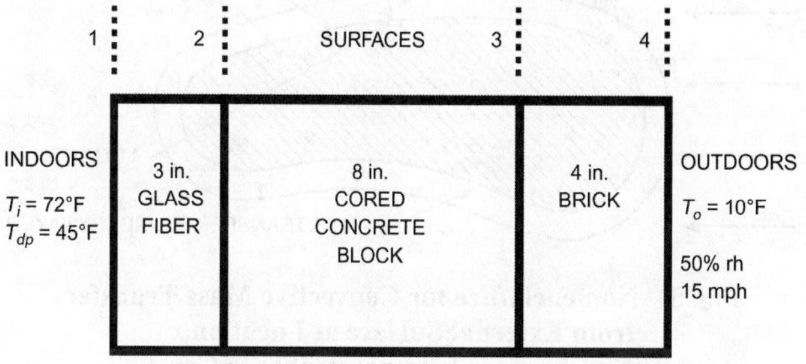

Fig. 4 Composite Wall for Example 4

Table 2 Material Values for Example 4

	L, in.	$\bar{\mu}$, perm·in.	k, Btu·in/h·ft²·°F	$1/h$, h·ft²·°F/Btu	Thermal Resistance, h·°F/Btu	Diffusion Resistance, h·in. of mercury/gr	Comment
Indoor surface		NA	NA	0.68	0.68	0	
Glass fiber batt	3	118	0.24	NA	12.5	0.03	
Concrete block	8	19	3.8	NA	2.1	0.42	
Fired clay brick	4	3.5	6.8	NA	0.59	1.14	Assume 70% rh
Outdoor surface		NA	NA	0.17	0.17	0	
Total, R_T and r_T					**16.04**	**1.59**	

$$h_M \equiv \frac{\dot{m}''_B}{\rho_{Bi} - \rho_{B\infty}} \quad (26)$$

where

h_M = local external mass transfer coefficient, ft/h
$\dot{m}''_B$ = mass flux of gas B from surface, $lb_m/ft^2 \cdot h$
ρ_{Bi} = density of gas B at interface (saturation density), lb_m/ft^3
$\rho_{B\infty}$ = density of component B outside boundary layer, lb_m/ft^3

If ρ_{Bi} and $\rho_{B\infty}$ are constant over the entire interfacial surface, the mass transfer rate from the surface can be expressed as

$$\dot{m}''_B = \bar{h}_M(\rho_{Bi} - \rho_{B\infty}) \quad (27)$$

where $\bar{h}_M$ is the average mass transfer coefficient, defined as

$$\bar{h}_M \equiv \frac{1}{A}\int_A h_m\, dA \quad (28)$$

Mass Transfer Coefficients for Internal Flows. Most internal convective mass transfer problems, such as those that occur in channels or in the cores of dehumidification coils, can be solved if an appropriate expression is available to relate the mass transfer flux (to or from the interfacial surface) to the difference between the concentration at the surface and the bulk concentration in the channel, as shown in Figure 6. This formulation leads to the definition of the mass transfer coefficient for internal flows:

$$h_M \equiv \frac{\dot{m}''_B}{\rho_{Bi} - \rho_{Bb}} \quad (29)$$

where

h_M = internal mass transfer coefficient, ft/h
$\dot{m}''_B$ = mass flux of gas B at interfacial surface, $lb_m/ft^2 \cdot h$
ρ_{Bi} = density of gas B at interfacial surface, lb_m/ft^3

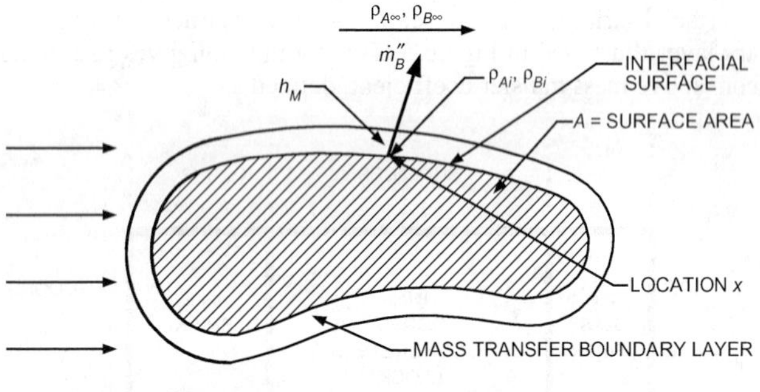

Fig. 5 Nomenclature for Convective Mass Transfer from External Surface at Location x Where Surface Is Impermeable to Gas A

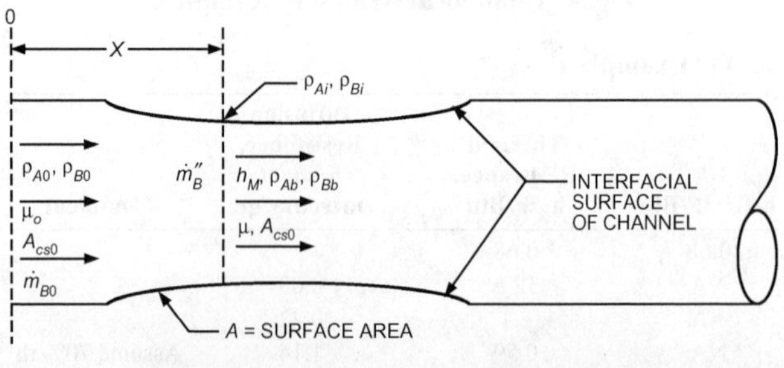

Fig. 6 Nomenclature for Convective Mass Transfer from Internal Surface Impermeable to Gas A

$\rho_{Bb} \equiv (1/\bar{u}_B A_{cs})\int_{A_{cs}} u_B \rho_B\, dA_{cs}$ = bulk density of gas B at location x
$\bar{u}_B \equiv (1/A_{cs})\int_A u_B\, dA_{cs}$ = average velocity of gas B at location x, fpm
A_{cs} = cross-sectional area of channel at station x, ft^2
u_B = velocity of component B in x direction, fpm
ρ_B = density distribution of component B at station x, lb_m/ft^3

Often, it is easier to obtain the bulk density of gas B from

$$\rho_{Bb} = \frac{\dot{m}_{Bo} + \int_A \dot{m}''_B dA}{\bar{u}_B A_{cs}} \quad (30)$$

where

$\dot{m}_{Bo}$ = mass flow rate of component B at station $x = 0$, lb_m/h
A = interfacial area of channel between station $x = 0$ and station $x = x$, ft^2

Equation (28) can be derived from the preceding definitions. The major problem is determining $\bar{u}_B$. If, however, analysis is restricted to cases where B is dilute and concentration gradients of B in the x direction are negligibly small, $\bar{u}_B \approx \bar{u}$. Component B is swept along in the x direction with an average velocity equal to the average velocity of the dilute mixture.

Analogy Between Convective Heat and Mass Transfer

Most expressions for the convective mass transfer coefficient h_M are determined from expressions for the convective heat transfer coefficient h.

For problems in internal and external flow where mass transfer occurs at the convective surface and where component B is dilute, Bird et al. (1960) and Incropera and DeWitt (1996) found that the Nusselt and Sherwood numbers are defined as follows:

$$\text{Nu} = f(X, Y, Z, \text{Pr}, \text{Re}) \quad (31)$$

$$\text{Sh} = f(X, Y, Z, \text{Sc}, \text{Re}) \quad (32)$$

and

$$\overline{\text{Nu}} = g(\text{Pr}, \text{Re}) \quad (33)$$

$$\overline{\text{Sh}} = g(\text{Sc}, \text{Re}) \quad (34)$$

where f in Equations (31) and (32) indicates a functional relationship among the dimensionless groups shown. The function f is the same in both equations. Similarly, g indicates a functional relationship that is the same in Equations (33) and (34). Pr and Sc are dimensionless Prandtl and Schmidt numbers, respectively, as defined in the Symbols section. The primary restrictions on the analogy are that the surface shapes are the same and that the temperature boundary conditions are analogous to the density distribution boundary conditions for component B when cast in dimensionless form. Several primary factors prevent the analogy from being perfect. In some cases, the Nusselt number was derived for smooth surfaces. Many mass transfer problems involve wavy, droplet-like, or roughened surfaces. Many Nusselt number relations are obtained for constant-temperature surfaces. Sometimes ρ_{Bi} is not constant over the entire surface because of varying saturation conditions and the possibility of surface dryout.

In all mass transfer problems, there is some blowing or suction at the surface because of condensation, evaporation, or transpiration of component B. In most cases, this blowing/suction has little effect on the Sherwood number, but the analogy should be examined closely if $v_i/u_\infty > 0.01$ or $v_i/\bar{u} > 0.01$, especially if the Reynolds number is large.

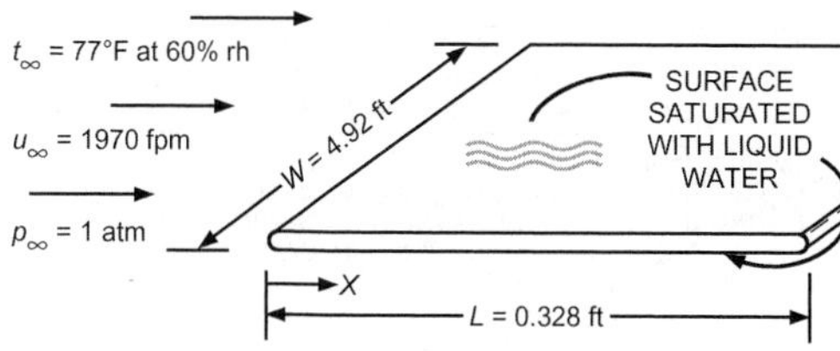

Fig. 7 Water-Saturated Flat Plate in Flowing Airstream

Example 5. Air at 77°F, 1 atm, and 60% rh flows at 32.8 ft/s (1970 ft/min), as shown in Figure 7. Find the rate of evaporation, rate of heat transfer to the water, and water surface temperature.

Solution: Heat transfer to water from air supplies the energy required to evaporate the water.

$$q = hA(t_\infty - t_s) = \dot{m}h_{fg} = h_M A(\rho_s - \rho_\infty)h_{fg}$$

where

h = convective heat transfer coefficient
h_M = convective mass transfer coefficient
A = 0.328 × 4.92 × 2 = 3.23 ft² = surface area (both sides)
$\dot{m}$ = evaporation rate
t_s, ρ_s = temperature and vapor density at water surface
t_∞, ρ_∞ = temperature and vapor density of airstream

This energy balance can be rearranged to give

$$\rho_s - \rho_\infty = \frac{h}{h_M}\left[\frac{(t_\infty - t_s)}{h_{fg}}\right]$$

The heat transfer coefficient h is found by first calculating the Nusselt number:

$$\text{Nu} = 0.664\text{Re}^{1/2}\text{Pr}^{1/3} \quad \text{for laminar flow}$$
$$\text{Nu} = 0.037\text{Re}^{4/5}\text{Pr}^{1/3} \quad \text{for turbulent flow}$$

The mass transfer coefficient h_M requires calculation of Sherwood number Sh, obtained using the analogy expressed in Equations (33) and (34):

$$\text{Sh} = 0.664\text{Re}^{1/2}\text{Pr}^{1/3} \quad \text{for laminar flow}$$
$$\text{Sh} = 0.037\text{Re}^{4/5}\text{Pr}^{1/3} \quad \text{for turbulent flow}$$

With Nu and Sh known,

$$h_M = \frac{\text{Sh}\,D_v}{L} \qquad h = \frac{\text{Nu}\,k}{L}$$

or

$$\frac{h}{h_M} = \frac{\text{Nu}\,k}{\text{Sh}\,D_v} = \left(\frac{\text{Pr}}{\text{Sc}}\right)^{1/3}\frac{k}{D_v}$$

This result is valid for both laminar and turbulent flow. Using this result in the preceding energy balance gives

$$\rho_s - \rho_\infty = \left(\frac{\text{Pr}}{\text{Sc}}\right)^{1/3}\frac{k}{D_v}\left[\frac{(t_\infty - t_s)}{h_{fg}}\right]$$

This equation must be solved for ρ_s. Then, water surface temperature t_s is the saturation temperature corresponding to ρ_s. Air properties Sc, Pr, D_v, and k are evaluated at film temperature $t_f = (t_\infty + t_s)/2$, and h_{fg} is evaluated at t_s. Because t_s appears in the right side and all the air properties also vary somewhat with t_s, iteration is required. Start by guessing t_s = 57.2°F (the dew point of the airstream), giving t_f = 67.1°F. At these temperatures, values on the right side are found in property tables or calculated as

k = 0.01485 Btu/h·ft·°F
Pr = 0.709
D_v = 0.9769 ft²/h = 0.01628 ft²/min [from Equation (10)]
ρ = 0.07435 lb$_m$/ft³
μ = 0.04376 lb$_m$/ft·h
Sc = $\mu/\rho D_v$ = 0.6025
h_{fg} = 1055.5 Btu/lb$_m$ (at 57.2°F)
ρ_∞ = 8.846 × 10⁻⁴ lb$_m$/ft³ (from psychrometric chart at 77°F, 60% rh)
t_s = 57.2°F (initial guess)

Solving yields ρ_s = 1.184 × 10⁻³ lb$_m$/ft³. The corresponding value of t_s = 70.9°F. Repeat the process using t_s = 70.9°F as the initial guess. The result is ρ_s = 0.977 × 10⁻³ lb$_m$/ft³ and t_s = 64.9°F. Continue iterations until ρ_s converges to 1.038 × 10⁻³ lb$_m$/ft³ and t_s = 66.9°F.

To solve for the rates of evaporation and heat transfer, first calculate the Reynolds number using air properties at t_f = (77 + 66.9)/2 = 72.0°F.

$$\text{Re}_L = \frac{\rho u_\infty L}{\mu} = \frac{(0.07435)(118{,}200)(0.328)}{0.04376} = 65{,}871$$

where L = 0.328 ft, the length of the plate in the direction of flow. Because Re_L < 500,000, flow is laminar over the entire length of the plate; therefore,

$$\text{Sh} = 0.664\text{Re}^{1/2}\text{Sc}^{1/3} = 144$$

$$h_M = \frac{\text{Sh}D_v}{L} = 7.15 \text{ fpm}$$

$$\dot{m} = h_M A(\rho_s - \rho_\infty) = 0.00354 \text{ lb/min}$$

$$q = \dot{m}\,h_{fg} = 3.74 \text{ Btu/min}$$

The same value for q would be obtained by calculating the Nusselt number and heat transfer coefficient h and setting $q = hA(t_\infty - t_s)$.

The kind of similarity between heat and mass transfer that results in Equations (31) to (34) can also be shown to exist between heat and momentum transfer. Chilton and Colburn (1934) used this similarity to relate Nusselt number to friction factor by the analogy

$$j_H = \frac{\text{Nu}}{\text{Re Pr}^{(1-n)}} = \text{St Pr}^n = \frac{f}{2} \qquad (35)$$

where n = 2/3, St = Nu/(Re Pr) is the Stanton number, and j_H is the Chilton-Colburn j-factor for heat transfer. Substituting Sh for Nu and Sc for Pr in Equations (33) and (34) gives the Chilton-Colburn j-factor for mass transfer, j_D:

$$j_D = \frac{\text{Sh}}{\text{Re Sc}^{(1-n)}} = \text{St}_m\text{Sc}^n = \frac{f}{2} \qquad (36)$$

where $\text{St}_m = \text{Sh}P_{Am}/(\text{Re Sc})$ is the Stanton number for mass transfer. Equations (35) and (36) are called the **Chilton-Colburn *j*-factor analogy**.

The power of the Chilton-Colburn j-factor analogy is represented in Figures 8 to 11. Figure 8 plots various experimental values of j_D from a flat plate with flow parallel to the plate surface. The solid line, which represents the data to near perfection, is actually $f/2$ from Blasius' solution of laminar flow on a flat plate (left-hand portion of the solid line) and Goldstein's solution for a turbulent boundary layer (right-hand portion). The right-hand part also represents McAdams' (1954) correlation of turbulent flow heat transfer coefficient for a flat plate.

A **wetted-wall column** is a vertical tube in which a thin liquid film adheres to the tube surface and exchanges mass by evaporation or absorption with a gas flowing through the tube. Figure 9 illustrates typical data on vaporization in wetted-wall columns, plotted as j_D versus Re. The point spread with variation in $\mu/\rho D_v$ results from Gilliland's finding of an exponent of 0.56, not 2/3, representing the effect of the Schmidt number. Gilliland's equation can be written as follows:

$$j_D = 0.023\,\text{Re}^{-0.17}\left(\frac{\mu}{\rho D_v}\right)^{-0.56} \qquad (37)$$

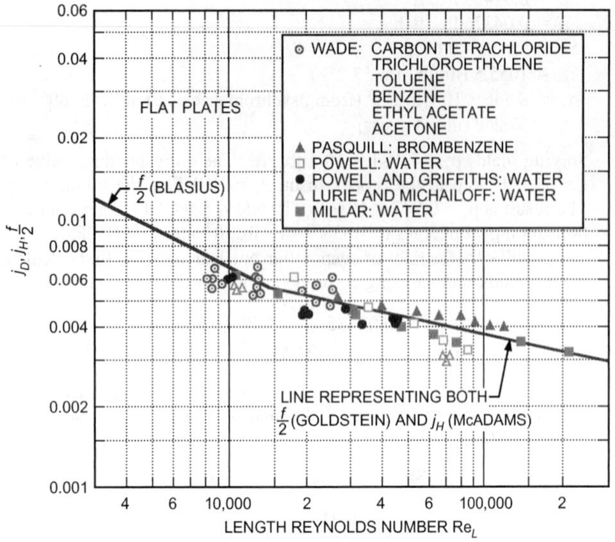

Fig. 8 Mass Transfer from Flat Plate

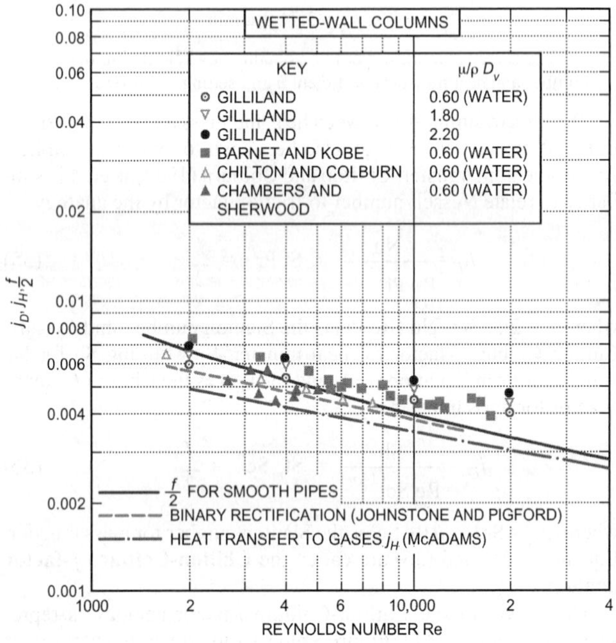

Fig. 9 Vaporization and Absorption in Wetted-Wall Column

Similarly, McAdams' (1954) equation for heat transfer in pipes can be expressed as

$$j_H = 0.023\ \text{Re}^{-0.20}\left(\frac{c_p\mu}{k}\right)^{-0.7} \tag{38}$$

This is represented by the dash-dot curve in Figure 9, which falls below the mass transfer data. The curve $f/2$, representing friction in smooth tubes, is the upper, solid curve.

Data for liquid evaporation from single cylinders into gas streams flowing transversely to the cylinders' axes are shown in Figure 10. Although the dash-dot line in Figure 10 represents the data, it is actually taken from McAdams (1954) as representative of a large collection of data on heat transfer to single cylinders placed transverse to airstreams. To compare these data with friction, it is necessary to distinguish between total drag and skin friction. Because the analogies are based on skin friction, normal pressure

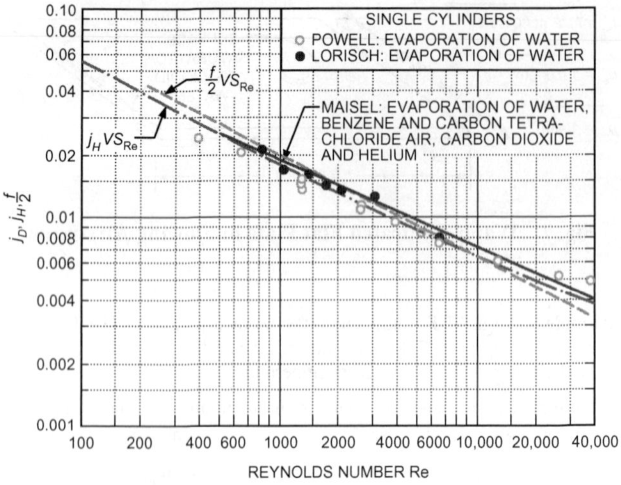

Fig. 10 Mass Transfer from Single Cylinders in Crossflow

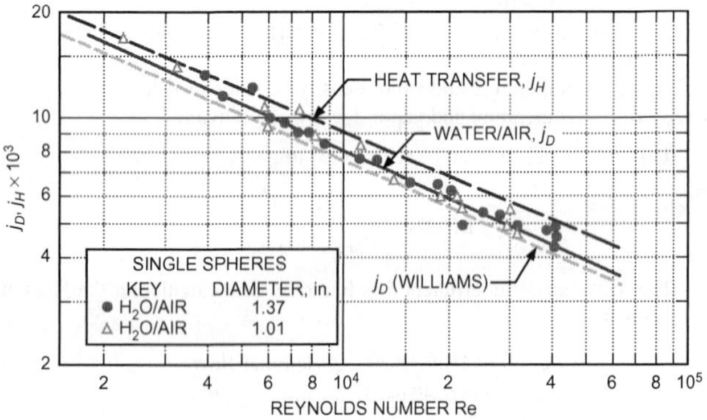

Fig. 11 Mass Transfer from Single Spheres

drag must be subtracted from the measured total drag. At Re = 1000, skin friction is 12.6% of the total drag; at Re = 31,600, it is only 1.9%. Consequently, values of $f/2$ at a high Reynolds number, obtained by the difference, are subject to considerable error.

In Figure 11, data on evaporation of water into air for single spheres are presented. The solid line, which best represents these data, agrees with the dashed line representing McAdams' correlation for heat transfer to spheres. These results cannot be compared with friction or momentum transfer because total drag has not been allocated to skin friction and normal pressure drag. Application of these data to air/water-contacting devices such as air washers and spray cooling towers is well substantiated.

When the temperature of the heat exchanger surface in contact with moist air is below the air's dew-point temperature, vapor condensation occurs. Typically, air dry-bulb temperature and humidity ratio both decrease as air flows through the exchanger. Therefore, sensible and latent heat transfer occur simultaneously. This process is similar to one that occurs in a spray dehumidifier and can be analyzed using the same procedure; however, this is not generally done.

Cooling coil analysis and design are complicated by the problem of determining transport coefficients h, h_M, and f. It would be convenient if heat transfer and friction data for dry heating coils could be used with the Colburn analogy to obtain the mass transfer coefficients, but this approach is not always reliable, and Guillory and McQuiston (1973) and Helmer (1974) show that the analogy is not consistently true. Figure 12 shows j-factors for a simple parallel-plate exchanger for different surface conditions with sensible heat transfer. Mass transfer j-factors and friction factors exhibit the same

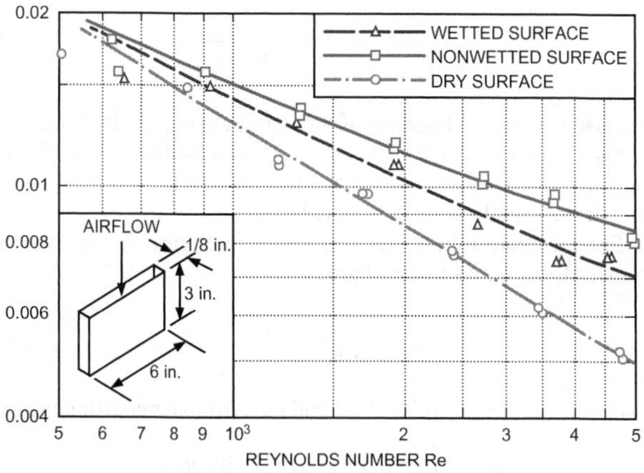

Fig. 12 Sensible Heat Transfer *j*-Factors for Parallel Plate Exchanger

behavior. Dry-surface *j*-factors fall below those obtained under dehumidifying conditions with the surface wet. At low Reynolds numbers, the boundary layer grows quickly; the droplets are soon covered and have little effect on the flow field. As the Reynolds number increases, the boundary layer becomes thin and more of the total flow field is exposed to the droplets. Roughness caused by the droplets induces mixing and larger *j*-factors.

The data in Figure 12 cannot be applied to all surfaces, because the length of the flow channel is also an important variable. However, water collecting on the surface is mainly responsible for breakdown of the *j*-factor analogy. The *j*-factor analogy is approximately true when surface conditions are identical. Under some conditions, it is possible to obtain a film of condensate on the surface instead of droplets. Guillory and McQuiston (1973) and Helmer (1974) related dry sensible *j*- and *f*-factors to those for wetted dehumidifying surfaces.

The equality of j_H, j_D, and $f/2$ for certain streamlined shapes at low mass transfer rates has experimental verification. For flow past bluff objects, j_H and j_D are much smaller than $f/2$, based on total pressure drag. The heat and mass transfer, however, still relate in a useful way by equating j_H and j_D.

Example 6. Using solid cylinders of volatile solids (e.g., naphthalene, camphor, dichlorobenzene) with airflow normal to these cylinders, Bedingfield and Drew (1950) found that the ratio between the heat and mass transfer coefficients could be closely correlated by the following relation:

$$\frac{h}{\rho h_M} = (0.294\ \text{Btu/lb}_m\cdot°\text{F})\left(\frac{\mu}{\rho D_v}\right)^{0.56}$$

For completely dry air at 70°F flowing at a velocity of 31 fps over a wet-bulb thermometer of diameter d = 0.300 in., determine the heat and mass transfer coefficients from Figure 10 and compare their ratio with the Bedingfield-Drew relation.

Solution: For dry air at 70°F and standard pressure, ρ = 0.075 lb$_m$/ft³, μ = 0.044 lb$_m$/h·ft, k = 0.0149 Btu/h·ft·°F, and c_p = 0.240 Btu/lb$_m$·°F. From Equation (10), D_v = 0.973 ft²/h. Therefore,

$$\text{Re}_{da} = \rho u_\infty d/\mu = 0.0749 \times 31 \times 3600 \times 0.300/(12 \times 0.044) = 4750$$

$$\text{Pr} = c_p\mu/k = 0.240 \times 0.044/0.0149 = 0.709$$

$$\text{Sc} = \mu/\rho D_v = 0.044/(0.0749 \times 0.973) = 0.604$$

From Figure 10 at Re$_{da}$ = 4750, read j_H = 0.0088, and j_D = 0.0099. From Equations (35) and (36),

$$h = j_H\rho c_p u_\infty/(\text{Pr})^{2/3}$$

$$= 0.0088 \times 0.0749 \times 0.240 \times 31 \times 3600/(0.709)^{2/3}$$

$$= 22.2\ \text{Btu/h}\cdot\text{ft}^2\cdot°\text{F}$$

$$h_M = j_D u_\infty/(\text{Sc})^{2/3} = 0.0099 \times 31 \times 3600/(0.604)^{2/3}$$

$$= 1550\ \text{ft/h}$$

$$h/\rho h_M = 22.2/(0.0749 \times 1550) = 0.191\ \text{Btu/lb}_m\cdot°\text{F}$$

From the Bedingfield-Drew relation,

$$h/\rho h_M = 0.294(0.604)^{0.56} = 0.222\ \text{Btu/lb}_m\cdot°\text{F}$$

Equations (36) and (37) are called the Reynolds analogy when Pr = Sc = 1. This suggests that $h/\rho h_M = c_p$ = 0.240 Btu/lb$_m$·°F. This close agreement is because the ratio Sc/Pr is 0.604/0.709 or 0.85, so that the exponent of these numbers has little effect on the ratio of the transfer coefficients.

The extensive developments for calculating heat transfer coefficients can be applied to calculate mass transfer coefficients under similar geometrical and flow conditions using the *j*-factor analogy. For example, Table 8 of Chapter 4 lists equations for calculating heat transfer coefficients for flow inside and normal to pipes. Each equation can be used for mass transfer coefficient calculations by equating j_H and j_D and imposing the same restriction to each stated in Table 8 of Chapter 4. Similarly, mass transfer experiments often replace corresponding heat transfer experiments with complex geometries where exact boundary conditions are difficult to model (Sparrow and Ohadi 1987a, 1987b).

The *j*-factor analogy is useful only at low mass transfer rates. As the rate increases, the movement of matter normal to the transfer surface increases the convective velocity. For example, if a gas is blown from many small holes in a flat plate placed parallel to an airstream, the boundary layer thickens, and resistance to both mass and heat transfer increases with increasing blowing rate. Heat transfer data are usually collected at zero or, at least, insignificant mass transfer rates. Therefore, if such data are to be valid for a mass transfer process, the mass transfer rate (i.e., the blowing) must be low.

The *j*-factor relationship $j_H = j_D$ can still be valid at high mass transfer rates, but neither j_H nor j_D can be represented by data at zero mass transfer conditions. Chapter 24 of Bird et al. (1960) and Eckert and Drake (1972) have detailed information on high mass transfer rates.

Lewis Relation

Heat and mass transfer coefficients are satisfactorily related at the same Reynolds number by equating the Chilton-Colburn *j*-factors. Comparing Equations (35) and (36) gives

$$\text{St Pr}^n = f/2 = \text{St}_m\text{Sc}^n$$

Inserting the definitions of St, Pr, St$_m$, and Sc gives

$$\frac{h}{\rho c_p \bar{u}}\left(\frac{c_p\mu}{k}\right)^{2/3} = \frac{h_M P_{Am}}{\bar{u}}\left(\frac{\mu}{\rho D_v}\right)^{2/3}$$

or

$$\frac{h}{h_M\rho c_p} = P_{Am}\left[\frac{(\mu/\rho D_v)}{(c_p\mu/k)}\right]^{2/3} = P_{Am}(\alpha/D_v)^{2/3} \qquad (39)$$

The quantity α/D_v is the **Lewis number Le**. Its magnitude expresses relative rates of propagation of energy and mass within a system. It is fairly insensitive to temperature variation. For air and water vapor mixtures, the ratio is (0.60/0.71) or 0.845, and $(0.845)^{2/3}$ is 0.894. At low diffusion rates, where the heat/mass transfer analogy is valid, P_{Am} is essentially unity. Therefore, for air and water vapor mixtures,

$$h/h_M \rho c_p \approx 1 \quad (40)$$

The ratio of the heat transfer coefficient to the mass transfer coefficient equals the specific heat per unit volume of the mixture at constant pressure. This relation [Equation (40)] is usually called the Lewis relation and is nearly true for air and water vapor at low mass transfer rates. It is generally not true for other gas mixtures because the ratio Le of thermal to vapor diffusivity can differ from unity. Agreement between wet-bulb temperature and adiabatic saturation temperature is a direct result of the nearness of the Lewis number to unity for air and water vapor.

The Lewis relation is valid in turbulent flow whether or not α/D_v equals 1 because eddy diffusion in turbulent flow involves the same mixing action for heat exchange as for mass exchange, and this action overwhelms any molecular diffusion. Deviations from the Lewis relation are, therefore, caused by a laminar boundary layer or a laminar sublayer and buffer zone where molecular transport phenomena are the controlling factors.

3. SIMULTANEOUS HEAT AND MASS TRANSFER BETWEEN WATER-WETTED SURFACES AND AIR

A simplified method used to solve simultaneous heat and mass transfer problems was developed using the Lewis relation, and it gives satisfactory results for most air-conditioning processes. Extrapolation to very high mass transfer rates, where the simple heat-mass transfer analogy is not valid, leads to erroneous results.

Enthalpy Potential

The water vapor concentration in the air is the humidity ratio W, defined as

$$W \equiv \frac{\rho_B}{\rho_A} \quad (41)$$

A mass transfer coefficient is defined using W as the driving potential:

$$\dot{m}''_B = K_M(W_i - W_\infty) \quad (42)$$

where the coefficient K_M is in $lb_m/h \cdot ft^2$. For dilute mixtures, $\rho_{Ai} \cong \rho_{A\infty}$; that is, the partial mass density of dry air changes by only a small percentage between interface and free stream conditions. Therefore,

$$\dot{m}''_B = \frac{K_M}{\rho_{Am}}(\rho_{Bi} - \rho_\infty) \quad (43)$$

where ρ_{Am} = mean density of dry air, lb_m/ft^3. Comparing Equation (43) with Equation (26) shows that

$$h_M = \frac{K_M}{\rho_{Am}} \quad (44)$$

The **humid specific heat** c_{pm} of the airstream is, by definition (Mason and Monchick 1965),

$$c_{pm} = (1 + W_\infty)c_p \quad (45a)$$

or

$$c_{pm} = (\rho/\rho_{A\infty})c_p \quad (45b)$$

where c_{pm} is in $Btu/lb_{da} \cdot °F$.

Substituting from Equations (44) and (45b) into Equation (40) gives

$$\frac{h\rho_{Am}}{K_M \rho_{A\infty} c_{pm}} = 1 \approx \frac{h}{K_M c_{pm}} \quad (46)$$

because $\rho_{Am} \cong \rho_{A\infty}$ because of the small change in dry-air density. Using a mass transfer coefficient with the humidity ratio as the driving force, the Lewis relation becomes ratio of heat to mass transfer coefficient equals humid specific heat.

For the plate humidifier illustrated in Figure 7, the total heat transfer from liquid to interface is

$$q'' = q''_A + \dot{m}''_B h_{fg} \quad (47)$$

Using the definitions of the heat and mass transfer coefficients gives

$$q'' = h(t_i - t_\infty) + K_M(W_i - W_\infty)h_{fg} \quad (48)$$

Assuming Equation (46) is valid gives

$$q'' = K_M[c_{pm}(t_i - t_\infty) + (W_i - W_\infty)h_{fg}] \quad (49)$$

The enthalpy of the air is approximately

$$h = c_{pa}(t - t_o) + Wh_s \quad (50)$$

The enthalpy h_s of the water vapor can be expressed by the ideal gas law as

$$h_s = c_{ps}(t - t_o) + h_{fgo} \quad (51)$$

where the base of enthalpy is taken as saturated water at temperature t_o. Combining Equations (50) and (51) gives

$$h = (c_{pa} + Wc_{ps})(t - t_o) + Wh_{fgo} = c_{pm}(t - t_o) + Wh_{fgo} \quad (52)$$

If small changes in the latent heat of vaporization of water with temperature are neglected when comparing Equations (50) and (52), the total heat transfer can be written as

$$q'' = K_M(h_i - h_\infty) \quad (53)$$

Where the driving potential for heat transfer is temperature difference and the driving potential for mass transfer is mass concentration or partial pressure, the driving potential for simultaneous transfer of heat and mass in an air water/vapor mixture is, to a close approximation, enthalpy.

Basic Equations for Direct-Contact Equipment

Air-conditioning equipment can be classified by whether the air and water used as a cooling or heating fluid are (1) in direct contact or (2) separated by a solid wall. Examples of the former are air washers and cooling towers; an example of the latter is a direct-expansion refrigerant (or water) cooling and dehumidifying coil. In both cases, the airstream is in contact with a water surface. Direct contact implies contact directly with the cooling (or heating) fluid. In the dehumidifying coil, contact is direct with condensate removed from the airstream, but is indirect with refrigerant flowing inside the coil tubes. These two cases are treated separately because the surface areas of direct-contact equipment cannot be evaluated.

For the direct-contact spray chamber air washer of cross-sectional area A_{cs} and length l (Figure 13), the steady mass flow rate of dry air per unit cross-sectional area is

$$\dot{m}_a/A_{cs} = G_a \quad (54)$$

and the corresponding mass flux of water flowing parallel with the air is

$$\dot{m}_L / A_{cs} = G_L \tag{55}$$

where

$\dot{m}_a$ = mass flow rate of air, lb/h
G_a = mass flux or flow rate per unit cross-sectional area for air, lb/h·ft²
$\dot{m}_L$ = mass flow rate of liquid, lb/h
G_L = mass flux or flow rate per unit cross-sectional area for liquid, lb/h·ft²

Because water is evaporating or condensing, G_L changes by an amount dG_L in a differential length dl of the chamber. Similar changes occur in temperature, humidity ratio, enthalpy, and other properties.

Because evaluating the true surface area in direct-contact equipment is difficult, it is common to work on a unit volume basis. If a_H and a_M are the areas of heat transfer and mass transfer surface per unit of chamber volume, respectively, the total surface areas for heat and mass transfer are

$$A_H = a_H A_{cs} l \quad \text{and} \quad A_M = a_M A_{cs} l \tag{56}$$

The basic equations for the process occurring in the differential length dl can be written for

Mass transfer

$$-dG_L = G_a\,dW = K_M a_M (W_i - W)dl \tag{57}$$

That is, the water evaporation rate, air moisture content increase, and mass transfer rate are all equal.

Heat transfer to air

$$G_a c_{pm} dt_a = h_a a_H (t_i - t_a)dl \tag{58}$$

Total energy transfer to air

$$G_a(c_{pm}dt_a + h_{fgo}dW) = [K_M a_M (W_i - W)h_{fg} + h_a a_H (t_i - t_a)]dl \tag{59}$$

Assuming $a_H = a_M$ and Le = 1, and neglecting small variations in h_{fg}, Equation (59) reduces to

$$G_a dh = K_M a_M (h_i - h)dl \tag{60}$$

The heat and mass transfer areas of spray chambers are assumed to be identical ($a_H = a_M$). Where packing materials, such as wood slats or Raschig rings, are used, the two areas may be considerably different because the packing may not be wet uniformly. The validity of the Lewis relation was discussed previously. It is not necessary to account for small changes in latent heat h_{fg} after making the two previous assumptions.

Energy balance

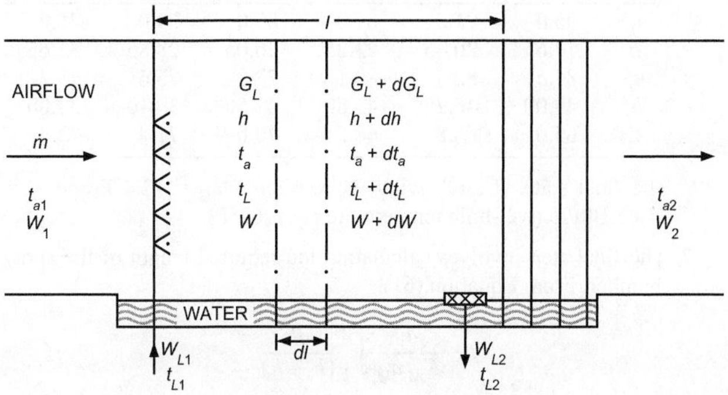

Fig. 13 Air Washer Spray Chamber

$$G_a dh = \pm G_L c_L dt_L \tag{61}$$

A minus sign refers to parallel flow of air and water; a plus refers to counterflow (water flow in the opposite direction from airflow).

The water flow rate changes between inlet and outlet as a result of the mass transfer. For exact energy balance, the term ($c_L t_L dG_L$) should be added to the right side of Equation (61). The percentage change in G_L is quite small in usual applications of air-conditioning equipment and, therefore, can be ignored.

Heat transfer to water

$$\pm G_L c_L dt_L = h_L a_H (t_L - t_i)dl \tag{62}$$

Equations (57) to (62) are the basic relations for solution of simultaneous heat and mass transfer processes in direct-contact air-conditioning equipment.

To facilitate use of these relations in equipment design or performance, three other equations can be extracted from the above set. Combining Equations (60), (61), and (62) gives

$$\frac{h - h_i}{t_L - t_i} = -\frac{h_L a_H}{K_M a_M} = -\frac{h_L}{K_M} \tag{63}$$

Equation (63) relates the enthalpy potential for total heat transfer through the gas film to the temperature potential for this same transfer through the liquid film. Physical reasoning leads to the conclusion that this ratio is proportional to the ratio of gas film resistance ($1/K_M$) to liquid film resistance ($1/h_L$). Combining Equations (58), (60), and (46) gives

$$\frac{dh}{dt_a} = \frac{h - h_i}{t_a - t_i} \tag{64}$$

Similarly, combining Equations (57), (58), and (46) gives

$$\frac{dW}{dt_a} = \frac{W - W_i}{t_a - t_i} \tag{65}$$

Equation (65) indicates that, at any cross section in the spray chamber, the instantaneous slope of the air path dW/dt_a on a psychrometric chart is determined by a straight line connecting the air state with the interface saturation state at that cross section. In Figure 14, state

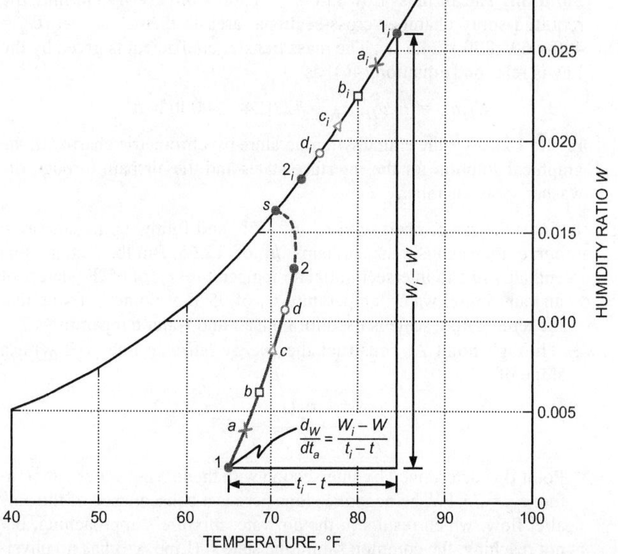

Fig. 14 Air Washer Humidification Process on Psychrometric Chart

1 represents the state of air entering the parallel-flow air washer chamber of Figure 13. The washer operates as a heating and humidifying apparatus, so the interface saturation state of the water at air inlet is the state designated 1_i. Therefore, the initial slope of the air path is along a line directed from state 1 to state 1_i. As the air is heated, the water cools and the interface temperature drops. Corresponding air states and interface saturation states are indicated by the letters *a*, *b*, *c*, and *d* in Figure 14. In each instance, the air path is directed toward the associated interface state. The interface states are derived from Equations (61) and (63). Equation (61) describes how air enthalpy changes with water temperature; Equation (63) describes how the interface saturation state changes to accommodate this change in air and water conditions. The solution for the interface state on the normal psychrometric chart of Figure 14 can be determined either by trial and error from Equations (61) and (63) or by a complex graphical procedure (Kusuda 1957).

Air Washers

Air washers are direct-contact apparatus used to (1) simultaneously change the temperature and humidity content of air passing through the chamber and (2) remove air contaminants such as dust and odors. Adiabatic spray washers, which have no external heating or chilling source, are used to cool and humidify air. Chilled-spray air washers have an external chiller to cool and dehumidify air. Heated-spray air washers, with an external heating source that provides additional energy for water evaporation, are used to humidify and possibly heat air.

Example 7. A parallel-flow air washer with the following design conditions is to be designed (see Figure 13).

Water temperature at inlet t_{L1} = 95°F
Water temperature at outlet t_{L2} = 75°F
Air temperature at inlet t_{a1} = 65°F
Air wet-bulb at inlet t'_{a1} = 45°F
Air mass flow rate per unit area G_a = 1200 lb/h·ft²
Spray ratio G_L/G_a = 0.70
Air heat transfer coefficient per cubic foot of chamber volume
$h_a a_H$ = 72 Btu/h·°F·ft³
Liquid heat transfer coefficient per cubic foot of chamber volume
$h_L a_H$ = 900 Btu/h·°F·ft³
Air volumetric flow rate Q = 6500 cfm

Solution: The air mass flow rate $\dot{m}_a$ = 6500 × 0.075 = 490 lb/min; the required spray chamber cross-sectional area is then $A_{cs} = \dot{m}_a/G_a$ = 490 × 60/1200 = 24.5 ft². The mass transfer coefficient is given by the Lewis relation [Equation (46)] as

$$K_M a_M = (h_a a_H)/c_{pm} = 72/0.24 = 300 \text{ lb/h·ft}^3$$

Figure 15 shows the enthalpy/temperature psychrometric chart with the graphical solution for the interface states and the air path through the washer spray chamber.

1. Enter bottom of chart with t'_{a1} of 45°F, and follow up to saturation curve to establish air enthalpy h_1 of 17.65 Btu/lb. Extend this enthalpy line to intersect initial air temperature t_{a1} of 65°F (state 1 of air) and initial water temperature t_{L1} of 95°F at point A. (Note that the temperature scale is used for both air and water temperatures.)
2. Through point A, construct the *energy balance* line A-B with a slope of

$$\frac{dh}{dt_L} = -\frac{c_L G_L}{G_a} = -0.7$$

Point B is determined by intersection with the leaving water temperature t_{L2} = 75°F. The negative slope here is a consequence of the parallel flow, which results in the air/water mixture's approaching, but not reaching, the common saturation state *s*. (Line A-B has no physical significance in representing any *air state* on the psychrometric chart. It is merely a construction line in the graphical solution.)
3. Through point A, construct the *tie-line* A-1_i having a slope of

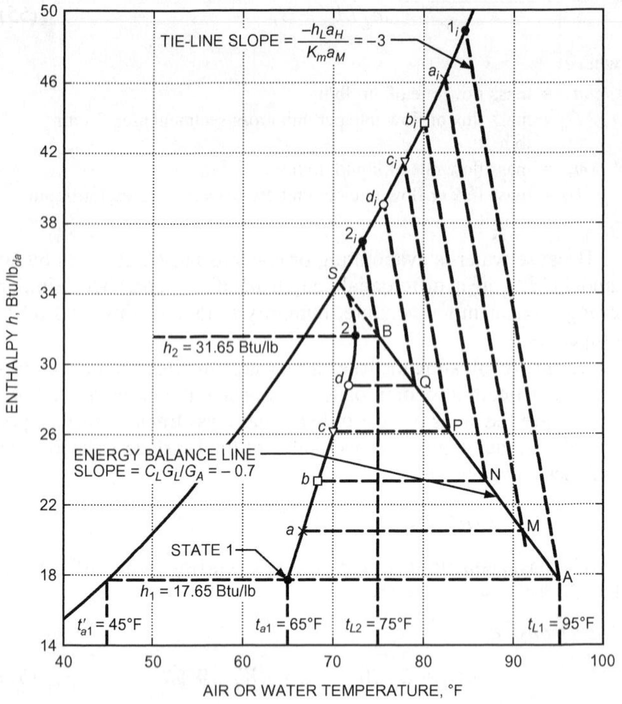

Fig. 15 Graphical Solution for Air-State Path in Parallel-Flow Air Washer

$$\frac{h - h_i}{t_L - t_i} = -\frac{h_L a_H}{K_M a_M} = -\frac{900}{300} = -3$$

The intersection of this line with the saturation curve gives the initial interface state 1_i at the chamber inlet. [Note how the energy balance line and tie-line, representing Equations (61) and (63), combine for a simple graphical solution on Figure 15 for the interface state.]

4. The initial slope of the air path can now be constructed, according to Equation (64), drawing line 1-*a* toward the initial interface state 1_i. (Length of line 1-*a* depends on the degree of accuracy required in the solution and the rate at which the slope of the air path changes.)
5. Construct the horizontal line *a*-M, locating point M on the energy-balance line. Draw a new tie-line (slope of −3 as before) from M to a_i locating interface state a_i. Continue the air path from *a* to *b* by directing it toward the new interface state a_i. (Note that the change in slope of the air path from 1-*a* to *a*-*b* is quite small, justifying the path incremental lengths used.)
6. Continue in the manner of step 5 until point 2, the final state of air leaving the chamber, is reached. In this example, six steps are used in the graphical construction, with the following results:

State	1	*a*	*b*	*c*	*d*	2
t_L	95.0	91.0	87.0	83.0	79.0	75.0
h	17.65	20.45	23.25	26.05	28.85	31.65
t_i	84.5	82.3	80.1	77.8	75.6	73.2
h_i	49.00	46.25	43.80	41.50	39.10	37.00
t_a	65.0	66.8	68.5	70.0	71.4	72.4

The final state of air leaving the washer is t_{a2} = 72.4°F and h_2 = 31.65 Btu/lb (wet-bulb temperature t'_{a2} = 67°F).

7. The final step involves calculating the required length of the spray chamber. From Equation (61),

$$l = \frac{G_a}{K_M a_M}\int_1^2 \frac{dh}{(h_i - h)}$$

The integral is evaluated graphically by plotting $1/(h_i - h)$ versus h, as shown in Figure 16. Any satisfactory graphical method can be

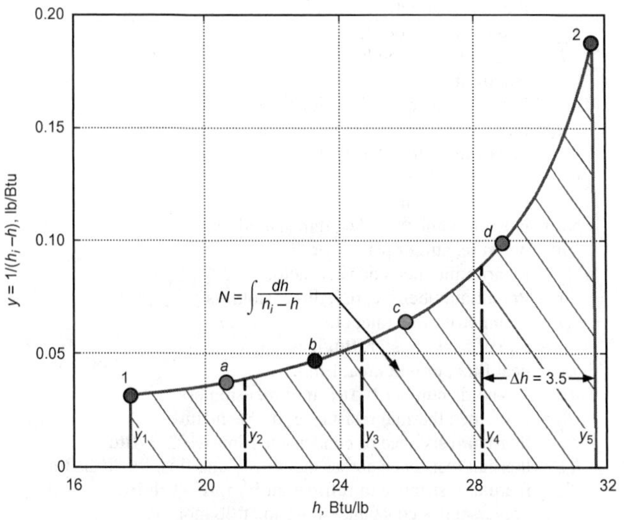

Fig. 16 Graphical Solution of $\int dh/(h_i - h)$

used to evaluate the area under the curve. Simpson's rule with four equal increments of Δh equal to 3.5 gives

$$N = \int_1^2 \frac{dh}{(h_i - h)} \approx (\Delta h/3)(y_1 + 4y_2 + 2y_3 + 4y_4 + y_5)$$

$$N = (3.5/3)[0.0319 + (4 \times 0.0400) + (2 \times 0.0553) + (4 \times 0.0865) + 0.1870] = 0.975$$

Therefore, the design length is $l = (1200/300)(0.975) = 3.9$ ft.

This method can also be used to predict performance of existing direct-contact equipment and to determine transfer coefficients when performance data from test runs are available. By knowing the water and air temperatures entering and leaving the chamber and the spray ratio, it is possible to determine by trial and error the proper slope of the tie-line necessary to achieve the measured final air state. The tie-line slope gives the ratio $h_L a_H / K_M a_M$; $K_M a_M$ is found from the integral relationship in Example 7 from the known chamber length l.

Additional descriptions of air spray washers and general performance criteria are given in Chapter 41 of the 2016 *ASHRAE Handbook—HVAC Systems and Equipment*.

Cooling Towers

A cooling tower is a direct-contact heat exchanger in which waste heat picked up by the cooling water from a refrigerator, air conditioner, or industrial process is transferred to atmospheric air by cooling the water. Cooling is achieved by breaking up the water flow to provide a large water surface for air, moving by natural or forced convection through the tower, to contact the water. Cooling towers may be counterflow, crossflow, or a combination of both.

The temperature of water leaving the tower and the packing depth needed to achieve the desired leaving water temperature are of primary interest for design. Therefore, the mass and energy balance equations are based on an overall coefficient K, which is based on (1) the enthalpy driving force from h at the bulk water temperature and (2) neglecting the film resistance. Combining Equations (60) and (61) and using the parameters described previously yields

$$G_L c_L dt = K_M a_M (h_i - h) dl = G_a dh = \frac{K_a dV(h' - h_a)}{A_{cs}} \quad (66)$$

or

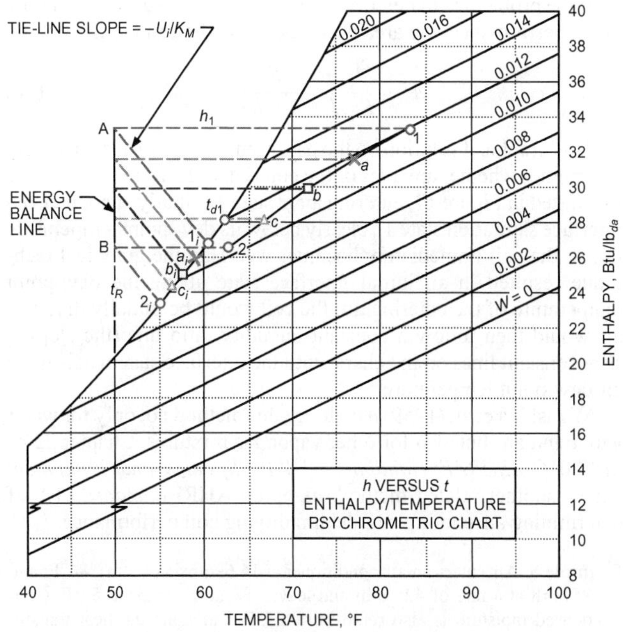

Fig. 17 Graphical Solution for Air-State Path in Dehumidifying Coil with Constant Refrigerant Temperature

$$\frac{K_a V}{\dot{m}_L} = \int_{t_1}^{t_2} \frac{c_L dt}{(h' - h_a)} \quad (67)$$

Chapter 40 of the 2016 *ASHRAE Handbook—HVAC Systems and Equipment* covers cooling tower design in detail.

Cooling and Dehumidifying Coils

When water vapor is condensed out of an airstream onto an extended-surface (finned) cooling coil, the simultaneous heat and mass transfer problem can be solved by the same procedure set forth for direct-contact equipment. The basic equations are the same, except that the true surface area of coil A is known and the problem does not have to be solved on a unit-volume basis. Therefore, if, in Equations (57), (58), and (60), $a_M dl$ or $a_H dl$ is replaced by dA/A_{cs}, these equations become the basic heat, mass, and total energy transfer equations for indirect-contact equipment such as dehumidifying coils. The energy balance shown by Equation (61) remains unchanged. The heat transfer from the interface to the refrigerant now encounters the combined resistances of the condensate film ($R_L = 1/h_L$); the metal wall and fins, if any (R_m); and the refrigerant film ($R_r = A/h_r A_r$). If this combined resistance is designated as $R_i = R_L + R_m + R_r = 1/U_i$, Equation (62) becomes, for a coil dehumidifier,

$$\pm \dot{m}_L c_L dt_L = U_i (t_L - t_i) dA \quad (68)$$

(plus sign for counterflow, minus sign for parallel flow).

The tie-line slope is then

$$\frac{h - h_i}{t_L - t_i} = \pm \frac{U_i}{K_M} \quad (69)$$

Figure 17 illustrates the graphical solution on a psychrometric chart for the air path through a dehumidifying coil with a constant refrigerant temperature. Because the tie-line slope is infinite in this case, the energy balance line is vertical. The corresponding interface and air states are denoted by the same letter symbols, and the solution follows the same procedure as in Example 7.

If the problem is to determine the required coil surface area for a given performance, the area is computed by the following relation:

$$A = \frac{\dot{m}_a}{K_M}\int_1^2 \frac{dh}{(h_i - h)} \tag{70}$$

This graphical solution on the psychrometric chart automatically determines whether any part of the coil is dry. Thus, in the example illustrated in Figure 17, entering air at state 1 initially encounters an interface saturation state 1_i, clearly below its dew-point temperature t_{d1}, so the coil immediately becomes wet. Had the graphical technique resulted in an initial interface state above the dew-point temperature of the entering air, the coil would be initially dry. The air would then follow a constant humidity ratio line (the sloping W = constant lines on the chart) until the interface state reached the air dew-point temperature.

Mizushina et al. (1959) developed this method not only for water vapor and air, but also for other vapor/gas mixtures. Chapter 23 of the 2016 *ASHRAE Handbook—HVAC Systems and Equipment* shows another related method, based on AHRI *Standard* 410, of determining air-cooling and dehumidifying coil performance.

Example 8. Air enters an air conditioner at 14.696 psia (1 atm), 86°F, and 85% rh at a rate of 425 cfm and leaves as saturated air at 57°F. Condensed moisture is also removed at 57°F. Calculate the heat transfer and moisture removal rate from the air.

Solution: Water mass flow is

$$\dot{m}_w = \dot{m}_a(W_1 - W_2)$$

and energy or heat transfer rate is

$$\dot{q}_{out} = \dot{m}_a(h_1 - h_2) - \dot{m}_w h_w$$

Properties of air both at inlet and exit states can be determined from the psychrometric chart as follows:

$$h_1 = 46.2 \text{ Btu/lb}_{da}, \quad W_1 = 0.023 \text{ lb}_{H_2O}/\text{lb}_{da}$$

$$\text{specific volume} = 14.3 \text{ ft}^3/\text{lb}_{da}$$

$$h_2 = 24.8 \text{ Btu/lb}_{da}, \quad W_2 = 0.010 \text{ lb}_{H_2O}/\text{lb}_{da}$$

Enthalpy of the condensate from saturated-water temperature table is

$$h_w = h_f \text{ at } 57°\text{F} = 25.28 \text{ Btu/lb}$$

Then,

$$\dot{m}_a = (425 \times 60)/14.3 = 1783 \text{ lb/h}$$

$$\dot{m}_w = (1783)(0.023 - 0.010) = 23.18 \text{ lb/h}$$

$$\dot{q}_{out} = (1783)(46.2 - 24.8) - (23.18)(25.28) = 37{,}570 \text{ Btu/h}$$

So, the air conditioner's heat transfer and moisture removal rates are 36,500 Btu/h and 23.18 lb/h, respectively.

4. SYMBOLS

A = surface area, ft²
a = constant that depends on units used; or surface area per unit volume, ft²/ft³
A_{cs} = cross-sectional area, ft²
b = exponent or constant, dimensionless
C = molal concentration of solute in solvent, lb mol/ft²
c_L = specific heat of liquid, Btu/lb·°F
c_p = specific heat at constant pressure, Btu/lb·°F
c_{pm} = specific heat of moist air at constant pressure, Btu/lb_{da}·°F
d = diameter, ft
D_v = diffusion coefficient (mass diffusivity), ft²/h
f = Fanning friction factor, dimensionless
G = mass flux, flow rate per unit of cross-sectional area, lb_m/h·ft²
g_c = gravitational constant, ft·$\text{lb}_m/\text{h}^2\cdot\text{lb}_f$
h = enthalpy, Btu/lb; or heat transfer coefficient, Btu/h·ft²·°F
h_{fg} = enthalpy of vaporization, Btu/lb_m
h_M = mass transfer coefficient, ft/h
J = diffusive mass flux, lb_m/h·ft²
J^* = diffusive molar flux, lb mol/h·ft²
j_D = Colburn mass transfer group = Sh/(ReSc$^{1/3}$), dimensionless
j_H = Colburn heat transfer group = Nu/(RePr$^{1/3}$), dimensionless
k = thermal conductivity, Btu/h·ft·°F
K_M = mass transfer coefficient, lb/h·ft²
L = characteristic length, ft
l = length, ft
Le = Lewis number = α/D_v, dimensionless
M = relative molecular weight, lb_m/lb
$\dot{m}$ = rate of mass transfer, lb/h
$\dot{m}''$ = mass flux, lb/h·ft²
$\dot{m}''^*$ = molar flux, lb mol/h·ft²
Nu = Nusselt number = hL/k, dimensionless
p = pressure, atm or psi
P_{Am} = logarithmic mean density factor
Pr = Prandtl number = $c_p\mu/k$, dimensionless
Q = volumetric flow rate, cfm
q = rate of heat transfer, Btu/h
q'' = heat flux per unit area, Btu/h·ft²
Re = Reynolds number = $\rho uL/\mu$, dimensionless
R_i = combined thermal resistance, ft²·°F·h/Btu
R_L = thermal resistance of condensate film, ft²·°F·h/Btu
R_m = thermal resistance across metal wall and fins, ft²·°F·h/Btu
R_r = thermal resistance of refrigerant film, ft²·°F·h/Btu
R_u = universal gas constant = 1545 lb_f·ft/lb mol·°R
Sc = Schmidt number = $\mu/\rho D_v$, dimensionless
Sh = Sherwood number = $h_M L/D_v$, dimensionless
St = Stanton number = $h/\rho c_p \bar{u}$, dimensionless
St_m = mass transfer Stanton number = $h_M P_{Am}/\bar{u}$, dimensionless
T = absolute temperature, °R
t = temperature, °F
u = velocity in x direction, fpm
U_i = overall conductance from refrigerant to air/water interface for dehumidifying coil, Btu/h·ft²·°F
V = fluid stream velocity, fpm
v = velocity in y direction, fpm
v_i = velocity normal to mass transfer surface for component i, ft/h
W = humidity ratio, $\text{lb}_w/\text{lb}_{da}$
X, Y, Z = coordinate direction, dimensionless
x, y, z = coordinate direction, ft

Greek

α = thermal diffusivity = $k/\rho c_p$, ft²/h
ε = Lennard-Jones energy parameter
ε_D = eddy mass diffusivity, ft²/h
θ = time parameter, dimensionless
μ = absolute (dynamic) viscosity, lb_m/ft·h
$\bar{\mu}$ = permeability, gr·in/h·ft²·in. Hg
ν = kinematic viscosity, ft²/h
ρ = mass density or concentration, lb_m/ft^3
σ = characteristic molecular diameter, nm
τ = time
τ_i = shear stress in the x-y coordinate plane, lb_f/ft^2
ω = mass fraction, lb/lb
$\Omega_{D,AB}$ = temperature function in Equation (9)

Subscripts

A = gas component of binary mixture
a = air property
Am = logarithmic mean
B = more dilute gas component of binary mixture
c = critical state
da = dry-air property or air-side transfer quantity
H = heat transfer quantity
i = air/water interface value
L = liquid
M = mass transfer quantity
m = mean value or metal
min = minimum
o = property evaluated at 0°F
s = water vapor property or transport quantity
w = water vapor
∞ = property of main fluid stream

Superscripts

* = on molar basis
– = average value
′ = wet bulb

REFERENCES

ASHRAE members can access *ASHRAE Journal* articles and ASHRAE research project final reports at technologyportal .ashrae.org. Articles and reports are also available for purchase by nonmembers in the online ASHRAE Bookstore at www.ashrae.org /bookstore.

AHRI. 2001. Forced-circulation air-cooling and air-heating coils. *Standard* 410-2001. Air-Conditioning, Heating, and Refrigeration Institute, Arlington, VA.

Barnet, W.I., and K.A. Kobe. 1941. Heat and vapor transfer in a wetted-wall tower. *Industrial & Engineering Chemistry* 33(4):436-442.

Bedingfield, G.H., Jr., and T.B. Drew. 1950. Analogy between heat transfer and mass transfer—A psychrometric study. *Industrial and Engineering Chemistry* 42:1164.

Bird, R.B., W.E. Stewart, and E.N. Lightfoot. 1960. *Transport phenomena*. John Wiley & Sons, New York.

Chambers, F.S., Jr., and T.K. Sherwood. 1937. Absorption of nitrogen dioxide by aqueous solution. *Industrial & Engineering Chemistry* 29:1415-1422.

Chilton, T.H., and A.P. Colburn. 1934. Mass transfer (absorption) coefficients. *Industrial & Engineering Chemistry* 26(11):1183-1187.

Eckert, E.R.G., and R.M. Drake, Jr. 1972. *Analysis of heat and mass transfer*. McGraw-Hill, New York.

Gilliland, E.R. 1934. Diffusion coefficients in gaseous systems. *Industrial & Engineering Chemistry* 26:681-685.

Goldstein, S. 1938. *Modern developments in fluid mechanics*, vols. 1 and 2. Oxford University Press, New York.

Guillory, J.L., and F.C. McQuiston. 1973. An experimental investigation of air dehumidification in a parallel plate heat exchanger. *ASHRAE Transactions* 79(2):146.

Helmer, W.A. 1974. *Condensing water vapor—Airflow in a parallel plate heat exchanger*. Ph.D. dissertation, Purdue University, West Lafayette, IN.

Hirschfelder, J.O., C.F. Curtiss, and R.B. Bird. 1954. *Molecular theory of gases and liquids*. John Wiley & Sons, New York.

Incropera, F.P., and D.P. DeWitt. 1996. *Fundamentals of heat and mass transfer*, 4th ed. John Wiley & Sons, New York.

Kusuda, T. 1957. Graphical method simplifies determination of aircoil, wet-heat-transfer surface temperature. *Refrigerating Engineering* 65:41.

Lorisch, W. 1929. Bestimmung von Wärmeübergangszahlen durch Diffusionsversuche. *Forschungsarbeiten auf dem Gebiete des Ingenieurwesens*. 322:46-68.

Lurie, M., and N. Michailoff. 1936. Evaporation from free water surfaces. *Industrial & Engineering Chemistry* 28(3):345-49.

Maisel, D.S., and J.K. Sherwood. 1950. Evaporation of liquids into turbulent gas streams. *Chemical Engineering Progress* 46:131-138.

Mason, E.A., and L. Monchick. 1965. Survey of the equation of state and transport properties of moist gases. In *Humidity and moisture*, vol. 3. Reinhold, New York.

McAdams, W.H. 1954. *Heat transmission*, 3rd ed. McGraw-Hill, New York.

Millar, F.G. 1937. Evaporation from free water surfaces. *Canadian Meteorological Memoirs* 1(2).

Mizushina, T., N. Hashimoto, and M. Nakajima. 1959. Design of cooler condensers for gas-vapour mixtures. *Chemical Engineering Science* 9:195.

Pasquill, F. 1943. Evaporation from a plane, free-liquid surface into a turbulent air stream. *Proceedings of the Royal Society of London, Ser. A*(182): 75-94.

Powell, R.W. 1940. Further experiments on the evaporation of water from saturated surfaces. *Transactions of the Institution of Chemical Engineers* 18:36-55.

Powell, R.W., and E. Griffiths. 1935. The evaporation of water from plane and cylindrical surfaces. *Transactions of the Institution of Chemical Engineers* 13:175-198.

Reid, R.C., and T.K. Sherwood. 1966. *The properties of gases and liquids: Their estimation and correlation*, 2nd ed. McGraw-Hill, New York.

Reid, R.C., J.M. Prausnitz, and B.E. Poling. 1987. *The properties of gases and liquids*, 4th ed. McGraw-Hill, New York.

Sherwood, T.K., and R.L. Pigford. 1952. *Absorption and extraction*. McGraw-Hill, New York.

Sparrow, E.M., and M.M. Ohadi. 1987a. Comparison of turbulent thermal entrance regions for pipe flows with developed velocity and velocity developing from a sharp-edged inlet. *ASME Transactions, Journal of Heat Transfer* 109:1028-1030.

Sparrow, E.M., and M.M. Ohadi. 1987b. Numerical and experimental studies of turbulent flow in a tube. *Numerical Heat Transfer* 11:461-476.

Treybal, R.E. 1980. *Mass transfer operations*, 3rd ed. McGraw-Hill, New York.

BIBLIOGRAPHY

Bennett, C.O., and J.E. Myers. 1982. *Momentum, heat and mass transfer*, 3rd ed. McGraw-Hill, New York.

DeWitt, D.P., and E.L. Cussler. 1984. *Diffusion, mass transfer in fluid systems*. Cambridge University Press, U.K.

Geankopolis, C.J. 1993. *Transport processes and unit operations*, 3rd ed. Prentice Hall, Englewood Cliffs, NJ.

Kays, W.M., and M.E. Crawford. 1993. *Convective heat and mass transfer*. McGraw-Hill, New York.

Mikielviez, J., and A.M.A. Rageb. 1995. Simple theoretical approach to direct-contact condensation on subcooled liquid film. *International Journal of Heat and Mass Transfer* 38(3):557.

Ohadi, M.M., and E.M. Sparrow. 1989. Heat transfer in a straight tube situated downstream of a bend. *International Journal of Heat and Mass Transfer* 32(2):201-212.

REFERENCES

ASHRAE members can access *ASHRAE Journal* articles and ASHRAE research project final reports at technologyportal.ashrae.org. Articles and reports are also available for purchase by nonmembers in the online ASHRAE Bookstore at www.ashrae.org/bookstore.

AMCA. 2014. Forced circulation air coolers and air heaters—Standard methods [illegible]. Air Conditioning, Heating, and Refrigeration Institute, Arlington, VA.

Bernot, W. [illegible] and K. [illegible]. [illegible]. Heat and vapor transfer [illegible] wetted-wall [illegible] [illegible] [illegible].

Bedingfield, C.H., Jr., and T.B. Drew. 1950. Analogy between heat transfer and mass transfer—A psychrometric study. *Industrial and Engineering Chemistry* [illegible].

[illegible]. Sherwood, and [illegible]. 1975. [illegible] [illegible] [illegible], New York.

Chilton, T.H., and A.P. Colburn. 1934. Mass transfer (absorption) coefficients—Prediction from data on heat transfer and fluid friction. *Industrial and Engineering Chemistry* 26:1183-1187.

[illegible] Colburn. [illegible].

[illegible] [illegible] 1964. [illegible].

[illegible] [illegible]. [illegible], New York.

Hirschfelder, J.O., C.F. Curtiss, and R.B. Bird. 1954. *Molecular theory of gases and liquids*. John Wiley & Sons, New York.

Kusuda, T. 1965. Calculation of the temperature of a flat-plate wet surface under adiabatic conditions with respect to the Lewis relation. In *Humidity and moisture*, [illegible].

Lemmon, E.W. and [illegible]. 20[illegible]. [illegible] [illegible].

[illegible] [illegible] Hinds. [illegible] Thermal conductivity [illegible].

[illegible] [illegible] 1964. [illegible].

Lewis, W.K. 1922. The evaporation of a liquid into a gas. *Transactions of ASME* 44:325-340.

Lienhard, J.H. 1983. *A heat transfer textbook*. Prentice-Hall, Englewood Cliffs, NJ.

Hausen, W.J. and P.J. DeWitt. 1990. *Fundamentals of heat and mass transfer*, 4th ed. John Wiley & Sons, New York.

[illegible] [illegible]. [illegible] [illegible] [illegible] [illegible] [illegible] [illegible] [illegible].

[illegible] [illegible]. [illegible] [illegible] [illegible] [illegible] [illegible] [illegible] [illegible] [illegible] 2:[illegible]-[illegible].

Bunton, M., and [illegible] Mikhailov. 19[illegible]. [illegible] [illegible] [illegible] [illegible] [illegible].

Mason, J., S. Hall, [illegible] [illegible]. [illegible] [illegible] [illegible] [illegible] [illegible] [illegible] [illegible] 46(11):[illegible].

Mason, E.A., and L. Monchick. 1965. Survey of the equation of state and transport properties of moist gases. In *Humidity and moisture*, vol. 3. Reinhold, New York.

McAdams, W.H. 1954. *Heat transmission*, 3rd ed. McGraw-Hill, New York.

Mills, E.A. 1962. Evaporation from free water surfaces. *Canadian Meteorological Memoirs* [illegible].

Mizushina, T., N. Hashimoto, and M. Nakajima. 1959. Design of cooler condensers for gas-vapour mixtures. *Chemical Engineering Science* 9:[illegible].

Parrott, J. 1964. [illegible] [illegible] [illegible] from a [illegible] [illegible] [illegible] [illegible]. [illegible] *Proceedings of the* [illegible] [illegible] [illegible].

Powell, R.W. 1940. Further experiments on the evaporation of water from saturated surfaces. *Transactions of the Institution of Chemical Engineers* 18:36-55.

[illegible] [illegible] [illegible] [illegible] [illegible] [illegible] [illegible] [illegible] [illegible] [illegible] [illegible] [illegible].

[illegible] [illegible] [illegible] [illegible] [illegible] [illegible] [illegible] [illegible].

Reid, R.C., J.M. Prausnitz, and [illegible]. [illegible] [illegible] [illegible] [illegible], New York.

[illegible] [illegible] [illegible] [illegible]. [illegible] [illegible] [illegible] [illegible].

Sparrow, E.M., and M.A. Ouuk. 1983. A prediction of turbulent thermal [illegible] [illegible] [illegible] [illegible] [illegible] [illegible] [illegible] [illegible] [illegible] [illegible].

Sparrow, E.M., and M.A. Ouuk. 1983. Numerical and experimental studies [illegible] [illegible] [illegible] [illegible] [illegible].

Treybal, R.E. 1980. *Mass-transfer operations*. McGraw-Hill, New York.

BIBLIOGRAPHY

[illegible] [illegible] Mickley. [illegible]. *Momentum, heat, and mass transfer*. McGraw-Hill, New York.

DeWitt, T.K., and [illegible] Chase. 1984. *Diffusion: Mass transfer in fluid systems*. Cambridge University Press, U.K.

[illegible]. [illegible] [illegible] [illegible] [illegible] [illegible]. Prentice Hall, Englewood Cliffs, NJ.

Kays, W.M., and M.E. Crawford. 1993. *Convective heat and mass transfer*. McGraw-Hill, New York.

Mitchell, [illegible] and M. [illegible] Ragan. 1991. [illegible] [illegible] [illegible] [illegible] [illegible] [illegible] [illegible] liquid film. [illegible] *Journal of Heat and Mass Transfer* [illegible].

[illegible] M. and E.M. Sparrow. 1983. Heat transfer [illegible] [illegible] [illegible] [illegible] [illegible] [illegible]. *International Journal of Heat and Mass Transfer* 26:201-[illegible].

CHAPTER 7

FUNDAMENTALS OF CONTROL

AUTOMATIC control systems are designed to maintain temperature, humidity, pressure, energy use, power, lighting levels, and safe levels of indoor contaminants. Automatic control primarily modulates actuators; stages modes of action; or sequences the mechanical and electrical equipment on and off to satisfy load requirements, provide safe equipment operation, and maintain safe building contaminant levels. Automatic control systems can use digital, pneumatic, mechanical, electrical, and electronic control devices. Human intervention often involves scheduling equipment operation and adjusting control set points, but also includes tracking trends and programming control logic algorithms to fulfill building needs.

This chapter focuses on the fundamental concepts and devices normally used by a control system designer. It covers (1) control fundamentals, including terminology; (2) types of control components; (3) methods of connecting components to form various individual control loops, subsystems, or networks; and (4) commissioning and operation. Chapter 47 of the 2015 *ASHRAE Handbook—HVAC Applications* discusses the design of controls for specific HVAC applications.

1. GENERAL

1.1 TERMINOLOGY

An **open-loop** control does not have a direct feedback link between the value of the controlled variable and the controller. Open-loop control anticipates the effect of an external variable on the system and adjusts its output to minimize the expected deviation of the controlled variable from its set point. An example is an outdoor thermostat arranged to control heat to a building in proportion to the calculated load caused by changes in outdoor temperature. In essence, the designer presumes a fixed relationship between outdoor air temperature. The actual space temperature has no effect on this controller. Because there is no feedback on the controlled variable (space temperature), the control is an open loop.

A **closed-loop** or **feedback** control measures actual changes in the controlled variable and actuates the controlled device to bring about a change. The corrective action may continue until the controlled variable is at set point or within a prescribed tolerance. This arrangement of having the controller respond to the value of the controlled variable is known as feedback.

Every closed loop must contain a sensor, a controller, and a controlled device that will affect the sensor reading(s). Figure 1 shows the components of the typical control loop. The **sensor** measures the controlled variable and transmits to the controller a signal (pneumatic, electric, or electronic) having a pressure, voltage, or current value related by a known function to the value of the variable being measured. The **controller** compares this value with the set point and signals to the controlled device for corrective action. A controller can be hardware or software. A hardware controller is an analog device (e.g., thermostat, humidistat, pressure control) that continuously receives and acts on data. A software controller is a digital device (e.g., digital algorithm) that receives and acts on data on a sample-rate basis.

The **controlled variable** is the temperature, humidity, pressure, or other condition being controlled.

The **set point** is the desired value of the controlled variable. The controller seeks to maintain this set point. The controlled device reacts to signals from the controller to vary the control agent.

The **controlled device** is typically a valve, damper, heating element, or variable-speed drive.

The **control agent** is the medium manipulated by the controlled device. It may be air or gas flowing through a damper; gas, steam, or water flowing through a valve; or an electric current.

The **process** is the HVAC apparatus being controlled, such as a coil, fan, or humidifier. It reacts to the control agent's output and effects the change in the controlled variable.

Both open and closed control loops can be represented in the form of a **block diagram**, in which each component is modeled and represented in its own block. Figure 2 is a block diagram of the closed loop shown in Figure 1. Information flow from one component to the next is shown by lines between the blocks. The figure shows the set point being compared to the controlled variable. The difference is the **error**. If the error persists, it may be called offset,

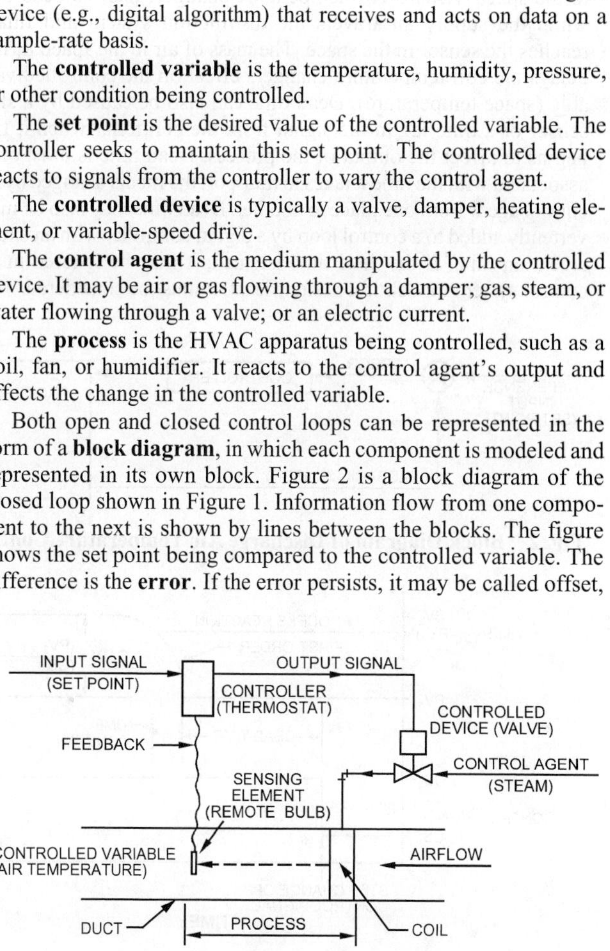

Fig. 1 Example of Feedback Control: Discharge Air Temperature Control

The preparation of this chapter is assigned to TC 1.4, Control Theory and Application.

drift, deviation, droop, or steady-state error. The error is fed into the controller, which sends an output signal to the controlled device (in this case, a valve that can change the amount of steam flow through the coil of Figure 1). The amount of steam flow is the input to the next block, which represents the process. From the process block comes the controlled variable, which is temperature. The controlled variable is sensed by the sensing element and fed to the controller as feedback, completing the loop.

Control loop performance is greatly affected by time lags, which are delay periods associated with seeing a control agent change reflected in the desired end-point condition. Time lags can cause control and modeling problems and should be understood and evaluated carefully. There are two types of time lags: first-order lags and dead time.

First-order lags involve the time it takes for the change to be absorbed by the system. If heat is supplied to a cold room, the room heats up gradually, even though heat may be applied at the maximum rate. The **time constant** is the unit of measure used to describe first-order lags and is defined as the time it takes for the controlled variable of a first-order, linear system to reach 63.2% of its final value when a step change in the input occurs. Components with small time constants alter their output rapidly to reflect changes in the input; components with a larger time constant are sluggish in responding to input changes.

Dead time (or time lag) is the time from when a change in the controller output is made to when the controlled variable exhibits a measurable response. Dead time can occur in the control loop of Figure 1 because of the transportation time of the air from the coil to the space. After a coil temperature changes, there is dead time while the supply air travels the distribution system and finally reaches the sensor in the space. The mass of air in the space further delays the coil temperature change's effect on the controlled variable (space temperature). Dead time can also be caused by a slow sensor or a time lag in the signal from the controller when it first begins to affect the output of the process. Dead time is most often associated with the time it takes to transport the media changed by the control agent from one place to another. Dead time may also be inadvertently added to a control loop by a digital controller with an excessive scan time. If the dead time is small, it may be ignored in the control system model; if it is significant, it must be considered.

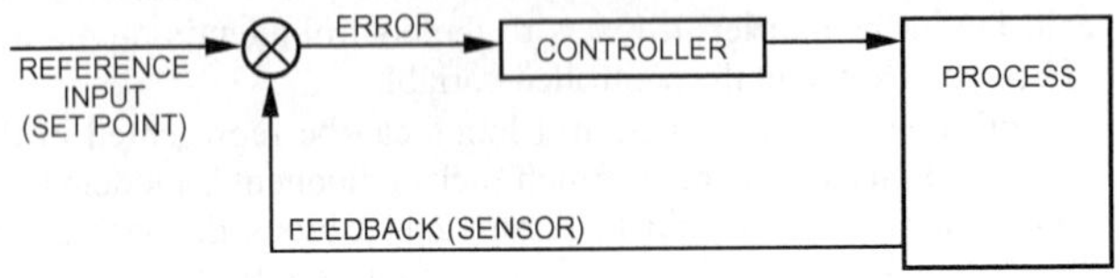

Fig. 2 Block Diagram of Discharge Air Temperature Control

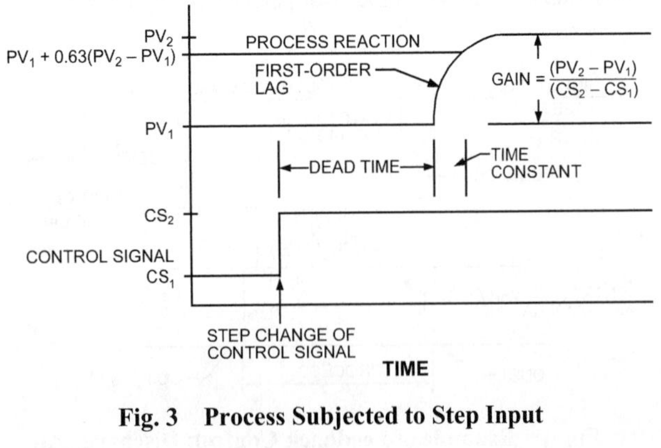

Fig. 3 Process Subjected to Step Input

Figure 1 depicts the mechanisms that create both first-order and dead-time lags, and Figure 3 shows the effect related to time. Dead time is the time it takes warmer air resulting from a higher set point to reach the space, followed by the first-order lag created by the wall on which the thermostat is mounted, and that of the temperature sensor (all of which warm gradually rather than all at once). The control loop must be tuned to account for the combined effect of each time lag. Note that, in most HVAC systems, the first-order lag element predominates.

The **gain** of a transfer function is the amount the output of the component changes per unit of change of input under steady-state conditions. If the element (valve, damper, and/or temperature/pressure differential) is linear, its gain remains constant. However, many control components are nonlinear and have gains that depend on the operating conditions. Figure 3 shows the response of the first-order-plus-dead-time process to a step change of the input signal. Note that the process shows no reaction during dead time, followed by a response that resembles a first-order exponential.

1.2 TYPES OF CONTROL ACTION

Control loops can be classified by the adjustability of the controlled device. A **two-position** controlled device has two operating states (e.g., open and closed), whereas a **modulating** controlled device has a continuous range of operating states (e.g., 0 to 100% open).

Two-Position Action

The control device shown in Figure 4 can be positioned only to a maximum or minimum state (i.e., on or off). Because two-position control is simple and inexpensive, it is used extensively for both industrial and commercial control. A typical home thermostat that starts and stops a furnace is an example.

Controller differential, as it applies to two-position control action, is the difference between a setting at which the controller operates to one position and a setting at which it operates to the other. Thermostat ratings usually refer to the differential (in degrees) that becomes apparent by raising and lowering the dial setting. This differential is known as the **manual differential** of the thermostat. When the same thermostat is applied to an operating system, the total change in temperature that occurs between a "turn-on" state and a "turn-off" state is usually different from the mechanical differential. The **operating differential** may be greater because of thermostat lag or hysteresis, or less because of heating or cooling anticipators built into the thermostat.

Anticipation Applied to Two-Position Action. This common variation of strictly two-position action is often used on room thermostats to reduce the operating differential. In heating thermostats, a heater element in the thermostat is energized during *on* periods, thus shortening the *on* time because the heater warms the thermostat (**heat anticipation**). The same anticipation action can be obtained in cooling thermostats by energizing a heater thermostat at *off* periods. In both cases, the percentage of *on* time is varied in proportion to the load, and the total cycle time remains relatively constant.

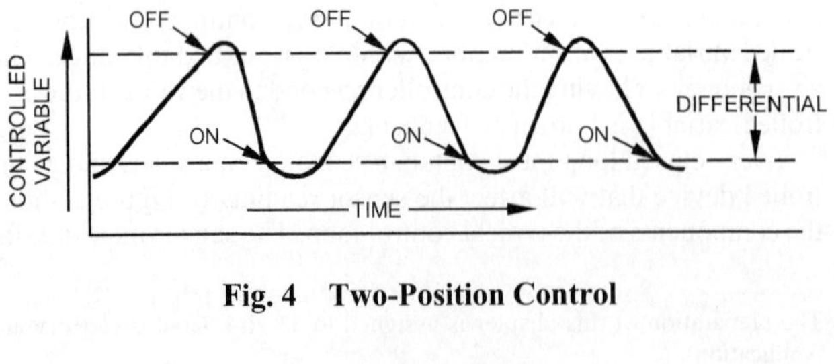

Fig. 4 Two-Position Control

Modulating Control

With modulating control, the controller's output can vary over its entire range. The following terms are used to describe this type of control:

- **Throttling range** is the amount of change in the controlled variable required to cause the controller to move the controlled device from one extreme to the other. It can be adjusted to meet job requirements. The throttling range is inversely proportional to proportional gain
- **Control point** is the actual value of the controlled variable at which the instrument is controlling. It varies within the controller's throttling range and changes with changing load on the system and other variables.
- **Offset**, or error signal, is the difference between the set point and actual control point under stable conditions. This is sometimes called drift, deviation, droop, or steady-state error.

In each of the following examples of modulating control, there is a set of parameters that quantifies the controller's response. The values of these parameters affect the control loop's speed, stability, and accuracy. In every case, control loop performance depends on matching (or **tuning**) the parameter values to the characteristics of the system under control.

Proportional Control. In proportional control, the controlled device is positioned proportionally in response to changes in the controlled variable (Figure 5). A proportional controller can be described mathematically by

$$V_p = K_p e + V_o \tag{1}$$

where

V_p = controller output
K_p = proportional gain parameter (inversely proportional to throttling range)
e = error signal or offset
V_o = offset adjustment parameter

The controller output is proportional to the difference between the sensed value, the controlled variable, and its set point. The controlled device is normally adjusted to be in the middle of its control range at set point by using an offset adjustment. This control is similar to that shown in Figure 5.

Proportional plus Integral (PI) Control. PI control improves on simple proportional control by adding another component to the control action that eliminates the offset typical of proportional control (Figure 6). Reset action may be described by

$$V_p = K_p e + K_i \int e \, d\theta + V_o \tag{2}$$

where

K_i = integral gain parameter
θ = time

The second term in Equation (2) implies that the longer error *e* exists, the more the controller output changes in attempting to eliminate the error. Proper selection of proportional and integral gain constants increases stability and eliminates offset, giving greater control accuracy.

Proportional-Integral-Derivative (PID) Control. This is PI control with a derivative term added to the controller. It varies with the value of the derivative of the error. The equation for PID control is

$$V_p = K_p e + K_i \int e \, d\theta + K_d \frac{de}{d\theta} + V_o \tag{3}$$

where

K_d = derivative gain parameter of controller
$de/d\theta$ = time derivative of error

Adding the derivative term gives some anticipatory action to the controller, which results in a faster response and greater stability. However, the derivative term also makes the controller more sensitive to noisy signals and harder to tune than a PI controller. Most HVAC control loops perform satisfactorily with PI control alone.

Adaptive Control. An adaptive controller adjusts the parameters that define its response as the dynamic characteristics of the process change. If the controller is PID based, then it adjusts feedback gains. An adaptive controller may be based on other feedback rules. The key is that it adjusts its parameters to match the characteristics of the process. When the process changes, the tuning parameters change to match it. Adaptive control is applied in HVAC systems because normal variations in operating conditions affect the characteristics relevant to tuning. For instance, the extent to which zone dampers are open or closed in a VAV system affects the way duct pressure responds to fan speed, and entering fluid temperatures at a coil affect the way the leaving temperature responds to the valve position. **Neural networks** and **self-learning performance-predictive** controllers are sophisticated adaptive controllers.

Fuzzy Logic. This type of control offers an alternative to traditional control algorithms. A fuzzy logic controller uses a series of "if-then" rules that emulates the way a human operator might control the process. Examples of fuzzy logic might include

- IF room temperature is high AND temperature is decreasing, THEN increase cooling a little.
- IF room temperature is high AND temperature is increasing, THEN increase cooling a lot.

The designer of a fuzzy logic controller must first define the rules and then define terms such as *high, increasing, decreasing, a lot,* and *a little.* Room temperature, for instance, might be mapped into a series of functions that include *very low, low, OK, high,* and *very high.* The "fuzzy" element is introduced when the functions overlap and the room temperature is, for example, 70% high and 30% OK. In this case, multiple rules are combined to determine the appropriate control action.

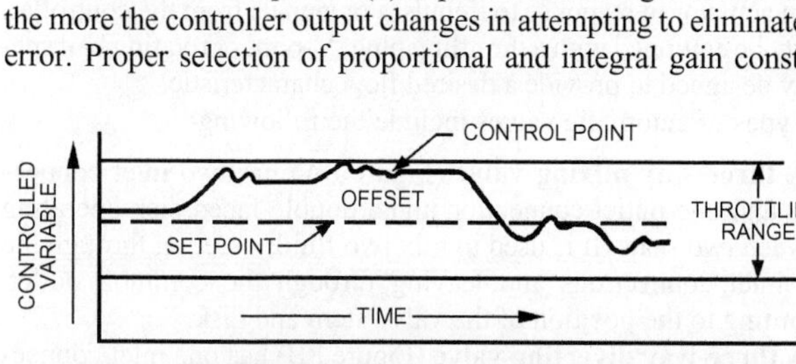

Fig. 5 Proportional Control Showing Variations in Controlled Variable as Load Changes

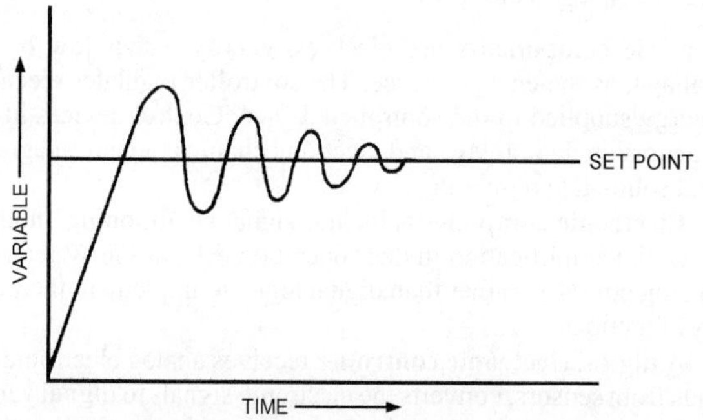

Fig. 6 Proportional plus Integral (PI) Control

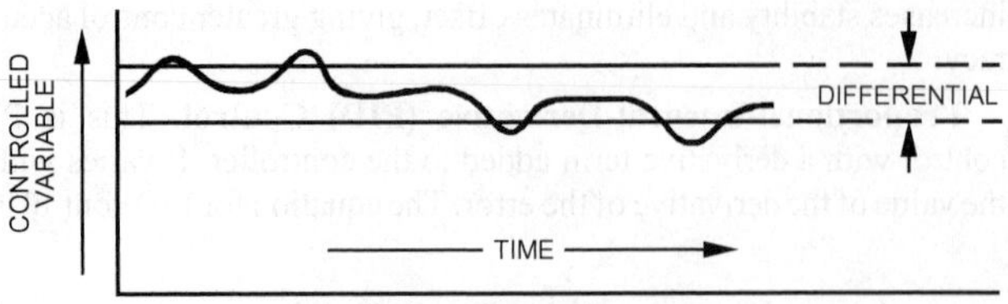

Fig. 7 Floating Control Showing Variations in Controlled Variable as Load Changes

Combinations of Two-Position and Modulating

Some control loops include two-position components in a system that exhibits nearly modulating response.

Timed Two-Position Control. This cycles a two-position heating or cooling element on and off quickly enough that the effect on the controlled temperature approximates a modulating device. In this case, a controller may adjust the duty cycle ("on-time" as a percentage of "cycle-time") as a modulating controlled variable. For example, an element may be turned on for two minutes and off for one minute when the deviation from set point is 3°F. Timed two-position action combines a modulating controller with a two-position controlled device.

Floating Control. This combines a modulating controlled device with a pair of two-position outputs. The controlled device has a continuous operating range, but the actuators that move it only turn on and off. The controller selects one of three operations: moving the controlled device toward its open position, moving it toward its closed position, or leaving the device in its current position. Control is accomplished by applying a pair of two-position contacts with a selected gap between their set points (Figure 7). Generally, a neutral zone between the two positions allows the controlled device to stop at any position when the controlled variable is within the differential of the controller. When the controlled variable falls outside the differential of the controller, the controller moves the controlled device in the proper direction. To function properly, the sensing element must react faster than the actuator drive time. If not, the control functions the same as a two-position control. When applied with a digital controller, floating-point control is also referred to as **tri-state control**.

Incremental Control. This variation of floating control varies the pulse action to open or close an actuator, depending on how close the controlled variable is to the set point. As the controlled variable comes close to the set point, the pulses become shorter. This allows closer control using floating motor actuators. When applied with a digital controller, incremental control is also referred to as **pulse-width-modulation (PWM) control**.

1.3 CLASSIFICATION OF CONTROL COMPONENTS BY ENERGY SOURCE

Control components may be classified according to the primary source of energy as follows:

- **Electric components** use electrical energy, either low or line voltage, as the energy source. The controller regulates electrical energy supplied to the controlled device. Control devices in this category include relays and electromechanical, electromagnetic, and solid-state regulating devices.

  Electronic components include signal conditioning, modulation, and amplification in their operation. Electronic systems use analog circuitry, rather than digital logic, to implement their control functions.

  A **digital electronic controller** receives analog electronic signals from sensors, converts the electronic signals to digital values, and performs mathematical operations on these values inside a microprocessor. Output from the digital controller takes the form of a digital value, which is then converted to an electronic signal to operate the actuator. The digital controller must sample its data because the microprocessor requires time for operations other than reading data. If the sampling interval for the digital controller is properly chosen to avoid second- and third-order harmonics, there will be no significant degradation in control performance from sampling.
- **Self-powered components** apply the power of the measured system to induce the necessary corrective action. The measuring system derives its energy from the process under control, without any auxiliary source of energy. Temperature changes at the sensor result in pressure or volume changes of the enclosed media that are transmitted directly to the operating device of the valve or damper. A component using a thermopile in a pilot flame to generate electrical energy is also self powered.
- **Pneumatic components** use compressed air, usually at a pressure of 15 to 20 psig, as an energy source. The air is generally supplied to the controller, which regulates the pressure supplied to the controlled device.

This method of classification can be extended to individual control loops and to complete control systems. For example, the room temperature control for a particular room that includes a pneumatic room thermostat and a pneumatically actuated reheat coil would be referred to as a pneumatic control loop. Many control systems use a combination of control components and are called **hybrid** systems.

Computers for Automatic Control

Computers perform the control functions in direct digital control (DDC) systems. Uses range from personal computers used as operator interfaces for DDC systems to embedded program microprocessors used to control variable-air-volume boxes, fan-coil units, heat pumps, and other terminal HVAC equipment. Other uses include primary HVAC equipment programmable controllers, distributed network controllers, and servers used to store DDC system trend data. Chapter 40 of the 2015 *ASHRAE Handbook—HVAC Applications* covers computer components and HVAC computer applications more extensively.

2. CONTROL COMPONENTS

2.1 CONTROL DEVICES

A control device is the component of a control loop used to vary the input (controlled variable). Both **valves** and **dampers** perform essentially the same function and must be properly sized and selected for the particular application. The control link to the valve or damper is called an **actuator** or **operator**, and uses electricity, compressed air, hydraulic fluid, or some other means to power the motion of the valve stem or damper linkage through its operating range. For additional information, see Chapter 36.

Valves

An automatic valve is designed to control the flow of steam, water, gas, or other fluids. It can be considered a variable orifice positioned by an actuator in response to impulses or signals from the controller. It may be equipped with a throttling plug, V-port, or rotating ball specially designed to provide a desired flow characteristic.

Types of automatic valves include the following:

A **three-way mixing valve** (Figure 8A) has two inlet connections and one outlet connection and a double-faced disk operating between two seats. It is used to mix two fluids entering through the two inlet connections and leaving through the common outlet, according to the position of the valve stem and disk.

A **three-way diverting valve** (Figure 8B) has one inlet connection and two outlet connections, and two separate disks and seats. It is used to divert flow to either of the outlets or to proportion the flow

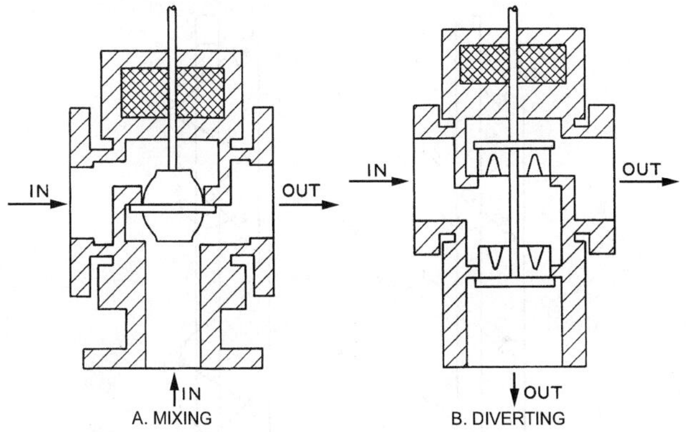

Fig. 8 Typical Three-Way Mixing and Diverting Globe Valves

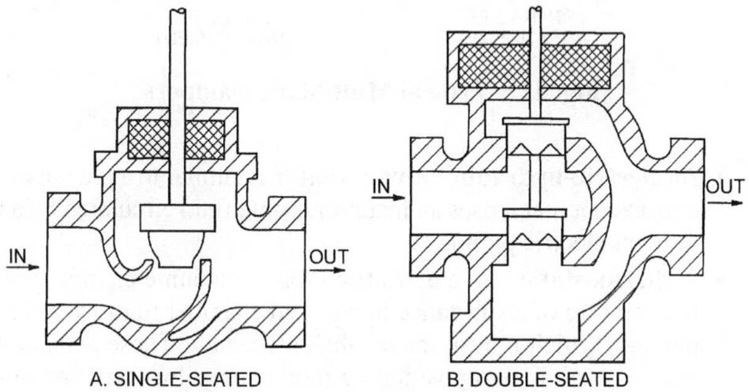

Fig. 9 Typical Single- and Double-Seated Two-Way Globe Valves

to both outlets. Three-way diverting valves are more expensive and have more complex applications, and generally are not used in typical HVAC systems.

A **two-way globe valve** may be either single or double seated. A **single-seated valve** (Figure 9A) is designed for tight shutoff. Appropriate disk materials for various pressures and media are used. A **double-seated** or **balanced valve** (Figure 9B) is designed so that the media pressure acting against the valve disk is essentially balanced, reducing the actuator force required. It is widely used where fluid pressure is too high to allow a single-seated valve to close or to modulate properly. It is not usually used where tight shutoff is required.

A **butterfly valve** consists of a heavy ring enclosing a disk that rotates on an axis at or near its center and is similar to a round single-blade damper. In principle, the disk seats against a ring machined within the body or a resilient liner in the body. Two butterfly valves can be used together to act like a three-way valve for mixing or diverting. In this arrangement, one valve is set up as normally open and the other is normally closed. In applications with pipe sizes 4 in. and above, butterfly valves are either two position or modulating, and they are less expensive than globe-style valves (see Chapter 47 of the 2016 *ASHRAE Handbook—HVAC Systems and Equipment* for information on globe valves).

A **ball valve** consists of a ball with a hole drilled through it, rotating in a valve body. Ball valves are increasingly popular because of their low cost and high close-off ratings. Features that provide flow characteristics similar to or better than globe valves are available.

Pressure-independent valves are control valves with integral pressure regulators. This allows the valve to maintain a constant flow at a given shaft position because the integral pressure regulator maintains a constant differential pressure across the valve's orifice, regardless of system pressure fluctuations.

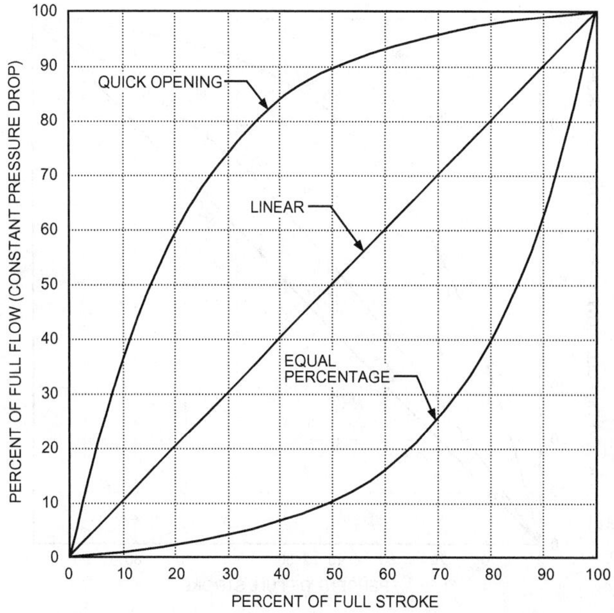

Fig. 10 Typical Flow Characteristics of Valves

Flow Characteristics. Valve performance is expressed in terms of its flow characteristics as it operates through its stroke, based on a constant pressure drop. Three common characteristics are shown in Figure 10 and are defined as follows:

- **Quick opening.** Maximum flow is approached rapidly as the device begins to open.
- **Linear.** Opening and flow are related in direct proportion.
- **Equal percentage.** Each equal increment of opening increases flow by an equal percentage over the previous value.

On a pressure-dependent valve, because pressure drop across the valve's orifice seldom remains constant as its opening changes, actual performance usually deviates from the published characteristic curve. The magnitude of deviation is determined by the overall design. For example, in a system arranged so that control valves or dampers can shut off all flow, pressure drop across a controlled device increases from a minimum at design conditions to total pressure drop at no flow. Figure 11 shows the extent of resulting deviations for a valve or damper designed with a linear characteristic, when selection is based on various percentages of total system pressure drop. To allow for adequate control by the valve, design pressure drop should be a reasonably large percentage of total system pressure drop at the valve (i.e., adequate valve authority) and the system should be designed and controlled so that pressure drop remains relatively constant. Hydronic piping circuits and valve authority are discussed in Chapters 13 and 47 of the 2016 *ASHRAE Handbook—HVAC Systems and Equipment*, respectively.

Selection and Sizing. Higher pressure drops for control devices are obtained by using smaller sizes, with a possible increase in size of other equipment in the system. Sizing control valves is discussed in Chapter 47 of the 2016 *ASHRAE Handbook—HVAC Systems and Equipment*.

Steam Valves. Steam-to-water and steam-to-air heat exchangers are typically controlled by regulating steam flow using a two-way throttling valve. One-pipe steam systems require a line-size, two-position valve for proper condensate drainage and steam flow; two-pipe steam systems can be controlled by two-position or modulating (throttling) valves. Maximum pressure drop for steam valves is a function of operating pressure and cannot be exceeded.

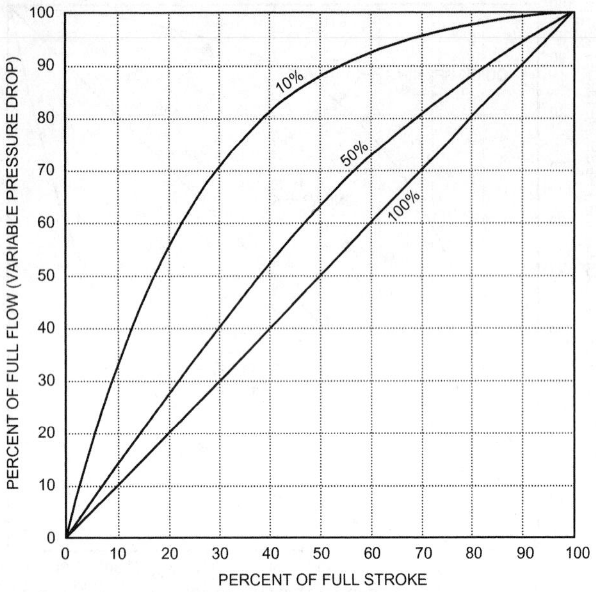

Fig. 11 Typical Valve Authority Performance Curves for Linear Devices at Various Percentages of Total System Pressure Drop

Water Valves. Valves for water service may be two- or three-way and two-position or proportional. Proportional valves are used most often, but two-position valves are not unusual and are sometimes essential. Variable-flow systems are designed to keep the pressure differential constant from supply to return. For valve selection, it is safer to assume that the pressure drop across the valve increases as it modulates from fully open to fully closed.

Equal-percentage valves provide better control at part load, particularly in hot-water coils because the coil's heat output is not linearly related to flow. As flow reduces, more heat is transferred with each unit of water, counteracting the reduction in flow. Equal-percentage valves can provide linear heat transfer from the coil with respect to the control signal.

Actuators. Valve actuators include the following general types:

- A **pneumatic valve actuator** consists of a spring-opposed, flexible diaphragm or bellows attached to the valve stem. An increase in air pressure above the minimum point of the spring range compresses the spring and simultaneously moves the valve stem. Springs of various pressure ranges can sequence the operation of two or more devices, if properly selected or adjusted. For example, a chilled-water valve actuator may modulate the valve from fully closed to fully open over a spring range of 9 to 13 psig, whereas a sequenced steam valve may actuate from 3 to 8 psig.

  Two-position pneumatic control is accomplished using a two-position pneumatic relay to apply either full air pressure or no pressure to the valve actuator. Pneumatic valves and valves with spring-return electric actuators can be classified as normally open or normally closed.

  A **normally open valve** assumes an open position, providing full flow, when all actuating force is removed.

  A **normally closed valve** assumes a closed position, stopping flow, when all actuating force is removed.

- **Double-acting** or **springless pneumatic valve actuators**, which use two opposed diaphragms or two sides of a single diaphragm, are generally limited to special applications involving large valves or high fluid pressure.

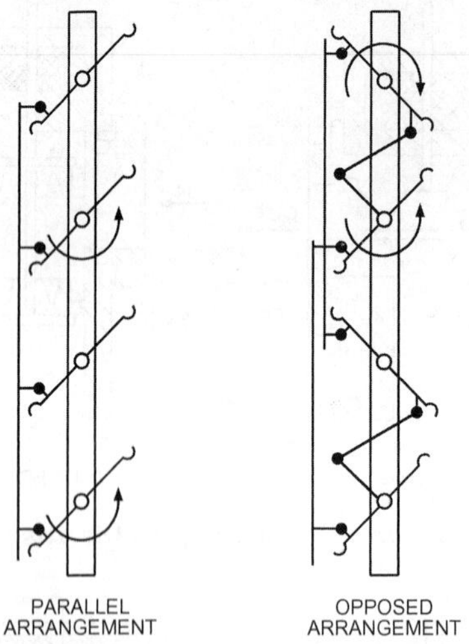

Fig. 12 Typical Multiblade Dampers

- An **electric-hydraulic valve actuator** is similar to a pneumatic one, except that it uses an incompressible fluid circulated by an internal electric pump.
- A **thermostatic valve actuator** uses the volume change with temperature of a substance in a sealed chamber to move a diaphragm, which in turn moves the valve shaft. These actuators can be used as two-position or modulating. In **wax thermostatic valves,** the volume change is caused by phase change (the wax melts or solidifies). The heat source is usually the environment or the fluid whose temperature is being controlled, but can also be a resistive element in the chamber receiving voltage from a controller.
- A **solenoid** consists of a magnetic coil operating a movable plunger. Most are for two-position operation, but modulating solenoid valves are available with a pressure equalization bellows or piston to achieve modulation. Solenoid valves are generally limited to relatively small sizes (up to 4 in.).
- An **electric actuator** operates the valve stem through a gear train and linkage. Electric motor actuators are classified in the following three types:
  - **Spring-return**, for two-position operation (energy drives the valve to one position and a spring returns the valve to its normal position) or for modulating operation (energy drives the valve to a variable position and a spring returns the valve to an open or closed position upon a signal or power failure). With spring-return electric actuators, on loss of actuator power, the spring positions the valve to its fail-safe (normal) position (either fully open or fully closed).
  - **Electronic fail-safe,** which uses a capacitor instead of a spring to drive the actuator to its fail-safe (normal) position. The fail-safe position can be set for fully open, fully closed, or anywhere in between at varying increments.
  - **Reversible**, for floating and proportional operation. The motor can run in either direction and can stop in any position. It is sometimes equipped with a return spring or an electronic fail-safe. In proportional-control applications, an integral feedback potentiometer for rebalancing the control circuit is also driven by the motor.

Dampers

Automatic dampers are used in air conditioning and ventilation to control airflow. They may be used (1) in a modulating application to maintain a controlled variable, such as mixed air temperature or supply air duct static pressure; or (2) for two-position control to initiate operation, such as opening minimum outdoor air dampers when a fan is started.

Multiblade dampers are typically available in two arrangements: parallel-blade and opposed-blade (Figure 12), although combinations of the two are manufactured. They are used to control flow through large openings typical of those in air handlers. Both types are adequate for two-position control.

When dampers are applied in modulating control loops, a nonlinear relationship between flow and stroke can lead to difficulties in tuning a control loop for performance. Nonlinearity is expressed as variation in the slope of the flow versus stroke curve. Perfect linearity is not required: if slope varies throughout the range of required flow by less than a factor of 2 from the slope at the point where the loop is tuned, nonlinearity is not likely to disrupt performance.

Parallel blades are used for modulating control when the design condition pressure drop of the damper is about 25% or more of the pressure in a subsystem (Figure 13A). **Opposed-blade dampers** are preferable for modulating control when the damper is about 15% or less of the pressure drop in a subsystem (Figure 13B). A subsystem is defined as a portion of the duct system between two relatively constant pressure points (e.g., the return air section between the mixed air and return plenum tee). A combination may be considered between 15 and 25% damper drop. **Single-blade dampers** are typically used for flow control in small terminal units.

In Figure 13, *A* is **authority**, which is the ratio of pressure drop across the fully open damper at design flow to total subsystem pressure drop, including fully open control damper pressure drop. The curves here are typical for ducted applications. The Air Movement and Control Association (AMCA *Standard* 500) defined a number of geometric arrangements of dampers for testing pressure losses. The curves in Figure 13 are those of an AMCA 5.3 geometry, which is a fully ducted arrangement with long sections of duct before and after a damper. Other geometric applications, such as plenum or wall-mounted dampers, exhibit different response curves (Felker and Felker 2009; van Becelaere et al. 2004).

Figure 14 shows two parallel-blade (PB) applications, two opposed-blade (OB) applications, and an "anti-PB" (aPB) arrangement. The response curves are not like those of the AMCA 5.3

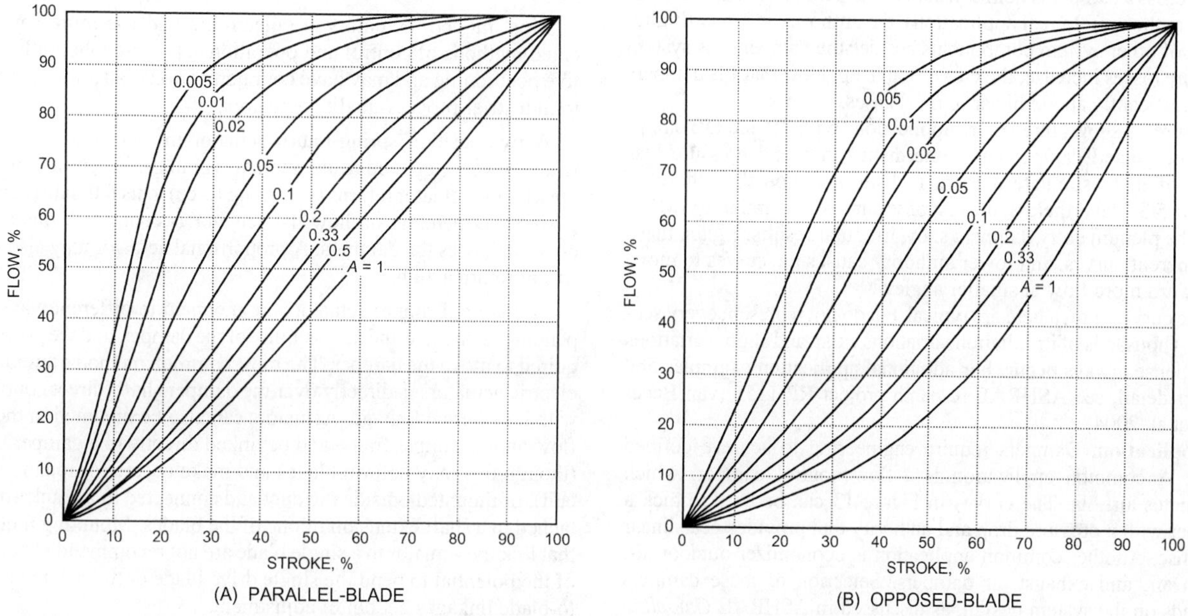

Fig. 13 Characteristic Curves of Installed Dampers in an AMCA 5.3 Geometry

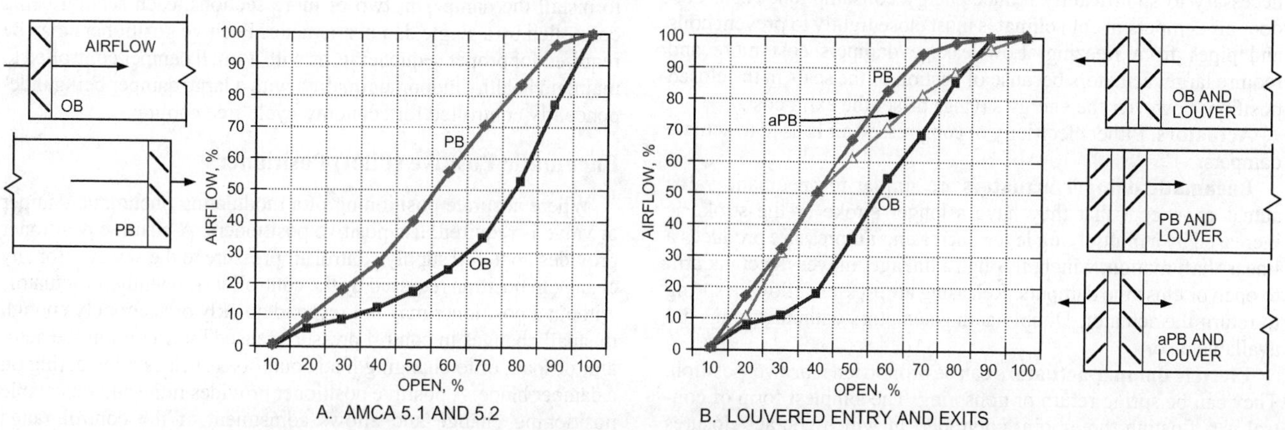

Fig. 14 Inherent Curves for Partially Ducted and Louvered Dampers (RP-1157)

Based on data in van Becelaere et al. (2004)

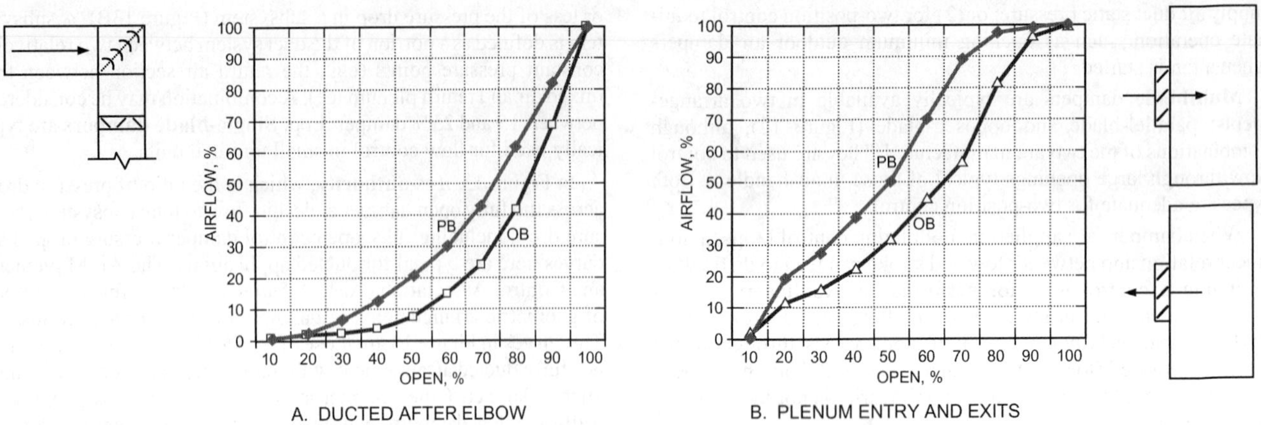

Fig. 15 Inherent Curves for Ducted and Plenum-Mounted Dampers (RP-1157)
Based on data in van Becelaere et al. (2004)

ducted application. These are "inherent" curves, where pressure drop across a damper is held constant as the damper rotates (so it has 100% authority). In real applications, the authority is lower (higher losses of other system components besides the damper). As system pressure losses increase, the curves move up. Note that PB dampers are significantly above linear in most cases.

Figure 15 shows three more applications with PB and OB dampers. The ducted damper has some disturbance and pressure loss ahead of it, to simulate a more realistic situation than those of AMCA 5.3. Nevertheless, the response curves are similar to AMCA 5.3. The plenum entry dampers show irregular results. Again, these are inherent curves, and lower authority causes the curves to move up toward more flow at smaller angles.

The curves shown here are typical, but do not represent every scenario. Thousands of installation variations exist, and slight variations in response always occur. For additional application examples and greater detail, see ASHRAE research project RP-1157 (van Becelaere et al. 2004).

Application. Dampers require engineering to achieve defined goals. A common application is a flow control damper, which modulates airflow. The curves in Figure 13 can be used to pick a damper with a pressure drop and authority that provides near-linear response. Another common application is economizer outdoor air, return air, and exhaust air dampers. Selection of these dampers depends on the system design, as discussed in ASHRAE *Guideline* 16-2014.

Damper leakage is a concern, particularly where tight shutoff is necessary to significantly reduce energy consumption. Also, outdoor air dampers in cold climates must close tightly to prevent coils and pipes from freezing. Low-leakage dampers cost more and require larger actuators because of friction of the seals in the closed position; however, the energy savings offset the extra cost.

Actuators. Either electricity or compressed air is used to actuate dampers.

Pneumatic damper actuators are similar to pneumatic valve actuators, except that they have a longer stroke or the stroke is increased by a multiplying lever. Increasing air pressure produces a linear shaft motion, which, through a linkage, moves the crank arm to open or close the dampers. Releasing air pressure allows a spring to return the actuator. Double-acting actuators without springs are available also.

Electric damper actuators can be proportional or two-position. They can be spring return or nonspring. The simplest form of control is a floating three-point controller, in which contact closures drive the motor clockwise or counterclockwise. In addition, a variety of standard electronic signals from electronic controllers or DDC systems, such as 4 to 20 mA, 2 to 10 V (dc), or 0 to 10 V (dc), can be used to control proportionally actuated dampers.

Most modern actuators are electronic and use more sophisticated methods of control and operation. They are inherently positive positioning and may have communications capabilities similar to industrial-process-quality actuators.

A two-position spring-return actuator moves in one direction when power is applied to its internal windings. When no power is present, the actuator returns (via spring force) to its fail-safe (normal) position. Depending on how the actuator is connected, this action opens or closes the dampers. A proportional actuator may also have spring-return action.

Mounting. Damper actuators are mounted in different ways, depending on the size and accessibility of the damper, and the power required to move the damper. The most common method of mounting electric actuators is directly over the damper shaft (direct coupling) with no external linkage. Actuators can also be mounted in the airflow on the damper frame and be linked directly to a damper blade (though this may deform blades and make access for repairs difficult), or mounted outside the duct and connected to a crank arm attached to a shaft extension of one of the blades. Mounting methods that link the actuator to a single blade are not recommended because of the potential to bend the single drive blade or to have the blade-to-blade linkages get out of adjustment.

Large dampers may require two or more actuators, which are usually mounted at separate points on the damper. An alternative is to install the damper in two or more sections, each section being controlled by a single damper actuator. Positive positioners may be required for proper sequencing, as with a small damper controlled to maintain healthy indoor air quality, with a large damper being independently controlled for economy-cycle free cooling.

Pneumatic Positive (Pilot) Positioners

Where accurate positioning of a modulating pneumatic damper or valve is required, use positive positioners. A positive positioner provides up to full supply control air pressure to the actuator for any change in position required by the controller. A pneumatic actuator without a positioner may not respond quickly or accurately enough to small changes in control pressure caused by friction in the actuator or load, or to changing load conditions such as wind acting on a damper blade. A positive positioner provides finite and repeatable positioning change and allows adjustment of the control range (spring range of the actuator) to provide a proper sequencing control of two or more control devices.

2.2 SENSORS AND TRANSMITTERS

A sensor responds to a change in the controlled variable. The response, which is a change in some physical or electrical property of the primary sensing element, is available for translation or amplification into a mechanical or electrical signal. This signal is sent to the controller.

Transmitters take the output of a sensor and convert the sensor's signal to an industry-standard signal type (e.g., 4 to 20 mA, 0 to 10 V, network protocol).

Chapter 47 of the 2015 *ASHRAE Handbook—HVAC Applications* and manufacturer's catalogs and tutorials include information on specific applications. In selecting a sensor for a specific application, consider the following:

- **Operating range of controlled variable.** The sensor must be capable of providing an adequate change in its output signal over the expected input range.
- **Compatibility of controller input.** Electronic and digital controllers accept various ranges and types of electronic signals. The sensor's signal must be compatible with the controller. If the controller's input requirements are unknown, it may be possible to use a transducer to convert the sensor signal to an industry-standard signal, such as 4 to 20 mA or 0 to 10 V (DC).
- **Accuracy, sensitivity, and repeatability.** For some control applications, the controlled variable must be maintained within a narrow band around a desired set point. Both the accuracy and sensitivity of the sensor selected must reflect this requirement. **Sensitivity** is the ratio of a change in output magnitude to the change of input that causes it, after steady state has been reached. **Repeatability** is closeness of agreement among repeated measurements of the same variable under the same conditions. However, even an accurate sensor cannot maintain the set point if (1) the controller is unable to resolve the input signal, (2) the controlled device cannot be positioned accurately, (3) the controlled device exhibits excessive hysteresis, or (4) disturbances drive its system faster than the controls can regulate it. See ASHRAE *Guideline* 13, clause 7.9, for a discussion on end-to-end accuracy.
- **Sensor response time.** Associated with a sensor/transducer arrangement is a response curve, which describes the response of the sensor output to change in the controlled variable. If the time constant of the process being controlled is short and stable and accurate control is important, then the sensor selected must have a fast response time.
- **Control agent properties and characteristics.** The control agent is the medium to which the sensor is exposed, or with which it comes in contact, for measuring a controlled variable such as temperature or pressure. If the agent corrodes the sensor or otherwise degrades its performance, a different sensor should be selected, or the sensor must be isolated or protected from direct contact with the control agent.
- **Ambient environment characteristics.** Even when the sensor's components are isolated from direct contact with the control agent, the ambient environment must be considered. The temperature and humidity range of the ambient environment must not reduce the sensor's accuracy. Likewise, the presence of certain gases, chemicals, and electromagnetic interference (EMI) can cause performance degradation. In such cases, a special sensor or transducer housing can be used to protect it. Special housings may also be required in wet, flammable, explosive, or corrosive environments.
- **Placement requirements.** The sensing element must be in the correct point(s) required for proper measurement. For instance, pipe wall thickness (schedule) affects the required length of water temperature or flow probes; sensors inside air ducts (especially low-temperature switches) should be long enough to compensate for air stratification; room temperature and humidity sensors should not be installed close to heat sources, on outer walls, in direct airstreams, or in areas where air stalls (e.g., behind furniture); single measurements of return air properties, no matter how accurate, are just averages and do not detect areas with simultaneous opposite extremes.

Temperature Sensors

Temperature-sensing elements generally detect changes in either (1) relative dimension (caused by differences in thermal expansion), (2) the state of a vapor or liquid, or (3) some electrical property. Within each category, there are various sensing elements to measure room, duct, water, and surface temperatures. Temperature-sensing technologies commonly used in HVAC applications are as follows:

- A **bimetal element** is composed of two thin strips of dissimilar metals fused together. Because the two metals have different coefficients of thermal expansion, the element bends and changes position as the temperature varies. Depending on the space available and the movement required, it may be straight, U-shaped, or wound into a spiral. This element is commonly used in room, insertion, and immersion thermostats.
- A **rod-and-tube element** consists of a high-expansion metal tube containing a low-expansion rod. One end of the rod is attached to the rear of the tube. The tube changes length with changes in temperature, causing the free end of the rod to move. This element is commonly used in certain insertion and immersion thermostats.
- A **sealed bellows element** is either vapor, gas, or liquid filled. Temperature changes vary the pressure and volume of the gas or liquid, resulting in a change in force or a movement.
- A **remote bulb element** is a bulb or capsule connected to a sealed bellows or diaphragm by a capillary tube; the entire system is filled with vapor, gas, or liquid. Temperature changes at the bulb cause volume or pressure changes that are conveyed to the bellows or diaphragm through the capillary tube. This element is useful where the temperature-measuring point is remote from the desired thermostat location.
- A **thermistor** is a semiconductor that changes electrical resistance with temperature. It has a negative temperature coefficient (i.e., resistance decreases as temperature increases). Its characteristic curve of temperature versus resistance is nonlinear over a wide range. Several techniques are used to convert its response to a linear change over a particular temperature range. With digital control, one technique is to store a computer look-up table that maps the temperature corresponding to the measured resistance. The table breaks the curve into small segments, and each segment is assumed to be linear over its range. Thermistors are used because of their relatively low cost, the large change in resistance possible for a small change in temperature, and their long-term stability.
- A **resistance temperature device (RTD)** also changes resistance with temperature. Most metallic materials increase in resistance with increasing temperature; over limited ranges, this variation is linear for certain metals (e.g., platinum, copper, tungsten, nickel/iron alloys). Platinum, for example, is linear within ±0.3% from 0 to 300°F. The RTD sensing element is available in several forms for surface or immersion mounting. Flat grid windings are used for measurements of surface temperatures. For direct measurement of fluid temperatures, the windings are encased in a stainless steel bulb to protect them from corrosion.

Humidity Sensors and Transmitters

Humidity sensors, or **hygrometers**, measure relative humidity, dew point, or absolute humidity of ambient or moving air. **Transmitters** convert the signal from the humidity sensor to an industry-standard output such as 0 to 10 V or 4 to 20 mA. Some transmitters compensate for temperature variations. Two types of sensors that detect relative humidity are mechanical hygrometers and electronic hygrometers.

Electronic hygrometers can use either resistance or capacitance sensing elements. The resistance element is a conductive grid coated with a hygroscopic substance. The grid's conductivity varies with the water retained; thus, resistance varies with relative humidity. The conductive element is arranged in an AC-excited Wheatstone bridge and responds rapidly to humidity changes.

The capacitance element is a stretched membrane of nonconductive film, coated on both sides with metal electrodes and mounted in a perforated plastic capsule. The response of the sensor's capacity to rising relative humidity is nonlinear. The signal is linearized and temperature is compensated in the amplifier circuit to provide an output signal as relative humidity changes from 0 to 100%.

The **chilled-mirror humidity sensor** determines dew point rather than relative humidity. Air flows across a small mirror in the sensor. A thermoelectric cooler lowers the surface temperature of the mirror until it reaches the dew point of the air. Condensation on the surface reduces the amount of light reflected from the mirror compared to a reference light level.

Dispersive infrared (DIR) technology can be used to sense absolute humidity or dew point. It is similar to technology used to sense carbon dioxide or other gases. Infrared water vapor sensors are optical sensors that detect the amount of water vapor in air based on the infrared light absorption characteristics of water molecules. Light absorption is proportional to the number of molecules present. An **infrared hygrometer** typically provides a value of absolute humidity or dew point, and can operate in diffusion or flow-through sample mode. This type of humidity sensor is unique in that the sensing element (a light detector and an infrared filter) is behind a transparent window and is never exposed directly to the sample environment. As a result, this sensor has excellent long-term stability, long life, and fast response time; is not subject to saturation; and operates equally well in very high or low humidity. Previously used solely for high-end applications, infrared hygrometers are now commonly used in HVAC applications because they cost about the same as mid-range-accuracy (1 to 3%) humidity sensors.

Pressure Transmitters and Transducers

A pneumatic pressure transmitter converts a change in absolute, gage, or differential pressure to a mechanical motion using a bellows, diaphragm, or Bourdon tube mechanism. When connected through appropriate links, this mechanical motion produces a change in air pressure to a controller. In some instances, sensing and control functions are combined in a single component, a pressure controller.

An electronic pressure transducer may use mechanical actuation of a diaphragm or Bourdon tube to operate a potentiometer or differential transformer. Another type uses a strain gage bonded to a diaphragm. The strain gage detects displacement resulting from the force applied to the diaphragm. Capacitance transducers are most often used for measurements below 1 in. of water because of their high sensitivity and repeatability. Electronic circuits provide temperature compensation and amplification to produce a standard output signal.

Flow Rate Sensors

Orifice plate, pitot-static tube, venturi, turbine, magnetic flow, thermal dispersion, vortex shedding, and ultrasonic meters are some of the technologies used to sense fluid flow. In general, pressure differential devices (orifice plates, venturi, and pitot tubes) are less expensive and simpler to use, but have limited range; thus, their accuracy depends on how they are applied and where in a system they are located.

More sophisticated flow devices, such as turbine, magnetic, and vortex shedding meters, usually have better range and are more accurate over a wide range. If an existing piping system is being considered for retrofit with a flow device, the expense of shutting down the system and cutting into a pipe must be considered. In this case, a noninvasive meter, such as an ultrasonic flow meter, may be cost effective.

There are two types of ultrasonic flow meters. One uses the Doppler effect, which is better for monitoring flow in slurry applications. The other type uses the transit time effect, which is more accurate at lower flows and with standard nonslurry fluids.

For air velocity metering, pitot-static tubes provide a naturally larger signal change at high velocities, with limitations on their application below 500 to 600 fpm. Vortex shedding for airflow applications has similar low-velocity limitations. Thermal dispersion sensors provide a naturally larger signal change at lower velocities without appreciable losses through velocities common in most ventilation systems, which makes them more suitable for applications below 1000 fpm.

Indoor Air Quality Sensors

Indoor air quality control can be divided into two categories: ventilation control and contamination protection. In spaces with dense populations and intermittent or highly variable occupancy, ventilation can be more efficiently applied by detecting changes in population or ventilation requirements [**demand-controlled ventilation (DCV)**]. This involves using time schedules and population counters, and measuring the indoor/outdoor differential levels of carbon dioxide (CO_2) or other contaminants in a space. Changes in differential CO_2 mirror changes in space population; thus, the amount of outdoor air introduced into the occupied space can then be controlled. Demand control helps maintain proper ventilation rates at all levels of occupancy. Control set-point levels for carbon dioxide are determined by the specific relationships between differential CO_2, rate of CO_2 production by occupants, the variable airflow rate required by the changing population, and a fixed amount of ventilation required to dilute building-generated contaminants unrelated to CO_2 production. ASHRAE *Standard* 62.1 and its user's manual (ASHRAE 2013) provide further information on ventilation for acceptable indoor air quality and DCV for single-zone systems.

Contamination protection sensors monitor levels of hazardous or toxic substances and issue warning signals and/or initiate corrective actions through the building automation system (BAS). Sensors are available for many different gases. The carbon monoxide (CO) sensor is one of the most common, and is often used in buildings wherever combustion occurs (e.g., parking garages). Refrigerant-specific sensors are used to measure, alarm, and initiate ventilation purging in enclosed spaces that house refrigeration equipment, to prevent occupant suffocation upon a refrigerant leak (see ASHRAE *Standard* 15 for more information). The type selected, substances monitored, and action taken in an alarm condition all depend on where these sensors are applied.

Lighting Level Sensors

Analog lighting level transmitters packaged in various configurations allow control of ambient lighting levels using building automation strategies for energy conservation. Examples include ceiling-mounted indoor light sensors used to measure room lighting levels; outdoor ambient lighting sensors used to control parking, general exterior, security, and sign lighting; and interior skylight sensors used to monitor and control light levels in skylight wells and other atrium spaces.

Power Sensing and Transmission

Passive electronic devices that sense the magnetic field around a conductor carrying current allow low-cost instrumentation of power circuits. A wire in the sensor forms an inductive coupling that powers the internal function and senses the level of the power signal. These devices can provide an analog output signal to monitor current flow or operate a switch at a user-set level to turn on an alarm or other device.

2.3 CONTROLLERS

An HVAC controller reads sensors' signals and regulates control devices to achieve one or more objectives, which may include maintaining comfort, minimizing energy use, and ensuring safe operation and environmental conditions. Controllers can use other sources of information to determine their output, such as schedules, tables, operator commands, and weather forecasts. Controllers may also collect data about the processes and their own operation to help monitor, diagnose, and tune the processes' operation. Digital controllers perform the control functions using a microprocessor and control algorithms. The sensors and controller can be combined in a single instrument, such as a room thermostat, or they may be separate devices.

Digital Controllers

Digital controls use microprocessors to execute software programs that are customized for use in commercial buildings. Controllers use sensors to measure values such as temperature and humidity, perform control routines in software programs, and exert control using output signals to actuators such as valves and electric or pneumatic actuators connected to dampers. The operator may enter parameters such as set points, proportional or integral gains, minimum on and off times, or high and low limits, but the control algorithms make the control decisions. The controller scans input devices, executes control algorithms, and then positions the output device(s), in a stepwise scheme. The controller calculates proper control signals digitally rather than using an analog circuit or mechanical change, as in electric/electronic and pneumatic controllers. Use of digital controls in building automation is referred to as direct digital control (DDC).

Digital controls can be used as stand-alones or can be integrated into building management systems (BMSs) through network communications. Simple controls may have a single control loop that can perform a single control function (e.g., temperature control of a unit ventilator); larger versions can control a larger number of loops or even perform complex strategies such as managing energy allocation to multiple processes and open loop controls, and balancing multiple objectives (e.g., comfort, energy consumption, equipment wear).

Advantages of digital controls include the following:

- Sequences or equipment can be modified by changing software, which reduces the cost and diversity of hardware necessary to achieve control.
- Features such as demand setback, reset, data logging, diagnostics, and time-clock integration can be added to the controller with small incremental cost.
- Precise, accurate control can be implemented, limited by the resolution of sensor and analog-to-digital (A/D) and digital-to-analog (D/A) conversion processes. PID and other control algorithms can be implemented mathematically and can adjust performance based on sophisticated algorithms.
- Controllers can communicate with each other using open or proprietary networking (e.g., Ethernet or RS-485) standards.

A single control that is fixed in functionality with flexibility to change set points and small configurations is called an **application-specific controller**. Many manufacturers include application-specific controls with their HVAC equipment, such as air-handling units and chillers.

Firmware and Software. Preprogrammed control routines, known as firmware, are sometimes stored in permanent memory such as programmable read-only memory (PROM) or electrically programmable read-only memory (EPROM), and the application or set points are stored in changeable memory such as electrically erasable programmable read-only memory (EEPROM). The operator can modify parameters such as set points, limits, and minimum *off* times within the control routines, but the primary program logic cannot be changed without replacing the memory chips.

User-programmable controllers allow the algorithms to be changed by the user. The programming language provided with the controller can vary from a derivation of a standard language to custom language developed by the controller's manufacturer, to graphically based programming. Preprogrammed routines for proportional, proportional plus integral, Boolean logic, timers, etc., are typically included in the language. Standard energy management routines may also be preprogrammed and may interact with other control loops where appropriate.

Digital controllers can have both preprogrammed firmware and user-programmed routines. These routines can automatically modify the firmware's parameters according to user-defined conditions to accomplish the control sequence designed by the control engineer.

Operator Interface. Some digital controllers (e.g., a programmable room thermostat) are designed for dedicated purposes and are adjustable only through manual switches and potentiometers mounted on the controller. This type of controller cannot be networked with other controllers. A **direct digital controller** can have manually adjustable features, but it is more typically adjusted either through a built-in LED or LCD display, a hand-held device, or a terminal or computer. The direct digital controller's digital communication allows remote connection to other controllers and to higher-level computing devices and host operating stations.

A **terminal** allows the user to communicate with the controller and, where applicable, to modify the program in the controller. Terminals can range from hand-held units with an LCD display and several buttons to a full-sized console with a video monitor and keyboard. The terminal can be limited in function to allow only display of sensor and parameter values, or powerful enough to allow changing or reprogramming the control strategies. In some instances, a terminal can communicate remotely with one or more controllers, thus allowing central displays, alarms, and commands. Usually, hand-held terminals are used by technicians for troubleshooting, and full-sized, fully functional terminals are used at a fixed location to monitor the entire digital control system. Standard Internet browsers can sometimes be used to access system information, complemented with online help and application libraries, plus cloud-based troubleshooting and graphic user interface design tools.

Electric/Electronic Controllers

For **two-position control**, the controller output may be a simple electrical contact that starts a fan or pump, or one that actuates a spring-return valve or damper actuator. Electrical contacts can be normally open (NO), normally closed (NC), or have one of each (double throw). An output that has three terminals (common, NO, and NC) is called single-pole, double-throw (SPDT). SPDTs simplify designs, because the same device can be used as NO or NC depending on the requirements of the application. In some cases, both contacts are used (e.g., to send a signal to one device or another, depending on whether the system is in cooling or heating mode). Both single-pole, single-throw (SPST) and SPDT circuits can be used for timed two-position action.

Floating control uses two NO output contacts with a neutral zone where neither contact is made. This control is used with reversible motors; it has a slow response and a wide throttling range.

Output for **floating control** is a SPDT switching circuit with a neutral zone where neither contact is made. This control is used with reversible motors; it has a slow response and a wide throttling range.

Pulse modulation control is an improvement over floating control. It provides closer control by varying the duration of the contact closure. As the actual condition moves closer to the set point, the pulse duration shortens for closer control. As the actual condition moves farther from the set point, the pulse duration lengthens.

Proportional control gives continuous or incremental changes in output signal to position an electrical actuator or controlled device.

Pneumatic Receiver-Controllers

Pneumatic receiver-controllers are normally combined with pneumatic elements that use a mechanical force or position reaction to the sensed variable to obtain a variable-output air pressure. Control is usually proportional, but other modes (e.g., proportional-plus-integral) can be used. These controllers are generally classified as nonrelay or relay, and as direct-acting or reverse-acting.

The nonrelay (single-pipe) pneumatic controller uses low-volume output. A relay (two-pipe) pneumatic controller actuates a relay device that amplifies the air volume available for control. The relay provides quicker response to a variable change.

Direct-acting controllers increase the output signal as the controlled variable increases. Reverse-acting controllers increase the output signal as the controlled variable decreases. For example, a reverse-acting pneumatic thermostat increases output pressure when the measured temperature drops and decreases output pressure when the measured temperature rises.

Thermostats

Thermostats combine sensing and control functions in a single device. Microprocessor-based thermostats have many of the following features.

- An **occupied/unoccupied** or **dual-temperature room thermostat** controls at another set-point temperature at night. It may be indexed (changed from occupied to unoccupied) individually or in a group by a manual switch, an electronic occupancy sensor, or time switch from a remote point. Some electric units have an individual clock and switch built into the thermostat.
- A **pneumatic day/night thermostat** uses a two-pressure air supply system (often 13 and 17 psig, or 15 and 20 psig). Changing pressure at a central point from one value to the other actuates switching devices in the thermostat that index it from occupied to unoccupied or vice versa.
- A **heating/cooling** or **summer/winter thermostat** can have its action reversed and its set point changed by indexing. It is used to actuate control devices (e.g., valves, dampers) that regulate a heating source at one time and a cooling source at another.
- A **multistage thermostat** operates two or more successive steps in sequence.
- A **submaster thermostat** has its set point raised or lowered over a predetermined range in accordance with variations in output from a master controller. The master controller can be a thermostat, manual switch, pressure controller, or similar device.
- A **dead-band thermostat** has a wide differential over which the thermostat remains neutral, requiring neither heating nor cooling. This differential may be adjustable up to 10°F. The thermostat then controls to maximum or minimum output over a small differential at the end of each dead band (Figure 16).

2.4 AUXILIARY CONTROL DEVICES

Auxiliary control devices for electric systems include the following:

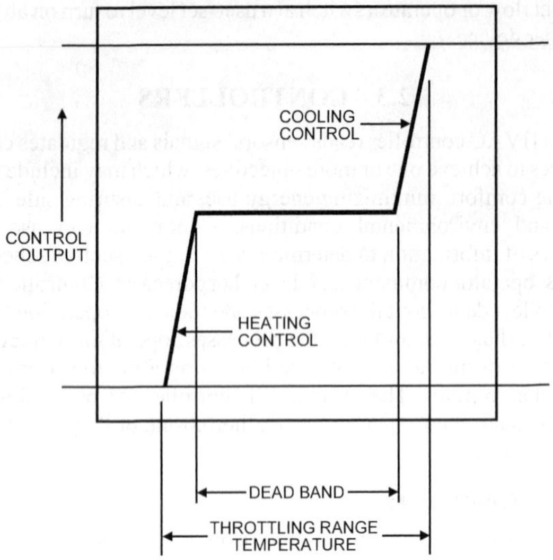

Fig. 16 Dead-Band Thermostat

Relays

Relays provide a means for one electrical source to switch to a different electrical circuit. The switched voltage may be the same or different. Relay configurations include several variations:

- Shape and number of electrical connections
- Optional override button and/or LED indication
- Base or panel mount
- Electromechanical or solid state
- Normally open or normally closed (or both)
- Latching or nonlatching

Electric relays can be used to start and stop electric heaters, burners, compressors, fans, pumps, or other apparatus for which the electrical load is too large to be handled directly by the controller. Other uses include time-delay and circuit-interlocking safety applications. Form letters are part of an industry consensus that defines the arrangement of contacts for relays and switches. The three most common types in HVAC are forms A, B, and C. Form A relays are single pole, single throw, normally open (SPST-NO). Form B relays are single pole, single throw, normally closed (SPST-NC). Form C relays are single pole, double throw (SPDT) and can be either normally open or normally closed, so control panels can be built using all form C (SPDT) relays. In small sizes, the added cost of the second contact is insignificant. As current ratings go up, forms A and B become more cost effective.

Time-delay relays, similar to control relays, include an adjustable time delay that is set using dipswitches and/or a knob. The device is either a delay-on-make (*on* delay) or delay-on-break (*off* delay). The time delay is either in seconds to minutes or minutes to hours. Uses include preventing multiple pieces of equipment from starting simultaneously and overloading the electrical supply, ensuring equipment completes its warm-up cycle, preventing triggering of nuisance alarms during short transitions (e.g., before equipment has reached enough speed for its status sensors to activate), and temporarily changing the mode of operation (e.g., thermostat override timer during unoccupied hours).

Power relays handle high-power switching of electrical loads in motor control centers and lighting control applications. They may be of open-frame construction or enclosed, single or multiple pole, panel mounted or field mounted, with or without auxiliary contacts.

Solid-state relays are optically isolated relays used to switch voltages up to 600 V with high amperage loads using a form A contact. They have a high surge dielectric strength, and reverse voltage protection. They operate using an input voltage of 4 to 32 V DC. These devices are easily affected by high temperatures and induced currents, but their life expectancy, measured in number of operations, is much greater than that of electromechanical switches, so they are used wherever switching every few minutes or seconds is required, as in pulse-width modulation (PWM) controls.

Control relay sockets are used with control relays to terminate all the wires that need to be connected to the relay. They may have either blade- or pin-type terminals. Sockets make wiring easier (without the relay getting in the way), provide a way to ensure equipment is not started until the system is commissioned, and allow relay replacement without redoing the wiring terminations.

Equipment Status

Auxiliary contacts are sometimes used to determine equipment status. The auxiliary contacts close when the starter's contactor closes, so they do not account for broken belts, couplings, or wires; locked rotors; flow obstructions; or missing power.

Differential pressure switches are used for status indication for air filters, fans, and pumps. Additionally, they can be used to provide flow and level status and in safety circuits to protect system components.

Current switches are current-sensing relays used to monitor the status of electrical devices. Typically, they have one or more adjustable current set points. They should be adjusted at start-up so that if the fan or pump motor coupling breaks, the current switch does not indicate *on* status.

Paddle switches indicate flow of water or air and are used to sense the status of pumps and fans.

Equipment with embedded controls such as boilers, chillers, terminal units, and variable-speed pumps and fans usually provide their status through contacts and over serial communication.

Limit switches convert mechanical motion into a switching action. Common applications include valve and damper position and proximity feedback.

Other Switches

Manual switches, either two-position or multiple-position with single or multiple poles, are used to switch equipment from one state to another.

Auxiliary switches on electric or electronic equipment, such as valve and damper actuators, sensors, and variable-speed controls are used to select a sequence or mode of operation.

Moisture switches are used to detect moisture in drain pains, under raised floors, and in containment areas to shut down equipment and/or alert operators before flooding or damage occurs.

Level switches (float, conductive probe, or ultrasonic) are used to start/stop equipment, either in normal operation, such as supply or drain pumps, or in protection circuits, as in boilers or chillers.

Time Switches

Time switches (mechanical or electronic) turn electrical loads on and off, based on a 24 h/7 day or 24 h/365 day schedule.

Analog time switches are set manually to control an electrical load. They have either normally open or normally closed contacts. Timing is either in minutes or hours, and may have an override hold feature to keep the load on or off continuously.

Digital time switches are set manually to control an electrical load and have either normally open or normally closed contacts. The timing function is either in minutes or hours, and sometimes combines a regular weekly calendar with a yearly exceptions calendar used for holidays and other special events. They may have an override hold feature to keep the load on or off continuously, and a flash or beeper option to notify the operator that the load will be turning off shortly.

Transducers

Transducers are devices that convert one signal (sensor reading or command) into a signal of another type that conveys some or all of the original information. Examples include pressure into voltage, voltage into current, voltage into contact closure, and rotational speed into pulse frequency. Transducers may convert proportional input to either proportional or two-position output.

The **electronic-to-pneumatic transducer (EPT** is used in many applications. It converts a proportional electronic output signal into a proportional pneumatic signal and can be used to combine electronic and pneumatic control components to form a control loop (Figure 17). Electronic components are used for sensing and signal conditioning, whereas pneumatic components are used for actuation. The electronic controller can be either analog or digital.

The EPT presents a special option for retrofit applications. An existing HVAC system with pneumatic controls can be retrofitted with electronic sensors and controllers while retaining the existing pneumatic actuators (Figure 18).

Signal transducers to change one standard signal into another. Variables usually transformed include voltage [0 to 10, 0 to 5, 2 to 10 V (DC)], current (4 to 20 mA), resistance (0 to 135 Ω), pressure (3 to 15, 0 to 20 psig), phase cut voltage [0 to 20 V (DC)], pulse-width modulation, and time duration pulse. Signal transducers allow use of an existing control device in a retrofit application.

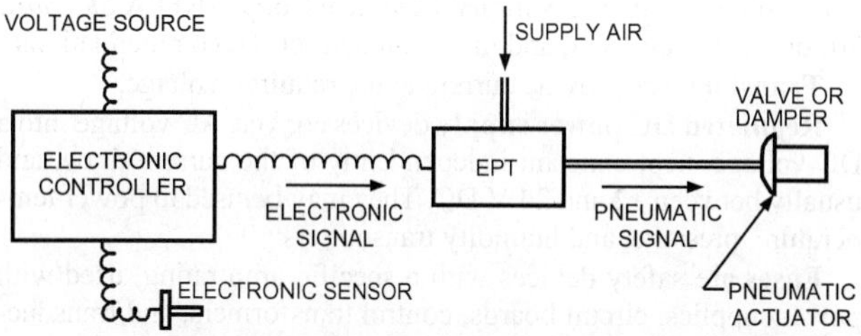

Fig. 17 Electronic and Pneumatic Control Components Combined with Electronic-to-Pneumatic Transducer (EPT)

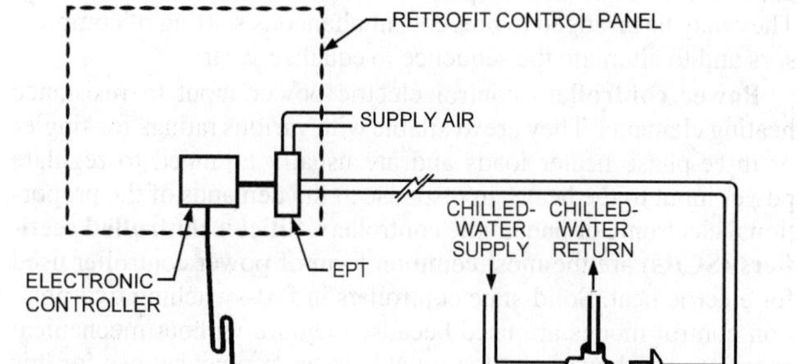

Fig. 18 Retrofit of Existing Pneumatic Control with Electronic Sensors and Controllers

Other Auxiliary Control Devices

Variable-frequency drives (VFDs) control AC motors' speed by using electronics to vary the frequency and voltage amplitude of the electrical input power. VFDs are commonly applied to fans, heat recovery wheels, pumps, and compressors.

Occupancy sensors are used to automatically adjust controlled variables (e.g., lighting, ventilation rate, temperature) based on occupancy.

Potentiometers are used for manual positioning of proportional control devices, for remote set-point adjustment of electronic controllers, and for position feedback.

Smoke detectors sense smoke and other combustion products in air moving through HVAC ducts. Through sampling tubes, selected based on duct size, they test air moving in the duct. For duct applications, using only photoelectric sensor heads is recommended. The device typically has two alarm contacts, used to shut down the associated equipment and provide remote indication, and a trouble contact, which monitors incoming power and removal of the detector head. Where a fire alarm system is installed, the smoke detectors must be listed for use with the fire alarm system. Addressable fire alarm systems may use a separate programmable relay for fan shutdown rather than a hard-wired connection to the detector.

Transient voltage surge suppressors (TVSSs), formerly called **lightning arrestors**, protect communication lines and critical power lines between buildings or at building entrance vaults against high-voltage transients caused by VFDs, motors, transmitters, and lightning. To be effective, they must be grounded to a grounding rod in compliance with the National Electrical Code® (NFPA *Standard* 70) or local equivalent, and the manufacturer's recommendations.

Transformers provide current at the required voltage.

Regulated DC power supply devices convert AC voltage into a DC voltage, kept constant independently of the current draw, and usually between 12 and 24 V DC. They may be used to power temperature, pressure, and humidity transmitters.

Fuses are safety devices with a specific amp rating, used with power supplies, circuit boards, control transformers, and transducers. They may be rated for either high or low inrush currents, and are available in slow-blow or fast-acting models.

Step controllers operate several switches in sequence using a proportional electric or pneumatic input signal. They are commonly used to control several steps of heating or refrigeration capacity. They may be arranged to prevent simultaneous starting of compressors and to alternate the sequence to equalize wear.

Power controllers control electric power input to resistance heating elements. They are available with various ratings for single- or three-phase heater loads and are usually arranged to regulate power input to the heater in response to the demands of the proportional electronic or pneumatic controllers. **Silicon controlled rectifiers (SCRs)** are the most common form of power controller used for electric heat. Solid-state controllers in fast-switching two-position control modes are used because they are without mechanical contacts, which wear out too quickly to be of practical use for this application, and can arc when power is applied or removed.

High-temperature limits are safety devices that shut down equipment when the temperature exceeds the high limit set point. They are typically set at 125 to 150°F for heating air applications and 195 to 205°F for hot-water applications. A manual or automatic reset reactivates the device once the condition has cleared.

Low-temperature limits for ducts are used to protect chilled-water and preheat coils from freezing. They typically have a 20 ft long vapor-charged sensing element, set at 35°F, that shuts down equipment when the temperature in any 12 or 18 in. section falls below its set point. They may be manually or automatically reset. The device must be mounted parallel to the coil tubes with capillary mounting clips for proper measurement. Limits may be either SPST or double-pole, double-throw (DPDT), with the second contact used to alert operators that the device has tripped.

Three- and **five-valve manifolds** protect water differential pressure sensors from overpressurization during installation, start-up, shutdown, system testing, and maintenance. Three-valve manifolds are comprised of two isolation valves and a bypass valve. A five-valve manifold includes two additional valves to allow online calibration. Depending on the application, snubbers may be required, as well.

Snubbers, made of brass or stainless steel, stop shocks and pulsations caused by fluid hammering and system surges. Two types of pressure snubbers are used in HVAC applications: porous and piston. A porous snubber has no moving parts and uses a porous material to stop device damage. A piston snubber uses a moving piston inside a tube that moves up and down to stop device damage and push away any sediment or scale that may clog the system's monitoring devices. Depending on the application, the type of piston to be used may need to be specified.

Steam pigtail siphons protect pressure transmitters from the high temperature of steam. They are typically made from steel or stainless steel of a specific length with a loop. The temperature of the medium being monitored determines the length and material. Most pressure devices have an operating temperature range of 0 to 200°F.

Thermostat guards are plastic or metal covers that protect switches, thermostat controllers, and sensors from damage, tampering, and unauthorized adjustment.

Enclosures/control panels may be used indoors or outdoors to protect equipment and people. In North America, enclosures are rated by the National Electrical Manufacturers Association (NEMA *Standard* 250) and Electrical and Electronic Manufacturer Association of Canada (EEMAC); elsewhere, they receive an ingress protection (IP) rating, which describes their degree of resistance to ingress of objects, dust, and water (IEC *Standard* 60529).

Pilot lights are replaceable incandescent or light-emitting diode (LED) lights that indicate the status or mode of operation of mechanical and electrical equipment. They are panel-mounted, and may be round or flat, of various colors, and powered using either AC or DC power. They are typically installed in an enclosure rated for the application under NEMA *Standard* 250, or with an appropriate IP rating.

Strobes use a high-intensity xenon flash tube to generate a high-intensity light that is visible in all directions. If this device is used in a safety application (e.g., refrigeration monitoring), in the United States, it must comply with UL *Standard* 1971 and the Americans with Disabilities Act (ADA), Title III; in Canada, with ULC *Standard* S526; elsewhere, it must meet requirements of British Standards Institution (BSI) *Standard* BS EN 54-23.

Horns provide an audible tone with a specified loudness rated in decibels (dB), and are mounted in a panel or junction box. The tone may be continuous, warbled, short beeps, or long beeps. The tone should be at least 10 dB above the ambient noise level in the area that the device is mounted. The operating voltage may be either DC or AC. When used in a life safety application, it must comply with NFPA *Standard* 72 or BSI *Standard* BS EN 54-3.

3. COMMUNICATION NETWORKS FOR BUILDING AUTOMATION SYSTEMS

A **building automation system (BAS)** is a centralized control and/or monitoring system for many or all building systems (e.g., HVAC, electrical, life safety, security). A BAS may link information from control systems actuated by different technologies.

One important characteristic of a BAS is the ability to share information. Information is transferred between (1) controllers to coordinate their action, (2) controllers and building operator interfaces to monitor and command systems, and (3) controllers and other computers for off-line calculation. This information is typically shared over communication networks. A BAS nearly always involves at least one network; often, two or more networks are interconnected to form an **internetwork**.

3.1 COMMUNICATION PROTOCOLS

A communication protocol is a set of rules that define exchange of information between devices on a communication network. These rules define the content and format of messages to be exchanged, what information it contains, how it is routed/received, what error detection and recovery is used, and what response is given. They also describe the addressing and naming used to identify devices as well as the interaction between them, how to respond to new devices, what to do when devices fail, and when/how often a device is allowed to initiate or respond to a new message.

Layering allows portions of the technology to be used by a wide variety of applications, and thus lowers the cost because of economies of scale. For example, one of the most widely used computer communication standards is the Institute of Electrical and Electronics Engineers (IEEE) *Standard* 802.3 (Ethernet). Ethernet is a general-purpose mechanism for exchanging information across a local area network (LAN). Ethernet networks are used for many applications, including e-mail, file transfer, web browsing, and building control systems. However, two devices on the same Ethernet may be completely unable to communicate because Ethernet does not define the content of messages to be exchanged.

Open protocols for building automation systems facilitate communication among devices from different suppliers. Although there is no commonly accepted definition of *openness*, IEEE *Standard* 802.3 defines three classes of protocols:

- **Standard protocol.** Published and controlled by a standards body.
- **Public protocol.** Published but controlled by a private organization.
- **Private protocol.** Unpublished; use and specification controlled by a private organization. Examples include the proprietary communications used by many building automation devices.

Multivendor communication is possible with any of these three classes, but the challenges vary. Specifying a standard or widely used public protocol can improve the chances for a competitive bidding process and provide economic options for future expansions. However, specifying a common protocol does not ensure that the requirement for interoperability is met. It is also necessary to specify the desired interaction between devices.

3.2 OSI NETWORK MODEL

ISO *Standard* 7498-1 presents a seven-layer model of information exchange called the Open Systems Interconnection (OSI) Reference Model (Figure 19).

Most computer networks, especially open networks, are based on this reference model. The layers can be thought of as steps in the translation of a message from something with meaning at the application layer, to something measurable at the physical layer, and back to meaningful information at the application layer.

The full seven-layer model does not apply to every network, but it is still used to describe the aspects that fit. When describing DDC networks that use the same technology throughout the system, the seven-layer model is relatively unimportant. For systems that use various technologies at different points in the network, the model helps to describe where and how the pieces are bound together.

7 Application Layer	Window between applications and network.
6 Presentation Layer	Coordinates representation of information between different applications.
5 Session Layer	Synchronizes and structures exchange of data messages between specific users.
4 Transport Layer	Converts data messages into packets for transmission, and converts received packets into messages. Responsible for data message error recognition and recovery, and ensures reliable delivery of messages.
3 Network Layer	Addressing and routing packets independent of media and topology.
2 Data Link Layer	Responsible for point-to-point reliability. Media access. Representation of bits and bytes as physical signals. Organizes bits into data packets.
1 Physical Layer	Electrical characteristics of devices and conductors.

Fig. 19 OSI Reference Model

3.3 NETWORK STRUCTURE

BAS Three-Tier Network Architecture

Often, a single BAS applies different network technologies at different points in the system. For example, a relatively low-speed, inexpensive network with relatively primitive functions may link a group of room controllers to a supervisory controller, while a faster, more sophisticated network links the supervisory controller to its peers and to one or more operator workstations. Figure 20 demonstrates the representation and interaction of a multitier BAS system architecture as described in ASHRAE *Guideline* 13-2015. The architecture model has three tiers. Tier 1 is the enterprise-level information technology (IT) network and provides access to user interfaces, dashboards, kiosks, and application interfaces. Tier 2 is the building network infrastructure and includes the building control network connectivity to the building IT network. Tier 3 is the control network and the associated controllers, equipment, sensors, and actuators.

The opposite extreme is completely **flat network architecture**, which links all devices through the same network. A flat architecture is more viable in small systems than in large ones, because economic constraints typically dictate that low-cost (and therefore low-speed) networks be used to connect field-level controllers. Because of their performance limitations, these networks do not scale well to large numbers of devices. As the cost of electronics for communication drops, flatter networks become more feasible.

Network structure can affect

- Opportunities for expansion of a BAS.
- Reliability and failure modes. It may be appropriate to separate sections of a network to isolate failures.
- How devices load the information-carrying capacity of the network. It can isolate one busy branch from the rest of the system, or isolate branches from the high-speed backbone.
- How and where information is displayed to operating personnel; web servers accessible through the Internet make BAS information available to anyone, anywhere, who has a standard web browser and access rights to view the server pages.
- System cost, because it determines the mix of low- and high-speed devices.
- System data security and access control.

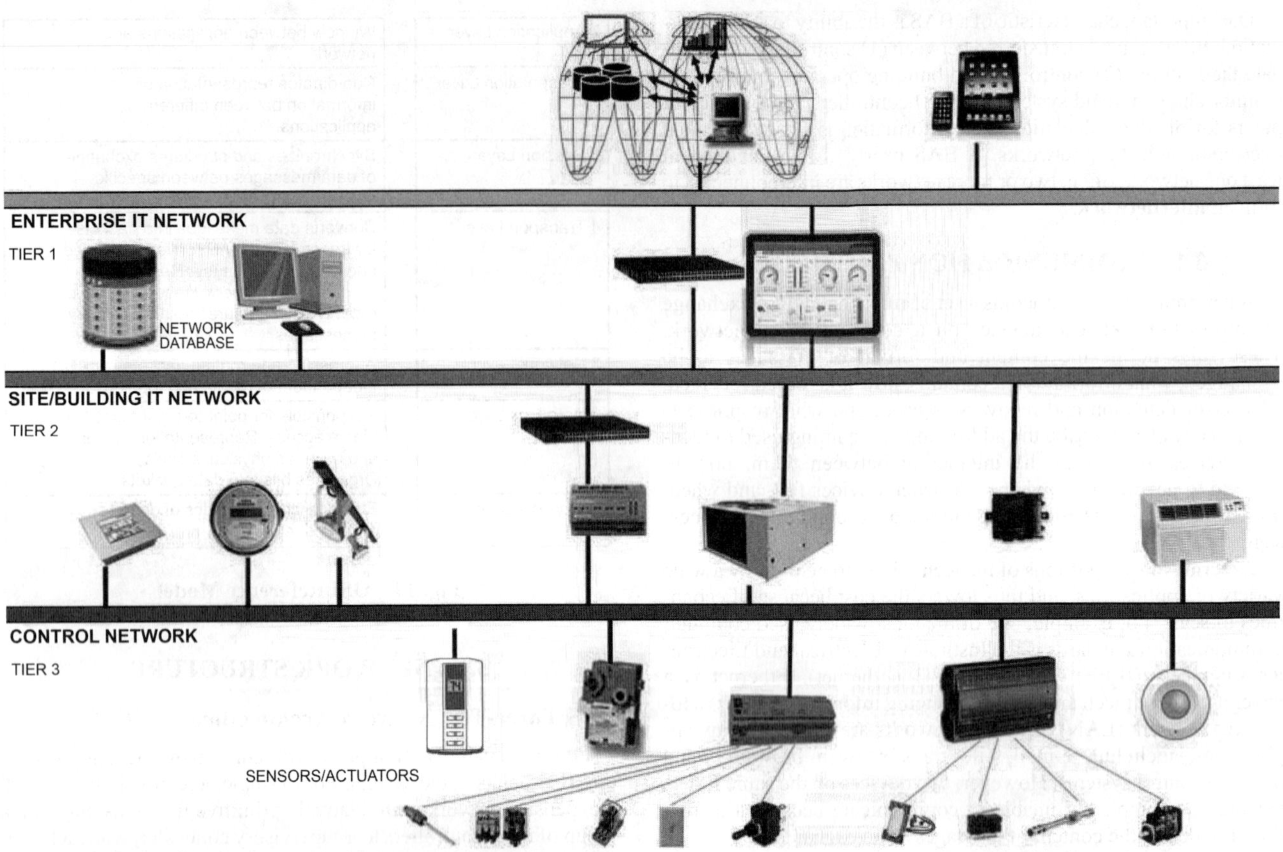

Fig. 20 Hierarchical Network for Three-Tier System Architecture

The relative merits of one structure versus another depend on the communication functions required, hardware and software available for the task, and cost. For a given job, there is probably more than one suitable structure. Product capabilities change quickly. Engineers who choose to specify network structure must be aware of new technologies to take advantage of the most cost-effective solutions.

Connections Between BAS Networks and Other Computer Networks

Some BAS networks use other networks to connect segments of the BAS. This occurs

- Within a building, using the information technology network
- Between buildings, using an intranet or the Internet
- Between buildings, using telephone lines, wireless links, or fiber optics

In each case, the link between BAS segments must be considered part of the BAS network when evaluating function, security, and performance. The link also raises new issues. The connecting segment is likely to be outside the control of the owner of the BAS, which could affect availability of service. Traffic and bandwidth issues may have to be addressed with the link administrator.

Using a dial-up connection to interact with a remote building or to serve a remote operator requires consideration of which segment may dial the other, what circumstances trigger the call, and security implications. Handling interbuilding communication through intranet or Internet connections, with the operator interface provided by a web browser communicating with a web server, has largely replaced dial-up connections.

Transmission Media

The transmission medium is the foundation of the network. It is usually, but not always, cable. The cable may be plenum rated or non-plenum rated, depending on the installation application. Where physical cable connection is not possible or practical, devices may transfer information using wireless technologies, such as radio waves or infrared light.

RS-485 is the data link layer standard most commonly used in BAS for communications inside a building. It works over a single shielded twisted pair, 18 to 24 gage, and can reach distances of up to 1500 ft between repeaters and up to 120 devices per segment. It has no polarity (i.e., no positive and negative wires), which reduces wiring errors, and in most cases is optically isolated at the controllers, allowing for different power sources without risk of short circuits.

ANSI/TIA/EIA *Standard* 568-B.1 provides IT cabling specifications for commercial buildings. This cabling is used for computers and telephone networks and can also be used for low-level BAS, access, security, or fire detection systems, but close work between the BAS and IT design and execution teams is required. The potential for third-party devices halting all network traffic discourages its use for control and security applications, as does the location of outlets prescribed in the standard (in occupied spaces instead of plenums and mechanical rooms where the controllers are). Also, IT network administrators are sometimes reluctant to allow connection of unfamiliar devices they cannot configure.

Cable length. Maximum length varies with cable type, transmission speed, and protocol.

100 Ω Balanced Twisted-Pair Communications Outlet/Connector. Each four-pair cable terminates on an eight-position modular jack, and all unshielded twisted-pair (UTP) and screened twisted-pair (ScTP) telecommunications outlets must meet the requirements of IEC *Standard* 60603-7, as well as ANSI/TIA/EIA *Standard* 568-B.2 and the terminal marking and mounting requirements of ANSI/TIA/EIA *Standard* 570-B.

Twisted-Pair Copper Cable. A twisted-pair cable consists of multiple twisted pairs (typically 24 gage) of wire covered by an overall sheath or jacket. Varying the number of twists for each pair relative to the other pairs in the cable can greatly reduce crosstalk (interference between signals on different pairs).

Screened twisted-pair (ScTP) cable is similar in construction to UTP data cabling, except that ScTP has a foil shield between the conductors and outer jacket, as well as a drain wire used to minimize interference-related problems. ScTP cable is preferred over UTP cable in environments where high immunity and/or low emissions are critical. It also allows less crosstalk than UTP. However, ScTP requires more labor-intensive installation, and any break or improper grounding of the shield reduces its overall effectiveness.

Category 3 cable connects hardware and patch cords that are rated to a maximum frequency of 16 MHz. This cable is rated up to 16 megabits per second. This category is usually the lowest level of cable installed and is used mainly for voice and low-speed networks.

Category 5 cable connects hardware and patch cords that are rated to a maximum frequency of 100 MHz. The actual data transmission rate varies with the compression scheme used. Category 5 was defined in ANSI/TIA/EIA *Standard* 568-A, but is no longer recognized in the new ANSI/TIA/EIA *Standard* 568-B.1.

Category 5e cable connects hardware and patch cords that are rated to a maximum frequency of 100 MHz. The actual data transmission rate varies with the compression or encoding scheme used. Category 5e, the lowest category recommended for data installations, is defined by ANSI/TIA/EIA *Standards* 568-B.1 and B.2. This cable is rated up to 100 megabits per second.

Category 6 cable connects hardware and patch cords that are rated to a maximum frequency of 250 MHz, though the actual data transmission rate varies with the compression scheme used. UTP or STP cable is currently the most common medium. This cable is rated up to 1 gigabit per second.

Category 6e cable connects hardware and patch cords that are rated to a maximum frequency of 250 MHz, though actual data transmission rate varies with the compression scheme used. With all Category 6 systems, an eight-position jack is mandatory in the work area.

Category 7 cable connects hardware and patch cords that are rated to a maximum frequency of 600 MHz, though actual data transmission rate varies with the compression scheme used. This category is still in development and uses a braided shield surrounding all four foil-shielded pairs to reduce noise and interference. Depending on future technological developments, the current RJ-45 connector will not be used in Category 7.

Fiber-Optic Cable. Fiber-optic cable uses glass or plastic fibers to transfer data in the form of light pulses, which are typically generated by either a laser or an LED. Fiber-optic cable systems are classified as either single-mode fiber or multimode fiber systems. Table 1 compares their characteristics.

Light in a fiber-optic system loses less energy than electrical signals traveling through copper and has no capacitance. This translates into greater transmission distances and dramatically higher data transfer rates, which impose no limits on a BAS. Fiber optics also have exceptional noise immunity. However, the necessary conversions between light-based signaling and electricity-based computing make fiber optics more expensive per device, which sometimes offsets its advantages.

Structured Cabling. ANSI/TIA/EIA *Standard* 568 allows cable planning and installation to begin before the network engineering is finalized. It supports both voice and data. The standard was written for the telecommunications industry, but cabling is gaining recognition as building infrastructure, and the standard is being applied to BAS networks as well.

Table 1 Comparison of Fiber Optic Technology

	Multimode Fiber	Single-Mode Fiber
Light source	LED	Laser
Cable designation (core/cladding diameter)	62.6/125	8.3/125
Transmission distance	6600 ft	98,000 ft
Data rate	>10 gigabit/s and increasing	Even higher
Relative cost	Less per connection, more per data rate	More per connection, less per data rate

ANSI/TIA/EIA *Standard* 568-B specifies **star topology** (each device individually cabled to a hub) because connectivity is more robust and management is simpler than for busses and rings. If the wires in a leg are shorted, only that leg fails, making fault isolation easier; with a bus, all drops would fail.

The basic structure specified is a **backbone**, which typically runs from floor to floor in a building and possibly between buildings. **Horizontal cabling** runs between the distribution frames on each floor and the information outlets in the work areas.

Wireless Networks. The rapid maturity of everyday wireless technologies, now widely used for mobile phones, Internet access, and even barcode replacement, has tremendously increased the ability to collect information from the physical world. Wireless technologies offer significant opportunities in sensors and controls for building operation, especially in reducing the cost of installing data acquisition and control devices. Installation costs typically represent 20 to 80% of the total cost of a sensor and control point in any HVAC system, so reducing or eliminating the cost of installation can have a dramatic effect on the overall installed system cost. Low-cost wireless sensors and control systems also make it economical to use more sensors, thereby establishing highly energy-efficient building operations and demand responsiveness that enhance the electric grid reliability.

Wireless sensors and control networks consist of sensor and control devices that are connected to a network using radio-frequency (RF) or optical (infrared) signals. Devices can communicate bidirectionally (i.e., transmitting and receiving) or one way (transmitting only). Most RF products transmit in the industrial, scientific, or medical frequency bands, which are set aside by the Federal Communication Commission (FCC) for use without an FCC license. Wireless sensor networks have different requirements than computer networks and, thus, different network topologies, and separate communication protocols have evolved for them. The simplest is the **point-to-point topology**, in which two nodes communicate directly with each other. The **point-to-multipoint** or **star topology** is an extension of the point-to-point configuration in which many nodes communicate with a central receiving or gateway node. In either topology, sensor nodes might have pure transmitters, which provide one-way communication only, or transceivers, which allow two-way communication and verification of the receipt of messages. Gateways provide a means to convert and pass data between protocols (e.g., from a wireless sensor network protocol to the wired Ethernet protocol).

The communication range of the point-to-point and star topologies is limited by the maximum communication range between the sensor node (from which the measured data originates) and the receiver node. This range can be extended by using repeaters, which receive transmissions from sensor nodes and then retransmit them, usually at higher power than the original transmissions. In the **mesh network topology**, each sensor node includes a transceiver that can communicate directly with any other node within its communication range. These networks connect many devices to many other devices, thus forming a mesh of nodes in which signals are transmitted between distant points via multiple hops. This approach decreases the distance over which each node must communicate and reduces each node's power use substantially, making them more compatible with onboard power sources such as batteries (Capehardt 2005).

3.4 SPECIFYING BUILDING AUTOMATION SYSTEM NETWORKS

Specifying a building automation system includes specifying a platform comprising the following components: field device (e.g., sensors, actuators), controllers (e.g., equipment and/or supervisory), and information management and network communication (e.g., security, diagnostics, maintenance). Many technologies can deliver many performance levels at many different prices. Building automation system design requires assessing the owner's risk tolerance against the proposed project budget. In some cases, new equipment must interface with existing devices, which may limit networking options. ASHRAE *Guideline* 13-2015 provides detailed information on how to specify a building automation system.

Communication Tasks

Determining network performance requirements means identifying and quantifying the communication functions required. Ehrlich and Pittel (1999) identified the following five basic communication tasks necessary to establish network requirements.

Data Exchange. What data passes between which devices? What control and optimization data passes between controllers? What update rates are required? What data does an operator need to reach? How much delay is acceptable in retrieving values? What update rates are required on "live" data displays? (Within one system, answers may vary according to data use.) Which set points and control parameters do operators need to adjust over the network?

Alarms and Events. Where do alarms originate? Where are they logged and displayed? How much delay is acceptable? Where are they acknowledged? What information must be delivered along with the alarm? (Depending on system design, alarm messages may be passed over the network along with the alarms.) Where are alarm summary reports required? How and where do operators need to adjust alarm limits, etc.?

Schedules. For HVAC equipment that runs on schedules, where can the schedules be read? Where can they be modified?

Trends. Where does trend data originate? Where is it stored? How much will be transmitted? Where is it displayed and processed? Which user interfaces can set and modify trend collection parameters?

Network Management. What network diagnostic and maintenance functions are required at which user interfaces? Data access and security functions may be handled as network management functions.

Bushby et al. (1999) refer to the same five communication tasks as **interoperability areas** and list many more specific considerations in each area. ASHRAE *Guideline* 13 also provides more detailed information that is helpful.

3.5 APPROACHES TO INTEROPERABILITY

Many approaches to interoperability have been proposed and applied, each with varying degrees of success under various circumstances. The field changes quickly as product lines emerge and standards develop and gain acceptance. The building automation world continues to evaluate options project by project.

Typically, an interoperable system uses one of two approaches: standard protocols or special-purpose gateways. With a standard, the supplier is responsible for compliance with the standard; the system specifier or integrator is responsible for interoperation. With a gateway, the supplier takes responsibility for interoperation. Where the job requires interoperation with existing equipment, gateways may be the only solution available. Bushby (1998) addressed this issue and some of the limitations associated with gateways. To date, interoperability by any method requires solid field engineering and capable system integration; the issues extend well beyond the selection of a communication protocol.

Table 2 Some Standard Communication Protocols Applicable to BAS

Protocol	Definition
BACnet®	ANSI/ASHRAE *Standard* 135-2012, EN/ ISO *Standard* 16484-5:2013
LonTalk	ANSI/CEA *Standard* 709.1
PROFIBUS FMS	EN 50170:2000 Volume 2
Konnex	EN 50090
MODBUS	Modbus Application Protocol Specification V1.1
ZigBee®	ZigBee® Commercial Building Automation Profile Specification

Standard Protocols

Table 2 lists some applicable standard protocols that have been used in BAS. Their different characteristics make some more suited to particular tasks than others. PROFIBUS (www.profibus.com) and MODBUS (www.modbus.org) were designed for low-cost industrial process control and automated manufacturing applications, but they have been applied to BAS. LonTalk defines a LAN technology but not messages that are to be exchanged for BAS applications. BACnet® or implementers' agreements, such as those made by members of LonMark International, are necessary to achieve interoperability with LonTalk devices. Konnex evolved from the European Installation Bus (EIB) and several other European protocols developed for residential applications, including multifamily housing. ZigBee® is an open communications standard for wireless devices developed by the ZigBee Alliance. Annex O of the BACnet standard (ANSI/ASHRAE *Standard* 135-2013) specifies using BACnet messaging with services described in the ZigBee specification. Martocci (2008) describes how a wireless ZigBee network can be integrated into a BACnet network.

BACnet is the only standard protocol developed specifically for commercial BAS applications. BACnet has been adopted as a national standard in the United States, Korea, and Japan, as a European standard, and as a world standard (EN/ISO *Standard* 16484-5). BACnet was designed to be used with non-BACnet networks. Principles of mapping are documented in Annex H of ANSI/ASHRAE *Standard* 135-2012.

Gateways and Interfaces

Rather than conforming to a published standard, a supplier can design a specific device to exchange data with another specific device. This typically requires cooperation between two manufacturers. In some cases, it can be simpler and more cost-effective than for both manufacturers to conform to an agreed-upon standard. The device can be either custom-designed or off the shelf. In either case, the communication tasks must be carefully specified to ensure that the gateway performs as needed.

Choosing a system that supports a variety of gateways may be a way to maintain a flexible position as products and standards continue to develop.

4. SPECIFYING BUILDING AUTOMATION SYSTEMS

Successful building automation system (BAS) installation depends in part on a clear description (specification) of what is required to meet the customer's needs. The specification should include descriptions of the products desired, or of the performance and features expected. Needed points or data objects should be listed. A control schematic shows the layout of each system to be controlled, including instrumentation and input/output objects and any hard-wired interlocks.

Writing a descriptive network specification requires knowledge of the details of network technology. To succeed with any specification, the designer must articulate the end user's needs. Typically, performance-based specification is the best value for the customer (Ehrlich and Pittel 1999).

The sequences of operation describe how the system should function and are the designer's primary method of communication to the control system programmer. A sequence should be written for each system to be controlled. In writing a sequence, be sure to describe all operational modes and ensure that all input/output (I/O) devices needed to implement the sequence are shown on the object list and drawings.

Annex A of ASHRAE *Guideline* 13-2015 shows a sample specification outline for a building automaton system. Information on specifying building automaton systems is in *MasterFormat* (CSI 2004): Division 23, Section 23 09 00, or in Division 25. Additional information on specifying BAS controls and sample sequences of control for air-handling systems can be found in ASHRAE *Guideline* 13.

5. COMMISSIONING

Commissioning controls can refer either to the proper configuration and tuning of a controller or, more broadly, a standard process of quality assurance to ensure that owner's requirements are met, design intent is achieved, and staff is well prepared for operation and maintenance. Because individual pieces of equipment are often tied together into larger systems, and sequences of operation on these systems (affecting safety, indoor air quality, comfort, and energy efficiency) are implemented through controls configuration and programming, building performance is highly dependent on the quality of controls design and implementation.

A successful control system requires proper start-up, testing, and documentation, not merely adjustment of a few parameters (set points and throttling ranges) and a few quick checks.

Because of the impact on building performance, controls have become a significant focus of the building commissioning process. The typical BAS system should be commissioned directly using an experienced, unbiased third party; this is an effective way to test and document HVAC system performance.

The commissioning process requires coordination between the owner, designers, and contractors, and is most effective when it begins before the start of design and continues for the life of the building. Issues are tracked and results are documented throughout the process. Design and construction specifications should include specific commissioning procedures. Review submittals for conformance to design. Check each control device to ensure that it is installed and connected according to approved drawings. Each connection should be verified, and all safeties and sequences tested. Performance assessment should continue after occupancy, especially for large equipment, to identify and address degradation over time. Chapter 43 of the 2015 *ASHRAE Handbook—HVAC Applications* and ASHRAE *Guideline* 1 explain more about commissioning.

Package controls of high-cost equipment (e.g., chillers, preassembled plants) or that may pose safety risks (e.g., boilers) should always be commissioned by factory-authorized service providers. Because factory-supplied equipment and controls are usually integrated into larger systems, some on-site commissioning is still appropriate.

5.1 TUNING

Systematic tuning of controllers improves performance of all controls and is particularly important for digital control. First, the controlled process should be controlled manually between various set points to evaluate the following questions:

- Is the process noisy (rapid fluctuations in controlled variable)?
- Is there appreciable hysteresis (backlash) in the actuator?
- How easy (or difficult) is it to maintain and change set point?
- In which operating region is the process most sensitive (highest gain)?

If the process cannot be controlled manually, the reason should be identified and corrected before the controller is tuned.

Tuning optimizes control parameters that determine steady-state and transient characteristics of the control system. HVAC processes are nonlinear, and characteristics change seasonally. Controllers tuned under one operating condition may become unstable as conditions change.

A well-tuned controller (1) minimizes steady-state error for set point, (2) responds with appropriate timing to disturbances, and (3) remains stable under all operating conditions. Tuning proportional controllers is a compromise between minimizing steady-state error and maintaining margins of stability. Proportional plus integral (PI) control minimizes this compromise because the integral action reduces steady-state error, and the proportional term determines the controller's response to disturbances.

As performance requirements have become more stringent, sequences of operation have become increasingly complex, and the task of tuning has also become more challenging. Some manufacturers now provide self-tuning routines to avoid the need for manual adjustment and help maintain performance with changing conditions.

Tuning Proportional, PI, and PID Controllers

Popular methods of determining proportional, PI, and PID controller tuning parameters include closed- and open-loop process identification methods and trial-and-error methods. For each method, carefully consider the resulting timing of system responses to avoid compromising safety or reducing the expected life of equipment. Two of the most widely used techniques for tuning these controllers are ultimate oscillation and first-order-plus-dead-time. There are many optimization calculations for these two techniques. The Ziegler-Nichols, which is given here, is well established.

Ultimate Oscillation (Closed-Loop) Method. The closed-loop method increases controller gain in proportional-only mode until the equipment continuously cycles after a set-point change (Figure 21, where $K_p = 40$). Proportional and integral terms are then computed from the cycle's period of oscillation and the K_p value that caused cycling. The ultimate oscillation method is as follows:

1. Adjust control parameters so that all are essentially off. This corresponds to a proportion band (gain) at its maximum (minimum), the integral time (repeats per minute) or integral gain to maximum (minimum), and derivative to its minimum.
2. Adjust manual output of the controller to give a measurement as close to midscale as possible.
3. Put controller in automatic.
4. Gradually increase proportional feedback (this corresponds to reducing the proportional band or increasing the proportional gain) until observed oscillations neither grow nor diminish in amplitude. If response saturates at either extreme, start over at Step 2 to obtain a stable response. If no oscillations are observed, change the set point and try again.

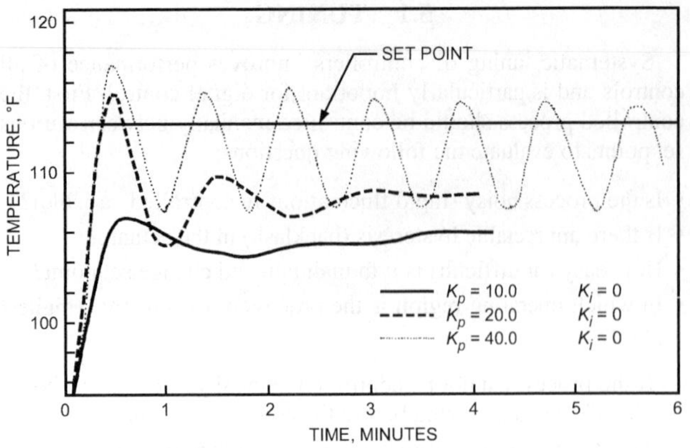

Fig. 21 Response of Discharge Air Temperature to Step Change in Set Points at Various Proportional Constants with No Integral Action

5. Record the proportional band as PB_u and the period of oscillations as T_u.
6. Use the recorded proportional band and oscillation period to calculate controller settings as follows:

Proportional only:

$$PB = 1.8(PB_u) \quad \text{percent} \tag{4}$$

Proportional plus integral (PI):

$$PB = 2.22(PB_u) \quad \text{percent} \tag{5}$$

$$T_i = 0.83T_u \quad \text{minute per repeat} \tag{6}$$

Proportional plus integral plus derivative (PID):

$$PB = 1.67(PB_u) \quad \text{percent} \tag{7}$$

$$T_i = 0.50T_u \quad \text{minute per repeat} \tag{8}$$

$$T_d = 0.125T_u \quad \text{minute} \tag{9}$$

First-Order-plus-Dead-Time (Open-Loop) Method. The open-loop method introduces a step change in input into the opened control loop. A graphical technique is used to estimate the process transfer function parameters. Proportional and integral terms are calculated from the estimated process parameters using a series of equations.

The value of the process variable must be recorded over time, and the dead time and time constant must be determined from it. This can be accomplished graphically, as seen in Figure 22. The first-order-plus-dead-time method is as follows:

1. Adjust controller manual output to give a midscale measurement.
2. Arrange to record the process variable over time.
3. Move the manual output of the controller by 10% as rapidly as possible to approximate a step change.
4. Record the value of the process variable over time until it reaches a new steady-state value.
5. Determine dead time and time constant.
6. Use dead time (TD) and time constant (TC) values to calculate PID values as follows:

$$\text{Gain} = \frac{\text{\% change in controlled variable}}{\text{\% change in control signal}} \tag{10}$$

Proportional only:

$$PB = \text{Gain}/(TC/TD) \tag{11}$$

Proportional plus integral (PI):

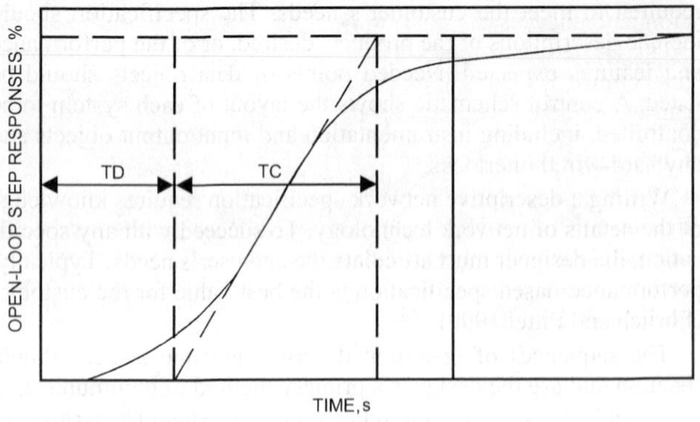

Fig. 22 Open-Loop Step Response Versus Time

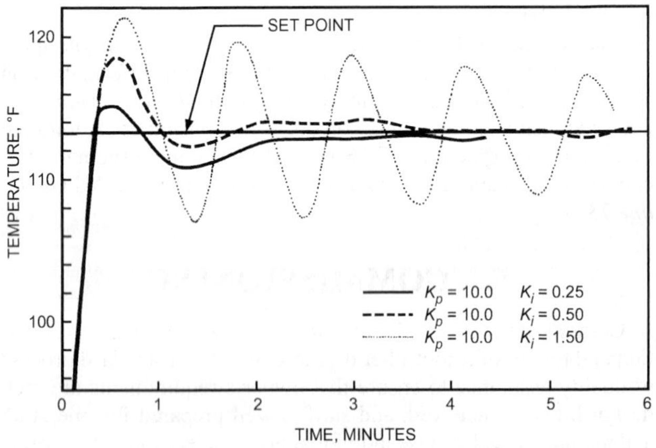

Fig. 23 Response of Discharge Air Temperature to Step Change in Set Points at Various Integral Constants with Fixed Proportional Constant

$$PB = 0.9(\text{Gain})/(TC/TD) \tag{12}$$

$$T_i = 3.33(TD) \tag{13}$$

Proportional-integral-derivative (PID):

$$PB = 1.2(\text{Gain})/(TC/TD) \tag{14}$$

$$T_i = 2(TD) \tag{15}$$

$$T_d = 0.5(TD) \tag{16}$$

Trial and Error. This method involves adjusting the gain of the proportion-only controller until the desired response to a set point is observed. Conservative tuning dictates that this response should have a small initial overshoot and quickly damp to steady-state conditions. Set-point changes should be made in the range where controller saturation, or output limit, is avoided. The integral term is then increased until changes in set point produce the same dynamic response as the controller under proportional control, but with the response now centered about the set point (Figure 23).

Tuning Digital Controllers

In tuning digital controllers, additional parameters may need to be specified. The digital controller sampling interval is critical because it can introduce harmonic distortion if not selected properly. This sampling interval is usually set at the factory and may not be adjustable. A controller sampling interval of about one-tenth of the controlled-process time constant usually provides adequate control. Many digital control algorithms include an error dead band to eliminate unnecessary control actions when the process is near set point. Hysteresis compensation is possible with digital controllers, but it must be carefully applied because overcompensation can cause continuous cycling of the control loop.

Computer Modeling of Control Systems

Each component of a control system can be represented by a transfer function, which is an idealized mathematical representation of the relationship between the input and output variables of the component. The transfer function must be sufficiently detailed to cover both the dynamic and static characteristics of the device. The dynamics are represented in the time domain by a differential equation. In environmental control, the transfer function of many of the components can be adequately described by a first-order differential equation, implying that the dynamic behavior is dominated by a single capacitance factor. For a solution, the differential equation is converted to its Laplace or z-transform.

For more information on computer modeling programs, see Chapter 40 of the 2015 *ASHRAE Handbook—HVAC Applications*.

5.2 CODES AND STANDARDS

AMCA. 2012. Laboratory methods of testing dampers for rating. ANSI/AMCA *Standard* 500-D-12. Air Movement and Control Association, Arlington Heights, IL.

ANSI/CTA. 2014. Control network protocol specification. ANSI/CEA *Standard* 709.1-C-2014. Consumer Electronics Association, Arlington, VA.

ANSI/CTA. 2015. Free-topology twisted-pair channel specification. ANSI/CTA *Standard* 709.3-R2015. Consumer Technology Association, Arlington, VA.

ANSI/CTA. 2014. Enhanced protocol for tunneling component network protocols over Internet protocol channels. ANSI/CTA *Standard* 852.1-A-2014. Consumer Technology Association, Arlington, VA.

ANSI/TIA/EIA. 2000. Commercial building telecommunications cabling standard. *Standard* 568-A. Telecommunications Industry Association, Arlington, VA.

ANSI/TIA/EIA. 2010. Commercial building telecommunications cabling standard—Part 1: General requirements. *Standard* 568-B.1-2-2010. Telecommunications Industry Association, Arlington, VA.

ANSI/TIA/EIA. 2010. Commercial building telecommunications cabling standard—Part 2: Balanced twisted pair telecommunications cabling and components standards. *Standard* 568-C.2-2010. Telecommunications Industry Association, Arlington, VA.

ANSI/TIA/EIA. 2011. Optical fiber cabling component standard. *Standard* 568-C.3-2011. Telecommunications Industry Association, Arlington, VA.

ANSI/TIA/EIA. 2009. Residential telecommunications infrastructure standard. *Standard* 570-B AMD1. Telecommunications Industry Association, Arlington, VA.

ASHRAE. 2013. Safety standard for refrigeration systems. ANSI/ASHRAE *Standard* 15-2013.

ASHRAE. 2016. Ventilation for acceptable indoor air quality. ANSI/ASHRAE *Standard* 62.1-2016.

ASHRAE. 2012. BACnet®—A data communication protocol for building automation and control networks. ANSI/ASHRAE Standard 135-2012, EN/ISO *Standard* 16484-5 (2013).

CENELEC. 2011. Home and building electronic systems. EN *Standard* 50090 (various parts).

EIA. 2003. Electrical characteristics of generators and receivers for use in balanced digital multipoint systems. TIA/EIA *Standard* 485-2003.

IEC. 2013. Degrees of protection provided by enclosures (IP code). *Standard* 60529:1989 + AMD1:1999 + AMD2:2013, consolidated version. International Electrotechnical Commission, Geneva.

IEC. 2011. Connectors for electronic equipment—Part 7: Detail specification for 8-way, unshielded, free and fixed connectors. *Standard* 60603-7:2008 + AMD1:2011. International Electrotechnical Commission, Geneva.

IEEE. 2008. Information technology—Telecommunications and information exchange between systems—Local and metropolitan area network—Specific requirements—Part 3: Carrier sense multiple access with collision detection (CSMA/CD) access method and physical layer specifications. *Standard* 802.3-2008. Institute of Electrical and Electronics Engineers, Piscataway, NJ.

ISO. 2004. Information technology—Open systems interconnection—Basic reference model: The basic model. ISO/IEC *Standard* 7498-1:1994. International Organization for Standardization, Geneva.

NEMA. 2014. Enclosures for electrical equipment (1000 volts maximum). *Standard* 250. National Electrical Manufacturers Association, Rosslyn, VA.

NFPA. 2017. National electrical code®. *Standard* 70-2017. National Fire Protection Association, Quincy, MA.

UL. 2002. Signaling devices for the hearing impaired. ANSI/UL *Standard* 1971. Underwriters Laboratories, Northbrook, IL.

REFERENCES

ASHRAE members can access ASHRAE Journal articles and ASHRAE research project final reports at technologyportal .ashrae.org. Articles and reports are also available for purchase by nonmembers in the online ASHRAE Bookstore at www.ashrae.org /bookstore.

ASHRAE. 2007. HVAC&R technical requirements for the commissioning process. *Guideline* 1.1-2007.

ASHRAE. 2015. Specifying building automation systems. *Guideline* 13-2015.

ASHRAE. 2014. Selecting outdoor, return, and relief dampers for air-side economizer systems. *Guideline* 16-2014.

ASHRAE. 2010. *Standard 62.1-2010 user's manual.*

ASHRAE. 2007. *Sequence of operation for common HVAC systems*. CD-ROM.

Bushby, S.T. 1998. Friend or foe? Communication gateways. *ASHRAE Journal* 40(4):50-53.

Bushby, S.T., H.M. Newman, and M.A. Applebaum. 1999. *GSA guide to specifying interoperable building automation and control systems using ANSI/ASHRAE* Standard *135-1995, BACnet*. NISTIR 6392. National Institute of Standards and Technology, Gaithersburg, MD. Available from National Technical Information Service, Springfield, VA.

Capehardt, B., and L. Capehardt. 2005. *Web based energy information and control system: Case studies and applications*, Ch. 27, Wireless Sensor Applications for Building Operation and Management. Fairmont Press and CRC, Boca Raton, FL.

CSI. 2004. *MasterFormat*. The Construction Specifications Institute, Alexandria, VA.

Ehrlich, P., and O. Pittel. 1999. Specifying interoperability. *ASHRAE Journal* 41(4):25-29.

Felker, L.G., and T.L. Felker. 2009. *Dampers and airflow control*. ASHRAE.

van Becelaere, R., H.J. Sauer, and F. Finaish. 2004. Flow resistance and modulating characteristics of control dampers. ASHRAE Research Project RP-1157, *Final Report*.

Martocci, J. 2008. Unplugged ZigBee® and BACnet connect. *ASHRAE Journal* 50(6):42-46.

ULC. 2016. Visible signaliing devices for fire alarm and signaling systems, including accessories. CAN/ULC *Standard* S526:2016-EN. Underwriters Laboratories of Canada, Toronto.

BIBLIOGRAPHY

Avery, G. 1989. Updating the VAV outside air economizer controls. *ASHRAE Journal* (April).

Avery, G. 1992. The instability of VAV systems. *Heating, Piping and Air Conditioning* (February).

BICSI. 1999. *LAN and internetworking design manual*, 3rd ed. Building Industry Consulting Service International, Tampa.

CEN. 1999. *Building control systems, Part 1: Overview and definitions*. prEN ISO16484-1. CEN, the European Committee for Standardization.

Haines, R.W., and D.C. Hittle. 2003. *Control systems for heating, ventilating and air conditioning*, 6th ed. Springer.

Hartman, T.B. 1993. *Direct digital controls for HVAC systems*. McGraw-Hill, New York.

Kettler, J.P. 1998. Controlling minimum ventilation volume in VAV systems. *ASHRAE Journal* (May).

Levenhagen, J.I., and D.H. Spethmann. 1993. *HVAC controls and systems*. McGraw-Hill, New York.

Lizardos, E., and K. Elovitz. 2000. Damper sizing using damper authority. *ASHRAE Journal* (April).

LonMark. 1998. *LonMark application layer interoperability guidelines*. LonMark Interoperability Association, Sunnyvale, CA.

LonMark. 1999. *LonMark functional profile: Space comfort controller*. 8500-10. LonMark Interoperability Association.

Newman, H.M. 1994. *Direct digital control for building systems: Theory and practice*. John Wiley & Sons, New York.

OPC Foundation. 1998. *What is OPC?* OPC Foundation, Boca Raton, FL. Available at opcfoundation.org/about/what-is-opc/.

Rose, M.T. 1990. *The open book: A practical perspective on OSI*. Prentice-Hall, Englewood Cliffs, NJ.

Seem, J.E., J.M. House, and R.H. Monroe. 1999. On-line monitoring and fault detection. *ASHRAE Journal* (July).

Starr, R. 1999. Pneumatic controls in a digital age. *Heating, Piping and Air Conditioning* (November).

Tillack, L., and J.B. Rishel. 1998. Proper control of HVAC variable speed pumps. *ASHRAE Journal* (November).

CHAPTER 8

SOUND AND VIBRATION

IF FUNDAMENTAL principles of sound and vibration control are applied in the design, installation, and use of HVAC&R systems, suitable levels of noise and vibration can be achieved with a high probability of user acceptance. This chapter introduces these fundamental principles, including characteristics of sound, basic definitions and terminology, human response to sound, acoustic design goals, and vibration isolation fundamentals. Chapter 48 of the 2015 *ASHRAE Handbook—HVAC Applications* and the references at the end of this chapter contain technical discussions, tables, and design examples helpful to HVAC designers.

1. ACOUSTICAL DESIGN OBJECTIVE

A primary objective in the design of HVAC systems and equipment is to evaluate noise and vibration to ensure that the acoustical environment in a given space is acceptable for various occupant activities. Sound and vibration are created by a **source**, are transmitted along one or more **paths**, and reach a **receiver**. Treatments and modifications can be applied to any or all of these elements to reduce unwanted noise and vibration, although it is usually most effective and least expensive to reduce noise at the source.

2. CHARACTERISTICS OF SOUND

Sound is a propagating disturbance in a fluid (gas or liquid) or in a solid. In fluid media, the disturbance travels as a longitudinal compression wave. Sound in air is called *airborne sound* or just *sound.* It is generated by a vibrating surface or turbulent fluid stream. In solids, sound can travel as bending, compressional, torsional, shear, or other waves, which, in turn, are sources of airborne sound. Sound in solids is generally called *structureborne sound.* In HVAC system design, both airborne and structureborne sound propagation are important.

Levels

The magnitude of sound and vibration physical properties are almost always expressed in *levels.* As shown in the following equations, the level L is based on the common (base 10) logarithm of a ratio of the magnitude of a physical property of power, intensity, or energy to a reference magnitude of the same type of property:

$$L = 10 \log\left(\frac{A}{A_{ref}}\right) \tag{1}$$

where A is the magnitude of the physical property of interest and A_{ref} is the reference value. Note that the ratio is dimensionless. In this equation, a factor of 10 is included to convert bels to decibels (dB).

The preparation of this chapter is assigned to TC 2.6, Sound and Vibration.

Sound Pressure and Sound Pressure Level

Sound waves in air are variations in pressure above and below atmospheric pressure. **Sound pressure** is measured in pascals (Pa) (SI units are used here rather than I-P because of international agreement). The human ear responds across a broad range of sound pressures; the threshold of hearing to the threshold of pain covers a range of approximately 10^{14}:1. Table 1 gives approximate values of sound pressure by various sources at specified distances from the source.

The range of sound pressure in Table 1 is so large that it is more convenient to use a scale proportional to the logarithm of this quantity. Therefore, the **decibel** (dB) scale is the preferred method of presenting quantities in acoustics, not only because it collapses a large range of pressures to a more manageable range, but also because its levels correlate better with human responses to the magnitude of sound than do sound pressures. Equation (1) describes levels of power, intensity, and energy, which are proportional to the square of other physical properties, such as sound pressure and vibration acceleration. Thus, the **sound pressure level** L_p corresponding to a sound pressure is given by

$$L_p = 10 \log\left(\frac{p}{p_{ref}}\right)^2 = 20 \log\left(\frac{p}{p_{ref}}\right) \tag{2}$$

where p is the root mean square (RMS) value of acoustic pressure in pascals. The root mean square is the square root of the time average of the square of the acoustic pressure ratio. The ratio p/p_{ref} is squared to give quantities proportional to intensity or energy. A

Table 1 Typical Sound Pressures and Sound Pressure Levels

Source	Sound Pressure, Pa	Sound Pressure Level, dB re 20 μPa	Subjective Reaction
Military jet takeoff at 100 ft	200	140	Extreme danger
Artillery fire at 10 ft	63.2	130	
Passenger jet takeoff at 50 ft	20	120	Threshold of pain
Loud rock band	6.3	110	Threshold of discomfort
Automobile horn at 10 ft	2	100	
Unmuffled large diesel engine at 130 ft	0.6	90	Very loud
Accelerating diesel truck at 50 ft	0.2	80	
Freight train at 100 ft	0.06	70	Loud
Conversational speech at 3 ft	0.02	60	
Window air conditioner at 3 ft	0.006	50	Moderate
Quiet residential area	0.002	40	Quiet
Whispered conversation at 6 ft	0.0006	30	
Buzzing insect at 3 ft	0.0002	20	Perceptible
Threshold of good hearing	0.00006	10	Faint
Threshold of excellent youthful hearing	0.00002	0	Threshold of hearing

reference quantity is needed so the term in parentheses is nondimensional. For sound pressure levels in air, the reference pressure p_{ref} is 20 μPa, which corresponds to the approximate threshold of hearing for a young person with good hearing exposed to a pure tone with a frequency of 1000 Hz.

The decibel scale is used for many different descriptors relating to sound: source strength, sound level at a specified location, and attenuation along propagation paths; each has a different reference quantity. For this reason, it is important to be aware of the context in which the term *decibel* or *level* is used. For most acoustical quantities, there is an internationally accepted reference value. A reference quantity is always implied even if it does not appear.

Sound pressure level is relatively easy to measure and thus is used by most noise codes and criteria. (The human ear and microphones are pressure sensitive.) Sound pressure levels for the corresponding sound pressures are also given in Table 1.

Frequency

Frequency is the number of oscillations (or cycles) completed per second by a vibrating object. The international unit for frequency is hertz (Hz) with dimension s^{-1}. When the motion of vibrating air particles is simple harmonic, the sound is said to be a **pure tone** and the sound pressure p as a function of time and frequency can be described by

$$p(t, f) = p_0 \sin(2\pi f t) \tag{3}$$

where f is frequency in hertz, p_0 is the maximum amplitude of oscillating (or acoustic) pressure, and t is time in seconds.

The **audible frequency range** for humans with unimpaired hearing extends from about 20 Hz to 20 kHz. In some cases, infrasound (<20 Hz) or ultrasound (>20 kHz) are important, but methods and instrumentation for these frequency regions are specialized and are not considered here.

Speed

The speed of a longitudinal wave in a fluid is a function of the fluid's density and bulk modulus of elasticity. In air, at room temperature, the speed of sound is about 1100 fps; in water, about 5000 fps. In solids, there are several different types of waves, each with a different speed. The speeds of **compressional, torsional,** and **shear waves** do not vary with frequency, and are often greater than the speed of sound in air. However, these types of waves are not the primary source of radiated noise because resultant displacements at the surface are small compared to the internal displacements. **Bending waves**, however, are significant sources of radiation, and their speed changes with frequency. At lower frequencies, bending waves are slower than sound in air, but can exceed this value at higher frequencies (e.g., above approximately 1000 Hz).

Wavelength

The wavelength of sound in a medium is the distance between successive maxima or minima of a simple harmonic disturbance propagating in that medium at a single instant in time. Wavelength, speed, and frequency are related by

$$\lambda = c/f \tag{4}$$

where

λ = wavelength, ft
c = speed of sound, fps
f = frequency, Hz

Sound Power and Sound Power Level

The **sound power** of a source is its rate of emission of acoustical energy and is expressed in watts. Sound power depends on operating conditions but not distance of observation location from the source or surrounding environment. Approximate sound power outputs for common sources are shown in Table 2 with corresponding sound power levels. For **sound power level L_w**, the power reference is 10^{-12} W or 1 picowatt. The definition of sound power level is therefore

$$L_w = 10 \log(w/10^{-12}) \tag{5}$$

where w is the sound power emitted by the source in watts. (Sound power emitted by a source is not the same as the power consumed by the source. Only a small fraction of the consumed power is converted into sound. For example, a loudspeaker rated at 100 W may be only 1 to 5% efficient, generating only 1 to 5 W of sound power.) Note that the sound power level is 10 times the logarithm of the ratio of the power to the reference power, and the sound pressure is 20 times the logarithm of the ratio of the pressure to the reference pressure.

Table 2 Examples of Sound Power Outputs and Sound Power Levels

Source	Sound Power, W	Sound Power Level, dB re 10^{-12} W
Large rocket launch (e.g., space shuttle)	10^8	200
Jet aircraft at takeoff	10^4	160
Large pipe organ	10	130
Small aircraft engine	1	120
Large HVAC fan	0.1	110
Heavy truck at highway speed	0.01	100
Voice, shouting	0.001	90
Garbage disposal unit	10^{-4}	80
Voice, conversation level	10^{-5}	70
Electronic equipment ventilation fan	10^{-6}	60
Office air diffuser	10^{-7}	50
Small electric clock	10^{-8}	40
Voice, soft whisper	10^{-9}	30
Rustling leaves	10^{-10}	20
Human breath	10^{-11}	10

Most mechanical equipment is rated in terms of sound power levels so that comparisons can be made using a common reference independent of distance and acoustical conditions in the room. AHRI *Standard* 370-2011 is a common source for rating large air-cooled outdoor equipment. AMCA *Publication* 303-79 provides guidelines for using sound power level ratings. Also, AMCA *Standards* 301-90 and 311-05 provide methods for developing fan sound ratings from laboratory test data. Note, however, some HVAC equipment has sound data available only in terms of sound pressure levels; for example, AHRI *Standard* 575-2008 is used for water-cooled chiller sound rating for indoor applications. In such cases, special care must be taken in predicting the sound pressure level in a specific room (e.g., manufacturer's sound pressure data may be obtained in large spaces nearly free of sound reflection, whereas an HVAC equipment room can often be small and very reverberant).

Sound Intensity and Sound Intensity Level

The **sound intensity** I at a point in a specified direction is the rate of flow of sound energy (i.e., power) through unit area at that point. The unit area is perpendicular to the specified direction, and the units of intensity are watts per square metre. (SI units are used here rather than I-P units because of international agreement on the definition.) **Sound intensity level L_I** is expressed in dB with a reference quantity of 10^{-12} W/m²; thus,

$$L_I = 10 \log(I/10^{-12}) \tag{6}$$

The instantaneous intensity I is the product of the pressure and velocity of air motion (e.g., particle velocity), as shown here:

$$I = pv \tag{7}$$

Both pressure and particle velocity are oscillating, with a magnitude and time variation. Usually, the time-averaged intensity I_{ave} (i.e., the net power flow through a surface area, often simply called "the intensity") is of interest.

Taking the time average of Equation (7) over one period yields

$$I_{ave} = \text{Real}\{pv\} \tag{8}$$

where Real is the real part of the complex (with amplitude and phase) quantity. At locations far from the source and reflecting surfaces,

$$I_{ave} \approx p^2/\rho_0 c \tag{9}$$

where p is the RMS sound pressure, ρ_0 is the density of air (0.075 lb/ft^3), and c is the acoustic phase speed in air (1100 fps). Equation (9) implies that the relationship between sound intensity and sound pressure varies with air temperature and density. Conveniently, the sound intensity level differs from the sound pressure level by less than 0.5 dB for temperature and densities normally experienced in HVAC environments. Therefore, sound pressure level is a good measure of the intensity level at locations far from sources and reflecting surfaces.

Note that all equations in this chapter that relate sound power level to sound pressure level are based on the assumption that sound pressure level is equal to sound intensity level.

Combining Sound Levels

To estimate the levels from multiple sources from the levels from each source, the intensities (not the levels) must be added. Thus, the levels must first be converted to find intensities, the intensities summed, and then converted to a level again, so the combination of multiple levels L_1, L_2, etc., produces a level L_{sum} given by

$$L_{sum} = 10 \log\left(\sum_i 10^{L_i/10}\right) \tag{10}$$

where, for sound pressure level L_p, $10^{L_i/10}$ is p_i^2/p_{ref}^2, and L_i is the sound pressure level for the ith source.

A simpler and slightly less accurate method is outlined in Table 3. This method, although not exact, results in errors of 1 dB or less. The process with a series of levels may be shortened by combining the largest with the next largest, then combining this sum with the third largest, then the fourth largest, and so on until the combination of the remaining levels is 10 dB lower than the combined level. The process may then be stopped.

The procedures in Table 3 and Equation (10) are valid if the individual sound levels are not highly correlated, which is true for most sounds encountered in HVAC systems. One notable exception is the pure tone. If two or more sound signals contain pure tones at the same frequency, the pressures (amplitude and phase) should be added and the level (20 log) taken of the sum to find the sound pressure level of the two combined tones. The combined sound level is a function of not only the level of each tone (i.e., amplitude of the pressure), but also the phase difference between the tones. Combined sound levels from two tones of equal amplitude and frequency can range from zero (if the tones are 180° out of phase) up to 6 dB greater than the level of either tone (if the tones are exactly in phase). When two tones of similar amplitude are very close in frequency but not exactly the same, the combined sound level oscillates as the tones move in and out of phase. This effect creates an audible "beating" with a period equal to the inverse of the difference in frequency between the two tones.

Table 3 Combining Two Sound Levels

Difference between levels to be combined, dB	0 to 1	2 to 4	5 to 9	10 and More
Number of decibels to add to highest level to obtain combined level	3	2	1	0

Measurements of sound levels generated by individual sources are made in the presence of background noise (i.e., noise from sources other than the ones of interest). Thus, the measurement includes noise from the source and background noise. To remove background noise, the levels are unlogged and the square of the background sound pressure subtracted from the square of the sound pressure for the combination of the source and background noise [see Equation (2)]:

$$L_p(\text{source}) = 10 \log\left(10^{L(\text{comb})/10} - 10^{L(\text{bkgd})/10}\right) \tag{11}$$

where L(bkgd) is the sound pressure level of the background noise, measured with the source of interest turned off. If the difference between the levels with the source on and off is greater than 10 dB, then background noise levels are low enough that the effect of background noise on the levels measured with the source on can be ignored.

Resonances

Acoustic resonances occur in enclosures, such as a room or HVAC plenum, and mechanical resonances occur in structures, such as the natural frequency of vibration of a duct wall. Resonances occur at discrete frequencies where system response to excitation is high. To prevent this, the frequencies at which resonances occur must be known and avoided, particularly by sources of discrete-frequency tones. Avoid aligning the frequency of tonal noise with any frequencies of resonance of the space into which the noise is radiated.

At resonance, multiple reflections inside the space form a standing wave pattern (called a **mode shape**) with nodes at minimum pressure and antinodes at maximum pressure. Spacing between nodes (minimum acoustic pressure) and antinodes (maximum acoustic pressure) is one-quarter of an acoustic wavelength for the frequency of resonance.

Absorption and Reflection of Sound

Sound incident on a surface, such as a ceiling, is either absorbed, reflected, or transmitted. **Absorbed sound** is the part of incident sound that is transmitted through the surface and either dissipated (as in acoustic tiles) or transmitted into the adjoining space (as through an intervening partition). The fraction of acoustic intensity incident on the surface that is absorbed is called the **absorption coefficient** α, as defined by the following equation:

$$\alpha = I_{abs}/I_{inc} \tag{12}$$

where I_{abs} is the intensity of absorbed sound and I_{inc} is the intensity of sound incident on the surface.

The absorption coefficient depends on the frequency and angle of incident sound. In frequency bands, the absorption coefficient of nearly randomly incident sound is measured in large reverberant rooms. The difference in the rates at which sound decays after the source is turned off is measured before and after the sample is placed in the reverberant room. The rate at which sound decays is related to the total absorption in the room via the Sabine equation:

$$T_{60} = 0.05(V/A) \tag{13}$$

where

T_{60} = reverberation time (time required for average sound pressure level in room to decay by 60 dB), s
V = volume of room, ft^3
A = total absorption in room, given by

$$A = \sum_i S_i \alpha_i$$

S_i = surface area for ith surface, ft^2
α_i = absorption coefficient for ith surface

Just as for absorption coefficients, reverberation time varies with frequency.

For sound to be incident on surfaces from all directions during absorption measurement, the room must be reverberant so that most of the sound incident on surfaces is reflected and bounced around the room in all directions. In a **diffuse sound field**, sound is incident on the absorbing sample equally from all directions. The Sabine equation applies only in a diffuse field.

Reflected sound superimposes on the incident sound, which increases the level of sound at and near the surfaces (i.e., the sound level near a surface is higher than those away from the surface in the free field). Because the energy in the room is related to the free-field sound pressure levels (see the section on Determining Sound Power for a discussion of free fields) and is often used to relate the sound power emitted into the room and the room's total absorption, it is important that sound pressure level measurements not be made close to reflecting surfaces, where the levels will be higher than in the free field. Measurements should be made at least one-quarter of a wavelength from the nearest reflecting surface (i.e., at a distance of $d \approx \lambda/4 \approx 275/f$, where d is in feet and f is frequency in Hz).

Room Acoustics

The characteristics of sound radiated into a room are affected by surfaces in the room that might absorb, reflect, or transmit sound. The changes of primary concern are the increase in sound levels from those that would exist without the room (i.e., in the open) and reverberation. Lower absorption leads to higher sound pressure levels away from the sources of noise (see the section on Sound Transmission Paths). With lower absorption, reverberation times may be longer. Reverberation can affect perception of music (e.g., in a concert hall) and speech intelligibility (e.g., in a lecture hall). Thus, when adding absorption to reduce a room's background HVAC-generated noise levels, it is important to be aware of the added absorption's effect on reverberation in the room.

Acoustic Impedance

Acoustic impedance z_a is the ratio of acoustic pressure p to particle velocity v:

$$z_a = p/v \tag{14}$$

For a wave propagating in free space far (more than ~3 ft) from a source, the acoustic impedance is

$$z_a \approx \rho_0 c \tag{15}$$

where ρ_0 is the density of air (0.075 lb/ft^3) and c is the sound speed in air (1100 fps).

Where acoustic impedance changes abruptly, some of the sound incident at the location of the impedance change is reflected. For example, inside an HVAC duct, the acoustic impedance is different from the free field acoustic impedance, so at the duct termination there is an abrupt change in the acoustic impedance from inside the duct to outside into the room, particularly at low frequencies. Thus, some sound inside the duct is reflected back into the duct (**end reflection**). Losses from end reflection are discussed in Chapter 48 of the 2015 *ASHRAE Handbook—HVAC Applications*.

3. MEASURING SOUND

Instrumentation

The basic instrument for measuring sound is a **sound level meter**, which comprises a microphone, electronic circuitry, and a display device. The microphone converts sound pressure at a point to an electronic signal, which is then processed and the sound pressure level displayed using analog or digital circuitry. Sound level meters are usually battery-operated, lightweight, handheld units with outputs that vary in complexity depending on cost and level of technology.

Time Averaging

Most sounds are not constant; pressure fluctuates from moment to moment and the level can vary quickly or slowly. Sound level meters can show time fluctuations of the sound pressure level using specified time constants (slow, fast, impulse), or can hold the maximum or minimum level recorded during some specified interval. All sound level meters perform some kind of time averaging. Some integrating sound level meters take an average of the sound pressure level over a user-definable time, then hold and display the result. The advantage of an integrating meter is that it is easier to read and more repeatable (especially if the measurement period is long). The quantity measured by the integrating sound level meter is the **equivalent continuous sound pressure level L_{eq}**, which is the level of the time average of the squared pressure:

$$L_{eq} = 10 \log\left[\frac{1}{T}\int_0^T \frac{p^2(t)}{p_{ref}^2}\,dt\right] \tag{16}$$

where $1/T\int_0^T dt$ is the time average (i.e., the sum $\int_0^T dt$ divided by the time over which the sum is taken).

Spectra and Analysis Bandwidths

Real sounds are much more complex than simple pure tones, where all the energy is at a single frequency. **Broadband sound** contains energy that usually covers most of the audible frequency range. Sometimes there are multiple, harmonically related tones. All sounds, however, can be represented as levels as a function of frequency using **frequency** or **spectral analysis**.

A **constant-bandwidth analysis** expresses a sound's energy content as a spectrum where each data point represents the same spectral width in frequency (e.g., 1 Hz). This is useful when an objectionable sound contains strong tones and the tones' frequencies must be accurately identified before remedial action is taken. A constant-bandwidth spectrum usually contains too much information for typical noise control work or for specifications of acceptable noise levels.

Measurements for most HVAC noise control work are usually made with filters that extract the energy in either **octave** or **one-third octave bands.** An octave band is a frequency band with an upper frequency limit twice that of its lower frequency limit. Octave and 1/3 octave bands are identified by their respective center frequencies, which are the geometric means of the upper and lower band limits (ANSI *Standards* S1.6 and S1.11):

$$f_c = \sqrt{f_{upper} f_{lower}}$$

Three 1/3 octave bands make up an octave band. Table 4 lists the upper, lower, and center frequencies for the preferred series of octave and 1/3 octave bands. For most HVAC sound measurements, filters for the range 20 to 5000 Hz are usually adequate.

Although octave band analysis is usually acceptable for rating acoustical environments in rooms, 1/3 octave band analysis is often useful in product development, in assessing transmission losses through partitions, and for remedial investigations.

Some sound level meters have standard broadband filters that simulate the frequency response to sound of the average human ear. The **A-weighting** filter, which simulates the response of the human ear to low levels of sound, is the most common (Figure 1 and Table 5). It deemphasizes the low-frequency portions of a sound spectrum, automatically compensating for the lower sensitivity of the human ear to low-frequency sounds.

The **C-weighting** filter weights the sound less as a function of frequency than the A-weighting, as shown in Figure 1. Because sound levels at low frequencies are attenuated by A-weighting but not by

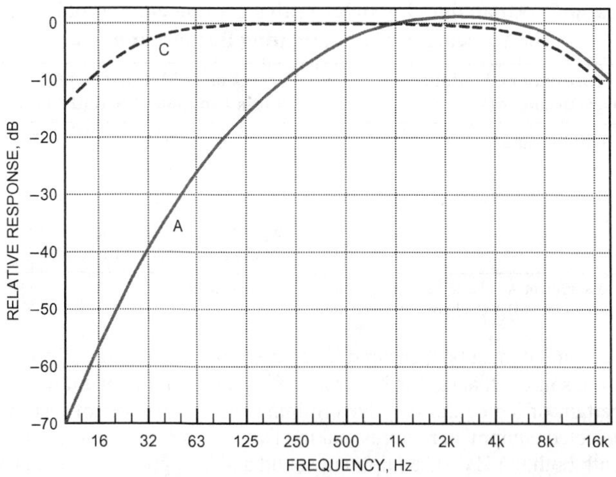

Fig. 1 Curves Showing A- and C-Weighting Responses for Sound Level Meters

Table 4 Midband and Approximate Upper and Lower Cutoff Frequencies for Octave and 1/3 Octave Band Filters

Octave Bands, Hz			1/3 Octave Bands, Hz		
Lower	Midband	Upper	Lower	Midband	Upper
			11.2	12.5	14
11.2	16	22.4	14	16	18
			18	20	22.4
			22.4	25	28
22.4	31.5	45	28	31.5	35.5
			35.5	40	45
			45	50	56
45	63	90	56	63	71
			71	80	90
			90	100	112
90	125	180	112	125	140
			140	160	180
			180	200	224
180	250	355	224	250	280
			280	315	355
			355	400	450
355	500	710	450	500	560
			560	630	710
			710	800	900
710	1,000	1,400	900	1,000	1,200
			1,120	1,250	1,400
			1,400	1,600	1,800
1,400	2,000	2,800	1,800	2,000	2,240
			2,240	2,500	2,800
			2,800	3,150	3,550
2,800	4,000	5,600	3,550	4,000	4,500
			4,500	5,000	5,600
			5,600	6,300	7,100
5,600	8,000	11,200	7,100	8,000	9,000
			9,000	10,000	11,200
			11,200	12,500	14,000
11,200	16,000	22,400	14,000	16,000	18,000
			18,000	20,000	22,400

C-weighting, these weightings can be used to estimate whether a particular sound has excessive low-frequency energy when a spectrum analyzer is not available. If the difference between C- and A-weighted levels for the sound exceeds about 20 dB, then the sound is likely to be annoying because of excessive low-frequency noise.

Table 5 A-Weighting for 1/3 Octave and Octave Bands

1/3 Octave Band Center Frequency, Hz	A-Weighting, dB	Octave Band Center Frequency, Hz	A-Weighting, dB
16	−56.7	16	−56.7
20	−50.5		
25	−44.7		
31.5	−39.4	31.5	−39.4
40	−34.6		
50	−30.2		
63	−26.2	63	−26.2
80	−22.5		
100	−19.1		
125	−16.1	125	−16.1
160	−13.4		
200	−10.9		
250	−8.6	250	−8.6
315	−6.6		
400	−4.8		
500	−3.2	500	−3.2
630	−1.9		
800	−0.8		
1000	0	1000	0
1250	+0.6		
1600	+1.0		
2000	+1.2	2000	+1.2
2500	+1.3		
3150	+1.2		
4000	+1.0	4000	+1.0
5000	+0.5		
6300	−0.1		
8000	−1.1	8000	−1.1
10,000	−2.5		

Table 6 Combining Decibels to Determine Overall Sound Pressure Level

Octave Band Frequency, Hz	Octave Band Level L_p, dB	$10^{L_p/10}$		
63	85	3.2×10^8	=	0.32×10^9
125	90	1.0×10^9	=	1.0×10^9
250	92	1.6×10^9	=	1.6×10^9
500	87	5.0×10^8	=	0.5×10^9
1000	82	1.6×10^8	=	0.16×10^9
2000	78	6.3×10^7	=	0.06×10^9
4000	65	3.2×10^6	=	0.003×10^9
8000	54	2.5×10^5	=	0.0002×10^9
				3.6432×10^9
				$10 \log (3.6 \times 10^9) = 96$ dB

Note that C-weighting provides some attenuation at very low and very high frequencies: C-weighting is not the same as no weighting (i.e., flat weighting).

Sound level meters are available in several accuracy grades specified by ANSI *Standard* S1.4. A type 1 meter has an accuracy of about ±1.0 dB from 50 to 4000 Hz. The general-purpose type 2 meter, which is less expensive, has a tolerance of about ±1.5 dB from 100 to 1000 Hz, and is adequate for most HVAC sound measurements.

Manually selecting filters sequentially to cover the frequency range from 20 to 5000 Hz is time consuming. An instrument that gives all filtered levels simultaneously is called a **real-time analyzer (RTA)**. It speeds up measurement significantly, and most models can save information to an internal or external digital storage device.

The process described in Equation (10) for adding a series of levels can be applied to a set of octave or 1/3 octave bands to calculate the overall broadband level (see Table 6 for an example). The

A-weighted sound level may be estimated using octave or 1/3 octave band levels by adding A-weightings given in Table 5 to octave or 1/3 octave band levels before combining the levels.

Sound Measurement Basics

The sound pressure level in an occupied space can be measured directly with a sound level meter, or estimated from published sound power data after accounting for room volume, distance from the source, and other acoustical factors (see the section on Sound Transmission Paths). Sound level meters measure sound pressure at the microphone location. Estimation techniques calculate sound pressure at a specified point in an occupied space. Measured or estimated sound pressure levels in frequency bands can then be plotted, analyzed, and compared with established criteria for acceptance.

Sound measurements must be done carefully to ensure repeatable and accurate results. Note that equipment noise varies significantly with the operation conditions. To make proper comparisons, HVAC unit conditions must be controlled under a reference condition (e.g., full load). Even so, sound levels may not be steady, particularly at low frequencies (250 Hz and lower), and can vary significantly with time. In these cases, both maximum (as measured on a meter with slow response) and average levels (over intervals established by various standards) should be recorded. Other important considerations for sound measurement procedures include

- Ambient sound pressure level with HVAC equipment off, with correction factors when HVAC levels are not significantly above ambient
- Number of locations for measurements, based on room volume, occupancy, etc.
- Duration of time-averaged measurements, statistical meter settings, etc.

Sophisticated sound measurements and their procedures should be carried out by individuals experienced in acoustic measurements. At present, there are only a few noise standards that can be used to measure interior sound levels from mechanical equipment (e.g., ASTM *Standards* E1573 and E1574). Most manuals for sound level meters include sections on how to measure sound, but basic methods that can help obtain acceptable measurements are included here.

Determining the sound spectrum in a room or investigating a noise complaint usually requires measuring sound pressure levels in the octave bands from 16 to 8000 Hz. In cases where tonal noise or rumble is the complaint, narrow-band or 1/3 octave band measurements are recommended because of their greater frequency resolution. Whatever the measurement method, remember that sound pressure levels can vary significantly from point to point in a room. In a room, each measurement point often provides a different value for sound pressure level, so the actual location of measurement is very important and must be detailed in the report. A survey could record the location and level of the loudest position, or could establish a few representative locations where occupants are normally situated. In general, the most appropriate height is 4 to 6 ft above the floor. Avoid the exact geometric center of the room and any location within 3 ft of a wall, floor, or ceiling. Wherever the location, it must be defined and recorded. If the meter has an integrating-averaging function, use a rotating boom to sample a large area, or slowly walk around the room, and the meter will determine the average sound pressure level for that path. However, take care that no extraneous sounds are generated by microphone movement or by walking; using a windscreen reduces extraneous noise generated by airflow over the moving microphone. Locations with noticeably higher-than-average sound levels should be recorded. See the section on Measurement of Room Sound Pressure Level for more details.

When measuring HVAC noise, **background noise** from other sources (occupants, wind, nearby traffic, elevators, etc.) must be determined. Sometimes the sound from a particular piece of HVAC equipment must be measured in the presence of background sound from sources that cannot be turned off, such as automobile traffic or certain office equipment. Determining the sound level of just the selected equipment requires making two sets of measurements: one with both the HVAC equipment sound and background sound, and another with only the background sound (with HVAC equipment turned off). This situation might also occur, for example, when determining whether noise exposure at the property line from a cooling tower meets a local noise ordinance.

Table 7 Guidelines for Determining Equipment Sound Levels in the Presence of Contaminating Background Sound

Measurement A minus Measurement B	Correction to Measurement A to Obtain Equipment Sound Level
10 dB or more	0 dB
6 to 9 dB	–1 dB
4 to 5 dB	–2 dB
Less than 4 dB	Equipment sound level is more than 2 dB below Measurement A

Measurement A = Tested equipment plus background sound
Measurement B = Background sound alone

The guidelines in Table 7 help determine the sound level of a particular machine in the presence of background sound. Equation (11) in the section on Combining Sound Levels may be used.

The uncertainty associated with correcting for background sound depends on the uncertainty of the measuring instrument and the steadiness of the sounds being measured. In favorable circumstances, it might be possible to extend Table 7. In particularly unfavorable circumstances, even values obtained from the table could be substantially in error.

Measuring sound emissions from a particular piece of equipment or group of equipment requires a measurement plan specific to the situation. The Air-Conditioning, Heating, and Refrigeration Institute (AHRI); Air Movement and Control Association International (AMCA); American Society of Testing and Materials (ASTM); American National Standards Institute (ANSI); and Acoustical Society of America (ASA) all publish sound level measurement procedures for various laboratory and field sound measurement situations.

Outdoor measurements are somewhat easier to make than indoor because there are typically few or no boundary surfaces to affect sound build-up or absorption. Nevertheless, important issues such as the effect of large, nearby sound-reflecting surfaces and weather conditions such as wind, temperature, and precipitation must be addressed. Where measurements are made close to extended surfaces (i.e., flat or nearly flat surfaces with dimensions more than four times the wavelength of the sound of interest), sound pressure levels can be significantly increased. These effects can be estimated through guidelines in many sources such as Harris (1991).

Measurement of Room Sound Pressure Level

In commissioning building HVAC systems, often a specified room noise criterion must demonstratively be met. Measurement procedures for obtaining the data to demonstrate compliance should also be specified to avoid confusion when different parties make measurements using different procedures. The problem is that most rooms exhibit significant point-to-point variation in sound pressure level.

When a noise has no audible tonal components, differences in measured sound pressure level at several locations in a room may be as high as 3 to 5 dB. However, when audible tonal components are present, especially at low frequencies, variations caused by standing waves that occur at frequencies of resonance may exceed 10 dB. These are generally noticeable to the average listener when moving through the room.

Although commissioning procedures usually set precise limits for demonstrating compliance, the outcome can unfortunately be controversial unless the measurement procedure has been specified in detail. In the absence of firm agreement in the industry on an acoustical measurement procedure for commissioning HVAC systems, possibilities include the new ANSI *Standard* S12.72-2015 on measuring ambient noise levels in a room, as well as AHRI *Standard* 885, which incorporates a "suggested procedure for field verification of NC/RC levels."

Measurement of Acoustic Intensity

Equation (8) for the time-averaged intensity (often called simply *intensity*) requires both the pressure and particle velocity. Pressure is easily measured with a microphone, but there is no simple transducer that converts particle velocity to a measurable electronic signal. Fortunately, particle velocity can be estimated from sound pressures measured at closely spaced (less than ~1/10 of an acoustic wavelength) locations, using Euler's equation:

$$v = -\frac{1}{i2\pi f\rho_0} \times \frac{\partial p}{\partial x} \approx -\frac{1}{i2\pi f\rho_0} \times \frac{p_2 - p_1}{x_2 - x_1} \quad (17)$$

where x_2 and x_1 are the locations of measurements of pressures p_2 and p_1, f is frequency in Hz, and ρ_0 is density of air. The spatial derivative of pressure ($\partial p/\partial x$) is approximated with ($\Delta p/\Delta x$) = $[(p_2 - p_1)/(x_2 - x_1)]$. Thus, intensity probes typically contain two closely spaced microphones that have nearly identical responses (i.e., are phase matched). Because intensity is a vector, it shows the direction of sound propagation along the line between the microphones, in addition to the magnitude of the sound. Also, because intensity is power/area, it is not sensitive to the acoustic nearfield (see the section on Typical Sources of Sound) or to standing waves where the intensity is zero. Therefore, unlike pressure measurement, intensity measurements can be made in the acoustic nearfield of a source or in the reverberant field in a room to determine the power radiated from the source. However, intensity measurements cannot be used in a diffuse field to determine the acoustic energy in the field, such as used for determining sound power using the reverberation room method.

4. DETERMINING SOUND POWER

The sound power of a source cannot be measured directly. Rather, it is calculated from several measurements of sound pressure or sound intensity created by a source in one of several test environments. The following four methods are commonly used.

Free-Field Method

A **free field** is a sound field where the effects of any boundaries are negligible over the frequency range of interest. In ideal conditions, there are no boundaries. Free-field conditions can be approximated in rooms with highly sound-absorbing walls, floor, and ceiling (**anechoic rooms**). In a free field, the sound power of a sound source can be determined from measurements of sound pressure level on an imaginary spherical surface centered on and surrounding the source. This method is based on the fact that, because sound absorption in air can be practically neglected at small distances from the sound source, all of the sound power generated by a source must flow through an imagined sphere with the source at its center. The intensity I of the sound (conventionally expressed in W/m^2) is estimated from measured sound pressure levels using the following equation:

$$I = (1 \times 10^{-12})10^{L_p/10} \quad (18)$$

where L_p is sound pressure level. The intensity at each point around the source is multiplied by that portion of the area of the imagined sphere associated with the measuring points. Total sound power W is the sum of these products for each point:

$$W = \sum_i I_i A_i \quad (19)$$

where A_i is the surface area (in m^2) associated with the ith measurement location.

ANSI *Standard* S12.55 describes various methods used to calculate sound power level under free-field conditions. Measurement accuracy is limited at lower frequencies by the difficulty of obtaining room surface treatments with high sound absorption coefficients at low frequencies. For example, a glass fiber wedge structure that gives significant absorption at 70 Hz must be at least 4 ft long.

The relationship between sound power level L_w and sound pressure level L_p for a nondirectional sound source in a free field at distance r in feet can be written as

$$L_w = L_p + 20 \log r + 0.7 \quad (20)$$

For directional sources, use Equation (19) to compute sound power.

Often, a completely free field is not available, and measurements must be made in a free field over a reflecting plane. This means that the sound source is placed on a hard floor (in an otherwise sound-absorbing room) or on smooth, flat pavement outdoors. Because the sound is then radiated into a hemisphere rather than a full sphere, the relationship for L_w and L_p for a nondirectional sound source becomes

$$L_w = L_p + 20 \log r - 2.3 \quad (21)$$

A sound source may radiate different amounts of sound power in different directions. A directivity pattern can be established by measuring sound pressure under free-field conditions, either in an anechoic room or over a reflecting plane in a hemianechoic space at several points around the source. The directivity factor Q is the ratio of the squared sound pressure at a given angle from the sound source to the squared sound pressure that would be produced by the same source radiating uniformly in all directions. Q is a function of frequency and direction. The section on Typical Sources of Sound in this chapter and Chapter 48 of the 2015 *ASHRAE Handbook—HVAC Applications* provide more detailed information on sound source directivity.

Reverberation Room Method

Another method to determine sound power places the sound source in a reverberation room. AHRI *Standard* 220 and ANSI *Standard* S12.58 give standardized methods for determining the sound power of HVAC equipment in reverberation rooms when the sound source contains mostly broadband sound or when tonal sound is prominent. These standards provide a method of qualifying the room to verify that sound power levels for both broadband and tonal noise sources can be accurately determined.

Some sound sources that can be measured by these methods are room air conditioners, refrigeration compressors, components of central HVAC systems, and air terminal devices. For ducted equipment, AHRI *Standard* 260 provides a method of test and AHRI *Standards* 270 and 370 provide test methods for measuring outdoor equipment. Compressors should be tested according to AHRI *Standard* 530. ANSI/ASHRAE *Standard* 130, and ANSI/AHRI *Standard* 880-2011 establish special measuring procedures for some of these units. AMCA *Standard* 300 is appropriate for testing fans that are not incorporated into equipment.

Two measurement methods may be used in reverberation rooms: direct and substitution. In **direct reverberation room measurement**, the sound pressure level is measured with the source in the reverberation room at several locations at a distance of at least 3 ft from the source and at least one-quarter of a wavelength from the surfaces of the room. The sound power level is calculated from the average of the sound pressure levels, using the reverberation time and the volume of the reverberation room.

The relationship between sound power level and sound pressure level in a reverberation room is given by

$$L_w = L_p + 10 \log V - 10 \log T_{60} - 29.4 \tag{22}$$

where

L_p = sound pressure level averaged over room, dB re 20 μPa
V = volume of room, ft³
T_{60} = room reverberation time (time required for a 60 dB decay), s

The **substitution** procedure implemented in most ASHRAE, AHRI, and AMCA test standards uses a calibrated **reference sound source (RSS)**. The sound power levels of noise radiated by an RSS are known by calibration using the free-field methodmethod or, in the case of AHRI *Standard* 250-2013, a hemi-anechoic room method.

The most common RSS is a small, vertically shafted direct-drive fan impeller that has no volute housing or scroll. The forward-curved impeller has a choke plate on its inlet face, causing the fan to operate in a rotating-stall condition that is very noisy. The reference source is designed to have a stable sound power level output from 63 to 8000 Hz and a relatively uniform frequency spectrum in each octave band.

Sound pressure level measurements are first made in the reverberant field (far from the RSS or source in question) with only the reference sound source operating in the test room. Then the reference source is turned off and the measurements are repeated with the given source in operation. Because the acoustical environment and measurement locations are the same for both sources, the differences in sound pressure levels measured represent differences in sound power level between the two sources.

Using this method, the relationship between sound power level and sound pressure level for the two sources is given by

$$L_w = L_p + (L_w - L_p)_{ref} \tag{23}$$

where

L_p = sound pressure level averaged over room, dB re 20 μPa
$(L_w - L_p)_{ref}$ = difference between sound power level and sound pressure level of reference sound source

Progressive Wave (In-Duct) Method

By attaching a fan to one end of a duct, sound energy is confined to a progressive wave field in the duct. Fan sound power can then be determined by measuring the sound pressure level inside the duct. Intensity is then estimated from the sound pressure levels (see the section on the Free-Field Method) and multiplied by the cross-sectional area of the duct to find the sound power. The method is described in detail in ASHRAE *Standard* 68 (AMCA *Standard* 330) for in-duct testing of fans. This method is not commonly used because of difficulties in constructing the required duct termination and in discriminating between fan noise and flow noise caused by the presence of the microphone in the duct.

Sound Intensity Method

The average sound power radiated by the source can be determined by measuring the sound intensity over the sphere or hemisphere surrounding a sound source (see the sections on Measurement of Acoustic Intensity and on the Free-Field Method). One advantage of this method is that, with certain limitations, sound intensity (and therefore sound power) measurements can be made in the presence of steady background noise in semireverberant environments and in the acoustic nearfield of sources. Another advantage is that by measuring sound intensity over surfaces that enclose a sound source, sound directivity can be determined. Also, for large sources, areas of radiation can be localized using intensity measurements. This procedure can be particularly useful in diagnosing sources of noise during product development.

International and U.S. standards that prescribe methods for making sound power measurements with sound intensity probes consisting of two closely spaced microphones include ANSI *Standard* S12.12 and ISO *Standards* 9614-1 and 9614-2. In some situations, the sound fields may be so complex that measurements become impractical. A particular concern is that small test rooms or those with somewhat flexible boundaries (e.g., sheet metal or thin drywall) can increase the radiation impedance for the source, which could affect the source's sound power output.

Measurement Bandwidths for Sound Power

Sound power is normally determined in octave or 1/3 octave bands. Occasionally, more detailed determination of the sound source spectrum is required: **narrowband analysis**, using either constant fractional bandwidth (1/12 or 1/24 octave) or constant absolute bandwidth (e.g., 1 Hz). The most frequently used analyzer types are digital filter analyzers for constant-percent bandwidth measurements and fast Fourier transform (FFT) analyzers for constant-bandwidth measurements. Narrowband analyses are used to determine the frequencies of pure tones and their harmonics in a sound spectrum.

5. CONVERTING FROM SOUND POWER TO SOUND PRESSURE

Designers are often required to use sound power level information of a source to predict the sound pressure level at a given location. Sound pressure at a given location in a room from a source of known sound power level depends on (1) room volume, (2) room furnishings and surface treatments, (3) magnitude of sound source(s), (4) distance from sound source(s) to point of observation, and (5) directivity of source.

The classic relationship between a single-point source sound power level and room sound pressure level at some frequency is

$$L_p = L_w + 10 \log(Q/4\pi r^2 + 4/R) + 10.3 \tag{24}$$

where

L_p = sound pressure level, dB re 20 μPa
L_w = sound power level, dB re 10^{-12} W
Q = directivity of sound source (dimensionless)
r = distance from source, ft
R = room constant, $S\alpha/(1 - \alpha)$
S = sum of all surface areas, ft²
α = average absorption coefficient of room surfaces at given frequency, given by

$$\sum_i S_i\alpha_i / \sum_i S_i$$

where S_i is area of ith surface and α_i is absorption coefficient for ith surface.

If the source is outdoors, far from reflecting surfaces, this relationship simplifies to

$$L_p = L_w + 10 \log(Q/4\pi r^2) + 10.3 \tag{25}$$

This relationship does not account for atmospheric absorption, weather effects, and barriers. Note that r^2 is present because the sound pressure in a free field decreases with $1/r^2$ (the inverse-square law; see the section on Sound Transmission Paths). Each time the distance from the source is doubled, the sound pressure level decreases by 6 dB.

For a simple source centered in a large, flat, reflecting surface, Q may be taken as 2. At the junction of two large flat surfaces, Q is 4; in a corner, Q is 8.

In most typical rooms, the presence of acoustically absorbent surfaces and sound-scattering elements (e.g., furniture) creates a relationship between sound power and sound pressure level that is difficult to predict. For example, hospital rooms, which have only a small amount of absorption, and executive offices, which have substantial absorption, are similar when the comparison is based on the same room volume and distance between the source and point of observation.

Using a series of measurements taken in typical rooms, Equation (26) was developed to estimate the sound pressure level at a chosen observation point in a normally furnished room. The estimate is accurate to ±2 dB (Schultz 1985).

$$L_p = L_w - 5 \log V - 3 \log f - 10 \log r + 25 \tag{26}$$

Equation (26) applies to a single sound source in the room itself, not to sources above the ceiling. With more than one source, total sound pressure level at the observation point is obtained by adding the contribution from each source in energy or power-like units, not decibels, and then converting back to sound pressure level [see Equation (10)]. Studies (Warnock 1997, 1998a, 1998b) indicate that sound sources above ceilings may not act as point sources, and Equation (26) may not apply (AHRI *Standard* 885).

6. SOUND TRANSMISSION PATHS

Sound from a source is transmitted along one or more paths to a receiver. Airborne and structureborne transmission paths are both of concern for the HVAC system designer. Sound transmission between rooms occurs along both airborne and structureborne transmission paths. Chapter 48 of the 2015 *ASHRAE Handbook—HVAC Applications* has additional information on transmission paths.

Spreading Losses

In a free field, the intensity I of sound radiated from a single source with dimensions that are not large compared to an acoustic wavelength is equal to the power W radiated by the source divided by the surface area A (expressed in m^2) over which the power is spread:

$$I = W/A \tag{27}$$

In the absence of reflection, the spherical area over which power spreads is $A = 4\pi(r/3.28)^2$, so that the intensity is

$$I = W/4\pi(r/3.28)^2 \tag{28}$$

where r is the distance from the source in feet (with a 3.28 ft/m conversion factor). Taking the level of the intensity (i.e., 10 log) and using Equation (20) to relate intensity to sound pressure levels leads to

$$L_p = L_w - 10 \log(4\pi r^2) + 10.3 \tag{29}$$

which becomes

$$L_p = L_w - 20 \log r - 0.7 = L_w - 10 \log(r^2) - 0.7 \tag{30}$$

Thus, the sound pressure level decreases as 10 log(r^2), or 6 dB per doubling of distance. This reduction in sound pressure level of sound radiated into the free field from a single source is called **spherical spreading loss**.

Direct Versus Reverberant Fields

Equation (24) relates the sound pressure level L_p in a room at distance r from a source to the sound power level L_w of the source. The first term in the brackets ($Q/4\pi r^2$) represents sound radiated directly from the source to the receiver, and includes the source's directivity Q and the spreading loss $1/4\pi r^2$ from the source to the observation location. The second term in the brackets, $4/R$, represents the reverberant field created by multiple reflections from room surfaces. The room constant is

$$R = \frac{\sum_i S_i \alpha_i}{1 - \bar{\alpha}} \tag{31}$$

where $\bar{\alpha}$ is the spatial average absorption coefficient,

$$\bar{\alpha} = \frac{\sum_i S_i \alpha_i}{\sum_i S_i} \tag{32}$$

At distances close enough to the source that $Q/4\pi r^2$ is larger than $4/R$, the direct field is dominant and Equation (24) can be approximated by

$$L_p = L_w + 10 \log\left(\frac{Q}{4\pi r^2}\right) + 10.3 \tag{33}$$

Equation (33) is independent of room absorption R, which indicates that adding absorption to the room will not change the sound pressure level. At distances far enough from the source that $Q/4\pi r^2$ is less than $4/R$, Equation (24) can be approximated by

$$L_p = L_w + 10 \log\left(\frac{4}{R}\right) + 10.3 = L_w - 10 \log R + 16.3 \tag{34}$$

Adding absorption to the room increases the room constant and thereby reduces the sound pressure level. The reduction in reverberant sound pressure levels associated with adding absorption in the room is approximated by

$$\text{Reduction} \approx 10 \log\left(\frac{R_2}{R_1}\right) \tag{35}$$

where R_2 is the room constant for the room with added absorption and R_1 is the room constant for the room before absorption is added. The distance from the source where the reverberant field first becomes dominant such that adding absorption to the room is effective is the critical distance r_c, obtained by setting $Q/4\pi r^2 = 4/R$. This leads to

$$r_c \approx 0.04\sqrt{QR} \tag{36}$$

where R is in ft^2 and r_c is in ft.

Airborne Transmission

Sound transmits readily through air, both indoors and outdoors. Indoor sound transmission paths include the direct line of sight between the source and receiver, as well as reflected paths introduced by the room's walls, floor, ceiling, and furnishings, which cause multiple sound reflection paths.

Outdoors, the effects of the reflections are small, unless the source is located near large reflecting surfaces. However, wind and temperature gradients can cause sound outdoors to refract (bend) and change propagation direction. Without strong wind and temperature gradients and at small distances, sound propagation outdoors follows the inverse square law. Therefore, Equations (20) and (21) can generally be used to calculate the relationship between sound power level and sound pressure level for fully free-field and hemispherical free-field conditions, respectively.

Ductborne Transmission

Ductwork can provide an effective sound transmission path because the sound is primarily contained within the boundaries of the ductwork and thus suffers only small spreading losses. Sound can transmit both upstream and downstream from the source. A special case of ductborne transmission is **crosstalk**, where sound is transmitted from one room to another via the duct path. Where duct geometry changes abruptly (e.g., at elbows, branches, and terminations), the resulting change in the acoustic impedance reflects sound, which increases propagation losses. Chapter 48 of the 2015 *ASHRAE Handbook—HVAC Applications* has additional information on losses for airborne sound propagation in ducts.

Room-to-Room Transmission

Room-to-room sound transmission generally involves both airborne and structureborne sound paths. The sound power incident on a room surface element undergoes three processes: (1) some sound energy is reflected from the surface element back into the source room, (2) a portion of the energy is lost through energy transfer into the material comprising the surface element, and (3) the remainder is transmitted through the surface element to the other room. Airborne sound is radiated as the surface element vibrates in the receiving room, and structureborne sound can be transmitted via the studs of a partition or the floor and ceiling surfaces.

Structureborne Transmission

Solid structures are efficient transmission paths for sound, which frequently originates as a vibration imposed on the transmitting structure. Typically, only a small amount of the input energy is radiated by the structure as airborne sound. With the same force excitation, a lightweight structure with little inherent damping radiates more sound than a massive structure with greater damping.

Flanking Transmission

Sound from the source room can bypass the primary separating element and get into the receiving room along other paths, called **flanking paths**. Common sound flanking paths include return air plenums, doors, and windows. Less obvious paths are those along floor and adjoining wall structures. Such flanking paths can reduce sound isolation between rooms. Flanking can explain poor sound isolation between spaces when the partition between them is known to provide very good sound insulation, and how sound can be heard in a location far from the source in a building. Determining whether flanking sound transmission is important and what paths are involved can be difficult. Experience with actual situations and the theoretical aspects of flanking transmission is very helpful. Sound intensity methods may be useful in determining flanking paths.

7. TYPICAL SOURCES OF SOUND

Whenever mechanical power is generated or transmitted, a fraction of the power is converted into sound power and radiated into the air. Therefore, virtually any major component of an HVAC system could be considered a sound source (e.g., fans, pumps, ductwork, piping, motors). The component's sound source characteristics depend on its construction, form of mechanical power, and integration with associated system components. The most important source characteristics include total sound power output L_w, frequency distribution, and radiation directivity Q. In addition, a vibrating HVAC system may be relatively quiet but transmit noise to connecting components, such as the unit casing, which may be serious sources of radiated noise. All of these characteristics vary with frequency.

Source Strength

For airborne noise, source strength should be expressed in terms of sound power levels. For structureborne noise (i.e., vibration), source strengths should be expressed in terms of free vibration levels (measured with the source free from any attachments). Because it is difficult to free a source from all attachments, measurements made with the source on soft mounts, with small mechanical impedances compared to the impedance of the source, can be used to obtain good approximations to free vibration levels.

Directivity of Sources

Noise radiation from sources can be directional. The larger the source, relative to an acoustic wavelength, the greater the potential of the source to be directional. Small sources tend to be nondirectional. The directivity of a source is expressed by the directivity factor Q as

$$Q = \frac{p^2(\theta)}{p_{ave}^2} \tag{37}$$

where $p^2(\theta)$ is the squared pressure observed in direction θ and p_{ave}^2 is the energy average of the squared pressures measured over all directions.

Acoustic Nearfield

Not all unsteady pressures produced by the vibrating surfaces of a source or directly by disturbances in flow result in radiated sound. Some unsteady pressures "cling" to the surface. Their magnitude decreases rapidly with distance from the source, whereas the magnitude of radiating pressures decreases far less rapidly. The region close to the source where nonradiating unsteady pressures are significant is called the **acoustic nearfield**. Sound pressure level measurements should not be made in the acoustic nearfield because it is difficult to relate sound pressure levels measured in the nearfield to radiated levels. In general, the nearfield for most sources extends no more than 3 ft from the source. However, at lower frequencies and for large sources, sound pressure level measurements should be made more than 3 ft from the source when possible.

Sound and vibration sources in HVAC systems are so numerous that it is impractical to provide a complete listing here. Major sources include rotating and reciprocating equipment such as compressors, fans, motors, pumps, air-handling units, water-source heat pumps (WSHPs, often used in hotels), rooftop units, and chillers.

Noise generation occurs from many mechanisms, including

- Vortex shedding, which can be tonal, at the trailing edges of fan blades. Levels of vortex shedding noise increase with velocity of flow v_b over the blade proportionate to $\log(v_b)$.
- Turbulence generated upstream of the fan and ingested into the fan. Levels of this broadband noise increase proportionate to $\log(v_0)$, where v_0 is the free-stream velocity of flow into the fan. Turbulence in the boundary layer on the surface of fan blades also causes broadband noise that increases proportionate to $\log(v_b)$. Flow that separates from blade surfaces can cause low-frequency noise. Nonuniform inflow to fans, created by obstructions, can produce tonal noise at frequencies of blade passage ($f_b = Nf_r$, where N is the number of blades and f_r is the rotation speed in rev/s) and integer multiples. Fan imbalance produces vibration at frequencies of shaft rotation and multiples. These low-frequency vibrations can couple to the structures to which the fan is attached, which can transmit the vibration over long distances and radiate low-frequency noise into rooms.
- Air and fluid sounds, such as those associated with flow through ductwork, piping systems, grilles, diffusers, terminal boxes, manifolds, and pressure-reducing stations.
- Turbulent flow inside ducts, which is a source of broadband noise. Levels increase proportionate to $\log(v_0)$. Sharp corners of elbows and branches can separate flow from duct walls, producing low-frequency noise.
- Excitation of surfaces (e.g., friction); movement of mechanical linkages; turbulent flow impacts on ducts, plenum panels, and pipes; and impacts within equipment, such as cams and valve slap. Broadband flow noise increases rapidly with flow velocity v

[60 to 80 log(v)], so reducing flow velocities can be very effective in reducing broadband noise.
- Magnetostriction (transformer hum), which becomes significant in motor laminations, transformers, switchgear, lighting ballasts, and dimmers. A characteristic of magnetostrictive oscillations is that their fundamental frequency is twice the electrical line frequency (120 Hz in a 60 Hz electrical distribution system.)

8. CONTROLLING SOUND

Terminology

The following noninterchangeable terms are used to describe the acoustical performance of many system components. ASTM *Standard* C634 defines additional terms.

Sound attenuation is a general term describing the reduction of the level of sound as it travels from a source to a receiver.

Insertion loss (IL) of a silencer or other sound-attenuating element, expressed in dB, is the decrease in sound pressure level or sound intensity level, measured at a fixed receiver location, when the sound-attenuating element is inserted into the path between the source and receiver. For example, if a straight, unlined piece of ductwork were replaced with a duct silencer, the sound level difference at a fixed location would be considered the silencer's insertion loss. Measurements are typically in either octave or 1/3 octave bands.

Sound transmission loss (TL) of a partition or other building element is equal to 10 times the logarithm of the ratio of the airborne sound power incident on the partition to the sound power transmitted by the partition and radiated on the other side, in decibels. Measurements are typically in octave or 1/3 octave bands. Chapter 48 of the 2015 *ASHRAE Handbook—HVAC Applications* defines the special case of breakout transmission loss through duct walls.

Noise reduction (NR) is the difference between the space-average sound pressure levels produced in two enclosed spaces or rooms (a receiving room and a source room) by one or more sound sources in the source room. An alternative, non-ASTM definition of NR is the difference in sound pressure levels measured upstream and downstream of a duct silencer or sound-attenuating element. Measurements are typically in octave or 1/3 octave bands. For partitions, NR is related to the transmission loss TL as follows:

$$\mathrm{NR} = \mathrm{TL} - 10\log\left(\frac{S}{R}\right) \tag{38}$$

where S is the partition's surface area and R is the room constant for the receiving room. Note that sound pressure levels measured close to the partition on the receiving side may be higher and should not be included in the space average used to compute the noise reduction.

Random-incidence sound absorption coefficient α is the fraction of incident sound energy absorbed by a surface exposed to randomly incident sound. It is measured in a reverberation room using 1/3 octave bands of broadband sound (ASTM *Standard* C423). The sound absorption coefficient of a material in a specific 1/3 octave band depends on the material's thickness, airflow resistivity, stiffness, and method of attachment to the supporting structure.

Scattering is the change in direction of sound propagation caused by an obstacle or inhomogeneity in the transmission medium. It results in the incident sound energy being dispersed in many directions.

Enclosures and Barriers

Enclosing a sound source is a common means of controlling airborne radiation from a source. Enclosure performance is expressed in terms of insertion loss. The mass of the enclosure panels combines with the stiffness (provided by compression) of the air trapped between the source and enclosure panel to produce a resonance. At resonance, the insertion loss may be negative, indicating that radiated noise levels are higher with the enclosure than without it. Therefore, the enclosure design should avoid aligning the enclosure resonance with frequencies commonly radiated from the source at high levels. At low frequencies, insertion loss of enclosures is more sensitive to stiffness of the enclosure panels than to the surface mass density of the panels. At high frequencies, the opposite is true.

The insertion loss of an enclosure may be severely compromised by openings or leaks. All penetrations must be sealed. Also, at higher frequencies, adding an enclosure creates a reverberant space between the outer surfaces of the source and the inner surfaces of the enclosure. To avoid build-up of reverberant noise, and thereby noise transmitted through the enclosure, add absorption inside the enclosure.

A barrier is a solid element that blocks line-of-sight transmission but does not totally enclose the source or receiver. Properly designed barriers can effectively block sound that propagates directly from the source to the receiver. Barrier performance is expressed in terms of insertion loss: in general, the greater the increase in the path over or around the barrier relative to the direct path between the source and receiver without the barrier, the greater the barrier's insertion losses. Thus, placing the barrier close to the source or receiver is better than midway between the two. The barrier must break the line of sight between the source and receiver to be effective. Insertion losses increase as the barrier extends further above the line of sight. Barriers are only effective in reducing levels for sound propagated directly from the source to the receiver; they do not reduce levels of sound reflected from surfaces in rooms that bypass the barrier. Therefore, barriers are less effective in reverberant spaces than in nonreverberant spaces.

Partitions

Partitions are typically either single- or double-leaf. **Single-leaf partitions** are solid homogeneous panels with both faces rigidly connected. Examples are gypsum board, plywood, concrete block, brick, and poured concrete. The transmission loss of a single-leaf partition depends mainly on its surface mass (mass per unit area): the heavier the partition, the less it vibrates in response to sound waves and the less sound it radiates on the side opposite the sound source. Surface mass can be increased by increasing the partition's thickness or its density.

The **mass law** is a semiempirical expression that can predict transmission loss for randomly incident sound for thin, homogeneous single-leaf panels below the critical frequency (discussed later in this section) for the panel. It is written as

$$\mathrm{TL} = 20\log(w_s f) - 33 \tag{39}$$

where

TL = transmission loss
w_s = surface mass of panel, lb/ft²
f = frequency, Hz

The mass law predicts that transmission loss increases by 6 dB for each doubling of surface mass or frequency. If sound is incident only perpendicularly on the panel (rarely found in real-world applications), TL is about 5 dB greater than that predicted by Equation (39).

Transmission loss also depends on stiffness and internal damping. The transmission losses of three single-leaf walls are shown in Figure 2. For 5/8 in. gypsum board, TL depends mainly on the surface mass of the wall at frequencies below about 1 kHz; agreement with the mass law is good. At higher frequencies, there is a dip in the TL curve called the **coincidence dip** because it occurs at the frequency where the wavelength of flexural vibrations in the wall coincides with the wavelength of sound on the panel surface. The lowest frequency where coincidence between the flexural and surface pressure waves can occur is called the **critical frequency** f_c:

$$f_c = \frac{c^2}{2\pi}\left(\frac{12\rho}{Eh^2}\right)^{1/2} \quad (40)$$

where

ρ = density of panel material, lb/ft³
E = Young's modulus of panel material, lb/ft²
h = thickness of outer panel of partition, ft
c = sound speed in air, ft/s

This equation indicates that increasing the material's stiffness and/or thickness reduces the critical frequency, and that increasing the material's density increases the critical frequency. For example, the 6 in. concrete slab weighs about 75 lb/ft² and has a coincidence frequency at 125 Hz. Thus, over most of the frequency range shown in Figure 2, the transmission loss for the 6 in. concrete slab is well below that predicted by mass law. The coincidence dip for the 25 gage steel sheet occurs at high frequencies not shown in the figure.

The **sound transmission class (STC) rating** of a partition or assembly is a single number rating often used to classify sound isolation for speech (ASTM *Standards* E90 and E413). To determine a partition's STC rating, compare transmission losses measured in 1/3 octave bands with center frequencies from 125 to 4000 Hz to the STC contour shown in Figure 3. This contour is moved up until either

- The sum of differences between TL values below the contour and the corresponding value on the contour is no more than 32, or
- One of the differences between the contour and a TL value is no greater than 8.

The STC is then the value on the contour at 500 Hz. As shown in Figure 3, the STC contour deemphasizes transmission losses at low frequencies, so the STC rating should not be used as an indicator of an assembly's ability to control sound that is rich in low frequencies. Most fan sound spectra have dominant low-frequency sound; therefore, to control fan sound, walls and slabs should be selected only on the basis of 1/3 octave or octave band sound transmission loss values, particularly at low frequencies.

Note also that sound transmission loss values for ceiling tile are inappropriate for estimating sound reduction between a sound source located in a ceiling plenum and the room below. See AHRI *Standard* 885 for guidance.

Walls with identical STC ratings may not provide identical sound insulation at all frequencies. Most single-number rating systems have limited frequency ranges, so designers should select partitions and floors based on their 1/3 octave or octave band sound transmission loss values instead, especially when frequencies below 125 Hz are important.

For a given total mass in a wall or floor, much higher values of TL can be obtained by forming a **double-leaf** construction where each layer is independently or resiliently supported so vibration transmission between them is minimized. As well as mass, TL for such walls depends on cavity depth. Mechanical decoupling of leaves reduces sound transmission through the panel, relative to the transmission that would occur with the leaves structurally connected. However, transmission losses for a double-leaf panel are less than the sum of the transmission losses for each leaf. Air in the cavity couples the two mechanically decoupled leaves. Also, resonances occur inside the cavity between the leaves, thus increasing transmission (decreasing transmission loss) through the partition. Negative effects at resonances can be reduced by adding sound-absorbing material inside the cavity. For further information, see Chapter 48 of the 2015 *ASHRAE Handbook—HVAC Applications*.

Transmission losses of an enclosure may be severely compromised by openings or leaks in the partition. Ducts that lead into or through a noisy space can carry sound to many areas of a building. Designers need to consider this factor when designing duct, piping, and electrical systems.

When a partition contains two different constructions (e.g., a partition with a door), the transmission loss TL_c of the composite partition may be estimated using the following equation:

$$TL_c = 10 \log\left[\frac{S_1 + S_2}{S_1\tau_1 + S_2\tau_2}\right] \quad (41)$$

where S_1 and S_2 are the surface areas of the two types of constructions, and τ_1 and τ_2 are the transmissibilities, where $\tau = 10^{-TL/10}$. For leaks, $\tau = 1$. For a partition with a transmission of 40 dB, a hole that covers only 1% of the surface area results in a composite transmission loss of 20 dB, a 20 dB reduction in the transmission loss without the hole. This shows the importance of sealing penetrations through partitions to maintain design transmission losses.

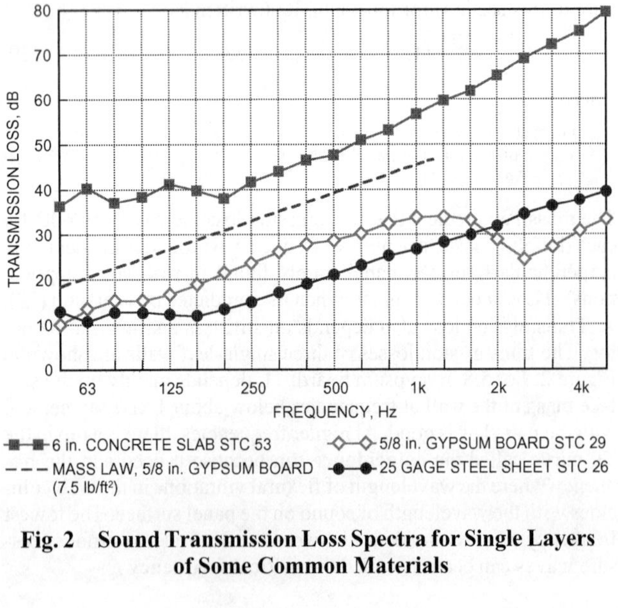

Fig. 2 Sound Transmission Loss Spectra for Single Layers of Some Common Materials

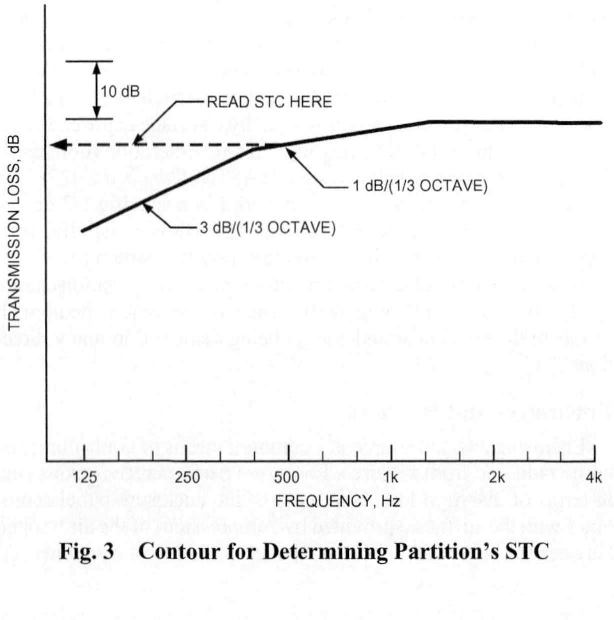

Fig. 3 Contour for Determining Partition's STC

Sound Attenuation in Ducts and Plenums

Most ductwork, even a sheet metal duct without acoustical lining or silencers, attenuates sound to some degree. The natural attenuation of unlined ductwork is minimal, but can, especially for long runs of rectangular ductwork, significantly reduce ductborne sound. Acoustic lining of ductwork can greatly attenuate sound propagation through ducts, particularly at middle to high frequencies. Chapter 48 of the 2015 *ASHRAE Handbook—HVAC Applications* has a detailed discussion of lined and unlined ductwork attenuation.

If analysis shows that lined ductwork will not reduce sound propagation adequately, commercially available sound attenuators (also known as **sound traps** or **duct silencers**) can be used. There are three types: dissipative, reactive, and active. The first two are commonly known as **passive attenuators**.

- **Dissipative silencers** use absorptive media such as glass or rock fiber as the principal sound-absorption mechanism. Thick, perforated sheet metal baffles filled with low-density fiber insulation restrict the air passage width within the attenuator housing. The fiber is sometimes protected from the airstream by cloths or films. This type of attenuator is most effective in reducing mid- and high-frequency sound energy.
- **Reactive silencers** (sometimes called **mufflers**) rely on changes in impedance to reflect energy back toward the source and away from the receiver. This attenuator type is typically used in HVAC systems serving hospitals, laboratories, or other areas with strict air quality standards. They are constructed only of metal, both solid and perforated. Chambers of specially designed shapes and sizes behind the perforated metal are tuned as resonators or expansion chambers to react with and reduce sound power at selected frequencies. When designed for a broad frequency range, they are usually not as effective as dissipative attenuators of the same length. However, they can be highly effective and compact if designed for a limited frequency range (e.g., for a pure tone).
- **Active silencer systems** use microphones, loudspeakers, and appropriate electronics to reduce in-duct sound by generating sound 180° out of phase that destructively interferes with the incident sound energy. Microphones sample the sound field in the duct and loudspeakers generate signals with phase opposite to the original noise. Controlled laboratory experiments have shown that active attenuators reduce both broadband and tonal sound, but are typically only effective in the 31.5 through 250 Hz octave bands. Active silencers are more effective for tonal than for broadband noise. Insertion losses of as much as 30 dB have been achieved under controlled conditions. Because the system's microphones and loudspeakers are mounted flush with the duct wall, there is no obstruction to airflow and therefore negligible pressure drop. Because active silencers are not effective in excessively turbulent airflow, their use is limited to relatively long, straight duct sections with an air velocity less than about 1500 fpm.

Silencers are available for fans, cooling towers, air-cooled condensers, compressors, gas turbines, and many other pieces of commercial and industrial equipment. HVAC silencers are normally installed on the intake or discharge side (or both) of a fan or air-handling unit. They may also be used on the receiver side of other noise generators such as terminal boxes, valves, and dampers.

Self-noise (i.e., noise generated by airflow through the silencer) can limit an attenuator's effective insertion loss for air velocities over about 2000 fpm. Sound power at the silencer outlet is a combination of the power of the noise attenuated by the silencer and the noise generated inside the silencer by flow. Thus, output power W_M is related to input power W_0 as follows:

$$W_M = W_0 10^{-\mathrm{IL}/10} + W_{SG} \tag{42}$$

where IL is the insertion loss and W_{SG} is the power of the self-noise. It is also important to determine the dynamic insertion loss at design airflow velocity through the silencer, because a silencer's insertion loss varies with flow velocity.

End reflection losses caused by abrupt area changes in duct cross section are sometimes useful in controlling propagation at low frequencies. Low-frequency noise reduction is inversely proportional to the cross-sectional dimension of the duct, with the end reflection effect maximized in smaller cross sections and when the duct length of the smaller cross section is several duct diameters. Note, however, that abrupt area changes can increase flow velocities, which increase broadband high-frequency noise.

Where space is available, a **lined plenum** can provide excellent attenuation across a broad frequency range, especially effective at low frequencies. The combination of end reflections at the plenum's entrance and exit, a large offset between the entrance and exit, and sound-absorbing lining on the plenum walls can result in an effective sound-attenuating device.

Chapter 48 of the 2015 *ASHRAE Handbook—HVAC Applications* has additional information on sound control.

Standards for Testing Duct Silencers

Attenuators and duct liner materials are tested according to ASTM *Standard* E477 in North America and ISO *Standard* 7235 elsewhere. These define acoustic and aerodynamic performance in terms of dynamic insertion loss, self-noise, and airflow pressure drop. Many similarities exist, but the ASTM and ISO standards produce differing results because of variations in loudspeaker location, orientation, duct termination conditions, and computation methods. Currently, no standard test methods are available to measure attenuation by active silencers, although it is easy to measure the effectiveness simply by turning the active silencer control system on and off.

Dynamic insertion loss is measured in the presence of both forward and reverse flows. Forward flow occurs when air and sound move in the same direction, as in a supply air or fan discharge system; reverse flow occurs when air and sound travel in opposite directions, as in a return air or fan intake system.

9. SYSTEM EFFECTS

The way the HVAC components are assembled into a system affects the sound level generated by the system. Many engineers believe that satisfactory noise levels in occupied spaces can be achieved solely by using a manufacturer's sound ratings as a design tool, without considering the system influence.

However, most manufacturers' sound data are obtained under standardized (ideal) laboratory test conditions. In the field, different configurations of connected ductwork, and interactions with other components of the installation, often significantly change the operating noise level. For example, uniform flow into or out of a fan is rare in typical field applications. Nonuniform flow conditions usually increase the noise generated by fans, and are difficult to predict. However, the increases can be large (e.g., approaching 10 dB), so it is desirable to design systems to provide uniform inlet conditions. One method is to avoid locating duct turns near the inlet or discharge of a fan. Furthermore, components such as dampers and silencers installed close to fan equipment can produce nonuniformities in the velocity profile at the entrance to the silencer, which results in a significantly higher-than-anticipated pressure drop across that component. The combination of these two system effects changes the operating point on the fan curve. As a result, airflow is reduced and must be compensated for by increasing fan speed, which may increase noise. Conversely, a well-designed damper or silencer can actually improve flow conditions, which may reduce noise levels.

10. HUMAN RESPONSE TO SOUND

Noise

Noise may be defined as any unwanted sound. Sound becomes noise when it

- Is too loud: the sound is uncomfortable or makes speech difficult to understand
- Is unexpected (e.g., the sound of breaking glass)
- Is uncontrolled (e.g., a neighbor's lawn mower)
- Happens at the wrong time (e.g., a door slamming in the middle of the night)
- Contains unwanted tones (e.g., a whine, whistle, or hum)
- Contains unwanted information or is distracting (e.g., an adjacent telephone conversation or undesirable music)
- Is unpleasant (e.g., a dripping faucet)
- Connotes unpleasant experiences (e.g., a mosquito buzz or a siren wail)
- Is any combination of the previous examples

To be noise, sound does not have to be loud, just unwanted. In addition to being annoying, loud noise can cause hearing loss, and, depending on other factors, can affect stress level, sleep patterns, and heart rate.

To increase privacy, broadband sound may be radiated into a room by an electronic sound-masking system that has a random noise generator, amplifier, and multiple loudspeakers. Noise from such a system can mask low-level intrusive sounds from adjacent spaces. This controlled sound may be referred to as *noise*, but not in the context of unwanted sound; rather, it is a broadband, neutral sound that is frequently unobtrusive. It is difficult to design air-conditioning systems to produce noise that effectively masks low-level intrusive sound from adjacent spaces without also being a source of annoyance.

Random noise is an oscillation, the instantaneous magnitude of which cannot be specified for any given instant. The instantaneous magnitudes of a random noise are specified only by probability distributions, giving the fraction of the total time that the magnitude, or some sequence of magnitudes, lies within a specified range (ANSI *Standard* S1.1). There are three types of random noise: white, pink, and red.

- **White noise** has a continuous frequency spectrum with equal energy per hertz over a specified frequency range. Because octave bands double in width for each successive band, for white noise the energy also doubles in each successive octave band. Thus white noise displayed on a 1/3 octave or octave band chart increases in level by 3 dB per octave.
- **Pink noise** has a continuous frequency spectrum with equal energy per constant-percentage bandwidth, such as per octave or 1/3 octave band. Thus pink noise appears on a 1/3 octave or octave band chart as a horizontal line.
- **Red noise** has a continuous frequency spectrum with octave band levels that decrease at a rate of 4 to 5 dB per octave with increasing frequency. Red noise is typical of noise from well-designed HVAC systems.

Predicting Human Response to Sound

Predicting the response of people to any given sound is, at best, only a statistical concept, and, at worst, very inaccurate. This is because response to sound is not only physiological but psychological and depends on the varying attitude of the listener. Hence, the effect of sound is often unpredictable. However, people respond adversely if the sound is considered too loud for the situation or if it sounds "wrong." Therefore, criteria are based on descriptors that account for level and spectrum shape.

Sound Quality

To determine the acoustic acceptability of a space to occupants, sound pressure levels in the space must be known. This, however, is often not sufficient; sound quality is important, too. Factors influencing sound quality include (1) loudness, (2) tone perception, (3) frequency balance, (4) harshness, (5) time and frequency fluctuation, and (6) vibration.

People often perceive sounds with tones (such as a whine or hum) as particularly annoying. A tone can cause a relatively low-level sound to be perceived as noise.

Loudness

The primary method for determining subjective estimations of loudness is to present sounds to a sample of listeners under controlled conditions. Listeners compare an unknown sound with a standard sound. (The accepted standard sound is a pure tone of 1000 Hz or a narrow band of random noise centered on 1000 Hz.) Loudness level is expressed in **phons**, and the loudness level of any sound in phons is equal to the sound pressure level in decibels of a standard sound deemed to be equally loud. Thus, a sound that is judged as loud as a 40 dB, 1000 Hz tone has a loudness level of 40 phons.

Average reactions of humans to tones are shown in Figure 4 (Robinson and Dadson 1956). The reaction changes when the sound is a band of random noise (Pollack 1952), rather than a pure tone (Figure 5). The figures indicate that people are most sensitive in the midfrequency range. The contours in Figure 4 are closer together at low frequencies, showing that at lower frequencies, people are less sensitive to sound level, but are more sensitive to *changes* in level.

Under carefully controlled experimental conditions, humans can detect small changes in sound level. However, for humans to describe a sound as being half or twice as loud requires changes in the overall sound pressure level of about 10 dB. For many people, a 3 dB change is the minimum perceptible difference. This means that halving the power output of the source causes a barely noticeable change in sound pressure level, and power output must be reduced by a factor of 10 before humans determine that loudness has been halved. Table 8 summarizes the effect of changes in sound levels for simple sounds in the frequency range of 250 Hz and higher.

The phon scale covers the large dynamic range of the ear, but does not fit a subjective linear loudness scale. Over most of the

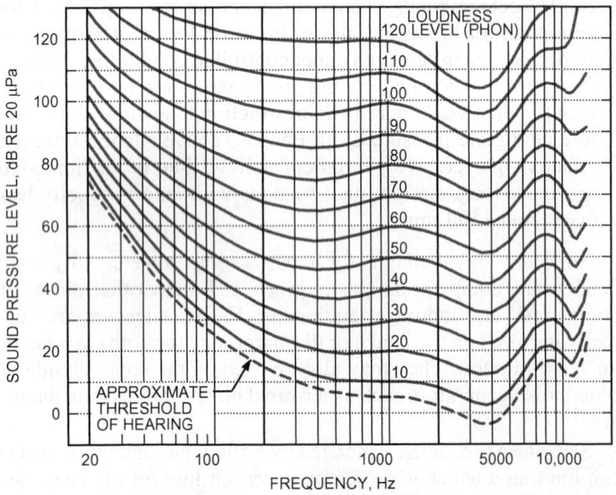

Fig. 4 Free-Field Equal Loudness Contours for Pure Tones
(Robinson and Dadson 1956)

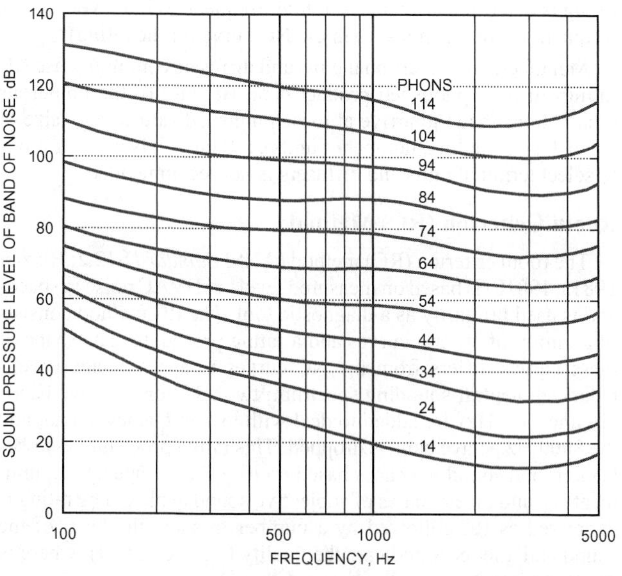

Fig. 5 Equal Loudness Contours for Relatively Narrow Bands of Random Noise

(Reprinted with permission from I. Pollack, *Journal of the Acoustical Society of America*, vol. 24, p. 533, 1952. Copyright 1952, Acoustical Society of America.)

Table 8 Subjective Effect of Changes in Sound Pressure Level, Broadband Sounds (Frequency ≥ 250 Hz)

Subjective Change	Objective Change in Sound Level (Approximate)
Much louder	More than +10 dB
Twice as loud	+10 dB
Louder	+5 dB
Just perceptibly louder	+3 dB
Just perceptibly quieter	–3 dB
Quieter	–5 dB
Half as loud	–10 dB
Much quieter	Less than –10 dB

audible range, a doubling of loudness corresponds to a change of approximately 10 phons. To obtain a quantity proportional to the loudness sensation, use a loudness scale based on the **sone**. One sone equals the loudness level of 40 phons. A rating of two sones corresponds to 50 phons, and so on. In HVAC, only the ventilation fan industry (e.g., bathroom exhaust and sidewall propeller fans) uses loudness ratings.

Standard objective methods for calculating loudness have been developed. ANSI *Standard* S3.4 calculates loudness or loudness level using 1/3 octave band sound pressure level data as a starting point. The loudness index for each 1/3 octave band is obtained from a graph or by calculation. Total loudness is then calculated by combining the loudnesses for each band according to a formula given in the standard. A graphic method using 1/3 octave band sound pressure levels to predict loudness of sound spectra containing tones is presented in Zwicker (ISO *Standard* 532) and German *Standard* DIN 45631. Because of its complexity, loudness has not been widely used in engineering practice in the past.

Acceptable Frequency Spectrum

The most acceptable frequency spectrum for HVAC sound is a balanced or neutral spectrum in which octave band levels decrease at a rate of 4 to 5 dB per octave with increasing frequency. This means that it is not too hissy (excessive high-frequency content) or too rumbly (excessive low-frequency content). Unfortunately, achieving a balanced sound spectrum is not always easy: there may be numerous sound sources to consider. As a design guide, Figure 6 shows the more common mechanical and electrical sound sources and frequency regions that control the indoor sound spectrum. Chapter 48 of the 2015 *ASHRAE Handbook—HVAC Applications* provides more detailed information on treating some of these sound sources.

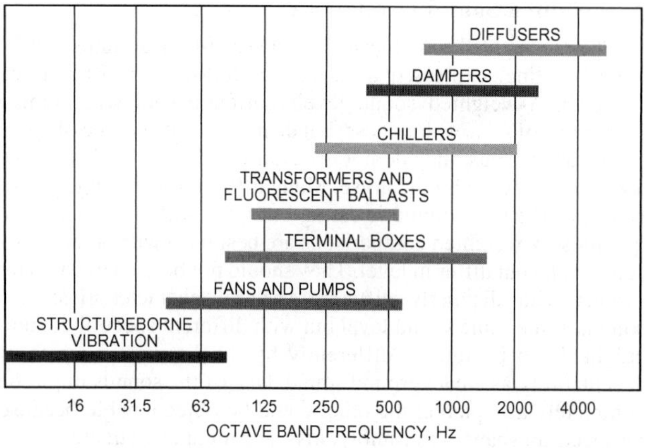

Fig. 6 Frequencies at Which Various Types of Mechanical and Electrical Equipment Generally Control Sound Spectra

11. SOUND RATING SYSTEMS AND ACOUSTICAL DESIGN GOALS

The degree of occupant satisfaction with the background noise level in any architectural space depends on the sound quality of the noise itself, the occupant's aural sensitivity, and specific task engagement. In most cases, background noise must be unobtrusive, meaning that the noise level must not be excessive enough to cause distraction or annoyance, or to interfere with, for example, music listening and speech intelligibility. In addition, the frequency content and temporal variations must not call attention to the noise intrusion, but rather present a bland and unobtrusive background. For critical listening conditions such as for music in a symphony hall or speech in grade schools, background noise must not exceed a relatively low exposure level. However, for speech and music in a high school gymnasium, a significantly higher background noise level will be tolerated. When low annoyance and distractions are a key factor, such as in open-plan offices for occupant productivity, a minimum acceptable background noise must be considered to effectively cover undesirable intruding sounds. Consequently, HVAC system sound control goals vary depending on the required use of the space.

To be unobtrusive, HVAC-related background noise should have the following properties:

- Frequency content that is broadband and smooth in nature, and at a level suitable for the use of the space
- No audible tones or other characteristics such as roar, whistle, hum, or rumble
- No significant time fluctuations in level or frequency such as throbbing or pulsing

Unfortunately, there is no standard process to easily characterize the effects of audible tones and level fluctuations, so currently available rating methods do not adequately address these issues.

Conventional approaches for rating sound in an occupied space include the following.

A-Weighted Sound Level (dBA)

The A-weighted sound level L_A is an easy-to-determine, single-number rating, expressed as a number followed by dBA (e.g., 40 dBA). A-weighted sound levels correlate well with human judgments of relative loudness, but do not indicate degree of spectral balance. Thus, they do not necessarily correlate well with the annoyance caused by the noise. Many different-sounding spectra can have the same numeric rating but quite different subjective qualities. A-weighted comparisons are best used with sounds that sound alike but differ in level. They should not be used to compare sounds with distinctly different spectral characteristics; two sounds at the same sound level but with different spectral content are likely to be judged differently by the listener in terms of acceptability as a background sound. One of the sounds might be completely acceptable; the other could be objectionable because its spectrum shape was rumbly, hissy, or tonal in character.

A-weighted sound levels are used extensively in outdoor environmental noise standards and for estimating the risk of damage to hearing for long-term exposures to noise, such as in industrial environments and other workplaces. In outdoor environmental noise standards, the principal sources of noise are vehicular traffic and aircraft, for which A-weighted criteria of acceptability have been developed empirically.

Outdoor HVAC equipment can create significant sound levels that affect nearby properties and buildings. Local noise ordinances often limit property line A-weighted sound levels and typically are more restrictive during nighttime hours.

Noise Criteria (NC) Method

The NC method remains the predominant design criterion used by HVAC engineers. This single-number rating is somewhat sensitive to the relative loudness and speech interference properties of a given sound spectrum. Its wide use derives in part from its ease of use and its publication in HVAC design textbooks. The method consists of a family of criterion curves now extending from 16 to 8000 Hz and a rating procedure based on speech interference levels (ANSI *Standard* S12.2-2008). The criterion curves define the limits of octave band spectra that must not be exceeded to meet acceptance in certain spaces. The NC curves shown in Figure 7 are in steps of 5 dB. NC-rating procedures for measured data use interpolation, rounded to the nearest dB.

The rating is expressed as NC followed by a number. For example, the spectrum shown is rated NC 43 because this is the lowest rating curve that falls entirely above the measured data. An NC 35 design goal is common for private offices. The background sound level meets this goal if no portion of its spectrum lies above the designated NC 35 curve.

The NC method is sensitive to level but has the disadvantage as a design criterion method that it does not require the sound spectrum to approximate the shape of the NC curves. Thus, many different sounds can have the same numeric rating, but rank differently on the basis of subjective sound quality. In many HVAC systems that do not produce excessive low-frequency sound, the NC rating correlates relatively well with occupant satisfaction if sound quality is not a significant concern or if the octave band levels have a shape similar to the nearest NC curves.

Two problems occur in using the NC procedure as a diagnostic tool. First, when the NC level is determined by a prominent peak in the spectrum, the actual level of resulting background sound may be quieter than that desired for masking unwanted speech and activity sounds, because the spectrum on either side of the tangent peak drops off too rapidly. Second, when the measured spectrum does not match the shape of the NC curve, the resulting sound might be rumbly (levels at low frequencies determine the NC rating and levels at high frequencies roll off faster than the NC curve) or hissy (the NC rating is determined by levels at high frequencies but levels at low frequencies are much less than the NC curve for the rating).

Manufacturers of terminal units and diffusers commonly use NC ratings in their published product data. Because of the numerous assumptions made to arrive at these published values (e.g., size of room, type of ceiling, number of units), relying solely on NC ratings to select terminal units and diffusers is not recommended.

Room Criterion (RC) Method

The room criterion (RC) method (ANSI *Standard* S12.2; Blazier 1981a, 1981b) is based on measured levels of HVAC noise in spaces and is used primarily as a diagnostic tool. The RC method consists of a family of criteria curves and a rating procedure. The shape of these curves differs from the NC curves to approximate a well-balanced, neutral-sounding spectrum; two additional octave bands (16 and 31.5 Hz) are added to deal with low-frequency sound, and the 8000 Hz octave band is dropped. This rating procedure assesses background sound in spaces based on its effect on speech communication, and on estimates of subjective sound quality. The rating is expressed as RC followed by a number to show the level of the sound and a letter to indicate the quality [e.g., RC 35(N), where N denotes neutral].

For a full explanation of RC curves and analysis procedures, see Chapter 48 of the 2015 *ASHRAE Handbook—HVAC Applications*.

Criteria Selection Guidelines

In general, these basic guidelines are important:

- Sound levels below NC or RC 35 are generally not detrimental to good speech intelligibility. Sound levels at or above these levels may interfere with or mask speech.
- Even if the occupancy sound is significantly higher than the anticipated background sound level generated by mechanical equipment, the sound design goal should not necessarily be raised to levels approaching the occupancy sound. This avoids occupants

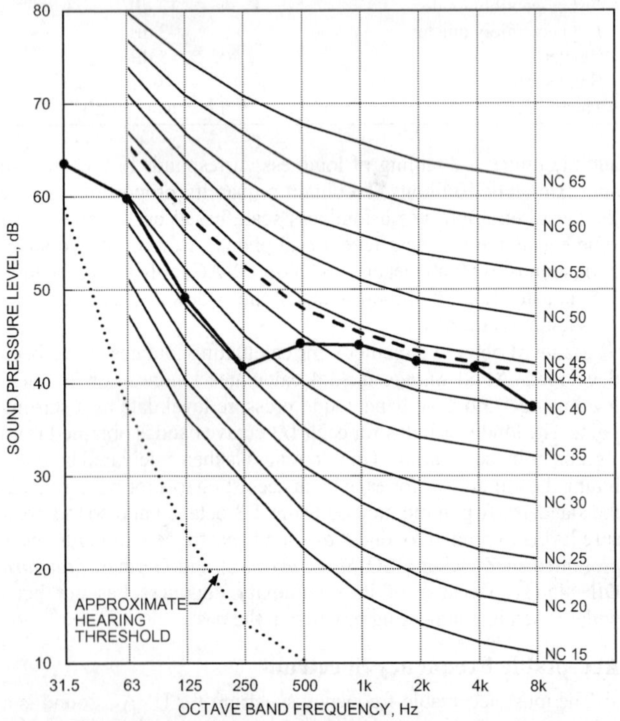

Fig. 7 NC (Noise Criteria) Curves and Sample Spectrum (Curve with Symbols)

having to raise their voices uncomfortably to be heard over the noise.

For full details and recommended background sound level criteria for different spaces, see Chapter 48 of the 2015 *ASHRAE Handbook—HVAC Applications*.

12. FUNDAMENTALS OF VIBRATION

A rigidly mounted machine transmits its internal vibratory forces directly to the supporting structure. However, by inserting resilient mountings (**vibration isolators**) between the machine and supporting structure, the magnitude of transmitted force can be dramatically reduced. Vibration isolators can also be used to protect sensitive equipment from floor vibration.

Single-Degree-of-Freedom Model

The simplest representation of a vibration isolation system is the single-degree-of-freedom model, shown in Figure 8. Only motion along the vertical axis is considered. The isolated system is represented by a mass and the isolator is represented by a spring, which is considered fixed to ground. Excitation (i.e., the vibratory forces generated by the isolated equipment, such as shaft imbalance in rotating machinery) is applied to the mass. This simple model is the basis for catalog information provided by most manufacturers of vibration isolation hardware.

Mechanical Impedance

Mechanical impedance Z_m is a structural property useful in understanding the performance of vibration isolators in a given installation. Z_m is the ratio of the force F applied to the structure divided by the velocity v of the structure's vibration response at the point of excitation:

$$Z_m = F/v \tag{43}$$

At low frequencies, the mechanical impedance of a vibration isolator is approximately equal to $k/2\pi f$, where k is the stiffness of the isolator (force per unit deflection) and f is frequency in Hz (cycles per second). Note that the impedance of the isolator is inversely proportional to frequency. This characteristic is the basis for an isolator's ability to block vibration from the supported structure. In the simple single-degree-of-freedom model, impedance of the isolated mass is proportional to frequency. Thus, as frequency increases, the isolator increasingly provides an impedance mismatch between the isolated structure and ground. This mismatch attenuates the forces imposed on the ground. However, at the system's particular natural frequency (discussed in the following section), the effects of the isolator are decidedly detrimental.

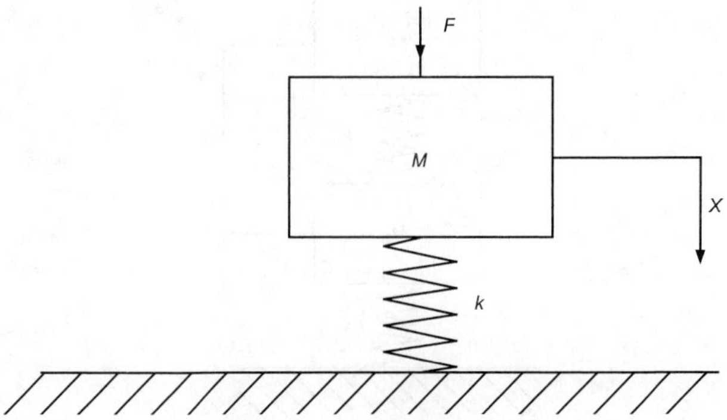

Fig. 8 Single-Degree-of-Freedom System

Natural Frequency

Using the single-degree-of-freedom model, the frequency at which the magnitude of the spring and mass impedances are equal is the **natural frequency f_n**. At this frequency, the mass's vibration response to the applied excitation is a maximum, and the isolator actually amplifies the force transmitted to ground. The natural frequency of the system (also called the **isolation system resonance**) is given approximately by

$$f_n = \frac{1}{2\pi}\sqrt{\frac{k}{M}} \tag{44}$$

where M is the mass of the equipment supported by the isolator. The stiffness k is in lb/in., and M equals the weight (lb_f) divided by the acceleration due to gravity, 386 in/sec^2.

This equation simplifies to

$$f_n = \frac{3.13}{\sqrt{\delta_{st}}} \tag{45}$$

where δ_{st} is the **isolator static deflection** (the incremental distance the isolator spring compresses under the weight of the supported equipment) in inches. Thus, to achieve the appropriate system natural frequency for a given application, it is customary to specify the corresponding isolator static deflection and the load to be supported at each of the mounting points.

The **transmissibility T** of this system is the ratio of the amplitudes of the force transmitted to the building structure to the exciting force produced inside the vibrating equipment. For disturbing frequency f_d, T is given by

$$T = \left|\frac{1}{1-(f_d/f_n)^2}\right| \tag{46}$$

The transmissibility equation is plotted in Figure 9.

It is important to note that T is inversely proportional to the square of the ratio of the disturbing frequency f_d to the system natural frequency f_n. At $f_d = f_n$, resonance occurs: the denominator of Equation (46) equals zero and transmission of vibration is theoretically infinite. In practice, transmissibility at resonance is limited by damping in the system, which is always present to some degree. Thus, the magnitude of vibration amplification at resonance always has a finite, though often dramatically high, value.

Note that vibration isolation (attenuation of force applied to ground) does not occur until the ratio of the disturbing frequency f_d

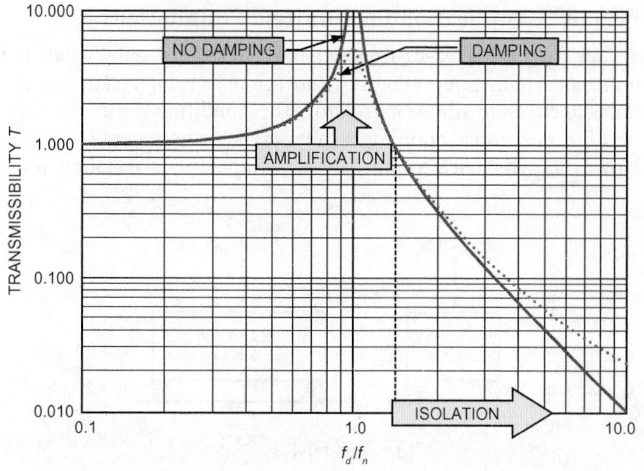

Fig. 9 Vibration Transmissibility T as Function of f_d/f_n

to the system natural frequency f_n is greater than 1.4. Above this ratio, vibration transmissibility decreases (attenuation increases) with the square of frequency.

In designing isolators, it is customary to specify a frequency ratio of at least 3.5, which corresponds to an isolation efficiency of about 90%, or 10% transmissibility. Higher ratios may be specified, but in practice this often does not greatly increase isolation efficiency, especially at frequencies above about 10 times the natural frequency. The reason is that wave effects and other nonlinear characteristics in real isolators cause a deviation from the theoretical curve that limits performance at higher frequencies.

To obtain the design objective of $f_d/f_n \approx 3.5$, the lowest frequency of excitation f_d is determined first. This is usually the shaft rotation rate in hertz (Hz; cycles/second). Because it is usually not possible to change the mass of the isolated equipment, the combined stiffness of the isolators is then selected such that

$$k = (2\pi f_d/3.5)^2 W_f/386 \tag{47}$$

where W_f is the weight of the mounted equipment in lb_f, and k is in lb_f/in. With four isolators, the stiffness of each isolator is k/4, assuming equal mass distribution.

For a given set of isolators, as shown by Equations (44) and (46), if equipment mass is increased, the resonance frequency decreases and isolation increases. In practice, the load-carrying capacity of isolators usually requires that their stiffness or their number be increased. Consequently, the static deflection and transmissibility may remain unchanged.

For example, as shown in Figure 10, a 1000 lb piece of equipment installed on isolators with stiffness k of 1000 lb_f/in. results in a 1 in. deflection and a system resonance frequency f_n of 3.13 Hz. If the equipment operates at 564 rpm (9.4 Hz) and develops an internal force of 100 lb_f, 12.5 lb_f is transmitted to the structure. If the total mass is increased to 10,000 lb by placing the equipment on a concrete inertia base and the stiffness of the springs is increased to 10,000 lb_f/in., the deflection is still 1 in., the resonance frequency of the system is maintained at 3.13 Hz, and the force transmitted to the structure remains at 12.5 lb_f.

The increased mass, however, reduces equipment displacement. The forces F generated inside the mounted equipment, which do not change when mass is added to the equipment, now must excite more mass with the same internal force. Therefore, because $F = Ma$, where a is acceleration, the maximum dynamic displacement of the mounted equipment is reduced by a factor of M_1/M_2, where M_1 and M_2 are the masses before and after mass is added, respectively.

Practical Application for Nonrigid Foundations

The single-degree-of-freedom model is valid only when the impedance of the supporting structure (ground) is high relative to the impedance of the vibration isolator. This condition is usually satisfied for mechanical equipment in on-grade or basement locations. However, when heavy mechanical equipment is installed on a structural floor, particularly on the roof of a building, significantly softer vibration isolators are usually required than in the on-grade or basement case. This is because the impedance of the supporting structure can no longer be ignored.

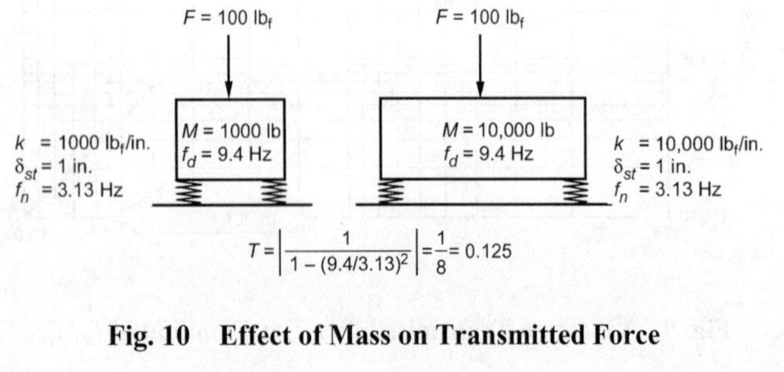

Fig. 10 Effect of Mass on Transmitted Force

For the two-degrees-of-freedom system in Figure 11, mass M_1 and isolator K_1 represent the supported equipment, and M_2 and K_2 represent the effective mass and stiffness of the floor structure. In this case, transmissibility refers to the vibratory force imposed on the floor, and is given by

$$T = \frac{1}{\left[1 - \left(\frac{f_d}{f_{n1}}\right)^2\right] - \frac{1}{\left(\frac{f_{n1}}{f_d}\right)^2 \frac{k_2}{k_1} - \frac{M_2}{M_1}}} \tag{48}$$

As in Equation (46), f_d is the forcing frequency. Frequency f_{n1} is the natural frequency of the isolated equipment with a rigid foundation [Equation (44)].

The implication of Equation (48) relative to Equation (46) is that a nonrigid foundation can severely alter the effectiveness of the isolation system. Figure 12 shows transmissibility of a floor structure with twice the stiffness of the isolator, and a floor effective mass half that of the isolated equipment. Comparing Figure 12 to Figure 9 shows that the nonrigid floor introduces a second resonance well above that of the isolation system assuming a rigid floor. Unless care is taken in the isolation system design, this secondary amplification can cause a serious sound or vibration problem.

As a general rule, it is advisable to design the system such that the static deflection of the isolator, under the applied equipment weight, is on the order of 10 times the incremental static deflection of the floor caused by the equipment weight (Figure 13). Above the rigid-foundation natural frequency f_{n1}, transmissibility is comparable to that of the simple single-degree-of-freedom model.

Other complicating factors exist in actual installations, which often depart from the two-degrees-of-freedom model. These include the effects of horizontal and rotational vibration. Given these complexities, it is often beneficial to collaborate with an experienced acoustical consultant or structural engineer when designing vibration isolation systems applied to flexible floor structures.

13. VIBRATION MEASUREMENT BASICS

Control of HVAC system sound and vibration are of equal importance, but measurement of vibration is often not necessary to determine sources or transmission paths of disturbing sound.

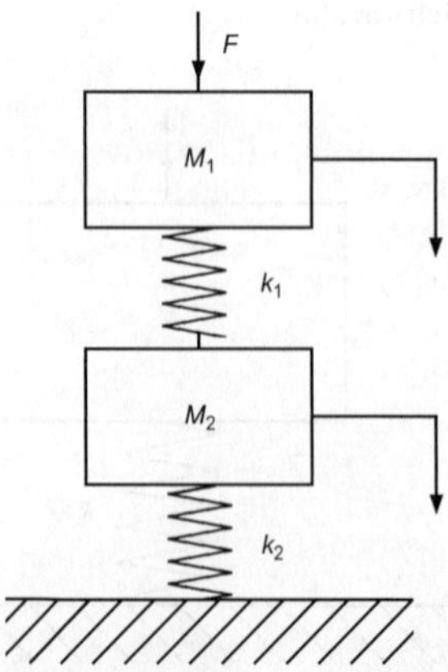

Fig. 11 Two-Degrees-of-Freedom System

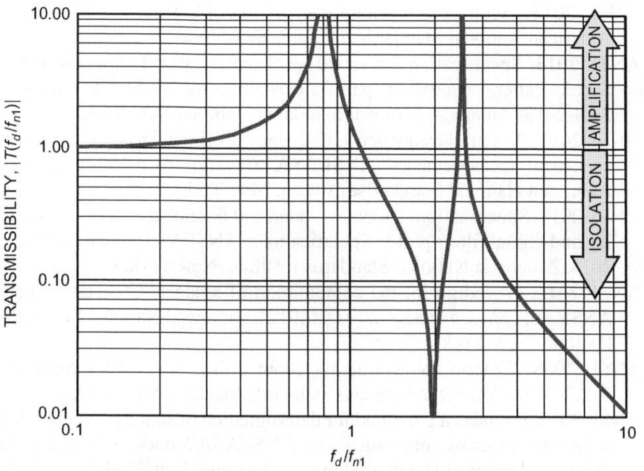

Fig. 12 Transmissibility T as Function of f_d/f_{n1} with $k_2/k_1 = 2$ and $M_2/M_1 = 0.5$

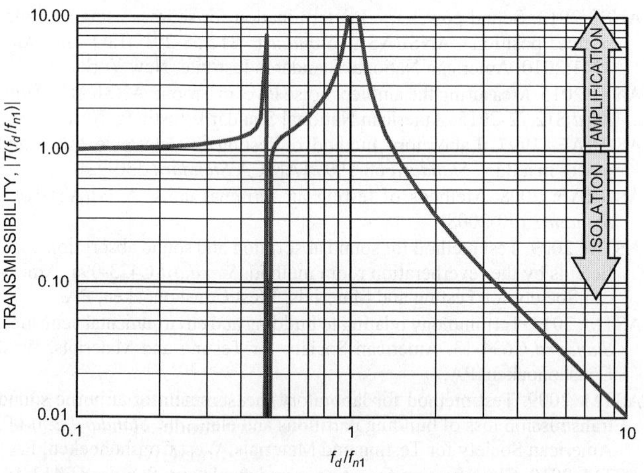

Fig. 13 Transmissibility T as Function of f_d/f_{n1} with $k_2/k_1 = 10$ and $M_2/M_1 = 40$

The typical vibrations measured are periodic motions of a surface. This surface displacement oscillates at one or more frequencies produced by mechanical equipment (e.g., rotating shafts or gears), thermal processes (e.g., combustion), or fluid-dynamic means (e.g., airflow through a duct or fan interactions with air).

A **transducer** detects displacement, velocity, or acceleration of a surface and converts the motion to electrical signals. Displacement transducers are often most appropriate for low-frequency measurements. For most HVAC applications, the transducer of choice is an **accelerometer**, which is rugged and compact. The accelerometer attaches to an amplifier, which connects to a meter, much like the microphone on a sound level meter. Readouts may be in acceleration level or decibels. The measurement also specifies whether the amplitude of the acceleration sinusoid is defined by its peak, peak-to-peak, or RMS level.

For steady-state (continuous) vibration, simple relationships exist between displacement, velocity, and acceleration; output can be specified as any of these, regardless of which transducer type is used. For a given frequency f,

$$a = (2\pi f)^2 d = (2\pi f)v \quad (49)$$

where a is acceleration, v is velocity, and d is displacement.

The simplest measure is the overall signal level as a function of time. This is analogous to the unfiltered sound pressure level. If a detailed frequency analysis is needed, there is a choice of filters similar to those available for sound measurements: octave band, 1/3 octave band, or 1/12 octave band. In addition, there are narrowband analyzers that use the fast Fourier transform (FFT) to analyze and filter a signal. Though widely used, they should only be used by a specialist for accurate results.

The most important issues in vibration measurement include (1) choosing a transducer with a frequency range appropriate to the measurement, (2) properly mounting the transducer to ensure that the frequency response claimed is achieved, and (3) properly calibrating the vibration measurement system for the frequency range of interest.

For more thorough descriptions of specialized vibration measurement and analysis methods, designers should consult other sources [e.g., Harris (1991)].

14. SYMBOLS

A = magnitude of physical property [Equation (1)], surface area, ft^2
a = acceleration, ft/s^2
c = speed of sound in air, 1100 fps
d = distance of measurement from nearest reflecting surface, or displacement, ft
d_f = deflection of foundation
d_I = deflection of mounts
E = Young's modulus, lb/ft^2
F = force applied to structure, lb_f
f = frequency, Hz
f_c = critical frequency, Hz
f_d = disturbing frequency, Hz
f_n = system natural frequency, Hz
f_r = rotation speed of fan blades, rev/s
h = thickness of outer panel of partition, in.
I = sound intensity, dB
I_{ave} = time-averaged sound intensity
k = stiffness of vibration isolator, lb_f/in.
L = level of magnitude of sound or vibration
L_{eq} = equivalent continuous sound pressure level
L_I = level of sound intensity
L_p = sound pressure level, dB
L_w = sound power level
M = mass of equipment supported by isolator (W_f/386), lb_m
M_1 = mass of equipment before additional mass added, lb_m
M_2 = mass of equipment after additional mass added, lb_m
N = number of fan blades
p = acoustic pressure
Q = directivity factor, dimensionless
R = room constant
r = distance between site of measurement and nondirectional sound source, ft
Re = real part of complex quantity
S = surface area, ft^2
t or T = time, s
T = system transmissibility
T_{60} = reverberation time
V = volume of room, ft^3
v = velocity
v_b = velocity of flow over fan blade, ft/s
v_0 = free stream velocity of flow into fan, ft/s
W = total sound power
w = sound power of source, W
W_0 = input power
W_f = weight of equipment, lb_f
W_M = output power
w_s = surface mass of panel, lb/ft^2
W_{SG} = power of self-noise
x = location of measurement of pressure p, Equation (17)
z_a = acoustic impedance, $lb_m/ft^2 \cdot s$ or $lb_f \cdot s/ft^3$
Z_f = impedance of foundation where isolator attached, $lb_f \cdot s$/ft

Z_I = isolator impedance, $lb_f \cdot s/ft$
Z_m = mechanical impedance of structure, $lb_f \cdot s/ft$

Greek

α = absorption coefficient
$\bar{\alpha}$ = average absorption coefficient of room surface at given frequency
δ_{st} = isolator static deflection, in.
θ = direction
λ = wavelength, ft
ρ = density, lb_m/ft^3

Subscripts

0 = maximum amplitude
abs = absorbed
ave = average
i = value for *i*th source
inc = incident
ref = reference magnitude of physical property [Equation (1)]
w = sound power

REFERENCES

ASHRAE members can access *ASHRAE Journal* articles and ASHRAE research project final reports at technologyportal.ashrae.org. Articles and reports are also available for purchase by nonmembers in the online ASHRAE Bookstore at www.ashrae.org/bookstore.

AHRI. 2014. Reverberation room qualification and testing procedures for determining sound power of HVAC equipment. ANSI/AHRI *Standard* 220-2014. Air-Conditioning, Heating, and Refrigeration Institute, Arlington, VA.

AHRI. 2013. Performance and calibration of reference sound sources. ANSI/AHRI *Standard* 250-2013 with Addendum 1. Air-Conditioning, Heating, and Refrigeration Institute, Arlington, VA.

AHRI. 2014. Sound rating of ducted air moving and conditioning equipment. ANSI/AHRI *Standard* 260 (I-P)-2012. Air-Conditioning, Heating, and Refrigeration Institute, Arlington, VA.

AHRI. 2014. Sound rating of outdoor unitary equipment. *Standard* 270-2015. Air-Conditioning, Heating, and Refrigeration Institute, Arlington, VA.

AHRI. 2014. Sound performance rating of large air-cooled outdoor refrigerating and air-conditioning equipment. ANSI/AHRI *Standard* 370-2015. Air-Conditioning, Heating, and Refrigeration Institute, Arlington, VA.

AHRI. 2014. Rating of sound and vibration for refrigerant compressors. ANSI/AHRI *Standard* 530-2011. Air-Conditioning, Heating, and Refrigeration Institute, Arlington, VA.

AHRI. 2008. Method of measuring machinery sound within an equipment space. ANSI/AHRI *Standard* 575-2008. Air-Conditioning, Heating, and Refrigeration Institute, Arlington, VA.

AHRI. 2011. Performance rating of air terminals. ANSI/AHRI *Standard* 880 (I-P)-2011 (with addendum 1). Air-Conditioning, Heating, and Refrigeration Institute, Arlington, VA.

AHRI. 2008. Procedure for estimating occupied space sound levels in the application of air terminals and air outlets. *Standard* 885-2008 (with addendum). Air-Conditioning, Heating, and Refrigeration Institute, Arlington, VA.

AMCA. 2014. Reverberant room method for sound testing of fans. ANSI/AMCA *Standard* 300-14. Air Movement and Control Association International, Inc., Arlington Heights, IL.

AMCA. 2014. Methods for calculating fan sound ratings from laboratory test data. *Standard* 301-14. Air Movement and Control Association International, Inc., Arlington Heights, IL.

AMCA. 2005. Certified ratings program—Product rating manual for fan sound performance. *Standard* 311-05. Air Movement and Control Association International, Inc., Arlington Heights, IL.

AMCA. 1997. Laboratory method of testing to determine the sound power in a duct. *Standard* 330-97 (ASHRAE *Standard* 68-1997). Air Movement and Control Association International, Inc., Arlington Heights, IL.

AMCA. 2012. Application of sound power level ratings for fans. *Publication* 303-79 (R2012). Air Movement and Control Association International, Inc., Arlington Heights, IL.

ANSI. 2015. Measuring the ambient noise level in a room. *Standard* S12.72-2015. American National Standards Institute, New York.

ANSI. 2013. Acoustical terminology. ANSI/ASA *Standard* S1.1-2013. American National Standards Institute, New York.

ANSI. 2013. Specification for sound level meters, part 1: Specifications; part 2: Pattern evaluation; part 3: Periodic tests. ANSI/IEC *Standard* S1.4-2013. American National Standards Institute, New York.

ANSI. 2011. Preferred frequencies, frequency levels, and band numbers for acoustical measurements. ANSI/ASA *Standard* S1.6-1984 (R2011). American National Standards Institute, New York.

ANSI. 2014. Specifications for octave-band and fractional octave-band analog and digital filters part 1: Specifications. ANSI/ASA *Standard* S1.11-2014. American National Standards Institute, New York.

ANSI. 2012. Procedure for the computation of loudness of steady sound. ANSI/ASA *Standard* S3.4-2007 (R2012). American National Standards Institute, New York.

ANSI. 2008. Criteria for evaluating room noise. ANSI/ASA *Standard* S12.2-2008. American National Standards Institute, New York.

ANSI. 2012. Engineering method for determination of sound power level of noise sources using sound intensity. ANSI/ASA *Standard* S12.12-1992 (R2012). American National Standards Institute, New York.

ANSI. 2012. Determination of sound power levels of noise sources using sound pressure—Precision methods for anechoic and hemi-anechoic rooms. ANSI/ASA *Standard* S12.55-2012/ISO *Standard* 3745:2012. American National Standards Institute, New York.

ANSI. 2012. Sound power level determination for sources using a single-source position. ANSI/ASA *Standard* S12.58-2012/ISO *Standard* 3741:2010. American National Standards Institute, New York.

ANSI. 2015. Measuring the ambient noise level in a room. ANSI/ASA *Standard* S12.72-2015. American National Standards Institute, New York.

ASHRAE. 1997. Laboratory method of testing to determine the sound power in a duct. *Standard* 68-1997 (AMCA *Standard* 330-92).

ASHRAE. 2008. Methods of testing air terminal units. ANSI/ASHRAE *Standard* 130-2008.

ASTM. 2009. Test method for sound absorption and sound absorption coefficients by the reverberation room method. *Standard* C423-09a. American Society for Testing and Materials, West Conshohocken, PA.

ASTM. 2013. Terminology relating to building and environmental acoustics. *Standard* C634-13. American Society for Testing and Materials, West Conshohocken, PA.

ASTM. 2009. Test method for laboratory measurement of airborne sound transmission loss of building partitions and elements. *Standard* E90-09. American Society for Testing and Materials, West Conshohocken, PA.

ASTM. 2010. Classification for rating sound insulation. *Standard* E413-10. American Society for Testing and Materials, West Conshohocken, PA.

ASTM. 2013. Test method for measuring acoustical and airflow performance of duct liner materials and prefabricated silencers. *Standard* E477-2013e1. American Society for Testing and Materials, West Conshohocken, PA.

ASTM. 2009. Test method for evaluating masking sound in open offices using A-weighted and one-third octave band sound pressure levels. *Standard* E1573-09. American Society for Testing and Materials, West Conshohocken, PA.

ASTM. 2014. Test method for measurement of sound in residential spaces. *Standard* E1574-98 (2014). American Society for Testing and Materials, West Conshohocken, PA.

Blazier, W.E., Jr. 1981a. Revised noise criteria for application in the acoustical design and rating of HVAC systems. *Noise Control Engineering Journal* 16(2):64-73.

Blazier, W. E., Jr. 1981b. Revised noise criteria for design and rating of HVAC systems. *ASHRAE Transactions* 87(1). *Paper* CH-81-06-2.

DIN. 1991. Procedure for calculating loudness level and loudness. German *Standard* DIN 45631. Deutsches Institut für Normung, Berlin.

Harris, C.M. 1991. *Handbook of acoustical measurements and noise control*, 3rd ed. Acoustical Society of America, Melville, NY.

ISO. 1975. Acoustics—Methods for calculating loudness level. *Standard* 532-1975. International Organization for Standardization, Geneva.

ISO. 2003. Acoustics—Laboratory measurement procedures for ducted silencers and air-terminal units—Insertion loss, flow noise and total pressure loss. *Standard* 7235-2003. International Organization for Standardization, Geneva.

ISO. 1993. Determination of sound power levels of noise sources using sound intensity—Part 1: Measurements at discrete points. *Standard* 9614-1. International Organization for Standardization, Geneva.

ISO. 1996. Acoustics—Determination of sound power levels of noise sources using sound intensity—Part 2: Measurement by scanning. *Standard* 9614-2. International Organization for Standardization, Geneva.

Pollack, I. 1952. The loudness of bands of noise. *Journal of the Acoustical Society of America* 24(9):533.

Robinson, D.W., and R.S. Dadson. 1956. A redetermination of the equal loudness relations for pure tones. *British Journal of Applied Physics* 7(5): 166.

Schultz, T.J. 1985. Relationship between sound power level and sound pressure level in dwellings and offices. *ASHRAE Transactions* 91(1):124-153. *Paper* 2865 (RP-339).

Warnock, A.C.C. 1997. Sound transmission through ceilings from air terminal devices in the plenum. ASHRAE Research Project RP-755, *Final Report*.

Warnock, A.C.C. 1998a. Sound pressure level vs. distance from sources in rooms. *ASHRAE Transactions* 104(1):643-649. *Paper* 4159 (RP-755).

Warnock, A.C.C. 1998b. Transmission of sound from air terminal devices through ceiling systems. *ASHRAE Transactions* 104(1):650-657. *Paper* 4160 (RP-755).

BIBLIOGRAPHY

AMCA. 2012. Application of sone ratings for non-ducted air moving devices. *Publication* 302-73 (R2012). Air Movement and Control Association International, Inc., Arlington Heights, IL.

ANSI. 2012. Determination of sound power levels of noise sources using sound pressure—Precision methods for reverberation rooms. ANSI/ASA *Standard* S12.51-2012/ISO *Standard* 3741:2010. American National Standards Institute, New York.

ANSI. 2010. Acoustical performance criteria, sound requirements, and guidelines for schools, part 1: Permanent schools. *Standard* S12.60-2010 (R2015). American National Standards Institute, New York.

ASHRAE. 2016. Ventilation for acceptable indoor air quality. *Standard* 62.1-2016.

ASHRAE. 2016. Ventilation and acceptable indoor air quality in low-rise residential buildings. *Standard* 62.2-2016.

Beranek, L.L. 1957. Revised criteria for noise in buildings. *Noise Control* 1:19.

Beranek, L.L. 1986. *Acoustics*, rev. ed. American Institute of Physics, Acoustical Society of America, New York.

Beranek, L.L. 1988. *Noise and vibration control*, rev. ed. Institute of Noise Control Engineering, Washington, D.C.

Beranek, L.L. 1989. Balanced noise criterion (NCB) curves. *Journal of the Acoustic Society of America* (86):650-654.

Beranek, L.L., and I.L. Ver. 2005. *Noise and vibration control engineering: Principles and applications*, 2nd ed. John Wiley & Sons, New York.

Bies, D.A., and C.H. Hansen. 2009. *Engineering noise control: Theory and practice*, 4th ed. E&F Spon, New York.

Blazier, W.E., Jr. 1995. Sound quality considerations in rating noise from heating, ventilating and air-conditioning (HVAC) systems in buildings. *Noise Control Engineering Journal* 43(3).

Blazier, W.E., Jr. 1997. RC Mark II: A refined procedure for rating the noise of heating, ventilating and air-conditioning (HVAC) systems in buildings. *Noise Control Engineering Journal* 45(6).

Broner, N. 1994. Low-frequency noise assessment metrics—What do we know? (RP-714). *ASHRAE Transactions* 100(2):380-388. *Paper* 3821 (RP-714).

Crede, C.E. 1951. *Vibration and shock isolation*. John Wiley & Sons, New York.

Ebbing, C.E., and W. Blazier, eds. 1998. *Application of manufacturers' sound data*. ASHRAE.

Harris, C.M., and C.E. Crede. 2001. *Shock and vibration handbook*, 5th ed. McGraw-Hill, New York.

ISO. 2002. Acoustics—Determination of sound power levels of noise sources using sound intensity—Part 3: Precision method for measurement by scanning. *Standard* 9614-3. International Organization for Standardization, Geneva.

Persson-Waye, K., R. Rylander, S. Benton, and H.G. Leventhall. 1997. Effects on performance and work quality due to low-frequency ventilation noise. *Journal of Sound and Vibration* 205(4):467-474.

Peterson, A.P.G., and E.E. Gross, Jr. 1974. *Handbook of noise measurement*. GenRad, Inc., Concord, MA.

Plunkett, R. 1958. Interaction between a vibratory machine and its foundation. *Noise Control* 4(1).

Schaffer, M.E. 2005. *A practical guide to noise and vibration control for HVAC systems*, 2nd ed. ASHRAE.

ISO. 1993. Acoustics—Determination of sound power levels of noise sources using sound intensity—Part 2: Measurement by scanning. *Standard* 9614-2. International Organization for Standardization, Geneva.
Pollack, I. 1952. The loudness of bands of noise. *Journal of the Acoustical Society of America* 24(9):533.
Robinson, D.W., and R.S. Dadson. 1956. A redetermination of the equal loudness relations for pure tones. *British Journal of Applied Physics* 7(5): 166-181.
Schultz, T.J. 1985. Relationship between sound power level and sound pressure level in dwellings and offices. *ASHRAE Transactions* 91(1):124-153. *Paper* 2868 (RP-339).
Warnock, A.C.C. 1997. Sound transmission through ceilings from air terminal devices in the plenum. ASHRAE *Research Project* RP-755, *Final Report*.
Warnock, A.C.C. 1998. Sound pressure level vs. distance from sources in rooms. *ASHRAE Transactions* 104(1):643-649. *Paper* 4158 (RP-755).
Warnock, A.C.C. 1998. Transmission of sound from air terminal devices through ceiling systems. *ASHRAE Transactions* 104(1):650-657. *Paper* 4159 (RP-755).

BIBLIOGRAPHY

AMCA. 2015. [illegible]
[illegible] Air Movement and Control Association International, [illegible].
ANSI. 2012. Determination of sound power levels of noise sources using sound pressure—Precision methods for reverberant test rooms. ANSI/ASA *Standard* S12.51-2012/ISO 3741:2010. American National Standards Institute, New York.
ANSI. 2010. Acoustical performance criteria, design requirements, and guidelines for schools, part 1: Permanent schools. *Standard* S12.60-2010/Part 1. American National Standards Institute, New York.
ASHRAE. 2016. Ventilation for acceptable indoor air quality. ANSI/ASHRAE *Standard* 62.1-2016.
ASHRAE. 2016. Ventilation and acceptable indoor air quality in low-rise residential buildings. *Standard* 62.2-2016.
Beranek, L.L. 1960. [illegible]
Beranek, L.L. 1986. *Acoustics*, rev. ed. American Institute of Physics, Acoustical Society of America, New York.
Beranek, L.L. 1988. *Noise and vibration control*, rev. ed. Institute of Noise Control Engineering, Washington, D.C.
Beranek, L.L. 1989. Balanced noise criterion (NCB) curves. *Journal of the Acoustical Society of America* 86(2):650-664.
Beranek, L.L., and I.L. Vér. 2005. *Noise and vibration control engineering: Principles and applications*, 2nd ed. John Wiley & Sons, New York.
Bies, D.A., and C.H. Hansen. 2009. *Engineering noise control: Theory and practice*, 4th ed. E & F Spon, New York.
Blazier, W.E., Jr. 1995. Sound quality considerations in rating noise from heating, ventilating and air-conditioning (HVAC) systems in buildings. *Noise Control Engineering Journal* 43(3).
Blazier, W.E., Jr. [illegible]
[illegible]
Broner, N. [illegible]
[illegible]
Crede, C.E. [illegible]
Ebbing, C., and W. Blazier, eds. 1998. *Application of manufacturers' sound data*. ASHRAE.
Harris, C.M., and C. [illegible] 2002. *Shock and vibration handbook*, 5th ed. McGraw-Hill, New York.
ISO. 2002. Acoustics—Determination of sound power levels of noise sources using sound intensity—Part 3: Precision method for measurement by scanning. *Standard* 9614-3. International Organization for Standardization, Geneva.
Persson-Waye, K., R. Rylander, S. Benton, and H.G. Leventhall. 1997. Effects on performance and work quality due to low frequency ventilation noise. *Journal of Sound and Vibration* 205(4):467-474.
Peterson, A.P.G., and E.E. Gross, Jr. 1972. *Handbook of noise measurement*. GenRad, Inc., Concord, MA.
Plunkett, R. 1958. Interaction between a vibratory machine and its foundation. *Noise Control* 4(1).
Schaffer, M.E. 2005. *A practical guide to noise and vibration control for HVAC systems*, 2nd ed. ASHRAE.

CHAPTER 9

THERMAL COMFORT

A principal purpose of HVAC is to provide conditions for human thermal comfort, "that condition of mind that expresses satisfaction with the thermal environment and is assessed by subjective evaluation" (ASHRAE *Standard* 55). This definition leaves open what is meant by "condition of mind" or "satisfaction," but it correctly emphasizes that judgment of comfort is a cognitive process involving many inputs influenced by physical, physiological, psychological, and other processes. This chapter summarizes the fundamentals of human thermoregulation and comfort in terms useful to the engineer for operating systems and designing for the comfort and health of building occupants.

The conscious mind appears to reach conclusions about thermal comfort and discomfort from direct temperature and moisture sensations from the skin, deep body temperatures, and the efforts necessary to regulate body temperatures (Berglund 1995; Gagge 1937; Hardy et al. 1971; Hensel 1973, 1981). In general, comfort occurs when body temperatures are held within narrow ranges, skin moisture is low, and the physiological effort of regulation is minimized.

Comfort also depends on behaviors that are initiated consciously or unconsciously and guided by thermal and moisture sensations to reduce discomfort. Some examples are altering clothing, altering activity, changing posture or location, changing the thermostat setting, opening a window, complaining, or leaving the space.

Surprisingly, although climates, living conditions, and cultures differ widely throughout the world, the temperature that people choose for comfort under similar conditions of clothing, activity, humidity, and air movement has been found to be very similar (Busch 1992; de Dear et al. 1991; Fanger 1972).

1. HUMAN THERMOREGULATION

Metabolic activities of the body result almost completely in heat that must be continuously dissipated and regulated to maintain normal body temperatures. Insufficient heat loss leads to overheating (**hyperthermia**), and excessive heat loss results in body cooling (**hypothermia**). Skin temperature greater than 113°F or less than 64.5°F causes pain (Hardy et al. 1952). Skin temperatures associated with comfort at sedentary activities are 91.5 to 93°F and decrease with increasing activity (Fanger 1967). In contrast, internal temperatures rise with activity. The temperature regulatory center in the brain is about 98.2°F at rest in comfort and increases to about 99.3°F when walking and 100.2°F when jogging. An internal temperature less than about 82°F can lead to serious cardiac arrhythmia and death, and a temperature greater than 110°F can cause irreversible brain damage. Therefore, careful regulation of body temperature is critical to comfort and health.

A resting adult produces about 350 Btu/h of heat. Because most of this is transferred to the environment through the skin, it is often convenient to characterize metabolic activity in terms of heat production per unit area of skin. For a resting person, this is about 18.4 Btu/h·ft^2 (50 kcal/h·m^2) and is called 1 **met**. This is based on the average male European, with a skin surface area of about 19.4 ft^2. For comparison, female Europeans have an average surface area of 17.2 ft^2. Systematic differences in this parameter may occur between ethnic and geographical groups. Higher metabolic rates are often described in terms of the resting rate. Thus, a person working at metabolic rate five times the resting rate would have a metabolic rate of 5 met.

The **hypothalamus**, located in the brain, is the central control organ for body temperature. It has hot and cold temperature sensors and is bathed by arterial blood. Because the recirculation rate of blood is rapid and returning blood is mixed together in the heart before returning to the body, arterial blood is indicative of the average internal body temperature. The hypothalamus also receives thermal information from temperature sensors in the skin and perhaps other locations as well (e.g., spinal cord, gut), as summarized by Hensel (1981).

The hypothalamus controls various physiological processes to regulate body temperature. Its control behavior is primarily proportional to deviations from set-point temperatures with some integral and derivative response aspects. The most important and often-used physiological process is regulating blood flow to the skin: when internal temperatures rise above a set point, more blood is directed to the skin. This **vasodilation** of skin blood vessels can increase skin blood flow by 15 times (from 0.56 L/h·ft^2 at resting comfort to 8.4 L/h·ft^2) in extreme heat to carry internal heat to the skin for transfer to the environment. When body temperatures fall below the set point, skin blood flow is reduced (**vasoconstricted**) to conserve heat. The effect of maximum vasoconstriction is equivalent to the insulating effect of a heavy sweater. At temperatures less than the set point, muscle tension increases to generate additional heat; where muscle groups are opposed, this may increase to visible shivering, which can increase resting heat production to 4.5 met.

At elevated internal temperatures, sweating occurs. This defense mechanism is a powerful way to cool the skin and increase heat loss from the core. The sweating function of the skin and its control is more advanced in humans than in other animals and is increasingly necessary for comfort at metabolic rates above resting level (Fanger 1967). Sweat glands pump perspiration onto the skin surface for evaporation. If conditions are good for evaporation, the skin can remain relatively dry even at high sweat rates with little perception of sweating. At skin conditions less favorable for evaporation, the sweat must spread on the skin around the sweat gland until the sweat-covered area is sufficient to evaporate the sweat coming to the surface. The fraction of the skin that is covered with water to account for the observed total evaporation rate is termed **skin wettedness** (Gagge 1937).

Humans are quite good at sensing skin moisture from perspiration (Berglund 1994; Berglund and Cunningham 1986), and skin moisture correlates well with warm discomfort and unpleasantness (Winslow et al. 1937). It is rare for a sedentary or slightly active person to be

The preparation of this chapter is assigned to TC 2.1, Physiology and Human Environment.

comfortable with a skin wettedness greater than 25%. In addition to the perception of skin moisture, skin wettedness increases the friction between skin and fabrics, making clothing feel less pleasant and fabrics feel more coarse (Gwosdow et al. 1986). This also occurs with architectural materials and surfaces, particularly smooth, nonhygroscopic surfaces.

With repeated intermittent heat exposure, the set point for the onset of sweating decreases and the proportional gain or temperature sensitivity of the sweating system increases (Gonzalez et al. 1978; Hensel 1981). However, under long-term exposure to hot conditions, the set point increases, perhaps to reduce the physiological effort of sweating. Perspiration, as secreted, has a lower salt concentration than interstitial body fluid or blood plasma. After prolonged heat exposure, sweat glands further reduce the salt concentration of sweat to conserve salt.

At the skin's surface, the water in sweat evaporates while the dissolved salt and other constituents remain and accumulate. Because salt lowers the vapor pressure of water and thereby impedes its evaporation, the accumulating salt results in increased skin wettedness. Some of the relief and pleasure of washing after a warm day is related to the restoration of a hypotonic sweat film and decreased skin wettedness. Other adaptations to heat are increased blood flow and sweating in peripheral regions where heat transfer is better. Such adaptations are examples of **integral control**.

Role of Thermoregulatory Effort in Comfort. Chatonnet and Cabanac (1965) compared the sensation of placing a subject's hand in relatively hot or cold water (86 to 100°F) for 30 s with the subject at different thermal states. When the person was overheated (hyperthermic), the cold water was pleasant and the hot water was very unpleasant, but when the subject was cold (hypothermic), the hand felt pleasant in hot water and unpleasant in cold water. Kuno (1995) describes similar observations during transient whole-body exposures to hot and cold environment. When a subject is in a state of thermal discomfort, any move away from the thermal stress of the uncomfortable environment is perceived as pleasant during the transition.

2. ENERGY BALANCE

Figure 1 shows the thermal interaction of the human body with its environment. The total metabolic rate M within the body is the metabolic rate required for the person's activity M_{act} plus the metabolic level required for shivering M_{shiv} (should shivering occur). Some of the body's energy production may be expended as external work W; the net heat production $M - W$ is transferred to the environment through the skin surface (q_{sk}) and respiratory tract (q_{res}) with any surplus or deficit stored (S), causing the body's temperature to rise or fall.

$$\begin{aligned} M - W &= q_{sk} + q_{res} + S \\ &= (C + R + E_{sk}) + (C_{res} + E_{res}) + (S_{sk} + S_{cr}) \end{aligned} \tag{1}$$

where

M = rate of metabolic heat production, Btu/h·ft²
W = rate of mechanical work accomplished, Btu/h·ft²
q_{sk} = total rate of heat loss from skin, Btu/h·ft²
q_{res} = total rate of heat loss through respiration, Btu/h·ft²
$C + R$ = sensible heat loss from skin, Btu/h·ft²
E_{sk} = total rate of evaporative heat loss from skin, Btu/h·ft²
C_{res} = rate of convective heat loss from respiration, Btu/h·ft²
E_{res} = rate of evaporative heat loss from respiration, Btu/h·ft²
S_{sk} = rate of heat storage in skin compartment, Btu/h·ft²
S_{cr} = rate of heat storage in core compartment, Btu/h·ft²

Heat dissipates from the body to the immediate surroundings by several modes of heat exchange: sensible heat flow $C + R$ from the skin; latent heat flow from sweat evaporation E_{rsw} and from evaporation of moisture diffused through the skin E_{dif}; sensible heat flow

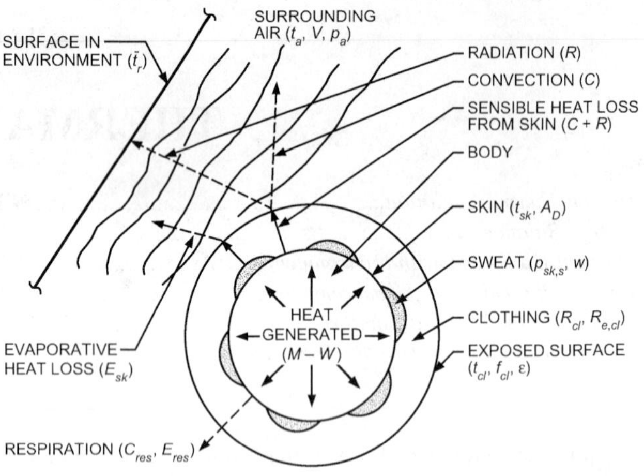

Fig. 1 Thermal Interaction of Human Body and Environment

during respiration C_{res}; and latent heat flow from evaporation of moisture during respiration E_{res}. Sensible heat flow from the skin may be a complex mixture of conduction, convection, and radiation for a clothed person; however, it is equal to the sum of the convection C and radiation R heat transfer at the outer clothing surface (or exposed skin).

Sensible and latent heat losses from the skin are typically expressed in terms of environmental factors, skin temperature t_{sk}, and skin wettedness w. Factors also account for thermal insulation and moisture permeability of clothing. The independent environmental variables can be summarized as air temperature t_a, mean radiant temperature $\bar{t}_r$, relative air velocity V, and ambient water vapor pressure p_a. The independent personal variables that influence thermal comfort are activity and clothing.

The rate of heat storage in the body equals the rate of increase in internal energy. The body can be considered as two thermal compartments: the skin and the core (see the Two-Node Model section under Prediction of Thermal Comfort). The storage rate can be written separately for each compartment in terms of thermal capacity and time rate of change of temperature in each compartment:

$$S_{cr} = \frac{(1 - \alpha_{sk}) m c_{p,\,b}}{A_D} \times \frac{dt_{cr}}{d\theta} \tag{2}$$

$$S_{sk} = \frac{\alpha_{sk} m c_{p,\,b}}{A_D} \times \frac{dt_{sk}}{d\theta} \tag{3}$$

where

α_{sk} = fraction of body mass concentrated in skin compartment
m = body mass, lb
$c_{p,b}$ = specific heat capacity of body = 0.834 Btu/lb·°F
A_D = DuBois surface area, ft²
t_{cr} = temperature of core compartment, °F
t_{sk} = temperature of skin compartment, °F
θ = time, h

The fractional skin mass α_{sk} depends on the rate $\dot{m}_{bl}$ of blood flowing to the skin surface.

3. THERMAL EXCHANGES WITH ENVIRONMENT

Fanger (1967, 1970), Gagge and Hardy (1967), Hardy (1949), and Rapp and Gagge (1967) give quantitative information on calculating heat exchange between people and the environment. This section summarizes the mathematical statements for various terms of heat exchange used in the heat balance equations (C, R, E_{sk}, C_{res},

E_{res}). Terms describing the heat exchanges associated with the thermoregulatory control mechanisms ($q_{cr,sk}$, M_{shiv}, E_{rsw}), values for the coefficients, and appropriate equations for M_{act} and A_D are presented in later sections.

Mathematical description of the energy balance of the human body combines rational and empirical approaches to describing thermal exchanges with the environment. Fundamental heat transfer theory is used to describe the various mechanisms of sensible and latent heat exchange, and empirical expressions are used to determine the values of coefficients describing these rates of heat exchange. Empirical equations are also used to describe the thermophysiological control mechanisms as a function of skin and core temperatures in the body.

Body Surface Area

The terms in Equation (1) have units of power per unit area and refer to the surface area of the nude body. The most useful measure of nude body surface area, originally proposed by DuBois and DuBois (1916), is described by

$$A_D = 0.108 m^{0.425} l^{0.725} \tag{4}$$

where

A_D = DuBois surface area, ft²
m = mass, lb
l = height, in.

A correction factor $f_{cl} = A_{cl}/A_D$ must be applied to the heat transfer terms from the skin (C, R, and E_{sk}) to account for the actual surface area A_{cl} of the clothed body. Table 7 presents f_{cl} values for various clothing ensembles. For a 68 in. tall, 154 lb man, A_D = 19.6 ft². All terms in the basic heat balance equations are expressed per unit DuBois surface area.

Sensible Heat Loss from Skin

Sensible heat exchange from the skin must pass through clothing to the surrounding environment. These paths are treated in series and can be described in terms of heat transfer (1) from the skin surface, through the clothing insulation, to the outer clothing surface, and (2) from the outer clothing surface to the environment.

Both convective C and radiative R heat losses from the outer surface of a clothed body can be expressed in terms of a heat transfer coefficient and the difference between the mean temperature t_{cl} of the outer surface of the clothed body and the appropriate environmental temperature:

$$C = f_{cl} h_c (t_{cl} - t_a) \tag{5}$$

$$R = f_{cl} h_r (t_{cl} - \bar{t}_r) \tag{6}$$

where

h_c = convective heat transfer coefficient, Btu/h·ft²·°F
h_r = linear radiative heat transfer coefficient, Btu/h·ft²·°F
f_{cl} = clothing area factor A_{cl}/A_D, dimensionless

The coefficients h_c and h_r are both evaluated at the clothing surface. Equations (5) and (6) are commonly combined to describe the total sensible heat exchange by these two mechanisms in terms of an operative temperature t_o and a combined heat transfer coefficient h:

$$C + R = f_{cl} h (t_{cl} - t_o) \tag{7}$$

where

$$t_o = \frac{h_r \bar{t}_r + h_c t_a}{h_r + h_c} \tag{8}$$

$$h = h_r + h_c \tag{9}$$

Based on Equation (8), operative temperature t_o can be defined as the average of the mean radiant and ambient air temperatures, weighted by their respective heat transfer coefficients.

The actual transport of sensible heat through clothing involves conduction, convection, and radiation. It is usually most convenient to combine these into a single thermal resistance value R_{cl}, defined by

$$C + R = (t_{sk} - t_{cl})/R_{cl} \tag{10}$$

where R_{cl} is the thermal resistance of clothing in ft²·°F·h/Btu.

Because it is often inconvenient to include the clothing surface temperature in calculations, Equations (7) and (10) can be combined to eliminate t_{cl}:

$$C + R = \frac{t_{sk} - t_o}{R_{cl} + 1/(f_{cl} h)} \tag{11}$$

where t_o is defined in Equation (8).

Evaporative Heat Loss from Skin

Evaporative heat loss E_{sk} from skin depends on the amount of moisture on the skin and the difference between the water vapor pressure at the skin and in the ambient environment:

$$E_{sk} = \frac{w(p_{sk,s} - p_a)}{R_{e,cl} + 1/(f_{cl} h_e)} \tag{12}$$

where

w = skin wettedness, dimensionless
$p_{sk,s}$ = water vapor pressure at skin, normally assumed to be that of saturated water vapor at t_{sk}, psi
p_a = water vapor pressure in ambient air, psi
$R_{e,cl}$ = evaporative heat transfer resistance of clothing layer (analogous to R_{cl}), ft²·psi·h/Btu
h_e = evaporative heat transfer coefficient (analogous to h_c), Btu/h·ft²·psi

Procedures for calculating $R_{e,cl}$ and h_e are given in the section on Engineering Data and Measurements. Skin wettedness is the ratio of the actual evaporative heat loss E_{sk} to the maximum possible evaporative heat loss E_{max} with the same conditions and a completely wet skin (w = 1). Skin wettedness is important in determining evaporative heat loss. Maximum evaporative potential E_{max} occurs when w = 1.

Evaporative heat loss from the skin is a combination of the evaporation of sweat secreted because of thermoregulatory control mechanisms E_{rsw} and the natural diffusion of water through the skin E_{dif}:

$$E_{sk} = E_{rsw} + E_{dif} \tag{13}$$

Evaporative heat loss by regulatory sweating is directly proportional to the rate of regulatory sweat generation:

$$E_{rsw} = \dot{m}_{rsw} h_{fg} \tag{14}$$

where

h_{fg} = heat of vaporization of water = 1045 Btu/lb at 86°F
$\dot{m}_{rsw}$ = rate at which regulatory sweat is generated, lb/h·ft²

The portion w_{rsw} of a body that must be wetted to evaporate the regulatory sweat is

$$w_{rsw} = E_{rsw}/E_{max} \tag{15}$$

With no regulatory sweating, skin wettedness caused by diffusion is approximately 0.06 for normal conditions. For large values of E_{max} or long exposures to low humidities, the value may drop to as low as 0.02, because dehydration of the outer skin layers alters its diffusive characteristics. With regulatory sweating, the 0.06 value applies only to the portion of skin not covered with sweat $(1 - w_{rsw})$; the diffusion evaporative heat loss is

$$E_{dif} = (1 - w_{rsw})0.06E_{max} \tag{16}$$

These equations can be solved for w, given the maximum evaporative potential E_{max} and the regulatory sweat generation E_{rsw}:

$$w = w_{rsw} + 0.06(1 - w_{rsw}) = 0.06 + 0.94E_{rsw}/E_{max} \tag{17}$$

Once skin wettedness is determined, evaporative heat loss from the skin is calculated from Equation (12), or by

$$E_{sk} = wE_{max} \tag{18}$$

To summarize, the following calculations determine w and E_{sk}:

E_{max}	Equation (12), with $w = 1.0$
E_{rsw}	Equation (14)
w	Equation (17)
E_{sk}	Equation (18) or (12)

Although evaporation from the skin E_{sk} as described in Equation (12) depends on w, the body does not directly regulate skin wettedness but, rather, regulates sweat rate $\dot{m}_{rsw}$ [Equation (14)]. Skin wettedness is then an indirect result of the relative activity of the sweat glands and the evaporative potential of the environment. Skin wettedness of 1.0 is the upper theoretical limit. If the aforementioned calculations yield a wettedness of more than 1.0, then Equation (14) is no longer valid because not all the sweat is evaporated. In this case, $E_{sk} = E_{max}$.

Skin wettedness is strongly correlated with warm discomfort and is also a good measure of thermal stress. Theoretically, skin wettedness can approach 1.0 while the body still maintains thermoregulatory control. In most situations, it is difficult to exceed 0.8 (Berglund and Gonzalez 1977). Azer (1982) recommends 0.5 as a practical upper limit for sustained activity for a healthy, acclimatized person.

Respiratory Losses

During respiration, the body loses both sensible and latent heat by convection and evaporation of heat and water vapor from the respiratory tract to the inhaled air. A significant amount of heat can be associated with respiration because air is inspired at ambient conditions and expired nearly saturated at a temperature only slightly cooler than t_{cr}.

The total heat and moisture losses through respiration are

$$q_{res} = C_{res} + E_{res} = \frac{\dot{m}_{res}(h_{ex} - h_a)}{A_D} \tag{19}$$

$$\dot{m}_{w,res} = \frac{\dot{m}_{res}(W_{ex} - W_a)}{A_D} \tag{20}$$

where

$\dot{m}_{res}$ = pulmonary ventilation rate, lb/h
h_{ex} = enthalpy of exhaled air, Btu/lb (dry air)
h_a = enthalpy of inspired (ambient) air, Btu/lb (dry air)
$\dot{m}_{w,res}$ = pulmonary water loss rate, lb/h
W_{ex} = humidity ratio of exhaled air, lb (water vapor)/lb (dry air)
W_a = humidity ratio of inspired (ambient) air, lb (water vapor)/lb (dry air)

Under normal circumstances, pulmonary ventilation rate is primarily a function of metabolic rate (Fanger 1970):

$$\dot{m}_{res} = K_{res}MA_D \tag{21}$$

where

M = metabolic rate, Btu/h·ft²
K_{res} = proportionality constant 3.33 lb/Btu

For typical indoor environments (McCutchan and Taylor 1951), the exhaled temperature and humidity ratio are given in terms of ambient conditions:

$$t_{ex} = 88.6 + 0.066t_a + 57.6W_a \tag{22}$$

$$W_{ex} = 0.0265 + 0.000036t_a + 0.2W_a \tag{23}$$

where ambient t_a and exhaled t_{ex} air temperatures are in °F. For extreme conditions, such as outdoor winter environments, different relationships may be required (Holmér 1984).

The humidity ratio of ambient air can be expressed in terms of total or barometric pressure p_t and ambient water vapor pressure p_a:

$$W_a = \frac{0.622p_a}{p_t - p_a} \tag{24}$$

Respiratory heat loss is often expressed in terms of sensible C_{res} and latent E_{res} heat losses. Two approximations are commonly used to simplify Equations (22) and (23) for that purpose. First, because dry respiratory heat loss is relatively small compared to the other terms in the heat balance, an average value for t_{ex} is determined by evaluating Equation (22) at standard conditions of 68°F, 50% rh, sea level. Second, noting in Equation (23) that there is only a weak dependence on t_a, the second term in Equation (23) and the denominator in Equation (24) are evaluated at standard conditions. Using these approximations and substituting latent heat h_{fg} and specific heat of air $c_{p,a}$ at standard conditions, C_{res} and E_{res} can be determined by

$$C_{res} = 0.0084M(93.2 - t_a) \tag{25}$$

$$E_{res} = 1.28M(0.851 - p_a) \tag{26}$$

where p_a is expressed in psi and t_a is in °F.

Alternative Formulations

Equations (11) and (12) describe heat loss from skin for clothed people in terms of clothing parameters R_{cl}, $R_{e,cl}$, and f_{cl}; parameters h and h_e describe outer surface resistances. Other parameters and definitions are also used. Although these alternative parameters and definitions may be confusing, note that information presented in one form can be converted to another form. Table 1 presents common parameters and their qualitative descriptions. Table 2 presents equations showing their relationship to each other. Generally, parameters related to dry or evaporative heat flows are not independent because they both rely, in part, on the same physical processes. The **Lewis relation** describes the relationship between convective heat transfer and mass transfer coefficients for a surface [see Equation (41) in Chapter 6]. The Lewis relation can be used to relate convective and evaporative heat transfer coefficients defined in Equations (5) and (12) according to

$$\text{LR} = h_e/h_c \tag{27}$$

where LR is the **Lewis ratio** and, at typical indoor conditions, equals approximately 205°F/psi. The Lewis relation applies to surface convection coefficients. Heat transfer coefficients that include the effects of insulation layers and/or radiation are still coupled, but the relationship may deviate significantly from that for a surface. The i terms in Tables 1 and 2 describe how the actual ratios of these parameters deviate from the ideal Lewis ratio (Oohori et al. 1984; Woodcock 1962).

Table 1 Parameters Used to Describe Clothing

Sensible Heat Flow

- R_{cl} = intrinsic clothing insulation: thermal resistance of a uniform layer of insulation covering entire body that has same effect on sensible heat flow as actual clothing.
- R_t = total insulation: total equivalent uniform thermal resistance between body and environment: clothing and boundary resistance.
- R_{cle} = effective clothing insulation: increased body insulation due to clothing as compared to nude state.
- R_a = boundary insulation: thermal resistance at skin boundary for nude body.
- $R_{a,cl}$ = outer boundary insulation: thermal resistance at outer boundary (skin or clothing).
- R_{te} = total effective insulation.
- h' = overall sensible heat transfer coefficient: overall equivalent uniform conductance between body (including clothing) and environment.
- h'_{cl} = clothing conductance: thermal conductance of uniform layer of insulation covering entire body that has same effect on sensible heat flow as actual clothing.
- F_{cle} = effective clothing thermal efficiency: ratio of actual sensible heat loss to that of nude body at same conditions.
- F_{cl} = intrinsic clothing thermal efficiency: ratio of actual sensible heat loss to that of nude body at same conditions including adjustment for increase in surface area due to clothing.

Evaporative Heat Flow

- $R_{e,cl}$ = evaporative heat transfer resistance of clothing: impedance to transport of water vapor of uniform layer of insulation covering entire body that has same effect on evaporative heat flow as actual clothing.
- $R_{e,t}$ = total evaporative resistance: total equivalent uniform impedance to transport of water vapor from skin to environment.
- F_{pcl} = permeation efficiency: ratio of actual evaporative heat loss to that of nude body at same conditions, including adjustment for increase in surface area due to clothing.

Parameters Relating Sensible and Evaporative Heat Flows

- i_{cl} = clothing vapor permeation efficiency: ratio of actual evaporative heat flow capability through clothing to sensible heat flow capability as compared to Lewis ratio.
- i_m = total vapor permeation efficiency: ratio of actual evaporative heat flow capability between skin and environment to sensible heat flow capability as compared to Lewis ratio.
- i_a = air layer vapor permeation efficiency: ratio of actual evaporative heat flow capability through outer air layer to sensible heat flow capability as compared to Lewis ratio.

Table 2 Relationships Between Clothing Parameters

Sensible Heat Flow

$$R_t = R_{cl} + 1/(hf_{cl}) = R_{cl} + R_a/f_{cl}$$
$$R_{te} = R_{cle} + 1/h = R_{cle} + R_a$$
$$h'_{cl} = 1/R_{cl}$$
$$h' = 1/R_t$$
$$h = 1/R_a$$
$$R_{a,cl} = R_a/f_{cl}$$
$$F_{cl} = h'/(hf_{cl}) = 1/(1 + f_{cl}hR_{cl})$$
$$F_{cle} = h'/h = f_{cl}/(1 + f_{cl}hR_{cl}) = f_{cl}F_{cl}$$

Evaporative Heat Flow

$$R_{e,t} = R_{e,cl} + 1/(h_e f_{cl}) = R_{e,cl} + R_{e,a}/f_{cl}$$
$$h_e = 1/R_{e,a}$$
$$h'_{e,cl} = 1/R_{e,cl}$$
$$h'_e = 1/R_{e,t} = f_{cl}F_{pcl}h_e$$
$$F_{pcl} = 1/(1 + f_{cl}h_e R_{e,cl})$$

Parameters Relating Sensible and Evaporative Heat Flows

$$i_{cl}\text{LR} = h'_{e,cl}/h'_{cl} = R_{cl}/R_{e,cl}$$
$$i_m\text{LR} = h'_e/h' = R_t/R_{e,t}$$
$$i_m = (R_{cl} + R_{a,cl})/[(R_{cl}/i_{cl}) + (R_{a,cl}/i_a)]$$
$$i_a\text{LR} = h_e/h$$
$$i_a = h_c/(h_c + h_r)$$

Table 3 Skin Heat Loss Equations

Sensible Heat Loss

$$C + R = (t_{sk} - t_o)/[R_{cl} + 1/(f_{cl}h)]$$
$$C + R = (t_{sk} - t_o)/R_t$$
$$C + R = F_{cle}h(t_{sk} - t_o)$$
$$C + R = F_{cl}f_{cl}h(t_{sk} - t_o)$$
$$C + R = h'(t_{sk} - t_o)$$

Evaporative Heat Loss

$$E_{sk} = w(p_{sk,s} - p_a)/[R_{e,cl} + 1/(f_{cl}h_e)]$$
$$E_{sk} = w(p_{sk,s} - p_a)/R_{e,t}$$
$$E_{sk} = wF_{pcl}f_{cl}h_e(p_{sk,s} - p_a)$$
$$E_{sk} = h'_e w(p_{sk,s} - p_a)$$
$$E_{sk} = h'wi_m\text{LR}(p_{sk,s} - p_a)$$

Depending on the combination of parameters used, heat transfer from the skin can be calculated using several different formulations (see Tables 2 and 3). If the parameters are used correctly, the end result will be the same regardless of the formulation used.

Total Skin Heat Loss

Total skin heat loss (sensible heat plus evaporative heat) can be calculated from any combination of the equations presented in Table 3. Total skin heat loss is used as a measure of the thermal environment; two combinations of parameters that yield the same total heat loss for a given set of body conditions (t_{sk} and w) are considered to be approximately equivalent. The fully expanded skin heat loss equation, showing each parameter that must be known or specified, is as follows:

$$q_{sk} = \frac{t_{sk} - t_o}{R_{cl} + R_{a,cl}} + \frac{w(p_{sk,s} - p_a)}{R_{e,cl} + 1/(\text{LR}h_c f_{cl})} \tag{28}$$

where t_o is the operative temperature and represents the temperature of a uniform environment ($t_a = \bar{t}_r$) that transfers dry heat at the same rate as in the actual environment [$t_o = (\bar{t}_r h_r + t_a h_c)/(h_c + h_r)$]. After rearranging, Equation (28) becomes

$$q_{sk} = F_{cl}f_{cl}h(t_{sk} - t_o) + w\text{LR}F_{pcl}h_c(p_{sk,s} - p_a) \tag{29}$$

This equation allows evaluation of the trade-off between any two or more parameters under given conditions. If the trade-off between two specific variables (e.g., operative temperature and humidity) is to be examined, then a simplified form of the equation suffices (Fobelets and Gagge 1988):

$$q_{sk} = h'[(t_{sk} + wi_m\text{LR}p_{sk,s}) - (t_o + wi_m\text{LR}p_a)] \tag{30}$$

Equation (30) can be used to define a combined temperature t_{com}, which reflects the combined effect of operative temperature and humidity for an actual environment:

$$t_{com} + wi_m\text{LR}p_{tcom} = t_o + wi_m\text{LR}p_a$$

or

$$t_{com} = t_o + wi_m\text{LR}p_a - wi_m\text{LR}p_{tcom} \tag{31}$$

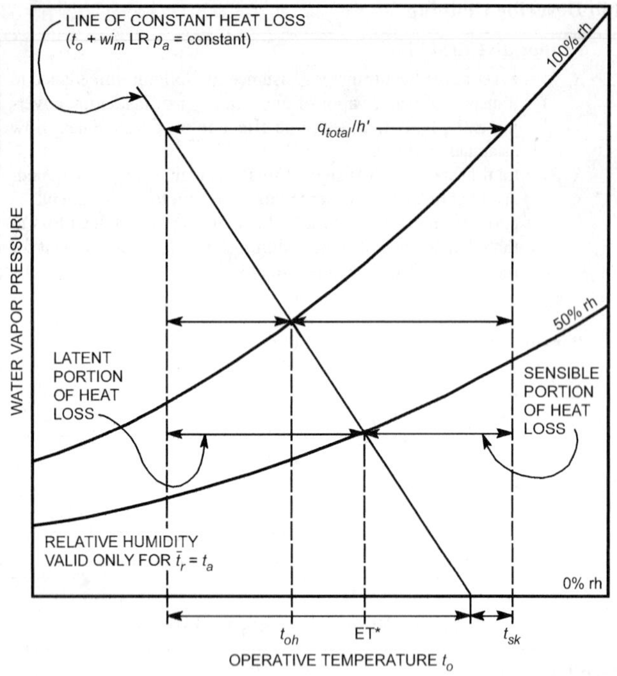

Fig. 2 Constant Skin Heat Loss Line and Its Relationship to t_{oh} and ET*

where p_{tcom} is a vapor pressure related in some fixed way to t_{com} and is analogous to $p_{wb,s}$ for t_{wb}. The term $wi_m \mathrm{LR} p_{tcom}$ is constant to the extent that i_m is constant, and any combination of t_o and p_a that gives the same t_{com} results in the same total heat loss.

Two important environmental indices, humid operative temperature t_{oh} and effective temperature ET*, can be represented in terms of Equation (31). The humid operative temperature is that temperature which at 100% rh yields the same total heat loss as for the actual environment:

$$t_{oh} = t_o + wi_m \mathrm{LR}(p_a - p_{oh,s}) \tag{32}$$

where $p_{oh,s}$ is saturated vapor pressure, in psi, at t_{oh}.

The effective temperature is the temperature at 50% rh that yields the same total heat loss from the skin as for the actual environment:

$$\mathrm{ET}^* = t_o + wi_m \mathrm{LR}(p_a - 0.5 p_{\mathrm{ET}^*,s}) \tag{33}$$

where $p_{\mathrm{ET}^*,s}$ is saturated vapor pressure, in psi, at ET*.

The psychrometric chart in Figure 2 shows a constant total heat loss line and the relationship between these indices. This line represents only one specific skin wettedness and permeation efficiency index. The relationship between indices depends on these two parameters (see the section on Environmental Indices).

4. ENGINEERING DATA AND MEASUREMENTS

Applying basic equations to practical problems of the thermal environment requires quantitative estimates of the body's surface area, metabolic requirements for a given activity and the mechanical efficiency for the work accomplished, evaluation of heat transfer coefficients h_r and h_c, and the general nature of clothing insulation used. This section provides the necessary data and describes how to measure the parameters of the heat balance equation.

Metabolic Rate and Mechanical Efficiency

Maximum Capacity. In choosing optimal conditions for comfort and health, the rate of work done during routine physical activities must be known, because metabolic power increases in proportion to exercise intensity. Metabolic rate varies over a wide range, depending on the activity, person, and conditions under which the activity is performed. Table 4 lists typical metabolic rates for an average adult (A_D = 19.6 ft²) for activities performed continuously. The highest power a person can maintain for any continuous period is approximately 50% of the maximal capacity to use oxygen (maximum energy capacity).

Table 4 Typical Metabolic Heat Generation for Various Activities

	Btu/h·ft²	met*
Resting		
Sleeping	13	0.7
Reclining	15	0.8
Seated, quiet	18	1.0
Standing, relaxed	22	1.2
Walking (on level surface)		
2.9 fps (2 mph)	37	2.0
4.4 fps (3 mph)	48	2.6
5.9 fps (4 mph)	70	3.8
Office Activities		
Reading, seated	18	1.0
Writing	18	1.0
Typing	20	1.1
Filing, seated	22	1.2
Filing, standing	26	1.4
Walking about	31	1.7
Lifting/packing	39	2.1
Driving/Flying		
Car	18 to 37	1.0 to 2.0
Aircraft, routine	22	1.2
Aircraft, instrument landing	33	1.8
Aircraft, combat	44	2.4
Heavy vehicle	59	3.2
Miscellaneous Occupational Activities		
Cooking	29 to 37	1.6 to 2.0
Housecleaning	37 to 63	2.0 to 3.4
Seated, heavy limb movement	41	2.2
Machine work		
sawing (table saw)	33	1.8
light (electrical industry)	37 to 44	2.0 to 2.4
heavy	74	4.0
Handling 110 lb bags	74	4.0
Pick and shovel work	74 to 88	4.0 to 4.8
Miscellaneous Leisure Activities		
Dancing, social	44 to 81	2.4 to 4.4
Calisthenics/exercise	55 to 74	3.0 to 4.0
Tennis, singles	66 to 74	3.6 to 4.0
Basketball	90 to 140	5.0 to 7.6
Wrestling, competitive	130 to 160	7.0 to 8.7

Sources: Compiled from various sources. For additional information, see Buskirk (1960), Passmore and Durnin (1967), and Webb (1964).
*1 met = 18.4 Btu/h·ft²

A unit used to express the metabolic rate per unit DuBois area is the **met**, defined as the metabolic rate of a sedentary person (seated, quiet): 1 met = 18.4 Btu/h·ft² = 50 kcal/h·m². A normal, healthy man at age 20 has a maximum capacity of approximately M_{act} = 12 met, which drops to 7 met at age 70. Maximum rates for women are on average about 30% lower. Long-distance runners and trained athletes have maximum rates as high as 20 met. An average 35-year-old who does not exercise has a maximum rate of about 10 met, and activities with M_{act} > 5 met are likely to prove exhausting.

Intermittent Activity. Often, people's activity consists of a mixture of activities or a combination of work/rest periods. A weighted average metabolic rate is generally satisfactory, provided that activities alternate frequently (several times per hour). For example, a person whose activities consist of typing 50% of the time, filing while seated 25% of the time, and walking about 25% of the time would have an average metabolic rate of 0.50 × 20 + 0.25 × 22 + 0.25 × 31 = 23 Btu/h·ft² (see Table 4).

Accuracy. Estimating metabolic rates is difficult. Values given in Table 4 indicate metabolic rates only for the specific activities listed. Some entries give a range and some a single value, depending on the data source. The level of accuracy depends on the value of M_{act} and how well the activity can be defined. For well-defined activities with $M_{act} < 1.5$ met (e.g., reading), Table 4 is sufficiently accurate for most engineering purposes. For values of $M_{act} > 3$, where a task is poorly defined or where there are various ways of performing a task (e.g., heavy machine work), the values may be in error by as much as ±50% for a given application. Engineering calculations should thus allow for potential variations.

Measurement. When metabolic rates must be determined more accurately than is possible with tabulated data, physiological measurements with human subjects may be necessary. The rate of metabolic heat produced by the body is most accurately measured by the rate of respiratory oxygen consumption and carbon dioxide production. An empirical equation for metabolic rate is given by Nishi (1981):

$$M = \frac{567(0.23\mathrm{RQ} + 0.77)Q_{O_2}}{A_D} \tag{34}$$

where

M = metabolic rate, Btu/h·ft²
RQ = respiratory quotient; molar ratio of Q_{CO_2} exhaled to Q_{O_2} inhaled, dimensionless
Q_{O_2} = volumetric rate of oxygen consumption at conditions (STPD) of 32°F, 14.7 psi, ft³/h

The exact value of the respiratory quotient RQ depends on a person's activity, diet, and physical condition. It can be determined by measuring both carbon dioxide and oxygen in the respiratory airflows, or it can be estimated with reasonable accuracy. A good estimate for the average adult is RQ = 0.83 for light or sedentary activities ($M < 1.5$ met), increasing proportionately to RQ = 1.0 for extremely heavy exertion ($M = 5.0$ met). Estimating RQ is generally sufficient for all except precision laboratory measurements because it does not strongly affect the value of the metabolic rate: a 10% error in estimating RQ results in an error of less than 3% in the metabolic rate.

A second, much less accurate, method of estimating metabolic rate physiologically is to measure the heart rate. Table 5 shows the relationship between heart rate and oxygen consumption at different levels of physical exertion for a typical person. Once oxygen consumption is estimated from heart rate information, Equation (34) can be used to estimate the metabolic rate. Other factors that affect heart rate include physical condition, heat, emotional factors, and muscles used. Astrand and Rodahl (1977) show that heart rate is only a very approximate measure of metabolic rate and should not be the only source of information where accuracy is required.

Table 5 Heart Rate and Oxygen Consumption at Different Activity Levels

Level of Exertion	Heart Rate, bpm	Oxygen Consumed, ft³/h
Light work	<90	<1
Moderate work	90 to 110	1 to 2
Heavy work	110 to 130	2 to 3
Very heavy work	130 to 150	3 to 4
Extremely heavy work	150 to 170	>4

Source: Astrand and Rodahl (1977).

Mechanical Efficiency. In the heat balance equation, the rate W of work accomplished must be in the same units as metabolism M and expressed in terms of A_D in Btu/h·ft². The mechanical work done by the muscles for a given task is often expressed in terms of the body's mechanical efficiency $\mu = W/M$. It is unusual for μ to be more than 0.05 to 0.10; for most activities, it is close to zero. The maximum value under optimal conditions (e.g., bicycle ergometer) is μ = 0.20 to 0.24 (Nishi 1981). It is common to assume that mechanical work is zero for several reasons: (1) mechanical work produced is small compared to metabolic rate, especially for office activities; (2) estimates for metabolic rates are often inaccurate; and (3) this assumption gives a more conservative estimate when designing air-conditioning equipment for upper comfort and health limits. More accurate calculation of heat generation may require estimating mechanical work produced for activities where it is significant (walking on a grade, climbing a ladder, bicycling, lifting, etc.). In some cases, it is possible to either estimate or measure the mechanical work. For example, a 200 lb person walking up a 5% grade at 4.4 fps (3 mph) would lift a 200 lb weight a height of 0.22 ft every second, for a work rate of 44 ft·lb$_f$/s, or 204 Btu/h. This rate of mechanical work would then be subtracted from M to determine the net heat generated.

Heat Transfer Coefficients

Values for the linearized radiative heat transfer coefficient, convective heat transfer coefficient, and evaporative heat transfer coefficient are required to solve the equations describing heat transfer from the body.

Radiative Heat Transfer Coefficient. The linearized radiative heat transfer coefficient can be calculated by

$$h_r = 4\varepsilon\sigma\frac{A_r}{A_D}\left(459.7 + \frac{t_{cl} + \bar{t}_r}{2}\right)^3 \tag{35}$$

where

h_r = radiative heat transfer coefficient, Btu/h·ft²·°F
ε = average emissivity of clothing or body surface, dimensionless
σ = Stefan-Boltzmann constant, 0.1712 × 10⁻⁸ Btu/h·ft²·°R⁴
A_r = effective radiation area of body, ft²

The ratio A_r/A_D is 0.70 for a sitting person and 0.73 for a standing person (Fanger 1967). Emissivity ε is close to unity (typically 0.95), unless special reflective materials are used or high-temperature sources are involved. It is not always possible to solve Equation (35) explicitly for h_r, because t_{cl} may also be unknown. Some form of iteration may be necessary if a precise solution is required. Fortunately, h_r is nearly constant for typical indoor temperatures, and a value of 0.83 Btu/h·ft²·°F suffices for most calculations. If emissivity is significantly less than unity, adjust the value by

$$h_r = 0.83\varepsilon \tag{36}$$

where ε represents the area-weighted average emissivity for the clothing/body surface.

Convective Heat Transfer Coefficient. Heat transfer by convection is usually caused by air movement within the living space or by body movements. Equations for estimating h_c under various conditions are presented in Table 6. Where two conditions apply (e.g., walking in moving air), a reasonable estimate can be obtained by taking the larger of the two values for h_c. Limits have been given to all equations. If no limits were given in the source, reasonable limits have been estimated. Be careful using these values for seated and reclining persons. The heat transfer coefficients may be accurate, but the effective heat transfer area may be substantially reduced through body contact with a padded chair or bed.

Table 6 Equations for Convection Heat Transfer Coefficients

Equation	Limits	Condition	Remarks/Sources
$h_c = 0.061V^{0.6}$ $h_c = 0.55$	$40 < V < 800$ $0 < V < 40$	Seated with moving air	Mitchell (1974)
$h_c = 0.475 + 0.044V^{0.67}$ $h_c = 0.90$	$30 < V < 300$ $0 < V < 30$	Reclining with moving air	Colin and Houdas (1967)
$h_c = 0.092V^{0.53}$	$100 < V < 400$	Walking in still air	V is walking speed (Nishi and Gagge 1970)
$h_c = (M - 0.85)^{0.39}$	$1.1 < M < 3.0$	Active in still air	Gagge et al. (1976)
$h_c = 0.146V^{0.39}$	$100 < V < 400$	Walking on treadmill in still air	V is treadmill speed (Nishi and Gagge 1970)
$h_c = 0.068V^{0.69}$ $h_c = 0.70$	$30 < V < 300$ $0 < V < 30$	Standing person in moving air	Developed from data presented by Seppänen et al. (1972)

Note: h_c in Btu/h·ft²·°F, V in fpm, and M in met, where 1 met = 18.4 Btu/h·ft².

Quantitative values of h_c are important, not only in estimating convection loss, but in evaluating (1) operative temperature t_o, (2) clothing parameters I_t and i_m, and (3) rational effective temperatures t_{oh} and ET*. All heat transfer coefficients in Table 6 were evaluated at or near 14.7 psia. These coefficients should be corrected as follows for atmospheric pressure:

$$h_{cc} = h_c(p_t/14.7)^{0.55} \tag{37}$$

where

h_{cc} = corrected convective heat transfer coefficient, Btu/h·ft²·°F
p_t = local atmospheric pressure, psia

The combined coefficient h is the sum of h_r and h_c, described in Equation (35) and Table 6, respectively. The coefficient h governs exchange by radiation and convection from the exposed body surface to the surrounding environment.

Evaporative Heat Transfer Coefficient. The evaporative heat transfer coefficient h_e for the outer air layer of a nude or clothed person can be estimated from the convective heat transfer coefficient using the Lewis relation given in Equation (27). If the atmospheric pressure is significantly different from the reference value (14.7 psia), the correction to the value obtained from Equation (27) is

$$h_{ec} = h_e(14.7/p_t)^{0.45} \tag{38}$$

where h_{ec} is the corrected evaporative heat transfer coefficient in Btu/h·ft²·°F.

Clothing Insulation and Permeation Efficiency

Thermal Insulation. The most accurate ways to determine clothing insulation are (1) measurements on heated mannikins (McCullough and Jones 1984; Olesen and Nielsen 1983) and (2) measurements on active subjects (Nishi et al. 1975). For most routine engineering work, estimates based on tables and equations in this section are sufficient. Thermal mannikins can measure the sensible heat loss from "skin" ($C + R$) in a given environment. Equation (11) can then be used to evaluate R_{cl} if environmental conditions are well defined and f_{cl} is measured. Evaluation of clothing insulation on subjects requires measurement of t_{sk}, t_{cl}, and t_o. Clothing thermal efficiency is calculated by

$$f_{cl} = \frac{t_{cl} - t_o}{t_{sk} - t_o} \tag{39}$$

Table 7 Typical Insulation and Permeation Efficiency Values for Western Clothing Ensembles

Ensemble Description[a]	I_{cl}, clo	I_t,[b] clo	f_{cl}	i_{cl}	i_m[b]
Walking shorts, short-sleeved shirt	0.36	1.02	1.10	0.34	0.42
Trousers, short-sleeved shirt	0.57	1.20	1.15	0.36	0.43
Trousers, long-sleeved shirt	0.61	1.21	1.20	0.41	0.45
Same as above, plus suit jacket	0.96	1.54	1.23		
Same as above, plus vest and T-shirt	1.14	1.69	1.32	0.32	0.37
Trousers, long-sleeved shirt, long-sleeved sweater, T-shirt	1.01	1.56	1.28		
Same as above, plus suit jacket and long underwear bottoms	1.30	1.83	1.33		
Sweat pants, sweat shirt	0.74	1.35	1.19	0.41	0.45
Long-sleeved pajama top, long pajama trousers, short 3/4 sleeved robe, slippers (no socks)	0.96	1.50	1.32	0.37	0.41
Knee-length skirt, short-sleeved shirt, panty hose, sandals	0.54	1.10	1.26		
Knee-length skirt, long-sleeved shirt, full slip, panty hose	0.67	1.22	1.29		
Knee-length skirt, long-sleeved shirt, half slip, panty hose, long-sleeved sweater	1.10	1.59	1.46		
Same as above, replace sweater with suit jacket	1.04	1.60	1.30	0.35	0.40
Ankle-length skirt, long-sleeved shirt, suit jacket, panty hose	1.10	1.59	1.46		
Long-sleeved coveralls, T-shirt	0.72	1.30	1.23		
Overalls, long-sleeved shirt, T-shirt	0.89	1.46	1.27	0.35	0.40
Insulated coveralls, long-sleeved thermal underwear, long underwear bottoms	1.37	1.94	1.26	0.35	0.39

Sources: McCullough and Jones (1984) and McCullough et al. (1989).
[a]All ensembles include shoes and briefs or panties. All ensembles except those with panty hose include socks unless otherwise noted.
[b]For $t_r = t_a$ and air velocity less than 40 fpm (I_a = 0.72 clo and i_m = 0.48 when nude).

The intrinsic clothing insulation can then be calculated from mannikin measurements, provided f_{cl} is measured and conditions are sufficiently well defined to determine h accurately:

$$R_{cl} = \frac{t_{sk} - t_o}{q} - \frac{1}{hf_{cl}} \tag{40}$$

where q is heat loss from the mannikin in Btu/h·ft².

Clothing insulation value may be expressed in clo units. To avoid confusion, the symbol I is used with the clo unit instead of the symbol R. The relationship between the two is

$$R = 0.88I \tag{41}$$

or 1.0 clo is equivalent to 0.88 ft²·°F·h/Btu.

Because clothing insulation cannot be measured for most routine engineering applications, tables of measured values for various clothing ensembles can be used to select an ensemble comparable to the one(s) in question. Table 7 gives values for typical indoor clothing ensembles. More detailed tables are presented by McCullough and Jones (1984) and Olesen and Nielsen (1983). Accuracies for I_{cl} on the order of ±20% are typical if good matches between ensembles are found. Values of thermal insulation and clothing area factors for clothing ensembles typical of the Arabian Gulf region may be found in Al-ajmi et al. (2008).

ASHRAE research project RP-1504 (Havenith et al. 2015) produced a database of static total and intrinsic clothing thermal insulation values and vapor permeability indices for non-Western ensembles. The report presents tabulated data for more than 40 ensembles from India, Pakistan, Indonesia, Kuwait, Nigeria, Ghana, and China. Table 8 gives values for a selection of these ensembles. Local regional thermal insulation values for the ensembles were also measured, together with data on the effects of air velocity, posture, and walking on the total thermal insulation values.

Table 8 Insulation and Permeability Values for a Selection of Non-Western Clothing Ensembles

Ensemble Description[a]	Country	I_{cl} clo	I_t, clo	f_{cl}	i_m
Shalwar (pants), kameez (shirt), scarf, sandals (f)	Pakistan	0.69	1.1	1.41	0.32
Shalwar (pants), kameez (shirt), socks, athletic shoes (m)	Pakistan	0.86	1.3	1.36	0.35
Dishdasha (thowb or caftan), short-sleeved t-shirt, long serwal (pants), tagiya (hat), iqal (cord), ghutra (headdress), socks, athletic shoes (m)	Kuwait	1.36	1.7	1.66	0.30
Full slip, double-layer abaya (dress), anta (head cover), hijab (headscarf), sandals (f)	Kuwait	1.27	1.7	1.65	0.33
Underskirt, blouse, sari, sandals (f)	India	0.74	1.2	1.46	0.33
Churidhar pants, churidhar dress, shawl, sandals (f)	India	0.58	1.1	1.28	0.36
Short shirt with long sleeves, long pants, boubou (wide-sleeved robe), kufi (hat), sandals (m)	Nigeria/ Ghana	1.40	1.7	1.96	0.42
Short shirt with long sleeves, long pants, sandals (f)	Nigeria/ Ghana	0.78	1.3	1.35	0.40
Long-sleeved shirt, skirt, headscarf, socks, athletic shoes (f)	Indonesia	0.97	1.4	1.43	0.31
Camisole, short-sleeved qipao (dress), sandals (f)	China	0.42	0.9	1.31	0.40

(f) = clothing traditionally worn by women
(m) = clothing traditionally worn by men
Source: Havenith et al. (2015). Values are the means of manikin-based measurements conducted in three laboratories. All ensembles include bra and panties (female) and briefs (male). For all women's ensembles, I_a = 0.64 clo; for all men's ensembles, I_a = 0.63 clo.

When a premeasured ensemble cannot be found to match the one in question, estimate the ensemble insulation from the insulation of individual garments. Table 9 lists common individual garments. The insulation of an ensemble is estimated from the individual values using a summation formula (McCullough and Jones 1984):

$$I_{cl} = 0.835 \sum_i I_{clu,i} + 0.161 \tag{42}$$

where $I_{clu,i}$ is the effective insulation of garment i, and I_{cl}, as before, is the insulation for the entire ensemble. A simpler and nearly as accurate summation formula is (Olesen 1985)

$$I_{cl} = \sum_i I_{clu,i} \tag{43}$$

Either Equation (42) or (43) gives acceptable accuracy for typical indoor clothing. The main source of inaccuracy is in determining the appropriate values for individual garments. Overall accuracies are on the order of ±25% if the tables are used carefully. If it is important to include a specific garment not included in Table 8, its insulation can be estimated by (McCullough and Jones 1984)

$$I_{clu,i} = (0.534 + 3.43x_f)(A_G/A_D) - 0.0549 \tag{44}$$

where

x_f = fabric thickness, in.
A_G = body surface area covered by garment, ft²

Values in Table 7 may be adjusted by information in Table 9 and a summation formula. Using this method, values of $I_{clu,i}$ for the selected items in Table 9 are then added to or subtracted from the ensemble value of I_{cl} in Table 7.

When a person is sitting, the chair generally has the effect of increasing clothing insulation by up to 0.15 clo, depending on the contact area A_{ch} between the chair and body (McCullough et al. 1994). A string webbed or beach chair has little or no contact area, and the insulation actually decreases by about 0.1 clo, likely because of compression of the clothing in the contact area. In contrast, a cushioned executive chair has a large contact area that can increase the intrinsic clothing insulation by 0.15 clo. For other chairs, the increase in intrinsic insulation ΔI_{cl} can be estimated from

Table 9 Garment Insulation Values

Garment Description[a]	$I_{clu,i}$, clo[b]	Garment Description[a]	$I_{clu,i}$, clo[b]	Garment Description[a]	$I_{clu,i}$, clo[b]
Underwear		Long-sleeved, flannel shirt	0.34	Long-sleeved (thin)	0.25
Men's briefs	0.04	Short-sleeved, knit sport shirt	0.17	Long-sleeved (thick)	0.36
Panties	0.03	Long-sleeved, sweat shirt	0.34	**Dresses and Skirts[c]**	
Bra	0.01	**Trousers and Coveralls**		Skirt (thin)	0.14
T-shirt	0.08	Short shorts	0.06	Skirt (thick)	0.23
Full slip	0.16	Walking shorts	0.08	Long-sleeved shirtdress (thin)	0.33
Half slip	0.14	Straight trousers (thin)	0.15	Long-sleeved shirtdress (thick)	0.47
Long underwear top	0.20	Straight trousers (thick)	0.24	Short-sleeved shirtdress (thin)	0.29
Long underwear bottoms	0.15	Sweatpants	0.28	Sleeveless, scoop neck (thin)	0.23
Footwear		Overalls	0.30	Sleeveless, scoop neck (thick)	0.27
Ankle-length athletic socks	0.02	Coveralls	0.49	**Sleepwear and Robes**	
Calf-length socks	0.03	**Suit Jackets and Vests (Lined)**		Sleeveless, short gown (thin)	0.18
Knee socks (thick)	0.06	Single-breasted (thin)	0.36	Sleeveless, long gown (thin)	0.20
Panty hose	0.02	Single-breasted (thick)	0.44	Short-sleeved hospital gown	0.31
Sandals/thongs	0.02	Double-breasted (thin)	0.42	Long-sleeved, long gown (thick)	0.46
Slippers (quilted, pile-lined)	0.03	Double-breasted (thick)	0.48	Long-sleeved pajamas (thick)	0.57
Boots	0.10	Sleeveless vest (thin)	0.10	Short-sleeved pajamas (thin)	0.42
Shirts and Blouses		Sleeveless vest (thick)	0.17	Long-sleeved, long wrap robe (thick)	0.69
Sleeveless, scoop-neck blouse	0.12	**Sweaters**		Long-sleeved, short wrap robe (thick)	0.48
Short-sleeved, dress shirt	0.19	Sleeveless vest (thin)	0.13	Short-sleeved, short robe (thin)	0.34
Long-sleeved, dress shirt	0.25	Sleeveless vest (thick)	0.22		

[a]"Thin" garments are summerweight; "thick" garments are winterweight. [b]1 clo = 0.88°F·ft²·h/Btu [c]Knee-length

$$\Delta I_{cl} = 6.95 \times 10^{-2} A_{ch} - 0.1 \tag{45}$$

where A_{ch} is in ft².

For example, a desk chair with a body contact area of 2.9 ft² has a ΔI_{cl} of 0.1 clo. This amount should be added to the intrinsic insulation of the standing clothing ensemble to obtain the insulation of the ensemble when sitting in the desk chair.

Although sitting increases clothing insulation, walking decreases it (McCullough and Hong 1994), as does air movement (Havenith and Nilsson 2004). The change in clothing insulation ΔI_{cl} can be estimated from the standing intrinsic insulation I_{cl} of the ensemble and the walking speed (Walkspeed) in steps per minute:

$$\Delta I_{cl} = -0.504 I_{cl} - 0.00281(\text{Walkspeed}) + 0.24 \tag{46}$$

For example, the clothing insulation of a person wearing a winter business suit with a standing intrinsic insulation of 1 clo would decrease by 0.52 clo when the person walks at 90 steps per minute (about 2.3 mph). Thus, when the person is walking, the intrinsic insulation of the ensemble would be 0.48 clo.

A correction for both walking and air speed for a person in normal or light clothing (0.6 clo $< I_{cl} <$ 1.4 clo, or 1.2 clo $< I_T <$ 2.0 clo, respectively) is given by Havenith and Nilsson (2004) and Havenith et al. (2012) as

$$\begin{aligned} I_{cl,r} &= I_{T,r} - \frac{1}{f_{cl}\, 0.155h} \\ &= \left[e^{[-0.281 \times (v_{ar} - 0.15) + 0.044 \times (v_{ar} - 0.15)^2 - 0.492w + 0.176w^2]} \times \left(I_{cl,static} + \frac{0.7}{f_{cl}} \right) \right] \\ &\quad - \frac{(0.92 e^{(-0.15 v_{ar} - 0.22 v_w)} - 0.0045)0.7}{f_{cl}} \end{aligned} \tag{47}$$

where

$I_{cl,r}$ = resultant intrinsic clothing insulation, clo
$I_{cl,static}$ = static intrinsic clothing insulation obtained from manikin or tables, clo
$I_{T,r}$ = resultant total insulation of clothing plus adjacent air layer
v_{ar} = wind speed relative to person, from 0.5 to 13 fps (if above this range, treat as 13 fps; if below this range, treat as 0.5 fps)
v_w = walking speed, from 0 to 4 fps (if above this range, treat as 4 fps)

Permeation Efficiency. Permeation efficiency data for some clothing ensembles are presented in terms of i_{cl} and i_m in Table 7. Values of i_m can be used to calculate $R_{e,t}$ using the relationships in Table 2. Ensembles worn indoors generally fall in the range $0.3 < i_m < 0.5$. Assuming $i_m = 0.4$ is reasonably accurate (McCullough et al. 1989) and may be used if a good match to ensembles in Table 7 cannot be made. The value of i_m or $R_{e,t}$ may be substituted directly into equations for body heat loss calculations (see Table 3). However, i_m for a given clothing ensemble is a function of the environment as well as the clothing properties. Unless i_m is evaluated at conditions very similar to the intended application, it is more rigorous to use i_{cl} to describe the permeation efficiency of the clothing. The value of i_{cl} is not as sensitive to environmental conditions; thus, given data are more accurate over a wider range of air velocity and radiant and air temperature combinations for i_{cl} than for i_m. Relationships in Table 2 can be used to determine $R_{e,cl}$ from i_{cl}, and $R_{e,cl}$ can then be used for body heat loss calculations (see Table 3). McCullough et al. (1989) found an average value of $i_{cl} = 0.34$ for common indoor clothing; this value can be used when other data are not available.

Measuring i_m or i_{cl} may be necessary if unusual clothing (e.g., impermeable or metallized) and/or extreme environments (e.g., high radiant temperatures, high air velocities) are to be addressed. There are three different methods for measuring the permeation efficiency of clothing: (1) using a wet mannikin to measure the effect of sweat evaporation on heat loss (McCullough 1986), (2) using permeation efficiency measurements on component fabrics as well as dry mannikin measurements (Umbach 1980), and (3) using measurements from sweating subjects (Holmer 1984; Nishi et al. 1975). For an overview, please see ISO *Standard* 9920.

Clothing Surface Area. Many clothing heat transfer calculations require that clothing area factor f_{cl} be known. The most reliable approach is to measure it using photographic methods (Olesen et al. 1982). Other than actual measurements, the best method is to use previously tabulated data for similar clothing ensembles. Table 7 is adequate for most indoor clothing ensembles. No good method of estimating f_{cl} for an ensemble from other information is available, although a rough estimate can be made by (McCullough and Jones 1984)

$$f_{cl} = 1.0 + 0.3 I_{cl} \tag{48}$$

Total Evaporative Heat Loss

The total evaporative heat loss (latent heat) from the body through both respiratory and skin losses, $E_{sk} + E_{res}$, can be measured directly from the body's rate of mass loss as observed by a sensitive scale:

$$E_{sk} + E_{res} = \frac{h_{fg}}{A_D} \times \frac{dm}{d\theta} \tag{49}$$

where

h_{fg} = latent heat of vaporization of water, Btu/lb
m = body mass, lb
θ = time, h

When using Equation (49), adjustments should be made for any food or drink consumed, body effluents (e.g., wastes), and metabolic weight losses. Metabolism contributes slightly to weight loss primarily because the oxygen absorbed during respiration is converted to heavier CO_2 and exhaled. It can be calculated by

$$\frac{dm_{ge}}{d\theta} = 2.2 Q_{O2}(0.1225\text{RQ} - 0.0891) \tag{50}$$

where

$dm_{ge}/d\theta$ = rate of mass loss due to respiratory gas exchange, lb/h
Q_{O_2} = oxygen uptake at STPD, ft³/h
RQ = respiratory quotient
0.1225 = density of CO_2 at STPD, lb/ft³
0.0891 = density of O_2 at STPD, lb/ft³
STPD = standard temperature and pressure of dry air at 32°F and 14.7 psi

Environmental Parameters

Thermal environment parameters that must be measured or otherwise quantified to obtain accurate estimates of human thermal response are divided into two groups: those that can be measured directly and those calculated from other measurements.

Directly Measured Parameters. Seven psychrometric parameters used to describe the thermal environment are (1) air temperature t_a, (2) wet-bulb temperature t_{wb}, (3) dew-point temperature t_{dp}, (4) water vapor pressure p_a, (5) total atmospheric pressure p_t, (6) relative humidity (rh), and (7) humidity ratio W_a. These parameters are discussed in detail in Chapter 1, and methods for measuring them are discussed in Chapter 36. Two other important parameters include air velocity V and mean radiant temperature $\bar{t}_r$. Air velocity measurements are also discussed in Chapter 36. The radiant temperature is the temperature of an exposed surface in the environment. The temperatures of individual surfaces are usually combined into a mean radiant temperature $\bar{t}_r$. Finally, globe temperature t_g, which can also be measured directly, is a good approximation of the operative temperature t_o and is also used with other measurements to calculate the mean radiant temperature.

Calculated Parameters. The **mean radiant temperature** $\bar{t}_r$ is a key variable in thermal calculations for the human body. It is the uniform temperature of an imaginary enclosure in which radiant heat transfer from the human body equals the radiant heat transfer in the actual nonuniform enclosure. Measurements of the globe temperature, air temperature, and air velocity can be combined to estimate the mean radiant temperature (see Chapter 36). Accuracy of $\bar{t}_r$ determined this way varies considerably, depending on the type of environment and accuracy of the individual measurements. Because the mean radiant temperature is defined with respect to the human body, the shape of the sensor is also a factor. The spherical shape of the globe thermometer gives a reasonable approximation of a seated person; an ellipsoid sensor gives a better approximation of the shape of a human, both upright and seated.

Mean radiant temperature can also be calculated from the measured temperature of surrounding walls and surfaces and their positions with respect to the person. Most building materials have a high emittance ε, so all surfaces in the room can be assumed to be black. The following equation is then used:

$$\bar{T}_r^4 = T_1^4 F_{p-1} + T_2^4 F_{p-2} + \cdots + T_N^4 F_{p-N} \tag{51}$$

where

$\bar{T}_r$ = mean radiant temperature, °R
T_N = surface temperature of surface N, °R
F_{p-N} = angle factor between a person and surface N

Because the sum of the angle factors is unity, the fourth power of mean radiant temperature equals the mean value of the surrounding surface temperatures to the fourth power, weighted by the respective angle factors. In general, angle factors are difficult to determine, although Figures 3A and 3B may be used to estimate them for rectangular surfaces. The angle factor normally depends on the position and orientation of the person (Fanger 1982).

If relatively small temperature differences exist between the surfaces of the enclosure, Equation (51) can be simplified to a linear form:

$$\bar{t}_r = t_1 F_{p-1} + t_2 F_{p-2} + \cdots + t_N F_{p-N} \tag{52}$$

Equation (52) always gives a slightly lower mean radiant temperature than Equation (51), but the difference is small. If, for example, half the surroundings ($F_{p-N} = 0.5$) has a temperature 10°F higher than the other half, the difference between the calculated mean radiant temperatures [according to Equations (51) and (52)] is only 0.4°F. If, however, this difference is 200°F, the mean radiant temperature calculated by Equation (52) is 20°F too low.

Mean radiant temperature may also be calculated from the plane radiant temperature t_{pr} in six directions (up, down, right, left, front, back) and for the projected area factors of a person in the same six directions. For a standing person, the mean radiant temperature may be estimated as

$$\begin{aligned}\bar{t}_r &= \{0.08[t_{pr}(\text{up}) + t_{pr}(\text{down})] + 0.23[t_{pr}(\text{right})\\ &\quad + t_{pr}(\text{left})] + 0.35[t_{pr}(\text{front}) + t_{pr}(\text{back})]\}\\ &\quad \div [2(0.08 + 0.23 + 0.35)]\end{aligned} \tag{53}$$

For a seated person,

$$\begin{aligned}\bar{t}_r &= \{0.18[t_{pr}(\text{up}) + t_{pr}(\text{down})] + 0.22[t_{pr}(\text{right})\\ &\quad + t_{pr}(\text{left})] + 0.30[t_{pr}(\text{front}) + t_{pr}(\text{back})]\}\\ &\quad \div [2(0.18 + 0.22 + 0.30)]\end{aligned} \tag{54}$$

The **plane radiant temperature** t_{pr}, introduced by Korsgaard (1949), is the uniform temperature of an enclosure in which the incident radiant flux on one side of a small plane element is the same as that in the actual environment. The plane radiant temperature

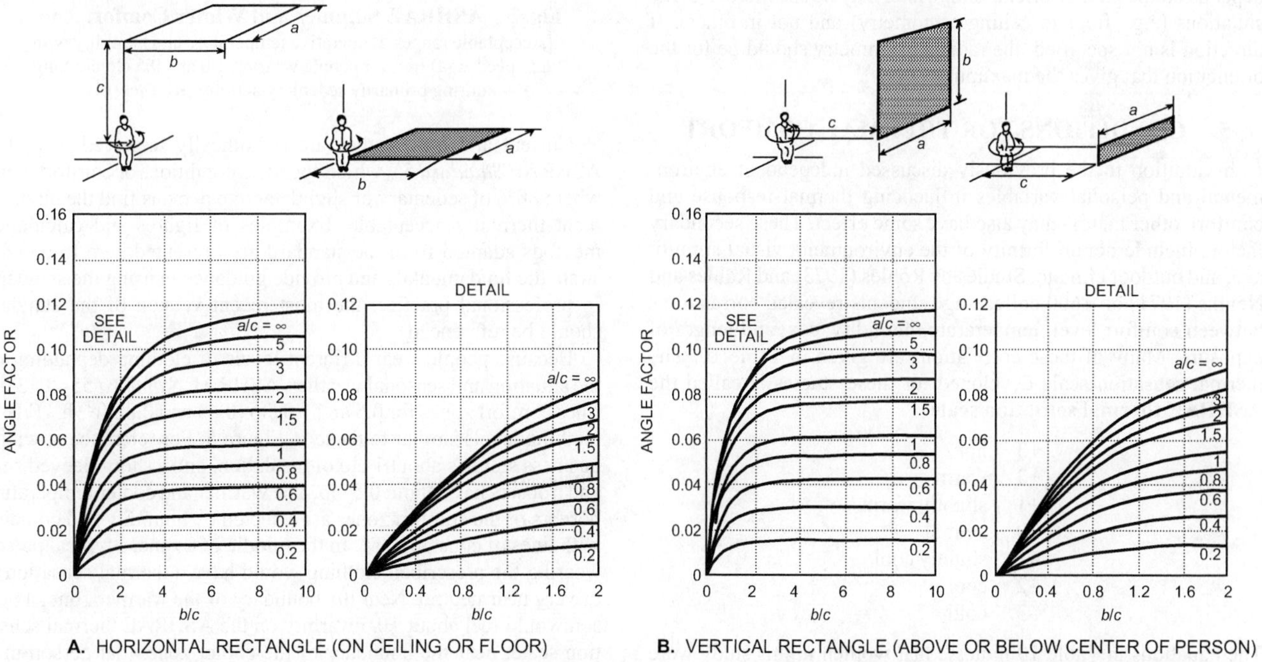

Fig. 3 Mean Value of Angle Factor Between Seated Person and Horizontal or Vertical Rectangle when Person Is Rotated Around Vertical Axis
(Fanger 1982)

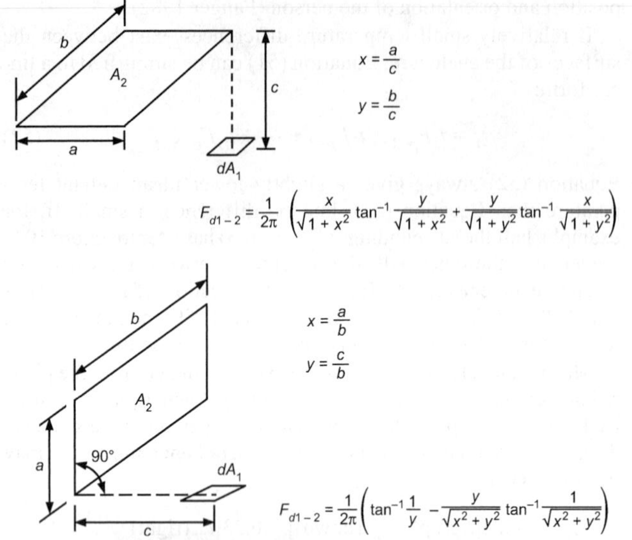

Fig. 4 Analytical Formulas for Calculating Angle Factor for Small Plane Element

describes thermal radiation in one direction, and its value thus depends on the direction. In comparison, mean radiant temperature $\bar{t}_r$ describes the thermal radiation for the human body from all directions. The plane radiant temperature can be calculated using Equations (50) and (51) with the same limitations. Area factors are determined from Figure 4.

The **radiant temperature asymmetry** Δt_{pr} is the difference between the plane radiant temperature of the opposite sides of a small plane element. This parameter describes the asymmetry of the radiant environment and is especially important in comfort conditions. Because it is defined with respect to a plane element, its value depends on the plane's orientation, which may be specified in some situations (e.g., floor to ceiling asymmetry) and not in others. If direction is not specified, the radiant asymmetry should be for the orientation that gives the maximum value.

5. CONDITIONS FOR THERMAL COMFORT

In addition to the previously discussed independent environmental and personal variables influencing thermal response and comfort, other factors may also have some effect. These secondary factors include nonuniformity of the environment, visual stimuli, age, and outdoor climate. Studies by Rohles (1973) and Rohles and Nevins (1971) on 1600 college-age students revealed correlations between comfort level, temperature, humidity, sex, and length of exposure. Many of these correlations are given in Table 10. The thermal sensation scale developed for these studies is called the **ASHRAE thermal sensation scale**:

+3	hot
+2	warm
+1	slightly warm
0	neutral
−1	slightly cool
−2	cool
−3	cold

The equations in Table 10 indicate that women in this study were more sensitive to temperature and less sensitive to humidity than the men, but in general about a 5.4°F change in temperature or a 0.44 psi change in water vapor pressure is necessary to change a thermal sensation vote by one unit or temperature category.

Table 10 Equations for Predicting Thermal Sensation Y of Men, Women, and Men and Women Combined

Exposure Period, h	Subjects	Regression Equations[a, b] t = dry-bulb temperature, °F p = vapor pressure, psi
1.0	Men	$Y = 0.122t + 1.61p - 9.584$
	Women	$Y = 0.151t + 1.71p - 12.080$
	Both	$Y = 0.136t + 1.71p - 10.880$
2.0	Men	$Y = 0.123t + 1.86p - 9.953$
	Women	$Y = 0.157t + 1.45p - 12.725$
	Both	$Y = 0.140t + 1.65p - 11.339$
3.0	Men	$Y = 0.118t + 2.02p - 9.718$
	Women	$Y = 0.153t + 1.76p - 13.511$
	Both	$Y = 0.135t + 1.92p - 11.122$

[a] Y values refer to the ASHRAE thermal sensation scale.
[b] For young adult subjects with sedentary activity and wearing clothing with a thermal resistance of approximately 0.5 clo, $\bar{t}_r < \bar{t}_a$ and air velocities < 40 fpm.

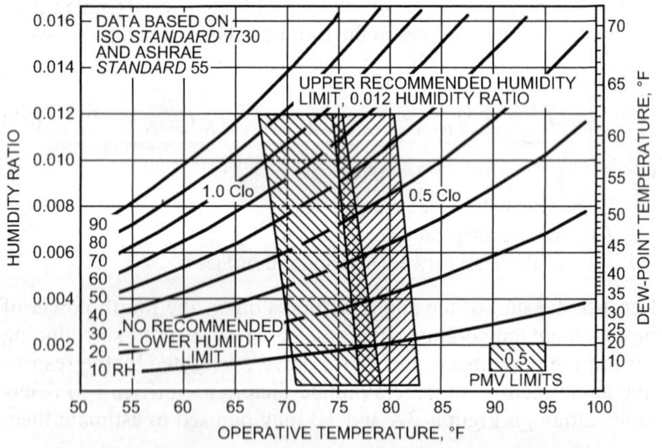

Fig. 5 ASHRAE Summer and Winter Comfort Zones

[Acceptable ranges of operative temperature and humidity with air speed ≤ 40 fpm for people wearing 1.0 and 0.5 clo clothing during primarily sedentary activity (≤1.1 met).]

Current and past studies are periodically reviewed to update ASHRAE *Standard* 55, which specifies conditions or comfort zones where 80% of sedentary or slightly active persons find the environment thermally acceptable. Examples of figures and calculation methods adapted from the standard are presented here to demonstrate the fundamentals and provide guidance in using the standard. In professional practice, the most recent version of the standard should be referenced.

Because people wear different levels of clothing depending on the situation and seasonal weather, ASHRAE *Standard* 55-2013 defines comfort zones for 0.5 and 1.0 clo (0.44 and 0.88 $ft^2 \cdot h \cdot °F/Btu$) clothing levels similar to those in Figure 5. For reference, a winter business suit has about 1 clo of insulation, and a short-sleeved shirt and trousers have about 0.5 clo. The warmer and cooler temperature borders of the comfort zones are affected by humidity and coincide with lines of constant ET*. In the middle of a zone, a typical person wearing the prescribed clothing would have a thermal sensation at or very near neutral. Near the boundary of the warmer zone, a person would feel about +0.5 warmer on the ASHRAE thermal sensation scale; near the boundary of the cooler zone, that person may have a thermal sensation of −0.5.

The comfort zone's temperature boundaries (T_{min}, T_{max}) can be adjusted by interpolation for clothing insulation levels (I_{cl}) between those in Figure 5 by using the following equations:

$$T_{min,I_{cl}} = \frac{(I_{cl} - 0.5\ \text{clo})T_{min,1.0\ \text{clo}} + (1.0\ \text{clo} - I_{cl})T_{min,0.5\ \text{clo}}}{0.5\ \text{clo}} \tag{55}$$

$$T_{max,I_{cl}} = \frac{(I_{cl} - 0.5\ \text{clo})T_{max,1.0\ \text{clo}} + (1.0\ \text{clo} - I_{cl})T_{max,0.5\ \text{clo}}}{0.5\ \text{clo}} \tag{56}$$

In general, comfort temperatures for other clothing levels can be approximated by decreasing the temperature borders of the zone by 1°F for each 0.1 clo increase in clothing insulation and vice versa. Similarly, a zone's temperatures can be decreased by 2.5°F per met increase in activity above 1.2 met.

The upper and lower humidity levels of the comfort zones are less precise, and ASHRAE *Standard* 55-2013 specifies no lower humidity limit for thermal comfort. Low humidity can dry the skin and mucous surfaces and lead to comfort complaints about dry nose, throat, eyes, and skin, typically when the dew point is less than 32°F. Liviana et al. (1988) found eye discomfort increased with time in low-humidity environments (dew point < 36°F). Green (1982) found that respiratory illness and absenteeism increase in winter with decreasing humidity and found that any increase in humidity from very low levels decreased absenteeism in winter.

At high humidity, too much skin moisture tends to increase discomfort (Berglund and Cunningham 1986; Gagge 1937), particularly skin moisture of physiological origin (water diffusion and perspiration). At high humidity, thermal sensation alone is not a reliable predictor of thermal comfort (Tanabe et al. 1987). The discomfort appears to be caused by the feeling of the moisture itself, increased friction between skin and clothing with skin moisture (Gwosdow et al. 1986), and other factors. To prevent warm discomfort, Nevins et al. (1975) recommended that, on the warm side of the comfort zone, the relative humidity not exceed 60%.

ASHRAE *Standard* 55-2013 specifies an upper humidity ratio limit of 0.012 $lb_w/lb_{dry\ air}$, which corresponds to a dew point of 62.2°F at standard pressure. This limit can be exceeded under certain circumstances if the standard's analytical comfort zone method is used.

The comfort zones of Figure 5 are for air speeds not to exceed 40 fpm. However, elevated air speeds can be used to improve comfort beyond the maximum temperature limit of this figure. The air speeds necessary to compensate for a temperature increase above the warm-temperature border are shown in Figure 6. The combination of air speed and temperature defined by the curves in this figure result in the same heat loss from the skin.

The amount of air speed increase is affected by the mean radiant temperature $\bar{t}_r$. The curves of Figure 6 are for different levels of $\bar{t}_r - t_a$. That is, when the mean radiant temperature is low and the air temperature is high, elevated air speed is less effective at increasing heat loss and a higher air speed is needed for a given temperature increase. Conversely, elevated air speed is more effective when the mean radiant temperature is high and air temperature is low; then, less of an air speed increase is needed. Figure 6 applies to lightly clothed individuals (clothing insulation between 0.5 and 0.7 clo) who are engaged in near-sedentary physical activity. The elevated air speed may be used to offset an increase in temperature by up to 5.4°F above the warm-temperature boundary of Figure 5.

Thermal Complaints

Unsolicited thermal complaints can increase a building's operation and maintenance (O&M) cost by requiring unscheduled maintenance to correct the problem.

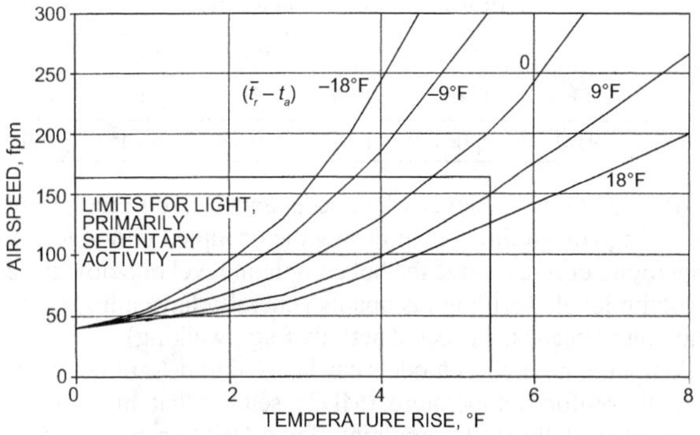

Fig. 6 Air Speed to Offset Temperatures Above Warm-Temperature Boundaries of Figure 5

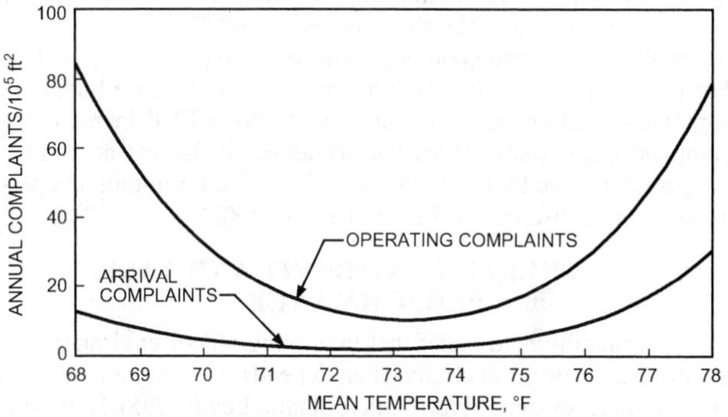

Fig. 7 Predicted Rate of Unsolicited Thermal Operating Complaints

Federspiel (1998) analyzed complaint data from 690 commercial buildings with a total of 23,500 occupants. The most common kind of unsolicited complaint was of temperature extremes. Complaints were rarely because of individual differences in preferred temperature, because 96.5% of the complaints occurred at temperatures less than 70°F or greater than 75°F; most complaints were caused by HVAC faults or poor control performance.

The hourly complaint rate per zone area of being too hot (ν_h) or too cold (ν_l) can be predicted from the HVAC system's operating parameters, specifically the mean space temperature (μ_T), standard deviation of the space temperature (σ_T), and the standard deviation of the rate of change in space temperature ($\sigma_{\dot{T}_H}$, $\sigma_{\dot{T}_L}$):

$$\nu_h = \frac{1}{2\pi}\left(\frac{\sigma^2_{\dot{T}H} + \sigma^2_{\dot{T}B}}{\sigma^2_{T_H} + \sigma^2_{T_B}}\right)^{1/2} \exp\left(-\frac{1}{2}\frac{(\mu_{T_B} - \mu_{T_H})^2}{(\sigma^2_{T_H} + \sigma^2_{T_B})}\right) \tag{57}$$

$$\nu_l = \frac{1}{2\pi}\left(\frac{\sigma^2_{\dot{T}L} + \sigma^2_{\dot{T}B}}{\sigma^2_{T_L} + \sigma^2_{T_B}}\right)^{1/2} \exp\left(-\frac{1}{2}\frac{(\mu_{T_B} - \mu_{T_L})^2}{(\sigma^2_{T_L} + \sigma^2_{T_B})}\right) \tag{58}$$

where the subscripts *H*, *L*, and *B* refer to too hot, too cold, and building (Federspiel 2001).

The building maintenance and space temperature records of six commercial buildings in Minneapolis, Seattle, and San Francisco were analyzed for the values of the *H* and *L* model parameters (Federspiel et al. 2003) of Table 11.Complaint rates predicted by the model for these building parameters are graphed in Figure 7. **Arrival complaints** occur when the temperature exceeds either the

Table 11 Model Parameters

Zone, ft²	μ_{T_H}, °F	σ_{T_H}, °F	$\sigma_{\dot{T}_H}$, °F/h	μ_{T_L}, °F	σ_{T_L}, °F	$\sigma_{\dot{T}_L}$, °F/h
4657	91.0	5.06	1.14	50.43	6.14	4.08

hot or cold complaint level when occupants arrive in the morning. **Operating complaints** occur during the occupied period when the temperature crosses above the hot complaint level or below the cold complaint level. Arriving occupants generally have a higher metabolic power because of recent activity (e.g., walking).

Complaint prediction models can be used to determine the minimum discomfort temperature (MDT) setting that minimizes the occurrences of thermal complaints for a building with known or measured HVAC system parameters σ_{T_B} and $\sigma_{\dot{T}_B}$. Similarly, complaint models can be used with building energy models and service call costs to determine the minimum cost temperature (MCT) where the operating costs are minimized. For example, the summer MDT and MCT in Sacramento, California, are 73 and 77°F for a commercial building at design conditions with σ_{T_B} = 0.6°F and $\sigma_{\dot{T}_B}$ = 1°F. For these conditions, temperatures below 73°F increase both cold complaints and energy costs, and those above 77°F increase hot complaints and costs. Thus, the economically logical acceptable temperature range for this building is 73 to 77°F for minimum operating cost and discomfort (Federspiel et al. 2003).

6. THERMAL COMFORT AND TASK PERFORMANCE

The generally held belief that improving indoor environmental quality enhances productivity often depends on indirect evidence, because direct evidence is difficult to obtain (Levin 1995). However, numerous studies have measured performance over a wide range of tasks and indoor environments [e.g., Berglund et al. (1990); Link and Pepler (1970); Niemelä et al. (2001); Pepler and Warner (1968); Roelofsen (2001); Seppänen et al. (2006); Wyon (1996)]. Task performance is generally highest at comfort conditions (Gonzalez 1975; Griffiths and McIntyre 1975), and a range of temperature at comfort conditions exists within which there is no significant further effect on performance (Federspiel 2001; Federspiel et al. 2002; McCartney and Humphreys 2002; Witterseh 2001).

Twenty-four studies were analyzed and normalized to quantify and generalize the effects of room temperature as a surrogate for thermal comfort on office task performance (Seppänen and Fisk 2006). Of these, 11 were field studies with data collected in working offices and 9 were conducted in controlled laboratory environments.

Most of the office field studies were performed in call centers; in these studies, the speed of work (e.g., average time per call) was used as a measure of work performance. Laboratory studies typically assessed work performance by evaluating the speed and accuracy with which subjects performed tasks, such as text processing and simple calculations, simulating aspects of office work.

The percentage of performance change per degree increase in temperature was calculated for all studies, positive values indicating increases in performance with increasing temperature, and negative values indicating decreases in performance with increasing temperature. A weighted average of the measured performance changes per degree change results in the curve shown in Figure 8. In averaging the measurements, work done by subjects in office field studies was assumed more representative of overall real-world performance and was weighted higher than performance changes in simulated computerized tasks.

Data points from 11 of the studies are also shown in Figure 8. Note the large amount of scatter in the individual studies about the line, indicating a high level of uncertainty.

However, as a first approximation, the performance versus temperature relationship in the graph may still be useful as a general

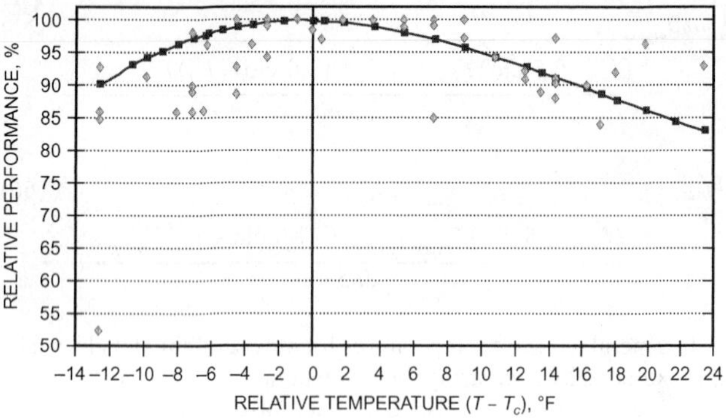

Fig. 8 Relative Performance of Office Work Performance versus Deviation from Optimal Comfort Temperature T_c

representation of real-world office work performance for the tasks performed in the studies, and helpful as a guide in design, operation, and cost analysis.

The results show that performance decreases as temperature deviates above or below a thermal comfort temperature range. As shown in Figure 8, at a temperature 16°F higher than optimal, average office task performance decreased to about 90% of the value at optimum temperature.

7. THERMAL NONUNIFORM CONDITIONS AND LOCAL DISCOMFORT

A person may feel thermally neutral as a whole but still feel uncomfortable if one or more parts of the body are too warm or too cold. Nonuniformities may be caused by a cold window, a hot surface, a draft, or a temporal variation of these. Even small variations in heat flow cause the thermal regulatory system to compensate, thus increasing the physiological effort of maintaining body temperatures. The boundaries of the comfort zones (see Figure 5) of ASHRAE *Standard* 55 provide a thermal acceptability level of 90% if the environment is thermally uniform. Because the standard's objective is to specify conditions for 80% acceptability, the standard allows nonuniformities to decrease acceptability by 10%. Fortunately for the designer and user, the effect of common thermal nonuniformities on comfort is quantifiable and predictable, as discussed in the following sections. Furthermore, most humans are fairly insensitive to small nonuniformities.

Asymmetric Thermal Radiation

Asymmetric or nonuniform thermal radiation in a space may be caused by cold windows, uninsulated walls, cold products, cold or warm machinery, or improperly sized heating panels on the wall or ceiling. In residential buildings, offices, restaurants, etc., the most common causes are cold windows or improperly sized or installed ceiling heating panels. At industrial workplaces, the reasons include cold or warm products, cold or warm equipment, etc.

Recommendations in ISO *Standard* 7730 and ASHRAE *Standard* 55 are based primarily on studies reported by Fanger et al. (1980). These standards include guidelines regarding the radiant temperature asymmetry from an overhead warm surface (heated ceiling) and a vertical cold surface (cold window). Among the studies conducted on the influence of asymmetric thermal radiation are those by Fanger and Langkilde (1975), McIntyre (1974, 1976), McIntyre and Griffiths (1975), McNall and Biddison (1970), and Olesen et al. (1972). These studies all used seated subjects, who were always in thermal neutrality and exposed only to the discomfort resulting from excessive asymmetry.

The subjects gave their reactions on their comfort sensation, and a relationship between the radiant temperature asymmetry

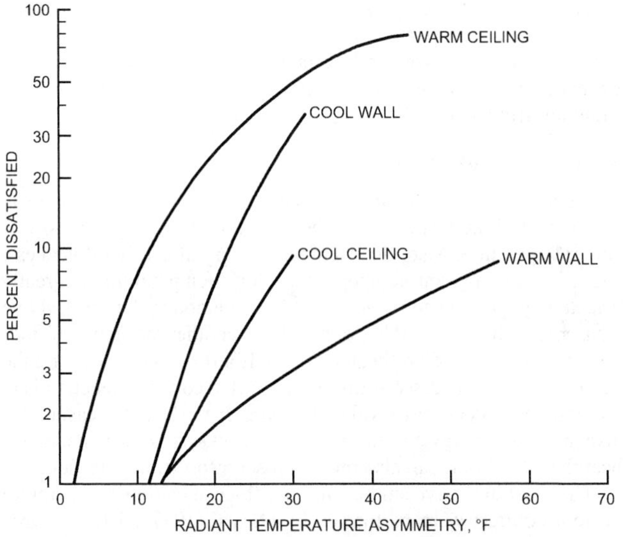

Fig. 9 Percentage of People Expressing Discomfort Caused by Asymmetric Radiation

and the number of subjects feeling dissatisfied was established (Figure 9). Radiant asymmetry, as defined in the section on Environmental Parameters, is the difference in radiant temperature of the environment on opposite sides of the person. More precisely, radiant asymmetry is the difference in radiant temperatures seen by a small flat element looking in opposite directions.

Figure 9 shows that people are more sensitive to asymmetry caused by an overhead warm surface than by a vertical cold surface. The influence of an overhead cold surface or a vertical warm surface is much less. These data are particularly important when using radiant panels to provide comfort in spaces with large cold surfaces or cold windows.

Loveday et al. (1998) used a series of controlled climate chamber studies to establish the design conditions required for thermal comfort for sedentary subjects conducting office work in combined chilled-ceiling and displacement ventilation environments. As part of this study, Hodder et al. (1998) found that the vertical radiant temperature asymmetry for the typical range of ceiling temperatures (71.6 to 54.5°F) encountered in practice in these combination environments had no effect on the overall thermal comfort of the seated occupants, and that existing guidance regarding toleration of radiant asymmetry in these environments remains valid.

Other studies of clothed persons in neutral environments found thermal acceptability unaffected by radiant temperature asymmetries of 18°F or less (Berglund and Fobelets 1987) and comfort unaffected by asymmetries of 36°F or less (McIntyre and Griffiths 1975).

Draft

Draft is an undesired local cooling of the human body caused by air movement. This is a serious problem, not only in many ventilated buildings but also in automobiles, trains, and aircraft. Draft has been identified as one of the most annoying factors in offices. When people sense draft, they often demand higher air temperatures in the room or that ventilation systems be stopped.

Fanger and Christensen (1986) aimed to establish the percentage of the population feeling draft when exposed to a given mean velocity. Figure 10 shows the percentage of subjects who felt draft on the head region (the dissatisfied) as a function of mean air velocity at the neck. The head region comprises head, neck, shoulders, and back. Air temperature significantly influenced the percentage of dissatisfied. There was no significant difference between responses

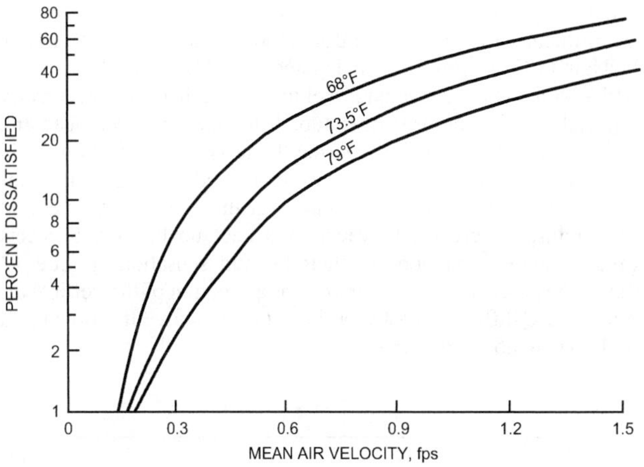

Fig. 10 Percentage of People Dissatisfied as Function of Mean Air Velocity

of men and women. The data in Figure 10 apply only to persons wearing normal indoor clothing and performing light, mainly sedentary work. Persons with higher activity levels are not as sensitive to draft (Jones et al. 1986).

A study of the effect of air velocity over the whole body found thermal acceptability unaffected in neutral environments by air speeds of 50 fpm or less (Berglund and Fobelets 1987). This study also found no interaction between air speed and radiant temperature asymmetry on subjective responses. Thus, acceptability changes and the percent dissatisfied because of draft and radiant asymmetry are independent and additive.

Fanger et al. (1989) investigated the effect of turbulence intensity on sensation of draft. Turbulence intensity significantly affects draft sensation, as predicted by the following model. This model can be used to quantify draft risk in spaces and to develop air distribution systems with a low draft risk.

$$PD = 0.021(93.2 - t_a)(V - 9.8)^{0.62}(0.0019V\,Tu + 3.14) \quad (59)$$

where PD is percent dissatisfied and Tu is the turbulence intensity (in percent) defined by

$$Tu = 100\,\frac{V_{sd}}{V} \quad (60)$$

For $V < 9.8$ fpm, insert $V = 9.8$, and for PD > 100%, insert PD = 100%. V_{sd} is the standard deviation of the velocity measured with an omnidirectional anemometer having a 0.2 s time constant.

The model extends the Fanger and Christensen (1986) draft chart model to include turbulence intensity. In this study, Tu decreases when V increases. Thus, the effects of V for the experimental data to which the model is fitted are $68 < t_a < 79$°F, $10 < V < 100$ fpm, and $0 < Tu < 70$%. Figure 11 gives more precisely the curves that result from intersections between planes of constant Tu and the surfaces of PD = 15%.

At thermal conditions above neutrality, air movement can be beneficial for thermal comfort. Arens et al. (2009) found people prefer more air movement under some conditions in office spaces. Applications of this include ceiling fans and personal environmental control systems in offices and transportation systems.

Vertical Air Temperature Difference

In most buildings, air temperature normally increases with height above the floor. If the gradient is sufficiently large, local warm discomfort can occur at the head and/or cold discomfort can occur at the feet, although the body as a whole is thermally neutral.

Among the few studies of vertical air temperature differences and the influence of thermal comfort reported are Eriksson (1975), McNair (1973), McNair and Fishman (1974), and Olesen et al. (1979). Subjects were seated in a climatic chamber and individually exposed to different air temperature differences between head and ankles (Olesen et al. 1979). During the tests, the subjects were in thermal neutrality because they were allowed to change the temperature level in the test room whenever they desired; the vertical temperature difference, however, was kept unchanged. Subjects gave subjective reactions to their thermal sensation; Figure 12 shows the percentage of dissatisfied as a function of the vertical air temperature difference between head (43 in. above the floor) and ankles (4 in. above the floor).

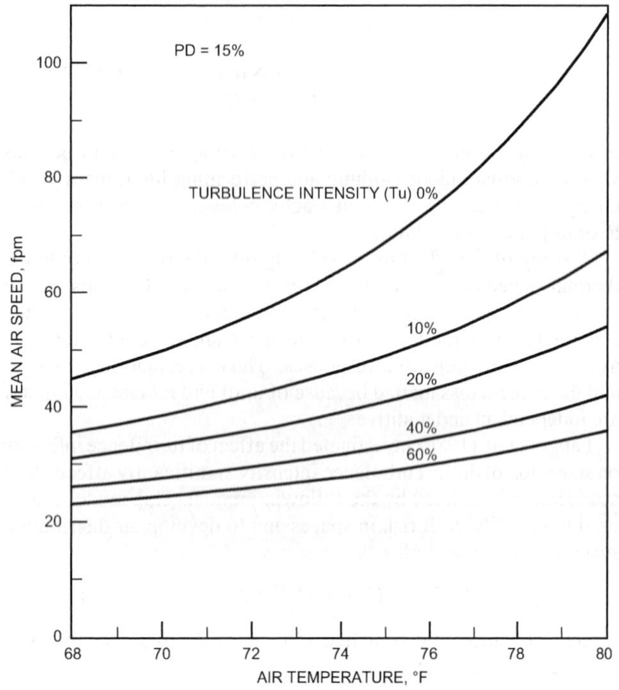

Fig. 11 Draft Conditions Dissatisfying 15% of Population (PD = 15%)

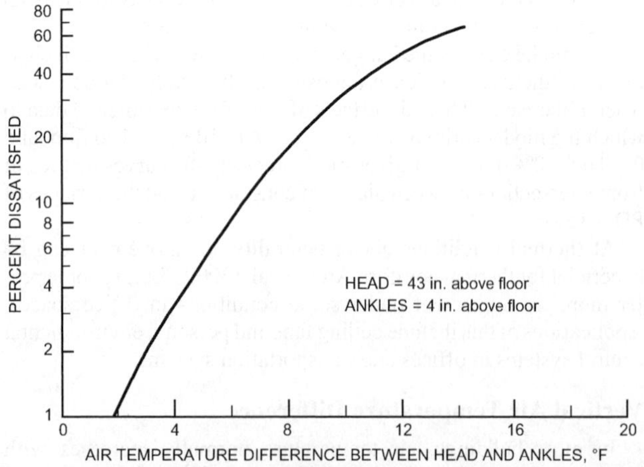

Fig. 12 Percentage of Seated People Dissatisfied as Function of Air Temperature Difference Between Head and Ankles

A head-level air temperature lower than that at ankle level is not as critical for occupants. Eriksson (1975) indicated that subjects could tolerate much greater differences if the head were cooler. This observation is verified in experiments with asymmetric thermal radiation from a cooled ceiling (Fanger et al. 1985).

Warm or Cold Floors

Because of direct contact between the feet and the floor, local discomfort of the feet can often be caused by a too-high or too-low floor temperature. Also, floor temperature significantly influences a room's mean radiant temperature. Floor temperature is greatly affected by building construction (e.g., insulation of the floor, above a basement, directly on the ground, above another room, use of floor heating, floors in radiant-heated areas). If a floor is too cold and the occupants feel cold discomfort in their feet, a common reaction is to increase the temperature level in the room; in the heating season, this also increases energy consumption. A radiant system, which radiates heat from the floor, can also prevent discomfort from cold floors.

The most extensive studies of the influence of floor temperature on foot comfort were performed by Olesen (1977a, 1977b), who, based on his own experiments and reanalysis of data from Nevins and Feyerherm (1967), Nevins and Flinner (1958), and Nevins et al. (1964), found that flooring material is important for people with bare feet (e.g., in swimming halls, gymnasiums, dressing rooms, bathrooms, bedrooms). Ranges for some typical floor materials are as follows:

Textiles (rugs)	70 to 82°F
Pine floor	72.5 to 82°F
Oak floor	76 to 82°F
Hard linoleum	75 to 82°F
Concrete	79 to 83°F

To save energy, insulating flooring materials (cork, wood, carpets), radiant heated floors, or floor heating systems can be used to eliminate the desire for higher ambient temperatures caused by cold feet. These recommendations should also be followed in schools, where children often play directly on the floor.

For people wearing normal indoor footwear, flooring material is insignificant. Olesen (1977b) found an optimal temperature of 77°F for sedentary and 73.5°F for standing or walking persons. At the optimal temperature, 6% of occupants felt warm or cold discomfort in the feet. Figure 13 shows the relationship between floor temperature and percent dissatisfied, combining data from experiments with seated and standing subjects. In all experiments, subjects were in thermal neutrality; thus, the percentage of dissatisfied is only related to discomfort caused by cold or warm feet. No significant difference

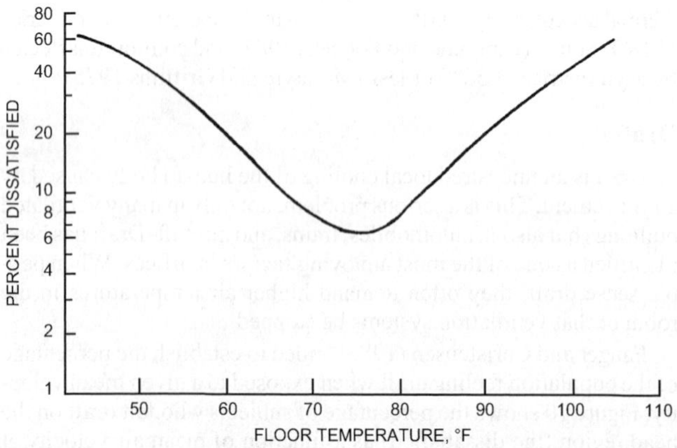

Fig. 13 Percentage of People Dissatisfied as Function of Floor Temperature

in preferred floor temperature was found between females and males.

8. SECONDARY FACTORS AFFECTING COMFORT

Temperature, air speed, humidity, their variation, and personal parameters of metabolism and clothing insulation are primary factors that directly affect energy flow and thermal comfort. However, many secondary factors, some of which are discussed in this section, may more subtly influence comfort.

Day-to-Day Variations

Fanger (1973) determined the preferred ambient temperature for each of a group of subjects under identical conditions on four different days. Because the standard deviation was only 1.0°F, Fanger concluded that comfort conditions for an individual can be reproduced and vary only slightly from day to day.

Age

Because metabolism decreases slightly with age, many have stated that comfort conditions based on experiments with young and healthy subjects cannot be used for other age groups. Fanger (1982), Fanger and Langkilde (1975), Langkilde (1979), Nevins et al. (1966), and Rohles and Johnson (1972) conducted comfort studies in Denmark and the United States on different age groups (mean ages 21 to 84). The studies revealed that the thermal environments preferred by older people do not differ from those preferred by younger people. The lower metabolism in older people is compensated for by a lower evaporative loss. Collins and Hoinville (1980) confirmed these results.

The fact that young and old people prefer the same thermal environment does not necessarily mean that they are equally sensitive to cold or heat. In practice, the ambient temperature level in the homes of older people is often higher than that for younger people. This may be explained by the lower activity level of elderly people, who are normally sedentary for a greater part of the day.

Adaptation

Many believe that people can acclimatize themselves by exposure to hot or cold surroundings, so that they prefer other thermal environments. Fanger (1982) conducted experiments involving subjects from the United States, Denmark, and tropical countries. The latter group was tested in Copenhagen immediately after their arrival by plane from the tropics, where they had lived all their lives. Other experiments were conducted for two groups exposed to cold daily. One group comprised subjects who had been doing sedentary work in cold surroundings (in the meat-packing industry) for 8 h daily for at least 1 year. The other group consisted of winter swimmers who bathed in the sea daily.

Only slight differences in preferred ambient temperature and physiological parameters in the comfort conditions were reported for the various groups. These results indicate that people cannot adapt to preferring warmer or colder environments, and therefore the same comfort conditions can likely be applied throughout the world. However, in determining the preferred ambient temperature from the comfort equations, a clo-value corresponding to local clothing habits should be used, such as those given in Table 8 and in Havenith et al. (2015). A comparison of field comfort studies from different parts of the world shows significant differences in clothing habits depending on, among other things, outdoor climate (Nicol and Humphreys 1972). According to these results, adaptation has little influence on preferred ambient temperature. In uncomfortable warm or cold environments, however, adaptation often has an influence. People used to working and living in warm climates can more easily accept and maintain a higher work performance in hot environments than people from colder climates.

Sex

Fanger (1982), Fanger and Langkilde (1975), and Nevins et al. (1966) used equal numbers of male and female subjects, so comfort conditions for the two sexes can be compared. The experiments show that men and women prefer almost the same thermal environments. Women's skin temperature and evaporative loss are slightly lower than those for men, and this balances the somewhat lower metabolism of women. The reason that women often prefer higher ambient temperatures than men may be partly explained by the lighter clothing often worn by women.

Seasonal and Circadian Rhythms

Because people cannot adapt to prefer warmer or colder environments, it follows that there is no difference between comfort conditions in winter and in summer. McNall et al. (1968) confirmed this in an investigation where results of winter and summer experiments showed no difference. On the other hand, it is reasonable to expect comfort conditions to alter during the day because internal body temperature has a daily rhythm, with a maximum late in the afternoon, and a minimum early in the morning.

In determining the preferred ambient temperature for each of 16 subjects both in the morning and in the evening, Fanger et al. (1974) and Ostberg and McNicholl (1973) observed no difference. Furthermore, Fanger et al. (1973) found only small fluctuations in preferred ambient temperature during a simulated 8 h workday (sedentary work). There is a slight tendency to prefer somewhat warmer surroundings before lunch, but none of the fluctuations are significant.

9. PREDICTION OF THERMAL COMFORT

Thermal comfort and thermal sensation can be predicted several ways. One way is to use Figure 5 and Table 10 and adjust for clothing and activity levels that differ from those of the figure. More numerical and rigorous predictions are possible by using the PMV-PPD and two-node models described in this section.

Steady-State Energy Balance

Fanger (1982) related comfort data to physiological variables. At a given level of metabolic activity M, and when the body is not far from thermal neutrality, mean skin temperature t_{sk} and sweat rate E_{rsw} are the only physiological parameters influencing heat balance. However, heat balance alone is not sufficient to establish thermal comfort. In the wide range of environmental conditions where heat balance can be obtained, only a narrow range provides thermal comfort. The following linear regression equations, based on data from Rohles and Nevins (1971), indicate values of t_{sk} and E_{rsw} that provide thermal comfort:

$$t_{sk,req} = 96.3 - 0.156(M - W) \tag{61}$$

$$E_{rsw,req} = 0.42\,(M - W - 18.43) \tag{62}$$

At higher activity levels, sweat loss increases and mean skin temperature decreases, both of which increase heat loss from the body core to the environment. These two empirical relationships link the physiological and heat flow equations and thermal comfort perceptions. By substituting these values into Equation (11) for $C + R$, and into Equations (17) and (18) for E_{sk}, Equation (1) (the energy balance equation) can be used to determine combinations of the six environmental and personal parameters that optimize comfort for steady-state conditions.

Fanger (1982) reduced these relationships to a single equation, which assumed all sweat generated is evaporated, eliminating clothing permeation efficiency i_{cl} as a factor in the equation. This assumption is valid for normal indoor clothing worn in typical indoor environments with low or moderate activity levels. At higher activity levels (M_{act} > 3 met), where a significant amount of sweating occurs even at optimum comfort conditions, this assumption may limit accuracy. The reduced equation is slightly different from the heat transfer equations developed here. The radiant heat exchange is expressed in terms of the Stefan-Boltzmann law (instead of using h_r), and diffusion of water vapor through the skin is expressed as a diffusivity coefficient and a linear approximation for saturated vapor pressure evaluated at t_{sk}. The combination of environmental and personal variables that produces a neutral sensation may be expressed as follows:

$$\begin{aligned} M - W = {} & 1.196 \times 10^{-9} f_{cl}[(t_{cl} + 460)^4 - (\bar{t}_r + 460)^4] + f_{cl} h_c (t_{cl} - t_a) \\ & + 0.97[5.73 - 0.022(M - W) - 6.9p_a] \\ & + 0.42[(M - W) - 18.43] + 0.0173M(5.87 - 6.9p_a) \\ & + 0.00077M(93.2 - t_a) \end{aligned} \tag{63}$$

where

$$\begin{aligned} t_{cl} = {} & 96.3 - 0.156(M - W) - R_{cl}\{(M - W) \\ & - 0.97[5.73 - 0.022(M - W) - 6.9p_a] \\ & - 0.42[(M - W) - 18.43] - 0.0173M(5.87 - 6.9p_a) \\ & - 0.00077M(93.2 - t_a)\} \end{aligned} \tag{64}$$

The values of h_c and f_{cl} can be estimated from tables and equations given in the section on Engineering Data and Measurements. Fanger used the following relationships:

$$h_c = \begin{cases} 0.361(t_{cl} - t_a)^{0.25} & 0.361(t_{cl} - t_a)^{0.25} > 0.151\sqrt{V} \\ 0.151\sqrt{V} & 0.361(t_{cl} - t_a)^{0.25} < 0.151\sqrt{V} \end{cases} \tag{65}$$

$$f_{cl} = \begin{cases} 1.0 + 0.2I_{cl} & I_{cl} < 0.5 \text{ clo} \\ 1.05 + 0.1I_{cl} & I_{cl} > 0.5 \text{ clo} \end{cases} \tag{66}$$

Figures 14 and 15 show examples of how Equation (63) can be used.

Equation (63) is expanded to include a range of thermal sensations by using a **predicted mean vote (PMV) index**. The PMV index predicts the mean response of a large group of people according to the ASHRAE thermal sensation scale. Fanger (1970) related PMV to the imbalance between actual heat flow from the body in a given environment and the heat flow required for optimum comfort at the specified activity by the following equation:

$$\text{PMV} = 3.155[0.303 \exp(-0.114M) + 0.028]L \tag{67}$$

where L is the thermal load on the body, defined as the difference between internal heat production and heat loss to the actual environment for a person hypothetically kept at comfort values of t_{sk} and E_{rsw} at the actual activity level. Thermal load L is then the difference between the left and right sides of Equation (63) calculated for the actual values of the environmental conditions. As part of this calculation, clothing temperature t_{cl} is found by iteration as

$$\begin{aligned} t_{cl} = {} & 96.3 - 0.156(M - W) \\ & - R_{cl}\{1.196 \times 10^{-9} f_{cl}[(t_{cl} + 460)^4 - (\bar{t}_r + 460)^4] \\ & + f_{cl} h_c (t_{cl} - t_a)\} \end{aligned} \tag{68}$$

After estimating the PMV with Equation (67) or another method, the **predicted percent dissatisfied (PPD)** with a condition can also be estimated. Fanger (1982) related the PPD to the PMV as follows:

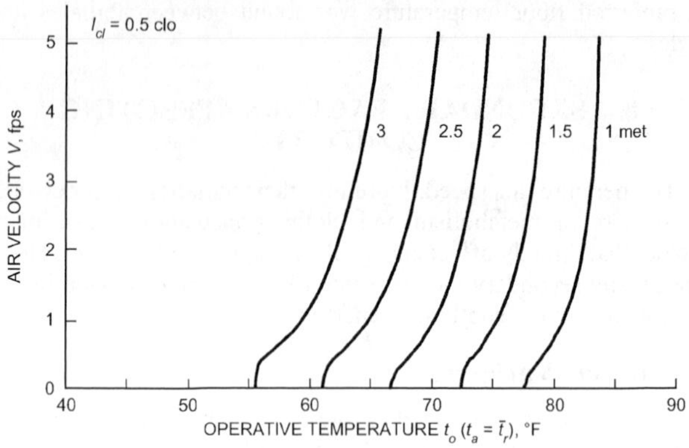

Fig. 14 Air Velocities and Operative Temperatures at 50% rh Necessary for Comfort (PMV = 0) of Persons in Summer Clothing at Various Levels of Activity

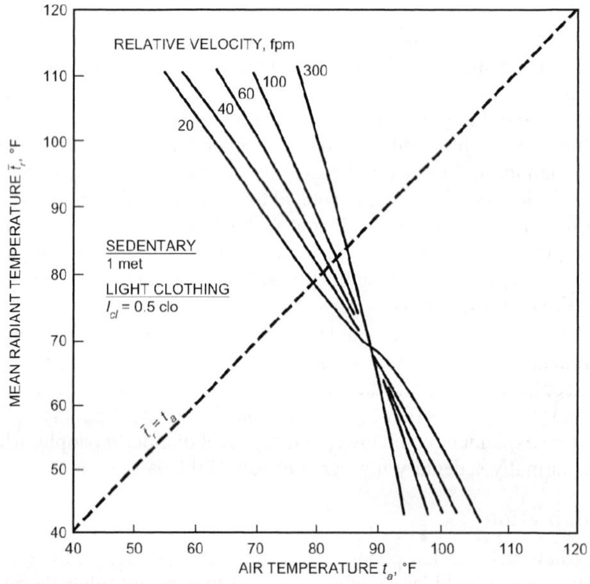

Fig. 15 Air Temperatures and Mean Radiant Temperatures Necessary for Comfort (PMV = 0) of Sedentary Persons in Summer Clothing at 50% rh

$$\text{PPD} = 100 - 95 \exp[-(0.03353\text{PMV}^4 + 0.2179\text{PMV}^2)] \tag{69}$$

where dissatisfied is defined as anybody not voting –1, +1, or 0. This relationship is shown in Figure 16. A PPD of 10% corresponds to the PMV range of ±0.5, and even with PMV = 0, about 5% of the people are dissatisfied.

The **PMV-PPD model** is widely used and accepted for design and field assessment of comfort conditions. ISO *Standard* 7730 includes a short computer listing that facilitates computing PMV and PPD for a wide range of parameters.

Two-Node Model

The PMV model is useful only for predicting steady-state comfort responses. The two-node model can be used to predict physiological responses or responses to transient situations, at least for low and moderate activity levels in cool to very hot environments (Gagge et al. 1971a, 1986). This model is a simplification of thermoregulatory models developed by Stolwijk and Hardy (1966). The simple, lumped parameter model considers a human as two

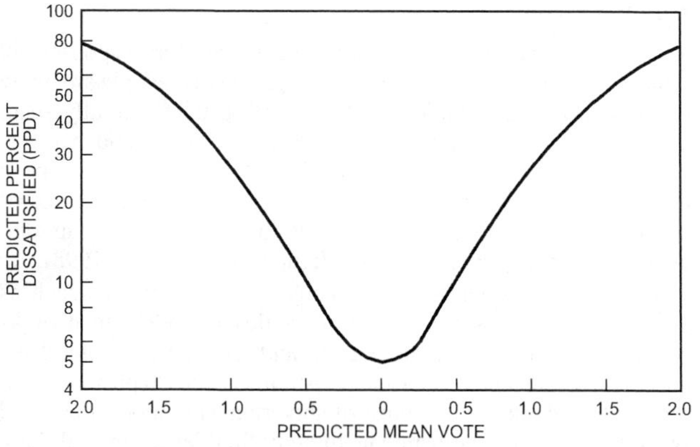

Fig. 16 Predicted Percentage of Dissatisfied (PPD) as Function of Predicted Mean Vote (PMV)

concentric thermal compartments that represent the skin and the core of the body.

The **skin compartment** simulates the epidermis and dermis and is about 1/16 in. thick. Its mass, which is about 10% of the total body, depends on the amount of blood flowing through it for thermoregulation. Compartment temperature is assumed to be uniform so that the only temperature gradients are between compartments. In a cold environment, blood flow to the extremities may be reduced to conserve the heat of vital organs, resulting in axial temperature gradients in the arms, legs, hands, and feet. Heavy exercise with certain muscle groups or asymmetric environmental conditions may also cause nonuniform compartment temperatures and limit the model's accuracy.

All the heat is assumed to be generated in the **core compartment**. In the cold, shivering and muscle tension may generate additional metabolic heat. This increase is related to skin and core temperature depressions from their set point values, or

$$M_{shiv} = [27.473(98.6 - t_c) + 8.277(91.4 - t_{sk}) - 0.1536(91.4 - t_{sk})^2]/\mathrm{BF}^{0.5} \tag{70}$$

where BF is percentage body fat and the temperature difference terms are set to zero if they become negative (Tikusis and Giesbrecht 1999).

The core loses energy when the muscles do work on the surroundings. Heat is also lost from the core through respiration. The rate of respiratory heat loss depends on sensible and latent changes in respired air and the ventilation rate as in Equations (19) and (20).

In addition, heat is conducted passively from the core to the skin. This is modeled as a massless thermal conductor ($K = 0.93$ Btu/h·ft²·°F). A controllable heat loss path from the core consists of pumping variable amounts of warm blood to the skin for cooling. This peripheral blood flow Q_{bl} in L/h·ft² depends on skin and core temperature deviations from their respective set points:

$$Q_{bl} = \frac{\mathrm{BFN} + c_{dil}(t_{cr} - 98.6)}{1 + S_{tr}(93.2 - t_{sk})} \tag{71}$$

The temperature terms can only be > 0. If the deviation is negative, the term is set to zero. For average persons, the coefficients BFN, c_{dil}, and S_{tr} are 0.585, 2.57, and 0.28. Further, skin blood flow Q_{bl} is limited to a maximum of 8.4 L/h·ft². A very fit and well-trained athlete could expect to have $c_{dil} = 9$.

Dry (sensible) heat loss q_{dry} from the skin flows through the clothing by conduction and then by parallel paths to the air and surrounding surfaces. Evaporative heat follows a similar path, flowing through the clothing and through the air boundary layer. Maximum evaporation E_{max} occurs if the skin is completely covered with sweat. The actual evaporation rate E_{sw} depends on the size w of the sweat film:

$$E_{sw} = wE_{max} \tag{72}$$

where w is E_{rsw}/E_{max}.

The rate of regulatory sweating E_{rsw} (rate at which water is brought to the surface of the skin in Btu/h·ft²) can be predicted by skin and core temperature deviations from their set points:

$$E_{rsw} = c_{sw}(t_b - t_{bset})\exp[(t_{sk} - 93.2)/19.3] \tag{73}$$

where $t_b = (1 - \alpha_{sk})t_{cr} + \alpha_{sk}t_{sk}$ and is the mean body temperature, $t_{bset} = 97.68$°F, and $c_{sw} = 20.43$ Btu/h·ft²·°F. The temperature deviation terms are set to zero when negative. The fraction of the total body mass considered to be thermally in the skin compartment is α_{sk}:

$$\alpha_{sk} = 0.0418 + \frac{0.745}{10.8Q_{bl} + 0.585} \tag{74}$$

Regulatory sweating Q_{rsw} in the model is limited to 0.1 L/h·ft² or 200 Btu/h·ft². E_{rsw} evaporates from the skin, but if E_{rsw} is greater than E_{max}, the excess drips off.

An energy balance on the core yields

$$M + M_{shiv} = W + q_{res} + (K + \mathrm{SkBF}c_{p,bl})(t_{cr} - t_{sk}) + m_{cr}c_{cr}\frac{dt_{cr}}{d\theta} \tag{75}$$

and for the skin,

$$(K + \mathrm{SkBF}c_{p,bl})(t_{cr} - t_{sk}) = q_{dry} + q_{evap} + m_{sk}c_{sk}\frac{dt_{sk}}{d\theta} \tag{76}$$

where c_{cr}, c_{sk}, and $c_{p,bl}$ are specific heats of core, skin, and blood (0.83, 0.83, and 1.0 Btu/lb·°F, respectively), and SkBF is $\rho_{bl}Q_{bl}$, where ρ_{bl} is density of blood (2.34 lb/L).

Equations (75) and (76) can be rearranged in terms of $dt_{sk}/d\theta$ and $dt_{cr}/d\theta$ and numerically integrated with small time steps (10 to 60 s) from initial conditions or previous values to find t_{cr} and t_{sk} at any time.

After calculating values of t_{sk}, t_{cr}, and w, the model uses empirical expressions to predict thermal sensation (TSENS) and thermal discomfort (DISC). These indices are based on 11-point numerical scales, where positive values represent the warm side of neutral sensation or comfort, and negative values represent the cool side. TSENS is based on the same scale as PMV, but with extra terms for ±4 (very hot/cold) and ±5 (intolerably hot/cold). Recognizing the same positive/negative convention for warm/cold discomfort, DISC is defined as

5	intolerable
4	limited tolerance
3	very uncomfortable
2	uncomfortable and unpleasant
1	slightly uncomfortable but acceptable
0	comfortable

TSENS is defined in terms of deviations of mean body temperature t_b from cold and hot set points representing the lower and upper limits for the zone of evaporative regulation: $t_{b,c}$ and $t_{b,h}$, respectively. The values of these set points depend on the net rate of internal heat production and are calculated by

$$t_{b,c} = \frac{0.34}{58.15}(M - W) + 97.34 \qquad (77)$$

$$t_{b,h} = \frac{0.608}{58.15}(M - W) + 98.0 \qquad (78)$$

TSENS is then determined by

$$\text{TSENS} = \begin{cases} 0.26(t_b - t_{b,c}) & t_b < t_{b,c} \\ 4.7\eta_{ev}(t_b - t_{b,c})/(t_{b,h} - t_{b,c}) & t_{b,c} \le t_b \le t_{b,h} \\ 4.7\eta_{ev} + 0.26(t_b - t_{b,h}) & t_{b,h} < t_b \end{cases} \qquad (79)$$

where η_{ev} is the evaporative efficiency (assumed to be 0.85).

DISC is numerically equal to TSENS when t_b is below its cold set point $t_{b,c}$ and it is related to skin wettedness when body temperature is regulated by sweating:

$$\text{DISC} = \begin{cases} 0.26(t_b - t_{b,c}) & t_b < t_{b,tc} \\ \dfrac{4.7(E_{rsw} - E_{rsw,req})}{E_{max} - E_{rsw,req} - E_{dif}} & t_{b,c} \le t_b \end{cases} \qquad (80)$$

where $E_{rsw,req}$ is calculated as in Fanger's model, using Equation (62).

Multisegment Thermal Physiology and Comfort Models

Unlike the two-node model, which represents the body as one cylinder with two nodes of core and skin, multisegment models divide the body into more segments (e.g., head, chest, hands, feet) and more tissue layers (e.g., core, muscle, fat, skin). They are intended to predict thermal physiology and thermal comfort in nonuniform [e.g., offices with displacement ventilation or underfloor air, radiant-cooled ceiling/floors, or natural and mixed-mode ventilation; personal environmental control (PEC) systems] and transient (e.g., occupants moving between different environments in offices, quick-responding PECs, automobiles) environments. Major multisegment physiological models include Fiala (1998), Fiala et al. (2003), Gordon (1974), Huizenga et al. (2001), Kraning and Gonzalez (1997), Smith (1991), Stolwijk (1971), Tanabe et al. (2002), Werner and Webb (1993), and Wissler (1964, 1985, 1988). These models mostly use finite-difference or finite-element methods, and include active thermoregulatory control in addition to passive heat transfer. They predict skin temperature for several local body segments, and central core temperature. They also predict other physiological parameters, such as segment sweat rate and skin wettedness, shivering, and cardiac blood flow.

Comfort is independently predicted from the output of physiological models. One comfort model, based on a review of literature addressing human sensation testing, uses an average of local skin temperatures and its time derivative to predict whole-body thermal sensation under stable and transient environments (Fiala 1998; Fiala et al. 2003). Another model uses the heat storage rate of the skin or core to predict whole-body thermal sensation under stable and transient environments (Wang 1994; Wang and Peterson 1992). The Berkeley comfort model predicts thermal sensation and comfort for each segment as well as for the whole body, using local skin temperatures, core temperature, and their time derivatives (Zhang 2003; Zhang et al. 2010a, 2010b, 2010c).

The equivalent homogeneous temperature (EHT) approach uses segmented electrical manikin measurements to determine the equivalent uniform environment for each body part (Nilsson 2007; Wyon et al. 1989). From these, comfortable environmental temperature ranges have been defined for each of the body segments. The EHT can determine comfort under nonuniform environments that are at steady state.

Adaptive Models

Adaptive models do not actually predict comfort responses but rather the almost constant conditions under which people are likely to be comfortable in buildings. In general, people naturally adapt and may also make various adjustments to themselves and their surroundings to reduce discomfort and physiological strain. It has been observed that, through adaptive actions, an acceptable degree of comfort in residences and offices is possible over a range of air temperatures from about 63 to 88°F (Humphreys and Nicol 1998).

Adaptive adjustments are typically conscious actions such as altering clothing, posture, activity schedules or levels, rate of working, diet, ventilation, air movement, and local temperature. They may also include unconscious longer-term changes to physiological set points and gains for control of shivering, skin blood flow, and sweating, as well as adjustments to body fluid levels and salt loss. However, only limited documentation and information on such changes is available.

An important driving force behind the adaptive process is the pattern of outdoor weather conditions and exposure to them. This is the principal input to adaptive models, which predict likely comfort temperatures t_c or ranges of t_c from monthly mean outdoor temperatures t_{out}. Humphreys and Nicol's (1998) model is based on data from a wide range of buildings, climates, and cultures:

$$t_c = 75.6 + 0.43(t_{out} - 71.6)\exp - \left(\frac{t_{out} - 71.6}{61.1}\right)^2 \qquad (81)$$

Adaptive models are useful to guide design and energy decisions, and to specify building temperature set points throughout the year. An ASHRAE-sponsored study (de Dear and Brager 1998) on adaptive models compiled an extensive database from field studies to study, develop, and test adaptive models. For climates and buildings where cooling and central heating are not required, the study suggests the following model:

$$t_{oc} = 54.1 + 0.31t_{out} \qquad (82)$$

where t_{oc} is the operative comfort temperature. The adaptive model boundary temperatures for 90% thermal acceptability are approximately t_{oc}+ 4.5°F and t_{oc} – 4°F according to ASHRAE *Standard* 55-2013.

In general, the value of using an adaptive model to specify set points or guide temperature control strategies is likely to increase with the freedom that occupants are given to adapt (e.g., by having flexible working hours, locations, or dress codes).

Zones of Comfort and Discomfort

The Two-Node Model section shows that comfort and thermal sensation are not necessarily the same variable, especially for a person in the zone of evaporative thermal regulation. Figures 17 and 18 show this difference for the standard combination of met-clo-air movement used in the standard effective temperature ET*. Figure 17 demonstrates that practically all basic physiological variables predicted by the two-node model are functions of ambient temperature and are relatively independent of vapor pressure. All exceptions occur at relative humidities above 80% and as the isotherms reach the ET* = 107°F line, where regulation by evaporation fails. Figure 18 shows that lines of constant ET* and wettedness are functions of both ambient temperature and vapor pressure. Thus, human thermal responses are divided into two classes: those in Figure 17, which respond only to heat stress from the environment, and those in Figure 18, which respond to both heat stress from the environment and the resultant heat strain (Stolwijk et al. 1968).

For warm environments, any index with isotherms parallel to skin temperature is a reliable index of thermal sensation alone, and not of

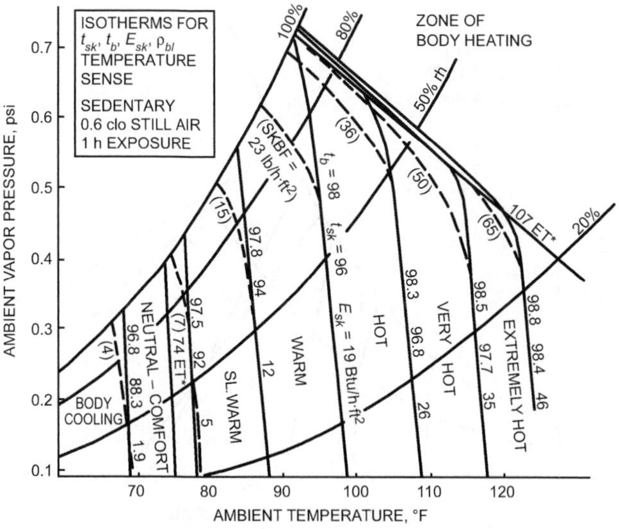

Fig. 17 Effect of Environmental Conditions on Physiological Variables

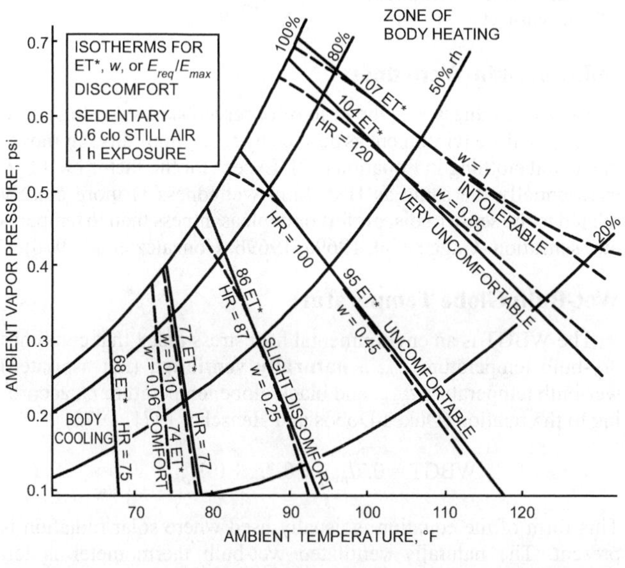

Fig. 18 Effect of Thermal Environment on Discomfort

discomfort caused by increased humidity. Indices with isotherms parallel to ET* are reliable indicators of discomfort or dissatisfaction with thermal environments. For a fixed exposure time to cold, lines of constant t_{sk}, ET*, and t_o are essentially identical, and cold sensation is no different from cold discomfort. For a state of comfort with sedentary or light activity, lines of constant t_{sk} and ET* coincide. Thus, comfort and thermal sensations coincide in this region as well. The upper and lower temperature limits for comfort at these levels can be specified either by thermal sensation (Fanger 1982) or by ET*, as is done in ASHRAE *Standard* 55, because lines of constant comfort and lines of coOnstant thermal sensation should be identical.

10. ENVIRONMENTAL INDICES

An environmental index combines two or more parameters (e.g., air temperature, mean radiant temperature, humidity, air velocity) into a single variable. Indices simplify description of the thermal environment and the stress it imposes. Environmental indices may be classified according to how they are developed. Rational indices are based on the theoretical concepts presented earlier. Empirical indices are based on measurements with subjects or on simplified relationships that do not necessarily follow theory. Indices may also be classified according to their application, generally either heat stress or cold stress.

Effective Temperature

Effective temperature ET* is probably the most common environmental index, and has the widest range of application. It combines temperature and humidity into a single index, so two environments with the same ET* should evoke the same thermal response even though they have different temperatures and humidities, as long as they have the same air velocities.

The original empirical effective temperature was developed by Houghten and Yaglou (1923). Gagge et al. (1971a, 1971b) defined a new effective temperature using a rational approach. Defined mathematically in Equation (33), this is the temperature of an environment at 50% rh that results in the same total heat loss E_{sk} from the skin as in the actual environment.

Because the index is defined in terms of operative temperature t_o, it combines the effects of three parameters ($\bar{t}_r$, t_a, and p_a) into a single index. Skin wettedness w and the permeability index i_m must be specified and are constant for a given ET* line for a particular situation. The two-node model is used to determine skin wettedness in the zone of evaporative regulation. At the upper limit of regulation, w approaches 1.0; at the lower limit, w approaches 0.06. Skin wettedness equals one of these values when the body is outside the zone of evaporative regulation. Because the slope of a constant ET* line depends on skin wettedness and clothing moisture permeability, effective temperature for a given temperature and humidity may depend on the person's clothing and activity. This difference is shown in Figure 19. At low skin wettedness, air humidity has little influence, and lines of constant ET* are nearly vertical. As skin wettedness increases because of activity and/or heat stress, the lines become more horizontal and the influence of humidity is much more pronounced. The ASHRAE comfort envelope shown in Figure 5 is described in terms of ET*.

Because ET* depends on clothing and activity, it is not possible to generate a universal ET* chart. A standard set of conditions representative of typical indoor applications is used to define a **standard effective temperature SET***, defined as the equivalent air temperature of an isothermal environment at 50% rh in which a subject, wearing clothing standardized for the activity concerned, has the same heat stress (skin temperature t_{sk}) and thermoregulatory strain (skin wettedness w) as in the actual environment.

Humid Operative Temperature

The **humid operative temperature t_{oh}** is the temperature of a uniform environment at 100% rh in which a person loses the same total amount of heat from the skin as in the actual environment. This index is defined mathematically in Equation (32). It is analogous to ET*, except that it is defined at 100% rh and 0% rh rather than at 50% rh. Figures 2 and 19 indicate that lines of constant ET* are also lines of constant t_{oh}. However, the values of these two indices differ for a given environment.

Heat Stress Index

Originally proposed by Belding and Hatch (1955), this rational index is the ratio of total evaporative heat loss E_{sk} required for thermal equilibrium (the sum of metabolism plus dry heat load) to maximum evaporative heat loss E_{max} possible for the environment, multiplied by 100, for steady-state conditions (S_{sk} and S_{cr} are zero) and with t_{sk} held constant at 95°F. The ratio E_{sk}/E_{max} equals skin wettedness w [Equation (18)]. When **heat stress index (HSI)** > 100, body heating occurs; when HSI < 0, body cooling occurs. Belding

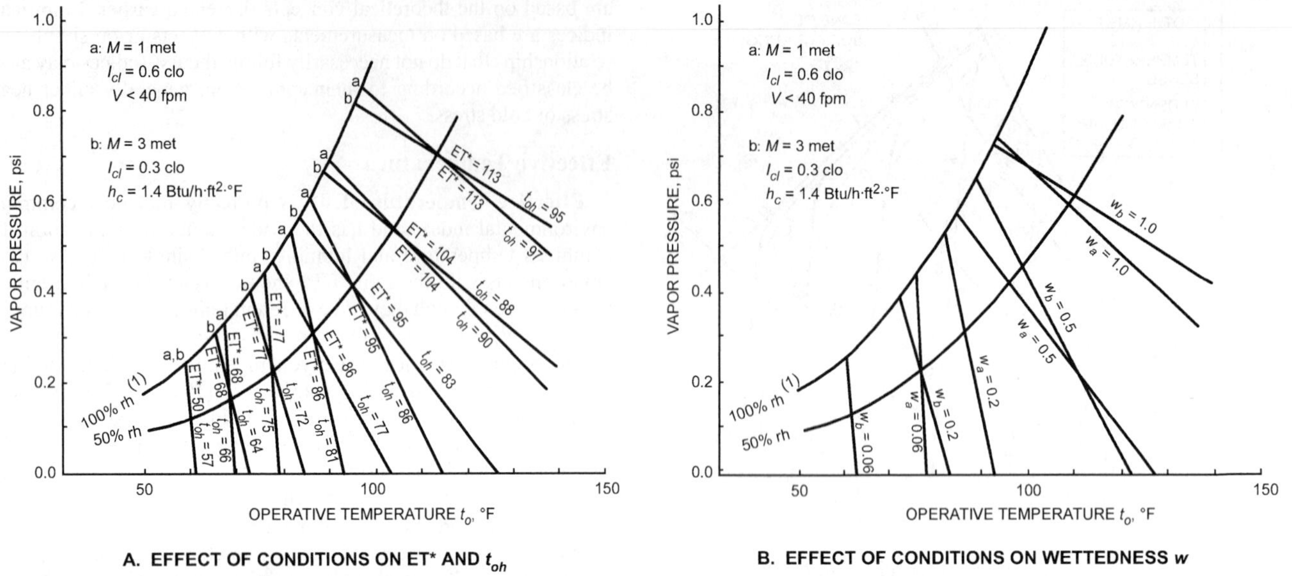

Fig. 19 Effective Temperature ET* and Skin Wettedness w
[Adapted from Gonzalez et al. (1978) and Nishi et al. (1975)]

Table 12 Evaluation of Heat Stress Index

Heat Stress Index	Physiological and Hygienic Implications of 8 h Exposures to Various Heat Stresses
0	*No* thermal strain.
10, 20, 30	*Mild to moderate* heat strain. If job involves higher intellectual functions, dexterity, or alertness, subtle to substantial decrements in performance may be expected. In performing heavy physical work, little decrement is expected, unless ability of individuals to perform such work under no thermal stress is marginal.
40, 50, 60	*Severe* heat strain involving a threat to health unless workers are physically fit. Break-in period required for men not previously acclimatized. Some decrement in performance of physical work is to be expected. Medical selection of personnel desirable, because these conditions are unsuitable for those with cardiovascular or respiratory impairment or with chronic dermatitis. These working conditions are also unsuitable for activities requiring sustained mental effort.
70, 80, 90	*Very severe* heat strain. Only a small percentage of the population may be expected to qualify for this work. Personnel should be selected (a) by medical examination, and (b) by trial on the job (after acclimatization). Special measures are needed to ensure adequate water and salt intake. Amelioration of working conditions by any feasible means is highly desirable, and may be expected to decrease the health hazard while increasing job efficiency. Slight "indisposition," which in most jobs would be insufficient to affect performance, may render workers unfit for this exposure.
100	The *maximum* strain tolerated daily by fit, acclimatized young men.

and Hatch (1955) limited E_{max} to 220 Btu/h·ft², which corresponds to a sweat rate of approximately 0.21 lb/h·ft². When t_{sk} is constant, loci of constant HSI coincide with lines of constant ET* on a psychrometric chart. Other indices based on wettedness have the same applications (Belding 1970; Gonzalez et al. 1978; ISO *Standard* 7933) but differ in their treatment of E_{max} and the effect of clothing. Table 12 describes physiological factors associated with HSI values.

Index of Skin Wettedness

Skin wettedness *w* is the ratio of observed skin sweating E_{sk} to the E_{max} of the environment as defined by t_{sk}, t_a, humidity, air movement, and clothing in Equation (12). Except for the factor of 100, it is essentially the same as HSI. Skin wettedness is more closely related to the sense of discomfort or unpleasantness than to temperature sensation (Gagge et al. 1969a, 1969b; Gonzalez et al. 1978).

Wet-Bulb Globe Temperature

The WBGT is an environmental heat stress index that combines dry-bulb temperature t_{db}, a **naturally ventilated** (not aspirated) wet-bulb temperature t_{nwb}, and black globe temperature t_g, according to the relation (Dukes-Dobos and Henschel 1971, 1973)

$$\text{WBGT} = 0.7t_{nwb} + 0.2t_g + 0.1t_a \quad (83)$$

This form of the equation is usually used where solar radiation is present. The naturally ventilated wet-bulb thermometer is left exposed to sunlight, but the air temperature t_a sensor is shaded. In enclosed environments, Equation (83) is simplified by dropping the t_a term and using a 0.3 weighting factor for t_g.

The black globe thermometer responds to air temperature, mean radiant temperature, and air movement, whereas the naturally ventilated wet-bulb thermometer responds to air humidity, air movement, radiant temperature, and air temperature. Thus, WBGT is a function of all four environmental factors affecting human environmental heat stress.

The WBGT index is widely used for estimating the heat stress potential of industrial environments (Davis 1976). In the United States, the National Institute of Occupational Safety and Health (NIOSH) developed criteria for a heat-stress-limiting standard (NIOSH 1986). ISO *Standard* 7243 also uses the WBGT. Figure 20 summarizes permissible heat exposure limits, expressed as working time per hour, for a fit individual, as specified for various WBGT levels. Values apply for normal permeable clothing (0.6 clo) and must be adjusted for heavy or partly vapor-permeable clothing. For example, the U.S. Air Force (USAF) recommended adjusting the measured WBGT upwards by 10°F for personnel wearing chemical protective clothing or body armor. This type of

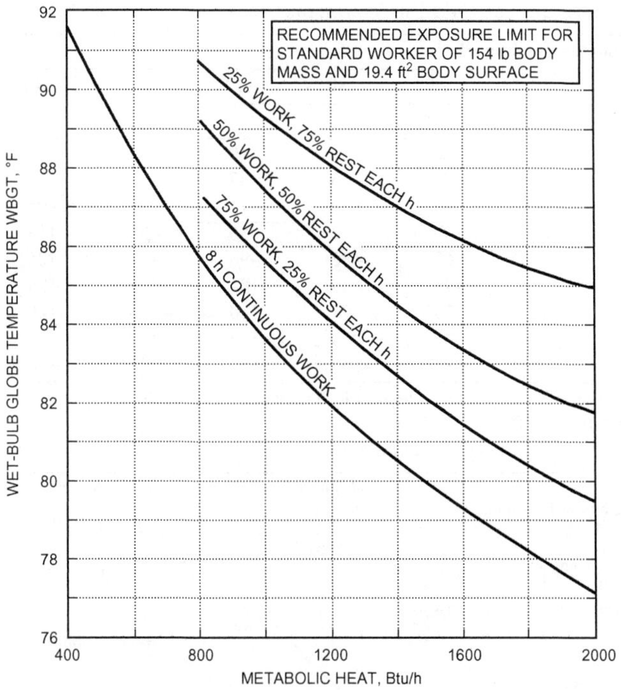

Fig. 20 Recommended Heat Stress Exposure Limits for Heat Acclimatized Workers
[Adapted from NIOSH (1986)]

clothing increases resistance to sweat evaporation about threefold (higher if it is totally impermeable), requiring an adjustment in WBGT level to compensate for reduced evaporative cooling at the skin.

Several mathematical models are available for predicting WBGT from environmental factors: air temperature, psychrometric wet-bulb temperature, mean radiant temperature, and air motion (Azer and Hsu 1977; Sullivan and Gorton 1976).

Wet-Globe Temperature

The WGT, introduced by Botsford (1971), is a simpler approach to measuring environmental heat stress than the WBGT. The measurement is made with a wetted globe thermometer called a Botsball, which consists of a 2.5 in. black copper sphere covered with a fitted wet black mesh fabric, into which the sensor of a dial thermometer is inserted. A polished stem attached to the sphere supports the thermometer and contains a water reservoir for keeping the sphere covering wet. This instrument is suspended by the stem at the site to be measured.

Onkaram et al. (1980) showed that WBGT can be predicted with reasonable accuracy from WGT for temperate to warm environments with medium to high humidities. With air temperatures between 68 and 95°F, dew points from 45 to 77°F (relative humidities above 30%), and wind speeds of 15 mph or less, the experimental regression equation (r = 0.98) in °F for an outdoor environment is

$$\text{WBGT} = 1.044(\text{WGT}) - 1.745 \qquad (84)$$

This equation should not be used outside the experimental range given because data from hot/dry desert environments show differences between WBGT and WGT that are too large (10°F and above) to be adjusted by Equation (84) (Matthew et al. 1986). At very low humidity and high wind, WGT approaches the psychrometric wet-bulb temperature, which is greatly depressed below t_a. However, in the WBGT, t_{nwb} accounts for only 70% of the index value, with the remaining 30% at or above t_a.

Wind Chill Index

The wind chill index (WCI) is an empirical index developed from cooling measurements obtained in Antarctica on a cylindrical flask partly filled with water (Siple and Passel 1945). The index describes the rate of heat loss from the cylinder by radiation and convection for a surface temperature of 91.4°F, as a function of ambient temperature and wind velocity. As originally proposed,

$$\text{WCI} = \frac{(10.45 - 0.447V + 6.686\sqrt{V})(91.4 - t_a)}{1.8} \qquad (85)$$

where V and t_a are in mph and °F, respectively, and WCI units are kcal/(h·m^2). Multiply WCI by 0.368 to convert to Btu/h·ft^2.The 91.4°F surface temperature was chosen to be representative of the mean skin temperature of a resting human in comfortable surroundings.

Some valid objections have been raised about this formulation. Cooling rate data from which it was derived were measured on a 2.24 in. diameter plastic cylinder, making it unlikely that WCI would be an accurate measure of heat loss from exposed flesh, which has different characteristics from plastic (curvature, roughness, and radiation exchange properties) and is invariably below 91.4°F in a cold environment. Moreover, values given by the equation peak at 56 mph, then decrease with increasing velocity.

Nevertheless, for velocities below 50 mph, this index reliably expresses combined effects of temperature and wind on subjective discomfort. For example, if the calculated WCI is less than 1400 and actual air temperature is above 14°F, there is little risk of frostbite during brief exposures (1 h or less), even for bare skin. However, at a WCI of 2000 or more, the probability is high that exposed flesh will begin to freeze in 1 min or less unless measures are taken to shield exposed skin (such as a fur ruff to break up wind around the face).

Rather than using the WCI to express the severity of a cold environment, meteorologists use an index derived from the WCI called the **equivalent wind chill temperature** $t_{eq,wc}$. This is the ambient temperature that would produce, in a calm wind (defined for this application as 4 mph), the same WCI as the actual combination of air temperature and wind velocity:

$$t_{eq,wc} = -0.0818(\text{WCI}) + 91.4 \qquad (86)$$

where $t_{eq,wc}$ is in °F (and frequently referred to as a **wind chill factor**), thus distinguishing it from WCI, which is given either as a cooling rate or as a plain number with no units. For velocities less than 4 mph, Equation (86) does not apply, and the wind chill temperature is equal to the air temperature.

Equation (86) does not imply cooling to below ambient temperature, but recognizes that, because of wind, the cooling rate is increased as though it were occurring at the lower equivalent wind chill temperature. Wind accelerates the rate of heat loss, so that the skin surface cools more quickly toward the ambient temperature. Table 13 shows a typical wind chill chart, expressed in equivalent wind chill temperature.

11. SPECIAL ENVIRONMENTS

Infrared Heating

Optical and thermal properties of skin must be considered in studies of the effects of infrared radiation in (1) producing changes in skin temperature and skin blood flow, and (2) evoking sensations of temperature and comfort (Hardy 1961). Although the body can be considered to have the properties of water, thermal sensation and heat transfer with the environment require a study of the skin and its interaction with visible and infrared radiation.

Table 13 Equivalent Wind Chill Temperatures of Cold Environments

Wind Speed, mph	Actual Thermometer Reading, °F											
	50	40	30	20	10	0	−10	−20	−30	−40	−50	−60
	Equivalent Wind Chill Temperature, °F											
0	50	40	30	20	10	0	−10	−20	−30	−40	−50	−60
5	48	37	27	16	6	−5	−15	−26	−36	−47	−57	−68
10	40	28	16	3	−9	−21	−34	−46	−58	−71	−83	−95
15	36	22	9	−5	−18	−32	−45	−59	−72	−86	−99	−113
20	32	18	4	−11	−25	−39	−53	−68	−82	−96	−110	−125
25	30	15	0	−15	−30	−44	−59	−74	−89	−104	−119	−134
30	28	13	−3	−18	−33	−48	−64	−79	−94	−110	−125	−140
35	27	11	−4	−20	−36	−51	−67	−83	−98	−114	−129	−145
40	26	10	−6	−22	−38	−53	−69	−85	−101	−117	−133	−148

Little danger: In less than 5 h, with dry skin. Maximum danger from false sense of security.	**Increasing danger:** Danger of freezing exposed flesh within 1 min.	**Great danger:** Flesh may freeze within 30 s.
(WCI < 1400)	(1400 ≤ WCI ≤ 2000)	(WCI > 2000)

Source: U.S. Army Research Institute of Environmental Medicine.
Notes: Cooling power of environment expressed as an equivalent temperature under calm conditions [Equation (86)].
Winds greater than 43 mph have little added chilling effect.

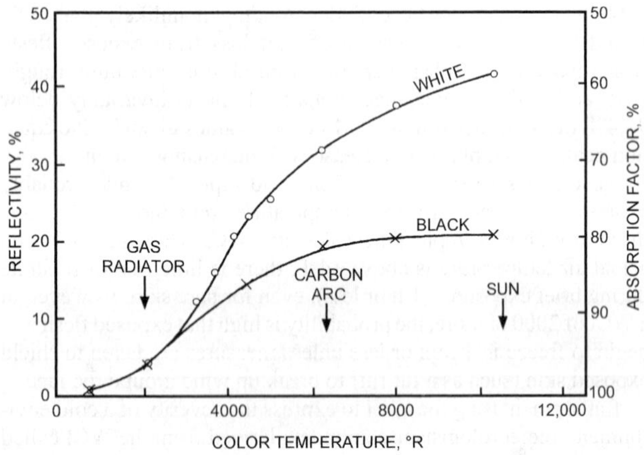

Fig. 21 Variation in Skin Reflection and Absorptivity for Blackbody Heat Sources

Figure 21 shows how skin reflectance and absorptance vary for a blackbody heat source at the temperature (in °R) indicated. These curves show that darkly pigmented skin is heated more by direct radiation from a high-intensity heater at 4500°R than is lightly pigmented skin. With low-temperature, low-intensity heating equipment used for total area heating, there is minimal, if any, difference. Also, in practice, clothing minimizes differences.

Changes in skin temperature caused by high-intensity infrared radiation depend on the thermal conductivity, density, and specific heat of living skin (Lipkin and Hardy 1954). Modeling skin heating with the heat transfer theory yields a parabolic relation between exposure time and skin temperature rise for nonpenetrating radiation:

$$t_{sf} - t_{si} = \Delta t = 2J\alpha\sqrt{\theta/(\pi k \rho c_p)} \qquad (87)$$

where

t_{sf} = final skin temperature, °F
t_{si} = initial skin temperature, °F
J = irradiance from source radiation temperatures, Btu/h·ft²
α = skin absorptance at radiation temperatures, dimensionless
θ = time, h
k = specific thermal conductivity of tissue, Btu/h·ft·°R
ρ = density, lb/ft³
c_p = specific heat, Btu/lb·°R

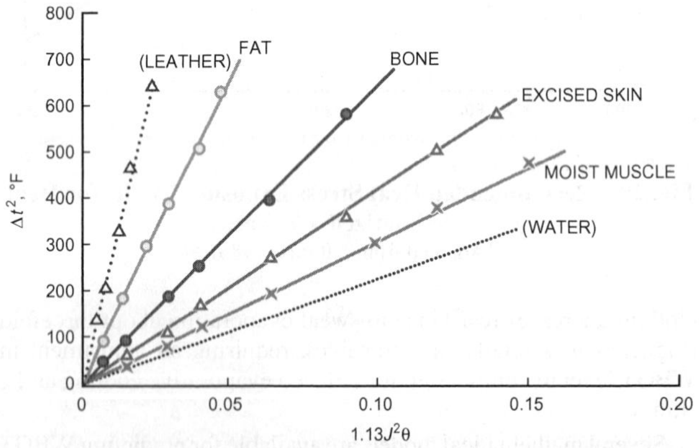

Fig. 22 Comparing Thermal Inertia of Fat, Bone, Moist Muscle, and Excised Skin to That of Leather and Water

Product $k\rho c_p$ is the physiologically important quantity that determines temperature elevation of skin or other tissue on exposure to nonpenetrating radiation. Fatty tissue, because of its relatively low specific heat, is heated more rapidly than moist skin or bone. Experimentally, $k\rho c_p$ values can be determined by plotting Δt^2 against $1.13J^2\theta$ (Figure 22). The relationship is linear, and the slopes are inversely proportional to the $k\rho c_p$ of the specimen. Comparing leather and water with body tissues suggests that thermal inertia values depend largely on tissue water content.

Living tissues do not conform strictly to this simple mathematical formula. Figure 23 compares excised skin with living skin with normal blood flow, and skin with blood flow occluded. For short exposure times, the $k\rho c_p$ of normal skin is the same as that in which blood flow has been stopped; excised skin heats more rapidly because of unavoidable dehydration that occurs postmortem. However, with longer exposure to thermal radiation, vasodilation increases blood flow, cooling the skin. For the first 20 s of irradiation, skin with normally constricted blood vessels has a $k\rho c_p$ value one-fourth that for skin with fully dilated vessels.

Skin temperature is the best single index of thermal comfort. The most rapid changes in skin temperature occur during the first 60 s of exposure to infrared radiation. During this initial period, thermal sensation and the heating rate of the skin vary with the quality of infrared radiation (color temperature in °R). Because radiant heat from a gas-fired heater is absorbed at the skin surface, the same unit level of absorbed radiation during the first 60 s of exposure can

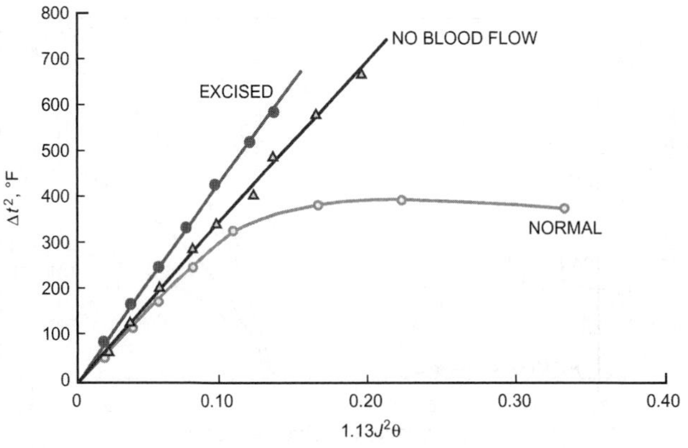

Fig. 23 Thermal Inertias of Excised, Bloodless, and Normal Living Skin

cause an even warmer initial sensation than penetrating solar radiation. Skin heating curves tend to level off after a 60 s exposure (Figure 23), which means that a relative balance is quickly created between heat absorbed, heat flow to the skin surface, and heat loss to the ambient environment. Therefore, the effects of radiant heating on thermal comfort should be examined for conditions approaching thermal equilibrium.

Stolwijk and Hardy (1966) described an unclothed subject's response for a 2 h exposure to temperatures of 41 to 95°F. Nevins et al. (1966) showed a relation between ambient temperatures and thermal comfort of clothed, resting subjects. For any given uniform environmental temperature, both initial physiological response and degree of comfort can be determined for a subject at rest.

Physiological implications for radiant heating can be defined by two environmental temperatures: (1) mean radiant temperature $\bar{t}_r$ and (2) ambient air temperature t_a. For this discussion on radiant heat, assume that (1) relative humidity is less than 50%, and (2) air movement is low and constant, with an equivalent convection coefficient of 0.51 Btu/h·ft²·°F.

The equilibrium equation, describing heat exchange between skin surface at mean temperature t_{sk} and the radiant environment, is given in Equation (28), and can be transformed to give (see Table 2)

$$M' - E_{sk} - F_{cle}[h_r(t_{sk} - \bar{t}_r) + h_c(t_{sk} - t_o] = 0 \qquad (88)$$

where M' is the net heat production $(M - W)$ less respiratory losses.

By algebraic transformation, Equation (88) can be rewritten as

$$M' + \text{ERF} \times F_{cle} = E_{sk} + (h_r + h_c)(t_{sk} - t_a)F_{cle} \qquad (89)$$

where $\text{ERF} = h_r(\bar{t}_r - t_a)$ is the effective radiant field and represents the additional radiant exchange with the body when $\bar{t}_r \neq t_a$.

The last term in Equation (89) describes heat exchange with an environment uniformly heated to temperature t_a. The term h_r, evaluated in Equation (35), is also a function of posture, for which factor A_r/A_D can vary from 0.67 for crouching to 0.73 for standing. For preliminary analysis, a useful value for h_r is 0.83 Btu/h·ft²·°F, which corresponds to a normally clothed (at 75°F) sedentary subject. Ambient air movement affects h_c, which appears only in the right-hand term of Equation (89).

Although the linear radiation coefficient h_r is used in Equations (88) and (89), the same definition of ERF follows if the fourth power radiation law is used. By this law, assuming emissivity of the body surface is unity, the ERF term in Equation (89) is

$$\text{ERF} = \sigma(A_r/A_D)[(\bar{t}_r - 460)^4 - (t_a + 460)^4]F_{cle} \qquad (90)$$

where σ is the Stefan-Boltzmann constant, 0.1712×10^{-8} Btu/h·ft²·°R⁴.

Because $\bar{t}_r$ equals the radiation of several surfaces at different temperatures $(T_1, T_2, \ldots, T_j)$,

$$\text{ERF} = (\text{ERF})_1 + (\text{ERF})_2 + \cdots + (\text{ERF})_j \qquad (91)$$

where

$\text{ERF}_j = \sigma(A_r/A_D)\alpha_j F_{m-j}(T_j^4 - T_a^4)F_{cle}$
α_j = absorptance of skin or clothing surface for source radiating at temperature T_j
F_{m-j} = angle factor to subject m from source j
T_a = ambient air temperature, °R

ERF is the sum of the fields caused by each surface T_j [e.g., T_1 may be an infrared beam heater; T_2, a heated floor; T_3, a warm ceiling; T_4, a cold plate glass window $(T_4 < T_a)$; etc.]. Only surfaces with T_j differing from T_a contribute to the ERF.

Comfort Equations for Radiant Heating

The **comfort equation for radiant heat** (Gagge et al. 1967a, 1967b) follows from definition of ERF and Equation (8):

$$t_o \text{ (for comfort)} = t_a + \text{ERF (for comfort)}/h \qquad (92)$$

Thus, operative temperature for comfort is the temperature of the ambient air plus a temperature increment ERF/h, a ratio that measures the effectiveness of the incident radiant heating on occupants. Higher air movement (which increases the value of h or h_c) reduces the effectiveness of radiant heating systems. Clothing lowers t_o for comfort and for thermal neutrality.

Values for ERF and h must be determined to apply the comfort equation for radiant heating. Table 3 may be used to estimate h. One method of determining ERF is to calculate it directly from radiometric data that give (1) radiation emission spectrum of the source, (2) concentration of the beam, (3) radiation from the floor, ceiling, and windows, and (4) corresponding angle factors involved. This analytical approach is described in Chapter 54 of the 2015 *ASHRAE Handbook—HVAC Applications*.

For direct measurement, a black globe, 6 in. in diameter, can measure the radiant field ERF for comfort, by the following relation:

$$\text{ERF} = (A_r/A_D)(1.07 + 0.169\sqrt{V})(t_g - t_a) \qquad (93)$$

where t_g is uncorrected globe temperature in °F and V is air movement in fpm. The average value of A_r/A_D is 0.7. For a black globe, ERF must be multiplied by α for the exposed clothing/skin surface. For a subject with 0.6 to 1.0 clo, t_o for comfort should agree numerically with t_a for comfort in Figure 5. When t_o replaces t_a in Figure 5, humidity is measured in vapor pressure rather than relative humidity, which refers only to air temperature.

Other methods may be used to measure ERF. The most accurate is by physiological means. In Equation (89), when M, $t_{sk} - t_a$, and the associated transfer coefficients are experimentally held constant,

$$\Delta E = \Delta \text{ERF} \qquad (94)$$

The variation in evaporative heat loss E (rate of weight loss) caused by changing the wattage of two T-3 infrared lamps is a measure in absolute terms of the radiant heat received by the body.

A third method uses a directional radiometer to measure ERF directly. For example, radiation absorbed at the body surface (in Btu/h·ft²) is

$$\text{ERF} = \alpha(A_i/A_D)J \qquad (95)$$

where irradiance J can be measured by a directional (Hardy-type) radiometer, α is the surface absorptance effective for the source used, and A_i is the projection area of the body normal to the directional irradiance. Equation (95) can be used to calculate ERF only for the simplest geometrical arrangements. For a human subject lying supine and irradiated uniformly from above, A_i/A_D is 0.3. Figure 21 shows variance of α for human skin with blackbody temperature (in °R) of the radiating source. When irradiance J is uneven and coming from many directions, as is usually the case, the previous physiological method can be used to obtain an effective A_i/A_D from the observed ΔE and $\Delta(\alpha J)$.

Personal Environmental Control (PEC) Systems

Because of the large interpersonal variability in thermal requirements, some occupants in any uniformly conditioned environment will be too warm at the same time as others are too cool. The ASHRAE 80% acceptability criterion reflects this physiological constraint. Only environments that respond to individual preferences are capable of thermally satisfying all occupants (Bauman et al. 1998). Such occupant-specific microenvironments may be conditioned with low energy input because their aggregate volume is smaller than the total space volume, and because heating or cooling the occupants themselves may be more energy efficient than space conditioning. Such designs require attention to the thermal sensitivities of different parts of the human body and to the physical properties of its microenvironment.

In warm conditions, the comfort of the head and hands dictates a person's overall discomfort; in cool conditions, the feet and hands dictate overall discomfort (Arens et al. 2006; Zhang 2003). Keeping the feet and hands warm is necessary to prevent discomfort from vasoconstriction in the limbs. However in warm conditions, the hands and wrists are important heat dissipaters, and cooling them is important. Arens et al. (2006) and Zhang (2003) suggest that a personal environmental control (PEC) system, also called **task-ambient conditioning (TAC)** or **personal ventilation (PV) systems**, that focuses directly on these body parts may offer an energy-efficient means for improving comfort in office environments.

PEC fan systems using either recirculated room air or outdoor air can provide comfort and improve perceived air quality (Amai et al. 2007; Arens et al. 2008, 2011; Dygert and Dang 2011; Melikov 2003; Russo and Khalifa 2011; Sekhar et al. 2005; Tham and Willem 2004; Yang et al. 2009, 2010; Zhang et al. 2010d). Air quality can also be improved, because fan flows above 60 fpm disrupt the body's thermal plume that carries pollutants upward to the breathing zone (Arens et al. 2008, 2011).

Using air movement for cooling has constraints. Strong airflow directed at the eyes might cause dry-eye discomfort and should be avoided (Melikov et al. 2011). However, a large percentage of office occupants in neutral and warm conditions prefer an increase in available air movement (Arens et al. 2009). A recent study of hemoglobin levels showed that air movement also reduces fatigue (Nishihara and Tanabe 2011; Tanabe and Nishihara 2004).

Foot heating is usually done by radiant heating or through contact with a heated surface. Efficiency of these systems depends greatly on confining the heating to the body surfaces without too much loss to the surrounding air.

Hands and wrists may both be heated and cooled by contact with conductive surfaces. Wrist cooling may not require actively cooled surfaces, because the skin is almost always at a higher temperature than surfaces in a normal environment.

Some researchers suggest that a PEC system can be part of an energy-saving strategy (Hoyt et al. 2009; Zhang et al. 2011) by keeping occupants comfortable while allowing the surrounding spaces to be less conditioned (Figure 24). The success of this strategy also depends on the length of time occupants are away from the PEC zone. Once steady state is reached, the change of sensations when moving from a comfortable environment to one less comfortable is much slower than the change on returning to comfortable conditions (Zhang et al. 2010a). For example, 10-min excursions climbing stairs were judged comfortable throughout, despite an 82°F stairwell temperature, whereas 15-min excursions climbing stairs became uncomfortable; occupants judged their status comfortable/acceptable within 30 s of returning to the PEC zone.

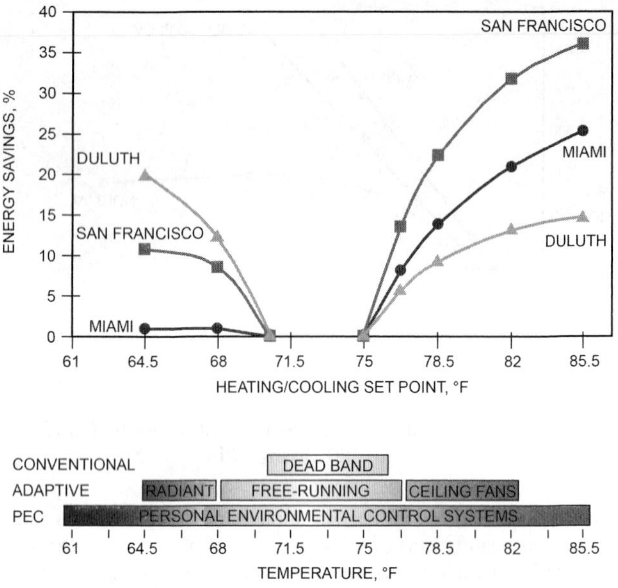

Fig. 24 Recommended Temperature Set Points for HVAC with PEC Systems and Energy Savings from Extending HVAC Temperature Set Points
[Based on Hoyt et al. (2009) and Zhang et al. (2011)]

Hot and Humid Environments

Tolerance limits to high temperature vary with the ability to (1) sense temperature, (2) lose heat by regulatory sweating, and (3) move heat from the body core by blood flow to the skin surface, where cooling is the most effective. many interrelating processes are involved in heat stress (Figure 25).

Skin surface temperatures of 113°F trigger pain receptors in the skin; direct contact with metal at this temperature is painful. However, because thermal insulation of the air layer around the skin is high, much higher dry-air temperatures can be tolerated (e.g., 185°F for brief periods in a sauna). For lightly clothed subjects at rest, tolerance times of nearly 50 min have been reported at 180°F db; 33 min at 200°F; 26 min at 220°F; and 24 min at 240°F. In each case, dew points were lower than 86°F. Short exposures to these extremely hot environments are tolerable because of cooling by sweat evaporation. However, when ambient vapor pressure approaches 0.87 psi (97°F dp, typically found on sweating skin), tolerance is drastically reduced. Temperatures of 122°F can be intolerable if the dew-point temperature is greater than 77°F, and both deep body temperature and heart rate rise within minutes (Gonzalez et al. 1978).

The rate at which and length of time a body can sweat are limited. The maximum rate of sweating for an average man is about 4 lb/h. If all this sweat evaporates from the skin surface under conditions of low humidity and air movement, maximum cooling is about 214 Btu/h·°F. However, because sweat rolls off the skin surface without evaporative cooling or is absorbed by or evaporated within clothing, a more typical cooling limit is 6 met (10 Btu/h·ft^2), representing approximately 2.2 lb/h of sweating for the average man.

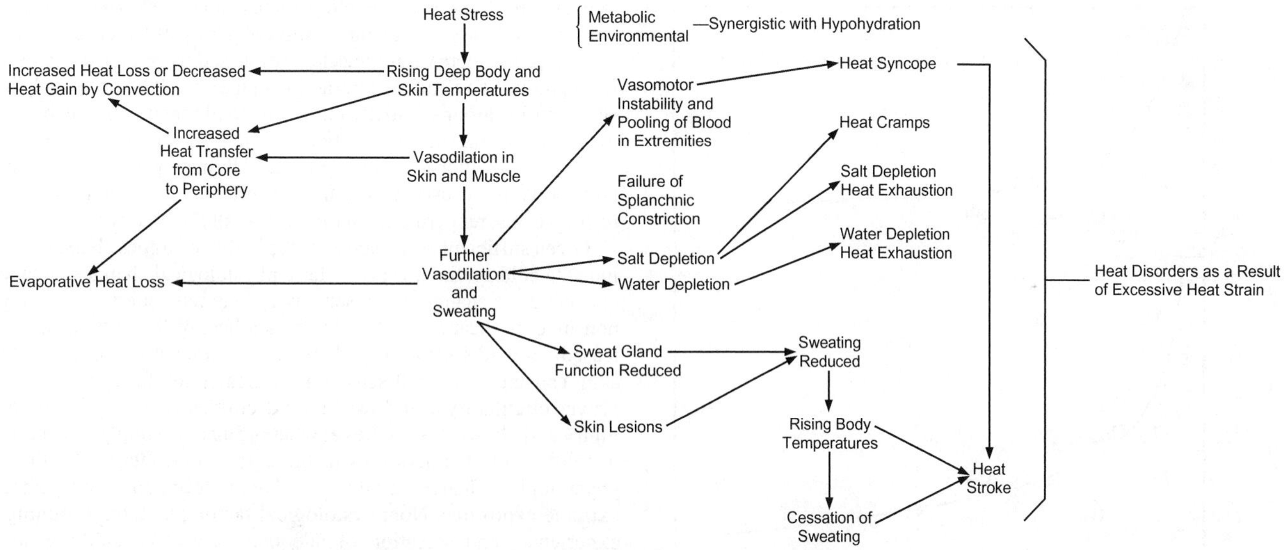

Fig. 25 Schematic Design of Heat Stress and Heat Disorders
[Modified by Buskirk (1960) from scale diagram by Belding (1967) and Leithead and Lind (1964)]

Thermal equilibrium is maintained by dissipation of resting heat production (1 met) plus any radiant and convective load. If the environment does not limit heat loss from the body during heavy activity, decreasing skin temperature compensates for the core temperature rise. Therefore, mean body temperature is maintained, although the gradient from core to skin is increased. Blood flow through the skin is reduced, but muscle blood flow necessary for exercise is preserved. The upper limit of skin blood flow is about 200 lb/h (Burton and Bazett 1936).

Body heat storage of 318 Btu (or a rise in t_b of 2.5°F) for an average-sized man represents an average voluntary tolerance limit. Continuing work beyond this limit increases the risk of heat exhaustion. Collapse can occur at about 635 Btu of storage (5°F rise); few individuals can tolerate heat storage of 872 Btu (6.8°F above normal).

The cardiovascular system affects tolerance limits. In normal, healthy subjects exposed to extreme heat, heart rate and cardiac output increase in an attempt to maintain blood pressure and supply of blood to the brain. At a heart rate of about 180 bpm, the short time between contractions prevents adequate blood supply to the heart chambers. As heart rate continues to increase, cardiac output drops, causing inadequate convective blood exchange with the skin and, perhaps more important, inadequate blood supply to the brain. Victims of this heat exhaustion faint or black out. Accelerated heart rate can also result from inadequate venous return to the heart caused by blood pooling in the skin and lower extremities. In this case, cardiac output is limited because not enough blood is available to refill the heart between beats. This occurs most frequently when an overheated individual, having worked hard in the heat, suddenly stops working. The muscles no longer massage the blood back past the valves in the veins toward the heart. Dehydration compounds the problem by reducing fluid volume in the vascular system.

If core temperature t_{cr} increases above 106°F, critical hypothalamic proteins can be damaged, resulting in inappropriate vasoconstriction, cessation of sweating, increased heat production by shivering, or some combination of these. Heat stroke damage is frequently irreversible and carries a high risk of death.

Another problem, hyperventilation, occurs mainly in hot/wet conditions, when too much CO_2 is washed from the blood. This can lead to tingling sensations, skin numbness, and vasoconstriction in the brain with occasional loss of consciousness.

Because a rise in heart rate or rectal temperature is essentially linear with ambient vapor pressure above a dew point of 77°F, these two changes can measure severe heat stress. Although individual heart rate and rectal temperature responses to mild heat stress vary, severe heat stress saturates physiological regulating systems, producing uniform increases in heart rate and rectal temperature. In contrast, sweat production measures stress under milder conditions but becomes less useful under more severe stress. The maximal sweat rate compatible with body cooling varies with (1) degree of heat acclimatization, (2) duration of sweating, and (3) whether the sweat evaporates or merely saturates the skin and drips off. Total sweat rates over 4.4 lb/h can occur in short exposures, but about 2.2 lb/h is an average maximum sustainable level for an acclimatized man.

Figure 26 shows the decline in heart rate, rectal temperature, and skin temperature when exercising subjects are exposed to 104°F over a period of days. Acclimatization can be achieved by working in the heat for 100 min each day: 30% improvement occurs after the first day, 50% after 3 days, and 95% after 6 or 7 days. Increased sweat secretion while working in the heat can be induced by rest. Although reducing salt intake during the first few days in the heat can conserve sodium, heat cramps may result. Working regularly in the heat improves cardiovascular efficiency, sweat secretion, and sodium conservation. Once induced, heat acclimatization can be maintained by as little as one workout a week in the heat; otherwise, it diminishes slowly over a 2- to 3-week period and disappears.

Extremely Cold Environments

Human performance in extreme cold ultimately depends on maintaining thermal balance. Subjective discomfort is reported by a 154 lb man with 19.4 ft² of body surface area when a heat debt of about 100 Btu is incurred. A heat debt of about 600 Btu is acutely uncomfortable; this represents a drop of approximately 4.7°F (or about 7% of total heat content) in mean body temperature.

This loss can occur during 1 to 2 h of sedentary activity outdoors. A sleeping individual will wake after losing about 300 Btu, decreasing mean skin temperature by about 5.5°F and deep body temperature by about 1°F. A drop in deep body temperature (e.g., rectal temperature) below 95°F threatens a loss of body temperature regulation, and 82.4°F is considered critical for survival, despite recorded survival from a deep body temperature of 64.4°F.

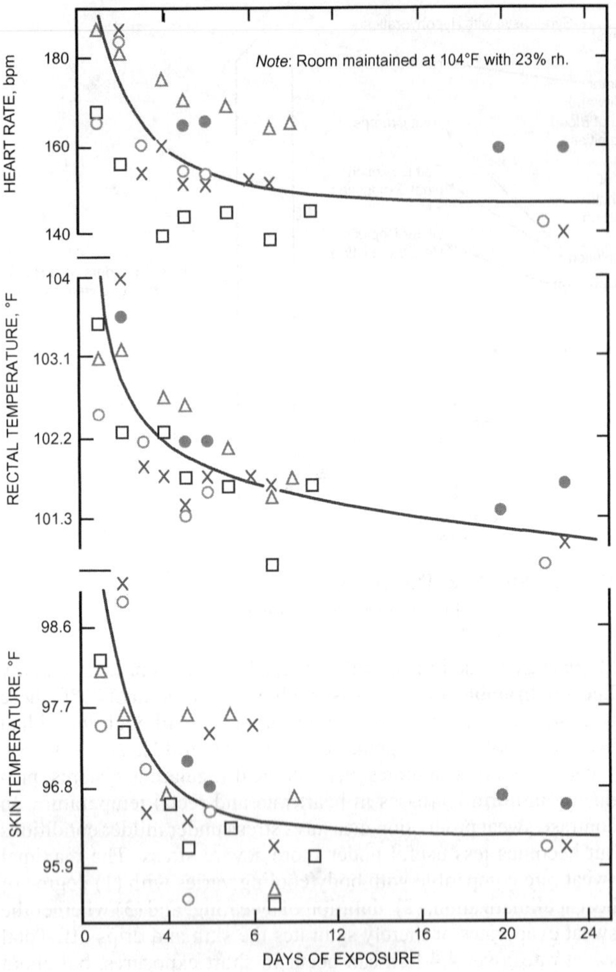

Fig. 26 Acclimatization to Heat Resulting from Daily Exposure of Five Subjects to Extremely Hot Room
(Robinson et al. 1943)

Activity level also affects human performance. Subjective sensations reported by sedentary subjects at a mean skin temperature of 92°F are comfortable; at 88°F, uncomfortably cold; at 86°F, shivering cold; and at 84°F, extremely cold. The critical subjective tolerance limit (without numbing) for mean skin temperature appears to be about 77°F. However, during moderate to heavy activity, subjects reported the same skin temperatures as comfortable. Although mean skin temperature is significant, the temperature of the extremities is more frequently the critical factor for comfort in the cold. Consistent with this, one of the first responses to cold exposure is vasoconstriction, which reduces circulatory heat input to the hands and feet. A hand-skin temperature of 68°F causes a report of uncomfortably cold; 59°F, extremely cold; and 41°F, painful. Identical verbal responses for the foot surface occur at approximately 2.7 to 3.5°F warmer temperatures.

An ambient temperature of –30°F is the lower limit for useful outdoor activity, even with adequate insulative clothing. At –60°F, almost all outdoor effort becomes exceedingly difficult; even with appropriate protective equipment, only limited exposure is possible. Reported exposures of 30 min at –103°F have occurred in the Antarctic without injury.

In response to extreme heat loss, maximal heat production becomes very important. When the less-efficient vasoconstriction cannot prevent body heat loss, shivering is an automatic, more efficient defense against cold. This can be triggered by low deep body temperature, low skin temperature, rapid change of skin temperature, or some combination of all three. Shivering is usually preceded by an imperceptible increase in muscle tension and by noticeable gooseflesh produced by muscle contraction in the skin. It begins slowly in small muscle groups, initially increasing total heat production by 1.5 to 2 times resting levels. As body cooling increases, the reaction spreads to additional body segments. Ultimately violent, whole-body shivering causes maximum heat production of about 6 times resting levels, rendering the individual totally ineffective.

Given sufficient cold exposure, the body undergoes changes that indicate cold acclimatization. These physiological changes include (1) endocrine changes (e.g., sensitivity to norepinephrine), causing nonshivering heat production by metabolism of free fatty acids released from adipose tissue; (2) improved circulatory heat flow to skin, causing an overall sensation of greater comfort; and (3) improved circulatory heat flow to the extremities, reducing the risk of injury and allowing activities at what ordinarily would be severely uncomfortable temperatures in the extremities. Generally, these physiological changes are minor and are induced only by repeated extreme exposures. Nonphysiological factors, including training, experience, and selection of adequate protective clothing, are more useful and may be safer than dependence on physiological changes.

Food energy intake requirements for adequately clothed subjects in extreme cold are only slightly greater than those for subjects living and working in temperate climates. This greater requirement results from added work caused by (1) carrying the weight of heavy clothing (energy cost for heavy protective footwear may be six times that of an equivalent weight on the torso); and (2) the inefficiency of walking in snow, snowshoeing, or skiing, which can increase energy cost up to 300%.

To achieve proper protection in low temperatures, a person must either maintain high metabolic heat production by activity or reduce heat loss by controlling the body's microclimate with clothing. Other protective measures include spot radiant heating, showers of hot air for work at a fixed site, and warm-air-ventilated or electrically heated clothing. Extremities (e.g., fingers and toes) are at greater risk than the torso because, as thin cylinders, they are particularly susceptible to heat loss and difficult to insulate without increasing the surface for heat loss. Vasoconstriction can reduce circulatory heat input to extremities by over 90%.

Although there is no ideal insulating material for protective clothing, radiation-reflective materials are promising. Insulation is primarily a function of clothing thickness; the thickness of trapped air, rather than fibers used, determines insulation effectiveness.

Protection for the respiratory tract seems unnecessary in healthy individuals, even at –50°F. However, asthmatics or individuals with mild cardiovascular problems may benefit from a face mask that warms inspired air. Masks are unnecessary for protecting the face because heat to facial skin is not reduced by local vasoconstriction, as it is for hands. If wind chill is great, there is always a risk of cold injury caused by freezing of exposed skin. Using properly designed torso clothing, such as a parka with a fur-lined hood to minimize wind penetration to the face, and 35 Btu/h of auxiliary heat to each hand and foot, inactive people can tolerate –67°F with a 10 mph wind for more than 6 h. As long as the skin temperature of fingers remains above 60°F, manual dexterity can be maintained and useful work performed without difficulty.

12. SYMBOLS

A = area, ft^2
BFN = neutral skin blood flow, lb/h·ft^2
c = specific heat, Btu/lb·°F
c_{dil} = specific heat (constant) for skin blood flow
c_{sw} = proportionality constant for sweat control, 30 Btu/h·ft^2·°F
C = convective heat loss, Btu/h·ft^2

$C + R$ = total sensible heat loss from skin, Btu/h·ft²
DISC = thermal discomfort
E = evaporative heat loss, Btu/h·ft²
ERF = effective radiant field, Btu/h·ft²
ET* = effective temperature based on 50% rh, °F
f_{cl} = clothing area factor, A_{cl}/A_D, dimensionless
F = thermal efficiency, or angle factor
h = enthalpy, Btu/lb (dry air), or heat transfer coefficient, Btu/h·ft²·°F
HSI = heat stress index
i = vapor permeation efficiency, dimensionless
I = thermal resistance in clo units, clo
J = irradiance, Btu/h·ft²
k = thermal conductivity of body tissue, Btu/h·ft·°F
K = effective conductance between core and skin, Btu/h·ft²·°F
K_{res} = proportionality constant, 3.33 lb/Btu
l = height, ft
L = thermal load on body, Btu/h·ft²
LR = Lewis ratio, °F/psi
m = mass, lb
$\dot{m}$ = mass flow, lb/h·ft²
M = metabolic heat production, Btu/h·ft²
p = water vapor pressure, psi
PD = percent dissatisfied
PMV = predicted mean vote
PPD = predicted percent dissatisfied
q = heat flow, Btu/h·ft²
Q = volume rate, ft³/h, or volume flow rate of blood per unit surface area, L/h·ft²
R = thermal resistance, ft²·°F·h/Btu, or radiative heat loss from skin, Btu/h·ft²
RQ = respiratory quotient, dimensionless
S = heat storage, Btu/h·ft²
SET* = standard effective temperature, °F
SkBF = skin blood flow, lb/h·ft²
t = temperature, °F
$\bar{t}_r$ = mean temperature, °F
T = absolute temperature, °R
TSENS = thermal sensation
Tu = turbulence intensity, %
V = air velocity, fpm
V_{sd} = standard deviation of velocity measured with omnidirectional anemometer with 0.2 s time constant
w = skin wettedness, dimensionless
W = external work accomplished, Btu/h·ft², or humidity ratio of air, lb (water vapor)/lb (dry air)
WBGT = wet-bulb globe temperature, °F
WCI = wind chill index, kcal/h·m²
WGT = wet-globe temperature, °F
x_f = fabric thickness, in.

Greek

α = skin absorptance, dimensionless
ε = emissivity, dimensionless
η_{ev} = evaporative efficiency, dimensionless
θ = time, h
μ = mechanical efficiency of body = W/M, dimensionless
μ_T = mean space temperature, °F
ν = unsolicited thermal complaint rate, complaints/h·zone area
ρ = density, lb/ft³
ρ_{bl} = density of blood, 2.34 lb/L
σ = Stefan-Boltzmann constant = 0.1712×10^{-8} Btu/h·ft²·°R⁴
σ_T = standard deviation of space temperature, °F
$\sigma_{\dot{T}_H}, \sigma_{\dot{T}_L}$ = standard deviation of rate of change of high and low space temperature, °F/h

Superscripts and Subscripts

$'$ = overall, net
a = ambient air
act = activity
b = of body tissue
B = building
b,c = lower limit for evaporative regulation zone
b,h = upper limit for evaporative regulation zone
bl = of blood
c = convection, or comfort
cc = corrected convection value
ch = between chair and body
cl = of clothed body or clothing
cle = of clothing, effective
clu,i = effective insulation of garment i
com = combined
cr = body core
cr,sk = from core to skin
D = DuBois value
db = dry bulb
dif = due to moisture diffusion through skin
dil = skin blood flow
dp = dew point
dry = sensible
e = evaporative, at surface
ec = at surface, corrected
eq,wc = equivalent wind chill
$evap$ = latent
ex = exhaled air
fg = vaporization of water
g = globe
G = covered by garment
ge = gas exchange
h = too hot
l = too cold
m = total
max = maximum
$m-j$ = from person to source j
N = of surface N
nwb = naturally ventilated wet bulb
o = operative
oc = operative comfort
oh = humid operation
out = monthly mean outside
p = at constant pressure
pcl = permeation
$p-N$ = between person and source N
pr = plane radiant
r = radiation, radiant
req = required
res = respiration
rsw = regulatory sweat
s = saturated
sf = final skin
$shiv$ = shivering
si = initial skin
sk = skin
sw = sweat
t = atmospheric, or total
tr = constriction constant for skin blood flow
wb = wet bulb
w,res = respiratory water loss

CODES AND STANDARDS

ASHRAE. 2013. Thermal environmental conditions for human occupancy. ANSI/ASHRAE *Standard* 55-2013.

ISO. 1989. Hot environments—Estimation of the heat stress on working man, based on the WBGT-index (wet bulb globe temperature). *Standard* 7243. International Organization for Standardization, Geneva.

ISO. 2005. Ergonomics of the thermal environment—Analytical determination and interpretation of thermal comfort using calculation of the PMV and PPD indices and local thermal comfort criteria. *Standard* 7730. International Organization for Standardization, Geneva.

ISO. 2004. Ergonomics of the thermal environment—Analytical determination and interpretation of heat stress using calculation of the predicted heat strain. *Standard* 7933. International Organization for Standardization, Geneva.

ISO. 2010. Ergonomics of the thermal environment—Estimation of thermal insulation and water vapour resistance of a clothing ensemble. *Standard* 9920 (R2010). International Organization for Standardization, Geneva.

REFERENCES

ASHRAE members can access *ASHRAE Journal* articles and ASHRAE research project final reports at technologyportal.ashrae.org. Articles and reports are also available for purchase by nonmembers in the online ASHRAE Bookstore at www.ashrae.org/bookstore.

Al-ajmi, F.F., D.L. Loveday, K.H. Bedwell, and G. Havenith. 2008. Thermal insulation and clothing area factors of typical Arabian Gulf clothing ensembles for males and females: measurements using thermal manikins. *Applied Ergonomics* 39(3):407-414.

Amai, H., S. Tanabe, T. Akimoto, and T. Genma. 2007. Thermal sensation and comfort with different task conditioning systems. *Building and Environment* 42(12):3955-3964.

Arens, E., H. Zhang, and C. Huizenga. 2006. Partial- and whole body thermal sensation and comfort, part I: Uniform environmental conditions. *Journal of Thermal Biology* 31:53-59.

Arens, E., H. Zhang, D. Kim, E. Buchberger, F. Bauman, C. Huizenga, and H. Higuchi. 2008. Impact of a task-ambient ventilation system on perceived air quality. *Proceedings of Indoor Air 2008*, Copenhagen.

Arens, E., S. Turner, H. Zhang, and G. Paliaga. 2009. Moving air for comfort. *ASHRAE Journal* 51(5):18-29.

Arens, E., H. Zhang, and W. Pasut. 2011. Thermal comfort and perceived air quality of a PEC system. *Proceedings of Indoor Air 2011*, Austin.

Astrand, P., and K. Rodahl. 1977. *Textbook of work physiology: Physiological bases of exercise.* McGraw-Hill, New York.

Azer, N.Z. 1982. Design guidelines for spot cooling systems: Part I—Assessing the acceptability of the environment. *ASHRAE Transactions* 88:1.

Azer, N.Z. and S. Hsu. 1977. OSHA heat stress standards and the WBGT index. *ASHRAE Transactions* 83(2):30.

Bauman, F.S., T.G. Carter, A.V. Baughman, and E. Arens. 1998. Field study of the impact of a desktop task/ambient conditioning system in office buildings. *ASHRAE Transactions* 104(1A).

Belding, H.D. 1967. Heat stress. In *Thermobiology*, A.H. Rose, ed. Academic Press, New York.

Belding, H.S. 1970. The search for a universal heat stress index. In *Physiological and behavioral temperature regulation*, J.D. Hardy, A.P. Gagge, and J.A.J. Stolwijk, eds. Springfield, IL.

Belding, H.S., and T.F. Hatch. 1955. Index for evaluating heat stress in terms of resulting physiological strains. *Heating, Piping and Air Conditioning* 207:239.

Berglund, L.G. 1994. Common elements in the design and operation of thermal comfort and ventilation systems. *ASHRAE Transactions* 100(1):776-781.

Berglund, L.G. 1995. Comfort criteria: Humidity and standards. *Proceedings of Pan Pacific Symposium on Building and Urban Environmental Conditioning in Asia* vol. 2, pp. 369-382. University of Nagoya, Japan.

Berglund, L.G., and D.J. Cunningham. 1986. Parameters of human discomfort in warm environments. *ASHRAE Transactions* 92(2):732-746.

Berglund, L.G., and A. Fobelets. 1987. A subjective human response to low level air currents and asymmetric radiation. *ASHRAE Transactions* 93(1):497-523.

Berglund, L.G., and R.R. Gonzalez. 1977. Evaporation of sweat from sedentary man in humid environments. *Journal of Applied Physiology* 42(5):767-772.

Berglund, L., R. Gonzales, and A. Gagge. 1990. Predicted human performance decrement from thermal discomfort and ET*. *Proceedings of Indoor Air '90*, Toronto, vol. 1, pp. 215-220.

Botsford, J.H. 1971. A wet globe thermometer for environmental heat measurement. *American Industrial Hygiene Association Journal* 32:1-10.

Burton, A.C., and H.C. Bazett. 1936. A study of the average temperature of the tissues, the exchange of heat and vasomotor responses in man, by a bath calorimeter. *American Journal of Physiology* 117:36.

Busch, J.F. 1992. A tale of two populations: Thermal comfort in air-conditioned and naturally ventilated offices in Thailand. *Energy and Buildings* 18:235-249.

Buskirk, E.R. 1960. Problems related to the caloric cost of living. *Bulletin of the New York Academy of Medicine* 26:365.

Chatonnet, J., and M. Cabanac. 1965. The perception of thermal comfort. *International Journal of Biometeorology* 9:183-193.

Colin, J., and Y. Houdas. 1967. Experimental determination of coefficient of heat exchange by convection of the human body. *Journal of Applied Physiology* 22:31.

Collins, K.J., and E. Hoinville. 1980. Temperature requirements in old age. *Building Services Engineering Research and Technology* 1(4):165-172.

Davis, W.J. 1976. Typical WBGT indexes in various industrial environments. *ASHRAE Transactions* 82(2):303.

de Dear, R.J., and G.S. Brager. 1998. Developing an adaptive model of thermal comfort and preference. *ASHRAE Technical Data Bulletin* 14(1):27-49.

de Dear, R., K. Leow, and A. Ameen. 1991. Thermal comfort in the humid tropics—Part I. *ASHRAE Transactions* 97(1):874-879.

DuBois, D., and E.F. DuBois. 1916. A formula to estimate approximate surface area, if height and weight are known. *Archives of Internal Medicine* 17:863-871.

Dukes-Dobos, F., and A. Henschel. 1971. The modification of the WBGT index for establishing permissible heat exposure limits in occupational work. HEW/USPHE/NIOSH *Report* TR-69.

Dukes-Dobos, F., and A. Henschel. 1973. Development of permissible heat exposure limits for occupational work. *ASHRAE Journal* 9:57.

Dygert, R.K., and T.Q. Dang. 2012. Experimental validation of local exhaust strategies for improved IAQ in aircraft cabins. *Building and Environment* 47:76-88.

Eriksson, H.A. 1975. Heating and ventilating of tractor cabs. Presented at the 1975 Winter Meeting, American Society of Agricultural Engineers, Chicago.

Fanger, P.O. 1967. Calculation of thermal comfort: Introduction of a basic comfort equation. *ASHRAE Transactions* 73(2):III.4.1.

Fanger, P.O. 1970. *Thermal comfort analysis and applications in environmental engineering.* McGraw-Hill, New York.

Fanger, P.O. 1972. *Thermal comfort.* McGraw-Hill, New York.

Fanger, P.O. 1973. The variability of man's preferred ambient temperature from day to day. *Archives des Sciences Physiologiques* 27(4):A403.

Fanger, P.O. 1982. *Thermal comfort: Analysis and applications in environmental engineering.* Robert E. Krieger, Malabar, FL.

Fanger, P.O., and N.K. Christensen. 1986. Perception of draught in ventilated spaces. *Ergonomics* 29(2):215-235.

Fanger, P.O., and G. Langkilde. 1975. Interindividual differences in ambient temperature preferred by seated persons. *ASHRAE Transactions* 81(2):140-147.

Fanger, P.O., J. Hojbjerre, and J.O.B. Thomsen. 1973. Man's preferred ambient temperature during the day. *Archives des Sciences Physiologiques* 27(4):A395-A402.

Fanger, P.O., J. Hojbjerre, and J.O.B. Thomsen. 1974. Thermal comfort conditions in the morning and the evening. *International Journal of Biometeorology* 18(1):16.

Fanger, P.O., L. Banhidi, B.W. Olesen, and G. Langkilde. 1980. Comfort limits for heated ceilings. *ASHRAE Transactions* 86(1):141-156.

Fanger, P.O., B.M. Ipsen, G. Langkilde, B.W. Olesen, N.K. Christensen, and S. Tanabe. 1985. Comfort limits for asymmetric thermal radiation. *Energy and Buildings.*

Fanger, P.O., A.K. Melikov, H. Hanzawa, and J. Ring. 1989. Turbulence and draft. *ASHRAE Journal* 31(4):18-25.

Federspiel, C.C. 1998. Statistical analysis of unsolicited thermal sensation complaints in commercial buildings. *ASHRAE Transactions* 104(1):912-923.

Federspiel, C.C. 2001. Estimating the frequency and cost of responding to building complaints. In *Indoor air quality handbook*, J. Spengler, J.M. Sammet, and J.F. McCarthy, eds. McGraw-Hill.

Federspiel, C., G. Liu, M. Lahiff, D. Faulkner, D. Dibartolomeo, W. Fisk, P. Price, and D. Sullivan. 2002. Worker performance and ventilation: Analysis of individual data for call-center workers. *Proceedings of Indoor Air 2002*, pp. 796-801.

Federspiel, C.C., R. Martin, and H. Yan. 2003. Thermal comfort models and "call-out" (complaint) frequencies. ASHRAE Research Project RP-1129, *Final Report.*

Fiala, D. 1998. *Dynamic simulation of human heat transfer and thermal comfort.* Ph.D. dissertation, Institute of Energy and Sustainable Development, DeMontfort University, Leicester, UK.

Fiala, D., K. Lomas, and M. Stohrer. 2003. First principles modeling of thermal sensation responses in steady state and transient boundary conditions. *ASHRAE Transactions* 109(1):179-186.

Fobelets, A.P.R., and A.P. Gagge. 1988. Rationalization of the ET* as a measure of the enthalpy of the human environment. *ASHRAE Transactions* 94:1.

Gagge, A.P. 1937. A new physiological variable associated with sensible and insensible perspiration. *American Journal of Physiology* 20(2):277-287.

Gagge, A.P., and J.D. Hardy. 1967. Thermal radiation exchange of the human by partitional calorimetry. *Journal of Applied Physiology* 23(2): 248-258.

Gagge, A.P., G.M. Rapp, and J.D. Hardy. 1967a. The effective radiant field and operative temperature necessary for comfort with radiant heating. *ASHRAE Transactions* 73(1):I.2.1.

Gagge, A.P., G.M. Rapp, and J.D. Hardy. 1967b. The effective radiant field and operative temperature necessary for comfort with radiant heating. *ASHRAE Journal* 9(5):63.

Gagge, A.P., J.A.J. Stolwijk, and B. Saltin. 1969a. Comfort and thermal sensation and associated physiological responses during exercise at various ambient temperatures. *Environmental Research* 2:209.

Gagge, A.P., J.A.J. Stolwijk, and Y. Nishi. 1969b. The prediction of thermal comfort when thermal equilibrium is maintained by sweating. *ASHRAE Transactions* 75(2):108.

Gagge, A.P., J. Stolwijk, and Y. Nishi. 1971a. An effective temperature scale based on a simple model of human physiological regulatory response. *ASHRAE Transactions* 77(1):247-262.

Gagge, A.P., A.C. Burton, and H.D. Bazett. 1971b. A practical system of units for the description of heat exchange of man with his environment. *Science* 94:428-430.

Gagge, A.P., Y. Nishi, and R.G. Nevins. 1976. The role of clothing in meeting FEA energy conservation guidelines. *ASHRAE Transactions* 82(2):234.

Gagge, A.P., A.P. Fobelets, and L.G. Berglund. 1986. A standard predictive index of human response to the thermal environment. *ASHRAE Transactions* 92(2B).

Gonzalez, R.R. 1975. Effects of ambient temperature and humidity on human performance. *Special Technical Report* 4. John B. Pierce Foundation Laboratory, New Haven, CT.

Gonzalez, R.R., L.G. Berglund, and A.P. Gagge. 1978. Indices of thermoregulatory strain for moderate exercise in the heat. *Journal of Applied Physiology* 44(6):889-899.

Gordon, R.G. 1974. *The responses of human thermoregulatory system in the cold*. PhD dissertation, University of California–Santa Barbara.

Green, G.H. 1982. Positive and negative effects of building humidification. *ASHRAE Transactions* 88(1):1049-1061.

Griffiths, T., and D. McIntyre. 1975. The effect of mental effect on subjective assessments on warmth. *Ergonomics* 18(1):29-32.

Gwosdow, A.R., J.C. Stevens, L. Berglund, and J.A.J. Stolwijk. 1986. Skin friction and fabric sensations in neutral and warm environments. *Textile Research Journal* 56:574-580.

Hardy, J.D. 1949. Heat transfer. In *Physiology of heat regulation and science of clothing*, L.H. Newburgh, ed. W.B. Saunders, London.

Hardy, J.D. 1961. Physiological effects of high intensity infrared heating. *ASHRAE Journal* 4:11.

Hardy, J.D., H.G. Wolf, and H. Goodell. 1952. *Pain sensations and reactions*. Williams and Wilkins, Baltimore.

Hardy, J.D., J.A.J. Stolwijk, and A.P. Gagge. 1971. Man. In *Comparative physiology of thermoregulation*, Chapter 5. Charles C. Thomas, Springfield, IL.

Havenith, G., and Nilsson H. 2004. Correction of clothing insulation for movement and wind effects, a meta-analysis. *European Journal of Applied Physiology* 92:636–640.

Havenith, G., D. Fiala, K. Błazejczyk, M. Richards, P. Bröde, I. Holmér, H. Rintamaki, Y. Benshabat, and G. Jendritzky. 2012. The UTCI-clothing model. *International Journal of Biometeorology* 56(3):461-470.

Havenith, G., K. Kuklane, J. Fan, S. Hodder, Y. Ouzzahra, K. Lundgren, Y. Au, and D. Loveday. 2015. A database of static clothing thermal insulation and vapor permeability values of non-Western ensembles for use in ASHRAE *Standard* 55, ISO 7730, and ISO 9920. *ASHRAE Transactions* 121(1).

Hensel, H. 1973. Temperature reception and thermal comfort. *Archives des Sciences Physiologiques* 27:A359-A370.

Hensel, H. 1981. *Thermoreception and temperature regulation*. Academic Press, London.

Hodder, S.G., D.L. Loveday, K.C. Parsons, and A.H. Taki. 1998. Thermal comfort in chilled ceiling and displacement ventilation environments: Vertical radiant temperature asymmetry effects. *Energy and Buildings* 27:167-173.

Holmér, I. 1984. Required clothing insulation (IREQ) as an analytical index of cold stress. *ASHRAE Transactions* 90(1B):1116-1128.

Houghten, F.C., and C.P. Yaglou. 1923. ASHVE *Research Report* 673. *ASHVE Transactions* 29:361.

Hoyt, T., H.L. Kwang, H. Zhang, E. Arens, and T. Webster. 2009. Energy savings from extended air temperature setpoints and reductions in room air mixing. *Proceedings of the International Conference on Environmental Ergonomics 2009*, August.

Huizenga, C., H. Zhang, and E. Arens. 2001. A model of human physiology and comfort for assessing complex thermal environments. *Building and Environment* 36(6):691-699.

Humphreys, M., and J.F. Nicol. 1998. Understanding the adaptive approach to thermal comfort. *ASHRAE Technical Data Bulletin* 14(1):1-14.

Jones, B.W., K. Hsieh, and M. Hashinaga. 1986. The effect of air velocity on thermal comfort at moderate activity levels. *ASHRAE Transactions* 92:2.

Korsgaard, V. 1949. Necessity of using a directional mean radiant temperature to describe thermal conditions in rooms. *Heating, Piping and Air Conditioning* 21(6):117-120.

Kraning, K., and R. Gonzalez. 1997. A mechanistic computer simulation of human work in heat that accounts for physical and physiological effects of clothing, aerobic fitness, and progressive dehydration. *Journal of Thermal Biology* 22:331-342.

Kuno, S. 1995. Comfort and pleasantness. In *Proceedings of Pan Pacific Symposium on Building and Urban Environmental Conditioning in Asia*, 2:383-392. University of Nagoya, Japan.

Langkilde, G. 1979. Thermal comfort for people of high age. In *Confort thermique: Aspects physiologiques et psychologiques*, INSERM, Paris 75:187-93.

Leithead, C.S., and A.R. Lind. 1964. *Heat stress and heat disorders*. Cassell & Co., London.

Levin, H. 1995. Preface. *Proceedings, Indoor Environment and Productivity Workshop*, Atlanta. H. Levin, ed. ASHRAE.

Link, J., and R. Pepler. 1970. Associated fluctuations in daily temperature, productivity and absenteeism (RP-57). *ASHRAE Transactions* 76(2): 326-337.

Lipkin, M. and J.D. Hardy 1954. Measurement of some thermal properties of human tissues. *Journal of Applied Physiology* 7:212.

Liviana, J.E., F.H. Rohles, and O.D. Bullock. 1988. Humidity, comfort and contact lenses. *ASHRAE Transactions* 94(1):3-11.

Loveday, D.L., K.C. Parsons, A.H. Taki, S.G. Hodder, and L.D. Jeal. 1998. Designing for thermal comfort in combined chilled ceiling/displacement ventilation environments. *ASHRAE Transactions* 104(1).

Matthew, W.H., G.J. Thomas, L.E. Armstrong, P.C. Szlyk, and I.V. Sils. 1986. Botsball (WGT) performance characteristics and their impact on the implementation of existing military hot weather doctrine. U.S. Army Reserves Institute of Environmental Medicine *Technical Report* T 9/86, April.

McCartney, K.J., and M.A. Humphreys. 2002. Thermal comfort and productivity. *Proceedings of Indoor Air 2002*, pp. 822-827.

McCullough, E.A. 1986. An insulation data base for military clothing. Institute for Environmental Research *Report* 86-01, Kansas State University, Manhattan.

McCullough, E.A., and S. Hong. 1994. A data base for determining the decrease in clothing insulation due to body motion. *ASHRAE Transactions* 100(1):765.

McCullough, E.A., and B.W. Jones. 1984. A comprehensive data base for estimating clothing insulation. IER Technical *Report* 84-01, Institute for Environmental Research, Kansas State University, Manhattan. ASHRAE Research Project RP-411, *Final Report*.

McCullough, E.A., B.W. Jones, and T. Tamura. 1989. A data base for determining the evaporative resistance of clothing. *ASHRAE Transactions* 95(2).

McCullough, E.A., B.W. Olesen, and S.W. Hong. 1994. Thermal insulation provided by chairs. *ASHRAE Transactions* 100(1):795-802.

McCutchan, J.W., and C.L. Taylor. 1951. Respiratory heat exchange with varying temperature and humidity of inspired air. *Journal of Applied Physiology* 4:121-135.

McIntyre, D.A. 1974. The thermal radiation field. *Building Science* 9:247-262.

McIntyre, D.A. 1977. Overhead radiation and comfort. *The Building Services Engineer* 44:226-232.

McIntyre, D.A., and I.D. Griffiths. 1975. The effects of uniform and asymmetric thermal radiation on comfort. *CLIMA 2000, 6th International Congress of Climatritics*, Milan.

McNair, H.P. 1973. A preliminary study of the subjective effects of vertical air temperature gradients. British Gas Corporation *Report* WH/T/R&D/73/94, London.

McNair, H.P., and D.S. Fishman. 1974. A further study of the subjective effects of vertical air temperature gradients. British Gas Corporation *Report* WH/T/R&D/73/94, London.

McNall, P.E., Jr., and R.E. Biddison. 1970. Thermal and comfort sensations of sedentary persons exposed to asymmetric radiant fields. *ASHRAE Transactions* 76(1):123.

McNall, P.E., P.W. Ryan, and J. Jaax. 1968. Seasonal variation in comfort conditions for college-age persons in the Middle West. *ASHRAE Transactions* 74(1):IV.2.1-9.

Melikov, A.K. 2003. Personalized ventilation. *Indoor Air* 14:157-167.

Melikov, A.K., V.S. Lyubenova, M. Skwarczynski, and J. Kaczmarczyk. 2011. Impact of air temperature, relative humidity, air movement and pollution on eye blinking. *Proceedings of Indoor Air 2011*, Austin.

Mitchell, D. 1974. Convective heat transfer in man and other animals. In *Heat loss from animals and man*, J.L. Monteith and L.E. Mount, eds. Butterworth Publishing, London.

Nevins, R.G., and A.M. Feyerherm. 1967. Effect of floor surface temperature on comfort: Part IV, Cold floors. *ASHRAE Transactions* 73(2):III.2.1.

Nevins, R.G., and A.O. Flinner. 1958. Effect of heated-floor temperatures on comfort. *ASHRAE Transactions* 64:175.

Nevins, R.G., K.B. Michaels, and A.M. Feyerherm. 1964. The effect of floor surface temperature on comfort: Part 1, college age males; Part II, college age females. *ASHRAE Transactions* 70:29.

Nevins, R.G., F.H. Rohles, Jr., W.E. Springer, and A.M. Feyerherm. 1966. Temperature-humidity chart for thermal comfort of seated persons. *ASHRAE Transactions* 72(1):283.

Nevins, R.G., R.R. Gonzalez, Y. Nishi, and A.P. Gagge. 1975. Effect of changes in ambient temperature and level of humidity on comfort and thermal sensations. *ASHRAE Transactions* 81(2).

Nicol, J.F., and M.A. Humphreys. 1972. Thermal comfort as part of a self-regulating system. *Proceedings of CIB Symposium on Thermal Comfort*, Building Research Station, London.

Niemelä, R., J. Railio, M. Hannula, S. Rautio, and K. Reijula. 2001. Assessing the effect of indoor environment on productivity. *Proceedings of CLIMA 2000 (CD-ROM)*, Napoli.

Nilsson, H.O. 2007. Thermal comfort evaluation with virtual manikin methods. *Building and Environment* 42:4000–4005.

NIOSH. 1986. Criteria for a recommended standard—Occupational exposure to hot environments, revised criteria. U.S. Dept. of Health and Human Services, USDHHS (NIOSH) *Publication* 86-113. Available from www.cdc.gov/NIOSH/docs/86-113/86-113.pdf.

Nishi, Y. 1981. Measurement of thermal balance of man. In *Bioengineering Thermal Physiology and Comfort*, K. Cena and J.A. Clark, eds. Elsevier New York.

Nishi, Y., and A.P. Gagge. 1970. Direct evaluation of convective heat transfer coefficient by naphthalene sublimation. *Journal of Applied Physiology* 29:830.

Nishi, Y., R.R. Gonzalez, and A.P. Gagge. 1975. Direct measurement of clothing heat transfer properties during sensible and insensible heat exchange with thermal environment. *ASHRAE Transactions* 81(2):183.

Nishihara, N., and S. Tanabe. 2011. Effect of individual control of air flow from task fan on task performance, fatigue and cerebral blood flow. *Proceedings of Indoor Air 2011*, Austin.

Olesen, B.W. 1977a. Thermal comfort requirements for floors. In *Proceedings of Commissions B1, B2, E1 of the IIR*, Belgrade, 337-343.

Olesen, B.W. 1977b. Thermal comfort requirements for floors occupied by people with bare feet. *ASHRAE Transactions* 83(2).

Olesen, B.W. 1985. A new and simpler method for estimating the thermal insulation of a clothing ensemble. *ASHRAE Transactions* 91(2).

Olesen, B.W., and R. Nielsen. 1983. *Thermal insulation of clothing measured on a moveable manikin and on human subjects.* Technical University of Denmark, Lyngby.

Olesen, S., J.J. Bassing, and P.O. Fanger. 1972. Physiological comfort conditions at sixteen combinations of activity, clothing, air velocity and ambient temperature. *ASHRAE Transactions* 78(2):199.

Olesen, B.W., M. Scholer, and P.O. Fanger. 1979. Vertical air temperature differences and comfort. In *Indoor climate,* P.O. Fanger and O. Valbjorn, eds. Danish Building Research Institute, Copenhagen.

Olesen, B.W., E. Sliwinska, T.L. Madsen, and P.O. Fanger. 1982. Effect of posture and activity on the thermal insulation of clothing. Measurement by a movable thermal manikin. *ASHRAE Transactions* 82(2):791-805.

Onkaram, B., L. Stroschein, and R.F. Goldman. 1980. Three instruments for assessment of WBGT and a comparison with WGT (Botsball). *American Industrial Hygiene Association* 41:634-641.

Oohori, T., L.G. Berglund, and A.P. Gagge. 1984. Comparison of current two-parameter indices of vapor permeation of clothing—As factors governing thermal equilibrium and human comfort. *ASHRAE Transactions* 90(2).

Ostberg, O., and A.G. McNicholl. 1973. The preferred thermal conditions for "morning" and "evening" types of subjects during day and night—Preliminary results. *Build International* 6(1):147-157.

Passmore, R., and J.V.G. Durnin. 1967. *Energy, work and leisure.* Heinemann Educational Books, London.

Pepler, R., and R. Warner. 1968. Temperature and learning: An experimental study. *ASHRAE Transactions* 74(2):211-219.

Rapp, G., and A.P. Gagge. 1967. Configuration factors and comfort design in radiant beam heating of man by high temperature infrared sources. *ASHRAE Transactions* 73(2):III.1.1.

Robinson, S., E.S. Turrell, H.S. Belding, and S.M. Horvath. 1943. Rapid acclimatization to work in hot climates. *American Journal of Physiology* 140:168-176.

Roelofsen, P. 2001. The design of workplace as a strategy for productivity enhancement. *Proceedings of CLIMA 2000*, Napoli.

Rohles, F.H., Jr. 1973. The revised modal comfort envelope. *ASHRAE Transactions* 79(2):52.

Rohles, F.H., Jr., and M.A. Johnson. 1972. Thermal comfort in the elderly. *ASHRAE Transactions* 78(1):131.

Rohles, F.H., Jr., and R.G. Nevins. 1971. The nature of thermal comfort for sedentary man. *ASHRAE Transactions* 77(1):239.

Russo, J.S., and H.E. Khalifa. 2011. Surface reactions on the human body: using personal ventilation to remove squalene oxidation products from the breathing zone with CFD. *Proceedings of Indoor Air 2011*, Austin.

Sekhar, S.C., N. Gong, K.W. Tham, K.W. Cheong, A.K. Melikov, D.P. Wyon, and P.O. Fanger. 2005. Findings of personalised ventilation studies in a hot and humid climate. *International Journal of HVAC&R Research* (now *Science and Technology for the Built Environment*) 11(4):603-620.

Seppänen, O., and W.J. Fisk. 2006. Some quantitative relations between indoor environmental quality and work performance and health. *International Journal of HVAC&R Research* (now *Science and Technology for the Built Environment*) 12(4):957-973.

Seppänen, O., P.E. McNall, D.M. Munson, and C.H. Sprague. 1972. Thermal insulating values for typical indoor clothing ensembles. *ASHRAE Transactions* 78(1):120-30.

Seppänen, O., W.J. Fisk, and Q.H. Lei. 2006. Effect of temperature on task performance in office environment. *Report* LBNL-60946. indoor.lbl.gov/sites/all/files/lbnl-60946.pdf.

Siple, P.A., and C.F. Passel. 1945. Measurements of dry atmospheric cooling in subfreezing temperatures. *Proceedings of the American Philosophical Society* 89:177.

Smith, C.E. 1991. *A transient, three-dimensional model of the human thermal system*. PhD dissertation, Kansas State University.

Stolwijk, J.A.J. 1971. A mathematical model of physiological temperature regulation in man. NASA Contractor *Report*, Yale University School of Medicine.

Stolwijk, J.A.J., and J.D. Hardy. 1966. Partitional calorimetric studies of response of man to thermal transients. *Journal of Applied Physiology* 21:967.

Stolwijk, J.A.J., A.P. Gagge, and B. Saltin. 1968. Physiological factors associated with sweating during exercise. *Journal of Aerospace Medicine* 39:1101.

Sullivan, C.D., and R.L. Gorton. 1976. A method of calculating WBGT from environmental factors. *ASHRAE Transactions* 82(2):279.

Tanabe, S., and N. Nishihara. 2004. Productivity and fatigue. *Indoor Air* 14(S-7):126-133.

Tanabe, S., K. Kimura, and T. Hara. 1987. Thermal comfort requirements during the summer season in Japan. *ASHRAE Transactions* 93(1):564-577.

Tanabe, S.-I., K. Kobayashi, J. Nakano, Y. Ozeki, and M. Konishi. 2002. Evaluation of thermal comfort using combined multi-node thermoregulation (65MN) and radiation models and computational fluid dynamics (CFD). *Energy and Building* 34(6):637-646.

Tham, K.W., and H.C. Willem. 2005. Temperature and ventilation effects on performance and neurobehavioral-related symptoms of tropically acclimatized call center operators near thermal neutrality. *ASHRAE Transactions* 111(2):687-698.

Tikusis, P., and G.G. Giesbrecht. 1999. Prediction of shivering heat production from core and mean skin temperatures. *European Journal of Applied Physiology* 79:221-229.

Umbach, K.H. 1980. Measuring the physiological properties of textiles for clothing. *Melliand Textilberichte* (English edition) G1:543-548.

Wang, X.L. 1994. *Thermal comfort and sensation under transient conditions*. Doctoral dissertation, Department of Energy Technology, Royal Institute of Technology, Stockholm.

Wang, X.L., and F. Peterson. 1992. Estimating thermal transient comfort. *ASHRAE Transactions* 98(1):182-188.

Webb, P. 1964. *Bioastronautics data base*. NASA.

Werner, J., and P. Webb. 1993. A six cylinder model of human thermoregulation for general use on personal computers. *Annals of Physiological Anthropology* 12(3):123-134.

Winslow, C.-E.A., L.P. Herrington, and A.P. Gagge. 1937. Relations between atmospheric conditions, physiological reactions and sensations of pleasantness. *American Journal of Hygiene* 26(1):103-115.

Wissler, E.H. 1964. A mathematical model of the human thermoregulatory system. *Bulletin of Mathematical Biophysics* 26:147-166.

Wissler, E.H. 1985. Mathematical simulation of human thermal behavior using wholebody models. In *Heat transfer in medicine and biology—Analysis and applications*, vol. 1, pp. 325-374, A. Shitzer and R.C. Eberhart, eds. Plenum Press, New York.

Wissler, E.H. 1988. A review of human thermal models. In *Environmental ergonomics*, I.B. Mekjavic, E.W. Banister, and J.B. Morrison, eds. Taylor and Francis, London.

Witterseh, T. 2001. *Environmental perception, SBS symptoms and performance of office work under combined exposure to temperature, noise and air pollution.* Ph.D. dissertation. International Center for Indoor Environment and Energy, Department of Mechanical Engineering, Technical University of Denmark.

Woodcock, A.H. 1962. Moisture transfer in textile systems. *Textile Research Journal* 8:628-633.

Wyon, D.P. 1996. Individual microclimate control: Required range, probable benefits and current feasibility. *Proceedings of Indoor Air '96,* Nagoya, Japan, vol. 2, pp. 27-36.

Wyon, D.P., S. Larsson, B. Forsgren, and I. Lundgren. 1989. Standard procedures for assessing vehicle climate with a thermal manikin. *SAE Technical Paper Series* 890049:1-11.

Yang, B., A. Melikov, and S.C. Sekhar. 2009. Performance evaluation of ceiling mounted personalized ventilation system. *ASHRAE Transactions* 115 (2):395-406.

Yang, B., S.C. Sekhar, and A. Melikov. 2010. Ceiling mounted personalized ventilation system integrated with a secondary air distribution system—A human response study in hot and humid climate. *Indoor Air—International Journal of Indoor Environment and Health* 20(4):309-319.

Zhang, H. 2003. *Human thermal sensation and comfort in transient and non-uniform thermal environments*. Ph.D. dissertation, University of California, Berkeley.

Zhang, H., E. Arens, C. Huizenga, and T. Han. 2010a. Thermal sensation and comfort models for non-uniform and transient environments: Part I: Local sensation of individual body parts. *Building and Environment* 45(2):380-388.

Zhang, H., E. Arens, C. Huizenga, and T. Han. 2010b. Thermal sensation and comfort models for non-uniform and transient environments: Part II: Local comfort of individual body parts. *Building and Environment,* 45(2):389-398.

Zhang, H., E. Arens, C. Huizenga, and T. Han. 2010c. Thermal sensation and comfort models for non-uniform and transient environments: Part III: Whole-body sensation and comfort. *Building and Environment* 45(2):399-410.

Zhang, H., E. Arens, D. Kim, E. Buchberger, F. Bauman, and C. Huizenga. 2010d. Comfort, perceived air quality, and work performance in a low-power task-ambient conditioning system. *Building and Environment* 45(1):29-39.

Zhang, H., E. Arens, and W. Pasut. 2011. Air temperature thresholds for indoor comfort and perceived air quality. *Building Research and Information* 39(2):134-144.

BIBLIOGRAPHY

Fanger, P.O., A. Melikov, H. Hanzawa, and J. Ring. 1988. Air turbulence and sensation of draught. *Energy and Buildings* 12:21-39.

Kroner, W.M., and J.A. Stark-Martin. 1994. Environmentally responsive workstations and office worker productivity. *ASHRAE Transactions* 100(2):750-755.

Li, R., S.C. Sekhar, and A. Melikov. 2011. Thermal comfort and indoor air quality in rooms with integrated personalized ventilation and underfloor air distribution systems. *HVAC&R Research* (now *Science and Technology for the Built Environment*) 17(5):829-846.

Niemelä, R., M. Hannula, S. Rautio, K. Reijula, and J. Railio. 2002. The effect of indoor air temperature on labour productivity in call centers—A case study. *Energy and Buildings* 34:759-764.

REHVA. 2006. Indoor climate and productivity in offices. *REHVA Guidebook* 6, pp. 29-34. P. Wargocki, and O. Seppänen, eds. Federation of European Heating and Air-Conditioning Associations, Brussels.

Schiavon, S., A. Melikov, and S.C. Sekhar. 2010. Energy analysis of the personalized ventilation system in hot and humid climates. *Energy and Buildings* 42:699-707.

Witherspoon, J.M., R.F. Goldman, and J.R. Breckenridge. 1971. Heat transfer coefficients of humans in cold water. *Journal de Physiologie* 63:459.

Wyon, D., I. Wyon, and F. Norin. 1996. Effects of moderate heat stress on driver vigilance in a moving vehicle. *Ergonomics* 39(1):61-75.

CHAPTER 10

INDOOR ENVIRONMENTAL HEALTH

INDOOR environmental health comprises those aspects of human health and disease that are determined by factors in the indoor environment. It also refers to the theory and practice of assessing and controlling factors in the indoor environment that can potentially affect health. The practice of indoor environmental health requires consideration of chemical, biological, physical and ergonomic hazards, and has the goal of increasing healthy indoor environments.

Diseases are caused by genetics and exposures [biological (biotic) and/or chemical or physical (abiotic)]. Despite a huge investment in DNA research in recent decades, few diseases can be solely explained by our genes. An interaction between genes and environmental exposures is needed, and understanding indoor environmental exposures is essential in this respect. Over a 70-year lifespan in a developed region, indoor air (in homes, schools, day cares, offices, shops, etc.) constitutes around 65% of the total lifetime exposure (in mass), whereas outdoor air, air during transportation, food, and liquid makes up the rest. For more vulnerable populations, such as newborns, the elderly, and the homebound ill, indoor air in homes makes up around 80% of the exposure.

It is essential for engineers and others involved in building design and operation to understand the fundamentals of indoor environmental health because the design, operation, and maintenance of buildings and their HVAC systems significantly affect the health of building occupants. In many cases, buildings and systems can be designed and operated to reduce the exposure of occupants to potential hazards. Unfortunately, neglecting to consider indoor environmental health can lead to conditions that create or worsen those hazards and increased associated exposure.

This chapter provides general background information and introduces important concepts of hazard recognition, analysis, and control. It also presents information on specific hazards, and describes sources of exposure to each hazard, potential health effects, relevant exposure standards and guidelines, and methods to control exposure.

This chapter also includes a brief introduction to the very broad and dynamic field of indoor environmental health. Thus, descriptions of potential hazards (and especially their controls) presented do not constitute a comprehensive, state-of-the-art review. Additional detail is available on many important topics in other ASHRAE Handbook chapters, including

- Chapter 9, Thermal Comfort, of this volume
- Chapter 11, Air Contaminants, of this volume
- Chapter 12, Odors, of this volume
- Chapter 16, Ventilation and Infiltration, of this volume
- Chapter 29, Air Cleaners for Particulate Contaminants, of the 2016 *ASHRAE Handbook—HVAC Systems and Equipment*
- Chapter 31, Ventilation of the Industrial Environment, of the 2015 *ASHRAE Handbook—HVAC Applications*
- Chapter 46, Air Cleaners for Gaseous Contaminants, of the 2015 *ASHRAE Handbook—HVAC Applications*

Other important sources of information from ASHRAE include the building ventilation and related requirements in *Standards* 62.1 and 62.2, as well as *Standard* 170 for health care occupancies and the *Indoor Air Quality Guide* (ASHRAE 2009). Additional details are available from governmental and private sources, including the U.S. Department of Health and Human Services' Centers for Disease Control and Prevention, U.S. Environmental Protection Agency, Occupational Safety and Health Administration, American Conference of Governmental Industrial Hygienists, National Institute for Occupational Safety and Health, parallel institutions in other countries, and the World Health Organization.

1. BACKGROUND

Evaluation of exposure incidents and laboratory studies with humans and animals have generated reasonable consensus on safe and unsafe workplace exposures for about 1000 chemicals and particles. Consequently, many countries regulate exposures of workers to these agents. However, chemical and particle concentrations that meet occupational health criteria usually exceed levels acceptable to occupants in nonindustrial spaces such as offices, schools, and residences, where exposure times often last longer and exposures may involve mixtures of many contaminants and where those exposed comprise a less robust population (e.g., infants, the elderly, the infirm) (NAS 1981).

The generally accepted broad definition of health is that in the constitution of the World Health Organization (WHO): "Health is a state of complete physical, mental, and social well-being and not merely the absence of disease or infirmity."

Another definition of health, more narrowly focused on air pollution, presented by the American Thoracic Society (ATS 1999) takes into account broader, societal decision-making processes in defining what constitutes an adverse health effect of air pollution. Key points of the ATS definition of adverse effects include

- **Biomarkers, or biological indicators (e.g., in blood, exhaled air, sputum) of environmental effects.** Because few markers have yet been sufficiently validated for use in defining thresholds, not all changes in biomarkers related to air pollution should be considered adverse effects.
- **Quality of life.** Adverse effects of air pollution can range from watering, stinging eyes to cardiopulmonary symptoms, and even psychiatric conditions.
- **Physiological impact.** Physical effects of pollution can be transitory or permanent, and appear alone or accompanied by other symptoms. The ATS minimum requirement for considering pollution to have an adverse effect is reversible damage accompanied

The preparation of this chapter is assigned to the Environmental Health Committee.

by other symptoms (reversible damage alone is not sufficient). Also, effects such as developmental damage to lungs, or exacerbation of age-related decay in function, must be considered.

- **Symptoms.** Not all increased occurrences of symptoms are considered adverse effects of air pollution: only those diminishing an individual's quality of life or changing a patient's clinical status should be considered adverse.
- **Clinical outcomes.** Detectable effects of air pollution on clinical tests should be considered adverse.
- **Mortality.** Any increase in mortality should be judged adverse.
- **Population health versus individual risk.** Any increase in the risk of an exposed population should be considered adverse, even if there is no immediate, outright illness.

Definitions of comfort vary. Comfort encompasses perception of the environment (e.g., hot/cold, humid/dry, noisy/quiet, bright/dark) and a value rating of affective implications (e.g., too hot, too cold). Rohles et al. (1989) noted that acceptability may represent a more useful concept of evaluating occupant response, because it allows progression toward a concrete goal. Acceptability is the foundation of a number of standards covering thermal comfort and acoustics, as well as odor comfort. Nevertheless, acceptability varies between climatic regions and cultures, and may change over time as expectations change.

Concern about the health effects associated with indoor air dates back several hundred years, and has increased significantly in recent decades. During the 1970s and 1980s, this attention was mainly a result of concerns about radon and lung cancer, and about increased reporting by building occupants of complaints about poor health associated with exposure to indoor air or sick building syndrome (SBS). More recently, interest has largely focused on asthma, allergies, and airway infections.

SBS encompasses a number of adverse health symptoms related to occupancy in a "sick" building or room, including mucosal irritation, fatigue, headache, and, occasionally, lower respiratory symptoms, and nausea. Large field studies (EPA 2012; Skov and Valbjorn 1987; Sundell et al. 1994) have shed light on the causes. Widespread occurrence of these symptoms prompted the World Health Organization to classify SBS symptoms (WHO 1983):

- General symptoms, such as headache, tiredness, nausea
- Mucous membrane symptoms in the nose, eyes, or throat, including coughing, sensations of dryness
- Skin symptoms: redness, itching, on upper body parts

Sick building syndrome is characterized by an absence of routine physical signs and clinical laboratory abnormalities with regard to sensory irritation and neurotoxic symptoms, while skin symptoms often can be objectively verified. Some investigations have sought to correlate SBS symptoms with reduced neurological and physiological performance. In controlled studies, SBS symptoms can reduce performance in susceptible individuals (Mølhave et al. 1986).

Building-related illnesses (BRIs) have similar symptoms, but include physical signs and abnormalities that can be more easily clinically identified (e.g., hypersensitivity illnesses, including hypersensitivity pneumonitis, humidifier fever, asthma, and allergic rhinitis).

Some illnesses associated with exposure in indoor environments are listed in Table 1.

Table 1 Selected Illnesses Related to Exposure in Buildings

Illness	Physical Examination	Laboratory Testing	Linkage	Causes/Exposures
Allergic rhinitis	Stuffy/runny nose, postnasal drip, pale or erythematous mucosa	Anterior and posterior rhinomanometry, acoustic rhinometry, nasal lavage, biopsy, rhinoscopy, immunoassay (IgE) or skin prick testing	Immunologic skin prick or immunoassay (IgE) or in vitro testing	Pollen and dust mites are common examples
Asthma	Coughing, wheezing, episodic dyspnea, wheezing on examination, chest tightness, temporal pattern at work	Spirometry peak expiratory flow diary, methacholine challenge, exhaled NO	Immunology testing: skin prick or immunoassay (IgE); physiology testing*	Pet dander, mold, environmental tobacco smoke, and dust mites are common examples
Organic dust toxic syndrome	Cough, dyspnea, chest tightness, feverishness	DLCO, TLC	Temporal pattern related to work	Gram-negative bacteria or endotoxin
Hypersensitivity pneumonitis	Cough, dyspnea, myalgia, weakness, rales, clubbing, feverishness	DLCO, FVC, TLC, CXR, lung biopsy	Immunology testing: IgG antibody to agents present, challenge testing, physiology testing (in acute forms): spirometry, DLCO	Causative agents include thermophilic actinomycetes; molds; mixed amoebae, fungi, and bacteria; avian proteins; certain metals and chemicals
Contact dermatitis	Dry skin, itching, scaling skin	Scaling, rash, eczema, biopsy	Patch testing; allergy testing	
Urticaria (hives)	Multiple swollen raised itchy areas of skin	Inspection, biopsy	Provocation testing	Skin irritation, foods, heat/cold, direct pressure, sunlight, drugs
Eye irritation	Eye itching, irritation, dryness	Tear-film break-up time, conjunctival staining (fluorescein)	Temporal pattern	VOCs and particulate matter are common examples
Nasal irritation	Stuffy, congested nose, rhinitis	Acoustic rhinometry, posterior and anterior rhinomanometry, nasal lavage, nasal biopsy	Temporal pattern	VOCs and particulate matter are common examples
Central nervous system symptoms	Headache, fatigue, irritability, difficulty concentrating	Neuropsychological testing	Temporal pattern (epidemiology)	Chemical compounds, noise, lighting, work stress, and carbon monoxide are common examples
Legionnaires' disease, Aspergillosis, *Pseudomonas* infection	Pneumonia, high fever, organ dysfunction	Environmental surveillance (water system monitoring), *Legionella pneumophila* identification from patient	Organism isolated from patient and source; immunology testing	*Legionella* (and other microorganism)-contaminated aerosols from water sources
Pontiac fever	Non-pneumonic flulike illness	Environmental surveillance (water system monitoring)		Range of microorganisms, chemicals

*(1) 10% decrement in FEV_1 across workday,
(2) peak flow changes suggestive of work relatedness
(3) methacholine reactivity resolving after six weeks away from exposure

DLCO = single breath carbon monoxide diffusing capacity
FVC = forced vital capacity
TLC = total lung capacity
CXR = chest X-ray
IgE = immunoassay
IgG = class G immunoglobulins
FEV_1 = forced expiratory volume in the first second

1.1 HEALTH SCIENCES RELEVANT TO INDOOR ENVIRONMENT

The study of health effects in indoor environments involves a number of scientific disciplines. A few are briefly described here to further the engineer's understanding of which health sciences may be applicable to a given environmental health problem.

Epidemiology and Biostatistics

Epidemiology studies the causes, distribution, and control of disease in a population. It represents the application of quantitative methods to evaluate health-related events and effects. Epidemiology is traditionally subdivided into observational and analytical components; the focus may be descriptive, or may attempt to identify causal relationships. Some classical criteria for determining causal relationships in epidemiology are consistency, temporality, plausibility, specificity, strength of association, and dose/response (Hill 1965).

Observational epidemiology studies are generally performed with a defined group of interest because of a specific exposure or risk factor. A control group is selected on the basis of similar criteria, but without the exposure or risk factor present. A prospective study (cohort study) consists of observations of a specific group over a long time.

Examples of epidemiological investigations are cross-sectional, experimental, and case-control studies. Observations conducted at one point in time are considered cross-sectional studies. In experimental studies, individuals are selectively exposed to a specific agent or condition. These studies are performed with the consent of the participants unless the condition is part of the usual working condition and it is known to be harmless. Control groups must be observed in parallel. Case-control studies are conducted by identifying individuals with the condition of interest and comparing factors of interest in individuals without that condition.

Industrial, Occupational, and Environmental Medicine or Hygiene

Industrial or occupational hygiene is about anticipating, recognizing, evaluating, controlling, and preventing conditions that may lead to illness or injury, or affect the well-being of workers, consumers, and/or communities. Important aspects include identifying hazardous exposures and physical stressors, determining methods for collecting and analyzing contaminant samples, evaluating measurement results, and developing suitable control measures. Occupational hygienists work closely with toxicologists for understanding chemical hazards, physicists for physical hazards (e.g., ionizing radiation), and physicians and microbiologists for biological hazards.

Microbiology

Buildings are more than inanimate physical entities, masses of inert material that remain relatively stable over time. The building and its occupants, contents, and surroundings constitute a dynamic tetrad in which all elements affect each other. In fact, a building is a dynamic combination of physical, chemical, and biological dimensions. Buildings can be described and understood as complex systems. Some new approaches, based on the frameworks, tools, and methods used by ecologists to understand ecosystems, can help engineers understand the processes and microbes continually occurring indoors and how they affect the building's inhabitants, durability, and function (Bassler 2009; Humphries 2012).

Building scientists need to understand the complex and bidirectional relationship between the physical/chemical parameters of a building and the microbiology of that environment. Attempting to control a single parameter (e.g., temperature) to regulate the growth of a single microbe (e.g., mold), for example, does not address the complexity of the system.

Microbiologists must recognize the importance of understanding all of the environmental variables that are present in a given habitat. Simply collecting microbes from surfaces or materials in a structure is not enough to understand the organisms' behavior and relationships in the context of the building. Collecting appropriate information about the building (**metadata**) such as air turnover rates and material composition is essential to understanding the microbial communities that live inside it. Microbiologists must also be ever mindful of the need to distinguish between the occurrence of a microbe and the activity (metabolome) of a microbe or microbial community.

Culture-independent (genetic) methods of identifying microorganisms in microbiology are rapidly changing our understanding of the occurrence and nature of microbes in indoor environments [see Microbiology of the Built Environment network (www.microbe.net)]. These methods have increased tenfold the number of known bacteria over the past decade. Efforts to better understand the relationship between the indoor environment and its microbial ecology are yielding new knowledge about the complexity of the indoor environment as an ecosystem (Corsi et al. 2012).

Viruses require living cells for replication, so abiotic building components, strictly speaking, do not serve as a source of viruses. Viruses in buildings come from the building's occupants. Building components or systems can provide surfaces that facilitate transmission (e.g., doorknobs), and some viruses can become airborne. A substantial body of literature compares airborne and other routes of transmission; from a building design and operations standpoint, though, avoid generalizations because transmission routes are not the same for all viruses.

Empirical data (Lowen et al. 2007) demonstrate that some airborne viruses (e.g., influenza) are inactivated more quickly at high humidity, and that low humidity rapidly reduces the size of respiratory droplets, thereby prolonging time aloft. Maintaining humidity in the range deemed comfortable to a majority of occupants reduces these effects that favor influenza transmission.

Much of the literature on fungi focuses on temperature and moisture, with some emphasis on moisture and nutrient availability, although there is sufficient nutrient content on most indoor surfaces: fungi can grow even on what appears to be clean glass. There is less literature on the factors determining bacterial species and survival indoors, in spite of the growing interest in the hygiene hypothesis and humans' intimate relationships with both beneficial and harmful bacteria (e.g., probiotics). See Flanigan et al. (2001) for details.

Moisture on many surfaces supports the life, reproduction, and evolution of microorganisms. The microorganisms themselves produce chemicals, some of which can alter the pH of the surface and subsequent surface chemistry. Many additional microbes arrive on human skin, which sheds on a regular basis. Skin cells and the oils and other chemicals in and on them, as well the bacteria living on them, end up on the floor, furniture, and even the walls and windows.

When bacteria colonize stable surfaces, they often form complex communities. The structure and composition of these communities depend not only on the organisms present, but also on the conditions surrounding them: the moisture, chemicals, and other particles present on the surface or in the air nearby. Some of these communities may even develop into **biofilms**, which are very stable communities that are resistant to many antimicrobial compounds and can shelter pathogenic microbes. Bacterial communities sense the presence of other bacteria, and when they are enough of them to collectively affect their host, they all excrete chemicals that collectively affect the host and, in the case of human hosts, can make the bacteria more infectious (Bassler 2009).

Toxicology

Toxicology studies the influence of chemicals, particles, ultrafine particles, and bioaerosols on health. All chemical substances may function as toxins, but low concentrations prevent many, but not all, of them from being harmful. Defining which component of the structure of a chemical predicts the harmful effect is of fundamental importance in toxicology. A second issue is defining the dose/response relationships of a chemical and the exposed population. Dose may refer to delivered dose (exposure presented to the target tissue) or absorbed dose (the dose actually absorbed by the body and available for metabolism). For many substances, the time of exposure may be most important: low-level exposure during a specific week during pregnancy, for instance, may be critical, whereas higher doses later may have less of an effect.

Because permission to conduct exposure of human subjects in experimental conditions is difficult to obtain, most toxicological literature is based on animal studies. Isolated animal systems (e.g., homogenized rat livers, purified enzyme systems, other isolated living tissues) are used to study the effects of chemicals, but extrapolation between dose level effects from animals to humans is problematic.

1.2 HAZARD RECOGNITION, ANALYSIS, AND CONTROL

Hazard recognition and analysis are conducted to determine the presence of hazardous materials or conditions as sources of potential problems. Research, inspection, and analysis determine how a particular hazard affects health. Exposure assessment, an element of hazard recognition, relies on qualitative, semiquantitative, or quantitative approaches. In many situations, air sampling can determine whether a hazardous material is present. An appropriate sampling strategy must be used to ensure validity of collected samples, determining worst-case (for compliance) or usual (average) exposures. Air sampling can be conducted to determine **time-weighted average (TWA)** exposures, which cover a defined period of time, or **short-term exposures**, which determine the magnitude of exposures to materials that are acutely hazardous. Samples may be collected for a single substance or a multicomponent mixture. Hazard analysis also characterizes the potential skin absorption or ingestion hazards of an indoor environment. Analyses of bulk material samples and surface wipe samples are also used to determine whether hazardous conditions exist. Physical agent characterization may require direct-reading sampling methods. After collection and analysis, the results must be interpreted and an appropriate control strategy developed to control, reduce, or eliminate the hazard.

A main problem today is identifying which hazards, and particularly which chemical compounds, to study, although chemicals mimicking hormones (often female hormones) are increasingly of interest.

Hazards are generally grouped into one of the following four classes of environmental stressors:

- **Chemical hazards.** Routes of exposure to airborne chemicals are inhalation (aspiration), dermal (skin) contact, dermal absorption, and ingestion. The degree of risk from exposure depends on the nature and potency of the toxic effects; the endocrine effects; susceptibility of the person exposed; and timing, magnitude, and/or duration of exposure. Airborne contaminants are very important because of their ease of dispersal from sources and the risk of exposure through the lungs or skin. Airborne chemical hazards can be gaseous (vapors or gases) or particulate (e.g., dusts, fumes, mists, aerosols, fibers). Some chemicals, such as semivolatile organic compounds (SVOCs), are both gaseous and particulate. For more information, see Chapter 11.
- **Biological hazards.** Bacteria, viruses, fungi, and other living or nonliving organisms that can cause acute and chronic illness in building occupants are classified as biological hazards in indoor environments. Routes of exposure are inhalation, dermal (skin) contact, and ingestion. The degree of risk from exposure depends on the nature and potency of the biological hazard, susceptibility of the person exposed, and magnitude and duration of exposure.
- **Physical hazards.** These include excessive levels of ionizing and nonionizing electromagnetic radiation, noise, vibration, illumination, temperature, and force.
- **Ergonomic hazards.** Tasks that involve repetitive motions, require excessive force, or must be carried out in awkward postures can damage muscles, nerves, and joints.

Hazard Control

Strategies for controlling exposures in the indoor environment include substitution (removal of the hazardous substance), isolation, disinfection, dilution ventilation, and air cleaning. Not all measures may be applicable to all types of hazards, but all hazards can be controlled by using one of them. Personal protective equipment and engineering, work practice, and administrative controls are used to apply these methods. Source removal or substitution, customarily the most effective measure, is not always feasible. Engineering controls (e.g., ventilation, air cleaning) may be effective for a range of hazards. Local exhaust ventilation is more effective for controlling point-source contaminants than is general dilution ventilation.

Hazard Analysis and Control Processes. The goal of hazard analysis and control processes is to prevent harm to people from hazards associated with buildings. Quantitative hazard analysis and control processes are practical and cost-effective. Preventing disease from hazards requires facility managers and owners to answer three simple, site-specific questions:

- What is the hazard?
- How can it be prevented from harming people?
- How can it be verified that the hazard has been prevented from harming people?

Seven principles comprise effective hazard analysis and control:

- Use process flow diagrams to perform systematic hazard analysis.
- Identify critical control points (process steps at which the hazard can be eliminated or prevented from harming people).
- Establish hazard control critical limits at each critical control point.
- Establish a hazard control monitoring plan for critical limits at critical control points.
- Establish hazard control corrective actions for each critical limit.
- Establish procedures to document all activities and results.
- Establish procedures to confirm that the plan (1) actually works under operating conditions (**validation**), (2) is implemented properly (**verification**), and (3) is periodically reassessed.

2. AIRBORNE CONTAMINANTS

Many airborne contaminants cause problems in both industrial and nonindustrial indoor environments. These include biological and nonbiological particles [e.g., synthetic vitreous fibers, asbestos, environmental tobacco smoke (ETS), combustion nuclei, dust (including human skin scales)], bioaerosols, and chemical gases and vapors. Airborne contaminants may enter the building from the outdoors or be released indoors by processes, building materials, furnishings, equipment, or occupant activities. In industrial environments, airborne contaminants are usually associated with the type of process that occurs in a specific setting, and exposures may be determined relatively easily by air sampling. Airborne contaminants in nonindustrial environments may result from emissions and/or shedding of building materials and systems; originate in outdoor air; or result from building operating and maintenance programs, procedures, or conditions. In general, compared to industrial settings, nonindustrial environments include many more contaminants with the potential to contribute to health-related problems. These contaminants are usually present in lower concentrations and often are more difficult to identify. More information on contaminant types, characteristics, typical levels, and measurement methods is presented in Chapter 11.

2.1 PARTICLES

Particulate matter can be solid or liquid; typical examples include dust, smoke, fumes, and mists. **Dusts** are particles of a size and density that will settle; their behavior is affected mostly by gravity. **Smoke**, **fumes**, and **mists** contain mixtures of overlapping particle sizes, many in the smaller ranges (<~0.1 μm) where gravity is less important than temperature, particle charge, and other factors in determining how long particles remain aloft.

Fibers are solid particles with length several times greater than their diameter, such as asbestos, manufactured mineral fibers, synthetic vitreous fibers, and refractory ceramic fibers. Bioaerosols of concern to human health range from 0.5 to 30 μm in diameter, but generally bacterial and fungal aerosols range from 2 to 8 μm in diameter because of agglomeration or rafting of cells or spores (Lighthart 1994).

Units of Measurement. The quantity of particles in the air is frequently reported as the mass concentration or count concentration in a given volume of air. Mass concentration units are milligrams per cubic metre of air sampled (mg/m^3) or micrograms per cubic metre of air sampled ($\mu g/m^3$). For conversion, $1\ mg/m^3 = 1000\ \mu g/m^3$. Mass units are widely used in industrial environments because these units are used to express occupational exposure limits.

Count concentration units are usually expressed as counts per cubic foot, cubic centimetre (cc), or cubic metre, and are specified for a given range of particle diameter. Count concentration measurements are generally used in environments such as office buildings and industrial cleanrooms.

General Health Effects of Exposure. Health effects of airborne particulate matter depend on several factors, including particle dimension, durability, dose, and toxicity of materials in the particle. Respirable particles vary in size from <1 to 10 μm (Alpaugh and Hogan 1988). Methods for measuring airborne particles are discussed in Chapter 11. **Durability** (how long the particle can exist in the biological system before it dissolves or is transported from the system) and **dose** (amount of exposure encountered by the worker) both affect relative toxicity. In some instances, very low exposures can cause adverse health effects (hazardous exposures), and in others, seemingly high exposures may not cause any adverse health effects (nuisance exposures).

Safety and health professionals are primarily concerned with particles smaller than 2 μm. Particles larger than 8 to 10 μm in aerodynamic diameter are primarily separated and retained by the upper respiratory tract. Intermediate sizes are deposited mainly in the conducting airways of the lungs, from which they are rapidly cleared and swallowed or coughed out. About 50% or less of the particles in inhaled air settle in the respiratory tract. Submicron particles penetrate deeper into the lungs, but many do not deposit and are exhaled. Nanoparticles (<100 nm diameter) can enter the blood and be transported to the brain or other organs (Mühlfeld et al. 2008).

Industrial Environments

Exposures and Exposure Sources. In industrial environments, airborne particles are generated by work-related activities (e.g., adding batch ingredients for a manufacturing process, applying asphalt in a roofing operation, drilling an ore deposit in preparation for blasting). The engineer must recognize sources of particle generation to appropriately address exposure concerns. Dusts are generated by handling, crushing, or grinding, and may become airborne during generation or handling. Any industrial process that produces dust fine enough (about 10 μm) to remain in the air long enough to be inhaled or ingested should be regarded as potentially hazardous. In determining worker exposure, the nature of particles released by the activity, local air movement caused by makeup air and exhaust, and worker procedures should be assessed for a complete evaluation (Burton 2000).

Health Effects of Industrial Exposures. Pneumoconiosis is a fibrous hardening of the lungs caused by irritation from inhaling dust in industrial settings. The most commonly known pneumoconioses are asbestosis, silicosis, and coal worker's pneumoconiosis.

Asbestosis results from inhalation of asbestos fibers found in the work environment. The U.S. Department of Health and Human Services (ATSDR 2001) characterizes the toxicological and adverse health effects of asbestos and indicates that asbestos-induced respiratory disease can generally take 10 to 20 years to develop, although there is evidence that early cases of asbestosis can develop in five to six years when fiber concentrations are very high. Asbestos fibers cause fibrosis (scarring) of lung tissue, which clinically manifests itself as dyspnea (shortness of breath) and a nonproductive, irritating cough. Asbestos fiber is both dimensionally respirable and durable in the respiratory system.

Silicosis, probably the most common of all industrial occupational lung diseases, is caused by inhalation of silica dust. Workers with silicosis usually are asymptomatic, even in the early stages of massive fibrosis (Leathart 1972). It is not considered a problem in nonindustrial indoor environments.

Coal worker's pneumoconiosis (**CWP**, also known as "black lung") results from inhalation of dust generated in coal-mining operations. The dust is composed of a combination of carbon and varying percentages of silica (usually <10%) (Alpaugh and Hogan 1988). Because of the confined underground work environment, exposures can be very high at times, thus creating very high doses. Data show that workers may develop CWP at exposures below the current dust standard of 1 mg/m^3.

Exposure Standards and Criteria. In the United States, the Occupational Safety and Health Administration (OSHA) has established permissible exposure limits (PELs) for many airborne particles. PELs are published in the Code of Federal Regulations (29CFR1910.1000, 29CFR1926.1101) under the authority of the Department of Labor. Table 2 lists PELs for several common workplace particles.

Exposure Control Strategies. Particulate or dust control strategies include source elimination or enclosure, local exhaust, general dilution ventilation, wetting, filtration, and use of personal protective devices such as respirators.

The most effective way to control exposures to particles is to totally eliminate them from the work environment. The best dust control method is total enclosure of the dust-producing process, with negative pressure maintained inside the entire enclosure by exhaust ventilation (Alpaugh and Hogan 1988).

Local exhaust ventilation as an exposure control strategy is most frequently used where particles are generated either in large volumes or with high velocities (e.g., lathe and grinding operations). High-velocity air movement captures the particles and removes them from the work environment.

Table 2 OSHA Permissible Exposure Limits (PELs) for Particles[a]

Substance	CAS[b] #	PEL
Cadmium	7440-43-9	0.005 mg/m^3
Manganese fume	7439-96-5	1.0 mg/m^3
Plaster of Paris	Nuisance	10.0 mg/m^3
Emery	Nuisance	10.0 mg/m^3
Grain dust	Nuisance	10.0 mg/m^3
Crystalline silica (as quartz)	14808-60-7	0.1 mg/m^3
Asbestos	1332-21-4	0.1 $fibers/cm^3$
Total dust	Nuisance	15.0 mg/m^3

Data from CFR (29CFR1910.1000, 29CFR1926.1101).
[a]See CFR for current values. [b]Chemical Abstract Survey

General dilution ventilation in the work environment reduces particulate exposure. This type of ventilation is used when particulate sources are numerous and widely distributed over a large area. This strategy is often the least effective means of control, and may be very costly if conditioned (warm or cold) air is exhausted and unconditioned air is introduced without benefit of air-side energy recovery. Ventilation and local exhaust for industrial environments are discussed more thoroughly in Chapters 31 and 32 of the 2015 *ASHRAE Handbook—HVAC Applications*.

Filtration can be an effective control strategy and may be less expensive than general ventilation, although increased pressure drop across a filter can add to variable fan power requirements, and maintenance adds to system operating cost.

Using personal protective equipment (e.g., a respirator) is appropriate as a primary control during intermittent maintenance or cleaning activities when other controls are not feasible. Respirators can also supplement good engineering and work practice controls to increase employee protection and comfort (Alpaugh and Hogan 1988). Consultation with an industrial hygienist or other qualified health professional is needed to ensure proper selection, fit, and use of respirators.

Synthetic Vitreous Fibers

Exposures and Exposure Sources. Fibers are defined as slender, elongated structures with substantially parallel sides (as distinguished from a dust, which is more spherical). Synthetic vitreous fibers (SVFs) are inorganic fibrous materials such as glass wool, mineral wool (also known as rock and slag wool), textile glass fibers, and refractory ceramic fibers. These fibers are used primarily in thermal and acoustical insulation products, but are also used for filtration, fireproofing, and other applications. Human exposure to SVFs occurs mostly during manufacture, fabrication and installation, and demolition of those products, because the installed products do not result in airborne fiber levels that could produce significant consumer exposure. Simultaneous exposure to other dusts (e.g., asbestos during manufacture, demolition products and bioaerosols during demolition) is also important.

Health Effects of Exposure. Possible effects of SVFs on health include the following.

Cancer. In October 2001, an international review by the International Agency for Research on Cancer (IARC) reevaluated the 1988 IARC assessment of SVFs and insulation glass wool and rock wool. This resulted in a downgrading of the classification of these fibers from Group 2B (possible carcinogen) to Group 3 (not classifiable as to the carcinogenicity in humans). IARC noted specifically that "Epidemiologic studies published during the 15 years since the previous IARC *Monograph*'s review of these fibers in 1988 provide no evidence of increased risks of lung cancer or mesothelioma (cancer of the lining of the body cavities) from occupational exposures during manufacture of these materials, and inadequate evidence of any overall cancer risk." IARC retained the Group 2B classification for special-purpose glass fibers and refractory ceramic fibers, but its review indicated that many of the previous studies need to be updated and reevaluated, because they did not include the National Toxicology Program's Report on Carcinogens and the State of California's listing of substances known to cause cancer.

Dermatitis. SVFs may cause an irritant contact dermatitis with dermal contact and embedding in the skin, or local inflammation of the conjunctiva when fibers contact the eye. Resin binders sometimes used to tie fibers together have, on rare occasions, been associated with allergic contact dermatitis.

Exposure Standards and Criteria. OSHA has not adopted specific occupational exposure standards for SVFs. A voluntary workplace health and safety program has been established with fibrous glass and rock and slag wool insulation industries under OSHA oversight. This Health and Safety Partnership Program established an 8 h, time-weighted average permissible exposure limit of 1 fiber per cubic centimetre for respirable SVFs.

Exposure Control Strategies. As with other particles, SVF exposure control strategies include engineering controls, work practices, and use of personal protective devices. Appropriate intervention strategies focus on source control.

Combustion Nuclei

Exposures and Sources. Combustion products include water vapor, carbon dioxide, heat, oxides of carbon and nitrogen, and combustion nuclei. Combustion nuclei, defined in this chapter as particulate products of combustion, can be hazardous in many situations. They may contain potential carcinogens such as polycyclic aromatic hydrocarbons (PAHs).

Polycyclic aromatic compounds (PACs) are the nitrogen-, sulfur-, and oxygen-heterocyclic analogs of PAHs and other related PAH derivatives. Depending on their relative molecular mass and vapor pressure, PACs are distributed between vapor and particle phases. In general, combustion particles are smaller (0.01 to 4 μm) than mechanically generated dusts.

Typical sources of combustion nuclei are tobacco smoke, fossil-fuel-based heating devices (e.g., unvented space heaters and gas ranges), and flue gas from improperly vented gas- or oil-fired furnaces and wood-burning fireplaces or stoves. Infiltration of outdoor combustion contaminants can also be a significant source of these contaminants in indoor air. Therefore, combustion nuclei are important in both industrial and nonindustrial settings.

Exposure Standards and Criteria. OSHA established exposure limits for several carcinogens categorized as combustion nuclei [i.e., benzo(a)pyrene, cadmium, nickel, benzene, *n*-nitrosodimethylamine]. These limits are established for industrial work environments and are not directly applicable to general indoor air situations. Underlying atherosclerotic heart disease may be exacerbated by carbon monoxide (CO) exposures.

Exposure Control Strategies. Exposure control strategies for combustion nuclei are similar in many ways to those for other particles. For combustion nuclei derived from space heating, air contamination can be avoided by proper installation and venting of equipment to ensure that these contaminants cannot enter the work or personal environment. Proper equipment maintenance is also essential to minimize exposures to combustion nuclei.

Particles in Nonindustrial Environments

Exposures and Sources. In the nonindustrial indoor environment, particle concentrations are greatly affected by the outdoor environment. Diesel engines emit large quantities of fine particulate matter. Indoor particle sources may include cleaning, resuspension of particles from carpets and other surfaces, construction and renovation debris, paper dust, deteriorated insulation, office equipment, and combustion processes (including cooking stoves, fires, and environmental tobacco smoke).

Although **asbestos** is commonly found in buildings constructed before the 1970s, it generally does not represent a respiratory hazard except to individuals who actively disturb it during maintenance and construction.

An important source of particulates, **environmental tobacco smoke (ETS)** from cigarettes consists of exhaled mainstream smoke from the smoker and, with conventional cigarettes, the sidestream smoke emitted from the smoldering tobacco. Approximately 70 to 90% of ETS results from sidestream smoke, which has a chemical composition somewhat different from mainstream smoke. More than 4700 compounds have been identified in laboratory-based studies, including known human toxic and carcinogenic compounds such as carbon monoxide, ammonia, formaldehyde, nicotine, tobacco-specific nitrosamines, benzo(a)pyrene, benzene, cadmium, nickel, and aromatic amines. Many of these constituents are more concentrated in sidestream smoke than in mainstream smoke (Glantz and Parmley 1991). In studies conducted in residences and office buildings with tobacco smoking permitted, ETS was a substantial source of many gaseous and particulate PACs (Offermann et al. 1991).

Increased use of electronic cigarettes (e-cigarettes or e-cigs) and vaping has generated a new potential concern for indoor air quality. Data are still limited on potential exposures and human health risks posed by the use of e-cigarettes indoors, especially among bystanders from secondhand and third-hand exposures (AIHA 2014). Although the literature generally supports findings that e-cigarette emissions and exposure risks are much less harmful than tobacco smoke (AIHA 2014), emissions from these devices are not contaminant free. Nicotine is present in most forms of e-cigarettes, but the concentration can vary greatly and has also been found in some products identified as not containing nicotine (Burstyn 2013; Czogala et al. 2013; FDA 2009; Villa et al. 2012). Propylene glycol and vegetable glycerin are used as delivery vehicles for nicotine and various flavoring ingredients, which can break down into acrolein, formaldehyde, and acetaldehyde in the vapor (Geiss et al. 2014; Goniewicz et al. 2013; Lauterbach et al. 2012; Uchiyama et al. 2013). Flavorings used in e-cigarettes are typically considered safe for food or ingestion, but the health effects of inhaling them as vapors have not thoroughly been evaluated (AIHA 2014; Offerman 2014). Characterizing the differences in exposure from traditional cigarettes and from e-cigarettes is an active area of research.

Health Effects of Exposure. The health effects of exposure to combustion nuclei depend on many factors, including concentration, toxicity, and individual susceptibility or sensitivity to the particular substance. Combustion-generated PACs include many PAHs and nitro-PAHs that have been shown to be carcinogenic in animals (NAS 1983). Other PAHs are biologically active as tumor promoters and/or cocarcinogens. Mumford et al. (1987) reported high exposures to PAH and aza-arenes for a population in China with very high lung cancer rates.

According to the U.S. EPA (2005) fine particulate matter (particles less than 2.5 μm in diameter, or $PM_{2.5}$) is associated with lung disease, asthma, and other respiratory problems. Short-term exposure may cause shortness of breath, eye and lung irritation, nausea, light-headedness, and possible allergy aggravations.

$PM_{2.5}$ has been calculated to have the highest impact on health of studied chronic air pollutants inhaled in residences. The metric used was the disability-adjusted life years (DALYs). DALYs are a measure of the morbidity (disability) and mortality (death) caused by exposure to contaminants or other risks. $PM_{2.5}$ accounts for nearly 90% of the DALYs lost through chronic air pollutants inhaled in residences. Additional contaminants in descending importance ranked by DALYs are secondhand smoke (SHS), radon (for smokers), formaldehyde (a major source is composite wood products), and acrolein (a major source is cooking fats) (Logue et al. 2011, 2012). This type of analysis provides a rationale as well as a value that can be monetized to guide practitioners and researchers in determining which indoor contaminants are most important for control. From this analysis, $PM_{2.5}$ is clearly the obvious first target in indoor air quality: it is the dominant contaminant of concern in most residences, and one of the easiest and least expensive to control (primarily with filtration with higher-efficiency filters).

ETS has been shown to be causally associated with lung cancer in adults and respiratory infections, asthma exacerbations, middle ear effusion (DHHS 1986; NRC 1986), and low birth weight (Martin and Bracken 1986). The U.S. Environmental Protection Agency classifies ETS as a known human carcinogen (EPA 1992). Health effects can also include heart disease, headache, and irritation. ETS is also a cause of sensory irritation and annoyance (odors and eye irritation).

Table 3 Primary and Secondary Standards for Particle Pollution

	Time Span	Primary	Secondary	Notes
$PM_{2.5}$	Annual	12 μg/m³	15 μg/m³	Annual mean, averaged over three years.
	24 h	35 μg/m³		98th percentile, averaged over three years.
PM_{10}	24 h	150 μg/m³		Not to be exceeded more than once per year on average over three years.

Exposure Standards. There are no established exposure guidelines for particles in nonindustrial indoor environments. The EPA's National Ambient Air Quality standard (NAAQS) established primary and secondary standards for particle pollution. **Primary standards** provide public health protection, including protecting the health of sensitive populations such as asthmatics, children, and the elderly. **Secondary standards** provide public welfare protection, including protection against decreased visibility and damage to animals, crops, vegetation, and buildings. Table 3 gives information on primary and secondary standards for $PM_{2.5}$ and PM_{10}.

Exposure Control Strategies. Particulate or dust control strategies for the nonindustrial environment include source elimination or reduction, good housekeeping, general dilution ventilation, and upgraded filtration. In general, source control is preferred. Combustion appliances must be properly vented and maintained. If a dust problem exists, identify the type of dust to develop an appropriate intervention strategy. Damp dusting and high-efficiency vacuum cleaners may be considered. Building spaces under construction or renovation should be properly isolated from occupied spaces to limit transport of dust and other contaminants. Minimizing idling of diesel-powered vehicles near buildings can reduce entry of fine particulate matter.

Control of ETS has been accomplished primarily through regulatory mandates on the practice of tobacco smoking indoors. Most U.S. states and E.U. member states have passed laws to control tobacco smoking in at least some public places, including public buildings, restaurants, and workplaces, and the FAA (2000) has prohibited smoking on all flights to and from the United States, as have many airlines throughout the world. Where tobacco smoking is permitted, appropriate local and general dilution ventilation can be used for control; however, the efficacy of ventilation is unproven (Repace 1984). Some studies indicate that extremely high ventilation rates may be needed to dilute secondhand smoke to minimal risk levels (Repace and Lowrey 1985, 1993).

Bioaerosols

Bioaerosols are airborne biological particles derived from viruses, bacteria, fungi, protozoa, algae, mites, plants, insects, and their by-products, fragments, and cell mass components. Bioaerosols are present in both indoor and outdoor environments. For the indoor environment, locations that provide appropriate temperature and moisture conditions and a food source for biological growth may become problematic.

In microbiology, **reservoirs** allow microorganisms to survive, **amplifiers** allow them to proliferate, and **disseminators** effectively distribute bioaerosols. Building components and systems may have only one factor, or all three; for instance, a cooling tower is an ideal location for growth and dispersal of microbial contaminants and can be the reservoir, amplifier, and disseminator for *Legionella* (harboring microorganisms in scale, allowing them to proliferate, and generating an aerosol).

Both the physical and biological properties of bioaerosols need to be understood. For a microorganism to cause illness in building occupants, it must be transported in sufficient dose to a susceptible occupant. Airborne infectious particles behave physically in the same way as any other aerosol-containing particles with similar size, density, and electrostatic charge. The major difference is that bioaerosols may cause disease by several mechanisms (infection, allergic disease, immunomodulation, irritation, toxicosis), depending on the organism, dose, and susceptibility of the exposed population. Although microorganisms exist normally in indoor environments, the presence of abundant moisture and nutrients in interior spaces results in the growth of fungi, bacteria, protozoa, algae, or even nematodes (Arnow et al. 1978; Morey and Jenkins 1989; Morey et al. 1986; Strindehag et al. 1988). Thus, humidifiers, water spray systems, and wet porous surfaces can be reservoirs and sites for growth. Excessive air moisture (Burge 1995) and floods (Hodgson et al. 1985) can also result in proliferation of these microorganisms indoors. Turbulence associated with the start-up of air-handling unit plenums may also elevate concentrations of bacteria and fungi in occupied spaces (Buttner and Stetzenbach 1999; Yoshizawa et al. 1987).

Building Surface and Material Sources. Floors and floor coverings can be reservoirs for organisms that are subsequently resuspended into the air. Routine activity, including walking and vacuuming (Buttner et al. 2002), may even promote resuspension (Cox 1987). Some viruses may persist up to eight weeks on nonporous surfaces (Mbithi et al. 1991).

Building Water System Sources. Although potable water is usually delivered to buildings free of biological hazards, once the water enters the facility it becomes the responsibility of facility managers and owners to ensure that its microbial and chemical quality does not degrade. In fact, biological hazards associated with processes in building water systems cause considerable disease. Most cases of legionellosis, for example, result from exposure to potable water in buildings (McCoy 2005; WHO 2007).

Nonpotable water is a well-known source of infective agents and of noninfective biological particles. Baylor et al. (1977) demonstrated the sequestering of small particles by foam and their subsequent dispersal through bubble bursting. This dispersal may take place in surf, river sprays, or artificial sources such as whirlpools.

Building Occupant Sources. People are an important source of bacteria and viruses in indoor air. Infected humans can release virulent agents from skin lesions or disperse them by coughing, sneezing, or talking. Other means for direct release include sprays of saliva and respiratory secretions during dental and respiratory therapy procedures. Large droplets can transmit infectious particles to those close to the disseminator, and smaller particles can remain airborne for short or very long distances (Moser et al. 1979). Droplet nuclei can be transported over long distances, resulting in infection transmission, as shown by studies of SARS in Hong Kong (Li et al. 2005a, 2005b). Studies of student dorms found lower ventilation associated with higher incidence of infectious diseases (Sun et al. 2011).

Health Effects. The presence of microorganisms in indoor environments may cause infective and/or allergic building-related illnesses (Burge 1989; Morey and Feeley 1988). Some microorganisms under certain conditions may produce microbial volatile organic chemicals (MVOCs) (Hyppel 1984; Mason et al. 2010) that are malodorous. Microorganisms must remain viable to cause infection, although nonviable particles may promote an allergic disease, which is an immunological response. An organism that does not remain virulent in the airborne state cannot cause infection, regardless of how many units of organisms are deposited in the human respiratory tract. Virulence depends on factors such as relative humidity, temperature, oxygen, pollutants, ozone, and ultraviolet light (Burge 1995), each of which can affect survival and virulence differently for different microorganisms. Harmful chemicals and fragments produced by microorganisms can also cause irritant responses and carry biologically active metabolites (e.g., allergens, ligands) that trigger inflammatory immune responses (Drummond and Brown 2011; Green et al. 2005).

A wide variety of bacteria, fungi, and protozoa are prevalent in building water systems and can cause disease by transmission through water and air. Clinically important microorganisms known to cause disease in health care facilities include the bacteria *Legionella*, *Pseudomonas*, and *Mycobacterium*; the fungi *Aspergillus* and *Fusarium*; and the protozoa *Cryptosporidium*, *Giardia*, and *Acanthamoeba*.

Fungal Pathogens. Many fungal genera are widely distributed in nature and are common in the soil and on decaying vegetation, dust, and other organic debris (Levetin 1995). Fungi that have a filamentous structure are called **molds**, and reproduce by spores. Mold spores are small (2 to 10 μm in diameter), readily dispersed by water splash and air currents, and may remain airborne for long periods of time (Lighthart and Stetzenbach 1994; Streifel et al. 1989).

Dampness and mold growth/colonization in buildings have long been thought to cause increased health problems for occupants (Institute of Medicine 2004). In recent decades, multiple high-profile incidents have generated great public concern about mold in buildings, but also conflicting opinions on which health effects can be caused by dampness and mold, and on how to determine the level of risk in a building. Published reviews and meta-analyses of the scientific literature have clarified the available scientific basis for defining these health risks (Bornehag et al. 2001; Fisk et al. 2007, 2010; Institute of Medicine 2004; Kreiger et al. 2010; Mendell et al. 2011; WHO 2009).

Health studies have led to a consensus among health scientists that the presence in buildings of (1) visible water damage, (2) damp materials, (3) visible mold growth/colonization, or (4) mold odor indicates an increased risk of respiratory disease for occupants. In addition, evidence is accumulating that the more extensive, widespread, or severe these indicators, the greater the health risks. Known health risks include development of asthma, allergies, and respiratory infections; triggering of asthma attacks; and increased wheeze, cough, difficulty breathing, and other symptoms. Associations with other kinds of health effects have not been substantiated, but also have not been ruled out. Available information also suggests that children are more sensitive to dampness and mold than adults. The specific dampness-related agents that cause these respiratory health effects, whether molds, bacteria, other microbial agents, or dampness-related chemical emissions, have not been identified.

There also is consensus that the traditional methods used to measure molds in air or dust do not reliably predict increased health risks. Some newer methods of measuring mold, although promising, have not been proven to be better predictors of health effects than simply assessing the presence of evident dampness or mold growth/colonization. Therefore, current practices for the collection, analysis, and interpretation of environmental samples for mold-derived aerosols cannot be used to quantify health risks posed by dampness and mold growth/colonization in buildings or to guide health-based actions. Also, current consensus does not justify the differentiation of some molds as toxic or especially hazardous to healthy individuals. The only types of evidence that have been related consistently to adverse health effects are the presence of current or past water damage, damp materials, visible mold, and mold odor, *not* the number or type of mold spores or the presence of other markers of mold growth/colonization in indoor air or dust.

Bacterial Pathogens. Diseases produced by the bacterial genus ***Legionella*** are collectively called legionelloses. More than 45 species have been identified, with over 20 isolated from both environmental and clinical sources. Conditions favorable for *Legionella* spp. growth include water temperatures of 77 to 108°F; stagnant conditions; presence of scale, sediment, and biofilms; and the presence of amoebas (Geary 2000). Diseases produced by *Legionella pneumophila* include Legionnaires' disease (pneumonia form) and

Pontiac fever (flulike form). *L. pneumophila* serogroup 1 is the most frequently isolated from nature and most frequently associated with disease. Infection rates are affected by the strain of *L. pneumophila* as well as host condition (e.g., tobacco smoking, excessive weight, age). Legionellosis is not rare, but it is rarely diagnosed, and is severely underreported, often lost among other causes of pneumonia. McCoy (2006) estimated that, every day in the United States, an average of about 11 people die from legionellosis, and another 57 are infected but survive, often with lifelong debilitation.

In a review of waterborne infections from building water systems, it was estimated that 1400 deaths occur each year in the United States from *Pseudomonas aeruginosa*, another waterborne bacteria commonly found in building water systems (Anaissie et al. 2002).

Viral Pathogens. Outbreaks of infection in indoor air may also be caused by **viruses**. Viruses are readily disseminated from infected individuals, but cannot reproduce outside a host cell. Therefore, they do not reproduce in building structures or air-handling components, but can be distributed throughout buildings through duct systems and on air currents. Human-to-human dispersal is common. In one example, most of the passengers in an airline cabin developed influenza following exposure to one acutely ill person (Moser et al. 1979). In this case, the plane had been parked on a runway for several hours with the ventilation system turned off. Severe acute respiratory syndrome (SARS), caused by a corona virus similar to the common cold, was assumed to result from large droplet transmission; however, in an outbreak in a high-rise apartment, airborne transmission was the primary mode of disease spread, likely through dissemination from a bathroom drain (Yu et al. 2004). Ventilation and airflows in buildings were shown to affect the transmission of SARS in this outbreak and another outbreak in a hospital ward (Li et al. 2005a, 2005b).

Infectious diseases are transmitted through three primary routes: (1) direct contact and fomites (i.e., inanimate objects that transport infectious organisms from one individual to another), (2) large droplets [generally with a mass median aerodynamic diameter (MMAD) > 10 μm], and (3) fine particles, sometimes called *droplet nuclei* (MMAD < 10 μm) (Mandell et al. 1999). Routes of disease transmission that are not related to the environment or to buildings (e.g., blood-borne, insect vectored) exist, but are beyond the scope of this chapter. Table 4 lists infections considered transmissible by air.

Nonviable Biological Substances. **Allergic reactions** are an immunological response to foreign glycol proteins. The causes of the rapid increase in allergies all over the world are not known, but indoor exposures to new chemicals (e.g., plasticisers, flame retardants, biocides, cleaning products) and alterations to the gut microflora driving immunomodulation are suspected, as well as reduced ventilation. When a person has acquired an allergy, an acute attack may develop after dermal contact or inhalation of particles containing allergens (e.g., enzymes, mite and cockroach excreta, pet dander, pollen). The severity of immunological reactions to bioaerosols can vary dramatically, from discomfort (allergic rhinitis and sinusitis) to life-threatening asthma. Allergy testing in conjunction with a carefully obtained history may be helpful in identifying an offending agent. In cases of more severe illness, it may be necessary to remove an affected individual from exposure, even after appropriate abatement and exposure control methods have been instituted in the building, though this is the purview of the clinicians, and not of building professionals.

Exposure Guidelines for Bioaerosols. At present, numerical guidelines for bioaerosol exposure in indoor environments and for infectious pathogens that can spread via airborne routes are not available for the following reasons (Morey 1990):

- Incomplete data on background concentrations and types of microorganisms indoors, especially as affected by geographical, seasonal, and building parameters
- Incomplete understanding of and ability to measure routes of exposure, internal dose, and intermediate and ultimate clinical effects
- Absence of epidemiological data relating bioaerosol exposure indoors to illness
- Enormous variability in types of microbial particles, including viable cells, dead spores, toxins, antigens, MVOCs, and viruses
- Large variation in human susceptibility to microbial particles, making estimates of health risk difficult

Exposure Control Strategies. Because of the wide variety of pathogens and sources, a range of bioaerosol exposure control strategies may be required. Typically, these strategies should focus on source control (including good housekeeping and proper HVAC system operation and maintenance), but dilution ventilation, local exhaust ventilation, disinfection procedures, space pressure control, and filtration may also be considered.

Moisture control is the key to mold growth/colonization control. Molds need both food and water to survive; because molds can digest most things, water is the key factor that limits mold growth. The presence of **water damage**, **dampness**, **visible mold**, or **mold odor** in schools, workplaces, residences, and other indoor environments is unhealthy. It is not recommended to measure indoor microorganisms or the presence of specific microorganisms to attempt to determine the level of health hazard or the need for urgent remediation. Instead, address water damage, dampness, visible mold, and mold odor by (1) identifying and correcting the **source of water** that may allow microbial growth or contribute to other problems, (2) rapidly drying or removing **damp materials**, and (3) cleaning or removing **mold colonies and mold-colonized (moldy) materials**, as rapidly and safely as possible, to protect the health and well being of building occupants, especially children. More detailed information may be found in Harriman et al. (2001) and ASHRAE's (2003) *Mold and Moisture Management in Buildings*.

ASHRAE *Standard* 188 and *Guideline* 12 provides environmental and operational guidance for safe operation of building water systems to minimize the risk of Legionnaires' disease.

2.2 GASEOUS CONTAMINANTS

Gaseous contaminants include both true gases (which have boiling points less than room temperature) and vapors of liquids with boiling points above normal indoor temperatures. It also includes both volatile organic compounds and inorganic air contaminants.

Volatile organic compounds (VOCs) include 4- to 16-carbon alkanes, chlorinated hydrocarbons, alcohols, aldehydes, ketones, esters, terpenes, ethers, aromatic hydrocarbons (such as benzene and toluene), and heterocyclic hydrocarbons. Also included are chlorofluorocarbons (CFCs) and hydrochlorofluorocarbons (HCFCs), which are still used as refrigerants in existing installations, although production and importation have been phased out for environmental protection (Calm and Domanski 2004). More information on classifications, characteristics, and measurement methods can be found in Chapter 11.

Inorganic gaseous air contaminants include ammonia, nitrogen oxides, ozone, sulfur dioxide, carbon monoxide, and carbon dioxide. Although the last two contain carbon, they are by tradition regarded as inorganic chemicals.

The most common units of measurement for gaseous contaminants are parts per million by volume (ppm) and milligrams per cubic metre (mg/m^3). For smaller quantities, parts per billion (ppb) and micrograms per cubic metre ($\mu g/m^3$) are used. The relationship between these units of measure is also described in Chapter 11.

Industrial Environments

Exposures and Sources. In the industrial environment, a wide variety of gaseous contaminants may be emitted as process

Table 4 Pathogens with Potential for Airborne Transmission

Pathogen	Aerosol Route of Transmission
Anthrax	Inhalation of spores
Arenaviruses	Inhalation of small particle aerosols from rodent excreta
Aspergillosis	Inhalation of airborne conidia (spores)
Blastomycosis	Conidia, inhaled in spore-laden dust
Brucellosis	Inhalation of airborne bacteria
Chickenpox/shingles (*Varicella zoster* virus)	Droplet or airborne spread of vesicle fluid or respiratory tract secretions
Coccidioidomycosis	Inhalation of infective arthroconidia
Adenovirus	Transmitted through respiratory droplets
Enteroviruses (Coxsackie virus)	Aerosol droplet spread
Cryptococcosis	Presumably by inhalation
Human parvovirus	Contact with infected respiratory secretions
Rotavirus	Possible respiratory spread
Norwalk virus	Airborne transmission from fomites
Hantavirus	Presumed aerosol transmission from rodent excreta
Histoplasmosis	Inhalation of airborne conidia
Influenza	Airborne spread predominates
Lassa virus	Aerosol contact with excreta of infected rodents
Legionellosis	Epidemiological evidence supports airborne transmission
Lymphocytic choriomeningitis	Oral or respiratory contact with virus contaminated excreta, food, or dust
Measles	Airborne by droplet spread
Melioidosis	Inhalation of soil dust
Meningitis (*Neisseria meningitidis*)	Respiratory droplets from nose and throat
(*Haemophilus influenzae*)	Droplet infection and discharges from nose and throat
(*Streptococcus pneumoniae*)	Droplet spread and contact with respiratory secretions
Mumps	Airborne transmission or droplet spread
Nocardia	Acquired through inhalation
Paracoccidioidomycosis	Presumably through inhalation of contaminated soil or dust
Whooping cough (*Bordetella pertussis*)	Direct contact with discharges from respiratory mucous membranes of infected persons by the airborne route
Plague (*Yersinia pestis*)	Rarely airborne droplets from human patients. In the case of deliberate use, plague bacilli would possibly be transmitted as an aerosol.
Pneumonia (*Streptococcus pneumoniae*)	Droplet spread
(*Mycoplasma pneumoniae*)	Probably droplet inhalation
(*Chlamydia pneumoniae*)	Possibilities include airborne spread
Psittacosis (*Chlamydia psittaci*)	Inhalation of agent from desiccated droppings, secretions, and dust from feathers of infected birds
Q fever (*Coxiella burnetti*)	Commonly through airborne dissemination of *Coxiellae* in dust
Rabies	Airborne spread has been demonstrated in a cave where bats were roosting, and in laboratory settings, but this occurs very rarely.
Rhinitis/common cold (rhinovirus, coronavirus, parainfluenza, respiratory syncytial virus)	Presumably inhalation of airborne droplets
Rubella	Droplet spread
Smallpox (*Variola major*)	Via respiratory tract (droplet spread)
Sporotrichosis	Pulmonary sporotrichosis presumably arises through inhalation of conidia
Staphylococcal diseases	Airborne spread rare, but has been demonstrated in patients with associated viral respiratory disease
Streptococcal diseases	Large respiratory droplets. Individuals with acute upper respiratory tract (especially nasal) infections are particularly likely to transmit infection.
Toxoplasmosis	Inhalation of sporulated oocysts was associated with one outbreak
Tuberculosis	Exposure to tubercle bacilli in airborne droplet nuclei
Tularaemia (*Francisella tularensis*)	By inhalation of dust from contaminated soil, grain, or hay

Source: Tang et al. (2006).
Note: Virtually all these pathogens are also transmissible by direct contact. Pathogens in **bold** are those considered to have potential for long-distance airborne transmission.

by-products (e.g., paints, solvents, and welding fumes) or as accidental spills and releases.

Health Effects of Industrial Exposures. Given that tens of thousands of contaminants are regularly used by industry, possible health effects can range from mild skin or eye irritation and headaches, to failure of major organs or systems and death.

Exposure standards and specific health effects for various industrial contaminants are discussed in the following section.

Exposure Standards. Occupational exposure standards or legal concentration limits are established by a country or by a widely recognized organization like the WHO, with specific clarifications or recommendations for each state, province, or territory. In the United States, the Occupational Safety and Health Administration (OSHA) sets permissible exposure limits (PELs) for toxic and hazardous substances, which are enforceable workplace regulatory standards. These are published yearly in the *Code of Federal Regulations* (29CFR1910, Subpart Z) and intermittently in the *Federal Register*. Most of the regulatory levels were derived from those recommended by the American Conference of Governmental Industrial Hygienists (ACGIH) and Agency for Toxic Substances and Disease Registry (ATSDR). The health effects on which these standards were based can be found in their publications. ACGIH reviews data on a regular basis and publishes annual revisions to their Threshold Limit Values (TLVs®).

The National Institute for Occupational Safety and Health (NIOSH), a research agency of the U.S. Department of Health and Human Service, conducts research and makes recommendations to prevent work-related illness and injury. NIOSH publishes the *Registry of Toxic Effects and Chemical Substances* (RTECS), as well as numerous criteria on recommended standards for occupational exposures. Some compounds not listed by OSHA are covered by NIOSH, and their recommended exposure limits (RELs) are sometimes lower than the legal requirements set by OSHA. The NIOSH *Pocket Guide to Chemical Hazards* (NIOSH 2007) condenses these references and is a convenient reference for engineering purposes.

The harmful effects of gaseous pollutants depend on both short-term peak concentrations and the time-integrated exposures received by the person. OSHA defined three periods for concentration averaging and assigned allowable levels that may exist in these categories in workplaces for over 490 compounds, mostly gaseous contaminants. Abbreviations for concentrations for the three averaging periods are

AMP = acceptable maximum peak (for a short exposure)
ACC = acceptable ceiling concentration (not to be exceeded during an 8 h shift, except for periods where an AMP applies)
TWA8 = time-weighted average (not to be exceeded in any 8 h shift of a 40 h week)

The respective levels are presented in Tables Z-1, Z-2, and Z-3 of 29CFR1910.1000, *Occupational safety and health standards: Air contaminants*.

In non-OSHA literature, the AMP is sometimes called a short-term exposure limit (STEL), and a TWA8 is sometimes called a threshold limit value (TLV). NIOSH (1997) also lists values for the toxic limit that is immediately dangerous to life and health (IDLH).

Standards differ for industrial and nonindustrial environments (EHD 1987). A Canadian National Task Force developed guideline criteria for residential indoor environments (Health Canada 2010), and the World Health Organization (WHO) published indoor air quality guidelines for Europe (WHO 2010). Table 5 compares some of these guidelines with occupational criteria for selected contaminants.

Exposure Control Strategies. Gaseous contaminant control strategies include eliminating or reducing sources, local exhaust, general dilution ventilation, and using personal protective devices such as respirators. The most effective control strategy is source control. If source control is not possible, local exhaust ventilation can often be the most cost-effective method of controlling airborne contaminants. General dilution ventilation is often the least effective means of control. Ventilation and local exhaust for industrial environments are discussed more thoroughly in Chapters 31 and 32 of the 2015 *ASHRAE Handbook—HVAC Applications*.

Nonindustrial Environments

Gaseous contaminants of concern in nonindustrial environments include organic compounds, refrigerants, and inorganic gases.

Volatile Organic Compounds.

Sources. Indoor sources of VOCs include building materials, furnishings, cleaning products, office and HVAC equipment, ETS [including products from e-cigarettes (vaping)], marijuana smoke, and people and their personal care products. Outdoor sources of VOCs may also enter the building through various airflow paths, including intake air and infiltration through the building envelope.

Health Effects. Potential adverse health effects of VOCs in nonindustrial indoor environments are not well understood, but may include (1) irritant effects, including perception of unpleasant odors, mucous membrane irritation, and exacerbation of asthma; (2) systemic effects, such as fatigue and difficulty concentrating; and (3) toxic, chronic effects, such as carcinogenicity (Girman 1989).

Chronic adverse health effects from VOC exposure are of concern because some VOCs commonly found in indoor air are human (benzene) or animal (chloroform, trichloroethylene, carbon tetrachloride, p-dichlorobenzene) carcinogens. Some other VOCs are also genotoxic. Theoretical risk assessment studies suggest that risk from chronic VOC exposures in residential indoor air is greater than that associated with exposure to VOCs in the outdoor air or in drinking water (McCann et al. 1987; Tancrede et al. 1987).

A biological model for acute human response to low levels of VOCs indoors is based on three mechanisms: sensory perception of the environment, weak inflammatory reactions, and environmental stress reaction (Mølhave 1991). A growing body of literature summarizes measurement techniques for the effects of VOCs on nasal (Koren 1990; Koren et al. 1992; Meggs 1994; Mølhave et al. 1993; Ohm et al. 1992) and ocular (Franck et al. 1993; Kjaergaard 1992; Kjaergaard et al. 1991) mucosa. It is not well known how different sensory receptions to VOCs are combined into perceived comfort and the sensation of air quality. This perception is apparently related to stimulation of the olfactory sense in the nasal cavity, the gustatory sense on the tongue, and the common chemical sense (Cain 1989; Mølhave 1991).

Cometto-Muñiz and Cain (1994a, 1994b) addressed the independent contribution of the trigeminal and olfactory nerves to the detection of airborne chemicals. Smell is experienced through olfactory nerve receptors in the nose. Nasal pungency, described as common chemical sensations such as prickling, irritation, tingling, freshness, stinging, and burning, is experienced through nonspecialized receptors of the trigeminal nerve in the face. Odor and pungency thresholds follow different patterns related to chemical concentration. Odor is often detected at much lower levels. A linear correlation between pungency thresholds of homologous series (of alcohols, acetates, ketones, and alkylbenzenes, all relatively nonreactive agents) suggests that nasal pungency relies on a physicochemical interaction with a susceptible biophase within the cell membrane. Through this nonspecific mechanism, low, subthreshold levels of a wide variety of VOCs, as found in many polluted indoor environments, may be additive in sensory impact to produce noticeable sensory irritation.

Exposure Standards. Few standards exist for exposure to VOCs in nonindustrial indoor environments. NIOSH, OSHA, and ACGIH have regulatory standards or recommended limits for industrial occupational exposures [ACGIH (annual); NIOSH 1992]. With few

Table 5 Comparison of Indoor Environment Standards and Guidelines

	Canadian[a]	WHO/Europe[b]	NAAQS/EPA[c]	NIOSH REL (TWA)[d]	OSHA (TWA)[d]	ACGIH (TWA)[d]
Acrolein				0.1 ppm[e] 0.3 ppm (15 min)	0.1 ppm	C 0.1 ppm, A4
Acetaldehyde				Ca: ALARA[f]	200 ppm	C 25 ppm, A2
Benzene	As low as possible	As low as possible		Ca: 0.1 ppm 1 ppm (15 min)	1 ppm 5 ppm (15 min)	0.5 ppm 2.5 ppm (15 min) Skin; A1; BEI
Formaldehyde	0.04 ppm (8 h) 0.1 ppm (1 h)	0.081 ppm (30 min)		0.016 ppm 0.1 ppm (15 min) Ca	0.75 ppm 2 ppm (15 min) Ca	C 0.3 ppm, A2
Carbon dioxide				5000 ppm 30,000 ppm (15 min)	5000 ppm	5000 ppm 30,000 ppm (15 min)
Carbon monoxide	10 ppm (24 h) 25 ppm (1 h)	6 ppm (24 h) 8 ppm (8 h) 28 ppm (1 h) 80 ppm (15 min)	9 ppm (8 h) 35 ppm (1 h)	35 ppm C 200 ppm	50 ppm	25 ppm
Nitrogen dioxide	0.011 ppm (24 h) 0.09 ppm (1 h)	0.2 ppb (1 yr)	0.1 ppm (three yr avg. of 98th percentile of daily max. 1 h avg.)	1 ppm (15 min)	C 5 ppm	0.2 ppm A4
Ozone	0.02 ppm (8 h)		0.070 ppm (annual fourth-highest daily maximum 8 h concentration, averaged over three years)	C 0.1 ppm	0.1 ppm	0.05 ppm (for heavy work) 0.2 ppm ($\leq$2 h) (light, moderate, or heavy work) A4
Particles < 2.5 MMAD[g]	As low as possible		12 to 15 $\mu g/m^3$ (1 yr) 35 $\mu g/m^3$ (24 h)		5 mg/m^3 (respirable fraction)	3 mg/m^3
Sulfur dioxide		0.047 ppm (24 h) 0.019 ppm (1 yr)	75 ppb (99th percentile of 1 h daily maximum concentrations over three years) 0.5 ppm (not to be exceeded more than once a year)	2 ppm (8 h) 5 ppm (15 min)	5 ppm	0.25 ppm (15 min) A4
Radon	200 Bq/m^3[h]	100 Bq/m^3 or <300 Bq/m^3 (annual)	4 pCi/L			4 working level months (WLM)

(*) Numbers in parentheses represent averaging periods
C = ceiling limit
Ca = carcinogen
A1 = confirmed human carcinogen
A2 = suspected human carcinogen
A4 = not classifiable as human carcinogen per ACGIH
BEI = Biological Exposure Indices
WLM = working level months
[a]Health Canada *Exposure Guidelines for Residential Indoor Air Quality*
[b]WHO Guidelines for Indoor Air Quality: Selected Pollutants.
[c]U.S. EPA National Ambient Air Quality Standards
[d]Value for 8 h TWA, unless otherwise noted
[e]Parts per million (10^6)
[f]As low as reasonably achievable
[g]Mass median aerodynamic diameter
[h]Mean in normal living areas

exceptions, concentrations observed in nonindustrial indoor environments fall well below (100 to 1000 times lower) published pollutant-specific occupational exposure limits. The California Office of Environmental Health Hazard Assessment (OEHHA 2016a) established chronic reference exposure limits (cRELs) for inhalation exposure to 80 compounds, including many VOCs found in indoor air, which can be used as guidelines for establishing appropriate IAQ criteria regarding specific VOCs of interest.

Total VOC (TVOC) concentrations were suggested as an indicator of the ability of combined VOC exposures to produce adverse health effects. This approach is no longer supported, because the irritant potential and toxicity of individual VOCs vary widely, and measured concentrations are highly dependent on the sampling and analytical methods used (Hodgson 1995). In controlled exposure experiments, odors become significant at roughly 3 mg/m^3. At 5 mg/m^3, objective effects were seen, in addition to subjective reports of irritation. Exposures for 50 min to 8 mg/m^3 of synthetic mixtures of 22 VOCs led to significant irritation of mucous membranes in the eyes, nose, and throat (Kjærgaard et al. 1991).

Exposure Control Strategies. VOC control strategies include source elimination or reduction, local exhaust, air cleaning, and general dilution ventilation. Several emission testing standards [e.g., BIFMA *Standard* M7.1; CDPH (2010)] have been established to promote the use and production of low-VOC-emission materials and products. Air-cleaning technologies include physical and chemical adsorption, photocatalytic oxidization, and dynamic botanical filtration (Wang 2011). Caution is needed to ensure that target pollutants are sufficiently removed and no by-products with adverse health effects are produced (Pei and Zhang 2011; Zhang et al. 2011). Ventilation requirements and other means of control of gaseous contaminants are discussed more thoroughly in Chapter 16 of this volume and Chapter 46 of the 2015 *ASHRAE Handbook—HVAC Applications*.

Semivolatile organic compounds (SVOCs) include phthalates, alkylphenols, flame retardants, polycyclic aromatic hydrocarbons (PAHs), polychlorinated biphenyls (PCBs), and pesticides. Many SVOCs are associated with adverse health outcomes in laboratory animal studies and in some environmental epidemiology studies.

Sources. Indoor sources of SVOCs include consumer products and building materials such as detergents, toys, lotions, nail polish, perfume, cosmetics, shampoo, electronic equipment (e.g., computers, televisions), pesticides, furniture foam or stuffing, shower curtains, vinyl flooring, and PVC products. In general, since the 1950s, levels of volatile organic compounds (VOCs) increased and then decreased. During this same period, levels of SVOCs, such as those used as plasticizers and flame retardants, have increased and remain high (Rudel and Perovich 2009; Weschler 2009). Table 6 lists compounds representative of SVOCs encountered indoors (Weschler and Nazaroff 2008).

Table 6 Selected SVOCs Found in Indoor Environments

Chemical Class	SVOC	CAS Number	Formula
Biocides and preservatives			
Antimicrobials	Triclosan	3380-34-5	$C_{12}H_7Cl_3O_2$
Antioxidants	Butylated hydroxytoluene (BHT)	128-37-0	$C_{15}H_{24}O$
Fungicides	Tributyltin oxide (TBTO)	56-35-9	$C_{24}H_{54}OSn_2$
Wood preservatives	Pentachlorophenol (PCP)	87-86-5	C_6HCl_5O
Combustion by-products			
Environmental tobacco smoke	Nicotine	54-11-5	$C_{10}H_{14}N_2$
Polychlorinated dibenzo-p-dioxins	2,3,7,8-Tetrachlorodibenzo-p-dioxin (TCDD)	1746-01-6	$C_{12}H_4Cl_4O_2$
Polycyclic aromatic hydrocarbons	Benzo[a]pyrene (BaP)	50-32-8	$C_{20}H_{12}$
	Phenanthrene	85-01-8	$C_{14}H_{10}$
	Pyrene	129-00-0	$C_{16}H_{10}$
Degradation products/residual monomers			
Phenols	Bisphenol A	80-05-7	$C_{15}H_{16}O_2$
Flame retardants			
Brominated flame retardants	2,2′,4,4′,5,5′-Hexabromodiphenyl ether (BDE-153)	68631-49-2	$C_{12}H_4Br_6O$
	2,2′,4,4′,5-Pentabromodiphenyl ether (BDE-99)	60348-60-9	$C_{12}H_5Br_5O$
	2,2′,4,4′-Tetrabromodiphenyl ether (BDE-47)	5436-43-1	$C_{12}H_6Br_4O$
Chlorinated flame retardants	Perchloropentacyclodecane (mirex)	2385-85-5	$C_{10}Cl_{12}$
Phosphate esters	Tris(chloropropyl) phosphate	13674-84-5	$C_9H_{18}Cl_3O_4P$
Heat transfer fluids			
Polychlorinated biphenyls (PCBs)	2,2′,5,5′-tetrachloro-1,1′-biphenyl (PCB 52)	35693-99-3	$C_{12}H_6Cl_4$
	2,2′,4,4′,5,5′-hexachloro-1,1′-biphenyl (PCB 153)	35065-27-1	$C_{12}H_4Cl_6$
Microbial emissions			
Sesquiterpenes	Geosmin	23333-91-7	$C_{12}H_{22}O$
Personal care products			
Musk compounds	Galaxolide	1222-05-5	$C_{18}H_{26}O$
Petrolatum constituents	n-Pentacosane	629-99-2	$C_{25}H_{52}$
Pesticides/termiticides/herbicides			
Carbamates	Propoxur	114-26-1	$C_{11}H_{15}NO_3$
Organochlorine pesticides	Chlordane	57-74-9	$C_{10}H_6Cl_8$
	p,p′-DDT	50-29-3	$C_{14}H_9Cl_5$
Organophosphate pesticides	Chlorpyrifos	2921-88-2	$C_9H_{11}Cl_3NO_3PS$
	Diazinon	333-41-5	$C_{12}H_{21}N_2O_3PS$
	Methyl parathion	298-00-0	$C_8H_{10}NO_5PS$
Pyrethroids	Cyfluthrin	68359-37-5	$C_{22}H_{18}Cl_2FNO_3$
	Cypermethrin	52315-07-8	$C_{22}H_{19}Cl_2NO_3$
	Permethrin	52645-53-1	$C_{21}H_{20}Cl_2O_3$
Synergists	Piperonyl butoxide	51-03-6	$C_{19}H_{30}O_5$
Plasticizers			
Adipate esters	Di(2-ethylhexyl) adipate (DEHA)	103-23-1	$C_{22}H_{42}O_4$
Phosphate esters	Triphenylphosphate (TPP)	115-86-6	$C_{18}H_{15}O_4P$
Phthalate esters	Butylbenzyl phthalate (BBzP)	85-68-7	$C_{19}H_{20}O_4$
	Dibutyl phthalate (DBP)	84-74-2	$C_{16}H_{22}O_4$
	Di(2-ethylhexyl) phthalate (DEHP)	117-81-7	$C_{24}H_{38}O_4$
Sealants			
Silicones	Tetradecamethylcycloheptasiloxane (D7)	107-50-6	$C_{14}H_{42}O_7Si_7$
Stain repellents, oil and water repellents			
Perfluorinated surfactants	N-ethyl perfluorooctane sulfonamidoethanol (EtFOSE)	1691-99-2	$C_{12}H_{10}F_{17}NO_3S$
	N-methylperfluorooctane sulfonamidoethanol (MeFOSE)	24448-09-7	$C_{11}H_8F_{17}NO_3S$
Surfactants (nonionic), emulsifiers, coalescing agents			
Alkylphenol ethoxylates	4-Nonylphenol	104-40-5	$C_{15}H_{24}O$
Coalescing agents	3-Hydroxy-2,2,4-Trimethylpentyl-1-Isobutyrate (Texanol)	25625-77-4	$C_{12}H_{24}O_3$
Terpene oxidation products			
	Pinonaldehyde	2704-78-1	$C_{10}H_{16}O_2$
Water disinfection products			
	3-Chloro-4-(dichloromethyl)-5-hydroxy-2(5H)-furanone (MX)	77439-76-0	$C_5H_3Cl_3O_3$
Waxes, polishes, and essential oils			
Fatty acids	Stearic acid (octadecanoic acid)	57-11-4	$C_{18}H_{36}O_2$
	Linoleic acid	60-33-3	$C_{18}H_{32}O_2$
Sesquiterpenes	Caryophyllene	87-44-5	$C_{15}H_{24}$

Source: Adapted from Table 1 of Weschler and Nazaroff (2008).

Health Effects. Exposures to SVOCs in nonindustrial indoor environments have been associated with adverse health effects in a number of recent studies. Exposures to these compounds have been linked to endocrine disruptions in both animals and in humans, poor semen quality (motility, number), birth abnormalities in anogenital distance, and premature sexual development (genital and reproductive anomalies such as hypospadias) (Hauser and Calafat 2005; Rogan and Ragan 2007; Swan 2008). Human exposure to SVOCs has also been studied by monitoring concentrations of metabolites in body fluids such as in urine or blood. Results show that people are exposed to multiple SVOCs everywhere, and that children often are more exposed than adults (EPA 2011). Biomonitoring data suggest that over 95% of the U.S. population is exposed to phthalates (Kato et al. 2004), and the body burden for polybrominated diphenyl ethers (PBDEs, used in flame retardants) in North Americans is 10 to 100 times higher than in Europeans because of the much higher indoor exposure of the U.S. population (Harrad et al. 2006; Sjodin et al. 2008).

When determining SVOC exposure pathways, remember that SVOCs can be either gaseous or condensed. They are redistributed from their original source to indoor air and subsequently to all interior surfaces, including airborne particles, settled dust, fixed surfaces, and human surfaces (Rudel and Perovich 2009; Weschler and Nazaroff 2008; Xu et al. 2010). Indeed, contaminated indoor environments have recently been recognized as a significant uptake pathway for SVOCs (Harrad et al. 2006; Xu et al. 2010). Exposure routes of SVOCs include diet, inhalation, dermal absorption, and oral ingestion of dust (Hauser and Calafat 2005; Weschler and Nazaroff 2008, 2012). Diet, the only pathway that is relatively insensitive to the indoor presence of SVOCs, is considered the dominant source for total intake (body burden) for many SVOCs. However, awareness is growing of potential exposure through inhalation, inadvertent ingestion, or skin adsorption (Hauser and Calafat 2005; Weschler and Nazaroff 2012). For some SVOCs, indoor exposures via these three pathways appear to be larger than that resulting from diet. Table 7 provides the indoor concentrations and body burden of selected semivolatile organic compounds.

Table 7 Indoor Concentrations and Body Burden of Selected Semivolatile Organic Compounds

Chemical	Typical Reported Concentrations in Indoor Environments: Air, ng/m³	Typical Reported Concentrations in Indoor Environments: Dust, μg/g	U.S. Body Burdens, 95th Percentile: in Blood, ng/g Serum; in Urine, μg/g Creatinine
Biocides and preservatives			
Triclosan	—	0.2 to 2	360 (urine)
Tributyltin oxide (TBTO)	—	0.01 to 0.1	—
Pentachlorophenol (PCP)	0.4 to 4	0.2 to 2	2.3 (urine)
Combustion by-products			
Nicotine	200 to 2000	10 to 100	2.2 (blood)
Benzo[a]pyrene (BaP)	0.02 to 0.2	0.2 to 2	0.18 (urine)
Phenanthrene	10 to 100	0.2 to 2	1.7 (urine)
Pyrene	1 to 10	0.2 to 2	0.24 (urine)
Degradation products/residual monomers			
Bisphenol A	0.5 to 5	0.2 to 2	11 (urine)
Flame retardants			
2,2′,4,4′,5,5′-Hexabromodiphenyl ether (BDE-153, hexa BDE)	0.002 to 0.02	0.03 to 0.3	0.44 (blood)
2,2′,4,4′,5-Pentabromodiphenyl ether (BDE-99, penta BDE)	0.03 to 0.3	0.4 to 4	0.28 (blood)
2,2′,4,4′-Tetrabromodiphenyl ether (BDE-47, tetra BDE)	0.06 to 0.6	0.3 to 3	1.1 (blood)
Perchloropentacyclodecane (Mirex)	—	—	0.41 (blood)
Tris(chloropropyl) phosphate	6 to 60	0.3 to 3	—
Heat transfer fluids			
2,2′,5,5′-tetrachloro-1,1′-biphenyl (PCB 52)	0.2 to 2.0	0.05 to 0.5	0.089 (blood)
2,2′,4,4′,5,5′-hexachloro-1,1′-biphenyl (PCB 153)	0.1 to 1.0	0.007 to 0.07	0.85 (blood)
Personal care products			
Galaxolide	25 to 250	0.5 to 5	—
Pesticides/termiticides/herbicides			
Propoxur	0.8 to 8	0.05 to 0.5	<1 (urine)
Chlordane	0.5 to 5	0.04 to 0.4	0.35 (blood)
p,p′-DDT	0.2 to 2	0.1 to 1	0.18 (blood)
Chlorpyrifos	1 to 10	0.08 to 0.8	9.2 (urine)
Diazinon	1 to 5	0.02 to 0.2	<1 (urine)
Methyl parathion	0.05 to 0.5	0.01 to 0.1	2.9 (urine)
Cyfluthrin	0.1 to 1.0	0.08 to 0.8	Common metabolite: 2.6 (urine)
Cypermethrin	—	0.08 to 0.8	
Permethrin	0.1 to 0.7	0.2 to 2	3.8 (urine)
Piperonyl butoxide	0.1 to 1.0	0.1 to 1.0	—
Plasticizers			
Di(2-ethylhexyl) adipate (DEHA)	5 to 15	2 to 10	—
Triphenylphosphate (TPP)	0.1 to 1	2 to 20	—
Butylbenzyl phthalate (BBzP)	5 to 80	15 to 150	90 (urine)
Dibutyl phthalate (DBP)	200 to 1200	20 to 200	81 (urine)
Di(2-ethylhexyl) phthalate (DEHP)	50 to 500	300 to 900	270 (urine)
Stain repellents, oil/water repellents			
N-ethyl perfluorooctane sulfonamidoethanol (EtFOSE)	0.5 to 3	30 to 500	Common metabolite (PFOS): 55 (blood)
N-methylperfluorooctane sulfonamidoethanol (MeFOSE)	0.5 to 5	30 to 300	
Surfactants (nonionic), emulsifiers, coalescing agents			
4-Nonlyphenol	40 to 400	0.8 to 8	1.4 (urine)
Texanol 2	500 to 5000	—	—

Source: Adapted from Table 2 of Weschler and Nazaroff (2008).

Exposure Standards. Few standards exist for exposure to SVOCs in nonindustrial indoor environments. NIOSH, OSHA, EPA, and ACGIH have regulatory standards or recommended limits for industrial occupational exposures for inhalation, some of which are given in Table 5. The California Environmental Protection Agency's Office of Environmental Health Hazard Assessment (OEHHA 2016b) maintains a list of VOCs and other chemicals known to the state to cause cancer or reproductive toxicity.

Lately, a new generation of scientific tools has emerged to rapidly measure responses from cells, tissues, and organisms following exposure to chemicals, including SVOCs. The goal of such methods is to rapidly screen and prioritize chemicals for more detailed toxicity testing (Judson et al. 2010). However, activities to compile exposure data to develop novel approaches and metrics to screen and evaluate chemicals based on biologically relevant human exposures are still in their initial stages.

Exposure Control Strategies. SVOC control strategies include source identification, elimination or reduction. Weschler and Nazaroff (2008) argued, based on theoretical considerations, that ventilation is not as effective in reducing indoor concentrations of SVOCs as it is in reducing indoor concentrations of VOCs. Although recent modeling studies indicate that ventilation has a limited ability to reduce indoor levels of most airborne SVOCs and thus the ability to reduce human exposures (Liang and Xu 2011; Xu et al. 2010), Weschler and Nazaroff (2008) showed that ventilation is generally ineffective in controlling human exposure because of the long-term persistence of condensed SVOCs. Laboratory studies have demonstrated the small impact that ventilation has on indoor airborne levels of di(2-ethylhexyl) phthalate (DEHP), a compound used as a plasticizer (Xu et al. 2010). Field studies are needed to evaluate the impact of ventilation on different types of SVOCs under realistic indoor conditions. Furthermore, there is also a lack of literature documenting SVOC exposure reductions via air cleaning. Table 7 shows indoor concentrations and body burdens of selected SVOCs.

Inorganic Gases.

Sources. Inorganic gases in the nonindustrial environment may come from a combination of outdoor air and indoor sources, including occupants (e.g., respiration, toiletries), processes (e.g., combustion, office equipment), and indoor air chemistry (e.g., reaction between ozone and alkenes).

Health Effects. **Carbon monoxide** is a chemical asphyxiant. Inhalation of CO causes a throbbing headache because hemoglobin has a greater affinity for CO than for oxygen (about 240 times greater), and because of a detrimental shift in the oxygen dissociation curve. Carbon monoxide inhibits oxygen transport in the blood by forming carboxyhemoglobin and inhibiting cytochrome oxidase at the cellular level. Cobb and Etzel (1991) suggested that CO poisoning at home represented a major preventable disease. Moolenaar et al. (1995) had similar findings, and suggested that motor vehicles and home furnaces were primary causes of mortality. Girman et al. (1998) identified both fatal outcomes and "episodes" and classed them by cause:

Cause	Fatal Outcomes, %	Nonfatal Episodes, %
Motor vehicles	35.9	30.6
Appliance combustion	34.8	39.9
Small appliances	4.5	5.2
Camping equipment	2.2	2.3
Fires	5.6	5.0
Grills/hibachis	13.4	13.3
Unknown	3.6	3.7

In a review of CO exposures in the United States from 2001 to 2003, the Centers for Disease Control (CDC 2005) found that nearly 500 people died and over 15,000 were treated in emergency departments each year after unintentional, non-fire-related CO exposures. Of cases with known sources, the most common source of CO was furnaces (18.5%), followed by motor vehicles (9.1%). Inappropriate use of portable generators, a growing problem, resulted in around 50 deaths per year from 2002 to 2005 (CPSC 2006).

Carbon dioxide can become dangerous not as a toxic agent but as a simple asphyxiant. When concentrations exceed 35,000 ppm, central breathing receptors are triggered and cause the sensation of shortness of breath. At progressively higher concentrations, central nervous system dysfunction begins because of displacement of oxygen. Measured concentrations of CO_2 in nonindustrial environments are typically below 1000 ppm, but can occasionally be as high as 2500 ppm, depending on occupant density and outdoor air ventilation rates (Persily 2015a). Nevertheless, much confusion exists regarding the significance of indoor CO_2 and its effects on occupant health and comfort (ASHRAE 2009).

Inhalation of **nitric oxide (NO)** causes methemoglobin formation, which adversely affects the body by interfering with oxygen transport at the cellular level. NO exposures of 3 ppm have been compared to carbon monoxide exposures of 10 to 15 ppm (Case et al. 1979, in EPA 1991).

Nitrogen dioxide (NO_2) is a corrosive gas with a pungent odor, with a reported odor threshold between 0.11 and 0.22 ppm. NO_2 has low water solubility, and is therefore inhaled into the deep lung, where it causes a delayed inflammatory response. Increased airway resistance has been reported at 1.5 to 2 ppm (Bascom 1996). NO_2 is reported to be a potential carcinogen through free radical production (Burgess and Crutchfield 1995). At high concentrations, NO_2 causes lung damage directly by its oxidant properties, and may cause health effects indirectly by increasing host susceptibility to respiratory infections. Health effects from exposures to ambient outdoor concentrations or in residential situations are inconsistent, especially in studies relating to exposures from gas cooking stoves (Samet et al. 1987). Indoor concentrations of NO_2 often exceed ambient concentrations because of the presence of strong indoor sources and a trend toward more energy-efficient (tighter) homes. Acute toxicity is seldom seen from NO_2 produced by unvented indoor combustion, because insufficient quantities of NO_2 are produced. Chronic pulmonary effects from exposure to combinations of low-level combustion pollutants are possible, however (Bascom et al. 1996).

Sulfur dioxide (SO_2) is a colorless gas with a pungent odor detected at about 0.5 ppm (EPA 1991). Because SO_2 is quite soluble in water, it readily reacts with moisture in the respiratory tract to irritate the upper respiratory mucosa. Concomitant exposure to fine particles, an individual's depth and rate of breathing, and preexisting disease can influence the degree of response to SO_2 exposure.

Ozone (O_3) is a pulmonary irritant and has been known to alter human pulmonary function at concentrations of approximately 0.12 ppm (Bates 1989). However, inhaling ozone at considerably lower concentrations (e.g., about 0.080 ppm) has been shown to decrease respiratory function in healthy children (Spektor et al. 1988a). Outdoor ozone levels as low as 0.020 ppm have been shown to increase mortality, and levels below 0.010 ppm may be required for safety (ASHRAE 2011). These levels are far below current federal NAAQS levels of 0.075 ppm. Reducing ozone levels indoors to as low as reasonably achievable (ALARA) levels by various means is recommended.

Products of ozone reactions are often more irritating than precursors. Ozone and isoprene react to form free radicals, formaldehyde, methacrolein, and methyl vinyl ketone. Ozone and terpenoids react to form free radicals, secondary ozonides, formaldehyde, acrolein, hydrogen peroxide, organic peroxides, dicarbonyls, carboxylic acids, and submicron particles.

Ozone reacts with many organic chemicals and airborne particulate matter commonly found indoors. Weschler (2006) summarizes current knowledge of these reactions and their products, which include both stable reaction products that may be more irritating than their chemical precursors (Mølhave et al. 2005; Tamas et al. 2006; Weschler and Shields 2000) and relatively short-lived products that are highly irritating and may also have chronic toxicity or carcinogenicity (Destaillats et al. 2006; Nazaroff et al. 2006; Weschler 2000; Wilkins et al. 2001; Wolkoff et al. 2000).

Chen et al. (2012) assessed the influence of indoor exposure to outdoor ozone on short-term mortality in U.S. communities. When air with ozone passes through loaded filters, the downstream concentrations of submicron-sized particles is higher than the upstream concentration. Ozone removal efficiencies on used filters change by one of at least two different removal mechanisms: reactions with compounds on the filter media after manufacturing, and reactions with compounds on captured particles (Beko et al. 2007).

The scientific literature is well developed in showing the effect of ozone on respiratory function and health effects of exposure to elevated levels of ozone (Lippmann 1993; Spektor et al. 1988b, 1991; Thurston et al. 1997). A critical review of the health effects of ozone is provided by Lippmann (1989).

Exposure to ozone at 0.060 to 0.080 ppm causes inflammation, bronchoconstriction, and increased airway responsiveness. The EPA's BASE study of over 100 randomly selected typical U.S. office buildings (Apte et al. 2007) found a clear statistical relationship between ambient ozone concentrations and building-related health symptoms, despite the fact that only one building had a workday average ambient ozone concentration greater than the then-current 8 h national ambient air quality standards [NAAQS; see EPA (2016a)] level of 0.080 ppm.

Ambient air ozone concentrations down to 0.020 ppm are associated with increased mortality (Bell et al. 2005). Several researchers have explored the relationship between ozone and mortality (Bates 2005; Goodman 2005; Ito et al. 2005; Levy et al. 2005).

Although ozone uptake (deposition velocity v_d) on diverse materials varies greatly (e.g., from 0.025 m/h for aluminum to 28 m/h for gypsum board), uptakes in a wide variety of building types and occupancies are within a fairly narrow range (between 0.9 and 1.5 m/h).

Inhalation exposures to gaseous oxides of nitrogen (NO_x), sulfur (SO_2), and ozone (O_3) occur in residential and commercial buildings. These air pollutants are of considerable concern because of the potential for acute and chronic respiratory tract health effects in exposed individuals, particularly individuals with preexisting pulmonary disease.

Exposure Standards and Guidelines. Currently, there are no specific U.S. government standards for nonindustrial occupational exposures to air contaminants. Occupational exposure criteria are health based; that is, they consider only healthy workers, and not necessarily individuals who may be unusually responsive to the effects of chemical exposures. The U.S. EPA's (2016a) NAAQS are also health-based standards designed to protect the general public from the effects of hazardous airborne pollutants (see Chapter 11). Table 8 is not meant as a health-based guideline for evaluating indoor exposures to inorganic gases; rather, it is intended for comparison and consideration by investigators of the indoor environment. These criteria may not be completely protective for all occupants.

Exposure Control Strategies. Inorganic gas contaminant control strategies include source elimination or reduction, local exhaust, space pressure control, general dilution ventilation, and gaseous air cleaning. Ventilation requirements and other means of control of gaseous contaminants are discussed more thoroughly in Chapter 16 of this volume and Chapter 46 of the 2015 *ASHRAE Handbook—HVAC Applications*.

The by-products of indoor air chemistry can be limited by using carbon-based filters in locations where outdoor ozone concentrations commonly approach or exceed the NAAQS.

Table 8 Inorganic Gas Comparative Criteria

Contaminant	ACGIH TWA[a]	U.S. EPA NAAQS[b]
Nitric oxide	25 ppm	0.100 ppm (1 h)[c]
Nitrogen dioxide	0.2 ppm	0.100 ppm (1 h)[c] 0.053 ppm[d]
Sulfur dioxide	0.25 ppm[e]	0.075 ppm (200 μg/m³)[f] 0.5 ppm (1333 μg/m³)[g]
Ozone	0.05 to 0.2 ppm	0.070 ppm (8 h in specified form)[h]

[a]TWA: 8 h time-weighted average (unless otherwise noted)
[b]National Ambient Air Quality Standards
[c]Three-year average of the 98th percentile of the daily maximum 1 h average
[d]Annual mean
[e]Ceiling value, not to be exceeded during any part of working exposure
[f]Three-year average of the 99th percentile of the daily maximum 1 h average
[g]Not to be exceeded more than once per year
[h]Annual fourth-highest daily maximum 8 h concentration, averaged over three years.

3. PHYSICAL AGENTS

Physical factors in the indoor environment include thermal conditions (temperature, moisture, air velocity, and radiant energy); mechanical energy (noise and vibration); and electromagnetic radiation, including ionizing (radon) and nonionizing [light, radiofrequency, and extremely low frequency (ELF)] magnetic and electric fields. Physical agents can act directly on building occupants, interact with indoor air quality factors, or affect human responses to the indoor environment. Though not categorized as indoor air quality factors, physical agents often affect perceptions of indoor air quality.

3.1 THERMAL ENVIRONMENT

The thermal environment affects human health in that it affects body temperature regulation and heat exchange with the environment. A normal, healthy, resting adult's internal or core body temperatures are very stable, with variations seldom exceeding 1°F. The internal temperature of a resting adult, measured orally, averages about 98.6°F; measured rectally, it is about 1°F higher. Core temperature is carefully modulated by an elaborate physiological control system. In contrast, skin temperature is basically unregulated and can (depending on environmental temperature) vary from about 88 to 96.8°F in normal environments and activities. It also varies between different parts of the skin, with the greatest range of variation in the hands and feet.

Range of Healthy Living Conditions

Environmental conditions for good thermal comfort minimize effort of the physiological control system. The control system regulates internal body temperature by varying the amount of blood flowing to different skin areas, thus increasing or decreasing heat loss to the environment. Additional physiological response includes secreting sweat, which can evaporate from the skin in warm or hot environments, or increasing the body's rate of metabolic heat production by shivering in the cold. For a resting person wearing trousers and a long-sleeved shirt, thermal comfort in a steady state is experienced in a still-air environment at 75°F. A zone of comfort extends about 3°F above and below this optimum level (Fanger 1970).

An individual can minimize the need for physiological (involuntary) responses to the thermal environment, which generally are perceived as uncomfortable, in various ways. In a cool or cold environment, these responses include increased clothing, increased activity, or seeking or creating an environment that is warmer. In a warm or hot environment, the amount of clothing or level of physical activity can be reduced, or an environment that is more

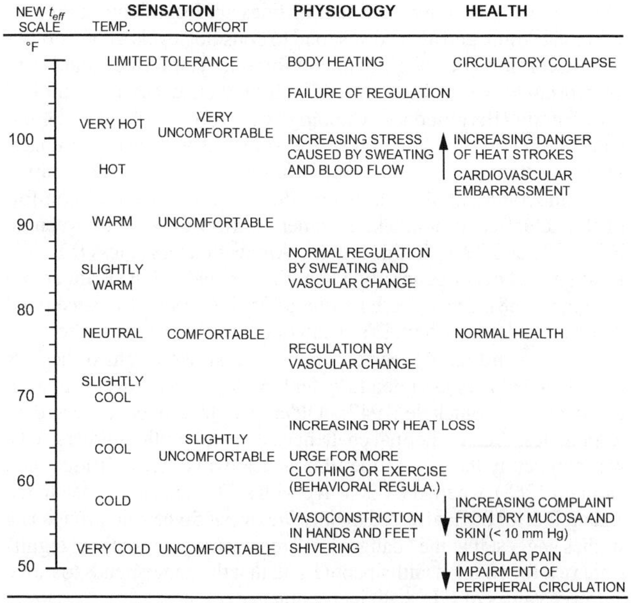

Fig. 1 Related Human Sensory, Physiological, and Health Responses for Prolonged Exposure

conducive to increased heat loss can be created. Some human responses to the thermal environment are shown in Figure 1.

Cardiovascular and other diseases and aging can reduce the capacity or ability of physiological processes to maintain internal body temperature through balancing heat gains and losses. Thus, some people are less able to deal with thermal challenges and deviations from comfortable conditions. Metabolic heat production tends to decrease with age, as a result of decreasing basal metabolism together with decreased physical activity. Metabolic heat production at age 80 is about 20% less than that at age 20, for comparable size and mass. People in their eighties, therefore, may prefer an environmental temperature about 3°F warmer than people in their twenties. Older people may have reduced capacity to secrete sweat and to increase their skin blood flow, and are therefore more likely to experience greater strain in warm and hot conditions, as well as in cool and cold conditions. However, the effect of age on metabolism and other factors related to thermal response varies considerably from person to person, and care should be taken in applying these generalizations to specific individuals.

Hypothermia

Hypothermia is defined as a core body temperature of less than 95°F. Hypothermia can result from environmental cold exposure, but may also be induced by other conditions, such as metabolic disorders and drug use. Occupational hypothermia occurs in workers in a cold environment when heat balance cannot be met while maintaining work performance. Elderly persons sitting inactive in a cool room may become hypothermic, because they often fail to observe a slow fall in body temperature (Nordic Conference on Cold 1991).

Deleterious effects of cold on work performance derive from peripheral vasoconstriction and cooling, which slows down the rate of nerve conduction and muscle contraction, and increases stiffness in tendons and connective tissues. This induces clumsiness and increases risk for injury (e.g., in occupational settings). Direct effects of cold include injuries from frostbite (skin freezes at 32 to 35.5°F) and a condition called **immersion foot**, in which the feet are exposed to wetness and temperatures of 34 to 50°F for more than 12 h, and vasoconstriction and low oxygen supply lead to edema and tissue damage.

Hyperthermia

In hyperthermia, body temperatures are above normal. A deep-body temperature increase of 4°Fabove normal does not generally impair body function. For example, it is not unusual for runners to have rectal temperatures of 104°F after a long race. An elevated body temperature increases metabolism. However, when body temperature increases above normal for reasons other than exercise, heat illness may develop. Heat illness represents a number of disorders from mild to fatal, which do not depend only on the hyperthermia in itself. In heat stroke, the most severe condition, the heat balance regulation system collapses, resulting in a rapid rise in body temperature. Central nervous system function deteriorates at deep body temperatures above 106 to 108°F. Convulsions may occur above such temperatures, and cells may be damaged. This condition is particularly dangerous for the brain, because lost neurons are not replaced. Thermoregulatory functions of sweating and peripheral vasodilation cease at about 110°F, after which body temperatures tend to rise rapidly if external cooling is not imposed (Blatteis 1998; Hales et al. 1996).

Seasonal Patterns

Ordinary seasonal changes in temperate climates are temporally associated with illness. Many acute and several chronic diseases vary in frequency or severity with time of year, and some are present only in certain seasons. Most countries report increased mortality from cardiovascular disease during colder winter months. Minor respiratory infections, such as colds and sore throats, occur mainly in fall and winter. More serious infections, such as pneumonia, have a somewhat shorter season in winter. Intestinal infections, such as dysentery and typhoid fever, are more prevalent in summer. Diseases transmitted by insects, such as encephalitis and endemic typhus, are limited to summer, because insects are active in warm temperatures only.

Hryhorczuk et al. (1992), Martinez et al. (1989), and others describe a correlation between weather and seasonal illnesses, but correlations do not necessarily establish a causal relationship. Daily or weekly mortality and heat stress in heat waves have a strong physiological basis directly linked to outdoor temperature. In indoor environments, which have well-controlled temperature and humidity, such temperature extremes and the possible adverse effects on health are strongly attenuated.

Climate Change

Impacts to human health can include the direct effects of climate change such as increased ambient temperatures, air pollution, and extreme weather. Additionally, indirect impacts of climate change may include vector-borne diseases and expanded habitats, industrial transitions, emerging industries (e.g., renewable energy, carbon sequestration, "green industries," toxic waste from PV cell fabrication, noise and flickering from wind turbines), increased use of pesticides, and changes in the built environment (Institute of Medicine 2014; NIOSH 2014).

In general, climate change can affect people from these perspectives:

- Amplification of known safety and health hazards such as severe weather events, heat, wildland fire, and infectious disease
- New, unanticipated, or unrecognized hazards (increased infectious disease vector ranges, increase in pesticide use)
- Hazards that result from responses to climate change such as the development of renewable energy, recycling, carbon sequestration, and material substitution (Kiefer and Watson 2015)

Increased Deaths in Heat Waves

The role of weather-induced ambient temperature extremes in producing discomfort, incapacity, and death has been studied extensively (Katayama and Momiyana-Sakamoto 1970). Military personnel, deep-mine workers, and other workers occupationally exposed to extremes of high and low temperature have been studied, but the importance of thermal stress affecting both the sick and healthy general population is not sufficiently appreciated. Collins and Lehmann (1953) studied weekly deaths over many years in large U.S. cities and demonstrated the effect of heat waves in producing conspicuous periods of excess mortality. Excess mortality caused by heat waves was of the same amplitude as that from influenza epidemics, but tended to last one week instead of the four to six weeks of influenza epidemics.

Ellis (1972) reviewed heat wave-related excess mortality in the United States. Mortality increases of 30% over background are common, especially in heat waves early in the summer. Much of the increase occurs in the population over age 65, more of it in women than in men, and many deaths are from cardiovascular, cerebrovascular, or respiratory causes (often exacerbated preexisting conditions). Oeschli and Buechley (1970) studied heat-related deaths in Los Angeles heat waves of 1939, 1955, and 1963. Kilbourne et al. (1982) suggested that the same risk factors (i.e., age, low income, and African-American derivation) persist in more recent heat death epidemics.

Among the most notable lethal heat waves in Europe are Athens in 1987 and 1988 (Giles et al. 1990), Seville in 1988 (Diaz et al. 2002), Valencia in 1991 and 1993 (Ballester et al. 1997), London in 1995 (Hajat et al. 2002), the Netherlands between 1979 and 1991 (Kunst et al. 1993), and Paris in 2003 (Thirion et al. 2005). In the 2003 Parisian heat wave, about 3000 people died.

The temperature/mortality relation varies greatly by latitude and climatic zone (McMichael et al. 2006). Occupants of hotter cities are more affected by colder temperatures, and occupants of colder cities are more affected by warmer temperatures. People living in urban environments are at greater risk than those in nonurban regions. Thermally inefficient housing and the so-called urban heat island effect amplify and extend the rise in temperatures (especially overnight).

Hardy (1971) showed the relationship of health data to comfort on a psychrometric diagram (Figure 2). The diagram contains ASHRAE effective temperature (ET*) lines and lines of constant skin moisture level or skin wettedness. Skin wettedness is defined as that fraction of the skin covered with water to account for the

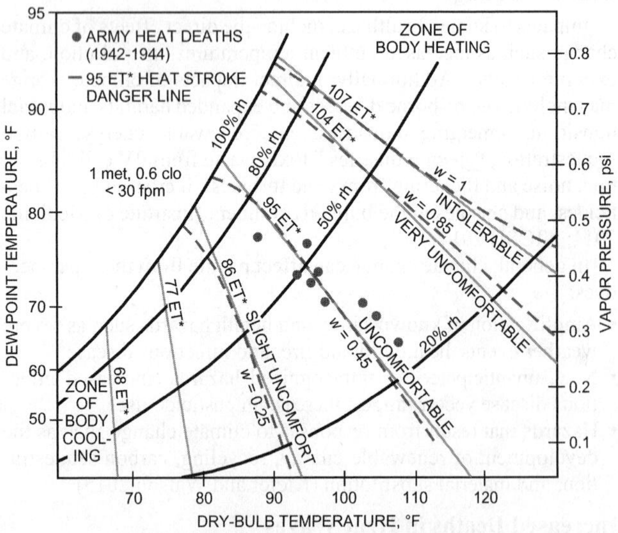

Fig. 2 Isotherms for Comfort, Discomfort, Physiological Strain, Effective Temperature (ET*), and Heat Stroke Danger Threshold

observed evaporation rate. The ET* lines are loci of constant physiological strain, and also correspond to constant levels of physiological discomfort (i.e., slightly uncomfortable, comfortable, and very comfortable) (Gonzalez et al. 1978). Skin wettedness, as an indicator of strain (Berglund and Cunningham 1986; Berglund and Gonzalez 1977) and the fraction of the skin wet with perspiration, is fairly constant along an ET* line. Numerically, ET* is the equivalent temperature at 50% rh that produces the strain and discomfort of the actual condition. The summer comfort range is between an ET* of 73 and 79°F. In this region, skin wettedness is less than 0.2. Heat strokes occur generally when ET* exceeds 93°F (Bridger and Helfand 1968). Thus, the ET* line of 95°F is generally considered dangerous. At this point, skin wettedness will be 0.4 or higher.

The dots in Figure 2 correspond to heat stroke deaths of healthy male U.S. soldiers assigned to sedentary duties in midwestern army camp offices (Shickele 1947). Older people can be expected to respond less well to thermal challenges than do healthy soldiers. This was apparently the case in the Illinois heat wave study (Bridger and Helfand 1968), where the first wave with a 33% increase in death rate and an ET* of 85°F affected mainly the over-65-year-old group. The studies suggest that the "danger line" represents a threshold of significant risk for young healthy people, and that the danger tends to move to lower values of ET* with increasing age.

Effects of Thermal Environment on Specific Diseases

Cardiovascular diseases are largely responsible for excess mortality during heat waves. For example, Burch and DePasquale (1962) found that heart disease patients with decompensation (i.e., inadequate circulation) were extremely sensitive to high temperatures, and particularly to moist heat. However, both cold and hot temperature extremes have been associated with increased coronary heart disease deaths and anginal symptoms (Teng and Heyer 1955).

Both acute and chronic respiratory diseases often increase in frequency and severity during extreme cold weather. No increase in these diseases has been noted in extreme heat. Additional studies of hospital admissions for acute respiratory illness show a negative correlation with temperature after removal of seasonal trends (Holland 1961). Symptoms of chronic respiratory disease (bronchitis, emphysema) increase in cold weather, probably because reflex constriction of the bronchi adds to the obstruction already present. Greenberg (1964) found evidence of cold sensitivity in asthmatics: emergency room treatments for asthma increased abruptly in local hospitals with early and severe autumn cold spells. Later cold waves with even lower temperatures produced no such effects, and years without early extreme cold had no asthma epidemics of this type. Patients with cystic fibrosis are extremely sensitive to heat because their reduced sweat gland function greatly diminishes their ability to cope with increased temperature (Kessler and Anderson 1951).

Itching and chapping of the skin are influenced by (1) atmospheric factors, particularly cold and dry air; (2) frequent washing or wetting of skin; and (3) low indoor humidities. Although skin itching is usually a winter cold-climate illness in the general population, it can be caused by excessive summer air conditioning (Gaul and Underwood 1952; Susskind and Ishihara 1965).

People suffering from chronic illness (e.g., heart disease) or serious acute illnesses that require hospitalization often manage to avoid serious thermal stress. Katayama and Momiyana-Sakamoto (1970) found that countries with the most carefully regulated indoor climates (e.g., Scandinavian countries, the United States) have only small seasonal fluctuations in mortality, whereas countries with less space heating and cooling exhibit greater seasonal swings in mortality. For example, mandatory air conditioning in retirement and assisted living homes in the southwest United States has virtually eliminated previously observed mortality increases during heat waves.

Table 9 Approximate Surface Temperature Limits to Avoid Pain and Injury

	Contact Time				
Material	**1 s**	**10 s**	**1 min**	**10 min**	**8 h**
Metal, water	149°F	133°F	124°F	118°F	109°F
Glass, concrete	176°F	151°F	129°F	118°F	109°F
Wood	248°F	190°F	140°F	118°F	109°F

Source: ISO *Standard* 13732-1:2006.

Injury from Hot and Cold Surfaces

The skin has cold, warm, and pain sensors to feed back thermal information about surface contacts. When the skin temperature rises above 113°F or falls below about 59°F, sensations from the skin's warm and cold receptors are replaced by those from pain receptors to warn of imminent thermal injury to tissue. The rate of change of skin temperature and not just the actual skin temperature may also be important in pain perception. Skin temperature and its rate of change depend on the temperature of the contact surface, its conductivity, and contact time. Table 9 gives approximate temperature limits to avoid pain and injury when contacting three classes of conductors for various contact times (ISO *Standard* 13732-1).

3.2 ELECTRICAL HAZARDS

Electrical current can cause burns, neural disturbances, and cardiac fibrillation (Billings 1975). The threshold of perception is about 5 mA for direct current, with a feeling of warmth at the contact site. The threshold is 1 mA for alternating current, which causes a tingling sensation.

Resistance of the current pathway through the body is a combination of core and skin resistance. The core is basically a saline volume conductor with very little resistance; therefore, the skin provides the largest component of the resistance. Skin resistance decreases with moisture. If the skin is moist, voltages as low as 2 V (AC) or 5 V (DC) are sufficient to be detected, and voltages as low as 20 V (AC) or 100 V (DC) can cause a 50% loss in muscular control.

The dangerous aspect of alternating electrical current is its ability to cause cardiac arrest by ventricular fibrillation. If a weak alternating current (100 mA for 2 s) passes through the heart (as it would in going from hand to foot), the current can force the heart muscle to fibrillate and lose the rhythmic contractions of the ventricles necessary to pump blood. Unconsciousness and death soon follow if medical aid cannot rapidly restore normal rhythm.

3.3 MECHANICAL ENERGIES

Vibration

Vibration in a building originates from both outside and inside the building. Outdoor sources include blasting operations, road traffic, overhead aircraft, underground railways, earth movements, and weather conditions. Indoor sources include doors closing, foot traffic, moving machinery, elevators, escalators, HVAC systems, and other building services. Vibration is an omnipresent, integral part of the built environment. The effects of vibration on building occupants depend on whether it is perceived by those persons and on factors related to the building, building location, occupants' activities, and perceived source and magnitude of vibration. Factors influencing the acceptability of building vibration are presented in Figure 3.

The combination of hearing, seeing, or feeling vibration determines human response. Components concerned with hearing and seeing are part of the visual environment of a room and can be assessed as such. The perception of mechanical vibration by feeling is generally through the cutaneous and kinesthetic senses at high frequencies, and through the vestibular and visceral senses at low frequencies. Because of this and the nature of vibration sources and

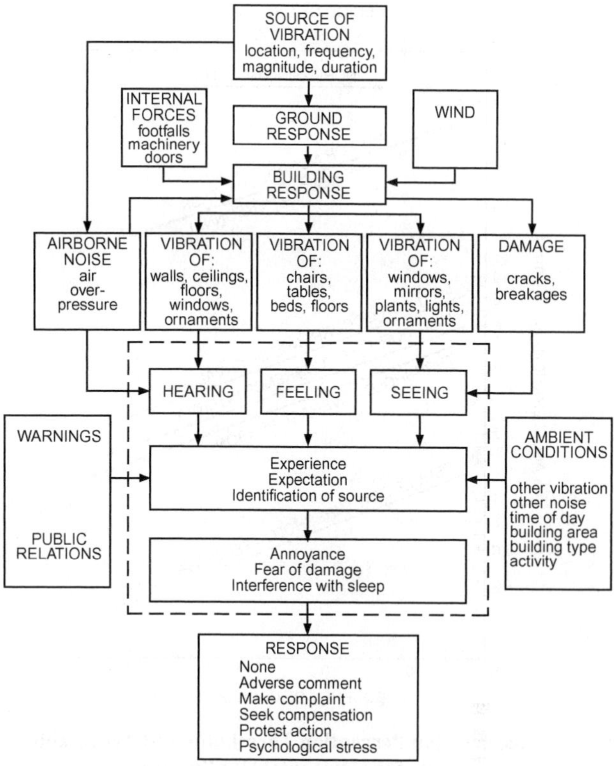

Fig. 3 Factors Affecting Acceptability of Building Vibration

building responses, building vibration may be conveniently considered in two categories: low-frequency vibrations less than 1 Hz and high-frequency vibrations of 1 to 80 Hz.

Measurement and Assessment. Human response to vibration depends on vibration of the body. The main vibrational characteristics are vibration level, frequency, axis (and area of the body), and exposure time. A root-mean-square (RMS) averaging procedure over the time of interest is often used to represent vibration acceleration ($ft/s^2 \cdot$ RMS). Vibration frequency is measured in cycles per second (Hz), and the vibration axis is usually considered in three orthogonal, human-centered translational directions: up-and-down, side-to-side, and fore-and-aft. Although the coordinate system is centered inside the body, in practice, vibration is measured at the human surface, and measurements are directly compared with relevant limit values or other data concerning human response.

Rotational motions of a building in roll, pitch, and yaw are usually about an axis of rotation some distance from the building occupants. For most purposes, these motions can be considered as the translational motions of the person. For example, a roll motion in a building about an axis of rotation some distance from a seated person has a similar effect as side-to-side translational motions of that person, etc.

Most methods assess building vibrations with RMS averaging and frequency analysis. However, human response is related to the time-varying characteristics of vibration as well. For example, many stimuli are transient, such as those caused by a train passing a building. The vibration event builds to a peak, followed by a decay in level over a total period of about 10 s. The nature of the time-varying event and how often it occurs during a day are important factors that might be overlooked if data are treated as steady-state and continuous.

Standard Limits

Low-Frequency Motion (1 Hz). The most commonly experienced form of slow vibration in buildings is building sway. This

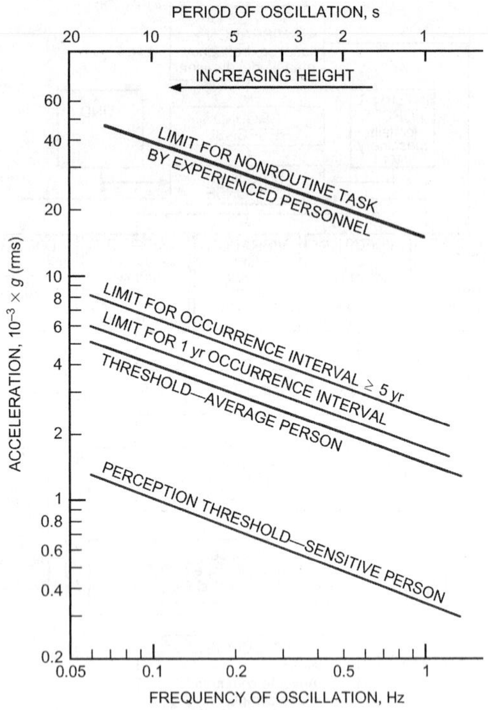

Fig. 4 Acceleration Perception Thresholds and Acceptability Limits for Horizontal Oscillations

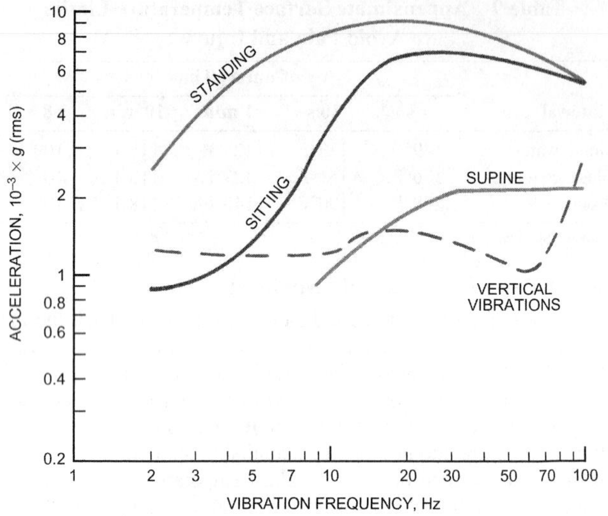

Fig. 5 Median Perception Thresholds to Horizontal (Solid Lines) and Vertical (Dashed Line) Vibrations

motion can be alarming to occupants if there is fear of building damage or injury. Whereas occupants of two-story wood frame houses accept occasional creaks and motion from wind storms or a passing heavy vehicle, such events are not as accepted by occupants of high-rise buildings. Detected motion in tall buildings can cause discomfort and alarm. The perception thresholds of normal, sensitive humans to low-frequency horizontal motion are given in Figure 4 (Chen and Robertson 1972; ISO *Standard* 6897). The frequency range is from 0.06 to 1 Hz or, conversely, for oscillations with periods of 1 to 17 s. The natural frequency of sway of the Empire State Building in New York City, for example, has a period of 8.3 s (Davenport 1988). The thresholds are expressed in terms of relative acceleration, which is the actual acceleration divided by the standard acceleration of gravity g (32.2 ft/s^2). The perception threshold to sway in terms of building accelerations decreases with increasing frequency and ranges from 0.16 to 0.06 ft/s^2.

For tall buildings, the highest horizontal accelerations generally occur near the top at the building's natural frequency of oscillation. Other parts of the building may have high accelerations at multiples of the natural frequency. Tall buildings always oscillate at their natural frequency, but the deflection is small and the motion undetectable. In general, short buildings have a higher natural frequency of vibration than taller ones. However, strong wind forces energize the oscillation and increase the horizontal deflection, speed, and accelerations of the structure.

ISO *Standard* 6897 states that building motions should not produce alarm and adverse comment from more than 2% of the building's occupants. The level of alarm depends on the interval between events. If noticeable building sway occurs for at least 10 min at intervals of 5 years or more, the acceptable acceleration limit is higher than if this sway occurs annually (Figure 4). For annual intervals, the acceptable limit is only slightly above the normal person's threshold of perception. Motion at the 5-year limit level is estimated to cause 12% to complain if it occurred annually. The recommended limits are for purely horizontal motion; rotational oscillations, wind noise, and/or visual cues of the building's motion exaggerate the sensation of motion, and, for such factors, the acceleration limit is lower.

The upper line in Figure 4 is intended for offshore fixed structures such as oil drilling platforms. The line indicates the level of horizontal acceleration above which routine tasks by experienced personnel would be difficult to accomplish on the structure. Because they are routinely in motion in three dimensions, Figure 4 does not apply to transportation vehicles.

High-Frequency Motion (1 to 80 Hz). Higher-frequency vibrations in buildings are caused by machinery, elevators, foot traffic, fans, pumps, and HVAC equipment. Further, the steel structures of modern buildings are good transmitters of high-frequency vibrations. Sensitivity to these higher-frequency vibrations is indicated in Figure 5 (data from Parsons and Griffin 1988), showing median perception thresholds to vertical and horizontal vibrations in the 2 to 100 Hz frequency range. The average perception threshold for vibrations of this type is from 0.03 to 0.3 ft/s^2, depending on frequency and on whether the person is standing, sitting, or lying down.

People detect horizontal vibrations at lower acceleration levels when lying down than when standing. However, a soft bed decouples and isolates a person fairly well from vibrations of the structure. The threshold to vertical vibrations is nearly constant at approximately 0.04 ft/s^2 for both sitting and standing positions from 2 to 100 Hz. This agrees with observations by Reiher and Meister (1931).

Many building spaces with critical work areas (surgery, precision laboratory work) are considered unacceptable if vibration is perceived by the occupants. In other situations and activities, perceived vibration may be acceptable. Parsons and Griffin (1988) found that accelerations twice the threshold level were unacceptable to occupants in their homes. A method of assessing acceptability in buildings is to compare the vibration with perception threshold values (Table 10).

Sound and Noise

In general terms, sound transmitted through air consists of oscillations in pressure above and below ambient atmospheric pressure. A vibrating object causes high- and low-pressure areas to be formed; these areas propagate away from the source. The entire mechanical energy spectrum includes infrasound and ultrasound as well as audible sound (Figure 6).

Health Effects. Hearing loss is generally considered the most undesirable effect of noise exposure, although there are other effects.

Table 10 Ratios of Acceptable to Threshold Vibration Levels

Place	Time	Continuous or Intermittent Vibration	Impulse or Transient Vibration Several Times per Day
Critical work areas	Day or night	1	1
Residential	Day/night	2 to 4/1.4	30 to 90/1.4 to 20
Office	Day or night	4	60 to 128
Workshop	Day or night	8	90 to 128

Note: Ratios for continuous or intermittent vibration and repeated impulse shock range from 0.7 to 1.0 for hospital operating theaters (room) and critical working areas. In other situations, impulse shock can generally be much higher than when vibration is more continuous.

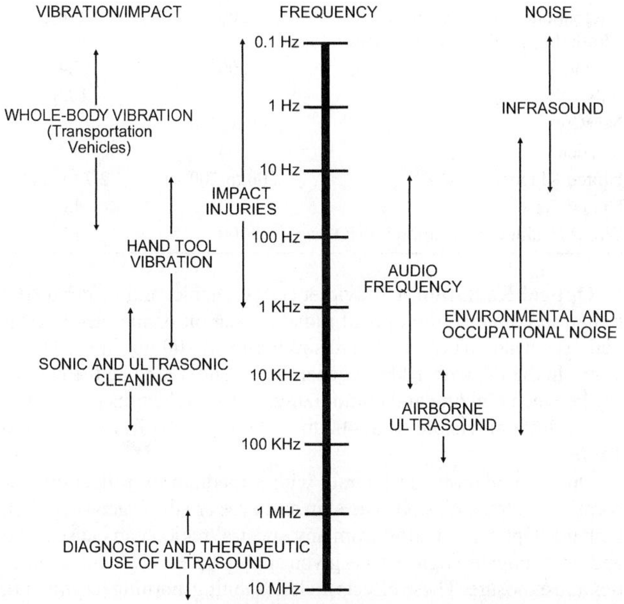

Fig. 6 Mechanical Energy Spectrum

Tinnitus, a ringing in the ears, is really the hearing of sounds that do not exist. It often accompanies hearing loss. **Paracusis** is a disorder where a sound is heard incorrectly; that is, a tone is heard, but has an inappropriate pitch. **Speech misperception** occurs when an individual mistakenly hears one sound for another (e.g., when the sound for *t* is heard as a *p*).

Hearing loss can be categorized as conductive, sensory, or neural. **Conductive** hearing loss results from a general decrease in the amount of sound transmitted to the inner ear. Excessive ear wax, a ruptured eardrum, fluid in the middle ear, or missing elements of bone structures in the middle ear are all associated with conductive hearing loss. These are generally not occupationally related and are generally reversible by medical or surgical means. **Sensory** hearing losses are associated with irreversible damage to the inner ear. Sensory hearing loss is further classified as (1) presbycusis, loss caused as the result of aging; (2) noise-induced hearing loss (industrial hearing loss and sociacusis, which is caused by noise in everyday life); and (3) nosoacusis, losses attributed to all other causes. **Neural** deficits are related to damage to higher centers of the auditory system.

Noise-induced hearing loss is believed to occur in the most sensitive individuals among those exposed for 8 h per day over a working lifetime at levels of 75 dBA, and for most people similarly exposed to 85 dBA.

Even when below levels that can cause adverse health effects, sound and noise can lead to reduced indoor environmental quality and potentially other unhealthy situations. For example, people often react to noisy mechanical equipment by shutting the equipment off

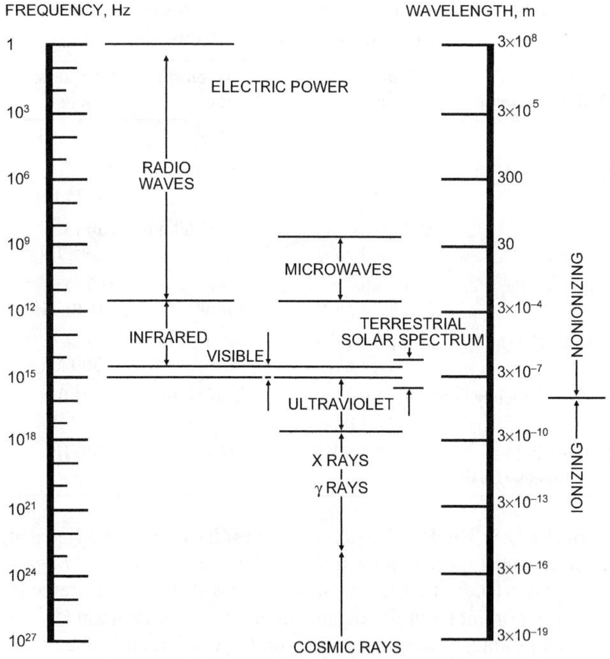

Fig. 7 Electromagnetic Spectrum

or blocking openings that provide a transmission pathway for the noise. Shutting off ventilation systems can lead to unhealthy indoor environments. Blocking some openings, such as those designed to provide combustion air, can also cause problems. Therefore, selecting components that are unlikely to lead to occupant dissatisfaction can be important in providing good indoor environmental quality.

For methods to address potential sound and noise problems, see Chapter 48 of the 2015 *ASHRAE Handbook—HVAC Applications*.

3.4 ELECTROMAGNETIC RADIATION

Radiation energy is emitted, transmitted, or absorbed in wave or particulate form. This energy consists of electric and magnetic forces, which, when disturbed in some manner, produce electromagnetic radiation. Electromagnetic radiation is grouped into a spectrum arranged by frequency and/or wavelength. The product of frequency and wavelength is the speed of light (1.9×10^5 miles per second). The spectrum includes ionizing, ultraviolet, visible, infrared, microwave, radio, and extremely low frequency (ELF) (Figure 7). Table 11 presents these electromagnetic radiations by their range of energies, frequencies, and wavelengths. The regions are not sharply delineated from each other and often overlap. It is convenient to divide these regions as listed in Table 11, because of the nature of the physical and biological effects.

Ionizing Radiation

Ionizing radiation is the part of the electromagnetic spectrum with very short wavelengths and high frequencies, and it has the ability to ionize matter. These ionizations tend to be very damaging to living matter. Background radiation that occurs naturally in the environment is from cosmic rays and naturally occurring radionuclides. It has not been established whether exposure at the low dose rate of average background levels is harmful to humans.

The basic standards for permissible air concentrations of radioactive materials are those of the National Committee on Radiation Protection, published by the National Bureau of Standards as *Handbook* 69 (NBS 1969). Industries operating under licenses

Table 11 Energy, Wavelength, and Frequency Ranges for Electromagnetic Radiation

Radiation Type	Energy Range	Wavelength Range	Frequency Range
Ionizing	>12.4 eV	<100 nm	>3.00 PHz
Ultraviolet (UV)	12.40 to 3.10 eV	100 to 400 nm	3.00 to 0.75 PHz
Visible	3.10 to 1.63 eV	400 to 760 nm	750 to 395 THz
Infrared (IR)	1.63 to 1.24 meV	760 nm to 1 mm	395 to 0.30 THz
Microwave (MW)	1.24 meV to 1.24 eV	1 mm to 1 m	300 GHz to 300 MHz
Radio-frequency (RF)	1.24 eV to 1.24 peV	1 m to 1 Mm	300 MHz to 300 Hz
Extremely low frequency (ELF)	<1.24 peV	>1 Mm	<300 Hz

from the U.S. Nuclear Regulatory Commission or state licensing agencies must meet requirements of the *Code of Federal Regulations*, Title 10, Part 20. Some states have additional requirements.

An important naturally occurring radionuclide is radon (^{222}Rn), a decay product of uranium in the soil (^{238}U). Radon is chemically inert. Details of units of measurement, typical radon levels, measurement methods and control strategies can be found in Chapter 11.

Health Effects of Radon. Radon is the leading cause of lung cancer among nonsmokers, according to EPA (2016b) estimates. Most information about radon's health risks comes from studies of workers in uranium and other underground mines. The radioactive decay of radon produces a series of radioactive isotopes of polonium, bismuth, and lead. Unlike their chemically inert radon parent, these progeny are chemically active and can attach to airborne particles that subsequently deposit in the lung, or deposit directly in the lung without attachment to particles. Some of these progeny, like radon, are alpha-particle emitters, which can cause cellular changes that may initiate lung cancer when they pass through lung cells (Samet 1989). Thus, adverse health effects associated with radon are caused by exposures to radon decay products, and the amount of risk is assumed to be directly related to the total exposure. Even though it is the radon progeny that present the possibility of adverse health risks, radon itself is usually measured and used as a surrogate for progeny measurements because of the expense involved in accurate measurements of radon progeny.

Exposure Standards. Many countries have established standards for exposure to radon. Some international action levels are listed in Table 12.

About 6% of U.S. homes (i.e., 5.8 million homes) have annual average radon concentrations exceeding 148 Bq/m^3 (4 pCi/L), approaching the action level (150 Bq/m^3) set by the U.S. Environmental Protection Agency (Marcinowski et al. 1994). Because there is no known safe level of exposure to radon, the EPA (2016b) also recommends that all homes be tested for radon, regardless of geographic location, and remedial measures be considered in homes with radon levels between 2 and 4 pCi/L.

Nonionizing Radiation

Ultraviolet radiation, visible light, and infrared radiation are components of sunlight and of all artificial light sources. Microwave and radio-frequency radiation are essential in a wide range of communication technologies and are also in widespread use for heating as in microwave ovens and heat sealers, and for heat treatments of various products. Power frequency fields are an essential and unavoidable consequence of the generation, transmission, distribution, and use of electrical power.

Table 12 2015 Action Levels for Radon Concentration Indoors

Country/Agency	Action Level Bq/m^3	Action Level pCi/L
Australia	200	5.4
Austria	200/400	5.4/10.8
Belgium	100/400	2.7/10.8
Canada	200	5.4
Czech Republic	200/400	5.4/10.8
P.R. China	200	5.4
European Union	<300	<8.1
Finland	200/400	5.4/10.8
Germany	100	2.7
International Commission on Radiological Protection (ICRP)	200	5.4
Ireland	200	5.4
Italy	—	10.8
Norway	100 to 200	2.7 to 5.4
Sweden	200	5.4
United Kingdom	100 to 200	2.7 to 5.4
United States	150	4.0
World Health Organization (WHO)	100	2.7

Optical Radiation. Ultraviolet (UV), visible, and infrared (IR) radiation compose the optical radiation region of the electromagnetic spectrum. The wavelengths range from 100 nm in the UV to 1 mm in the IR, with 100 nm generally considered to be the boundary between ionizing and nonionizing. UV wavelengths range from 100 to 400 nm, visible from 400 to 760 nm, and IR from 760 nm to 1 mm.

Optical radiation can interact with a medium by reflection, absorption, or transmission. The skin and eyes are the organs at risk in humans. Optical radiation from any spectral region can cause acute and/or chronic biologic effects given appropriate energy characteristics and exposure. These effects include tanning, burning (erythema), premature "aging," and skin cancer; and dryness, irritation, cataracts, and blindness in the eyes.

The region of the electromagnetic spectrum visible to humans is known as light. There can be biological, behavioral, psychological, and health effects from exposure to light. Assessment of these effects depends on the purpose and application of the illumination. Individual susceptibility varies, with other environmental factors (air quality, noise, chemical exposures, and diet) acting as modifiers. It is difficult, therefore, to generalize potential hazards. **Light pollution** is the presence of unwanted light.

Light penetrating the retina not only allows the exterior world to be seen, but, like food and water, is also used in a variety of metabolic processes. Darkness stimulates the pineal gland to secrete melatonin, which regulates the human biological clock. This, in turn, influences reproductive cycles, sleeping, eating patterns, activity levels, and moods. The color of light affects the way the objects appear. Distortion of color rendition may result in disorientation, headache, dizziness, nausea, and fatigue.

As the daylight shortens, the human body may experience a gradual slowing down, loss of energy, and a need for more sleep. It becomes harder to get to work, and depression or even withdrawal may take place. This type of seasonal depression, brought on by changes in light duration and intensity, is called **seasonal affective disorder (SAD)**. Sufferers also complain of anxiety, irritability, headache, weight gain, and lack of concentration and motivation. This problem is treated through manipulation of environmental lighting (exposure to full-spectrum lighting for extended periods, 12 h/day).

Radio-Frequency Radiation. Just as the body absorbs infrared and light energy, which can affect thermal balance, it can also absorb

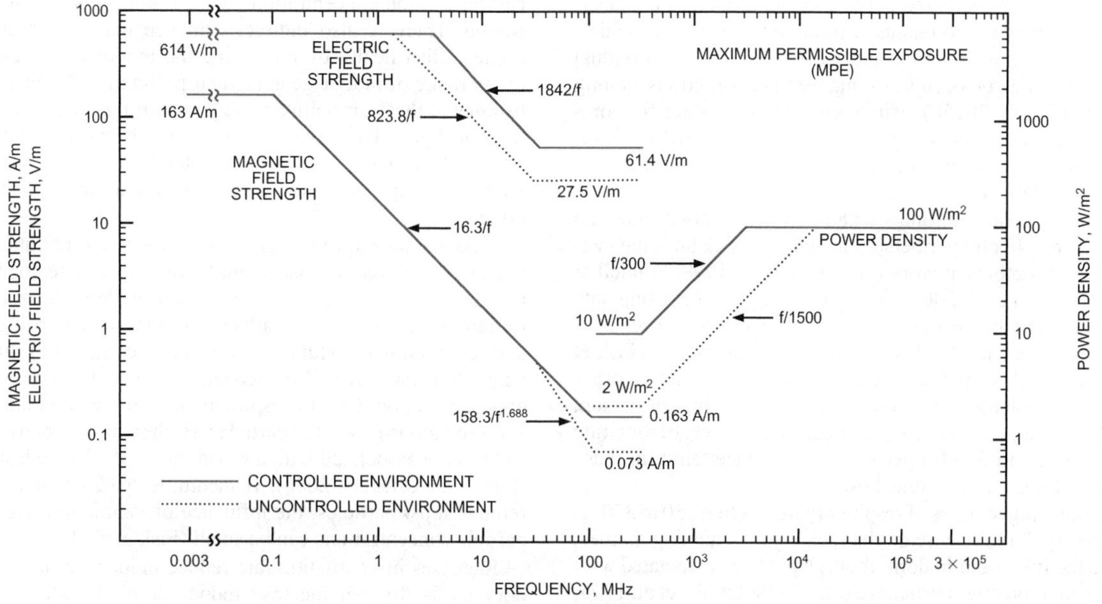

Fig. 8 Maximum Permissible Levels of Radio Frequency Radiation for Human Exposure
(Adapted from ANSI/IEEE *Standard* C95.1-2005)

other longer-wavelength electromagnetic radiation. For comparison, visible light has wavelengths in the range 0.4 to 0.7 μm and infrared from 0.7 to 10 μm, whereas the wavelength of K and X band radar is 12 and 28.6 mm. The wavelength of radiation in a typical microwave oven is 120 mm. Infrared is absorbed within 1 mm of the surface (Murray 1995).

The heat of absorbed radiation raises skin temperature and, if sufficient, is detected by the skin's thermoreceptors, warning the person of possible thermal danger. With increasing wavelength, radiation penetrates deeper into the body. Energy can thus be deposited well beneath the skin's thermoreceptors, making the person less able or slower to detect and be warned of the radiation (Justesen et al. 1982). Physiologically, these longer waves only heat the tissue and, because the heat may be deeper and less detectable, the maximum power density of such waves in occupied areas is regulated (ANSI *Standard* C95.1) (Figure 8). Maximum allowed power densities are less than half of sensory threshold values.

3.5 ERGONOMICS

Ergonomics is the scientific study of the relationship between humans and their work environments to achieve optimum adjustment in terms of efficiency, health, and well-being. Ergonomic designs of tools, chairs, etc., help workers interact more comfortably and efficiently with their environment. In ergonomically designed systems, productivity typically increases and the worker enjoys a healthier working experience. More recently, researchers have distinguished intrinsic ergonomics from extrinsic, or traditional, ergonomics. Intrinsic ergonomics considers how the interface between an individual and the environment affects and relies on specific body parts (e.g., muscles, tendons, bones) and work practices such as force of application, relaxation intervals, styles, and strength reserves that are not adequately considered in simple analyses of the physical environment.

The goals of ergonomic programs range from making work safe and humane, to increasing human efficiency, to creating human well-being. The successful application of ergonomic factors is measured by improved productivity, efficiency, safety, and acceptance of the resultant system design. The design engineer uses not only engineering skills, but also the principles of anatomy, orthopedics, physiology, medicine, psychology, and sociology to apply ergonomics to a design.

Implementing ergonomic principles in the workplace helps minimize on-the-job stress and strain, and prevents cumulative trauma disorders (CTDs). These disorders are subtle injuries that can affect the muscles, tendons, and nerves at body joints, especially the hands, wrists, elbows, shoulders, neck, back, and knees. Carpal tunnel syndrome is an example of a CTD. CTDs most frequently occur as a result of strain from performing the same task on a continuous or repetitive basis. This strain can slowly build over time, until the worker experiences pain and difficulty using the injured part of the body. Higher risks of developing CTDs are encountered when the work task requires repetitive motions, excessive force, or awkward postures. The ergonomics engineer addresses these risk factors by analyzing the task thoroughly and minimizing the repetitive motion, excessive force, and awkward posture.

Poor space ergonomics (Hartkopf and Loftness 1999) and consequent occupant interventions may also directly affect indoor conditions. For example, inappropriate use of cabinets, closets, furniture, partitions, room equipment or other obstructions may block air supply or exhaust vents, reduce airflow rates and temperature or humidity regulation, and disturb airflow (Lee and Awbi 2004). These kinds of problems are often attributed to poor space layout and ventilation design, but usually originate from lack of space availability, such as small room dimensions and high occupant densities. Reduced ventilation rates deteriorate conditions for indoor environmental health, working, and comfort. They may be encountered in overstaffed offices (Mahdavi and Unzeitig 2005) or in demanding environments such as hospital operating theatres (Balaras et al. 2006). The interaction between ergonomics and indoor environmental quality is increasingly important as personalized environmental control systems, such as personal ventilation systems (PVSs), are used to provide customized environment for occupants. This area requires further research.

3.6 OUTDOOR AIR VENTILATION AND HEALTH

Increased outdoor air ventilation reduces indoor concentrations of indoor-generated air pollutants, although the extent of reduction varies; in some cases, increased outdoor air ventilation can increase indoor levels of outdoor pollutants. Ventilation rates vary considerably from building to building and over time within individual buildings, depending on occupancy and weather conditions, among other factors (Persily 2015b). Minimum ventilation rates for commercial and residential buildings are specified in ASHRAE *Standards* 62.1 and 62.2, respectively, and for health care facilities in ASHRAE *Standard* 170.

Occupants of office buildings with higher ventilation rates (up to approximately 40 cfm per person) have fewer sick building syndrome (SBS) symptoms at work (Seppänen et al. 1999; Sundell et al. 2011; Wargocki et al. 2002). Statistical analysis of existing data provided a central estimate of the average relationship between SBS symptom prevalence in office workers and ventilation rate (Fisk et al. 2009). This analysis indicates a 23% increase in symptom prevalence as the ventilation rate drops from 21 to 11 cfm per person, and a 29% decrease in symptom prevalence rates as ventilation rate increases from 21 to 53 cfm per person. The uncertainty in these central estimates is considerable, however.

Substantially higher rates of respiratory illness (e.g., 50 to 370%) in high-density buildings (e.g., barracks, jails, nursing homes, health care facilities) and in dorm rooms have been associated with very low ventilation rates (Brundage et al. 1988; Drinka et al. 1996; Hoge et al. 1994; Seppänen et al. 1999; Sun et al. 2011), presumably because lower ventilation rates are likely to result in higher airborne concentrations of infectious viruses and bacteria. Only a few studies have been performed. In a literature review by a multidisciplinary panel (Li et al. 2007), a broader set of evidence was considered to evaluate the role of both ventilation rates and indoor airflow patterns in respiratory disease. The review panel concluded that "there is strong and sufficient evidence" to demonstrate that lower ventilation rates and indoor airflow from infected to uninfected people are associated with increased transmission of infectious diseases "such as measles, tuberculosis, chickenpox, influenza, smallpox, and SARS."

In offices, a 35% decrease in short-term absence was associated with a doubling of ventilation rate from 25 to 50 cfm per person (Milton et al. 2000). In elementary-grade classrooms, on average, for each 100 ppm decrease in the difference between indoor and outdoor CO_2 concentrations, there was a 1 to 2% relative decrease in the absence rate (Shendell et al. 2004). Given the relationship of CO_2 concentrations with ventilation rates, for each 2.1 cfm per person increase in ventilation rate, the relative decrease in absence rates was estimated to be 1 to 4%. This relationship applied over an estimated ventilation rate range of 5 to 30 cfm per person, and should not be applied outside those limits. Data relating building ventilation rates and absence rates are very limited.

In residences, very little research has been conducted on the relationship of ventilation rates with the health of occupants. A Norwegian study (Oie et al. 1999) of young children found that low home ventilation rates were not associated with an increase in bronchial obstruction (i.e., reduced breathing airflows) in children. However, the increase in risk of bronchial obstruction resulting from other factors, such as building dampness, was moderately to markedly higher in homes with ventilation rates below 0.5 air changes per hour (ach). In other words, having low ventilation rates increased the health risks from some building conditions (e.g., dampness) associated with indoor pollutant emissions. Bornehag et al. (2005) studied 390 single-family homes and found that children in homes with very low ventilation rates (0.05 to 0.24 ach) had twice as many allergic symptoms compared to those in homes with high ventilation rates (0.44 to 1.44 ach). However, Emenius et al. (2004) found that the risk of recurrent wheezing in children was not different for houses with measured air exchange rates above and below 0.5 ach. Another residential study (Norback et al. 1995) found that the risk of having asthma symptoms was increased in homes with higher indoor carbon dioxide concentrations, which indicate less ventilation per person. There is also indirect evidence that ventilation rates of homes affect health by modifying the indoor concentrations of a broad range of indoor-generated air pollutants. Because exposures to some of these air pollutants (e.g., environmental tobacco smoke, formaldehyde) have been linked with adverse health (California EPA 1997; DHHS 2006; Mendell 2006; WHO 2002), it is likely that increased home ventilation rates would reduce the associated health effects.

Indoor concentrations of some outdoor air pollutants can be increased with an increased ventilation rate. Ozone concentrations may be the one of most concern: higher outdoor air ozone concentrations are associated with adverse respiratory and irritation effects and several other health effects (Hubbell et al. 2005). Increases in ventilation rates can also increase indoor concentrations of, and exposures to, outdoor air respirable particles, while reducing exposures to indoor-generated particles. Higher outdoor particle concentrations are associated with a broad range of adverse health effects (Pope and Dockery 2006). If incoming outdoor air is filtered to remove most particles, the influence of ventilation rate on indoor particle concentrations can be small (Fisk et al. 2002).

Increases in ventilation rate reduce indoor humidity when outdoor air is dry but increase indoor humidity when outdoor air humidity is high and the building mechanical systems also do not dehumidify sufficiently to counteract the effects of increased moisture entry. Some studies have found that levels of house dust mites or allergens from mites, which are associated with allergy and asthma symptoms, decrease with higher ventilation rates, but findings have not been consistent (Fisk 2009). Where increased ventilation results in high indoor humidity, dust mite allergen levels and the risk of indoor mold growth/colonization problems also increase.

Overall, increases in ventilation rate diminish exposures to various indoor-generated air pollutants and might increase exposures to some outdoor air pollutants. On balance, the scientific literature points to improvements in health with increased ventilation rates. Appropriate air-cleaning methods should be used to remove excessive pollutants in the outdoor ventilation air, as required in ASHRAE *Standards* 62.1 and 61.2.

REFERENCES

ASHRAE members can access *ASHRAE Journal* articles and ASHRAE research project final reports at technologyportal.ashrae.org. Articles and reports are also available for purchase by nonmembers in the online ASHRAE Bookstore at www.ashrae.org/bookstore.

AIHA. 2014. *White paper: Electronic cigarettes in the indoor environment*. American Industrial Hygiene Association, Falls Church, VA. www.aiha.org/government-affairs/PositionStatements/Electronc%20Cig%20Document_Final.pdf.

Alpaugh, E.L., and T.J. Hogan. 1988. *Fundamentals of industrial hygiene*, 3rd ed. National Safety Council, Itasca, IL.

Anaissie, E.J., S.R. Penzak, and M.C. Dignani. 2002. The hospital water supply as a source of nosocomial infections: A plea for action. *Archives of Internal Medicine* 162(13):1483-1492.

ANSI/IEEE. 2005. Safety levels with respect to human exposure to radio frequency electromagnetic radiation, 3 kHz to 300 GHz. ANSI/IEEE *Standard* C95.1-2005. American National Standards Institute, New York.

Apte, M.G., I.S.H. Buchanan, and M.J. Mendell. 2007. Outdoor ozone and building related symptoms in the BASE study. *Report* LBNL-62419. Lawrence Berkeley National Laboratory, Berkeley, CA.

Arnow, P.M., J.N. Fink, D.P. Schlueter, J.J. Barboriak, G. Mallison, S.I. Said, S. Martin, G.F. Unger, G.T. Scanlon, and V.P. Kurup. 1978. Early detection of hypersensitivity pneumonitis in office workers. *American Journal of Medicine* 64(2):237-242.

ASHRAE. 2003. *Mold and moisture management in buildings*.

ASHRAE. 2009. *Indoor air quality guide: Best practices for design, construction, and commissioning*.

ASHRAE. 2011. *Environmental Health Committee (EHC) emerging issue report: Ozone and indoor chemistry*. www.ashrae.org/File%20Library /docLib/Committees/EHC/EmergingIssues/EHC_Emerging_Issue-Ozone andIndoorAirChemistry.pdf.

ASHRAE. 2000. Minimizing the risk of legionellosis associated with building water systems. *Guideline* 12-2000.

ASHRAE. 2016. Ventilation for acceptable indoor air quality. ANSI/ ASHRAE *Standard* 62.1-2016.

ASHRAE. 2010. Ventilation for acceptable indoor air quality in low rise residential buildings. ANSI/ASHRAE *Standard* 62.2 -2010.

ASHRAE. 2013. Ventilation of health care facilities. ANSI/ASHRAE/ ASHE *Standard* 170-2013.

ASHRAE. 2015. Legionellosis: Risk management for building water systems. ANSI/ASHRAE *Standard* 188-2015.

ATS. 1999. Pulmonary rehabilitation. *American Journal of Respiratory and Critical Care Medicine* 159:1666-1682.

ATSDR. 2001. *Toxicological profile for asbestos*. Agency for Toxic Substances and Disease Registry, U.S. Department of Health and Human Services, Washington, D.C.

Balaras, C.A., E. Dascalaki, and A. Gaglia. 2006. HVAC and indoor thermal conditions in hospital operating rooms, *Energy and Buildings* 39(4): 454-470.

Ballester, F., D. Corella, S. Perez-Hoyos, M. Saez, and A. Hervas. 1997. Mortality as a function of temperature: A study in Valencia, Spain, 1991-1993. *International Journal of Epidemiology* 26(3):551-561.

Bascom, R.A. 1996. Environmental factors and respiratory hypersensitivity: The Americas. *Toxicology Letters* 86:115-130.

Bascom, R., P. Bromberg, D.A. Costa, R. Devlin, D.W. Dockery, M.W. Frampton, W. Lambert, J.M. Samet, F.E. Speizer, and M. Utell. 1996. Health effects of outdoor pollution, parts I and II. *American Journal of Respiratory and Critical Care Medicine* 153:3-50, 477-489.

Bassler, B. 2009. *How bacteria communicate*. Lecture available at www.ted .com/talks/lang/en/bonnie_bassler_on_how_bacteria_communicate.html.

Bates, D.V. 2005 Ambient ozone and mortality. *Epidemiology*. 16:427-429

Baylor, E.R., V. Peters, and M.B. Baylor. 1977. Water-to-air transfer of virus. *Science* 252:763.

Beko, G., G. Clausen, and C.J. Weschler. 2007. Further studies of oxidation processes on filter surfaces: Evidence for oxidation products and the influence of time in service. *Atmospheric Environment* 41 (2007):5202-5212.

Bell, M.L., F. Dominnici, and J.M. Samet. 2005. A meta-analysis of time-series studies of ozone and mortality with comparison to the National Morbidity, Mortality, and Air Pollution Study. *Epidemiology* 16:436-445.

Berglund, L.G., and D. Cunningham. 1986. Parameters of human discomfort in warm environments. *ASHRAE Transactions* 92(2).

Berglund, L.G., and R.R. Gonzalez. 1977. Evaporation of sweat from sedentary man in humid environments. *Journal of Applied Physiology, Respiratory, Environmental and Exercise Physiology* 42(5):767-772.

BIFMA. 2011. Standard method for testing VOC emissions from office furniture systems, components, and seating. ANSI/BIFMA *Standard* M7.1-2011 (RA 2016). Business and Institutional Furniture Manufacturers Association, Grand Rapids, MI.

Billings, C.E. 1975. Electrical shock. In *Textbook of medicine*. Saunders, Philadelphia.

Blatteis, C.M., ed. 1998. *Physiology and pathophysiology of temperature regulation*. World Scientific, Singapore.

Bornehag, C.G., G. Blomquist, F. Gyntelberg, B. Jarvholm, P. Malmberg, L. Nordvall, A. Nielsen, G. Pershagen, and J. Sundell. 2001. Dampness in buildings and health: Nordic interdisciplinary review of the scientific evidence on associations between exposure to "dampness" in buildings and health effects (NORDDAMP). *Indoor Air* 11(2):72-86.

Bornehag, C.G., J. Sundell, L. Hagerhed-Engman, and T. Sigsgaard. 2005. Association between ventilation rates in 390 Swedish homes and allergic symptoms in children. *Indoor Air* 15(4):275-280.

Bridger, C.A., and L.A. Helfand. 1968. Mortality from heat during July 1966 in Illinois. *International Journal of Biometeorology* 12:51.

Brundage, J.F., R.M. Scott, W.M. Lednar, D.W. Smith, and R.N. Miller. 1988. Building-associated risk of febrile acute respiratory diseases in Army trainees. *Journal of the American Medical Association* 259:2108.

Burch, G.E., and N.P. DePasquale. 1962. *Hot climates, man and his heart*. Charles C. Thomas, Springfield, IL.

Burge, H.A. 1989. In *Occupational medicine: State of the art reviews*, vol. 4, *Problem buildings: Building-associated illness and the sick building syndrome*, pp. 713-721. J.E. Cone and M.J. Hodgson, eds. Hanley and Belfus, Philadelphia.

Burge, H.A. 1995. *Bioaerosols*. Lewis, Chelsea, MI.

Burgess, J.L., and C.D. Crutchfield. 1995. Quantitative respirator fit tests of Tucson fire fighters and measures of negative pressure excursions during exertion. *Applied Occupational and Environmental Hygiene* 10(1):29-36.

Burstyn, I. 2013. Peering through the mist: What does the chemistry of contaminants in electronic cigarettes tell us about health risks? public health.drexel.edu/SiteData/docs/ms08/f90349264250e603/ms08.pdf.

Burton, D.J. 2000. *Industrial ventilation: A self-directed learning workbook*, 4th ed. Carr, North Bountiful, UT.

Buttner, M.P., and L.D. Stetzenbach. 1999. Dispersal of fungal spores from three types of air handling system duct material. *Aerobiologia* 15:1-8.

Buttner, M.P., P. Cruz-Perez, L.D. Stetzenbach, P.J. Garrett, and A.E. Luedtke. 2002. Measurement of airborne fungal spore dispersal from three types of flooring materials. *Aerobiologia* 18:1-11.

Cain, W.S. 1989. *Perceptual characteristics of nasal irritation*. National Danish Institute on Occupational Health, Copenhagen.

California EPA. 1997. Health effects of exposure to environmental tobacco smoke. *Final Report*, California Environmental Protection Agency, Office of Environmental Health Hazard Assessment.

Calm, J.M., and P.A. Domanski. 2004. R-22 replacement status. *ASHRAE Journal* 46(8):29-39.

CDC. 2005. Unintentional non-fire-related carbon monoxide exposures—United States, 2001-2003. *Morbidity and Mortality Weekly Report* 54(2): 36-39.

CDPH. 2010. *Standard method for the testing and evaluation of volatile organic chemical emissions from indoor sources using environmental chambers*, v. 1.1. California Department of Public Health. www.cal-iaq .org/phocadownload/cdph-iaq_standardmethod_v1_1_2010%20new11 10.pdf.

CFR. Annual. *Occupational safety and health standards: Air contaminants*. 29CFR1910.1000. U.S. Government Printing Office, Washington, D.C.

CFR. Annual. *Occupational safety and health standards: Asbestos*. 29CFR1926.1101. U.S. Government Printing Office, Washington, D.C.

Chen, P.W., and L.E. Robertson. 1972. Human perception thresholds of horizontal motion. *ASCE Journal*, Structure Division, August.

Chen, C., B. Zhao, and C.J. Weschler. 2012. Assessing the influence of indoor exposure to "outdoor ozone" on the relationship between ozone and short-term mortality in U.S. communities. *Environmental Health Perspectives* 120:235-240. dx.doi.org/10.1289/ehp.1103970.

Cobb, N., and R.A. Etzel. 1991. Unintentional carbon monoxide-related deaths in the United States, 1979 through 1988. *Journal of the American Medical Association* 266:659-663.

Collins, S.D., and J. Lehmann. 1953. Excess deaths from influenza and pneumonia and from important chronic diseases during epidemic periods, 1918-51. *Public Health Monograph* 20.10, U.S. Public Health Service *Publication* 213.

Cometto-Muñiz, J.E., and W.S. Cain. 1994a. Sensory reactions of nasal pungency and odor to volatile organic compounds: The alkylbenzenes. *American Industrial Hygiene Association Journal* 55(9):811-817.

Cometto-Muñiz, J.E., and W.S. Cain. 1994b. Perception of odor and nasal pungency from homologous series of volatile organic compounds. *Indoor Air* 4:140-145.

Corsi, R.L., K.A. Kinney, and H. Levin. 2012. Microbiomes of built environments: 2011 symposium highlights and workgroup recommendations. *Indoor Air* 22(3):171-172.

Cox, C.S. 1987. *The aerobiological pathway of microorganisms*. John Wiley & Sons, New York.

CPSC. 2006. *Portable generators: Legal memorandum and staff briefing package for ANPR*. Consumer Product Safety Commission, Washington, D.C.

Czogala, J., M.L. Goniewicz, B. Fidelus, W. Zielinska-Danch, W. Travers, and A. Sobczak. 2013. Secondhand exposure to vapors from electronic cigarettes. *Nicotine and Tobacco Research*. dx.doi.org/10.1093/ntr/ntt203.

Davenport, A.G. 1988. The response of supertall buildings to wind. In *Second century of the skyscraper*, pp. 705-726. L. Beedle, ed. Van Nostrand Reinhold, New York.

Destaillats, H., M.M. Lunden, B.C. Singer, B.K. Coleman, A.T. Hodgson, C.J. Weschler, and W.W. Nazaroff. 2006. Indoor secondary pollutants from household product emissions in the presence of ozone: A bench-scale chamber study. *Environmental Science & Technology* 40:4421-4428.

DHHS. 1986. The health consequences of involuntary smoking. A report of the surgeon general. DHHS *Publication* (PHS) 87-8398. U.S. Department of Health and Human Services, Public Health Services, Office of the Assistant Secretary for Health, Office of Smoking and Health.

DHHS. 2006. *The health consequences of involuntary exposure to tobacco smoke: A report of the Surgeon General*. Department of Health and Human Services, Centers for Disease Control and Prevention, Coordinating Center for Health Promotion, National Center for Chronic Disease Prevention and Health Promotion, Office on Smoking and Health, Washington, D.C.

Diaz, J., R. Garcia, F. Velazquez de Castro, E. Hernandez, C. Lopez, and A. Otero. 2002. Effects of extremely hot days on people older than 65 years in Seville (Spain) from 1986 to 1997. *International Journal of Biometeorology* 46(3):145-149.

Drinka, P.J., P. Krause, M. Schilling, B.A. Miller, P. Shult, and S. Gravenstein. 1996. Report of an outbreak: Nursing home architecture and influenza-A attack rates. *Journal of the American Geriatric Society* 44(8): 910-913.

Drummond, R.A., and G.D. Brown. 2011. The role of Dectin-1 in the host defence against fungal infections. *Current Opinion in Microbiology* 14: 392-399.

EHD. 1987. *Exposure guidelines for residential indoor air quality*. EHD-TR-156. Environmental Health Directorate, Health Protection Branch. Ottawa, ON.

Ellis, F.P. 1972. Mortality from heat illness and heat aggravated illness in the United States. *Environmental Research* 5.

Emenius, G., M. Svartengren, J. Korsgard, L. Nordvall, G. Pershagen, and M. Wickman. 2004. Building characteristics, indoor air quality and recurrent wheezing in very young children (BAMSE). *Indoor Air* 14(1): 34-42.

EPA. 1991. Introduction to indoor air quality, a reference manual. *Report* EPA 400/3-91/003.

EPA. 1992. *Respiratory health effects of passive smoking: Lung cancer and other disorders, review draft*. EPA/600-6-90/006F. Office of Research and Development, Washington, D.C.

EPA. 2005. IAQ tools for schools—IAQ reference guide. *Report* 402-K-95-001. U.S. Environmental Protection Agency, Washington, D.C.

EPA. 2011. Exposure-based chemical prioritization workshop: Semi-volatile organic compounds. Indoor Environment Workshop, Research Triangle Park, NC. epa.gov/ncct/expocast/svoc_agenda.html.

EPA. 2012. *Building assessment survey and evaluation (BASE) study*. U.S. Environmental Protection Agency, Washington, D.C. www.epa.gov/indoor-air-quality-iaq/building-assessment-survey-and-evaluation-study.

EPA. 2016a. *National ambient air quality standards (NAAQS)*. U.S. Environmental Protection Agency, Washington, D.C. www.epa.gov/criteria-air-pollutants/naaqs-table.

EPA. 2016b. *Health risk of radon*. U.S. Environmental Protection Agency, Washington, D.C. www.epa.gov/radon/health-risk-radon.

FAA. 2000. Prohibition of smoking on scheduled passenger flights: Final rules. 14CFR121, 129, and 135. *Federal Register* 65(112):36, 776-36, 780.

Fanger, P.O. 1970. *Thermal comfort*. Teknisk Forlag, Copenhagen.

FDA. 2009. Summary of results: Laboratory analysis of electronic cigarettes conducted by FDA. U.S. Food and Drug Administration, Silver Spring, MD. www.fda.gov/NewsEvents/PublicHealthFocus/ucm173146.htm.

Fisk, W.J. 2009. Do residential indoor humidity control measures reduce the risks of house dust mites? *Proceedings of Healthy Buildings 2009*, Syracuse, NY.

Fisk, W.J., D. Faulkner, J. Palonen, and O. Seppanen. 2002. Performance and costs of particle air filtration technologies. *Indoor Air* 12(4):223-234.

Fisk, W.J., Q. Lei-Gomez, and M.J. Mendell. 2007. Meta-analyses of the associations of respiratory health effects with dampness and mold in homes. *Indoor Air* 17(4):284-295.

Fisk, W.J., A.G. Mirer, and M.J. Mendell. 2009. Quantitative relationship of sick building syndrome symptoms with ventilation rates. *Indoor Air* 19(2):159-165.

Fisk, W.J., E. Eliseeva, and M.J. Mendell. 2010. Association of residential dampness and mold with respiratory tract infections and bronchitis: a meta-analysis. *Environmental Health* 9:72.

Flannigan, B., R.A. Samson, and J.D. Miller. 2001. *Microorganisms in home and indoor work environments*. Taylor and Francis, New York.

Franck, C., P. Skov, and O. Bach. 1993. Prevalence of objective eye manifestations in people working in office buildings with different prevalences of the sick building syndrome compared with the general population. *International Archives of Occupational and Environmental Health* 65:65-69.

Gaul, L.E., and G.B. Underwood. 1952. Relation of dew point and barometric pressure to chapping of normal skin. *Journal of Investigative Dermatology* 19:9.

Geary, D.F. 2000. New guidelines on *Legionella*. *ASHRAE Journal* 44(9): 44-49.

Geiss, O., I. Bianchi, F. Barhona, and J. Barrero-Moreno. 2014. Characterisation of mainstream and passive vapours emitted by selected electronic cigarettes. *International Journal of Hygiene and Environmental Health* 281:169-180.

Giles, B., C. Balafoutis, and P. Maheras. 1990. Too hot for comfort: The heatwaves in Greece in 1987 and 1988. *International Journal of Biometeorology* 34:98-104.

Girman, J.R. 1989. Volatile organic compounds and building bake-out. In *Occupational medicine: State of the art reviews*, vol. 4, *Problem buildings: Building-associated illness and the sick building syndrome*, pp. 695-712. J.E. Cone and M.J. Hodgson, eds. Hanley and Belfus, Philadelphia.

Girman, J., Y.-L. Chang, S.B. Hayward, and K.S. Liu. 1998. Causes of unintentional deaths from carbon monoxide poisonings in California. *Western Journal of Medicine* 168(3):158-165.

Glantz, S.A., and W.W. Parmley. 1991. Passive smoking and heart disease epidemiology, physiology, and biochemistry. *Circulation* 83:633-642.

Goniewicz, M.L., J. Knysak, M. Gawron, L. Kosmider, A. Sobczak, J. Kurek, A Prokopowicz, M. Jablonska-Czapla, C. Rosik-Dulewska, C. Havel, P. Jacob III, and N. Benowitz. 2014. Levels of selected carcinogens and toxicants in vapour from electronic cigarettes. *Tobacco Control* 23:133-139. dx.doi.org/10.1136/tobaccocontrol-2012-050859.

Gonzalez, R.R., L.G. Berglund, and A.P. Gagge. 1978. Indices of thermoregulatory strain for moderate exercise. *Journal of Applied Physiology: Respiratory Environmental and Exercise Physiology* 44(6):889-899.

Goodman, S.N. 2005. The methodologic ozone effect. *Epidemiology* 16: 430-435.

Green, B.J., J.K. Sercombe, and E.R. Tovey. 2005. Fungal fragments and undocumented conidia function as new aeroallergen sources. *Journal of Allergy and Clinical Imumunology* 115:1043-1048. www.jacionline.org/article/S0091-6749(05)00362-3/fulltext.

Greenberg, L. 1964. Asthma and temperature change. *Archives of Environmental Health* 8:642.

Hajat, S., R.S. Kovats, R.W. Atkinson, and A. Haines. 2002. Impact of hot temperatures on death in London: A time series approach. *Journal of Epidemiology and Community Health* 56(5):367-372.

Hales, J.B.S., R.W. Hubbard, and S.L. Graffin. 1996. Limits of heat tolerance. Chapter 15 in *Handbook of physiology*, sect. 4, *Environmental physiology*. M.J. Fregly and C.M. Blatteis, eds. *American Physiological. Society,* Bethesda, MD.

Hardy, J.D. 1971. Thermal comfort and health. *ASHRAE Journal* 13:43.

Harrad, S., S. Hazrati, and C. Ibarra. 2006. Concentrations of polychlorinated biphenyls in indoor air and polybrominated diphenyl ethers in indoor air and dust in Birmingham, United Kingdom: Implications for human exposure. *Environmental Science & Technology* 40(15):4633-4638.

Harriman, L., G. Brundrett, and R. Kittler. 2001. *Humidity control design guide for commercial and institutional buildings*. ASHRAE.

Hartkopf, V., and V. Loftness. 1999. Global relevance of total building performance. *Automation in Construction* 8(4):377-393.

Hauser, R., and A.M. Calafat. 2005. Phthalates and human health. *Occupational and Environmental Medicine* 62(11):806-818.

Health Canada. 2015. *Residential indoor air quality guidelines*. healthycanadians.gc.ca/healthy-living-vie-saine/environment-environnement/air/guidelines-lignes-directrices-eng.php.

Hill, A.B. 1965. The environment and disease: Association or causation? *Proceedings of the Royal Society of Medicine* 58:295-300. www.ncbi.nlm.nih.gov/pmc/articles/PMC1898525/pdf/procrsmed00196-0010.pdf.

Hodgson, A.T. 1995. A review and a limited comparison of methods for measuring total volatile organic compounds in indoor air. *Indoor Air* 5(4):247.

Hodgson, M.J., P.R. Morey, M. Attfield, W. Sorenson, J.N. Fink, W.W. Rhodes, and G.S. Visvesvara. 1985. *Archives of Environmental Health* 40:96.

Hoge, C.W., M.R. Reichler, E.A. Dominguez, J.C. Bremer, T.D. Mastro, K.A. Hendricks, D.M. Musher, J.A. Elliott, R.R. Facklam, and R.F. Breiman. 1994. An epidemic of pneumococcal disease in an overcrowded, inadequately ventilated jail. *New England Journal of Medicine* 331(10): 643-648.

Holland, W.W. 1961. Influence of the weather on respiratory and heart disease. *Lancet* 2:338.

Hryhorczuk, D.O., L.J. Frateschi, J.W. Lipscomb, and R. Zhang. 1992. Use of the scan statistic to detect temporal clustering of poisonings. *Journal of Toxicology—Clinical Toxicology* 30:459-465.

Hubbell, B.J., A. Hallberg, D.R. McCubbin, and E. Post. 2005. Health-related benefits of attaining the 8-hr ozone standard. *Environmental Health Perspectives* 113(1):73-82.

Humphries, C. 2012. Indoor ecosystems. *Science* 335:648-650.

Hyppel, A. 1984. Fingerprint of a mould odor. *Proceedings of the 3rd International Conference on Indoor Air Quality and Climate*, Stockholm, Sweden, vol. 3, pp. 443-447. B. Berglund, T. Lindvall, and J. Sundell, eds.

Institute of Medicine. 2004. *Damp indoor spaces and health*. National Academies Press, Washington, D.C. www.nap.edu/openbook.php?isbn=0309091934.

Institute of Medicine. 2011. *Climate change, the indoor environment, and health*. National Academies Press, Washington, D.C.

ISO. 1984. Guidelines for the evaluation of the response of occupants of fixed structures, especially buildings and off-shore structures, to low-frequency horizontal motion (0.063 to 1 Hz). *Standard* 6897 (RA 2015). International Organization for Standardization, Geneva.

ISO. 2006. Ergonomics of the thermal environment—Methods for the assessment of human responses to contact with surfaces—Part 1: Hot surfaces. *Standard* 13732-1:2006 (RA 2010). International Organization for Standardization, Geneva.

Ito, K., S.F. DeLeon, and M. Lippmann. 2005. Associations between ozone and daily mortality: analysis and meta-analysis. *Epidemiology* 16:446-457.

Judson, R.S., K.A. Houck, R.J. Kavlock, T.B. Knudsen, M.T. Martin, H.M. Mortensen, D.M. Reif, D.M. Rotroff, I. Shah, A.M. Richard, and D.J. Dix. 2010. In vitro screening of environmental chemicals for targeted testing prioritization: The ToxCast project. *Environmental Health Perspectives* 118(4):485-492. www.ncbi.nlm.nih.gov/pmc/articles/PMC2854724/.

Justesen, D.R., E.R. Adair, J.C. Stevens, and V. Bruce-Wolfe. 1982. A comparative study of human sensory thresholds: 2450 MHz microwaves vs. far-infrared radiation. *Bioelectromagnetics* 3:117-125.

Katayama, K. and M. Momiyana-Sakamoto. 1970. A biometeorological study of mortality from stroke and heart diseases. *Meteorological Geophysics* 21:127.

Kato, K., M.J. Silva, J.A. Reidy, D. Hurtz, N.A. Malek, L.L. Needham, H. Nakazawa, D.B. Barr, and A.M. Calafat. 2004. Mono(2-ethyl-5-hydroxyhexyl) phthalate and mono-(2-ethyl-5-oxohexyl) phthalate as biomarkers for human exposure assessment to di-(2-ethylhexyl) phthalate. *Environmental Health Perspectives* 112(3):327-330. www.ncbi.nlm.nih.gov/pmc/articles/PMC1241862/pdf/ehp0112-000327.pdf.

Kessler, W.R., and W.R. Anderson. 1951. Heat prostration in fibrocystic disease of pancreas and other conditions. *Pediatrics* 8:648.

Kiefer, M., and J. Watson. 2015. Ill wind: Climate change and industrial hygiene. *The Synergist* (November).

Kilbourne, E.M., T.S. Jones, K. Choi, and S.B. Thacker. 1982. Risk factors for heatstroke: A case-control study. *Journal of the American Medical Association* 247(24):3332-3336.

Kjaergaard, S. 1992. Assessment methods and causes of eye irritation in humans in indoor environments. In *Chemical, microbiological, health, and comfort aspects of indoor air quality*, H. Knoeppel and P. Wolkoff, eds., pp. 115-127. Energy Cost Savings Council, European Economic Community, and European Atomic Energy Council, Brussels.

Kjaergaard, S., L. Mølhave, and O.F. Pedersen. 1991. Human reactions to a mixture of indoor pollutants. *Atmospheric Environment* 25:1417-1426.

Koren, H. 1990. The inflammatory response of the human upper airways to volatile organic compounds. *Proceedings of Indoor Air '90*, vol. 1, pp. 325-330.

Koren, H., D.E. Graham, and R.B. Devlin. 1992. Exposure of humans to a volatile organic mixture III: Inflammatory response. *Archives of Environmental Health* 47:39-44.

Krieger, J., D.E. Jacobs, P.J. Ashley, A. Baeder, G.L. Chew, D. Dearborn, H.P. Hynes, J.D. Miller, R. Morley, F. Rabito, and D.C. Zeldin. 2010. Housing interventions and control of asthma-related indoor biologic agents: A review of the evidence. *Journal of Public Health Management and Practice* 16(5):S11-S20. www.ncbi.nlm.nih.gov/pmc/articles/PMC3934496/.

Kunst, A.E., C.W. Looman, and J.P. Mackenbach. 1993. Outdoor air temperature and mortality in The Netherlands: A time-series analysis. *American Journal of Epidemiology* 137(3):331-341.

Lauterbach, J.H., M. Laugesen, and B.B. Ross. 2012. Suggested protocol for estimation of harmful and potentially harmful constituents in mainstream aerosols generated by electronic nicotine delivery systems (ENDS). *Toxicologist* 126:1.

Leathart, G.L. 1972. Clinical aspects of respiratory disease because of mining. In *Medicine in the mining industry*, J.M. Rogan, ed. Heinemann Medical, London.

Lee, H., and H.B. Awbi. 2004. Effect of internal partitioning on indoor air quality of rooms with mixing ventilation—Basic study. *Building and Environment* 39(2):127-141.

Levetin, E. 1995. Fungi. In *Bioaerosols*, H.A. Burge, ed. CRC Press, Lewis Publishers, Boca Raton, FL.

Levy, J.I., S.M. Chemerynski, and J.A. Sarnat. 2005. Ozone exposure and mortality: An empirical Bayes meta-regression analysis. *Epidemiology* 16:458-468

Li, Y., X. Huang, I.T. Yu, T.W. Wong, and H. Qian. 2005a. Role of air distribution in SARS transmission during the largest nosocomial outbreak in Hong Kong. *Indoor Air* 15:83-95.

Li, Y., S. Duan, I.T. Yu, and T.W. Wong. 2005b. Multi-zone modeling of probable SARS virus transmission by airflow between flats in Block E, Amoy Gardens. *Indoor Air* 15:96-111.

Li, Y., G.M. Leung, J.W. Tang, X. Yang, C.Y.H. Chao, J.Z. Lin, J.W. Lu, P.V. Nielsen, J. Niu, H. Qian, A C. Sleigh, H.-J.J. Su, J. Sundell, T.W. Wong, and P.L. Yuen. 2007. Role of ventilation in airborne transmission of infectious agents in the built environment—A multidisciplinary systematic review. *Indoor Air* 17(1):2-18.

Liang, Y., and Y. Xu. 2011. Indoor fate model of phthalate plasticizer. *Proceedings of Indoor Air 2011*, Austin, TX.

Lighthart, B. 1994. Physics of bioaerosols. In *Atmospheric microbial aerosols: Theory and applications*, pp. 5-27. B. Lighthart and J. Mohr, eds. Chapman and Hall, New York.

Lighthart, B., and L.D. Stetzenbach. 1994. Distribution of microbial aerosol. In *Atmospheric microbial aerosols: Theory and applications*, pp. 68-98. B. Lighthart and J. Mohr, eds. Chapman and Hall, New York.

Lippmann, M. 1989. Health effects of ozone: A critical review. *Journal of the Air Pollution Control Association* 39:672-695.

Lippmann, M. 1993. Health effects of tropospheric ozone: Implications of recent research findings to ambient air quality standards. *Journal of Exposure Analysis and Environmental Epidemiology* 3:103-129.

Logue, J.M., T.E. McKone, M.H. Sherman, and B.C. Singer. 2011. Hazard assessment of chemical air contaminants measured in residences. *Indoor Air* 21(2):92-109.

Logue, J.M., P.N. Price, M.H. Sherman, and B.C. Singer. 2012. A method to estimate the chronic health impact of air pollutants in U.S. residences. *Environmental Health Perspectives* 120:216-222. dx.doi.org/10.1289/ehp.1104035.

Lowen, A.C., S. Mubareka, J. Steel, and P. Palese. 2007. Influenze virus transmission is dependent on relative humidity and temperature. *PLoS Pathology* 3(10). dx.doi.org/10.1371/journal.ppat.0030151.

Mahdavi, A., and U. Unzeitig. 2005. Occupancy implications of spatial, indoor-environmental, and organizational features of office spaces. *Building and Environment* 40(1):113-123.

Mandell, G.L., J.E. Bennett, and R. Dolin, eds. 1999. *Principles and practice of infectious disease*. G. Churchill Livingstone, New York.

Marcinowski, F., R.M. Lucas, and W.M. Yeager. 1994. National and regional distributions of airborne radon concentrations in U.S. homes. *Health Physics* 66(6):699-706.

Martin, T.R., and M.B. Bracken. 1986. Association of low birth weight with passive smoke exposure in pregnancy. *American Journal of Epidemiology* 124(4):633-642.

Martinez, B.F., M.L. Kirk, J.L. Annest, K.J. Lui, E.M. Kilbourne, and S.M. Smith. 1989. Geographic distribution of heat-related deaths among elderly persons: Use of county-level dot maps for injury surveillance and epidemiologic research. *Journal of the American Medical Association* 262:2246-2250.

Mason, S., D. Cortes, and W.E. Horner. 2010. Detection of gaseous effluents and by-products of fungal growth that affects environments. *HVAC&R Research* (now *Science and Technology for the Built Environment*) 16:109-121.

Mbithi, J.N., V.S. Springthorpe, and S.A. Sattar. 1991. Effect of relative humidity and air temperature on survival of hepatitis A virus on environmental surfaces. *Applied and Environmental Microbiology* 57(5):1394-1399.

McCann, J., L. Horn, J. Girman, and A.V. Nero. 1987. *Short-term bioassays in the analysis of complex mixtures V*, pp. 325-354. Plenum Press, New York.

McCoy, W.F. 2005. *Preventing legionellosis*. International Water Association Publishing, London.

McCoy, W.F. 2006. Legionellosis: Why the problem continues. *ASHRAE Journal* 45(1):24-27.

McMichael, A.J., R.E. Woodruff, and S. Hales. 2006. Climate change and human health: Present and future risks. *The Lancet* 367(9513):859-869.

Meggs, W.J. 1994. RADS and RUDS—The toxic induction of asthma and rhinitis. *Journal of Toxicology—Clinical Toxicology.* 32:487-501.

Mendell, M.J. 2006. Indoor residential chemical exposures as risk factors for asthma and allergy in infants and children: a review. *Healthy Buildings 2006*, vol. 1, pp. 151-156.

Mendell, M.J., A.G. Mirer, K. Cheung, M. Tong, and J. Douwes. 2011. Respiratory and allergic health effects of dampness, mold, and dampness-related agents: A review of the epidemiologic evidence. *Environmental Health Perspectives* 119(6):748-756. www.ncbi.nlm.nih.gov/pmc/articles/PMC3114807/.

Milton, D.K., P.M. Glencross, and M.D. Walters. 2000. Risk of sick leave associated with outdoor air supply rate, humidification, and occupant complaints. *Indoor Air* 10(4):212-221.

Mølhave, L. 1991. Volatile organic compounds, indoor air quality and health. *Indoor Air* 1(4):357-376.

Mølhave, L., R. Bach, and O.F. Pederson. 1986. Human reactions to low concentrations of volatile organic compounds. *Environment International* 12:167-175.

Mølhave, L., Z. Liu, A.H. Jorgensen, O.F. Pederson, and S. Kjaergard. 1993. Sensory and physiologic effects on humans of combined exposures to air temperatures and volatile organic compounds. *Indoor Air* 3:155-169.

Mølhave, L., S.K. Kjaergaard, T. Sigsgaard, and M. Lebowitz. 2005. Interaction between ozone and airborne particulate matter in office air. *Indoor Air* 15:383-392.

Moolenaar, R.L., R.A. Etzel, and R.G. Parrish. 1995. Unintentional deaths from carbon monoxide poisoning in New Mexico, 1980 to 1988: A comparison of medical examiner and national mortality data. *Western Journal of Medicine* 163(5):431-434.

Morey, P.R. 1990. The practitioner's approach to indoor air quality investigations. *Proceedings of the Indoor Air Quality International Symposium*, American Industrial Hygiene Association, Akron, OH.

Morey, P.R., and J.C. Feeley. 1988. *ASTM Standardization News* 16:54.

Morey, P.R., and B.A. Jenkins. 1989. What are typical concentrations of fungi, total volatile organic compounds, and nitrogen dioxide in an office environment? *Proceedings of IAQ '89, The Human Equation: Health and Comfort*, pp. 67-71.

Morey, P.R., M.J. Hodgson, W.G. Sorenson, G.J. Kullman, W.W. Rhodes, and G.S. Visvesvara. 1986. Environmental studies in moldy office buildings. *ASHRAE Transactions* 93(1B):399-419.

Moser, M.R., T.R. Bender, H.S. Margolis, G.R. Noble. A.P. Kendal, and D.G. Ritter. 1979. An outbreak of influenza aboard a commercial airliner. *American Journal of Epidemiology* 110:1-6.

Mühlfeld, C., P. Gehr, and B. Rothen-Rutishauser. 2008. Translocation and cellular entering mechanisms of nanoparticles in the respiratory tract. *Swiss Medical Weekly* 138(27-28):387-391.

Mumford, J.L., X.Z. He, R.S. Chapman, S.R. Cao, D.B. Harris, K.M. Li, Y.L. Xian, W.Z. Jiang, C.W. Xu, J.C. Chang, W.E. Wilson, and M. Cooke. 1987. Lung cancer and indoor air pollution in Xuan Wei, China. *Science* 235:217-220.

Murray, W. 1995. Nonionizing electromagnetic energies. Chapter 14 in *Patty's industrial hygiene and toxicology*, vol. 3B, pp. 623-727. R.L. Harris, L.J. Cralley, and L.V. Cralley, eds. John Wiley & Sons, Hoboken, NJ.

NAS. 1981. *Indoor pollutants*. National Research Council/National Academy of Sciences, Committee on Indoor Pollutants. National Academy of Sciences Press, Washington, D.C.

NAS. 1983. *Polycyclic aromatic hydrocarbons: Evaluation of sources and effects*. National Academy Press, Washington, D.C.

Nazaroff, W.W., B.K. Coleman, H. Destaillats, A. Hodgson, D.T.L. Liu, M.M. Lunden, B.C. Singer, and C.J. Weschler. 2006. Indoor air chemistry: Cleaning agents, ozone and toxic air contaminants. *Final Report*, ARB Contract 01-336. California Environmental Protection Agency, Air Resources Board, Sacramento.

NBS. 1969. Maximum permissible body burdens and maximum permissible concentrations of radionuclides in air and in water for occupational exposure. *Handbook* 69. U.S. Department of Commerce, National Bureau of Standards (now National Institute of Standards and Technology), Washington, D.C. www.orau.org/ptp/Library/NBS/NBS%2069.pdf.

NIOSH. 1992. NIOSH recommendations for occupational safety and health compendium of policy documents and statements. DHHS (NIOSH) *Publication* 92-100. U.S. Department of Health and Human Services, Public Health Service, Centers for Disease Control, National Institute for Occupational Safety and Health, Atlanta.

NIOSH. 2007. NIOSH pocket guide to chemical hazards. DHHS (NIOSH) *Publication* 2005-149. U.S. Department of Labor, Occupational Safety and Health Administration, Washington, D.C. www.cdc.gov/niosh/npg/.

NIOSH. 2014. *Climate change and occupational safety and health*. U.S. Department of Health and Human Services. National Institute for Occupational Safety and Health, Washington, D.C.

NIOSH. Annual. *Annual registry of toxic effects of chemical substances*. U.S. Department of Health and Human Services, National Institute for Occupational Safety and Health, Washington, D.C.

Norback, D., E. Bjornnson, C. Janson, J. Widstron, and G. Bowman. 1995. Asthma symptoms and volatile organic compounds, formaldehyde, and carbon dioxide in dwellings. *Occupational and Environmental Medicine* 52(6):388-395.

Nordic Conference on Cold. 1991. Cold physiology and cold injuries. *Arctic Medical Research* (now *International Journal of Circumpolar Health*) 50(6).

NRC. 1986. *Environmental tobacco smoke: Measuring exposures and assessing health effects*. National Research Council. National Academy Press, Washington, D.C.

OEHHA. 2016a. *Air toxicology and epidemiology: All chronic reference exposure levels (cRELs)*. California Environmental Protection Agency, Office of Environmental Health Hazard Assessment, Sacramento. www.oehha.ca.gov/air/general-info/oehha-acute-8-hour-and-chronic-reference-exposure-level-rel-summary.

OEHHA. 2016b. *Chemicals known to the state to cause cancer or reproductive toxicity*. California Environmental Protection Agency, Office of Environmental Health Hazard Assessment, Sacramento. www.oehha.ca.gov/media/downloads/proposition-65/p65single080516.pdf.

Oeschli, F.W., and R.W. Buechley. 1970. Excess mortality associated with three Los Angeles September hot spells. *Environmental Research* 3:277.

Offerman, F.J. 2014. The hazards of e-cigarettes. *ASHRAE Journal* 53(6): 38-44.

Offermann, F.J., S.A. Loiselle, A.T. Hodgson, L.A. Gundel, and J.M. Daisey. 1991. A pilot study to measure indoor concentrations and emission rates of polycyclic aromatic hydrocarbons. *Indoor Air* 4:497-512.

Ohm, M., J.E. Juto, and K. Andersson. 1992. Nasal hyper-reactivity and sick building syndrome. *IAQ '92: Environments for People*. ASHRAE.

Oie, L., P. Nafstad, G. Botten, P. Magnus, and J.K. Jaakkola. 1999. Ventilation in homes and bronchial obstruction in young children. *Epidemiology* 10(3):294-299.

Parsons, K.C. and M.J. Griffin. 1988. Whole-body vibration perception thresholds. *Journal of Sound and Vibration* 121(2):237-258.

Pei, J., and J.S. Zhang. 2011. A critical review of catalytic oxidization and chemisorption methods for indoor formaldehyde removal. *HVAC&R Research* (now *Science and Technology for the Built Environment*) 17(4).

Persily, A.K. 2015a. Indoor carbon dioxide concentrations in ventilation and indoor air quality standards. *Proceedings of 36th AIVC Conference Effective Ventilation in High Performance Buildings*, Madrid. www.aivc.org/resource/indoor-carbon-dioxide-concentrations-ventilation-and-indoor-air-quality-standards.

Persily, A. 2015b. Field measurements of ventilation rates. *Indoor Air* 26(1): 97-111. dx.doi.org/10.1111/ina.12193.

Pope, C.A., 3rd, and D.W. Dockery. 2006. Health effects of fine particulate air pollution: lines that connect. *Journal of the Air & Waste Management Association* 56(6):709-742.

Reiher, H., and F.J. Meister. 1931. The sensitivities of the human body to vibrations. *Forschung* VDI 2:381-386. 1946 translation of *Report* Fts616RE. Headquarters Air Material Command, Wright Field, Dayton, OH.

Repace, J.L. 1984. Effect of ventilation on passive smoking in a model workplace. *Proceedings of an Engineering Foundation Conference on Management of Atmospheres in Tightly Enclosed Spaces*, Santa Barbara.

Repace, J.L., and A.H. Lowrey. 1985. An indoor air quality standard for ambient tobacco smoke based on carcinogenic risk. *New York State Journal of Medicine* 85:381-383.

Repace, J.L., and A.H. Lowrey. 1993. An enforceable indoor air quality standard for environmental tobacco smoke in the workplace. *Risk Analysis* 13(4).

Rogan, W.J., and N.B. Ragan. 2007. Some evidence of effects of environmental chemicals on the endocrine system in children. *International Journal of Hygiene and Environmental Health* 210(5):659-667.

Rohles, F.H., J.A. Woods, and P.R. Morey. 1989. Indoor environmental acceptability: Development of a rating scale. *ASHRAE Transactions* 95(1): 23-27.

Rudel, R.A., and L.J. Perovich. 2009. Endocrine disrupting chemicals in indoor and outdoor air. *Atmospheric Environment* 43:170-181.

Samet, J.M. 1989. Radon and lung cancer. *Journal of the National Cancer Institute* 81:145.

Samet, J.M., M.C. Marbury, and J.D. Spengler. 1987. Health effects and sources of indoor air pollution. *American Review of Respiratory Disease* 136:1486-1508.

Seppänen, O.A., W.J. Fisk, and M.J. Mendell. 1999. Association of ventilation rates and CO_2 concentrations with health and other responses in commercial and institutional buildings. *Indoor Air* 9(4):226-252.

Shendell, D.G., R. Prill, W.J. Fisk, M.G. Apte, D. Blake, and D. Faulkner. 2004. Associations between classroom CO_2 concentrations and student attendance in Washington and Idaho. *Indoor Air* 14(5):333-341.

Shickele, E. 1947. Environment and fatal heat stroke. *Military Surgeon* 100: 235.

Sjodin, A., O. Papke, E. McGahee, J.F. Focant, R.S. Jones, T. Pless-Mulloli, L.M.L. Toms, T. Herrmann, J. Muller, L.L. Needham, and D.G. Patterson. 2008. Concentration of polybrominated diphenyl ethers (PBDEs) in household dust from various countries. *Chemosphere* 73(1):S131-S136.

Skov, P., and O. Valbjorn. 1987. Danish indoor climate, study group: The sick building syndrome in the office environment: The Danish town hall study. *Environment International* 13:339-349.

Spektor, D.M., M. Lippmann, G.D. Thurston, P.J. Lioy, J. Stecko, G. O'Connor, E. Garshick, F.E. Speizer, and C. Hayes. 1988a. Effects of ambient ozone on respiratory function in healthy adults exercising outdoors. *American Review of Respiratory Disease* 138:821-828.

Spektor, D.M., M. Lippmann, P.J. Lioy, G.D. Thurston, K. Citak, D.J. James, N. Bock, F.E. Speizer, and C. Hayes. 1988b. Effects of ambient ozone on respiratory function in active normal children. *American Review of Respiratory Disease* 137:313-320.

Spektor, D.M., G.D. Thurston, J. Mao, D. He, C. Hayes, and M. Lippmann. 1991. Effects of single and multi-day ozone exposures on respiratory function in active normal children. *Environmental Research* 55:107-122.

Streifel, A.J., D. Vesley, F.S. Rhame, and B. Murray. 1989. Control of airborne fungal spores in a university hospital. *Environment International* 15:221.

Strindehag, O., I. Josefsson, and E. Hennington. 1988. *Healthy Buildings '88,* Stockholm, vol. 3, pp. 611-620.

Sun, Y., Z. Wang, Y. Zhang. and J. Sundel. 2011. In China, students in crowded dormitories with a low ventilation rate have more common colds: Evidence for airborne transmission. *PLoS One* 6(11):e27140.

Sundell, J., T. Lindvall, B. Stenberg, and S. Wall. 1994. Sick building syndrome (SBS) in office workers and facial skin symptoms among VDT-workers in relation to building and room characteristics: Two case-referent studies. *Indoor Air* 4(2):83-94.

Sundell, J., H. Levin, W.W. Nazaroff, W.S. Cain, W.J. Fisk, D.T. Grimsrud, F. Gyntelberg, Y. Li, A.K. Persily, A.C. Pickering, J.M. Samet, J.D. Spengler, S.T. Taylor, and C.J. Weschler. 2011. Ventilation rates and health: multidisciplinary review of the scientific literature. *Indoor Air* 21(3):191-204.

Susskind, R.R., and M. Ishihara. 1965. The effects of wetting on cutaneous vulnerability. *Archives of Environmental Health* 11:529.

Swan, S.H. 2008. Environmental phthalate exposure in relation to reproductive outcomes and other health endpoints in humans. *Environmental Research* 108(2):177-184.

Tamas, G., C.J. Weschler, J. Toftum, and P.O. Fanger. 2006. Influence of ozone-limonene reactions on perceived air quality. *Indoor Air* 16: 168-178.

Tancrede, M., R. Wilson, L. Ziese, and E.A.C. Crouch. 1987. *Atmospheric Environment* 21:2187.

Tang, J.W., Y. Li, I. Eames, P.K.S. Chan, and G.L. Ridgway. 2006. Factors involved in the aerosol transmission of infection and control of ventilation in health care premises. *Journal of Hospital Infection* 64(2):100-114.

Teng, H.C., and H.E. Heyer, eds. 1955. The relationship between sudden changes in the weather and acute myocardial infarction. *American Heart Journal* 49:9.

Thirion, X., D. Debensason, J.C. Delaroziere, and J.L. San Marco. 2005. August 2003: Reflections on a French summer disaster. *Journal of Contingencies and Crisis Management* 13(4):153-158.

Thurston, G.D., M. Lippmann, M.B. Scott, and J.M. Fine. 1997. Summertime haze air pollution and children with asthma. *American Journal of Respiratory and Critical Care Medicine* 155:654-660.

Uchiyama, S., K. Ohta, Y. Inaba, and N. Kunugita. 2013. Determination of carbonyl compounds generated from the e-cigarette using coupled silica cartridges impregnated with hydroquinone and 2,4-dinitrophenylhydrazine, followed by high-performance liquid chromatography. *Analytical Sciences* 29(12):1219-1222.

Villa, A.F., P. Sauvic, V. Gazin, and R. Garnier. 2012. Electronic cigarettes: Risk assessment. *Clinical Toxicology* 50(4):309-310.

Wang, Z. 2011. Dynamic botanical filtration system for indoor air purification. *Mechanical and Aerospace Engineering—Dissertations*. Paper 63.

Wargocki, P., J. Sundell, W. Bischof, G. Brundrett, P.O. Fanger, F. Gyntelberg, S.O. Hanssen, P. Harrison, A. Pickering, O. Seppänen, and P. Wouters. 2002. Ventilation and health in non-industrial indoor environments: report from a European multidisciplinary scientific consensus meeting (EUROVEN). *Indoor Air* 12(2):113-128.

Weschler, C.J. 2000. Ozone in indoor environments: Concentration and chemistry. *Indoor Air* 10:269.

Weschler, C.J. 2006. Ozone's impact on public health: Contributions from indoor exposures to ozone and products of ozone-initiated chemistry. *Environmental Health Perspectives* 114:1489-1496.

Weschler, C.J. 2009. Changes in indoor pollutants since the 1950s. *Atmospheric Environment* 43:153-159.

Weschler, C.J., and W.W. Nazaroff. 2008. Semivolatile organic compounds in indoor environments, *Atmospheric Environment* 42:9018-9040.

Weschler, C.J., and W.W. Nazaroff. 2012. SVOC exposure indoors: Fresh look at dermal pathways. *Indoor Air* (published online, Mar. 2, 2012).

Weschler, C.J., and H.C. Shields. 2000. The influence of ventilation on reactions among indoor pollutants: Modeling and experimental observations. *Indoor Air* 10:92-100.

WHO. 1983. Indoor air pollutants: Exposure and health effects. *EURO Reports and Studies* 78. World Health Organization, Copenhagen.

WHO. 2002. *Concise international chemical assessment document 40—Formaldehyde*. World Health Organization, Geneva.

WHO. 2007. *Legionella and the prevention of Legionellosis.* World Health Organization, Geneva.

WHO. 2009. Health effects associated with dampness and mould. Chapter 4 in *Guidelines for indoor air quality: Dampness and mould.* World Health Organization Europe, Copenhagen. www.euro.who.int/__data/assets/pdf_file/0017/43325/E92645.pdf.

WHO. 2010. *WHO guidelines for indoor air quality: Selected pollutants.* World Health Organization, Bonn. www.euro.who.int/__data/assets/pdf_file/0009/128169/e94535.pdf.

Wilkins, C.K., P.A. Clausen, P. Wolkoff, S.T. Larsen, M. Hammer, K. Larsen, V. Hansen, and G.D. Nielsen. 2001. Formation of strong airway irritants in mixtures of isoprene/ozone and isoprene/ozone/nitrogen dioxide. *Environmental Health Perspectives* 109:937-941.

Wolkoff, P., P.A. Clausen, C.K. Wilkins, and G.D. Nielsen. 2000. Formation of strong airway irritants in terpene/ozone mixtures. *Indoor Air* 10:82-91.

Xu, Y., E.A. Cohen Hubal, and J.C. Little. 2010. Predicting residential exposure to phthalate plasticizer emitted from vinyl flooring—Sensitivity, uncertainty, and implications for biomonitoring. *Environmental Health Perspectives* 118(2):253-258.

Yoshizawa, S., F. Surgawa, S. Ozawo, Y. Kohsaka, and A. Matsumae. 1987. *Proceedings of the 4th International Conference on Indoor Air Quality and Climate*, Berlin, vol. 1, pp. 627-631.

Yu, I.T., Y. Li, T.W. Wong, W. Tam, A.T. Chan, J.H. Lee, D.Y. Leung, and T. Ho. 2004. Evidence of airborne transmission of the severe acute respiratory syndrome virus. *New England Journal of Medicine* 350(17):1731-1739.

Zhang, Y., J. Mo, Y. Li, J. Sundell, P. Wargocki, J. Zhang, J. Little, R. Corsi, Q. Deng, M. Leung, J. Siegel, L. Fang, W. Chen, J. Li, and Y. Sun. 2011. Effectiveness and problems of commonly-used indoor air cleaning techniques—A literature review. *Atmospheric Environment*.

BIBLIOGRAPHY

ACGIH. 1999. *Bioaerosols: Assessment and control*. American Conference of Government Industrial Hygienists, Cincinnati, OH.

ACSM. 2007. Exertional heat illness during training and competition. *Medicine & Science in Sports & Exercise* 39(3):556-572. dx.doi.org/10.1249/MSS.0b013e31802fa199.

Anderson, H.A., D. Higgins, L.P. Hanrahan, P. Sarow, and J. Schirmer. 1991. Mesothelioma among employees with likely contact with in-place asbestos-containing building materials. *Annals of the New York Academy of Sciences* 643:550-572.

ASHRAE. 2013. Safety standard for refrigeration systems. *Standard* 15-2013.

ASHRAE. 2013. Designation and safety classification of refrigerants. ANSI/ASHRAE *Standard* 34-2013.

ATS. 2000. What constitutes an adverse health effect of air pollution? *American Journal of Respiratory and Critical Care Medicine* 161(2):665-673.

Bates, D.V. 1989. Ozone—Myth and reality. *Environmental Research* 50:230-237.

Burge, S., A. Hedge, S. Wilson, J.H. Bass, and A. Robertson. 1987. Sick building syndrome: A study of 4373 office workers. *Annals of Occupational Hygiene* 31:493-504.

Cain, W.S., J.M. Samet, and M.J. Hodgson. 1995. The quest for negligible health risk from indoor air. *ASHRAE Journal* 37(7):38.

CEN. *Surface temperatures of touchable parts, a draft proposal*. TC 114 N 122 D/E. European Standards Group.

Crandall, M.S., and W.K. Sieber. 1996. The NIOSH indoor environmental evaluation experience: Part one, building evaluations. *Applied Occupational and Environmental Hygiene*.

Edwards, J.H. 1980. Microbial and immunological investigations and remedial action after an outbreak of humidifier fever. *British Journal of Industrial Medicine* 37:55-62.

EPA. 2001. Mold remediation in schools and commercial buildings. *Report* 402-K-01-001. U.S. Environmental Protection Agency, Washington, D.C.

EPA. 2009. National primary drinking water regulations. *Standard* 816-F-09-004. U.S. Environmental Protection Agency, Washington, D.C. nepis.epa.gov/Exe/ZyPURL.cgi?Dockey=P1005EJT.txt.

Hathaway, G.J., N.H. Proctor, J.P. Hughes, and M.L. Fischman, eds. 1991. *Proctor and Hughes' chemical hazards in the workplace*, 3rd ed. Van Nostrand Reinhold, New York.

Hodgson, M.J., P.R. Morey, J.S. Simon, T.D. Waters, and J.N. Fink. 1987. An outbreak of recurrent acute and chronic hypersensitivity pneumonitis in office workers. *American Journal of Epidemiology* 125:631-638.

Lauterbach, J.H., and M. Laugesen. 2012. Comparison of toxicant levels in mainstream aerosols generated by Ruyan® electronic nicotine delivery systems (ENDS) and conventional cigarette products. *Toxicologist* 126:1.

Lilienfeld, D.E. 1991. Asbestos-associated pleural mesothelioma in school teachers: A discussion of four cases. *Annals of the New York Academy of Sciences* 643:454-486.

Liu, K.S., J. Wesolowski, F.Y. Huang, K. Sexton, and S.B. Hayward. 1991. Irritant effects of formaldehyde exposure in mobile homes. *Environmental Health Perspectives* 94:91-94.

Miller, J.D., and J. Day. 1997. Indoor mold exposure: Epidemiology, consequences and immunotherapy. *Journal of the Canadian Society of Allergy and Clinical Immunology* 2(1):25-32.

Morey, P.R. 1988. Experience on the contribution of structure to environmental pollution. In *Architectural design and indoor microbial pollution*, pp. 40-80. R.B. Kundsin, ed. Oxford University Press, New York.

Russi, M., W. Buchta, M. Swift, L. Budnick, M. Hodgson, D. Berube, and G. Kelefant. 2008. *Guidance for occupational health services in medical centers*. American College of Occupational and Environmental Medicine, Elk Grove Village, IL. www.acoem.org/uploadedFiles/Public_Affairs/Policies_And_Position_Statements/Guidelines/Guidelines/MCOHGuidance.pdf.

Schulman, J.H., and E.M. Kilbourne. 1962. Airborne transmission of influenza virus infection in mice. *Nature* 195:1129.

Spengler, J.D., H.A. Burge, and H.J. Su. 1992. Biological agents and the home environment. *Bugs, Mold and Rot (I): Proceedings of the Moisture Control Workshop*, E. Bales and W.B. Rose, eds., pp. 11-18. Building Thermal Envelope Council, National Institute of Building Sciences, Washington, D.C.

Tansey, M.R., and C.B. Fliermans. 1978. Pathogenic species of thermophilic and thermotolerant fungi in reactor effluents of the Savannah River Plant. *DOE Symposium Series CONF-77114: Energy and Environmental Stress in Aquatic Systems Symposium*, pp. 663-690. J.H. Thorpe and J.W. Gibbons, eds.

Zenz, C., ed. 1988. *Occupational safety in industry, occupational medicine, principles and practical applications*. Year Book Medical Publishers, Chicago.

CHAPTER 11

AIR CONTAMINANTS

AIR contamination is a concern for ventilation engineers when it causes problems for building occupants. Engineers need to understand the vocabulary used by the air sampling and building air cleaning industry. This chapter focuses on the types and levels of air contaminants that might enter ventilation systems or be found as indoor contaminants. Industrial contaminants are included only for special cases. Because it is not a building air concern, the effects of refrigerants on the atmosphere are not included in this chapter; see Chapter 29 for discussion of this topic.

Air is composed mainly of gases. The major gaseous components of clean, dry air near sea level are approximately 21% oxygen, 78% nitrogen, 1% argon, and 0.04% carbon dioxide. Normal outdoor air contains varying amounts of other materials (permanent atmospheric impurities) from natural processes such as wind erosion, sea spray evaporation, volcanic eruption, and metabolism or decay of organic matter. The concentration of permanent atmospheric impurities varies, but is usually lower than that of anthropogenic (i.e., caused by human activities) air contaminants.

Anthropogenic outdoor air contaminants are many and varied, originating from numerous types of human activity. Electric-power-generating plants, various modes of transportation, industrial processes, mining and smelting, construction, and agriculture generate large amounts of contaminants. These outdoor air contaminants can also be transmitted to the indoor environment. In addition, the indoor environment can exhibit a wide variety of local contaminants, both natural and anthropogenic.

Contaminants that present particular problems in the indoor environment include allergens (e.g., dust mite or cat antigen), tobacco smoke, radon, and formaldehyde.

Air composition may be changed accidentally or deliberately. In sewers, sewage treatment plants, agricultural silos, sealed storage vaults, tunnels, and mines, the oxygen content of air can become so low that people cannot remain conscious or survive. Concentrations of people in confined spaces (theaters, survival shelters, submarines) require that carbon dioxide given off by normal respiratory functions be removed and replaced with oxygen. Pilots of high-altitude aircraft, breathing at greatly reduced pressure, require systems that increase oxygen concentration. Conversely, for divers working at extreme depths, it is common to increase the percentage of helium in the atmosphere and reduce nitrogen and sometimes oxygen concentrations.

At atmospheric pressure, oxygen concentrations less than 12% or carbon dioxide concentrations greater than 5% are dangerous, even for short periods. Lesser deviations from normal composition can be hazardous under prolonged exposures. Chapter 10 further details environmental health issues.

Although lack of oxygen can be a danger in confined spaces, it is unlikely ever to be a problem in naturally and mechanically ventilated buildings. Although the amount of oxygen consumed approximates the amount of carbon dioxide produced by respiration, the level of oxygen in the air is so much greater than that of carbon dioxide to start with that there is effectively no change in oxygen content between air intake and exhaust.

1. CLASSES OF AIR CONTAMINANTS

Air contaminants are generally classified as either particles or gases. Particles dispersed in air are also known as **aerosols**. In common usage, the terms *aerosol*, *airborne particle*, and *particulate air contaminant* are interchangeable. The distinction between particles and gases is important when determining removal strategies and equipment. Although the motion of particles is described using the same equations used to describe gas movement, even the smallest particles are much larger and heavier than individual gas molecules, and have a much lower diffusion rate. Conversely, particles are typically present in much fewer numbers than even trace levels of contaminant gases.

The **particulate** class covers a vast range of particle sizes, from dust large enough to be visible to the eye to submicroscopic particles that elude most filters. Particles may be liquid, solid, or have a solid core surrounded by liquid. The following traditional particulate contaminant classifications arise in various situations, and overlap. They are all still in common use.

- **Dusts**, **fumes**, and **smokes** are mostly solid particulate matter, although smoke often contains liquid particles.
- **Mists**, **fogs**, and **smogs** are mostly suspended liquid particles smaller than those in dusts, fumes, and smokes.
- **Bioaerosols** include primarily intact and fragmentary viruses, bacteria, fungal spores, and plant and animal allergens; their primary effect is related to their biological origin. Common indoor particulate allergens (dust mite allergen, cat dander, house dust, etc.) and endotoxins are included in the bioaerosol class.
- Particulate contaminants may be defined by their size, such as **coarse**, **fine**, or **ultrafine**; **visible** or **invisible**; or **macroscopic**, **microscopic**, or **submicroscopic**.
- Particles may be described using terms that relate to their interaction with the human respiratory system, such as **inhalable** and **respirable**

The **gaseous** class covers chemical contaminants that can exist as free molecules or atoms in air. Molecules and atoms are smaller than particles and may behave differently as a result. This class covers two important subclasses:

The preparation of this chapter is assigned to TC 2.3, Gaseous Air Contaminants and Gas Contaminant Removal Equipment, in conjunction with TC 2.4, Particulate Air Contaminants and Particulate Contaminant Removal Equipment.

- **Gases**, which are naturally gaseous under ambient indoor or outdoor conditions (i.e., their boiling point is less than ambient temperature at ambient pressure)
- **Vapors**, which are normally solid or liquid under ambient indoor or outdoor conditions (i.e., their boiling point is greater than ambient temperature at ambient pressure), but which evaporate readily

Through evaporation, liquids change into vapors and mix with the surrounding atmosphere. Like gases, they are formless fluids that expand to occupy the space or enclosure in which they are confined.

Air contaminants can also be classified according to their sources; properties; or the health, safety, and engineering issues faced by people exposed to them. Any of these can form a convenient classification system because they allow grouping of applicable standards, guidelines, and control strategies. Most such special classes include both particulate and gaseous contaminants.

This chapter also covers background information for selected special air contaminant classes (Chapter 10 deals with applicable indoor health and comfort regulations).

- Outdoor air contaminants
- Industrial air contaminants
- Nonindustrial indoor air contaminants and indoor air quality
- Flammable gases and vapors
- Combustible dusts
- Radioactive contaminants
- Soil gases

In the 2016 *ASHRAE Handbook—HVAC Systems and Equipment*, Chapter 29 discusses particulate air contaminant removal, and Chapter 30 covers industrial air cleaning. Chapter 46 in the 2015 *ASHRAE Handbook—HVAC Applications* deals with gaseous contaminant removal.

2. PARTICULATE CONTAMINANTS

2.1 PARTICULATE MATTER

Airborne particulate contamination ranges from dense clouds of desert dust storms to completely invisible and dilute cleanroom particles. It may be anthropogenic or completely natural. It is often a mixture of many different components from several different sources. A much more extensive discussion of particulate contamination is available from the U.S. Environmental Protection Agency (EPA 2016a).

Particles occur in a variety of different shapes, including spherical, irregular, and fibers, which are defined as particles with aspect ratio (length-to-width ratio) greater than 3. In describing particle size ranges, *size* is the diameter of an assumed spherical particle.

Solid Particles

Dusts are solid particles projected into the air by natural forces such as wind, volcanic eruption, or earthquakes, or by mechanical processes such as crushing, grinding, demolition, blasting, drilling, shoveling, screening, and sweeping. Some of these forces produce dusts by reducing larger masses, whereas others disperse materials that have already been reduced. Particles are not considered to be dust unless they are smaller than about 100 μm. Dusts can be mineral, such as rock, metal, or clay; vegetable, such as grain, flour, wood, cotton, or pollen; or animal, including wool, hair, silk, feathers, and leather. *Dust* is also used as a catch-all term (house dust, for example) that can have broad meaning.

Fumes are solid particles formed by condensation of vapors of solid materials. Metallic fumes are generated from molten metals and usually occur as oxides because of the highly reactive nature of finely divided matter. Fumes can also be formed by sublimation, distillation, or chemical reaction. Such processes create submicrometre airborne primary particles that may agglomerate into larger particle (1 to 2 μm) clusters if aged at high concentration.

Bioaerosols are airborne biological materials, including viruses and intact and fragmentary bacteria, pollen, fungi, and bacterial and fungal spores. Individual **viruses (virions)** typically range in size from 0.02 to 0.4 μm, although filioviruses (e.g., ebola) may be longer than 1 μm. Viruses usually occur as aggregates (droplet nuclei) and are associated with sputum or saliva. Therefore, in air they generally appear to be much larger than their true size. Most individual **bacteria** range between 0.4 and 5 μm and may be found singly or as aggregates. Intact individual **fungal** and **bacterial** spores are usually 2 to 10 μm, whereas **pollen** grains are 10 to 100 μm, with many common varieties in the 20 to 40 μm range. The size range of **allergens** varies widely: the allergenic molecule is very small, but the source of the allergen (mite feces or cat dander) may be quite large. See the section on Bioaerosols for more detailed discussion.

Liquid Particles

Mists are aggregations of small airborne droplets of materials that are ordinarily liquid at normal temperatures and pressure. They can be formed by atomizing, spraying, mixing, violent chemical reactions, evolution of gas from liquid, or dissolved gas escaping when pressure is released.

Fogs are clouds of fine airborne droplets, usually formed by condensation of vapor, which remain airborne longer than mists. Fog nozzles are named for their ability to produce extra-fine droplets, as compared with mists from ordinary spray devices. Many droplets in fogs or clouds are microscopic and submicroscopic and serve as a transition stage between larger mists and vapors. The volatile nature of most liquids reduces the size of their airborne droplets from the mist to the fog range and eventually to the vapor phase, until the air becomes saturated with that liquid. If solid material is suspended or dissolved in the liquid droplet, it remains in the air as particulate contamination. For example, sea spray evaporates fairly rapidly, generating a large number of fine salt particles that remain suspended in the atmosphere.

Complex Particles

Smokes are small solid and/or liquid particles produced by incomplete combustion of organic substances such as tobacco, wood, coal, oil, and other carbonaceous materials. The term *smoke* is applied to a mixture of solid, liquid, and gaseous products, although technical literature distinguishes between such components as soot or carbon particles, fly ash, cinders, tarry matter, unburned gases, and gaseous combustion products. Smoke particles vary in size, the smallest being much less than 1 μm in diameter. The average is often in the range of 0.1 to 0.3 μm.

Environmental tobacco smoke (ETS) consists of a suspension of 0.01 to 1.0 μm (mass median diameter of 0.3 μm) solid and liquid particles that form as the superheated vapors leaving burning tobacco condense, agglomerate into larger particles, and age. Numerous gaseous contaminants are also produced, including carbon monoxide.

Smog commonly refers to air pollution; it implies an airborne mixture of smoke particles, mists, and fog droplets of such concentration and composition as to impair visibility, in addition to being irritating or harmful. The composition varies among different locations and at different times. The term is often applied to haze caused by a sunlight-induced photochemical reaction involving materials in automobile exhausts. Smog is often associated with temperature inversions in the atmosphere that prevent normal dispersion of contaminants.

Sizes of Airborne Particles

Particle size can be defined in several different ways. These depend, for example, on the source or method of generation, visibility, effects, or measurement instrument. Ambient atmospheric particulate contamination is classified by aerosol scientists and the EPA by source mode, with common usage now recognizing three primary modes: coarse, fine, and ultrafine.

Coarse-mode aerosol particles are largest, and are generally formed by mechanical breaking up of solids. They generally have a minimum size of 1 to 3 μm (EPA 2009a). Coarse particles also include bioaerosols such as mold spores, pollen, animal dander, and dust mite particles that can affect the immune system. Coarse-mode particles are predominantly primary, natural, and chemically inert. Road dust is a good example. Chemically, coarse particles tend to contain crustal material components such as silicon compounds, iron, aluminum, sea salt, and vegetative particles.

Fine-mode particles are generally secondary particles formed from chemical reactions or condensing gases. They have a maximum size of about 1 to 3 μm. Fine particles are usually more chemically complex than coarse-mode particles and result from human activity, particularly combustion. Smoke is a good example. Chemically, fine aerosols typically include sulfates, organics, ammonium, nitrates, carbon, lead, and some trace constituents. The modes overlap, and their definitions are not precise.

Recently, there has been increased interest in even smaller contaminants, known as **ultrafine**-mode particles. Ultrafines have a maximum size of 0.1 μm (100 nm) (EPA 2009a). They are complex particles for which the biggest source is reaction of gases with other particles. They also form as a result of degradation of larger particles. Natural sources include volcanic eruptions, ocean spray, and smoke from wildfires. Sources involving human activity include tobacco smoke, burning of fossil fuels, and emissions from cooking and office machines. Engineered ultrafines, often referred to as **nanoparticles**, have a variety of applications, particularly in the medical field (Moghini et al. 2005). The U.S. National Nanotechnology Initiative (NNI 2008) uses the same size definition for nanoparticles as given above for ultrafine particles. Figure 1 shows a typical distribution, including the chemical species present in each of the three modes.

The size of a particle determines where in the human respiratory system particles are deposited, and various samplers collect particles that penetrate more or less deeply into the lungs. Figure 2 shows the relative deposition efficiencies of various sizes of particles in the human nasal and respiratory systems. The **inhalable mass** is made up of particles that may deposit anywhere in the respiratory system, and is represented by a sample with a median cut point of 100 μm. Most of the inhalable mass is captured in the nasal passages. The **thoracic particle mass** is the fraction that can penetrate to the respiratory airways and is represented by a sample with a median cut point of 10 μm (PM_{10}). The **respirable particle mass** is the fraction that can penetrate to the gas-exchange region of the lungs, which ACGIH (1989) defines as having a median cut point of 4 μm. The EPA no longer uses the term *respirable*. Their current concern is with particles having a median cut point of 2.5 μm ($PM_{2.5}$) (this definition includes both fine and ultrafine particles as discussed above), and with smaller particles such as PM_1.

Particles differ in density, and may be irregular in shape. It is useful to characterize mixed aerosol size in terms of some standard particle. The **aerodynamic (equivalent) diameter** of a particle, defined as the diameter of a unit-density sphere having the same gravitational settling velocity as the particle in question (Willeke and Baron 1993), is commonly used as the standard particle size. Samplers that fractionate particles based on their inertial properties, such as impactors and cyclones, naturally produce results as functions of the aerodynamic diameters. Samplers that use other sizing principles, such as optical particle counters, must be calibrated to give aerodynamic diameter.

The tendency of particles to settle on surfaces is of interest. Figure 3 shows the sizes of typical indoor airborne solid and liquid particles. Particles smaller than 0.1 μm behave like gas molecules, exhibiting irregular motion from collisions with air molecules and having no measurable settling velocity. Particles in the range from 0.1 to 1 μm have calculable settling velocities, but they are so low that settling is usually negligible, because normal air currents counteract any settling. By number, over 99.9% of the particles in a typical atmosphere are below 1 μm (i.e., fewer than 1 particle in every 1000 is larger than 1 μm). Particles between 1 and 10 μm settle in still air at constant and appreciable velocity. However, normal air currents keep them in suspension for appreciable periods. Particles larger than 10 μm settle fairly rapidly and can be found suspended in air only near their source or under strong wind conditions. Exceptions are lint and other light, fibrous materials, such as portions of some weed seeds, which remain suspended longer because their aerodynamic behavior is similar to that of smaller particles (they have aerodynamic diameters smaller than their physical dimensions suggest.)

Table 1 shows settling times for various types of particles. Most individual particles 10 μm or larger are visible to the naked eye under favorable conditions of lighting and contrast. Smaller particles are visible only in high concentrations. Cigarette smoke (with an average particle size less than 0.5 μm) and clouds are common examples. Direct fallout in the vicinity of the dispersing stack or flue and other nuisance problems of air pollution involve larger particles.

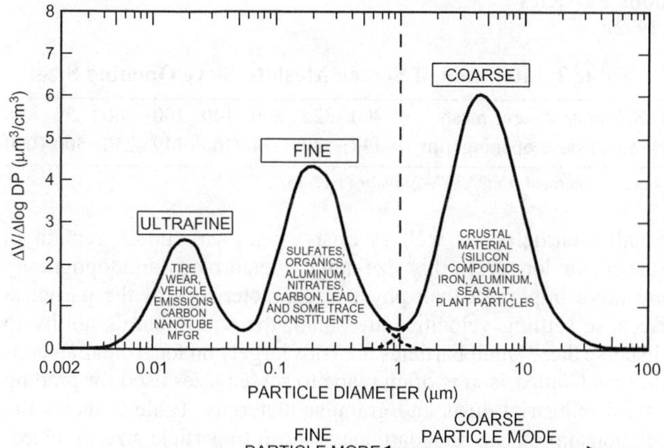

Fig. 1 Typical Outdoor Aerosol Composition by Particle Size Fraction
(adapted from Wilson and Suh 1997)

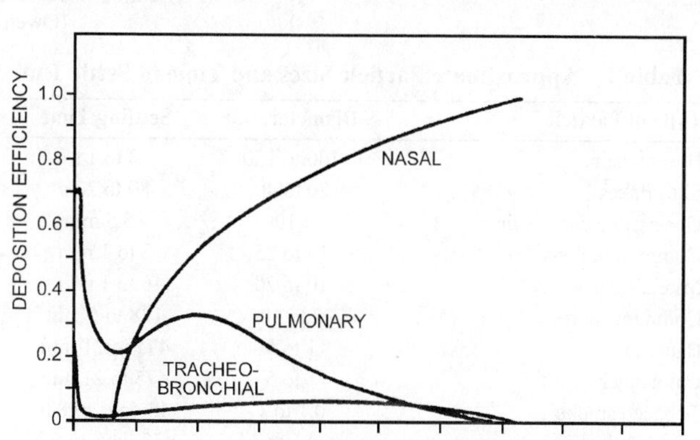

Fig. 2 Relative Deposition Efficiencies of Different-Sized Particles in the Three Main Regions of the Human Respiratory System, Calculated for Moderate Activity Level
(Task Group on Lung Dynamics 1966)

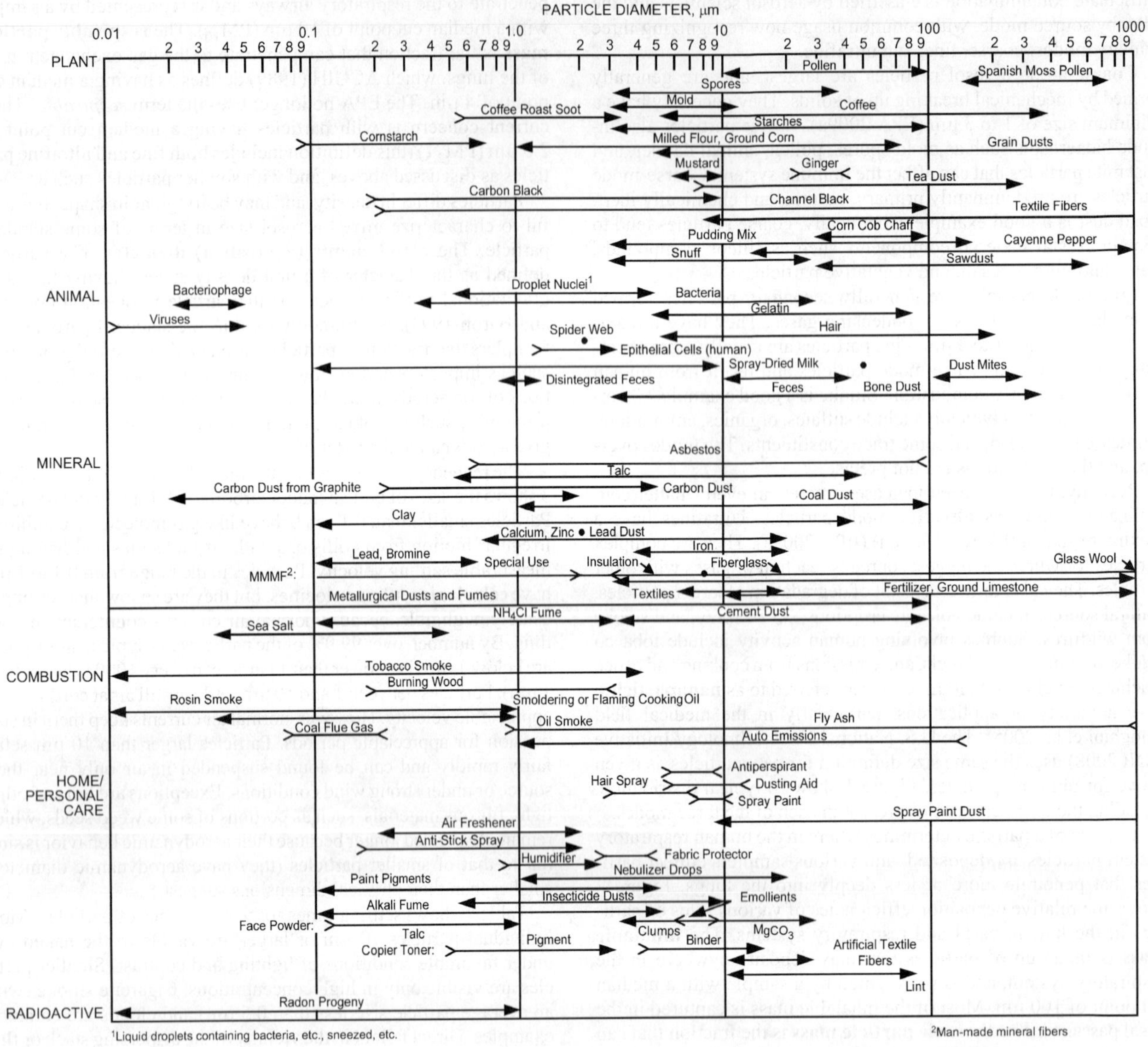

Fig. 3 Sizes of Indoor Particles
(Owen et al. 1992)

Table 1 Approximate Particle Sizes and Time to Settle 1 m

Type of Particle	Diameter, μm	Settling Time
Human hair	100 to 150	3 to 1 s
Skin flakes	20 to 40	80 to 20 s
Observable dust in air	>10	<5.5 min
Common pollens	15 to 25	2 to 1 min
Mite allergens	10 to 20	6 to 1 min
Common spores	2 to 10	128 to 6 min
Bacteria	1 to 5	475 to 21 min
Cat dander	1 to 5	475 to 21 min
Tobacco smoke	0.1 to 1	13 days to 8 h
Metal and organic fumes	<0.1 to 1	>13 days to 8 h
Cell debris	0.01 to 1	171 days to 8 h
Viruses	<0.1	>13 days

Note: Spores, bacteria, and virus sizes are for the typical complete unit. As entrained in the air, they may be smaller (fragments) or larger (attached to debris, enclosed in sputum, etc.)
Based on information obtained from J.D. Spengler, Harvard School of Public Health, 1982.

Table 2 Relation of Screen Mesh to Sieve Opening Size

U.S. Standard sieve mesh	400	325	200	140	100	60	35	18
Nominal sieve opening, μm	37	44	74	105	149	250	500	1000

Source: Excerpted from ASTM *Standard* E11-15.

Smaller particles, as well as mists, fogs, and fumes, remain in suspension longer. In this size range, meteorology and topography are more important than physical characteristics of the particles. Because settling velocities are small, the atmosphere's ability to disperse these small particles depends largely on local weather conditions. Comparison is often made to screen sizes used for grading useful industrial dusts and granular materials. Table 2 shows the relationship of U.S. standard sieve mesh to particle size in micrometers. Particles above 40 μm are known as the screen sizes, and those below are known as the subscreen or microscopic sizes.

Particle Size Distribution

The particle size distribution in any sample can be expressed in several different ways. Figure 4 shows particle count data for typical

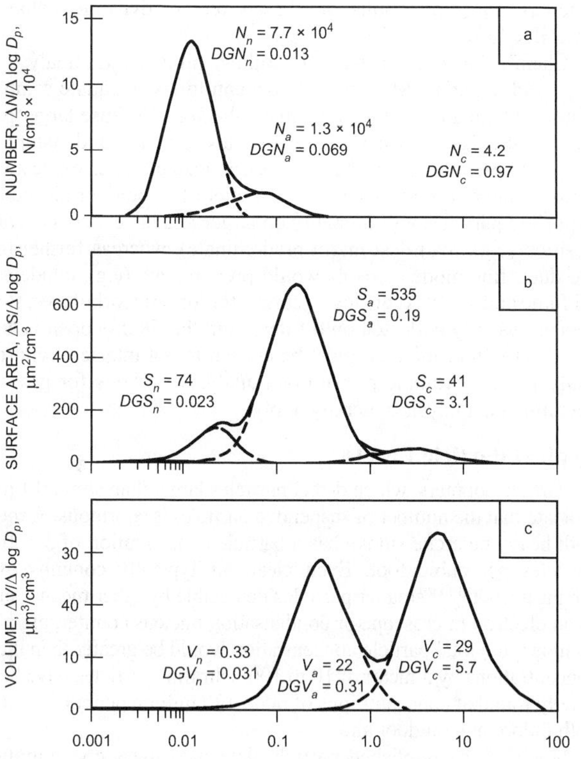

Data are plotted by particle number *N* (plot A), surface area *S* (plot B), and volume *V* (plot C). D_p is particle diameter in microns. Legends show geometric mean diameters (*DG*) for each distribution, and particle number, surface area, or volume in mode.

Fig. 4 Typical Urban Outdoor Distributions of Ultrafine or Nuclei (n) Particles, Fine or Accumulation (a) Particles, and Coarse (c) Particles
(Whitby 1978)

coarse and fine atmospheric contamination plotted to show particle number, total particle surface area, and total particle volume as a function of particle size.

Note the differences between the three curves. Figure 4 demonstrates that particles 0.1 μm or less in diameter typically make up about 80% of the number of particles in the atmosphere but contribute only about 1% of the volume or mass. Also, 0.1% of the number of particles larger than 1 μm typically carry 70% of the total mass, which is the direct result of the mass of a spherical particle increasing as the cube of its diameter. Although most of the mass is contributed by intermediate and larger particles, over 80% of the area (staining) contamination is supplied by particles less than 1 μm in diameter, which is in the center of the respirable particle size range and is the size most likely to remain in the lungs (see Figure 2 and Chapter 10). Of possible concern to the HVAC industry is the fact that most of the staining effect on ceilings, walls, windows, and light fixtures results from particles less than 1 μm in diameter. Fouling of heat transfer devices and rotating equipment involves particles in this size range and larger. Suspended particles in urban air are predominantly smaller than 1 μm (aerodynamic diameter) and have a distribution that is approximately log-normal.

Units of Measurement

The quantity of particulate matter in the air can be determined as a mass or particle count in a given volume of air. Mass units are milligrams per cubic metre of air sampled (mg/m³) or micrograms per cubic metre of air sampled (μg/m³); 1 mg/m³ = 1000 μg/m³. Particle counts are usually quoted for volumes of 0.1 ft³, 1 ft³, 1 L, or 1 m³ and are specified for a given range of particle diameter.

Harmful Effects of Particulate Contaminants

Particulate contaminants can be damaging to people, the buildings in which they live and work, and materials and artifacts in these buildings.

Effects on People. Harmful effects of nonviable particles on people include toxicity, irritation, and odor. Effects of viable particles are covered in the section on Bioaerosols and in Chapter 10.

Dusts produced in industrial processes can be highly toxic (see Chapter 10). Most nonviable particles encountered outdoors and in commercial and residential buildings are of lower toxicity. Their impact depends on particle size and amount present. Larger coarse and fine particles trapped before reaching the lungs are likely to cause irritation if present in sufficient quantity. Smaller fine and ultrafine particles that reach the lungs are more of an issue. There have been concerns for many years about the long-term effects on the lungs of exposure to particles, but the first support for an association between airborne coarse particles and incidence of asthma and hospital admissions for respiratory problems did not come until the 1990s (Pope 1991). Other studies have shown that chronic exposure to fine particles can affect both the heart and lungs (Pope et al. 2002), and identified fine particles as a priority chronic hazard in U.S. homes (Logue et al. 2011). Ultrafine particles, which have much higher number concentrations and surface areas than fine particles and can adsorb gaseous contaminants, may also be health issues (Delfino et al. 2005; Soutas et al. 2005). More information on health effects of particulate matter can be found in Chapter 10.

Particulate contaminants are not odorous in themselves but can become so by adsorbing odorous gaseous contaminants such as nitrogen and sulfur oxides from combustion processes. Such particles can be trapped by HVAC filters and may release the odor later on.

Effects on Materials. Damage depends on the size of the particles, with larger particles having the potential for settling on and abrading materials, and smaller particles having the potential for soiling both horizontal and vertical surfaces. Both size ranges are of concern for HVAC components, and their impacts can be reduced by using filters. Finishes and furnishings in occupied buildings can require more frequent maintenance if soiling is not effectively controlled. Artworks and artifacts in galleries and museums can be permanently damaged by exposure to both abrasive and soiling particles; for details, see Chapter 23 of the 2015 *ASHRAE Handbook—HVAC Applications*.

Measurement of Airborne Particles

Suitable methods for determining the quantity of particulate matter in the air vary, depending on the amount present and on the size of particles involved. **Direct gravimetric measurement**, in which a dusty air sample is drawn through a preweighed filter, is a common technique in industrial workplaces that often contain significant numbers of large particles. If the total airstream is drawn through the test filter, the sample is known as the **total mass**; if a size-selective inlet is used on the filter, the sample is characterized by the inlet used ($PM_{2.5}$, PM_{10}, respirable, etc.). Gravimetric methods have the advantage of providing an integrated sample (over the sample duration) and of providing a direct measure of the mass concentration (mass/volume). In general, gravimetric methods are not real-time, although some innovative samplers use secondary methods (e.g., beta attenuation, crystal vibration frequency changes) to infer mass on a real-time basis. Further, gravimetric methods require increasing test effort (sample duration and balance quality) as the mass concentration drops toward office and indoor air levels.

Normal daily activities of individuals cause higher personal exposures to both particles and gas contaminants than would be expected from measurements of undisturbed air. Personal activities frequently bring individuals close to air contaminant sources, and also generate particles. Sampling near a person requires special care because the degree of exposure also depends on particle transport as air flows around the body because of convective forces, air turbulence, and obstructions nearby (Rodes and Thornburg 2004).

Optical particle counters (OPCs) are widely used and likely to become more so. They are very convenient and provide real-time, size-selective data. Individual aerosol particles are illuminated with a bright light as they singly pass through the OPC viewing volume. Each particle scatters light, which is collected to produce a voltage pulse in the detector. The pulse size is proportional to the particle size, and the electronics of the OPC assign counts to size ranges based on the pulse size. ASHRAE *Standard* 52.2 defines a laboratory method for assessing the performance of media filters using an OPC to measure particle counts up- and downstream of the filter in 12 size ranges between 0.3 and 10 μm. Filters tested are reported with their **minimum efficiency reporting value (MERV)** number based on the count data. It is important to sample isokinetically in fast-moving airstreams, such as found in air ducts. This involves sizing the OPC sampling inlet so that the speed of sampled air entering the device is the same as that of air moving past the OPC. If this is not done, the OPC samples inaccurately, capturing too few particles when sampling speed is greater than surrounding air speed, and too many when sampling speed is less than that of the surrounding air.

Counters are also used to test cleanrooms for compliance with the U.S. General Services Administration's (GSA) *Federal Standard* 209E and ISO *Standard* 14644-1. Cleanrooms are defined in terms of the number of particles in certain size ranges that they contain; for more information, see Chapter 18 of the 2015 *ASHRAE Handbook—HVAC Applications*.

Modern OPCs use laser light scattering to continuously count and size airborne particles and, depending on design, can detect particles down to 0.1 μm (ASTM *Standard* F50). Like all aerosol instruments, OPCs should be used with awareness of their limitations. They report particle size from a calibration curve that was developed from a particle having particular optical properties. Actual ambient aerosol particle size is usually close to that indicated by an OPC, but significant errors are possible. Further, many OPCs were developed for cleanroom applications and can become overloaded in other applications. In general, they do not inform the user when they are out of range.

A **condensation nucleus counter (CNC)** can count particles to below 0.01 μm. These particles, present in great numbers in the atmosphere, serve as nuclei for condensation of water vapor (Scala 1963). CNCs provide total particle numbers, and cannot directly provide particle sizing information.

Another indirect method measures the **optical density** of the collected dust, based on the projected area of the particles. Dust particles can be sized with graduated scales or optical comparisons using a standard microscope. The lower limit for sizing with the light-field microscope is approximately 0.9 μm, depending on the vision of the observer, dust color, and available contrast. This size can be reduced to about 0.4 μm by using oil-immersion objective techniques. Dark-field microscopic techniques reveal particles smaller than these, to a limit of approximately 0.1 μm. Smaller submicroscopic dusts can be sized and compared with the aid of an electron microscope.

Other sizing techniques may take into account velocity of samplings in calibrated devices and actual settlement measurements in laboratory equipment. The electron microscope and sampling instruments such as the cascade impactor have been successful in sizing particulates, including fogs and mists. Each method of measuring particle size distribution gives a different value for the same size particle, because different properties are actually measured. For example, a microscopic technique may measure longest dimension, whereas impactor results are based on aerodynamic behavior (ACGIH 2001).

Chemical analysis of particles follows protocols for analysis of any solid material. At industrial concentrations, adequate samples can be obtained from ducts and dust collectors. Because larger particles settle faster than smaller particles, the size and nature of deposited particles often change as suspended particles move away from a source. For instance, near the inlet of an outdoor air intake, deposited particles will probably be larger and have a coarse composition (e.g., road dust might predominate), whereas further into the duct, fine-mode aerosols would predominate (e.g., condensed oil fume and soot). At the lower concentrations of workplaces, samples are usually collected onto filters, and the filter deposit is analyzed. The filter material must be chosen to not interfere with the analysis. After sample preparation, analysis methods for gaseous contaminant analysis generally apply.

Typical Particle Levels

Particle counters, which detect particles larger than about 0.1 μm, indicate that the number of suspended particles is enormous. A room with heavy cigarette smoke has a particle concentration of 3×10^{10} particles per cubic foot. Even clean air typically contains over 10^6 particles/ft^3. If smaller particles detectable by other means, such as an electron microscope or condensation nucleus counter, are also included, the total particle concentration would be greater than these concentrations by a factor of 10 to 100. Ultrafine particles have been widely found at concentrations of 60 to 120 million per cubic foot in both indoor and outdoor air.

Much of the published particle data uses mass concentration rather than number concentration, because the EPA outdoor limits are expressed in these units (see Table 12). Typical daytime average levels of outdoor PM_{10} and $PM_{2.5}$ in school or residential areas may be 10 to 30 μg/m^3 (Fromme et al. 2008; Williams et al. 2000), and $PM_{2.5}$ in heavy traffic areas in large cities can be >100 μg/m^3 (Cassidy et al. 2007; Han et al. 2005). In indoor environments with few internal sources, such as offices, indoor concentrations in both size ranges tend to be smaller than outdoors because of HVAC filters. However, in schools, where activity levels are higher and indoor sources are present, indoor PM_{10} and $PM_{2.5}$ may be higher than outdoors (Fromme et al. 2008).

Indoor particle levels in buildings are influenced by the number of people and their activities, building materials and construction, outdoor conditions, ventilation rate, and the air-conditioning and filtration system. Wallace (1996) reviewed the effect of outdoor particle penetration and activities on indoor concentrations, and Riley et al. (2002) discussed the influence of air exchange rates and filtration on indoor concentrations in residential and commercial buildings. ASHRAE research project RP-1281 investigated factors affecting the penetration of fine and ultrafine particles into nonresidential buildings (Facciola et al. 2006). For further information, see the section on Commercial, Institutional, and Residential Indoor Air Contaminants.

Bioaerosols

Bioaerosol refers to any airborne biological (generally microscopic) particulate matter. Though often thought of as originating as microorganisms (fungi, bacteria, viruses, protozoa, algae), bioaerosols may also be derived from plants (pollen and plant fragments) and animals (hair, dander, and saliva from dogs and cats; dust mites). In addition to the intact organisms (e.g., bacteria), their parts (fungal spores and fragments), components (endotoxins, allergens), and products (dust mite antigen-containing fecal pellets and fungal mycotoxins) may be included in the definition. The antigen or toxin to which the body reacts may be quite small; only trace amounts are required for many allergic or toxic reactions. Public interest has focused on airborne microorganisms responsible for diseases and infections, primarily bacteria and viruses. These are discussed in more detail in Chapter 10, including sources, transmission and health effects.

Bioaerosols are universally present in both indoor and outdoor environments. Although the organisms that are sources of bioaerosols are living, reproducing organisms, bioaerosols themselves do not have to be alive to cause allergic, toxic, or inflammatory responses. In fact, as little as 1 to 10% of outdoor bioaerosol is thought to be viable (Jaenicke 1998; Tong and Lighthart 1999). Furthermore, fragments of bioaerosols may be transported while attached to inert particles, and may be important from an exposure standpoint.

Problems of concern to engineers occur when microorganisms grow and reproduce indoors, or when large amounts of bioaerosol enter a building from outdoors. Buildings are not sterile, nor are they meant to be. The presence of bacteria and fungi outdoors in soil, water, and atmospheric habitats is normal. For example, spores of the fungus *Cladosporium* are commonly found on leaves and dead vegetation and are almost always found in outdoor air samples. Often, they are found in variable numbers in indoor air, depending on the amount of outdoor air that infiltrates into interior spaces or is brought in by the HVAC system. Outdoor microorganisms and pollen can also enter on shoes and clothing and be transferred to other surfaces in buildings. Through infiltration, pollens can be quite problematic indoors, often depending on the season. Pollens discharged by weeds, grasses, and trees (Hewson et al. 1967; Jacobson and Morris 1977; Solomon and Mathews 1978) can cause hay fever. Bioaerosols have properties of special interest to air-cleaning equipment designers (see Chapter 29 of the 2016 *ASHRAE Handbook—HVAC Systems and Equipment*).

Some bioaerosols originate indoors. Many allergens, such as cat, dog, and dust mite allergens, either originate indoors or have indoor reservoirs (e.g., bedding and fleecy materials). Much attention has been given to fungi, which include yeasts, molds (filamentous fungi), and mildews, as well as large mushrooms, puffballs, and bracket fungi. All fungi depend on external sources of organic material for both energy requirements and carbon skeletons, but very small quantities can be sufficient. Thus, they increase in number when supplied with a suitable food source such as very small quantities of dirt/dust, paper, or wood. Sufficient nutrients are almost always readily available in buildings. For growth to occur, sufficient water must also be available in the material. Adequate moisture content of a material may be attained when the relative humidity is high (typically, the equilibrium relative humidity of a porous material with the surrounding air is greater than 60%), on water incursion from a roof leak or condensation, or when water spills. Note that controlling humidity in a space per se is not sufficient to limit fungal growth; the moisture content of the substrate material must be controlled. Some species of mold that often grow on water-damaged building materials are listed in Table 3.

Mycotoxins are secondary metabolites produced by some filamentous fungi, Some are very toxic (e.g., aflatoxin) and some are beneficial (e.g., penicillin). There are hundreds of different mycotoxins, and more are being identified all the time. Mycotoxins can cause disease and death in humans and other animals, primarily when consumed in foods. However, inhalation exposure of fungal spores and fragments containing mycotoxins has been raised as a potential concern as a bioaerosol contaminant.

Bacteria are much simpler organisms than fungi, and generally require more water for growth, often growing in liquids or periodically wetted surfaces. Whereas fungi actively release spores into the environment from contaminated surfaces, bacteria are generally aerosolized by reentrainment of the water in which they are growing. Cooling towers, evaporative condensers, and domestic water service systems all provide water and nutrients for amplification of bacteria such as *Legionella pneumophila*. Growth of bacterial populations to excessive concentrations is generally associated with inadequate preventive maintenance or leaks creating standing water. *Legionella* is well studied, and ASHRAE *Standard* 188-2015 discusses its risk management.

Table 3 Common Molds on Water-Damaged Building Materials

Mold Species	Mold Species
Alternaria alternata	*Memnoniella echinata*
Aspergillus sydowii	*Paecilomyces variotii*
Aspergillus versicolor	*Penicillium aurantogriseum*
Chaetomium globusum	*Penicillium chrysogenum*
Cladosporium cladosporioides	*Penicillium citrinum*
Cladosporium sphaerospermum	*Penicillium commune*
Eurotium herbariorum	*Stachybotrys chartarum*
Eurotium repens	*Ulocladium chartarum*

Source: Health Canada (2004).

Drain pans and cooling coils may also be sources of bacteria. Growth can occur in the water and the organism then can become aerosolized in water droplets. The most common source of bacteria as bioaerosols, especially in closed occupied spaces, may be droplet nuclei caused by actions such as sneezing, or carried on human or animal skin scales.

Endotoxins are components of the cell walls of a fairly large group of bacteria classified as Gram negative (i.e., crystal violet dye, used in a Gram stain test, does not affect their color). Endotoxin exposure has been associated with a number of adverse health effects. Humidifier fever has been associated with inhalation of endotoxins (Teeuw et al. 1994).

Units of Measurement. Microorganisms such as bacteria and molds are usually measured either as total culturable or total countable bioaerosol. **Culturable** (viable) bioaerosols are those that can be grown in a laboratory culture. Results are normally reported as number of colony-forming units (CFU) per unit sample volume (m^3 for air samples), area (cm^2 for surface samples) or mass (g for bulk samples).

Countable bioaerosols (viable plus nonviable) include all particles that can be identified and counted under a microscope. Results are reported as number of particles per unit sample volume, area, or mass.

Allergens are usually expressed as their weight (in ng) per unit volume; endotoxins are expressed as EU or endotoxin units.

Sampling. Sampling when bioaerosols are suspected as a contaminant may include direct plating of observed microbial growth, collection of bulk or surface samples, or air sampling. Surface sampling is useful for bioaerosol detection, because the surface may constitute a long-time duration sampler. The principles of sampling and analysis for bioaerosols are presented in depth by Macher (1999). AIHA (1996) gives assessment guidelines for collecting microbiological particulates.

The same principles that affect collection of an inert particulate aerosol sample also govern air sampling for microorganisms. Air sampling is not likely to yield useful data and information unless the sample collected is representative of exposure, and appropriate control samples are collected. The most representative samples are those collected in breathing zones over the range of aerosol concentrations. Personal sampling (in the breathing zone of a worker) is generally preferable, but area sampling (e.g., on a table) over representative periods is more commonly performed. Some investigators attempt to replicate exposure conditions through disturbance of the environment (semiaggressive sampling), such as occurs when walking on carpets, slamming doors, and opening books or file cabinets.

The sampling method selected affects the measured count. Methods that rely on counting analysis usually report higher concentrations than those that use culturing analysis, because of inclusion of nonviable particles. There is no single, ideal bioaerosol sampler, but rather several complementary techniques that may be appropriate in any particular application. Collection directly on **filter paper** is simple and direct, but may dehydrate some organisms and underestimate exposure for live counting techniques. **Glass impingers** are an effective and standard method, but may overestimate exposure because liquid contact and agitation can break clusters into smaller individual organisms, which are then each counted as a separate entity. **Slit-to-agar samplers** may give a more accurate culturable colony count, but do not measure nonculturable organisms or fragments, parts, or components. In general, culture plate impactors, including multiple- and single-stage devices as well as slit-to-agar samplers, are most useful in office environments where low concentrations of bacteria and fungi are expected. Some multihole impactors require application of a positive hole correction factor to the raw counts to compensate for multiple organisms focused aerodynamically and landing in the same place on the media. Because not all microorganisms can grow on the same media, impactors that separate samples must be collected for each. Liquid impingement subculturing allows plating one sample on multiple media. Filter cassette samplers are useful for some hardy microorganisms or components (e.g., endotoxins) and allergen analyses. Filter cassettes can also be used for spore counts.

Nonculture methods for fungal spores and pollen grains generally involve exposing an adhesive-coated glass slide or plate for a specific time period, then counting calibrated areas under the microscope, and calculating the number in a measured volume of air. Measurement methods for pollen are not discussed further here, because data are widely available in the public domain.

Some viruses, bacteria, algae, and protozoa are more difficult to culture than fungi, and air-sampling methodology for these organisms may not be practical. For example, *Legionella* requires special nutrients and conditions for growth, and thus may be difficult to recover from air. To further complicate the issue, not all fungi grow on any one media, so media selection may be important.

Rank-order assessment is used to interpret air-sampling data for microorganisms (Macher 1999). Individual organisms are listed in descending order of abundance for a complainant indoor site and for one or more control locations. The predominance of one or more microbes in the complainant site, but not in the control sites or outdoors, suggests the presence of a source for that organism. An example is shown in Table 4.

Recently, quantitative real-time **polymerase chain reaction (PCR)** (Mullis 1990) testing has been developed for routine diagnosis of specific microorganisms in clinical microbiology laboratories (Espy 2006) and for mold determination in residential and commercial venues. PCR is a molecular technique for multiplying a specific strand of DNA or RNA millions of times by manipulating the chemical nature of the cell. Once multiplied (or amplified), the target DNA can be detected through a variety of methods.

PCR-based methods eliminate the need to culture organisms for detection, and remedy shortcomings of traditional techniques by allowing rapid, sensitive, and specific identification of the pathogens of concern rather than indicator organisms. Traditional culturing can take anywhere from 3 to 7 days, whereas real-time PCR can often be run in 10 to 24 h (Yang and Rothman 2004).

Table 4 Example Case of Airborne Fungi in Building and Outdoor Air

Location	CFU/m^3	Rank Order Taxa
Outdoors	210	*Cladosporium* > *Fusarium* > *Epicoccum* > *Aspergillus*
Complainant office #1	2500	*Tritirachium* > *Aspergillus* > *Cladosporium*
Complainant office #2	3000	*Tritirachium* > *Aspergillus* > *Cladosporium*

Notes: CFU/m^3 = colony-forming units per cubic metre of air. Culture media, for this example, was malt extract agar (ACGIH 1989).

U.S. Environmental Protection Agency (EPA) and Department of Housing and Urban Development (HUD) researchers have developed a metric called the environmental relative moldiness index (ERMI) to objectively describe the home mold burden (Vesper et al. 2007). A DNA-based analysis called mold-specific quantitative PCR (MSQPCR) of 36 molds, including 26 species associated with homes with water damage and 10 found in homes independent of water damage, forms the basis of the ERMI.

Controlling Exposures to Particulate Matter

Control of airborne particulate levels may be achieved by one of four methods:

- Reduction of source emissions
- Capture of emissions at the source using local exhaust
- Dilution using mechanical ventilation
- Removal from ventilation air by filtration

Of these, filtration is of particular importance to HVAC&R. This topic is covered in detail in Chapter 29 in the 2016 *ASHRAE Handbook—HVAC Systems and Equipment*.

Control of bioaerosols is a complex issue because of their capacity for growth and dispersion. However, in general, particulate removal devices and controls are effective in collecting and removing bioaerosols, including allergens (Foarde et al. 1994). Control may also be achieved by ultraviolet irradiation, as described in Chapter 60 of the 2015 *ASHRAE Handbook—HVAC Applications*.

3. GASEOUS CONTAMINANTS

The terms **gas** and **vapor** are both used to describe the gaseous state of a substance. *Gas* is the correct term for describing any pure substance or mixture that naturally exists in the gaseous state at normal atmospheric conditions. That is, its vapor pressure is greater than ambient pressure at ambient temperature. Examples are oxygen, helium, ammonia, and nitrogen. *Vapor* is used to describe a substance in the gaseous state whose natural state is a liquid or solid at normal atmospheric conditions. The vapor pressure is below ambient pressure at ambient temperature. Examples include benzene, carbon tetrachloride, and water. Differences between the two classes reflect their preferred states:

- For a strong source, the concentration of a gas in air in a confined space can rise above one atmosphere. Thus, even nontoxic gases can be lethal if they completely fill a space, displacing the oxygen necessary for survival.
- Vapors can never exceed their saturated vapor pressure in air. The most familiar example of a vapor is water, with relative humidity expressing the air concentration as a percentage of the saturated vapor pressure.
- Vapors, because their natural state is liquid or solid (low vapor pressure), tend to condense on surfaces and be adsorbed.

Gaseous contaminants can also usefully be divided into organic and inorganic types. **Organic** compounds include all chemicals based on a skeleton of carbon atoms. Because carbon atoms easily combine to form chain, branched, and ring structures, there is a wide variety of organic compounds. Despite the variety, they have similarities that can be used in sampling, analysis, and removal. Chemists subclassify organic compounds based on families having similar structure and predictable properties. Organic gaseous contaminants include gases such as methane, but the majority are vapors.

All other gaseous contaminants are classified as **inorganic**. Most inorganic air contaminants of interest to ventilation engineers are gases (mercury is an important exception). Major chemical families of inorganic and organic gaseous contaminants, with examples of specific compounds, are shown in Table 5, along with information

Table 5 Major Chemical Families of Gaseous Air Contaminants

No. Family	Examples	Other Information
Inorganic Contaminants		
1. Single-element atoms and molecules	Chlorine, radon, mercury	Chlorine is a strong respiratory irritant used as a disinfectant; outdoor sources include seawater, chlorinated pools, and road salt. Radon is an important soil gas. Mercury is the vapor in fluorescent light bulbs and tubes.
2. Oxidants	Ozone, nitrogen dioxide, hydrogen peroxide	Corrosive; respiratory irritants.
3. Reducing agents	Carbon monoxide	Toxic; fuel combustion product.
4. Acid gases	Carbon dioxide, hydrogen chloride, hydrogen fluoride, hydrogen sulfide, nitric acid, sulfur dioxide, sulfuric acid	Carbon dioxide and hydrogen sulfide are only weakly acidic. Hydrogen sulfide is the main agent in sewer gas. Other members are corrosive and respiratory irritants. Some are important outdoor contaminants.
5. Nitrogen compounds	Ammonia, hydrazine, nitrous oxide	Ammonia is used in cleaning products; it is a strong irritant. Hydrazine is used as an anticorrosion agent. Nitrous oxide (laughing gas) is used as an anesthetic.
6. Miscellaneous	Arsine, phosphine	Used in the semiconductor industry.
Organic Contaminants		
7. *n*-Alkanes	Methane, propane, *n*-butane, *n*-hexane, *n*-heptane, *n*-octane, *n*-nonane, *n*-decane, *n*-undecane, *n*-dodecane	*n*-Alkanes are linear molecules and relatively easily identified analytically. Along with the far more numerous branched alkanes, they are components of solvents such as mineral spirits.
8. Branched alkanes	2-methyl pentane, 2-methyl hexane	Numerous; members are difficult to separate and identify. Many occur as components of products such as gasoline, kerosene, mineral spirits, etc.
9. Alkenes and cyclic hydrocarbons	Ethylene, butadiene, 1-octene, cyclohexane, 4-phenyl cyclohexene (4-PC)	Ethylene gas is produced by ripening fruit (and used in the fruit industry). Some liquid members are components of gasoline, etc. 4-PC is responsible for "new carpet" odor.
10. Chlorofluorocarbons	R-11 (trichlorofluoromethane), R-12 (dichlorodifluoromethane), R-114 (dichlorotetrafluoroethane)	Widely used as refrigerants; are being phased out because of their ozone-depleting potential.
11. Chlorinated hydrocarbons	Carbon tetrachloride, chloroform, dichloromethane, 1,1,1-trichloroethane, trichloroethylene, tetrachloroethylene, *p*-dichlorobenzene	Dichlorobenzene, an aromatic chemical, is a solid used as an air freshener. Others shown here are liquids and effective nonpolar solvents. Some are used as degreasers or in the dry-cleaning industry.
12. Halide compounds	Methyl bromide, methyl iodide	Low combustibility; some are used as flame retardants.
13. Alcohols	Methanol, ethanol, 2-propanol (isopropanol), 3-methyl 1-butanol, ethylene glycol, 2-butoxyethanol, phenol, texanol	Strongly polar. Some (including 2-butoxyethanol and texanol) are used as solvents in water-based products. Phenol is used as a disinfectant. 3-methyl 1-butanol is emitted by some molds.
14. Ethers	Ethyl ether, methyl tertiary butyl ether (MTBE), 2-butoxyethanol	Ethyl ether and 2-butoxyethanol are used as solvents. MTBE is added to gasoline to improve combustion in vehicle motors.
15. Aldehydes	Formaldehyde, acetaldehyde, acrolein, benzaldehyde	Formaldehyde, acetaldehyde, and acrolein have unpleasant odors and are strong irritants formed during combustion of fuels and tobacco.
16. Ketones	2-propanone (acetone), 2-butanone (MEK), methyl isobutyl ketone (MIBK), 2-hexanone	Medium-polarity chemicals; some are useful solvents. Acetone and 2-hexanone are emitted by some molds.
17. Esters	Ethyl acetate, vinyl acetate, butyl acetate, texanol	Medium-polarity chemicals; some have pleasant odors and are added as fragrances to consumer products.
18. Nitrogen compounds other than amines	Nitromethane, acetonitrile, acrylonitrile, urea, hydrogen cyanide, peroxyacetal nitrite (PAN)	Includes several different types of chemicals with few common properties. Acetonitrile is used as a solvent; urea is a metabolic product; PAN is found in vehicle exhaust.
19. Aromatic hydrocarbons	Benzene, toluene, *p*-xylene, styrene, 1,2,4 trimethyl benzene, naphthalene, benz-α-pyrene	Benzene, toluene, and xylene are widely used as solvents and in manufacturing, and are ubiquitous in indoor air. Naphthalene is used as moth repellent.
20. Terpenes	α-pinene, limonene	A variety of terpenes are emitted by wood. The two listed here have pleasant odors and are used as fragrances in cleaners, perfumes, etc.
21. Heterocylics	Ethylene oxide, tetrahydrofuran, 3-methyl furan, 1,4-dioxane, pyridine, nicotine	Most are of medium polarity. Ethylene oxide is used as a disinfectant. Tetrahydrofuran and pyridine are used as solvents. Nicotine is a component of tobacco smoke.
22. Organophosphates	Malathion, tabun, sarin, soman	Listed are components of agricultural pesticides and occur as outdoor air contaminants.
23. Amines	Trimethylamine, ethanolamine, cyclohexylamine, morpholine	Typically have unpleasant odors detectable at very low concentrations. Some (cyclohexylamine and morpholine) are used as antioxidants in boilers.
24. Monomers	Vinyl chloride, ethylene, methyl methacrylate, styrene	Potential to be released from their respective polymers (PVC, polythene, perspex, polystyrene) if materials are heated.
25. Mercaptans and other sulfur compounds	Bis-2-chloroethyl sulfide (mustard gas), ethyl mercaptan, dimethyl disulfide	Sulfur-containing chemicals typically have unpleasant odors detectable at very low concentrations. Ethyl mercaptan is added to natural gas so that gas leaks can be detected by odor. Mustard gas has been used in chemical warfare.
26. Organic acids	Formic acid, acetic acid, butyric acid	Formic and acetic acids (vinegar) are emitted by some types of wood. Butyric acid is a component of "new car" odor.
27. Miscellaneous	Phosgene, siloxanes	Phosgene is a toxic gas released during combustion of some chlorinated organic chemicals. Siloxanes occur widely in consumer products, including adhesives, sealants, cleaners, and hair and skin care products.

about occurrence and use. Some organics belong to more than one class and carry the attributes of both.

Another useful gaseous contaminant classification is polar versus nonpolar. There is a continuous distribution between these extremes. For **polar** compounds, charge separation occurs between atoms, which affects physical characteristics as well as chemical reactivity. Water is one of the best examples of a polar compound, and consequently polar gaseous contaminants tend to be soluble in water. **Nonpolar** compounds are much less soluble in water, but dissolve in nonpolar liquids. This classification provides the basis for dividing consumer products that contain organic compounds into water-based and solvent-based. Contaminant classes in Table 5 that are strongly polar include acid gases, chemicals containing oxygen (e.g., alcohols, aldehydes, ketones, esters, organic acids), and some nitrogen-containing chemicals. Nonpolar classes include all hydrocarbons (alkyl, alkene, cyclic, aromatic), chlorinated hydrocarbons, terpenes, and some sulfur-containing chemicals.

Because no single sampling and analysis method applies to every (or even most) potential contaminant, having some idea what the contaminants and their properties might be is very helpful. Contaminants have sources, and consideration of the locale, industries, raw materials, cleaners, and consumer products usually provides some guidance regarding probable contaminants. Material safety data sheets (MSDS) provide information on potentially harmful chemicals that a product contains, but the information is often incomplete. Once a potential contaminant has been identified, the *Merck Index* (Budavi 1996), the *Toxic Substances Control Act Chemical Substance Inventory* (EPA 1979), *Dangerous Properties of Industrial Materials* (Sax and Lewis 1988), and *Handbook of Environmental Data on Organic Chemicals* (Verschueren 1996) are all useful in identifying and gathering information on contaminant properties, including some known by trade names only. Chemical and physical properties can be found in reference books such as the *Handbook of Chemistry and Physics* (Lide 1996). Note that a single chemical compound, especially an organic one, may have several scientific names. To reduce confusion, the Chemical Abstracts Service (CAS) assigns each chemical a unique five- to nine-digit identifier number. Table 6 shows CAS numbers and some physical properties for selected gaseous contaminants. The volatility designation for organic chemicals (VVOC, VOC, SVOC) is explained in the section on Volatile Organic Compounds. Volatilities, expressed more exactly in boiling point and saturated vapor pressure data, are important in predicting airborne concentrations of gaseous contaminants in cases of spillage or leakage of liquids. For example, because of its much higher volatility, ammonia requires more rigorous safety precautions than ethylene glycol when used as a heat exchange fluid. In laboratories where several acids are stored, hydrochloric acid (hydrogen chloride) usually causes more corrosion than sulfuric or nitric acids because its greater gaseous concentration results in escape of more chemical. Additional chemical and physical properties for some of the chemicals in Tables 5 and 6 can be found in Chapter 33.

Harmful Effects of Gaseous Contaminants

Harmful effects may be divided into four categories: toxicity, irritation, odor, and material damage.

Toxicity. The harmful effects of gaseous pollutants on a person depend on both short-term peak concentrations and the time-integrated exposure received by the person. Toxic effects are generally considered to be proportional to the exposure dose, although individual response variation can obscure the relationship. The allowable concentration for short exposures is higher than that for long exposures. Safe exposure limits have been set for a number of common gaseous contaminants in industrial settings. This topic is covered in more detail in the section on Industrial Air Contaminants and in Chapter 10.

A few gaseous contaminants are also capable of causing cancer. Formaldehyde has recently been declared a known human carcinogen by the U.S. National Toxicology Program (NTP 2011), based on an earlier report issued by the International Agency for Research in Cancer (IARC 2004). The NTP also stated that styrene is "reasonably anticipated to be a human carcinogen" (NTP 2011).

Gaseous contaminants can also be responsible for chronic health effects when exposure to low levels occurs over a long period of time. Acetaldehyde, acrolein, benzene, 1,3-butadiene, 1,4-dichlorobenzene, formaldehyde, naphthalene, and nitrogen dioxide have recently been identified as priority chronic hazards in U.S. homes (Logue et al. 2011). More information on health effects of gaseous contaminants can be found in Chapter 10.

Irritation. Although gaseous pollutants may have no discernible continuing health effects, exposure may cause physical irritation to building occupants. This phenomenon has been studied principally in laboratories and nonindustrial work environments, and is discussed in more detail in the section on Nonindustrial Indoor Air Contaminants and in Chapter 10.

Odors. Gaseous contaminant problems often appear as complaints about odors, and these usually are the result of concentrations considerably below industrial exposure limits. Odors are discussed in more detail in Chapter 12. Note that controlling gaseous contaminants because they constitute a nuisance odor is fundamentally different from controlling a contaminant because it has a demonstrated health effect. Odor control frequently can use limited-capacity "peak-shaving" technology to drop peaks of odorous compounds below the odor threshold. Later reemission at a low rate is neither harmful nor noticed. Such an approach may not be acceptable for control of toxic materials.

Damage to Materials. Material damage from gaseous pollutants includes corrosion, embrittlement, and discoloration. Because these effects usually involve chemical reactions that need water, material damage from air pollutants is less severe in the relatively dry indoor environment than outdoors, even at similar gaseous contaminant concentrations. Contaminants that can corrode HVAC systems include seawater, acid gases (chlorine, hydrogen fluoride, hydrogen sulfide, nitrogen oxides and sulfur oxides), ammonia, and ozone. Corrosion from these gases can also cause electrical, electronic, and telephone switching systems to malfunction (ISA 1985).

Some dry materials can be significantly damaged. These effects are most serious in museums, because any loss of color or texture changes the essence of the object. Libraries and archives are also vulnerable, as are pipe organs and textiles. Consult Chapter 23 in the 2015 *ASHRAE Handbook—HVAC Applications* for additional information and an exhaustive reference list.

Units of Measurement

Concentrations of gaseous contaminants are usually expressed in the following units:

ppm = parts of contaminant by volume per million parts of air by volume

ppb = parts of contaminant by volume per billion parts of air by volume

1000 ppb = 1 ppm

mg/m^3 = milligrams of contaminant per cubic metre of air

$\mu g/m^3$ = micrograms of contaminant per cubic metre of air

Conversions between ppm and mg/m^3 are

$$\text{ppm} = [0.6699(459.7 + t)/Mp]\ (\text{mg/m}^3) \tag{1}$$

$$\text{mg/m}^3 = [1.493(Mp)/(459.7 + t)]\ (\text{ppm}) \tag{2}$$

where

M = relative molecular weight of contaminant

Table 6 Characteristics of Selected Gaseous Air Contaminants

	Chemical and Physical Properties				
Contaminant	Table 5 Family	CAS[a] number	Volatility[b]	M[c]	Usage
Inorganic Contaminants					
Ammonia	5	7664-41-7	Gas	17	145.1,[d] 145.2[e]
Arsine	6	7784-42-1	Gas	78	
Carbon dioxide	4	124-38-9	Gas	44	145.2
Carbon monoxide	3	630-08-0	Gas	28	145.2
Chlorine	1	7782-50-5	Gas	71	145.1, 145.2
Hydrogen chloride	4	7647-01-0	Gas	37	145.2
Hydrogen fluoride	4	7664-39-3	Vapor	20	
Hydrogen sulfide	4	7783-06-4	Gas	34	145.1, 145.2
Mercury	1	7439-97-6	Vapor	201	
Nitric acid	4	7697-37-2	Vapor	63	
Nitric oxide	5	10102-43-9	Gas	30	145.1
Nitrogen dioxide	2	10102-44-0	Vapor	46	145.1, 145.2
Ozone	2	10028-15-6	Gas	48	145.1, 145.2
Sulfur dioxide	4	7446-09-5	Gas	64	145.1, 145.2
Organic Contaminants					
1,1,1-trichloroethane	11	71-55-6	VOC	133	IAQ[f]
1,2,4-trimethylbenzene	19	95-63-6	VOC	120	IAQ
2-butanone (MEK)	16	78-93-3	VVOC	72	145.1, 145.2, IAQ
2-butoxyethanol	13, 14	111-76-2	VOC	118	IAQ
4-phenyl cyclohexene	9, 19	4994-16-5	SVOC	158	IAQ
β-pinene	20	127-91-3	VOC	136	IAQ
Acetaldehyde	15	75-07-0	VVOC	44	145.1, 145.2
Acetic acid	26	64-19-7	VOC	60	
Acetone	16	67-64-1	VVOC	58	145.2, IAQ
Acrolein	15	107-02-8	VOC	56	
Benzene	19	71-43-2	VOC	78	145.2, IAQ
Butyl acetate	17	123-86-4	VOC	116	IAQ
Carbon disulfide	25	75-15-0	VVOC	76	IAQ
Carbon tetrachloride	11	56-23-5	VOC	154	
Chloroform	11	67-66-3	VVOC	119	IAQ
Cyclohexane	9	110-82-7	VVOC	84	145.2
Cyclohexylamine	9, 23	108-91-8	VOC	99	
Cyclopentane	9	287-92-3	VVOC	70	145.2
Dichlorodifluoromethane	10	75-71-8	VVOC	121	
Dichloromethane	12	75-09-2	VVOC	85	145.1, 145.2, IAQ
Dimethyl disulfide	25	624-92-0	VVOC	94	IAQ
Dimethylmethylphosphate	22	756-79-6	VOC	124	145.2
Ethanol	13	64-17-5	VVOC	46	145.2, IAQ
Ethyl acetate	17	141-78-6	VVOC	88	IAQ
Ethylene glycol	13	107-21-1	VOC	62	
Ethylene oxide	21	75-21-8	VVOC	44	
Formaldehyde	15	50-00-0	VVOC	30	145.1, 145.2, IAQ
Hexanal	15	66-25-1	VOC	100	145.2
Hydrogen cyanide	18	74-90-8	VVOC	27	
Isobutane	8	75-28-5	VVOC	58	IAQ
Isobutanol	13	78-83-1	VOC	74	145.1, 145.2
Isopropanol	13	67-63-0	VVOC	60	145.2, IAQ
Limonene	20	5989-27-5	VOC	136	IAQ
Malathion	17, 22	121-75-5	VOC	330	
Methane	7	74-82-8	Gas	16	
Methanol	13	67-56-1	VVOC	32	
Methyl isobutyl ketone	16	108-10-1	VOC	100	IAQ
Methyl tertiary butyl ether	14	1634-04-4	VVOC	88	IAQ
Morpholine	21, 23	110-91-8	VOC	87	
Naphthalene	19	91-20-3	VOC	128	IAQ
n-decane	7	124-18-5	VOC	142	IAQ
n-dodecane	7	112-40-3	VOC	170	IAQ
n-hexane	7	110-54-3	VVOC	86	145.1, 145.2
n-heptane	7	142-82-5	VOC	100	
Nicotine	21	54-11-5	SVOC	162	
N-methylpyrrholidone	16, 21	872-50-4	VOC	99	145.2
n-nonane	7	111-84-2	VOC	128	IAQ
n-octane	7	111-65-9	VOC	114	IAQ
n-undecane	7	1120-21-4	VOC	156	IAQ
p-dichlorobenzene	11, 19	106-46-7	VOC	147	IAQ
Phenol	13	108-95-2	VOC	94	IAQ
Phosgene	27	75-44-5	VVOC	90	
Propane	7	74-98-6	VVOC	44	IAQ
Siloxanes	27	Various	VOC	various	IAQ
Styrene	9, 19	100-42-5	VOC	104	IAQ
Tetrachloroethylene	11	127-18-4	VOC	166	145.1, 145.2, IAQ
Toluene	19	108-88-3	VOC	92	145.1, 145.2, IAQ
Toluene diisocyanate	18	584-84-9	SVOC	174	
Trichloroethylene	11	79-01-6	VOC	131	IAQ
Trichlorofluoromethane	10	75-69-4	VVOC	137	IAQ
Vinyl chloride monomer	24	75-01-4	VVOC	63	

[a]CAS = Chemical Abstracts Services.
[b]Volatility of organic chemicals complies with Table 9. VVOC adopted from the list produced by Salthammer (2016). Volatility of inorganic chemicals is gas if boiling point is less than 68°F, and vapor if boiling point is greater than 68°F.
[c]M = molecular weight.
[d]Listed as a challenge gas for laboratory testing of gas-phase filter granular media using ASHRAE *Standard* 145.1.
[e]Listed as a challenge gas for testing full-size gas-phase filters using ASHRAE *Standard* 145.2.
[f]Commonly found in buildings and may impact indoor air quality (IAQ) (taken from list in Table 10).

p = mixture pressure, psia
t = mixture temperature, °F

Concentration data are often reduced to standard temperature and pressure (i.e., 77°F and 14.7 psia)), in which case,

$$\text{ppm} = (24.46/M)\ (\text{mg/m}^3) \quad (3)$$

Using the 70°F standard temperature more familiar to engineers results in a conversion factor between ppm and mg/m³ of 24.14 in Equation (3). A temperature of 32°F gives a corresponding conversion factor of 22.41. These calculations show that variations in indoor temperature are likely to impact conversion factors by 1% or less, and can probably be ignored. However, outdoor temperatures may result in conversion factors in Equations (1) and (2) that differ by 10% from indoor ones, so that indoor and outdoor data may need to be converted separately using the appropriate factors. The differences in the conversion factors are caused by the fact that gases contract and become denser as temperatures decrease. Concentrations expressed in ppm are temperature independent, because

Table 7 Gaseous Contaminant Sample Collection Techniques

Technique*	Advantages	Disadvantages
Active Methods		
1. Direct flow to detectors	Real-time readout, continuous monitoring possible Several pollutants possible with one sample (when coupled with chromatograph, spectroscope, or multiple detectors)	Average concentration must be determined by integration No preconcentration possible before detector; sensitivity may be inadequate On-site equipment often complicated, expensive, intrusive, and requires skilled operator
2. Capture by pumped flow through colorimetric detector tubes, papers, or tapes	Very simple, relatively inexpensive equipment and materials Immediate readout Integration over time	One pollutant per sample Relatively high detection limit Poor precision Requires multiple tubes, papers, or tapes for high concentrations or long-term measurements
3. Capture by pumped flow through solid adsorbent; subsequent desorption for concentration measurement	On-site sampling equipment relatively simple and inexpensive Preconcentration and integration over time inherent in method Several pollutants possible with one sample	Sampling media and desorption techniques are compound-specific Interaction between captured compounds and between compounds and sampling media; bias may result Gives only average over sampling period, no peaks Subsequent concentration measurement required
4. Collection in evacuated containers	Very simple on-site equipment No pump (silent) Several pollutants possible with one sample	Subsequent concentration measurement required Gives average over sampling period; no peaks Finite volume requires multiple containers for long-term or continuous measurement
5. Collection in nonrigid containers (specialized, commercially available sampling bags)	Simple, inexpensive on-site equipment (pumps required) Several pollutants possible with one sample	Cannot hold some pollutants Subsequent concentration measurement required Gives average over sampling period; no peaks Finite volume requires multiple containers for long-term or continuous measurement
6. Cryogenic condensation	Wide variety of organic pollutants can be captured Minimal problems with interferences and media interaction Several pollutants possible with one sample	Water vapor interference Subsequent concentration measurement required Gives average over sampling period; no peaks
7. Liquid impingers (bubblers)	Integration over time Several pollutants possible with one sample if appropriate liquid chosen	May be noisy Subsequent concentration measurement required Gives average over sampling period; no peaks
Passive Methods		
8. Passive colorimetric badges	Immediate readout possible Simple, unobtrusive, inexpensive No pumps, mobile; may be worn by occupants to determine average exposure	One pollutant per sample Relatively high detection limit Poor precision May require multiple badges for higher concentrations or long-term measurement
9. Passive diffusional samplers	Simple, unobtrusive, inexpensive No pumps, mobile; may be worn by occupants to determine average exposure	Subsequent concentration measurement required Gives average over sampling period; no peaks Poor precision

Sources: ATC (1990), Lodge (1988), NIOSH (1977, 1994), and Taylor et al. (1977).
*All techniques except 1, 2, and 8 require laboratory work after completion of field sampling. Only first technique is adaptable to continuous monitoring and able to detect short-term excursions.

both the contaminant gas and the diluting air contract. However, concentrations expressed in mg/m^3 increase as temperature decreases, leading to lower ratios of ppm to mg/m^3.

Equations (1) to (3) are strictly true only for ideal gases, but generally are acceptable for dilute vaporous contaminants dispersed in ambient air.

Measurement of Gaseous Contaminants

The concentration of contaminants in air must be measured to determine whether indoor air quality conforms to occupational health standards (in industrial environments) and is acceptable (in nonindustrial environments).

Measurement methods for airborne chemicals that are important industrially have been published by several organizations, including NIOSH (1994) and OSHA (1995). Methods typically involve sampling air with pumps for several hours to capture contaminants on a filter or in an adsorbent tube, followed by laboratory analysis for detection and determination of contaminant concentration. Concentrations measured in this way can usefully be compared to 8 h industrial exposure limits.

Measurement of gaseous contaminants at the lower levels acceptable for indoor air is not always as straightforward. Relatively costly analytical equipment may be needed, and it must be calibrated and operated by experienced personnel.

Currently available sample collection techniques are listed in Table 7, with information about their advantages and disadvantages. Analytical measurement techniques are shown in Table 8, with information on the types of contaminants to which they apply. Tables 7 and 8 provide an overview of gaseous contaminant sampling and analysis, with the intent of allowing informed interaction with specialists.

Techniques 1, 2, and 8 in Table 7 combine sampling and analysis in one piece of equipment and give immediate, on-site results. The other sampling methods require laboratory analysis after the field work. Equipment using the first technique can be coupled with a

Table 8 Analytical Methods to Measure Gaseous Contaminant Concentration

Method	Description	Typical Application (Family)
Gas chromatography (using the following detectors)	Separation of gas mixtures by time of passage down absorption column	
Flame ionization	Change in flame electrical resistance caused by ions of pollutant	Volatile, nonpolar organics (7-27)
Flame photometry	Measures light produced when pollutant is ionized by a flame	Sulfur (25), phosphorous (22) compounds
Photoionization	Measures ion current for ions created by ultraviolet light	Most organics (7-27), except methane
Electron capture	Radioactively generated electrons attach to pollutant atoms; current measured	Halogenated organics (11, 12) Nitrogenated organics (18, 23)
Mass spectroscopy	Pollutant molecules are charged, passed through electrostatic magnetic fields in vacuum; path curvature depends on mass of molecule, allowing separation and counting of each type	Volatile organics (7-27 with boiling point <149°F)
Infrared spectroscopy, including Fourier transform IR (FTIR) and photoacoustic IR	Absorption of infrared light by pollutant gas in a transmission cell; a range of wavelengths is used, allowing identification and measurement of individual pollutants	Acid gases (4, 26), carbon monoxide (3) Many organics; any gas with an absorption band in the infrared (7-27)
High-performance liquid chromatography (HPLC)	Pollutant is captured in a liquid, which is then passed through a liquid chromatograph (analogous to a gas chromatograph)	Aldehydes (15), ketones (16) Phosgene (27) Nitrosamines (18, 23) Cresol, phenol (13)
Colorimetry	Chemical reaction with pollutant in solution yields a colored product whose light absorption is measured	Ozone (2) Oxides of nitrogen (2) Formaldehyde (15)
Fluorescence and pulsed fluorescence	Pollutant atoms are stimulated by a monochromatic light beam, often ultraviolet; they emit light at characteristic fluorescent wavelengths, whose intensity is measured	Sulfur dioxide (4) Carbon monoxide (3)
Chemiluminescence	Reaction (usually with a specific injected gas) results in photon emission proportional to concentration	Ozone (2) Nitrogen compounds (5, 18, 23) Some organics (7-27)
Electrochemical	Pollutant is bubbled through reagent/water solution, changing its conductivity or generating a voltage	Ozone (2) Hydrogen sulfide (4) Acid gases (4, 26)
Titration	Pollutant is absorbed into water and known quantities of acid or base are added to achieve neutrality	Acid gases (4, 26) Basic gases (5, 23)
Ultraviolet absorption	Absorption of UV light by a cell through which the polluted air passes is measured	Ozone (2) Aromatics (19) Sulfur dioxide (4) Oxides of nitrogen (2) Carbon monoxide (3)
Atomic absorption	Contaminant is burned in a hydrogen flame; a light beam with a spectral line specific to the pollutant is passed through the flame; optical absorption of the beam is measured	Mercury vapor (1)
Surface acoustic wave, flexural plate wave, etc.	Contaminant adsorption on a substrate alters the resonant vibration frequency or vibration transmittance characteristics	
Chemiresistor (metal oxide)	Contaminant interacts with coated metal oxide surface at high temperature, changing the resistance to electrical current	Carbon monoxide (3), hydrogen sulfide (4), organic vapors (7-27)

Sources: ATC (1990), Lodge (1988), NIOSH (1977, 1994), and Taylor et al. (1977).

data logger to perform continuous monitoring and to obtain average concentrations over a time period. Most of the sample collection techniques can capture several contaminants. Several allow pollutants to accumulate or concentrate over time so that very low concentrations can be measured.

Some analytical measurement techniques are specific for a single pollutant, whereas others can provide concentrations for many contaminants simultaneously. Note that formaldehyde requires different measurement methods from other volatile organic compounds.

Measurement instruments used in industrial situations should be able to detect contaminants of interest at about one-tenth of **threshold limit value (TLV)** levels, published annually by ACGIH. If odors are of concern, detection sensitivity must be at odor threshold levels. Procedures for evaluating odor levels are given in Chapter 12.

Note that information in Tables 7 and 8 is not sufficient in itself to allow preparation of a measurement protocol. ASHRAE's *Guideline* 27 provides guidance on developing a test protocol, including criteria for deciding whether to use instantaneous measurement or integrated sampling techniques, selection of locations to test, and information to obtain about the test building (building and air-handling system layout, space occupancy and use patterns, environmental conditions and HVAC operating parameters during the test period, etc.). The guideline also presents practical information on test equipment use.

3.1 VOLATILE ORGANIC COMPOUNDS

The entire range of organic indoor pollutants has been categorized by volatility, as indicated in Table 9 (WHO 1989). No sharp limits

Table 9 Classification of Indoor Organic Contaminants by Volatility

Description	Abbre-viation	Boiling Point Range, °F
Very volatile (gaseous) organic compounds	VVOC	<32 to 120–212
Volatile organic compounds	VOC	120–212 to 460–500
Semivolatile organics (pesticides, polynuclear aromatic compounds, plasticizers)	SVOC	460–500 to 720–750

Source: WHO (1989).
Notes:
Polar compounds and VOCs with higher mol weight appear at higher end of each boiling-point range.
The EPA uses a different definition of VOC for regulatory purposes.

exist between the categories, which are defined by boiling-point ranges. Volatile organic compounds (VOCs) have attracted considerable attention in nonindustrial environments. They have boiling points in the range of approximately 120 to 480°F and vapor pressures greater than about 4×10^{-5} to 4×10^{-6} in. Hg. [Note that the EPA has a specific regulatory definition of VOCs (*Code of Federal Regulations* 40CFR51.100) that must be consulted if regulated U.S. air emissions are the matter of interest. Although similar to the definition here, it is more complex, with some excluded compounds and specified test methods.]

Sources of VOCs include solvents, reagents, and degreasers in industrial environments; and furniture, furnishings, wall and floor finishes, cleaning and maintenance products, and office and hobby activities in nonindustrial environments. Which gas contaminants are likely in an industrial environment can usually best be identified from the nature of the industrial processes, and that is the recommended first step. This discussion focuses on indoor VOCs because they are usually more difficult to identify and quantify.

Berglund et al. (1988) found that the sources of VOCs in nonindustrial indoor environments are confounded by the variable nature of emissions from potential sources. Emissions of VOCs from indoor sources can be classified by their presence and rate patterns. For example, emissions are continuous and regular from building materials and furnishings (e.g., carpet and composite-wood furniture), whereas emissions from other sources can be continuous but irregular (e.g., paints used in renovation work), intermittent and regular (e.g., VOCs in combustion products from gas stoves or cleaning products), or intermittent and irregular (e.g., VOCs from carpet shampoos) (Morey and Singh 1991).

Many "wet" emission sources (paints and adhesives) have very high emission rates immediately after application, but rates drop steeply with time until the product has cured or dried. New "dry" materials (carpets, wall coverings, and furnishings) also emit chemicals at higher rates until aged. Decay of these elevated VOC concentrations to normal constant-source levels can take weeks to months, depending on emission rates, surface areas of materials, and ventilation protocols. Renovation can cause similar increases of somewhat lower magnitude. The total VOC concentration in new office buildings at the time of initial occupancy can be 50 to 100 times that present in outdoor air (Sheldon et al. 1988a, 1988b). In new office buildings with adequate outdoor air ventilation, these ratios often fall to less than 5:1 after 4 or 5 months of aging. In older buildings with continuous, regular, and irregular emission sources, indoor/outdoor ratios of total VOCs may vary from nearly 1:1, when maximum amounts of outdoor air are being used in HVAC systems, to greater than 10:1 during winter and summer months, when minimum amounts of outdoor air are being used (Morey and Jenkins 1989; Morey and Singh 1991).

Although direct VOC emissions are usually the primary source of VOCs in a space, some materials act as sinks for emissions and then become secondary sources as they reemit adsorbed chemicals (Berglund et al. 1988). Adsorption may lower the peak concentrations achieved, but the subsequent desorption prolongs the presence of indoor air pollutants. Sink materials include carpet, fabric partitions, and other fleecy materials, as well as ceiling tiles and wallboard. The type of material and compound affects the rate of adsorption and desorption (Colombo et al. 1991). Experiments conducted in an IAQ test house confirmed the importance of sinks when trying to control the level of indoor VOCs (Tichenor et al. 1991). Longer periods of increased ventilation lessen sink and reemission effects. Early models used empirically derived adsorption and desorption rates to predict the behavior of sinks. A better modeling approach uses intrinsic characteristics of the adsorbed contaminant and the sink material (Little and Hodgson 1996). ASHRAE research project RP-1321 refined and extended this approach to enable prediction of IAQ in spaces containing sink materials (Yang et al. 2010).

VanOsdell (1994) reviewed research studies of indoor VOCs as part of ASHRAE research project RP-674, and found more than 300 compounds had been identified indoors and that there was no agreement on a short list of key VOCs. The large number of VOCs usually found indoors, and the impossibility of identifying all of them in samples, led to the concept of **total VOC (TVOC)**. Some researchers have used TVOC to represent the sum of all detected VOCs. TVOC concentrations are often reported as everything detected in the air by analysis methods such as photoionization detectors (PID) or flame ionization detectors (FID). Therefore, all methods for TVOC determination are intrinsically of low to moderate accuracy because of variations in detector response to different classes of VOCs. Despite the limitations, TVOC can be useful, and is widely used for mixed-contaminant atmospheres. Both theoretical and practical limitations of the TVOC approach have been discussed (Hodgson 1995; Otson and Fellin 1993). Wallace et al. (1991) showed that individual VOC concentrations in homes and buildings are two to five times those of outdoors, and personal TVOC exposures resulting from normal daily activities were estimated to be two to three times greater than general indoor air concentrations.

Personal activities frequently bring individuals close to air contaminant sources. In addition, exposure from contaminated air jets depends on the complex airflows around the body, including the main flow stream, air turbulence, and obstructions nearby (Rodes et al. 1991). Individual organic compounds seldom exceed 0.05 mg/m^3 (50 μg/m^3) in indoor air. An upper extreme average concentration of TVOCs in normally occupied houses is approximately 20 mg/m^3.

The EPA's Large Buildings Study (Brightman et al. 1996) developed the VOC sample target list shown in Table 10 to identify common VOCs that should be measured. Lists of common indoor VOCs prepared by other organizations are similar.

Because chlorofluorocarbons (CFCs) are hydrocarbons with some hydrogen atoms replaced by chlorine and fluorine atoms, they are classed as organic chemicals. They have been widely used as heat transfer gases in refrigeration applications, blowing agents, and propellants in aerosol products (including medications and consumer products) and as expanders in plastic foams. Exposure to CFCs and HCFCs occurs mainly through inhalation, and can occur from leaks in refrigeration equipment or during HVAC maintenance.

Volatile organic compounds produced by microorganisms as they grow are referred to as **microbial VOCs (MVOCs)**. Of particular interest are those emitted by fungi contaminating water-damaged buildings. Usually, mixtures of MVOCs that are common to many different species (as well as to industrial chemicals) are produced. However, there are also compounds specific to a particular genus or species. Analysis for MVOCs is generally by gas chromatography/mass spectrometry (GC/MS) with thermal desorption.MVOCs include a variety of chemical classes including alcohols, ketones, organic acids, and heterocyclic compounds, among others. Many

Table 10 VOCs Commonly Found in Buildings*

Benzene	Styrene
m-, *p*-xylene	*p*-dichlorobenzene
1,2,4-trimethylbenzene	*n*-undecane
n-octane	*n*-nonane
n-decane	Ethyl acetate
n-dodecane	Dichloromethane
Butyl acetate	1,1,1-trichloroethane
Chloroform	Tetrachloroethylene
Trichloroethylene	Carbon disulfide
Trichlorofluoromethane	Acetone
Dimethyl disulfide	2-butanone
Methyl isobutyl ketone	Methyl tertiary butyl ether
Limonene	Naphthalene
α-,β-pinene	4-phenyl cyclohexene
Propane	Butane
2-butoxyethanol	Ethanol
Isopropanol	Phenol
Formaldehyde	Siloxanes
Toluene	

Source: Brightman et al. (1996).
*Properties of these VOCs can be found in Table 6.

have extremely low odor thresholds. Examples in Table 5 include acetone, ethanol, 3-methyl 1-butanol, 2-hexanone, and 3-methyl furan. More information on MVOCs can be found in Horner and Miller (2003).

It is not known whether exposure to MVOCs is likely to cause adverse health effects on its own, because MVOCs are not likely to comprise the sole exposure. However, many are quite objectionable and may be irritating. At the very least, they may indicate a potential mold growth problem in a building, and often cause complaints about air quality. Note that MVOCs are distinct from fungal mycotoxins, which are nonvolatile and therefore not odorous.

Controlling Exposure to VOCs

Much can be done to reduce building occupants' exposures to emissions of VOCs from building materials and products and to prevent outdoor VOCs from being brought into buildings. In most cases, the economically and technically preferred hierarchy for indoor contaminant reduction is (1) source control, (2) dilution with ventilation air, and (3) air filtration (local exhaust is seldom used in commercial buildings, though it is common in industrial facilities). Chapter 46 of the 2015 *ASHRAE Handbook—HVAC Applications* provides a full discussion.

3.2 SEMIVOLATILE ORGANIC COMPOUNDS

Semivolatile organic compounds (SVOCs) are organic chemicals with boiling points ranging from approximately 460 to 750°F and vapor pressures of 1.5×10^{-13} to 1.5×10^{-3} psia. Low vapor pressures mean that SVOCs are present in the air in lower concentrations than VOCs, and tend to outgas more slowly and condense more readily, sticking to floors, furniture, and clothing and remaining in the surroundings for longer periods of time. Indoor SVOCs are of special interest today because of growing concerns about their effects on health.

The SVOC group includes a number of familiar chemical types, including

- Polychlorinated biphenyls (PCBs), once in common use as flame retardants but now largely banned
- Polycyclic aromatic hydrocarbons (PAHs), originating from indoor and outdoor combustion sources and traffic emissions
- Phthalates, widely used as plasticizers to improve flexibility and durability of plastics in consumer products and food packaging
- Chlorine- and phosphate-containing organic pesticides
- Organic phosphates, chlorine-containing compounds, and polybrominated diphenyl ethers (PBDEs) used as flame retardants

Many SVOCs are more common indoors than outdoors. They can be the active ingredients in cleaning products and personal care products, and major additives in materials such as floor coverings, furnishings, electronic components, foams, and food containers. They also occur in antimicrobials, sealants (e.g., silicones), heat transfer agents, and pesticides (Weschler and Nazaroff 2008). More than a thousand high-production-volume organic chemicals are produced or imported into the United States in amounts greater than one million pounds per year (EPA 2007), including a number of SVOCs. SVOCs may persist in the indoor environment for years after introduction. Exposures can occur via inhalation, ingestion, and dermal pathways through both gaseous and adsorption onto suspended particulate matter and floor dust (Weschler and Nazaroff 2010).

Selected SVOCs, such as PAHs, have long histories of known health effects. However, more recently, effects on the indoor environment from use of SVOCs in commercial products are becoming more widely understood. SVOC health impacts generally are chronic, with increasing and cumulative body burdens. Potential health consequences include endocrine disruption (Adibi et al. 2003; Apelberg et al. 2007), cancer (Bostrom et al. 2002), allergy (Bornehag et al. 2004), and neurodevelopment and behavioral problems (e.g., autism, attention deficit disorder) (Howdeshell 2002; Jacobson and Jacobson 1996).

Indoor concentrations depend on the SVOC and the source, but in general range between 0.002 and 5000 ng/m^3 (Weschler and Nazaroff 2008). In one study, a major source of brominated flame retardants in office buildings was found to be computer servers (Batterman et al. 2010), with the median concentration in settled dust being 8754 ng/g. One distribution route was through the HVAC system. SVOCs are not easily detected, and few can be measured by common sampling and analytical methods for indoor environmental monitoring. Improved standard measurement methodologies are currently being developed to help understand the extent of the prevalence of SVOCs in the indoor environment and the associated health risks from exposure.

3.3 INORGANIC GASES

Several inorganic gases are of concern because of their effects on human health and comfort and on materials. These include carbon dioxide, carbon monoxide, oxides of nitrogen, sulfur dioxide, ozone, and ammonia. Most have both outdoor and indoor sources.

Carbon dioxide (CO_2) or **carbonic acid** gas is produced by human respiration. It is not normally considered to be a toxic air contaminant, but it can be a simple asphyxiant (by oxygen displacement) in confined spaces such as submarines. CO_2 is found in the ambient environment at 330 to 370 ppm. Levels in the urban environment may be higher because of emissions from gasoline and, more often, diesel engines. Measurement of CO_2 in occupied spaces has been widely used to evaluate the amount of outdoor air supplied to indoor spaces. In ASHRAE *Standard* 62.1, a level of 1000 to 1200 ppm (or 700 ppm above outdoor air) has been suggested as being representative of delivery rates of 15 cfm per person of outdoor air when CO_2 is measured at equilibrium concentrations and at occupant densities of 10 people per 1000 ft^2 of floor space. Measuring CO_2 level before it has reached steady-state conditions can lead to inaccurate conclusions about the amount of outdoor air used in the building.

Carbon monoxide (CO) is an odorless, colorless, and tasteless gas produced by incomplete combustion of hydrocarbons. It is a common ambient air pollutant and is very toxic. Common indoor sources of CO include gas stoves, kerosene lanterns and heaters, mainstream and sidestream tobacco smoke, woodstoves, and unvented or improperly vented combustion sources. Building makeup air intakes located at street level or near parking garages can entrain CO from automobiles and carry it to the indoor environment. Air containing carbon monoxide may also enter the building directly if the indoor space is at negative pressure relative to outdoors. Major predictors of indoor CO concentrations are indoor fossil fuel sources, such as gas furnaces, hot water heaters, and other combustion appliances; attached garages; and weather inversions. Carbon monoxide can be a problem in indoor ice skating arenas where gasoline- or propane-powered resurfacing machines are used. Levels in homes only rarely exceed 5 ppm. In one sample of randomly selected homes, 10% failed a backdrafting test (Conibear et al. 1996). Under backdrafting conditions, indoor CO sources may contribute to much higher, dangerous levels of CO.

Oxides of nitrogen (NO_x) indoors result mainly from cooking appliances, pilot lights, and unvented heaters. Sources generating CO often produce nitric oxide (NO) and nitrogen dioxide (NO_2), as well. Underground or attached parking garages can also contribute to indoor concentrations of NO_x. An unvented gas cookstove contributes approximately 0.025 ppm of nitrogen dioxide to a home. During cooking, 0.2 to 0.4 ppm peak levels may be reached (Samet et al. 1987). Ambient air pollution from vehicle exhausts in urban locations can contribute NO_x to the indoor environment in makeup air. Oxides of nitrogen also are present in mainstream and sidestream tobacco smoke; NO and NO_2 are of most concern.

Sulfur dioxide (SO_2) can result from emissions of kerosene space heaters; combustion of fossil fuels such as coal, heating oil, and gasoline; or burning any material containing sulfur. Thus, sulfur dioxide is a common ambient air pollutant in many urban areas.

Ozone (O_3) is an oxidant that forms outdoors at ground level when hydrocarbons (usually from fossil fuels) and oxides of nitrogen react with ultraviolet radiation in sunlight to produce photochemical smog.

Indoor ozone mainly comes from outdoor air through infiltration or mechanical ventilation, which makes the indoor ozone concentration change in a similar pattern to that of outdoor ozone, both daily and seasonally. Indoor ozone concentrations from this source are typically about 20 to 30% of outdoor values for moderate-ventilation rooms and about 50 to 70% of outdoor values for highly ventilated rooms (Weschler et al. 1989). In addition, indoor devices such as electronic air cleaners (Boelter and Davidson 1997), photocopiers, and laser printers (Allen et al. 1978; Valuntaite and Girgzdiene 2007; Worthan and Black 1999) are important indoor ozone sources. Ozone can also form when ozone-generating devices marketed as portable air cleaners and ionizers are used in the indoor environment (Esswein and Boeniger 1994), though use of such devices is now banned in some jurisdictions.

Indoor ozone can react with many indoor VOCs (especially those with unsaturated carbon/carbon bonds), surfaces of furniture, and other building materials such as carpet and HVAC ventilation duct. These can all serve as indoor ozone sinks, but almost all ozone-initiated indoor chemical reactions lead to secondary pollution. Ozone can react with many indoor terpenes to form aerosol particles (Vartiainen et al. 2006; Weschler and Shields 1999); presence of ozone and d-limonene can lead to many hydroperoxides, such as hydrogen peroxide (H_2O_2) (Li et al. 2002). Field and laboratory experiments show that reaction of ozone with indoor surfaces, household products, and building materials generates aldehydes and submicron particles (Aokia and Tanabe 2007; Destaillats et al. 2006; Wang and Morrison 2006). Interaction between ozone and carpet can also generate other aldehydes (Morrison and Nazaroff 2002). Exposure of ventilation ducts (including liner, duct sealing caulk, and neoprene) to ozone could increase emission of aldehydes (Morrison et al. 1998). A number of the secondary contaminants are toxic or act as respiratory irritants.

Ammonia (NH_3) is a colorless gas with a sharp and intensely irritating odor. It is lighter than air and readily soluble in water. Ammonia is itself a refrigerant and fertilizer and is also a high-volume industrial chemical used in the manufacture of a wide variety of products (e.g., nitrogen fertilizers, nitric acid, synthetic fibers, explosives, and many others). In nature, ammonia is an animal metabolism by-product formed by decomposition of uric acid. As an indoor air contaminant, ammonia generally originates in synthetic cleaners and as a metabolic by-product.

Mercury is a naturally occurring element found in air, water, and soil. It exists in several forms: elemental or metallic mercury (a shiny, silver-white metal liquid at room temperature and a colorless, odorless gas if heated), inorganic mercury compounds, and organic mercury compounds.

Mercury is classified as a hazardous air pollutant under the Clean Air Act. Exposures to mercury can affect the human nervous system and harm the brain, heart, kidneys, lungs, and immune system.

One concern is breathing mercury vapor, which can occur when elemental mercury or products containing elemental mercury release mercury to the air, particularly in warm or poorly ventilated indoor spaces. Typically, mercury is released into the atmosphere in one of three forms: elemental mercury, which can remain in the atmosphere for up to a year and travel globally before being transformed; particle-bound mercury; or oxidized mercury [sometimes called ionic or reactive gaseous mercury (RGM)].

Exposure is most likely to occur during mining, production, and transportation of mercury, as well as mining and refining of gold and silver ores. Coal-burning power plants are the largest human-caused source of mercury emissions to the air in the United States, accounting for over 50% of all domestic human-caused mercury emissions (EPA 2017). Mercury is commonly found in thermometers, manometers, barometers, gages, valves, switches, batteries, and high-intensity discharge (HID) lamps. It is also used in dental amalgams, preservatives, heat transfer technology, pigments, catalysts, and lubricating oils.

The U.S. Occupational Health and Safety Administration (OSHA) set a mercury permissible exposure limit (PEL) of 0.1 mg/m^3 (8 h time-weighted average [TWA]). Some state OSHA programs regulate a stricter mercury vapor limit of 0.05 mg/m^3 (8 h TWA). Additionally, the American Conference of Governmental Industrial Hygienists (ACGIH) recommends a guideline of 0.025 mg/m^3.

Mercury hazards are addressed in specific standards for the general industry, shipyard employment, and the construction industry.

Controlling Exposures to Inorganic Gases

As for VOCs, the three main methods of control for inorganic gaseous contaminants are (1) source control, (2) ventilation control, and (3) removal by filters. Chapter 46 of the 2015 *ASHRAE Handbook—HVAC Applications* provides more detail on these methods.

4. AIR CONTAMINANTS BY SOURCE

Some air contaminants are commonly encountered and addressed as groups or single components originating from a source or having other common characteristics. Outdoor air contaminants, though widely varied between locations, are regulated uniformly across the United States and can usefully be considered as a separate category worthy of common consideration. Radioactive air contaminants also vary widely, but they too have many commonalities. This section addresses the commonalities and characteristics of air contaminants as a function of source or their common characteristics.

4.1 OUTDOOR AIR CONTAMINANTS

The total amount of suspended particulate matter in the atmosphere can influence the loading rate of air filters and their selection. The amount of soot that falls in U.S. cities ranges from 20 to 200 ton/mi^2 per month. Soot fall data indicate effectiveness of smoke

Table 11 Typical U.S. Outdoor Concentrations of Selected Gaseous Air Contaminants

Inorganic Air Contaminants[a]

Inorganic Name	CAS Number	Period of Average	Arithmetic Mean Concentration	
			mg/m³	ppb
Carbon monoxide	630-08-0	1 year (2008)	2 mg/m³	2 ppm
Nitrogen dioxide	10102-44-0	1 year (2008)	29 μg/m³	15 ppb
Ozone	10028-15-6	3 years (2006-2008)	149 μg/m³	76 ppb

Organic Air Contaminants[b]

VOC Name	CAS Number	Number of Sites Tested	Frequency Detected, % of Sites	Arithmetic Mean Concentration	
				μg/m³	ppb
Chloromethane	74-87-3	87	99	2.6	1.3
Benzene	71-43-2	67	99	3.0	0.94
Acetone	67-64-1	67	98	8.6	3.6
Acetaldehyde	75-07-0	86	98	3.4	1.9
Toluene	108-88-3	69	96	5.1	1.4
Formaldehyde	50-00-0	99	95	3.9	3.2
Phenol	108-95-2	40	93	1.6	0.42
m- and *p*-xylenes	1330-20-7	69	92	3.2	0.74
Ethanol	64-17-5	13	92	32	17
Dichlorodifluoro-methane	75-71-8	87	91	7.1	1.4
o-xylene	95-47-6	69	89	1.2	0.28
Nonanal	124-19-6	40	89	1.1	0.19
2-butanone	78-93-3	66	88	1.4	0.48
1,2,4-trimethylbenzene	95-63-6	69	87	1.2	0.24
Ethylbenzene	100-41-4	69	84	0.9	0.21
n-decane	124-18-5	69	80	0.97	0.17
n-hexane	110-54-3	38	75	1.7	0.48
Tetrachloroethene	127-18-4	69	73	1.1	0.16
4-ethyltoluene	622-96-8	69	72	0.53	0.11
n-undecane	1120-21-4	69	70	0.6	0.094
Nonane	111-84-2	69	66	0.59	0.11
1,1,1-trichloroethane	71-55-6	66	65	0.88	0.16
Styrene	100-42-5	69	61	0.39	0.092
Ethyl acetate	141-78-6	66	58	0.43	0.12
Octane	111-65-9	68	56	0.44	0.094
1,3,5-trimethylbenzene	108-67-8	69	56	0.41	0.083
Hexanal	66-25-1	40	53	0.65	0.16

Sources:
[a]EPA (2009b). Note that only statistically viable data sets were used to calculate national average concentrations, so numbers may not be fully representative.
[b]EPA (1997).
ppb = parts per 10^9

abatement and proper combustion methods, and serve as comparative indices of such control programs. However, the data are of limited value to the ventilating and air-conditioning engineer, because they do not accurately represent airborne soot concentrations.

Concentrations of outdoor pollutants are important, because they may determine indoor concentrations in the absence of indoor sources. Table 11 presents typical urban outdoor concentrations of some common gaseous pollutants. Higher levels might be found if the building under consideration were located near a major source of contamination, such as a power plant, a refinery, freeway, or a sewage treatment plant. Note that levels of sulfur dioxide and nitrogen dioxide, which are often attached to particles, may be reduced by about half by building filtration systems. Also, ozone is a reactive gas that can be significantly reduced by contact with ventilation system components (e.g., ductwork or other metal surfaces) (Weschler et al. 1989).

Table 12 National Ambient Air Quality Standards for the United States

Contaminant	Primary or Secondary Standard	Averaging Time	Level	Details
Carbon monoxide	Primary	1 h	35 ppm	Not to be exceeded more than once per year
		8 h	9 ppm	
Nitrogen dioxide	Primary	1 h	100 ppb	98th percentile, averaged over 3 years
	Primary/ secondary	1 yr	53 ppb	Annual mean
Ozone	Primary/ secondary	8 h	70 ppb	Annual fourth-highest daily maximum 8 h concentration, averaged over 3 years
Sulfur dioxide	Primary	1 h	75 ppb	99th percentile of 1 h daily maximum concentrations, averaged over 3 years
	Secondary	3 h	500 ppb	Not to be exceeded more than once per year
Particulate, $PM_{2.5}$[a]	Primary/ secondary	24 h	35 μg/m³	98th percentile, averaged over 3 years
		1 yr	15 μg/m³	Annual mean, averaged over 3 years
Particulate, PM_{10}[b]	Primary/ secondary	24 h	150 μg/m³	Not to be exceeded more than once per year on average over 3 years
Lead (Pb) in particles	Primary/ secondary	3 mo	0.15 μg/m³	Not to be exceeded

Source: Adapted from EPA (2015). For details, see www.epa.gov/criteria-air-pollutants/naaqs-table.
[a]$PM_{2.5}$ = particulates below 2.5 μm diameter.
[b]PM_{10} = particulates below 10 μm diameter.
ppb = parts per 10^9

The U.S. Environmental Protection Agency identifies several important outdoor contaminants as criteria pollutants. The list includes carbon monoxide, nitrogen dioxide, ozone, sulfur dioxide, suspended particulate matter in two size ranges, and lead (Pb) particulate matter. Standards set for these contaminants are of two types: primary, which are intended to provide health protection; and secondary, which provide welfare and environmental protection. Current standards are shown in Table 12. Levels of these contaminants are measured at a large number of locations in the United States and published by the EPA each year (*Code of Federal Regulations* 40CFR50).

Daily concentrations of VOCs in outdoor air can vary drastically (Ekberg 1994). These variations derive from vehicle traffic density, wind direction, industrial emissions, and photochemical reactions.

4.2 INDUSTRIAL AIR CONTAMINANTS

Many industrial processes produce significant quantities of air contaminants in the form of dusts, fumes, smokes, mists, vapors, and gases. Particulate and gaseous contaminants are best controlled at the source, so that they are neither dispersed through the factory nor allowed to increase to toxic concentration levels. Dilution ventilation is much less effective than local exhaust for reducing contamination from point-source emissions, and is used for control only when sources are distributed and not amenable to capture by an exhaust hood. For sources generating high levels of contaminants, it may also be necessary to provide equipment that reduces the amount of material discharged to the atmosphere (e.g., a dust collector for particulate contaminants and/or a high-dwell-time gas-phase media bed for gaseous contaminants). Control methods are covered in Chapters 29 and 30 of the 2016 *ASHRAE Handbook—*

HVAC Systems and Equipment and Chapters 32 and 46 of the 2015 *ASHRAE Handbook—HVAC Applications*.

Reducing concentrations of all contaminants to zero is not economically feasible. Absolute control of all contaminants cannot be maintained, and workers can assimilate small quantities of various toxic materials without injury. The science of industrial hygiene is based on the facts that most air contaminants become toxic only if their concentration exceeds a maximum allowable limit for a specified period, and that workers can "detoxify" by being away from the workplace for a period of time. Allowable limits for work environments are covered in Chapter 10. Some commercial workspaces must also comply with OSHA.

Although the immediately dangerous to life and health (IDLH) toxicity limit is rarely a factor in HVAC design, HVAC engineers should consider it when deciding how much recirculation is needed in a given system. Ventilation airflow must never be so low that the concentration of any gaseous contaminant could rise to the IDLH level. Another toxic effect that may influence design is loss of sensory acuity because of gaseous contaminant exposure. For example, high concentrations of hydrogen sulfide, which has a very unpleasant odor, effectively eliminate a person's ability to smell the gas. Carbon monoxide, which has no odor to alert people to its presence, affects psychomotor responses and could be a problem in working environments such as air traffic control towers and vehicle repair shops. Clearly, waste anesthetic gases should not be allowed to reach levels in operating suites such that the alertness of any of the personnel is affected. NIOSH recommendations are frequently based on such subtle effects.

4.3 COMMERCIAL, INSTITUTIONAL, AND RESIDENTIAL INDOOR AIR CONTAMINANTS

Indoor air quality in residences, offices, and other indoor, nonindustrial environments is a widespread concern (NRC 1981; Spengler et al. 1982). Exposure to indoor pollutants can be as important as exposure to outdoor pollutants because a large portion of the population spends up to 90% of their time indoors and because indoor pollutant concentrations are frequently higher than corresponding outdoor contaminant levels.

For facilities such as hospitals and clinics, where occupants may have more vulnerable immune systems, it is essential to remove air contaminants, especially viable organisms, to prevent any possibility of respiratory issues. Therefore, it is important to understand the specific health care facility and its patient population when designing the HVAC system.

In schools and research institutes, good indoor air quality is key for teachers, staff, and students for peak productivity and the greatest opportunity for success. EPA (2016b) provides IAQ guidance for these applications.

Indoor air quality is also important in museums and galleries. Particulate contaminants in air can permanently damage valuable collectibles through abrasion or soiling, and gaseous pollutants may cause damage through chemical attacks; see Chapter 23 of the 2015 *ASHRAE Handbook—HVAC Applications* for details.

Symptoms of exposure to indoor pollutants include coughing; sneezing; eye, throat, and skin irritation; nausea; breathlessness; drowsiness; headaches; and depression. Rask (1988) suggests that when 20% of a single building's occupants suffer such irritations, the structure is suffering from **deficient indoor air quality (DIAQ)**, previously referred to as **sick building syndrome (SBS)**. Case studies of such occurrences have consisted of analyses of questionnaires submitted to building occupants, measurements of contaminant levels, or both. Some attempts to relate irritations to gaseous contaminant concentrations are reported (Berglund et al. 1986; Cain et al. 1986; Lamm 1986; Mølhave et al. 1982). The correlation of reported complaints with gaseous pollutant concentrations is not strong; many factors affect these less serious responses to pollution. In general, physical irritation does not occur at odor threshold concentrations.

Symptoms of exposure include coughing; sneezing; eye, throat, and skin irritation; nausea; breathlessness; drowsiness; headaches; and depression. Rask (1988) suggests that when 20% of a single building's occupants suffer such irritations, the structure is suffering from **sick building syndrome (SBS)**. Case studies of such occurrences have consisted of analyses of questionnaires submitted to building occupants, measurements of contaminant levels, or both. Some attempts to relate irritations to gaseous contaminant concentrations are reported (Berglund et al. 1986; Cain et al. 1986; Lamm 1986; Mølhave et al. 1982). The correlation of reported complaints with gaseous pollutant concentrations is not strong; many factors affect these less serious responses to pollution. In general, physical irritation does not occur at odor threshold concentrations.

Characterization of indoor air quality has been the subject of numerous recent studies. ASHRAE *Indoor Air Quality (IAQ) Conference Proceedings* discuss indoor air quality problems and some practical controls. ASHRAE *Standard* 62.1 addresses many indoor air quality concerns. Table 13 shows sources, source locations, and typical indoor and outdoor concentration ranges of several key contaminants found in indoor environments. Chapter 10 has further information on indoor health issues.

Knowledge of sources frequently present in different types of buildings can be useful when investigating the causes of DIAQ. Common nonindustrial indoor sources are discussed in some detail here. Technical advances allow generation rates to be measured for several of these sources. These rates are necessary inputs for design of filter control equipment; full details are given in Chapter 46 of the 2015 *ASHRAE Handbook—HVAC Applications*.

Building materials and **furnishing** sources have been well studied. Particleboard, which is usually made from wood chips bonded with a phenol-formaldehyde or other resin, is widely used in current construction, especially for mobile homes, carpet underlay, and case goods. These materials, along with ceiling tiles, carpeting, wall coverings, office partitions, adhesives, and paint finishes, emit formaldehyde and other VOCs. Latex also contains mercury and emits mercury vapor. Although emission rates for these materials decline steadily with age, the half-life of emissions is surprisingly long. Black and Bayer (1986), Mølhave et al. (1982), and Nelms et al. (1986) report on these sources.

Ventilation systems may be a source of VOCs (Mølhave and Thorsen 1990). The interior of the HVAC system can have large areas of porous material used as acoustical liner that can adsorb odorous compounds, or these compounds can deposit on HVAC system surfaces. These materials can also hold nutrients and, with moisture, can become a reservoir for microorganisms. Microbial contaminants produce characteristic VOCs [microbial VOCs (MVOCs)] associated with their metabolism. Other HVAC components, such as condensate drain pans, fouled cooling coils, and some filter media, may support microbiological life. Deodorants, sealants, and encapsulants are also sources of VOCs in HVAC systems.

Equipment sources in commercial and residential spaces have generation rates that are usually substantially lower than in the industrial environment. Because these sources are rarely hooded, emissions go directly to the occupants. In commercial spaces, the chief sources of gaseous contaminants are office equipment, including dry-process copiers (ozone); liquid-process copiers (VOCs); diazo printers (ammonia and related compounds); carbonless copy paper (formaldehyde); correction fluids, inks, and adhesives (various VOCs); and spray cans, cosmetics, and so forth (Miksch et al. 1982). Three-dimensional (3D) printers can also be a source of particles and vapors (Azimi et al. 2016; Davis et al. 2016). Medical and dental activities generate pollutants from the escape of anesthetic gases

Table 13 Sources and Indoor and Outdoor Concentrations of Selected Indoor Contaminants

Contaminant	Sources of Indoor Contaminants	Typical Indoor Concentration	Typical Outdoor Concentration	Locations
Carbon monoxide	Combustion equipment, engines, faulty heating systems	0.5 to 5 ppm[a] (without gas stoves) 5 to 15 ppm[a] (with gas stoves)	2 ppm[a]	Indoor ice rinks, homes, cars, vehicle repair shops, parking garages
$PM_{2.5}$	Stoves, fireplaces, cigarettes, condensation of volatiles, aerosol sprays, cooking	7 to 10 μg/m[3a]	<10 μg/m[3a]	Homes, offices, cars, public facilities, bars, restaurants
PM_{10}	Combustion, heating system, cooking	40 to 60 μg/m[3a]	60 μg/m[3a]	Homes, offices, transportation, restaurants
Organic vapors	Combustion, solvents, resin products, pesticides, aerosol sprays, cleaning products, building materials, paints	Different for each VOC[c] (2 to 5 times outdoor levels)	See Table 11	Homes, restaurants, public facilities, offices, hospitals
Nitrogen dioxide	Combustion, gas stoves, water heaters, gas-fired dryers, cigarettes, engines	<8 ppb[a] (without combustion appliances) >15 ppb with combustion appliances)	15 ppb[a]	Homes, indoor ice rinks
Nitric oxide	Combustion, gas stoves, water heaters, gas-fired dryers, cigarettes, engines		Various	Homes, any building with combustion source
Sulfur dioxide	Heating system	20 μg/m[3b]	<20 μg/m[3b] 3 ppb[a]	Mechanical/furnace rooms
Formaldehyde	Insulation, product binders, pressed wood products, carpets	0.1 to 0.3 ppm[a]	NA	Homes, schools, offices
Radon and progeny	Building materials, groundwater, soil	1.3 pCi/L[a]	4 pCi/L[a]	Homes, schools
Carbon dioxide	Combustion appliances, humans, pets	600 to 1000 ppm[c]	300 to 500 ppm[c]	Indoors and outdoors
Biological contaminants	Humans, pets, rodents, insects, plants, fungi, humidifiers, air conditioners	NA	NA (lower than indoor levels)	Homes, hospitals, schools, offices, public facilities
Ozone	Electric arcing, electronic air cleaners, copiers, printers	42 ppb[d]	70 ppb[a]	Airplanes, offices, homes

Sources: [a]EPA (2011).
[b]NRC (1981).
[c]Seppänen et al. (1999) and ASHRAE *Standard* 62.1, Appendix C.
[d]Weschler (2000).
NA = not applicable
ppb = parts per 10^9

(nitrous oxide and isoflurane) and from sterilizers (ethylene oxide). The potential for asphyxiation is always a concern when compressed gases are present, even if that gas is nitrogen. In residences, the main sources of equipment-derived pollutants are gas ranges, wood stoves, printers, and kerosene heaters. Venting is helpful, but some pollutants escape into the occupied area. The pollutant contribution by gas ranges is somewhat mitigated by the fact that they operate for shorter periods than heaters. The same is true of showers, which can contribute to radon and halocarbon concentrations indoors.

Cleaning agents and **other consumer products** can act as contaminant sources. Commonly used liquid detergents, waxes, polishes, spot removers, and cosmetics contain organic solvents that volatilize slowly or quickly. Mothballs and other pest control agents emit organic vapors. Black and Bayer (1986), Knoeppel and Schauenburg (1989), and Tichenor (1989) report data on the release of these volatile organic compounds (VOCs). Field studies show that such products contribute significantly to indoor pollution; however, a large variety of compounds is in use, and few studies have been made that allow calculation of typical emission rates. Pesticides, both those applied indoors and those applied outdoors to control termites, also pollute building interiors.

Tobacco smoke is a prevalent and potent source of indoor air pollutants in residences, but not as much of a pollutant source in commercial buildings. Traditionally, almost all tobacco smoke arises from cigarette smoking. **Environmental tobacco smoke (ETS)**, sometimes called secondhand smoke, is the aged and diluted combination of sidestream smoke (smoke from the lit end of a cigarette and smoke that escapes from the filter between puffs) and mainstream smoke (smoke exhaled by a smoker). With the increasing popularity of the use of **electronic smoking devices ("e-cigarettes")** and cannabis legalization in some jurisdictions, ASHRAE *Standard* 62.1 (2016) extended its definition of ETS to include smoke produced from combustion of cannabis and controlled substances, and the emissions produced by electronic smoking devices. E-cigarette regulations differ across jurisdictions. The effects of tobacco smoke have been well studied: emission factors for ETS components, the ratio of ETS components to marker compounds, and apportionment of ETS components in indoor air are reported in the literature by Heavner et al. (1996), Hodgson et al. (1996), Martin et al. (1997), and Nelson et al. (1994). The emission profiles, exposure, and health risks of e-cigarette use are the subject of recent studies (Cooke et al. 2015; Herrington and Myers 2014; Pisinger and Døssing 2014). However, the available data are limited and often inconsistent, indicating a need for further research. Some background information on e-cigarettes can be found in Baker (2016).

Occupants, both humans and animals, emit a wide array of pollutants by breath, sweat, and flatus. Some of these emissions are conversions from solids or liquids within the body. Many volatile organics emitted are, however, reemissions of pollutants inhaled earlier, with the tracheobronchial system acting like a physical adsorber for gases, or as a filter for particles.

Floor dust, which typically contains much larger particles and fibers than the air, has been found to be a sink (adsorption medium) and secondary emission source for VOCs. Floor dust is a mixture of organic and inorganic particles, hair and skin scales, and textile fibers. The fiber portion of floor dust has been shown to contain as much as 169 ppm TVOC, and the particle portion 148 ppm (Gyntelberg et al. 1994). These VOCs were correlated to the prevalence of irritative (sore throat) and cognitive (concentration problems) symptoms among building occupants. One hundred eighty-eight compounds were identified from thermal desorption of office dust at 250°F (Wilkins et al. 1993). Household dust was found to be similar in composition (Wolkoff and Wilkins 1994).

Contaminants from other sources include chloroform from water; tetrachloroethylene and 1,1,1-trichloroethane from cleaning solvents; methylene chloride from paint strippers, fresheners, cleaners, and polishers; α-pinene and limonene from floor waxes; and 1-methoxy-2-propanol from spray carpet cleaners. Formaldehyde, a major VOC, has many sources, but pressed-wood products appear to be the most significant.

4.4 FLAMMABLE GASES AND VAPORS

Use of flammable materials is widespread. Flammable gases and vapors (as defined in NFPA *Standard* 30) can be found at hazardous levels in sewage treatment plants, sewage and utility tunnels, dry-cleaning plants, automobile garages, and industrial finishing process plants.

A flammable liquid's vapor pressure and volatility or rate of evaporation determine its ability to form an explosive mixture. These properties can be expressed by the **flash point**, which is the temperature to which a flammable liquid must be heated to produce a flash when a small flame is passed across the surface of the liquid. Depending on the test methods, either the open- or closed-cup flash point may be listed. The higher the flash point, the more safely the liquid can be handled. Liquids with flash points higher than 100°F are called **combustible**, whereas those under 100°F are described as **flammable**. Those with flash points less than 70°F should be regarded as highly flammable.

In addition to having a low flash point, the air/vapor or air/gas mixture must have a concentration in the flammable (explosive) range before it can be ignited. The **flammable (explosive) range** is the range between the upper and lower explosive limits, expressed as percent by volume in air. Concentrations of material above the higher range or below the lower range will not explode. Flashpoint and explosive range data for many chemicals are listed in the *Fire Protection Guide to Hazardous Materials*, published by the National Fire Protection Association (NFPA 2010). Data for a small number of representative chemicals are shown in Table 14.

In designing ventilation systems to control flammable gases and vapors, the engineer must consider the following.

Most safety authorities and fire underwriters prefer to limit concentrations to 20 to 25% of the lower explosive limit of a material. The resulting safety factor of 4 or 5 allows latitude for imperfections in air distribution and variations of temperature or mixture and guards against unpredictable or unrecognized sources of ignition. Operation at concentrations above the upper explosive limit should be allowed only in rare instances, and after taking appropriate precautions. Some guidance is provided in American Petroleum Institute documents [e.g., API (2009)]. To reach the upper explosive limit, the flammable gas or vapor must pass through the active explosive range, in which any source of ignition can cause an explosion. In addition, a drop in gas concentration caused by unforeseen dilution or reduced evaporation rate may place a system in the dangerous explosive range.

In occupied places where ventilation is applied for proper health control, the danger of an explosion is minimized. In most instances, flammable gases and vapors are also toxic, and maximum allowable concentrations are far below the material's lower explosive limit (LEL). For example, proper ventilation for acetone vapors keeps the concentration below the occupational exposure limit of 500 ppm (0.05% by volume). Acetone's LEL is 2.5% by volume. Proper location of exhaust and supply ventilation equipment depends primarily on how a contaminant is given off and on other problems of the process, and secondarily on the relative density of flammable vapor.

If the specific density of the explosive mixture is the same as that of air, cross drafts, equipment movement, and temperature differentials may cause sufficient mixing to produce explosive concentrations and disperse these throughout the atmosphere. In reasonably still air, heavier-than-air vapors may pool at floor level. Therefore, the engineer must either provide proper exhaust and supply air patterns to control hazardous material, preferably at its source, or offset the effects of drafts, equipment movement, and

Table 14 Flammable Limits of Some Gases and Vapors

		Flammable Limits, % by Volume	
Gas or Vapor	**Flash Point,* °F**	**Lower**	**Upper**
Acetone	0	2.5	12.8
Ammonia	Gas	15	28
Benzene (benzol)	12	1.2	7.8
n-Butane	–26	1.9	8.5
Carbon disulfide	–22	1.3	50
Carbon monoxide	Gas	12.5	74
1,2-Dichloroethylene	36	5.6	12.8
Diethylether	–49	1.9	36
Ethyl alcohol	55	3.3	19
Ethylene	Gas	2.7	36
Gasoline	–45	1.4	7.6
Hydrogen	Gas	4.0	75
Hydrogen sulfide	Gas	4.3	44
Isopropyl alcohol	53	2.0	12.7
Methyl alcohol	52	6.0	36
Methyl ethyl ketone	16	1.4	11.4
Natural gas (variable)	Gas	3.8 to 6.5	13 to 17
Naphtha	Less than 0	1.1	5.9
Propane	Gas	2.1	9.5
Toluene (toluol)	40	0.1	7.1
o-Xylene	90	0.9	6.7

*Measured by closed-cup method

convection currents by providing good distribution of exhaust and supply air for general dilution and exhaust. The intake duct should be positioned so that it does not bring in exhaust gases or emissions from ambient sources.

Adequate ventilation minimizes the risk of or prevents fires and explosions and is necessary, regardless of other precautions, such as elimination of the ignition sources, safe building construction, and the use of automatic alarm and extinguisher systems.

Chapter 32 of the 2015 *ASHRAE Handbook—HVAC Applications* gives more details about equipment for control of combustible materials. Some design, construction, and ventilation issues are also addressed by NFPA *Standard* 30.

4.5 COMBUSTIBLE DUSTS

Many organic and some mineral dusts can produce dust explosions (Bartnecht 1989). Explosive dusts are potential hazards whenever uncontrolled dust escapes, and often, a primary explosion results from a small amount of dust in suspension that has been exposed to a source of ignition. Explosibility limits for combustible dusts differ from those for flammable gases and flammable vapors because of the interaction between dust layers and suspended dust. In addition, the pressure and vibration created by an explosion can dislodge large accumulations of dust on horizontal surfaces, creating a larger secondary explosion.

For ignition, dust clouds require high temperatures and sufficient dust concentration. These temperatures and concentrations and the minimum spark energy can be found in Avallone et al. (2007). Several methods can be used to prevent ignition of dust material (Jaeger and Siwek 1999; Siwek 1997):

- Limit the temperature of deposited product.
- Avoid potentially explosive combustible substance/air mixtures.
- Introduce inert gas in the area to lower the oxygen volume content below the limiting oxygen concentration (LOC) or maximum allowable oxygen concentration (MOC), so that ignition of the mixture cannot occur. Adding inert dusts (e.g., rock salt, sodium sulfate) also works; in general, inert dust additions of more than 50% by weight are necessary. It is also possible to

replace flammable solvents and cleaning agents with nonflammable halogenated hydrocarbons or water, or flammable pressure transmission fluids with halocarbon oils.

- Avoid effective ignition sources: eliminate heat sources (hot surfaces or smoldering material) and sources of sparks or electrostatic discharge.

Proper exhaust ventilation design can also be used for preventing high-dust conditions. Forced ventilation allows use of greater amounts of air and selective air circulation in areas surrounding the equipment. Its use and calculation of the minimum volume flow rate for supply and exhaust air are subject to certain requirements, covered in Chapter 32 of the 2015 *ASHRAE Handbook—HVAC Applications.* Ventilation systems and equipment chosen must prevent dust pocketing inside the equipment. When local exhaust ventilation is used, separation equipment should be installed as close to the dust source as possible to prevent transport of dust in the exhaust system.

4.6 RADIOACTIVE AIR CONTAMINANTS

Radioactive contaminants (Jacobson and Morris 1977) can be particulate or gaseous in nature. Many radioactive materials would be chemically toxic if present in high concentrations; however, in most cases, the radioactivity necessitates limiting their concentration in air.

Most radioactive air contaminants affect the body when they are absorbed and retained. This is known as the **internal radiation hazard**. Airborne radioactive particulates can eventually enter the food chain and thus the human body. Radioactive material deposited on the ground increases **external radiation exposure**. However, except for fallout from nuclear weapons or a serious reactor accident, such exposure is insignificant.

Radioactive air contaminants can emit alpha, beta, or gamma rays. **Alpha rays**, although of higher energy, penetrate tissue poorly and present no hazard, except when the material is deposited inside or on the body. **Beta rays** are somewhat more penetrating and can be both an internal and an external hazard. Penetration of **gamma rays** depends on their energy, which varies with radioactive element or isotope.

There is a distinction between the radioactive material itself and the radiation it emits. Radioactive materials present distinctive problems. High concentrations of radioactivity can generate enough heat to damage filtration equipment or ignite the material spontaneously. Most radioactive materials are hazardous at much lower concentrations than those for ordinary materials; thus, special electronic instruments that respond to radioactivity must be used to detect these hazardous levels.

Radioactive particles can be removed from air by devices such as HEPA and ULPA filters, and radioactive gases by impregnated carbon or alumina and absorption traps, but the gamma radiation from such collected material can penetrate outside of the material. This distinction is frequently overlooked.

The amount of radioactive material in air is measured in becquerels (Bq) per cubic metre [1 Bq = 27.027 picocuries (pCi)], and the dose of radiation from deposited material is measured in rads.

The ventilation engineer faces difficulty in dealing with radioactive air contamination because of the extremely low permissible concentrations for radioactive materials. For some sensitive industrial plants, such as those in the photographic industry, contaminants must be kept from entering the plant. If radioactive materials are handled inside the plant, the problem is to collect the contaminated air as close to the source as possible, and then remove the contaminant from the air with a high degree of efficiency, before discharging the air to the outdoors. Filters are generally used for particulate materials, but venturi scrubbers, wet washers, and other devices can be used as prefilters to meet special needs.

Design of equipment and systems for control of radioactive particulates and gases in nuclear laboratories, power plants, and fuel-processing facilities is a highly specialized technology. Careful attention must be given to the reliability, as well as the contaminant-removal ability, of equipment under the special environmental stresses involved. More information on these procedures can be found in Chapter 46 of the 2015 *ASHRAE Handbook—HVAC Applications* and in various publications of the U.S. Department of Energy [see, e.g., DOE (2006)].

Radon

A major source of airborne radioactive exposure to the population comes from radon. Radon (Rn) is a naturally occurring, chemically inert, colorless, odorless, tasteless radioactive gas. It is produced from radioactive decay of radium, which is formed through several intermediate steps of decay of uranium and thorium. Radon is widely found in the natural environment, because uranium salt precursors are widespread. Radon-222 is the most common isotope of radon. The EPA has developed a map of the United States that shows predicted radon concentrations throughout the country (EPA 2016c).

As a gas, radon (before it decays) can move limited distances through very small spaces, such as those between particles of soil and rock, and enter indoor environments (Nazaroff et al. 1988; Tanner 1980). Additional but secondary sources of indoor radon include groundwater (radon is quite soluble in water) and radium-containing building materials.

Radon gas enters a house or building primarily through cracks, joints, and other holes in concrete foundations; directly through porous concrete blocks; through joints and openings in crawlspace ceilings; and through leakage points in HVAC ductwork embedded in slab floors or located in crawlspaces. Pressure-driven flow is the dominant radon entry mechanism in houses with elevated radon concentrations (Nazaroff et al. 1987). Pressure differences are caused by several factors, including thermal stack effect, wind, and operation of HVAC equipment. Rn can also diffuse directly through substructural materials (e.g., concrete). The diffusive Rn entry rate is often a significant portion of the total entry rate into residences.

Typical Radon Levels. The outdoor radon concentration is about 15 Bq/m^3 (0.4 pCi/L). The annual average concentration of radon in U.S. homes is about 46 Bq/m^3 (1.25 pCi/L) (EPA 1989). Although several sources of radon may contribute to the annual indoor average, pressure-driven flow of soil gas is the principal source for elevated concentrations. Nonmunicipal water supplies can be a source of elevated indoor radon, but only in isolated instances.

Measurement Methods. Indoor concentrations of radon can vary hourly, daily, and seasonally by a factor of 10 to 20 (Turk et al. 1990). Thus, long-term measurements (3 months to 1 year) generally provide more reliable estimates of the average indoor concentration. Two widely used techniques are the short-term charcoal canister (measuring for up to 7 days), and the long-term alpha-track methods (kept in place for 90 days to 1 year). Generally, short-term measurements should only be used as a screening technique to determine whether long-term measurement is necessary. When interpreting the results, consider the great uncertainties in measurement accuracy with these devices (up to 50% at the radon levels typically found in homes), as well as the natural variability of radon concentrations.

Ideally, long-term measurements should be the basis for decisions about installing radon mitigation systems, and short-term measurements should only be used as a screening method to identify buildings with radon concentrations that are very high, justifying immediate remedial action. In practice, short-term measurements at the time a building is sold are the basis for most decisions about remedial action.

Control. Exposure to indoor radon may be reduced by (1) inhibiting its entry into the building or (2) removing or diluting radon decay products in indoor air. The most effective and energy-efficient control measures are generally those that reduce radon entry rates (Henschel 1993). Chapter 46 of the 2015 *ASHRAE Handbook—HVAC Applications* provides more detail on these measures.

4.7 SOIL GASES

The radioactive gas radon (Rn) is the best-known soil gas, but other gaseous contaminants may enter buildings along with radon from surrounding soil. Methane from landfills has reached explosive levels in some buildings. Potentially toxic or carcinogenic VOCs, including chlorinated hydrocarbons in the soil because of spills, improper disposal, leaks from storage tanks, and disposal in landfills, can also be transported into buildings (Garbesi and Sextro 1989; Hodgson et al. 1992; Kullman and Hill 1990; Wood and Porter 1987). Pesticides applied to soil beneath or adjacent to houses have also been detected in indoor air (Livingston and Jones 1981; Wright and Leidy 1982). The broad significance of health effects of exposure to these soil contaminants is not well understood.

Although soil gases generally have limited effects when diffusion is the primary mechanism driving entry, there are situations where advective processes are dominant. In such cases, effects on indoor air can be significant (Adomait and Fugler 1997). Pressure-driven airflow produced by thermal or wind drivers on the building affects entry of soil gas into the structure. Soil permeability to vapors, soil gas concentration, and soil-to-building pressure differential are the largest factors influencing indoor concentrations of these gases.

Techniques that reduce Rn entry from soil should also be effective in reducing entry of other soil gases into buildings. Other approaches (e.g., increasing ventilation in the building, such as by slightly opening a window) may help reduce house negative pressure (created by stack effect) with respect to soil gas pressure. Increased ventilation should be used with caution, and only after establishing for the house in question that it will not increase negative pressure where the soil gas enters.

REFERENCES

ACGIH. 1989. *Guidelines for the assessment of bioaerosols in the indoor environment*. American Conference of Governmental Industrial Hygienists, Cincinnati, OH.

ACGIH. Annual. *TLVs® and BEIs®: Threshold limit values for chemical substances and physical agents*. American Conference of Governmental Industrial Hygienists, Cincinnati, OH.

ACGIH. 2001. *Air sampling instruments*, 9th ed. American Conference of Governmental Industrial Hygienists, Cincinnati, OH.

Adibi, J.J., F.P. Perera, W. Jedrychowski, D.E. Camann, D. Barr, R. Jacek, and R.M. Whyatt. 2003. Prenatal exposures to phthalates among women in New York City and Krakow, Poland. *Environmental Health Perspectives* 111:1719-1722.

Adomait, M., and D. Fugler. 1997. Method to evaluate soil gas VOC influx into houses. *Proceedings of the Air and Waste Management Association's 90th Annual Meeting*, Toronto.

AIHA. 1996. *Field guide for the determination of biological contaminants in environmental samples.* American Industrial Hygiene Association, Fairfax, VA.

Allen, R.J., R.A. Wadden, and E.D. Ross. 1978. Characterization of potential indoor sources of ozone. *American Industrial Hygiene Association Journal* 39:4666-4671.

Aoki, T., and S. Tanabe. 2007. Generation of sub-micron particles and secondary pollutants from building materials by ozone reaction. *Atmospheric Environment* 41:3139-3150.

API. 2009. Management of hazards associated with location of process plant permanent buildings. *Recommended Practice* RP 752. American Petroleum Institute, Washington, D.C.

ASHRAE. 2012. Method of testing general ventilation air-cleaning devices for removal efficiency by particle size. ANSI/ASHRAE *Standard* 52.2-2012.

ASHRAE. 2016. Ventilation for acceptable indoor air quality. ANSI/ASHRAE *Standard* 62.1-2016.

ASHRAE. 2015. Laboratory test method for assessing the performance of gas-phase air-cleaning systems: Loose granular media. ANSI/ASHRAE *Standard* 145.1-2015.

ASHRAE. 2011. Laboratory test method for assessing the performance of gas-phase air-cleaning systems: Air-cleaning devices. ANSI/ASHRAE *Standard* 145.2-2011.

ASHRAE. 2015. Risk management for building water systems. ANSI/ASHRAE *Standard* 188-2015.

ASHRAE. 2017. Measurement procedures for gaseous contaminants in commercial buildings. ASHRAE *Guideline* 27-2017.

ASTM. 2015. Standard specification for woven wire test sieve cloth and test sieves. ASTM *Standard* E11-15. American Society for Testing and Materials, West Conshohocken, PA.

ASTM. 2007. Practice for continuous sizing and counting of airborne particles in dust-controlled areas and cleanrooms using instruments capable of detecting single sub-micrometer and larger particles. ASTM *Standard* F50-07. American Society for Testing and Materials, West Conshohocken, PA.

ATC. 1990. *Technical assistance document for sampling and analysis of toxic organic compounds in ambient air*. Environmental Protection Agency, Research Triangle Park, NC.

Avallone, E.A., T. Baumeister, and A. Sadegh. 2007. *Marks' standard handbook for mechanical engineers*, 11th ed. McGraw-Hill, New York.

Azimi, P., D. Zhao, C. Pouzet, N.E. Crain, and B. Stephens. 2016. Emissions of ultrafine particles and volatile organic compounds from commercially available desktop three-dimensional printers with multiple filaments. *Environmental Science and Technology* 50:1260-1268.

Baker, W.A. 2016. Origins and evolution of e-cigarettes. *ASHRAE Journal* 58(4): 78-80.

Bartnecht, W. 1989. *Dust explosions: Course, prevention, protection*. Springer-Verlag, Berlin.

Batterman, S., C. Godwin, S. Chernyak, J. Chunrong, and S. Charles. 2010. Brominated flame retardants in offices in Michigan, U.S.A. *Environment International* 36(6):548-556.

Berglund, B., U. Berglund, and T. Lindvall. 1986. Assessment of discomfort and irritation from the indoor air. *IAQ '86: Managing Indoor Air for Health and Energy Conservation*, pp. 138-149. ASHRAE.

Berglund, B., I. Johansson, and T. Lindvall. 1988. Adsorption and desorption of organic compounds in indoor materials. In *Healthy Buildings '88*, vol. 3, pp. 299-309. B. Berglund and T. Lindvall, eds. Swedish Council for Building Research, Stockholm.

Black, M.S., and C.W. Bayer. 1986. Formaldehyde and other VOC exposures from consumer products. *IAQ '86: Managing Indoor Air for Health and Energy Conservation*. ASHRAE.

Boelter, K.J., and J.H. Davidson. 1997. Ozone generation by indoor electrostatic air cleaners. *Aerosol Science and Technology* 27:689-708.

Bornehag, C.G., J. Sundell, C.J. Weschler, T. Sigsgaard, B. Lundgren, M. Hasselgren, and L. Hagerhed-Engman. 2004. The association between asthma and allergic symptoms in children and phthalates in house dust: A nested case-control study. *Environmental Health Perspectives* 112: 1393-1397.

Bostrom, C.E, P. Gerde, A. Handberg, B. Jernstrom, C. Johansson, T. Kyrklund, A. Rannug, M. Tornqvist, K. Victorin, and R. Westerholm. 2002. Cancer risk assessment, indicators, and guidelines for polycyclic aromatic hydrocarbons in the ambient air. *Environmental Health Perspectives* 110(S-3):451-489.

Brightman, H.S., S.E. Womble, E.L. Ronca, and J.R. Girman. 1996. Baseline information on indoor air quality in large buildings (BASE '95). *Proceedings of Indoor Air '96*, vol. 3, pp. 1033-1038.

Budavi, S., ed. 1996. *The Merck index*, 12th ed. Merck and Company, White Station, NJ.

Cain, W.S., L.C. See, and T. Tosun. 1986. Irritation and odor from formaldehyde chamber studies, 1986. *IAQ '86: Managing Indoor Air for Health and Energy Conservation*. ASHRAE.

Cassidy, B.E., M.A. Alabanza-Akers, T.A. Akers, D.B. Hall, P.B. Ryan, C.W. Bayer, and L.P. Naeher. 2007. Particulate matter and carbon monoxide multiple regression models using environmental characteristics in a high diesel-use area of Baguio City, Philippines. *Science of The Total Environment* 381(1-3):47-58.

CFR. Annual. National primary and secondary ambient air quality standards. 40CFR50. *Code of Federal Regulations,* U.S. Government Printing Office, Washington, D.C.

CFR. Annual. Protection of environment: Requirements for preparation, adoption, and submittal of implementation plans. 40CFR51.100. *Code of Federal Regulations*, Government Printing Office, Washington, D.C.

Colombo, A., M. DeBortoli, H. Knöppel, H. Schauenburg, and H. Vissers. 1991. Small chamber tests and headspace analysis of volatile organic compounds emitted from household products. *Indoor Air* 1:13-21.

Conibear, S., S. Geneser, and B.W. Carnow. 1996. Carbon monoxide levels and sources found in a random sample of households in Chicago during the 1994-1995 heating season. *Proceedings of IAQ '95*, pp. 111-118. ASHRAE.

Cooke, A., J. Fergeson, A. Bulkhi, and T.B. Casale. 2015. The electronic cigarette: The good, the bad, and the ugly. *Journal of Allergy Clinical Immunology: In Practice* 3(4):498-505.

Davis, A., M. Black, Q. Zhang, J.P.S. Wong, and R. Weber. 2016. Fine particulate and chemical emissions from desktop 3D printers. *ASHRAE Annual Conference Papers*.

Delfino, R.J., C. Soutas, and S. Malik. 2005. Potential role of ultrafine particles in associations between airborne particle mass and cardiovascular health. *Environmental Health Perspectives* 113:934-945.

Destaillats, H., M.M. Lunden, B.C. Singer, B.K. Coleman, A.T. Hodgson, C.J. Weschler, and W.W. Nazaroff. 2006. Indoor secondary pollutants from household product emissions in the presence of ozone: A bench-scale chamber study. *Environmental Science and Technology* 40:4421-4428.

DOE. 2006. *Transportation Emergency Preparedness Program emergency responder radioactive material quick reference sheet*. U.S. Department of Energy, Washington, D.C. energy.gov/em/downloads/emergency-responder-radioactive-material-quick-reference-sheet-0.

Ekberg, L.E. 1994. Outdoor air contaminants and indoor air quality under transient conditions. *Indoor Air* 4:189-196.

EPA. 1979. *Toxic substances control act chemical substance inventory*, vol. I-IV. U.S. Environmental Protection Agency, Office of Toxic Substances, Washington, D.C.

EPA. 1989. *Radon and radon reduction technology*. EPA-600/9-89/006a, 1:4-15. U.S. Environmental Protection Agency, Washington, D.C.

EPA. 1997. *Data from the Building Assessment Survey and Evaluation (BASE) study*. U.S. Environmental Protection Agency, Washington, D.C. www.epa.gov/iaq/base/obtain_data.html.

EPA. 2005. *2005 national emissions inventory (NEI) data*. U.S. Environmental Protection Agency, Washington, D.C.

EPA. 2007. *High production volume (HPV) challenge*. U.S. Environmental Protection Agency, Washington, D.C. www.epa.gov/chemrtk/index.htm.

EPA. 2009a. *Policy assessment for the review of the particulate matter National Ambient Air Quality Standards*. U.S. Environmental Protection Agency, Washington, D.C. www3.epa.gov/ttn/naaqs/standards/pm/data/PreliminaryDraftPA091609.pdf.

EPA. 2009b. *Data from the air quality system measurements*. U.S. Environmental Protection Agency, Washington, D.C. www.epa.gov/ttri/airs/airsaqs/detaildata/AQIndex.htm.

EPA. 2011. *Air pollutants*. U.S. Environmental Protection Agency, Washington, D.C. www.epa.gov/air/airpollutants.html.

EPA. 2015. *National ambient air quality standards (NAAQS)*. U.S. Environmental Protection Agency, Washington, D.C. Available from www.epa.gov/criteria-air-pollutants/naaqs-table.

EPA. 2016a. *Particulate matter (PM) pollution*. U.S. Environmental Protection Agency, Washington, D.C. www.epa.gov/pm-pollution.

EPA. 2016b. *EPA guidance and tools for schools*. U.S. Environmental Protection Agency, Washington, D.C.

EPA. 2016c. *EPA map of radon zones*. U.S. Environmental Protection Agency, Washington, D.C. www.epa.gov/radon/epa-map-radon-zones.

EPA. 2017. *International cooperation: Mercury emissions: The global context*. Environmental Protection Agency, Washington, D.C. www.epa.gov/international-cooperation/mercury-emissions-global-context.

Espy, M.J., J.R. Uhl, L.M. Sloan, S.P. Buckwalter, M.F. Jones, E.A. Vetter, J.D.C. Yao, N.L. Wengenack, J.E. Rosenblatt, F.R. Cockerill III, and T.F. Smith. 2006. Real-time PCR in clinical microbiology: Applications for routine laboratory testing. *Clinical Microbiology Reviews* 19(1):165-256. cmr.asm.org/content/19/1/165.full.

Esswein, E.J., and M.F. Boeniger. 1994. Effect of an ozone generating air purifying device on reducing concentrations of formaldehyde in air. *Applied Occupational Environmental Hygiene* 9(2).

Facciola, N.A., J. Zhai, D. Toohey, and S.L. Miller. 2006. Identification, classification, and correlation of ultrafine indoor airborne particulate matter with outdoor values. ASHRAE Research Project RP-1281, *Final Report*.

Foarde, K.K., D.W. VanOsdell, J.J. Fischer, and K.E. Lee. 1994. Investigate and identify indoor allergens and biological toxins that can be removed by filtration. ASHRAE Research Project RP-760, *Final Report*.

Fromme, H., J. Diemer, S. Dietrich, J. Cyrys, J. Heinrich, W. Lang, M. Kiranoglu, and D. Twardella. 2008. Chemical and morphological properties of particulate matter (PM_{10}, $PM_{2.5}$) in school classrooms and outdoor air. *Atmospheric Environment* 42(27):6597-6605.

Garbesi, K., and R.G. Sextro. 1989. Modeling and field evidence of pressure-driven entry of soil gas into a home through permeable below-grade walls. *Environment Science and Technology* 23:1481-1487.

GSA. 1992. Airborne particulate cleanliness classes in cleanrooms and clean zones. *Federal Standard* 209E. U.S. General Services Administration, Washington, D.C.

Gyntelberg, F., P. Suadicami, J.W. Nielsen, P. Skov, O. Valbjorn, T. Nielsen, T.O. Schneider, O. Jorgenson, P. Wolkoff, C. Wilkins, S. Gravesen, and S. Nom. 1994. Dust and the sick-building syndrome. *Indoor Air* 4:223-238.

Han, X., M. Aguilar-Villalobos, J. Allen, C. Carlton, R. Robinson, C. Bayer, and L.P. Naeher. 2005. Traffic-related occupational exposures to $PM_{2.5}$, CO, and VOCs in Trujillo, Peru. *International Journal of Occupational and Environmental Health* 11:276-288.

Health Canada. 2004. *Fungal contamination in public buildings: Health effects and investigation methods.* Health Canada, Ottawa.

Heavner, D.L., W.T. Morgan, and M.W. Ogden. 1996. Determination of volatile organic compounds and respirable particulate matter in New Jersey and Pennsylvania homes and workplaces. *Environment International* 22:159-183.

Henschel, D.B. 1993. *Radon reduction techniques for existing detached houses—Technical guidance*, 3rd ed. EPA/625/R-93/011.

Herrington, J.S., and C. Myers. 2015. Electronic cigarette solutions and resultant aerosol profiles. *Journal of Chromatography A* 1418:192-199.

Hewson, E.W., W.W. Payne, A.L. Cole, J.B. Harrington, Jr., and W.R. Solomon. 1967. Air pollution by ragweed pollen. *Journal of the Air Pollution Control Association* 17(10):651.

Hodgson, A.T. 1995. A review and a limited comparison of methods for measuring total volatile organic compounds in indoor air. *Indoor Air* 5(4):247.

Hodgson, A.T., K. Garbesi, R.G. Sextro, and J.M. Daisey. 1992. Soil gas contamination and entry of volatile organic compounds into a house near a landfill. *Journal of the Air and Waste Management Association* 42:277-283.

Hodgson, A.T., J.M. Daisey, K.R.R. Mahanama, J.T. Brinke, and L.E. Alevantis. 1996. Use of volatile tracers to determine the contribution of environmental tobacco smoke to concentrations of volatile organic compounds in smoking environments. *Environment International* 22:295-307.

Horner, W.E., and J.D. Miller. 2003. Microbial volatile organic compounds with emphasis on those arising from filamentous fungal contaminants of buildings (RP-1072). *ASHRAE Transactions* 109(1):215-231.

Howdeshell, K.L. 2002. A model of the development of the brain as a construct of the thyroid system. *Environmental Health Perspectives* 110 (S-3):337-348.

IARC. 2004. *Monographs on the Evaluation of Carcinogenic Risks to Humans* 88. International Agency for Research in Cancer, Lyon, France.

ISA. 1985. Environmental conditions for process measurement and control systems: airborne contaminants. *Standard* S71.04. International Society of Automation, Research Triangle Park, NC.

ISO. 2015. Cleanrooms and associated controlled environments—Part 1: Classification of air cleanliness by particle concentration. *Standard* 14644-1. International Organization for Standardization, Geneva.

Jacobson, J.L., and S.W. Jacobson. 1996. Intellectual impairment in children exposed to polychlorinated biphenyl *in utero*. *New England Journal of Medicine* 335:783-789.

Jacobson, A.R., and S.C. Morris. 1977. The primary pollutants, viable particulates, their occurrence, sources and effects. In *Air pollution*, 3rd ed., p. 169. Academic Press, New York.

Jaeger, N., and R. Siwek. 1999. Prevent explosions of combustible dusts. *Chemical Engineering Progress* 95(6).

Jaenicke, R. 1998. Biological aerosols in the atmosphere. Plenary Lecture, Fifth International Aerosol Conference, Edinburgh, Scotland.

Knoeppel, H., and H. Schauenburg. 1989. Screening of household products for the emission of volatile organic compounds. *Environment International* 15:413-418.

Kullman, G.J., and R.A. Hill 1990. Indoor air quality affected by abandoned gasoline tanks. *Applied Occupational Environmental Hygiene* 5:36-37.

Lamm, S.H. 1986. Irritancy levels and formaldehyde exposures in U.S. mobile homes. In *Indoor air quality in cold climates*, pp. 137-147. Air and Waste Management Association, Pittsburgh, PA.

Li, T.-H., B.J. Turpin, H.C. Shields, and C.J. Weschler. 2002. Indoor hydrogen peroxide derived from ozone/d-limonene reactions. *Environmental Science and Technology* 36:3295-3302.

Lide, D.R., ed. 1996. *Handbook of chemistry and physics*, 77th ed. CRC Press, Boca Raton, FL.

Little, J.C., and A.T. Hodgson. 1996. A strategy for characterizing homogeneous diffusion-controlled indoor sources and sinks. ASTM *Special Technical Publication* STP 1287, pp. 294-304. American Society for Testing and Materials, West Conshohocken, PA.

Livingston, J.M., and C.R. Jones. 1981. Living area contamination by chlordane used for termite treatment. *Bulletin of Environmental Contaminant Toxicology* 27:406-411.

Lodge, J.E., ed. 1988. *Methods of air sampling and analysis*, 3rd ed. Lewis, Chelsea, MD.

Logue, J.M., T.E. McKone, M.H. Sherman, and B.C. Singer. 2011. Hazard assessment of chemical air contaminants measured in residences. *Indoor Air* 21:92-109.

Macher, J., ed. 1999. *Bioaerosols: Assessment and control.* American Conference of Governmental Industrial Hygienists, Cincinnati, Ohio.

Martin, P., D.L. Heavner, P.R. Nelson, K.C. Maiolo, C.H. Risner, P.S. Simmons, W.T. Morgan, and M.W. Ogden. 1997. Environmental tobacco smoke (ETS): A market cigarette study. *Environment International* 23(1):75-90.

Miksch, R.R., C.D. Hollowell, and H.E. Schmidt. 1982. Trace organic chemical contaminants in office spaces. *Atmospheric Environment* 8: 129-137.

Moghini, S.M., A.C. Hunter, and J.C. Murray. 2005. Nanomedicine: Current status and future prospects. *The FASEB Journal* 19(3):311-330.

Mølhave, L., and M. Thorsen. 1990. A model for investigations of ventilation systems as sources for volatile organic compounds in indoor climate. *Atmospheric Environment* 25A:241-249.

Mølhave, L., L. Anderson, G.R. Lundquist, and O. Nielson. 1982. Gas emission from building materials. *Report* 137. Danish Building Research Institute, Copenhagen.

Morey, P.R., and B.A. Jenkins. 1989. What are typical concentrations of fungi, total volatile organic compounds, and nitrogen dioxide in an office environment. *Proceedings of IAQ '89, The Human Equation: Health and Comfort*, pp. 67-71. ASHRAE.

Morey, P.R., and J. Singh. 1991. Indoor air quality in non-industrial occupational environments. In *Patty's industrial hygiene and toxicology*, 4th ed.

Morrison, G.C., and W.W. Nazaroff. 2002. Ozone interactions with carpet: Secondary emissions of aldehydes. *Environmental Science and Technology* 36:2185-2192.

Morrison, G.C., W.W. Nazaroff, J.A. Cano-Ruiz, A.T. Hodgson, and M.P. Modera. 1998. Indoor air quality impacts of ventilation ducts: Ozone removal and emission of volatile organic compounds. *Journal of Air and Waste Management Association* 48:941-949.

Mullis, K.B. 1990. The unusual origin of the polymerase chain reaction. *Scientific American* 262:56-65.

Nazaroff, W.W., S.R. Lewis, S.M. Doyle, B.A. Moed, and A.V. Nero. 1987. Experiments on pollutant transport from soil into residential basements by pressure-driven air flow. *Environment Science and Technology* 21:459.

Nazaroff, W.W., B.A. Moed, and R.G. Sextro. 1988. Soil as a source of indoor radon: Generation, migration and entry. In *Radon and its decay products in indoor air*, pp. 57-112. Wiley, New York.

Nelms, L.H., M.A. Mason, and B.A. Tichenor. 1986. The effects of ventilation rates and product loading on organic emission rates from particleboard. *IAQ '86: Managing Indoor Air for Health and Energy Conservation*, pp. 469-485. ASHRAE.

Nelson, P.R., P. Martin, M.W. Ogden, D.L. Heavner, C.H. Risner, K.C. Maiolo, P.S. Simmons, and W.T. Morgan. 1994. Environmental tobacco smoke characteristics of different commercially available cigarettes. *Proceedings of the Fourth International Aerosol Conference*, vol. 1, pp. 454-455.

NFPA. 2010. *The fire protection guide to hazardous materials*, 14th ed. National Fire Protection Association, Quincy, MA.

NFPA. 2015. Flammable and combustible liquids code. NFPA *Standard* 30. National Fire Protection Association, Quincy, MA.

NIOSH. 1977. *NIOSH manual of sampling data sheets*. U.S. Department of Health and Human Services, National Institute for Occupational Safety and Health, Washington, D.C.

NIOSH. 2016. *NIOSH manual of analytical methods*, 5th ed. M.E. Cassellini and P.F. O'Connor, eds. DHHS (NIOSH) *Publication* 94-113.

NNI. 2008. *Size of the nanoscale*. National Nanotechnology Initiative. www.nano.gov/nanotech-101/nanotechnology-facts.

NRC. 1981. *Indoor pollutants*. National Research Council, National Academy Press, Washington, D.C.

NTP. 2011. *Report on carcinogens*, 12th ed. U.S. Department of Health and Human Services, National Toxicology Program, Research Triangle Park, NC.

OSHA. 1995. *OSHA computerized information system chemical sampling information*. U.S. Government Printing Office, Washington, D.C.

Otson, R., and P. Fellin. 1993. TVOC measurements: Relevance and limitations. *Proceedings of Indoor Air '93*, vol. 2, pp. 281-285.

Owen, M.K., D.S. Ensor, and L.E. Sparks. 1992. Airborne particle sizes and sources found in indoor air. *Atmospheric Environment* 26A(12):2149-2162.

Pisinger, C., and M. Døssing. 2014. A systematic review of health effects of electronic cigarettes. *Preventive Medicine* 69:248-260.

Pope, C.A. 1991. Respiratory hospital admissions associated with PM_{10} pollution in Utah, Salt Lake, and Cache valleys. *Archives of Environmental Health* 46:90-97.

Pope, C.A., R.T. Burnett, and M.J. Thun. 2002. Lung cancer, cardiopulmonary mortality, and long-term exposure to fine particulate air pollution. *Journal of the American Medical Association* 287:1132-1141.

Rask, D. 1988. Indoor air quality and the bottom line. *Heating, Piping and Air Conditioning* 60(10).

Riley, W.J., T.E. McKone, A.C.K. Lai, and W.W. Nazaroff. 2002. Indoor particulate matter of outdoor origin: Importance of size-dependent removal mechanisms. *Environmental Science and Technology* 36:200-207.

Rodes, C.E., and J. W. Thornburg. 2004. Breathing zone exposure assessment. Ch. 5 in *Aerosols handbook: Measurement, dosimetry, and health effects*. L.S. Ruzer and N.H. Harley, eds. CRC Press, Boca Raton, FL.

Rodes, C.E., R.M. Kamens, and R.W. Wiener. 1991. The significance and characteristics of the personal activity cloud on exposure assessment methods for indoor contaminants. *Indoor Air* 2:123-145.

Salthammer, T. 2016. Very volatile organic compounds: An understudied class of indoor air pollutants. *Indoor Air* 26:25-38.

Samet, J.M., M.C. Marbury, and J.D. Spengler. 1987. Health effects and sources of indoor air pollution. *American Review of Respiratory Disease* 136:1486-1508.

Sax, N.I., and R.J. Lewis, Sr. 1988. *Dangerous properties of industrial materials*, 6th ed, 3 vol. Van Nostrand Reinhold, New York.

Scala, G.F. 1963. A new instrument for the continuous measurement of condensation nuclei. *Analytical Chemistry* 35(5):702.

Seppänen, O.A., W.J. Fisk, and M.J. Mendell. 1999. Association of ventilation rates and CO2 concentrations with health and other responses in commercial and institutional buildings. *Indoor Air* 9:226-252.

Sheldon, L., R.W. Handy, T. Hartwell, R.W. Whitmore, H. Zelon, and E.D. Pellizzari. 1988a. *Indoor air quality in public buildings*, vol. I. EPA/600/S6-88/009a. Environmental Protection Agency, Washington, D.C.

Sheldon, L., H. Zelon, J. Sickles, C. Easton, T. Hartwell, and L. Wallace. 1988b. *Indoor air quality in public buildings*, vol. II. EPA/600/S688/009b. Environmental Protection Agency, Research Triangle Park, NC.

Siwek, R. 1997. Dusts: Explosion protection. In *Perry's chemical handbook for chemical engineering*, 7th ed. McGraw-Hill, New York.

Solomon, W.R., and K.P. Mathews. 1978. Aerobiology and inhalant allergens. In *Allergy: Principles and practices*. Mosley, St. Louis.

Soutas, C., R.J. Delfino, and M. Singh. 2005. Exposure assessment for atmospheric ultrafine particles (UFPs) and implications in epidemiological research. *Environmental Health Perspectives* 113:947-955.

Spengler, J., C. Hallowell, D. Moschandreas, and O. Fanger. 1982. Environment international. *Indoor air pollution*. Pergamon Press, Oxford, U.K.

Tanner, A.B. 1980. Radon migration in the ground: A supplementary review. In *Natural radiation environment*, vol. III. U.S. Department of Commerce, NTIS, Springfield, VA.

Task Group on Lung Dynamics. 1966. Deposition and retention models for internal dosimetry of the human respiratory tract. *Health Physics* 12(2):173-207.

Taylor, D.G., R.E. Kupel, and J.M. Bryant. 1977. *Documentation of the NIOSH validation tests*. U.S. National Institute for Occupational Safety and Health, Washington, D.C.

Teeuw, K.B., C.M.J.E. Vandenbroucke-Grauls, and J. Verhoef. 1994. Airborne gram-negative bacteria and endotoxin in sick building syndrome. *Archives of Internal Medicine* 154:2339-2345.

Tichenor, B.A. 1989. Measurement of organic compound emissions using small test chambers. *Environment International* 15:389-396.

Tichenor, B.A., G. Guo, J.E. Dunn, L.E. Sparks, and M.A. Mason. 1991. The interaction of vapour phase organic compounds with indoor sinks. *Indoor Air* 1:23-35.

Tong, Y., and B. Lighthart. 1999. Diurnal distribution of total and culturable atmospheric bacteria at a rural site. *Aerosol Science and Technology* 30:246-254.

Turk, B.H., R.J. Prill, D.T. Grimsrud, B.A. Moed, and R.G. Sextro. 1990. Characterizing the occurrence, sources and variability of radon in Pacific Northwest homes. *Journal of the Air and Waste Management Association* 40:498-506.

Valuntaite, V., and R. Girgzdiene. 2007. Investigation of ozone emission and dispersion from photocopying machines. *Journal of Environmental Engineering and Landscape Management* XV(2):61-67.

VanOsdell, D.W. 1994. Evaluation of test methods for determining the effectiveness and capacity of gas-phase air filtration equipment for indoor air applications—Phase I: Literature review and test recommendations (RP-674). *ASHRAE Transactions* 100(2):511-523.

Vartiainen, E., M. Kulmala, T.M. Ruuskanen, R. Taipale, J. Rinne, and H. Vehkamaki. 2006. Formation and growth of indoor air aerosol particles as a result of D-limonene oxidation. *Atmospheric Environment* 40:7882-7892.

Verschueren, K. 1996. *Handbook of environmental data on organic chemicals*, 3rd ed. Van Nostrand Reinhold, New York.

Vesper, S.J., C. McKinstry, R.A. Haugland, Y. Iossifova, G. LeMasters, L. Levin, G.K.K. Hershey, M. Villareal, D.I. Bernstein, and T. Reponen. 2007. Relative moldiness index as predictor of childhood respiratory illness. *Journal of Exposure Science and Environmental Epidemiology* 17:88-94.

Wallace, L. 1996. Indoor particles: A review. *Journal of the Air Waste Management Association* 46:98-126.

Wallace, L.A., E. Pellizzari, and C. Wendel. 1991. Total volatile organic concentrations in 2700 personal, indoor, and outdoor air samples collected in the US EPA Team Studies. *Indoor Air* 4:465-477.

Wang, H., and G.C. Morrison. 2006. Ozone-initiated secondary emission rates of aldehydes from indoor surfaces in four homes. *Environmental Science and Technology* 40:5263-5268.

Weschler, C.J. 2000. Ozone in indoor environments: Concentration and chemistry. *Indoor Air* 10:269-288.

Weschler, C.J., and W.W. Nazaroff. 2008. Semivolatile organic compounds in indoor environments. *Atmospheric Environment* 42(40):9018-9040.

Weschler, C.J., and W.W. Nazaroff. 2010. SVOC partitioning between the gas phase and settled dust indoors. *Atmospheric Environment* 44(30):3609-3620.

Weschler, C.J., and H.C. Shields. 1999. Indoor ozone/terpene reactions as a source of indoor particles. *Atmospheric Environment* 33:2301-2312.

Weschler, C.J., H.C. Shields, and D.V. Naik. 1989. Indoor ozone exposures. *Journal of the Air Pollution Control Association* 39:1562-1568.

Whitby, K.T. 1978. The physical characteristics of sulfur aerosols. *Atmospheric Environment* 12:135-159.

WHO. 1989. Indoor air quality: Organic pollutants. *Euro Report and Studies* 111. World Health Organization, Regional Office for Europe, Copenhagen.

Wilkins, C.K., P. Wolkoff, F. Gyntelberg, P. Skov, and O. Valbjørn. 1993. Characterization of office dust by VOCs and TVOC release—Identification of potential irritant VOCs by partial least squares analysis. *Indoor Air* 3:283-290.

Willeke, K., and P.A. Baron, eds. 1993. *Aerosol measurement—Principles, techniques and applications*. Van Nostrand Reinhold, New York.

Williams, R., J. Suggs, R. Zweidinger, G. Evans, J. Creason, R. Kwok, C. Rodes, P. Lawless, and L. Sheldon. 2000. The 1998 Baltimore Particulate Matter Epidemiology—Exposure Study: Part 1. Comparison of Ambient, Residential Outdoor, Indoor and Apartment Particulate Matter Monitoring. *Journal of Exposure Analysis and Environmental Epidemiology* 10(6 Part 1):518-532.

Wilson, W.E., and H.H. Suh. 1997. Fine particles and coarse particles: Concentration relationships relevant to epidemiological studies. *Journal of the Air and Waste Management Association* 47(12):1238-1249.

Wolkoff, P., and C.K. Wilkins. 1994. Indoor VOCs from household floor dust: Comparison of headspace with desorbed VOCs; method for VOC release determination. *Indoor Air* 4:248-254.

Wood, J.A., and M.L. Porter. 1987. Hazardous pollutants in class II landfills. *Journal of the Air Pollution Control Association* 37:609-615.

Worthan, A.W., and M.S. Black. 1999. Emissions from office equipment. *International Conference on Digital Printing Technologies*, pp. 459-462.

Wright, C.G., and R.B. Leidy. 1982. Chlordane and heptachlor in the ambient air of houses treated for termites. *Bulletin of Environmental Contaminant Toxicology* 28:617-623.

Yang, S., and R.E. Rothman. 2004. PCR-based diagnostics for infectious diseases: Uses, limitations, and future applications in acute-care settings. *The Lancet Infectious Diseases* 4(6):337-348.

Yang, X., J. Zhang, and Q. Deng. 2010. Modeling VOC sorption of building materials and its impact on indoor air quality. ASHRAE Research Project RP-1321, *Final Report*.

BIBLIOGRAPHY

ACGIH. 1985. *Particle size-selective sampling in the workplace*. American Conference of Governmental Industrial Hygienists, Cincinnati, OH.

Apte, M.G., I.S.H. Buchanan, and M.J. Mendell. 2007/2008. Outdoor ozone and building related symptoms in the base study. *Indoor Air* 18(2).

ASHRAE. 2016. Designation and safety classification of refrigerants. ANSI/ASHRAE *Standard* 34-2016.

ASTM. 1990. Biological contaminants in indoor environments. *Special Technical Publication* STP 1071. American Society for Testing and Materials, West Conshohocken, PA.

Barbaree, J.M., B.S. Fields, J.C. Feeley, G.W. Gorman, and W.T. Martin. 1986. Isolation of protozoa from water associated with a Legionellosis outbreak and demonstration of intracellular multiplication of *Legionella pneumophila*. *Applied Environmental Microbiology* 51:422-424.

Buchanan I.S.H, M.J. Mendell, A. Mirer, and M.G. Apte. 2008. Air filter materials, outdoor ozone and building-related symptoms in the BASE study. *Indoor Air* 18(2).

Burge, H.A. 1995. *Bioaerosols*. Lewis, Chelsea, MA.

Code of Federal Regulations. Annual. Occupational safety and health standards. 29CFR1900. *Code of Federal Regulations*, U.S. Government Printing Office, Washington, D.C.

EPA. 1982. *Air quality criteria for particulate matter and sulfur*. EPA-600/8-82-029b.

EPA. 1999. *Indoor air quality for schools: Actions to improve indoor air quality*. EPA 402-F-99-008.

EPA. 2009. Integrated science assessment for particulate matter. *Final Report*. Environmental Protection Agency, Office of Research and Development, Washington, D.C. cfpub.epa.gov/ncea/risk/recordisplay.cfm?deid=216546.

Fliermans, C.B. 1985. Ecological niche of *Legionella pneumophila*. *Critical Reviews of Microbiology* 11:75-116.

Hodgson, A.T., K. Garbesi, R.G. Sextro, and J.M. Daisey. 1988. Transport of volatile organic compounds from soil into a residential basement. *Paper* 88-95B.1, *Proceedings of the 81st Annual Meeting of the Air Pollution Control Association*. Air Pollution Control Association, Pittsburgh, PA. Also LBL *Report* 25267. Lawrence Berkeley National Laboratory, CA.

Milton, D.K., R.J. Gere, H.A. Feldman, and I.A. Greaves. 1990. Endotoxin measurement: Aerosol sampling and application of a new limulus method. *American Industrial Hygiene Association Journal* 51:331.

CHAPTER 12

ODORS

VARIOUS factors make odor control an important consideration in ventilation engineering: (1) contemporary construction methods result in buildings that allow less air infiltration through the building envelope; (2) indoor sources of odors associated with modern building materials, furnishings, and office equipment have increased; (3) outdoor air is often polluted; and (4) energy costs encourage lower ventilation rates at a time when requirements for a relatively odor-free environment are greater than ever.

Since Yaglou et al.'s (1936) classic studies, the philosophy behind ventilation of nonindustrial buildings has mainly been to provide indoor air that is acceptable to occupants. Air is evaluated by the olfactory sense, although the general chemical sense, which is sensitive to irritants in the air, also plays a role.

This chapter reviews how odoriferous substances are perceived. Chapter 46 of the 2015 *ASHRAE Handbook—HVAC Applications* covers control methods. Chapter 10 of this volume has more information on indoor environmental health.

1. ODOR SOURCES

Outdoor sources of odors include automotive and diesel exhausts, hazardous waste sites, sewage treatment plants, compost piles, refuse facilities, printing plants, refineries, chemical plants, and many other stationary and mobile sources. These sources produce both inorganic compounds (e.g., ammonia and hydrogen sulfide) and volatile organic compounds (VOCs), including some that evaporate from solid or liquid particulate matter. Odors emitted by outdoor sources eventually enter the indoor environment.

Indoor sources also emit odors. Sources include tobacco products, bathrooms and toilets, building materials (e.g., adhesives, paints, caulks, processed wood, carpets, plastic sheeting, insulation board), consumer products (e.g., food, toiletries, cleaning materials, polishes), hobby materials, fabrics, and foam cushions. In offices, offset printing processes, copiers, and computer printers may produce odors. Electrostatic processes may emit ozone. Humans emit a wide range of odorants, including acetaldehyde, ammonia, ethanol, hydrogen sulfide, and mercaptans.

Mildew and other decay processes often produce odors in occupied spaces (home and office), damp basements, and ventilation systems (e.g., from wetted air-conditioning coils and spray dehumidifiers).

Chapter 46 of the 2015 *ASHRAE Handbook—HVAC Applications* gives further information on contaminant sources and generation rates.

2. SENSE OF SMELL

Olfactory Stimuli

Organic substances with molecular weights greater than 300 are generally odorless. Some substances with molecular weights less than 300 are such potent olfactory stimuli that they can be perceived at concentrations too low to be detected with direct-reading instruments. Trimethylamine, for example, can be recognized as a fishy odor by a human at a concentration of about 10^{-4} ppm.

Table 1 shows **odor detection threshold concentrations** for selected compounds. The **threshold limit value** (TLV) is the concentration of a compound that should have no adverse health consequences if a worker is regularly exposed for 8 h periods (ACGIH, revised annually). Table 1 also includes the ratio of the TLV to the odor threshold for each compound. For ratios greater than 1, most occupants can detect the odor and leave the area long before the compound becomes a health risk. As the ratio increases, the safety factor provided by the odor also increases. Table 1 is not a comprehensive list of the chemicals found in indoor air. AIHA (1989) and EPA (1992) list odor thresholds for selected chemicals.

Olfactory sensitivity often makes it possible to detect potentially harmful substances at concentrations below dangerous levels so that they can be eliminated. Foul-smelling air is often assumed to be unhealthy. In reality, however, there is little correlation between odor perception and toxicity, and there is considerable individual variation in the perception of pleasantness/unpleasantness of odors. When symptoms such as nausea, headache, and loss of appetite are caused by an unpleasant odor, it may not matter whether the air is toxic but whether the odor is perceived to be unpleasant, associated

Table 1 Odor Thresholds, ACGIH TLVs, and TLV/Threshold Ratios of Selected Gaseous Air Pollutants

Compound	Odor Threshold,[a] ppmv	TLV,[b] ppmv	Ratio
Acetaldehyde	0.067	25-C	360
Acetone	62	500	8.1
Acetonitrile	1600	20	0.013
Acrolein	1.8	0.1-C	0.06
Ammonia	17	25	1.5
Benzene	61	0.5	0.01
Benzyl chloride	0.041	1	24
Carbon tetrachloride	250	5	0.02
Chlorine	0.08	0.5	6
Chloroform	192	10	0.05
Dioxane	12	20	1.7
Ethylene dichloride	26	10	0.4
Hydrogen sulfide	0.0094	10	1064
Methanol	160	200	1.25
Methylene chloride	160	50	0.3
Methyl ethyl ketone	16	200	12.5
Phenol	0.06	5	83
Sulfur dioxide	2.7	2	0.74
Tetrachloroethane	7.3	1	0.14
Tetrachloroethylene	47	25	0.5
Toluene	1.6	20	13
Trichloroethylene	82	10	0.1
Xylene (isomers)	20	100	5

Sources: ACGIH (updated annually), AIHA (1989).
[a]All thresholds are detection thresholds (ED_{50}).
[b]All TLVs are 8 h time-weighted averages, except those shown with -C, which are 15 min ceiling values.

The preparation of this chapter is assigned to TC 2.3, Gaseous Air Contaminants and Gas Contaminant Removal Equipment.

with an unpleasant experience, or simply felt to be out of appropriate context. The magnitude of the symptoms is related to the magnitude of the odor, but even a room with a low but recognizable odor can make occupants uneasy. Several papers review sensory irritation and its relation to indoor air pollution (Cain and Cometto-Muñiz 1995; Cometto-Muñiz and Cain 1992; Cometto-Muñiz et al. 1997; Shams Esfandabad 1993).

Anatomy and Physiology

The **olfactory receptors** lie in the **olfactory cleft**, which is high in the nasal cavity. About five million olfactory **neurons** (a small cluster of nerve cells inside the nasal cavity above the bridge of the nose) each send an **axon** (an extension of the neuron) into the olfactory bulb of the brain. Information received from the receptors is passed to various central structures of the brain (e.g., olfactory cortex, hippocampus, amygdala). One sniff of an odorant can often evoke a complex, emotion-laden memory, such as a scene from childhood.

The surrounding nasal tissue contains other diffusely distributed nerve endings of the trigeminal nerve that also respond to airborne vapors. These receptors mediate the chemosensory responses such as tickling, burning, cooling, and, occasionally, painful sensations that accompany olfactory sensations. Most odorous substances at sufficient concentration also stimulate these nerve endings.

Olfactory Acuity

The olfactory acuity of the population is normally distributed. Most people have an average ability to smell substances or to respond to odoriferous stimuli, a few people are very sensitive or hypersensitive, and a few others are insensitive, including some who are totally unable to smell (**anosmic**). The olfactory acuity of an individual varies with the odorant.

Hormonal factors, which often influence emotional states, can modulate olfactory sensitivity. Although the evidence is not uniformly compelling, research has found that (1) the sensitivity of females varies during the menstrual cycle, reaching a peak just before and during ovulation (Schneider 1974); (2) females are generally more sensitive than males, but this difference only emerges around the time of sexual maturity (Koelega and Koster 1974); (3) sensitivity is altered by some diseases (Schneider 1974); and (4) various hormones and drugs (e.g., estrogen, alcohol) alter sensitivity (Engen et al. 1975; Schneider 1974).

Other factors that may affect olfactory perception include the individual's olfactory acuity, the magnitude of flow rate toward olfactory receptors, temperature, and relative humidity. Olfactory acuity can also vary with age (Stevens et al. 1989; Wysocki and Gilbert 1989), genetics (Wysocki and Beauchamp 1984), exposure history (Dalton and Wysocki 1996; Wysocki et al. 1997), and disease or injury (Cowart et al. 1993, 1997). Humans are able to perceive a large number of odors, yet untrained individuals are able to name only a few (Ruth 1986).

Individuals who are totally unable to detect odors are relatively rare (Cowart et al. 1997). A more common occurrence is an inability to detect one or a very limited number of odors, a condition known as **specific anosmia**. Although the huge number of possible chemicals makes for an untestable hypothesis, it has been posited that most, if not all, individuals have a specific anosmia to one or more compounds (Wysocki and Beauchamp 1984). The fact that individuals with specific anosmias have normal olfactory acuity for all other odors suggests that such anosmias may be caused by genetic differences.

In olfactory science, **adaptation** refers to decreased sensitivity or responsiveness to an odor after prolonged exposure. This exposure can selectively impair the perception of the exposure odorant, but there are also examples of cross-adaptation, where exposure to one odorant can result in adaptation to other odors as well. Adaptation can occur in the short term, where perception of a room's odor begins to fade within seconds of entering the room (Cometto-Muñiz and Cain 1995; Pierce et al. 1996). With long-term adaptation, an individual who habitually returns to the same environment does not smell odors that are quite discernible to a naive observer. This effect appears to shift both the threshold and the **suprathreshold** (stimuli above the threshold level) response to the odor (Dalton and Wysocki 1996). This is an important phenomenon for indoor air quality (IAQ) personnel to be aware of because it is often one of the biggest reasons for variations in detectability or response in real-world environments and makes the choice of test population or panelists for air quality evaluations a critical one.

3. FACTORS AFFECTING ODOR PERCEPTION

Humidity and Temperature

Temperature and humidity can both affect the perception of odors. Cain et al. (1983) reported that a combination of high temperature (78°F) and high humidity exacerbates odor problems. Berglund and Cain (1989) found that air was generally perceived to be fresher and less stuffy with decreasing temperature and humidity. Fang et al. (1998a, 1998b) and Toftum et al. (1998) found little or no increase in odor intensity with increasing enthalpy (temperature and humidity), but reported a very significant decrease in odor acceptability with increasing enthalpy.

Not all researchers have supported these findings. Kerka and Humphreys (1956) reported a decrease in odor intensity with increasing humidity. Berg-Munch and Fanger (1982) found no increase in odor intensity with increasing temperature (73.5 to 89.5°F). Clausen et al. (1985) found no significant change in odor intensity with increasing relative humidity (30% to 80%).

Although the findings are not homogeneous, they do show that temperature and humidity can act together to affect one's perception of odors. Air that is cooler and drier is generally perceived to be fresher and more acceptable even if odor intensity is not affected.

Sorption and Release of Odors

Because furnishings and interior surfaces absorb (and later desorb) odors during occupancy, spaces frequently retain normal occupancy odor levels long after occupancy has ceased. This is observed when furnaces or radiators, after a long shutdown, are heated at winter start-up and when evaporator coils warm up. The rate of desorption can be decreased by decreasing temperature and relative humidity, and increased (as for cleaning) by the reverse.

Environmental tobacco smoke may desorb from surfaces long after smoking has taken place. This phenomenon has caused many hotels to establish nonsmoking rooms.

Where the odor source is intrinsic to the materials (as in linoleum, paint, rubber, and upholstery), reducing the relative humidity decreases the rate of odor release. Quantitative values should not be used without considering the sorption/desorption phenomenon.

Emotional Responses to Odors

There can be considerable variation between individuals regarding the perceived pleasantness or unpleasantness of a given odor. Responses to odors may be determined by prior experiences and can include strong emotional reactions. This is because one of the brain structures involved in the sense of smell is the **amygdala**, a regulator of emotional behaviors (Frey 1995). Some IAQ complaints can involve emotional responses completely out of proportion to the concentration of the odorant or the intensity of the odor it produces.

Two theories describe physiological reasons for these strong responses. One of these is **kindling**, in which repeated, intermittent stimuli amplify nerve responses. The other is **response facilitation**, in which an initial stimulus perceived as strong is facilitated (becomes greater) rather than adapted to (Frey 1995).

Because of this emotional aspect, IAQ complaints involving odors can be very difficult to solve, especially if they are coming from a few sensitized individuals. It is important to respond quickly to complaints to minimize the risk of kindling or response facilitation.

4. ODOR SENSATION ATTRIBUTES

Odor sensation has four components or attributes: detectability, intensity, character, and hedonic tone.

Detectability (or **threshold**) is the minimum concentration of an odorant that provokes detection by some predetermined segment of the population. Two types of thresholds exist: detection and recognition.

The **detection threshold** is the lowest level that elicits response by a segment of the population. If that segment is 50%, the detection threshold is denoted by ED_{50}. **Recognition threshold** is the lowest level at which a segment of the population can recognize a given odor. Thresholds can be attributed to 100%, which includes all olfactory sensitivities, or to 10%, which includes only the most sensitive segment of the population. Threshold values are not physical constants, but statistical measurements of best estimates.

Intensity is a quantitative aspect of a descriptive analysis, stating the degree or magnitude of the perception elicited. Intensity of the perceived odor is, therefore, the strength of the odoriferous sensation. Detection threshold values and, most often, odor intensity determine the need for indoor odor controls.

Character defines the odor as similar to some familiar smell (e.g., fishy, sour, flowery). **Hedonics**, or the hedonic tone of an odor, is the degree to which an odor is perceived as pleasant or unpleasant. Hedonic judgments include both a *category* judgment (pleasant, neutral, unpleasant) and a *magnitude* judgment (very unpleasant, slightly pleasant).

Important questions are

- What is the minimum concentration of odorant that can be detected?
- How does perceived odor magnitude grow with concentration above the threshold?

No universal method has been accepted to measure either the threshold or perceived magnitude of the odor above threshold. However, guidelines and conventions simplify the choice of methods.

Detectability

Perception of weak odoriferous signals is probabilistic: at one moment odor may be perceptible, and at the next moment it may not. Factors affecting this phenomenon include moment-to-moment variability in the number of molecules striking the olfactory receptors, variability in which of the receptors are stimulated, concentration of the odor, the individual's style of breathing, and the individual's previous experience with the odor. The combined effect of these factors may prevent an individual from perceiving an odor during the entire time of the stimulus. During odor evaluation, dilution to detection or recognition threshold values allows determination of the largest number of dilutions that still allows half of the panelists to detect or recognize the odor.

Determination of Odor Thresholds. Odor threshold testing is over a century old. The process is complex, and several different methods are used. Partly because of variations in measurement techniques, reported threshold values can vary by several orders of magnitude for a given substance. To minimize variation caused by experimental techniques, a standard set of criteria has been developed for the panel, presentation apparatus, and presentation method (AIHA 1989; EPA 1992).

The **panel** should

- Include at least six members per group.
- Be selected based on odor sensitivity. Factors to be considered include anosmia, pregnancy, drug use, and smoking.
- Be calibrated to document individual and group variability.

Considerations for the **presentation apparatus** include

- Vapor modality: choice of a gas/air mixture, water vapor, or other substance.
- Diluent: choice of diluent (e.g., air, nitrogen), how it is treated, and what its source is.
- Presentation mode: delivery systems can be nose ports, vents into which the head is inserted, flasks, or whole rooms.
- Analytic measurement of odorant concentration.
- System calibration: flow rate should be approximately 0.1 cfm; face velocity should be low enough to be barely perceptible to the panelists.

Criteria for the **presentation method** include

- Threshold type: detection or recognition.
- Concentration presentation: this must take adaptation into account. Presenting ascending concentrations or allowing longer periods between concentrations helps avoid adaptation.
- Number of trials: test/retest reliability for thresholds is low. Increasing the number of trials helps correct for this.
- Forced-choice procedure: panelists must choose between the stimuli and one or two blanks. This helps eliminate false positive responses.
- Concentration steps: odorant should be presented successively at concentrations no more than three times the preceding one.

For more details regarding psychophysical procedures, ways to sample odoriferous air, handling samples, means of stimulus presentation, and statistical procedures, consult ASTM (1996).

Intensity

Psychophysical Power Law. The relation between **perceived odor magnitude *S*** and **concentration *C*** conforms to a power function:

$$S = kC^n \tag{1}$$

where

S = perceived intensity (magnitude) of sensation
k = characteristic constant
C = odorant concentration
n = exponent of psychophysical function (slope on a log-log scale)

This exemplifies the psychophysical power law, also called **Stevens' law** (Stevens 1957). In the olfactory realm, $n < 1.0$. Accordingly, a given percentage change in odorant concentration causes a smaller percentage change in perceived odor magnitude.

Scaling Methods. There are various ways to scale perceived magnitude, but a **category scale**, which can be either number- or word-categorized, is common. Numerical values on this scale do not reflect ratio relations among magnitudes (e.g., a value of 2 does not represent a perceived magnitude twice as great as a value of 1). Table 2 gives four examples of category scales.

Although category scaling procedures can be advantageous in the field, **ratio scaling** is used frequently in the laboratory (Cain and Moskowitz 1974). Ratio scaling requires observers to assign numbers proportional to perceived magnitude. For example, if the observer is instructed to assign the number 10 to one concentration and a subsequently presented concentration seems three times as strong, the observer calls it 30; if another seems half as strong, the observer assigns it 5. This procedure, called **magnitude estimation**, was used to derive the power function for butanol (Figure 1). Ratio scaling techniques allow for such relationships because they require subjects to produce numbers to match perceived sensations in which the numbers emitted reflect the ratio relations among the sensations.

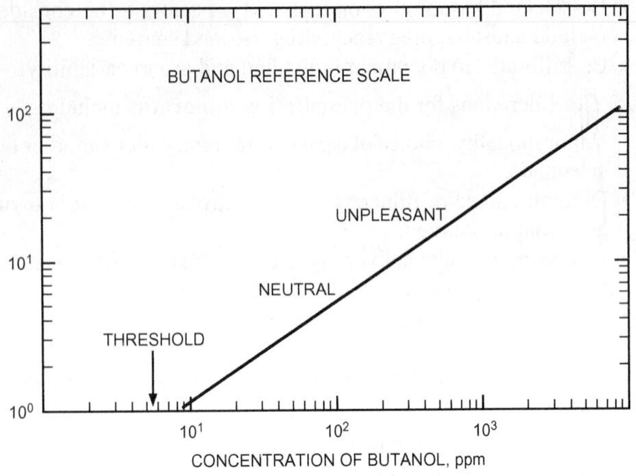

Fig. 1 Standardized Function Relating Perceived Magnitude to Concentration of 1-Butanol
(Moskowitz et al. 1974)

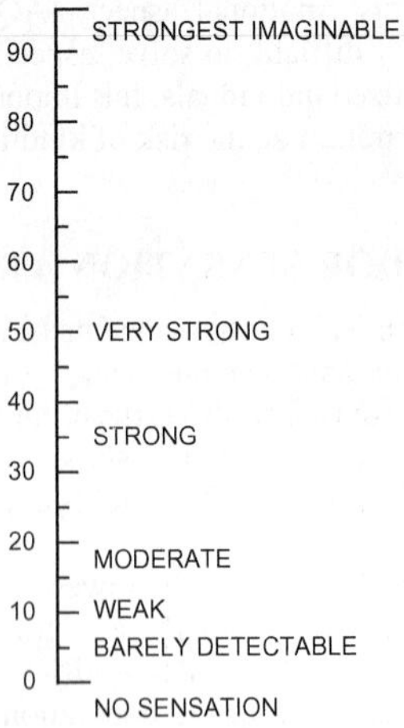

Subjects use a cursor (on a computer screen) or a pencil to mark the location on the scale that represents their judgment of intensity. They do not see numbers, only labels, and can place the mark anywhere on the scale.

Fig. 2 Labeled Magnitude Scale

Table 2 Examples of Category Scales

Number Category		Word Category	
Scale I	Scale II	Scale I	Scale II
0	0	None	None at all
1	1	Threshold	Just detectable
2	2.5	Very slight	Very mild
3	5	Slight	Mild
4	7.5	Slight-moderate	Mild-distinct
5	10	Moderate	Distinct
6	12.5	Moderate-strong	Distinct-strong
7	15	Strong	Strong

Source: Meilgaard et al. (1987).

The **labeled magnitude scale** is a hybrid of category and ratio scales (Green et al. 1996). This scale is intended to yield ratio-level data with a true zero and an orderly relationship among the scale values, such that any stimulus can be expressed as being proportionately more or less intense than another. Because it allows subjects to use natural-language descriptors to scale perceived experience, it often requires less training than ratio scales and produces absolute intensity estimates of perceived sensation (Figure 2).

A fourth way to measure suprathreshold odor intensity is to **match the intensity of odorants**. An observer can be given a concentration series of a matching odorant (e.g., 1-butanol) to choose the member that matches most closely the intensity of an *unknown* odorant. The matching odorant can be generated by a relatively inexpensive olfactometer such as that shown in Figure 3. Figure 4 shows, in logarithmic coordinates, functions for various odorants obtained by matching (Dravnieks and Laffort 1972). The left-hand ordinate expresses intensity in terms of concentration of butanol, and the right-hand ordinate expresses intensity in terms of perceived magnitude. The two ordinates are related by the function in Figure 1, the standardized function for butanol. The matching method illustrated here has been incorporated into ASTM *Standard* E544.

Character

The quality or character of an odor is difficult to assess quantitatively. A primary difficulty is that odors can vary along many dimensions. One way to assess quality is to ask panelists to judge the similarity between a test sample and various reference samples, using a five-point category scale. For some applications, reference odorants can be chosen to represent only the portion of the qualitative range relevant to the problem under investigation (e.g., animal odors). Another procedure is to ask panelists to assess the degree of

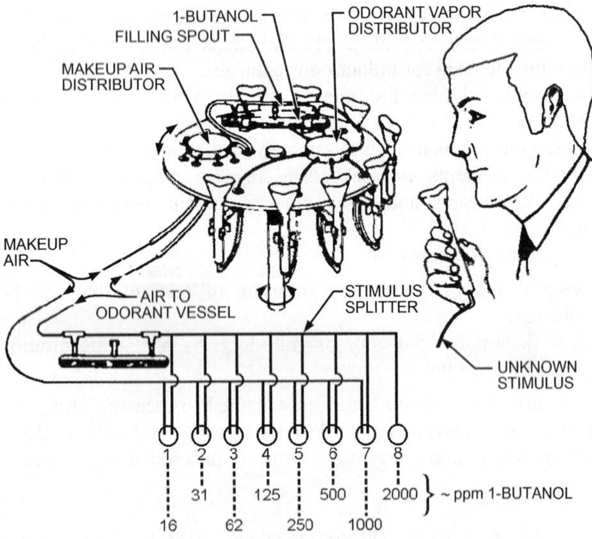

Fig. 3 Panelist Using Dravnieks Binary Dilution Olfactometer
(Dravnieks 1975)

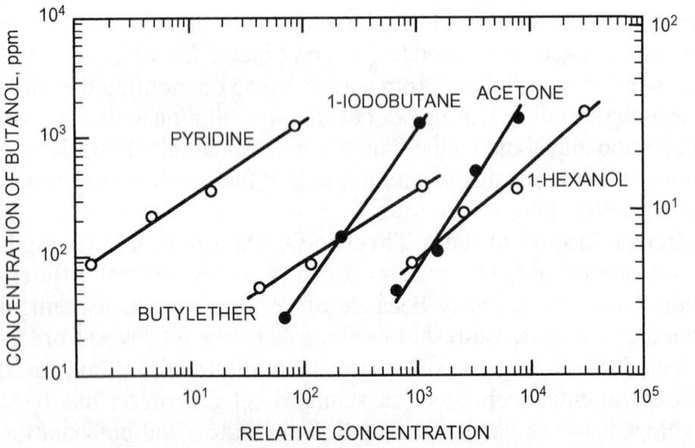

Fig. 4 Matching Functions Obtained with Dravnieks Olfactometer
(Cain 1978; Dravnieks and Laffort 1972)

association between a test sample's quality and certain verbal descriptors (e.g., sweaty, woody, chalky, sour).

The number of odorant descriptors and descriptors to be used have been subjects of disagreement (Harper et al. 1968). The number of descriptors varies from a minimum of seven (Amoore 1962) to as many as 830 used by an ASTM subcommittee. An atlas of odor characters, containing 146 descriptors, was compiled for 180 chemicals by ASTM (1985).

An odor can be characterized either by an open-ended word description or by multidimensional scaling. **Multidimensional scaling** is based on similarity and dissimilarity judgments in comparison to a set of standard odors or to various descriptors.

In some cases, the interest may be merely whether an odor's quality has changed as a result of some treatment (e.g., use of a bacteriostat). Under these circumstances, samples of air taken before and after treatment can be compared directly (using a simple scale of similarity) or indirectly (with appropriate verbal descriptors).

Hedonics

The acceptability or pleasantness of an odor can be measured psychophysically in the same way as odor intensity. Both ratio and category scaling procedures can be adapted to odor acceptability.

Odors do not always cause adverse reactions. Products are manufactured to elicit favorable responses. Acceptance tests may involve product comparison (frequently used in the perfume industry) or a hedonic scale. The premise of acceptance tests is that the larger the segment of subjects accepting the odor, the better the odor. A hedonic scale that allows for negative as well as positive responses is likely to better determine how acceptable the odor is.

All persons exposed to a given odor are not likely to agree on its acceptability. Acceptability of a given odor to a person is based on a complex combination of associations and is not simply a characteristic of the odor itself (Beck and Day 1991). Responses to odors are determined by both **bottom-up factors** (attributes or properties of the odorant) and **top-down factors** (expectations, attitudes, and associations from prior experience stored in memory, and appropriateness of the odor in its present context). Both factors are activated when an individual detects an odor, and the individual's ultimate response (e.g., perception of intensity, hedonics, irritation, or symptoms) is a joint function of both (Dalton 1996; Dalton et al. 1997). In some cases, the interpretation provided by the top-down process appears to override the outcome from the bottom-up process, resulting in complaints, symptoms, and reports of illness.

5. DILUTION OF ODORS BY VENTILATION

The size of the exponent n in Stevens' law [Equation (1)] varies from one odorant to another, ranging from less than 0.2 to about 0.7 (Cain and Moskowitz 1974). This determines the **slope** or **dose response** of the odor intensity/odorant concentration function and has important consequences for malodor control. A low slope value indicates an odor that requires greater relative dilution for the odor to dissipate; a high slope value indicates an odor that can be more quickly reduced by ventilation. For example, an exponent of 0.7 implies that, to reduce perceived intensity by a factor of 5, the concentration must be reduced by a factor of 10; an exponent of 0.2 would require a reduction in concentration by a factor of more than 3000 for the same reduction in perceived magnitude. Examples of compounds with low slope values include hydrogen sulfide, butyl acetate, and amines. Compounds with high slope values include ammonia and aldehydes.

The ability of ventilation to control odors also depends on the strength of the source generating the odorant(s) and the nature of the odor. An odorant with a stronger source requires proportionately more ventilation to achieve the same reduction in concentration. Odors that are perceived as unpleasant may require substantially greater reduction before being perceived as acceptable. In addition, some sources, such as painted walls and flooring materials, may show increased emission rates in response to increased ventilation rates, which further complicates the issue (Gunnarsen 1997).

6. ODOR CONCENTRATION

Analytical Measurement

Performance data on control of specific odorants can be obtained using suitable analytical methods. Detectors can sense substances in amounts as little as 1 ng. Air contains many minor components, so gas chromatographic separation of the components must precede detection. Because odor thresholds for some compounds are low, preconcentration of the minor components is necessary. **Preconcentration** consists of adsorption or absorption by a stable, sufficiently nonvolatile material, followed by thermal desorption or extraction. NIOSH (1993) reviews techniques for sampling and analysis of VOCs in indoor air.

Mass spectrometry can be used with **gas chromatography** to identify constituents of complex mixtures. The chromatograph resolves a mixture into its constituents, and the spectrometer provides identification and concentration of selected constituents.

Several other detectors are sufficiently sensitive and specific to detect resolved components. **Hydrogen flame ionization detectors** respond adequately and nearly mass-proportionally to almost all hydrocarbons, though their responses to organic chemicals containing other atoms (e.g., oxygen) are more variable. **Flame photometric detectors** can pinpoint with equal sensitivity compounds that contain sulfur; many sulfur compounds are strongly odorous and are of interest in odor work. A **Coulson conductometric detector** is specifically and adequately sensitive to ammonia and organic nitrogen compounds. **Thermal conductivity detectors** are generally not sensitive enough for analytical work on odors.

Frequently, a **sniffing port** (Dravnieks and Krotoszynski 1969; Dravnieks and O'Donnell 1971) is installed in parallel with the detector(s). Part of the resolved effluent exhausts through the port and allows components that are particularly odorous or carry some relevant odor quality to be annotated. Usually, only a fraction of all components studied exhibits odors.

Airborne VOCs cause odors, but the correlation between indoor VOC concentrations and odor complaints in indoor environments is poor. Considerable work has been done on **artificial noses**, which may offer objective determination of odorants (Bartlett et al. 1997; Freund and Lewis 1995; Moy et al. 1994; Taubes 1996). However, because the physicochemical correlates of olfaction are poorly understood, no simple analytical means to predict an odorant's perceived quality and intensity exists. Moreover, because acceptability of an odorant depends strongly on context, it is unlikely that analytical instruments will supplant human evaluation.

Odor Units

Odor concentration can be expressed as the number of unit volumes that a unit volume of odorous sample occupies when diluted to the odor threshold with nonodorous air. If a sample of odorous air can be reduced to threshold by a tenfold dilution with pure air, the concentration of the original sample is said to be 10 odor units. Hence, odor units are equivalent to multiples of threshold concentrations. Odor units are not units of perceived magnitude.

Odor units are widely used to express legal limits for emission of odoriferous materials. For example, the law may state that a factory operation may not cause the ambient odor level to exceed 15 odor units. For every odorant (chemical), odor units and parts per million (ppm) are proportional. The proportionality constant varies from one odorant to another, depending on the number of ppm needed to evoke a threshold response. Perceived odor magnitude (intensity), however, does not grow proportionally with concentration expressed in ppm. Therefore, it cannot grow proportionally with concentration expressed in odor units. For example, a sample of 20 odor units is always perceived as less than twice as strong as a sample of 10 odor units. Moreover, because the psychophysical function (slope) varies from one odorant to another, samples of two odorants, each at 20 odor units, may have unequal perceived intensities.

Although odor units are not equivalent to units of perceived magnitude, they can be useful. Most indoor and outdoor contaminants are complex mixtures, so that the actual concentration of the odoriferous portion of a sample cannot be expressed with certainty. Thus, the odor unit is a useful measure of concentration of the mixture when evaluating, for example, the efficiency of a filter or ventilation system to remove or dilute the odor.

7. OLF UNITS

Sometimes IAQ scientists cannot successfully resolve complaints about air in offices, schools, and other nonindustrial environments. Customarily, complaints are attributed to elevated pollutant concentrations; frequently, however, such high concentrations are not found, yet complaints persist.

Assuming that the inability to find a difference between air pollutant levels in buildings with registered complaints and those without complaints is due to inadequacies of prevailing measurement techniques, Fanger and others changed the focus from chemical analysis to sensory analysis (Fanger 1987, 1988; Fanger et al. 1988). Fanger quantified air pollution sources by comparing them with a well-known source: a sedentary person in thermal comfort. A new unit, the **olf**, was defined as the emission rate of air pollutants (bioeffluents) from a standard person. A **decipol** is one olf ventilated at a rate of 20 cfm of unpolluted air.

To use these units, Fanger generated a curve that relates the percentage of persons dissatisfied with air polluted by human bioeffluents as a function of the outdoor air ventilation rate and obtained the following expression:

$$D = 395\exp(-3.66q^{0.36}) \quad \text{for} \quad q \geq 0.332$$
$$D = 100 \quad \text{for} \quad q < 0.332 \qquad (2)$$

where

D = percentage of persons dissatisfied
q = ventilation/emission ratio, cfm per olf

This curve (Figure 5) is based on experiments involving more than 1000 European subjects (Fanger and Berg-Munch 1983). Experiments with American (Cain et al. 1983) and Japanese (Iwashita et al. 1990) subjects show very similar results.

The idea behind the olf is to express both human and nonhuman sensory sources in a single unit: equivalent standard persons (i.e., in olfs). A room should therefore be ventilated to handle the total sensory load from persons and building. The olf concept is used in European publications for ventilation (CEN 1998; ECA 1992) to determine required ventilation and in several national standards, including the Norwegian Building Code. Table 3 shows the sensory loads from different pollution sources used in CEN (1998).

Example. Office, low-polluting building, occupancy 0.007 persons/ft².

Occupants	0.007 olf/ft²
Building	0.01 olf/ft²
Total sensory load	0.017 olf/ft²

30% dissatisfied requires 8 cfm per olf ventilation rate (Figure 5).
Required ventilation: 8 × 0.017 = 0.14 cfm/ft².

The sensory load on the air in a space can be determined from Figure 5 by measuring the outdoor ventilation rate and determining the percent dissatisfied, using an untrained panel with a minimum of

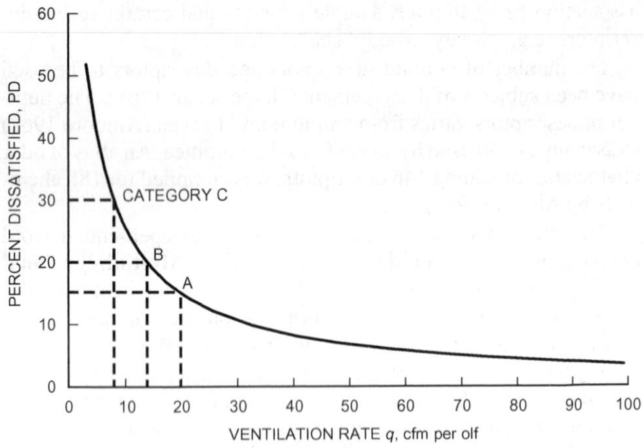

Fig. 5 Percentage of Dissatisfied Persons as a Function of Ventilation Rate per Standard Person (i.e., per Olf)
(CEN 1998)

Table 3 Sensory Pollution Load from Different Pollution Sources

Source	Sensory Load
Sedentary person (1 to 1.5 met)	1 olf
Person exercising	
Low level (3 met)	4 olf
Medium level (6 met)	10 olf
Children, kindergarten (3 to 6 yrs)	1.2 olf
Children, school (4 to 16 yrs)	1.3 olf
Low-polluting building	0.01 olf/ft²
Non-low-polluting building	0.02 olf/ft²

Source: CEN (1998).

20 impartial persons (Gunnarsen and Fanger 1992). The panel judges the acceptability of the air just after entering the space. The required ventilation rate depends on the desired percentage of occupant satisfaction. In ASHRAE *Standard* 62.1, 80% acceptability (20% dissatisfied) is the goal; European guidelines offer three quality levels: 15%, 20%, and 30% dissatisfied.

Although this system has much to offer from a theoretical standpoint, its use is controversial in some areas. Problems have been found in cultural differences among panel members and access to outdoor air for dilution (Aizlewood et al. 1996). The trend is now to use untrained panels, as described in the previous paragraph. Knudsen et al. (1998) showed that, for some building materials, the curve giving the relation between percent dissatisfied and ventilation rate is less steep than that in Figure 5, whereas it is steeper for others. The sensory load in this case depends on the ventilation rate. The constant sensory loads in Table 3 should therefore be seen as a first approximation.

REFERENCES

ASHRAE members can access *ASHRAE Journal* articles and ASHRAE research project final reports at technologyportal .ashrae.org. Articles and reports are also available for purchase by nonmembers in the online ASHRAE Bookstore at www.ashrae.org /bookstore.

ACGIH. Annually. *TLVs® and BEIs®*. American Conference of Governmental Industrial Hygienists, Cincinnati, OH.

AIHA. 1989. *Odor thresholds for chemicals with established occupational health standards*. American Industrial Hygiene Association, Akron, OH.

Aizlewood, C.E., G.J Raw, and N.A. Oseland. 1996. Decipols: Should we use them? *Indoor Built Environment* 5:263-269.

Amoore, J.E. 1962. The stereochemical theory of olfaction, 1: Identification of seven primary odors. *Proceedings of the Scientific Section of the Toilet Goods Association* 37:1-12.

ASHRAE. 2016. Ventilation for acceptable indoor air quality. ANSI/ ASHRAE *Standard* 62.1-2016.

ASTM. 1985. Atlas of odor character profiles. *Data Series* 61. American Society for Testing and Materials, West Conshohocken, PA.

ASTM. 1996. Sensory testing methods, 2nd ed. E. Chambers IV and M.B. Wolf, eds. *Document* MNL26-EB. American Society for Testing and Materials, West Conshohocken, PA.

ASTM. 2004. Standard practices for referencing suprathreshold odor intensity. *Standard* E544-1999 (2004). American Society for Testing and Materials, West Conshohocken, PA.

Bartlett, P., J. Elliott, and J. Gardner. 1997. Electronic noses and their applications in the food industry. *Food Technology* 51(12):44-48.

Beck, L., and V. Day. 1991. New Jersey's approach to odor problems. *Transactions: Recent developments and current practices and odor regulations control and technology*, D.R. Derenzo and A. Gnyp, eds. Air and Waste Management Association, Pittsburgh, PA.

Berglund, L., and W.S. Cain. 1989. Perceived air quality and the thermal environment. *Proceedings of IAQ '89: The Human Equation: Health and Comfort*, San Diego, pp. 93-99.

Berg-Munch, B., and P.O. Fanger. 1982. The influence of air temperature on the perception of body odour. *Environment International* 8:333-335.

Cain, W.S. 1978. The odoriferous environment and the application of olfactory research. In *Handbook of perception*, vol. 6, *Tasting and smelling*, pp. 197-199, C.C. Carterette and M.P. Friedman, eds. Academic Press, New York.

Cain, W.S., and J.E. Cometto-Muñiz. 1995. Irritation and odors as indicators of indoor pollution. *Occupational Medicine* 10(1):133-135.

Cain, W.S., and H.R. Moskowitz. 1974. Psychophysical scaling of odor. In *Human responses to environmental odors*, pp. 1-32, A. Turk, J.W. Johnston, and D.G. Moulton, eds. Academic Press, New York.

Cain, W.S., B.P. Leaderer, R. Isseroff, L.G. Berglund, R.I. Huey, E.D. Lipsitt, and D. Perlman. 1983. Ventilation requirements in buildings—I: Control of occupancy odor and tobacco smoke odor. *Atmospheric Environment* 17:1183-1197.

CEN. 1998. Ventilation for buildings: Design criteria for the indoor environment. *Technical Report* CR1752. European Committee for Standardization, Brussels.

Clausen, G., P.O Fanger, W.S. Cain, and B.P. Leaderer. 1985. The influence of aging particle filtration and humidity on tobacco smoke odour. *Proceedings of CLIMA 2000*, vol. 4, pp. 345-349. Copenhagen.

Cometto-Muñiz, J.E., and W.S. Cain. 1992. Sensory irritation, relation to indoor air pollution in sources of indoor air contaminants—Characterizing emissions and health effects. In *Annals of the New York Academy of Sciences*, vol. 641: *Sources of indoor air contaminants: Characterizing emissions and health impacts.*

Cometto-Muñiz, J.E., and W.S. Cain. 1995. Olfactory adaptation. In *Handbook of olfaction and gustation*, R.L. Doty, ed. Marcel Dekker, New York.

Cometto-Muñiz, J.E., W.S. Cain, and H.K. Hudnell. 1997. Agonistic sensory effects of airborne chemicals in mixtures: Odor, nasal pungency and eye irritation. *Perception and Psychophysics* 59(5):665-674.

Cowart, B.J., K. Flynn-Rodden, S.J. McGeady, and L.D. Lowry. 1993. Hyposmia in allergic rhinitis. *Journal of Allergy and Clinical Immunology* 91:747-751.

Cowart, B.J., I.M. Young, R.S. Feldman, and L.D. Lowry. 1997. Clinical disorders of smell and taste. *Occupational Medicine* 12:465-483.

Dalton, P. 1996. Odor perception and beliefs about risk. *Chemical Senses* 21:447-458.

Dalton, P., and C.J. Wysocki. 1996. The nature and duration of adaptation following long-term exposure to odors. *Perception & Psychophysics* 58(5):781-792.

Dalton, P., C.J. Wysocki, M.J. Brody, and H.J. Lawley. 1997. The influence of cognitive bias on the perceived odor, irritation and health symptoms from chemical exposure. *International Archives of Occupational and Environmental Health* 69:407-417.

Dravnieks, A. 1975. Evaluation of human body odors, methods and interpretations. *Journal of the Society of Cosmetic Chemists* 26:551.

Dravnieks, A., and., and B. Krotoszynski. 1969. Analysis and systematization of data for odorous compounds in air. *ASHRAE Symposium Bulletin: Odor and odorants: The engineering view.*

Dravnieks, A., and P. Laffort. 1972. Physicochemical basis of quantitative and qualitative odor discrimination in humans. *Olfaction and Taste IV: Proceedings of the Fourth International Symposium*, pp. 142-148. D. Schneider, ed. Wissenschaftliche Verlagsgesellschaft mbH, Stuttgart.

Dravnieks, A., and A. O'Donnell. 1971. Principles and some techniques of high resolution headspace analysis. *Journal of Agricultural and Food Chemistry* 19:1049.

ECA. 1992. Guidelines for ventilation requirements in buildings. European Collaborative Action *Indoor Air Quality and its Impact on Man*: *Report* 11. EUR 14449 EN. Office for Official Publications of the European Committees, Luxembourg.

Engen, T., R.A. Kilduff, and N.J. Rummo. 1975. The influence of alcohol on odor detection. *Chemical Senses and Flavor* 1:323.

EPA. 1992. *Reference guide to odor thresholds for hazardous air pollutants listed in the* Clean Air Act Amendments of 1990. EPA/600/R-92/047. Office of Research and Development, U.S. Environmental Protection Agency, Washington, D.C.

Fang, L., G. Clausen, and P.O. Fanger. 1998a. Impact of temperature and humidity on the perception of indoor air quality. *Indoor Air* 8(2):80-90.

Fang, L., G. Clausen, and P.O. Fanger. 1998b. Impact of temperature and humidity on perception of indoor air quality during immediate and longer whole-body exposures. *Indoor Air* 8(4):276-284.

Fanger, P.O. 1987. A solution to the sick building mystery. *Indoor Air '87, Proceedings of the International Conference on Indoor Air and Climate.* Institute of Water, Soil and Air Hygiene, Berlin.

Fanger, P.O. 1988. Introduction of the olf and decipol units to quantify air pollution perceived by humans indoors and outdoors. *Energy and Buildings* 12:1-6.

Fanger, P.O., and B. Berg-Munch. 1983. Ventilation and body odor. *Proceedings of Engineering Foundation Conference on Management of Atmospheres in Tightly Enclosed Spaces,* pp. 45-50. ASHRAE.

Fanger, P.O., J. Lauridsen, P. Bluyssen, and G. Clausen. 1988. Air pollution sources in offices and assembly halls quantified by the olf unit. *Energy and Buildings* 12:7-19.

Freund, M.S., and N.S. Lewis. 1995. A chemically diverse conduction polymer-based "electronic nose." *Proceedings of the National Academy of Sciences* 92:2652-2656.

Frey, A.F. 1995. A review of the nature of odour perception and human response. *Indoor Environment* 4:302-305.

Green, B.G., P. Dalton, B. Cowart, G. Shaffer, K.R. Rankin, and J. Higgins. 1996. Evaluating the "labeled magnitude scale" for measuring sensations of taste and smell. *Chemical Senses* 21(3):323-334.

Gunnarsen, L. 1997. The influence of area-specific rate on the emissions from construction products. *Indoor Air* 7:116-120.

Gunnarsen, L., and P.O. Fanger. 1992. Adaptation to indoor air pollution. *Energy and Buildings* 18:43-54.

Harper, R., E.C. Bate Smith, and D.G. Land. 1968. *Odour description and odour classification.* American Elsevier, New York. Distributors for Churchill Livingston Publishing, Edinburgh, Scotland.

Iwashita, G., K. Kimura, S. Tanabe, S. Yoshizawa, and K. Ikeda. 1990. Indoor air quality assessment based on human olfactory sensation. *Journal of Architecture, Planning and Environmental Engineering* 410:9-19.

Kerka, W.F., and C.M. Humphreys. 1956. Temperature and humidity effect on odour perception. *ASHRAE Transactions* 62:531-552.

Knudsen, H.N., O. Valbjørn, and P.A. Nielsen. 1998. Determination of exposure-response relationships for emissions from building products. *Indoor Air* 8(4):264-275.

Koelega, H.S., and E.P. Koster. 1974. Some experiments on sex differences in odor perception. In *Annals of the New York Academy of Sciences*, vol. 237: *Evaluation, Utilization, and Control*, p. 234.

Meilgaard, M., G.V. Civille, and B.T. Carr. 1987. *Sensory evaluation techniques.* CRC Press, Boca Raton, FL.

Moskowitz, H.R., A. Dravnieks, W.S. Cain, and A. Turk. 1974. Standardized procedure for expressing odor intensity. *Chemical Senses and Flavor* 1:235.

Moy, L., T. Tan, and J.W. Gardner. 1994. Monitoring the stability of perfume and body odors with an "electronic nose." *Perfumer and Flavorist* 19: 11-16.

NIOSH. 1993. Case studies—Indoor environmental quality "from the ground up." *Applied Occupational and Environmental Hygiene* 8: 677-680.

Norwegian Building Code. 1996. Oslo, Statens Hygningstekniske Eur.

Pierce, J.J.D., C.J. Wysocki, E.V. Aronov, J.B. Webb, and R.M. Boden. 1996. The role of perceptual and structural similarity in cross adaptation. *Chemical Senses* 21:223-227.

Ruth, J.H. 1986. Odor thresholds and irritation levels of several chemical substances: A review. *American Industrial Hygiene Association Journal* 47:142-151.

Schneider, R.A. 1974. Newer insights into the role and modifications of olfaction in man through clinical studies. In *Annals of the New York Academy of Sciences*, vol. 237: *Evaluation, Utilization, and Control*, p. 217.

Shams Esfandabad, H. 1993. *Perceptual analysis of odorous irritants in indoor air*. Ph.D. dissertation, Department of Psychology, Stockholm University.

Stevens, J.C., W.S. Cain, F.T. Schiet, and M.W. Oatley. 1989. Olfactory adaptation and recovery in old age. *Perception* 18(22):265-276.

Stevens, S.S. 1957. On the psychophysical law. *Psychological Review* 64:153.

Taubes, G. 1996. The electronic nose. *Discover* (September):40-50.

Toftum, J., A.S. Jørgensen, and P.O. Fanger. 1998. Upper limits for air humidity for preventing warm respiratory discomfort. *Energy and Buildings* 28(1):15-23.

Wysocki, C.J., and G.K. Beauchamp. 1984. Ability to smell androstenone is genetically determined. *Proceeding of the National Academy of Sciences of the United States of America* 81:4899-4902.

Wysocki, C.J., and A.N. Gilbert. 1989. *National Geographic* smell survey: Effects of age are heterogeneous. In *Annals of the New York Academy of Sciences*, vol. 561: *Nutrition and the Chemical Senses in Aging: Recent Advances and Current Research*, pp. 12-28. C.L. Murphy, W.S. Cain, and D.M. Hegsted, eds.

Wysocki, C.J., P. Dalton, P., M.J. Brody, and H.J. Lawley. 1997. Acetone odor and irritation thresholds obtained from acetone-exposed factory workers and from control (occupationally non-exposed) subjects. *American Industrial Hygiene Association Journal* 58:704-712.

Yaglou, C.P., E.C. Riley, and D.I. Coggins. 1936. Ventilation requirements. *ASHRAE Transactions* 42:133-162.

BIBLIOGRAPHY

ACGIH. 1988. *Advances in air sampling*. American Conference of Government Industrial Hygienists, Cincinnati, OH.

Clemens, J.B., and R.G. Lewis. 1988. Sampling for organic compounds. *Principles of Environmental Sampling* 20:147-157.

Moschandreas, D.J., and S.M. Gordon. 1991. Volatile organic compounds in the indoor environment: Review of characterization methods and indoor air quality studies. In *Organic chemistry of the atmosphere*. CRC Press, Boca Raton, FL.

CHAPTER 13

INDOOR ENVIRONMENTAL MODELING

THIS chapter presents two common indoor environmental modeling methods to calculate airflows and contaminant concentrations in buildings: computational fluid dynamics (CFD) and multizone network airflow modeling. Discussion of each method includes its mathematical background, practical modeling advice, model validation, and application examples.

Each modeling method has strengths and weaknesses for studying different aspects of building ventilation, energy, and indoor air quality (IAQ). CFD modeling can be used for a microscopic view of a building or its components by solving Navier-Stokes equations to obtain detailed flow field information and pollutant concentration distributions within a space. Its strengths include the rigorous application of fundamental fluid mechanics and the detailed nature of the airflow, temperature, and contaminant concentration results. However, these results require significant time, both for the analyst to create a model and interpret the results and for the computer to solve the equations. This time cost typically limits CFD to applications involving single rooms and steady-state solutions.

In contrast, multizone airflow and pollutant transport modeling can yield a macroscopic view of a building by solving a network of mass balance equations to obtain airflows and average pollutant concentrations in different zones of a whole building. This entire process takes much less time, making whole-building modeling, including various mechanical systems, possible over time periods as long as a year. This method's limitations include far less-detailed results (e.g., no internal-room airflow details, a single contaminant concentration for each room), which poorly approximate some modeling scenarios (e.g., atria, stratified rooms).

Although modeling software is widely available, successful application of either indoor environmental modeling method is still challenging. A strong grasp of fundamental building physics and detailed knowledge of the building space being modeled are both necessary. (Also see Chapters 1, 3, 4, 6, 9, 11, 16, and 24 of this volume.) Successful modeling also starts with planning that considers the project's objectives, resources, and available information. When modeling existing buildings, taking measurements may significantly improve the modeling effort. Modeling is particularly useful when known and unknown elements are combined, such as an existing building under unusual circumstances (e.g., fire, release of an airborne hazard). However, even for hypothetical buildings (e.g., in the design stage), knowledge gained from a good modeling effort can be valuable to planning and design efforts.

The preparation of this chapter is assigned to TC 4.10, Indoor Environmental Modeling.

1. COMPUTATIONAL FLUID DYNAMICS

Computational fluid dynamic (CFD) modeling quantitatively predicts thermal/fluid physical phenomena in an indoor space. The conceptual model interprets a specific problem of the indoor environment through a mathematical form of the conservation law and situation-specific information (boundary conditions). The governing equations remain the same for all indoor environment applications of airflow and heat transfer, but boundary conditions change for each specific problem: for example, room layout may be different, or speed of the supply air may change. In general, a boundary condition defines the physical problem at specific positions. Often, physical phenomena are complicated by simultaneous heat flows (e.g., heat conduction through the building enclosure, heat gains from heated indoor objects, solar radiation through building fenestration), phase changes (e.g., condensation and evaporation of water), chemical reactions (e.g., combustion), and mechanical movements (e.g., fans, occupant movements).

CFD involves solving coupled partial differential equations, which must be worked simultaneously or successively. No analytical solutions are available for indoor environment modeling. Computer-based numerical procedures are the only means of generating complete solutions of these sets of equations.

CFD code is more than just a numerical procedure of solving governing equations; it can be used to solve fluid flow, heat transfer, chemical reactions, and even thermal stresses. Unless otherwise implemented, CFD does not solve acoustics and lighting, which are also important parameters in indoor environment analysis. Different CFD codes have different capabilities: a simple code may solve only laminar flow, whereas a complicated one can handle a far more complex (e.g., compressible) flow.

Mathematical and Numerical Background

Airflow in natural and built environments is predominantly turbulent, characterized by randomness, diffusivity, dissipation, and relatively large Reynolds numbers (Tennekes and Lumley 1972). Turbulence is not a fluid property, as are viscosity and thermal conductivity, but a phenomenon caused by flow motion. Research on turbulence began during the late nineteenth century (Reynolds 1895) and has been intensively pursued in academia and industry. For further information, see Corrsin's (1961) overview; Hinze's (1975) and Tennekes and Lumley's (1972) classic monographs; and Bernard and Wallace (2002), Mathieu and Scott (2000), and Pope (2000).

Indoor airflow, convective heat transfer, and species dispersion are controlled by the governing equations for mass, momentum in each flow direction, energy (**Navier-Stokes equation**), and contaminant distribution. A common form is presented in Equation (1), relating the change in time of a variable at a location to the amount of variable flux (e.g., momentum, mass, thermal energy). Essentially, transient changes plus convection equals diffusion plus sources:

$$\frac{\partial}{\partial t}(\rho\phi) + \frac{\partial}{\partial x_j}(\rho U_j \phi) = \frac{\partial}{\partial x_j}\left(\Gamma_\phi \frac{\partial \phi}{\partial x_j}\right) + S_\phi \qquad (1)$$

where

t = time, s
ρ = density, lb/ft³
ϕ = transport property (e.g., air velocity, temperature, species concentration) at any point
x_j = distance in j direction, ft
U_j = velocity in j direction, fpm
Γ_ϕ = generalized diffusion coefficient or transport property of fluid flow
S_ϕ = source or sink

Local turbulence is expressed as a variable diffusion coefficient called the **turbulent viscosity**, often calculated from the equations for turbulent kinetic energy and its dissipation rate. The total description of flow, therefore, consists of eight differential equations, which are coupled and nonlinear. These equations contain first and second derivatives that express the convection, diffusion, and source of the variables. The equations can also be numerically solved [see the section on Large Eddy Simulation (LES)].

Direct solution of differential equations for the room's flow regime is not possible, but a numerical method can be applied. The differential equations are transformed into finite-volume equations formulated around each grid point, as shown in Figure 1. Convection and diffusion terms are developed for all six surfaces around the control volume, and the source term is formulated for the volume (see Figure 1B).

Assuming a room is typically divided into 90 × 90 × 90 cells, the eight differential equations are replaced by eight difference equations in each point, giving a total of 5.8×10^6 equations with the same number of unknown variables.

The numerical method typically involves 3000 iterations, which means that a total of 17×10^9 grid point calculations are made for the prediction of a flow field. This method obviously depends heavily on computers: the first predictions of room air movement were made in the 1970s, and have since increased dramatically in popularity, especially because computation cost has decreased by a factor of 10 every eight years. Baker et al. (1994), Chen and Jiang (1992), Nielsen (1975), and Williams et al. (1994a, 1994b) show early CFD predictions of flow in ventilated rooms, and Jones and Whittle (1992) discuss status and capabilities in the 1990s. Russell and Surendran (2000) review recent work on the subject.

Turbulent flow is a three-dimensional, random process with a wide spectrum of scales in time and space, initiated by flow instabilities at high Reynolds numbers; the energy involved dissipates in a cascading fashion (Mathieu and Scott 2000). Statistical analysis is used to quantify the phenomenon. At a given location and time, the instantaneous velocity u_i is

$$u_i = \bar{u}_i + u_i' \qquad (2)$$

where $\bar{u}_i$ is the ensemble average of v for steady flow, and u_i' is fluctuation velocity. Through measurement, u_i' is obtained as the standard deviation of u_i. The turbulence intensity TI is

$$\text{TI} \equiv \frac{u_i}{\bar{u}_i} \times 100 \text{ in percent} \qquad (3)$$

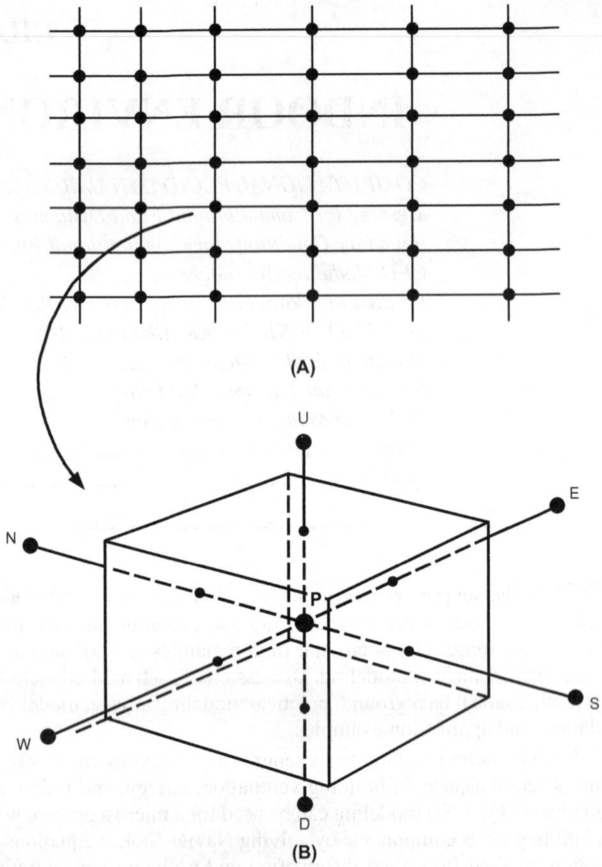

Fig. 1 (A) Grid Point Distribution and (B) Control Volume Around Grid Point P

The turbulent kinetic energy k per unit mass is

$$k = \frac{1}{2}\bar{u}_i'^2 = \frac{1}{2}(u_1'^2 + u_2'^2 + u_3'^2) \qquad (4)$$

To quantify length and time, velocity correlations and higher moments of u_i are commonly used (Monin and Yaglom 1971). Those scales are essential to characterize turbulent flows and their energy transport mechanisms. With its turbulent kinetic energy extracted from the mean flow, large eddies cascade energy to smaller eddies. In the smallest eddies, viscous dissipation of the turbulent kinetic energy occurs. By equating the total amount of energy transfer to its dissipation rate ε, based on Kolmogorov's theory (Tennekes and Lumley 1972), a length scale η is defined as

$$\eta \equiv \left(\frac{\nu^3}{\varepsilon}\right)^{\frac{1}{4}} \qquad (5)$$

where ν is the fluid's kinematic viscosity. The Kolmogorov length scale η is used to determine the smallest dissipative scale of a turbulent flow; it is important in determining the requirements of grid size [see the sections on Large Eddy Simulation (LES) and Direct Numerical Simulation (DNS)].

For an incompressible fluid, the governing equations of the turbulent flow motion are

$$\frac{\partial u_i}{\partial x_i} = 0 \qquad (6)$$

$$\rho\frac{\partial u_i}{\partial t}+\rho u_j\frac{\partial u_i}{\partial x_j} = -\frac{\partial P}{\partial x_i}+\frac{\partial \tau_{ij}}{\partial x_j} \quad (7)$$

where t is time, ρ is the fluid density, P is pressure, and τ_{ij} is the viscous stress tensor defined as

$$\tau_{ij} \equiv 2\mu s_{ij} \quad (8)$$

where μ is the dynamic viscosity and s_{ij} is the strain rate tensor, defined as

$$s_{ij} \equiv \frac{1}{2}\left(\frac{\partial u_i}{\partial x_j}+\frac{\partial u_j}{\partial x_i}\right) \quad (9)$$

From Equations (6), (8), and (9), Equation (7) is rewritten as

$$\rho\frac{\partial u_i}{\partial t}+\rho\frac{\partial(u_i u_j)}{\partial x_j} = -\frac{\partial P}{\partial x_i}+\frac{\partial(2\mu s_{ij})}{\partial x_j} \quad (10)$$

Taking the ensemble average by using Equation (2), Equation (6) becomes

$$\frac{\partial \bar{u}_i}{\partial x_i} = 0 \quad (11)$$

Considering Equation (2), Equation (10) becomes the **Reynolds-averaged Navier-Stokes (RANS) equation** (Wilcox 1998):

$$\rho\frac{\partial \bar{u}_i}{\partial t}+\rho\bar{u}_j\frac{\partial \bar{u}_i}{\partial x_j} = -\frac{\partial \bar{P}}{\partial x_i}+\frac{\partial\left(2\mu\bar{s}_{ij}-\rho\overline{u_i'u_j'}\right)}{\partial x_j} \quad (12)$$

The right-hand term $-\rho\overline{u_i'u_j'}$ is called the **Reynolds stress tensor**. To compute the mean flow of turbulent fluid motion, this additional term causes the famous closure problem because of ensemble averaging, and must be calculated. Much turbulence research focuses on the closure problem by proposing various turbulence models.

Reynolds-Averaged Navier-Stokes (RANS) Approaches

The most intuitive approach to calculate Reynolds stresses is to adopt the mixing-length hypotheses originated by Prandtl. Many variants of the algebraic models and their applicability for various types of turbulent flows (e.g., free shear flows, wakes, jets) are collected and provided by Wilcox (1998).

Because of the importance of turbulent kinetic energy k in the turbulent energy budget, many researchers have developed models based on k and other derived turbulence quantities for calculating the Reynolds stresses. To solve the closure problem, the number of the additional equation(s) in turbulence models ranges from zero (Chen and Xu 1998) to seven [Reynolds stress model (RSM) for three-dimensional flows (Launder et al. 1975)]; all equations in these approaches are time-averaged. Two-equation variants of the k-ε model (where ε is the dissipation rate of turbulent kinetic energy) are popular in industrial applications, mostly for simulating steady mean flows and scalar species transport (Chen et al. 1990; Horstman 1988; Spalart 2000). A widely used method is predicting eddy viscosity μ_t from a two-equation k-ε turbulence model, as in Launder and Spalding (1974). Nielsen (1998) discusses modifications for room airflow. The k-ε turbulence model is only valid for fully developed turbulent flow.

Flow in a room will not always be at a high Reynolds number (i.e., fully developed everywhere in the room), but good predictions are generally obtained in areas with a certain velocity level. Low-turbulence effects can be predicted near wall regions with, for example, a Launder-Sharma (1974) low-Reynolds-number model.

More elaborate models, such as the Reynolds stress model (RSM), can also predict turbulence. This model closes the equation system with additional transport equations for Reynolds stresses [see Launder (1989)]; it is superior to the standard k-ε model because anisotropic effects of turbulence are taken into account. For example, the wall-reflection terms damp turbulent fluctuations perpendicular to the wall and convert energy to fluctuations parallel to the wall. This effect may be important for predicting a three-dimensional wall jet flow (Schälin and Nielsen 2004).

In general, RSM gives better results than the standard k-ε model for mean flow prediction, but improvements are not always significant, especially for the velocity fluctuations (Chen 1996; Kato et al. 1994). Murakami et al. (1994) compared the k-ε model, algebraic model (simplified RSM), and RSM in predicting room air movement induced by a horizontal nonisothermal jet. RSM's prediction of mean velocity and temperature profiles in the jet showed slightly better agreement with experiments than the k-ε model's prediction.

Large Eddy Simulation (LES)

For intrinsically transient flow fields, time-dependent RANS simulations often fail to resolve the flow field temporally. Large eddy simulation (LES) directly calculates the time-dependent large eddy motion while resolving the more universally small-scale motion using subgrid scale (SGS) modeling. LES has progressed rapidly since its inception four decades ago (Ferziger 1977; Smagorinsky 1963; Spalart 2000), when it was mainly a research tool that required enormous computing resources; modern computers can now implement LES for relatively simple geometries in building airflow applications (Emmerich and McGrattan 1998; Lin et al. 2001). For an excellent introduction to this promising CFD technique, see Ferziger (1977).

Filtering equations differentiate mathematically between large and small eddies. For example,

$$\bar{f}(r) = \int_{R^3} f(r')G_\Delta(r,r')dr' \quad (13)$$

where $G_\Delta(r,r')$ is a filter function with a filter with length scale Δ. $G_\Delta(r,r')$ integrates to 1 and decays to 0 for scales smaller than Δ (Chester et al. 2001). To resolve the SGS stresses, an analog to the RANS approach for the Reynolds stress is implemented as

$$u_i = \langle u_i\rangle + \langle u_i'\rangle \quad (14)$$

where $\langle u_i\rangle$ is the filtered average defined by Equation (13) and $\langle u_i'\rangle$ is the subgrid scale velocity, which is calculated through subgrid modeling. Filtering Equation (6) and (7) gives

$$\frac{\partial\langle u_i\rangle}{\partial x_i} = 0 \quad (15)$$

$$\rho\frac{\partial\langle u_i\rangle}{\partial t}+\rho\frac{\partial\langle u_iu_j\rangle}{\partial x_j} = -\frac{\partial\langle p\rangle}{\partial x_i}+\frac{\partial\langle 2\mu s_{ij}\rangle}{\partial x_j} \quad (16)$$

Based on Equation (14), the $\langle u_iu_j\rangle$ term in Equation (16) becomes,

$$\begin{aligned}\langle u_iu_j\rangle &= \langle\langle u_i\rangle\langle u_j\rangle\rangle + \langle\langle u_i'\rangle\langle u_j\rangle\rangle \\ &\quad + \langle\langle u_i\rangle\langle u_j'\rangle\rangle + \langle\langle u_i'\rangle\langle u_j'\rangle\rangle\end{aligned} \quad (17)$$

The last three terms that contain the subgrid velocity are therefore the subject of modeling (Ferziger 1977). Breuer (1998) and Spalart (2000) describe some of the many other subgrid models and their performance. The latest developments of LES and its related techniques, such as the detached eddy simulation (DES), are described in detail by Spalart (2000).

Direction Numerical Simulation (DNS)

Direct numerical simulation (DNS) is used to study turbulent flow. This method is very accurate (sometimes better than experiments), and is used to benchmark performance of other CFD techniques. Because of its stringent requirements on grid, especially in the normal direction within the boundary layer (Grötzbach 1983), DNS is used to study spatially and temporally confined flows with simple geometry (Spalart 2000). Notwithstanding these limits, DNS also has been used to explore more complicated geometry, such as flow over a wavy wall (Cherukat et al. 1998), and flow mechanisms, such as multiphase flow (Ling et al. 1998) and droplet evaporation (Mashayek 1998).

1.1 MESHING FOR COMPUTATIONAL FLUID DYNAMICS

The first step in conducting a CFD analysis for a fluid region of interest is to divide the region into a large number of smaller regions called **cells**. The collection of cells that makes up the domain of interest is typically called the **mesh** or **grid**, and the process of dividing up the domain is called **meshing**, **gridding**, **grid generation**, or **discretization** of the computational domain.

Meshes can be structured or unstructured, depending on the connectivity of the cells in the mesh to one another. Individual cell shape varies, and each shape has advantages and disadvantages. These shapes range from triangles and quadrilaterals for two-dimensional (2D) geometry, to tetrahedrals (four-sided triangular-based shapes) and hexahedrons (typically six-sided boxes) for three-dimensional (3D) geometry. Wedges (a triangle swept into a three-dimensional shape) and rectangular-based pyramids can also be used to transition between the triangular sides of the tetrahedrals and quadrilateral sides of the hexahedrons.

Structured Grids

Structured grids have consistent geometrical regularity, wherein families of grid lines (in one direction) do not cross each other. Figure 2 shows examples of structured grids. These grids can be further subclassified as orthogonal and nonorthogonal.

Orthogonal structured grids, the simplest scheme, are based on Cartesian/polar-cylindrical coordinate systems. A curved or sloped boundary in the CFD domain is typically approximated by stepwise boundary. Figure 2A shows a meshed 2D domain for flow through a 90° elbow using a Cartesian orthogonal coordinate system. Cells outside the elbow are blocked from CFD analysis or turned into cells that do not participate in the flow field. The stairstep approach to representing the curved surface can lead to numerical errors at curved walls. Finer grids are needed to more accurately represent the curved/sloped boundary. The effect of reducing local grid size in one region (grid refinement) may propagate to other sections of the domain and result in an increase in the number of model cells. This, together with the blocked cells outside the flow domain, creates a burden on computing resources. The stepwise approximation of the boundary may also result in errors that negatively affect the CFD solution.

Modeling curved/sloped surfaces is possible by using the geometrical flexibility of the **nonorthogonal** grid, also known as **body-fitted** or **boundary-fitted grid**. An example of a 2D body-fitted nonorthogonal structured grid for a 90° elbow is shown in Figure 2B. Using the body-fitting method, geometric details are accurately represented without using stepwise approximation. An orthogonal grid can be structured (i.e., a single block, as in Figure 2), block-structured, or overlapping-structured.

A **block-structured** grid consists of a group of meshed regions (blocks) that collectively form the entire region of interest. This is typically referred to as a **multiblock domain**. The blocks may have a fine grid at the region of interest, to provide more details for flow field analysis, and a coarser grid away from the region of interest. Figure 3 shows block-structured grid for 2D flow through a 90° elbow connected to a rectangular duct. The grid is fine close to the solid surfaces, and is refined at point A, where flow separation is expected. This grid refinement is propagated through blocks 2 and 3. Interblock interfaces could have matching grids, as between blocks 1 and 2, or a nonmatching interface, as between blocks 2 and 3. The nonmatching interface is used to transfer from coarse to finer grid or vice versa. Numerical inaccuracies can occur where blocks are joined together with nonmatching mesh lines. The relative difference in mesh size on either side of the interface is important. Also, there is additional computational overhead associated with managing the nonconformal interface.

At the interface of the block-structured grid, the ratio of cell size change (i.e., large to small cells) between two blocks is recommended to be no more than two (Ferziger and Peric 1997), because transporting field variables from a fine to a coarse mesh or vice versa allows inaccuracies to enter the solution. If flow in a domain travels from a group of four cells to a single cell, the flow detail represented by the four cells is lost. In some cases, this rule can be bent, but this is best done by an experienced CFD modeler.

Structured grids simplify programming for the CFD code developer and provide regular structure for the matrix of algebraic equations. However, they may not adequately describe complex geometries, and it can be difficult to control grid distribution in the region of interest without propagating through the whole analyzed domain.

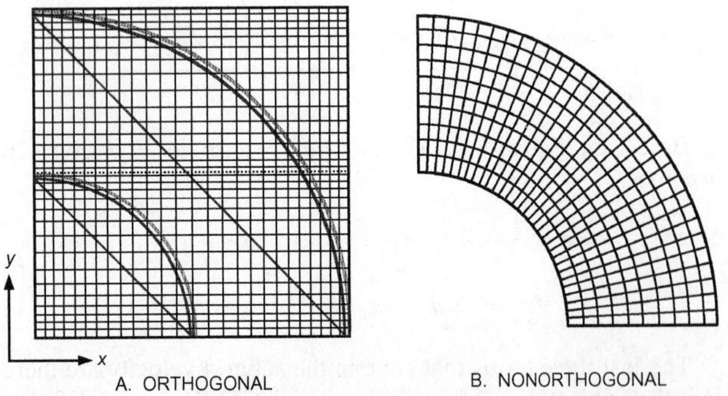

Fig. 2 Two-Dimensional CFD Structured Grid Model for Flow Through 90° Elbow

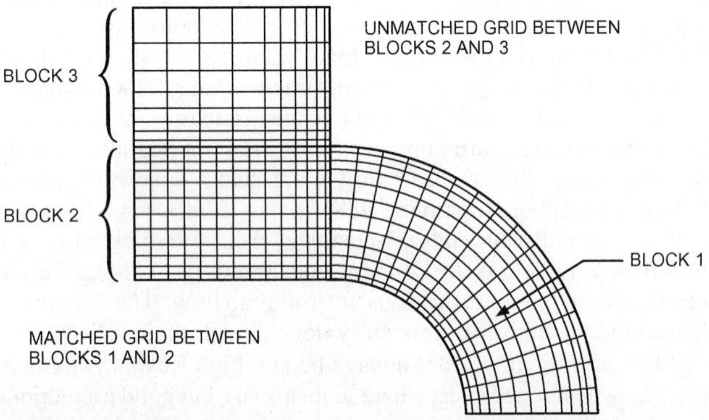

Fig. 3 Block-Structured Grid for Two-Dimensional Flow Simulation Through 90° Elbow Connected to Rectangular Duct

These structured grid types are mainly associated with finite-difference methods. The examples in Figures 2 and 3 are called the **physical planes**. Finite-difference methods require a uniform rectangular grid called the **computational plane**. The governing equations must be transformed to give one-to-one correspondences between the physical and computational planes. After analysis of the computational plane, the results are transferred back to the corresponding point on the physical plane. Using data transformation increases the programming efforts and computing costs for CFD. Anderson (1995) has more information on transformation methods.

Unstructured Grids

Unstructured grids (Figure 4) are flexible: they can represent complex geometry boundaries, and can be easily refined in the region of interest without propagating to the rest of the domain. Elements of different shapes can be used in the domain. Either matching or nonmatching nodes can be used between neighboring elements. Figure 4A is an unstructured grid using tetrahedral elements, whereas Figure 4B uses hexahedral elements; note that both have a meshing zone near the pipe wall to resolve the boundary layer. Unlike structured grids, the matrix of algebraic equation does not have a regular diagonal structure and has a slower solver than a structured grid solver (Ferzinger and Peric 1997).

Unstructured grids are mostly used for finite-element and finite-volume methods. No transformations are required for finite-volume methods, and analysis can be performed directly on the physical plane of the unstructured grid.

Grid Quality

Grid quality measures include the shape of the individual cells, the size of the cell relative to flow field features of interest, and the jump in grid size from one block to the next.

Cell quality is important. Values for variables stored at centers of cells must be interpolated to the face of the cell, which allows calculation of fluxes at faces of control volumes. A poor-quality mesh gives less accurate interpolations and can affect the quality of the simulation result by the introducing numerical inaccuracies. Mildly poor grids can increase convergence times; in extreme cases, local poor cell quality can result in overall flow field inaccuracies or cause the simulation to diverge and not reach a solution at all.

The examples in Figures 2 to 4 show clean, nonskewed cell shapes: the triangles do not lean over and the quadrilaterals have corners that do not vary significantly from 90°. In many practical meshes, the individual cells become distorted from these ideal shapes (e.g., because four-sided shapes may not fit well into wedge-shaped corners). The amount of distortion is typically referred to as **skewness**. Different CFD codes allow different levels of skewness, and the solver's overall sensitivity to skewness may be affected by the method of numerical discretization.

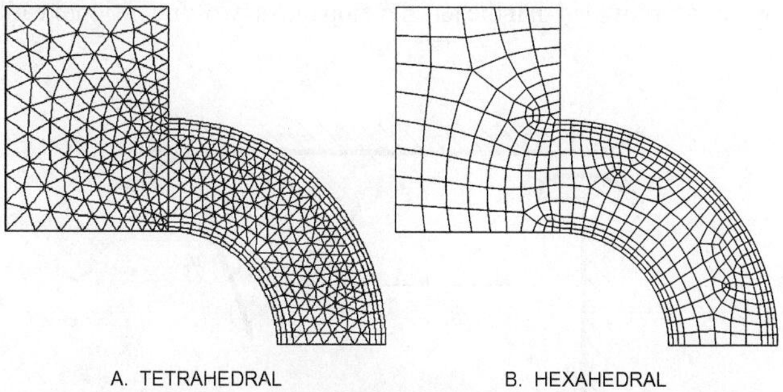

Fig. 4 Unstructured Grid for Two-Dimensional Meshing Scheme Flow Simulation Through 90° Elbow Connected to Rectangular Duct

Grid cell size may be partially determined by the level of geometric detail needed. Cells need to be small enough to resolve the smallest geometric features of the domain. If cell size is too large, any curved elements cannot be represented by a series of straight lines.

In addition, a CFD solution's ability to resolve flow field features is limited by the grid resolution. If a grid has cell sizes of 0.4 in., then flow field features smaller than 0.8 in. cannot be solved. Therefore, sharp gradients of flow field variables necessitate a finer mesh. The additional cells in the finer mesh are required to resolve the rapid change in the flow field variable. Additionally, fine grid resolution at walls is important for methods that use the law of the wall (see the Wall/Surface Boundary Conditions section), because fluxes and shear at the wall require accurate calculations of gradients.

Many CFD codes can start with a coarse mesh and add cells as necessary in particular regions, which can save computational time in the set-up and test simulation phases.

When generating a mesh, it is important to determine whether the mesh itself will affect the simulation and generate erroneous results. Figure 5 shows three circles with different meshing schemes. Figure 5A shows a grid on the circle that has a pincushion-like look; this mesh distorts the flow field in the "corners," because the four corner cells have two sides on the perimeter of the circle, whereas the rest of the cells around the circumference have only one. If this mesh is used to simulate flow down a pipe, flow velocity in the corner cells is adversely affected by the additional friction that these cells experience. Figure 5B shows the same geometry, but with a structured mesh created by placing a square in the center of the circle and drawing rays diagonally out from the corners. These rays and the circle's perimeter define other meshing blocks. If cut halfway through the horizontal or vertical centerline, the mesh can be stretched out into a rectangle. Finally, Figure 5C shows an unstructured mesh over the same geometry. The meshes in Figures 5B and 5C influence results less significantly than that in Figure 5A.

Immersed Boundary Grid Generation

The preceding discussion assumes that a 2D or 3D computer model already exists for the geometry, architecture, or region of interest, and that the geometry can be imported into a gridding software package. The grid is then overlaid onto that geometry.

In immersed boundary grid generation, a model is not required to exist a priori. This simplifies gridding and geometry generation in one step: the orthogonal structured grid is created within a block and then the geometry (represented by blanked-out sections of cells within the meshed block) is overlaid (see Figure 1A). Groups of meshed blocks with overlaid architecture can be assembled to generate more complicated computational domains.

Although this technique can yield high-quality meshes for simple geometrical features (blocked representation), more sophisticated grid-generation techniques may be needed to grid complicated domains.

Grid Independence

The level of grid independence from the flow field solution is important to determine in advance. It may be sufficient to demonstrate

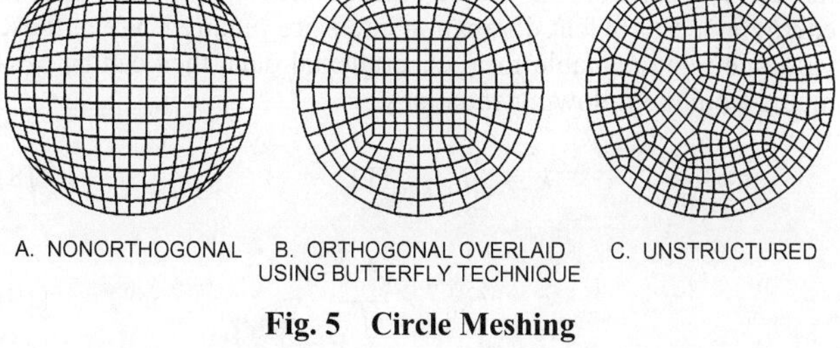

Fig. 5 Circle Meshing

that grids of similar resolution applied to similar problems give sufficiently low levels of uncertainty.

Grid independence can be achieved experimentally by using successive grid refinements in areas with sharp gradients or cell skewness. This allows solutions obtained with coarser and finer grids to be compared. If results of two successive trials are comparable, then both models are grid-independent. In some cases, experienced CFD practitioners may be able to identify a sufficiently grid-independent solution without trials, but new CFD users should not assume a solution is grid independent: different levels of grid can yield results different enough to make conclusions drawn from the flow field unreliable.

1.2 BOUNDARY CONDITIONS FOR COMPUTATIONAL FLUID DYNAMICS

Boundary conditions are integral to CFD modeling's ability to solve the general Navier-Stokes equations for a particular problem in an indoor environment. Boundary conditions specify physical and/or chemical characteristics at the model's perimeters. These characteristics could be constant throughout the analysis or time-dependent in transient analyses. This section discusses applying boundary conditions for CFD modeling of subsonic fluid flow.

Excluding free surface flow, most boundary conditions can be classified as either **Dirichlet** (variable values specified at the boundary node) or **Neumann** (variable derivatives are required at the boundary, and the boundary condition must be discretized to provide the required equation). Free surface flow requires moving boundary conditions, such as **kinematic** and **dynamic**.

Every model has walls, and most have at least one inlet and one outlet boundary. Some cases of natural convection heat transfer (e.g., CFD modeling of an enclosure with heated and cooled sides, modeling of convection from an object such as cylinder in a large fluid medium) may not require an inlet or outlet in the model. Typical boundary condition types for HVAC applications are inlets, outlets, walls or surfaces, symmetry surfaces, and fixed sources or sinks.

Inlet Boundary Conditions

Special attention must be paid to inlet boundary conditions, because supply diffusers are usually dominant sources of momentum that create airflow patterns responsible for temperature and concentration distributions.

Inlet boundary conditions may be velocity, pressure, or mass flow. When details of flow distribution are unknown, a constant-pressure boundary or constant flow rate can be specified. The pressure inlet boundary requires specifying static pressure for incompressible flow. Stagnation pressure and stagnation temperature should be specified at the pressure boundary for compressible flow. In both conditions, velocity components at the boundary are obtained by extrapolation.

The mass flow inlet condition requires specifying the mass flow rate and temperature for incompressible flow at the boundary. Velocities and pressure are calculated by extrapolation at inlet boundaries.

Experimentally measured values of turbulence quantities at the inlet boundary are also required for accurate CFD simulation for turbulent flow. For the k-ε turbulence model, turbulent kinetic energy k and turbulent dissipation rate ε are required. When these values are not available from experimental data, they can be estimated from the following equations:

$$k = \frac{3}{2}(U_{ref}\mathrm{TI})^2 \tag{18}$$

$$\varepsilon = C_\mu^{3/4} \times \frac{k^{3/2}}{l} \tag{19}$$

$$l = 0.07L \tag{20}$$

where U_{ref} is the mean stream velocity, TI is turbulence intensity, l is the turbulence length scale, C_μ is the k-ε turbulence model constant ($C_\mu = 0.0845$), and L is the characteristic length of the inlet (for a duct, L is the equivalent radius).

For indoor environmental modeling, the inlet boundary is especially important because of the potentially complex geometry of supply diffusers designed to produce particular performance characteristics. Detailed diffuser modeling is possible for limited regions near the diffuser, but is not very practical in room-flow simulations: including the small geometric details of the diffuser in the room model results in a mesh with so many cells that current computation resources cannot efficiently find a solution. Therefore, most room airflow simulations should use simplified diffuser modeling that replicates diffuser performance without explicitly modeling the fine geometric details of the diffuser.

Other simplifications are possible. The most obvious method is replacing the actual diffuser with a less-complicated diffuser geometry, such as a slot opening, that supplies the same flow momentum and airflow rate to the space as the actual diffuser does (Nielsen 1992; Srebric and Chen 2002). Simplified methods are classified as jet momentum modeling either (1) at air supply devices or (2) in front of air supply devices (Fan 1995). Modeling at the supply device has several variations, including the slot and momentum models; variations of modeling in front of the diffuser include prescribed velocity, box, and diffuser specification (Srebric and Chen 2001, 2002). The most widely used methods are the momentum, box, and prescribed velocity methods.

The **momentum** method decouples the momentum and mass boundary conditions for the diffuser (Chen and Moser 1991). The diffuser is represented with an opening that has the same gross area, mass flux, and momentum flux as a real diffuser. This model allows source terms in the conservation equations to be specified over the real diffuser area. Air supply velocity for the momentum source is calculated from the mass flow rate $\dot{m}$ and the diffuser effective area A_0:

$$U_0 = \frac{\dot{m}}{\rho A_0} \tag{21}$$

The momentum method is very simple, but might not work well for certain types of diffusers (Srebric and Chen 2002).

The **box** method is based on the wall jet flow generated close to the diffuser (Nielsen 1992; Srebric and Chen 2002). Figure 6 shows the location of boundary conditions around the diffuser. Details of flow immediately around the supply opening are ignored, and the supplied jet is described by values along surfaces a and b. There are two advantages of this method compared to the detailed diffuser simulations: (1) the box method does not require as fine a grid as fully numerical prediction of the wall jet development; and (2) two-dimensional predictions can be made for three-dimensional supply openings, provided that the jets develop into a two-dimensional wall

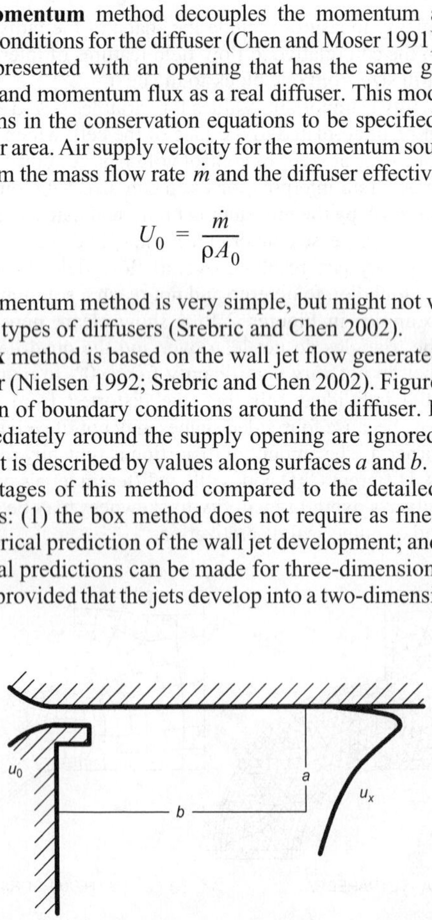

Fig. 6 Boundary Condition Locations Around Diffuser Used in Box Method

jet or free jet at a certain distance from the openings. Data for velocity distribution in a wall (or free) jet generated by different commercial diffusers can be obtained from diffuser catalogues or design guide books, Chapter 20, and textbooks [e.g., Awbi (1991), Etheridge and Sandberg (1996), and Rajaratnam (1976)].

The **prescribed velocity** method has also been used in numerical prediction of room air movement. Figure 7 shows the method's details. Inlet profiles are given as boundary conditions of a simplified slot diffuser, represented by only a few grid points. All variables except velocities u and w are predicted in a volume close to the diffuser (x_a, y_b) as well as in the rest of the room. Velocities u and w are prescribed in the volume in front of the diffuser as the fixed analytical values obtained for a wall jet from the diffuser, or they are given as measured values in front of the diffuser (Gosman et al. 1980; Nielsen 1992).

For a more detailed description of simplified methods and their applicability to common supply diffusers, see Chen and Srebric (2000). Figure 8 shows how real diffusers can be simplified by the momentum method and box method in CFD simulations (Srebric 2000).

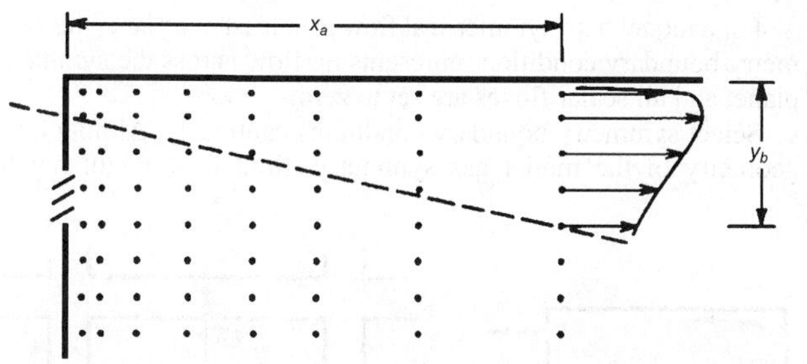

Fig. 7 Prescribed Velocity Field Near Supply Opening

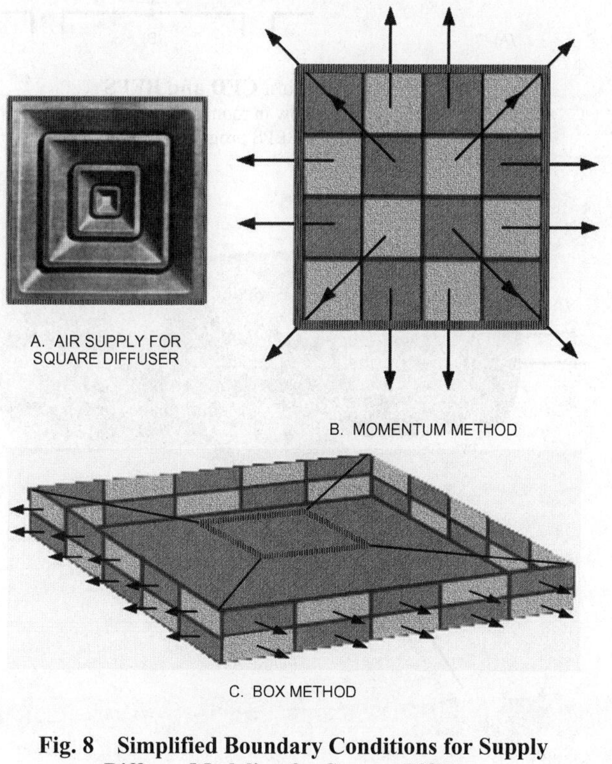

Fig. 8 Simplified Boundary Conditions for Supply Diffuser Modeling for Square Diffuser

Outlet Boundary Conditions

A mass flow rate or constant pressure can be specified for an outlet boundary condition. The outlet flow rate or pressure boundary is extrapolated to determine the boundary velocity, which needs to be corrected during calculations to satisfy mass conservation in the analyzed domain. Some commercial CFD codes require turbulence values at outlet boundary conditions. These values are used when reversed flow occurs at the outlet pressure boundary.

Wall/Surface Boundary Conditions

Wall boundary conditions represent the wet, solid perimeter of the CFD model. All velocity components are set equal to wall velocity for no-slip wall conditions, and to zero for a stationary wall. This is an example of a Dirichlet boundary condition. Wall roughness for both types of flow regimes (laminar and turbulent) should be specified. At the wall, both regimes have laminar flow. For turbulent flow, the wall turbulent boundary layer consists of three sublayers as presented in Figure 9 (Wilcox 1998): a thin, viscous sublayer followed by the log-law layer and the defect layer. Turbulent flow modeling requires very fine mesh inside the boundary layer. This requires extensive computational hardware, which is very costly, but the resource requirements can be reduced by using empirical wall functions in the near wall region instead of directly applying the k-ε turbulence model with a very fine mesh.

Turbulent flow near a wall can be categorized as **laminar** (viscous sublayer) or **turbulent** (log-law layer), depending on the dimensionless distance Y^+ from the wall, defined as

$$Y^+ = \frac{\Delta Y_p}{\nu}\sqrt{\frac{\tau_w}{\rho}} \qquad (22)$$

where ΔY_p is the distance from the wall to the center of the first cell, τ_w is wall shear stress, ρ is fluid density, and ν is the fluid kinematic viscosity.

The viscous sublayer is very thin ($Y^+ < 5$), and is typically smaller than the first cell ($2\Delta Y_p$). For the viscous sublayer, as shown in Figure 9,

$$u^+ = Y^+ \qquad (23)$$

where u^+ is the dimensionless mean velocity ($u^+ = U_P/u_t$, $u_t = \sqrt{\tau_w/\rho}$, and U_P is the is the velocity parallel to the wall at ΔY_p).

In practical terms, most important layer is the turbulent log-law sublayer, which is characterized by the following dimensionless velocity profile:

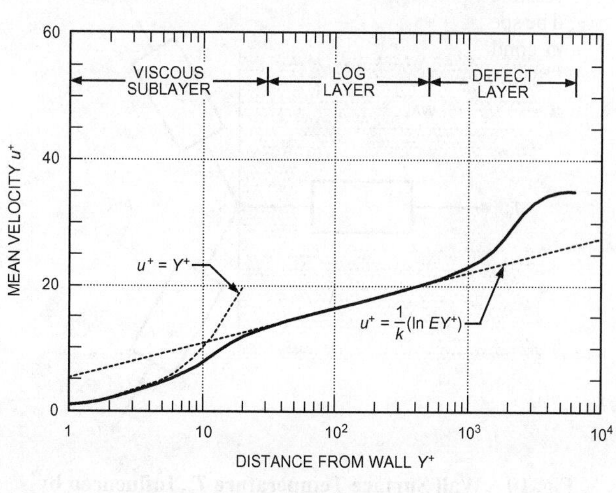

Fig. 9 Typical Velocity Distribution in Near-Wall Region

$$u^+ = \frac{1}{\kappa}(\ln EY^+) \qquad (24)$$

where κ is Von Karman's constant (κ = 0.41), and E is a constant depending on the wall roughness (E = 9.8 for hydraulically smooth walls).

The size of the log-law layer is typically $30 < Y^+ < 500$ (Versteeg and Malalasekera 1995). The turbulent kinetic energy k and turbulent dissipation rate ε use the following functions in the log-law layer:

$$k = \frac{u_\tau^2}{\sqrt{C_\mu}} \quad \text{and} \quad \varepsilon = \frac{u_\tau^3}{\kappa y} \qquad (25)$$

where C_μ is the k-ε turbulence model constant.

Overall, wall functions are of great practical importance because they allow significant savings of computational time. However, assumptions used to derive the wall functions [i.e., Prandtl mixing hypothesis, Boussinesq eddy viscosity assumption, fully developed flow, and no pressure gradients or other momentum sources (constant shear stresses)] restrict their application to a certain class of flows. For indoor airflow applications, these assumptions are acceptable, and wall functions are widely used. However, predicted heat transfer in the near-wall region tends to be incorrect, depending on the control volume size at the wall (Yuan et al. 1994). Heat transfer calculation can be improved with more accurate temperature profile equations or use of prescribed empirical values for the convective heat transfer coefficient h.

Surface temperature and heat transfer are often complicated variables of time and position. However, many CFD simulations use steady-state boundary conditions for a typical or design day. Boundary conditions for surface temperature and heat transfer are illustrated in Figure 10, showing how surface temperature T_s depends on heat transfer to and from the surroundings, on radiation to and from the surfaces in the room, and on the air temperature close to the surface.

Boundary conditions for temperature or energy flux can be found from measurements, manual energy calculations, or a **building energy performance simulation (BEPS)** program. BEPS predicts both energy flow in the building structure and radiation plus detailed dynamic energy flow and consumption of the whole building during a period of time (Figure 11). There are different ways to exchange heat transfer information between BEPS and CFD programs (Zhai et al. 2002); the best method is to transfer surface temperatures from BEPS to CFD, and convective heat transfer coefficients and air temperature from CFD to BEPS, to achieve a unique solution (Zhai and Chen 2003).

Dynamic simulations can be structured in different ways. A BEPS program can be connected to a separate CFD program, which predicts energy flow in selected situations. A CFD program can also be extended to find a combined solution of radiation, conduction, and thermal storage parallel to solving the flow field; this is often called a conjugate heat transfer model. Another possibility is to use additional CFD code in selected rooms as an extension of a large BEPS program. Examples of conjugate heat transfer and combined models are available in Beausoleil-Morrison (2000), Chen (1988), Kato et al. (1995), Moser et al. (1995), Nielsen and Tryggvason (1998), Srebric (2000), and Zhai and Chen (2003).

The simplest way to account for heat transfer at CFD boundaries is to prescribe wall temperatures obtained from on-site measurements. Using a turbulence model without wall functions is also recommended when heat and mass flows from surfaces are the important parameters. Predictions of actual flow at surfaces are more accurate than analytical values found from wall functions.

Symmetry Surface Boundary Conditions

For a model with symmetrical flow in at least one plane, the symmetry boundary condition represents no flow across the symmetry plane, and all scalar fluxes are set to zero.

Select symmetry boundary conditions cautiously. Although the geometry of the model has symmetry, fluid flow might not be

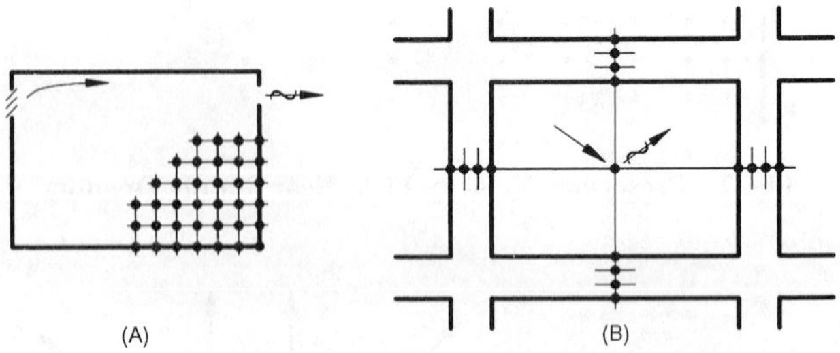

Fig. 11 Combination CFD and BEPS
The CFD program predicts flow in room based on heat flux calculated by BEPS program.

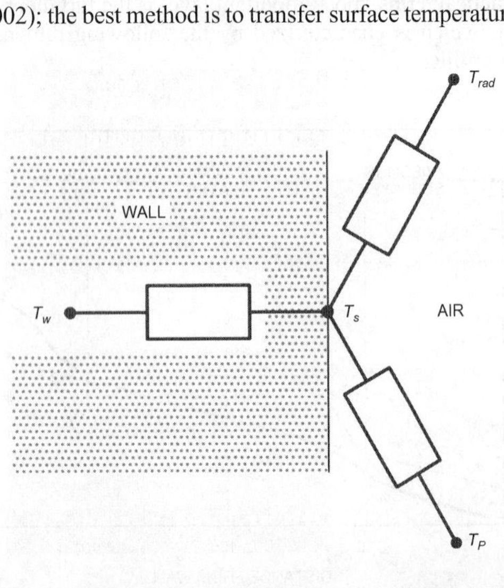

Fig. 10 Wall Surface Temperature T_s, Influenced by Conduction T_w, Radiation T_{rad}, and Local Air Temperature T_P

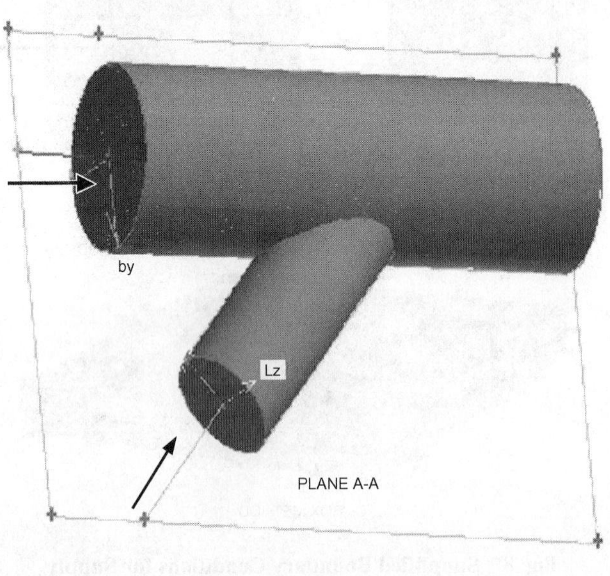

Fig. 12 Duct with Symmetry Geometry

symmetrical at the geometry symmetry plane. In Figure 12, the geometry is symmetrical at plane A-A, but the flow is asymmetrical because of flow instability at the merged flow region.

Zhang et al. (2000) studied the symmetry pattern for a 28 by 16.4 by 10 ft room, with air supplied through a slot at the ceiling and along the 16.4 ft long side. Return air exited through a slot at the floor along the same side wall as the inlet air. Velocity on one side of the symmetry plane was up to two times higher than on the other side, at the symmetrical location.

Fixed Sources and Sinks

Fixed sources are boundary conditions specified as fixed values of the calculated parameter or as mass/momentum/heat/contaminant fluxes. Examples include heat flux from a wall to simulate solar radiation, total heat flow in the occupied zone to simulate heat dissipation from occupants, momentum source from an operating fan, and species generation rate from contaminant sources. These sources could be placed anywhere in the CFD calculation domain, and can vary with time. Fixed-value sources/sinks usually use the wall functions if the source/sink is given as a fixed value, whereas fixed-flux sources/sinks do not use wall functions. These boundary conditions could also be associated with blockages in the flow domain (e.g., furniture, occupants, or other flow obstacles).

Modeling Considerations

Pressure boundary conditions are used when there is not enough information to specify the flow distribution, and the boundary pressure is known or assumed. Pressure boundaries are mostly used for buoyancy-driven flow and external flow applications. In inlet/outlet pressure boundary conditions, the stagnation pressure, temperature, concentration, and turbulence quantities k and ε are required. For external flow away from the wall, the free-stream k and ε can be set to zero. A pressure boundary velocity cannot be specified, but must be determined by the CFD code from interior conditions relative to the pressure boundary condition (inflow or outflow condition is possible).

When using different boundary conditions, be aware that most boundary conditions are just approximations of real physical phenomena. It is the user's responsibility to evaluate adequacy and influence of different boundary conditions on the accuracy of CFD simulation solutions.

1.3 CFD MODELING APPROACHES

Some steps are common to developing all types of CFD models and can increase the likelihood of getting a reasonable result with appropriate computing time.

Planning

Planning a CFD simulation is perhaps the most important step. During this phase, a clear understanding of what is being investigated is important. If the simulation is about thermal comfort in a room, some details about unoccupied space regions may be simplified: there may be little point in determining the thermal comfort in an unoccupied zone. If the purpose is to gain insight into a flow field, then some effort to estimate flow patterns helps during early modeling decisions and later evaluation of results.

During planning, a decision of whether to conduct a steady-state or transient simulation must be made. Transient simulations present time-accurate results, such as filling a tank, whereas steady-state simulations represent conditions after the flow field has been flowing long enough to reach equilibrium. It is important to recognize that some flows are inherently unsteady. The effect of choosing a steady-state solver to model unsteady flow should be considered during this process.

The physics to be examined should also be determined. Turbulence, heat transfer, species transport, and radiation phenomena can be evaluated during CFD modeling.

The final stage of planning is to determine how to represent the boundary conditions and flow physics. Diffusers, thermal sources leading to plumes, and contaminant sources are all important flow details that need to be appropriately represented.

Dimensional Accuracy and Faithfulness to Details

Highly detailed representation of architecture in a CFD model can significantly add to grid and computational costs. Often, high detail is not required. For instance, including doorknobs on a door will not likely change the simulation results greatly except immediately around the doorknob itself. However, if the room is negatively pressurized, significant flow through a crack beneath the door can cause a jet to propagate into the room, so accurately representing effects of flow through the crack is important. If the simulation is intended to assess thermal comfort in a laboratory with fume hoods, then the fume hood sash details may not be very important. However, if the purpose of the simulation is to evaluate fume hood capture performance, the sash opening detail can be important.

For complicated models, it can be helpful to evaluate and include the potential modifications for subsequent simulations before completing the geometry. This allows the simulation to be modified without breaking the grid and geometry, which can be the most time-consuming step of simulation. Preparing the grid for future simulations may reduce overall costs for later simulations.

CFD Simulation Steps

The basic mechanical steps in CFD simulation are as follows:

1. Create the geometry (a 3D model of the simulation environment)
2. Generate the grid
3. Define surfaces and volumes and implement boundary conditions
4. Execute the simulation
5. Evaluate the simulation and conduct quality checks to determine whether CFD simulation is complete; refine the grid, change discretization, and continue to solve
6. Postprocess/analyze the simulation to extract desired information
7. Modify the simulation and redo as required

During planning, a large set of physical phenomena (e.g., turbulence, heat transfer, radiation, species transport, combustion) may need to be included within the simulation(s). When executing the simulation itself, starting with a minimal set of physics and then increasing the level of complexity has advantages. For example, for flow in a room with a large convective and radiant heat source from which a contaminant is escaping (e.g., an industrial furnace), (1) solve the fluid velocity field with turbulence, (2) calculate energy to get a temperature distribution, (3) add radiation to redistribute some thermal energy, and (4) track the contaminant by adding species transport equations to the simulation.

This stepped approach allows the modeler to build on previous flow field solutions and ensure that each new set of physics is starting from a reasonable estimate of the flow field. It has particular advantages for complicated models or increasing the probability of success for new users.

1.4 VERIFICATION, VALIDATION, AND REPORTING RESULTS

It is important to document and assess the credibility of CFD simulations through verification, validation, and reporting of results. The American Institute of Aeronautics and Astronautics (AIAA 1998) defines *verification* as "the process of determining that a (physical/mathematical) model implementation accurately represents the developer's conceptual description of the model and the solution on the model," and *validation* as "the process of determining the degree to which a (CFD) model is an accurate representation of the real world from the perspective of the intended uses of the model."

Verification ensures that a CFD code can accurately and correctly solve the equations used in the conceptual model; it does not imply that the computational results represent physical reality. Generally, verification is done during code development. Because very few HVAC engineers who do indoor environment analysis develop CFD codes, this section focuses mostly on code applications, not development. In addition, time and money available for simulation are usually limited, which requires that verification and validation be realistically achievable. Therefore, this section refines the definitions of verification, validation, and reporting of results:

- **Verification** identifies relevant physical phenomena for analysis and provides instructions on how to assess whether a particular CFD code can account for those physical phenomena.
- **Validation** provides instructions on how to demonstrate the coupled ability of a user and a CFD code to accurately conduct representative indoor environmental simulations with available experimental data.
- **Reporting** results provides instructions on how to summarize results so that others can make informed assessments of the value and quality of the CFD work.

Therefore, verification should represent physical realities, although the cases can be very simple, containing only one (or a few) flow and heat transfer features of the complete system. The validation cases should be close to reality and include the flow and heat transfer characteristics that need to be analyzed, although approximations may be used in the validation.

This section describes a procedure developed by Chen and Srebric (2002) for verification, validation, and reporting of CFD results, but its intent is not to develop standards. The extent of CFD's capability in modeling has not yet been developed to the point where standards can be written (AIAA 1998).

Verification

The basic physical phenomena of the indoor environment are airflow, heat transfer (conduction, convection, and radiation), mass transfer (species concentrations and solid and liquid particles), and chemical reactions (combustion). Therefore, the first step of verification is to identify benchmark cases with one or more flow and heat transfer features of those basic phenomena.

In some indoor regions, airflow can be laminar or weakly turbulent. The overall flow features are often considered as turbulent. Most indoor airflows are turbulent because of the high Rayleigh number Ra, and sometimes high Reynolds number Re, defined as

$$Ra = \beta g\, \Delta T L^2 / \nu k \quad (26)$$

$$Re = UL/\nu \quad (27)$$

In most rooms, Ra ranges from 10^9 to 10^{12} and Re from 10^4 to 10^7 if room height is used as the characteristic length L. Experiments have found that turbulence occurs when Ra > 10^9 and/or Re > 10^4.

Turbulence modeling approximations, which require more complex numerical schemes so that a converged solution can be achieved, must be made for CFD to solve the flow fields.

The ability of a CFD code to simulate airflow in an indoor environment and the fidelity of the computer model to the physical realities may vary, and should be assessed. Predicting indoor physical phenomena may require auxiliary flow and heat transfer models. The following aspects require special attention:

- Basic flow and heat transfer (convection, diffusion, conduction, and/or radiation)
- Turbulence models
- Auxiliary heat transfer and flow models
- Numerical methods
- Assessing CFD predictions

Whether a CFD code can be used to simulate an indoor environment depends on the flow and heat transfer features. For an indoor space with a baseboard heater, a CFD code that can solve natural convection flow may be sufficient. If a radiator replaces the baseboard heater, a radiation model is needed. When heat transfer through the walls must be considered, the code should have a conjugate heat transfer feature. When a duct supplies fresh air, room airflow becomes mixed convection, which requires the capability of mixed convection simulation. For indoor air quality studies, the code should be able to solve species concentrations. The more realistic the model is, the more complex the flow and heat transfer.

To verify a CFD code's capability of simulating the indoor environment of interest, review the code's manual and any libraries or examples provided by the developer to illustrate successful applications. Discussing the particular application with the code developer can ensure that the physical models required for the application are all available. However, even if a code has been found capable of simulating the physical phenomena in the indoor environment in the past, repeating the verification is helpful because success relies on the joint function of the user and the CFD code.

Hands-on verification usually starts with the simplest cases, which contain only one or two flow features and have been thoroughly tested to minimize uncertainties and errors. After successful verification, further simulations can be performed for more realistic cases, which may contain many key features of physical phenomena in an indoor space. The Reynolds or Rayleigh numbers can then be similar to those in reality.

Often, verification data are from high-precision experimental measurements. The quantity and quality of the experimental data are usually accompanied by quantified errors. They are generally accurate, have few human errors, cover a large area of interest in the CFD community, and are widely used for testing CFD simulations. These experimental data contain detailed information, such as boundary and initial conditions, and are usually two-dimensional.

Different cases represent different flow characteristics. Ideally, verification should be done for all flow features, but in practice, two to three important cases may be sufficient for most indoor environmental analyses.

Turbulence Model Identification. With a verification case identified, the next step is to identify a suitable turbulence model. These are divided into two groups: large eddy simulations (LES), and turbulent transport models [Reynolds-averaged Navier-Stokes (RANS) equation modeling]. LES divides turbulent flow into large-scale motion (calculated in LES) and small-scale motion (which must be modeled because of its effect on large-scale motion). Using a suitable subgrid scale model for the simulation is the most important factor, because the subgrid's accuracy and efficiency determines how correct and useful the LES is.

RANS models are more common in indoor airflow simulation. In general, eddy viscosity models are accurate for simple airflows, and Reynolds stress models are needed for complex flows. Complex flow exists in a flow domain with complex geometry, such as room and air supply diffuser geometry. Many CFD studies compare different turbulence models, so users may consult the literature for reported studies that are close to the case in question. The k-ε model is inaccurate for flows with adverse pressure gradient, which seriously limits its general usefulness. If comparisons for a particular case are not available, start with simple, popular models, such as the standard k-ε model (Launder and Spalding 1974), moving to progressively more complicated models if necessary. Vendors have made selecting different turbulence models as easy as a simple mouse click. However, a user should understand the principle of the model, its suitability for the problem to be solved, and the corresponding changes needed in using the model.

Identifying Auxiliary Heat Transfer and Flow Models. The indoor environment consists of very complicated physical phenomena, with radiative, conductive, and convective heat transfer almost always occurring simultaneously, and sometimes also including combustion, participating media radiation, and particle transport in multiple phases (air/liquid, air/solid, and air/liquid/solid). It is important to verify whether these physical phenomena can be modeled by a CFD code.

Separate verification of auxiliary models and turbulence models reduces the possibility of error. According to AIAA (1998), an error is "a recognizable deficiency in any phase or activity of modeling and simulation that is not due to lack of knowledge." A complex problem may be verified by separating it into several components that have analytical solutions. For example, a combined conductive, convective, and radiative heat transfer process can be verified by separating it into a conductive and radiative problem, and a convective problem. The two problems can then be verified by the relevant analytical solutions. Another example is liquid particle trajectory in indoor air quality simulations that involve condensation, evaporation, and collision, as well as strong interaction with airflow turbulence. The physical phenomena should be verified separately.

Verification does not ensure the correctness of the combined process. Therefore, uncertainty exists in the combined process. **Uncertainty** is a potential deficiency in any phase or activity of modeling caused by lack of knowledge; no highly accurate solutions are available. This may be addressed during validation.

Verification of numerical methods involves investigating the discretization of the continuous space and time (if transient) into finite intervals. The variables are computed at only a finite number of locations (**grid points**), so the continuous information contained in the solution of differential equations is replaced with discrete values. When a Cartesian mesh system is used for sloped or curved surfaces, the true geometry is not represented in the calculation because it would introduce an error. Thus, for sloped or curved surfaces, similar geometries must be verified rather restricting the simulation to empty rectangular rooms.

Different discretization schemes can be verified by comparing the results obtained from two different schemes. For example, to verify an unstructured grid system, Cartesian coordinates can be used as a reference. Case geometry should be simple, such as a rectangular room. Then, the two schemes should generate the same results. If the code has only one grid system, the discretization scheme verification can be combined with model verification.

Refining Grid Size and Time Step. Because CFD discretizes partial differential equations into discretized equations, this introduces an error. Verification of grid size and time step is done to reduce error to a level acceptable for the particular application. The time step applies only to transient flow simulation. Therefore, it is not sufficient to perform CFD computations on a single fixed grid. The difference in grid size and time step between two cases should be large enough to identify differences in CFD results. The common method is to repeat the computation by doubling the grid number, and compare the two solutions (Wilcox 1998). It is very important to separate numerical error from turbulence-model error, because the merits of different turbulence models cannot be objectively evaluated unless the discretization error of the numerical algorithm is known.

The geometry of an indoor space can be very complicated, and computer speed and capacity are still insufficient for simulating an indoor environment with very fine grid sizes (over a few million grids) and time steps (tens of thousands). Verification estimates the discretization error of the numerical solution. Theoretically, when grid size and time step approach zero, the discretization error of the numerical solution becomes negligible. For LES, when grid size and time step become small, flow in the subgrid scale is isotropic and the results become more accurate. When grid size is much smaller than the Kolmogorov length scale, the LES turns into a direct-numerical simulation.

Numerical Schemes, Iteration, and Convergence. A numerical scheme is important in CFD code to obtain a fast, accurate, and stable solution. A higher-order differencing scheme should be more accurate than a lower-order scheme for simple cases, such as those suggested for turbulence model verification. However, be aware of the limitations of various differencing schemes. For example, the central differencing scheme (accurate to the second order) is used for small Peclet numbers ($Pe < 2$), and the upwind scheme [accurate to the first order (but accounts for transportiveness)] is used for a high Peclet number. The Peclet number, the ratio of convection to conduction, is defined as

$$Pe = LU\rho C_p / k \tag{28}$$

where C_p is specific heat.

Solution algorithms in CFD codes can be quite different, ranging from SIMPLE in conventional program with iteration, to the fast Fourier transformation for solving the Poisson pressure equation in LES without iteration. Iteration is normally needed in two situations: (1) globally for boundary value problems (i.e., over the entire domain), or (2) within each time step for transient physical phenomena. Criteria can be set to determine whether a converged solution is reached, such as a specified absolute and relative residual tolerance. The **residual** is the imbalance of solved variables (e.g., velocities, mass flow, energy, turbulence quantities, species concentrations). For indoor environment modeling, a CFD solution has converged if

$$\text{Residual for mass} = \frac{\text{Sum of absolute residuals in each cell}}{\text{Total mass inflow}} < 0.1\%$$

$$\text{Residual for energy} = \frac{\text{Sum of absolute residuals in each cell}}{\text{Total heat gains}} < 1\%$$

Similar convergence criteria can be defined for other solved variables, such as species concentration and turbulence parameters. Note that, for natural convection in a room, net mass flow is zero. Therefore, convergence has most likely been reached if there is little change (no change in the fourth digit) in the major dependent variables (temperature, velocities, and concentrations) within the last 100 iterations. However, a small relaxation factor can always give a false indication of convergence (Anderson et al. 1984).

To obtain stable and converged results, iteration often uses relaxation factors for different variables solved, such as underrelaxation factors and false time steps. Underrelaxation factors differ only slightly from false-time-steps.

Assessing CFD Predictions. A detailed qualitative and quantitative comparison of CFD results with data from experiments, analytical solutions, and direct numerical simulations is an important final step. All error analyses should be discussed in this section as well. The results indicate whether the CFD code can be used for indoor environment modeling.

Although this procedure divides verification into several parts, they often are integrated. The turbulence model and numerical technique must work together to obtain a correct CFD prediction for the flow features selected. However, it is necessary to break them down into individual items in some types of verifications, such as in CFD code development. Indoor environment designers often use commercial software, and it is logical to assume that the codes were verified during development. However, the verifications (if any) may have used different flows that are irrelevant to indoor airflow. In addition, a user may not fully understand the code's functions. It is imperative for the user to reverify a CFD code's capabilities for indoor environment simulations. This helps the user become more familiar with the code and eliminates human errors in using the code.

Generally, verification cases are not proprietary or restricted for security reasons; the data are usually available from the literature. It is strongly recommended that verification be reported when publishing CFD studies. This is especially helpful in eliminating user errors, because most CFD codes may have been validated by those cases. There are many examples of failed CFD simulations caused by user mistakes. Verification should be done for the following parameters:

- All variables solved by the governing equations (e.g., velocity, temperature, species concentrations)
- Boundary conditions (e.g., heat flux, mass inflow and outflow rates)

With these items verified, a CFD code should be able to correctly compute airflow and heat transfer encountered in an indoor environment. The level of accuracy depends on the criteria used in the verification. If the code failed to compute the flow correctly, the problem may be that (1) the code is incapable of solving the indoor airflows, (2) the code has bugs, or (3) there are errors in the user input data that defines the problem to be solved.

Validation

Validation demonstrates the ability of both the user and the code to accurately predict representative indoor environmental applications for which some sort of reliable data are available. It estimates how accurately the user can apply the code in simulating a full, real-world indoor environment problem, and gives the user the confidence to use the code for further applications, such as a design tool. A CFD code may solve the physical models selected to describe the real world, but may give inaccurate results because the selected models do not represent physical reality. For example, an indoor environment may simultaneously involve conduction, convection, and radiation, but a user may misinterpret the problem as purely convection. The CFD prediction may be correct for the convection part but fail to describe the complete physics involved. It is obviously a problem on the user's side, which validation process also tries to eliminate.

Note that *validation* addresses a complete flow and heat transfer system, or several subsystems that, together, represent a complete system. Although the procedure is almost the same, *verification* addresses only one of the flow aspects in an indoor environment.

The basic idea of validation is to identify suitable experimental data, to make sure that all important phenomena in the problem are correctly modeled, and to quantify the error and uncertainty in the CFD simulation. Because the primary role of CFD in indoor environment modeling is to serve as a high-fidelity tool for design and analysis, it is essential to have a systematic, rational, and affordable code validation process. Validation focuses on

- Confirming the capabilities of the turbulence model and other auxiliary models in predicting all the important physical phenomena associated with an indoor environment, before applying the CFD model for design and evaluation of a similar indoor environment category
- Confirming correctness of the discretization method, grid resolution, and numerical algorithm for flow simulation
- Confirming the user's knowledge of the CFD code and understanding of the basic physics involved

Ideally, validation should be performed for a complete indoor environment system that includes all important airflow and heat transfer physics and a full geometric configuration. Experimental data for a complete system can be obtained from on-site measurements or experiments in an environmental chamber. The data usually have a fairly high degree of uncertainty and large errors, and may contain little information about initial and boundary conditions. Reasonable assumptions are needed to make CFD simulation feasible.

Often, experimental data may not be available for a complete indoor environment system. In this case, validations for several subsystems or an incomplete system can be used. A subsystem represents some of the flow features in an indoor environment to be analyzed. The overall effect of several subsystems is equivalent to a complete system. For example, a complete indoor environment system consists of airflow and heat transfer in a room with occupants, furniture, and a forced air unit. If a user can correctly simulate several subsystems such as airflow and heat transfer (1) around a person, (2) in a room with obstacles, and (3) in a room with a forced air unit, the validation is acceptable. In the same example, an incomplete system for this environment can consist of airflow and heat transfer in a room with an occupant and a forced-air unit. Furniture, although it affects the indoor environment, is not as important as the other components, so validation with an incomplete system is acceptable. In either case, the key is that validation should lead to a solid confirmation of the combined capabilities of the user and code.

Although validation is for a complete indoor environment system, it is not necessary to start with a very complicated case if alternatives are available. Reliability is better for

- A simpler geometry, rather than a complicated one
- Convection, rather than combined convection, conduction, and radiation
- Single-phase flows, rather than multiphase flows
- Chemically inert materials, rather than chemically reactive materials

For complex physical phenomena in an indoor space, input data for CFD analysis may involve too much guesswork or imprecision. The available computer power may not be sufficient for high numerical accuracy, and the scientific knowledge base may be inadequate.

Complete system validation should be broken down into steps:

1. Setting up building geometry, and then placing inlets and outlets. Isothermal flow indicates the airflow pattern.
2. Adding heat transfer. Species concentration, particle trajectory, etc., should be considered later.

This progressive simulation procedure not only builds user confidence in performing the simulation, but also discovers some potential errors in the simulation.

If a CFD code has multiple choices, simple, popular models should be considered as the starting point for validation. The starting point can be as basic as

- Standard k-ε model
- No-auxiliary-flow and heat transfer models
- Structured mesh system
- Upwind scheme
- SIMPLE algorithm

The way of measuring real-world accuracy of the representation is to systematically compare CFD simulations to experimental data. The indoor environment systems used in validation are usually complicated, and the corresponding experimental data may contain bias errors and random errors, which should be reported as part of the validation. If the errors are unknown, a report on the equipment used in the measurements is helpful in assessing data quality. Although desirable, it is expensive and time-consuming to obtain good-quality data for a complete system. Therefore, reporting the CFD validation of the complete system cannot be overemphasized.

The criteria for accuracy when conducting a validation depend on the application. Very high accuracy, although desirable, is not essential because most design changes are incremental variations from a baseline. As long as the predicted trends are consistent, then less-than-perfect accuracy should be acceptable. The validation process should be flexible, allowing varying levels of accuracy, and be tolerant of incremental improvements as time and funding permit. The level of agreement achieved with the test data, taking into the account measurement uncertainties, should be reviewed in light of the CFD application requirements. For example, validation for modeling air temperature in a fire simulation requires much lower minimum accuracy than that for a thermal comfort study for an indoor environment.

If validation cases are simple and represent a subsystem of a complex indoor airflow, the validation criteria should be more restrictive than those for the complete system. The criteria can also be selective. For example, if correct prediction of air velocity is more important, the criteria for heat transfer may be relaxed. Although air velocity and temperature are interrelated, one parameter's effect on the other may be second-order. This allows a fast, less detailed model to be used, such as standard k-ε model, rather than a detailed but slower model, such as low-Reynolds-number model for heat transfer calculation in boundary layers.

Reporting CFD Results

Reporting involves summarizing CFD simulation results, while providing sufficient information on the value and quality of the CFD work. This is an important quality assurance strategy for CFD analysis of the indoor environment.

It is recommended to start with verification and then proceed to validation. In principle, reports for technical audiences should include the information discussed in the verification and validation sections, such as

- Experimental design
- CFD models and auxiliary heat transfer and flow models
- Boundary conditions
- Numerical methods
- Comparison of the CFD results with the data
- Drawing conclusions

The reporting format, however, can be flexible. If a report were intended for nontechnical readers, including only the last two items would be sufficient.

Experimental Design. Thermal and flow conditions of the test environment should be described in enough detail that other people could repeat the simulation. This can be as simple as a reference to the literature or a description of cases in the report. An analysis of uncertainties and errors in the experimental data or a short description of the experimental procedure and equipment should also be included.

CFD Models and Auxiliary Heat Transfer and Flow Models. CFD includes hundreds of different models of LES and RANS. Many popular turbulence models have been widely used and reported, making it unnecessary to provide detailed formulation. When reporting CFD results, it is important to specify which turbulence model is used. If the model has not been widely reported, detailed information (including why the model was selected) should be presented.

Indoor environment analysis may require auxiliary heat transfer and flow models. For example, a building may use porous material as insulation. Heat transfer through the insulation combines conduction, convection, and radiation (too complex a process for limited computer resources to simulate in detail). Instead, a lumped-parameter model may be used to combine the heat transfer processes and obtain accurate CFD results for the indoor environment. Therefore, it should be described in the CFD analysis report.

Boundary Conditions. Accurate specification of boundary conditions is crucial, because they indicate how the user interprets the specific physical phenomena into a computer model or mathematical equations that can be solved by the code. This interpretation requires the most skill in CFD modeling. Therefore, detailed description of boundary conditions can help others make informed assessments of the simulation's quality. Include the following information:

- **Geometry settings** (the size of the computational domain along with sizes and locations of all solid objects represented in the model). If there is an external wall involved that cannot be considered adiabatic, external ambient conditions (e.g., ambient temperature, external radiation temperature, convective heat transfer coefficient) should be reported as well.
- **Inlet**. Airflow from a diffuser greatly affects a room's airflow pattern. Diffuser geometry, and approximations are often used in a complete system to make indoor airflow solvable. Therefore, the CFD report should give detailed information on the approximations used, as well as the set boundary conditions for the inlet. In some situations, the exact location of an inlet may be difficult to identify (e.g., air infiltration from the outdoors to an indoor space could be through the cracks of windows and doors). Conditions may differ from one window to another. Also, infiltration flow rate can be difficult to estimate because wind magnitude and direction change over time. Furthermore, turbulence parameters for the inlet are generally unknown, and should be estimated. Therefore, how these "inlet" conditions are specified should be clearly stated.
- **Outlet**. An outlet has little effect on room airflow. However, conditions set for the outlet often can significantly influence numerical stability. For example, the outlet may become an inlet during iteration of a calculation. If the default outlet temperature is 32°F, this could lead to a diverged solution.
- **Walls**. Rigid surfaces in an indoor space, such as walls, ceilings, floors, and furniture surfaces, are all considered as walls. Very close to the wall, airflow is laminar, and convective heat transfer often occurs in this region between the flow and surfaces. Many turbulence models cannot accurately handle the laminar sublayer, so ad hoc solutions, such as damping functions, are often used. How a CFD code treats wall boundary conditions greatly affects the accuracy of numerical results. Even if the indoor space is large and the wall effect seems small, accurate prediction of heat transfer from the walls to room air is still important.
- **Open boundary**. When the area of interest is a part of the indoor space, the computational domain does not have to align with a rigid surface; instead, an "open" boundary can be defined. Depending on the inside and outside pressure difference, air may flow in or out across the open boundary.
- **Source/sink**. This boundary condition fixes thermal or dynamic parameters (e.g., heat flux from a wall to simulate solar radiation, total heat flow in the occupied zone to simulate heat dissipation from occupants, momentum source from an operating fan, species generation rate from contaminant sources) in a defined region. Describe the location, size, and parameter being specified.
- **Coupling between a micro and a macro model**. For a large indoor space, CFD analysis may be divided into micro and macro simulations. The micro simulation zooms into a particular area to reveal details of flow and thermal characteristic on a small scale compared with that for the entire space of interest. This allows finer-resolution examination of details of flow in that area. The macro simulation is applied to the entire flow system, and may use the results of the micro simulation so that a coarser grid system can be used. This coupling is usually a complicated procedure that should be detailed in the report.
- **Other approximations.** Approximations are almost always involved when representing the real world in a computer model. For example, when the surface temperature distribution of a heated object is not uniform, the CFD simulation may choose to neglect temperature variation on the surface. When designing a large stadium, it may not be feasible to simulate each individual spectator; instead, the model may combine all the spectators into a human

layer. There are numerous examples in indoor environment modeling that need to be approximated in a CFD simulation. All approximations should be reported.

Numerical Methods. It is essential to report the numerical methods used in the analysis, although the report can be brief if the technique is popular and widely available from the literature. The numerical technique includes discretization technique, grid size and quality, time step, numerical schemes, iteration number, and convergence criteria. The report should briefly state why the technique was used, and how suitable it is to the problem under consideration. It is also important to provide the quality indices of the mesh of a body-fitted coordinate, because mesh quality affects the prediction's accuracy. Typically, these indices include normal distances from solid surfaces to the centers of the first adjacent cells, maximum scale ratios of each two neighboring cells in each coordinate, and smallest angle of mesh cells. The first index determines the prediction of boundary layer flows, and the other two indicate whether unacceptable numerical errors are introduced into the simulation. Because a coarse grid introduces more numerical viscosity, grid-refinement study is essential to achieving a grid-independent solution, and should be included in the CFD report. Although it may not be realistic to conduct grid refinement for the complete system, it should be conducted for benchmark cases, to estimate the errors introduced in the complete system.

If different numerical schemes have been tested, the results should be reported. Knowing the performance of different numerical schemes helps identify whether a numerical scheme or turbulence model causes a discrepancy between the CFD results and experimental data. Iteration number and convergence criteria are interrelated. It is better to use the sum of the absolute residual at each cell for all the variables as convergence criteria. The relaxation method and values should also be reported.

Comparison of Results with Data. The most important part of the report is comparing experimental data with analysis results. Qualitative values, such as airflow pattern, should be compared first, followed by first-order parameters, such as air velocity, temperature, and species concentrations. In general, both CFD results and experimental data are more accurate for first-order parameters. Second-order parameters, such as turbulence kinetic energy, Reynolds stresses, and heat fluxes, usually have greater uncertainties and errors than the first-order parameters in both the results and the experimental data, so seeking perfect agreement for these parameters is unnecessary.

It is insufficient to describe the comparison between CFD results and experimental data as *excellent*, *good*, *fair*, *poor*, or *unacceptable*. For example, a 20% difference can be considered excellent for a complex flow problem, but rather poor for two-dimensional forced convection in an empty room. Therefore, the comparison should be quantitative. The most useful information from comparison is how to interpret discrepancies. If there is little discrepancy, it is important to know why a turbulence model that uses approximations can predict the physical phenomena so well. The comparison should clearly state the uncertainties and errors of the experimental data, if they are known.

Conclusions. The most important findings of the CFD analysis should be presented as its conclusions, which should have broad applicability to indoor environment simulation. The report may also recommend measures for further improvements in CFD analyses.

2. MULTIZONE NETWORK AIRFLOW AND CONTAMINANT TRANSPORT MODELING

Multizone or network models are used to address airflow, contaminant transport, heat transfer, or some combination thereof. This section presents the mathematical and numerical background of network airflow and contaminant transport models. Thermal network models are addressed in Chapter 19.

2.1 MULTIZONE AIRFLOW MODELING

Theory

Network airflow models idealize a building as a collection of zones, such as rooms, hallways, and duct junctions, joined by flow paths representing doors, windows, fans, ducts, etc. Thus, the user assembles a building description by connecting zones via the appropriate flow paths.

The network model predicts zone-to-zone airflows based on the pressure-flow characteristics of the path models, and pressure differences across the paths. Three types of forces drive flow through the paths: wind, temperature differences (stack effect), and mechanical devices such as fans.

As shown in Figure 13, airflow network models resemble electrical networks. Airflow corresponds to electric current, with zone pressure acting like the voltage at an electrical node. Flow paths correspond to resistors and other electrical elements, including active elements like batteries (fans).

Unlike CFD models, network models do not prescribe details of airflow in zones. Thus, at any given time, each network zone is characterized by a single pressure. Pressure in the zone varies according to height, for example, using the simple hydrostatic relationship $P + \rho gh$ = constant. Air density ρ is determined by the equation of state $\rho = P/(R_{air}T)$, based on the zone reference pressure P, temperature T, and the gas constant of the air mixture R_{air}. Zone temperature is given either directly by the user, or by an independent thermal model. The gas constant is typically assumed to be that of dry air, but can be made a function of other non-trace constituents as well (e.g., water vapor).

This lack of detail in the network zone models makes CFD preferable for predicting thermal comfort, or designing displacement ventilation systems, where airflow patterns in a room control the quantities of interest (Emmerich 1997).

In network airflow modeling, flow path models provide most of the modeling detail. Typically, the airflow rate $F_{j,i}$ from zone j to zone i, in lb/min, is some function of the pressure drop $P_j - P_i$ along the flow path:

$$F_{j,i} = f(P_j - P_i) \tag{29}$$

Various models represent different types of flow paths, but they are typically nonlinear. For example, the power-law model is commonly implemented as

$$Q = C(\Delta P)^n \tag{30}$$

where

$Q = F/\rho$ = volumetric airflow rate, cfm

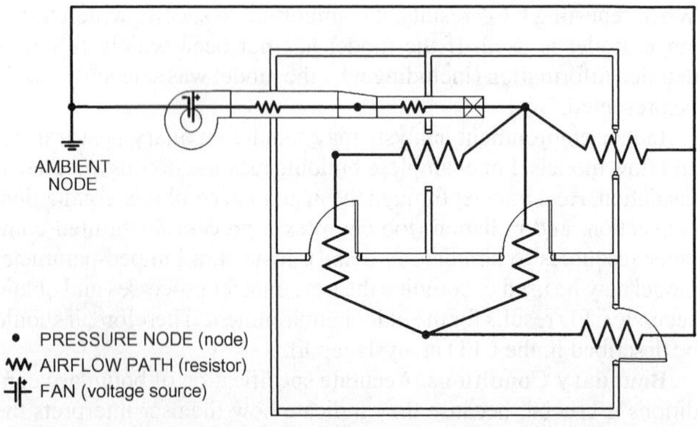

Fig. 13 Airflow Path Diagram

ΔP = pressure drop across opening, psi
C = flow coefficient, $\text{psi}^{1/n} \cdot \text{ft}^3/\text{s}$
n = flow exponent (typically 0.5 to 0.6)
ρ = density of air in flow path, lb/ft^3

$\Delta P_{j,i}$ is assumed to be governed by the Bernoulli equation, which accounts for static pressure on each side of the flow path and pressure differences through the flow path caused by density and height changes. Static pressure at flow path connections depends on the zone pressures, again after accounting for height-dependent pressure changes in the zones. Where a flow path connects to the building facade, the pressure also may depend on pressure imposed by wind (see Chapters 16 and 24). Typically, the calculated pressure drop through a flow path neglects heat transfer and changes in kinetic energy, but this is not an inherent limitation of the model.

The power law model is based on engineering equations for orifice flow (see Chapter 16). Models for duct system components (e.g., dampers, bends, transitions) also follow the power law, with flow coefficient C given by tables (see Chapter 21). Other models describe the flow through doors and windows, fans, and so on (Dols and Walton 2002; Fuestel 1998).

The network airflow model combines the flow element and zone relations by enforcing mass conservation at each zone. The mass of air m_i in zone i is given by the ideal gas law

$$m_i = \rho_i V_i = \frac{P_i V_i}{R_{air} T_i} \tag{31}$$

where

m_i = mass of air in zone i, lb
ρ_i = zone density, lb/ft^3
V_i = zone volume, ft^3
P_i = zone pressure, psi
T_i = zone temperature, °F
R_{air} = gas constant for air = 0.06856 Btu/lb·°F

For a transient solution, the principle of conservation of mass states that

$$\frac{\partial m_i}{\partial t} = \rho_i \frac{\partial V_i}{\partial t} + V_i \frac{\partial \rho_i}{\partial t} = \sum_j F_{j,i} + F_i \tag{32}$$

$$\frac{\partial m_i}{\partial t} \approx \frac{1}{\Delta t}\left[\left(\frac{P_i V_i}{R_{air} T_i}\right)_t - (m_i)_{t-\Delta t}\right] \tag{33}$$

where

$F_{j,i}$ = airflow rate between zones j and i (positive values indicate flows from j to i; negative values indicate flows from i to j), lb/min
F_i = nonflow processes that could add or remove significant quantities of air flows from j to i; negative values indicate flows from i to j

However, airflows are typically calculated for steady-state conditions. This is reasonable for most cases where driving forces change slowly compared to the airflow (e.g., because of the building's large thermal mass, or because rate-limited actuators change damper and fan settings slowly compared to the rate at which the airflow system reestablishes a steady state). Under this quasi-steady assumption, mass conservation in zone i reduces to

$$\sum_j F_{j,i} = 0 \tag{34}$$

This model was based on the assumption that airflows were quiescent and that the zones' resistance to airflow was negligible relative to the resistance imposed by the airflow paths that connect the zones. Hence, the model enforces conservation of mass in each zone, but does not conserve momentum. This means it cannot model some effects, such as the suction that develops in one branch of a duct junction because of flow in another branch (see Chapter 21), or effects of zone geometry (e.g., short-circuiting of a room when a ventilation supply duct blows air directly into a return air intake). For momentum-based effects, a CFD model of the room is preferable to a network model.

Solution Techniques

In a nodal formulation of the network airflow problem, zone pressures drive the problem. Specifically, the solution algorithm chooses one reference pressure for each zone, and then finds the driving pressure drops across each flow path, after accounting for changes of height in both zones and flow paths. Applying the element pressure/flow relations yields each path's mass flow. Finally, these flows are summed for each zone to determine whether mass conservation is satisfied.

This approach leads to a set of algebraic mass balance equations that must be satisfied simultaneously for any given point in time. Because airflows depend nonlinearly on node pressures, these equations are nonlinear, and therefore must be solved iteratively using a nonlinear equation solver. The simultaneous set of mass balance equations is typically solved using the **Newton-Raphson method** to "correct" the zone reference pressures until the simultaneous mass balance of all flows is achieved. This method requires a **correction vector**, which depends on the partial derivatives of relationships between flow and pressure for all flow connections. Therefore, these flow-pressure relationships must be first-order differentiable (Feustel 1998; Walton 1989).

The Newton-Raphson method begins with an initial guess of the pressures. A new estimated vector of all zone pressures $\{\mathbf{P}\}^*$ is computed from the current estimate of pressures $\{\mathbf{P}\}$ by

$$\{\mathbf{P}\}^* = \{\mathbf{P}\} - \{\mathbf{C}\} \tag{35}$$

where the correction vector $\{\mathbf{C}\}$ is computed by the matrix relationship

$$[\mathbf{J}]\{\mathbf{C}\} = \{\mathbf{B}\} \tag{36}$$

where $\{\mathbf{B}\}$ is a column vector of total flow into each zone, with each element given by

$$\mathbf{B}_i = \sum_j F_{j,i} \tag{37}$$

[J] is the square (i.e., N by N for a network of N zones) Jacobian matrix whose elements are given by

$$\mathbf{J}_{i,j} = \sum_i \frac{\partial F_{j,i}}{\partial P_j} \tag{38}$$

In Equations (37) and (38), $F_{j,i}$ and $\partial F_{j,i}/\partial P_j$ are evaluated using the current estimate of pressure $\{\mathbf{P}\}$.

Equation (35) represents a set of linear equations which must be solved iteratively until a convergent solution of the set of zone pressures is achieved. In its full form, **[J]** requires computer memory for N^2 values, and a standard Gauss elimination solution has execution time proportional to N^3. Sparse matrix methods can be used to reduce both the storage and execution time requirements. Two solution methods for the linear equations have been successfully implemented: **Skyline** (also called the **profile method**) and **preconditioned conjugate gradient (PCG)**, which may be useful for problems with many zones and junctions (Dols and Walton 2002). The number of iterations needed to find a solution may be reduced by applying descent-based techniques to Newton-Raphson (Dennis and Schnabel 1996). Under a fairly modest set of conditions, line search methods are guaranteed to converge to a unique solution (Lorenzetti 2002).

2.2 CONTAMINANT TRANSPORT MODELING

Fundamentals

Multizone contaminant transport models generally address transport of contaminants by advection via interzone airflows and mechanical system flows while accounting for some or all of the following: contaminant generation by various sources or chemical reaction, removal by filtration, chemical reaction, radiochemical decay, settling, or sorption of contaminants.

Unlike CFD models, the details of contaminant distribution within a zone are not modeled: each zone is considered well-mixed and characterized by a single concentration at any given point in time. Therefore, the well-mixed assumption's applicability to the mixing time and pattern of airflow in a zone should be considered. For example, the well-mixed assumption may be quite appropriate for zones with a mixing time well within the solution time step of interest (e.g., long-term off-gassing of building materials in common ventilation system configurations with relatively steady airflows). However, if a zone is characterized by steep concentration gradients and the time step of interest is relatively short (e.g., a chemical release in a relatively large zone), CFD analysis might be more appropriate. This is especially true if the reason for analysis is to resolve concentration gradients within the zone.

Solution Techniques

Generally, the goal is to solve a set of mass balance equations for each contaminant in each zone.

The mass of contaminant α in zone i is

$$m_{\alpha,i} = m_i C_{\alpha,i} \tag{39}$$

where m_i is the mass of air in zone i and $C_{\alpha,i}$ is the concentration mass fraction of α (lb of α/lb of air).

Contaminant is removed from zone i by

- Outward airflows from the zone at a rate of $\Sigma_j F_{i,j} C_{\alpha,j}$, where $F_{i,j}$ is the rate of air flow from zone i to zone j
- Removal at the rate $C_{\alpha,i} R_{\alpha,i}$ where $R_{\alpha,i}$ (lb of air/s) is a removal coefficient
- First-order chemical reactions with other contaminants $C_{\beta,i}$ (lb of β/lb of air) at rate $m_i \Sigma_\beta \kappa_{\alpha,\beta} C_{\beta,i}$, where $\kappa_{\alpha,\beta}$(1/s) is the kinetic reaction coefficient in zone i between species α and β

Contaminant is added to the zone by

- Inward airflows at rate $\Sigma_j (1 - \eta_{\alpha,j,i}) F_{j,i} C_{\alpha,j}$ where $\eta_{\alpha,j,i}$ is the filter efficiency in the path from zone j to zone i
- Generation at rate $G_{\alpha,i}$ (lb of α/s)
- Reactions of other contaminants

Conservation of contaminant mass for each species and assuming trace dispersal (i.e., $m_{\alpha,i} \ll m_i$) produces the following basic equation for contaminant dispersal for a given zone in a building:

$$\frac{dm_{\alpha,i}}{dt} = -R_{\alpha,i} C_{\alpha,i} - \sum_j F_{i,j} C_{\alpha,i} + \sum_j F_{i,j} (1 - \eta_{\alpha,j,i}) C_{\alpha,j} + m_i \sum_\beta \kappa_{\alpha,\beta} C_{\beta,i} + G_{\alpha,i} \tag{40}$$

This equation must be developed and solved for all zones to determine each contaminant's concentration. The various techniques for solving the ensuing set of equations can be categorized by the fundamental control volume used to develop them (i.e., Eulerian or Lagrangian), and by whether the analysis is geared towards solving the steady-state or dynamic system, or determining analytical solutions via eigen-analysis (Axley 1987, 1988; Dols and Walton 2002; Rodriguez and Allard 1992).

2.3 MULTIZONE MODELING APPROACHES

Simulation Planning

Planning can improve results and reduce the amount of input effort required in multizone simulations. The most important steps are determining what aspects of flow and contaminant transport are being studied, and what driving forces are likely to be most important.

One of the first decisions is defining zones in the model. The level of detail needed depends on both the building and scenario being modeled. For a study of contaminant transport from a garage into a house, separate zone models of clothes closets or kitchen cabinets are unnecessary and typically would only be needed if, for example, the source of the contaminant were inside the closet or cabinet. Because zones are typically broken where there are obstructions to air movement and/or differences in air properties, often a doorway between adjacent rooms is an appropriate place to define zones. Therefore, usually, a good starting point is to consider each room as a separate zone, and then model smaller enclosures in more detail or subdivide nonuniform rooms as necessary. On the other hand, sometimes the problem statement allows several rooms to be grouped together as a single zone. This is usually done to save user input time, because multizone models of even very large buildings can be quickly simulated on a desktop PC. HVAC system zoning also provides cues about how to group zones. Considering the primary driving forces (natural, mechanical, etc.) and the relative resistance of the flow elements that connect the zones to these forces can also be helpful. Starting with the assumption that each room is a zone, these changes can be made as the physics of the problem allow.

The type of simulation must also be determined. Are only airflow data necessary, or are contaminant concentrations also needed? Are the flow and contaminant transport problems steady-state, cyclical, or transient? Note that they may not be the same. Some models can simulate steady-state flow and transient contaminant transport.

During planning, the required model input data and boundary condition information must be specified, with the level of detail depending on the problem. Some items to consider are exterior envelope and interzonal leakage, weather conditions, wind pressure profiles, contaminant characteristics, contaminant source types and strengths, mechanical system flow rates, control algorithms, occupancy, and zone volumes.

Steps

The following process is typical of that used by experienced modelers to help catch mistakes and verify that the model is as intended. Always remember to save and test the model often.

1. **Input zones and building geometry**, using just enough detail to capture necessary information.
2. **Determine and specify building leakage.** This information may be obtained from blower door or tracer gas tests of the actual building, or estimated based on published data (see Chapter 16). Perform the following tests:
   - *Simulated blower door test*: Within the model, set all interior doors in the building to *open* and put a large pressurization fan in an exterior wall. Pressurize the building and use the fan's flow rate and consequent pressure difference across the exterior wall to calculate the leakage area per area of exterior wall. Verify specification of the proper amount of leakage on all walls by comparing inputs with data from an actual building or the literature. This is especially important when specifying individual leakage paths. If a result does not make sense, adjust leakage paths to see their effect on overall leakage.
   - *Simulation with typical weather boundary conditions.* Verify that the resulting infiltration rate is realistic.

3. **Check stack effects.** Remove the blower door fan from the model, specify a very cold outdoor temperature, and run a simulation. Check the location of the **neutral pressure level**, which is the collection of points on the building envelope where the pressure difference with the outdoors is zero. The points usually form a plane at the building's midheight, though it may be a bit higher if roof leakage occurs with no corresponding floor leakage. A very high or low neutral pressure level could indicate large unintended leaks, probably somewhere near the neutral pressure level. (Note that, in complex operating systems or scenarios, the neutral pressure level may not form a plane and could change with time.)
4. **Specify wind and wind pressure profiles** on exterior leakage paths: Some programs allow wind specification, but this has no effect unless the wind pressure profile for each path is also specified. Perform the following tests:
   - *Run a simulation with no stack effect or mechanical system, and a high wind.* Flow should be visible through each exterior path. This allows quick identification of paths that may be missing a wind pressure profile.
   - *Verify that inflows and outflows are as prescribed* for the wind pressure profile. (For example, inflow on the windward side, outflow for walls at negative pressure) This helps verify that the pressure profile is correctly input and that the building and wind are oriented properly.
   - *Try other terrain conditions* to see if changing this variable significantly affects results.
5. **Input air-handling system(s)** (if any). Again, use only as much detail as is necessary. For small buildings, it may be reasonable to represent the air-handling system as a simple fan through an exterior wall for ventilation. For internal distribution from zone to zone, HVAC system flows in and out of each zone must be specified. Duct details should be included only if they are an important aspect of the problem. Sometimes supply and return vents can be placed in plenums or other locations where duct leakage is expected, to approximate duct leakage. However, if pressure-driven leakage must be modeled, the ducts should be specified in detail. Keep in mind that leakage in VAV systems, for example, should be separately specified upstream and downstream of the VAV box. Perform the following tests:
   - *Run a simulation with no stack or wind driving forces* and check outdoor, return, and exhaust air volumes to verify that the outside air is properly defined. This is a common beginner's mistake because there are several ways to specify outside air (e.g., setting a percentage of outside air, or scheduling outside air when the default may be 100%), and they may override one another. Also note that the amount of return air specified must equal or exceed the recirculation air needed. Otherwise, outdoor air may be used to make up the difference.
   - *Verify a realistic pressure difference across walls.* For example, a 0.2 in. of water pressure difference would not occur in a real house, and probably indicates problems with either the system or leakage input. It is important that the magnitude of the pressure differences makes sense for the situation being modeled.
6. **Specify contaminants.** Contaminant sources are usually specified on either a mass or volume basis, although numerical counts (e.g., of particles, spores) can also be modeled and can typically be interchanged with mass units. Model refinement is often most appropriate and desirable near the contaminant source, where large concentration gradients are present. Simulation tests for pressure and velocity suggest the expected accuracy when a contaminant is added to the system. Transport of contaminants, particularly aerosols, is also influenced by other mechanisms, for which coefficients are specified in the basic transport equations.
   - *Verify that the model predicts conservation of contaminant mass* across multiple zones.
   - *Use experimental tracer analysis* using dynamically similar, nontoxic materials (if desired and feasible).
7. **Run a sensitivity analysis:** Deviations in some variables may need to be considered. Depending on the source of the input data and type of simulation, it is often good to know how the system performs over a range of certain variables. Possible items to consider include
   - *Formal sensitivity analysis*, if resources permit.
   - *Leakage dependence*, tested under a range of values. If conclusions are too leakage-dependent and leakage test data are not available, then a range of possible results should be considered.
   - *System pressure balance.* In a building with multiple air-handling systems, their design flow rates may imply perfect balance between systems; however, in real buildings, the balance will never be perfect, which can drive contaminants into shafts and distribute them through the building. Pressurizing or depressurizing a floor slightly compared to others (by specifying slightly imbalanced system flows) can illustrate how big this effect is.
   - *Weather effects*, which can be particularly important when studying infiltration or trying to maintain a pressure differential somewhere in the system. Verify that the system can accommodate the expected range of outdoor conditions.

2.4 VERIFICATION AND VALIDATION

Verification and validation of multizone models are similar in many regards to that of CFD models. Because the number of cases a complex multizone model can simulate is unlimited, Herrlin (1992) concluded that absolute validation is impossible. However, validation is still important to identify and eliminate large errors and to establish the model's range of applicability. Therefore, a model's performance should be evaluated under a variety of situations, with the recognition that predictions will always have a degree of uncertainty.

Herrlin lists three techniques of model validation:

- **Analytical verification** (comparison to simple analytically solved cases)
- **Intermodel comparison** (comparison of one model to another)
- **Empirical validation** (comparison to experimental tests)

Herrlin also discussed some specific difficulties in validating multizone airflow models, including input uncertainty (particularly of air leakage distribution) and attempting to simulate processes that cannot be modeled (e.g., using a steady-state airflow model to simulate dynamic airflow).

ASTM *Standard* D5157 provides information on establishing evaluation objectives, choosing data sets for evaluation, statistical tools for assessing model performance, and considerations in applying statistical tools. It stresses that data used for the evaluation process should be independent of the data used to develop the model. Also, sufficiently detailed information should be available for both the measured pollutant concentrations and the required input parameters. *Standard* D5157 also discusses the fact that model validation consists of multiple evaluations, with each evaluation assessing performance in specific situations.

Analytical Verification

Analytical verifications of multizone modeling tools are routinely performed to check the numerical solution. Analytical test cases are simple forms of problems that can be solved analytically to compare the model with an exact solution. For multizone models, these include airflow elements in series and parallel; stack effect; wind pressure effect; fan and duct elements; contaminant generation, dispersal, filtration, and deposition; and simple kinetic reactions. These tests are typically performed by model developers, but may be repeated by the user to develop confidence in the model and to verify the user's familiarity with the model. Such tests are not routinely published, but some were described by Walton (1989).

Unfortunately, most buildings are too complicated for the equations describing airflow and pollutant transport to be solved analytically. Therefore, analytical verification is of limited value in determining the adequacy of a multizone IAQ model for practical applications.

Intermodel Comparison

Intermodel comparison provides a relative check of different models' assumptions and numerical solutions. As with analytical verification, this is of limited value in evaluating a model's adequacy for practical applications. Generally, intermodel comparisons are not essential to a user, although good comparisons allow empirical validation conclusions to be generalized beyond the specific model studied.

Haghighat and Megri (1996) reported good agreement between CONTAM [the predecessor of CONTAMW (Dols and Walton 2002)], COMIS (Feustel et al. 1989), AIRNET (Walton 1989), CBSAIR (Haghighat and Rao 1991), and BUS (Tuomaala 1993) for airflow predictions for a four-zone model. The model building was two stories tall, with power-law flow elements for leakage. A single set of temperatures and wind-induced pressures was simulated. Model predictions for zone pressures and flow rates were within 5% and 13%, respectively.

Orme (2000) also found good agreement overall between CONTAM, COMIS, MZAP (unpublished), and BREEZE (BRE 1994) airflow predictions for a three-story building model. Power-law airflow elements were used to connect the four interior zones with each other and the ambient zone. A single wind speed and ambient temperature condition were applied. Note that both of these intermodel comparisons tested models for only a very limited range of conditions.

Empirical Validation

Empirical validation compares model assumptions and numerical solutions to indoor environmental problems of practical interest. However, the standard is only as accurate or realistic as the measurements used to produce it. Not only do all models have uncertainty, but all measurements do as well. Differences between model predictions and measurements could stem from errors in either set of data. As discussed in the section on CFD Modeling Approaches, comparison depends on the numerical model's capabilities and limiting assumptions, as well as the modeler's knowledge of both the model being applied and the indoor environment being modeled.

It is essential to apply valid statistical tools when interpreting comparisons of measurements and predictions. ASTM *Standard* D5157 provides three statistical tools for evaluating accuracy of IAQ predictions, and two additional statistical tools for assessing bias. Values for these statistical criteria are provided to indicate whether model performance is adequate. Note that the criteria and specific values in *Standard* D5157 are not ultimate arbiters of model accuracy, but they provide a useful template for the type of statistical analysis needed. Other valid statistical criteria may be substituted, with values appropriate for the accuracy needed for a specific project.

ASTM *Standard* D5157 suggests the following for assessing agreement between predictions:

- The correlation coefficient of predictions versus measurements should be 0.9 or greater.
- The line of regression between predictions and measurements should have a slope between 0.75 and 1.25 and an intercept less than 25% of the average measured concentration.

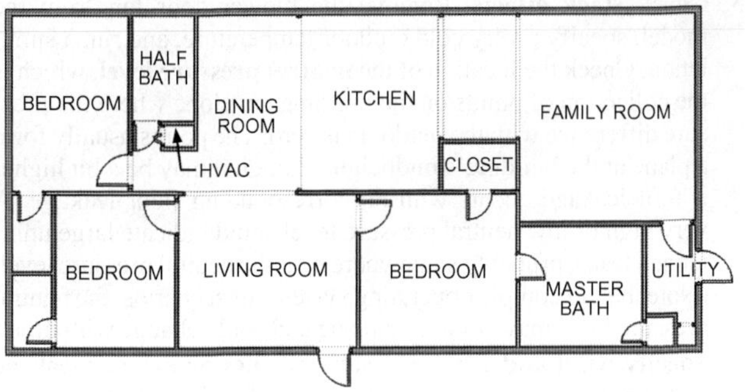

Fig. 14 Floor Plan of Living Area Level of Manufactured House

- The **normalized mean square error (NMSE)** should be less than 0.25. NMSE is calculated as

$$\mathrm{NMSE} = \sum_{i=1}^{N} (C_{pi} - C_{oi})^2 / (n\bar{C}_o\bar{C}_p) \tag{41}$$

where C_p is the predicted concentration and C_o is the observed concentration.

For assessing bias,

1. The **normalized** or **fractional bias FB of mean concentrations** should be 0.25 or lower, and is calculated as

$$\mathrm{FB} = 2(\bar{C}_p - \bar{C}_o)/(\bar{C}_p + \bar{C}_o) \tag{42}$$

2. The **fractional bias FS of variance** should be 0.5 or lower. FS is calculated as

$$\mathrm{FS} = 2(\sigma^2\bar{C}_p - \sigma^2\bar{C}_o)/(\sigma^2\bar{C}_p + \sigma^2\bar{C}_o) \tag{43}$$

Emmerich (2001) reviewed the research literature for reports of empirical multizone model validation for residential-scale buildings. Few reviewed reports used either the ASTM *Standard* D5157 measures or other limited statistical evaluations to evaluate the results. However, for those cases with sufficient published data, Emmerich calculated several statistical measures from *Standard* D5157. Although these measures specifically address concentrations, they have been used to compare predicted and measured airflow rates also. Table 1 summarizes these published multizone model validation efforts.

There are many published validations for residential buildings, but far fewer for large commercial buildings because of the significant effort and cost involved in detailed measuring of a large building. Commercial studies are available by Furbringer et al. (1993), Said and MacDonald (1991), and Upham (1997).

Example 1. Ventilation Characterization of a New Manufactured House. Develop a multizone model to investigate various ventilation strategies of a new double-wide manufactured home consisting of three levels: crawlspace, living area, and attic. The crawlspace is divided into two sections by an insulated plastic belly; the region above the belly contains HVAC ductwork, and the volume below vents to the outdoors. The living area is shown in Figure 14. The attic comprises the volume above the vaulted ceiling, with five roof vents and eave vents spanning the perimeter of the house. Figure 15 provides a schematic of the house, showing connections between the levels and the air distribution system.

The building has an automated data acquisition system for monitoring air temperatures, building pressures, weather, and HVAC operation. The instrumentation system also has an automated tracer gas system for continuous monitoring of building air change rates. The tracer gas system injects sulfur hexafluoride into the house every 4 to 6 h, allows it to mix to a uniform concentration, and then monitors the

Table 1 Summary of Multizone Model Validation Reports

Reference	Test Building	Model	Parameter Evaluated	R	m	B	NMSE	FB
Bassett 1990	Five houses	CONTAM	Zone air change rates	0.91	1.31	–0.23	0.35	0.08
			Interzone airflows	0.27	0.10	1.34	2.98	0.37
Blomsterberg et al. 1999	Houses and apartment flats	COMIS	Average whole-house air change rates	0.98	1.04	–0.03	0.01	0.01
			Average room air change rates	0.72	0.70	0.32	0.24	0.03
Borchiellini et al. 1995	Two test houses	COMIS	Average interzone airflows	0.84	0.60	0.18	0.41	–0.24
Emmerich and Nabinger 2000	Single-zone test house	CONTAM	0.3 to 5.0 μm particle concentrations	0.94 to 0.99	0.84 to 1.02	–0.25 to 0.29	0.04 to 0.19	–0.26 to 0.16
Koontz et al. 1992	Test chamber	CONTAM	Methylene chloride concentration	0.98	1.08	0.07	0.20	0.16
	Two-zone research house	CONTAM	Transient CO concentration (zone 1)	0.94	0.70	0.14	0.15	0.06
			Transient CO concentration (zone 2)	0.98	0.85	0.26	0.02	–0.11
Haghighat and Megri 1996	Multizone laboratory	CONTAM	Interzone airflows	0.96	0.90	0.10	0.18	0.002
	House	CONTAM	Room airflows	0.96	0.84	0.14	0.04	–0.02
Lansari et al. 1996	Two-story house with garage	CONTAM	Tracer gas concentrations in garage	0.97	1.07	0.10	0.01	–0.03
			Tracer gas concentrations in other rooms	0.92	0.94	0.18	0.12	–0.27
Sextro et al. 1999	Three-story test building	CONTAM	Tracer gas concentrations	0.97	1.04	0.14	0.10	0.16
Yoshino et al. 1995	Three-room test house	COMIS	Air change rates	0.79	0.87	NA	NA	NA
			Tracer gas concentrations	0.98	1.06	NA	NA	NA
Zhao et al. 1998	Test house	COMIS	Room air change rates	0.72	0.92	NA	NA	NA
			Tracer gas concentrations	0.93	0.93	NA	NA	NA

Source: Emmerich (2001).
Note: R = correlation coefficient; m = slope of regression line; B = ratio of intercept of regression line to average measured value; NMSE = normalized mean square error; FB = fractional bias.

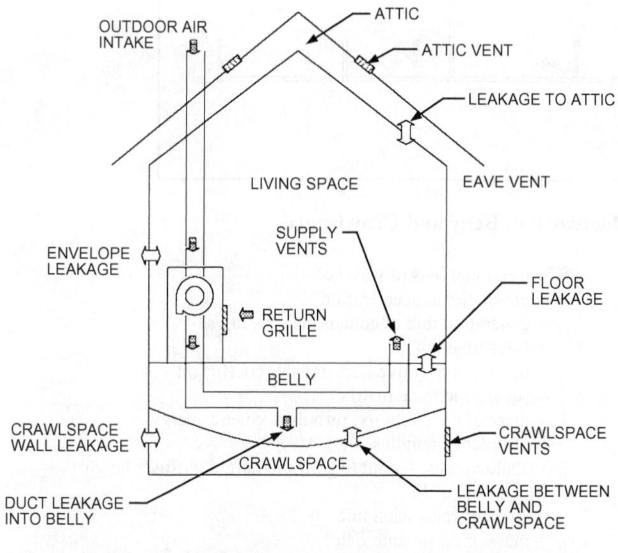

Fig. 15 Schematic of Ventilation System and Envelope Leakage

concentration decay in all the major zones of the building. Air change rates are then calculated based on the tracer gas decay rate in the living space.

Model Description. The model contains four levels: crawlspace, belly volume, living area (Figure 16), and attic. The duct modeling capabilities (see Figure 17 depicting belly level) were used to model the forced-air system. Leakage values of model airflow paths are listed in Table 2. Leaks in the living space envelope include the exterior wall and interfaces between the ceiling and wall, floor and wall, and the walls at the corners. In addition, there are two types of windows, the exterior doors, and the living space floor, which contains openings into the belly. There are also interior airflow paths, including leaks in the walls, doorframes, and open doors. Note that for all the tests and simulations performed, all interior doors were open. The attic has leakage in its floor (i.e., the ceiling of the living space), as well as the two types of attic vents to the outdoors. The crawlspace has leaks to the outdoors in the walls, vents in the front and rear of the house, and an access door. The model also includes a leak from the crawlspace into the belly. Finally, the duct leak into the belly, based on the described measurement, is included in the model.

Results. Tracer gas decay tests were simulated using the multizone model. Figure 18 shows the results of one of these simulations 30 min after injection of the tracer gas. The darker the shading, the higher the tracer gas concentration.

Figure 19A shows the measured and predicted air change rates with the forced-air system off as a function of indoor/outdoor air temperature difference under low wind speed conditions. Values predicted with the model are in good agreement with the measurements, particularly at low values of ΔT, but tend to underpredict by around 20% at higher values. Note that in all reported measurements and predictions, the outdoor air intake on the forced-air system and the window inlet vents are closed.

Figure 19B plots the measured and predicted air change rates with the forced-air system on, again for low wind speeds. Under positive temperature differences, the measured air change rates are actually lower than with the system off, which might not be expected with significant duct leakage. Airflow measurements indicate that the system moves about 950 cfm, but about 265 cfm is lost through duct leakage into the belly. Some of this airflow returns to the living space through leaks in the floor, but some flows through the crawlspace to the outdoors, which tends to depressurize the house. A significant air change rate is seen at zero ΔT, but this is not unexpected given the duct leakage. At higher values of ΔT, the stack effect "competes" with duct leakage into the belly, decreasing the air change rate into the house. This effect has actually been proposed as a means of controlling airflow and

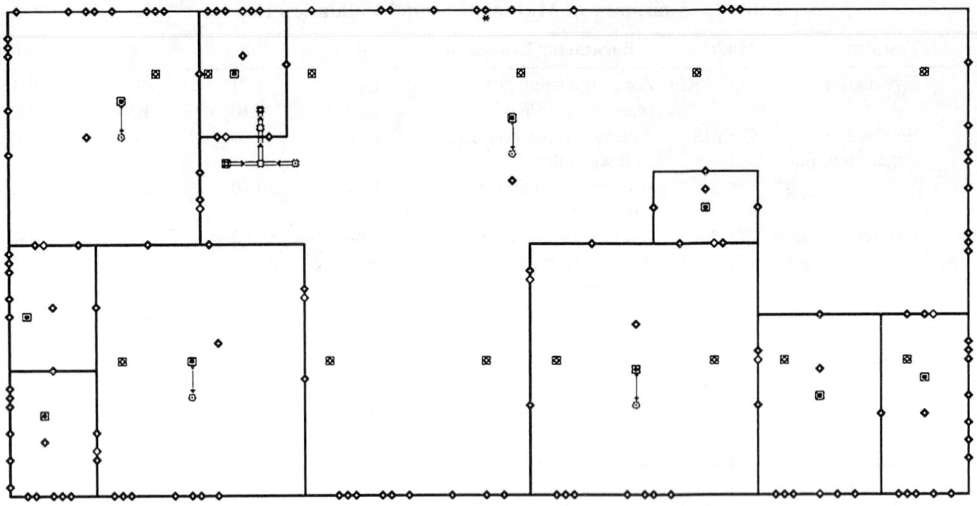

Fig. 16 Multizone Representation of First Floor

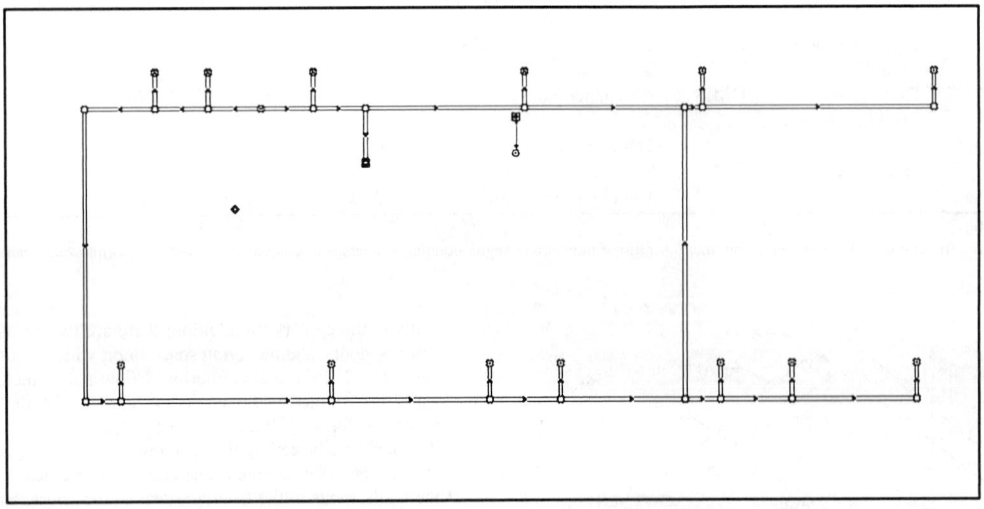

Fig. 17 Multizone Representation of Ductwork in Belly and Crawlspace

contaminant entry from crawlspaces (Phaff and De Gids 1994). Overall, with the fan on, the agreement between the predicted and measured air change rates is quite good.

2.5 SYMBOLS

A_0 = diffuser effective area
B = ratio of intercept of regression line to average measured value
$\{\mathbf{B}\}$ = column vector of total flow into each zone
$\{\mathbf{C}\}$ = correction vector
C = flow coefficient, $\text{psi}^{1/n} \cdot \text{ft}^3/\text{s}$; concentration mass fraction
C_o = observed concentration
c_p = concentration in air
C_p = specific heat; predicted concentration
c_R = mean concentration in return openings
$C_{\alpha,i}$ = concentration mass fraction of α, lb_α/lb of air
C_μ = k-ε turbulence model constant
E = constant depending on wall roughness (9.8 for hydraulically smooth walls)
f = [see Equation (29)]
FB = fractional bias of mean concentrations
F_i = nonflow processes that could add or remove significant quantities of air
$F_{j,i}$ = mass flow rate from zone j to zone i, lb/min
FS = fractional bias of variance
g = gravitational acceleration
$G_{\alpha,i}$ = generation rate of contaminant α, lb_α/s
G_Δ = filter function
h = height; convective heat transfer coefficient
$[\mathbf{J}]$ = square Jacobian matrix
k = thermal conductivity; turbulent kinetic energy
l = turbulence length scale
L = characteristic length (e.g., room height, diffuser height)
m = mass of air, lb
M = slope of regression line
m_i = mass of air in zone i, lb
$\dot{m}$ = mass flow rate
n = flow exponent (typically 0.5 to 0.6)
NMSE = normalized mean square error
P = pressure
ΔP = pressure drop across opening, psi
$\{\mathbf{P}\}$ = estimated pressures
$\{\mathbf{P}^*\}$ = estimated vector of all zone pressures
Pe = Peclet number (ratio of convection to conduction)
P_i, P_j = zone pressure, psi
Q = volumetric airflow rate, F/ρ, cfm
R = removal coefficient; correlation coefficient
R_{air} = gas constant of air, 0.06856 Btu/lb·°F

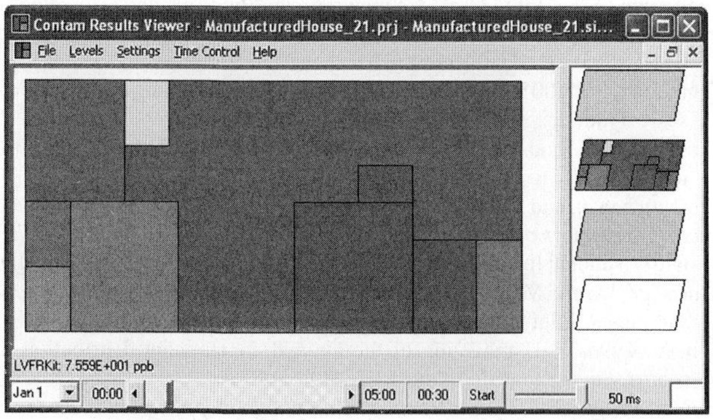

Fig. 18 Test Simulation of Concentration of Tracer Gas Decay in Manufactured House 30 min After Injection

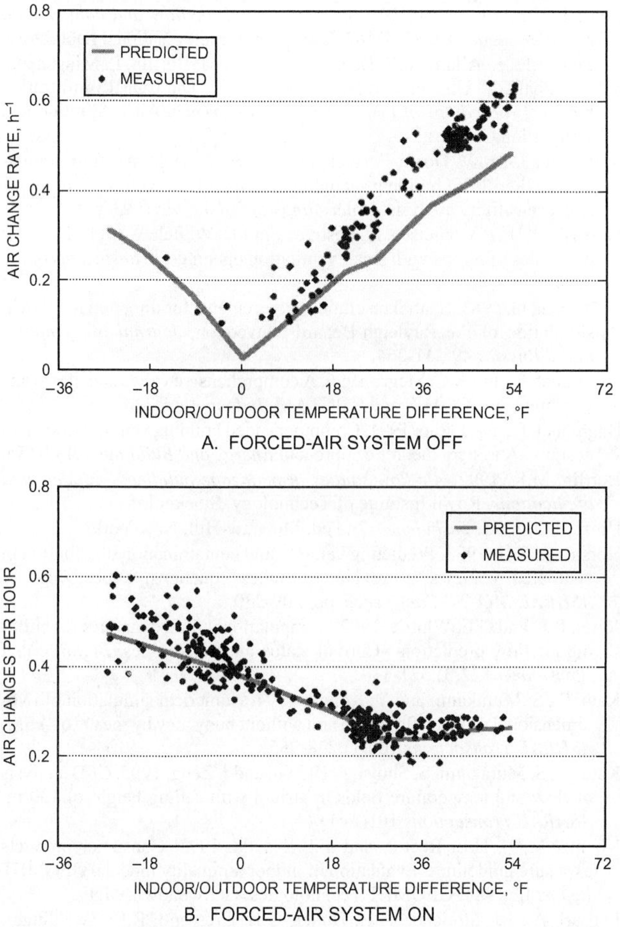

Fig. 19 Measured and Predicted Air Change Rates for Wind Speeds less than 4.5 mph

Ra = Rayleigh number
Re = Reynolds number
s_{ij} = strain rate tensor
S_ϕ = source or sink
t = time, s
T = temperature, °F
ΔT = temperature change
TI = turbulence intensity, %
T_s = surface temperature
T_i = zone temperature, °F

Table 2 Leakage Values of Model Airflow Components

	Exterior Airflow Paths	ELA at 0.016 in. of water
Living space envelope	Exterior wall	0.002 in²/ft²
	Ceiling wall interface	0.038 in²/ft²
	Floor wall interface	0.059 in²/ft
	Window #1	0.78 in²
	Window #2	0.30 in²
	Corner interface	0.038 in²/ft
	Exterior doors	2.90 in²
	Living space floor to belly volume	0.053 in²/ft²
Interior airflow paths	Interior walls	0.029 in²/ft²
	Bedroom doorframe	6.36 in²
	Open interior doors	6.5 by 3 ft
	Bathroom doorframe	5.12 in²
	Interior doorframe	3.88 in²
	Closet doorframe	0.71 in²
Attic	Attic floor	0.029 in²/ft²
	Roof vents	1.45 ft²
	Eave vents	5.0 in²/ft
Crawlspace and belly	Exterior walls of crawlspace	0.36 in²/ft²
	Rear crawlspace vents	50 in²
	Front crawlspace vents	72 in²
	Crawlspace access door	32 in²
	Crawlspace to belly	40 in²
	Duct leak into belly	5 in²

U = velocity
u_i = instantaneous velocity
$\bar{u}_i$ = ensemble average of ν for steady flow
u_i' = fluctuation velocity
u_j = velocity in j direction, fpm
U_P = velocity parallel to wall at ΔY_p
U_{ref} = mean stream velocity
U_0 = air supply velocity for momentum source
V_i = zone volume, ft³
x_i = distance in i direction, ft
x_j = distance in j direction, ft
Y^+ = dimensionless distance from wall
ΔY_p = distance from wall to center of first cell

Greek

α, β = contaminants
Γ_ϕ = generalized diffusion coefficient or transport property of fluid flow
ε = dissipation rate of turbulent kinetic energy
η = Kolmogorov length scale; filter efficiency
κ = von Karmann's constant (0.41)
$\kappa_{\alpha,\beta}$ = kinetic reaction coefficient between α and β
μ = dynamic viscosity
μ_t = eddy viscosity
ν = kinematic viscosity
ρ = density, lb/ft³
ρ_i = zone density, lb/ft³
σ = standard deviation
τ_{ij} = viscous tensor stress
τ_w = wall shear stress
ϕ = transport property (1 for mass continuity, momentum, temperature, or species concentration)

REFERENCES

ASHRAE members can access *ASHRAE Journal* articles and ASHRAE research project final reports at technologyportal .ashrae.org. Articles and reports are also available for purchase by nonmembers in the online ASHRAE Bookstore at www.ashrae.org /bookstore.

AIAA. 1998. Guide for the verification and validation of computational fluid dynamics simulations. AIAA *Standard* G-077-1998. American Institute of Aeronautics and Astronautics, Reston, VA.

Anderson, J.D., Jr. 1995. *Computational fluid dynamics: The basics with applications*. McGraw-Hill, New York.

Anderson, D.A., J.C. Tannehill, and R.H. Pletcher. 1984. *Computational fluid dynamics and heat transfer*. Hemisphere, Washington, D.C.

ASTM. 1997. Standard guide for statistical evaluation of indoor air quality models. *Standard* D5157-97(2003)e1. American Society for Testing and Materials, West Conshohocken, PA.

Awbi, H.B. 1991. *Ventilation of buildings*. Chapman & Hall, London.

Axley, J.A. 1987. *Indoor air quality modeling, phase II report.* NBSIR 87-3661. National Institute of Standards and Technology, Gaithersburg, MD.

Axley, J.A. 1988. *Progress toward a general analytical method for predicting indoor air pollution in buildings—Indoor air quality modeling, phase III report.* NBSIR 88-3814. National Institute of Standards and Technology, Gaithersburg, MD.

Baker, A.J., P.T. Williams, and R.M. Kelso. 1994. Numerical calculation of room air motion—Part 1. *ASHRAE Transactions* 100(1):514-530.

Bassett, M. 1990. Infiltration and leakage paths in single family houses—A multizone infiltration case study. *AIVC Technical Note* 27. Air Infiltration and Ventilation Centre, Brussels, Belgium.

Beausoleil-Morrison, I. 2000. *The adaptive coupling of heat and air flow modelling with dynamic whole-building.* Ph.D. dissertation, Department of Mechanical Engineering, University of Strathclyde, Glasgow.

Bernard, P.S., and J.M. Wallace. 2002. *Turbulent flow: Analysis, measurement, and prediction.* John Wiley & Sons, Hoboken, NJ.

Blomsterberg, A., T. Carlsson, C. Svensson, and J. Kronvall. 1999. Air flows in dwellings—Simulations and measurements. *Energy and Buildings* 30:87-95.

Borchiellini, R., M. Cali, and M. Torchio. 1995. Experimental evaluation of COMIS results for ventilation of a detached house. *ASHRAE Transactions* 101(1).

BRE. 1994. *BREEZE 6.0 user manual.* Building Research Establishment, Garston, U.K.

Breuer, M. 1998. Large eddy simulation of the subcritical flow past a circular cylinder: Numerical and modeling aspects. *International Journal of Numerical Methods in Fluids* 28:1281-1302.

Chen, Q. 1988. *Indoor airflow, air quality and energy consumption of buildings*. Ph.D. dissertation, Delft University of Technology, The Netherlands.

Chen, Q. 1996. Prediction of room air motion by Reynolds-stress models. *Building and Environment* 31(3):233-244.

Chen, Q., and Z. Jiang. 1992. Significant questions in predicting room air motion. *ASHRAE Transactions* 98(1):929-939.

Chen, Q., and A. Moser. 1991. Simulation of a multiple-nozzle diffuser. *Proceedings of the 12th AIVC Conference* 2:1-14.

Chen, Q., A. Moser, and A. Huber. 1990. Prediction of buoyant, turbulent flow by a low Reynolds-number k-ε model. *ASHRAE Transactions* 96(1):564-573.

Chen, Q., and J. Srebric. 2000. Simplified diffuser boundary conditions for numerical room airflow models. ASHRAE Research Project (RP) 1009, *Final Report.*

Chen, Q., and J. Srebric. 2002. A procedure for verification, validation, and reporting of indoor environment CFD analyses. *International Journal of HVAC&R Research* (now *Science and Technology for the Built Environment)* 8(2):201-216.

Chen, Q., and W. Xu. 1998. A zero-equation turbulence model for indoor airflow simulation. *Energy and Buildings* 28(2):137-144.

Cherukat, P., Y. Na, and T. J. Hanratty. 1998. Direct numerical simulation of a fully developed turbulent flow over a wavy wall. *Theoretical and Computational Fluid Dynamics* 11:109-134.

Chester, S., F. Charlette, and C. Meneveau. 2001. Dynamic model for LES without test filtering: Quantifying the accuracy of Taylor series approximations. *Theoretical and Computational Fluid Dynamics* 15:165-181.

Corrsin, S. 1961. Turbulent flow. *American Scientist* 49:300-325.

Dennis, J.E., and R.B. Schnabel. 1996. *Numerical methods for unconstrained optimization and nonlinear equations.* Society for Industrial and Applied Mathematics, Philadelphia.

Dols, W.S., and G. Walton. 2002. *CONTAMW 2.0 user manual.* NISTIR 6921. National Institute of Standards and Technology, Gaithersburg, MD.

Emmerich, S.J. 1997. *Use of computational fluid dynamics to analyze indoor air quality issues*. NISTIR 5997. National Institute of Standards and Technology, Gaithersburg, MD.

Emmerich, S.J. 2001. Validation of multizone IAQ modeling of residential-scale buildings: A review. *ASHRAE Transactions* 107.

Emmerich, S.J., and K.B. McGrattan. 1998. Application of a large eddy simulation model to study room airflow *ASHRAE Transactions* 104(1):1-9.

Emmerich, S.J., and S.J. Nabinger. 2000. *Measurement and simulation of the IAQ impact of particle air cleaner in a single-zone building.* NISTIR 6461. National Institute of Standards and Technology, Gaithersburg, MD.

Etheridge, D., and M. Sandberg. 1996. *Building ventilation, theory and measurements.* John Wiley & Sons, Chichester, NY.

Fan, Y. 1995. CFD modeling of the air and contaminant distribution in rooms. *Energy and Buildings* 23:33-39.

Fanger, P.O. 1972. *Thermal comfort: Analysis and application in environmental engineering.* McGraw-Hill.

Ferziger, J.H. 1977. Large eddy numerical simulations of turbulent flows. *AIAA Journal* 15(9):1261-1267.

Ferziger, J., and M. Peric. 1997. *Computational methods for fluid dynamics*. Springer, New York.

Feustel, H.E. 1998. *COMIS—An international air-flow and contaminant transport model.* LBNL 42182. Lawrence Berkeley National Laboratory.

Feustel, H.E., F. Allard, V.B. Dorer, M. Grosso, M. Herrlin, L. Mingsheng, J.C. Phaff, Y. Utsumi, and H. Yoshino. 1989. The COMIS infiltration model. *Proceedings of the 10th AIVC Conference,* Air Infiltration and Ventilation Centre.

Furbringer J.-M., V. Dorer, F. Huck, and A. Weber. 1993. Air flow simulation of the LESO building including a comparison with measurements and a sensitivity analysis. *Proceedings of Indoor Air 1993*, p. 5.

Gosman, A.D., P.V. Nielsen, A. Restivo, and J.H. Whitelaw. 1980. The flow properties of rooms with small ventilation openings. *Transactions of the ASME.*

Grötzbach, G. 1983. Spatial resolution requirements for direction numerical simulation of the Rayleigh-Bénard convection. *Journal of Computational Physics* 49:241-264.

Haghighat, F., and A.C. Megri. 1996. A comprehensive validation of two airflow models—COMIS and CONTAM. *Indoor Air* 6:278-288.

Haghighat, F., and J. Rao. 1991. Computer-aided building ventilation system design—A system theoretic approach. *Energy and Buildings* 1:147-155.

Herrlin, M.K. 1992. *Air-flow studies in multizone buildings—Models and applications.* Royal Institute of Technology, Stockholm.

Hinze, J.O. 1975. *Turbulence*, 2nd ed. McGraw-Hill, New York.

Horstman, R.H. 1988. Predicting velocity and contamination distribution in ventilated volumes using Navier-Stokes equations. *Proceedings of ASHRAE IAQ '88 Conference,* pp. 209-230.

Jones, P.J., and G.E. Whittle. 1992. Computational fluid dynamics for building air flow prediction—Current status and capabilities. *Building and Environment* 27(3):321-338.

Kato, S., S. Murakami, and Y. Kondo. 1994. Numerical simulation of two-dimensional room airflow with and without buoyancy by means of ASM. *ASHRAE Transactions* 100(1):238-255.

Kato, S., S. Murakami, S. Shoya, F. Hanyu, and J. Zeng. 1995. CFD analysis of flow and temperature fields in atrium with ceiling height of 130 m. *ASHRAE Transactions* 101(2):1144-1157.

Koontz, M.D., H.E. Rector, and N.L. Nagda. 1992. Consumer products exposure guidelines: Evaluation of indoor air quality models. GEOMET *Report* IE-1980. GEOMET Technologies, Germantown, MD.

Lansari, A., J.J. Streicher, A.H. Huber, G.H. Crescenti, R.B. Zweidinger, J.W. Duncan, C.P. Weisel, and R.M. Burton. 1996. Dispersion of automotive alternative fuel vapors within a residence and its attached garage. *Indoor Air* 6:118-126.

Launder, B.E. 1989. Second-moment closure: Present . . . and future? *International Journal of Heat and Fluid Flow* 10:282-300.

Launder, B.E., and D.B. Spalding. 1974. The numerical computation of turbulent flows. *Computer Methods in Applied Mechanics and Engineering* 3:269-289.

Launder, B.E., G.J. Reece, and W. Rodi. 1975. Progress in the development of a Reynolds-stress turbulence closure. *Journal of Fluid Mechanics* 68(3):537-566.

Launder, B.E., and B.I. Sharma. 1974. Application of the energy dissipation model of turbulence to the calculation of flow near a spinning disc. *Letters in Heat and Mass Transfer* 1(2):131-138.

Lin, C.H., M.F. Ahlers, A.K. Davenport, L.M. Sedgwick, R.H. Horstman, and J.C. Yu. 2001. *A numerical model for airborne disease transmission in a 767-300 passenger cabin.* Final report to the National Institute for Occupational Safety and Health, contract no. 200-2000-08001. Boeing Commercial Airplanes Group.

Lin, C.H., T. Han, and C.A. Koromilas. 1992. Effect of HVAC design parameters on passenger thermal comfort. SAE *Paper* No. 920264. Society of Automotive Engineers, Warrendale, PA.

Ling, W., J.N. Chung, T.R. Troutt, and C.T. Crowe. 1998. Direct numerical simulation of a three-dimensional temporal mixing layer with particle dispersion. *Journal of Fluid Mechanics* 358:61-85.

Lorenzetti, D.M. 2002. Computational aspects of nodal multizone airflow systems. *Building and Environment* 37:1083-1090.

Mashayek, F. 1998. Direct numerical simulation of evaporating droplet dispersion in forced low Mach number turbulence. *International Journal of Heat and Mass Transfer* 41(17):2601-2617.

Mathieu, J., and J. Scott. 2000. *An introduction to turbulent flow*. Cambridge University.

Monin, A.S., and A.M. Yaglom. 1971. *Statistical fluid mechanics*, vol. 1. MIT Press, Cambridge.

Moser, A., F. Off, A. Schälin, and X. Yuan. 1995. Numerical modeling of heat transfer by radiation and convection in an atrium with thermal inertia. *ASHRAE Transactions* 101(2):1136-1143.

Murakami, S. Kato, and R. Ooka. 1994. Comparison of numerical predictions of horizontal nonisothermal jet in a room with three turbulence models—k-ε, EVM, ASM, and DSM. *ASHRAE Transactions* 100(2): 697-706.

Nielsen, P.V. 1975. Prediction of air flow and comfort in air conditioned spaces. *ASHRAE Transactions* 81(2):247-259.

Nielsen, P.V. 1992. The description of supply openings in numerical models for room air distribution. *ASHRAE Transactions* 98(1):963-971.

Nielsen, P.V. 1995. Air flow in an exposition pavilion studied by scale-model experiments and computational fluid dynamics. *ASHRAE Transactions* 101(2):1118-1126.

Nielsen. P.V. 1998. The selection of turbulence models for prediction of room airflow. *ASHRAE Transactions* 104(1B):1119-1127.

Nielsen, P.V., and T. Tryggvason. 1998. Computational fluid dynamics and building energy performance simulation. *Proceedings of ROOMVENT '98: Sixth International Conference on Air Distribution in Rooms*, Stockholm, 1:101-107.

Orme, M. 2000. Applicable input data for a proposed ventilation modeling data guide. *ASHRAE Transactions* 106(2).

Phaff, H.J.C., and W.F. deGids. 1994. The air lock floor. *Proceedings of 5th Air Infiltration and Ventilation Centre Conference*. Air Infiltration and Ventilation Centre, Brussels, Belgium.

Pope, S.B. 2000. *Turbulent flows*. Cambridge University.

Rajaratnam, N. 1976. *Turbulent jets*. Elsevier, Amsterdam.

Reynolds, O. 1895. On the dynamical theory of incompressible viscous fluids and the determination of the criterion. *Philosophical Transactions of the Royal Society, London* A(186):123.

Rodriguez, E.A., and F. Allard. 1992. Coupling COMIS airflow model with other transfer phenomena. *Energy and Buildings* 18:147-157.

Russell, M.B., and P.N. Surendran. 2000. Use of computational fluid dynamics to aid studies of room air distribution: A review of some recent work. *Proceedings of CIBSE A: Building Services Engineering Research and Technology* 21(4):241-247.

Said, M.N., and R.A. MacDonald. 1991. An evaluation of a network smoke control model. *ASHRAE Transactions* 97(1):275-282.

Schälin, A., and P.V. Nielsen. 2004. Impact of turbulence anisotropy near walls in room air flow. *Indoor Air* 14(3):159-168. dx.doi.org/10.1111/j.1600-0668.2004.00201e.x.

Sextro, R.G., J.M. Daisey, H.E. Feustel, D.J. Dickerhoff, and C. Jump. 1999. Comparison of modeled and measured tracer gas concentrations in a multizone building. *Proceedings of Indoor Air '99*, vol. 1.

Smagorinsky, J. 1963. General circulation experiments with primitive equations. *Monthly Weather Review* 91:99-165.

Spalart, P.R. 2000. Strategies for turbulence modeling and simulations. *International Journal of Heat and Fluid Flow* 21:252-263.

Srebric, J. 2000. *Simplified methodology for indoor environment design*. Ph.D. dissertation, Department of Architecture, Massachusetts Institute of Technology, Cambridge.

Srebric, J., and Q. Chen. 2001. A method of test to obtain diffuser data for CFD modeling of room airflow. *ASHRAE Transactions* 107(2):108-116.

Srebric, J., and Q. Chen. 2002. Simplified numerical models for complex air supply diffusers. *International Journal of HVAC&R Research* (now *Science and Technology for the Built Environment*) 8(3): 277-294.

Tennekes, H., and J. L. Lumley. 1972. *A first course in turbulence*. MIT Press, Cambridge.

Tuomaala, P. 1993. New building air flow simulation model: Theoretical bases. *Building Services Engineering Research and Technology* 14: 151-157.

Upham, R.D. 1997. *A validation study of multizone air flow and contaminant migration simulation program CONTAM as applied to tall buildings*. M.S. thesis. The Pennsylvania State University, University Park.

Versteeg, H., and W. Malalasekera. 1995. *An introduction to computational fluid dynamics: The finite volume method*. Prentice Hall, Old Tappan, NJ.

Walton, G.N. 1989. *AIRNET—A computer program for building network airflow modeling*. NISTIR 89-4072. National Institute of Standards and Technology, Gaithersburg, MD.

Wilcox, D.C. 1998. *Turbulence modeling for CFD*, 2nd ed. DCW Industries, La Cañada, CA.

Williams, P.T., A.J. Baker, and R.M. Kelso. 1994a. Numerical calculation of room air motion—Part 2. *ASHRAE Transactions* 100(1):531-548.

Williams, P.T., A.J. Baker, and R.M. Kelso. 1994b. Numerical calculation of room air motion—Part 3. *ASHRAE Transactions* 100(1):549-564.

Yoshino, H., Z. Yun, H. Kobayashi, and Y. Utsumi. 1995. Simulation and measurement of air infiltration and pollutant transport using a passive solar test house. *ASHRAE Transactions* 101(1).

Yuan, X., A. Moser, and P. Suter. 1994. Wall functions for numerical simulations of turbulent natural convection. *Proceedings of the 10th International Heat Transfer Conference*, Brighton, U.K., pp. 191-196.

Zhai, Z., and Q. Chen. 2003. Solution characters of iterative coupling between energy simulation and CFD programs. *Energy and Buildings* 35(5):493-505.

Zhai, Z., Q. Chen, P. Haves, and J.H. Klems. 2002. On approaches to couple energy simulation and computational fluid dynamics programs. *Building and Environment* 37:857-864.

Zhang, G., S. Morsing, B. Bjerg, K. Svidt, and J.S. Strom. 2000. Test room for validation of airflow patterns estimated by computational fluid dynamics. *Journal of Agricultural Engineering Research* 76:141-148.

Zhao, Y., H. Yoshino, and H. Okuyama. 1998. Evaluation of the COMIS model by comparing simulation and measurement of airflow and pollutant concentration. *Indoor Air* 8:123-130.

BIBLIOGRAPHY

Feustel, H.E., and B.V. Smith. 1997. *COMIS 3.0 user's guide*. Lawrence Berkeley National Laboratory.

Jiang, Y., D. Alexander, H. Jenkins, R. Arthur, and Q. Chen. 2003. Natural ventilation in buildings: measurement in a wind tunnel and numerical simulation with large eddy simulation. *Journal of Wind Engineering and Industrial Aerodynamics* 91(3):331-353.

Jiang, Y., and Q. Chen. 2001. Study of natural ventilation in buildings by large eddy simulation. *Journal of Wind Engineering and Industrial Aerodynamics*. 89(13):1155-1178.

Jiang, Y., and Q. Chen. 2002. Effect of fluctuating wind direction on cross natural ventilation in building from large eddy simulation. *Building and Environment* 37(4):379-386.

Jiang, Y., and Q. Chen. 2003. Buoyancy-driven single-sided natural ventilation in buildings with large openings. *International Journal of Heat and Mass Transfer* 46(6):973-988.

Jiang, Y., M. Su, and Q. Chen. 2003. Using large eddy simulation to study airflows in and around buildings. *ASHRAE Transactions* 109(2).

Liddament, M., and C. Allen. 1983. The validation and comparison of mathematical models of air infiltration. *AIC Technical Note* 11. Air Infiltration Centre, Brussels, Belgium.

Spalart, P.R., and S.R. Allmaras. 1994. A one-equation turbulence model for aerodynamic flows. *La Recherche Aérospatiale* 1:5.

Su, M., Q. Chen, and C.-M. Chiang. 2001. Comparison of different subgrid-scale models of large eddy simulation for indoor airflow modeling. *Journal of Fluids Engineering* 123:628-639.

CHAPTER 14

CLIMATIC DESIGN INFORMATION

THIS chapter and the data on the accompanying CD-ROM provide the climatic design information for 8118 locations in the United States, Canada, and around the world. This is an increase of 1675 stations from the 2013 *ASHRAE Handbook—Fundamentals*. As in the previous edition, the large number of stations made printing the whole tables impractical. Consequently, the complete table of design conditions for only Atlanta, GA, appears in this printed chapter to illustrate the table format. However, a subset of the table elements most often used is presented in the Appendix at the end of this chapter for selected stations representing major urban centers in the United States, Canada, and around the world. The complete data tables for all 8118 stations are contained on the CD-ROM that accompanies this book.

This climatic design information is commonly used for design, sizing, distribution, installation, and marketing of heating, ventilating, air-conditioning, and dehumidification equipment, as well as for other energy-related processes in residential, agricultural, commercial, and industrial applications. These summaries include values of dry-bulb, wet-bulb, and dew-point temperature, and wind speed with direction at various frequencies of occurrence. Also included are monthly degree-days to various bases, parameters to calculate clear-sky irradiance, and monthly averages of daily all-sky solar radiation. Sources of other climate information of potential interest to ASHRAE members are described later in this chapter.

Design information in this chapter was developed largely through research project RP-1699 (Roth 2017). The information includes design values of dry-bulb with mean coincident wet-bulb temperature, design wet-bulb with mean coincident dry-bulb temperature, and design dew-point with mean coincident dry-bulb temperature and corresponding humidity ratio. These data allow the designer to consider various operational peak conditions. Design values of wind speed facilitate the design of smoke management systems in buildings (Lamming and Salmon 1996, 1998).

Warm-season temperature and humidity conditions are based on annual percentiles of 0.4, 1.0, and 2.0. Cold-season conditions are based on annual percentiles of 99.6 and 99.0. The use of annual percentiles to define design conditions ensures that they represent the same probability of occurrence in any climate, regardless of the seasonal distribution of extreme temperature and humidity.

Monthly precipitation data are also included. They are used mostly to determine climate zones for ASHRAE *Standard* 169, but may also be helpful in developing green technologies such as vegetative roofs.

The clear-sky solar radiation model introduced in the 2009 edition and slightly modified in the 2013 edition is unchanged in its general formulation. However, the site-specific coefficients have been recalculated, based on the latest atmospheric information available. Additionally, all-sky solar radiation values have been added; these are useful in assessing solar technologies (solar heating, photovoltaics), which are typically necessary in the quest for designing net-zero buildings.

Design conditions are provided for locations for which long-term hourly observations were available (1990-2014 for most stations in the United States and Canada). Compared to the 2013 chapter, the number of U.S. stations increased from 1406 to 1952 (39% increase); Canadian stations increased from 562 to 765 (36% increase); and stations in the rest of the world increased from 4475 to 5401 (21% increase; see Figure 1 for map).

1. CLIMATIC DESIGN CONDITIONS

Table 1 shows climatic design conditions for Atlanta, GA, to illustrate the format of the data available on the CD-ROM. A limited subset of these data for 1445 of the 8118 locations for 21 annual data elements is provided for convenience in the Appendix.

The top part of the table contains station information as follows:

- Name of the observing station, state (USA) or province (Canada), country.
- World Meteorological Organization (WMO) station identifier.
- Weather Bureau Army Navy (WBAN) number (99999 denotes missing).
- Latitude of station, °N/S.
- Longitude of station, °E/W.
- Elevation of station, ft.
- Standard pressure at elevation, in psia (see Chapter 1 for equations used to calculate standard pressure).
- Time zone, h ± UTC.
- Time zone code (e.g., NAE = Eastern Time, USA and Canada). The CD-ROM contains a list of all time zone codes used in the tables.
- Period analyzed (e.g., 90-14 = data from 1990 to 2014 were used).

Annual Design Conditions

Annual climatic design conditions are contained in the first three sections following the top part of the table. They contain information as follows:

Annual Heating and Humidification Design Conditions.

- Coldest month (i.e., month with lowest average dry-bulb temperature; 1 = January, 12 = December).
- Dry-bulb temperature corresponding to 99.6 and 99.0% annual cumulative frequency of occurrence (cold conditions), °F.
- Dew-point temperature corresponding to 99.6 and 99.0% annual cumulative frequency of occurrence, °F; corresponding humidity ratio, calculated at standard atmospheric pressure at elevation of station, grains of moisture per lb of dry air; mean coincident dry-bulb temperature, °F.
- Wind speed corresponding to 0.4 and 1.0% cumulative frequency of occurrence for coldest month, mph; mean coincident dry-bulb temperature, °F.
- Mean wind speed coincident with 99.6% dry-bulb temperature, mph; corresponding most frequent wind direction, degrees from north (east = 90°).

Annual Cooling, Dehumidification, and Enthalpy Design Conditions.

- Hottest month (i.e., month with highest average dry-bulb temperature; 1 = January, 12 = December).

The preparation of this chapter is assigned to TC 4.2, Climatic Information.

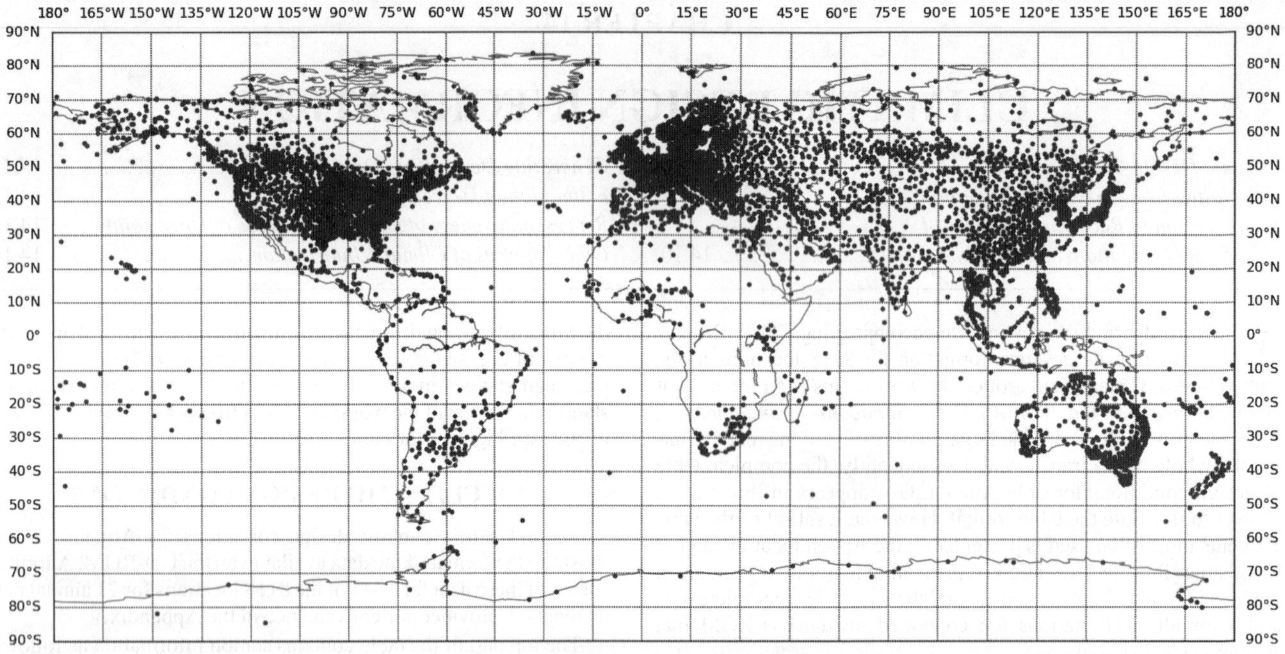

Fig. 1 Locations of Weather Stations

- Daily temperature range for hottest month, °F [defined as mean of the difference between daily maximum and daily minimum dry-bulb temperatures for hottest month].
- Dry-bulb temperature corresponding to 0.4, 1.0, and 2.0% annual cumulative frequency of occurrence (warm conditions), °F; mean coincident wet-bulb temperature, °F.
- Wet-bulb temperature corresponding to 0.4, 1.0, and 2.0% annual cumulative frequency of occurrence, °F; mean coincident dry-bulb temperature, °F.
- Mean wind speed coincident with 0.4% dry-bulb temperature, mph; corresponding most frequent wind direction, degrees true from north (east = 90°).
- Dew-point temperature corresponding to 0.4, 1.0, and 2.0% annual cumulative frequency of occurrence, °F; corresponding humidity ratio, calculated at the standard atmospheric pressure at elevation of station, grains of moisture per lb of dry air; mean coincident dry-bulb temperature, °F.
- Enthalpy corresponding to 0.4, 1.0, and 2.0% annual cumulative frequency of occurrence, Btu/lb; mean coincident dry-bulb temperature, °F.
- Extreme maximum wet-bulb temperature, °F.

Extreme Annual Design Conditions.

- Wind speed corresponding to 1.0, 2.5, and 5.0% annual cumulative frequency of occurrence, mph.
- Mean and standard deviation of extreme annual minimum and maximum dry-bulb temperature, °F.
- 5-, 10-, 20-, and 50-year return period values for minimum and maximum extreme dry-bulb temperature, °F.
- Mean and standard deviation of extreme annual minimum and maximum wet-bulb temperature, °F.
- 5-, 10-, 20-, and 50-year return period values for minimum and maximum extreme wet-bulb temperature, °F.

Monthly Design Conditions

Monthly design conditions are divided into subsections as follows:

Temperatures, Degree-Days, and Degree-Hours.

- Average temperature, °F. This parameter is a prime indicator of climate and is also useful to calculate heating and cooling degree-days to any base.
- Standard deviation of average daily temperature, °F. This parameter is useful to calculate heating and cooling degree-days to any base. Its use is explained in the section on Estimation of Degree-Days.
- Heating and cooling degree-days (bases 50 and 65°F). These parameters are useful in energy estimating methods. They are also used to classify locations into climate zones in ASHRAE *Standard* 169.
- Cooling degree-hours (bases 74 and 80°F). These are used in various standards, such as *Standard* 90.2-2004.

Wind.

- Monthly average wind speed, mph. This parameter is useful to estimate the wind potential at a site; however, the local topography may significantly alter this value, so close attention is needed.

Precipitation.

- Average precipitation, in. This parameter is used to calculate climate zones for *Standard* 169, and is of interest in some green building technologies (e.g., vegetative roofs).
- Standard deviation of precipitation, in. This parameter indicates the variability of precipitation at the site.
- Minimum and maximum precipitation, in. These parameters give extremes of precipitation and are useful for green building technologies and stormwater management.

Monthly Design Dry-Bulb, Wet-Bulb, and Mean Coincident Temperatures.

These values are derived from the same analysis that results in the annual design conditions. The monthly summaries are useful when seasonal variations in solar geometry and intensity, building or facility occupancy, or building use patterns require consideration. In particular, these values can be used when determining air-conditioning loads during periods of maximum solar radiation. The values listed in the tables include

- Dry-bulb temperature corresponding to 0.4, 2.0, 5.0, and 10.0% cumulative frequency of occurrence for indicated month, °F; mean coincident wet-bulb temperature, °F.
- Wet-bulb temperature corresponding to 0.4, 2.0, 5.0, and 10.0% cumulative frequency of occurrence for indicated month, °F; mean coincident dry-bulb temperature, °F.

For a 30-day month, the 0.4, 2.0, 5.0 and 10.0% values of occurrence represent the value that occurs or is exceeded for a total of 3, 14, 36, or 72 h, respectively, per month on average over the period of record. Monthly percentile values of dry- or wet-bulb temperature may be higher or lower than the annual design conditions corresponding to the same nominal percentile, depending on the month and the seasonal distribution of the parameter at that location. Generally, for the hottest or most humid months of the year, the monthly percentile value exceeds the design condition for the same element corresponding to the same nominal percentile. For example, Table 1 shows that the annual 0.4% design dry-bulb temperature at Atlanta, GA, is 94.0°F; the 0.4% monthly dry-bulb temperature exceeds 94.0°F for June, July, and August, with values of 94.5, 97.6, and 97.4°F, respectively. Fifth and tenth percentiles are also provided to give a greater range in the frequency of occurrence, in particular providing less extreme options to select for design calculations.

A general, very approximate rule of thumb is that the *n*% annual cooling design condition is roughly equivalent to the 5*n*% monthly cooling condition for the hottest month; that is, the 0.4% annual design dry-bulb temperature is roughly equivalent to the 2% monthly design dry-bulb temperature for the hottest month; the 1% annual value is roughly equivalent to the 5% monthly value for the hottest month, and the 2% annual value is roughly equivalent to the 10% monthly value for the hottest month.

Mean Daily Temperature Range. These values are useful in calculating daily dry- and wet-bulb temperature profiles, as explained in the section on Generating Design-Day Data. Three kinds of profile are defined:

- Mean daily temperature range for month indicated, °F (defined as mean of difference between daily maximum and minimum dry-bulb temperatures).
- Mean daily dry- and wet-bulb temperature ranges coincident with the 5% monthly design dry-bulb temperature. This is the difference between daily maximum and minimum dry- or wet-bulb temperatures, respectively, averaged over all days where the maximum daily dry-bulb temperature exceeds the 5% monthly design dry-bulb temperature.
- Mean daily dry- and wet-bulb temperature ranges coincident with the 5% monthly design wet-bulb temperature. This is the difference between daily maximum and minimum dry- or wet-bulb temperatures, respectively, averaged over all days where the maximum daily wet-bulb temperature exceeds the 5% monthly design wet-bulb temperature.

Clear-Sky Solar Irradiance. Clear-sky irradiance parameters are useful in calculating solar-related air conditioning loads for any time of any day of the year. Parameters are provided for the 21st day of each month. The 21st of the month is usually a convenient day for solar calculations because June 21 and December 21 represent the solstices (longest and shortest days) and March 21 and September 21 are close to the equinox (days and nights have the same length). Parameters listed in the tables are

- Clear-sky optical depths for beam and diffuse irradiances, which are used to calculate beam and diffuse irradiance as explained in the section on Calculating Clear-Sky Solar Radiation.
- Clear-sky beam normal and diffuse horizontal irradiances at solar noon. These two values can be calculated from the clear-sky optical depths but are listed here for convenience.

All-Sky Solar Radiation. All-sky solar radiation parameters are useful for evaluating the potential of solar technologies (e.g., solar heating, photovoltaics), which are valuable in the design of net-zero energy buildings. Parameters listed in the tables are

- Monthly average daily global radiation on a horizontal surface. This is a traditional way to characterize the solar resource at a site.
- Standard deviation of monthly average daily radiation on a horizontal surface. This parameter gives an idea of the year-to-year variability of the solar resource at the site.

Data Sources

The following primary sources of observational data sets were used in calculating design values:

- For most Canadian stations, meteorological data were obtained directly from Environment Canada (climate.weather.gc.ca) for the years 1982-2014.
- Data were obtained from the U.S. Climate Reference Network (CRN) (www.ncdc.noaa.gov/crn) (Diamond et al. 2013).
- Most stations, including some in Canada with inadequate data, were sourced through the Integrated Surface Database (ISD) from NOAA (www.ncdc.noaa.gov) (Smith et al. 2011) for the years 1982-2015.

In most cases, the period of record used in the calculations spanned 25 years (1990 to 2014). This choice of period is a compromise between trying to derive design conditions from the longest possible period of record, and using the most recent data to capture climatic or land-use trends from the past two decades. The actual number of years used in the calculations for a given station depends on the amount of missing data, and, as discussed in the next section, may be as little as 8 years. The first and last years of the period of record used to calculate design conditions are listed in the top section of the tables of climatic design conditions, as shown in Table 1 for Atlanta. For a limited number of stations, years as far back as 1982 or as recent as 2015 were used instead of 1990 to 2014 because that time frame lacked the necessary data.

Precipitation data were derived from a number of sources, including station data from the Global Historical Climatology Network, version 2 (GHCN 2015) and the United Nations Food and Agriculture Organization (FAO 2011), as well as gridded data from the Global Precipitation Climatology Centre, version 7 (GPCC 2015), and the Global Precipitation Climate Project (GPCP).

Clear-sky solar irradiance parameters listed in the tables constitute a simple parameterization of the more sophisticated REST2 broadband clear-sky radiation model (Gueymard 2008; Gueymard and Thevenard 2009; Thevenard 2009). The REST2 model requires detailed knowledge of various atmospheric constituents, such as aerosols, water vapor, or ozone. To extend applicability of the model to the whole world, multiple data sets, mainly derived from space observations and reanalysis models, were used to obtain these inputs. These sources of data have changed or have been updated since the 2013 edition, which explains the coincident changes in site-specific coefficients. Water vapor, ozone, and ground albedo data are now derived from the National Aeronatucis and Space Administration (NASA) Modern-Era Retrospective Analysis for Research and Applications, version 2 (MERRA-2) reanalysis dataset (Molod et al. 2015), corrected for elevation in the case of water vapor (Gueymard and Thevenard 2009). The period of data is now uniform and longer, from 2000 to 2014. An exception is nitrogen dioxide, for which a database from Ozone Monitoring Instrument (OMI) satellite observations (aura.gsfc.nasa.gov/omi.html) is used

Table 1 Design Conditions for Atlanta, GA, USA (see Table 1A for Nomenclature)

ATLANTA HARTSFIELD-JACKSON, GA, USA

WMO#: **722190**

Lat: **33.640N** Long: **84.430W** Elev: **1027** StdP: **14.16** Time Zone: **-5.00 (NAE)** Period: **90-14** WBAN: **13874**

Annual Heating and Humidification Design Conditions

	Coldest Month	Heating DB		Humidification DP/MCDB and HR						Coldest month WS/MCDB				MCWS/PCWD to 99.6% DB		
				99.6%			99%			0.4%		1%				
		99.6%	99%	DP	HR	MCDB	DP	HR	MCDB	WS	MCDB	WS	MCDB	MCWS	PCWD	
	(a)	(b)	(c)	(d)	(e)	(f)	(g)	(h)	(i)	(j)	(k)	(l)	(m)	(n)	(o)	
(1)	1	21.9	26.5	4.9	7.3	29.3	9.3	9.2	32.8	24.8	39.7	23.3	39.2	11.8	320	(1)

Annual Cooling, Dehumidification, and Enthalpy Design Conditions

	Hottest Month	Hottest Month DB Range	Cooling DB/MCWB						Evaporation WB/MCDB						MCWS/PCWD to 0.4% DB		
			0.4%		1%		2%		0.4%		1%		2%				
			DB	MCWB	DB	MCWB	DB	MCWB	WB	MCDB	WB	MCDB	WB	MCDB	MCWS	PCWD	
	(a)	(b)	(c)	(d)	(e)	(f)	(g)	(h)	(i)	(j)	(k)	(l)	(m)	(n)	(o)	(p)	
(2)	7	16.7	94.0	74.2	91.6	73.8	89.5	73.3	77.3	88.3	76.3	86.5	75.4	84.8	8.7	300	(2)

	Dehumidification DP/MCDB and HR									Enthalpy/MCDB						Extreme Max WB	
	0.4%			1%			2%			0.4%		1%		2%			
	DP	HR	MCDB	DP	HR	MCDB	DP	HR	MCDB	Enth	MCDB	Enth	MCDB	Enth	MCDB		
	(a)	(b)	(c)	(d)	(e)	(f)	(g)	(h)	(i)	(j)	(k)	(l)	(m)	(n)	(o)	(p)	
(3)	74.3	133.3	81.3	73.4	128.9	80.3	72.6	125.5	79.6	41.3	88.3	40.3	86.7	39.5	85.4	82.4	(3)

Extreme Annual Design Conditions

	Extreme Annual WS				Extreme Annual Temperature				n-Year Return Period Values of Extreme Temperature								
					Mean		Standard Deviation		n=5 years		n=10 years		n=20 years		n=50 years		
	1%	2.5%	5%		Min	Max	Min	Max	Min	Max	Min	Max	Min	Max	Min	Max	
	(n)	(o)	(p)		(b)	(c)	(d)	(e)	(f)	(g)	(h)	(i)	(j)	(k)	(l)	(m)	
(4)	21.3	18.9	17.0	DB	15.0	96.6	4.6	3.7	11.6	99.3	8.9	101.4	6.3	103.5	3.0	106.2	(4)
(5)				WB	12.6	79.0	4.4	1.5	9.5	80.1	6.9	81.0	4.4	81.8	1.2	82.9	(5)

Monthly Climatic Design Conditions

				Annual	Jan	Feb	Mar	Apr	May	Jun	Jul	Aug	Sep	Oct	Nov	Dec	
				(d)	(e)	(f)	(g)	(h)	(i)	(j)	(k)	(l)	(m)	(n)	(o)	(p)	
(6)	Temperatures, Degree-Days and Degree-Hours		DBAvg	63.0	44.5	48.0	54.9	62.6	70.5	77.3	80.1	79.5	73.9	63.6	53.5	46.4	(6)
(7)			DBStd	14.60	9.66	8.88	9.00	7.40	6.17	4.51	3.50	3.84	5.47	7.07	8.10	8.82	(7)
(8)			HDD50	653	224	132	55	6	0	0	0	0	0	4	56	176	(8)
(9)			HDD65	2640	635	477	329	127	25	1	0	0	7	111	352	576	(9)
(10)			CDD50	5391	54	76	205	385	636	819	933	914	717	425	161	66	(10)
(11)			CDD65	1901	0	1	14	56	195	370	468	449	273	67	7	1	(11)
(12)			CDH74	16445	0	3	103	435	1509	3337	4488	4173	2014	360	22	1	(12)
(13)			CDH80	6151	0	0	8	66	419	1333	1922	1726	637	40	0	0	(13)
(14)	Wind		WSAvg	8.2	9.2	9.4	9.5	8.8	7.9	7.3	7.0	6.7	7.5	7.8	8.2	8.9	(14)
(15)	Precipitation		PrecAvg	50.80	4.70	4.80	5.80	4.30	4.30	3.60	5.00	3.70	3.40	3.10	3.90	4.30	(15)
(16)			PrecMax	64.90	10.20	12.80	11.70	11.90	8.40	7.40	8.50	8.70	6.10	7.50	7.20	9.90	(16)
(17)			PrecMin	37.70	1.70	0.80	2.40	1.50	0.40	1.00	0.70	0.50	0.70	0.10	0.90	0.70	(17)
(18)			PrecStd	7.20	2.10	2.70	2.70	2.40	2.30	1.80	2.20	2.20	1.60	2.10	1.60	2.40	(18)
(19)	Monthly Design Dry Bulb and Mean Coincident Wet Bulb Temperatures	0.4%	DB		70.5	73.4	80.8	85.0	90.2	94.5	97.6	97.4	92.8	83.5	77.4	72.3	(19)
(20)			MCWB		60.8	61.3	62.6	66.5	71.3	72.9	74.8	74.3	72.0	68.3	64.1	63.1	(20)
(21)		2%	DB		66.3	69.1	76.9	82.0	87.0	92.0	94.1	93.7	89.0	80.9	73.3	68.6	(21)
(22)			MCWB		58.7	58.8	60.6	64.9	69.8	72.9	74.7	74.6	71.4	66.7	61.8	61.6	(22)
(23)		5%	DB		63.0	65.9	73.5	79.2	84.6	89.8	91.6	90.9	86.4	78.2	70.3	64.6	(23)
(24)			MCWB		57.2	56.9	59.1	63.4	68.8	72.5	74.3	74.2	70.7	64.7	60.6	59.0	(24)
(25)		10%	DB		59.5	62.7	69.8	76.1	82.1	87.4	89.1	88.3	83.8	75.3	67.1	60.9	(25)
(26)			MCWB		53.9	54.5	57.7	61.8	67.8	71.9	74.2	73.4	70.2	64.1	58.4	55.2	(26)
(27)	Monthly Design Wet Bulb and Mean Coincident Dry Bulb Temperatures	0.4%	WB		64.2	65.5	66.4	70.8	74.9	77.3	78.9	78.4	76.4	72.0	69.2	66.7	(27)
(28)			MCDB		67.5	67.9	72.8	79.2	83.3	88.4	89.6	89.9	86.1	78.8	71.8	69.8	(28)
(29)		2%	WB		61.6	62.4	64.1	68.3	72.7	75.9	77.5	77.2	74.6	70.2	66.1	63.5	(29)
(30)			MCDB		64.6	66.6	71.5	76.3	82.3	86.5	88.3	88.4	83.2	75.9	70.0	66.4	(30)
(31)		5%	WB		58.6	59.5	62.1	66.4	71.3	74.9	76.5	76.2	73.5	68.7	63.5	60.3	(31)
(32)			MCDB		61.9	64.0	70.0	74.4	80.6	85.0	86.7	86.1	80.9	73.8	67.7	64.1	(32)
(33)		10%	WB		55.2	56.3	60.0	64.5	69.9	73.8	75.4	75.2	72.6	66.9	60.5	56.3	(33)
(34)			MCDB		58.3	60.6	67.0	72.3	78.6	83.1	84.9	84.2	79.5	72.3	65.4	59.8	(34)
(35)	Mean Daily Temperature Range		MDBR		17.3	18.2	19.2	19.8	18.2	17.2	16.7	16.4	16.5	18.1	18.7	16.6	(35)
(36)		5% DB	MCDBR		19.5	20.9	22.5	22.0	20.1	20.1	20.2	19.5	19.1	20.4	20.9	19.5	(36)
(37)			MCWBR		13.6	13.3	11.0	9.5	7.5	6.6	6.1	6.0	6.8	8.9	11.7	13.2	(37)
(38)		5% WB	MCDBR		16.0	17.5	17.9	18.2	17.3	17.3	17.5	16.8	15.3	14.9	16.8	16.8	(38)
(39)			MCWBR		13.2	13.8	11.0	9.8	7.7	6.9	6.4	6.1	6.9	8.9	12.9	13.6	(39)
(40)	Clear-Sky Solar Irradiance		taub		0.310	0.315	0.347	0.386	0.440	0.473	0.515	0.515	0.417	0.363	0.333	0.311	(40)
(41)			taud		2.538	2.521	2.453	2.324	2.213	2.168	2.066	2.052	2.312	2.460	2.484	2.554	(41)
(42)			Ebn,noon		288	298	295	286	270	260	249	246	268	277	276	281	(42)
(43)			Edh,noon		26	29	34	40	46	48	53	52	39	31	27	24	(43)
(44)	All-Sky Solar Radiation		RadAvg		852	1054	1407	1751	1904	1954	1858	1726	1496	1275	963	738	(44)
(45)			RadStd		50	122	109	126	164	162	134	103	148	163	82	73	(45)

Nomenclature: See separate page

Table 1A Nomenclature for Tables of Climatic Design Conditions

CDD*n*	Cooling degree-days base n°F, °F-day
CDH*n*	Cooling degree-hours base n°F, °F-hour
DB	Dry-bulb temperature, °F
DBAvg	Average daily dry-bulb temperature, °F
DBSD	Standard deviation of average daily dry-bulb temperature, °F
DP	Dew-point temperature, °F
Ebn,noon	Clear-sky beam normal irradiances at solar noon, Btu/h·ft²
Edh,noon	Clear-sky diffuse horizontal irradiance at solar noon, Btu/h·ft²
Elev	Elevation, ft
Enth	Enthalpy, Btu/lb base 0°F and 1 atm pressure
HDD*n*	Heating degree-days base n°F, °F-day
HR	Humidity ratio, $gr_{moisture}/lb_{dry\ air}$
Lat	Latitude, °N
Long	Longitude, °E
MCDB	Mean coincident dry-bulb temperature, °F
MCDBR	Mean coincident dry-bulb temp. range, °F
MCWB	Mean coincident wet-bulb temperature, °F
MCWBR	Mean coincident wet-bulb temp. range, °F
MCWS	Mean coincident wind speed, mph
MDBR	Mean dry-bulb temp. range, °F
PCWD	Prevailing coincident wind direction, ° (0 = North; 90 = East)
Period	Years used to calculate the design conditions
PrecAvg	Average precipitation, in.
PrecMax	Maximum precipitation, in.
PrecMin	Minimum precipitation, in.
PrecStd	Standard deviation of precipitation, in.
RadAvg	Monthly mean daily all-sky radiation, Btu/ft²·day
RadStd	Standard deviation of monthly mean daily radiation, Btu/ft²·day
StdP	Standard pressure at station elevation, psi
taub	Clear-sky optical depth for beam irradiance
taud	Clear-sky optical depth for diffuse irradiance
Time Zone	Hours ahead or behind UTC, and time zone code
WB	Wet-bulb temperature, °F
WBAN	Weather Bureau Army Navy number
WMO#	Station identifier from the World Meteorological Organization
WS	Wind speed, mph
WSAvg	Monthly average wind speed, mph

Note: Numbers *(1)* to *(45)* and letters *(a)* to *(p)* are row and column references to quickly point to an element in the table. For example, the 5% design wet-bulb temperature for July can be found in row *(31)*, column *(k)*.

over the period 2005 to 2014. Pressure is estimated from station's elevation.

Aerosol turbidity data (in the form of separate evaluations of aerosol optical depth and Ångström exponent) received special attention, because they are the primary inputs that affect the accuracy of direct and diffuse irradiance predictions under clear skies. Spaceborne retrievals of aerosol optical depth at various wavelengths from NASA's Multi-angle Imaging SpectroRadiometer (MISR; www-misr.jpl.nasa.gov) and two Moderate Resolution Imaging Spectroradiometer (MODIS; modis-atmos.gsfc.nasa.gov) instruments were used between 2000 and 2014 and compared to reference data from a large number of ground-based sites, mostly from the Aerosol Robotic Network (AERONET; aeronet.gsfc.nasa.gov), after appropriate scale-height corrections to remove artifacts from the effect of elevation (Gueymard and Thevenard 2009). Regional corrections of the satellite data were devised to remove as much bias as possible, compared to the reference ground-based data. To fill missing data or correct biased satellite observations, modeled aerosol datasets were used, including 10 years (2003 to 2012) of simulated monthly-average aerosol optical depth from the Monitoring Atmospheric Composition and Climate (MACC) reanalysis model (Eskes et al. 2015; Inness et al. 2013) and 13 years (2002 to 2014) of MERRA-2 reanalysis data (Molod et al. 2015). Results from the REST2 model (Gueymard 2008) were then fitted to the simple two-parameter model described in this chapter. The fits enable a concise formulation requiring tabulation, on a monthly basis, of only two parameters per station, referred to here as the clear-sky beam and diffuse optical depths. Details about the fitting procedure can be found in Thevenard and Gueymard (2013).

Global horizontal irradiance at the surface, and its standard deviation, were calculated from the Clouds and the Earth's Radiant Energy System (CERES) Energy Balanced and Filled (EBAF) dataset (ceres.larc.nasa.gov/products.php?product=EBAF-Surface). From the available 1°×1° dataset, a bilinear interpolation, without altitude adjustment, was made given the station latitude and longitude for the period 2000 to 2014.

Calculation of Design Conditions

Values of ambient dry-bulb, dew-point, and wet-bulb temperature and wind speed corresponding to the various annual percentiles represent the value that is exceeded on average by the indicated percentage of the total number of hours in a year (8760). The 0.4, 1.0, 2.0, and 5.0% values are exceeded on average 35, 88, 175, and 438 h per year, respectively, for the period of record. The design values occur more frequently than the corresponding nominal percentile in some years and less frequently in others. The 99.0 and 99.6% (cold-season) values are defined in the same way but are usually viewed as the values for which the corresponding weather element is less than the design condition for 88 and 35 h, respectively.

Simple design conditions were obtained by binning hourly data into frequency tables, then deriving from the binned data the design condition having the probability of being exceeded a certain percentage of the time. Mean coincident values were obtained by double-binning the hourly data into joint frequency matrices, then calculating the mean coincident value corresponding to the simple design condition.

Coincident temperature ranges were also obtained by double-binning daily temperature ranges (daily maximum minus minimum) versus maximum daily temperature. The mean coincident daily range was then calculated by averaging all bins above the simple design condition of interest.

The weather data sets used for the calculations often contain missing values (either isolated records, or because some stations report data only every third hour). Gaps up to 6 h were filled by linear interpolation to provide as complete a time series as possible. Dry-bulb temperature, dew-point temperature, station pressure, and humidity ratio were interpolated. However, wind speed and direction were not interpolated because of their more stochastic and unpredictable nature.

Some stations in the ISD data set also provide data that were not recorded at the beginning of the hour. When data at the exact hour were missing, they were replaced by data up to 0.5 h before or after, when available.

Finally, psychrometric quantities such as wet-bulb temperature or enthalpy are not contained in the weather data sets. They were calculated from dry-bulb temperature, dew-point temperature, and station pressure using the psychrometric equations in Chapter 1.

Measures were taken to ensure that the number and distribution of missing data, both by month and by hour of the day, did not introduce significant biases into the analysis. Annual cumulative frequency distributions were constructed from the relative frequency distributions compiled for each month. Each individual month's data were included if they met the following screening criteria for completeness and unbiased distribution of missing data after data filling:

- The number of hourly dry-bulb temperature values for the month, after filling by interpolation, had to be at least 85% of the total hours for the month.
- The difference between the number of day and nighttime dry-bulb temperature observations had to be less than 60.

Although the nominal period of record selected for this analysis was 25 years (1990 to 2014 for most stations), some variation and gaps in observed data meant that some months' data were unusable because of incompleteness. Some months were also eliminated during additional quality control checks. A station's dry-bulb temperature design conditions were calculated only if there were data from at least 8 months that met the quality control and screening criteria from the period of record for each month of the year. For example, there had to be 8 months each of January, February, March, etc. for which data met the completeness screening criteria. These criteria were ascertained from results of RP-1171 (Hubbard et al. 2004) and were the same as used in calculating the design conditions in the 2001 to 2013 editions of the *ASHRAE Handbook—Fundamentals*.

Dew-point temperature, wet-bulb temperature, and enthalpy design conditions were calculated for a given month only if the number of dew-point, wet-bulb, or enthalpy values was greater than 85% of the minimum number of dry-bulb temperature values defined previously; wind speed and direction conditions were calculated for a given month only if the number of values was greater than 28.3% (i.e., one-third of 85%) the minimum number of dry-bulb temperature values. For example, a month of January was included in calculations if the number of dry-bulb temperature values exceeded 85% of 744 h, or 633 h. The month was included in calculation of dew-point temperature design conditions only if dew-point temperature was present for at least 85% of 633 h, or 538 h. The month was included in calculation of wind speed design conditions only if wind speed was present for at least 28.3% of 633 h, or 179 h.

Annual dry-bulb temperature extremes were calculated only for years that were 85% complete. At least 8 annual extremes were required to calculate the mean and standard deviation of extreme annual dry-bulb temperatures.

Daily minimum and maximum temperatures were calculated only for complete days; so were daily temperature ranges and mean coincident temperature ranges.

Details about quality checks and other steps taken during data processing to ensure results as free from error as possible are detailed in Roth (2017).

Differences from Previously Published Design Conditions

- Climatic design conditions in this chapter are generally similar to those in previous editions, because similar if not identical analysis procedures were used. There are some differences, however, owing to a more recent period of record (generally 1990-2014 versus 1982-2006). For example, when compared to the 2009 edition, 99.6% heating dry-bulb temperatures have increased by 0.09°F on average, and 0.4% cooling dry-bulb temperatures have increased by 0.15°F on average. Similar trends are observed for other design temperatures. The root mean square differences are 1.13°F for the 99.6% heating dry-bulb values and 0.65°F for 0.4% cooling dry-bulb. The increases noted here are generally consistent with the discussion in the section on Effects of Climate Change.
- Further details concerning differences between design conditions in the 2013, 2009, and 2005 editions are described in Thevenard (2009) and Thevenard and Gueymard (2013). Differences between the 2005 and the 2001 editions are described in Thevenard et al. (2005). Differences between the 1993 and previous editions are described in Colliver et al. (2000).

Applicability and Characteristics of Design Conditions

Climatic design values in this chapter represent different psychrometric conditions. Design data based on dry-bulb temperature represent peak occurrences of the sensible component of ambient outdoor conditions. Design values based on wet-bulb temperature are related to the enthalpy of the outdoor air. Conditions based on dew point relate to the peaks of the humidity ratio. The designer, engineer, or other user must decide which set(s) of conditions and probability of occurrence apply to the design situation under consideration. Additional sources of information on frequency and duration of extremes of temperature and humidity are provided in the section on Other Sources of Climatic Information. Further information is available from Harriman et al. (1999). This section discusses the intended use of design conditions in the order they appear in Table 1.

Annual Heating and Humidification Design Conditions. The month with the lowest mean dry-bulb temperature is used, for example, to determine the time of year where the maximum heating load occurs.

The 99.6 and 99.0% design conditions are often used in sizing heating equipment.

The humidification dew-point and mean coincident dry-bulb temperatures and humidity ratio provide information for cold-season humidification applications.

Wind design data provide information for estimating peak loads accounting for infiltration: extreme wind speeds for the coldest month, with the mean coincident dry-bulb temperature; and mean wind speed and direction coincident to the 99.6% design dry-bulb temperature.

Annual Cooling, Dehumidification, and Enthalpy Design Conditions. The month with the highest mean dry-bulb temperature is used, for example, to determine the time of year where the maximum sensible cooling load occurs, not taking into account solar loads.

The mean daily dry-bulb temperature range for the hottest month is the mean difference between the daily maximum and minimum temperatures during the hottest month and is calculated from the extremes of the hourly temperature observations. The true maximum and minimum temperatures for any day generally occur between hourly readings. Thus, the mean maximum and minimum temperatures calculated in this way are about 1°F less extreme than the mean daily extreme temperatures observed with maximum and minimum thermometers. This results in the true daily temperature range generally about 2°F greater than that calculated from hourly data. The mean daily dry-bulb temperature range is used in cooling load calculations.

The 0.4, 1.0, and 2.0% dry-bulb temperatures and mean coincident wet-bulb temperatures often represent conditions on hot, mostly sunny days. These are often used in sizing cooling equipment such as chillers or air-conditioning units.

Design conditions based on wet-bulb temperature represent extremes of the total sensible plus latent heat of outdoor air. This information is useful for design of cooling towers, evaporative coolers, and outdoor-air ventilation systems.

The mean wind speed and direction coincident with the 0.4% design dry-bulb temperature is used for estimating peak loads accounting for infiltration.

Design conditions based on dew-point temperatures are directly related to extremes of humidity ratio, which represent peak moisture loads from the weather. Extreme dew-point conditions may occur on days with moderate dry-bulb temperatures, resulting in high relative humidity. These values are especially useful for humidity control applications, such as desiccant cooling and dehumidification, cooling-based dehumidification, and outdoor-air ventilation systems. The values are also used as a check point when analyzing the behavior of cooling systems at part-load conditions, particularly when such systems are used for humidity control as a secondary function. Humidity ratio values are calculated from the corresponding dew-point temperature and the standard pressure at the location's elevation.

Annual enthalpy design conditions give the annual enthalpy for the cooling season; this is used for calculating cooling loads caused by infiltration and/or ventilation into buildings. Enthalpy represents the total heat content of air (the sum of its sensible and latent energies). Cooling loads can be calculated knowing the conditions of both the outdoor ambient and the building's interior air.

The extreme maximum wet-bulb temperature provides the highest wet-bulb temperature observed over the entire period of record and is the most extreme condition observed during the data record for evaporative processes such as cooling towers. For most locations, the extreme maximum wet-bulb value is significantly higher than the 0.4% wet-bulb (discussed previously) and should be used only for design of critical applications where an occasional short-duration capacity shortfall is not acceptable.

Extreme Annual Design Conditions. Extreme annual design wind speeds are used in designing smoke management systems.

The mean and standard deviation of the extreme annual maximum and minimum dry-bulb temperatures are used to calculate the probability of occurrence of very extreme conditions. These can be required for design of equipment to ensure continuous operation and serviceability regardless of whether the heating or cooling loads are being met. These values were calculated from extremes of hourly temperature observations. The true maximum and minimum temperatures for any day generally occur between hourly readings. Thus, the mean maximum and minimum temperatures calculated in this way are about 1°F less extreme than the mean daily extreme temperatures observed with maximum and minimum thermometers.

The 5-, 10-, 20- and 50-year return periods for maximum and minimum extreme dry-bulb temperature are also listed in the table. Return period (or recurrence interval) is defined as the reciprocal of the annual probability of occurrence. For instance, the 50-year return period maximum dry-bulb temperature has a probability of occurring or being exceeded of 2.0% (i.e., 1/50) each year. This statistic does not indicate how often the condition will occur in terms of the number of hours each year (as in the design conditions based on percentiles) but describes the probability of the condition occurring at all in any year. The following method can be used to estimate the return period (recurrence interval) of extreme temperatures:

$$T_n = M + IFs \tag{1}$$

where

T_n = n-year return period value of extreme dry-bulb temperature to be estimated, years
M = mean of annual extreme maximum or minimum dry-bulb temperatures, °F
s = standard deviation of annual extreme maximum or minimum dry-bulb temperatures, °F
I = 1 if maximum dry-bulb temperatures are being considered
= –1 if minimum dry-bulb temperatures are being considered

$$F = -\frac{\sqrt{6}}{\pi}\left\{0.5772 + \ln\left[\ln\left(\frac{n}{n-1}\right)\right]\right\}$$

For example, the 50-year return period extreme maximum dry-bulb temperature estimated for Atlanta, GA, is 106.2°F (according to Table 1, M = 96.6°F, s = 3.7, and n = 50; I = 1). Similarly, the 50-year return period extreme minimum dry-bulb temperature for Atlanta, GA, is 3.0°F [M = 15.0°F, s = 4.6, and n = 50; I = –1]. The n-year return periods can be obtained for most stations using ASHRAE's Weather Data Viewer 6.0 (ASHRAE 2017), which is discussed in the section on Other Sources of Climatic Information.

New in 2017 are the parameters required to calculate the 5-, 10-, 20- and 50-year return periods for maximum and minimum extreme wet-bulb temperature. The maximum conditions in particular may be useful in determining very extreme wet-bulb temperatures during which evaporative systems may have to operate.

Calculation of the n-year return period is based on assumptions that annual maxima and minima are distributed according to the Gumbel (Type 1 Extreme Value) distribution and are fitted with the method of moments (Lowery and Nash 1970). The uncertainty or standard error using this method increases with standard deviation, value of return period, and decreasing length of the period of record. It can be significant. For instance, the standard error in the 50-year return period maximum dry-bulb temperature estimated at a location with a 12-year period of record can be 5°F or more. Thus, the uncertainties of return period values estimated in this way are greater for stations with fewer years of data than for stations with the complete period of record from 1990 to 2014.

Temperatures, Degree-Days, and Degree-Hours. Monthly average temperatures and standard deviation of daily average temperatures are calculated using the averages of the minimum and maximum temperatures for each complete day within the period analyzed. They are used to estimate heating and cooling degree-days to any base, as explained in the section on Estimation of Degree-Days.

Heating and cooling degree-days (base 50 or 65°F) are calculated as the sum of the differences between daily average temperatures and the base temperature. For example the number of **heating degree-days (HDD)** in the month is calculated as

$$\text{HDD} = \sum_{i=1}^{N} (T_{base} - \overline{T}_i)^+ \tag{2}$$

where N is the number of days in the month, T_{base} is the reference temperature to which the degree-days are calculated, and $\overline{T}_i$ is the mean daily temperature calculated by adding the maximum and minimum temperatures for the day, then dividing by 2. The + superscript indicates that only positive values of the bracketed quantity are taken into account in the sum. Similarly, monthly **cooling degree-days (CDD)** are calculated as

$$\text{CDD} = \sum_{i=1}^{N} (\overline{T}_i - T_{base})^+ \tag{3}$$

Degree-days are used in energy estimating methods, and to classify stations into climate zones for ASHRAE *Standard* 169.

Monthly Design Dry-Bulb and Mean Coincident Wet-Bulb Temperatures. These values provide design conditions for processes driven by dry-bulb air temperature. In particular, air-conditioning cooling loads are generally based on dry-bulb design conditions (plus clear-sky solar irradiance).

Monthly Design Wet-Bulb and Mean Coincident Dry-Bulb Temperatures. Wet-bulb design conditions are of use in analysis of evaporative coolers, cooling towers, and other equipment involving evaporative transfer. Note also that air wet-bulb temperature and enthalpy are closely related, so applications with large ventilation flow rates may have maximum cooling requirements under high wet-bulb conditions.

Mean Daily Temperature Range. Mean daily range values are computed using all days of the month, as opposed to coincident values that derive from design days. Mean daily range values have been published in previous Handbook editions and are included for completeness. Coincident daily range values should be used for generating design-day profiles.

Clear-Sky Solar Irradiance. Clear-sky solar irradiance data are used in load calculation methods. **Beam normal irradiance** refers to solar radiation emanating directly from the solar disk and measured

Table 2 Approximate Astronomical Data for 21st Day of Each Month

Month	Jan	Feb	Mar	Apr	May	Jun	Jul	Aug	Sep	Oct	Nov	Dec
Day of year	21	52	80	111	141	172	202	233	264	294	325	355
E_o, Btu/h·ft^2	447	443	437	429	423	419	420	424	430	437	444	447
Equation of time (ET), min	–10.6	–14.0	–7.9	1.2	3.7	–1.3	–6.4	–3.6	6.9	15.5	13.8	2.2
Declination δ, degrees	–20.1	–11.2	–0.4	11.6	20.1	23.4	20.4	11.8	–0.2	–11.8	–20.4	–23.4

perpendicularly to the rays of the sun. **Diffuse horizontal irradiance** refers to solar radiation emanating from the sky dome, sun excluded, and measured on a horizontal surface. Because the beam and diffuse irradiances vary during the course of the day, current load calculation methods require their estimation at various times, which can be done with the method described in the section on Calculating Clear-Sky Solar Radiation. The method uses the clear-sky optical depths τ_b and τ_d, listed in Table 1 as *taub* and *taud*, respectively, as inputs. Clear-sky beam normal and diffuse horizontal irradiances at solar noon are also listed in Table 1 for convenience.

All-Sky Solar Radiation. All-sky solar radiation data are used in the design of solar energy systems (either thermal or photovoltaic). **Monthly average daily radiation on the horizontal** refers to average amount of solar radiation received on a horizontal surface during the course of a day, for the month under consideration. The **standard deviation of monthly average daily radiation on the horizontal** is the standard deviation of the previous monthly quantity, calculated over the period of record used for the Handbook, and is an indicator of the year-to-year variability of solar radiation.

2. CALCULATING CLEAR-SKY SOLAR RADIATION

Knowledge of clear-sky solar radiation at various times of year and day is required by several calculation methods for heat gains in HVAC loads and solar energy applications. The tables of climatic design conditions include the parameters required to calculate clear-sky beam and diffuse solar irradiances using the equations in the following section. The section on Transposition to Receiving Surfaces of Various Orientations explains how to use these values to calculate clear-sky solar radiation incident on arbitrary surfaces.

Note that in all equations in this section, *angles are expressed in degrees*. This includes the arguments appearing in trigonometric functions.

Solar Constant and Extraterrestrial Solar Radiation

The **solar constant E_{sc}** is defined as the intensity of solar radiation on a surface normal to the sun's rays, just beyond the earth's atmosphere, at the average earth-sun distance. One frequently used value is that proposed by the World Meteorological Organization in 1981, E_{sc} = 433.3 Btu/h·ft^2 (Iqbal 1983).

Because the earth's orbit is slightly elliptical, the **extraterrestrial radiant flux E_o** varies throughout the year, reaching a maximum of 447.6 Btu/h·ft^2 near the beginning of January, when the earth is closest to the sun (aphelion) and a minimum of 419.1 Btu/h·ft^2 near the beginning of July, when the earth is farthest from the sun (perihelion). Extraterrestrial solar irradiance incident on a surface normal to the sun's ray can be approximated with the following equation:

$$E_o = E_{sc}\left\{1 + 0.033\cos\left[360°\frac{(n-3)}{365}\right]\right\} \quad (4)$$

where *n* is the day of year (1 for January 1, 32 for February 1, etc.) and the argument inside the cosine is in degrees. Table 2 tabulates values of E_o for the 21st day of each month.

Table 3 Time Zones in United States and Canada

Time Zone Name	TZ (Hours ± UTC)	Local Standard Meridian Longitude (°E)
Newfoundland standard time	–3.5	–52.5
Atlantic standard time	–4	–60
Eastern standard time	–5	–75
Central standard time	–6	–90
Mountain standard time	–7	–105
Pacific standard time	–8	–120
Alaska standard time	–9	–135
Hawaii-Aleutian standard time	–10	–150

Equation of Time and Solar Time

The earth's orbital velocity also varies throughout the year, so **apparent solar time (AST)**, as determined by a solar time sundial, varies somewhat from the **mean time** kept by a clock running at a uniform rate. This variation is called the **equation of time (ET)** and is approximated by the following formula (Iqbal 1983):

$$\begin{aligned} ET = 2.2918[0.0075 + 0.1868\cos(\Gamma) - 3.2077\sin(\Gamma) \\ - 1.4615\cos(2\Gamma) - 4.089\sin(2\Gamma)] \end{aligned} \quad (5)$$

with ET expressed in minutes and

$$\Gamma = 360°\frac{n-1}{365} \quad (6)$$

Table 2 tabulates the values of ET for the 21st day of each month.

The conversion between local standard time and solar time involves two steps: the equation of time is added to the local standard time, and then a longitude correction is added. This longitude correction is four minutes of time per degree difference between the **local (site) longitude** and the longitude of the **local standard meridian (LSM)** for that time zone; hence, AST is related to the **local standard time (LST)** as follows:

$$AST = LST + ET/60 + (LON - LSM)/15 \quad (7)$$

where

AST = apparent solar time, decimal hours
LST = local standard time, decimal hours
ET = equation of time in minutes, from Table 2 or Equation (5)
LSM = longitude of local standard time meridian, °E of Greenwich (negative in western hemisphere)
LON = longitude of site, °E of Greenwich

Most standard meridians are found every 15° from 0° at Greenwich, U.K., with a few exceptions, such as the province of Newfoundland in Canada. Standard meridian longitude is related to time zone as follows:

$$LSM = 15TZ \quad (8)$$

where TZ is the time zone, expressed in hours ahead or behind **coordinated universal time (UTC)**. TZ is listed for each station on the CD-ROM accompanying this book. Table 3 lists time zones and standard time meridians for the United States and Canada.

If **daylight saving time** (DST) is to be used, rather than local standard time, an additional correction has to be performed. In most locales, local standard time can be obtained from daylight savings time by subtracting one hour:

$$LST = DST - 1 \tag{9}$$

where DST is in decimal hours.

Declination

Because the earth's equatorial plane is tilted at an angle of 23.45° to the orbital plane, the **solar declination** δ (the angle between the earth/sun line and the equatorial plane) varies throughout the year, as shown in Figure 2. This variation causes the changing seasons with their unequal periods of daylight and darkness. Declination can be obtained from astronomical or nautical almanacs; however, for most engineering applications, the following equation provides sufficient accuracy:

$$\delta = 23.45 \sin\left(360° \frac{n + 284}{365}\right) \tag{10}$$

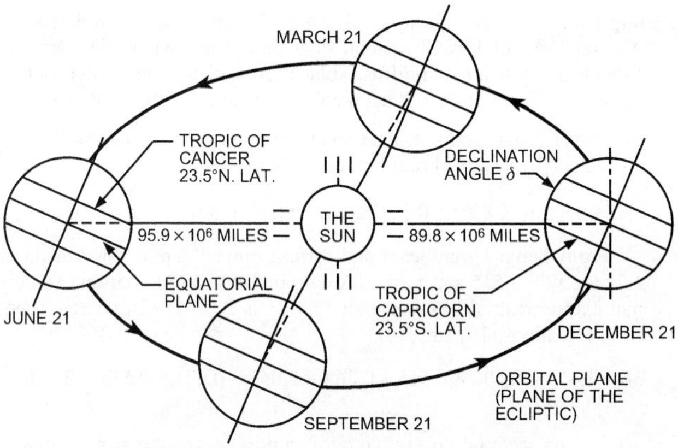

Fig. 2 Motion of Earth around Sun

where δ is in degrees and the argument inside the sine is also in degrees. Table 2 provides δ for the 21st day of each month.

Sun Position

The sun's position in the sky is conveniently expressed in terms of the solar altitude above the horizontal and the solar azimuth measured from the south (Figure 3). The solar altitude angle β is defined as the angle between the horizontal plane and a line emanating from the sun. Its value ranges from 0° when the sun is on the horizon, to 90° if the sun is directly overhead. Negative values correspond to night times. The solar azimuth angle ϕ is defined as angular displacement from south of the projection, on the horizontal plane, of the earth/sun line. By convention, it is counted positive for afternoon hours and negative for morning hours.

Solar altitude and azimuth angles, in turn, depend on the local latitude L (°N, negative in the southern hemisphere); the solar declination δ, which is a function of the date [see Table 2 or Equation (10)]; and the hour angle H, defined as the angular displacement of the sun east or west of the local meridian caused by the rotation of the earth, and expressed in degrees as

$$H = 15(AST - 12) \tag{11}$$

where AST is the apparent solar time [Equation (7)]. H is zero at solar noon, positive in the afternoon, and negative in the morning.

Equation (12) relates the solar altitude angle β to L, δ, and H:

$$\sin\beta = \cos L \cos\delta \cos H + \sin L \sin\delta \tag{12}$$

Note that at solar noon, $H = 0$ and the sun reaches its maximum altitude in the sky:

$$\beta_{max} = 90° - |L - \delta| \tag{13}$$

The azimuth angle ϕ is uniquely determined by its sine and cosine, given in Equations (14) and (15):

$$\sin\phi = \sin H \cos\delta / \cos\beta \tag{14}$$

$$\cos\phi = (\cos H \cos\delta \sin L - \sin\delta \cos L)/\cos\beta \tag{15}$$

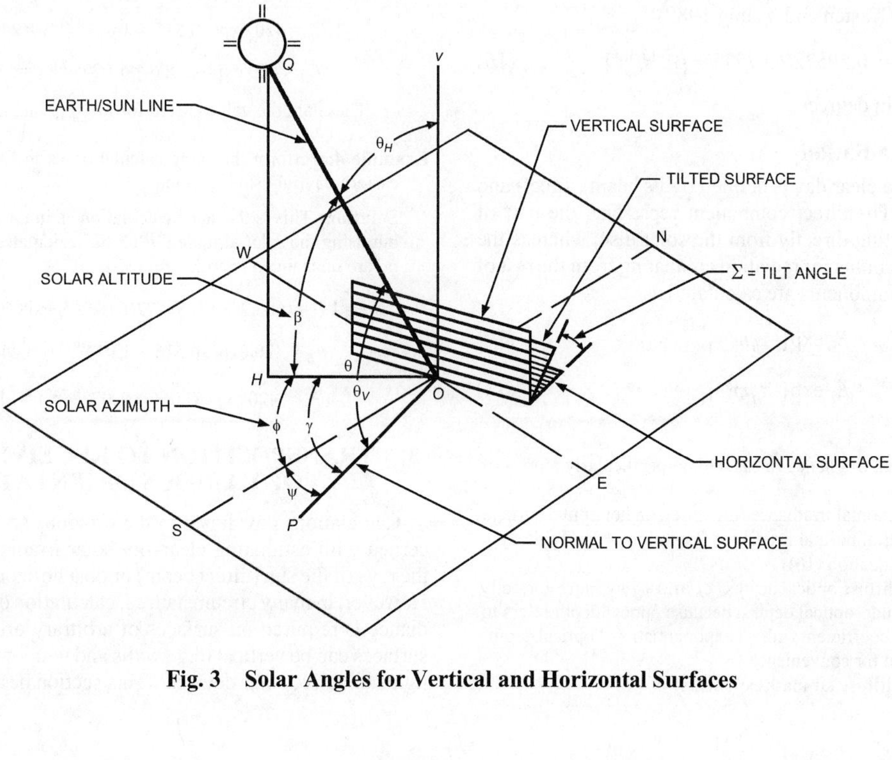

Fig. 3 Solar Angles for Vertical and Horizontal Surfaces

Example 1. Calculate the position of the sun in Atlanta, GA, for July 21 at noon solar time.

Solution: From Table 1, Atlanta is at latitude $L = 33.64°N$. From Table 2 or Equation (10), declination $\delta = 20.44°$.

Solar altitude is given by Equation (13):

$$\beta = 90 - |33.64 - 20.44| = 76.80°$$

At solar noon, the sun is due south, so the azimuth angle ϕ is simply 0°.

Example 2. Perform the same calculation as in Example 1, but for 3:00 PM eastern daylight saving time.

Solution: Compared to Example 1, a few extra steps are required to calculate AST. From Table 1, for Atlanta, LON = 84.43°W = –84.43°E and TZ = –5.00. Also, from Table 1 or Equation (5), ET = –6.4 min. Then, from Equation (8):

$$LSM = 15(-5.00) = -75°$$

Because 3 PM daylight saving time is 2 PM standard time, or hour 14, Equation (7) leads to

$$AST = 14 - 6.4/60 + [(-84.43) - (-75)]/15 = 13.27 \text{ h}$$

Then, from Equation (11):

$$H = 15(13.27 - 12) = 18.97°$$

Solar altitude is given by Equation (12), using the same latitude and declination as in Example 1:

$$\sin\beta = \cos(33.64°)\cos(20.44°)\cos(18.97°) + \sin(33.64°)\sin(20.44°) = 0.931$$

Therefore, $\beta = 68.62°$.

Solar azimuth is obtained through Equations (14) and (15):

$$\sin\phi = \sin(18.97°)\cos(20.44°)/\cos(68.62°) = 0.836$$

$$\cos\phi = [\cos(18.97°)\cos(20.44°)\sin(33.64°) - \sin(20.44°)\cos(33.64°)]/\cos(68.62°) = 0.549$$

Therefore, $\phi = 56.69°$.

Air Mass

The relative air mass m is the ratio of the mass of atmosphere in the actual earth/sun path to the mass that would exist if the sun were directly overhead. Air mass is solely a function of solar altitude β and is obtained from (Kasten and Young 1989)

$$m = 1/[\sin\beta + 0.50572(6.07995 + \beta)^{-1.6364}] \tag{16}$$

where β is expressed in degrees.

Clear-Sky Solar Radiation

Solar radiation on a clear day is defined by its beam (direct) and diffuse components. The direct component represents the part of solar radiation emanating directly from the solar disc, whereas the diffuse component accounts for radiation emanating from the rest of the sky. These two components are calculated as

$$E_b = E_o \exp[-\tau_b m^{ab}] \tag{17}$$

$$E_d = E_o \exp[-\tau_d m^{ad}] \tag{18}$$

where

E_b = beam normal irradiance (measured perpendicularly to rays of the sun)
E_d = diffuse horizontal irradiance (measured on horizontal surface)
E_o = extraterrestrial normal irradiance [Equation (4) or Table 2]
m = air mass [Equation (16)]
τ_b and τ_d = beam and diffuse optical depths (τ_b and τ_d are more correctly termed pseudo-optical depths, because optical depth refers to an air mass coefficient without exponentiation; "optical depth" is used here for convenience.)
ab and ad = beam and diffuse air mass exponents

Values of τ_b and τ_d are location-specific, and vary during the year. They embody the dependence of clear-sky solar radiation on local conditions, such as elevation, precipitable water, aerosols, ozone, and surface reflectance. In previous editions, their average values were determined through ASHRAE research projects RP-1453 (Thevenard 2009) and RP-1613 (Thevenard and Gueymard 2013). For this edition, the results are from RP-1699 (Roth 2017), and are tabulated for the 21st day of each month for all the locations in the tables of climatic design conditions. Values for other days of the year should be found by interpolation.

Air mass exponents ab and ad are correlated to τ_b and τ_d through the following empirical relationships:

$$ab = 1.454 - 0.406\,\tau_b - 0.268\,\tau_d + 0.021\,\tau_b\tau_d \tag{19}$$

$$ad = 0.507 + 0.205\,\tau_b - 0.080\,\tau_d - 0.190\,\tau_b\tau_d \tag{20}$$

Equations (17) to (20) describe a simple parameterization of a sophisticated broadband radiation model and provide accurate predictions of E_b and E_d, even at sites where the atmosphere is very hazy or humid most of the time.

Example 3. Calculate clear-sky beam and diffuse solar irradiance in Atlanta, GA, for July 21 at noon solar time. Note that Table 1 already lists clear-sky beam and diffuse solar irradiance for solar noon. Calculations are shown here to illustrate the application of the method.

Solution: From Example 1, at solar noon on July 21 in Atlanta solar altitude is $\beta = 76.80°$. From Equation (16):

$$m = 1/[\sin(76.80°) + 0.50572(6.07995 + 76.80)^{-1.6364}] = 1.027$$

From Table 1, the beam and diffuse optical depths for Atlanta in July are $\tau_b = 0.515$ and $\tau_d = 2.066$. From Table 2 or Equation (4), normal extraterrestrial irradiance on July 21 is $E_o = 420$ Btu/h·ft². Then, from Equations (19) and (20)

$$ab = 1.454 - 0.406 \times 0.515 - 0.268 \times 2.066 + 0.021 \times 0.515 \times 2.066 = 0.714$$

$$ad = 0.507 + 0.205 \times 0.515 - 0.080 \times 2.066 - 0.190 \times 0.515 \times 2.066 = 0.245$$

and from Equations (17) and (18),

$$E_b = 420 \exp(-0.515 \times 1.027^{0.714}) = 249 \text{ Btu/h·ft}^2$$

$$E_d = 420 \exp(-2.066 \times 1.027^{0.245}) = 53 \text{ Btu/h·ft}^2$$

These are the values listed for $Eb_{n,noon}$ and $Edh_{,noon}$ in Table 1.

Example 4. Perform the same calculation as in Example 3, but for 3 PM eastern daylight saving time.

Solution: This is the same calculation as in the solution of Example 3, but using the solar altitude $\beta = 68.62°$ calculated in Example 2 (ab and ad are unchanged from Example 3):

$$m = 1/[\sin(68.62°) + 0.50572(6.07995 + 68.62)^{-1.6364}] = 1.073$$

$$E_b = 420 \exp(-0.515 \times 1.073^{0.714}) = 244 \text{ Btu/h·ft}^2$$

$$E_d = 420 \exp(-2.066 \times 1.073^{0.245}) = 51 \text{ Btu/h·ft}^2$$

3. TRANSPOSITION TO RECEIVING SURFACES OF VARIOUS ORIENTATIONS

Calculations developed in the previous section are chiefly concerned with estimating clear-sky solar irradiance either normal to the rays of the sun (direct beam) or on a horizontal surface (diffuse). However, in many circumstances, calculation of clear-sky solar irradiance is required on surfaces of arbitrary orientations. Receiving surfaces can be vertical (e.g., walls and windows) or tilted (e.g., skylights or active solar devices). This section describes **transposition**

Table 4 Surface Orientations and Azimuths, Measured from South

Orientation	N	NE	E	SE	S	SW	W	NW
Surface azimuth ψ	180°	−135°	−90°	−45°	0	45°	90°	135°

models that enable calculating solar irradiance on any surface, knowing beam normal and diffuse horizontal irradiance.

Solar Angles Related to Receiving Surfaces

The orientation of a receiving surface is best characterized by its tilt angle and its azimuth, shown in Figure 3. The tilt angle Σ (also called **slope**) is the angle between the surface and the horizontal plane. Its value lies between 0 and 180°. Most often, slopes are between 0° (horizontal) and 90° (vertical). Values above 90° correspond to surfaces facing the ground. The surface azimuth ψ is defined as the displacement from south of the projection, on the horizontal plane, of the normal to the surface. Surfaces that face west have a positive surface azimuth; those that face east have a negative surface azimuth. Surface azimuths for common orientations are summarized in Table 4. Note that, in this chapter, surface azimuth is defined as relative to south in both the northern and southern hemispheres. Other presentations and software use relative-to-north or relative-to-equator; care is required.

The surface-solar azimuth angle γ is defined as the angular difference between the solar azimuth ϕ and the surface azimuth ψ:

$$\gamma = \phi - \psi \tag{21}$$

Values of γ greater than 90° or less than −90° indicate that the surface is in the shade.

Finally, the angle between the line normal to the irradiated surface and the earth-sun line is called the angle of incidence θ. It is important in fenestration, load calculations, and solar technology because it affects the intensity of the direct component of solar radiation striking the surface and the surface's ability to absorb, transmit, or reflect the sun's rays. Its value is given by

$$\cos\theta = \cos\beta\cos\gamma\sin\Sigma + \sin\beta\cos\Sigma \tag{22}$$

Note that for vertical surfaces ($\Sigma = 90°$) Equation (22) simplifies to

$$\cos\theta = \cos\beta\cos\gamma \tag{23}$$

whereas for horizontal surfaces ($\Sigma = 0°$) it simplifies to

$$\theta = 90 - \beta \tag{24}$$

Example 5. For Atlanta, GA, on July 21 at 3 PM eastern daylight saving time, find the angle of incidence at a vertical widow facing 60° west of south.

Solution: The azimuth of the receiving surface is $\psi = +60°$. According to Example 2, solar azimuth angle is $\phi = 56.69°$. Then, Equation (21) gives the surface-solar azimuth angle as

$$\gamma = 56.69° - 60° = -3.31°$$

Still from Example 2, solar altitude angle is $\beta = 68.62°$. Equation (23) leads to

$$\cos\theta = \cos(68.62°)\cos(-3.31°) = 0.364$$

Therefore, $\theta = 68.66°$.

Example 6. For the same conditions as in Example 5, find the angle of incidence at a skylight tilted at 30° and facing 60° west of south.

Solution: The azimuth of the receiving surface is still $\psi = +60°$, but its slope is $\Sigma = 30°$. Other angles are unchanged from Example 5. Equation (22) now applies:

$$\cos\theta = \cos(68.62°)\cos(-3.31°)\sin(30°) + \sin(68.62°)\cos(30°) = 0.988$$

which leads to $\theta = 8.74°$.

Calculation of Clear-Sky Solar Irradiance Incident On Receiving Surface

Total clear-sky irradiance E_t reaching the receiving surface is the sum of three components: the beam component $E_{t,b}$ originating from the solar disc; the diffuse component $E_{t,d}$, originating from the sky dome; and the ground-reflected component $E_{t,r}$ originating from the ground in front of the receiving surface. Thus,

$$E_t = E_{t,b} + E_{t,d} + E_{t,r} \tag{25}$$

Only a simple method for computing all the factors on the right side of Equation (25) is presented here. More elaborate methods, particularly with regard to the calculating the diffuse component, can be found in Gueymard (1987) and Perez et al. (1990).

Beam Component. The beam component is obtained from a straightforward geometric relationship:

$$E_{t,b} = E_b\cos\theta \tag{26}$$

where θ is the angle of incidence. This relationship is valid only when $\cos\theta > 0$; otherwise, $E_{t,b} = 0$.

Diffuse Component. The diffuse component is more difficult to estimate because of the anisotropic nature of diffuse radiation: some parts of the sky, such as the circumsolar disc or the horizon, tend to be brighter than the rest of the sky, which makes the development of a simplified model challenging. For vertical surfaces, Stephenson (1965) and Threlkeld (1963) showed that the ratio Y of clear-sky diffuse irradiance on a vertical surface to clear-sky diffuse irradiance on the horizontal is a simple function of the angle of incidence θ:

$$E_{t,d} = E_d Y \tag{27}$$

with

$$Y = \max(0.45,\ 0.55 + 0.437\cos\theta + 0.313\cos^2\theta) \tag{28}$$

For a nonvertical surface with slope Σ, the following simplified relationships are sufficient for most applications described in this volume:

$$E_{t,d} = E_d(Y\sin\Sigma + \cos\Sigma) \qquad \text{if } \Sigma \le 90° \tag{29}$$

$$E_{t,d} = E_d Y\sin\Sigma \qquad \text{if } \Sigma > 90° \tag{30}$$

where Y is calculated for a *vertical surface* having the same azimuth as the receiving surface considered.

Note that Equations (27) to (30) are appropriate for clear-sky conditions, but should not be used for cloudy skies.

Ground-Reflected Component. Ground-reflected irradiance for surfaces of all orientations is given by

$$E_{t,r} = (E_b\sin\beta + E_d)\rho_g\frac{1-\cos\Sigma}{2} \tag{31}$$

where ρ_g is ground reflectance, often taken to be 0.2 for a typical mixture of ground surfaces. Table 5 provides estimates of ρ_g for other surfaces, including in the presence of snow.

Example 7. Find the direct, diffuse and ground-reflected components of clear-sky solar irradiance on the window in Example 5.

Solution: Clear-sky beam normal irradiance E_b and diffuse horizontal irradiance E_d were calculated in Example 4 as E_b = 244 Btu/h·ft² and E_d = 51 Btu/h·ft². Example 2 provided the solar altitude as $\beta = 68.62°$ and Example 5 provided the angle of incidence as $\theta = 68.66°$. The surface slope is $\Sigma = 90°$, and ground reflectance is assumed to be 0.2. Substituting these values into Equations (26), (27), (28), and (31) leads to

$$E_{t,b} = 244\cos(68.66°) = 89 \text{ Btu/h·ft}^2$$

$$Y = \max[0.45,\ 0.55 + 0.437\cos(68.66°) + 0.313\cos^2(68.66°)] = 0.750$$

$$E_{t,d} = 51 \times 0.750 = 38 \text{ Btu/h}\cdot\text{ft}^2$$

$$E_{t,r} = [244 \sin(68.62°) + 51]0.2\frac{1+\cos(68.62°)}{2} = 38 \text{ Btu/h}\cdot\text{ft}^2$$

Example 8. Find the direct, diffuse and ground-reflected components of clear-sky solar irradiance on the skylight in Example 6.

Solution: This example uses the same values as Example 7, except that the surface slope is $\Sigma = 30°$ and the angle of incidence, calculated in Example 6, is $\theta = 8.74°$. The clear-sky irradiance components are then calculated from Equations (26), (29) and (31); the ratio Y is calculated for a *vertical* surface having the same azimuth as the receiving surface, so the value calculated in Example 7 is unchanged.

$$E_{t,b} = 244 \cos(8.74°) = 241 \text{ Btu/h}\cdot\text{ft}^2$$

$$E_{t,d} = 51[0.750 \sin(30°) + \cos(30°)] = 64 \text{ Btu/h}\cdot\text{ft}^2$$

$$E_{t,r} = [244 \sin(68.62°) + 51]0.2\frac{1+\cos(68.62°)}{2} = 38 \text{ Btu/h}\cdot\text{ft}^2$$

4. GENERATING DESIGN-DAY DATA

This section provides procedures for generating 24 h temperature data sequences suitable as input to many HVAC analysis methods, including the radiant time series (RTS) cooling load calculation procedure described in Chapter 18.

Temperatures. Table 6 gives a normalized daily temperature profile in fractions of daily temperature range. Recent research projects RP-1363 (Hedrick 2009) and RP-1453 (Thevenard 2009) have shown that this profile is representative of both dry-bulb and wet-bulb temperature variation on typical design days. To calculate hourly temperatures, subtract the Table 6 fraction of the dry- or wet-bulb daily range from the dry- or wet-bulb design temperature (limiting by saturation in the case of the wet-bulb). This procedure is applicable to annual or monthly data and is shown in Example 9. Table 7 specifies the input values to be used for generating several design-day types.

Because daily temperature variation is driven by heat from the sun, the profile in Table 6 is, strictly speaking, specified in terms of solar time. Typical HVAC calculations (e.g., hourly cooling loads) are performed in local time, reflecting building operation schedules. The difference between local and solar time can easily be 1 or 2 h, depending on site longitude and whether daylight saving time is in effect. This difference can be included by accessing the temperature profile using apparent solar time (AST) calculated with Equation (7), as shown in Example 9.

Additional Moist-Air Properties. Once hourly dry-bulb and wet-bulb temperatures are known, additional moist air properties (e.g., dew-point temperature, humidity ratio, enthalpy) can be derived using the psychrometric chart, equations in Chapter 1, or psychrometric software.

Table 5 Ground Reflectance of Foreground Surfaces

Foreground Surface	Reflectance
Water (near normal incidences)	0.07
Coniferous forest (winter)	0.07
Asphalt, new	0.05
weathered	0.10
Bituminous and gravel roof	0.13
Dry bare ground	0.2
Weathered concrete	0.2 to 0.3
Green grass	0.26
Dry grassland	0.2 to 0.3
Desert sand	0.4
Light building surfaces	0.6
Snow-covered surfaces:	
Typical city center	0.2
Typical urban site	0.4
Typical rural site	0.5
Isolated rural site	0.7

Source: Adapted from Thevenard and Haddad (2006).

Example 9. Deriving Hourly Design-Day Temperatures. Calculate hourly temperatures for Atlanta, GA, for a July dry-bulb design day using the 5% design conditions.

Solution: From Table 1, the July 5% dry-bulb design conditions for Atlanta are DB = 91.6°F and MCWB = 74.3°F. Daily range values are MCDBR = 20.2°F and MCWBR = 6.1°F. Daylight saving time is in effect for Atlanta in July. Apparent solar time (AST) for hour 1 local daylight saving time (LDT) is –0.73. The nearest hour to the AST is 23, yielding a Table 6 profile value of 0.75. Then $t_{db,1} = 91.6 - 0.75 \times 20.2 = 76.5$°F. Similarly, $t_{wb,1} = 74.3 - 0.75 \times 6.1 = 69.7$°F. With psychrometric formulas, derive $t_{dp,1} = 66.7$°F. Table 8 shows results of this procedure for all 24 h.

5. ESTIMATION OF DEGREE-DAYS

Monthly Degree-Days

The tables of climatic design conditions in this chapter list heating and cooling degree-days (bases 50 and 65°F). Although 50 and 65°F represent the most commonly used bases for the calculation of degree-days, calculation to other bases may be necessary. With that goal in mind, the tables also provide two parameters (monthly average temperature T, and standard deviation of daily average temperature s_d) that enable estimation of degree-days to any base with reasonable accuracy.

The calculation method was established by Schoenau and Kehrig (1990). Heating degree days HDD_b to base T_b are expressed as

$$HDD_b = Ns_d[Z_bF(Z_b) + f(Z_b)] \quad (32)$$

where N is the number of days in the month and Z_b is the difference between monthly average temperature $\bar{T}$ and base temperature T_b, normalized by the standard deviation of the daily average temperature s_d:

$$Z_b = \frac{T_b - \bar{T}}{s_d} \quad (33)$$

Function f is the normal (Gaussian) probability density function with mean 0 and standard deviation 1, and function F is the equivalent cumulative normal probability function:

$$f(Z) = \frac{1}{\sqrt{2\pi}}\exp\left(\frac{-Z^2}{2}\right) \quad (34)$$

$$F(Z) = \int_{-\infty}^{Z} f(z)dz \quad (35)$$

Table 6 Fraction of Daily Temperature Range

Time, h	Fraction	Time, h	Fraction	Time, h	Fraction
1	0.88	9	0.55	17	0.14
2	0.92	10	0.38	18	0.24
3	0.95	11	0.23	19	0.39
4	0.98	12	0.13	20	0.50
5	1.00	13	0.05	21	0.59
6	0.98	14	0.00	22	0.68
7	0.91	15	0.00	23	0.75
8	0.74	16	0.06	24	0.82

Table 7 Input Sources for Design-Day Generation

Design Day Type	Design Conditions	Daily Ranges	Limits
Dry-bulb			
Annual	0.4, 1, or 2% annual cooling DB/MCWB	Hottest month 5% DB MCDBR/MCWBR	Hourly wet-bulb temp. = min(dry-bulb temp., wet-bulb temp.)
Monthly	0.4, 2, 5, or 10% DB/MCWB for month	5% DB MCDBR/MCWBR for month	
Wet-bulb			
Annual	0.4, 1, or 2% annual cooling WB/MCDB	Hottest month 5% WB MCDBR/MCWBR	Hourly dry-bulb temp. = max(dry-bulb temp., wet-bulb temp.)
Monthly	0.4, 2, 5, or 10% WB/MCDB for month	5% WB MCDBR/MCWBR for month	

Table 8 Derived Hourly Temperatures for Atlanta, GA for July for 5% Design Conditions, °F

Hour (LDT)	t_{db}	t_{wb}	t_{dp}	Hour (LDT)	t_{db}	t_{wb}	t_{dp}
1	76.5	69.7	66.7	13	87.0	72.9	66.9
2	75.0	69.3	66.7	14	89.0	73.5	67.0
3	76.5	69.7	66.7	15	90.6	74.0	67.1
4	73.8	68.9	66.7	16	91.6	74.3	67.1
5	73.0	68.7	66.7	17	91.6	74.3	67.1
6	72.4	68.5	66.7	18	90.4	73.9	67.1
7	71.8	68.3	66.8	19	88.8	73.4	67.0
8	71.4	68.2	66.8	20	86.8	72.8	66.9
9	71.8	68.3	66.8	21	83.7	71.9	66.8
10	73.2	68.7	66.7	22	81.5	71.3	66.8
11	76.7	69.8	66.7	23	79.7	70.7	66.8
12	80.5	70.9	66.8	24	77.9	70.2	66.7

LDT = Local daylight saving time.

Both *f* and *F* are readily available as built-in functions in many scientific calculators or spreadsheet programs, so their manual calculation is rarely warranted.

Cooling degree days CDD_b to base T_b are calculated by the same equation:

$$CDD_b = Ns_d[Z_b F(Z_b) + f(Z_b)] \tag{36}$$

except that Z_b is now expressed as

$$Z_b = \frac{\overline{T} - T_b}{s_d} \tag{37}$$

Alternative Equations. The following formulas from ISO *Standard* 15927-6 give results very similar to Equations (32) and (36) but are somewhat simpler:

$$HDD_b = \frac{N(T_b - \overline{T})}{1 - \exp(-\sqrt{2\pi}(T_b - \overline{T})/s_d)} \tag{38}$$

$$CDD_b = \frac{N(\overline{T} - T_b)}{1 - \exp(-\sqrt{2\pi}(\overline{T} - T_b)/s_d)} \tag{39}$$

When $\overline{T} = T_b$, the right-hand side of these equations become $Ns_d/\sqrt{2\pi}$.

Annual Degree-Days

Annual degree-days are simply the sum of monthly degree days over the twelve months of the year.

Example 10. Calculate heating and cooling degree-days (base 59°F) for Atlanta for the month of October.

Solution: For October in Atlanta, Table 1 provides $\overline{T}$ = 63.6°Fand s_d = 7.07°F. For heating degree-days, Equation (33) provides Z_b = (59 – 63.6)/7.07 = –0.651. From a scientific calculator or a spreadsheet program $f(Z_b)$ = 0.323, and $F(Z_b)$ = 0.258. Equation (32) then gives

$$HDD_{59} = 31 \times 7.07[-0.651 \times 0.258 + 0.323] = 34.0\text{°F-day.}$$

For cooling degree-days, Z_b = 0.651. Note that $f(-Z_b) = f(Z_b)$ and $F(-Z_b) = 1 - F(Z_b)$, hence

$$f(Z_b) = 0.323 \quad \text{and} \quad F(Z_b) = 0.742$$

and

$$CDD_{59} = 31 \times 7.07(0.651 \times 0.742 + 0.323) = 176.6\text{°F-day.}$$

For most stations, the monthly degree-days calculated with this method are within 9°F-day of the observed values.

6. REPRESENTATIVENESS OF DATA AND SOURCES OF UNCERTAINTY

Representativeness of Data

The climatic design information in this chapter was obtained by direct analysis of observations from the indicated locations. Design values reflect an estimate of the cumulative frequency of occurrence of the weather conditions at the recording station, either for single or jointly occurring elements, for several years into the future. Several sources of uncertainty affect the accuracy of using the design conditions to represent other locations or periods.

The most important of these factors is spatial representativeness. Most of the observed data for which design conditions were calculated were collected from airport observing sites, the majority of which are flat, grassy, open areas, away from buildings and trees or other local influences. Temperatures recorded in these areas may be significantly different from built-up areas where the design conditions are being applied. For example, the maximum urban heat island intensity may be 18°F or more (Oke 1987), although intraurban variability is typically quite large. Urban microclimate is affected by the three-dimensional density of building construction, usually represented by the ratio of building height to street width(*H*/*W*); by type and extent of plant cover; and by anthropogenic heat emissions from buildings and vehicles. Significant variations can also occur with changes in local elevation, even if elevations differ by a few hundred feet, or in the vicinity of large bodies of water. It should be emphasized that such variations are not constant in time: intraurban differences in temperature and humidity fluctuate not only in predictable diurnal patterns, but also in response to changes in synoptic conditions and wind direction. Urban heat islands, for example, are typically prominent on clear nights with little or no wind, and are weaker or nonexistent in windy conditions and during daytime. Therefore, judgment must always be used in assessing the representativeness of the design conditions. Consult an applied climatologist regarding estimating design conditions for locations not listed in this chapter. For online references to applied climatologists in the United States, see wcdirectory.ametsoc.org/certified-consulting-meteorologists; in Canada, consult cmos.ca/client/roster/clientRosterView.html?clientRosterId=190. Also, GIS-compatible files (KML format) are provided as a special feature in ASHRAE Handbook Online. This allows use of the data in a GIS environment such as Google Earth or ArcGIS, which provides capabilities to overlay various layers of information such as elevation, land use, and bodies of water. This type of information can greatly assist in determining the most representative location to use for an application.

Table 9 Locations Representing Various Climate Types

Cold Snow Forest	Dry	Warm Rainy	Tropical Rainy
Portland, ME	Amarillo, TX	Huntsville, AL	Key West, FL
Grand Island, NE	Bakersfield, CA	Wilmington, NC	West Palm Beach, FL
Minot, ND	Sacramento, CA	Portland, OR	
Indianapolis, IN	Phoenix, AZ	Quillayute, WA	

Depending on a site's specific geographic location and setting (e.g., proximity to large body of water or hills), the data in this chapter for the nearest weather station may not be representative of the actual climate experienced at the project site. In these instances, it may be beneficial to obtain climate data using procedures developed by ASHRAE research project RP-1561 (Qiu et al. 2016). The methodologies provide a protocol for using state-of-the-art mesoscale modeling techniques to derive meteorological conditions specific to the study area. The research project included the methodology based on the Weather Research and Forecasting (WRF) model designed to develop site-specific climate data where standard weather stations are unavailable or not representative of site conditions. The methodology was evaluated by using observations in various geographic regions, including coastal, mountain valley, mountain plateau, and major cities. A simplified procedure was developed; it is freely available at klimaat.github.io/emspy/.

The underlying data also depend on the method of observation. During the 1990s, most data gathering in the United States and Canada was converted to automated systems designated either an automated surface observation system (ASOS) or an automated weather observing system (AWOS). This change improved completeness and consistency of available data. However, changes have resulted from the inherent differences in type of instrumentation, instrumentation location, and processing procedures between the prior manual systems and ASOS. These effects were investigated in ASHRAE research project RP-1226 (Belcher and DeGaetano 2004). Comparison of one-year ASOS and manual records revealed some biases in dry-bulb temperature, dew-point temperature, and wind speed. These biases are judged to be negligible for HVAC engineering purposes; the tabulated design conditions in this chapter were derived from mixed automated and manual data as available. Changes in the location of the observing instruments often have a larger effect than changes in instrumentation. On the other hand, ASOS measurements of sky coverage and ceiling height differ markedly from manual observations and are incompatible with solar radiation models used in energy simulation software. An updated solar model, compatible with ASOS data, was developed as part of RP-1226. The ASOS-based model was found less accurate than models based on manually observed data when compared to measured solar radiation.

Weather conditions vary from year to year and, to some extent, from decade to decade because of the inherent variability of climate. Similarly, values representing design conditions vary depending on the period of record used in the analysis. Thus, because of short-term climatic variability, there is always some uncertainty in using design conditions from one period to represent another period. Typically, values of design dry-bulb temperature vary less than 2°F from decade to decade, but larger variations can occur. Differing periods used in the analysis can lead to differences in design conditions between nearby locations at similar elevations. Design conditions may show trends in areas of increasing urbanization or other regions experiencing extensive changes to land use. Longer-term climatic change brought by human or natural causes may also introduce trends into design conditions. This is discussed further in the section on Effects of Climate Change.

Wind speed and direction are very sensitive to local exposure features such as terrain and surface cover. The original wind data used to calculate the wind speed and direction design conditions in Table 1 are often representative of a flat, open exposure, such as at airports. Wind engineering methods, as described in Chapter 24, can be used to account for exposure differences between airport and building sites. This is a complex procedure, best undertaken by an experienced applied climatologist or wind engineer with knowledge of the exposure of the observing and building sites and surrounding regions.

Uncertainty from Variation in Length of Record

ASHRAE research project RP-1171 (Hubbard et al. 2004) investigated the uncertainty associated with the climatic design conditions in the 2001 *ASHRAE Handbook—Fundamentals*. The main objectives were to determine how many years are needed to calculate reliable design values and to look at the frequency and duration of episodes exceeding the design values.

Design temperatures in the 1997 and 2001 editions were calculated for locations for which there were at least 8 years of sufficient data; the criterion for using 8 years was based on unpublished work by TC 4.2. RP-1171 analyzed data records from 14 U.S. locations (Table 9) representing four different climate types. The dry-bulb temperatures corresponding to the five annual percentile design temperatures (99.6, 99, 0.4, 1, and 2%) from the 33-year period 1961-1993 (period used for the 2001 edition's U.S. stations) were calculated for each location. The temperatures corresponding to the same percentiles for each contiguous subperiod ranging from 1 to 33 years in length was calculated, and the standard deviation of the differences between the resulting design temperature from each subperiod and the entire 33-year period was calculated. For instance, for a 10-year period, the dry-bulb values corresponding to each of the 23 subperiods 1961-1970, 1962-1971, ... 1984-1993 were calculated and the standard deviation of differences with the dry-bulb value for the same percentile from the 33-year period calculated. The standard deviation values represent a measure of uncertainty of the design temperatures relative to the design temperature for the entire period of record.

The results for the five annual percentiles are summarized in Figures 4A to 4E, each of which shows how the uncertainty (the average standard deviation for each of the locations in each climate type) varies with length of period.

To the degree that the differences used to calculate the standard deviations are distributed normally, the short-period design temperatures can be expected to lie within one standard deviation of the long-term design temperature 68% of the time. For example, from Figure 4A, the uncertainty for the cold snow forest for a 1-year period is 6.5°F. This can be interpreted that the probability is 68% that the difference in a 99.6% dry-bulb in any given year will be within 6.5°F of the long-term 99.6% dry-bulb. Similarly, there is a 68% probability that the 99.6% dry-bulb from any 10-year period will be within 1.8°F of the long-term value for a location of the cold snow forest climate type.

The uncertainty for the cold season is higher than for the warm season. For example, the uncertainty for the 99.6% dry-bulb for a 10-year period ranges from 1.1 to 1.8°F for the five climate types, whereas the uncertainty for the 0.4% dry-bulb for a 10-year period ranges from 0.7 to 1.1°F.

A variety of other general characteristics of uncertainty are evident from an inspection of Figure 4. For example, the highest uncertainty of any climate type for a 10-year period is 2.0°F for the cold snow forest 99% dry-bulb case. The smallest uncertainty is 0.4°F for the tropical rainy 1% and 2% dry-bulb cases.

Based on these results, it was concluded that using a minimum of 8 years of data would provide reliable (within ±1.8°F) climatic design calculations for most stations.

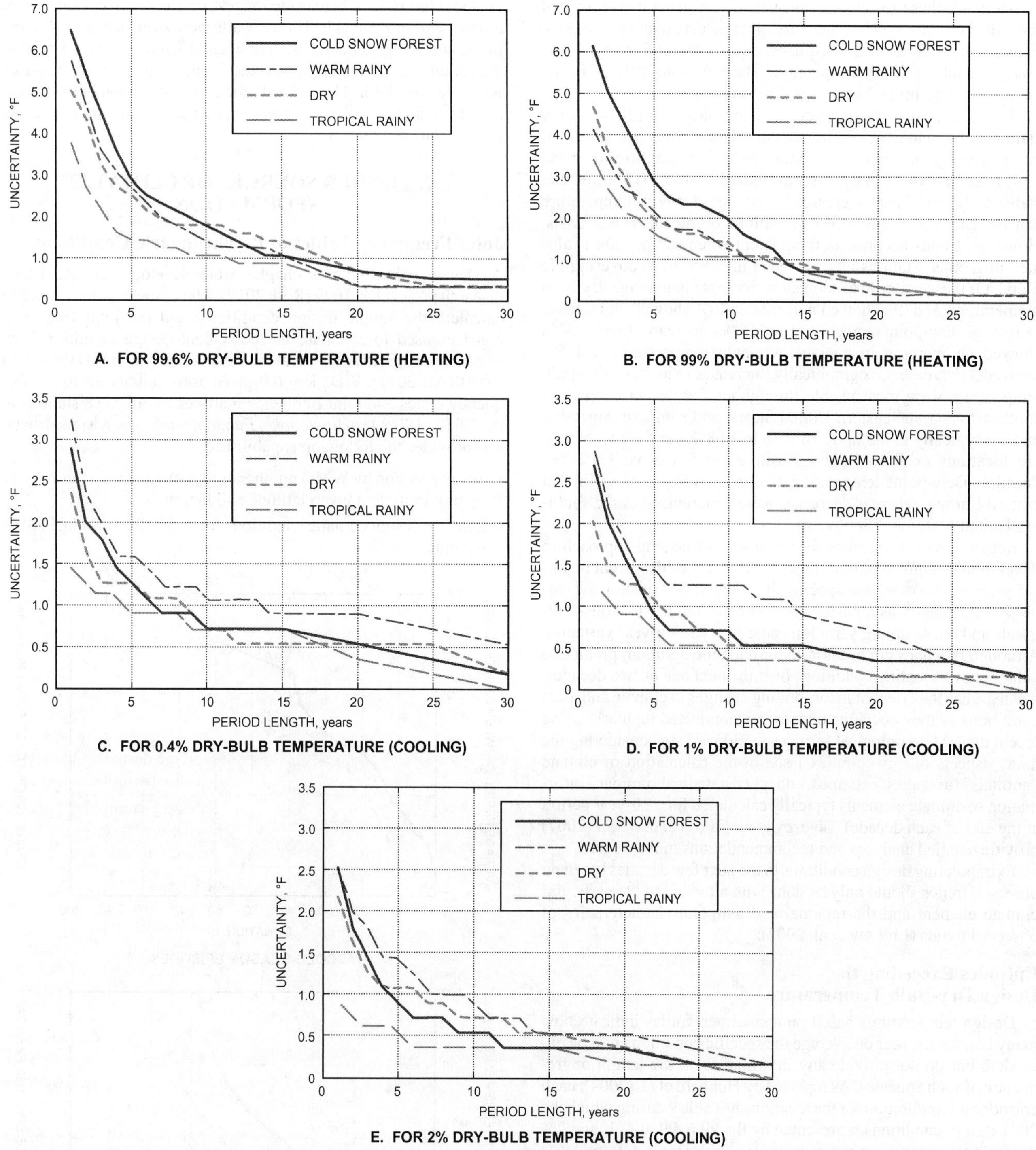

Fig. 4 Uncertainty versus Period Length for Various Dry-Bulb Temperatures, by Climate Type

Effects of Climate Change

The evidence is unequivocal that the climate system is warming globally (IPCC 2007). The most frequently observed effects relate to increases in average, and to some degree, extreme temperatures.

This is partly shown by the results of an analysis of design conditions conducted as part of calculating the values for the 2009 edition of this chapter (Thevenard 2009). For 1274 observing sites worldwide with suitably complete data from 1977 to 2006, selected design conditions were compared between the period 1977-1986 and 1997-2006. The results, averaged over all locations, are as follows:

- The 99.6% annual dry-bulb temperature increased 2.74°F
- The 0.4% annual dry-bulb increased 1.42°F
- Annual dew point increased by 0.99°F
- Heating degree-days (base 65°F) decreased by 427°F-days
- Cooling degree-days (base 50°F) increased by 245°F-days

Although these results are consistent with general warming of the world climate system, there are other effects that undoubtedly contribute, such as increased urbanization around many of the observing sites (airports, typically). There was no attempt in the analysis to determine the reasons for the changes.

A more recent study by Thevenard and Shephard (2014), using stations used in the 2013 edition of this chapter, looked at trends for yearly average dry-bulb temperature and other quantities over the 1986 to 2010 period using statistical methods. The study showed that statistically significant increases in average dry-bulb temperature can be detected in only 19% of stations on an individual basis. However, trends become more apparent when stations are evaluated in groups. Stations were grouped in 5°×5° cells covering the globe. Of these cells, 44% showed an increase in average dry-bulb temperature, and 2% showed a decrease; 26% showed an increase in average dew-point temperature and 10% a decrease; finally, 34% showed an increase in average wet-bulb temperature, and 5% showed a decrease. Geographically, increases in average dry-bulb temperature were most visible throughout Europe, in China and southeast Asia, the eastern United States, and southern Australia, and are typically in the range of 0.36 to 1.08°F per decade. Northern locations exhibited higher positive trends (above 1.8°F per decade). Dew-point temperature increases were most visible in eastern Europe, whereas decreases were experienced in the southern United States and South America.

Regardless of the reasons for increases, the general approach of developing design conditions based on analysis of the recent record (25 years, in this case) was specifically adopted for updating the values in this chapter as a balance between accounting for long-term trends and the sampling variation caused by year-to-year variation. Although this does not necessarily provide the optimum predictive value for representing conditions over the next one or two decades, it at least has the effect of incorporating changes in climate and local conditions as they occur, as updates are conducted regularly using recent data. Meteorological services worldwide are considering the many aspects of this complex issue in the calculation of climate "normals" (averages, extremes, and other statistical summary information of climate elements typically calculated for a 30-year period at the end of each decade). Livezey et al. (2007) and WMO (2007) provide detailed analyses and recommendations in this regard.

Extrapolating design conditions to the next few decades based on observed trends should only be done with attention to the particular climate element and the regional and temporal characteristics of observed trends (Livezey et al. 2007).

Episodes Exceeding the Design Dry-Bulb Temperature

Design temperatures based on annual percentiles indicate how many hours each year on average the specific conditions will be exceeded, but do not provide any information on the length or frequency of such episodes. As reported by Hubbard et al. (2004), each episode and its duration for the locations in Table 9 during which the 2001 design conditions represented by the 99.6, 99, 0.4, 1, and 2% dry-bulb temperatures were exceeded (i.e., were more extreme) was tabulated and their frequency of occurrence analyzed. The measure of frequency is the average number of episodes per year or its reciprocal, the average period between episodes.

Cold- and warm-season results are presented in Figures 5A and 5B, respectively, for Indianapolis, IN, as a representative example. The duration for the 10-year period between episodes more extreme than the 99.6% design dry bulb is 37 h, and 62 h for the 99% design dry bulb. For the warm season, the 10-year period durations corresponding to the 0.4, 1, and 2% design dry bulb, are about 10, 12, and 15 h, respectively.

Although the results in Hubbard et al. (2004) varied somewhat among the locations analyzed, generally the longest cold-season episodes last days, whereas the longest warm-season episodes were always shorter than 24 h. These results were seen at almost all locations, and are general for the continental United States. The only exception was Phoenix, where the longest cold-season episodes were less than 24 h. This is likely the result of the southern latitude and dry climate, which produces a large daily temperature range, even in the cold season.

7. OTHER SOURCES OF CLIMATIC INFORMATION

Joint Frequency Tables of Psychrometric Conditions

Design values in this chapter were developed by ASHRAE research project RP-1699 (Roth 2017). The frequency tables used to calculate the simple design conditions, and the joint frequency matrices used to calculate the coincident design conditions, are available in ASHRAE's Weather Data Viewer 6.0 (WDView 6.0) (ASHRAE 2017). WDView 6.0 gives users full access to the frequency tables and joint frequency matrices for all 8118 stations in the 2017 *ASHRAE Handbook—Fundamentals* via a spreadsheet, and provides the following capabilities:

- Select a station by WMO number or region/country/state/name or by proximity to a given latitude and longitude.
- Retrieve design climatic conditions for a specified station, in SI or I-P units.

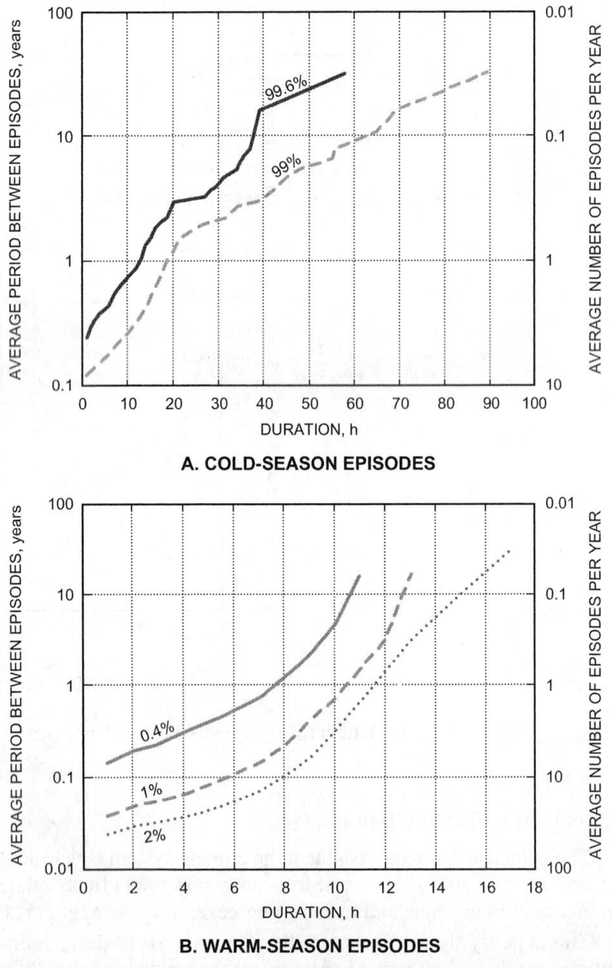

Fig. 5 Frequency and Duration of Episodes Exceeding Design Dry-Bulb Temperature for Indianapolis, IN

- Display frequency vectors and joint frequency matrices in the form of numerical tables.
- Display frequency distribution and the cumulative frequency distribution functions in graphical form.
- Display joint frequency functions in graphical form.
- Display the table of years and months used for the calculation.
- Display hourly binned dry-bulb temperature data.
- Calculate heating and cooling degree-days to any base, using the method of Schoenau and Kehrig (1990).

The **Engineering Weather Data CD** (NCDC 1999), an update of Air Force *Manual* 88-29, was compiled by the U.S. Air Force 14th Weather Squadron. This CD contains several tabular and graphical summaries of temperature, humidity, and wind speed information for hundreds of locations in the United States and around the world. In particular, it contains detailed joint frequency tables of temperature and humidity for each month, binned at 1°F and 3 h local time-of-day intervals. This CD is available from NCDC: www.ncdc.noaa.gov /nespls/olstore.prodspecific?prodnum=5005.

The **International Station Meteorological Climate Summary (ISMCS)** is a CD-ROM containing climatic summary information for over 7000 locations around the world (NCDC 1996). A table providing the joint frequency of dry-bulb temperature and wet-bulb temperature depression is provided for the locations with hourly observations. It can be used as an aid in estimating design conditions for locations for which no other information is available. The CD is available at gcmd.nasa.gov/records/GCMD_gov.noaa.ncdc.C00268 .html. A web version of this product is now available free of charge from NCDC at www7.ncdc.noaa.gov/CDO/cdoselect.cmd?data setabbv=SUMMARIES. This service is also available via gis.ncdc .noaa.gov/map/viewer.

The monthly frequency distribution of dry-bulb temperatures and mean coincident wet-bulb temperatures for 134 Canadian locations is available from Environment Canada (1983-1987).

Degree Days and Climate Normals

The 1981 to 2010 climate normals for over 6000 United States locations are available online (free of charge) from the National Climatic Data Center: gis.ncdc.noaa.gov/map/viewer/.

The Canadian Climate Normals (updated every 10 years; the most recent values are for the 1981-2010 period) can be found at climate.weather.gc.ca/climate_normals/index_e.html.

The *Climatography of the United States* No. 20 (CLIM20), monthly station climate summaries for 1971 to 2000 are climatic station summaries of particular interest to engineering, energy, industry, and agricultural applications (NCDC 2004). These summaries contain a variety of statistics for temperature, precipitation, snow, freeze dates, and degree-day elements for 4273 stations. The statistics include means, medians (precipitation and snow elements), extremes, mean number of days exceeding threshold values, and heating, cooling, and growing degree-days for various temperature bases. Also included are probabilities for monthly precipitation and freeze data. Information on this product can be found at www .ncdc.noaa.gov/oa/documentlibrary/pdf/eis/clim20eis.pdf. Note that this is for 1971 to 2000 and not for the 1981 to 2010 period (latest normals) noted previously.

Heating and cooling degree-day and degree-hour data for 3677 locations from 115 countries were developed by Crawley (1994) from the Global Daily Summary (GDS) version 1.0 and the International Station Meteorological Climate Summary (ISMCS) version 4.0 data.

Typical Year Data Sets

Software is available to simulate the annual energy performance of buildings requiring a 1-year data set (8760 h) of weather conditions. Many data sets in different record formats have been developed to meet this requirement. The data represent a typical year with respect to weather-induced energy loads on a building. No explicit effort was made to represent extreme conditions, so these files do not represent design conditions.

The National Renewable Energy Laboratory's (NREL) TMY3 data set (Wilcox and Marion 2008) contains data for 1020 U.S. locations. TMY3, along with the 1991-2010 National Solar Radiation Data Base (NSRDB) (NREL 2011), contains hourly solar radiation [global, beam (direct), and diffuse] and meteorological data for 1454 stations; TMY3 is available at rredc.nrel.gov/solar/old_data/nsrdb /1991-2005/tmy3/, and the NSRDB at www.ncdc.noaa.gov/land -based-station-data/solar-radiation/. These were produced using an objective statistical algorithm to select the most typical month from the long-term record. A more recent source of *gridded* weather, solar radiation, and environmental TMY data with a visual and dynamic interface is available from maps.nrel.gov/nsrdb-viewer. The solar radiation data are derived from satellite data, and the environmental data are downscaled from the MERRA reanalysis data set derived from a large climate forecasting model (Rienecker et al. 2011). The grid spacing for this source of data is about 2.5 miles, and currently covers North America up to 50° N, as well as a part of South America down to 10° S. Various types of TMY data are available there, currently for the period 1998 to 2014, as well as each historical year within that time period, with anticipated annual updates.

Canadian Weather Year for Energy Calculation (CWEC) files for 47 Canadian locations were developed for use with the Canadian National Energy Code, using the TMY algorithm and software (Environment Canada 1993). Files for 75 locations are now available.

ASHRAE's International Weather for Energy Calculations (IWEC2) data set (Huang et al. 2014) contains typical-year weather data for 3012 international locations outdoor of the United States and Canada. The IWEC2s were developed through ASHRAE RP-1477, which used the same source of raw weather data (ISD; Lott et al. 2001) as used for the design condition tables in this chapter, but for a slightly earlier time period of 12 to 25 years ending in 2009. The IWEC2 data set is available on a DVD from the ASHRAE Climate Data Center at www.ashrae.org/resources--publications /bookstore/climate-data-center#iwec; individual files and country sets are also available online from commercial resellers.

Sequences of Extreme Temperature and Humidity Durations

Colliver (1997) and Colliver et al. (1998) compiled extreme sequences of 1-, 3-, 5-, and 7-day duration for 239 U.S. and 144 Canadian locations based independently on the following five criteria: high dry-bulb temperature, high dew-point temperature, high enthalpy, low dry-bulb temperature, and low wet-bulb depression. For the criteria associated with high values, the sequences are selected according to annual percentiles of 0.4, 1.0, and 2.0. For the criteria corresponding to low values, annual percentiles of 99.6, 99.0, and 98.0 are reported. Although these percentiles are identical to those used to select annual heating and cooling design temperatures, the maximum or minimum temperatures within each sequence are significantly more extreme than the corresponding design temperatures. The data included for each hour of a sequence are solar radiation, dry-bulb and dew-point temperature, atmospheric pressure, and wind speed and direction. Accompanying information allows the user to go back to the source data and obtain sequences with different characteristics (e.g., different probability of occurrence, windy conditions, low or high solar radiation). These extreme sequences are available on CD (ASHRAE 1997).

These sequences were developed primarily to assist the design of heating or cooling systems having a finite capacity before regeneration is required or of systems that rely on thermal mass to limit loads.

The information is also useful where information on the hourly weather sequence during extreme episodes is required for design.

Global Weather Data Source Web Page

Because of growing demand for more comprehensive global coverage of weather data for HVAC applications around the world, ASHRAE sponsored research project RP-1170 (Plantico 2001) to construct a Global Weather Data Sources (GWDS) web page. Many national climate services and other climate data sources are making more information available over the Internet. The purpose of RP-1170 was to provide ASHRAE membership with easy access to major sources of international weather data through one consolidated online system. This web page was later updated to better use the resources of the World Meteorological Organization (WMO) and NCDC. The GWDS web page is accessible at www.ncdc.noaa.gov/oa/ashrae/gwds-title.html.

Observational Data Sets

For detailed designs, custom analysis of the most appropriate long-term weather record is best. National weather services are generally the best source of long-term observational data. The National Climatic Data Center (NCDC), in conjunction with U.S. Air Force and Navy partners in Asheville's Federal Climate Complex (FCC), developed the global Integrated Surface Data (Lott 2004; Lott et al. 2001) to address a pressing need for an integrated global database of hourly land surface climatological data. The database of over 20,000 stations contains hourly and some daily summary data from as early as 1900 (many stations beginning in the 1948-1973 timeframe), is operationally updated each day with the latest available data, and is now being further integrated with various data sets from the United States and other countries to further expand the spatial and temporal coverage of the data. For access to ISD, go to www.ncdc.noaa.gov/isd or, for a GIS interface, gis.ncdc.noaa.gov/map/viewer/. For a complete review of ISD and all of its products, go to www.ncdc.noaa.gov/isd.

The National Solar Radiation Database (NSRDB) (www.ncdc.noaa.gov/land-based-station-data/solar-radiation/; maps.nrel.gov/nsrdb-viewer) and Canadian Weather Energy and Engineering Data Sets (CWEEDS) (Environment Canada 1993) provide long-term hourly data, including solar radiation values for the United States and Canada. A previous version of the NSRDB required a modified solar radiation model because of the implementation of automated observing systems that do not report traditional cloud elements. The current NSRDB Data Viewer (maps.nrel.gov/nsrdb-viewer), which is mentioned earlier in the section on Typical Year Data Sets, also contains both solar radiation and environmental data for every year from 1998 through 2014 covering North America up to 50° North, and South America down to 10° South. The solar radiation data are derived from GOES satellites and the environmental data are downscaled from MERRA reanalysis data set.

Considerable information about weather and climate services and data sets is available elsewhere online. Information supplementary to this chapter may also be posted on the ASHRAE Technical Committee 4.2 website, the link to which is available from the ASHRAE website (www.ashrae.org).

REFERENCES

ASHRAE members can access *ASHRAE Journal* articles and ASHRAE research project final reports at technologyportal.ashrae.org. Articles and reports are also available for purchase by nonmembers in the online ASHRAE Bookstore at www.ashrae.org/bookstore.

ASHRAE. 1997. *Design weather sequence viewer* 2.1. (CD-ROM).

ASHRAE. 2017. *Weather data viewer, version 6.0*. (CD-ROM).

ASHRAE. 2013. Climatic data for building design standards. ANSI/ASHRAE *Standard* 169-2013.

Belcher, B.N., and A.T. DeGaetano. 2004. Integration of ASOS weather data into building energy calculations with emphasis on model-derived solar radiation (RP-1226). ASHRAE Research Project, *Final Report*.

Colliver, D.G. 1997. Sequences of extreme temperature and humidity for design calculations (RP-828). ASHRAE Research Project, *Final Report*.

Colliver, D.G., R.S. Gates, H. Zhang, and K.T. Priddy. 1998. Sequences of extreme temperature and humidity for design calculations. *ASHRAE Transactions* 104(1A):133-144.

Colliver, D.G., R.S. Gates, T.F. Burkes, and H. Zhang. 2000. Development of the design climatic data for the 1997 *ASHRAE Handbook—Fundamentals*. *ASHRAE Transactions* 106(1).

Crawley, D.B. 1994. *Development of degree day and degree hour data for international locations*. D.B. Crawley Consulting, Washington, D.C.

Diamond, H., T. Karl, M. Palecki, C. Baker, J. Bell, R. Leeper, D. Easterling, J. Lawrimore, T. Meyers, M. Helfert, G. Goodge, and P. Thorne. 2013. U.S. Climate Reference Network after one decade of operations: Status and assessment. *Bulletin of the American Meteorological Society* 94(4): 485-498.

Environment Canada. 1983-1987. *Principal station data*. PSD 1 to 134. Atmospheric Environment Service, Downsview, Ontario.

Eskes, H., et al. 2015. Validation of reactive gases and aerosols in the MACC global analysis and forecast system. *Geoscientific Model Development* 8(11):3523-3543. www.geosci-model-dev.net/8/3523/2015/gmd-8-3523-2015-discussion.html.

FAO. 2011. *Climate impact on agriculture*. Food and Agriculture Organization of the United Nations, Rome.

GHCN. 2015. *Global historical climatology network—Daily*. National Climatic Data Center, National Oceanic and Atmospheric Administration, Asheville, NC. www.ncdc.noaa.gov/oa/climate/ghcn-daily/ and ftp.ncdc.noaa.gov/pub/data/ghcn/daily/.

GPCC. 2015. *GPCC Full Data Reanalysis Version 7*. Global Precipitation Climatology Centre, Deutscher Wetterdienst, Offenbach am Main, Germany. ftp.dwd.de/pub/data/gpcc/html/fulldata_v7_doi_download.html.

Gueymard, C.A. 1987. An anisotropic solar irradiance model for tilted surfaces and its comparison with selected engineering algorithms. *Solar Energy* 38:367-386. Erratum, *Solar Energy* 40:175 (1988).

Gueymard, C.A. 2008. REST2: High performance solar radiation model for cloudless-sky irradiance, illuminance and photosynthetically active radiation—Validation with a benchmark dataset. *Solar Energy* 82:272-285.

Gueymard, C.A., and D. Thevenard. 2009. Monthly average clear-sky broadband irradiance database for worldwide solar heat gain and building cooling load calculations. *Solar Energy* 83:1998-2018.

Harriman, L.G., D.G. Colliver, and H.K. Quinn. 1999. New weather data for energy calculations. *ASHRAE Journal* 41(3):31-38.

Hedrick, R. 2009. Generation of hourly design-day weather data (RP-1363). ASHRAE Research Project, *Final Report* (Draft).

Huang, Y.J., F.X. Su, D.H. Seo, and M. Krarti. 2014. Development of ASHRAE IWEC2 weather files from the Integrated Surface Hourly (ISH) data base of historical weather data for 3,012 international locations. *ASHRAE Transactions* 120(1):340-355.

Hubbard, K., K. Kunkel, A. DeGaetano, and K. Redmond. 2004. Sources of uncertainty in the calculation of the design weather conditions in the *ASHRAE Handbook of Fundamentals* (RP-1171). ASHRAE Research Project, *Final Report*.

Inness, A., et al. 2013. The MACC reanalysis: An 8 yr data set of atmospheric composition. *Atmospheric Chemistry and Physics* 13(8):4073-4109. www.atmos-chem-phys.net/13/4073/2013/acp-13-4073-2013-discussion.html.

IPCC. 2007. *Fourth assessment report: Summary for policy makers*. International Panel on Climate Change, World Meteorological Organization, Geneva. www.ipcc.ch/pdf/assessment-report/ar4/wg1/ar4-wg1-spm.pdf.

Iqbal, M. 1983. *An introduction to solar radiation*. Academic Press, Toronto.

ISO. 2007. Hygrothermal performance of buildings—Calculation and presentation of climatic data—Part 6: Accumulated temperature differences (degree days). *Standard* 15927-6. International Organization for Standardization, Geneva.

Kasten, F., and T. Young. 1989. Revised optical air mass tables and approximation formula. *Applied Optics* 28:4735-4738.

Lamming, S.D., and J.R. Salmon. 1996. Wind data for design of smoke control systems (RP-816). ASHRAE Research Project, *Final Report*.

Lamming, S.D., and J.R. Salmon. 1998. Wind data for design of smoke control systems. *ASHRAE Transactions* 104(1A):742-751.

Livezey, R.E., K.Y. Vinnikov, M.M. Timofeyeva, R. Tinker, and H.M. Van Den Dool. 2007. Estimation and extrapolation of climate normals and climatic trends. *Journal of Applied Meteorology and Climatology* 46: 1759-1776.

Lott, J.N. 2004. The quality control of the integrated surface hourly database. 84th American Meteorological Society Annual Meeting, Seattle, WA. ams.confex.com/ams/pdfpapers/71929.pdf.

Lott, J.N., R. Baldwin, and P. Jones. 2001. The FCC Integrated Surface Hourly Database, a new resource of global climate data. NCDC *Technical Report* 2001-01. National Climatic Data Center, Asheville, NC. ftp.ncdc.noaa.gov/pub/data/techrpts/tr200101/tr2001-01.pdf.

Lowery, M.D., and J.E. Nash. 1970. A comparison of methods of fitting the double exponential distribution. *Journal of Hydrology* 10(3):259-275.

Molod, A., L. Takacs, M. Suarez, and J. Bacmeister. 2015. Development of the GEOS-5 atmospheric general circulation model: Evolution from MERRA to MERRA2. *Geoscientific Model Development* 8:1339-1356.

NCDC. 1996. *International station meteorological climate summary (ISMCS)*. National Climatic Data Center, Asheville, NC.

NCDC. 1999. *Engineering weather data*. National Climatic Data Center, Asheville, NC.

NCDC. 2004. Monthly station climate summaries. In *Climatography of the U.S.* #20. National Climatic Data Center, Asheville, NC.

NREL. 2011. National solar radiation database, 1991-2010 update: User's manual. *Technical Report* NREL/TP-581-41364. National Renewable Energy Laboratory, Golden, CO. rredc.nrel.gov/solar/old_data/nsrdb/1991-2010/.

Oke, T.R. 1987. *Boundary layer climates*, 2nd ed. Methuen, London.

Perez, R., P. Ineichen, R. Seals, J. Michalsky, and R. Stewart. 1990. Modeling daylight availability and irradiance components from direct and global irradiance. *Solar Energy* 44(5):271-289.

Plantico, M. 2001. Identify and characterize international weather data sources (RP-1170). ASHRAE Research Project, *Final Report*.

Rienecker, M.M., et al. 2011. MERRA: NASA's Modern-Era Retrospective Analysis for Research and Applications. *Journal of Climate* 24:3624-3648. journals.ametsoc.org/doi/full/10.1175/JCLI-D-11-00015.1.

Qiu, X., M. Roth, H. Corbett-Hains, and F. Yang. 2016. Mesoscale climate modeling procedure development and performance evaluation (RP-1561). *ASHRAE Transactions* 122(2).

Roth, M. 2017. Updating climatic design data in the 2017 *ASHRAE Handbook—Fundamentals* (RP-1699). ASHRAE Research Project RP-1699, *Final Report* (in preparation).

Schoenau, G.J., and R.A. Kehrig. 1990. A method for calculating degree-days to any base temperature. *Energy and Buildings* 14:299-302.

Smith, A., N. Lott, and R. Vose. 2011. The integrated surface database: Recent developments and partnerships. *Bulletin of the American Meteorological Society* 92(6):704.

Stephenson, D.G. 1965. Equations for solar heat gain through windows. *Solar Energy* 9(2):81-86.

Thevenard, D. 2009. Updating the ASHRAE climatic data for design and standards (RP-1453). ASHRAE Research Project, *Final Report*.

Thevenard, D., and C. Gueymard. 2013. Updating climatic design data in Chapter 14 of the 2013 *Handbook of Fundamentals* (RP-1613). ASHRAE Research Project RP-1613, *Final Report*.

Thevenard, D., and K. Haddad. 2006. Ground reflectivity in the context of building energy simulation. *Energy and Buildings* 38(8):972-980.

Thevenard, D., and M. Shephard. 2014. Temperature trends for locations listed in the tables of climatic design conditions in the 2013 *ASHRAE Handbook—Fundamentals*. *ASHRAE Transactions* 120(2).

Thevenard, D., J. Lundgren, and R. Humphries. 2005. Updating the climatic design conditions in the *ASHRAE Handbook of Fundamentals* (RP-1273). ASHRAE Research Project, *Final Report*.

Threlkeld, J.L. 1963. Solar irradiation of surfaces on clear days. *ASHRAE Transactions* 69:24.

Wilcox, S., and W. Marion. 2008. Users manual for TMY3 data sets. *Technical Report* NREL/TP-581-43156. National Renewable Energy Laboratory, Golden, CO. www.nrel.gov/docs/fy08osti/43156.pdf.

WMO. 2007. The role of climatological normals in a changing climate. *Technical Document* 1377. World Meteorological Organization, Geneva.

BIBLIOGRAPHY

ASHRAE. 2013. Weather data for building design standards. ANSI/ASHRAE *Standard* 169-2013.

Environment Canada. 2013. *Canadian 1971-2000 climate normals*. Meteorological Service of Canada, Downsview, Ontario. climate.weatheroffice.ec.gc.ca.

NCDC. 2002. Monthly normals of temperature, precipitation, and heating and cooling degree-days. In *Climatography of the United States* #81. National Climatic Data Center, Asheville, NC.

NCDC. 2002. Annual degree-days to selected bases (1971-2000). In *Climatography of the United States* #81. National Climatic Data Center, Asheville, NC.

NCDC. 2003. *Data documentation for data set 3505 (DSI-3505) integrated surface hourly (ISH) data*. National Climatic Data Center, Asheville, NC.

Thevenard, D., and R. Humphries. 2005. The calculation of climatic design conditions in the 2005 *ASHRAE Handbook—Fundamentals*. *ASHRAE Transactions* 111(1):457-466.

APPENDIX: DESIGN CONDITIONS FOR SELECTED LOCATIONS (Go to CD-ROM to access additional station tables.)

Meaning of acronyms:
DB: Dry bulb temperature, °F — *WB: Wet bulb temperature, °F*
MCWB: Mean coincident wet bulb temperature, °F
Lat: Latitude, ° — *Long: Longitude, °* — *Elev: Elevation, ft*
DP: Dew point temperature, °F — *HR: Humidity ratio, grains of moisture per lb of dry air* — *WS: Wind speed, mph*
MCDB: Mean coincident dry bulb temperature, °F — *HDD and CDD 65: Annual heating and cooling degree-days, base 65°F, °F-day*

Station	Lat	Long	Elev	Heating DB		Cooling DB/MCWB						Evaporation WB/MCDB				Dehumidification DP/HR/MCDB						Extreme Annual WS			Heat./Cool. Degree-Days	
				99.6%	99%	0.4% DB	0.4% MCWB	1% DB	1% MCWB	2% DB	2% MCWB	0.4% WB	0.4% MCDB	1% WB	1% MCDB	0.4% DP	0.4% HR	0.4% MCDB	1% DP	1% HR	1% MCDB	1%	2.5%	5%	HDD	CDD 65
United States of America																										*542 sites, 1410 more on CD-ROM*
Alabama																										*11 sites, 28 more on CD-ROM*
AUBURN UNIVERSITY REGIONAL	32.616N	85.433W	776	23.2	27.5	93.4	73.5	91.2	73.9	90.1	73.6	77.6	88.3	76.6	86.7	74.8	134.1	81.5	73.3	127.4	80.3	17.9	15.8	13.1	2416	1916
BIRMINGHAM SHUTTLESWORTH INTL	33.566N	86.745W	615	20.8	25.1	95.6	74.6	93.2	74.5	91.1	74.2	78.4	88.5	77.5	87.5	75.9	138.7	82.8	74.7	133.0	81.8	18.5	16.5	14.6	2610	2054
CAIRNS AAF	31.267N	85.717W	301	26.8	29.8	95.6	76.2	93.4	76.0	91.4	75.6	80.5	88.7	79.3	87.7	78.8	151.2	83.6	77.2	143.2	82.1	17.5	15.2	12.8	1797	2378
DOTHAN REGIONAL	31.317N	85.450W	374	27.4	30.9	96.4	75.7	93.9	75.3	91.9	75.0	79.8	89.5	78.6	88.0	77.4	144.3	83.3	76.3	139.3	82.5	19.7	17.6	15.6	1735	2521
HUNTSVILLE INTL	34.644N	86.786W	624	18.7	22.9	95.3	75.0	92.9	74.6	90.7	74.0	78.4	88.4	77.5	87.4	75.9	138.6	82.7	74.8	133.4	81.7	20.4	18.2	16.3	3052	1846
MAXWELL AFB	32.383N	86.350W	171	25.6	29.6	97.5	76.1	95.5	76.3	93.5	76.3	80.2	91.2	79.3	90.2	77.4	143.4	84.2	76.6	139.6	83.6	18.0	15.8	13.1	1957	2546
MOBILE REGIONAL	30.688N	88.246W	215	27.7	31.1	94.1	76.8	92.2	76.5	90.5	76.1	80.1	88.5	79.1	87.2	78.0	146.4	83.4	77.1	142.0	82.5	20.0	17.9	16.2	1642	2516
MONTGOMERY REGIONAL	32.300N	86.408W	202	24.3	27.9	96.8	76.0	94.7	75.9	92.7	75.6	79.6	90.7	78.5	89.1	76.6	139.9	84.1	75.7	135.4	83.1	18.7	16.5	14.3	2109	2352
NORTHEAST ALABAMA AP	33.967N	86.083W	569	18.8	22.6	93.4	74.4	91.2	74.4	90.0	74.2	78.0	89.0	77.0	87.7	74.8	133.2	83.5	73.3	126.3	82.1	16.6	14.1	12.2	3179	1590
NORTHWEST ALABAMA REGIONAL	34.744N	87.600W	540	19.8	23.8	96.2	75.4	93.7	75.1	91.4	74.7	78.9	89.6	77.9	88.4	76.0	138.7	83.6	75.0	133.8	82.5	18.9	16.8	14.7	2997	1906
TUSCALOOSA REGIONAL	33.212N	87.616W	150	22.5	26.6	97.3	75.4	94.6	75.7	92.4	75.4	79.4	90.1	78.4	88.9	76.8	140.4	83.3	75.4	134.0	82.5	17.2	15.0	12.8	2450	2200
Alaska																										*7 sites, 120 more on CD-ROM*
BRYANT AAF	61.266N	149.653W	388	-19.6	-14.0	74.8	60.3	71.6	58.9	68.3	57.1	61.7	72.6	59.6	69.5	56.3	68.6	65.4	54.9	65.1	62.6	19.3	14.6	11.5	10677	5
ELMENDORF AFB	61.253N	149.794W	212	-15.4	-10.6	74.2	58.7	71.6	57.8	68.2	56.4	60.7	70.3	59.3	67.6	57.2	70.3	61.2	55.5	66.0	60.4	19.6	16.3	13.1	10324	12
FAIRBANKS INTL	64.804N	147.876W	432	-42.8	-38.6	81.2	60.9	78.1	59.8	74.8	58.5	63.2	77.0	61.5	74.0	58.3	73.7	65.5	56.5	69.1	64.3	16.9	14.3	12.0	13577	69
JUNEAU INTL	58.357N	134.564W	16	4.7	8.9	73.9	59.5	70.1	58.0	66.5	56.5	61.0	71.3	59.4	67.4	57.2	69.9	61.3	56.0	66.8	60.4	26.5	23.4	19.6	8377	3
LAKE HOOD SEAPLANE BASE	61.178N	149.966W	90	-8.2	-3.7	74.0	59.5	70.7	58.1	67.9	56.7	61.0	71.4	59.4	68.1	56.5	68.3	63.3	55.1	64.7	62.3	18.4	15.9	12.9	9741	15
MERRILL FIELD	61.217N	149.855W	138	-10.7	-7.0	73.2	59.3	70.6	58.2	68.1	56.9	61.2	70.5	59.7	67.9	57.2	70.0	62.8	55.5	65.8	62.2	15.5	12.3	10.5	9961	13
TED STEVENS ANCHORAGE INTL	61.169N	150.028W	120	-8.7	-4.5	71.5	58.9	68.4	57.4	66.0	56.2	60.4	69.0	58.9	66.3	56.4	68.2	62.9	55.2	65.1	61.7	20.8	18.6	16.6	10115	5
Arizona																										*9 sites, 14 more on CD-ROM*
CASA GRANDE MUNICIPAL	32.950N	111.767W	1462	31.7	34.9	108.5	69.5	106.5	69.1	104.5	68.6	74.0	92.9	73.2	93.9	70.2	117.3	79.4	67.9	108.3	79.6	20.5	17.7	15.1	1498	3575
DAVIS-MONTHAN AFB	32.167N	110.883W	2704	32.4	35.5	105.2	65.2	102.8	64.9	100.4	64.6	72.6	85.5	71.7	86.1	70.0	122.2	76.2	68.3	115.0	76.8	20.6	18.2	16.1	1457	3222
FLAGSTAFF PULLIAM AP	35.144N	111.666W	7003	3.9	9.4	85.8	55.3	83.5	54.9	81.3	54.7	61.4	72.6	60.2	72.2	58.3	94.7	63.8	56.8	89.6	63.1	24.8	20.7	18.3	6801	129
LUKE AFB	33.550N	112.367W	1085	34.8	37.3	110.9	70.0	108.6	69.9	106.4	69.6	76.3	94.1	75.3	93.9	72.5	125.6	81.2	70.5	116.9	82.8	20.7	18.0	15.8	1222	4041
PHOENIX SKY HARBOR INTL	33.428N	112.004W	1107	39.2	41.8	110.3	69.5	108.3	69.3	106.4	69.0	75.7	95.0	74.9	94.6	71.3	120.2	82.0	69.4	112.8	84.1	18.8	16.4	13.5	912	4636
PRESCOTT MUNICIPAL	34.652N	112.421W	5042	17.7	20.8	94.5	60.6	92.1	60.1	90.1	59.7	66.5	80.9	65.3	79.5	63.0	104.2	70.4	61.3	98.0	69.7	21.4	18.7	16.9	4145	1021
TUCSON INTL	32.131N	110.955W	2549	31.8	34.4	105.8	66.0	103.6	65.7	101.4	65.4	72.5	87.9	71.8	87.5	69.3	118.2	76.3	68.1	113.5	76.7	21.5	18.8	16.7	1401	3310
WINDOW ROCK AP	35.658N	109.061W	6739	0.1	5.2	89.8	56.2	87.7	55.7	85.1	55.0	61.6	75.5	60.5	74.7	57.9	92.2	63.4	56.7	88.5	63.4	25.7	21.2	18.3	6395	306
YUMA INTL AP	32.650N	114.600W	207	42.3	44.8	111.0	72.6	108.9	72.3	107.5	71.7	79.3	96.4	78.1	95.4	75.1	132.7	86.9	73.2	124.4	87.8	21.0	18.6	16.6	657	4749
Arkansas																										*11 sites, 20 more on CD-ROM*
BENTONVILLE MUNICIPAL	36.350N	94.217W	1296	10.1	15.9	96.6	74.5	92.6	74.4	90.2	74.1	77.5	90.0	76.4	88.5	73.3	130.1	84.2	72.6	126.9	83.3	19.6	17.5	15.7	4043	1437
CLINTON NATL	34.727N	92.239W	258	20.6	24.5	98.8	77.0	96.0	77.0	93.4	76.6	80.1	92.0	79.1	90.8	77.1	142.4	85.5	76.0	137.3	84.6	19.3	17.2	15.6	2897	2207
DRAKE FIELD	36.010N	94.169W	1251	10.4	16.3	95.9	74.3	92.8	74.4	90.4	74.3	77.9	88.9	76.8	87.9	74.7	136.3	83.4	73.3	129.5	82.1	20.8	18.7	16.9	3962	1426
FORT SMITH REGIONAL	35.333N	94.363W	449	17.9	22.4	100.3	75.8	97.3	76.2	94.5	75.9	79.6	92.4	78.5	90.9	76.4	139.9	84.7	75.3	134.9	83.9	20.4	17.9	16.0	3122	2131
GRIDER FIELD	34.175N	91.935W	206	22.4	25.8	97.5	77.5	95.2	77.3	93.0	76.9	80.4	91.7	79.4	90.9	77.4	143.4	85.7	76.4	138.6	84.9	19.4	17.5	15.8	2745	2223
JONESBORO MUNICIPAL	35.831N	90.646W	262	17.1	20.7	97.1	76.9	94.7	76.2	92.6	75.8	80.0	91.4	78.8	90.1	77.0	141.9	85.4	75.4	134.4	84.2	22.6	19.4	17.4	3504	1958
LITTLE ROCK AFB	34.917N	92.150W	311	18.1	22.2	99.8	77.3	97.0	77.5	94.3	77.2	81.3	91.7	80.1	90.7	78.9	151.9	85.3	77.3	143.9	84.7	18.3	16.0	13.5	3135	2098
NORTH LITTLE ROCK MUNICIPAL	34.835N	92.260W	563	18.4	23.2	95.4	76.6	93.0	76.3	90.9	75.6	79.1	90.2	78.1	88.8	76.0	138.9	84.7	75.0	134.1	83.9	18.4	16.5	14.7	3175	1937
ROGERS MUNICIPAL	36.372N	94.107W	1353	9.9	15.7	95.1	73.3	91.9	73.7	89.8	73.2	76.9	88.2	75.7	86.9	73.3	130.3	82.6	72.4	126.2	81.9	22.2	19.3	17.3	4046	1429
SMITH FIELD	36.191N	94.491W	1193	10.2	16.1	97.2	74.3	93.1	74.3	90.5	74.1	77.4	90.4	76.3	88.8	73.2	129.1	84.5	72.5	125.8	83.7	23.5	20.3	18.2	3954	1489
TEXARKANA REGIONAL	33.454N	94.007W	361	23.8	27.2	99.3	75.7	96.8	75.9	94.2	75.8	79.4	91.2	78.4	90.0	76.4	139.5	84.0	75.4	134.8	83.2	18.8	16.8	14.8	2448	2369
California																										*55 sites, 60 more on CD-ROM*
ALAMEDA	37.772N	122.298W	7	40.4	42.4	81.1	64.0	77.2	62.9	73.9	62.0	66.5	78.6	65.2	76.3	62.4	84.4	68.9	61.0	80.0	67.9	20.3	17.7	15.7	2508	160
BEALE AFB	39.133N	121.433W	113	31.1	33.9	101.1	70.3	98.2	69.1	95.2	67.9	73.0	95.9	71.3	93.3	64.8	92.1	82.2	63.2	87.1	79.7	23.3	19.4	16.9	2398	1548
BOB HOPE AP	34.201N	118.358W	775	38.8	41.1	97.6	67.9	94.1	66.8	91.1	66.4	72.6	89.6	71.0	87.4	66.8	101.5	77.7	65.7	97.5	76.8	18.2	14.8	12.7	1381	1449
BROWN FIELD MUNICIPAL	32.572N	116.979W	515	39.0	41.5	89.5	64.1	85.2	64.6	82.0	64.6	71.1	81.9	69.6	79.2	67.6	103.5	75.4	66.2	98.2	74.0	16.3	13.0	11.9	1647	667
CAMARILLO AP	34.217N	119.083W	77	37.5	39.7	86.2	62.2	82.4	63.1	79.9	63.1	69.1	79.1	67.8	77.6	64.9	92.5	73.6	63.7	88.7	71.7	25.0	20.0	16.2	1819	421
CAMP PENDLETON MCAS	33.300N	117.350W	75	31.9	34.7	92.0	65.8	87.9	65.3	84.3	65.2	71.5	83.5	70.2	81.9	67.6	101.7	76.8	66.0	96.0	75.9	16.6	14.0	12.3	1818	679
CASTLE AFB	37.383N	120.567W	191	30.0	31.9	102.5	69.6	99.9	68.2	97.7	67.3	72.1	96.0	70.7	94.3	64.5	91.4	74.4	63.3	87.6	72.7	20.4	17.6	14.6	2384	1762
DESERT RESORTS REGIONAL	33.627N	116.159W	-118	31.1	34.4	111.5	72.2	109.1	71.7	107.1	71.2	79.7	97.0	78.2	96.8	75.0	130.6	88.8	73.0	121.7	89.0	20.2	17.8	15.7	1092	3915
EL TORO MCAS	33.667N	117.733W	384	43.2	45.3	91.9	67.8	88.9	67.5	86.0	66.8	71.7	86.1	70.4	84.5	66.4	98.5	79.1	65.0	93.8	77.8	15.5	12.3	10.6	1111	1172
FRESNO YOSEMITE INTL	36.780N	119.719W	333	31.9	34.1	103.7	70.3	101.0	69.0	98.5	68.0	73.4	97.3	71.7	94.9	65.3	94.5	85.7	63.0	87.2	84.0	18.4	16.4	14.5	2216	2166
FULLERTON MUNICIPAL	33.872N	117.979W	96	39.8	42.8	95.0	66.9	91.3	66.8	88.3	66.3	72.3	87.3	70.9	85.0	66.9	99.2	78.9	65.8	95.4	77.8	12.8	10.9	10.1	1113	1352
HAWTHORN MUNICIPAL	33.923N	118.334W	63	44.5	45.8	87.9	62.8	84.0	63.0	81.1	63.5	69.7	79.6	68.6	77.9	66.2	96.7	74.4	64.6	91.3	72.3	16.2	13.9	12.4	1105	819
HAYWARD EXECUTIVE	37.654N	122.115W	43	36.8	38.9	87.1	65.2	82.4	64.1	78.5	63.3	67.6	81.7	66.0	78.9	62.6	85.0	71.6	61.2	80.8	69.3	19.4	17.6	16.1	2542	293
IMPERIAL COUNTY AP	32.834N	115.579W	-58	35.7	37.9	111.3	72.8	109.1	72.4	107.5	72.1	81.0	97.2	79.5	96.3	77.0	140.4	88.3	75.0	131.0	88.9	26.0	22.0	18.7	937	4164

(Go to CD-ROM to access additional station tables.)

Meaning of acronyms:
DB: Dry bulb temperature, °F — *WB: Wet bulb temperature, °F*
MCWB: Mean coincident wet bulb temperature, °F
Lat: Latitude, ° — *DP: Dew point temperature, °F* — *MCDB: Mean coincident dry bulb temperature, °F*
Long: Longitude, ° — *HR: Humidity ratio, grains of moisture per lb of dry air*
Elev: Elevation, ft — *WS: Wind speed, mph* — *HDD and CDD 65: Annual heating and cooling degree-days, base 65°F, °F-day*

Station	Lat	Long	Elev	Heating DB		Cooling DB/MCWB						Evaporation WB/MCDB				Dehumidification DP/HR/MCDB						Extreme Annual WS			Heat./Cool. Degree-Days	
						0.4%		1%		2%		0.4%		1%		0.4%			1%							
				99.6%	99%	DB	MCWB	DB	MCWB	DB	MCWB	WB	MCDB	WB	MCDB	DP	HR	MCDB	DP	HR	MCDB	1%	2.5%	5%	HDD	CDD 65
LEMOORE NAS	36.333N	119.950W	232	28.0	31.0	103.4	70.7	100.6	69.7	98.4	68.7	73.8	97.1	71.9	95.8	65.6	95.4	87.4	63.0	86.8	84.7	20.8	18.0	15.6	2296	1836
LIVERMORE MUNICIPAL	37.693N	121.814W	393	30.6	33.1	98.7	67.6	94.8	66.0	90.9	64.8	69.5	93.5	67.8	90.3	60.9	81.0	76.1	59.2	76.1	72.6	19.3	17.8	16.3	2671	836
LOMPOC AP	34.667N	120.467W	88	32.4	35.5	81.7	61.1	77.4	60.9	74.1	60.4	65.3	75.7	63.8	73.7	61.2	81.1	69.4	59.3	75.6	67.8	20.3	18.5	17.1	2809	60
LONG BEACH AP	33.812N	118.146W	31	41.6	43.7	91.4	66.2	87.8	66.3	84.5	65.6	72.0	83.0	70.5	81.0	68.6	105.2	75.9	67.0	99.5	75.0	16.8	14.1	12.3	1188	1098
LOS ANGELES INTL	33.938N	118.389W	97	44.9	46.8	83.8	63.1	80.4	63.9	77.8	64.1	70.0	77.4	68.8	75.7	67.3	100.8	73.8	66.1	96.4	72.7	20.0	17.4	16.0	1287	614
LOS ANGELES ONTARIO INTL	34.056N	117.600W	949	38.4	40.6	100.2	69.7	97.5	68.4	94.6	67.8	73.5	93.1	71.9	91.1	67.6	105.2	80.3	65.7	98.1	78.3	21.7	18.0	15.8	1381	1797
MARCH AFB	33.900N	117.250W	1536	32.1	35.0	101.3	67.9	98.8	66.9	95.9	66.2	72.1	93.7	70.7	91.8	65.8	100.6	78.1	63.8	93.9	75.3	18.0	15.6	13.1	1895	1584
MCCLELLAN-PALOMAR AP	33.128N	117.279W	328	42.9	44.8	83.8	62.0	80.7	63.8	77.9	64.0	70.2	77.1	69.0	75.4	67.5	102.4	74.3	66.2	97.8	73.1	13.5	12.0	10.7	1623	536
MEADOWS FIELD	35.434N	119.054W	489	32.6	35.3	102.9	70.4	100.4	69.2	98.1	68.2	73.4	96.9	71.7	95.4	65.0	94.2	87.4	62.6	86.3	85.1	18.4	15.8	13.0	2050	2319
MINETA SAN JOSE INTL	37.359N	121.924W	51	35.5	37.7	91.4	66.1	87.8	65.3	83.9	64.3	68.9	85.9	67.5	83.0	62.8	85.6	75.6	61.3	81.0	73.9	19.5	17.9	16.2	2143	624
MIRAMAR MCAS	32.867N	117.133W	477	39.1	41.4	90.8	65.9	87.5	65.9	84.1	65.5	71.5	83.4	70.3	81.6	67.7	103.5	76.2	66.2	98.2	74.9	15.3	12.6	11.2	1489	845
MODESTO CITY-COUNTY AP	37.624N	120.951W	73	30.7	33.3	101.4	69.9	98.2	68.4	95.4	67.1	71.8	96.4	70.1	94.2	62.6	85.0	83.4	60.5	78.9	80.6	19.1	17.0	15.4	2362	1631
MOFFETT FEDERAL AIRFIELD	37.406N	122.048W	39	36.0	38.5	88.1	65.5	83.7	64.5	80.5	64.1	68.2	82.5	66.8	79.8	63.0	86.3	73.9	61.4	81.5	71.9	18.8	17.0	15.4	2190	467
MONTEREY REGIONAL	36.588N	121.845W	165	36.6	38.8	78.7	59.9	73.5	59.2	71.1	58.9	63.0	72.0	61.9	70.2	59.4	76.1	65.2	58.0	72.2	64.1	16.8	14.6	12.6	3231	50
MONTGOMERY FIELD	32.816N	117.139W	417	40.7	43.0	90.3	65.4	86.5	64.9	83.3	64.9	71.2	82.8	69.7	80.3	67.2	101.6	76.4	65.9	97.1	74.8	15.7	12.9	11.9	1465	854
NAPA COUNTY AP	38.210N	122.285W	14	29.2	31.8	91.1	65.8	86.5	64.8	82.4	63.9	68.4	86.1	66.7	82.8	61.4	81.3	74.5	60.3	78.1	72.8	21.3	19.1	17.5	3182	242
NORTH ISLAND NAS	32.700N	117.200W	26	44.8	46.2	84.6	64.0	81.3	65.2	78.9	65.8	71.2	77.8	70.0	76.6	69.1	107.0	74.9	67.5	101.1	73.9	18.7	16.5	14.5	1118	783
OAKLAND INTL	37.721N	122.221W	6	36.6	38.9	83.4	64.2	79.1	63.0	75.0	62.2	66.5	78.1	65.1	75.4	62.7	85.1	69.2	61.1	80.6	68.1	23.6	20.1	18.3	2692	164
PALM SPRINGS INTL	33.822N	116.504W	409	41.1	43.5	111.4	70.7	109.2	70.4	107.6	69.9	78.7	98.3	77.1	97.1	73.1	124.7	90.7	71.2	116.9	91.0	23.0	20.0	17.9	757	4394
POINT ARGUELLO	34.580N	120.650W	106	45.7	47.6	71.6	N/A	67.9	N/A	65.5	N/A	N/A	N/A	N/A	N/A	N/A	N/A	N/A	N/A	N/A	N/A	41.6	34.9	31.9	3405	23
POINT MUGU NAS	34.117N	119.117W	13	38.9	41.0	81.5	61.2	78.4	62.4	75.4	62.9	69.5	75.4	67.9	73.9	67.5	101.2	72.3	65.5	94.1	71.4	23.2	19.1	16.6	2078	213
PORTERVILLE MUNICIPAL	36.029N	119.063W	442	30.1	33.5	100.5	70.0	99.2	69.3	97.1	68.1	72.8	96.6	71.1	94.3	63.7	89.8	85.9	62.6	86.2	84.7	12.9	11.4	10.4	2520	1704
REDDING MUNICIPAL	40.518N	122.299W	497	28.5	30.9	105.3	68.4	102.0	67.1	99.1	66.0	71.4	96.5	69.9	94.8	63.5	89.2	79.9	61.3	82.6	78.1	25.0	19.8	16.8	2702	1889
RIVERSIDE MUNICIPAL	33.952N	117.439W	804	36.4	38.7	100.2	69.3	97.7	68.4	94.8	67.4	72.9	93.3	71.4	91.7	66.0	98.8	81.5	63.9	91.7	79.1	19.0	16.1	13.3	1448	1718
SACRAMENTO EXECUTIVE	38.507N	121.495W	15	30.9	33.6	100.1	69.8	96.9	68.4	93.6	67.2	72.3	95.5	70.3	92.6	63.6	88.0	83.5	61.5	81.6	79.4	20.1	17.9	15.8	2491	1222
SACRAMENTO INTL	38.696N	121.590W	23	30.3	33.2	100.5	70.4	97.6	69.3	94.6	68.0	72.9	96.2	71.1	93.7	64.0	89.5	84.4	62.6	85.0	82.6	23.9	19.8	17.4	2496	1364
SACRAMENTO MATHER AP	38.567N	121.300W	99	27.7	30.1	101.2	68.8	98.2	67.4	94.8	66.5	70.9	96.8	69.3	93.6	61.3	81.4	75.4	59.9	77.4	75.8	20.6	17.0	13.7	2771	1190
SACRAMENTO MCCLELLAN AFB	38.667N	121.400W	77	30.1	33.0	102.1	70.0	99.3	68.7	95.8	67.4	72.2	97.7	70.5	95.0	63.2	87.0	79.6	61.3	81.2	78.7	20.8	17.6	14.9	2323	1588
SALINAS MUNICIPAL	36.664N	121.608W	74	33.9	36.4	83.2	62.1	78.6	61.0	75.0	60.7	65.0	77.5	63.6	74.5	60.6	79.2	67.6	59.2	75.4	66.4	20.7	18.6	17.0	2707	112
SAN BERNARDINO INTL	34.095N	117.235W	1159	33.9	36.5	102.9	69.7	100.2	69.5	97.4	68.8	74.5	95.1	73.0	93.6	68.1	107.7	83.1	66.1	100.5	83.3	16.7	12.9	10.9	1652	1811
SAN DIEGO INTL	32.734N	117.183W	15	45.0	46.9	83.7	64.7	80.6	65.5	78.3	65.6	71.1	77.6	69.9	76.2	68.5	104.8	74.6	67.4	100.9	73.8	16.9	15.1	12.9	1171	715
SAN FRANCISCO INTL	37.620N	122.365W	8	39.5	41.6	82.6	62.7	77.9	62.0	74.3	61.4	65.6	77.2	64.2	74.3	61.4	81.3	68.4	60.1	77.7	67.2	28.5	25.5	23.3	2679	157
SAN LUIS OBISPO CO REGIONAL	35.237N	120.641W	200	34.0	36.3	89.1	64.0	84.3	63.2	81.2	62.8	67.3	82.8	65.8	80.2	61.5	82.2	71.3	60.5	79.2	70.1	25.0	22.3	19.6	2223	294
SANTA BARBARA MUNICIPAL	34.426N	119.843W	9	35.0	37.0	82.9	63.3	79.7	63.7	77.0	63.1	68.4	77.0	67.0	75.4	64.9	92.1	71.5	63.7	88.3	70.1	18.9	16.3	13.1	2224	218
SANTA MARIA PUBLIC AP	34.899N	120.449W	242	33.2	35.5	84.2	61.9	80.0	61.3	76.6	60.8	66.0	78.0	64.4	75.7	61.4	82.0	69.0	60.0	77.8	67.9	24.3	20.5	18.3	2668	115
SONOMA COUNTY AP	38.504N	122.810W	114	28.9	31.2	94.7	66.4	90.9	65.7	87.2	64.4	69.1	89.9	67.4	87.1	61.0	80.4	75.7	59.2	75.4	73.3	17.1	15.0	12.6	2986	366
SOUTHERN CALIFORNIA LOGISTICS	34.583N	117.383W	2885	27.6	30.5	100.7	65.3	98.4	64.7	96.0	63.9	69.8	88.4	68.4	88.2	64.5	101.2	76.9	61.9	92.1	78.6	22.7	18.9	16.7	2661	1911
STOCKTON METROPOLITAN	37.889N	121.226W	26	30.3	32.7	101.1	70.0	97.9	68.8	94.8	67.9	73.2	96.1	70.8	94.0	64.6	91.3	84.8	61.6	82.0	80.2	22.7	19.3	17.3	2448	1393
TRAVIS AFB	38.267N	121.933W	62	30.0	33.0	99.0	67.7	95.1	66.6	91.1	65.6	70.4	93.2	68.6	90.2	62.7	85.3	73.6	60.8	79.8	72.2	28.8	26.8	24.9	2516	993
VISALIA MUNICIPAL	36.317N	119.400W	295	29.8	32.4	100.0	71.8	98.7	70.9	96.5	69.9	74.7	95.4	73.0	93.4	67.8	103.4	85.2	65.5	95.3	84.5	15.4	12.5	10.9	2509	1641
WILLIAM J FOX AP	34.741N	118.212W	2338	21.3	24.7	102.8	65.8	100.3	64.4	98.0	63.5	68.3	96.3	66.9	95.0	58.0	78.4	80.6	55.2	70.6	80.5	29.9	27.0	24.9	2937	1890
Colorado																									*10 sites, 30 more on CD-ROM*	
BUCKLEY AFB	39.717N	104.750W	5663	0.4	7.2	93.2	58.4	90.6	58.4	88.0	58.3	63.9	77.8	62.5	77.4	60.8	98.5	65.8	58.8	91.6	65.4	24.1	20.1	17.4	5798	687
CENTENNIAL AP	39.570N	104.849W	5883	-0.1	5.8	91.9	59.5	89.9	59.2	87.2	58.8	64.8	80.3	63.2	78.8	60.9	99.7	68.1	58.7	91.9	67.5	24.7	20.9	18.4	6052	628
COLORADO SPRINGS MUNICIPAL	38.810N	104.688W	6181	1.4	7.0	90.9	58.7	88.3	58.4	85.7	58.3	63.4	78.5	62.3	77.4	59.5	95.7	65.9	58.2	91.3	65.5	28.2	24.8	21.0	6117	505
DENVER INTL	39.833N	104.658W	5414	-0.8	5.3	94.8	59.7	92.2	59.7	89.5	59.5	64.8	80.9	63.7	80.5	60.7	97.1	67.9	59.1	91.6	67.6	27.1	23.7	20.0	5935	812
DENVER STAPLETON	39.750N	104.867W	5288	-1.4	5.1	93.9	60.7	91.2	60.0	88.5	59.6	64.5	81.8	63.4	80.7	60.1	94.7	67.2	58.5	89.1	67.0	24.3	19.7	17.2	5667	721
FORT COLLINS DOWNTOWN	40.588N	105.042W	4939	-2.6	4.8	90.1	60.9	87.2	60.4	84.4	60.1	64.6	80.7	63.6	80.0	59.7	92.1	69.7	58.4	87.9	69.2	20.0	16.8	13.6	6096	462
FORT COLLINS LOVELAND MUNI	40.450N	105.017W	5015	-0.2	5.5	93.5	60.9	90.9	60.8	88.3	60.5	65.4	82.5	64.2	82.0	61.0	96.7	69.9	58.6	88.5	69.6	25.9	21.4	18.0	6196	624
GRAND JUNCTION REGIONAL	39.134N	108.540W	4858	3.7	9.3	97.7	61.2	95.2	60.3	92.7	59.7	65.1	84.9	64.0	83.8	60.7	95.1	68.0	58.7	88.3	68.5	23.6	19.5	17.0	5481	1228
GREELEY-WELD COUNTY AP	40.436N	104.632W	4697	-7.8	0.0	96.6	62.6	92.6	62.2	90.0	62.1	67.2	84.7	65.9	84.1	62.6	101.1	73.2	60.8	94.9	72.1	28.2	24.0	19.4	6579	643
PUEBLO MEMORIAL	38.290N	104.498W	4720	0.0	6.5	98.5	62.2	95.8	61.9	93.1	61.6	66.8	84.9	65.8	84.1	62.7	101.9	69.0	61.3	96.6	69.0	28.7	24.7	20.4	5488	951
Connecticut																									*5 sites, 5 more on CD-ROM*	
BRADLEY INTL	41.938N	72.683W	190	4.8	9.8	91.4	73.2	88.4	71.8	85.6	70.3	76.2	86.5	74.7	83.8	73.2	124.1	80.2	71.9	118.9	79.0	22.7	19.3	17.4	5843	789
HARTFORD-BRAINARD AP	41.736N	72.651W	19	8.2	12.2	90.9	73.1	88.2	72.2	85.1	70.7	76.6	85.7	75.2	83.3	73.7	125.7	80.2	72.6	120.9	79.2	19.2	17.5	15.7	5500	863
IGOR SIKORSKY MEMORIAL	41.158N	73.129W	5	11.4	15.6	87.9	73.1	84.9	71.7	82.5	70.6	76.1	83.2	74.9	81.0	73.8	126.1	79.5	72.8	121.6	78.3	24.3	20.7	18.5	5230	858
WATERBURY-OXFORD AP	41.483N	73.133W	726	3.2	8.8	87.6	72.9	83.7	71.1	81.3	69.5	75.4	83.2	73.7	80.4	72.9	125.4	78.9	72.0	121.7	77.8	19.5	17.0	14.9	6416	468
WINDHAM AP	41.742N	72.184W	247	3.6	9.3	89.7	73.2	86.5	71.9	83.8	70.4	76.1	84.9	74.6	82.2	73.2	124.6	79.5	72.3	120.8	78.5	19.2	17.0	15.3	5950	642

(Go to CD-ROM to access additional station tables.)

(Go to CD-ROM to access additional station tables.)

Meaning of acronyms:
DB: Dry bulb temperature, °F — *WB: Wet bulb temperature, °F*
MCWB: Mean coincident wet bulb temperature, °F
Lat: Latitude, °
DP: Dew point temperature, °F
MCDB: Mean coincident dry bulb temperature, °F
Long: Longitude, °
HR: Humidity ratio, grains of moisture per lb of dry air
HDD and CDD 65: Annual heating and cooling degree-days, base 65°F, °F-day
Elev: Elevation, ft
WS: Wind speed, mph

Station	Lat	Long	Elev	Heating DB		Cooling DB/MCWB						Evaporation WB/MCDB				Dehumidification DP/HR/MCDB						Extreme Annual WS			Heat./Cool. Degree-Days	
						0.4%		1%		2%		0.4%		1%		0.4%			1%							
				99.6%	99%	DB	MCWB	DB	MCWB	DB	MCWB	WB	MCDB	WB	MCDB	DP	HR	MCDB	DP	HR	MCDB	1%	2.5%	5%	HDD	CDD 65
Delaware																										*2 sites, 3 more on CD-ROM*
DOVER AFB	39.133N	75.467W	28	14.7	18.7	92.5	75.7	90.0	74.8	87.3	74.0	78.7	87.0	77.5	85.5	76.7	139.4	82.3	75.2	132.4	80.9	24.7	20.9	18.7	4461	1194
NEW CASTLE AP	39.673N	75.601W	79	13.8	17.7	92.3	75.1	89.4	73.8	86.8	72.9	78.0	87.5	76.7	85.2	75.4	133.4	81.9	74.2	128.1	80.6	24.7	20.8	18.6	4684	1160
Florida																										*32 sites, 45 more on CD-ROM*
CECIL FIELD	30.219N	81.876W	81	30.3	34.0	96.1	76.7	93.9	76.4	92.0	75.9	79.6	89.6	78.6	88.5	77.2	142.1	82.7	76.2	137.1	82.1	19.0	16.9	15.0	1164	2730
CRAIG MUNICIPAL	30.336N	81.515W	41	32.7	36.1	94.3	77.0	92.2	76.8	90.4	76.6	80.0	88.8	79.1	87.8	77.6	143.8	83.5	76.9	140.2	82.9	19.0	17.4	15.8	1158	2745
DAYTONA BEACH INTL	29.183N	81.048W	31	35.5	39.6	92.7	76.9	90.9	76.8	89.3	76.7	80.0	88.1	79.1	87.1	77.6	143.7	83.6	76.9	140.3	83.0	20.3	18.0	16.2	728	3020
FT LAUDERDALE HOLLYWOOD INTL	26.072N	80.154W	11	47.8	52.0	91.8	78.3	90.6	78.3	89.8	78.2	81.1	87.9	80.4	87.2	79.3	151.9	84.7	78.6	148.4	84.3	21.9	19.6	18.1	124	4609
GAINESVILLE REGIONAL	29.692N	82.276W	123	29.6	33.2	93.8	75.9	92.2	75.8	90.6	75.5	79.5	87.9	78.5	86.8	77.3	142.8	82.6	76.4	138.5	81.9	18.3	16.3	14.2	1148	2670
HOMESTEAD AFB	25.483N	80.383W	5	46.0	50.2	91.2	79.2	90.4	79.0	89.6	78.9	81.4	87.5	80.7	87.0	79.4	152.8	84.0	79.1	150.9	83.8	20.1	18.1	16.3	144	4228
JACKSONVILLE INTL	30.495N	81.694W	26	29.5	32.8	94.5	77.2	92.7	76.9	90.9	76.5	79.9	89.4	79.1	88.2	77.4	142.7	83.3	76.7	139.3	82.6	20.1	17.9	16.1	1303	2629
JACKSONVILLE NAS	30.233N	81.667W	20	34.2	37.5	95.8	76.8	93.7	76.3	91.9	76.0	80.4	88.4	79.4	87.8	78.7	149.1	83.7	77.3	142.0	83.1	20.9	18.6	16.7	946	3259
KENNEDY SPACE CENTER	28.617N	80.683W	10	39.2	43.1	91.7	78.1	90.4	78.0	89.3	77.8	80.7	87.5	79.9	86.6	79.2	151.5	83.6	78.3	147.2	83.2	18.7	16.7	14.7	525	3176
MACDILL AFB	27.850N	82.517W	14	38.8	43.0	93.3	78.4	92.2	78.1	91.0	77.8	82.2	88.7	81.3	87.9	80.6	159.1	85.1	79.5	152.9	84.6	18.9	16.9	15.4	491	3653
MAYPORT NAF	30.400N	81.417W	16	35.2	39.0	93.9	77.2	91.6	77.1	89.9	76.8	80.5	88.4	79.5	87.6	78.7	148.8	85.0	77.2	141.7	84.1	21.4	18.7	16.7	1007	2961
MELBOURNE INTL	28.101N	80.644W	27	38.6	43.0	91.9	77.5	90.4	77.5	89.5	77.5	80.3	87.8	79.5	87.1	78.5	148.2	84.0	77.3	141.9	83.5	20.9	18.9	17.6	462	3473
MIAMI EXECUTIVE	25.648N	80.433W	10	45.6	49.6	92.8	77.9	91.4	77.7	90.5	77.6	80.4	87.9	79.8	87.4	78.9	149.9	83.2	77.5	143.1	83.0	20.7	18.8	17.5	164	4147
MIAMI INTL	25.791N	80.316W	29	48.8	52.6	91.9	77.6	90.8	77.6	89.8	77.5	80.3	86.9	79.7	86.8	78.4	147.6	83.5	77.6	143.7	83.3	20.0	18.3	16.7	113	4578
NAPLES MUNICIPAL	26.152N	81.775W	9	43.6	47.5	91.6	77.7	90.5	77.8	89.7	77.8	80.9	87.4	80.1	87.0	79.1	151.3	84.2	78.2	146.5	83.7	18.9	17.0	15.2	273	3807
ORLANDO EXECUTIVE	28.545N	81.333W	108	38.9	43.2	93.5	76.1	92.4	75.9	91.0	75.7	79.7	86.6	78.8	86.0	78.4	148.3	82.4	77.1	141.6	81.6	19.4	17.6	15.9	505	3543
ORLANDO INTL	28.434N	81.325W	90	38.3	42.3	93.8	76.5	92.4	76.2	91.1	75.9	79.6	87.3	78.8	86.5	77.7	144.6	81.7	77.1	141.3	81.2	20.3	18.2	16.5	529	3405
ORLANDO SANFORD INTL	28.780N	81.244W	55	36.9	40.9	94.4	75.7	92.9	75.5	91.2	75.4	79.0	88.0	78.3	87.1	76.9	140.5	82.0	76.0	136.0	81.5	20.1	17.9	16.1	617	3342
PAGE FIELD	26.585N	81.861W	15	42.7	46.6	93.5	76.7	92.4	76.7	91.2	76.7	80.2	88.0	79.4	87.3	78.2	146.6	83.1	77.4	142.4	82.6	18.6	16.8	15.0	267	3943
PALM BEACH INTL	26.685N	80.099W	19	44.5	48.5	91.7	77.7	90.4	77.7	89.3	77.7	80.2	87.8	79.5	87.2	78.0	145.7	83.6	77.3	142.4	83.4	22.6	19.9	18.4	208	4138
PANAMA CITY BAY COUNTY INTL	30.212N	85.683W	21	31.8	35.7	92.8	76.8	91.1	76.9	90.1	76.7	81.4	87.0	80.2	86.4	79.5	153.1	83.9	78.9	150.0	83.7	18.7	16.7	15.0	1242	2847
PENSACOLA INTL	30.478N	87.187W	112	30.0	33.8	93.9	77.5	92.0	77.3	90.3	77.0	81.0	88.4	80.0	87.4	79.1	151.8	84.4	78.1	146.4	83.6	20.1	18.1	16.4	1422	2706
PENSACOLA NAS	30.350N	87.317W	28	29.6	33.1	93.1	78.7	91.3	78.5	90.0	78.1	81.9	88.5	80.8	87.7	80.1	156.2	85.5	79.0	150.6	84.8	20.6	18.4	16.6	1474	2618
SARASOTA BRADENTON INTL	27.401N	82.559W	28	39.6	44.1	92.4	78.5	91.1	78.4	90.3	78.2	82.6	88.6	81.4	87.5	81.2	162.2	86.5	79.5	153.2	85.0	20.7	18.4	16.6	456	3477
SOUTHWEST FLORIDA INTL	26.536N	81.755W	31	41.3	45.4	93.4	76.6	92.2	76.6	91.0	76.5	80.2	87.4	79.4	86.8	78.8	149.8	82.7	77.4	142.6	82.3	20.3	18.1	16.1	306	3743
ST PETE-CLEARWATER INTL	27.911N	82.688W	11	42.2	45.4	92.2	77.6	91.0	77.6	90.2	77.4	81.4	86.9	80.4	86.4	80.0	155.7	84.2	79.0	150.5	83.6	20.9	18.8	17.1	443	3672
TALLAHASSEE REGIONAL	30.393N	84.353W	55	26.2	29.7	96.2	76.1	94.2	75.6	92.4	75.3	79.7	89.0	78.8	87.8	77.4	142.9	82.8	76.5	138.4	82.1	18.2	16.1	13.7	1493	2662
TAMPA INTL	27.962N	82.540W	19	39.6	43.4	92.5	77.0	91.3	77.0	90.3	77.0	80.4	87.9	79.8	87.5	78.4	147.5	84.9	77.5	142.9	84.1	18.1	16.0	13.6	505	3609
TAYLOR FIELD	29.167N	82.233W	87	29.6	33.9	93.2	75.2	91.4	75.3	90.6	75.1	78.6	87.8	78.0	87.4	75.7	134.8	82.4	75.2	132.4	82.1	18.0	15.3	12.6	1043	2756
TYNDALL AFB	30.067N	85.583W	17	31.5	35.5	91.3	78.8	90.2	78.8	89.0	78.5	82.5	87.4	81.5	86.8	81.3	162.5	85.3	80.0	155.8	84.9	20.5	18.3	16.4	1324	2644
VENICE	27.070N	82.450W	0	41.8	45.8	88.1	76.4	86.9	77.0	86.2	77.2	82.1	83.7	80.9	83.6	81.8	165.4	83.0	80.2	156.9	82.4	28.0	23.8	19.8	477	3009
VERO BEACH REGIONAL	27.651N	80.420W	28	38.8	43.2	91.8	77.6	90.5	77.7	89.4	77.7	80.3	88.0	79.7	87.3	78.4	147.6	84.2	77.4	142.5	83.7	20.4	18.5	17.0	414	3460
Georgia																										*19 sites, 27 more on CD-ROM*
ATHENS BEN EPPS AP	33.948N	83.328W	785	22.6	26.5	95.4	74.6	93.1	74.0	90.7	73.6	77.7	88.9	76.8	87.4	74.7	133.9	81.8	73.8	129.5	80.6	18.2	16.1	13.6	2755	1804
ATLANTA HARTSFIELD-JACKSON	33.640N	84.430W	1027	21.9	26.5	94.0	74.2	91.6	73.8	89.5	73.3	77.3	88.3	76.3	86.5	74.3	133.3	81.3	73.4	128.9	80.3	21.3	18.9	17.0	2640	1901
ATLANTA REGIONAL	33.355N	84.567W	798	19.4	23.4	93.4	73.8	91.3	73.6	89.8	73.4	77.5	87.4	76.5	86.0	74.9	134.9	81.2	73.5	128.2	79.6	17.3	15.0	12.3	3002	1578
AUGUSTA REGIONAL	33.364N	81.963W	132	22.6	26.1	97.3	76.0	94.9	75.6	92.6	75.2	79.4	90.7	78.3	89.1	76.5	139.1	83.4	75.5	134.2	82.4	18.8	16.5	14.1	2384	2074
COLUMBUS AP	32.516N	84.942W	392	25.9	29.6	96.4	74.6	94.2	74.4	92.3	74.1	78.2	89.3	77.3	88.0	75.3	134.6	82.1	74.4	130.6	81.2	18.4	16.3	14.1	2047	2359
DANIEL FIELD	33.467N	82.039W	423	27.2	29.9	96.8	74.4	93.9	73.7	91.8	73.4	77.5	89.1	76.9	87.9	74.8	132.2	80.8	73.4	126.4	79.8	16.6	14.5	12.5	2106	2329
DEKALB-PEACHTREE AP	33.875N	84.302W	1002	21.1	25.5	94.2	73.6	91.8	73.3	90.2	72.8	76.9	88.0	75.9	86.4	73.4	129.1	79.3	73.0	127.0	79.0	18.6	16.5	14.0	2867	1816
DOBBINS AFB	33.917N	84.517W	1068	19.5	24.5	93.1	74.4	91.1	74.2	89.2	73.6	77.3	87.7	76.3	86.3	74.4	133.9	81.2	73.4	129.3	80.2	18.9	16.7	14.5	2924	1757
FULTON COUNTY AP	33.779N	84.521W	840	21.2	25.7	94.1	74.4	91.9	74.0	90.1	73.5	77.4	88.4	76.5	86.9	74.4	132.7	81.6	73.3	127.9	80.6	17.6	15.4	13.1	2807	1765
HUNTER AAF	32.017N	81.133W	41	27.9	31.7	95.6	77.3	93.3	76.9	91.2	76.6	81.1	88.3	79.9	88.0	79.3	152.0	83.6	77.5	143.2	82.9	19.2	16.8	14.7	1610	2579
LAWSON AAF	32.332N	84.989W	232	22.5	25.9	96.7	75.9	94.6	75.8	92.4	75.5	80.3	89.6	79.0	89.0	77.9	146.4	83.7	76.6	139.8	82.6	17.0	14.5	12.3	2312	2074
LEE GILMER MEMORIAL	34.272N	83.830W	1275	21.3	26.1	92.5	73.3	90.5	73.1	88.4	72.5	76.4	86.4	75.4	85.0	73.4	130.3	79.6	72.7	127.1	79.1	19.0	16.9	15.2	3006	1643
MIDDLE GEORGIA REGIONAL	32.685N	83.653W	343	23.9	27.4	96.6	75.3	94.4	75.1	92.3	74.7	79.0	90.0	78.0	88.7	76.2	138.5	83.0	75.3	134.1	82.0	18.2	16.1	13.5	2265	2153
MOODY AFB	30.967N	83.200W	233	29.1	32.6	96.1	76.5	94.2	76.2	92.6	75.8	80.1	90.6	78.9	89.4	77.4	143.7	83.8	76.4	138.8	82.9	17.8	15.3	12.8	1433	2667
RICHARD B RUSSELL REGIONAL	34.348N	85.161W	639	19.4	23.4	95.8	74.5	93.2	73.9	91.1	73.8	78.0	89.6	77.1	88.3	75.0	134.4	82.0	73.7	128.7	81.1	16.2	13.3	11.8	3030	1777
ROBINS AFB	32.633N	83.600W	294	24.8	28.0	97.0	75.8	94.9	75.8	92.7	75.2	79.7	90.4	78.4	88.9	77.1	142.7	83.5	75.7	135.8	82.4	19.4	16.8	14.3	2135	2228
SAVANNAH HILTON HEAD INTL	32.130N	81.210W	46	27.6	30.8	95.5	77.1	93.3	76.8	91.3	76.2	80.2	89.5	79.2	88.3	78.0	145.6	83.5	77.0	140.9	82.6	18.9	16.8	15.2	1723	2465

Meaning of acronyms:
DB: Dry bulb temperature, °F — WB: Wet bulb temperature, °F — MCWB: Mean coincident wet bulb temperature, °F
Lat: Latitude, ° — DP: Dew point temperature, °F — MCDB: Mean coincident dry bulb temperature, °F
Long: Longitude, ° — HR: Humidity ratio, grains of moisture per lb of dry air — HDD and CDD 65: Annual heating and cooling degree-days, base 65°F, °F-day
Elev: Elevation, ft — WS: Wind speed, mph

Station	Lat	Long	Elev	Heating DB		Cooling DB/MCWB						Evaporation WB/MCDB				Dehumidification DP/HR/MCDB						Extreme Annual WS			Heat./Cool. Degree-Days	
						0.4%		1%		2%		0.4%		1%		0.4%			1%							
				99.6%	99%	DB	MCWB	DB	MCWB	DB	MCWB	WB	MCDB	WB	MCDB	DP	HR	MCDB	DP	HR	MCDB	1%	2.5%	5%	HDD	CDD 65
SW GEORGIA REGIONAL	31.536N	84.194W	190	26.6	29.6	96.8	75.9	94.7	75.7	92.7	75.4	79.7	90.4	78.5	88.8	77.2	142.4	83.1	75.9	136.4	82.2	18.4	16.4	14.2	1746	2547
VALDOSTA REGIONAL	30.783N	83.277W	198	27.7	30.8	96.6	76.6	94.5	76.2	92.7	75.8	80.2	90.0	79.2	88.8	77.6	144.6	83.1	76.9	141.1	82.5	16.5	14.0	12.4	1477	2627
Hawaii																										*4 sites, 8 more on CD-ROM*
HILO INTL	19.719N	155.053W	38	61.6	62.8	85.7	74.0	84.7	73.7	83.9	73.4	76.5	82.0	75.8	81.5	75.0	131.5	79.2	74.0	127.2	78.5	16.7	14.9	12.8	0	3245
HONOLULU INTL	21.324N	157.929W	7	62.5	64.5	89.4	73.8	88.5	73.4	87.7	73.0	77.1	84.5	76.2	83.8	74.9	130.9	81.0	73.7	125.6	80.3	22.5	20.4	18.9	0	4656
KALAELOA	21.317N	158.067W	33	60.4	62.5	90.1	73.4	88.8	73.2	87.9	73.0	77.4	84.9	76.3	84.2	75.1	131.9	81.5	73.5	124.7	80.5	18.2	16.4	14.7	0	4214
KANEOHE MCAS	21.450N	157.768W	24	64.0	65.9	84.9	74.3	84.1	74.1	83.4	73.8	77.0	81.6	76.1	81.3	75.3	132.9	79.8	74.3	128.5	79.5	18.5	16.7	15.4	0	4190
Idaho																										*7 sites, 14 more on CD-ROM*
BOISE AP	43.567N	116.241W	2814	9.4	15.9	98.6	63.8	95.7	62.8	92.8	61.9	66.1	92.0	64.7	90.2	57.5	78.3	71.5	55.1	71.8	71.6	22.0	19.1	17.1	5414	1007
CALDWELL INDUSTRIAL AP	43.650N	116.633W	2429	9.6	15.7	97.0	66.2	93.1	64.7	90.6	63.8	68.2	92.3	66.4	90.0	59.1	82.0	78.5	56.7	75.0	77.6	22.1	19.2	17.0	5739	692
COEUR D'ALENE AP	47.767N	116.817W	2307	5.8	10.4	91.3	63.1	88.5	62.6	84.2	61.1	66.3	85.6	64.3	83.4	59.2	81.7	72.0	56.8	75.0	70.6	22.3	18.9	16.8	6875	316
IDAHO FALLS REGIONAL	43.516N	112.067W	4729	-6.6	-0.3	92.1	60.9	89.6	60.5	86.7	59.6	64.7	83.2	63.0	81.9	58.7	87.9	71.0	56.2	80.3	68.9	27.2	24.3	20.7	7672	288
LEWISTON-NEZ PERCE CO REGL	46.375N	117.016W	1436	13.0	18.8	98.5	65.3	95.0	64.5	91.4	63.2	67.8	91.9	66.1	89.8	60.0	81.6	72.7	57.7	75.1	72.0	20.9	17.9	15.1	5044	868
MAGIC VALLEY REGIONAL	42.482N	114.487W	4151	7.6	12.0	95.0	62.6	92.2	62.1	89.8	61.6	66.3	88.7	64.7	86.1	58.8	86.4	74.6	56.6	79.6	74.2	27.9	24.6	20.9	6029	775
POCATELLO REGIONAL	42.920N	112.571W	4452	-2.0	3.8	94.9	61.4	91.8	60.8	88.8	60.0	65.2	86.3	63.5	84.5	58.7	86.9	70.7	55.8	78.2	70.5	28.6	25.5	22.6	6941	440
Illinois																										*14 sites, 48 more on CD-ROM*
ABRAHAM LINCOLN CAPITAL	39.845N	89.684W	594	1.1	6.9	92.6	76.7	90.4	75.6	88.0	74.1	79.5	89.5	77.9	87.3	76.5	141.4	86.2	75.0	134.3	84.3	24.7	21.4	19.1	5328	1144
AURORA MUNICIPAL	41.770N	88.481W	710	-4.9	0.7	90.7	74.1	88.2	73.2	85.5	72.0	77.7	87.1	76.0	84.3	74.8	134.0	83.4	73.1	126.2	81.3	26.0	23.0	19.9	6537	729
CHICAGO MIDWAY INTL	41.786N	87.752W	612	0.5	6.1	91.9	74.7	89.4	73.1	86.6	72.0	77.8	87.8	76.0	85.3	74.9	133.6	84.0	72.9	125.0	82.0	24.4	21.0	19.1	5850	1057
CHICAGO O'HARE INTL	41.995N	87.934W	662	-1.0	4.4	91.3	74.2	88.5	72.9	85.9	71.6	77.5	87.3	75.7	84.7	74.5	132.2	83.5	72.8	124.7	81.4	24.6	21.0	19.1	6190	882
CHICAGO ROCKFORD INTL	42.193N	89.093W	730	-5.4	0.3	90.9	74.4	88.0	72.9	85.4	71.6	77.8	87.0	75.8	84.0	75.0	134.8	83.3	73.2	126.5	81.7	24.5	20.9	18.9	6589	786
DECATUR AP	39.834N	88.866W	675	1.9	7.3	93.1	76.6	90.7	75.5	88.3	74.3	79.4	89.4	77.8	87.5	76.4	141.5	86.0	74.9	134.0	84.1	24.7	21.5	19.6	5388	1105
DUPAGE COUNT AP	41.914N	88.246W	754	-2.5	2.6	90.2	74.6	87.8	73.5	84.6	71.8	77.9	86.8	76.0	84.0	75.0	135.1	83.8	73.1	126.6	81.5	24.8	21.6	19.3	6430	750
GLENVIEW NAS	42.083N	87.817W	653	-0.7	4.8	93.7	75.0	90.2	73.3	87.1	72.1	77.9	90.2	76.2	87.0	74.2	130.7	85.1	72.4	123.1	83.6	20.2	18.0	16.2	6104	909
GREATER PEORIA REGIONAL	40.668N	89.684W	650	-0.9	4.3	92.0	76.5	89.6	75.2	87.0	73.6	79.3	88.3	77.5	86.5	76.6	142.1	85.3	74.8	133.7	83.2	23.1	19.7	17.8	5733	1057
QUAD CITY INTL	41.465N	90.523W	592	-3.5	1.8	92.4	76.2	89.7	74.9	87.1	73.2	79.1	88.8	77.4	86.5	76.3	140.5	85.3	74.6	132.4	83.2	23.9	20.2	18.2	6091	988
QUINCY REGIONAL	39.937N	91.192W	769	0.4	5.6	93.1	76.5	90.3	75.4	87.7	74.1	78.9	89.1	77.5	87.1	76.0	139.6	85.3	74.4	132.3	83.6	24.3	20.7	18.7	5497	1119
SCOTT AFB	38.550N	89.850W	459	7.2	12.1	95.2	77.7	92.7	76.9	90.3	75.9	80.7	90.2	79.2	88.6	78.1	148.5	85.8	76.7	141.4	84.5	22.7	19.6	17.5	4617	1413
ST LOUIS DOWNTOWN AP	38.571N	90.157W	413	8.6	12.7	95.4	76.6	92.7	76.3	90.4	75.2	79.9	90.5	78.3	88.9	77.0	142.9	85.4	75.1	133.9	83.9	20.8	18.6	16.6	4569	1432
U OF ILLINOIS WILLARD AP	40.040N	88.278W	754	-0.4	4.9	91.4	75.5	89.6	74.8	86.9	73.4	79.2	87.8	77.4	85.9	76.7	143.1	85.1	74.8	134.2	82.7	27.5	24.6	21.4	5693	973
Indiana																										*8 sites, 9 more on CD-ROM*
EVANSVILLE REGIONAL	38.044N	87.521W	400	9.0	14.6	94.0	76.1	91.7	75.6	89.5	74.7	79.2	89.9	78.0	88.3	76.2	138.7	85.1	75.0	133.0	83.7	20.5	18.2	16.3	4388	1452
FORT WAYNE INTL	40.971N	85.206W	791	-0.5	5.4	90.8	74.5	88.1	73.0	85.5	71.7	77.6	87.0	75.8	84.1	74.7	133.8	83.0	73.1	126.8	81.1	25.1	21.8	19.2	5978	826
GRISSOM AFB	40.650N	86.150W	812	-1.4	5.5	90.6	75.4	88.0	74.0	85.6	72.8	79.4	85.9	77.4	84.2	77.8	148.7	83.1	75.5	137.5	81.0	25.9	22.6	19.5	5868	899
INDIANAPOLIS INTL	39.732N	86.279W	790	2.6	8.6	91.3	75.0	88.9	74.0	86.5	72.8	78.1	87.5	76.6	85.3	75.3	136.7	83.7	73.9	130.2	82.0	24.9	21.4	19.0	5249	1106
MONROE COUNTY AP	39.133N	86.617W	844	3.9	9.8	91.4	74.9	89.6	74.9	87.1	73.4	78.4	86.9	77.2	85.9	75.5	138.0	83.3	74.5	133.1	82.2	19.5	17.3	15.6	5071	1026
PURDUE UNIVERSITY AP	40.412N	86.937W	599	0.6	6.3	91.6	75.6	89.5	74.3	86.9	72.8	78.5	87.9	76.9	85.7	75.7	137.7	84.5	74.1	130.2	82.3	22.7	19.8	18.0	5526	998
SOUTH BEND INTL	41.707N	86.316W	773	0.4	6.3	90.4	74.0	87.7	72.4	85.0	71.1	77.2	86.1	75.3	83.7	74.5	132.6	82.8	72.7	124.6	80.5	24.0	20.5	18.5	6160	799
TERRE HAUTE INTL	39.452N	87.309W	575	2.2	8.8	92.5	76.2	90.1	75.6	87.8	74.2	79.2	88.6	77.7	86.8	76.5	141.2	85.1	74.9	133.5	83.2	22.5	19.3	17.7	5170	1084
Iowa																										*9 sites, 46 more on CD-ROM*
AMES MUNICIPAL	41.991N	93.619W	955	-6.4	-1.5	90.9	76.2	88.3	74.7	85.8	73.1	79.1	87.3	77.2	85.4	76.7	144.1	84.9	74.7	134.7	82.6	26.3	23.5	20.2	6625	808
ANKENY REGIONAL	41.691N	93.566W	910	-3.7	1.0	93.0	75.6	90.3	75.1	87.8	73.7	79.3	88.1	77.4	86.8	76.9	145.1	84.8	74.5	133.6	83.2	22.9	19.6	17.7	6125	975
BOONE MUNICIPAL	42.049N	93.848W	1160	-5.7	0.2	91.2	76.5	89.5	75.8	86.1	73.5	80.2	87.9	78.1	85.2	77.5	149.6	85.4	75.4	139.1	83.0	26.2	23.4	20.3	6484	878
DAVENPORT MUNICIPAL	41.614N	90.591W	753	-6.9	-1.4	91.1	75.0	88.2	73.9	85.8	72.6	77.9	87.7	76.4	85.6	75.0	135.0	84.3	73.3	127.2	82.8	26.7	24.0	20.6	6474	878
DES MOINES INTL	41.534N	93.653W	957	-4.3	0.6	92.8	76.2	89.7	75.0	87.1	73.4	78.7	88.8	77.2	86.6	75.9	140.2	85.3	74.3	132.6	83.7	25.5	22.3	19.5	6147	1066
DUBUQUE REGIONAL	42.398N	90.704W	1056	-8.1	-2.7	88.4	75.0	85.6	73.3	83.1	71.4	77.5	85.3	75.6	82.6	75.2	137.6	82.5	73.3	128.7	80.5	25.8	22.8	19.9	7042	641
SIOUX GATEWAY AP	42.391N	96.379W	1095	-7.1	-2.5	92.9	75.2	90.1	74.3	87.4	73.0	78.8	88.3	77.2	86.7	76.2	142.3	85.2	74.2	133.1	83.6	28.5	25.1	22.0	6733	914
THE EASTERN IOWA AP	41.883N	91.717W	868	-8.2	-2.6	90.4	76.3	87.6	74.5	84.8	72.7	78.6	86.7	76.9	84.6	76.3	141.9	84.1	74.5	133.2	82.0	26.7	23.7	20.5	6755	774
WATERLOO MUNICIPAL	42.554N	92.401W	868	-9.5	-4.5	91.0	75.5	88.1	73.7	85.5	72.3	78.5	87.0	76.6	84.6	76.1	140.9	84.4	74.1	131.5	82.0	26.1	23.4	20.2	7016	769
Kansas																										*10 sites, 22 more on CD-ROM*
COLONEL JAMES JABARA AP	37.746N	97.221W	1421	6.7	11.0	100.0	73.6	97.2	73.9	93.2	73.6	77.4	91.0	76.4	90.0	73.4	130.8	83.5	72.5	126.9	82.4	27.8	25.1	22.8	4504	1632
FORBES FIELD	38.950N	95.664W	1067	3.5	8.9	99.0	76.0	94.8	75.4	91.4	74.6	78.9	91.8	77.7	90.4	75.2	137.7	85.8	73.6	130.0	84.0	26.2	23.6	20.5	4977	1422
JOHNSON COUNTY EXECUTIVE	38.850N	94.739W	1070	4.3	9.2	96.5	75.5	92.7	75.3	90.1	74.9	78.9	89.7	77.7	88.6	75.4	138.6	85.3	74.5	134.2	84.1	23.3	20.1	18.3	4837	1413
LAWRENCE MUNICIPAL	39.008N	95.212W	832	3.4	8.6	99.2	76.6	95.5	75.8	92.0	75.4	79.8	92.3	78.3	90.8	76.3	141.4	87.1	74.8	134.5	85.6	25.1	21.9	19.2	4991	1475
MANHATTAN REGIONAL	39.135N	96.679W	1056	1.9	7.5	100.2	75.3	97.0	75.3	93.1	74.6	78.5	92.5	77.5	91.5	74.9	136.1	85.6	73.3	128.7	83.6	24.1	20.5	18.3	5145	1486
MARSHALL AIRFIELD	39.050N	96.767W	1065	4.8	9.2	100.7	75.0	96.8	75.1	93.6	74.8	78.8	91.6	77.5	90.5	75.5	139.1	85.0	74.0	132.2	83.6	24.4	20.6	18.5	4940	1593
MCCONNELL AFB	37.617N	97.267W	1371	8.3	12.8	100.2	72.7	97.2	73.3	93.8	73.4	77.7	90.0	76.6	88.8	74.8	137.4	82.1	73.2	129.6	81.3	27.4	24.8	22.2	4284	1745
PHILIP BILLARD MUNICIPAL	39.073N	95.626W	876	4.0	8.9	98.3	75.9	94.9	75.9	91.8	75.0	79.1	91.6	77.9	90.4	75.5	138.0	86.0	74.2	132.1	84.8	23.2	20.0	18.1	4885	1506

(Go to CD-ROM to access additional station tables.)

(Go to CD-ROM to access additional station tables.)

Meaning of acronyms:
DB: Dry bulb temperature, °F — *WB: Wet bulb temperature, °F*
MCWB: Mean coincident wet bulb temperature, °F
Lat: Latitude, ° — *DP: Dew point temperature, °F* — *MCDB: Mean coincident dry bulb temperature, °F*
Long: Longitude, ° — *HR: Humidity ratio, grains of moisture per lb of dry air* — *HDD and CDD 65: Annual heating and cooling degree-days, base 65°F, °F-day*
Elev: Elevation, ft — *WS: Wind speed, mph*

Station	Lat	Long	Elev	Heating DB		Cooling DB/MCWB						Evaporation WB/MCDB				Dehumidification DP/HR/MCDB						Extreme Annual WS			Heat./Cool. Degree-Days	
						0.4%		1%		2%		0.4%		1%		0.4%			1%							
				99.6%	99%	DB	MCWB	DB	MCWB	DB	MCWB	WB	MCDB	WB	MCDB	DP	HR	MCDB	DP	HR	MCDB	1%	2.5%	5%	HDD	CDD 65
SALINA MUNICIPAL	38.800N	97.650W	1269	4.3	9.2	101.9	73.5	98.8	73.7	95.3	73.2	77.3	92.4	76.1	91.0	73.1	129.1	83.9	72.1	124.3	83.0	28.1	25.2	22.6	4799	1706
WICHITA EISENHOWER NATL	37.648N	97.430W	1321	7.6	12.3	101.1	73.2	97.8	73.6	94.4	73.5	77.6	90.7	76.6	89.9	74.2	134.2	83.7	72.9	128.2	82.2	28.3	25.7	23.5	4444	1743
Kentucky																									*8 sites, 9 more on CD-ROM*	
BLUE GRASS AP	38.041N	84.606W	980	8.8	14.1	91.5	74.0	89.2	73.6	87.0	72.7	77.3	87.2	76.0	85.3	74.3	132.8	82.6	73.1	127.5	81.0	20.7	18.4	16.5	4535	1197
BOWLING GREEN AP	36.965N	86.424W	528	12.4	17.6	94.1	75.1	91.6	75.0	89.6	74.5	78.4	88.8	77.4	87.5	75.4	135.6	83.9	74.3	130.9	82.7	19.8	17.8	15.8	3979	1475
BOWMAN FIELD	38.228N	85.664W	540	10.7	16.3	93.4	75.1	91.2	74.7	89.3	73.9	78.4	88.4	77.3	87.2	75.5	136.1	83.2	74.5	131.7	82.4	18.5	16.5	14.4	4156	1486
CAMPBELL AAF	36.667N	87.483W	573	12.0	17.7	94.6	76.1	92.1	75.8	90.2	75.3	79.4	89.3	78.3	87.8	77.0	143.8	83.4	75.5	136.3	82.5	20.2	17.7	15.6	3773	1615
CINCINNATI NORTHERN KY INTL	39.043N	84.672W	869	5.9	11.9	91.6	74.3	89.0	73.4	86.7	72.5	77.5	87.0	76.1	85.0	74.6	133.8	82.5	73.3	128.1	80.8	21.6	18.9	17.0	4918	1115
HENDERSON CITY-COUNTY AP	37.800N	87.683W	387	8.8	14.3	93.4	76.3	91.2	75.9	90.1	75.3	79.4	91.3	78.0	89.2	75.4	135.1	86.9	74.5	130.9	85.8	21.3	18.8	16.7	4473	1396
LAKE CUMBERLAND REGIONAL	37.054N	84.615W	927	12.2	18.0	94.1	74.6	91.3	74.0	90.0	73.5	77.9	90.0	76.5	87.8	73.5	128.9	82.6	72.9	126.5	81.8	17.9	15.5	12.6	3945	1388
LOUISVILLE INTL	38.181N	85.739W	488	11.0	16.6	94.2	75.3	91.8	75.0	89.5	74.2	78.7	89.2	77.5	87.9	75.8	137.3	85.0	74.4	130.8	83.3	21.0	18.7	16.8	4057	1604
Louisiana																									*12 sites, 16 more on CD-ROM*	
ALEXANDRIA ESLER REGIONAL	31.395N	92.291W	118	26.0	28.4	98.0	76.7	95.6	77.0	93.5	76.9	80.3	89.9	79.5	89.7	78.0	146.1	83.7	77.0	141.3	83.3	16.3	13.6	11.9	1988	2533
ALEXANDRIA INTL	31.335N	92.559W	84	27.0	29.9	97.4	76.9	95.1	77.0	93.0	76.7	80.4	89.6	79.5	89.5	78.5	148.5	84.1	77.0	141.1	83.5	18.8	16.8	14.6	1850	2659
BARKSDALE AFB	32.500N	93.667W	166	24.6	27.6	99.0	75.5	96.4	75.8	93.9	76.0	79.3	90.7	78.4	89.5	76.5	139.1	83.2	75.4	134.1	82.4	20.3	18.1	16.1	2238	2424
BATON ROUGE METROPOLITAN	30.537N	91.147W	64	28.4	31.6	94.8	77.4	93.3	77.4	91.8	77.0	80.4	88.8	79.7	88.1	78.4	148.0	83.7	77.5	143.3	83.0	18.8	16.7	14.7	1576	2721
LAFAYETTE REGIONAL	30.205N	91.988W	38	30.2	33.7	94.8	77.7	93.1	77.5	91.5	77.2	80.5	88.7	79.9	88.2	78.8	149.5	83.7	77.7	144.0	83.2	20.3	18.3	16.5	1443	2857
LAKE CHARLES REGIONAL	30.125N	93.228W	9	30.5	33.8	94.7	77.7	93.0	77.7	91.4	77.6	81.3	88.5	80.4	87.6	79.4	152.6	84.1	78.6	148.3	83.6	20.3	18.2	16.5	1434	2849
LAKEFRONT AP	30.049N	90.029W	9	36.0	39.2	93.5	78.7	92.6	78.4	91.1	77.9	81.4	89.7	80.6	88.8	79.3	151.9	86.0	78.7	148.9	85.6	26.2	23.1	19.9	1072	3385
LOUIS ARMSTRONG NEW ORLEANS	29.993N	90.251W	4	33.3	36.6	94.2	77.9	92.5	77.7	91.0	77.4	80.6	88.8	80.1	88.2	78.5	147.9	84.5	77.8	144.7	84.0	20.9	18.8	17.0	1255	3000
MONROE REGIONAL	32.516N	92.041W	79	25.4	28.4	98.3	77.7	95.8	77.4	93.6	77.1	80.8	91.6	80.0	90.8	78.1	146.6	85.3	77.1	141.7	84.5	19.1	17.1	15.0	2183	2506
NEW ORLEANS NAS	29.817N	90.017W	2	31.2	34.5	93.1	77.6	91.6	77.4	90.3	77.2	81.2	87.5	80.1	86.9	79.4	152.6	83.6	78.4	147.5	83.2	18.6	16.4	14.1	1375	2728
SHREVEPORT DOWNTOWN AP	32.543N	93.745W	179	26.5	29.1	99.5	76.2	97.1	76.1	94.6	76.0	79.4	91.1	78.5	89.9	76.6	139.6	83.0	75.5	134.5	82.7	18.8	16.7	14.8	2173	2654
SHREVEPORT REGIONAL	32.447N	93.824W	254	25.9	29.0	99.2	75.7	96.7	76.0	94.4	76.0	79.3	91.2	78.5	90.0	76.3	138.8	83.4	75.6	135.2	82.8	19.9	17.8	16.1	2093	2612
Maine																									*5 sites, 24 more on CD-ROM*	
AUBURN LEWISTON MUNICIPAL	44.050N	70.283W	288	-5.9	0.1	87.8	71.2	83.6	69.7	81.1	67.6	73.8	83.4	71.7	80.4	70.5	113.4	78.6	69.6	109.8	77.3	20.8	18.5	16.4	7585	314
BANGOR INTL	44.798N	68.819W	148	-7.0	-1.8	87.7	70.5	84.2	69.0	81.1	67.0	73.0	83.2	71.2	80.6	69.7	109.8	77.9	68.0	103.3	75.4	23.4	19.8	17.9	7614	360
BRUNSWICK NAS	43.900N	69.933W	70	-2.2	2.3	86.2	70.3	82.8	68.9	80.3	67.1	73.4	82.1	71.4	79.6	70.4	112.1	77.9	68.7	105.8	75.7	23.5	19.8	17.7	7180	369
PORTLAND INTL JETPORT	43.650N	70.300W	45	0.5	5.2	86.7	71.2	83.3	69.9	80.2	68.1	73.9	83.2	72.1	80.0	70.8	113.6	78.5	69.3	107.9	76.2	23.2	19.6	17.5	6930	382
SANFORD SEACOAST REGIONAL	43.394N	70.708W	244	-6.1	0.3	89.7	71.7	85.7	70.0	82.2	68.1	74.5	85.2	72.4	82.3	71.6	117.9	80.9	69.7	110.3	78.6	20.9	18.5	16.3	7423	366
Maryland																									*3 sites, 10 more on CD-ROM*	
ANDREWS AFB	38.817N	76.867W	282	15.1	18.7	94.1	75.0	91.0	74.0	88.5	72.9	78.0	88.5	76.6	86.3	75.1	133.2	81.8	73.5	125.9	80.2	24.2	20.5	18.2	4378	1251
BALTIMORE-WASHINGTON INTL	39.167N	76.683W	156	14.6	18.4	94.2	74.8	91.4	74.0	88.6	72.8	77.7	88.9	76.5	86.4	74.9	131.5	81.7	73.7	126.1	80.3	22.0	18.9	16.8	4491	1268
THOMAS POINT	38.900N	76.440W	0	18.2	22.0	86.9	76.4	84.9	75.9	83.1	75.2	81.9	83.3	80.0	81.9	81.5	164.0	82.5	79.4	152.7	81.0	37.6	31.6	26.5	4135	1245
Massachusetts																									*11 sites, 14 more on CD-ROM*	
BARNSTABLE MUNICIPAL	41.669N	70.280W	55	10.3	15.4	84.2	72.9	81.5	71.5	79.3	70.4	75.6	81.1	74.3	78.7	73.5	124.7	77.8	72.8	121.7	77.0	24.7	21.2	19.1	5791	526
BOSTON LOGAN INTL	42.361N	71.011W	12	8.5	13.4	90.6	72.6	87.6	71.6	84.3	70.0	75.8	85.7	74.2	83.0	72.6	121.0	80.4	71.3	115.3	78.6	26.8	24.0	20.7	5512	776
BUZZARDS BAY	41.400N	71.030W	0	13.1	17.2	76.4	N/A	74.7	N/A	73.4	N/A	N/A	N/A	N/A	N/A	N/A	N/A	N/A	N/A	N/A	N/A	44.0	38.2	33.9	5411	339
CHATHAM MUNICIPAL	41.688N	69.993W	68	12.1	17.4	83.0	72.8	80.7	71.7	78.4	70.6	75.2	80.1	73.9	78.0	73.3	124.2	77.6	72.5	120.6	76.6	20.4	17.9	16.1	5598	493
LAWRENCE MUNICIPAL	42.717N	71.124W	149	4.9	9.8	90.5	73.0	87.9	71.9	84.2	70.2	75.7	85.5	74.3	83.2	72.7	121.8	79.9	71.8	118.3	79.3	20.4	18.1	16.2	6007	684
MARTHAS VINEYARD AP	41.393N	70.615W	68	9.8	14.4	84.1	72.5	81.4	71.3	79.2	70.2	75.3	80.9	74.0	78.8	73.3	124.0	78.1	72.4	120.4	76.9	26.0	23.4	20.3	5777	451
NEW BEDFORD REGIONAL	41.676N	70.958W	80	8.6	12.4	88.2	73.4	84.5	71.5	82.0	70.2	75.9	83.9	74.5	81.0	73.3	124.0	78.9	72.4	120.5	77.9	23.1	19.8	17.8	5770	586
NORWOOD MEMORIAL	42.191N	71.174W	50	3.1	9.0	90.6	73.5	87.9	72.4	84.4	70.4	76.6	86.0	75.0	83.1	73.4	124.4	79.9	72.5	120.5	79.0	20.3	18.0	16.1	6140	606
PLYMOUTH MUNICIPAL	41.910N	70.729W	149	6.1	10.3	88.7	73.0	85.3	71.7	82.3	70.0	75.8	84.3	74.3	81.4	73.1	123.8	79.0	72.3	120.1	78.1	23.4	19.8	17.8	6052	575
SOUTH WEYMOUTH NAS	42.150N	70.933W	161	5.9	10.4	91.2	73.8	87.7	72.3	84.7	70.7	76.9	86.8	74.9	83.8	74.1	127.9	81.9	72.2	119.7	79.4	18.5	16.5	14.5	5832	646
WORCESTER REGIONAL	42.271N	71.873W	1000	2.4	7.1	85.8	70.9	83.2	69.5	80.6	68.0	73.7	81.5	72.3	79.3	71.4	120.2	77.1	70.0	114.6	75.7	25.9	23.0	19.8	6603	485
Michigan																									*15 sites, 72 more on CD-ROM*	
BISHOP INTL	42.967N	83.749W	770	-0.2	4.5	89.4	73.4	86.6	71.7	84.0	70.1	76.0	85.4	74.1	83.2	72.9	125.7	81.9	71.2	118.3	79.2	23.9	20.4	18.4	6692	610
DETROIT COLEMAN YOUNG INTL	42.409N	83.010W	626	5.2	9.6	90.6	73.4	88.0	71.9	85.4	70.5	76.3	86.2	74.5	83.7	73.1	125.9	81.7	71.6	119.4	80.1	20.5	18.6	17.1	5977	883
DETROIT METRO WAYNE COUNTY AP	42.231N	83.331W	631	3.3	8.2	90.3	74.0	87.4	72.5	84.7	70.9	76.8	86.4	74.9	83.5	73.7	128.6	82.2	72.1	121.7	80.1	25.0	21.5	19.1	6066	821
GERALD R FORD INTL	42.883N	85.524W	803	2.8	7.3	89.2	73.1	86.5	71.6	83.9	70.1	76.2	85.2	74.4	82.8	73.4	128.1	81.2	71.5	119.9	79.0	24.9	21.3	19.1	6544	663
GROSSE ILE MUNICIPAL	42.099N	83.161W	587	6.5	9.8	89.8	74.5	86.1	73.7	83.5	72.6	77.9	84.9	76.2	82.9	75.3	135.5	81.8	73.4	126.9	79.9	20.9	18.7	16.8	5887	858
JACKSON COUNTY AP	42.267N	84.467W	998	0.5	5.4	88.6	73.2	85.9	71.8	83.2	70.2	75.9	84.7	74.2	82.3	73.1	127.7	80.8	71.6	121.1	79.2	20.2	18.3	16.8	6596	581
KALAMAZOO BATTLE CREEK INTL	42.235N	85.552W	868	2.5	7.4	90.2	73.1	87.7	71.7	84.3	70.2	76.1	85.4	74.5	83.2	73.0	126.4	81.5	71.9	121.8	80.1	21.7	19.0	17.2	6288	731
LANSING CAPITAL REGION INTL	42.780N	84.579W	841	-0.5	4.7	89.0	73.2	86.2	71.6	83.5	70.0	76.0	85.2	74.2	82.6	73.1	126.8	81.4	71.3	119.1	79.0	24.1	20.4	18.5	6774	579
MBS INTL	43.533N	84.080W	660	0.4	4.7	89.4	73.0	86.3	71.2	83.6	70.0	75.9	85.4	74.1	82.8	73.0	125.3	81.2	71.3	118.4	78.9	24.5	20.9	18.9	6854	586
MUSKEGON COUNTY AP	43.171N	86.237W	625	5.5	9.4	86.2	72.2	83.7	70.7	81.6	69.6	75.3	82.5	73.8	80.4	73.0	125.5	79.6	71.4	118.7	78.0	25.2	22.7	19.9	6565	538
OAKLAND COUNTY INTL	42.665N	83.418W	976	1.0	5.4	89.7	73.0	86.4	71.1	83.7	69.6	75.3	84.9	73.5	82.3	72.4	124.4	80.8	70.6	116.9	78.5	24.1	20.6	18.6	6632	654

Meaning of acronyms:
DB: Dry bulb temperature, °F — *WB: Wet bulb temperature, °F* — *Lat: Latitude, °* — *Long: Longitude, °* — *Elev: Elevation, ft*
MCWB: Mean coincident wet bulb temperature, °F — *DP: Dew point temperature, °F* — *HR: Humidity ratio, grains of moisture per lb of dry air* — *WS: Wind speed, mph*
MCDB: Mean coincident dry bulb temperature, °F — *HDD and CDD 65: Annual heating and cooling degree-days, base 65°F, °F-day*

Station	Lat	Long	Elev	Heating DB		Cooling DB/MCWB						Evaporation WB/MCDB				Dehumidification DP/HR/MCDB						Extreme Annual WS			Heat./Cool. Degree-Days	
						0.4%		1%		2%		0.4%		1%		0.4%			1%							
				99.6%	99%	DB	MCWB	DB	MCWB	DB	MCWB	WB	MCDB	WB	MCDB	DP	HR	MCDB	DP	HR	MCDB	1%	2.5%	5%	HDD	CDD 65
SELFRIDGE ANGB	42.608N	82.818W	580	1.7	6.8	90.0	74.0	86.5	72.1	83.9	70.8	76.5	85.5	74.6	83.0	73.4	126.9	81.3	72.1	121.4	79.7	21.6	19.3	17.6	6413	663
ST CLAIR COUNTY INTL	42.911N	82.529W	640	0.0	5.0	89.9	73.5	85.9	71.3	82.3	69.6	75.9	84.5	73.9	81.8	73.0	125.3	79.8	72.0	121.0	78.7	18.7	16.6	14.7	6800	458
WEST MICHIGAN REGIONAL	42.746N	86.097W	689	6.8	10.1	89.5	73.4	86.4	71.9	83.6	70.7	76.2	85.3	74.5	83.0	73.1	125.9	81.6	72.0	121.6	80.0	25.6	22.1	19.1	6218	663
WILLOW RUN AP	42.233N	83.533W	777	1.0	6.4	91.2	73.8	88.3	72.4	85.5	70.7	76.8	87.2	74.9	84.3	73.4	127.7	82.1	72.1	122.1	80.4	24.7	21.3	19.0	6342	733
Minnesota																										*11 sites, 87 more on CD-ROM*
ANOKA COUNTY AP	45.150N	93.217W	912	-8.8	-4.5	90.2	74.8	87.7	73.7	83.9	71.7	78.1	85.9	75.8	83.4	75.2	136.8	82.9	73.1	127.1	80.4	23.1	19.7	17.7	7530	617
CRYSTAL AP	45.062N	93.351W	861	-9.5	-6.0	90.7	73.4	88.1	72.0	84.5	69.9	76.9	86.9	74.7	84.2	73.3	127.8	83.5	71.9	121.6	81.5	21.1	19.0	17.2	7599	724
DULUTH INTL	46.837N	92.183W	1433	-17.2	-12.0	84.2	69.7	81.1	67.1	78.2	65.3	72.6	81.1	70.0	78.0	69.4	114.1	78.0	67.1	105.0	75.3	24.9	21.4	19.2	9286	218
FLYING CLOUD AP	44.832N	93.471W	907	-10.6	-6.3	90.8	74.2	88.2	72.7	85.0	70.9	77.6	87.4	75.4	84.2	74.7	134.2	83.9	72.4	124.3	81.8	21.8	19.2	17.4	7415	807
MANKATO MUNICIPAL	44.217N	93.917W	1021	-12.3	-8.2	89.9	73.7	86.3	71.9	83.5	70.6	77.0	85.5	74.7	83.0	73.5	129.4	82.3	72.2	123.6	80.9	26.8	24.1	20.8	7705	628
MINNEAPOLIS-ST PAUL INTL	44.883N	93.229W	872	-10.6	-5.8	90.8	73.3	87.8	72.0	84.9	70.2	76.9	87.2	74.8	84.0	73.7	129.4	83.5	71.7	120.9	81.2	24.0	20.6	18.8	7477	782
ROCHESTER INTL	43.904N	92.492W	1304	-12.4	-7.6	87.7	73.3	84.7	71.7	82.2	70.3	76.8	84.3	74.6	81.7	74.3	134.5	81.8	72.2	124.9	79.7	28.2	25.4	23.2	7832	528
SKY HARBOR AP	46.722N	92.043W	610	-10.5	-6.3	86.2	71.9	82.3	69.3	80.5	68.0	75.3	82.8	72.8	79.4	72.9	124.8	79.1	71.5	119.0	77.7	28.3	25.0	21.5	8561	310
SOUTH ST PAUL MUNICIPAL	44.857N	93.033W	820	-8.8	-4.4	90.8	73.1	88.1	71.6	84.6	69.8	77.1	86.2	74.9	83.6	74.5	132.8	82.6	72.2	123.0	80.4	18.8	16.7	14.8	7371	770
ST CLOUD REGIONAL	45.543N	94.051W	1009	-16.8	-11.3	89.4	72.5	86.3	70.7	83.4	68.7	76.2	85.4	74.0	83.0	73.2	128.1	82.1	70.9	118.0	79.5	23.7	20.1	18.1	8425	484
ST PAUL DOWNTOWN AP	44.932N	93.056W	700	-10.0	-5.8	90.6	73.8	87.9	72.5	84.3	70.5	77.3	86.6	75.2	84.0	74.4	132.0	83.5	72.3	122.8	81.3	23.2	20.1	18.3	7465	753
Mississippi																										*6 sites, 13 more on CD-ROM*
HATTIESBURG-LAUREL AP	31.467N	89.333W	293	25.0	27.7	96.6	75.7	93.1	75.1	91.1	74.9	78.5	89.8	77.7	88.9	75.3	133.9	83.1	74.6	130.9	82.6	16.5	13.8	12.0	2086	2273
JACKSON INTL	32.321N	90.078W	330	23.6	26.9	96.3	76.1	94.2	76.1	92.3	75.9	79.6	90.2	78.5	88.7	77.0	142.1	83.7	76.1	137.8	82.8	18.5	16.4	14.2	2272	2315
KEESLER AFB	30.417N	88.917W	33	30.6	34.7	94.3	80.2	92.2	79.4	90.6	78.8	83.6	90.3	82.2	88.4	81.7	164.9	87.3	80.9	160.6	86.4	18.5	16.6	14.8	1432	2800
KEY FIELD	32.335N	88.744W	294	22.6	26.1	96.1	75.8	93.9	75.9	92.0	75.7	79.7	89.4	78.5	88.2	77.1	142.8	83.6	76.1	137.8	82.6	18.5	16.5	14.5	2351	2161
MERIDIAN NAS MCCAIN FIELD	32.550N	88.567W	271	22.5	26.6	96.8	76.2	94.6	76.2	92.6	75.9	80.0	90.8	78.8	89.7	77.1	142.5	85.6	75.8	136.2	83.9	16.5	13.0	11.3	2343	2232
TUPELO REGIONAL	34.262N	88.771W	361	19.5	23.8	96.2	76.0	93.8	75.7	91.7	75.5	79.3	89.9	78.3	88.7	76.4	139.7	84.0	75.4	135.0	83.2	18.9	16.8	15.2	2911	2010
Missouri																										*9 sites, 16 more on CD-ROM*
CAPE GIRARDEAU REGIONAL	37.225N	89.571W	336	10.1	15.9	94.4	77.0	92.3	76.7	90.2	75.9	80.2	90.1	78.8	88.5	77.4	144.3	86.4	76.0	137.5	84.6	21.9	19.3	17.5	4193	1513
COLUMBIA REGIONAL	38.817N	92.218W	893	3.6	9.2	94.7	75.7	91.7	75.9	89.0	74.9	79.4	89.4	77.9	87.8	76.5	143.0	85.6	75.1	136.0	84.0	24.0	20.5	18.5	4917	1276
CR WHEELER DOWNTOWN	39.121N	94.597W	742	5.8	10.2	97.3	76.1	94.1	75.7	91.3	75.2	79.5	91.6	78.2	89.8	76.1	140.0	86.8	74.8	133.8	85.7	22.1	19.4	18.0	4567	1663
JEFFERSON CITY MEMORIAL	38.591N	92.156W	573	6.5	11.6	96.1	75.9	92.8	75.2	90.4	74.6	79.4	89.9	77.9	88.5	76.6	141.4	85.0	74.9	133.5	83.4	20.8	18.4	16.4	4574	1444
JOPLIN REGIONAL	37.147N	94.502W	980	8.7	14.0	97.4	74.8	94.4	75.3	91.6	74.8	78.5	90.3	77.6	89.4	75.3	137.5	85.5	74.0	131.7	84.1	25.1	22.0	19.5	4044	1669
KANSAS CITY INTL	39.297N	94.731W	1005	2.4	7.5	96.0	76.5	92.7	76.1	89.7	75.4	79.9	90.5	78.3	88.9	76.9	145.5	86.7	75.3	137.5	85.4	25.4	22.8	20.0	5027	1376
LAMBERT-ST LOUIS INTL	38.753N	90.374W	531	7.5	12.7	96.2	76.7	93.5	76.1	91.1	75.0	79.5	90.9	78.2	89.3	76.3	140.0	86.0	74.9	133.4	85.1	23.3	19.9	18.0	4403	1676
SPIRIT OF ST LOUIS AP	38.657N	90.656W	462	6.2	11.7	95.5	77.1	92.8	76.3	90.4	75.2	79.8	90.7	78.3	89.0	76.8	142.0	85.7	75.2	134.2	84.5	20.6	18.4	16.5	4672	1398
SPRINGFIELD-BRANSON REGIONAL	37.240N	93.390W	1259	7.1	12.8	95.5	74.0	92.4	74.1	89.6	74.0	77.7	88.7	76.6	87.5	74.5	135.4	83.4	73.4	130.1	82.2	23.6	20.4	18.5	4428	1406
Montana																										*7 sites, 18 more on CD-ROM*
BERT MOONEY AP	45.965N	112.501W	5506	-17.3	-9.1	87.9	57.4	84.7	56.4	81.7	55.9	60.3	79.3	58.9	77.7	54.5	77.8	62.6	52.2	71.3	61.9	20.9	18.7	16.6	9095	79
BILLINGS LOGAN INTL	45.807N	108.542W	3581	-9.5	-3.2	94.7	62.7	91.3	61.9	88.1	61.4	66.3	85.2	64.6	83.8	60.3	89.2	72.0	58.1	82.3	70.7	27.6	24.7	21.7	6738	648
BOZEMAN YELLOWSTONE INTL	45.788N	111.161W	4427	-15.1	-7.7	92.1	61.1	88.7	60.4	85.2	59.4	64.3	83.2	62.5	81.7	58.1	85.2	69.1	55.9	78.5	68.1	21.2	18.2	15.3	8172	237
GREAT FALLS	47.450N	111.383W	3709	-13.8	-6.9	90.6	60.3	87.3	59.5	84.1	58.9	63.5	82.6	61.8	80.6	57.3	80.5	66.9	55.2	74.4	67.6	31.3	27.2	24.7	7706	333
GREAT FALLS INTL	47.473N	111.382W	3664	-16.2	-9.5	92.5	60.9	89.1	60.2	85.6	59.3	64.0	84.4	62.3	82.3	57.8	81.7	67.1	55.6	75.5	66.9	31.4	27.4	24.7	7557	336
MALMSTROM AFB	47.517N	111.183W	3472	-14.9	-8.5	94.5	62.7	90.8	61.5	87.4	60.5	65.8	87.0	63.7	84.6	58.5	83.4	71.7	56.3	76.7	69.8	30.9	27.1	24.4	6875	483
MISSOULA INTL	46.921N	114.093W	3192	-3.5	3.3	93.1	61.8	89.8	61.2	86.3	60.2	64.7	85.3	63.2	83.8	58.3	81.8	68.4	56.2	75.8	67.5	20.9	18.5	16.4	7353	336
Nebraska																										*5 sites, 37 more on CD-ROM*
CENTRAL NEBRASKA REGIONAL	40.961N	98.314W	1840	-3.2	1.9	95.6	74.0	92.4	73.2	89.4	72.0	77.6	89.2	76.0	87.8	74.3	137.2	84.3	72.5	129.1	82.7	28.8	25.8	23.1	6092	1054
EPPLEY AIRFIELD	41.310N	95.899W	982	-3.2	1.4	94.8	76.0	91.8	75.3	88.9	73.8	79.4	89.5	77.6	87.7	76.5	143.4	86.1	74.7	134.7	84.1	26.5	23.9	20.6	6024	1165
LINCOLN MUNICIPAL	40.851N	96.748W	1190	-2.6	2.0	96.6	74.9	93.3	74.5	90.4	73.6	78.4	90.5	77.0	89.0	75.1	137.8	85.7	73.4	130.0	83.9	27.2	24.5	21.0	5969	1191
NORTH OMAHA AP	41.367N	96.017W	1332	-6.1	-0.1	94.0	75.0	90.9	74.6	88.0	73.0	77.7	89.0	76.3	87.3	74.4	135.3	84.2	72.9	128.2	83.0	23.3	19.2	17.8	5981	1093
OFFUTT AFB	41.117N	95.917W	1047	-2.5	1.7	95.0	76.5	91.4	75.8	89.0	74.5	80.0	89.3	78.2	87.4	77.4	148.2	85.1	75.5	138.7	83.6	24.7	20.8	18.5	5950	1166
Nevada																										*3 sites, 14 more on CD-ROM*
MCCARRAN INTL	36.072N	115.163W	2180	31.7	34.3	108.5	67.5	106.3	66.7	104.1	65.9	72.5	96.1	71.1	94.4	66.0	103.9	81.4	63.5	95.0	83.3	25.6	22.6	19.7	1962	3557
NELLIS AFB	36.250N	115.033W	1870	28.5	31.7	109.2	67.3	107.2	66.7	104.9	65.9	72.3	94.9	71.1	94.7	66.1	103.3	80.1	63.5	94.1	83.3	26.9	24.0	20.4	2072	3454
RENO TAHOE INTL	39.484N	119.771W	4410	13.1	18.0	96.4	61.4	93.8	60.4	91.3	59.2	63.9	89.4	62.3	87.9	55.0	75.8	71.5	51.7	67.2	72.0	25.7	21.3	18.7	4961	872
New Hampshire																										*4 sites, 11 more on CD-ROM*
CONCORD MUNICIPAL	43.195N	71.501W	346	-3.0	2.1	90.0	71.3	87.0	69.8	84.1	68.5	74.6	84.9	72.9	82.2	71.6	118.0	78.0	70.0	111.9	76.8	21.0	18.6	16.5	7061	477
JAFFREY-SILVER RANCH AP	42.805N	72.004W	1040	-2.3	2.1	87.1	70.0	83.8	68.6	81.3	67.2	73.0	81.4	71.6	79.2	70.6	116.9	75.9	69.8	113.8	75.2	16.3	13.6	12.0	7280	379

(Go to CD-ROM to access additional station tables.)

(Go to CD-ROM to access additional station tables.)

Meaning of acronyms:
DB: Dry bulb temperature, °F *WB: Wet bulb temperature, °F*
MCWB: Mean coincident wet bulb temperature, °F
Lat: Latitude, °
DP: Dew point temperature, °F
MCDB: Mean coincident dry bulb temperature, °F
Long: Longitude, °
HR: Humidity ratio, grains of moisture per lb of dry air
Elev: Elevation, ft
WS: Wind speed, mph
HDD and CDD 65: Annual heating and cooling degree-days, base 65°F, °F-day

Station	Lat	Long	Elev	Heating DB		Cooling DB/MCWB						Evaporation WB/MCDB				Dehumidification DP/HR/MCDB						Extreme Annual WS			Heat./Cool. Degree-Days	
						0.4%		1%		2%		0.4%		1%		0.4%			1%							
				99.6%	99%	DB / MCWB		DB / MCWB		DB / MCWB		WB / MCDB		WB / MCDB		DP / HR / MCDB			DP / HR / MCDB			1%	2.5%	5%	HDD / CDD 65	
MANCHESTER-BOSTON REGIONAL	42.933N	71.438W	225	2.2	7.2	91.1	71.9	88.5	70.6	85.6	69.3	75.3	85.5	73.6	83.0	72.3	120.6	79.8	71.0	115.1	78.3	19.8	17.8	15.8	6207	732
PORTSMOUTH INTL	43.083N	70.817W	100	2.7	7.7	89.5	72.5	86.0	71.1	82.8	69.5	75.3	85.1	73.5	82.0	72.3	120.2	79.6	70.8	114.0	77.8	23.4	19.9	17.7	6396	556
																									7 sites, 7 more on CD-ROM	
New Jersey																										
ATLANTIC CITY INTL	39.449N	74.567W	60	12.3	16.5	92.3	75.2	89.3	73.8	86.5	72.7	77.9	87.6	76.6	84.9	75.2	132.5	81.9	74.1	127.7	80.6	25.0	21.6	18.9	4806	1035
MCGUIRE AFB	40.017N	74.600W	131	11.7	15.9	92.9	75.4	90.3	74.5	87.7	73.2	78.5	87.4	77.1	86.1	76.4	138.4	82.6	74.6	130.2	81.2	23.5	20.0	17.9	4849	1073
MILLVILLE MUNICIPAL	39.367N	75.067W	70	11.6	16.2	92.1	75.0	89.4	74.0	86.9	72.8	78.0	87.1	76.7	85.0	75.4	133.3	81.5	74.3	128.5	80.5	20.3	18.2	16.3	4845	1057
MONMOUTH EXECUTIVE	40.183N	74.133W	159	11.6	16.0	91.0	73.9	88.4	72.7	84.5	71.3	76.8	86.9	75.2	84.3	73.3	124.5	80.8	72.4	120.8	80.2	24.9	21.5	19.0	5052	919
NEWARK LIBERTY INTL	40.683N	74.169W	7	12.8	16.9	94.3	74.4	91.2	73.0	88.3	71.9	77.5	88.4	76.2	85.6	74.6	129.6	82.1	73.3	123.9	80.8	25.1	22.0	19.4	4633	1270
TETERBORO AP	40.850N	74.061W	9	11.9	16.1	92.6	74.1	89.9	72.9	87.3	71.5	77.1	87.3	75.6	84.7	74.0	126.7	80.8	72.8	121.8	79.9	20.7	18.5	16.8	4915	1090
TRENTON MERCER AP	40.277N	74.816W	184	11.8	16.1	92.6	74.3	89.9	73.2	87.3	72.3	77.2	87.9	75.8	85.0	74.0	127.5	81.1	72.9	123.0	80.0	20.3	18.1	16.3	4916	1057
																									8 sites, 20 more on CD-ROM	
New Mexico																										
ALAMOGORDO-WHITE SANDS AP	32.840N	105.991W	4200	20.7	24.9	99.8	63.5	98.6	63.7	95.2	63.2	70.7	86.5	69.2	85.0	66.2	113.0	75.0	64.4	106.1	74.4	22.5	18.9	16.6	2897	1909
ALBUQUERQUE INTL	35.042N	106.616W	5310	18.3	21.9	95.5	59.9	93.3	59.7	91.0	59.5	65.2	81.4	64.3	80.6	61.4	99.4	68.0	60.1	94.6	68.9	28.3	24.7	20.6	3956	1438
CANNON AFB	34.383N	103.317W	4295	13.7	18.2	98.5	63.2	95.5	63.2	93.0	63.6	70.5	80.9	69.2	81.0	68.4	122.6	71.6	66.4	114.3	70.8	29.3	26.0	23.1	3718	1442
CLOVIS MUNICIPAL	34.433N	103.083W	4216	12.2	17.6	97.3	64.1	94.6	63.9	91.4	63.9	69.4	84.8	68.4	84.3	65.5	110.3	73.8	63.9	104.3	72.5	32.0	27.4	24.5	4053	1247
FOUR CORNERS REGIONAL	36.744N	108.229W	5495	7.8	12.3	95.9	59.6	93.3	59.1	91.0	58.9	64.6	81.4	63.6	81.2	61.1	98.7	67.1	58.9	91.4	67.4	25.2	21.9	18.8	5271	988
HOLLOMAN AFB	32.850N	106.100W	4158	18.7	22.1	99.8	62.7	97.5	62.5	95.2	62.3	68.6	84.6	67.8	84.0	65.3	109.4	71.1	63.7	103.1	71.7	24.8	20.5	17.9	3217	1838
ROSWELL INTL AIR CENTER	33.308N	104.508W	3649	17.7	21.6	101.1	64.4	98.5	64.7	96.2	64.6	70.7	86.6	69.6	85.7	67.1	114.2	74.1	65.9	109.4	73.6	26.6	22.7	18.9	3095	1976
WHITE SANDS	32.383N	106.483W	4081	18.4	22.5	99.0	63.7	96.5	63.9	94.2	63.8	69.8	87.4	68.9	86.1	65.9	111.2	72.1	64.6	106.4	72.3	18.7	16.2	13.3	2946	1811
																									19 sites, 26 more on CD-ROM	
New York																										
ALBANY INTL	42.743N	73.809W	312	-0.3	4.7	88.9	72.6	86.1	71.0	83.4	69.7	75.3	84.8	73.7	82.0	72.4	121.2	79.9	70.9	115.3	78.4	23.9	20.3	18.3	6473	639
AMBROSE LIGHT	40.460N	73.830W	0	13.7	17.9	84.0	N/A	80.9	N/A	78.4	N/A	N/A	N/A	N/A	N/A	N/A	N/A	N/A	N/A	N/A	N/A	43.1	37.8	33.9	4850	720
BUFFALO NIAGARA INTL	42.941N	78.736W	716	3.5	7.4	86.3	71.2	83.9	69.9	81.6	68.9	74.7	81.7	73.1	80.2	72.3	122.9	78.9	70.5	115.4	77.5	27.0	24.1	20.6	6460	580
CHAUTAUQUA COUNTY AP	42.150N	79.250W	1723	0.6	4.8	82.4	69.7	81.1	68.6	78.8	66.9	72.3	80.0	70.6	77.8	70.1	118.1	77.4	68.0	109.9	75.3	21.4	18.9	17.2	7185	304
DUTCHESS COUNTY AP	41.627N	73.884W	166	2.7	8.4	91.3	73.5	88.4	72.3	85.6	70.9	76.4	86.8	75.0	84.2	73.2	124.0	81.2	72.1	119.6	80.1	18.6	16.9	14.4	6003	725
ELMIRA CORNING REGIONAL	42.159N	76.892W	955	-0.1	4.8	89.6	71.5	86.4	69.9	83.7	68.7	74.3	84.5	72.7	82.3	71.5	120.3	79.4	69.8	113.7	77.7	20.3	18.0	16.0	6726	470
GREATER BINGHAMTON AP	42.207N	75.980W	1595	0.0	4.5	85.2	69.8	82.3	68.3	79.8	67.2	72.6	80.8	71.1	78.6	70.0	117.3	76.5	68.5	111.0	75.0	20.7	18.6	16.9	7033	403
GREATER ROCHESTER INTL	43.117N	77.677W	539	2.8	7.1	88.5	73.0	85.6	71.0	82.9	69.6	75.3	84.6	73.4	81.9	72.3	122.0	80.3	70.6	114.9	78.0	25.3	21.5	19.0	6466	571
GRIFFIS AIRFIELD	43.234N	75.412W	519	-5.7	0.7	87.9	72.0	85.1	70.2	82.5	68.7	74.6	84.1	72.8	81.5	71.6	118.8	79.7	69.9	112.3	77.7	23.0	19.5	17.3	6992	485
JOHN F KENNEDY INTL	40.639N	73.762W	11	14.1	18.0	89.9	73.0	86.6	71.7	83.9	70.9	76.6	84.1	75.4	81.9	74.5	128.9	80.2	73.3	123.7	78.7	27.5	24.8	21.9	4777	1014
LAGUARDIA AP	40.779N	73.880W	11	14.3	18.4	92.5	73.9	89.6	72.5	86.9	71.4	76.8	86.9	75.5	84.2	74.0	126.7	80.9	72.8	121.5	80.1	27.0	24.4	21.1	4493	1284
LONG ISLAND MACARTHUR AP	40.794N	73.102W	84	11.9	15.9	88.6	73.5	85.7	71.9	83.1	71.0	76.6	83.7	75.3	81.3	74.5	129.4	79.7	73.3	123.9	78.4	24.3	20.6	18.7	5199	839
NIAGARA FALLS INTL	43.108N	78.938W	585	2.8	6.9	87.8	72.4	85.2	71.0	82.5	69.5	75.2	83.7	73.6	81.5	72.5	123.0	79.7	71.2	117.5	78.3	26.5	23.6	20.3	6595	581
ONEIDA COUNTY AP	43.145N	75.384W	711	-4.8	1.2	87.1	72.4	84.2	70.6	81.8	69.0	75.0	83.1	73.2	80.7	72.5	123.4	79.0	70.6	115.7	77.4	20.8	18.7	17.1	7010	471
PLATTSBURGH INTL	44.650N	73.467W	234	-8.7	-2.7	86.8	71.0	83.0	69.5	80.3	68.2	73.9	82.2	72.2	79.9	71.2	115.9	78.5	69.6	109.8	76.8	20.6	18.3	16.3	7534	374
REPUBLIC AP	40.734N	73.417W	81	12.4	17.0	89.9	73.8	86.3	71.9	83.6	71.3	76.6	84.3	75.4	81.9	74.6	129.8	79.9	73.2	123.6	78.4	24.5	20.9	18.8	5039	911
STEWART INTL	41.500N	74.100W	491	3.5	9.1	90.2	72.2	87.0	71.3	84.1	69.8	75.8	84.9	74.1	82.7	73.0	124.9	80.2	71.9	120.1	78.8	24.7	20.9	18.9	5940	713
SYRACUSE HANCOCK INTL	43.111N	76.104W	413	-0.7	4.9	89.2	73.0	86.4	71.2	83.7	69.8	75.2	85.6	73.5	82.6	72.0	120.3	80.8	70.3	113.4	78.8	24.4	20.6	18.4	6495	625
WESTCHESTER COUNTY AP	41.067N	73.708W	379	9.2	13.5	89.6	73.4	86.4	71.8	83.8	70.5	76.2	84.8	74.6	82.2	73.4	125.8	79.4	72.4	121.7	78.4	22.9	19.1	17.0	5471	773
																									14 sites, 55 more on CD-ROM	
North Carolina																										
ALBERT J ELLIS AP	34.833N	77.617W	96	20.6	24.8	94.7	77.0	91.4	76.1	90.2	75.5	79.9	90.7	78.4	88.5	77.0	140.9	84.9	75.2	132.8	83.1	19.8	17.4	15.4	2950	1737
ASHEVILLE REGIONAL	35.432N	82.538W	2117	15.4	19.7	88.0	71.2	85.7	70.4	83.6	69.7	73.8	83.0	72.8	81.5	71.3	124.9	77.1	70.2	120.2	76.2	22.7	19.2	17.2	4076	857
CHARLOTTE DOUGLAS INTL	35.224N	80.955W	728	21.6	25.3	94.2	74.7	91.8	74.1	89.6	73.4	77.3	88.6	76.2	86.9	74.2	131.1	81.4	73.2	126.8	80.3	18.5	16.3	13.9	3041	1690
FAYETTEVILLE REGIONAL	34.991N	78.880W	186	22.9	26.7	96.3	75.9	93.4	74.9	91.2	74.4	78.7	89.6	77.8	88.2	75.7	135.5	81.9	75.0	132.4	81.3	20.4	17.9	15.9	2705	1984
HICKORY REGIONAL	35.743N	81.382W	1143	20.0	24.0	92.4	72.7	90.0	72.4	87.8	71.7	76.0	85.7	74.9	84.4	73.2	128.8	79.5	72.2	124.3	78.6	17.4	14.8	12.8	3454	1378
NEW RIVER MCAS	34.708N	77.440W	26	23.4	26.8	93.0	78.0	90.7	77.2	88.7	76.4	80.3	88.7	79.1	87.5	78.4	147.6	84.7	76.8	139.8	83.3	20.4	18.0	16.1	2536	1924
PIEDMONT TRIAD INTL	36.097N	79.943W	890	19.3	22.8	92.5	74.1	90.3	73.5	88.1	72.7	76.8	87.6	75.5	85.5	73.5	128.9	80.9	72.6	125.0	79.8	20.2	17.9	16.0	3533	1454
PITT-GREENVILLE AP	35.633N	77.383W	25	20.8	24.9	95.0	76.1	92.9	75.1	90.8	74.5	78.9	90.5	77.6	88.0	75.4	133.3	82.6	74.8	130.4	82.0	18.7	16.4	14.0	2994	1867
POPE AFB	35.174N	79.009W	218	21.1	25.0	97.1	76.3	94.6	75.7	91.8	74.8	79.9	88.9	78.5	87.8	77.6	144.6	82.9	76.5	139.1	82.2	19.0	16.7	14.5	2817	2034
RALEIGH-DURHAM INTL	35.892N	78.782W	416	20.4	24.2	95.0	75.5	92.5	75.0	90.1	74.3	78.2	89.8	77.3	88.2	75.2	134.2	82.7	74.2	129.6	81.4	18.9	16.7	14.7	3208	1685
SEYMOUR-JOHNSON AFB	35.344N	77.965W	109	22.7	26.5	96.6	76.2	93.7	75.7	91.3	75.1	80.1	88.3	78.9	87.1	78.4	148.1	82.2	77.1	141.6	81.6	19.3	16.9	14.9	2685	2013
SIMMONS AAF	35.133N	78.933W	244	22.4	26.2	96.7	75.7	94.0	75.2	91.4	74.5	78.9	89.7	77.8	88.1	76.3	138.6	82.4	75.2	133.4	81.5	18.2	15.6	12.9	2741	2034
SMITH REYNOLDS AP	36.134N	80.222W	970	20.2	24.4	92.2	73.7	90.2	73.0	88.1	72.4	76.5	86.9	75.4	85.2	73.3	128.3	80.1	72.5	124.7	79.4	17.8	15.3	12.8	3416	1469
WILMINGTON INTL	34.268N	77.900W	38	24.7	27.9	93.5	77.9	91.2	77.0	89.0	76.3	80.1	88.9	79.0	87.1	77.8	144.6	83.9	76.8	139.7	82.9	20.8	18.5	16.7	2364	2020
																									6 sites, 10 more on CD-ROM	
North Dakota																										
BISMARCK MUNICIPAL	46.783N	100.757W	1651	-17.5	-12.2	93.1	69.9	89.4	68.9	86.1	67.6	74.5	85.9	72.2	84.1	70.9	121.2	81.8	68.4	110.8	78.7	27.1	24.2	20.7	8452	529
GRAND FORKS AFB	47.967N	97.400W	913	-20.1	-15.5	89.6	72.2	86.1	70.2	83.3	68.5	76.5	83.7	73.7	82.0	74.4	133.0	80.3	71.8	121.6	78.3	28.1	25.1	22.1	9311	420
GRAND FORKS INTL	47.943N	97.184W	842	-21.4	-16.6	89.0	71.7	85.9	69.5	83.2	67.9	74.9	84.6	72.6	82.3	71.7	120.8	81.2	69.2	110.8	78.6	26.8	24.2	20.9	9363	418

(Go to CD-ROM to access additional station tables.)

Meaning of acronyms:
DB: Dry bulb temperature, °F *WB: Wet bulb temperature, °F* *Lat: Latitude, °* *Long: Longitude, °* *Elev: Elevation, ft*
MCWB: Mean coincident wet bulb temperature, °F *DP: Dew point temperature, °F* *HR: Humidity ratio, grains of moisture per lb of dry air* *WS: Wind speed, mph*
MCDB: Mean coincident dry bulb temperature, °F *HDD and CDD 65: Annual heating and cooling degree-days, base 65°F, °F-day*

Station	Lat	Long	Elev	Heating DB		Cooling DB/MCWB						Evaporation WB/MCDB				Dehumidification DP/HR/MCDB						Extreme Annual WS			Heat./Cool. Degree-Days	
						0.4%		1%		2%		0.4%		1%		0.4%			1%							
				99.6%	99%	DB	MCWB	DB	MCWB	DB	MCWB	WB	MCDB	WB	MCDB	DP	HR	MCDB	DP	HR	MCDB	1%	2.5%	5%	HDD	CDD 65
HECTOR INTL	46.925N	96.811W	900	-18.7	-13.9	90.0	72.3	87.0	70.3	84.3	68.7	75.4	85.3	73.4	83.4	72.3	123.7	82.3	69.9	113.7	80.1	28.1	25.3	23.0	8740	551
MINOT AFB	48.417N	101.350W	1667	-22.3	-17.3	90.5	68.9	87.0	68.1	83.7	66.3	73.2	84.2	70.9	81.6	70.1	117.6	78.8	67.6	107.8	76.7	29.4	26.3	23.4	9348	355
MINOT INTL	48.255N	101.273W	1665	-18.1	-13.2	90.5	69.3	86.9	68.2	83.7	66.2	73.5	84.0	71.1	81.9	70.2	118.4	79.9	67.6	107.9	77.6	27.9	24.9	21.9	8794	431
Ohio																										*13 sites, 21 more on CD-ROM*
AKRON-CANTON REGIONAL	40.917N	81.433W	1208	3.1	8.2	88.6	72.6	86.0	71.4	83.5	69.9	75.4	84.4	73.7	82.0	72.6	126.3	80.5	71.2	120.2	78.1	23.3	19.9	18.1	5993	703
CINCINNATI MUNICIPAL LUNKEN	39.103N	84.419W	490	8.2	13.8	92.7	75.1	90.1	74.3	87.8	73.4	78.1	88.0	76.8	86.1	75.3	134.9	82.8	74.0	129.1	81.4	20.4	18.2	16.4	4755	1123
CLEVELAND HOPKINS INTL	41.405N	81.853W	770	4.6	10.0	89.4	73.6	86.8	72.2	84.2	70.9	76.1	85.3	74.6	83.1	73.1	126.7	81.2	71.8	120.7	79.5	24.6	21.0	18.9	5801	786
FAIRFIELD COUNTY AP	39.756N	82.657W	869	2.3	9.4	90.5	73.9	88.3	73.1	85.9	71.7	77.0	86.9	75.4	84.2	73.5	128.7	81.5	72.5	124.3	80.4	20.0	17.7	15.9	5449	816
FINDLAY AP	41.014N	83.669W	800	1.1	6.9	90.3	73.5	87.8	72.2	85.1	70.6	76.5	86.3	74.7	83.5	73.2	127.2	82.4	71.9	121.5	80.4	25.1	21.7	19.3	5912	807
JMCOX DAYTON INTL	39.906N	84.219W	1000	2.3	8.5	90.3	73.8	87.9	72.8	85.5	71.3	76.5	86.3	75.1	84.1	73.4	128.8	82.0	72.2	123.5	80.5	24.8	21.4	19.0	5481	952
MANSFIELD LAHM REGIONAL	40.820N	82.518W	1295	1.5	7.0	88.0	72.8	85.6	71.5	83.2	70.1	75.5	84.4	74.0	82.1	72.9	128.0	80.4	71.4	121.6	78.7	24.2	20.7	18.7	6110	670
OHIO STATE UNIVERSITY AP	40.078N	83.078W	905	4.4	9.9	90.5	73.5	88.2	72.7	85.8	71.3	76.5	86.4	75.0	84.0	73.2	127.5	81.6	72.2	123.4	80.2	22.1	19.2	17.3	5450	928
PORT COLUMBUS INTL	39.991N	82.881W	810	5.5	11.0	91.3	73.7	89.0	72.7	86.6	71.5	76.7	87.1	75.3	84.7	73.5	128.6	81.3	72.3	123.2	80.3	23.1	19.4	17.3	5185	1055
RICKENBACKER INTL	39.817N	82.933W	744	6.8	12.0	92.7	74.3	90.4	73.3	88.2	72.3	79.7	86.1	77.5	85.8	78.5	152.3	84.1	75.1	135.4	80.9	23.5	19.6	17.4	5025	1137
TOLEDO EXPRESS AP	41.589N	83.801W	669	1.5	7.0	91.2	74.1	88.4	72.3	85.7	70.9	77.0	86.9	75.2	84.1	73.9	129.7	82.3	72.3	122.7	80.1	24.5	20.8	18.6	6050	808
WRIGHT-PATTERSON AFB	39.833N	84.050W	823	3.2	9.6	91.1	74.4	88.6	73.2	86.2	71.8	77.0	86.8	75.5	84.9	74.1	131.3	81.5	72.7	125.2	80.1	22.5	19.4	17.4	5363	928
YOUNGSTOWN-WARREN REGIONAL	41.254N	80.674W	1180	3.3	8.1	88.2	72.4	85.6	70.7	83.2	69.4	74.9	84.2	73.3	81.8	72.0	123.8	79.6	70.5	117.2	77.5	21.1	18.8	17.0	6159	582
Oklahoma																										*9 sites, 33 more on CD-ROM*
HENRY POST AAF	34.650N	98.400W	1189	15.7	20.2	103.5	72.5	100.3	72.8	97.4	72.6	77.3	91.1	76.3	90.2	73.7	131.3	82.1	72.6	126.3	81.3	25.9	22.9	20.2	3154	2270
LAWTON-FORT SILL REGIONAL	34.558N	98.417W	1069	16.2	20.0	104.5	72.7	101.8	72.8	99.2	73.3	77.9	92.3	76.8	91.3	73.5	129.8	82.9	72.8	126.8	82.3	26.2	23.3	20.2	3157	2375
RICHARD L JONES JR AP	36.039N	95.984W	638	14.3	18.5	101.6	75.3	99.0	76.3	96.1	76.2	79.4	93.6	78.4	92.3	75.4	136.4	85.3	74.7	133.1	84.8	19.8	17.8	16.1	3513	2084
STILLWATER REGIONAL	36.162N	97.089W	984	12.1	17.7	102.5	74.4	99.5	74.9	96.7	74.8	78.9	93.4	77.8	92.1	75.0	136.3	86.2	73.4	128.8	84.1	24.8	22.1	19.7	3610	2072
TINKER AFB	35.417N	97.383W	1291	13.8	18.5	100.4	73.5	97.4	73.6	94.6	73.9	78.1	90.2	77.0	89.3	74.9	137.5	83.4	73.4	130.3	82.1	26.5	24.0	20.9	3387	1997
TULSA INTL	36.199N	95.887W	650	13.5	18.3	100.4	75.2	97.6	75.6	94.8	75.5	79.2	92.4	78.2	91.1	75.5	136.6	85.6	74.4	131.7	84.8	24.7	21.7	19.5	3450	2108
VANCE AFB	36.333N	97.917W	1306	10.3	15.6	101.9	73.1	99.4	73.3	96.6	73.5	77.5	91.7	76.5	90.5	73.9	132.9	82.1	72.8	127.8	81.4	27.9	25.1	22.4	3920	1960
WILEY POST AP	35.534N	97.647W	1297	13.8	18.6	100.4	73.3	98.3	73.5	95.1	73.6	77.4	91.1	76.3	90.0	73.3	129.8	83.6	72.5	126.2	82.7	27.2	25.0	22.9	3473	2111
WILL ROGERS WORLD AP	35.389N	97.601W	1285	14.5	19.1	100.7	73.7	97.9	74.0	95.0	74.0	77.8	91.1	76.9	90.2	74.3	134.2	83.9	73.2	129.2	82.5	27.7	25.1	22.9	3420	2016
Oregon																										*9 sites, 29 more on CD-ROM*
AURORA STATE AP	45.249N	122.769W	196	25.2	28.1	91.4	67.1	88.1	66.6	83.9	65.1	69.8	86.1	68.1	84.3	63.7	88.9	75.1	62.6	85.6	73.4	18.2	15.9	12.9	4461	375
CORVALLIS MUNICIPAL	44.500N	123.283W	250	24.7	27.5	92.7	67.0	89.7	66.0	85.5	64.4	68.8	88.5	67.2	86.7	61.2	81.5	75.6	59.1	75.4	74.6	19.7	17.7	16.0	4306	393
EUGENE AP	44.128N	123.221W	353	22.9	26.9	91.8	66.7	88.0	65.7	84.3	64.5	68.9	87.5	67.2	84.7	62.1	84.6	74.6	60.4	79.4	72.5	19.5	17.3	15.7	4664	282
MCMINNVILLE MUNICIPAL	45.195N	123.134W	159	25.8	28.1	92.2	66.7	88.4	66.0	84.2	64.7	68.9	87.3	67.2	85.2	62.4	84.8	73.4	60.8	80.0	72.3	20.6	17.6	15.4	4654	301
PORTLAND INTL	45.596N	122.609W	19	25.0	29.0	91.2	67.5	87.1	66.4	83.4	65.2	69.5	86.8	68.0	84.2	63.2	86.8	75.2	61.8	82.4	73.3	23.7	19.7	17.4	4232	447
PORTLAND-HILLSBORO AP	45.541N	122.949W	204	22.7	26.5	91.7	67.8	88.0	66.9	83.8	65.3	70.2	87.6	68.1	84.9	63.7	89.0	76.5	61.6	82.5	73.3	18.6	16.5	13.9	4792	276
ROBERTS FIELD	44.256N	121.139W	3043	5.1	12.0	93.1	61.4	90.2	60.7	87.0	59.4	63.6	88.2	62.0	85.8	54.9	71.7	66.9	52.8	66.4	66.6	20.9	18.7	16.7	6541	238
ROGUE VALLEY INTL	42.381N	122.872W	1297	22.8	26.0	99.0	67.1	95.5	65.7	92.3	64.6	68.9	94.1	67.4	91.4	60.3	81.9	74.1	58.3	76.2	73.8	18.2	15.3	12.3	4262	864
SALEM MUNICIPAL	44.905N	123.001W	205	23.7	27.3	92.2	66.9	88.1	65.9	84.3	64.6	68.8	88.3	67.2	85.1	61.7	82.8	73.4	60.1	78.1	72.3	20.9	18.2	16.1	4503	341
Pennsylvania																										*14 sites, 18 more on CD-ROM*
ALLEGHENY COUNTY AP	40.355N	79.922W	1248	6.7	10.9	89.2	72.1	86.5	70.9	84.2	69.7	75.0	84.4	73.5	82.3	72.3	125.2	79.6	70.7	118.6	78.0	20.5	18.4	16.7	5389	838
ALTOONA-BLAIR COUNTY AP	40.296N	78.320W	1480	6.4	10.4	88.3	71.8	85.5	70.6	82.9	69.5	74.7	84.0	73.2	81.8	72.0	124.9	79.7	70.3	118.0	77.8	23.4	19.5	17.3	5881	619
BUTLER COUNTY AP	40.777N	79.950W	1247	3.1	8.8	88.2	72.0	84.5	70.4	82.3	69.0	74.7	83.7	73.1	81.7	72.2	124.6	80.1	70.4	117.0	77.7	18.2	15.9	13.3	6100	561
CAPITAL CITY AP	40.217N	76.851W	340	12.3	16.2	92.3	74.0	89.5	72.5	86.9	71.5	76.5	87.0	75.2	84.9	73.3	125.3	80.5	72.3	121.1	79.6	20.4	18.1	16.0	5009	1066
ERIE INTL	42.080N	80.183W	730	6.1	10.4	86.7	73.0	84.2	71.7	81.9	70.6	75.3	82.8	73.8	81.2	72.8	125.0	80.6	71.2	118.3	78.7	24.4	21.1	19.2	6035	668
HARRISBURG INTL	40.196N	76.772W	312	11.7	15.7	92.4	75.1	89.5	73.8	86.8	72.6	77.9	87.8	76.4	85.4	75.0	132.9	83.0	73.4	125.6	81.0	25.6	22.5	19.0	5030	1119
LEHIGH VALLEY INTL	40.651N	75.449W	390	8.7	13.0	91.0	73.7	88.3	72.5	85.7	71.3	76.6	86.5	75.2	83.9	73.6	127.0	81.0	72.4	121.7	79.8	22.4	19.0	17.0	5482	851
NORTHEAST PHILADELPHIA AP	40.082N	75.011W	100	13.4	17.7	93.2	74.8	90.5	73.6	88.1	72.5	77.8	88.5	76.3	86.1	74.9	131.1	82.4	73.2	123.9	80.5	22.1	19.0	17.3	4692	1194
PHILADELPHIA INTL	39.868N	75.231W	10	14.5	18.6	93.6	74.9	90.9	74.0	88.3	72.6	78.1	88.5	76.7	86.0	75.3	132.5	82.5	74.0	126.7	81.1	24.8	21.0	18.9	4425	1357
PITTSBURGH INTL	40.485N	80.214W	1203	5.6	10.4	89.2	72.0	86.6	70.7	84.3	69.6	75.1	84.6	73.5	82.1	72.1	124.3	79.7	70.8	118.5	78.0	22.8	19.4	17.4	5532	785
READING REGIONAL	40.367N	75.967W	344	9.9	14.2	92.6	74.4	89.7	73.2	86.9	72.0	77.1	88.0	75.6	85.0	73.5	126.2	81.6	72.6	122.4	80.6	22.8	19.3	17.5	5170	1000
WASHINGTON COUNTY AP	40.133N	80.283W	1185	2.7	8.8	88.3	71.2	85.5	69.9	82.7	68.6	74.2	83.3	72.6	81.8	71.7	122.5	80.2	70.0	115.5	77.9	19.0	16.8	14.5	5958	540
WILKES-BARRE SCRANTON INTL	41.334N	75.727W	930	4.7	9.4	89.1	71.7	86.2	70.2	83.6	68.9	74.6	84.2	73.1	81.9	71.8	121.5	78.7	70.3	115.4	77.3	20.2	18.0	16.1	6007	653
WILLOW GROVE NAS	40.200N	75.150W	361	12.5	16.6	91.9	73.9	89.4	72.6	86.8	71.5	77.1	87.5	75.5	84.9	73.9	127.9	82.5	72.5	121.9	80.8	19.4	16.9	14.7	4935	1034
Rhode Island																										*1 site, 10 more on CD-ROM*
T F GREEN AP	41.722N	71.433W	60	8.8	13.3	90.1	73.2	86.7	71.8	83.9	70.4	76.3	85.3	74.8	82.1	73.6	125.5	80.1	72.4	120.3	78.7	24.2	20.5	18.5	5481	765

(Go to CD-ROM to access additional station tables.)

(Go to CD-ROM to access additional station tables.)

Meaning of acronyms:
DB: Dry bulb temperature, °F *WB: Wet bulb temperature, °F*
MCWB: Mean coincident wet bulb temperature, °F
Lat: Latitude, °
DP: Dew point temperature, °F
MCDB: Mean coincident dry bulb temperature, °F
Long: Longitude, °
HR: Humidity ratio, grains of moisture per lb of dry air
Elev: Elevation, ft
WS: Wind speed, mph
HDD and CDD 65: Annual heating and cooling degree-days, base 65°F, °F-day

Station	Lat	Long	Elev	Heating DB		Cooling DB/MCWB						Evaporation WB/MCDB				Dehumidification DP/HR/MCDB						Extreme Annual WS			Heat./Cool. Degree-Days	
						0.4%		1%		2%		0.4%		1%		0.4%			1%							
				99.6%	99%	DB / MCWB		DB / MCWB		DB / MCWB		WB / MCDB		WB / MCDB		DP / HR / MCDB			DP / HR / MCDB			1%	2.5%	5%	HDD / CDD 65	
South Carolina																									*6 sites, 13 more on CD-ROM*	
CHARLESTON INTL	32.899N	80.040W	40	27.5	30.9	94.3	78.0	92.2	77.5	90.3	76.9	80.7	89.1	79.8	87.9	78.6	148.8	84.4	77.6	143.7	83.5	20.5	18.3	16.5	1845	2379
COLUMBIA METROPOLITAN	33.942N	81.118W	225	23.4	27.0	97.1	75.4	94.6	74.8	92.5	74.5	78.5	89.7	77.6	88.5	75.8	136.2	82.3	74.9	131.7	81.4	19.5	16.9	14.8	2432	2202
FLORENCE REGIONAL	34.185N	79.724W	146	24.1	27.3	96.1	76.6	93.5	75.9	91.4	75.4	79.3	90.6	78.3	88.8	76.5	138.8	83.5	75.4	133.8	82.3	19.4	17.6	15.6	2396	2114
FOLLY ISLAND	32.680N	79.890W	10	31.6	35.1	87.5	77.9	86.2	78.0	85.1	77.7	80.5	85.0	79.7	84.3	79.3	151.9	84.3	78.2	146.6	83.3	33.0	26.2	23.0	1878	2157
GREENVILLE-SPARTANBURG INTL	34.884N	82.221W	943	21.9	25.6	94.4	73.7	91.8	73.4	89.5	72.7	77.0	87.8	75.8	85.9	74.0	131.3	80.3	73.0	127.0	79.5	19.2	17.1	15.4	3016	1642
SHAW AFB	33.967N	80.467W	241	23.7	27.2	96.0	75.7	93.4	75.4	91.2	75.0	79.2	89.9	78.1	88.2	76.5	139.5	83.3	75.3	134.0	82.0	19.6	17.4	15.4	2435	2066
South Dakota																									*3 sites, 21 more on CD-ROM*	
ELLSWORTH AFB	44.150N	103.100W	3278	-8.2	-2.8	95.2	66.4	91.4	65.7	88.2	65.1	71.2	85.8	69.4	83.9	66.6	110.6	77.5	64.5	102.7	75.8	35.4	30.0	25.9	7028	678
RAPID CITY REGIONAL	44.043N	103.054W	3160	-8.8	-3.4	96.7	66.0	92.7	65.7	89.0	64.9	71.1	85.5	69.4	84.4	66.7	110.8	78.1	64.7	103.1	75.8	35.2	30.6	26.2	7069	659
SIOUX FALLS REGIONAL	43.578N	96.754W	1428	-11.3	-6.5	91.5	73.7	88.4	72.9	85.6	71.3	77.4	86.7	75.5	84.9	74.7	137.1	83.7	72.7	127.7	81.7	27.3	24.5	21.1	7510	739
Tennessee																									*7 sites, 6 more on CD-ROM*	
CHATTANOOGA AP	35.031N	85.201W	671	19.6	23.7	95.0	74.5	92.6	74.2	90.4	73.6	77.7	88.8	76.8	87.3	74.9	133.9	81.5	73.8	129.3	80.7	17.9	16.0	13.6	3093	1790
MCGHEE TYSON AP	35.818N	83.986W	962	17.1	21.6	92.7	73.9	90.4	73.5	88.3	72.9	77.1	87.5	76.0	85.8	74.0	131.5	81.4	73.0	127.1	80.4	20.6	17.8	15.3	3532	1525
MCKELLAR-SIPES REGIONAL	35.593N	88.917W	433	15.7	19.9	95.1	76.5	92.8	76.5	90.8	76.0	79.9	90.3	78.7	88.8	77.0	142.8	85.8	75.7	136.5	84.3	19.7	17.8	15.9	3436	1739
MEMPHIS INTL	35.056N	89.987W	254	19.5	23.8	96.6	76.9	94.4	76.4	92.5	76.0	79.9	91.5	78.8	90.0	76.7	140.6	85.8	75.6	135.3	85.0	20.5	18.4	16.7	2884	2266
MILLINGTON MUNICIPAL	35.350N	89.867W	320	18.6	23.1	99.2	80.3	96.9	78.7	93.5	77.4	82.9	95.1	81.2	92.4	79.4	154.6	89.3	78.7	150.9	88.6	18.2	16.1	13.6	3065	2125
NASHVILLE INTL	36.119N	86.689W	600	15.4	19.9	94.6	74.8	92.3	74.6	90.2	73.9	78.1	88.9	77.0	87.7	75.1	134.5	82.9	73.9	129.3	81.8	19.0	17.0	15.3	3491	1736
TRI-CITIES REGIONAL	36.473N	82.404W	1500	13.5	17.9	90.2	71.8	88.0	71.3	86.0	70.8	75.0	84.9	73.9	83.6	72.1	125.5	79.0	71.0	121.0	77.9	18.9	16.5	13.6	4177	1036
Texas																									*51 sites, 101 more on CD-ROM*	
ABILENE REGIONAL	32.411N	99.682W	1790	20.1	24.6	100.3	70.4	98.1	70.5	95.9	70.7	75.5	89.1	74.6	88.2	72.1	127.0	79.9	71.1	122.4	79.3	26.3	23.9	20.8	2444	2488
AL MANGHAM JR REGIONAL	31.578N	94.709W	355	25.0	27.6	99.1	75.7	96.8	75.8	93.2	75.6	79.0	90.1	78.3	89.5	76.5	140.1	82.3	75.2	134.1	81.7	18.5	16.3	14.0	2144	2460
AMARILLO RICK HUSBAND INTL	35.230N	101.704W	3604	10.1	15.8	98.6	65.4	95.8	65.8	93.2	65.8	71.2	86.4	70.1	85.6	67.2	114.3	75.2	66.0	109.6	74.3	30.1	26.7	24.4	4043	1471
ANGELINA COUNTY AP	31.236N	94.754W	288	26.9	29.7	99.0	76.1	96.5	76.4	94.3	76.3	79.9	90.4	79.1	89.4	77.3	143.8	82.8	76.7	140.8	82.5	17.8	16.1	14.2	1831	2709
AUSTIN-BERGSTROM INTL	30.183N	97.680W	480	26.7	30.2	100.2	74.1	98.2	74.4	96.2	74.5	78.5	88.9	78.0	88.3	76.4	140.0	81.1	75.5	135.9	80.5	20.9	18.8	17.0	1634	3005
BROWNSVILLE INTL	25.914N	97.423W	24	38.7	42.5	95.7	77.8	94.5	77.8	93.3	77.8	80.9	88.0	80.3	87.6	79.3	152.3	83.0	78.6	148.6	82.7	26.3	23.9	20.8	509	4073
CORPUS CHRISTI INTL	27.774N	97.512W	44	34.6	38.3	96.8	77.6	95.3	77.7	93.7	77.6	81.0	89.5	80.3	88.6	79.1	151.2	83.3	78.4	147.6	83.0	27.4	25.0	23.1	826	3625
CORPUS CHRISTI NAS	27.683N	97.283W	18	37.2	41.5	92.8	79.3	91.6	79.4	90.8	79.3	82.4	88.0	81.6	87.4	81.2	162.1	84.7	80.1	156.2	84.4	26.2	23.9	20.9	705	3752
DALLAS EXECUTIVE	32.681N	96.868W	658	24.9	28.0	101.7	74.1	99.4	74.6	97.2	74.4	78.1	91.7	77.3	90.8	74.8	133.8	82.3	73.5	127.5	81.4	22.7	19.4	17.5	2112	2854
DALLAS FORT WORTH INTL	32.898N	97.019W	560	23.3	27.6	101.4	74.2	99.1	74.5	96.9	74.6	78.5	91.4	77.7	90.7	75.4	135.7	83.7	74.3	131.0	82.8	26.1	23.7	20.6	2161	2878
DALLAS HENSLEY FIELD NAS	32.733N	96.967W	492	21.5	27.2	99.6	75.5	97.5	75.4	95.3	75.0	79.0	92.0	77.9	91.2	75.4	135.5	85.6	74.2	130.1	84.2	20.6	18.7	17.0	2171	2723
DALLAS LOVE FIELD	32.852N	96.856W	440	24.7	28.7	101.5	74.7	99.3	75.2	97.2	74.9	79.1	92.6	78.0	91.3	75.4	135.1	84.4	74.5	131.2	83.6	23.0	20.3	18.7	2031	3024
DEL RIO INTL	29.378N	100.927W	999	31.5	34.6	102.1	71.9	100.1	72.1	98.3	72.2	77.6	89.4	76.9	88.7	74.9	135.7	81.4	73.8	130.5	81.0	20.8	18.6	16.9	1269	3534
DRAUGHON-MILLER CENTRAL TEXAS	31.150N	97.417W	682	25.1	28.0	100.1	74.0	98.9	74.0	96.8	74.0	77.9	90.6	77.2	89.9	74.8	133.9	81.7	73.4	127.3	80.9	25.1	22.5	20.1	1978	2767
DYESS AFB ABILENE	32.417N	99.850W	1788	19.1	23.4	102.4	72.0	100.1	71.8	98.0	71.7	76.8	91.5	75.6	90.5	73.2	131.7	81.0	72.1	127.1	80.4	26.9	24.4	21.1	2509	2644
EASTERWOOD FIELD	30.589N	96.365W	305	28.4	31.7	100.0	75.4	98.0	75.6	95.9	75.5	79.7	90.6	78.6	88.9	77.2	143.2	83.1	76.3	139.0	82.2	20.5	18.5	16.8	1568	3100
EL PASO INTL	31.811N	106.376W	3918	25.1	28.4	101.1	64.1	98.8	63.7	96.6	63.6	69.9	86.3	69.1	85.4	66.3	112.3	73.2	65.1	107.4	73.4	27.2	23.5	19.5	2300	2521
FORT WORTH ALLIANCE AP	32.973N	97.318W	685	21.2	25.4	102.3	73.9	100.0	74.4	97.7	74.2	78.2	92.4	77.3	91.4	74.6	133.0	83.5	73.3	127.1	82.3	23.4	20.7	18.8	2397	2716
FORT WORTH NAS	32.767N	97.450W	608	24.1	28.1	102.5	73.1	100.2	73.6	98.0	73.7	78.2	92.2	77.3	91.2	74.6	132.6	83.3	73.4	127.0	82.5	24.7	21.7	19.5	2092	2978
FT WORTH MEACHAM INTL	32.819N	97.361W	687	22.5	26.8	101.5	73.9	99.3	74.5	97.1	74.3	78.4	91.6	77.5	90.8	75.1	135.3	83.5	74.0	130.1	82.4	23.3	20.3	18.6	2241	2778
GALVESTON SCHOLES INTL	29.273N	94.859W	5	36.5	39.6	92.0	79.1	90.9	79.2	90.0	79.1	81.9	87.7	81.2	87.1	80.9	160.3	84.5	79.4	152.5	84.5	25.5	22.7	20.1	990	3344
GEORGE BUSH INTERCONTINENTAL	29.980N	95.360W	95	31.1	34.1	97.5	76.4	95.5	76.5	93.8	76.5	80.1	88.8	79.4	88.1	78.0	146.1	82.8	77.3	142.5	82.4	20.0	18.1	16.4	1340	3123
GEORGETOWN MUNICIPAL	30.679N	97.679W	787	26.5	28.3	99.0	72.8	96.9	72.9	94.5	72.9	76.9	88.5	76.1	87.7	73.4	127.8	79.8	73.0	125.9	79.7	21.0	18.8	17.1	1948	2688
HOOKS MEMORIAL	30.068N	95.556W	152	29.7	32.9	98.7	75.7	96.2	76.0	93.5	76.2	80.2	88.1	79.4	87.6	78.8	150.4	82.5	77.4	143.1	82.1	17.7	15.9	13.6	1458	3016
HOUSTON ELLINGTON AP	29.617N	95.167W	32	34.1	37.0	96.8	78.1	94.9	78.5	93.0	78.5	82.1	88.8	81.3	88.0	81.1	161.8	84.1	79.4	152.9	83.3	19.8	18.1	16.4	1167	3197
JACK BROOKS REGIONAL	29.951N	94.021W	16	31.6	35.0	95.0	77.7	93.2	77.9	91.7	77.9	81.5	88.9	80.5	87.9	79.4	152.9	84.7	78.7	149.0	83.9	21.5	19.2	17.6	1328	2948
KILLEEN MUNICIPAL	31.083N	97.683W	841	26.3	28.9	100.0	74.0	98.9	74.1	96.8	74.1	77.5	91.8	76.9	91.0	73.4	127.9	82.3	72.9	126.1	82.1	22.1	19.8	18.2	1889	2861
LACKLAND AFB	29.383N	98.583W	690	29.7	33.1	100.4	74.1	99.0	74.1	96.9	74.1	80.0	88.1	78.8	87.0	78.5	151.8	82.1	77.0	144.5	81.6	20.8	18.7	16.9	1359	3278
LAREDO INTL	27.544N	99.463W	494	36.2	39.2	104.7	74.5	102.4	74.3	100.4	74.2	79.4	91.5	78.6	90.6	77.1	143.6	82.7	75.7	136.9	82.6	24.4	21.2	19.8	783	4454
LAUGHLIN AFB	29.367N	100.783W	1082	30.7	34.3	104.3	72.0	102.0	72.5	99.9	72.6	78.9	90.0	77.5	89.9	76.5	143.7	83.3	74.6	134.7	81.9	23.9	20.5	18.5	1179	3710
LONGVIEW EAST TEXAS REGIONAL	32.385N	94.712W	365	25.5	28.1	100.2	74.9	97.9	75.2	95.2	75.3	78.8	90.4	78.1	89.6	75.9	137.0	82.2	75.2	133.9	81.8	20.3	18.1	16.3	2121	2628
LUBBOCK INTL	33.666N	101.823W	3254	15.9	20.2	99.4	66.2	97.1	66.9	94.7	66.9	72.6	87.8	71.4	86.8	68.6	118.7	76.8	67.5	114.2	75.8	29.0	26.0	23.5	3256	1915
MCALLEN INTL	26.176N	98.240W	100	38.6	42.1	100.4	75.9	99.0	76.4	97.4	76.3	80.3	90.7	79.6	89.1	78.4	148.1	82.2	77.5	143.4	82.0	24.9	22.8	20.5	532	4502
MCGREGOR EXECUTIVE	31.485N	97.316W	592	24.8	27.7	101.7	74.4	99.5	74.6	97.4	74.5	78.4	91.9	77.7	91.6	75.1	134.7	83.1	73.4	127.2	82.2	23.6	20.6	18.7	2087	2794
MCKINNEY NATL	33.190N	96.591W	586	20.8	25.0	101.0	74.3	99.1	75.0	96.9	74.9	78.4	91.7	77.7	90.9	75.2	134.9	82.8	74.1	130.2	82.0	23.7	20.3	18.3	2511	2546
MIDLAND INTL	31.948N	102.209W	2862	20.5	24.4	101.1	66.7	98.6	67.1	96.5	67.3	73.0	87.9	72.0	86.9	69.4	120.4	76.0	68.4	116.0	75.9	26.9	24.2	20.9	2554	2392
NEW BRAUNFELS MUNICIPAL	29.709N	98.046W	645	28.3	31.4	100.3	73.7	98.6	73.9	96.6	73.9	78.1	88.9	77.4	88.0	75.5	136.9	80.3	75.0	134.6	80.1	23.7	20.5	18.6	1510	3061
PORT ARANSAS	27.830N	97.050W	0	37.5	41.6	86.2	78.0	85.4	78.2	85.0	78.1	80.5	83.8	80.2	83.7	79.5	152.9	83.1	79.0	150.4	82.9	38.5	32.3	26.8	795	3088

(Go to CD-ROM to access additional station tables.)

Meaning of acronyms:
DB: Dry bulb temperature, °F *WB: Wet bulb temperature, °F*
MCWB: Mean coincident wet bulb temperature, °F
Lat: Latitude, °
DP: Dew point temperature, °F
MCDB: Mean coincident dry bulb temperature, °F
Long: Longitude, °
HR: Humidity ratio, grains of moisture per lb of dry air
HDD and CDD 65: Annual heating and cooling degree-days, base 65°F, °F-day
Elev: Elevation, ft
WS: Wind speed, mph

Station	Lat	Long	Elev	Heating DB		Cooling DB/MCWB						Evaporation WB/MCDB				Dehumidification DP/HR/MCDB						Extreme Annual WS			Heat./Cool. Degree-Days	
						0.4%		1%		2%		0.4%		1%		0.4%			1%							
				99.6%	99%	DB	MCWB	DB	MCWB	DB	MCWB	WB	MCDB	WB	MCDB	DP	HR	MCDB	DP	HR	MCDB	1%	2.5%	5%	HDD	CDD 65
RANDOLPH AFB	29.533N	98.262W	728	28.5	31.9	100.2	73.7	98.6	73.7	96.5	73.8	78.4	88.2	77.7	87.5	76.4	141.4	80.6	75.4	136.6	80.1	21.5	19.2	17.6	1455	3103
REESE AFB LUBBOCK	33.600N	102.050W	3337	14.7	19.4	101.0	67.0	97.8	67.3	95.1	67.2	73.2	87.2	72.0	86.7	69.5	122.9	78.7	67.9	116.4	77.6	27.4	24.1	20.6	3182	1831
ROBERT GRAY AFF	31.067N	97.833W	1015	25.7	29.7	100.4	73.0	99.0	73.2	96.8	73.3	77.7	89.9	76.9	88.9	75.0	136.3	81.0	73.6	130.0	80.0	23.9	20.7	18.8	1802	2906
SABINE PASS	29.670N	94.050W	3	32.3	36.2	89.0	77.4	87.5	77.6	86.6	77.6	80.6	85.4	80.1	85.1	79.4	152.8	83.9	78.4	147.6	83.7	34.7	27.1	23.6	1428	2660
SAN ANGELO REGIONAL	31.352N	100.495W	1916	22.2	26.0	101.7	70.0	99.5	69.8	97.3	69.8	75.1	89.1	74.2	88.2	71.7	125.7	79.4	70.6	121.1	78.8	24.6	21.3	19.3	2185	2642
SAN ANTONIO INTL	29.544N	98.484W	789	29.9	33.0	99.3	73.5	97.6	73.5	95.8	73.8	78.1	88.0	77.4	87.1	76.0	139.8	80.2	75.2	136.3	80.0	20.6	18.7	16.9	1380	3222
SAN MARCOS REGIONAL	29.891N	97.864W	597	27.6	30.2	99.8	74.0	98.8	74.1	96.7	74.1	78.3	90.3	77.6	89.9	75.2	135.0	83.0	73.9	129.3	82.3	24.6	21.3	19.2	1622	3032
STINSON MUNICIPAL	29.339N	98.472W	571	30.6	33.8	101.1	73.6	99.3	73.9	97.3	73.6	78.7	88.9	78.0	88.2	76.3	140.3	81.7	75.3	135.6	80.8	18.9	17.2	15.8	1274	3399
VALLEY INTL	26.228N	97.654W	34	37.1	41.1	98.8	77.3	97.2	77.4	95.8	77.4	81.0	89.4	80.3	88.8	79.3	152.4	82.8	78.8	149.8	82.7	27.6	24.9	22.9	578	4104
VICTORIA REGIONAL	28.861N	96.930W	115	31.4	34.5	97.9	76.5	95.9	76.6	94.1	76.6	80.3	88.0	79.8	87.5	78.7	149.6	82.3	78.0	146.1	82.0	24.3	20.9	19.1	1164	3247
WACO REGIONAL	31.619N	97.228W	500	24.6	28.2	101.3	74.3	99.2	74.7	97.2	74.8	78.5	91.1	77.9	90.4	75.6	136.5	82.0	74.8	132.9	81.6	24.2	20.9	19.1	2008	2904
WICHITA FALL REGIONAL	33.979N	98.493W	1017	18.6	22.7	103.8	72.6	101.2	72.7	98.6	72.9	77.6	91.8	76.6	90.9	73.8	130.7	82.8	72.7	126.0	81.8	27.1	24.5	21.7	2793	2546
WILLIAM P HOBBY AP	29.638N	95.282W	44	33.6	36.7	96.0	77.1	94.1	77.1	92.6	77.0	80.4	89.0	79.7	88.2	78.5	148.2	83.3	77.5	143.1	82.8	20.6	18.6	16.9	1139	3222
Utah																										*5 sites, 10 more on CD-ROM*
HILL AFB	41.117N	111.967W	4789	8.7	12.2	93.9	60.9	91.3	60.2	89.2	59.8	64.5	84.7	63.3	84.2	58.1	86.3	71.6	55.3	77.9	72.5	23.7	20.3	18.5	5977	953
LOGAN-CACHE AP	41.787N	111.853W	4454	-5.8	0.3	94.8	61.6	92.2	61.0	89.9	60.4	65.1	85.2	63.9	84.3	59.5	89.6	69.9	56.8	81.4	69.5	20.0	16.7	13.2	7196	507
PROVO MUNICIPAL	40.219N	111.723W	4497	7.5	11.9	94.6	62.4	91.2	62.1	89.7	61.8	66.3	87.0	65.0	85.2	59.4	89.4	75.0	57.1	82.3	74.7	24.1	20.1	17.5	5972	778
SALT LAKE CITY INTL	40.778N	111.969W	4225	9.9	14.4	98.0	62.5	95.4	61.9	92.9	61.4	66.2	87.3	65.1	86.3	60.3	91.6	72.2	57.9	84.0	72.8	24.9	20.9	18.4	5466	1262
ST GEORGE MUNICIPAL	37.100N	113.600W	2936	25.2	27.8	106.2	66.2	103.4	65.2	100.4	64.3	69.1	93.5	68.1	92.7	63.2	96.9	75.8	61.0	89.6	77.5	26.7	23.1	19.4	2974	2721
Vermont																										*1 site, 6 more on CD-ROM*
BURLINGTON INTL	44.468N	73.150W	330	-7.3	-1.8	88.3	71.3	85.4	69.8	82.5	68.4	74.3	83.7	72.6	81.3	71.3	116.9	78.6	69.6	110.1	77.2	23.2	20.0	18.2	7227	525
Virginia																										*18 sites, 35 more on CD-ROM*
DANVILLE REGIONAL	36.573N	79.336W	571	18.3	21.7	93.9	74.5	91.3	74.1	89.6	73.4	77.7	89.1	76.5	87.1	74.5	131.7	82.3	73.2	126.2	80.9	18.6	16.4	14.0	3649	1440
DAVISON AAF	38.717N	77.183W	73	15.1	19.2	96.0	75.7	93.1	74.7	90.5	73.7	79.1	90.5	77.5	88.2	75.8	135.4	84.3	74.5	129.4	82.5	21.4	18.1	15.0	4229	1357
DINWIDDIE COUNTY	37.183N	77.500W	193	16.3	19.4	98.0	77.0	94.8	76.1	91.5	74.8	80.5	91.6	79.0	90.5	77.4	143.4	85.9	75.3	133.8	83.7	17.9	15.6	12.8	3682	1610
LANGLEY AFB	37.083N	76.360W	10	20.8	24.9	92.8	76.2	90.5	75.5	88.3	74.7	79.4	86.9	78.2	85.8	77.4	142.6	82.1	76.1	136.2	81.5	23.9	20.3	18.4	3415	1584
LESSBURG EXECUTIVE	39.078N	77.558W	389	14.2	18.2	95.0	76.3	92.2	75.0	90.3	74.2	79.1	90.4	77.8	88.3	75.5	135.4	82.9	74.8	132.4	82.3	22.5	18.8	16.2	4431	1347
LYNCHBURG REGIONAL	37.321N	79.207W	940	15.8	19.7	92.1	73.8	89.6	73.0	87.1	72.0	76.4	86.9	75.2	85.1	73.4	128.6	80.5	72.3	123.9	79.3	17.5	15.4	12.9	4192	1112
MANSAS REGIONAL	38.721N	77.515W	192	11.7	16.1	93.0	74.2	90.7	73.9	88.4	72.9	77.3	88.3	75.9	86.6	73.4	125.1	82.0	72.6	121.6	81.3	21.4	18.6	16.2	4826	1075
NEWPORT NEWS WILLIAMSBURG	37.132N	76.493W	42	20.4	24.3	94.5	77.1	92.0	76.1	89.9	75.2	79.4	90.3	78.2	88.2	76.7	139.4	84.0	75.3	133.0	82.8	20.3	18.4	16.8	3408	1638
NORFOLK INTL	36.903N	76.192W	30	22.9	26.6	93.7	76.7	91.3	76.0	88.9	75.0	79.1	88.5	78.0	87.0	76.7	139.1	83.0	75.5	133.8	81.7	24.4	20.7	18.7	3165	1715
NORFOLK NAS	36.937N	76.289W	17	24.0	27.6	94.4	77.1	91.9	76.3	89.9	75.6	79.9	89.7	78.5	87.9	77.2	141.7	84.1	75.8	134.8	83.0	25.3	21.8	19.1	2972	1889
OCEANA NAS	36.817N	76.033W	23	21.9	25.9	92.9	77.3	90.4	76.3	88.2	75.4	79.4	88.9	78.2	86.8	76.9	140.3	83.9	75.5	133.6	82.3	24.7	20.9	18.9	3262	1594
QUANTICO MCAF	38.504N	77.305W	10	17.0	20.5	92.6	76.3	90.2	75.6	87.9	74.6	79.5	88.9	77.9	87.1	76.8	139.5	85.2	75.1	131.9	83.2	20.1	17.6	15.7	4129	1376
RICHMOND INTL	37.505N	77.320W	164	18.5	22.1	95.1	75.7	92.7	75.1	90.1	74.0	78.4	89.3	77.4	87.8	75.7	135.2	82.8	74.5	129.8	81.5	20.9	18.7	16.7	3634	1564
ROANOKE-BLACKSBURG REGIONAL	37.317N	79.974W	1175	16.8	20.6	92.2	72.7	89.7	71.9	87.3	71.1	75.3	86.4	74.3	84.9	72.2	124.4	79.4	71.1	119.9	78.5	23.0	19.2	16.9	3961	1239
RONALD REAGAN WASHINGTON NATL	38.848N	77.034W	10	17.9	21.6	94.7	75.5	92.0	74.7	89.4	73.5	78.4	89.1	77.3	87.4	75.7	134.4	83.2	74.4	128.7	82.0	23.3	20.0	18.0	3901	1587
SHENANDOAH VALLEY REGIONAL	38.264N	78.896W	1201	11.8	16.4	93.2	73.8	90.9	73.4	88.7	72.7	78.2	87.1	76.7	85.8	75.3	138.7	82.4	73.5	130.1	80.3	17.6	15.3	12.6	4467	1129
VIRGINIA TECH MONTGOMERY EXEC	37.208N	80.408W	2132	11.0	15.9	89.7	72.8	86.5	71.2	83.9	70.5	75.9	83.6	74.4	81.9	73.3	133.9	78.7	72.3	129.7	78.0	20.1	17.7	15.4	4798	787
WASHINGTON DULLES INTL	38.941N	77.464W	290	13.3	17.3	93.5	74.6	90.9	73.7	88.3	72.7	77.5	88.8	76.3	86.4	74.3	129.7	81.7	73.2	124.8	80.5	21.4	18.7	16.7	4591	1188
Washington																										*20 sites, 28 more on CD-ROM*
ARLINGTON MUNICIPAL	48.161N	122.159W	137	19.5	24.5	82.0	66.0	79.3	64.4	75.3	63.0	67.4	80.3	65.6	77.4	62.7	85.5	74.0	60.9	80.2	71.3	20.8	18.0	15.6	5401	62
BELLINGHAM INTL	48.794N	122.537W	149	19.2	23.7	79.4	65.3	76.2	63.9	73.2	62.2	66.7	77.6	64.9	74.6	62.3	84.4	71.8	60.8	79.9	69.3	25.4	20.7	18.3	5339	56
BREMERTON NATL	47.483N	122.767W	444	22.6	26.6	85.6	65.1	81.7	63.5	78.8	62.2	66.5	82.6	64.8	79.6	60.8	80.8	71.9	57.9	72.7	68.7	19.4	17.0	15.0	5641	98
FAIRCHILD AFB	47.633N	117.650W	2461	5.2	11.2	91.8	62.0	89.0	61.3	85.6	60.5	64.9	84.5	63.3	83.0	59.0	81.7	68.0	56.6	74.7	66.2	24.4	20.5	18.2	6792	401
FELTS FIELD	47.683N	117.321W	1953	8.5	14.2	94.4	64.9	91.0	63.7	87.9	62.7	67.4	89.3	65.5	86.6	60.2	83.6	71.8	57.5	75.8	71.4	20.0	17.5	15.1	6122	464
GRAY AFF	47.083N	122.583W	300	20.0	24.5	87.5	65.5	83.1	64.2	79.6	62.8	67.2	83.5	65.5	80.1	61.5	82.6	68.8	60.6	79.8	68.6	18.5	16.0	13.3	5164	153
KING COUNTY INTL AP	47.530N	122.301W	18	25.8	29.4	85.6	65.3	81.9	64.0	79.0	62.7	66.8	82.7	65.2	79.2	61.2	80.8	69.5	59.6	76.2	69.5	18.4	16.3	13.9	4354	268
MCCHORD AFB	47.150N	122.483W	322	20.5	24.5	86.3	65.2	82.4	63.7	79.2	62.5	66.8	82.6	65.2	79.7	61.3	82.1	69.8	59.6	77.2	68.4	20.3	17.8	15.6	5161	134
OLYMPIA REGIONAL	46.973N	122.903W	188	20.4	24.3	87.3	66.0	83.3	64.7	79.7	63.4	67.9	84.5	66.0	80.9	61.7	82.7	71.3	60.2	78.4	69.7	18.8	16.5	14.3	5377	110
PAINE FIELD	47.908N	122.280W	606	25.0	28.9	80.1	63.5	76.3	62.2	73.1	61.0	65.3	76.9	63.5	73.8	61.0	81.8	68.5	59.1	76.4	67.6	24.5	20.2	17.5	5192	81
PEARSON FIELD	45.621N	122.657W	30	24.1	27.2	90.7	66.4	87.2	65.8	83.0	64.6	69.1	86.0	67.4	83.8	63.0	86.1	74.2	61.2	80.8	72.9	16.4	13.3	11.8	4416	382
SANDERSON FIELD	47.238N	123.141W	271	22.3	25.8	87.4	65.2	82.9	64.3	79.0	62.7	67.2	83.5	65.4	80.4	61.2	81.5	69.7	59.6	77.0	68.6	20.4	18.3	16.4	5491	100
SEATTLE-TACOMA INTL	47.444N	122.314W	370	25.4	29.5	85.3	65.1	81.6	63.8	78.2	62.7	66.9	82.4	65.1	78.9	61.1	81.6	70.2	59.7	77.4	68.6	20.4	18.2	16.3	4705	196
SOUTHWEST WASHINGTON REGIONAL	46.117N	122.894W	20	22.9	26.8	87.9	67.2	82.3	65.5	79.4	63.9	68.7	83.9	66.8	81.0	63.0	86.1	75.1	61.2	80.7	72.3	17.2	14.9	12.7	4832	182
SPOKANE INTL	47.622N	117.528W	2353	5.1	11.2	92.9	62.8	89.6	61.8	86.2	60.6	65.2	86.9	63.6	84.8	58.0	78.3	68.5	55.9	72.6	68.0	25.6	21.9	19.0	6627	461
TACOMA NARROWS AP	47.268N	122.576W	292	27.3	30.9	83.6	64.3	80.3	62.9	76.7	61.7	66.0	80.7	64.2	77.1	60.9	80.7	68.5	59.2	75.8	67.2	19.5	17.3	15.4	4792	145
TRI-CITIES AP	46.267N	119.117W	407	10.2	16.4	99.2	69.4	96.2	67.8	92.6	66.7	71.7	93.7	69.7	91.6	64.1	91.0	79.4	62.5	85.9	77.4	24.8	20.8	18.2	4945	815

(Go to CD-ROM to access additional station tables.)

(Go to CD-ROM to access additional station tables.)

Meaning of acronyms:
DB: Dry bulb temperature, °F — *WB: Wet bulb temperature, °F*
MCWB: Mean coincident wet bulb temperature, °F
Lat: Latitude, °
DP: Dew point temperature, °F
MCDB: Mean coincident dry bulb temperature, °F
Long: Longitude, °
HR: Humidity ratio, grains of moisture per lb of dry air
HDD and CDD 65: Annual heating and cooling degree-days, base 65°F, °F-day
Elev: Elevation, ft
WS: Wind speed, mph

Station	Lat	Long	Elev	Heating DB		Cooling DB/MCWB						Evaporation WB/MCDB				Dehumidification DP/HR/MCDB						Extreme Annual WS			Heat./Cool. Degree-Days	
						0.4%		1%		2%		0.4%		1%		0.4%			1%							
				99.6%	99%	DB	MCWB	DB	MCWB	DB	MCWB	WB	MCDB	WB	MCDB	DP	HR	MCDB	DP	HR	MCDB	1%	2.5%	5%	HDD	CDD 65
WALLA WALLA REGIONAL	46.095N	118.287W	1166	11.0	17.3	98.5	66.3	94.7	64.9	91.0	63.8	68.4	92.8	66.6	90.3	60.5	82.1	73.7	57.8	74.6	72.6	24.3	20.2	17.9	4810	934
WEST POINT	47.660N	122.440W	10	29.6	33.1	70.5	61.0	68.1	60.3	66.2	59.5	62.5	67.3	61.2	65.8	60.5	78.7	64.3	59.2	75.2	63.0	36.8	31.1	26.3	4927	9
YAKIMA AIR TERMINAL	46.568N	120.543W	1064	8.3	13.8	96.4	66.2	93.3	65.4	89.9	63.9	68.4	91.1	66.6	89.1	60.3	81.2	75.8	58.0	74.7	74.3	22.6	18.9	16.2	5845	556
3 sites, 12 more on CD-ROM																										
West Virginia																										
HUNTINGTON TRI-STATE AP	38.365N	82.555W	824	10.8	15.8	91.7	73.8	89.2	73.3	86.9	72.4	77.3	86.6	75.9	84.7	74.6	133.5	81.6	73.2	127.3	80.1	16.8	14.7	12.6	4398	1143
MID-OHIO VALLEY REGIONAL	39.345N	81.439W	831	8.6	13.6	90.6	73.8	88.1	72.8	85.8	71.6	76.7	86.2	75.3	84.0	73.8	130.0	81.1	72.5	124.3	79.6	18.3	16.0	13.8	4886	943
YEAGER AP	38.379N	81.590W	910	10.7	15.8	91.2	73.1	88.8	72.6	86.5	71.8	76.6	85.9	75.3	84.1	73.9	130.8	80.5	72.7	125.2	79.0	17.3	14.7	12.2	4402	1078
14 sites, 42 more on CD-ROM																										
Wisconsin																										
APPLETON INTL	44.267N	88.517W	917	-6.0	-0.3	88.4	75.2	84.9	72.8	82.3	70.9	77.8	85.3	75.5	82.6	75.2	136.7	81.6	73.0	127.0	79.6	24.7	21.7	19.0	7210	608
AUSTIN STRAUBEL INTL	44.479N	88.137W	687	-7.9	-2.8	88.0	73.7	85.0	71.7	82.4	70.1	76.3	84.8	74.3	82.0	73.4	127.6	81.4	71.6	119.5	79.6	23.8	20.2	18.2	7590	480
CENTRAL WISCONSIN AP	44.783N	89.667W	1277	-11.0	-7.3	86.5	72.3	83.6	70.5	81.2	68.1	74.3	83.2	72.0	80.6	71.7	122.7	81.2	69.6	114.2	78.8	23.1	19.8	17.7	8303	361
CHIPPEWA VALLEY REGIONAL	44.867N	91.488W	885	-13.1	-8.0	90.0	73.1	86.7	71.0	84.0	69.2	75.9	85.4	73.9	83.0	72.9	126.3	81.5	70.9	117.7	79.5	20.1	18.0	16.3	7843	587
DANE COUNTY REGIONAL	43.141N	89.345W	866	-6.3	-1.2	89.3	74.1	86.6	72.4	83.9	71.0	76.9	86.2	74.9	83.3	73.9	130.3	83.0	72.1	122.7	80.6	21.5	19.0	17.2	7083	640
FOND DU LAC COUNTY AP	43.769N	88.491W	807	-6.3	-1.0	88.9	73.5	85.8	71.5	82.8	70.1	76.3	85.2	74.3	82.6	73.1	126.6	82.1	71.9	121.5	80.4	23.6	20.2	18.3	7173	601
GENERAL MITCHELL INTL	42.955N	87.904W	670	-1.0	3.6	89.6	74.4	86.4	72.3	83.4	70.6	76.6	86.4	74.8	83.3	73.5	127.6	82.0	71.8	120.6	80.4	24.9	21.8	19.5	6676	693
KENOSHA REGIONAL	42.595N	87.938W	743	-2.4	2.2	90.3	74.3	87.5	73.2	84.0	71.2	77.0	86.9	75.1	83.8	73.4	127.7	82.0	72.3	123.0	80.8	24.8	21.5	19.2	6735	629
LA CROSSE MUNICIPAL	43.879N	91.253W	652	-9.2	-4.2	91.3	74.9	88.4	73.0	85.7	71.4	77.8	87.4	75.7	85.0	74.8	133.7	83.6	72.7	124.1	81.5	23.2	19.7	18.0	7026	820
MANITOWOC COUNTY AP	44.133N	87.667W	651	-4.3	0.5	84.7	71.7	81.9	70.4	79.5	68.4	74.9	82.7	72.7	79.7	72.4	122.7	80.3	70.3	114.3	77.6	24.1	20.7	18.8	7573	354
SHEBOYGAN	43.750N	87.690W	577	-1.8	2.8	83.0	71.5	79.5	70.6	76.6	69.8	76.4	79.3	74.2	76.9	75.5	136.3	77.3	73.4	126.8	75.8	41.1	33.8	28.4	7248	340
SHEBOYGAN COUNTY MEMORIAL	43.769N	87.851W	746	-4.5	0.1	88.4	73.9	84.5	71.4	81.9	70.0	76.0	85.0	74.0	82.1	73.0	125.9	81.5	71.6	120.0	79.2	24.1	20.5	18.5	7469	446
WAUSAU DOWNTOWN AP	44.929N	89.628W	1200	-12.0	-7.1	87.6	71.7	84.4	69.4	81.8	67.6	74.4	83.2	72.5	80.8	71.8	122.8	79.0	69.8	114.5	77.4	20.4	18.1	16.2	8025	455
WITTMAN REGIONAL	43.984N	88.557W	782	-6.2	-1.6	88.5	73.6	85.4	71.6	82.4	70.1	76.3	85.0	74.3	82.5	73.2	126.9	81.6	71.9	121.4	80.1	23.0	19.9	18.0	7343	571
2 sites, 21 more on CD-ROM																										
Wyoming																										
CASPER-NATRONA COUNTY INTL	42.898N	106.474W	5313	-8.5	-1.0	94.0	59.6	91.2	59.0	88.4	58.5	63.2	82.8	61.8	81.9	57.6	86.3	66.5	55.4	79.7	66.0	32.3	28.2	25.6	7308	469
CHEYENNE REGIONAL	41.150N	104.817W	6130	-4.1	2.6	89.5	58.1	86.9	57.6	84.0	57.2	62.6	77.3	61.5	76.8	58.5	92.3	65.9	56.9	86.9	65.2	33.4	28.7	25.6	7056	355
Canada — *100 sites, 665 more on CD-ROM*																										
13 sites, 114 more on CD-ROM																										
Alberta																										
BOW ISLAND	49.730N	111.450W	2679	-20.7	-14.4	88.8	64.4	85.4	63.2	81.9	62.3	68.3	82.6	66.2	79.9	63.5	96.9	74.9	61.2	89.1	72.4	28.5	24.9	21.7	8604	200
CALGARY INTL	51.120N	114.010W	3606	-19.2	-12.8	83.4	60.9	79.8	59.9	76.5	58.8	64.1	77.6	62.0	75.9	59.1	85.4	70.0	56.7	78.3	67.1	27.0	23.1	20.2	9197	67
CANADIAN OLYMPIC PARK UPPER	51.080N	114.220W	4052	-17.2	-11.6	82.5	59.4	78.8	58.1	75.3	57.2	63.4	75.1	61.2	73.4	59.2	87.5	68.2	56.7	79.6	65.5	22.8	19.7	17.2	9071	74
EDMONTON CITY CENTRE AWOS	53.570N	113.520W	2203	-20.1	-14.5	83.2	64.4	79.9	62.8	76.8	61.0	66.5	79.6	64.6	76.7	61.9	89.8	72.6	59.7	82.9	70.3	22.4	19.3	16.9	9423	132
EDMONTON INTL	53.310N	113.580W	2373	-26.7	-20.6	82.1	64.3	78.7	62.9	75.8	61.0	67.1	78.4	65.0	75.8	62.8	93.5	73.3	60.5	86.1	70.8	22.9	19.8	17.3	10473	45
EDMONTON NAMAO AWOS	53.670N	113.470W	2257	-22.2	-16.6	82.1	64.3	78.8	62.5	75.6	60.6	66.3	78.5	64.4	75.9	61.8	89.7	72.2	59.7	83.1	69.7	22.9	19.9	17.3	10060	67
FORT MCMURRAY CS	56.650N	111.210W	1210	-30.5	-25.5	83.7	63.8	80.0	61.8	77.0	60.2	66.5	78.4	64.5	75.3	62.5	88.6	69.8	60.3	81.7	68.0	19.4	16.7	14.5	11244	75
GRANDE PRAIRIE	55.180N	118.880W	2195	-32.7	-24.4	81.8	62.2	78.3	60.6	75.2	59.0	64.5	77.8	62.5	74.8	59.8	83.2	69.0	57.6	76.9	66.6	25.3	22.0	18.9	10674	47
LACOMBE CDA 2	52.450N	113.760W	2822	-25.6	-19.0	82.6	64.8	79.0	63.1	75.9	61.3	67.3	78.7	65.0	76.1	63.0	95.8	73.8	60.6	87.8	71.1	21.0	18.1	15.5	10318	41
LETHBRIDGE CDA	49.700N	112.770W	2986	-18.1	-12.1	89.1	62.4	85.4	61.4	81.9	60.7	66.3	81.2	64.3	79.1	61.3	90.6	72.7	58.9	83.0	70.3	29.8	26.5	23.5	8108	205
MEDICINE HAT RCS	50.030N	110.720W	2346	-19.5	-13.4	91.5	62.7	88.0	61.6	84.5	61.0	66.0	82.9	64.2	81.2	60.4	85.4	71.6	58.2	79.1	69.8	24.1	20.8	18.2	8497	322
RED DEER	52.180N	113.890W	2968	-25.6	-18.8	82.3	63.1	78.8	61.4	75.7	60.0	65.6	78.4	63.5	75.5	60.6	88.1	72.0	58.6	81.9	69.5	20.0	18.0	16.1	10309	42
SPRINGBANK	51.100N	114.370W	3940	-24.5	-17.9	80.4	60.1	76.8	58.3	73.7	57.5	62.4	75.7	60.4	73.3	57.2	80.7	68.3	55.2	75.1	65.3	24.8	21.2	18.6	10296	8
27 sites, 71 more on CD-ROM																										
British Columbia																										
ABBOTSFORD	49.030N	122.360W	194	18.1	22.9	85.6	67.4	81.9	66.0	78.5	64.5	69.0	83.1	67.0	79.7	63.3	87.8	75.9	61.6	82.5	73.3	20.3	17.1	14.5	5240	145
AGASSIZ RCS	49.240N	121.760W	63	18.7	23.1	86.2	68.5	82.8	67.3	79.6	66.1	70.9	82.6	68.9	80.1	66.5	97.7	77.6	64.6	91.3	74.9	22.7	17.7	13.9	5142	209
BALLENAS ISLAND	49.350N	124.160W	42	30.3	32.9	74.4	66.3	72.1	65.3	70.2	64.1	67.7	72.6	66.1	70.9	65.6	94.8	71.0	64.1	89.6	69.3	35.5	30.5	26.9	4772	102
COMOX	49.720N	124.900W	84	23.5	27.1	80.2	64.0	76.7	62.9	73.6	61.6	65.5	76.9	64.0	74.0	61.2	80.8	68.8	59.9	77.3	67.5	30.0	25.7	21.8	5561	102
DISCOVERY ISLAND	48.420N	123.230W	62	29.6	34.1	72.8	N/A	69.2	N/A	66.3	N/A	N/A	N/A	N/A	N/A	N/A	N/A	N/A	N/A	N/A	N/A	36.2	28.3	22.0	4995	18
ENTRANCE ISLAND	49.210N	123.810W	25	29.5	32.3	74.5	64.8	72.0	63.9	69.9	63.0	65.7	71.0	64.6	70.1	63.4	87.3	69.7	62.0	83.3	68.5	31.9	27.9	25.0	4848	104
ESQUIMALT HARBOUR	48.430N	123.440W	10	27.3	30.7	71.8	60.6	68.7	59.5	66.1	58.6	62.1	68.8	60.9	66.6	59.4	75.5	64.3	58.2	72.5	62.9	22.0	18.9	16.6	5475	11
HOWE SOUND PAM ROCKS	49.490N	123.300W	23	26.9	30.3	76.4	66.3	73.5	64.8	71.3	64.0	68.0	73.8	66.4	71.7	65.6	94.7	72.0	64.0	89.3	70.1	39.9	35.0	29.6	4769	139
KAMLOOPS	50.700N	120.450W	1133	-3.2	4.0	93.3	64.8	89.5	63.7	85.5	62.3	66.6	88.2	64.9	85.2	59.4	78.9	70.8	57.6	73.8	69.8	22.9	20.2	18.1	6359	501
KELOWNA	49.960N	119.380W	1421	0.8	7.3	91.6	64.7	88.1	63.5	84.4	62.1	66.7	86.0	64.8	83.4	60.1	81.6	71.0	58.2	76.4	69.6	17.7	14.6	12.2	7009	252
MALAHAT	48.570N	123.530W	1200	21.6	25.6	81.8	63.2	78.2	61.9	75.1	60.8	65.9	78.1	64.1	74.8	60.8	83.3	73.0	59.2	78.6	70.2	14.8	12.7	10.8	5857	173
PENTICTON	49.460N	119.600W	1130	7.8	12.7	91.2	65.7	87.8	64.5	84.5	63.2	67.4	86.8	65.7	84.1	60.3	81.4	73.4	58.6	76.5	72.3	23.3	20.4	18.2	6166	410
PITT MEADOWS CS	49.210N	122.690W	16	19.2	23.5	86.4	67.7	82.7	66.3	79.2	65.0	69.2	82.8	67.3	79.9	64.1	89.5	74.9	62.3	84.1	71.9	12.2	10.2	8.9	5382	141
POINT ATKINSON	49.330N	123.260W	46	28.7	31.9	76.2	N/A	73.8	N/A	71.9	N/A	N/A	N/A	N/A	N/A	N/A	N/A	N/A	N/A	N/A	N/A	30.1	25.7	21.9	4380	185
PRINCE GEORGE	53.880N	122.680W	2267	-22.4	-13.7	82.5	61.6	78.7	60.0	75.1	58.3	63.2	78.7	61.2	75.3	57.4	76.3	66.5	55.7	71.8	64.9	21.9	18.8	16.7	9244	40
SANDHEADS CS	49.110N	123.300W	36	25.9	29.8	72.0	N/A	70.1	N/A	68.3	N/A	N/A	N/A	N/A	N/A	N/A	N/A	N/A	N/A	N/A	N/A	30.4	26.8	23.8	4982	53
SUMMERLAND CS	49.560N	119.650W	1490	6.8	12.6	91.2	63.8	87.9	63.0	84.4	61.9	66.7	84.8	64.9	82.4	60.6	83.3	72.1	58.5	77.3	70.7	18.3	14.5	11.9	6306	458

(Go to CD-ROM to access additional station tables.)

Meaning of acronyms:
DB: Dry bulb temperature, °F · *WB: Wet bulb temperature, °F* · *MCWB: Mean coincident wet bulb temperature, °F*
Lat: Latitude, ° · *DP: Dew point temperature, °F* · *MCDB: Mean coincident dry bulb temperature, °F*
Long: Longitude, ° · *HR: Humidity ratio, grains of moisture per lb of dry air* · *HDD and CDD 65: Annual heating and cooling degree-days, base 65°F, °F-day*
Elev: Elevation, ft · *WS: Wind speed, mph*

Station	Lat	Long	Elev	Heating DB		Cooling DB/MCWB						Evaporation WB/MCDB				Dehumidification DP/HR/MCDB						Extreme Annual WS			Heat./Cool. Degree-Days	
						0.4%		1%		2%		0.4%		1%		0.4%			1%							
				99.6%	99%	DB	MCWB	DB	MCWB	DB	MCWB	WB	MCDB	WB	MCDB	DP	HR	MCDB	DP	HR	MCDB	1%	2.5%	5%	HDD	CDD 65
VANCOUVER HARBOUR CS	49.300N	123.120W	8	26.8	30.5	78.5	64.2	75.9	63.0	73.5	62.0	65.7	75.6	64.4	74.3	61.3	81.1	70.8	60.1	77.5	69.0	N/A	N/A	N/A	4829	127
VANCOUVER INTL	49.190N	123.180W	14	21.0	25.8	77.2	65.2	74.5	64.2	72.3	63.0	66.5	75.0	65.1	73.0	62.9	85.9	71.4	61.6	81.9	69.8	24.1	20.5	17.8	5240	83
VERNON	50.220N	119.190W	1581	2.3	8.2	91.2	65.2	87.5	64.1	83.6	62.7	67.4	84.8	65.6	82.9	62.0	88.1	70.6	60.0	82.0	69.1	17.3	13.1	10.9	6787	369
VICTORIA GONZALES CS	48.410N	123.320W	200	26.6	30.7	76.3	62.4	72.0	60.8	68.9	59.4	63.8	73.4	62.0	69.8	60.0	78.0	66.2	58.8	74.5	64.6	27.7	23.8	20.8	5170	40
VICTORIA HARTLAND CS	48.530N	123.460W	506	25.3	29.1	83.2	65.7	79.9	64.2	76.7	63.1	67.9	79.6	66.2	76.7	63.7	89.9	72.3	62.1	84.9	70.2	20.7	17.8	15.3	5142	171
VICTORIA INTL	48.650N	123.430W	64	24.7	27.9	80.1	63.8	76.3	62.5	73.3	61.1	64.7	77.8	63.1	74.6	59.1	75.1	68.4	57.9	71.8	67.3	20.3	17.0	14.5	5413	46
VICTORIA UNIVERSITY CS	48.460N	123.300W	197	27.2	30.9	80.5	64.6	77.0	63.4	73.9	62.3	66.7	77.2	65.0	74.1	62.9	86.4	70.0	61.3	81.5	68.1	12.6	11.0	9.6	4990	64
WEST VANCOUVER	49.350N	123.190W	558	21.6	26.2	80.7	65.1	77.3	64.3	74.4	63.2	67.3	77.7	65.6	75.0	63.1	88.3	72.8	61.6	83.7	70.9	10.9	9.2	7.7	5398	136
WHITE ROCK CAMPBELL SCI	49.020N	122.780W	43	22.4	26.7	76.7	65.9	73.8	64.5	71.6	63.4	67.4	74.5	65.7	72.1	64.6	91.4	71.5	62.9	86.0	69.2	13.9	11.3	9.2	5018	55
YOHO PARK	51.440N	116.340W	5256	-21.8	-15.8	77.9	56.7	74.1	55.3	70.3	53.9	58.5	72.9	56.7	70.5	53.4	73.9	60.4	51.6	69.1	58.9	23.6	21.2	19.5	11693	2
Manitoba																										*1 site, 41 more on CD-ROM*
WINNIPEG INTL	49.910N	97.240W	783	-25.7	-21.4	86.5	70.3	83.5	68.6	80.7	66.9	73.4	83.1	71.0	80.4	70.2	114.3	79.6	67.6	104.6	76.6	28.4	25.1	22.4	10365	286
New Brunswick																										*3 sites, 19 more on CD-ROM*
FREDERICTON INTL	45.870N	66.540W	68	-9.8	-5.1	85.9	69.8	82.5	67.9	79.6	66.2	72.1	82.1	70.3	79.1	68.8	106.1	76.6	67.2	100.4	74.7	22.2	19.3	17.3	8253	257
MONCTON INTL	46.110N	64.680W	232	-8.0	-3.5	83.6	69.7	80.5	67.6	77.8	66.1	71.9	80.0	70.2	77.3	69.2	108.2	75.9	67.6	102.4	74.2	28.3	24.6	21.6	8397	199
SAINT JOHN	45.320N	65.890W	357	-8.1	-3.1	79.2	65.8	76.3	64.2	73.5	62.6	68.4	75.4	66.6	72.8	65.9	96.8	71.3	64.3	91.5	69.1	27.7	23.9	21.1	8445	60
Newfoundland and Labrador																										*1 site, 41 more on CD-ROM*
ST JOHN'S INTL	47.620N	52.750W	461	4.8	8.6	76.6	66.4	73.9	65.0	71.4	63.8	69.1	73.7	67.3	71.7	67.5	102.7	71.9	65.5	95.7	69.9	35.3	30.1	27.1	8629	60
Northwest Territories																										*1 site, 45 more on CD-ROM*
YELLOWKNIFE	62.460N	114.440W	675	-40.8	-36.9	77.7	60.9	74.7	59.4	71.9	58.3	63.0	72.9	61.3	71.2	59.1	76.8	66.5	57.2	71.6	65.2	20.8	18.5	16.6	14687	66
Nova Scotia																										*3 sites, 34 more on CD-ROM*
HALIFAX STANFIELD INTL	44.880N	63.500W	477	-0.8	3.0	82.2	68.7	79.1	66.9	76.3	65.4	71.2	78.2	69.5	75.6	69.0	108.6	74.1	67.5	102.7	72.1	28.1	24.3	21.2	7655	199
SHEARWATER	44.630N	63.500W	144	1.0	4.9	79.2	67.1	76.3	65.4	73.4	64.3	69.9	75.0	68.2	72.9	68.3	104.4	71.8	66.6	98.3	70.1	26.7	23.2	20.6	7529	130
SYDNEY	46.170N	60.050W	203	0.2	4.7	81.6	68.5	78.6	67.0	75.5	65.4	70.8	78.5	69.0	75.6	68.2	104.2	74.6	66.5	98.3	72.4	27.9	24.5	21.7	8092	158
Nunavut																										*1 site, 60 more on CD-ROM*
IQALUIT CLIMATE	63.750N	68.540W	110	-32.0	-29.4	64.3	54.6	58.7	52.1	54.7	49.6	55.6	63.3	52.6	58.0	50.9	55.5	58.0	48.8	51.3	55.8	29.5	25.6	22.4	17043	1
Ontario																										*21 sites, 75 more on CD-ROM*
BEAUSOLEIL	44.850N	79.870W	600	-12.4	-5.9	85.9	74.0	82.6	71.7	79.7	70.3	75.9	82.6	73.9	79.9	73.9	129.2	79.5	71.9	120.8	77.2	14.0	12.1	10.7	7909	382
BELLE RIVER	42.300N	82.700W	602	6.5	10.6	88.6	75.3	85.7	74.0	82.8	72.4	79.3	84.3	77.0	82.4	78.2	150.0	82.3	75.4	136.1	80.1	28.8	25.3	22.2	6023	762
ERIEAU	42.250N	81.900W	584	5.3	9.3	80.3	73.2	78.5	72.0	77.0	71.1	76.1	78.1	74.5	76.8	75.5	136.5	77.5	73.7	128.4	76.1	28.4	25.0	22.0	6502	507
GUELPH TURFGRASS INSTITUTE	43.547N	80.215W	1066	-6.6	-1.1	85.6	71.1	82.5	69.6	79.9	67.9	73.6	81.7	71.8	79.3	71.3	120.1	77.7	69.5	112.7	75.9	19.0	16.9	15.1	7981	275
HAMILTON INTL	43.170N	79.940W	780	-0.7	4.1	87.1	72.4	84.2	71.1	81.3	69.5	74.9	83.4	73.1	81.1	72.3	123.0	79.2	70.6	115.9	77.4	27.2	23.2	20.6	7066	449
LONDON INTL	43.030N	81.150W	912	-0.8	3.9	86.4	72.4	83.5	71.0	80.9	69.3	74.7	82.8	73.0	80.7	72.2	123.1	79.3	70.4	115.8	77.3	23.8	21.0	18.7	7097	430
NORTH BAY	46.360N	79.420W	1215	-17.4	-12.0	82.3	68.1	79.4	66.5	76.8	65.1	71.2	78.5	69.3	75.3	68.9	111.0	74.4	67.1	104.4	72.8	22.3	19.5	17.5	9272	227
OTTAWA INTL	45.320N	75.670W	374	-11.5	-6.3	87.1	71.3	84.2	69.5	81.2	68.0	73.9	83.1	72.0	80.3	71.0	115.8	78.7	69.2	108.9	76.7	22.6	19.9	17.8	8070	434
PETERBOROUGH TRENT U	44.350N	78.300W	709	-8.3	-2.5	87.4	70.4	84.0	68.8	81.2	67.1	72.8	83.2	71.1	80.5	69.6	111.6	77.6	68.0	105.5	76.2	13.8	12.0	10.7	7782	319
PORT WELLER	43.250N	79.220W	259	8.9	12.6	84.4	73.0	81.7	71.7	79.2	70.5	75.8	80.9	74.0	78.7	74.3	129.5	78.9	72.6	121.9	77.0	31.6	27.7	24.3	6291	558
REGION OF WATERLOO INTL	43.460N	80.380W	1055	-5.0	0.7	87.0	71.5	84.0	70.1	81.0	68.5	73.9	83.1	72.3	80.8	71.2	119.8	78.1	69.6	113.1	76.6	25.7	22.5	19.9	7634	332
SAULT STE MARIE	46.480N	84.510W	630	-12.2	-6.8	83.1	70.0	79.9	68.0	77.1	66.2	72.1	79.8	70.0	77.1	69.4	110.7	76.5	67.6	103.7	74.1	22.9	19.7	17.5	8893	162
SUDBURY	46.630N	80.800W	1143	-17.8	-12.3	84.2	68.3	80.9	66.3	78.0	64.5	70.8	80.1	68.9	76.9	67.8	106.5	74.4	65.9	99.8	72.8	22.6	20.0	18.0	9385	223
THUNDER BAY CS	48.370N	89.330W	654	-19.9	-15.2	84.5	68.4	81.3	66.2	78.1	64.7	70.8	80.3	68.5	77.2	67.3	102.8	76.7	65.2	95.5	73.7	21.1	18.8	16.7	9945	145
TIMMINS	48.570N	81.380W	967	-27.7	-21.6	85.3	67.9	81.6	65.3	78.4	64.0	70.6	81.0	68.3	77.8	66.9	102.7	75.5	65.0	95.8	73.3	18.7	17.4	14.5	10768	158
TORONTO BILLY BISHOP	43.630N	79.400W	252	3.8	8.4	83.1	70.9	80.3	69.9	77.5	68.9	74.0	79.4	72.4	77.5	72.3	120.6	77.1	70.7	114.0	75.6	29.7	26.2	23.2	6627	432
TORONTO BUTTONVILLE	43.860N	79.370W	650	-3.4	1.8	88.9	72.2	85.5	70.3	82.4	68.8	74.4	85.0	72.5	82.2	71.0	117.1	79.8	69.3	110.2	77.8	21.1	18.7	16.8	7232	475
TORONTO PEARSON INTL	43.680N	79.630W	569	-0.5	4.1	88.4	72.4	85.2	70.6	82.1	69.1	74.7	84.6	72.9	82.2	71.6	119.3	80.1	69.8	111.9	78.2	27.3	23.6	20.9	6907	547
TRENTON	44.120N	77.530W	283	-7.0	-1.6	84.5	71.8	81.8	70.3	79.4	68.9	74.3	81.3	72.6	79.2	71.9	119.1	78.6	70.2	112.5	76.8	23.4	20.4	17.9	7450	375
WINDSOR	42.280N	82.960W	622	4.0	8.6	89.5	73.6	86.7	72.2	84.2	70.7	76.2	85.7	74.4	83.1	73.3	126.6	81.6	71.6	119.6	79.3	25.5	22.5	20.1	6158	788
Prince Edward Island																										*1 site, 6 more on CD-ROM*
CHARLOTTETOWN	46.290N	63.120W	159	-4.3	0.1	80.4	69.4	77.8	67.4	75.3	65.9	71.2	77.7	69.5	75.2	69.0	107.1	75.0	67.3	100.9	73.2	26.5	22.9	20.3	8230	194
Québec																										*22 sites, 81 more on CD-ROM*
BAGOTVILLE	48.330N	71.000W	522	-21.6	-16.8	84.8	67.0	81.3	65.3	78.0	64.0	70.0	79.6	68.0	77.2	66.6	100.0	73.7	64.9	93.9	72.0	26.9	23.6	21.0	10092	183
BIG TROUT LAKE	53.820N	89.900W	730	-34.0	-29.8	80.6	65.7	77.5	63.8	74.4	62.5	68.5	76.4	66.3	74.1	65.7	97.4	72.2	63.3	89.3	69.8	20.3	17.9	15.9	13229	94
JONQUIERE	48.430N	71.140W	445	-22.4	-16.9	84.2	67.6	80.8	66.1	77.6	64.8	71.1	79.4	69.2	76.7	68.4	106.0	75.2	66.5	99.1	72.8	23.3	20.8	18.7	9914	177
LA BAIE	48.300N	70.920W	498	-22.4	-17.8	84.4	67.4	80.7	66.2	77.4	64.9	71.0	79.5	69.0	76.7	68.2	105.7	74.8	66.3	98.7	72.6	22.8	20.1	17.8	10224	128
LAC SAINT-PIERRE	46.180N	72.920W	53	-11.6	-6.4	82.3	70.0	79.6	68.6	77.3	67.3	72.7	78.8	71.1	77.0	70.6	112.7	76.5	69.0	106.8	75.1	30.1	26.8	23.9	8230	359
L'ACADIE	45.290N	73.350W	144	-11.8	-7.1	86.2	70.8	83.4	69.7	80.8	68.3	74.4	82.0	72.4	79.4	71.8	118.2	78.9	70.1	111.5	76.7	23.0	19.8	17.0	7936	412
L'ASSOMPTION	45.810N	73.430W	69	-14.1	-8.6	86.8	71.4	83.8	69.6	81.0	68.1	74.2	82.9	72.2	80.0	71.4	116.2	78.6	69.6	109.3	76.7	18.8	16.3	14.3	8288	380
LENNOXVILLE	45.370N	71.820W	594	-13.7	-7.9	84.9	70.7	82.2	69.2	79.7	67.7	73.6	81.2	71.7	79.0	71.2	117.6	77.7	69.2	109.8	75.7	20.0	17.6	15.5	8253	272

(Go to CD-ROM to access additional station tables.)

(Go to CD-ROM to access additional station tables.)

Meaning of acronyms:
DB: Dry bulb temperature, °F *WB: Wet bulb temperature, °F*
MCWB: Mean coincident wet bulb temperature, °F
Lat: Latitude, °
DP: Dew point temperature, °F
MCDB: Mean coincident dry bulb temperature, °F
Long: Longitude, °
HR: Humidity ratio, grains of moisture per lb of dry air
HDD and CDD 65: Annual heating and cooling degree-days, base 65°F, °F-day
Elev: Elevation, ft
WS: Wind speed, mph

Station	Lat	Long	Elev	Heating DB		Cooling DB/MCWB						Evaporation WB/MCDB				Dehumidification DP/HR/MCDB						Extreme Annual WS			Heat./Cool. Degree-Days	
						0.4%		1%		2%		0.4%		1%		0.4%			1%							
				99.6%	99%	DB	MCWB	DB	MCWB	DB	MCWB	WB	MCDB	WB	MCDB	DP	HR	MCDB	DP	HR	MCDB	1%	2.5%	5%	HDD	CDD 65
MONT-JOLI	48.610N	68.210W	172	-10.7	-6.6	80.3	67.6	77.2	65.7	74.5	64.1	69.3	77.5	67.3	75.0	66.0	96.5	74.6	64.1	90.2	72.3	28.4	25.1	22.4	9511	130
MONT-ORFORD	45.310N	72.240W	2776	-19.4	-13.4	77.2	65.4	74.3	64.0	71.6	62.9	69.0	73.6	66.8	70.7	67.5	112.1	71.3	65.6	104.7	69.0	35.1	30.3	27.2	10186	96
MONTREAL MCTAVISH	45.510N	73.580W	238	-7.5	-2.5	86.2	71.4	83.4	69.6	81.0	68.1	73.9	82.7	72.0	79.9	71.0	115.1	79.0	69.3	108.7	77.3	11.2	9.8	8.8	7463	547
MONTREAL MIRABEL INTL	45.680N	74.040W	270	-14.8	-9.3	85.2	71.4	82.4	69.4	79.8	67.9	73.5	82.2	71.6	79.5	70.6	113.7	78.9	68.7	106.6	76.4	18.6	16.0	13.9	8509	323
MONTREAL ST-HUBERT	45.520N	73.420W	90	-10.2	-5.4	86.1	71.8	83.4	70.0	80.9	68.6	74.3	82.6	72.4	80.1	71.6	116.9	78.9	69.8	109.9	77.2	25.2	22.2	19.8	7945	423
MONTREAL TRUDEAU INTL	45.470N	73.740W	118	-9.5	-4.6	86.0	71.7	83.3	69.9	80.9	68.4	73.8	82.7	72.0	80.0	70.8	114.2	78.8	69.3	108.1	77.2	25.7	22.4	19.9	7771	490
NICOLET	46.230N	72.660W	26	-14.1	-9.0	83.8	72.2	81.0	70.4	78.5	68.8	74.3	81.1	72.3	78.6	72.0	118.3	78.6	70.1	111.0	76.3	21.1	18.1	15.7	8436	302
POINTE-AU-PERE INRS	48.510N	68.470W	16	-7.2	-2.6	73.5	65.4	70.7	63.7	68.3	61.9	67.3	71.8	64.9	69.4	65.3	93.4	70.6	62.9	85.8	68.2	28.7	25.2	22.4	9554	20
QUEBEC CITY JEAN LESAGE INTL	46.800N	71.380W	197	-12.0	-7.4	83.7	69.5	81.2	68.3	78.4	66.5	72.8	80.6	70.8	77.9	70.1	111.5	77.5	68.1	104.1	75.2	22.3	19.8	17.8	8783	247
SAINTE-FOY U LAVAL	46.780N	71.290W	300	-11.6	-6.9	84.3	69.1	81.5	67.3	78.7	65.7	72.4	80.3	70.4	77.5	69.8	110.8	76.3	68.0	104.1	74.3	20.8	17.9	15.2	8675	270
SHERBROOKE	45.440N	71.690W	792	-17.2	-11.5	83.8	70.0	81.1	68.3	78.7	66.9	72.6	80.4	70.7	78.2	69.9	113.3	77.5	68.1	106.1	75.0	20.4	17.8	15.5	8843	185
ST-ANICET 1	45.120N	74.290W	161	-12.3	-7.0	87.0	72.8	84.3	71.2	81.7	69.6	75.5	83.7	73.7	81.4	72.9	122.7	80.4	71.1	115.4	78.2	20.7	18.0	15.9	7950	393
STE-ANNE-DE-BELLEVUE 1	45.430N	73.930W	128	-10.8	-5.5	86.0	71.2	83.3	69.8	80.7	68.3	74.2	82.4	72.3	79.7	71.5	116.9	78.6	69.9	110.4	76.3	19.8	17.5	15.6	7928	416
TROIS-RIVIERES	46.350N	72.520W	20	-11.6	-6.8	81.2	70.3	79.0	69.4	76.9	68.3	73.2	78.2	71.6	76.7	71.4	115.8	76.5	69.8	109.8	75.2	24.1	20.9	18.5	8298	332
VARENNES	45.720N	73.380W	59	-10.3	-5.7	86.5	71.2	83.5	69.6	80.9	68.1	74.2	82.5	72.3	80.0	71.5	116.5	78.8	69.8	109.7	76.8	24.5	21.2	18.9	8059	373
Saskatchewan																										*5 sites, 47 more on CD-ROM*
MOOSE JAW CS	50.330N	105.540W	1893	-22.2	-17.3	89.2	65.5	85.4	64.6	81.8	63.4	71.0	80.8	68.4	78.8	67.9	109.9	76.5	65.2	99.8	72.9	27.5	24.6	22.0	9705	209
PRINCE ALBERT	53.210N	105.670W	1405	-32.2	-26.3	84.0	66.1	80.6	64.4	77.7	62.6	68.5	79.9	66.4	77.3	64.4	95.5	73.7	62.4	88.9	71.3	20.8	18.5	16.7	11167	120
REGINA RCS	50.430N	104.670W	1894	-26.1	-21.2	87.9	67.2	83.9	65.3	80.7	63.8	71.1	82.1	68.3	79.1	67.5	108.4	76.8	64.6	97.9	73.9	28.1	25.1	22.5	10393	199
SASKATOON INTL	52.170N	106.700W	1654	-29.5	-24.0	86.4	66.1	82.8	64.6	79.5	63.4	69.3	81.2	67.2	78.6	65.3	99.6	75.0	63.2	92.1	72.4	24.9	21.9	19.5	10628	166
SASKATOON KERNEN FARM	52.150N	106.550W	1673	-28.3	-23.0	87.2	63.8	83.4	62.4	80.2	61.0	68.9	80.5	66.5	76.9	65.1	98.8	74.6	62.6	90.3	71.6	24.0	21.2	19.0	10626	182
Yukon Territory																										*1 site, 17 more on CD-ROM*
WHITEHORSE	60.710N	135.070W	2317	-39.4	-30.2	78.3	57.5	74.1	56.0	70.4	54.4	58.8	74.7	57.0	71.6	52.3	63.3	61.2	50.5	59.4	60.3	23.0	20.7	18.6	12188	13
Albania																										*1 site, 0 more on CD-ROM*
TIRANA RINAS	41.415N	19.721E	126	26.9	29.6	93.6	73.2	91.6	73.9	89.5	73.7	82.3	86.1	79.9	84.8	81.0	161.8	84.3	78.8	150.3	82.9	17.5	14.7	12.7	2757	1236
Algeria																										*3 sites, 38 more on CD-ROM*
CONSTANTINE BOUDIAF INTL	36.276N	6.620E	2265	31.1	32.9	102.0	68.4	98.5	68.3	95.1	67.7	72.5	91.7	71.0	90.0	67.3	109.3	78.3	65.8	103.5	77.6	22.2	18.9	16.5	2984	1540
DAR EL BEIDA	36.691N	3.215E	82	35.2	37.3	95.3	72.3	92.4	72.5	89.7	72.5	78.0	87.2	76.7	85.7	75.4	133.4	82.3	73.8	126.3	81.4	23.3	20.1	17.4	1772	1614
ORAN INTL	35.624N	0.621W	295	35.9	38.8	93.7	69.9	90.5	70.4	87.9	70.7	76.7	85.1	75.5	83.5	73.8	127.4	80.9	73.2	124.6	80.4	26.0	22.1	19.2	1621	1643
Argentina																										*15 sites, 42 more on CD-ROM*
CORDOBA INTL	31.324S	64.208W	1604	31.6	34.4	94.8	70.7	91.6	70.3	89.2	69.8	76.8	87.4	75.0	84.9	73.8	133.8	81.9	71.9	125.3	80.1	25.5	22.7	20.2	1737	1350
CORRIENTES INTL	27.446S	58.762W	203	39.6	42.6	98.5	76.0	96.4	76.2	93.6	75.6	80.9	90.6	79.8	89.4	78.6	149.6	86.6	77.2	142.5	85.0	22.0	19.0	16.6	712	2943
EL PLUMERILLO	32.832S	68.793W	2310	30.7	33.6	96.4	67.4	93.5	67.3	91.3	66.9	72.7	88.3	71.3	87.0	67.9	111.9	81.1	66.3	105.4	79.8	18.1	15.2	13.0	2191	1653
EZEIZA INTL	34.822S	58.536W	67	31.8	34.2	92.9	72.6	89.9	71.8	87.6	71.1	76.4	86.5	74.9	84.5	73.6	125.3	81.2	71.9	118.3	79.3	21.3	18.7	16.6	2126	1202
JORGE NEWBERY INTL	34.559S	58.416W	18	39.5	42.4	88.1	73.8	85.9	73.4	83.9	72.4	77.3	84.3	75.8	82.7	75.2	132.1	82.4	73.5	124.8	80.8	24.8	21.9	19.6	1604	1369
MAR DEL PLATA	37.934S	57.573W	71	29.8	32.0	87.9	70.1	84.4	68.8	80.9	67.8	73.5	81.6	71.9	79.1	71.4	116.1	76.4	69.8	109.7	74.9	24.4	22.0	19.6	3343	433
PARANA	31.795S	60.480W	243	36.5	38.9	94.1	73.7	91.5	72.7	89.2	72.0	78.1	88.8	76.4	86.5	74.9	132.0	84.6	73.3	125.1	82.4	23.7	20.9	18.4	1500	1646
POSADAS INTL	27.386S	55.971W	430	40.8	43.7	97.0	75.2	95.1	75.1	93.3	74.9	79.8	90.7	78.8	89.7	76.9	142.3	86.3	75.5	135.8	84.7	18.4	15.8	13.7	572	3190
RESISTENCIA INTL	27.450S	59.056W	173	35.2	38.8	98.9	75.4	96.7	75.8	94.4	75.6	80.8	91.0	79.7	89.7	78.3	147.9	86.4	77.1	141.7	85.3	19.9	17.0	15.1	837	2875
ROSARIO	32.904S	60.785W	85	30.6	33.7	93.6	73.8	91.4	73.0	89.2	72.3	78.3	88.1	76.5	85.7	75.4	133.4	83.8	73.6	125.7	81.8	24.7	22.1	18.9	1821	1450
SALTA AP	24.856S	65.486W	4088	30.0	32.4	91.6	65.2	89.0	65.6	86.1	65.6	72.0	82.7	70.9	81.0	69.1	124.7	76.1	68.1	120.3	75.3	16.7	14.2	12.2	1671	1034
SAN JUAN	31.571S	68.418W	1959	28.1	30.9	100.4	67.5	97.9	67.3	95.3	66.6	72.1	92.4	70.8	90.6	66.0	103.0	80.6	64.5	97.6	80.0	30.6	25.9	22.5	2095	2082
SAN MIGUEL DE TUCUMAN	26.841S	65.105W	1495	37.6	40.6	97.3	74.0	94.9	74.0	92.1	73.5	79.3	90.4	78.0	88.8	76.4	145.6	86.9	75.0	138.9	85.4	19.4	16.0	13.2	1011	2270
SANTIAGO DEL ESTERO	27.766S	64.310W	656	30.5	34.5	102.5	74.3	99.5	73.9	96.7	73.4	79.4	92.1	78.0	91.0	76.2	140.0	86.2	74.8	133.4	84.0	22.6	18.8	16.3	1057	2697
SAUCE VIEJO	31.712S	60.812W	56	32.8	36.0	95.2	75.6	92.5	74.5	89.9	73.5	79.7	89.6	78.1	87.4	77.0	140.7	85.6	75.3	132.9	83.7	33.2	27.5	23.7	1456	1881
Armenia																										*1 site, 5 more on CD-ROM*
YEREVAN EREBUNI	40.133N	44.467E	3740	8.4	12.7	97.0	70.7	94.7	69.8	91.8	68.7	72.9	93.3	71.1	91.5	66.1	110.7	87.7	64.2	103.5	84.6	22.4	18.8	15.5	4932	1388
Australia																										*25 sites, 500 more on CD-ROM*
ADELAIDE INTL	34.945S	138.531E	20	39.0	41.0	97.2	65.0	93.1	64.3	89.2	63.4	70.7	83.5	69.0	82.5	66.9	99.1	75.3	64.6	91.3	74.0	25.6	23.0	20.8	2080	861
BRISBANE ARCHERFIELD	27.570S	153.008E	63	41.7	44.0	91.2	73.1	88.6	72.6	86.4	71.9	77.2	85.7	76.0	83.7	75.1	131.8	80.2	73.8	126.1	79.6	20.6	18.4	16.5	649	1923
BRISBANE INTL	27.383S	153.117E	16	42.5	45.0	87.6	72.7	85.5	73.3	84.0	72.4	77.4	83.0	76.3	81.8	75.6	133.9	80.7	74.6	129.6	80.0	22.2	19.7	17.7	600	1825
CANBERRA	35.307S	149.195E	1886	26.1	28.2	93.1	64.1	89.3	63.2	85.5	62.3	68.3	81.2	66.8	79.4	65.0	99.4	71.4	63.0	92.5	69.9	23.4	21.0	18.9	3687	491
CANTERBURY RACECOURSE	33.900S	151.117E	10	38.8	40.6	90.5	68.0	86.5	68.4	83.3	68.0	73.7	82.3	72.4	80.4	71.1	114.7	77.2	69.9	109.9	76.2	22.8	18.7	16.5	1610	932
GOLD COAST	28.164S	153.505E	21	42.9	46.0	84.6	74.0	83.3	73.6	82.2	72.9	77.4	81.8	76.2	80.8	75.9	135.6	80.2	74.8	130.4	79.5	21.9	20.1	18.4	570	1697
GOLD COAST SEAWAY	27.933S	153.433E	10	49.3	51.4	87.0	73.3	84.7	72.9	83.0	72.5	77.4	81.9	76.2	80.9	76.2	136.9	79.5	74.9	130.9	78.7	29.3	25.5	22.6	335	2004
JANDAKOT AP	32.100S	115.883E	102	35.3	37.7	97.6	67.9	94.4	67.4	91.0	66.6	73.5	86.8	71.1	85.2	69.7	109.7	77.9	67.0	99.6	75.5	23.0	20.5	18.6	1692	1254
KENT TOWN	34.917S	138.617E	167	40.5	42.4	99.8	66.2	95.4	65.4	91.4	64.3	70.8	87.3	69.0	85.8	66.4	97.9	75.6	63.7	89.0	74.0	18.5	16.4	14.7	1916	1087
LAVERTON RAAF	37.867S	144.750E	66	35.4	37.4	95.0	66.1	89.6	65.2	84.5	64.3	70.0	83.1	68.3	81.4	66.4	97.3	74.2	64.4	90.8	72.2	26.3	23.2	20.8	2981	429

Meaning of acronyms:

DB: Dry bulb temperature, °F *WB: Wet bulb temperature, °F* *Lat: Latitude, °* *Long: Longitude, °* *Elev: Elevation, ft*
MCWB: Mean coincident wet bulb temperature, °F *DP: Dew point temperature, °F* *HR: Humidity ratio, grains of moisture per lb of dry air* *WS: Wind speed, mph*
MCDB: Mean coincident dry bulb temperature, °F *HDD and CDD 65: Annual heating and cooling degree-days, base 65°F, °F-day*

Station	Lat	Long	Elev	Heating DB 99.6%	Heating DB 99%	Cooling DB/MCWB 0.4% DB	0.4% MCWB	1% DB	1% MCWB	2% DB	2% MCWB	Evaporation WB/MCDB 0.4% WB	0.4% MCDB	1% WB	1% MCDB	Dehumidification DP/HR/MCDB 0.4% DP	0.4% HR	0.4% MCDB	1% DP	1% HR	1% MCDB	Extreme Annual WS 1%	2.5%	5%	Heat./Cool. Degree-Days HDD	CDD 65
MELBOURNE INTL	37.673S	144.843E	434	37.2	39.0	95.1	64.7	90.1	63.8	85.8	63.3	69.4	82.0	67.5	80.9	65.9	97.1	73.1	63.7	89.8	70.9	30.9	27.5	24.1	2993	483
MELBOURNE MOORABBIN	37.976S	145.102E	50	36.8	39.1	93.6	66.7	88.8	65.6	84.0	65.0	70.9	82.3	69.1	80.4	68.3	104.1	73.5	65.9	95.5	72.5	26.0	23.2	20.9	2856	418
MELBOURNE REGIONAL OFFICE	37.817S	144.967E	105	40.5	42.4	94.8	65.9	90.2	65.0	85.6	64.3	70.2	83.3	68.4	81.7	66.3	97.3	74.8	64.3	90.7	73.2	16.6	14.3	12.3	2264	632
MOUNT LOFTY	34.967S	138.700E	2395	36.4	37.7	88.0	60.9	84.3	59.4	80.9	58.1	65.4	77.7	63.4	76.5	62.1	91.1	67.6	59.3	82.3	65.9	34.1	30.1	26.6	4598	331
NEWCASTLE NOBBYS SIGNAL	32.918S	151.799E	108	45.9	47.6	86.7	67.4	81.7	67.4	78.4	68.7	74.2	78.0	73.1	76.6	73.2	123.7	75.8	72.0	118.8	75.0	37.2	32.5	29.2	1065	1020
PERTH INTL	31.940S	115.967E	67	38.9	41.1	99.0	66.9	95.7	66.7	92.5	66.2	72.3	87.6	70.6	86.0	68.0	103.0	76.9	66.1	96.5	75.6	24.8	22.1	20.1	1390	1462
PERTH METRO	31.917S	115.867E	82	38.9	41.2	97.4	68.6	94.0	67.8	90.7	67.1	72.9	86.7	71.1	85.6	68.7	105.9	78.0	67.0	99.8	76.1	18.0	15.9	14.2	1327	1409
SCORESBY RESEARCH INSTITUTE	37.867S	145.250E	262	36.1	38.1	93.4	66.8	89.3	66.1	85.3	65.4	70.7	84.7	68.9	82.5	66.7	99.1	74.7	64.5	91.6	72.9	18.0	16.0	14.2	2944	488
SWANBOURNE	31.950S	115.767E	135	43.6	45.5	95.3	68.2	91.2	67.8	87.6	67.4	73.9	83.9	72.1	81.7	71.1	115.2	78.1	69.3	108.3	75.8	28.6	24.6	21.5	1127	1284
SYDNEY BANKSTOWN	33.924S	150.988E	29	38.0	40.0	92.8	69.1	88.6	68.8	85.0	68.2	74.0	84.1	72.5	81.7	71.1	114.9	77.6	69.9	110.0	76.0	21.8	19.1	17.1	1639	1007
SYDNEY INTL	33.946S	151.177E	21	43.5	45.0	91.3	66.8	86.4	68.2	83.3	68.0	73.7	81.4	72.5	79.7	71.6	116.9	76.4	70.2	111.2	75.5	29.3	26.1	23.4	1205	1192
SYDNEY OBSERVATORY HILL	33.850S	151.200E	131	45.1	46.5	88.1	67.7	84.0	68.4	81.2	68.5	73.5	81.1	72.3	79.2	71.1	115.3	76.9	70.1	111.1	76.0	N/A	N/A	N/A	1137	1109
SYDNEY OLYMPIC PARK ARCHERY	33.833S	151.067E	13	42.2	43.9	92.4	67.7	88.4	67.6	84.9	67.4	73.2	82.4	71.9	80.7	70.6	112.9	76.3	69.3	107.6	75.2	20.3	17.0	14.9	1324	1168
TUGGERANONG ISABELLA PLAINS	35.417S	149.100E	1929	25.4	27.4	93.1	64.7	89.1	63.9	85.4	62.8	68.4	82.1	67.0	80.2	65.4	101.0	70.8	63.2	93.3	70.1	18.5	16.3	14.5	3710	512
WILLIAMTOWN	32.795S	151.834E	31	39.1	41.2	93.9	69.3	89.4	69.3	85.6	68.8	74.6	84.3	73.3	81.8	72.0	118.7	77.3	71.0	114.4	76.4	26.6	23.1	20.6	1463	1063
Austria																									*5 sites, 89 more on CD-ROM*	
GUMPOLDSKIRCHEN	48.033N	16.283E	764	14.6	18.5	88.3	70.8	84.9	69.0	81.8	67.4	71.9	85.7	70.1	82.7	67.2	102.9	78.6	65.5	96.8	76.6	17.8	14.8	12.7	5349	488
TULLN	48.321N	16.112E	575	11.8	16.9	89.0	70.8	85.6	69.1	82.5	67.5	72.3	86.1	70.3	82.9	67.6	103.5	79.5	65.9	97.5	77.0	26.5	23.0	20.2	5577	408
WIEN HOHE WARTE	48.250N	16.367E	656	15.2	19.2	88.1	71.4	84.8	69.5	81.8	67.9	72.5	85.8	70.6	82.7	67.8	104.5	79.9	66.1	98.7	77.6	21.8	18.7	16.4	5305	487
WIEN INNERE STADT	48.200N	16.367E	561	17.6	21.3	89.2	71.9	86.1	70.3	83.1	68.7	73.5	86.7	71.7	83.7	69.0	108.8	80.4	67.4	102.9	78.6	19.7	17.2	15.5	4830	695
WIEN SCHWECHAT	48.110N	16.570E	600	13.4	17.4	88.2	69.2	85.0	68.0	82.1	66.7	71.0	84.0	69.5	81.8	66.6	100.0	75.9	64.8	94.1	74.5	27.2	24.1	21.5	5509	437
Belarus																									*6 sites, 13 more on CD-ROM*	
BREST	52.108N	23.898E	468	-0.2	6.4	86.4	67.9	82.9	66.3	79.7	64.7	69.9	81.6	68.2	79.3	66.1	98.0	74.0	64.5	92.5	72.5	18.4	15.8	13.7	6742	273
GOMEL	52.527N	31.017E	472	-5.0	1.2	87.1	68.3	83.8	67.1	80.6	65.5	70.6	82.1	69.0	79.9	66.7	99.9	74.5	65.2	94.9	73.0	19.6	16.6	15.1	7366	322
GRODNO	53.600N	24.050E	440	-2.9	3.4	83.9	67.7	80.3	65.9	77.2	64.1	69.8	79.6	67.9	77.3	66.5	99.0	75.3	64.5	92.2	72.1	23.2	20.4	17.8	7383	165
MINSK 1	53.864N	27.540E	748	-3.2	2.8	84.5	67.5	81.5	65.8	78.6	64.4	69.6	80.6	67.7	77.9	65.9	98.3	75.3	64.1	92.0	72.6	18.4	16.0	14.0	7667	208
MOGILEV	53.950N	30.067E	630	-7.2	-1.4	84.0	67.7	80.5	66.1	77.3	64.8	69.7	80.5	67.9	77.4	66.1	98.5	74.9	64.3	92.4	72.4	21.9	19.4	17.4	8037	174
VITEBSK	55.127N	30.350E	682	-6.8	-0.9	83.4	67.4	80.2	66.0	77.0	64.2	69.4	80.0	67.5	76.9	65.7	97.2	74.2	64.1	91.9	72.1	18.1	15.9	14.0	7982	195
Belgium																									*3 sites, 16 more on CD-ROM*	
ANTWERP INTL	51.189N	4.460E	39	20.3	24.1	84.8	69.0	81.0	67.3	77.7	65.5	70.5	81.8	68.6	78.6	66.5	97.7	75.9	64.7	91.7	73.6	21.8	18.8	16.6	4988	196
BRUSSELS NATL	50.901N	4.484E	184	20.3	24.0	84.4	68.2	80.7	66.9	77.2	65.1	69.8	81.3	68.0	78.2	65.7	95.6	74.6	64.1	90.2	72.5	24.8	21.4	18.7	5148	177
UCCLE	50.800N	4.350E	331	21.0	24.5	84.1	67.6	80.5	66.1	77.1	64.3	69.3	80.5	67.4	77.7	65.4	94.9	74.1	63.6	89.1	71.8	20.6	17.8	15.5	5093	203
Benin																									*1 site, 5 more on CD-ROM*	
COTONOU CAJEHOUN	6.357N	2.384E	19	71.6	73.0	91.3	80.7	90.0	80.8	89.7	80.8	84.0	88.8	83.1	87.8	82.6	169.9	88.1	82.0	166.9	87.5	18.0	16.5	15.6	0	6156
Bolivia																									*3 sites, 0 more on CD-ROM*	
COCHABAMBA AP	17.421S	66.177W	8360	35.5	37.6	86.1	59.1	84.3	58.5	82.6	58.1	63.0	78.7	62.1	77.6	58.8	101.5	68.0	57.4	96.6	65.6	20.3	17.3	12.8	919	505
EL ALTO INTL	16.513S	68.192W	13325	23.1	25.0	64.1	42.7	62.5	42.4	61.0	42.2	48.3	56.9	47.5	55.8	44.9	73.4	50.0	44.4	72.1	49.5	19.0	16.9	14.9	7014	0
VIRU VIRU INTL	17.645S	63.135W	1225	48.6	51.6	94.9	74.5	93.1	74.9	91.4	75.2	78.9	87.9	78.2	87.0	76.9	146.7	82.9	75.6	140.4	81.3	29.3	25.8	22.9	157	3957
Bosnia and Herzegovina																									*3 sites, 5 more on CD-ROM*	
BJELASNICA	43.704N	18.257E	6791	-1.7	2.7	67.1	53.5	64.3	52.5	61.9	51.9	56.8	62.6	55.0	61.0	54.2	80.7	59.6	52.4	75.5	57.7	73.7	66.3	58.6	10823	2
SARAJEVO	43.825N	18.331E	1708	8.7	13.9	91.5	67.4	88.0	67.4	84.5	66.5	70.9	85.1	69.1	82.9	66.2	102.8	78.5	64.4	96.6	75.3	17.9	13.9	10.9	5599	426
SARAJEVO-BJELAVE	43.867N	18.433E	2093	11.6	15.9	91.3	67.3	87.8	66.6	84.4	65.5	71.0	84.4	68.6	82.3	66.2	104.2	79.7	63.7	95.6	75.5	12.3	10.5	9.1	5358	519
Brazil																									*30 sites, 21 more on CD-ROM*	
AFONSO PENA AP	25.528S	49.176W	2988	37.1	40.9	87.6	68.2	85.7	68.4	83.8	68.4	73.6	80.4	72.4	79.3	71.8	131.4	75.8	70.4	125.1	74.4	19.6	17.0	14.7	1129	1066
ANAPOLIS AB	16.229S	48.964W	3728	55.8	57.6	91.2	65.9	89.3	66.6	87.5	67.3	75.0	81.6	74.3	81.1	73.4	143.0	78.2	72.0	136.0	77.2	16.7	14.4	12.8	14	2937
ARACAJU AP	10.984S	37.070W	23	69.8	71.4	89.8	79.9	89.2	79.6	88.0	79.2	81.1	87.0	80.5	86.7	79.2	151.6	84.9	78.9	150.1	84.9	18.1	16.5	15.4	0	5548
BELEM VAL DE CANS INTL	1.379S	48.476W	54	73.0	73.2	91.8	78.7	91.4	78.5	90.0	78.4	82.5	86.7	81.8	86.4	81.0	161.4	85.1	80.7	159.9	84.9	18.7	15.6	13.5	0	6120
BELO HORIZONTE AP	19.851S	43.951W	2589	52.0	54.0	91.3	68.3	89.5	68.3	87.8	68.3	72.9	82.8	72.2	82.1	70.4	123.2	74.7	69.9	121.3	74.3	14.2	12.3	11.4	39	2839
BRASILIA INTL	15.863S	47.913W	3479	51.0	53.2	90.0	63.6	88.2	64.3	87.0	64.7	71.7	79.5	70.9	78.9	69.9	125.3	73.9	68.5	119.3	73.0	16.8	14.4	13.0	24	2566
CAMPO GRANDE AB	20.469S	54.673W	1833	46.5	50.4	97.2	72.5	95.4	72.9	93.6	73.2	79.0	89.7	78.2	88.8	76.7	149.1	83.9	75.5	142.9	82.2	23.0	21.2	19.1	115	4557
CONFINS INTL	19.634S	43.969W	2715	51.4	53.3	89.6	68.1	87.8	68.5	86.0	68.6	74.8	81.2	73.6	80.8	73.3	137.1	77.6	71.7	129.8	76.3	17.0	14.9	13.4	107	2237
CUIABA INTL	15.653S	56.117W	617	55.4	58.9	100.7	71.8	98.9	72.0	97.2	72.7	82.4	88.7	80.9	87.1	80.9	164.0	85.3	79.2	155.2	83.8	17.3	14.4	12.6	22	6018
EDUARDO GOMES INTL	3.039S	60.050W	264	71.2	71.4	96.5	79.3	95.0	78.8	93.5	78.7	83.2	90.3	82.3	89.2	81.0	162.9	85.0	80.8	161.5	84.6	13.6	11.6	10.0	0	6123
FLORIANOPOLIS INTL	27.670S	48.547W	20	46.1	49.4	89.8	77.4	87.8	77.0	85.8	76.0	79.6	86.1	78.6	84.5	77.5	143.1	82.3	77.0	140.7	81.8	18.7	16.5	14.7	388	2343
FORTALEZA INTL	3.776S	38.533W	82	73.0	73.3	89.8	76.9	89.4	76.7	88.2	76.2	80.0	84.6	79.2	84.2	79.1	151.3	81.9	78.4	148.0	81.5	22.4	20.3	18.5	0	6054
GOIANIA AP	16.632S	49.221W	2450	54.5	56.9	95.4	67.5	93.5	68.3	91.8	68.9	76.2	85.7	75.5	84.9	73.7	137.5	79.1	73.3	135.5	78.7	17.7	15.2	12.5	5	4260
LONDRINA AP	23.334S	51.130W	1867	46.3	49.8	93.2	71.1	91.3	71.4	89.6	71.7	78.1	84.1	77.1	83.4	76.9	150.3	80.6	75.5	143.1	79.4	15.1	13.0	11.5	215	2929
MACAPA INTL	0.051N	51.072W	56	73.0	73.2	95.2	79.8	94.8	79.8	93.4	79.9	82.4	90.8	81.7	90.2	80.4	158.0	87.0	79.2	151.7	85.5	18.4	16.3	14.6	0	6490

(Go to CD-ROM to access additional station tables.)

(Go to CD-ROM to access additional station tables.)

Meaning of acronyms:
DB: Dry bulb temperature, °F — *WB: Wet bulb temperature, °F*
MCWB: Mean coincident wet bulb temperature, °F
Lat: Latitude, °
DP: Dew point temperature, °F
MCDB: Mean coincident dry bulb temperature, °F
Long: Longitude, °
HR: Humidity ratio, grains of moisture per lb of dry air
HDD and CDD 65: Annual heating and cooling degree-days, base 65°F, °F-day
Elev: Elevation, ft
WS: Wind speed, mph

Station	Lat	Long	Elev	Heating DB		Cooling DB/MCWB						Evaporation WB/MCDB				Dehumidification DP/HR/MCDB						Extreme Annual WS			Heat./Cool. Degree-Days	
						0.4%		1%		2%		0.4%		1%		0.4%			1%							
				99.6%	99%	DB	MCWB	DB	MCWB	DB	MCWB	WB	MCDB	WB	MCDB	DP	HR	MCDB	DP	HR	MCDB	1%	2.5%	5%	HDD	CDD 65
MACEIO INTL	9.511S	35.792W	387	65.8	66.4	91.5	77.9	89.9	77.2	89.4	77.0	80.4	86.5	79.6	85.7	79.0	152.7	83.2	78.4	149.4	82.7	17.4	16.0	14.5	0	4836
MANAUS AB	3.146S	59.986W	267	72.2	73.1	94.8	78.5	93.4	78.5	92.1	78.4	81.0	88.6	80.5	88.3	79.1	152.7	84.6	78.8	150.8	84.4	12.8	11.4	9.9	0	6219
NATAL AB	5.911S	35.248W	169	69.5	70.0	91.1	77.9	89.9	77.4	89.3	77.3	80.1	85.8	79.5	85.5	78.9	151.0	83.0	77.9	145.7	82.3	22.4	20.5	18.8	0	5606
PORTO ALEGRE INTL	29.994S	51.171W	11	39.0	42.4	94.8	76.5	91.6	75.5	89.4	74.6	79.6	89.0	78.3	87.1	77.2	141.4	83.1	75.6	134.0	81.4	20.9	18.1	15.8	879	2051
PORTO VELHO INTL	8.709S	63.902W	294	65.8	68.0	96.8	76.0	95.2	76.4	93.6	77.0	82.3	87.9	81.6	87.5	80.9	162.4	84.1	80.5	160.2	83.9	13.5	11.4	9.7	1	6018
RECIFE INTL	8.126S	34.924W	33	70.4	71.5	93.2	80.7	91.8	79.7	91.2	79.4	81.7	90.4	80.9	89.4	79.2	151.5	87.2	78.7	149.1	86.8	19.5	18.0	16.4	0	6068
RIO GALEAO TOM JOBIN INTL	22.809S	43.244W	28	58.8	60.5	98.5	77.1	95.4	76.6	93.3	76.6	82.4	89.8	81.2	88.4	80.7	159.5	86.1	79.2	151.5	84.6	18.7	16.5	14.3	11	4330
RIO SANTOS DUMONT AP	22.910S	43.163W	11	61.1	62.7	93.3	77.2	91.1	76.9	89.3	76.6	79.9	87.7	79.2	86.7	77.4	142.5	84.0	77.0	140.7	83.7	18.7	16.5	14.5	7	4082
SALVADOR INTL	12.911S	38.331W	64	69.4	70.1	90.2	80.0	89.6	79.7	88.2	79.1	81.5	87.4	80.7	87.0	79.8	154.9	85.3	79.0	150.8	84.9	19.8	18.1	16.4	0	5433
SAO LUIS INTL	2.585S	44.234W	178	73.1	73.5	93.0	79.0	91.7	78.4	91.1	78.1	81.8	87.2	81.0	86.9	80.6	160.2	84.8	79.4	153.7	83.7	20.8	18.8	17.2	0	6486
SAO PAULO CONGONHAS AP	23.627S	46.655W	2631	48.2	50.4	89.9	68.3	88.0	68.4	86.2	68.3	73.8	81.8	72.7	80.8	71.7	129.0	77.9	70.2	122.5	76.1	17.8	15.7	14.0	382	2093
SAO PAULO INTL	23.432S	46.470W	2459	46.1	48.4	91.0	70.7	88.2	70.4	86.4	70.1	76.0	82.9	74.8	81.7	74.8	143.0	78.0	73.3	135.7	76.9	16.4	14.4	13.0	396	1916
TERESINA AP	5.060S	42.823W	219	71.4	72.7	101.9	73.0	100.4	73.8	98.9	74.3	81.0	88.2	80.4	88.1	79.2	152.8	83.2	78.9	151.3	83.1	11.5	9.9	8.9	0	7254
VIRACOPOS INTL	23.007S	47.135W	2170	48.1	50.4	91.7	69.6	90.0	69.8	88.2	69.8	75.3	83.5	74.5	82.8	73.5	135.2	77.2	72.0	128.4	76.2	25.1	22.9	21.1	178	2557
VITORIA AP	20.258S	40.286W	11	62.2	64.0	93.4	77.9	91.8	77.3	90.6	77.1	80.9	87.1	80.0	86.1	79.2	151.7	83.4	78.8	149.3	83.0	23.1	20.8	18.5	0	4697
																										4 sites, 33 more on CD-ROM
Bulgaria																										
CHERNI VRAH	42.583N	23.267E	7520	-2.4	1.1	63.2	51.7	60.6	51.0	58.4	50.2	54.3	59.2	52.8	57.6	52.4	77.5	56.3	50.8	73.1	54.8	63.4	54.0	44.4	11500	0
PLOVDIV	42.068N	24.851E	597	13.6	18.5	94.7	69.3	91.5	69.1	89.2	68.2	72.9	87.8	71.2	85.5	68.3	106.1	78.5	66.5	99.8	76.5	25.1	21.8	18.5	4556	1007
SOFIA	42.695N	23.406E	1742	8.9	14.1	91.4	66.2	87.8	65.6	84.5	65.2	69.6	83.1	68.2	81.4	64.9	98.3	74.5	64.0	95.4	73.6	21.1	18.2	15.7	5476	536
VARNA	43.232N	27.825E	230	15.6	19.5	89.4	72.1	86.3	71.7	84.2	70.9	76.2	84.5	74.4	82.6	73.5	125.9	81.3	71.7	118.1	79.8	27.5	22.5	18.7	4567	782
																										2 sites, 7 more on CD-ROM
Burkina Faso																										
BOBO DIOULASSO	11.160N	4.331W	1511	65.2	67.3	100.7	68.5	99.3	68.6	98.0	68.8	78.9	89.7	78.1	88.7	76.1	144.5	83.8	75.4	140.6	83.0	16.6	14.8	13.5	0	6224
OUAGADOUGOU INTL	12.353N	1.512W	1037	61.1	63.2	105.5	68.5	103.9	68.7	102.3	69.1	79.6	92.1	78.9	91.2	77.0	146.0	83.3	75.6	139.3	82.8	17.1	15.0	13.4	0	6961
																										1 site, 1 more on CD-ROM
Chad																										
N'DJAMENA INTL	12.134N	15.034E	968	55.6	58.6	109.4	71.5	107.7	71.2	105.9	70.8	82.9	93.9	81.7	92.7	80.6	164.5	87.7	79.0	156.2	86.8	20.6	17.9	15.9	1	7005
																										2 sites, 11 more on CD-ROM
Chile																										
CERRO MORENO INTL	23.444S	70.445W	455	49.9	51.6	75.5	66.0	74.4	65.2	73.4	64.5	67.9	73.0	66.6	72.1	66.0	97.4	71.7	64.4	92.2	69.9	20.1	18.3	16.7	1281	315
SANTIAGO PUDAHUEL INTL	33.393S	70.786W	1555	30.1	32.1	89.4	63.0	87.5	62.8	85.7	62.6	66.2	84.1	65.1	83.2	59.0	78.9	71.9	57.4	74.5	70.7	19.1	17.3	15.6	2675	475
																										87 sites, 327 more on CD-ROM
China																										
ANQING	30.617N	116.967E	207	28.2	30.4	96.2	80.9	94.4	80.7	92.4	80.1	83.3	91.6	82.4	90.7	81.1	162.9	88.3	80.2	158.0	87.5	17.6	15.5	13.8	2835	2390
ANYANG	36.050N	114.133E	642	16.3	19.7	95.7	73.8	93.2	75.0	90.8	75.0	82.0	89.1	80.6	87.4	80.2	160.6	86.7	78.7	152.8	85.3	16.7	14.4	12.4	4243	1787
BAITA	40.851N	111.824E	3556	-9.6	-4.2	89.7	63.3	87.0	62.8	84.3	62.2	69.8	81.1	68.2	78.4	66.5	111.5	73.9	64.7	104.5	74.1	20.2	16.9	14.3	7970	611
BAODING	38.733N	115.483E	56	13.5	16.8	95.5	72.7	92.7	73.2	90.3	73.4	80.7	88.3	79.1	86.4	78.6	148.8	85.5	77.0	140.8	84.1	14.2	11.9	9.9	4738	1727
BAOJI	34.350N	107.133E	2001	21.1	23.7	95.1	71.1	92.6	70.6	90.0	70.5	76.6	87.6	75.2	85.8	73.6	134.9	82.9	72.2	128.4	81.4	13.9	11.6	9.8	4216	1468
BEIJING CAPITAL INTL	40.080N	116.585E	116	11.9	15.0	95.0	71.6	92.3	72.0	89.8	72.2	80.7	86.9	79.0	85.2	79.0	151.2	84.3	77.2	142.1	82.6	22.5	18.5	15.2	5121	1567
BENGBU	32.850N	117.300E	92	22.9	25.7	96.1	79.7	93.9	79.0	91.5	77.7	82.9	91.1	81.9	90.0	80.8	160.7	88.0	79.8	155.0	87.2	16.1	13.9	12.2	3424	2062
BENXI	41.317N	123.783E	607	-8.2	-4.2	88.3	71.3	86.1	71.1	84.1	70.7	76.3	83.2	75.0	81.8	74.2	130.8	80.3	72.8	124.6	79.0	14.4	12.0	10.5	7363	893
CANGZHOU	38.333N	116.833E	36	15.1	18.1	93.6	73.7	91.4	74.3	89.4	74.1	81.3	87.9	79.8	86.1	79.5	153.5	85.6	78.1	146.0	84.0	19.5	16.3	13.9	4769	1668
CHANGCHUN LONGJIA	43.996N	125.681E	706	-14.0	-9.6	87.7	69.2	85.4	69.6	83.0	69.1	75.6	82.0	74.0	80.4	73.6	128.4	79.6	71.9	121.1	78.1	23.3	19.7	16.8	8701	759
CHANGDE	29.050N	111.683E	115	30.1	32.1	97.6	80.1	95.5	80.0	93.3	79.5	83.4	91.9	82.2	90.9	81.1	162.5	88.9	80.0	156.2	87.8	13.9	11.5	9.6	2656	2403
CHANGSHA	28.117N	112.783E	394	29.9	31.9	97.5	78.9	95.6	78.9	93.6	78.7	82.0	91.1	81.1	90.3	79.9	157.3	86.9	78.8	151.9	86.0	14.7	12.6	11.2	2628	2500
CHAOYANG	41.550N	120.450E	577	-2.3	1.6	92.6	70.1	89.9	70.1	87.5	69.7	77.9	85.6	76.2	83.4	75.7	137.2	82.5	74.1	129.9	80.8	18.6	16.1	14.0	6640	1158
CHENGDE	40.967N	117.917E	1388	-0.8	2.5	91.6	68.8	88.8	68.8	86.3	68.3	75.8	84.0	74.3	82.4	73.4	131.0	80.4	71.8	123.9	78.8	15.9	12.5	10.0	6860	936
CHENGDU SHUANGLIU	30.579N	103.947E	1625	33.4	35.4	93.0	77.0	91.0	76.2	88.2	74.9	80.6	87.9	79.2	86.1	78.8	159.1	85.3	77.3	150.8	83.6	12.7	10.1	8.6	2434	1833
CHIFENG	42.300N	118.833E	1860	-4.7	-1.5	91.2	67.1	88.2	66.3	85.7	65.6	72.9	83.8	71.3	81.4	69.7	116.9	78.4	68.1	110.6	77.1	18.4	15.7	13.5	7593	801
CHONGQING JIANGBEI INTL	29.719N	106.642E	1365	37.0	38.9	99.0	76.9	96.6	77.2	94.2	77.0	81.0	90.5	80.1	89.5	78.8	157.6	86.0	77.7	151.7	85.1	12.1	10.2	8.9	2108	2341
DALIAN INTL	38.966N	121.539E	107	10.0	13.3	88.2	74.2	86.1	73.3	84.1	72.7	79.0	83.7	77.8	82.0	77.4	143.2	81.3	76.6	139.3	80.6	23.0	20.4	18.1	5549	1154
DANDONG	40.050N	124.333E	46	2.9	6.6	85.9	74.4	83.5	73.4	81.4	72.6	78.2	82.2	76.8	80.2	77.1	141.4	80.4	75.7	134.5	78.7	19.0	16.5	14.4	6498	824
DATONG	40.083N	113.417E	3458	-5.3	-1.8	89.6	63.5	86.7	62.8	84.2	62.6	70.2	80.3	68.8	78.6	67.4	114.7	74.3	65.7	107.9	73.5	21.0	18.0	15.5	7561	641
DEZHOU	37.433N	116.317E	72	17.1	19.7	93.6	75.7	91.3	75.8	89.4	75.2	82.1	88.7	80.4	86.8	80.2	156.9	86.6	78.6	148.9	85.2	16.5	14.3	12.4	4492	1738
FUZHOU CHANGLE INTL	25.935N	119.663E	46	40.3	42.4	96.0	80.0	93.8	79.7	91.8	79.3	81.9	91.7	81.0	90.0	79.2	151.8	87.3	78.7	149.5	86.4	23.2	20.5	18.0	1265	2953
GANYU	34.850N	119.133E	33	19.3	22.2	91.9	79.5	89.3	78.4	87.0	77.9	82.8	89.0	81.7	87.2	81.1	161.8	87.1	80.0	156.0	85.8	16.3	14.0	12.2	4150	1544
GUANGZHOU BAIYUN INTL	23.392N	113.299E	50	42.4	44.4	96.6	79.2	94.8	79.1	93.1	78.9	81.9	89.0	81.3	88.3	80.4	158.1	85.3	79.2	151.9	84.5	16.1	13.8	11.9	693	3790
GUIYANG LONGDONGBAO INTL	26.539N	106.801E	3736	26.4	28.8	86.6	70.1	84.7	69.9	82.9	69.4	73.5	81.9	72.4	80.4	71.1	131.9	77.3	70.1	127.5	76.1	14.7	12.7	11.3	3122	1180
HAIKOU	20.000N	110.250E	79	51.3	54.1	95.1	80.3	93.6	80.1	92.2	79.9	82.4	90.5	81.7	89.4	80.4	158.5	86.1	79.8	155.1	85.4	17.6	15.1	13.2	187	4551
HANGZHOU XIAOSHAN INTL	30.228N	120.432E	23	28.2	30.3	97.9	79.4	95.9	79.4	93.5	79.1	82.5	91.0	81.5	90.1	80.7	159.3	86.2	79.2	151.5	85.4	15.7	13.4	11.6	2810	2328
HARBIN	45.933N	126.567E	386	-18.0	-13.9	88.5	68.7	85.9	69.7	83.4	69.1	75.4	82.5	74.0	80.7	73.2	125.3	79.4	71.8	119.2	78.2	17.0	14.8	12.9	9392	720
HEFEI LUOGANG	31.780N	117.298E	108	24.4	26.8	96.1	81.9	93.8	81.2	91.7	80.2	84.0	92.3	82.8	90.8	82.1	167.7	89.5	80.7	160.1	88.2	16.2	13.9	12.1	3279	2148

Meaning of acronyms:
DB: Dry bulb temperature, °F — *WB: Wet bulb temperature, °F*
MCWB: Mean coincident wet bulb temperature, °F
Lat: Latitude, °
DP: Dew point temperature, °F
MCDB: Mean coincident dry bulb temperature, °F
Long: Longitude, °
HR: Humidity ratio, grains of moisture per lb of dry air
Elev: Elevation, ft
WS: Wind speed, mph
HDD and CDD 65: Annual heating and cooling degree-days, base 65°F, °F-day

Station	Lat	Long	Elev	Heating DB		Cooling DB/MCWB						Evaporation WB/MCDB				Dehumidification DP/HR/MCDB						Extreme Annual WS			Heat./Cool. Degree-Days	
						0.4%		1%		2%		0.4%		1%		0.4%			1%							
				99.6%	99%	DB	MCWB	DB	MCWB	DB	MCWB	WB	MCDB	WB	MCDB	DP	HR	MCDB	DP	HR	MCDB	1%	2.5%	5%	HDD	CDD 65
JINAN TSINAN	36.683N	116.983E	190	16.9	20.0	95.1	73.8	92.8	74.0	90.6	73.6	80.6	89.3	79.5	87.6	78.3	147.7	85.6	77.2	142.3	84.9	19.9	16.9	14.5	4078	1942
JINGDEZHEN	29.300N	117.200E	197	29.6	31.8	97.2	79.6	95.4	79.3	93.6	78.8	81.9	92.1	81.1	90.8	79.4	153.8	86.5	78.7	150.1	85.9	11.8	9.8	8.5	2386	2567
JINGZHOU JIANGLING	30.333N	112.183E	108	28.9	30.9	95.1	81.8	93.3	81.0	91.5	79.9	83.5	92.0	82.5	90.9	81.4	163.8	89.2	80.3	158.0	88.3	15.0	13.0	11.3	2838	2234
JINZHOU	41.133N	121.117E	230	3.3	6.7	89.2	71.2	86.9	71.1	84.8	70.7	78.1	83.4	76.6	81.8	76.6	139.6	81.6	75.0	132.5	79.9	19.8	17.0	14.9	6289	1112
JIXI	45.300N	130.917E	897	-12.7	-9.2	86.8	69.1	84.1	68.6	81.5	68.1	74.3	81.4	72.6	79.4	72.0	122.5	77.9	70.5	116.0	76.6	24.5	21.1	18.4	9406	513
KUNMING WUJIABA	24.992N	102.744E	6217	33.2	35.5	82.4	61.5	80.5	61.5	78.8	61.8	67.7	75.8	67.0	74.6	65.5	118.9	70.7	64.7	115.7	69.9	20.4	17.7	15.4	2072	641
LANZHOU	36.050N	103.883E	4980	11.6	14.3	90.7	64.5	87.9	63.3	85.4	62.3	68.5	83.4	67.1	81.5	64.1	107.9	76.2	62.5	101.8	74.3	9.7	7.8	7.0	5516	811
LIANGJIANG	25.218N	110.039E	570	33.8	36.0	95.2	77.8	93.4	77.6	91.6	77.5	80.8	88.5	80.0	87.5	79.0	153.8	84.0	78.3	150.2	83.4	16.1	14.0	12.2	1854	2706
LINGXIAN	37.333N	116.567E	62	12.9	16.4	95.1	74.4	92.4	75.1	90.0	75.1	82.0	88.2	80.5	86.8	80.5	158.5	86.2	78.8	149.9	84.5	18.3	15.7	13.6	4642	1657
LIUZHOU	24.350N	109.400E	318	38.1	40.5	95.5	78.1	94.0	78.1	92.6	77.9	81.0	90.0	80.3	89.1	78.7	151.0	84.9	78.1	147.7	84.6	11.4	9.7	8.6	1262	3400
MENGJIN	34.817N	112.433E	1093	20.1	22.7	94.9	71.6	92.2	72.1	89.7	72.3	80.0	87.8	78.7	85.8	78.0	151.7	84.8	76.7	145.0	82.9	19.6	16.2	13.7	3948	1676
MUDANJIANG	44.500N	129.667E	1006	-15.7	-11.8	88.3	70.0	85.7	68.9	83.0	68.3	74.3	83.0	72.7	80.6	71.6	121.1	79.2	70.2	115.3	77.8	19.4	16.1	13.4	9268	621
NANCHANG CHANGBEI INTL	28.865N	115.900E	143	30.7	32.7	96.6	80.0	94.9	79.8	93.0	79.6	82.8	90.8	81.9	90.0	80.9	161.2	87.0	79.9	156.1	86.6	12.7	11.1	9.7	2449	2636
NANJING LUKOU	31.742N	118.862E	49	23.4	26.3	96.2	80.1	93.9	79.8	91.6	79.1	82.8	91.1	81.8	89.8	80.8	160.1	87.6	79.8	154.8	86.7	17.1	14.9	13.1	3340	2039
NANNING WUXU INTL	22.608N	108.172E	421	40.7	43.0	95.1	79.1	93.4	79.0	91.8	78.7	81.9	89.5	81.1	88.4	80.1	158.7	85.5	79.2	153.9	84.6	14.2	12.1	10.4	887	3527
NEIJIANG	29.583N	105.050E	1171	36.5	38.5	95.6	78.7	93.3	78.0	91.0	77.1	81.2	91.0	80.2	89.4	78.8	156.3	86.9	77.8	151.1	85.7	11.5	9.5	7.9	2193	2088
QINGDAO INTL	36.266N	120.374E	33	17.2	19.8	91.0	74.9	88.0	74.6	85.9	73.8	80.3	84.9	79.1	83.3	79.0	150.8	83.0	77.9	145.1	81.9	23.7	20.9	18.5	4489	1440
QINGJIANG	33.600N	119.033E	62	21.1	24.7	92.8	80.8	90.8	79.7	88.8	78.3	82.9	90.0	81.8	88.5	81.0	161.3	87.5	79.9	155.7	86.5	14.6	12.3	11.0	3767	1735
QIQIHAR SANJIAZI	47.240N	123.918E	477	-18.6	-14.7	89.5	69.3	86.3	68.6	83.8	68.1	74.9	82.0	73.2	80.7	72.8	123.7	79.2	70.9	115.9	77.5	19.8	16.7	14.5	9714	732
SHANGHAI BAOSHAN	31.400N	121.467E	13	28.3	30.7	95.5	79.9	93.3	79.6	91.0	79.2	82.0	90.3	81.1	89.0	79.9	155.5	86.7	79.1	150.9	85.7	16.7	14.8	13.4	2875	2148
SHANGHAI HONGQIAO INTL	31.198N	121.336E	10	26.7	29.8	96.7	80.8	93.6	80.7	91.7	80.0	83.7	90.9	82.4	89.4	82.2	167.8	87.8	80.7	159.4	86.6	20.6	18.2	16.2	2880	2255
SHANTOU	23.400N	116.683E	10	45.0	47.7	93.5	80.8	91.7	80.6	90.0	80.1	83.5	89.2	82.5	87.8	82.3	168.6	87.1	80.9	160.7	85.5	18.5	16.0	14.0	606	3393
SHAOGUAN	24.667N	113.600E	223	35.9	38.2	95.6	78.4	93.9	78.2	92.3	77.9	80.9	90.0	80.1	88.8	78.7	150.2	84.6	78.0	146.9	84.0	15.8	13.7	11.9	1393	3113
SHENGYANG TAOXIAN	41.640N	123.483E	198	-11.4	-7.4	89.5	73.2	87.4	73.2	85.6	72.2	78.6	85.1	77.0	83.4	76.8	140.5	83.5	75.1	132.7	81.5	22.8	19.4	16.7	7468	1012
SHENYANG	41.733N	123.517E	141	-9.5	-5.2	88.6	73.5	86.6	72.6	84.7	71.9	78.0	84.4	76.5	82.7	76.2	137.3	82.0	74.7	130.5	80.4	21.2	18.0	15.4	7402	982
SHENZHEN BAO'AN INTL	22.639N	113.811E	13	44.7	47.3	93.2	79.4	91.6	79.3	90.4	79.2	83.9	87.9	82.7	86.8	82.8	171.0	86.3	82.1	167.4	85.9	17.9	15.9	14.1	453	3994
SHIJIAZHUANG	38.067N	114.350E	344	17.1	19.9	96.9	71.4	94.0	72.9	91.4	73.2	80.8	88.5	79.2	86.9	78.7	151.0	86.2	77.0	142.5	84.4	13.0	10.7	9.1	4361	1876
SIPING	43.183N	124.333E	548	-10.1	-6.4	87.9	70.5	85.6	70.4	83.7	70.0	76.5	82.6	75.1	81.1	74.7	132.5	80.2	73.2	126.0	79.0	18.9	16.3	13.9	8044	864
TAI SHAN	36.256N	117.105E	5039	1.7	5.5	72.8	63.0	71.0	63.3	69.7	63.8	69.6	70.1	68.4	69.0	69.5	131.1	69.9	68.2	125.4	68.8	39.9	35.2	31.6	8047	82
TAIYUAN WUSU INTL	37.747N	112.628E	2575	5.1	8.8	92.4	67.6	89.7	67.8	87.6	67.3	75.5	84.5	73.7	82.7	73.2	135.7	80.8	71.3	127.3	78.6	20.7	17.3	14.3	5744	1006
TANGSHAN	39.650N	118.100E	95	7.8	11.4	92.2	73.5	89.8	73.4	87.7	72.9	80.1	86.8	78.4	84.8	78.1	146.5	84.5	76.6	139.0	82.8	17.8	14.5	12.1	5347	1446
TIANJIN	39.100N	117.167E	16	13.0	16.1	93.9	73.7	91.5	73.9	89.2	73.4	80.9	87.6	79.4	85.7	79.1	151.1	85.5	77.5	143.1	83.9	20.3	16.6	13.7	4910	1681
TIANJIN BINHAI INTL	39.124N	117.346E	10	12.2	15.6	93.7	73.7	91.6	73.5	89.6	73.4	81.6	86.9	80.0	85.5	80.5	158.5	85.2	78.8	149.5	83.2	23.1	19.6	16.7	4966	1657
URUMQI DIWOPU	43.907N	87.474E	2125	-11.4	-7.5	95.4	64.3	93.2	63.9	91.0	63.3	68.4	86.0	66.9	84.5	64.0	96.5	71.9	61.1	87.1	72.1	16.3	12.7	10.5	7739	1394
WEIFANG	36.767N	119.183E	72	12.8	15.7	93.9	75.5	91.3	75.2	88.9	74.5	81.4	88.9	79.9	86.4	79.3	152.4	86.0	78.1	146.2	84.4	20.1	17.3	15.1	4847	1466
WENZHOU	28.017N	120.667E	23	34.3	37.0	93.0	81.2	91.2	80.7	89.6	80.0	82.5	90.7	81.6	89.0	80.2	157.1	86.8	79.7	154.0	85.9	14.4	12.2	11.0	1937	2350
WUHAN TIANHE	30.784N	114.208E	113	27.5	29.9	97.0	81.7	95.1	81.1	93.1	80.6	84.6	92.3	83.4	90.9	82.7	171.0	89.3	81.7	165.6	88.5	15.7	13.3	11.5	2878	2389
WUHUXIAN	31.150N	118.583E	52	26.4	28.7	97.2	81.3	95.1	80.7	92.8	80.1	83.5	92.6	82.4	91.6	81.2	162.6	88.8	80.1	156.3	87.6	16.7	14.3	12.4	3058	2208
WULUMUQI	43.783N	87.617E	3015	-7.7	-3.9	92.1	61.4	89.3	60.9	86.8	60.4	64.4	82.8	63.3	81.7	59.2	84.0	68.3	57.3	78.4	68.6	16.7	13.2	11.0	7823	977
XIAMEN GAOQI INTL	24.544N	118.128E	59	44.2	46.1	94.6	79.3	92.8	79.3	91.1	78.9	82.0	88.1	81.2	87.4	80.7	159.9	85.1	79.5	153.4	84.4	19.7	17.3	15.4	813	3188
XIANYANG	34.447N	108.752E	1572	17.3	20.8	97.1	73.5	94.9	73.2	91.8	72.9	79.4	89.9	78.0	88.1	76.9	148.6	85.8	75.2	140.2	84.5	18.3	15.7	13.4	4245	1630
XIHUA	33.783N	114.517E	174	21.9	24.5	95.3	78.0	93.1	78.4	90.9	77.3	83.4	91.1	82.0	89.2	81.5	164.6	88.7	80.1	157.3	87.2	12.3	10.5	9.2	3720	1847
XINGTAI	37.183N	114.367E	604	18.9	21.4	96.7	72.1	93.8	73.0	91.5	73.5	81.1	89.0	79.7	87.2	79.0	153.9	86.1	77.6	146.6	85.2	12.1	10.1	8.9	4188	1911
XINING	36.617N	101.767E	7421	0.9	4.1	81.7	59.3	78.8	57.7	76.1	56.5	62.7	75.3	61.0	72.5	59.0	98.8	66.7	57.3	92.8	65.3	12.2	9.9	7.8	7559	88
XINYANG	32.133N	114.050E	377	23.7	26.1	94.6	79.5	92.4	78.5	90.3	77.5	82.0	90.5	81.0	89.2	79.9	157.2	87.0	78.8	151.6	86.1	17.5	14.8	12.8	3403	1926
XINZHENG INTL	34.520N	113.841E	495	20.4	22.9	95.6	74.2	93.3	75.0	91.0	75.0	82.3	88.8	80.8	87.4	80.6	161.8	86.8	79.0	153.3	85.3	18.5	15.3	12.8	3883	1802
XUZHOU	34.283N	117.150E	138	20.5	23.5	94.7	78.5	92.5	77.6	90.2	76.6	82.5	90.6	81.4	88.9	80.4	158.9	87.8	79.3	152.9	86.5	14.1	12.1	10.7	3829	1870
YANGJIANG	21.867N	111.967E	72	44.6	46.9	91.5	79.7	90.0	79.4	88.8	79.2	81.9	86.8	81.4	86.2	80.8	160.3	84.2	80.1	156.8	83.9	19.5	16.6	14.5	503	3666
YANJI	42.883N	129.500E	584	-8.1	-4.4	87.9	70.7	85.0	69.5	82.2	68.5	74.9	83.1	73.1	79.8	72.5	122.9	79.6	71.0	116.6	77.6	23.1	19.8	16.8	8523	533
YICHANG	30.733N	111.367E	845	30.2	32.2	96.5	79.9	94.2	78.9	91.9	77.8	82.6	91.6	81.4	90.2	80.3	162.2	88.0	79.1	156.1	86.6	9.9	8.5	7.4	2649	2204
YINCHUAN	38.483N	106.217E	3648	2.5	6.4	90.9	65.9	88.6	65.4	86.2	64.5	71.7	83.4	70.0	81.7	68.2	118.9	78.1	66.4	111.4	76.9	18.3	14.1	11.6	6209	921
YINGKOU	40.667N	122.200E	13	0.3	4.0	86.8	75.2	84.9	74.3	83.3	73.6	78.5	83.7	77.2	82.3	76.9	140.2	82.4	75.6	133.9	80.9	22.2	19.3	17.1	6532	1107
YUEYANG	29.383N	113.083E	171	29.9	32.0	94.0	80.9	92.6	80.3	91.2	79.8	83.0	91.0	81.8	89.8	80.8	160.9	89.0	79.7	154.9	87.7	15.9	13.9	12.2	2638	2402
YUNCHENG	35.117N	111.067E	1235	16.3	19.8	97.6	72.3	95.1	72.4	92.6	72.0	78.5	90.3	77.3	88.9	75.4	139.4	85.6	73.9	132.4	84.4	19.6	16.4	14.0	4178	1881
ZHANGJIAKOU	40.783N	114.883E	2382	1.5	4.7	91.5	65.7	88.6	65.5	86.0	65.2	72.9	83.1	71.5	81.1	70.0	120.6	78.4	68.2	113.4	77.6	16.5	13.9	11.9	6673	981
ZHANJIANG	21.217N	110.400E	92	45.7	48.2	92.9	79.8	91.6	80.0	90.3	79.9	82.5	88.1	81.9	87.3	81.0	161.8	85.1	80.5	159.1	84.8	18.2	15.5	13.6	398	4012
ZHAOQING GAOYAO	23.050N	112.467E	39	43.4	45.5	95.2	79.0	93.7	78.9	92.2	78.8	81.6	89.8	80.9	88.7	79.6	153.7	85.1	79.0	150.8	84.6	15.4	13.0	11.2	686	3756
ZUNYI	27.700N	106.883E	2772	30.7	32.7	90.8	72.8	88.9	72.4	87.0	72.1	75.5	85.5	74.7	84.2	72.9	135.6	79.8	72.2	132.2	79.0	10.3	8.7	7.4	2943	1540

(Go to CD-ROM to access additional station tables.)

(Go to CD-ROM to access additional station tables.)

Meaning of acronyms:
DB: Dry bulb temperature, °F *WB: Wet bulb temperature, °F*
MCWB: Mean coincident wet bulb temperature, °F
Lat: Latitude, °
DP: Dew point temperature, °F
MCDB: Mean coincident dry bulb temperature, °F
Long: Longitude, °
HR: Humidity ratio, grains of moisture per lb of dry air
Elev: Elevation, ft
WS: Wind speed, mph
HDD and CDD 65: Annual heating and cooling degree-days, base 65°F, °F-day

Station	Lat	Long	Elev	Heating DB		Cooling DB/MCWB						Evaporation WB/MCDB				Dehumidification DP/HR/MCDB						Extreme Annual WS			Heat./Cool. Degree-Days	
						0.4%		1%		2%		0.4%		1%		0.4%			1%							
				99.6%	99%	DB	MCWB	DB	MCWB	DB	MCWB	WB	MCDB	WB	MCDB	DP	HR	MCDB	DP	HR	MCDB	1%	2.5%	5%	HDD	CDD 65
Colombia																										*5 sites, 1 more on CD-ROM*
ALFONSO BONILLA ARAGON INTL	3.543N	76.382W	3162	64.0	64.4	89.9	71.7	89.1	71.6	87.7	71.5	73.9	85.1	73.1	84.6	70.7	127.5	79.1	69.9	124.0	77.9	14.9	13.2	11.8	0	3952
ELDORADO INTL	4.702N	74.147W	8361	38.4	40.9	70.2	56.1	69.5	56.0	68.2	55.8	59.4	65.8	58.8	65.1	57.5	96.7	61.8	56.9	94.6	61.4	17.6	15.2	13.5	2999	0
ERNESTO CORTIZZOS INTL	10.890N	74.781W	98	73.0	73.6	93.6	81.1	92.8	81.0	91.5	80.5	83.6	89.1	82.8	88.3	82.5	169.9	86.0	81.2	162.9	85.3	24.3	21.6	19.0	0	6611
JOSE MARIA CORDOVA INTL	6.165N	75.423W	7028	50.1	51.7	75.0	60.7	73.7	60.2	73.4	60.1	63.6	70.4	62.8	69.8	61.2	105.3	64.9	60.9	104.3	64.5	17.9	14.2	12.2	705	43
RAFAEL NUNEZ AP	10.442N	75.513W	4	73.8	75.0	91.5	81.7	90.0	81.0	89.7	80.8	83.0	88.7	82.4	88.1	81.0	161.1	86.9	80.8	159.9	86.7	18.6	16.0	13.8	0	6535
Congo																										*1 site, 1 more on CD-ROM*
BRAZZAVILLE MAYA MAYA INTL	4.252S	15.253E	1048	64.4	66.1	93.5	76.2	92.4	76.2	91.3	76.1	78.9	87.9	78.2	87.1	76.9	145.6	82.5	75.6	139.4	81.5	13.1	11.3	9.8	0	5124
Costa Rica																										*1 site, 0 more on CD-ROM*
JUAN SANTAMARIA INTL	9.994N	84.209W	3021	62.3	63.1	87.5	69.4	86.0	68.8	84.5	68.8	75.5	80.2	74.7	79.7	74.0	141.9	77.8	73.3	138.7	77.3	23.4	21.3	19.2	0	3305
Côte d'Ivoire																										*1 site, 2 more on CD-ROM*
ABIDJAN	5.261N	3.926W	21	70.2	71.6	91.2	81.5	89.9	80.9	89.3	80.7	84.0	88.1	83.2	87.2	82.8	171.3	85.5	82.5	169.4	85.3	16.0	14.3	13.2	0	5838
Croatia																										*2 sites, 14 more on CD-ROM*
ZAGREB MAKSIMIR	45.817N	16.033E	420	14.4	19.3	90.7	70.7	87.6	69.6	84.8	68.6	72.4	86.0	71.0	84.3	68.1	104.9	78.2	66.5	99.0	76.9	12.6	10.6	9.1	4881	633
ZAGREB PLESO	45.743N	16.069E	353	12.1	17.2	91.0	71.3	87.9	70.2	85.1	69.3	73.5	86.3	72.0	84.1	69.6	110.2	79.6	67.9	103.9	78.0	18.8	15.9	13.2	5086	570
Cuba																										*3 sites, 6 more on CD-ROM*
CAMAGUEY INTL	21.420N	77.848W	413	58.8	61.2	92.8	74.5	91.5	74.8	90.4	74.8	79.1	85.8	78.3	85.2	77.3	144.4	81.6	76.7	141.5	81.1	21.1	18.7	16.6	8	4820
HAVANA JOSE MARTI INTL	22.989N	82.409W	210	50.2	53.6	91.6	77.0	90.9	77.0	89.7	77.0	81.8	86.7	80.6	86.3	80.6	160.4	85.2	79.1	152.2	84.0	20.9	18.5	16.5	54	4146
SANTIAGO ANTONIO MACEO INTL	19.970N	75.835W	249	65.4	67.1	89.7	77.6	88.6	77.7	88.0	77.7	81.1	85.6	80.4	85.5	80.4	159.1	84.2	79.0	152.1	83.7	18.3	15.8	13.9	0	5157
Czech Republic																										*5 sites, 35 more on CD-ROM*
BRNO-TURANY	49.151N	16.694E	778	10.3	14.3	87.5	68.4	84.1	67.0	80.9	65.6	70.3	83.0	68.7	80.7	66.1	99.1	75.7	64.5	93.4	73.9	22.6	19.6	17.4	6067	345
OSTRAVA MOSNOV	49.696N	18.111E	844	5.1	10.6	86.8	68.4	83.2	67.1	80.0	65.5	70.1	82.5	68.4	80.1	66.1	99.1	74.5	64.5	93.6	73.1	22.6	20.0	17.9	6392	228
PRAHA-KBELY	50.117N	14.533E	937	9.3	14.0	85.5	67.1	82.1	66.1	79.1	64.8	69.6	80.5	67.9	78.0	66.0	99.3	73.1	64.5	94.0	71.5	20.4	17.6	15.2	6132	257
PRAHA-LIBUS	50.000N	14.450E	996	10.4	14.8	87.2	66.6	83.6	65.5	80.3	64.1	68.7	81.8	67.2	79.3	64.6	94.7	72.3	63.1	89.8	70.8	15.8	13.6	11.8	6080	279
PRAHA-RUZYNE	50.101N	14.260E	1247	8.5	13.4	85.3	66.6	81.8	65.3	78.4	64.0	68.4	80.4	66.8	78.2	64.4	94.7	73.5	62.8	89.5	70.9	26.4	22.4	19.3	6540	187
Denmark																										*4 sites, 45 more on CD-ROM*
DROGDEN FYR	55.533N	12.717E	20	22.5	24.8	72.1	65.1	70.1	64.0	68.4	63.0	66.6	70.4	65.2	68.7	64.9	92.4	68.8	63.7	88.4	67.5	39.5	34.3	31.2	6130	54
KOEBENHAVNS KASTRUP	55.618N	12.656E	17	19.6	22.6	78.0	64.9	75.3	63.9	72.7	62.7	67.4	73.9	65.7	72.0	65.0	92.7	70.4	63.4	87.5	68.7	27.9	25.1	22.6	6324	98
ROSKILDE	55.586N	12.131E	146	15.6	19.4	78.6	64.9	75.3	63.8	72.8	62.7	67.7	74.0	65.8	72.2	65.7	95.2	70.9	63.6	88.3	68.9	27.7	24.6	22.0	6681	60
VAERLOSE	55.767N	12.343E	59	14.4	19.2	79.9	65.1	76.8	64.3	73.4	62.9	67.9	74.0	66.1	73.1	66.0	96.0	70.4	64.1	89.8	68.6	26.5	23.1	20.4	6775	72
Dominican Republic																										*2 sites, 4 more on CD-ROM*
LAS AMERICAS INTL	18.430N	69.669W	59	64.5	66.1	91.5	79.5	90.0	79.3	89.6	79.2	82.6	88.5	81.7	87.7	80.9	160.6	87.6	80.0	156.3	86.9	16.7	14.4	13.2	0	5212
SANTO DOMINGO	18.433N	69.883W	46	67.6	68.9	90.7	80.9	89.7	80.8	89.0	80.5	83.3	88.5	82.4	88.0	81.8	165.6	87.6	80.8	160.2	86.9	14.4	12.2	10.0	0	5503
Ecuador																										*2 sites, 2 more on CD-ROM*
JOSE JOAQUIN DE OLMEDO INTL	2.157S	79.884W	19	66.0	66.6	91.3	75.1	89.8	75.2	89.2	75.1	79.7	85.7	78.4	85.0	78.5	148.0	83.8	76.8	139.7	81.5	16.1	14.3	13.1	0	4999
QUITO PARQUE BICENTENARIO	0.141S	78.488W	9228	44.2	45.1	71.4	53.3	70.0	53.4	69.4	53.4	58.1	65.8	57.3	65.0	55.5	93.0	60.8	54.2	88.8	59.1	17.1	15.2	13.5	2535	0
Egypt																										*6 sites, 22 more on CD-ROM*
ALEXANDRIA INTL	31.184N	29.949E	-6	44.6	46.4	91.8	72.3	89.4	74.0	87.6	74.7	78.2	86.3	77.2	85.3	75.5	133.5	83.5	74.8	130.2	83.1	21.9	19.1	17.3	814	2433
ASSIUT	27.047N	31.012E	772	40.5	42.4	106.0	69.0	103.6	68.9	101.0	68.3	73.5	95.2	72.0	94.3	67.7	104.6	82.1	65.2	95.9	81.6	22.6	20.2	18.3	853	3806
CAIRO INTL	30.122N	31.406E	382	46.2	48.1	100.7	70.2	98.4	70.7	96.2	70.9	77.3	89.7	76.2	88.4	73.8	127.8	81.9	73.1	124.8	81.4	20.9	18.1	16.1	619	3397
LUXOR INTL	25.671N	32.707E	294	42.4	44.5	109.8	73.1	107.9	72.8	106.1	72.3	76.0	104.1	74.9	103.1	66.5	98.5	92.0	64.7	92.6	92.3	15.6	13.6	11.8	476	5117
PORT SAID	31.267N	32.300E	20	49.6	51.5	89.9	77.6	88.2	77.7	87.6	77.6	80.6	86.9	79.7	86.0	79.0	150.5	85.0	77.4	142.5	84.3	23.3	20.9	19.0	497	2914
PORT SAID EL GAMIL	31.283N	32.233E	20	49.3	51.2	89.4	77.8	87.9	77.6	86.7	76.9	80.4	86.6	79.3	85.7	78.6	148.7	84.9	77.3	142.2	84.4	25.5	22.6	20.6	554	2751
Estonia																										*1 site, 22 more on CD-ROM*
TALLINN	59.413N	24.833E	131	-1.3	4.8	80.0	66.4	76.6	64.4	73.3	62.7	68.3	76.3	66.2	73.4	65.6	94.9	72.0	63.4	87.9	69.8	20.6	18.2	16.2	8206	74
Finland																										*2 sites, 70 more on CD-ROM*
HELSINKI VANTAA	60.317N	24.963E	179	-6.2	-0.4	80.7	64.7	77.4	62.9	74.8	61.6	67.4	76.3	65.4	73.9	64.4	91.0	70.7	62.3	84.5	68.8	23.0	20.4	18.2	8458	95
ISOSAARI	60.100N	25.067E	23	0.6	6.8	72.9	66.1	70.8	64.9	68.7	63.5	67.7	71.5	65.9	69.7	66.0	96.0	70.6	64.2	90.0	68.6	35.4	31.6	28.0	8073	55

(Go to CD-ROM to access additional station tables.)

Meaning of acronyms:
DB: Dry bulb temperature, °F *WB: Wet bulb temperature, °F*
MCWB: Mean coincident wet bulb temperature, °F
Lat: Latitude, °
DP: Dew point temperature, °F
MCDB: Mean coincident dry bulb temperature, °F
Long: Longitude, °
HR: Humidity ratio, grains of moisture per lb of dry air
HDD and CDD 65: Annual heating and cooling degree-days, base 65°F, °F-day
Elev: Elevation, ft
WS: Wind speed, mph

Station	Lat	Long	Elev	Heating DB		Cooling DB/MCWB						Evaporation WB/MCDB				Dehumidification DP/HR/MCDB						Extreme Annual WS			Heat./Cool. Degree-Days	
						0.4%		1%		2%		0.4%		1%		0.4%			1%							
				99.6%	99%	DB	MCWB	DB	MCWB	DB	MCWB	WB	MCDB	WB	MCDB	DP	HR	MCDB	DP	HR	MCDB	1%	2.5%	5%	HDD	CDD 65
France																										*14 sites, 163 more on CD-ROM*
CAP COURONNE	43.333N	5.050E	89	26.8	32.7	87.3	72.7	85.0	72.2	83.0	71.3	76.7	83.7	75.3	82.1	74.5	129.6	81.4	73.1	123.3	79.9	38.3	33.6	29.9	2841	1021
CAP FERRAT	43.683N	7.333E	472	39.3	41.4	84.4	72.3	82.6	72.3	80.9	71.8	76.3	81.2	75.1	80.1	74.7	132.0	79.8	73.4	126.5	78.7	27.2	22.1	18.0	2286	1008
CAP POMEGUES	43.267N	5.300E	230	29.4	35.2	83.5	71.6	81.1	71.5	79.3	70.7	75.5	79.6	74.2	78.3	74.2	128.9	78.0	72.8	122.6	77.0	52.5	46.3	40.0	2741	823
LYON-BRON	45.727N	4.944E	659	22.0	25.0	91.7	67.7	88.2	67.2	85.0	66.6	70.4	84.8	69.1	83.1	65.9	97.7	75.2	64.5	93.1	74.2	25.0	21.5	18.7	4269	663
LYON-SAINT EXUPERY	45.726N	5.091E	821	21.3	24.4	90.6	67.9	87.3	67.4	84.0	66.6	70.5	84.0	69.1	82.2	66.2	99.4	75.8	64.7	94.4	73.9	23.7	20.5	17.7	4435	597
MARSEILLE PROVENCE	43.436N	5.214E	74	27.5	30.0	91.1	69.9	88.7	69.5	86.4	68.9	74.1	83.9	72.7	82.9	71.2	115.5	79.6	69.4	108.4	78.4	35.8	31.2	27.1	2908	1159
NICE COTE D'AZUR	43.658N	7.216E	12	35.5	37.5	85.1	72.7	83.3	72.4	81.8	71.9	76.5	81.8	75.0	80.9	74.8	130.5	80.5	73.0	122.4	79.8	26.8	22.9	18.9	2490	984
PARIS CHARLES DE GAULLE	49.013N	2.550E	392	22.8	25.9	87.5	67.8	83.6	66.4	80.0	65.2	70.0	82.4	68.3	79.6	66.0	97.4	74.7	64.3	91.6	72.9	25.3	21.9	19.3	4599	309
PARIS LE BOURGET	48.969N	2.441E	218	23.6	26.5	87.9	67.7	84.0	66.4	80.4	65.2	70.0	83.1	68.1	79.9	65.8	95.8	73.9	64.0	90.1	72.2	21.5	19.0	16.7	4484	303
PARIS ORLY	48.725N	2.359E	291	23.0	26.3	87.9	68.0	84.2	66.9	80.7	65.4	70.2	83.2	68.6	80.2	66.3	97.8	74.6	64.5	91.9	73.0	23.8	20.6	18.1	4601	329
PARIS-MONTSOURIS	48.817N	2.333E	253	26.4	28.7	88.1	68.2	84.3	67.1	80.8	65.4	70.3	84.0	68.4	80.5	65.8	96.0	75.3	64.0	90.2	73.4	16.3	14.3	12.8	4127	423
TOULOUSE BLAGNAC	43.629N	1.364E	499	25.2	28.1	91.7	69.2	88.2	68.4	85.3	67.5	72.1	85.1	70.7	83.2	68.1	105.1	77.5	66.5	99.4	76.1	23.9	20.9	18.6	3638	719
TRAPPES	48.767N	2.000E	551	23.2	26.1	86.3	67.3	82.4	65.9	79.0	64.6	69.2	81.5	67.5	78.5	65.4	95.8	73.4	63.7	90.3	71.2	15.1	13.3	11.8	4802	249
VELIZY-VILLACOUBLAY	48.774N	2.202E	584	23.2	26.2	86.0	67.2	82.4	66.0	78.9	64.6	69.4	81.4	67.7	78.4	65.5	96.3	74.0	63.9	90.9	72.1	20.8	18.3	16.3	4860	279
Gabon																										*1 site, 0 more on CD-ROM*
LIBREVILLE INTL	0.459N	9.412E	39	71.4	72.3	89.2	81.3	88.1	80.9	87.6	80.7	82.9	86.5	82.2	85.7	82.3	168.4	85.9	81.0	161.1	84.6	15.2	13.7	12.3	0	5425
Ga																										*1 site, 0 more on CD-ROM*
BANJUL INTL	13.338N	16.652W	95	61.9	63.1	100.0	68.5	96.9	68.4	94.9	69.8	81.8	88.7	81.0	87.8	80.3	157.6	86.3	79.1	151.7	85.1	19.2	17.4	15.4	0	5654
Georgia																										*1 site, 7 more on CD-ROM*
TBILISI	41.667N	44.950E	1624	21.2	24.6	94.9	71.1	92.3	70.5	89.6	70.1	75.1	88.5	73.0	86.9	71.0	121.5	83.2	68.5	111.2	80.7	42.7	35.3	30.3	4114	1283
Germany																										*28 sites, 117 more on CD-ROM*
BERLIN DAHLEM	52.467N	13.300E	167	10.4	15.6	84.7	66.3	81.1	64.7	78.1	63.4	68.4	79.8	66.7	77.4	64.7	92.0	72.1	62.9	86.2	70.0	16.5	14.5	13.1	6102	213
BERLIN SCHONEFELD	52.380N	13.523E	157	7.6	13.1	85.9	66.5	82.3	64.8	78.9	63.5	68.5	80.4	66.8	78.4	64.7	92.0	72.1	62.9	86.2	70.3	24.9	21.5	18.9	6273	201
BERLIN TEGEL	52.560N	13.288E	122	9.7	15.4	86.1	65.6	82.5	64.4	79.2	62.8	68.0	80.4	66.3	78.2	64.2	90.4	71.7	62.4	84.7	69.9	23.3	20.6	18.3	5970	264
BERLIN TEMPELHOF	52.473N	13.404E	167	10.8	15.4	86.0	66.1	82.3	64.7	79.1	63.4	68.2	80.5	66.6	78.4	64.3	90.9	71.8	62.5	85.0	70.1	23.2	20.4	18.1	5910	265
BREMEN	53.048N	8.787E	14	15.1	18.8	84.1	67.0	80.4	65.7	77.0	64.0	69.1	79.7	67.1	76.6	65.4	94.0	73.1	63.8	88.5	70.7	25.8	22.6	19.9	6048	157
CELLE	52.591N	10.022E	129	13.4	17.8	86.4	66.3	82.8	65.0	79.3	63.6	68.4	81.8	66.8	79.2	64.1	90.0	71.4	62.4	84.7	71.2	20.4	17.6	15.3	5807	229
DRESDEN	51.133N	13.767E	755	8.1	13.5	85.7	65.9	81.9	64.8	78.7	63.5	68.2	81.0	66.4	77.9	63.7	90.8	71.6	62.3	86.3	70.7	21.6	18.6	16.3	6094	243
DUSSELDORF	51.289N	6.767E	147	14.1	19.7	85.3	67.3	82.1	65.6	78.9	64.2	69.0	81.2	67.4	78.8	64.9	92.5	73.1	63.3	87.4	71.5	23.3	20.5	18.2	5271	251
ESSEN MULHEIM	51.400N	6.967E	528	14.3	19.5	82.8	66.7	79.8	65.2	76.7	63.7	68.3	79.1	66.6	77.2	64.5	92.5	72.4	62.8	87.1	70.2	21.6	18.8	16.5	5720	186
FRANKFURT AM MAIN	50.026N	8.543E	364	16.2	20.4	88.5	66.4	84.8	65.6	81.6	64.6	69.5	82.0	67.9	79.3	66.0	97.2	72.2	64.2	91.0	71.7	22.7	19.6	16.9	5447	350
FURSTENFELDBRUCK	48.206N	11.267E	1703	4.8	10.2	84.3	66.0	80.7	64.6	77.4	63.0	67.4	81.0	65.8	78.4	62.5	90.2	73.9	60.9	85.1	71.2	24.9	20.7	17.3	6670	147
GUTERSLOH	51.923N	8.306E	236	16.2	20.9	86.4	66.6	82.4	65.5	78.9	64.3	69.2	81.2	67.5	78.3	65.4	94.6	72.3	63.9	89.6	71.0	22.0	18.9	16.6	5523	219
HAMBURG FUHLSBUTTEL	53.630N	9.988E	53	11.1	16.0	82.1	66.1	78.7	64.5	75.3	62.9	68.0	78.5	66.0	75.5	64.2	90.2	71.7	62.5	84.6	70.1	22.7	20.2	18.2	6324	110
HANNOVER	52.461N	9.685E	183	9.2	14.5	84.0	66.9	80.6	65.3	77.3	63.7	68.7	79.7	67.0	77.3	65.0	93.0	72.0	63.2	87.2	70.8	22.7	20.0	17.8	6063	144
HEIDELBERG	49.393N	8.652E	358	17.3	21.5	89.9	68.8	86.3	67.5	82.8	65.7	70.9	84.3	69.3	82.3	66.5	98.8	74.9	64.7	92.7	74.0	18.5	15.9	13.9	4897	497
ITZEHOE	53.983N	9.567E	85	14.7	18.8	83.2	65.7	79.0	65.0	75.5	63.9	68.5	78.3	66.8	75.6	65.4	94.0	72.3	63.5	87.8	70.4	21.0	18.1	15.9	6274	112
KOLN BONN	50.866N	7.143E	302	17.1	20.8	86.5	67.3	82.7	65.9	79.4	64.4	69.5	81.9	67.5	78.6	65.4	94.9	73.9	63.8	89.5	71.9	20.0	17.4	15.4	5495	211
LEIPZIG HALLE	51.424N	12.236E	465	8.0	13.4	85.7	66.5	81.9	65.3	78.7	63.8	68.4	80.8	66.7	78.2	64.0	90.9	72.9	62.6	86.4	71.2	27.9	24.2	21.1	6108	216
LEIPZIG-HOLZHAUSEN	51.317N	12.450E	495	12.2	17.2	86.5	66.8	83.0	65.2	79.6	64.2	68.8	81.2	67.3	78.3	64.9	94.0	72.0	63.4	89.1	70.9	14.5	12.7	11.3	5704	276
MUNICH	48.354N	11.786E	1487	8.6	13.9	85.9	66.5	82.2	65.5	79.0	64.2	68.2	80.4	66.9	78.5	64.4	95.7	71.6	62.8	90.4	70.5	25.0	21.1	18.2	6285	195
NORVENICH	50.831N	6.658E	386	18.1	22.4	87.2	67.1	83.1	66.0	79.5	64.4	69.2	82.3	67.5	79.5	64.8	93.2	73.5	63.2	88.1	71.9	22.0	18.4	15.8	5208	235
NURNBERG	49.499N	11.078E	1046	6.1	12.3	86.3	65.2	82.9	64.2	79.7	62.6	67.5	80.3	66.1	77.9	63.8	92.0	70.3	62.2	86.9	69.1	20.7	17.6	15.1	6311	231
POTSDAM	52.383N	13.067E	328	9.2	14.0	85.5	66.0	81.8	64.9	78.7	63.8	68.5	80.6	66.8	78.2	64.8	92.9	71.3	62.8	86.5	70.2	24.0	21.0	18.6	6186	214
QUICKBORN	53.733N	9.883E	56	14.5	18.7	82.9	66.0	79.2	65.2	75.8	63.8	68.7	78.0	66.9	75.4	65.6	94.7	71.3	63.9	89.1	69.6	19.7	16.8	14.8	6229	101
ROTH	49.218N	11.100E	1268	8.5	13.8	87.8	66.8	84.1	65.2	80.7	64.0	68.4	82.7	66.9	80.2	64.1	93.8	71.4	62.5	88.7	70.7	17.5	14.6	12.4	6373	207
STUTTGART FILDERSTADT	48.690N	9.222E	1276	9.1	14.1	84.8	66.0	81.7	65.1	78.5	63.9	68.0	81.3	66.5	78.7	63.3	91.3	73.5	62.0	87.0	71.9	20.9	17.8	15.1	6281	191
STUTTGART SCHNARREN	48.833N	9.200E	1033	11.3	15.8	85.2	67.3	82.0	65.5	79.0	64.3	69.0	81.1	67.4	78.7	64.8	95.5	73.7	63.3	90.5	72.4	20.3	17.2	14.7	5674	288
WUNSTORF	52.457N	9.427E	187	15.0	19.1	86.4	66.5	82.5	65.4	79.0	63.8	68.7	81.9	67.0	79.0	64.3	90.9	72.3	62.6	85.6	71.6	23.1	20.3	18.0	5615	229
Greece																										*3 sites, 26 more on CD-ROM*
ATHINAI HELLINIKON	37.882N	23.735E	69	35.2	37.9	96.4	70.0	93.5	69.8	91.5	70.0	76.3	88.6	74.9	87.4	72.1	118.9	84.3	70.8	113.8	83.3	22.0	19.6	17.7	1976	2073
ELEFSIS	38.064N	23.556E	143	33.5	35.8	98.4	69.1	95.3	68.8	93.3	68.2	72.7	89.0	71.6	88.5	67.9	103.2	79.8	66.1	96.8	79.0	22.4	19.9	18.1	2190	2133
THESSALONIKI MAKEDONIA	40.520N	22.971E	22	26.5	29.7	94.6	71.0	91.6	71.0	89.5	70.2	74.8	87.9	73.4	86.4	70.2	111.1	82.9	68.6	105.2	81.4	25.7	21.2	18.2	3173	1537
Guatemala																										*1 site, 3 more on CD-ROM*
LA AURORA INTL	14.583N	90.527W	4952	51.6	53.5	82.5	64.0	80.8	64.1	79.2	64.1	68.3	76.6	67.5	75.3	66.3	116.6	70.3	64.8	110.8	69.1	26.2	22.8	20.8	111	1271

(Go to CD-ROM to access additional station tables.)

(Go to CD-ROM to access additional station tables.)

Meaning of acronyms:
DB: Dry bulb temperature, °F *WB: Wet bulb temperature, °F*
MCWB: Mean coincident wet bulb temperature, °F
Lat: Latitude, °
DP: Dew point temperature, °F
MCDB: Mean coincident dry bulb temperature, °F
Long: Longitude, °
HR: Humidity ratio, grains of moisture per lb of dry air
Elev: Elevation, ft
WS: Wind speed, mph
HDD and CDD 65: Annual heating and cooling degree-days, base 65°F, °F-day

Station	Lat	Long	Elev	Heating DB		Cooling DB/MCWB						Evaporation WB/MCDB				Dehumidification DP/HR/MCDB						Extreme Annual WS			Heat./Cool. Degree-Days	
						0.4%		1%		2%		0.4%		1%		0.4%			1%							
				99.6%	99%	DB	MCWB	DB	MCWB	DB	MCWB	WB	MCDB	WB	MCDB	DP	HR	MCDB	DP	HR	MCDB	1%	2.5%	5%	HDD	CDD 65
Honduras																										*2 sites, 1 more on CD-ROM*
RAMON VILLEDA MORALES INTL	15.453N	87.924W	91	64.0	65.8	98.4	78.3	96.4	78.7	94.8	78.8	83.2	90.8	82.3	89.5	81.0	161.7	86.4	80.7	159.8	86.0	18.6	16.4	14.3	0	5770
TONCONTIN INTL	14.061N	87.217W	3294	53.2	55.3	89.7	66.7	87.9	67.4	86.2	67.4	72.7	81.8	71.9	81.1	70.1	125.3	75.6	69.6	123.1	75.0	20.4	17.8	15.6	19	2718
Hong Kong																										*2 sites, 4 more on CD-ROM*
HONG KONG INTL	22.309N	113.915E	28	47.9	50.3	93.2	79.7	91.7	79.3	91.0	79.1	81.8	88.0	81.1	87.4	80.4	157.7	86.4	79.2	151.5	85.6	23.6	20.7	18.6	324	4222
HONG KONG OBSERVATORY	22.300N	114.167E	203	49.3	51.6	90.0	79.7	89.0	79.6	88.1	79.4	81.3	86.8	80.9	86.3	79.9	156.2	84.7	79.2	152.9	84.4	19.3	16.6	14.5	426	3556
Hungary																										*3 sites, 33 more on CD-ROM*
BUDAORS	47.450N	18.967E	433	11.8	15.8	87.8	68.2	84.8	67.4	82.0	66.5	70.3	84.0	68.9	81.5	65.5	95.8	75.8	64.3	91.6	74.6	31.2	26.0	20.8	5530	443
BUDAPEST FERIHEGY	47.437N	19.256E	495	10.6	15.5	91.5	71.5	88.0	69.5	84.5	67.9	73.4	87.1	71.4	83.9	68.4	106.4	79.7	67.6	103.4	78.1	27.9	23.1	19.2	5589	515
BUDAPEST PESTSZENTLORINC	47.433N	19.183E	456	14.3	17.9	91.7	68.8	88.3	67.7	85.2	66.5	71.0	85.3	69.4	84.1	66.5	99.1	75.8	64.8	93.5	74.3	16.7	14.3	12.2	5213	670
India																										*36 sites, 46 more on CD-ROM*
AHMEDABAD	23.077N	72.635E	189	51.5	53.7	108.5	73.4	106.1	73.1	104.1	73.2	83.6	93.0	82.6	90.9	81.7	166.2	87.4	80.7	160.7	86.3	15.1	13.4	11.9	20	6294
AKOLA	20.700N	77.033E	925	53.9	56.4	109.7	71.5	107.7	71.0	105.8	70.9	80.6	91.5	79.7	89.4	78.3	151.9	84.0	77.4	147.6	83.0	9.5	7.6	6.6	2	6429
AURANGABAD	19.863N	75.398E	1911	51.4	53.9	104.2	73.1	102.5	72.9	100.7	72.3	80.0	95.4	78.3	91.7	76.4	148.1	85.6	75.4	142.7	83.2	16.6	14.0	12.1	10	5044
BANGALURU	12.967N	77.583E	3022	59.5	60.9	93.6	67.9	92.2	67.7	90.7	67.7	74.5	84.3	73.6	83.2	72.0	132.7	77.8	71.1	128.6	76.9	12.1	10.0	8.7	0	3888
BELGAUM	15.859N	74.618E	2487	55.4	57.6	97.3	66.6	95.5	66.7	93.9	67.0	75.5	84.9	74.6	83.3	73.2	135.4	78.7	72.5	132.0	77.8	18.2	16.2	13.9	0	4004
BHOPAL	23.287N	77.337E	1719	49.2	51.5	107.2	71.4	105.1	70.9	102.9	70.7	79.3	88.7	78.5	87.3	77.3	151.7	82.6	76.6	147.8	81.6	19.7	17.6	15.1	110	4932
BHUBANESHWAR	20.244N	85.818E	138	57.1	59.1	102.3	80.8	99.9	80.5	97.7	80.1	85.2	94.1	84.5	92.9	83.3	175.2	88.9	82.6	170.9	88.3	22.0	19.1	17.2	1	6084
BIKANER	28.000N	73.300E	735	42.9	45.4	111.5	70.6	109.2	71.5	106.9	72.3	82.6	93.9	81.6	93.0	80.1	160.6	86.9	79.1	155.3	86.5	14.8	11.7	9.1	319	6236
CHENNAI INTL	12.994N	80.181E	52	67.8	69.4	102.0	78.6	99.3	78.5	97.2	78.4	83.2	91.4	82.3	90.1	81.0	161.5	86.8	80.5	158.9	86.4	18.0	16.0	14.1	0	6894
COIMBATORE INTL	11.031N	77.044E	1324	64.9	66.5	97.3	71.6	96.0	72.2	94.4	72.7	78.2	88.3	77.4	87.0	76.2	143.6	81.0	75.4	139.8	80.4	19.9	18.1	16.3	0	5651
CWC VISHAKHAPATNAM WALTAIR	17.700N	83.300E	217	68.0	69.4	92.9	80.9	91.6	81.6	90.7	81.4	84.6	90.0	83.9	89.3	83.3	175.2	89.0	82.4	170.4	88.5	17.5	14.9	12.9	0	6207
DEVI AHILYA BAI HOLKAR INTL	22.722N	75.801E	1850	48.9	51.4	105.2	68.0	103.2	68.0	101.1	67.9	78.0	86.7	77.2	85.4	76.1	145.9	80.9	75.4	142.5	80.2	22.7	20.4	18.7	80	4750
GUWAHATI INTL	26.106N	91.586E	162	51.4	53.2	94.7	80.8	93.1	80.7	91.7	80.5	84.4	91.1	83.6	90.0	82.7	171.5	88.1	81.9	167.0	87.3	10.9	9.2	7.7	102	4370
GWALIOR	26.293N	78.228E	617	42.6	44.6	110.5	73.7	108.4	73.8	106.1	73.7	83.4	91.9	82.6	90.8	81.5	167.6	87.4	80.7	163.3	86.6	9.7	7.7	6.5	345	5445
HYDERABAD BEGUMPET AP	17.452N	78.461E	1742	56.5	58.8	105.0	71.1	102.6	71.1	100.6	71.1	78.2	88.9	77.2	87.6	75.6	143.0	81.9	74.9	139.7	81.0	16.6	14.2	12.8	1	5586
JABALPUR	23.178N	80.052E	1624	47.0	49.3	108.4	69.3	106.4	69.2	104.1	69.6	79.9	87.9	79.1	86.6	78.1	155.1	82.9	77.4	151.3	82.2	9.3	7.6	6.8	152	5126
JAIPUR	26.824N	75.812E	1263	44.8	47.2	108.4	70.4	106.1	70.4	103.9	70.5	81.9	87.5	81.0	87.0	80.8	167.8	83.8	79.7	161.8	83.5	17.0	14.0	12.0	298	5370
JAMSHEDPUR	22.813N	86.169E	505	50.1	52.3	107.9	72.6	105.2	73.0	102.3	73.7	82.8	92.1	81.9	90.5	80.7	162.6	86.5	79.9	158.3	85.5	9.7	7.7	6.7	44	5569
JODHPUR	26.251N	73.049E	717	47.8	49.9	108.7	70.3	106.3	71.0	104.2	71.4	81.5	90.2	80.7	89.6	79.7	158.1	85.2	78.8	153.5	84.5	11.1	8.5	7.3	136	6083
KOLKATA BOSE INTL	22.655N	88.447E	16	52.3	54.3	100.0	81.0	98.0	81.0	96.3	80.6	85.4	94.4	84.6	93.2	83.2	173.8	90.3	82.6	169.8	89.6	14.1	12.1	10.7	36	5612
KOZHIKODE	11.250N	75.783E	16	72.6	73.6	94.0	82.4	93.0	81.8	92.1	81.3	84.0	91.8	83.3	91.0	81.8	165.4	89.9	81.0	161.2	88.9	12.6	10.3	8.1	0	6450
LUCKNOW	26.761N	80.889E	410	44.1	46.3	107.9	73.6	105.7	73.5	102.6	74.7	84.8	93.8	84.1	92.6	82.7	173.5	89.0	82.3	171.0	88.6	14.9	12.9	11.1	347	5055
MANGALURU INTL	12.961N	74.890E	337	69.4	70.8	93.9	76.8	92.8	76.9	91.9	76.6	80.9	88.4	80.3	87.7	79.1	152.9	84.2	78.4	149.5	83.7	17.6	14.5	13.1	0	6006
MUMBAI SHIVAJI INTL	19.089N	72.868E	37	62.3	64.6	96.6	72.9	94.8	73.4	93.2	73.9	82.1	87.9	81.5	87.3	80.7	159.7	85.6	80.0	155.7	85.1	16.1	14.3	13.2	0	6257
NAGPUR AMBEDKAR INTL	21.092N	79.047E	1033	52.5	55.1	111.5	72.7	109.5	72.6	107.4	72.2	81.9	90.4	80.8	89.5	80.4	163.9	85.7	78.9	156.0	84.5	17.0	13.8	11.9	10	5972
NELLORE	14.450N	79.983E	66	68.9	70.2	105.3	80.5	102.8	80.7	100.6	80.4	84.1	96.7	83.3	95.1	81.5	164.3	88.6	80.7	159.9	88.2	11.2	8.8	7.5	0	7386
NEW DELHI INDIRA GANDHI INTL	28.567N	77.103E	777	42.4	44.4	109.8	72.3	107.7	72.2	105.4	72.3	84.9	91.7	83.7	90.5	83.9	183.1	87.6	82.4	173.9	87.0	17.6	14.9	13.2	526	5347
NEW DELHI SAFDARJUNG	28.585N	77.206E	705	42.8	44.7	108.2	73.3	105.5	73.8	103.1	74.0	83.7	93.6	83.1	92.6	81.7	169.3	88.3	80.9	165.0	87.7	15.6	13.2	11.1	480	5082
PATIALA	30.333N	76.467E	823	41.0	43.0	107.2	77.2	104.6	76.8	101.6	76.8	85.2	93.1	84.6	92.8	83.5	180.6	89.3	82.7	176.1	88.9	8.7	7.1	5.7	721	4414
PATNA	25.591N	85.088E	170	46.0	48.1	106.1	73.5	103.7	73.7	100.6	75.0	84.1	93.1	83.5	91.8	82.3	169.0	87.9	81.5	164.6	87.2	14.3	12.8	11.5	261	5206
PUNE INTL	18.583N	73.917E	1942	49.6	51.7	100.8	67.8	99.0	67.6	97.2	67.7	76.4	85.9	75.6	84.4	74.2	137.4	79.1	73.6	134.3	78.5	11.3	9.1	7.5	13	4275
RAJKOT	22.309N	70.780E	441	53.3	55.8	106.0	72.2	104.0	72.0	102.0	72.9	82.2	91.8	81.3	89.8	80.3	160.0	84.7	79.6	156.3	84.1	22.7	19.8	18.0	11	6211
SOLAPUR	17.628N	75.935E	1584	59.8	62.3	105.9	72.6	104.1	73.0	102.2	72.5	80.0	92.3	78.7	90.3	77.2	150.3	84.9	76.1	144.8	83.5	6.8	5.5	5.2	0	6325
SURAT	21.200N	72.833E	39	57.4	59.7	100.2	72.6	97.6	73.2	95.4	73.6	82.8	89.3	82.3	88.7	81.3	162.9	86.3	80.7	159.6	85.7	12.1	10.3	8.5	1	6165
THIRUVANANTHAPURAM	8.483N	76.950E	210	71.9	73.0	93.1	78.6	92.1	78.4	91.2	78.2	81.8	89.1	81.1	88.3	79.9	156.3	85.9	79.2	152.5	85.3	11.7	9.7	7.8	0	6160
TIRUCHIRAPPALLI	10.765N	78.710E	288	68.0	69.5	102.4	78.7	100.8	78.4	99.9	78.2	81.9	95.0	81.0	93.6	79.2	152.9	86.1	78.4	149.3	85.5	24.9	21.7	19.0	0	7289
Indonesia																										*8 sites, 50 more on CD-ROM*
BALI NGURAH RAI INTL	8.748S	115.167E	14	71.3	73.0	90.6	79.9	89.7	79.6	89.1	79.5	81.8	87.3	81.0	86.7	80.4	158.0	85.8	79.2	151.6	84.6	19.5	17.2	15.0	0	6087
HASANUDDIN INTL	5.062S	119.554E	47	68.3	69.9	93.7	75.3	92.9	75.7	91.7	76.4	81.9	87.4	81.2	87.0	80.8	160.3	84.1	79.8	155.1	83.5	14.8	12.9	11.3	0	5948
JUANDA INTL	7.380S	112.787E	10	69.7	71.3	93.4	75.9	92.4	76.1	91.5	76.4	80.5	87.8	80.0	87.2	78.8	149.5	83.8	78.1	146.2	83.5	18.7	16.5	14.2	0	6287
MEDAN POLONIA INTL	3.558N	98.672E	114	72.6	73.1	93.6	78.7	92.8	78.8	91.6	78.8	81.4	89.2	80.8	88.5	79.2	152.1	85.2	78.9	150.5	84.9	13.9	12.0	10.9	0	6218
MINANGKABAU INTL	0.875S	100.352E	9	70.4	71.6	90.0	78.6	89.4	78.6	88.7	78.4	80.9	87.6	80.2	86.9	79.0	150.6	85.2	78.3	147.0	84.6	13.7	11.6	9.9	0	5700
SAM RATULANGI INTL	1.549N	124.926E	264	69.2	70.6	91.5	76.0	90.7	76.2	89.8	76.4	79.8	87.1	79.2	86.4	77.5	144.3	83.2	77.2	143.1	82.9	16.7	13.5	11.0	0	5560
SOEKARNO HATTA INTL	6.126S	106.656E	34	71.9	73.1	93.2	77.9	91.8	78.2	91.4	78.2	81.9	88.3	81.3	87.8	80.5	158.3	86.2	79.2	151.7	84.8	20.4	17.7	15.5	0	6245
SYARIF KASIM II INTL	0.461N	101.445E	102	71.6	72.3	94.3	79.5	93.4	79.5	92.6	79.4	82.4	91.0	81.7	90.2	79.9	156.0	88.2	79.2	152.0	87.3	12.0	10.0	8.9	0	6336

(Go to CD-ROM to access additional station tables.)

Meaning of acronyms:
DB: Dry bulb temperature, °F *WB: Wet bulb temperature, °F*
MCWB: Mean coincident wet bulb temperature, °F
Lat: Latitude, °
DP: Dew point temperature, °F
MCDB: Mean coincident dry bulb temperature, °F
Long: Longitude, °
HR: Humidity ratio, grains of moisture per lb of dry air
Elev: Elevation, ft
WS: Wind speed, mph
HDD and CDD 65: Annual heating and cooling degree-days, base 65°F, °F-day

Station	Lat	Long	Elev	Heating DB 99.6%	Heating DB 99%	Cooling DB/MCWB 0.4% DB	0.4% MCWB	1% DB	1% MCWB	2% DB	2% MCWB	Evaporation WB/MCDB 0.4% WB	0.4% MCDB	1% WB	1% MCDB	Dehumidification DP/HR/MCDB 0.4% DP	0.4% HR	0.4% MCDB	1% DP	1% HR	1% MCDB	Extreme Annual WS 1%	2.5%	5%	Heat./Cool. Degree-Days HDD 65	CDD 65
Iran, Islamic Republic of																										*17 sites, 50 more on CD-ROM*
ABADAN	30.371N	48.228E	10	39.1	42.0	118.3	72.5	116.4	72.2	114.5	71.6	83.6	95.1	81.3	95.4	80.9	160.7	90.5	77.4	142.6	89.7	23.4	20.6	18.1	748	5964
AHVAZ	31.337N	48.762E	66	40.6	42.9	118.1	73.6	116.3	73.2	114.5	72.6	82.7	96.7	80.1	99.5	79.2	151.7	91.2	75.2	132.5	91.6	19.4	16.4	14.1	772	5987
ARAK	34.138N	49.847E	5452	3.6	11.1	97.7	61.0	95.5	60.4	93.4	59.6	65.5	89.9	63.3	89.1	56.3	83.0	79.5	53.1	73.7	75.6	19.0	17.1	14.5	4363	1611
BANDAR ABBASS INTL	27.218N	56.378E	22	48.3	51.4	107.4	75.1	104.1	77.5	102.0	78.5	87.9	95.5	87.2	94.8	86.2	192.1	92.9	85.6	187.9	92.7	19.7	17.1	15.4	133	5853
BANDAR ANZALI	37.467N	49.467E	-85	34.2	36.7	87.5	77.7	86.2	77.3	84.9	76.6	80.3	85.4	79.2	84.4	78.8	148.8	84.4	77.5	142.7	83.5	26.6	21.7	17.1	2705	1600
HAMEDAN	34.850N	48.533E	5738	-0.3	6.3	96.0	62.2	94.0	61.2	91.9	60.5	66.1	90.5	64.0	88.6	56.6	84.7	79.0	53.9	76.7	78.0	23.0	19.2	16.3	5097	1000
ISFAHAN SHAHID BEHESHTI INTL	32.751N	51.862E	5072	17.4	21.0	102.4	62.7	100.5	61.9	98.5	61.5	65.7	97.0	64.1	95.8	53.5	73.5	80.9	50.4	65.5	76.1	22.8	18.9	15.9	3627	1900
KASHAN	33.895N	51.577E	3465	23.0	27.4	107.6	67.2	105.4	66.6	103.2	65.9	71.0	101.1	69.3	99.6	60.3	89.0	89.7	57.4	79.9	88.3	17.1	13.5	11.1	2665	3327
KERMAN	30.274N	56.951E	5736	19.1	22.7	100.5	61.1	98.7	60.3	96.7	59.8	63.8	94.0	62.4	93.5	51.8	70.9	73.6	49.4	64.6	71.9	24.2	20.5	17.2	2911	1855
MASHHAD INTL	36.235N	59.641E	3263	15.5	21.0	98.9	64.1	96.9	63.7	94.9	62.9	70.6	91.8	68.4	90.3	62.9	96.9	83.8	60.2	87.8	80.8	20.1	17.4	15.1	3688	1885
MEHRABAD INTL	35.689N	51.313E	3962	25.5	28.6	101.9	64.5	99.3	64.2	97.2	63.7	71.4	90.7	68.7	91.9	64.5	105.3	86.6	60.5	91.3	83.0	24.6	21.4	17.3	2865	2787
SHAHID ASHRAFI ESFAHANI	34.346N	47.158E	4284	17.8	21.9	103.8	63.9	101.8	63.3	99.4	62.1	67.9	98.5	65.8	96.6	55.5	77.0	78.5	53.2	70.7	76.4	21.3	18.3	16.0	3697	1832
SHIRAZ SHAHID DASTGHAIB INTL	29.539N	52.589E	4920	28.0	30.2	102.6	64.1	100.8	63.3	98.9	62.6	68.5	94.9	66.8	94.2	59.1	90.1	86.4	55.8	79.7	83.1	20.4	17.1	14.2	2467	2565
TABRIZ INTL	38.134N	46.235E	4459	10.8	15.5	96.6	62.2	93.6	61.5	91.5	61.0	65.1	88.6	64.0	87.0	57.3	82.9	73.4	55.6	77.7	73.8	23.5	21.0	18.2	4763	1482
URMIA	37.668N	45.069E	4344	10.5	14.8	91.7	63.8	89.6	63.8	87.5	63.2	67.5	85.4	66.3	84.3	61.2	95.0	76.9	59.3	88.8	76.2	19.9	15.6	12.5	5184	823
ZAHEDAN INTL	29.476N	60.907E	4520	22.7	26.3	102.4	61.6	100.5	60.9	98.6	59.8	65.6	93.1	63.3	94.9	55.0	76.2	77.3	50.9	65.4	69.3	25.8	22.0	18.7	2126	2644
ZANJAN	36.774N	48.359E	5382	6.3	11.5	93.7	60.7	91.3	60.9	88.9	60.0	65.2	86.8	63.7	84.7	57.3	85.6	74.5	55.8	81.1	73.1	25.8	21.6	17.8	5289	818
Ireland																										*2 sites, 15 more on CD-ROM*
CASEMENT	53.302N	6.451W	319	26.4	29.1	72.8	63.3	70.0	61.9	67.8	60.7	64.8	70.2	63.3	68.2	62.7	86.2	67.3	61.1	81.5	65.7	32.3	28.5	25.3	5666	13
DUBLIN	53.421N	6.270W	242	27.1	29.9	71.4	62.6	68.9	61.3	66.8	60.1	64.1	69.1	62.6	67.2	61.9	83.7	66.4	60.5	79.5	65.0	30.1	26.9	24.0	5696	7
Israel																										*2 sites, 5 more on CD-ROM*
TEL AVIV BEN GURION	32.011N	34.887E	135	42.4	44.5	95.2	69.0	91.8	71.8	89.9	73.0	78.7	87.6	77.4	86.6	75.6	134.6	84.6	74.7	130.5	83.9	22.1	19.5	17.4	940	2589
TEL AVIV SDE DOV	32.117N	34.783E	43	45.1	47.7	88.5	74.2	86.8	75.6	85.9	75.5	80.0	85.1	78.8	84.4	78.5	148.1	84.1	77.0	140.9	83.5	26.0	21.4	18.2	879	2410
Italy																										*16 sites, 77 more on CD-ROM*
BARI KAROL WOJTYLA	41.133N	16.767E	177	33.6	35.6	93.2	72.3	89.8	71.9	87.5	71.3	77.4	85.6	75.6	84.1	75.1	132.7	81.9	73.1	123.8	80.7	20.8	18.1	15.8	2668	1241
BOLOGNA	44.535N	11.289E	123	24.4	26.8	93.9	72.3	91.4	71.9	89.2	71.2	76.2	87.5	74.4	85.8	72.9	122.8	82.5	71.2	115.5	80.8	16.2	13.9	12.0	3834	1227
CATANIA FONTANAROSSA	37.467N	15.066E	39	34.8	37.2	93.9	73.8	91.1	73.5	88.2	73.1	79.2	85.9	77.6	85.1	77.3	142.3	82.5	75.4	133.4	81.5	22.0	18.9	16.5	1978	1492
CATANIA SIGONELLA	37.400N	14.917E	102	33.7	35.9	98.9	72.0	95.7	71.8	93.1	71.7	76.8	88.2	75.5	87.3	73.7	125.9	81.3	71.9	118.4	80.7	21.6	18.8	16.7	1937	1782
FIRENZE PERETOLA	43.810N	11.205E	144	26.5	29.8	95.4	71.3	93.0	71.0	89.9	70.1	75.5	88.0	73.8	86.2	71.8	118.0	80.5	69.9	110.7	79.7	18.5	15.7	13.5	3000	1307
GENOVA SESTRI	44.412N	8.842E	13	34.2	37.2	85.9	73.4	84.0	74.2	82.3	73.8	78.9	82.1	77.4	81.2	77.5	143.3	81.1	75.8	134.8	80.1	25.2	22.6	20.4	2440	1165
GRAZZANISE	41.061N	14.082E	29	30.4	32.4	91.2	74.6	89.1	74.3	86.4	73.9	80.5	85.9	78.7	84.4	79.0	150.6	84.4	76.9	140.3	83.0	21.8	18.4	15.5	2761	1141
MILANO LINATE	45.445N	9.277E	353	23.3	26.3	91.7	74.6	89.6	73.4	87.5	72.3	77.2	87.7	75.5	85.5	74.0	128.3	82.6	72.2	120.9	81.0	15.6	12.2	9.9	3856	1141
NAPOLI CAPODICHINO	40.884N	14.291E	236	34.0	36.2	91.3	73.6	89.3	73.5	87.4	73.3	79.0	85.9	77.3	84.5	77.0	142.0	83.2	75.1	133.0	81.9	19.5	16.4	14.0	2297	1424
PALERMO FALCONE-BORSELLINO	38.176N	13.091E	65	44.2	46.0	91.6	72.3	88.0	73.4	85.8	74.4	79.6	84.1	78.3	83.3	78.5	148.3	82.9	76.8	139.9	82.0	29.6	26.0	22.8	1438	1753
PRATICA DI MARE	41.659N	12.445E	41	33.5	35.6	87.8	73.6	85.9	73.9	84.2	74.4	79.2	83.5	77.8	82.6	77.4	142.7	82.7	75.6	134.4	81.3	22.7	19.5	17.0	2428	1098
ROMA CIAMPINO	41.799N	12.595E	427	30.1	32.2	93.1	71.0	90.7	70.9	88.0	70.2	76.5	83.5	75.0	82.7	74.9	132.8	80.1	73.1	125.0	78.8	24.5	20.2	16.8	2832	1225
ROMA LEONARDO DA VINCI	41.804N	12.251E	15	31.6	33.6	88.1	71.5	86.2	72.1	84.5	72.0	77.5	82.9	76.1	81.9	75.6	133.9	80.7	74.2	127.8	79.8	24.2	20.8	18.0	2668	1030
TORINO BRIC DELLA CROCE	45.033N	7.733E	2329	23.1	26.2	82.7	69.1	80.6	68.3	78.6	67.2	73.5	78.2	71.7	76.9	71.9	128.6	75.8	70.0	120.3	74.9	19.5	15.6	12.2	4680	510
TORINO CASELLE	45.201N	7.650E	989	21.6	24.6	87.7	72.2	85.6	71.0	83.1	69.7	74.7	83.5	73.1	81.9	71.9	122.4	78.5	70.2	115.2	77.5	14.4	11.2	9.3	4386	718
TRIESTE	45.650N	13.750E	66	28.8	32.0	89.1	73.9	86.6	73.6	84.8	72.5	77.5	85.8	75.7	84.5	74.8	130.5	84.8	72.6	121.2	83.1	27.2	22.9	19.2	3153	1197
Jamaica																										*1 site, 1 more on CD-ROM*
NORMAN MANLEY INTL	17.936N	76.788W	10	72.0	73.3	91.8	78.8	91.4	78.8	90.2	78.5	82.6	86.8	81.8	86.8	81.6	164.6	84.8	80.6	159.1	84.6	30.2	27.3	24.4	0	6455
Japan																										*65 sites, 133 more on CD-ROM*
AKITA	39.717N	140.100E	72	23.2	24.9	88.9	75.7	86.1	74.7	83.5	73.6	77.6	85.0	76.5	83.5	75.6	134.2	81.5	74.4	129.0	80.7	27.3	23.7	20.7	5032	935
ASAHIKAWA	43.750N	142.367E	459	0.6	4.6	85.4	72.2	82.5	70.1	80.1	68.7	74.6	82.3	72.8	79.6	72.1	120.8	79.2	70.5	114.1	77.3	19.4	16.3	13.7	7687	441
ASHIYA	33.883N	130.653E	98	30.4	32.2	90.3	78.4	88.2	78.4	86.4	77.9	80.1	86.4	79.3	85.4	78.7	149.5	84.4	77.3	142.6	83.0	23.1	20.2	18.0	3080	1517
ATSUGI NAS	35.450N	139.450E	167	30.3	32.1	91.5	77.8	89.6	77.0	87.7	76.6	79.2	87.0	78.5	85.9	77.2	142.6	82.6	76.6	139.6	82.5	23.6	20.7	18.4	3007	1607
CHIBA	35.600N	140.100E	20	32.7	34.1	90.5	78.2	88.7	77.7	87.0	77.1	79.8	87.3	79.0	86.1	77.7	144.2	84.3	76.9	140.2	83.5	27.1	23.1	19.7	2921	1594
FUJISAN	35.367N	138.733E	12393	-19.6	-16.1	53.4	41.4	50.6	40.5	48.2	39.5	46.6	48.9	45.1	47.0	45.8	73.1	47.0	44.4	69.3	45.6	65.4	57.7	51.3	15985	0
FUKUOKA	33.586N	130.451E	32	31.9	33.7	93.2	78.1	91.4	77.8	89.5	77.1	80.0	88.3	79.2	87.3	77.4	142.5	84.3	77.0	140.6	83.9	20.8	18.5	16.6	2757	1908
FUKUYAMA	34.450N	133.250E	9	27.3	29.1	93.3	77.5	91.4	77.4	89.7	77.0	79.2	89.5	78.3	88.3	76.4	137.5	84.1	75.5	133.5	83.7	13.4	11.5	9.8	3332	1738
FUSHIKI	36.800N	137.050E	43	27.7	29.3	92.2	76.9	89.5	76.8	86.8	76.1	79.3	87.0	78.2	85.9	77.2	141.6	83.9	76.0	136.2	82.8	16.8	14.4	12.3	3956	1330
FUTENMA	26.267N	127.750E	247	51.9	53.5	90.0	79.5	89.5	79.5	88.1	79.3	82.3	86.3	81.2	85.7	80.9	162.2	85.0	80.0	157.0	84.3	25.3	21.6	19.1	334	3366
GIFU	35.394N	136.870E	128	26.2	28.1	94.6	78.0	91.7	77.2	89.5	76.4	79.9	88.1	78.9	87.0	77.4	143.4	82.3	77.0	141.2	82.2	18.3	15.9	13.7	3550	1662
HAMAMATSU	34.750N	137.703E	150	30.5	32.2	91.4	78.1	88.2	77.6	86.4	76.9	80.0	86.5	79.1	85.0	78.7	149.9	83.3	77.3	142.9	82.2	21.5	19.6	17.8	2884	1609
HIMEJI	34.833N	134.667E	130	28.1	29.7	92.2	77.8	90.4	77.4	88.6	76.8	79.5	88.5	78.6	87.1	77.1	141.8	83.8	76.3	137.9	83.2	18.5	15.8	13.7	3377	1670
HIROSHIMA	34.400N	132.467E	177	30.7	32.3	92.8	77.7	91.1	77.3	89.4	76.7	79.3	88.6	78.6	87.5	76.9	141.0	83.9	76.1	137.4	83.5	20.6	18.1	16.1	2957	1881

(Go to CD-ROM to access additional station tables.)

(Go to CD-ROM to access additional station tables.)

Meaning of acronyms:
DB: Dry bulb temperature, °F *WB: Wet bulb temperature, °F*
MCWB: Mean coincident wet bulb temperature, °F

Lat: Latitude, °
DP: Dew point temperature, °F
MCDB: Mean coincident dry bulb temperature, °F

Long: Longitude, °
HR: Humidity ratio, grains of moisture per lb of dry air

Elev: Elevation, ft
WS: Wind speed, mph
HDD and CDD 65: Annual heating and cooling degree-days, base 65°F, °F-day

Station	Lat	Long	Elev	Heating DB		Cooling DB/MCWB						Evaporation WB/MCDB				Dehumidification DP/HR/MCDB						Extreme Annual WS			Heat./Cool. Degree-Days	
						0.4%		1%		2%		0.4%		1%		0.4%			1%							
				99.6%	99%	DB	MCWB	DB	MCWB	DB	MCWB	WB	MCDB	WB	MCDB	DP	HR	MCDB	DP	HR	MCDB	1%	2.5%	5%	HDD	CDD 65
IIZUKA	33.650N	130.700E	124	28.8	30.7	92.4	78.0	90.7	77.8	88.7	77.1	79.8	88.8	78.9	87.3	77.4	143.1	83.8	76.6	139.3	83.1	15.9	13.6	11.9	3119	1705
IRUMA	35.842N	139.411E	295	26.4	28.2	93.5	77.6	91.4	77.1	88.2	76.1	79.5	88.9	78.5	87.4	77.1	142.6	83.3	75.6	135.4	82.2	22.4	19.1	16.6	3609	1414
KADENA AB	26.350N	127.767E	157	48.4	51.4	91.6	80.2	90.0	80.0	89.5	79.9	83.5	87.2	82.6	86.2	82.7	171.4	85.3	82.0	167.7	84.9	26.6	22.4	19.8	389	3385
KAGOSHIMA	31.550N	130.550E	104	34.6	36.6	92.3	78.4	90.7	78.0	89.2	77.7	80.2	88.0	79.6	87.1	78.3	147.3	84.4	77.5	143.4	84.2	19.9	17.1	15.0	1953	2328
KANAZAWA	36.583N	136.633E	111	29.8	31.1	91.7	76.6	89.8	76.4	87.8	75.9	78.7	87.2	77.8	86.4	76.2	137.6	83.7	75.2	132.8	83.0	26.4	22.5	19.5	3623	1484
KANSAI INTL	34.433N	135.233E	26	35.3	37.0	91.4	77.7	89.7	77.3	87.9	77.1	80.0	86.4	79.3	85.5	78.5	148.2	84.0	77.2	141.8	83.3	27.7	24.0	21.1	2738	1932
KOBE	34.700N	135.217E	100	32.2	34.1	91.7	77.2	89.8	76.9	88.0	76.5	79.6	86.8	78.9	85.9	77.6	143.9	83.5	76.8	140.3	83.3	21.8	18.7	16.3	2844	1943
KOCHI	33.567N	133.550E	16	30.7	32.5	91.3	77.5	89.7	77.2	88.1	76.8	79.9	86.7	79.1	85.7	78.2	146.3	83.4	77.3	142.3	82.9	12.1	10.2	8.8	2490	1907
KOMATSU	36.395N	136.407E	36	28.5	30.2	91.8	76.3	89.6	76.2	87.6	75.9	78.9	87.1	77.9	86.0	76.8	139.8	83.3	75.3	133.0	82.4	25.6	21.9	19.0	3777	1363
KUMAGAYA	36.150N	139.383E	104	28.2	29.9	95.8	77.8	93.3	77.2	90.5	76.1	79.6	90.8	78.6	89.2	76.9	140.7	82.9	76.0	136.3	82.9	17.9	15.2	13.0	3344	1620
KUMAMOTO	32.817N	130.700E	129	29.1	31.1	94.2	77.6	92.4	77.2	90.5	76.6	79.8	88.7	79.0	87.6	77.5	143.9	83.4	76.8	140.2	83.0	16.1	13.7	11.9	2697	2085
KURE	34.233N	132.550E	17	32.0	33.7	90.5	77.3	89.0	76.9	87.3	76.3	78.7	87.2	77.9	86.1	76.2	136.8	83.5	75.4	133.3	83.0	16.7	14.2	12.2	2891	1789
KYOTO	35.017N	135.733E	153	30.6	32.1	95.0	76.4	93.0	76.0	90.8	75.5	78.3	89.9	77.4	88.6	75.3	133.2	83.3	74.4	129.3	83.0	12.1	10.8	9.6	3137	1916
MATSUYAMA	33.850N	132.783E	113	32.0	33.7	92.2	76.6	90.7	76.3	89.1	75.9	78.3	88.0	77.5	87.0	75.7	134.8	82.7	74.8	130.8	82.5	13.3	11.6	10.0	2821	1847
MINAMITORISHIMA	24.290N	153.979E	22	64.4	65.7	89.5	79.4	88.6	79.1	87.7	78.9	80.9	86.9	80.3	86.3	79.2	151.5	84.8	78.6	148.6	84.5	27.0	24.4	22.2	0	4948
MIYAZAKI	31.933N	131.417E	49	31.8	34.0	92.8	78.1	90.6	78.1	88.6	77.8	80.3	87.5	79.6	86.7	78.5	148.3	83.8	77.7	144.2	83.3	20.7	17.7	15.2	2239	1986
NAGANO	36.667N	138.200E	1378	20.0	22.2	91.2	74.4	88.8	73.7	86.2	72.7	76.0	87.2	74.9	85.3	72.9	128.4	80.9	71.9	124.2	80.1	17.6	15.5	13.7	4893	1176
NAGASAKI	32.733N	129.867E	118	33.5	35.4	91.0	77.9	89.3	77.8	87.6	77.4	80.1	86.4	79.3	85.6	78.4	148.3	83.8	77.7	144.6	83.3	17.3	14.5	12.4	2440	1930
NAGOYA	35.255N	136.924E	52	28.4	30.2	95.2	77.1	93.1	76.6	91.0	76.1	79.2	88.5	78.4	87.5	77.1	141.3	82.6	75.6	134.2	82.1	22.1	19.1	16.6	3207	1887
NAHA	26.196N	127.646E	12	55.0	55.6	90.0	79.6	89.5	79.6	88.1	79.7	81.9	86.3	81.2	85.9	80.7	159.4	85.9	79.2	151.8	84.8	30.0	26.1	23.2	211	3676
NARA	34.700N	135.833E	358	28.2	29.5	93.3	76.8	91.5	76.5	89.4	75.9	78.6	89.1	77.7	87.8	76.0	137.6	82.5	75.0	133.2	81.9	10.0	8.7	7.5	3498	1589
NAZE	28.383N	129.500E	26	49.2	50.7	91.2	78.9	90.0	78.8	88.9	78.6	80.8	87.7	80.1	86.9	78.8	149.8	84.9	78.2	146.4	84.5	16.5	14.4	12.7	627	2910
NIIGATA	37.900N	139.017E	19	28.9	30.3	91.1	77.1	88.9	76.5	86.4	75.8	78.8	87.4	77.7	86.1	76.3	137.2	84.1	75.2	132.3	83.3	22.7	19.8	17.2	4019	1327
NYUTABARU	32.084N	131.451E	259	30.0	32.2	91.2	78.0	88.2	78.3	86.3	78.0	80.5	86.0	79.6	85.0	79.0	152.2	83.5	78.5	149.4	83.1	22.2	18.5	15.5	2449	1732
OITA	33.233N	131.617E	44	31.3	33.2	92.3	77.6	90.5	77.3	88.6	76.8	79.3	88.1	78.5	86.9	77.1	141.1	83.6	76.2	136.8	82.9	15.9	13.8	12.1	2760	1761
OKAYAMA	34.667N	133.917E	61	30.0	31.7	94.0	77.3	92.2	76.9	90.4	76.4	79.0	89.5	78.3	88.1	76.4	138.1	83.1	75.6	134.5	83.1	21.9	18.6	15.8	3112	1931
OMAEZAKI	34.600N	138.217E	154	32.4	34.2	86.6	78.6	85.3	78.1	84.0	77.4	80.1	84.2	79.3	83.2	79.1	151.7	82.6	78.2	147.1	81.9	27.6	25.2	22.9	2618	1520
ONAHAMA	36.950N	140.900E	17	27.9	29.6	84.4	75.5	82.4	75.1	80.7	74.3	77.2	81.9	76.4	80.7	75.8	135.0	80.0	75.0	131.4	79.3	18.4	16.0	14.0	3851	907
OSAKA	34.683N	135.517E	272	33.3	34.8	93.9	76.6	92.1	76.3	90.4	75.9	78.9	88.7	78.1	87.8	76.3	138.6	83.9	75.4	134.6	83.6	19.3	16.4	14.2	2761	2090
OSAKA INTL	34.786N	135.438E	50	29.9	31.7	94.7	77.9	92.8	77.3	91.0	76.8	79.8	89.5	79.0	88.3	77.2	141.9	83.9	76.7	139.3	83.7	18.7	16.5	14.5	3105	1920
OTARU	43.183N	141.017E	86	14.9	17.0	82.8	72.0	79.9	70.2	77.4	69.0	73.7	80.7	72.2	78.0	71.3	115.8	77.6	70.0	110.6	76.7	18.0	15.5	13.6	6654	405
OZUKI	34.045N	131.052E	13	31.6	33.4	90.0	78.5	88.2	78.5	87.4	78.4	80.5	87.0	79.7	85.9	78.9	149.9	85.4	77.4	142.5	83.7	25.4	21.8	18.8	3068	1596
SAPPORO	43.067N	141.333E	86	14.1	16.5	84.6	72.6	81.9	70.9	79.4	69.3	74.6	82.1	73.1	79.6	72.2	119.4	79.3	70.7	113.4	77.9	21.9	18.8	16.3	6437	537
SENDAI	38.267N	140.900E	144	25.5	27.3	88.6	76.0	85.8	75.1	83.3	74.0	77.6	84.8	76.6	83.0	75.6	134.6	81.1	74.7	130.4	80.3	22.7	19.2	16.5	4474	902
SHIMOFUSA	35.799N	140.011E	98	28.4	30.3	92.4	78.5	89.9	77.5	87.9	77.1	79.9	88.2	79.0	86.6	77.4	142.8	83.9	77.0	141.0	83.4	20.9	18.1	15.7	3262	1492
SHIMONOSEKI	33.950N	130.933E	64	34.9	36.9	89.9	78.2	88.3	77.8	86.8	77.3	79.8	86.7	79.0	85.8	77.8	144.6	84.2	76.9	140.5	83.6	22.3	19.3	16.8	2575	1796
SHIZUHAMA	34.813N	138.298E	23	31.6	33.4	89.9	78.4	87.9	78.5	86.0	77.7	80.6	86.2	79.8	85.0	79.1	151.0	83.6	78.6	148.4	83.2	23.9	21.5	19.3	2740	1564
SHIZUOKA	34.983N	138.400E	52	31.7	33.6	91.2	77.5	88.9	77.2	87.0	76.6	79.7	87.1	78.9	85.8	77.7	144.1	83.6	76.8	140.1	83.1	14.1	12.2	11.2	2602	1682
SUMOTO	34.333N	134.900E	369	32.1	33.6	89.3	77.8	87.5	77.4	85.6	76.9	79.5	86.0	78.6	84.8	77.7	145.8	83.2	76.8	141.4	82.3	15.4	13.1	11.5	3135	1558
TADOTSU	34.283N	133.750E	16	31.9	33.7	92.6	77.1	90.8	76.7	89.0	76.3	79.2	87.8	78.2	87.1	76.9	140.0	83.7	75.7	134.3	83.4	16.4	14.1	12.2	2953	1858
TAKAMATSU	34.317N	134.050E	46	31.4	33.1	93.9	77.3	92.1	77.1	90.1	76.8	79.3	89.1	78.6	88.1	76.9	140.1	83.7	76.1	136.4	83.4	17.9	15.3	13.3	2953	1917
TOKUSHIMA	34.067N	134.567E	21	33.0	34.6	91.9	77.8	90.1	77.5	88.4	77.0	79.8	88.0	78.9	86.8	77.4	142.8	84.2	76.6	138.7	83.5	20.1	17.4	15.3	2756	1858
TOKYO	35.683N	139.767E	118	33.6	35.1	92.3	77.4	90.4	76.8	88.5	76.1	79.0	88.4	78.2	87.0	76.4	138.5	84.2	75.6	134.4	84.0	18.7	16.3	14.3	2800	1742
TOKYO INTL	35.552N	139.780E	35	33.7	35.4	91.3	78.5	89.4	77.7	87.5	77.4	79.9	87.3	79.1	86.0	77.4	142.6	84.1	77.0	140.7	83.7	28.2	25.1	22.5	2836	1621
TOYAMA	36.717N	137.200E	57	27.6	29.3	92.8	77.8	90.5	77.3	88.0	76.5	79.8	88.2	78.7	86.7	77.5	143.4	84.4	76.5	138.2	83.3	20.4	17.3	14.7	3856	1418
TSUIKI	33.685N	131.040E	55	28.3	30.1	91.0	78.6	88.2	78.5	86.4	77.9	80.7	86.6	79.8	85.7	79.1	151.2	84.4	78.4	147.6	83.9	23.2	20.3	18.0	3333	1503
UTSUNOMIYA	36.550N	139.867E	460	24.6	26.4	92.4	77.7	90.0	77.0	87.5	75.9	79.1	89.1	78.1	87.1	76.4	140.1	83.6	75.5	135.8	82.7	20.8	17.4	14.6	3841	1343
WAKAYAMA	34.233N	135.167E	59	32.9	34.4	92.1	76.5	90.2	76.5	88.6	76.4	79.3	87.5	78.5	86.6	77.1	141.2	84.7	76.2	136.8	84.1	24.2	20.5	17.8	2784	1917
YOKOHAMA	35.433N	139.650E	140	33.2	34.6	90.7	77.8	88.8	77.1	87.0	76.4	79.3	87.1	78.3	85.7	77.2	142.4	83.6	76.3	137.8	82.9	21.0	18.5	16.1	2868	1589
YOKOSUKA	35.283N	139.667E	161	35.5	37.2	93.3	78.6	89.8	77.4	87.4	76.7	80.1	88.8	78.8	86.4	77.4	143.6	84.1	76.8	140.4	83.7	29.1	25.2	22.2	2514	1688
YOKOTA AB	35.750N	139.350E	466	25.1	27.2	93.2	78.5	91.1	77.7	88.1	76.3	79.9	89.2	78.8	87.4	77.3	144.5	83.7	76.7	141.5	83.3	21.2	18.3	15.8	3568	1394
Jordan																						*3 sites, 6 more on CD-ROM*				
AMMAN	31.973N	35.992E	2555	34.0	36.8	96.8	65.5	93.6	64.9	91.6	64.6	72.1	86.7	70.4	85.0	68.0	113.2	78.0	66.1	106.0	76.6	22.3	18.9	16.4	2146	2064
IRBID MET	32.550N	35.850E	2031	35.1	37.9	93.9	67.3	91.3	66.9	89.0	66.8	74.2	84.6	72.6	82.3	71.4	124.8	78.6	69.9	118.8	76.4	19.0	16.7	14.7	1975	1926
QUEEN ALIA INTL	31.723N	35.993E	2395	30.6	33.3	98.6	67.6	95.4	66.2	93.3	66.0	73.1	90.0	71.4	88.5	68.0	112.7	79.8	66.1	105.1	79.3	26.3	22.3	19.9	2437	1492

(Go to CD-ROM to access additional station tables.)

Meaning of acronyms:
DB: Dry bulb temperature, °F *WB: Wet bulb temperature, °F*
MCWB: Mean coincident wet bulb temperature, °F
Lat: Latitude, °
DP: Dew point temperature, °F
MCDB: Mean coincident dry bulb temperature, °F
Long: Longitude, °
HR: Humidity ratio, grains of moisture per lb of dry air
Elev: Elevation, ft
WS: Wind speed, mph
HDD and CDD 65: Annual heating and cooling degree-days, base 65°F, °F-day

Station	Lat	Long	Elev	Heating DB		Cooling DB/MCWB						Evaporation WB/MCDB				Dehumidification DP/HR/MCDB						Extreme Annual WS			Heat./Cool. Degree-Days	
						0.4%		1%		2%		0.4%		1%		0.4%			1%							
				99.6%	99%	DB	MCWB	DB	MCWB	DB	MCWB	WB	MCDB	WB	MCDB	DP	HR	MCDB	DP	HR	MCDB	1%	2.5%	5%	HDD	CDD 65
Kazakhstan																									*6 sites, 75 more on CD-ROM*	
ALMATY	43.233N	76.933E	2792	-4.3	1.0	93.5	65.1	90.9	64.4	87.9	63.7	68.7	85.6	67.1	84.1	63.0	95.7	74.8	61.1	89.3	73.9	14.1	11.5	9.5	6455	859
ASTANA INTL	51.022N	71.467E	1165	-27.0	-21.9	90.1	63.9	86.4	63.0	83.2	62.2	67.2	81.1	65.8	79.5	63.0	89.8	70.8	61.2	84.3	69.8	26.9	23.1	20.1	10323	344
KARAGANDY INTL	49.671N	73.334E	1765	-26.9	-20.4	89.7	62.1	86.1	61.3	82.7	60.1	65.2	80.6	63.8	78.8	60.8	84.9	68.6	59.0	79.6	67.5	27.5	23.3	20.1	10123	299
PAVLODAR	52.195N	77.074E	410	-30.9	-24.7	91.4	65.1	87.8	64.7	84.4	63.6	69.0	82.3	67.4	80.7	64.9	93.5	73.6	62.9	87.2	72.6	23.1	19.9	17.3	10306	442
SHYMKENT	42.364N	69.479E	1385	2.9	8.7	100.0	66.2	97.1	65.4	95.0	64.9	69.6	91.9	68.1	90.3	62.4	88.6	78.2	60.5	82.7	76.8	17.9	15.2	13.3	4646	1556
TARAZ	42.850N	71.300E	2139	-4.3	1.5	96.5	64.3	93.5	63.7	91.1	63.1	67.2	87.9	66.0	87.2	61.0	86.8	72.0	59.2	81.3	72.0	24.8	18.8	14.2	5721	1095
Kenya																									*2 sites, 15 more on CD-ROM*	
MOMBASA INTL	4.035S	39.594E	200	68.2	69.5	91.6	77.3	90.7	77.2	89.8	77.0	79.7	86.3	79.2	85.6	77.9	146.0	82.3	77.3	143.3	81.9	20.9	18.9	17.4	0	5465
NAIROBI JOMO KENYATTA INTL	1.319S	36.928E	5327	50.1	52.1	84.3	60.4	82.7	60.5	81.3	60.9	66.0	74.3	65.3	73.7	63.9	108.8	67.3	63.0	105.2	66.5	21.0	18.8	16.9	152	1062
Korea, Democratic People's Republic of																									*7 sites, 20 more on CD-ROM*	
CHONGJIN	41.783N	129.817E	141	9.6	12.4	81.4	72.6	79.1	71.6	77.1	70.8	75.3	79.1	73.8	77.2	74.1	127.7	77.8	72.6	121.5	76.3	16.7	13.1	10.3	6796	417
HAMHUNG	39.933N	127.550E	72	8.8	12.2	88.7	75.0	85.9	74.1	83.1	72.6	78.1	85.2	76.5	82.7	76.0	136.2	81.9	74.7	130.3	80.2	18.0	14.8	11.8	5736	762
KAESONG	37.967N	126.567E	230	9.0	12.3	87.7	77.3	85.3	75.7	83.2	74.5	79.8	84.9	78.4	82.6	78.3	148.4	82.3	77.2	142.8	81.1	20.6	17.5	14.5	5509	1026
NAMPO	38.717N	125.383E	154	9.0	12.4	86.4	77.9	84.3	76.5	82.5	75.2	79.7	84.6	78.4	82.5	78.2	147.1	82.8	77.1	141.9	81.3	21.9	18.2	15.2	5693	1050
PYONGYANG SUNAN INTL	39.224N	125.670E	117	5.6	9.2	88.2	75.9	86.2	75.0	84.3	74.0	79.0	85.2	77.7	83.1	77.2	142.0	82.5	76.1	136.7	81.2	15.6	13.0	10.9	5838	1114
SINUIJU	40.100N	124.383E	23	4.0	7.6	87.5	75.3	85.0	74.1	82.8	73.3	78.7	83.9	77.2	81.5	77.2	141.7	81.6	75.9	135.5	79.9	16.7	14.1	12.0	6266	945
WONSAN	39.183N	127.433E	118	13.6	16.9	89.0	74.3	86.1	73.5	83.4	72.6	77.9	84.6	76.5	82.5	76.0	136.6	81.4	74.7	130.6	79.9	17.3	14.3	12.0	5252	822
Korea, Republic of																									*27 sites, 32 more on CD-ROM*	
BUSAN	35.100N	129.033E	233	23.0	26.0	88.1	77.8	86.2	77.2	84.3	76.4	79.8	85.0	78.7	83.8	78.2	147.8	83.0	77.1	142.3	82.4	22.1	18.9	16.5	3351	1291
BUSAN GIMHAE INTL	35.180N	128.938E	6	21.0	23.1	91.1	78.5	88.2	77.7	86.2	76.7	80.1	87.4	79.2	86.1	78.5	147.8	85.3	77.1	140.9	83.8	19.7	17.1	15.4	3776	1415
CHANGWON	35.170N	128.573E	121	23.0	26.0	90.3	77.8	88.0	77.1	85.8	76.1	79.7	86.7	78.6	85.3	77.6	144.3	83.8	76.6	139.1	82.9	14.4	12.4	11.4	3542	1435
CHEONGJU	36.633N	127.450E	194	12.8	16.2	91.0	76.3	88.7	74.9	86.5	73.7	78.8	86.1	77.6	84.6	76.9	141.1	82.3	75.6	135.1	81.5	14.0	11.7	9.9	4782	1359
CHEONGJU INTL	36.717N	127.499E	191	8.2	12.1	91.6	79.1	89.5	77.5	87.4	76.4	80.9	88.1	79.5	86.2	79.0	151.8	84.8	77.4	143.4	83.0	16.0	13.4	11.6	5130	1303
DAEGU	35.883N	128.617E	200	19.7	22.5	93.7	75.4	91.2	74.7	88.9	73.8	78.3	87.3	77.3	86.2	76.1	137.4	82.1	75.0	132.2	81.7	16.7	14.4	12.5	3933	1551
DAEGU AB	35.894N	128.659E	116	17.4	19.8	94.7	77.8	91.6	76.7	89.5	75.6	80.0	89.1	79.0	87.5	77.4	143.1	83.7	76.9	140.7	83.4	19.9	17.2	14.8	4193	1482
DAEJEON	36.300N	127.400E	256	12.8	16.2	90.6	77.4	88.2	75.9	86.1	74.6	79.7	86.7	78.3	84.8	77.7	145.5	83.1	76.6	140.1	81.9	15.6	12.7	10.8	4827	1252
GIMPO INTL	37.558N	126.791E	58	8.3	11.8	89.8	76.6	87.7	76.0	85.7	74.2	80.0	85.3	78.8	83.8	78.9	150.1	82.3	77.2	142.0	81.1	18.2	15.8	13.8	5404	1177
GWANGJU	35.167N	126.900E	243	20.3	23.0	90.7	77.0	88.6	76.1	86.6	75.0	78.9	86.4	78.0	85.2	77.0	141.8	82.4	76.0	137.3	82.0	16.3	13.9	11.9	4069	1462
GWANGJU INTL	35.126N	126.809E	39	19.3	21.5	93.4	79.3	91.1	78.1	88.2	76.6	80.7	88.8	79.7	87.6	78.9	150.3	84.4	77.3	142.4	83.1	16.9	14.5	12.7	4295	1509
INCHEON	37.467N	126.633E	230	13.7	17.1	87.9	76.5	85.5	75.3	83.4	74.1	79.4	84.2	77.8	82.6	78.0	146.9	82.0	76.4	139.1	80.7	20.0	16.8	14.4	4862	1148
JEJU	33.517N	126.533E	75	32.7	34.4	89.7	77.5	87.8	77.4	86.1	77.0	80.3	86.0	79.1	85.0	78.7	149.2	84.5	77.4	142.7	83.5	22.8	19.7	16.8	2965	1481
JEJU INTL	33.511N	126.493E	118	31.9	33.7	89.6	79.2	87.6	79.6	85.8	78.8	82.6	86.1	81.1	84.7	82.1	167.6	85.7	80.5	158.9	84.2	27.6	24.5	21.9	3168	1368
JEONJU	35.833N	127.117E	205	16.3	19.6	91.8	76.8	89.7	76.0	87.5	74.5	79.6	86.2	78.4	85.1	77.9	146.1	82.7	76.7	140.0	81.8	12.9	11.3	9.8	4386	1470
JINJU	35.167N	128.033E	98	16.8	19.4	91.3	76.7	89.0	76.0	86.6	75.0	79.3	86.7	78.3	85.1	77.4	143.1	82.7	76.4	138.3	82.0	15.0	12.6	10.8	4306	1303
OSAN AB	37.091N	127.030E	38	8.4	12.1	91.4	79.3	89.2	77.9	86.3	76.1	82.1	86.1	80.5	85.2	81.0	161.1	83.3	79.2	151.5	82.3	18.8	16.2	14.0	5173	1276
POHANG	35.988N	129.420E	70	19.2	21.5	93.2	78.6	90.9	77.8	87.8	76.6	80.3	89.7	79.2	87.7	77.4	143.0	84.6	76.9	140.4	84.2	21.5	18.7	16.6	4027	1234
PYEONGTAEK A511	36.967N	127.033E	52	9.3	12.6	91.1	78.5	88.2	76.9	86.2	75.5	80.8	86.7	79.4	84.9	79.2	151.9	83.0	78.3	147.2	82.4	17.9	15.3	13.2	5172	1262
SEOGWIPO	33.250N	126.567E	167	33.0	35.1	88.7	79.6	87.1	79.1	85.5	78.4	81.2	86.2	80.4	85.3	79.8	155.8	84.8	79.0	151.2	84.0	17.6	15.1	13.3	2492	1629
SEOUL AB	37.446N	127.114E	92	5.3	10.3	91.7	77.6	89.5	76.3	86.4	74.4	79.4	88.0	78.2	86.0	77.1	141.6	83.7	75.6	134.3	81.7	13.9	11.7	10.1	5240	1207
SEOUL CITY	37.567N	126.967E	285	11.5	15.2	89.8	75.4	87.6	73.9	85.5	72.9	78.6	85.5	77.2	83.7	76.7	140.5	82.1	75.3	134.0	81.0	15.2	13.3	11.8	4831	1325
SEOUL SINYONGSAN	37.533N	126.967E	95	10.8	13.9	91.7	77.3	89.6	76.0	87.4	75.3	79.4	87.9	78.4	86.1	77.2	142.1	83.0	76.5	138.6	82.4	14.1	11.7	10.0	4716	1433
SUWON	37.267N	126.983E	115	11.6	15.2	89.9	77.0	87.6	75.6	85.5	74.3	79.2	85.4	78.1	84.0	77.5	143.7	82.1	76.4	138.4	81.3	14.0	11.9	10.3	4991	1281
ULSAN	35.593N	129.352E	45	21.5	24.3	91.7	76.6	89.3	76.1	86.9	75.3	78.9	87.0	77.9	85.7	76.8	139.7	82.7	75.7	134.5	82.4	15.3	13.3	11.8	3750	1303
WANDO	34.400N	126.700E	115	24.9	27.4	88.3	78.6	86.3	77.7	84.2	76.7	79.9	85.9	78.9	84.6	78.2	147.1	83.8	77.2	142.3	82.6	26.8	23.1	20.3	3773	1270
YEOSU	34.733N	127.750E	220	23.5	26.1	86.8	77.2	84.9	76.5	83.1	75.9	79.4	83.5	78.3	82.5	78.3	147.9	81.8	77.1	142.4	80.9	27.0	23.4	20.7	3633	1253
Kyrgyzstan																									*1 site, 8 more on CD-ROM*	
BISHKEK	42.850N	74.533E	2493	-0.2	5.2	95.3	66.6	92.7	65.1	90.1	64.2	71.1	90.2	68.4	86.9	64.3	99.1	81.1	61.7	90.2	77.4	17.1	14.1	11.4	5434	1152
Latvia																									*1 site, 19 more on CD-ROM*	
RIGA	56.967N	24.050E	85	-2.5	4.8	84.0	68.2	80.6	67.4	77.2	65.0	70.8	79.9	68.8	77.0	67.8	102.6	75.7	65.9	95.9	73.3	20.3	18.1	16.2	7421	168
Lebanon																									*1 site, 2 more on CD-ROM*	
BEIRUT RAFIC HARIRI INTL	33.821N	35.488E	87	46.6	49.2	90.6	74.2	88.3	75.6	87.4	75.7	80.3	86.9	79.2	85.8	78.6	148.8	85.9	77.2	141.9	84.9	23.2	19.0	16.0	718	2688
Libyan Arab Jamahiriya																									*3 sites, 5 more on CD-ROM*	
BENINA INTL	32.097N	20.269E	433	44.3	46.1	98.7	69.2	95.3	68.9	92.6	68.4	76.7	85.4	75.5	84.2	74.6	131.6	80.4	73.2	125.5	79.8	34.6	31.3	28.6	1090	2453
MISRATA	32.417N	15.050E	105	46.9	48.6	98.3	70.7	94.0	70.5	90.5	70.8	79.5	85.1	78.4	84.3	78.0	146.2	83.1	76.8	140.1	82.4	29.4	24.0	21.2	807	2535
TRIPOLI INTL	32.664N	13.159E	263	40.3	42.4	107.5	73.3	103.9	72.2	100.3	71.5	80.1	95.4	77.8	91.3	76.5	139.3	86.4	74.3	129.5	84.4	23.4	21.3	18.9	1136	3037

(Go to CD-ROM to access additional station tables.)

(Go to CD-ROM to access additional station tables.)

Meaning of acronyms:
DB: Dry bulb temperature, °F *WB: Wet bulb temperature, °F*
MCWB: Mean coincident wet bulb temperature, °F
Lat: Latitude, °
DP: Dew point temperature, °F
MCDB: Mean coincident dry bulb temperature, °F
Long: Longitude, °
HR: Humidity ratio, grains of moisture per lb of dry air
HDD and CDD 65: Annual heating and cooling degree-days, base 65°F, °F-day
Elev: Elevation, ft
WS: Wind speed, mph

Station	Lat	Long	Elev	Heating DB		Cooling DB/MCWB						Evaporation WB/MCDB				Dehumidification DP/HR/MCDB						Extreme Annual WS			Heat./Cool. Degree-Days	
						0.4%		1%		2%		0.4%		1%		0.4%			1%							
				99.6%	99%	DB / MCWB		DB / MCWB		DB / MCWB		WB / MCDB		WB / MCDB		DP / HR / MCDB			DP / HR / MCDB			1%	2.5%	5%	HDD / CDD 65	
Lithuania																									*2 sites, 8 more on CD-ROM*	
KAUNAS	54.883N	23.833E	253	-1.7	4.4	83.1	67.8	79.8	66.0	76.7	64.2	70.0	79.5	67.9	76.3	66.8	99.4	74.2	64.8	92.7	72.0	21.0	18.6	16.4	7380	151
VILNIUS INTL	54.634N	25.286E	646	-2.7	3.2	83.7	66.8	80.3	65.3	77.0	63.7	69.5	78.9	67.4	75.8	66.3	99.4	73.2	64.5	93.1	71.0	22.4	19.5	17.2	7692	159
Macao																									*1 site, 0 more on CD-ROM*	
MACAU INTL	22.150N	113.592E	20	45.3	48.1	91.3	80.7	89.7	80.4	88.2	80.2	82.7	87.3	82.0	86.3	81.0	161.4	85.3	80.8	160.1	85.2	25.0	22.1	19.8	508	3626
Macedonia, the former Yugoslav Republic of																									*1 site, 6 more on CD-ROM*	
SKOPJE ALEXANDER THE GREAT	41.962N	21.621E	781	10.5	17.2	96.8	68.6	93.5	68.1	91.0	67.3	71.4	89.6	70.1	87.8	66.0	98.6	76.3	64.5	93.4	74.9	19.4	16.7	13.8	4623	984
Madagascar																									*1 site, 3 more on CD-ROM*	
IVATO	18.797S	47.479E	4198	46.3	48.2	85.9	67.4	84.1	67.5	82.5	67.5	73.6	80.1	72.2	79.2	71.7	137.0	77.1	70.0	129.4	75.5	16.7	15.2	13.7	529	1298
Malaysia																									*6 sites, 18 more on CD-ROM*	
KOTA KINABALU INTL	5.937N	116.051E	10	73.0	73.4	92.9	82.4	91.7	81.8	91.2	81.6	83.8	91.1	83.1	90.5	82.0	166.3	90.5	80.8	160.2	89.7	14.1	11.6	9.8	0	6284
KUALA LUMPUR SUBANG	3.131N	101.549E	90	72.9	73.5	94.7	79.3	93.4	79.1	92.8	78.9	82.6	90.1	81.7	89.1	80.7	159.8	87.2	79.5	153.8	85.8	13.4	11.7	10.2	0	6629
KUANTAN	3.775N	103.209E	58	71.1	71.8	93.3	80.2	92.2	80.0	91.5	79.9	82.8	89.8	82.0	89.1	80.9	160.6	87.9	80.3	157.8	87.3	13.3	11.7	10.2	0	6044
KUCHING INTL	1.485N	110.347E	89	71.6	72.3	93.2	78.6	91.8	78.7	91.2	78.7	81.4	88.7	80.6	88.0	79.2	152.0	85.4	78.8	150.0	84.9	12.0	10.5	9.3	0	5898
SANDAKAN	5.901N	118.059E	46	73.2	73.9	92.8	79.7	91.5	79.5	90.5	79.5	81.9	88.4	81.3	87.8	80.2	156.8	86.4	79.2	151.8	85.2	14.4	12.6	11.6	0	6238
TAWAU	4.313N	118.122E	57	71.8	72.8	90.9	78.9	89.9	79.0	89.4	79.0	81.7	87.6	81.0	87.2	80.0	156.0	86.4	79.1	151.3	85.6	12.3	11.2	9.8	0	5841
Mali																									*1 site, 0 more on CD-ROM*	
BAMAKO-SENOU INTL	12.534N	7.950W	1247	58.9	61.2	104.4	67.5	103.2	67.7	101.9	68.0	80.7	88.8	79.3	87.7	79.0	157.5	83.6	77.4	149.2	82.1	18.1	15.5	13.7	0	6328
Mauritania																									*1 site, 1 more on CD-ROM*	
NOUAKCHOTT	18.098N	15.948W	7	55.2	57.4	106.2	68.4	103.4	68.2	100.0	68.0	83.9	86.8	82.4	86.0	83.4	174.4	85.0	81.7	164.9	84.1	21.1	18.9	17.2	4	5374
Mexico																									*18 sites, 22 more on CD-ROM*	
ACAPULCO INTL	16.757N	99.754W	13	66.6	69.4	91.8	79.9	91.5	79.8	91.0	79.5	82.3	90.4	81.4	89.2	80.3	157.4	88.4	79.1	151.0	87.0	18.4	16.1	13.7	0	5904
CANCUN INTL	21.037N	86.877W	20	55.7	58.8	93.3	80.7	91.7	80.2	91.3	80.1	82.8	90.2	82.0	89.3	80.8	160.3	87.5	80.4	157.8	87.2	21.2	18.4	16.5	5	5145
CHETUMAL INTL	18.505N	88.327W	39	60.1	63.3	93.4	80.3	92.1	80.2	91.1	80.1	82.7	89.9	81.9	89.1	80.7	159.9	88.1	79.8	154.8	87.1	23.5	23.0	22.3	0	5867
GUADALAJARA INTL	20.522N	103.311W	5016	35.4	37.6	91.7	60.4	89.9	59.6	88.1	59.0	68.2	80.2	67.4	78.9	64.7	110.4	72.0	64.2	108.4	71.6	21.9	18.0	14.1	633	1297
GUANAJUATO INTL	20.983N	101.483W	5956	39.3	42.6	93.5	58.5	91.4	58.4	89.5	58.4	67.4	79.5	66.4	77.8	64.7	114.4	67.5	64.1	112.0	67.2	23.1	20.7	17.5	480	1430
HERMOSILLO INTL	29.096N	111.048W	627	40.7	43.2	109.0	73.0	106.4	73.5	104.4	73.1	80.7	95.7	79.7	94.6	77.3	145.3	85.3	76.6	142.1	85.0	18.1	15.4	13.2	379	4827
MAZATLAN INTL	23.161N	106.266W	38	46.8	49.8	93.2	77.9	91.7	77.5	91.2	77.3	82.2	89.1	81.1	87.8	80.5	158.7	87.2	79.1	151.1	85.9	21.6	17.2	14.8	56	3835
MERIDA INTL	20.937N	89.658W	38	56.8	60.4	101.8	75.8	99.0	76.0	97.2	76.0	82.7	88.9	81.8	88.4	82.0	167.0	84.4	80.6	159.1	83.6	22.7	19.7	17.8	2	5896
MEXICO CITY INTL	19.436N	99.072W	7316	37.6	40.9	84.5	54.7	82.5	54.3	80.7	54.1	60.9	72.5	60.2	71.4	57.5	93.1	62.7	57.2	91.9	62.5	22.2	18.8	16.7	1045	368
MONTERREY INTL	25.778N	100.107W	1278	37.5	41.0	101.9	73.4	100.0	73.3	98.3	73.5	79.5	93.8	78.6	92.2	75.6	140.7	84.6	75.2	138.8	84.3	25.1	21.9	18.7	666	3855
PUERTO VALLARTA INTL	20.680N	105.254W	23	57.4	59.3	91.8	80.3	91.5	80.2	91.0	80.0	82.4	89.8	81.5	88.9	80.7	159.3	87.5	79.2	151.7	86.2	17.3	14.8	13.0	1	4629
SAN LUIS POTOSI INTL	22.254N	100.931W	6035	32.7	35.9	89.9	58.5	87.7	58.7	85.6	58.7	65.7	77.1	64.7	76.1	62.9	107.8	67.2	62.3	105.4	66.9	21.8	18.6	16.1	1200	775
TAMPICO INTL	22.296N	97.866W	80	50.4	53.6	93.4	80.1	91.8	79.9	91.3	79.8	83.5	89.7	81.9	88.6	81.9	166.6	89.0	80.4	158.4	87.3	33.4	26.6	22.4	138	4609
TAPACHULA	14.917N	92.250W	387	68.0	69.6	95.8	78.8	94.6	78.7	93.5	78.7	82.8	91.4	81.9	90.7	80.5	160.5	89.3	79.4	155.0	88.3	23.2	14.8	10.6	0	6268
TIJUANA INTL	32.541N	116.970W	489	42.5	44.3	90.0	68.5	86.3	67.6	84.0	66.9	73.4	84.9	71.6	82.3	69.7	111.4	80.3	68.0	104.6	77.5	18.3	15.6	13.8	1268	909
TOLUCA INTL	19.337N	99.566W	8466	28.3	30.5	79.0	53.8	77.1	53.4	75.2	53.0	60.7	69.9	59.3	68.6	57.6	97.5	62.8	57.0	95.5	62.4	19.6	17.1	14.4	3196	3
TORREON INTL	25.568N	103.411W	3688	38.9	42.3	100.4	69.1	98.4	68.7	96.6	68.4	76.1	92.3	74.5	91.1	71.6	134.0	86.6	69.7	125.6	83.5	19.9	15.2	12.3	567	3687
VERACRUZ INTL	19.146N	96.187W	90	58.7	60.8	95.2	80.3	93.4	80.3	91.8	79.9	82.6	91.7	81.6	90.2	80.4	158.6	87.6	79.1	151.7	85.9	43.8	32.7	23.3	6	4937
Moldova, Republic of																									*1 site, 1 more on CD-ROM*	
CHISINAU	47.017N	28.983E	568	6.3	11.3	90.4	67.6	87.1	66.8	84.3	65.9	70.7	83.4	69.2	81.5	66.6	100.1	75.8	65.2	95.1	74.4	16.5	13.9	11.9	5758	718
Mongolia																									*1 site, 59 more on CD-ROM*	
CHINGGIS KHAAN INTL	47.843N	106.767E	4364	-33.0	-29.0	87.7	60.3	83.8	58.9	80.1	57.7	63.8	78.1	62.1	75.8	59.3	88.7	67.7	57.4	82.8	66.7	23.0	19.8	16.9	12689	177
Morocco																									*11 sites, 9 more on CD-ROM*	
AGADIR AL MASSIRA INTL	30.325N	9.413W	250	40.9	43.1	101.9	67.7	94.9	66.4	89.8	66.1	72.5	87.0	71.4	84.6	68.3	105.1	75.6	67.7	102.8	75.2	21.1	18.1	15.9	708	1688
CASABLANCA ANFA	33.557N	7.660W	203	43.6	45.8	85.5	70.7	81.6	71.3	79.2	71.2	75.1	80.0	73.9	78.6	73.5	125.7	78.0	72.2	120.1	76.5	14.4	12.3	11.1	1144	1166
CASABLANCA MOHAMMED V INTL	33.367N	7.590W	656	37.3	39.5	96.7	70.6	91.7	70.4	87.9	69.8	74.2	88.3	72.8	85.7	70.2	113.7	78.0	69.3	110.2	76.8	21.7	18.7	16.5	1469	1424
FES-SAISS	33.927N	4.978W	1900	33.5	35.5	103.2	67.9	99.6	67.9	96.4	67.5	72.4	92.5	70.7	91.1	66.2	103.7	80.3	64.4	97.3	78.1	22.7	18.6	15.6	2161	1577
INEZGANE	30.381N	9.546W	89	41.0	43.6	95.4	66.9	89.3	65.8	84.2	65.2	72.4	83.7	71.3	79.9	69.7	109.7	75.3	68.4	104.8	73.8	23.6	19.5	16.2	939	1168
MARRAKECH MENARA	31.607N	8.036W	1535	39.2	41.4	107.6	69.0	103.8	68.9	100.2	68.5	73.5	96.0	71.9	93.9	66.9	104.6	79.7	65.9	101.1	78.3	16.6	14.0	11.8	1116	2574
MEKNES BASSATINE	33.879N	5.515W	1890	36.2	38.8	102.2	69.7	98.3	69.5	94.6	68.9	74.7	92.8	72.7	90.3	68.9	114.1	85.9	67.0	106.4	82.1	18.9	16.2	14.1	1975	1565
OUJDA ANGADS	34.787N	1.924W	1535	33.6	35.9	100.3	69.0	96.6	69.2	93.3	68.8	74.6	90.5	73.3	87.8	70.1	117.1	80.4	68.8	112.0	79.3	26.1	22.4	20.0	2000	1616
RABAT SALE INTL	34.051N	6.752W	276	40.7	42.6	91.2	70.7	86.0	70.2	82.4	70.5	75.6	83.2	73.9	80.7	73.4	125.3	79.9	71.8	118.5	77.8	19.0	16.3	14.2	1444	981
TANGIER IBN BATOUTA	35.727N	5.917W	62	39.4	42.4	91.8	70.5	89.4	70.3	86.3	69.9	73.6	85.4	72.6	83.6	70.0	110.6	78.5	69.0	106.7	77.8	32.9	29.0	25.7	1428	1315
TETOUAN SANIA RAMEL	35.594N	5.320W	10	43.1	45.6	91.4	68.8	88.0	68.8	85.5	68.8	75.5	81.4	74.5	80.2	73.7	125.6	78.3	72.8	121.7	77.7	25.7	23.0	20.8	1127	1504
Mozambique																									*1 site, 0 more on CD-ROM*	
MAPUTO INTL	25.921S	32.573E	145	53.4	55.3	95.7	74.7	92.7	74.7	89.9	74.7	80.0	88.3	79.0	86.9	77.6	144.3	83.6	76.9	140.7	83.0	34.0	28.7	23.4	31	3561
Netherlands																									*6 sites, 37 more on CD-ROM*	

Meaning of acronyms:
DB: Dry bulb temperature, °F — WB: Wet bulb temperature, °F — MCWB: Mean coincident wet bulb temperature, °F
Lat: Latitude, ° — DP: Dew point temperature, °F — MCDB: Mean coincident dry bulb temperature, °F
Long: Longitude, ° — HR: Humidity ratio, grains of moisture per lb of dry air
Elev: Elevation, ft — WS: Wind speed, mph — HDD and CDD 65: Annual heating and cooling degree-days, base 65°F, °F-day

Station	Lat	Long	Elev	Heating DB		Cooling DB/MCWB						Evaporation WB/MCDB				Dehumidification DP/HR/MCDB						Extreme Annual WS			Heat./Cool. Degree-Days	
				99.6%	99%	0.4%		1%		2%		0.4%		1%		0.4%			1%			1%	2.5%	5%	HDD / CDD 65	
						DB	MCWB	DB	MCWB	DB	MCWB	WB	MCDB	WB	MCDB	DP	HR	MCDB	DP	HR	MCDB				HDD	CDD
AMSTERDAM SCHIPHOL	52.309N	4.764E	-11	20.8	24.5	82.0	67.6	78.1	66.2	74.7	64.5	69.3	78.6	67.4	75.5	66.2	96.5	73.1	64.5	90.8	70.8	30.2	26.3	23.1	5272	128
HOEK VAN HOLLAND	51.983N	4.100E	46	22.7	26.0	80.9	66.7	76.4	65.2	73.0	64.4	69.1	77.0	67.3	73.7	66.4	97.5	72.0	64.8	92.1	70.0	35.9	32.1	29.2	4962	126
IJMUIDEN	52.467N	4.567E	13	20.5	24.6	78.0	65.7	74.4	64.1	71.3	63.6	68.1	73.9	66.6	70.8	66.3	96.8	70.0	65.1	92.9	68.4	41.7	36.7	33.5	5257	92
ROTTERDAM THE HAGUE	51.957N	4.437E	-15	20.8	24.6	82.5	67.8	78.5	66.4	75.2	64.6	69.6	79.2	67.7	75.9	66.3	97.0	73.5	64.7	91.3	71.3	27.2	23.6	20.8	5223	128
VALKENBURG	52.167N	4.433E	3	20.7	24.4	80.8	67.4	76.7	65.6	73.3	64.0	69.0	77.4	67.1	74.1	66.1	96.2	72.5	64.4	90.7	70.2	29.4	25.9	22.9	5294	101
WOENSDRECHT AB	51.449N	4.342E	63	18.2	22.7	84.4	67.6	80.1	66.3	76.7	64.7	69.8	80.0	68.0	77.0	66.3	97.1	73.2	64.6	91.5	71.5	21.8	18.9	16.6	5334	140
New Zealand																										*4 sites, 35 more on CD-ROM*
AUCKLAND AERO AWS	37.000S	174.800E	23	40.0	42.1	77.3	67.4	75.7	66.5	74.2	65.8	70.1	74.2	68.9	73.0	68.7	105.5	72.3	67.4	100.6	71.4	28.3	24.9	22.2	2199	282
AUCKLAND INTL	37.008S	174.792E	23	39.2	41.3	78.3	67.8	76.6	66.9	74.9	66.0	70.5	74.8	69.1	73.4	69.4	108.1	73.1	67.8	102.1	71.6	28.2	25.3	22.7	2193	309
CHRISTCHURCH AP AWS	43.483S	172.517E	121	27.6	29.4	81.7	61.8	77.9	60.5	74.4	59.4	64.5	75.3	63.0	72.4	61.2	80.9	66.4	59.8	77.2	65.1	25.5	22.6	20.2	4675	89
CHRISTCHURCH INTL	43.489S	172.532E	123	26.9	28.7	82.4	62.4	78.7	60.8	75.1	59.8	64.9	76.0	63.4	73.2	61.1	80.8	66.9	59.7	76.9	65.4	25.2	22.4	20.1	4715	100
Nicaragua																										*1 site, 0 more on CD-ROM*
MANAGUA INTL	12.141N	86.168W	194	67.9	69.6	96.8	75.7	95.3	75.5	94.6	75.4	79.9	88.5	79.2	87.9	77.4	143.3	83.2	77.1	142.2	83.0	18.6	16.4	14.5	0	6263
Niger																										*1 site, 12 more on CD-ROM*
NIAMEY DIORI HAMANI INTL	13.482N	2.184E	732	60.7	62.6	108.1	68.9	107.2	68.8	105.6	68.8	80.7	91.3	79.8	90.6	78.6	152.8	84.8	77.2	145.5	84.3	20.7	17.9	15.7	0	7649
Norway																										*2 sites, 117 more on CD-ROM*
HAKADAL	60.117N	10.833E	558	-2.3	3.0	79.8	63.8	76.7	62.4	73.4	60.7	66.5	74.3	64.6	73.1	64.0	91.2	69.0	61.4	83.0	66.7	17.9	15.1	12.9	8124	79
OSLO-BLINDERN	59.942N	10.720E	318	6.2	10.2	80.1	63.2	76.7	61.9	73.5	60.2	65.6	74.7	63.9	72.9	62.2	84.7	68.4	60.6	79.9	67.0	17.8	15.4	13.4	7528	98
Oman																										*1 site, 20 more on CD-ROM*
AL BURAIMI	24.233N	55.783E	981	49.7	52.2	113.2	70.7	111.4	70.3	109.7	70.2	81.3	91.9	79.9	93.1	79.0	156.4	87.2	76.6	143.7	88.1	18.3	16.0	14.1	128	6761
Pakistan																										*3 sites, 25 more on CD-ROM*
BENAZIR BHUTTO INTL	33.617N	73.099E	1668	35.8	37.8	106.0	72.9	102.9	73.0	100.4	72.9	82.5	93.6	81.5	92.2	79.7	164.0	88.4	78.9	159.5	87.8	29.1	23.3	20.9	1150	3679
JINNAH INTL	24.907N	67.161E	100	50.2	53.3	102.0	72.9	98.8	73.5	96.8	74.2	82.8	92.0	82.1	90.9	80.8	160.4	87.6	79.9	156.0	87.3	21.8	19.0	17.2	43	5846
LAHORE ALLAMA IQBAL INTL	31.522N	74.404E	712	37.4	40.6	109.8	74.1	107.5	74.0	104.2	73.9	84.5	94.0	83.5	92.7	82.5	174.1	89.9	81.0	165.5	88.8	17.9	14.2	12.1	800	4695
Palestinian Territory, Occupied																										*1 site, 0 more on CD-ROM*
JERUSALEM ATAROT	31.867N	35.217E	2490	33.4	35.9	91.6	65.0	89.2	64.9	86.6	64.6	71.1	83.7	69.5	81.1	67.7	111.6	75.6	66.2	106.0	73.2	21.1	18.9	17.3	2327	1421
Panama																										*2 sites, 0 more on CD-ROM*
PANAMA PACIFICO INTL	8.917N	79.600W	43	71.9	73.2	95.0	77.7	93.5	77.5	92.9	77.4	81.8	89.1	81.0	88.2	80.0	155.7	86.8	79.0	151.0	85.9	18.1	16.1	14.3	0	6418
TOCUMEN INTL	9.071N	79.383W	135	69.5	70.8	93.4	77.6	92.1	77.1	91.5	76.9	81.7	88.1	80.8	87.6	80.3	157.8	85.3	79.1	151.5	84.3	17.3	14.6	12.6	0	6053
Paraguay																										*1 site, 3 more on CD-ROM*
SILVIO PETTIROSSI INTL	25.240S	57.519W	292	41.2	44.7	98.9	75.0	97.0	75.3	95.1	75.3	80.1	90.5	79.5	89.8	77.4	143.9	84.9	76.8	141.0	84.6	23.2	21.0	18.9	462	3796
Peru																										*8 sites, 5 more on CD-ROM*
AREQUIPA INTL	16.341S	71.583W	8405	42.7	44.3	75.3	52.5	73.8	51.7	73.3	51.5	58.5	69.8	57.5	68.6	55.1	88.7	60.8	53.7	84.4	60.0	20.1	16.9	15.1	2049	3
CHICLAYO INTL	6.787S	79.828W	97	58.8	59.3	90.0	75.5	89.2	75.2	87.5	74.4	78.1	86.5	76.7	85.3	75.4	133.5	83.9	73.7	125.9	83.1	23.3	21.5	20.0	2	2927
CUSCO INTL	13.536S	71.939W	10860	32.2	34.0	73.5	50.3	71.9	49.9	71.0	49.6	54.4	68.4	53.6	67.4	49.3	78.7	58.4	48.4	76.0	57.3	18.0	15.1	13.0	3602	0
HUANCHACO INTL	8.081S	79.109W	106	57.7	58.6	82.4	74.0	80.8	73.4	79.1	72.1	74.5	81.4	73.6	80.3	71.8	117.9	80.2	71.2	115.7	79.7	15.4	14.2	13.3	235	1208
IQUITOS INTL	3.785S	73.309W	306	66.3	68.4	93.5	79.5	92.7	79.5	91.4	79.3	81.2	90.3	80.8	89.8	78.8	151.2	87.8	78.0	147.3	87.0	12.6	10.0	8.7	0	5502
LIMA CALLAO INTL	12.022S	77.114W	113	57.2	58.0	83.9	72.9	82.0	72.0	80.4	71.5	74.4	81.0	73.1	79.9	71.9	118.5	79.4	70.2	111.7	77.4	17.7	15.7	14.1	327	1402
PIURA INTL	5.206S	80.616W	116	60.5	61.5	93.3	77.7	91.8	77.1	90.8	76.7	79.6	90.1	78.7	89.4	76.8	140.4	85.1	75.6	134.4	85.2	18.5	16.9	15.4	0	4295
PUCALLPA INTL	8.378S	74.574W	513	64.0	66.2	94.7	79.2	93.4	79.1	92.3	78.8	80.6	91.2	80.0	90.4	77.4	145.4	85.4	77.2	144.2	85.3	14.4	12.1	10.0	1	5655
Philippines																										*10 sites, 44 more on CD-ROM*
CAGAYAN DE ORO	8.483N	124.650E	20	71.8	73.0	94.3	81.5	93.3	81.3	92.5	81.1	83.8	91.7	83.2	91.1	81.7	164.9	90.2	80.9	160.7	89.8	10.7	8.4	6.7	0	6482
FRANCISCO BANGOY INTL	7.126N	125.646E	96	73.0	73.5	93.1	80.4	91.8	80.3	91.4	80.2	82.8	90.1	82.2	89.5	80.8	160.5	88.6	80.2	157.5	88.0	17.5	13.5	11.4	0	6394
GENERAL SANTOS INTL	6.050N	125.100E	436	72.9	73.4	95.1	81.1	93.8	80.9	92.8	80.7	82.7	91.7	82.2	91.0	80.3	160.0	88.9	79.8	157.3	88.5	13.6	11.9	10.7	0	6395
ILOILO	10.713N	122.541E	27	73.0	73.9	94.6	81.8	93.3	81.6	92.0	81.3	83.3	91.6	82.7	90.9	81.0	161.2	88.9	80.4	158.1	88.7	16.4	14.3	12.6	0	6408
MACTAN CEBU INTL	10.308N	123.979E	31	74.0	74.9	91.7	81.1	90.7	80.8	89.9	80.7	83.5	88.4	82.8	87.8	82.3	168.2	86.7	81.6	164.3	86.4	18.6	16.1	13.9	0	6359
MANILA	14.583N	120.983E	43	73.7	74.8	94.2	79.5	93.0	79.5	91.8	79.3	82.7	89.7	81.9	88.9	80.8	160.3	87.5	80.0	156.2	86.8	18.7	15.4	12.9	0	6708
NINOY AQUINO INTL	14.509N	121.020E	75	71.2	72.3	95.1	78.9	93.5	78.7	92.6	78.6	83.1	88.4	82.3	87.4	82.1	167.6	86.1	80.9	161.1	84.9	29.8	22.0	17.4	0	6386
SANGLEY POINT AB	14.495N	120.904E	8	72.2	74.1	95.2	83.4	93.9	83.0	92.8	82.6	84.4	93.0	83.8	92.1	81.9	166.1	90.1	81.6	164.2	89.9	18.7	16.2	14.2	0	6805
SCIENCE GARDEN	14.650N	121.050E	151	68.5	70.0	95.3	79.3	94.0	79.2	92.7	79.1	81.9	90.2	81.4	89.5	79.9	156.1	86.2	79.2	152.5	85.4	12.3	10.4	8.6	0	6105
ZAMBOANGA INTL	6.922N	122.060E	33	72.8	73.7	93.4	81.5	92.6	81.3	91.7	81.0	82.8	91.0	82.2	90.4	80.7	159.5	88.9	80.0	155.9	88.2	12.1	10.8	9.4	0	6533
Poland																										*13 sites, 63 more on CD-ROM*
GDANSK LECHA WALESY	54.378N	18.466E	489	4.9	10.4	80.9	66.3	77.3	64.8	74.9	63.6	68.7	77.3	66.9	75.0	65.9	97.4	72.9	64.1	91.2	70.9	25.4	21.3	18.5	7102	93
GDANSK-SWIBNO	54.333N	18.933E	30	1.4	9.1	78.5	67.0	74.6	65.0	71.5	63.7	68.5	75.9	66.5	72.5	65.9	95.5	71.7	63.9	89.1	70.1	22.9	19.4	16.7	7003	62
HEL	54.600N	18.817E	10	15.6	19.3	77.7	68.5	74.8	66.8	72.4	65.5	70.0	75.5	68.2	73.2	67.8	102.2	73.4	66.3	96.8	71.1	21.5	18.5	16.4	6462	104
KATOWICE	50.233N	19.033E	932	5.2	10.6	85.5	67.9	82.0	66.0	78.9	64.6	69.5	80.6	67.8	78.7	65.8	98.6	74.1	64.2	93.1	71.9	18.8	16.4	14.3	6605	192
KRAKOW BALICE	50.078N	19.785E	791	3.5	8.8	86.1	68.7	82.6	67.2	79.3	65.7	70.5	82.3	68.9	79.9	66.5	100.4	75.5	64.9	94.8	73.1	21.4	18.6	16.3	6527	233
LODZ	51.733N	19.400E	623	5.5	10.6	85.9	67.4	82.4	65.9	79.1	64.4	69.7	80.6	68.0	78.4	66.3	99.0	73.6	64.5	93.1	71.7	20.2	17.7	15.6	6650	228

(Go to CD-ROM to access additional station tables.)

(Go to CD-ROM to access additional station tables.)

Meaning of acronyms:
DB: Dry bulb temperature, °F *WB: Wet bulb temperature, °F*
MCWB: Mean coincident wet bulb temperature, °F

Lat: Latitude, °
DP: Dew point temperature, °F
MCDB: Mean coincident dry bulb temperature, °F

Long: Longitude, °
HR: Humidity ratio, grains of moisture per lb of dry air
HDD and CDD 65: Annual heating and cooling degree-days, base 65°F, °F-day

Elev: Elevation, ft
WS: Wind speed, mph

Station	Lat	Long	Elev	Heating DB		Cooling DB/MCWB						Evaporation WB/MCDB				Dehumidification DP/HR/MCDB						Extreme Annual WS			Heat./Cool. Degree-Days	
						0.4%		1%		2%		0.4%		1%		0.4%			1%							
				99.6%	99%	DB	MCWB	DB	MCWB	DB	MCWB	WB	MCDB	WB	MCDB	DP	HR	MCDB	DP	HR	MCDB	1%	2.5%	5%	HDD	CDD 65
LUBLIN RADAWIEC	51.217N	22.400E	787	2.2	8.0	84.3	68.4	80.9	67.2	77.8	65.5	70.6	80.7	68.7	78.1	67.0	102.3	75.9	65.3	96.1	73.2	19.1	16.6	14.4	6967	191
POZNAN LAWICA	52.421N	16.826E	308	7.6	13.0	86.4	66.9	82.9	65.5	80.1	64.3	69.6	81.7	67.9	79.0	66.0	96.9	72.8	64.3	91.3	71.6	21.5	18.8	16.6	6338	247
RACIBORZ	50.050N	18.200E	676	4.8	10.4	85.9	68.3	82.4	66.8	79.1	65.5	70.2	81.1	68.5	78.9	66.6	100.3	75.1	64.9	94.6	73.1	22.3	19.3	16.7	6301	220
SZCZECIN	53.400N	14.617E	23	10.4	15.8	84.4	68.0	80.8	66.4	77.6	65.1	70.5	80.4	68.5	77.2	67.1	99.8	74.7	65.4	93.9	72.6	21.0	18.6	16.5	6233	179
TERESPOL	52.067N	23.617E	449	-0.9	5.8	85.7	68.8	82.1	67.5	79.0	65.5	71.1	81.6	69.1	78.6	67.5	102.9	75.4	65.8	96.7	73.5	16.6	14.5	13.1	6933	219
WARSZAWA OKECIE	52.166N	20.967E	362	3.6	9.6	85.9	68.5	82.4	66.7	79.1	64.9	70.5	81.6	68.9	78.8	66.9	100.3	74.6	65.5	95.4	73.2	22.4	19.7	17.5	6620	250
WROCLAW STRACHOWICE	51.103N	16.886E	404	6.9	12.7	86.5	68.0	83.2	66.6	80.0	65.3	70.1	82.0	68.4	79.2	66.3	98.2	74.5	64.6	92.6	72.5	20.3	17.6	15.5	6159	245
Portugal																									*1 site, 33 more on CD-ROM*	
LISBOA	38.767N	9.133W	344	40.3	42.4	92.8	68.6	89.1	67.5	85.4	66.6	70.8	87.0	69.4	83.3	66.6	99.2	72.6	65.5	95.2	72.2	18.7	16.5	14.5	1858	1022
Puerto Rico																									*2 sites, 3 more on CD-ROM*	
JOSE APONTE DE LA TORRE AP	18.255N	65.641W	33	68.4	70.0	89.9	78.4	89.4	78.1	88.2	77.7	81.3	86.8	80.6	86.2	79.2	151.9	84.4	78.9	150.1	84.2	18.3	16.6	15.5	0	5760
LUIS MUNOZ MARIN INTL	18.433N	66.011W	8	69.7	70.6	91.6	77.4	89.8	77.8	88.9	77.8	80.9	86.6	80.1	86.3	79.1	151.0	83.8	78.3	146.8	83.5	20.5	18.9	17.6	0	5692
Qatar																									*1 site, 1 more on CD-ROM*	
DOHA INTL	25.261N	51.565E	35	53.3	55.4	111.3	71.9	109.2	72.4	107.2	73.0	88.0	95.3	87.2	94.9	86.3	192.4	93.2	85.6	187.9	93.1	23.1	20.6	18.2	102	6706
Romania																									*8 sites, 46 more on CD-ROM*	
BUCURESTI BANEASA	44.503N	26.102E	297	8.5	13.6	93.6	69.7	90.8	69.1	87.8	68.1	73.1	86.2	71.4	84.6	69.8	110.6	76.5	67.9	103.7	74.5	18.5	15.7	13.2	5387	738
BUCURESTI HENRI COANDA INTL	44.571N	26.085E	314	7.0	12.4	93.3	70.5	89.9	70.4	87.6	69.1	73.8	86.4	72.2	85.1	70.2	112.3	77.0	68.3	105.0	75.8	22.8	18.4	15.8	5314	800
CLUJ NAPOCA	46.785N	23.686E	1036	5.6	10.8	87.8	68.6	84.6	67.4	81.8	66.2	71.1	83.0	69.2	80.7	67.5	104.9	75.8	65.7	98.5	73.5	17.0	13.7	11.2	6224	338
CONSTANTA	44.217N	28.650E	46	15.8	19.6	86.3	74.2	84.1	73.0	82.1	72.1	77.9	82.7	75.6	81.2	76.5	138.5	81.1	73.9	126.5	79.4	26.3	22.3	17.7	4632	856
CRAIOVA	44.318N	23.889E	626	9.7	14.5	93.3	70.3	90.1	69.7	87.3	69.0	74.3	86.5	72.5	84.5	70.7	115.9	79.0	68.8	108.2	77.1	25.0	20.0	17.3	5141	849
IASI	47.178N	27.621E	397	3.5	9.3	91.6	69.8	88.2	68.7	85.4	67.8	73.0	84.8	71.2	82.9	69.5	110.1	78.2	67.7	103.2	76.0	19.9	16.7	14.8	5771	651
MIHAIL KOGALNICEANU	44.362N	28.488E	353	12.2	16.0	91.3	70.9	88.0	69.8	85.7	69.3	75.1	82.8	73.4	81.6	73.3	125.5	77.8	71.4	117.3	76.6	25.1	21.2	19.0	5078	791
TIMISOARA TRAIAN VUIA	45.810N	21.338E	348	11.1	15.8	93.4	69.8	90.1	69.4	87.4	68.1	73.1	85.7	71.4	83.7	69.9	111.4	76.5	68.0	104.2	75.0	18.9	15.8	13.4	5111	685
Russian Federation																									*62 sites, 540 more on CD-ROM*	
ARKHANGELSK TALAGI	64.600N	40.717E	62	-27.1	-20.3	81.6	67.0	77.3	64.4	73.4	62.4	69.1	78.2	66.7	75.0	65.9	95.8	73.5	63.4	87.5	70.9	18.0	15.7	14.0	11188	84
ASTRAKHAN	46.283N	47.983E	-69	-2.1	4.0	97.1	70.1	94.2	69.4	91.2	68.8	74.5	86.9	72.7	85.6	71.0	113.8	79.5	68.9	105.9	77.9	23.2	20.2	17.7	6042	1265
BALANDINO	55.306N	61.503E	769	-20.5	-15.1	87.4	66.7	83.8	65.6	80.4	64.4	69.8	81.4	68.0	79.0	66.1	98.8	73.9	64.3	92.7	72.5	23.0	20.3	17.9	10015	265
BARNAUL	53.364N	83.539E	837	-28.9	-23.1	86.2	65.9	83.1	64.9	80.4	63.7	69.7	80.3	67.7	78.0	66.1	99.3	74.6	64.2	92.6	73.2	23.5	20.0	17.6	10514	295
BOLSHOYE SAVINO	57.915N	56.021E	404	-23.4	-17.0	85.8	68.6	82.2	66.5	78.7	64.6	70.3	81.5	68.5	79.4	66.4	98.5	76.0	64.5	92.2	73.6	22.5	20.0	17.8	10332	198
BOLVANSKIY	70.450N	59.083E	40	-26.6	-23.1	57.2	52.9	53.2	50.5	49.7	47.7	53.9	56.6	50.6	52.8	52.1	58.0	55.2	49.0	51.5	52.0	38.2	34.1	31.0	15996	0
BRYANSK	53.214N	34.176E	663	-7.8	-1.9	84.6	67.6	81.1	65.5	78.3	64.3	69.3	80.6	67.4	77.7	65.4	96.2	73.8	63.6	90.3	72.0	19.8	17.1	15.5	8106	231
CHEREPOVETS	59.267N	38.017E	374	-21.2	-15.4	82.9	68.0	79.1	66.3	75.5	64.1	70.1	79.6	68.0	76.3	66.7	99.7	75.1	64.8	93.1	72.3	19.7	16.6	14.1	9925	101
CHERTOVITSKOYE	51.814N	39.230E	514	-11.6	-5.7	91.3	66.6	87.2	65.6	82.7	64.4	69.5	82.2	67.9	80.8	64.9	93.9	73.3	64.0	91.0	72.4	22.2	18.9	16.4	7876	385
CHITA KADALA	52.026N	113.306E	2272	-35.1	-31.4	87.7	66.4	84.1	64.6	80.6	62.8	69.6	82.6	67.3	79.0	65.4	102.1	74.7	63.1	94.1	71.8	22.1	18.9	16.5	12615	183
GUMRAK	48.783N	44.346E	482	-8.2	-3.4	95.6	65.7	91.9	65.3	88.3	64.6	69.2	85.3	67.8	84.1	64.5	92.5	73.4	62.8	86.9	72.8	27.0	23.9	21.5	7327	847
IRKUTSK	52.268N	104.389E	1675	-32.1	-25.8	83.8	64.0	80.5	63.5	77.2	62.1	67.9	78.1	66.1	75.6	64.5	96.8	71.6	62.7	90.7	69.9	22.4	19.4	16.8	11892	96
IZHEVSK	56.833N	53.450E	522	-20.8	-14.9	85.3	67.8	81.9	66.0	78.7	64.6	69.8	81.4	68.2	79.1	65.9	97.4	75.0	64.2	91.6	73.0	21.6	18.4	15.9	10155	223
KALUGA	54.550N	36.367E	652	-13.5	-7.2	83.0	66.7	80.0	65.5	77.0	64.5	69.7	78.6	67.7	76.2	66.4	99.7	74.7	64.5	93.2	72.3	20.5	16.8	14.8	8725	140
KAZAN	55.606N	49.279E	414	-18.1	-12.2	87.6	67.8	83.9	66.8	80.5	65.2	70.3	82.0	68.7	79.7	66.4	98.6	75.8	64.6	92.7	73.7	24.4	21.9	20.2	9414	328
KEMEROVO	55.270N	86.107E	863	-29.0	-23.7	84.1	66.2	80.7	64.8	77.4	63.4	69.2	78.6	67.3	76.6	66.0	99.1	73.6	64.1	92.5	71.8	23.8	21.0	18.8	11184	206
KHABAROVSK	48.528N	135.188E	246	-22.2	-18.8	86.6	72.2	83.9	71.1	80.8	69.5	75.4	82.0	73.5	80.1	73.5	125.9	78.1	71.5	117.5	76.7	24.4	21.1	18.8	10906	408
KHRABROVO	54.890N	20.593E	43	2.5	8.6	82.7	67.9	78.9	65.9	75.6	64.1	70.1	78.6	68.0	76.0	67.5	101.1	74.5	64.8	92.1	71.3	21.1	18.1	16.2	6885	131
KIROV	58.567N	49.567E	518	-20.3	-14.7	85.1	68.7	81.7	66.6	78.5	64.8	70.2	81.7	68.6	79.1	66.4	98.9	74.9	64.7	93.4	73.2	13.7	12.0	10.8	10066	226
KOLTSOVO	56.743N	60.803E	764	-23.3	-18.0	85.4	67.1	82.0	65.4	78.7	63.9	70.0	80.7	68.0	78.3	66.4	100.0	74.3	64.4	93.2	72.5	20.3	17.9	15.9	10572	173
KRASNODAR	45.035N	39.171E	118	5.6	12.0	94.0	72.4	91.0	71.6	87.7	70.4	75.5	87.8	73.7	85.7	71.8	117.8	81.8	69.9	110.6	79.7	23.0	20.5	18.6	5098	973
KRASNOYARSK	56.000N	92.883E	909	-28.6	-23.9	83.1	65.0	79.9	63.7	76.6	62.3	68.0	78.2	66.2	75.7	64.5	94.1	72.3	62.6	87.9	70.4	22.7	18.8	15.8	11257	122
KRASNOYARSK MININO	56.067N	92.733E	770	-33.9	-28.9	84.1	66.6	80.8	65.3	77.6	63.7	69.2	79.8	67.2	77.1	65.5	97.0	74.2	63.7	90.8	71.9	15.9	13.6	11.8	11099	183
KURGAN	55.467N	65.400E	243	-26.6	-21.0	88.5	66.6	84.9	65.8	81.6	64.7	70.0	82.9	68.4	80.5	65.7	95.8	74.4	64.2	90.6	72.8	23.6	20.7	18.2	10516	303
KURSK	51.767N	36.167E	810	-7.9	-2.3	87.4	67.3	83.8	65.9	80.6	64.7	69.7	81.7	68.1	79.6	65.7	97.8	74.3	64.1	92.4	72.8	18.6	16.5	14.8	7834	369
KURUMOCH	53.505N	50.164E	477	-16.2	-10.4	90.0	66.8	86.4	65.9	83.2	64.7	70.4	82.3	68.9	80.8	66.5	99.3	75.1	64.7	93.1	73.1	23.2	20.6	18.3	8907	439
MAGNITOGORSK	53.350N	59.083E	1260	-21.3	-16.6	87.3	65.3	83.8	64.0	80.7	62.9	68.0	81.2	66.4	79.4	63.5	91.7	73.5	61.8	86.4	71.9	22.1	18.8	16.3	10346	261
MAKHACHKALA	43.000N	47.500E	-61	9.3	15.1	88.9	73.7	86.5	73.8	84.4	73.1	77.8	84.8	76.5	83.5	75.6	133.8	83.0	74.0	126.6	81.9	24.1	20.8	18.1	4943	1047
MOSCOW BIBIREVO	55.833N	37.617E	515	-7.9	-2.2	85.4	69.6	82.0	68.1	78.7	66.4	71.6	82.5	69.6	79.2	67.8	104.1	77.1	66.0	97.8	74.9	9.2	7.7	7.0	8333	248
MOSCOW SHEREMETYEVO	55.973N	37.415E	622	-11.2	-5.7	86.0	66.5	82.4	65.3	78.8	64.5	69.2	79.1	67.3	77.5	66.0	98.2	73.6	64.2	91.9	71.7	20.6	18.3	16.4	8741	216
MOSCOW VNUKOVO	55.592N	37.261E	685	-9.7	-4.2	85.7	66.8	82.1	65.7	78.7	64.6	69.5	80.1	67.5	77.8	66.0	98.3	74.2	64.2	92.2	72.4	20.9	18.5	16.4	8664	230
MURMANSK	68.782N	32.751E	266	-26.0	-20.2	75.6	61.0	71.4	58.8	67.4	57.0	62.8	71.7	60.3	68.6	59.0	75.2	66.6	56.4	68.3	63.9	23.4	20.2	17.4	11988	18
NIZHNY NOVGOROD STRIGINO	56.217N	43.817E	269	-16.2	-10.0	86.2	68.2	82.7	66.8	79.4	65.4	70.4	81.8	68.7	79.6	66.5	98.5	75.0	64.7	92.5	73.1	16.6	14.5	12.9	9044	241
NIZHNY TAGIL	57.883N	60.067E	853	-24.1	-19.4	83.0	66.8	79.8	65.1	76.8	63.5	69.2	79.7	67.3	77.0	65.5	97.2	73.9	63.6	90.9	71.8	16.5	14.3	12.7	10971	112

(Go to CD-ROM to access additional station tables.)

Meaning of acronyms:
DB: Dry bulb temperature, °F *WB: Wet bulb temperature, °F*
MCWB: Mean coincident wet bulb temperature, °F
Lat: Latitude, °
DP: Dew point temperature, °F
MCDB: Mean coincident dry bulb temperature, °F
Long: Longitude, °
HR: Humidity ratio, grains of moisture per lb of dry air
HDD and CDD 65: Annual heating and cooling degree-days, base 65°F, °F-day
Elev: Elevation, ft
WS: Wind speed, mph

Station	Lat	Long	Elev	Heating DB		Cooling DB/MCWB						Evaporation WB/MCDB				Dehumidification DP/HR/MCDB						Extreme Annual WS			Heat./Cool. Degree-Days	
						0.4%		1%		2%		0.4%		1%		0.4%			1%							
				99.6%	99%	DB	MCWB	DB	MCWB	DB	MCWB	WB	MCDB	WB	MCDB	DP	HR	MCDB	DP	HR	MCDB	1%	2.5%	5%	HDD	CDD 65
NOVOKUZNETSK	53.817N	86.883E	1010	-27.5	-22.4	84.8	66.8	81.6	65.4	78.6	64.4	69.6	80.0	67.7	77.9	66.1	99.8	74.7	64.1	92.9	72.4	26.0	21.6	18.5	10695	189
NOVOSIBIRSK TOLMACHEVO	55.013N	82.651E	365	-33.0	-27.2	85.7	66.0	82.4	64.7	79.2	63.3	69.1	79.9	67.5	77.5	65.8	96.5	73.1	64.0	90.5	71.8	22.7	19.5	17.0	11102	219
OMSK	54.967N	73.311E	311	-27.4	-22.3	87.9	65.8	84.3	64.8	80.9	63.6	69.2	81.9	67.5	79.7	64.8	92.8	73.5	63.0	87.2	72.0	23.0	19.7	17.3	10874	294
ORENBURG	51.796N	55.457E	387	-21.6	-15.3	94.4	67.0	90.9	66.2	87.1	65.1	70.4	86.0	68.6	84.2	65.4	95.0	75.9	63.3	88.4	74.1	23.2	20.5	18.2	9158	574
ORYOL	52.933N	36.000E	643	-10.4	-4.4	86.7	68.1	83.1	66.9	80.0	65.3	70.2	81.4	68.7	79.6	66.5	100.0	75.9	64.9	94.5	73.6	22.3	19.3	17.2	8064	298
PENZA	53.133N	45.017E	571	-16.9	-11.1	89.6	68.0	85.7	67.1	82.2	65.6	70.6	83.2	69.0	81.3	66.4	99.4	75.9	64.7	93.5	73.9	22.3	20.5	18.9	8842	339
PSKOV	57.817N	28.333E	148	-9.6	-2.5	83.7	68.5	80.3	66.6	77.0	64.6	70.4	80.5	68.3	77.4	66.7	98.6	75.4	64.7	91.9	72.9	16.4	14.1	12.2	8165	155
ROSTOV-NA-DONU	47.250N	39.817E	256	0.2	5.3	94.9	70.4	91.2	69.9	87.7	68.4	73.9	88.1	72.2	85.2	69.7	110.4	80.4	67.9	103.3	78.3	27.8	24.5	21.3	6121	921
RYAZAN	54.633N	39.700E	518	-11.6	-5.9	86.5	67.9	82.8	66.3	79.5	64.9	70.2	81.6	68.4	79.1	66.5	99.5	75.3	64.7	93.3	72.7	16.6	13.9	12.1	8545	282
SARATOV TSENTRALNY	51.565N	46.047E	499	-10.5	-5.5	91.8	67.7	88.0	66.8	84.5	65.8	70.3	84.5	69.0	82.9	66.0	97.7	74.9	64.4	92.2	73.7	22.7	19.9	17.5	8079	649
SMOLENSK	54.750N	32.067E	784	-7.8	-2.2	82.3	67.9	79.1	66.1	76.1	64.6	69.5	78.9	67.7	76.7	66.2	99.3	74.3	64.5	93.4	72.0	16.0	13.8	12.0	8433	149
SOCHI INTL	43.450N	39.957E	89	28.5	31.2	87.4	75.0	84.6	74.1	82.7	73.4	77.9	83.9	76.3	82.5	75.6	134.4	82.2	74.2	128.1	80.9	16.7	14.6	13.1	3511	917
ST PETERSBURG PULKOVO	59.800N	30.263E	79	-9.0	-3.5	82.8	67.3	79.1	65.6	75.7	63.8	69.5	79.4	67.3	76.3	66.0	96.0	74.5	64.1	89.7	72.1	20.2	17.3	15.2	8555	127
STAVROPOL INTL	45.109N	42.113E	1486	-0.2	6.4	92.5	67.3	89.3	66.5	85.8	65.9	70.7	84.8	69.2	82.4	66.2	102.0	76.8	64.5	96.2	75.1	28.0	23.9	20.8	6002	734
SURGUT	61.344N	73.402E	200	-40.3	-35.5	84.0	65.4	80.5	63.8	76.7	62.9	67.9	78.6	66.0	75.9	64.3	90.9	71.9	62.4	84.9	71.1	22.4	19.8	17.5	13306	150
TOMSK	56.500N	84.917E	456	-33.4	-27.7	83.5	67.5	80.5	65.9	77.5	64.4	70.0	79.2	68.2	77.2	66.8	100.4	74.2	64.9	93.7	72.6	17.7	14.1	11.2	11499	176
TRUBCHEVSK	52.583N	33.767E	584	-9.1	-2.8	86.0	68.9	82.4	67.4	79.2	66.1	71.4	81.1	69.5	79.0	68.0	105.1	77.1	66.1	98.4	74.8	19.1	16.1	13.1	7879	243
TULA	54.233N	37.617E	666	-12.3	-6.3	86.1	68.1	82.5	66.4	79.5	65.3	70.1	81.5	68.4	79.2	66.3	99.3	75.4	64.7	93.8	73.5	15.9	13.7	11.9	8491	251
TVER	56.883N	35.867E	449	-13.0	-7.1	85.1	67.1	81.4	66.0	78.0	64.4	69.6	80.4	67.8	77.8	65.9	97.2	73.7	64.3	91.7	72.0	18.8	16.4	14.5	8766	193
TYUMEN	57.117N	65.433E	335	-25.9	-20.8	85.2	67.2	82.0	65.8	78.9	64.7	70.0	81.0	68.3	78.3	66.2	97.7	75.1	64.5	92.0	73.6	14.2	12.4	11.3	10798	213
UFA	54.558N	55.874E	449	-24.2	-18.4	88.3	69.0	85.3	67.6	82.1	66.2	71.4	83.8	69.6	81.7	67.1	101.2	77.5	65.2	94.9	75.5	22.3	19.0	16.5	9806	290
ULAN-UDE	51.808N	107.438E	1690	-34.0	-29.2	88.7	64.7	84.6	63.7	81.1	62.4	68.2	81.9	66.5	79.2	63.8	94.4	73.0	62.1	88.9	71.4	23.0	19.6	16.9	12387	245
VELIKIYE LUKI	56.350N	30.620E	348	-8.5	-2.3	82.4	66.5	79.5	65.7	76.5	64.3	69.5	78.3	67.3	76.0	66.2	97.9	74.0	64.2	91.1	71.3	18.7	16.4	14.3	8265	134
VLADIKAVKAZ	43.033N	44.683E	2306	5.7	11.1	87.6	68.6	84.4	67.8	81.3	66.6	71.7	82.6	70.1	80.3	68.3	113.2	77.5	66.5	106.4	75.8	12.0	9.6	7.7	6066	480
VLADIMIR	56.117N	40.350E	564	-13.8	-8.3	85.0	69.4	81.4	68.0	78.1	66.4	71.9	81.5	69.6	78.9	68.5	106.8	77.9	66.1	98.3	75.1	19.5	17.4	15.5	8968	228
VLADIVOSTOK	43.117N	131.933E	600	-13.4	-8.7	82.8	70.3	80.0	69.0	76.9	67.7	73.7	79.3	71.9	76.3	71.9	120.5	75.8	70.3	114.0	74.0	28.8	24.8	21.7	8953	298
VORONEZH	51.700N	39.217E	489	-10.3	-4.8	90.2	68.1	86.7	67.2	83.1	65.7	70.7	84.3	69.1	81.9	66.4	99.0	75.0	64.9	94.0	73.9	17.6	15.4	13.6	7651	499
YELABUGA	55.767N	52.067E	299	-19.7	-13.8	87.7	68.7	83.8	67.4	80.5	65.5	70.8	83.3	69.0	80.9	66.6	99.2	75.9	64.8	92.9	74.2	28.0	22.2	19.3	9575	317
Saudi Arabia																									*9 sites, 19 more on CD-ROM*	
ABHA	18.240N	42.657E	6858	43.7	46.1	88.2	55.7	87.4	55.7	85.9	56.0	67.8	75.6	66.7	74.6	65.8	123.6	71.8	64.4	117.6	71.3	20.8	18.6	16.7	864	1475
DHAHARAN KING ABDULAZIZ	26.265N	50.152E	84	46.2	48.4	113.4	74.2	111.3	74.2	109.4	74.0	88.4	96.6	86.8	96.0	86.4	193.6	93.6	84.5	181.6	92.9	24.6	22.0	19.8	312	6187
GASSIM PRINCE ABDULAZIZ	26.300N	43.767E	2126	37.8	41.3	113.1	69.3	111.3	67.8	109.7	66.9	72.3	104.9	71.1	104.4	65.9	103.4	75.5	62.8	92.5	74.3	20.0	17.6	15.3	742	5388
JEDDAH KING ABDULAZIZ INTL	21.680N	39.157E	48	60.4	62.3	105.7	74.7	103.8	75.6	101.9	76.2	85.8	95.1	84.4	93.8	83.9	177.9	92.4	82.3	168.6	90.9	21.7	19.4	17.5	1	6863
KHAMIS MUSHAIT KING KHALED AB	18.297N	42.804E	6778	45.1	47.8	89.5	59.7	88.1	59.4	87.4	59.2	67.2	76.7	66.1	75.3	64.5	117.6	72.0	62.9	111.0	71.3	21.5	19.2	17.0	563	1876
MAKKAH	21.433N	39.767E	787	61.3	64.0	113.3	75.9	111.4	75.6	109.6	75.5	83.9	101.1	82.5	99.9	80.2	161.2	95.5	78.4	151.8	94.7	13.2	11.3	9.6	1	8694
MEDIAN PRINCE ABDULAZIZ INTL	24.553N	39.705E	2151	48.5	51.6	113.3	66.5	111.5	65.8	109.8	65.2	72.2	98.9	70.2	99.8	64.0	96.7	83.0	60.9	86.6	79.5	20.7	18.2	16.1	137	6846
RIYADH KING SALMAN AB	24.710N	46.725E	2082	42.7	46.0	112.5	66.8	111.1	66.1	109.5	65.4	70.3	99.5	68.8	99.9	64.2	97.1	73.3	61.2	87.2	71.4	20.7	18.3	16.2	497	6058
TABUK	28.365N	36.619E	2551	35.4	37.6	106.0	66.0	103.8	65.1	101.9	64.5	69.7	97.5	68.1	95.6	59.4	83.2	81.2	57.5	77.4	80.9	22.9	19.1	15.8	1182	3839
Senegal																									*1 site, 7 more on CD-ROM*	
LEOPOLD SEDAR SENGHOR INTL	14.740N	17.490W	85	62.3	62.9	90.0	73.7	88.2	77.0	87.6	77.6	82.4	85.6	81.3	84.9	81.0	161.8	84.0	80.6	159.5	83.7	21.4	19.4	17.8	0	4356
Sei																									*2 sites, 26 more on CD-ROM*	
BEOGRAD	44.800N	20.467E	433	16.1	19.9	93.7	70.4	90.7	69.7	87.7	68.5	72.8	87.9	71.3	86.2	68.1	104.8	80.1	66.4	98.8	77.1	16.5	14.0	11.8	4404	998
BEOGRAD SURCIN	44.818N	20.309E	335	13.7	17.7	94.0	70.2	91.0	70.3	87.7	68.9	73.4	87.6	71.9	85.5	69.3	109.1	79.6	67.7	103.1	77.8	22.3	19.0	16.4	4739	820
Singapore																									*1 site, 2 more on CD-ROM*	
SINGAPORE CHANGI INTL	1.350N	103.994E	22	73.6	74.8	91.8	79.5	91.3	79.5	90.0	79.3	81.9	87.2	81.5	86.8	80.8	159.8	85.0	80.3	157.2	84.5	15.6	13.8	12.1	0	6489
Slovakia																									*1 site, 17 more on CD-ROM*	
BRATISLAVA-STEFANIK	48.170N	17.213E	436	12.5	17.4	90.2	69.1	87.2	67.9	84.0	66.5	70.9	85.4	69.4	83.3	66.3	98.3	76.3	64.6	92.6	74.9	23.3	20.3	17.8	5386	534
South Africa																									*8 sites, 55 more on CD-ROM*	
BLOEMFONTEIN INTL	29.093S	26.302E	4458	23.1	25.4	92.8	59.9	90.3	59.7	88.1	59.7	67.4	79.2	66.4	78.5	64.4	107.0	70.8	62.8	101.1	69.9	20.1	17.5	15.4	2506	906
CAPE TOWN INTL	33.965S	18.602E	151	39.1	41.3	88.9	67.4	85.6	66.5	82.4	65.6	70.3	81.9	69.1	80.0	66.6	98.5	73.3	65.8	95.6	72.6	30.1	27.3	24.7	1574	742
DE AAR	30.667S	24.017E	4222	30.7	33.1	94.5	60.9	92.5	60.6	90.5	60.3	68.1	80.2	66.7	78.9	65.0	108.5	70.9	63.7	103.4	70.3	27.6	24.1	21.2	2048	1372
DURBAN INTL	29.970S	30.951E	33	48.4	50.5	86.8	75.0	84.9	74.4	83.6	73.9	77.7	83.5	76.6	82.2	75.6	134.0	80.9	75.0	131.6	80.5	24.7	22.1	19.9	254	1984
EAST LONDON	33.036S	27.826E	435	46.3	48.1	87.2	68.1	83.9	68.9	81.0	69.2	74.8	81.6	73.6	79.4	72.9	124.1	78.4	71.7	118.9	76.9	27.3	24.0	21.4	747	1042
JOHANNESBURG INTL	26.139S	28.246E	5558	32.2	35.5	84.2	58.8	82.3	59.1	80.4	59.5	66.9	74.9	65.6	73.8	64.5	111.9	70.2	62.9	105.9	68.7	21.0	18.8	16.8	1969	483
PORT ELIZABETH INTL	33.985S	25.617E	226	41.4	44.2	84.6	66.1	81.3	67.2	79.0	67.6	72.8	78.4	71.7	77.0	71.3	116.5	75.6	69.9	110.9	74.6	32.5	28.8	25.6	1194	722
PRETORIA	25.733S	28.183E	4337	37.2	39.2	90.2	63.2	88.0	63.0	86.2	63.1	69.8	80.7	68.8	79.5	66.9	116.4	72.8	65.9	112.4	72.5	11.9	10.0	8.9	1060	1556
Spain																									*14 sites, 25 more on CD-ROM*	
A CORUNA	43.367N	8.417W	220	40.1	42.3	78.4	66.4	75.4	65.3	73.1	64.4	68.0	75.3	66.8	72.8	65.5	95.0	70.6	64.5	91.6	69.5	22.7	19.9	17.6	2515	219

(Go to CD-ROM to access additional station tables.)

(Go to CD-ROM to access additional station tables.)

Meaning of acronyms:
DB: Dry bulb temperature, °F *WB: Wet bulb temperature, °F*
MCWB: Mean coincident wet bulb temperature, °F
Lat: Latitude, °
DP: Dew point temperature, °F
MCDB: Mean coincident dry bulb temperature, °F
Long: Longitude, °
HR: Humidity ratio, grains of moisture per lb of dry air
HDD and CDD 65: Annual heating and cooling degree-days, base 65°F, °F-day
Elev: Elevation, ft
WS: Wind speed, mph

Station	Lat	Long	Elev	Heating DB		Cooling DB/MCWB						Evaporation WB/MCDB				Dehumidification DP/HR/MCDB						Extreme Annual WS			Heat./Cool. Degree-Days	
						0.4%		1%		2%		0.4%		1%		0.4%			1%							
				99.6%	99%	DB	MCWB	DB	MCWB	DB	MCWB	WB	MCDB	WB	MCDB	DP	HR	MCDB	DP	HR	MCDB	1%	2.5%	5%	HDD	CDD 65
ALICANTE	38.282N	0.558W	142	37.9	40.5	90.8	70.2	88.2	70.8	86.4	71.3	77.6	83.4	76.2	82.7	75.6	134.7	80.9	74.1	128.0	80.3	23.0	20.1	17.5	1616	1593
BARCELONA EL PRAT	41.297N	2.078E	12	34.9	37.1	87.4	74.5	85.2	74.1	83.7	73.5	77.9	84.2	76.4	82.8	75.6	133.9	82.3	74.1	127.3	81.2	22.2	19.1	16.9	2344	1163
BILBAO	43.301N	2.911W	138	31.7	33.9	89.9	69.4	85.6	68.4	82.0	67.3	72.9	83.5	71.1	80.2	70.0	110.8	75.9	68.2	104.2	74.2	22.1	18.6	16.0	2740	642
GRAN CANARIA	27.932N	15.387W	78	56.8	57.7	86.3	67.7	83.4	68.2	81.2	69.1	74.8	79.4	73.6	78.5	73.3	124.1	78.1	71.8	117.7	77.0	33.1	31.2	29.4	113	1965
MADRID BARAJAS	40.494N	3.567W	2000	25.0	27.6	97.6	65.6	95.3	64.8	93.0	64.2	70.0	92.5	67.9	88.5	61.9	89.0	78.3	60.2	83.9	76.5	21.5	18.7	16.4	3547	1182
MALAGA	36.675N	4.499W	52	39.3	41.9	95.2	68.2	91.4	68.3	87.9	67.8	75.2	82.9	74.1	81.7	72.9	122.3	79.6	71.6	117.0	79.2	22.8	20.3	18.0	1457	1596
MURCIA	38.000N	1.167W	203	36.5	39.1	96.9	71.3	94.4	71.0	92.2	70.8	76.5	88.2	75.2	86.4	73.6	125.9	80.4	72.2	119.9	79.8	17.7	15.3	13.3	1592	2016
PALMA DE MALLORCA	39.550N	2.733E	26	32.4	35.2	91.7	72.6	89.3	72.6	87.0	72.6	78.2	84.9	76.7	83.8	75.8	135.1	82.0	74.8	130.3	81.5	22.8	19.8	17.4	2274	1280
SEVILLA	37.418N	5.893W	111	35.6	38.2	102.6	72.1	100.3	71.2	97.1	69.9	76.2	96.0	74.3	92.6	71.5	116.9	80.4	69.7	109.8	79.0	19.7	17.2	15.2	1527	2218
TORREJON AB	40.497N	3.446W	2026	23.3	26.4	97.1	67.4	95.0	66.2	92.8	65.0	71.2	93.8	69.1	90.1	62.7	91.8	82.6	60.9	86.1	79.4	21.8	18.8	16.4	3779	1070
VALENCIA	39.489N	0.482W	225	33.5	35.8	91.8	69.5	89.4	70.5	87.4	70.9	76.6	84.3	75.4	83.3	73.9	127.4	81.2	73.1	123.8	80.8	23.8	20.5	17.5	1958	1502
VALLADOLID	41.633N	4.750W	2411	25.1	27.3	93.8	64.7	90.9	64.1	87.6	63.3	67.2	87.4	65.7	85.5	60.8	87.1	71.7	59.3	82.4	70.1	17.6	14.7	12.5	4311	652
ZARAGOZA AB	41.666N	1.042W	863	28.1	30.4	97.2	70.2	94.4	69.2	91.2	68.3	72.8	90.9	71.1	88.0	67.8	105.4	78.3	66.0	98.9	77.2	29.6	26.6	23.9	3066	1277
Sri Lanka																										*1 site, 0 more on CD-ROM*
BANDARANAIKE INTL	7.181N	79.866E	29	69.8	71.6	91.6	76.3	90.1	77.3	89.6	77.6	81.7	87.5	81.0	87.0	80.1	156.5	86.1	79.1	151.4	85.2	18.9	17.4	15.8	0	6129
Sweden																										*4 sites, 211 more on CD-ROM*
GOTEBORG	57.717N	12.000E	7	10.4	14.9	80.3	64.5	77.4	63.8	74.3	62.3	67.5	75.8	65.8	73.5	64.6	91.2	71.4	62.9	85.7	69.3	18.4	15.8	13.8	6514	114
MALMO	55.567N	13.067E	69	14.6	18.9	79.7	66.0	76.9	65.1	73.7	63.6	68.5	75.7	66.7	73.2	65.9	95.6	71.5	64.3	90.3	69.9	20.0	17.5	15.5	6310	85
STOCKHOLMN BROMMA	59.354N	17.942E	47	5.0	10.5	80.6	64.2	77.3	62.7	74.6	61.6	67.2	75.4	65.4	73.0	64.4	90.7	69.9	62.6	84.9	68.6	19.3	17.0	15.3	7469	99
UPPSALA	59.897N	17.589E	68	-1.9	4.3	80.1	65.2	76.8	63.4	73.7	62.0	67.2	76.1	65.3	73.5	64.1	89.8	70.2	62.2	83.8	68.4	21.7	19.1	16.9	8059	55
Switzerland																										*3 sites, 62 more on CD-ROM*
BERN-ZOLLIKOFEN	46.983N	7.467E	1860	14.3	18.2	85.4	67.0	82.2	66.2	79.0	64.8	68.4	81.5	67.2	79.3	63.9	95.4	73.3	62.8	91.5	72.1	16.5	13.0	10.9	6028	230
LAEGEREN	47.483N	8.400E	2766	12.7	16.5	79.4	63.3	76.1	62.1	73.4	61.2	65.2	75.2	63.8	73.2	61.5	90.6	69.1	60.3	86.5	67.6	25.4	22.0	19.4	7001	127
ZUERICH-FLUNTERN	47.383N	8.567E	1829	17.0	20.6	84.4	66.8	81.2	65.5	78.1	64.2	68.2	80.6	66.9	78.1	64.2	96.1	72.4	62.9	92.0	70.8	19.1	15.5	12.3	5756	269
Syrian Arab Republic																										*5 sites, 7 more on CD-ROM*
ALEPPO INTL	36.181N	37.224E	1276	28.3	30.6	102.8	67.9	100.2	67.5	97.4	67.4	73.3	90.9	72.0	89.5	68.1	108.1	81.5	66.5	102.3	80.4	23.5	21.2	18.9	2693	2511
DAMASCUS INTL	33.412N	36.516E	2020	25.9	28.7	103.5	65.7	100.5	64.9	98.5	64.6	70.4	87.3	69.1	86.2	66.4	104.9	74.0	64.7	98.8	73.1	27.8	24.2	21.6	2588	2105
DARAA	32.600N	36.100E	1781	33.5	36.1	97.2	66.8	94.6	67.0	92.1	67.2	73.1	87.9	71.8	85.8	69.2	114.5	77.2	68.0	109.9	76.7	20.1	16.9	14.4	2051	1957
HAMA	35.117N	36.750E	994	29.8	32.6	102.7	69.6	99.9	69.1	97.5	68.3	73.5	93.4	72.1	92.3	67.4	104.3	83.4	65.6	98.1	81.7	16.2	13.0	10.5	2306	2547
LATAKIA	35.533N	35.767E	23	39.2	41.7	91.1	72.6	89.2	74.8	87.7	75.6	79.7	86.8	78.8	85.8	77.4	142.6	85.3	76.5	138.1	84.6	22.1	18.2	15.0	1282	2164
Taiwan																										*19 sites, 19 more on CD-ROM*
GANGSHAN	22.783N	120.262E	34	49.9	52.2	91.8	80.9	91.2	80.8	89.9	80.4	82.7	88.6	82.2	88.1	81.0	161.1	86.3	80.6	159.2	86.1	19.4	16.4	14.3	143	4071
HENGCHUN	22.000N	120.750E	79	60.8	62.4	90.8	80.3	89.9	80.1	89.0	79.8	82.2	87.8	81.6	87.3	80.8	160.3	85.5	80.0	156.4	85.2	24.8	21.6	19.0	10	4742
HSINCHU	24.818N	120.939E	26	48.4	50.3	91.7	82.3	90.7	81.9	89.7	81.4	84.0	89.6	82.9	88.8	82.5	169.3	88.7	81.0	161.3	87.7	30.2	26.8	24.2	496	3323
HSINCHU CITY	24.833N	121.000E	89	48.4	50.6	91.7	80.0	90.6	79.8	89.4	79.5	81.7	89.0	80.9	88.3	79.7	154.6	86.3	78.8	150.2	85.7	23.1	20.7	18.3	480	3262
KAOHSIUNG	22.633N	120.283E	95	55.2	57.3	90.9	80.9	90.0	80.7	89.1	80.5	82.6	88.8	81.9	88.1	80.9	160.9	86.8	80.1	156.8	86.3	14.4	12.3	11.1	55	4575
KAOHSIUNG INTL	22.577N	120.350E	26	53.8	56.5	91.8	80.0	91.4	80.0	90.0	79.5	82.3	87.9	81.6	87.5	80.8	160.1	86.0	80.3	157.4	85.7	18.8	16.0	13.9	57	4698
KEELUNG	25.150N	121.800E	10	50.9	52.7	93.0	78.6	91.3	78.4	89.9	78.4	80.9	87.7	80.2	87.2	79.2	151.8	84.5	78.4	147.3	84.3	19.8	17.0	15.1	426	3316
KINMEN	24.428N	118.359E	93	44.8	46.6	91.3	83.2	89.8	82.7	88.9	82.3	85.0	89.2	84.0	88.5	84.1	179.5	88.3	82.7	170.8	87.2	20.9	18.6	16.6	894	2865
MATSU NANGAN	26.160N	119.958E	223	40.1	42.1	88.9	81.9	87.6	81.6	86.1	80.8	82.8	87.0	81.9	85.9	81.7	166.3	86.5	80.7	160.8	85.6	34.0	30.3	26.9	1795	2155
PINGTUNG NORTH	22.700N	120.482E	97	52.0	54.8	93.9	81.1	93.2	80.9	91.8	80.4	82.8	91.0	82.0	90.1	80.8	160.3	87.1	80.0	156.1	86.5	16.5	13.7	11.6	72	4520
PINGTUNG SOUTH	22.672N	120.462E	78	53.3	55.3	94.9	81.2	93.5	80.8	92.7	80.5	83.0	91.4	82.2	90.5	80.8	160.7	87.6	80.2	157.3	86.9	16.5	13.9	11.8	57	4721
TAICHUNG	24.186N	120.654E	377	46.3	48.6	93.6	82.1	92.9	82.0	91.6	81.5	84.1	91.8	83.2	90.9	82.2	170.1	90.3	80.9	162.6	89.1	20.7	17.9	16.0	326	3744
TAICHUNG AP	24.265N	120.621E	663	46.3	48.2	89.9	80.9	89.2	80.7	88.0	80.4	82.9	87.6	81.9	87.0	81.7	169.3	87.1	80.5	162.4	86.4	27.6	23.5	21.0	562	2974
TAINAN	22.950N	120.206E	63	50.4	53.3	92.3	81.9	91.5	81.7	90.1	81.1	83.6	89.9	82.8	89.1	82.0	167.0	88.5	80.9	160.9	87.5	21.0	18.4	16.4	131	4275
TAIPEI	25.033N	121.517E	30	49.7	51.7	94.9	80.4	93.4	80.0	92.1	79.6	81.9	91.8	81.1	90.7	79.2	151.7	87.4	78.4	147.8	86.8	16.8	15.0	13.6	394	3758
TAIPEI SONGSHAN	25.069N	121.552E	18	49.6	51.6	95.2	79.7	93.5	79.6	92.8	79.6	82.4	90.7	81.6	89.4	80.5	158.5	86.6	79.2	151.6	85.6	20.0	17.7	16.0	393	3805
TAIWAN TAOYUAN INTL	25.078N	121.233E	107	48.4	50.4	94.6	80.1	93.0	80.4	91.4	80.0	83.3	89.7	82.3	88.7	81.1	162.0	86.8	80.7	159.9	86.4	29.0	26.6	24.6	475	3493
TAOYUAN	25.056N	121.243E	151	47.7	49.6	93.2	82.8	91.7	82.2	90.9	81.8	84.5	91.0	83.4	90.2	82.7	171.4	90.0	81.2	163.1	88.8	27.1	24.0	21.8	594	3252
WU-CHI OBSERVATORY	24.250N	120.517E	16	50.6	52.5	91.1	81.2	90.2	80.9	89.3	80.6	82.5	89.4	81.8	88.8	80.4	158.1	88.1	79.8	154.5	87.6	31.6	28.5	25.8	347	3574
Tajikistan																										*1 site, 7 more on CD-ROM*
DUSHANBE	38.543N	68.825E	2575	14.4	21.0	100.2	66.0	98.2	65.6	95.6	65.1	72.6	92.4	70.4	90.2	66.0	105.6	84.6	63.5	96.6	81.9	14.6	12.0	10.0	3498	1668

Meaning of acronyms:
DB: Dry bulb temperature, °F — *WB: Wet bulb temperature, °F* — *MCWB: Mean coincident wet bulb temperature, °F*
Lat: Latitude, ° — *DP: Dew point temperature, °F* — *MCDB: Mean coincident dry bulb temperature, °F*
Long: Longitude, ° — *HR: Humidity ratio, grains of moisture per lb of dry air*
Elev: Elevation, ft — *WS: Wind speed, mph* — *HDD and CDD 65: Annual heating and cooling degree-days, base 65°F, °F-day*

Station	Lat	Long	Elev	Heating DB		Cooling DB/MCWB						Evaporation WB/MCDB				Dehumidification DP/HR/MCDB						Extreme Annual WS			Heat./Cool. Degree-Days	
						0.4%		1%		2%		0.4%		1%		0.4%			1%							
				99.6%	99%	DB	MCWB	DB	MCWB	DB	MCWB	WB	MCDB	WB	MCDB	DP	HR	MCDB	DP	HR	MCDB	1%	2.5%	5%	HDD	CDD 65
Tanzania, United Republic of																										*1 site, 3 more on CD-ROM*
DAR ES SALAAM INTL	6.878S	39.203E	182	64.6	65.9	91.7	78.2	91.1	78.0	89.9	77.6	80.3	87.2	79.8	86.6	78.9	151.0	83.1	78.2	147.4	82.5	20.6	18.8	17.5	0	5319
Thailand																										*2 sites, 72 more on CD-ROM*
BANGKOK INTL	13.913N	100.607E	9	67.2	69.7	99.0	79.4	97.6	79.5	96.5	79.4	85.3	92.9	84.3	91.8	83.6	175.9	89.7	82.5	169.6	88.5	17.3	15.0	13.3	0	7194
PHUKET	7.883N	98.400E	13	74.8	75.5	94.0	78.6	92.9	78.5	92.0	78.4	81.5	89.3	80.9	88.7	79.5	153.1	84.9	78.9	150.2	84.5	10.1	9.5	8.5	0	6853
Togo																										*1 site, 1 more on CD-ROM*
LOME-TOKOIN	6.166N	1.255E	72	70.9	72.0	91.8	79.0	91.3	79.5	90.0	79.5	82.8	87.5	82.3	87.0	82.0	167.2	85.1	80.9	161.2	84.7	18.6	16.8	15.6	0	6157
Tunisia																										*1 site, 14 more on CD-ROM*
TUNIS-CARTHAGE INTL	36.851N	10.227E	22	41.3	43.3	100.1	72.5	96.4	72.5	93.2	72.1	78.3	88.5	77.0	87.1	75.5	133.7	82.7	73.9	126.6	81.9	25.3	22.5	19.9	1351	2275
Turkey																										*18 sites, 47 more on CD-ROM*
ADANA INCIRLIK	37.000N	35.417E	217	33.2	35.5	97.6	71.9	95.1	72.6	93.2	73.1	79.7	89.1	78.6	87.7	77.3	143.0	83.6	76.1	137.4	83.0	19.5	17.0	14.9	1859	2423
ADANA SAKIRPASA	36.982N	35.280E	65	34.0	37.3	98.2	72.0	95.2	73.3	93.4	74.0	79.7	89.7	78.8	88.4	77.2	141.7	83.8	75.6	134.5	82.7	17.6	15.2	13.5	1654	2665
ANKARA ETIMESGUT	39.950N	32.689E	2653	12.3	16.5	94.8	64.0	91.5	63.8	88.2	62.8	68.3	86.4	66.5	84.0	62.2	92.3	76.4	60.2	86.0	74.6	18.9	16.2	13.8	5042	800
ANTALYA	36.899N	30.800E	177	35.5	37.6	100.9	68.2	98.3	68.2	95.0	68.6	79.5	87.3	78.5	86.4	77.2	142.4	85.2	75.6	135.0	84.3	23.8	20.4	17.3	1791	2321
BURSA	40.183N	29.067E	328	26.3	28.5	93.9	71.6	91.4	71.2	89.1	70.4	74.8	88.7	73.4	87.1	70.2	112.6	82.8	68.7	106.8	81.3	16.3	13.8	11.9	3445	1201
DIYARBAKIR	37.894N	40.201E	2251	15.4	21.1	104.4	66.6	102.5	66.3	100.4	66.2	73.3	97.1	71.1	95.7	64.6	99.2	89.8	62.0	90.5	86.4	20.3	17.6	15.2	3851	2186
ERZURUM	39.957N	41.170E	5763	-20.4	-15.1	86.8	58.8	84.1	58.5	81.0	58.1	63.0	79.6	61.3	78.1	56.8	85.4	72.1	55.0	79.8	69.5	22.7	20.4	18.2	8893	146
ESENBOGA	40.128N	32.995E	3125	5.1	11.9	92.9	62.9	89.6	62.5	86.4	61.8	66.5	84.8	64.8	83.3	59.4	85.1	73.8	57.6	79.6	72.6	19.7	17.0	14.9	5705	525
ESKISEHIR	39.784N	30.582E	2581	12.7	17.3	91.8	66.5	89.3	65.9	86.2	64.8	70.8	86.2	69.1	83.4	66.0	105.5	78.2	64.1	98.7	77.1	19.6	17.4	15.5	5125	632
GAZIANTEP OGUZELI	36.947N	37.479E	2315	23.3	26.5	102.3	69.9	100.1	69.1	97.4	68.3	74.2	97.2	72.5	95.6	66.3	105.7	90.6	64.2	98.0	88.7	18.8	16.5	14.3	3443	2122
ISTANBUL ATATURK	40.977N	28.821E	163	28.7	31.7	89.4	70.5	87.1	70.1	84.6	69.5	76.1	82.1	74.5	81.2	73.9	127.1	79.5	72.0	119.0	78.5	25.0	22.3	20.2	3260	1285
IZMIR ADNAN MENDERES	38.292N	27.157E	412	27.4	30.1	98.8	69.2	96.5	68.7	94.2	68.2	72.7	91.2	71.2	89.6	66.7	99.8	79.4	64.8	93.4	78.8	26.1	23.8	22.1	2777	1857
IZMIR CIGLI	38.513N	27.010E	16	28.8	31.7	98.3	70.5	95.3	70.1	93.3	69.6	74.4	90.6	72.9	89.4	69.6	108.8	82.5	67.7	101.8	81.6	22.4	20.1	18.1	2433	1871
KAYSERI	38.770N	35.495E	3463	3.2	9.7	93.9	63.1	91.1	62.5	87.8	61.5	66.4	85.5	64.7	84.2	59.9	87.6	73.1	57.6	80.6	71.9	20.3	16.5	13.2	5530	537
KONYA	37.979N	32.562E	3381	10.5	15.5	93.5	61.8	91.1	61.6	88.0	60.8	65.3	85.4	63.4	84.3	58.4	82.6	72.5	55.7	74.9	70.1	24.5	21.0	18.7	5047	899
MALATYA ERHAC	38.435N	38.091E	2828	11.5	16.2	100.4	66.8	98.3	65.5	95.3	65.0	72.2	94.3	69.6	91.5	64.1	99.6	90.5	60.8	88.5	85.1	22.3	19.3	16.5	4675	1488
SAMSUN	41.283N	36.300E	13	30.4	32.5	83.5	72.1	81.9	71.7	80.5	71.3	75.0	80.9	73.8	79.9	73.0	122.4	79.5	71.7	117.1	78.8	16.7	13.8	11.7	3398	800
VAN	38.468N	43.332E	5480	8.3	11.7	84.1	65.4	82.1	65.4	80.4	65.2	71.3	80.1	69.1	79.0	68.2	127.5	78.8	65.6	116.3	77.8	19.3	16.1	13.0	6268	398
Turkmenistan																										*1 site, 20 more on CD-ROM*
ASHGABAT	37.987N	58.361E	692	17.9	23.2	104.4	67.0	102.3	66.8	100.2	66.7	73.5	94.4	71.9	92.6	66.2	99.1	85.5	64.4	92.8	84.7	20.7	18.1	15.8	3339	2717
Ukraine																										*15 sites, 33 more on CD-ROM*
CHERNIHIV	51.467N	31.250E	463	-2.9	2.2	87.3	68.3	84.0	67.2	80.8	65.8	70.8	83.0	69.1	80.4	66.7	100.1	76.0	65.2	94.8	74.0	18.9	16.8	15.2	7242	355
DNEPROPETROVSK	48.600N	34.967E	469	0.2	5.2	92.4	69.8	88.8	68.6	85.6	67.4	72.3	86.0	70.8	84.2	68.1	104.9	78.2	66.5	99.1	76.2	24.3	21.4	19.2	6528	698
DONETSK	48.067N	37.767E	738	-1.9	3.4	91.7	66.9	88.1	66.4	84.6	65.5	70.5	83.5	68.9	81.5	66.3	99.7	74.9	64.7	94.1	73.3	25.7	22.4	19.5	6811	601
KHARKIV INTL	49.925N	36.290E	508	-2.8	2.1	91.0	67.4	87.1	66.3	83.9	65.4	70.1	83.1	68.7	81.1	66.1	98.0	74.6	64.6	92.8	74.0	21.1	18.7	16.9	7017	550
KHERSON	46.633N	32.567E	177	4.0	9.3	93.7	70.1	90.2	68.9	87.0	67.7	72.5	86.6	71.0	84.4	68.6	105.6	76.5	66.9	99.6	75.5	20.3	17.2	14.5	5798	793
KIEV ZHULIANY INTL	50.402N	30.451E	586	1.3	6.5	87.7	68.6	84.4	67.6	81.3	66.0	71.0	82.3	69.5	80.4	67.6	103.5	76.0	66.0	97.8	74.2	18.9	16.4	14.3	6762	430
KRYVYI RIH	48.033N	33.217E	407	0.0	5.1	91.7	69.0	88.2	67.6	85.2	66.6	71.5	84.8	69.9	83.0	67.3	102.0	76.7	65.6	96.1	75.0	24.5	21.6	18.6	6483	613
LUHANSK	48.567N	39.250E	203	-5.1	1.1	94.5	69.0	90.7	68.2	87.1	67.1	71.8	86.7	70.3	85.2	67.3	101.0	77.0	65.7	95.4	75.6	16.2	14.0	12.1	6628	666
LVIV INTL	49.813N	23.956E	1071	1.3	7.0	84.5	68.1	81.5	66.6	78.7	65.1	70.1	81.1	68.1	78.1	66.3	100.8	75.1	64.5	94.7	73.0	20.8	17.9	15.8	6870	213
MARIUPOL'	47.033N	37.500E	230	3.5	8.5	89.7	70.4	86.6	70.0	84.0	69.2	74.6	83.7	72.9	82.0	71.8	118.5	79.5	69.9	110.8	78.4	28.9	25.2	21.9	6230	747
ODESA INTL	46.427N	30.676E	172	8.3	13.6	90.1	69.1	87.4	68.4	84.2	67.6	73.4	82.1	71.8	80.7	70.8	114.3	77.5	68.9	106.7	76.2	23.4	20.3	18.1	5604	743
POLTAVA	49.600N	34.550E	525	-1.7	3.5	89.3	68.3	85.9	67.1	82.8	66.0	71.0	83.4	69.5	81.6	66.9	100.8	76.7	65.3	95.5	75.0	20.4	17.3	14.7	6924	510
SIMFEROPOL INTL	45.052N	33.975E	639	9.7	14.3	92.2	68.5	89.2	67.8	85.8	66.8	72.1	83.1	70.4	81.9	69.0	109.1	76.3	66.8	101.0	74.2	28.4	24.7	21.6	5313	718
VINNYTSIA	49.233N	28.600E	978	-1.8	4.4	85.5	67.3	82.3	66.0	79.6	65.0	69.8	81.4	68.2	78.9	65.9	98.9	74.9	64.4	93.8	72.8	23.0	19.6	17.1	7092	283
ZAPORIZHIA INTL	47.867N	35.316E	373	0.4	5.4	93.3	68.4	89.8	67.6	86.3	66.6	71.8	85.0	70.2	83.5	68.0	104.2	76.5	66.3	98.1	74.7	21.3	18.9	16.9	6343	719
United Arab Emirates																										*5 sites, 3 more on CD-ROM*
ABU DHABI INTL	24.433N	54.651E	88	53.3	55.4	112.9	73.4	110.4	73.9	107.9	74.1	87.0	95.5	85.9	94.6	84.6	182.5	92.2	84.0	178.9	92.0	21.0	18.8	17.0	49	6616
AL AIN INTL	24.262N	55.609E	869	51.7	53.6	114.8	73.0	113.1	73.0	111.4	72.9	84.1	96.7	82.6	96.5	81.8	170.7	90.4	79.2	156.3	90.1	23.0	20.2	18.1	74	7141
BATEEN	24.428N	54.458E	16	56.5	58.6	111.3	74.0	109.0	74.5	106.1	75.1	87.6	94.7	86.6	94.2	86.0	190.7	92.5	84.6	181.6	92.1	20.5	18.1	16.1	24	6695
DUBAI INTL	25.255N	55.364E	34	55.6	57.5	109.5	74.3	107.3	74.8	104.8	75.5	86.6	95.2	85.7	94.5	84.5	181.6	92.1	83.8	177.4	92.1	20.1	17.9	16.2	29	6651
SHARJAH INTL	25.329N	55.517E	111	50.3	53.1	111.6	74.7	109.5	75.1	107.5	75.7	86.1	97.8	85.0	96.7	83.8	177.9	92.3	82.4	169.7	91.6	18.5	16.2	14.3	75	6285
United Kingdom																										*25 sites, 223 more on CD-ROM*
AUGHTON	53.550N	2.917W	184	26.8	29.3	76.0	63.3	72.3	62.1	68.9	60.6	64.9	73.3	63.4	70.2	62.0	83.8	67.0	60.5	79.2	65.7	25.7	22.9	20.4	5748	33
BINGLEY NO2	53.817N	1.867W	876	24.9	27.2	74.6	63.1	71.0	61.2	67.8	59.6	64.6	71.2	62.6	68.8	62.1	86.0	66.8	60.2	80.5	64.7	27.3	23.6	20.8	6439	17
BIRMINGHAM	52.454N	1.748W	327	23.2	26.3	79.2	64.1	75.5	62.6	72.8	61.4	65.9	75.6	64.3	72.7	62.7	86.2	69.0	61.0	81.2	67.2	22.0	19.5	17.6	5584	55
BRISTOL	51.383N	2.719W	622	26.2	28.2	76.9	63.7	73.2	62.3	69.9	61.1	65.6	73.2	63.7	70.2	62.9	87.7	67.3	61.2	82.5	65.3	26.7	23.5	21.2	5508	38
BRISTOL WEATHER CENTRE	51.467N	2.600W	36	28.5	31.1	80.1	65.0	76.6	63.0	73.4	61.9	66.7	75.8	64.8	72.6	63.5	87.8	69.4	61.9	82.8	67.7	22.9	19.7	17.2	4670	106

(Go to CD-ROM to access additional station tables.)

(Go to CD-ROM to access additional station tables.)

Meaning of acronyms:
DB: Dry bulb temperature, °F *WB: Wet bulb temperature, °F*
MCWB: Mean coincident wet bulb temperature, °F
Lat: Latitude, °
DP: Dew point temperature, °F
MCDB: Mean coincident dry bulb temperature, °F
Long: Longitude, °
HR: Humidity ratio, grains of moisture per lb of dry air
Elev: Elevation, ft
WS: Wind speed, mph
HDD and CDD 65: Annual heating and cooling degree-days, base 65°F, °F-day

Station	Lat	Long	Elev	Heating DB		Cooling DB/MCWB						Evaporation WB/MCDB				Dehumidification DP/HR/MCDB						Extreme Annual WS			Heat./Cool. Degree-Days	
						0.4%		1%		2%		0.4%		1%		0.4%			1%							
				99.6%	99%	DB	MCWB	DB	MCWB	DB	MCWB	WB	MCDB	WB	MCDB	DP	HR	MCDB	DP	HR	MCDB	1%	2.5%	5%	HDD	CDD 65
CARDIFF WEATHER CENTRE	51.483N	3.183W	171	30.2	32.2	79.2	64.8	75.7	63.4	72.8	61.9	66.6	76.0	64.8	72.8	63.2	87.3	69.5	61.8	83.1	67.8	26.1	22.9	20.1	4554	103
CHURCH LAWFORD	52.367N	1.333W	348	24.3	26.9	79.6	65.5	75.8	63.4	72.7	61.9	66.9	75.8	64.9	73.1	63.8	89.9	69.3	61.9	83.8	67.6	21.0	18.3	16.1	5583	54
CILFYNYDD	51.633N	3.300W	636	24.5	27.3	78.0	64.3	74.2	62.2	70.8	60.9	65.9	74.9	63.8	71.0	62.8	87.5	68.3	61.2	82.6	65.8	25.7	22.2	19.4	5899	40
CROSBY	53.500N	3.067W	30	25.9	28.9	75.9	64.8	72.0	63.3	69.0	62.0	66.5	73.0	64.7	69.9	64.3	90.4	68.5	62.6	85.1	66.9	38.5	33.4	29.7	5230	34
EDINBURGH	55.950N	3.373W	135	22.6	26.2	71.9	61.9	69.3	60.9	66.6	59.1	63.7	69.7	62.1	67.1	61.1	80.9	66.0	59.7	76.9	64.5	27.8	24.2	21.2	6161	7
EMLEY MOOR	53.617N	1.667W	850	26.1	27.8	74.7	63.5	71.1	61.7	68.3	60.3	64.9	71.7	63.0	69.2	62.2	86.4	67.7	60.4	80.9	65.7	33.1	28.8	24.3	6289	25
GLASGOW	55.872N	4.433W	26	21.3	24.9	73.6	62.7	70.1	61.1	67.7	59.9	64.5	71.1	62.7	68.0	62.2	83.8	67.5	60.5	78.9	66.0	28.4	24.7	21.5	6077	12
GRAVESEND-BROADNESS	51.467N	0.300E	10	27.7	29.8	81.9	67.2	78.3	65.5	75.1	63.8	69.1	78.8	67.0	75.3	65.5	94.4	72.7	63.7	88.4	70.8	26.5	22.6	19.9	4701	134
HAWARDEN	53.178N	2.978W	45	24.2	27.2	77.2	64.8	73.6	63.4	70.7	62.0	66.6	73.9	64.8	71.6	64.0	89.2	69.4	62.0	83.2	67.7	23.1	20.4	18.0	5428	33
KENLEY	51.300N	0.083W	558	26.2	28.4	79.2	64.4	75.8	62.9	72.7	61.6	66.2	75.6	64.5	72.7	62.9	87.5	68.8	61.4	83.1	67.5	23.2	20.6	18.3	5358	76
LECONFIELD	53.867N	0.433W	23	25.3	28.2	76.8	64.8	73.6	63.2	70.9	61.7	66.2	73.7	64.5	71.5	63.4	87.5	69.1	61.8	82.5	67.1	27.0	23.5	20.9	5668	31
LEEDS BRADFORD	53.866N	1.661W	681	25.2	28.1	75.1	64.1	71.5	61.9	68.2	60.3	65.1	71.9	63.1	69.5	62.5	86.8	68.2	60.8	81.5	65.7	28.6	24.7	21.6	6182	22
LEEDS WEATHER CENTRE	53.800N	1.550W	154	27.7	29.8	79.1	64.3	75.4	62.5	72.3	61.1	65.7	75.7	64.0	73.0	62.1	83.9	69.5	60.5	79.2	67.4	28.9	24.5	21.0	5306	74
LIVERPOOL JOHN LENNON	53.334N	2.850W	80	28.0	30.0	77.0	63.9	73.4	62.4	70.2	61.3	65.4	73.9	63.8	71.1	62.5	84.7	68.7	60.8	79.9	67.4	29.1	25.2	22.2	5166	50
LONDON HEATHROW	51.478N	0.461W	83	27.5	29.8	82.9	65.4	79.2	63.9	76.1	62.7	67.3	78.8	65.6	75.5	63.3	87.3	70.6	61.9	83.1	69.3	23.0	20.3	18.0	4641	167
LONDON WC CLERKENWELL	51.522N	0.112W	128	30.9	32.8	82.8	65.0	79.2	63.6	76.0	62.3	67.0	78.1	65.5	75.5	62.9	86.3	71.0	61.5	82.0	69.7	20.7	18.5	16.5	4180	222
MANCHESTER	53.354N	2.275W	257	24.7	28.0	77.9	64.1	74.2	62.5	71.3	61.2	65.5	74.4	64.0	71.8	62.5	85.5	68.7	60.9	80.7	66.8	24.7	21.9	19.5	5550	49
NORTHOLT	51.553N	0.418W	124	25.1	27.7	82.7	65.3	79.0	63.9	75.7	62.5	67.3	78.5	65.5	75.2	63.2	87.3	70.5	61.8	82.9	69.1	22.9	20.4	18.2	4945	127
NOTTINGHAM EAST MIDLANDS	52.831N	1.328W	306	25.2	28.2	79.1	64.4	75.4	62.6	72.0	61.2	66.1	75.9	64.4	72.4	62.8	86.4	69.5	61.0	81.0	67.6	27.6	24.2	21.3	5440	67
VALLEY ANGLESEY	53.248N	4.535W	37	29.1	31.4	73.3	63.1	69.5	61.0	66.4	59.6	64.0	70.4	62.4	66.8	61.8	82.5	65.2	60.7	79.2	63.7	38.7	33.6	30.0	5165	18
Uruguay																										*2 sites, 11 more on CD-ROM*
CARRASCO INTL	34.838S	56.031W	105	34.1	37.1	89.2	71.4	86.0	70.6	82.8	69.9	75.7	83.2	74.0	80.5	73.5	125.3	79.0	71.9	118.3	77.0	27.2	23.0	20.6	2170	853
MONTEVIDEO PRADO	34.850S	56.200W	52	37.4	39.8	88.8	72.5	86.2	71.6	83.9	71.0	75.6	84.3	74.3	82.1	72.9	122.5	79.7	71.8	117.6	78.7	22.8	19.3	17.0	1987	1032
Uzbekistan																										*3 sites, 18 more on CD-ROM*
NAMANGAN	40.983N	71.583E	1555	15.8	20.3	98.3	70.1	96.0	69.4	94.0	68.8	73.6	91.6	72.0	90.9	67.4	106.7	85.5	65.4	99.4	83.9	16.2	12.3	9.6	4023	2009
SAMARKAND	39.701N	66.984E	2224	12.7	18.5	97.2	66.0	95.0	65.5	93.0	64.8	69.3	90.9	67.8	89.4	62.2	90.8	77.4	60.3	84.9	75.9	21.2	18.5	15.8	3991	1541
TASHKENT INTL	41.258N	69.281E	1417	13.8	18.2	101.6	67.4	98.9	66.6	96.8	66.1	72.3	92.9	70.2	91.3	65.1	97.8	84.0	62.9	90.5	80.4	14.0	11.8	10.1	3801	1903
Venezuela																										*2 sites, 6 more on CD-ROM*
JUAN VICENTE GOMEZ INTL	7.841N	72.440W	1312	67.8	69.3	95.4	74.1	94.4	73.9	93.2	73.7	78.6	88.4	77.5	87.6	76.5	144.9	81.4	75.2	138.9	80.6	26.5	23.2	21.2	0	5934
SIMON BOLIVAR INTL	10.603N	66.991W	235	69.4	70.8	93.1	82.5	91.7	81.9	91.1	81.7	85.8	89.8	84.5	88.9	84.6	183.2	88.0	83.8	178.5	87.5	9.5	7.7	7.2	0	6077
Viet Nam																										*4 sites, 25 more on CD-ROM*
DA NANG INTL	16.044N	108.199E	33	62.1	63.4	97.1	78.9	95.3	79.0	93.6	79.1	82.3	90.1	81.6	89.3	80.4	158.2	86.7	79.6	153.6	85.8	16.8	14.2	12.1	6	5259
HAI PHONG PHU LIEN	20.800N	106.633E	381	49.5	51.5	93.1	83.8	91.5	83.5	90.1	82.8	85.8	90.6	84.6	89.5	84.5	183.8	89.6	83.4	177.1	88.2	14.6	11.9	10.0	323	3933
HO CHI MINH TAN SON NHAT INTL	10.819N	106.652E	33	68.0	69.9	96.0	78.4	94.6	78.4	93.3	78.3	82.4	89.1	81.8	88.4	80.8	160.2	85.3	80.3	157.4	85.0	21.4	17.2	14.5	0	6476
NOI BAI INTL	21.221N	105.807E	39	49.9	51.8	96.8	81.3	94.9	81.4	93.2	81.3	84.8	90.9	83.8	90.0	83.8	177.1	88.2	82.5	169.5	87.4	15.6	13.6	11.9	313	4286
Zimbabwe																										*1 site, 1 more on CD-ROM*
HARARE INTL	17.932S	31.093E	4887	43.2	45.3	88.0	61.6	86.1	61.5	84.3	61.4	68.4	77.5	67.7	76.5	66.3	116.6	70.4	65.5	113.1	69.9	19.8	17.3	15.5	629	1372

CHAPTER 15

FENESTRATION

FENESTRATION is an architectural term that refers to the arrangement, proportion, and design of window, skylight, and door systems in a building. Fenestration can serve as a physical and/or visual connection to the outdoors, as well as a means to admit solar radiation for daylighting and heat gain to a space. Fenestration can be fixed or operable, and operable units can allow natural ventilation to a space and egress in low-rise buildings.

Fenestration affects building energy use through four basic mechanisms: thermal heat transfer, solar heat gain, air leakage/ventilation/exchange, and daylighting. Fenestration can be used to positively influence a building's energy performance by (1) using glazing and framing to minimize conductive heat loss, (2) using glazing and shading strategies to control solar heat gain to supplement heating and minimize cooling requirements, (3) specifying low-air-leakage fenestration products, (4) integrating fenestration into natural ventilation strategies that can reduce energy use for cooling and outdoor air requirements, and (5) using daylight to offset lighting requirements.

Today's designers and builders; minimum energy standards and codes; green building standards, codes, and rating programs; and energy efficiency incentive programs are seeking more from fenestration systems and giving credit for high-performing products. Window, skylight, and door manufacturers are responding with new and improved products to meet these demands. With the widespread use of simulation software, designing to improve thermal performance of fenestration products has become much easier. Through participation in rating and certification programs that require the use of this software, fenestration manufacturers can take credit for these improvements through certified ratings.

A designer should consider architectural and code requirements, thermal performance, daylight performance, air leakage, energy and environmental impacts, economic criteria, and human comfort when selecting fenestration. Typically, a wide range of fenestration products is available that meet the specifications for a project. Refining the specifications to improve energy performance and enhance a living or work space can result in lower energy costs, increased productivity, and improved thermal and visual comfort.

The preparation of this chapter is assigned to TC 4.5, Fenestration.

1. FENESTRATION COMPONENTS

Fenestration components include glazing material, either glass or plastic; framing, insulation, mullions, muntin bars, dividers, and opaque door slabs; and indoor and outdoor shading devices such as louvered blinds, drapes, roller shades, lightshelves, metal grills, and awnings. In this chapter, **fenestration** and **fenestration systems** refer to the basic assemblies and components of window, skylight, and door systems that are part of the building envelope.

1.1 GLAZING UNITS

Most fenestration currently manufactured using glass contains a glazing system that is packaged in the form of a **glazing unit**. A glazing unit consists of two or more glazing layers that are held apart by an edge seal. Figure 1 shows the construction of a typical double-glazing unit.

The most common glazing material is glass, although polymer (plastic) is sometimes used, either in the form of intermediate films bonded to glass, or as stand-alone glazing material popular in some skylight products. Both may be clear, tinted, coated, laminated,

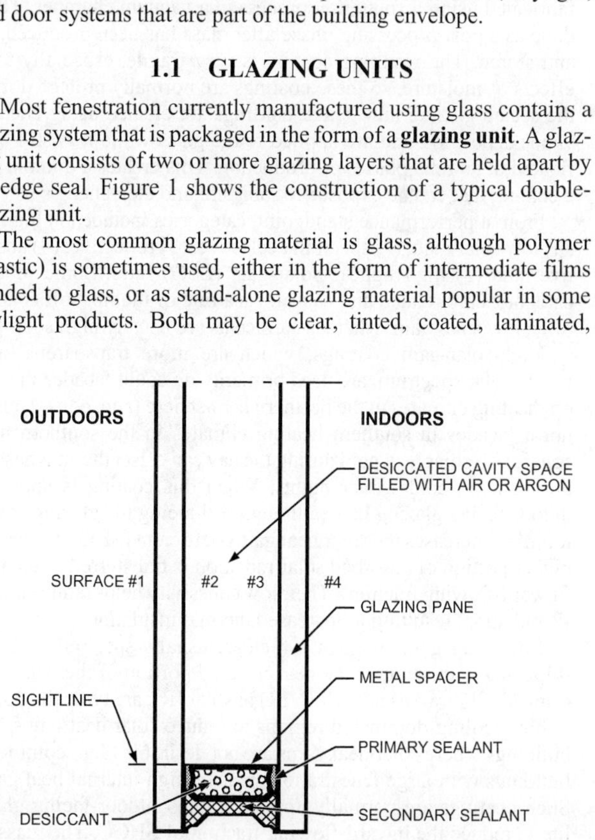

Fig. 1 Construction Details of Typical Double-Glazing Unit

tempered, patterned, or obscured, and polymer types can be easily shaped, textured, and profiled using several processing options. Clear glazing material transmits more than 75% of the incident solar radiation and more than 85% of the visible light. Body-tinted glass containing a pigment is available in many colors, all of which differ in the amount of solar radiation and visible light they transmit and absorb. Some coated glazing materials are highly reflective (e.g., mirrors), whereas others have very low reflectance. Some **spectrally selective glazing** products include coatings that have a visible light transmittance more than double their solar transmittance; these are desirable for good daylighting while minimizing cooling loads. Coatings that reduce radiant heat exchange are called **low-emissivity (low-e) coatings**. Laminated glass is made of two panes of glass adhered together. The interlayer between the two panes of glass is typically plastic and may be clear, tinted, or coated. Tempered glass is designed for safety and shatters into pebble-sized pieces when broken. Patterned glass is a durable ceramic frit applied to a glass surface in a decorative pattern. Obscured glass is translucent and is typically used in privacy applications.

Low-e coated glass is energy efficient, improves daylighting potential, and enhances occupant comfort. Thus, it is now used in the vast majority of fenestration products. Low-e coatings are typically applied to one of the protected internal surfaces of the glazing unit (surface #2 or #3 in Figure 1), but some manufacturers now offer double- or triple-glazed products with an additional low-e coating on the exposed room-side surface (surface #4 in Figure 1, or what would be #6 in triple glazing). Low-e coatings can also be applied to thin plastic films for use either as one of the middle layers in glazing units with three or more layers (stretched and held in place by a spacer system), or surface-applied film, where the exposed low-e coating is protected by a very thin, thermal-IR (TIR) transparent protective layer.

A wide variety of low-e coatings are used today. Physically, they can be divided into either soft- or hard-coat types. **Soft-coat low-e** is fabricated using a sputtering process in a vacuum chamber. This is done as a post-processing phase after glass has been produced, cut, and stored. The resulting coating is very fragile, especially to the effects of moisture, so these coatings are normally protected inside the sealed glazing unit. **Hard coatings** are created using chemical vapor deposition and are applied to the glass while it is still being floated in its final phases of production. This creates a durable low-e coating that can be exposed to moisture and elements.

From a performance standpoint, categories include (1) high versus low solar gain, (2) spectrally selective, (3) reflective, (4) absorptive, and (5) high light-to-solar-gain (LSG) ratio. Some of these categories are related and causal. As a rule of thumb, soft coats are often low solar gain, whereas hard coats are usually high solar gain.

High-solar-gain coatings, which are more transparent to the whole solar spectrum, are used primarily on south facades in northern heating climates in the northern hemisphere (and, conversely, on north facades in southern heating climates in the southern hemisphere), so solar heat gain during the day can offset thermal heat loss during long, cold winter nights. When this coating is applied to indoor-facing glazing lites (although still facing the glazing cavity), it further increases the solar heat gain coefficient (SHGC), because a higher portion of absorbed solar radiation is transferred to the room (inward-flowing fraction). Their low emissivity helps reduce thermal IR radiation, resulting in increased thermal insulation.

Low-solar-gain coatings, which are usually spectrally selective [blocking admission of the near infrared portion of the solar spectrum, also known as near IR (NIR) or solar IR], are typically applied in hot, cooling-dominated regions to reduce solar heat gains, or in buildings where solar heat gains are not desirable (e.g., commercial buildings with large fenestration areas or high internal heat gains). Such coatings are normally applied to the outdoor-facing glazing lite to reduce the inward-flowing fraction of SHGC. The glass surface's low emissivity also reduces thermal IR radiation heat transfer and therefore increases thermal resistance of the fenestration product. Although the majority of low-e coatings are applied to the glazing surface facing the glazing cavity, increasing numbers of durable coatings are being applied to the room-facing glazing surface. This further improves thermal performance (U-factor) by substantially reducing thermal IR radiation heat transfer on the room side of the window. However, in building spaces with higher indoor humidity levels in cold climates, this approach may significantly increase the risk of moisture condensation on glass surfaces. A new class of low-e surface-applied films may be applied as a retrofit measure to the indoor-facing glass surface; these films can perform similarly to low-e coated glass, so their use is more likely to be as an easy retrofit measure, removing the need to replace glass or sash.

In addition to low-e, **fill gases** such as argon, krypton, and xenon are used in lieu of air in the gap between glass panes. These fill gases reduce convective heat transfer across the glazing cavity. Krypton and xenon also reduce gap width, because their optimal gap widths are nearly half that of air.

The main requirements of the edge seal are to exclude moisture, provide a desiccant for the sealed space, and retain the glazing unit's structural integrity. Further, the edge seal isolates the cavity between the glazing materials, thereby reducing the number of surfaces to be cleaned, and creating an enclosure suitable for nondurable low-e coatings and/or fill gases. The edge seal is composed of a spacer, single- or multilevel sealant, and desiccant.

The **spacer** separates glazing layers and provides a surface for primary and secondary sealant adhesion. Several types of spacers are used, each of which provides different heat transfer properties, depending on spacer material and geometry.

Heat transfer at the edge of the glazing unit is greater than at its center because of (1) heat flow through the spacer system and (2) convective flow, which creates an area of higher convective heat transfer as the gas turns from one glazing to the other. To minimize this heat flow, warm-edge spacers have been developed that reduce edge heat transfer by using materials (e.g., stainless steel, galvanized steel, tin-plated steel, polymers, foamed silicone) of lower thermal conductivity than the typical aluminum alloy from which spacers have often been made. Fusing or bending the corners of the spacer minimizes moisture and hydrocarbon vapor transmission from the gap space.

Several different sealant configurations are used in glazing unit construction. In **dual-seal construction**, a primary seal minimizes moisture transmission and gas escape. A secondary seal provides structural integrity between the lites of the glazing unit, and ensures long-term adhesion and greater resistance to solvents, oils, and short-term water immersion. In typical dual-seal construction, the primary seal is made of compressed polyisobutylene (PIB), and the secondary seal is made of silicone, polysulfide, or polyurethane. **Single-seal construction** depends on a single sealant to adhere the glazing to the spacer and to minimize moisture transmission and gas escape. Single-seal construction is generally more cost effective than dual-seal systems. **Dual-seal-equivalent (DSE)** materials take advantage of advanced cross-linking polymers that provide low moisture transmission and structural properties equivalent to dual-seal systems.

Desiccants are used to absorb moisture trapped in the glazing unit during assembly or that gradually diffuses through seals after construction. Typical desiccants include molecular sieve, silica gel, or a matrix of both materials.

1.2 FRAMING

The three main categories of fenestration framing materials are wood, metal, and polymers. Wood has good structural integrity and insulating value but low resistance to weather, moisture, warpage, and organic degradation (from mold and insects). Metal is durable and has excellent structural characteristics, but it has very poor

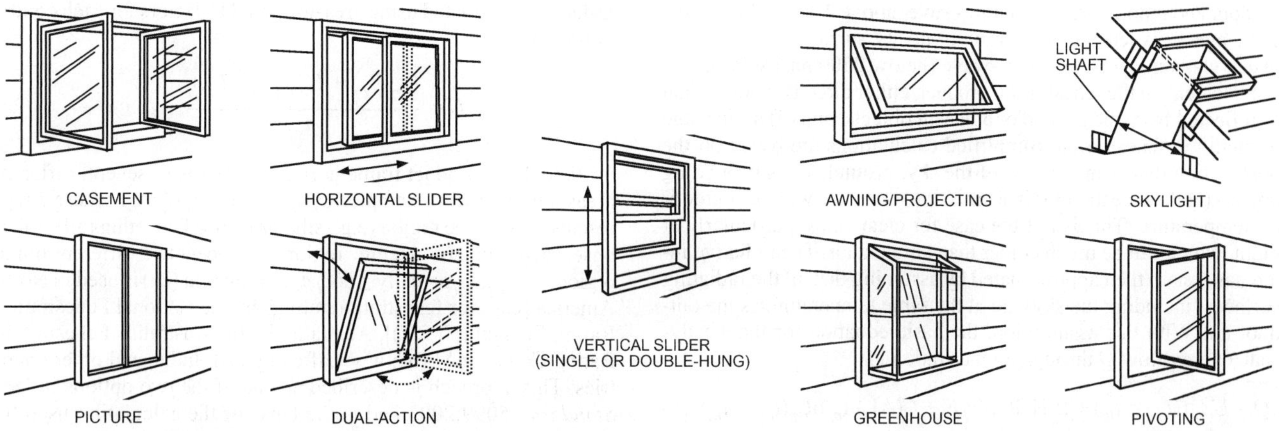

Fig. 2 Various Framing Configurations for Residential Fenestration

thermal performance. The metal of choice in fenestration is almost exclusively aluminum alloy, because of its ease of manufacture, low cost, and low mass, but aluminum alloy has a thermal conductivity roughly 1000 times that of wood or polymers. Steel is sometimes used. Although lower in its thermal conductivity, the overall U-factor of a steel frame is similar to that of an aluminum frame of the same geometry. The poor thermal performance of metal-frame fenestration can be improved with a thermal break (a nonmetal component that separates the metal frame exposed to the outdoors from the surfaces exposed to the indoors). However, to be most effective, there must be thermal breaks in all operable sashes as well as in the frame. Polymer frames are made of extruded vinyl [unplasticized PVC (uPVC)] or pultruded fiberglass (glass-reinforced polyester). Their thermal and structural performance is similar to that of wood. Vinyl frames for large fenestration must be reinforced, which degrades their thermal performance slightly and substantially increases their weight. Polymer frames are generally hollow and thus can also be filled with polyurethane insulation, which reduces convective and radiative heat transfer, thereby achieving a better thermal performance than wood.

Manufacturers sometimes combine these materials as clad units (e.g., vinyl-clad aluminum, aluminum-clad wood, vinyl-clad wood) to increase durability, improve thermal performance, or improve aesthetics. In addition, curtain wall systems for commercial buildings may be structurally glazed, and the outdoor "framing" is simply rubber gaskets or silicone.

Generally, the framing system categorizes residential fenestration, as shown by the examples of traditional basic types in Figure 2. The glazing system can be mounted either directly in the frame (a direct-glazed or direct-set fenestration, which is not operable) or in a sash that moves in the frame (for an operating fenestration). In operable fenestration, a weather-sealing system between the frame and sash reduces air and water leakage.

1.3 SHADING

Shading devices are available in a wide range of products that differ greatly in their appearance and energy performance. They include louvered shades (e.g., venetian blinds, vertical blinds, louvered shutters), roller shades, solar screens, cellular shades, awnings, roller shutters, draperies (curtains), roman shades, perforated panels, etc. Shades can be positioned as indoor, outdoor, or between-glazing products. When shades are applied after the fenestration unit was installed, a popular retrofit measure, these products are called **fenestration attachments**. When a fenestration unit is sold with matched shading as a complete assembly, the shade is called **integral**. Materials used include metal, wood, polymer, woven, and nonwoven fabrics.

The ability of shading devices to control solar gains depends mainly on the location of the device. Shades on the outdoor side of the glazing can effectively reduce solar heat gains, but need more frequent maintenance and are often difficult to adjust. Conversely, indoor devices are ubiquitous and easier to maintain and operate, but may not be as effective in providing significant solar heat gain control, depending on the glazing type, shade properties, and control (Barnaby et al. 2009; Lee and Selkowitz 1995; Moeseke et al. 2007; Shen and Tzempelikos 2012; Tzempelikos and Athienitis 2007; Wright et al. 2009a). Shading devices often do not produce any significant improvement in a fenestration system's U-factor (Barnaby et al. 2009; Wright et al. 2009b). However, several classes of insulating shades (e.g., roller shutters, cellular shades, window quilts) can provide substantial insulating value and be used as an effective retrofit option to improve thermal resistance, especially if they are sealed tightly around the perimeter, and are not porous to air.

Shading devices are well suited to deal with daylighting, privacy, views, glare, and thermal comfort issues. Some products, such as properly adjusted venetian blinds, are quite versatile in this respect. Motorized shading devices can be adjusted under changing outdoor conditions to reduce glare, maximize daylight, reduce internal temperatures (Newsham 1994; Reinhart 2004), or improve thermal comfort to building occupants (Bessoudo et al. 2010) while also providing increased hours of view to the outdoor (Rao and Tzempelikos 2012).

Shading of vertical fenestration is not confined to the use of shading devices. Building elements such as window reveals, side fins, and overhangs can also offer effective shading. Metal grilles with fixed louvers mounted horizontally at the top of a fenestration can block solar gain while still letting some light through, thereby avoiding the negative impacts of solid structural overhangs that act as thermal bridges in the building envelope and reduce daylight. Light shelves can provide shading and also redirect sunlight deeper into the room to provide a more even spatial distribution of daylight in a space. Metal perforated panels are a suitable compromise between completely cutting out views and alleviating glare and overillumination issues. Outdoor vegetative shading is particularly effective in reducing solar heat gain while enhancing the outdoor scene, but may be hard to maintain and also not be persistent over multiple years.

2. DETERMINING FENESTRATION ENERGY FLOW

Energy flows through fenestration via (1) conductive and convective heat transfer caused by the temperature difference between outdoor and indoor air; (2) net long-wave (above 2500 nm) radiative exchange between the fenestration and its surroundings and between glazing layers; (3) short-wave (below 2500 nm) solar radiation incident on the fenestration product, either directly from the sun or reflected from the ground or adjacent objects; and (4) air leakage through the fenestration. Simplified calculations are based on the observation that temperatures of the sky, ground, and surrounding objects (and hence their radiant emission) correlate with the outdoor air temperature. This is not the case for clear skies, particularly at night, which can be much colder than ambient air. The radiative interchanges are then approximated by assuming that all the radiating surfaces (including the sky) are at the same temperature as the outdoor air. With this assumption, the basic equation for the steady-state energy flow Q through a fenestration is

$$Q = UA_{pf}(t_{out} - t_{in}) + (\text{SHGC})A_{pf}E_t + C(\text{AL})A_{pf}\rho C_p(t_{out} - t_{in}) \quad (1)$$

where

Q = instantaneous energy flow, Btu/h
U = overall coefficient of heat transfer (U-factor), Btu/h·ft²·°F
A_{pf} = total projected area of fenestration (product's rough opening in wall or roof less installation clearances), ft²
t_{in} = indoor air temperature, °F
t_{out} = outdoor air temperature, °F
SHGC = solar heat gain coefficient, dimensionless; also known as *g*-value in Europe
E_t = incident total irradiance, Btu/h·ft²
C = constant, 60 min/h
AL = air leakage at current conditions, cfm/ft²
ρ = air density, lb_m/ft^3
C_p = specific heat of air, $Btu/lb_m \cdot °F$

Here, the first term on the right-hand side of Equation (1) represents heat transfer resulting from a temperature difference across the fenestration, the second term represents heat transfer caused by solar radiation, and the last term represents heat transfer caused by air leakage. The sections on U-factor (Thermal Transmittance), Solar Heat Gain Coefficient and Visible Transmittance, and Air Leakage discuss these topics, respectively.

The main justification for Equation (1) is its simplicity, achieved by collecting all the linked radiative, conductive, and convective energy transfer processes into U and SHGC. Note, however, that the values of U and SHGC vary because (1) convective heat transfer rates vary as fractional powers of temperature differences or free-stream speeds, (2) variations in temperature caused by weather or climate are small on the absolute temperature scale (°R) that controls radiative heat transfer rates, (3) fenestration systems always involve at least two thermal resistances in series, and (4) solar heat gain coefficients depend on solar incident angle and spectral distribution. Using U and SHGC values taken from product ratings causes some error in calculating Q. Of the two, the larger error results from the use of normal-incidence SHGC.

3. U-FACTOR (THERMAL TRANSMITTANCE)

In the absence of sunlight, air infiltration, and moisture condensation, the first term on the right side of Equation (1) represents the heat transfer rate through a fenestration system. Most fenestration systems consist of transparent multipane glazing units and opaque elements comprising the sash and frame (hereafter called **frame**). The glazing unit's heat transfer paths are subdivided into center-of-glass, edge-of-glass, and frame contributions (denoted by subscripts *cg*, *eg*, and *f*, respectively). Consequently, the total rate of heat transfer through a fenestration system can be calculated knowing the separate contributions of these three paths. (When present, glazing dividers, such as decorative grilles and muntin bars, also affect heat transfer, and their contribution must be considered.) The overall U-factor is estimated using area-weighted U-factors for each contribution by

$$U = \frac{U_{cg}A_{cg} + U_{eg}A_{eg} + U_fA_f}{A_{pf}} \quad (2a)$$

Note that a product frame normally consists of several different areas, and that, for example, U_fA_f is really $\sum U_{fi}A_{fi}$, where i represents each frame region (e.g., sill, jamb, head, meeting rail). Likewise, each "edge of glazing" region is adjacent to a different frame region, so $U_{eg}A_{eg}$ is really $\sum U_{egi}A_{egi}$. Equation (2a) is used in North America [e.g., for fenestration ratings by the National Fenestration Rating Council (NFRC)], Australia [by the Australian Fenestration Rating Council (AFRC; www.afrc.org.au)], India, and other countries. This approach is described as one of the two options in ISO *Standard* 15099:2003 and is the basis of the calculation used by the Lawrence Berkeley National Lab WINDOW program (LBNL 2016), a widely used software tool for modeling fenestration products' solar-optical and thermal performance. ASHRAE-derived environmental conditions, as used by the NFRC, are applied when Equation (2a) is used. These environmental conditions are detailed in Table 2.

When a fenestration product has glazed surfaces in only one direction, the sum of the areas equals the projected area A_{pf}. Skylights, greenhouse/garden windows, bay/bow windows, etc., because they extend beyond the plane of the wall/roof, have greater surface area for heat loss than fenestration with a similar glazing option and frame material; consequently, U-factors for such products are greater than for the nonprojecting versions. When the slope of a multiglazed fenestration product varies from vertical, the gas in the glazing cavity begins to exhibit vortices that also increase heat flow per unit area. This results in a further U-Factor penalty for products rated at a slope (such as skylights).

In Europe and in some other parts of the world, U-factor is calculated differently: instead of the area-based, edge-of-glass term of Equation (2a), a linear thermal transmittance term Ψ_g is used to describe heat transfer near the perimeter of the glass area. This length-weighted method follows an alternative standard, ISO *Standard* 10077-2:2012, and is also described as second option in ISO *Standard* 15099.

$$U = (U_{cg}A_{cg} + \Psi_g l_g + U_fA_f)/A_{pf} \quad (2b)$$

where l_g is the perimeter length of the entire vision area, delimited by the sightline. ISO *Standards* 10077-2 and 10077-1:2006 use simpler algorithms than ISO *Standard* 15099. In many fenestration systems, this leads to a different apparent U-factor, depending on which standard was followed. In a globalized economy, it is essential that designers and specifiers are aware of this lack of harmonization and that straight conversion between these standards is not possible.

Comparison Between Area-Weighted and Length-Weighted Methods

Glazing units (double- and triple-pane, many with low-e coatings and noble gas fills) were modeled for U-factor and reviewed by Curcija (2005) and van Dijk (2003). The studies showed that ISO 10077 versus NFRC differences in glazing U-factor can be as great as 0.05 Btu/h·ft²·°F. These discrepancies are larger than the precision with which U-factors are reported for ratings under the European and NFRC systems. Therefore, for some glazing systems a noticeable difference in U-factor will be seen.

In addition to differences between center-of-glass U-factors obtained by the two methods, it is important to note that large differences can occur in frame U-factors; ISO *Standard* 15099/NFRC frame U-factors can be ~0.2 Btu/h·ft²·°F greater than their ISO *Standard* 10077-2 equivalents. Although such differences are diluted when a whole-system, area-weighted calculation is performed, it cannot be assumed that these differences are negligible in all cases. Use ISO *Standard* 10077-based U-factors with caution and, for code compliance purposes in the United States, Canada, Australia, and some other countries, seek certifications based on NFRC procedures and environmental conditions. Refer to building codes for detailed requirements concerning NFRC compliance.

3.1 DETERMINING FENESTRATION U-FACTORS

Center-of-Glass U-Factor

For single glazing, U-factors depend strongly on indoor and outdoor film coefficients. The U-factor for single glazing is

$$U_{single\ glazing} = \frac{1}{1/h_o + 1/h_i + L/k} \tag{3}$$

where

h_o, h_i = outdoor and indoor respective glazing surface heat transfer coefficients, Btu/h·ft²·°F
L = glazing thickness, in.
k = thermal conductivity of glass, Btu·in/h·ft²·°F

For other fenestration, values for U_{cg} at standard indoor and outdoor conditions depend on glazing construction features such as the number of glazing lights, gas space dimensions, orientation relative to vertical, emissivity of each surface, and composition of fill gas. Several computer programs can be used to estimate glazing unit heat transfer for a wide range of glazing construction. The National Fenestration Rating Council (NFRC) calls for LBNL WINDOW 7.4 (LBNL 2016) as a standard calculation method for center of glazing.

Heat flow across the central glazed portion of a multipane unit must consider both convective and radiative transfer in the gas space, and may be considered one-dimensional. Convective heat transfer is estimated based on high-aspect-ratio, natural convection correlations for vertical and inclined air layers (El Sherbiny et al. 1982; Shewen 1986; Wright 1996a). Radiative heat transfer (ignoring gas absorption) is quantified using a more fundamental approach. Computational methods solving the combined heat transfer problem have been devised by Hollands and Wright (1982), Rubin (1982a, 1982b), and Rubin et al. (1998).

Figure 3 shows the effect of gas space width on U_{cg} for vertical double- and triple-paned glazing units. U-factors are plotted for air, argon, and krypton fill gases and for high (uncoated) and low (coated) values of surface emissivity. The optimum gas space width is 0.5 in. for air and argon, and 5/16 in. for krypton. Greater widths have no significant effect on U_{cg}. Greater glazing unit thicknesses decrease U_o because the length of the shortest heat flow path through the frame increases. A low-emissivity coating combined with krypton gas fill offers significant potential for reducing heat transfer in narrow-gap-width glazing units.

Edge-of-Glass U-Factor

The edge-of-glass area is typically taken to be a band 2.5 in. wide around the sightline. The width of this area is determined from the extent of two-dimensional heat transfer effects in current computer models, which are based on conduction-only analysis. In reality, because of convective and radiative effects, this area may extend beyond 2.5 in. (Beck et al. 1995; Curcija and Goss 1994; Wright and Sullivan 1995a), and depends on the type of glazing unit and its thickness. The edge region may also extend farther in opaque systems such as spandrel panels. The appropriate edge width to use can be determined using finite-element heat transfer modeling, as described by Curcija and Goss (1994).

In low-conductivity frames, most heat flow at the edge-of-glass and frame area is through the spacer, so the type of spacer has a greater impact on the edge-of-glass and frame U-factor. In metal frames, the edge-of-glass and frame U-factor varies little with the type of spacer (metal or insulating) because there is a significant heat flow through the highly conductive frame near the edge-of-glass area.

Frame U-Factor

Fenestration frame elements consist of all structural members exclusive of glazing units and include sash, jamb, head, and sill members; meeting rails and stiles; mullions; and other glazing dividers. Estimating the rate of heat transfer through the frame is complicated by the (1) variety of fenestration products and frame configurations, (2) different combinations of materials used for frames, (3) different sizes available, and, to a lesser extent, (4) glazing unit width and spacer type. Internal dividers or grilles have little effect on the fenestration U-factor, provided there is at least a 1/8 in. gap between the divider and each glazing.

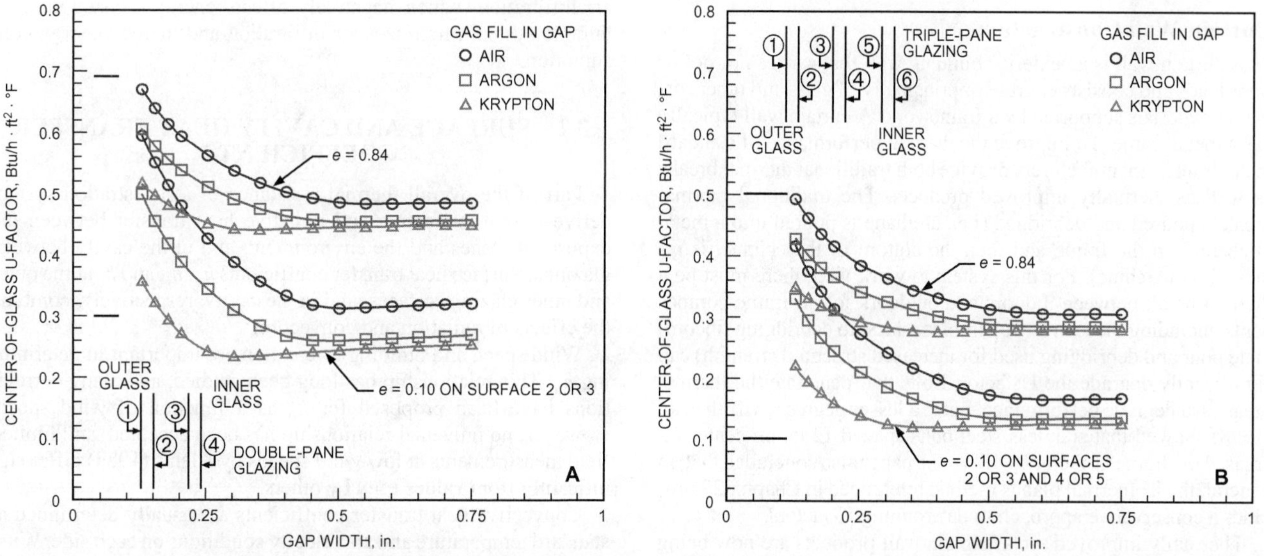

Fig. 3 Center-of-Glass U-Factor for Vertical Double- and Triple-Pane Glazing Units
Gas fill is assumed to be 90% argon, 10% air.

Table 1 Representative Fenestration Frame U-Factors in Btu/h·ft²·°F, Vertical Orientation

		Product Type/Number of Glazing Layers																
		Operable			Fixed			Garden Window		Plant-Assembled Skylight			Curtain Wall[e]			Sloped/Overhead Glazing[e]		
Frame Material	Type of Spacer	1[b]	2[c]	3[d]	1[b]	2[c]	3[d]	1[b]	2[c]	1[b]	2[c]	3[d]	1[f]	2[g]	3[h]	1[f]	2[g]	3[h]
Aluminum without thermal break	All	2.38	2.27	2.20	1.92	1.80	1.74	1.88	1.83	7.85	7.02	6.87	3.01	2.96	2.83	3.05	3.00	2.87
Aluminum with thermal break[a]	Metal	1.20	0.92	0.83	1.32	1.13	1.11			6.95	5.05	4.58	1.80	1.75	1.65	1.82	1.76	1.66
	Insulated	N/A	0.88	0.77	N/A	1.04	1.02			N/A	4.75	4.12	N/A	1.63	1.51	N/A	1.64	1.52
Aluminum-clad wood/ reinforced vinyl	Metal	0.60	0.58	0.51	0.55	0.51	0.48			4.86	3.93	3.66						
	Insulated	N/A	0.55	0.48	N/A	0.48	0.44			N/A	3.75	3.43						
Wood/vinyl	Metal	0.55	0.51	0.48	0.55	0.48	0.42	0.90	0.85	2.50	2.08	1.78						
	Insulated	N/A	0.49	0.40	N/A	0.42	0.35	N/A	0.83	N/A	2.02	1.71						
Insulated fiberglass/ vinyl	Metal	0.37	0.33	0.32	0.37	0.33	0.32											
	Insulated	N/A	0.32	0.26	N/A	0.32	0.26											
Structural glazing	Metal												1.80	1.27	1.04	1.82	1.28	1.05
	Insulated												N/A	1.02	0.75	N/A	1.02	0.75

Note: This table should only be used as an estimating tool for early phases of design.
[a]Depends strongly on width of thermal break. Value given is for 3/8 in.
[b]Single glazing corresponds to individual glazing unit thickness of 1/8 in. (nominal).
[c]Double glazing corresponds to individual glazing unit thickness of 3/4 in. (nominal).
[d]Triple glazing corresponds to individual glazing unit thickness of 1 3/8 in. (nominal).
[e]Glass thickness in curtainwall and sloped/overhead glazing is 1/4 in.
[f]Single glazing corresponds to individual glazing unit thickness of 1/4 in. (nominal).
[g]Double glazing corresponds to individual glazing unit thickness of 1 in. (nominal).
[h]Triple glazing corresponds to individual glazing unit thickness of 1 3/4 in. (nominal).
N/A Not applicable.

Computer simulations show that frame heat loss in most fenestration is controlled by a single component or controlling resistance, and only changes in this component significantly affect frame heat loss (EEL 1990). For example, the frame U-factor for thermally broken aluminum fenestration products is largely controlled by the depth of the thermal break material in the heat flow direction. For aluminum frames without a thermal break, the indoor film coefficient provides most of the resistance to heat flow. For vinyl- and wood-framed fenestrations, the controlling resistance is the shortest distance between the indoor and outdoor surfaces, which usually depends on the thickness of the sealed glazing unit.

Carpenter and McGowan (1993) experimentally validated frame U-factors for a variety of fixed and operable fenestration product types, sizes, and materials using computer modeling techniques. Table 1 lists frame U-factors for a variety of frame and spacer materials and glazing unit thicknesses. Frame and edge U-factors are normally determined by two-dimensional, finite-element computer simulation.

Curtain Wall Construction

A curtain wall is an exterior building wall that carries no roof or floor loads and consists entirely or principally of glass and other surfacing materials supported by a framework. A curtain wall typically has a metal frame. To improve the thermal performance of standard metal frames, manufacturers provide both traditional thermal breaks as well as thermally improved products. The traditional thermal break is poured and debridged (i.e., urethane is poured into a metal U-channel in the frame and then the bottom of the channel is removed by machine). For this system to work well, there must be a thermal break between indoors and outdoors for all frame components, including those in any operable sash. Skip debridging (incomplete pour and debridging used for increased structural strength) can significantly degrade the U-factor. Bolts that penetrate the thermal break also degrade performance, but to a lesser degree. Griffith et al. (1998) showed that stainless steel bolts spaced 12 in. on center increased the frame U-factor by 18%. The paper also concluded that, in general, the isothermal planes method referenced in Chapter 27 provides a conservative approach to determining U-factors.

Thermally improved metal curtain wall products are now being used more widely. In these products, most of the metal frame tends to be located on the indoor side with only a metal cap exposed on the outdoor side. Plastic spacers isolate the glazing assembly from both the outdoor metal cap and the indoor metal frame. These products can have significantly better thermal performance than standard metal frames, but it is important to minimize the number and area of the bolts that penetrate from outdoor to indoor. Curtain wall systems using structural silicone glazing (SSG) can also provide better thermal performance than dry-glazed bolted systems. Silicone sealants, with a typical thermal conductivity of 2.42 Btu·in/h·ft²·°F and a dimension of 1/4 in. between the glass and aluminum are considered thermal breaks per NFRC *Technical Document* 100 (NFRC 2014a). Work by Carbary et al. (2009) demonstrates that SSG systems have lower U-factors than comparable nonbroken or thermally improved dry-glazed systems, resulting in frame temperatures closer to interior ambient conditions.

A more recent development is the use of fiberglass as the framing material for curtain walls. Fiberglass provides the strength needed for taller buildings while having a U-factor equal to or lower than that of other nonmetal materials (e.g., wood, vinyl).

An important consideration in any curtain wall system is durability. Sealants or gaskets that degrade or fail over time allow additional air infiltration, which negatively affects energy consumption. A durable system minimizes air infiltration and thereby energy consumption.

3.2 SURFACE AND CAVITY HEAT TRANSFER COEFFICIENTS

Part of the overall thermal resistance of a fenestration system derives from convective and radiative heat transfer between the exposed surfaces and the environment, and in the cavity between glazings. Surface heat transfer coefficients h_o, h_i, and h_c at the outer and inner glazing surfaces, and in the cavity, respectively, combine the effects of radiation and convection.

Wind speed and building orientation are important in determining h_o. This relationship has long been studied, and many correlations have been proposed for h_o as a function of wind speed. However, no universal relationship has been accepted, and limited field measurements at low wind speeds by Klems (1989) differ significantly from values used by others.

Convective heat transfer coefficients are usually determined at standard temperature and air velocity conditions on each side. Wind speed can vary from less than 0.5 mph for calm weather, free convection conditions, to over 65 mph for storm conditions. A nominal value of 4.6 Btu/h·ft²·°F corresponding to a 12.3 mph wind is often

Table 2 Indoor Surface Heat Transfer Coefficient h_i in Btu/h·ft²·°F, Vertical Orientation (Still Air Conditions)

Glazing ID[a]	Glazing Type	Glazing Height, ft	Winter Conditions[b] Glazing Temp., °F	Winter Conditions[b] Temp. Diff., °F	Winter Conditions[b] h_i, Btu/h·ft²·°F	Summer Conditions[c] Glazing Temp., °F	Summer Conditions[c] Temp. Diff., °F	Summer Conditions[c] h_i, Btu/h·ft²·°F
1	Single glazing	2	17	53	1.41	89	14	1.41
		4	17	53	1.31	89	14	1.33
		6	17	53	1.25	89	14	1.29
5	Double glazing with	2	45	25	1.36	89	14	1.41
	1/2 in. air space	4	45	25	1.27	89	14	1.33
		6	45	25	1.22	89	14	1.29
23	Double glazing with	2	56	14	1.31	87	12	1.38
	e = 0.1 on surface 2 and	4	56	14	1.23	87	12	1.31
	1/2 in. argon space	6	56	14	1.19	87	12	1.27
43	Triple glazing with	2	63	7	1.25	93	18	1.45
	e = 0.1 on surfaces 2 and 5	4	63	7	1.18	93	18	1.36
	and 1/2 in. argon spaces	6	63	7	1.15	93	18	1.32

Notes:
[a]Glazing ID refers to fenestration assemblies in Table 4.
[b]Winter conditions: room air temperature t_i = 69.8°F, outdoor air temperature t_o = 0.4°F, no solar radiation
[c]Summer conditions: room air temperature t_i = 75.2°F, outdoor air temperature t_o = 89.6°F, direct solar irradiance E_D = 248.2 Btu/h·ft²
$h_i = h_{ic} + h_{iR} = 0.3(\Delta T/L)^{0.25} + \varepsilon\sigma(T_i^4 - T_g^4)/\Delta T$, where $\Delta T = T_i - T_g$, °R; L = glazing height, ft; T_g = glazing temperature, °R, σ = Stefan-Boltzmann constant, and ε = surface emissivity.

used to represent winter design conditions. At low wind speeds, h_o varies with outdoor air and surface temperature, orientation to vertical, and air moisture content. The overall surface heat transfer coefficient can be as low as 1.2 Btu/h·ft²·°F (Yazdanian and Klems 1993).

For natural convection and radiation at the indoor surface of a vertical fenestration product, surface coefficient h_i depends on the indoor air and glazing surface temperatures and on the emissivity of the glazing surface. Table 2 shows the variation of h_i for winter (t_i = 69.8°F) and summer (t_i = 75.2°F) design conditions, for a range of glazing system types and heights. Designers often use h_i = 1.46 Btu/h·ft²·°F, which corresponds to t_i = 69.8°F, a glazing temperature of 15°F, and emissivity of e_g = 0.84 (uncoated glass). For summer conditions, the same value (h_i = 1.46 Btu/h·ft²·°F) is normally used, and corresponds approximately to a glazing temperature of 95°F, t_i = 75.2°F, and e_g = 0.84. For winter conditions, this most closely approximates single glazing with clear glass that is 2 ft tall, but it overestimates the value as the glazing unit conductance decreases and height increases. For summer conditions, this value approximates all types of glass that are 2 ft tall but, again, is less accurate as glass height increases. If the indoor surface of the glass has a low-e coating, h_i values are about halved at both winter and summer conditions.

Heat transfer between the glazing surface and its environment is driven not only by local air temperatures but also by radiant temperatures to which the surface is exposed. The radiant temperature of the indoor environment is generally assumed to be equal to the indoor air temperature. This is a safe assumption where a small fenestration is exposed to a large room with surface temperatures equal to the air temperature, but it is not valid in rooms where the fenestration is exposed to other large areas of glazing surfaces (e.g., greenhouse, atrium) or to other cooled or heated surfaces (Parmelee and Huebscher 1947).

The radiant temperature of the outdoor environment is frequently assumed to be equal to the outdoor air temperature. This assumption may be in error, because additional radiative heat loss occurs between a fenestration and the clear sky (Berdahl and Martin 1984). Therefore, for clear-sky conditions, some effective outdoor temperature $t_{o,e}$ should replace t_o in Equation (1). For methods of determining $t_{o,e}$, see, for example, work by AGSL (1992). Note that a fully cloudy sky is assumed in ASHRAE design conditions.

The air space in a glazing unit constructed using glass with no reflective coating on the air space surfaces has a coefficient h_s of 1.3 Btu/h·ft²·°F. When a reflective coating is applied to an air space surface, h_s can be selected from Table 3 by first calculating the effective air space emissivity $e_{s,e}$ by Equation (4):

$$e_{s,e} = \frac{1}{1/e_o + 1/e_i - 1} \tag{4}$$

where e_o and e_i are the hemispherical emissivities of the two air space surfaces. Hemispherical emissivity of ordinary uncoated glass is 0.84 over a wavelength range of 0.4 to 40 μm.

Table 4 lists computed U-factors, using winter design conditions, for a variety of generic fenestration products, based on ASHRAE-sponsored research involving laboratory testing and computer simulations. In the past, test data were used to provide more accurate results for specific products (Hogan 1988). Computer simulations (with validation by testing) are now accepted as the standard method for accurate product-specific U-factor determination. The simulation methodologies are specified in NFRC *Technical Document* 100 (NFRC 2014a) and are based on algorithms published in ISO *Standard* 15099. The *International Energy Conservation Code* and various state energy codes in the United States, the National Energy Code in Canada, and ASHRAE *Standards* 90.1 and 90.2 all reference these standards. Fenestration must be rated in accordance with the NFRC standards for code compliance. Use of Table 4 should be limited to that of an estimating tool for the early phases of design.

Values in Table 4 are for vertical installation and for skylights and other sloped installations with glazing surfaces sloped 20° from the horizontal. Data are based on center-of-glass and edge-of-glass component U-factors and assume that there are no dividers. However, they apply only to the specific design conditions described in the table's footnotes, and are typically used only to determine peak load conditions for sizing heating equipment. Although these U-factors have been determined for winter conditions, they can also be used to estimate heat gain during peak cooling conditions, because conductive gain, which is one of several variables, is usually a small portion of the total heat gain for fenestration in direct sunlight. Glazing designs and framing materials may be compared in choosing a fenestration system that needs a specific winter design U-factor.

Table 4 lists 48 glazing types, with multiple glazing categories appropriate for sealed glazing units and the addition of storm sash to other glazing units. No distinction is made between flat and domed units such as skylights. For acrylic domes, use an average gas-space width to determine the U-factor. Note that garden window and sloped/pyramid/barrel vault skylight U-factors are approximately twice those of other similar products. Although this is partially because of the difference in slope in the case of sloped/pyramid/barrel vault skylights, it is largely because these products project out

Table 3 Air Space Coefficients for Horizontal Heat Flow

Air Space Thickness, in.	Air Space Temp., °F	Air Temp. Diff., °F	Air Space Coefficient h_s, Btu/h·ft²·°F Effective Emissivity $e_{s,e}$ 0.82	0.72	0.40	0.20	0.10	0.05
0.5	5	10	0.88	0.82	0.60	0.46	0.39	0.35
		25	0.90	0.83	0.61	0.48	0.41	0.37
		55	1.00	0.93	0.71	0.57	0.50	0.47
		70	1.05	0.98	0.76	0.62	0.55	0.51
		90	1.10	1.03	0.81	0.67	0.60	0.57
	32	10	1.00	0.92	0.66	0.50	0.42	0.38
		25	1.01	0.93	0.67	0.51	0.43	0.39
		55	1.08	1.00	0.74	0.57	0.49	0.45
		70	1.12	1.04	0.78	0.62	0.53	0.49
		90	1.17	1.09	0.83	0.67	0.58	0.54
	50	10	1.09	1.00	0.71	0.53	0.44	0.39
		25	1.10	1.01	0.72	0.54	0.44	0.40
		55	1.14	1.05	0.76	0.58	0.49	0.44
		70	1.18	1.09	0.80	0.62	0.53	0.48
		90	1.23	1.14	0.85	0.67	0.57	0.53
	85	10	1.28	1.16	0.81	0.59	0.48	0.42
		25	1.28	1.17	0.81	0.59	0.48	0.43
		55	1.30	1.19	0.84	0.62	0.51	0.45
		70	1.33	1.21	0.86	0.64	0.53	0.47
		90	1.36	1.25	0.90	0.67	0.56	0.51
	120	10	1.48	1.35	0.92	0.66	0.52	0.46
		25	1.49	1.35	0.92	0.66	0.52	0.46
		55	1.50	1.37	0.94	0.67	0.54	0.47
		70	1.51	1.38	0.95	0.68	0.55	0.48
		90	1.53	1.40	0.97	0.70	0.57	0.50
0.4	5	10	0.96	0.89	0.67	0.54	0.47	0.43
		55	1.00	0.93	0.71	0.57	0.50	0.47
		90	1.07	1.01	0.78	0.64	0.58	0.54
0.4	32	10	1.09	1.00	0.74	0.58	0.50	0.46
		55	1.11	1.03	0.76	0.60	0.52	0.48
		90	1.15	1.07	0.81	0.64	0.56	0.52
	50	10	1.18	1.09	0.79	0.61	0.52	0.48
		55	1.19	1.10	0.81	0.63	0.54	0.49
		90	1.22	1.13	0.84	0.66	0.57	0.52
	85	10	1.37	1.26	0.90	0.68	0.57	0.51
		55	1.38	1.26	0.91	0.69	0.58	0.52
		90	1.40	1.26	0.93	0.70	0.59	0.54
	120	10	1.58	1.45	1.02	0.75	0.62	0.55
		55	1.59	1.45	1.02	0.76	0.62	0.56
		90	1.60	1.46	1.03	0.77	0.63	0.57
0.3	5	<90	1.10	1.03	0.81	0.68	0.61	0.57
	32	<90	1.23	1.15	0.89	0.72	0.64	0.60
	50	<90	1.32	1.23	0.94	0.76	0.67	0.62
	85	<90	1.52	1.41	1.06	0.84	0.72	0.67
	120	<90	1.74	1.61	1.18	0.92	0.78	0.72
0.25	5	<90	1.20	1.13	0.91	0.77	0.70	0.67
	32	<90	1.34	1.26	0.99	0.83	0.75	0.71
	50	<90	1.43	1.34	1.05	0.87	0.78	0.74
	85	<90	1.64	1.53	1.18	0.96	0.84	0.79
	120	<90	1.87	1.74	1.31	1.04	0.91	0.84
0.2	5	<90	1.36	1.29	1.07	0.93	0.86	0.83
	32	<90	1.50	1.42	1.16	1.00	0.92	0.88
	50	<90	1.61	1.52	1.23	1.05	0.95	0.91
	85	<90	1.83	1.71	1.36	1.14	1.03	0.97
	120	<90	2.07	1.93	1.51	1.24	1.10	1.04

from the surface of the wall or roof. For instance, the skylight surface area, which includes the curb, can vary from 13 to 240% greater than the rough opening area, depending on the size and mounting method. Unless otherwise noted, all multiple-glazed units are filled with dry air. Argon units are assumed to be filled with 90% argon (Elmahdy and Yusuf 1995). U-factors for CO_2-filled units are similar to argon fills. For spaces up to 1/2 in., argon/SF_6 (sulfur hexafluoride) mixtures up to 70% SF_6 are generally the same as argon fills. Use of krypton gas can provide U-factors lower than those for argon for glazing spaces less than 1/2 in.

Table 4 provides data for six values of hemispherical emissivity and for 1/4 and 1/2 in. gas space widths. Emissivity of various low-e glasses varies considerably between manufacturers and processes. When emissivity is between the listed values, interpolation may be used. When manufacturers' data are not available for low-e glass, assume that glass with a pyrolytic (hard) coating has a maximum emissivity of 0.20 and that glass with a sputtered (soft) coating has a maximum emissivity of 0.10. Tinted glass does not change the winter U-factor. Also, some surface-coated reflective glass may have an emissivity less than 0.84. Values listed are for glass units using aluminum edge spacers. If an insulated or nonmetallic spacer is used, the U-factors are approximately 0.03 Btu/h·ft²·°F lower.

Fenestration product types are subdivided first by vertical versus sloped installation and then into two general categories: manufactured and site assembled. **Manufactured products** are delivered as complete units to the site. These products are typically installed in low-rise residential and small commercial/institutional/industrial buildings. Use the operable category for vertical sliders, horizontal sliders, casement, awning, pivoted, and dual-action windows, and for sliding and swinging glass doors. For picture windows, use the fixed category. For products that project out from the surface of the wall, use the garden window category. For skylights, use the sloped skylight category.

Site-assembled products have frame extrusions that are assembled on site, and then glazing is added. These products are typically installed in high-rise residential and larger commercial/institutional/industrial buildings. Curtain walls are typically made up of vision (transparent) and spandrel (opaque) panels. Table 4 contains representative U-factors for the vision panel (including mullions) for these assemblies. The spandrel portion of curtain walls usually consists of a metal pan filled with insulation and covered with a sheet of glass or other weatherproof covering. Although the U-factor in the center of the spandrel panel can be quite low, the metal pan is a thermal bridge, significantly increasing the U-factor of the assembly. Two-dimensional simulation, validated by testing of a curtain wall having an aluminum frame with a thermal break, found that the U-factor for the edge of the spandrel panel (the 2 1/2 in. band around the perimeter adjacent to the frame) was 40% of the way toward the U-factor of the frame. The U-factor was 0.06 Btu/h·ft²·°F for the center of the spandrel, 0.45 for the edge of the spandrel, and 1.06 for the frame (Carpenter and Elmahdy 1994). Two-dimensional heat transfer analysis or physical testing is recommended to determine the U-factor of spandrel panels. Use the sloped/overhead glazing category for sloped glazing panels comparable to curtain walls.

Physical testing of double-glazed units showed U-factors of 1.0 Btu/h·ft²·°F for a thermally broken aluminum pyramidal skylight and 1.3 Btu/h·ft²·°F for an aluminum-frame half-round barrel

Table 4 U-Factors for Various Fenestration Products in Btu/h·ft²·°F

Product Type		Glass Only		Vertical Installation: Operable (including sliding and swinging glass doors)					Vertical Installation: Fixed				
ID	Frame Type / Glazing Type	Center of Glass	Edge of Glass	Aluminum Without Thermal Break	Aluminum with Thermal Break	Reinforced Vinyl/ Aluminum Clad Wood	Wood/ Vinyl	Insulated Fiberglass/ Vinyl	Aluminum Without Thermal Break	Aluminum with Thermal Break	Reinforced Vinyl/ Aluminum Clad Wood	Wood/ Vinyl	Insulated Fiberglass/ Vinyl
	Single Glazing												
1	1/8 in. glass	1.04	1.04	1.23	1.07	0.93	0.91	0.85	1.12	1.07	0.98	0.98	1.04
2	1/4 in. acrylic/polycarbonate	0.88	0.88	1.10	0.94	0.81	0.80	0.74	0.98	0.92	0.84	0.84	0.88
3	1/8 in. acrylic/polycarbonate	0.96	0.96	1.17	1.01	0.87	0.86	0.79	1.05	0.99	0.91	0.91	0.96
	Double Glazing												
4	1/4 in. air space	0.55	0.64	0.81	0.64	0.57	0.55	0.50	0.68	0.62	0.56	0.56	0.55
5	1/2 in. air space	0.48	0.59	0.76	0.58	0.52	0.50	0.45	0.62	0.56	0.50	0.50	0.48
6	1/4 in. argon space	0.51	0.61	0.78	0.61	0.54	0.52	0.47	0.65	0.59	0.53	0.52	0.51
7	1/2 in. argon space	0.45	0.57	0.73	0.56	0.50	0.48	0.43	0.60	0.53	0.48	0.47	0.45
	Double Glazing, *e* = 0.60 on surface 2 or 3												
8	1/4 in. air space	0.52	0.62	0.79	0.61	0.55	0.53	0.48	0.66	0.59	0.54	0.53	0.52
9	1/2 in. air space	0.44	0.56	0.72	0.55	0.49	0.48	0.43	0.59	0.53	0.47	0.47	0.44
10	1/4 in. argon space	0.47	0.58	0.75	0.57	0.51	0.50	0.45	0.61	0.55	0.49	0.49	0.47
11	1/2 in. argon space	0.41	0.54	0.70	0.53	0.47	0.45	0.41	0.56	0.50	0.44	0.44	0.41
	Double Glazing, *e* = 0.40 on surface 2 or 3												
12	1/4 in. air space	0.49	0.60	0.76	0.59	0.53	0.51	0.46	0.63	0.57	0.51	0.51	0.49
13	1/2 in. air space	0.40	0.54	0.69	0.52	0.47	0.45	0.40	0.55	0.49	0.44	0.43	0.40
14	1/4 in. argon space	0.43	0.56	0.72	0.54	0.49	0.47	0.42	0.58	0.52	0.46	0.46	0.43
15	1/2 in. argon space	0.36	0.51	0.66	0.49	0.44	0.42	0.37	0.52	0.46	0.40	0.40	0.36
	Double Glazing, *e* = 0.20 on surface 2 or 3												
16	1/4 in. air space	0.45	0.57	0.73	0.56	0.50	0.48	0.43	0.60	0.53	0.48	0.47	0.45
17	1/2 in. air space	0.35	0.50	0.65	0.48	0.43	0.41	0.37	0.51	0.45	0.39	0.39	0.35
18	1/4 in. argon space	0.38	0.52	0.68	0.51	0.45	0.43	0.39	0.54	0.47	0.42	0.42	0.38
19	1/2 in. argon space	0.30	0.46	0.61	0.45	0.39	0.38	0.33	0.47	0.41	0.35	0.35	0.30
	Double Glazing, *e* = 0.10 on surface 2 or 3												
20	1/4 in. air space	0.42	0.55	0.71	0.54	0.48	0.46	0.41	0.57	0.51	0.45	0.45	0.42
21	1/2 in. air space	0.32	0.48	0.63	0.46	0.41	0.39	0.34	0.49	0.42	0.37	0.37	0.32
22	1/4 in. argon space	0.35	0.50	0.65	0.48	0.43	0.41	0.37	0.51	0.45	0.39	0.39	0.35
23	1/2 in. argon space	0.27	0.44	0.59	0.42	0.37	0.36	0.31	0.44	0.38	0.33	0.32	0.27
	Double Glazing, *e* = 0.05 on surface 2 or 3												
24	1/4 in. air space	0.41	0.54	0.70	0.53	0.47	0.45	0.41	0.56	0.50	0.44	0.44	0.41
25	1/2 in. air space	0.30	0.46	0.61	0.45	0.39	0.38	0.33	0.47	0.41	0.35	0.35	0.30
26	1/4 in. argon space	0.33	0.48	0.64	0.47	0.42	0.40	0.35	0.49	0.43	0.38	0.37	0.33
27	1/2 in. argon space	0.25	0.42	0.57	0.41	0.36	0.34	0.30	0.43	0.36	0.31	0.31	0.25
	Triple Glazing												
28	1/4 in. air spaces	0.38	0.52	0.67	0.49	0.43	0.43	0.38	0.53	0.47	0.42	0.42	0.38
29	1/2 in. air spaces	0.31	0.47	0.61	0.44	0.38	0.38	0.34	0.47	0.41	0.36	0.36	0.31
30	1/4 in. argon spaces	0.34	0.49	0.63	0.46	0.41	0.40	0.36	0.50	0.44	0.38	0.38	0.34
31	1/2 in. argon spaces	0.29	0.45	0.59	0.42	0.37	0.36	0.32	0.45	0.40	0.34	0.34	0.29
	Triple Glazing, *e* = 0.20 on surface 2, 3, 4, or 5												
32	1/4 in. air spaces	0.33	0.48	0.62	0.45	0.40	0.39	0.35	0.49	0.43	0.37	0.37	0.33
33	1/2 in. air spaces	0.25	0.42	0.56	0.39	0.34	0.33	0.29	0.42	0.36	0.31	0.31	0.25
34	1/4 in. argon spaces	0.28	0.45	0.58	0.41	0.36	0.36	0.31	0.45	0.39	0.33	0.33	0.28
35	1/2 in. argon spaces	0.22	0.40	0.54	0.37	0.32	0.31	0.27	0.39	0.33	0.28	0.28	0.22
	Triple Glazing, *e* = 0.20 on surfaces 2 or 3 and 4 or 5												
36	1/4 in. air spaces	0.29	0.45	0.59	0.42	0.37	0.36	0.32	0.45	0.40	0.34	0.34	0.29
37	1/2 in. air spaces	0.20	0.39	0.52	0.35	0.31	0.30	0.26	0.38	0.32	0.26	0.26	0.20
38	1/4 in. argon spaces	0.23	0.41	0.54	0.37	0.33	0.32	0.28	0.40	0.34	0.29	0.29	0.23
39	1/2 in. argon spaces	0.17	0.36	0.49	0.33	0.28	0.28	0.24	0.35	0.29	0.24	0.24	0.17
	Triple Glazing, *e* = 0.10 on surfaces 2 or 3 and 4 or 5												
40	1/4 in. air spaces	0.27	0.44	0.58	0.40	0.36	0.35	0.31	0.44	0.38	0.32	0.32	0.27
41	1/2 in. air spaces	0.18	0.37	0.50	0.34	0.29	0.28	0.25	0.36	0.30	0.25	0.25	0.18
42	1/4 in. argon spaces	0.21	0.39	0.53	0.36	0.31	0.31	0.27	0.38	0.33	0.27	0.27	0.21
43	1/2 in. argon spaces	0.14	0.34	0.47	0.30	0.26	0.26	0.22	0.32	0.27	0.21	0.21	0.14
	Quadruple Glazing, *e* = 0.10 on surfaces 2 or 3 and 4 or 5												
44	1/4 in. air spaces	0.22	0.40	0.54	0.37	0.32	0.31	0.27	0.39	0.33	0.28	0.28	0.22
45	1/2 in. air spaces	0.15	0.35	0.48	0.31	0.27	0.26	0.23	0.33	0.27	0.22	0.22	0.15
46	1/4 in. argon spaces	0.17	0.36	0.49	0.33	0.28	0.28	0.24	0.35	0.29	0.24	0.24	0.17
47	1/2 in. argon spaces	0.12	0.32	0.45	0.29	0.25	0.24	0.20	0.31	0.25	0.20	0.20	0.12
48	1/4 in. krypton spaces	0.12	0.32	0.45	0.29	0.25	0.24	0.20	0.31	0.25	0.20	0.20	0.12

Notes:

1. All heat transmission coefficients in this table include film resistances and are based on winter conditions of 0°F outdoor air temperature and 70°F indoor air temperature, with 15 mph outdoor air velocity and zero solar flux. Except for single glazing, small changes in indoor and outdoor temperatures do not significantly affect overall U-factors. Coefficients are for vertical position except skylight values, which are for 20° from horizontal with heat flow up.

2. Glazing layer surfaces are numbered from outdoor to indoor. Double, triple, and quadruple refer to number of glazing panels. All data are based on 1/8 in. glass, unless otherwise noted. Thermal conductivities are: 0.53 Btu/h·ft·°F for glass, and 0.11 Btu/h·ft·°F for acrylic and polycarbonate.

3. Standard spacers are metal. Edge-of-glass effects are assumed to extend over the 2 1/2 in. band around perimeter of each glazing unit.

Table 4 U-Factors for Various Fenestration Products in Btu/h·ft²·°F (*Concluded*)

Vertical Installation							Sloped Installation								
Garden Windows		Curtain Wall			Glass Only (Skylights)		Manufactured Skylight				Site-Assembled Sloped/Overhead Glazing				
Aluminum Without Thermal Break	Wood/ Vinyl	Aluminum Without Thermal Break	Aluminum with Thermal Break	Structural Glazing	Center of Glass	Edge of Glass	Aluminum Without Thermal Break	Aluminum with Thermal Break	Reinforced Vinyl/ Aluminum Clad Wood	Wood/ Vinyl	Aluminum Without Thermal Break	Aluminum with Thermal Break	Structural Glazing	ID	
2.50	2.10	1.21	1.10	1.10	1.19	1.19	1.77	1.70	1.61	1.42	1.35	1.34	1.25	1	
2.24	1.84	1.06	0.96	0.96	1.03	1.03	1.60	1.54	1.45	1.31	1.20	1.20	1.10	2	
2.37	1.97	1.13	1.03	1.03	1.11	1.11	1.68	1.62	1.53	1.39	1.27	1.27	1.18	3	
1.72	1.32	0.77	0.67	0.63	0.58	0.66	1.10	0.96	0.92	0.84	0.80	0.83	0.66	4	
1.62	1.22	0.71	0.61	0.57	0.57	0.65	1.09	0.95	0.91	0.84	0.79	0.82	0.65	5	
1.66	1.26	0.74	0.63	0.59	0.53	0.63	1.05	0.91	0.87	0.80	0.76	0.80	0.62	6	
1.57	1.17	0.68	0.58	0.54	0.53	0.63	1.05	0.91	0.87	0.80	0.76	0.80	0.62	7	
1.68	1.28	0.74	0.64	0.60	0.54	0.63	1.06	0.92	0.88	0.81	0.77	0.80	0.63	8	
1.56	1.16	0.68	0.57	0.53	0.53	0.63	1.05	0.91	0.87	0.80	0.76	0.80	0.62	9	
1.60	1.20	0.70	0.60	0.56	0.49	0.60	1.01	0.87	0.83	0.76	0.72	0.77	0.58	10	
1.51	1.11	0.65	0.55	0.51	0.49	0.60	1.01	0.87	0.83	0.76	0.72	0.77	0.58	11	
1.63	1.23	0.72	0.62	0.58	0.51	0.61	1.03	0.89	0.85	0.78	0.74	0.78	0.60	12	
1.50	1.10	0.64	0.54	0.50	0.50	0.61	1.02	0.88	0.84	0.77	0.73	0.78	0.59	13	
1.54	1.14	0.67	0.56	0.52	0.44	0.56	0.96	0.83	0.78	0.72	0.68	0.74	0.54	14	
1.44	1.04	0.61	0.50	0.46	0.46	0.58	0.98	0.85	0.80	0.74	0.70	0.75	0.56	15	
1.57	1.17	0.68	0.58	0.54	0.46	0.58	0.98	0.85	0.80	0.74	0.70	0.75	0.56	16	
1.43	1.03	0.60	0.50	0.45	0.46	0.58	0.98	0.85	0.80	0.74	0.70	0.75	0.56	17	
1.47	1.07	0.62	0.52	0.48	0.39	0.53	0.91	0.78	0.74	0.68	0.64	0.70	0.50	18	
1.35	0.95	0.55	0.45	0.41	0.40	0.54	0.92	0.79	0.75	0.68	0.64	0.71	0.51	19	
1.53	1.13	0.66	0.56	0.51	0.44	0.56	0.96	0.83	0.78	0.72	0.68	0.74	0.54	20	
1.38	0.98	0.57	0.47	0.43	0.44	0.56	0.96	0.83	0.78	0.72	0.68	0.74	0.54	21	
1.43	1.03	0.60	0.50	0.45	0.36	0.51	0.88	0.75	0.71	0.65	0.61	0.68	0.47	22	
1.30	0.90	0.53	0.43	0.38	0.38	0.52	0.90	0.77	0.73	0.67	0.63	0.69	0.49	23	
1.51	1.11	0.65	0.55	0.51	0.42	0.55	0.94	0.81	0.76	0.70	0.66	0.72	0.52	24	
1.35	0.95	0.55	0.45	0.41	0.43	0.56	0.95	0.82	0.77	0.71	0.67	0.73	0.53	25	
1.40	1.00	0.58	0.48	0.44	0.34	0.49	0.86	0.73	0.69	0.63	0.59	0.66	0.45	26	
1.27	0.87	0.51	0.41	0.37	0.36	0.51	0.88	0.75	0.71	0.65	0.61	0.68	0.47	27	
see note 7	see note 7	0.61	0.51	0.46	0.39	0.53	0.90	0.75	0.71	0.64	0.62	0.69	0.48	28	
		0.55	0.45	0.40	0.36	0.51	0.87	0.72	0.68	0.61	0.60	0.67	0.45	29	
		0.58	0.48	0.43	0.35	0.50	0.86	0.71	0.67	0.60	0.59	0.66	0.44	30	
		0.53	0.43	0.38	0.33	0.48	0.84	0.69	0.65	0.59	0.57	0.65	0.42	31	
see note 7	see note 7	0.57	0.47	0.42	0.34	0.49	0.85	0.70	0.66	0.59	0.58	0.65	0.43	32	
		0.50	0.40	0.35	0.31	0.47	0.82	0.67	0.63	0.57	0.56	0.63	0.41	33	
		0.53	0.43	0.37	0.28	0.45	0.80	0.64	0.60	0.54	0.53	0.61	0.38	34	
		0.47	0.37	0.32	0.27	0.44	0.79	0.63	0.59	0.53	0.52	0.60	0.37	35	
see note 7	see note 7	0.53	0.43	0.38	0.29	0.45	0.81	0.65	0.61	0.55	0.54	0.62	0.39	36	
		0.46	0.36	0.30	0.27	0.44	0.79	0.63	0.59	0.53	0.52	0.60	0.37	37	
		0.48	0.38	0.33	0.24	0.42	0.76	0.60	0.57	0.50	0.49	0.58	0.35	38	
		0.43	0.33	0.28	0.22	0.40	0.74	0.58	0.55	0.49	0.48	0.57	0.33	39	
see note 7	see note 7	0.52	0.42	0.37	0.27	0.44	0.79	0.63	0.59	0.53	0.52	0.60	0.37	40	
		0.44	0.34	0.29	0.25	0.42	0.77	0.61	0.57	0.51	0.50	0.59	0.36	41	
		0.46	0.36	0.31	0.21	0.39	0.73	0.57	0.54	0.48	0.47	0.56	0.32	42	
		0.40	0.30	0.25	0.20	0.39	0.72	0.56	0.53	0.47	0.46	0.55	0.31	43	
		0.47	0.37	0.32	0.22	0.40	0.74	0.58	0.55	0.49	0.48	0.57	0.33	44	
see note 7	see note 7	0.41	0.31	0.26	0.19	0.38	0.71	0.55	0.52	0.46	0.45	0.54	0.30	45	
		0.43	0.33	0.28	0.18	0.37	0.70	0.54	0.51	0.45	0.44	0.54	0.29	46	
		0.39	0.29	0.23	0.16	0.35	0.68	0.52	0.49	0.43	0.42	0.52	0.28	47	
		0.39	0.29	0.23	0.13	0.33	0.65	0.49	0.46	0.40	0.40	0.50	0.25	48	

4. Product sizes are described in Figure 4, and frame U-factors are from Table 1.
5. Use $U = 0.6$ Btu/(h·ft²·°F) for glass block with mortar but without reinforcing or framing.
6. Use of this table should be limited to that of an estimating tool for early phases of design.
7. Values for triple- and quadruple-glazed garden windows are not listed, because these are not common products.
8. U-factors in this table were determined using NFRC 100-91. They have not been updated to the current rating methodology in NFRC 100 (2014a).

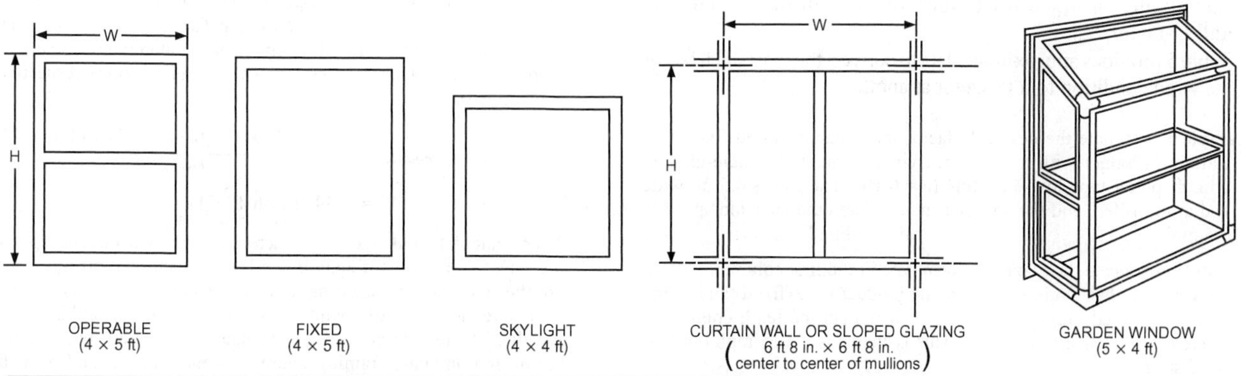

Frame Material	Frame Width, inches					
	Operable	Fixed	Garden Window	Skylight	Curtain Wall	Sloped/Overhead Glazing
Aluminum without thermal break	1.5	1.3	1.75	0.7	2.25	2.25
Aluminum with thermal break	2.1	1.3	N/A	0.7	2.25	2.25
Aluminum-clad wood/reinforcing vinyl	2.8	1.6	N/A	0.9	N/A	N/A
Wood/vinyl	2.8	1.6	1.75	0.9	N/A	N/A
Insulated fiberglass/vinyl	3.1	1.8	N/A	N/A	N/A	N/A
Structural glazing	N/A	N/A	N/A	N/A	2.25	2.5

Fig. 4 Frame Widths for Standard Fenestration Units

vault (both normalized to a rough opening of 8 ft by 8 ft). Until more conclusive results are available, U-factors for these systems can be estimated by multiplying the site-assembled sloped/overhead glazing values in Table 4 by the ratio of total product surface area (including curbs) to rough opening area. These ratios range from 1.2 to 2.0 for low-slope skylights, 1.4 to 2.1 for pyramid assemblies sloped at 45°, and 1.7 to 2.9 for semicircular barrel vault assemblies.

U-factors in Table 4 are based on definitions of the six product types, frame sizes, and proportion of frame to glass area shown in Figure 4. Four of the products are manufactured type. Sizes are as defined in NFRC *Technical Document* 100 (2014a): operable and fixed (nonoperable) glazing units are 20 ft^2 in area, and the overall size corresponds to a 4 ft by 5 ft fenestration product. The garden window category is 20 ft^2 in projected area (35 ft^2 in surface area) and 5 ft wide by 4 ft high by 15 in. deep. The manufactured skylight category is a nominal 16 ft^2 in area, corresponding to a 4 ft by 4 ft skylight. The nominal dimensions of a roof-mounted skylight correspond to centerline spacing of roof framing members; consequently, the rough opening dimensions are 3 ft 10.5 in. by 3 ft 10.5 in. The curtain wall and sloped/overhead glazing categories are a nominal 43 ft^2 in area, representing repeating 6 ft 8 in. by 6 ft 8 in. panels. The nominal dimensions correspond to centerline spacing of the head and sill and vertical mullions.

Six frame types are listed (although not all for any one category) in order of improving thermal performance. The most conservative assumption is to use the frame category of aluminum frame without a thermal break (although there are products on the market that have higher U-factors). The aluminum frame with a thermal break is for frames having at least a 3/8 in. thermal break between the indoors and outdoors for all members including both the frame and the operable sash, if applicable. Some products are available with significantly wider thermal breaks, which achieve considerable improvement. The aluminum-clad wood/reinforced vinyl category represents vinyl-frame products, such as sliding glass doors or large windows that have extensive metal reinforcing within the frame and wood products with extensive metal, usually on the outdoor surface of the frame. Both of these factors provide short circuits, which degrade the thermal performance of the frame material. The wood/vinyl frame category represents the improved thermal performance that is possible if the thermal short circuits from the previous frame

Table 5 Glazing U-Factors for Various Wind Speeds in $Btu/h \cdot ft^2 \cdot °F$

Wind Speed, mph		
15	7.5	0
0.10	0.10	0.10
0.20	0.20	0.19
0.30	0.29	0.28
0.40	0.38	0.37
0.50	0.47	0.45
0.60	0.56	0.53
0.70	0.65	0.61
0.80	0.74	0.69
0.90	0.83	0.78
1.00	0.92	0.86
1.10	1.01	0.94
1.20	1.10	1.02
1.30	1.19	1.10

category do not exist. Insulated fiberglass/vinyl represents fiberglass or vinyl frames that do not have metal reinforcing and whose frame cavities are filled with insulation. For several site-assembled product types, there is a structural glazing frame category that represents products where sheets of glass are butt-glazed to each other using a sealant only, and framing members are not exposed to the exterior. For glazing with a steel frame, use aluminum frame values. For aluminum fenestration with wood trim or vinyl cladding, use the values for aluminum. Frame type refers to the primary unit; therefore, when storm sash is added over another fenestration product, use values given for the nonstorm product.

To estimate the overall U-factor of a fenestration product that differs significantly from the assumptions given in Table 4 and/or Figure 4, first determine the area that is frame/sash, center-of-glass, and edge-of-glass (based on a 2 1/2 in. band around the perimeter of each glazing unit). Next, determine the appropriate component U-factors. These can be taken either from the standard values listed in italics in Table 4 for glass, from the values in Table 1 for frames, or from some other source such as test data or computed factors. Finally, multiply the area and the component U-factors, sum these products, and then divide by the rough opening in the building envelope where this product will fit to obtain the overall U-factor U_o.

Table 5 provides approximate data to convert the overall U-factor at one wind condition to a U-factor at another.

Example 1. Estimate the design U-factor for a manufactured fixed fenestration product with a reinforced vinyl frame and double-glazing with a sputter-type low-e coating (e = 0.10). The gap is 0.5 in. wide and argon-filled, and the spacer is metal. The outdoor wind speed is 7.5 mph.

Solution: Locate the glazing system type in the first column of Table 4 (ID = 23), then find the appropriate product type (fixed) and frame type (reinforced vinyl). The U-factor listed (in the tenth column of U-factors) is 0.33 Btu/h·ft²·°F. This U-factor is for 15 mph outdoor wind speed.

From Table 5, interpolate 0.33 in the 15 mph column to the corresponding value in the 7.5 mph column.

$$\frac{0.33 - 0.30}{0.40 - 0.30} = \frac{U_{7.5\text{ mph}} - 0.29}{0.38 - 0.29}$$

$$U_{7.5\text{ mph}} = 0.32\text{ Btu/h·ft}^2\text{·°F}$$

Example 2. Estimate a representative U-factor for a wood-framed, 38 by 82 in. swinging French door with eight 11 by 16 in. panes (true divided panels), each consisting of clear double-glazing with a 0.25 in. air space and a metal spacer.

Solution: Without more detailed information, assume that the dividers have the same U-factor as the frame and that the divider edge has the same U-factor as the edge-of-glass. Calculate center-of-glass, edge-of-glass, and frame areas:

$$A_{cg} = 8[(11 - 5)(16 - 5)] = 528\text{ in}^2$$

$$A_{eg} = 8(11 \times 16) - 528 = 880\text{ in}^2$$

$$A_f = (38 \times 82) - 8(11 \times 16) = 1708\text{ in}^2$$

Select center-of-glass, edge-of-glass, and frame U-factors. These component U-factors are 0.55 and 0.64 (from Table 4, glazing ID = 4, U-factor columns 1 and 2) and 0.51 Btu/h·ft²·°F (from Table 1, wood frame, metal spacer, operable, double-glazing), respectively. From Equation (2),

$$U_{french\ door} = \frac{(0.55 \times 528) + (0.64 \times 880) + (0.51 \times 1708)}{(38 \times 82)}$$

$$= 0.55\text{ Btu/h·ft}^2\text{·°F}$$

Example 3. Estimate the overall average U-factor for a multifloor curtain wall assembly that is part vision glass and part opaque spandrel. The typical floor-to-floor height is 12 ft, and the building module is 4 ft as reflected in the spacing of the mullions both horizontally and vertically. For a representative section 4 ft wide and 12 ft tall, one of the modules is glazed and the other two are opaque. The mullions are aluminum frame with a thermal break 3 in. wide and centered on the module. The glazing unit is double glazing with a pyrolytic low-e coating (e = 0.40) and has a 1/2 in. gap filled with air and a metal spacer. The spandrel panel has a metal pan backed by R-20 insulation and no intermediate reinforcing members.

Solution: It is necessary to calculate the U-factor for the glazed module and for the opaque spandrel modules, and then to do an area-weighted average to determine the average U-factor for the overall curtain wall assembly.

First, calculate the overall U-factor for the glazed module. Calculate center-of-glass, edge-of-glass, and frame areas. The glazed area is 45 by 45 in. (48 in. module, 1.5 in. of mullions on each edge).

$$A_{cg} = (45 - 5)(45 - 5) = 1600\text{ in}^2$$

$$A_{eg} = (45 \times 45) - 1600 = 425\text{ in}^2$$

$$A_f = (48 \times 48) - (45 \times 45) = 279\text{ in}^2$$

Select center-of-glass, edge-of-glass, and frame U-factors. These component U-factors are 0.40 and 0.54 (from Table 4, ID = 13, columns 1 and 2) and 1.75 Btu/h·ft²·°F (from Table 1, aluminum frame with a thermal break, metal spacer, curtain wall, double glazing), respectively. From Equation (2),

$$U_{glazing\ module} = \frac{(0.40 \times 1600) + (0.54 \times 425) + (1.75 \times 279)}{(48 \times 48)}$$

$$= 0.59\text{ Btu/h·ft}^2\text{·°F}$$

Then, calculate the overall U-factor for the two opaque spandrel modules. The center-of-spandrel, edge-of spandrel, and frame areas are the same as the glazed module. The frame U-factor is the same. Calculate the center-of-spandrel U-factor. In this particular case, the R-value of the insulation does not need to be rated, because there are no intermediate framing members penetrating it and providing thermal short circuits. When the resistance of the insulation (20 ft²·°F·h/Btu) is added to the exterior air film resistance of 0.17 and the interior air film resistance of 0.68 ft²·°F·h/Btu (from Table 1, Chapter 26), the total resistance is 20.85 ft²·°F·h/Btu, and the U-factor is 1/20.85 = 0.05 Btu/h·ft²·°F. The edge-of-spandrel U-factor is 40% of the way to the frame U-factor, which is 0.05 + [0.40 × (1.75 – 0.05)] = 0.73 Btu/h·ft²·°F.

$$U_{opaque\ spandrel\ module} = \frac{(0.05 \times 1600) + (0.73 \times 425) + (1.75 \times 279)}{(48 \times 48)}$$

$$= 0.38\text{ Btu/h·ft}^2\text{·°F}$$

Finally, calculate the overall average U-factor for the curtain wall assembly, including the one module of vision glass and the two modules of opaque spandrel.

$$U_{curtain\ wall} = \frac{[0.59 \times (48 \times 48)] + [0.38 \times 2 \times (48 \times 48)]}{3 \times (48 \times 48)}$$

$$= 0.45\text{ Btu/h·ft}^2\text{·°F}$$

Note that even with double glazing having a low-e coating and with R-20 in the opaque areas, this curtain wall with metal pans only has an overall R-value of approximately 2.

Example 4. Estimate the U-factor for a semicircular barrel vault that is 18 ft wide, 9 ft tall, and 30 ft long mounted on a 6 in. curb. The barrel vault has an aluminum frame without a thermal break. The glazing is double with a 1/2 in. gap width filled with air and a low-e coating (e = 0.20).

Solution: An approximation can be made by multiplying the U-factor for a site-assembled sloped/overhead glazing product having the same frame and glazing features by the ratio of the surface area (including the curb) of the barrel vault to the rough opening area in the roof that the barrel vault fits over. First, determine the surface area (including the curb) of the barrel vault:

Area of the curved portion of the barrel vault
= (π × diameter/2) × length
= (3.14 × 18/2) × 30 = 848 ft²

Area of the two ends of the barrel vault
= 2 × (π × radius²)/2 = πr^2
= 3.14 × 9² = 254 ft²

Area of the curb
= perimeter × curb height
= (18 + 30 + 18 + 30) × 6/12 = 48 ft²

Total surface area of the barrel vault
= 848 + 254 + 48 = 1150 ft²

Second, determine the rough opening area in the roof that the barrel vault fits over:
= length × width
= 18 × 30 = 540 ft²

Third, determine the ratio of the surface area to the rough opening area:
= 1150/540 = 2.13

Fourth, determine the U-factor from Table 4 of a site-assembled sloped/overhead glazing product having the same frame and glazing features.

The U-factor is 0.70 Btu/h·ft²·°F (ID = 17, 12th column on the second page of Table 4).

Fifth, determine the estimated U-factor of the barrel vault.

$$U_{barrel\ vault} = U_{sloped\ overhead\ glazing} \times \text{surface area/rough opening for the barrel vault}$$
$$= 0.70 \times 2.13 = 1.49 \text{ Btu/h·ft}^2\text{·°F}$$

3.3 REPRESENTATIVE U-FACTORS FOR DOORS

Doors are often an overlooked component in the thermal integrity of the building envelope. Although entry doors (swinging, revolving, etc.) represent a small portion of the building envelope of residential, commercial, and institutional buildings, their U-factor is usually many times higher than that of the walls or ceilings. In some commercial and industrial buildings, vehicular access doors (upward-acting doors) represent a significant area of heat loss. Table 6 contains representative U-factors for swinging doors determined through computer simulation (Carpenter and Hogan 1996). These are generic values, and product-specific values determined in accordance with standards should be used whenever available. NFRC *Technical Document* 100 (NFRC 2014a) gives procedures for evaluating the performance of entry and vehicular access doors. Tables 7 to 9 contain representative U-factors for revolving, emergency exit, garage, and aircraft hangar doors determined through testing (McGowan et al. 2006).

Swinging doors can be divided into two categories: slab and stile-and-rail. A stile-and-rail door is a swinging door with a full-glass insert supported by horizontal rails and vertical stiles. The stiles and rails are typically either solid wood members or extruded aluminum or vinyl, as shown in Figure 5. Most residential doors are slab type with solid wood, steel, or a fiberglass skin over foam insulation in a wood frame with aluminum sill. The edges of the steel skin door are normally wood to provide a thermal break. In commercial construction, doors are either steel skin over foam insulation in a steel frame (i.e., utility doors) or a full glass door made up of aluminum stiles, rails, and frame (i.e., entrance doors). The most important factors affecting door U-factor are material construction, glass size, and glass type. Frame depth, slab width, and number of panels have a minor effect on door performance. Side lites and double doors have U-factors similar to a single door of the same construction. For wood slab doors in a wood frame, the glazing area has little effect on the U-factor. For an insulated steel slab in a wood frame, however, glazing area strongly affects U-factor. Typical commercial insulated slab doors have a U-factor approximately twice that of residential insulated doors, the prime reason being thermal bridging of the slab edge and the steel frame. Stile-and-rail doors, even if thermally broken, have U-factors 50% higher than a full-glass commercial steel slab door.

There are three generic types of upward-acting doors:

- Rolling (also called roll-up) doors consist of small metal slats of approximately 2.5 in. in height that travel in vertical guides and roll up around a metal barrel to open.
- Sectional (also called garage) doors consist of a series of approximately 18 to 32 in. high sections that travel in vertical tracks to open.
- Folding (also called biparting) doors, commonly used in aircraft hangars, have two large sections that also travel in vertical tracks to open, but fold together when the door is fully open.

There is a wide range in the design of insulated upward-acting doors. Factors affecting heat transfer include insulation thickness, section/slat design, and section/slat interface design (which may

Table 6 Design U-Factors of Swinging Doors in Btu/h·ft²·°F

Door Type (Rough Opening = 38 × 82 in.)	No Glazing	Single Glazing	Double Glazing with 1/2 in. Air Space	Double Glazing with e = 0.10, 1/2 in. Argon
Slab Doors				
Wood slab in wood frame[a]	0.46			
6% glazing (22 × 8 in. lite)	—	0.48	0.46	0.44
25% glazing (22 × 36 in. lite)	—	0.58	0.46	0.42
45% glazing (22 × 64 in. lite)	—	0.69	0.46	0.39
More than 50% glazing		Use Table 4 (operable)		
Insulated steel slab with wood edge in wood frame[b]	0.16			
6% glazing (22 × 8 in. lite)	—	0.21	0.19	0.18
25% glazing (22 × 36 in. lite)	—	0.39	0.26	0.23
45% glazing (22 × 64 in. lite)	—	0.58	0.35	0.26
More than 50% glazing		Use Table 4 (operable)		
Foam insulated steel slab with metal edge in steel frame[c]	0.37			
6% glazing (22 × 8 in. lite)	—	0.44	0.41	0.39
25% glazing (22 × 36 in. lite)	—	0.55	0.48	0.44
45% glazing (22 × 64 in. lite)	—	0.71	0.56	0.48
More than 50% glazing		Use Table 4 (operable)		
Cardboard honeycomb slab with metal edge in steel frame	0.61			
Stile-and-Rail Doors				
Sliding glass doors/French doors		Use Table 4 (operable)		
Site-Assembled Stile-and-Rail Doors				
Aluminum in aluminum frame	—	1.32	0.93	0.79
Aluminum in aluminum frame with thermal break	—	1.13	0.74	0.63

Notes:
[a]Thermally broken sill (add 0.03 Btu/h·ft²·°F for non-thermally broken sill)
[b]Non-thermally broken sill
[c]Nominal U-factors are through center of insulated panel before consideration of thermal bridges around edges of door sections and because of frame.

Table 7 Design U-Factors for Revolving Doors in Btu/h·ft²·°F

Type	Size (Width × Height)	U-Factor
3-wing	8 × 7 ft	0.79
	10 × 8 ft	0.80
4-wing	7 × 6.5 ft	0.63
	7 × 7.5 ft	0.64
Open*	82 × 84 in.	1.32

*U-factor of open door determined using NFRC *Technical Document* 100-91. It has not been updated to current rating methodology in NFRC *Technical Document* 100 (2014a).

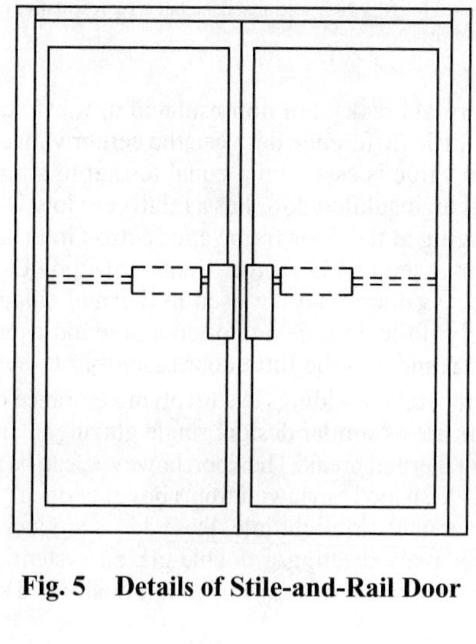

Fig. 5 Details of Stile-and-Rail Door

Table 8 Design U-Factors for Double-Skin Steel Emergency Exit Doors in Btu/h·ft²·°F

Core Insulation		Rough Opening Size	
Thickness, in.	Type	3 ft × 6 ft 8 in.	6 ft × 6 ft 8 in.
1 3/8*	Honeycomb kraft paper	0.57	0.52
	Mineral wool, steel ribs	0.44	0.36
	Polyurethane foam	0.34	0.28
1 3/4*	Honeycomb kraft paper	0.57	0.54
	Mineral wool, steel ribs	0.41	0.33
	Polyurethane foam	0.31	0.26
1 3/8	Honeycomb kraft paper	0.60	0.55
	Mineral wool, steel ribs	0.47	0.39
	Polyurethane foam	0.37	0.31
1 3/4	Honeycomb kraft paper	0.60	0.57
	Mineral wool, steel ribs	0.44	0.37
	Polyurethane foam	0.34	0.30

*With thermal break

Table 9 Design U-Factors for Double-Skin Steel Sectional, Tilt-Up, and Aircraft Hangar Doors in Btu/h·ft²·°F

Insulation		Sectional or Tilt-Up[a]	Aircraft Hangar	
Thickness, in.	Type	9 × 7 ft	72 × 12 ft[b]	240 × 50 ft[c]
1 3/4	Polyurethane, thermally broken	0.28		
1 3/8	Extruded polystyrene, steel ribs	0.39		
	Expanded polystyrene, steel ribs	0.36		
2	Extruded polystyrene, steel ribs	0.33		
	Expanded polystyrene, steel ribs	0.31		
3	Extruded polystyrene, steel ribs	0.28		
	Expanded polystyrene, steel ribs	0.27		
4	Extruded polystyrene, steel ribs	0.25		
	Expanded polystyrene, steel ribs	0.24		
6	Extruded polystyrene, steel ribs	0.21		
	Expanded polystyrene, steel ribs	0.21		
4	Expanded polystyrene		0.25	0.16
	Mineral wool, steel ribs		0.25	0.16
	Extruded polystyrene		0.23	0.15
6	Expanded polystyrene		0.21	0.13
	Mineral wool, steel ribs		0.23	0.13
	Extruded polystyrene		0.20	0.12
—	Uninsulated	1.15[d]	1.10	1.23

Notes:
[a]U-factor determined using NFRC *Technical Document* 100-91. Not updated to current rating methodology in NFRC (2014a) *Technical Document* 100-2014.
[b]Typical size for a small private airplane (single- or twin-engine.)
[c]Typical hangar door for a midsized commercial jet airliner.
[d]U-factor determined for 10 × 10 ft sectional door, but is representative of similar products of different sizes.

include a thermal break). For noninsulated upward-acting doors, there is very little difference between the center value and the total value: the value is essentially equal to that of single glazing. The center of an insulated door has a relatively low U-factor, but thermal bridging at the door frame and section interfaces can affect the door assembly U-factor. Center-of-door U-factors for vehicular access doors may be used in thermal calculations for buildings only if the door design or door size indicates little difference with respect to the total door assembly U-factor.

Many commercial buildings use revolving entrance doors. Most of these doors are of similar design: single glazing in an aluminum frame without thermal break. The door, however, can be in two positions: closed (X-shaped as viewed from above) or open (+-shaped as viewed from above). At nighttime, these doors are locked in the X position, effectively creating a double-glazed system. During the daytime, the door revolves and is often left positioned so that there is only one glazing between the indoors and outdoors (+ position). U-factors are given in Table 7 for both positions.

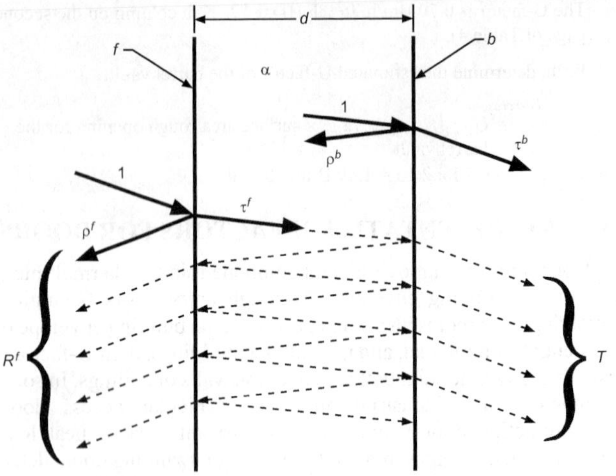

Fig. 6 Optical Properties of a Single Glazing Layer

4. SOLAR HEAT GAIN AND VISIBLE TRANSMITTANCE

Fenestration solar heat gain has two components. First is **directly transmitted solar radiation**. The quantity of radiation entering the fenestration directly is governed by the solar transmittance of the glazing system, and is determined by multiplying the incident irradiance by the glazing area and its solar transmittance. The second component is the inward flowing fraction of **absorbed solar radiation**, radiation that is absorbed in the glazing and framing materials of the fenestration, some of which is subsequently conducted, convected, or radiated to the interior of the building.

Visible transmittance is the solar radiation transmitted through fenestration weighted with respect to the photopic response of the human eye. It physically represents the perceived clearness of the fenestration, and is likely different from the solar transmittance of the same fenestration.

The underlying physics behind solar heat gain and visible transmittance can be very complex, but a rudimentary understanding is required if technologies such as low-e coatings are to be discussed. Accurately calculating the solar heat gain and visible transmittance of a fenestration system, including the effects of angular and spectral dependence, in the presence of multiple glazing and shade layers, is very complex. Refer to ISO *Standard* 15099 or the ASHRAE Handbook Online supplemental features for this chapter for complete details of how to do this calculation. Software such as LBNL WINDOW 7 (LBNL 2016) incorporate these advanced calculations and can be used for more detailed fenestration analysis.

4.1 SOLAR-OPTICAL PROPERTIES OF GLAZING

Optical Properties of Single Glazing Layers

Radiation passing from one medium into another is partly transmitted and partly reflected at the interface between the two media. Further, as this radiation passes through either medium, an additional fraction is absorbed because of the absorptivity of the material. Materials that do not absorb radiation completely, such as air or glass, are classified as being transparent or translucent. Translucent glazings exhibit sufficient light-diffusing properties that images of objects viewed through it are blurred. Opaque glazings transmit no perceptible light.

If solar radiation incident on glazing is considered, the **transmittance** T, **reflectance** R, and **absorptance** $\mathcal{A}$ of the glazing layer contain the effects of multiple reflections between the two interfaces of the layer as well as the effects of absorption during the passage through the layer of each interreflection (Figure 6). For radiation incident on the front side of the glazing, the reflectance is called the **front reflectance** R^f. The **back reflectance** R^b (not shown in Figure 6) is the reflectance of the layer for radiation incident on back side b.

The transmittance, reflectance, and absorptance of a layer are formally defined as the fractions of incident flux that transmit, reflect, and are absorbed by the layer, respectively, including the effects of interreflection. Their sum equals unity, as shown in Equation (5).

$$T + R + \mathcal{A} = 1 \qquad (5)$$

The layer has a thickness d and is characterized by **transmissivity** τ and **reflectivity** ρ of each of the two surfaces and by the **absorptivity** α of the glazing layer of thickness d. In general, τ and ρ are characteristics of the interface between the material and the adjacent medium; they may in principle be different for the two surfaces (e.g., for a coated surface, or where a material layer is adjacent to another material rather than air). Physical arguments, however, dictate that T^f and T^b for the layer be the same (and the f and b superscripts are therefore omitted). R^f and R^b will be different given similar variations in coatings or adjacent materials, and examination of Equation (5) shows that $\mathcal{A}^f$ and $\mathcal{A}^b$ may be different as well. Uncoated glass has the same front and back properties.

Angular Variations. The interfacial properties τ and ρ, and consequently layer properties T, R, and $\mathcal{A}$, also depend on the incident angle θ of the radiation incident on the layer. Figure 7 shows the optical properties of common window glass as a function of incidence angle. This variation of properties is small for incident angles below 40° but becomes significant at larger angles. Chapter 14 provides details on calculating the direction and magnitude of solar flux that is incident on a glazing system.

Rubin (1985) measured broadband transmittance and reflectances for many uncoated (monolithic) glass substrates, including tinted substrates at various thicknesses. These formed the basis for Figure 8, which compares the properties of glasses of different thickness and composition. As the incident angle increases from zero, transmittance decreases, reflectance increases, and absorptance first increases because of the lengthened optical path and then decreases as more incident radiation is reflected. Although the shapes of the property curves are superficially similar, note that both the magnitude of the transmittance at normal incidence and the angle at which the transmittance changes significantly vary with glass type and thickness.

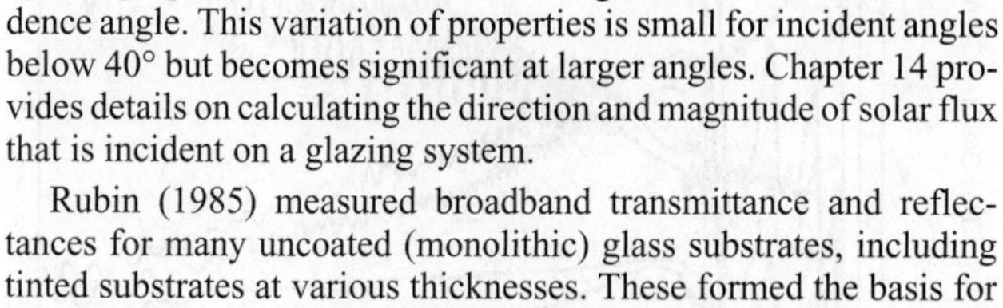

Fig. 7 Transmittance and Reflectance of Glass Plate
(Refractive index $n = 1.55$, thickness $t = 1/8$ in., absorptance $\alpha = 0.0003$ in.)

Wong (2016) normalized the measured solar transmittance (Rubin 1985) for 0.25 in. substrates. Two distinct sets of regressions coefficients appear to be adequate to represent the angular variation for a wide range of clear and tinted substrates. The result of the normalization is shown in Figure 9. These two distinct sets of regression coefficients were incorporated into the then WINDOW4 program (Finlayson et al. 1994) and all subsequent versions of that software. Note that tinted substrates considered here do not have as strong a spectrally selectively behavior as the high-performance tints described in Carmody et al. (2004).

The three curves all have slightly different shapes. For coated glasses or for multiple-pane glazing systems, this difference is more pronounced. One cannot assume that all glazings or glazing systems have a universal angular dependence.

ADOPT (1996) is a two-parameter model that describes the angular-dependent optical properties of glazing systems. It has been validated (Karlsson et al. 2001) against actual measurements (Rubin et al. 1999). Models have been developed from the ADOPT project, and validation of its accuracies at discrete angles of incidence had been reported (Hutchins et al. 2001; Rubin et al. 1998). The Simple Window Model (Arasteh et al. 2009) offers correlations for single-, double-, and triple-glazed systems for use in building energy simulation. The normalized transmittance curve is shown in Figure 10 below.

Angular performance is important when peak gains and annual energy performance are considered. In North America, peak summertime solar gains occur with east- and west-facing vertical

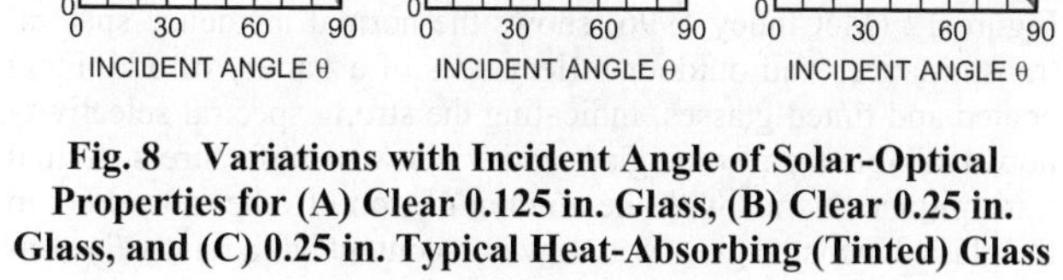

Fig. 8 Variations with Incident Angle of Solar-Optical Properties for (A) Clear 0.125 in. Glass, (B) Clear 0.25 in. Glass, and (C) 0.25 in. Typical Heat-Absorbing (Tinted) Glass

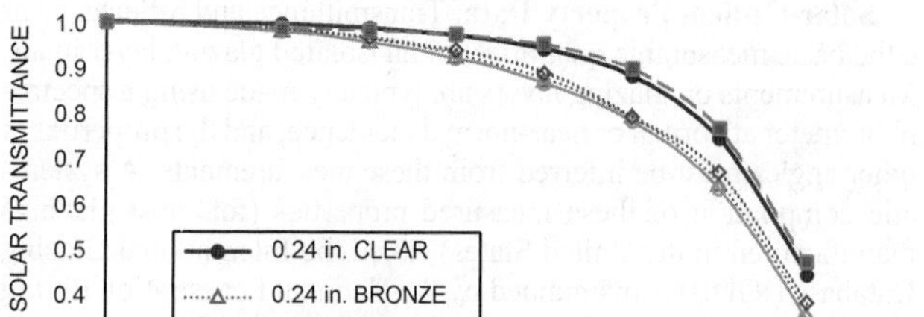

Fig. 9 Normalized Solar Transmittance for Five Common Glass Substrates as Function of Incidence Angle in Degrees

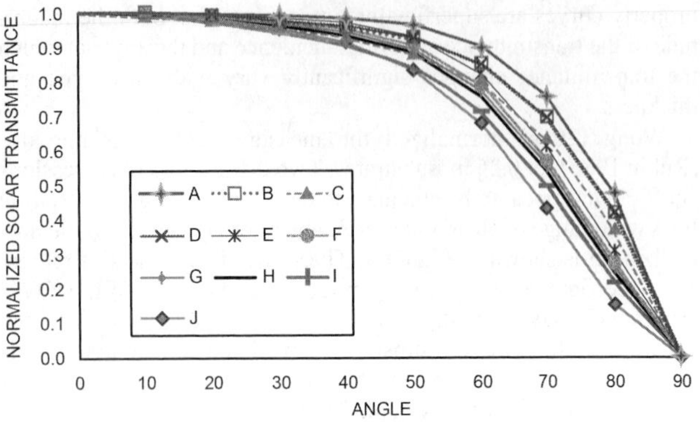

Fig. 10 Normalized Solar Transmittance, as Function of Incidence Angle in Degrees, for 10 Glazing Systems (Single-, Double-. and Triple-Pane) as Developed for Simple Window Model
(Arasteh et al. 2009)

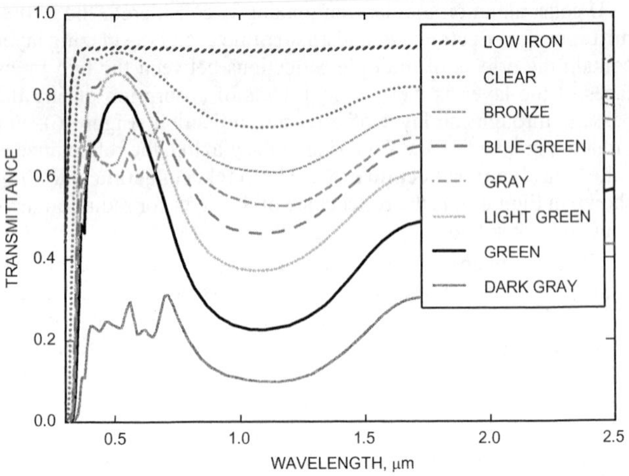

Fig. 11 Spectral Transmittances of Commercially Available Glazings
(Kruis 2015)

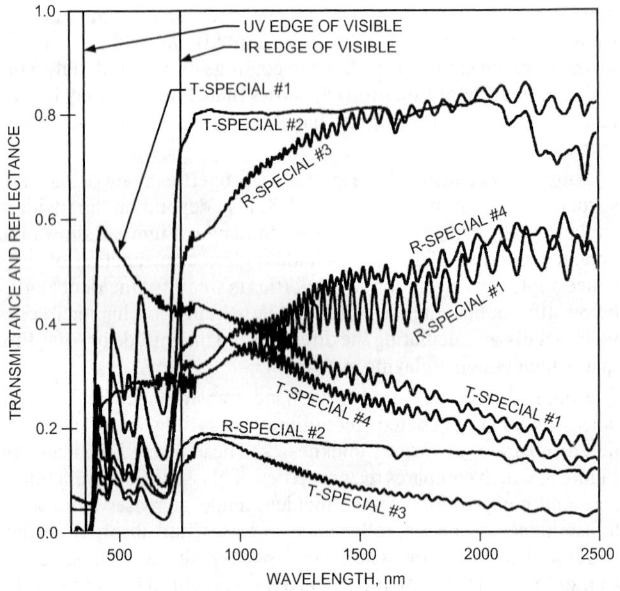

Fig. 12 Spectral Transmittances and Reflectances of Strongly Spectrally Selective Commercially Available Glazings
(McCluney 1996)

glazings at angles of incidence ranging from about 25 to 55°. The peak solar gain for horizontal glazings occurs typically at relatively small angles of incidence (midday sun high in sky in summer). For north- and south-facing vertical glazings, peak summertime solar gains occur at angles of incidence greater than about 40°. Angles of incidence important for annual energy performance calculations range from 5° to over 80° for east- and west-facing vertical and for horizontal glazings. This range is only slightly diminished for south-facing glazings. For north-facing glazings, the direct beam solar gains are small and their angles of incidence range from 62 to 86° (McCluney 1994a).

Spectral Variations. Many glazing systems have optical properties that are *spectrally selective* (i.e., they vary across the electromagnetic spectrum with wavelength λ). Ordinary clear float glass possesses this property, but to a modest degree that is seldom of much concern in load calculations. Tinted and coated glass can exhibit strong spectral selectivity, a desirable property for certain applications, and this effect must be accounted for in solar heat gain determinations.

Figure 11 (McCluney 1993) shows the normal incidence spectral transmittances of several common commercially available glazings. Figure 12 (McCluney 1996) shows the normal incidence spectral transmittances and outdoor reflectances of a variety of additional coated and tinted glasses, indicating the strong spectral selectivity now available from some glass and window manufacturers. Actual transmittance varies with the amount of iron or other absorbers in the glass. Uncoated glass with low iron content has a relatively constant spectral transmittance over the entire solar spectrum.

Solar-Optical Property Data. Transmittance and reflectance ar e the basic measurable quantities for an isolated glazing layer in air. Measurements on glazing layers are typically made using a spectrophotometer at normal or near-normal incidence, and the properties at other angles must be inferred from these measurements. A systematic compilation of these measured properties (for most glazings manufactured in the United States) called the International Glazing Database (IGDB) is maintained by the National Fenestration Rating Council and is available on the Internet at www.nfrc.org or from windows.lbl.gov/materials/IGDB/default.htm (LBNL 2016; NFRC 2014b). For uncoated glazings, layer properties can also be determined from first principles [e.g., McCluney (1994b)].

Advances in modeling complex glazing layers (e.g., screens, woven shades, blinds, some types of drapes) have led to the establishment of the Complex Glazing Database (CGDB 2016). Designed to support the LBNL (2016) WINDOW program and similar software, the CGDB contains detailed information on the angular and spectral properties of such materials, for total and diffuse transmittance and reflectance. The CGDB is being expanded to include products from many international manufacturers. More information may be found in the section on Shading and Fenestration Attachments.

Obtaining the necessary basic information about the solar-optical properties of coated glass requires spectrophotometric measurements. Alternatively, an approximation procedure is described by Finlayson and Arasteh (1993). Coated glazing properties should vary from these estimates by no more than ±20% at 60° incidence (Rubin et al. 1999). It is currently not practical to determine the solar-optical properties of coated glazings from first principles.

Optical Properties of Glazing Systems

The optical properties of glazing systems (multiple glazing layers) are affected by interreflections between layers in addition to the specular and angular properties of the individual layers.

Consequently, the effect of a particular layer on the overall properties may not only depend on its solar-optical properties, but also on its position in the assembly. It is therefore necessary to expand glazing layer considerations to apply to the overall properties of systems and subsystems of glazing layers. The properties of any subsystem can be calculated by using recursion relations (LBNL 2016).

Spectral Averaging of Glazing System Properties. The solar-optical properties of a glazing are the wavelength-integrated (or total) transmittance, reflectance, and absorptance of the glazing to incident solar radiation. If the spectral optical properties $T(\lambda)$, $R(\lambda)$, and $\mathcal{A}(\lambda)$ of the glazing and the spectral irradiance $E(\lambda)$ incident on the glazing are known, the solar optical properties can be calculated using ASTM *Standards* E971, E972, and E1084, as well as NFRC *Technical Document* 300 (NFRC 2014c).

$$X = \frac{\int_{\lambda_{min}}^{\lambda_{max}} E_{STD}(\lambda) X(\lambda) d\lambda}{\int_{\lambda_{min}}^{\lambda_{max}} E_{STD}(\lambda) d\lambda} \tag{6}$$

where

$X(\lambda)$ = $T(\lambda)$, $R(\lambda)$, or $\mathcal{A}(\lambda)$
$E_{STD}(\lambda)$ = standard solar distribution
X = total T, R, or $\mathcal{A}$ to standard solar distribution

For multiple-layer glazing systems, the spectral averaging should in general be applied to the system spectral properties at each angle. Because all glazing layer properties are to some extent both angle and wavelength dependent, and because these equations are nonlinear in the glazing properties, this is the only procedure that is valid in principle.

Many glazings do not have strong spectral selectivity over the solar spectrum, so their spectral optical properties can be considered constant, even if the source spectrum changes substantially. In these cases, the transmitted spectral irradiance can be determined by multiplying the incident irradiance by the solar transmittance obtained with the standard solar distribution. For special combinations of climate and location, it may be desirable to use variant solar spectra as weighting functions, which requires an appropriate spectral solar radiation model (Gueymard 2007). It is still difficult, and seldom necessary, to perform radiative calculations using a detailed, time-dependent solar spectrum and the spectral glazing properties. Such additional calculations might only be justified in the case of glazings with strong spectral selectivity (Gueymard and DuPont 2009).

Angular Averaging of Glazing System Properties. It is relatively simple to account for angular dependence in beam solar radiation, because at a given time the radiation is incident from a single, easily determined direction. However, for diffuse solar and ground-reflected radiation, the situation is more complicated. In principle, energy flow through the glazing should equal the sum of individual energy flows caused by incident radiation from each direction.

Although such calculations can be done for specific sky conditions using detailed sky data or models, the labor involved is worthwhile only for very specific purposes. Usually, a drastically simplifying assumption is made. Both sky and ground radiation are assumed to be **ideally diffuse** (i.e., to have a sky radiance that is independent of direction). Diffuse properties are then determined by integrating over all directions. See the section on Diffuse Radiation under Solar Heat Gain Coefficient for more details. In addition, the spectral dependence is assumed to be the same as for beam solar radiation.

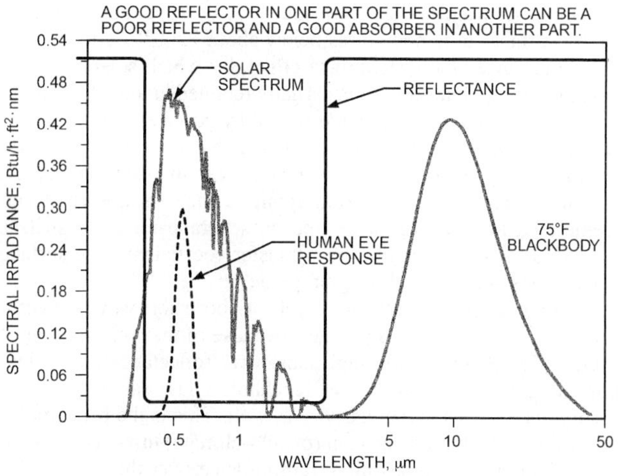

Fig. 13 Solar Spectrum, Human Eye Response Spectrum, Scaled Blackbody Radiation Spectrum, and Idealized Glazing Reflectance Spectrum

$$X_D = \frac{\iint_{hem} X(\theta)\cos\theta \, d\varpi}{\iint_{hem} \cos\theta \, d\varpi} = 2\int_0^{\pi/2} X(\theta)\cos\theta \, d\theta \tag{7}$$

where

$X(\theta)$ = $T(\theta)$, $R(\theta)$, or $\mathcal{A}(\theta)$
ϖ = solid angle of integration
X_D = total T, R, or $\mathcal{A}$ of standard solar distribution

More careful consideration must be given to these quantities for tilted glazings or for direction-dependent shading (e.g., overhangs, venetian blinds) when greater accuracy is desired.

Spectrally Selective Glazing and Glazing Systems. Spectrally selective glazing shows strong changes in its optical properties with variations in wavelength over the spectrum. The spectral range from 0.3 to over 50 μm contains radiation from both the sun and sky incident on fenestration systems. The majority of this radiation is called **short-wave** or **solar** radiation. About 99% of the energy in the solar spectrum is between 0.3 to 3.5 μm. The spectral range from 3.5 to over 50 μm is called **long-wave**, **infrared**, or **thermal** radiation, which contains radiation from the sun and sky, but also from warm bodies both outside and inside the building. In Figure 13, the solar spectrum for an air mass $m = 1.5$ (corresponding to a solar altitude of 41.8°) represents short-wave radiation, with thermal radiation represented by a blackbody source at 75°F. The latter has been scaled up to better compare it with the shape of the solar spectrum. The reflectance spectrum shown is an idealization of typical glazing reflectance. Figure 13 clearly shows the separation of the solar spectrum from the long-wave spectrum characteristic of radiant emission from an indoor pane of a multiple-pane glazing system.

Figure 13 also shows the human eye spectral response (called the human photopic visibility function). To the human eye, the glazing represented in the figure does not appear very reflective. It is also strongly transmitting for solar radiation, including the visible portion. The glazing is, however, nearly opaque to long-wave radiation, demonstrating that visual perception of a material is a poor indicator of its overall spectral characteristics. The glazing system reflectance depicted in Figure 13 is good for admitting solar radiation while preventing the escape of long-wave radiation emitted by surfaces inside the room, a good design for cold sunny days.

Almost all window glass is opaque to long-wave radiation emitted by surfaces at temperatures below about 2200°F. This characteristic produces the **greenhouse effect**, by which solar radiation passing through fenestration is partially retained indoors by the following mechanism. Radiation absorbed by surfaces in the room is emitted as long-wavelength radiation, which cannot escape directly through the glass because of its opaqueness to radiation beyond 4.5 μm. Instead, radiation from room surfaces is absorbed and reemitted to both sides as determined by several parameters, such as the indoor and outdoor film heat transfer coefficients, the surface emissivities, and other glazing properties.

A good long-wave reflector can be a poor short-wave reflector and a good short-wave transmitter. Because of the conservation of energy ($T + R + \mathcal{A} = 1.0$), high long-wave reflectance means low transmittance and absorptance. Kirchhoff's law shows that low absorptance means low emissivity as well. This is the principle of operation of the high-solar-gain (or cold-climate) **low-e coating** on glass. Such a coating has high transmittance over the entire solar spectrum, producing high solar heat gain while being highly reflective to long-wave infrared radiation emitted by the indoor surfaces, reflecting this radiation inward. The term *low-e* refers to a low emissivity over the long-wavelength portion of the spectrum.

Figure 14 shows hypothetical glazing systems with performance tuned to specific climates. In this case, the sharp **reflectance edge** that the ideal high-solar-gain, cold-climate low-e coating exhibits just past the end of the solar spectrum in Figure 13 is shifted closer to the edge of the visible portion of the spectrum, thereby increasing the solar near-infrared (NIR) reflectance of the glazing. This results in a drop in the hot-climate transmittance to the right of the visible portion of the spectrum. The effect is to reflect the near-infrared portion of the solar spectrum outdoors, reducing solar gain, while still admitting visible light in the wavelength region below about 0.8 μm. This low-solar-gain, hot-climate coating also exhibits low emissivity over the long-wave spectrum, and is therefore also properly termed a low-e coating. To distinguish the cold- from the hot-climate version, a glazing with this type of spectral response is often termed **selective low-e**. This is something of a misnomer, because both hot- and cold-climate glazings are spectrally selective. Another term is **high-solar-gain, low-e** glazing system for cold climates, contrasted with **low-solar-gain, low-e** glazing system for hot climates.

The reduced infrared transmittance for the hot-climate glazing is ideally achieved by high reflectance and low absorptance (meaning also low emissivity). It can also be done with high infrared absorptance, if the flow of absorbed solar radiation to the interior of the building can be reduced, introducing a second approach to the construction of a hot-climate, low-solar-gain glazing system. In this case, the outer pane of a multiple-pane glazing system is made to have good visible transmittance but high absorptance over the solar infrared spectrum. To protect the interior of the building from the heat of this absorbed radiation, additional glazings, gas spaces, and cold-climate or low-solar-gain, low-e coatings are added.

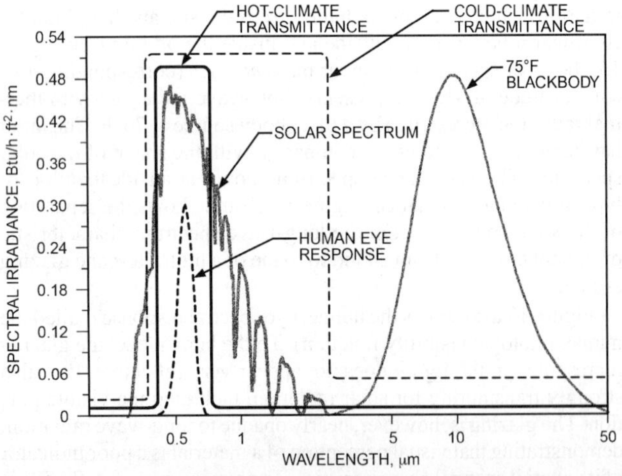

Fig. 14 Demonstration of Two Spectrally Selective Glazing Concepts, Showing Ideal Spectral Transmittances for Glazings Intended for Hot and Cold Climates

By this means, radiation, conduction, and convection of heat from the hot outer pane to the interior ones and to the interior of the building are reduced because of the coating, the gas space, and the additional panes. Such a glazing system for hot climates is insulated primarily *not* to protect the building from conductive heat losses in winter but to protect the interior from solar radiant heat absorbed by the hot outer pane in summer. Many manufacturers offer this kind of nonreflecting, spectrally selective glazing system for commercial and residential buildings having large cooling loads. Figure 14 shows that glazings intended for hot climates should have (1) high transmittance over the visible portion of the spectrum to let daylight in for both illumination and view and (2) low transmittance over all other portions of the spectrum to reduce solar heat gain. In contrast, glazings intended for very cold climates should have high transmittance over the whole solar spectrum, from 0.38 to over 3.5 μm, for maximum admission of solar radiant heat gain and light. In addition, glazings for cold climates should have low transmittance over the long-wavelength portion of the spectrum to block radiant heat emitted by the relatively warm indoor surfaces of buildings, preventing its escape to the outdoors.

Extreme spectral selectivity in glazing systems in the visible portion of the spectrum can produce an unwanted color shift in transmitted light. The color of transmitted light and its color-rendering properties should be considered in the design.

When discussing spectral behavior of fenestration, it is important to understand the relationship between the solar spectrum and the resulting broadband solar-optical properties of glazing systems. A brief introduction is provided here.

Calculation of a glazing system's SHGC (see the section on Solar Heat Gain Coefficient) requires calculating broadband solar transmittance and absorptance. It is influenced by the solar spectrum and the spectral selectivity achieved through the combination of coatings and substrates that make up the glazing system. These two glazing attributes contribute strongly to spectral variations displayed by glazing systems.

To understand any spectral selectivity associated with a glazing layer, it is also necessary to have a good understanding of the spectral distribution of solar radiation. Typically, this is known as a **solar spectrum** or **weighting function,** whose wavelengths range from 300 to 2500 nm. Although there is energy at thermal wavelengths much longer than 2500 nm, glass and polymer layers are opaque to such wavelengths. Of available solar energy, the **direct normal irradiance (DNI)** exhibits the strongest intensity.

Accurate representation of the solar spectrum is essential to calculate broadband solar-optical properties of glazings, which in turn are used to calculate SHGC. It can also be used to compare the solar control characteristics of different glazing layers. Gueymard and Kambezidis (2004) reviewed ways to mathematically describe the atmospheric processes of scattering and absorption, to better consider the effect of atmospheric attenuation of extraterrestrial solar irradiation. This enables more realistic modeling of the DNI spectrum.

Over the past decade, better understanding of atmospheric phenomena that govern the attenuation of extraterrestrial solar radiation has led to updates of reference solar spectra. Because high-quality observational data have become more readily available, many aspects of the scattering and absorption process can now be modeled with increasing confidence. Reference spectra range from the original ASTM *Standard* E891-1989 (RA 1992) spectrum as referred to in the WINDOW4 documentation (Finlayson et al. 1993), through the use of ISO *Standard* 9845 as discussed in Rubin et al. (1998) and finally ASTM *Standard* G173-2003 (RA 2008) in the latest NFRC (2014c) *Technical Document* 300-2014.

Note that the solar spectrum referenced by NFRC *Technical Document* 300 (2014c) is identical to that used by the LBNL (2016) WINDOW program for NFRC certification purposes. At present, the DNI spectrum is used to calculate both broadband transmittance and reflectance.

Increased availability of high-quality observational data means it is now possible to develop mathematical models of the attenuation of solar radiation caused by scattering and absorption by aerosols and gases in the atmosphere. Several updates of the solar spectra have been published as a result of better consideration of atmospheric phenomena that govern the attenuation of extraterrestrial solar radiation.

ASTM *Standards* G173 and G197 are examples of recent standards based on version 2.9.2 of the Simple Model of the Atmospheric Radiative Transfer of Sunshine (SMARTS) atmospheric transmission code for the photovoltaic industry (Gueymard and Kambezidis 2004). *Standards* G173 and G197 use angles of tilt (from the horizontal) of 37 and 20°, respectively, which are different from those used in earlier standards such as ASTM *Standard* E891 and ISO *Standard* 9845.

Standards G173 and G197 are regarded as superior solar spectra because of their ability to consider more atmospheric interactions. They have better resolution (2002 wavelengths of information) than older standards (120 wavelengths).

Development and review of newly created solar spectra are ongoing, but there has not yet been a thorough analysis on the influence played by different spectra on the calculated broadband solar transmittance and reflectance. It has been found that some glazing systems (Gueymard and Kambezidis 2004; Lyons et al. 2010), especially those that exhibit strong spectral selectivity, are more sensitive to the choice of solar spectrum compared with glazings having less selective behavior (Gueymard and du Pont 2009). In addition, there has not been any clear guidance on how trapezoidal integration deals with improved resolutions introduced through the newer *Standards* G173 and G197 spectra (Finlayson et al. 1993; ISO *Standard* 15099; Rubin et al. 1998). Most spectral measurements for coated and monolithic glazing layers only have 111 and 441 records respectively, as required by the NFRC.

4.2 SOLAR HEAT GAIN COEFFICIENT

The concept of the solar heat gain coefficient is best shown for the case of a single glass pane in direct sunlight. If $E_D = E_{DN}\cos\theta$ is the direct solar irradiance incident on the glass, with T the solar transmittance, $\mathcal{A}$ the solar absorptance, and N the **inward-flowing fraction** of the absorbed radiation, then the total solar gain (per unit area) q_b that enters the space because of incident solar radiation is

$$q_b = E_D(T + N\mathcal{A}) \tag{8}$$

in units of energy flux per unit area, Btu/h·ft^2.

The inward-flowing fraction is thermal in origin; it depends on heat transfer properties of the assembly rather than on its optical properties. Absorbed solar radiation, including ultraviolet, visible, and infrared radiation from the sun and sky, is turned into heat inside the absorbing material. In fenestration, the glazing system temperature rises as a result to some approximately equilibrium value at which energy gains from absorbed radiation are balanced by equal losses. Absorbed solar radiation is dissipated through conduction, convection, and radiation. Some heat leaves the building, and the remainder goes indoors, adding to the directly transmitted solar radiation. The magnitude of the inward-flowing fraction depends on the nature of the air boundary layers adjacent to both sides of the glazing, including any gas between the panes of a multiple-pane glazing system (N_i is often used to distinguish the inward-flowing fraction from the outward-flowing fraction, N_o. However, because only the inward-flowing fraction is used here, the subscript i is dropped for clarity).

The quantity in parenthesis in Equation (8) is called the **solar heat gain coefficient (SHGC)**, also known as ***g*-value** or **total solar energy transmittance** in Europe. The total solar gain power per unit area (from direct beam radiation) can therefore be computed using the following equation:

$$q_b = E_D \mathrm{SHGC} \tag{9}$$

The SHGC is needed to determine the solar heat gain through a fenestration's glazing system, and should be included along with U-factor and other instantaneous performance properties in any manufacturer's description of a fenestration's energy performance.

Calculation of Solar Heat Gain Coefficient

Because the optical properties $\mathcal{A}$ and T vary with the angle of incidence and wavelength, the solar heat gain coefficient is also a function of these variables. In the most general way, the solar heat gain power per unit area $q(\theta)$ and the solar heat gain coefficient SHGC(θ,λ) are defined as

$$\begin{aligned} q(\theta) &= \int_{\lambda} E_D(\lambda)[T(\theta,\lambda) + N\mathcal{A}(\theta,\lambda)]d\lambda \\ &= \int_{\lambda} E_D(\lambda)\mathrm{SHGC}(\theta,\lambda)d\lambda \end{aligned} \tag{10}$$

where

$E_D(\lambda)$ = incident solar spectral irradiance
$T(\theta,\lambda)$ = spectral transmittance of glazing system
$\mathcal{A}(\theta,\lambda)$ = total spectral absorptance of glazing system

Here, the angle- and wavelength-dependent solar heat gain coefficient is given by

$$\mathrm{SHGC}(\theta,\lambda) = T(\theta,\lambda) + N\mathcal{A}(\theta,\lambda) \tag{11}$$

Combined with Equation (6), this becomes the wavelength-averaged solar heat gain coefficient:

$$\mathrm{SHGC}(\theta) = \frac{\int_{\lambda_{min}}^{\lambda_{max}} E_D(\lambda)[T(\theta,\lambda) + N(\lambda)\mathcal{A}(\theta,\lambda)]d\lambda}{\int_{\lambda_{min}}^{\lambda_{max}} E_D(\lambda)d\lambda} \tag{12}$$

Equations (10) to (12) indicate the preferred way of determining the solar gain of glazing systems and calculating the solar heat gain coefficient. Computer programs such as LBNL (2016) WINDOW are available to assist in the calculation. In WINDOW, the overall system optical properties at a given incident angle are calculated for each wavelength and the results averaged following Equation (12). The ASTM *Standard* G173 spectrum for direct irradiance is generally used in the averaging. The wavelength-averaged properties (at a given incident angle) can then be used in Equation (9). This approach has been adopted by the National Fenestration Rating Council in NFRC (2014d) *Technical Document* 200 for rating, certifying, and labeling fenestration for energy performance and by the Canadian Standards Association (CSA *Standard* A440.2). The method is valid for strongly spectrally selective (as well as nonselective) glazing systems.

When a glazing system is not strongly spectrally selective, the solar-weighted spectral broadband values of the optical properties can be used, and the integral over wavelength shown in Equations (10) and (12) is not needed. In this case, each glazing layer has its own individual inward-flowing fraction of the absorbed radiation for that layer. With the glazings numbered from the outdoors inward, and k the glazing index, the SHGC is given by

$$\text{SHGC}(\theta) = T^f(\theta) + \sum_{k=1}^{L} N_k \mathcal{A}_k^f(\theta) \quad (13)$$

where

T^f = front transmittance of glazing system

L = number of glazing layers

$\mathcal{A}_k^f$ = absorptance of layer k as part of the composite L-layer system (Finlayson et al 1993; Rubin et al. 1998). This is *different* from the individual, stand-alone absorptance of layer k.

N_k = inward-flowing fraction for layer k

The inward-flowing fractions can be calculated from simplified heat transfer models, using the following equation:

$$N_k = U\sum_{j=k}^{1} R_{j-1,j} \quad (14)$$

where

$\sum R_{j-1,j}$ = sum of resistances from exterior air node up to center of kth glazing layer

Thus, the inward-flowing fraction of layer k is essentially the U-factor of the fenestration times the thermal resistance from the center of the kth layer to the outdoors. In more complicated multilayer glazing systems, it is advisable to perform a detailed heat transfer analysis of the system to determine the values of N_k, because the effective heat transfer coefficients and U depend (weakly) on the glazing layer temperatures and other environmental conditions [e.g., Finlayson et al. (1993), LBNL (2016), Wright (1995a)].

Diffuse Radiation

For incident diffuse radiation, the hemispherical average solar heat gain coefficient must be used. This may be calculated by combining Equation (12) with Equation (7) as follows:

$$\langle \text{SHGC}(\theta)\rangle_D = \frac{\iint_{hem} \text{SHGC}(\theta)\cos\theta\, d\varpi}{\iint_{hem} \cos\theta\, d\varpi} = 2\int_0^{\pi/2} \text{SHGC}(\theta)\cos\theta\, d\theta \quad (15)$$

Equivalently, T and $\mathcal{A}$ in Equation (13) can be hemispherically averaged using Equation (7) so that

$$\langle \text{SHGC}\rangle_D = \langle T^f\rangle_D + \sum_{k=1}^{L} N_k \langle \mathcal{A}_k^f\rangle_D \quad (16)$$

In any case, N_k is unaffected in averaging, because it does not depend on incident angle or wavelength. In contrast, T and $\mathcal{A}$ do depend on wavelength. The spectral distribution of diffuse light is notably different from that of direct radiation. However, under usual clear-sky conditions, the fractional amount of diffuse radiation is relatively low compared to that of its direct counterpart, so that the error introduced by neglecting this difference is low in general.

Solar Gain Through Frame and Other Opaque Elements

Figure 15 shows the mechanisms by which fenestration provides solar gain. It is assumed that all of the directly transmitted solar radiation is absorbed at indoor surfaces, where it is converted to heat. Solar gain also enters a building through opaque elements such as the frame and any mullion or dividers that are part of the fenestration system, because part of the solar energy absorbed at the surfaces of these elements is redirected to the indoor side by heat transfer.

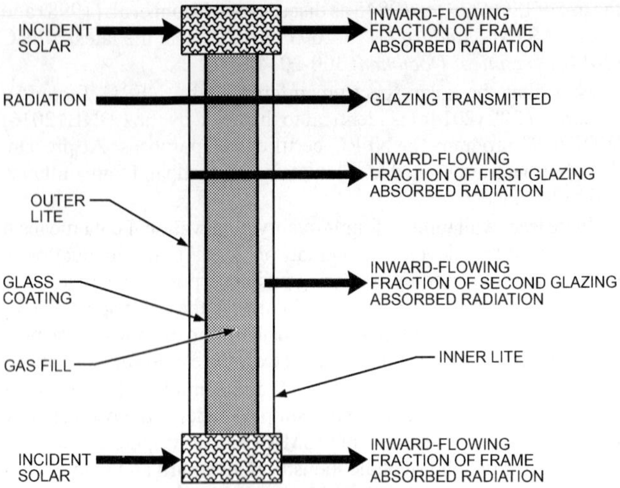

Fig. 15 Components of Solar Radiant Heat Gain with Double-Pane Fenestration, Including Both Frame and Glazing Contributions

The solar heat gain coefficient of the fenestration system can be calculated while accounting for solar gain through the opaque elements by area-weighting the solar heat gain coefficients of the glazing, frame, and M divider elements. Thus,

$$\text{SHGC} = \frac{\text{SHGC}_g A_g + \text{SHGC}_f A_f + \sum_{i=1}^{M} A_i \text{SHGC}_i}{A_g + A_f + \sum_{i=1}^{M} A_i} \quad (17)$$

where SHGC_g, SHGC_f, and SHGC_i are the solar heat gain coefficients of the glazed area, frame, and ith divider, respectively. A_g, A_f, and A_i are the corresponding projected areas.

In some cases, it is useful to have an overall SHGC for the opaque elements only, which is defined by

$$\text{SHGC}_{op} = \frac{\text{SHGC}_f A_f + \sum_{i=1}^{M} A_i \text{SHGC}_i}{A_{op}} \quad (18)$$

where

$$A_{op} = A_f + \sum_{i=1}^{M} A_i$$

SHGC_f can be estimated (ISO *Standard* 15099:2003; Wright 1995b) using

$$\text{SHGC}_f = \alpha_f^s\left(\frac{U_f}{h_f}\right)\left(\frac{A_f}{A_{surf}}\right) \quad (19)$$

where α_f^s is the solar absorptance of the outdoor surface of the frame, U_f is the frame U-factor, and h_f is the heat transfer coefficient (radiative plus convective) between the frame and the outdoor environment. The projected-to-surface area ratio (A_f/A_{surf}) corrects for the fact that U_f is based on projected area A_f, whereas h_f is based on the exposed outdoor frame surface area A_{surf}. SHGC_i can be calculated in the same way:

$$\text{SHGC}_i = \alpha_i^s\left(\frac{U_i}{h_i}\right)\left(\frac{A_i}{A_{surf,i}}\right) \quad (20)$$

The outdoor-side heat transfer coefficients h_f and h_i can be estimated using

$$h_f \text{ or } h_i = h_{co} + 4\sigma e_f t_{out}^3 \quad (21)$$

where h_{co} is the convective heat transfer coefficient between the frame (or divider) surface and the outdoor environment, e_f is the emissivity (long-wave) of the outdoor frame (or divider) surface, t_{out} is the outdoor temperature, and σ is the Stefan-Boltzmann constant.

Solar Heat Gain Coefficient, Visible Transmittance, and Spectrally Averaged Solar-Optical Property Values

Table 10 lists visible transmittance, solar transmittance, front and back reflectance, and solar heat gain coefficients for common glazing and window systems. The ID number for each entry in Table 10 refers to an ID number in Table 4, and the window systems therefore include windows with aluminum or metal frames and windows with other frames that have a lower conductivity (e.g., thermally broken aluminum, wood, vinyl, and fiberglass). As can be seen in Table 10, total window solar heat gain coefficient varies with type of operator, size of fenestration product, and type of frame.

The glazing T_v, T_{sol}, R^f, R^b, and SHGC values have been calculated using manufacturers' spectral data following methods described in Finlayson and Arasteh (1993) and Wright (1995b), and using the 1.5 air mass spectrum found in ASTM *Standard* G173. Glazing values are given for 1/8 and 1/4 in. glass and vary with glass thickness and manufacturer. Values shown are averages and may vary by ±0.05. It is recommended that actual values be determined using detailed spectral data from NFRC (2014b). The front reflectance is that of the unit to the outdoors, and the back reflectance is that to the room side.

Visible transmittances are provided in Table 10 for center-glazing values at normal incidence and for total window values at normal incidence. A rule of thumb is to select a glazing unit whose visible transmittance is 1.5 to 2.0 times greater than its solar heat gain coefficient, especially if daylighting strategies will be used in the building. For maximum light with minimum solar gain, some fenestration products have visible transmittances 2.5 times their SHGCs. For energy calculations on a daylit building, visible transmittance for the entire window should be used. The visible transmittance of a window can be calculated by multiplying the fraction of glazing area by the center-glazing visible transmittance.

Solar heat gain coefficients are provided for center-glazing and total window values. Center-glazing solar heat gain coefficients are given at normal incidence (0°) and at 40°, 50°, 60°, 70°, and 80° incidence angles. For angles other than those listed, straight-line interpolation can be used between the two closest angles for which values are shown. Total window solar heat gain coefficients assume normal incidence. The operable and fixed window sizes in Table 4 were used. To calculate the frame area, frame heights shown in Figure 4 for aluminum and aluminum-clad wood/wood/vinyl were used. The frame area for aluminum windows is 11% for operable size, and 10% for fixed. The frame area for other frames is 20% for the operable size and 12% for fixed. The ratio of projected frame dimension (PFD) to frame surface area is assumed to be 1.0, based on Wright (1995b). In reality, for most frames this ratio is in the range 0.7 to 0.9, because frames cannot simultaneously be flush with both outdoor and indoor glass surfaces. The PFD is defined by the sight line, which is the intersection of the opaque frame (which could be indoors or outdoors) and the vision area.

Frame solar heat gain coefficients used to determine the total window solar heat gain coefficients are calculated according to the section on Solar Gain Through Frame and Other Opaque Elements. Frame U-factors are taken from Table 1. Frame absorptance is assumed to be 0.5 (this is the default NFRC value for commercial frames; however, note that NFRC procedures stipulate 0.3 for residential frames). The outdoor convective film coefficient is 2.64 Btu/h·ft²·°F, corresponding to a wind speed of 6.3 mph. For the aluminum window, the frame solar heat gain coefficient is 0.14 for the operable window and 0.11 for the fixed. For the other frames, the frame solar heat gain coefficient varies between 0.02 and 0.07 for the various lower-conductivity frame types. A frame solar heat gain coefficient of 0.04 is used for the operable window, and 0.03 for the fixed. These values correspond directly to the aluminum-clad wood/reinforced vinyl frames.

Solar transmittances and front and back reflectances are also center-glazing values and are given at normal incidence (0°) and at 40°, 50°, 60°, 70°, and 80° incidence angles. The effective inward-flowing fraction of absorbed radiation for the entire system (not layer-specific values) can be determined from Equation (9) by inserting the solar transmittance and corresponding SHGC.

Example 5. Estimate the overall visible light transmittance for an operable wood casement window with clear, uncoated 1/4 in. double glazing. The operable window has 27% frame area with a wood frame.

Solution: The center-glazing visible light transmittance is 0.78 (see Table 10, glazing ID = 5b, first column). The overall visible light transmittance is

$$T_v = 0.27(0) + 0.73(0.78) = 0.57$$

Airflow Windows

If properly managed, airflow between panes of a double-glazed window can improve fenestration performance. In normal use, a venetian blind is located between the glazing layers. Ventilation air from the room enters the double-glazed cavity, flows over the blind, and can be exhausted from the building or returned through the ducts to the central HVAC system.

These systems can control window heat transfer under many different operating conditions. During sunny winter days, the blind acts as a solar air collector; heat removed by the moving air can be used elsewhere in the building. Furthermore, the window acts as a heat exchanger when sunlit so that the indoor glazing temperature nearly equals the room air temperature and improves thermal comfort (also see the section on Occupant Comfort and Acceptance). In the summer, the window can have a very low solar heat gain coefficient if the blinds are appropriately placed, because the majority of solar gains are removed from the window.

Brandle and Boehm (1982) and Sodergren and Bostrom (1971) give details on airflow windows.

Skylights

Skylight solar heat gain strongly depends on the configuration of the space below or adjacent to (i.e., in sloped applications) the skylight formed by the skylight curb and any associated light well.

Five aspects must be considered: (1) transmittance and absorptance of the skylight unit, (2) transmitted solar flux that reaches the aperture of the light well, (3) whether that aperture is covered by a diffuser, (4) transmitted solar flux that strikes the walls of the light well, and (5) reflectance of the walls of the light well. Data for flat skylights, which may be considered as sloped glazings, are found in Tables 4 and 11.

The following categories of skylights all admit daylight from the roof plane but differ markedly in their design.

Domed Skylights. Solar and total heat gains for domed skylights can be determined by the same procedure used for windows. Table 11 gives SHGCs for plastic domed skylights at normal incidence (Shutrum and Ozisik 1961). Manufacturers' literature has further details. Given the poorly defined incident angle conditions for domed skylights, it is best to use these values without correction for incident angle, together with the correct (angle-dependent) value of incident solar irradiance. Results should be considered approximate. In the absence of other data, these values may also be used to make estimates for skylights on slanted roofs.

Table 10 Visible Transmittance T_v, Solar Heat Gain Coefficient (SHGC), Solar Transmittance T, Front Reflectance R^f, Back Reflectance R^b, and Layer Absorptance $\mathcal{A}_n^f$ for Glazing and Window Systems

Glazing System					Center-of-Glazing Properties							Total Window SHGC at Normal Incidence				Total Window T_v at Normal Incidence			
					Incidence Angles							Aluminum		Other Frames		Aluminum		Other Frames	
ID	Glass Thick., in.		Center Glazing T_v		Normal 0.00	40.00	50.00	60.00	70.00	80.00	Hemis., Diffuse	Operable	Fixed	Operable	Fixed	Operable	Fixed	Operable	Fixed
Uncoated Single Glazing																			
1a	1/8	CLR	0.90	SHGC	0.86	0.84	0.82	0.78	0.67	0.42	0.78	0.78	0.79	0.70	0.76	0.80	0.81	0.72	0.79
				T	0.83	0.82	0.80	0.75	0.64	0.39	0.75								
				R^f	0.08	0.08	0.10	0.14	0.25	0.51	0.14								
				R^b	0.08	0.08	0.10	0.14	0.25	0.51	0.14								
				$\mathcal{A}_1^f$	0.09	0.10	0.10	0.11	0.11	0.11	0.10								
1b	1/4	CLR	0.88	SHGC	0.81	0.80	0.78	0.73	0.62	0.39	0.73	0.74	0.74	0.66	0.72	0.78	0.79	0.70	0.77
				T	0.77	0.75	0.73	0.68	0.58	0.35	0.69								
				R^f	0.07	0.08	0.09	0.13	0.24	0.48	0.13								
				R^b	0.07	0.08	0.09	0.13	0.24	0.48	0.13								
				$\mathcal{A}_1^f$	0.16	0.17	0.18	0.19	0.19	0.17	0.17								
1c	1/8	BRZ	0.68	SHGC	0.73	0.71	0.68	0.64	0.55	0.34	0.65	0.67	0.67	0.59	0.65	0.61	0.61	0.54	0.60
				T	0.65	0.62	0.59	0.55	0.46	0.27	0.56								
				R^f	0.06	0.07	0.08	0.12	0.22	0.45	0.12								
				R^b	0.06	0.07	0.08	0.12	0.22	0.45	0.12								
				$\mathcal{A}_1^f$	0.29	0.31	0.32	0.33	0.33	0.29	0.31								
1d	1/4	BRZ	0.54	SHGC	0.62	0.59	0.57	0.53	0.45	0.29	0.54	0.57	0.57	0.50	0.55	0.48	0.49	0.43	0.48
				T	0.49	0.45	0.43	0.39	0.32	0.18	0.41								
				R^f	0.05	0.06	0.07	0.11	0.19	0.42	0.10								
				R^b	0.05	0.68	0.66	0.62	0.53	0.33	0.10								
				$\mathcal{A}_1^f$	0.46	0.49	0.50	0.51	0.49	0.41	0.48								
1e	1/8	GRN	0.82	SHGC	0.70	0.68	0.66	0.62	0.53	0.33	0.63	0.64	0.64	0.57	0.62	0.73	0.74	0.66	0.72
				T	0.61	0.58	0.56	0.52	0.43	0.25	0.53								
				R^f	0.06	0.07	0.08	0.12	0.21	0.45	0.11								
				R^b	0.06	0.07	0.08	0.12	0.21	0.45	0.11								
				$\mathcal{A}_1^f$	0.33	0.35	0.36	0.37	0.36	0.31	0.35								
1f	1/4	GRN	0.76	SHGC	0.60	0.58	0.56	0.52	0.45	0.29	0.54	0.55	0.55	0.49	0.53	0.68	0.68	0.61	0.67
				T	0.47	0.44	0.42	0.38	0.32	0.18	0.40								
				R^f	0.05	0.06	0.07	0.11	0.20	0.42	0.10								
				R^b	0.05	0.06	0.07	0.11	0.20	0.42	0.10								
				$\mathcal{A}_1^f$	0.47	0.50	0.51	0.51	0.49	0.40	0.49								
1g	1/8	GRY	0.62	SHGC	0.70	0.68	0.66	0.61	0.53	0.33	0.63	0.64	0.64	0.57	0.62	0.55	0.56	0.50	0.55
				T	0.61	0.58	0.56	0.51	0.42	0.24	0.53								
				R^f	0.06	0.07	0.08	0.12	0.21	0.44	0.11								
				R^b	0.06	0.07	0.08	0.12	0.21	0.44	0.11								
				$\mathcal{A}_1^f$	0.33	0.36	0.37	0.37	0.37	0.32	0.35								
1h	1/4	GRY	0.46	SHGC	0.59	0.57	0.55	0.51	0.44	0.28	0.52	0.54	0.54	0.48	0.52	0.41	0.41	0.37	0.40
				T	0.46	0.42	0.40	0.36	0.29	0.16	0.38								
				R^f	0.05	0.06	0.07	0.10	0.19	0.41	0.10								
				R^b	0.05	0.06	0.07	0.10	0.19	0.41	0.10								
				$\mathcal{A}_1^f$	0.49	0.52	0.54	0.54	0.52	0.43	0.51								
1i	1/4	BLUGRN	0.75	SHGC	0.62	0.59	0.57	0.54	0.46	0.30	0.55	0.57	0.57	0.50	0.55	0.67	0.68	0.60	0.66
				T	0.49	0.46	0.44	0.40	0.33	0.19	0.42								
				R^f	0.06	0.06	0.07	0.11	0.20	0.43	0.11								
				R^b	0.06	0.06	0.07	0.11	0.20	0.43	0.11								
				$\mathcal{A}_1^f$	0.45	0.48	0.49	0.49	0.47	0.38	0.48								
Reflective Single Glazing																			
1j	1/4	SS on CLR 8%	0.08	SHGC	0.19	0.19	0.19	0.18	0.16	0.10	0.18	0.18	0.18	0.16	0.17	0.07	0.07	0.06	0.07
				T	0.06	0.06	0.06	0.05	0.04	0.03	0.05								
				R^f	0.33	0.34	0.35	0.37	0.44	0.61	0.36								
				R^b	0.50	0.50	0.51	0.53	0.58	0.71	0.52								
				$\mathcal{A}_1^f$	0.61	0.61	0.60	0.58	0.52	0.37	0.57								
1k	1/4	SS on CLR 14%	0.14	SHGC	0.25	0.25	0.24	0.23	0.20	0.13	0.23	0.24	0.24	0.21	0.22	0.12	0.13	0.11	0.12
				T	0.11	0.10	0.10	0.09	0.07	0.04	0.09								
				R^f	0.26	0.27	0.28	0.31	0.38	0.57	0.30								
				R^b	0.44	0.44	0.45	0.47	0.52	0.67	0.46								
				$\mathcal{A}_1^f$	0.63	0.63	0.62	0.60	0.55	0.39	0.60								

Table 10 Visible Transmittance T_v, Solar Heat Gain Coefficient (SHGC), Solar Transmittance T, Front Reflectance R^f, Back Reflectance R^b, and Layer Absorptance $\mathcal{A}_n^f$ for Glazing and Window Systems (*Continued*)

					Center-of-Glazing Properties							Total Window SHGC at Normal Incidence				Total Window T_v at Normal Incidence			
	Glazing System				Incidence Angles							Aluminum		Other Frames		Aluminum		Other Frames	
ID	Glass Thick., in.		Center Glazing T_v		Normal 0.00	40.00	50.00	60.00	70.00	80.00	Hemis., Diffuse	Operable	Fixed	Operable	Fixed	Operable	Fixed	Operable	Fixed
1l	1/4	SS on CLR 20%	0.20	SHGC	0.31	0.30	0.30	0.28	0.24	0.16	0.28	0.29	0.29	0.26	0.28	0.18	0.18	0.16	0.18
				T	0.15	0.15	0.14	0.13	0.11	0.06	0.13								
				R^f	0.21	0.22	0.23	0.26	0.34	0.54	0.25								
				R^b	0.38	0.38	0.39	0.41	0.48	0.64	0.41								
				$\mathcal{A}_1^f$	0.64	0.64	0.63	0.61	0.56	0.40	0.60								
1m	1/4	SS on GRN 14%	0.12	SHGC	0.25	0.25	0.24	0.23	0.21	0.14	0.23	0.24	0.24	0.21	0.22	0.11	0.11	0.10	0.11
				T	0.06	0.06	0.06	0.06	0.04	0.03	0.06								
				R^f	0.14	0.14	0.16	0.19	0.27	0.49	0.18								
				R^b	0.44	0.44	0.45	0.47	0.52	0.67	0.46								
				$\mathcal{A}_1^f$	0.80	0.80	0.78	0.76	0.68	0.48	0.75								
1n	1/4	TI on CLR 20%	0.20	SHGC	0.29	0.29	0.28	0.27	0.23	0.15	0.27	0.27	0.27	0.24	0.26	0.18	0.18	0.16	0.18
				T	0.14	0.13	0.13	0.12	0.09	0.06	0.12								
				R^f	0.22	0.22	0.24	0.26	0.34	0.54	0.26								
				R^b	0.40	0.40	0.42	0.44	0.50	0.65	0.43								
				$\mathcal{A}_1^f$	0.65	0.65	0.64	0.62	0.57	0.40	0.62								
1o	1/4	TI on CLR 30%	0.30	SHGC	0.39	0.38	0.37	0.35	0.30	0.20	0.35	0.36	0.36	0.32	0.35	0.27	0.27	0.24	0.26
				T	0.23	0.22	0.21	0.19	0.16	0.09	0.20								
				R^f	0.15	0.15	0.17	0.20	0.28	0.50	0.19								
				R^b	0.32	0.33	0.34	0.36	0.43	0.60	0.36								
				$\mathcal{A}_1^f$	0.63	0.65	0.64	0.62	0.57	0.40	0.62								
Uncoated Double Glazing																			
5a	1/8	CLR CLR	0.81	SHGC	0.76	0.74	0.71	0.64	0.50	0.26	0.66	0.69	0.70	0.62	0.67	0.72	0.73	0.65	0.71
				T	0.70	0.68	0.65	0.58	0.44	0.21	0.60								
				R^f	0.13	0.14	0.16	0.23	0.36	0.61	0.21								
				R^b	0.13	0.14	0.16	0.23	0.36	0.61	0.21								
				$\mathcal{A}_1^f$	0.10	0.11	0.11	0.12	0.13	0.13	0.11								
				$\mathcal{A}_2^f$	0.07	0.08	0.08	0.08	0.07	0.05	0.07								
5b	1/4	CLR CLR	0.78	SHGC	0.70	0.67	0.64	0.58	0.45	0.23	0.60	0.64	0.64	0.57	0.62	0.69	0.70	0.62	0.69
				T	0.61	0.58	0.55	0.48	0.36	0.17	0.51								
				R^f	0.11	0.12	0.15	0.20	0.33	0.57	0.18								
				R^b	0.11	0.12	0.15	0.20	0.33	0.57	0.18								
				$\mathcal{A}_1^f$	0.17	0.18	0.19	0.20	0.21	0.20	0.19								
				$\mathcal{A}_2^f$	0.11	0.12	0.12	0.12	0.10	0.07	0.11								
5c	1/8	BRZ CLR	0.62	SHGC	0.62	0.60	0.57	0.51	0.39	0.20	0.53	0.57	0.57	0.50	0.55	0.55	0.56	0.50	0.55
				T	0.55	0.51	0.48	0.42	0.31	0.14	0.45								
				R^f	0.09	0.10	0.12	0.16	0.27	0.49	0.15								
				R^b	0.12	0.13	0.15	0.21	0.35	0.59	0.19								
				$\mathcal{A}_1^f$	0.30	0.33	0.34	0.36	0.37	0.34	0.33								
				$\mathcal{A}_2^f$	0.06	0.06	0.06	0.06	0.05	0.03	0.06								
5d	1/4	BRZ CLR	0.47	SHGC	0.49	0.46	0.44	0.39	0.31	0.17	0.41	0.45	0.45	0.40	0.43	0.42	0.42	0.38	0.41
				T	0.38	0.35	0.32	0.27	0.20	0.08	0.30								
				R^f	0.07	0.08	0.09	0.13	0.22	0.44	0.12								
				R^b	0.10	0.11	0.13	0.19	0.31	0.55	0.17								
				$\mathcal{A}_1^f$	0.48	0.51	0.52	0.53	0.53	0.45	0.50								
				$\mathcal{A}_2^f$	0.07	0.07	0.07	0.07	0.06	0.04	0.07								
5e	1/8	GRN CLR	0.75	SHGC	0.60	0.57	0.54	0.49	0.38	0.20	0.51	0.55	0.55	0.49	0.53	0.67	0.68	0.60	0.66
				T	0.52	0.49	0.46	0.40	0.30	0.13	0.43								
				R^f	0.09	0.10	0.12	0.16	0.27	0.50	0.15								
				R^b	0.12	0.13	0.15	0.21	0.35	0.60	0.19								
				$\mathcal{A}_1^f$	0.34	0.37	0.38	0.39	0.39	0.35	0.37								
				$\mathcal{A}_2^f$	0.05	0.05	0.05	0.04	0.04	0.03	0.04								
5f	1/4	GRN CLR	0.68	SHGC	0.49	0.46	0.44	0.39	0.31	0.17	0.41	0.45	0.45	0.40	0.43	0.61	0.61	0.54	0.60
				T	0.39	0.36	0.33	0.29	0.21	0.09	0.31								
				R^f	0.08	0.08	0.10	0.14	0.23	0.45	0.13								
				R^b	0.10	0.11	0.13	0.19	0.31	0.55	0.17								
				$\mathcal{A}_1^f$	0.49	0.51	0.05	0.53	0.52	0.43	0.50								
				$\mathcal{A}_2^f$	0.05	0.05	0.05	0.05	0.04	0.03	0.05								

Table 10 Visible Transmittance T_v, Solar Heat Gain Coefficient (SHGC), Solar Transmittance T, Front Reflectance R^f, Back Reflectance R^b, and Layer Absorptance $\mathcal{A}_n^f$ for Glazing and Window Systems (*Continued*)

Glazing System					Center-of-Glazing Properties: Incidence Angles							Total Window SHGC at Normal Incidence: Aluminum		Total Window SHGC at Normal Incidence: Other Frames		Total Window T_v at Normal Incidence: Aluminum		Total Window T_v at Normal Incidence: Other Frames	
ID	Glass Thick., in.		Center Glazing T_v		Normal 0.00	40.00	50.00	60.00	70.00	80.00	Hemis., Diffuse	Operable	Fixed	Operable	Fixed	Operable	Fixed	Operable	Fixed
5g	1/8	GRY CLR	0.56	SHGC	0.60	0.57	0.54	0.48	0.37	0.20	0.51	0.55	0.55	0.49	0.53	0.50	0.50	0.45	0.49
				T	0.51	0.48	0.45	0.39	0.29	0.12	0.42								
				R^f	0.09	0.09	0.11	0.16	0.26	0.48	0.14								
				R^b	0.12	0.13	0.15	0.21	0.34	0.59	0.19								
				$\mathcal{A}_1^f$	0.34	0.37	0.39	0.40	0.41	0.37	0.37								
				$\mathcal{A}_2^f$	0.05	0.06	0.06	0.05	0.05	0.03	0.05								
5h	1/4	GRY CLR	0.41	SHGC	0.47	0.44	0.42	0.37	0.29	0.16	0.39	0.43	0.43	0.38	0.42	0.36	0.37	0.33	0.36
				T	0.36	0.32	0.29	0.25	0.18	0.07	0.28								
				R^f	0.07	0.07	0.08	0.12	0.21	0.43	0.12								
				R^b	0.10	0.11	0.13	0.18	0.31	0.55	0.17								
				$\mathcal{A}_1^f$	0.51	0.54	0.56	0.57	0.56	0.47	0.53								
				$\mathcal{A}_2^f$	0.07	0.07	0.07	0.06	0.05	0.03	0.06								
5i	1/4	BLUGRN CLR	0.67	SHGC	0.50	0.47	0.45	0.40	0.32	0.17	0.43	0.46	0.46	0.41	0.44	0.60	0.60	0.54	0.59
				T	0.40	0.37	0.34	0.30	0.22	0.10	0.32								
				R^f	0.08	0.08	0.10	0.14	0.24	0.46	0.13								
				R^b	0.11	0.11	0.14	0.19	0.31	0.55	0.17								
				$\mathcal{A}_1^f$	0.47	0.49	0.50	0.51	0.50	0.42	0.48								
				$\mathcal{A}_2^f$	0.06	0.06	0.06	0.05	0.04	0.03	0.05								
5j	1/4	HI-P GRN CLR	0.59	SHGC	0.39	0.37	0.35	0.31	0.25	0.14	0.33	0.36	0.36	0.32	0.35	0.53	0.53	0.47	0.52
				T	0.28	0.26	0.24	0.20	0.15	0.06	0.22								
				R^f	0.06	0.07	0.08	0.12	0.21	0.43	0.11								
				R^b	0.10	0.11	0.13	0.19	0.31	0.55	0.17								
				$\mathcal{A}_1^f$	0.62	0.65	0.65	0.65	0.62	0.50	0.63								
				$\mathcal{A}_2^f$	0.03	0.03	0.03	0.03	0.02	0.01	0.03								
Reflective Double Glazing																			
5k	1/4	SS on CLR 8%, CLR	0.07	SHGC	0.13	0.12	0.12	0.11	0.10	0.06	0.11	0.13	0.13	0.11	0.12	0.06	0.06	0.06	0.06
				T	0.05	0.05	0.04	0.04	0.03	0.01	0.04								
				R^f	0.33	0.34	0.35	0.37	0.44	0.61	0.37								
				R^b	0.38	0.37	0.38	0.40	0.46	0.61	0.40								
				$\mathcal{A}_1^f$	0.61	0.61	0.60	0.58	0.53	0.37	0.56								
				$\mathcal{A}_2^f$	0.01	0.01	0.01	0.01	0.01	0.01	0.01								
5l	1/4	SS on CLR 14%, CLR	0.13	SHGC	0.17	0.17	0.16	0.15	0.13	0.08	0.16	0.17	0.16	0.14	0.15	0.12	0.12	0.10	0.11
				T	0.08	0.08	0.08	0.07	0.05	0.02	0.07								
				R^f	0.26	0.27	0.28	0.31	0.38	0.57	0.30								
				R^b	0.34	0.33	0.34	0.37	0.44	0.60	0.36								
				$\mathcal{A}_1^f$	0.63	0.64	0.64	0.63	0.61	0.56	0.60								
				$\mathcal{A}_2^f$	0.02	0.02	0.02	0.02	0.02	0.02	0.02								
5m	1/4	SS on CLR 20%, CLR	0.18	SHGC	0.22	0.21	0.21	0.19	0.16	0.09	0.20	0.21	0.21	0.18	0.20	0.16	0.16	0.14	0.16
				T	0.12	0.11	0.11	0.09	0.07	0.03	0.10								
				R^f	0.21	0.22	0.23	0.26	0.34	0.54	0.25								
				R^b	0.30	0.30	0.31	0.34	0.41	0.59	0.33								
				$\mathcal{A}_1^f$	0.64	0.64	0.63	0.62	0.57	0.41	0.61								
				$\mathcal{A}_2^f$	0.03	0.03	0.03	0.03	0.02	0.02	0.03								
5n	1/4	SS on GRN 14%, CLR	0.11	SHGC	0.16	0.16	0.15	0.14	0.12	0.08	0.14	0.16	0.16	0.14	0.14	0.10	0.10	0.09	0.10
				T	0.05	0.05	0.05	0.04	0.03	0.01	0.04								
				R^f	0.14	0.14	0.16	0.19	0.27	0.49	0.18								
				R^b	0.34	0.33	0.34	0.37	0.44	0.60	0.36								
				$\mathcal{A}_1^f$	0.80	0.80	0.79	0.76	0.69	0.49	0.76								
				$\mathcal{A}_2^f$	0.01	0.01	0.01	0.01	0.01	0.01	0.01								
5o	1/4	TI on CLR 20%, CLR	0.18	SHGC	0.21	0.20	0.19	0.18	0.15	0.09	0.18	0.20	0.20	0.18	0.19	0.16	0.16	0.14	0.16
				T	0.11	0.10	0.10	0.08	0.06	0.03	0.09								
				R^f	0.22	0.22	0.24	0.27	0.34	0.54	0.26								
				R^b	0.32	0.31	0.32	0.35	0.42	0.59	0.35								
				$\mathcal{A}_1^f$	0.65	0.66	0.65	0.63	0.58	0.41	0.62								
				$\mathcal{A}_2^f$	0.02	0.02	0.02	0.02	0.02	0.01	0.02								
5p	1/4	TI on CLR 30%, CLR	0.27	SHGC	0.29	0.28	0.27	0.25	0.20	0.12	0.25	0.27	0.27	0.24	0.26	0.24	0.24	0.22	0.24
				T	0.18	0.17	0.16	0.14	0.10	0.05	0.15								
				R^f	0.15	0.15	0.17	0.20	0.29	0.51	0.19								
				R^b	0.27	0.27	0.28	0.31	0.40	0.58	0.31								
				$\mathcal{A}_1^f$	0.64	0.64	0.63	0.62	0.58	0.43	0.61								
				$\mathcal{A}_2^f$	0.04	0.04	0.04	0.04	0.03	0.02	0.04								

Table 10 Visible Transmittance T_v, Solar Heat Gain Coefficient (SHGC), Solar Transmittance T, Front Reflectance R^f, Back Reflectance R^b, and Layer Absorptance $\mathcal{A}_n^f$ for Glazing and Window Systems (*Continued*)

	Glazing System				Center-of-Glazing Properties							Total Window SHGC at Normal Incidence				Total Window T_v at Normal Incidence			
					Incidence Angles							Aluminum		Other Frames		Aluminum		Other Frames	
ID	Glass Thick., in.		Center Glazing T_v		Normal 0.00	40.00	50.00	60.00	70.00	80.00	Hemis., Diffuse	Operable	Fixed	Operable	Fixed	Operable	Fixed	Operable	Fixed
Low-e Double Glazing, e = 0.2 on surface 2																			
17a	1/8	LE CLR	0.76	SHGC	0.65	0.64	0.61	0.56	0.43	0.23	0.57	0.59	0.60	0.53	0.58	0.68	0.68	0.61	0.67
				T	0.59	0.56	0.54	0.48	0.36	0.18	0.50								
				R^f	0.15	0.16	0.18	0.24	0.37	0.61	0.22								
				R^b	0.17	0.18	0.20	0.26	0.38	0.61	0.24								
				$\mathcal{A}_1^f$	0.20	0.21	0.21	0.21	0.20	0.16	0.20								
				$\mathcal{A}_2^f$	0.07	0.07	0.08	0.08	0.07	0.05	0.07								
17b	1/4	LE CLR	0.73	SHGC	0.60	0.59	0.57	0.51	0.40	0.21	0.53	0.55	0.55	0.49	0.53	0.65	0.66	0.58	0.64
				T	0.51	0.48	0.46	0.41	0.30	0.14	0.43								
				R^f	0.14	0.15	0.17	0.22	0.35	0.59	0.21								
				R^b	0.15	0.16	0.18	0.23	0.35	0.57	0.22								
				$\mathcal{A}_1^f$	0.26	0.26	0.26	0.26	0.25	0.19	0.25								
				$\mathcal{A}_2^f$	0.10	0.11	0.11	0.11	0.10	0.07	0.10								
Low-e Double Glazing, e = 0.2 on surface 3																			
17c	1/8	CLR LE	0.76	SHGC	0.70	0.68	0.65	0.59	0.46	0.24	0.61	0.64	0.64	0.57	0.62	0.68	0.68	0.1	0.67
				T	0.59	0.56	0.54	0.48	0.36	0.18	0.50								
				R^f	0.17	0.18	0.20	0.26	0.38	0.61	0.24								
				R^b	0.15	0.16	0.18	0.24	0.37	0.61	0.22								
				$\mathcal{A}_1^f$	0.11	0.12	0.13	0.13	0.14	0.15	0.12								
				$\mathcal{A}_2^f$	0.14	0.14	0.14	0.13	0.11	0.07	0.13								
17d	1/4	CLR LE	0.73	SHGC	0.65	0.63	0.60	0.54	0.42	0.21	0.56	0.59	0.60	0.53	0.58	0.65	0.66	0.58	0.64
				T	0.51	0.48	0.46	0.41	0.30	0.14	0.43								
				R^f	0.15	0.16	0.18	0.23	0.35	0.57	0.22								
				R^b	0.14	0.15	0.17	0.22	0.35	0.59	0.21								
				$\mathcal{A}_1^f$	0.17	0.19	0.20	0.21	0.22	0.22	0.19								
				$\mathcal{A}_2^f$	0.17	0.17	0.17	0.15	0.13	0.07	0.16								
17e	1/8	BRZ LE	0.58	SHGC	0.57	0.54	0.51	0.46	0.35	0.18	0.48	0.52	0.52	0.46	0.51	0.52	0.52	0.46	0.51
				T	0.46	0.43	0.41	0.36	0.26	0.12	0.38								
				R^f	0.12	0.12	0.14	0.18	0.28	0.50	0.17								
				R^b	0.14	0.15	0.17	0.23	0.35	0.60	0.21								
				$\mathcal{A}_1^f$	0.31	0.34	0.35	0.37	0.38	0.35	0.34								
				$\mathcal{A}_2^f$	0.11	0.11	0.10	0.10	0.08	0.04	0.10								
17f	1/4	BRZ LE	0.45	SHGC	0.45	0.42	0.40	0.35	0.27	0.14	0.38	0.42	0.42	0.37	0.40	0.40	0.41	0.36	0.40
				T	0.33	0.30	0.28	0.24	0.17	0.07	0.26								
				R^f	0.09	0.09	0.10	0.14	0.23	0.44	0.13								
				R^b	0.13	0.14	0.16	0.21	0.34	0.58	0.20								
				$\mathcal{A}_1^f$	0.48	0.51	0.52	0.54	0.53	0.45	0.50								
				$\mathcal{A}_2^f$	0.11	0.11	0.10	0.09	0.07	0.04	0.09								
17g	1/8	GRN LE	0.70	SHGC	0.55	0.52	0.50	0.44	0.34	0.17	0.46	0.50	0.51	0.45	0.49	0.62	0.63	0.56	0.62
				T	0.44	0.41	0.38	0.33	0.24	0.11	0.36								
				R^f	0.11	0.11	0.13	0.17	0.27	0.48	0.16								
				R^b	0.14	0.15	0.17	0.23	0.35	0.60	0.21								
				$\mathcal{A}_1^f$	0.35	0.38	0.39	0.41	0.42	0.37	0.38								
				$\mathcal{A}_2^f$	0.11	0.10	0.10	0.09	0.07	0.04	0.09								
17h	1/4	GRN LE	0.61	SHGC	0.41	0.39	0.36	0.32	0.25	0.13	0.34	0.38	0.38	0.34	0.36	0.54	0.55	0.49	0.54
				T	0.29	0.26	0.24	0.21	0.15	0.06	0.23								
				R^f	0.08	0.08	0.09	0.13	0.22	0.43	0.13								
				R^b	0.13	0.14	0.16	0.21	0.34	0.58	0.20								
				$\mathcal{A}_1^f$	0.53	0.57	0.58	0.59	0.58	0.48	0.56								
				$\mathcal{A}_2^f$	0.10	0.09	0.09	0.08	0.06	0.03	0.08								
17i	1/8	GRY LE	0.53	SHGC	0.54	0.51	0.49	0.44	0.33	0.17	0.46	0.50	0.50	0.44	0.48	0.47	0.48	0.42	0.47
				T	0.43	0.40	0.38	0.33	0.24	0.11	0.35								
				R^f	0.11	0.11	0.13	0.17	0.27	0.48	0.16								
				R^b	0.14	0.15	0.17	0.22	0.35	0.60	0.21								
				$\mathcal{A}_1^f$	0.36	0.39	0.40	0.42	0.42	0.38	0.39								
				$\mathcal{A}_2^f$	0.10	0.10	0.10	0.09	0.07	0.04	0.09								

Table 10 Visible Transmittance T_v, Solar Heat Gain Coefficient (SHGC), Solar Transmittance T, Front Reflectance R^f, Back Reflectance R^b, and Layer Absorptance $\mathcal{A}_n^f$ for Glazing and Window Systems (*Continued*)

ID	Glass Thick., in.	Glazing System	Center Glazing T_v		Center-of-Glazing Properties: Incidence Angles Normal 0.00	40.00	50.00	60.00	70.00	80.00	Hemis., Diffuse	Total Window SHGC at Normal Incidence: Aluminum Operable	Aluminum Fixed	Other Frames Operable	Other Frames Fixed	Total Window T_v at Normal Incidence: Aluminum Operable	Aluminum Fixed	Other Frames Operable	Other Frames Fixed
17j	1/4	GRY LE	0.37	SHGC	0.39	0.37	0.35	0.31	0.24	0.13	0.33	0.36	0.36	0.32	0.35	0.33	0.33	0.30	0.33
				T	0.27	0.25	0.23	0.20	0.14	0.06	0.21								
				R^f	0.09	0.09	0.11	0.14	0.23	0.44	0.14								
				R^b	0.13	0.14	0.16	0.22	0.34	0.58	0.20								
				$\mathcal{A}_1^f$	0.55	0.58	0.59	0.59	0.58	0.48	0.56								
				$\mathcal{A}_2^f$	0.09	0.09	0.08	0.07	0.06	0.03	0.08								
17k	1/4	BLUGRN LE	0.62	SHGC	0.45	0.42	0.40	0.35	0.27	0.14	0.37	0.42	0.42	0.37	0.40	0.55	0.56	0.50	0.55
				T	0.32	0.29	0.27	0.23	0.17	0.07	0.26								
				R^f	0.09	0.09	0.10	0.14	0.23	0.44	0.13								
				R^b	0.13	0.14	0.16	0.21	0.34	0.58	0.20								
				$\mathcal{A}_1^f$	0.48	0.51	0.53	0.54	0.54	0.45	0.51								
				$\mathcal{A}_2^f$	0.11	0.10	0.10	0.09	0.07	0.03	0.09								
17l	1/4	HI-P GRN LE	0.55	0.241	0.34	0.31	0.30	0.26	0.20	0.11	0.28	0.32	0.32	0.28	0.30	0.49	0.50	0.44	0.48
				T	0.22	0.19	0.18	0.15	0.10	0.04	0.17								
				R^f	0.07	0.07	0.08	0.11	0.20	0.41	0.11								
				R^b	0.13	0.14	0.16	0.21	0.33	0.58	0.20								
				$\mathcal{A}_1^f$	0.64	0.67	0.68	0.68	0.66	0.53	0.65								
				$\mathcal{A}_2^f$	0.08	0.07	0.06	0.06	0.04	0.02	0.06								
Low-e Double Glazing, e = 0.1 on surface 2																			
21a	1/8	LE CLR	0.76	SHGC	0.65	0.64	0.62	0.56	0.43	0.23	0.57	0.59	0.60	0.53	0.58	0.68	0.68	0.61	0.67
				T	0.59	0.56	0.54	0.48	0.36	0.18	0.50								
				R^f	0.15	0.16	0.18	0.24	0.37	0.61	0.22								
				R^b	0.17	0.18	0.20	0.26	0.38	0.61	0.24								
				$\mathcal{A}_1^f$	0.20	0.21	0.21	0.21	0.20	0.16	0.20								
				$\mathcal{A}_2^f$	0.07	0.07	0.08	0.08	0.07	0.05	0.07								
21b	1/4	LE CLR	0.72	SHGC	0.60	0.59	0.57	0.51	0.40	0.21	0.53	0.55	0.55	0.49	0.53	0.64	0.65	0.58	0.63
				T	0.51	0.48	0.46	0.41	0.30	0.14	0.43								
				R^f	0.14	0.15	0.17	0.22	0.35	0.59	0.21								
				R^b	0.15	0.16	0.18	0.23	0.35	0.57	0.22								
				$\mathcal{A}_1^f$	0.26	0.26	0.26	0.26	0.25	0.19	0.25								
				$\mathcal{A}_2^f$	0.10	0.11	0.11	0.11	0.10	0.07	0.10								
Low-e Double Glazing, e = 0.1 on surface 3																			
21c	1/8	CLR LE	0.75	SHGC	0.60	0.58	0.56	0.51	0.40	0.22	0.52	0.55	0.55	0.49	0.53	0.67	0.68	0.60	0.66
				T	0.48	0.45	0.43	0.37	0.27	0.13	0.40								
				R^f	0.26	0.27	0.28	0.32	0.42	0.62	0.31								
				R^b	0.24	0.24	0.26	0.29	0.38	0.58	0.28								
				$\mathcal{A}_1^f$	0.12	0.13	0.14	0.14	0.15	0.15	0.13								
				$\mathcal{A}_2^f$	0.14	0.15	0.15	0.16	0.16	0.10	0.15								
21d	1/4	CLR LE	0.72	SHGC	0.56	0.55	0.52	0.48	0.38	0.20	0.49	0.51	0.52	0.46	0.50	0.64	0.65	0.58	0.63
				T	0.42	0.40	0.37	0.32	0.24	0.11	0.35								
				R^f	0.24	0.24	0.25	0.29	0.38	0.58	0.28								
				R^b	0.20	0.20	0.22	0.26	0.34	0.55	0.25								
				$\mathcal{A}_1^f$	0.19	0.20	0.21	0.22	0.23	0.22	0.21								
				$\mathcal{A}_2^f$	0.16	0.17	0.17	0.17	0.16	0.10	0.16								
21e	1/8	BRZ LE	0.57	SHGC	0.48	0.46	0.44	0.40	0.31	0.17	0.42	0.44	0.44	0.39	0.43	0.51	0.51	0.46	0.50
				T	0.37	0.34	0.32	0.27	0.20	0.08	0.30								
				R^f	0.18	0.17	0.19	0.22	0.30	0.50	0.21								
				R^b	0.23	0.23	0.25	0.29	0.37	0.57	0.28								
				$\mathcal{A}_1^f$	0.34	0.37	0.38	0.39	0.39	0.35	0.37								
				$\mathcal{A}_2^f$	0.11	0.12	0.12	0.12	0.11	0.07	0.11								
21f	1/4	BRZ LE	0.45	SHGC	0.39	0.37	0.35	0.31	0.24	0.13	0.33	0.36	0.36	0.32	0.35	0.40	0.41	0.36	0.40
				T	0.27	0.24	0.22	0.19	0.13	0.05	0.21								
				R^f	0.12	0.12	0.13	0.16	0.24	0.44	0.16								
				R^b	0.19	0.20	0.22	0.25	0.34	0.55	0.24								
				$\mathcal{A}_1^f$	0.51	0.54	0.55	0.56	0.55	0.46	0.53								
				$\mathcal{A}_2^f$	0.10	0.10	0.10	0.10	0.09	0.05	0.10								

Table 10 Visible Transmittance T_v, Solar Heat Gain Coefficient (SHGC), Solar Transmittance T, Front Reflectance R^f, Back Reflectance R^b, and Layer Absorptance $\mathcal{A}_n^f$ for Glazing and Window Systems (*Continued*)

	Glazing System				Center-of-Glazing Properties: Incidence Angles							Total Window SHGC at Normal Incidence: Aluminum		Other Frames		Total Window T_v at Normal Incidence: Aluminum		Other Frames	
ID	Glass Thick., in.		Center Glazing T_v		Normal 0.00	40.00	50.00	60.00	70.00	80.00	Hemis., Diffuse	Operable	Fixed	Operable	Fixed	Operable	Fixed	Operable	Fixed
21g	1/8	GRN LE	0.68	SHGC	0.46	0.44	0.42	0.38	0.30	0.16	0.40	0.42	0.43	0.38	0.41	0.61	0.61	0.54	0.60
				T	0.36	0.32	0.30	0.26	0.18	0.08	0.28								
				R^f	0.17	0.16	0.17	0.20	0.29	0.48	0.20								
				R^b	0.23	0.23	0.25	0.29	0.37	0.57	0.27								
				$\mathcal{A}_1^f$	0.38	0.41	0.42	0.43	0.43	0.38	0.40								
				$\mathcal{A}_2^f$	0.10	0.11	0.11	0.11	0.10	0.06	0.10								
21h	1/4	GRN LE	0.61	SHGC	0.36	0.33	0.31	0.28	0.22	0.12	0.30	0.34	0.34	0.30	0.32	0.54	0.55	0.49	0.54
				T	0.24	0.21	0.19	0.16	0.11	0.05	0.18								
				R^f	0.11	0.10	0.11	0.14	0.22	0.43	0.14								
				R^b	0.19	0.20	0.22	0.25	0.34	0.55	0.24								
				$\mathcal{A}_1^f$	0.56	0.59	0.61	0.61	0.59	0.48	0.58								
				$\mathcal{A}_2^f$	0.09	0.09	0.09	0.08	0.08	0.04	0.08								
21i	1/8	GRY LE	0.52	SHGC	0.46	0.44	0.42	0.38	0.30	0.16	0.39	0.42	0.43	0.38	0.41	0.46	0.47	0.42	0.46
				T	0.35	0.32	0.30	0.25	0.18	0.08	0.28								
				R^f	0.16	0.16	0.17	0.20	0.28	0.48	0.20								
				R^b	0.23	0.23	0.25	0.29	0.37	0.57	0.27								
				$\mathcal{A}_1^f$	0.39	0.42	0.43	0.44	0.44	0.38	0.41								
				$\mathcal{A}_2^f$	0.10	0.11	0.11	0.11	0.10	0.06	0.10								
21j	1/4	GRY LE	0.37	SHGC	0.34	0.32	0.30	0.27	0.21	0.12	0.28	0.32	0.32	0.28	0.30	0.33	0.33	0.30	0.33
				T	0.23	0.20	0.18	0.15	0.11	0.04	0.17								
				R^f	0.11	0.11	0.12	0.15	0.23	0.44	0.15								
				R^b	0.20	0.20	0.22	0.25	0.34	0.55	0.24								
				$\mathcal{A}_1^f$	0.58	0.60	0.61	0.61	0.59	0.48	0.59								
				$\mathcal{A}_2^f$	0.08	0.08	0.08	0.08	0.07	0.04	0.08								
21k	1/4	BLUGRN LE	0.62	SHGC	0.39	0.37	0.34	0.31	0.24	0.13	0.33	0.36	0.36	0.32	0.35	0.55	0.56	0.50	0.55
				T	0.28	0.25	0.23	0.20	0.14	0.06	0.22								
				R^f	0.12	0.12	0.13	0.16	0.24	0.44	0.16								
				R^b	0.23	0.23	0.25	0.28	0.37	0.57	0.27								
				$\mathcal{A}_1^f$	0.51	0.54	0.56	0.56	0.55	0.46	0.53								
				$\mathcal{A}_2^f$	0.08	0.09	0.08	0.08	0.08	0.05	0.08								
21l	1/4	HI-P GRN W/LE CLR	0.57	SHGC	0.31	0.30	0.29	0.26	0.21	0.12	0.27	0.29	0.29	0.26	0.28	0.51	0.51	0.46	0.50
				T	0.22	0.21	0.19	0.17	0.12	0.06	0.18								
				R^f	0.07	0.07	0.09	0.13	0.22	0.46	0.12								
				R^b	0.23	0.23	0.24	0.28	0.37	0.57	0.27								
				$\mathcal{A}_1^f$	0.67	0.68	0.67	0.66	0.62	0.46	0.65								
				$\mathcal{A}_2^f$	0.04	0.05	0.05	0.05	0.04	0.03	0.04								
Low-e Double Glazing, e = 0.05 on surface 2																			
25a	1/8	LE CLR	0.72	SHGC	0.41	0.40	0.38	0.34	0.27	0.14	0.36	0.38	0.38	0.34	0.36	0.64	0.65	0.58	0.63
				T	0.37	0.35	0.33	0.29	0.22	0.11	0.31								
				R^f	0.35	0.36	0.37	0.40	0.47	0.64	0.39								
				R^b	0.39	0.39	0.40	0.43	0.50	0.66	0.42								
				$\mathcal{A}_1^f$	0.24	0.26	0.26	0.27	0.28	0.23	0.26								
				$\mathcal{A}_2^f$	0.04	0.04	0.04	0.04	0.03	0.03	0.04								
25b	1/4	LE CLR	0.70	SHGC	0.37	0.36	0.34	0.31	0.24	0.13	0.32	0.34	0.34	0.30	0.33	0.62	0.63	0.56	0.62
				T	0.30	0.28	0.27	0.23	0.17	0.08	0.25								
				R^f	0.30	0.30	0.32	0.35	0.42	0.60	0.34								
				R^b	0.35	0.35	0.35	0.38	0.44	0.60	0.37								
				$\mathcal{A}_1^f$	0.34	0.35	0.35	0.36	0.35	0.28	0.34								
				$\mathcal{A}_2^f$	0.06	0.07	0.07	0.06	0.06	0.04	0.06								
25c	1/4	BRZ W/LE CLR	0.42	SHGC	0.26	0.25	0.24	0.22	0.18	0.10	0.23	0.25	0.25	0.22	0.23	0.37	0.38	0.34	0.37
				T	0.18	0.17	0.16	0.14	0.10	0.05	0.15								
				R^f	0.15	0.16	0.17	0.21	0.29	0.51	0.20								
				R^b	0.34	0.34	0.35	0.37	0.44	0.60	0.37								
				$\mathcal{A}_1^f$	0.63	0.63	0.63	0.61	0.57	0.42	0.60								
				$\mathcal{A}_2^f$	0.04	0.04	0.04	0.04	0.03	0.03	0.04								

Table 10 Visible Transmittance T_v, Solar Heat Gain Coefficient (SHGC), Solar Transmittance T, Front Reflectance R^f, Back Reflectance R^b, and Layer Absorptance $\mathcal{A}^f_n$ for Glazing and Window Systems (*Continued*)

Glazing System					Center-of-Glazing Properties							Total Window SHGC at Normal Incidence				Total Window T_v at Normal Incidence			
					Incidence Angles							Aluminum		Other Frames		Aluminum		Other Frames	
ID	Glass Thick., in.		Center Glazing T_v		Normal 0.00	40.00	50.00	60.00	70.00	80.00	Hemis., Diffuse	Operable	Fixed	Operable	Fixed	Operable	Fixed	Operable	Fixed
25d	1/4	GRN W/LE CLR	0.60	SHGC	0.31	0.30	0.28	0.26	0.21	0.12	0.27	0.29	0.29	0.26	0.28	0.53	0.54	0.48	0.53
				T	0.22	0.21	0.20	0.17	0.13	0.06	0.18								
				R^f	0.10	0.10	0.12	0.16	0.25	0.48	0.15								
				R^b	0.35	0.34	0.35	0.37	0.44	0.60	0.37								
				$\mathcal{A}^f_1$	0.64	0.64	0.64	0.63	0.59	0.43	0.62								
				$\mathcal{A}^f_2$	0.05	0.05	0.05	0.05	0.04	0.03	0.05								
25e	1/4	GRY W/LE CLR	0.35	SHGC	0.24	0.23	0.22	0.20	0.16	0.09	0.21	0.23	0.23	0.20	0.21	0.31	0.32	0.28	0.31
				T	0.16	0.15	0.14	0.12	0.09	0.04	0.13								
				R^f	0.12	0.13	0.15	0.18	0.26	0.49	0.17								
				R^b	0.34	0.34	0.35	0.37	0.44	0.60	0.37								
				$\mathcal{A}^f_1$	0.69	0.69	0.68	0.67	0.62	0.45	0.66								
				$\mathcal{A}^f_2$	0.03	0.03	0.03	0.03	0.03	0.02	0.03								
25f	1/4	BLUE W/LE CLR	0.45	SHGC	0.27	0.26	0.25	0.23	0.18	0.11	0.24	0.26	0.25	0.22	0.24	0.40	0.41	0.36	0.40
				T	0.19	0.18	0.17	0.15	0.11	0.05	0.16								
				R^f	0.12	0.12	0.14	0.17	0.26	0.49	0.16								
				R^b	0.34	0.34	0.35	0.37	0.44	0.60	0.37								
				$\mathcal{A}^f_1$	0.66	0.66	0.65	0.64	0.60	0.44	0.63								
				$\mathcal{A}^f_2$	0.04	0.04	0.04	0.04	0.04	0.03	0.04								
25g	1/4	HI-P GRN W/LE CLR	0.53	SHGC	0.27	0.26	0.25	0.23	0.18	0.11	0.23	0.26	0.25	0.22	0.24	0.47	0.48	0.42	0.47
				T	0.18	0.17	0.16	0.14	0.10	0.05	0.15								
				R^f	0.07	0.07	0.09	0.13	0.22	0.46	0.12								
				R^b	0.35	0.34	0.35	0.38	0.44	0.60	0.37								
				$\mathcal{A}^f_1$	0.71	0.72	0.71	0.69	0.64	0.47	0.68								
				$\mathcal{A}^f_2$	0.04	0.04	0.04	0.04	0.03	0.02	0.04								
Triple Glazing																			
29a	1/8	CLR CLR CLR	0.74	SHGC	0.68	0.65	0.62	0.54	0.39	0.18	0.57	0.62	0.62	0.55	0.60	0.66	0.67	0.59	0.65
				T	0.60	0.57	0.53	0.45	0.31	0.12	0.49								
				R^f	0.17	0.18	0.21	0.28	0.42	0.65	0.25								
				R^b	0.17	0.18	0.21	0.28	0.42	0.65	0.25								
				$\mathcal{A}^f_1$	0.10	0.11	0.12	0.13	0.14	0.14	0.12								
				$\mathcal{A}^f_2$	0.08	0.08	0.09	0.09	0.08	0.07	0.08								
				$\mathcal{A}^f_3$	0.06	0.06	0.06	0.06	0.05	0.03	0.06								
29b	1/4	CLR CLR CLR	0.70	SHGC	0.61	0.58	0.55	0.48	0.35	0.16	0.51	0.56	0.56	0.50	0.54	0.62	0.63	0.56	0.62
				T	0.49	0.45	0.42	0.35	0.24	0.09	0.39								
				R^f	0.14	0.15	0.18	0.24	0.37	0.59	0.22								
				R^b	0.14	0.15	0.18	0.24	0.37	0.59	0.22								
				$\mathcal{A}^f_1$	0.17	0.19	0.20	0.21	0.22	0.21	0.19								
				$\mathcal{A}^f_2$	0.12	0.13	0.13	0.13	0.12	0.08	0.12								
				$\mathcal{A}^f_3$	0.08	0.08	0.08	0.08	0.06	0.03	0.08								
29c	1/4	HI-P GRN CLR CLR	0.53	SHGC	0.32	0.29	0.27	0.24	0.18	0.10	0.26	0.30	0.30	0.26	0.29	0.47	0.48	0.42	0.47
				T	0.20	0.17	0.15	0.12	0.07	0.02	0.15								
				R^f	0.06	0.07	0.08	0.11	0.20	0.41	0.11								
				R^b	0.13	0.14	0.16	0.22	0.35	0.57	0.20								
				$\mathcal{A}^f_1$	0.64	0.67	0.68	0.68	0.66	0.53	0.65								
				$\mathcal{A}^f_2$	0.06	0.06	0.05	0.05	0.05	0.03	0.05								
				$\mathcal{A}^f_3$	0.04	0.04	0.04	0.03	0.02	0.01	0.04								
Triple Glazing, e = 0.2 on surface 2																			
32a	1/8	LE CLR CLR	0.68	SHGC	0.60	0.58	0.55	0.48	0.35	0.17	0.51	0.55	0.55	0.49	0.53	0.61	0.61	0.54	0.60
				T	0.50	0.47	0.44	0.38	0.26	0.10	0.41								
				R^f	0.17	0.19	0.21	0.27	0.41	0.64	0.25								
				R^b	0.19	0.20	0.22	0.29	0.42	0.63	0.26								
				$\mathcal{A}^f_1$	0.20	0.20	0.20	0.21	0.21	0.17	0.20								
				$\mathcal{A}^f_2$	0.08	0.08	0.08	0.09	0.08	0.07	0.08								
				$\mathcal{A}^f_3$	0.06	0.06	0.06	0.06	0.05	0.03	0.06								

Table 10 Visible Transmittance T_v, Solar Heat Gain Coefficient (SHGC), Solar Transmittance T, Front Reflectance R^f, Back Reflectance R^b, and Layer Absorptance $\mathcal{A}_n^f$ for Glazing and Window Systems (*Continued*)

ID	Glass Thick., in.	Glazing System	Center Glazing T_v		Center-of-Glazing Properties, Incidence Angles: Normal 0.00	40.00	50.00	60.00	70.00	80.00	Hemis., Diffuse	Total Window SHGC at Normal Incidence: Aluminum Operable	Aluminum Fixed	Other Frames Operable	Other Frames Fixed	Total Window T_v at Normal Incidence: Aluminum Operable	Aluminum Fixed	Other Frames Operable	Other Frames Fixed
32b	1/4	LE CLR CLR	0.64	SHGC	0.53	0.50	0.47	0.41	0.29	0.14	0.44	0.49	0.49	0.43	0.47	0.57	0.58	0.51	0.56
				T	0.39	0.36	0.33	0.27	0.17	0.06	0.30								
				R^f	0.14	0.15	0.17	0.21	0.31	0.53	0.20								
				R^b	0.16	0.16	0.19	0.24	0.36	0.57	0.22								
				$\mathcal{A}_1^f$	0.28	0.31	0.31	0.34	0.37	0.31	0.31								
				$\mathcal{A}_2^f$	0.11	0.11	0.11	0.11	0.10	0.08	0.11								
				$\mathcal{A}_3^f$	0.08	0.08	0.08	0.07	0.05	0.03	0.07								
Triple Glazing, e = 0.2 on surface 5																			
32c	1/8	CLR CLR LE	0.68	SHGC	0.62	0.60	0.57	0.49	0.36	0.16	0.52	0.57	0.57	0.50	0.55	0.61	0.61	0.54	0.60
				T	0.50	0.47	0.44	0.38	0.26	0.10	0.41								
				R^f	0.19	0.20	0.22	0.29	0.42	0.63	0.26								
				R^b	0.18	0.19	0.21	0.27	0.41	0.64	0.25								
				$\mathcal{A}_1^f$	0.11	0.12	0.13	0.14	0.15	0.15	0.13								
				$\mathcal{A}_2^f$	0.09	0.10	0.10	0.10	0.10	0.08	0.10								
				$\mathcal{A}_3^f$	0.11	0.11	0.11	0.10	0.08	0.04	0.10								
32d	1/4	CLR CLR LE	0.64	SHGC	0.56	0.53	0.50	0.44	0.32	0.15	0.47	0.51	0.52	0.46	0.50	0.57	0.58	0.1	0.56
				T	0.39	0.36	0.33	0.27	0.17	0.06	0.30								
				R^f	0.16	0.16	0.19	0.24	0.36	0.57	0.22								
				R^b	0.14	0.15	0.17	0.21	0.31	0.53	0.20								
				$\mathcal{A}_1^f$	0.17	0.19	0.20	0.21	0.22	0.22	0.19								
				$\mathcal{A}_2^f$	0.13	0.14	0.14	0.14	0.13	0.10	0.13								
				$\mathcal{A}_3^f$	0.15	0.16	0.15	0.14	0.12	0.05	0.14								
Triple Glazing, e = 0.1 on surface 2 and 5																			
40a	1/8	LE CLR LE	0.62	SHGC	0.41	0.39	0.37	0.32	0.24	0.12	0.34	0.38	0.38	0.34	0.36	0.55	0.56	0.50	0.55
				T	0.29	0.26	0.24	0.20	0.13	0.05	0.23								
				R^f	0.30	0.30	0.31	0.34	0.41	0.59	0.33								
				R^b	0.30	0.30	0.31	0.34	0.41	0.59	0.33								
				$\mathcal{A}_1^f$	0.25	0.27	0.28	0.30	0.32	0.27	0.28								
				$\mathcal{A}_2^f$	0.07	0.08	0.08	0.08	0.07	0.06	0.07								
				$\mathcal{A}_3^f$	0.08	0.09	0.09	0.09	0.07	0.04	0.08								
40b	1/4	LE CLR LE	0.59	SHGC	0.36	0.34	0.32	0.28	0.21	0.10	0.30	0.34	0.34	0.30	0.32	0.53	0.53	0.47	0.52
				T	0.24	0.21	0.19	0.16	0.10	0.03	0.18								
				R^f	0.34	0.34	0.35	0.38	0.44	0.61	0.37								
				R^b	0.23	0.23	0.25	0.28	0.36	0.56	0.27								
				$\mathcal{A}_1^f$	0.24	0.25	0.26	0.28	0.30	0.25	0.26								
				$\mathcal{A}_2^f$	0.10	0.11	0.11	0.11	0.10	0.07	0.10								
				$\mathcal{A}_3^f$	0.09	0.09	0.09	0.08	0.07	0.03	0.08								
Triple Glazing, e = 0.05 on surface 2 and 4																			
40c	1/8	LE LE CLR	0.58	SHGC	0.27	0.25	0.24	0.21	0.16	0.08	0.23	0.26	0.25	0.22	0.25	0.52	0.52	0.46	0.51
				T	0.18	0.17	0.16	0.13	0.08	0.03	0.14								
				R^f	0.41	0.41	0.42	0.44	0.50	0.65	0.44								
				R^b	0.46	0.45	0.46	0.48	0.53	0.68	0.47								
				$\mathcal{A}_1^f$	0.27	0.28	0.28	0.29	0.30	0.24	0.28								
				$\mathcal{A}_2^f$	0.12	0.12	0.12	0.12	0.11	0.07	0.12								
				$\mathcal{A}_3^f$	0.02	0.02	0.02	0.02	0.01	0.01	0.02								
40d	1/4	LE LE CLR	0.55	SHGC	0.26	0.25	0.23	0.21	0.16	0.08	0.22	0.25	0.25	0.21	0.24	0.49	0.0	0.44	0.48
				T	0.15	0.14	0.12	0.10	0.07	0.02	0.12								
				R^f	0.33	0.33	0.34	0.37	0.43	0.60	0.36								
				R^b	0.39	0.38	0.38	0.40	0.46	0.61	0.40								
				$\mathcal{A}_1^f$	0.34	0.36	0.36	0.37	0.36	0.28	0.35								
				$\mathcal{A}_2^f$	0.15	0.15	0.15	0.14	0.12	0.08	0.14								
				$\mathcal{A}_3^f$	0.03	0.03	0.03	0.03	0.02	0.01	0.03								

KEY:
CLR = clear, BRZ = bronze, GRN = green, GRY = gray, BLUGRN = blue-green, SS = stainless steel reflective coating, TI = titanium reflective coating
Reflective coating descriptors include percent visible transmittance as *x*%.
HI-P GRN = high-performance green tinted glass, LE = low-emissivity coating

T_v = visible transmittance, T = solar transmittance, SHGC = solar heat gain coefficient, and H. = hemispherical SHGC
ID #s refer to U-factors in Table 4, except for products 49 and 50.

Table 11 Solar Heat Gain Coefficients for Domed Horizontal Skylights

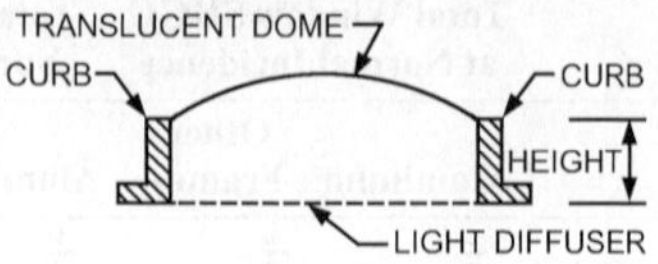

Dome	Light Diffuser (Translucent)	Curb Height, in.	Curb Width-to-Height Ratio	Solar Heat Gain Coefficient	Visible Transmittance
Clear	Yes	0	∞	0.53	0.56
τ = 0.86	τ = 0.58	9	5	0.50	0.58
		12	2.5	0.44	0.59
Clear		0	∞	0.86	0.91
τ = 0.86	None	9	5	0.77	0.91
		12	2.5	0.70	0.91
Translucent		0	∞	0.50	0.46
τ = 0.52	None	12	2.5	0.40	0.32
Translucent		0	∞	0.30	0.25
τ = 0.27	None	9	5	0.26	0.21
		12	2.5	0.24	0.18

Sources: Laouadi et al. (2003), Schutrum and Ozisik (1961).

Tubular Daylighting Devices (TDDs). Tubular daylighting devices collect and channel daylight (diffuse sky and sunbeam light) from the roof of a building into interior spaces (Figure 16). TDDs are also known as **mirror light pipes** or **tubular skylights**. They are an alternative to conventional skylights and have the advantages of energy savings (small area relative to the amount of useful light they admit), lower solar heat gains, relative ease of installation, and tube lengths (depending on the tube length-to-diameter ratio) of up to 42 ft. TDD technologies undergo continuous development to meet the increasing needs for high standards of energy efficiency in buildings and glare-free lighting. The energy-saving potential of TDDs is well recognized (Allen 1997; Carter 2008; Laouadi 2004), and TDDs are encouraged or mandated, particularly in commercial buildings [CEC 2010; see also U.S. Green Building Council's (USGBC) Leadership in Energy and Environmental Design (LEED) program]. A variant known as a hybrid TDD (HTDD) is available from some manufacturers. In an HTDD, more than one material or geometry is present along the length of the tube (e.g., a round tube that transitions to a square ceiling diffuser).

The natural daylight that TDDs deliver is beneficial to the visual comfort, health, and well-being of building occupants (Boyce et al. 2003; Carter and Al-Marwaee 2009). The daylighting performance (light output) of a TDD depends on many location and material parameters, but a typical device can illuminate an area of up to 300 ft^2. The area of coverage depends on the height of the ceiling: the higher the ceiling, the more widely the light will be uniformly distributed.

TDD Components. TDDs typically consist of (1) a collector on the roof to gather sunbeams and diffuse sky light, (2) a hollow pipe guide in the plenum/attic space to channel light downwards, and (3) a light diffuser at ceiling level to spread light indoors (see Figure 16).

The **collector** is usually a single- or multilayer transparent glass or plastic dome projecting above the plane of the roof. It may also include passive or active geometries (e.g., static or tracking reflectors) or some optical devices (e.g., prisms, diffusing elements) to enhance the device's lighting output, especially at low sun altitude angles (Laouadi 2013).

Straight **guides** (tubes) are common, but nonlinear light guides with bent sections (Figure 16) are sometimes needed to suit the geometry of a building. The guide can be rigid or flexible, and is typically made from an aluminum sheet with highly reflective interior coatings, which are sometimes spectrally selective. This measure reduces solar heat transmission while preserving light transmission. Coating materials with a reflectivity exceeding 99% are commercially available. Vertical pipes without bends are more efficient than bent guides for low incidence angles (<60°; e.g., summer noon), and less efficient for higher incidence angles (e.g., winter noon) (Laouadi et al. 2013a).

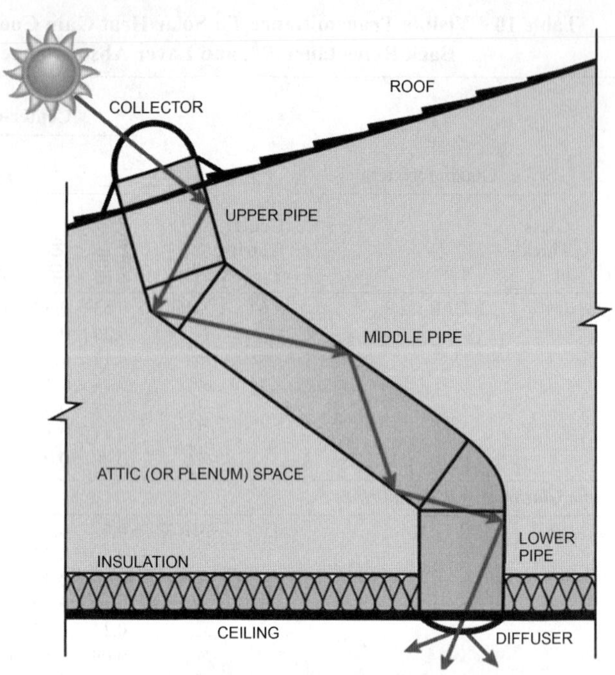

Fig. 16 Generalized Tubular Daylighting Device
(NRCC 2011)

Diffusers in the ceiling plane of TDDs are usually hemispherical or flat with single- or multilayer glass or poly(methyl methacrylate (PMMA, also known as acrylic) or polycarbonate. Diffusers typically use one of three types of glazing: prismatic, diffusing, or lensed. **Prismatic** glazing consists of arrays or layers of micro replicated shapes (conical prisms, ridges, wedges, etc.), which reflect, refract, and redirect the incoming light based on the angle of incidence. Typical prismatic diffusers are made of acrylic or polycarbonate sheets with conical prisms. **Diffusing** glazing consists of very fine particles, pigments, or films applied to clear glass or plastic sheets to make the glazing look opal (white). The scattering properties depend on the refractive index and the size of the microstructures used. **Lensed** glazing is comprised of arrays of diverging lenses (e.g., Fresnel lenses) that are very thin so that little light is lost by absorption.

Performance Metrics. Various theoretical and empirical models have been developed to predict the daylighting performance of TDDs [e.g., CIE (2006), Zhang and Muneer (2000)]. ASHRAE research project RP-1415 developed and validated models for the prediction of the optical and thermal performance of complex TDDs (Laouadi et al. 2013b, 2013c, 2013d). Several metrics were proposed, including

- **Visible transmittance (VT):** calculated or measured at a standard incidence angle, or averaged over a predetermined number of incidence angles. Angle of incidence is the angle between the entering ray and the axis of the upper tube section.
- **Normalized intensity distribution:** an index that treats TDDs as lighting luminaire systems. TDD intensity distribution is important for lighting energy calculation and spatial arrangement of TDDs.

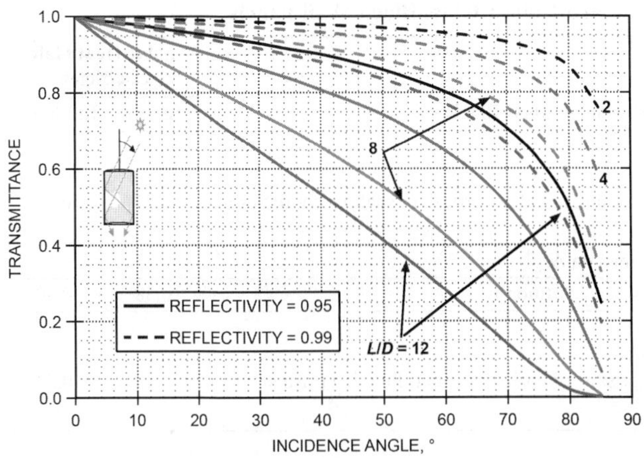

Fig. 17 Transmittance of Straight Tube (Light Pipe) as Function of Reflectivity and Aspect Ratio (Length/Diameter)

- **Daylighting area coverage (DAC):** portion of the work plane surface area under a daylight illuminance equal or greater than the recommended task illuminance under CIE standard clear sky conditions. DAC is an important parameter for TDD product rating and selection, and spatial arrangement that guarantees capital cost reduction (with minimum number of TDDs).
- **Spacing ratio (SR):** maximum distance between two pairs of TDDs, normalized by the ceiling height of buildings. SR is calculated based on the illuminance uniformity criterion on the work plane surface.
- **Solar heat gain coefficient (SHGC):** normalized solar heat gains penetrating the indoor space through a TDD system when sunbeam light is incident on the TDD pipe aperture at a standard angle.
- **Thermal transmittance (U-factor):** heat loss from a TDD to the outdoors per unit surface area and temperature difference between the indoor and outdoor environments under standard thermal conditions.

Simplified Single-Angle Solar and Visible Analysis. The following simplified equations are presented only as a guide to solar-optical behavior of a TDD. Real-world TDD performance is a function of many location-specific and season-dependent factors (especially solar angle of incidence) which lead to the final, effective SHGC and VT being a somewhat complex weighted average.

For a given input solar ray and angle of incidence, the visible (or solar) transmittance of a TDD is the product of the individual visible (or solar) transmittances of the collecting dome *c*, the tube *t*, and the ceiling diffuser *d*:

$$T_{TDD} = t_c t_t t_d$$

Of the three terms on the right-hand side of the equation, tube transmittance t_t is by far the most sensitive to the incidence angle of the ray (Figure 17) and the presence of any optical element in the collector, which may change the angle of the incident ray. The equation also assumes that multiple interreflections between TDD components make a negligible contribution to the overall system transmittance and throughput of light. This is approximately true for large aspect ratios. The solar heat gain coefficient of the TDD is the sum of the (solar) transmittance plus an indirect, thermal term that is analogous to the inward-flowing fraction of solar heat gain from a general glazing system. The fraction of original, outdoor solar power incident on the diffuser is

$$I_d/I_s = t_c t_t$$

Table 12 Performance Characteristics of Typical TDDs

Glazing of Collector/ Diffuser	Single/ Single Layer	Double/ Double Layer	Double/ Single Layer	Single/ Double Layer	Single/ Triple Layer
Visible transmittance*	0.77	0.63	0.72	0.66	0.58
SHGC* (10 in. insulation above ceiling)	0.32	0.24	0.27	0.28	0.24
SHGC* (10 in. insulation under roof)	0.34	0.33	0.32	0.35	0.34
U-factor, Btu/h·ft²·°F (10 in. insulation above ceiling)	0.62	0.38	0.62	0.38	0.27
U-factor (10 in. insulation under roof)	1.34	0.83	0.83	1.34	1.33

*VT and SHGC calculated at solar incidence angle of 50° at due south; this angle is close to annual averaged incidence angle (48.84°) of NFRC *Standard* 203-2014.

where I_s and I_d are the solar fluxes (W/m²) incident on the collector dome and diffuser respectively.

The fraction of incident solar radiation energy absorbed in the diffuser is α_d of which approximately half is transferred downward by convection and radiation into the building. The other half is transferred upward to the column of air in the tube. The fraction of this power that is transferred inward is equal to $0.5t_c t_t \alpha_d$.

Thus the solar heat gain coefficient of the TDD system, and where all optical parameters are determined for the solar spectrum, is approximately

$$SHGC_{TDD} = T_{TDD} + 0.5t_c t_t \alpha_d = t_c t_t (t_d + 0.5\alpha_d)$$

The National Fenestration Rating Council (NFRC) sets the model sizes and environmental conditions for the product rating of TDDs. At the time of writing, NFRC ratings are based on physical testing only, after a former NFRC simulation procedure for U-factor of TDDs was retired in 2012. TDD ratings for U-factor follow NFRC (2014a) *Technical Document* 100. Ratings for SHGC follow NFRC (2014e) *Technical Document* 201-2014, whereas ratings for VT follow NFRC (2014f) *Technical Document* 203-2014, which in turn references ASTM *Standard* E1175-87 (RA 2015).

Table 12 shows the computed optical and thermal characteristics of a typical TDD made up of a 1/8 in. PMMA collector and a 1/8 in. polycarbonate diffuser with an NFRC standard-size pipe of 14 in. diameter and aspect ratio of 2.14. The tube reflectivity is 99% and 76% for the visible and solar spectrum, respectively. The NFRC *Technical Document* 100 boundary conditions (NFRC 2014a) are used for the U-factor calculation. The table shows that, although the number of layers in the collector or diffuser has only a small effect on visible transmittance, as expected it has a significant effect on thermal performance. The table does not show any best arrangement, but provides information that can help a designer select an arrangement that best suits a particular application in residential or commercial buildings.

Practical Guidelines. When selecting TDDs, specifiers should consider the following:

- **Visible transmittance:** products with the highest visible transmittance should be selected for daylighting.
- **Solar heat gain coefficient:** ideally, for heating-dominated climates, TDDs would have moderate to high SHGC. However, most available TDDs have medium to low SHGC (<0.40) by design, because ENERGY STAR (www.energystar.gov) requires SHGC ≤ 0.40 except in the northern U.S. climate zone. Some indicative, real-world solar heat gain coefficients are given in Table 12. All exceed the minimum performance defined by ENERGY STAR (i.e., rated SHGC is lower than the ENERGY STAR upper limit).

Table 13 Solar Heat Gain Coefficients for Standard Hollow Glass Block Wall Panels

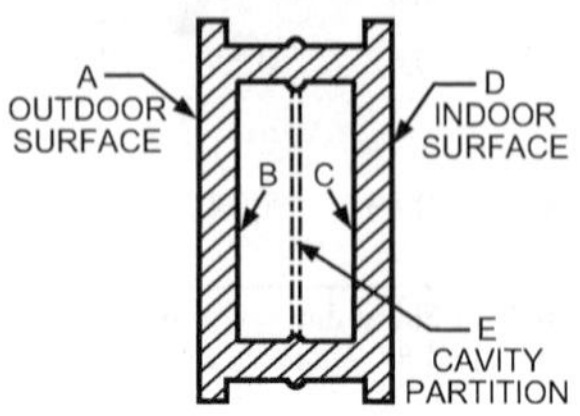

Type of Glass Block[a]	Description of Glass Block	Solar Heat Gain Coefficient In Sun	Solar Heat Gain Coefficient In Shade[b]
Type I	Glass colorless or aqua A, D: Smooth B, C: Smooth or wide ribs, or flutes horizontal or vertical, or shallow configuration E: None	0.57	0.35
Type IA	Same as Type I except ceramic enamel on A	0.23	0.17
Type II	Same as Type I except glass fiber screen partition E	0.38	0.30
Type III	Glass colorless or aqua A, D: Narrow vertical ribs or flutes. B, C: Horizontal light-diffusing prisms, or horizontal light-directing prisms E: Glass fiber screen	0.29	0.23
Type IIIA	Same as Type III except E: Glass fiber screen with green ceramic spray coating or glass fiber screen and gray glass or glass fiber screen with light-selecting prisms	0.22	0.16
Type IV	Same as Type I except reflective oxide coating on A	0.14	0.10

[a]All values are for 7 3/4 by 7 3/4 by 3 7/8 in. block, set in light-colored mortar. For 11 3/4 by 11 3/4 by 3 7/8 in. block, increase coefficients by 15%, and for 5 3/4 by 5 3/4 by 3 7/8 in. block reduce coefficients by 15%.

[b]For NE, E, and SE panels in shade, add 50% to values listed for panels in shade.

- **U-factor:** the lower the U-factor, the better. ENERGY STAR-qualified TDDs must achieve a U-factor of ≤ 0.27 Btu/h·ft²·°F in the northern U.S. climate zone. This is relaxed somewhat as one moves to progressively warmer climates, leading to a threshold of 0.40 Btu/h·ft²·°F in the southern climate zone. Products that are insulated above the ceiling perform considerably better than those with insulation under the roof.
- **Tubular daylighting devices:** TDDs should have multipane ceiling diffusers when insulation is placed at ceiling level (e.g., residential buildings) or multipane collectors when insulation is placed at roof level (e.g., commercial buildings) to reduce thermal losses. In residential applications, a multipane ceiling diffuser is the single most effective measure to reduce the overall U-factor of a TDD. This is because tubes typically penetrate an unconditioned attic zone. In winter, heat loss from tube cavity to attic zone can be severe, and disproportionately large in comparison with the TDD's cross-sectional area, if the ceiling diffuser is only single-glazed.
- **Spacing ratio (SR):** SR relates to the normalized luminous intensity distribution of TDDs. To minimize capital cost (number of TDDs), select TDDs with higher spacing ratios. For ideally diffusing TDDs, SR varies from 1 to 1.5 for illuminance uniformity (minimum to average ratio) of 0.95 to 0.8, respectively.

Installation. Installation methods vary depending on roof type (asphalt shingles, roof tiles, membranes, metallic roofing, etc.). TDD assemblies must be installed to resist air and water infiltration, and damage from wind, hail, and snow load. Manufacturers' instructions provide specific details. Attention to detail is required when the roof is replaced.

Glass Block Walls

Glass block can be used for light transmission through outdoor walls when optical clarity for view is unnecessary. Table 13 describes a variety of glass block patterns and gives solar heat gain coefficients to be applied to solar irradiances so that approximate instantaneous solar heat gains can be calculated (Smith and Pennington 1964). Table 4, footnote 6, provides a representative U-factor for glass block. Note that the U-factor for glass block is poor when compared to double glazing with a low-emissivity coating.

Convection and low-temperature radiative heat gain for all hollow glass block panels fall within a narrow range. Differences in SHGCs are largely the result of differences in transmittance of glass blocks for solar radiation. Solar heat gain coefficients for any particular glass block pattern vary depending on orientation and time of day. The SHGC for western exposures in the morning (shaded) is depressed because of heat storage in the block, whereas the SHGC for eastern exposures in the afternoon (shaded) is elevated as stored heat is dissipated. Time lag effects from heat storage are estimated by using solar gains and air-to-air temperature differences for one hour earlier than the time for which the load calculation is made.

Calorimeter tests of Type 1A glass block showed little difference in solar heat gains between glass block with either black or white ceramic enamel on the exterior of the block. White and black ceramic enamel surfaces represent the two extremes for reflecting or absorbing solar energy; therefore, glass block with enamel surfaces of other colors should have solar heat gain coefficients between these values. Because glass blocks are good examples of strongly angularly selective fenestrations, appropriate caution must be taken.

Plastic Materials for Glazing

Generally, factors outlined for glass apply also to glazing materials such as acrylic, polycarbonate, polystyrene, or other plastic panels. If solar transmittance, absorptance, and reflectance are known, the SHGC can be calculated in the same way as for glass. These properties can be obtained from the manufacturer or be determined by simple laboratory tests. The National Fenestration Rating Council developed standards for testing the optical properties of glazing (NFRC 2014d, 2014g).

In selecting plastic panels for glazing, concerns include possible deterioration from the sun, expansion and contraction because of temperature extremes, and possible damage from abrasion.

4.3 CALCULATION OF SOLAR HEAT GAIN

To calculate solar energy fluxes, first calculate the incident angle θ from the local standard time and the longitude. The direct normal solar irradiance E_{DN}, diffuse sky irradiance E_d, ground-reflected radiation E_r, and total incident irradiance E_t can then be determined. Note that the latter two are assumed to be ideally diffuse radiation. Calculation methods for these parameters are described in Chapter 14.

Solar energy flow through a fenestration may be divided into two parts: opaque (q_{op}) and glazing (q_s) portions. The glazing solar energy flux q_s can be split into that from incident beam radiation

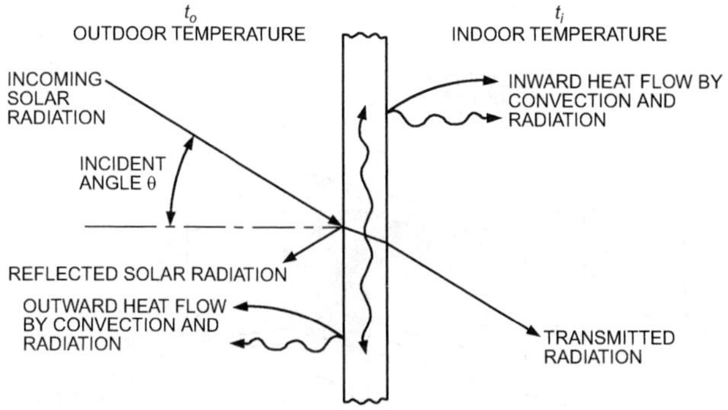

Fig. 18 Instantaneous Heat Balance for Sunlit Glazing Material

(q_b) and incident diffuse radiation (q_d), which includes both diffuse sky radiation and radiation scattered (reflected) from the ground:

$$q_s = q_b + q_d \tag{22}$$

The net heat balance that would occur for a sunlit glazing if there were no diffuse radiation is shown in Figure 18. This net heat balance does not include any of the heat flows resulting from indoor/outdoor temperature differences. The heat balance is pictured as superimposed on the thermal effect. This superposition picture should not be carried too far, however, because the heat flows indicated in Figure 18 as resulting from convection and radiation depend in part on processes that are nonlinear with respect to temperature, so that in reality the two effects cannot be separated. To calculate them, the actual glazing (and other) temperatures are needed, not simply the incremental temperature rise caused by sunlight.

Figure 18 shows that the glazing solar energy flow from beam radiation consists of two parts:

$$q_b = q_{bt} + q_{ba} \tag{23}$$

where

q_{bt} = glazing solar energy flux caused by transmitted incident beam radiation

q_{ba} = glazing solar energy flux caused by inward heat flow of absorbed beam radiation

The glazing solar energy flux caused by incident beam radiation is calculated from

$$q_b = E_{DN} \cos\theta \, \mathrm{SHGC}(\theta) \tag{24}$$

where the beam solar heat gain coefficient is given by Equation (12) or (13). If, instead, the solar radiant and heat fluxes are needed separately, calculate the glazing transmitted solar flux (solar radiation traveling in the incident direction) from

$$q_{bt} = E_{DN} \cos\theta \, T(\theta) \tag{25}$$

and the inward-flowing absorbed solar flux (heat) from

$$q_{ba} = E_{DN} \cos\theta \sum_{k=1}^{L} N_k \mathcal{A}_k^f(\theta) \tag{26}$$

Values of $T(\theta)$ and $\mathcal{A}^f(\theta)$ in these equations can be found in Table 10, and determination of N_k is discussed in the section on Calculation of Solar Heat Gain Coefficient.

For diffuse radiation,

$$q_d = q_{dt} + q_{da} \tag{27}$$

where

q_{dt} = glazing solar energy flux caused by transmitted incident diffuse radiation

q_{da} = glazing solar energy flux caused by inward heat flow of absorbed diffuse radiation

Glazing solar energy flux caused by diffuse incident radiation is calculated from

$$q_d = (E_d + E_r)\langle \mathrm{SHGC} \rangle_D \tag{28}$$

where the hemispherically averaged solar heat gain coefficient is calculated from Equation (15). Solar radiant and heat fluxes can be separately calculated from

$$q_{dt} = (E_d + E_r)\langle T \rangle_D \tag{29}$$

which is diffusely distributed solar radiation (note that effects of finite glazing size and thickness are neglected), and

$$q_{da} = (E_d + E_r) \sum_{k=1}^{L} N_k \langle \mathcal{A}_k^f \rangle_D \tag{30}$$

Opaque Fenestration Elements

The opaque portion solar energy flux is calculated from

$$q_{op} = (E_{DN} \cos\theta + E_d + E_r)\mathrm{SHGC}_{op} \tag{31}$$

where SHGC_{op} is obtained from Equation (18).

Example 6. Calculate the solar energy flux through the glazing system ID 25a given $\theta = 60°$, $E_{DN} = 190$ Btu/h·ft², and $E_d = 50$ Btu/h·ft².

Solution: The solar heat gain coefficients are SHGC(60°) = 0.34, and $\mathrm{SHGC}_D = 0.36$ (see Table 10, glazing ID 25a, 5th and 8th columns).

$$\begin{aligned} q_s &= q_b + q_d \\ &= E_{DN}\cos(60)\mathrm{SHGC}(60) + (E_d + E_r)\langle \mathrm{SHGC} \rangle_D \\ &= (190.0)\cos(60)(0.34) + (50)(0.36) = 50.3 \text{ Btu/h·ft}^2 \end{aligned}$$

5. SHADING AND FENESTRATION ATTACHMENTS

5.1 SHADING

The most effective way to reduce the solar load on fenestration is to intercept direct radiation from the sun before it reaches the glazing system. Fenestration products fully shaded from the outdoors reduce solar heat gain by as much as 80%. Fenestration can be shaded by roof overhangs, vertical and horizontal architectural projections, awnings, heavily proportioned outdoor louvers, or a variety of vegetative shades, including trees, hedges, and trellis vines. In all outdoor shading structures, it is necessary to consider the structures' geometry relative to changing sun position to determine the times and quantities of direct sunlight penetration. A detailed discussion of the effectiveness of outdoor shading is given in Ewing and Yellott (1976).

The general effect of shading is to attenuate solar radiation. Some of the beam radiation may reach the fenestration unaffected by the shade, and this is accounted for by the unshaded fraction F_u. Assuming that the shade does not transmit or diffuse solar radiation, the solar heat gain of the fenestration can be approximated by modifying Equation (22):

$$q_s = F_u q_b + q_{d,shaded} \tag{32}$$

Here, the term $q_{d,shaded}$ indicates that a new SHGC must be determined to account for the fact that the shading device restricts the amount of sky-diffuse radiation on the fenestration system. More

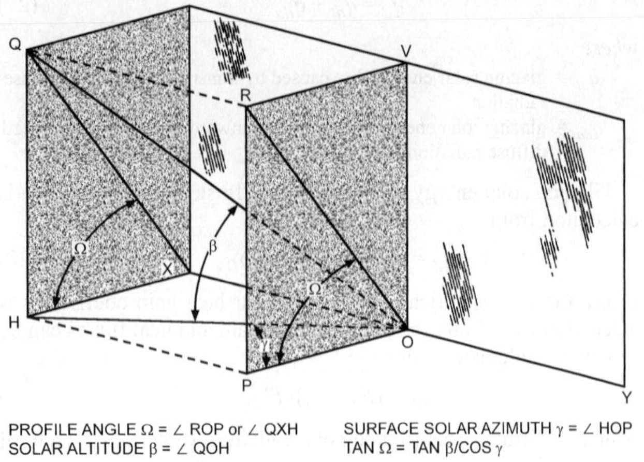

Fig. 19 Profile Angle for South-Facing Horizontal Projections

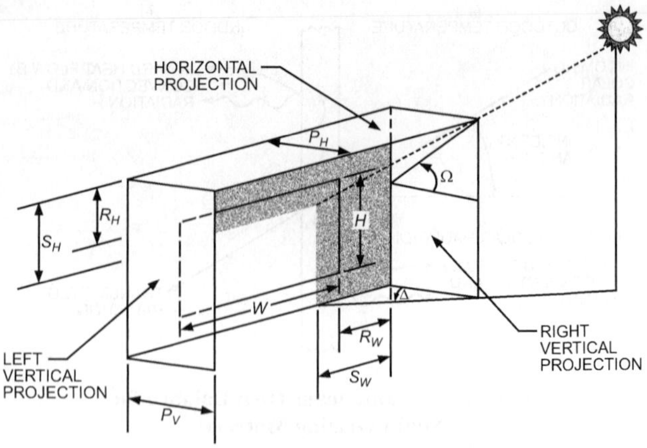

Fig. 20 Vertical and Horizontal Projections and Related Profile Angles for Vertical Surface Containing Fenestration

complex models are required for situations where the shade is partially transmitting and diffusing in nature.

Overhangs and Glazing Unit Recess: Horizontal and Vertical Projections

In the northern hemisphere, horizontal projections can considerably reduce solar heat gain on south, southeast, and southwest exposures during late spring, summer, and early fall. On east and west exposures during the entire year, and on south exposures in winter, the solar altitude is generally so low that, to be effective, horizontal projections must be excessively long. On the other hand, recessing the fenestration deeper back into the wall achieves the same effect as a horizontal projection.

The ability of horizontal projections to intercept the direct component of solar radiation depends on their geometry and the profile or shadow-line angle Ω (Figure 19), defined as the angular difference between a horizontal plane and a plane tilted about a horizontal axis in the plane of the fenestration until it includes the sun. The vertical profile angle Ω can be calculated by

$$\tan \Omega = \tan \beta / \cos \gamma \tag{33}$$

where

β = solar altitude angle
γ = solar azimuth

The shadow width S_W and shadow height S_H (Figure 20) produced by the vertical and horizontal projections (P_V and P_H), respectively, can be calculated using the surface solar azimuth γ and the vertical profile angle Ω determined by Equation (33).

$$S_W = P_V\,|\tan \gamma| \tag{34}$$

$$S_H = P_H \tan \Omega \tag{35}$$

When the surface solar azimuth γ is greater than 90° and less than 270°, the fenestration product is completely in the shade; thus, $S_W = W + R_w$ and sunlit area $A_{SL} = 0$.

The sunlit (A_{SL}) and shaded (A_{SH}) areas of the fenestration product are variable during the day and can be calculated for each moment using the following relations:

$$A_{SL} = [W - (S_W - R_W)][H - (S_H - R_H)] \tag{36}$$

$$A_{SH} = A - A_{SL} \tag{37}$$

where A is total fenestration product area.

For software-based or multiple calculations, McCluney (1990) describes an algorithm that can be used to calculate the unshaded fraction of a window equipped with overhangs, awnings, or side fins.

Example 7. A window facing 30° south of west (wall azimuth ψ = +60°) in a building at 33.65°N latitude, and 84.42°W longitude is 72.5 in. wide and 247.5 in. high. The depth of the horizontal projection is 96 in. At 3:00 PM on July 21, it is calculated that the hour angle $H = 15 \times (13.27 - 12) = 19.03°$; and the declination δ = 20.60°.

The solar altitude β is calculated to be:

$$\sin \beta = \cos(33.65)\cos(20.60)\cos(19.03) + \sin(33.65)\sin(20.60)$$

$$\beta = 68.7°$$

The solar azimuth ϕ is

$$\cos \phi = [\sin(68.68)\sin(33.65) - \sin(20.60)]/[\cos(68.68)\cos(33.65)]$$

$$\phi = 57.1°$$

Thus, the wall solar azimuth is γ = 57.1 – 60 = –2.9°.

(a) Find the sunlit and shaded area of the window.

(b) Find the depth of the projections necessary to fully shade the window.

Solution:

(a) Using Equation (34), the width of the vertical projection shadow is

$$S_W = 0\,|\tan(-2.9)| = 0 \text{ in.}$$

Using Equation (33), the profile angle for the horizontal projection is

$$\tan \Omega = \tan(68.7)/\cos(2.9)$$

$$\Omega = 68.7°$$

Using Equation (35), the height of the horizontal projection shadow is

$$S_H = 96\tan(68.7) = 246 \text{ in.}$$

Using Equations (36) and (37), the sunlit and shaded areas of the window are now

$$A_{SL} = [72.5 - (0 - 0)][247.5 - (246 - 0)]/144 = 0.76 \text{ ft}^2$$

$$A_{SH} = (72.5 \times 247.5)/144 - 0.76 = 123.8 \text{ ft}^2$$

(b) The shadow length necessary to fully shade the given window $S_{H(fs)}$ and $S_{W(fs)}$ from the horizontal and vertical projection are given by (see Figure 20)

$$S_{H(fs)} = 247.5 + 0 = 247.5 \text{ in.}$$

$$S_{W(fs)} = 72.5 + 0 = 72.5 \text{ in.}$$

Thus, using Equations (34) and (35),

$$P_{H(fs)} = 247.5\cot(68.7) = 96.6 \text{ in.}$$

$$P_{W(fs)} = 72.5|\cot(-2.9)| = 1431 \text{ in.}$$

For this example, because both horizontal and vertical projections do not need to fully shade the window, a horizontal projection of 96.6 in. is satisfactory. Also, to accurately analyze the influence of external projections, an hour-by-hour calculation must be performed over the periods of the year for which shading is desired.

5.2 FENESTRATION ATTACHMENTS

Fenestration attachments generally consist of items that can be used as part of a system to provide solar and daylighting control, as well as privacy, aesthetics, and comfort for building occupants. Attachments also include other devices that, though not intended for solar control, affect the solar and visual performance of the fenestration system. Attachments to the indoor side of fenestration can include horizontal louvers (venetian blinds), vertical louvers, roller shades, insect screens, and drapery. Between glazings of multiglazed fenestration, horizontal louvers and roller shades may be incorporated. On the outdoor side, insect screens can be added, as well as horizontal louvers in the plane of the fenestration.

Fenestrations with shading devices have a degree of thermal and optical complexity far greater than that of unshaded fenestrations, and are referred to as **complex fenestration**.

In unshaded fenestration, individual glazing layers can only communicate thermally with adjacent layers. This is not the case for complex fenestration. A fenestration layer such as a screen or louvered blind is not sealed, and allows convective heat transfer between nonadjacent layers. Similarly, shading layers are inherently diathermanous (i.e., they transmit both long- and short-wave radiation). Radiative heat transfer, therefore, can also occur between nonadjacent layers. For example, for a window with indoor venetian blinds, heat transfer occurs between the indoor glass and the blind, the indoor glass and the room, and between the blind and the room. Therefore, methods described previously for determining the U-factor and inward-flowing fractions of fenestration systems cannot be applied to complex fenestration (Collins and Wright 2006; Wright 2008).

Also, complex fenestration can have a **nonspecular optical element.** This is an element for which light (or short-wave infrared radiation) incident on the element from a single spatial direction does not emerge traveling in a single transmitted direction and/or a single reflected direction. Examples of nonspecular elements are shades, drapes, blinds, honeycombs, figured glass, ground glass, and other diffusers, lenses, prisms, and holographic glazings.

Two methods have been developed that allow the analysis of complex fenestration. The first method was proposed by Klems (1994a, 1994b, 2001), and relies on measurement of the bidirectional transmittance and reflectance of each glazing layer, and on calorimetrically determined values of inward flowing fraction, as input to a matrix calculation. It is a physically based and highly accurate approach that is also computationally and experimentally intensive. For details of this approach, see Chapter 31 of the 2005 *ASHRAE Handbook—Fundamentals*. The second method, developed through ASHRAE-sponsored research (Wright et al. 2008), is an empirically based approach that uses readily available information about the system geometry and material properties, and is designed to fit into established fenestration analysis methodology. The methodology has been shown to accurately predict complex fenestration performance from easily obtained data regarding shade geometry and material.

In contrast to these two methods, a simplified approach is presented in the following section for calculating the approximate SHGC for a selection of the more common shading elements and glazing systems.

Simplified Methodology

Considering only the approximate total heat flux through the fenestration, measurements made on a fenestration under one set of conditions can often be extrapolated to other fenestrations and conditions to give an adequate answer. In this case, heat flux through the center-glass region is represented by

$$q = E_{DN}\cos(\theta)\text{SHGC}(\theta)\text{IAC}(\theta, \Omega) + (E_d + E_r)\langle\text{SHGC}\rangle_D\text{IAC}_D \tag{38}$$

where the solar heat gain coefficients are for the center-glass region of an unshaded glazing, and may be calculated using methods described previously, or obtained from Table 10. The **indoor solar attenuation coefficient (IAC)** represents the fraction of heat flow that enters the room, some energy having been excluded by the shading. Depending on the type of shade, it may vary angularly and with shade type and geometry. The IAC is defined as

$$\begin{aligned}\text{IAC}(\theta, \Omega) &= \frac{\text{SHGC}(\theta, \Omega)_{cg,\,shaded}}{\text{SHGC}(\theta)_{cg}}\\ \text{IAC}_D &= \frac{\langle\text{SHGC}\rangle_{D,\,cg,\,shaded}}{\langle\text{SHGC}\rangle_{D,\,cg}}\end{aligned} \tag{39}$$

where Ω is either the horizontal or vertical profile angle.

IAC values presented in the following sections have been determined using the ASHWAT models (Wright et al. 2008), which have been validated, with calorimetric results showing prediction of fenestration performance to within 5% (Figure 21).

Because shading layers generally have a small effect on the U-factor of complex fenestration systems (Wright et al. 2008), in this simplified analysis, the effects of shading devices on U-factor are ignored. System U-factor is assumed to be similar to that of the same glazing (minus the shade) and can be determined from Table 4.

Note that this simplified approach applies only to the SHGC of the center-glass region of the fenestration product. Results from this analysis must be combined with the methods provided in the Solar Heat Gain Coefficient and Solar Heat Gain sections.

Slat-Type Sunshades

Slat-type sunshades consist of horizontal or vertically oriented louvers in located in the plane of the fenestration. They can be installed on the outdoor and indoor side of the fenestration, or between glazings in a multilayered glazing system. The transmitted solar radiation may consist of straight-through, transmitted diffuse, and reflected-through components.

The geometry considered is shown in Figure 22, with slat width w, slat crown c, slat spacing s, and slat angle ϕ. The ratios of w/s and w/c are assumed constant at 1.2 and 16 respectively, which are representative of many commercially available products. The profile angle Ω can represent either the vertical profile Ω_V or the horizontal profile Ω_H. The vertical profile angle is used for horizontal louvered shades, and is calculated using Equation (33). The horizontal profile angle is used for vertical louvered shades and is equal to the wall surface solar azimuth γ.

Tables 14A to 14G presents IAC values at profile angles of 0 and 60° for various glazing and shade combinations. IAC varies with profile angle where the profile angle can be the vertical profile (for horizontal louvers) or horizontal profile (for vertical louvers). The variation of IAC with profile angle can be determined from

$$\text{IAC}(\theta,\Omega) = \text{IAC}_0 + \text{IAC}_x \times \min(1.2\,\Omega, 60)/60 \tag{40}$$

Barnaby et al. (2009), Collins et al. (2008), Huang et al. (2006), Kotey et al. (2009a), and Wright et al. (2008) contain more

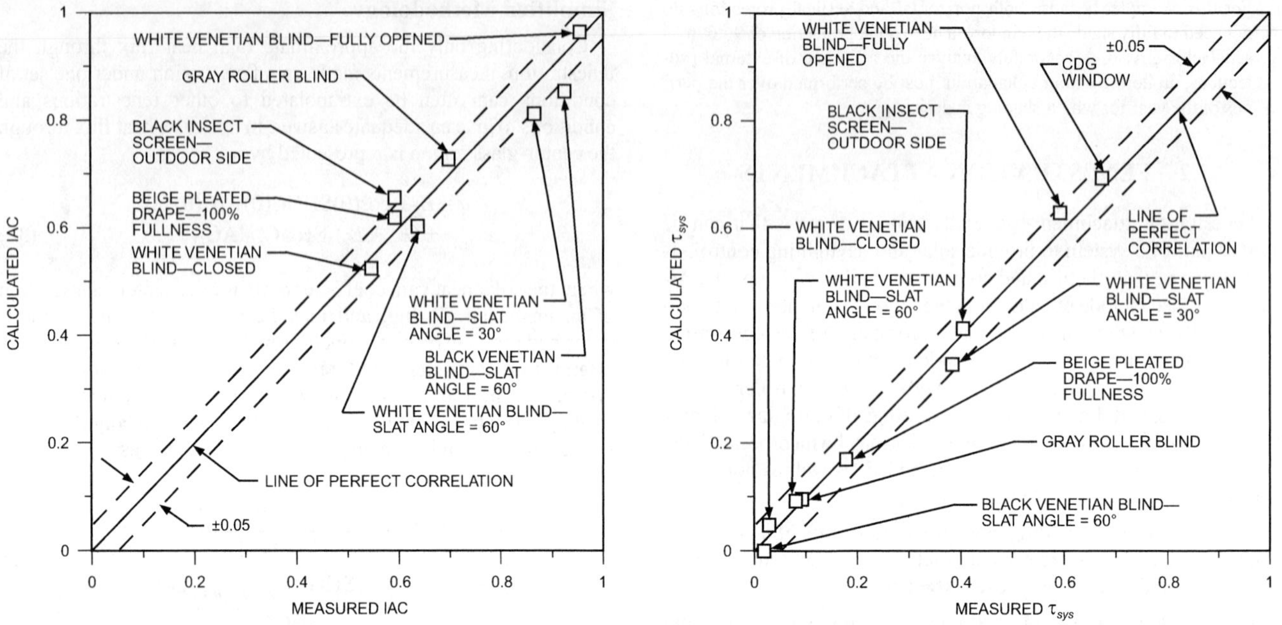

Fig. 21 Comparison of IAC and Solar Transmission Values from ASHWAT Model Versus Measurements
(Normal incidence; various shading layers attached to conventional double-glazed window)
(Wright et al. 2009a)

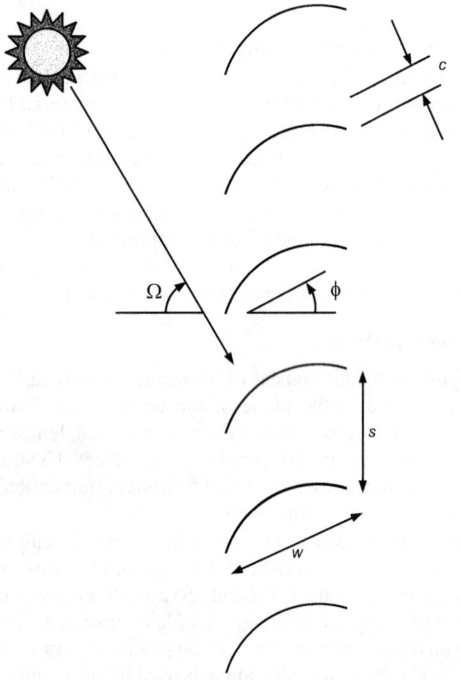

Fig. 22 Geometry of Slat-Type Sunshades

comprehensive discussions of models used to determine IACs of louvered sunshades.

Example 8. Calculate the SHGC of glazing system ID 25a if a horizontally louvered shade is added (a) on the indoor side, (b) between the glazings, and (c) on the outdoor side. The shade material has a reflectance of 0.60 and the shades are installed in the open position (0°). $\theta = 60°$ and $\Omega_V = 40°$. Also consider (d) vertical louvers located on the indoor side of the glazing with $\Omega_H = 40°$.

Solution: Use Equations (39) and (40) and values from Table 14E. From Example 6, SHGC(60°) = 0.34, and $SHGC_D = 0.36$.

(a) Indoor shade

$$\begin{aligned} IAC(60,40) &= IAC_0 + (IAC_{60} - IAC_0) \times \min(1.2\Omega,\ 60)/60 \\ &= 0.99 + (0.87 - 0.99) \times \frac{40}{60} \\ &= 0.91 \end{aligned}$$

$$\begin{aligned} SHGC(\theta,\Omega)_{cg,\ shaded} &= IAC(60,40) \times SHGC(\theta)_{cg} \\ &= 0.91 \times 0.34 \\ &= 0.31 \end{aligned}$$

$$\begin{aligned} SHGC_{D,\ cg,\ shaded} &= IAC_D \times SHGC_{D,\ cg} \\ &= 0.93 \times 0.36 \\ &= 0.33 \end{aligned}$$

(b) Louvers between glazings

$$\begin{aligned} IAC(60,40) &= IAC_0 + (IAC_{60} - IAC_0) \times \min(1.2\Omega,\ 60)/60 \\ &= 0.97 + (0.68 - 0.97) \times \frac{40}{60} \\ &= 0.78 \end{aligned}$$

$$\begin{aligned} SHGC(\theta,\Omega)_{cg,\ shaded} &= IAC(60,40) \times SHGC(\theta)_{cg} \\ &= 0.78 \times 0.34 \\ &= 0.27 \end{aligned}$$

$$\begin{aligned} SHGC_{D,\ cg,\ shaded} &= IAC_D \times SHGC_{D,\ cg} \\ &= 0.82 \times 0.36 \\ &= 0.30 \end{aligned}$$

(c) Outdoor louvers

$$\begin{aligned} IAC(60,40) &= IAC_0 + (IAC_{60} - IAC_0) \times \min(1.2\Omega,\ 60)/60 \\ &= 0.94 + (0.15 - 0.94) \times \frac{40}{60} \\ &= 0.41 \end{aligned}$$

$$\begin{aligned} SHGC(\theta,\Omega)_{cg,\ shaded} &= IAC(60,40) \times SHGC(\theta)_{cg} \\ &= 0.41 \times 0.34 \\ &= 0.14 \end{aligned}$$

$$\begin{aligned} SHGC_{D,\ cg,\ shaded} &= IAC_D \times SHGC_{D,\ cg} \\ &= 0.51 \times 0.36 \\ &= 0.18 \end{aligned}$$

(d) Vertical louvers

For the given conditions, results are the same as for part (a).

Drapery

Drapery fabrics can be classified in terms of their solar-optical properties as having specific values of fabric transmittance and reflectance. Fabric reflectance is the major factor in determining the ability of a fabric to reduce solar heat gain. Based on their appearance, draperies can also be classified by yarn color as dark, medium, and light and by weave as closed, semiopen, and open. The apparent color of a fabric is determined by the reflectance of the yarn itself. Drapery fabrics are classified into nine types, rated by openness and yarn reflectances (Figures 23 and 24).

The solar-optical properties of drapery fabrics can be determined accurately by laboratory tests (Collins et al. 2011; Kotey et al. 2009b; Yellott 1963), and manufacturers can usually supply solar transmittance and reflectance values for their products. In addition to these properties, the openness factor (ratio of the open area between the fibers to the total area of the fabric) is a useful property that can be measured exactly (Keyes 1967; Pennington and Moore 1967). Visual estimations of openness and yarn reflectance, interpreted through Figures 23 and 24, are valuable in judging the effectiveness of drapes for (1) protection from excessive radiant energy from either sunlight or sun-heated glazing, (2) brightness control, (3) providing either outward view or privacy, and (4) sound control.

To understand drapery layer solar-optical properties, the **fullness** of the drapery is needed. As simplified in Figure 25, the pleating of the drape is assumed to be square, with pleat depth *w* and width *s*. For 100% fullness, the width of fabric used is twice the width of the fenestration. If the drapery is hung flat, like a fenestration product shade, the fullness is 0%.

Table 14G presents IAC and radiant heat transfer fraction F_R values for typical glazing and shade combinations. For these types of shades, the IAC value is not strongly influenced by the incident angle of irradiation; therefore, a constant value of IAC can be used.

Kotey et al. (2009b, 2009c, 2011) and Wright et al. (2009a) contain more comprehensive discussions of models used to determine IACs of draperies.

Example 9. Calculate the SHGC of glazing system ID 25a if a drapery is added on the indoor side. The fabric has an openness factor of 0.05 and a yarn reflectance of 0.60, and the drapery has 100% fullness.

Solution: In Figure 24, these lines intersect in the area of designator III_L. Fabric is closed and light in color, with probable fabric reflectance of 0.52 and fabric transmittance of 0.30.

From Table 14G, both IAC and $IAC_D = 0.68$.

$$SHGC(\theta,\Omega)_{cg,\ shaded} = IAC \times SHGC(\theta)_{cg}$$

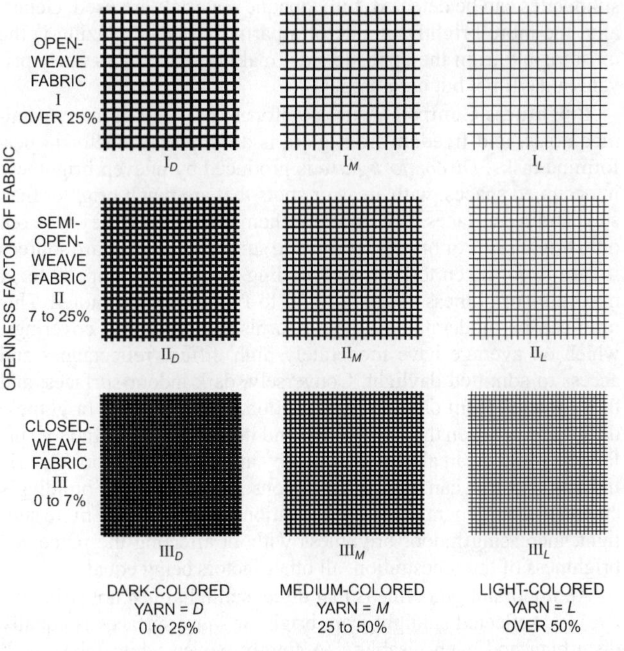

NOTE: Classes may be approximated by eye. With closed fabrics, no objects are visible through the material, but large light or dark areas may show. Semiopen fabrics do not allow details to be seen, and large objects are clearly defined. Open fabrics allow details to be seen, and the general view is relatively clear with no confusion of vision. The yarn color or shade of light or dark may be observed to determine whether the fabric is light, medium, or dark.

Fig. 23 Designation of Drapery Fabrics

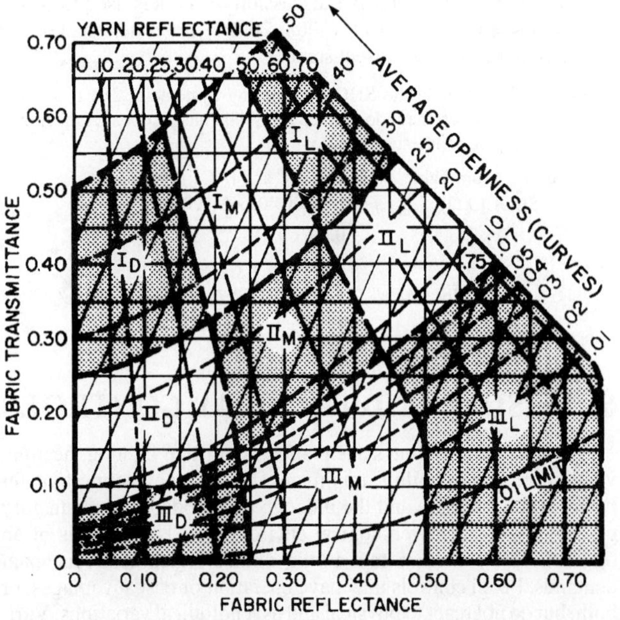

Fig. 24 Drapery Fabric Properties

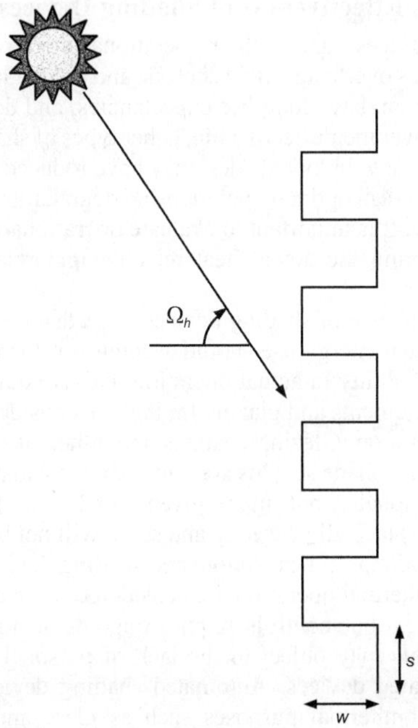

Fig. 25 Geometry of Drapery Fabrics

$$= 0.68 \times 0.34$$
$$= 0.23$$
$$SHGC_{D,\,cg,\,shaded} = IAC_D \times SHGC_{D,\,cg}$$
$$= 0.68 \times 0.36$$
$$= 0.25$$

Roller Shades and Insect Screens

In general, both roller shades and insect screens are equivalent to drapery of 0% fullness. Appropriately, much of the methodology applied to drapery fabrics applies for these devices as well.

Table 14G presents IAC for typical glazing and shade combinations. For these types of shades, the IAC value is not strongly influenced by the incident angle of irradiation; therefore, a constant value of IAC can be used.

For a more comprehensive discussion of models used to determine IACs, see Kotey et al. (2008, 2009d) for roller shades and Kotey et al. (2009e) for insect screens.

Example 10. Calculate the SHGC of glazing system ID 25a if a roller shade is added on the indoor side. The shade has an openness factor of 0.0 and a yarn reflectance of 0.65.

Solution: From Table 14G, both IAC and $IAC_D = 0.60$.

$$SHGC(\theta,\Omega)_{cg,\,shaded} = IAC(60,40) \times SHGC(\theta)_{cg}$$
$$= 0.60 \times 0.34$$
$$= 0.20$$
$$SHGC_{D,\,cg,\,shaded} = IAC_D \times SHGC_{D,\,cg}$$
$$= 0.60 \times 0.36$$
$$= 0.22$$

6. VISUAL AND THERMAL CONTROLS

The ideal fenestration system allows optimum lighting, heating, ventilation, and visibility; minimizes moisture and sound transfer between the outdoors and the indoors; and produces a satisfactory physiological and psychological environment. The controls of an optimum system react to varying climatological and occupant demands. Fixed controls may have operation or cost advantages, or both, but do not react to physical and psychological variations. Variable controls are, therefore, more effective in energy conservation and environmental satisfaction.

Operational Effectiveness of Shading Devices

Shading devices vary in their operational effectiveness. Some devices, such as overhangs, light shelves, and tinted glazings, do not require operation, have long life expectancies, and do not degrade significantly over their effective life. Other types of shading devices, especially operable indoor shades, may have reduced effectiveness because of less than optimal operation and degradation of effectiveness over time. It is important to evaluate operational effectiveness when considering the actual heat rejection potential of shading devices.

The performance of shading devices for reducing peak cooling loads and annual energy use should account for operational effectiveness or reliability in actual operation. Passive devices, such as architectural elements and glazing tinting, are considered 100% effective in operation. Glazing coatings and adherent films may degrade over time. Shade screens are removable and may be assumed to operate seasonally, but in any given population of users, some will remain in place all year long and some will not be installed or removed at optimum times. Automated shading devices controlled for optimum thermal operation are considered more effective than manual devices, but controls require ongoing maintenance, and some occupants may object to the lack of personal control with totally automated devices. Automated shading devices may also operate for nonthermal purposes such as glare and daylighting optimization, and this may reduce thermal effectiveness. Manually operated devices are subject to wide variation in use effectiveness, and this diversity in effective use should be considered when evaluating performance.

Indoor Shading Devices

Although thermal comfort of occupants may be paramount to the HVAC designer, other factors that should be considered, some of which may be more important to the user, include the following:

Radiant Energy Protection. Unshaded fenestration products become sources of radiant heat by transmitting short-wave solar radiation and by emitting long-wave radiation to dissipate some of the absorbed solar energy. In winter, glazing temperatures usually fall below room air temperature, which may produce thermal discomfort to occupants near the fenestration. In summer, individuals seated near unshaded fenestration may experience discomfort from both direct solar rays and long-wave radiation emitted by sun-heated glazing. In winter, loss of heat by radiation to cold glazing can also cause discomfort. Tightly woven, highly reflective drapes minimize such discomfort; drapes with high openness factors are less effective because they allow short- and long-wave radiation to pass more freely. Light-colored shading devices with maximum total surface usually provide the best protection because they absorb less heat and tend to lose heat readily by convection to the conditioned air.

Outward Vision. Outward vision is normally desirable in both business and living spaces. Open-weave, dark-colored fabrics of uniform pattern allow maximum outward vision, whereas uneven pattern weaves reduce the ability to see out. A semiopen weave modifies the view without completely obscuring the outdoors. Tightly woven fabrics block outward vision completely.

Privacy. Venetian blinds, either vertical or horizontal, can be adjusted and, when completely closed, afford full privacy. When draperies are closed, the degree of privacy is determined by their color and tightness of weave and the source of the principal illumination. To obscure the view so completely that not even shadows or silhouettes can be detected, fully opaque materials are used. Generally, the more brightly lit side of a partially shaded glazing is the most visible from the opposite side, making the indoors fairly private in daytime, but not at night.

Brightness Control. Visual comfort is essential in many occupied areas, and freedom from glare is an important factor in performing tasks. *Discomfort glare* is produced by uneven brightness in occupied spaces, with areas or spots that are much brighter than surrounding surfaces. Fenestrations themselves, when they look out onto bright skies or brightly reflecting surfaces, can be glare sources if care is not taken to keep surrounding brightness comparable. A maximum brightness ratio of about 3 to 1 is sometimes quoted. This ratio can be moderated by indoor furnishings and wall coverings, which on average have moderately high diffuse reflectances and access to admitted daylight. Conversely, dark indoor surfaces, and those shaded from daylight illumination, accentuate the brightness difference between the fenestration and its surroundings. Indoor surface brightness can also be elevated by ample use of indoor electric lighting, but this can have adverse consequences for the building's energy use. In general, larger fenestration apertures admit more sunlight, increasing indoor brightness without affecting the perceived brightness of the fenestration, all other factors being equal.

An important guideline is that direct sunlight must not strike the eye, and reflected sunlight from bright or shiny surfaces is equally disturbing and even disabling. A tightly woven white fabric with high solar transmittance attains such brilliance when illuminated by direct sunshine that, by contrast with its surroundings, it creates excessive glare. Off-white colors should be used so their surface brightness is not too great. Venetian blinds allow considerable light to enter by interreflection between slats. When two shading devices are used, the one on the indoors (away from the fenestration product) should be darker and more open. With this arrangement, the indoor

Table 14A IAC Values for Louvered Shades: Uncoated Single Glazings

		Glazing ID:	1a	1b	1c	1d	1e	1f	1g	1h	1i
Louver Location	Louver Reflection	φ	IAC_0 (IAC_{60})/IAC_{diff}, F_R[d]								
Indoor Side	0.15	Worst[a]	0.98 (0.97)/0.86 0.92	0.98 (0.97)/0.86 0.91	0.98 (0.96)/0.86 0.88	0.97 (0.95)/0.87 0.82	0.98 (0.96)/0.87 0.87	0.97 (0.95)/0.87 0.82	0.98 (0.96)/0.87 0.87	0.97 (0.95)/0.87 0.81	0.97 (0.95)/0.87 0.83
		0°	0.98 (0.78)/0.87 0.69	0.98 (0.79)/0.87 0.68	0.98 (0.80)/0.88 0.66	0.97 (0.82)/0.88 0.64	0.98 (0.80)/0.88 0.66	0.97 (0.82)/0.89 0.63	0.98 (0.80)/0.88 0.66	0.97 (0.82)/0.89 0.63	0.97 (0.82)/0.88 0.64
		Excluded Beam[b]	0.73 (0.78)/0.87 0.43	0.74 (0.79)/0.87 0.43	0.75 (0.80)/0.88 0.42	0.77 (0.82)/0.88 0.41	0.76 (0.80)/0.88 0.42	0.77 (0.82)/0.88 0.41	0.76 (0.80)/0.88 0.42	0.78 (0.82)/0.88 0.41	0.77 (0.82)/0.88 0.41
		45°	0.80 (0.74)/0.83 0.47	0.80 (0.75)/0.83 0.46	0.81 (0.76)/0.84 0.45	0.82 (0.78)/0.85 0.44	0.81 (0.77)/0.84 0.45	0.83 (0.79)/0.85 0.43	0.81 (0.77)/0.84 0.45	0.83 (0.79)/0.85 0.43	0.82 (0.78)/0.85 0.44
		Closed	0.70 (0.70)/0.73 0.44	0.70 (0.70)/0.74 0.44	0.72 (0.72)/0.75 0.42	0.74 (0.74)/0.76 0.4	0.72 (0.72)/0.75 0.42	0.74 (0.74)/0.77 0.4	0.72 (0.72)/0.75 0.42	0.74 (0.74)/0.77 0.4	0.74 (0.74)/0.76 0.4
Indoor Side	0.50	Worst[a]	0.98 (0.96)/0.80 0.94	0.97 (0.96)/0.80 0.93	0.97 (0.96)/0.81 0.89	0.97 (0.95)/0.83 0.83	0.97 (0.96)/0.82 0.88	0.97 (0.95)/0.83 0.83	0.97 (0.96)/0.82 0.88	0.97 (0.95)/0.83 0.82	0.97 (0.95)/0.83 0.84
		0°	0.98 (0.70)/0.83 0.74	0.97 (0.70)/0.84 0.73	0.97 (0.72)/0.84 0.71	0.97 (0.75)/0.86 0.67	0.97 (0.73)/0.85 0.7	0.97 (0.76)/0.86 0.67	0.97 (0.73)/0.85 0.7	0.97 (0.76)/0.86 0.66	0.97 (0.75)/0.86 0.67
		Excluded Beam[b]	0.59 (0.70)/0.82 0.5	0.60 (0.70)/0.83 0.5	0.63 (0.72)/0.84 0.48	0.67 (0.75)/0.85 0.46	0.64 (0.73)/0.84 0.48	0.67 (0.76)/0.85 0.46	0.64 (0.73)/0.84 0.48	0.67 (0.76)/0.85 0.46	0.67 (0.75)/0.85 0.46
		45°	0.69 (0.58)/0.74 0.53	0.70 (0.59)/0.75 0.52	0.72 (0.62)/0.76 0.5	0.75 (0.66)/0.79 0.48	0.73 (0.63)/0.77 0.5	0.75 (0.67)/0.79 0.47	0.73 (0.63)/0.77 0.5	0.75 (0.67)/0.79 0.47	0.75 (0.66)/0.79 0.48
		Closed	0.51 (0.49)/0.58 0.46	0.52 (0.50)/0.58 0.45	0.55 (0.53)/0.61 0.43	0.60 (0.58)/0.65 0.4	0.56 (0.54)/0.62 0.42	0.60 (0.59)/0.65 0.4	0.56 (0.54)/0.62 0.42	0.61 (0.59)/0.66 0.39	0.60 (0.58)/0.65 0.4
Indoor Side	0.80	Worst[a]	0.97 (0.96)/0.73 0.95	0.97 (0.96)/0.74 0.94	0.97 (0.95)/0.76 0.9	0.96 (0.95)/0.78 0.85	0.97 (0.95)/0.76 0.89	0.96 (0.95)/0.79 0.84	0.97 (0.95)/0.76 0.89	0.96 (0.95)/0.79 0.83	0.96 (0.95)/0.78 0.85
		0°	0.97 (0.60)/0.78 0.82	0.97 (0.61)/0.79 0.81	0.97 (0.64)/0.80 0.78	0.96 (0.68)/0.82 0.73	0.97 (0.65)/0.81 0.77	0.96 (0.69)/0.83 0.72	0.97 (0.65)/0.81 0.77	0.96 (0.69)/0.83 0.72	0.96 (0.68)/0.82 0.73
		Excluded Beam[b]	0.45 (0.60)/0.77 0.66	0.47 (0.61)/0.77 0.65	0.51 (0.64)/0.79 0.61	0.57 (0.68)/0.81 0.56	0.52 (0.65)/0.79 0.59	0.57 (0.69)/0.81 0.55	0.52 (0.65)/0.79 0.59	0.58 (0.69)/0.82 0.55	0.57 (0.68)/0.81 0.56
		45°	0.59 (0.42)/0.66 0.66	0.60 (0.43)/0.67 0.65	0.63 (0.48)/0.69 0.61	0.67 (0.54)/0.73 0.56	0.64 (0.49)/0.70 0.59	0.68 (0.55)/0.73 0.55	0.64 (0.49)/0.70 0.59	0.68 (0.56)/0.73 0.55	0.68 (0.54)/0.73 0.56
		Closed	0.33 (0.29)/0.43 0.52	0.35 (0.31)/0.44 0.51	0.40 (0.37)/0.49 0.46	0.47 (0.44)/0.54 0.41	0.42 (0.38)/0.50 0.45	0.48 (0.45)/0.55 0.41	0.42 (0.38)/0.50 0.45	0.49 (0.46)/0.55 0.41	0.47 (0.44)/0.54 0.42
Outdoor Side	0.15	Worst[a]	0.93 (0.89)/0.36 0.98	0.93 (0.89)/0.36 0.97	0.93 (0.89)/0.36 0.95	0.93 (0.89)/0.37 0.92	0.93 (0.89)/0.36 0.94	0.93 (0.89)/0.37 0.91	0.93 (0.89)/0.36 0.94	0.93 (0.89)/0.37 0.91	0.93 (0.89)/0.37 0.92
		0°	0.93 (0.05)/0.41 0.9	0.93 (0.06)/0.41 0.89	0.93 (0.06)/0.42 0.87	0.93 (0.06)/0.42 0.84	0.93 (0.06)/0.42 0.87	0.93 (0.06)/0.42 0.84	0.93 (0.06)/0.42 0.87	0.93 (0.07)/0.42 0.83	0.93 (0.06)/0.42 0.84
		Excluded Beam[b]	0.04 (0.05)/0.39 0.77	0.04 (0.06)/0.40 0.76	0.04 (0.06)/0.40 0.74	0.05 (0.06)/0.40 0.72	0.04 (0.06)/0.40 0.74	0.05 (0.06)/0.40 0.72	0.04 (0.06)/0.40 0.74	0.05 (0.07)/0.40 0.72	0.05 (0.06)/0.40 0.72
		45°	0.20 (0.04)/0.29 0.83	0.20 (0.04)/0.30 0.82	0.21 (0.04)/0.30 0.81	0.21 (0.05)/0.30 0.78	0.21 (0.04)/0.30 0.8	0.21 (0.05)/0.30 0.78	0.21 (0.04)/0.30 0.8	0.21 (0.05)/0.30 0.77	0.21 (0.05)/0.30 0.78
		Closed	0.03 (0.03)/0.11 0.65	0.03 (0.04)/0.11 0.65	0.04 (0.04)/0.11 0.65	0.04 (0.05)/0.12 0.64	0.04 (0.04)/0.11 0.64	0.05 (0.05)/0.12 0.64	0.04 (0.04)/0.11 0.64	0.05 (0.05)/0.12 0.64	0.04 (0.05)/0.12 0.64
Outdoor Side	0.50	Worst[a]	0.94 (0.95)/0.44 0.98	0.94 (0.95)/0.44 0.97	0.94 (0.95)/0.44 0.95	0.94 (0.95)/0.44 0.92	0.94 (0.95)/0.44 0.94	0.94 (0.95)/0.44 0.91	0.94 (0.95)/0.44 0.94	0.94 (0.95)/0.44 0.91	0.94 (0.95)/0.44 0.92
		0°	0.94 (0.15)/0.50 0.96	0.94 (0.15)/0.50 0.96	0.94 (0.15)/0.50 0.93	0.94 (0.15)/0.50 0.9	0.94 (0.15)/0.50 0.92	0.94 (0.15)/0.50 0.89	0.94 (0.15)/0.50 0.92	0.94 (0.15)/0.50 0.89	0.94 (0.15)/0.50 0.9
		Excluded Beam[b]	0.08 (0.15)/0.48 0.92	0.08 (0.15)/0.48 0.91	0.09 (0.15)/0.48 0.89	0.09 (0.15)/0.48 0.85	0.09 (0.15)/0.48 0.88	0.09 (0.15)/0.48 0.85	0.09 (0.15)/0.48 0.88	0.09 (0.15)/0.48 0.84	0.09 (0.15)/0.48 0.85
		45°	0.26 (0.07)/0.36 0.93	0.26 (0.07)/0.36 0.92	0.26 (0.07)/0.36 0.89	0.26 (0.07)/0.37 0.86	0.26 (0.07)/0.36 0.89	0.26 (0.07)/0.37 0.85	0.26 (0.07)/0.36 0.89	0.26 (0.07)/0.37 0.85	0.26 (0.07)/0.37 0.86
		Closed	0.05 (0.03)/0.14 0.8	0.05 (0.03)/0.14 0.8	0.05 (0.03)/0.14 0.77	0.05 (0.04)/0.15 0.75	0.05 (0.04)/0.14 0.77	0.06 (0.04)/0.15 0.74	0.05 (0.04)/0.14 0.77	0.06 (0.04)/0.15 0.74	0.05 (0.04)/0.15 0.75

Table 14A IAC Values for Louvered Shades: Uncoated Single Glazings (*Continued*)

		Glazing ID:	1a	1b	1c	1d	1e	1f	1g	1h	1i
Outdoor Side	0.80	Worst[a]	0.95 (1.02)/0.54 0.98	0.95 (1.02)/0.54 0.98	0.95 (1.01)/0.54 0.95	0.95 (1.00)/0.54 0.92	0.95 (1.01)/0.54 0.95	0.95 (1.00)/0.54 0.91	0.95 (1.01)/0.54 0.95	0.95 (1.00)/0.54 0.91	0.95 (1.01)/0.54 0.92
		0°	0.95 (0.28)/0.61 0.98	0.95 (0.28)/0.61 0.97	0.95 (0.28)/0.61 0.95	0.95 (0.28)/0.61 0.91	0.95 (0.28)/0.61 0.94	0.95 (0.28)/0.61 0.91	0.95 (0.28)/0.61 0.94	0.95 (0.28)/0.61 0.91	0.95 (0.28)/0.61 0.91
		Excluded Beam[b]	0.17 (0.28)/0.59 0.97	0.17 (0.28)/0.59 0.96	0.17 (0.28)/0.58 0.94	0.17 (0.28)/0.58 0.9	0.17 (0.28)/0.58 0.93	0.17 (0.28)/0.58 0.89	0.17 (0.28)/0.58 0.93	0.17 (0.28)/0.59 0.89	0.17 (0.28)/0.59 0.9
		45°	0.34 (0.12)/0.46 0.97	0.34 (0.12)/0.46 0.96	0.34 (0.12)/0.46 0.94	0.34 (0.12)/0.46 0.9	0.34 (0.12)/0.46 0.93	0.34 (0.12)/0.46 0.9	0.34 (0.12)/0.46 0.93	0.34 (0.12)/0.46 0.89	0.35 (0.12)/0.46 0.9
		Closed	0.08 (0.04)/0.21 0.93	0.08 (0.04)/0.21 0.92	0.09 (0.04)/0.20 0.89	0.09 (0.04)/0.21 0.86	0.09 (0.04)/0.20 0.89	0.09 (0.04)/0.21 0.85	0.09 (0.04)/0.20 0.89	0.09 (0.04)/0.21 0.85	0.09 (0.04)/0.21 0.86
Sheer		100%	0.7 0.5	0.71 0.49	0.72 0.47	0.74 0.45	0.72 0.47	0.74 0.44	0.72 0.47	0.74 0.44	0.74 0.45

Notes:
[a]Louvers track so that profile angle equals negative slat angle and maximum direct beam is admitted.
[b]Louvers track to block direct beam radiation. When negative slat angles result, slat defaults to 0°.
[c]Glazing cavity width equals original cavity width plus slat width.
[d]F_R is radiant fraction; ratio of radiative heat transfer to total heat transfer, on room side of glazing system.

Table 14B IAC Values for Louvered Shades: Uncoated Double Glazings

		Glazing ID:	5a	5b	5c	5d	5e	5f	5g	5h	5i
Louver Location	Louver Reflection	φ	IAC_0 (IAC_{60})/IAC_{diff}, F_R[d]								
Indoor Side	0.15	Worst[a]	0.99 (0.98)/0.92 0.87	0.99 (0.98)/0.92 0.84	0.99 (0.97)/0.92 0.84	0.98 (0.97)/0.93 0.79	0.99 (0.97)/0.92 0.83	0.98 (0.97)/0.93 0.78	0.99 (0.97)/0.92 0.83	0.98 (0.97)/0.93 0.78	0.98 (0.97)/0.93 0.79
		0°	0.99 (0.88)/0.93 0.67	0.99 (0.89)/0.93 0.65	0.99 (0.89)/0.93 0.65	0.98 (0.90)/0.93 0.62	0.99 (0.89)/0.93 0.65	0.98 (0.90)/0.94 0.62	0.99 (0.89)/0.93 0.65	0.98 (0.90)/0.94 0.62	0.98 (0.90)/0.93 0.62
		Excluded Beam[b]	0.84 (0.88)/0.93 0.42	0.84 (0.89)/0.93 0.41	0.84 (0.89)/0.93 0.41	0.86 (0.90)/0.93 0.4	0.85 (0.89)/0.93 0.41	0.86 (0.90)/0.93 0.4	0.85 (0.89)/0.93 0.41	0.86 (0.90)/0.93 0.4	0.86 (0.90)/0.93 0.4
		45°	0.88 (0.85)/0.90 0.45	0.88 (0.85)/0.90 0.44	0.88 (0.85)/0.90 0.44	0.89 (0.87)/0.91 0.42	0.88 (0.86)/0.90 0.44	0.89 (0.87)/0.91 0.42	0.88 (0.86)/0.90 0.44	0.89 (0.87)/0.91 0.42	0.89 (0.87)/0.91 0.42
		Closed	0.81 (0.81)/0.83 0.41	0.82 (0.82)/0.84 0.4	0.82 (0.82)/0.84 0.4	0.83 (0.84)/0.85 0.38	0.82 (0.82)/0.84 0.4	0.83 (0.84)/0.85 0.38	0.82 (0.82)/0.84 0.4	0.83 (0.84)/0.85 0.38	0.83 (0.84)/0.85 0.38
Indoor Side	0.50	Worst[a]	0.98 (0.97)/0.86 0.88	0.98 (0.97)/0.87 0.86	0.98 (0.97)/0.87 0.85	0.98 (0.97)/0.88 0.8	0.98 (0.97)/0.87 0.84	0.98 (0.97)/0.89 0.79	0.98 (0.97)/0.87 0.84	0.98 (0.97)/0.89 0.79	0.98 (0.97)/0.88 0.8
		0°	0.98 (0.80)/0.89 0.71	0.98 (0.82)/0.90 0.69	0.98 (0.81)/0.90 0.69	0.98 (0.84)/0.91 0.65	0.98 (0.82)/0.90 0.68	0.98 (0.84)/0.91 0.65	0.98 (0.82)/0.90 0.68	0.98 (0.84)/0.91 0.65	0.98 (0.84)/0.91 0.65
		Excluded Beam[b]	0.70 (0.80)/0.88 0.48	0.72 (0.82)/0.89 0.47	0.72 (0.81)/0.89 0.47	0.75 (0.84)/0.90 0.45	0.73 (0.82)/0.89 0.46	0.76 (0.84)/0.90 0.45	0.73 (0.82)/0.89 0.46	0.76 (0.84)/0.90 0.45	0.75 (0.84)/0.90 0.45
		45°	0.78 (0.70)/0.82 0.5	0.80 (0.72)/0.83 0.49	0.79 (0.72)/0.83 0.48	0.82 (0.76)/0.85 0.46	0.80 (0.73)/0.84 0.48	0.82 (0.76)/0.85 0.46	0.80 (0.73)/0.84 0.48	0.82 (0.76)/0.85 0.46	0.82 (0.76)/0.85 0.46
		Closed	0.63 (0.63)/0.69 0.42	0.66 (0.65)/0.71 0.4	0.65 (0.65)/0.71 0.4	0.70 (0.70)/0.74 0.38	0.66 (0.66)/0.71 0.4	0.70 (0.70)/0.75 0.38	0.66 (0.66)/0.71 0.4	0.70 (0.70)/0.75 0.38	0.70 (0.70)/0.74 0.38
Indoor Side	0.80	Worst[a]	0.97 (0.96)/0.80 0.9	0.97 (0.96)/0.81 0.87	0.97 (0.96)/0.81 0.87	0.97 (0.96)/0.84 0.81	0.97 (0.96)/0.82 0.86	0.97 (0.96)/0.84 0.8	0.97 (0.96)/0.82 0.86	0.97 (0.96)/0.84 0.8	0.97 (0.96)/0.84 0.81
		0°	0.97 (0.71)/0.84 0.78	0.97 (0.73)/0.85 0.75	0.97 (0.73)/0.85 0.75	0.97 (0.77)/0.87 0.7	0.97 (0.73)/0.85 0.74	0.97 (0.77)/0.87 0.7	0.97 (0.73)/0.85 0.74	0.97 (0.77)/0.87 0.7	0.97 (0.77)/0.87 0.71
		Excluded Beam[b]	0.57 (0.71)/0.83 0.6	0.60 (0.73)/0.84 0.58	0.60 (0.73)/0.84 0.58	0.65 (0.77)/0.86 0.54	0.61 (0.73)/0.84 0.57	0.66 (0.77)/0.86 0.53	0.61 (0.73)/0.84 0.57	0.66 (0.77)/0.86 0.53	0.65 (0.77)/0.86 0.54
		45°	0.68 (0.56)/0.74 0.6	0.71 (0.60)/0.76 0.58	0.70 (0.59)/0.76 0.58	0.74 (0.65)/0.79 0.54	0.71 (0.60)/0.76 0.57	0.75 (0.66)/0.79 0.53	0.71 (0.60)/0.76 0.57	0.75 (0.66)/0.79 0.53	0.74 (0.65)/0.79 0.54
		Closed	0.47 (0.45)/0.55 0.46	0.51 (0.50)/0.59 0.43	0.50 (0.49)/0.58 0.43	0.57 (0.56)/0.64 0.4	0.51 (0.50)/0.59 0.43	0.57 (0.57)/0.64 0.39	0.51 (0.50)/0.59 0.43	0.57 (0.57)/0.65 0.39	0.57 (0.56)/0.64 0.4
Between Glazings[c]	0.15	Worst[a]	0.97 (0.98)/0.66 0.93	0.97 (0.99)/0.67 0.91	0.96 (0.97)/0.67 0.91	0.95 (0.96)/0.69 0.88	0.95 (0.97)/0.67 0.91	0.95 (0.95)/0.69 0.88	0.95 (0.97)/0.67 0.91	0.95 (0.95)/0.69 0.88	0.95 (0.96)/0.69 0.88
		0°	0.97 (0.50)/0.70 0.81	0.97 (0.51)/0.71 0.8	0.96 (0.52)/0.70 0.8	0.95 (0.55)/0.72 0.78	0.95 (0.52)/0.70 0.79	0.95 (0.55)/0.72 0.78	0.95 (0.52)/0.70 0.79	0.95 (0.55)/0.72 0.78	0.95 (0.55)/0.72 0.78
		Excluded Beam[b]	0.43 (0.50)/0.69 0.66	0.45 (0.51)/0.69 0.66	0.46 (0.52)/0.69 0.66	0.49 (0.55)/0.71 0.65	0.46 (0.52)/0.69 0.65	0.49 (0.55)/0.71 0.65	0.46 (0.52)/0.69 0.65	0.49 (0.55)/0.71 0.65	0.49 (0.55)/0.71 0.65
		45°	0.54 (0.47)/0.62	0.55 (0.48)/0.63	0.56 (0.49)/0.63	0.58 (0.52)/0.65	0.56 (0.49)/0.63	0.58 (0.52)/0.65	0.56 (0.49)/0.63	0.59 (0.52)/0.65	0.58 (0.52)/0.65

Table 14B IAC Values for Louvered Shades: Uncoated Double Glazings (*Continued*)

		Glazing ID:	5a	5b	5c	5d	5e	5f	5g	5h	5i
			0.7	0.7	0.7	0.69	0.69	0.68	0.69	0.68	0.69
		Closed	0.42 (0.45)/0.50 0.65	0.44 (0.47)/0.51 0.65	0.44 (0.47)/0.52 0.65	0.47 (0.50)/0.54 0.64	0.45 (0.48)/0.52 0.64	0.48 (0.51)/0.54 0.64	0.45 (0.48)/0.52 0.64	0.48 (0.51)/0.54 0.64	0.47 (0.50)/0.54 0.64
Between Glazings[c]	0.50	Worst[a]	0.97 (1.01)/0.67 0.94	0.97 (1.02)/0.67 0.92	0.96 (1.00)/0.67 0.92	0.95 (0.98)/0.69 0.89	0.95 (0.99)/0.68 0.92	0.95 (0.98)/0.69 0.89	0.95 (0.99)/0.68 0.92	0.95 (0.98)/0.69 0.89	0.95 (0.98)/0.69 0.89
		0°	0.97 (0.49)/0.71 0.84	0.97 (0.50)/0.72 0.83	0.96 (0.51)/0.72 0.83	0.95 (0.54)/0.73 0.8	0.95 (0.52)/0.72 0.82	0.95 (0.55)/0.73 0.8	0.95 (0.52)/0.72 0.82	0.95 (0.55)/0.73 0.8	0.95 (0.54)/0.73 0.8
		Excluded Beam[b]	0.38 (0.49)/0.70 0.72	0.39 (0.50)/0.70 0.71	0.40 (0.51)/0.70 0.71	0.44 (0.54)/0.72 0.69	0.41 (0.52)/0.71 0.71	0.45 (0.55)/0.72 0.69	0.41 (0.52)/0.71 0.71	0.45 (0.55)/0.72 0.69	0.44 (0.54)/0.72 0.69
		45°	0.51 (0.38)/0.61 0.75	0.52 (0.40)/0.62 0.74	0.53 (0.41)/0.62 0.73	0.56 (0.45)/0.64 0.72	0.53 (0.42)/0.62 0.73	0.56 (0.46)/0.64 0.71	0.53 (0.42)/0.62 0.73	0.56 (0.46)/0.64 0.71	0.56 (0.45)/0.64 0.72
		Closed	0.32 (0.32)/0.42 0.67	0.33 (0.33)/0.43 0.66	0.35 (0.35)/0.44 0.66	0.39 (0.39)/0.47 0.65	0.36 (0.36)/0.45 0.66	0.39 (0.40)/0.48 0.65	0.36 (0.36)/0.45 0.66	0.40 (0.40)/0.48 0.65	0.39 (0.39)/0.47 0.66
Between Glazings[c]	0.80	Worst[a]	0.97 (1.04)/0.68 0.94	0.97 (1.04)/0.68 0.93	0.96 (1.02)/0.69 0.93	0.95 (1.01)/0.70 0.9	0.96 (1.02)/0.69 0.93	0.95 (1.00)/0.70 0.9	0.96 (1.02)/0.69 0.93	0.95 (1.00)/0.70 0.89	0.95 (1.01)/0.70 0.9
		0°	0.97 (0.49)/0.73 0.89	0.97 (0.50)/0.74 0.88	0.96 (0.51)/0.74 0.87	0.95 (0.55)/0.75 0.84	0.96 (0.52)/0.74 0.87	0.95 (0.55)/0.75 0.84	0.96 (0.52)/0.74 0.87	0.95 (0.55)/0.75 0.84	0.95 (0.55)/0.75 0.84
		Excluded Beam[b]	0.35 (0.49)/0.72 0.82	0.36 (0.50)/0.72 0.81	0.37 (0.51)/0.72 0.8	0.42 (0.55)/0.74 0.76	0.38 (0.52)/0.72 0.79	0.42 (0.55)/0.74 0.76	0.38 (0.52)/0.72 0.79	0.42 (0.55)/0.74 0.76	0.42 (0.55)/0.74 0.77
		45°	0.50 (0.32)/0.60 0.83	0.51 (0.33)/0.61 0.81	0.52 (0.35)/0.62 0.8	0.55 (0.40)/0.64 0.77	0.53 (0.36)/0.62 0.8	0.55 (0.41)/0.64 0.77	0.53 (0.36)/0.62 0.8	0.56 (0.41)/0.64 0.77	0.55 (0.40)/0.64 0.77
		Closed	0.24 (0.20)/0.36 0.74	0.25 (0.22)/0.37 0.73	0.27 (0.25)/0.39 0.71	0.32 (0.30)/0.43 0.69	0.28 (0.26)/0.40 0.71	0.33 (0.31)/0.43 0.69	0.28 (0.26)/0.40 0.71	0.33 (0.31)/0.43 0.69	0.32 (0.30)/0.43 0.69
Outdoor Side	0.15	Worst[a]	0.93 (0.89)/0.35 0.95	0.93 (0.89)/0.36 0.94	0.93 (0.89)/0.36 0.93	0.93 (0.89)/0.36 0.9	0.93 (0.89)/0.36 0.93	0.93 (0.89)/0.36 0.89	0.93 (0.89)/0.36 0.93	0.93 (0.89)/0.36 0.89	0.93 (0.89)/0.36 0.9
		0°	0.93 (0.05)/0.41 0.9	0.93 (0.05)/0.41 0.88	0.93 (0.05)/0.41 0.88	0.93 (0.05)/0.41 0.84	0.93 (0.05)/0.41 0.87	0.93 (0.06)/0.41 0.84	0.93 (0.05)/0.41 0.87	0.93 (0.06)/0.41 0.84	0.93 (0.05)/0.41 0.84
		Excluded Beam[b]	0.03 (0.05)/0.39 0.78	0.03 (0.05)/0.39 0.77	0.03 (0.05)/0.39 0.76	0.03 (0.05)/0.39 0.73	0.03 (0.05)/0.39 0.76	0.03 (0.06)/0.39 0.73	0.03 (0.05)/0.39 0.76	0.04 (0.06)/0.40 0.73	0.03 (0.05)/0.39 0.73
		45°	0.19 (0.03)/0.29 0.84	0.19 (0.03)/0.29 0.82	0.20 (0.03)/0.29 0.82	0.20 (0.04)/0.29 0.79	0.20 (0.03)/0.29 0.81	0.20 (0.04)/0.29 0.78	0.20 (0.03)/0.29 0.81	0.20 (0.04)/0.30 0.78	0.20 (0.04)/0.29 0.79
		Closed	0.02 (0.02)/0.10 0.66	0.02 (0.02)/0.10 0.66	0.02 (0.03)/0.10 0.65	0.03 (0.03)/0.11 0.64	0.03 (0.03)/0.10 0.65	0.03 (0.03)/0.11 0.64	0.03 (0.03)/0.10 0.65	0.03 (0.03)/0.11 0.64	0.03 (0.03)/0.11 0.64
Outdoor Side	0.50	Worst[a]	0.94 (0.98)/0.44 0.95	0.94 (0.98)/0.44 0.94	0.94 (0.97)/0.44 0.93	0.94 (0.96)/0.44 0.9	0.94 (0.96)/0.44 0.93	0.94 (0.95)/0.44 0.9	0.94 (0.96)/0.44 0.93	0.94 (0.95)/0.44 0.89	0.94 (0.96)/0.44 0.9
		0°	0.94 (0.14)/0.50 0.94	0.94 (0.14)/0.50 0.93	0.94 (0.15)/0.50 0.92	0.94 (0.15)/0.50 0.89	0.94 (0.15)/0.50 0.92	0.94 (0.15)/0.50 0.88	0.94 (0.15)/0.50 0.92	0.94 (0.15)/0.50 0.88	0.94 (0.15)/0.50 0.89
		Excluded Beam[b]	0.07 (0.14)/0.48 0.91	0.07 (0.14)/0.48 0.9	0.08 (0.15)/0.48 0.89	0.08 (0.15)/0.48 0.85	0.08 (0.15)/0.48 0.88	0.08 (0.15)/0.48 0.85	0.08 (0.15)/0.48 0.88	0.08 (0.15)/0.48 0.84	0.08 (0.15)/0.48 0.85
		45°	0.25 (0.06)/0.36 0.92	0.25 (0.06)/0.36 0.9	0.25 (0.06)/0.36 0.9	0.25 (0.07)/0.36 0.86	0.25 (0.06)/0.36 0.89	0.25 (0.07)/0.36 0.85	0.25 (0.06)/0.36 0.89	0.25 (0.07)/0.36 0.85	0.25 (0.07)/0.36 0.86
		Closed	0.04 (0.02)/0.14 0.82	0.04 (0.03)/0.14 0.81	0.04 (0.03)/0.14 0.8	0.04 (0.03)/0.14 0.76	0.04 (0.03)/0.14 0.79	0.05 (0.03)/0.14 0.76	0.04 (0.03)/0.14 0.79	0.05 (0.03)/0.14 0.76	0.04 (0.03)/0.14 0.76
Outdoor Side	0.80	Worst[a]	0.95 (1.08)/0.55 0.95	0.95 (1.07)/0.55 0.94	0.95 (1.04)/0.55 0.93	0.95 (1.02)/0.54 0.9	0.95 (1.04)/0.55 0.93	0.95 (1.02)/0.54 0.9	0.95 (1.04)/0.55 0.93	0.95 (1.02)/0.54 0.89	0.95 (1.03)/0.54 0.9
		0°	0.95 (0.29)/0.62 0.95	0.95 (0.29)/0.61 0.94	0.95 (0.28)/0.61 0.94	0.95 (0.28)/0.61 0.9	0.95 (0.28)/0.61 0.93	0.95 (0.28)/0.61 0.9	0.95 (0.28)/0.61 0.93	0.95 (0.28)/0.61 0.89	0.95 (0.28)/0.61 0.9
		Excluded Beam[b]	0.16 (0.29)/0.59 0.94	0.16 (0.29)/0.59 0.93	0.16 (0.28)/0.59 0.92	0.16 (0.28)/0.59 0.89	0.16 (0.28)/0.59 0.92	0.16 (0.28)/0.59 0.88	0.16 (0.28)/0.59 0.92	0.16 (0.28)/0.59 0.88	0.16 (0.28)/0.59 0.89
		45°	0.34 (0.12)/0.47 0.95	0.34 (0.12)/0.47 0.93	0.33 (0.12)/0.47 0.93	0.33 (0.12)/0.46 0.89	0.33 (0.12)/0.46 0.92	0.33 (0.12)/0.46 0.88	0.33 (0.12)/0.46 0.92	0.33 (0.12)/0.46 0.88	0.34 (0.12)/0.46 0.89
		Closed	0.08 (0.04)/0.21 0.92	0.08 (0.04)/0.21 0.9	0.08 (0.04)/0.21 0.89	0.08 (0.04)/0.21 0.86	0.08 (0.04)/0.21 0.89	0.08 (0.04)/0.21 0.85	0.08 (0.04)/0.21 0.89	0.08 (0.04)/0.21 0.85	0.08 (0.04)/0.21 0.86

Notes:
[a]Louvers track so that profile angle equals negative slat angle and maximum direct beam is admitted.
[b]Louvers track to block direct beam radiation. When negative slat angles result, slat defaults to 0°.
[c]Glazing cavity width equals original cavity width plus slat width.
[d]F_R is radiant fraction; ratio of radiative heat transfer to total heat transfer, on room side of glazing system.

Table 14C IAC Values for Louvered Shades: Coated Double Glazings with 0.2 Low-e

		Glazing ID:	17a	17b	17c	17d	17e	17f	17g	17h	17i	17j	17k
Louver Location	Louver Reflection	φ	IAC_0 (IAC_{60})/IAC_{diff}, F_R[d]										
Indoor Side	0.15	Worst[a]	0.99 (0.98)/0.94 0.86	0.99 (0.98)/0.94 0.83	0.99 (0.98)/0.94 0.83	0.99 (0.98)/0.94 0.79	0.99 (0.98)/0.94 0.81	0.99 (0.98)/0.95 0.76	0.99 (0.98)/0.94 0.8	0.99 (0.98)/0.95 0.75	0.99 (0.98)/0.94 0.8	0.99 (0.98)/0.95 0.75	0.99 (0.98)/0.95 0.76
		0°	0.99 (0.91)/0.95 0.66	0.99 (0.91)/0.95 0.64	0.99 (0.91)/0.95 0.65	0.99 (0.92)/0.95 0.63	0.99 (0.92)/0.95 0.63	0.99 (0.93)/0.95 0.61	0.99 (0.92)/0.95 0.63	0.99 (0.93)/0.95 0.6	0.99 (0.92)/0.95 0.63	0.99 (0.93)/0.95 0.6	0.99 (0.93)/0.95 0.61
		Excluded Beam[b]	0.87 (0.91)/0.94 0.41	0.88 (0.91)/0.95 0.41	0.88 (0.91)/0.95 0.41	0.89 (0.92)/0.95 0.41	0.88 (0.92)/0.95 0.41	0.90 (0.93)/0.95 0.4	0.88 (0.92)/0.95 0.41	0.90 (0.93)/0.95 0.4	0.88 (0.92)/0.95 0.41	0.90 (0.93)/0.95 0.4	0.90 (0.93)/0.95 0.4
		45°	0.90 (0.88)/0.92 0.44	0.91 (0.89)/0.93 0.43	0.91 (0.89)/0.93 0.44	0.92 (0.89)/0.93 0.43	0.91 (0.89)/0.93 0.43	0.92 (0.90)/0.93 0.42	0.91 (0.89)/0.93 0.43	0.92 (0.90)/0.93 0.42	0.91 (0.89)/0.93 0.43	0.92 (0.90)/0.93 0.42	0.92 (0.90)/0.93 0.42
		Closed	0.85 (0.85)/0.87 0.4	0.86 (0.86)/0.88 0.39	0.85 (0.86)/0.88 0.4	0.86 (0.87)/0.88 0.39	0.86 (0.86)/0.88 0.39	0.87 (0.88)/0.89 0.37	0.86 (0.86)/0.88 0.39	0.87 (0.88)/0.89 0.37	0.86 (0.86)/0.88 0.39	0.87 (0.88)/0.89 0.37	0.87 (0.88)/0.89 0.37
Indoor Side	0.50	Worst[a]	0.98 (0.98)/0.88 0.87	0.98 (0.98)/0.89 0.84	0.98 (0.98)/0.89 0.84	0.98 (0.98)/0.90 0.8	0.98 (0.98)/0.90 0.82	0.98 (0.98)/0.91 0.76	0.98 (0.98)/0.90 0.81	0.98 (0.98)/0.91 0.76	0.98 (0.98)/0.90 0.81	0.98 (0.98)/0.91 0.76	0.98 (0.98)/0.91 0.77
		0°	0.98 (0.83)/0.91 0.7	0.98 (0.85)/0.91 0.68	0.98 (0.85)/0.91 0.68	0.98 (0.86)/0.92 0.66	0.98 (0.85)/0.92 0.67	0.98 (0.87)/0.93 0.63	0.98 (0.85)/0.92 0.66	0.98 (0.87)/0.93 0.63	0.98 (0.85)/0.92 0.66	0.98 (0.87)/0.93 0.63	0.98 (0.87)/0.93 0.64
		Excluded Beam[b]	0.74 (0.83)/0.90 0.47	0.76 (0.85)/0.91 0.46	0.76 (0.85)/0.91 0.46	0.79 (0.86)/0.92 0.45	0.77 (0.85)/0.91 0.45	0.80 (0.87)/0.92 0.44	0.77 (0.85)/0.91 0.45	0.80 (0.87)/0.92 0.44	0.77 (0.85)/0.91 0.45	0.81 (0.87)/0.92 0.44	0.80 (0.87)/0.92 0.44
		45°	0.81 (0.74)/0.85 0.49	0.83 (0.76)/0.86 0.48	0.83 (0.76)/0.86 0.48	0.84 (0.79)/0.87 0.47	0.83 (0.77)/0.86 0.47	0.86 (0.81)/0.88 0.45	0.83 (0.77)/0.87 0.47	0.86 (0.81)/0.88 0.45	0.83 (0.77)/0.87 0.47	0.86 (0.81)/0.88 0.45	0.86 (0.81)/0.88 0.45
		Closed	0.67 (0.67)/0.73 0.41	0.70 (0.70)/0.75 0.39	0.70 (0.70)/0.75 0.4	0.73 (0.73)/0.78 0.38	0.71 (0.71)/0.76 0.39	0.75 (0.75)/0.79 0.37	0.72 (0.71)/0.76 0.38	0.76 (0.75)/0.79 0.37	0.72 (0.71)/0.76 0.38	0.76 (0.76)/0.80 0.37	0.75 (0.75)/0.79 0.37
Indoor Side	0.80	Worst[a]	0.98 (0.97)/0.82 0.88	0.98 (0.97)/0.83 0.85	0.98 (0.97)/0.83 0.85	0.98 (0.97)/0.85 0.82	0.98 (0.97)/0.84 0.83	0.98 (0.97)/0.86 0.78	0.98 (0.97)/0.84 0.83	0.98 (0.97)/0.87 0.77	0.98 (0.97)/0.84 0.83	0.98 (0.97)/0.87 0.77	0.98 (0.97)/0.87 0.78
		0°	0.98 (0.74)/0.86 0.76	0.98 (0.76)/0.87 0.74	0.98 (0.76)/0.87 0.74	0.98 (0.79)/0.88 0.71	0.98 (0.77)/0.88 0.72	0.98 (0.81)/0.89 0.68	0.98 (0.77)/0.88 0.72	0.98 (0.81)/0.89 0.68	0.98 (0.77)/0.88 0.72	0.98 (0.81)/0.89 0.68	0.98 (0.81)/0.89 0.68
		Excluded Beam[b]	0.61 (0.74)/0.84 0.59	0.64 (0.76)/0.86 0.56	0.64 (0.76)/0.86 0.56	0.68 (0.79)/0.87 0.54	0.66 (0.77)/0.86 0.55	0.71 (0.81)/0.88 0.51	0.66 (0.77)/0.87 0.54	0.71 (0.81)/0.89 0.51	0.66 (0.77)/0.87 0.54	0.72 (0.81)/0.89 0.51	0.71 (0.81)/0.88 0.51
		45°	0.71 (0.60)/0.77 0.59	0.74 (0.64)/0.79 0.56	0.74 (0.64)/0.79 0.56	0.77 (0.68)/0.81 0.54	0.75 (0.66)/0.80 0.55	0.79 (0.71)/0.83 0.51	0.75 (0.66)/0.80 0.54	0.79 (0.71)/0.83 0.51	0.75 (0.66)/0.80 0.54	0.79 (0.72)/0.83 0.51	0.79 (0.71)/0.83 0.51
		Closed	0.51 (0.50)/0.59 0.44	0.55 (0.54)/0.63 0.42	0.55 (0.55)/0.63 0.42	0.60 (0.60)/0.67 0.4	0.57 (0.57)/0.65 0.41	0.64 (0.64)/0.70 0.38	0.58 (0.57)/0.65 0.4	0.64 (0.64)/0.70 0.38	0.58 (0.57)/0.65 0.4	0.64 (0.64)/0.70 0.38	0.64 (0.64)/0.70 0.38
Between Glazings[c]	0.15	Worst[a]	0.97 (1.02)/0.78 0.92	0.98 (1.02)/0.78 0.9	0.96 (0.96)/0.59 0.91	0.96 (0.96)/0.60 0.89	0.95 (0.95)/0.60 0.9	0.95 (0.95)/0.62 0.87	0.95 (0.95)/0.60 0.9	0.95 (0.95)/0.62 0.87	0.95 (0.95)/0.60 0.9	0.95 (0.95)/0.62 0.87	0.95 (0.95)/0.62 0.87
		0°	0.97 (0.66)/0.80 0.8	0.98 (0.67)/0.81 0.79	0.96 (0.39)/0.63 0.79	0.96 (0.40)/0.64 0.78	0.95 (0.41)/0.64 0.79	0.95 (0.44)/0.65 0.77	0.95 (0.41)/0.64 0.79	0.95 (0.44)/0.65 0.77	0.95 (0.41)/0.64 0.79	0.95 (0.44)/0.65 0.77	0.95 (0.44)/0.65 0.77
		Excluded Beam[b]	0.59 (0.66)/0.79 0.66	0.60 (0.67)/0.80 0.66	0.33 (0.39)/0.62 0.66	0.34 (0.40)/0.62 0.66	0.35 (0.41)/0.62 0.65	0.38 (0.44)/0.64 0.65	0.36 (0.41)/0.63 0.65	0.39 (0.44)/0.64 0.65	0.36 (0.41)/0.63 0.65	0.39 (0.44)/0.64 0.65	0.38 (0.44)/0.64 0.65
		45°	0.67 (0.62)/0.74 0.69	0.68 (0.63)/0.75 0.69	0.46 (0.36)/0.54 0.7	0.46 (0.37)/0.55 0.7	0.47 (0.38)/0.55 0.7	0.50 (0.41)/0.57 0.69	0.47 (0.38)/0.56 0.7	0.50 (0.41)/0.57 0.69	0.47 (0.38)/0.56 0.7	0.50 (0.41)/0.58 0.69	0.49 (0.41)/0.57 0.69
		Closed	0.57 (0.60)/0.64 0.65	0.58 (0.61)/0.65 0.65	0.32 (0.34)/0.40 0.64	0.33 (0.35)/0.41 0.64	0.34 (0.36)/0.42 0.64	0.37 (0.40)/0.44 0.64	0.35 (0.37)/0.42 0.64	0.38 (0.40)/0.45 0.64	0.35 (0.37)/0.42 0.64	0.38 (0.40)/0.45 0.64	0.37 (0.39)/0.44 0.64
Between Glazings[c]	0.50	Worst[a]	0.97 (1.03)/0.75 0.92	0.97 (1.03)/0.75 0.91	0.96 (1.01)/0.61 0.91	0.96 (1.01)/0.62 0.89	0.96 (1.00)/0.62 0.91	0.95 (0.99)/0.64 0.87	0.95 (0.99)/0.62 0.9	0.95 (0.98)/0.64 0.87	0.95 (0.99)/0.62 0.9	0.95 (0.98)/0.64 0.87	0.95 (0.99)/0.64 0.88
		0°	0.97 (0.61)/0.79 0.83	0.97 (0.62)/0.79 0.82	0.96 (0.41)/0.66 0.83	0.96 (0.42)/0.67 0.82	0.96 (0.43)/0.67 0.82	0.95 (0.45)/0.68 0.8	0.95 (0.43)/0.67 0.82	0.95 (0.46)/0.68 0.8	0.95 (0.43)/0.67 0.82	0.95 (0.46)/0.69 0.8	0.95 (0.45)/0.68 0.8
		Excluded Beam[b]	0.49 (0.61)/0.77 0.7	0.50 (0.62)/0.78 0.7	0.31 (0.41)/0.65 0.72	0.32 (0.42)/0.65 0.72	0.33 (0.43)/0.65 0.71	0.36 (0.45)/0.67 0.7	0.33 (0.43)/0.66 0.71	0.37 (0.46)/0.67 0.7	0.33 (0.43)/0.66 0.71	0.37 (0.46)/0.67 0.7	0.36 (0.45)/0.67 0.7

Table 14C IAC Values for Louvered Shades: Coated Double Glazings with 0.2 Low-e (*Continued*)

		Glazing ID:	17a	17b	17c	17d	17e	17f	17g	17h	17i	17j	17k
		45°	0.61 (0.49)/0.69 0.73	0.62 (0.50)/0.70 0.72	0.45 (0.31)/0.55 0.75	0.46 (0.32)/0.56 0.74	0.47 (0.33)/0.56 0.74	0.49 (0.37)/0.58 0.72	0.47 (0.34)/0.56 0.74	0.50 (0.37)/0.58 0.72	0.47 (0.34)/0.56 0.74	0.50 (0.37)/0.58 0.72	0.49 (0.37)/0.58 0.72
		Closed	0.42 (0.42)/0.52 0.66	0.43 (0.43)/0.53 0.66	0.25 (0.25)/0.35 0.67	0.26 (0.26)/0.36 0.66	0.28 (0.27)/0.37 0.66	0.31 (0.31)/0.40 0.66	0.28 (0.28)/0.38 0.66	0.32 (0.32)/0.41 0.65	0.28 (0.28)/0.38 0.66	0.32 (0.32)/0.41 0.65	0.31 (0.31)/0.40 0.66
Between Glazings[c]	0.80	Worst[a]	0.97 (1.05)/0.72 0.94	0.97 (1.05)/0.72 0.92	0.97 (1.05)/0.65 0.92	0.97 (1.05)/0.66 0.9	0.96 (1.04)/0.66 0.91	0.96 (1.02)/0.67 0.88	0.96 (1.03)/0.66 0.91	0.95 (1.02)/0.67 0.88	0.96 (1.03)/0.66 0.91	0.95 (1.02)/0.68 0.88	0.96 (1.02)/0.67 0.88
		0°	0.97 (0.55)/0.77 0.88	0.97 (0.56)/0.78 0.86	0.97 (0.45)/0.71 0.88	0.97 (0.46)/0.72 0.86	0.96 (0.46)/0.72 0.87	0.96 (0.49)/0.73 0.84	0.96 (0.47)/0.72 0.86	0.95 (0.49)/0.73 0.83	0.96 (0.47)/0.72 0.86	0.95 (0.50)/0.73 0.83	0.96 (0.49)/0.73 0.84
		Excluded Beam[b]	0.40 (0.55)/0.75 0.8	0.41 (0.56)/0.76 0.78	0.31 (0.45)/0.69 0.82	0.32 (0.46)/0.70 0.81	0.33 (0.46)/0.70 0.8	0.37 (0.49)/0.71 0.77	0.34 (0.47)/0.70 0.8	0.37 (0.49)/0.71 0.77	0.34 (0.47)/0.70 0.8	0.37 (0.50)/0.71 0.77	0.37 (0.49)/0.71 0.77
		45°	0.55 (0.37)/0.65 0.81	0.56 (0.39)/0.65 0.79	0.47 (0.28)/0.58 0.83	0.48 (0.29)/0.58 0.81	0.49 (0.31)/0.59 0.81	0.51 (0.34)/0.61 0.77	0.49 (0.31)/0.59 0.8	0.51 (0.35)/0.61 0.77	0.49 (0.31)/0.59 0.8	0.52 (0.35)/0.61 0.77	0.51 (0.34)/0.61 0.78
		Closed	0.29 (0.25)/0.41 0.72	0.30 (0.27)/0.42 0.71	0.21 (0.17)/0.33 0.75	0.22 (0.18)/0.34 0.73	0.24 (0.20)/0.35 0.72	0.27 (0.25)/0.38 0.7	0.24 (0.21)/0.36 0.72	0.28 (0.25)/0.39 0.7	0.24 (0.21)/0.36 0.72	0.28 (0.26)/0.39 0.69	0.27 (0.25)/0.38 0.7
Outdoor Side	0.15	Worst[a]	0.93 (0.89)/0.35 0.95	0.93 (0.89)/0.35 0.93	0.93 (0.89)/0.35 0.93	0.93 (0.89)/0.35 0.91	0.93 (0.89)/0.35 0.92	0.93 (0.89)/0.35 0.88	0.93 (0.89)/0.35 0.91	0.93 (0.89)/0.35 0.88	0.93 (0.89)/0.35 0.91	0.93 (0.89)/0.36 0.88	0.93 (0.89)/0.35 0.88
		0°	0.93 (0.04)/0.41 0.9	0.93 (0.04)/0.41 0.88	0.93 (0.04)/0.41 0.89	0.93 (0.04)/0.41 0.87	0.93 (0.04)/0.41 0.87	0.93 (0.05)/0.41 0.84	0.93 (0.04)/0.41 0.87	0.93 (0.05)/0.41 0.83	0.93 (0.04)/0.41 0.87	0.93 (0.05)/0.41 0.83	0.93 (0.05)/0.41 0.84
		Excluded Beam[b]	0.02 (0.04)/0.39 0.8	0.02 (0.04)/0.39 0.79	0.02 (0.04)/0.39 0.8	0.02 (0.04)/0.39 0.78	0.02 (0.04)/0.39 0.77	0.03 (0.05)/0.39 0.74	0.02 (0.04)/0.39 0.77	0.03 (0.05)/0.39 0.74	0.02 (0.04)/0.39 0.77	0.03 (0.05)/0.39 0.74	0.03 (0.05)/0.39 0.74
		45°	0.19 (0.02)/0.28 0.84	0.19 (0.02)/0.29 0.83	0.19 (0.02)/0.28 0.84	0.19 (0.02)/0.29 0.82	0.19 (0.02)/0.29 0.82	0.19 (0.03)/0.29 0.79	0.19 (0.03)/0.29 0.81	0.20 (0.03)/0.29 0.78	0.19 (0.03)/0.29 0.81	0.20 (0.03)/0.29 0.78	0.19 (0.03)/0.29 0.79
		Closed	0.02 (0.02)/0.09 0.67	0.02 (0.02)/0.09 0.66	0.02 (0.02)/0.09 0.67	0.02 (0.02)/0.09 0.66	0.02 (0.02)/0.09 0.66	0.02 (0.02)/0.10 0.65	0.02 (0.02)/0.09 0.66	0.02 (0.03)/0.10 0.65	0.02 (0.02)/0.09 0.66	0.02 (0.03)/0.10 0.65	0.02 (0.02)/0.10 0.65
Outdoor Side	0.50	Worst[a]	0.94 (0.98)/0.43 0.95	0.94 (0.98)/0.43 0.93	0.94 (0.99)/0.44 0.93	0.94 (0.98)/0.44 0.91	0.94 (0.97)/0.43 0.92	0.94 (0.95)/0.43 0.88	0.94 (0.96)/0.43 0.91	0.94 (0.95)/0.43 0.88	0.94 (0.96)/0.43 0.91	0.94 (0.95)/0.43 0.88	0.94 (0.96)/0.43 0.88
		0°	0.94 (0.14)/0.50 0.94	0.94 (0.14)/0.50 0.92	0.94 (0.14)/0.50 0.92	0.94 (0.14)/0.50 0.9	0.94 (0.14)/0.49 0.91	0.94 (0.14)/0.49 0.87	0.94 (0.14)/0.49 0.91	0.94 (0.14)/0.49 0.87	0.94 (0.14)/0.49 0.91	0.94 (0.14)/0.49 0.87	0.94 (0.14)/0.49 0.88
		Excluded Beam[b]	0.07 (0.14)/0.47 0.91	0.07 (0.14)/0.47 0.9	0.07 (0.14)/0.48 0.9	0.07 (0.14)/0.48 0.88	0.07 (0.14)/0.47 0.88	0.07 (0.14)/0.47 0.85	0.07 (0.14)/0.47 0.88	0.07 (0.14)/0.47 0.84	0.07 (0.14)/0.47 0.88	0.08 (0.14)/0.47 0.84	0.07 (0.14)/0.47 0.85
		45°	0.25 (0.06)/0.36 0.92	0.25 (0.06)/0.36 0.9	0.25 (0.06)/0.36 0.91	0.25 (0.06)/0.36 0.88	0.25 (0.06)/0.36 0.89	0.25 (0.06)/0.36 0.85	0.25 (0.06)/0.36 0.88	0.25 (0.06)/0.36 0.85	0.25 (0.06)/0.36 0.88	0.25 (0.06)/0.36 0.85	0.25 (0.06)/0.36 0.85
		Closed	0.04 (0.02)/0.13 0.84	0.04 (0.02)/0.13 0.82	0.04 (0.02)/0.13 0.83	0.04 (0.02)/0.13 0.81	0.04 (0.02)/0.13 0.81	0.04 (0.03)/0.13 0.77	0.04 (0.02)/0.13 0.8	0.04 (0.03)/0.14 0.77	0.04 (0.02)/0.13 0.8	0.04 (0.03)/0.14 0.77	0.04 (0.03)/0.14 0.77
Outdoor Side	0.80	Worst[a]	0.95 (1.07)/0.55 0.95	0.95 (1.07)/0.55 0.93	0.95 (1.08)/0.55 0.93	0.95 (1.08)/0.55 0.91	0.95 (1.04)/0.55 0.92	0.95 (1.02)/0.54 0.88	0.95 (1.04)/0.54 0.91	0.95 (1.02)/0.54 0.88	0.95 (1.04)/0.54 0.91	0.95 (1.02)/0.54 0.88	0.95 (1.03)/0.54 0.88
		0°	0.95 (0.28)/0.61 0.95	0.95 (0.28)/0.61 0.93	0.95 (0.29)/0.62 0.93	0.95 (0.28)/0.61 0.91	0.95 (0.28)/0.61 0.92	0.95 (0.28)/0.61 0.88	0.95 (0.28)/0.61 0.91	0.95 (0.28)/0.61 0.88	0.95 (0.28)/0.61 0.91	0.95 (0.28)/0.61 0.88	0.95 (0.28)/0.61 0.88
		Excluded Beam[b]	0.16 (0.28)/0.59 0.94	0.16 (0.28)/0.59 0.92	0.16 (0.29)/0.59 0.92	0.16 (0.28)/0.59 0.9	0.16 (0.28)/0.59 0.91	0.16 (0.28)/0.58 0.87	0.16 (0.28)/0.59 0.9	0.16 (0.28)/0.58 0.87	0.16 (0.28)/0.59 0.9	0.16 (0.28)/0.58 0.87	0.16 (0.28)/0.59 0.87
		45°	0.34 (0.12)/0.47 0.94	0.34 (0.12)/0.47 0.92	0.34 (0.12)/0.47 0.92	0.34 (0.12)/0.47 0.9	0.33 (0.12)/0.46 0.91	0.33 (0.12)/0.46 0.88	0.33 (0.12)/0.46 0.91	0.33 (0.12)/0.46 0.87	0.33 (0.12)/0.46 0.91	0.33 (0.12)/0.46 0.87	0.33 (0.12)/0.46 0.88
		Closed	0.08 (0.04)/0.21 0.92	0.08 (0.04)/0.21 0.9	0.08 (0.04)/0.21 0.91	0.08 (0.04)/0.21 0.88	0.08 (0.04)/0.21 0.89	0.08 (0.04)/0.20 0.85	0.08 (0.04)/0.21 0.88	0.08 (0.04)/0.20 0.85	0.08 (0.04)/0.21 0.88	0.08 (0.04)/0.20 0.85	0.08 (0.04)/0.20 0.85

Notes: [a]Louvers track so that profile angle equals negative slat angle and maximum direct beam is admitted.
[b]Louvers track to block direct beam radiation. When negative slat angles result, slat defaults to 0°.
[c]Glazing cavity width equals original cavity width plus slat width.
[d]F_R is radiant fraction; ratio of radiative heat transfer to total heat transfer, on room side of glazing system.

Table 14D IAC Values for Louvered Shades: Coated Double Glazings with 0.1 Low-e

		Glazing ID:	21a	21b	21c	21d	21e	21f	21g	21h	21i	21j	21k
Louver Location	Louver Reflection	ϕ	IAC_0 (IAC_{60})/IAC_{diff}, F_R[d]										
Indoor Side	0.15	Worst[a]	0.99 (0.98)/0.94 0.85	0.99 (0.98)/0.95 0.82	0.99 (0.98)/0.95 0.82	0.99 (0.98)/0.95 0.8	0.99 (0.98)/0.95 0.8	0.99 (0.98)/0.95 0.75	0.99 (0.98)/0.95 0.79	0.99 (0.98)/0.95 0.75	0.99 (0.98)/0.95 0.79	0.99 (0.98)/0.95 0.75	0.99 (0.98)/0.95 0.76
		0°	0.99 (0.92)/0.95 0.66	0.99 (0.92)/0.95 0.64	0.99 (0.93)/0.96 0.64	0.99 (0.93)/0.96 0.63	0.99 (0.93)/0.96 0.63	0.99 (0.93)/0.96 0.61	0.99 (0.93)/0.96 0.63	0.99 (0.94)/0.96 0.6	0.99 (0.93)/0.96 0.63	0.99 (0.94)/0.96 0.6	0.99 (0.93)/0.96 0.61
		Excluded Beam[b]	0.89 (0.92)/0.95 0.41	0.89 (0.92)/0.95 0.41	0.90 (0.93)/0.95 0.41	0.90 (0.93)/0.96 0.41	0.90 (0.93)/0.95 0.4	0.91 (0.93)/0.96 0.4	0.90 (0.93)/0.96 0.4	0.91 (0.94)/0.96 0.4	0.90 (0.93)/0.96 0.4	0.91 (0.94)/0.96 0.4	0.91 (0.93)/0.96 0.4
		45°	0.92 (0.89)/0.93 0.44	0.92 (0.90)/0.93 0.43	0.92 (0.90)/0.93 0.43	0.93 (0.91)/0.94 0.43	0.92 (0.91)/0.94 0.43	0.93 (0.91)/0.94 0.42	0.93 (0.91)/0.94 0.42	0.93 (0.91)/0.94 0.41	0.93 (0.91)/0.94 0.42	0.93 (0.91)/0.94 0.41	0.93 (0.91)/0.94 0.42
		Closed	0.86 (0.87)/0.88 0.4	0.87 (0.87)/0.89 0.39	0.87 (0.88)/0.89 0.39	0.88 (0.88)/0.90 0.39	0.88 (0.88)/0.89 0.38	0.89 (0.89)/0.90 0.37	0.88 (0.88)/0.90 0.38	0.89 (0.89)/0.90 0.37	0.88 (0.88)/0.90 0.38	0.89 (0.89)/0.90 0.37	0.89 (0.89)/0.90 0.37
Indoor Side	0.50	Worst[a]	0.99 (0.98)/0.89 0.86	0.99 (0.98)/0.90 0.84	0.99 (0.98)/0.91 0.83	0.99 (0.98)/0.91 0.81	0.99 (0.98)/0.91 0.81	0.99 (0.98)/0.92 0.76	0.99 (0.98)/0.91 0.8	0.99 (0.98)/0.92 0.76	0.99 (0.98)/0.91 0.8	0.99 (0.98)/0.92 0.76	0.99 (0.98)/0.92 0.76
		0°	0.99 (0.85)/0.92 0.7	0.99 (0.86)/0.92 0.68	0.99 (0.87)/0.93 0.67	0.99 (0.87)/0.93 0.66	0.99 (0.87)/0.93 0.66	0.99 (0.89)/0.94 0.63	0.99 (0.87)/0.93 0.66	0.99 (0.89)/0.94 0.63	0.99 (0.87)/0.93 0.66	0.99 (0.89)/0.94 0.63	0.99 (0.89)/0.94 0.64
		Excluded Beam[b]	0.77 (0.85)/0.91 0.47	0.79 (0.86)/0.92 0.46	0.79 (0.87)/0.92 0.46	0.81 (0.87)/0.92 0.45	0.80 (0.87)/0.92 0.45	0.82 (0.89)/0.93 0.44	0.80 (0.87)/0.92 0.45	0.82 (0.89)/0.93 0.44	0.80 (0.87)/0.92 0.45	0.82 (0.89)/0.93 0.44	0.82 (0.89)/0.93 0.44
		45°	0.83 (0.77)/0.86 0.49	0.84 (0.79)/0.87 0.48	0.85 (0.79)/0.88 0.48	0.86 (0.81)/0.88 0.47	0.85 (0.80)/0.88 0.47	0.87 (0.82)/0.89 0.45	0.86 (0.80)/0.88 0.47	0.87 (0.83)/0.89 0.45	0.86 (0.80)/0.88 0.47	0.87 (0.83)/0.89 0.45	0.87 (0.82)/0.89 0.45
		Closed	0.71 (0.70)/0.75 0.41	0.73 (0.73)/0.77 0.39	0.74 (0.73)/0.78 0.39	0.75 (0.75)/0.79 0.38	0.75 (0.75)/0.79 0.39	0.77 (0.77)/0.81 0.37	0.75 (0.75)/0.79 0.38	0.78 (0.78)/0.81 0.37	0.75 (0.75)/0.79 0.38	0.78 (0.78)/0.81 0.37	0.77 (0.77)/0.81 0.37
Indoor Side	0.80	Worst[a]	0.98 (0.97)/0.84 0.88	0.98 (0.97)/0.85 0.85	0.98 (0.97)/0.86 0.84	0.98 (0.97)/0.87 0.82	0.98 (0.97)/0.86 0.82	0.98 (0.97)/0.88 0.77	0.98 (0.97)/0.86 0.81	0.98 (0.97)/0.88 0.77	0.98 (0.97)/0.86 0.81	0.98 (0.97)/0.88 0.77	0.98 (0.97)/0.88 0.78
		0°	0.98 (0.76)/0.87 0.76	0.98 (0.78)/0.88 0.74	0.98 (0.79)/0.89 0.73	0.98 (0.81)/0.89 0.71	0.98 (0.80)/0.89 0.72	0.98 (0.83)/0.90 0.68	0.98 (0.81)/0.89 0.71	0.98 (0.83)/0.90 0.68	0.98 (0.81)/0.89 0.71	0.98 (0.83)/0.90 0.68	0.98 (0.83)/0.90 0.68
		Excluded Beam[b]	0.64 (0.76)/0.86 0.59	0.67 (0.78)/0.87 0.56	0.69 (0.79)/0.88 0.56	0.71 (0.81)/0.89 0.54	0.70 (0.80)/0.88 0.55	0.73 (0.83)/0.90 0.52	0.70 (0.81)/0.88 0.54	0.74 (0.83)/0.90 0.52	0.70 (0.81)/0.88 0.54	0.74 (0.83)/0.90 0.52	0.73 (0.83)/0.90 0.52
		45°	0.74 (0.64)/0.79 0.59	0.76 (0.67)/0.81 0.57	0.77 (0.68)/0.81 0.56	0.79 (0.71)/0.83 0.54	0.78 (0.70)/0.82 0.55	0.80 (0.74)/0.84 0.52	0.78 (0.70)/0.82 0.55	0.81 (0.74)/0.84 0.52	0.78 (0.70)/0.82 0.55	0.81 (0.74)/0.84 0.51	0.81 (0.74)/0.84 0.52
		Closed	0.54 (0.53)/0.62 0.45	0.59 (0.58)/0.66 0.42	0.60 (0.59)/0.67 0.42	0.63 (0.62)/0.69 0.4	0.62 (0.61)/0.68 0.41	0.66 (0.66)/0.72 0.38	0.62 (0.62)/0.69 0.41	0.67 (0.66)/0.72 0.38	0.62 (0.62)/0.69 0.41	0.67 (0.67)/0.72 0.38	0.66 (0.66)/0.72 0.38
Between Glazings[c]	0.15	Worst[a]	0.98 (1.01)/0.80 0.91	0.98 (1.01)/0.80 0.9	0.96 (0.99)/0.60 0.9	0.96 (0.99)/0.61 0.89	0.96 (0.98)/0.61 0.89	0.95 (0.97)/0.63 0.87	0.95 (0.98)/0.61 0.89	0.95 (0.97)/0.63 0.86	0.95 (0.98)/0.61 0.89	0.95 (0.97)/0.63 0.86	0.95 (0.97)/0.62 0.87
		0°	0.98 (0.69)/0.82 0.8	0.98 (0.70)/0.83 0.79	0.96 (0.40)/0.64 0.79	0.96 (0.40)/0.65 0.78	0.96 (0.42)/0.65 0.78	0.95 (0.44)/0.66 0.77	0.95 (0.42)/0.65 0.78	0.95 (0.45)/0.66 0.77	0.95 (0.42)/0.65 0.78	0.95 (0.45)/0.66 0.77	0.95 (0.44)/0.66 0.77
		Excluded Beam[b]	0.63 (0.69)/0.81 0.66	0.64 (0.70)/0.82 0.66	0.34 (0.40)/0.63 0.66	0.35 (0.40)/0.63 0.65	0.36 (0.42)/0.64 0.65	0.39 (0.44)/0.65 0.65	0.37 (0.42)/0.64 0.65	0.39 (0.45)/0.65 0.65	0.37 (0.42)/0.64 0.65	0.40 (0.45)/0.65 0.65	0.39 (0.44)/0.65 0.65
		45°	0.71 (0.66)/0.77 0.69	0.71 (0.67)/0.78 0.69	0.47 (0.36)/0.55 0.7	0.47 (0.37)/0.56 0.7	0.48 (0.38)/0.56 0.69	0.50 (0.41)/0.58 0.69	0.49 (0.39)/0.57 0.69	0.51 (0.42)/0.58 0.68	0.49 (0.39)/0.57 0.69	0.51 (0.42)/0.58 0.68	0.50 (0.41)/0.58 0.69
		Closed	0.61 (0.64)/0.68 0.65	0.63 (0.65)/0.69 0.65	0.33 (0.35)/0.41 0.64	0.34 (0.36)/0.41 0.64	0.35 (0.37)/0.42 0.64	0.38 (0.40)/0.45 0.64	0.35 (0.37)/0.43 0.64	0.38 (0.40)/0.45 0.64	0.35 (0.37)/0.43 0.64	0.38 (0.40)/0.45 0.64	0.38 (0.40)/0.45 0.64
Between Glazings[c]	0.50	Worst[a]	0.97 (1.03)/0.77 0.92	0.97 (1.03)/0.78 0.9	0.97 (1.06)/0.63 0.91	0.97 (1.06)/0.63 0.89	0.96 (1.05)/0.64 0.9	0.95 (1.03)/0.65 0.87	0.96 (1.04)/0.64 0.89	0.95 (1.03)/0.65 0.87	0.96 (1.04)/0.64 0.89	0.95 (1.03)/0.65 0.87	0.95 (1.03)/0.65 0.87
		0°	0.97 (0.65)/0.81 0.83	0.97 (0.66)/0.81 0.82	0.97 (0.42)/0.68 0.83	0.97 (0.42)/0.68 0.82	0.96 (0.44)/0.69 0.82	0.95 (0.46)/0.69 0.8	0.96 (0.44)/0.69 0.81	0.95 (0.46)/0.70 0.8	0.96 (0.44)/0.69 0.81	0.95 (0.47)/0.70 0.79	0.95 (0.46)/0.69 0.8
		Excluded Beam[b]	0.54 (0.65)/0.80 0.7	0.55 (0.66)/0.80 0.7	0.32 (0.42)/0.66 0.72	0.32 (0.42)/0.67 0.71	0.34 (0.44)/0.67 0.71	0.37 (0.46)/0.68 0.7	0.34 (0.44)/0.67 0.71	0.37 (0.46)/0.68 0.7	0.34 (0.44)/0.67 0.71	0.38 (0.47)/0.68 0.7	0.37 (0.46)/0.68 0.7

Table 14D IAC Values for Louvered Shades: Coated Double Glazings with 0.1 Low-e (*Continued*)

		Glazing ID:	21a	21b	21c	21d	21e	21f	21g	21h	21i	21j	21k
		45°	0.64 (0.54)/0.72 0.73	0.65 (0.55)/0.73 0.72	0.47 (0.31)/0.56 0.75	0.47 (0.32)/0.57 0.74	0.48 (0.34)/0.58 0.74	0.50 (0.37)/0.59 0.72	0.49 (0.34)/0.58 0.73	0.51 (0.37)/0.59 0.72	0.49 (0.34)/0.58 0.73	0.51 (0.38)/0.59 0.72	0.50 (0.37)/0.59 0.72
		Closed	0.47 (0.47)/0.56 0.66	0.48 (0.48)/0.57 0.66	0.26 (0.25)/0.36 0.67	0.27 (0.26)/0.37 0.66	0.28 (0.28)/0.38 0.66	0.32 (0.32)/0.41 0.65	0.29 (0.29)/0.39 0.66	0.32 (0.32)/0.41 0.65	0.29 (0.29)/0.39 0.66	0.33 (0.32)/0.42 0.65	0.32 (0.32)/0.41 0.66
Between Glazings[c]	0.80	Worst[a]	0.97 (1.04)/0.74 0.93	0.97 (1.04)/0.75 0.92	0.97 (1.12)/0.67 0.91	0.97 (1.12)/0.68 0.9	0.96 (1.11)/0.68 0.9	0.96 (1.09)/0.69 0.88	0.96 (1.11)/0.68 0.9	0.96 (1.09)/0.69 0.88	0.96 (1.11)/0.68 0.9	0.95 (1.09)/0.69 0.88	0.96 (1.09)/0.69 0.88
		0°	0.97 (0.60)/0.79 0.88	0.97 (0.60)/0.80 0.86	0.97 (0.46)/0.73 0.87	0.97 (0.46)/0.73 0.86	0.96 (0.47)/0.73 0.86	0.96 (0.50)/0.74 0.84	0.96 (0.48)/0.73 0.86	0.96 (0.50)/0.74 0.83	0.96 (0.48)/0.73 0.86	0.95 (0.50)/0.74 0.83	0.96 (0.50)/0.74 0.84
		Excluded Beam[b]	0.45 (0.60)/0.78 0.8	0.46 (0.60)/0.78 0.79	0.33 (0.46)/0.71 0.82	0.33 (0.46)/0.71 0.81	0.35 (0.47)/0.71 0.8	0.38 (0.50)/0.72 0.77	0.35 (0.48)/0.72 0.79	0.38 (0.50)/0.72 0.77	0.35 (0.48)/0.72 0.79	0.39 (0.50)/0.72 0.77	0.38 (0.50)/0.72 0.77
		45°	0.59 (0.43)/0.68 0.81	0.59 (0.44)/0.68 0.8	0.49 (0.29)/0.60 0.82	0.50 (0.30)/0.60 0.81	0.51 (0.31)/0.61 0.8	0.53 (0.35)/0.62 0.78	0.51 (0.32)/0.61 0.8	0.53 (0.35)/0.63 0.77	0.51 (0.32)/0.61 0.8	0.53 (0.36)/0.63 0.77	0.53 (0.35)/0.62 0.78
		Closed	0.33 (0.30)/0.44 0.73	0.34 (0.31)/0.45 0.72	0.22 (0.17)/0.34 0.75	0.23 (0.18)/0.35 0.74	0.25 (0.21)/0.37 0.72	0.28 (0.25)/0.40 0.7	0.25 (0.22)/0.37 0.72	0.29 (0.26)/0.40 0.7	0.25 (0.22)/0.37 0.72	0.29 (0.26)/0.41 0.7	0.28 (0.25)/0.40 0.7
Outdoor Side	0.15	Worst[a]	0.93 (0.90)/0.35 0.94	0.93 (0.90)/0.35 0.93	0.93 (0.90)/0.35 0.92	0.93 (0.90)/0.35 0.91	0.93 (0.89)/0.35 0.91	0.93 (0.89)/0.35 0.88	0.93 (0.89)/0.35 0.9	0.93 (0.89)/0.36 0.88	0.93 (0.89)/0.35 0.9	0.93 (0.89)/0.36 0.88	0.93 (0.89)/0.35 0.88
		0°	0.93 (0.04)/0.41 0.9	0.93 (0.04)/0.41 0.88	0.93 (0.04)/0.41 0.88	0.93 (0.04)/0.41 0.87	0.93 (0.04)/0.41 0.87	0.93 (0.05)/0.41 0.84	0.93 (0.04)/0.41 0.86	0.93 (0.05)/0.41 0.84	0.93 (0.04)/0.41 0.86	0.93 (0.05)/0.41 0.83	0.93 (0.05)/0.41 0.84
		Excluded Beam[b]	0.02 (0.04)/0.39 0.8	0.02 (0.04)/0.39 0.79	0.02 (0.04)/0.39 0.79	0.02 (0.04)/0.39 0.78	0.02 (0.04)/0.39 0.77	0.03 (0.05)/0.39 0.74	0.02 (0.04)/0.39 0.77	0.03 (0.05)/0.39 0.74	0.02 (0.04)/0.39 0.77	0.03 (0.05)/0.39 0.74	0.03 (0.05)/0.39 0.74
		45°	0.19 (0.02)/0.29 0.84	0.19 (0.02)/0.29 0.83	0.19 (0.02)/0.29 0.83	0.19 (0.02)/0.29 0.82	0.19 (0.02)/0.29 0.81	0.20 (0.03)/0.29 0.79	0.19 (0.03)/0.29 0.81	0.20 (0.03)/0.29 0.78	0.19 (0.03)/0.29 0.81	0.20 (0.03)/0.29 0.78	0.20 (0.03)/0.29 0.79
		Closed	0.02 (0.02)/0.09 0.67	0.02 (0.02)/0.09 0.66	0.02 (0.02)/0.09 0.67	0.02 (0.02)/0.09 0.66	0.02 (0.02)/0.09 0.66	0.02 (0.02)/0.10 0.65	0.02 (0.02)/0.09 0.66	0.02 (0.03)/0.10 0.65	0.02 (0.02)/0.09 0.66	0.02 (0.03)/0.10 0.65	0.02 (0.02)/0.10 0.65
Outdoor Side	0.50	Worst[a]	0.94 (1.02)/0.44 0.94	0.94 (1.01)/0.44 0.93	0.94 (1.01)/0.44 0.92	0.94 (1.01)/0.44 0.91	0.94 (0.98)/0.44 0.91	0.94 (0.96)/0.44 0.88	0.94 (0.98)/0.44 0.91	0.94 (0.96)/0.44 0.88	0.94 (0.98)/0.44 0.91	0.94 (0.96)/0.44 0.88	0.94 (0.97)/0.44 0.88
		0°	0.94 (0.14)/0.50 0.94	0.94 (0.14)/0.50 0.92	0.94 (0.14)/0.50 0.92	0.94 (0.14)/0.50 0.9	0.94 (0.14)/0.50 0.9	0.94 (0.14)/0.50 0.87	0.94 (0.14)/0.50 0.9	0.94 (0.14)/0.50 0.87	0.94 (0.14)/0.50 0.9	0.94 (0.14)/0.50 0.87	0.94 (0.14)/0.50 0.88
		Excluded Beam[b]	0.07 (0.14)/0.48 0.91	0.07 (0.14)/0.48 0.9	0.07 (0.14)/0.48 0.89	0.07 (0.14)/0.48 0.88	0.07 (0.14)/0.48 0.88	0.08 (0.14)/0.48 0.85	0.07 (0.14)/0.48 0.87	0.08 (0.14)/0.48 0.84	0.07 (0.14)/0.48 0.87	0.08 (0.14)/0.48 0.84	0.08 (0.14)/0.48 0.85
		45°	0.25 (0.06)/0.37 0.92	0.25 (0.06)/0.37 0.9	0.25 (0.06)/0.37 0.9	0.25 (0.06)/0.37 0.89	0.25 (0.06)/0.36 0.88	0.25 (0.06)/0.36 0.85	0.25 (0.06)/0.36 0.88	0.25 (0.06)/0.36 0.85	0.25 (0.06)/0.36 0.88	0.25 (0.06)/0.36 0.85	0.25 (0.06)/0.36 0.85
		Closed	0.04 (0.02)/0.14 0.84	0.04 (0.02)/0.14 0.82	0.04 (0.02)/0.14 0.83	0.04 (0.02)/0.14 0.81	0.04 (0.02)/0.14 0.8	0.04 (0.03)/0.14 0.77	0.04 (0.02)/0.14 0.8	0.04 (0.03)/0.14 0.77	0.04 (0.02)/0.14 0.8	0.04 (0.03)/0.14 0.77	0.04 (0.03)/0.14 0.77
Outdoor Side	0.80	Worst[a]	0.95 (1.14)/0.56 0.94	0.95 (1.12)/0.56 0.93	0.95 (1.13)/0.56 0.92	0.95 (1.12)/0.56 0.91	0.95 (1.07)/0.55 0.91	0.95 (1.04)/0.55 0.88	0.95 (1.07)/0.55 0.91	0.95 (1.04)/0.54 0.88	0.95 (1.07)/0.55 0.91	0.95 (1.03)/0.54 0.88	0.95 (1.05)/0.55 0.88
		0°	0.95 (0.29)/0.62 0.95	0.95 (0.29)/0.62 0.93	0.95 (0.29)/0.62 0.92	0.95 (0.29)/0.62 0.91	0.95 (0.28)/0.61 0.91	0.95 (0.28)/0.61 0.88	0.95 (0.28)/0.61 0.91	0.95 (0.28)/0.61 0.88	0.95 (0.28)/0.61 0.91	0.95 (0.28)/0.61 0.88	0.95 (0.28)/0.61 0.88
		Excluded Beam[b]	0.17 (0.29)/0.60 0.94	0.17 (0.29)/0.60 0.92	0.17 (0.29)/0.60 0.91	0.17 (0.29)/0.60 0.9	0.16 (0.28)/0.59 0.9	0.16 (0.28)/0.59 0.87	0.16 (0.28)/0.59 0.9	0.16 (0.28)/0.59 0.87	0.16 (0.28)/0.59 0.9	0.16 (0.28)/0.59 0.87	0.16 (0.28)/0.59 0.87
		45°	0.35 (0.13)/0.49 0.94	0.35 (0.13)/0.48 0.92	0.35 (0.13)/0.48 0.92	0.35 (0.13)/0.48 0.9	0.34 (0.12)/0.47 0.9	0.34 (0.12)/0.46 0.88	0.34 (0.12)/0.47 0.9	0.34 (0.12)/0.46 0.87	0.34 (0.12)/0.47 0.9	0.34 (0.12)/0.46 0.87	0.34 (0.12)/0.47 0.88
		Closed	0.08 (0.04)/0.22 0.92	0.08 (0.04)/0.22 0.9	0.08 (0.04)/0.22 0.9	0.08 (0.04)/0.22 0.89	0.08 (0.04)/0.21 0.88	0.08 (0.04)/0.21 0.85	0.08 (0.04)/0.21 0.88	0.08 (0.04)/0.21 0.85	0.08 (0.04)/0.21 0.88	0.08 (0.04)/0.21 0.85	0.08 (0.04)/0.21 0.85

Notes: [a]Louvers track so that profile angle equals negative slat angle and maximum direct beam is admitted.
[b]Louvers track to block direct beam radiation. When negative slat angles result, slat defaults to 0°.
[c]Glazing cavity width equals original cavity width plus slat width.
[d]F_R is radiant fraction; ratio of radiative heat transfer to total heat transfer, on room side of glazing system.

Table 14E IAC Values for Louvered Shades: Double Glazings with 0.05 Low-e

		Glazing ID:	25a	25b	25c	26d	25e	25f
Louver Location	Louver Reflection	ϕ	IAC_0 (IAC_{60})/IAC_{diff}, F_R[d]					
Indoor Side	0.15	Worst[a]	0.99 (0.99)/0.95 0.84	0.99 (0.98)/0.95 0.81	0.99 (0.98)/0.96 0.74	0.99 (0.98)/0.96 0.76	0.99 (0.98)/0.96 0.72	0.99 (0.98)/0.96 0.76
		0°	0.99 (0.93)/0.96 0.65	0.99 (0.93)/0.96 0.64	0.99 (0.94)/0.96 0.6	0.99 (0.94)/0.96 0.61	0.99 (0.95)/0.96 0.59	0.99 (0.94)/0.96 0.61
		Excluded Beam[b]	0.90 (0.93)/0.96 0.41	0.91 (0.93)/0.96 0.4	0.92 (0.94)/0.96 0.39	0.92 (0.94)/0.96 0.4	0.92 (0.95)/0.96 0.39	0.92 (0.94)/0.96 0.4
		45°	0.93 (0.91)/0.94 0.43	0.93 (0.91)/0.94 0.43	0.94 (0.93)/0.95 0.41	0.94 (0.92)/0.95 0.42	0.94 (0.93)/0.95 0.41	0.94 (0.92)/0.95 0.42
		Closed	0.88 (0.88)/0.90 0.39	0.89 (0.89)/0.90 0.39	0.90 (0.90)/0.91 0.36	0.90 (0.90)/0.91 0.37	0.90 (0.91)/0.92 0.36	0.90 (0.90)/0.91 0.37
Indoor Side	0.50	Worst[a]	0.99 (0.98)/0.91 0.86	0.99 (0.98)/0.92 0.82	0.99 (0.98)/0.93 0.75	0.99 (0.98)/0.93 0.77	0.99 (0.98)/0.93 0.73	0.99 (0.98)/0.93 0.77
		0°	0.99 (0.87)/0.93 0.69	0.99 (0.89)/0.94 0.67	0.99 (0.91)/0.95 0.63	0.99 (0.90)/0.94 0.64	0.99 (0.91)/0.95 0.62	0.99 (0.90)/0.94 0.64
		Excluded Beam[b]	0.80 (0.87)/0.92 0.47	0.82 (0.89)/0.93 0.46	0.85 (0.91)/0.94 0.44	0.85 (0.90)/0.94 0.44	0.86 (0.91)/0.94 0.43	0.84 (0.90)/0.94 0.45
		45°	0.85 (0.80)/0.88 0.49	0.87 (0.83)/0.90 0.48	0.89 (0.85)/0.91 0.45	0.89 (0.85)/0.91 0.46	0.89 (0.86)/0.91 0.45	0.89 (0.85)/0.91 0.46
		Closed	0.74 (0.74)/0.79 0.4	0.77 (0.77)/0.81 0.39	0.81 (0.81)/0.84 0.37	0.80 (0.80)/0.83 0.37	0.82 (0.82)/0.85 0.36	0.80 (0.80)/0.83 0.38
Indoor Side	0.80	Worst[a]	0.98 (0.98)/0.86 0.87	0.98 (0.98)/0.88 0.84	0.98 (0.97)/0.90 0.76	0.98 (0.98)/0.90 0.78	0.98 (0.97)/0.90 0.74	0.98 (0.98)/0.89 0.78
		0°	0.98 (0.80)/0.89 0.76	0.98 (0.83)/0.91 0.73	0.98 (0.86)/0.92 0.68	0.98 (0.85)/0.92 0.69	0.98 (0.86)/0.92 0.66	0.98 (0.85)/0.92 0.69
		Excluded Beam[b]	0.69 (0.80)/0.88 0.59	0.73 (0.83)/0.90 0.56	0.78 (0.86)/0.91 0.52	0.77 (0.85)/0.91 0.53	0.78 (0.86)/0.92 0.51	0.77 (0.85)/0.91 0.53
		45°	0.78 (0.69)/0.82 0.59	0.81 (0.73)/0.84 0.57	0.84 (0.78)/0.87 0.52	0.83 (0.77)/0.86 0.53	0.84 (0.79)/0.87 0.51	0.83 (0.77)/0.86 0.54
		Closed	0.60 (0.59)/0.67 0.45	0.65 (0.65)/0.71 0.42	0.71 (0.71)/0.76 0.39	0.70 (0.70)/0.75 0.4	0.72 (0.72)/0.77 0.38	0.70 (0.69)/0.75 0.4
Between Glazings[c]	0.15	Worst[a]	0.97 (1.00)/0.80 0.91	0.97 (0.99)/0.81 0.89	0.95 (0.96)/0.80 0.86	0.95 (0.96)/0.80 0.86	0.94 (0.95)/0.80 0.85	0.96 (0.96)/0.80 0.86
		0°	0.97 (0.71)/0.82 0.79	0.97 (0.72)/0.82 0.78	0.95 (0.73)/0.82 0.76	0.95 (0.73)/0.82 0.77	0.94 (0.73)/0.82 0.76	0.96 (0.73)/0.82 0.77
		Excluded Beam[b]	0.66 (0.71)/0.82 0.65	0.67 (0.72)/0.82 0.65	0.69 (0.73)/0.81 0.65	0.69 (0.73)/0.81 0.65	0.70 (0.73)/0.81 0.64	0.69 (0.73)/0.81 0.65
		45°	0.73 (0.69)/0.78 0.68	0.73 (0.69)/0.78 0.68	0.75 (0.71)/0.78 0.67	0.75 (0.71)/0.78 0.67	0.75 (0.72)/0.79 0.67	0.75 (0.71)/0.78 0.67
		Closed	0.65 (0.67)/0.70 0.65	0.66 (0.68)/0.71 0.65	0.68 (0.70)/0.72 0.64	0.68 (0.70)/0.72 0.64	0.69 (0.71)/0.73 0.64	0.68 (0.70)/0.72 0.64
Between Glazings[c]	0.50	Worst[a]	0.97 (1.01)/0.79 0.92	0.97 (1.00)/0.79 0.9	0.95 (0.97)/0.80 0.86	0.95 (0.98)/0.80 0.87	0.94 (0.96)/0.80 0.85	0.95 (0.98)/0.80 0.87
		0°	0.97 (0.68)/0.82 0.82	0.97 (0.69)/0.82 0.81	0.95 (0.71)/0.82 0.79	0.95 (0.71)/0.82 0.79	0.94 (0.72)/0.82 0.78	0.95 (0.71)/0.82 0.79

Table 14E IAC Values for Louvered Shades: Double Glazings with 0.05 Low-e (*Continued*)

		Glazing ID:	25a	25b	25c	26d	25e	25f
		Excluded Beam[b]	0.58 (0.68)/0.81 0.7	0.60 (0.69)/0.81 0.7	0.64 (0.71)/0.81 0.68	0.63 (0.71)/0.81 0.69	0.65 (0.72)/0.81 0.68	0.63 (0.71)/0.81 0.69
		45°	0.68 (0.59)/0.74 0.73	0.69 (0.61)/0.75 0.72	0.71 (0.65)/0.76 0.7	0.71 (0.64)/0.76 0.71	0.72 (0.66)/0.77 0.7	0.71 (0.64)/0.76 0.71
		Closed	0.52 (0.52)/0.60 0.66	0.54 (0.54)/0.61 0.66	0.59 (0.59)/0.65 0.65	0.58 (0.58)/0.64 0.66	0.60 (0.60)/0.65 0.65	0.58 (0.58)/0.64 0.66
Between Glazings[c]	0.80	Worst[a]	0.97 (1.02)/0.77 0.93	0.97 (1.01)/0.78 0.91	0.95 (0.98)/0.79 0.87	0.95 (0.98)/0.79 0.88	0.94 (0.97)/0.79 0.86	0.95 (0.99)/0.79 0.88
		0°	0.97 (0.65)/0.81 0.87	0.97 (0.67)/0.82 0.86	0.95 (0.70)/0.82 0.83	0.95 (0.69)/0.82 0.83	0.94 (0.71)/0.82 0.82	0.95 (0.69)/0.82 0.84
		Excluded Beam[b]	0.51 (0.65)/0.80 0.8	0.53 (0.67)/0.81 0.79	0.59 (0.70)/0.81 0.76	0.58 (0.69)/0.81 0.76	0.60 (0.71)/0.81 0.75	0.58 (0.69)/0.81 0.76
		45°	0.64 (0.50)/0.71 0.81	0.65 (0.53)/0.73 0.8	0.69 (0.59)/0.74 0.76	0.68 (0.58)/0.74 0.77	0.69 (0.60)/0.75 0.76	0.68 (0.58)/0.74 0.77
		Closed	0.39 (0.36)/0.49 0.73	0.42 (0.39)/0.51 0.73	0.49 (0.47)/0.57 0.7	0.48 (0.46)/0.56 0.71	0.51 (0.49)/0.58 0.7	0.48 (0.46)/0.56 0.71
Outdoor Side	0.15	Worst[a]	0.93 (0.92)/0.36 0.94	0.93 (0.92)/0.36 0.92	0.93 (0.90)/0.36 0.87	0.93 (0.89)/0.36 0.88	0.93 (0.90)/0.36 0.86	0.93 (0.89)/0.36 0.89
		0°	0.93 (0.05)/0.41 0.89	0.93 (0.05)/0.41 0.87	0.93 (0.06)/0.41 0.82	0.93 (0.05)/0.41 0.83	0.93 (0.06)/0.42 0.81	0.93 (0.05)/0.41 0.84
		Excluded Beam[b]	0.03 (0.05)/0.39 0.78	0.03 (0.05)/0.39 0.77	0.04 (0.06)/0.40 0.72	0.03 (0.05)/0.39 0.73	0.04 (0.06)/0.40 0.71	0.03 (0.05)/0.39 0.74
		45°	0.20 (0.03)/0.29 0.83	0.20 (0.03)/0.29 0.82	0.20 (0.04)/0.30 0.77	0.20 (0.03)/0.29 0.78	0.20 (0.04)/0.30 0.76	0.20 (0.03)/0.29 0.78
		Closed	0.02 (0.02)/0.10 0.66	0.02 (0.02)/0.10 0.66	0.03 (0.03)/0.11 0.64	0.03 (0.03)/0.10 0.65	0.03 (0.04)/0.11 0.64	0.03 (0.03)/0.10 0.65
Outdoor Side	0.50	Worst[a]	0.94 (1.08)/0.45 0.94	0.94 (1.06)/0.45 0.92	0.94 (0.99)/0.44 0.87	0.94 (0.96)/0.44 0.88	0.94 (0.98)/0.44 0.86	0.94 (0.97)/0.44 0.89
		0°	0.94 (0.15)/0.51 0.93	0.94 (0.15)/0.51 0.91	0.94 (0.15)/0.50 0.86	0.94 (0.15)/0.50 0.87	0.94 (0.15)/0.50 0.85	0.94 (0.15)/0.50 0.88
		Excluded Beam[b]	0.08 (0.15)/0.49 0.9	0.08 (0.15)/0.49 0.88	0.08 (0.15)/0.48 0.83	0.08 (0.15)/0.48 0.84	0.08 (0.15)/0.48 0.82	0.08 (0.15)/0.48 0.85
		45°	0.26 (0.06)/0.38 0.91	0.26 (0.06)/0.38 0.89	0.26 (0.07)/0.37 0.84	0.25 (0.06)/0.36 0.85	0.26 (0.07)/0.37 0.82	0.25 (0.06)/0.36 0.85
		Closed	0.04 (0.03)/0.15 0.82	0.04 (0.03)/0.15 0.81	0.05 (0.03)/0.14 0.75	0.04 (0.03)/0.14 0.76	0.05 (0.03)/0.14 0.74	0.04 (0.03)/0.14 0.76
Outdoor Side	0.80	Worst[a]	0.95 (1.25)/0.59 0.94	0.95 (1.21)/0.58 0.92	0.95 (1.08)/0.56 0.87	0.95 (1.04)/0.55 0.88	0.95 (1.06)/0.55 0.86	0.95 (1.05)/0.55 0.89
		0°	0.95 (0.30)/0.64 0.94	0.95 (0.30)/0.64 0.92	0.95 (0.29)/0.62 0.88	0.95 (0.28)/0.61 0.88	0.95 (0.29)/0.61 0.86	0.95 (0.28)/0.61 0.89
		Excluded Beam[b]	0.18 (0.30)/0.62 0.93	0.18 (0.30)/0.62 0.91	0.17 (0.29)/0.60 0.86	0.16 (0.28)/0.59 0.87	0.17 (0.29)/0.59 0.85	0.17 (0.28)/0.59 0.88
		45°	0.37 (0.13)/0.51 0.93	0.37 (0.13)/0.50 0.91	0.35 (0.13)/0.48 0.86	0.34 (0.12)/0.47 0.87	0.35 (0.13)/0.47 0.85	0.34 (0.12)/0.47 0.88
		Closed	0.09 (0.04)/0.24 0.91	0.09 (0.04)/0.24 0.89	0.09 (0.04)/0.22 0.83	0.08 (0.04)/0.21 0.85	0.09 (0.04)/0.21 0.82	0.08 (0.04)/0.21 0.85

Notes: [a]Louvers track so that profile angle equals negative slat angle and maximum direct beam is admitted.
[b]Louvers track to block direct beam radiation. When negative slat angles result, slat defaults to 0°.
[c]Glazing cavity width equals original cavity width plus slat width.
[d]F_R is radiant fraction; ratio of radiative heat transfer to total heat transfer, on room side of glazing system.

Table 14F IAC Values for Louvered Shades: Triple Glazing

		Glazing ID:	29a	29b	32a	32b	32c	32d	40a	40b	40c	40d
Louver Location	Louver Reflection	ϕ	IAC_0 (IAC_{60})/IAC_{diff}, F_R[d]									
Indoor Side	0.15	Worst[a]	0.99 (0.98)/0.94 0.82	0.99 (0.98)/0.95 0.78	0.99 (0.98)/0.95 0.8	0.99 (0.98)/0.96 0.75	1.00 (1.00)/0.97 0.76	1.00 (1.00)/0.97 0.71	1.00 (1.00)/0.98 0.73	1.00 (1.00)/0.98 0.67	0.99 (0.99)/0.96 0.78	0.99 (0.99)/0.96 0.73
		0°	0.99 (0.92)/0.95 0.65	0.99 (0.93)/0.95 0.62	0.99 (0.94)/0.96 0.64	0.99 (0.94)/0.96 0.61	1.00 (0.96)/0.98 0.6	1.00 (0.96)/0.98 0.56	1.00 (0.96)/0.98 0.58	1.00 (0.97)/0.99 0.54	0.99 (0.95)/0.97 0.63	0.99 (0.95)/0.97 0.6
		Excluded Beam[b]	0.88 (0.92)/0.95 0.41	0.89 (0.93)/0.95 0.4	0.90 (0.94)/0.96 0.41	0.91 (0.94)/0.96 0.4	0.93 (0.96)/0.97 0.39	0.93 (0.96)/0.98 0.36	0.94 (0.96)/0.98 0.37	0.95 (0.97)/0.98 0.35	0.92 (0.95)/0.97 0.4	0.93 (0.95)/0.97 0.4
		45°	0.91 (0.89)/0.93 0.43	0.92 (0.90)/0.93 0.43	0.93 (0.91)/0.94 0.43	0.93 (0.92)/0.95 0.42	0.95 (0.93)/0.96 0.41	0.95 (0.94)/0.97 0.38	0.95 (0.94)/0.97 0.39	0.96 (0.95)/0.97 0.37	0.94 (0.92)/0.95 0.42	0.94 (0.93)/0.96 0.41
		Closed	0.86 (0.87)/0.88 0.39	0.87 (0.88)/0.89 0.38	0.88 (0.89)/0.90 0.39	0.89 (0.90)/0.91 0.37	0.91 (0.91)/0.93 0.37	0.92 (0.92)/0.94 0.35	0.92 (0.93)/0.94 0.36	0.93 (0.94)/0.95 0.33	0.90 (0.90)/0.92 0.38	0.91 (0.91)/0.92 0.37
Indoor Side	0.50	Worst[a]	0.98 (0.98)/0.90 0.83	0.98 (0.98)/0.91 0.79	0.99 (0.98)/0.91 0.81	0.99 (0.98)/0.92 0.76	0.99 (0.99)/0.92 0.77	1.00 (1.00)/0.93 0.72	0.99 (1.00)/0.93 0.74	1.00 (1.00)/0.95 0.68	0.99 (0.98)/0.92 0.79	0.99 (0.98)/0.93 0.74
		0°	0.98 (0.86)/0.92 0.68	0.98 (0.87)/0.93 0.65	0.99 (0.88)/0.93 0.67	0.99 (0.90)/0.94 0.64	0.99 (0.89)/0.94 0.62	1.00 (0.91)/0.95 0.58	0.99 (0.91)/0.95 0.6	1.00 (0.92)/0.96 0.56	0.99 (0.89)/0.94 0.66	0.99 (0.91)/0.95 0.63
		Excluded Beam[b]	0.77 (0.86)/0.91 0.46	0.80 (0.87)/0.92 0.45	0.80 (0.88)/0.93 0.45	0.83 (0.90)/0.94 0.44	0.81 (0.89)/0.94 0.42	0.83 (0.91)/0.95 0.39	0.83 (0.91)/0.95 0.4	0.86 (0.92)/0.96 0.37	0.82 (0.89)/0.93 0.45	0.84 (0.91)/0.94 0.44
		45°	0.83 (0.78)/0.87 0.48	0.85 (0.81)/0.88 0.46	0.85 (0.81)/0.89 0.47	0.87 (0.84)/0.90 0.45	0.86 (0.82)/0.90 0.43	0.88 (0.84)/0.91 0.4	0.88 (0.84)/0.91 0.41	0.90 (0.87)/0.93 0.38	0.87 (0.83)/0.90 0.46	0.89 (0.85)/0.91 0.45
		Closed	0.71 (0.72)/0.77 0.39	0.74 (0.75)/0.79 0.38	0.75 (0.76)/0.80 0.39	0.78 (0.79)/0.82 0.37	0.76 (0.76)/0.81 0.35	0.79 (0.80)/0.83 0.33	0.78 (0.80)/0.83 0.34	0.82 (0.83)/0.86 0.31	0.77 (0.78)/0.81 0.38	0.80 (0.81)/0.84 0.36
Indoor Side	0.80	Worst[a]	0.98 (0.97)/0.85 0.84	0.98 (0.97)/0.87 0.8	0.98 (0.97)/0.86 0.82	0.98 (0.97)/0.88 0.77	0.99 (0.99)/0.87 0.79	0.99 (0.99)/0.89 0.73	0.99 (0.99)/0.88 0.75	0.99 (0.99)/0.90 0.69	0.98 (0.98)/0.87 0.8	0.98 (0.98)/0.89 0.75
		0°	0.98 (0.78)/0.88 0.74	0.98 (0.81)/0.89 0.7	0.98 (0.81)/0.89 0.72	0.98 (0.84)/0.91 0.68	0.99 (0.81)/0.90 0.67	0.99 (0.83)/0.91 0.62	0.99 (0.83)/0.91 0.64	0.99 (0.86)/0.93 0.59	0.98 (0.82)/0.90 0.71	0.98 (0.85)/0.92 0.67
		Excluded Beam[b]	0.66 (0.78)/0.87 0.56	0.70 (0.81)/0.89 0.53	0.69 (0.81)/0.88 0.55	0.74 (0.84)/0.90 0.52	0.69 (0.81)/0.89 0.49	0.73 (0.83)/0.90 0.45	0.72 (0.83)/0.90 0.46	0.77 (0.86)/0.92 0.42	0.71 (0.82)/0.89 0.54	0.76 (0.85)/0.91 0.51
		45°	0.75 (0.67)/0.80 0.56	0.78 (0.71)/0.83 0.53	0.77 (0.71)/0.82 0.55	0.81 (0.75)/0.85 0.52	0.77 (0.70)/0.83 0.49	0.80 (0.74)/0.85 0.44	0.80 (0.74)/0.85 0.46	0.83 (0.78)/0.87 0.42	0.79 (0.73)/0.84 0.54	0.82 (0.77)/0.86 0.51
		Closed	0.57 (0.58)/0.65 0.42	0.62 (0.64)/0.70 0.4	0.61 (0.63)/0.69 0.41	0.67 (0.68)/0.74 0.38	0.60 (0.62)/0.69 0.35	0.66 (0.67)/0.73 0.31	0.65 (0.66)/0.72 0.33	0.71 (0.72)/0.77 0.29	0.64 (0.65)/0.71 0.4	0.69 (0.71)/0.76 0.38
Between Glazings[c]	0.15	Worst[a]	0.97 (1.01)/0.63 0.9	0.97 (1.02)/0.64 0.87	0.98 (1.05)/0.76 0.88	0.98 (1.05)/0.77 0.85	0.97 (1.01)/0.60 0.79	0.98 (1.02)/0.62 0.74	0.98 (1.05)/0.73 0.75	0.99 (1.05)/0.75 0.7	0.98 (1.04)/0.71 0.87	0.99 (1.04)/0.73 0.84
		0°	0.97 (0.44)/0.66 0.79	0.97 (0.46)/0.68 0.78	0.98 (0.62)/0.78 0.78	0.98 (0.63)/0.80 0.77	0.97 (0.40)/0.64 0.59	0.98 (0.42)/0.66 0.56	0.98 (0.57)/0.76 0.57	0.99 (0.60)/0.78 0.54	0.98 (0.55)/0.74 0.78	0.99 (0.58)/0.76 0.76
		Excluded Beam[b]	0.36 (0.44)/0.65 0.66	0.38 (0.46)/0.67 0.65	0.52 (0.62)/0.77 0.66	0.54 (0.63)/0.79 0.65	0.32 (0.40)/0.63 0.34	0.35 (0.42)/0.65 0.33	0.48 (0.57)/0.75 0.33	0.50 (0.60)/0.77 0.33	0.46 (0.55)/0.73 0.65	0.49 (0.58)/0.75 0.65
		45°	0.48 (0.41)/0.59 0.7	0.50 (0.43)/0.60 0.69	0.62 (0.58)/0.72 0.69	0.64 (0.60)/0.73 0.68	0.45 (0.37)/0.56 0.43	0.47 (0.40)/0.58 0.41	0.58 (0.54)/0.69 0.4	0.60 (0.57)/0.71 0.39	0.57 (0.52)/0.68 0.69	0.59 (0.55)/0.69 0.68
		Closed	0.36 (0.41)/0.46 0.64	0.38 (0.43)/0.48 0.64	0.51 (0.57)/0.61 0.65	0.53 (0.58)/0.63 0.65	0.32 (0.37)/0.43 0.31	0.34 (0.40)/0.45 0.31	0.46 (0.53)/0.57 0.32	0.49 (0.55)/0.60 0.32	0.45 (0.51)/0.56 0.64	0.48 (0.53)/0.58 0.64
Between Glazings[c]	0.50	Worst[a]	0.97 (1.06)/0.65 0.9	0.98 (1.06)/0.66 0.88	0.98 (1.08)/0.74 0.89	0.98 (1.08)/0.75 0.86	0.97 (1.07)/0.63 0.8	0.98 (1.07)/0.65 0.75	0.98 (1.09)/0.72 0.77	0.99 (1.09)/0.74 0.71	0.98 (1.08)/0.71 0.88	0.99 (1.08)/0.72 0.85
		0°	0.97 (0.45)/0.69 0.83	0.98 (0.47)/0.71 0.81	0.98 (0.58)/0.78 0.81	0.98 (0.60)/0.79 0.79	0.97 (0.42)/0.68 0.66	0.98 (0.44)/0.69 0.62	0.98 (0.55)/0.77 0.62	0.99 (0.57)/0.78 0.59	0.98 (0.54)/0.75 0.81	0.99 (0.56)/0.77 0.79

Table 14F IAC Values for Louvered Shades: Triple Glazing (*Continued*)

		Glazing ID:	29a	29b	32a	32b	32c	32d	40a	40b	40c	40d
		Excluded Beam[b]	0.33 (0.45)/0.68 0.71	0.34 (0.47)/0.69 0.7	0.44 (0.58)/0.77 0.7	0.46 (0.60)/0.78 0.69	0.30 (0.42)/0.66 0.46	0.32 (0.44)/0.68 0.43	0.41 (0.55)/0.75 0.42	0.43 (0.57)/0.77 0.4	0.40 (0.54)/0.74 0.7	0.42 (0.56)/0.75 0.69
		45°	0.47 (0.35)/0.59 0.74	0.49 (0.37)/0.60 0.73	0.57 (0.47)/0.68 0.72	0.59 (0.48)/0.69 0.71	0.45 (0.32)/0.57 0.51	0.47 (0.35)/0.59 0.48	0.55 (0.44)/0.66 0.47	0.56 (0.46)/0.68 0.44	0.54 (0.43)/0.65 0.72	0.56 (0.45)/0.67 0.71
		Closed	0.28 (0.29)/0.39 0.66	0.29 (0.31)/0.41 0.66	0.38 (0.40)/0.50 0.66	0.40 (0.41)/0.51 0.66	0.25 (0.27)/0.37 0.36	0.27 (0.29)/0.39 0.35	0.35 (0.37)/0.48 0.35	0.37 (0.39)/0.49 0.34	0.34 (0.36)/0.46 0.66	0.36 (0.38)/0.48 0.65
Between Glazings[c]	0.80	Worst[a]	0.97 (1.11)/0.68 0.91	0.98 (1.11)/0.69 0.89	0.97 (1.11)/0.73 0.9	0.98 (1.11)/0.73 0.87	0.98 (1.12)/0.67 0.81	0.98 (1.12)/0.69 0.76	0.98 (1.12)/0.72 0.79	0.99 (1.12)/0.73 0.73	0.98 (1.11)/0.71 0.89	0.99 (1.11)/0.72 0.86
		0°	0.97 (0.48)/0.74 0.87	0.98 (0.49)/0.75 0.85	0.97 (0.55)/0.78 0.85	0.98 (0.56)/0.79 0.83	0.98 (0.47)/0.73 0.75	0.98 (0.48)/0.74 0.7	0.98 (0.54)/0.78 0.71	0.99 (0.55)/0.79 0.66	0.98 (0.53)/0.77 0.85	0.99 (0.54)/0.78 0.82
		Excluded Beam[b]	0.32 (0.48)/0.72 0.81	0.33 (0.49)/0.73 0.79	0.38 (0.55)/0.76 0.78	0.39 (0.56)/0.77 0.76	0.31 (0.47)/0.71 0.63	0.32 (0.48)/0.72 0.59	0.37 (0.54)/0.76 0.58	0.38 (0.55)/0.77 0.54	0.36 (0.53)/0.75 0.78	0.38 (0.54)/0.76 0.76
		45°	0.48 (0.31)/0.61 0.82	0.49 (0.32)/0.62 0.79	0.54 (0.37)/0.65 0.79	0.55 (0.38)/0.66 0.77	0.47 (0.30)/0.60 0.65	0.49 (0.32)/0.62 0.6	0.52 (0.36)/0.65 0.59	0.54 (0.37)/0.66 0.55	0.52 (0.35)/0.64 0.79	0.53 (0.36)/0.65 0.77
		Closed	0.22 (0.19)/0.36 0.73	0.23 (0.21)/0.37 0.72	0.27 (0.24)/0.41 0.71	0.29 (0.26)/0.42 0.7	0.21 (0.18)/0.35 0.49	0.22 (0.20)/0.37 0.46	0.26 (0.23)/0.40 0.45	0.28 (0.25)/0.41 0.43	0.25 (0.23)/0.39 0.72	0.27 (0.24)/0.40 0.7
Outdoor Side	0.15	Worst[a]	0.93 (0.90)/0.35 0.92	0.93 (0.90)/0.35 0.9	0.93 (0.90)/0.35 0.91	0.93 (0.89)/0.35 0.88	0.93 (0.90)/0.35 0.83	0.93 (0.90)/0.35 0.78	0.93 (0.90)/0.35 0.81	0.93 (0.89)/0.35 0.75	0.93 (0.89)/0.35 0.9	0.93 (0.89)/0.35 0.87
		0°	0.93 (0.04)/0.41 0.88	0.93 (0.05)/0.41 0.86	0.93 (0.04)/0.40 0.88	0.93 (0.04)/0.41 0.85	0.93 (0.04)/0.41 0.77	0.93 (0.04)/0.41 0.72	0.93 (0.04)/0.40 0.76	0.93 (0.04)/0.41 0.7	0.93 (0.04)/0.40 0.87	0.93 (0.04)/0.40 0.84
		Excluded Beam[b]	0.02 (0.04)/0.39 0.78	0.02 (0.05)/0.39 0.76	0.02 (0.04)/0.39 0.79	0.02 (0.04)/0.39 0.77	0.02 (0.04)/0.39 0.59	0.02 (0.04)/0.39 0.55	0.02 (0.04)/0.39 0.59	0.02 (0.04)/0.39 0.55	0.02 (0.04)/0.39 0.79	0.02 (0.04)/0.39 0.77
		45°	0.19 (0.02)/0.29 0.83	0.19 (0.03)/0.29 0.81	0.19 (0.02)/0.28 0.83	0.19 (0.02)/0.28 0.81	0.19 (0.02)/0.29 0.67	0.19 (0.02)/0.29 0.63	0.19 (0.02)/0.28 0.66	0.19 (0.02)/0.28 0.62	0.19 (0.02)/0.28 0.83	0.19 (0.02)/0.28 0.8
		Closed	0.02 (0.02)/0.09 0.66	0.02 (0.02)/0.09 0.66	0.01 (0.02)/0.09 0.67	0.02 (0.02)/0.09 0.66	0.02 (0.02)/0.09 0.36	0.02 (0.02)/0.09 0.35	0.01 (0.01)/0.09 0.37	0.01 (0.02)/0.09 0.35	0.01 (0.01)/0.09 0.67	0.01 (0.02)/0.09 0.66
Outdoor Side	0.50	Worst[a]	0.94 (1.00)/0.44 0.92	0.94 (0.99)/0.44 0.9	0.94 (0.99)/0.44 0.91	0.94 (0.99)/0.44 0.88	0.94 (1.00)/0.44 0.84	0.94 (1.00)/0.44 0.79	0.94 (1.00)/0.44 0.81	0.94 (0.99)/0.44 0.75	0.94 (0.99)/0.44 0.9	0.94 (0.99)/0.43 0.87
		0°	0.94 (0.14)/0.50 0.92	0.94 (0.14)/0.50 0.89	0.94 (0.14)/0.50 0.91	0.94 (0.14)/0.50 0.88	0.94 (0.14)/0.50 0.83	0.94 (0.14)/0.50 0.78	0.94 (0.14)/0.50 0.81	0.94 (0.14)/0.50 0.75	0.94 (0.14)/0.50 0.9	0.94 (0.14)/0.50 0.87
		Excluded Beam[b]	0.07 (0.14)/0.48 0.89	0.07 (0.14)/0.48 0.86	0.07 (0.14)/0.48 0.88	0.07 (0.14)/0.48 0.85	0.07 (0.14)/0.48 0.78	0.07 (0.14)/0.48 0.73	0.07 (0.14)/0.48 0.76	0.07 (0.14)/0.48 0.7	0.07 (0.14)/0.48 0.88	0.07 (0.14)/0.47 0.85
		45°	0.24 (0.06)/0.36 0.9	0.25 (0.06)/0.36 0.87	0.24 (0.06)/0.36 0.89	0.24 (0.06)/0.36 0.86	0.24 (0.06)/0.36 0.8	0.24 (0.06)/0.36 0.74	0.24 (0.06)/0.36 0.78	0.24 (0.06)/0.36 0.72	0.24 (0.06)/0.36 0.88	0.24 (0.06)/0.36 0.85
		Closed	0.04 (0.02)/0.14 0.82	0.04 (0.02)/0.14 0.79	0.03 (0.02)/0.13 0.82	0.04 (0.02)/0.13 0.79	0.03 (0.02)/0.14 0.65	0.04 (0.02)/0.14 0.61	0.03 (0.02)/0.13 0.65	0.03 (0.02)/0.13 0.6	0.03 (0.02)/0.13 0.82	0.03 (0.02)/0.13 0.79
Outdoor Side	0.80	Worst[a]	0.95 (1.11)/0.56 0.92	0.95 (1.10)/0.56 0.9	0.95 (1.10)/0.56 0.91	0.95 (1.08)/0.55 0.88	0.95 (1.11)/0.56 0.84	0.95 (1.10)/0.56 0.79	0.95 (1.10)/0.56 0.81	0.95 (1.09)/0.55 0.75	0.95 (1.10)/0.55 0.9	0.95 (1.08)/0.55 0.87
		0°	0.95 (0.29)/0.62 0.93	0.95 (0.29)/0.62 0.9	0.95 (0.29)/0.62 0.92	0.95 (0.29)/0.62 0.89	0.95 (0.29)/0.62 0.84	0.95 (0.29)/0.62 0.79	0.95 (0.29)/0.62 0.82	0.95 (0.29)/0.62 0.76	0.95 (0.29)/0.62 0.9	0.95 (0.29)/0.62 0.87
		Excluded Beam[b]	0.16 (0.29)/0.60 0.91	0.16 (0.29)/0.60 0.88	0.16 (0.29)/0.60 0.9	0.16 (0.29)/0.59 0.87	0.15 (0.29)/0.60 0.82	0.15 (0.29)/0.60 0.76	0.15 (0.29)/0.60 0.79	0.15 (0.29)/0.60 0.73	0.15 (0.29)/0.60 0.89	0.15 (0.29)/0.59 0.86
		45°	0.33 (0.13)/0.48 0.92	0.33 (0.13)/0.48 0.89	0.33 (0.12)/0.48 0.91	0.33 (0.12)/0.47 0.88	0.33 (0.13)/0.48 0.83	0.33 (0.13)/0.48 0.77	0.33 (0.12)/0.48 0.8	0.33 (0.12)/0.47 0.74	0.33 (0.12)/0.48 0.9	0.33 (0.12)/0.47 0.87
		Closed	0.08 (0.04)/0.22 0.89	0.08 (0.04)/0.22 0.87	0.08 (0.04)/0.21 0.89	0.08 (0.04)/0.21 0.86	0.08 (0.04)/0.22 0.79	0.08 (0.04)/0.22 0.74	0.08 (0.04)/0.21 0.77	0.08 (0.04)/0.21 0.71	0.08 (0.04)/0.21 0.88	0.08 (0.04)/0.21 0.85

Notes: [a]Louvers track so that profile angle equals negative slat angle and maximum direct beam is admitted.
[b]Louvers track to block direct beam radiation. When negative slat angles result, slat defaults to 0°.
[c] Glazing cavity width equals original cavity width plus slat width.
[d]F_R is radiant fraction; ratio of radiative heat transfer to total heat transfer, on room side of glazing system.

Table 14G IAC Values for Draperies, Roller Shades, and Insect Screens

Drapery													
		Glazing ID:	**1a**	**1b**	**1c**	**1d**	**1e**	**1f**	**1g**	**1h**	**1i**		
Shade	**Fabric Designator**	**Fullness**	IAC, F_R[d]										
Dark Closed Weave	III_D	100%	0.71, 0.50	0.71, 0.49	0.72, 0.47	0.74, 0.45	0.72, 0.47	0.74, 0.44	0.72, 0.47	0.74, 0.44	0.74, 0.45		
Medium Closed Weave	III_M	100%	0.59, 0.53	0.60, 0.52	0.62, 0.49	0.65, 0.46	0.63, 0.49	0.66, 0.46	0.63, 0.49	0.66, 0.45	0.65, 0.46		
Light Closed Weave	III_L	100%	0.45, 0.62	0.46, 0.60	0.50, 0.56	0.55, 0.50	0.51, 0.54	0.56, 0.50	0.51, 0.54	0.56, 0.49	0.55, 0.51		
Dark Semiopen Weave	II_D	100%	0.75, 0.55	0.75, 0.54	0.76, 0.52	0.78, 0.49	0.76, 0.52	0.78, 0.49	0.76, 0.52	0.78, 0.49	0.78, 0.49		
Medium Semiopen Weave	II_M	100%	0.65, 0.63	0.66, 0.62	0.68, 0.59	0.70, 0.55	0.68, 0.58	0.71, 0.54	0.68, 0.58	0.71, 0.54	0.70, 0.55		
Light Semiopen Weave	II_L	100%	0.56, 0.79	0.57, 0.77	0.60, 0.71	0.64, 0.65	0.61, 0.70	0.65, 0.64	0.61, 0.70	0.65, 0.63	0.64, 0.65		
Dark Open Weave	I_D	100%	0.80, 0.63	0.80, 0.62	0.81, 0.60	0.82, 0.57	0.82, 0.59	0.83, 0.56	0.82, 0.59	0.83, 0.56	0.82, 0.57		
Medium Open Weave	I_M	100%	0.71, 0.73	0.72, 0.72	0.73, 0.69	0.76, 0.64	0.74, 0.68	0.76, 0.63	0.74, 0.68	0.76, 0.63	0.76, 0.64		
Light Open Weave	I_L	100%	0.64, 0.87	0.65, 0.85	0.68, 0.80	0.71, 0.73	0.68, 0.78	0.71, 0.72	0.68, 0.78	0.72, 0.71	0.71, 0.73		
Sheer		100%	0.73, 0.89	0.73, 0.88	0.75, 0.83	0.77, 0.77	0.75, 0.82	0.78, 0.76	0.75, 0.82	0.78, 0.75	0.77, 0.77		
		Glazing ID:	**5a**	**5b**	**5c**	**5d**	**5e**	**5f**	**5g**	**5h**	**5i**		
Dark Closed Weave	III_D	100%	0.81, 0.46	0.82, 0.45	0.82, 0.44	0.83, 0.42	0.82, 0.44	0.83, 0.42	0.82, 0.44	0.84, 0.42	0.83, 0.42		
Medium Closed Weave	III_M	100%	0.70, 0.48	0.72, 0.46	0.72, 0.46	0.75, 0.43	0.72, 0.46	0.75, 0.43	0.72, 0.46	0.75, 0.43	0.75, 0.43		
Light Closed Weave	III_L	100%	0.57, 0.54	0.60, 0.52	0.59, 0.52	0.64, 0.47	0.60, 0.51	0.65, 0.47	0.60, 0.51	0.65, 0.47	0.64, 0.47		
Dark Semiopen Weave	II_D	100%	0.84, 0.51	0.85, 0.50	0.85, 0.49	0.86, 0.47	0.85, 0.49	0.86, 0.47	0.85, 0.49	0.86, 0.46	0.86, 0.47		
Medium Semiopen Weave	II_M	100%	0.75, 0.57	0.76, 0.55	0.76, 0.55	0.79, 0.51	0.76, 0.55	0.79, 0.51	0.76, 0.55	0.79, 0.51	0.79, 0.52		
Light Semiopen Weave	II_L	100%	0.65, 0.70	0.68, 0.67	0.67, 0.67	0.71, 0.61	0.68, 0.66	0.72, 0.60	0.68, 0.66	0.72, 0.60	0.72, 0.61		
Dark Open Weave	I_D	100%	0.88, 0.59	0.88, 0.57	0.88, 0.57	0.89, 0.54	0.88, 0.57	0.89, 0.54	0.88, 0.57	0.89, 0.54	0.89, 0.54		
Medium Open Weave	I_M	100%	0.79, 0.68	0.80, 0.65	0.80, 0.65	0.82, 0.61	0.80, 0.65	0.82, 0.60	0.80, 0.65	0.82, 0.60	0.82, 0.61		
Light Open Weave	I_L	100%	0.72, 0.79	0.74, 0.76	0.73, 0.76	0.77, 0.69	0.74, 0.75	0.77, 0.69	0.74, 0.75	0.77, 0.68	0.77, 0.69		
Sheer		100%	0.78, 0.83	0.8, 0.8	0.8, 0.8	0.82, 0.73	0.8, 0.79	0.82, 0.73	0.8, 0.79	0.82, 0.73	0.82, 0.74		
		Glazing ID:	**17a**	**17b**	**17c**	**17d**	**17e**	**17f**	**17g**	**17h**	**17i**	**17j**	**17k**
Dark Closed Weave	III_D	100%	0.85, 0.45	0.86, 0.43	0.86, 0.44	0.87, 0.43	0.86, 0.43	0.88, 0.41	0.87, 0.42	0.88, 0.40	0.87, 0.42	0.88, 0.40	0.88, 0.41
Medium Closed Weave	III_M	100%	0.74, 0.47	0.76, 0.45	0.76, 0.45	0.79, 0.44	0.77, 0.44	0.80, 0.42	0.78, 0.44	0.80, 0.41	0.78, 0.44	0.80, 0.41	0.80, 0.42
Light Closed Weave	III_L	100%	0.60, 0.52	0.64, 0.50	0.64, 0.50	0.68, 0.47	0.66, 0.48	0.71, 0.44	0.66, 0.48	0.71, 0.44	0.66, 0.48	0.71, 0.44	0.71, 0.45
Dark Semiopen Weave	II_D	100%	0.88, 0.50	0.89, 0.48	0.88, 0.49	0.89, 0.47	0.89, 0.48	0.90, 0.45	0.89, 0.47	0.90, 0.45	0.89, 0.47	0.90, 0.45	0.90, 0.45
Medium Semiopen Weave	II_M	100%	0.78, 0.56	0.8, 0.54	0.8, 0.54	0.82, 0.52	0.81, 0.52	0.83, 0.49	0.81, 0.52	0.83, 0.49	0.81, 0.52	0.83, 0.49	0.83, 0.49
Light Semiopen Weave	II_L	100%	0.68, 0.68	0.71, 0.64	0.71, 0.64	0.74, 0.61	0.72, 0.62	0.76, 0.57	0.73, 0.62	0.77, 0.57	0.73, 0.62	0.77, 0.57	0.76, 0.57
Dark Open Weave	I_D	100%	0.90, 0.58	0.91, 0.56	0.91, 0.56	0.91, 0.55	0.91, 0.55	0.92, 0.52	0.91, 0.55	0.92, 0.52	0.91, 0.55	0.92, 0.52	0.92, 0.52
Medium Open Weave	I_M	100%	0.81, 0.66	0.83, 0.64	0.83, 0.64	0.85, 0.61	0.84, 0.62	0.86, 0.58	0.84, 0.62	0.86, 0.58	0.84, 0.62	0.86, 0.58	0.86, 0.58
Light Open Weave	I_L	100%	0.74, 0.77	0.76, 0.73	0.76, 0.73	0.79, 0.69	0.77, 0.71	0.81, 0.65	0.78, 0.71	0.81, 0.65	0.78, 0.71	0.81, 0.65	0.81, 0.65
Sheer		100%	0.8, 0.81	0.82, 0.77	0.82, 0.78	0.84, 0.74	0.83, 0.75	0.85, 0.7	0.83, 0.75	0.85, 0.69	0.83, 0.75	0.85, 0.69	0.85, 0.7
		Glazing ID:	**21a**	**21b**	**21c**	**21d**	**21e**	**21f**	**21g**	**21h**	**21i**	**21j**	**21k**
Dark Closed Weave	III_D	100%	0.87, 0.44	0.88, 0.43	0.88, 0.43	0.88, 0.42	0.88, 0.42	0.89, 0.40	0.88, 0.42	0.89, 0.40	0.88, 0.42	0.89, 0.40	0.89, 0.40
Medium Closed Weave	III_M	100%	0.77, 0.46	0.79, 0.45	0.79, 0.45	0.81, 0.43	0.80, 0.43	0.82, 0.41	0.80, 0.43	0.82, 0.41	0.80, 0.43	0.82, 0.41	0.82, 0.41
Light Closed Weave	III_L	100%	0.64, 0.52	0.67, 0.49	0.68, 0.49	0.70, 0.47	0.69, 0.47	0.73, 0.45	0.70, 0.47	0.73, 0.44	0.70, 0.47	0.73, 0.44	0.73, 0.45
Dark Semiopen Weave	II_D	100%	0.89, 0.49	0.90, 0.48	0.90, 0.48	0.90, 0.47	0.90, 0.47	0.91, 0.45	0.90, 0.47	0.91, 0.45	0.90, 0.47	0.91, 0.45	0.91, 0.45
Medium Semiopen Weave	II_M	100%	0.8, 0.55	0.82, 0.53	0.82, 0.53	0.83, 0.51	0.83, 0.52	0.85, 0.49	0.83, 0.51	0.85, 0.49	0.83, 0.51	0.85, 0.49	0.85, 0.49
Light Semiopen Weave	II_L	100%	0.71, 0.67	0.74, 0.64	0.74, 0.63	0.76, 0.61	0.75, 0.61	0.78, 0.57	0.76, 0.61	0.78, 0.57	0.76, 0.61	0.78, 0.57	0.78, 0.57
Dark Open Weave	I_D	100%	0.92, 0.57	0.92, 0.56	0.92, 0.55	0.92, 0.54	0.92, 0.54	0.93, 0.52	0.92, 0.54	0.93, 0.52	0.92, 0.54	0.93, 0.52	0.93, 0.52
Medium Open Weave	I_M	100%	0.83, 0.65	0.85, 0.63	0.85, 0.63	0.86, 0.61	0.86, 0.61	0.87, 0.58	0.86, 0.61	0.87, 0.58	0.86, 0.61	0.87, 0.58	0.87, 0.58
Light Open Weave	I_L	100%	0.76, 0.77	0.78, 0.73	0.79, 0.72	0.81, 0.69	0.80, 0.70	0.82, 0.65	0.80, 0.69	0.82, 0.65	0.80, 0.69	0.82, 0.65	0.82, 0.66
Sheer		100%	0.82, 0.81	0.83, 0.77	0.84, 0.76	0.85, 0.74	0.85, 0.74	0.86, 0.7	0.85, 0.74	0.86, 0.69	0.85, 0.74	0.86, 0.69	0.86, 0.7

Table 14G IAC Values for Draperies, Roller Shades, and Insect Screens (*Continued*)

		Glazing ID:	25a	25b	25c	26d	25e	25f
Dark Closed Weave	III$_D$	100%	0.88, 0.43	0.89, 0.42	0.90, 0.40	0.90, 0.40	0.91, 0.39	0.90, 0.40
Medium Closed Weave	III$_M$	100%	0.80, 0.45	0.82, 0.44	0.85, 0.41	0.84, 0.41	0.85, 0.40	0.84, 0.42
Light Closed Weave	III$_L$	100%	0.68, 0.51	0.72, 0.48	0.76, 0.44	0.76, 0.45	0.77, 3	0.76, 0.45
Dark Semiopen Weave	II$_D$	100%	0.91, 0.48	0.91, 0.47	0.92, 0.44	0.92, 0.45	0.92, 0.43	0.92, 0.45
Medium Semiopen Weave	II$_M$	100%	0.83, 0.54	0.85, 0.52	0.87, 0.48	0.86, 0.49	0.87, 0.47	0.86, 0.49
Light Semiopen Weave	II$_L$	100%	0.75, 0.66	0.78, 0.63	0.81, 0.57	0.81, 0.58	0.82, 0.55	0.81, 0.58
Dark Open Weave	I$_D$	100%	0.93, 0.56	0.93, 0.55	0.94, 0.51	0.94, 0.52	0.94, 0.50	0.94, 0.52
Medium Open Weave	I$_M$	100%	0.86, 0.65	0.87, 0.62	0.89, 0.57	0.89, 0.58	0.89, 0.56	0.89, 0.59
Light Open Weave	I$_L$	100%	0.79, 0.75	0.82, 0.72	0.85, 0.65	0.84, 0.66	0.85, 0.63	0.84, 0.67
Sheer		100%	0.84, 0.8	0.86, 0.76	0.88, 0.69	0.88, 0.7	0.89, 0.67	0.88, 0.71

		Glazing ID:	29a	29b
Dark Closed Weave	III$_D$	100%	0.86, 0.44	0.87, 0.42
Medium Closed Weave	III$_M$	100%	0.77, 0.45	0.80, 0.43
Light Closed Weave	III$_L$	100%	0.65, 0.50	0.69, 0.47
Dark Semiopen Weave	II$_D$	100%	0.89, 0.48	0.90, 0.47
Medium Semiopen Weave	II$_M$	100%	0.81, 0.54	0.83, 0.51
Light Semiopen Weave	II$_L$	100%	0.72, 0.65	0.76, 0.60
Dark Open Weave	I$_D$	100%	0.91, 0.56	0.92, 0.54
Medium Open Weave	I$_M$	100%	0.84, 0.64	0.85, 0.60
Light Open Weave	I$_L$	100%	0.77, 0.73	0.80, 0.69
Sheer		100%	0.83, 0.78	0.85, 0.73

		Glazing ID:	32a	32b	32c	32d
Dark Closed Weave	III$_D$	100%	0.89, 0.43	0.90, 0.41	0.91, 0.42	0.92, 0.39
Medium Closed Weave	III$_M$	100%	0.80, 0.44	0.83, 0.42	0.82, 0.42	0.84, 0.39
Light Closed Weave	III$_L$	100%	0.69, 0.48	0.73, 0.45	0.69, 0.44	0.73, 0.40
Dark Semiopen Weave	II$_D$	100%	0.91, 0.47	0.92, 0.46	0.93, 0.46	0.94, 0.43
Medium Semiopen Weave	II$_M$	100%	0.83, 0.52	0.85, 0.50	0.84, 0.50	0.86, 0.46
Light Semiopen Weave	II$_L$	100%	0.75, 0.62	0.79, 0.58	0.75, 0.58	0.79, 0.52
Dark Open Weave	I$_D$	100%	0.93, 0.55	0.93, 0.53	0.95, 0.53	0.95, 0.50
Medium Open Weave	I$_M$	100%	0.86, 0.62	0.87, 0.59	0.87, 0.59	0.88, 0.54
Light Open Weave	I$_L$	100%	0.80, 0.71	0.83, 0.66	0.80, 0.66	0.82, 0.60
Sheer		100%	0.84, 0.75	0.87, 0.7	0.85, 0.71	0.87, 0.65

		Glazing ID:	40a	40b	40c	40d
Dark Closed Weave	III$_D$	100%	0.93, 0.41	0.94, 0.37	0.90, 0.42	0.91, 0.40
Medium Closed Weave	III$_M$	100%	0.84, 0.40	0.87, 0.37	0.82, 0.43	0.85, 0.41
Light Closed Weave	III$_L$	100%	0.73, 0.42	0.77, 0.38	0.71, 0.47	0.76, 0.44
Dark Semiopen Weave	II$_D$	100%	0.94, 0.45	0.95, 0.41	0.92, 0.46	0.93, 0.45
Medium Semiopen Weave	II$_M$	100%	0.86, 0.48	0.89, 0.44	0.85, 0.51	0.87, 0.48
Light Semiopen Weave	II$_L$	100%	0.78, 0.55	0.82, 0.49	0.77, 0.60	0.80, 0.56
Dark Open Weave	I$_D$	100%	0.96, 0.51	0.96, 0.47	0.94, 0.54	0.94, 0.52
Medium Open Weave	I$_M$	100%	0.88, 0.56	0.90, 0.51	0.87, 0.60	0.89, 0.57
Light Open Weave	I$_L$	100%	0.82, 0.63	0.85, 0.57	0.81, 0.69	0.84, 0.64
Sheer		100%	0.86, 0.68	0.89, 0.61	0.86, 0.73	0.88, 0.68

Roller Shades and Insect Screens

Shade/Screen	Openness	Refl./Trans.									
		Glazing ID:	**1a**	**1b**	**1c**	**1d**	**1e**	**1f**	**1g**	**1h**	**1i**
Light Translucent	0.14	0.60/0.25	0.44, 0.74	0.45, 0.72	0.49, 0.66	0.55, 0.59	0.51, 0.65	0.56, 0.59	0.51, 0.65	0.57, 0.58	0.55, 0.6
White Opaque	0.00	0.65/0.00	0.34, 0.45	0.35, 0.44	0.4, 0.41	0.47, 0.38	0.42, 0.4	0.48, 0.38	0.42, 0.4	0.49, 0.38	0.47, 0.38
Dark Opaque	0.00	0.20/0.00	0.64, 0.48	0.65, 0.47	0.67, 0.45	0.69, 0.43	0.67, 0.45	0.7, 0.42	0.67, 0.45	0.7, 0.42	0.69, 0.43
Light Gray Translucent	0.10	0.31/0.15	0.61, 0.57	0.62, 0.57	0.64, 0.54	0.68, 0.51	0.65, 0.53	0.68, 0.5	0.65, 0.53	0.69, 0.5	0.68, 0.51
Dark Gray Translucent	0.14	0.17/0.19	0.71, 0.58	0.72, 0.58	0.73, 0.55	0.76, 0.52	0.74, 0.55	0.76, 0.52	0.74, 0.55	0.76, 0.52	0.76, 0.52
Reflective White Opaque	0.00	0.84/0.00	0.3, 0.71	0.32, 0.68	0.38, 0.6	0.45, 0.53	0.39, 0.58	0.46, 0.52	0.39, 0.58	0.47, 0.52	0.45, 0.53
Reflective White Translucent	0.07	0.75/0.16	0.23, 0.42	0.25, 0.41	0.31, 0.38	0.39, 0.36	0.33, 0.37	0.4, 0.35	0.33, 0.37	0.41, 0.35	0.39, 0.36
Outdoor Insect Screen			0.64, 0.98	0.64, 0.98	0.64, 0.95	0.64, 0.92	0.64, 0.95	0.64, 0.91	0.64, 0.95	0.64, 0.91	0.64, 0.92
Indoor Insect Screen			0.88, 0.81	0.88, 0.8	0.89, 0.78	0.9, 0.75	0.89, 0.78	0.9, 0.75	0.89, 0.78	0.9, 0.75	0.9, 0.76
		Glazing ID:	**5a**	**5b**	**5c**	**5d**	**5e**	**5f**	**5g**	**5h**	**5i**
Light Translucent	0.14	0.60/0.25	0.55, 0.65	0.58, 0.62	0.58, 0.62	0.63, 0.56	0.58, 0.61	0.64, 0.56	0.58, 0.61	0.64, 0.56	0.63, 0.56
White Opaque	0.00	0.65/0.00	0.48, 0.4	0.52, 0.39	0.51, 0.39	0.57, 0.37	0.52, 0.39	0.58, 0.37	0.52, 0.39	0.58, 0.36	0.57, 0.37
Dark Opaque	0.00	0.20/0.00	0.76, 0.44	0.77, 0.43	0.77, 0.43	0.8, 0.41	0.78, 0.43	0.8, 0.41	0.78, 0.43	0.8, 0.4	0.8, 0.41
Light Gray Translucent	0.10	0.31/0.15	0.72, 0.53	0.74, 0.51	0.74, 0.51	0.77, 0.48	0.74, 0.51	0.77, 0.48	0.74, 0.51	0.77, 0.48	0.77, 0.48
Dark Gray Translucent	0.14	0.17/0.19	0.81, 0.54	0.82, 0.53	0.82, 0.53	0.84, 0.5	0.82, 0.52	0.84, 0.5	0.82, 0.52	0.84, 0.5	0.84, 0.5
Reflective White Opaque	0.00	0.84/0.00	0.43, 0.6	0.47, 0.55	0.46, 0.56	0.54, 0.5	0.47, 0.55	0.55, 0.49	0.47, 0.55	0.55, 0.49	0.54, 0.5
Reflective White Translucent	0.07	0.75/0.16	0.37, 0.38	0.42, 0.36	0.41, 0.36	0.49, 0.34	0.42, 0.36	0.5, 0.34	0.42, 0.36	0.5, 0.34	0.49, 0.34
Outdoor Insect Screen			0.64, 0.96	0.64, 0.94	0.64, 0.94	0.64, 0.91	0.64, 0.94	0.64, 0.9	0.64, 0.94	0.64, 0.9	0.64, 0.91
Indoor Insect Screen			0.92, 0.78	0.93, 0.77	0.93, 0.76	0.93, 0.74	0.93, 0.76	0.93, 0.74	0.93, 0.76	0.93, 0.73	0.93, 0.74

Table 14G IAC Values for Draperies, Roller Shades, and Insect Screens (*Continued*)

		Glazing ID:	17a	17b	17c	17d	17e	17f	17g	17h	17i	17j	17k
Light Translucent	0.14	0.60/0.25	0.58, 0.63	0.62, 0.6	0.62, 0.6	0.67, 0.56	0.64, 0.58	0.69, 0.53	0.64, 0.57	0.7, 0.53	0.64, 0.57	0.7, 0.53	0.7, 0.53
White Opaque	0.00	0.65/0.00	0.52, 0.39	0.56, 0.38	0.57, 0.38	0.61, 0.37	0.59, 0.37	0.65, 0.36	0.59, 0.37	0.65, 0.36	0.59, 0.37	0.65, 0.35	0.65, 0.36
Dark Opaque	0.00	0.20/0.00	0.8, 0.43	0.82, 0.42	0.82, 0.42	0.83, 0.41	0.82, 0.41	0.84, 0.39	0.82, 0.41	0.84, 0.39	0.82, 0.41	0.84, 0.39	0.84, 0.39
Light Gray Translucent	0.10	0.31/0.15	0.76, 0.52	0.78, 0.5	0.78, 0.5	0.8, 0.48	0.78, 0.49	0.81, 0.46	0.79, 0.49	0.82, 0.46	0.79, 0.49	0.82, 0.46	0.81, 0.46
Dark Gray Translucent	0.14	0.17/0.19	0.84, 0.53	0.85, 0.52	0.85, 0.52	0.86, 0.5	0.86, 0.51	0.87, 0.48	0.86, 0.51	0.88, 0.48	0.86, 0.51	0.88, 0.48	0.87, 0.48
Reflective White Opaque	0.00	0.84/0.00	0.46, 0.57	0.52, 0.53	0.52, 0.53	0.58, 0.5	0.54, 0.51	0.61, 0.47	0.55, 0.51	0.62, 0.46	0.55, 0.51	0.62, 0.46	0.61, 0.47
Reflective White Translucent	0.07	0.75/0.16	0.41, 0.37	0.47, 0.36	0.47, 0.36	0.53, 0.35	0.49, 0.35	0.57, 0.34	0.5, 0.35	0.58, 0.34	0.5, 0.35	0.58, 0.33	0.57, 0.34
Outdoor Insect Screen			0.64, 0.95	0.64, 0.93	0.64, 0.94	0.64, 0.91	0.64, 0.92	0.64, 0.89	0.64, 0.92	0.64, 0.89	0.64, 0.92	0.64, 0.89	0.64, 0.89
Indoor Insect Screen			0.94, 0.77	0.94, 0.76	0.94, 0.76	0.94, 0.74	0.94, 0.75	0.95, 0.72	0.94, 0.75	0.95, 0.72	0.94, 0.75	0.95, 0.72	0.95, 0.72

		Glazing ID:	21a	21b	21c	21d	21e	21f	21g	21h	21i	21j	21k
Light Translucent	0.14	0.60/0.25	0.61, 0.63	0.65, 0.59	0.66, 0.59	0.69, 0.56	0.68, 0.57	0.72, 0.53	0.68, 0.57	0.72, 0.53	0.68, 0.57	0.72, 0.53	0.72, 0.53
White Opaque	0.00	0.65/0.00	0.55, 0.39	0.6, 0.38	0.61, 0.38	0.64, 0.37	0.63, 0.37	0.67, 0.36	0.63, 0.37	0.67, 0.36	0.63, 0.37	0.68, 0.35	0.67, 0.36
Dark Opaque	0.00	0.20/0.00	0.82, 0.43	0.84, 0.42	0.84, 0.42	0.85, 0.41	0.85, 0.41	0.86, 0.39	0.85, 0.41	0.86, 0.39	0.85, 0.41	0.86, 0.39	0.86, 0.39
Light Gray Translucent	0.10	0.31/0.15	0.78, 0.51	0.8, 0.5	0.8, 0.5	0.82, 0.48	0.81, 0.48	0.83, 0.46	0.81, 0.48	0.83, 0.46	0.81, 0.48	0.83, 0.46	0.83, 0.46
Dark Gray Translucent	0.14	0.17/0.19	0.86, 0.53	0.87, 0.51	0.87, 0.51	0.88, 0.5	0.88, 0.5	0.89, 0.48	0.88, 0.5	0.89, 0.48	0.88, 0.5	0.89, 0.48	0.89, 0.48
Reflective White Opaque	0.00	0.84/0.00	0.5, 0.56	0.55, 0.53	0.56, 0.52	0.6, 0.5	0.58, 0.51	0.63, 0.47	0.59, 0.5	0.64, 0.47	0.59, 0.5	0.64, 0.47	0.64, 0.47
Reflective White Translucent	0.07	0.75/0.16	0.44, 0.36	0.5, 0.35	0.51, 0.35	0.56, 0.35	0.54, 0.35	0.6, 0.34	0.54, 0.35	0.6, 0.34	0.54, 0.35	0.6, 0.33	0.6, 0.34
Outdoor Insect Screen			0.64, 0.95	0.64, 0.93	0.64, 0.93	0.64, 0.91	0.64, 0.92	0.64, 0.89	0.64, 0.91	0.64, 0.89	0.64, 0.91	0.64, 0.89	0.64, 0.89
Indoor Insect Screen			0.94, 0.77	0.95, 0.75	0.95, 0.75	0.95, 0.74	0.95, 0.74	0.95, 0.72	0.95, 0.74	0.95, 0.72	0.95, 0.74	0.95, 0.72	0.95, 0.72

		Glazing ID:	25a	25b	25c	26d	25e	25f
Light Translucent	0.14	0.60/0.25	0.66, 0.62	0.71, 0.58	0.75, 0.53	0.75, 0.54	0.77, 0.52	0.74, 0.55
White Opaque	0.00	0.65/0.00	0.6, 0.38	0.66, 0.37	0.71, 0.35	0.7, 0.36	0.72, 0.35	0.7, 0.36
Dark Opaque	0.00	0.20/0.00	0.85, 0.42	0.86, 0.41	0.88, 0.39	0.88, 0.39	0.88, 0.38	0.87, 0.39
Light Gray Translucent	0.10	0.31/0.15	0.81, 0.5	0.83, 0.49	0.86, 0.46	0.85, 0.46	0.86, 0.45	0.85, 0.47
Dark Gray Translucent	0.14	0.17/0.19	0.88, 0.52	0.89, 0.51	0.9, 0.47	0.9, 0.48	0.91, 0.47	0.9, 0.48
Reflective White Opaque	0.00	0.84/0.00	0.55, 0.55	0.61, 0.52	0.68, 0.47	0.67, 0.48	0.69, 0.46	0.66, 0.48
Reflective White Translucent	0.07	0.75/0.16	0.5, 0.36	0.57, 0.35	0.64, 0.33	0.62, 0.34	0.65, 0.33	0.62, 0.34
Outdoor Insect Screen			0.65, 0.95	0.65, 0.93	0.64, 0.88	0.64, 0.89	0.64, 0.87	0.64, 0.89
Indoor Insect Screen			0.95, 0.76	0.96, 0.75	0.96, 0.72	0.96, 0.72	0.96, 0.71	0.96, 0.72

		Glazing ID:	29a	29b
Light Translucent	0.14	0.60/0.25	0.64, 0.6	0.68, 0.56
White Opaque	0.00	0.65/0.00	0.58, 0.38	0.63, 0.37
Dark Opaque	0.00	0.20/0.00	0.82, 0.42	0.84, 0.41
Light Gray Translucent	0.10	0.31/0.15	0.78, 0.5	0.81, 0.48
Dark Gray Translucent	0.14	0.17/0.19	0.86, 0.52	0.87, 0.5
Reflective White Opaque	0.00	0.84/0.00	0.53, 0.53	0.59, 0.49
Reflective White Translucent	0.07	0.75/0.16	0.48, 0.36	0.55, 0.35
Outdoor Insect Screen			0.64, 0.94	0.64, 0.91
Indoor Insect Screen			0.94, 0.76	0.95, 0.74

		Glazing ID:	32a	32b	32c	32d	40a	40b	40c	40d
Light Translucent	0.14	0.60/0.25	0.67, 0.58	0.72, 0.54	0.67, 0.52	0.71, 0.46	0.7, 0.49	0.75, 0.43	0.69, 0.56	0.74, 0.52
White Opaque	0.00	0.65/0.00	0.62, 0.37	0.68, 0.36	0.62, 0.33	0.67, 0.3	0.67, 0.31	0.72, 0.29	0.65, 0.37	0.71, 0.36
Dark Opaque	0.00	0.20/0.00	0.85, 0.41	0.87, 0.4	0.87, 0.4	0.89, 0.38	0.89, 0.39	0.91, 0.36	0.87, 0.41	0.88, 0.39
Light Gray Translucent	0.10	0.31/0.15	0.81, 0.49	0.84, 0.47	0.82, 0.46	0.85, 0.43	0.85, 0.44	0.87, 0.41	0.83, 0.48	0.85, 0.46
Dark Gray Translucent	0.14	0.17/0.19	0.88, 0.51	0.89, 0.49	0.9, 0.49	0.91, 0.45	0.91, 0.47	0.92, 0.43	0.89, 0.5	0.91, 0.48
Reflective White Opaque	0.00	0.84/0.00	0.57, 0.51	0.64, 0.47	0.57, 0.44	0.63, 0.39	0.61, 0.41	0.68, 0.36	0.6, 0.5	0.67, 0.46
Reflective White Translucent	0.07	0.75/0.16	0.53, 0.35	0.61, 0.34	0.52, 0.28	0.59, 0.26	0.58, 0.27	0.65, 0.25	0.56, 0.35	0.64, 0.34
Outdoor Insect Screen			0.64, 0.92	0.64, 0.9	0.64, 0.86	0.64, 0.8	0.64, 0.83	0.64, 0.77	0.64, 0.91	0.64, 0.88
Indoor Insect Screen			0.95, 0.75	0.96, 0.73	0.95, 0.7	0.95, 0.67	0.96, 0.68	0.96, 0.64	0.96, 0.74	0.96, 0.72

Notes: [a]Louvers track so that profile angle equals negative slat angle and maximum direct beam is admitted.
[b]Louvers track to block direct beam radiation. When negative slat angles result, slat defaults to 0°.
[c]Glazing cavity width equals original cavity width plus slat width.
[d]F_R is radiant fraction; ratio of radiative heat transfer to total heat transfer, on room side of glazing system.

Table 15 Summary of Environmental Control Capabilities of Draperies

Item	Designator (Figure 23)								
	I_D	I_M	I_L	II_D	II_M	II_L	III_D	III_M	III_L
1. Protection from direct solar radiation and long-wave radiation to or from window areas	Fair	Fair	Fair	Fair	Good	Good	Fair	Good	Good
2. Effectiveness in allowing outward vision through fenestration	Good	Good	Fair	Fair	Fair	Some	None	None	None
3. Effectiveness in attaining privacy (limiting inward vision from outdoors)	None	None	Poor[a] Good[a]	Poor	Fair	Fair[a] Good[a]	Good[b]	Good[b]	Good[b]
4. Protection against excessive brightness and glare from sunshine and external objects	Mild	Mild	Mild[c] Poor[c]	Good	Good	Good[c] Poor[c]	Good	Good	Good[c] Poor[c]
5. Effectiveness in modifying unattractive or distracting view out of window	Little	Little	Some	Some	Good	Good	Blocks	Blocks	Blocks

[a]Good when bright illumination is on viewing side.
[b]To obscure view completely, material must be completely opaque.
[c]Poor rating applies to white fabric in direct sunlight. Use off-white color to avoid excessive transmitted light.

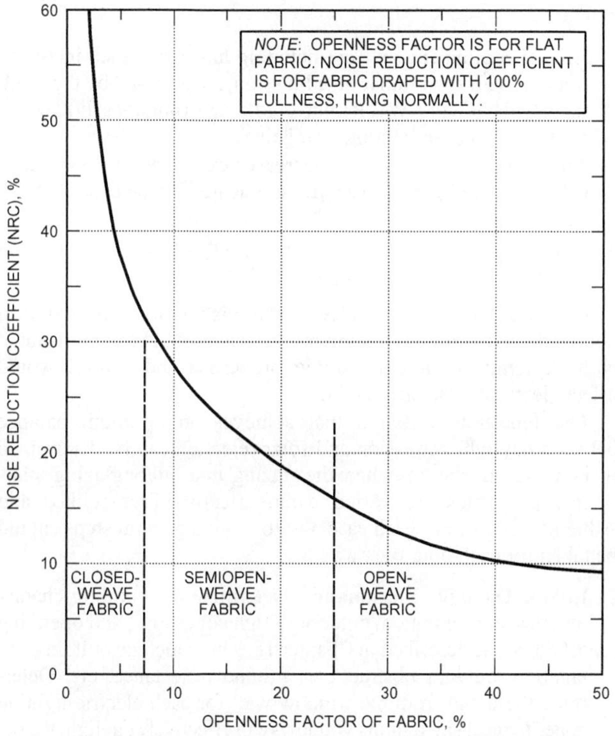

Fig. 26 Noise Reduction Coefficient Versus Openness Factor for Draperies

device can be used to control brightness for the other shading devices and, when used alone, to reduce brightness while still allowing some view of the outdoors.

View Modification. When the view is unattractive or distracting, draperies modify the view to some degree, depending on fabric weave and color (summarized in Table 15), but the fenestration product remains as an effective connection to the outdoors.

Sound Control. Indoor shading devices, particularly draperies, can absorb some sounds originating in the room but have little or no effect in preventing outdoor sounds from entering. For excessive internally generated sound, the usual remedy is to apply acoustical treatment to the ceiling and other room surfaces. Although these materials can be effective in controlling sound, they are often located on the two horizontal surfaces (ceiling and floor) and leave the opposing vertical surfaces of glazing and bare wall to reflect sound. The noise reduction coefficient (NRC = average absorptance coefficient at four frequencies) for venetian blinds is about 0.10, compared to 0.02 for glass and 0.03 for plaster. For drapery fabrics at 100% fullness, NRC ranges from 0.10 to 0.65, depending on the tightness of weave. Class III (tightly woven) fabrics have NRC values of 0.35 to 0.65. Figure 26 shows the relationship between NRC and openness factor for fabrics of normal weight.

Double Drapery

Double draperies (two sets of drapery covering the same area) have a light, open weave on the fenestration product side for outward vision and daylight when desired and a heavy, closed weave or opaque drapery on the room side to block out sunlight and provide privacy when desired. When properly selected and used, double draperies can provide a reduced U-factor and a lowered IAC. The reduced U-factor results principally from adding a semiclosed air space to the barrier.

To most effectively reduce solar heat gain, drapery exposed to sunlight should have high reflectance and low transmittance. The light, open-weave drapery should be opened when the heavy drapery is closed to prevent entry of sunlight.

Properly used double draperies give (1) extreme flexibility of vision and light intensity, (2) a lowered U-factor and IAC, and (3) improved comfort, because the room-side drapery is more nearly at room temperature. Table 14 gives characteristics of individual draperies. For large areas, the IAC should be calculated in detail to determine the cooling load.

7. AIR LEAKAGE

Infiltration Through Fenestration

Air infiltration through fenestration products affects occupant comfort and energy consumption. Infiltration is the uncontrolled inward leakage of air caused by pressure effects of wind or differences in air density, such as stack effect. Infiltration should not be confused with ventilation. Although fenestration products can be operated to intentionally provide natural ventilation and increase comfort, infiltration should be reasonably minimized to avoid unpleasant accompanying problems. If additional air is required, controlled ventilation is preferable to infiltration. Mechanical ventilation provides air in a comfortable manner and when desired. For infiltration, however, peak supply is more likely to occur as an uncomfortable draft and when least desired, such as during a storm or the coldest weather.

ASHRAE/IES *Standard* 90.1, ASHRAE's energy standard for all buildings other than low-rise residential buildings, establishes an air leakage maximum of 0.06 cfm/ft^2 for curtain wall and storefront fenestration and 0.2 cfm/ft^2 of gross fenestration product area for most other products (1.0 cfm/ft^2 for glazed swinging entrance doors and revolving doors, 0.4 cfm/ft^2 for nonswinging opaque doors, and 0.3 cfm/ft^2 for unit skylights). This air leakage is as determined in accordance with NFRC *Technical Document* 400 (NFRC 2014h) and ASTM *Standard* E283 and allows direct comparison of all fenestration products: operable and fixed, windows and doors.

Most manufactured fenestration products achieve these reasonable standards of maximum air infiltration. However, products that do not completely seal, such as jalousie windows or doors, are not likely to do so and are most appropriate for installation in unconditioned spaces.

For products achieving this infiltration standard, energy consumption caused by infiltration is likely to be significantly less than energy associated with U-factor and solar heat gain coefficient. Also, although overall air infiltration is a significant component in determining a building's heating and cooling loads, infiltration through fenestration products meeting the standard is generally likely to be a small portion of that total.

Indoor Air Movement

Because supply air grilles are frequently located directly below fenestration products, air sweeps the indoor glazing surface. Heated supply air should be directed away from the glazing to prevent large temperature differences between the center and edges of the glazing. These thermal effects must be considered, particularly when annealed glass is used and air is forced over the glass surface during the heating season. Direct flow of heated air over the glass surface can increase the heat transfer coefficient and temperature difference, causing a substantial increase in heat loss, as well as leading to thermally induced stress and risk of glass breakage.

Systems designed predominantly for cooling lower the glazing temperature and rapidly pick up the cooling load. Both tend to improve comfort conditions. However, the air-conditioned space has an increased net heat gain caused by increases in (1) solar heat gain coefficient (SHGC) caused by delivery of more of the absorbed heat to the indoor space, (2) fenestration U-factor because of the greater convection effect at the indoor surface, and (3) air-to-air temperature difference because supply air rather than room air is in contact with the indoor glazing surface. The principal increase in heat gain with clear glazing is the result of increased U-factor and air-to-air temperature difference.

8. DAYLIGHTING

8.1 DAYLIGHT PREDICTION

Daylighting is the illumination of building interiors with sunlight and sky light and is known to affect visual performance, lighting quality, health, human performance, and energy efficiency. In many European countries with predominantly cloudy skies, codes regulate minimum window size, minimum daylight factor, and window position to provide views to all occupants and to create a minimum indoor brightness level. Daylighting also provides back-up indoor illumination in the event of power outages. Daylighting may have some positive or negative health effects on the skin, eyes, hormone secretion, and mood. Its intensity, spectral content, and diurnal and temporal variation may be used to combat jet lag, sick building syndrome, and other health problems.

In terms of energy efficiency, daylighting can provide substantial whole-building energy reductions in nonresidential buildings through the use of electric lighting controls. Daylight admission can displace the need for electric lighting at the perimeter zone with vertical windows (sidelighting) and at the core zone with skylights (toplighting) and special core sunlighting systems designed to bring sunlight to core spaces and distribute it as necessary, with good lighting quality. Lighting and its associated cooling energy use constitute 30 to 40% of a nonresidential building's energy use. Energy use reductions can be achieved, perhaps less reliably, in residential buildings with manual or automated switching of electric lights on and off to match space occupancy. For internal-load-dominated buildings, daylight admission must be balanced against solar heat admission to achieve optimum energy efficiency. Because heat gains through the building envelope from solar radiation typically define peak load conditions, daylighting is also a very effective method of decreasing peak demand. Daylighting can not only decrease annual operating costs through energy efficiency, but may also reduce capital cost by mechanical system downsizing.

For daylighting designs using direct-beam sunlight entry, take care to avoid overheating and glare. Such problems can be avoided by carefully controlling or eliminating direct beam entry through orientation and shading of daylighting apertures, optical management components, and other architectural features.

For conventional sidelit nonresidential buildings, three basic relationships for daylight optimization are given as functions of (1) glazing properties and (2) fenestration area as a percent of the gross wall area:

1. Annual cooling energy use (including fan energy use) increases linearly with solar radiation admission, as indicated by the product of SHGC and WWR, but is affected (nonlinearly) by decreases in electric lighting heat gains.
2. Annual lighting energy use decreases exponentially/asymptotically with daylight admission, as indicated by the product of T_v and WWR.
3. Annual heating energy use (including fan energy use) increases linearly with decreased lighting heat gains.

Figure 27 shows the first two relationships for a prototypical nonresidential building. A similar relationship can be demonstrated with skylights. Different shading properties and control would affect electricity use differently.

The fenestration design that achieves an optimum balance between daylight admission and solar rejection can be determined by iterative calculations where the glazing area and/or glazing solar-optical properties are varied parametrically (Tzempelikos and Athienitis 2005). For each case, the following general steps should be taken for each hour over a year:

1. **Indoor Daylight Illuminance.** Determine the building characteristics, configuration, outdoor design conditions, and operating schedules as described in Chapter 18. These include building orientation, outdoor obstructions, ground reflectance, etc. Determine the depth from the window wall for each electric lighting zone. Typical sidelighting windows can effectively daylight the perimeter zone to a depth of 1.5 times the head height of the window. In private offices, one dimming zone is typically cost effective, whereas in open-plan offices, two zones are cost effective.

   Select a typical task location in each of the lighting zones. Determine indoor daylight illuminance from all window and skylight sources at these locations. Indoor illuminance may be determined using computer simulation tools or physical scale models. Comprehensive explanations of simple and computer-based tools are available (IEA 1999). The majority of these tools can model simple box geometry with noncomplex fenestration systems. Some advanced simulation tools, such as Radiance (Ward 1990) and Adeline (Erhorn and Dirksmöller 2000), can model complex geometry and fenestration systems with adequate bidirectional solar-optical data, but this capability is not routine.
2. **Lighting Energy Use.** Determine the type of lamps, ballasts, and control system to be used in the perimeter zones. Determine whether the lamp can be dimmed or switched. For example, LED and fluorescent lamps can be dimmed, but metal halides cannot be switched or dimmed. Cold, outdoor applications of some lamps may prevent switching. For electronic dimming ballasts, obtain dimming power and light output characteristics. Obtain control

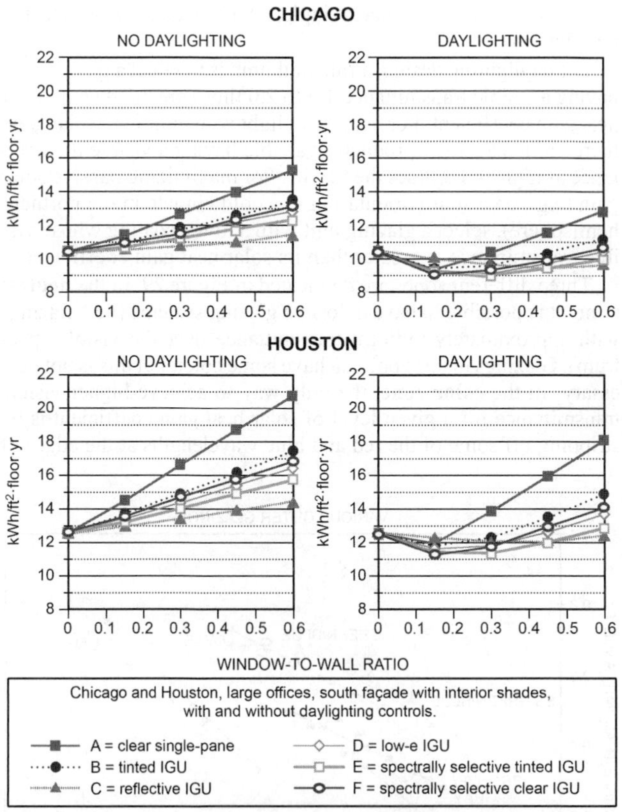

Fig. 27 Window-to-Wall Ratio Versus Annual Electricity Use in kWh/ft^2·floor·year

specifications to determine how the system will respond to available light; dead-band ranges, response times, and commissioning affect the sensitivity and accuracy of the system. The type of switching (on/off, bilevel, multilevel, and continuous dimming controls) are dictated by both the type of lamp and space use.

Determine the task illuminance design set point for each zone. Determine the percentage electric lighting power reduction $F_{daylight}$ that will result with automatic daylight controls, and apply to the installed wattage. Simplified methods for calculating lighting power reductions based on task illuminance levels are given in Robbins (1986). More sophisticated programs (Choi and Mistrick 1999) model commercially available photosensor dimming control systems (typically located in the ceiling above the work plane task) more rigorously; the spectral and bidirectional response of the photosensor to incident flux is used to determine voltage output, which is then used by the ballast controller algorithm to determine the lighting power reduction. Response delays and commissioning set points further affect this predicted output. Lights may also be switched manually, but there are very few modeling prediction tools for manual switching (Reinhart 2004). Field tests (Jennings et al. 1999) indicate that with bilevel switching, 45% of the lighting zone-hours were at less than full-power lighting, with 28% at only one-third of full lighting output levels. Manual switching occurred less in public spaces. Occupancy and other types of switching may occur as well and should be accounted for as a confounding effect with any daylighting controls.

3. **Mechanical Energy Use.** Determine mechanical energy use caused by fenestration loads and reduced electric lighting heat gains. Fenestration heat gains and losses may be computed using the section on Determining Fenestration Energy Flow. Instantaneous lighting heat gains q_{el}, described in Chapter 18, must be multiplied by the power reduction factor $F_{daylight}$.

Mechanical loads and energy use may then be determined as described in Chapter 18. Many studies have investigated the magnitude of change in heating and cooling energy use associated with reductions of lighting energy use in nonresidential buildings, as will be realized with daylighting controls. In a DOE-2.1E simulation study (Sezgen and Koomey 1998), the greatest savings were generated in hospitals, large offices, and large hotels; for every $1.00 saved through lighting energy efficiency, additional savings as a result of reduced HVAC were $0.26, $0.16, and $0.14, respectively. These results emphasize the need to include HVAC effects when assessing the effects of daylighting. Simplified design tools are available to conduct such parametric runs for preliminary analysis. Skylighting tools based on regressions using DOE-2 data or simplified DOE-2 procedures are also available [American Architectural Manufacturers Association (AAMA) 1987; Heschong et al. 1998]. More comprehensive building energy prediction tools combined with daylighting algorithms, such as DOE-2.1E (Winkelmann 1983), implement hour-by-hour calculations using existing weather data and enable evaluation of glare, visual comfort, and quality of light as well (Hitchcock et al. 2008; Lee and Selkowitz 1995; Ochoa and Capeluto 2009; Tzempelikos and Athienitis 2007).

In the United States, a general rule has been that the fenestration area should be at least 20% of the floor area. In Europe, a similar rule was based on a minimum illumination value on the normal work plane from a standard overcast sky condition. In general, it is more energy efficient to use larger fenestration areas to elevate indoor surface brightness as a glare reduction strategy than to increase indoor electric lighting levels. As fenestration area increases, indoor brightness increases while fenestration brightness remains the same. Of course, mitigating considerations include increased cost and heat transfer with larger fenestration. The latter problem can be mitigated with multiple-pane fenestration and special coatings to reduce solar gain without serious loss of light transmission, as discussed in the section on Selecting Fenestration. Orientation and shading can also be effective at mitigating glare and overheating problems.

The secondary visual benefit of fenestration is the amount and quality of light it produces in the work environment. One general rule determined the need for auxiliary electric light by assuming that daylight was adequate for a depth of two and one-half times the height of the fenestration product into the room based on a normal sill height. To prevent excessive glare, all fenestration should have sun controls. Variable and removable controls are often more effective in daylighting than fixed controls.

For more accurate evaluation of daylight distribution in a space, several prediction tools, such as the *Recommended Practice of Daylighting* (IES 1999), are available. This practice shows a simple way of calculating the daylight distribution on the work plane from windows and skylights with and without controls. Many other daylight prediction tools calculate illuminance from radiant flux transfer or ray tracing. The Illuminating Engineering Society's Daylighting Committee, Subcommittee on Daylighting Metrics, identified various instantaneous and annual measures of daylighting performance in building spaces. New techniques and improved computer tools are being developed to help calculate these measures, and various building code bodies and energy incentive programs are expected to specify daylighting performance metrics for compliance with these programs.

Any or all of the various daylight prediction tools can be used to compare the relative value of daylight distribution from alternative fenestration systems, but ultimately the designer must evaluate costs and benefits to choose between alternative designs. This may be based on energy use or, more properly, on overall costs and benefits to the client. Also, the risk of total loss of productivity from an electric brown-out in a space with no natural ventilation or daylight may be as important as the benefits of many energy-saving schemes.

8.2 LIGHT TRANSMITTANCE AND DAYLIGHT USE

When daylight is to be the primary lighting system, the minimum expected daylight in the building must be calculated for the building performance cycle and integrated into lighting calculations. IES (1999) gives daylight design and calculation procedures. In some glazing applications, such as artists' studios and showrooms, maximum transmittance may be required for adequate daylighting, and care is needed to maintain good color rendering when glazing tints and coatings are used. Regular clear glass, produced by float, plate, or sheet process, may be the logical choice.

When daylight is a supplementary light source, electric lighting can be designed independently of the daylight system. However, adequate switching must be included in the electric distribution to substitute available daylight for electric lighting by automatic or prescribed manual control whenever practical. Photosensitive controls automatically adjust shading devices to provide uniform illumination and reduce energy consumption. Manual control is less effective.

Buildings with large areas of glazing usually have glazing units with clear, tinted, or reflective coatings. Tinted and reflecting units reduce the brightness contrast between fenestration products and other room surfaces and provide a relatively glare-free environment for most daylight conditions.

Table 10 lists typical approximate solar energy transmittances and daylight transmittances for various glass types. Manufacturers' literature has more appropriate type-specific values.

The color of glazing chosen for a building depends largely on where and how it is used. For commercial building lobbies, showroom fenestration products, and other areas where maximum visibility from outdoors to indoors is required, regular clear glass is generally best. Clear glass with a low-e coating is also suitable for these locations, including for retail storefronts, because it only decreases light transmittance by about 10%. For other glazing areas, tinted or coated glass may best complement the indoor colors. Bronze, gray, and reflective-film glasses also give some privacy to building occupants during daylight hours. Patterned, fritted, etched, or sandblasted glass that diffuses lighting is available. In warm climates, tinted outer glazing in an insulated double-pane system can have solar heat gain rejection benefits, while providing good color-rendering illumination of the interior without apparent color.

The primary purpose of a fenestration product is not just to save energy but to provide a view of the outdoors and bring useful daylight indoors. The light-transmitting properties of fenestration systems are therefore of great importance. It is conceivable that one could design a fenestration product with excellent solar heat gain performance for hot climates (meaning a very low solar heat gain coefficient) but very poor view and daylight illumination performance. If this problem is bad enough, it can cause occupants to turn on electric lights indoors during the daytime, which adds to the electric bill and possibly causes problems of thermal discomfort as well.

The light-transmitting property of a fenestration product is called the visible **transmittance** T_v. It is similar to the solar-weighted solar transmittance, except that an additional weighting function is needed, in this case to account for the spectral response of the human eye.

In most applications, it is important to have high visible transmittance. In cooler climates, good solar heat gain is also important for offsetting wintertime heating costs. In warmer climates, low solar heat gain is good for offsetting summertime cooling costs. In the latter situation, it is difficult to have both high visible transmittance and a low solar heat gain coefficient. Figures 28 and 29 show plots of visible transmittance versus SHGC for several glazing systems covering a range of spectral selectivities (McCluney 1996). The data are for normal incidence and a single, ASTM standard solar spectral distribution.

For daylighting design, a rule of thumb is to select a glazing unit having a visible transmittance 1.5 to 2.0 times greater than its solar heat gain coefficient. For maximum light with minimum solar gain, there are fenestration products available having a visible transmittance as high as 3.0 times the SHGC. For maximizing passive solar gain (e.g., on a south orientation in a cold climate in the northern hemisphere), select a glazing unit with a low-e coating whose visible transmittance is greater than its solar heat gain coefficient.

Three different zones are delineated in Figure 29. In the **neutral zone**, it is possible to have colorless glazing systems (i.e., glazings with approximately uniform transmittance over the visible spectrum). Glazings in this zone can have some color, but this is not necessary. In the **color zone**, the only way to achieve higher visible transmittance for a given level of solar heat gain coefficient is by stripping off some of the red and blue wavelengths at the edges of

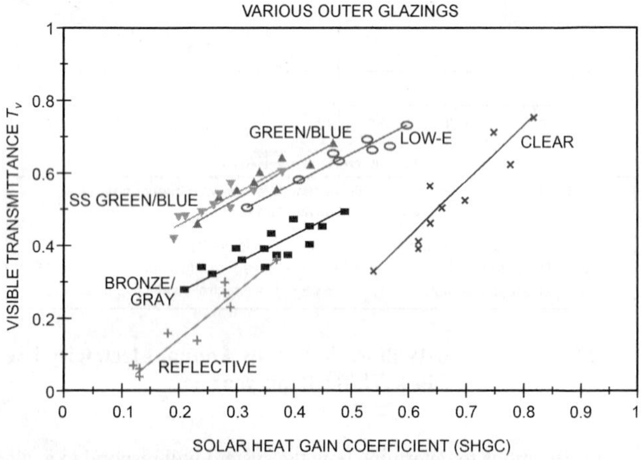

Fig. 28 Visible Transmittance Versus SHGC for Several Glazings with Different Spectral Selectivities

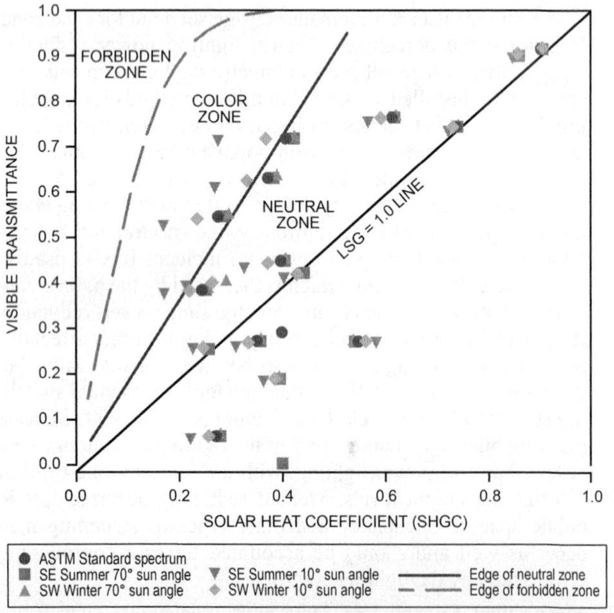

Fig. 29 Visible Transmittance Versus SHGC at Various Spectral Selectivities
(McCluney 1996)

Table 16 Spectral Selectivity of Several Glazings

Glazing	T_v	SHGC	LSG
Reflective blue-green	0.33	0.38	0.87
Film on clear glass	0.19	0.22	0.86
Green tinted, medium	0.75	0.69	1.09
Green low-e	0.71	0.49	1.45
Sun-control low-e + green	0.36	0.23	1.56
Super low-e + clear	0.71	0.40	1.77
Super low-e + green	0.60	0.30	2.00

the human spectral response function with a spectrally selective glazing transmittance, imparting color to the transmitted radiation (or by otherwise altering the spectral transmittance and hence the color over the visible portion of the spectrum). In the **forbidden zone**, no combination of visible transmittance and solar heat gain coefficient is possible for normal incidence and for the solar spectral distribution used. (Changing the solar spectral distribution used to calculate T_v and SHGC shifts the transition curves somewhat. A low solar altitude angle, direct-beam spectrum will move the curves to the left on the plot in Figure 29.) Glazings that transmit more solar radiant heat than light cluster on the lower portion of the plot.

The T_v versus SHGC chart can be a useful tool for illustrating the degree of spectral selectivity attained by a glazing system. These concepts lead to an index of spectral selectivity that can be useful. It is called the **light-to-solar-gain ratio (LSG)** (McCluney and Jindra 2001), defined as

$$\text{LSG} = \frac{T_v}{\text{SHGC}} \tag{41}$$

Some characteristic values for T_v, SHGC, and LSG are given in Table 16 for several different glazings, using the ASTM standard spectral distribution at normal incidence to calculate the values.

The LSG can be useful in spotting errors in calculating the SHGC. Values of SHGC that lie outside reasonable ranges can be spotted fairly quickly and used to identify possible problems in calculations or measurements. In general, it is very difficult and therefore unlikely to have a useful glazing system for buildings with an LSG value greater than 3.0. Values below 0.3 should be particularly suspect, because they indicate a glazing that transmits considerably more heat than light and would be unlikely candidates for general use. Generally, a high value of LSG is desired for residential buildings in hot climates, to maximize daylight admission with minimal solar heat gain. This is also true for internal-load-dominated nonresidential buildings in many climates, because solar gain rejection is often desired for such buildings, even in cool or cold climates. Provided that the fenestration product has a low-e coating, an LSG value somewhat below 1.0 is appropriate in cold climates for residential buildings and nonresidential buildings without strong internal cooling loads.

9. SELECTING FENESTRATION

Because fenestration systems provide so many functions, and because environmental conditions and user needs vary widely, it is difficult to make a completely optimal selection of a fenestration system. Considering aesthetics and cost, visual and comfort performance, annual energy costs, peak-load consequences, and acoustic characteristics, the choice is seldom optimal. The HVAC system designer, fortunately, has a more restricted range of interests, mainly dealing with the energy consequences of a particular fenestration selection. This section therefore focuses on fenestration energy performance determination.

9.1 ANNUAL ENERGY PERFORMANCE

Instantaneous energy performance indices (e.g., U-factor, solar heat gain coefficient, visible transmittance, air leakage) are typically used to compare fenestration systems under a fixed set of conditions. However, the absolute and relative effect of these indices on a building's heating and cooling load can fluctuate as environmental conditions change. Further, internal loads from electric lighting fluctuate as automatic controls dim or turn off electric lighting in response to available daylight. As a result, these indices alone are not good indicators of the annual energy performance attributable to the fenestration. Such energy performance is difficult to quantify in and of itself because of numerous dynamic responses between the fenestration system and the total environment in which it is installed. The four basic mechanisms of fenestration energy performance (thermal transfer, solar heat gains, air leakage, and daylighting) should all be taken into account but are not independent of many other parameters that influence performance. As a result, the annual energy performance of fenestration systems can be accurately determined only when many variables are considered. Building type and orientation, climate (weather, temperature, wind speed), microclimate (shading from adjacent buildings, trees, terrain), occupant usage patterns, and certain HVAC parameters can significantly affect the annual energy effects of fenestration systems.

For these reasons, the most effective means of establishing fenestration annual energy performance is through detailed, dynamic, hourly computer simulations for the specific building and climate of interest. Because instantaneous performance of fenestration often varies by differing magnitudes as climatic conditions change, the most accurate simulation results are obtained when these variances are accounted for in a building energy simulation computer program. After constructing the simulation model following the procedures defined in Chapters 17 and 18 (for residential and commercial construction, respectively), specific changes to the fenestration system can be modeled, and the annual energy performance changes attributable to fenestration can be quantified. These analytical techniques do not consider issues of performance durability for the various instantaneous indices and should only be used as an initial annual energy performance indicator (Mathis and Garries 1995).

Simplified Techniques for Rough Estimates of Fenestration Annual Energy Performance

Although dynamic hourly modeling is certainly the most accurate technique for determining fenestration annual energy performance, and software for hourly modeling now runs on most desktop and laptop computers, it is not always available to decision makers and end users of fenestration products, simply because users may not want to make the necessary inputs to run the analysis. Under these circumstances, it may be useful to assess the relative importance of, or balance the trade-off between, the known instantaneous performance indices of U-factor, SHGC, T_v, and air leakage, for any given fenestration system when considering heating, cooling, and lighting loads for many different building types and climates. Huang et al. (1999) and Mitchell et al. (1999, 2012) describe personal computer programs to run this simplified analysis for residential windows.

Broad generalizations can be made for some classifications of building types and climates. For instance, with large commercial buildings, which require substantial cooling energy use during daytime occupied hours because of high internal loads, significant thermal mass, or high orientation dependency, low SHGC is important to reduce the cooling load. Also, an evaluation of commercial fenestration annual energy use can take into account the trade-off between electric lighting and the natural daylighting benefits associated with a particular fenestration system. However, low U-factor is also important because commercial buildings have bimodal operation: they can have significant heating energy consumption during morning warm-up, which occurs during unoccupied predawn hours, before people arrive and lights and equipment are turned on, and before any passive solar gain. In low-rise, detached residential buildings, electric lighting loads are typically very small in comparison to the heating and cooling loads because of high envelope-dependent energy use, egress requirements, and occupant usage patterns. The slight energy benefits of daylighting may be neglected altogether when using light-emitting diode (LED) lighting, which reduces residential light loads substantially. Despite these generalizations, the problem still exists of balancing and assessing the effect of each of the remaining parameters to establish seasonal or annual energy performance for cases in which detailed computer modeling is not performed. Furthermore, in all building types, the fact that energy savings afforded by daylighting are small does not negate the desirability of well-controlled natural light: daylighting without glare or excessive contrast is an important amenity.

Developing simplified annual energy performance indices for fenestration typically involves using instantaneous fenestration performance indices to quantify building- and climate-independent scalars of annual or seasonal energy performance for rating purposes. Many of these performance indices can be relatively independent of building type, climate, distribution of products, orientation, and other items needed for hourly dynamic building energy analyses. These normalized, scalar-based approaches are also limited in accuracy for the same reasons. A further limitation of the simplified techniques is that they do not have broad applicability to varied building types (e.g., commercial versus residential buildings). The usefulness of these scalar-based approaches can be increased when limiting the comparison to a single building type. Currently, simplified techniques for characterizing fenestration annual energy performance are applicable only to fenestration systems for detached residential buildings and are not appropriate for use with multifamily residential or commercial building fenestration systems.

Where a building function requires controlling outdoor air through a door opening, evaluation of the fenestration annual energy performance involving the resulting air exchange cannot be based on instantaneous indices, but must be based on an annualized process. Evaluate an automated door product designed to limit door-opening, door-open, and door-closing times for its air exchange, air leakage, and thermal transmittance properties, and compare its performance to that of a conventionally operating automated insulated sectional door complying with U-factor and air leakage requirements. Because a door product limiting air exchange is specified in terms of the number of opening and closing cycles per day averaged over a one-year period, not only can its annual energy performance be assessed, but its heating and cooling savings can also be estimated with respect to the sectional door, assuming the same number of average cycles per day and a similar door-open time.

Simplified Residential Annual Energy Performance Ratings

Annual energy performance (AEP) ratings can provide a simple means of product comparisons for consumers. These ratings have been derived with many assumptions, usually to suit local climatic conditions.

The Canadian Standards Association (CSA *Standard* A440.2) developed a simplified energy rating applicable to residential heating in the Canadian climate, which was adopted in the 1995 *National Energy Code for Houses*. The standard also provides for specific energy ratings to compare products by orientation and climate.

In the United States, where heating and cooling are both significant, NFRC is developing a rating system that includes both effects (Arasteh et al. 2000; Crooks et al. 1995). NFRC's (2014i) *Technical Document* 901 provides guidance on how fenestration affects heating and cooling energy consumption in single-family residences.

In Australia, the Window Energy Rating Scheme (WERS; www.wers.net) publishes simplified, consumer-friendly AEP ratings for heating and cooling performance of residential windows. It displays regression-based AEP rankings as stars, on a scale of 0 to 10; one rating is for cooling performance, and another for heating. Ten stars for either heating and cooling corresponds to the "perfect" window for that purpose. As inputs, WERS uses U-factor and SHGC, determined using procedures licensed from the NFRC and the Australian Fenestration Rating Council (AFRC; www.afrc.org.au).

9.2 CONDENSATION RESISTANCE

Water vapor condenses in a film on fenestration surfaces that are at temperatures below the dew-point temperature of the indoor air. If the surface temperature is below freezing, frost forms. Sometimes, condensation occurs first, and ice from the condensed water forms when temperatures drop below freezing. Condensation frequently occurs on single glazing and on aluminum frames without a thermal break. The edge seal creates a thermal bridge at the perimeter of the glazing unit.

Circulation of fill gas caused by temperature differences in the glazing unit cavity contributes to the condensation problem at the bottom of the indoor glazing (Curcija and Goss 1994, 1995; Wright 1996b; Wright and Sullivan 1995a, 1995b). In winter, fill gas near the indoor glazing is warmed and flows up, while gas near the outdoor glazing is cooled and flows down. The descending gas becomes progressively colder until it reaches the bottom of the cavity. There, the gas turns and flows to the indoor glazing, resulting in higher heat transfer rates at the bottom. Thus, the bottom edge of the indoor glazing is cooled both by edge-seal conduction and by fill-gas convection. The combined effect of these two heat transfer mechanisms is shown in Figure 30. The surface isotherms show a wider band of cold glazing at the bottom of the window. Typical condensation patterns match these isotherms. The vertical indoor surface temperature profile also shows the effect of edge-seal conduction and that the minimum indoor surface temperature is near the bottom edge of the glazing.

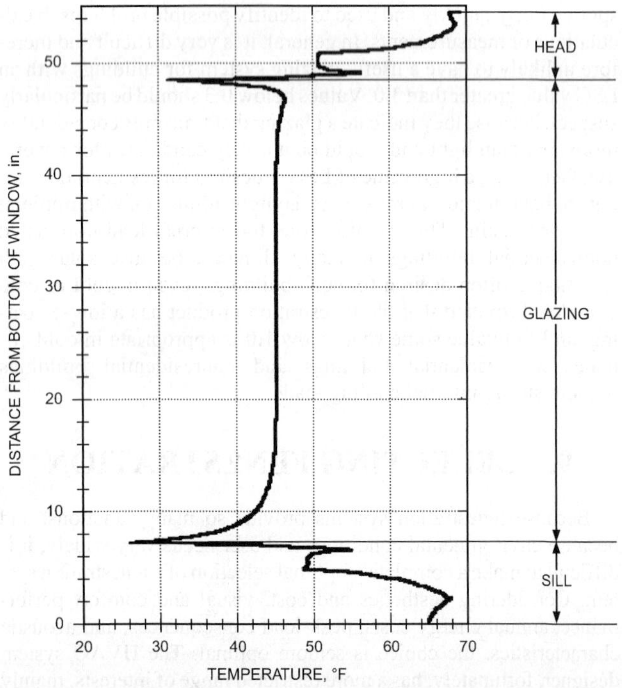

Fig. 30 Temperature Distribution on Indoor Surfaces of Glazing Unit

Condensation on fenestration and surrounding structures can cause extensive structural, aesthetic, and health problems. Specific examples include peeling of paint, rotting of wood, saturation of insulation, and mold growth. Ice can render doors and windows inoperable and prevent egress during an emergency.

Energy-efficient housing has been accompanied by reduced ventilation. The resulting increase in indoor humidity has contributed to the condensation problem. However, the solution does not lie in the reduction of humidity levels to a minimum. Relative humidity below 20% and above 70% can increase health risks and reduce comfort. Generally, a minimum of 30% rh should be maintained, and 40% to 50% is more desirable (Sterling et al. 1985). Consequently, a better solution is to improve the fenestration product so interior surface temperatures are warmer and condensation does not occur or is minimized.

Minimum indoor surface temperatures can be quantified in a variety of ways. De Abreu et al. (1996), Elmahdy (1996), Griffith et al. (1996), Sullivan et al. (1996), and Zhao et al. (1996) demonstrated good agreement between detailed two-dimensional numerical simulation and surface temperature measurements using thermographs. Curcija et al. (1996) and Wright and Sullivan (1995c) developed simplified simulation models to predict condensation resistance. Center-glass and bottom-edge surface temperatures that can be expected for two different glazing systems exposed to a range of outdoor temperature are shown in Figure 31. Both glazing systems include insulating foam edge seals. High-performance glazing systems (e.g., low-e/argon and insulated spacers) allow significantly higher indoor humidity levels.

Current measures of condensation resistance of a fenestration system are the **condensation resistance (CR)** as defined by NFRC 500 (2014j) and its user guide (2014h), the **condensation resistance factor (CRF)** as defined by AAMA (1988), or the **temperature index (I)**, as defined in CSA *Standards* A440 and A440.1.

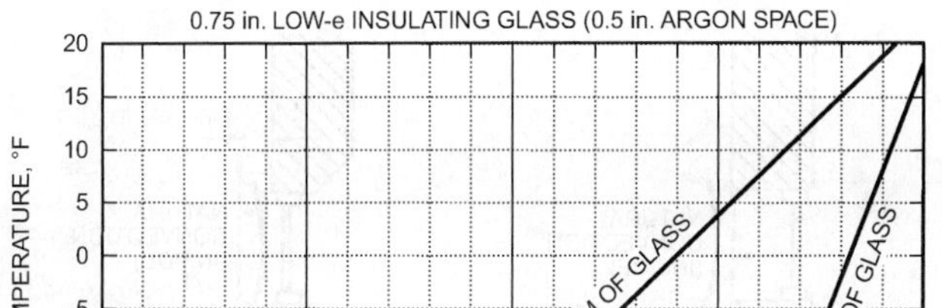

Fig. 31 Minimum Indoor Surface Temperatures Before Condensation Occurs

Note that the temperature index method in CSA *Standard* A440 stipulates that the test is performed on the fenestration with all the cracks *not* sealed. This represents a major difference between the CSA *Standard* A440 method and the AAMA and NFRC methods. There are some merits of leaving cracks unsealed during testing for condensation resistance. In particular, any inherent deficiencies in fenestration design may result in uncontrolled air leakage through the fenestration. This air leakage could not be detected or dealt with in the simulation models, and can only be seen in the results of the determined temperature index. On the other hand, there is some financial benefit to the window manufacturer in testing the fenestration for condensation resistance with cracks sealed, because one test can determine R-value and condensation resistance.

Research shows that air leakage does affect the temperature index (measure of condensation resistance as determined by CSA *Standard* A440). Elmahdy (2001, 2003) showed that sealing cracks during testing artificially improves the temperature index, compared to the results of the same window tested with cracks unsealed.

Condensation resistance is a measure of condensation potential, based on both area and temperature weighting and expressed as a minimum of center-of-glazing, edge-of-glazing, and frame CRs. The novelty of this index is that it is determined using computer simulation tools unless the overall thermal performance cannot be validated with testing. If thermal performance cannot be validated, a testing option for determining CR is used.

The other two standards define the values by a single dimensionless number as

$$\text{CRF or } I = \frac{t - t_c}{t_h - t_c} \tag{42}$$

where t_h and t_c are the warm- and cold-side temperatures, respectively. Figure 32 can be used to determine the acceptable range of CRF/*I* for a specific climatic zone.

The two standards differ in the methods used to determine temperature. The CSA test procedure is based on thermocouple measurements at the coldest location on the frame plus three locations on the glazing, each 3/8 in. above the bottom sightline. The AAMA procedure specifies two separate factors: one for the frame (CRF_F), which uses weighted frame temperature obtained from surface temperature measurements at predetermined and roving locations on the frame, and one for the glazing unit (CRF_G), which uses the average of six temperatures measured at predetermined locations near the top, middle, and bottom of the glazed area.

Indoor details can significantly alter the potential for condensation on fenestration surfaces. Items such as venetian blinds, roll blinds, insect screens, and drapes increase thermal resistance between the indoor space and fenestration and lower the temperature of the fenestration surfaces. These fenestration treatments do not prevent migration of moisture, so they can cause increased condensation. Figure 33 shows different situations that affect the potential for condensation. Note that window reveal plays an important role. If the window is placed near the outside of the wall, the increase in the outdoor film coefficient and decrease in the indoor film coefficient cause colder window surfaces. This effect is more pronounced near the corners of the recess where the indoor film coefficient is locally suppressed because air movement is restricted. Also, blinds should be placed at least 4 in. from the plane of the wall to allow some natural convection between the window and the blind.

Air leakage, especially in operable sections of fenestration, is another important cause of low surface temperature. Leakage near edge-of-glass sections can further increase the potential for condensation. However, the drier outdoor air decreases relative humidity near leakage sites and, in some cases, offsets the undesirable effect of lower surface temperatures. The net effect of air leakage cannot readily be determined experimentally or with simulation.

9.3 OCCUPANT COMFORT AND ACCEPTANCE

Human thermal comfort is an immediate sensation that reflects building occupants' perceived response to many physical factors. Unlike much building design that is based primarily on long-term energy and economic considerations, comfort-related design focuses on, and must take heed of, short-term responses of the body's physiology to its surroundings.

Fenestration influences thermal comfort through a combination of three mechanisms: long-wave radiation exchange, absorption of solar radiation, and convective draft effects (Figure 34). An understanding of these phenomena is important to help designers evaluate the benefits of improved fenestration and create comfortable buildings. Although it is well understood that high-performance fenestration can reduce building energy consumption, a better understanding of their effect on comfort might lead to further savings. For example, Hawthorne and Reilly (2000) suggest that significant energy consumption is caused by the standard practice of using perimeter duct distribution in houses to mitigate potential discomfort caused by fenestration. They found that perimeter heating is often not necessary when high-performance fenestration is installed and that heating energy savings of 10 to 15% could result from installing a simpler, less expensive duct system. Better windows can allow thermostat settings to be lowered with no loss

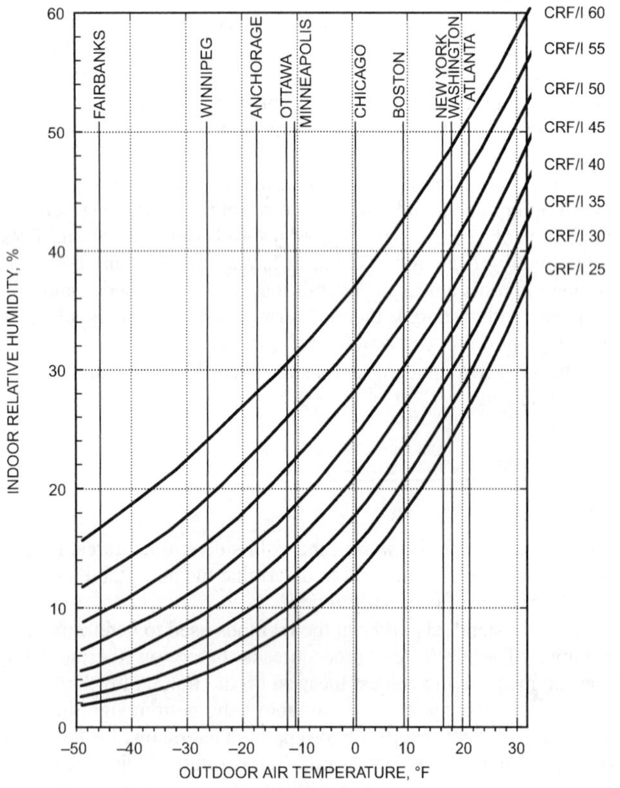

Fig. 32 Minimum Condensation Resistance Requirements (t_h = 68°F)

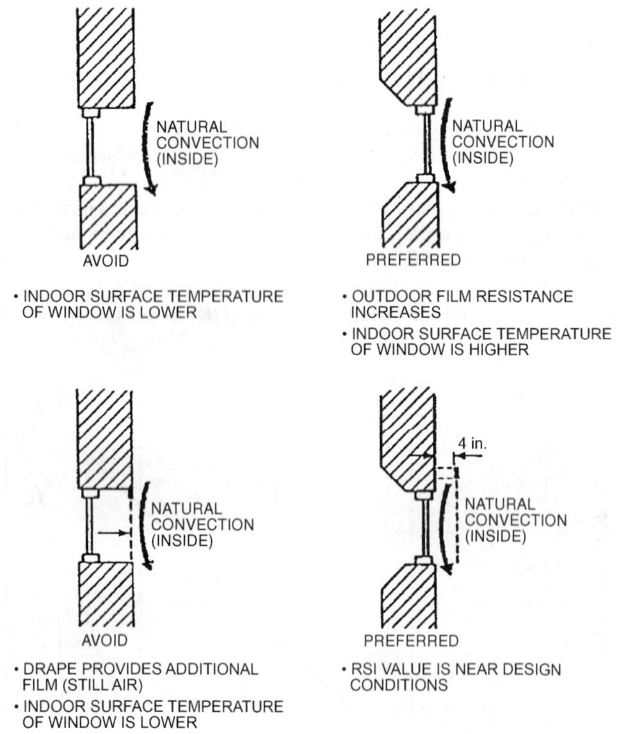

Fig. 33 Location of Fenestration Product Reveals and Blinds/Drapes and Their Effect on Condensation Resistance

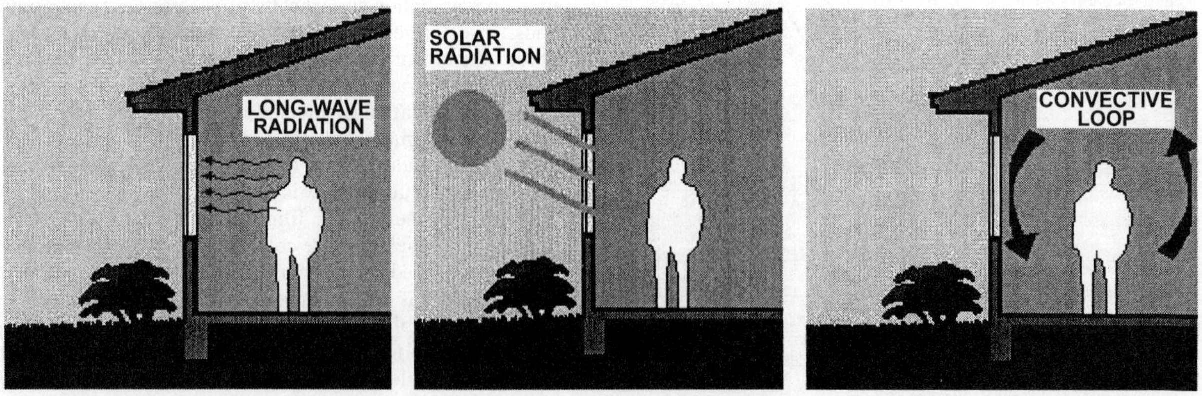

Fig. 34 Fenestration Effects on Thermal Comfort: Long-Wave Radiation, Solar Radiation, Convective Draft

of comfort. Another simulation study (Lyons et al. 2000) examined the relative magnitudes of a residential window's physical influences under a wide variety of winter and summer climates, glazing parameters, and clothing levels. They found that

- Long-wave, thermal radiation influences of the window dominate unless direct sun strikes the occupant
- Direct solar load has a major influence on perceptions of comfort
- For most residential-size windows, draft effects are generally small

With all but highly insulating fenestration, the indoor surface temperature of the fenestration is heavily influenced by outdoor conditions, and this temperature can significantly affect radiant heat exchange between an occupant and the environment. If this heat exchange moves outside the acceptable range, discomfort results. Mean radiant temperature (MRT) is commonly used to simplify the characterization of the radiant environment. On a cold day, the indoor surface temperature can easily drop below 15°F for a clear single-pane window and below 40°F for a clear, double-pane window. If the occupant is sitting sufficiently near the window, MRT could drop to 55°F for the single-pane case and 62°F for the double-pane case. Based on ASHRAE *Standard* 55, even use of the clear double-pane window could result in discomfort. [This example assumes an outdoor air temperature of 0°F, indoor air temperature of 72°F, nonwindow surface temperatures of 72°F, occupant/window view factor of 0.3, 0.9 clo (standard winter indoor clothing), and activity level of 1 met.] In addition to the MRT effect, a cold indoor glazing surface can induce a downward draft that increases air movement, contributing to further discomfort. If direct solar radiation strikes the glazing or occupant, the situation is much more complex. Conversely, for a double-pane window with a low-e coating and a triple-pane window with two low-e coatings, the net results would be MRTs of 67°F and 69°F, respectively. Both of these would satisfy the ASHRAE *Standard* 55 criteria for comfort.

In winter, the warming effect of sunlight on skin and clothing is often welcome, depending on the compounding effect of other factors such as air temperature. Fenestration also absorbs and transmits a significant amount of solar radiation. Because of such absorption, solar-heated fenestration may improve MRT for a nearby person. The premise of passive solar design is that occupants will welcome, or at least tolerate, solar gain in exchange for savings on heating energy. However, it is desirable that the onset of discomfort be able to be predicted; otherwise, the energy-saving design may be defeated if occupants draw shades to prevent overheating.

In summer, solar-heated glazing may become uncomfortably hot and, in commercial premises, actually devalue rented space near windows. The indoor surface of body-tinted, heat-absorbing glass can routinely reach temperatures above 120°F in summer conditions, raising MRT by as much as 15°F. This can be ameliorated by adding a second glazing on the indoors. Transmitted radiation often causes discomfort if it falls directly on the occupant. A person sitting near a window in direct solar radiation can experience heat gain equivalent to a 20°F rise in MRT (Arens et al. 1986). Similarly, in residential applications, the perceived need for solar control is affected both by the contribution of window surfaces to MRT and by overheating from direct solar load.

Advances in fenestration technology, especially high-performance glazings, mean that the designer has a choice of potential glazing systems. On the basis of annual energy performance for heating, cooling, and lighting, these alternatives may give similar outcomes. However, because they represent different combinations of U-factor, SHGC, and indoor glazing surface temperature, their comfort outcomes may differ considerably. Research continues to develop tools to help designers evaluate such difficult trade-offs. In the meantime, several general rules of thumb may be followed:

- In heating-dominated climates, fenestration with the lowest U-factor tends to give the best comfort outcomes. However, there is likely to be a trade-off between the twin goals of maximizing instantaneous comfort and minimizing annual energy consumption.
- In cooling-dominated climates or for orientations where cooling loads are of concern, fenestration with the lowest rise in surface temperature for a given SHGC tends to give the best comfort outcomes.

Table 17 Sound Transmittance Loss for Various Types of Glass

Type of Glass	Sound Transmittance Loss, dB
1/8 in. double-strength sheet glass	24
1/4 in. plate or float glass	27
1/2 in. plate glass	32
3/4 in. plate glass	35
1 in. plate glass	36
1/4 in. laminated glass (9/20 in. plastic interlayer)	30
1 in. double glass	32
1/2 in. laminated glass (9/20 in. plastic interlayer)	34
Multiple-glazing unit, 6 in. air space, 1/4 in. plate or float glass	40

Sound Reduction

Proper acoustical treatment of outdoor walls can decrease noise levels in certain areas. The airtightness of a wall is the primary factor to consider in reducing sound transmission from outdoors. Once walls and fenestration products are tight, the choice of glazing and draperies becomes important. Draperies do not prevent sound from coming through the fenestration; they act as an absorber for sound that does penetrate. Table 17 lists average sound transmission losses for various types of glass. These averages apply for the frequency range of 125 to 4000 Hz and were determined by tests based on ASTM *Standard* E90.

Strength and Safety

In addition to its thermal, visual, and aesthetic functions, glazing for building exteriors must also perform well structurally. Wind loads are specified in most building codes, and these requirements may be adequate for many structures. However, detailed wind tunnel tests should be run for tall or unusually shaped buildings and for buildings where the surroundings create unusual wind patterns. The strength of annealed, heat-strengthened, tempered, laminated, and insulated glass is given in ASTM *Standard* E1300.

Thermal expansion and contraction can break ordinary annealed glass. This expansion and contraction can be caused by solar radiation onto partly shaded glazing, by heat traps from drop ceilings and tight-fitting drapes, or by HVAC ducts incorrectly directed toward the glazing. High-performance tinted and reflective glasses with low-e coatings are usually more vulnerable to thermal stress breakage than clear glass. Heat treating (heat strengthening or fully tempering) the glass resists thermal stress breakage. Heat-strengthened glass, although not a safety glass, is usually preferred to tempered (safety) glass because it typically has less distortion and is much less likely to have spontaneous breakage, which can occur on very rare occasions in tempered glass. Consult the glass manufacturer or fabricator for information on thermal stress performance.

Building codes may require glass in certain positions to perform with certain breakage characteristics, which can be satisfied by tempered, laminated, or wired glass. In this case, glass should meet *Code of Federal Regulations* 16CFR1201 or other appropriate breakage performance requirements.

Life-Cycle Costs

Alternative building shells should be compared to ensure satisfactory energy use and total energy budget compliance, if required. ASHRAE *Standards* 90.1 and 90.2 should be used as a starting point. A life-cycle cost model should be developed for each system considered. See Chapter 37 of the 2015 *ASHRAE Handbook—HVAC Applications*.

9.4 DURABILITY

Service life and long-term performance of fenestration systems depend on the durability of all the system's components. Representative samples of glazing units are usually tested (for seal durability) according to test methods to ensure the integrity of the seal. Failure of glazing units is usually indicated by loss of adhesion of sealant to the glazing; as a result, fogging occurs inside the glazing cavity.

For argon-filled units, seal failure means a loss of argon and, hence, degradation in the unit's thermal characteristics. Extensive study of the durability of glazing units filled with argon gas (Elmahdy and Yusuf 1995) indicated that, under normal conditions, argon loss by diffusion through the sealant is very small. However, when cracks or pinholes exist in the sealant, most of the argon gas escapes, which implies that stringent quality control procedures are essential for production of durable glazing units.

Degradation of organic materials and other chemical components in glazing units as a result of exposure to ultraviolet radiation is also a factor affecting durability and service life of fenestration systems. Low-e coatings on glass tend to enhance the appearance of chemical deposits on the glass surface. Also, inserting muntin bars in glazing cavities may result in excessive rates of unit failure during ultraviolet volatile (fogging) tests unless strict quality assurance processes are implemented. Current ASTM (United States) and CGSB (Canada) durability standards are being reviewed to reflect the emergence of new technologies in the fenestration industry.

A 15-year correlation study of insulating glazing units products by the Insulating Glass Manufacturers Association (IGMA) found that long-term performance and durability of glazing units correlated well with the test level to which the unit's construction had been manufactured under ASTM *Standard* E2190's specification for sealed glazing units. Units showing the highest percentage of resistance to seal failure were those tested in conformance with the ASTM *Standard* E2190 class CBA standard. Units that did not qualify to the A level showed a definite correlation to a higher percentage of failure. Field correlation studies found that units glazed in compliance with IGMA recommendations perform for longer periods than units not constructed properly, having deficiencies in the glazing system, or not meeting ASTM requirements.

Durability of fenestration systems also depends on durability of other system components, such as weatherstripping, gaskets, glazing tapes, air seals, and hardware. Wear of these elements with time and use may result in excessive air and water leakage, which affects overall performance and service life of the system. Excessive water leakage may cause damage to the fenestration product, especially the edge seal, as well as the wall section where the product is mounted. Excessive air leakage may lead to frost build-up and condensation on fenestration surfaces.

Studies conducted at the National Research Council of Canada (Elmahdy 1995) and elsewhere (Patenaude 1995) showed that, when windows are tested at high pressure and temperature differentials, they experience air leakage rates exceeding those determined at 0.3 in. of water and zero temperature differential (conditions used in rating window air leakage in U.S. and Canadian standards). In other studies (CANMET 1991, 1993), pressure and motion cycling on windows resulted in excessive degradation in almost all performance factors, particularly condensation resistance, ease of operation, and air and water leakage.

To predict long-term performance, unit construction for glazing units should be tested and certified in accordance with ASTM *Standard* E2190 class CBA level and the requirements of IGMA or equivalent.

Durability may also affect long-term energy performance. Consequently, NFRC now requires third-party certification for sealed-glass units.

9.5 SUPPLY AND EXHAUST AIRFLOW WINDOWS

Airflow windows allow air to flow between glass panes of multilayered glazing units, to improve the window assembly's thermal performance.

Exhaust air windows allow indoor air to flow between the inner two panes of a triple-glazed window. In the cooling season, this airflow helps reduce the cooling load by transferring heat to the flowing air and discharging it to the outdoors. During the heating season, heat loss through the outer pane of the window comes mostly from exhaust airflow, which helps reduce thermal transmission loss through the window. In addition, exhaust airflow helps maintain the inner pane surface temperature close to the indoor air temperature, thus improving the thermal comfort of occupants (Haddad and Elmahdy 1998, 1999).

The **supply air window** allows outdoor air to flow between the outer two panes of a triple-glazed window and into the building. The airflow helps reduce the heating load when heat picked up by the flowing air finds its way back into the indoor space. In the cooling season, the supply air window may increase the cooling load when heat is picked up from the outer glass pane and delivered into the indoor space.

Haddad and Elmahdy (1998, 1999) provide results of computer models comparing thermal performance of supply and exhaust airflow windows with conventional windows in various locations in North America.

9.6 CODES AND STANDARDS

National Fenestration Rating Council (NFRC)

The National Fenestration Rating Council (NFRC) was formed in 1989 to respond to a need for fair, accurate, and credible ratings for fenestration products. NFRC has developed rating procedures for U-factor [NFRC (2014a) *Technical Document* 100], solar heat gain coefficient and visible transmittance [NFRC (2014d) *Technical Document* 200], optical properties [NFRC (2014c) *Technical Document* 300], air leakage [NFRC (2014f) *Technical Document* 400], and condensation resistance [NFRC (2014j) *Technical Document* 500]. To provide certified ratings, manufacturers follow the requirements in the NFRC Product Certification Program (PCP), which involves working with laboratories accredited to the NFRC Laboratory Accreditation Program (LAP), and independent certification and inspection agencies accredited through the NFRC Certification Agency Program (CAP).

NFRC (2014a) *Technical Document* 100 was the first NFRC rating procedure approved and thus the first NFRC procedure adopted into energy codes in the United States. It requires using a combination of state-of-the-art computer simulations and improved thermal testing to determine U-factors for the whole product. The next step is product certification. NFRC has a series of checks and balances to ensure that the rating system is accurately and uniformly used. Products and their ratings are authorized for certification by an NFRC-licensed independent certification and inspection agency (IA). Finally, two labels are required: the temporary label, which contains the product ratings, and a permanent label, which allows tracking back to the IA and information in the NFRC *Product Directory*. In addition to informing the buyer, the temporary label provides the building inspector with information necessary to verify energy code compliance. The permanent label provides access to energy rating information for a future owner, property manager, building inspector, lending agency, or building energy rating organization.

This process has noteworthy features that make it superior to previous fenestration energy rating systems and correct past problems:

- The procedures provide a means for manufacturers to take credit for all the nuances and refinement in their product design and a common basis for others to compare product claims.
- Involvement of independent laboratories and the IA provides architects, engineers, designers, contractors, consumers, building officials, and utility representatives with greater confidence that the information is unbiased.
- Requiring simulation and testing provides an automatic check on accuracy. This also remedies a shortcoming of previous energy code requirements that relied on testing alone, which allowed manufacturers to perform several tests and then use the best one for code purposes.
- The certification process indicates that the manufacturer is consistently producing the product that was rated. This corrects a past concern that manufacturers were able to make an exceptionally high-quality sample and obtain a good rating in a test but not consistently produce that product.
- A readily visible temporary label can be used by the building inspector to quickly verify compliance with the energy code.
- A permanent label enables future access to energy rating information.

Although the NFRC program is similar for other fenestration characteristics, there are differences worth noting. Solar heat gain coefficient and visible transmittance ratings [NFRC (2014d) *Technical Document* 200], referenced in several codes, and condensation resistance ratings [NFRC (2014j) *Technical Document* 500] are based on simulation alone. Optical properties [NFRC (2014c) *Technical Document* 300] and emissivity [NFRC (2014g) *Technical Document* 301] are based on measurements by the manufacturer, with independent verification. Air leakage ratings [NFRC (2014h) *Technical Document* 400] are based on testing alone. For site-assembled fenestration products (e.g., curtain walls, window walls), an NFRC label certificate fulfills the labeling requirements and serves the certification purpose. A separate NFRC label certificate is required for each "individual product" in a particular project.

United States Energy Policy Act (EPAct)

In the United States, the 1992 Energy Policy Act (EPAct) required the development of national fenestration energy rating systems and specified NFRC as the preferred developer. (The U.S. Department of Energy was to establish procedures if NFRC did not.) Although this recognition provided an impetus for NFRC to develop the desired procedures and programs, the EPAct sections on energy codes have been a key factor in their implementation.

EPAct set baselines for state energy codes. The ICC 2015 *International Energy Conservation Code® (IECC®)* and ASHRAE/IES *Standard* 90.1-2016, Energy Standard for Buildings Except Low-Rise Residential Buildings, are the current successors to the versions cited in the 1992 legislation. The majority of states have adopted the predecessors to the 2015 *IECC* (including the 2012, 2009, 2006, 2003, 2000, and 1998 *IECC* and the CABO 1995 *Model Energy Code*) and to ASHRAE/IES *Standard* 90.1-2016 (i.e., ASHRAE/IES *Standard* 90.1-2013/2010/2007/2004/2001/1999/1989) into their codes either directly or by reference when adopting a building code published by one of the three national code organizations in the United States. The ICC 2015 *International Building Code* (the U.S. model building code jointly developed by ICBO, BOCA, and SBCCI) references the 2015 *IECC*.

ICC's 2015 *International Energy Conservation Code*

The ICC's 2015 *IECC* references NFRC (2014a) *Technical Document* 100 for U-factor (as did the 2012, 2009, 2006, 2003, 2000, and 1998 *IECC* and the 1995 *Model Energy Code*) and NFRC (2014d) *Technical Document* 200 for solar heat gain coefficient (SHGC) (as did the 2012, 2009, 2006, 2003, 2000, and 1998 *IECC*). Sections C303.1.1 and R303.1.3, which cover all occupancies, require U-factors and SHGCs and visible transmittances (T_vs) of fenestration products (windows, doors, and skylights) to be determined in accordance with NFRC *Technical Documents* 100 and 200 by an accredited independent laboratory, and labeled and certified by the manufacturer. The language does not specify NFRC accreditation; however, it requires both the use of the NFRC rating procedure by an independent entity, and labeling and certification. Sections C402.4.3 and R402.4.3 cite NFRC (2014h) *Technical Document* 400, and others for air leakage testing.

ASHRAE/IES *Standard* 90.1-2016

In 1999, ASHRAE and IES published a comprehensive update to *Standard* 90.1-1989 that included fenestration rating, labeling, and certification criteria in Sections 5.2.2 and 5.2.3. U-factors were to be determined in accordance with NFRC (2014a) *Technical Document* 100, solar heat gain coefficient and visible transmittance in accordance with NFRC (2014d) *Technical Document* 200, and air leakage in accordance with NFRC (2014h) *Technical Document* 400.

In 2001, ASHRAE and IES made nominal modifications to *Standard* 90.1. The most significant changes for the 2004 version were in the lighting section, with fenestration rating, labeling, and certification criteria found in Sections 5.8.2.

The 2007 revision included substantial increases in stringency for the building envelope, including both opaque assemblies and fenestration. The NFRC references remained unchanged.

The 2010 update had limited changes to the fenestration U-factor and SHGC criteria, but called for reduced air leakage. The standard began to address fenestration orientation and daylighting: in the northern hemisphere, vertical fenestration must have more area on the south side than on either the east or west side. Spaces with tall ceilings and under a roof must have a minimum skylight area for daylighting purposes. Exceptions are provided to the SHGC requirements for dynamic glazing.

The 2013 version made significant changes to fenestration U-factor and SHGC criteria. The standard expanded the consideration of daylighting by establishing criteria for a minimum VT/SHGC ratio where there is automatic control of lighting in daylight zones.

The 2016 update further changed the requirements for fenestration U-factors in most climate zones, and for SHGC in a few climate zones. Limited modifications were made to the fenestration orientation criteria.

For further information on U.S. energy codes, the Building Codes Assistance Project (BCAP) publishes a bimonthly summary entitled "Status of State Energy Codes," which provides information on current codes and pending legislation. For additional information, contact BCAP at www.bcap-energy.org.

ASHRAE/USGBC/IES *Standard* 189.1-2014

In 2006, ASHRAE, the U.S. Green Building Council (USGBC), and IES embarked on a project to develop a baseline standard for high-performance, green buildings that would apply to all buildings except low-rise residential buildings. Their *Standard* 189.1-2009 addresses sustainable sites, energy and water efficiency, the building's effect on the atmosphere, materials and resources, and indoor environmental quality (IEQ). The standard is not a rating system, but it is hoped that it will be integrated into future building rating systems.

Energy-efficiency goals for the first version of *Standard* 189.1 were to achieve a 30% additional energy savings beyond that in ASHRAE/IES *Standard* 90.1-2007. *Standard* 189.1 builds on *Standard* 90.1, but the prescriptive option in *Standard* 189.1 substitutes more stringent values in the tables and adds other criteria. For example, the prescriptive option requires that, in the northern hemisphere, vertical fenestration on the west, south, and east be shaded by a device or devices with a 0.50 projection factor (e.g., an overhang that is one-half as wide as the window is tall).

There were subsequent updates in 2011 and 2014.

ICC's 2015 *International Green Construction Code™*

The ICC's 2012 *International Green Construction Code™* (*IgCC™*) is an overlay code to ICC's 2012 *IECC*. The fenestration criteria call for a 10% reduction in U-factor and SHGC from the 2012 *IECC*. The prescriptive option requires that, in the northern hemisphere, vertical fenestration on the west, south, and east be shaded by a device with a 0.25 projection factor (e.g., an overhang that is one-quarter as wide as the window is tall). The *IgCC* also allows ASHRAE/USGBC/IES *Standard* 189.1 as a compliance option.

After publication of the 2015 *International Green Construction Code*, ASHRAE and USGBC began investigating the possibilities for greater alignment between the *IgCC* and *Standard* 189.1.

Canadian Standards Association (CSA)

In Canada, the Canadian Standards Association (CSA) promulgates fenestration energy rating standards. CSA *Standard* A440.2 addresses most fenestration products, and CSA *Standard* A453 addresses doors. These are companion standards to NFRC (2014a) *Technical Document* 100. NFRC and CSA established a Thermal Harmonization Task Force to attempt to harmonize their fenestration energy rating standards.

Building Code of Australia/National Construction Code

In Australia, the Australian Building Codes Board maintains the *National Construction Code*, which includes the *Building Code of Australia* (BCA). The code is divided into separate volumes for residential and commercial construction. Sections 2 and 3 (residential) and Section J (commercial) set out various compliance paths for building envelope performance. Section J of the *National Construction Code* covers energy efficiency provisions for nonresidential building stock in Australia. To demonstrate compliance with Section J2 of the *National Construction Code*, the U-factor and SHGC of fenestration systems are to be rated in accordance to with Australian Fenestration Rating Council (AFRC; www.afrc.org.au), which adopts the same technical procedures as NFRC. Users should note that the energy provisions for fenestration systems are based on an energy-flow approach and do not have an upper limit for fenestration area as a percentage of gross wall area.

Complex Glazings and Window Coverings

In North America, the European Union, and Australia, fenestration rating programs are being extended to include shading devices and other nonspecular, "complex" glazing layers. These rating schemes rely on expanded capabilities of existing modeling software and measurements of basic material properties, supported by a set of industry-consensus assumptions about fitting details. However, such calculations can also be performed in "expert" mode to serve the needs of building energy modelers who require exact, rather than generalized, details.

9.7 SYMBOLS

a = absorptance in a layer, considered as an isolated layer
A = total projected area of a fenestration product; apparent solar constant
$\mathcal{A}$ = absorptance in a layer or a collection of layers (system or subsystem)
e = hemispherical emissivity
E_d = diffuse sky irradiance
E_D = direct irradiance
E_{DN} = direct normal irradiance
E_r = diffuse ground reflected irradiance
E_t = total irradiance
F_R = radiant fraction
h = surface heat transfer coefficient
k = thermal conductivity
L = glass thickness
n = refractive index
P_H = horizontal projection depth
P_V = vertical projection depth
q = instantaneous energy flux
Q = instantaneous energy flow
R = reflectance of a layer or collection of layers (system or subsystem)
R_H = height of opaque surface between fenestration product and horizontal projection
R_W = width of opaque surface between fenestration product and vertical projection
S_H = shadow height
S_W = shadow width
SHGC = solar heat gain coefficient
t = relative temperature
T = absolute temperature; transmittance of layer or collection of layers (system or subsystem)
U = overall coefficient of heat transfer
W = fenestration product width

Greek

α = material absorptivity
β = solar altitude angle
γ = surface solar azimuth
Δ = vertical projection profile angle
δ = declination
θ = incident angle
λ = wavelength
ξ = refractive angle
ρ_g = ground reflectivity
Σ = surface tilt
τ = transmissivity
ϕ = solar azimuth
Ω = horizontal projection profile angle
ϖ = solid angle

REFERENCES

ASHRAE members can access *ASHRAE Journal* articles and ASHRAE research project final reports at technologyportal.ashrae.org. Articles and reports are also available for purchase by nonmembers in the online ASHRAE Bookstore at www.ashrae.org/bookstore.

AAMA. 1987. *Skylight handbook: Design guidelines*. American Architectural Manufacturers Association, Schamberg, IL.

AAMA. 1988. Voluntary test method for thermal transmittance and condensation resistance of windows, doors and glazed wall sections. *Publication* AAMA 1503.1-88. American Architectural Manufacturers Association, Schamberg, IL.

ADOPT. 1996. *Angle-dependent optical properties*. Commission of the European Communities, Standards, Measurement and Testing Programme, DG XII, Contract SMT4-CT96-2138. Coordinator A. Roos, University of Uppsala, Sweden.

AGSL. 1992. *Vision3: Glazing system thermal analysis—User manual*. Department of Mechanical Engineering, University of Waterloo, Ontario.

Allen, T. 1997. Conventional and tubular skylights: An evaluation of the daylighting systems at two ACT commercial buildings. *Proceedings of the 22nd National Passive Solar Conference*, Washington, D.C., pp. 97-129.

Arasteh, D., J. Huang, R. Mitchell, B. Clear, and C. Kohler. 2000. A database of window annual energy use in typical North American single family houses. *ASHRAE Transactions* 106(1):562-574.

Arasteh, D., C. Kohler, and B. Griffith. 2009. Modeling windows in EnergyPlus with simple performance indices. *Report* LBNL-2804E. Lawrence Berkeley National Laboratory.

Arens, E.A., R. Gonzalez, and L. Berglund. 1986. Thermal comfort under an extended range of environmental conditions. *ASHRAE Transactions* 92(1).

ASHRAE. 2013. Thermal environmental conditions for human occupancy. ANSI/ASHRAE *Standard* 55-2013.

ASHRAE. 2016. Energy standard for buildings except low-rise residential buildings. ANSI/ASHRAE/IES *Standard* 90.1-2016.

ASHRAE. 2007. Energy-efficient design of low-rise residential buildings. ANSI/ASHRAE *Standard* 90.2-2007.

ASHRAE. 2014. Standard for the design of high-performance green buildings except low-rise residential buildings. ANSI/ASHRAE/USGBC/IES *Standard* 189.1-2014.

ASTM. 2009. Recommended practice for laboratory measurements of airborne sound transmission loss of building partitions. *Standard* E90-09. American Society for Testing and Materials, West Conshohocken, PA.

ASTM. 2012. Standard test method for determining rate of air leakage through exterior windows, curtain walls, and doors under specified pressure differences across the specimen. *Standard* E283-04 (2012). American Society for Testing and Materials, West Conshohocken, PA.

ASTM. 1992. Tables for terrestrial direct normal solar spectral irradiance tables for air mass 1.5. *Standard* E891-1989 (1992). Withdrawn 1999. American Society for Testing and Materials, West Conshohockehn, PA.

ASTM. 2011. Standard practice for calculation of photometric transmittance and reflectance of materials to solar radiation. *Standard* E971-11. American Society for Testing and Materials, West Conshohocken, PA.

ASTM. 2013. Standard test method for solar photometric transmittance of sheet materials using sunlight. *Standard* E972-92 (2013). American Society for Testing and Materials, West Conshohocken, PA.

ASTM. 2015. Standard test method for solar transmittance (terrestrial) of sheet materials using sunlight. *Standard* E1084-86 (2015). American Society for Testing and Materials, West Conshohocken, PA.

ASTM. 2015. Standard test method for determining solar or photopic reflectance, transmittance, and absorptance of materials using a large diameter integrating sphere. *Standard* E1175-87 (2015). American Society for Testing and Materials, West Conshohocken, PA.

ASTM. 2016. Standard practice for determining load resistance of glass in buildings. *Standard* E1300-16. American Society for Testing and Materials, West Conshohocken, PA.

ASTM. 2010. Standard specification for insulated glass unit performance and evaluation. *Standard* E2190-10. American Society for Testing and Materials, West Conshohocken, PA.

ASTM. 2012. Standard tables for reference solar spectral irradiances: Direct normal and hemispherical on 37° tilted surface. *Standard* G173-03 (2012). American Society for Testing and Materials, West Conshohocken, PA.

Barnaby, C.S., J.L. Wright, and M.R. Collins. 2009. Improving load calculations for fenestration with shading devices. *ASHRAE Transactions* 115(2):130-144.

Beck, F.A., B.T. Griffith, D. Turler, and D. Arasteh. 1995. Using infrared thermography for the creation of a window surface temperature database to validate computer heat transfer models. *Proceedings of Windows Innovations Conference '95*, Toronto, ON.

Berdahl, P., and M. Martin. 1984. Emissivity of clear skies. *Solar Energy* 32(5).

Bessoudo, M., A. Tzempelikos, A.K. Athienitis, and R. Zmeureanu. 2010. Indoor thermal environmental conditions near glazed facades with shading devices—Part I: Experiments and building thermal model. *Building and Environment* 45:2506-2516.

Boyce, P. C. Hunter, and O. Howlett. 2003. The benefits of daylight through windows. www.lrc.rpi.edu/programs/daylighting/pdf/DaylightBenefits.pdf. Lighting Research Center. New York.

Brandle, K., and R.F. Boehm. 1982. Airflow windows: Performance and applications. *Proceedings of Thermal Performance of the Exterior Envelopes of Buildings II*, ASHRAE/DOE Conference, ASHRAE Special Project SP-38.

CANMET. 1991. *A study of the long term performance of operating and fixed windows subjected to pressure cycling*. Catalogue M91-7/214-1993E. Efficiency and Alternative Energy Technology Branch, CANMET, Ottawa, ON.

CANMET. 1993. *Long term performance of operating windows subjected to motion cycling*. Catalogue M91-7/235-1993E. Efficiency and Alternative Energy Technology Branch, CANMET, Ottawa, ON.

Carbary, L., V. Hayez, A. Wolf, and M. Bhandari. 2009. Comparisons of thermal performance and energy consumptions of facades used in commercial buildings. *Proceedings of Glass Performance Days 2009*, pp. 89-94.

Carmody, J., S. Selkowitz, E.S. Lee, and D. Arasteh. 2004. *Window systems for high-performance buildings*. W.W. Norton & Company.

Carpenter, S., and A. Elmahdy. 1994. Thermal performance of complex fenestration systems. *ASHRAE Transactions* 100(2):1179-1186.

Carpenter, S., and J. Hogan. 1996. Recommended U-factors for swinging, overhead and revolving doors. *ASHRAE Transactions* 102(1):955-959.

Carpenter, S., and A. McGowan. 1993. Effect of framing systems on the thermal performance of windows. *ASHRAE Transactions* 99(1):907-914.

Carter, D.J. 2008. Tubular guidance systems for daylight: UK case studies. *Building Research & Information* 36(5):520-535.

Carter, D.J,. and M. Al-Marwaee. 2009. User attitudes toward tubular daylight guidance systems. *Lighting Research and Technology* 41:71-88.

CEC. 2010. 2008 Building energy efficiency standards for residential and nonresidential buildings. *California Code of Regulations*, Title 24, Part 6. California Energy Commission.

CGDB. 2016. *Complex glazing database*. Lawrence Berkeley National Laboratory. windows.lbl.gov/software/CGDB/index.html.

Choi, A.S., and R.G. Mistrick. 1999. Analysis of daylight responsive dimming system performance. *Building and Environment* 34:231-243.

CIE. 2006. Tubular daylight guidance systems, CIE *Technical Report* 173:2006. Technical Committee TC3-38, International Commission on Illumination, Austria.

Code of Federal Regulations. Annual. *Safety standard for architectural glazing materials.* 16CFR1201. U.S. Government Printing Office, Washington, D.C.

Collins, M.R., and J.L. Wright. 2006. Calculating center-glass performance indices of windows with a diathermanous layer. *ASHRAE Transactions* 112(2):22-29.

Collins, M.R., S.H. Tasnim, and J.L. Wright. 2008. Determination of convective heat transfer for glazing systems with between-the-glass louvered shades. *International Journal of Heat and Mass Transfer* 51:2742-2751.

Collins, M.R., J.L. Wright, and N.A. Kotey. 2011. Measuring off-normal solar optical properties of flat shading materials. *Journal of Measurement* (45):79-93.

Crooks, B.P., J. Larsen, R. Sullivan, D. Arasteh, and S. Selkowitz. 1995. NFRC efforts to develop a residential fenestration annual energy rating methodology. *Proceedings of Windows Innovations Conference '95*, Toronto, ON. Lawrence Berkeley Laboratory *Publication* 36896.

CSA. 2000. Windows. CAN/CSA *Standard* A440-00. Canadian Standards Association, Etobicoke, ON.

CSA. 2005. Windows/User selection guide to CSA *Standard* CAN/CSA-A440-00. CAN/CSA *Special Publication* A440.1-00 (R2005). Canadian Standards Association, Etobicoke, ON.

CSA. 2014. Fenestration energy performance. CAN/CSA *Standard* A440.2. Canadian Standards Association, Etobicoke, ON.

CSA. 2000. Energy performance evaluation of swinging doors. CAN/CSA *Standard* A453-95 (R2000). Canadian Standards Association, Etobicoke, ON.

Curcija, D.C. 2005. *Discrepancies between ISO window simulation standards.* Technical report to ISO TC 163, Subcommittee 2, Working Group 9. November 23, 2005.

Curcija, D., and W.P. Goss. 1994. Two-dimensional finite-element model of heat transfer in complete fenestration systems. *ASHRAE Transactions* 100(2):1207-1221.

Curcija, D., and W.P. Goss. 1995. Three-dimensional finite element model of heat transfer in complete fenestration systems. *Proceedings of Windows Innovations Conference '95*, Toronto, ON.

Curcija, D., W.P. Goss, J.P. Power, and Y. Zhao. 1996. "Variable-h" model for improved prediction of surface temperatures in fenestration systems. *Technical Report*, University of Massachusetts at Amherst.

de Abreu, P., R.A. Fraser, H.F. Sullivan, and J.L. Wright. 1996. A study of insulated glazing unit surface temperature profiles using two-dimensional computer simulation. *ASHRAE Transactions* 102(2):497-507.

EEL. 1990. *FRAME/VISION window performance modelling and sensitivity analysis*. Institute for Research in Construction, National Research Council of Canada, Ottawa.

Elmahdy, A.H. 1995. Air leakage characteristics of windows subjected to simultaneous temperature and pressure differentials. *Proceedings of Windows Innovations Conference '95*, CANMET.

Elmahdy, H. 1996. Surface temperature measurement of insulating glass units using infrared thermography. *ASHRAE Transactions* 102(2):489-496.

Elmahdy, A.H. 2001. To seal or not to seal? A critical look at the effects of air leakage on the condensation resistance of windows. *The Whole-Life Performance of Façades*, Bath, U.K.

Elmahdy, A.H. 2003. Quantification of air leakage effects on the condensation resistance of windows. *ASHRAE Transactions* 109(1):600-606.

Elmahdy, A.H., and S.A. Yusuf. 1995. Determination of argon concentration and assessment of the durability of high-performance insulating glass units filled with argon gas. *ASHRAE Transactions* 101(2):1026-1037.

El Sherbiny, S.M., K.G.T. Hollands, and G.D. Raithby. 1982. Heat transfer by natural convection across vertical and inclined air layers. *Journal of Heat Transfer* 104:96-102.

Erhorn, H., and M. Dirksmöller, eds. 2000. *Documentation of the software package ADELINE 3*. Fraunhofer Institut für Bauphysik, Stuttgart.

Ewing, W.B., and J.I. Yellott. 1976. Energy conservation through the use of exterior shading of fenestration. *ASHRAE Transactions* 82(1):703-733.

Finlayson, E.U., and D. Arasteh. 1993. WINDOW 4.0: Documentation of calculation procedures. *Publication* LBL-33943/UC-350, Lawrence Berkeley Laboratory, Energy & Environment Division, Berkeley, CA.

Griffith, B.T., D. Turler, and D. Arasteh. 1996. Surface temperatures of insulated glazing units: Infrared thermography laboratory measurements. *ASHRAE Transactions* 102(2):479-488.

Griffith, B., E. Finlayson, M. Yazdanian, and D. Arasteh. 1998. The significance of bolts in the thermal performance of curtain-wall frames for glazed facades. *ASHRAE Transactions* 105(1):1063-1069.

Gueymard, C.A. 2007. Advanced solar irradiance model and procedure for spectral solar heat gain calculation. *ASHRAE Transactions* 113(1):149-164.

Gueymard, C.A., and W.C. DuPont. 2009. Spectral effects on the transmittance, solar heat gain, and performance rating of glazing systems. *Solar Energy* 83:940-953.

Gueymard, C.A., and H.D. Kambezidis. 2004. Solar spectral radiation. Ch. 5 in *Solar radiation and daylight models*, T. Muneer, ed., pp. 221-301. Elsevier Butterworth-Heinemann, Oxford.

Haddad, K.H., and A.H. Elmahdy. 1998. Comparison of the thermal performance of a conventional window and a supply-air window. *ASHRAE Transactions* 104(1A):1261-1270.

Haddad, K.H., and A.H. Elmahdy. 1999. Comparison of the thermal performance of an exhaust-air window and a supply-air window. *ASHRAE Transactions* 105(2):918-926.

Hawthorne, W.A., and S. Reilly. 2000. The impact of glazing selection on residential duct design and comfort. *ASHRAE Transactions* 106(1):553-561.

Heschong, L., D. Mahone, F. Rubinstein, and J. McHugh. 1998. *Skylighting guidelines*. The Heschong Mahone Group, Sacramento, CA.

Hitchcock, R.J., R. Mitchell, M. Yazdanian, E. Lee, and C. Huigenza. 2008. COMFEN—A commercial fenestration/façade design tool. *Proceedings of SimBuild 2008*, pp. 246-252.

Hogan, J.F. 1988. A summary of tested glazing U-values and the case for an industry wide testing program. *ASHRAE Transactions* 94(2).

Hollands, K.G.T. and J.L. Wright. 1982. Heat loss coefficients and effective $\tau\alpha$ products for flat plate collectors with diathermous covers. *Solar Energy* 30:211-216.

Huang, J., R. Mitchell, D. Arasteh, and S. Selkowitz. 1999. Residential fenestration performance analysis using RESFEN 3.1. *Thermal Performance of the Exterior Envelopes of Buildings VII*, ASHRAE.

Huang, N.Y.T., J.L. Wright, and M.R. Collins. 2006. Thermal resistance of a window with an enclosed venetian blind: Guarded heater plate measurements. *ASHRAE Transactions* 112(2):13-21.

Hutchins, M.G., A.J. Topping, C. Anderson, F. Olive, P.A. van Nijnatten, P. Polato, A. Roos, and M. Rubin. 2001. Angle-dependent optical properties of coated glass products: results of an inter-laboratory comparison of spectral transmittance and reflectance. *Thin Solid Films* 392(2):269.

ICC. 2015. *International building code® (IBC®)*. International Code Council, Washington, D.C.

ICC. 2015. *International energy conservation code® (IECC®)*. International Code Council, Washington, D.C.

ICC. 2015. *International green construction code™ (IgCC™)*. International Code Council, Washington, D.C.

IEA. 1999. *Daylighting simulation: Methods, algorithms, and resources.* IEA SHC Task 21/ECBCS Annex 29. LBNL-44296, Lawrence Berkeley National Laboratory. www.iea-shc.org.

IES. 1999. *IES recommended practice of daylighting.* IES RP-5-99. Illuminating Engineering Society, New York.

ISO. 2015. Solar energy—Reference solar spectral irradiance at the ground at different receiving conditions—Part 1: Direct normal and hemispherical solar irradiance for air mass 1,5. *Standard* 9845-1992 (2005). International Organization for Standardization, Geneva.

ISO. 2006. Thermal performance of windows, doors and shutters—Calculation of thermal transmittance—Part 1: General. *Standard* 10077-1. International Organization for Standardization, Geneva.

ISO. 2012. Thermal performance of windows, doors and shutters—Calculation of thermal transmittance—Part 2: Numerical method for frames. *Standard* 10077-2. International Organization for Standardization, Geneva.

ISO. 2003. Thermal performance of windows, doors and shading devices—Detailed calculations. *Standard* 15099. International Organization for Standardization, Geneva.

Jennings, J.D., F.M. Rubinstein, D. DiBartolomeo, and S. Blanc. 1999. *Comparison of control options in private offices in an advanced lighting controls testbed*. LBNL-43096, Lawrence Berkeley National Laboratory, Berkeley, CA.

Karlsson, J., M. Rubin, and A. Roos. 2001. Evaluation of some models for the angle-dependent total solar energy transmittance of glazing materials. *Solar Energy* 71(1).

Keyes, M.W. 1967. Analysis and rating of drapery materials used for indoor shading. *ASHRAE Transactions* 73(1):8.4.1.

Klems, J.H. 1989. U-values, solar heat gain, and thermal performance: Recent studies using the MoWiTT. *ASHRAE Transactions* 95(1):609-617.

Klems, J.H. 1994a. A new method for predicting the solar heat gain of complex fenestration systems: I. Overview and derivation of the matrix layer calculation. *ASHRAE Transactions* 100(1):1065-1072.

Klems, J.H. 1994b. A new method for predicting the solar heat gain of complex fenestration systems: II. Detailed description of the matrix layer calculation. *ASHRAE Transactions* 100(1):1073-1086.

Klems, J.H. 2001. *Solar heat gain through fenestration systems containing shading: Procedures for estimating performance from minimal data.* LBNL-46682. Windows and Daylighting Group, Lawrence Berkeley National Laboratory, Berkeley, CA.

Kotey, N.A., J.L. Wright, and M.R. Collins. 2008. *Proceedings of the 3rd Annual Canadian Solar Buildings Conference*, Fredericton, NB. Solar Energy Society of Canada.

Kotey, N.A., M.R. Collins, J.L. Wright, and T. Jiang. 2009a. A simplified method for calculating the effective solar optical properties of a venetian blind layer for building energy simulation. *ASME Journal of Solar Energy Engineering* 131(2).

Kotey, N.A., J.L. Wright, and M.R. Collins. 2009b. Determination of angle-dependent solar optical properties of drapery fabrics. *ASHRAE Transactions* 115(2).

Kotey, N.A., J.L. Wright, and M.R. Collins. 2009c. A detailed model to determine the effective solar optical properties of draperies. *ASHRAE Transactions* 115(1).

Kotey, N.A., J.L. Wright, and M.R. Collins. 2009d. Determination of angle-dependent solar optical properties of roller blind materials. *ASHRAE Transactions* 115(1).

Kotey, N.A., J.L. Wright, and M.R. Collins. 2009e. Determination of angle-dependent solar optical properties of insect screens. *ASHRAE Transactions* 115(1).

Kotey, N.A., J.L. Wright, and M.R. Collins. 2011. A method for determining the effective longwave radiative properties of pleated draperies. *HVAC&R Research* (now *Science and Technology for the Built Environment*) 17(5):660-669.

Kruis, N. 2016. Representative layer-by-layer descriptions for fenestration systems with specified bulk properties such as U-factor and SHGC. ASHRAE Research Project RP-1588, *Report*.

Laouadi, A. 2004. Design with SkyVision: A computer tool to predict daylighting performance of skylights. *CIB World Building Conference*, Toronto, pp. 1-11.

Laouadi, A. 2013. Advanced performance prediction of tubular daylighting devices: New research from the National Research Council of Canada takes an in-depth look inside TDDs. *Lighting Design and Application* (September):52.

Laouadi, A., A.D. Galasiu, M.R. Atif, and A. Haqqani. 2003. SkyVision: A software tool to calculate the optical characteristics and daylighting performance of skylights. *Building Simulation, 8th IBPSA Conference*, Eindhoven, Netherlands, pp. 705-712.

Laouadi, A., H.H. Saber, A.D. Galasiu, and C. Arsenault. 2013a. Optical model for tubular hollow light guides (1415-RP). *HVAC&R Research* (now *Science and Technology for the Built Environment*) 19(3):324-334.

Laouadi, A., A.D. Galasiu, H.H. Saber, and C. Arsenault. 2013b. Tubular daylighting devices- part I: development of an optical model (1415-RP). *HVAC&R Research* (now *Science and Technology for the Built Environment*) 19(5):536-556.

Laouadi, A., C. Arsenault, H.H. Saber, and A.D. Galasiu. 2013c. Tubular daylighting devices- part II: validation of the optical model (1415-RP). *HVAC&R Research* (now *Science and Technology for the Built Environment*) 19(5):557-572.

Laouadi, A., H.H. Saber, A.D. Galasiu, and C. Arsenault. 2013d. Tubular daylighting devices—Development and validation of a thermal model (1415-RP). *HVAC&R Research* (now *Science and Technology for the Built Environment*) 19(5):513-535.

LBNL. 2016. *WINDOW 7*. Windows and Daylighting Group, Lawrence Berkeley Laboratory, Berkeley, CA. windows.lbl.gov/software/window/window.html.

Lee, E., and S.E. Selkowitz. 1995. The design and evaluation of integrated envelope and lighting control strategies for commercial buildings. *ASHRAE Transactions* 101(1):326-342.

Lyons, P.R., D.A. Arasteh, and C. Huizenga. 2000. Window performance for human thermal comfort. *ASHRAE Transactions* 106(1):594-602.

Lyons, P., J. Wong, and M. Bhandari. 2010. A comparison of window modeling methods in Energyplus 4.0. SimBuild 2010, New York.

Mathis, R.C., and R. Garries. 1995. Instant, annual life: A discussion on the current practice and evolution of fenestration energy performance rating. *Proceedings of Windows Innovations Conference '95*, Toronto, ON.

McCluney, R. 1990. Awning shading algorithm update. *ASHRAE Transactions* 96(1):34-38.

McCluney, R. 1993. Sensitivity of optical properties and solar gain of spectrally selective glazing systems to changes in solar spectrum. *Solar '93*, 22nd American Solar Energy Society Conference, Washington, D.C.

McCluney, R. 1994a. Angle of incidence and diffuse radiation influences on glazing system solar gain. *Proceedings Solar '94 Conference*, American Solar Energy Society, San Jose, CA.

McCluney, R. 1994b. *Introduction to radiometry and photometry*. Artech House, Boston.

McCluney, R. 1996. Sensitivity of fenestration solar gain to source spectrum and angle of incidence. *ASHRAE Transactions* 102(2):112-122.

McCluney, R., and P. Jindra. 2001. *Industry guide to selecting the best residential window options for the Florida climate*. FSEC-PF-358-01. Florida Solar Energy Center, University of Central Florida, Cocoa.

McGowan, A, R. Jutras, G. Riopel, and M. Hanam. 2006. Heat transfer through roll-up doors, revolving doors and opaque non-residential swinging, sliding and rolling doors. ASHRAE Research Project RP-1236, *Final Report*.

Mitchell, R., J. Huang, D. Arasteh, R. Sullivan, and S. Phillip. 1999. *RESFEN 3.1: A PC program for calculating the heating and cooling energy use of windows in residential buildings—Program description.* LBNL-40682 Rev. BS-371. Lawrence Berkeley National Laboratory, Berkeley, CA.

Mitchell, R., M. Yazdanian, L. Zhu, D. Arasteh, and J. Huang. 2012. *RESFEN6: Program description*. LBNL-40682 Rev. Lawrence Berkeley National Laboratory, Berkeley, CA.

Moeseke, G., I. Bruyere, and A.D. Herde. 2007. Impact of control rules on the efficiency of shading devices and free cooling for office buildings. *Building and Environment* 42:784-793.

Newsham, G.R. 1994. Manual control of window blinds and electric lighting: implications for comfort and energy consumption. *Indoor Environment 3,* pp. 135-144.

NFRC. 2014a. Procedure for determining fenestration product U-factors. *Technical Document* 100-2014. National Fenestration Rating Council, Silver Spring, MD.

NFRC. 2014b. *Spectral data library*. Available from www.nfrc.org/software.aspx. National Fenestration Rating Council, Silver Spring, MD.

NFRC. 2014c. Standard test method for determining the solar optical properties of glazing materials and systems. *Technical Document* 300-2014. National Fenestration Rating Council, Silver Spring, MD.

NFRC. 2014d. Procedure for determining fenestration product solar heat gain coefficient and visible transmittance at normal incidence. *Technical Document* 200-2014. National Fenestration Rating Council, Silver Spring, MD.

NFRC. 2014e. Procedure for interim standard test method for measuring he solar heat gain coefficient of fenestration systems using calorimetry hot box methods. *Technical Document* 201-2014. National Fenestration Rating Council, Silver Spring, MD.

NRFC. 2014f. Procedure for determining visible transmittance of tubular daylighting devices. *Technical Document* 203-2014. National Fenestration Rating Council, Silver Spring, MD.

NFRC. 2014g. Standard test method for emittance of specular surfaces using spectromteric measurements. *Technical Document* 301-2014. National Fenestration Rating Council, Silver Spring, MD.

NFRC. 2014h. Procedure for determining fenestration product air leakage. *Technical Document* 400-2014. National Fenestration Rating Council, Silver Spring, MD.

NFRC. 2014i. Guidelines to estimate the effects of fenestration on heating and cooling energy consumption in single family residences. *Technical Document* 901-2014. National Fenestration Rating Council, Silver Spring, MD.

NFRC. 2014j. Procedure for determining fenestration product condensation resistance values. *Technical Document* 500-2014. National Fenestration Rating Council, Silver Spring, MD.

NFRC. 2014k. User guide to the procedure for determining fenestration product condensation resistance rating values. *Technical Document* 501-2014. National Fenestration Rating Council, Silver Spring, MD.

NRCC. 2011. Tubular daylighting devices: An alternative to skylights. *Construction Innovation* 16(1). National Research Council Canada, Ottawa.

Ochoa, C.E., and I.G. Capeluto. 2009. Advice tool for early design stages of intelligent facades based on energy and visual comfort approach. *Energy and Buildings* 41(5):480-488.

Parmelee, G.V., and R.G. Huebscher. 1947. Forced convection heat transfer from flat surfaces. *ASHVE Transactions*, pp. 245-284.

Patenaude, A. 1995. Air infiltration rate of windows under temperature and pressure differentials. *Proceedings of Windows Innovations Conference '95*, Toronto, ON.

Pennington, C.W., and G.L. Moore. 1967. Measurement and application of solar properties of drapery shading materials. *ASHRAE Transactions* 73(1):8.3.1.

Rao, S.R., and A. Tzempelikos. 2012. The impact of a combined dynamic shading system on the thermal performance of building perimeter zones. *ASHRAE Transactions* 118(1):265-273.

Reinhart, C.F. 2004. Lightswitch-2002: A model for manual and automated control of electric lighting and blinds. *Solar Energy* 77(2004):15-28.

Robbins, C.L. 1986. *Daylighting: Design and analysis*. Van Nostrand Reinhold, New York.

Rubin, M. 1982a. Solar optical properties of windows. *Energy Research* 6: 122-133.

Rubin, M. 1982b. Calculating heat transfer through windows. *Energy Research* 6:341-349.

Rubin, M. 1985. Optical constants and bulk optical properties of soda lime silica glasses for windows. *Solar Energy Materials* 12:275-288.

Rubin, M., K. von Rottkay, and R. Powles. 1998. Window optics. *Solar Energy* 62(3):149-161.

Rubin, M., R. Powles, and K. von Rottkay. 1999. Models for the angle-dependent optical properties of coated glazing materials. *Solar Energy* 66(4):267-276.

Schutrum, L.F., and N. Ozisik. 1961. Solar heat gains through domed skylights. *ASHRAE Journal*, pp. 51-60.

Sezgen, O., and J.G. Koomey. 1998. *Interactions between lighting and space conditioning energy use in U.S. commercial buildings.* LBNL-39795, Lawrence Berkeley National Laboratory, Berkeley, CA. eetd.lbl.gov/sites/all/files/lbnl-39795.pdf.

Shen, H., and A. Tzempelikos. 2012. Daylighting and energy analysis of private offices with automated interior roller shades. *Solar Energy 86*, pp. 681-704.

Shewen, E.C. 1986. *A Peltier-effect technique for natural convection heat flux measurement applied to the rectangular open cavity.* Ph.D. dissertation. Department of Mechanical Engineering, University of Waterloo, ON.

Smith, W.A., and C.W. Pennington. 1964. Shading coefficients for glass block panels. *ASHRAE Journal* 5(12):31.

Sodergren, D., and T. Bostrom. 1971. Ventilating with the exhaust air window. *ASHRAE Journal* 13(4):51.

Sterling, E.M., A. Arundel, and T.D. Sterling. 1985. Criteria for human exposure in occupied buildings. *ASHRAE Transactions* 91(1).

Sullivan, H.F., J.L. Wright, and R.A. Fraser. 1996. Overview of a project to determine the surface temperatures of insulated glazing units: Thermographic measurement and two-dimensional simulation. *ASHRAE Transactions* 102(2):516-522.

Tzempelikos, A., and A.K. Athienitis. 2005. Integrated daylighting and thermal analysis of office buildings. *ASHRAE Transactions* 111(1):227-238.

Tzempelikos, A., and A.K. Athienitis. 2007. The impact of shading design and control on building cooling and lighting demand. *Solar Energy* 81(3), 369-382.

van Dijk, D. 2003. *Comparison of standards on thermal, solar and/or light properties of windows and window components*. TNO Building and Construction Research, Delft, Netherlands. April 8.

Ward, G.W. 1990. Visualization. *Lighting Design + Application* 20(6):4-20.

Winkelmann, F.C. 1983. *Daylighting calculation in DOE-2*. LBNL-11353. Lawrence Berkeley National Laboratory, Berkeley, CA.

Wong, J.C.S. 2016. Personal communication.

Wright, J.L. 1995a. *VISION4 glazing system thermal analysis: Reference manual.* Advanced Glazing System Laboratory, University of Waterloo.

Wright, J.L. 1995b. Summary and comparison of methods to calculate solar heat gain. *ASHRAE Transactions* 101(1):802-818.

Wright, J.L. 1996a. A correlation to quantify convective heat transfer between window glazings. *ASHRAE Transactions* 102(1):940-946.

Wright, J.L. 1996b. A simplified numerical method for assessing the condensation resistance of windows. *ASHRAE Transactions* 104(1):1222-1229.

Wright, J.L. 2008. Calculating centre-glass performance indices of glazing systems with shading devices. *ASHRAE Transactions* 114(2):199-209.

Wright, J.L., and H.F. Sullivan. 1995a. A two-dimensional numerical model for glazing system thermal analysis. *ASHRAE Transactions* 101(1):819-831.

Wright, J.L., and H.F. Sullivan. 1995b. A two-dimensional numerical model for natural convection in a vertical, rectangular window cavity. *ASHRAE Transactions* 100(2):1193-1206.

Wright, J.L., and H.F. Sullivan. 1995c. A simplified method for the numerical condensation resistance analysis of windows. *Proceedings of Windows Innovations Conference '95*, Toronto, ON.

Wright, J.L., N.Y.T. Huang, and M.R. Collins. 2008. Thermal resistance of a window with an enclosed venetian blind: A simplified model. *ASHRAE Transactions* 114(1):471-482.

Wright, J.L., M.R. Collins, and N. Kotey. 2009a. Solar gain through windows with shading devices: Simulations versus measurements. *ASHRAE Transactions* 115(2):18-30.

Wright, J.L., C. Barnaby, M.R. Collins, and N. Kotey. 2009b. Improving load calculations for fenestrations with shading devices. ASHRAE Research Project RP-1311, *Final Report*.

Yazdanian, M., and J.H. Klems. 1993. Measurement of the exterior convective film coefficient for windows in low-rise buildings. *ASHRAE Transactions* 100(1):1087-1096.

Yellott, J.I. 1963. Selective reflectance—A new approach to solar heat control. *ASHRAE Transactions* 69:418.

Zhang, X., and T. Muneer. 2000. Mathematical model for the performance of lightpipes. *Lighting Research and Technology* 32(3):141-146.

Zhao, Y., D. Curcija, and W.P. Goss. 1996. Condensation resistance validation project—Detailed computer simulations using finite element methods. *ASHRAE Transactions* 102(2):508-515.

BIBLIOGRAPHY

Wright, J.L., and N.A. Kotey. 2006. Solar absorption by each element in a glazing/shading layer array. *ASHRAE Transactions* 112(2):3-12.

Zhao, Y., D. Curcija, and W.P. Goss. 1999. Convective heat transfer correlations for fenestration glazing cavities: A review. *ASHRAE Transactions* 105(2).

CHAPTER 16

VENTILATION AND INFILTRATION

PROVIDING a comfortable and healthy indoor environment for building occupants is the primary concern of HVAC engineers. Comfort and indoor air quality (IAQ) depend on many factors, including thermal regulation; control of internal and external sources of pollutants; supply of acceptable air; removal of unacceptable air; occupants' activities and preferences; and proper construction, operation, and maintenance of building systems. Proper ventilation and infiltration are only part of achieving acceptable indoor air quality and thermal comfort. HVAC designers, occupants, and building owners must be aware of and address other factors as well. Further information on indoor environmental health may be found in Chapter 10. Changing ventilation and infiltration rates to solve thermal comfort problems and reduce energy consumption can affect indoor air quality and may be against building code or other regulations, so any changes should be approached with care and be under the direction of a registered professional engineer with expertise in HVAC analysis and design.

HVAC design engineers and others concerned with building ventilation and indoor air quality should obtain a copy of ASHRAE *Standard* 62.1 or 62.2, or those for specific applications (e.g., *Standard* 170 for health care), whichever is most relevant to the project. These standards are reviewed regularly and contain ventilation design and evaluation requirements for commercial and institutional (*Standard* 62.1) and residential (*Standard* 62.2) buildings, respectively. When designing a new building or analyzing an existing building, check which version of *Standard* 62 has been adopted by the local code authority. An existing building may be required to meet the current version of the standard, or allowed to comply with an older version. The last chapter of each year's *ASHRAE Handbook* (Chapter 39 of this volume) has a list of current standards.

This chapter addresses commercial and institutional buildings, where ventilation concerns usually dominate (though infiltration should not be ignored), and single- and multifamily residences, where infiltration has traditionally been considered most important but ventilation issues have received increased attention in recent years. Basic concepts and terminology for both are presented before more advanced analytical and design techniques are given. Ventilation of industrial buildings is covered in Chapter 31 of the 2015 *ASHRAE Handbook—HVAC Applications*. However, many of the fundamental ideas and terminology presented in this chapter can also be applied to industrial buildings.

Sustainable Building Standards and Rating Systems

Good indoor air quality is necessary for maintaining health and high productivity. Consequently, sustainable building standards such as ASHRAE *Standard* 189.1 and building rating systems, such as U.S. Green Building Council's (USGBC) Leadership in Energy and Environmental Design™ (LEED®) program, place great importance on creating and maintaining acceptable IAQ. In fact, the LEED rating system was first developed to address IAQ concerns, and roughly one-quarter of the available credit points for new commercial buildings are still IAQ related. Preparers of such rating systems, like others, have struggled with how to characterize complex ventilation and infiltration issues. These issues are addressed in detail by many portions of this chapter; separate ASHRAE design guides, manuals, books, and standards; and the references cited; these sources also provide methods to demonstrate the effectiveness of various HVAC systems and techniques in providing good IAQ in residential, commercial, and other buildings. In all designs, care is needed to eliminate excessive ventilation (e.g., beyond that needed for IAQ or by an air-side economizer) to avoid inappropriately increasing energy use. Increasing the ventilation rate above that required by *Standard* 62.1, for example, does not necessarily increase the acceptability of the indoor air quality.

1. BASIC CONCEPTS AND TERMINOLOGY

Outdoor air that flows through a building is often used to dilute and remove indoor air contaminants. However, the energy required to condition this outdoor air can be a significant portion of the total space-conditioning load. The magnitude of outdoor airflow into the building must be determined to size the HVAC equipment properly, and to evaluate energy consumption (if required). For buildings without mechanical cooling and dehumidification, proper ventilation and infiltration airflows are important for providing acceptable IAQ and better thermal comfort for occupants. ASHRAE *Standard* 55 specifies conditions under which 80% or more of the occupants in a space will find it thermally acceptable. Chapter 9 of this volume also addresses thermal comfort.

Airflow into buildings and between zones also affects fires, smoke movement, and safe occupant egress. Smoke management is addressed in Chapter 53 of the 2015 *ASHRAE Handbook—HVAC Applications*.

Ventilation and Infiltration

Air exchange of outdoor air with air already in a building can be divided into two broad classifications: ventilation and infiltration.

Ventilation is intentional introduction of air from the outdoors into a building; it is further subdivided into natural and mechanical ventilation. **Natural ventilation** is the flow of air through open windows, doors, grilles, and other planned building envelope penetrations. **Mechanical** (or **forced**) ventilation, shown in Figure 1, is the intentional movement of air into and out of a building using fans, ductwork, intake louvers, and exhaust grilles, for example.

Infiltration is the flow of outdoor air into a building through cracks and other unintentional openings and through the normal use

The preparation of this chapter is assigned to TC 4.3, Ventilation Requirements and Infiltration.

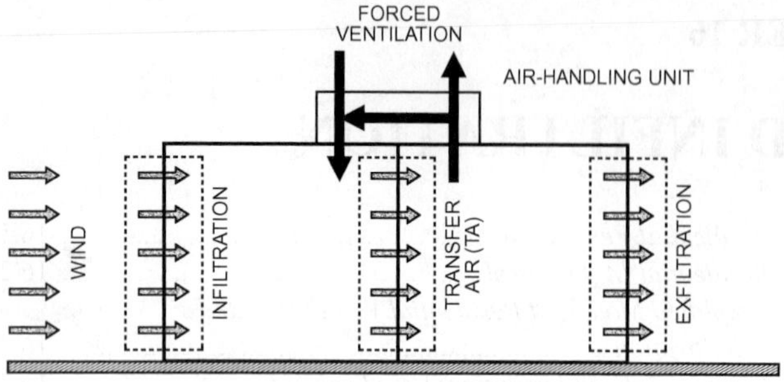

Fig. 1 Two-Space Building with Mechanical Ventilation, Infiltration, and Exfiltration

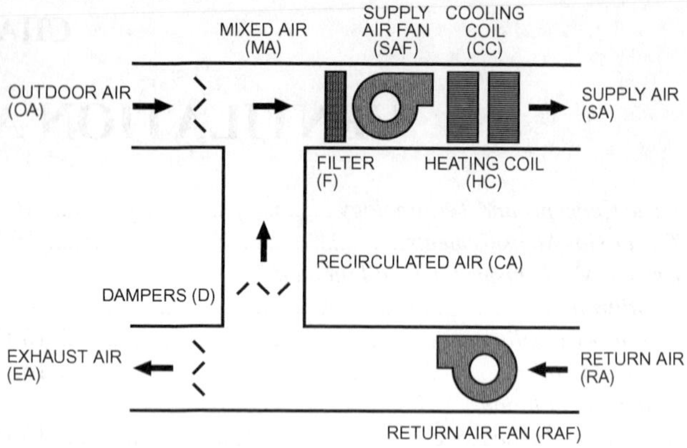

Fig. 2 Simple All-Air Air-Handling Unit with Associated Airflows

of exterior doors for entrance and egress. Infiltration is also known as **air leakage** into a building. **Exfiltration**, depicted in Figure 1, is leakage of indoor air out of a building through similar types of openings. Like natural ventilation, infiltration and exfiltration are driven by natural and/or artificial pressure differences. These forces are discussed in detail in the section on Driving Mechanisms for Ventilation and Infiltration. **Transfer air** is air that moves from one interior space to another, either intentionally or not.

Ventilation and infiltration differ significantly in how they affect energy consumption, air quality, and thermal comfort, and can each vary with weather conditions, HVAC system operation, and building use. Although one mode may be expected to dominate in a particular building, both must be considered in the proper design and operation of an HVAC system. Seasonal weather and other transient factors must be considered, as well.

Ventilation Air

Ventilation air is air used to provide acceptable indoor air quality. It may be composed of mechanical or natural ventilation, infiltration, suitably treated recirculated air, transfer air, or an appropriate combination, although the allowable means of providing ventilation air varies in standards and guidelines.

Modern commercial and institutional buildings normally have mechanical ventilation and are usually intended to be pressurized somewhat to reduce or eliminate infiltration. Mechanical ventilation has the greatest potential for control of air exchange when the system is properly designed, installed, and operated; it should provide acceptable indoor air quality and thermal comfort when ASHRAE *Standards* 55 and 62.1's requirements are followed, although issues (e.g., unusually strong pollutant sources) can still result in unacceptable indoor environment conditions. Mechanical ventilation equipment and systems are described in Chapters 1, 4, and 10 of the 2016 *ASHRAE Handbook—HVAC Systems and Equipment*.

In commercial and institutional buildings, natural ventilation (e.g., through uncontrolled use of manually operated windows) may not be desirable from the points of view of energy conservation, comfort, security, or control of airborne pollen or other pollutants in some climates and locations. In commercial and institutional buildings with mechanical cooling and ventilation, an automatically controlled air- or water-side economizer may be preferable to operable windows for taking advantage of cool outdoor conditions when interior cooling is required. When moderate outdoor temperatures occur, an air-side economizer control scheme may not only increase the rate of ventilation but also operate the cooling equipment to optimize energy use (**hybrid** or **mixed mode**).

Infiltration may be significant in commercial and institutional buildings too, especially in tall, leaky, or partially pressurized buildings and in lobby and loading dock areas. The joint between roof decking and outer walls is often particularly leaky in commercial and other large buildings, and should be properly detailed, constructed, and inspected.

In most of the United States, residential buildings have historically relied on infiltration and natural ventilation to meet their ventilation air needs. Neither is reliable for ventilation air purposes because they depend on weather conditions, building construction, occupants, and maintenance. Natural ventilation, usually through operable windows and screened doors, is more likely to allow occupants to control indoor airborne contaminants and interior air temperature, but it can have a substantial energy cost if used while the residence's heating or cooling equipment is operating. Opened windows and doors also may lead to security, noise, or other concerns.

In place of or in addition to operable windows, small exhaust fans should be provided for localized venting of residential spaces with high pollutant levels or moisture (e.g., kitchens, bathrooms). Not all local building codes require that such exhaust be vented to the outdoors, but it is required by ASHRAE *Standard* 62.2. Instead, a local code may allow the air to be treated and returned to the space or to be discharged to an attic space. Poor maintenance of these recirculating treatment devices can make nonducted vents ineffective for ventilation purposes. Warm exhaust air can hold much moisture, so condensation in attics should be avoided. If not already required by code, consider venting attached garages and other storage spaces to the outdoors, as well.

Increasingly, building codes require general mechanical ventilation in residences. Heat recovery heat exchangers are popular for reducing energy consumption, especially in cold climates. Residential buildings with low rates of infiltration and natural ventilation, including most new buildings, require mechanical ventilation at rates given in ASHRAE *Standard* 62.2.

Forced-Air Distribution Systems

Figure 2 shows a simple **air-handling unit (AHU)** or **air handler** that conditions air for a building. Air brought back to the air handler from the conditioned space is **return air (RA)**. The return air either is discharged to the environment [**exhaust air (EA)**] or is reused [**recirculated air (CA)**]. Air brought in intentionally from the environment is **outdoor air (OA)**. Because outdoor air may need treatment to be acceptable for use in a building, it should not be called "fresh air." Outdoor and recirculated air are combined to form **mixed air (MA)**, which is then conditioned and delivered to the spaces served as **supply air (SA)**. Any portion of the mixed air that intentionally or unintentionally circumvents conditioning is **bypass air (BA)**. Because of the wide variety of air-handling systems, the airflows shown in Figure 2 may not all be present in a particular system as defined here. Also, more complex systems may have additional airflows.

In HVAC design, volumetric airflow rates Q are normally reported in cubic feet per minute (cfm). The incorrect term "volume" should not be used to describe airflow rates.

Outdoor Air Fraction

The outdoor airflow introduced to a building or zone by an air-handling unit can also be described by the **outdoor air fraction** X_{oa}, which is the ratio of the volumetric flow rate Q of outdoor air brought in by the air handler to the total supply airflow rate:

$$X_{oa} = \frac{Q_{oa}}{Q_{sa}} = \frac{Q_{oa}}{Q_{ma}} = \frac{Q_{oa}}{Q_{oa} + Q_{ca}} \tag{1}$$

When expressed as a percentage, the outdoor air fraction is called the **percent outdoor air**. The design outdoor airflow rate Q_{oa} for a building's or zone's ventilation system is found by applying the requirements of ASHRAE *Standard* 62.1 or 62.2 to that specific building, occupancy, and HVAC system. The supply airflow rate Q_{sa} is that required to meet the thermal load. The outdoor air fraction and percent outdoor air then describe the degree of recirculation, where a low value indicates a high rate of recirculation, and a high value shows little recirculation. Conventional all-air air-handling systems for commercial and institutional buildings often have approximately 10 to 40% outdoor air.

100% outdoor air means no recirculation of return air through the air-handling system. Instead, all the supply air is treated outdoor air, also known as **makeup air (KA)**, and all return air is discharged directly to the outdoors as **relief air (LA)**, via separate or centralized exhaust fans or relief dampers and grilles. An air-handling unit that provides exclusively 100% outdoor air to offset air that is exhausted is typically called a **makeup air unit (MAU)**.

When outdoor air via mechanical ventilation is used to provide ventilation air, as is common in commercial and institutional buildings and increasingly in residences, this outdoor air is usually delivered to spaces as all or part of the supply air. With a variable-air-volume (VAV) system, the outdoor air fraction of the supply air may need to be increased when supply airflow is reduced to meet a particular thermal load. In some HVAC systems, such as a dedicated outdoor air system (DOAS), conditioned outdoor air may be delivered separately from the way the spaces' loads are handled (Mumma and Shank 2001).

Room Air Movement

Air movement within spaces affects the diffusion of ventilation air and, therefore, indoor air quality and comfort. Two distinct flow patterns are commonly used to characterize air movement in rooms: displacement flow and entrainment flow. **Displacement flow**, shown in Figure 3, is the movement of air within a space in a piston- or plug-type motion. Ideally, no mixing of the room air occurs, which is desirable for removing pollutants generated within a space. Air mixing does occur, however, to various degrees. A laminar-flow air distribution system that is intended to sweep air across a space with reduced turbulence and mixing may produce a high degree of displacement flow and thus more effective pollutant removal. The pollutants' buoyancy and occupants' thermal comfort are concerns when deciding on the intended direction of airflow.

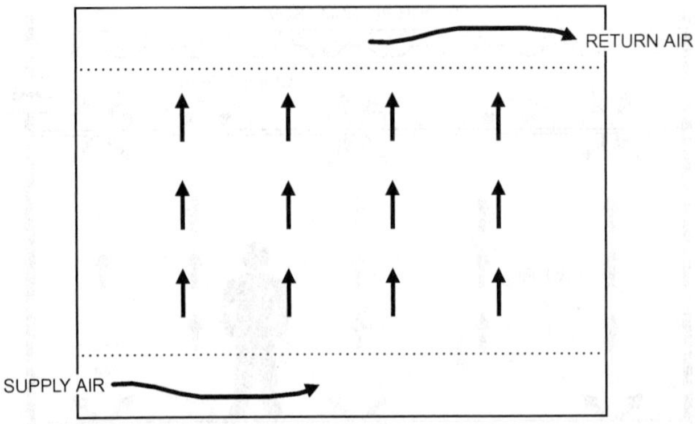

Fig. 3 Displacement Flow Within a Space

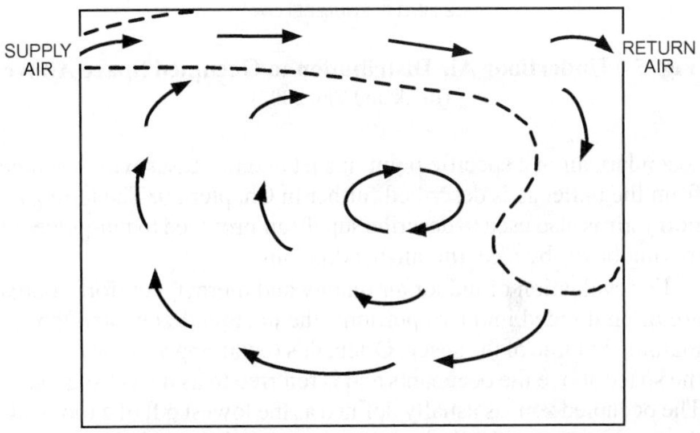

Fig. 4 Entrainment Flow Within a Space

Entrainment flow, shown in Figure 4, is also known as **conventional mixing**. Systems with ceiling-based supply air diffusers and return air grilles are common examples of air distribution systems that produce entrainment flow. Airborne pollutants are removed by dilution by the ventilation air that is delivered as all or part of the supply air. Entrainment flow with very poor mixing in the room has been called **short-circuiting flow** because much of the supply air leaves the room without mixing with room air. There is little evidence that properly designed, installed, and operated air distribution systems exhibit substantial short circuiting, although poorly designed, installed, or operated systems may short circuit (especially ceiling-based systems in heating mode) to a higher degree (Offermann and Int-Hout 1989).

Theoretical perfect mixing occurs when supply air is instantly and evenly distributed throughout a space. Perfect mixing is also known as **complete** or **uniform mixing**; the air may be called **well stirred** or **well mixed**. This theoretical performance is approached by entrainment flow systems that have good mixing and by displacement flow systems that allow too much mixing (Rock et al. 1995). The outdoor air requirements given in the minimum ventilation rate in breathing zone table of ASHRAE *Standard* 62.1 assume delivery of ventilation air with perfect mixing within spaces. For more detailed information on space air diffusion, see Chapter 20.

Underfloor air distribution (UFAD or **UAD)**, as shown in Figure 5, is a hybrid method of conditioning and ventilating spaces (Bauman and Daly 2003). Air is introduced through a floor plenum, with or without branch ductwork or terminal units, and delivered to a space by floor-mounted diffusers. These diffusers encourage air mixing near the floor to temper the supply air for thermal comfort. The combined air then moves vertically through the space, with reduced mixing, toward returns or exhausts placed in or near the ceiling. This vertical upward movement of the air is in the same direction as the thermal and contaminant plumes created by occupants and common equipment. The ventilating performance of UFAD systems is thus often between floor-to-ceiling displacement flow and uniform mixing.

Supply air that enters a space through a diffuser, grille, or nozzle is also known as **primary air**. An air **jet** is formed as this primary air leaves the supply air outlet. **Secondary air** is the room air entrained into the jet. **Total air** is the combination of primary and

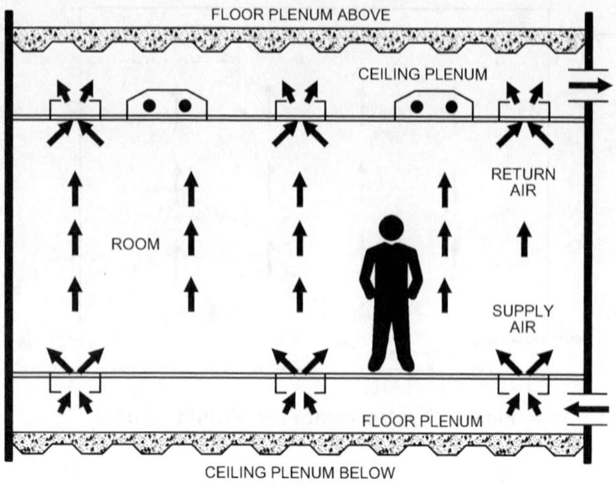

Fig. 5 Underfloor Air Distribution to Occupied Space Above
(Rock and Zhu 2002)

secondary air at a specific point in a jet and increases with distance from the outlet as is described further in Chapter 20. The term **primary air** is also used to describe supply air provided to fan-powered mixing boxes by a central air-handling unit.

For evaluation of indoor air quality and thermal comfort, rooms are often divided into two portions: the **occupied zone** and the remaining volume of the space. Often, this remaining volume is solely the space above the occupants and is referred to as the **ceiling zone**. The occupied zone is usually defined as the lowest 6 ft of a room, although layers near the floor and walls are sometimes deducted from it; when these deductions are made, the occupied zone is sometimes renamed the **breathing zone**. Ceiling and floor plenums are not normally included in the occupied or ceiling zones. **Thermal zones** are different from these room air zones, and are defined for HVAC subsystems and their controls.

Air Change Rate

The **air change** (or **exchange**) **rate** ***I*** compares airflow to the space's volume and is

$$I = Q/V \tag{2}$$

where

Q = volumetric flow rate of air into space, cfm
V = interior volume of space, ft^3

The air change rate has units of 1/time, usually h^{-1}. When the time unit is hours, the air change rate is also called **air changes per hour (ACH)**, with units of h^{-1}. The air change rate may be defined for several different situations. For example, the air change rate for an entire building or thermal zone served by an air-handling unit compares the amount of outdoor air brought into the building or zone to the total interior volume. This **nominal air change rate** I_N is

$$I_N = Q_{oa}/V \tag{3}$$

where Q_{oa} is the outdoor airflow rate including ventilation and infiltration. I_N describes the outdoor air ventilation rate entering a building or zone. It does not describe recirculation or the distribution of ventilation air to each space in a building or zone.

For a particular space, the **space air exchange rate** I_S compares the supply airflow rate Q_{sa} to the volume of that space:

$$I_S = Q_{sa}/V \tag{4}$$

For a particular space or zone, I_S includes recirculated as well as any outdoor air in the supply air, and is used frequently in evaluating supply air outlet performance and space air mixing.

Time Constants

Time constants τ, which have units of time (usually in hours or seconds), are also used to describe ventilation and infiltration. One time constant is the time required for one air change in a building, zone, or space if ideal displacement flow existed. It is the inverse of the air change rate:

$$\tau = 1/I = V/Q \tag{5}$$

The **nominal time constant** compares the interior volume of a building or zone to the volumetric outdoor airflow rate:

$$\tau_N = V/Q_{oa} \tag{6}$$

Like the nominal air change rate, τ_N does not describe recirculation of air in a building or zone, or characterize the distribution of the outdoor air to individual spaces in a building or zone.

The **space time constant** compares the interior volume of a particular space to the total supply airflow rate to that space. The space time constant is the inverse of the space air change rate:

$$\tau_S = V/Q_{sa} \tag{7}$$

The space time constant includes the effect of recirculated air that is part of the supply air as well as that of outdoor air introduced to the space through the supply air. If infiltration is significant in a space, then the infiltration flow rate should be included when determining both the space air change rate and the space time constant.

Averaging Time-Varying Ventilation Rates

When assessing time-varying ventilation in terms of controlling indoor air quality, the quantity of interest is often the temporal average rather than the peak. The concept of **effective ventilation** (Sherman and Wilson 1986; Yuill 1986, 1991) describes the proper ventilation rate averaging process. In this concept, the average (effective) rate is the steady-state rate that yields the same average contaminant concentration over the period of interest in the occupied space as does the actual sequence of time-varying discrete ventilation rates over the same period and in the same space. This effective rate is only equal to the simple arithmetic average rate when the discrete ventilation rates are constant over the period of interest and the contaminant concentration has reached its steady-state value. Simple arithmetic averaging of instantaneous ventilation rates or concentrations cannot generally be used to determine these averages because of the nonlinear response of indoor concentrations to ventilation rate variations.

An important constraint in the effective ventilation concept is that the contaminant source strength F must be constant over the period of interest or must be uncorrelated with the ventilation rate. These conditions are satisfied in many residential and commercial buildings because the emission rates of many contaminants that are controlled by whole-building ventilation systems vary slowly. Sherman and Wilson (1986) describe how to deal with pollutants that have stepped but otherwise constant emission rates. Pollutants such as carbon monoxide, radon, and formaldehyde, whose emission rates can be affected by ventilation, cannot be properly characterized with this concept and require more complex analyses. For constant-source-strength pollutants, the relationship between effective air change rate, effective ventilation rate, volumetric flow, source strength, average concentration, and time-averaged effective turnover time is given by

$$I_m = \frac{\bar{Q}}{V} = \frac{F}{V\bar{C}} = \frac{1}{\bar{\tau}_e} \tag{8}$$

The time-averaged effective turnover time $\bar{\tau}_e$ in Equation (8) represents the characteristic time for the concentration in the occupied space to approach steady state over the period of interest. It can be determined from a sequence of discrete, instantaneous ventilation air change rates I_i using the following (Sherman and Wilson 1986):

$$\bar{\tau}_e = \frac{1}{N}\sum_{i=1}^{N}\tau_{e,i} \quad (9)$$

$$\text{for } I_i > 0, \tau_{e,i} = \frac{1-\exp(-I_i\Delta t)}{I_i} + \tau_{e,i-1}\exp(-I_i\Delta t) \quad (10)$$

$$\text{for } I_i = 0, \tau_{e,i} = \Delta t + t_{e,i-1} \quad (11)$$

where

Δt = length of each discrete time period
$\bar{\tau}_e$ = time-averaged effective turnover time
$\tau_{e,i}$ = instantaneous turnover time in period i
$\tau_{e,i-1}$ = instantaneous turnover time in previous period

ASHRAE *Standard* 62.2 provides a set of factors to help calculate the annual effective air exchange rate.

Age of Air

The **age of air** θ_{age} (Sandberg 1981) is the length of time t that some quantity of outdoor air has been in a building, zone, or space. The "youngest" air is at the point where outdoor air enters the building by mechanical or natural ventilation, or through infiltration (Grieve 1989). The "oldest" air may be at some location in the building or in the exhaust air. When the characteristics of the air distribution system are varied, age of air is inversely correlated with quality of outdoor air delivery. Units are of time, usually in seconds or minutes, so it is not a true efficiency or effectiveness measure. The age of air concept, however, has gained wide acceptance in Europe.

The age of air can be evaluated for existing buildings using tracer gas methods. Using either the decay (step-down) or growth (step-up) tracer gas method and assuming perfect mixing, the zone average or **nominal age of air** $\theta_{age,N}$ can be determined by taking concentration measurements in the exhaust air. The **local age of air** $\theta_{age,L}$ is evaluated through tracer gas measurements at any desired point in a space, such as at a worker's desk. When time-dependent data of tracer gas concentration are available, the age of air can be calculated from

$$\theta_{age} = \int_{t=0}^{\infty}\frac{C_{in}-C}{C_{in}-C_o}\,dt \quad (12)$$

where C_{in} is the concentration of tracer gas being injected.

Because evaluation of the age of air requires integration to infinite time, an exponential tail is usually added to the known concentration data (Farrington et al. 1990).

Air Change Effectiveness

Ventilation effectiveness is a description of an air distribution system's ability to remove internally generated pollutants from a building, zone, or space. **Air change effectiveness** is a description of an air distribution system's ability to deliver ventilation air to a building, zone, or space. The HVAC design engineer usually does not have knowledge or control of actual pollutant sources within buildings, so the minimum prescribed ventilation rates of ASHRAE *Standard* 62.1 define outdoor air requirements for typical, expected building uses. For most projects, therefore, air change effectiveness is of more relevance to HVAC system design than ventilation effectiveness. Various definitions for air change effectiveness have been proposed. The specific measure that meets local code requirements must be determined, if any is needed at all.

Air change effectiveness measures ε_I are nondimensional gages of ventilation air delivery. One common definition of air change effectiveness is the ratio of a time constant to an age of air:

$$\varepsilon_I = \tau/\theta_{age} \quad (13)$$

The **nominal air change effectiveness** $\varepsilon_{I,N}$ shows the effectiveness of outdoor air delivery to the entire building, zone, or space:

$$\varepsilon_{I,N} = \tau_N/\theta_{age,N} \quad (14)$$

where the nominal time constant τ_N is usually calculated from measured airflow rates.

The **local air change effectiveness** $\varepsilon_{I,L}$ shows the effectiveness of outdoor air delivery to one specific point in a space:

$$\varepsilon_{I,L} = \tau_N/\theta_{age,L} \quad (15)$$

where τ_N is found either through airflow measurements or from tracer gas concentration data. An $\varepsilon_{I,L}$ value of 1.0 indicates that the air distribution system delivers air equivalent to that of a system with perfectly mixed air in the spaces. A value less than 1.0 shows less than perfect mixing with some degree of stagnation. A value of $\varepsilon_{I,L}$ greater than 1.0 suggests that a degree of plug or displacement flow is present at that point (Rock 1992).

An HVAC design engineer often assumes that a properly designed, installed, operated, and maintained air distribution system provides an air change effectiveness of about 1. However, the zone air distribution table of ASHRAE *Standard* 62.1 provides some estimates of effectiveness for operating in heating or cooling mode, and with various air distribution techniques. These values are then adjusted for commercial and institutional building design when the ventilation rate procedure (VRP) is used. If the IAQ procedure of *Standard* 62.1 is used, then actual pollutant sources and the air change effectiveness must be known for the successful design of HVAC systems that have fixed ventilation airflow rates.

ASHRAE *Standard* 129 describes a method for measuring air change effectiveness of mechanically vented spaces and buildings with limited air infiltration, exfiltration, and air leakage with surrounding indoor spaces.

2. TRACER GAS MEASUREMENTS

The only reliable way to determine an existing building's air change rate is to measure it. Several tracer gas measurement procedures exist (e.g., ASTM *Standard* E741 test method), all involving an inert or nonreactive gas used to label the indoor air (Charlesworth 1988; Dietz et al. 1986; Fisk et al. 1989; Fortmann et al. 1990; Harrje et al. 1981, 1990; Hunt 1980; Lagus 1989; Lagus and Persily 1985; Persily 1988; Persily and Axley 1990; Sherman 1989a, 1989b, 1990; Sherman et al. 1980). The tracer is released into the building in a specified manner, and the concentration of the tracer in the building is measured through time and related to the building's air change rate. Various tracer gases and associated concentration detection devices have been used. Desirable qualities of a tracer gas are detectability, nonreactivity, nontoxicity, neutral buoyancy, relatively low concentration in ambient air, and low cost (Hunt 1980).

All tracer gas measurement techniques are based on a mass balance of the tracer gas in the building. Assuming the outdoor concentration is zero and the indoor air is well mixed, this total balance takes the following form:

$$V\frac{dC}{dt} = F(t) - Q(t)C(t) \quad (16)$$

where

V = volume of space being tested, ft^3

$C(t)$ = tracer gas concentration at time t
dC/dt = time rate of change of concentration, min
$F(t)$ = tracer gas injection rate at time t, cfm
$Q(t)$ = airflow rate out of building at time t, cfm
t = time, min

In Equation (16), density differences between indoor and outdoor air are generally ignored for moderate climates; therefore, Q also refers to the airflow rate into the building. Although Q is often referred to as the infiltration rate, any measurement includes both mechanical and natural ventilation in addition to infiltration. The ratio of Q to the volume V being tested has units of 1/time, often converted to ACH, and is the air change rate I described previously in this chapter.

Equation (16) is based on the assumptions that (1) no unknown tracer gas sources exist, (2) airflow out of the building is the dominant means of removing the tracer gas from the space so the tracer gas does not react chemically in the space and/or is not adsorbed onto or absorbed by interior surfaces or air cleaners, and (3) the tracer gas concentration in the building can be represented by a single value (i.e., the tracer gas is uniformly mixed within the space). In such tracer gas experiments, box-type fans are often operated in rooms to enhance mixing.

Three different tracer gas procedures are used to measure air change rates: (1) decay or growth, (2) constant concentration, and (3) constant injection.

Decay or Growth

Decay. The simplest tracer gas measurement technique is the decay method, also known as the step-down method. A small amount of tracer gas is injected into the space and is allowed to mix with the interior air. After the injection, $F = 0$ and then the solution to Equation (16) is

$$C(t) = C_o e^{-It} \tag{17}$$

where C_o is the concentration of the tracer in the space at $t = 0$.

Equation (17) is generally used to solve for I by measuring the tracer gas concentration periodically during the decay and then fitting the data to the logarithmic form of Equation (17):

$$\ln C(t) = \ln C_o - It \tag{18}$$

Like all tracer gas techniques, the decay method has advantages and disadvantages. One advantage is that, because logarithms of concentration are taken, only relative concentrations are needed, which can simplify calibration of concentration-measuring equipment. Also, the tracer gas injection rate need not be measured, although it must be controlled so that the tracer gas concentrations are within the range of the concentration-measuring device. The concentration-measuring equipment can be located on site, or building samples can be collected in suitable containers (e.g., grab bags) and analyzed elsewhere.

The most serious problem with the decay technique is imperfect mixing of tracer gas with interior air, both at initial injection and during decay. Equations (16) and (17) assume that the tracer gas concentration within the building is uniform at any particular time. If the tracer is not well mixed, this assumption is not appropriate and the determination of I is subject to errors. It is difficult to estimate the magnitude of errors caused by poor mixing, and there has been little analysis of this problem. Sometimes a two-zone model is applied to a room, and a mixing coefficient selected, to estimate the effect of poor mixing [e.g., Rock (1992)].

Growth. The growth or step-up method is similar to the decay method except that the initial tracer gas concentration is low and the injected tracer gas is increased suddenly during the test.

Constant Concentration

In the constant concentration technique, the tracer gas injection rate is adjusted to maintain a constant concentration within the building. If the concentration is truly constant, then Equation (16) reduces to

$$Q(t) = F(t)/C \tag{19}$$

There is less experience with this technique than with the decay procedure, and an increasing number of applications for it exist (Bohac et al. 1985; Collet 1981; Fortmann et al. 1990; Kumar et al. 1979; Walker and Forest 1995; Walker and Wilson 1998; Wilson and Walker 1993).

Because tracer gas injection is continuous, no initial mixing period is required. Another advantage is that tracer gas injection into each zone of the building can be separately controlled; thus, the amount of outdoor air flowing into each zone can be determined. This procedure is best suited for longer-term continuous monitoring of fluctuating infiltration rates. One disadvantage is that it requires measurement of absolute tracer concentrations and injection rates. Also, imperfect mixing of the tracer and interior air causes a delay in the response of the concentration to changes in the injection rate.

Constant Injection

In the constant-injection procedure, the tracer is injected at a constant rate, and the solution to Equation (16) becomes

$$C(t) = (F/Q)(1 - e^{-It}) \tag{20}$$

After sufficient time, the transient term reduces to zero, the concentration attains equilibrium, and Equation (20) reduces to

$$Q = F/C \tag{21}$$

Equation (21) is valid only when air change rate I and airflow rate Q are constant; thus, this technique is only appropriate for systems at or near equilibrium. It is particularly useful in spaces with mechanical ventilation or with high air change rates. Constant injection requires measurement of absolute concentrations and injection rates.

Dietz et al. (1986) used a special case of the constant-injection technique, using permeation tubes as a tracer gas source. The tubes release the tracer at an ideally constant rate into the building being tested, and a sampling tube packed with an adsorbent collects the tracer from the interior air at a constant rate by diffusion. After a sampling period of one week or more, the sampler is removed and analyzed to determine the average tracer gas concentration in the building during the sampling period.

Solving Equation (16) for C and taking the time average gives

$$\langle C \rangle = \langle F/Q \rangle = F \langle 1/Q \rangle \tag{22}$$

where $\langle \ldots \rangle$ denotes time average. Note that the time average of dC/dt is assumed to equal zero.

Equation (22) shows that the average tracer concentration $\langle C \rangle$ and injection rate F can be used to calculate the average of the inverse airflow rate. The average of the inverse is less than the inverse of the actual average, with the magnitude of this difference depending on the distribution of airflow rates during the measurement period. Sherman and Wilson (1986) calculated these differences to be about 20% for one-month averaging periods. Differences greater than 30% have been measured when occupant airing of houses caused large changes in air change rate; errors from 5 to 30% were measured when the variation was caused by weather effects (Bohac et al. 1987). Longer averaging periods and large changes in air change rates during the measurement periods generally lead to larger differences between the average inverse change rate and the inverse of the actual average rate.

Multizone Air Change Measurement

Equation (16) assumes a single, well-mixed enclosure, and the techniques described are for single-zone measurements. Multizone measurement techniques address airflow between internal zones and between the exterior and individual internal zones (Fortmann et al. 1990; Harrje et al. 1985, 1990; Sherman and Dickerhoff 1989). These techniques are important when considering the transport of pollutants from one room of a building to another. A theoretical development is provided by Sinden (1978a). Multizone measurements typically use either multiple tracer gases for the different zones or the constant-concentration technique. A proper uncertainty analysis is essential in all multizone flow determination (Charlesworth 1988; D'Ottavio et al. 1988).

3. DRIVING MECHANISMS FOR VENTILATION AND INFILTRATION

Natural ventilation and infiltration are driven by pressure differences across the building envelope caused by wind and air density differences. Mechanical air-moving systems also induce pressure differences across the envelope through operation of appliances, such as combustion devices, leaky forced-air thermal distribution systems, and mechanical ventilation systems. The indoor/outdoor pressure difference at a location depends on the magnitude of these driving mechanisms as well as on the characteristics of the openings in the building envelope.

Stack Pressure

Stack pressure is the hydrostatic pressure caused by the weight of a column of air located inside or outside a building. It can also occur within a flow element, such as a duct or chimney that has vertical separation between its inlet and outlet. The hydrostatic pressure in the air depends on density and the height of interest above a reference point.

Air density is a function of local barometric pressure, temperature, and humidity ratio, as described in Chapter 1. As a result, standard conditions should not be used to calculate the density. For example, a building site at 5000 ft has air density that is about 20% less than if the building were at sea level. An air temperature increase from –20 to 70°F causes a similar air density difference. Combined, these elevation and temperature effects can reduce air density about 45%. Moisture effects on density are generally much less but can be significant if the change in elevation is great (e.g., in a natural draft cooling tower). Saturated air at 105°F has a density about 5% less than that of dry air at the same pressure.

Assuming the air temperature and humidity ratio are constant over the height of interest, the stack pressure decreases linearly as the distance above the reference point increases. For a single column of air, the stack pressure can be calculated as

$$p_s = p_r - 0.00598\rho g H \tag{23}$$

where

p_s = stack pressure, in. of water
p_r = stack pressure at reference height, in. of water
g = gravitational acceleration, 32.2 ft/s²
ρ = indoor or outdoor air density, lb_m/ft^3
H = height above reference plane, ft
0.00598 = unit conversion factor, in. of water·ft·s^2/lb_m

For tall buildings or when significant temperature stratification occurs indoors, Equation (23) should be modified to include the density gradient over the height of the building.

Temperature, and thus air density differences between indoors and outdoors cause stack pressure differences that drive airflows across the building envelope; the **stack effect** is this buoyancy phenomenon. Sherman (1991) showed that any single-zone building can be treated as an equivalent box from the point of view of stack effect; if there is air leakage, follow the power law as described in the section on Residential Air Leakage. The building is then characterized by an effective stack height and neutral pressure level (NPL) or leakage distribution, as described in the section on Neutral Pressure Level. Once calculated, these parameters can be used in physical, single-zone models to estimate infiltration.

Neglecting vertical density gradients, the stack pressure difference for a horizontal leak at any vertical location is

$$\Delta p_s = 0.00598(\rho_o - \rho_i)g(H_{NPL} - H)$$
$$= 0.00598\rho_o\left(\frac{T_i - T_o}{T_i}\right)g(H_{NPL} - H) \tag{24}$$

where

T_o = absolute outdoor temperature, °R
T_i = absolute indoor temperature, °R
ρ_o = outdoor air density, lb/ft³
ρ_i = indoor air density, lb/ft³
H_{NPL} = height of neutral pressure level above reference plane without any other driving forces, ft

Chastain and Colliver (1989) showed that, when there is stratification, the average of the vertical distribution of temperature differences is more appropriate to use in Equation (24) than the localized temperature difference near the opening of interest.

By convention, stack pressure differences are positive when the building is pressurized relative to outdoors, which causes flow out of the building. Therefore, absent other driving forces and assuming no stack effect within the flow elements themselves, when indoor air is warmer than outdoors, the base of the building is depressurized and the top is pressurized relative to outdoors; when indoor air is cooler than outdoors, the reverse is true. At some elevation in the building, with such conditions, the pressure indoors is equal to the outdoors: this height is the neutral pressure level.

Absent other driving forces, the location of the NPL is influenced by leakage distribution over the building exterior and by interior compartmentation. As a result, the NPL is not necessarily at the mid-height of the building; with effective horizontal barriers in tall buildings, it is also possible to have more than one NPL. NPL location and leakage distribution are described in the Combining Driving Forces and Neutral Pressure Level sections.

For a penetration through the building envelope for which (1) there is vertical separation between its inlet and outlet and (2) air inside the flow element is not at the indoor or outdoor temperature (e.g., in a chimney), more complex analyses than Equation (24) are required to determine the stack effect at any location on the building envelope.

Wind Pressure

When wind impinges on and flows around and over a building, it creates a distribution of static pressures on the building's exterior surfaces that depends on the wind direction, wind speed, air density, surface orientation, and surrounding conditions. Wind pressures are generally positive with respect to the static pressure in the undisturbed airstream on the windward side of a building and negative on the leeward sides and roof. However, these pressures depend highly on wind speed, angle, turbulence, the surroundings, and building shape. Static pressures over building surfaces are almost proportional to the velocity head of the undisturbed airstream. The wind pressure or velocity head is given by the Bernoulli equation, assuming no height change or pressure losses:

$$p_w = 0.0129 C_p \rho \frac{U^2}{2} \tag{25}$$

where

p_w = wind surface pressure relative to outdoor static pressure in undisturbed flow, in. of water

ρ = outdoor air density, lb_m/ft^3 (about 0.075 at or near sea level)
U = wind speed, mph
C_p = wind surface pressure coefficient, dimensionless
0.0129 = unit conversion factor, in. of water·$ft^3/lb_m \cdot mph^2$

C_p is a function of location on the building envelope and wind direction. Chapter 24 provides additional information on values of C_p.

Most pressure coefficient data are for winds approaching perpendicularly to upwind building surfaces. Unfortunately, for a real building, this fixed wind direction rarely occurs, and when the wind is not normal to the upwind wall, these pressure coefficients do not apply. Walker and Wilson (1994) developed a harmonic trigonometric function to interpolate between the surface average pressure coefficients on a wall that were measured with the wind normal to each of the four building surfaces. This function was developed for low-rise buildings three stories or less in height. For each wall of the building, C_p is given by

$$C_p(\phi) = 1/2\{[C_p(1) + C_p(2)](\cos^2\phi)^{1/4} + [C_p(1) - C_p(2)](\cos\phi)^{3/4} + [C_p(3) + C_p(4)](\sin^2\phi)^2 + [C_p(3) - C_p(4)]\sin\phi\} \quad (26)$$

where

$C_p(1)$ = pressure coefficient when wind is at 0°
$C_p(2)$ = pressure coefficient when wind is at 180°
$C_p(3)$ = pressure coefficient when wind is at 90°
$C_p(4)$ = pressure coefficient when wind is at 270°
ϕ = wind angle measured clockwise from the normal to wall 1

Because the cosine term in Equation (26) can be negative, its sign must be tracked. When cos(ϕ) is negative, subtract the value of the absolute of cos(ϕ) to the 3/4 power.

The measured data used to develop the harmonic function from Akins et al. (1979) and Wiren (1985) show that typical values for the pressure coefficients are $C_p(1) = 0.6$, $C_p(2) = -0.3$, and $C_p(3) = C_p(4) = -0.65$. Because of geometry effects on flow around a building, application of this interpolation function is limited to low-rise buildings of rectangular plan on flat, featureless sites, with the longest wall less than three times the length of the shortest wall. For less regular buildings or sites, simple correlations are inadequate and building-specific pressure coefficients are required; computational fluid dynamic models are often used. Chapter 24 discusses wind pressures for complex building shapes and for high-rise buildings in more detail.

The wind speed most commonly available for infiltration calculations is that measured at the local weather station, typically the nearest airport. This wind speed needs to be corrected for reductions caused by the difference between the height where the wind speed is measured and the height of the building, and reductions caused by shelter effects.

The reference wind speed used to determine pressure coefficients is usually the wind speed at the eave height for a low-rise building and the building height for a high-rise building. However, meteorological wind speed measurements are made at a different height, typically 33 ft for official weather stations, and at a different location than for the buildings of interest. The difference in terrain between the measurement station and the building under study must also be addressed. Chapter 24 shows how to calculate the effective wind speed U_H from the reference wind speed U_{met} using boundary layer theory and estimates of terrain effects.

In addition to the reduction in wind pressures caused by reduced wind speed, the effects of local shelter also act to reduce wind pressures. The shielding effects of trees, shrubbery, and other buildings within several building heights, horizontally, of a particular building produce large-scale turbulence eddies that not only reduce effective wind speed but also alter wind direction. Local geological features or gaps between neighboring large buildings can, at times, greatly increase wind velocity. Thus, meteorological wind speed data must be adjusted carefully when applied to specific buildings and their locations.

Infiltration rates measured by Wilson and Walker (1991) for a row of houses showed reductions in airflow rates of up to a factor of three when the wind changed direction from perpendicular to parallel to the row. They recommended estimating wind shelter for winds perpendicular to each side of the building and then using the interpolation function in Equation (27) to find the wind shelter for intermediate wind angles:

$$s = \frac{1}{2}\{[s(1) + s(2)]\cos^2\phi + [s(1) - s(2)]\cos\phi + [s(3) + s(4)]\sin^2\phi + [s(3) - s(4)]\sin\phi\} \quad (27)$$

where

s = shelter factor for the particular wind direction ϕ
$s(i)$ = shelter factor when wind is normal to wall i (i = 1 to 4, for four sides of a building)

Although this method gives a realistic variation of wind shelter effects with wind direction, estimates for numerical values of wind shelter factor s for each of the four cardinal directions must be provided. Table 8 in the section on Residential Calculation Examples lists typical shelter factors. The wind speed used in Equation (25) is then given by

$$U = sU_H \quad (28)$$

The magnitude of pressure differences found on the surfaces of buildings varies rapidly with time because of turbulent fluctuations in the wind (Etheridge and Nolan 1979; Grimsrud et al. 1979). However, using average wind pressures to calculate pressure differences is usually sufficient to calculate average infiltration values.

Mechanical Systems

Operation of mechanical equipment, such as supply or exhaust systems and vented combustion devices, affects pressure differences across the building envelope and thus air change rates. Interior static pressure adjusts such that the sum of all airflows through openings in the building envelope plus equipment-induced airflows balances to zero. To predict these changes in pressure differences and airflow rates caused by mechanical equipment, the location of each opening in the envelope and relationship between pressure difference and airflow rate for each opening must be known. The interaction between mechanical ventilation system operation and envelope airtightness has been discussed for low-rise buildings (Nylund 1980) and for office buildings (Persily and Grot 1985a; Tamura and Wilson 1966, 1967a).

Air exhausted from a building by a whole-building exhaust system must be balanced by increasing airflow into the building through other openings or the air-handling systems. As pressures vary, air leakage at some locations changes from outflow to inflow. When using makeup air and no dedicated exhaust, the situation is reversed and envelope inflows may become outflows. Thus, the effects of a mechanical system on a building must be considered. Depressurization caused by an improperly designed exhaust system can increase the rate of radon entry into a building and can interfere with proper operation of combustion device venting or other exhaust systems. Pollutant entry can be increased from garages and other attached storage spaces. Depressurization can also force moist outdoor air through the building envelope; for example, during the cooling season in hot, humid climates, moisture may condense in the building envelope and cause rust, rot, or mold. A similar phenomenon, but in reverse, can occur during the heating, and potentially humidifying, season in cold climates if the building is pressurized. Active pressure control is often recommended, as is proper use of moisture retarders, drainage, and drying of in situ building materials.

The interaction between mechanical systems and the building envelope also pertains to systems serving zones of buildings. Performance of zone-specific exhaust or pressurization systems is affected by leakage in partitions between zones as well as through exterior walls.

Mechanical systems can also create infiltration-driving forces in single-zone buildings. Specifically, some single-family houses with central forced-air duct systems have many distributed supply registers, yet only one central return grille. When insufficiently undercut internal doors are closed in these houses, large positive indoor-to-outdoor pressure differentials are created for rooms with only supply registers, whereas the room or hallway with the return grille tends to depressurize relative to the outdoors. This is caused by the resistance of the internal door undercuts, often partially blocked by carpeting, to flow from the supply register to the return; the magnitudes of the indoor/outdoor pressure differentials created average 0.012 to 0.024 in. of water (Modera et al. 1991). Balanced airflow systems with ducted air return and distributed grilles or adequately sized transfer grilles (where still allowed by fire code) reduce this effect significantly.

Building envelope airtightness and interzonal airflow resistance can also affect performance of mechanical systems. The actual airflow rate delivered by these systems, particularly ventilation systems, depends on the pressure differences they work against. This effect is the same as the interaction of a fan with its associated ductwork, which is discussed in Chapter 21 of this volume and Chapter 21 of the 2016 *ASHRAE Handbook—HVAC Systems and Equipment*. The building envelope and its leakage should be considered part of the ductwork in determining the pressure drop of the system.

Duct leakage can cause similar problems. Supply leaks to the outdoors tend to depressurize the building; return leaks from the outdoors tend to pressurize it. Keeping these ducts within the conditioned buildings, and sealing all ducts well with durable materials and high-quality construction methods, significantly reduces this problem.

Combining Driving Forces

Pressure differences caused by wind, stack effect, and mechanical systems are considered in combination by adding them together and then determining the resulting airflow rate through each building envelope. The airflows must be determined in this manner, as opposed to adding the airflow rates caused by the separate driving forces, because the airflow rate through each opening is not linearly related to pressure difference.

For uniform indoor air temperatures, the total pressure difference across each leak can be written in terms of a reference wind parameter P_U and stack effect parameter P_T common to all leaks:

$$P_U = \rho_o \frac{U_H^2}{2} \tag{29}$$

$$P_T = g\rho_o[(T_i - T_o)/T_i] \tag{30}$$

where T is absolute air temperature in °R.

The pressure difference across each leak, with positive pressures for flow into the building, is then given by

$$\Delta p = 0.0129 s^2 C_p P_U + H P_T + \Delta p_I \tag{31}$$

where Δp_I is the pressure that acts to balance inflows and outflows, including mechanical system flows. Equation (31) can then be applied to every leak for the building with appropriate values of C_p, s, and H. Thus, each leak is defined by its pressure coefficient, shelter, and height. Where indoor pressures are not uniform, more complex and often numerical analyses are required.

Neutral Pressure Level

The neutral pressure level (NPL) varies and is that height or heights in the building envelope where, at that particular instant, there is no indoor-to-outdoor pressure difference. Internal partitions, stairwells, elevator shafts, utility ducts, chimneys, vents, operable windows, and mechanical supply and exhaust systems complicate the prediction of NPL location. An opening with a large area relative to the total building leakage causes the NPL to shift toward the opening. In particular, chimneys and openings at or above roof height raise the NPL in small buildings. Exhaust systems increase the height of the NPL; outdoor air supply systems lower it.

Figure 6 qualitatively shows the addition of driving forces for a building with uniform openings above and below mid-height and without significant internal resistance to airflow. The slopes of the pressure lines are a function of the densities of the indoor and outdoor air. In Figure 6A, with indoor air warmer than outdoor and pressure differences caused solely by thermal forces, the NPL is at mid-height, with inflow through lower openings and outflow through higher openings. For the low air velocities typical in and around buildings, the direction of flow is always from the higher to the lower-pressure region.

Figure 6B presents qualitative uniform pressure differences caused by wind alone, with opposing effects on the windward and leeward sides. When temperature difference and wind effects both exist, the pressures caused by each are added together to determine the total pressure difference across the building envelope. In Figure 6B, there is no NPL because no locations on the building envelope have zero pressure difference. Figure 6C shows the combination, where the wind force of Figure 6B has just balanced the thermal force of Figure 6A, causing no pressure difference at the top windward or bottom leeward side.

The relative importance of wind and stack pressures in a building depends on building height, internal resistance to vertical airflow, location and flow resistance characteristics of envelope openings, local terrain, and the immediate shielding of the building. The taller the building and the smaller its internal resistances to airflow, the stronger the stack effect. The stack effect can be reduced by effectively sealing the building internally between floors, typically by gasketing elevator and stairway doors, and sealing pipe, duct, and electrical penetrations; these measures, when done by code-approved means, also typically reduce undesired smoke migration during fire events. Gasketing interior doors, especially those from exterior spaces or to elevator lobbies, in tall buildings can also help restrict air leakage paths.

The effect of mechanical ventilation on envelope pressure differences is more complex and depends on both the direction of ventilation flow (exhaust or supply) and the differences in these ventilation flows among the zones of the building. If mechanically supplied outdoor air is provided uniformly to each story, the change in the exterior wall pressure difference pattern is uniform. With a nonuniform supply of outdoor air (e.g., to one story only), the extent of pressurization varies from story to story and depends on internal airflow resistance. Pressurizing all levels uniformly has little effect on pressure differences across floors and vertical shaft enclosures, but pressurizing individual stories increases the pressure drop across these internal separations. Pressurizing the ground level is often used in tall buildings in winter to reduce negative air pressures across entries; vestibules and revolving doors are also used to limit air leakage. Vestibules may also be used for elevator lobbies and stair towers to reduce air and smoke movement vertically through tall buildings.

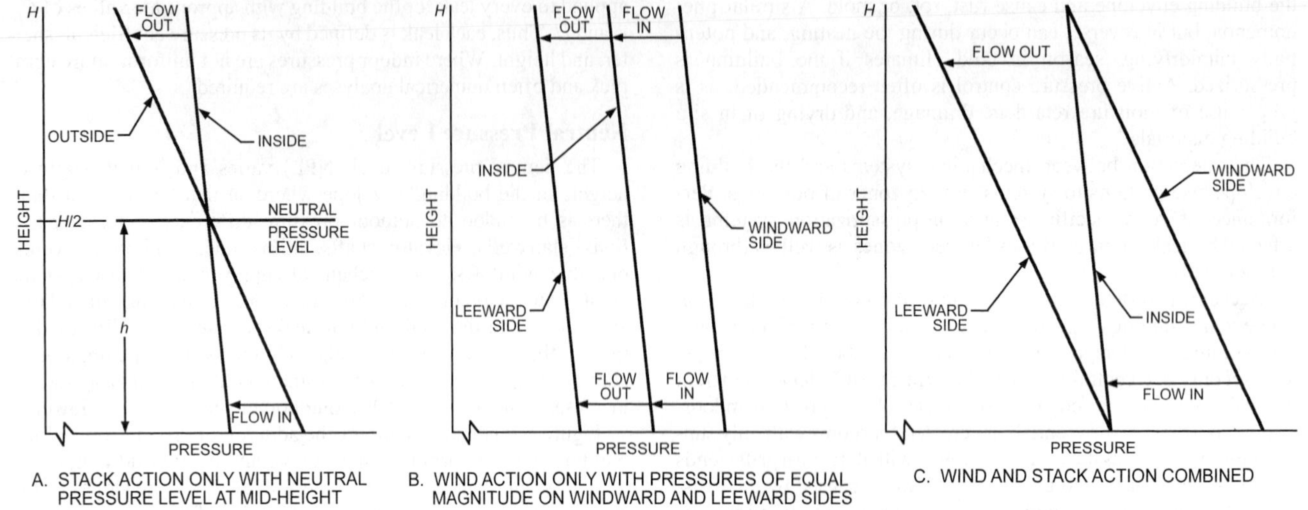

Fig. 6 Distribution of Indoor and Outdoor Pressures over Height of Building

Available data on the NPL in various kinds of buildings are limited. In tall buildings studied by Tamura and Wilson (1966, 1967b), the NPL varied from 0.3 to 0.7 of total building height. For houses, especially those with chimneys, the NPL is usually above mid-height. Operating a combustion heat source that vents to the outdoors raises the NPL further, sometimes above the ceiling (Shaw and Brown 1982).

Thermal Draft Coefficient

Compartmentation of a building also affects the NPL location. Equation (24) provides a maximum stack pressure difference, given no internal airflow resistance. The sum of pressure differences across the exterior wall at the bottom and top of the building, as calculated by these equations, equals the total theoretical draft for the building. The sum of actual top and bottom pressure differences, divided by the total theoretical draft pressure difference, equals the **thermal draft coefficient**. The value of the thermal draft coefficient depends on the airflow resistance of exterior walls relative to the airflow resistance between floors. For a building without internal partitions, the total theoretical draft is achieved across the exterior walls (Figure 7A), and the thermal draft coefficient equals 1. In a building with airtight separations between each floor, each story acts independently, its own stack effect being unaffected by that of any other floor (Figure 7B). The theoretical draft is minimized in this case, and each story has its own NPL.

Real multistory buildings are neither open inside, nor airtight between stories. Vertical air passages, stairwells, elevators, and other service shafts allow airflow between floors. Figure 7C represents a heated building with uniform openings in the exterior wall, through each floor, and into the vertical shaft at each story. Between floors, the slope of the line representing the indoor pressure is the same as that shown in Figure 7A, and the discontinuity at each floor (Figure 7B) represents the pressure difference across it. Some of the pressure difference maintains flow through openings in the floors and vertical shafts. As a result, the pressure difference across the exterior wall at any level is less than it would be with no internal flow resistance.

Maintaining airtightness between floors and from floors to vertical shafts is a way to control indoor/outdoor pressure differences because of the stack effect and, therefore, infiltration and exfiltration. Good separation is also conducive to proper operation of mechanical ventilation and smoke management systems. However, care is needed to avoid creating pressure differences that could prevent

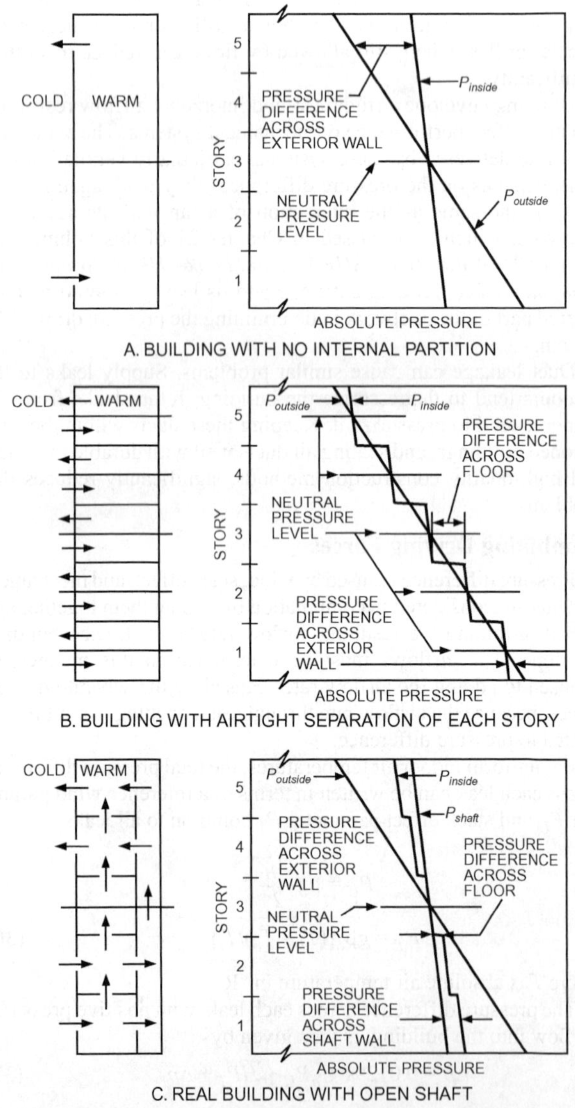

Fig. 7 Compartmentation Effect in Buildings

egress doors from opening in an emergency. Tamura and Wilson (1967a) showed that when vertical shaft leakage is at least two times envelope leakage, the thermal draft coefficient is almost one and the effect of compartmentation is negligible. Measurements of pressure differences in three tall office buildings by Tamura and Wilson (1967b) indicated that the thermal draft coefficient ranged from 0.8 to 0.9 with ventilation systems off. Modern internal sealing techniques should result in much less vertical leakage.

4. INDOOR AIR QUALITY

Outdoor air requirements for creating and maintaining acceptable indoor air quality (IAQ) have long been debated, and different rationales have produced radically different ventilation standards (Grimsrud and Teichman 1989; Janssen 1989; Klauss et al. 1970; Yaglou et al. 1936; Yaglou and Witheridge 1937). Historically, the major considerations have included the rate of outdoor air admission required to control airborne moisture, carbon dioxide (CO_2), odors, and tobacco smoke generated by occupants. These considerations have led to prescriptions of minimum rates of outdoor air supply per occupant or by unit floor area, or both. More recently, a major concern has been maintaining acceptable indoor concentrations of various additional pollutants that are not generated primarily by occupants. Engineering experience and field studies indicate that an outdoor air supply of about 20 cfm per person is very likely to provide acceptable perceived indoor air quality in office spaces, whereas lower rates may lead to increased sick building syndrome symptoms (Apte et al. 2000; Mendell 1993; Seppanen et al. 1999; Sundell et al. 2011). Information on contaminants can be found in Chapter 11, and odors are addressed in Chapter 12.

Indoor pollutant concentrations depend on the strength of pollutant sources and the total rate of pollutant removal. Pollutant sources include outdoor air; indoor sources such as occupants, furnishings, and appliances; lack of cleanliness as well as use of cleaning and other products; soil adjacent to the building; and building materials themselves, especially when new. Pollutant removal processes include dilution with cleaner outdoor air, local exhaust ventilation, deposition on surfaces, chemical reactions, and air-cleaning processes. If (1) general building ventilation is the only significant pollutant removal process, (2) indoor air is thoroughly mixed, and (3) pollutant source strength and ventilation rate have been stable for a sufficient period, then the steady-state indoor concentration of a specific pollutant is given by

$$C_i = C_o + 10^6 S/Q_{oa} \tag{32}$$

where

C_i = steady-state indoor concentration, ppm
C_o = outdoor concentration, ppm
S = total pollutant source strength, cfm
Q_{oa} = ventilation rate, cfm

Variation in pollutant source strengths, rather than variation in ventilation rate, is considered the largest cause of building-to-building variation in concentrations of pollutants that are not generated by occupants. Turk et al. (1989) found that a lack of correlation between average indoor respirable particle concentrations and whole-building outdoor ventilation rate indicated that source strength, high outdoor concentrations, building volume, and removal processes are important. Because pollutant source strengths are highly variable, maintaining minimum ventilation rates does not ensure acceptable indoor air quality in all situations. The lack of health-based concentration standards for many indoor air pollutants, primarily because of the lack of health data, makes the specification of minimum ventilation rates difficult.

In cases of high contaminant source strengths, such as with indoor sanding, spray painting, or smoking, impractically high rates of dilution ventilation are required to control contaminant levels, and other methods of control are more effective. Removal or reduction of contaminant sources is the most effective means of control. Controlling a localized source by means of local exhaust, such as paint booths, laboratory fume hoods, range hoods, or bathroom exhaust fans, as well as filtration and absorption, may also be effective [e.g., Rock (2006)].

Some particles can be removed with various types of air filters. Gaseous contaminants with higher molecular weight can often be controlled with activated carbon or alumina pellets impregnated with a substance such as potassium permanganate. Chapter 29 of the 2016 *ASHRAE Handbook—HVAC Systems and Equipment* has information on air cleaning.

Protection from Extraordinary Events

The design, operation and maintenance of a building's ventilation system and envelope, as well as other factors, can significantly affect the building's potential vulnerability to extraordinary threats, which range from intentional releases of chemical or biological agents inside or outside a building, to releases of chemicals in industrial or transportation accidents, to natural disasters. ASHRAE (2003) addresses several key steps to manage risk from extraordinary incidents, including

- Evaluate the risk to a facility of an extraordinary incident
- Assess the building's vulnerability
- Determine the degree of acceptable vulnerability
- Consider protective measures or options in relation to new, renovated, and existing buildings

Persily (2004) details how ventilation affects buildings' vulnerability to airborne chemical and biological releases, as well as some strategies for using ventilation, particularly involving airtightness and pressurizing the building interior to protect against outdoor releases, to increase the level of building protection against such incidents. Persily et al. (2007) evaluate retrofit options for protecting buildings from airborne threats; approaches considered include enhanced particle filtration, sorbent-based gaseous air cleaning, ventilation system recommissioning, building envelope airtightening, building pressurization, relocation of outdoor air intakes, shelter-in-place (SIP), isolation of vulnerable spaces such as lobbies, and system shutdown and purge cycles. The filtration and air cleaning options have the advantage of always being operational as long as the systems are properly designed, installed, and maintained. However, the lack of standard test methods is a critical issue in application of some air-cleaning technologies. Building envelope air sealing and pressurization can be quite effective in protecting against outdoor releases as long as effective filtration against the contaminant of concern is also in place. Protection provided by operational changes such as system shutdown and purging depends heavily on timing; if timing is inappropriate, occupant exposure may be increased. Isolating vulnerable zones and other system-related modifications depend on building layout and system design, and careful implementation is necessary for effectiveness under the range of conditions that exist in buildings. Finally, many retrofits can also increase energy efficiency and improve indoor air quality, which should be included in a life-cycle cost comparison of different options to the degree possible. Chapter 59 of the 2015 *ASHRAE Handbook—HVAC Applications* addresses extraordinary events further.

5. THERMAL LOADS

Outdoor air introduced into a building constitutes a large part of the total space-conditioning load, which is one reason to limit air change rates to the minimum required. Air exchange typically represents 20 to 50% of a modern, ventilation-code-compliant building's thermal load in nontemperate climates. The effect on heating loads tends to be much larger than on cooling loads (McDowell et al. 2003). Chapters 17 and 18 address thermal loads in more detail.

Air exchange increases a building's thermal load in several ways. First, incoming air must be heated or cooled from the outdoor air temperature to the indoor or supply air temperature. The rate of energy consumption by this sensible heating or cooling is

$$q_s = 60Q\rho c_p \Delta T \quad (33)$$

where

q_s = sensible heat load, Btu/h
Q = airflow rate, cfm
ρ = air density, lb_m/ft^3 (about 0.075 at or near sea level)
c_p = specific heat of air, $Btu/lb_m \cdot °F$ (about 0.24)
ΔT = temperature difference between indoors and outdoors, °F

and at or near sea-level air density, with an adjustment for typical room air humidity, this equation is commonly presented for design use as

$$q_s = 1.1Q\Delta t \quad (34)$$

Equations (33) and (34) are known as the **sensible heat equation**. HVAC designers typically assume sea-level air pressure for locations with altitudes of 2000 ft or lower. A method to adjust for elevation is provided in Chapter 18.

Air exchange also modifies the moisture content of the air in a building. The rate of energy consumption associated with these latent loads, to add or remove water from the air and neglecting the energy associated with any condensate, is

$$q_l = 60Q\rho\Delta W(1061 + 0.444T) \quad (35)$$

where

q_l = latent heat load, Btu/h
ΔW = humidity ratio difference between indoors and outdoors, lb_m water/lb_m dry air
T = average of indoor and outdoor temperatures, °F

Equation (35) is known as the **latent heat equation**. When at or near sea level, and for common comfort air temperatures, the right-hand side of Equation (35) is approximately $4840Q\Delta W$.

Example 1. A makeup air unit (MAU) is to condition 5000 cfm of outdoor air in the winter for a building in Atlanta, Georgia. If the air is to be delivered directly to the occupied spaces at 75°F and 30% rh, how much sensible and latent heat must be added to this ventilation air at winter design conditions?

Solution: From the weather data tables provided on the CD included with this volume, Atlanta is at an elevation of about 1000 ft. Because this is below the rule-of-thumb cutoff of 2000 ft for assuming sea-level conditions, air density is assumed to be 0.075 lb_m/ft^3. Also from the Atlanta data table, the winter 99% design dry-bulb (db) temperature is 26.4°F, but a mean coincident wet bulb is not provided. However, for humidification design, a dew-point temperature of 9.1°F is given along with its 32.2°F mean coincident dry bulb (MCDB). Using these data, a 1°F dew point is assumed as the 99% mean coincident dew point.

From ASHRAE's sea-level psychrometric chart and the winter design conditions, the desired humidity ratio W of the 75°F, 30% rh makeup air is about 0.0056 lb_mw/lb_mda. For the very dry outdoor air, with a dew point of 1°F, a problem occurs: the standard sea-level psychrometric chart does not extend below 32°F. Designers often assume that air below this temperature has $W = 0$, and this assumption gives conservative results. However, both high- and low-temperature psychrometric charts are available from ASHRAE, as is a table of moist air properties at standard conditions in Chapter 1. From this table, saturated air at 1°F, which is also its dew point, has a humidity ratio of 0.0008298 lb_mw/lb_mda. With 5000 cfm of outdoor air to be conditioned, and using the sensible and latent heat equations for sea level, the energy needed to condition this outdoor air is

$$q_s = 1.1Q\Delta T = 1.1 \times 5000 \text{ cfm}(75 - 26.4°\text{F}) = 267{,}300 \text{ Btu/h}$$

and

$$q_l = 4840Q\Delta W = 4840 \times 5000 \text{ cfm}(0.0056 - 0.0008298 \text{ lb}_m\text{w/lb}_m\text{da}) = 115{,}439 \text{ Btu/h} \approx 115{,}000 \text{ Btu/h}$$

Thus, the MAU's heating coil and humidifier, neglecting fan heat, need to be sized to provide at least a net 267,300 Btu/h of sensible heat, and 115,000 Btu/h of latent heat. Humidification can be provided by cold water, warm water, or steam, so a more precise psychrometric analysis is needed to size the heating coil correctly after the humidification method is selected and it is decided whether the humidifier will be placed before or after the heating coil.

As Example 1 shows, ventilation loads are substantial. They are often 50% or more of the total space conditioning loads in modern, well-insulated, high-occupancy commercial buildings in less temperate climates. When cooling outdoor air, substantial moisture usually must be removed from the ventilation air; reheat or regenerative heat recovery may be required in all but dry climates.

Effect on Envelope Insulation

Air exchange also can affect a building's thermal load by altering performance of the envelope insulation system. Airflow through insulation can decrease the thermal load through heat exchange between infiltrating or exfiltrating air and the insulation. Conversely, air moving in and out of the insulation from the outdoors can increase the thermal load. Experimental and numerical studies demonstrate that significant thermal coupling can occur between air leakage and insulation layers, thereby modifying the heat transmission in building envelopes. In particular, research (Bankvall 1987; Berlad et al. 1978; Lecompte 1987; Wolf 1966) shows that convective airflow through air-permeable insulation in an envelope assembly may degrade its effective thermal resistance. This R-value degradation occurs when outdoor air moves through and/or around the insulation within the wall cavity and returns to the outdoors without reaching the conditioned space. A literature review by Powell et al. (1989) summarized the findings about air movement effects on the effective thermal resistance of porous insulation under various conditions. The effect of such airflow on insulation system performance is difficult to quantify, but should be considered. Airflow within the insulation system can also decrease the system's performance because of moisture condensation in and on the insulation.

Even if air flows only through cracks instead of through the insulation, the actual heating/cooling load from the combined effect of conduction and airflow heat transfer can be lower than the heating/cooling load calculated by Equation (33). This reduction in total heating/cooling load is a consequence of the thermal coupling between conduction and convection heat transfer and is called **infiltration heat recovery (IHR)**. Using a computer simulation, Kohonen et al. (1987) found that the conduction/infiltration thermal interaction reduced total heating load by 15%. Several experimental studies (e.g., Claridge and Bhattacharyya 1990; Claridge et al. 1988; Liu and Claridge 1992a, 1992b, 1992c, 1995; Timusk et al. 1992), using a test cell under both steady-state and dynamic conditions, found that the actual energy attributed to air infiltration can be 20 to 80% of the values given by Equation (35). Judkoff et al. (1997) measured heat recovery in a mobile home under steady-state conditions, and found that up to 40% heat recovery occurs during exfiltration through the envelope. Buchanan and Sherman (2000) performed two- and three-dimensional computational fluid dynamics (CFD) simulations to study the fundamental physics of the IHR process and developed a simple macro-scale mathematical model based on the steady-state one-dimensional convection-diffusion equation to predict a heat recovery factor. Their results show that the traditional method may overpredict the infiltration energy load. Using physical experiments, ASHRAE research project RP-1169 (Ackerman et al. 2006) showed that thermal resistances are affected by infiltration and exfiltration, but, on a net basis, the IHR effect can be neglected.

Infiltration Degree-Days

Heating and cooling degree-days (HDDs and CDDs) are a simple way to characterize the severity of a particular climate. Heating and cooling degree-day values are based on sensible temperature data, but infiltration loads are both sensible and latent. **Infiltration degree days (IDDs)** more fully describe a climate and can be used to estimate heat loss or gain from infiltration in residences (Sherman 1986). Total infiltration degree-days is the sum of the heating and cooling infiltration degree-days and is calculated from hour-by-hour weather data and base conditions using weather weighted by infiltration rate. The selection of base conditions is an important part of the calculation of the IDDs. ASHRAE *Standard* 119 lists IDDs for many locations with a particular set of base conditions.

6. NATURAL VENTILATION

Natural ventilation is the flow of outdoor air caused by wind and thermal pressures through intentional openings in a building's shell. Under some circumstances, it can effectively control temperature, contaminants, and possibly airborne moisture in mild climates, but it is not considered practical in hot and humid climates in the summer or in cold climates during the winter. Temperature control by natural ventilation is often the only means of providing some cooling when mechanical air conditioning is not available. The arrangement, location, and control of ventilation openings should combine the driving forces of wind and temperature to achieve a desired ventilation rate and good distribution of ventilation air through the building. However, intentional openings cannot always guarantee adequate temperature and humidity control or indoor air quality because of the dependence on natural wind and stack effects to drive the flow (Wilson and Walker 1992). Using night ventilation and the building's thermal mass effect may be effective for reducing conventional cooling energy consumption in some buildings and climates if moisture condensation can be controlled. Axley (2001a) and the Chartered Institute of Building Services Engineers (CIBSE 2005) reviewed natural ventilation in commercial buildings, including potential advantages and problems, natural ventilation components and system designs, and recommended design and analysis approaches.

Natural Ventilation Openings

Natural ventilation openings include (1) operable windows, clerestories, doors, and skylights; (2) roof ventilators; (3) stacks; and (4) specially designed inlet or outlet openings such as OA louvers and EA grilles, ventilation penthouses or shafts, chimneys, windcatchers, and roof monitors.

Operable windows transmit light, and provide ventilation when opened. They may open by sliding vertically or horizontally; by tilting on horizontal pivots at or near the center; or by swinging on pivots at the top, bottom, or side. The type of pivoting used is important for weather protection and affects airflow rate. Exterior doors, often with insect screens, can also provide a path for natural ventilation; as with operable windows, security concerns must be considered.

Roof ventilators provide a weather-resistant air outlet. Capacity is determined by the ventilator's location on the roof; the resistance to airflow of the ventilator and its ductwork; the ventilator's ability to use kinetic wind energy to induce flow by centrifugal or ejector action; and the height of the draft.

Natural-draft or gravity roof ventilators can be stationary, pivoting, oscillating, or rotating. Selection criteria include appearance, ruggedness, corrosion resistance, stormproofing features, dampers and operating mechanisms, noise, cost, and maintenance. Natural ventilators can be supplemented with power-driven supply or exhaust fans; their motors need only be energized when the natural exhaust capacity is too low. Gravity ventilator dampers can be manual or controlled by thermostat or wind velocity.

A natural-draft roof ventilator should be positioned so that it receives full, unrestricted wind. Turbulence created by surrounding obstructions, including higher adjacent buildings, impairs a ventilator's ejector action. Inlets can be conical or bell-mouthed to increase their flow coefficients. The opening area at any inlet should be increased if screens, grilles, or other structural members cause flow resistance. Building air inlets, most effectively installed at the lowest levels, should be larger than the combined throat areas of all roof ventilators.

Stacks or **vertical flues** should be located where wind can act on them from any direction. Without wind, stack effect alone removes some air from the rooms with inlets. Much practical experience with natural ventilation from before the adoption of modern air-conditioning appears in publications by ASHVE (a predecessor society to ASHRAE).

Ceiling Heights

In buildings that use natural ventilation, floor-to-ceiling heights are often increased well beyond the normal 8 to 10 ft. Higher ceilings, as seen in buildings constructed before air conditioning was available, allow warm air and contaminants to rise above the occupied portions of rooms. Air is then exhausted from the ceiling zones, and outdoor air is introduced near the floors; a degree of floor-to-ceiling displacement airflow is thus desirable when using natural ventilation during the cooling season.

Required Flow for Indoor Temperature Control

The ventilation airflow rate required to remove a given amount of heat from a building can be calculated from Equations (33) and (35) if the quantity of heat to be removed and the indoor/outdoor temperature and humidity ratio differences are known.

Airflow Through Large Intentional Openings

The relationship describing the airflow through a large intentional opening is based on the Bernoulli equation with steady, incompressible flow. The general form that includes stack, wind, and mechanical ventilation pressures across the opening is

$$Q = 776 C_D A \sqrt{2\Delta p/\rho} \qquad (36)$$

where

Q = airflow rate, cfm
C_D = discharge coefficient for opening, dimensionless
A = cross-sectional area of opening, ft^2
ρ = air density, lb$_m$/ft^3
Δp = pressure difference across opening, in. of water
776 = unit conversion factor

The discharge coefficient C_D is a dimensionless number that depends on the geometry of the opening and the Reynolds number of the flow.

Flow Caused by Wind Only

Aspects of wind that affect the ventilation rate include average speed, prevailing direction, seasonal and daily variation in speed and direction, terrain, and local obstructions such as nearby buildings, hills, trees, and shrubbery. Liddament (1988) reviewed the relevance of wind pressure as a driving mechanism. A multiflow path simulation model was developed and used to illustrate the effects of wind on air change rate.

Average wind speeds may be lower in summer than in winter; directional frequency is also a function of season. Natural ventilation systems are often designed for wind speeds of one-half the seasonal average. Equation (37) shows the rate of air forced through ventilation inlet openings by wind or determines the proper size of openings to produce given airflow rates:

$$Q = 88.0 C_v A U \quad (37)$$

where

Q = airflow rate, cfm
C_v = effectiveness of openings (C_v is assumed to be 0.5 to 0.6 for perpendicular winds and 0.25 to 0.35 for diagonal winds)
A = free area of inlet openings, ft²
U = wind speed, mph
88.0 = unit conversion factor

Air intakes should be placed in exterior high-pressure regions, and air reliefs should be placed in exterior low-pressure regions, but because of wind variations, these static locations will, at times, not be optimal. Other considerations include flow control when wind speed is high, and security. Air intakes should face directly into the prevailing wind. If they are not advantageously placed, flow will be less than that predicted by Equation (37); if intakes are unusually well placed, flow will be slightly more. Desirable air relief locations are (1) on the leeward side of the building directly opposite the intake; (2) on the roof, in the low-pressure area caused by flow separation; (3) on a side perpendicular to the windward face, where low-pressure areas occur; (4) in a dormer on the leeward side; (5) in roof ventilators; or (6) by stacks. Chapter 24 gives a general description of the wind pressure distribution on a building, but transient computational modeling will likely be required.

Flow Caused by Thermal Forces Only

If building internal resistance is not significant, flow caused by stack effect can be expressed by

$$Q = 60 C_D A \sqrt{2g \Delta H_{NPL}(T_i - T_o)/T_i} \quad (38)$$

where

Q = airflow rate, cfm
C_D = discharge coefficient for opening
ΔH_{NPL} = height from midpoint of lower opening to NPL, ft
T_i = absolute indoor temperature, °R
T_o = absolute outdoor temperature, °R

Equation (38) applies when $T_i > T_o$. If $T_i < T_o$, replace T_i in the denominator with T_o, and replace $(T_i - T_o)$ in the numerator with $(T_o - T_i)$. If there is thermal stratification, use an average temperature for T_i. If the building has more than one opening for natural ventilation's airflow, the relief and intake areas are considered equal. The discharge coefficient C_D accounts for all viscous effects such as surface drag and interfacial mixing.

Estimating ΔH_{NPL} is difficult for naturally ventilated buildings. If one window or door represents a large fraction (approximately 90%) of the total opening area in the envelope, then the NPL is at the mid-height of that aperture, and ΔH_{NPL} equals one-half the height of the aperture. For this condition, flow through the opening is bidirectional (i.e., air from the warmer side flows through the top of the opening, and air from the colder side flows through the bottom). Interfacial mixing occurs across the counterflow interface, and the orifice coefficient can be calculated by (Kiel and Wilson 1986):

$$C_D = 0.40 + 0.0025|T_i - T_o| \quad (39)$$

If enough other openings are available, airflow through the opening will be unidirectional, and mixing cannot occur. A discharge coefficient of $C_D = 0.65$ should then be used. Additional information on stack-driven airflows for natural ventilation can be found in Foster and Down (1987).

The greatest flow per unit area of openings is obtained when the intake and relief areas are equal; Equations (38) and (39) are based on this equality. Increasing the relief area over intake area (or vice versa) increases airflow but not in proportion to the added area.

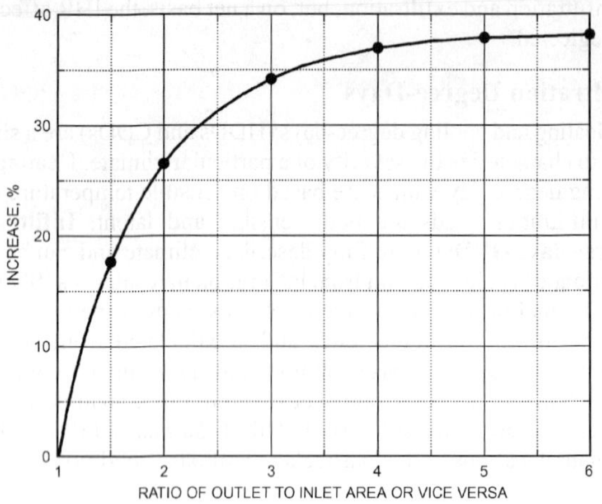

Fig. 8 Increase in Airflow by Increasing Area of One Opening

When openings are unequal, use the smaller area in Equation (38) and add the increase as determined from Figure 8.

Natural Ventilation Guidelines

Several general guidelines should be observed in designing for natural ventilation. Some of these may conflict with other climate-responsive strategies such as using orientation and shading devices to minimize solar gain, with building codes that encourage compartmentalization to restrict fire and smoke movement, or with other design considerations.

System selection

- In hot, humid climates, use mechanical cooling. If mechanical cooling is not available, air velocities should be maximized in the occupied zones of rooms.
- In hot, arid climates, consider evaporative cooling. Airflow throughout the building should be maximized for structural cooling, particularly at night when the outdoor air temperature is low.

Building and surroundings characteristics

- Topography, landscaping, and surrounding buildings should be used to redirect airflow and give maximum exposure to breezes. Vegetation can funnel breezes and avoid wind dams, which reduce the driving pressure differential around the building. Site objects should not obstruct air intakes' openings.
- The building should be shaped to expose maximum shell openings to breezes.
- Architectural elements such as wing walls, parapets, and overhangs should be used to promote airflow into the building interior.
- The long façade of the building and the majority of door and window openings should be oriented with respect to prevailing summer breezes. If there is no prevailing direction, openings should be sufficient to provide ventilation regardless of wind direction.

Opening locations

- Windows should be located in opposing pressure zones. Two openings on opposite sides of a space increase ventilation flow. Openings on perpendicular sides of the building force air to change direction, providing ventilation to a greater area. The benefits of the window arrangement depend on the air relief location relative to the direction of the intake's airstream.
- If a room has only one exterior wall, better airflow is achieved with two widely spaced windows.
- If openings are at the same level and near the ceiling, much of the flow may bypass the occupied portion of a room and be less effective in removing contaminants from there.

- Vertical distance between openings is required to take advantage of stack effect; the greater the vertical distance, the greater the ventilation rate.
- Openings near the NPL are least effective for thermally induced natural ventilation. If the building has only one large opening, the NPL tends to move to that level, which reduces pressure across the opening.

Opening characteristics

- Greatest airflow per unit area of total opening is obtained by having openings of nearly equal areas. An inlet window smaller than the outlet creates higher inlet velocities. An outlet smaller than the inlet creates lower but more uniform airspeeds through the room.
- Openings with areas much larger than calculated are sometimes desirable when anticipating increased occupancy or very hot weather.
- In one room, horizontally separated windows are generally better than vertically separated windows. They produce more airflow over a wider range of wind directions and are most beneficial in locations where prevailing wind patterns shift.
- Window openings should be accessible to and operable by occupants, unless fully automated. For secondary fire egress, operable windows may be required.
- Intake and exhaust openings should not be obstructed by draperies, furniture, or nearby indoor partitions, for example. Partitions can be placed to split and redirect airflow but should not restrict flow between the building's inlets and outlets. Vertical airshafts or open staircases, where allowable by fire code, can be used to increase and take advantage of stack effects. Enclosed staircases intended for evacuation or safe haven during a fire must not be used for ventilation.

Methods and tools have been developed in recent years to move the art of designing natural ventilation systems beyond the application of simple rules of thumb to engineered design (Axley et al. 2002; CIBSE 2005; Emmerich et al. 2012).

Hybrid Ventilation

Successful application of purely natural ventilation systems for cooling may be very limited in hot or humid climates, such as in much of the United States, by thermal comfort issues and the need for reliability. However, hybrid (or mixed-mode) ventilation systems or operational strategies offer the possibility of saving energy in a greater number of buildings and climates by combining natural ventilation systems with mechanical equipment (Emmerich 2006). The **air-side economizer** is one form of hybrid ventilation control scheme, and enjoys wide use in commercial, industrial, and institutional buildings in appropriate climates. The report of the International Energy Agency's (IEA) Annex 35 describes the principles of hybrid ventilation technologies, control strategies, design and analysis methods, and case studies (Heiselberg 2002). Integrated multizone airflow and thermal modeling is recommended when designing natural and hybrid ventilation systems (Axley 2001a; Dols et al. 2014; Li and Heiselberg 2003).

7. RESIDENTIAL AIR LEAKAGE

Most infiltration in U.S. low-rise residential buildings is dominated by unintentional envelope leakage. However, new construction tends toward tighter building envelopes; where mechanical or natural ventilation is not provided, it is possible for a residence to be too "tight," especially if indoor sources of pollutants are not adequately controlled.

Envelope Leakage Measurement

A building's envelope leakage can be measured with **pressurization testing,** commonly called a **blower-door test**. A fan pressurization test is relatively quick and inexpensive, and it characterizes building envelope airtightness independent of weather conditions; some jurisdictions now mandate that buildings be tested and rated. In this procedure, a large, variable-flow fan or blower is mounted in a door or window and induces a large, roughly uniform pressure difference across the building shell [ASTM *Standards* E779 and E1827; Canadian General Standards Board (CGSB) *Standard* 149.10; ISO *Standard* 9972]. The airflow required to maintain this pressure difference is then measured. The leakier the building is, the more airflow is necessary to induce a specific indoor/outdoor pressure difference. The airflow rate is generally measured at a series of pressure differences ranging from about 0.04 to 0.30 in. of water. Depressurization tests are also used.

The results of a pressurization test, therefore, consist of several combinations of pressure difference and airflow rate data. An example of typical data is shown in Figure 9. These data points characterize the air leakage of a building and are generally converted to a single value that is reported as the building's airtightness. There are several different measures of airtightness, most of which involve fitting the data to a curve describing the relationship between the airflow Q through an opening in the building envelope and the pressure difference Δp across it. This relationship is called the **leakage function** of the opening. The form of the leakage function depends on the geometry of the opening. Background theoretical material relevant to leakage functions may be found in Chastain et al. (1987), Etheridge (1977), Hopkins and Hansford (1974), Kronvall (1980), and Walker et al. (1997).

Openings in a building envelope are usually not uniform in geometry, and wind varies, so generally flow never becomes fully developed. Each opening in the building envelope, however, is often described by Equation (40), commonly called the **power law equation:**

$$Q = c(\Delta p)^n \tag{40}$$

where

Q = airflow through opening, cfm
c = flow coefficient, cfm/(in. of water)^n
n = pressure exponent, dimensionless

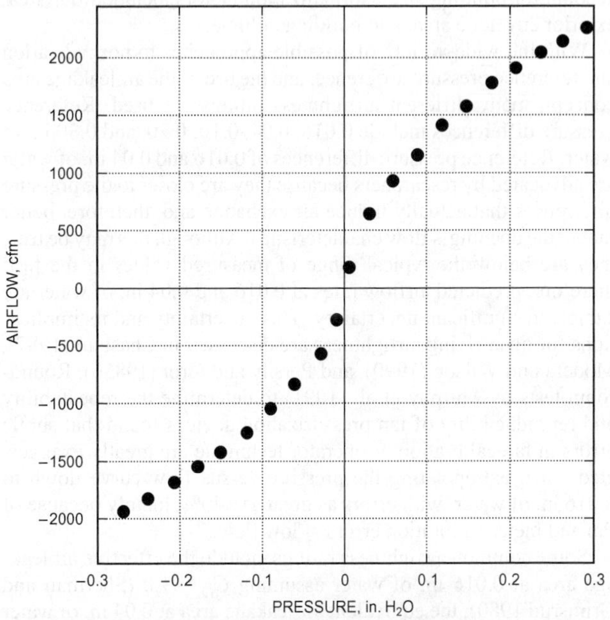

Fig. 9 Airflow Rate Versus Pressure Difference Data from Whole-House Pressurization Test

Sherman (1992a) showed how the power law can be developed analytically by looking at developing laminar flow in short pipes. Equation (40) only approximates the relationship between Q and Δp. Measurements of single cracks (Honma 1975; Kreith and Eisenstadt 1957) show that n can vary if Δp changes over a wide range. Additional investigation of pressure and flow data for simple cracks by Chastain et al. (1987) indicated the importance of adequately characterizing the three-dimensional geometry of openings and the entrance and exit effects. Walker et al. (1997) showed that, for the arrays of cracks in a building envelope over the range of pressures acting during infiltration, n is constant. A typical value for n is about 0.65. Values for c and n can be determined for a building by using fan pressurization testing.

Airtightness Ratings

In some cases, the predicted airflow rate is converted to an **equivalent** or **effective air leakage area** as follows:

$$A_L = 0.186 Q_r \frac{\sqrt{\rho/2\Delta p_r}}{C_D} \tag{41}$$

where

A_L = equivalent or effective air leakage area, in²
Q_r = predicted airflow rate at Δp_r (from curve fit to pressurization test data), cfm
ρ = air density, lb_m/ft^3
Δp_r = reference pressure difference, in. of water
C_D = discharge coefficient
0.186 = unit conversion factor

All openings in the building shell are combined into an overall opening area and discharge coefficient for the building when the equivalent or effective air leakage area is calculated. Some users of the leakage area approach set $C_D = 1$. Others set $C_D \approx 0.6$, which is the discharge coefficient for a sharp-edged orifice. The air leakage area of a building is, therefore, the area of an orifice with an assumed value of C_D that would produce the same amount of leakage as the building envelope at the reference pressure.

An airtightness rating, whether based on an air leakage area or a predicted airflow rate, is generally normalized by some factor to account for building size. Normalization factors include floor area, exterior envelope area, and building volume.

With the wide variety of possible approaches to normalization and reference pressure difference, and the use of the air leakage area concept, many different airtightness ratings are used. Reference pressure differences include 0.016, 0.04, 0.10, 0.20, and 0.30 in. of water. Reference pressure differences of 0.016 and 0.04 in. of water are advocated by researchers because they are closer to the pressure differences that actually induce air exchange and, therefore, better model the opening's flow characteristics. Although this may be true, they are below the typical range of measured values in the test; therefore, predicted airflow rates at 0.016 and 0.04 in. of water are subject to significant uncertainty. This uncertainty and its implications for quantifying airtightness are discussed in Chastain (1987), Modera and Wilson (1990), and Persily and Grot (1985b). Round-robin tests by Murphy et al. (1991) to determine the repeatability and reproducibility of fan pressurization devices found that subtle errors in fan calibration or operator technique are greatly exaggerated when extrapolating the pressure versus flow curve down to 0.016 in. of water, with errors as great as ±40%, mainly because of fan and meter calibration errors at low flow.

Some common airtightness ratings include the effective air leakage area at 0.016 in. of water assuming $C_D = 1.0$ (Sherman and Grimsrud 1980); the equivalent air leakage area at 0.04 in. of water assuming $C_D = 0.611$ (CGSB *Standard* 149.10); and the airflow rate at 0.20 in. of water, divided by the building volume to give units of air changes per hour (Blomsterberg and Harrje 1979).

Conversion Between Ratings

Air leakage areas at one reference pressure difference can be converted to air leakage areas at another reference pressure difference by

$$A_{r,2} = A_{r,1}\left(\frac{C_{D,1}}{C_{D,2}}\right)\left(\frac{\Delta p_{r,2}}{\Delta p_{r,1}}\right)^{n-0.5} \tag{42}$$

where

$A_{r,1}$ = air leakage area at reference pressure difference $\Delta p_{r,1}$, in²
$A_{r,2}$ = air leakage area at reference pressure difference $\Delta p_{r,2}$, in²
$C_{D,1}$ = discharge coefficient used to calculate $A_{r,1}$
$C_{D,2}$ = discharge coefficient used to calculate $A_{r,2}$
n = pressure exponent from Equation (40)

Air leakage area at one reference pressure difference can be converted to airflow rate at some other reference pressure difference by

$$Q_{r,2} = 5.39 C_{D,1} A_{r,2}\sqrt{\frac{2}{\rho}}(\Delta p_{r,1})^{0.5-n}(\Delta p_{r,2})^n \tag{43}$$

where

$Q_{r,2}$ = airflow rate at reference pressure difference $\Delta p_{r,2}$, cfm
5.39 = unit conversion factor

Flow coefficient c in Equation (40) may be converted to air leakage area by

$$A_L = \frac{c}{5.39 C_D}\sqrt{\frac{\rho}{2}}\,\Delta p_r^{(n-0.5)} \tag{44}$$

Finally, air leakage area may be converted to flow coefficient c in Equation (40) with

$$c = 5.39 C_D A_L \sqrt{\frac{2}{\rho}}(\Delta p_r)^{0.5-n} \tag{45}$$

Equations (42) to (45) require assumption of a value for n, unless n is reported with the measurement results. When whole-building pressurization test data are fitted to Equation (40), the value of n generally is between 0.6 and 0.7. Therefore, using a value of n in this range is often reasonable.

Building Air Leakage Data

Fan pressurization measures a building's leakage behavior that ideally varies little with time and weather conditions. In reality, unless wind and temperature differences during the measurement period are sufficiently mild, pressure differences induced by weather during the blower door test cause measurement errors. Modera and Wilson (1990) and Persily (1982) studied the effects of wind speed on pressurization test results. Several experimental studies also showed variations of about 20 to 40% over a year in the measured airtightness in the homes studied (Kim and Shaw 1986; Persily 1982; Warren and Webb 1986).

Figure 10 summarizes envelope leakage measured in North American housing (Sherman and Dickerhoff 1998) and from several European and Canadian sources (AIVC 1994). This figure shows the large range of measured envelope tightness but also shows typical and extreme values in the housing stock.

ASHRAE *Standard* 62.2 establishes air leakage performance levels for residential buildings. These levels are in terms of effective annual average infiltration rate Q_{inf}, which is based on normalized leakage area NL:

$$\text{NL} = 0.1\left(\frac{\text{ELA}}{A_{floor}}\right)\left(\frac{H}{H_r}\right)^{0.4} \tag{46}$$

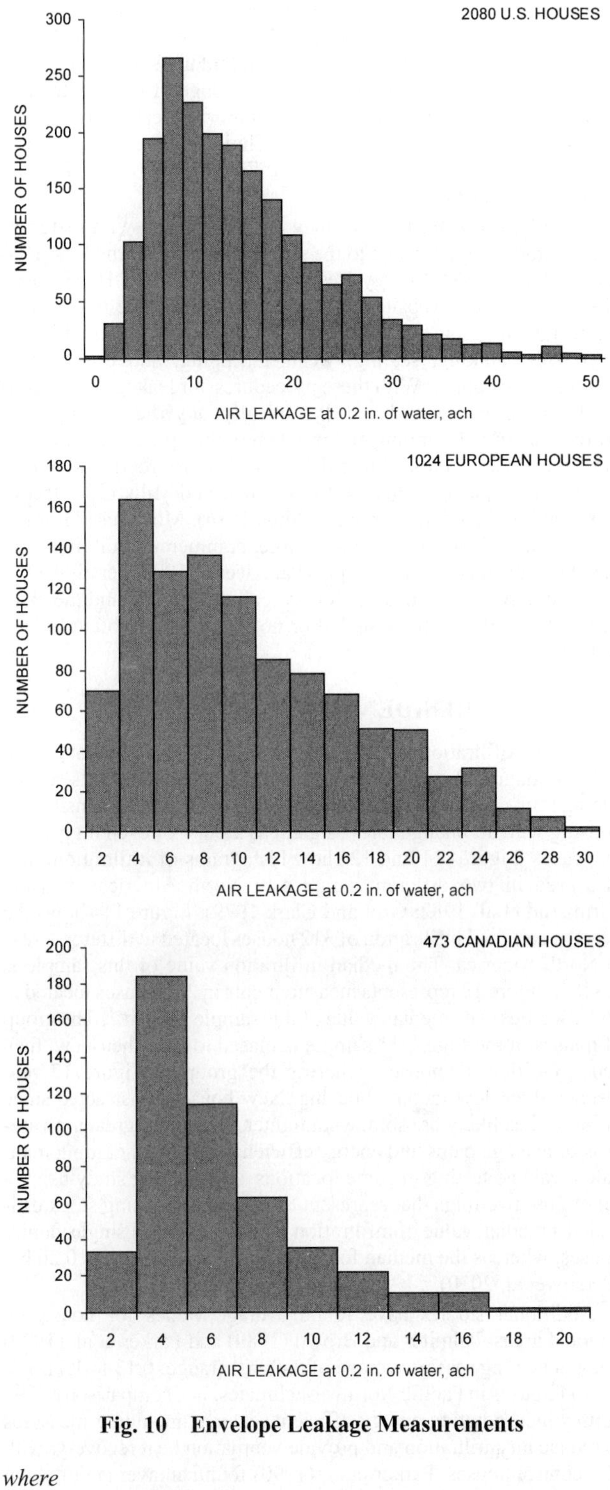

Fig. 10 Envelope Leakage Measurements

where

NL = normalized leakage
H_r = reference height, 8.2 ft
H = vertical distance from lowest above-grade floor to highest ceiling, ft
ELA = effective leakage area, ft^2, using 0.0006 psi reference pressure

$$\text{ELA} = (L_{press} - L_{depress})/2$$

where

L_{press} = leakage area from pressurization, ft^2
$L_{depress}$ = leakage area from depressurization, ft^2

Air Leakage of Building Components

The fan pressurization procedure discussed in the section on Envelope Leakage Measurement allows whole-building air leakage to be measured. The location and size of individual openings in building envelopes are extremely important because they influence the air infiltration rate of a building as well as the envelope's heat and moisture transfer characteristics. Additional test procedures for pressure-testing individual building components such as windows, walls, and doors are discussed in ASTM *Standards* E283 and E783 for laboratory and field tests, respectively.

Leakage Distribution

Dickerhoff et al. (1982) and Harrje and Born (1982) studied air leakage of individual building components and systems. The following points summarize the percentages of whole-building air leakage area that they found associated with various components and systems. Values in parentheses include the range determined for each component and the mean of the range.

Walls (18 to 50%; 35%). Both interior and exterior walls contribute to the leakage of the structure. Leakage can occur between the sill plate and the floor or foundation; through cracks below the bottom of the gypsum wallboard, around and through electrical boxes, and through plumbing penetrations; and into the attic at the top plates of walls. Holes drilled through the top plates into the attic for passage of wiring are often unsealed.

Ceiling Details (3 to 30%; 18%). Leakage across the top ceiling of the heated space is particularly insidious because it reduces the effectiveness of insulation on the attic floor and contributes to infiltration heat loss. Ceiling leakage also reduces the effectiveness of ceiling insulation in buildings without attics. Recessed lighting, plumbing, and other penetrations leading to the attic are some particular areas of concern, as are intentional openings such as access hatches or for whole-house fans.

Forced-Air Heating and/or Cooling Systems (3 to 28%; 18%). The location of the heating or cooling equipment, air handler, or ductwork in conditioned or unconditioned spaces; the venting arrangement of a fuel-burning device; and the existence and location of a combustion air supply all affect air leakage. Modera et al. (1991) and Robison and Lambert (1989), among others, found that the variability of leakage in ducts passing through unconditioned spaces is high, the coefficient of variation being about 50%. Field studies also showed that in situ repairs can eliminate one-quarter to two-thirds of the observed leakage (Cummings and Tooley 1989; Cummings et al. 1990; Jump et al. 1996; Robison and Lambert 1989). The 18% contribution of ducts to total leakage significantly underestimates their effect because, during system operation, pressure differentials across duct leaks are approximately ten times higher than typical pressure differences across envelope leaks (Modera 1989; Modera et al. 1991) and result in large (factors of two to three), changes in ventilation rate (Cummings et al. 1990; Walker 1999; Walker et al. 1999).

Windows and Doors (6 to 22%; 15%). More variation in window leakage is seen among window types (e.g., casement versus double-hung) than among new windows of the same type from different manufacturers (Weidt et al. 1979). Windows that seal by compressing the weather strip (casements, awnings) often show significantly lower leakage than windows with sliding seals. Leakage around the frames of windows also can be significant if not properly sealed, typically with controlled-expansion foam, during their installation. The door between a residence and an attached garage, or an enclosed hallway in multiunit housing, also needs gasketing to reduce air leakage as well as smoke and other pollutants' movement.

Fireplaces (0 to 30%; 12%). When a fireplace is not in use, poorly fitting dampers allow indoor air to escape. Glass doors may not seal the fireplace structure more tightly than a closed damper does. Chimney caps or fireplace plugs (with signs that warn they are in place) effectively reduce leakage through a cold fireplace but may not be allowed by fire code. The gap between a metal fireplace insert and the surrounding wall, tiles, or brick is often another leakage path if not properly sealed.

Exhaust Vents from Conditioned Spaces (2 to 12%; 5%). Exhaust ducts going from conditioned spaces to the outdoors frequently have either no dampers or dampers that do not close properly. The gap between the duct and the wall or roof penetration often needs sealing, as well.

Diffusion Through Walls and Ceilings (<1%). Compared to infiltration through holes and other openings in the structure, diffusion through well-constructed walls and ceilings is not an important flow mechanism. At 0.02 in. of water, the permeability of building materials produces an air change rate of less than 0.01 ach by wall diffusion in a typical house. Proper installation of an air-retarding membrane can help minimize this air leakage path.

Component Leakage Areas. Individual building component leakage areas vary widely from house to house. Typical variability for an individual component is about a factor of 10, depending on the component's construction and installation. Testing should establish the installed leakage of a component in critical applications such as energy-efficient manufactured housing.

Multifamily Building Leakage

Leakage distribution is particularly important in multifamily apartment buildings. These buildings often cannot be treated as single zones because of the internal resistance between apartments. Moreover, leakage between apartments varies widely, from very small for well-constructed buildings with air/moisture retarders and well-sealed wall and floor penetrations between units, to as high as 60% of the total apartment leakage in older, tall apartment buildings of masonry construction (Diamond et al. 1986; Modera et al. 1991). RDH (2013) reviewed the current state of airtightness in multifamily buildings, including testing requirements and techniques, performance targets, and current airtightness levels.

Controlling Air Leakage

New Buildings. It is much easier and more cost-effective to build a tight building than to tighten an existing building. Elmroth and Levin (1983), Eyre and Jennings (1983), Marbek Resource Consultants (1984), and Nelson et al. (1985) provide information and construction details on airtight building design for houses. The economic paybacks for basic "weatherization" improvements are often the most attractive of all energy conservation measures in buildings where no actions have been taken previously.

A continuous **air infiltration retarder**, formerly known as an air barrier, can be an effective way to reduce air leakage through walls, around window and door frames, and at joints between major building elements. Take particular care to ensure its continuity at all wall, floor, and ceiling joints; at window and door frames; and at all penetrations of the retarder such as electrical boxes, plumbing connections, and utility service penetrations. Joints in the **air/vapor retarder** must be lapped and sealed. Plastic vapor retarders installed in the ceiling should be tightly sealed to the vapor retarder in the outer walls and should be continuous over the interior walls. A seal at the top of the interior walls reduces leakage into the attic; the plate on top of the studs generally gives a poor seal. In cold climates, the air infiltration retarder can be installed either on the inside of the wall framing, in which case it usually functions as a vapor retarder as well, or on the outside of the wall framing, in which case it should have a permeance rating high enough to allow diffusion of water vapor from the wall. For a discussion of moisture transfer in building envelopes, see Chapters 25 and 26.

Existing Buildings. Air leakage paths must first be located before the envelope of an existing building can be tightened. As discussed earlier, air leakage into and out of buildings is caused by not only windows and doors but also a wide range of unexpected and unobvious construction defects. Many important leakage routes can be very difficult to find. A variety of techniques developed to locate leakage paths are described in ASTM *Standard* E1186 and Charlesworth (1988).

Once leakages are located, they can be repaired with materials and techniques appropriate to the size and location of the leak. Diamond et al. (1982), Energy Resource Center (1982), Harrje et al. (1979), and many websites and online videos include information on airtightening or "weatherization" in existing residential buildings with caulking, sealing, weatherstripping, and use of door sweeps, for example. With these procedures, air leakage of residential buildings can be reduced dramatically: anywhere from 5% to more than 50%, depending on the extent of the tightening effort and the experience of those doing the work (Blomsterberg and Harrje 1979; Giesbrecht and Proskiw 1986; Harrje and Mills 1980; Jacobson et al. 1986; Verschoor and Collins 1986). Much less information is available for airtightening large, commercial buildings, but the same general principles apply (Parekh et al. 1991; Persily 1991); the joint between corrugated floor or ceiling decking and the exterior walls is often poorly sealed or not at all, and is often hidden from easy view.

8. RESIDENTIAL VENTILATION

Typical infiltration rates in housing in North America vary by an order of magnitude, from tightly constructed housing with seasonal average air change rates as low as 0.1 h^{-1} to loosely constructed housing with air change rates as great as 2.0 h^{-1} or even higher in a few cases. Figures 11 and 12 show histograms of infiltration rates measured in two different samples of North American housing (Grimsrud et al. 1982; Grot and Clark 1979). Figure 11 shows the average seasonal infiltration of 312 houses located in different areas in North America. The median infiltration value of this sample is 0.5 h^{-1}. Figure 12 represents measurements in 266 houses located in 16 U.S. cities. The median value of this sample is 0.9 h^{-1}. The group of houses in the Figure 11 sample is biased toward then-new, then "energy-efficient" houses, whereas the group in Figure 12 represents older, low-income housing. New houses constructed since these studies likely are somewhat tighter because of greater awareness of leakage paths and energy efficiency efforts, including mandated leakage testing in some locations. A modeling study using a set of 209 dwellings that represent 80% of U.S. housing stock estimated a median value of infiltration of 0.44 h^{-1} for all single-family houses, whereas the median for those built since 1990 was 0.26 h^{-1} (Persily et al. 2010).

Additional studies have found average values for houses in regional areas. Palmiter and Brown (1989) and Parker et al. (1990) found a heating season average of 0.40 h^{-1} (range: 0.13 to 1.11 h^{-1}) for 134 houses in Pacific Northwest climates. In a comparison of 292 houses incorporating energy-efficient features, including measures to reduce air infiltration and provide ventilation heat recovery, with 331 control houses, Parker et al. (1990) found an average of about 0.25 h^{-1} (range: 0.02 to 1.63 h^{-1}) for the energy-efficient houses versus 0.49 h^{-1} (range: 0.05 to 1.63 h^{-1}) for the control group. Ek et al. (1990) found an average of 0.5 h^{-1} (range: 0.26 to 1.09 h^{-1}) for 93 double-wide manufactured homes in the Pacific Northwest. Canadian housing stock has been characterized by Riley (1990) and Yuill and Comeau (1989). Although these studies do not represent random samples of North American housing, they indicate the distribution of infiltration rates expected in a group of buildings.

The influence of occupants on infiltration has not been measured directly and varies widely. These influences are, for example, operation of doors, windows, and small exhaust fans. Desrochers and Scott (1985) estimated that they add an average of 0.10 to 0.15 h^{-1} to the unoccupied values. Kvisgaard and Collet (1990) found that, in 16 Danish dwellings, occupants on average provided 63% of the total air change rate.

Ventilation air for houses in the United States has traditionally been provided with the assumption occupants will use windows and exhaust fans when needed, and that the building envelope is leaky enough so that infiltration will suffice. Possible difficulties with this approach include occupant error, low infiltration when natural forces (temperature difference and wind) are weak; unnecessary energy consumption when these forces are strong; drafts in cold climates; lack of control of ventilation rates to meet changing needs; poor humidity control; potential for interstitial condensation from exfiltration in cold climates or infiltration in hot humid climates; and lack of opportunity to recover energy used to condition ventilation air. The solution to these concerns is to have a tight building envelope and a properly designed and operated mechanical ventilation system with automatic control.

ASHRAE *Standard* 62.2 and the National Building Code of Canada (NRCC 2010) encourage tighter envelope construction. Hamlin (1991) found a 30% increase in airtightness of tract-built Canadian houses between 1982 and 1989. Also, 82% of newer houses had natural air change rates below 0.3 h^{-1} in March. Yuill (1991) derived a

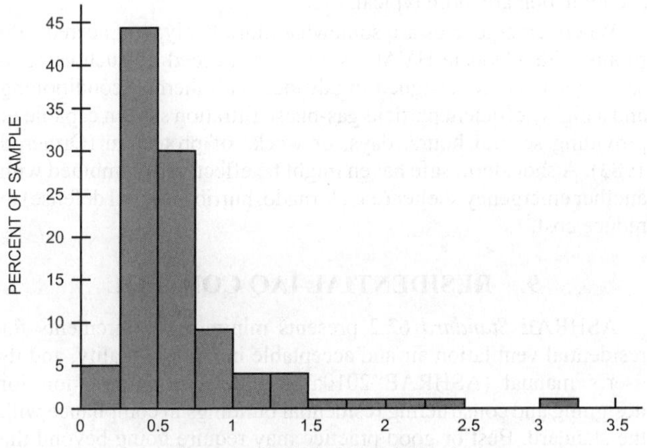

Fig. 11 Histogram of Infiltration Values for Then-New Construction

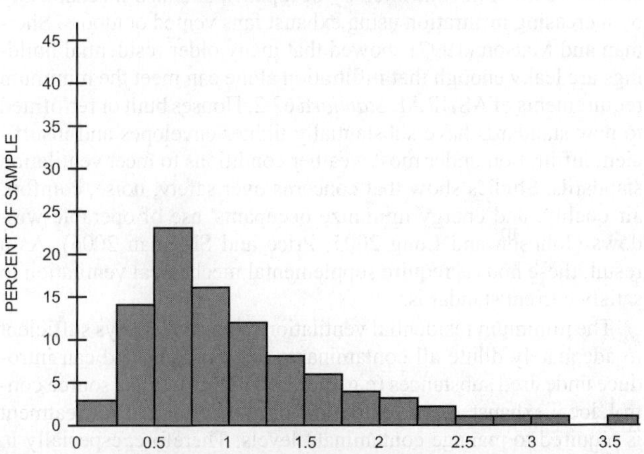

Fig. 12 Histogram of Infiltration Values for Low-Income Housing

procedure to show the extent to which infiltration contributes toward meeting ventilation air requirements. As a result, the National Building Code of Canada has requirements for mechanical ventilation capability in all new dwelling units.

Canadian Standards Association (CSA) *Standard* F326 expands the requirements for residential mechanical ventilation systems to include air distribution within the house, thermal comfort, minimum temperatures for equipment and ductwork, system controls, pressurization and depressurization of the dwelling, installation requirements, and verification of compliance. Verification can be by design or by test, but the total rate of outdoor air delivery must be measured.

Mechanical ventilation is required by ASHRAE *Standard* 62.2 and by building code in some U.S. states; some details of these requirements are described in this chapter. The net benefit of using controlled mechanical ventilation has been demonstrated and studied in various energy-efficient and advanced housing programs (Barley 2001; Palmiter et al. 1991; Riley 1990). Systems can be characterized as local or central; exhaust, supply, or balanced; with forced-air or radiant/hydronic heating/cooling systems; with or without heat recovery; and with continuous operation or with control by occupants, pollutant sensing, timers, or humidity. Note that not all combinations are viable. Various options are described by Fisk et al. (1984), Hekmat et al. (1986), Holton et al. (1997), Lubliner et al. (1997), Palmiter et al. (1991), Reardon and Shaw (1997), Sherman and Matson (1997), Sibbitt and Hamlin (1991), and Yuill et al. (1991).

The simplest systems use bathroom and kitchen fans to exhaust moisture and pollutants outdoors, and to depressurize to augment infiltration. Noise, installed capacity, durability under high or continuous operation, air movement from all rooms (especially bedrooms), envelope moisture, combustion safety, and energy efficiency issues need to be addressed. Many present bath and kitchen fans are ineffective ventilators because of poor installation and design, and many fail to exhaust outdoors. However, properly specified and installed exhaust fans can form part of good whole-house ventilation systems and are so specified in many building codes.

Some systems use their central air-handling unit blower to induce air from the outdoors and distribute it. However, the blower operates intermittently if thermostatically controlled and thus provides little ventilation in mild weather. Continuous blower operation increases energy consumption. If the blower operates continuously when the heat source is off, the combination of lower mixed-air temperature and high air speed can cause cold air drafts when in heating mode. To offset these problems, some systems use variable-speed blowers, which allow operation at lower speeds during mild weather. Others use a timer to cycle the blower when thermostatic demands are inadequate for ventilation purposes (Rudd 1998).

Central exhaust systems use leakage paths and, in some cases, intentional, controllable, and filtered openings in the building envelope for admitting makeup air. Such systems may be suitable for retrofit in existing houses. Energy can be recovered from the exhaust airstream to precondition makeup air or to warm potable water using a heat pump, for example.

For new houses with tightly constructed envelopes, balanced ventilation with passive heat recovery (e.g., air-to-air heat exchangers, heat recovery ventilators) can be appropriate in some climates. Fan-induced, filtered outdoor and exhaust airflow at nearly equal rates through a heat exchanger, where heat and sometimes moisture is transferred between the airstreams. This typically reduces the energy required to condition ventilation air by 60 to 80% (Cutter 1987). Concerns associated with these systems include airflow balance, leakage between streams, biological contamination of wet surfaces, frosting, and initial and maintenance costs.

Air-side economizers, which allow outdoor air to be up to 100% of the supply air at appropriate times, are not typically used in small buildings with low internal heat gains relative to the building envelope. Because of heat transfer through building envelopes, these small buildings quickly require heating or cooling as the outdoor air temperature falls or rises. Consequently, from an energy conservation point of view, small envelope-load-dominated buildings do not benefit as much as internal-load-dominated buildings in cool climates from daytime use of air-side economizers; night ventilation of residences during the cooling season may be very attractive, though, when the outdoor humidity ratio is low. Ventilation rates increase dramatically when air-side economizers are in operation, so the extra moisture introduced or removed must be considered.

The type of ventilation system can be selected based on house leakage class as defined in ASHRAE *Standard* 119. Balanced air-to-air systems with heat recovery are optimal for tight houses (leakage classes A to C in the standard). The leakier the house, the larger the contribution from infiltration and the less effective heat recovery ventilation will be. Tightening the envelope beyond the level of ASHRAE *Standard* 62.2 may be warranted in extremely cold climates to better use the heat recovery effect (Sherman and Matson 1997). In mild climates, these systems can also effectively be used in leakage classes D to F. Central exhaust systems should not be used for leakage classes A to C unless special air intakes are provided; otherwise their operation may depressurize the house enough to cause backdrafting through fossil-fueled appliances without closed-combustion systems. Unbalanced systems (either supply or exhaust) are optimal for leakage classes D to F. Ventilation systems are normally not needed for leakage classes G to J, but when they are needed, an unbalanced system is usually the best choice. More discussion of mechanical systems for residences is available in Russell et al. (2005); some information on practices outside North America can be found in McWilliams and Sherman (2005).

Shelter in Place

The most fundamental function of a house is to provide shelter from outdoor conditions. A first response to poor outdoor air quality is to go indoors. Closing windows and other air intakes and turning off exhaust fans reduces air exchange with the outdoors, decreasing the immediate intrusion of outdoor air into the home. However, because no home is perfectly airtight, closing doors and windows does not eliminate intrusion. Because all indoor air ultimately comes from outdoors, indoor air quality eventually comes to dynamic equilibrium with outdoor conditions in an idealized, unoccupied building. The tighter the building, the longer the time needed to come to equilibrium.

The delay time (the time it takes to completely change the air in a building) is determined by the ventilation rate. The effectiveness of sheltering within the home thus depends on envelope tightness. For a home with 0.35 air changes per hour, the delay time is roughly 3 h. For a very tight house without mechanical ventilation, the delay time can easily be twice as long. Most houses in the United States are leakier and thus could have a delay time of about one hour (Sherman and Matson 1997).

Reactive gases in outdoor air, such as ozone, can be decreased to some degree by the building envelope. For other outdoor contaminants, the building envelope serves to delay, not reduce, their introduction into the indoor environment. Such a delay is not very helpful at reducing exposures to outdoor contaminants that persist over days, but can be an effective strategy for short-duration (e.g., less than a few hours) sources. In houses without indoor sources, ozone levels tend to be higher in houses that do not have air conditioners than in those with air conditioners; ozone levels also are higher when windows are open than when they are closed (Weschler 2000). For outdoor exposure times shorter than the delay time, the house serves as a reservoir of cleaner air of that particular pollutant. After the outdoor contaminant is gone, windows can be opened to flush out pollutants that entered or were internally generated during the exposure period.

Safe Havens

Simply going indoors may not be sufficient for highly unusual but potentially lethal events. Chemical spills or fires, explosions, bioterrorism, or similar toxic air pollutant releases can temporarily create dangerous outdoor conditions that render other air quality issues insignificant. With sufficient warning, occupants should leave the vicinity, but the unexpected nature of these events means that the only viable alternative may be to shelter in place.

This strategy may work for short-term releases of airborne toxins. Homes are often too leaky to provide the protection needed for longer-duration events, but individual rooms can be temporarily sealed to become safe havens. A safe haven should be chosen to have as little contact as possible with outer walls, and preferably be on the side of the house farthest downwind from the source. Impermeable tape can be used to seal leaks, cracks, seams, register grilles, and doors, with thick plastic sheeting used to span larger gaps (Sorensen and Vogt 2001). If such a shelter has an air change rate of 0.15 h^{-1} with the house, it can take 4 to 6 h for contaminated outdoor air to affect significantly the safe haven. With very well-sealed, occupied spaces, the air quality inside degrades because of the occupants and materials within, especially rapidly for smaller spaces with higher occupant density. Suffocation is remotely possible, but thermal stress and odor accumulation are more typical.

Where emergencies are somewhat more likely, engineered safe rooms with adequate HVAC systems are needed. In such cases, a safe haven can be designed in advance with thermal conditioning and a highly efficient particle/gas-phase filtration system capable of providing several hours, days, or weeks of protection (Ormerod 1983). A short-term safe haven might be effectively combined with another emergency shelter (e.g., tornado, hurricane, civil defense) to reduce cost.

9. RESIDENTIAL IAQ CONTROL

ASHRAE *Standard* 62.2 presents minimum requirements for residential ventilation air and acceptable indoor air quality, and its user's manual (ASHRAE 2010a) has detailed information for designing and constructing residential buildings in compliance with the standard. Best or good practice may require going beyond the standard's minima. This section describes good practice; however, it presumes that the minimum requirements of 62.2 are met as well.

Traditionally, ventilation air for residences has been provided by natural ventilation controlled by occupants, and also mechanically by increasing infiltration using exhaust fans vented outdoors. Sherman and Matson (1997) showed that many older residential buildings are leaky enough that infiltration alone can meet the minimum requirements of ASHRAE *Standard* 62.2. Houses built or retrofitted to new standards have substantially tighter envelopes and insufficient infiltration under most weather conditions to meet ventilation standards. Studies show that concerns over safety, noise, comfort, air quality, and energy minimize occupants' use of operable windows (Johnson and Long 2005; Price and Sherman 2006). As a result, these houses require supplemental mechanical ventilation to satisfy current standards.

The minimum residential ventilation rate is not always sufficient to adequately dilute all contaminants (e.g., radon), and can introduce undesired substances (e.g., pollen). In these cases, source control, local exhaust, extra ventilation, or more effective air treatment is required to manage contaminant levels. Therefore, especially in single-family dwellings, occupants must be responsible for monitoring and controlling contaminant sources in and around their indoor environments, as well as for operating their dwelling units to meet their individual needs. Increasingly, residences are also used for business or hobby purposes, which may introduce air contaminants not addressed in *Standard* 62.2; portions of these residences may require ventilation air as required by *Standard* 62.1 or industrial guidelines.

Source Control

When considering how much whole-house ventilation should be supplied, both typical and unusual sources of indoor pollution should be controlled first to limit the required ventilation rate. This can be done either by mitigating the source itself or by using local exhaust to extract contaminants before they can mix into the indoor environment. Typical sources that should be considered include the following.

Clothes Dryers and Central Vacuum Systems. Clothes dryer exhaust is heavily laden with moisture and laundry by-products such as flammable lint and various gaseous contaminants. Many moisture problems have been traced to clothes dryers vented indoors or to attics, crawlspaces, garages, or other inappropriate locations. Exhaust from clothes dryers, which is typically about 150 cfm, must be vented directly to the outdoors. Similarly, central vacuum systems must be vented directly outdoors to exhaust the finer particles that pass through their filters.

Combustion. Water and carbon dioxide are always produced during combustion of hydrocarbons in air. Dangerous compounds are created, as well. All these products of combustion must be vented directly outdoors, preferably using sealed combustion or direct-vent equipment. Venting must meet or exceed all applicable codes. For buildings with naturally aspirated combustion appliances, excessive depressurization of the building by exhaust systems must be avoided to eliminate backdrafting. Consider a depressurization safety test, such as described in ASTM *Standard* E1998 or CGSB *Standard* 51.71. Fireplace combustion products should be isolated from the occupied space using tight-fitting doors and outdoor air intakes, when necessary. Flues and chimneys must be designed and installed to disperse combustion products well away from air intakes and operable windows, for example. Chapter 35 of the 2016 *ASHRAE Handbook—HVAC Systems and Equipment* has more information on venting systems. Exhaust hoods and fans for ranges and cooktops must vent outdoors.

Carbon monoxide is one of the most unwelcome indoor contaminants, and in significant concentration, poses an imminent threat to life. It can come from virtually any source of combustion, including from motorized vehicles and generators (Emmerich et al. 2013). Even combustion appliances that meet manufacturers' specifications can interact with the building and emit carbon monoxide. At least one carbon monoxide alarm meeting safety standards such as CSA *Standard* 6.19 should be installed near sleeping areas in each dwelling, including each unit of multifamily residential buildings, that has combustion appliances (e.g., fireplaces, stoves, furnaces, water heaters) within the pressure boundary, or has attached garages or storage sheds. Carbon monoxide alarms also should be considered for nonresidential buildings: poisonings have occurred in many building types, including hotels, motels, stores, restaurants, nursing homes, dormitories, laundromats, and schools.

Garages. Garages and storage spaces often contain many sources of contaminants. Doors between them and occupied spaces must be well sealed with gaskets or weatherstripping, including their sills, and possibly be self closing. Depressurized sections of HVAC systems for the regularly occupied portions of residences, such as the systems' air handlers or return or intake ducts, should not be located in garages. If such sections must pass through garages, they must be well sealed and never have registers or grilles installed in the garages or storage spaces; if such spaces need conditioning, they must use their own isolated systems. Take care to ensure that there is a good pressure barrier between the garage and the occupied space, typically using an air/moisture retarder such as heavy polyethylene as well as excellent sealing of the door between. Carbon monoxide sources may be present in garages, so pressure barriers, fire-rated compartmentation, and ventilation of attached residences are life-safety measures. Separate ventilation systems that slightly depressurize attached garages and storage spaces and that exhaust directly outdoors should be considered, especially when these support spaces are tightly constructed or are in cold climates. Several studies (Batterman et al. 2006; Emmerich et al. 2003; Fugler 2004) of contaminant sources and transport in garages found that, in some cases, significant fractions of infiltration air enter houses from attached garages, and that modern residential garages are tighter than older garages to reduce energy consumption and to improve comfort; garages were previously assumed to be leaky enough to avoid many related IAQ problems.

Particulates. The ventilation system should be designed such that return and any outdoor air is well filtered before passing through the thermal conditioning components of the HVAC system. Pressure drops associated with this filtration must be considered in the design and installation of the air-handling system. Particulate filters or air cleaners should have a minimum efficiency of 60% for 0.125 in. particles, which is equivalent to a MERV 6 designated filter according to ASHRAE *Standard* 52.2.

Microbiologicals. Because ventilation can increase the source as well as removal rates of various air pollutants, it is, at best, moderately effective at reducing exposures to many airborne microbiologicals. Ventilation can, however, be part of the moisture balance that is critical to retarding fungal growth on surfaces and spores released into the air, depending on indoor and outdoor conditions.

Radon and Other Soil Gases. Buildings are exposed to gases and water that migrate through the soil into occupied spaces through cracks or other leaks. Soil gases vary with time and conditions, and can contain toxins from pesticides, landfills, fuels, or sewers, but the highest-profile pollutant in this category is radon and its radioactive-decay-produced "daughters." Source control measures, such as differential pressure control and ground-to-building airtightening, are far more effective than ventilation mechanisms at controlling exposure to soil gas in buildings. See Chapter 11 for more information.

Volatile Organic Compounds (VOCs). VOCs are ubiquitous in modern life. Examples of products that emit VOCs include manufactured wood products, paints, stains, varnishes, solvents, pesticides, adhesives, wood preservatives, waxes, polishes, cleansers, lubricants, sealants, dyes, air fresheners, fuels, plastics, copy machines, printers, tobacco products, perfumes, cooking by-products, and dry-cleaned clothes. Whenever possible, VOCs and other toxic compounds should be stored outside the occupied space in loosely constructed or ventilated enclosures such as garden sheds or detached garages, and away from occupied buildings' ventilation intakes and operable windows. When unusual amounts of such compounds are present, consider using additional ventilation should be considered (e.g., extra ventilation during and for a while after construction projects). Reduced-VOC-emitting products are often available.

Outdoor Air. Outdoor air may at times contain unacceptably high levels of pollutants, including ozone, pollen, carbon monoxide, particulate matter, odors, or toxic agents. At such times, it may be impossible to provide acceptable indoor air quality using solely outdoor air, and increased ventilation rates can actually decrease indoor air quality. In locations where this problem may be anticipated, provide automatic or manual controls to allow temporary reduction of the ventilation rate. If these events are frequent, consider a means to more effectively clean recirculated air during these times.

Local Exhaust

After source elimination, the single most important source control mechanism in dwellings is local exhaust. Kitchens, utility rooms, bathrooms, and other spaces designed to allow specific contaminant releases should be provided with local exhaust that is vented to the outdoors. Workshops, recreation rooms, smoking areas, art studios, greenhouses, and hobby rooms may also require local ventilation and/or air cleaning to remove contaminants generated by the activities involved. Contaminants of concern should be evaluated to determine how much additional ventilation is required. Many of these rooms can be adequately ventilated by following the requirements for kitchens or bathrooms. If unvented combustion appliances must be used, rooms with these appliances should also meet general ventilation requirements for kitchens, because such appliances generate significant amounts of moisture and, often, ultrafine particles, even when operating properly.

Mechanical exhaust (i.e., a fan with ducting to the outdoors) with adequate makeup air is the preferred method for providing local ventilation. Normally, such an exhaust system is designed to operate intermittently under manual control to send contaminated air outdoors when occupants recognize the need for ventilation. However, in many circumstances, a continuous, lower-flow-rate exhaust can work as well. Specific provisions for intermittent versus continuous exhaust rates are typically included in ventilation standards such as ASHRAE *Standard* 62.2; some example information is provided here.

Continuous Local Mechanical Exhaust. A continuously operating mechanical exhaust system is intended to operate without occupant intervention. This exhaust may be part of a balanced whole-building mechanical ventilation system. The system should be designed to operate during all hours in which the dwelling is occupied. Override control, to provide higher exhaust rates when needed, should be provided. The minimum delivered ventilation should be at least that given in Table 1.

Intermittent Local Mechanical Exhaust. An intermittently operating local mechanical exhaust is intended to be operated as needed by the occupant. Shutoff timers, occupancy controls, multiple-speed fans, and switching integral with room lighting are helpful, provided they do not impede occupant control. The minimum airflow rate should be at least that given in Table 2.

Alternatives. Cleaning recirculated air can sometimes be substituted for local exhaust, if it can be shown to be effective and reliable in removing contaminants of concern. Natural ventilation is not generally a suitable method for local exhaust and ventilation air needs in many climates and spaces. Using natural ventilation can cause reentrainment problems when contaminated exhaust or exfiltrating air reenters the building. In milder climates, natural ventilation may be acceptable when the contaminant of concern is related to odor rather than health or safety. Purpose-designed passive exhaust systems have shown acceptable ventilation in some European settings, and may be considered in lieu of mechanical systems. Axley (2001b) discusses evaluation and design of passive residential ventilation systems further.

Whole-House Ventilation

Although control of significant sources of pollution in a dwelling is important, whole-house ventilation through centrally introduced, conditioned, and distributed outdoor air may still be needed. Each dwelling should be provided with outdoor air according to code adopted by the local jurisdiction; general guidance according to ASHRAE *Standard* 62.2 is given in Table 3 of this chapter. The rate is the sum of the Area-Based and Occupancy-Based columns. Design occupancy expectations in the United States can be based on the number of bedrooms as follows: first bedroom, two persons; each additional bedroom, one person. Additional ventilation should be considered when occupant densities exceed one person per 250 ft^2.

Natural whole-house ventilation that relies on occupant operation should not be used to make up any part of the minimum total whole-house ventilation air requirement. However, because occupancy and sources vary significantly, the capacity to ventilate above minimum rates can be provided by operable exterior openings such as doors and windows.

Table 1 Continuous Exhaust Airflow Rates

Application	Airflow Rate	Notes
Enclosed kitchen	5 ach	Based on kitchen volume
Restroom	20 cfm	Not less than 2 ach

Table 2 Intermittent Exhaust Airflow Rates

Application	Airflow Rate	Notes
Kitchen	100 cfm	With a vented range hood
	300 cfm	With other exhaust fans, including downdraft
Restroom	50 cfm	Not less than 2 ach

Table 3 Total Ventilation Air Requirements

Area Based	Occupancy Based
3 cfm/100 ft^2 of floor space	7.5 cfm per person, based on normal occupancy

Air Distribution

Ventilation air should be provided to each habitable room through mechanical and natural air distribution. If a room does not have a balance between air supply and return or exhaust, pathways for transfer air should be provided. These pathways may be door undercuts, transfer ducts with grilles, or simply grilles where ducts are not necessary; however, building codes must be checked, because compartmentation requirements for limiting fire and smoke movement may restrict transfer air means or require rated fire and smoke dampers, for example.

In houses without central air handlers, special provisions to distribute outdoor air may be required. Rooms in which occupants spend many continuous hours, such as bedrooms, may require special consideration. Local and whole-house ventilation equipment should be chosen to be energy efficient, easy to maintain, reliable, durable, and quiet. Consider using heat recovery, especially in cold climates.

Selection Principles for Residential Ventilation Systems

Occupant comfort, energy efficiency, ease of use, service life, initial and life-cycle costs, value-added features, and indoor environmental quality should be considered when selecting a strategy and system. Poorly designed, installed, or maintained HVAC and related systems can be potential contributors to poor indoor air quality. For example, occupants may not use the ventilation systems as intended if operation results in thermal or acoustical discomfort or excessive energy use. The resulting lack of ventilation might produce poor indoor air quality. Therefore, careful design, construction, commissioning, operation, and maintenance is necessary to provide optimum effectiveness.

All exhaust, supply, or air handler fans have the potential to change the pressure of an indoor space relative to the outdoors. High-flow fans, such as in the air handler and with some cooking exhausts, can cause significant depressurization, particularly in tightly constructed homes. Considering these effects is essential in design. Excessive depressurization of the living space relative to outdoors may cause backdrafting of combustion appliances and increased migration of contaminants such as radon or other soil gases, car exhaust, or insulation particles into the living space. Depressurization can also result in increased moisture intrusion into building cavities in warm, moist climates and may cause more structural damage and fungal growth. Pressurization of the living space can cause condensation in building cavities in cold climates, also resulting in structural damage. Excess pressure can best be prevented by balancing ventilation and exhaust systems and tightly sealing duct systems. In addition, adequate pathways must be available for all return air to the air-handling devices.

Occupant activities, operation of exhaust fans, and leaky ducts may depressurize the structure. Options to address backdrafting concerns include

- Using combustion appliances with sealed combustion systems
- Locating combustion appliances in a ventilated room isolated from depressurized zones by well-sealed partitions
- Providing supply or makeup air to balance exhaust from the zone
- Testing to ensure that depressurization is not excessive

The system must also be designed, built, operated, and maintained in a way that discourages growth of biological contaminants. Typical precautions include sloping condensate drain pans toward the drain, keeping condensate drains free of obstructions, keeping cooling coils free of dirt and other obstructions, maintaining humidifiers, and checking for and eliminating any cause of moisture inside ducts. Additional information on residential ventilation system design and IAQ control may be found in ASHRAE *Guideline* 24.

10. SIMPLIFIED MODELS OF RESIDENTIAL VENTILATION AND INFILTRATION

This section describes several calculation procedures, ranging from simple estimation techniques to more physical models. Orme (1999) provides a more thorough review of simplified models. For energy modeling or code compliance, a particular building's air change rate cannot be reliably deduced from the building's construction or age, or from a simple visual inspection. Some measurement is necessary, such as a pressurization test of envelope airtightness or a detailed quantification of the leakage sites and their magnitude. The air change rate of a building may be calculated given (1) the location and leakage function for every opening in the building envelope and between major building zones, (2) the wind pressure coefficients over the building envelope, and (3) any mechanical ventilation airflow rates. These data are generally unavailable for all except very simple structures or extremely well studied buildings. Therefore, their values must be assumed. The appropriateness of these assumptions influences the accuracy of predictions of air change rates.

Empirical Models

These models of residential infiltration are based on statistical fits of infiltration rate data for specific houses. They use pressurization test results to account for house airtightness and take the form of simple relations between infiltration rate, an airtightness rating, and, in most cases, weather conditions. Empirical models account for envelope infiltration only and do not include intentional ventilation. In one approach, the calculated air change rate at 0.20 in. of water based on a pressurization test is simply divided by a constant approximately equal to 20 (Sherman 1987). This technique does not account for the effect of infiltration-driving mechanisms on air exchange. Empirical models that do account for weather effects have been developed by Kronvall (1980), Reeves et al. (1979), and Shaw (1981).

The latter two models account for building air leakage using the values of c and n from Equation (40). The only other data required are wind speed and temperature difference. These empirical models predict long-term (one-week) infiltration rates very well in the houses from which they were developed; they do not, however, work as well in other houses because of the building-specific nature of leakage distribution, wind pressure, and internal partitioning. Persily (1986) and Persily and Linteris (1983) compared measured and predicted house infiltration rates for these and other models. The average long-term differences between measurements and predictions are generally about 40%, although individual predictions can be inaccurate by 100% or more (Persily 1986; Walker and Wilson 1998).

Multizone Models

Multicell models of airflow in buildings treat buildings as a series of interconnected zones and assume that air within each zone is well mixed. Several such models have been developed by Allard and Herrlin (1989), Etheridge and Alexander (1980), Feustel and Raynor-Hoosen (1990), Herrlin (1985), Liddament and Allen (1983), Walton (1984, 1989), and Walton and Dols (2003). They are all based on a mass balance for each zone of the building. These mass balances are used to solve for interior static pressures in the building by requiring that inflows and outflows for each zone balance to zero. The user must provide information describing building envelope leakage, values to account for wind pressure on the building envelope, temperatures for each zone, and any mechanical ventilation airflow rates. Wind pressure coefficient data in the literature, air leakage measurement results from the building or its components, and air leakage data from research can be used as estimates. These models not only solve for whole-building and individual zone air change rates, but also determine airflow rates and pressure differences between zones. These interzone airflow rates are useful for predicting pollutant transport within buildings with well mixed zones. Chapter 13 has more details on multizone airflow and IAQ modeling.

Single-Zone Models

Several procedures have been developed to calculate building air change rates that are based on physical models of the building interior as a single zone. These single-zone models are only appropriate for buildings with minimal internal resistance to airflow, and are therefore inappropriate for large, multizone buildings. Some models of this type have been developed by Cole et al. (1980), Sherman and Grims-rud (1980), Walker and Wilson (1998), and Warren and Webb (1980). The section on Residential Calculation Examples uses both basic and enhanced models (Bradley 1993; CHBA 1994; Hamlin and Pushka 1994; Palmiter and Bond 1994; Walker and Wilson 1998).

The **basic model** uses effective air leakage area A_L at 0.016 in. of water, which can be obtained from a whole-building pressurization test. The **enhanced model** uses pressurization test results to characterize house air leakage through leakage coefficient c and pressure exponent n. The enhanced model improves on the basic model by using a power law to represent envelope leakage, including a flue as a separate leakage path, and having separate wind effects for houses with crawlspaces or basements instead of slab-on-grade foundations.

For both models, the user must provide the wind speed, the temperature difference, information on the distribution of leakage over the building envelope, a wind shelter parameter or local shielding for the basic model, and a terrain coefficient. The predictive accuracy of the enhanced model can be very good, typically ±10% when parameters are well known for the building in question (Palmiter and Bond 1994; Sherman and Modera 1986; Walker and Wilson 1998). All models' results are sensitive to the user-provided data, and some of these parameters are often quite difficult to determine.

Superposition of Wind and Stack Effects

Simplified physical models of infiltration solve the problem of two natural driving forces (wind and stack) separately and then combine them in a process called **superposition**. Superposition is necessary because each physical process can affect internal and external air pressures on the building's envelope, and can cause interactions between physical processes that are otherwise independent. An exact solution is impossible, because (1) detailed properties of all the building leaks are unknown and (2) leakage is a nonlinear process. Therefore, most modelers have developed a simplified superposition process to combine stack and wind effects. Sherman (1992b) compared various superposition procedures and derived a generalized superposition equation involving simple leakage distribution parameters, and showed that the result is always subadditive. Typically, only 35% of infiltration from the smaller effect can be added to the larger effect. Depending on the specific building and conditions, that percentage could go as high as 85% or as low as zero. Walker and Wilson (1993) compared several superposition techniques to measured data. Sherman, as well as Walker and Wilson, found quadrature, shown in Equation (47), to be a robust superposition technique:

$$Q = \sqrt{Q_s^2 + Q_w^2} \tag{47}$$

The following sections discuss how superposition is combined with calculation of wind and stack flows to determine total flow.

Residential Calculation Examples

Basic Model. The following calculations are based on the Sherman and Grimsrud (1980) model, which uses the effective air leakage area at 0.016 in. of water. This leakage area can be obtained from a whole-building pressurization test. Using effective air leakage area, the airflow rate from infiltration is

$$Q = A_L\sqrt{C_s|\Delta T| + C_w U^2} \tag{48}$$

where

Q = airflow rate, cfm
A_L = effective air leakage area, in²
C_s = stack coefficient, cfm²/in⁴·°F
ΔT = average indoor-outdoor temperature difference for time interval of calculation, °F
C_w = wind coefficient, cfm²/in⁴·mph²
U = average wind speed measured at local weather station for time interval of calculation, mph

Table 4 shows values of Cs for one-, two-, and three-story houses. The value of wind coefficient Cw depends on the local shelter class of the building (Table 5) and the building height. Table 6 shows values of Cw for one-, two-, and three-story houses in shelter classes 1 to 5. In calculating values in Tables 4 and 6, the following assumptions were made:

- Terrain used for converting meteorological to local wind speeds is that of a rural area with scattered obstacles
- $R = 0.5$ (half the building leakage in the walls)
- $X = 0$ (equal amounts of leakage in the floor and ceiling)
- Heights of one-, two-, and three-story buildings = 8, 16, and 24 ft, respectively

Table 4 Basic Model Stack Coefficient C_s

	House Height (Stories)		
	One	Two	Three
Stack coefficient	0.0150	0.0299	0.0449

Table 5 Local Shelter Classes

Shelter Class	Description
1	No obstructions or local shielding
2	Typical shelter for an isolated rural house
3	Typical shelter caused by other buildings across street from building under study
4	Typical shelter for urban buildings on larger lots where sheltering obstacles are more than one building height away
5	Typical shelter produced by buildings or other structures immediately adjacent (closer than one house height: e.g., neighboring houses on same side of street, trees, bushes)

Example 2. Estimate the infiltration at winter design conditions for a two-story house in Lincoln, Nebraska. The house has effective air leakage area of 77 in² and volume of 12,000 ft³, and the predominant wind is perpendicular to the street (shelter class 3). The indoor air temperature is 68°F.

Solution: The 99% design temperature for Lincoln is –2°F. Assume a design wind speed of 15 mph. From Equation (48), with C_s = 0.0299 from Table 4 and C_w = 0.0086 from Table 6, the airflow rate caused by infiltration is

$$Q = 77\sqrt{(0.0299)(70) + (0.0086)(15^2)} = 155 \text{ cfm} = 9300 \text{ ft}^3\text{/h}$$

From Equation (2), air change rate I is equal to Q divided by the building volume:

$$I = (9300 \text{ ft}^3\text{/h})/12{,}000 \text{ ft}^3 = 0.78 \text{ h}^{-1} = 0.78 \text{ ach}$$

Example 3. Predict the average infiltration during a one-week period in January for a one-story house in Portland, Oregon. During this period, the average indoor/outdoor temperature difference is 30°F, and average wind speed is 6 mph. The house has volume of 9000 ft³ and effective air leakage area of 107 in², and it is located in an area with buildings and trees within 30 ft in most directions (shelter class 4).

Solution: From Equation (48), the airflow rate caused by infiltration is

$$Q = 107\sqrt{(0.0150)(30) + (0.0039)(6^2)} = 82.2 \text{ cfm} = 4930 \text{ ft}^3\text{/h}$$

The air change rate is therefore

$$I = 4930/9000 = 0.55 \text{ h}^{-1} = 0.55 \text{ ach}$$

Example 4. Estimate the average infiltration over the heating season in a two-story house with volume of 11,000 ft³ and leakage area of 131 in². The house is located on a lot with several large trees but no other close buildings (shelter class 3). Average wind speed during the heating season is 7 mph, and the average indoor/outdoor temperature difference is 36°F.

Solution: From Equation (48), the airflow rate from infiltration is

$$Q = 131\sqrt{(0.0299)(36) + (0.0086)(7^2)} = 160 \text{ cfm} = 9620 \text{ ft}^3\text{/h}$$

The average air change rate is therefore

$$I = 9620/11{,}000 = 0.87 \text{ h}^{-1} = 0.87 \text{ ach}$$

Enhanced Model. This section presents a simple, single-zone approach to calculating air infiltration rates in houses based on the Walker and Wilson (1998) model. The airflow rate from stack and wind infiltration is

$$Q_s = cC_s\Delta T^n \tag{49}$$

$$Q_w = cC_w(sU)^{2n} \tag{50}$$

where

Q_s = stack airflow rate, cfm

Table 6 Basic Model Wind Coefficient C_w

	House Height (Stories)		
Shelter Class	One	Two	Three
1	0.0119	0.0157	0.0184
2	0.0092	0.0121	0.0143
3	0.0065	0.0086	0.0101
4	0.0039	0.0051	0.0060
5	0.0012	0.0016	0.0018

Q_w = wind airflow rate, cfm
c = flow coefficient, cfm/(in. of water)^n
C_s = stack coefficient, (in. of water/°F)^n
C_w = wind coefficient, (in. of water/mph^2)^n
s = shelter factor
ΔT = indoor – outdoor temperature difference, °F
n = pressure exponent

In calculating tabulated values of C_s, C_w, and s, the assumptions were

- Each story is 8 ft high.
- The flue is 6 in. in diameter and reaches 6 ft above the upper ceiling.
- The flue is unsheltered.
- Half of envelope leakage (not including the flue) is in the walls and one-quarter each is at the floor and ceiling, respectively.
- $n = 0.67$

The following examples use typical values for terrain factors, house height, and wind speed measurement height, wind speed multiplier G given in Table 7, and use a relationship based on equations found in Chapter 24.

Example 5. Estimate the infiltration at winter design conditions for a two-story slab-on-grade house with a flue in Lincoln, Nebraska. The house has a flow coefficient of c = 4370 cfm/(in. of water)^n and a pressure exponent of n = 0.67 (corresponding to effective leakage area of 77 in^2 at 0.016 in. of water). The building volume is 12,000 ft^3. The 97.5% design temperature is –2°F, and design wind speed is 15 mph.

Solution: For a slab-on-grade two-story house with a flue, Table 8 gives C_s = 0.001478 (in. of water/°F)^n and C_w = 0.001313 (in. of water/mph^2)^n. The house is maintained at 68°F indoors. The building wind speed is determined by taking the design wind speed U_{met} and applying by the wind speed multiplier G from Table 7:

$$U = GU_{met} = 0.59(15) = 8.9 \text{ mph}$$

From Table 5, the shelter class for a typical urban house is 4. Table 9 gives the shelter factor for a two-story house with a flue and shelter class 4 as s = 0.64. The stack flow is calculated using Equation (49):

$$Q_s = 4370(0.001478)[68 - (-2)]^{0.67} = 111 \text{ cfm}$$

The wind flow is calculated using Equation (50):

$$Q_w = (4370)(0.001313)(0.64 \times 8.9)^{1.34} = 59 \text{ cfm}$$

Substituting Q_s and Q_w into Equation (47) gives Q = 126 cfm = 7560 ft^3/h. From Equation (2), air change rate I is equal to Q divided by the building volume:

$$I = (7560 \text{ ft}^3/\text{h})/12{,}000 \text{ ft}^3 = 0.63 \text{ h}^{-1} = 0.63 \text{ ach}$$

Example 6. Estimate the average infiltration over a one-week cold-weather period for a single-story house with a crawlspace in Redmond, Washington. The house has a flow coefficient of c = 6890 cfm/(in. of water)^n and a pressure exponent of n = 0.6 (corresponding to effective leakage area of 107 in^2 at 0.016 in. of water). The building volume is 9000 ft^3. During this period, the average indoor-to-outdoor temperature difference is 29°F, and wind speed is 6 mph. The house is electrically heated and has no flue.

Solution: For a single-story house with no flue, C_s =0.000891 (in. of water/°F)^n. For a crawlspace, C_w = 0.001074 (in. of water/mph^2)^n. From Table 7, for a one-story house, G = 0.48.

$$U = GU_{met} = 0.48(6) = 2.9 \text{ mph}$$

Table 9 gives shelter factor s = 0.50 for a house with no flue and shelter class 4. Stack flow is calculated using Equation (49):

$$Q_s = 6890(0.000891)(29)^{0.6} = 46 \text{ cfm}$$

Wind flow is calculated using Equation (50):

$$Q_w = (6890)(0.001074)(0.50 \times 2.9)^{1.34} = 12 \text{ cfm}$$

Substituting Q_s and Q_w into Equation (47) gives Q = 48 cfm = 2880 ft^3/h. From Equation (2), air change rate I is equal to Q divided by the building volume:

$$I = (2880 \text{ ft}^3/\text{h})/9000 \text{ ft}^3 = 0.32 \text{ h}^{-1} = 0.32 \text{ ach}$$

Example 7. Estimate the infiltration for a three-story house in San Francisco, California. The house has a flow coefficient of c = 8740 cfm/(in. of water)^{n}and a pressure exponent of n = 0.67 (corresponding to effective leakage area of 155 in^2 at 0.016 in. of water). The building volume is 14,200 ft^3. The indoor/outdoor temperature difference is 9°Fand wind speed is 10 mph. The house has a flue and a crawlspace.

Solution: For a three-story house with a flue, C_s = 0.001791 (in. of water/°F)^n. For a crawlspace, C_w = 0.001295 (in. of water/mph^2)^n. From Table 7, for a three-story house, G = 0.67.

$$U = GU_{met} = 0.67(10) = 6.7 \text{ mph}$$

The prevailing wind blows along the row of houses parallel to the street, so the house has a shelter class of 5. Table 9 gives the shelter factor for a three-story house with a flue and shelter class 5 as s = 0.43.

$$Q_s = 8740(0.001791)(9)^{0.67} = 68 \text{ cfm}$$

$$Q_w = 8740(0.001295)(0.43 \times 6.7)^{1.34} = 47 \text{ cfm}$$

Substituting Q_s and Q_w in Equation (47) gives Q = 83 cfm = 4960 ft^3/h. The air changes per hour are

$$I = (4960 \text{ ft}^3/\text{h})/(14{,}200 \text{ ft}^3) = 0.35 \text{ h}^{-1} = 0.35 \text{ ach}$$

Table 7 Enhanced Model Wind Speed Multiplier G

	House Height (Stories)		
	One	Two	Three
Wind speed multiplier G	0.48	0.59	0.67

Table 8 Enhanced Model Stack and Wind Coefficients

	One-Story		Two-Story		Three-Story	
	No Flue	With Flue	No Flue	With Flue	No Flue	With Flue
C_s	0.000891	0.001144	0.001308	0.001478	0.001641	0.001791
C_w for slab-on-grade	0.001313	0.001194	0.001432	0.001313	0.001432	0.001402
C_w for crawl-space	0.001074	0.001074	0.001194	0.001194	0.001271	0.001295

Table 9 Enhanced Model Shelter Factor s

Shelter Class	No Flue	One-Story with Flue	Two-Story with Flue	Three-Story with Flue
1	1.00	1.10	1.07	1.06
2	0.90	1.02	0.98	0.97
3	0.70	0.86	0.81	0.79
4	0.50	0.70	0.64	0.61
5	0.30	0.54	0.47	0.43

Combining Residential Infiltration and Mechanical Ventilation

Significant infiltration and mechanical ventilation often occur simultaneously in residences. The pressure difference from Equation (31) can be used for each building leak, and the flow network (including mechanical ventilation) for the building can be solved to find the airflow through all the leaks while accounting for the effect of the mechanical ventilation. However, for simplified models, natural infiltration and mechanical ventilation are usually determined separately and require a superposition method to combine the flow rates.

Sherman (1992b) compared various procedures and derived a generalized superposition equation that involves simple leakage distribution parameters. The result is always subadditive. For small, unbalanced fans, typically only half the mechanically introduced outdoor airflow contributes to the total, but this fraction can be anywhere between 0 and 100%, depending on leakage distribution. When the makeup air fan's flow rate is large, infiltration may be ignored, because the building becomes either neutrally or positively pressurized.

In special cases when the leakage distribution is known and highly skewed, it may be necessary to work through the superposition method in more detail. For example, in a wind-dominated situation, a makeup air fan has a much bigger effect than an exhaust fan on changing the total ventilation rate; the same is true for houses with high neutral pressure levels in cold climates. For the general case, when details are not known or can be assumed to be broad and typical, the following superposition gives good results:

$$Q_{comb} = Q_{bal} + \sqrt{Q_{unbal}^2 + Q_{infiltration}^2} \tag{51}$$

Typical Practice

The preceding sections on estimating infiltration in low-rise residences represent current analytical techniques typically used for research and remediation purposes, but most small residential buildings are designed and constructed without direct involvement of ventilation engineers. Contractors, who typically prepare these buildings' designs, are required to follow mandates in various codes and standards, and they apply experience-based rules of thumb when determining, for example, exhaust needs. Often, leaky buildings or air quality problems result. Research and experience have shown that tightening building envelopes and using mechanical ventilation with heat recovery can improve indoor air quality and reduce energy consumption. Retaining the services of a ventilation engineer before construction begins is advisable in some situations.

11. COMMERCIAL AND INSTITUTIONAL AIR LEAKAGE

Envelope Leakage

ASTM *Standard* E779 and CGSB *Standard* 149.10 include methods to measure the airtightness of building envelopes of single-zone buildings. Although many multizone buildings can be treated as single-zone buildings for testing by opening interior doors or by inducing equal pressures in adjacent zones, these standards provide no guidelines for dealing with problems arising in tall buildings, such as stack and wind effects. Tall buildings require refinement and extensions of established procedures because they have obstacles to accurate measurement not present in small buildings, including large envelope leakage area, interfloor leakage, vertical shafts, and large wind and stack pressures. Chapter 4 in the 2015 *ASHRAE Handbook—HVAC Applications* discusses tall buildings and their challenges in detail.

For conducting a pressurization test in a large building, the building's own air-handling equipment sometimes can be used to induce test pressures, as described in CGSB *Standard* 149.15. In other cases, a large fan is brought to the building to perform the test, as described by CIBSE *Standard* TM23. ASHRAE RP-1478's final report (Anis and Brennan 2014) discusses how to test the envelope leakage of large commercial buildings.

In the past, building envelopes of large commercial buildings were often assumed to be quite airtight. Tamura and Shaw (1976a) found that, assuming a flow exponent n of 0.65 in Equation (40), air leakage measurements in eight Canadian office buildings with sealed windows ranged from 0.120 to 0.480 cfm/ft^2. Persily and Grot (1986) performed whole-building pressurization tests in large office buildings that showed that pressurization airflow rate divided by building volume was relatively low compared to that of houses. However, if these airflow rates are normalized by building envelope area instead of by volume, the results indicate envelope airtightness levels similar to those in typical North American houses. The same study also looked at eight U.S. office buildings and found air leakage ranging from 0.213 to 1.028 cfm/ft^2 at 0.30 in. of water. This means that the office buildings' envelopes were leakier than expected. Typical air leakage values per unit wall area at 0.30 in. of water were 0.10, 0.30, and 0.60 cfm/ft^2 for tight, average, and leaky walls, respectively (Tamura and Shaw 1976a).

Emmerich and Persily (2014) summarized available measured airtightness data for almost 400 buildings, including about 70 constructed between 2000 and 2010. The average air leakage for the buildings was 20% tighter than the average for the 228 buildings included in a similar 2011 analysis. The data were analyzed to determine factors that affect airtightness (e.g., building type, height). Recent additions to the database, previously reported by Emmerich and Persily (2005), include numerous buildings constructed to meet the specifications of sustainable building programs such as U.S. Green Building Council's LEED® rating system, as well as buildings designed and constructed with air retarders. The overall average airtightness reported was 0.72 cfm/ft^2 for six-sided (i.e., including slabs and basement surfaces) envelope surface areas at 0.0109 psi. The data show only weak trends related to year of construction, height, floor area, wall construction, or building type, but do demonstrate that buildings designed and constructed with attention to airtightness are much tighter than typical commercial buildings. The analysis found that the 79 buildings with air retarders had an average air leakage almost 70% less than the average for the 290 buildings not specified as having air retarders, thus demonstrating the critical need to design and construct commercial buildings with dedicated air retarders to support sustainable building design. However, the wide variation among the measures taken to limit or reduce air leakage among these buildings and the lack of detailed descriptions of the air retarders make it difficult to predict a specific level of airtightness that will result from use of a specific air retarder approach.

In the United States, commercial building construction practices are addressed by various standards, codes, and green building program requirements, and Table 10 summarizes some of the relevant air leakage limits from these requirements. Both ASHRAE *Standards* 90.1 and 189.1 require **continuous air barriers (CABs)** for most commercial buildings. Since 2010, *Standard* 90.1 requires the CAB to meet either a material tightness limit (0.004 cfm/ft^2 under a pressure differential of 0.30 in. of water) or an assembly tightness limit (0.04 cfm/ft^2 under a pressure differential of 0.30 in. of water), but it does not include a whole-building tightness limit or a requirement for whole-building pressurization testing. The building commissioning requirements of *Standard* 189.1-2014 include a whole-building test demonstrating the building meets a tightness limit of 0.25 cfm/ft^2 under a pressure differential of 0.30 in. of water or the implementation of a rigorous envelope commissioning program.

The 2012 International Energy Conservation Code® (IECC®) (ICC 2012a) has requirements with options for a CAB with material or assembly tightness or a whole-building test. The 2012 International Green Construction Code® (IgCC®) (ICC 2012b) includes the same requirements as the 2012 IECC but also includes a whole-building testing requirement consistent with the U.S. Army Corps of Engineers (USACE 2009) value. Many U.S. state building codes currently or will include requirements for continuous air barriers either through reference to IECC, IGCC, ASHRAE *Standard* 90.1 or 189.1, or their own independent requirements; a current list of requirements is available at www.airbarrier.org.

Since 2009, the USACE has required that conditioned buildings be built or retrofitted to include a continuous air barrier to control air leakage through the building envelope (USACE 2009). The

Table 10 Summary of Building Airtightness Data

	Air Leakage, cfm/ft² at 0.30 in. of water		
Standard or Code	Material	Assembly	Whole Building*
ASHRAE 90.1	0.004	0.04	—
ASHRAE 189.1	0.004	0.04	0.25
IECC	0.004	0.04	0.39
IgCC	Same as IECC	Same as IECC	0.25
USACE	0.004	—	0.25
GSA	0.004	0.04	0.40

Notes: IECC= International Energy Conservation Code
IgCC = International Green Construction Code
USACE = U.S. Army Corps of Engineers
GSA = U.S. General Services Administration
*Whole-building limits are based on six-sided enclosure, including slab and below-grade walls.

specification requires whole-building testing with a maximum leakage of 0.25 cfm/ft² at 0.30 in. of water based on the six-sided building enclosure area (including slab and subgrade walls). The average tightness for a set of 285 new and retrofitted USACE buildings was reported to be 0.18 cfm/ft² (Zhivov 2013). Also, the U.S. General Services Administration (GSA 2010) since 2010 requires all new U.S. federal buildings for the Public Buildings Service to include an air barrier with the whole building having an air leakage rate of not more than 0.39 cfm/ft² at 0.30 in. of water.

Grot and Persily (1986) also found that eight recently constructed office buildings had infiltration rates ranging from 0.1 to 0.6 ach when outdoor air intakes were deactivated. Infiltration rates exhibited varying degrees of weather dependence, generally much lower than that measured in houses. Infiltration in commercial buildings can have many negative consequences, including reduced thermal comfort, interference with proper operation of mechanical ventilation systems, degraded indoor air quality, moisture damage of building envelope components, and increased energy consumption. These results suggest strongly that commercial buildings' envelopes require tighter construction, and that continuous air barrier systems should be used in the enclosures of all conditioned buildings. Since 1997, the Building Environment and Thermal Envelope Council of the National Institute of Building Sciences has sponsored several symposia on air barriers for buildings in North American climates. Others have also published articles on the importance of limiting air leakage in commercial buildings (Anis 2001; Ask 2003; Fennell and Haehnel 2005).

Envelope leakage in commercial buildings also depends on HVAC system operation. Often, commercial buildings and their HVAC systems are in operation during normal daytime business hours but switch into "unoccupied" operation at nights and on weekends and holidays. If pressurized while their HVAC systems operate, infiltration is often very low or even eliminated in buildings with tight envelopes. However, in unoccupied mode, this pressurization is often lost, so infiltration and potentially moisture intrusion may be significant at times.

Air Leakage Through Internal Partitions

In large buildings, air leakage associated with internal partitions becomes very important. Walls, doors, floors, ceilings, plenums, chases, transfer ducts and grilles, and elevator and stairway enclosures are the major separations of concern in these buildings. Their leakage characteristics are needed in multizone models to predict infiltration through exterior walls and airflow patterns in a building. These internal resistances are also important in the event of a fire to predict smoke movement patterns and evaluate smoke management systems.

Table 11 gives air leakage areas calculated at 0.30 in. of water with C_D = 0.65 for different internal partitions of commercial buildings (Klote et al. 2012). Figure 13 presents examples of measured

Table 11 Air Leakage Areas for Internal Partitions in Commercial Buildings (at 0.30 in. of water and C_D = 0.65)

Construction Element	Wall Tightness	Area Ratio
		A_L/A_w
Stairwell walls	Tight	0.14 × 10⁻⁴
	Average	0.11 × 10⁻³
	Loose	0.35 × 10⁻³
Elevator shaft walls	Tight	0.18 × 10⁻³
	Average	0.84 × 10⁻³
	Loose	0.18 × 10⁻²
		A_L/A_f
Floors	Average	0.52 × 10⁻⁴

A_L = air leakage area A_w = wall area A_f = floor area

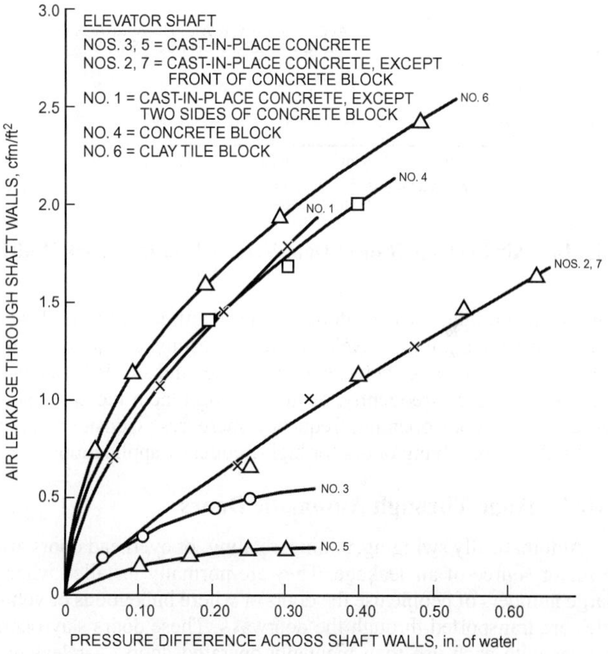

Fig. 13 Air Leakage Rates of Elevator Shaft Walls

air leakage rates of elevator shaft walls (Tamura and Shaw 1976b), the type of data used to derive the values in Table 11. Consult Chapter 53 of the 2015 *ASHRAE Handbook—HVAC Applications* for performance models and applications of smoke control systems. As with the exterior shell, making significant effort to seal unintentional openings in internal partitions in large buildings can improve thermal comfort and energy efficiency, as well as improve the building's performance in a fire.

Leakage paths, intentional or otherwise, at the top of elevator shafts are often equivalent to orifice areas of 620 to 1550 in². Air leakage rates through stair tower and elevator doors are shown in Figure 14 as a function of average crack width around the door. Sealing elevator and stair doors well, and possibly using indoor vestibules for them, can reduce air as well as smoke flow rates significantly. Air leakage areas associated with other openings in commercial buildings are also important for air movement calculations. These include interior doors and partitions, suspended ceilings in buildings where space above the ceiling is used for air supply or return, and other components of the air distribution system.

Air Leakage Through Exterior Doors

Door infiltration depends on the type and use of door, room, and building, and on air speed and pressure differentials. In residences

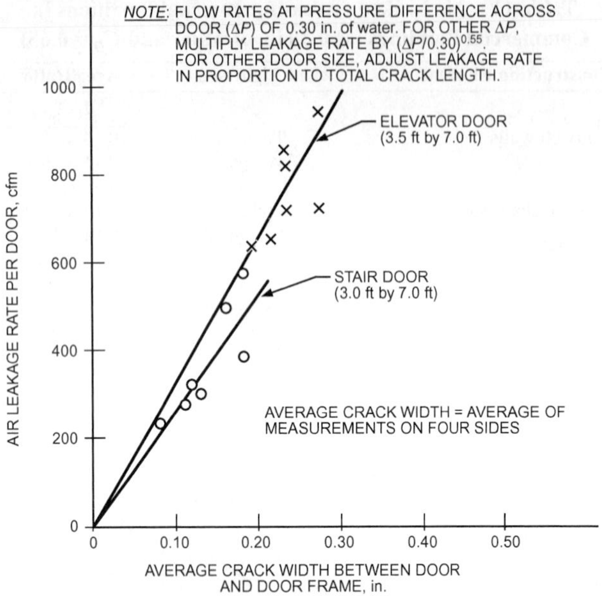

Fig. 14 Air Leakage Rate of Door Versus Average Crack Width

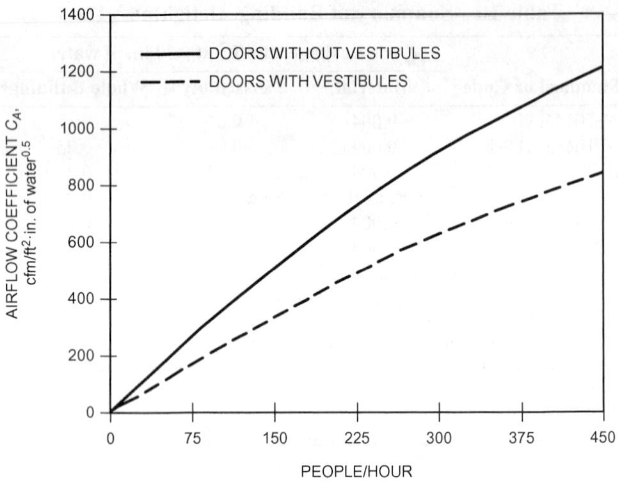

Fig. 15 Airflow Coefficient for Automatic Doors

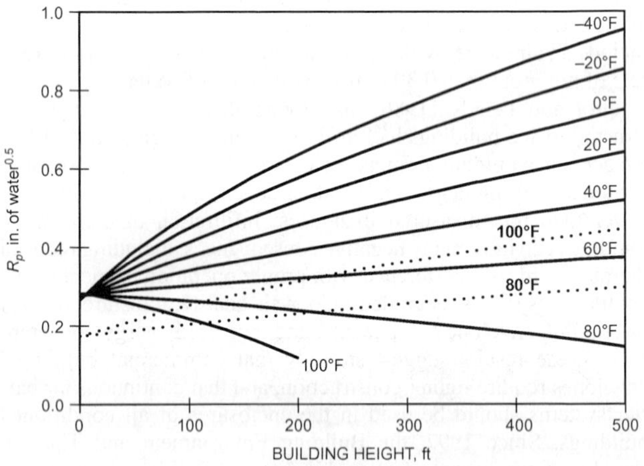

Fig. 16 Pressure Factor for Automatic Doors

and small buildings where doors are used infrequently, a closed door is assumed, and air exchange can be estimated based on air leakage through cracks between door, frame, and sill. Where exterior door are used frequently, airflow through them increases significantly as door-opening frequency increases. Consider using vestibules or revolving doors for high-frequency applications.

Air Leakage Through Automatic Doors

Automatically swinging, sliding, rotating, or overhead doors are a major source of air leakage. They are normally installed where large numbers of people use the doors or where bulk goods or vehicles are transported through the doorways. These doors stay open longer with each use than manually operated doors. Air leakage through an automatic door can be reduced by installing a vestibule. However, pairs of automatic doors on the inside and outside of a vestibule normally have overlapping open periods, even when used by only one person at a time. Therefore, it is important that designers include airflow through automatic doors when calculating heating and cooling loads in adjacent spaces.

To calculate the average airflow rate through an automatic door, the designer must consider the area of the door, the pressure difference across it, the discharge coefficient of the door when it is open, and the fraction of time that it is open. Obtaining the discharge coefficient is complicated by the fact that it changes as the door opens and closes.

To simplify this calculation, ASHRAE research project RP-763 (Yuill 1996) developed Figure 15 to combine the discharge coefficients of doors as they open and close with the fraction of time that doors are open at a particular level of use. This figure presents an overall airflow coefficient as a function of the number of people using a door per hour. To obtain the average infiltration rate through an automatic door, multiply this coefficient by the door's opening area and by the square root of the pressure difference between the outdoor and indoor air at the door's location. The pressure difference across a door in a building is difficult to predict accurately and depends on wind pressure on the building, stack effect caused by the indoor/outdoor temperature difference, and effects of air-handling system operation. It also depends on leakage characteristics of the building's exterior walls and of internal partitions.

Two simplified design methods are presented here. The first method uses practical assumptions to determine design values for R_p, the square root of the pressure difference across the automatic door, given in Figure 16. The second method requires explicit calculation of envelope pressures.

In Figure 16, airflows shown for outdoor air temperatures of 80 and 100°F, represented by dotted lines, are outward flows. They intercept the vertical axis at a lower point than the other lines because wind pressure coefficients on the building's downwind face, where the greatest outward flows occur, are lower than on the upward face. In many buildings, air pressure in the building is controlled by varying the flow rate through return or exhaust fan(s) or by controlling the relief air dampers. These systems are usually set to maintain a pressure slightly above ambient in the lobby, but in a large building, multiple sensors may be used to regulate air pressure on each floor independently, for example. Subtracting the interior pressure maintained from the wind pressure gives the net pressure for estimating airflow through an exterior door.

Method 1. For the first method, the infiltration rate through the automatic door is

$$Q = C_A A R_p \tag{52}$$

where

Q = airflow rate, cfm

C_A = airflow coefficient from Figure 15, cfm/ft²·in. of water$^{0.5}$
A = area of the door opening, ft²
R_p = pressure factor from Figure 16, in. of water$^{0.5}$

Method 2. Airflow Q is

$$Q = C_A A \sqrt{\Delta p} \tag{53}$$

where

Q = airflow rate, cfm
C_A = airflow coefficient from Figure 15, cfm/ft²·in. of water$^{0.5}$
A = area of the door opening, ft²
Δp = pressure difference across door, in. of water

To find Δp, it is necessary to find the pressure differential created by both wind and stack effect. To give the largest possible pressure difference across the door, there are no interactions between the two natural pressures:

$$\Delta p = p_w - \Delta p_s \tag{54}$$

where

p_w = wind-induced surface pressure relative to static pressure, in. of water
Δp_s = pressure difference caused by stack effect, in. of water

Example Calculations

Find the maximum possible winter infiltration through an automatic door on the ground floor of a 20-story building. The area of the door is 36 × 84 in. = 3024 in² = 21 ft². Each floor is 13 ft high. Approximately 300 people per hour pass through the door. The design wind conditions are 15 mph, indoor temperature is 70°F, and outdoor temperature is 20°F. The airflow coefficient from Figure 15, using the line for doors without vestibules, is approximately 920 cfm/[ft²·(in. of water)$^{0.5}$].

Method 1:

The pressure factor from Figure 16 is 0.5 in. of water$^{0.5}$. Equation (52) gives the door's airflow as

$$Q = 920(21)0.5 = 9660 \text{ cfm}$$

Method 2:

The worst possible case for wind surface pressure coefficient C_p at any point and in any position on the ground floor of the building is inferred from the figures in Chapter 24 to be about 0.75. Using this in Equation (25), together with the specified wind speed, results in p_w = 0.082 in. of water. Assume that H is one-half the door height (42 in.). To have maximum pressure across the door, assume the neutral pressure plane is located halfway up the building such that

$$H_{NPL} = \frac{1}{2}(20 \text{ stories})\frac{13 \text{ ft}}{\text{story}} = 130 \text{ ft}$$

Substituting these values into Equation (24) gives Δp_s = –0.19 in. of water. This is the maximum stack pressure difference given no internal resistance to airflow. To find the actual stack pressure difference, it is necessary to multiply this by a draft coefficient. For this example, the coefficient is assumed to be 0.9, which is the highest value that has been found for tall buildings. Therefore, Δp_s = 0.9(–0.19 in. of water) = –0.17 in. of water. The total pressure is then Δp = 0.082 – (–0.17) = 0.252 in. of water. Substituting into Equation (53),

$$Q = 920(21)\sqrt{0.252} = 9700 \text{ cfm}$$

If the building has a vestibule, the airflow coefficient is read from Figure 15 using the line for doors with vestibules, and it is approximately 626 cfm/ft²·in. of water$^{0.5}$, reducing airflow to 6600 cfm into the building.

Standard-sized revolving doors are often used where there is high use, but typically not where people would often be carrying large bags or pushing carts. Dols et al. (2014) applied a coupled building energy and airflow simulation tool to simulate airflow through entry doors in a prototype medium office building created by Ng et al. (2012) and found that using a vestibule reduced infiltration through the building entrance by 23%. More information on predicting infiltration rates through standard and extra-large revolving doors is still needed.

Air Exchange Through Air Curtains

Air curtains are jets of air projected across envelope openings with the intention of reducing air exchange and the entrance of dust and insects, for example. They are commonly applied to loading dock doorways and high-use building entrances. Performance of air curtains strongly depends on factors such as jet characteristics, wind, and building pressurization. More discussion on air curtain performance is available in the research literature and in Chapter 20 of the 2016 *ASHRAE Handbook—HVAC Systems and Equipment.*

12. COMMERCIAL AND INSTITUTIONAL VENTILATION

ASHRAE *Standard* 62.1 contains requirements on ventilation and indoor air quality for commercial, institutional, and high-rise residential buildings. These requirements address system and equipment issues, design ventilation rates, commissioning and systems start-up, and operation and maintenance. The user's manual for *Standard* 62.1-2010 (ASHRAE 2010b) provides details to help design, install, and operate building systems to meet requirements. The design requirements include two alternative procedures:

- The prescriptive **ventilation rate procedure (VRP)** contains a table of outdoor air ventilation requirements for a variety of space types, with adjustments for air distribution in rooms and systems serving multiple spaces. These requirements consist of both a per-person rate and a per-floor-area rate. Minimum outdoor air ventilation rates are based, in part, on research by Berg-Munch et al. (1986), Cain et al. (1983), Iwashita et al. (1989), and Yaglou et al. (1936), as well as years of experience of designers and building operators.
- The performance **indoor air quality procedure (IAQP)** seeks acceptable indoor air quality by controlling indoor contaminant concentrations through source control, air cleaning, and ventilation. It allows for either or both improved indoor air quality and reduced energy consumption. Chapter 29 of the 2016 *ASHRAE Handbook—HVAC Systems and Equipment* has information on air cleaning.

The ventilation rate procedure is by far the more commonly used because of its prescriptive nature.

Combining source control and local exhaust, as opposed to dilution with ventilation air, is the method of choice in many industrial environments. Industrial ventilation is discussed in Chapters 31 and 32 of the 2015 *ASHRAE Handbook—HVAC Applications* and in *Industrial Ventilation: A Manual of Recommended Practice* (ACGIH 2016). Ventilation of medical facilities, where high indoor air quality is expected, is discussed in ASHRAE *Standard* 62.1, Chapter 8 of the 2015 *ASHRAE Handbook—HVAC Applications*, and other publications [e.g., FGI (2014)].

Commercial and institutional building ventilation systems are typically designed to provide slight pressurization to reduce infiltration. This pressurization is achieved by having the outdoor or makeup airflow rate higher than the exhaust or relief airflow rate. In these buildings, infiltration is therefore usually neglected in HVAC design except in areas such as lobbies and loading docks, where infiltration can be important because of doors. However, as discussed previously, this little to no infiltration may only be achieved in practice with very tight envelope construction (e.g., including a continuous air barrier). As discussed in the section on Driving Mechanisms for Ventilation and Infiltration, wind and stack effect can also cause significant infiltration and exfiltration. Ventilation airflow rates for commercial and institutional buildings are typically determined using procedures in ASHRAE *Standard* 62.1. In these procedures for designing mechanical ventilation systems, no credit is given for infiltration. However, weather-driven pressure differentials may be significant and need to be considered when designing the ventilation system.

Ventilation Rate Procedure

Per ASHRAE *Standard* 62.1, the design ventilation rate is determined starting with a table of minimum ventilation requirements for different space types. These requirements are expressed as an outdoor airflow rate per occupant or per unit floor area, or often both, depending on space type. These ventilation rates are based on air pollutants generated by people, activities, and building materials and furnishings. The rates are then adjusted for various parameters (e.g., multiple zones, type of room air distribution).

The HVAC designer faces several challenges in designing an air distribution system to deliver outdoor air to building occupants. The first is to determine whether the outdoor air is acceptable for use, and to design a system for cleaning the air if it is not acceptable. A second is to design an air intake and distribution system that will *deliver* the required level of outdoor air to the occupied portions of the building, and not just *admit* it to an air handler. This outdoor air must be delivered not only at design conditions, but throughout the year. The task is complicated by weather-related variations in indoor/outdoor pressure difference. Other complications include pressure variations caused by building components such as intermittent exhaust fans or dirty filters, and probably most significantly by supply flow variations associated with variable-air-volume (VAV) systems (Janu et al. 1995; Mumma and Wong 1990). This delivery issue is related to the discussion in the section on Air Change Effectiveness.

Multiple Spaces

Many commercial and institutional buildings have multiple-zone, recirculating ventilation systems wherein one or more conventional air handlers condition a mixture of outdoor and recirculated air (**supply air**) to more than one ventilation zone. Each zone may have a different outdoor air fraction required by ASHRAE *Standard* 62.1, but each air handler can typically only provide one outdoor air fraction. Therefore, the zone that requires the greatest outdoor air fraction (the **critical zone**) defines the outdoor air intake rate of the air handler. Consequently, all other zones receive more outdoor air than their minimum requirement. These zones can be considered to have unused ventilation air, which could be returned to the air handler and recirculated; thus, the outdoor air fraction at the air handler could be reduced while still meeting the needs of the critical zone. A method to address multiple-zone recirculating systems, based on the system ventilation efficiency equation (SVEE), is provided in the ventilation rate procedure of *Standard* 62.1. ASHRAE-sponsored research experimentally tested the validity of this equation and confirmed that the SVEE is a valid predictor of ventilation distribution in a building (Yuill et al. 2012).

Secondary Path Systems. Some systems circulate unused ventilation air through paths other than through the central air handler. Common examples include transfer fans and fan-powered boxes. Warden (1995) suggested that *Standard* 62.1 should allow for the increased distribution efficiency that is possible with these systems, and presented a generalized SVEE that includes secondary air paths. A form of this equation is given in Equation (A-3) of ASHRAE *Standard* 62.1-2010.

Equation (A-3) depends on the ventilating ability of the secondary air E_r. The standard previously described E_r in terms of the proportion of average system return air directly recirculated from the critical zone. Yuill et al. (2008) argued that the formulation of Equation (A-3) implicitly defines E_r as a descriptor of the vitiation of the secondary air, and presented a formal definition of E_r, a version of which was adopted for *Standard* 62.1. Under this definition, if secondary air is drawn from an area that is less contaminated than the building average, values of E_r greater than 1 are possible. Yuill et al. (2012) measured E_r in several locations in an office building and found results ranging from 0.74 to 1.01. Results in the same building could have ranged from 0.14 to 1.13 if the fan-powered boxes had been located differently.

Survey of Ventilation Rates in Office Buildings

Relatively few measurements of as-built office building ventilation performance have been conducted, and those data generally have not used consistent measurement methods or involved representative collections of buildings. The U.S. Environmental Protection Agency (EPA) Building Assessment Survey and Evaluation (BASE) study involved indoor environmental measurements, including ventilation, in 100 randomly selected office buildings using a standardized protocol (EPA 2003). Persily et al. (2005) analyzed the BASE data and found that outdoor air ventilation rates measured using duct traverses at air handler intakes were higher than might be expected, with a mean of about 117 cfm per person. However, these elevated values are partially explained by low occupant density (mean of about four persons per 1000 ft^2) and high outdoor air fractions (mean of about 35%). Considering only values that correspond to minimum outdoor air intake, the mean ventilation rate was 23 cfm per workstation. About one-half the ventilation rates under minimum outdoor air intake were below 20 cfm per person. Another key outcome of this study is documentation of measured airflow rates that are quite different from their design values. This finding highlights the need for good system commissioning and maintenance to achieve design intent. Designing and configuring systems to encourage regular maintenance by providing easy access to key system components is also important.

13. OFFICE BUILDING EXAMPLE

Ventilation and infiltration principles from this chapter, *Standard* 62.1-2010, and elsewhere are applied to a conventional office building in Atlanta, Georgia. The infiltration, local exhaust, or ventilation airflow rates determined can be used later in the design process (1) as input for the heating and cooling load calculations; (2) for sizing fans, ducts, and dampers; and (3) for inclusion in the construction documents' air-handling units (AHUs) schedules and specifications.

This example relies on the 2010 edition of ASHRAE *Standard* 62.1; because this and other standards are updated frequently, users should check for the latest edition.

Location

The example building is about 8 mi northeast of downtown Atlanta, and is close to a major highway and its access roads. Atlanta's climate is hot and humid in the summer, and has relatively mild winters. The average annual outdoor air temperature is about 60.6°F and the heating degree-days per year, base 65°F (HDD_{65}), are about 3265 (Rock 2005). From Chapter 14, the winter 99% design outdoor air (OA) temperature is 23°F, whereas the 1% cooling dry-bulb temperature is 91°F, with a mean coincident wet-bulb temperature of 74°F. The 99.6 and 0.4% design wind speeds are 12 mph in the winter and 9 mph in the summer, both from the northwest. Warm and humid winds also travel north from the Gulf of Mexico, and occasionally the wind is from the Atlantic Ocean from the southeast.

Building

The approximately 30,500 ft^2 building is a two-story, flat-roofed, slab-on-grade commercial office building with a substantial roof overhang in each direction. Materials and construction quality are average commercial grade. Double-paned windows, and similar spandrel glass, are fixed in their metal curtain wall frames; all windows are nonoperable. The remaining portions of the exterior walls are brick. There are relatively few exterior doors, as described later in this example. The building is surrounded by black asphalt driveways, a parking lot, and some vegetation. The nearby highway is across a parallel two-lane access road, to the northwest.

Occupancy

The building is occupied during normal weekday business hours, and occasionally for special weekend events. Night and weekend thermostat setbacks are used. On the perimeter of the building are mostly single-person offices and conference rooms. The core of the building is mainly open plan with cubicle workspaces, as well as various support rooms, restrooms, two stair towers, and an elevator. There is a large mailroom on the first floor and a lunchroom on the second. Occupant density is high during workdays. The overhead fluorescent lighting is typical of such office buildings, and there are significant computing, printing, and copying equipment loads. Smoking is not allowed in the building.

The building is owner occupied. Owners generally have long-term interests in minimizing costs, and in maximizing indoor air quality and thermal comfort so that workers' productivity is high.

Infiltration

For this example, assume a conventional all-air overhead HVAC system, and that the building is well sealed. Consequently, a slightly positive overall building pressurization is assumed during occupied hours. Because water condensation in the exterior envelope of the building is possible, air pressurization should be as low as is practical, and continuous air and moisture retarders should be installed. As a more expensive alternative to slight pressurization, the automatic control system could actively manage the dampers' positions and fans' operation to maintain an average neutral pressurization, relative to the outdoors. In either case, a good assumption is that infiltration is minimized, the windows and spandrel glass are fixed and well sealed, and the exterior doors are normally kept closed. During high-wind conditions beyond design, windward perimeter spaces may have some infiltration loads, but under nonpeak outdoor temperatures, a well-zoned HVAC system should have enough capacity to handle these extra loads. If both the OA temperature and wind are extreme, then these upwind perimeter spaces may become slightly uncomfortable. These extreme conditions are expected to occur only a few hours in a typical year.

Spaces with exterior doors can experience significant infiltration loads when people enter and leave. First-floor vestibules on the north and south sides of the building help limit this infiltration through the two main entrances. The double doors from stair tower #2 have infrequent use, and a high level of thermal comfort in stair towers is not typically expected. Thus, brief infiltration surges in stair tower #2 are deemed acceptable. However, the doors from the parking lot to the mailroom are frequently used by staff for shipping, receiving, entrance, and egress, and infiltration loads on the vestibules and mailroom are of concern. Many designers choose to ignore these extra loads in pressurized buildings, because they are transient and not easily characterized; the systems' capacities are likely sufficient to minimize uncomfortable conditions in these spaces. In this example, however, the HVAC designer is concerned about summertime airborne moisture, especially in the mailroom where books and other publications are stored, because strong, humid, southerly winds easily overcome a slight indoor pressurization when the large doors to the parking lot are open.

This chapter and many of its supporting references describe detailed methods for estimating infiltration or air leakage. Typically, pressure differences, openings' coefficients, and hour-by-hour weather data are required to perform these transient calculations, usually using a computer program separate from that used for thermal load calculations. For HVAC design purposes for a building similar to the example, an air change rate of unconditioned outdoor air through infiltration, per space, expressed in air changes per hour or airflow rate (in cfm) is of more immediate use. Either value is then entered into the load calculation program. Unfortunately, accurate air changes per hour are difficult, if not impossible, to predict, so design estimates must be made. For example,

North Vestibule

- Gross floor area ≈ 11 ft × 13 ft = 143 ft^2
- Room volume ≈ 143 ft^2 × 9 ft = 1287 ft^3
- $ACH_{inf} \approx 1.0$, so
- $Q_{inf} \approx (1287\ \text{ft}^3 \times 1.0)/60\ \text{min/h} \approx 22\ \text{cfm}_{oa}$

Either 1.0 ach or 22 cfm of infiltration is then used as input for the load calculation program for this space. The 1.0 ach assumption was made by the designer during on-site observation that these particular manually operated exterior doors have low usage. If passage rates were known, Yuill's (1996) flow rate estimation method would have been used instead.

South Vestibule

- Gross floor area ≈ 8 ft × 10 ft = 80 ft^2
- Room volume ≈ 80 ft^2 × 9 ft = 720 ft^3
- $ACH_{inf} \approx 2.0$, so
- $Q_{inf} \approx (720\ \text{ft}^3 \times 2.0)/60\ \text{min/h} \approx 24\ \text{cfm}_{oa}$

In practice, this back entrance from the parking lot on the southeast side of the building is the primary means of entrance and egress, and as such, the estimated infiltration for it is increased to 2.0 ach, compared to the north vestibule's 1.0 ach.

In colder U.S. climates, it is common practice for low-cost commercial buildings to have only space heating, and not cooling, in stair towers and vestibules. However, for this building in the Southeast, the designer decided to provide cooling for these vestibules. Thus, the estimated infiltration rates are applied to both the heating and cooling load calculations for these spaces. The building's mailroom, which also has exterior doors, is to be heated and cooled, too.

Mailroom

- Gross floor area ≈ (51 ft × 22 ft) + (33 ft × 10 ft) = 1452 ft^2
- Room volume ≈ 1452 ft^2 × 9 ft = 13,068 ft^3
- $ACH_{inf} \approx 0.5$, so
- $Q_{inf} \approx (13{,}068\ \text{ft}^3 \times 0.5)/60\ \text{min/h} \approx 109\ \text{cfm}_{oa}$

Even though the mailroom has only a single layer of doors to the outdoors, and not a vestibule, the designer estimated the infiltration at a lower rate (0.5 ach) than those for the vestibules. This is because of the mailroom's large interior volume relative to its exterior doorway's area.

Note that *no* estimate of air changes will be accurate at all times; this portion of HVAC design is still largely an art because of the many unknowns and variability of weather and building use. For improved energy conservation, all exterior doors must be extremely well weatherstripped and have automatic closers. A sign indicating that the doors should be kept closed when not in use should be placed on the mailroom's exterior doors. High-quality gaskets and sealants for the windows and spandrel glass are also required to minimize infiltration.

Local Exhausts

(This section assumes that ANSI/ASHRAE *Standard* 62.1-2010 has been adopted into the local building code without modification.) At least 10 rooms require direct, powered air exhaust: two restrooms per floor, a darkroom, three designated photocopy spaces, and two janitors' closets. The restrooms have three flushable fixtures each, so from Table 6-4 of *Standard* 62.1-2010, with intermittent use, each restroom requires

$$Q_{ea} = 3\ \text{units} \times 50\ \text{cfm/unit} = 150\ \text{cfm}$$

Also from Table 6-4, the darkroom on the second floor needs

Gross floor area ≈ 10 ft × 15 ft = 150 ft^2

$$Q_{ea} = 150 \text{ ft}^2 \times 1.00 \text{ cfm/ft}^2 = 150 \text{ cfm}$$

Similarly, the designated photocopy areas need 0.50 $\text{cfm}_{ea}/\text{ft}^2$, so

$$\text{First floor, plan east: } \approx 80 \text{ ft}^2 \times 0.50 \text{ cfm/ft}^2 = 40 \text{ cfm}_{ea}$$

$$\text{First floor, plan southwest: } \approx 160 \text{ ft}^2 \times 0.50 \text{ cfm/ft}^2 = 80 \text{ cfm}_{ea}$$

$$\text{Second floor, plan east: } \approx 112 \text{ ft}^2 \times 0.50 \text{ cfm/ft}^2 = 56 \text{ cfm}_{ea}$$

The two small janitors' closets, one on each floor, also require exhaust:

$$60 \text{ ft}^2 \times 1.00 \text{ cfm/ft}^2 = 60 \text{ cfm}_{ea}$$

These local exhaust airflow rates are then entered into the load calculation program. They are room loads, attached to each particular space, and are *not* combined and entered as systems-level loads. The load calculation program evaluates the room loads, appropriately combines them, and then finds the systems-level loads for various peak hours.

Some local code authorities amend the requirements of *Standard* 62.1, or have not yet adopted the most current version, so significant deviations from these examples are possible. For example, in much of the United States, janitorial closets and photocopy rooms have not been required to have local exhausts. *Standard* 62.1-2010 recognized that these spaces can be significant sources of airborne pollutants, and some direct exhaust from each of them can be very beneficial for improving indoor air quality.

Ventilation

(This section also assumes that ANSI/ASHRAE *Standard* 62.1-2010 has been adopted into local code without changes.) Ventilation air is needed to maintain acceptable indoor air quality. The example building is well sealed, natural ventilation is not used, and no credit for any infiltration is taken toward ventilation air requirements, as is typical for conventional commercial buildings. Thus, minimum ventilation air required by *Standard* 62.1 is provided mechanically through the building's AHUs. Because smoking is not allowed in the building, no extra ventilation for environmental tobacco smoke (ETS) is needed. However, considering outdoor air pollution from the major highway nearby as well as metropolitan Atlanta's smog, some outdoor air pretreatment may be considered later in the design process.

Standard 62.1 has two methods for determining needed ventilation airflow rates: the performance IAQ procedure (IAQP), and the prescriptive ventilation rate procedure (VRP). Most HVAC designers of conventional buildings with normal occupancies and outdoor air conditions use the VRP, which is appropriate for this example building.

Required ventilation air, which is solely conditioned outdoor air, is admitted to this building through two air-handling units; each AHU serves one floor. Flow rates of outdoor air are input values for, and carried through to the results of, the load calculation simulation. Energy needed to condition the outdoor air ultimately is a systems-level load, because all of this ventilation air is conditioned by the AHUs before its introduction to the building.

Commercial load calculation programs often provide suggested values of ventilation airflow rates and occupancy schedules, but may not have been updated to reflect the latest VRP requirements and procedures of *Standard* 62.1. As such, it is difficult to present an example here; instead, a sample check using some assumed values for the first-floor executive director's office is given. It is assumed that this room is a separate thermal zone because of its use and its location on the southwest corner of the building and thus two afternoon solar exposures.

Executive Director's Office

- Gross floor area ≈ 12 ft × 21 ft = 252 ft^2
- Room volume ≈ 252 ft^2 × 9 ft = 2268 ft^3
- Assumed supply air Q_{sa} = 412 cfm

The supply airflow rate was estimated using 300 ft^2/ton, a sensible heat factor of 0.9, a cooling supply (55°F) to room (75°F) air temperature difference of 20°F, 12,000 Btu/h per ton of cooling, and the sensible heat equation 1.1 × cfm_{sa} × ΔT. From Table 6-1 of *Standard* 62.1-2010, the office's population P can be estimated as

$$P = 252 \text{ ft}^2 \times 5 \text{ occupants}/1000 \text{ ft}^2 = 1.26$$

In this case, however, there is only one regular occupant of the space. The needed ventilation airflow rate to the breathing zone V_{bz} is then found from the table as follows:

$$V_{bz} = R_p P_z + R_a A_z$$

$$V_{bz} = (5 \text{ cfm/person} \times 1 \text{ person}) + (0.06 \text{ cfm/ft}^2 \times 252 \text{ ft}^2) = 20.12 \text{ cfm}$$

where

R_p = outdoor airflow rate required per person, from *Standard* 62.1's Table 6-1, cfm
P_z = zone population (largest number of people expected to occupy the zone during typical use)
R_a = outdoor airflow rate required per unit area, from *Standard* 62.1's Table 6-1, cfm
A_z = occupiable floor area of zone, ft^2

Note that *Standard* 62.1's VRP includes a building component $R_a A_z$, as well as the traditional per-person people component.

Because this is a conventional office building, with ceiling plenums and no raised floors, overhead air supply and return is assumed. The cooling mode, not heating, is dominant in this and most other U.S. office buildings that have high internal heat gains and well-sealed and insulated envelopes. From the standard's Table 6-2, with ceiling supply of cool air, the zone air distribution effectiveness E_z is estimated as 1.0. From Equation (6-2) of the standard, the design zone outdoor airflow rate V_{oz} is then

$$V_{oz} = V_{bz}/E_z = 20.12 \text{ cfm}/1.0 = 20.12 \text{ cfm}$$

But this is still not the amount of outdoor air that must be conditioned by the air handler: the rate must be adjusted for inefficiencies and recirculation in the air distribution system.

Because single-duct VAV with terminal reheat air distribution systems were initially planned by the designer, *Standard* 62.1's multiple-zone recirculating systems adjustment is needed. For this thermal zone, the primary outdoor air fraction Z_p for its VAV terminal unit and downstream is

$$Z_p = V_{oz}/V_{pz} = 20.12 \text{ cfm}/412 \text{ cfm} = 0.05, \text{ or } 5\%$$

However, for VAV systems, the minimum expected primary airflow rate should be used. In this case, 412 cfm is the peak design airflow rate. Designers often assume about 30% of this peak flow as the minimum in VAV systems, so for this space, 412 × 0.3 = 124 cfm. The adjusted primary outdoor air fraction is then

$$Z_p = V_{oz}/V_{pz} = 20.12 \text{ cfm}/124 \text{ cfm} = 0.16, \text{ or } 16\%$$

The preceding calculations need to be performed for every thermal zone on each air handler. Then, for each system, the highest primary outdoor air fraction is used to estimate the air distribution systems' ventilation effectiveness; the 62.1 user's manual (ASHRAE 2010b) includes a spreadsheet for doing these calculations. Increasingly, load calculation programs include the necessary routines and data.

For the purposes of this example, 0.16 is assumed to be the maximum Z_p, so, from Table 6.3 of *Standard* 62.1, the system ventilation efficiency E_v is 0.9. If, instead, the standard's Appendix A method for determining E_v were used, a value closer to 1.0 for perfect mixing would likely result for this example's conventional overhead all-air cooling system. Table 6-3's value of 0.9 is likely somewhat conservative, but is obtained quickly for design purposes.

Next, the uncorrected outdoor air intake flow rate V_{ou} is needed; *Standard* 62.1's Equation (6-6) includes diversity factor D to adjust the people component of the flow rate. All zones' flow rates are needed to perform this calculation. For this example, the uncorrected outdoor air intake flow rate for the first floor's AHU was estimated from floor area, an occupancy of 5 people per 1000 ft², and 20 cfm per person, and is assumed to be 1525 cfm. The adjusted outdoor air intake flow rate V_{ot} for this AHU is then

$$V_{ot} = V_{ou}/E_v = 1525 \text{ cfm}/0.9 = 1700 \text{ cfm}_{oa}$$

After load calculations are complete, these assumed airflow rates can be replaced with actual values for each zone, and the outdoor airflow rate can be updated. Repeating the load calculations may be necessary. The final value of the adjusted outdoor air intake flow rate is then reported on the AHU's equipment schedule so that testing, adjusting, and balancing (TAB) personnel and others can use this information to ensure that the system admits the desired flow rate of ventilation air. The information is also used to select air cleaners, dampers, coils, ducts, and fans.

For more examples on determining ventilation air rates for commercial buildings, see the user's manual for *Standard* 62.1 (ASHRAE 2010b). For low-rise residential buildings, consult ASHRAE *Standard* 62.2 and its user's manual (ASHRAE 2010a).

14. SYMBOLS

A = area, ft² or in²
c = flow coefficient, cfm/(in. of water)^n
c_p = specific heat, Btu/lb$_m$·°F
C = concentration, ppm
$\overline{C}$ = time averaged concentration
C_A = airflow coefficient for automatic doors, cfm/ft²·in. of water$^{0.5}$
C_D = discharge coefficient
C_p = pressure coefficient
C_s = stack flow coefficient, cfm²/in⁴·°F or (in. of water/°F)^n
C_v = effectiveness of openings
C_w = wind flow coefficient, cfm²/in⁴·mph² or (in. of water/mph²)^n
E = system efficiency
ELA = effective leakage area
F = tracer gas injection rate, cfm
$\overline{F}$ = time-averaged contaminant source strength, cfm
f = fractional on-time
g = gravitational acceleration, ft/s²
G = wind speed multiplier, Table 7
h = specific enthalpy, Btu/lb$_m$
H = height, ft
i = hour of year
I = air change rate, 1/time
I_i = instantaneous air change rate, 1/time
I_m = effective air change rate, 1/time
IDD = infiltration degree-days, °F·day/yr
L = leakage area, ft² or in²
n = pressure exponent
N = number of discrete time periods in period of interest
NL = normalized leakage
p = pressure, in. of water
P = parameter, or number of people
q = heat rate, Btu/h
Q = volumetric flow rate, cfm
$\overline{Q}$ = effective volumetric flow rate, cfm
R = outdoor airflow rate, cfm
s = shelter factor
S = source strength, cfm
t = time
T = temperature, °F or °R
U = wind speed, mph
V = volume, ft³, or ventilation airflow rate, cfm
W = humidity ratio, lb$_m$ water/lb$_m$ dry air
ε_I = air change effectiveness
θ_{age} = age of air, s, min, or h
ρ = air density, lb$_m$/ft³
τ = time constant, s, min, or h
ϕ = wind angle, degrees

Subscripts

a = area
b = base
ba = bypass air
bz = breathing zone
c = calculated
ca = recirculated air
da = dry air
$depress$ = depressurization
e = effective
ea = exhaust air
f = floor
i = indoor or time counter for summation (instantaneous)
inf = infiltration
H = building height, eaves or roof
ka = makeup air
l = latent
la = relief air
L = leakage or local
ma = mixed air
met = meteorological station location
n = normalized
N = nominal
NPL = neutral pressure level
o = outdoor, initial condition, or reference
oa = outdoor air
ot = adjusted outdoor air
ou = uncorrected outdoor air
oz = zone outdoor
p = pressure, or primary
$press$ = pressurization
r = reference
s = sensible or stack
sa = supply air
S = space or source
w = wind or water
v = ventilation
z = zone

REFERENCES

ASHRAE members can access *ASHRAE Journal* articles and ASHRAE research project final reports at technologyportal.ashrae.org. Articles and reports are also available for purchase by nonmembers in the online ASHRAE Bookstore at www.ashrae.org/bookstore.

ACGIH. 2016. *Industrial ventilation: A manual of recommended practice*, 29th ed. American Conference of Governmental Industrial Hygienists, Cincinnati, OH.

Ackerman, M.Y., J.D. Dale, and D.J. Wilson. 2006. Infiltration heat recovery, part 1: Field studies in an instrumented test building (RP-1169). *ASHRAE Transactions* 112(2):597-608. *Paper* QC-06-056.

AIVC. 1994. An analysis and data summary of the AIVC's numerical database. *Technical Note* 44. International Energy Agency Air Infiltration and Ventilation Centre, Sint-Stevens-Woluwe, Belgium.

Akins, R.E., J.A. Peterka, and J.E. Cermak. 1979. Averaged pressure coefficients for rectangular buildings, vol. 1, *Proceedings of the Fifth International Wind Engineering Conference*, Fort Collins, pp. 369-380.

Allard, F., and M. Herrlin. 1989. Wind-induced ventilation. *ASHRAE Transactions* 95(2):722-728. *Paper* VA-89-10-2.

Anis, W. 2001. The impact of airtightness on system design. *ASHRAE Journal* 43(12):31-35.

Anis, W., and T. Brennan. 2014. Measuring airtightness of mid and high-rise non-residential buildings. ASHRAE Research Project RP-1478, *Final Report*.

Apte, M.G., W.J. Fisk, and J.M. Daisey. 2000. Associations between indoor CO_2 concentrations and sick building syndrome symptoms in US office buildings: An analysis of the 1994-1996 BASE study data. *Indoor Air* 10(4):246-257.

ASHRAE. 2003. Risk management guidance for health, safety and environmental security under extraordinary incidents. *Report*, Presidential Ad Hoc Committee for Building Health and Safety Under Extraordinary Incidents.

ASHRAE. 2010a. Standard *62.2-2010 user's manual*.

ASHRAE. 2010b. Standard *62.1-2010 user's manual*.

ASHRAE. 2012. Method of testing general ventilation air-cleaning devices for removal efficiency by particle size. ANSI/ASHRAE *Standard* 52.2-2012.

ASHRAE. 2013. Thermal environmental conditions for human occupancy. ASHRAE *Standard* 55-2013.

ASHRAE. 2010. Ventilation for acceptable indoor air quality. ANSI/ASHRAE *Standard* 62.1-2010.

ASHRAE. 2016. Ventilation and acceptable indoor air quality in low-rise residential buildings. ANSI/ASHRAE *Standard* 62.2-2016.

ASHRAE. 2016. Energy standard for buildings except low-rise residential buildings. ANSI/ASHRAE *Standard* 90.1-2016.

ASHRAE. 2004. Air leakage performance for detached single-family residential building. ANSI/ASHRAE *Standard* 119-1988 (RA 2004) (withdrawn).

ASHRAE. 2002. Measuring air-change effectiveness. ANSI/ASHRAE *Standard* 129-97 (RA 2002).

ASHRAE. 2013. Ventilation of health care facilities. ANSI/ASHRAE/ASHE *Standard* 170-2013.

ASHRAE. 2014. Standard for the design of high-performance green buildings. ANSI/ASHRAE/IES/USGBC *Standard* 189.1-2014.

ASHRAE. 2015. Ventilation and indoor air quality in low-rise residential buildings. ASHRAE *Guideline* 24-2015.

Ask, A. 2003. Ventilation and air leakage. *ASHRAE Journal* 45(11):28-36.

ASTM. 2012. Test method for determining rate of air leakage through exterior windows, curtain walls, and doors under specified pressure differences across the specimen. *Standard* E283-04 (R2012). American Society for Testing and Materials, West Conshohocken, PA.

ASTM. 2011. Test method for determining air change in a single zone by means of a tracer gas dilution. *Standard* E741-11. American Society for Testing and Materials, West Conshohocken, PA.

ASTM. 2010. Test method for determining air leakage rate by fan pressurization. *Standard* E779-10. American Society for Testing and Materials, West Conshohocken, PA.

ASTM. 2010. Test method for field measurement of air leakage through installed exterior windows and doors. *Standard* E783-02 (R2010). American Society for Testing and Materials, West Conshohocken, PA.

ASTM. 2009. Practices for air leakage site detection in building envelopes and air barrier systems. *Standard* E1186-03 (R2009). American Society for Testing and Materials, West Conshohocken, PA.

ASTM. 2011. Test methods for determining airtightness of buildings using an orifice blower door. *Standard* E1827-11. American Society for Testing and Materials, West Conshohocken, PA.

ASTM. 2011. Guide for assessing depressurization-induced backdrafting and spillage from vented combustion appliances. *Standard* E1998-11. American Society for Testing and Materials, West Conshohocken, PA.

Axley, J.W. 2001a. *Application of natural ventilation for U.S. commercial buildings—Climate suitability, design strategies and methods, modeling studies*. GCR-01-820, National Institute of Standards and Technology, Gaithersburg, MD.

Axley, J.W. 2001b. Residential passive ventilation systems: Evaluation and design. *Technical Note* 54. International Energy Agency Air Infiltration and Ventilation Centre, Sint-Stevens-Woluwe, Belgium.

Axley, J., S. Emmerich, S. Dols, and G. Walton. 2002. An approach to the design of natural and hybrid ventilation systems for cooling buildings. *Proceedings of the 9th International Conference on Indoor Air Quality and Climate*, Monterey, CA. Available at www.nist.gov/manuscript-publication-search.cfm?pub_id=860870.

Bankvall, C.G. 1987. Air movements and thermal performance of the building envelope. In *Thermal insulation: Materials and systems*, pp. 124-131. F.J. Powell and S.L. Mathews, eds. American Society for Testing and Materials, West Conshohocken, PA.

Barley, D. 2001. *Overview of residential ventilation activities in the Building America Program (phase I)*. NREL/TP-550-30107, National Renewable Energy Laboratory, Golden, CO.

Batterman, S., G. Hatzivasilis, and C. Jia. 2006. Concentrations and emissions of gasoline and other vapors from residential vehicle garages. *Atmospheric Environment* 40:1828-1844.

Bauman, F., and A. Daly. 2003. *Underfloor air distribution design guide*. ASHRAE.

Berg-Munch, B., G. Clausen, and P.O. Fanger. 1986. Ventilation requirements for the control of body odor in spaces occupied by women. *Environmental International* 12(1-4):195.

Berlad, A.L., N. Tutu, Y. Yeh, R. Jaung, R. Krajewski, R. Hoppe and F. Salzano. 1978. Air intrusion effects on the performance of permeable insulation systems. In *Thermal insulation performance*, STP 718, pp. 181-194. D. McElroy and R. Tye, eds. American Society for Testing and Materials, West Conshohocken, PA.

Blomsterberg, A.K., and D.T. Harrje. 1979. Approaches to evaluation of air infiltration energy losses in buildings. *ASHRAE Transactions* 85(1):797. *Paper* PH-79-10-1.

Bohac, D.L., D.T. Harrje, and L.K. Norford. 1985. Constant concentration infiltration measurement technique: An analysis of its accuracy and field measurements, 176. *Proceedings of the ASHRAE/DOE/BTECC Conference on the Thermal Performance of the Exterior Envelopes of Buildings III,* Clearwater Beach, FL.

Bohac, D.L., D.T. Harrje, and G.S. Horner. 1987. Field study comparisons of constant concentration and PFT infiltration measurements. *Proceedings of the 8th IEA Conference of the Air Infiltration and Ventilation Centre*, Überlingen, Germany, pp. 47-62.

Bradley, B. 1993. Implementation of the AIM-2 infiltration model in HOT-2000. *Report*, for Natural Resources Canada.

Buchanan, C.R., and M.H. Sherman. 2000. A mathematical model for infiltration heat recovery. *Proceedings of the 21st IEA Conference of the Air Infiltration and Ventilation Centre*, The Hague, Netherlands. *Report* LBNL-44294. Lawrence Berkeley National Laboratory, Berkeley, CA.

Cain, W.S., B. Leaderer, R. Isseroff, L. Berglund, R. Huey, and E. Lipsitt. 1983. Ventilation requirements in buildings—I. Control of occupancy odor and tobacco smoke odor. *Atmospheric Environment* 17(6):1183-1197.

CGSB. 2005. Depressurization test. CAN/CGSB *Standard* 51.71-2005. Canadian General Standards Board, Ottawa, ON.

CGSB. 1986. Determination of the airtightness of building envelopes by the fan depressurization method. *Standard* 149.10-M86. Canadian General Standards Board, Ottawa, ON.

CGSB. 1996. Determination of the overall envelope airtightness of buildings by the fan pressurization method using the building's air handling systems. *Standard* 149.15-96. Canadian General Standards Board, Ottawa, ON.

Charlesworth, P.S. 1988. Measurement of air exchange rates. Chapter 2 in *Air exchange rate and airtightness measurement techniques—An applications guide.* International Energy Agency Air Infiltration and Ventilation Centre, Sint-Stevens-Woluwe, Belgium.

Chastain, J.P. 1987. *Pressure gradients and the location of the neutral pressure axis for low-rise structures under pure stack conditions*. Unpublished M.S. thesis. University of Kentucky, Lexington.

Chastain, J.P., and D.G. Colliver. 1989. Influence of temperature stratification on pressure differences resulting from the infiltration stack effect. *ASHRAE Transactions* 95(1):256-268. *Paper* 3230.

Chastain, J.P., D.G. Colliver, and P.W. Winner, Jr. 1987. Computation of discharge coefficients for laminar flow in rectangular and circular openings. *ASHRAE Transactions* 93(2):2259-2283. *Paper* NT-87-27-1.

CHBA. 1994. *HOT2000 technical manual*. Canadian Home Builders Association, Ottawa, ON.

CIBSE. 2000. Testing buildings for air leakage. *Standard* TM-23. Chartered Institution of Building Services Engineers, London.

CIBSE. 2005. *Natural ventilation in non-domestic buildings*. Chartered Institution of Building Services Engineers, London.

Claridge, D.E., and S. Bhattacharyya. 1990. The measured impact of infiltration in a test cell. *ASME Journal of Solar Energy Engineering* 112: 123-126.

Claridge, D.E., M. Krarti, and S. Bhattacharyya. 1988. Preliminary measurements of the energy impact of infiltration in a test cell. *Proceedings of the Fifth Annual Symposium on Improving Building Energy Efficiency in Hot and Humid Climates*, pp. 308-317.

Cole, J.T., T.S. Zawacki, R.H. Elkins, J.W. Zimmer, and R.A. Macriss. 1980. Application of a generalized model of air infiltration to existing homes. *ASHRAE Transactions* 86(2):765. *Paper* DV-80-09-2.

Collet, P.F. 1981. Continuous measurements of air infiltration in occupied dwellings. *Proceedings of the 2nd IEA Conference of the Air Infiltration Centre*, Stockholm, p. 147.

CSA. 2016. Residential carbon monoxide alarming devices. CAN/CSA *Standard* C6.19-01 (R2016). Canadian Standards Association, Toronto.

CSA. 2014. Residential mechanical ventilation systems. CAN/CSA-F326-M91 (R2014). Canadian Standards Association, Toronto.

Cummings, J.B., and J.J. Tooley, Jr. 1989. Infiltration and pressure differences induced by forced air systems in Florida residences. *ASHRAE Transactions* 96(20):551-560. *Paper* VA-89-05-4.

Cummings, J.B., J.J. Tooley, Jr., and R. Dunsmore. 1990. Impacts of duct leakage on infiltration rates, space conditioning energy use and peak electrical demand in Florida homes. *Proceedings of the ACEEE Summer Study*, Pacific Grove, CA. American Council for an Energy-Efficient Economy, Washington, D.C.

Cutter. 1987. Air-to-air heat exchangers. In *Energy design update.* Cutter Information Corporation, Arlington, MA.

Desrochers, D., and A.G. Scott. 1985. Residential ventilation rates and indoor radon daughter levels. *Transactions of the APCA Specialty Conference, Indoor Air Quality in Cold Climates: Hazards and Abatement Measures*, Ottawa, p. 362.

Diamond, R.C., J.B. Dickinson, R.D. Lipschutz, B. O'Regan, and B. Shohl. 1982. The house doctor's manual. *Report* PUB-3017. Lawrence Berkeley National Laboratory, Berkeley, CA.

Diamond, R.C., M.P. Modera, and H.E. Feustel. 1986. Ventilation and occupant behaviour in two apartment buildings. *Proceedings of the 7th IEA Conference of the Air Infiltration and Ventilation Centre*, Stratford-upon-Avon, U.K. *Report* LBL-21862. Lawrence Berkeley National Laboratory, Berkeley, CA.

Dickerhoff, D.J., D.T. Grimsrud, and R.D. Lipschutz. 1982. Component leakage testing in residential buildings. *Proceedings of the American Council for an Energy-Efficient Economy, 1982 Summer Study*, Santa Cruz, CA. *Report* LBL 14735. Lawrence Berkeley National Laboratory, Berkeley, CA.

Dietz, R.N., R.W. Goodrich, E.A. Cote, and R.F. Wieser. 1986. Detailed description and performance of a passive perfluorocarbon tracer system for building ventilation and air exchange measurement. In *Measured air leakage of buildings*, STP 904, p. 203. H.R. Trechsel and P.L. Lagus, eds. American Society for Testing and Materials, West Conshohocken, PA.

Dols, W. S., L. Wang, S. J. Emmerich, and B. J. Polidoro. 2014. Development and application of an updated whole-building coupled thermal, airflow and contaminant transport simulation program (TRNSYS/CONTAM). *Journal of Building Performance Simulation*: 1-21.

D'Ottavio, T.W., G.I. Senum, and R.N. Dietz. 1988. Error analysis techniques for perfluorocarbon tracer derived multizone ventilation rates. *Building and Environment* 23(40).

Ek, C.W., S.A. Anisko, and G.O. Gregg. 1990. Air leakage tests of manufactured housing in the Northwest United States. In *Air change rate and airtightness in buildings*, STP 1067, pp. 152-164. M.H. Sherman, ed. American Society for Testing and Materials, West Conshohocken, PA.

Elmroth, A., and P. Levin. 1983. *Air infiltration control in housing*. International Energy Agency Air Infiltration Centre, Sint-Stevens-Woluwe, Belgium.

Emmerich, S.J. 2006. Simulated performance of natural and hybrid ventilation systems in an office building. *HVAC&R Research* (now *Science and Technology for the Built Environment*) 12(4):975-1004.

Emmerich, S.J., and A.K. Persily. 2005. Airtightness of commercial buildings in the U.S. *Proceedings of the 26th IEA Conference of the Air Infiltration and Ventilation Centre*, Brussels, pp 65-70.

Emmerich, S.J., and A.K. Persily. 2014. Analysis of US commercial building envelope air leakage database to support sustainable building design. *International Journal of Ventilation* 12(4):331-344. Available at www.nist.gov/manuscript-publication-search.cfm?pub_id=914293.

Emmerich, S.J., J.E. Gorfain, and C. Howard-Reed. 2003. Air and pollutant transport from attached garages to residential living spaces—Literature review and field test. *International Journal of Ventilation* 2(3):265-276.

Emmerich, S.J., W. S. Dols, and B. Polidoro. 2012. Application of a natural ventilation system design tool to a school building. *Proceeding of SimBuild 2012*, pp. 185-192. Available at www.nist.gov/customcf/get_pdf.cfm?pub_id=911004.

Emmerich, S.J., A.K. Persily, and L. Wang. 2013. Modeling and measuring the effects of portable gasoline powered generator exhaust on indoor carbon monoxide level. *Technical Note* (NIST TN) 1781. U.S. Department of Commerce, National Institute of Standards and Technology. Available at www.nist.gov/manuscript-publication-search.cfm?pub_id=912197.

Energy Resource Center. 1982. *How to house doctor*. University of Illinois, Chicago.

EPA. 2003. *A standardized EPA protocol for characterizing indoor air quality in large office buildings*. U.S. Environmental Protection Agency, Washington, D.C. Available from www.epa.gov/indoor-air-quality-iaq/standardized-epa-protocol-characterizing-indoor-air-quality-large-office.

Etheridge, D.W. 1977. Crack flow equations and scale effect. *Building and Environment* 12:181.

Etheridge, D.W., and D.K. Alexander. 1980. The British gas multi-cell model for calculating ventilation. *ASHRAE Transactions* 86(2):808. *Paper* DV-80-09-4.

Etheridge, D.W., and J.A. Nolan. 1979. Ventilation measurements at model scale in a turbulent flow. *Building and Environment* 14(1):53.

Eyre, D., and D. Jennings. 1983. *Air-vapour barriers—A general perspective and guidelines for installation*. Energy, Mines, and Resources Canada, Ottawa, ON.

Farrington, R., D. Martin, and R. Anderson. 1990. A comparison of displacement efficiency, decay time constant, and age of air for isothermal flow in an imperfectly mixed enclosure. *Proceedings of the ACEEE 1990 Summer Study on Energy Efficiency in Buildings*, pp. 4.35-4.43. American Council for an Energy-Efficient Economy, Washington, D.C.

Fennell, H.C., and J. Haehnel. 2005. Setting airtightness standards. *ASHRAE Journal* 47(9):26-31.

Feustel, H.E., and A. Raynor-Hoosen, eds. 1990. Fundamentals of the multizone air flow model—COMIS. *Technical Note* 29. International Energy Agency Air Infiltration and Ventilation Centre, Sint-Stevens-Woluwe, Belgium.

FGI. 2014. *Guidelines for design and construction of hospital and healthcare facilities*. American Institute of Architects, Facilities Guidelines Institute, and U.S. Department of Health and Human Services, Washington, D.C.

Fisk, W.J., R.K. Spencer, D.T. Grimsrud, F.J. Offermann, B. Pedersen, and R. Sextro. 1984. Indoor air quality control techniques: A critical review. *Report* LBL-16493. Lawrence Berkeley National Laboratory, Berkeley, CA.

Fisk, W.J., R.J. Prill, and O. Steppanen. 1989. A multi-tracer technique for studying rates of ventilation, air distribution patterns and air exchange efficiencies. *Proceedings of Conference on Building Systems—Room Air and Air Contaminant Distribution*, pp. 237-240. ASHRAE.

Fortmann, R.C., N.L. Nagda, and H.E. Rector. 1990. Comparison of methods for the measurement of air change rates and interzonal airflows to two test residences. In *Air change rate and airtightness in buildings*, STP 1067, pp. 104-118. M.H. Sherman, ed. American Society of Testing and Materials, West Conshohocken, PA.

Foster, M.P., and M.J. Down. 1987. Ventilation of livestock buildings by natural convection. *Journal of Agricultural Engineering Research* 37:1.

Fugler, D. 2004. Garage performance testing. *CMHC Research Highlights* (April). Canada Mortgage and Housing Corporation, Ottawa, ON.

Giesbrecht, P., and G. Proskiw. 1986. An evaluation of the effectiveness of air leakage sealing. In *Measured air leakage of buildings*, STP 904, p. 312. H.R. Trechsel and P.L. Lagus, eds. American Society for Testing and Materials, West Conshohocken, PA.

Grieve, P.W. 1989. *Measuring ventilation using tracer-gases*. Brüel and Kjær, Denmark.

Grimsrud, D.T., and K.Y. Teichman. 1989. The scientific basis of *Standard* 62-1989. *ASHRAE Journal* 31(10):51-54.

Grimsrud, D.T., M.H. Sherman, R.C. Diamond, P.E. Condon, and A.H. Rosenfeld. 1979. Infiltration-pressurization correlations: Detailed measurements in a California house. *ASHRAE Transactions* 85(1):851. *Paper* PH-79-10-5.

Grimsrud, D.T., M.H. Sherman, and R.C. Sonderegger. 1982. Calculating infiltration: Implications for a construction quality standard. *Proceedings of the ASHRAE/DOE Conference on the Thermal Performance of the Exterior Envelope of Buildings II*, Las Vegas, p. 422.

Grot, R.A., and R.E. Clark. 1979. Air leakage characteristics and weatherization techniques for low-income housing. *Proceedings of the ASHRAE/DOE Conference on the Thermal Performance of the Exterior Envelopes of Buildings*, p. 178. Orlando, FL.

Grot, R.A., and A.K. Persily. 1986. Measured air infiltration and ventilation rates in eight large office buildings. In *Measured air leakage of buildings*, STP 904, p. 151. H.R. Trechsel and P.L. Lagus, eds. American Society for Testing and Materials, West Conshohocken, PA.

GSA. 2010. *Facilities standards for the public buildings service*. PBS-P100. U.S. General Services Administration, Washington, D.C.

Hamlin, T.L. 1991. Ventilation and airtightness in new, detached Canadian housing. *ASHRAE Transactions* 97(2):904-910. *Paper* IN-91-12-3.

Hamlin, T., and W. Pushka. 1994. Predicted and measured air change rates in houses with predictions of occupant IAQ comfort. *Proceedings of the 15th IEA Air Infiltration and Ventilation Centre Conference*, Buxton, U.K., pp. 771-775.

Harrje, D.T., and G.J. Born. 1982. Cataloguing air leakage components in houses. *Proceedings of the ACEEE 1982 Summer Study*, Santa Cruz, CA. American Council for an Energy-Efficient Economy, Washington, D.C.

Harrje, D.T., and T.A. Mills, Jr. 1980. Air infiltration reduction through retrofitting. In *Building air change rate and infiltration measurements*. STP 719, p. 89. C.M. Hunt, J.C. King, and H.R. Trechsel, eds. American Society for Testing and Materials, West Conshohocken, PA.

Harrje, D.T., G.S. Dutt, and J. Beyea. 1979. Locating and eliminating obscure but major energy losses in residential housing. *ASHRAE Transactions* 85(2):521. *Paper* DE-79-03-1.

Harrje, D.T., R.A. Grot, and D.T. Grimsrud. 1981. Air infiltration site measurement techniques. *Proceedings of the 2nd IEA Conference of the Air Infiltration Centre*, p. 113. Stockholm, Sweden.

Harrje, D.T., G.S. Dutt, D.L. Bohac, and K.J. Gadsby. 1985. Documenting air movements and infiltration in multicell buildings using various tracer-gas techniques. *ASHRAE Transactions* 91(2):2012-2027. *Paper* HI-85-40-3.

Harrje, D.T., R.N. Dietz, M. Sherman, D.L. Bohac, T.W. D'Ottavio, and D.J. Dickerhoff. 1990. Tracer gas measurement systems compared in a multifamily building. In *Air change rate and airtightness in buildings*, STP 1067, pp. 5-12. M.H. Sherman, ed. American Society for Testing and Materials, West Conshohocken, PA.

Heiselberg, P. 2002. Principles of hybrid ventilation. *Final Report*, International Energy Agency Energy Conservation in Buildings and Community Systems, Annex 35. Hybrid Ventilation Centre, Aalborg University, Denmark.

Hekmat, D., H.E. Feustel, and M.P. Modera. 1986. Impacts of ventilation strategies on energy consumption and indoor air quality in single-family residences. *Energy and Buildings* 9(3):239.

Herrlin, M.K. 1985. MOVECOMP: A static-multicell-airflow-model. *ASHRAE Transactions* 91(2B):1989. *Paper* HI-85-40-1.

Holton, J.K., M.J. Kokayko, and T.R. Beggs. 1997. Comparative ventilation system evaluations. *ASHRAE Transactions* 103(2):675-692. *Paper* PH-97-08-1.

Honma, H. 1975. *Ventilation of dwellings and its disturbances*. Faibo Grafiska, Stockholm, Sweden.

Hopkins, L.P., and B. Hansford. 1974. Air flow through cracks. *Building Service Engineer* 42(September):123.

Hunt, C.M. 1980. Air infiltration: A review of some existing measurement techniques and data. In *Building air change rate and infiltration measurements*, STP 719, p. 3. C.M. Hunt, J.C. King, and H.R. Trechsel, eds. American Society for Testing and Materials, West Conshohocken, PA.

ICC. 2012a. *International energy conservation code®* (IECC®). International Code Council, Washington, D.C.

ICC. 2012b. *International green construction code®* (IgCC®). International Code Council, Washington, D.C.

ISO. 2006. Thermal performance of buildings—Determination of air permeability of buildings—Fan pressurization method. *Standard* 9972-2006. International Organization for Standardization, Geneva.

Iwashita, G., K. Kimura., et al. 1989. Pilot study on addition of olf units for perceived air pollution sources. *Proceedings of the SHASE Annual Meeting*, pp. 3221-3324. Society of Heating, Air-Conditioning and Sanitary Engineers of Japan, Tokyo.

Jacobson, D.I., G.S. Dutt, and R.H. Socolow. 1986. Pressurization testing, infiltration reduction, and energy savings. In *Measured air leakage of buildings*, STP 904, p. 265. H.R. Trechsel and P.L. Lagus, eds. American Society for Testing and Materials, West Conshohocken, PA.

Janssen, J.E. 1989. Ventilation for acceptable indoor air quality. *ASHRAE Journal* 31(10):40-48.

Janu, G.J., J.D. Wegner, and C.G. Nesler. 1995. Outdoor airflow control for VAV systems. *ASHRAE Journal* 37(4):62-68.

Johnson, T., and T. Long. 2005. Determining the frequency of open windows in residences: A pilot study in Durham, North Carolina during varying temperature conditions. *Journal of Exposure Analysis and Environmental Epidemiology* 15(4):329-349.

Judkoff, R., J.D. Balcomb, C.E. Handcock, G. Barker, and K. Subbarao. 1997. Side-by-side thermal tests of modular offices: A validation study of the STEM method. *Report*. National Renewable Energy Laboratory, Golden, CO.

Jump, D.A., I.S. Walker, and M.P. Modera. 1996. Field measurements of efficiency and duct retrofit effectiveness in residential forced air distribution systems. *Proceedings of the 1996 ACEEE Summer Study*, pp. 1.147-1.156. American Council for an Energy-Efficient Economy, Washington, D.C.

Kiel, D.E., and D.J. Wilson. 1986. Gravity driven airflows through open doors, 15.1. *Proceedings of the 7th IEA Conference of the Air Infiltration and Ventilation Centre*, Stratford-upon-Avon, U.K.

Kim, A.K., and C.Y. Shaw. 1986. Seasonal variation in airtightness of two detached houses. In *Measured air leakage of buildings*, STP 904, p. 17. H.R. Trechsel and P.L. Lagus, eds. American Society for Testing and Materials, West Conshohocken, PA.

Klauss, A.K., R.H. Tull, L.M. Roots, and J.R. Pfafflin. 1970. History of the changing concepts in ventilation requirements. *ASHRAE Journal* 12(6):51-55.

Klote, J.H., J.A. Milke, P.G. Turnbull, A. Kashef, and M.J. Ferreira. 2012. *Handbook of smoke control engineering*. ASHRAE.

Kohonen, R., T. Ojanen, and M. Virtanen. 1987. Thermal coupling of leakage flows and heating load of buildings. *Proceedings of the 8th IEA Air Infiltration and Ventilation Centre Conference*, Überlingen, Germany, pp. 10.1-10.22.

Kreith, F., and R. Eisenstadt. 1957. Pressure drop and flow characteristics of short capillary tubes at low Reynolds numbers. *ASME Transactions*, pp. 1070-1078.

Kronvall, J. 1980. *Correlating pressurization and infiltration rate data—Tests of an heuristic model*. Lund Institute of Technology, Division of Building Technology, Lund, Sweden.

Kumar, R., A.D. Ireson, and H.W. Orr. 1979. An automated air infiltration measuring system using SF6 tracer gas in constant concentration and decay methods. *ASHRAE Transactions* 85(2):385. *Paper* DE-2553.

Kvisgaard, B., and P.F. Collet. 1990. The user's influence on air change. In *Air change rate and airtightness in buildings*, STP 1067, pp. 67-76. M.H. Sherman, ed. American Society for Testing and Materials, West Conshohocken, PA.

Lagus, P.L. 1989. Tracer measurement instrumentation suitable for infiltration, air leakage, and airflow pattern characterization. *Proceedings of the Conference on Building Systems—Room Air and Air Contaminant Distribution*, pp. 97-102. ASHRAE.

Lagus, P., and A.K. Persily. 1985. A review of tracer-gas techniques for measuring airflows in buildings. *ASHRAE Transactions* 91(2B):1075. *Paper* HI-85-2-1.

Lecompte, J.G.N. 1987. The influence of natural convection in an insulated cavity on thermal performance of a wall. In *Insulation materials, testing, and applications*. American Society for Testing and Materials, West Conshohocken, PA.

Li, Y., and P. Heiselberg. 2003. Analysis methods for natural and hybrid ventilation—A critical literature review and recent developments. *International Journal of Ventilation* 1(4):3-20.

Liddament, M.W. 1988. The calculation of wind effect on ventilation. *ASHRAE Transactions* 94(2):1645-1660. *Paper* OT-88-13-1.

Liddament, M., and C. Allen. 1983. The validation and comparison of mathematical models of air infiltration. *Technical Note* 11. International Energy Agency Air Infiltration and Ventilation Centre, Sint-Stevens-Woluwe, Belgium.

Liu, M., and D.E. Claridge. 1992a. The measured energy impact of infiltration under dynamic conditions. *Proceedings of the 8th Symposium on Improving Building Systems in Hot and Humid Climates*, Dallas.

Liu, M., and D.E. Claridge. 1992b. The measured energy impact of infiltration in a test cell. *Proceedings of the 8th Symposium on Improving Building Systems in Hot and Humid Climates*, Dallas.

Liu, M., and D.E. Claridge. 1992c. The energy impact of combined solar radiation/infiltration/conduction effects in walls and attics. *Proceedings of the Thermal Performance of Exterior Envelopes of Buildings, 5th ASHRAE/DOE/BTECC Conference*, Clearwater Beach, FL.

Liu, M., and D.E. Claridge. 1995. Experimental methods for identifying infiltration heat recovery in building. *Proceedings of the Thermal Performance of Exterior Envelopes of Buildings, 6th ASHRAE/DOE/BTECC Conference*, Clearwater Beach, FL.

Lubliner, M., D.T. Stevens, and B. Davis. 1997. Mechanical ventilation in HUD-code manufactured housing in the Pacific Northwest. *ASHRAE Transactions* 103(1):693-705. *Paper* PH-97-08-2.

Marbek Resource Consultants. 1984. *Air sealing homes for energy conservation*. Energy, Mines and Resources Canada, Buildings Energy Technology Transfer Program, Ottawa, ON.

McDowell, T.P., S. Emmerich, J.W. Thornton, and G. Walton. 2003. Integration of airflow and energy simulation using CONTAM and TRNSYS. *ASHRAE Transactions* 109(2):757-770. *Paper* KC-03-10-2.

McWilliams, J., and M. Sherman. 2005. Review of literature related to residential ventilation requirements. *Paper* LBNL-57236. Lawrence Berkeley National Laboratory, Berkeley, CA.

Mendell, M.J. 1993. Non-specific symptoms in office workers: A review and summary of the epidemiologic literature. *Indoor Air* 3 (4):227-236.

Modera, M.P. 1989. Residential duct system leakage: Magnitude, impacts, and potential for reduction. *ASHRAE Transactions* 96(2):561-569. *Paper* VA-89-05-5.

Modera, M.P., and D.J. Wilson. 1990. The effects of wind on residential building leakage measurements. In *Air change rate and airtightness in buildings*, STP 1067, pp. 132-145. M.H. Sherman, ed. Lawrence Berkeley National Laboratory, Berkeley, CA. *Report* LBL-24195.

Modera, M.P., D. Dickerhoff, R. Jansky, and B. Smith. 1991. Improving the energy efficiency of residential air distribution systems in California. *Report* LBL-30866. Lawrence Berkeley National Laboratory, Berkeley, CA.

Mumma, S.A., and K.M. Shank. 2001. Achieving dry outside air in an energy efficient manner. *ASHRAE Transactions* 107(1):553-561. *Paper* AT-01-07-2.

Mumma, S.A., and Y.M. Wong. 1990. Analytical evaluation of outdoor airflow rate variation vs. supply airflow rate variation in VAV systems when the outside air damper position is fixed. *ASHRAE Transactions* 90(1):1197-1208.

Murphy, W.E., D.G. Colliver, and L.R. Piercy. 1991. Repeatability and reproducibility of fan pressurization devices in measuring building air leakage. *ASHRAE Transactions* 97(2):885-895. *Paper* IN-91-12-1.

Nelson, B.D., D.A. Robinson, and G.D. Nelson. 1985. Designing the envelope—Guidelines for buildings (SP-49). *Proceedings of the ASHRAE/DOE/BTECC Conference—Thermal Performance of the Exterior Envelopes of Buildings III*, Florida, pp. 1117-1122.

Ng, L.C., A. Musser, A.K. Persily, and S.J. Emmerich. 2012. Airflow and indoor air quality models of DOE reference commercial buildings. *Technical Note* 1734. National Institute of Standards and Technology, Gaithersburg, MD.

NRCC. 2010. *National Building Code of Canada*. National Research Council of Canada, Ottawa, ON.

Nylund, P.O. 1980. Infiltration and ventilation. *Report* D22:1980. Swedish Council for Building Research, Stockholm.

Offermann, F., and D. Int-Hout. 1989. Ventilation effectiveness measurements of three supply/return air configurations. *Environment International* 15(1-6):585-592.

Orme, M. 1999. Applicable models for air infiltration and ventilation calculations. *Technical Note* 51. International Energy Agency Air Infiltration and Ventilation Centre, Sint-Stevens-Woluwe, Belgium.

Ormerod, R. 1983. *Nuclear shelters: A guide to design*. Architectural Press, London.

Palmiter, L., and T. Bond. 1994. Modeled and measured infiltration II—A detailed case study of three homes. *Report* TR 102511. Electric Power Research Institute, Palo Alto, CA.

Palmiter, L., and I. Brown. 1989. The Northwest residential infiltration survey: Description and summary of results. *Proceedings of the ASHRAE/DOE/BTECC/CIBSE Conference—Thermal Performance of the Exterior Envelopes of Buildings IV*, Florida, pp. 445-457.

Palmiter, L., I.A. Brown, and T.C. Bond. 1991. Measured infiltration and ventilation in 472 all-electric homes. *ASHRAE Transactions* 97(2):979-987. *Paper* IN-91-15-3.

Parekh, A., K. Ruest, and M. Jacobs. 1991. Comparison of airtightness, indoor air quality and power consumption before and after air-sealing of high-rise residential buildings. *Proceedings of the 12th IEA Conference of the Air Infiltration and Ventilation Centre*, Sint-Stevens-Woluwe, Belgium.

Parker, G.B., M. McSorley, and J. Harris. 1990. The Northwest residential infiltration survey: A field study of ventilation in new houses in the Pacific Northwest. In *Air change rate and airtightness in buildings*, STP 1067, pp. 93-103. M.H. Sherman, ed. American Society for Testing and Materials, West Conshohocken, PA.

Persily, A. 1982. Repeatability and accuracy of pressurization testing. *Proceedings of the ASHRAE/DOE Conference, Thermal Performance of the Exterior Envelopes of Buildings II*, Las Vegas.

Persily, A.K. 1986. Measurements of air infiltration and airtightness in passive solar homes. In *Measured air leakage of buildings*, STP 904, p. 46. H.R. Trechsel and P.L. Lagus, eds. American Society for Testing and Materials, West Conshohocken, PA.

Persily, A.K. 1988. Tracer gas techniques for studying building air exchange. *Report* NBSIR 88-3708. National Institute of Standards and Technology, Gaithersburg, MD.

Persily, A.K. 1991. Design guidelines for thermal envelope integrity in office buildings. *Proceedings of the 12th IEA Conference of the Air Infiltration and Ventilation Centre*, Ottawa, ON.

Persily, A.K. 2004. Building ventilation and pressurization as a security tool. *ASHRAE Journal* 46 (9):18-24.

Persily, A.K., and J. Axley. 1990. Measuring airflow rates with pulse tracer techniques. In *Air change rate and airtightness in buildings*, pp. 31-51. STP 1067. M.H. Sherman, ed. American Society for Testing and Materials, West Conshohocken, PA.

Persily, A.K., and R.A. Grot. 1985a. The airtightness of office building envelopes. *Proceedings of the ASHRAE/DOE/BTECC Conference on the Thermal Performance of the Exterior Envelopes of Buildings III*, Clearwater Beach, FL, p. 125.

Persily, A.K., and R.A. Grot. 1985b. Accuracy in pressurization data analysis. *ASHRAE Transactions* 91(2B):105. *Paper* HI-85-03-2.

Persily, A.K., and R.A. Grot. 1986. Pressurization testing of federal buildings. In *Measured air leakage of buildings*, STP 904, p. 184. H.R. Trechsel and P.L. Lagus, eds. American Society for Testing and Materials, West Conshohocken, PA.

Persily, A.K., and G.T. Linteris. 1983. A comparison of measured and predicted infiltration rates. *ASHRAE Transactions* 89(2):183. *Paper* DC-83-04-1.

Persily, A.K., J. Gorfain, and G. Brunner. 2005. Ventilation design and performance in U.S. office buildings. *ASHRAE Journal* 47(4):30-35.

Persily, A.K., R.E. Chapman, S. Emmerich, W.S. Dols, H. Davis, P. Lavappa, and A. Rushing. 2007. Building retrofits for increased protection against airborne chemical and biological releases. NISTIR *Report* 7379. National Institute of Standards and Technology, Gaithersburg, MD.

Persily, A.K., A. Musser, and S. Emmerich. 2010. Modeled infiltration rate distributions for U.S. housing. *Indoor Air* 20(6):473-485.

Powell, F., M. Krarti, and A. Tuluca. 1989. Air movement influence on the effective thermal resistance of porous insulations: A literature survey. *Journal of Thermal Insulation* 12:239-251.

Price, P.N., and M.H. Sherman. 2006. Ventilation behavior and household characteristics in new California houses. *Report* LBNL-59620.

RDH. 2013. *Air leakage control in multi-unit residential buildings*. Canada Mortgage and Housing Corporation.

Reardon, J.T., and C.-Y. Shaw. 1997. Evaluation of five simple ventilation strategies suitable for houses without forced-air heating. *ASHRAE Transactions* 103(1):731-744. *Paper* PH-97-08-5.

Reeves, G., M.F. McBride, and C.F. Sepsy. 1979. Air infiltration model for residences. *ASHRAE Transactions* 85(1):667. *Paper* PH-79-07A-1.

Riley, M. 1990. Indoor air quality and energy conservation: The R-2000 home program experience. *Proceedings of Indoor Air '90: International Conference on Indoor Air Quality and Climate*, Ottawa, vol. 5, p. 143.

Robison, P.E., and L.A. Lambert. 1989. Field investigation of residential infiltration and heating duct leakage. *ASHRAE Transactions* 95(2):542-550. *Paper* VA-89-05-3.

Rock, B.A. 1992. *Characterization of transient pollutant transport, dilution, and removal for the study of indoor air quality*. Ph.D. dissertation, University of Colorado at Boulder. University Microfilms International.

Rock, B.A. 2005. A user-friendly model and coefficients for slab-on-grade load and energy calculations. *ASHRAE Transactions* 111(2):122-136. *Paper* 4795.

Rock, B.A. 2006. *Ventilation for environmental tobacco smoke*. Elsevier Science, New York, and ASHRAE.

Rock, B.A., and D. Zhu. 2002. *Designer's guide to ceiling-based air diffusion*. ASHRAE.

Rock, B.A., M.J. Brandemuehl, and R. Anderson. 1995. Toward a simplified design method for determining the air change effectiveness. *ASHRAE Transactions* 101(1):217-227. *Paper* 3852.

Rudd, A.F. 1998. Design/sizing methodology and economic evaluation of central-fan-integrated supply ventilation systems. *ACEEE 1998 Summer Study on Energy Efficiency in Buildings*. 23-28 August, Pacific Grove, CA. American Council for an Energy Efficient Economy, Washington, D.C.

Russell, M., M. Sherman, and A. Rudd. 2005. Review of residential ventilation technologies. *Paper* LBNL-576. Lawrence Berkeley National Laboratory, Berkeley, CA.

Sandberg, M.H. 1981. What is ventilation efficiency? *Building and Environment* 16:123-135.

Seppanen, O.A., W.J. Fisk and M.J. Mendell. 1999. Association of ventilation rates and CO_2 concentrations with health and other responses in commercial and institutional buildings. *Indoor Air* 9(4):226-252.

Shaw, C.Y. 1981. A correlation between air infiltration and air tightness for a house in a developed residential area. *ASHRAE Transactions* 87(2):333. *Paper* CI-2655.

Shaw, C.Y., and W.C. Brown. 1982. Effect of a gas furnace chimney on the air leakage characteristic of a two-story detached house. *Proceedings of the 3rd IEA Conference of the Air Infiltration Centre*, London.

Sherman, M.H. 1986. Infiltration degree-days: A statistic for quantifying infiltration-related climate. *ASHRAE Transactions* 92(2):161-181. *Paper* 2986.

Sherman, M.H. 1987. Estimation of infiltration from leakage and climate indications. *Energy and Buildings* 10(1):81.

Sherman, M.H. 1989a. Uncertainty in airflow calculations using tracer gas measurements. *Building and Environment* 24(4):347-354.

Sherman, M.H. 1989b. On the estimation of multizone ventilation rates from tracer gas measurements. *Building and Environment* 24(4):355-362.

Sherman, M.H. 1990. Tracer gas techniques for measuring ventilation in a single zone. *Building and Environment* 25(4):365-374.

Sherman, M.H. 1991. Single-zone stack-dominated infiltration modeling. *Proceedings of the 12th IEA Conference of the Air Infiltration and Ventilation Centre*, Ottawa, ON, pp. 297-314.

Sherman, M.H. 1992a. A power law formulation of laminar flow in short pipes. *Journal of Fluids Engineering* 114:601-605. *Report* LBL-29414, Lawrence Berkeley National Laboratory, Berkeley, CA.

Sherman, M.H. 1992b. Superposition in infiltration modeling. *Indoor Air* 2:101-114.

Sherman, M.H., and D. Dickerhoff. 1989. Description of the LBL multi-tracer measurement system. *Proceedings of the ASHRAE/DOE/BTECC/CIBSE Conference—Thermal Performance of the Exterior Envelopes of Buildings IV*, pp. 417-432.

Sherman, M.H., and D.J. Dickerhoff. 1998. Airtightness of U.S. dwellings. *ASHRAE Transactions* 104(2):1359-1367. *Paper* TO-98-25-1.

Sherman, M.H., and D.T. Grimsrud. 1980. Infiltration-pressurization correlation: Simplified physical modeling. *ASHRAE Transactions* 86(2):778. *Paper* DV-80-09-3.

Sherman, M.H., and N. Matson. 1997. Residential ventilation and energy characteristics. *ASHRAE Transactions* 103(1):717-730. *Paper* PH-97-08-4.

Sherman, M.H., and M.P. Modera. 1986. Comparison of measured and predicted infiltration using the LBL infiltration model. In *Measured air leakage of buildings*, STP 904, p. 325. H.R. Trechsel and P.L. Lagus, eds. American Society for Testing and Materials, West Conshohocken, PA.

Sherman, M.H., and D.J. Wilson. 1986. Relating actual and effective ventilation in determining indoor air quality. *Building and Environment* 21(3/4):135.

Sherman, M.H., D.T. Grimsrud, P.E. Condon, and B.V. Smith. 1980. Air infiltration measurement techniques. *Proceedings of the 1st IEA Conference of the Air Infiltration Centre*, London. *Report* LBL-10705. Lawrence Berkeley National Laboratory, Berkeley, CA.

Sibbitt, B.E., and T. Hamlin. 1991. *Meeting Canadian residential ventilation standard requirements with low-cost systems*. Canada Mortgage and Housing Corporation, Ottawa, ON.

Sinden, F.W. 1978a. Wind, temperature and natural ventilation—Theoretical considerations. *Energy and Buildings* 1(3):275.

Sinden, F.W. 1978b. Multi-chamber theory of air infiltration. *Building and Environment* 13:21-28.

Sorensen, J.H., and B.M. Vogt. 2001. Will duct tape and plastic really work? Issues related to expedient sheltering-in-place. *Report* ORNL/TM-2001/154. Oak Ridge National Laboratory, Oak Ridge, TN.

Sundell, J., H. Levin, W.W. Nazaroff, W.S. Cain, W.J. Fisk, D.T. Grimsrud, and F. Gyntelberg. 2011. Ventilation rates and health: Multidisciplinary review of the scientific literature. *Indoor Air* 21(3):191-204.

Tamura, G.T., and C.Y. Shaw. 1976a. Studies on exterior wall air tightness and air infiltration of tall buildings. *ASHRAE Transactions* 82(1):122. *Paper* DA-2388.

Tamura, G.T., and C.Y. Shaw. 1976b. Air leakage data for the design of elevator and stair shaft pressurization system. *ASHRAE Transactions* 82(2):179. *Paper* SE-2413.

Tamura, G.T., and A.G. Wilson. 1966. Pressure differences for a nine-story building as a result of chimney effect and ventilation system operation. *ASHRAE Transactions* 72(1):180.

Tamura, G.T., and A.G. Wilson. 1967a. Pressure differences caused by chimney effect in three high buildings. *ASHRAE Transactions* 73(2):II.1.1.

Tamura, G.T., and A.G. Wilson. 1967b. Building pressures caused by chimney action and mechanical ventilation. *ASHRAE Transactions* 73(2):II.2.1.

Timusk, J., A.L. Seskus, and K. Linger. 1992. A systems approach to extend the limit of envelope performance. *Proceedings of the 6th ASHRAE/DOE/BTECC Conference—Thermal Performance of Exterior Envelopes of Buildings*, Clearwater Beach, FL.

Turk, B.T., D.T. Grimsrud, J.T. Brown, K.L. Geisling-Sobotka, J. Harrison, and R.J. Prill. 1989. Commercial building ventilation rates and particle concentrations. *ASHRAE Transactions* 95(1):422-433. *Paper* 3248.

USACE. 2009. U.S. Army Corps of Engineers air leakage test protocol for building envelopes. Air Barrier Association of America, Walpole, MA, and U.S. Army Corps of Engineers.

Verschoor, J.D., and J.O. Collins. 1986. Demonstration of air leakage reduction program in navy family housing. In *Measured air leakage of buildings*, STP 904, p. 294. H.R. Trechsel and P.L. Lagus, eds. American Society for Testing and Materials, West Conshohocken, PA.

Walker, I.S. 1999. Distribution system leakage impacts on apartment building ventilation rates. *ASHRAE Transactions* 105(1):943-950. *Paper* CH-99-14-2.

Walker, I.S., and T.W. Forest. 1995. Field measurements of ventilation rates in attics. *Building and Environment* 30(3):333-347.

Walker, I.S., and D.J. Wilson. 1993. Evaluating models for superposition of wind and stack effects in air infiltration. *Building and Environment* 28(2):201-210.

Walker, I.S., and D.J. Wilson. 1994. Practical methods for improving estimates of natural ventilation rates. *Proceedings of the 15th IEA Conference of the Air Infiltration and Ventilation Centre*, Buxton, U.K., pp. 517-526.

Walker, I.S., and D.J. Wilson. 1998. Field validation of algebraic equations for stack and wind driven air infiltration calculations. *International Journal of HVAC&R Research* (now *Science and Technology for the Built Environment*) 4(2):119-140.

Walker, I.S., D.J. Wilson., and M.H. Sherman. 1997. A comparison of the power law to quadratic formulations for air infiltration calculations. *Energy and Buildings* 27(3).

Walker, I., M. Sherman, J. Siegel, D. Wang, C. Buchanan, and M. Modera. 1999. Leakage diagnostics, sealant longevity, sizing and technology transfer in residential thermal distribution systems: Part II. *Report* LBNL-42691.

Walton, G.N. 1984. A computer algorithm for predicting infiltration and interroom airflows. *ASHRAE Transactions* 90(1B):601. *Paper* AT-84-11-3.

Walton, G.N. 1989. Airflow network models for element-based building airflow modeling. *ASHRAE Transactions* 95(2):611-620. *Paper* VA-89-06-5.

Walton, G., and W.S. Dols. 2003. CONTAM 2.1 supplemental user guide and program documentation. NISTIR *Report* 7049, National Institute of Standards and Technology, Gaithersburg, MD.

Warden, D. 1995. Outdoor air: Calculation and delivery. *ASHRAE Journal* 37(6):54-63.

Warren, P.R., and B.C. Webb. 1980. The relationship between tracer gas and pressurization techniques in dwellings. *Proceedings of the 1st IEA Conference of the Air Infiltration Centre*, London.

Warren, P.R., and B.C. Webb. 1986. Ventilation measurements in housing. CIBSE Symposium, Natural Ventilation by Design. Chartered Institution of Building Services Engineers, London.

Weidt, J.L., J. Weidt, and S. Selkowitz. 1979. Field air leakage of newly installed residential windows. *Proceedings of the ASHRAE/DOE Conference—Thermal Performance of the Exterior Envelopes of Buildings* Orlando, FL, p. 149.

Weschler, C.J. 2000. Ozone in indoor environments: Concentration and chemistry. *Indoor Air* 10:269-288.

Wilson, D.J., and I.S. Walker. 1991. Wind shelter effects on air infiltration for a row of houses. *Proceedings of the 12th IEA Conference of the Air Infiltration and Ventilation Centre*, Ottawa, ON, pp. 335-346.

Wilson, D.J., and I.S. Walker. 1992. Feasibility of passive ventilation by constant area vents to maintain indoor air quality in houses. *Proceedings of Indoor Air Quality '92, ASHRAE/ACGIH/AIHA Conference*, San Francisco.

Wilson, D.J., and I.S. Walker. 1993. Infiltration data from the Alberta Home Heating Research Facility. *Technical Note* 41. Air Infiltration and Ventilation Centre, Sint-Stevens-Woluwe, Belgium.

Wiren, B.G. 1984. Wind pressure distributions and ventilation losses for a single-family house as influenced by surrounding buildings—A wind tunnel study. *Proceedings of the Air Infiltration Centre Wind Pressure Workshop*, Brussels, pp. 75-101.

Wolf, S. 1966. A theory of the effects of convective air flow through fibrous thermal insulation. *ASHRAE Transactions* 72(1):III 2.1-III 2.9.

Yaglou, C.P., and W.N. Witheridge. 1937. Ventilation requirements. *ASHVE Transactions* 43:423.

Yaglou, C.P., E.C. Riley, and D.I. Coggins. 1936. Ventilation requirements. *ASHVE Transactions* 42:133.

Yuill, G.K. 1986. The variation of the effective natural ventilation rate with weather conditions. *Proceedings of the Solar Energy Society of Canada Renewable Energy Conference '86*, pp. 70-75.

Yuill, G.K. 1991. The development of a method of determining air change rates in detached dwellings for assessing indoor air quality. *ASHRAE Transactions* 97(2):896-903. *Paper* IN-91-12-2.

Yuill, G.K. 1996. Impact of high use automatic doors on infiltration. ASHRAE Research Project RP-763, *Final Report*.

Yuill, G.K., and G.M. Comeau. 1989. Investigation of the indoor air quality, air tightness and air infiltration rates of a random sample of 78 houses in Winnipeg. *Proceedings of IAQ '89, The Human Equation—Health and Comfort*, pp. 122-127. ASHRAE.

Yuill, G.K., M.R. Jeanson, and C.P. Wray. 1991. Simulated performance of demand-controlled ventilation systems using carbon dioxide as an occupancy indicator. *ASHRAE Transactions* 97(2):963-968. *Paper* IN-91-15-1.

Yuill, D.P., G.K. Yuill, and A.H. Coward. 2008. Measurement and analysis of vitiation of secondary air in air distribution systems (RP-1276). *HVAC&R Research* (now *Science and Technology for the Built Environment*) 14(3):345-357.

Yuill, D.P., G.K. Yuill, and A.H. Coward. 2012. Experimental validation of the multiple-zone system ventilation efficiency equation of ANSI/ASHRAE *Standard* 62.1 (RP-1276). *HVAC&R Research* (now *Science and Technology for the Built Environment*) 18(3).

Zhivov, A. 2013. Air tightness in new and retrofitted US army buildings. Air Barrier Association of America, Walpole, MA.

BIBLIOGRAPHY

AIVC. [Ongoing]. *AIRBASE bibliographic database*. International Energy Agency Air Infiltration and Ventilation Centre, Sint-Stevens-Woluwe, Belgium. www.aivc.org/resources/airbase.

Brennan, T., W. Turner, G. Fisher, B. Thompson, and B. Ligman. 1992. Fan pressurization of school buildings. *Proceedings of Thermal Performance of the Exterior Envelopes of Buildings V*, pp. 643-645. ASHRAE.

Colliver, D.G., W.E. Murphy, and W. Sun. 1992. Evaluation of the techniques for the measurement of air leakage of building components. ASHRAE Research Project RP-438, *Final Report*. University of Kentucky, Lexington.

Lamming, S., and J. Salmon. 1998. Wind data for design of smoke control systems (RP-816). *ASHRAE Transactions* 104(1):742-751. *Paper* 4171.

Lstiburek, J.W. 2005. Understanding air barriers. *ASHRAE Journal* 47(7): 24-30.

Persily, A.K., W.S. Dols, S.J. Nabinger, and S. Kirchner. 1991. Preliminary results of the environmental evaluation of the Federal Records Center in Overland, Missouri. NISTIR *Report* 4634. National Institute of Standards and Technology, Gaithersburg, MD.

Potter, N. 2001. Air tightness testing—A guide for clients and contractors. *Technical Note* 19/2001. Building Services Research and Information Association, Bracknell, U.K.

Sherman, M.H. 1995. The use of blower door data. *Indoor Air* 5:215-224.

Yuill, D.P., G.K. Yuill, and A.H. Coward. 2007. A study of multiple space effects on ventilation system efficiency in *Standard* 62.1-2004 and experimental validation of the multiple spaces equation. ASHRAE Research Project RP-1276, *Final Report*.

Yuill, D.P., G.K. Yuill, and A.H. Coward. 2009. Experimental validation of the multiple spaces equation of ASHRAE *Standard* 62.1. ASHRAE Research Project RP-1276, *Final Report*.

CHAPTER 17

RESIDENTIAL COOLING AND HEATING LOAD CALCULATIONS

THIS chapter covers cooling and heating load calculation procedures for residential buildings, including detailed heat-balance methods that serve as the basis for cooling load calculation. Simple cooling load procedures, suitable for hand calculations, are provided for typical cases. Straightforward heating load calculation procedures are also included.

Procedures in this chapter are based on the same fundamentals as the nonresidential methods in Chapter 18. However, many characteristics distinguish residential loads, and Chapter 18's procedures should be applied with care to residential applications.

Additional information about residential heating and cooling is found in Chapter 1 of the 2015 *ASHRAE Handbook—HVAC Applications* and Chapter 10 of the 2016 *ASHRAE Handbook—HVAC Systems and Equipment.*

1. RESIDENTIAL FEATURES

With respect to heating and cooling load calculation and equipment sizing, the following unique features distinguish residences from other types of buildings:

- **Smaller Internal Heat Gains.** Residential system loads are primarily imposed by heat gain or loss through structural components and by air leakage or ventilation. Internal heat gains, particularly those from occupants and lights, are small compared to those in commercial or industrial structures.
- **Varied Use of Spaces.** Use of spaces in residences is more flexible than in commercial buildings. Localized or temporary temperature excursions are often tolerable.
- **Fewer Zones.** Residences are generally conditioned as a single zone or, at most, a few zones. Typically, a thermostat located in one room controls unit output for multiple rooms, and capacity cannot be redistributed from one area to another as loads change over the day. This results in some hour-to-hour temperature variation or swing that has a significant moderating effect on peak loads, because of heat storage in building components.
- **Greater Distribution Losses.** Residential ducts are frequently installed in attics or other unconditioned buffer spaces. Duct leakage and heat gain or loss can require significant increases in unit capacity. Residential distribution gains and losses cannot be neglected or estimated with simple rules of thumb.
- **Partial Loads.** Most residential cooling systems use units of relatively small capacity (about 12,000 to 60,000 Btu/h cooling, 40,000 to 120,000 Btu/h heating). Because loads are largely determined by outdoor conditions, and few days each season are design days, the unit operates at partial load during most of the season; thus, an oversized unit is detrimental to good system performance, especially for cooling in areas of high wet-bulb temperature.

The preparation of this chapter is assigned to TC 4.1, Load Calculation Data and Procedures.

- **Dehumidification Issues.** Dehumidification occurs during cooling unit operation only, and space condition control is usually limited to use of room thermostats (sensible heat-actuated devices). Excessive sensible capacity results in short-cycling and severely degraded dehumidification performance.

In addition to these general features, residential buildings can be categorized according to their exposure:

- **Single-Family Detached.** A house in this category usually has exposed walls in four directions, often more than one story, and a roof. The cooling system is a single-zone, unitary system with a single thermostat. Two-story houses may have a separate cooling system for each floor. Rooms are reasonably open and generally have a centralized air return. In this configuration, both air and load from rooms are mixed, and a load-leveling effect, which requires a distribution of air to each room that is different from a pure commercial system, results. Because the amount of air supplied to each room is based on the load for that room, proper load calculation procedures must be used.
- **Multifamily.** Unlike single-family detached units, multifamily units generally do not have exposed surfaces facing in all directions. Rather, each unit typically has a maximum of three exposed walls and possibly a roof. Each living unit has a single unitary cooling system or a single fan-coil unit and the rooms are relatively open to one another. This configuration does not have the same load-leveling effect as a single-family detached house.
- **Other.** Many buildings do not fall into either of the preceding categories. Critical to the designation of a single-family detached building is well-distributed exposure so there is not a short-duration peak; however, if fenestration exposure is predominantly east or west, the cooling load profile resembles that of a multifamily unit. On the other hand, multifamily units with both east and west exposures or neither east nor west exposure exhibit load profiles similar to single-family detached.

2. CALCULATION APPROACH

Variations in the characteristics of residences can lead to surprisingly complex load calculations. Time-varying heat flows combine to produce a time-varying load. The relative magnitude and pattern of the heat flows depends on the building characteristics and exposure, resulting in a building-specific load profile. In general, an hour-by-hour analysis is required to determine that profile and find its peak.

In theory, cooling and heating processes are identical; a common analysis procedure should apply to either. Acceptable simplifications are possible for heating; however, for cooling, different approaches are used.

Heating calculations use simple worst-case assumptions: no solar or internal gains, and no heat storage (with all heat losses evaluated instantaneously). With these simplifications, the heating problem is reduced to a basic $UA\Delta t$ calculation. The heating procedures in this chapter use this long-accepted approach, and thus differ only in details from prior methods put forth by ASHRAE and others.

The cooling procedures in this chapter were extensively revised in 2005, based on the results of ASHRAE research project RP-1199, also supported by the Air-Conditioning Contractors of America (ACCA) (Barnaby et al. 2004, 2005). Although the complexity of residential cooling load calculations has been understood for decades, prior methods used a cooling load temperature difference/cooling load factor (CLTD/CLF) form requiring only hand-tractable arithmetic. Without such simplification, the procedures would not have been used; an approximate calculation was preferable to none at all. The simplified approaches were developed using detailed computer models and/or empirical data, but only the simplifications were published. Now that computing power is routinely available, it is appropriate to promulgate 24 h, equation-based procedures.

3. OTHER METHODS

Several residential load calculation methods have been published in North America over the last 30 years. All use the $UA\Delta t$ heating formulation and some variation of the CLTD/CLF approach for cooling.

- **ACCA.** *Manual J*, 8th edition (ACCA 2016) is widely used in the United States. Cooling loads are calculated using semiempirical heat gain factors derived from experimental data taken at the University of Illinois in the 1950s. These factors, associated overview, and references are found in the 1985 and earlier editions of the *ASHRAE Handbook—Fundamentals*. The 8th edition retains the underlying factors but provides increased flexibility in their application, in addition to other extensions.
- **ASHRAE.** The 1989 to 2001 editions of the *ASHRAE Handbook—Fundamentals* contain an updated method based on ASHRAE research project RP-342 (McQuiston 1984). In this work, cooling factors were re-derived using a transfer-function building model that included temperature-swing effects.
- **F280.** This Canadian adaptation of the CLTD/CLF procedure (CAN/CSA *Standard* F280) also uses cooling methods based on ASHRAE RP-342. Heating procedures include detailed ground heat loss estimates.

A key common element of all cooling methods is attention to temperature swing, via empirical data or suitable models. Throughout the literature, it is repeatedly emphasized that direct application of nonresidential methods (based on a fixed set point) results in unrealistically high cooling loads for residential applications.

4. RESIDENTIAL HEAT BALANCE (RHB) METHOD

A 24 h procedure is required to accurately determine the cooling load profile of a residence. The heat balance (HB) method allows detailed simulation of space temperatures and heat flows. ASHRAE research project RP-1199 adapted HB to residential applications, resulting in the residential heat balance (RHB) method. Although RHB provides the technical basis for this chapter, it is a computer-only technique and is not documented here. HB is described in Chapter 18 and Pedersen et al. 1998; Barnaby et al. (2004, 2005) document RHB enhancements.

RP-1199 produced an implementation of the RHB method, called ResHB (Barnaby et al. 2004). This application is derived from the ASHRAE *Toolkit for Building Load Calculations* (Pedersen et al. 2001) and has the following features:

- **Multizone.** Whereas the original *Toolkit* code supported a single zone, ResHB can analyze projects that include multiple systems, zones, and rooms.
- **Temperature swing.** ResHB calculates cooling load with temperature swing. That is, the code searches for sensible capacity sufficient to hold the space temperature within a specified excursion above the set point.
- **Master/slave control.** ResHB allows control of cooling output in "slave" rooms based on the cooling requirements of a "master" room, where the thermostat is located. Rooms with incompatible load profiles will exhibit poor temperature control.
- **Residential defaults.** ResHB includes default values suitable for residential problems.

In its current form, ResHB is a research-oriented reference implementation of RHB. ResHB FORTRAN source code is available under license from ASHRAE.

5. RESIDENTIAL LOAD FACTOR (RLF) METHOD

The procedure presented in this chapter is the residential load factor (RLF) method. RLF is a simplified procedure derived from detailed ResHB analysis of prototypical buildings across a range of climates. The method is tractable by hand but is best applied using a spreadsheet. Two main applications are anticipated:

- **Education and training.** The transparency and simplicity of RLF make it suitable for use in introductory courses on building load calculations.
- **Quick load estimates.** In situations where detailed analysis is impractical, the RLF method is a possible alternative. For example, the method might be implemented as a spreadsheet on a handheld device and used for on-site sizing of replacement cooling equipment.

Note that, although room-by-room calculations are possible with the RLF method, computerized methods based on RHB are more suitable for performing full room-level calculations required for equipment selection and distribution system design.

RLF was derived from several thousand ResHB cooling load results (Barnaby and Spitler 2005; Barnaby et al. 2004). A range of climates and building types were analyzed. Statistical regression techniques were used to find values for the load factors tabulated in later sections. Factor values were validated by comparing ResHB versus RLF results for buildings not involved in the regression analysis. Within its range of applicability, RLF cooling loads are generally within 10% of those calculated with ResHB. The RLF derivation was repeated for 2009 using the updated temperature profile and clear-sky model (see Chapter 14), resulting in minor revisions to load factors and other coefficients. Additional revisions to Chapter 14 occurred in 2013 and 2017; those changes would alter RLF values very little, so the 2009 factors are retained.

The RLF method should not be applied to situations outside the range of underlying cases, as shown in Table 1.

Note that the RLF calculation sequence involves two distinct steps. First, the cooling and heating load factors (CFs and HFs) are derived for all project component types. These factors are then applied to the individual components by a single multiplication. (The two-step approach is demonstrated in the Load Calculation Example section.) For a specific location and representative constructions, CFs and HFs can be precalculated and used repeatedly. In essence, the structure of RLF allows assembling location-specific versions of the rigid tables found in prior editions, and also documents the equations used to generate tabulated values. Using these equations, a complete implementation of the RLF method, including CF and HF calculation, is well within the capabilities of current PC spreadsheet applications.

6. COMMON DATA AND PROCEDURES

The following guidelines, data requirements, and procedures apply to all load calculation approaches, whether heating or cooling, hand-tractable or computerized.

Table 1 RLF Limitations

Item	Valid Range	Notes
Latitude	20 to 60°N	Also approximately valid for 20 to 60°S with N and S orientations reversed for southern hemisphere.
Date	July 21	Application must be summer peaking. Buildings in mild climates with significant SE/S/SW glazing may experience maximum cooling load in fall or even winter. Use RHB if local experience indicates this is a possibility.
Elevation	Less than 6500 ft	RLF factors assume 164 ft elevation. With elevation-corrected C_s, method is acceptably accurate except at very high elevations.
Climate	Warm/hot	Design-day average outdoor temperature assumed to be above indoor design temperature.
Construction	Lightweight residential construction (wood or metal framing, wood or stucco siding)	May be applied to masonry veneer over frame construction; results are conservative. Use RHB for structural masonry or unconventional construction.
Fenestration area	0 to 15% of floor area on any façade, 0 to 30% of floor area total	Spaces with high fenestration fraction should be analyzed with RHB.
Fenestration tilt	Vertical or horizontal	Skylights with tilt less than 30° can be treated as horizontal. Buildings with significant sloped glazing areas should be analyzed with RHB.
Occupancy	Residential	Applications with high internal gains and/or high occupant density should be analyzed with RHB or nonresidential procedures.
Temperature swing	3°F	
Distribution losses	Typical	Applications with extensive duct runs in unconditioned spaces should be analyzed with RHB.

General Guidelines

Design for Typical Building Use. In general, residential systems should be designed to meet representative maximum-load conditions, not extreme conditions. Normal occupancy should be assumed, not the maximum that might occur during an occasional social function. Intermittently operated ventilation fans should be assumed to be off. These considerations are especially important for cooling-system sizing.

Building Codes and Standards. This chapter presentation is necessarily general. Codes and regulations take precedence; consult local authorities to determine applicable requirements.

Designer Judgment. Designer experience with local conditions, building practices, and prior projects should be considered when applying the procedures in this chapter. For equipment-replacement projects, occupant knowledge concerning performance of the existing system can often provide useful guidance for achieving a successful design.

Verification. Postconstruction commissioning and verification are important steps in achieving design performance. Designers should encourage pressurization testing and other procedures that allow identification and repair of construction shortcomings.

Uncertainty and Safety Allowances. Residential load calculations are inherently approximate. Many building characteristics are estimated during design and ultimately determined by construction quality and occupant behavior. These uncertainties apply to all calculation methods, including first-principles procedures such as RHB. It is therefore tempting to include safety allowances for each aspect of a calculation. However, this practice has a compounding effect and often produces oversized results. Typical conditions should be assumed; safety allowances, if applied at all, should be added to the final calculated loads rather than to intermediate components. In addition, temperature swing provides a built-in safety factor for sensible cooling: a 20% capacity shortfall typically results in a temperature excursion of at most about one or two degrees.

Basic Relationships

Common air-conditioning processes involve transferring heat via air transport or leakage. The sensible, latent, and total heat conveyed by air on a volumetric basis is

$$q_s = C_s Q \Delta t \quad (1)$$

$$q_l = C_l Q \Delta W \quad (2)$$

$$q_t = C_t Q \Delta h \quad (3)$$

$$q_t = q_s + q_l \quad (4)$$

where

q_s, q_l, q_t = sensible, latent, total heat transfer rates, Btu/h
C_s = air sensible heat factor, Btu/h·°F·cfm (1.1 at sea level)
C_l = air latent heat factor, Btu/h·cfm (4840 at sea level)
C_t = air total heat factor, Btu/h·cfm per Btu/lb enthalpy h (4.5 at sea level)
Q = air volumetric flow rate, cfm
Δt = air temperature difference across process, °F
ΔW = air humidity ratio difference across process, lb_w/lb_{da}
Δh = air enthalpy difference across process, Btu/lb

The heat factors C_s, C_l, and C_t are elevation dependent. The sea-level values in the preceding definitions are appropriate for elevations up to about 1000 ft. Procedures are provided in Chapter 18 for calculating adjusted values for higher elevations.

Design Conditions

The initial step in the load calculation is selecting indoor and outdoor design conditions.

Indoor Conditions. Indoor conditions assumed for design purposes depend on building use, type of occupancy, and/or code requirements. Chapter 9 and ASHRAE *Standard* 55 define the relationship between indoor conditions and comfort.

Typical practice for cooling is to design for indoor conditions of 75°F db and a maximum of 50 to 65% rh. For heating, 68°F db and 30% rh are common design values. These conditions are the default values used throughout this chapter.

Outdoor Conditions. Outdoor design conditions for load calculations should be selected from location-specific climate data in Chapter 14, or according to local code requirements as applicable.

Cooling. The 1% design dry-bulb temperature and mean coincident wet bulb temperature from Chapter 14 climate data are generally appropriate. As previously emphasized, oversized cooling equipment results in poor system performance. Extremely hot events are necessarily of short duration (conditions always moderate each night); therefore, sacrificing comfort under typical conditions to meet occasional extremes is not recommended.

Load calculations also require the hottest-month dry-bulb temperature daily range, and wind speed. These values can also be found in Chapter 14, although wind speed is commonly assumed to be 7.5 mph.

Typical buildings in middle latitudes generally experience maximum cooling requirements in midsummer (July in the northern hemisphere and January in the southern hemisphere). For this reason, the

RLF method is based on midsummer solar gains. However, this pattern does not always hold. Buildings at low latitudes or with significant south-facing glazing (north-facing in the southern hemisphere) should be analyzed at several times of the year using the RHB method. Local experience can provide guidance as to when maximum cooling is probable. For example, it is common for south-facing buildings in mild northern-hemisphere climates to have peak cooling loads in the fall because of low sun angles. Chapter 14 contains monthly temperature data to support calculations for any time of year.

Heating. General practice is to use the 99% design dry-bulb temperature from Chapter 14. Heating load calculations ignore solar and internal gains, providing a built-in safety factor. However, the designer should consider two additional factors:

- Many locations experience protracted (several-day) cold periods during which the outdoor temperature remains below the 99% value.
- Wind is a major determinant of infiltration. Residences with significant leakage (e.g., older houses) may have peak heating demand under conditions other than extreme cold, depending on site wind patterns.

Depending on the application and system type, the designer should consider using the 99.6% value or the mean minimum extreme as the heating design temperature. Alternatively, the heating load can be calculated at the 99% condition and a safety factor applied when equipment is selected. This additional capacity can also serve to meet pickup loads under nonextreme conditions.

Adjacent Buffer Spaces. Residential buildings often include unconditioned buffer spaces such as garages, attics, crawlspaces, basements, or enclosed porches. Accurate load calculations require the adjacent air temperature.

In many cases, a simple, conservative estimate is adequate, especially for heating calculations. For example, it is generally reasonable to assume that, under heating design conditions, adjacent uninsulated garages, porches, and attics are at outdoor temperature. Another reasonable assumption is that the temperature in an adjacent, unheated, *insulated* room is the mean of the indoor and outdoor temperatures.

In cases where a temperature estimate is required, a steady-state heat balance analysis yields the following:

$$t_b = \frac{C_s Q t_o + \sum A_x U_x t_x + q}{C_s Q + \sum A_x U_x} \tag{5}$$

where

t_b = buffer space temperature, °F
Q = buffer space infiltration/ventilation flow rate, cfm
t_o = outdoor air temperature, °F
A_x = area of xth buffer space surface, ft²
U_x = U-factor of xth buffer space surface, Btu/h·ft²·°F
t_x = air temperature at outside of xth buffer space surface, °F (typically, outdoor air temperature for exterior surfaces, conditioned space temperature for surfaces between buffer space and house, or ground temperature for below-grade surfaces)
q = additional buffer space heat gains, Btu/h (e.g., solar gains or distribution system losses)

Building Data

Component Areas. To perform load calculations efficiently and reliably, standard methods must be used for determining building surface areas. For fenestration, the definition of component area must be consistent with associated ratings.

Gross area. It is both efficient and conservative to derive gross surface areas from outer building dimensions, ignoring wall and floor thicknesses. Thus, floor areas should be measured to the outside of adjacent exterior walls or to the centerline of adjacent partitions. When apportioning to rooms, façade area should be divided at partition centerlines. Wall height should be taken as floor-to-floor.

Using outer dimensions avoids separate accounting of floor edge and wall corner conditions. Further, it is standard practice in residential construction to define floor area in terms of outer dimensions, so outer-dimension takeoffs yield areas that can be readily checked against building plans (e.g., the sum of room areas should equal the plan floor area). Although outer-dimension procedures are recommended as expedient for load calculations, they are not consistent with rigorous definitions used in building-related standards (e.g., ASTM *Standard* E631). However, the inconsistencies are not significant in the load calculation context.

Fenestration area. Fenestration includes exterior windows, skylights, and doors. Fenestration U-factor and SHGC ratings (see Table 2) are based on the entire product area, including frames. Thus, for load calculations, fenestration area is the area of the rough opening in the wall or roof, less installation clearances (projected product area A_{pf}). Installation clearances can be neglected; it is acceptable to use the rough opening as an approximation of A_{pf}.

Net area. Net surface area is the gross surface area less fenestration area (rough opening or A_{pf}) contained within the surface.

Volume. Building volume is expediently calculated by multiplying floor area by floor-to-floor height. This produces a conservative estimate of enclosed air volume, because wall and floor volumes are included in the total. More precise calculations are possible but are generally not justified in this context.

Construction Characteristics.

U-factors. Except for fenestration, construction U-factors should be calculated using procedures in Chapter 27, or taken from manufacturer's data, if available. U-factors should be evaluated under heating (winter) conditions.

Fenestration. Fenestration is characterized by U-factor and solar heat gain coefficient (SHGC), which apply to the entire assembly (including frames). If available, rated values should be used, determined according to procedures set forth by National Fenestration Rating Council (NFRC), Canadian Standards Association (CSA), or other specifying body (see Chapter 15). Ratings can be obtained from product literature, product label, or online listings (NFRC 2017). For unrated products (e.g., in existing construction), the U-factor and SHGC can be estimated using Table 2 or tables in Chapter 15. Note that fenestration U-factors are evaluated under heating (winter) design conditions but are used in this chapter for both heating and cooling calculations.

Relatively few types of glazing are encountered in residential applications. Single-glazed clear, double-glazed clear, and double-glazed low-emissivity ("low-e") glass predominate. Single-glazed is now rare in new construction but common in older homes. Triple-glazing, reflective glass, and heat-absorbing glass are encountered occasionally. Acrylic or glass skylights are common. Multipane low-e insulated glazing is available in high- and low-solar-gain variants, as discussed in Chapter 15. Low-solar is now the more common for new construction in all parts of the United States.

Properties of windows equipped with storm windows should be estimated from data for a similar configuration with an additional pane. For example, data for clear, double-glazed should be used for a clear single-glazed window with a storm window.

Fenestration interior and exterior shading must be included in cooling load calculations, as discussed in the Cooling Load section.

Table 2 shows representative window U-factor and SHGC values for common glazing and frame combinations. Consult Chapter 15 for skylight characteristics.

Load Components

Below-Grade Surfaces. For cooling calculations, heat flow into the ground is usually ignored because it is difficult to quantify.

Table 2 Typical Fenestration Characteristics[a]

					Frame									
					Operable					Fixed				
Glazing Type	Glazing Layers	ID[b]	Property[c,d]	Center of Glazing	Aluminum	Aluminum with Thermal Break	Reinforced Vinyl/Aluminum Clad Wood	Wood/Vinyl	Insulated Fiberglass/Vinyl	Aluminum	Aluminum with Thermal Break	Reinforced Vinyl/Aluminum Clad Wood	Wood/Vinyl	Insulated Fiberglass/Vinyl
Clear	1	1a	*U*	1.04	1.27	1.08	0.90	0.89	0.81	1.13	1.07	0.98	0.98	0.94
			SHGC	0.86	0.75	0.75	0.64	0.64	0.64	0.78	0.78	0.75	0.75	0.75
	2	5a	*U*	0.48	0.81	0.60	0.53	0.51	0.44	0.64	0.57	0.50	0.50	0.48
			SHGC	0.76	0.67	0.67	0.57	0.57	0.57	0.69	0.69	0.67	0.67	0.67
	3	29a	*U*	0.31	0.67	0.46	0.40	0.39	0.34	0.49	0.42	0.36	0.35	0.34
			SHGC	0.68	0.60	0.60	0.51	0.51	0.51	0.62	0.62	0.60	0.60	0.60
Low-e, low-solar	2	25a	*U*	0.30	0.67	0.47	0.41	0.39	0.33	0.48	0.41	0.36	0.35	0.33
			SHGC	0.41	0.37	0.37	0.31	0.31	0.31	0.38	0.38	0.36	0.36	0.36
	3	40c	*U*	0.27	0.64	0.43	0.37	0.36	0.31	0.45	0.39	0.33	0.32	0.31
			SHGC	0.27	0.25	0.25	0.21	0.21	0.21	0.25	0.25	0.24	0.24	0.24
Low-e, high-solar	2	17c	U	0.35	0.71	0.51	0.44	0.42	0.36	0.53	0.46	0.40	0.39	0.37
			SHGC	0.70	0.62	0.62	0.52	0.52	0.52	0.64	0.64	0.61	0.61	0.61
	3	32c	*U*	0.33	0.69	0.47	0.41	0.40	0.35	0.50	0.44	0.38	0.37	0.36
			SHGC	0.62	0.55	0.55	0.46	0.46	0.46	0.56	0.56	0.54	0.54	0.54
Heat-absorbing	1	1c	*U*	1.04	1.27	1.08	0.90	0.89	0.81	1.13	1.07	0.98	0.98	0.94
			SHGC	0.73	0.64	0.64	0.54	0.54	0.54	0.66	0.66	0.64	0.64	0.64
	2	5c	*U*	0.48	0.81	0.60	0.53	0.51	0.44	0.64	0.57	0.50	0.50	0.48
			SHGC	0.62	0.55	0.55	0.46	0.46	0.46	0.56	0.56	0.54	0.54	0.54
	3	29c	*U*	0.31	0.67	0.46	0.40	0.39	0.34	0.49	0.42	0.36	0.35	0.34
			SHGC	0.34	0.31	0.31	0.26	0.26	0.26	0.31	0.31	0.30	0.30	0.30
Reflective	1	1l	*U*	1.04	1.27	1.08	0.90	0.89	0.81	1.13	1.07	0.98	0.98	0.94
			SHGC	0.31	0.28	0.28	0.24	0.24	0.24	0.29	0.29	0.27	0.27	0.27
	2	5p	*U*	0.48	0.81	0.60	0.53	0.51	0.44	0.64	0.57	0.50	0.50	0.48
			SHGC	0.29	0.27	0.27	0.22	0.22	0.22	0.27	0.27	0.26	0.26	0.26
	3	29c	*U*	0.31	0.67	0.46	0.40	0.39	0.34	0.49	0.42	0.36	0.35	0.34
			SHGC	0.34	0.31	0.31	0.26	0.26	0.26	0.31	0.31	0.30	0.30	0.30

[a]Data are from Chapter 15, Tables 4 and 14 for selected combinations. [b]ID = Chapter 15 glazing type identifier. [c]U = U-factor, Btu/h·ft²·°F. [d]SHGC = solar heat gain coefficient.

Surfaces adjacent to the ground are modeled as if well insulated on the outside, so there is no overall heat transfer, but diurnal heat storage effects are included. Heating calculations must include loss via slabs and basement walls and floors, as discussed in the Heating Load section.

Infiltration. Infiltration is generally a significant component of both cooling and heating loads. Refer to Chapter 16 for a detailed discussion of residential air leakage. The simplified residential models found in that chapter can be used to calculate infiltration rates for load calculations. Infiltration should be evaluated for the entire building, not individual rooms or zones.

Natural infiltration leakage rates are modified by mechanical pressurization caused by unbalanced ventilation or duct leakage. These effects are discussed in the section on Combined Ventilation and Infiltration Airflow.

Leakage rate. Air leakage rates are specified either as airflow rate Q_i, or air exchanges per hour (ACH), related as follows:

$$Q_i = \text{ACH}(V/60) \tag{6}$$

$$\text{ACH} = \frac{60Q_i}{V} \tag{7}$$

where

Q_i = infiltration airflow rate, cfm
ACH = air exchange rate, changes/h
V = building volume, ft³

Infiltration airflow rate depends on two factors:

- Building effective leakage area (envelope leaks plus other air leakage paths, notably flues) and its distribution among ceilings, walls, floors, and flues.
- Driving pressure caused by buoyancy (stack effect) and wind.

Using the simplifying assumptions presented in Chapter 16, these factors can be evaluated separately and combined using Equation (8).

$$Q_i = A_L \text{IDF} \tag{8}$$

where

A_L = building effective leakage area (including flue) at reference pressure difference = 0.016 in. of water, assuming discharge coefficient C_D = 1, in²
IDF = infiltration driving force, cfm/in²

The following sections provide procedures for determining A_L and IDF.

Leakage area. As discussed in Chapter 16, there are several interconvertible ways to characterize building leakage, depending on reference pressure differences and assumed discharge coefficient. This formulation uses the effective leakage area at 0.016 in. of water, assuming C_D = 1, designated A_L (Sherman and Grimsrud 1980).

The only accurate procedure for determining A_L is by measurement using a pressurization test (commonly called a blower door test). Numerous field studies have shown that visual inspection is not adequate for obtaining even a crude estimate of leakage.

For buildings in design, a pressurization test is not possible and leakage area must be assumed for design purposes. Leakage can be estimated using tabulated component leakage areas found in Chapter 16. A simpler approach is based on an assumed average leakage per unit of building surface area:

$$A_L = A_{es}A_{ul} \quad (9)$$

where

A_{es} = building exposed surface area, ft²
A_{ul} = unit leakage area, in²/ft² (from Table 3)

A_{ul} is the leakage area per unit surface area; suitable design values are found in Table 3. Field experience indicates that the level of care applied to reducing leakage often depends on winter conditions, because cold-air leakage is readily detected. Thus, lower A_{ul} values are expected in colder climates. Note that the A_{ul} value doubles at each reduced construction quality step in Table 3; very high infiltration loads are typical in older houses.

In Equation (9), A_{es} is the total building surface area at the envelope pressure boundary, defined as all above-grade surface area that separates the outdoors from conditioned or semiconditioned space. Table 4 provides guidance for evaluating A_{es}.

IDF. To determine IDF, use the Chapter 16 methods cited previously. As a further simplification, Barnaby and Spitler (2005) derived the following relationship that yields results approximately equal to the AIM-2 model (Walker and Wilson 1990, 1998; Chapter 16's enhanced model) at design conditions:

$$\text{IDF} = \frac{I_0 + H|\Delta t|[I_1 + I_2(A_{L,flue}/A_L)]}{1000} \quad (10)$$

where

I_0, I_1, I_2 = coefficients, as follows:

	Cooling 7.5 mph	Heating 15 mph
I_0	343	698
I_1	0.88	0.81
I_2	0.28	0.53

H = building average stack height, ft (typically 8 to 10 ft per story)
Δt = difference between indoor and outdoor temperatures, °F
$A_{L,flue}$ = flue effective leakage area at reference pressure difference = 0.016 in. of water, assuming C_D = 1, in² (total for flues serving furnaces, domestic water heaters, fireplaces, or other vented equipment, evaluated assuming associated equipment is not operating and with dampers in closed position; see Chapter 16)

Building stack height H is the average height difference between the ceiling and floor (or grade, if the floor is below grade). Thus, for buildings with vented crawlspaces, the crawlspace height is not included. For basement or slab-on-grade construction, H is the average height of the ceiling above grade. Generally, there is significant leakage between basements and spaces above, so above-grade basement height should be included whether or not the basement is fully conditioned. With suitable adjustments for grade level, H can also be estimated as V/A_{cf} (conditioned floor area).

Equation (10) is valid for typical suburban residential wind sheltering, $A_{L,flue} < A_L/2$, and at any elevation. Table 5 shows IDF values derived with Equation (10), assuming $A_{L,flue}$ = 0.

Verification of leakage. A postconstruction pressurization test is strongly recommended to verify that design leakage assumptions are actually achieved. Excess leaks should be located and repaired.

Allocation of infiltration to rooms. Total building infiltration should typically be allocated to rooms according to room volume; that is, it should be assumed that each room has the same air exchange rate as the whole building. In reality, leakage varies by room and over time, depending on outdoor temperature and wind conditions. These effects can either increase or decrease room leakage. In addition, system air mixing tends to redistribute localized leakage to all rooms. Thus, in most cases, there is no reasonable way to assign more or less leakage to specific rooms.

An exception is leaky, multistory houses. The preferable and cost-effective response is mitigation of the leakage. If repair is not possible, then for heating load calculation purposes, some leakage can be differentially assigned to lower story and/or windward rooms in proportion to exposed surface area (i.e., adjustment using an "exposure factor").

Multifamily buildings. Usually, the simplified methods in Chapter 16 and this section do not apply to multifamily residences. However, they can be used for row houses that are full building height and have more than one exposed façade. For apartment units subdivided within a former detached residence, the entire building should be analyzed and the resulting exchange rate applied to the apartment volume. In other multifamily structures, infiltration is determined by many factors, including overall building height and degree of sealing between apartments. For low-rise construction, an upper bound for the infiltration rate can be found by evaluating the entire building. As building height increases, leakage problems can be magnified, as discussed in Chapter 16. Estimating leakage rates may require advice from a high-rise infiltration specialist.

Ventilation.

Whole-building ventilation. Because of energy efficiency concerns, residential construction has become significantly tighter over

Table 3 Unit Leakage Areas

Construction	Description	A_{ul}, in²/ft²
Tight	Construction supervised by air-sealing specialist	0.01
Good	Carefully sealed construction by knowledgeable builder	0.02
Average	Typical current production housing	0.04
Leaky	Typical pre-1970 houses	0.08
Very leaky	Old houses in original condition	0.15

Table 4 Evaluation of Exposed Surface Area

Situation	Include	Exclude
Ceiling/roof combination (e.g., cathedral ceiling without attic)	Gross surface area	
Ceiling or wall adjacent to attic	Ceiling or wall area	Roof area
Wall exposed to ambient	Gross wall area (including fenestration area)	
Wall adjacent to unconditioned buffer space (e.g., garage or porch)	Common wall area	Exterior wall area
Floor over open or vented crawlspace	Floor area	Crawlspace wall area
Floor over sealed crawlspace	Crawlspace wall area	Floor area
Floor over conditioned or semiconditioned basement	Above-grade basement wall area	Floor area
Slab floor		Slab area

Table 5 Typical IDF Values, cfm/in²

H, ft	Heating Design Temperature, °F					Cooling Design Temperature, °F		
	−40	−20	0	20	40	85	95	105
8	1.40	1.27	1.14	1.01	0.88	0.41	0.48	0.55
10	1.57	1.41	1.25	1.09	0.92	0.43	0.52	0.61
12	1.75	1.55	1.36	1.16	0.97	0.45	0.55	0.66
14	1.92	1.70	1.47	1.24	1.02	0.47	0.59	0.71
16	2.10	1.84	1.58	1.32	1.06	0.48	0.62	0.76
18	2.27	1.98	1.69	1.40	1.11	0.50	0.66	0.82
20	2.45	2.12	1.80	1.48	1.15	0.52	0.69	0.87
22	2.62	2.27	1.91	1.55	1.20	0.54	0.73	0.92
24	2.80	2.41	2.02	1.63	1.24	0.55	0.76	0.98

the last several decades. Natural leakage rates are often insufficient to maintain acceptable indoor air quality. ASHRAE *Standard* 62.2 specifies the required minimum whole-building ventilation rate as

$$Q_v = 0.03A_{cf} + 7.5(N_{br} + 1) \tag{11}$$

where

Q_v = required ventilation flow rate, cfm
A_{cf} = building conditioned floor area, ft^2
N_{br} = number of bedrooms (not less than 1)

Certain mild climates are exempted from this standard; local building authorities ultimately dictate actual requirements. In addition, *Standard* 62.2 specifies alternative methods for determining ventilation requirements that may result in smaller Q_v values. Whole-building ventilation is expected to become more common because of a combination of regulation and consumer demand. The load effect of Q_v must be included in both cooling and heating calculations.

Heat recovery. Heat recovery devices should be considered part of mechanical ventilation systems. These appliances are variously called heat recovery ventilators (HRVs) or energy recovery ventilators (ERVs) and integrate with residential distribution systems, as described in Chapter 26 of the 2016 *ASHRAE Handbook—HVAC Systems and Equipment*. Either sensible heat or total heat (enthalpy) can be exchanged between the exhaust and intake airstreams. ERV/HRV units are characterized by their sensible and total effectiveness.

Local mechanical exhaust. Kitchen and bathroom exhaust fans are required by *Standard* 62.2 and are typically present. Exhaust fans that operate intermittently by manual control are generally not included in load calculations. Continuously operating ventilation should be included. Note that exhaust fans induce load only through enhanced infiltration because of building depressurization (see the section on Combined Ventilation and Infiltration Airflow for further discussion).

Combustion Air. Fuel-fired boilers, furnaces, and domestic water heaters require combustion air. If the combustion air source is within the building envelope (including in semiconditioned basements), additional infiltration and heating load are induced. Locating the equipment outside of conditioned space (e.g., in a garage or vented mechanical closet) or using sealed-combustion equipment eliminates this load.

Combustion air requirements for new forced-draft equipment can be estimated at 0.25 cfm per 1000 Btu/h or about 25 cfm for a 100,000 Btu/h heating appliance. The requirements for existing natural draft equipment should be estimated at twice that amount. In many cases, these quantities are relatively small and can be neglected.

For cooling load calculations, heating equipment is assumed to be not operating, leaving only any domestic water heaters, for which the combustion air requirements are generally neglected.

Combined Ventilation and Infiltration Airflow. Mechanical pressurization modifies the infiltration leakage rate. To assess this effect, overall supply and exhaust flow rates must be determined and then divided into "balanced" and "unbalanced" components.

$$Q_{bal} = \min(Q_{sup}, Q_{exh}) \tag{12}$$

$$Q_{unbal} = \max(Q_{sup}, Q_{exh}) - Q_{bal} \tag{13}$$

where

Q_{bal} = balanced airflow rate, cfm
Q_{sup} = total ventilation supply airflow rate, cfm
Q_{exh} = total ventilation exhaust airflow rate (including any combustion air requirements), cfm
Q_{unbal} = unbalanced airflow rate, cfm

Note that unbalanced duct leakage can produce additional pressurization or depressurization. This effect is discussed in the section on Distribution Losses.

Airflow components can be combined with infiltration leakage as follows (Palmiter and Bond 1991; Sherman 1992):

$$Q_{vi} = \max(Q_{unbal}, Q_i + 0.5Q_{unbal}) \tag{14}$$

where

Q_{vi} = combined infiltration/ventilation flow rate (not including balanced component), cfm
Q_i = infiltration leakage rate assuming no mechanical pressurization, cfm

Ventilation/infiltration load. The cooling or heating load from ventilation and infiltration is calculated as follows:

$$q_{vi,s} = C_s[Q_{vi} + (1 - \varepsilon_s)Q_{bal,hr} + Q_{bal,oth}]\Delta t \tag{15}$$

$$q_{vi,l} = C_l(Q_{vi} + Q_{bal,oth})\Delta W \quad \text{(no HRV/ERV)} \tag{16}$$

$$q_{vi,t} = C_{t6}[Q_{vi} + (1 - \varepsilon_t)Q_{bal,hr} + Q_{bal,oth}]\Delta h \tag{17}$$

$$q_{vi,l} = q_{vi,t} - q_{vi,s} \tag{18}$$

where

$q_{vi,s}$ = sensible ventilation/infiltration load, Btu/h
ε_s = HRV/ERV sensible effectiveness
$Q_{bal,hr}$ = balanced ventilation flow rate via HRV/ERV equipment, cfm
$Q_{bal,oth}$ = other balanced ventilation supply airflow rate, cfm
Δt = indoor/outdoor temperature difference, °F
ΔW = indoor/outdoor humidity ratio difference
$q_{vi,t}$ = total ventilation/infiltration load, Btu/h
ε_t = HRV/ERV total effectiveness
Δh = indoor/outdoor enthalpy difference, Btu/lb
$q_{vi,l}$ = latent ventilation/infiltration load, Btu/h

Distribution Losses. Air leakage and heat losses from duct systems frequently impose substantial equipment loads in excess of building requirements. The magnitude of losses depends on the location of duct runs, their surface areas, surrounding temperatures, duct wall insulation, and duct airtightness. These values are usually difficult to accurately determine at the time of preconstruction load calculations, and must be estimated using assumed values, so that selected equipment capacity is sufficient.

Good design and workmanship both reduce duct losses. In particular, locating duct runs within the conditioned envelope (above dropped hallway ceilings, for example) substantially eliminates duct losses. Specific recommendations are found in Chapter 10 of the 2016 *ASHRAE Handbook—HVAC Systems and Equipment*. Good workmanship and correct materials are essential to achieve low leakage. Many common sealing techniques, notably duct tape, have been shown to fail in a few years. Well-constructed duct systems show leakage rates of 5% of fan flow from supply and return runs, whereas 11% or more on each side is more typical. Because of the potentially large load impact of duct leakage, postconstruction verification of airtightness is strongly recommended.

Duct losses can be estimated using models specified in ASHRAE *Standard* 152, Francisco and Palmiter (1999), and Palmiter and Francisco (1997). The allowance for distribution losses is calculated as follows:

$$q_d = F_{dl} q_{bl} \tag{19}$$

where

q_d = distribution loss, Btu/h
F_{dl} = duct loss/gain factor, from Table 6 *or* ASHRAE *Standard* 152 design efficiencies *or* a detailed model
q_{bl} = total building load, Btu/h

Table 6 shows typical duct loss/gain factors calculated for the conditions indicated. These values can provide guidance for hand

Table 6 Typical Duct Loss/Gain Factors

		1 Story						2 or More Stories					
	Supply/Return Leakage	**11%/11%**			**5%/5%**			**11%/11%**			**5%/5%**		
Duct Location	**Insulation ft²·h·°F/Btu**	**R-0**	**R-4**	**R-8**	**R-0**	**R-4**	**R-8**	**R-0**	**R-4**	**R-8**	**R-0**	**R-4**	**R-8**
Conditioned space		No loss (F_{dl} = 0)											
Attic	C	1.26	0.71	0.63	0.68	0.33	0.27	1.02	0.66	0.60	0.53	0.29	0.25
	H/F	0.49	0.29	0.25	0.34	0.16	0.13	0.41	0.26	0.24	0.27	0.14	0.12
	H/HP	0.56	0.37	0.34	0.34	0.19	0.16	0.49	0.35	0.33	0.28	0.17	0.15
Basement	C	0.12	0.09	0.09	0.07	0.05	0.04	0.11	0.09	0.09	0.06	0.04	0.04
	H/F	0.28	0.18	0.16	0.19	0.10	0.08	0.24	0.17	0.15	0.16	0.09	0.08
	H/HP	0.23	0.17	0.16	0.14	0.09	0.08	0.20	0.16	0.15	0.12	0.08	0.07
Crawlspace	C	0.16	0.12	0.11	0.10	0.06	0.05	0.14	0.12	0.11	0.08	0.06	0.05
	H/F	0.49	0.29	0.25	0.34	0.16	0.13	0.41	0.26	0.24	0.27	0.14	0.12
	H/HP	0.56	0.37	0.34	0.34	0.19	0.16	0.49	0.35	0.33	0.28	0.17	0.15

Values calculated for ASHRAE *Standard* 152 default duct system surface area using model of Francisco and Palmiter (1999). Values are provided as guidance only; losses can differ substantially for other conditions and configurations. Assumed surrounding temperatures:

Cooling (C): t_o = 95°F, t_{attic} = 120°F, t_b = 68°F, t_{crawl} = 72°F Heating/furnace (H/F) and heating/heating pump (H/HP): t_o = 32°F, t_{attic} = 32°F, t_b = 64°F, t_{crawl} = 32°F

estimates, and illustrate the need for achieving low duct leakage. To the extent conditions differ from those shown, specific calculations should be made using a method cited previously. Note also that Table 6 cooling factors represent sensible gain only. Duct leakage may also introduce significant latent gain; see ASHRAE *Standard* 152.

7. COOLING LOAD

A cooling load calculation determines total sensible cooling load from heat gain (1) through opaque surfaces (walls, floors, ceilings, and doors), (2) through transparent fenestration surfaces (windows, skylights, and glazed doors), (3) caused by infiltration and ventilation, and (4) because of occupancy. The latent portion of the cooling load is evaluated separately. Although the entire structure may be considered a single zone, equipment selection and system design should be based on room-by-room calculations. For proper design of the distribution system, the conditioned airflow required by each room must be known.

Peak Load Computation

To select a properly sized cooling unit, the peak or maximum load (block load) for each zone must be computed. The block load for a single-family detached house with one central system is the sum of all the room loads. If the house has a separate system for each zone, each zone block load is required. When a house is zoned with one central cooling system, the system size is based on the entire house block load, whereas zone components, such as distribution ducts, are sized using zone block loads.

In multifamily structures, each living unit has a zone load that equals the sum of the room loads. For apartments with separate systems, the block load for each unit establishes the system size. Apartment buildings having a central cooling system with fan-coils in each apartment require a block load calculation for the complete structure to size the central system; each unit load establishes the size of the fan-coil and air distribution system for each apartment. One of the methods for nonresidential buildings discussed in Chapter 18 may be used to calculate the block load.

Opaque Surfaces

Heat gain through walls, floors, ceilings, and doors is caused by (1) the air temperature difference across such surfaces and (2) solar gains incident on the surfaces. The heat capacity of typical construction moderates and delays building heat gain. This effect is modeled in detail in the computerized RHB method, resulting in accurate simultaneous load estimates.

Table 7 Opaque Surface Cooling Factor Coefficients

Surface Type	OF_t	OF_b, °F	OF_r
Ceiling or wall adjacent to vented attic	0.62	$25.7\,\alpha_{roof} - 8.1$	−0.19
Ceiling/roof assembly	1	$68.9\,\alpha_{roof} - 12.6$	−0.36
Wall (wood frame) or door with solar exposure	1	14.8	−0.36
Wall (wood frame) or door (shaded)	1	0	−0.36
Floor over ambient	1	0	−0.06
Floor over crawlspace	0.33	0	−0.28
Slab floor (see Slab Floor section)			

α_{roof} = roof solar absorptance (see Table 8).

Table 8 Roof Solar Absorptance α_{roof}

	Color			
Material	**White**	**Light**	**Medium**	**Dark**
Asphalt shingles	0.75	0.75	0.85	0.92
Tile	0.30	0.40	0.80	0.80
Metal	0.35	0.50	0.70	0.90
Elastomeric coating	0.30			

Source: Summarized from Parker et al. (2000).

The RLF method uses the following to estimate cooling load:

$$q_{opq} = A \times CF_{opq} \tag{20}$$

$$CF_{opq} = U(OF_t \Delta t + OF_b + OF_r DR) \tag{21}$$

where

q_{opq} = opaque surface cooling load, Btu/h
A = net surface area, ft²
CF = surface cooling factor, Btu/h·ft²
U = construction U-factor, Btu/h·ft²·°F
Δt = cooling design temperature difference, °F
OF_t, OF_b, OF_r = opaque-surface cooling factors (see Table 7)
DR = cooling daily range, °F

OF factors, found in Table 7, represent construction-specific physical characteristics. OF_t values less than 1 capture the buffering effect of attics and crawlspaces, OF_b represents incident solar gain, and OF_r captures heat storage effects by reducing the effective temperature difference. Note also that CF can be viewed as CF = U × CLTD, the formulation used in prior residential and nonresidential methods.

Table 7 factors for walls are simplified in two ways. First, the values do not depend on wall orientation. This has minimal effect on total load, because residences typically have a mix of exposures.

Second, only wood frame construction is included. The wood frame values can be used for heavier construction (e.g., masonry), but this overpredicts the wall's contribution to cooling load and is thus conservative.

Slab Floors

Slab floors produce a slight reduction in cooling load, as follows:

$$q_{opq} = A \times \text{CF}_{slab} \tag{22}$$

$$\text{CF}_{slab} = 0.59 - 2.5h_{srf} \tag{23}$$

where

A = area of slab, ft²
CF_{slab} = slab cooling factor, Btu/h·ft²
h_{srf} = effective surface conductance, including resistance of slab covering material such as carpet $=1/(R_{cvr} + 0.68)$, Btu/h·ft²·°F. Representative R_{cvr} values are found in Chapter 6 of the 2016 *ASHRAE Handbook—HVAC Systems and Equipment.*
0.59 = constant, Btu/h·ft²
2.5 = factor, °F

Surfaces Adjacent to Buffer Space

Heat gain from adjacent unconditioned or semiconditioned spaces can be calculated based on the partition U-factor and temperature difference. Buffer space air temperature t_b can be estimated using procedures discussed in the section on Adjacent Buffer Spaces. Generally, simple approximations are sufficient. If the partition surface is large and/or poorly insulated, buffer temperature should be calculated with more care.

Transparent Fenestration Surfaces

Cooling load associated with nondoor fenestration is calculated as follows:

$$q_{fen} = A \times \text{CF}_{fen} \tag{24}$$

$$\text{CF}_{fen} = U(\Delta t - 0.46\text{DR}) + \text{PXI} \times \text{SHGC} \times \text{IAC} \times \text{FF}_s \tag{25}$$

where

q_{fen} = fenestration cooling load, Btu/h
A = fenestration area (including frame), ft²
CF_{fen} = surface cooling factor, Btu/h·ft²
U = fenestration NFRC *heating* U-factor, Btu/h·ft²·°F
Δt = cooling design temperature difference, °F
PXI = peak exterior irradiance, including shading modifications, Btu/h·ft² [see Equations (26) or (27)]
SHGC = fenestration rated or estimated NFRC solar heat gain coefficient
IAC = interior shading attenuation coefficient, Equation (29)
FF_s = fenestration solar load factor, Table 13

Peak Exterior Irradiance (PXI). Although solar gain occurs throughout the day, RP-1199 regression studies (Barnaby et al. 2004) showed that the cooling load contribution of fenestration correlates well with the peak-hour irradiance incident on the fenestration exterior. PXI is calculated as follows:

$$\text{PXI} = T_x E_t \text{ (unshaded fenestration)} \tag{26}$$

$$\text{PXI} = T_x [E_d + (1 - F_{shd}) E_D] \text{ (shaded fenestration)} \tag{27}$$

where

PXI = peak exterior irradiance, Btu/h·ft²
E_t, E_d, E_D = peak total, diffuse, and direct irradiance (Table 9 or 10), Btu/h·ft²
T_x = transmission of exterior attachment (insect screen or shade screen)
F_{shd} = fraction of fenestration shaded by permanent overhangs, fins, or environmental obstacles

Table 9 Peak Irradiance Equations

Horizontal surfaces

$$E_t = 258.7 + 3.233L - 0.0572L^2$$

$$E_d = \min(E_t, 53.9)$$

$$E_D = E_t - E_d$$

Vertical surfaces

$$\phi = \left|\frac{\psi}{180}\right| \text{ (normalized exposure, 0 – 1)}$$

$$E_t = 134.2 + 393\phi - 1630\phi^3 + 1011\phi^4 + 11.17\phi L + 0.0452\phi L^2 - 4.086L - 0.1956L^2 + [0.2473L^2/(\phi + 1)]$$

$$E_d = \min\left(112.9 - 11.96\phi^2 + 0.0958\phi L - \frac{36.74\sqrt[4]{L}}{\phi + 1}\right)$$

$$E_D = E_t - E_d$$

where

E_t, E_d, E_D = peak hourly total, diffuse, and direct irradiance, Btu/h·ft²
L = site latitude, °N
ψ = exposure (surface azimuth), ° from south (–180 to +180)

Table 10 Peak Irradiance, Btu/h·ft²

Exposure		Latitude								
		20°	25°	30°	35°	40°	45°	50°	55°	60°
North	E_D	38	34	31	31	33	37	44	53	65
	E_d	35	31	27	24	21	18	15	13	11
	E_t	73	64	58	55	53	55	59	66	75
Northeast/Northwest	E_D	140	140	140	141	142	143	145	147	150
	E_d	50	47	44	42	39	37	35	33	32
	E_t	190	187	184	182	181	180	180	181	182
East/West	E_D	158	166	174	181	187	192	198	202	206
	E_d	59	56	54	52	50	49	47	46	45
	E_t	217	223	228	233	237	241	245	248	251
Southeast/Southwest	E_D	76	95	112	129	144	158	171	183	193
	E_d	63	61	59	58	56	55	54	53	52
	E_t	139	156	172	186	200	213	225	236	245
South	E_D	0	6	36	64	90	115	139	161	181
	E_d	39	62	61	60	59	58	57	56	56
	E_t	39	69	97	123	149	173	196	217	237
Horizontal	E_D	247	250	250	248	243	234	223	210	193
	E_d	54	54	54	54	54	54	54	54	54
	E_t	300	304	304	302	297	288	277	263	247

For horizontal or vertical surfaces, peak irradiance values can be obtained from Table 10 for primary exposures, or from Table 9 equations for any exposure. Skylights with slope less than 30° from horizontal should be treated as horizontal. Steeper, nonvertical slopes are not supported by the RLF method.

Exterior Attachments. Common window coverings can significantly reduce fenestration solar gain. Table 11 shows transmission values for typical attachments.

Permanent Shading. The shaded fraction F_{shd} can be taken as 1 for any fenestration shaded by adjacent structures during peak hours. Simple overhang shading can be estimated using the following:

$$F_{shd} = \min\left[1, \max\left(0, \frac{\text{SLF} \times D_{oh} - X_{oh}}{h}\right)\right] \tag{28}$$

where

SLF = shade line factor from Table 12
D_{oh} = depth of overhang (from plane of fenestration), ft
X_{oh} = vertical distance from top of fenestration to overhang, ft
h = height of fenestration, ft

The shade line factor (SLF) is the ratio of the vertical distance a shadow falls beneath the edge of an overhang to the depth of the overhang, so the shade line equals the SLF times the overhang depth. Table 12 shows SLFs for July 21 averaged over the hours of greatest solar intensity on each exposure.

More complex shading situations should be analyzed with the RHB method.

Fenestration Solar Load Factors. Fenestration solar load factors FF_s depend on fenestration exposure and are found in Table 13. The values represent the fraction of transmitted solar gain that contributes to peak cooling load. It is thus understandable that morning (east) values are lower than afternoon (west) values. Higher values are included for multifamily buildings with limited exposure.

Interior Shading. Interior shading significantly reduces solar gain and is ubiquitous in residential buildings. Field studies show that a large fraction of windows feature some sort of shading; for example, James et al. (1997) studied 368 houses and found interior shading in 80% of audited windows. Therefore, in all but special circumstances, interior shading should be assumed when calculating cooling loads. In the RLF method, the interior attenuation coefficient (IAC) model is used, as described in Chapter 15. Residential values from that chapter are consolidated in Table 14. IAC values for many other configurations are found in Chapter 15, Tables 14A to 14G.

In some cases, it is reasonable to assume that a shade is partially open. For example, drapes are often partially open to admit daylight. IAC values are computed as follows:

$$IAC = 1 + F_{cl}(IAC_{cl} - 1) \tag{29}$$

where

IAC = interior attenuation coefficient of fenestration with partially closed shade
F_{cl} = shade fraction closed (0 to 1)
IAC_{cl} = interior attenuation coefficient of fully closed configuration (from Table 14 or Chapter 15, Tables 14A to 14G)

Table 11 Exterior Attachment Transmission

Attachment	T_x
None	1.0
Exterior insect screen	0.64 (see Chapter 15, Table 13G)
Shade screen	Manufacturer shading coefficient (SC) value, typically 0.4 to 0.6

Table 12 Shade Line Factors (SLFs)

	Latitude								
Exposure	20°	25°	30°	35°	40°	45°	50°	55°	60°
North	2.8	2.1	1.4	1.5	1.7	1.0	0.8	0.9	0.8
Northeast/Northwest	1.4	1.5	1.6	1.2	1.3	1.3	0.9	0.9	0.8
East/West	1.2	1.2	1.1	1.1	1.1	1.0	1.0	0.9	0.8
Southeast/Southwest	2.1	1.8	2.0	1.7	1.5	1.6	1.4	1.2	1.1
South	20.0	14.0	6.9	4.7	3.3	2.7	2.1	1.7	1.4

Note: Shadow length below overhang = SLF × D_{oh}.

Table 13 Fenestration Solar Load Factors FF_s

Exposure	Single Family Detached	Multifamily
North	0.44	0.27
Northeast	0.21	0.43
East	0.31	0.56
Southeast	0.37	0.54
South	0.47	0.53
Southwest	0.58	0.61
West	0.56	0.65
Northwest	0.46	0.57
Horizontal	0.58	0.73

Infiltration and Ventilation

See the Common Data and Procedures section.

Internal Gain

The contributions of occupants, lighting, and appliance gains to peak sensible and latent loads can be estimated as

$$q_{ig,s} = 464 + 0.7A_{cf} + 75N_{oc} \tag{30}$$

$$q_{ig,l} = 68 + 0.07A_{cf} + 41N_{oc} \tag{31}$$

where

$q_{ig,s}$ = sensible cooling load from internal gains, Btu/h
$q_{ig,l}$ = latent cooling load from internal gains, Btu/h
A_{cf} = conditioned floor area of building, ft²
N_{oc} = number of occupants (if unknown, estimate as $N_{br} + 1$)

Equations (30) and (31) and their coefficients are derived from Building America (2004) load profiles evaluated at 4:00 PM, as documented by Barnaby and Spitler (2005). Predicted gains are typical for U.S. homes. Further allowances should be considered when unusual lighting intensities or other equipment are in continuous use during peak cooling hours. In critical situations where intermittent high occupant density or other internal gains are expected, a parallel cooling system should be considered.

For room-by-room calculations, $q_{ig,s}$ should be evaluated for the entire conditioned area, and allocated to kitchen and living spaces.

Air Distribution System: Heat Gain

See the Common Data and Procedures section.

Total Latent Load

The latent cooling load is the result of three predominant moisture sources: outdoor air (infiltration and ventilation), occupants, and miscellaneous sources, such as cooking, laundry, and bathing. These components, discussed in previous sections, combine to yield the total latent load:

$$q_l = q_{vi,l} + q_{ig,l} \tag{32}$$

where

q_l = total latent load, Btu/h

Table 14 Interior Attenuation Coefficients (IAC_{cl})

		Drapes			Roller Shades			Blinds	
		Open-Weave	Closed-Weave		Opaque		Translucent		
Glazing Layers	Glazing Type (ID*)	Light	Dark	Light	Dark	White	Light	Medium	White
1	Clear (1a)	0.64	0.71	0.45	0.64	0.34	0.44	0.74	0.66
	Heat absorbing (1c)	0.68	0.72	0.50	0.67	0.40	0.49	0.76	0.69
2	Clear (5a)	0.72	0.81	0.57	0.76	0.48	0.55	0.82	0.74
	Low-e high-solar (17c)	0.76	0.86	0.64	0.82	0.57	0.62	0.86	0.79
	Low-e low-solar (25a)	0.79	0.88	0.68	0.85	0.60	0.66	0.88	0.82
	Heat absorbing (5c)	0.73	0.82	0.59	0.77	0.51	0.58	0.83	0.76

*Chapter 15 glazing identifier

$q_{vi,l}$ = ventilation/infiltration latent gain, Btu/h, from Equation (16) or (18)

$q_{ig,l}$ = internal latent gain, Btu/h, from Equation (31)

Additional latent gains may be introduced through return duct leakage and specific atypical sources. These may be estimated and included. Lstiburek and Carmody (1993) provide data for household moisture sources; however, again note that Equation (31) adequately accounts for normal gains.

Because air conditioning systems are usually controlled by a thermostat, latent cooling is a side effect of equipment operation. During periods of significant latent gain but mild temperatures, there is little cooling operation, resulting in unacceptable indoor humidity. Multispeed equipment, combined temperature/humidity control, and dedicated dehumidification should be considered to address this condition.

Summary of RLF Cooling Load Equations

Table 15 contains a brief list of equations used in the cooling load calculation procedure described in this chapter.

8. HEATING LOAD

Calculating a residential heating load involves estimating the maximum heat loss of each room or space to be heated and the simultaneous maximum (block) heat loss for the building, while maintaining a selected indoor air temperature during periods of design outdoor weather conditions. As discussed in the section on Calculation Approach, heating calculations use conservative assumptions, ignoring solar and internal gains, and building heat storage. This leaves a simple steady-state heat loss calculation, with the only significant difficulty being surfaces adjacent to grade.

Exterior Surfaces Above Grade

All above-grade surfaces exposed to outdoor conditions (walls, doors, ceilings, fenestration, and raised floors) are treated identically, as follows:

$$q = A \times \text{HF} \tag{33}$$

$$\text{HF} = U\Delta t \tag{34}$$

where HF is the heating load factor in Btu/h·ft².

Two ceiling configurations are common:

- For **ceiling/roof combinations** (e.g., flat roof or cathedral ceiling), the U-factor should be evaluated for the entire assembly.
- For **well-insulated ceilings (or walls) adjacent to vented attic space**, the U-factor should be that of the insulated assembly only (the roof is omitted) and the attic temperature assumed to equal the heating design outdoor temperature. The effect of attic radiant barriers can be neglected. In cases where the ceiling or wall is not well insulated, the adjacent buffer space procedure (see the section on Surfaces Adjacent to Buffer Space) can be used.

Below-Grade and On-Grade Surfaces

The Heating Load Calculations section of Chapter 18 includes simplified procedures for estimating heat loss through below-grade walls and below- and on-grade floors. Those procedures are applicable to residential buildings. In more detailed work, Bahnfleth and Pedersen (1990) show a significant effect of the area-to-perimeter ratio. For additional generality and accuracy, see also methods described or cited in Beausoleil-Morrison and Mitalas (1997), CAN/CSA *Standard* F280, HRAI (2014), and Krarti and Choi (1996).

Surfaces Adjacent to Buffer Space

Heat loss to adjacent unconditioned or semiconditioned spaces can be calculated using a heating factor based on the partition temperature difference:

$$\text{HF} = U(t_i - t_b) \tag{35}$$

Buffer space air temperature t_b can be estimated using procedures discussed in the section on Adjacent Buffer Spaces. Generally, simple approximations are sufficient except where the partition surface is poorly insulated.

Crawlspaces and basements are cases where the partition (the house floor) is often poorly insulated; they also involve heat transfer to the ground. Most codes require crawlspaces to be adequately vented year round. However, work highlighting problems with venting crawlspaces (DeWitt 2003) has led to application of sealed crawlspaces with insulated perimeter walls. Equation (5) may be applied to basements and crawlspace by including appropriate ground-related terms in the heat balance formulation. For example, when including below-grade walls, $A_x = A_{bw}$, $U_x = U_{avg,bw}$, and $t_x = t_{gr}$ should be included as applicable in the summations in Equation (5). Losses from piping or ducting should be included as additional buffer space heat gain. Determining the ventilation or infiltration rate for crawlspaces and basements is difficult. Latta and Boileau (1969) estimated the air exchange rate for an uninsulated basement at 0.67 ach under winter conditions. Field measurements of eight ventilated crawlspaces summarized in Palmiter and Francisco (1996) yielded a median flow rate of 4.6 ach. Clearly, crawlspace infiltration rates vary widely, depending on vent configuration and operation.

Ventilation and Infiltration

Infiltration of outdoor air causes both sensible and latent heat loss. The energy required to raise the temperature of outdoor infiltrating air to indoor air temperature is the sensible component; energy associated with net loss of moisture from the space is the latent component. Determining the volumetric flow Q of outdoor air

Table 15 Summary of RLF Cooling Load Equations

Load Source	Equation	Tables and Notes
Exterior opaque surfaces	$q_{opq} = A \times \text{CF}$	
	$\text{CF} = U(\text{OF}_t\Delta t + \text{OF}_b + \text{OF}_r\text{DR})$	OF factors from Table 7
Exterior transparent surfaces	$q_{fen} = A \times \text{CF}$	PXI from Table 9 or 10 plus adjustments
	$\text{CF} = U(\Delta t - 0.46\text{DR}) + \text{PXI} \times \text{SHGC} \times \text{IAC} \times \text{FF}_s$	FF_s from Table 13
Partitions to unconditioned space	$q = AU\Delta t$	Δt = temperature difference across partition
Ventilation/infiltration	$q_s = C_sQ\Delta t$	See Common Data and Procedures section
Occupants and appliances	$q_{ig,s} = 464 + 0.7A_{cf} + 75N_{oc}$	
Distribution	$q_d = F_{dl}\Sigma q$	F_{dl} from Table 6
Total sensible load	$q_s = q_d + \Sigma q$	
Latent load	$q_l = q_{vi,l} + q_{ig,l}$	
Ventilation/infiltration	$q_{vi,l} = C_l Q\Delta W$	
Internal gain	$q_{ig,l} = 68 + 0.07A_{cf} + 41N_{oc}$	

entering the building is discussed in the Common Data and Procedures section and in Chapter 16. Determining the resulting sensible and latent loads is discussed in the Ventilation/Infiltration Load subsection.

Humidification

In many climates, humidification is required to maintain comfortable indoor relative humidity under heating conditions. The latent ventilation and infiltration load calculated, assuming desired indoor humidity conditions, equals the sensible heat needed to evaporate water at a rate sufficient to balance moisture losses from air leakage. Self-contained humidifiers provide this heat from internal sources. If the heat of evaporation is taken from occupied space or the distribution system, the heating capacity should be increased accordingly.

Pickup Load

For intermittently heated buildings and night thermostat setback, additional heat is required to raise the temperature of air, building materials, and material contents to the specified temperature. The rate at which this additional heat must be supplied is the pickup load, which depends on the structure's heat capacity, its material contents, and the time in which these are to be heated.

Because the design outdoor temperature is generally much lower than typical winter temperatures, under most conditions excess heating capacity is available for pickup. Therefore, many engineers make no pickup allowance except for demanding situations. If pickup capacity is justified, the following guidance can be used to estimate the requirement.

Relatively little rigorous information on pickup load exists. Building simulation programs can predict recovery times and required equipment capacities, but a detailed simulation study is rarely practical. Armstrong et al. (1992a, 1992b) developed a model for predicting recovery from setback and validated it for a church and two office buildings. Nelson and MacArthur (1978) studied the relationship between thermostat setback, furnace capacity, and recovery time. Hedrick et al. (1992) compared Nelson and MacArthur's results to tests for two test houses and found that the furnace oversizing required for a 2 h recovery time ranges from 20 to 120%, depending on size of setback, building mass, and heating Δt (colder locations require less oversizing on a percentage basis).

The designer should be aware that there are trade-offs between energy savings from thermostat setback and energy penalties incurred by oversizing equipment. Koenig (1978) studied a range of locations and suggested that 30% oversizing allows recovery times less than 4 h for nearly the entire heating season and is close to optimum from an energy standpoint.

The preceding guidance applies to residential buildings with fuel-fired furnaces. Additional considerations may be important for other types of heating systems. For air-source heat pumps with electric resistance auxiliary heat, thermostat setback may be undesirable (Bullock 1978).

Thermostats with optimum-start algorithms, designed to allow both energy savings and timely recovery to the daytime set point, are becoming routinely available and should be considered in all cases.

Summary of Heating Load Procedures

Table 16 lists equations used in the heating load calculation procedures described in this chapter.

9. LOAD CALCULATION EXAMPLE

A single-family detached house with floor plan shown in Figure 1 is located in Atlanta, GA, USA. Construction characteristics are documented in Table 17. Using the RLF method, find the block (whole-house) design cooling and heating loads. A furnace/air-conditioner forced-air system is planned with a well-sealed and well-insulated (R-8 wrap) attic duct system.

Solution

Design Conditions. Table 18 summarizes design conditions. Typical indoor conditions are assumed. Outdoor conditions are determined from Chapter 14.

Table 16 Summary of Heating Load Calculation Equations

Load Source	Equation	Tables and Notes
Exterior surfaces above grade	$q = UA\Delta t$	$\Delta t = t_i - t_o$
Partitions to unconditioned buffer space	$q = UA\Delta t$	Δt = temp. difference across partition
Walls below grade	$q = U_{avg,bw} A(t_{in} - t_{gr})$	
Floors on grade	$q = F_p p \Delta t$	See Chapter 18, Equations (41) and (42)
Floors below grade	$q = U_{avg,bf} A(t_{in} - t_{gr})$	See Chapter 18, Equations (37) and (38)
Ventilation/infiltration	$q_{vi} = C_s Q \Delta t$	From Common Data and Procedures section
Total sensible load	$q_s = \Sigma q$	

Table 17 Example House Characteristics

Component	Description	Factors
Roof/ceiling	Flat wood frame ceiling (insulated with R-30 fiberglass) beneath vented attic with medium asphalt shingle roof	U = 0.031 Btu/h·ft²·°F α_{roof} = 0.85 (Table 8)
Exterior walls	Wood frame, exterior wood sheathing, interior gypsum board, R-13 fiberglass insulation	U = 0.090 Btu/h·ft²·°F
Doors	Wood, solid core	U = 0.40 Btu/h·ft²·°F
Floor	Slab on grade with heavy carpet over rubber pad; R-5 edge insulation to 3 ft below grade	R_{cvr} = 1.2 ft²·h·°F/Btu (Table 3, Chapter 6, 2016 *ASHRAE Handbook—HVAC Systems and Equipment*) F_p = 0.5 Btu/h·ft·°F (estimated from Chapter 18, Table 24)
Windows	Low-e/low-solar in wood frames. Half fixed, half operable with insect screens (except living room picture window, which is fixed). 2 ft eave overhang on east and west with eave edge at same height as top of glazing for all windows. Allow for typical closed-weave light drape interior shading, half closed.	Fixed: U = 0.35 Btu/h·ft²·°F; SHGC = 0.36 (Table 2) Operable: U = 0.39 Btu/h·ft²·°F; SHGC = 0.31 (Table 2); T_x = 0.64 (Table 11) IAC_{cl} = 0.68 (Table 14)
Construction	Good	A_{ul} = 0.02 in²/ft² (Table 3)

Table 18 Example House Design Conditions

Item	Heating	Cooling	Notes
Latitude	—	—	33.64°N
Elevation	—	—	1027 ft
Indoor temperature	68°F	75°F	
Indoor relative humidity	N/A	50%	No humidification
Outdoor temperature	26°F	92°F	Cooling: 1% value (91.5°F rounded) Heating: 99% (26.5°F rounded conservatively)
Daily range	N/A	17°F	(16.7°F rounded)
Outdoor wet bulb	N/A	74°F	MCWB* at 1%
Wind speed	15 mph	7.5 mph	Default assumption
Design Δt	42°F	17°F	
Moisture difference		0.0050 lb/lb	Psychrometric chart

*MCWB = mean coincident wet bulb.

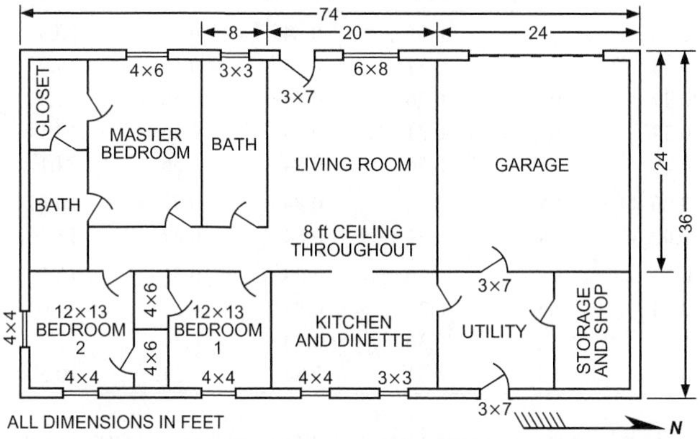

Fig. 1 Example House

Table 19 Example House Component Quantities

Component	Quantity	Notes
Ceiling	2088 ft^2	Overall area less garage area (74 × 36) – (24 × 24)
Doors	42 ft^2	2 (each 3 by 7 ft)
Windows	154 ft^2	
Walls, exposed exterior	1376 ft^2 gross, 1180 ft^2 net	Wall height = 8 ft
Walls, garage	384 ft^2	
Floor area	2088 ft^2	
Floor perimeter	220 ft	Include perimeter adjacent to garage
Total exposed surface	3848 ft^2	Wall gross area (including garage wall) plus ceiling area
Volume	16,704 ft^3	

Component Quantities. Areas and lengths required for load calculations are derived from plan dimensions (Figure 1). Table 19 summarizes these quantities.

Opaque Surface Factors. Heating and cooling factors are derived for each component condition. Table 20 shows the resulting factors and their sources.

Window Factors. Deriving cooling factors for windows requires identifying all unique glazing configurations in the house. Equation (25) input items indicate that the variations for this case are exposure, window height (with overhang shading), and frame type (which determines U-factor, SHGC, and the presence of insect screen). CF derivation for all configurations is summarized in Table 21.

For example, CF for operable 3 ft high windows facing west (the second row in Table 21) is derived as follows:

- U-factor and SHGC are found in Table 2.
- Each operable window is equipped with an insect screen. From Table 11, $T_x = 0.64$ for this arrangement.
- Overhang shading is evaluated with Equation (28). For west exposure and latitude 34°, Table 12 shows SLF = 1.1. Overhang depth (D_{oh}) is 2 ft and the window-overhang distance (X_{oh}) is 0 ft. With window height h of 3 ft, $F_s = 0.73$ (73% shaded).
- PXI depends on peak irradiance and shading. Approximating site latitude as 35°N, Table 10 shows $E_D = 181$ and $E_d = 52$ Btu/h·ft^2 for west exposure. Equation (27) combines these values with T_x and F_s to find PXI = 0.64[52 + (1 – 0.73)181] = 65 Btu/h·ft^2.
- All windows are assumed to have some sort of interior shading in the half-closed position. Use Equation (29) with $F_{cl} = 0.5$ and $IAC_{cl} = 0.68$ (per Table 17) to derive IAC = 0.84.
- FF_s is taken from Table 13 for west exposure.
- Finally, inserting the preceding values into Equation (25) gives CF = 0.39(17 – 0.46 × 17) + 65 × 0.31 × 0.84 × 0.56 = 13 Btu/h·ft^2.

Envelope Loads. Given the load factors and component quantities, heating and cooling loads are calculated for each envelope element, as shown in Table 22.

Infiltration and Ventilation. From Table 3, A_{ul} for this house is 0.02 in^2/ft^2 of exposed surface area. Applying Equation (9) yields $A_L = A_{es} \times A_{ul} = 3848 \times 0.02 = 77$ in^2. Using Table 5, estimate heating and cooling IDF to be 1.0 and 0.48 cfm/in^2, respectively [alternatively, Equation (10) could be used to find IDF values]. Apply Equation (8) to find the infiltration leakage rates and Equation (7) to convert the rate to air changes per hour:

$$Q_{i,h} = 77 \times 1.0 = 77 \text{ cfm } (0.28 \text{ ach})$$

$$Q_{i,c} = 77 \times 0.48 = 36 \text{ cfm } (0.13 \text{ ach})$$

Calculate the ventilation outdoor air requirement with Equation (11) using $A_{cf} = 2088$ ft^2 and $N_{br} = 3$, resulting in $Q_v = 93$ cfm. For design purposes, assume that this requirement is met by a mechanical system with balanced supply and exhaust flow rates ($Q_{unbal} = 0$).

Find the combined infiltration/ventilation flow rates by summing the balanced ventilation flow with net infiltration flow derived with Equation (14):

$$Q_{vi,h} = 93 + \max(0, 77 + 0.5 \times 0) = 170 \text{ cfm}$$

$$Q_{vi,c} = 93 + \max(0, 36 + 0.5 \times 0) = 129 \text{ cfm}$$

At Atlanta's elevation of 1027 ft, elevation adjustment of heat factors results in a small (4%) reduction in air heat transfer; thus, adjustment is unnecessary, resulting in $C_s = 1.10$ Btu/h·°F·cfm. Use Equation (15) with $Q_{bal,hr} = 0$ and $Q_{bal,oth} = 0$ to calculate the sensible infiltration/ventilation loads:

$$q_{vi,s,h} = 1.1 \times 170 \times 42 = 7854 \text{ Btu/h}$$

$$q_{vi,s,c} = 1.1 \times 129 \times 17 = 2412 \text{ Btu/h}$$

Table 20 Example House Opaque Surface Factors

Component	U, Btu/h·ft²·°F or F_p, Btu/h·ft·°F	Heating HF	Heating Reference	Cooling OF_t	Cooling OF_b	Cooling OF_r	Cooling CF	Cooling Reference
Ceiling	0.031	1.30	Equation (34)	0.62	13.75	–0.19	0.65	Table 7 Equation (21)
Wall	0.090	3.78		1	14.80	–0.36	2.31	
Garage wall	0.090	3.78		1	0.00	–0.36	0.98	
Door	0.400	16.80		1	14.80	–0.36	10.27	
Floor perimeter	0.500	21.00	Chapter 18, Equation (42)					
Floor area				0.59	–2.5/(0.68 + 1.20) = –1.33		–0.74	Equation (23)

Table 21 Example House Window Factors

Exposure	Height, ft	Frame	U, Btu/h·ft²·°F Table 2	HF Eq. (34)	T_x Table 11	F_{shd} Eq. (28)	PXI Eq. (27)	SHGC Table 2	IAC Eq. (29)	FF_s Table 13	CF Eq. (25)
West	3	Fixed	0.35	14.7	1	0.73	101	0.36	0.84	0.56	20.3
	3	Operable	0.39	16.4	0.64	0.73	65	0.31	0.84	0.56	13.0
	6	Fixed	0.35	14.7	1	0.37	166	0.36	0.84	0.56	31.3
	6	Operable	0.39	16.4	0.64	0.37	106	0.31	0.84	0.56	19.1
	8	Fixed	0.35	14.7	1	0.28	182	0.36	0.84	0.56	34.1
South	4	Fixed	0.35	14.7	1	0.00	124	0.36	0.84	0.47	20.8
	4	Operable	0.39	16.4	0.64	0.00	79	0.31	0.84	0.47	13.3
East	3	Fixed	0.35	14.7	1	0.73	101	0.36	0.84	0.31	12.7
	3	Operable	0.39	16.4	0.64	0.73	65	0.31	0.84	0.31	8.8
	4	Fixed	0.35	14.7	1	0.55	133	0.36	0.84	0.31	15.7
	4	Operable	0.39	16.4	0.64	0.55	85	0.31	0.84	0.31	10.5

Table 22 Example House Envelope Loads

Component	HF	CF	Quantity, ft² or ft	Heating Load, Btu/h	Cooling Load, Btu/h
Ceiling	1.30	0.65	2088	2714	1363
Wall	3.78	2.31	1180	4460	2727
Garage wall	3.78	0.98	384	1452	376
Door	16.8	10.27	42	706	431
Floor perimeter	21.0		220	4620	
Floor area		–0.74	2088		–1545
W-Fixed-3	14.7	20.3	4.5	66	91
W-Operable-3	16.4	13.0	4.5	74	58
W-Fixed-6	14.7	31.3	12	176	376
W-Operable-6	16.4	19.1	12	197	229
W-Fixed-8	14.7	34.1	48	706	1636
S-Fixed-4	14.7	20.8	8	118	167
S-Operable-4	16.4	13.3	8	131	106
E-Fixed-3	14.7	12.7	4.5	66	57
E-Operable-3	16.4	8.8	4.5	74	40
E-Fixed-4	14.7	15.7	24	353	377
E-Operable-4	16.4	10.5	24	394	251
Envelope totals				16,306	6742

Table 23 Example House Total Sensible Loads

Item	Heating Load, Btu/h	Cooling Load, Btu/h
Envelope	16,306	6,742
Infiltration/ventilation	7,854	2,412
Internal gain		2,226
Subtotal	24,160	11,380
Distribution loss	3,141	3,073
Total sensible load	27,301	14,453

Internal Gain. Apply Equation (30) to find the sensible cooling load from internal gain:

$$q_{ig,s} = 464 + 0.7 \times 2088 + 75(3 + 1) = 2226 \text{ Btu/h}$$

Distribution Losses and Total Sensible Load. Table 23 summarizes the sensible load components. Distribution loss factors F_{dl} are estimated (from Table 6) at 0.13 for heating and 0.27 for cooling.

Latent Load. Use Equation (16) with C_l = 4840 Btu/h·cfm, $Q_{vi,c}$ = 129 cfm, $Q_{bal,oth}$ = 0, and ΔW = 0.0050 to calculate the infiltration/ ventilation latent load = 3122 Btu/h. Use Equation (31) to find the latent load from internal gains = 378 Btu/h. Therefore, the total latent cooling load is 2565 Btu/h.

10. SYMBOLS

A = area, ft²; ground surface temperature amplitude, °F
A_L = building effective leakage area (including flue) at 0.016 in. of water, assuming C_D = 1, in²
C_l = air latent heat factor, 4840 Btu/h·cfm at sea level
C_s = air sensible heat factor, 1.1 Btu/h·cfm·°F at sea level
C_t = air total heat factor, 4.5 Btu/h·cfm·(Btu/lb) at sea level
CF = cooling load factor, Btu/h·ft²
D_{oh} = depth of overhang (from plane of fenestration), ft
DR = daily range of outdoor dry-bulb temperature, °F
E = peak irradiance for exposure, Btu/h·ft²
F_{dl} = distribution loss factor
F_p = heat loss coefficient per unit length of perimeter, Btu/h·ft·°F
F_{shd} = shaded fraction
FF = coefficient for CF_{fen}
G = internal gain coefficient
h_{srf} = effective surface conductance, including resistance of slab covering material such as carpet, $1/(R_{cvr} + 0.68)$ Btu/h·ft²·°F
Δh = indoor/outdoor enthalpy difference, Btu/lb
H = height, ft
HF = heating (load) factor, Btu/h·ft²
I = infiltration coefficient
IAC = interior shading attenuation coefficient
IDF = infiltration driving force, cfm/in²

k = conductivity, Btu/h·ft·°F
LF = load factor, Btu/h·ft^2
OF = coefficient for CF_{opq}
p = perimeter or exposed edge of floor, ft
PXI = peak exterior irradiance, including shading modifications, Btu/h·ft^2
q = heating or cooling load, Btu/h
Q = air volumetric flow rate, cfm
R = insulation thermal resistance, ft^2·h·°F/Btu
SHGC = fenestration rated or estimated NFRC solar heat gain coefficient
SLF = shade line factor
t = temperature, °F
T_x = solar transmission of exterior attachment
Δt = design dry-bulb temperature difference (cooling or heating), °F
U = construction U-factor, Btu/h·ft^2·°F (for fenestration, NFRC rated *heating* U-factor)
w = width, ft
ΔW = indoor-outdoor humidity ratio difference, lb_w/lb_{da}
V = building volume, ft^3
X_{oh} = vertical distance from top of fenestration to overhang, ft
z = depth below grade, ft
α_{roof} = roof solar absorptance
ε = heat/energy recovery ventilation (HRV/ERV) effectiveness

Subscripts

avg = average
b = base (as in OF_b), basement, building, buffer
bal = balanced
bf = basement floor
bl = building load
bw = basement wall
br = bedrooms
ceil = ceiling
cf = conditioned floor
cl = closed
cvr = floor covering
d = diffuse, distribution
D = direct
da = dry air
dl = distribution loss
env = envelope
es = exposed surface
exh = exhaust
fen = fenestration
floor = floor
gr = ground
hr = heat recovery
i = infiltration
in = indoor
ig = internal gain
l = latent
o = outdoor
oc = occupant
oh = overhang
opq = opaque
oth = other
pf = projected product
r = daily range (as in OF_r)
rhb = calculated with RHB method
s = sensible or solar
shd = shaded
slab = slab
srf = surface
sup = supply
t = total or temperature (as in OF_t)
ul = unit leakage
unbal = unbalanced
v = ventilation
vi = ventilation/infiltration
w = water
wall = wall
x = *x*th buffer space surface

REFERENCES

ASHRAE members can access *ASHRAE Journal* articles and ASHRAE research project final reports at technologyportal.ashrae.org. Articles and reports are also available for purchase by nonmembers in the online ASHRAE Bookstore at www.ashrae.org/bookstore.

ACCA. 2016. *Manual J residential load calculations*, 8th ed., v. 2.5. Air Conditioning Contractors of America, Arlington, VA.

Armstrong, P.R., C.E. Hancock, and J.R. Seem. 1992a. Commercial building temperature recovery—Part 1: Design procedure based on a step response model (RP-491). *ASHRAE Transactions* 98(1):381-396.

Armstrong, P.R., C.E. Hancock, and J.R. Seem. 1992b. Commercial building temperature recovery—Part 2: Experiments to verify step response model (RP-491). *ASHRAE Transactions* 98(1):397-410.

ASHRAE. 2013. Thermal environmental conditions for human occupancy. ANSI/ASHRAE *Standard* 55-2013.

ASHRAE. 2016. Ventilation and acceptable indoor air quality in low-rise residential buildings. ANSI/ASHRAE *Standard* 62.2-2016.

ASHRAE. 2014. Method of test for determining the design and seasonal efficiencies of residential thermal distribution systems. ANSI/ASHRAE *Standard* 152-2014.

ASTM. 1998. Standard terminology of building constructions. *Standard* E631-93a (1998)e1. American Society for Testing and Materials, West Conshohocken, PA.

Bahnfleth, W.P., and C.O. Pedersen 1990. A three-dimensional numerical study of slab-on-grade heat transfer. *ASHRAE Transactions* 96(2):61-72.

Barnaby, C.S., and J.D. Spitler. 2005. Development of the residential load factor method for heating and cooling load calculations. *ASHRAE Transactions* 111(1):291-307.

Barnaby, C.S., J.D. Spitler, and D. Xiao. 2004. Updating the ASHRAE/ACCA residential heating and cooling load calculation procedures and data (RP-1199). ASHRAE Research Project, *Final Report*.

Barnaby, C.S., J.D. Spitler, and D. Xiao. 2005. The residential heat balance method for heating and cooling load calculations (RP-1199). *ASHRAE Transactions* 111(1):308-319.

Beausoleil-Morrison, I., and G. Mitalas. 1997. BASESIMP: A residential-foundation heat-loss algorithm for incorporating into whole-building energy-analysis programs. *Proceedings of Building Simulation '97*, Prague.

Building America. 2004. *Building America research benchmark definition*, v. 3.1. Available at www.nrel.gov/docs/fy05osti/36429.pdf.

Bullock, C.E. 1978. Energy savings through thermostat setback with residential heat pumps. *ASHRAE Transactions* 84(2):352-363.

CSA Group. 2012. Determining the required capacity of residential space heating and cooling appliances. CAN/CSA *Standard* F280-12. CSA Group, Mississauga, ON, Canada.

DeWitt, C. 2003. Crawlspace myths. *ASHRAE Journal* 45:20-26.

Francisco, P.W., and L. Palmiter. 1999 (rev. 2003). *Improvements to ASHRAE* Standard *152P*. Ecotope, Inc., Seattle, WA.

Hedrick, R.L., M.J. Witte, N.P. Leslie, and W.W. Bassett. 1992. Furnace sizing criteria for energy-efficient setback strategies. *ASHRAE Transactions* 98(1):1239-1246.

HRAI. 2014. *Residential heat loss and gain calculations: Student reference guide.* Heating, Refrigerating and Air Conditioning Institute of Canada. Mississauga, ON.

James, P., J. Cummings, J. Sonne, R. Vieira, and J. Klongerbo. 1997. The effect of residential equipment capacity on energy use, demand, and runtime. *ASHRAE Transactions* 103(2):297-303.

Koenig, K. 1978. Gas furnace sizing requirements for residential heating using thermostat night setback. *ASHRAE Transactions* 84(2):335-351.

Krarti, M., and S. Choi 1996. Simplified method for foundation heat loss calculation. *ASHRAE Transactions* 102(1):140-152.

Latta, J.K., and G.G. Boileau. 1969. Heat losses from house basements. *Canadian Building* 19(10):39.

Lstiburek, J.L., and J. Carmody. 1993. *Moisture control handbook*. Van Nostrand Reinhold, New York.

McQuiston, F.C. 1984. A study and review of existing data to develop a standard methodology for residential heating and cooling load calculations (RP-342). *ASHRAE Transactions* 90(2A):102-136.

Nelson, L.W., and J.W. MacArthur. 1978. Energy savings through thermostat setback. *ASHRAE Transactions* 84(2):319-334.

NFRC. 2017. *NFRC certified products directory.* National Fenestration Rating Council, Greenbelt, MD. www.nfrc.org or search.nfrc.org.

Palmiter, L., and T. Bond. 1991. Interaction of mechanical systems and natural infiltration. *Proceedings of the 12th AIVC Conference on Air Movement and Ventilation Control Within Buildings.* Air Infiltration and Ventilation Centre, Coventry, U.K.

Palmiter, L., and P. Francisco. 1996. Modeled and measured infiltration: Phase III. A detailed case study of three homes. Electric Power Research Institute *Report* TR-106288. Palo Alto, CA.

Palmiter, L., and P. Francisco. 1997. Development of a practical method of estimating the thermal efficiency of residential forced-air distribution systems. Electric Power Research Institute *Report* TR-107744. Palo Alto, CA.

Parker, D.S., J.E.R. McIlvaine, S.F. Barkaszi, D.J. Beal, and M.T. Anello. 2000. *Laboratory testing of the reflectance properties of roofing materials.* FSEC-CR670-00. Florida Solar Energy Center, Cocoa.

Pedersen, C.O., D.E. Fisher, J.D. Spitler, and R.J. Liesen. 1998. *Cooling and heating load calculation principles*. ASHRAE.

Pedersen, C.O., R.J. Liesen, R.K. Strand, D.E. Fisher, L. Dong, and P.G. Ellis. 2001. *Toolkit for building load calculations*. ASHRAE.

Sherman, M.H. 1992. Superposition in infiltration modeling. *Indoor Air* 2: 101-114.

Sherman, M.H., and D.T. Grimsrud. 1980. Infiltration-pressurization correlation: Simplified physical modeling. *ASHRAE Transactions* 86(2):778.

Walker, I.S., and D.J. Wilson. 1990. The Alberta air infiltration model. The University of Alberta, Department of Mechanical Engineering, *Technical Report* 71.

Walker, I.S., and D.J. Wilson. 1998. Field validation of equations for stack and wind driven air infiltration calculations. *International Journal of HVAC&R Research* (now *Science and Technology for the Built Environment*) 4(2).

CHAPTER 18

NONRESIDENTIAL COOLING AND HEATING LOAD CALCULATIONS

HEATING and cooling load calculations are the primary design basis for most heating and air-conditioning systems and components. These calculations affect the size of piping, ductwork, diffusers, air handlers, boilers, chillers, coils, compressors, fans, and every other component of systems that condition indoor environments. Cooling and heating load calculations can significantly affect first cost of building construction, comfort and productivity of occupants, and operating cost and energy consumption.

Simply put, heating and cooling loads are the rates of energy input (heating) or removal (cooling) required to maintain an indoor environment at a desired temperature and humidity condition. Heating and air conditioning systems are designed, sized, and controlled to accomplish that energy transfer. The amount of heating or cooling required at any particular time varies widely, depending on external (e.g., outdoor temperature) and internal (e.g., number of people occupying a space) factors.

Peak design heating and cooling load calculations, which are this chapter's focus, seek to determine the maximum rate of heating and cooling energy transfer needed at any point in time. Similar principles, but with different assumptions, data, and application, can be used to estimate building energy consumption, as described in Chapter 19.

This chapter discusses common elements of cooling load calculation (e.g., internal heat gain, ventilation and infiltration, moisture migration, fenestration heat gain) and two methods of heating and cooling load estimation: heat balance (HB) and radiant time series (RTS).

1. COOLING LOAD CALCULATION PRINCIPLES

Cooling loads result from many conduction, convection, and radiation heat transfer processes through the building envelope and from internal sources and system components. Building components or contents that may affect cooling loads include the following:

- **External:** Walls, roofs, windows, skylights, doors, partitions, ceilings, and floors
- **Internal:** Lights, people, appliances, and equipment
- **Infiltration:** Air leakage and moisture migration
- **System:** Outdoor air, duct leakage and heat gain, reheat, fan and pump energy, and energy recovery

1.1 TERMINOLOGY

The variables affecting cooling load calculations are numerous, often difficult to define precisely, and always intricately interrelated. Many cooling load components vary widely in magnitude, and possibly direction, during a 24 h period. Because these cyclic changes in load components often are not in phase with each other, each component must be analyzed to establish the maximum cooling load for a building or zone. A **zoned system** (i.e., one serving several independent areas, each with its own temperature control) needs to provide no greater total cooling load capacity than the largest hourly sum of simultaneous zone loads throughout a design day; however, it must handle the peak cooling load for each zone at its individual peak hour. At some times of day during heating or intermediate seasons, some zones may require heating while others require cooling. The zones' ventilation, humidification, or dehumidification needs must also be considered.

Heat Flow Rates

In air-conditioning design, the following four related heat flow rates, each of which varies with time, must be differentiated.

Space Heat Gain. This instantaneous rate of heat gain is the rate at which heat enters into and/or is generated within a space. Heat gain is classified by its mode of entry into the space and whether it is sensible or latent. **Entry modes** include (1) solar radiation through transparent surfaces; (2) heat conduction through exterior walls and roofs; (3) heat conduction through ceilings, floors, and interior partitions; (4) heat generated in the space by occupants, lights, and appliances; (5) energy transfer through direct-with-space ventilation and infiltration of outdoor air; and (6) miscellaneous heat gains. **Sensible heat** is added directly to the conditioned space by conduction, convection, and/or radiation. **Latent heat** gain occurs when moisture is added to the space (e.g., from vapor emitted by occupants and equipment). To maintain a constant humidity ratio, water vapor must condense on the cooling apparatus and be removed at the same rate it is added to the space. The amount of energy required to offset latent heat gain essentially equals the product of the condensation rate and latent heat of condensation. In selecting cooling equipment, distinguish between sensible and latent heat gain: every cooling apparatus has different maximum removal capacities for sensible versus latent heat for particular operating conditions. In extremely dry climates, humidification may be required, rather than dehumidification, to maintain thermal comfort.

Radiant Heat Gain. Radiant energy must first be absorbed by surfaces that enclose the space (walls, floor, and ceiling) and objects in the space (furniture, etc.). When these surfaces and objects become warmer than the surrounding air, some of their heat transfers to the air by convection. The composite heat storage capacity of these surfaces and objects determines the rate at which their respective surface temperatures increase for a given radiant input, and thus governs the relationship between the radiant portion of heat gain and its corresponding part of the space cooling load (Figure 1). The thermal storage effect is critical in differentiating between instantaneous heat gain for a given space and its cooling load at that moment. Predicting

The preparation of this chapter is assigned to TC 4.1, Load Calculation Data and Procedures.

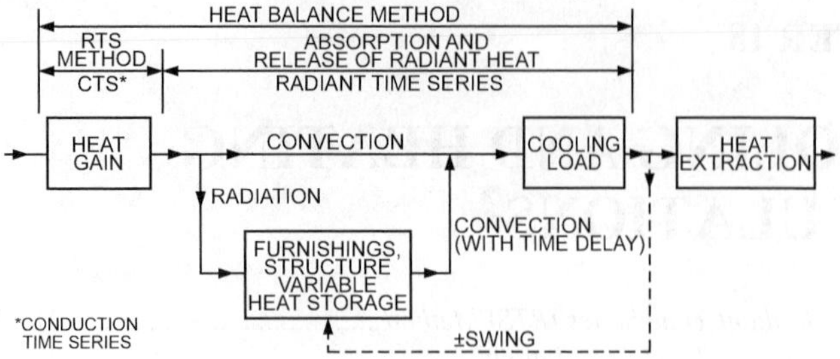

Fig. 1 Origin of Difference Between Magnitude of Instantaneous Heat Gain and Instantaneous Cooling Load

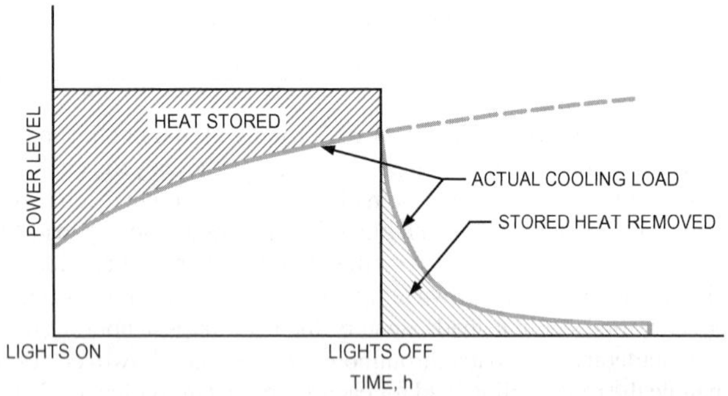

Fig. 2 Thermal Storage Effect in Cooling Load from Lights

the nature and magnitude of this phenomenon to estimate a realistic cooling load for a particular set of circumstances has long been of interest to design engineers; the Bibliography lists some early work on the subject.

Space Cooling Load. This is the rate at which sensible and latent heat must be removed from the space to maintain a constant space air temperature and humidity. The sum of all space instantaneous heat gains at any given time does not necessarily (or even frequently) equal the cooling load for the space at that same time.

Space Heat Extraction Rate. The rates at which sensible and latent heat are removed from the conditioned space equal the space cooling load only if the room air temperature and humidity are constant. Along with the intermittent operation of cooling equipment, control systems usually allow a minor cyclic variation or swing in room temperature; humidity is often allowed to float, but it can be controlled. Therefore, proper simulation of the control system gives a more realistic value of energy removal over a fixed period than using values of the space cooling load. However, this is primarily important for estimating energy use over time; it is not needed to calculate design peak cooling load for equipment selection.

Cooling Coil Load. The rate at which energy is removed at a cooling coil serving one or more conditioned spaces equals the sum of instantaneous space cooling loads (or space heat extraction rate, if it is assumed that space temperature and humidity vary) for all spaces served by the coil, plus any system loads. System loads include fan heat gain, duct heat gain, and outdoor air heat and moisture brought into the cooling equipment to satisfy the ventilation air requirement.

Time Delay Effect

Energy absorbed by walls, floor, furniture, etc., contributes to space cooling load only after a time lag. Some of this energy is still present and reradiating even after the heat sources have been switched off or removed, as shown in Figure 2.

There is always significant delay between the time a heat source is activated, and the point when reradiated energy equals that being instantaneously stored. This time lag must be considered when calculating cooling load, because the load required for the space can be much lower than the instantaneous heat gain being generated, and the space's peak load may be significantly affected.

Accounting for the time delay effect is the major challenge in cooling load calculations. Several methods, including the two presented in this chapter, have been developed to take the time delay effect into consideration.

1.2 COOLING LOAD CALCULATION METHODS

This chapter presents two load calculation methods that vary significantly from previous methods. The technology involved, however (the principle of calculating a heat balance for a given space) is not new. The first of the two methods is the **heat balance (HB) method**; the second is **radiant time series (RTS)**, which is a simplification of the HB procedure. Both methods are explained in their respective sections.

Cooling load calculation of an actual, multiple-room building requires a complex computer program implementing the principles of either method.

Cooling Load Calculations in Practice

Load calculations should accurately describe the building. All load calculation inputs should be as accurate as reasonable, without using safety factors. Introducing compounding safety factors at multiple levels in the load calculation results in an unrealistic and oversized load.

Variation in heat transmission coefficients of typical building materials and composite assemblies, differing motivations and skills of those who construct the building, unknown infiltration rates, and the manner in which the building is actually operated are some of the variables that make precise calculation impossible. Even if the designer uses reasonable procedures to account for these factors, the calculation can never be more than a good estimate of the actual load. Frequently, a cooling load must be calculated before every parameter in the conditioned space can be properly or completely defined. An example is a cooling load estimate for a new building with many floors of unleased spaces for which detailed partition requirements, furnishings, lighting, and layout cannot be predefined. Potential tenant modifications once the building is occupied also must be considered. Load estimating requires proper engineering judgment that includes a thorough understanding of heat balance fundamentals.

Perimeter spaces exposed to high solar heat gain often need cooling during sunlit portions of traditional heating months, as do completely interior spaces with significant internal heat gain. These spaces can also have significant heating loads during nonsunlit hours or after periods of nonoccupancy, when adjacent spaces have cooled below interior design temperatures. The heating loads involved can be estimated conventionally to offset or to compensate for them and prevent overheating, but they have no direct relationship to the spaces' design heating loads.

Correct design and sizing of air-conditioning systems require more than calculation of the cooling load in the space to be conditioned. The type of air-conditioning system, ventilation rate, reheat, fan energy, fan location, duct heat loss and gain, duct leakage, heat extraction lighting systems, type of return air system, and any sensible or latent heat recovery all affect system load and component sizing. Adequate system design and component sizing require that system performance be analyzed as a series of psychrometric processes.

System design could be driven by either sensible or latent load, and both need to be checked. In a sensible-load-driven space (the most common case), the cooling supply air has surplus capacity to dehumidify, but this is usually permissible. For a space driven by latent load (e.g., an auditorium), supply airflow based on sensible load is likely not to have enough dehumidifying capability, so subcooling and reheating or some other dehumidification process is needed.

This chapter is primarily concerned with a given space or zone in a building. When estimating loads for a group of spaces (e.g., for an air-handling system that serves multiple zones), the assembled zones must be analyzed to consider (1) the simultaneous effects taking place; (2) any diversification of heat gains for occupants, lighting, or other internal load sources; (3) ventilation; and/or (4) any other unique circumstances. With large buildings that involve more than a single HVAC system, simultaneous loads and any additional diversity also must be considered when designing the central equipment that serves the systems. Methods presented in this chapter are expressed as hourly load summaries, reflecting 24 h input schedules and profiles of the individual load variables. Specific systems and applications may require different profiles.

1.3 DATA ASSEMBLY

Calculating space cooling loads requires detailed building design information and weather data at design conditions. Generally, the following information should be compiled.

Building Characteristics. Building materials, component size, external surface colors, and shape are usually determined from building plans and specifications.

Configuration. Determine building location, orientation, and external shading from building plans and specifications. Shading from adjacent buildings can be determined from a site plan or by visiting the proposed site, but its probable permanence should be carefully evaluated before it is included in the calculation. The possibility of abnormally high ground-reflected solar radiation (e.g., from adjacent water, sand, or parking lots) or solar load from adjacent reflective buildings should not be overlooked.

Outdoor Design Conditions. Obtain appropriate weather data, and select outdoor design conditions. Chapter 14 provides information for many weather stations; note, however, that these design dry-bulb and mean coincident wet-bulb temperatures may vary considerably from data traditionally used in various areas. Use judgment to ensure that results are consistent with expectations. Also, consider prevailing wind velocity and the relationship of a project site to the selected weather station.

Recent research projects have greatly expanded the amount of available weather data (e.g., ASHRAE 2012). In addition to the conventional dry bulb with mean coincident wet bulb, data are now available for wet bulb and dew point with mean coincident dry bulb. Peak space load generally coincides with peak solar or peak dry bulb, but peak system load often occurs at peak wet-bulb temperature. The relationship between space and system loads is discussed further in following sections of the chapter.

To estimate conductive heat gain through exterior surfaces and infiltration and outdoor air loads at any time, applicable outdoor dry- and wet-bulb temperatures must be used. Chapter 14 gives monthly cooling load design values of outdoor conditions for many locations. These are generally midafternoon conditions; for other times of day, the daily range profile method described in Chapter 14 can be used to estimate dry- and wet-bulb temperatures. Peak cooling load is often determined by solar heat gain through fenestration; this peak may occur in winter months and/or at a time of day when outdoor air temperature is not at its maximum.

Indoor Design Conditions. Select indoor dry-bulb temperature, indoor relative humidity, and ventilation rate. Include permissible variations and control limits. Consult ASHRAE *Standard* 90.1 for energy-savings conditions, and *Standard* 55 for ranges of indoor conditions needed for thermal comfort.

Internal Heat Gains and Operating Schedules. Obtain planned density and a proposed schedule of lighting, occupancy, internal equipment, appliances, and processes that contribute to the internal thermal load.

Areas. Use consistent methods for calculation of building areas. For fenestration, the definition of a component's area must be consistent with associated ratings.

Gross surface area. It is efficient and conservative to derive gross surface areas from outer building dimensions, ignoring wall and floor thicknesses and avoiding separate accounting of floor edge and wall corner conditions. Measure floor areas to the outside of adjacent exterior walls or to the centerline of adjacent partitions. When apportioning to rooms, façade area should be divided at partition centerlines. Wall height should be taken as floor-to-floor height.

The outer-dimension procedure is expedient for load calculations, but it is not consistent with rigorous definitions used in building-related standards. The resulting differences do not introduce significant errors in this chapter's procedures.

Fenestration area. As discussed in Chapter 15, fenestration ratings [U-factor and solar heat gain coefficient (SHGC)] are based on the entire product area, including frames. Thus, for load calculations, fenestration area is the area of the rough opening in the wall or roof.

Net surface area. Net surface area is the gross surface area less any enclosed fenestration area.

2. INTERNAL HEAT GAINS

Internal heat gains from people, lights, motors, appliances, and equipment can contribute the majority of the cooling load in a modern building. As building envelopes have improved in response to more restrictive energy codes, internal loads have increased because of factors such as increased use of computers and the advent of dense-occupancy spaces (e.g., call centers). Internal heat gain calculation techniques are identical for both heat balance (HB) and radiant time series (RTS) cooling-load calculation methods, so internal heat gain data are presented here independent of calculation methods.

2.1 PEOPLE

Table 1 gives representative rates at which sensible heat and moisture are emitted by humans in different states of activity. In high-density spaces, such as auditoriums, these sensible and latent heat gains comprise a large fraction of the total load. Even for short-term occupancy, the extra sensible heat and moisture introduced by people may be significant. See Chapter 9 for detailed information; however, Table 1 summarizes design data for common conditions.

The conversion of sensible heat gain from people to space cooling load is affected by the thermal storage characteristics of that space because some percentage of the sensible load is radiant energy. Latent heat gains are usually considered instantaneous, but research is yielding practical models and data for the latent heat storage of and release from common building materials.

2.2 LIGHTING

Because lighting is often a major space cooling load component, an accurate estimate of the space heat gain it imposes is needed. Calculation of this load component is not straightforward; the rate of cooling load from lighting at any given moment can be quite different from the heat equivalent of power supplied instantaneously to those lights, because of heat storage.

Instantaneous Heat Gain from Lighting

The primary source of heat from lighting comes from light-emitting elements, or lamps, although significant additional heat may be generated from ballasts and other appurtenances in the

Table 1 Representative Rates at Which Heat and Moisture Are Given Off by Human Beings in Different States of Activity

Degree of Activity	Location	Total Heat, Btu/h Adult Male	Total Heat, Btu/h Adjusted, M/F[a]	Sensible Heat, Btu/h	Latent Heat, Btu/h	% Sensible Heat that is Radiant[b] Low V	% Sensible Heat that is Radiant[b] High V
Seated at theater	Theater	390	350	245	105	60	27
Seated, very light work	Offices, hotels, apartments	450	400	245	155		
Moderately active office work	Offices, hotels, apartments	475	450	250	200		
Standing, light work; walking	Department store; retail store	550	450	250	200	58	38
Walking, standing	Drug store, bank	550	500	250	250		
Sedentary work	Restaurant[c]	490	550	275	275		
Light bench work	Factory	800	750	275	475		
Moderate dancing	Dance hall	900	850	305	545	49	35
Walking 3 mph; light machine work	Factory	1000	1000	375	625		
Bowling[d]	Bowling alley	1500	1450	580	870		
Heavy work	Factory	1500	1450	580	870	54	19
Heavy machine work; lifting	Factory	1600	1600	635	965		
Athletics	Gymnasium	2000	1800	710	1090		

Notes:
1. Tabulated values are based on 75°F room dry-bulb temperature. For 80°F room dry bulb, total heat remains the same, but sensible heat values should be decreased by approximately 20%, and latent heat values increased accordingly.
2. Also see Table 4, Chapter 9, for additional rates of metabolic heat generation.
3. All values are rounded to nearest 5 Btu/h.

[a] Adjusted heat gain is based on normal percentage of men, women, and children for the application listed, and assumes that gain from an adult female is 85% of that for an adult male, and gain from a child is 75% of that for an adult male.
[b] Values approximated from data in Table 6, Chapter 9, where V is air velocity with limits shown in that table.
[c] Adjusted heat gain includes 60 Btu/h for food per individual (30 Btu/h sensible and 30 Btu/h latent).
[d] Figure one person per alley actually bowling, and all others as sitting (400 Btu/h) or standing or walking slowly (550 Btu/h).

luminaires. Generally, the instantaneous rate of sensible heat gain from electric lighting may be calculated from

$$q_{el} = 3.41 W F_{ul} F_{sa} \tag{1}$$

where

q_{el} = heat gain, Btu/h
W = total light wattage, W
F_{ul} = lighting use factor
F_{sa} = lighting special allowance factor
3.41 = conversion factor

The **total light wattage** is obtained from the ratings of all lamps installed, both for general illumination and for display use. Ballasts are not included, but are addressed by a separate factor. Wattages of magnetic ballasts are significant; the energy consumption of high-efficiency electronic ballasts might be insignificant compared to that of the lamps.

The **lighting use factor** is the ratio of wattage in use, for the conditions under which the load estimate is being made, to total installed wattage. For commercial applications such as stores, the use factor is generally 1.0.

The **special allowance factor** is the ratio of the lighting fixtures' power consumption, including lamps and ballast, to the nominal power consumption of the lamps. For incandescent lights, this factor is 1. For fluorescent lights, it accounts for power consumed by the ballast as well as the ballast's effect on lamp power consumption. The special allowance factor can be less than 1 for electronic ballasts that lower electricity consumption below the lamp's rated power consumption. Use manufacturers' values for system (lamps + ballast) power, when available.

For high-intensity-discharge lamps (e.g. metal halide, mercury vapor, high- and low-pressure sodium vapor lamps), the actual lighting system power consumption should be available from the manufacturer of the fixture or ballast. Ballasts available for metal halide and high-pressure sodium vapor lamps may have special allowance factors from about 1.3 (for low-wattage lamps) down to 1.1 (for high-wattage lamps).

An alternative procedure is to estimate the lighting heat gain on a per-square-foot basis. Such an approach may be required when final lighting plans are not available. Table 2 shows the maximum lighting power density (LPD) (lighting heat gain per square foot) allowed by ASHRAE *Standard* 90.1-2013 for a range of space types.

In addition to determining the lighting heat gain, the fraction of lighting heat gain that enters the conditioned space may need to be distinguished from the fraction that enters an unconditioned space; of the former category, the distribution between radiative and convective heat gain must be established.

Fisher and Chantrasrisalai (2006) and Zhou et al. (2016) experimentally studied 12 luminaire types and recommended several categories of luminaires, as shown in Table 3. The table provides a range of design data for the conditioned space fraction, short-wave radiative fraction, and long-wave radiative fraction under typical operating conditions: airflow rate of 1 cfm/ft², supply air temperature between 59 and 62°F, and room air temperature between 72 and 75°F. The recommended fractions in Table 3 are based on lighting heat input rates range of 0.9 to 2.6 W/ft². For higher design power input, the lower bounds of the space and short-wave fractions should be used; for design power input below this range, the upper bounds of the space and short-wave fractions should be used. The **space fraction** in the table is the fraction of lighting heat gain that goes to the room; the fraction going to the plenum can be computed as 1 – the space fraction. The **radiative fraction** is the radiative part of the lighting heat gain that goes to the room. The convective fraction of the lighting heat gain that goes to the room is 1 – the radiative fraction. Using values in the middle of the range yields sufficiently accurate results. However, values that better suit a specific situation may be determined according to the notes for Table 3.

Table 3's data apply to both ducted and nonducted returns. However, application of the data, particularly the ceiling plenum fraction, may vary for different return configurations. For instance, for a room with a ducted return, although a portion of the lighting energy initially dissipated to the ceiling plenum is quantitatively equal to the plenum fraction, a large portion of this energy would likely end up as the conditioned space cooling load and a small portion would end up as the cooling load to the return air.

If the space airflow rate is different from the typical condition (i.e., about 1 cfm/ft²), Figure 3 can be used to estimate the lighting heat gain parameters. Design data shown in Figure 3 are only applicable for the recessed fluorescent luminaire without lens.

Although design data presented in Table 3 and Figure 3 can be used for a vented luminaire with side-slot returns, they are likely not applicable for a vented luminaire with lamp compartment returns, because in the latter case, all heat convected in the vented luminaire

Table 2 Lighting Power Densities Using Space-by-Space Method

Common Space Types[a]	LPD, W/ft²
Atrium	
≤40 ft high	0.03/ft total height
>40 ft high	0.40 + 0.02/ft total height
Audience Seating Area	
In auditorium	0.63
In convention center	0.82
In gymnasium	0.65
In motion picture theater	1.14
In penitentiary	0.28
In performing arts theater	2.43
In religious building	1.53
In sports arena	0.43
All other audience seating areas	0.43
Banking Activity Area	1.01
Breakroom (*See* Lounge/Breakroom)	
Classroom/Lecture Hall/Training Room	
In penitentiary	1.34
All other classrooms/lecture halls/ training rooms	1.24
Conference/Meeting/Multipurpose Room	1.23
Confinement Cells	0.81
Copy/Print Room	0.72
Corridor[b]	
In facility for visually impaired (and not used primarily by staff)[c]	0.92
In hospital	0.99
In manufacturing facility	0.41
All other corridors	0.66
Courtroom	1.72
Computer Room	1.71
Dining Area	
In penitentiary	0.96
In facility for visually impaired (and not used primarily by staff)[c]	2.65
In bar/lounge or leisure dining	1.07
In cafeteria or fast food dining	0.65
In family dining	0.89
All other dining areas	0.65
Electrical/Mechanical Room[f]	0.42
Emergency Vehicle Garage	0.56
Food Preparation Area	1.21
Guest Room	0.91
Laboratory	
In or as classroom	1.43
All other laboratories	1.81
Laundry/Washing Area	0.60

Common Space Types[a]	LPD, W/ft²
Loading Dock, Interior	0.47
Lobby	
In facility for the visually impaired (and not used primarily by staff)[c]	1.80
For elevator	0.64
In hotel	1.06
In motion picture theater	0.59
In performing arts theater	2.00
All other lobbies	0.90
Locker Room	0.75
Lounge/Breakroom	
In health care facility	0.92
All other lounges/breakrooms	0.73
Enclosed and ≤250 ft²	1.11
Enclosed and >250 ft²	1.11
Open plan	0.98
Office	
Enclosed	1.11
Open plan	0.98
Parking Area, Interior	0.19
Pharmacy Area	1.68
Restroom	
In facility for the visually impaired (and not used primarily by staff)[c]	1.21
All other restrooms	0.98
Sales Area[d]	1.44
Seating Area, General	0.54
Stairway	
Space containing stairway determines LPD and control requirements for stairway.	
Stairwell	0.69
Storage Room	
<50 ft²	1.24
All other storage rooms	0.63
Vehicular Maintenance Area	0.67

Building-Specific Space Types*	LPD, W/ft²
Facility for Visually Impaired[c]	
Chapel (used primarily by residents)	2.21
Recreation room/common living room (and not used primarily by staff)	2.41
Automotive (*See* Vehicular Maintenance Area)	
Convention Center, Exhibit Space	1.45
Dormitory/Living Quarters	0.38
Fire Station, Sleeping Quarters	0.22
Gymnasium/Fitness Center	
Exercise area	0.72
Playing area	1.20
Health Care Facility	
Exam/treatment room	1.66
Imaging room	1.51
Medical supply room	0.74
Nursery	0.88
Nurses' station	0.71
Operating room	2.48
Patient room	0.62
Physical therapy room	0.91
Recovery room	1.15
Library	
Reading area	1.06
Stacks	1.71
Manufacturing Facility	
Detailed manufacturing area	1.29
Equipment room	0.74
Extra-high-bay area (>50 ft floor-to-ceiling height)	1.05
High-bay area (25 to 50 ft floor-to-ceiling height)	1.23
Low bay area (<25 ft floor-to-ceiling height)	1.19
Museum	
General exhibition area	1.05
Restoration room	1.02
Performing Arts Theater, Dressing Room	0.61
Post Office, Sorting Area	0.94
Religious Buildings	
Fellowship hall	0.64
Worship/pulpit/choir area	1.53
Retail Facilities	
Dressing/fitting room	0.71
Mall concourse	1.10
Sports Arena, Playing Area	
For Class I facility	3.68
For Class II facility	2.40
For Class III facility	1.80
For Class IV facility	1.20
Transportation Facility	
In baggage/carousel area	0.53
In airport concourse	0.36
At terminal ticket counter	0.80
Warehouse—Storage Area	
For medium to bulky, palletized items	0.58
For smaller, hand-carried items[e]	0.95

Source: ASHRAE *Standard* 90.1-2013.

[a]In cases where both a common space type and a building-specific type are listed, the building-specific space type applies.

[b]In corridors, extra lighting power density allowance is granted when corridor width is <8 ft and is not based on room/corridor ratio (RCR).

[c]A facility for the visually impaired one that can be documented as being designed to comply with light levels in ANSI/IES RP-28 and is (or will be) licensed by local/state authorities for either senior long-term care, adult daycare, senior support, and/or people with special visual needs.

[d]For accent lighting, see section 9.6.2(b) of ASHRAE *Standard* 90.1-2013.

[e]Sometimes called a picking area.

[f]An additional 0.53 W/ft² is allowed *only* if this additional lighting is controlled separately from the base allowance of 0.42 W/ft².

is likely to go directly to the ceiling plenum, resulting in zero convective fraction and a much lower space fraction. Therefore, the design data should only be used for a configuration where conditioned air is returned through the ceiling grille or luminaire side slots.

For other luminaire types, it may be necessary to estimate the heat gain for each component as a fraction of the total lighting heat gain by using judgment to estimate heat-to-space and heat-to-return percentages.

Table 3 Lighting Heat Gain Parameters for Typical Operating Conditions

Luminaire Category	Space Fraction	Radiative Fraction	Notes
Recessed fluorescent luminaire without lens	0.64 to 0.74	0.48 to 0.68	• Use middle values in most situations • May use higher space fraction, and lower radiative fraction for luminaire with side-slot returns • May use lower values of both fractions for direct/indirect luminaire • May use higher values of both fractions for ducted returns
Recessed fluorescent luminaire with lens	0.40 to 0.50	0.61 to 0.73	• May adjust values in the same way as for recessed fluorescent luminaire without lens
Downlight compact fluorescent luminaire	0.12 to 0.24	0.95 to 1.0	• Use middle or high values if detailed features are unknown • Use low value for space fraction and high value for radiative fraction if there are large holes in luminaire's reflector
Downlight incandescent luminaire	0.70 to 0.80	0.95 to 1.0	• Use middle values if lamp type is unknown • Use low value for space fraction if standard lamp (i.e. A-lamp) is used • Use high value for space fraction if reflector lamp (i.e. BR-lamp) is used
Non-in-ceiling fluorescent luminaire	1.0	0.5 to 0.57	• Use lower value for radiative fraction for surface-mounted luminaire • Use higher value for radiative fraction for pendant luminaire
Recessed LED troffer partial aperture diffuser	0.49 to 0.64	0.37 to 0.47	• Use middle value in most cases. • May use higher space fraction for ducted return configuration and lower space fraction for high supply air temperature. • May use higher radiant value for ducted return configuration and lower value for large supply airflow rate.
Recessed LED troffer uniform diffuser	0.44 to 0.66	0.32 to 0.41	• Use middle value in most cases. • May use higher space fraction for smaller supply airflow rate and lower value for larger supply airflow rate. • May use higher radiant value for ducted return configuration and lower value for larger supply airflow rate.
Recessed high-efficacy LED troffer	0.59	0.51	
Recessed LED downlight	0.40 to 0.56	0.15 to 0.18	• Use middle value in most cases. • May use higher space fraction value for high supply air temperature and lower value for smaller air flowrate. • May use higher radiant value for dimming control and lower value for large supply air flowrate.
Recessed LED retrofit kit 2×4	0.41 to 0.53	0.31 to 0.42	• Use middle value in most cases. • May use higher space fraction value for large supply air flowrate and lower value for ducted return configuration. • May use higher radiant value for ducted return configuration and lower value for larger supply airflow rate.
Recessed LED color tuning fixture	0.53 to 0.56	0.40 to 0.42	Use middle value in most cases.
High-bay LED fixture	1.0	0.42 to 0.51	Use middle value in most cases.
Linear pendant LED fixture	1.0	0.55 to 0.60	Use middle value in most cases.

Sources: Fisher and Chantrasrisalai (2006); Zhou et al. 2016.

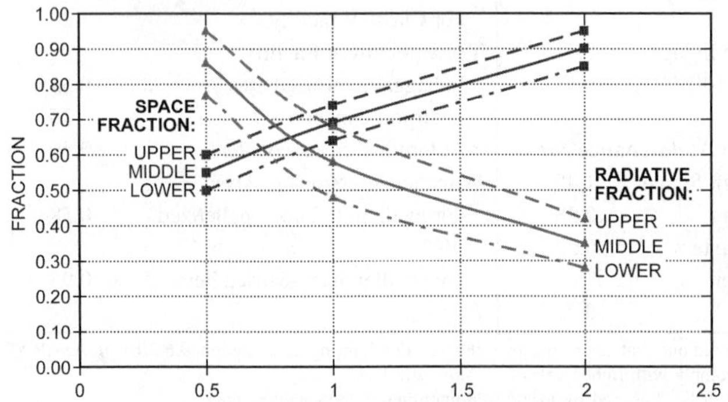

Fig. 3 Lighting Heat Gain Parameters for Recessed Fluorescent Luminaire Without Lens
(Fisher and Chantrasrisalai 2006)

Because of the directional nature of downlight luminaires, a large portion of the short-wave radiation typically falls on the floor. When converting heat gains to cooling loads in the RTS method, the solar **radiant time factors (RTFs)** may be more appropriate than nonsolar RTFs. (Solar RTFs are calculated assuming most solar radiation is intercepted by the floor; nonsolar RTFs assume uniform distribution by area over all interior surfaces.) This effect may be significant for rooms where lighting heat gain is high and for which solar RTFs are significantly different from nonsolar RTFs.

2.3 ELECTRIC MOTORS

Instantaneous sensible heat gain from equipment operated by electric motors in a conditioned space is calculated as

$$q_{em} = 2545(P/E_M)F_{UM}F_{LM} \quad (2)$$

where

q_{em} = heat equivalent of equipment operation, Btu/h
P = motor power rating, hp
E_M = motor efficiency, decimal fraction <1.0
F_{UM} = motor use factor, 1.0 or decimal fraction <1.0
F_{LM} = motor load factor, 1.0 or decimal fraction <1.0
2545 = conversion factor, Btu/h·hp

The motor use factor may be applied when motor use is known to be intermittent, with significant nonuse during all hours of operation

Table 4A Minimum Nominal Full-Load Efficiency for 60 Hz NEMA General-Purpose Electric Motors (Subtype I) Rated 600 V or Less (Random Wound)*

	Open Drip-Proof Motors			Totally Enclosed Fan-Cooled Motors		
Number of Poles ⇒	2	4	6	2	4	6
Synchronous Speed (RPM) ⇒	3600	1800	1200	3600	1800	1200
Motor Horsepower						
1	77.0	85.5	82.5	77.0	85.5	82.5
1.5	84.0	86.5	86.5	84.0	86.5	87.5
2	85.5	86.5	87.5	85.5	86.5	88.5
3	85.5	89.5	88.5	86.5	89.5	89.5
5	86.5	89.5	89.5	88.5	89.5	89.5
7.5	88.5	91.0	90.2	89.5	91.7	91.0
10	89.5	91.7	91.7	90.2	91.7	91.0
15	90.2	93.0	91.7	91.0	92.4	91.7
20	91.0	93.0	92.4	91.0	93.0	91.7
25	91.7	93.6	93.0	91.7	93.6	93.0
30	91.7	94.1	93.6	91.7	93.6	93.0
40	92.4	94.1	94.1	92.4	94.1	94.1
50	93.0	94.5	94.1	93.0	94.5	94.1
60	93.6	95.0	94.5	93.6	95.0	94.5
75	93.6	95.0	94.5	93.6	95.4	94.5
100	93.6	95.4	95.0	94.1	95.4	95.0
125	94.1	95.4	95.0	95.0	95.4	95.0
150	94.1	95.8	95.4	95.0	95.8	95.8
200	95.0	95.8	95.4	95.4	96.2	95.8

Source: ASHRAE *Standard* 90.1-2013.
*Nominal efficiencies established in accordance with NEMA *Standard* MG1. Design A and Design B are National Electric Manufacturers Association (NEMA) design class designations for fixed-frequency small and medium AC squirrel-cage induction motors.

(e.g., overhead door operator). For conventional applications, its value is 1.0.

The motor load factor is the fraction of the rated load delivered under the conditions of the cooling load estimate. Equation (2) assumes that both the motor and driven equipment are in the conditioned space. If the motor is outside the space or airstream,

$$q_{em} = 2545PF_{UM}F_{LM} \tag{3}$$

When the motor is inside the conditioned space or airstream but the driven machine is outside,

$$q_{em} = 2545P\left(\frac{1.0 - E_M}{E_M}\right)F_{UM}F_{LM} \tag{4}$$

Equation (4) also applies to a fan or pump in the conditioned space that exhausts air or pumps fluid outside that space.

Table 4A and 4B gives minimum efficiencies and related data representative of typical electric motors from ASHRAE *Standard* 90.1-2013. If electric motor load is an appreciable portion of cooling load, the motor efficiency should be obtained from the manufacturer. Also, depending on design, maximum efficiency might occur anywhere between 75 to 110% of full load; if under- or overloaded, efficiency could vary from the manufacturer's listing.

Overloading or Underloading

Heat output of a motor is generally proportional to motor load, within rated overload limits. Because of typically high no-load motor current, fixed losses, and other reasons, F_{LM} is generally assumed to be unity, and no adjustment should be made for underloading or overloading unless the situation is fixed and can be accurately established, and reduced-load efficiency data can be obtained from the motor manufacturer.

Table 4B Minimum Average Full-Load Efficiency for Polyphase Small Electric Motors*

	Full-Load Efficiency for Motors Manufactured on or after March 9, 2015, %		
	Open Motors		
Number of Poles ⇒	2	4	6
Synchronous Speed (RPM) ⇒	3600	1800	1200
Motor Horsepower			
0.25	65.6	69.5	67.5
0.33	69.5	73.4	71.4
0.50	73.4	78.2	75.3
0.75	76.8	81.1	81.7
1	77.0	83.5	82.5
1.5	84.0	86.5	83.8
2	85.5	86.5	N/A
3	85.5	86.9	N/A

*Average full-load efficiencies established in accordance with 10 CFR 431.

Radiation and Convection

Unless the manufacturer's technical literature indicates otherwise, motor heat gain normally should be equally divided between radiant and convective components for the subsequent cooling load calculations.

2.4 APPLIANCES

A cooling load estimate should take into account heat gain from all appliances (electrical, gas, or steam). Because of the variety of appliances, applications, schedules, use, and installations, estimates can be very subjective. Often, the only information available about heat gain from equipment is that on its nameplate, which can overestimate actual heat gain for many types of appliances, as discussed in the section on Office Equipment.

Cooking Appliances

These appliances include common heat-producing cooking equipment found in conditioned commercial kitchens. Marn (1962) concluded that appliance surfaces contributed most of the heat to commercial kitchens and that when appliances were installed under an effective hood, the cooling load was independent of the fuel or energy used for similar equipment performing the same operations.

Gordon et al. (1994) and Smith et al. (1995) found that gas appliances may exhibit slightly higher heat gains than their electric counterparts under wall-canopy hoods operated at typical ventilation rates. This is because heat contained in combustion products exhausted from a gas appliance may increase the temperatures of the appliance and surrounding surfaces, as well as the hood above the appliance, more so than the heat produced by its electric counterpart. These higher-temperature surfaces radiate heat to the kitchen, adding moderately to the radiant gain directly associated with the appliance cooking surface.

Marn (1962) confirmed that, where appliances are installed under an effective hood, only radiant gain adds to the cooling load; convective and latent heat from cooking and combustion products are exhausted and do not enter the kitchen. Gordon et al. (1994) and Smith et al. (1995) substantiated these findings. Chapter 33 of the 2015 ASHRAE *Handbook—HVAC Applications* has more information on kitchen ventilation.

Sensible Heat Gain for Hooded Cooking Appliances. To establish a heat gain value, nameplate energy input ratings may be used with appropriate usage and radiation factors. Where specific rating data are not available (nameplate missing, equipment not yet purchased, etc.), representative heat gains listed in Tables 5A to 5E (Swierczyna et al. 2008, 2009) for a wide variety of commonly encountered equipment items. In estimating appliance load, probabilities of simultaneous use and operation for different appliances located in the same space must be considered.

Radiant heat gain from hooded cooking equipment can range from 15 to 45% of the actual appliance energy consumption (Gordon et al. 1994; Smith et al. 1995; Swierczyna et al. 2008; Talbert et al. 1973). This ratio of heat gain to appliance energy consumption may be expressed as a radiation factor, and it is a function of both appliance type and fuel source. The radiation factor F_R is applied to the average rate of appliance energy consumption, determined by applying usage factor F_U to the nameplate or rated energy input. Marn (1962) found that radiant heat temperature rise can be substantially reduced by shielding the fronts of cooking appliances. Although this approach may not always be practical in a commercial kitchen, radiant gains can also be reduced by adding side panels or partial enclosures that are integrated with the exhaust hood.

Heat Gain from Meals. For each meal served, approximately 50 Btu/h of heat, of which 75% is sensible and 25% is latent, is transferred to the dining space.

Heat Gain for Generic Appliances. The average rate of appliance energy consumption can be estimated from the nameplate or rated energy input q_{input} by applying a duty cycle or usage factor F_U. Thus, sensible heat gain q_s for generic electric, steam, and gas appliances installed under a hood can be estimated using one of the following equations:

$$q_s = q_{input} F_U F_R \tag{5}$$

or

$$q_s = q_{input} F_L \tag{6}$$

where F_L is the ratio of sensible heat gain to the manufacturer's rated energy input. However, ASHRAE research (Swierczyna et al. 2008, 2009) showed the design value for heat gain from a hooded appliance at idle (ready-to-cook) conditions based on its energy consumption rate is, at best, a rough estimate. When appliance heat

Table 5A Recommended Rates of Radiant and Convective Heat Gain from Unhooded Electric Appliances During Idle (Ready-to-Cook) Conditions

	Energy Rate, Btu/h		Rate of Heat Gain, Btu/h				Usage Factor	Radiation Factor
Appliance	Rated	Standby	Sensible Radiant	Sensible Convective	Latent	Total	F_U	F_R
Cabinet: hot serving (large), insulated[a]	6,800	1,200	400	800	0	1,200	0.18	0.33
hot serving (large), uninsulated	6,800	3,500	700	2,800	0	3,500	0.51	0.20
proofing (large)[a]	17,400	1,400	1,200	0	200	1,400	0.08	0.86
proofing (small 15-shelf)	14,300	3,900	0	900	3,000	3,900	0.27	0.00
Cheesemelter[b]	8,200	3,300	1,500	1,800	0	3,300	0.41	0.45
Coffee brewing urn	13,000	1,200	200	300	700	1,200	0.09	0.17
Drawer warmers, 2-drawer (moist holding)[a]	4,100	500	0	0	200	200	0.12	0.00
Egg cooker[b]	8,100	850	200	650	0	850	0.10	0.26
Espresso machine*	8,200	1,200	400	800	0	1,200	0.15	0.33
Food warmer: steam table (2-well-type)	5,100	3,500	300	600	2,600	3,500	0.69	0.09
Freezer (small)	2,700	1,100	500	600	0	1,100	0.41	0.45
Fryer, countertop, open deep fat[b]	15,700	1,500	700	800	0	1,500	0.09	0.47
Griddle, countertop[b]	27,300	6,100	2,900	3,200	0	6,100	0.22	0.48
Hot dog roller[b]	5,500	4,200	900	3,300	0	4,200	0.77	0.22
Hot plate: single element, high speed	3,800	3,400	1,100	2,300	0	3,400	0.89	0.32
Hot-food case (dry holding)[a]	31,100	2,500	900	1,600	0	2,500	0.08	0.36
Hot-food case (moist holding)[a]	31,100	3,300	900	1,800	600	3,300	0.11	0.27
Induction hob, countertop[b]	17,100	0	0	0	0	0	0.00	0.00
Microwave oven: commercial	5,800	0	0	0	0	0	0.00	0.00
Oven: countertop conveyorized bake/finishing[b]	17,100	13,500	2,500	11,000	0	13,500	0.79	0.18
Panini[b]	6,100	2,300	700	1,600	0	2,300	0.37	0.29
Popcorn popper[b]	2,900	400	100	300	0	400	0.14	0.24
Rapid-cook oven (quartz-halogen)[a]	41,000	0	0	0	0	0	0.00	0.00
Rapid-cook oven (microwave/convection)[b]	19,400	3,900	300	3,600	0	3,900	0.20	0.08
Reach-in refrigerator[a]	4,800	1,200	300	900	0	1,200	0.25	0.25
Refrigerated prep table[a]	2,000	900	600	300	0	900	0.45	0.67
Rice cooker[b]	5,300	300	50	250	0	300	0.05	0.17
Soup warmer[b]	2,700	1,300	0	200	1,100	1,300	0.49	0.00
Steamer (bun)[b]	5,100	700	100	600	0	700	0.13	0.16
Steamer, countertop[b]	28,300	1,200	0	800	400	1,200	0.04	0.00
Toaster: 4-slice pop up (large): cooking	6,100	3,000	200	1,400	1,000	2,600	0.49	0.07
contact (vertical)[b]	8,900	2,600	600	2,000	0	2,600	0.29	0.24
conveyor (large)	32,800	10,300	3,000	7,300	0	10,300	0.31	0.29
small conveyor[b]	6,000	5,800	1,200	4,600	0	5,800	0.98	0.21
Tortilla grill[b]	7,500	3,600	900	2,700	0	3,600	0.47	0.25
Waffle iron[b]	9,200	900	200	700	0	900	0.10	0.22

Sources: Swierczyna et al. (2008, 2009); with the following exceptions as noted.
[a]Swierczyhna et al. (2009) only.
[b]Additions and updates from ASHRAE research project RP-1631 (Kong and Zhang 2016; Kong et al 2016).

gain measurements during idle conditions were regressed against energy consumption rates for gas and electric appliances, the appliances' emissivity, insulation, and surface cooling (e.g., through ventilation rates) scattered the data points widely, with large deviations from the average values. Because large errors could occur in the heat load calculation for specific appliance lines by using a general radiation factor, heat gain values in Table 5 should be applied in the HVAC design.

Table 5 lists usage factors, radiation factors, and load factors based on appliance energy consumption rate for typical electrical, steam, and gas appliances under standby (idle or ready-to-cook) and cooking conditions, hooded and unhooded.

Warewashing Applications. Typically, hot-water sanitizing and conveyor-type dish machines have either a dishwasher/condensing hood or direct-connected ductwork. If the ventilation is not operating properly, there are significant sensible and latent gains to the space. Chemical sanitizing and vapor reduction models are typically unhooded; consequently, the dish machines produce internal gains that must be accounted for and managed by the building HVAC system.

Table 5B Recommended Rates of Radiant and Convective Heat Gain from Unhooded Electric Appliances during Cooking Conditions

	Energy Rate, Btu/h		Rate of Heat Gain, Btu/h					
Appliance	Rated	Cooking	Sensible Radiant	Sensible Convective	Latent	Total	Usage Factor F_U	Radiation Factor F_R
Cheesemelter	8,200	9,300	1,500	3,700	2,000	7,200	1.13	0.16
Egg cooker	8,100	4,100	200	1,300	2,200	3,700	0.50	0.05
Fryer, countertop, open deep fryer	15,700	13,000	700	1,700	5,600	8,000	0.83	0.05
Griddle, countertop	27,300	11,200	2,900	2,200	4,400	9,500	0.41	0.26
Hot dog roller	5,500	5,400	900	2,100	2,300	5,300	0.99	0.17
Hot plate, single burner	3,800	3,400	1,100	2,100	200	3,400	0.90	0.32
Induction hob, countertop	17,100	2,200	0	1,100	1,100	2,200	0.13	0.00
Oven, conveyor	17,100	14,600	2,500	8,400	700	11,600	0.86	0.17
Microwave	5,800	8,100	0	3,200	3,400	6,600	1.39	0.00
Rapid cook	19,400	7,900	300	4,200	2,600	7,100	0.41	0.04
Panini grill	6,100	4,700	700	2,400	500	3,600	0.76	0.14
Popcorn popper	2,900	2,000	100	800	700	1,600	0.68	0.05
Rice cooker	5,300	4,000	50	300	200	550	0.75	0.01
Soup warmer	2,700	2,900	0	300	2,400	2,700	1.05	0.00
Steamer (bun)	5,100	2,700	100	800	1,700	2,600	0.53	0.04
Steamer, countertop	28,300	26,400	0	1,700	23,700	25,400	0.93	0.00
Toaster, conveyor	6,000	5,800	1,200	3,300	1,300	5,800	0.98	0.21
Vertical	8,900	6,300	600	2,400	1,100	4,100	0.71	0.10
Tortilla grill	7,500	7,500	900	4,300	2,300	7,500	1.00	0.12
Waffle maker	9,200	4,000	200	1,200	1,900	3,300	0.44	0.05

Source: ASHRAE research project RP-1631 (Zhang et al. 2015).

Table 5C Recommended Rates of Radiant Heat Gain from Hooded Electric Appliances During Idle (Ready-to-Cook) Conditions

	Energy Rate, Btu/h		Rate of Heat Gain, Btu/h		
Appliance	Rated	Standby	Sensible Radiant	Usage Factor F_U	Radiation Factor F_R
Broiler: underfired 3 ft	36,900	30,900	10,800	0.84	0.35
Cheesemelter*	12,300	11,900	4,600	0.97	0.39
Fryer, kettle	99,000	1,800	500	0.02	0.28
Open deep-fat, 1-vat	47,800	2,800	1,000	0.06	0.36
Pressure	46,100	2,700	500	0.06	0.19
Griddle, double-sided 3 ft (clamshell down)*	72,400	6,900	1,400	0.10	0.20
(Clamshell up)*	72,400	11,500	3,600	0.16	0.31
Flat 3 ft	58,400	11,500	4,500	0.20	0.39
Small 3 ft*	30,700	6,100	2,700	0.20	0.44
Induction cooktop*	71,700	0	0	0.00	0.00
Induction wok*	11,900	0	0	0.00	0.00
Oven, combi: combi-mode*	56,000	5,500	800	0.10	0.15
Convection mode	56,000	5,500	1,400	0.10	0.25
Oven, convection, full-sized	41,300	6,700	1,500	0.16	0.22
Half-sized*	18,800	3,700	500	0.20	0.14
Pasta cooker*	75,100	8,500	0	0.11	0.00
Range top, top off/oven on*	16,600	4,000	1,000	0.24	0.25
3 elements on/oven off	51,200	15,400	6,300	0.30	0.41
6 elements on/oven off	51,200	33,200	13,900	0.65	0.42
6 elements on/oven on	67,800	36,400	14,500	0.54	0.40
Range, hot-top	54,000	51,300	11,800	0.95	0.23
Rotisserie*	37,900	13,800	4,500	0.36	0.33
Salamander*	23,900	23,300	7,000	0.97	0.30
Steam kettle, large (60 gal) simmer lid down*	110,600	2,600	100	0.02	0.04
Small (40 gal) simmer lid down*	73,700	1,800	300	0.02	0.17
Steamer, compartment, atmospheric*	33,400	15,300	200	0.46	0.01
Tilting skillet/braising pan	32,900	5,300	0	0.16	0.00

*Items with an asterisk appear only in Swierczyna et al. (2009); all others appear in both Swierczyna et al. (2008) and (2009).

Table 5D Recommended Rates of Radiant Heat Gain from Hooded Gas Appliances during Idle (Ready-to-Cook) Conditions

Appliance	Energy Rate, Btu/h Rated	Energy Rate, Btu/h Standby	Rate of Heat Gain, Btu/h Sensible Radiant	Usage Factor F_U	Radiation Factor F_R
Broiler: batch*	95,000	69,200	8,100	0.73	0.12
Chain (conveyor)	132,000	96,700	13,200	0.73	0.14
Overfired (upright)*	100,000	87,900	2,500	0.88	0.03
Underfired 3 ft	96,000	73,900	9,000	0.77	0.12
Fryer: doughnut	44,000	12,400	2,900	0.28	0.23
Open deep-fat, 1 vat	80,000	4,700	1,100	0.06	0.23
Pressure	80,000	9,000	800	0.11	0.09
Griddle: double sided 3 ft, clamshell down*	108,200	8,000	1,800	0.07	0.23
Clamshell up*	108,200	14,700	4,900	0.14	0.33
Flat 3 ft	90,000	20,400	3,700	0.23	0.18
Oven: combi: combi-mode*	75,700	6,000	400	0.08	0.07
Convection mode	75,700	5,800	1,000	0.08	0.17
Convection, full-size	44,000	11,900	1,000	0.27	0.08
Conveyor (pizza)	170,000	68,300	7,800	0.40	0.11
Deck	105,000	20,500	3,500	0.20	0.17
Rack mini-rotating*	56,300	4,500	1,100	0.08	0.24
Pasta cooker*	80,000	23,700	0	0.30	0.00
Range top: top off/oven on*	25,000	7,400	2,000	0.30	0.27
3 burners on/oven off	120,000	60,100	7,100	0.50	0.12
6 burners on/oven off	120,000	120,800	11,500	1.01	0.10
6 burners on/oven on	145,000	122,900	13,600	0.85	0.11
Range: wok*	99,000	87,400	5,200	0.88	0.06
Rethermalizer*	90,000	23,300	11,500	0.26	0.49
Rice cooker*	35,000	500	300	0.01	0.60
Salamander*	35,000	33,300	5,300	0.95	0.16
Steam kettle: large (60 gal) simmer lid down*	145,000	5,400	0	0.04	0.00
Small (10 gal) simmer lid down*	52,000	3,300	300	0.06	0.09
Medium (40 gal) simmer lid down	100,000	4,300	0	0.04	0.00
Steamer: compartment: atmospheric*	26,000	8,300	0	0.32	0.00
Tilting skillet/braising pan	104,000	10,400	400	0.10	0.04

*Items with an asterisk appear only in Swierczyna et al. (2009); all others appear in both Swierczyna et al. (2008) and (2009).

Table 5E Recommended Rates of Radiant Heat Gain from Hooded Solid-Fuel Appliances during Idle (Ready-to-Cook) Conditions

Appliance	Rated	Standby Energy Rate, Btu/h	Rate of Sensible Heat Gain, Btu/h	Usage Factor F_U	Radiation Factor F_R
Broiler: solid fuel: charcoal	40 lb	42,000	6200	N/A	0.15
Broiler: solid fuel: wood (mesquite)	40 lb	49,600	7000	N/A	0.14

Source: Swierczyna (2008).

Table 5F Recommended Rates of Radiant and Convective Heat Gain from Warewashing Equipment during Idle (Standby) or Washing Conditions

Appliance	Energy Rate, Btu/h Rated	Energy Rate, Btu/h Standby/Washing	Unhooded Sensible Radiant	Unhooded Sensible Convective	Unhooded Latent	Unhooded Total	Hooded Sensible Radiant	Usage Factor F_U	Radiation Factor F_R
Dishwasher: conveyor type, hot-water sanitizing, washing	46,800	N/A	0	12,100	47,000	59,100	0	N/A	0.00
Standby	46,800	5,700	0	1,600	4,100	5,700	0	0.12	0.00
Dishwasher: conveyor type, chemical sanitizing, washing	46,800	43,600	0	11,100	35,400	46,500	0	0.93	0.00
Standby	46,800	5,700	0	1,600	4,100	5,700	0	0.12	0.00
Dishwasher: door type, hot-water sanitizing, washing	60,100	18,500	0	7,600	25,200	32,800	0	0.31	0.00
With heat recovery and vapor reduction	51,900	27,100	0	5,800	13,100	18,900	0	0.52	0.00
Standby	18,400	1,200	0	2,280	4,170	6,450	0	0.35	0.00
Dishwasher: door type, chemical sanitizing, washing	30,000	15,600	0	3,900	13,200	17,100	0	0.52	0.00
Standby	18,400	1,200	0	900	300	1,200	0	0.07	0.00
Dishwasher: door type, chemical sanitizing, dump and fill, washing	6,100	3,000	0	2,900	4,200	7,100	0	0.49	0.00
Standby	6,100	3,000	0	0	0	0	0	0.49	0.00
Pot and pan washer: door type, hot-water sanitizing, washing	53,200	36,400	0	6,000	23,500	29,500	0	0.68	0.00
With heat recovery and vapor reduction	53,200	35,200	0	5,500	19,000	24,500	0	0.66	0.00
Dishwasher: under-counter type, hot-water sanitizing, washing	28,500	7,600	800	3,200	6,900	10,900	800	0.27	0.11
With heat recovery and vapor reduction	26,600	22,800	0	2,000	1,100	3,100	0	0.86	0.00
Standby	26,600	1,700	800	500	400	1,700	800	0.06	0.47
Dishwasher: under-counter type, chemical sanitizing, washing	28,500	6,900	0	2,200	4,900	7,100	0	0.24	0.00
Standby	26,600	1,700	800	500	400	1,700	0	0.06	0.47
Booster heater	130,000	0	500	0	0	0	500	0	N/A

Sources: PG&E (2010-2016), Swierczyna et al. (2008) and (2009).

Sensible radiant and convective gains are affected by dishwasher insulation, and latent convective gains are affected by door seals. Heat loads may vary.

Recirculating Systems. Cooking appliances ventilated by recirculating systems or "ductless" hoods should be treated as unhooded appliances when estimating heat gain. In other words, all energy consumed by the appliance and all moisture produced by cooking is introduced to the kitchen as a sensible or latent cooling load.

Recommended Heat Gain Values. Table 5 lists recommended rates of heat gain from typical commercial cooking appliances. Data in the "hooded" columns assume installation under a properly designed exhaust hood connected to a mechanical fan exhaust system operating at an exhaust rate for complete capture and containment of the thermal and effluent plume. Improperly operating hood systems load the space with a significant convective component of the heat gain.

Hospital and Laboratory Equipment

Hospital and laboratory equipment items are major sources of sensible and latent heat gains in conditioned spaces. Care is needed in evaluating the probability and duration of simultaneous usage when many components are concentrated in one area, such as a laboratory, an operating room, etc. Commonly, heat gain from equipment in a laboratory ranges from 15 to 70 Btu/h·ft^2 or, in laboratories with outdoor exposure, as much as four times the heat gain from all other sources combined.

Medical Equipment. It is more difficult to provide generalized heat gain recommendations for medical equipment than for general office equipment because medical equipment is much more varied in type and in application. Some heat gain testing has been done, but the equipment included represents only a small sample of the type of equipment that may be encountered.

Data presented for medical equipment in Table 6 are relevant for portable and bench-top equipment. Medical equipment is very specific and can vary greatly from application to application. The data are presented to provide guidance in only the most general sense. For large equipment, such as MRI, heat gain must be obtained from the manufacturer.

Laboratory Equipment. Equipment in laboratories is similar to medical equipment in that it varies significantly from space to space. Chapter 16 of the 2015 *ASHRAE Handbook—HVAC Applications* discusses heat gain from equipment, which may range from 5 to 25 W/ft^2 in highly automated laboratories. Table 7 lists some values for laboratory equipment, but, as with medical equipment, it is for general guidance only. Wilkins and Cook (1999) also examined laboratory equipment heat gains.

Table 6 Recommended Heat Gain from Typical Medical Equipment

Equipment	Nameplate, W	Peak, W	Average, W
Anesthesia system	250	177	166
Blanket warmer	500	504	221
Blood pressure meter	180	33	29
Blood warmer	360	204	114
ECG/RESP	1440	54	50
Electrosurgery	1000	147	109
Endoscope	1688	605	596
Harmonical scalpel	230	60	59
Hysteroscopic pump	180	35	34
Laser sonics	1200	256	229
Optical microscope	330	65	63
Pulse oximeter	72	21	20
Stress treadmill	N/A	198	173
Ultrasound system	1800	1063	1050
Vacuum suction	621	337	302
X-ray system	968		82
	1725	534	480
	2070		18

Source: Hosni et al. (1999).

Office Equipment

Computers, printers, copiers, etc., can generate very significant heat gains, sometimes greater than all other gains combined. ASHRAE research project RP-822 developed a method to measure the actual heat gain from equipment in buildings and the radiant/convective percentages (Hosni et al. 1998; Jones et al. 1998). This methodology was then incorporated into ASHRAE research project RP-1055 and applied to a wide range of equipment (Hosni et al. 1999) as a follow-up to independent research by Wilkins and McGaffin (1994) and Wilkins et al. (1991). Komor (1997) found similar results. Analysis of measured data showed that results for office equipment could be generalized, but results from laboratory and hospital equipment proved too diverse. The following general guidelines for office equipment are a result of these studies

Nameplate Versus Measured Energy Use. Nameplate data rarely reflect the actual power consumption of office equipment. Actual power consumption is assumed to equal total (radiant plus convective) heat gain, but its ratio to the nameplate value varies widely. ASHRAE research project RP-1055 (Hosni et al. 1999) found that, for general office equipment with nameplate power consumption of less than 1000 W, the actual ratio of total heat gain to nameplate ranged from 25 to 50%, but when all tested equipment is considered, the range is broader. Generally, if the nameplate value is the only information known and no actual heat gain data are available for similar equipment, it is conservative to use 50% of nameplate as heat gain and more nearly correct if 25% of nameplate is used. Much better results can be obtained, however, by considering heat gain to be predictable based on the type of equipment. However, if the device has a mainly resistive internal electric load (e.g., a space heater), the nameplate rating may be a good estimate of its peak energy dissipation.

Table 7 Recommended Heat Gain from Typical Laboratory Equipment

Equipment	Nameplate, W	Peak, W	Average, W
Analytical balance	7	7	7
Centrifuge	138	89	87
	288	136	132
	5500	1176	730
Electrochemical analyzer	50	45	44
	100	85	84
Flame photometer	180	107	105
Fluorescent microscope	150	144	143
	200	205	178
Function generator	58	29	29
Incubator	515	461	451
	600	479	264
	3125	1335	1222
Orbital shaker	100	16	16
Oscilloscope	72	38	38
	345	99	97
Rotary evaporator	75	74	73
	94	29	28
Spectronics	36	31	31
Spectrophotometer	575	106	104
	200	122	121
	N/A	127	125
Spectro fluorometer	340	405	395
Thermocycler	1840	965	641
	N/A	233	198
Tissue culture	475	132	46
	2346	1178	1146

Source: Hosni et al. (1999).

Table 8A Recommended Heat Gain for Typical Desktop Computers

Description	Nameplate Power,[a] W	Peak Heat Gain,[b, d] W
Manufacturer 1		
3.0 GHz processor, 4 GB RAM, $n = 1$	NA	83
3.3 GHz processor, 8 GB RAM, $n = 8$	NA	50
3.5 GHz processor, 8 GB RAM, $n = 2$	NA	42
3.6 GHz processor, 16 GB RAM, $n = 2$	NA	66
3.3 GHz processor, 16 GB RAM, $n = 2$	NA	52
4.0 GHz processor, 16 GB RAM, $n = 1$	NA	83
3.3 GHz processor, 8 GB RAM, $n = 1$	NA	84
3.7 GHz processor, 32 GB RAM, $n = 1$	750	116
	NA	102
3.5 GHz processor, 16 GB RAM, $n = 3$[c]	550	144
	NA	93
Manufacturer 2		
3.6 GHz processor, 32 GB RAM, $n = 8$	NA	80
3.6 GHz processor, 16 GB RAM, $n = 1$	NA	78
3.4 GHz processor, 32 GB RAM, $n = 1$	NA	72
3.4 GHz processor, 24 GB RAM, $n = 1$	NA	86
3.50 GHz processor, 4 GB RAM, $n = 1$	NA	26
3.3 GHz processor, 8 GB RAM, $n = 1$	NA	78
3.20 GHz processor, 8 GB RAM, $n = 1$	NA	61
3.20 GHz processor, 4 GB RAM, $n = 1$	NA	44
2.93 GHz processor, 16 GB RAM, $n = 1$	NA	151
2.67 GHz processor, 8 GB RAM, $n = 1$	NA	137
Average 15-min peak power consumption (range)	82 (26-151)	

Source: Bach and Sarfraz (2017)

n = number of tested equipment of same configuration.

[a]Nameplate for desktop computer is present on its power supply, which is mounted inside desktop, hence not accessible for most computers, where NA = not available.

[b]For equipment peak heat gain value, highest 15-min interval of recorded data is listed in tables.

[c]For tested equipment with same configuration, increasing power supply size does not increase average power consumption.

[d]Approximately 90% convective heat gain and 10% radiative heat gain.

Table 8B Recommended Heat Gain for Typical Laptops and Laptop Docking Station

Equipment	Description	Nameplate Power,[a] W	Peak Heat Gain,[b, c] W
Laptop computer	Manufacturer 1, 2.6 GHz processor, 8 GB RAM, $n = 1$	NA	46
	Manufacturer 2, 2.4 GHz processor, 4 GB RAM, $n = 1$	NA	59
Average 15-min peak power consumption (range)		53 (46-59)	
Laptop with docking station	Manufacturer 1, 2.7 GHz processor, 8 GB RAM, $n = 1$	NA	38
	1.6 GHz processor, 8 GB RAM, $n = 2$	NA	45
	2.0 GHz processor, 8 GB RAM, $n = 1$	NA	50
	2.6 GHz processor, 4 GB RAM, $n = 1$	NA	51
	2.4 GHz processor, 8 GB RAM, $n = 1$	NA	40
	2.6 GHz processor, 8 GB RAM, $n = 1$	NA	35
	2.7 GHz processor, 8 GB RAM, $n = 1$	NA	59
	3.0 GHz processor, 8 GB RAM, $n = 3$	NA	70
	2.9 GHz processor, 32 GB RAM, $n = 3$	NA	58
	3.0 GHz processor, 32 GB RAM, $n = 1$	NA	128
	3.7 GHz processor, 32 GB RAM, $n = 1$	NA	63
	3.1 GHz processor, 32 GB RAM, $n = 1$	NA	89
Average 15-min peak power consumption (range)		61 (26-151)	

Source: Bach and Sarfraz (2017)

n = number of tested equipment of same configuration.

[a]Voltage and amperage information for laptop computer and laptop docking station is available on power supply nameplates; however, nameplate does not provide information on power consumption, where NA = not available.

[b]For equipment peak heat gain value, the highest 15-min interval of recorded data is listed in tables.

[c]Approximately 75% convective heat gain and 25% radiative heat gain.

Table 8C Recommended Heat Gain for Typical Tablet PC

Description	Nameplate Power,[a] W	Peak Heat Gain,[b] W
1.7 GHz processor, 4 GB RAM, $n = 1$	NA	42
2.2 GHz processor, 16 GB RAM, $n = 1$	NA	40
2.3 GHz processor, 8 GB RAM, $n = 1$	NA	30
2.5 GHz processor, 8 GB RAM, $n = 1$	NA	31
Average 15-min peak power consumption (range)	36 (31-42)	

Source: Bach and Sarfraz (2017)

n = number of tested equipment of same configuration.

[a]Voltage and amperage information for tablet PC is available on power supply nameplate; however, nameplate does not provide information on power consumption, where NA = not available.

[b]For equipment peak heat gain value, highest 15-min interval of recorded data is listed in tables.

Computers. Based on tests by Hosni et al. (1999) and Wilkins and McGaffin (1994), nameplate values on computers should be ignored when performing cooling load calculations. Tables 8A, 8B, and 8C (Bach and Sarfraz 2017) present typical heat gain values for computers of varying types and models.

Monitors. Table 8D shows typical values for various sizes and types.

Flat-panel monitors have replaced CRT monitors in almost all workplaces. Power consumption, and thus heat gain, for flat-panel displays are significantly lower than for CRTs.

Laser Printers. Hosni et al. (1999) found that power consumption, and therefore the heat gain, of laser printers depended largely on the level of throughput for which the printer was designed. Smaller printers tend to be used more intermittently, and larger printers may run continuously for longer periods.

Table 9 presents data on typical printers. These data can be applied by taking the value for continuous operation and then applying an appropriate diversity factor. This would likely be most appropriate for larger open office areas. Another approach, which may be appropriate for a single room or small area, is to take the value that most closely matches the expected operation of the printer with no diversity.

Copiers. Bach and Sarfraz (2017) also tested photocopy machines, including desktop and office (freestanding high-volume copiers) models. Larger machines used in production environments were not addressed. Table 9 summarizes the results. Desktop copiers rarely operate continuously, but office copiers frequently operate continuously for periods of an hour or more. Large, high-volume photocopiers often include provisions for exhausting air outdoors; if so equipped, the direct-to-space or system makeup air heat gain needs to be included in the load calculation. Also, when the air is dry, humidifiers are often operated near copiers to limit static electricity; if this occurs during cooling mode, their load on HVAC systems should be considered.

Miscellaneous Office Equipment. Table 10 presents data on miscellaneous office equipment such as vending machines and other equipment tested by Bach and Sarfraz (2017).

Diversity. The ratio of measured peak electrical load at equipment panels to the sum of the maximum electrical load of each individual item of equipment is the usage diversity. A small, one- or two-person office containing equipment listed in Tables 8 to 10 usually

Table 8D Recommended Heat Gain for Typical Monitors

Description[a]	Nameplate Power, W	Peak Heat Gain,[b, c] W
Manufacturer 1		
1397 mm LED flat screen, n = 1 (excluded from average because atypical size)	240	50
686 mm LED flat screen, n = 2	40	26
546 mm LED flat screen, n = 2	29	25
Manufacturer 2		
1270 mm 3D LED flat screen, n = 1 (excluded from average because atypical size)	94	49
Manufacturer 3		
864 mm LCD curved screen, n = 1 (excluded from average because atypical size and curved)	130	48
584 mm LED flat screen, n = 3	50	17
584 mm LED flat screen, n = 1	38	21
584 mm LED flat screen, n = 1	38	14
Manufacturer 4		
610 mm LED flat screen, n = 1	42	25
Manufacturer 5		
600 mm LED flat screen, n = 1	26	17
546 mm LED flat screen, n = 1	29	22
Manufacturer 6		
546 mm LED flat screen, n = 1	28	24
Average 15-min peak power consumption (range)	21 (14-26)	

Source: Bach and Sarfraz (2017)
n = number of tested equipment of same configuration.
[a]Screens with atypical size and shape are excluded for calculating average 15-min peak power consumption.
[b]For equipment peak heat gain value, highest 15-min interval of recorded data is listed in tables.
[c]Approximately 60% convective heat gain and 40% radiative heat gain.

Table 9 Recommended Heat Gain for Typical Printers

Equipment	Description	Max. Printing Speed, Pages per Minute	Nameplate Power, W	Peak Heat Gain,[a] W
Multifunction printer (copy, print, scan)	Large, multiuser, office type	40	1010	540 (Idle 29 W)
		30	1300	303 (Idle 116 W)
		28	1500	433 (Idle 28 W)
Average 15-min peak power consumption (range)		425 (303-540)		
	Multiuser, medium-office type	35	900	732 (Idle 18 W)
	Desktop, small-office type	25	470	56 (Idle 3 W)
Monochrome printer	Desktop, medium-office type	55	1000	222
		45	680	61
Average 15-min peak power consumption (range)		142 (61-222)		
Color printer	Desktop, medium-office type	40	620	120
Laser printer	Desktop, small-office type	14	310	89
		24	495	67
		26	1090	65
Average 15-min peak power consumption (range)		74 (65-89)		
Plotter	Manufacturer 1		1600	571
	Manufacturer 2		270	173
Average 15-min peak power consumption (range)		372 (173-571)		
Fax machine	Medium		1090	92
	Small		600	46
Average 15-min peak power consumption (range)		69 (46-92)		

Source: Bach and Sarfraz (2017)
[a]Approximately 70% convective heat gain and 30% radiative heat gain.

contributes heat gain to the space at the sum of the appropriate listed values. Progressively larger areas with many equipment items always experience some degree of usage diversity resulting from whatever percentage of such equipment is not in operation at any given time.

Wilkins and McGaffin (1994) measured diversity in 23 areas within five different buildings totaling over 275,000 ft^2. Diversity was found to range between 37 and 78%, with the average (normalized based on area) being 46%. Figure 4 shows the relationship between nameplate, sum of peaks, and actual electrical load with diversity accounted for, based on the average of the total area tested. Data on actual diversity can be used as a guide, but diversity varies significantly with occupancy. The proper diversity factor for an office of call center operators is different from that for an office of sales representatives who travel regularly.

ASHRAE research project RP-1093 derived diversity profiles for use in energy calculations (Abushakra et al. 2004; Claridge et al. 2004). Those profiles were derived from available measured data sets for a variety of office buildings, and indicated a range of peak weekday diversity factors for lighting ranging from 70 to 85% and for receptacles (appliance load) between 42 and 89%.

Heat Gain per Unit Area. Bach and Sarfraz (2017), Wilkins and Hosni (2000, 2011) and Wilkins and McGaffin (1994) summarized research on a heat gain per unit area basis. Diversity testing showed that the actual heat gain per unit area, or load factor, ranged from 0.44 to 1.08 W/ft^2, with an average (normalized based on area) of 0.81 W/ft^2. Spaces tested were fully occupied and highly automated, comprising 21 unique areas in five buildings, with a computer and monitor at every workstation. Table 11 presents a range of load factors with a subjective description of the type of space to which they would apply. The medium load density is likely to be appropriate for most standard office spaces. Medium/heavy or heavy load densities

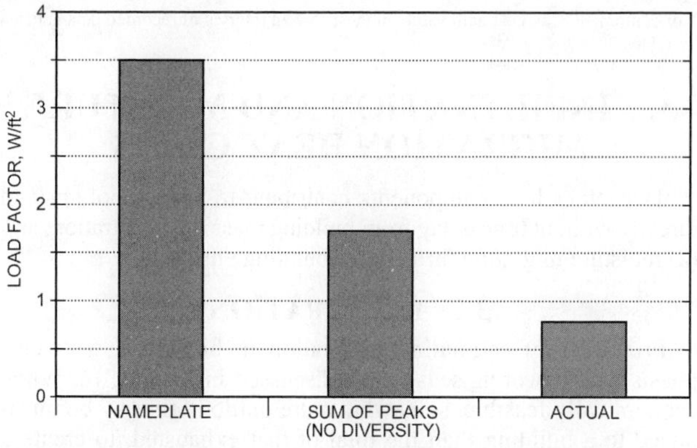

Fig. 4 Office Equipment Load Factor Comparison
(Wilkins and McGaffin 1994)

may be encountered but can be considered extremely conservative estimates even for densely populated and highly automated spaces. Table 12 indicates applicable diversity factors.

Radiant/Convective Split. ASHRAE research project RP-1482 (Hosni and Beck 2008) examined the radiant/convective split for common office equipment; the most important differentiating feature is whether the equipment had a cooling fan. Footnotes in Tables 8 and 9 summarize those results.

Table 10 Recommended Heat Gain for Miscellaneous Equipment

Equipment	Nameplate Power,[a] W	Peak Heat Gain,[b] W
Vending machine		
Drinks, 280 to 400 items	NA	940
Snacks	NA	54
Food (e.g., for sandwiches)	NA	465
Thermal binding machine, 2 single documents up to 340 pages	350	28.5
Projector, resolution 1024 × 768	340	308
Paper shredder, up to 28 sheets	1415	265
Electric stapler, up to 45 sheets	NA	1.5
Speakers	220	15
Temperature-controlled electronics soldering station	95	16
Cell phone charger	NA	5
Battery charger		
40 V	NA	19
AA	NA	5.5
Microwave oven, 7 to 9 gal	1000 to 1550	713 to 822
Coffee maker		
Single cup	1400	385
Up to 12 cups	950	780
With grinder	1350	376
Coffee grinder, up to 12 cups	NA	73
Tea kettle, up to 6 cups	1200	1200
Dorm fridge, 3.1 ft^3	NA	57
Freezer, 18 ft^3	130	125
Fridge, 18 to 28 ft^3	NA	387 to 430
Ice maker and dispenser, 20 lb bin capacity	NA	658
Top mounted bottled water cooler	NA	114 to 350
Cash register	25	9
Touch screen computer, 15 in. standard LCD and 2.2 GHz processor	NA	58
Self-checkout machine	NA	15

Source: Bach and Sarfraz (2017)
[a]For some equipment, nameplate power consumption is not available, where NA = not available.
[b]For equipment peak heat gain value, highest 15-min interval of recorded data is listed in tables.

Table 11 Recommended Load Factors for Various Types of Offices

Type of Use	Load Factor*, W/ft^2	Description
100% laptop, docking station		
light	0.34	167 ft^2/workstation, all laptop docking station use, 1 printer per 10
medium	0.46	125 ft^2/workstation, all laptop docking station use, 1 printer per 10
50% laptop, docking station		
light	0.44	167 ft^2/workstation, 50% laptop docking station/50% desktop, 1 printer per 10
medium	0.59	125 ft^2/workstation, 50% laptop docking station/50% desktop, 1 printer per 10
100% desktop		
light	0.54	167 ft^2/workstation, all desktop use, 1 printer per 10
medium	0.72	125 ft^2/workstation, all desktop use, 1 printer per 10
100% laptop, docking station		
2 screens	0.69	125 ft^2/workstation, all laptop docking station use, 2 screens, 1 printer per 10
100% desktop		
2 screens	0.84	125 ft^2/workstation, all laptop use, 2 screens, 1 printer per 10
3 screens	0.96	125 ft^2/workstation, all desktop use, 3 screens, 1 printer per 10
100% desktop		
heavy, 2 screens	1.02	85 ft^2/workstation, all desktop use, 2 screens, 1 printer per 8
heavy, 3 screens	1.16	85 ft^2/workstation, all desktop use, 3 screens, 1 printer per 8
100% laptop, docking station		
full on, 2 screens	1.14	85 ft^2/workstation, all laptop docking use, 2 screens, 1 printer per 8, no diversity
100% desktop		
full on, 2 screens	1.33	85 ft^2/workstation, all desktop use, 2 screens, 1 printer per 8, no diversity
full on, 3 screens	1.53	85 ft^2/workstation, all desktop use, 3 screens, 1 printer per 8, no diversity

Source: Bach and Sarfraz (2017)
*Medium-office type monochrome printer is used for load factor calculator with 15-min peak power consumption of 142 W.

Table 12 Diversity Factor for Different Equipment

Equipment	Diversity Factor, %	Diversity Factor,[a] %
Desktop PC	75	75
Laptop docking station	70	NA
Notebook computer	75[b]	75
Screen	70	60
Printer	45	NA

Source: Bach and Sarfraz (2017)
[a]2013 *ASHRAE Handbook—Fundamentals*
[b]Insufficient data from RP-1742; values based on previous data from 2013 *ASHRAE Handbook—Fundamentals* and judgment of Bach and Sarfraz (2017).

3. INFILTRATION AND MOISTURE MIGRATION HEAT GAINS

Two other load components contribute to space cooling load directly without time delay from building mass: (1) infiltration, and (2) moisture migration through the building envelope.

3.1 INFILTRATION

Principles of estimating infiltration in buildings, with emphasis on the heating season, are discussed in Chapter 16. When economically feasible, somewhat more outdoor air may be introduced to a building than the total of that exhausted, to create a slight overall positive pressure in the building relative to the outdoors. Under these conditions, air usually exfiltrates, rather than infiltrates, through the building envelope and thus effectively eliminates infiltration sensible and latent heat gains. However, there is concern, especially in some climates, that water may condense within the building envelope; actively managing space air pressures to reduce this condensation problem, as well as infiltration, may be needed.

When positive air pressure is assumed, most designers do not include infiltration in cooling load calculations for commercial buildings. However, including some infiltration for spaces such entry areas or loading docks may be appropriate, especially when those spaces are on the windward side of buildings. But the downward stack effect, as occurs when indoor air is denser than the outdoor, might eliminate infiltration to these entries on lower floors of tall buildings; infiltration may occur on the upper floors during cooling conditions if makeup air is not sufficient.

Infiltration also depends on wind direction and magnitude, temperature differences, construction type and quality, and occupant use of exterior doors and operable windows. As such, it is impossible to accurately predict infiltration rates. Designers usually predict overall rates of infiltration using the number of **air changes per**

hour (ACH). A common guideline for climates and buildings typical of at least the central United States is to estimate the ACHs for winter heating conditions, and then use half that value for the cooling load calculations.

Standard Air Volumes

Because the specific volume of air varies appreciably, calculations are more accurate when made on the basis of air mass instead of volume. However, volumetric flow rates are often required for selecting coils, fans, ducts, etc.; basing volumes on measurement at standard conditions may be used for accurate results. One standard value is 0.075 lb_{da}/ft^3 (13.33 ft^3/lb). This density corresponds to about 60°F at saturation and 69°F dry air (at 14.696 psia). Because air usually passes through the equipment at a density close to standard for locations below about 1000 ft, the accuracy desired normally requires no correction. When airflow is to be measured at a particular condition or point, such as at a coil entrance or exit, the corresponding specific volume can be read from the sea-level psychrometric chart. For higher elevations, the mass flow rates of air must be adjusted and higher-elevation psychrometric charts or algorithms must be used.

Heat Gain Calculations Using Standard Air Values

Air-conditioning design often requires the following information:

1. Total heat

Total heat gain q_t corresponding to the change of a given standard flow rate Q_s through an enthalpy difference Δh is

$$q_t = 60 \times 0.075 Q_s \Delta h = 4.5 Q_s \Delta h \quad (7)$$

where 60 = min/h, 0.075 = lb_{da}/ft^3.

This total heat equation can also be expressed as

$$q_t = C_t Q_s \Delta h$$

where C_t = 4.5 is the air total heat factor, in Btu/h·cfm per Btu/lb.

2. Sensible heat

Sensible heat gain q_s corresponding to the change of dry-bulb temperature Δt for given airflow (standard conditions) Q_s is

$$q_s = 60 \times 0.075(0.24 + 0.45W) Q_s \Delta t \quad (8)$$

where

0.24 = specific heat of dry air, Btu/lb·°F
W = humidity ratio, lb_w/lb_{da}
0.45 = specific heat of water vapor, Btu/lb·°F

The specific heats are for a range from about –100 to 200°F. When W = 0, the value of 60 × 0.075 (0.24 + 0.45W) = 1.08; when W = 0.01, the value is 1.10; when W = 0.02, the value is 1.12; and when W = 0.03, the value is 1.14. Because a value of W = 0.01 approximates conditions found in many air-conditioning problems, the sensible heat change (in Btu/h) has traditionally been found as

$$q_s = 1.10 Q_s \Delta t \quad (9)$$

This sensible heat equation can also be expressed as

$$q_s = C_s Q_s \Delta t$$

where C_s = 1.1 is the air sensible heat factor, in Btu/h·cfm·°F.

3. Latent heat

Latent heat gain q_l corresponding to the change of humidity ratio ΔW (in $lb_{m,w}/lb_{m,da}$) for given airflow (standard conditions) Q_s is

$$q_l = 60 \times 0.075 \times 1076 Q_s \Delta W = 4840 Q_s \Delta W \quad (10)$$

where 1076 Btu/lb is the approximate heat content of 50% rh vapor at 75°F less the heat content of water at 50°F. A common design condition for the space is 50% rh at 75°F, and 50°F is normal condensate temperature from cooling and dehumidifying coils.

This latent heat equation can also be expressed as

$$q_l = C_l Q_s \Delta W$$

where C_l = 4840 is the air latent heat factor, in Btu/h·cfm. When ΔW is in $gr_w/lb_{m,da}$, C_l = 0.69 Btu/h·cfm.

4. Elevation correction for total, sensible, and latent heat equations

The constants 4.5, 1.10, and 4840 are useful in air-conditioning calculations at sea level (14.696 psia) and for normal temperatures and moisture ratios. For other conditions, more precise values should be used. For an elevation of 5000 ft (12.2 psia), appropriate values are 3.74, 0.92, and 4027. Equations (8) to (10) can be corrected for elevations other than sea level by multiplying them by the ratio of pressure at sea level divided by the pressure at actual altitude. This can be derived from Equation (3) in Chapter 1 as

$$C_{x,alt} = C_{x,0} P/P_0$$

where $C_{x,0}$ is any sea-level C value and P/P_0 = [1 – (elevation × 6.8754 × 10^{-6})]$^{5.2559}$, where elevation is in feet.

Elevation Correction Examples

To correct the C values for El Paso, Texas, the elevation listed in the appendix of Chapter 14 is 3918 ft. C values for Equations (7) to (10) can be corrected using Equation (3) in Chapter 1 as follows:

$$C_{t,3918} = 4.5 \times [1 - (3918 \times 6.8754 \times 10^{-6})]^{5.2559} = 3.90$$

$$C_{s,3918} = 1.10 \times [1 - (3918 \times 6.8754 \times 10^{-6})]^{5.2559} = 0.95$$

$$C_{l,3918} = 4840 \times [1 - (3918 \times 6.8754 \times 10^{-6})]^{5.2559} = 4193$$

To correct the C values for Albuquerque, New Mexico, the elevation listed in the appendix of Chapter 14 is 5310 ft. C values for Equations (7) to (10) can be corrected as follows:

$$C_{t,5310} = 4.5 \times [1 - (5310 \times 6.8754 \times 10^{-6})]^{5.2559} = 3.70$$

$$C_{s,5310} = 1.10 \times [1 - (5310 \times 6.8754 \times 10^{-6})]^{5.2559} = 0.90$$

$$C_{l,5310} = 4840 \times [1 - (5310 \times 6.8754 \times 10^{-6})]^{5.2559} = 3981$$

3.2 LATENT HEAT GAIN FROM MOISTURE DIFFUSION

Diffusion of moisture through building materials is a natural phenomenon that is always present. Chapters 25 to 27 cover principles, materials, and specific methods used to control moisture. Moisture transfer through walls and roofs is often neglected in comfort air conditioning because the actual rate is quite small and the corresponding latent heat gain is insignificant. Permeability and permeance values for various building materials are given in Chapter 26. Vapor retarders should be specified and installed in the proper location to keep moisture transfer to a minimum, and to minimize condensation within the envelope. Moisture migration up through slabs-on-grade and basement floors has been found to be significant, but has historically not been addressed in cooling load calculations. Under-slab continuous moisture retarders and drainage can reduce upward moisture flow.

Some industrial applications require low moisture to be maintained in a conditioned space. In these cases, the latent heat gain accompanying moisture transfer through walls and roofs may be greater than any other latent heat gain. This gain is computed by

$$q_{l_m} = (M/7000) A \Delta p_v (h_g - h_f) \quad (11)$$

where

q_{l_m} = latent heat gain from moisture transfer, Btu/h
M = permeance of wall or roof assembly, perms or grains/(ft^2·h·in. Hg)

7000 = grains/lb
A = area of wall or roof surface, ft^2
Δp_v = vapor pressure difference, in. Hg
h_g = enthalpy at room conditions, Btu/lb
h_f = enthalpy of water condensed at cooling coil, Btu/lb
$h_g - h_f$ = 1076 Btu/lb when room temperature is 75°F and condensate off coil is 50°F

3.3 OTHER LATENT LOADS

Moisture sources within a building (e.g., shower areas, swimming pools or natatoriums, arboretums) can also contribute to latent load. Unlike sensible loads, which correlate to supply air quantities required in a space, latent loads usually only affect cooling coils sizing or refrigeration load. Because air from showers and some other moisture-generating areas is exhausted completely, those airborne latent loads do not reach the cooling coil and thus do not contribute to cooling load. However, system loads associated with ventilation air required to make up exhaust air must be recognized, and any recirculated air's moisture must be considered when sizing the dehumidification equipment.

For natatoriums, occupant comfort and humidity control are critical. In many instances, size, location, and environmental requirements make complete exhaust systems expensive and ineffective. Where recirculating mechanical cooling systems are used, evaporation (latent) loads are significant. Chapter 5 of the 2015 *ASHRAE Handbook—HVAC Applications* provides guidance on natatorium load calculations.

4. FENESTRATION HEAT GAIN

For spaces with neutral or positive air pressurization, the primary weather-related variable affecting cooling load is solar radiation. The effect of solar radiation is more pronounced and immediate on exposed, nonopaque surfaces. Chapter 14 includes procedures for calculating clear-sky solar radiation intensity and incidence angles for weather conditions encountered at specific locations. That chapter also includes some useful solar equations. Calculation of solar heat gain and conductive heat transfer through various glazing materials and associated mounting frames, with or without interior and/or exterior shading devices, is discussed in Chapter 15. This chapter covers application of such data to overall heat gain evaluation, and conversion of calculated heat gain into a composite cooling load for the conditioned space.

4.1 FENESTRATION DIRECT SOLAR, DIFFUSE SOLAR, AND CONDUCTIVE HEAT GAINS

For fenestration heat gain, use the following equations:

Direct beam solar heat gain q_b:

$$q_b = AE_{t,b}\,\mathrm{SHGC}(\theta)\mathrm{IAC}(\theta,\Omega) \tag{12}$$

Diffuse solar heat gain q_d:

$$q_d = A(E_{t,d} + E_{t,r})\langle\mathrm{SHGC}\rangle_D\,\mathrm{IAC}_D \tag{13}$$

Conductive heat gain q_c:

$$q_c = UA(T_{out} - T_{in}) \tag{14}$$

Total fenestration heat gain Q:

$$Q = q_b + q_d + q_c \tag{15}$$

where

A = window area, ft^2
$E_{t,b}$, $E_{t,d}$, and $E_{t,r}$ = beam, sky diffuse, and ground-reflected diffuse irradiance, calculated using equations in Chapter 14
SHGC(θ) = beam solar heat gain coefficient as a function of incident angle θ; may be interpolated between values in Table 10 of Chapter 15
$\langle\mathrm{SHGC}\rangle_D$ = diffuse solar heat gain coefficient (also referred to as hemispherical SHGC); from Table 10 of Chapter 15
T_{in} = indoor temperature, °F
T_{out} = outdoor temperature, °F
U = overall U-factor, including frame and mounting orientation from Table 4 of Chapter 15, Btu/h·ft^2·°F
IAC(θ.Ω) = indoor solar attenuation coefficient for beam solar heat gain coefficient; = 1.0 if no indoor shading device. IAC(θ.Ω) is a function of shade type and, depending on type, may also be a function of beam solar angle of incidence θ and shade geometry
IAC_D = indoor solar attenuation coefficient for diffuse solar heat gain coefficient; = 1.0 if not indoor shading device. IAC_D is a function of shade type and, depending on type, may also be a function of shade geometry

If specific window manufacturer's SHGC and U-factor data are available, those should be used. For fenestration equipped with indoor shading (blinds, drapes, or shades), the indoor solar attenuation coefficients IAC(θ.Ω) and IAC_D are listed in Tables 14A to 14G of Chapter 15.

Note that, as discussed in Chapter 15, fenestration ratings (U-factor and SHGC) are based on the entire product area, including frames. Thus, for load calculations, fenestration area is the area of the entire opening in the wall or roof.

4.2 EXTERIOR SHADING

Nonuniform exterior shading, caused by roof overhangs, side fins, or building projections, requires separate hourly calculations for the externally shaded and unshaded areas of the window in question, with the indoor shading SHGC still used to account for any internal shading devices. The areas, shaded and unshaded, depend on the location of the shadow line on a surface in the plane of the glass. Sun (1968) developed fundamental algorithms for analysis of shade patterns. McQuiston and Spitler (1992) provide graphical data to facilitate shadow line calculation.

Equations for calculating shade angles [Chapter 15, Equations (34) to (37)] can be used to determine the shape and area of a moving shadow falling across a given window from external shading elements during the course of a design day. Thus, a subprofile of heat gain for that window can be created by separating its sunlit and shaded areas for each hour.

5. HEAT BALANCE METHOD

Cooling load estimation involves calculating a surface-by-surface conductive, convective, and radiative heat balance for each room surface and a convective heat balance for the room air. These principles form the foundation for all methods described in this chapter. The heat balance (HB) method solves the problem directly instead of introducing transformation-based procedures. The advantages are that it contains no arbitrarily set parameters, and no processes are hidden from view.

Some computations required by this rigorous approach require the use of computers. The heat balance procedure is not new. Many energy calculation programs have used it in some form for many years. The first implementation that incorporated all the elements to form a complete method was NBSLD (Kusuda 1967). The heat balance procedure is also implemented in both the BLAST and TARP energy analysis programs (Walton 1983). Before ASHRAE research project RP-875, the method had never been described completely or in a form applicable to cooling load calculations. The papers resulting from RP-875 describe the heat balance procedure in detail (Liesen and Pedersen 1997; McClellan and Pedersen 1997; Pedersen et al. 1997).

The HB method is codified in the software called Hbfort that accompanies *Cooling and Heating Load Calculation Principles* (Pedersen et al. 1998).

ASHRAE research project RP-1117 constructed two model rooms for which cooling loads were physically measured using extensive instrumentation (Chantrasrisalai et al. 2003; Eldridge et al. 2003; Iu et al. 2003). HB calculations closely approximated measured cooling loads when provided with detailed data for the test rooms.

5.1 ASSUMPTIONS

All calculation procedures involve some kind of model; all models require simplifying assumptions and, therefore, are approximate. The most fundamental assumption is that air in the thermal zone can be modeled as **well mixed**, meaning its temperature is uniform throughout the zone. ASHRAE research project RP-664 (Fisher and Pedersen 1997) established that this assumption is valid over a wide range of conditions.

The next major assumption is that the surfaces of the room (walls, windows, floor, etc.) can be treated as having

- Uniform surface temperatures
- Uniform long-wave (LW) and short-wave (SW) irradiation
- Diffuse radiating surfaces
- One-dimensional heat conduction within

The resulting formulation is called the **heat balance (HB) model**. Note that the assumptions, although common, are quite restrictive and set certain limits on the information that can be obtained from the model.

5.2 ELEMENTS

Within the framework of the assumptions, the HB can be viewed as four distinct processes:

1. Outdoor-face heat balance
2. Wall conduction process
3. Indoor-face heat balance
4. Air heat balance

Figure 5 shows the relationship between these processes for a single opaque surface. The top part of the figure, inside the shaded box, is repeated for each surface enclosing the zone. The process for transparent surfaces is similar, but the absorbed solar component appears in the conduction process block instead of at the outdoor face, and the absorbed component splits into inward- and outward-flowing fractions. These components participate in the surface heat balances.

Outdoor-Face Heat Balance

The heat balance on the outdoor face of each surface is

$$q''_{\alpha sol} + q''_{LWR} + q''_{conv} - q''_{ko} = 0 \tag{16}$$

where

$q''_{\alpha sol}$ = absorbed direct and diffuse solar radiation flux (q/A), Btu/h·ft²
q''_{LWR} = net long-wave radiation flux exchange with air and surroundings, Btu/h·ft²
q''_{conv} = convective exchange flux with outdoor air, Btu/h·ft²
q''_{ko} = conductive flux (q/A) into wall, Btu/h·ft²

All terms are positive for net flux to the face except q''_{ko}, which is traditionally taken to be positive from outdoors to inside the wall.

Each term in Equation (16) has been modeled in several ways, and in simplified methods the first three terms are combined by using the sol-air temperature.

Wall Conduction Process

The wall conduction process has been formulated in more ways than any of the other processes. Techniques include

- Numerical finite difference
- Numerical finite element
- Transform methods
- Time series methods

This process introduces part of the time dependence inherent in load calculation. Figure 6 shows surface temperatures on the indoor and outdoor faces of the wall element, and corresponding conductive heat fluxes away from the outer face and toward the indoor face. All four quantities are functions of time. Direct formulation of the

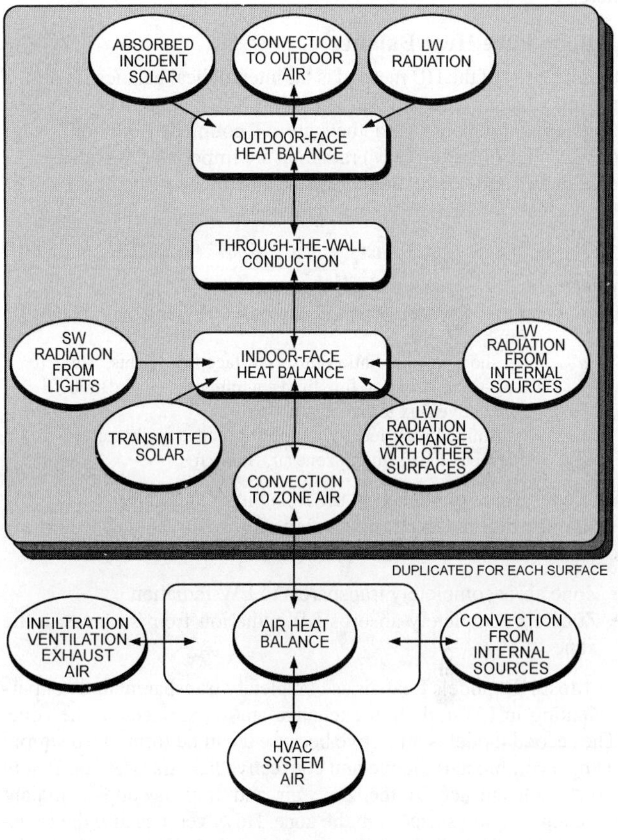

Fig. 5 Schematic of Heat Balance Processes in Zone

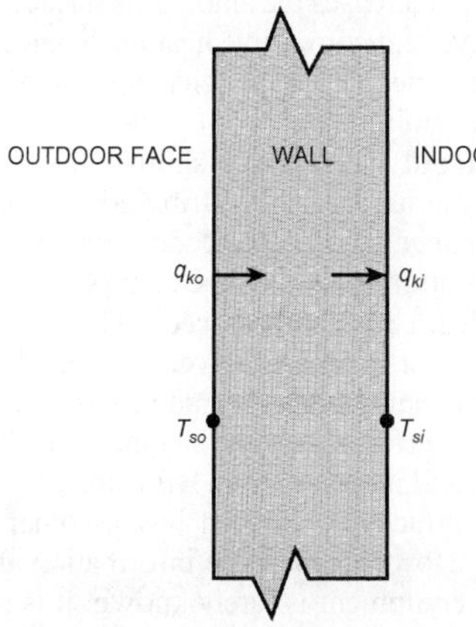

Fig. 6 Schematic of Wall Conduction Process

process uses temperature functions as input or known quantities, and heat fluxes as outputs or resultant quantities.

In some models, surface heat transfer coefficients are included as part of the wall element, making the temperatures in question the indoor and outdoor air temperatures. This is not a desirable formulation, because it hides the heat transfer coefficients and prohibits changing them as airflow conditions change. It also prohibits treating the internal long-wave radiation exchange appropriately.

Because heat balances on both sides of the element induce both the temperature and heat flux, the solution must deal with this simultaneous condition. Two computational methods that have been used widely are finite difference and conduction transfer function methods. Because of the computational time advantage, the conduction transfer function formulation has been selected for presentation here.

Indoor-Face Heat Balance

The heart of the HB method is the internal heat balance involving the inner faces of the zone surfaces. This heat balance has many heat transfer components, and they are all coupled. Both long-wave (LW) and short-wave (SW) radiation are important, as well as wall conduction and convection to the air. The indoor-face heat balance for each surface can be written as follows:

$$q''_{LWX} + q''_{SW} + q''_{LWS} + q''_{ki} + q''_{sol} + q''_{conv} = 0 \quad (17)$$

where

q''_{LWX} = net long-wave radiant flux exchange between zone surfaces, Btu/h·ft²
q''_{SW} = net short-wave radiation flux to surface from lights, Btu/h·ft²
q''_{LWS} = long-wave radiation flux from equipment in zone, Btu/h·ft²
q''_{ki} = conductive flux through wall, Btu/h·ft²
q''_{sol} = transmitted solar radiative flux absorbed at surface, Btu/h·ft²
q''_{conv} = convective heat flux to zone air, Btu/h·ft²

These terms are explained in the following paragraphs.

LW Radiation Exchange Among Zone Surfaces. The limiting cases for modeling internal LW radiation exchange are

- Zone air is completely transparent to LW radiation
- Zone air completely absorbs LW radiation from surfaces in the zone

Most HB models treat air as completely transparent and not participating in LW radiation exchange among surfaces in the zone. The second model is attractive because it can be formulated simply using a combined radiative and convective heat transfer coefficient from each surface to the zone air and thus decouples radiant exchange among surfaces in the zone. However, because the transparent air model allows radiant exchange and is more realistic, the second model is inferior.

Furniture in a zone increases the amount of surface area that can participate in radiative and convective heat exchanges. It also adds thermal mass to the zone. These two changes can affect the time response of the zone cooling load.

SW Radiation from Lights. The short-wavelength radiation from lights is usually assumed to be distributed over the surfaces in the zone in some manner. The HB procedure retains this approach but allows the distribution function to be changed.

LW Radiation from Internal Sources. The traditional model for this source defines a radiative/convective split for heat introduced into a zone from equipment. The radiative part is then distributed over the zone's surfaces in some manner. This model is not completely realistic, and it departs from HB principles. In a true HB model, equipment surfaces are treated just as other LW radiant sources in the zone. However, because information about the surface temperature of equipment is rarely known, it is reasonable to keep the radiative/convective split concept even though it ignores the true nature of the radiant exchange. ASHRAE research project RP-1055 (Hosni et al. 1999) determined radiative/convective splits for many additional equipment types, as listed in footnotes for Tables 8 and 9.

Transmitted Solar Heat Gain. Chapter 15's calculation procedure for determining transmitted solar energy through fenestration uses the solar heat gain coefficient (SHGC) directly rather than relating it to double-strength glass, as is done when using a shading coefficient (SC). The difficulty with this plan is that the SHGC includes both transmitted solar and inward-flowing fraction of the solar radiation absorbed in the window. With the HB method, this latter part should be added to the conduction component so it can be included in the indoor-face heat balance.

Transmitted solar radiation is also distributed over surfaces in the zone in a prescribed manner. It is possible to calculate the actual position of beam solar radiation, but this involves partial surface irradiation, which is inconsistent with the rest of the zone model, which assumes uniform conditions over an entire surface.

Using SHGC to Calculate Solar Heat Gain

The total solar heat gain through fenestration consists of directly transmitted solar radiation plus the inward-flowing fraction of solar radiation that is absorbed in the glazing system. Both parts contain beam and diffuse contributions. Transmitted radiation goes directly onto surfaces in the zone and is accounted for in the surface indoor heat balance. The zone heat balance model accommodates the resulting heat fluxes without difficulty. The second part, the inward-flowing fraction of the absorbed solar radiation, interacts with other surfaces of the enclosure through long-wave radiant exchange and with zone air through convective heat transfer. As such, it depends both on geometric and radiative properties of the zone enclosure and convection characteristics inside and outside the zone. The **solar heat gain coefficient (SHGC)** combines the transmitted solar radiation and the inward-flowing fraction of the absorbed radiation. The SHGC is defined as

$$\text{SHGC} = \tau + \sum_{k=1}^{n} N_k \alpha_k \quad (18)$$

where

τ = solar transmittance of glazing
α_k = solar absorptance of the kth layer of the glazing system
n = number of layers
N_k = inward-flowing fraction of absorbed radiation in the kth layer

Note that Equation (18) is written generically. It can be written for a specific incidence angle and/or radiation wavelength and integrated over the wavelength and/or angle, but the principle is the same in each case. Refer to Chapter 15 for the specific expressions.

Unfortunately, the inward-flowing fraction N interacts with the zone in many ways. This interaction can be expressed as

$N = f$(indoor convection coefficient, outdoor convection coefficient, glazing system overall heat transfer coefficient, zone geometry, zone radiation properties)

The only way to model these interactions correctly is to combine the window model with the zone heat balance model and solve both simultaneously. This has been done recently in some energy analysis programs, but is not generally available in load calculation procedures. In addition, the SHGC used for rating glazing systems is based on specific values of the indoor, outdoor, and overall heat transfer coefficients and does not include any zonal long-wavelength radiation considerations. So, the challenge is to devise a way to use SHGC values within the framework of heat balance calculation in the most accurate way possible, as discussed in the following paragraphs.

Using SHGC Data. The normal incidence SHGC used to rate and characterize glazing systems is not sufficient for determining solar heat gain for load calculations. These calculations require

Table 13 Single-Layer Glazing Data Produced by WINDOW 7.4.6

Parameter	Incident Angle 0	10	20	30	40	50	60	70	80	90	Diffuse (Hemis.)
V_{tc}	0.899	0.899	0.898	0.896	0.889	0.870	0.822	0.705	0.441	0	0.822
R_{fv}	0.083	0.083	0.083	0.085	0.091	0.109	0.156	0.272	0.536	1	0.148
R_{bv}	0.083	0.083	0.083	0.085	0.091	0.109	0.156	0.272	0.536	1	0.148
T_{sol}	0.834	0.833	0.831	0.827	0.818	0.797	0.749	0.637	0.389	0	0.753
R_f	0.075	0.075	0.075	0.077	0.082	0.099	0.143	0.253	0.506	1	0.136
R_b	0.075	0.075	0.075	0.077	0.082	0.099	0.143	0.253	0.506	1	0.136
A_{bs1}	0.091	0.092	0.094	0.096	0.100	0.104	0.108	0.110	0.105	0	0.101
SHGC	0.861	0.860	0.859	0.855	0.847	0.827	0.781	0.669	0.424	0	0.783

Source: LBL (2015).

solar heat gain as a function of the incident solar angle to determine the hour-by-hour gain profile. Thus, it is necessary to use angular SHGC values and also diffuse SHGC values. These can be obtained from the WINDOW 7.4.6 program (LBL 2015). This program does a detailed optical and thermal simulation of a glazing system and, when applied to a single clear layer, produces the information shown in Table 13.

Table 13 shows the parameters as a function of incident solar angle and also the diffuse values. The specific parameters shown are

V_{tc} = transmittance in visible spectrum
R_{fv} and R_{bv} = front and back surface visible reflectances
T_{sol} = solar transmittance [τ in Equations (18), (19), and (20)]
R_f and R_b = front and back surface solar reflectances
A_{bs1} = solar absorptance for layer 1, which is the only layer in this case [α in Equations (18), (19), and (20)]
SHGC = solar heat gain coefficient at center of glazing

The parameters used for heat gain calculations are T_{sol}, A_{bs}, and SHGC. For the specific convective conditions assumed in WINDOW 7.4.6 program, the inward-flowing fraction of the absorbed solar can be obtained by rearranging Equation (18) to give

$$N_k\alpha_k = \text{SHGC} - \tau \qquad (19)$$

This quantity, when multiplied by the appropriate incident solar intensity, provides the amount of absorbed solar radiation that flows inward. In the heat balance formulation for zone loads, this heat flux is combined with that caused by conduction through glazing and included in the surface heat balance.

The outward-flowing fraction of absorbed solar radiation is used in the heat balance on the outdoor face of the glazing and is determined from

$$(1 - N_k)\alpha_k = \alpha_k - N_k\alpha_k = \alpha_k - (\text{SHGC} - \tau) \qquad (20)$$

If there is more than one layer, the appropriate summation of absorptances must be done.

There is some potential inaccuracy in using the WINDOW 7.4.6 SHGC values because the inward-flowing fraction part was determined under specific conditions for the indoor and outdoor heat transfer coefficients. However, the program can be run with indoor and outdoor coefficients of one's own choosing. Normally, however, this effect is not large, and only in highly absorptive glazing systems might cause significant error.

For solar heat gain calculations, then, it seems reasonable to use the generic window property data that comes from WINDOW 7.4.6. Considering Table 13, the procedure is as follows:

1. Determine angle of incidence for the glazing.
2. Determine corresponding SHGC.
3. Evaluate $N_k\alpha_k$ using Equation (18).
4. Multiply T_{sol} by incident beam radiation intensity to get transmitted beam solar radiation.
5. Multiply $N_k\alpha_k$ by incident beam radiation intensity to get inward-flowing absorbed heat.
6. Repeat steps 2 to 5 with diffuse parameters and diffuse radiation.
7. Add beam and diffuse components of transmitted and inward-flowing absorbed heat.

This procedure is incorporated into the HB method so the solar gain is calculated accurately for each hour.

Table 10 in Chapter 15 contains SHGC information for many additional glazing systems. That table is similar to Table 13 but is slightly abbreviated. Again, the information needed for heat gain calculations is T_{sol}, SHGC, and A_{bs}.

The same caution about the indoor and outdoor heat transfer coefficients applies to the information in Table 10 in Chapter 15. Those values were also obtained with specific indoor and outdoor heat transfer coefficients, and the inward-flowing fraction N is dependent upon those values.

Convection to Zone Air. Indoor convection coefficients presented in past editions of this chapter and used in most load calculation procedures and energy programs are based on very old, natural convection experiments and do not accurately describe heat transfer coefficients in a mechanically ventilated zone. In previous load calculation procedures, these coefficients were buried in the procedures and could not be changed. A heat balance formulation keeps them as working parameters. In this way, research results such as those from ASHRAE research project RP-664 (Fisher 1998) can be incorporated into the procedures. It also allows determining the sensitivity of the load calculation to these parameters.

Air Heat Balance

In HB formulations aimed at determining cooling loads, the capacitance of air in the zone is neglected and the air heat balance is done as a quasisteady balance in each time period. Four factors contribute to the air heat balance:

$$q_{conv} + q_{CE} + q_{IV} + q_{sys} = 0 \qquad (21)$$

where

q_{conv} = convective heat transfer from surfaces, Btu/h
q_{CE} = convective parts of internal loads, Btu/h
q_{IV} = sensible load caused by infiltration and ventilation air, Btu/h
q_{sys} = heat transfer to/from HVAC system, Btu/h

Convection from zone surfaces q_{conv} is the sum of all the convective heat transfer quantities from the indoor-surface heat balance. This comes to the air through the convective heat transfer coefficient on the surfaces.

The **convective parts of the internal loads q_{CE}** is the companion to q''_{LWS}, the radiant contribution from internal loads [Equation (17)]. It is added directly to the air heat balance. This also violates the tenets of the HB approach, because surfaces producing internal loads exchange heat with zone air through normal convective processes. However, once again, this level of detail is generally not included in the heat balance, so it is included directly into the air heat balance instead.

In keeping with the well-mixed model for zone air, any air that enters directly to a space through **infiltration or ventilation** q_{IV} is immediately mixed with the zone's air. The amount of infiltration or natural ventilation air is uncertain. Sometimes it is related to the indoor/outdoor temperature difference and wind speed; however it is determined, it is added directly to the air heat balance.

Conditioned air that enters the zone from the HVAC system and provides q_{sys} is also mixed directly with the zone air. For commercial HVAC systems, ventilation air is most often provided using outdoor air as part of this mixed-in conditioned air; ventilation air is thus normally a system load rather than a direct-to-space load. An exception is where infiltration or natural ventilation is used to provide all or part of the ventilation air, as discussed in Chapter 16.

5.3 GENERAL ZONE FOR LOAD CALCULATION

The HB procedure is tailored to a single thermal zone, shown in Figure 7. The definition of a thermal zone depends on how the fixed temperature is controlled. If air circulated through an entire building or an entire floor is uniformly well stirred, the entire building or floor could be considered a thermal zone. On the other hand, if each room has a different control scheme, each room may need to be considered as a separate thermal zone. The framework needs to be flexible enough to accommodate any zone arrangement, but the heat balance aspect of the procedure also requires that a complete zone be described. This zone consists of four walls, a roof or ceiling, a floor, and a "thermal mass surface" (described in the section on Input Required). Each wall and the roof can include a window (or skylight in the case of the roof). This makes a total of 12 surfaces, any of which may have zero area if it is not present in the zone to be modeled.

The heat balance processes for this general zone are formulated for a 24 h steady-periodic condition. The variables are the indoor and outdoor temperatures of the 12 surfaces plus either the HVAC system energy required to maintain a specified air temperature or the air temperature, if system capacity is specified. This makes a total of 25 × 24 = 600 variables. Although it is possible to set up the problem for a simultaneous solution of these variables, the relatively weak coupling of the problem from one hour to the next allows a double iterative approach. One iteration is through all the surfaces in each hour, and the other is through the 24 h of a day. This procedure automatically reconciles nonlinear aspects of surface radiative exchange and other heat flux terms.

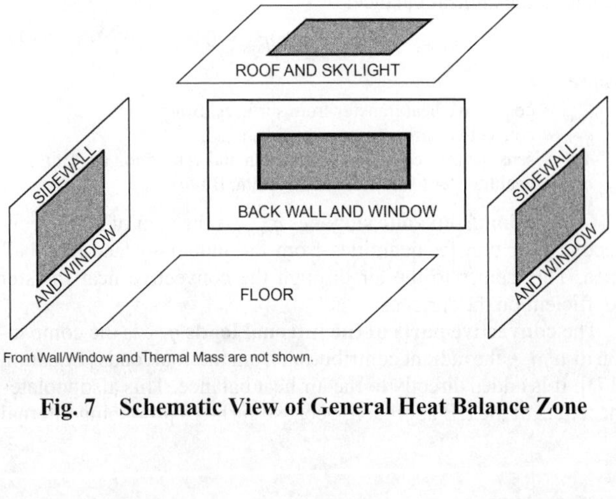

Fig. 7 Schematic View of General Heat Balance Zone

5.4 MATHEMATICAL DESCRIPTION

Conduction Process

Because it links the outdoor and indoor heat balances, the wall conduction process regulates the cooling load's time dependence. For the HB procedure presented here, wall conduction is formulated using **conduction transfer functions (CTFs)**, which relate conductive heat fluxes to current and past surface temperatures and past heat fluxes. The general form for the indoor heat flux is

$$q''_{ki}(t) = -Z_o T_{si,\theta} - \sum_{j=1}^{nz} Z_j T_{si,\theta-j\delta} + Y_o T_{so,\theta} + \sum_{j=1}^{nz} Y_j T_{so,\theta-j\delta} + \sum_{j=1}^{nq} \Phi_j q''_{ki,\theta-j\delta} \qquad (22)$$

For outdoor heat flux, the form is

$$q''_{ko}(t) = -Y_o T_{si,\theta} - \sum_{j=1}^{nz} Y_j T_{si,\theta-j\delta} + X_o T_{so,\theta} + \sum_{j=1}^{nz} X_j T_{so,\theta-j\delta} + \sum_{j=1}^{nq} \Phi_j q''_{ko,\theta-j\delta} \qquad (23)$$

where

X_j = outdoor CTF, $j = 0,1,\ldots nz$
Y_j = cross CTF, $j = 0,1,\ldots nz$
Z_j = indoor CTF, $j = 0,1,\ldots nz$
Φ_j = flux CTF, $j = 1,2,\ldots nq$
θ = time
δ = time step
T_{si} = indoor-face temperature, °F
T_{so} = outdoor-face temperature, °F
q''_{ki} = conductive heat flux on indoor face, Btu/h·ft²
q''_{ko} = conductive heat flux on outdoor face, Btu/h·ft²

The subscript following the comma indicates the time period for the quantity in terms of time step δ. Also, the first terms in the series have been separated from the rest to facilitate solving for the current temperature in the solution scheme.

The two summation limits *nz* and *nq* depend on wall construction and also somewhat on the scheme used for calculating the CTFs. If $nq = 0$, the CTFs are generally referred to as **response factors**, but then theoretically *nz* is infinite. Values for *nz* and *nq* are generally set to minimize the amount of computation. A development of CTFs can be found in Hittle and Pedersen (1981).

Heat Balance Equations

The primary variables in the heat balance for the general zone are the 12 indoor face temperatures and the 12 outdoor face temperatures at each of the 24 h, assigning *i* as the surface index and *j* as the hour index, or, in the case of CTFs, the sequence index. Thus, the primary variables are

$T_{so_{i,j}}$ = outdoor face temperature, $i = 1,2,\ldots,12$; $j = 1,2,\ldots, 24$

$T_{si_{i,j}}$ = indoor face temperature, $i = 1,2,\ldots,12$; $j = 1,2,\ldots, 24$

In addition, q_{sys_j} = cooling load, $j = 1,2,\ldots, 24$.

Equations (16) and (23) are combined and solved for T_{so} to produce 12 equations applicable in each time step:

$$T_{so_{i,j}} = \left(\sum_{k=1}^{nz} T_{si_{i,j-k}} Y_{i,k} - \sum_{k=1}^{nz} T_{so_{i,j-k}} Z_{i,k} - \sum_{k=1}^{nq} \Phi_{i,k} q''_{ko_{i,j-k}} \right. \tag{24}$$

$$\left. + q''_{\alpha sol_{i,j}} + q''_{LWR_{i,j}} + T_{si_{i,j}} Y_{i,0} + T_{o_j} h_{co_{i,j}} \right) / (Z_{i,0} + h_{co_{i,j}})$$

where

T_o = outdoor air temperature

h_{co} = outdoor convection coefficient, introduced by using $q''_{conv} = h_{co}(T_o - T_{so})$

Equation (24) shows the need to separate $Z_{i,0}$, because the contribution of current surface temperature to conductive flux can be collected with the other terms involving that temperature.

Equations (17) and (22) are combined and solved for T_{si} to produce the next 12 equations:

$$T_{si_{i,j}} = \left(T_{si_{i,j}} Y_{i,0} + \sum_{k-1}^{nz} T_{so_{i,j-k}} Y_{i,k} \right.$$

$$- \sum_{k=1}^{nz} T_{si_{i,j-k}} Z_{i,k} + \sum_{k=1}^{nq} \Phi_{i,k} q''_{ki_{i,j-k}} + T_{a_j} h_{ci_j} + q''_{LWS} \tag{25}$$

$$\left. + q''_{LWX} + q''_{SW} + q''_{sol} e \right) / (Z_{i,0} + h_{ci_{i,j}})$$

where

T_a = zone air temperature

h_{ci} = convective heat transfer coefficient indoors, obtained from $q''_{conv} = h_{ci}(T_a - T_{si})$

Note that in Equations (24) and (25), the opposite surface temperature at the current time appears on the right-hand side. The two equations could be solved simultaneously to eliminate those variables. Depending on the order of updating the other terms in the equations, this can have a beneficial effect on solution stability.

The remaining equation comes from the air heat balance, Equation (21). This provides the cooling load q_{sys} at each time step:

$$q_{sys_j} = \sum_{i=1}^{12} A_i h_{ci}(T_{si_{i,j}} - T_{a_j}) + q_{CE} + q_{IV} \tag{26}$$

In Equation (26), the convective heat transfer term is expanded to show the interconnection between the surface temperatures and the cooling load.

Overall HB Iterative Solution

The iterative HB procedure consists of a series of initial calculations that proceed sequentially, followed by a double iteration loop, as shown in the following steps:

1. Initialize areas, properties, and face temperatures for all surfaces, 24 h.
2. Calculate incident and transmitted solar flux for all surfaces and hours.
3. Distribute transmitted solar energy to all indoor faces, 24 h.
4. Calculate internal load quantities for all 24 h.
5. Distribute LW, SW, and convective energy from internal loads to all surfaces for all hours.
6. Calculate infiltration and direct-to-space ventilation loads for all hours.
7. Iterate the heat balance according to the following scheme:

```
For Day = 1 to Maxdays
    For j = 1 to 24                {hours in the day}
        For SurfaceIter = 1 to MaxIter
            For i = 1 to 12            {The twelve zone surfaces}
                Evaluate Equations (33) and (34)
            Next i
        Next SurfaceIter
        Evaluate Equation (35)
    Next j
If not converged, Next Day
```

8. Display results.

Generally, four or six surface iterations are sufficient to provide convergence. The convergence check on the day iteration should be based on the difference between the indoor and outdoor conductive heat flux terms q_k. A limit, such as requiring the difference between all indoor and outdoor flux terms to be less than 1% of either flux, works well.

5.5 INPUT REQUIRED

Previous methods for calculating cooling loads attempted to simplify the procedure by precalculating representative cases and grouping the results with various correlating parameters. This generally tended to reduce the amount of information required to apply the procedure. With heat balance, no precalculations are made, so the procedure requires a fairly complete description of the zone.

Global Information. Because the procedure incorporates a solar calculation, some global information is required, including latitude, longitude, time zone, month, day of month, directional orientation of the zone, and zone height (floor to floor). Additionally, to take full advantage of the flexibility of the method to incorporate, for example, variable outdoor heat transfer coefficients, things such as wind speed, wind direction, and terrain roughness may be specified. Normally, these variables and others default to some reasonable set of values, but the flexibility remains.

Wall Information (Each Wall). Because the walls are involved in three of the fundamental processes (external and internal heat balance and wall conduction), each wall of the zone requires a fairly large set of variables. They include

- Facing angle with respect to solar exposure
- Tilt (degrees from horizontal)
- Area
- Solar absorptivity outdoors
- Long-wave emissivity outdoors
- Short-wave absorptivity indoors
- Long-wave emissivity indoors
- Exterior boundary temperature condition (solar versus nonsolar)
- External roughness
- Layer-by-layer construction information

Again, some of these parameters can be defaulted, but they are changeable, and they indicate the more fundamental character of the HB method because they are related to true heat transfer processes.

Window Information (Each Window). The situation for windows is similar to that for walls, but the windows require some additional information because of their role in the solar load. Necessary parameters include

- Area
- Normal solar transmissivity
- Normal SHGC
- Normal total absorptivity
- Long-wave emissivity outdoors
- Long-wave emissivity indoor
- Surface-to-surface thermal conductance

- Reveal (for solar shading)
- Overhang width (for solar shading)
- Distance from overhang to window (for solar shading)

Roof and Floor Details. The roof and floor surfaces are specified similarly to walls. The main difference is that the ground outdoor boundary condition will probably be specified more often for a floor.

Thermal Mass Surface Details. An "extra" surface, called a thermal mass surface, can serve several functions. It is included in radiant heat exchange with the other surfaces in the space but is only exposed to the indoor air convective boundary condition. As an example, this surface would be used to account for movable partitions in a space. Partition construction is specified layer by layer, similar to specification for walls, and those layers store and release heat by the same conduction mechanism as walls. As a general definition, the extra thermal mass surface should be sized to represent all surfaces in the space that are exposed to the air mass, except the walls, roof, floor, and windows. In the formulation, both sides of the thermal mass participate in the exchange.

Internal Heat Gain Details. The space can be subjected to several internal heat sources: people, lights, electrical equipment, and infiltration. Infiltration energy is assumed to go immediately into the air heat balance, so it is the least complicated of the heat gains. For the others, several parameters must be specified. These include the following fractions:

- Sensible heat gain
- Latent heat gain
- Short-wave radiation
- Long-wave radiation
- Energy that enters the air immediately as convection
- Activity level of people
- Lighting heat gain that goes directly to the return air

Radiant Distribution Functions. As mentioned previously, the generally accepted assumptions for the HB method include specifying the distribution of radiant energy from several sources to surfaces that enclose the space. This requires a distribution function that specifies the fraction of total radiant input absorbed by each surface. The types of radiation that require distribution functions are

- Long-wave, from equipment and lights
- Short-wave, from lights
- Transmitted solar

Other Required Information. Additional flexibility is included in the model so that results of research can be incorporated easily. This includes the capability to specify such things as

- Heat transfer coefficients/convection models
- Solar coefficients
- Sky models

The amount of input information required may seem extensive, but many parameters can be set to default values in most routine applications. However, all parameters listed can be changed when necessary to fit unusual circumstances or when additional information is obtained.

6. RADIANT TIME SERIES (RTS) METHOD

The radiant time series (RTS) method is a simplified method for performing design cooling load calculations that is derived from the heat balance (HB) method. It effectively replaces all other simplified (non-heat-balance) methods, such as the transfer function method (TFM), the cooling load temperature difference/cooling load factor (CLTD/CLF) method, and the total equivalent temperature difference/time averaging (TETD/TA) method.

This method was developed to offer an approach that is rigorous, yet does not require iterative calculations, and that quantifies each component's contribution to the total cooling load. In addition, it is desirable for the user to be able to inspect and compare the coefficients for different construction and zone types in a form showing their relative effect on the result. These characteristics of the RTS method make it easier to apply engineering judgment during cooling load calculation.

The RTS method is suitable for peak design load calculations, but it should not be used for annual energy simulations because of its inherent limiting assumptions. Although simple in concept, RTS involves too many calculations for practical use as a manual method, although it can easily be implemented in a simple computerized spreadsheet, as shown in the examples. For a manual cooling load calculation method, refer to the CLTD/CLF method in Chapter 28 of the 1997 *ASHRAE Handbook—Fundamentals*.

6.1 ASSUMPTIONS AND PRINCIPLES

Design cooling loads are based on the assumption of **steady-periodic conditions** (i.e., the design day's weather, occupancy, and heat gain conditions are identical to those for preceding days such that the loads repeat on an identical 24 h cyclical basis). Thus, the heat gain for a particular component at a particular hour is the same as 24 h prior, which is the same as 48 h prior, etc. This assumption is the basis for the RTS derivation from the HB method.

Cooling load calculations must address two time-delay effects inherent in building heat transfer processes:

- Delay of conductive heat gain through opaque massive exterior surfaces (walls, roofs, or floors)
- Delay of radiative heat gain conversion to cooling loads.

Exterior walls and roofs conduct heat because of temperature differences between outdoor and indoor air. In addition, solar energy on exterior surfaces is absorbed, then transferred by conduction to the building interior. Because of the mass and thermal capacity of the wall or roof construction materials, there is a substantial time delay in heat input at the exterior surface becoming heat gain at the interior surface.

As described in the section on Cooling Load Principles, most heat sources transfer energy to a room by a combination of convection and radiation. The convective part of heat gain immediately becomes cooling load. The radiative part must first be absorbed by the finishes and mass of the interior room surfaces, and becomes cooling load only when it is later transferred by convection from those surfaces to the room air. Thus, radiant heat gains become cooling loads over a delayed period of time.

6.2 OVERVIEW

Figure 8 gives an overview of the RTS method. When calculating solar radiation, transmitted solar heat gain through windows, sol-air temperature, and infiltration, RTS is exactly the same as previous simplified methods (TFM and TETD/TA). Important areas that differ from previous simplified methods include

- Computation of conductive heat gain
- Splitting of all heat gains into radiant and convective portions
- Conversion of radiant heat gains into cooling loads

The RTS method accounts for both conduction time delay and radiant time delay effects by multiplying hourly heat gains by 24 h time series. The time series multiplication, in effect, distributes heat gains over time. Series coefficients, which are called **radiant time factors** and **conduction time factors**, are derived using the HB method. Radiant time factors reflect the percentage of an earlier

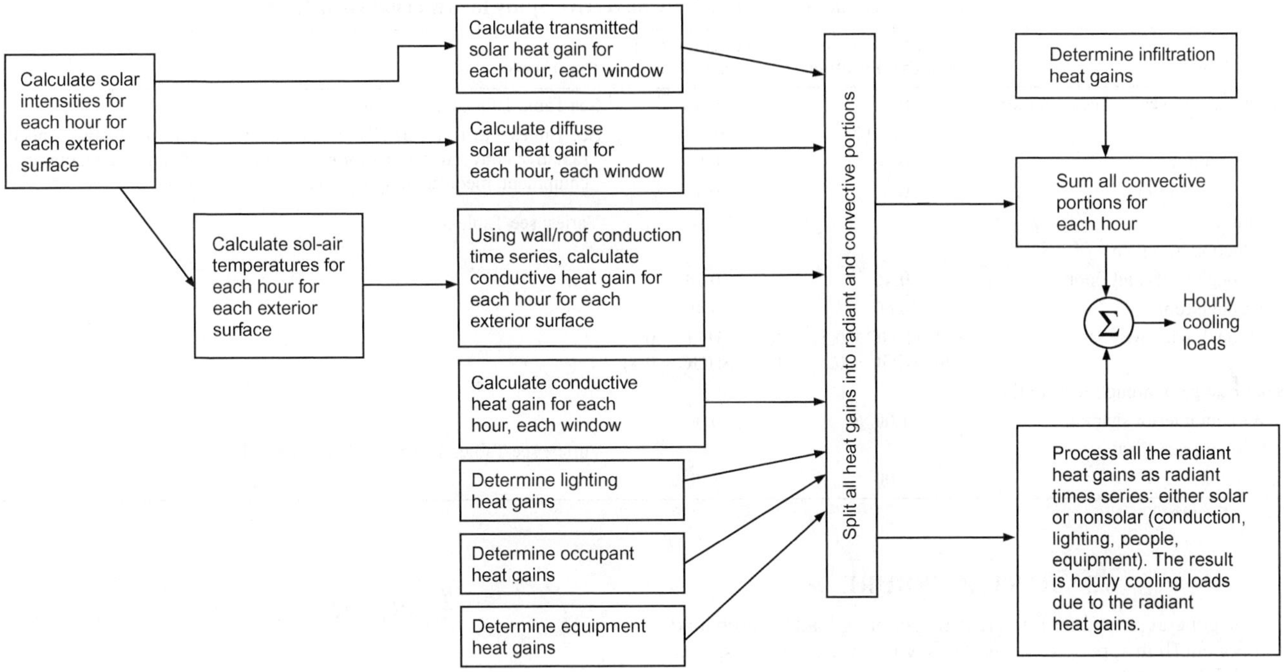

Fig. 8 Overview of Radiant Time Series Method

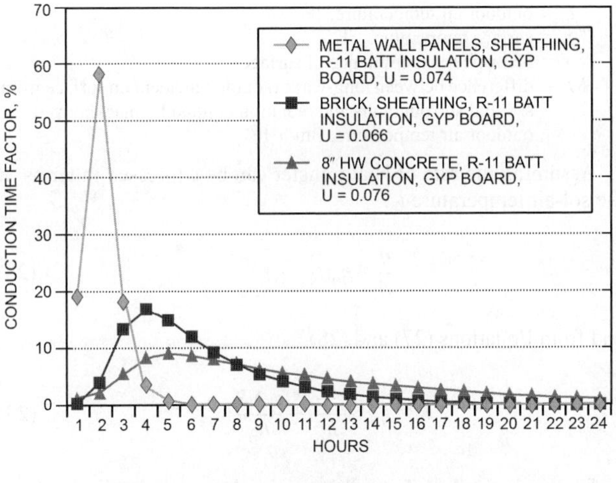

Fig. 9 CTS for Light to Heavy Walls

radiant heat gain that becomes cooling load during the current hour. Likewise, conduction time factors reflect the percentage of an earlier heat gain at the exterior of a wall or roof that becomes heat gain indoors during the current hour. By definition, each radiant or conduction time series must total 100%.

These series can be used to easily compare the time-delay effect of one construction versus another. This ability to compare choices is of particular benefit during design, when all construction details may not have been decided. Comparison can show the magnitude of difference between the choices, allowing the engineer to apply judgment and make more informed assumptions in estimating the load.

Figure 9 shows conduction time series (CTS) values for three walls with similar U-factors but with light to heavy construction. Figure 10 shows CTS for three walls with similar construction but with different amounts of insulation, thus with significantly different U-factors. Figure 11 shows RTS values for zones varying from light to heavy construction.

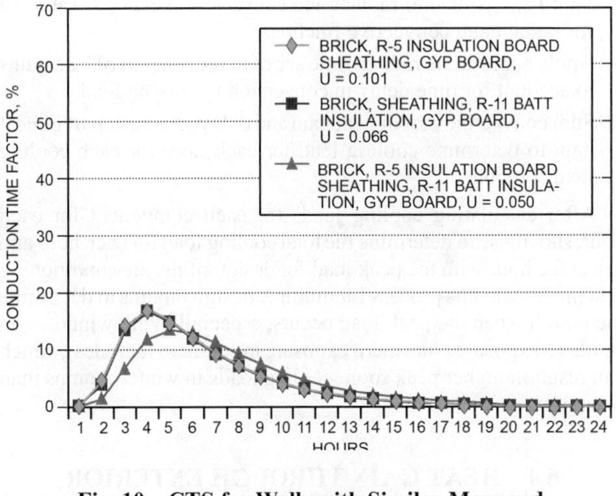

Fig. 10 CTS for Walls with Similar Mass and Increasing Insulation

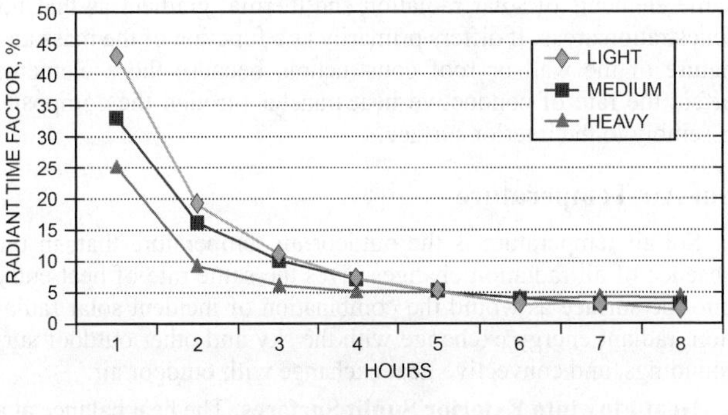

Fig. 11 RTS for Light to Heavy Construction

Table 14 Recommended Radiative/Convective Splits for Internal Heat Gains

Heat Gain Type	Recommended Radiative Fraction	Recommended Convective Fraction	Comments
Occupants, typical office conditions	0.60	0.40	See Table 1 for other conditions.
Equipment	0.1 to 0.8	0.9 to 0.2	See Tables 6 to 12 for details of equipment heat gain and recommended radiative/convective splits for motors, cooking appliances, laboratory equipment, medical equipment, office equipment, etc.
Office, with fan	0.10	0.90	
Without fan	0.30	0.70	
Lighting			Varies; see Table 3.
Conduction heat gain			
Through walls and floors	0.46	0.54	
Through roof	0.60	0.40	
Through windows	0.33 (SHGC > 0.5) 0.46 (SHGC < 0.5)	0.67 (SHGC > 0.5) 0.54 (SHGC < 0.5)	
Solar heat gain through fenestration			
Without interior shading	1.00	0.00	
With interior shading			Varies; see Tables 14A to 14G in Chapter 15.
Infiltration	0.00	1.00	

Source: Nigusse (2007).

6.3 RTS PROCEDURE

The general procedure for calculating cooling load for each load component (lights, people, walls, roofs, windows, appliances, etc.) with RTS is as follows:

1. Calculate 24 h profile of component heat gains for design day (for conduction, first account for conduction time delay by applying conduction time series).
2. Split heat gains into radiant and convective parts (see Table 14 for radiant and convective fractions).
3. Apply appropriate radiant time series to radiant part of heat gains to account for time delay in conversion to cooling load.
4. Sum convective part of heat gain and delayed radiant part of heat gain to determine cooling load for each hour for each cooling load component.

After calculating cooling loads for each component for each hour, sum those to determine the total cooling load for each hour and select the hour with the peak load for design of the air-conditioning system. Repeat this process for multiple design months to determine the month when the peak load occurs, especially with windows on southern exposures (northern exposure in southern latitudes), which can result in higher peak room cooling loads in winter months than in summer.

6.4 HEAT GAIN THROUGH EXTERIOR SURFACES

Heat gain through exterior opaque surfaces is derived from the same elements of solar radiation and thermal gradient as that for fenestration areas. It differs primarily as a function of the mass and nature of the wall or roof construction, because those elements affect the rate of conductive heat transfer through the composite assembly to the interior surface.

Sol-Air Temperature

Sol-air temperature is the outdoor air temperature that, in the absence of all radiation changes gives the same rate of heat entry into the surface as would the combination of incident solar radiation, radiant energy exchange with the sky and other outdoor surroundings, and convective heat exchange with outdoor air.

Heat Flux into Exterior Sunlit Surfaces. The heat balance at a sunlit surface gives the heat flux into the surface q/A as

$$\frac{q}{A} = \alpha E_t + h_o(t_o - t_s) - \varepsilon \Delta R \tag{27}$$

where

α = absorptance of surface for solar radiation
E_t = total solar radiation incident on surface, Btu/h·ft²
h_o = coefficient of heat transfer by long-wave radiation and convection at outer surface, Btu/h·ft²·°F
t_o = outdoor air temperature, °F
t_s = surface temperature, °F
ε = hemispherical emittance of surface
ΔR = difference between long-wave radiation incident on surface from sky and surroundings and radiation emitted by blackbody at outdoor air temperature, Btu/h·ft²

Assuming the rate of heat transfer can be expressed in terms of the sol-air temperature t_e,

$$\frac{q}{A} = h_o(t_e - t_s) \tag{28}$$

and from Equations (27) and (28),

$$t_e = t_o + \frac{\alpha E_t}{h_o} - \frac{\varepsilon \Delta R}{h_o} \tag{29}$$

For **horizontal surfaces** that receive long-wave radiation from the sky only, an appropriate value of ΔR is about 20 Btu/h·ft², so that if $\varepsilon = 1$ and $h_o = 3.0$ Btu/h·ft²·°F, the long-wave correction term is about 7°F (Bliss 1961).

Because **vertical surfaces** receive long-wave radiation from the ground and surrounding buildings as well as from the sky, accurate ΔR values are difficult to determine. When solar radiation intensity is high, surfaces of terrestrial objects usually have a higher temperature than the outdoor air; thus, their long-wave radiation compensates to some extent for the sky's low emittance. Therefore, it is common practice to assume $\varepsilon \Delta R = 0$ for vertical surfaces.

Tabulated Temperature Values. The sol-air temperatures in Example Cooling and Heating Load Calculations section have been calculated based on $\varepsilon \Delta R/h_o$ values of 7°F for horizontal surfaces and 0°F for vertical surfaces; total solar intensity values used for the calculations were calculated using equations in Chapter 14.

Surface Colors. Sol-air temperature values are given in the Example Cooling and Heating Load Calculations section for two values of the parameter α/h_o; the value of 0.15 is appropriate for a

Table 15 Solar Absorptance Values of Various Surfaces

Surface	Absorptance
Brick, red (Purdue) [a]	0.63
Paint	
Red[b]	0.63
Black, matte[b]	0.94
Sandstone[b]	0.50
White acrylic[a]	0.26
Sheet metal, galvanized	
New[a]	0.65
Weathered[a]	0.80
Shingles	
Gray[b]	0.82
Brown[b]	0.91
Black[b]	0.97
White[b]	0.75
Concrete[a,c]	0.60 to 0.83

[a]Incropera and DeWitt (1990). [b]Parker et al. (2000). [c]Miller (1971).

light-colored surface, whereas 0.30 represents the usual maximum value for this parameter (i.e., for a dark-colored surface or any surface for which the permanent lightness cannot reliably be anticipated). Solar absorptance values of various surfaces are included in Table 15.

This procedure was used to calculate the sol-air temperatures included in the Examples section. Because of the tedious solar angle and intensity calculations, using a simple computer spreadsheet or other software for these calculations can reduce the effort involved.

Calculating Conductive Heat Gain Using Conduction Time Series

In the RTS method, conduction through exterior walls and roofs is calculated using CTS values. Wall and roof conductive heat input at the exterior is defined by the familiar conduction equation as

$$q_{i,\theta\text{-}n} = UA(t_{e,\theta\text{-}n} - t_{rc}) \quad (30)$$

where

$q_{i,\theta-n}$ = conductive heat input for surface n hours ago, Btu/h
U = overall heat transfer coefficient for surface, Btu/h·ft²·°F
A = surface area, ft²
$t_{e,\theta-n}$ = sol-air temperature n hours ago, °F
t_{rc} = presumed constant room air temperature, °F

Conductive heat gain through walls or roofs can be calculated using conductive heat inputs for the current hours and past 23 h and conduction time series:

$$q_\theta = c_0 q_{i,\theta} + c_1 q_{i,\theta\text{-}1} + c_2 q_{i,\theta\text{-}2} + c_3 q_{i,\theta\text{-}3} + \cdots + c_{23} q_{i,\theta\text{-}23} \quad (31)$$

where

q_θ = hourly conductive heat gain for surface, Btu/h
$q_{i,\theta}$ = heat input for current hour
$q_{i,\theta-n}$ = heat input n hours ago
c_0, c_1, etc.=conduction time factors

Conduction time factors for representative wall and roof types are included in Tables 16 and 17. Those values were derived by first calculating conduction transfer functions for each example wall and roof construction. Assuming steady-periodic heat input conditions for design load calculations allows conduction transfer functions to be reformulated into periodic response factors, as demonstrated by Spitler and Fisher (1999a). The periodic response factors were further simplified by dividing the 24 periodic response factors by the respective overall wall or roof U-factor to form the conduction time series. The conduction time factors can then be used in Equation (31) and provide a way to compare time delay characteristics between different wall and roof constructions. Construction material data used in the calculations for walls and roofs in Tables 16 and 17 are listed in Table 18.

Heat gains calculated for walls or roofs using periodic response factors (and thus CTS) are identical to those calculated using conduction transfer functions for the steady periodic conditions assumed in design cooling load calculations. The methodology for calculating periodic response factors from conduction transfer functions was originally developed as part of ASHRAE research project RP-875 (Spitler and Fisher 1999b; Spitler et al. 1997). For walls and roofs that are not reasonably close to the representative constructions in Tables 16 and 17, CTS coefficients may be computed with a computer program such as that described by Iu and Fisher (2004). For walls and roofs with thermal bridges, the procedure described by Karambakkam et al. (2005) may be used to determine an equivalent wall construction, which can then be used as the basis for finding the CTS coefficients. When considering the level of detail needed to make an adequate approximation, remember that, for buildings with windows and internal heat gains, the conduction heat gains make up a relatively small part of the cooling load. For heating load calculations, the conduction heat loss may be more significant.

The tedious calculations involved make a simple computer spreadsheet or other computer software a useful labor saver.

6.5 HEAT GAIN THROUGH INTERIOR SURFACES

Whenever a conditioned space is adjacent to a space with a different temperature, heat transfer through the separating physical section must be considered. The heat transfer rate is given by

$$q = UA(t_b - t_i) \quad (32)$$

where

q = heat transfer rate, Btu/h
U = coefficient of overall heat transfer between adjacent and conditioned space, Btu/h·ft²·°F
A = area of separating section concerned, ft²
t_b = average air temperature in adjacent space, °F
t_i = air temperature in conditioned space, °F

U-values can be obtained from Chapter 27. Temperature t_b may differ greatly from t_i. The temperature in a kitchen or boiler room, for example, may be as much as 15 to 50°F above the outdoor air temperature. Actual temperatures in adjoining spaces should be measured, when possible. Where nothing is known except that the adjacent space is of conventional construction, contains no heat sources, and itself receives no significant solar heat gain, $t_b - t_i$ may be considered the difference between the outdoor air and conditioned space design dry-bulb temperatures minus 5°F. In some cases, air temperature in the adjacent space corresponds to the outdoor air temperature or higher.

Floors

For floors directly in contact with the ground or over an underground basement that is neither ventilated nor conditioned, sensible heat transfer may be neglected for cooling load estimates because usually there is a heat loss rather than a gain. An exception is in hot climates (i.e., where average outdoor air temperature exceeds indoor design condition), where the positive soil-to-indoor temperature difference causes sensible heat gains (Rock 2005). In many climates and for various temperatures and local soil conditions, moisture transport up through slabs-on-grade and basement floors is also significant, and contributes to the latent heat portion of the cooling load.

6.6 CALCULATING COOLING LOAD

The **instantaneous cooling load** is the rate at which heat energy is convected to the zone air at a given point in time. Computation of cooling load is complicated by the radiant exchange between

Table 16 Wall Conduction Time Series (CTS)

	Curtain Walls						Stud Walls			
	Spandrel Glass, R-10 Insulation Board, Gyp. Board	Spandrel Glass, R-20 Insulation Board, Gyp. Board	Metal Wall Panel, R-10 Insulation Board, Gyp. Board	Metal Wall Panel, R-20 Insulation Board, Gyp. Board	1 in. Stone, R-10 Insulation Board, Gyp. Board	1 in. Stone, R-20 Insulation Board, Gyp. Board	Metal Wall Panel, Sheathing, R-11 Batt Insulation, Gyp. Board	Metal Wall Panel, Sheathing, R-22 Batt Insulation, Gyp. Board	1 in. Stone, Sheathing, R-11 Batt Insulation, Gyp. Board	1 in. Stone, Sheathing, R-22 Batt Insulation, Gyp. Board
Wall Number	**1**	**2**	**3**	**4**	**5**	**6**	**7**	**8**	**9**	**10**
U, Btu/h·ft²·°F	**0.076**	**0.043**	**0.076**	**0.043**	**0.076**	**0.043**	**0.074**	**0.041**	**0.073**	**0.041**
Total R	**13.2**	**23.2**	**13.2**	**23.1**	**13.2**	**23.2**	**13.6**	**24.6**	**13.6**	**24.7**
Hour	**Conduction Time Factors, %**						**Conduction Time Factors, %**			
0	18.0	3.4	25.0	5.4	8.3	1.4	19.3	5.6	6.5	1.6
1	57.1	35.9	56.1	40.9	44.0	22.3	57.5	45.0	41.1	24.9
2	19.8	36.8	15.2	33.8	31.2	35.9	18.7	34.4	32.7	37.3
3	4.0	15.9	3.0	13.4	11.6	23.2	3.7	11.1	13.3	21.9
4	0.8	5.5	0.6	4.5	3.5	10.7	0.7	2.9	4.5	9.2
5	0.2	1.8	0.1	1.4	1.0	4.2	0.1	0.7	1.4	3.4
6	0.0	0.6	0.0	0.4	0.3	1.5	0.0	0.2	0.4	1.2
7	0.0	0.2	0.0	0.1	0.1	0.5	0.0	0.0	0.1	0.4
8	0.0	0.1	0.0	0.0	0.0	0.2	0.0	0.0	0.0	0.1
9	0.0	0.0	0.0	0.0	0.0	0.1	0.0	0.0	0.0	0.0
10	0.0	0.0	0.0	0.0	0.0	0.0	0.0	0.0	0.0	0.0
11	0.0	0.0	0.0	0.0	0.0	0.0	0.0	0.0	0.0	0.0
12	0.0	0.0	0.0	0.0	0.0	0.0	0.0	0.0	0.0	0.0
13	0.0	0.0	0.0	0.0	0.0	0.0	0.0	0.0	0.0	0.0
14	0.0	0.0	0.0	0.0	0.0	0.0	0.0	0.0	0.0	0.0
15	0.0	0.0	0.0	0.0	0.0	0.0	0.0	0.0	0.0	0.0
16	0.0	0.0	0.0	0.0	0.0	0.0	0.0	0.0	0.0	0.0
17	0.0	0.0	0.0	0.0	0.0	0.0	0.0	0.0	0.0	0.0
18	0.0	0.0	0.0	0.0	0.0	0.0	0.0	0.0	0.0	0.0
19	0.0	0.0	0.0	0.0	0.0	0.0	0.0	0.0	0.0	0.0
20	0.0	0.0	0.0	0.0	0.0	0.0	0.0	0.0	0.0	0.0
21	0.0	0.0	0.0	0.0	0.0	0.0	0.0	0.0	0.0	0.0
22	0.0	0.0	0.0	0.0	0.0	0.0	0.0	0.0	0.0	0.0
23	0.0	0.0	0.0	0.0	0.0	0.0	0.0	0.0	0.0	0.0
Total Percentage	100	100	100	100	100	100	100	100	100	100
Layer ID from outdoors to indoors (See Table 18)	F01	F01	F01	F01	F01	F01	F01	F01	F01	F01
	F09	F09	F08	F08	F10	F10	F08	F08	F10	F10
	F04	F04	F04	F04	F04	F04	G03	G03	G03	G03
	I02	I02	I02	I02	I02	I02	I04	I04	I04	I04
	F04	I02	F04	I02	F04	I02	G01	I04	G01	I04
	G01	F04	G01	F04	I02	F04	F02	G01	F02	G01
	F02	G01	F02	G01	F02	G01	0	F02	0	F02
	0	F02	0	F02	0	F02	0	0	0	0
	0	0	0	0	0	0	0	0	0	0
	0	0	0	0	0	0	0	0	0	0

surfaces, furniture, partitions, and other mass in the zone. Most heat gain sources transfer energy by both convection and radiation. Radiative heat transfer introduces a time dependency to the process that is not easily quantified. Radiation is absorbed by thermal masses in the zone and then later transferred by convection into the space. This process creates a time lag and dampening effect. The convective portion, on the other hand, is assumed to immediately become cooling load in the hour in which that heat gain occurs.

Heat balance procedures calculate the radiant exchange between surfaces based on their surface temperatures and emissivities, but they typically rely on estimated "radiative/convective splits" to determine the contribution of internal loads, including people, lighting, appliances, and equipment, to the radiant exchange. RTS further simplifies the HB procedure by also relying on an estimated radiative/convective split of wall and roof conductive heat gain instead of simultaneously solving for the instantaneous convective and radiative heat transfer from each surface, as in the HB procedure.

Thus, the cooling load for each load component (lights, people, walls, roofs, windows, appliances, etc.) for a particular hour is the sum of the convective portion of the heat gain for that hour plus the time-delayed portion of radiant heat gains for that hour and the previous 23 h. Table 14 contains recommendations for splitting each of the heat gain components into convective and radiant portions.

RTS converts the radiant portion of hourly heat gains to hourly cooling loads using radiant time factors, the coefficients of the

Table 16 Wall Conduction Time Series (CTS) (*Continued*)

	Stud Walls				EIFS					
	Wood Siding, Sheathing, R-11 Batt Insulation, 1/2 in. Wood	Wood Siding, Sheathing, R-22 Batt Insulation, 1/2 in. Wood	1 in. Stucco, Sheathing, R-11 Batt Insulation, Gyp. Board	1 in. Stucco, Sheathing, R-22 Batt Insulation, Gyp. Board	EIFS, R-5 Insulation Board, Sheathing, Gyp. Board	EIFS, R-10 Insulation Board, Sheathing, Gyp. Board	EIFS, R-5 Insulation Board, Sheathing, R-11 Batt Insulation, Gyp. Board	EIFS, R-5 Insulation Board, Sheathing, R-22 Batt Insulation, Gyp. Board	EIFS, R-5 Insulation Board, Sheathing, 8 in. LW CMU, Gyp. Board	EIFS, R-10 Insulation Board, Sheathing, 8 in. LW CMU, Gyp. Board
Wall Number	**11**	**12**	**13**	**14**	**15**	**16**	**17**	**18**	**19**	**20**
***U*, Btu/h·ft²·°F**	**0.071**	**0.040**	**0.073**	**0.076**	**0.040**	**0.118**	**0.054**	**0.034**	**0.093**	**0.063**
Total *R*	**14.1**	**25.2**	**13.8**	**24.8**	**8.5**	**13.4**	**18.6**	**29.7**	**10.8**	**15.8**
Hour	**Conduction Time Factors, %**				**Conduction Time Factors, %**					
0	6.4	1.5	5.7	1.3	11.9	6.0	2.6	0.5	1.0	1.3
1	40.7	24.3	40.4	23.8	48.8	40.7	25.2	11.9	2.0	1.8
2	32.4	36.3	33.6	37.6	26.3	31.6	30.7	25.9	5.8	4.5
3	13.5	21.9	13.7	22.5	8.8	13.2	19.5	22.9	8.7	7.3
4	4.7	9.8	4.6	9.6	2.8	5.1	10.6	15.4	9.3	8.3
5	1.6	3.9	1.4	3.5	0.9	2.0	5.5	9.5	8.9	8.2
6	0.5	1.5	0.4	1.2	0.3	0.8	2.9	5.7	8.1	7.7
7	0.2	0.5	0.1	0.4	0.1	0.3	1.5	3.4	7.2	7.0
8	0.0	0.2	0.0	0.1	0.0	0.1	0.8	2.0	6.5	6.4
9	0.0	0.1	0.0	0.0	0.0	0.0	0.4	1.2	5.7	5.8
10	0.0	0.0	0.0	0.0	0.0	0.0	0.2	0.7	5.1	5.3
11	0.0	0.0	0.0	0.0	0.0	0.0	0.1	0.4	4.5	4.8
12	0.0	0.0	0.0	0.0	0.0	0.0	0.1	0.2	4.0	4.3
13	0.0	0.0	0.0	0.0	0.0	0.0	0.0	0.1	3.6	3.9
14	0.0	0.0	0.0	0.0	0.0	0.0	0.0	0.1	3.2	3.5
15	0.0	0.0	0.0	0.0	0.0	0.0	0.0	0.1	2.8	3.2
16	0.0	0.0	0.0	0.0	0.0	0.0	0.0	0.0	2.5	2.9
17	0.0	0.0	0.0	0.0	0.0	0.0	0.0	0.0	2.2	2.6
18	0.0	0.0	0.0	0.0	0.0	0.0	0.0	0.0	2.0	2.4
19	0.0	0.0	0.0	0.0	0.0	0.0	0.0	0.0	1.8	2.1
20	0.0	0.0	0.0	0.0	0.0	0.0	0.0	0.0	1.6	1.9
21	0.0	0.0	0.0	0.0	0.0	0.0	0.0	0.0	1.4	1.8
22	0.0	0.0	0.0	0.0	0.0	0.0	0.0	0.0	1.2	1.6
23	0.0	0.0	0.0	0.0	0.0	0.0	0.0	0.0	1.1	1.4
Total Percentage	100	100	100	100	100	100	100	100	100	100
Layer ID from outdoors to indoors (See Table 18)	F01	F01	F01	F01	F01	F01	F01	F01	F01	F01
	F11	F11	F07	F07	F06	F06	F06	F06	F06	F06
	G02	G02	G03	G03	I01	I01	I01	I01	I01	I01
	I04	I04	I04	I04	G03	I01	G03	G03	G03	I01
	G01	I04	G01	I04	F04	G03	I04	I04	M03	G03
	F02	G01	F02	G01	G01	F04	G01	I04	F04	M03
	0	F02	0	F02	F02	G01	F02	G01	G01	F04
	0	0	0	0	0	F02	0	F02	F02	G01
	0	0	0	0	0	0	0	0	0	F02
	0	0	0	0	0	0	0	0	0	0

radiant time series. Radiant time factors are used to calculate the cooling load for the current hour on the basis of current and past heat gains. The radiant time series for a particular zone gives the time-dependent response of the zone to a single pulse of radiant energy. The series shows the portion of the radiant pulse that is convected to zone air for each hour. Thus, r_0 represents the fraction of the radiant pulse convected to the zone air in the current hour r_1 in the previous hour, and so on. The radiant time series thus generated is used to convert the radiant portion of hourly heat gains to hourly cooling loads according to the following equation:

$$Q_{r,\theta} = r_0 q_{r,\theta} + r_1 q_{r,\theta-1} + r_2 q_{r,\theta-2} + r_3 q_{r,\theta-3} + \cdots + r_{23} q_{r,\theta-23} \quad (33)$$

where

$Q_{r,\theta}$ = radiant cooling load Q_r for current hour θ, Btu/h
$q_{r,\theta}$ = radiant heat gain for current hour, Btu/h
$q_{r,\theta-n}$ = radiant heat gain n hours ago, Btu/h
r_0, r_1, etc. = radiant time factors

The radiant cooling load for the current hour, which is calculated using RTS and Equation (33), is added to the convective portion to determine the total cooling load for that component for that hour.

Radiant time factors are generated by a heat-balance-based procedure. A separate series of radiant time factors is theoretically required for each unique zone and for each unique radiant energy distribution function assumption. For most common design applications, RTS variation depends primarily on the overall massiveness of the construction and the thermal responsiveness of the surfaces the radiant heat gains strike.

Table 16 Wall Conduction Time Series (CTS) (*Continued*)

	Brick Walls								
	Brick, R-5 Insulation Board, Sheathing, Gyp. Board	**Brick, R-10 Insulation Board, Sheathing, Gyp. Board**	**Brick, Sheathing, R-11 Batt Insulation, Gyp. Board**	**Brick, Sheathing, R-22 Batt Insulation, Gyp. Board**	**Brick, R-5 Insulation Board, Sheathing, R-11 Batt Insulation, Gyp. Board**	**Brick, R-5 Insulation Board, Sheathing, R-22 Batt Insulation, Gyp. Board**	**Brick, R-5 Insulation Board, 8 in. LW CMU**	**Brick, R-10 Insulation Board, 8 in. LW CMU**	**Brick, 8 in. LW CMU, R-11 Batt Insulation, Gyp. Board**
Wall Number	**21**	**22**	**23**	**24**	**25**	**26**	**27**	**28**	**29**
***U*, Btu/h·ft²·°F**	**0.101**	**0.067**	**0.066**	**0.038**	**0.050**	**0.028**	**0.103**	**0.068**	**0.061**
Total *R*	**9.9**	**14.9**	**15.1**	**26.1**	**20.1**	**36.1**	**9.7**	**14.7**	**16.4**
Hour	**Conduction Time Factors, %**								
0	0.2	0.1	0.2	0.1	0.1	0.4	0.6	0.8	1.6
1	4.8	3.0	4.1	1.6	1.5	0.5	0.8	0.8	1.5
2	13.9	11.1	13.3	8.5	6.8	2.0	2.6	2.1	1.9
3	16.7	15.5	16.6	14.5	11.7	5.3	5.5	4.5	3.3
4	14.9	15.0	14.8	15.2	13.3	8.2	7.6	6.6	5.0
5	12.0	12.7	11.8	13.1	12.7	9.7	8.7	7.9	6.2
6	9.2	10.1	9.2	10.6	11.1	10.1	9.0	8.4	6.9
7	7.0	7.8	7.1	8.3	9.2	9.6	8.7	8.4	7.1
8	5.3	6.0	5.4	6.5	7.5	8.8	8.2	8.0	7.0
9	4.0	4.6	4.2	5.0	5.9	7.8	7.4	7.4	6.7
10	3.0	3.5	3.2	3.9	4.7	6.8	6.6	6.7	6.3
11	2.3	2.6	2.4	3.0	3.6	5.8	5.8	6.0	5.9
12	1.7	2.0	1.9	2.3	2.8	4.9	5.0	5.3	5.4
13	1.3	1.5	1.4	1.8	2.2	4.1	4.3	4.7	5.0
14	1.0	1.1	1.1	1.4	1.7	3.4	3.7	4.1	4.5
15	0.7	0.9	0.8	1.1	1.3	2.8	3.1	3.5	4.1
16	0.5	0.7	0.6	0.8	1.0	2.3	2.6	3.0	3.7
17	0.4	0.5	0.5	0.6	0.8	1.9	2.2	2.6	3.4
18	0.3	0.4	0.4	0.5	0.6	1.5	1.9	2.2	3.0
19	0.2	0.3	0.3	0.4	0.5	1.2	1.6	1.9	2.7
20	0.2	0.2	0.2	0.3	0.4	1.0	1.3	1.6	2.5
21	0.1	0.2	0.2	0.2	0.3	0.8	1.1	1.4	2.2
22	0.1	0.1	0.1	0.2	0.2	0.6	0.9	1.1	2.0
23	0.1	0.1	0.1	0.1	0.2	0.5	0.7	1.0	1.8
Total Percentage	100	100	100	100	100	100	100	100	100
Layer ID from outdoors to indoors (See Table 18)	F01	F01	F01	F01	F01	F01	F01	F01	F01
	M01	M01	M01	M01	M01	M01	M01	M01	M01
	F04	F04	F04	F04	F04	F04	F04	F04	F04
	I01	I01	G03	G03	I01	I01	I01	I01	M03
	G03	I01	I04	I04	G03	I01	M03	I01	I04
	F04	G03	G01	I04	I04	G03	F02	M03	G01
	G01	F04	F02	G01	G01	I04	0	F02	F02
	F02	G01	0	F02	F02	I04	0	0	0
	0	F02	0	0	0	G01	0	0	0
	0	0	0	0	0	F02	0	0	0

One goal in developing RTS was to provide a simplified method based directly on the HB method; thus, it was deemed desirable to generate RTS coefficients directly from a heat balance. A heat balance computer program was developed to do this: Hbfort, which is included as part of *Cooling and Heating Load Calculation Principles* (Pedersen et al. 1998). The RTS procedure is described by Spitler et al. (1997). The procedure for generating RTS coefficients may be thought of as analogous to the custom weighting factor generation procedure used by DOE 2.1 (Kerrisk et al. 1981; Sowell 1988a, 1988b). In both cases, a zone model is pulsed with a heat gain. With DOE 2.1, the resulting loads are used to estimate the best values of the transfer function method weighting factors to most closely match the load profile. In the procedure described here, a unit periodic heat gain pulse is used to generate loads for a 24 h period. As long as the heat gain pulse is a unit pulse, the resulting loads are equivalent to the RTS coefficients.

Two different radiant time series are used: **solar**, for direct transmitted solar heat gain (radiant energy assumed to be distributed to the floor and furnishings only) and **nonsolar**, for all other types of heat gains (radiant energy assumed to be uniformly distributed on all internal surfaces). Nonsolar RTS apply to radiant heat gains from people, lights, appliances, walls, roofs, and floors. Also, for diffuse solar heat gain and direct solar heat gain from fenestration with indoor shading (blinds, drapes, etc.), the nonsolar RTS should be used. Radiation from those sources is assumed to be more uniformly

Table 16 Wall Conduction Time Series (CTS) (*Continued*)

	Brick Walls								
	Brick, 8 in. LW CMU, R-22 Batt Insulation, Gyp. Board	**Brick, R-5 Insulation Board, 8 in. HW CMU, Gyp. Board**	**Brick, R-10 Insulation Board, 8 in. HW CMU, Gyp. Board**	**Brick, R-5 Insulation Board, Brick**	**Brick, R-10 Insulation Board, Brick**	**Brick, R-5 Insulation Board, 8 in. LW Concrete, Gyp. Board**	**Brick, R-10 Insulation Board, 8 in. LW Concrete, Gyp. Board**	**Brick, R-5 Insulation Board, 12 in. HW Concrete, Gyp. Board**	**Brick, R-10 Insulation Board, 12 in. HW Concrete, Gyp. Board**
Wall Number	**30**	**31**	**32**	**33**	**34**	**35**	**36**	**37**	**38**
***U*, Btu/h·ft²·°F**	**0.036**	**0.111**	**0.071**	**0.124**	**0.077**	**0.091**	**0.062**	**0.097**	**0.062**
Total *R*	**27.4**	**9.0**	**14.0**	**8.1**	**13.0**	**11.0**	**16.0**	**10.3**	**16.0**
Hour	**Conduction Time Factors, %**								
0	1.9	1.8	2.0	0.9	1.0	3.3	3.4	3.8	3.9
1	1.8	1.7	1.9	1.3	1.2	3.1	3.3	3.8	3.8
2	1.8	2.4	2.3	3.3	2.8	3.0	3.2	3.7	3.8
3	2.7	3.8	3.4	5.8	5.0	3.1	3.2	3.7	3.8
4	4.0	5.1	4.6	7.3	6.6	3.4	3.4	3.8	3.8
5	5.4	6.0	5.5	8.0	7.5	3.8	3.7	3.9	3.9
6	6.2	6.5	6.1	8.2	7.8	4.2	4.1	4.1	4.0
7	6.7	6.6	6.3	7.9	7.7	4.6	4.4	4.2	4.2
8	6.8	6.6	6.3	7.5	7.4	4.8	4.6	4.3	4.3
9	6.6	6.4	6.2	6.9	6.9	5.0	4.8	4.4	4.4
10	6.4	6.1	6.0	6.2	6.4	5.1	4.9	4.5	4.5
11	6.0	5.7	5.7	5.6	5.8	5.1	5.0	4.5	4.5
12	5.6	5.3	5.4	5.0	5.2	5.1	4.9	4.6	4.5
13	5.2	4.9	5.0	4.4	4.6	5.0	4.9	4.6	4.5
14	4.8	4.6	4.7	3.8	4.1	4.9	4.8	4.5	4.5
15	4.4	4.2	4.3	3.3	3.6	4.7	4.7	4.5	4.5
16	4.0	3.8	4.0	2.9	3.2	4.6	4.6	4.3	4.3
17	3.7	3.5	3.7	2.5	2.8	4.4	4.4	4.3	4.3
18	3.4	3.2	3.4	2.2	2.4	4.2	4.3	4.2	4.2
19	3.1	2.9	3.1	1.9	2.1	4.1	4.1	4.2	4.2
20	2.8	2.6	2.9	1.6	1.8	3.9	4.0	4.1	4.1
21	2.5	2.4	2.6	1.4	1.6	3.7	3.9	4.0	4.1
22	2.3	2.1	2.4	1.2	1.4	3.6	3.7	4.0	4.0
23	2.1	1.9	2.2	1.0	1.2	3.4	3.6	3.9	3.9
Total Percentage	100	100	100	100	100	100	100	100	100
Layer ID from outdoors to indoors (See Table 18)	F01	F01	F01	F01	F01	F01	F01	F01	F01
	M01	M01	M01	M01	M01	M01	M01	M01	M01
	F04	F04	F04	F04	F04	F04	F04	F04	F04
	M03	I01	I01	I01	I01	I01	I01	I01	I01
	I04	M05	I01	M01	I01	M13	I01	M16	I01
	I04	G01	M05	F02	M01	F04	M13	F04	M16
	G01	F02	G01	0	F02	G01	F04	G01	F04
	F02	0	F02	0	0	F02	G01	F02	G01
	0	0	0	0	0	0	F02	0	F02
	0	0	0	0	0	0	0	0	0

distributed onto all room surfaces. Effect of beam solar radiation distribution assumptions is addressed by Hittle (1999).

Representative solar and nonsolar RTS data for light, medium, and heavyweight constructions are provided in Tables 19 and 20. Those were calculated using the Hbfort computer program (Pedersen et al. 1998) with zone characteristics listed in Table 21. Customized RTS values may be calculated using the HB method where the zone is not reasonably similar to these typical zones or where more precision is desired.

ASHRAE research project RP-942 compared HB and RTS results over a wide range of zone types and input variables (Rees et al. 2000; Spitler et al. 1998). In general, total cooling loads calculated using RTS closely agreed with or were slightly higher than those of the HB method with the same inputs. The project examined more than 5000 test cases of varying zone parameters. The dominating variable was overall thermal mass, and results were grouped into lightweight, U.S. medium-weight, U.K. medium-weight, and heavyweight construction. Best agreement between RTS and HB results was obtained for light- and medium-weight construction. Greater differences occurred in heavyweight cases, with RTS generally predicting slightly higher peak cooling loads than HB. Greater differences also were observed in zones with extremely high internal radiant loads and large glazing areas or with a very lightweight exterior envelope. In this case, heat balance calculations predict that some of the internal radiant load will be transmitted to the outdoor environment and

Table 16 Wall Conduction Time Series (CTS) (*Continued*)

	Brick Walls		Concrete Block Walls						
	Brick, 8 in. HW Concrete, R-11 Batt Insulation, Gyp. Board	Brick, 8 in. HW Concrete, R-22 Batt Insulation, Gyp. Board	8 in. LW CMU, R-11 Batt Insulation, Gyp. Board	8 in. LW CMU, R-22 Batt Insulation, Gyp. Board	8 in. LW CMU w/Fill Insulation, R-11 Batt Insulation, Gyp. Board	8 in. LW CMU w/Fill Insulation, R-22 Batt Insulation, Gyp. Board	1 in. Stucco, 8 in. HW CMU, R-11 Batt Insulation, Gyp. Board	1 in. Stucco, 8 in. HW CMU, R-22 Batt Insulation, Gyp. Board	8 in. LW CMU w/Fill Insulation
Wall Number	**39**	**40**	**41**	**42**	**43**	**44**	**45**	**46**	**47**
***U*, Btu/h·ft²·°F**	**0.067**	**0.038**	**0.067**	**0.039**	**0.059**	**0.036**	**0.073**	**0.040**	**0.186**
Total *R*	**14.8**	**26.1**	**14.9**	**25.9**	**17.0**	**28.0**	**13.8**	**24.8**	**5.4**
Hour	**Conduction Time Factors, %**		**Conduction Time Factors, %**						
0	3.4	3.5	0.2	0.2	0.6	0.8	0.5	0.5	0.7
1	3.3	3.4	4.6	1.9	1.6	1.0	2.3	1.2	10.4
2	3.3	3.3	13.3	8.8	5.7	3.4	8.0	5.1	20.6
3	3.6	3.5	15.8	13.9	9.5	7.1	11.6	9.6	19.5
4	4.0	3.8	14.0	14.1	10.8	9.4	11.7	11.3	14.8
5	4.4	4.2	11.4	12.3	10.3	9.8	10.5	10.8	10.5
6	4.7	4.5	9.0	10.0	9.3	9.3	9.1	9.6	7.3
7	4.8	4.7	7.0	8.1	8.1	8.3	7.7	8.3	5.0
8	4.9	4.8	5.5	6.4	7.0	7.4	6.5	7.1	3.5
9	4.9	4.9	4.3	5.1	6.0	6.5	5.5	6.0	2.4
10	4.9	4.9	3.4	4.1	5.1	5.6	4.6	5.1	1.6
11	4.8	4.8	2.6	3.2	4.4	4.9	3.9	4.3	1.1
12	4.7	4.7	2.0	2.6	3.7	4.3	3.3	3.7	0.8
13	4.6	4.6	1.6	2.1	3.2	3.7	2.8	3.1	0.5
14	4.5	4.5	1.3	1.6	2.7	3.2	2.3	2.7	0.4
15	4.4	4.4	1.0	1.3	2.3	2.8	2.0	2.3	0.2
16	4.2	4.3	0.8	1.0	2.0	2.4	1.6	1.9	0.2
17	4.1	4.2	0.6	0.8	1.7	2.1	1.4	1.6	0.1
18	4.0	4.1	0.5	0.7	1.5	1.8	1.2	1.4	0.1
19	3.9	4.0	0.4	0.5	1.2	1.6	1.0	1.2	0.1
20	3.8	3.9	0.3	0.4	1.1	1.4	0.8	1.0	0.0
21	3.7	3.8	0.2	0.3	0.9	1.2	0.7	0.8	0.0
22	3.6	3.7	0.2	0.3	0.8	1.1	0.6	0.7	0.0
23	3.5	3.6	0.1	0.2	0.7	0.9	0.5	0.6	0.0
Total Percentage	100	100	100	100	100	100	100	100	100
Layer ID from outdoors to indoors (See Table 18)	F01	F01	F01	F01	F01	F01	F01	F01	F01
	M01	M01	M03	M03	M08	M08	F07	F07	M08
	F04	F04	I04	I04	I04	I04	M05	M05	F02
	M15	M15	G01	I04	G01	I04	I04	I04	0
	I04	I04	F02	G01	F02	G01	G01	I04	0
	G01	I04	0	F02	0	F02	F02	G01	0
	F02	G01	0	0	0	0	0	F02	0
	0	F02	0	0	0	0	0	0	0
	0	0	0	0	0	0	0	0	0
	0	0	0	0	0	0	0	0	0

never becomes cooling load in the space. RTS does not account for energy transfer out of the space to the environment, and thus predicted higher cooling loads.

ASHRAE research project RP-1117 built two model rooms for which cooling loads were physically measured using extensive instrumentation. The results agreed with previous simulations (Chantrasrisalai et al. 2003; Eldridge et al. 2003; Iu et al. 2003). HB calculations closely approximated measured cooling loads when provided with detailed data for the test rooms. RTS overpredicted measured cooling loads in tests with large, clear, single-glazed window areas with bare concrete floor and no furnishings or internal loads. Tests under more typical conditions (venetian blinds, carpeted floor, office-type furnishings, and normal internal loads) provided good agreement between HB, RTS, and measured loads.

7. HEATING LOAD CALCULATIONS

Techniques for estimating design heating load for commercial, institutional, and industrial applications are essentially the same as for those estimating design cooling loads for such uses, with the following exceptions:

- Temperatures outdoor conditioned spaces are generally lower than maintained space temperatures.
- Credit for solar or internal heat gains is not included
- Thermal storage effect of building structure or content is ignored.

Table 16 Wall Conduction Time Series (CTS) (*Continued*)

	Concrete Block Walls		Precast and Cast-in-Place Block Walls							
	8 in. LW CMU w/Fill Insulation, Gyp. Board	12 in. LW CMU w/Fill Insulation, Gyp. Board	4 in. LW Concrete. R-5 Board Insulation, Gyp. Board	4 in. LW Concrete. R-10 Board Insulation, Gyp. Board	4 in. LW Concrete. R-11 Batt Insulation, Gyp. Board	4 in. LW Concrete. R-22 Batt Insulation, Gyp. Board	4 in. LW Concrete. R-10 Board Insulation, 4 in. LW Concrete	4 in. LW Concrete. R-20 Board Insulation, 4 in. LW Concrete	EIFS, R-5 Insulation Board, 8 in. LW Concrete, Gyp. Board	EIFS, R-10 Insulation Board, 8 in. LW Concrete, Gyp. Board
Wall Number	**48**	**49**	**50**	**51**	**52**	**53**	**54**	**55**	**56**	**57**
U, Btu/h·ft²·°F	**0.147**	**0.121**	**0.119**	**0.075**	**0.073**	**0.041**	**0.077**	**0.044**	**0.115**	**0.073**
Total R	**6.8**	**8.3**	**8.4**	**13.4**	**13.6**	**24.6**	**13.0**	**23.0**	**8.7**	**13.7**
Hour	**Conduction Time Factors, %**		**Conduction Time Factors, %**							
0	0.2	1.0	0.7	0.3	0.4	0.1	0.7	0.9	2.2	2.4
1	3.6	1.1	10.4	7.1	8.4	3.8	0.9	0.8	2.2	2.4
2	11.8	2.6	19.7	17.4	18.2	13.6	2.8	1.6	3.2	3.1
3	15.5	5.0	18.1	18.1	17.9	17.5	5.6	3.7	4.6	4.2
4	14.6	7.1	13.9	14.6	14.2	15.6	7.7	5.9	5.7	5.2
5	12.2	8.3	10.2	11.1	10.7	12.3	8.7	7.4	6.2	5.7
6	9.7	8.5	7.4	8.2	7.9	9.4	8.9	8.2	6.3	5.9
7	7.5	8.3	5.4	6.1	5.9	7.0	8.6	8.3	6.2	5.9
8	5.8	7.7	3.9	4.5	4.3	5.3	8.0	8.1	6.0	5.8
9	4.5	7.0	2.8	3.3	3.2	3.9	7.3	7.6	5.7	5.6
10	3.5	6.3	2.1	2.5	2.4	3.0	6.5	6.9	5.4	5.3
11	2.7	5.6	1.5	1.8	1.7	2.2	5.7	6.3	5.1	5.1
12	2.0	4.9	1.1	1.3	1.3	1.6	5.0	5.6	4.8	4.8
13	1.6	4.3	0.8	1.0	0.9	1.2	4.3	4.9	4.5	4.6
14	1.2	3.8	0.6	0.7	0.7	0.9	3.7	4.3	4.2	4.3
15	0.9	3.3	0.4	0.5	0.5	0.7	3.2	3.7	3.9	4.1
16	0.7	2.9	0.3	0.4	0.4	0.5	2.7	3.2	3.7	3.9
17	0.6	2.5	0.2	0.3	0.3	0.4	2.3	2.8	3.5	3.6
18	0.4	2.2	0.2	0.2	0.2	0.3	1.9	2.4	3.2	3.4
19	0.3	1.9	0.1	0.2	0.2	0.2	1.6	2.0	3.0	3.3
20	0.3	1.7	0.1	0.1	0.1	0.2	1.4	1.7	2.8	3.1
21	0.2	1.5	0.1	0.1	0.1	0.1	1.1	1.5	2.6	2.9
22	0.1	1.3	0.0	0.1	0.1	0.1	0.9	1.2	2.5	2.7
23	0.1	1.1	0.0	0.0	0.0	0.1	0.8	1.0	2.3	2.6
Total Percentage	100	100	100	100	100	100	100	100	100	100
Layer ID from outdoors to indoors (See Table 18)	F01	F01	F01	F01	F01	F01	F01	F01	F01	F01
	M08	M09	M11	M11	M11	M11	M11	M11	F06	F06
	F04	F04	I01	I01	I04	I04	I02	I02	I01	I01
	G01	G01	F04	I01	G01	I04	M11	I02	M13	I01
	F02	F02	G01	F04	F02	G01	F02	M11	G01	M13
	0	0	F02	G01	0	F02	0	F02	F02	G01
	0	0	0	F02	0	0	0	0	0	F02
	0	0	0	0	0	0	0	0	0	0
	0	0	0	0	0	0	0	0	0	0
	0	0	0	0	0	0	0	0	0	0

Thermal bridging effects on wall and roof conduction are greater for heating loads than for cooling loads, and greater care must be taken to account for bridging effects on U-factors used in heating load calculations.

Heat losses (negative heat gains) are thus considered to be instantaneous, heat transfer essentially conductive, and latent heat treated only as a function of replacing space humidity lost to the exterior environment.

This simplified approach is justified because it evaluates worst-case conditions that can reasonably occur during a heating season. Therefore, the near-worst-case load is based on the following:

- Design interior and exterior conditions
- Including infiltration and/or ventilation
- No solar effect (at night or on cloudy winter days)
- Before the periodic presence of people, lights, and appliances has an offsetting effect

Typical commercial and retail spaces have nighttime unoccupied periods at a setback temperature where little to no ventilation is required, building lights and equipment are off, and heat loss is primarily through conduction and infiltration. Before being occupied, buildings are warmed to the occupied temperature (see the following discussion). During occupied time, building lights, equipment, and people cooling loads can offset conduction heat loss, although some perimeter heat may be required, leaving infiltration and ventilation as the primary heating loads. Ventilation heat load may be

Table 16 Wall Conduction Time Series (CTS) (*Concluded*)

	Precast and Cast-in-Place Block Walls								
	8 in. LW Concrete. R-11 Batt Insulation, Gyp. Board	8 in. LW Concrete. R-22 Batt Insulation, Gyp. Board	EIFS, R-10 Insulation Board, 8 in. HW Concrete, Gyp. Board	EIFS, R-20 Insulation Board, 8 in. HW Concrete, Gyp. Board	8 in. HW Concrete. R-11 Batt Insulation, Gyp. Board	8 in. HW Concrete, R-22 Batt Insulation, Gyp. Board	12 in. HW Concrete, R-19 Batt Insulation, Gyp. Board	12 in. HW Concrete, R-38 Batt Insulation, Gyp. Board	12 in. HW Concrete
Wall Number	**58**	**59**	**60**	**61**	**62**	**63**	**64**	**65**	**66**
U, Btu/h·ft²·°F	0.068	0.039	0.082	0.045	0.076	0.041	0.047	0.025	0.549
Total R	14.7	25.7	12.1	22.1	13.1	24.2	21.4	40.5	1.8
Hour	**Conduction Time Factors, %**								
0	1.4	1.6	2.8	2.9	1.1	1.2	2.5	2.7	1.2
1	1.6	1.6	3.0	2.9	2.1	1.5	2.4	2.6	1.9
2	3.2	2.4	4.2	3.5	5.5	3.8	2.7	2.5	4.3
3	5.6	4.3	5.2	4.5	8.2	6.9	3.6	2.8	6.6
4	7.2	6.2	5.6	5.2	8.9	8.4	4.7	3.5	7.8
5	7.7	7.2	5.6	5.5	8.6	8.6	5.5	4.3	8.1
6	7.7	7.4	5.5	5.5	7.9	8.1	5.9	5.1	7.9
7	7.3	7.3	5.3	5.4	7.1	7.4	6.0	5.5	7.4
8	6.8	6.9	5.2	5.2	6.4	6.7	5.9	5.8	6.8
9	6.2	6.4	5.0	5.0	5.7	6.1	5.7	5.8	6.2
10	5.6	5.9	4.8	4.9	5.1	5.4	5.5	5.7	5.6
11	5.1	5.4	4.6	4.7	4.6	4.9	5.2	5.5	5.0
12	4.7	4.9	4.4	4.5	4.1	4.4	5.0	5.3	4.5
13	4.2	4.5	4.3	4.4	3.7	3.9	4.7	5.1	4.0
14	3.8	4.1	4.1	4.2	3.3	3.5	4.4	4.8	3.6
15	3.5	3.7	3.9	4.1	2.9	3.2	4.2	4.6	3.2
16	3.2	3.4	3.8	3.9	2.6	2.8	4.0	4.3	2.9
17	2.9	3.1	3.6	3.8	2.3	2.5	3.7	4.1	2.6
18	2.6	2.8	3.5	3.6	2.1	2.3	3.5	3.9	2.3
19	2.4	2.6	3.4	3.5	1.9	2.0	3.3	3.6	2.0
20	2.1	2.4	3.2	3.4	1.7	1.8	3.1	3.4	1.8
21	1.9	2.2	3.1	3.3	1.5	1.6	3.0	3.2	1.6
22	1.8	2.0	3.0	3.1	1.3	1.5	2.8	3.1	1.5
23	1.6	1.8	2.9	3.0	1.2	1.3	2.6	2.9	1.3
Total Percentage	100	100	100	100	100	100	100	100	100
Layer ID from outdoors to indoors (See Table 18)	F01	F01	F01	F01	F01	F01	F01	F01	F01
	M13	M13	F06	F06	M15	M15	M16	M16	M16
	I04	I04	I02	I02	I04	I04	I05	I05	F02
	G01	I04	M15	I02	G01	I04	G01	I05	0
	F02	G01	G01	M15	F02	G01	F02	G01	0
	0	F02	F02	G01	0	F02	0	F02	0
	0	0	0	F02	0	0	0	0	0
	0	0	0	0	0	0	0	0	0
	0	0	0	0	0	0	0	0	0
	0	0	0	0	0	0	0	0	0

offset with heat recovery equipment. These loads (conduction loss, warm-up load, and ventilation load) may not be additive when sizing building heating equipment, and it is prudent to analyze each load and their interactions to arrive at final equipment sizing for heating.

7.1 HEAT LOSS CALCULATIONS

The general procedure for calculation of design heat losses of a structure is as follows:

1. Select outdoor design conditions: temperature, humidity, and wind direction and speed.
2. Select indoor design conditions to be maintained.
3. Estimate temperature in any adjacent unheated spaces.
4. Select transmission coefficients and compute heat losses for walls, floors, ceilings, windows, doors, and foundation elements.
5. Compute heat load through infiltration and any other outdoor air introduced directly to the space.
6. Sum the losses caused by transmission and infiltration.

Outdoor Design Conditions

The ideal heating system provides enough heat to match the structure's heat loss. However, weather conditions vary considerably from year to year, and heating systems designed for the worst weather conditions on record would have a great excess of capacity most of the time. A system's failure to maintain design conditions

Table 17 Roof Conduction Time Series (CTS)

	Sloped Frame Roofs								
	Metal Roof, R-19 Batt Insulation, Gyp. Board	Metal Roof, R-38 Batt Insulation, Gyp. Board	Metal Roof, R-19 Batt Insulation, Suspended Acoustical Ceiling	Metal Roof, R-38 Batt Insulation, Suspended Acoustical Ceiling	Metal Roof, R-19 Batt Insulation	Metal Roof, R-38 Batt Insulation	Asphalt Shingles, Wood Sheathing, R-19 Batt Insulation, Gyp. Board	Asphalt Shingles, Wood Sheathing, R-38 Batt Insulation, Gyp. Board	Slate or Tile, Wood Sheathing, R-19 Batt Insulation, Gyp. Board
Roof Number	**1**	**2**	**3**	**4**	**5**	**6**	**7**	**8**	**9**
***U*, Btu/h·ft²·°F**	**0.0438**	**0.0239**	**0.0399**	**0.0227**	**0.0449**	**0.0242**	**0.0414**	**0.0231**	**0.0421**
Total *R*	**22.85**	**41.91**	**25.07**	**44.12**	**22.29**	**41.35**	**24.18**	**43.24**	**23.78**
Hour	**Conduction Time Factors, %**								
1	6.4	0.3	10.1	0.5	26.6	1.9	0.9	0.0	0.8
2	44.2	10.9	55.6	14.8	61.0	27.5	16.5	2.6	16.6
3	32.7	28.5	27.3	32.1	11.2	34.7	30.1	13.3	32.8
4	11.6	25.9	5.7	24.3	1.1	19.1	23.5	21.0	25.0
5	3.6	16.2	1.0	13.6	0.1	9.0	14.0	20.2	13.6
6	1.1	8.9	0.2	7.1	0.0	4.2	7.5	15.5	6.4
7	0.3	4.6	0.0	3.7	0.0	1.9	3.8	10.6	2.8
8	0.1	2.3	0.0	1.9	0.0	0.9	1.9	6.7	1.2
9	0.0	1.2	0.0	1.0	0.0	0.4	0.9	4.1	0.5
10	0.0	0.6	0.0	0.5	0.0	0.2	0.5	2.5	0.2
11	0.0	0.3	0.0	0.3	0.0	0.1	0.2	1.4	0.1
12	0.0	0.1	0.0	0.1	0.0	0.0	0.1	0.8	0.0
13	0.0	0.1	0.0	0.1	0.0	0.0	0.1	0.5	0.0
14	0.0	0.0	0.0	0.0	0.0	0.0	0.0	0.3	0.0
15	0.0	0.0	0.0	0.0	0.0	0.0	0.0	0.2	0.0
16	0.0	0.0	0.0	0.0	0.0	0.0	0.0	0.1	0.0
17	0.0	0.0	0.0	0.0	0.0	0.0	0.0	0.1	0.0
18	0.0	0.0	0.0	0.0	0.0	0.0	0.0	0.0	0.0
19	0.0	0.0	0.0	0.0	0.0	0.0	0.0	0.0	0.0
20	0.0	0.0	0.0	0.0	0.0	0.0	0.0	0.0	0.0
21	0.0	0.0	0.0	0.0	0.0	0.0	0.0	0.0	0.0
22	0.0	0.0	0.0	0.0	0.0	0.0	0.0	0.0	0.0
23	0.0	0.0	0.0	0.0	0.0	0.0	0.0	0.0	0.0
24	0.0	0.0	0.0	0.0	0.0	0.0	0.0	0.0	0.0
Total Percentage	100	100	100	100	100	100	100	100	100
Layer ID from outdoors to indoors (See Table 18)	F01	F01	F01	F01	F01	F01	F01	F01	F01
	F08	F08	F08	F08	F08	F08	F12	F12	F14
	G03	G03	G03	G03	G03	G03	G05	G05	G05
	F05	F05	F05	F05	F05	F05	F05	F05	F05
	I05	I05	I05	I05	I05	I05	I05	I05	I05
	G01	I05	F05	I05	F03	I05	F05	I05	F05
	F03	G01	F16	F05	0	F03	G01	F05	G01
	0	F03	F03	F16	0	0	F03	G01	F03
	0	0	0	F03	0	0	0	F03	0
	0	0	0	0	0	0	0	0	0
	0	0	0	0	0	0	0	0	0
	0	0	0	0	0	0	0	0	0
	0	0	0	0	0	0	0	0	0
	0	0	0	0	0	0	0	0	0

during brief periods of severe weather usually is not critical. However, close regulation of indoor temperature may be critical for some occupancies or industrial processes. Design temperature data and discussion of their application are given in Chapter 14. Generally, the 99% temperature values given in the tabulated weather data are used. However, caution is needed, and local conditions should always be investigated. In some locations, outdoor temperatures are commonly much lower and wind velocities higher than those given in the tabulated weather data.

Indoor Design Conditions

The main purpose of the heating system is to maintain indoor conditions that make most of the occupants comfortable. Keep in mind, however, that the purpose of heating load calculations is to

Table 17 Roof Conduction Time Series (CTS) (*Continued*)

	Sloped Frame Roofs			Wood Deck				Metal Deck Roofs	
	Slate or Tile, Wood Sheathing, R-38 Batt Insulation, Gyp. Board	Wood Shingles, Wood Sheathing, R-19 Batt Insulation, Gyp. Board	Wood Shingles, Wood Sheathing, R-38 Batt Insulation, Gyp. Board	Membrane, Sheathing, R-10 Insulation Board, Wood Deck	Membrane, Sheathing, R-20 Insulation Board, Wood Deck	Membrane, Sheathing, R-10 Insulation Board, Wood Deck, Suspended Acoustical Ceiling	Membrane, Sheathing, R-20 Insulation Board, Wood Deck, Suspended Acoustical Ceiling	Membrane, Sheathing, R-10 Insulation Board, Metal Deck	Membrane, Sheathing, R-20 Insulation Board, Metal Deck
Roof Number	**10**	**11**	**12**	**13**	**14**	**15**	**16**	**17**	**18**
***U*, Btu/h·ft²·°F**	**0.0233**	**0.0405**	**0.0229**	**0.0695**	**0.0411**	**0.0582**	**0.0369**	**0.0799**	**0.0445**
Total *R*	**42.84**	**24.69**	**43.75**	**14.40**	**24.34**	**17.17**	**27.12**	**12.51**	**22.46**
Hour	**Conduction Time Factors, %**			**Conduction Time Factors, %**				**Conduction Time Factors, %**	
1	0.0	0.6	0.0	0.3	0.1	0.9	1.2	18.0	3.3
2	2.5	11.6	1.7	6.9	2.1	2.7	1.5	60.0	38.1
3	14.0	24.2	9.7	17.2	10.0	7.8	4.3	18.4	37.6
4	22.8	22.1	17.0	17.7	15.4	10.1	7.6	3.0	14.6
5	21.4	15.6	18.1	14.3	15.2	9.8	8.8	0.5	4.5
6	15.7	10.0	15.5	10.9	12.7	8.8	8.6	0.1	1.3
7	10.1	6.2	11.9	8.2	10.1	7.8	8.0	0.0	0.4
8	6.0	3.8	8.5	6.2	7.9	6.9	7.2	0.0	0.1
9	3.4	2.3	5.9	4.6	6.1	6.1	6.5	0.0	0.0
10	1.9	1.4	4.0	3.5	4.7	5.4	5.9	0.0	0.0
11	1.0	0.8	2.6	2.6	3.6	4.8	5.3	0.0	0.0
12	0.6	0.5	1.7	2.0	2.8	4.2	4.7	0.0	0.0
13	0.3	0.3	1.1	1.5	2.2	3.7	4.3	0.0	0.0
14	0.2	0.2	0.7	1.1	1.7	3.3	3.8	0.0	0.0
15	0.1	0.1	0.5	0.8	1.3	2.9	3.4	0.0	0.0
16	0.0	0.1	0.3	0.6	1.0	2.6	3.1	0.0	0.0
17	0.0	0.0	0.2	0.5	0.8	2.3	2.8	0.0	0.0
18	0.0	0.0	0.1	0.3	0.6	2.0	2.5	0.0	0.0
19	0.0	0.0	0.1	0.3	0.5	1.8	2.2	0.0	0.0
20	0.0	0.0	0.1	0.2	0.4	1.5	2.0	0.0	0.0
21	0.0	0.0	0.0	0.1	0.3	1.4	1.8	0.0	0.0
22	0.0	0.0	0.0	0.1	0.2	1.2	1.6	0.0	0.0
23	0.0	0.0	0.0	0.1	0.2	1.1	1.5	0.0	0.0
24	0.0	0.0	0.0	0.1	0.1	0.9	1.3	0.0	0.0
Total Percentage	100	100	100	100	100	100	100	100	100
Layer ID from outdoors to indoors (See Table 18)	F01	F01	F01	F01	F01	F01	F01	F01	F01
	F14	F15	F15	F13	F13	F13	F13	F13	F13
	G05	G05	G05	G03	G03	G03	G03	G03	G03
	F05	F05	F05	I02	I02	I02	I02	I02	I02
	I05	I05	I05	G06	I02	G06	I02	F08	I02
	I05	F05	I05	F03	G06	F05	G06	F03	F08
	F05	G01	F05	0	F03	F16	F05	0	F03
	G01	F03	G01	0	0	F03	F16	0	0
	F03	0	F03	0	0	0	F03	0	0
	0	0	0	0	0	0	0	0	0
	0	0	0	0	0	0	0	0	0
	0	0	0	0	0	0	0	0	0
	0	0	0	0	0	0	0	0	0
	0	0	0	0	0	0	0	0	0

obtain data for sizing the heating system components. In many cases, the system will rarely be called upon to operate at the design conditions. Therefore, the use and occupancy of the space are general considerations from the design temperature point of view. Later, when the building's energy requirements are computed, the actual conditions in the space and outdoor environment, including internal heat gains, must be considered.

The indoor design temperature should be selected at the lower end of the acceptable temperature range, so that the heating equipment will not be oversized. Even properly sized equipment operates under partial load, at reduced efficiency, most of the time; therefore, any oversizing aggravates this condition and lowers overall system efficiency. A maximum design dry-bulb temperature of 70°F is recommended for most occupancies. The indoor design value of relative

Table 17 Roof Conduction Time Series (CTS) (*Continued*)

	Metal Deck Roofs							Concrete Roofs	
	Membrane, Sheathing, R-10 Insulation Board, Metal Deck, Suspended Acoustical Ceiling	Membrane, Sheathing, R-20 Insulation Board, Metal Deck, Suspended Acoustical Ceiling	Membrane, Sheathing, R-15 Insulation Board, Metal Deck	Membrane, Sheathing, R-30 Insulation Board, Metal Deck	Membrane, Sheathing, R-25 Insulation Board, Metal Deck	2 in. Concrete Roof Ballast, Membrane, Sheathing, R-15 Insulation Board, Metal Deck	2 in. Concrete Roof Ballast, Membrane, Sheathing, R-30 Insulation Board, Metal Deck	Membrane, Sheathing, R-15 Insulation Board, 4 in. LW Concrete	Membrane, Sheathing, R-30 Insulation Board, 4 in. LW Concrete
Roof Number	**19**	**20**	**21**	**22**	**23**	**24**	**25**	**26**	**27**
U, Btu/h·ft²·°F	**0.0654**	**0.0331**	**0.0572**	**0.0309**	**0.0438**	**0.0526**	**0.0295**	**0.0539**	**0.0299**
Total R	**15.29**	**30.21**	**17.48**	**32.40**	**22.85**	**19.03**	**33.95**	**18.56**	**33.48**
Hour	**Conduction Time Factors, %**							**Conduction Time Factors, %**	
1	4.8	0.2	8.6	0.3	6.4	0.4	0.1	0.6	0.8
2	40.0	8.8	52.5	12.8	44.2	10.1	1.3	2.2	0.9
3	34.7	26.6	29.8	31.1	32.7	21.9	8.1	7.9	2.5
4	13.8	26.3	7.3	25.5	11.6	19.5	14.7	11.2	5.9
5	4.6	17.3	1.5	14.7	3.6	14.2	15.8	11.2	8.6
6	1.4	9.8	0.3	7.7	1.1	10.1	14.0	10.0	9.6
7	0.4	5.2	0.1	3.9	0.3	7.1	11.4	8.7	9.4
8	0.1	2.7	0.0	2.0	0.1	5.0	8.8	7.5	8.7
9	0.0	1.4	0.0	1.0	0.0	3.5	6.7	6.4	7.8
10	0.0	0.7	0.0	0.5	0.0	2.5	5.0	5.5	6.9
11	0.0	0.4	0.0	0.2	0.0	1.7	3.7	4.7	6.0
12	0.0	0.2	0.0	0.1	0.0	1.2	2.8	4.0	5.2
13	0.0	0.1	0.0	0.1	0.0	0.9	2.0	3.4	4.5
14	0.0	0.1	0.0	0.0	0.0	0.6	1.5	2.9	3.9
15	0.0	0.0	0.0	0.0	0.0	0.4	1.1	2.5	3.4
16	0.0	0.0	0.0	0.0	0.0	0.3	0.8	2.2	2.9
17	0.0	0.0	0.0	0.0	0.0	0.2	0.6	1.8	2.5
18	0.0	0.0	0.0	0.0	0.0	0.2	0.4	1.6	2.2
19	0.0	0.0	0.0	0.0	0.0	0.1	0.3	1.4	1.9
20	0.0	0.0	0.0	0.0	0.0	0.1	0.2	1.2	1.6
21	0.0	0.0	0.0	0.0	0.0	0.1	0.2	1.0	1.4
22	0.0	0.0	0.0	0.0	0.0	0.0	0.1	0.9	1.2
23	0.0	0.0	0.0	0.0	0.0	0.0	0.1	0.7	1.1
24	0.0	0.0	0.0	0.0	0.0	0.0	0.1	0.6	0.9
Total Percentage	100	100	100	100	100	100	100	100	100
Layer ID from outdoors to indoors (See Table 18)	F01	F01	F01	F01	F01	F01	F01	F01	F01
	F13	F13	F13	F13	F08	M17	M17	F13	F13
	G03	G03	G03	G03	G03	F13	F13	G03	G03
	I02	I02	I03	I03	F05	G03	G03	I03	I03
	F08	I02	F08	I03	I05	I03	I03	M11	I03
	F05	F08	F03	F08	G01	F08	I03	F03	M11
	F16	F05	0	F03	F03	F03	F08	0	F03
	F03	F16	0	0	0	0	F03	0	0
	0	F03	0	0	0	0	0	0	0
	0	0	0	0	0	0	0	0	0
	0	0	0	0	0	0	0	0	0
	0	0	0	0	0	0	0	0	0
	0	0	0	0	0	0	0	0	0
	0	0	0	0	0	0	0	0	0

humidity should be compatible with a healthful environment and the thermal and moisture integrity of the building envelope. A minimum relative humidity of 30% is recommended for most situations.

Calculation of Transmission Heat Losses

Exterior Surface Above Grade. All above-grade surfaces exposed to outdoor conditions (walls, doors, ceilings, fenestration, and raised floors) are treated identically, as follows:

$$q = A \times \text{HF} \tag{34}$$

$$\text{HF} = U\,\Delta t \tag{35}$$

where HF is the heating load factor in Btu/h·ft².

Below-Grade Surfaces. An approximate method for estimating below-grade heat loss [based on the work of Latta and Boileau (1969)] assumes that the heat flow paths shown in Figure 12 can be

Table 17 Roof Conduction Time Series (CTS) (*Concluded*)

	Concrete Roofs									
	Membrane, Sheathing, R-15 Insulation Board, 6 in. LW Concrete	Membrane, Sheathing, R-30 Insulation Board, 6 in. LW Concrete	Membrane, Sheathing, R-15 Insulation Board, 8 in. LW Concrete	Membrane, Sheathing, R-30 Insulation Board, 8 in. LW Concrete	Membrane, Sheathing, R-15 Insulation Board, 6 in. HW Concrete	Membrane, Sheathing, R-30 Insulation Board, 6 in. HW Concrete	Membrane, Sheathing, R-15 Insulation Board, 8 in. HW Concrete	Membrane, Sheathing, R-30 Insulation Board, 8 in. HW Concrete	Membrane, 6 in. HW Concrete, R-19 Batt Insulation, Suspended Acoustical Ceiling	Membrane, 6 in. HW Concrete, R-38 Batt Insulation, Suspended Acoustical Ceiling
Roof Number	28	29	30	31	32	33	34	35	36	37
***U*, Btu/h·ft²·°F**	0.0523	0.0294	0.0509	0.0297	0.0558	0.0304	0.0553	0.0303	0.0420	0.0233
Total *R*	19.10	34.02	19.65	33.64	17.93	32.85	18.09	33.02	23.78	42.84
Hour	**Conduction Time Factors, %**									
1	1.5	1.9	2.4	1.5	2.0	2.3	2.6	2.8	1.4	1.6
2	1.7	1.7	2.3	1.4	2.4	2.2	2.6	2.7	2.3	1.6
3	3.4	2.0	2.6	1.5	4.6	2.7	3.5	2.8	5.7	2.6
4	6.0	3.2	3.7	2.6	6.5	4.1	4.8	3.4	8.0	4.8
5	7.5	4.9	4.9	4.6	7.0	5.4	5.7	4.3	8.2	6.5
6	7.8	6.2	5.7	6.4	6.8	6.2	5.9	5.0	7.8	7.3
7	7.6	6.9	6.1	7.4	6.5	6.4	5.9	5.5	7.2	7.4
8	7.1	7.0	6.1	7.8	6.1	6.3	5.7	5.6	6.6	7.1
9	6.5	6.9	6.0	7.6	5.7	6.1	5.5	5.6	6.0	6.7
10	6.0	6.5	5.8	7.2	5.3	5.8	5.3	5.5	5.5	6.2
11	5.5	6.1	5.5	6.7	5.0	5.5	5.0	5.3	5.0	5.7
12	5.0	5.7	5.2	6.1	4.7	5.2	4.8	5.1	4.6	5.3
13	4.6	5.2	5.0	5.5	4.4	4.8	4.6	4.9	4.2	4.8
14	4.2	4.8	4.7	5.0	4.1	4.5	4.4	4.7	3.8	4.4
15	3.8	4.4	4.4	4.5	3.8	4.3	4.2	4.5	3.5	4.0
16	3.5	4.1	4.1	4.0	3.6	4.0	4.0	4.3	3.2	3.7
17	3.2	3.7	3.9	3.6	3.4	3.8	3.8	4.1	2.9	3.4
18	2.9	3.4	3.7	3.2	3.1	3.5	3.6	3.9	2.6	3.1
19	2.6	3.1	3.4	2.9	2.9	3.3	3.4	3.7	2.4	2.8
20	2.4	2.9	3.2	2.6	2.8	3.1	3.3	3.6	2.2	2.6
21	2.2	2.6	3.0	2.3	2.6	2.9	3.1	3.4	2.0	2.4
22	2.0	2.4	2.9	2.1	2.4	2.7	3.0	3.2	1.8	2.2
23	1.8	2.2	2.7	1.9	2.3	2.6	2.8	3.1	1.7	2.0
24	1.7	2.0	2.5	1.7	2.1	2.4	2.7	3.0	1.5	1.8
Total Percentage	100	100	100	100	100	100	100	100	100	100
Layer ID from outdoors to indoors (See Table 18)	F01	F01	F01	F01	F01	F01	F01	F01	F01	F01
	F13	F13	F13	F13	F13	F13	F13	F13	F13	F13
	G03	G03	G03	G03	G03	G03	G03	G03	M14	M14
	I03	I03	I03	I03	I03	I03	I03	I03	F05	F05
	M12	I03	M13	I03	M14	I03	M15	I03	I05	I05
	F03	M12	F03	M13	F03	M14	F03	M15	F16	I05
	0	F03	0	F03	0	F03	0	F03	F03	F16
	0	0	0	0	0	0	0	0	0	F03
	0	0	0	0	0	0	0	0	0	0
	0	0	0	0	0	0	0	0	0	0
	0	0	0	0	0	0	0	0	0	0
	0	0	0	0	0	0	0	0	0	0
	0	0	0	0	0	0	0	0	0	0

used to find the steady-state heat loss to the ground surface, as follows:

$$\text{HF} = U_{avg}(t_{in} - t_{gr}) \tag{36}$$

where

U_{avg} = average U-factor for below-grade surface from Equation (38) or (39), Btu/h·ft²·°F
t_{in} = below-grade space air temperature, °F
t_{gr} = design ground surface temperature from Equation (37), °F

The effect of soil heat capacity means that none of the usual external design air temperatures are suitable values for t_{gr}. Ground surface temperature fluctuates about an annual mean value by amplitude A, which varies with geographic location and surface cover. The minimum ground surface temperature, suitable for heat loss estimates, is therefore

$$t_{gr} = \bar{t}_{gr} - A \tag{37}$$

Table 18 Thermal Properties and Code Numbers of Layers Used in Wall and Roof Descriptions for Tables 16 and 17

Layer ID	Description	Thickness, in.	Conductivity, Btu·in/h·ft²·°F	Density, lb/ft³	Specific Heat, Btu/lb·°F	Resistance R, ft²·°F·h/Btu	Mass, lb/ft²	Thermal Capacity, Btu/ft²·°F	Notes
F01	Outdoor surface resistance	—	—	—	—	0.25	—	—	1
F02	Indoor vertical surface resistance	—	—	—	—	0.68	—	—	2
F03	Indoor horizontal surface resistance	—	—	—	—	0.92	—	—	3
F04	Wall air space resistance	—	—	—	—	0.87	—	—	4
F05	Ceiling air space resistance	—	—	—	—	1.00	—	—	5
F06	EIFS finish	0.375	5.00	116.0	0.20	0.08	3.63	0.73	6
F07	1 in. stucco	1.000	5.00	116.0	0.20	0.20	9.67	1.93	6
F08	Metal surface	0.030	314.00	489.0	0.12	0.00	1.22	0.15	7
F09	Opaque spandrel glass	0.250	6.90	158.0	0.21	0.04	3.29	0.69	8
F10	1 in. stone	1.000	22.00	160.0	0.19	0.05	13.33	2.53	9
F11	Wood siding	0.500	0.62	37.0	0.28	0.81	1.54	0.43	10
F12	Asphalt shingles	0.125	0.28	70.0	0.30	0.44	0.73	0.22	
F13	Built-up roofing	0.375	1.13	70.0	0.35	0.33	2.19	0.77	
F14	Slate or tile	0.500	11.00	120.0	0.30	0.05	5.00	1.50	
F15	Wood shingles	0.250	0.27	37.0	0.31	0.94	0.77	0.24	
F16	Acoustic tile	0.750	0.42	23.0	0.14	1.79	1.44	0.20	11
F17	Carpet	0.500	0.41	18.0	0.33	1.23	0.75	0.25	12
F18	Terrazzo	1.000	12.50	160.0	0.19	0.08	13.33	2.53	13
G01	5/8 in. Gyp. Board	0.625	1.11	50.0	0.26	0.56	2.60	0.68	
G02	5/8 in. plywood	0.625	0.80	34.0	0.29	0.78	1.77	0.51	
G03	1/2 in. fiberboard sheathing	0.500	0.47	25.0	0.31	1.06	1.04	0.32	14
G04	1/2 in. wood	0.500	1.06	38.0	0.39	0.47	1.58	0.62	15
G05	1 in. wood	1.000	1.06	38.0	0.39	0.94	3.17	1.24	15
G06	2 in. wood	2.000	1.06	38.0	0.39	1.89	6.33	2.47	15
G07	4 in. wood	4.000	1.06	38.0	0.39	3.77	12.67	4.94	15
I01	R-5, 1 in. insulation board	1.000	0.20	2.7	0.29	5.00	0.23	0.07	16
I02	R-10, 2 in. insulation board	2.000	0.20	2.7	0.29	10.00	0.45	0.13	16
I03	R-15, 3 in. insulation board	3.000	0.20	2.7	0.29	15.00	0.68	0.20	16
I04	R-11, 3 1/2 in. batt insulation	3.520	0.32	1.2	0.23	11.00	0.35	0.08	17
I05	R-19, 6 1/4 in. batt insulation	6.080	0.32	1.2	0.23	19.00	0.61	0.14	17
I06	R-30, 9 1/2 in. batt insulation	9.600	0.32	1.2	0.23	30.00	0.96	0.22	17
M01	4 in. brick	4.000	6.20	120.0	0.19	0.65	40.00	7.60	18
M02	6 in. LW concrete block	6.000	3.39	32.0	0.21	1.77	16.00	3.36	19
M03	8 in. LW concrete block	8.000	3.44	29.0	0.21	2.33	19.33	4.06	20
M04	12 in. LW concrete block	12.000	4.92	32.0	0.21	2.44	32.00	6.72	21
M05	8 in. concrete block	8.000	7.72	50.0	0.22	1.04	33.33	7.33	22
M06	12 in. concrete block	12.000	9.72	50.0	0.22	1.23	50.00	11.00	23
M07	6 in. LW concrete block (filled)	6.000	1.98	32.0	0.21	3.03	16.00	3.36	24
M08	8 in. LW concrete block (filled)	8.000	1.80	29.0	0.21	4.44	19.33	4.06	25
M09	12 in. LW concrete block (filled)	12.000	2.04	32.0	0.21	5.88	32.00	6.72	26
M10	8 in. concrete block (filled)	8.000	5.00	50.0	0.22	1.60	33.33	7.33	27
M11	4 in. lightweight concrete	4.000	3.70	80.0	0.20	1.08	26.67	5.33	
M12	6 in. lightweight concrete	6.000	3.70	80.0	0.20	1.62	40.00	8.00	
M13	8 in. lightweight concrete	8.000	3.70	80.0	0.20	2.16	53.33	10.67	
M14	6 in. heavyweight concrete	6.000	13.50	140.0	0.22	0.44	70.00	15.05	
M15	8 in. heavyweight concrete	8.000	13.50	140.0	0.22	0.48	93.33	20.07	
M16	12 in. heavyweight concrete	12.000	13.50	140.0	0.22	0.89	140.0	30.10	
M17	2 in. LW concrete roof ballast	2.000	1.30	40	0.20	1.54	6.7	1.33	28

Notes: The following notes give sources for the data in this table.

1. Chapter 26, Table 1 for 7.5 mph wind
2. Chapter 26, Table 1 for still air, horizontal heat flow
3. Chapter 26, Table 1 for still air, downward heat flow
4. Chapter 26, Table 3 for 1.5 in. space, 90°F, horizontal heat flow, 0.82 emittance
5. Chapter 26, Table 3 for 3.5 in. space, 90°F, downward heat flow, 0.82 emittance
6. EIFS finish layers approximated by Chapter 26, Table 4 for 3/8 in. cement plaster, sand aggregate
7. Chapter 33, Table 3 for steel (mild)
8. Chapter 26, Table 4 for architectural glass
9. Chapter 26, Table 4 for marble and granite
10. Chapter 26, Table 4, density assumed same as Southern pine
11. Chapter 26, Table 4 for mineral fiberboard, wet molded, acoustical tile
12. Chapter 26, Table 4 for carpet and rubber pad, density assumed same as fiberboard
13. Chapter 26, Table 4, density assumed same as stone
14. Chapter 26, Table 4 for nail-base sheathing
15. Chapter 26, Table 4 for Southern pine
16. Chapter 26, Table 4 for expanded polystyrene
17. Chapter 26, Table 4 for glass fiber batt, specific heat per glass fiber board
18. Chapter 26, Table 4 for clay fired brick
19. Chapter 26, Table 4, 16 lb block, 8 × 16 in. face
20. Chapter 26, Table 4, 19 lb block, 8 × 16 in. face
21. Chapter 26, Table 4, 32 lb block, 8 × 16 in. face
22. Chapter 26, Table 4, 33 lb normal weight block, 8 × 16 in. face
23. Chapter 26, Table 4, 50 lb normal weight block, 8 × 16 in. face
24. Chapter 26, Table 4, 16 lb block, vermiculite fill
25. Chapter 26, Table 4, 19 lb block, 8 × 16 in. face, vermiculite fill
26. Chapter 26, Table 4, 32 lb block, 8 × 16 in. face, vermiculite fill
27. Chapter 26, Table 4, 33 lb normal weight block, 8 × 16 in. face, vermiculite fill
28. Chapter 26, Table 4 for 40 lb/ft³ LW concrete

Table 19 Representative Nonsolar RTS Values for Light to Heavy Construction

	Light						Medium						Heavy						Interior Zones					
																			Light		Medium		Heavy	
	With Carpet			No Carpet			With Carpet			No Carpet			With Carpet			No Carpet								
% Glass	10%	50%	90%	10%	50%	90%	10%	50%	90%	10%	50%	90%	10%	50%	90%	10%	50%	90%	With Carpet	No Carpet	With Carpet	No Carpet	With Carpet	No Carpet
Hour	Radiant Time Factor, %																							
0	47	50	53	41	43	46	46	49	52	31	33	35	34	38	42	22	25	28	46	40	46	31	33	21
1	19	18	17	20	19	19	18	17	16	17	16	15	9	9	9	10	9	9	19	20	18	17	9	9
2	11	10	9	12	11	11	10	9	8	11	10	10	6	6	5	6	6	6	11	12	10	11	6	6
3	6	6	5	8	7	7	6	5	5	8	7	7	4	4	4	5	5	5	6	8	6	8	5	5
4	4	4	3	5	5	5	4	3	3	6	5	5	4	4	4	5	5	4	4	5	3	6	4	5
5	3	3	2	4	3	3	2	2	2	4	4	4	4	3	3	4	4	4	3	4	2	4	4	4
6	2	2	2	3	3	2	2	2	2	4	3	3	3	3	3	4	4	4	2	3	2	4	3	4
7	2	1	1	2	2	2	1	1	1	3	3	3	3	3	3	4	4	4	2	2	1	3	3	4
8	1	1	1	1	1	1	1	1	1	3	2	2	3	3	3	4	3	3	1	1	1	3	3	4
9	1	1	1	1	1	1	1	1	1	2	2	2	3	3	2	3	3	3	1	1	1	2	3	3
10	1	1	1	1	1	1	1	1	1	2	2	2	3	2	2	3	3	3	1	1	1	2	3	3
11	1	1	1	1	1	1	1	1	1	2	2	2	2	2	2	3	3	3	1	1	1	2	2	3
12	1	1	1	1	1	1	1	1	1	1	1	1	2	2	2	3	3	3	1	1	1	1	2	3
13	1	1	1	0	1	0	1	1	1	1	1	1	2	2	2	3	3	2	1	1	1	1	2	3
14	0	0	1	0	1	0	1	1	1	1	1	1	2	2	2	3	2	2	1	0	1	1	2	3
15	0	0	1	0	0	0	1	1	1	1	1	1	2	2	2	2	2	2	0	0	1	1	2	3
16	0	0	0	0	0	0	1	1	1	1	1	1	2	2	2	2	2	2	0	0	1	1	2	3
17	0	0	0	0	0	0	1	1	1	1	1	1	2	2	2	2	2	2	0	0	1	1	2	2
18	0	0	0	0	0	0	1	1	1	1	1	1	2	2	1	2	2	2	0	0	1	1	2	2
19	0	0	0	0	0	0	0	1	0	0	1	1	2	2	1	2	2	2	0	0	1	0	2	2
20	0	0	0	0	0	0	0	0	0	0	1	1	2	1	1	2	2	2	0	0	0	0	2	2
21	0	0	0	0	0	0	0	0	0	0	1	1	2	1	1	2	2	2	0	0	0	0	2	2
22	0	0	0	0	0	0	0	0	0	0	1	0	1	1	1	2	2	2	0	0	0	0	1	2
23	0	0	0	0	0	0	0	0	0	0	0	0	1	1	1	2	2	1	0	0	0	0	1	2
	100	100	100	100	100	100	100	100	100	100	100	100	100	100	100	100	100	100	100	100	100	100	100	100

Table 20 Representative Solar RTS Values for Light to Heavy Construction

	Light						Medium						Heavy					
	With Carpet			No Carpet			With Carpet			No Carpet			With Carpet			No Carpet		
% Glass	10%	50%	90%	10%	50%	90%	10%	50%	90%	10%	50%	90%	10%	50%	90%	10%	50%	90%
Hour	Radiant Time Factor, %																	
0	53	55	56	44	45	46	52	54	55	28	29	29	47	49	51	26	27	28
1	17	17	17	19	20	20	16	16	15	15	15	15	11	12	12	12	13	13
2	9	9	9	11	11	11	8	8	8	10	10	10	6	6	6	7	7	7
3	5	5	5	7	7	7	5	4	4	7	7	7	4	4	3	5	5	5
4	3	3	3	5	5	5	3	3	3	6	6	6	3	3	3	4	4	4
5	2	2	2	3	3	3	2	2	2	5	5	5	2	2	2	4	4	4
6	2	2	2	3	2	2	2	1	1	4	4	4	2	2	2	3	3	3
7	1	1	1	2	2	2	1	1	1	4	3	3	2	2	2	3	3	3
8	1	1	1	1	1	1	1	1	1	3	3	3	2	2	2	3	3	3
9	1	1	1	1	1	1	1	1	1	3	3	3	2	2	2	3	3	3
10	1	1	1	1	1	1	1	1	1	2	2	2	2	2	2	3	3	3
11	1	1	1	1	1	1	1	1	1	2	2	2	2	2	1	3	3	2
12	1	1	1	1	1	0	1	1	1	2	2	2	2	1	1	2	2	2
13	1	1	0	1	0	0	1	1	1	2	2	2	2	1	1	2	2	2
14	1	0	0	0	0	0	1	1	1	1	1	1	2	1	1	2	2	2
15	1	0	0	0	0	0	1	1	1	1	1	1	1	1	1	2	2	2
16	0	0	0	0	0	0	1	1	1	1	1	1	1	1	1	2	2	2
17	0	0	0	0	0	0	1	1	1	1	1	1	1	1	1	2	2	2
18	0	0	0	0	0	0	1	1	1	1	1	1	1	1	1	2	2	2
19	0	0	0	0	0	0	0	0	1	1	1	1	1	1	1	2	2	2
20	0	0	0	0	0	0	0	0	1	1	1	1	1	1	1	2	2	2
21	0	0	0	0	0	0	0	0	0	0	0	0	1	1	2	2	1	2
22	0	0	0	0	0	0	0	0	0	0	0	0	1	1	1	2	1	1
23	0	0	0	0	0	0	0	0	0	0	0	0	1	1	1	2	1	1
	100	100	100	100	100	100	100	100	100	100	100	100	100	100	100	100	100	100

Table 21 RTS Representative Zone Construction for Tables 19 and 20

Construction Class	Exterior Wall	Roof/Ceiling	Partitions	Floor	Furnishings
Light	Steel siding, 2 in. insulation, air space, 3/4 in. gyp.	4 in. LW concrete, ceiling air space, acoustic tile	3/4 in. gyp., air space, 3/4 in. gyp.	Acoustic tile, ceiling air space, 4 in. LW concrete	1 in. wood @ 50% of floor area
Medium	4 in. face brick, 2 in. insulation, air space, 3/4 in. gyp.	4 in. HW concrete, ceiling air space, acoustic tile	3/4 in. gyp., air space, 3/4 in. gyp.	Acoustic tile, ceiling air space, 4 in. HW concrete	1 in. wood @ 50% of floor area
Heavy	4 in. face brick, 8 in. HW concrete air space, 2 in. insulation, 3/4 in. gyp.	8 in. HW concrete, ceiling air space, acoustic tile	3/4 in. gyp., 8 in. HW concrete block, 3/4 in. gyp.	Acoustic tile, ceiling air space, 8 in. HW concrete	1 in. wood @ 50% of floor area

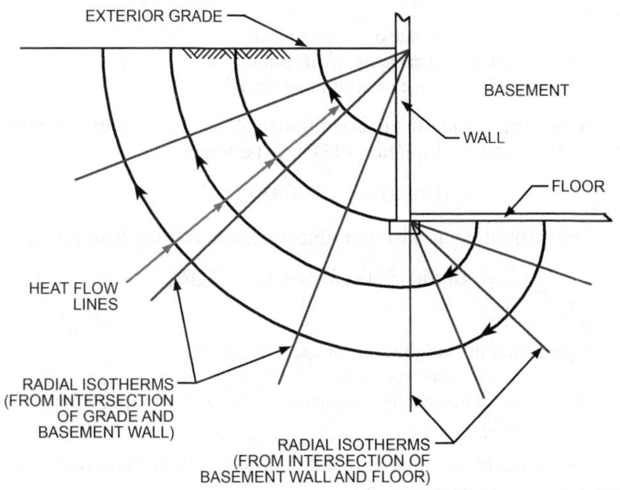

Fig. 12 Heat Flow from Below-Grade Surface

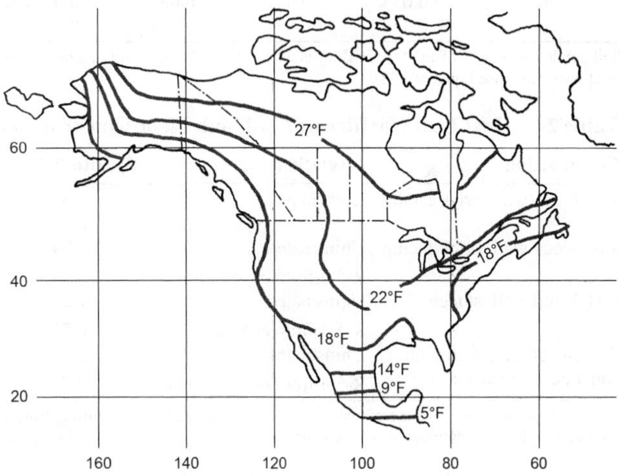

Fig. 13 Ground Temperature Amplitude

where

$\bar{t}_{gr}$ = mean ground temperature, °F, estimated from the annual average air temperature or from well-water temperatures, shown in Figure 18 of Chapter 34 in the 2011 *ASHRAE Handbook—HVAC Applications*

A = ground surface temperature amplitude, °F, from Figure 13 for North America

Figure 14 shows depth parameters used in determining U_{avg}. For walls, the region defined by z_1 and z_2 may be the entire wall or any portion of it, allowing partially insulated configurations to be analyzed piecewise.

The below-grade wall average U-factor is given by

$$U_{avg,bw} = \frac{2k_{soil}}{\pi(z_2 - z_1)} \times \left[\ln\left(z_2 + \frac{2k_{soil}R_{other}}{\pi}\right) - \ln\left(z_1 + \frac{2k_{soil}R_{other}}{\pi}\right)\right] \tag{38}$$

where

$U_{avg,bw}$ = average U-factor for wall region defined by z_1 and z_2, Btu/h·ft²·°F

k_{soil} = soil thermal conductivity, Btu/h·ft·°F

R_{other} = total resistance of wall, insulation, and indoor surface resistance, h·ft²·°F/Btu

z_1, z_2 = depths of top and bottom of wall segment under consideration, ft (Figure 14)

The value of soil thermal conductivity k varies widely with soil type and moisture content. A typical value of 0.8 Btu/h·ft·°F has been used previously to tabulate U-factors, and R_{other} is approximately 1.47 h·ft²·°F/Btu for uninsulated concrete walls. For these parameters, representative values for $U_{avg,bw}$ are shown in Table 22.

The average below-grade floor U-factor (where the entire basement floor is uninsulated or has uniform insulation) is given by

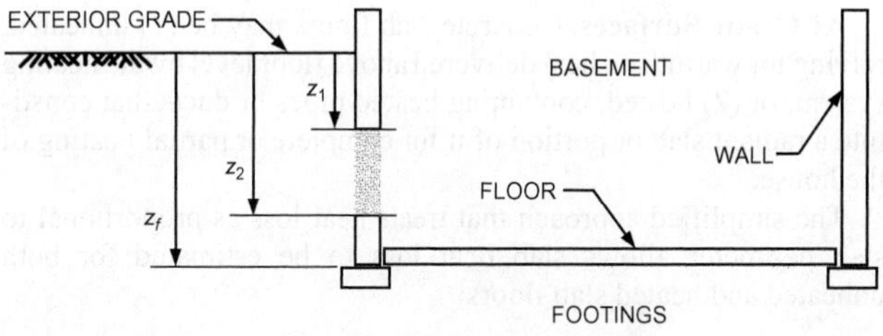

Fig. 14 Below-Grade Parameters

Table 22 Average U-Factor for Basement Walls with Uniform Insulation

Depth, ft	$U_{avg,bw}$ from Grade to Depth, Btu/h·ft²·°F			
	Uninsulated	R-5	R-10	R-15
1	0.432	0.135	0.080	0.057
2.6	0.331	0.121	0.075	0.054
3	0.273	0.110	0.070	0.052
4	0.235	0.101	0.066	0.050
5	0.208	0.094	0.063	0.048
6	0.187	0.088	0.060	0.046
7	0.170	0.083	0.057	0.044
8	0.157	0.078	0.055	0.043

Soil conductivity = 0.8 Btu/h·ft·°F; insulation is over entire depth. For other soil conductivities and partial insulation, use Equation (38).

$$U_{avg,bf} = \frac{2k_{soil}}{\pi w_b} \times \left[\ln\left(\frac{w_b}{2} + \frac{z_f}{2} + \frac{k_{soil}R_{other}}{\pi}\right) - \ln\left(\frac{z_f}{2} + \frac{k_{soil}R_{other}}{\pi}\right)\right] \tag{39}$$

where

w_b = basement width (shortest dimension), ft

Table 23 Average U-Factor for Basement Floors

z_f (Depth of Floor Below Grade), ft	$U_{avg,bf}$, Btu/h·ft²·°F			
	w_b (Shortest Width of Basement), ft			
	20	24	28	32
1	0.064	0.057	0.052	0.047
2	0.054	0.048	0.044	0.040
3	0.047	0.042	0.039	0.036
4	0.042	0.038	0.035	0.033
5	0.038	0.035	0.032	0.030
6	0.035	0.032	0.030	0.028
7	0.032	0.030	0.028	0.026

Soil conductivity is 0.8 Btu/h·ft·°F; floor is uninsulated. For other soil conductivities and insulation, use Equation (38).

Table 24 Heat Loss Coefficient F_p of Slab Floor Construction

Construction	Insulation	F_p, Btu/h·ft·°F
8 in. block wall, brick facing	Uninsulated	0.68
	R-5.4 from edge to footer	0.50
4 in. block wall, brick facing	Uninsulated	0.84
	R-5.4 from edge to footer	0.49
Metal stud wall, stucco	Uninsulated	1.20
	R-5.4 from edge to footer	0.53
Poured concrete wall with duct near perimeter*	Uninsulated	2.12
	R-5.4 from edge to footer	0.72

*Weighted average temperature of heating duct was assumed at 110°F during heating season (outdoor air temperature less than 65°F).

z_f = floor depth below grade, ft (see Figure 14)

Representative values of $U_{avg,bf}$ for uninsulated basement floors are shown in Table 23.

At-Grade Surfaces. Concrete slab floors may be (1) unheated, relying for warmth on heat delivered above floor level by the heating system, or (2) heated, containing heated pipes or ducts that constitute a radiant slab or portion of it for complete or partial heating of the house.

The simplified approach that treats heat loss as proportional to slab perimeter allows slab heat loss to be estimated for both unheated and heated slab floors:

$$q = p \times \mathrm{HF} \quad (40)$$

$$\mathrm{HF} = F_p \Delta t \quad (41)$$

where

q = heat loss through perimeter, Btu/h
F_p = heat loss coefficient per foot of perimeter, Btu/h·ft·°F, Table 24
p = perimeter (exposed edge) of floor, ft

Surfaces Adjacent to Buffer Space. Heat loss to adjacent unconditioned or semiconditioned spaces can be calculated using a heating factor based on the partition temperature difference:

$$\mathrm{HF} = U(t_{in} - t_b) \quad (42)$$

Infiltration

Infiltration of outdoor air through openings into a structure is caused by thermal forces, wind pressure, and negative pressure (planned or unplanned) with respect to the outdoors created by mechanical systems. Typically, in building design, if the mechanical systems are designed to maintain positive building pressure, infiltration need not be considered except in ancillary spaces such as entryways and loading areas.

Infiltration is treated as a room load and has both sensible and latent components. During winter, this means heat and humidity loss because cold, dry air must be heated to design temperature and moisture must be added to increase the humidity to design condition. Typically, during winter, controlling indoor humidity is not a factor and infiltration is reduced to a simple sensible component. Under cooling conditions, both sensible and latent components are added to the space load to be treated by the air conditioning system.Procedures for estimating the infiltration rate are discussed in Chapter 16. The infiltration rate is reduced to a volumetric flow rate at a known dry bulb/wet bulb condition. Along with indoor air condition, the following equations define the infiltration sensible and latent loads.

$$q_s\,(\mathrm{Btu/h}) = 60(\mathrm{cfm}/v)c_p\,(t_{in} - t_o) \quad (43)$$

where

cfm = volume flow rate of infiltrating air
c_p = specific heat capacity of air, Btu/lb$_m$·°F
v = specific volume of infiltrating air, ft³/lb$_m$

Assuming standard air conditions (59°F and sea-level conditions) for v and c_p, Equation (43) may be written as

$$q_s\,(\mathrm{Btu/h}) = 1.10(\mathrm{cfm})(t_{in} - t_o) \quad (44)$$

The infiltrating air also introduces a latent heating load given by

$$q_l\,(\mathrm{Btu/h}) = 60(\mathrm{cfm}/v)(W_{in} - W_o)D_h \quad (45)$$

where

W_{in} = humidity ratio for indoor space air, lb$_w$/lb$_a$
W_o = humidity ratio for outdoor air, lb$_w$/lb$_a$
D_h = change in enthalpy to convert 1 lb water from vapor to liquid, Btu/lb$_w$

For standard air and nominal indoor comfort conditions, the latent load may be expressed as

$$q_l = 4840(\mathrm{cfm})(W_{in} - W_o) \quad (46)$$

The coefficients 1.10 in Equation (44) and 4840 in Equation (46) are given for standard conditions. They depend on temperature and altitude (and, consequently, pressure).

7.2 HEATING SAFETY FACTORS AND LOAD ALLOWANCES

Before mechanical cooling became common in the second half of the 1900s, and when energy was less expensive, buildings included much less insulation; large, operable windows; and generally more infiltration-prone assemblies than the energy-efficient and much tighter buildings typical of today. Allowances of 10 to 20% of the net calculated heating load for piping losses to unheated spaces, and 10 to 20% more for a warm-up load, were common practice, along with other occasional safety factors reflecting the experience and/or concern of the individual designer. Such measures are less conservatively applied today with newer construction. A combined warm-up/safety allowance of 20 to 25% is fairly common but varies depending on the particular climate, building use, and type of construction. Engineering judgment must be applied for the particular project. Armstrong et al. (1992a, 1992b) provide a design method to deal with warm-up and cooldown load.

7.3 OTHER HEATING CONSIDERATIONS

Calculation of design heating load estimates has essentially become a subset of the more involved and complex estimation of cooling loads for such spaces. Chapter 19 discusses using the heating load estimate to predict or analyze energy consumption over time. Special provisions to deal with particular applications are covered in the 2015 *ASHRAE Handbook—HVAC Applications* and the 2016 *ASHRAE Handbook—HVAC Systems and Equipment*.

The 1989 *ASHRAE Handbook—Fundamentals* was the last edition to contain a chapter dedicated only to heating load. Its contents were incorporated into this volume's Chapter 17, which describes

Table 25 Common Sizing Calculations in Other Chapters

Subject	Volume/Chapter	Equation(s)
Duct heat transfer	ASTM *Standard* C680	
Piping heat transfer	Fundamentals Ch. 4	Table 2
Pump power	Systems Ch. 44	(3), (4)
Moist-air sensible heating and cooling	Fundamentals Ch. 1	(43)
Moist-air cooling and dehumidification	Fundamentals Ch. 1	(45)
Air mixing	Fundamentals Ch. 1	(46)
Space heat absorption and moist-air moisture gains	Fundamentals Ch. 1	(48)
Adiabatic mixing of water injected into moist air	Fundamentals Ch. 1	(47)

steady-state conduction and convection heat transfer and provides, among other data, information on losses through basement floors and slabs.

8. SYSTEM HEATING AND COOLING LOAD EFFECTS

The heat balance (HB) or radiant time series (RTS) methods are used to determine cooling loads of rooms within a building, but they do not address the plant size necessary to reject the heat. Principal factors to consider in determining the plant size are ventilation, heat transport equipment, and air distribution systems. Some of these factors vary as a function of room load, ambient temperature, and control strategies, so it is often necessary to evaluate the factors and strategies dynamically and simultaneously with the heat loss or gain calculations.

Detailed analysis of system components and methods calculating their contribution to equipment sizing are beyond the scope of this chapter, which is general in nature. Table 25 lists the most frequently used calculations in other chapters and volumes.

8.1 ZONING

Organization of building rooms into zones as defined for load calculations and air-handling units has no effect on room cooling loads. However, specific grouping and ungrouping of rooms into zones may cause peak system loads to occur at different times during the day or year, and may significantly affect heat removal equipment sizes.

For example, if each room is cooled by a separate heat removal system, the total capacity of the heat transport systems equals the sum of peak room loads. Conditioning all rooms by a single heat transport system (e.g., a variable-volume air handler) requires less capacity (equal to the simultaneous peak of the combined rooms load, which includes some rooms at off-peak loads). This may significantly reduce equipment capacity, depending on the configuration of the building.

8.2 VENTILATION

Consult ASHRAE *Standard* 62.1 and building codes to determine the required quantity of ventilation air for an application, and the various methods of achieving acceptable indoor air quality. The following discussion is confined to the effect of mechanical ventilation on sizing heat removal equipment. Where natural ventilation is used, through operable windows or other means, it is considered as infiltration and is part of the direct-to-room heat gain. Where ventilation air is conditioned and supplied through the mechanical system, its sensible and latent loads are applied directly to heat transport and central equipment, and do not affect room heating and cooling loads. If the mechanical ventilation rate sufficiently exceeds exhaust airflows, air pressure may be positive and infiltration from envelope openings and outdoor wind may not be included in the load calculations. Chapter 16 includes more information on ventilating commercial buildings.

Depending on ventilation requirements and local climate conditions, peak cooling coil loads may occur at peak dehumidification or enthalpy conditions instead of design dry-bulb conditions. Coil loads should be checked against all those peak conditions.

8.3 AIR HEAT TRANSPORT SYSTEMS

Heat transport equipment is usually selected to provide adequate heating or cooling for the peak load condition. However, selection must also consider maintaining desired indoor conditions during all occupied hours, which requires matching the rate of heat transport to room peak heating and cooling loads. Automatic control systems normally vary the heating and cooling system capacity during these off-peak hours of operation.

On/Off Control Systems

On/off control systems, common in residential and light commercial applications, cycle equipment on and off to match room load. They are adaptable to heating or cooling because they can cycle both heating and cooling equipment. In their purest form, their heat transport matches the combined room and ventilation load over a series of cycles.

Variable-Air-Volume Systems

Variable-air-volume (VAV) systems have airflow controls that adjust cooling airflow to match the room cooling load. Damper leakage or minimum airflow settings may cause overcooling, so most VAV systems are used in conjunction with separate heating systems. These may be duct-mounted heating coils, or separate radiant or convective heating systems.

The amount of heat added by the heating systems during cooling becomes part of the room cooling load. Calculations must determine the minimum airflow relative to off-peak cooling loads. The quantity of heat added to the cooling load can be determined for each terminal by Equation (8) using the minimum required supply airflow rate and the difference between supply air temperature and the room indoor heating design temperature.

Constant-Air-Volume Reheat Systems

In constant-air-volume (CAV) reheat systems, all supply air is cooled to remove moisture and then heated to avoid overcooling rooms. *Reheat* refers to the amount of heat added to cooling supply air to raise the supply air temperature to the temperature necessary for picking up the sensible load. The quantity of heat added can be determined by Equation (8).

With a constant-volume reheat system, heat transport system load does not vary with changes in room load, unless the cooling coil discharge temperature is allowed to vary. Where a minimum circulation rate requires a supply air temperature greater than the available design supply air temperature, reheat adds to the cooling load on the heat transport system. This makes the cooling load on the heat transport system larger than the room peak load.

Mixed Air Systems

Mixed air systems change the supply air temperature to match the cooling capacity by mixing airstreams of different temperatures; examples include multizone and dual-duct systems. Systems that cool the entire airstream to remove moisture and to reheat some of the air before mixing with the cooling airstream influence load on the heat transport system in the same way a reheat system does. Other systems separate the air paths so that mixing of hot- and cold-deck airstreams does not occur. For systems that mix hot and cold airstreams, the contribution to the heat transport system load is determined as follows.

1. Determine the ratio of cold-deck flow to hot-deck flow from

$$\frac{Q_h}{Q_c} = (T_c - T_r)/(T_r - T_h)$$

2. From Equation (9), the hot-deck contribution to room load during off-peak cooling is

$$q_{rh} = 1.1Q_h(T_h - T_r)$$

where

Q_h = heating airflow, cfm
Q_c = cooling airflow, cfm
T_c = cooling air temperature, °F
T_h = heating air temperature, °F
T_r = room or return air temperature, °F
q_{rh} = heating airflow contribution to room load at off-peak hours, Btu/h

Heat Gain from Fans

Fans that circulate air through HVAC systems add energy to the system through the following processes:

- Increasing velocity and static pressure adds kinetic and potential energy
- Fan inefficiency in producing airflow and static pressure adds sensible heat (fan heat) to the airflow
- Inefficiency of motor and drive dissipates sensible heat

The power required to provide airflow and static pressure can be determined from the first law of thermodynamics with the following equation:

$$P_A = 0.000157Vp$$

where

P_A = air power, hp
V = flow rate, cfm
p = pressure, in. of water

at standard air conditions with air density = 0.075 lb/ft^3 built into the multiplier 0.000157. The power necessary at the fan shaft must account for fan inefficiencies, which may vary from 50 to 70%. This may be determined from

$$P_F = P_A/\eta_F$$

where

P_F = power required at fan shaft, hp
η_F = fan efficiency, dimensionless

The power necessary at the input to the fan motor must account for fan motor inefficiencies and drive losses. Fan motor efficiencies generally vary from 80 to 95%, and drive losses for a belt drive are 3% of the fan power. This may be determined from

$$P_M = (1 + \text{DL})\,P_F/E_M E_D$$

where

P_M = power required at input to motor, hp
E_D = belt drive efficiency, dimensionless
E_M = fan motor efficiency, dimensionless
P_F = power required at fan shaft, hp
DL = drive loss, dimensionless

Almost all the energy required to generate airflow and static pressure is ultimately dissipated as heat in the building and HVAC system; a small portion is discharged with any exhaust air. Generally, it is assumed that all the heat is released at the fan rather than dispersed to the remainder of the system. The portion of fan heat released to the airstream depends on the location of the fan motor and drive: if they are within the airstream, all the energy input to the fan motor is released to the airstream. If the fan motor and drive are outdoor the airstream, the energy is split between the airstream and the room housing the motor and drive. Therefore, the following equations may be used to calculate heat generated by fans and motors:

If motor and drive are **outside** the airstream,

$$q_{fs} = 2545P_F$$

$$q_{fr} = 2545(P_M - P_F)$$

If motor and drive are **inside** the airstream,

$$q_{fs} = 2545P_M$$

$$q_{fr} = 0.0$$

where

P_F = power required at fan shaft, hp
P_M = power required at input to motor, hp
q_{fs} = heat release to airstream, Btu/h
q_{fr} = heat release to room housing motor and drive, Btu/h
2545 = conversion factor, Btu/h·hp

Supply airstream temperature rise may be determined from psychrometric formulas or Equation (8).

Variable- or adjustable-frequency drives (VFDs or AFDs) often drive fan motors in VAV air-handling units. These devices release heat to the surrounding space. Refer to manufacturers' data for heat released or efficiencies. The disposition of heat released is determined by the drive's location: in the conditioned space, in the return air path, or in a nonconditioned equipment room. These drives, and other electronic equipment such as building control, data processing, and communications devices, are temperature sensitive, so the rooms in which they are housed require cooling, frequently year round.

Duct Surface Heat Transfer

Heat transfer across the duct surface is one mechanism for energy transfer to or from air inside a duct. It involves conduction through the duct wall and insulation, convection at inner and outer surfaces, and radiation between the duct and its surroundings. Chapter 4 presents a rigorous analysis of duct heat loss and gain, and Chapter 23 addresses application of analysis to insulated duct systems.

The effect of duct heat loss or gain depends on the duct routing, duct insulation, and its surrounding environment. Consider the following conditions:

- For duct run within the area cooled or heated by air in the duct, heat transfer from the space to the duct has no effect on heating or cooling load, but beware of the potential for condensation on cold ducts.
- For duct run through unconditioned spaces or outdoors, heat transfer adds to the cooling or heating load for the air transport system but not for the conditioned space.
- For duct run through conditioned space not served by the duct, heat transfer affects the conditioned space as well as the air transport system serving the duct.
- For an extensive duct system, heat transfer reduces the effective supply air differential temperature, requiring adjustment through air balancing to increase airflow to extremities of the distribution system.

Duct Leakage

Air leakage from supply ducts can considerably affect HVAC system energy use. Leakage reduces cooling and/or dehumidifying capacity for the conditioned space, and must be offset by increased airflow (sometimes reduced supply air temperatures), unless leaked air enters the conditioned space directly. Supply air leakage into a ceiling return plenum or leakage from unconditioned spaces into return ducts also affects return air temperature and/or humidity.

Determining leakage from a duct system is complex because of the variables in paths, fabrication, and installation methods. Refer to Chapter 21 and publications from the Sheet Metal and Air Conditioning Contractors' National Association (SMACNA) for methods of determining leakage. In general, good-quality ducts and post-installation duct sealing provide highly cost-effective energy savings, with improved thermal comfort and delivery of ventilation air.

Ceiling Return Air Plenum Temperatures

The space above a ceiling, when used as a return air path, is a ceiling return air plenum, or simply a **return plenum**. Unlike a traditional ducted return, the plenum may have multiple heat sources in the air path. These heat sources may be radiant and convective loads from lighting and transformers; conduction loads from adjacent walls, roofs, or glazing; or duct and piping systems within the plenum.

As heat from these sources is picked up by the unducted return air, the temperature differential between the ceiling cavity and conditioned space is small. Most return plenum temperatures do not rise more than 1 to 3°F above space temperature, thus generating only a relatively small thermal gradient for heat transfer through plenum surfaces, except to the outdoors. This yields a relatively large-percentage reduction in space cooling load by shifting plenum loads to the system. Another reason plenum temperatures do not rise more is leakage into the plenum from supply air ducts, and, if exposed to the roof, increasing levels of insulation.

Where the ceiling space is used as a return air plenum, energy balance requires that heat picked up from the lights into the return air (1) become part of the cooling load to the return air (represented by a temperature rise of return air as it passes through the ceiling space), (2) be partially transferred back into the conditioned space through the ceiling material below, and/or (3) be partially lost from the space through floor surfaces above the plenum. If the plenum has one or more exterior surfaces, heat gains through them must be considered; if adjacent to spaces with different indoor temperatures, partition loads must be considered, too. In a multistory building, the conditioned space frequently gains heat through its floor from a similar plenum below, offsetting the floor loss. The radiant component of heat leaving the ceiling or floor surface of a plenum is normally so small, because of relatively small temperature differences, that all such heat transfer is considered convective for calculation purposes (Rock and Wolfe 1997).

Figure 15 shows a schematic of a typical return air plenum. The following equations, using the heat flow directions shown in Figure 15, represent the heat balance of a return air plenum design for a typical interior room in a multifloor building:

$$q_1 = U_c A_c (t_p - t_r) \tag{47}$$

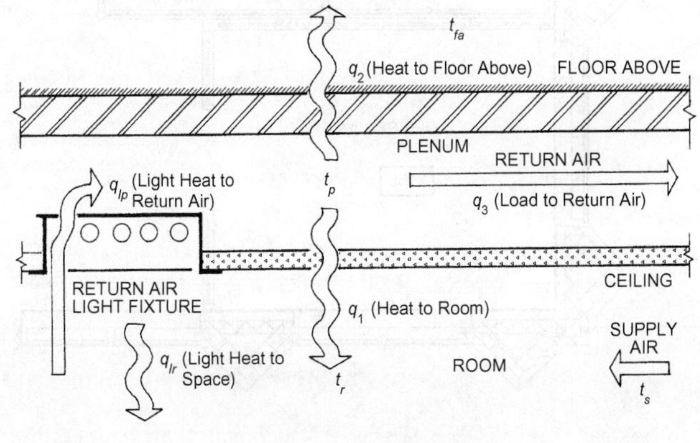

Fig. 15 Schematic Diagram of Typical Return Air Plenum

$$q_2 = U_f A_f (t_p - t_{fa}) \tag{48}$$

$$q_3 = 1.1Q(t_p - t_r) \tag{49}$$

$$q_{lp} - q_2 - q_1 - q_3 = 0 \tag{50}$$

$$Q = \frac{q_r + q_1}{1.1(t_r - t_s)} \tag{51}$$

where

q_1 = heat gain to space from plenum through ceiling, Btu/h
q_2 = heat loss from plenum through floor above, Btu/h
q_3 = heat gain "pickup" by return air, Btu/h
Q = return airflow, cfm
q_{lp} = light heat gain to plenum via return air, Btu/h
q_{lr} = light heat gain to space, Btu/h
q_f = heat gain from plenum below, through floor, Btu/h
q_w = heat gain from exterior wall, Btu/h
q_r = space cooling load, including appropriate treatment of q_{lr}, q_f, and/or q_w, Btu/h
t_p = plenum air temperature, °F
t_r = space air temperature, °F
t_{fa} = space air temperature of floor above, °F
t_s = supply air temperature, °F

By substituting Equations (47), (48), (49), and (51) into heat balance Equation (50), t_p can be found as the resultant return air temperature or plenum temperature. The results, although rigorous and best solved by computer, are important in determining the cooling load, which affects equipment size selection, future energy consumption, and other factors.

Equations (47) to (51) are simplified to illustrate the heat balance relationship. Heat gain into a return air plenum is not limited to heat from lights. Exterior walls directly exposed to the ceiling space can transfer heat directly to or from return air. For single-story buildings or the top floor of a multistory building, roof heat gain or loss enters or leaves the ceiling plenum rather than the conditioned space directly. The supply air quantity calculated by Equation (51) is only for the conditioned space under consideration, and is assumed to equal the return air quantity.

The amount of airflow through a return plenum above a conditioned space may not be limited to that supplied into the space; it will, however, have no noticeable effect on plenum temperature if the surplus comes from an adjacent plenum operating under similar conditions. Where special conditions exist, Equations (47) to (51) must be modified appropriately. Finally, although the building's thermal storage has some effect, the amount of heat entering the return air is small and may be considered as convective for calculation purposes.

Ceiling Plenums with Ducted Returns

Compared to those in unducted plenum returns, temperatures in ceiling plenums that have well-sealed return or exhaust air ducts float considerably. In cooling mode, heat from lights and other equipment raises the ceiling plenum's temperature considerably. Solar heat gain through a poorly insulated roof can drive the ceiling plenum temperature to extreme levels, so much so that heat gains to uninsulated supply air ducts in the plenum can dramatically decrease available cooling capacity to the rooms below. In cold weather, much heat is lost from warm supply ducts. Thus, insulating supply air ducts and sealing them well to minimize air leaks are highly desirable, if not essential. Appropriately insulating roofs and plenums' exterior walls and minimizing infiltration are also key to lowering total building loads and improving HVAC system performance.

Underfloor Air Distribution Systems

Room cooling loads determined by methods in this chapter cannot model two distinguishing aspects of the thermal performance of underfloor air distribution (UFAD) systems under cooling operation:

- Room air stratification: UFAD systems supply cool air at the floor and extract warmer air at the ceiling, thus creating vertical thermal stratification. Cooling load models assume a well-mixed uniform space temperature.
- Underfloor air supply plenums: cool supply air flowing through the underfloor plenum is exposed to heat gain from both the concrete slab (conducted from the warm return air on the adjacent floor below in a multistory building) and the raised floor panels (conducted from the warmer room above).

Extensive simulation and experimental research led to the development of a whole-building energy simulation program capable of modeling energy performance and load calculations for UFAD systems (Bauman et al. 2007; Webster et al. 2008). Previously, it was thought that cooling loads for UFAD and overhead (OH) mixing systems were nearly identical. However, energy modeling studies show that the UFAD cooling load is generally higher than that calculated in the same building for a well-mixed system (Schiavon et al. 2010a). The difference is primarily caused by the thermal storage effect of the lighter-weight raised-floor panels compared to the greater mass of a structural floor slab. Schiavon et al. (2010b) showed that the presence of the raised floor reduces the slab's ability to store heat, thereby producing higher peak cooling loads for a raised-floor system than for one without a raised floor. A second contributing factor is that the raised-floor surface above the underfloor plenum tends to be cooler (except when illuminated by the sun) than most other room surfaces, producing a room surface temperature distribution resembling a chilled radiant floor system, which has a different peak cooling load than an all-air system (Feng et al. 2012). The precise magnitude of difference in design cooling loads between OH and UFAD systems is still under investigation, but mainly depends on zone orientation and floor level, and possibly the effects of furniture. Methods for determining UFAD cooling loads will be updated as additional research results become available. For more information about simplified approaches to UFAD cooling load calculations, see the ASHRAE *Underfloor Air Distribution (UFAD) Design Guide* (ASHRAE 2013), Bauman et al. (2010), and Schiavon et al. (2010c).

Plenums in Load Calculations

Currently, most designers include ceiling and floor plenums within neighboring occupied spaces when thermally zoning a building. However, temperatures in these plenums, and the way that they behave, are significantly different from those of occupied spaces. Thus, they should be defined as a separate thermal zone. Most hand and computer-based load calculation routines, though, currently do not allow floating air temperatures or humidities; assuming a constant air temperature in plenums, attics, and other unconditioned spaces is a poor, but often necessary, assumption. The heat balance method does allow floating space conditions, and when fully implemented in design load software, should allow more accurate modeling of plenums and other complex spaces.

8.4 CENTRAL PLANT

Piping

Losses must be considered for piping systems that transport heat. For water or hydronic piping systems, heat is transferred through the piping and insulation (see Chapter 23 for ways to determine this transfer). However, distribution of this transferred heat depends on the fluid in the pipe and the surrounding environment.

Consider a heating hot-water pipe. If the pipe serves a room heater and is routed through the heated space, any heat loss from the pipe adds heat to the room. Heat transfer to the heated space and heat loss from the piping system is null. If the piping is exposed to ambient conditions en route to the heater, the loss must be considered when selecting the heating equipment; if the pipe is routed through a space requiring cooling, heat loss from the piping also becomes a load on the cooling system.

In summary, the designer must evaluate both the magnitude of the pipe heat transfer and the routing of the piping.

Pumps

Calculating heat gain from pumps is addressed in the section on Electric Motors. For pumps serving hydronic systems, disposition of heat from the pumps depends on the service. For chilled-water systems, energy applied to the fluid to generate flow and pressure becomes a chiller load. For condenser water pumps, pumping energy must be rejected through the cooling tower. The magnitude of pumping energy relative to cooling load is generally small.

9. EXAMPLE COOLING AND HEATING LOAD CALCULATIONS

To illustrate the cooling and heating load calculation procedures discussed in this chapter, an example problem has been developed based on the ASHRAE headquarters building located in Atlanta, Georgia. This example is a two-story office building of approximately 35,000 ft^2, including a variety of common office functions and occupancies. In addition to demonstrating calculation procedures, a hypothetical design/construction process is discussed to illustrate (1) application of load calculations and (2) the need to develop reasonable assumptions when specific data are not yet available, as often occurs in everyday design processes.

Table 26 summarizes RTS load calculation procedures.

9.1 SINGLE-ROOM EXAMPLE

Calculate the peak heating and cooling loads for the office room shown in Figure 16, for Atlanta, Georgia. The room is on the second floor of a two-story building and has two vertical exterior exposures, with a flat roof above.

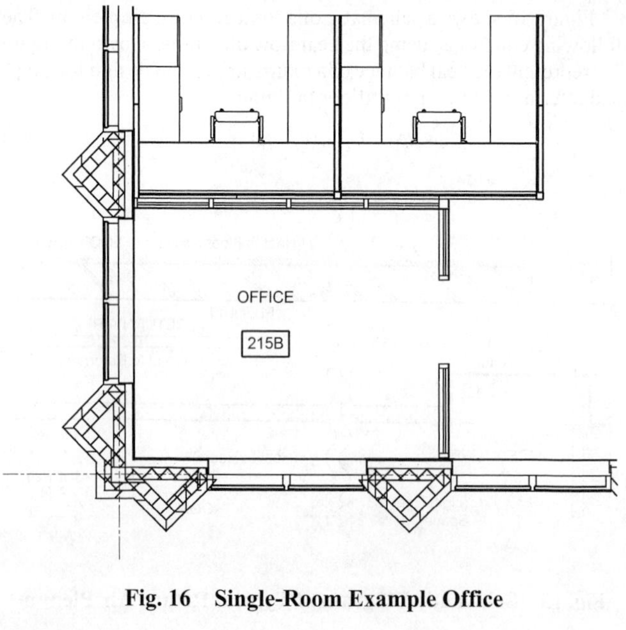

Fig. 16 Single-Room Example Office

Table 26 Summary of RTS Load Calculation Procedures

Equation	Equation No. in Chapter
External Heat Gain	
Sol-Air Temperature	
$t_e = t_o + \frac{\alpha E_t}{h_o} - \frac{\varepsilon \Delta R}{h_o}$	(29)
where	
t_e = sol-air temperature, °F	
t_o = outdoor air temperature, °F	
a = absorptance of surface for solar radiation	
E_t = total solar radiation incident on surface, Btu/h·ft²	
h_o = coefficient of heat transfer by long-wave radiation and convection at outer surface, Btu/h·ft²·°F	
ε = hemispherical emittance of surface	
ΔR = difference between long-wave radiation incident on surface from sky and surroundings and radiation emitted by blackbody at outdoor air temperature, Btu/h·ft²; 20 for horizontal surfaces; 0 for vertical surfaces	
Wall and Roof Transmission	
$q_\theta = c_0 q_{i,\theta} + c_1 q_{i,\theta\text{-}1} + c_2 q_{i,\theta\text{-}2} + \dots + c_{23} q_{i,\theta\text{-}23}$	(31)
$q_{i,\theta\text{-}n} = UA(t_{e,\theta\text{-}n} - t_{rc})$	(30)
where	
q_θ = hourly conductive heat gain for surface, Btu/h	
$q_{i,\theta}$ = heat input for current hour	
$q_{i,\theta\text{-}n}$ = conductive heat input for surface n hours ago, Btu/h	
c_0, c_1, etc. = conduction time factors	
U = overall heat transfer coefficient for surface, Btu/h·ft²·°F	
A = surface area, ft²	
Fenestration Transmission	
$q_c = UA(T_{out} - T_{in})$	(14)
where	
q = fenestration transmission heat gain, Btu/h	
U = overall U-factor, including frame and mounting orientation from Table 4 of Chapter 15, Btu/h·ft²·°F	
A = window area, ft²	
T_{in} = indoor temperature, °F	
T_{out} = outdoor temperature, °F	
Fenestration Solar	
T_{out} = outdoor temperature, °F	
$q_b = AE_{t,b}\,\text{SHGC}(\theta)\text{IAC}(\theta,\Omega)$	(12)
$q_d = A(E_{t,d} + E_{t,r})\langle \text{SHGC} \rangle_D\, \text{IAC}_D$	(13)
where	
q_b = beam solar heat gain, Btu/h	
q_d = diffuse solar heat gain, Btu/h	
A = window area, ft²	
$E_{t,b}$, $E_{t,d}$, and $E_{t,r}$ = beam, sky diffuse, and ground-reflected diffuse irradiance, calculated using equations in Chapter 14	
SHGC(θ) = beam solar heat gain coefficient as a function of incident angle θ; may be interpolated between values in Table 10 of Chapter 15	
IAC(θ.Ω) = indoor solar attenuation coefficient for beam solar heat gain coefficient; = 1.0 if no indoor shading device. IAC(θ.Ω) is a function of shade type and, depending on type, may also be a function of beam solar angle of incidence θ and shade geometry	
IAC_D = indoor solar attenuation coefficient for diffuse solar heat gain coefficient; = 1.0 if not indoor shading device. IAC_D is a function of shade type and, depending on type, may also be a function of shade geometry	
Partitions, Ceilings, Floors Transmission	
$q = UA(t_b - t_i)$	(32)
where	
q = heat transfer rate, Btu/h	
U = coefficient of overall heat transfer between adjacent and conditioned space, Btu/h·ft²·°F	
A = area of separating section concerned, ft²	
t_b = average air temperature in adjacent space, °F	
t_i = air temperature in conditioned space, °F	
Internal Heat Gain	
Occupants	
$q_s = q_{s,per} N$	
$q_l = q_{l,per} N$	
where	
q_s = occupant sensible heat gain, Btu/h	
q_l = occupant latent heat gain, Btu/h	
$q_{l,per}$ = latent heat gain per person, Btu/h·person; see Table 1	
N = number of occupants	
Lighting	
$q_{el} = 3.41 W F_{ul} F_{sa}$	(1)
where	
q_{el} = heat gain, Btu/h	
W = total light wattage, W	
F_{ul} = lighting use factor	
F_{sa} = lighting special allowance factor	
3.41 = conversion factor	
Electric Motors	
$q_{em} = 2545(P/E_M)F_{UM}F_{LM}$	(2)
where	
q_{em} = heat equivalent of equipment operation, Btu/h	
P = motor power rating, hp	
E_M = motor efficiency, decimal fraction <1.0	
F_{UM} = motor use factor, 1.0 or decimal fraction <1.0	
F_{LM} = motor load factor, 1.0 or decimal fraction <1.0	
2545 = conversion factor, Btu/h·hp	
Hooded Cooking Appliances	
$q_s = q_{input} F_U F_R$	
where	
q_s = sensible heat gain, Btu/h	
q_{input} = nameplate or rated energy input, Btu/h	
F_U = usage factor; see Tables 5B, 5C, 5D	
F_R = radiation factor; see Tables 5B, 5C, 5D	
For other appliances and equipment, find q_s for	
Unhooded cooking appliances: Table 5A	
Other kitchen equipment: Table 5E	
Hospital and laboratory equipment: Tables 6 and 7	
Computers, printers, scanners, etc.: Tables 8 and 9	
Miscellaneous office equipment: Table 10	
Find q_l for	
Unhooded cooking appliances: Table 5A	
Other kitchen equipment: Table 5E	
Ventilation and Infiltration Air Heat Gain	
$q_s = 1.10 Q_s \Delta t$	(9)
$q_l = 60 \times 0.075 \times 1076 Q_s \Delta W = 4840 Q_s \Delta W$	(10)
where	
q_s = sensible heat gain due to infiltration, Btu/h	

Table 26 Summary of RTS Load Calculation Procedures (*Concluded*)

Equation	Equation No. in Chapter
q_l = latent heat gain due to infiltration, Btu/h Q_s = infiltration airflow at standard air conditions, cfm t_o = outdoor air temperature, °F t_i = indoor air temperature, °F W_o = outdoor air humidity ratio, lb/lb W_i = indoor air humidity ratio, lb/lb 1.10 = air sensible heat factor at standard air conditions, Btu/h·cfm 4840 = air latent heat factor at standard air conditions, Btu/h·cfm	
Instantaneous Room Cooling Load	
$Q_s = \Sigma Q_{i,r} + \Sigma Q_{i,c}$ $Q_l = \Sigma q_{i,l}$	
where Q_s = room sensible cooling load, Btu/h $Q_{i,r}$ = radiant portion of sensible cooling load for current hour, resulting from heat gain element i, Btu/h $Q_{i,c}$ = convective portion of sensible cooling load, resulting from heat gain element i, Btu/h Q_l = room latent cooling load, Btu/h $q_{i,l}$ = latent heat gain for heat gain element i, Btu/h	
Radiant Portion of Sensible Cooling Load	
$Q_{i,r} = Q_{r,\theta}$	
$Q_{r,\theta} = r_0 q_{r,\theta} + r_1 q_{r,\theta-1} + r_2 q_{r,\theta-2} + r_3 q_{r,\theta-3} + \cdots + r_{23} q_{r,\theta-23}$	(33)
where $Q_{r,\theta}$ = radiant cooling load Q_r for current hour θ, Btu/h $q_{r,\theta}$ = radiant heat gain for current hour, Btu/h $q_{r,\theta-n}$ = radiant heat gain n hours ago, Btu/h r_0, r_1, etc. = radiant time factors; see Table 19 for radiant time factors for nonsolar heat gains: wall, roof, partition, ceiling, floor, fenestration transmission heat gains, and occupant, lighting, motor, appliance heat gain. Also used for fenestration diffuse solar heat gain; see Table 20 for radiant time factors for fenestration beam solar heat gain.	
$q_{r,\theta} = q_{i,s} F_r$	
where $q_{i,s}$ = sensible heat gain from heat gain element i, Btu/h F_r = fraction of heat gain that is radiant.	
Data Sources: Wall transmission: see Table 14 Roof transmission: see Table 14 Floor transmission: see Table 14 Fenestration transmission: see Table 14 Fenestration solar heat gain: see Table 14, Chapter 18 and Tables 14A to 14G, Chapter 15 Lighting: see Table 3 Occupants: see Tables 1 and 14 Hooded cooking appliances: see Tables 5B, 5C, and 5D Unhooded cooking appliances: see Table 5A Other appliances and equipment: see Tables 5E, 8, 9, 10, and 14 Infiltration: see Table 14 Lighting: see Table 3	
Convective Portion of Sensible Cooling Load	
$Q_{i,c} = q_{i,c}$	
where $q_{i,c}$ is convective portion of heat gain from heat gain element i, Btu/h.	
$q_{i,c} = q_{i,s}(1 - F_r)$	
where $q_{i,s}$ = sensible heat gain from heat gain element i, Btu/h F_r = fraction of heat gain that is radiant; see row for radiant portion for sources of radiant fraction data for individual heat gain elements	

Room Characteristics

Area: 130 ft^2.

Floor: Carpeted 5 in. concrete slab on metal deck above a conditioned space.

Roof: Flat metal deck topped with rigid closed-cell polyisocyanurate foam core insulation (R = 30), and light-colored membrane roofing. Space above 9 ft suspended acoustical tile ceiling is used as a return air plenum. Assume 30% of cooling load from the roof is directly absorbed in the return airstream without becoming room load. Use roof U = 0.032 Btu/h·ft^2·°F.

Spandrel wall: Spandrel bronze-tinted glass, opaque, backed with air space, rigid mineral fiber insulation (R = 5.0), mineral fiber batt insulation (R = 13), and 5/8 in. gypsum wall board. Use spandrel wall U = 0.077 Btu/h·ft^2·°F.

Brick wall: Light-brown-colored face brick (4 in.), lightweight concrete block (6 in.), rigid continuous insulation (R = 5), mineral fiber batt insulation (R = 13), and gypsum wall board (5/8 in.). Use brick wall U = 0.08 Btu/h·ft^2·°F.

Windows: Double glazed, 1/4 in. bronze-tinted outdoor pane, 1/2 in. air space and 1/4 in. clear indoor pane with light-colored interior miniblinds. Window normal solar heat gain coefficient (SHGC) = 0.49. Windows are nonoperable and mounted in aluminum frames with thermal breaks having overall combined U = 0.56 Btu/h·ft^2·°F (based on Type 5d from Tables 4 and 10 of Chapter 15). Indoor attenuation coefficients (IACs) for indoor miniblinds are based on light venetian blinds (assumed louver reflectance = 0.8 and louvers positioned at 45° angle) with heat-absorbing double glazing (Type 5d from Table 14B of Chapter 15), IAC(0) = 0.74, IAC(60) = 0.65, IAD(diff) = 0.79, and radiant fraction = 0.54. Each window is 6.25 ft wide by 6.4 ft tall for an area per window = 40 ft^2.

South exposure:	Orientation	= 30° east of true south
	Window area	= 40 ft^2
	Spandrel wall area	= 60 ft^2
	Brick wall area	= 60 ft^2
West exposure:	Orientation	= 60° west of south
	Window area	= 40 ft^2
	Spandrel wall area	= 60 ft^2
	Brick wall area	= 40 ft^2

Occupancy: 1 person from 8:00 AM to 5:00 PM.

Lighting: One 4-lamp pendant fluorescent 8 ft type. The fixture has four 32 W T-8 lamps plus electronic ballasts (special allowance factor 0.85 per manufacturer's data), for a total of 110 W for the room. Operation is from 7:00 AM to 7:00 PM. Assume 0% of cooling load from lighting is directly absorbed in the return airstream without becoming room load, per Table 3.

Table 27 Monthly/Hourly 5% Design Temperatures for Hartsfield-Jackson Atlanta International Airport, °F

	January		February		March		April		May		June		July		August		September		October		November		December	
Hour	db	wb	db	wb	db	wb	db	wb	db	wb	db	wb	db	wb	db	wb	db	wb	db	wb	db	wb	db	wb
1	45.8	45.2	47.5	45.2	53.7	49.4	59.8	55.0	66.9	62.2	72.1	66.7	73.8	68.9	73.7	68.9	69.6	64.7	60.2	56.9	51.9	50.3	47.4	47.4
2	45.1	44.7	46.7	44.7	52.8	49.0	59.0	54.7	66.1	61.9	71.3	66.4	73.0	68.7	73.0	68.7	68.8	64.4	59.4	56.5	51.1	49.8	46.7	46.7
3	44.5	44.3	46.0	44.3	52.1	48.7	58.3	54.4	65.5	61.7	70.7	66.2	72.4	68.5	72.4	68.5	68.3	64.2	58.8	56.2	50.4	49.5	46.1	46.1
4	43.9	43.9	45.4	43.9	51.5	48.3	57.6	54.1	64.9	61.5	70.1	66.0	71.8	68.3	71.8	68.3	67.7	64.0	58.2	56.0	49.8	49.1	45.5	45.5
5	43.5	43.5	45.0	43.6	51.0	48.1	57.2	53.9	64.5	61.3	69.7	65.9	71.4	68.2	71.4	68.2	67.3	63.9	57.8	55.8	49.4	48.9	45.1	45.1
6	43.9	43.9	45.4	43.9	51.5	48.3	57.6	54.1	64.9	61.5	70.1	66.0	71.8	68.3	71.8	68.3	67.7	64.0	58.2	56.0	49.8	49.1	45.5	45.5
7	45.3	44.8	46.9	44.8	53.0	49.1	59.2	54.8	66.3	62.0	71.5	66.5	73.2	68.7	73.2	68.7	69.0	64.5	59.6	56.6	51.3	50.0	46.9	46.9
8	48.6	47.1	50.4	47.1	56.9	51.0	62.9	56.4	69.7	63.3	74.9	67.6	76.7	69.8	76.5	69.8	72.3	65.7	63.1	58.1	54.8	51.9	50.2	49.2
9	52.3	49.7	54.4	49.6	61.1	53.1	67.1	58.2	73.5	64.7	78.7	68.9	80.5	70.9	80.2	70.9	75.9	67.0	67.0	59.8	58.8	54.2	53.9	51.7
10	55.6	52.0	58.0	51.8	65.0	54.9	70.8	59.8	77.0	66.0	82.2	70.0	83.9	72.0	83.5	71.9	79.1	68.1	70.4	61.3	62.4	56.2	57.2	54.0
11	58.5	54.1	61.1	53.8	68.3	56.6	74.1	61.2	80.0	67.1	85.2	71.0	87.0	72.9	86.4	72.8	82.0	69.1	73.5	62.7	65.5	57.9	60.1	56.0
12	60.5	55.4	63.2	55.2	70.6	57.7	76.3	62.2	82.0	67.8	87.2	71.6	89.0	73.5	88.4	73.4	83.9	69.8	75.5	63.5	67.6	59.1	62.1	57.3
13	62.0	56.5	64.9	56.2	72.4	58.6	78.1	62.9	83.6	68.4	88.8	72.2	90.6	74.0	89.9	73.9	85.4	70.4	77.2	64.3	69.3	60.0	63.6	58.3
14	63.0	57.2	65.9	56.9	73.5	59.1	79.2	63.4	84.6	68.8	89.8	72.5	91.6	74.3	90.9	74.2	86.4	70.7	78.2	64.7	70.3	60.6	64.6	59.0
15	63.0	57.2	65.9	56.9	73.5	59.1	79.2	63.4	84.6	68.8	89.8	72.5	91.6	74.3	90.9	74.2	86.4	70.7	78.2	64.7	70.3	60.6	64.6	59.0
16	61.8	56.4	64.6	56.1	72.2	58.4	77.9	62.8	83.4	68.4	88.6	72.1	90.4	73.9	89.7	73.8	85.3	70.3	77.0	64.2	69.0	59.9	63.4	58.2
17	60.3	55.3	63.0	55.0	70.4	57.6	76.1	62.1	81.8	67.8	87.0	71.6	88.8	73.4	88.2	73.4	83.7	69.7	75.3	63.5	67.4	59.0	61.9	57.2
18	58.3	53.9	60.9	53.7	68.1	56.5	73.9	61.1	79.8	67.0	85.0	70.9	86.8	72.8	86.2	72.8	81.8	69.1	73.3	62.6	65.3	57.8	59.9	55.8
19	55.4	51.9	57.7	51.7	64.7	54.8	70.6	59.7	76.8	65.9	82.0	69.9	83.7	71.9	83.3	71.9	79.0	68.0	70.2	61.2	62.1	56.0	57.0	53.9
20	53.3	50.4	55.5	50.3	62.3	53.6	68.2	58.7	74.6	65.1	79.8	69.2	81.5	71.3	81.2	71.2	76.9	67.3	68.0	60.3	59.9	54.8	54.9	52.4
21	51.5	49.2	53.6	49.1	60.2	52.6	66.2	57.8	72.7	64.4	77.9	68.6	79.7	70.7	79.4	70.7	75.1	66.7	66.2	59.4	58.0	53.7	53.1	51.2
22	49.7	48.0	51.7	47.9	58.2	51.6	64.2	56.9	70.9	63.7	76.1	68.0	77.9	70.2	77.6	70.1	73.4	66.1	64.3	58.6	56.1	52.6	51.3	50.0
23	48.4	47.0	50.2	46.9	56.6	50.9	62.7	56.3	69.5	63.2	74.7	67.6	76.5	69.7	76.3	69.7	72.1	65.6	62.9	58.0	54.6	51.8	50.0	49.1
24	47.0	46.0	48.8	46.0	55.1	50.1	61.2	55.6	68.1	62.7	73.3	67.1	75.0	69.3	74.9	69.3	70.7	65.1	61.5	57.4	53.2	51.0	48.6	48.2

Equipment: One computer and a personal printer are used, for which an allowance of 1 W/ft^2 is to be accommodated by the cooling system, for a total of 130 W for the room. Operation is from 8:00 AM to 5:00 PM.

Infiltration: For purposes of this example, assume the building is maintained under positive pressure during peak cooling conditions and therefore has no infiltration. Assume that infiltration during peak heating conditions is equivalent to one air change per hour.

Weather data: Per Chapter 14, for Atlanta, Georgia, latitude = 33.64, longitude = 84.43, elevation = 1027 ft above sea level, 99.6% heating design dry-bulb temperature = 21.9°F. For cooling load calculations, use 5% dry-bulb/coincident wet-bulb monthly design day profile calculated per Chapter 14. See Table 27 for temperature profiles used in these examples.

Indoor design conditions: 72°F for heating; 75°F with 50% rh for cooling.

Cooling Loads Using RTS Method

Traditionally, simplified cooling load calculation methods have estimated the total cooling load at a particular design condition by independently calculating and then summing the load from each component (walls, windows, people, lights, etc). Although the actual heat transfer processes for each component do affect each other, this simplification is appropriate for design load calculations and useful to the designer in understanding the relative contribution of each component to the total cooling load.

Cooling loads are calculated with the RTS method on a component basis similar to previous methods. The following example parts illustrate cooling load calculations for individual components of this single room for a particular hour and month. Equations used are summarized in Table 26.

Part 1. Internal cooling load using radiant time series. Calculate the cooling load from lighting at 3:00 PM for the previously described office.

Solution: First calculate the 24 h heat gain profile for lighting, then split those heat gains into radiant and convective portions, apply the appropriate RTS to the radiant portion, and sum the convective and radiant cooling load components to determine total cooling load at the designated time. Using Equation (1), the lighting heat gain profile, based on the occupancy schedule indicated is

$$
\begin{array}{ll}
q_1 = (110\text{ W})3.41(0\%) = 0 & q_{13} = (110\text{ W})3.41(100\%) = 375 \\
q_2 = (110\text{ W})3.41(0\%) = 0 & q_{14} = (110\text{ W})3.41(100\%) = 375 \\
q_3 = (110\text{ W})3.41(0\%) = 0 & q_{15} = (110\text{ W})3.41(100\%) = 375 \\
q_4 = (110\text{ W})3.41(0\%) = 0 & q_{16} = (110\text{ W})3.41(100\%) = 375 \\
q_5 = (110\text{ W})3.41(0\%) = 0 & q_{17} = (110\text{ W})3.41(100\%) = 375 \\
q_6 = (110\text{ W})3.41(0\%) = 0 & q_{18} = (110\text{ W})3.41(100\%) = 375 \\
q_7 = (110\text{ W})3.41(100\%) = 375 & q_{19} = (110\text{ W})3.41(0\%) = 0 \\
q_8 = (110\text{ W})3.41(100\%) = 375 & q_{20} = (110\text{ W})3.41(0\%) = 0 \\
q_9 = (110\text{ W})3.41(100\%) = 375 & q_{21} = (110\text{ W})3.41(0\%) = 0 \\
q_{10} = (110\text{ W})3.41(100\%) = 375 & q_{22} = (110\text{ W})3.41(0\%) = 0 \\
q_{11} = (110\text{ W})3.41(100\%) = 375 & q_{23} = (110\text{ W})3.41(0\%) = 0 \\
q_{12} = (110\text{ W})3.41(100\%) = 375 & q_{24} = (110\text{ W})3.41(0\%) = 0
\end{array}
$$

The convective portion is simply the lighting heat gain for the hour being calculated times the convective fraction for non-in-ceiling fluorescent luminaire (pendant), from Table 3:

$$Q_{c,15} = (375)(43\%) = 161.3 \text{ Btu/h}$$

The radiant portion of the cooling load is calculated using lighting heat gains for the current hour and past 23 h, the radiant fraction from Table 3 (57%), and radiant time series from Table 19, in accordance with Equation (33). From Table 19, select the RTS for medium-weight construction, assuming 50% glass and carpeted floors as representative of the described construction. Thus, the radiant cooling load for lighting is

$$
\begin{aligned}
Q_{r,15} &= r_0(0.48)q_{15} + r_1(0.48)q_{14} + r_2(0.48)q_{13} + r_3(0.48)q_{12} + \cdots \\
&\quad + r_{23}(0.48)q_{16} \\
&= (0.49)(0.57)(375) + (0.17)(0.57)(375) \\
&\quad + (0.09)(0.57)(375) + (0.05)(0.57)(375) + (0.03)(0.57)(375) \\
&\quad + (0.02)(0.57)(375) + (0.02)(0.57)(375) + (0.01)(0.57)(375) \\
&\quad + (0.01)(0.57)(375) + (0.01)(0.57)\ (0) + (0.01)(0.57)(0) \\
&\quad + (0.01)(0.57)(0) + (0.01)(0.57)(0) + (0.01)(0.57)(0) \\
&\quad + (0.01)(0.5748)(0) + (0.01)(0.57)(0) + (0.01)(0.57)(0) \\
&\quad + (0.01)(0.57)(0)
\end{aligned}
$$

Table 28 Cooling Load Component: Lighting, Btu/h

Hour	Usage Profile, %	Heat Gain	Heat Gain: Convective 43%	Heat Gain: Radiant 57%	Nonsolar RTS Zone Type 8, %	Radiant Cooling Load	Total Sensible Cooling Load	% Lighting to Return 0%	Room Sensible Cooling Load
1	0	—	—	—	49	26	26	—	26
2	0	—	—	—	17	26	26	—	26
3	0	—	—	—	9	24	24	—	24
4	0	—	—	—	5	21	21	—	21
5	0	—	—	—	3	19	19	—	19
6	0	—	—	—	2	17	17	—	17
7	100	375	161	214	2	120	281	—	281
8	100	375	161	214	1	154	315	—	315
9	100	375	161	214	1	171	332	—	332
10	100	375	161	214	1	180	341	—	341
11	100	375	161	214	1	184	345	—	345
12	100	375	161	214	1	186	347	—	347
13	100	375	161	214	1	188	349	—	349
14	100	375	161	214	1	188	349	—	349
15	100	375	161	214	1	190	352	—	352
16	100	375	161	214	1	192	354	—	354
17	100	375	161	214	1	195	356	—	356
18	100	375	161	214	1	197	358	—	358
19	0	—	—	—	1	94	94	—	94
20	0	—	—	—	1	60	60	—	60
21	0	—	—	—	0	43	43	—	43
22	0	—	—	—	0	34	34	—	34
23	0	—	—	—	0	30	30	—	30
24	0	—	—	—	0	28	28	—	28
		4,501	1,936	2,566	100	2,566	4,501	—	4,501

$+ (0.01)(0.57)(0) + (0.01)(0.57)(0) + (0.00)(0.57)(0)$
$+ (0.00)(0.57)(375) + (0.00)(0.57)(375)$
$+ (0.00)(0.57)(375) = 190.3$ Btu/h

The total lighting cooling load at the designated hour is thus

$$Q_{light} = Q_{c,15} + Q_{r,15} = 161.3 + 190.3 = 351.6 \text{ Btu/h}$$

See Table 28 for the office's lighting usage, heat gain, and cooling load profiles.

Part 2. Wall cooling load using sol-air temperature, conduction time series and radiant time series. Calculate the cooling load contribution from the spandrel wall section facing 60° west of south at 3:00 PM local standard time in July for the previously described office.

Solution: Determine the wall cooling load by calculating (1) sol-air temperatures at the exterior surface, (2) heat input based on sol-air temperature, (3) delayed heat gain through the mass of the wall to the interior surface using conduction time series, and (4) delayed space cooling load from heat gain using radiant time series.

First, calculate the sol-air temperature at 3:00 PM local standard time (LST) (4:00 PM daylight saving time) on July 21 for a vertical, dark-colored wall surface, facing 60° west of south, located in Atlanta, Georgia (latitude = 33.64, longitude = 84.43), solar clear sky optical depth for beam irradiance τ_b ("taub") = 0.515 and τ_d ("taud") for diffuse irradiance = 2.066 from monthly Atlanta weather data for July (Table 1 in Chapter 14). From Table 27, the calculated outdoor design temperature for that month and time is 91.6°F. The ground reflectivity is assumed $\rho_g = 0.2$.

Sol-air temperature is calculated using Equation (30). For the dark-colored wall, $\alpha/h_o = 0.30$, and for vertical surfaces, $\varepsilon\Delta R/h_o = 0$. The solar irradiance E_t on the wall must be determined using the equations in Chapter 14:

Solar Angles:

ψ = southwest orientation = +60°

Σ = surface tilt from horizontal (where horizontal = 0°) = 90° for vertical wall surface

3:00 PM LST = hour 15

Calculate solar altitude, solar azimuth, surface solar azimuth, and incident angle as follows:

From Table 2 in Chapter 14, solar position data and constants for July 21 are

$ET = -6.4$ min
$\delta = 20.4°$
$E_o = 419.8$ Btu/h·ft²

Local standard meridian (LSM) for Eastern Time Zone = 75°.

Apparent solar time AST

$$\begin{aligned} AST &= LST + ET/60 + (LSM - LON)/15 \\ &= 15 + (-6.4/60) + [(75 - 84.43)/15] \\ &= 14.2647 \end{aligned}$$

Hour angle H, degrees

$$\begin{aligned} H &= 15(AST - 12) \\ &= 15(14.2647 - 12) \\ &= 33.97° \end{aligned}$$

Solar altitude β

$$\begin{aligned} \sin\beta &= \cos L \cos\delta \cos H + \sin L \sin\delta \\ &= \cos(33.64)\cos(20.4)\cos(33.97) + \sin(33.64)\sin(20.4) \\ &= 0.841 \\ \beta &= \sin^{-1}(0.841) = 57.2° \end{aligned}$$

Solar azimuth ϕ

$$\begin{aligned} \cos\phi &= (\sin\beta \sin L - \sin\delta)/(\cos\beta \cos L) \\ &= [(\sin(57.2)\sin(33.64) - \sin(20.4)]/[\cos(57.2)\cos(33.64)] \\ &= 0.258 \\ \phi &= \cos^{-1}(0.253) = 75.05° \end{aligned}$$

Surface-solar azimuth γ

$$\begin{aligned} \gamma &= \phi - \psi \\ &= 75.05 - 60 \\ &= 15.05° \end{aligned}$$

Incident angle θ

$$\begin{aligned} \cos\theta &= \cos\beta \cos g \sin\Sigma + \sin\beta \cos\Sigma \\ &= \cos(57.2)\cos(15.05)\sin(90) + \sin(57.2)\cos(90) \end{aligned}$$

$= 0.523$

$\theta = \cos^{-1}(0.523) = 58.45°$

Beam normal irradiance E_b

$E_b = E_o \exp(-\tau_b m^{ab})$

m = relative air mass

$= 1/[\sin\beta + 0.50572(6.07995 + \beta)^{-1.6364}]$, β expressed in degrees

$= 1.18905$

ab = beam air mass exponent

$= 1.454 - 0.406\tau_b - 0.268\tau_d + 0.021\tau_b\tau_d$

$= 0.713566$

$E_b = 419.8 \exp[-0.440(1.18905^{0.713566})]$

$= 234.4$ Btu/h·ft²

Surface beam irradiance $E_{t,b}$

$E_{t,b} = E_b \cos\theta$

$= (234.4)\cos(58.5)$

$= 122.7$ Btu/h·ft²

Ratio Y of sky diffuse radiation on vertical surface to sky diffuse radiation on horizontal surface

$Y = 0.55 + 0.437\cos\theta + 0.313\cos^2\theta$

$= 0.55 + 0.437\cos(58.45) + 0.313\cos^2(58.45)$

$= 0.8644$

Diffuse irradiance E_d – Horizontal surfaces

$E_d = E_o \exp(-\tau_d m^{ad})$

ad = diffuse air mass exponent

$= 0.507 + 0.205\tau_b - 0.080\tau_d - 0.190\tau_b\tau_d$

$= 0.245137$

$E_d = E_o \exp(-\tau_d m^{ad})$

$= 419.8 \exp[-2.066(1.8905^{0.245137})]$

$= 48.6$ Btu/h·ft²

Diffuse irradiance E_d – Vertical surfaces

$E_{t,d} = E_d Y$

$= (48.6)(0.864)$

$= 42.0$ Btu/h·ft²

Ground reflected irradiance $E_{t,r}$

$E_{t,r} = (E_b \sin\beta + E_d)\rho_g(1 - \cos\Sigma)/2$

$= [234.4\sin(57.2) + 48.6](0.2)[1 - \cos(90)]/2$

$= 24.6$ Btu/h·ft²

Total surface irradiance E_t

$E_t = E_D + E_d + E_r$

$= 122.7 + 42.0 + 24.6$

$= 189.3$ Btu/h·ft²

Sol-air temperature [from Equation (29)]:

$T_e = t_o + \alpha E_t/h_o - \varepsilon\Delta R/h_o$

$= 91.6 + (0.30)(189.3) - 0$

$= 148.39°F$

This procedure is used to calculate the sol-air temperatures for each hour on each surface. Because of the tedious solar angle and intensity calculations, using a simple computer spreadsheet or other computer software can reduce the effort involved. A spreadsheet was used to calculate a 24 h sol-air temperature profile for the data of this example. See Table 29A for the solar angle and intensity calculations and Table 29B for the sol-air temperatures for this wall surface and orientation.

Conductive heat gain is calculated using Equations (30) and (31). First, calculate the 24 h heat input profile using Equation (30) and the sol-air temperatures for a southwest-facing wall with dark exterior color:

$q_{i,1} = (0.077)(60)(73.9 - 75) = -5$ Btu/h
$q_{i,2} = (0.077)(60)(73 - 75) = -9$
$q_{i,3} = (0.077)(60)(72.4 - 75) = -12$
$q_{i,4} = (0.077)(60)(71.8 - 75) = -15$
$q_{i,5} = (0.077)(60)(71.4 - 75) = -17$
$q_{i,6} = (0.077)(60)(72.8 - 75) = -10$
$q_{i,7} = (0.077)(60)(77.4 - 75) = 11$
$q_{i,8} = (0.077)(60)(84.1 - 75) = 42$
$q_{i,9} = (0.077)(60)(90.8 - 75) = 73$
$q_{i,10} = (0.077)(60)(96.7 - 75) = 100$
$q_{i,11} = (0.077)(60)(101.5 - 75) = 122$
$q_{i,12} = (0.077)(60)(105.5 - 75) = 141$
$q_{i,13} = (0.077)(60)(122.4 - 75) = 219$
$q_{i,14} = (0.077)(60)(139.6 - 75) = 298$
$q_{i,15} = (0.077)(60)(150.7 - 75) = 350$
$q_{i,16} = (0.077)(60)(153.7 - 75) = 363$
$q_{i,17} = (0.077)(60)(147.7 - 75) = 336$
$q_{i,18} = (0.077)(60)(131.7 - 75) = 262$
$q_{i,19} = (0.077)(60)(103.1 - 75) = 130$
$q_{i,20} = (0.077)(60)(81.7 - 75) = 31$
$q_{i,21} = (0.077)(60)(79.8 - 75) = 22$
$q_{i,22} = (0.077)(60)(78.0 - 75) = 14$
$q_{i,23} = (0.077)(60)(76.5 - 75) = 7$
$q_{i,24} = (0.077)(60)(75.1 - 75) = 0$

Next, calculate wall heat gain using conduction time series. The preceding heat input profile is used with conduction time series to calculate the wall heat gain. From Table 16, the most similar wall construction is wall number 1. This is a spandrel glass wall that has similar mass and thermal capacity. Using Equation (31), the conduction time factors for wall 1 can be used in conjunction with the 24 h heat input profile to determine the wall heat gain at 3:00 PM LST:

$$\begin{aligned} q_{15} &= c_0 q_{i,15} + c_1 q_{i,14} + c_2 q_{i,13} + c_3 q_{i,12} + \cdots + c_{23} q_{i,16} \\ &= (0.18)(350) + (0.58)(298) + (0.20)(219) + (0.04)(141) \\ &\quad + (0.00)(122) + (0.00)(100) + (0.00)(73) + (0.00)(42) \\ &\quad + (0.00)(11) + (0.00)(-10) + (0.00)(-17) + (0.00)(-15) \\ &\quad + (0.00)(-12) + (0.00)(-9) + (0.00)(-5) + (0.00)(0) \\ &\quad + (0.00)(7) + (0.00)(14) + (0.00)(22) + (0.00)(31) \\ &\quad + (0.00)(130) + (0.00)(262) + (0.00)(336) + (0.00)(363) \\ &= 285 \text{ Btu/h} \end{aligned}$$

Because of the tedious calculations involved, a spreadsheet is used to calculate the remainder of a 24 h heat gain profile indicated in Table 29B for the data of this example.

Finally, calculate wall cooling load using radiant time series. Total cooling load for the wall is calculated by summing the convective and radiant portions. The convective portion is simply the wall heat gain for the hour being calculated times the convective fraction for walls from Table 14 (54%):

$$Q_c = (285)(0.54) = 154 \text{ Btu/h}$$

The radiant portion of the cooling load is calculated using conductive heat gains for the current and past 23 h, the radiant fraction for walls from Table 14 (46%), and radiant time series from Table 19, in accordance with Equation (33). From Table 19, select the RTS for medium-weight construction, assuming 50% glass and carpeted floors as representative for the described construction. Use the wall heat gains from Table 29B for 24 h design conditions in July. Thus, the radiant cooling load for the wall at 3:00 PM is

$$\begin{aligned} Q_{r,15} &= r_0(0.46)q_{i,15} + r_1(0.46)\,q_{i,14} + r_2(0.46)\,q_{i,13} + r_3(0.46)\,q_{i,12} \\ &\quad + \cdots + r_{23}(0.46)\,q_{i,16} \\ &= (0.49)(0.46)(285) + (0.17)(0.46)(214) + (0.09)(0.46)(150) \\ &\quad + (0.05)(0.46)(119) + (0.03)(0.46)(96) + (0.02)(0.46)(69) \\ &\quad + (0.02)(0.46)(39) + (0.01)(0.46)(11) + (0.01)(0.46)(-8) \\ &\quad + (0.01)(0.46)(-15) + (0.01)(0.46)(-14) + (0.01)(0.46)(-12) \\ &\quad + (0.01)(0.46)(-9) + (0.01)(0.46)(-4) + (0.01)(0.46)(1) \\ &\quad + (0.01)(0.46)(8) + (0.01)(0.46)(15) + (0.01)(0.46)(27) \\ &\quad + (0.01)(0.46)(58) + (0.01)(0.46)(147) + (0.00)(0.46)(257) \\ &\quad + (0.00)(0.46)(329) + (0.00)(0.46)(353) + (0.00)(0.46)(337) \\ &= 93 \text{ Btu/h} \end{aligned}$$

The total wall cooling load at the designated hour is thus

$$Q_{wall} = Q_c + Q_{r15} = 154 + 93 = 247 \text{ Btu/h}$$

Again, a simple computer spreadsheet or other software is necessary to reduce the effort involved. A spreadsheet was used with the heat gain profile to split the heat gain into convective and radiant portions, apply RTS to the radiant portion, and total the convective and radiant loads to determine a 24 h cooling load profile for this example, with results in Table 29B.

Part 3. Window cooling load using radiant time series. Calculate the cooling load contribution, with and without indoor shading (venetian blinds) for the window area facing 60° west of south at 3:00 PM in July for the conference room example.

Table 29A Conduction: Wall Component of Solar Irradiance (Month 7)

						Direct Beam Solar			Diffuse Solar Heat Gain					
Local Standard Hour	Apparent Solar Time	Hour Angle H	Solar Altitude β	Solar Azimuth ϕ	Solar Air Mass m	Beam Normal E_b, Btu/h·ft²	Surface Incident Angle θ	Surface Direct, Btu/h·ft²	Diffuse Horizontal E_d, Btu/h·ft²	Ground Diffuse, Btu/h·ft²	Y Ratio	Sky Diffuse, Btu/h·ft²	Subtotal Diffuse, Btu/h·ft²	Total Surface Irradiance, Btu/h·ft²
1	0.26	–176	–36	–175	—	0.0	117.4	0.0	0.0	0.0	0.4500	0.0	0.0	0.0
2	1.26	–161	–33	–159	—	0.0	130.9	0.0	0.0	0.0	0.4500	0.0	0.0	0.0
3	2.26	–146	–27	–144	—	0.0	144.5	0.0	0.0	0.0	0.4500	0.0	0.0	0.0
4	3.26	–131	–19	–132	—	0.0	158.1	0.0	0.0	0.0	0.4500	0.0	0.0	0.0
5	4.26	–116	–9	–122	—	0.0	171.3	0.0	0.0	0.0	0.4500	0.0	0.0	0.0
6	5.26	–101	3	–113	16.91455	8.7	172.5	0.0	6.7	0.7	0.4500	3.0	3.7	3.7
7	6.26	–86	14	–105	3.98235	105.6	159.5	0.0	23.1	4.9	0.4500	10.4	15.3	15.3
8	7.26	–71	27	–98	2.22845	168.6	145.9	0.0	34.0	10.9	0.4500	15.3	26.2	26.2
9	8.26	–56	39	–90	1.58641	205.2	132.3	0.0	41.5	17.1	0.4500	18.7	35.8	35.8
10	9.26	–41	51	–81	1.27776	227.3	118.8	0.0	46.8	22.5	0.4500	21.1	43.5	43.5
11	10.26	–26	63	–67	1.11740	240.4	105.6	0.0	50.2	26.5	0.4553	22.9	49.4	49.4
12	11.26	–11	74	–39	1.04214	247.0	92.6	0.0	52.1	28.9	0.5306	27.6	56.5	56.5
13	12.26	4	76	16	1.02872	248.2	80.2	42.1	52.4	29.4	0.6332	33.2	62.6	104.7
14	13.26	19	69	57	1.07337	244.2	68.7	88.9	51.3	27.9	0.7505	38.5	66.4	155.2
15	14.2647	33.97	57.2	75.05	1.18905	234.4	58.45	122.7	48.6	24.6	0.8644	42.0	66.6	189.3
16	15.26	49	45	86	1.41566	217.0	50.4	138.3	44.3	19.7	0.9555	42.3	62.0	200.3
17	16.26	64	32	94	1.86186	188.2	45.8	131.3	37.9	13.9	1.0073	38.1	52.0	183.3
18	17.26	79	20	102	2.89735	139.7	45.5	97.9	28.7	7.7	1.0100	29.0	36.7	134.6
19	18.26	94	8	109	6.84406	55.0	49.7	35.6	15.3	2.3	0.9631	14.8	17.1	52.6
20	19.26	109	–3	117	—	0.0	57.5	0.0	0.0	0.0	0.8755	0.0	0.0	0.0
21	20.26	124	–14	127	—	0.0	67.5	0.0	0.0	0.0	0.7630	0.0	0.0	0.0
22	21.26	139	–23	138	—	0.0	79.0	0.0	0.0	0.0	0.6452	0.0	0.0	0.0
23	22.26	154	–30	151	—	0.0	91.3	0.0	0.0	0.0	0.5403	0.0	0.0	0.0
24	23.26	169	–35	167	—	0.0	104.2	0.0	0.0	0.0	0.4618	0.0	0.0	0.0

Table 29B Conduction: Wall Component of Sol-Air Temperatures, Heat Input, Heat Gain, Cooling Load (Month 7)

							Heat Gain, Btu/h					
Local Standard Hour	Total Surface Irradiance, Btu/h·ft²	Outdoor Temp., °F	Sol-Air Temp., °F	Indoor Temp., °F	Heat Input, Btu/h	CTS Type 1, %	Total	Convective 54%	Radiant 46%	Nonsolar RTS Zone Type 8, %	Radiant Cooling Load, Btu/h	Total Cooling Load, Btu/h
1	0.0	73.8	73.8	75	–6	18	1	1	1	49	15	16
2	0.0	73.0	73.0	75	–9	57	–4	–2	–2	17	12	10
3	0.0	72.4	72.4	75	–12	20	–8	–5	–4	9	10	5
4	0.0	71.8	71.8	75	–15	4	–12	–6	–5	5	8	2
5	0.0	71.4	71.4	75	–17	1	–14	–8	–7	3	7	–1
6	3.7	71.8	72.9	75	–10	0	–15	–8	–7	2	6	–2
7	15.3	73.2	77.8	75	13	0	–7	–4	–3	2	6	3
8	26.2	76.7	84.6	75	44	0	13	7	6	1	11	18
9	35.8	80.5	91.2	75	75	0	41	22	19	1	18	40
10	43.5	83.9	97.0	75	101	0	70	38	32	1	27	65
11	49.4	87.0	101.8	75	124	0	97	52	45	1	36	88
12	56.5	89.0	106.0	75	143	0	120	65	55	1	43	108
13	104.7	90.6	122.0	75	217	0	150	81	69	1	53	134
14	155.2	91.6	138.2	75	292	0	211	114	97	1	70	184
15	189.3	91.6	148.4	75	339	0	278	150	128	1	91	241
16	200.3	90.4	150.5	75	349	0	325	175	149	1	111	286
17	183.3	88.8	143.8	75	318	0	337	182	155	1	122	305
18	134.6	86.8	127.2	75	241	0	311	168	143	1	122	290
19	52.6	83.7	99.5	75	113	0	238	129	110	1	108	237
20	0.0	81.5	81.5	75	30	0	134	72	62	1	80	153
21	0.0	79.7	79.7	75	22	0	56	30	26	0	53	84
22	0.0	77.9	77.9	75	13	0	28	15	13	0	36	51
23	0.0	76.5	76.5	75	7	0	16	9	7	0	26	35
24	0.0	75.0	75.0	75	0	0	8	4	4	0	20	24

Solution: First, calculate the 24 h heat gain profile for the window, then split those heat gains into radiant and convective portions, apply the appropriate RTS to the radiant portion, then sum the convective and radiant cooling load components to determine total window cooling load for the time. The window heat gain components are calculated using Equations (12) to (14). From Part 2, at hour 15 LST (3:00 PM):

$$E_{t,b} = 133.6 \text{ Btu/h·ft}^2$$
$$E_{t,d} = 36.6 \text{ Btu/h·ft}^2$$
$$E_r = 25.7 \text{ Btu/h·ft}^2$$
$$\theta = 58.45°$$

From Chapter 15, Table 10, for glass type 5d,

Table 30 Window Component of Heat Gain (No Blinds or Overhang) (Month7)

	Beam Solar Heat Gain						Diffuse Solar Heat Gain							Conduction Heat Gain		
Local Std. Hour	Beam Normal, Btu/h·ft²	Surface Incident Angle	Surface Beam, Btu/h·ft²	Beam SHGC	Adjusted Beam IAC	Beam Solar Heat Gain, Btu/h	Diffuse Hor. E_d, Btu/h·ft²	Ground Diffuse, Btu/h·ft²	Y Ratio	Sky Diffuse, Btu/h·ft²	Subtotal Diffuse, Btu/h·ft²	Hemis. SHGC	Diffuse Solar Heat Gain, Btu/h	Outdoor Temp., °F	Conduction Heat Gain, Btu/h	Total Window Heat Gain, Btu/h
1	0.0	117.4	0.0	0.000	1.000	0	0.0	0.0	0.4500	0.0	0.0	0.410	0	73.8	–27	–27
2	0.0	130.9	0.0	0.000	1.000	0	0.0	0.0	0.4500	0.0	0.0	0.410	0	73.0	–45	–45
3	0.0	144.5	0.0	0.000	1.000	0	0.0	0.0	0.4500	0.0	0.0	0.410	0	72.4	–58	–58
4	0.0	158.1	0.0	0.000	1.000	0	0.0	0.0	0.4500	0.0	0.0	0.410	0	71.8	–72	–72
5	0.0	171.3	0.0	0.000	1.000	0	0.0	0.0	0.4500	0.0	0.0	0.410	0	71.4	–81	–81
6	8.7	172.5	0.0	0.000	0.000	0	6.7	0.7	0.4500	3.0	3.7	0.410	61	71.8	–72	–10
7	105.6	159.5	0.0	0.000	0.000	0	23.1	4.9	0.4500	10.4	15.3	0.410	251	73.2	–40	211
8	168.6	145.9	0.0	0.000	0.000	0	34.0	10.9	0.4500	15.3	26.2	0.410	430	76.7	38	468
9	205.2	132.3	0.0	0.000	0.000	0	41.5	17.1	0.4500	18.7	35.8	0.410	586	80.5	123	710
10	227.3	118.8	0.0	0.000	0.000	0	46.8	22.5	0.4500	21.1	43.5	0.410	714	83.9	199	913
11	240.4	105.6	0.0	0.000	0.000	0	50.2	26.5	0.4553	22.9	49.4	0.410	810	87.0	269	1079
12	247.0	92.6	0.0	0.000	0.000	0	52.1	28.9	0.5306	27.6	56.5	0.410	927	89.0	314	1241
13	248.2	80.2	42.1	0.166	1.000	280	52.4	29.4	0.6332	33.2	62.6	0.410	1026	90.6	349	1655
14	244.2	68.7	88.9	0.321	1.000	1140	51.3	27.9	0.7505	38.5	66.4	0.410	1088	91.6	372	2600
15	234.4	58.4	122.7	0.398	1.000	1952	48.6	24.6	0.8644	42.0	66.6	0.410	1092	91.6	372	3416
16	217.0	50.4	138.3	0.438	1.000	2422	44.3	19.7	0.9555	42.3	62.0	0.410	1017	90.4	345	3784
17	188.2	45.8	131.3	0.448	1.000	2355	37.9	13.9	1.0073	38.1	52.0	0.410	853	88.8	309	3517
18	139.7	45.5	97.9	0.449	1.000	1758	28.7	7.7	1.0100	29.0	36.7	0.410	602	86.8	264	2624
19	55.0	49.7	35.6	0.441	1.000	627	15.3	2.3	0.9631	14.8	17.1	0.410	280	83.7	195	1101
20	0.0	57.5	0.0	0.403	0.000	0	0.0	0.0	0.8755	0.0	0.0	0.410	0	81.5	146	146
21	0.0	67.5	0.0	0.330	0.000	0	0.0	0.0	0.7630	0.0	0.0	0.410	0	79.7	105	105
22	0.0	79.0	0.0	0.185	0.000	0	0.0	0.0	0.6452	0.0	0.0	0.410	0	77.9	65	65
23	0.0	91.3	0.0	0.000	1.000	0	0.0	0.0	0.5403	0.0	0.0	0.410	0	76.5	34	34
24	0.0	104.2	0.0	0.000	1.000	0	0.0	0.0	0.4618	0.0	0.0	0.410	0	75.0	0	0

$$\text{SHGC}(\theta) = \text{SHGC}(58.45) = 0.3978 \text{ (interpolated)}$$

$$\langle \text{SHGC} \rangle_D = 0.41$$

From Chapter 15, Table 14B, for light-colored blinds (assumed louver reflectance = 0.8 and louvers positioned at 45° angle) on double-glazed, heat-absorbing windows (Type 5d from Table 13B of Chapter 15), IAC(0) = 0.74, IAC(60) = 0.65, IAC(diff) = 0.79, and radiant fraction = 0.54. Without blinds, IAC = 1.0. Therefore, window heat gain components for hour 15, without blinds, are

$$q_{b15} = AE_{t,b}\,\text{SHGC}(\theta)(\text{IAC}) = (40)(133.6)(0.3978)(1.00) = 2126 \text{ Btu/h}$$

$$q_{d15} = A(E_{t,d} + E_r)\langle\text{SHGC}\rangle_D(\text{IAC}) = (40)(36.6 + 25.7)(0.41)(1.00) = 1021 \text{ Btu/h}$$

$$q_{c15} = UA(t_{out} - t_{in}) = (0.56)(40)(91.9 - 75) = 379 \text{ Btu/h}$$

This procedure is repeated to determine these values for a 24 h heat gain profile, shown in Table 30.

Total cooling load for the window is calculated by summing the convective and radiant portions. For windows with indoor shading (blinds, drapes, etc.), the direct beam, diffuse, and conductive heat gains may be summed and treated together in calculating cooling loads. However, in this example, the window does not have indoor shading, and the direct beam solar heat gain should be treated separately from the diffuse and conductive heat gains. The direct beam heat gain, without indoor shading, is treated as 100% radiant, and solar RTS factors from Table 20 are used to convert the beam heat gains to cooling loads. The diffuse and conductive heat gains can be totaled and split into radiant and convective portions according to Table 14, and nonsolar RTS factors from Table 19 are used to convert the radiant portion to cooling load.

The solar beam cooling load is calculated using heat gains for the current hour and past 23 h and radiant time series from Table 20, in accordance with Equation (38). From Table 20, select the solar RTS for medium-weight construction, assuming 50% glass and carpeted floors for this example. Using Table 30 values for direct solar heat gain, the radiant cooling load for the window direct beam solar component is

$$\begin{aligned} Q_{b,15} &= r_0 q_{b,15} + r_1 q_{b,14} + r_2 q_{b,13} + r_3 q_{b,12} + \ldots + r_{23} q_{b,16} \\ &= (0.54)(2126) + (0.16)(1234) + (0.08)(302) + (0.04)(0) \\ &\quad + (0.03)(0) + (0.02)(0) + (0.01)(0) + (0.01)(0) + (0.01)(0) \\ &\quad + (0.01)(0) + (0.01)(0) + (0.01)(0) + (0.01)(0) + (0.01)(0) \\ &\quad + (0.01)(0) + (0.01)(0) + (0.01)(0) + (0.01)(0) + (0.01)(0) \\ &\quad + (0.00)(0) + (0.00)(865) + (0.00)(2080) + (0.00)(2656) \\ &\quad + (0.00)(2670) = 1370 \text{ Btu/h} \end{aligned}$$

This process is repeated for other hours; results are listed in Table 31.

For diffuse and conductive heat gains, the radiant fraction according to Table 14 is 46%. The radiant portion is processed using nonsolar RTS coefficients from Table 19. The results are listed in Tables 30 and 31. For 3:00 PM, the diffuse and conductive cooling load is 1297 Btu/h.

The total window cooling load at the designated hour is thus

$$Q_{window} = Q_b + Q_{diff+cond} = 1370 + 1297 = 2667 \text{ Btu/h}$$

Again, a computer spreadsheet or other software is commonly used to reduce the effort involved in calculations. The spreadsheet shown in Table 30 is expanded in Table 31 to include splitting the heat gain into convective and radiant portions, applying RTS to the radiant portion, and totaling the convective and radiant loads to determine a 24 h cooling load profile for a window without indoor shading.

If the window has an indoor shading device, it is accounted for with the indoor attenuation coefficients (IAC), the radiant fraction, and the RTS type used. If a window has no indoor shading, 100% of the direct beam energy is assumed to be radiant and solar RTS factors are used. However, if an indoor shading device is present, the direct beam is assumed to be interrupted by the shading device, and a portion immediately becomes cooling load by convection. Also, the energy is assumed to be radiated to all surfaces of the room, therefore nonsolar RTS values are used to convert the radiant load into cooling load.

IAC values depend on several factors: (1) type of shading device, (2) position of shading device relative to window, (3) reflectivity of shading device, (4) angular adjustment of shading device, as well as (5) solar position relative to the shading device. These factors are discussed

Table 31 Window Component of Cooling Load (No Blinds or Overhang) (Month 7)

	Unshaded Direct Beam Solar Cooling Load (IFAC = 1)						Shaded Direct Beam (AC < 1.0) + Diffuse + Conduction Cooling Load									
Local Standard Hour	Beam Solar Heat Gain, Btu/h	Convective 0%, Btu/h	Radiant 100%, Btu/h	Solar RTS Zone Type 8, %	Radiant, Btu/h	Cooling Load, Btu/h	Beam Solar Heat Gain, Btu/h	Diffuse Heat Gain, Btu/h	Conduction Heat Gain, Btu/h	Total Heat Gain, Btu/h	Convective 54%, Btu/h	Radiant 46%, Btu/h	Nonsolar RTS Zone 8, %	Radiant, Btu/h	Cooling Load, Btu/h	Window Cooling Load, Btu/h
1	0	0	0	54	105	105	0	0	–27	–27	–15	–12	49	61	46	151
2	0	0	0	16	105	105	0	0	–45	–45	–24	–21	17	51	26	132
3	0	0	0	8	105	105	0	0	–58	–58	–31	–27	9	43	11	117
4	0	0	0	4	105	105	0	0	–72	–72	–39	–33	5	35	–4	101
5	0	0	0	3	105	105	0	0	–81	–81	–44	–37	3	27	–17	88
6	0	0	0	2	105	105	0	61	–72	–10	–6	–5	2	36	30	136
7	0	0	0	1	105	105	0	251	–40	211	114	97	2	85	199	305
8	0	0	0	1	103	103	0	430	38	468	253	215	1	157	410	512
9	0	0	0	1	91	91	0	586	123	710	383	326	1	235	618	710
10	0	0	0	1	72	72	0	714	199	913	493	420	1	309	803	874
11	0	0	0	1	47	47	0	810	269	1079	583	496	1	375	958	1005
12	0	0	0	1	24	24	0	927	314	1241	670	571	1	438	1108	1132
13	280	0	280	1	157	157	0	1026	349	1375	743	633	1	495	1238	1395
14	1140	0	1140	1	660	660	0	1088	372	1460	789	672	1	540	1328	1989
15	1952	0	1952	1	1259	1259	0	1092	372	1464	791	673	1	563	1353	2612
16	2422	0	2422	1	1722	1722	0	1017	345	1362	736	627	1	555	1291	3013
17	2355	0	2355	1	1869	1869	0	853	309	1162	627	534	1	513	1140	3009
18	1758	0	1758	1	1638	1638	0	602	264	866	468	398	1	435	902	2540
19	627	0	627	1	989	989	0	280	195	475	256	218	1	320	577	1566
20	0	0	0	0	461	461	0	0	146	146	79	67	1	204	283	744
21	0	0	0	0	273	273	0	0	105	105	57	48	0	150	207	480
22	0	0	0	0	183	183	0	0	65	65	35	30	0	115	150	333
23	0	0	0	0	135	135	0	0	34	34	18	15	0	92	110	246
24	0	0	0	0	112	112	0	0	0	0	0	0	0	74	74	186

in detail in Chapter 15. For this example with venetian blinds, the IAC for beam radiation is treated separately from the diffuse solar gain. The direct beam IAC must be adjusted based on the profile angle of the sun. At 3:00 PM in July, the profile angle of the sun relative to the window surface is 58°. Calculated using Equation (38) from Chapter 15, the beam IAC = 0.653. The diffuse IAC is 0.79. Thus, the window heat gains, with light-colored blinds, at 3:00 PM are

$$q_{b15} = AE_D\,\text{SHGC}(\theta)(\text{IAC}) = (40)(133.6)(0.3978)(0.653) = 1388 \text{ Btu/h}$$

$$q_{d15} = A(E_d + E_r)\langle\text{SHGC}\rangle_D(\text{IAC})_D = (40)(36.6 + 25.7)(0.41)(0.79)$$

$$= 807 \text{ Btu/h}$$

$$q_{c15} = UA(t_{out} - t_{in}) = (0.56)(40)(91.9 - 75) = 379 \text{ Btu/h}$$

Because the same radiant fraction and nonsolar RTS are applied to all parts of the window heat gain when indoor shading is present, those loads can be totaled and the cooling load calculated after splitting the radiant portion for processing with nonsolar RTS. This is shown by the spreadsheet results in Table 32. The total window cooling load with venetian blinds at 3:00 PM = 2171 Btu/h.

Part 4. Window cooling load using radiant time series for window with overhang shading. Calculate the cooling load contribution for the previous example with the addition of a 10 ft overhang shading the window.

Solution: In Chapter 15, methods are described and examples provided for calculating the area of a window shaded by attached vertical or horizontal projections. For 3:00 PM LST IN July, the solar position calculated in previous examples is

$$\text{Solar altitude } \beta = 57.2°$$

$$\text{Solar azimuth } \phi = 75.1°$$

$$\text{Surface-solar azimuth } \gamma = 15.1°$$

From Chapter 15, Equation (32), profile angle Ω is calculated by

$$\tan \Omega = \tan \beta / \cos \gamma = \tan(57.2)/\cos(15.1) = 1.6087$$

$$\Omega = 58.1°$$

From Chapter 15, Equation (34), shadow height S_H is

$$S_H = P_H \tan \Omega = 10(1.6087) = 16.1 \text{ ft}$$

Because the window is 6.4 ft tall, at 3:00 PM the window is completely shaded by the 10 ft deep overhang. Thus, the shaded window heat gain includes only diffuse solar and conduction gains. This is converted to cooling load by separating the radiant portion, applying RTS, and adding the resulting radiant cooling load to the convective portion to determine total cooling load. Those results are in Table 33. The total window cooling load = 1098 Btu/h.

Part 5. Room cooling load total. Calculate the sensible cooling loads for the previously described office at 3:00 PM in July.

Solution: The steps in the previous example parts are repeated for each of the internal and external loads components, including the southeast-facing window, spandrel and brick walls, the southwest-facing brick wall, the roof, people, and equipment loads. The results are tabulated in Table 34. The total room sensible cooling load for the office is 3674 Btu/h at 3:00 PM in July. When this calculation process is repeated for a 24 h design day for each month, it is found that the peak room sensible cooling load actually occurs in July at hour 14 (2:00 PM solar time) at 3675 Btu/h as indicated in Table 35.

Although simple in concept, these steps involved in calculating cooling loads are tedious and repetitive, even using the "simplified" RTS method; practically, they should be performed using a computer spreadsheet or other program. The calculations should be repeated for multiple design conditions (i.e., times of day, other months) to determine the maximum cooling load for mechanical equipment sizing. Example spreadsheets for computing each cooling load component using conduction and radiant time series are available from ASHRAE. To illustrate the full building example discussed previously, those individual component spreadsheets have been compiled to allow calculation of cooling and heating loads on a room by room basis as well as for a "block" calculation for analysis of overall areas or buildings where detailed room-by-room data are not available.

Table 32 Window Component of Cooling Load (with Blinds, No Overhang) (Month 7)

	Unshaded Direct Beam Solar Cooling Load (IFAC = 1)						Shaded Direct Beam (AC < 1.0) + Diffuse + Conduction Cooling Load									
Local Standard Hour	Beam Solar Heat Gain Btu/h	Convective 0%, Btu/h	Radiant 100%, Btu/h	Solar RTS Zone Type 8, %	Radiant, Btu/h	Cooling Load, Btu/h	Beam Solar Heat Gain, Btu/h	Diffuse Heat Gain, Btu/h	Conduction Heat Gain, Btu/h	Total Heat Gain, Btu/h	Convective 46%, Btu/h	Radiant 54%, Btu/h	Nonsolar RTS Zone 8, %	Radiant, Btu/h	Cooling Load, Btu/h	Window Cooling Load, Btu/h
1	0	0	0	1	0	0	0	0	–27	–27	–12	–15	49	101	88	88
2	0	0	0	0	0	0	0	0	–45	–45	–21	–24	17	87	66	66
3	0	0	0	0	0	0	0	0	–58	–58	–27	–31	9	78	51	51
4	0	0	0	0	0	0	0	0	–72	–72	–33	–39	5	69	36	36
5	0	0	0	0	0	0	0	0	–81	–81	–37	–44	3	60	23	23
6	0	0	0	0	0	0	0	48	–72	–23	–11	–13	2	69	58	58
7	0	0	0	0	0	0	0	199	–40	158	73	85	2	115	188	188
8	0	0	0	0	0	0	0	340	38	378	174	204	1	186	360	360
9	0	0	0	0	0	0	0	463	123	586	270	317	1	264	534	534
10	0	0	0	0	0	0	0	564	199	763	351	412	1	335	686	686
11	0	0	0	0	0	0	0	640	269	909	418	491	1	396	814	814
12	0	0	0	0	0	0	0	732	314	1046	481	565	1	450	932	932
13	0	0	0	0	0	0	182	810	349	1342	617	725	1	547	1164	1164
14	0	0	0	0	0	0	741	860	372	1973	907	1065	1	749	1657	1657
15	0	0	0	0	0	0	1274	863	372	2509	1154	1355	1	971	2125	2125
16	0	0	0	0	0	0	1618	804	345	2767	1273	1494	1	1135	2408	2408
17	0	0	0	0	0	0	1610	674	309	2593	1193	1400	1	1167	2360	2360
18	0	0	0	0	0	0	1232	475	264	1972	907	1065	1	1033	1941	1941
19	0	0	0	0	0	0	452	221	195	868	399	469	1	707	1106	1106
20	0	0	0	0	0	0	0	0	146	146	67	79	1	404	471	471
21	0	0	0	0	0	0	0	0	105	105	48	57	0	273	321	321
22	0	0	0	0	0	0	0	0	65	65	30	35	0	198	228	228
23	0	0	0	0	0	0	0	0	34	34	15	18	0	153	169	169
24	0	0	0	0	0	0	0	0	0	0	0	0	0	123	123	123

Table 33 Window Component of Cooling Load (with Blinds and Overhang) (Month 7)

	Overhang and Fins Shading Calculations						Shaded Direct Beam (AC < 1.0) + Diffuse + Conduction Cooling Load								
Local Standard Hour	Surface Solar Azimuth	Profile Angle	Shadow Width, ft	Shadow Height, ft	Direct Sunlit Area, ft^2	Beam Solar Heat Gain, Btu/h	Diffuse Heat Gain, Btu/h	Conduction Heat Gain, Btu/h	Total Heat Gain, Btu/h	Convective 54%, Btu/h	Radiant 46%, Btu/h	Nonsolar RTS Zone 8, %	Radiant, Btu/h	Cooling Load, Btu/h	Window Cooling Load, Btu/h
1	–235	52	0.0	0.0	0.0	0	0	–27	–27	–15	–12	49	55	40	40
2	–219	40	0.0	0.0	0.0	0	0	–45	–45	–24	–21	17	44	20	20
3	–204	29	0.0	0.0	0.0	0	0	–58	–58	–31	–27	9	36	5	5
4	–192	19	0.0	0.0	0.0	0	0	–72	–72	–39	–33	5	29	–10	–10
5	–182	9	0.0	0.0	0.0	0	0	–81	–81	–44	–37	3	21	–22	–22
6	–173	–3	0.0	0.0	0.0	0	48	–72	–23	–13	–11	2	28	16	16
7	–165	–15	0.0	0.0	0.0	0	199	–40	158	85	73	2	68	154	154
8	–158	–28	0.0	0.0	0.0	0	340	38	378	204	174	1	129	333	333
9	–150	–43	0.0	0.0	0.0	0	463	123	586	317	270	1	196	513	513
10	–141	–58	0.0	0.0	0.0	0	564	199	763	412	351	1	260	672	672
11	–127	–73	0.0	0.0	0.0	0	640	269	909	491	418	1	317	808	808
12	–99	–87	0.0	0.0	0.0	0	732	314	1046	565	481	1	371	936	936
13	–44	80	0.0	6.4	0.0	0	810	349	1160	626	534	1	420	1046	1046
14	–3	69	0.0	6.4	0.0	0	860	372	1232	665	567	1	456	1121	1121
15	15	58	0.0	6.4	0.0	0	863	372	1235	667	568	1	474	1141	1141
16	26	48	0.0	6.4	0.0	0	804	345	1149	620	528	1	468	1088	1088
17	34	38	0.0	6.4	0.0	0	674	309	983	531	452	1	432	963	963
18	42	26	0.0	4.9	9.4	291	475	264	1030	556	474	1	434	990	990
19	49	12	0.0	2.2	26.5	300	221	195	716	386	329	1	364	751	751
20	57	–6	0.0	0.0	0.0	0	0	146	146	79	67	1	214	293	293
21	67	–32	0.0	0.0	0.0	0	0	105	105	57	48	0	151	208	208
22	78	–64	0.0	0.0	0.0	0	0	65	65	35	30	0	112	148	148
23	91	87	0.0	0.0	0.0	0	0	34	34	18	15	0	88	106	106
24	107	67	0.0	0.0	0.0	0	0	0	0	0	0	0	69	69	69

Table 34 Single-Room Example Cooling Load (July 3:00 PM) for ASHRAE Example Office Building, Atlanta, GA

2017 ASHRAE FUNDAMENTALS EXAMPLE-IP UNITS						rev 2016-07-31		02-Aug-16
	Burdell Engineering Associates							George P. Burdell, P.E.
09N021	ASHRAE Example Office Building							Atlanta, Georgia
ROOM NO./NAME:		215B	Office Example - July 3 pm - not peak - Table 34					
	Length:	13	feet				Infiltration cfm	
	Width:	10	feet	Area	130	sq. feet	Cooling:	Heating:
	Ceiling Height:	9	feet	Volume	1170	cubic feet	0	19.5
INTERNAL LOADS:			Btuh/person:	Lighting,	Equipment,	Inside Design Conditions:		
		# People:	Sensible:	watts:	watts:	Cooling:	DB, F	75
	Over-ride Room Input:	1	250	110	130		RH	50%
	Default:	1	Latent:	143	130	Heating:	DB, F	72
	Use:	1	200	110	130	Outside Cooling Weather:		
EXPOSURES:		North	South	East	West	A - GA - ATLANTA HARTSFIELD-JACKSON - 5%		
	Nominal Azimuth:	-180	0	-90	90	Heating 99.6%, F:		21.9
	Actual Azimuth:	-210	-30	-120	60	Supply	Cooling, F	57
	Tilt:	90	90	90	90	Air:	Heating, F	100
	Type 1 Wall Area, sf:	0	60	0	40	Brick pilasters		
	Type 2 Wall Area, sf:	0	60	0	60	Spandrel panels		
	No. Type 1 Windows:	0	0	0	0	Dbl glazed, low-E, bronze		
	No. Type 2 Windows:	0	1	0	1	Dbl glz, low-E, brnz 10' ohng		
	Roof Area, sf:	130	30%	= Roof % to RA		26%	= Lights % to RA	
ROOM LOADS:		Peak Rm.Sens. Occurs:			Room	Ret. Air	Room	Room
		Month:	7	Per Unit	Sensible	Sensible	Latent	Sensible
		Hour:	15	Cooling	Cooling:	Cooling:	Cooling	Heating:
INTERNAL LOADS:			No. People:	Btuh/pers	Btuh	Btuh	Btuh	Btuh
		People:	1	234	234		200	
			watts:	Btuh/room sf				
		Lighting:	110	2.0	263			
		Lighting % to RA:	26%	0.7		92		
		Equipment:	130	3.3	429			
ENVELOPE LOADS:								
			Roof Area,sf	Btuh/roof sf				
ROOF:	0.032	U factor	130	1.0	132			208
		Roof % to RA:	30%			57		
WALLS:			Wall Area,sf	Btuh/wall sf				
	Wall Type 1:	Brick pilasters						
0.08	U factor	North	0	0.0	-			-
		South	60	1.7	103			240
		East	0	0.0	-			-
		West	40	1.2	47			160
	Wall Type 2	Spandrel panels						
0.077	U factor	North	0	0.0	-			-
		South	60	2.9	173			231
		East	0	0.0	-			-
		West	60	4.0	241			231
WINDOWS:			Window Area,sf:	Btuh/win sf				
	Window Type 1:	Dbl glazed, low-E, bronze						
40	sf/window	North	0	0.0	-			-
49%	SHGF(0)	South	0	0.0	-			-
0.56	U factor	East	0	0.0	-			-
74%	IAC	West	0	0.0	-			-
	Window Type 2:	Dbl glz, low-E, brnz 10' ohng						
40	sf/window	North	0	0.0	-			-
49%	SHGF(0)	South	40	24.1	962			1,122
0.56	U factor	East	0	0.0	-			-
74%	IAC	West	40	28.5	1,141			1,122
INFILTRATION LOADS:			cfm	Btuh/cfm				
		Cooling, Sensible:	0	0.0	-			
		Cooling, Latent:	0	0.0			-	
		Heating:	19.5	55.1				1,075
					-----	-----	-----	-----
			ROOM LOAD TOTALS =		3,724	149	200	4,391
				COOLING CFM =	188		HEATING CFM =	143
				CFM/SF =	1.4			
BLOCK LOADS:		TOTAL ROOM SENS+RA+LATENT =			4,073		ROOM HTG:	4,391
Peak Block Load Occurs:		OUTSIDE AIR:		OA Sensible:	-		OA Heating:	-
Month:	7	OA cfm =	0	OA Latent:	-			-----
Hour:	15	FAN HEAT:	0	HP to S. Air:	-		TOT HEATING,btuh=	4,391
		PUMP HEAT:	0	HP to CHW:	-		Heating btuh/sf =	33.8
					-----	tons	sf/ton	
		TOTAL BLOCK COOLING LOAD, btuh =			4,073	0.3	383	

Table 35 Single-Room Example Peak Cooling Load (Sept. 5:00 PM) for ASHRAE Example Office Building, Atlanta, GA

2017 ASHRAE FUNDAMENTALS EXAMPLE-IP UNITS						rev 2016-07-31		02-Aug-16
	Burdell Engineering Associates							George P. Burdell, P.E.
09N021	ASHRAE Example Office Building							Atlanta, Georgia
ROOM NO./NAME:		215B	Office Example - Table 35					
	Length:	13	feet				Infiltration cfm	
	Width:	10	feet	Area	130	sq. feet	Cooling:	Heating:
	Ceiling Height:	9	feet	Volume	1170	cubic feet	0	19.5
INTERNAL LOADS:			Btuh/person:	Lighting,	Equipment,	Inside Design Conditions:		
		# People:	Sensible:	watts:	watts:	Cooling:	DB, F	75
	Over-ride Room Input:	1	250	110	130		RH	50%
	Default:	1	Latent:	143	130	Heating:	DB, F	72
	Use:	1	200	110	130	Outside Cooling Weather:		
EXPOSURES:		North	South	East	West	A - GA - ATLANTA HARTSFIELD-JACKSON - 5%		
	Nominal Azimuth:	-180	0	-90	90	Heating 99.6%, F:		21.9
	Actual Azimuth:	-210	-30	-120	60	Supply	Cooling, F	57
	Tilt:	90	90	90	90	Air:	Heating, F	100
	Type 1 Wall Area, sf:	0	60	0	40	Brick pilasters		
	Type 2 Wall Area, sf:	0	60	0	60	Spandrel panels		
	No. Type 1 Windows:	0	0	0	0	Dbl glazed, low-E, bronze		
	No. Type 2 Windows:	0	1	0	1	Dbl glz, low-E, brnz 10' ohng		
	Roof Area, sf:	130	30%	= Roof % to RA		26%	= Lights % to RA	
ROOM LOADS:		Peak Rm.Sens. Occurs:			Room	Ret. Air	Room	Room
		Month:	8	Per Unit	Sensible	Sensible	Latent	Sensible
		Hour:	14	Cooling	Cooling:	Cooling:	Cooling	Heating:
INTERNAL LOADS:			No. People:	Btuh/pers	Btuh	Btuh	Btuh	Btuh
		People:	1	232	232		200	
			watts:	Btuh/room sf				
		Lighting:	110	2.0	262			
		Lighting % to RA:	26%	0.7		92		
		Equipment:	130	3.3	427			
ENVELOPE LOADS:								
			Roof Area,sf	Btuh/roof sf				
ROOF:	0.032	U factor	130	0.9	123			208
		Roof % to RA:	30%			53		
WALLS:			Wall Area,sf	Btuh/wall sf				
	Wall Type 1:	Brick pilasters						
0.08	U factor	North	0	0.0	-			-
		South	60	1.7	102			240
		East	0	0.0	-			-
		West	40	0.9	34			160
	Wall Type 2	Spandrel panels						
0.077	U factor	North	0	0.0	-			-
		South	60	4.0	241			231
		East	0	0.0	-			-
		West	60	3.3	200			231
WINDOWS:			Window Area,sf:	Btuh/win sf				
	Window Type 1:	Dbl glazed, low-E, bronze						
40	sf/window	North	0	0.0	-			-
49%	SHGF(0)	South	0	0.0	-			-
0.56	U factor	East	0	0.0	-			-
74%	IAC	West	0	0.0	-			-
	Window Type 2:	Dbl glz, low-E, brnz 10' ohng						
40	sf/window	North	0	0.0	-			-
49%	SHGF(0)	South	40	25.9	1,037			1,122
0.56	U factor	East	0	0.0	-			-
74%	IAC	West	40	28.0	1,120			1,122
INFILTRATION LOADS:			cfm	Btuh/cfm				
		Cooling, Sensible:	0	0.0	-			
		Cooling, Latent:	0	0.0			-	
		Heating:	19.5	55.1				1,075
					-----	-----	-----	-----
			ROOM LOAD TOTALS =		3,777	145	200	4,391
				COOLING CFM =	191		HEATING CFM =	143
				CFM/SF =	1.5			
BLOCK LOADS:		TOTAL ROOM SENS+RA+LATENT =			4,122		ROOM HTG:	4,391
Peak Block Load Occurs:		OUTSIDE AIR:		OA Sensible:	-		OA Heating:	-
Month:	8	OA cfm =	0	OA Latent:	-			-----
Hour:	14	FAN HEAT:	0	HP to S. Air:	-		TOT HEATING,btuh=	4,391
		PUMP HEAT:	0	HP to CHW:	-		Heating btuh/sf =	33.8
					-----	tons	sf/ton	
		TOTAL BLOCK COOLING LOAD, btuh =			4,122	0.3	378	

9.2 SINGLE-ROOM EXAMPLE PEAK HEATING LOAD

Although the physics of heat transfer that creates a heating load is identical to that for cooling loads, a number of traditionally used simplifying assumptions facilitate a much simpler calculation procedure. As described in the Heating Load Calculations section, design heating load calculations typically assume a single outdoor temperature, with no heat gain from solar or internal sources, under steady-state conditions. Thus, space heating load is determined by computing the heat transfer rate through building envelope elements ($UA\Delta T$) plus heat required because of outdoor air infiltration.

Part 6. Room heating load. Calculate the room heating load for the previous described office, including infiltration airflow at one air change per hour.

Solution: Because solar heat gain is not considered in calculating design heating loads, orientation of similar envelope elements may be ignored and total areas of each wall or window type combined. Thus, the total spandrel wall area = 60 + 60 = 120 ft^2, total brick wall area = 60 + 40 = 100 ft^2, and total window area = 40 + 40 = 80 ft^2. For this example, use the U-factors that were used for cooling load conditions.

In some climates, higher prevalent winds in winter should be considered in calculating U-factors (see Chapter 25 for information on calculating U-factors and surface heat transfer coefficients appropriate for local wind conditions). The 99.6% heating design dry-bulb temperature for Atlanta is 21.9°F and the indoor design temperature is 72°F. The room volume with a 9 ft ceiling = 9 × 130 = 1170 ft^3. At one air change per hour, the infiltration airflow = 1 × 1170/60 = 19.5 cfm. Thus, the heating load is

Windows:	0.56 × 80 × (72 – 21.9)	=	2244 Btu/h
Spandrel wall:	0.077 × 120 × (72 – 21.9)	=	463
Brick wall:	0.08 × 100 × (72 – 21.9)	=	401
Roof:	0.032 × 130 × (72 – 21.9)	=	208
Infiltration:	19.5 × 1.1 × (72 – 21.9)	=	1075
Total room heating load:			4391 Btu/h

9.3 WHOLE-BUILDING EXAMPLE

Because a single-room example does not illustrate the full application of load calculations, a multistory, multiple-room example building has been developed to show a more realistic case. A hypothetical project development process is described to illustrate its effect on the application of load calculations.

Table 36 Block Load Example: Envelope Area Summary, ft²

	Floor Area	Brick Areas				Spandrel/Soffit Areas				Window Areas			
		North	South	East	West	North	South	East	West	North	South	East	West
First floor	19,000	680	560	400	400	1400	1350	1040	360	600	1000	120	360
Second floor	15,700	510	390	300	300	1040	920	540	540	560	840	360	360
Building total	34,700	1190	950	700	700	2440	2270	1580	900	1160	1840	480	720

Design Process and Shell Building Definition

A development company has acquired a piece of property in Atlanta, GA, to construct an office building. Although no tenant or end user has yet been identified, the owner/developer has decided to proceed with the project on a speculative basis. They select an architectural design firm, who retains an engineering firm for the mechanical and electrical design.

At the first meeting, the developer indicates the project is to proceed on a fast-track basis to take advantage of market conditions; he is negotiating with several potential tenants who will need to occupy the new building within a year. This requires preparing **shell-and-core** construction documents to obtain a building permit, order equipment, and begin construction to meet the schedule.

The shell-and-core design documents will include finished design of the building exterior (the **shell**), as well as permanent interior elements such as stairs, restrooms, elevator, electrical rooms and mechanical spaces (the **core**). The primary mechanical equipment must be sized and installed as part of the shell-and-core package in order for the project to meet the schedule, even though the building occupant is not yet known.

The architect selects a two-story design with an exterior skin of tinted, double-glazed vision glass; opaque, insulated spandrel glass, and brick pilasters. The roof area extends beyond the building edge to form a substantial overhang, shading the second-floor windows. Architectural drawings for the shell-and-core package (see Figures 17 to 22) include plans, elevations, and skin construction details, and are furnished to the engineer for use in "block" heating and cooling load calculations. Mechanical systems and equipment must be specified and installed based on those calculations. (*Note*: Full-size, scalable electronic versions of the drawings in Figures 17 to 22, as well as detailed lighting plans, are available from ASHRAE at www.ashrae.org and in the ASHRAE Handbook Online version of this chapter, on the Additional Features tab.)

The HVAC design engineer meets with the developer's operations staff to agree on the basic HVAC systems for the project. Based on their experience operating other buildings and the lack of specific information on the tenant(s), the team decides on two variable-volume air-handling units (AHUs), one per floor, to provide operating flexibility if one floor is leased to one tenant and the other floor to someone else. Cooling will be provided by an air-cooled chiller located on grade across the parking lot. Heating will be provided by electric resistance heaters in parallel-type fan-powered variable-air-volume (VAV) terminal units. The AHUs must be sized quickly to confirm the size of the mechanical rooms on the architectural plans. The AHUs and chiller must be ordered by the mechanical subcontractor within 10 days to meet the construction schedule. Likewise, the electric heating loads must be provided to the electrical engineers to size the electrical service and for the utility company to extend services to the site.

The mechanical engineer must determine the (1) peak airflow and cooling coil capacity for each AHU, (2) peak cooling capacity required for the chiller, and (3) total heating capacity for sizing the electrical service.

Solution: First, calculate "block" heating and cooling loads for each floor to size the AHUs, then calculate a block load for the whole building determine chiller and electric heating capacity.

Based on the architectural drawings, the HVAC engineer assembles basic data on the building as follows:

Location: Atlanta, GA. Per Chapter 14, latitude = 33.64, longitude = 84.43, elevation = 1027 ft above sea level, 99.6% heating design dry-bulb temperature = 21.9°F. For cooling load calculations, use 5% dry-bulb/coincident wet-bulb monthly design day profile from Chapter 14 (on CD-ROM). See Table 27 for temperature profiles used in these examples.

Indoor design conditions: 72°F for heating; 75°F with 50% rh for cooling.

Building orientation: Plan north is 30° west of true north.

Gross area per floor: 19,000 ft² first floor and 15,700 ft² second floor.

Total building gross area: 34,700 ft².

Windows: Bronze-tinted, double-glazed. Solar heat gain coefficients, U-factors are as in the single-room example.

Walls: Part insulated spandrel glass and part brick-and-block clad columns. The insulation barrier in the soffit at the second floor is similar to that of the spandrel glass and is of lightweight construction; for simplicity, that surface is assumed to have similar thermal heat gain/loss to the spandrel glass. Construction and insulation values are as in single-room example.

Roof: Metal deck, topped with board insulation and membrane roofing. Construction and insulation values are as in the single-room example.

Floor: 5 in. lightweight concrete slab on grade for first floor and 5 in. lightweight concrete on metal deck for second floor

Total areas of building exterior skin, as measured from the architectural plans, are listed in Table 36.

The engineer needs additional data to estimate the building loads. Thus far, no tenant has yet been signed, so no interior layouts for population counts, lighting layouts, or equipment loads are available. To meet the schedule, assumptions must be made on these load components. The owner requires that the system design must be flexible enough to provide for a variety of tenants over the building's life. Based on similar office buildings, the team agrees to base the block load calculations on the following assumptions:

Occupancy: 7 people per 1000 ft² = 143 ft²/person
Lighting: 1.1 W/ft²
Tenant's office equipment: 1 W/ft²

Normal use schedule is assumed at 100% from 7:00 AM to 7:00 PM and unoccupied/off during other hours.

With interior finishes not finalized, the owner commits to using light-colored interior blinds on all windows. The tenant interior design could include carpeted flooring or acoustical tile ceilings in all areas, but the more conservative assumption, from a peak load standpoint, is chosen: carpeted flooring and no acoustical tile ceilings (no ceiling return plenum).

For block loads, the engineer assumes that the building is maintained under positive pressure during peak cooling conditions and that infiltration during peak heating conditions is equivalent to one air change per hour in a 12 ft deep perimeter zone around the building.

To maintain indoor air quality, outdoor air must be introduced into the building. Air will be ducted from roof intake hoods to the AHUs where it will be mixed with return air before being cooled and dehumidified by the AHU's cooling coil. ASHRAE *Standard* 62.1 is

Table 37 Block Load Example—First Floor Loads for ASHRAE Example Office Building, Atlanta, GA

2017 ASHRAE FUNDAMENTALS EXAMPLE-IP UNITS						rev 2016-07-31		02-Aug-16
	Burdell Engineering Associates							George P. Burdell, P.E.
09N021	ASHRAE Example Office Building							Atlanta, Georgia
ROOM NO./NAME:		AHU-1	First Floor Block Load - Table 37					
	Length:	190	feet				Infiltration cfm	
	Width:	100	feet	Area	19000	sq. feet	Cooling:	Heating:
	Ceiling Height:	9	feet	Volume	171000	cubic feet	0	0
INTERNAL LOADS:			Btuh/person:	Lighting,	Equipment,	Inside Design Conditions:		
		# People:	Sensible:	watts:	watts:	Cooling:	DB, F	75
Over-ride Room Input:		0	250	0	0		RH	50%
	Default:	133	Latent:	20900	19000	Heating:	DB, F	72
	Use:	133	200	20900	19000	Outside Cooling Weather:		
EXPOSURES:		North	South	East	West	A - GA - ATLANTA HARTSFIELD-JACKSON - 5%		
Nominal Azimuth:		-180	0	-90	90	Heating 99.6%, F:		21.9
Actual Azimuth:		-210	-30	-120	60	Supply	Cooling, F	57
	Tilt:	90	90	90	90	Air:	Heating, F	100
Type 1 Wall Area, sf:		680	560	400	400	Brick pilasters		
Type 2 Wall Area, sf:		1400	1350	1040	360	Spandrel panels		
No. Type 1 Windows:		15	25	3	9	Dbl glazed, low-E, bronze		
No. Type 2 Windows:		0	0	0	0	Dbl glz, low-E, brnz 10' ohng		
Roof Area, sf:		0	0%	= Roof % to RA		0%	= Lights % to RA	
ROOM LOADS:		Peak Rm.Sens. Occurs:			Room	Ret. Air	Room	Room
		Month:	9	Per Unit	Sensible	Sensible	Latent	Sensible
		Hour:	12	Cooling	Cooling:	Cooling:	Cooling	Heating:
INTERNAL LOADS:			No. People:	Btuh/pers	Btuh	Btuh	Btuh	Btuh
		People:	133	231	30,657		26,600	
			watts:	Btuh/room sf				
		Lighting:	20,900	3.5	66,822			
		Lighting % to RA:	0%	0.0		-		
		Equipment:	19,000	3.3	62,263			
ENVELOPE LOADS:								
			Roof Area,sf	Btuh/roof sf				
ROOF:	0.032	U factor	-	0.0	-			-
		Roof % to RA:	0%			-		
WALLS:			Wall Area,sf	Btuh/wall sf				
	Wall Type 1:	Brick pilasters						
0.08	U factor	North	680	0.0	(8)			2,725
		South	560	0.9	492			2,244
		East	400	0.6	247			1,603
		West	400	0.0	19			1,603
	Wall Type 2	Spandrel panels						
0.077	U factor	North	1400	1.2	1,654			5,401
		South	1350	4.9	6,623			5,208
		East	1040	2.2	2,269			4,012
		West	360	1.4	506			1,389
WINDOWS:			Window Area,sf:	Btuh/win sf				
	Window Type 1:	Dbl glazed, low-E, bronze						
40	sf/window	North	600	16.7	10,014			16,834
49%	SHGF(0)	South	1000	58.8	58,776			28,056
0.56	U factor	East	120	19.4	2,332			3,367
74%	IAC	West	360	22.1	7,943			10,100
	Window Type 2:	Dbl glz, low-E, brnz 10' ohng						
40	sf/window	North	0	0.0	-			-
49%	SHGF(0)	South	0	0.0	-			-
0.56	U factor	East	0	0.0	-			-
74%	IAC	West	0	0.0	-			-
INFILTRATION LOADS:			cfm	Btuh/cfm				
		Cooling, Sensible:	0	0.0	-			
		Cooling, Latent:	0	0.0			-	
		Heating:	0	0.0				-
					-----	-----	-----	-----
				ROOM LOAD TOTALS =	250,609	-	26,600	82,542
				COOLING CFM =	12,657		HEATING CFM =	2,680
				CFM/SF =	0.7			
BLOCK LOADS:		TOTAL ROOM SENS+RA+LATENT =			267,482		ROOM HTG:	82,542
Peak Block Load Occurs:		OUTSIDE AIR:		OA Sensible:	46,523		OA Heating:	146,593
Month:	8	OA cfm =	2660	OA Latent:	65,570			-----
Hour:	15	FAN HEAT:	15	HP to S. Air:	38,191		TOT HEATING,btuh=	229,135
		PUMP HEAT:	0	HP to CHW:	-		Heating btuh/sf =	12.1
					-----	tons	sf/ton	
		TOTAL BLOCK COOLING LOAD, btuh -			417,766	34.8	546	

Table 38 Block Load Example—Second Floor Loads for ASHRAE Example Office Building, Atlanta, GA

2017 ASHRAE FUNDAMENTALS EXAMPLE-IP UNITS						rev 2016-07-31		02-Aug-16
	Burdell Engineering Associates							George P. Burdell, P.E.
09N021	ASHRAE Example Office Building							Atlanta, Georgia
ROOM NO./NAME:		AHU-2	2nd Floor Block Load - with 10' overhang and no roof/lights to RA					
	Length:	157	feet				Infiltration cfm	
	Width:	100	feet	Area	15700	sq. feet	Cooling:	Heating:
	Ceiling Height:	9	feet	Volume	141300	cubic feet	0	863
INTERNAL LOADS:			Btuh/person:	Lighting,	Equipment,	Inside Design Conditions:		
		# People:	Sensible:	watts:	watts:	Cooling:	DB, F	75
Over-ride Room Input:		0	250	0	0		RH	50%
	Default:	110	Latent:	17270	15700	Heating:	DB, F	72
	Use:	110	200	17270	15700	Outside Cooling Weather:		
EXPOSURES:		North	South	East	West	A - GA - ATLANTA HARTSFIELD-JACKSON - 5%		
Nominal Azimuth:		-180	0	-90	90	Heating 99.6%, F:		21.9
Actual Azimuth:		-210	-30	-120	60	Supply	Cooling, F	57
	Tilt:	90	90	90	90	Air:	Heating, F	100
Type 1 Wall Area, sf:		510	390	300	300	Brick pilasters		
Type 2 Wall Area, sf:		1040	920	540	540	Spandrel panels		
No. Type 1 Windows:		0	0	0	0	Dbl glazed, low-E, bronze		
No. Type 2 Windows:		14	21	9	9	Dbl glz, low-E, brnz 10' ohng		
Roof Area, sf:		15700	0%	= Roof % to RA		0%	= Lights % to RA	
ROOM LOADS:		Peak Rm.Sens. Occurs:			Room	Ret. Air	Room	Room
		Month:	7	Per Unit	Sensible	Sensible	Latent	Sensible
		Hour:	14	Cooling	Cooling:	Cooling:	Cooling	Heating:
INTERNAL LOADS:			No. People:	Btuh/pers	Btuh	Btuh	Btuh	Btuh
		People:	110	232	25,520		22,000	
			watts:	Btuh/room sf				
		Lighting:	17,270	3.5	55,499			
		Lighting % to RA:	0%	0.0		-		
		Equipment:	15,700	3.3	51,610			
ENVELOPE LOADS:								
			Roof Area,sf	Btuh/roof sf				
ROOF:	0.032	U factor	15,700	1.4	22,509			25,170
		Roof % to RA:	0%			-		
WALLS:			Wall Area,sf	Btuh/wall sf				
	Wall Type 1:	Brick pilasters						
0.08	U factor	North	510	0.8	427			2,044
		South	390	1.5	591			1,563
		East	300	1.7	505			1,202
		West	300	0.9	265			1,202
	Wall Type 2	Spandrel panels						
0.077	U factor	North	1040	2.2	2,293			4,012
		South	920	3.4	3,137			3,549
		East	540	2.6	1,413			2,083
		West	540	3.1	1,654			2,083
WINDOWS:			Window Area,sf:	Btuh/win sf				
	Window Type 1:	Dbl glazed, low-E, bronze						
40	sf/window	North	0	0.0	-			-
49%	SHGF(0)	South	0	0.0	-			-
0.56	U factor	East	0	0.0	-			-
74%	IAC	West	0	0.0	-			-
	Window Type 2:	Dbl glz, low-E, brnz 10' ohng						
40	sf/window	North	560	25.1	14,073			15,711
49%	SHGF(0)	South	840	25.9	21,774			23,567
0.56	U factor	East	360	24.5	8,821			10,100
74%	IAC	West	360	28.0	10,092			10,100
INFILTRATION LOADS:			cfm	Btuh/cfm				
		Cooling, Sensible:	0	0.0	-			
		Cooling, Latent:	0	0.0			-	
		Heating:	863	55.1				47,560
					-----	-----	-----	-----
				ROOM LOAD TOTALS =	220,181	-	22,000	149,948
				COOLING CFM =	11,120		HEATING CFM =	4,868
				CFM/SF =	0.7			
BLOCK LOADS:		TOTAL ROOM SENS+RA+LATENT =			242,181		ROOM HTG:	149,948
Peak Block Load Occurs:		OUTSIDE AIR:		OA Sensible:	40,172		OA Heating:	121,242
Month:	7	OA cfm =	2200	OA Latent:	53,409			-----
Hour:	14	FAN HEAT:	10	HP to S. Air:	25,461		TOT HEATING,btuh=	271,190
		PUMP HEAT:	0	HP to CHW:	-		Heating btuh/sf =	17.3
					-----	tons	sf/ton	
		TOTAL BLOCK COOLING LOAD, btuh -			361,223	30.1	522	

the design basis for ventilation rates; however, no interior tenant layout is available for application of *Standard* 62.1 procedures. Based on past experience, the engineer decides to use 20 cfm of outdoor air per person for sizing the cooling coils and chiller.

Block load calculations were performed using the RTS method, and results for the first and second floors and the entire building are summarized in Tables 37, 38, and 39. Based on these results, the engineer performs psychrometric coil analysis, checks capacities versus vendor catalog data, and prepares specifications and schedules for the equipment. This information is released to the contractor with the shell-and-core design documents. The air-handling units and chiller are purchased, and construction proceeds.

Tenant Fit Design Process and Definition

About halfway through construction, a tenant agrees to lease the entire building. The tenant will require a combination of open and enclosed office space with a few common areas, such as conference/ training rooms, and a small computer room that will operate on a 24 h basis. Based on the tenant's space program, the architect prepares interior floor plans and furniture layout plans, and the electrical engineer prepares lighting design plans. Those drawings are furnished to the HVAC engineer to prepare detailed design documents. The first step in this process is to prepare room-by-room peak heating and cooling load calculations, which will then be used for design of the air distribution systems from each of the VAV air handlers already installed.

The HVAC engineer must perform a room-by-room "takeoff" of the architect's drawings. For each room, this effort identifies the floor area, room function, exterior envelope elements and areas, number of occupants, and lighting and equipment loads.

The tenant layout calls for a dropped acoustical tile ceiling throughout, which will be used as a return air plenum. Typical 2 by 4 ft fluorescent, recessed, return-air-type lighting fixtures are selected. Based on this, the engineer assumes that 20% of the heat gain from lighting will be to the return air plenum and not enter rooms directly. Likewise, some portion of the heat gain from the roof will be extracted via the ceiling return air plenum. From experience, the engineer understands that return air plenum paths are not always predictable, and decides to credit only 30% of the roof heat gain to the return air, with the balance included in the room cooling load.

For the open office areas, some areas along the building perimeter will have different load characteristics from purely interior spaces because of heat gains and losses through the building skin.

Table 39 Block Load Example—Overall Building Loads for ASHRAE Example Office Building, Atlanta, GA

2017 ASHRAE FUNDAMENTALS EXAMPLE-IP UNITS						rev 2016-07-31		02-Aug-16
	Burdell Engineering Associates						George P. Burdell, P.E.	
09N021	ASHRAE Example Office Building							Atlanta, Georgia
ROOM NO./NAME:		Building	Building Block Load - 10' Overhang - no lights/roof to RA-Table 39					
	Length:	347	feet				Infiltration cfm	
	Width:	100	feet	Area	34700	sq. feet	Cooling:	Heating:
	Ceiling Height:	9	feet	Volume	312300	cubic feet	0	1726
INTERNAL LOADS:			Btuh/person:	Lighting,	Equipment,	Inside Design Conditions:		
		# People:	Sensible:	watts:	watts:	Cooling:	DB, F	75
	Over-ride Room Input:	0	250	0	0		RH	50%
	Default:	243	Latent:	38170	34700	Heating:	DB, F	72
	Use:	243	200	38170	34700	Outside Cooling Weather:		
EXPOSURES:		North	South	East	West	A - GA - ATLANTA HARTSFIELD-JACKSON - 5%		
	Nominal Azimuth:	-180	0	-90	90	Heating 99.6%, F:		21.9
	Actual Azimuth:	-210	-30	-120	60	Supply	Cooling, F	57
	Tilt:	90	90	90	90	Air:	Heating, F	100
	Type 1 Wall Area, sf:	1190	950	700	700	Brick pilasters		
	Type 2 Wall Area, sf:	2440	2270	1580	900	Spandrel panels		
	No. Type 1 Windows:	15	25	3	9	Dbl glazed, low-E, bronze		
	No. Type 2 Windows:	14	21	9	9	Dbl glz, low-E, brnz 10' ohng		
	Roof Area, sf:	15700	0%	= Roof % to RA		0%	= Lights % to RA	
ROOM LOADS:		Peak Rm.Sens. Occurs:			Room	Ret. Air	Room	Room
		Month:	7	Per Unit	Sensible	Sensible	Latent	Sensible
		Hour:	15	Cooling	Cooling:	Cooling:	Cooling	Heating:
INTERNAL LOADS:			No. People:	Btuh/pers	Btuh	Btuh	Btuh	Btuh
		People:	243	234	56,741		48,600	
			watts:	Btuh/room sf				
		Lighting:	38,170	3.6	123,287			
		Lightiing % to RA:	0%	0.0		-		
		Equipment:	34,700	3.3	114,422			
ENVELOPE LOADS:								
			Roof Area,sf	Btuh/roof sf				
ROOF:	0.032	U factor	15,700	1.5	22,777			25,170
		Roof % to RA:	0%			-		
WALLS:			Wall Area,sf	Btuh/wall sf				
	Wall Type 1:	Brick pilasters						
0.08	U factor	North	1190	1.0	1,231			4,770
		South	950	1.7	1,625			3,808
		East	700	1.8	1,225			2,806
		West	700	1.2	817			2,806
	Wall Type 2	Spandrel panels						
0.077	U factor	North	2440	2.4	5,901			9,413
		South	2270	2.9	6,536			8,757
		East	1580	2.5	3,891			6,095
		West	900	4.0	3,621			3,472
WINDOWS:			Window Area,sf:	Btuh/win sf				
	Window Type 1:	Dbl glazed, low-E, bronze						
40	sf/window	North	600	27.4	16,443			16,834
49%	SHGF(0)	South	1000	25.2	25,159			28,056
0.56	U factor	East	120	24.5	2,934			3,367
74%	IAC	West	360	54.5	19,637			10,100
	Window Type 2:	Dbl glz, low-E, brnz 10' ohng						
40	sf/window	North	560	25.1	14,082			15,711
49%	SHGF(0)	South	840	24.1	20,207			23,567
0.56	U factor	East	360	23.4	8,435			10,100
74%	IAC	West	360	28.5	10,270			10,100
INFILTRATION LOADS:			cfm	Btuh/cfm				
		Cooling, Sensible:	0	0.0	-			
		Cooling, Latent:	0	0.0			-	
		Heating:	1726	55.1				96,120
					-----	-----	-----	-----
			ROOM LOAD TOTALS =		459,241	-	48,600	280,050
			COOLING CFM =		23,194	HEATING CFM =		9,093
			CFM/SF =		0.7			
BLOCK LOADS:		TOTAL ROOM SENS+RA+LATENT =			507,841		ROOM HTG:	280,050
Peak Block Load Occurs:		OUTSIDE AIR:		OA Sensible:	88,744		OA Heating:	267,835
Month:	7	OA cfm =	4860	OA Latent:	117,985			-----
Hour:	15	FAN HEAT:	25	HP to S. Air:	63,652	TOT HEATING,btuh=		547,885
		PUMP HEAT:	5	HP to CHW:	12,730	Heating btuh/sf =		15.8
					-----	tons	sf/ton	
		TOTAL BLOCK COOLING LOAD, btuh =			790,953	65.9	526	

Although those perimeter areas are not separated from other open office spaces by walls, the engineer knows from experience that they must be served by separate control zones to maintain comfort conditions.

Room-by-Room Cooling and Heating Loads

The room-by-room results of RTS method calculations, including the month and time of day of each room's peak cooling load, as well as peak heating loads for each room and all input data, are available at www.ashrae.org and in the ASHRAE Handbook Online version of this chapter (on the Additional Features tab) in spreadsheet format similar to Table 39. These results are used by the HVAC engineer to select and design room air distribution devices and to schedule airflow rates for each space. That information is incorporated into the tenant fit drawings and specifications issued to the contractor.

Conclusions

The example results illustrate issues that should be understood and accounted for in calculating heating and cooling loads:

- First, peak room cooling loads occur at different months and times, depending on the exterior exposure of the room. Calculation of cooling loads for a single point in time may miss the peak and result in inadequate cooling for that room.
- Often, in real design processes, not all data are known. Reasonable assumptions based on past experience must be made.
- Heating and air-conditioning systems often serve spaces whose use changes over the life of a building. Assumptions used in heating and cooling load calculations should consider reasonable possible uses over the life of the building, not just the first use of the space.
- The relative importance of each cooling and heating load component varies, depending on the portion of the building being considered. Characteristics of a particular window may have little effect on the entire building load, but could have a significant effect on the supply airflow to the room where the window is located and thus on the comfort of the occupants of that space.

10. PREVIOUS COOLING LOAD CALCULATION METHODS

Procedures described in this chapter are the most current and scientifically derived means for estimating cooling load for a defined building space, but methods in earlier editions of the ASHRAE Handbook are valid for many applications. These earlier procedures are simplifications of the heat balance principles, and their use requires experience to deal with atypical or unusual circumstances. In fact, any cooling or heating load estimate is no better than the assumptions used to define conditions and parameters such as physical makeup of the various envelope surfaces, conditions of occupancy and use, and ambient weather conditions. Experience of the practitioner can never be ignored.

The primary difference between the HB and RTS methods and the older methods is the newer methods' direct approach, compared to the simplifications necessitated by the limited computer capability available previously.

The **transfer function method (TFM)**, for example, required many calculation steps. It was originally designed for energy analysis with emphasis on daily, monthly, and annual energy use, and thus was more oriented to average hourly cooling loads than peak design loads.

The **total equivalent temperature differential method with time averaging (TETD/TA)** has been a highly reliable (if subjective) method of load estimating since its initial presentation in the 1967 *Handbook of Fundamentals*. Originally intended as a manual method of calculation, it proved suitable only as a computer application because of the need to calculate an extended profile of hourly heat gain values, from which radiant components had to be averaged over a time representative of the general mass of the building involved. Because perception of thermal storage characteristics of a given building is almost entirely subjective, with little specific information for the user to judge variations, the TETD/TA method's primary usefulness has always been to the experienced engineer.

The **cooling load temperature differential method with solar cooling load factors (CLTD/CLF)** attempted to simplify the two-step TFM and TETD/TA methods into a single-step technique that proceeded directly from raw data to cooling load without intermediate conversion of radiant heat gain to cooling load. A series of factors were taken from cooling load calculation results (produced by more sophisticated methods) as "cooling load temperature differences" and "cooling load factors" for use in traditional conduction ($q = UA\Delta t$) equations. The results are approximate cooling load values rather than simple heat gain values. The simplifications and assumptions used in the original work to derive those factors limit this method's applicability to those building types and conditions for which the CLTD/CLF factors were derived; the method should not be used beyond the range of applicability.

Although the TFM, TETD/TA, and CLTD/CLF procedures are not republished in this chapter, those methods are not invalidated or discredited. Experienced engineers have successfully used them in millions of buildings around the world. The accuracy of cooling load calculations in practice depends primarily on the availability of accurate information and the design engineer's judgment in the assumptions made in interpreting the available data. Those factors have much greater influence on a project's success than does the choice of a particular cooling load calculation method.

The primary benefit of HB and RTS calculations is their somewhat reduced dependency on purely subjective input (e.g., determining a proper time-averaging period for TETD/TA; ascertaining appropriate safety factors to add to the rounded-off TFM results; determining whether CLTD/CLF factors are applicable to a specific unique application). However, using the most up-to-date techniques in real-world design still requires judgment on the part of the design engineer and care in choosing appropriate assumptions, just as in applying older calculation methods.

REFERENCES

ASHRAE members can access *ASHRAE Journal* articles and ASHRAE research project final reports at technologyportal.ashrae .org. Articles and reports are also available for purchase by nonmembers in the online ASHRAE Bookstore at www.ashrae.org/bookstore.

Abushakra, B., J.S. Haberl, and D.E. Claridge. 2004. Overview of literature on diversity factors and schedules for energy and cooling load calculations (1093-RP). *ASHRAE Transactions* 110(1):164-176.

Armstrong, P.R., C.E. Hancock, III, and J.E. Seem. 1992a. Commercial building temperature recovery—Part I: Design procedure based on a step response model. *ASHRAE Transactions* 98(1):381-396.

Armstrong, P.R., C.E. Hancock, III, and J.E. Seem. 1992b. Commercial building temperature recovery—Part II: Experiments to verify the step response model. *ASHRAE Transactions* 98(1):397-410.

ASHRAE. 2013. Thermal environmental conditions for human occupancy. ANSI/ASHRAE *Standard* 55-2013.

ASHRAE. 2016. Ventilation for acceptable indoor air quality. ANSI/ ASHRAE *Standard* 62.1-2016.

ASHRAE. 2016. Energy standard for building except low-rise residential buildings. ANSI/ASHRAE/IES *Standard* 90.1-2016.

ASHRAE. 2012. Updating the climatic design conditions in the *ASHRAE Handbook—Fundamentals* (RP-1613). ASHRAE Research Project, *Final Report*.

ASHRAE. 2013. *Underfloor air distribution (UFAD) design guide*, 2nd ed.

ASTM. 2008. Practice for estimate of the heat gain or loss and the surface temperatures of insulated flat, cylindrical, and spherical systems by use of computer programs. *Standard* C680-08. American Society for Testing and Materials, West Conshohocken, PA.

Bach, C., and O. Sarfraz. 2017. Update to measurements of office heat gain data. ASHRAE Research Project RP-1742, *Progress Report*.

Bauman, F., T. Webster, P. Linden, and F. Buhl. 2007. Energy performance of UFAD systems. CEC-500-2007-050, *Final Report* to CEC PIER Buildings Program. Center for the Built Environment, University of California, Berkeley. www.energy.ca.gov/2007publications/CEC-500-2007-050/CEC-500-2007-050.PDF.

Bauman, F., S. Schiavon, T. Webster, and K.H. Lee. 2010. Cooling load design tool for UFAD systems. *ASHRAE Journal* (September):62-71. escholarship.org/uc/item/9d8430v3.

Bliss, R.J.V. 1961. Atmospheric radiation near the surface of the ground. *Solar Energy* 5(3):103.

CFR. Annual. Energy efficiency program for certain commercial and industrial equipment. *Code of Federal Regulations* 10 CFR 431. U.S. Government Publishing Office, Washington, D.C. www.ecfr.gov.

Chantrasrisalai, C., D.E. Fisher, I. Iu, and D. Eldridge. 2003. Experimental validation of design cooling load procedures: The heat balance method. *ASHRAE Transactions* 109(2):160-173.

Claridge, D.E., B. Abushakra, J.S. Haberl, and A. Sreshthaputra. 2004. Electricity diversity profiles for energy simulation of office buildings (RP-1093). *ASHRAE Transactions* 110(1):365-377.

Eldridge, D., D.E. Fisher, I. Iu, and C. Chantrasrisalai. 2003. Experimental validation of design cooling load procedures: Facility design (RP-1117). *ASHRAE Transactions* 109(2):151-159.

Feng, J., S. Schiavon, and F. Bauman. 2012. Comparison of zone cooling load for radiant and air conditioning systems. Proceedings of the International Conference on Building Energy and Environment. Boulder, CO. escholarship.org/uc/item/9g24f38j.

Fisher, D.R. 1998. New recommended heat gains for commercial cooking equipment. *ASHRAE Transactions* 104(2):953-960.

Fisher, D.E., and C. Chantrasrisalai. 2006. Lighting heat gain distribution in buildings (RP-1282). ASHRAE Research Project, *Final Report*.

Fisher, D.E., and C.O. Pedersen. 1997. Convective heat transfer in building energy and thermal load calculations. *ASHRAE Transactions* 103(2): 137-148.

Gordon, E.B., D.J. Horton, and F.A. Parvin. 1994. Development and application of a standard test method for the performance of exhaust hoods with commercial cooking appliances. *ASHRAE Transactions* 100(2).

Hittle, D.C. 1999. The effect of beam solar radiation on peak cooling loads. *ASHRAE Transactions* 105(2):510-513.

Hittle, D.C., and C.O. Pedersen. 1981. Calculating building heating loads using the frequency of multi-layered slabs. *ASHRAE Transactions* 87(2): 545-568.

Hosni, M.H., and B.T. Beck. 2008. Update to measurements of office equipment heat gain data (RP-1482). ASHRAE Research Project, *Progress Report*.

Hosni, M.H., B.W. Jones, J.M. Sipes, and Y. Xu. 1998. Total heat gain and the split between radiant and convective heat gain from office and laboratory equipment in buildings. *ASHRAE Transactions* 104(1A):356-365.

Hosni, M.H., B.W. Jones, and H. Xu. 1999. Experimental results for heat gain and radiant/convective split from equipment in buildings. *ASHRAE Transactions* 105(2):527-539.

Incropera, F.P., and D.P. DeWitt. 1990. *Fundamentals of heat and mass transfer*, 3rd ed. Wiley, New York.

Iu, I., and D.E. Fisher. 2004. Application of conduction transfer functions and periodic response factors in cooling load calculation procedures. *ASHRAE Transactions* 110(2):829-841.

Iu, I., C. Chantrasrisalai, D.S. Eldridge, and D.E. Fisher. 2003. Experimental validation of design cooling load procedures: The radiant time series method (RP-1117). *ASHRAE Transactions* 109(2):139-150.

Jones, B.W., M.H. Hosni, and J.M. Sipes. 1998. Measurement of radiant heat gain from office equipment using a scanning radiometer. *ASHRAE Transactions* 104(1B):1775-1783.

Karambakkam, B.K., B. Nigusse, and J.D. Spitler. 2005. A one-dimensional approximation for transient multi-dimensional conduction heat transfer in building envelopes. *Proceedings of the 7th Symposium on Building Physics in the Nordic Countries*, The Icelandic Building Research Institute, Reykjavik, vol. 1, pp. 340-347.

Kerrisk, J.F., N.M. Schnurr, J.E. Moore, and B.D. Hunn. 1981. The custom weighting-factor method for thermal load calculations in the DOE-2 computer program. *ASHRAE Transactions* 87(2):569-584.

Komor, P. 1997. Space cooling demands from office plug loads. *ASHRAE Journal* 39(12):41-44.

Kong, M., and J. Zhang. 2016. Life-cycle cost and benefit analysis of utilizing hoods for light-duty cooking appliances in commercial kitchens (RP-1631, part 2). *Science and Technology for the Built Environment* 22(6): 866-882.

Kong, M., J. Zhang, B. Guo, and K. Han. 2016. Measurements of grease emission and heat generation rates of electric countertop appliances (RP-1631, part 1). *Science and Technology for the Built Environment* 22(6): 845-865.

Kusuda, T. 1967. *NBSLD, the computer program for heating and cooling loads for buildings*. BSS 69 and NBSIR 74-574. National Bureau of Standards.

Latta, J.K., and G.G. Boileau. 1969. Heat losses from house basements. *Canadian Building* 19(10):39.

LBL. 2015. *WINDOW 7.4.6: A PC program for analyzing window thermal performance for fenestration products*. LBL-48255. Windows and Daylighting Group. Lawrence Berkeley Laboratory, Berkeley.

Liesen, R.J., and C.O. Pedersen. 1997. An evaluation of inside surface heat balance models for cooling load calculations. *ASHRAE Transactions* 103(2):485-502.

Marn, W.L. 1962. Commercial gas kitchen ventilation studies. *Research Bulletin* 90(March). Gas Association Laboratories, Cleveland, OH.

McClellan, T.M., and C.O. Pedersen. 1997. Investigation of outdoor heat balance models for use in a heat balance cooling load calculation procedure. *ASHRAE Transactions* 103(2):469-484.

McQuiston, F.C., and J.D. Spitler. 1992. *Cooling and heating load calculation manual*, 2nd ed. ASHRAE.

Miller, A. 1971. *Meteorology*, 2nd ed. Charles E. Merrill, Columbus.

Nigusse, B.A. 2007. *Improvements to the radiant time series method cooling load calculation procedure*. Ph.D. dissertation, Oklahoma State University.

Parker, D.S., J.E.R. McIlvaine, S.F. Barkaszi, D.J. Beal, and M.T. Anello. 2000. *Laboratory testing of the reflectance properties of roofing material*. FSEC-CR670-00. Florida Solar Energy Center, Cocoa.

Pedersen, C.O., D.E. Fisher, and R.J. Liesen. 1997. Development of a heat balance procedure for calculating cooling loads. *ASHRAE Transactions* 103(2):459-468.

Pedersen, C.O., D.E. Fisher, J.D. Spitler, and R.J. Liesen. 1998. *Cooling and heating load calculation principles*. ASHRAE.

PG&E. 2010-2016. *Dishwashing machine performance reports: Application of ASTM F2474, standard test method for heat gain to space performance of commercial kitchen ventilation/appliance systems*. PG&E Food Service Technology Center, San Ramon, CA. www.fishnick.com /publications/appliancereports/dishmachines/.

Rees, S.J., J.D. Spitler, M.G. Davies, and P. Haves. 2000. Qualitative comparison of North American and U.K. cooling load calculation methods. *International Journal of Heating, Ventilating, Air-Conditioning and Refrigerating Research* 6(1):75-99.

Rock, B.A. 2005. A user-friendly model and coefficients for slab-on-grade load and energy calculation. *ASHRAE Transactions* 111(2):122-136.

Rock, B.A., and D.J. Wolfe. 1997. A sensitivity study of floor and ceiling plenum energy model parameters. *ASHRAE Transactions* 103(1):16-30.

Schiavon, S., F. Bauman, K.H. Lee, and T. Webster. 2010a. Simplified calculation method for design cooling loads in underfloor air distribution (UFAD) systems. *Energy and Buildings* 43(1-2):517-528. escholarship .org/uc/item/5w53c7kr.

Schiavon, S., K.H. Lee, F. Bauman, and T. Webster. 2010b. Influence of raised floor on zone design cooling load in commercial buildings. *Energy and Buildings* 42(5):1182-1191. escholarship.org/uc/item/2bv611dt.

Schiavon, S., F. Bauman, K.H. Lee, and T. Webster. 2010c. Development of a simplified cooling load design tool for underfloor air distribution systems. *Final Report* to CEC PIER Program, July. escholarship.org/uc/item /6278m12z.

Smith, V.A., R.T. Swierczyna, and C.N. Claar. 1995. Application and enhancement of the standard test method for the performance of commercial kitchen ventilation systems. *ASHRAE Transactions* 101(2).

Sowell, E.F. 1988a. Cross-check and modification of the DOE-2 program for calculation of zone weighting factors. *ASHRAE Transactions* 94(2).

Sowell, E.F. 1988b. Load calculations for 200,640 zones. *ASHRAE Transactions* 94(2):716-736.

Spitler, J.D., and D.E. Fisher. 1999a. Development of periodic response factors for use with the radiant time series method. *ASHRAE Transactions* 105(2):491-509.

Spitler, J.D., and D.E. Fisher. 1999b. On the relationship between the radiant time series and transfer function methods for design cooling load calculations. *International Journal of Heating, Ventilating, Air-Conditioning and Refrigerating Research* (now *Science and Technology for the Built Environment*) 5(2):125-138.

Spitler, J.D., D.E. Fisher, and C.O. Pedersen. 1997. The radiant time series cooling load calculation procedure. *ASHRAE Transactions* 103(2).

Spitler, J.D., S.J. Rees, and P. Haves. 1998. Quantitive comparison of North American and U.K. cooling load calculation procedures—Part 1: Methodology, Part II: Results. *ASHRAE Transactions* 104(2):36-46, 47-61.

Sun, T.-Y. 1968. Shadow area equations for window overhangs and side-fins and their application in computer calculation. *ASHRAE Transactions* 74(1):I-1.1 to I-1.9.

Swierczyna, R., P. Sobiski, and D. Fisher. 2008. Revised heat gain and capture and containment exhaust rates from typical commercial cooking appliances (RP-1362). ASHRAE Research Project, *Final Report*.

Swierczyna, R., P.A. Sobiski, and D.R. Fisher. 2009. Revised heat gain rates from typical commercial cooking appliances from RP-1362. *ASHRAE Transactions* 115(2):138-160.

Talbert, S.G., L.J. Canigan, and J.A. Eibling. 1973. An experimental study of ventilation requirements of commercial electric kitchens. *ASHRAE Transactions* 79(1):34.

Walton, G. 1983. *Thermal analysis research program reference manual*. National Bureau of Standards.

Webster, T., F. Bauman, F. Buhl, and A. Daly. 2008. Modeling of underfloor air distribution (UFAD) systems. SimBuild 2008, University of California, Berkeley.

Wilkins, C.K., and M.R. Cook. 1999. Cooling loads in laboratories. *ASHRAE Transactions* 105(1):744-749.

Wilkins, C.K., and M.H. Hosni. 2000. Heat gain from office equipment. *ASHRAE Journal* 42(6):33-44.

Wilkins, C.K., and M. Hosni. 2011. Plug load design factors. *ASHRAE Journal* 53(5):30-34.

Wilkins, C.K., and N. McGaffin. 1994. Measuring computer equipment loads in office buildings. *ASHRAE Journal* 36(8):21-24.

Wilkins, C.K., R. Kosonen, and T. Laine. 1991. An analysis of office equipment load factors. *ASHRAE Journal* 33(9):38-44.

Zhou, X., S.J. Lochhead, Z. Zhong, and C.V. Huynh. 2016. Low energy LED lighting heat distribution in buildings. ASHRAE Research Project RP-1681, *Final Report*.

BIBLIOGRAPHY

Alereza, T., and J.P. Breen, III. 1984. Estimates of recommended heat gain due to commercial appliances and equipment. *ASHRAE Transactions* 90(2A):25-58.

ASHRAE. 1975. *Procedure for determining heating and cooling loads for computerized energy calculations, algorithms for building heat transfer subroutines*.

ASHRAE. 1979. *Cooling and heating load calculation manual*.

BLAST Support Office. 1991. *BLAST user reference*. University of Illinois, Urbana–Champaign.

Buffington, D.E. 1975. Heat gain by conduction through exterior walls and roofs—Transmission matrix method. *ASHRAE Transactions* 81(2):89.

Burch, D.M., B.A. Peavy, and F.J. Powell. 1974. Experimental validation of the NBS load and indoor temperature prediction model. *ASHRAE Transactions* 80(2):291.

Burch, D.M., J.E. Seem, G.N. Walton, and B.A. Licitra. 1992. Dynamic evaluation of thermal bridges in a typical office building. *ASHRAE Transactions* 98:291-304.

Butler, R. 1984. The computation of heat flows through multi-layer slabs. *Building and Environment* 19(3):197-206.

Ceylan, H.T., and G.E. Myers. 1985. Application of response-coefficient method to heat-conduction transients. *ASHRAE Transactions* 91:30-39.

Chiles, D.C., and E.F. Sowell. 1984. A counter-intuitive effect of mass on zone cooling load response. *ASHRAE Transactions* 91(2A):201-208.

Chorpening, B.T. 1997. The sensitivity of cooling load calculations to window solar transmission models. *ASHRAE Transactions* 103(1).

Clarke, J.A. 1985. *Energy simulation in building design*. Adam Hilger Ltd., Boston.

Davies, M.G. 1996. A time-domain estimation of wall conduction transfer function coefficients. *ASHRAE Transactions* 102(1):328-208.

Falconer, D.R., E.F. Sowell, J.D. Spitler, and B.B. Todorovich. 1993. Electronic tables for the ASHRAE load calculation manual. *ASHRAE Transactions* 99(1):193-200.

Harris, S.M., and F.C. McQuiston. 1988. A study to categorize walls and roofs on the basis of thermal response. *ASHRAE Transactions* 94(2):688-714.

Hittle, D.C. 1981. *Calculating building heating and cooling loads using the frequency response of multilayered slabs*, Ph.D. dissertation, Department of Mechanical and Industrial Engineering, University of Illinois, Urbana–Champaign.

Hittle, D.C., and R. Bishop. 1983. An improved root-finding procedure for use in calculating transient heat flow through multilayered slabs. *International Journal of Heat and Mass Transfer* 26:1685-1693.

Kimura and Stephenson. 1968. Theoretical study of cooling loads caused by lights. *ASHRAE Transactions* 74(2):189-197.

Kusuda, T. 1969. Thermal response factors for multilayer structures of various heat conduction systems. *ASHRAE Transactions* 75(1):246.

Mast, W.D. 1972. Comparison between measured and calculated hour heating and cooling loads for an instrumented building. ASHRAE *Symposium Bulletin* 72(2).

McBridge, M.F., C.D. Jones, W.D. Mast, and C.F. Sepsey. 1975. Field validation test of the hourly load program developed from the ASHRAE algorithms. *ASHRAE Transactions* 1(1):291.

Mitalas, G.P. 1968. Calculations of transient heat flow through walls and roofs. *ASHRAE Transactions* 74(2):182-188.

Mitalas, G.P. 1969. An experimental check on the weighting factor method of calculating room cooling load. *ASHRAE Transactions* 75(2):22.

Mitalas, G.P. 1972. Transfer function method of calculating cooling loads, heat extraction rate, and space temperature. *ASHRAE Journal* 14(12):52.

Mitalas, G.P. 1973. Calculating cooling load caused by lights. *ASHRAE Transactions* 75(6):7.

Mitalas, G.P. 1978. Comments on the Z-transfer function method for calculating heat transfer in buildings. *ASHRAE Transactions* 84(1):667-674.

Mitalas, G.P., and J.G. Arsenault. 1970. Fortran IV program to calculate Z-transfer functions for the calculation of transient heat transfer through walls and roofs. *Use of Computers for Environmental Engineering Related to Buildings*, pp. 633-668. National Bureau of Standards, Gaithersburg, MD.

Mitalas, G.P., and K. Kimura. 1971. A calorimeter to determine cooling load caused by lights. *ASHRAE Transactions* 77(2):65.

Mitalas, G.P., and D.G. Stephenson. 1967. Room thermal response factors. *ASHRAE Transactions* 73(2):III.2.1.

Nevins, R.G., H.E. Straub, and H.D. Ball. 1971. Thermal analysis of heat removal troffers. *ASHRAE Transactions* 77(2):58-72.

NFPA. 2012. Health care facilities code. *Standard* 99-2012. National Fire Protection Association, Quincy, MA.

Ouyang, K., and F. Haghighat. 1991. A procedure for calculating thermal response factors of multi-layer walls—State space method. *Building and Environment* 26(2):173-177.

Peavy, B.A. 1978. A note on response factors and conduction transfer functions. *ASHRAE Transactions* 84(1):688-690.

Peavy, B.A., F.J. Powell, and D.M. Burch. 1975. Dynamic thermal performance of an experimental masonry building. NBS *Building Science Series* 45 (July).

Romine, T.B., Jr. 1992. Cooling load calculation: Art or science? *ASHRAE Journal*, 34(1):14.

Rudoy, W. 1979. Don't turn the tables. *ASHRAE Journal* 21(7):62.

Rudoy, W., and F. Duran. 1975. Development of an improved cooling load calculation method. *ASHRAE Transactions* 81(2):19-69.

Seem, J.E., S.A. Klein, W.A. Beckman, and J.W. Mitchell. 1989. Transfer functions for efficient calculation of multidimensional transient heat transfer. *Journal of Heat Transfer* 111:5-12.

Sowell, E.F., and D.C. Chiles. 1984a. Characterization of zone dynamic response for CLF/CLTD tables. *ASHRAE Transactions* 91(2A):162-178.

Sowell, E.F., and D.C. Chiles. 1984b. Zone descriptions and response characterization for CLF/CLTD calculations. *ASHRAE Transactions* 91(2A): 179-200.

Spitler, J.D. 1996. *Annotated guide to load calculation models and algorithms.* ASHRAE.

Spitler, J.D., F.C. McQuiston, and K.L. Lindsey. 1993. The CLTD/SCL/CLF cooling load calculation method. *ASHRAE Transactions* 99(1): 183-192.

Spitler, J.D., and F.C. McQuiston. 1993. Development of a revised cooling and heating calculation manual. *ASHRAE Transactions* 99(1):175-182.

Stephenson, D.G. 1962. Method of determining non-steady-state heat flow through walls and roofs at buildings. *Journal of the Institution of Heating and Ventilating Engineers* 30:5.

Stephenson, D.G., and G.P. Mitalas. 1967. Cooling load calculation by thermal response factor method. *ASHRAE Transactions* 73(2):III.1.1.

Stephenson, D.G., and G.P. Mitalas. 1971. Calculation of heat transfer functions for multi-layer slabs. *ASHRAE Transactions* 77(2):117-126.

Sun, T.-Y. 1968. Computer evaluation of the shadow area on a window cast by the adjacent building. *ASHRAE Journal* (September).

Todorovic, B. 1982. Cooling load from solar radiation through partially shaded windows, taking heat storage effect into account. *ASHRAE Transactions* 88(2):924-937.

Todorovic, B. 1984. Distribution of solar energy following its transmittal through window panes. *ASHRAE Transactions* 90(1B):806-815.

Todorovic, B. 1987. The effect of the changing shade line on the cooling load calculations. In ASHRAE videotape, *Practical applications for cooling load calculations*.

Todorovic, B. 1989. *Heat storage in building structure and its effect on cooling load; Heat and mass transfer in building materials and structure.* Hemisphere Publishing, New York.

Todorovic, B., and D. Curcija. 1984. Calculative procedure for estimating cooling loads influenced by window shading, using negative cooling load method. *ASHRAE Transactions* 2:662.

Todorovic, B., L. Marjanovic, and D. Kovacevic. 1993. Comparison of different calculation procedures for cooling load from solar radiation through a window. *ASHRAE Transactions* 99(2):559-564.

Wilkins, C.K. 1998. Electronic equipment heat gains in buildings. *ASHRAE Transactions* 104(1B):1784-1789.

York, D.A., and C.C. Cappiello. 1981. *DOE-2 engineers manual* (Version 2.1A). Lawrence Berkeley Laboratory and Los Alamos National Laboratory.

11. BUILDING EXAMPLE DRAWINGS

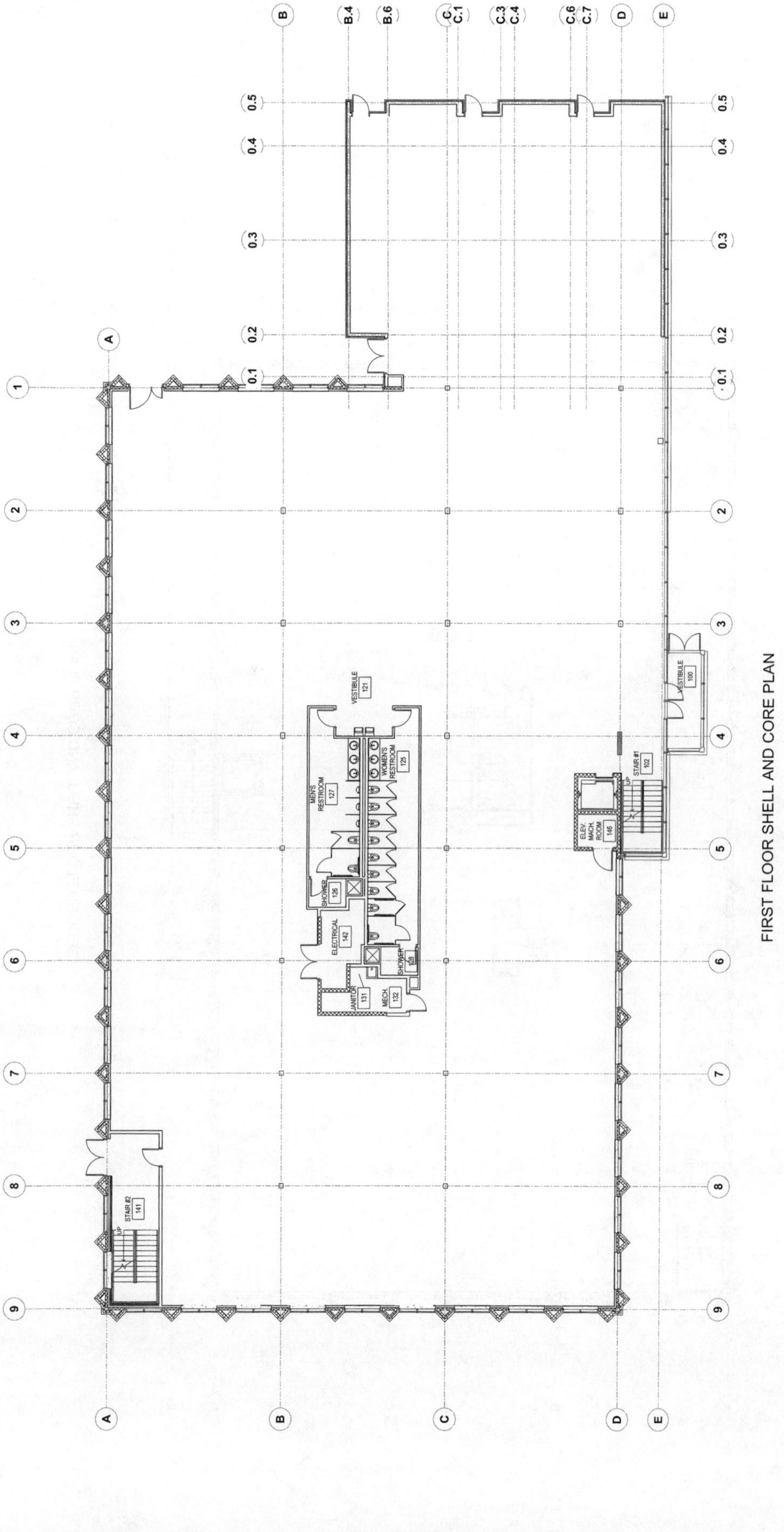

Fig. 17 First Floor Shell and Core Plan
(not to scale)

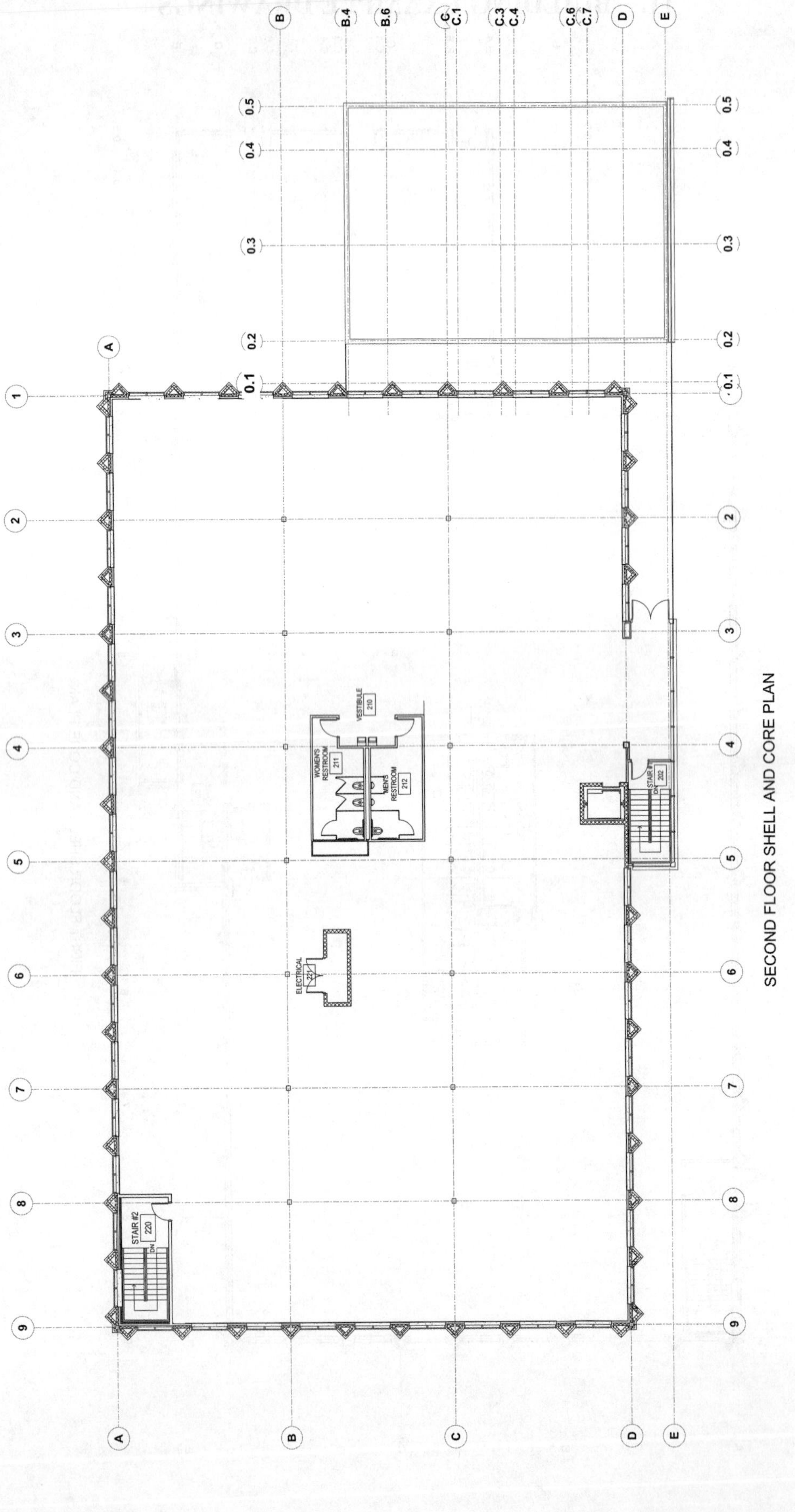

Fig. 18 Second Floor Shell and Core Plan
(not to scale)

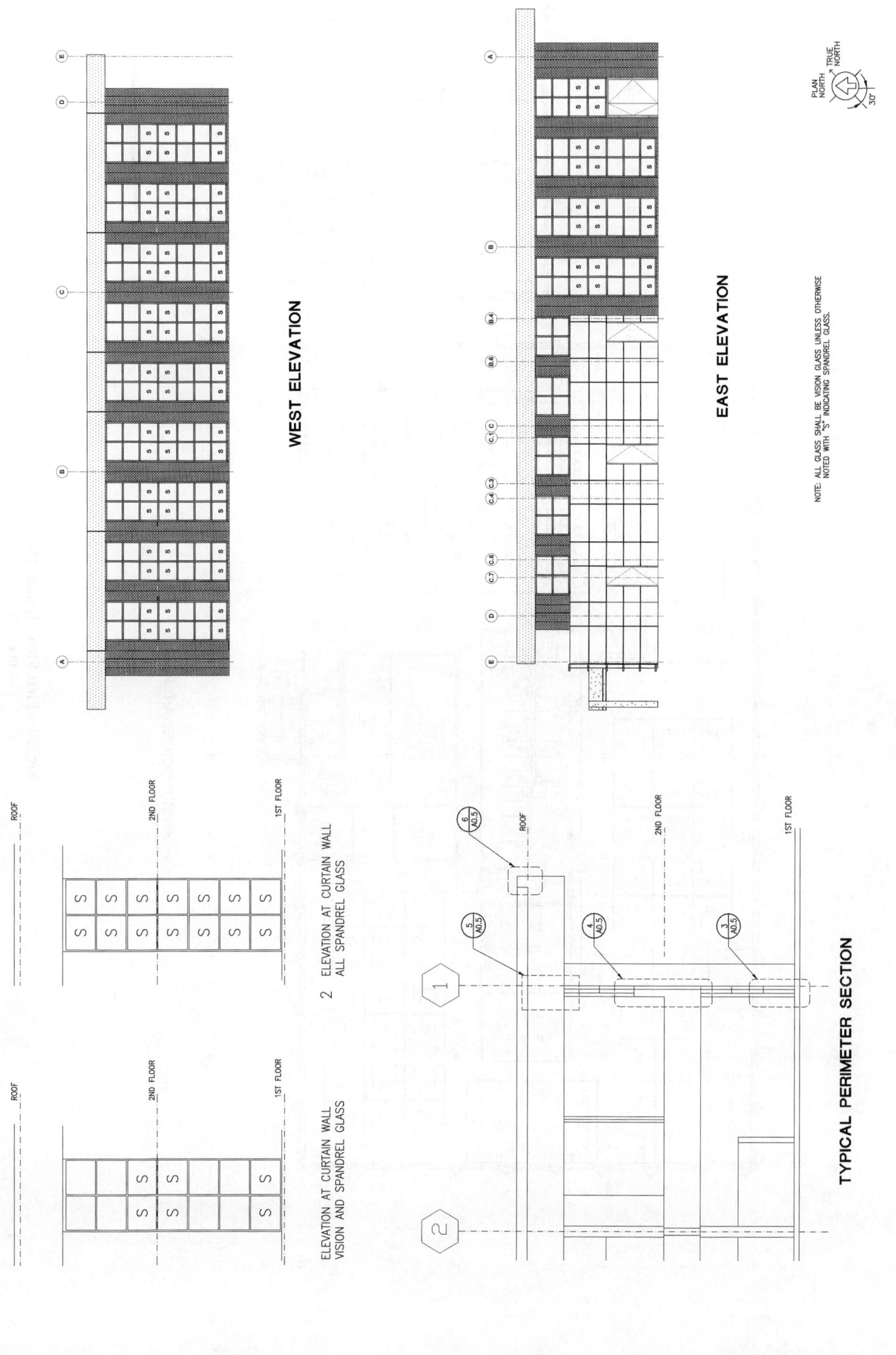

Fig. 19 East/West Elevations, Elevation Details, and Perimeter Section
(not to scale)

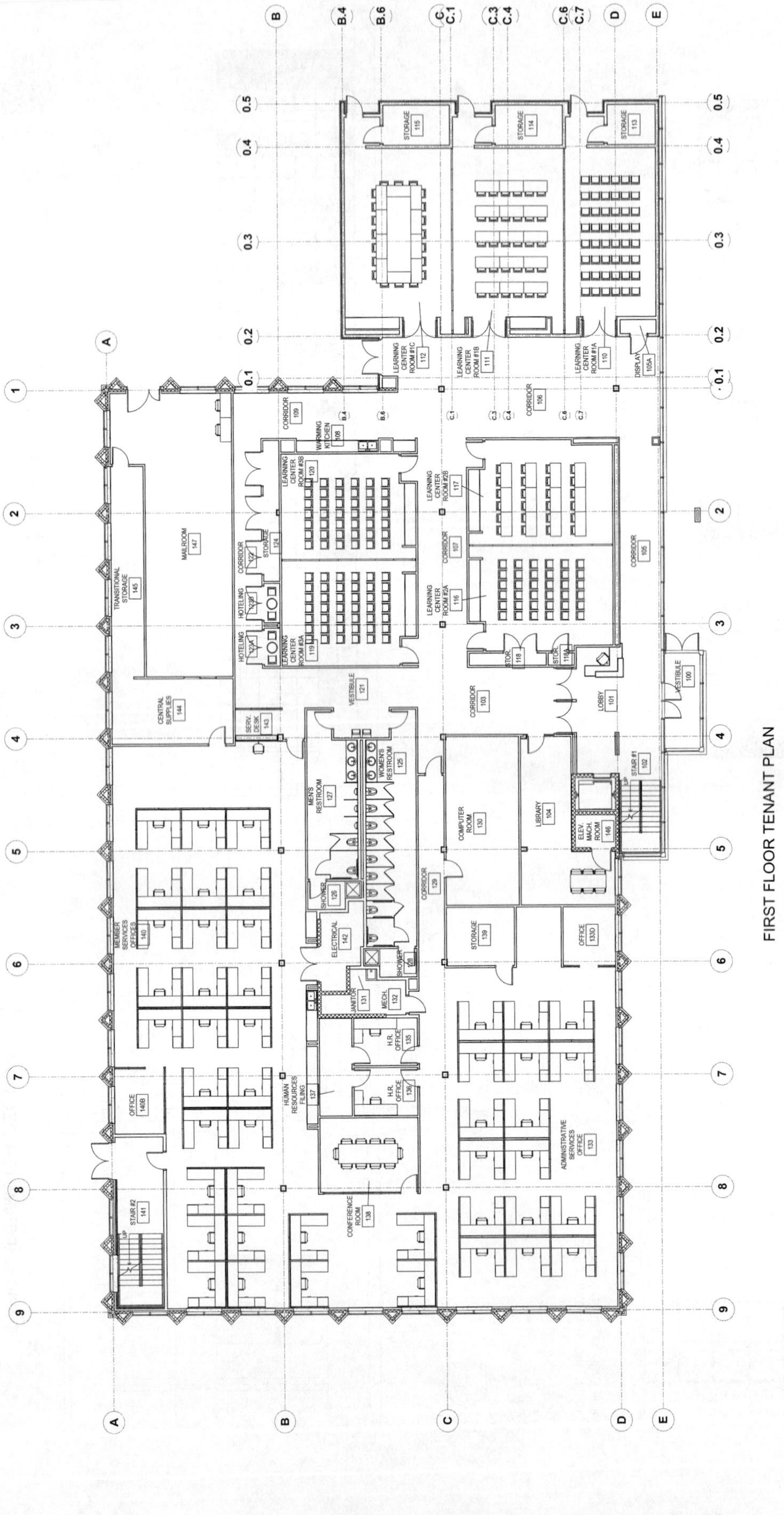

Fig. 20 First Floor Tenant Plan
(not to scale)

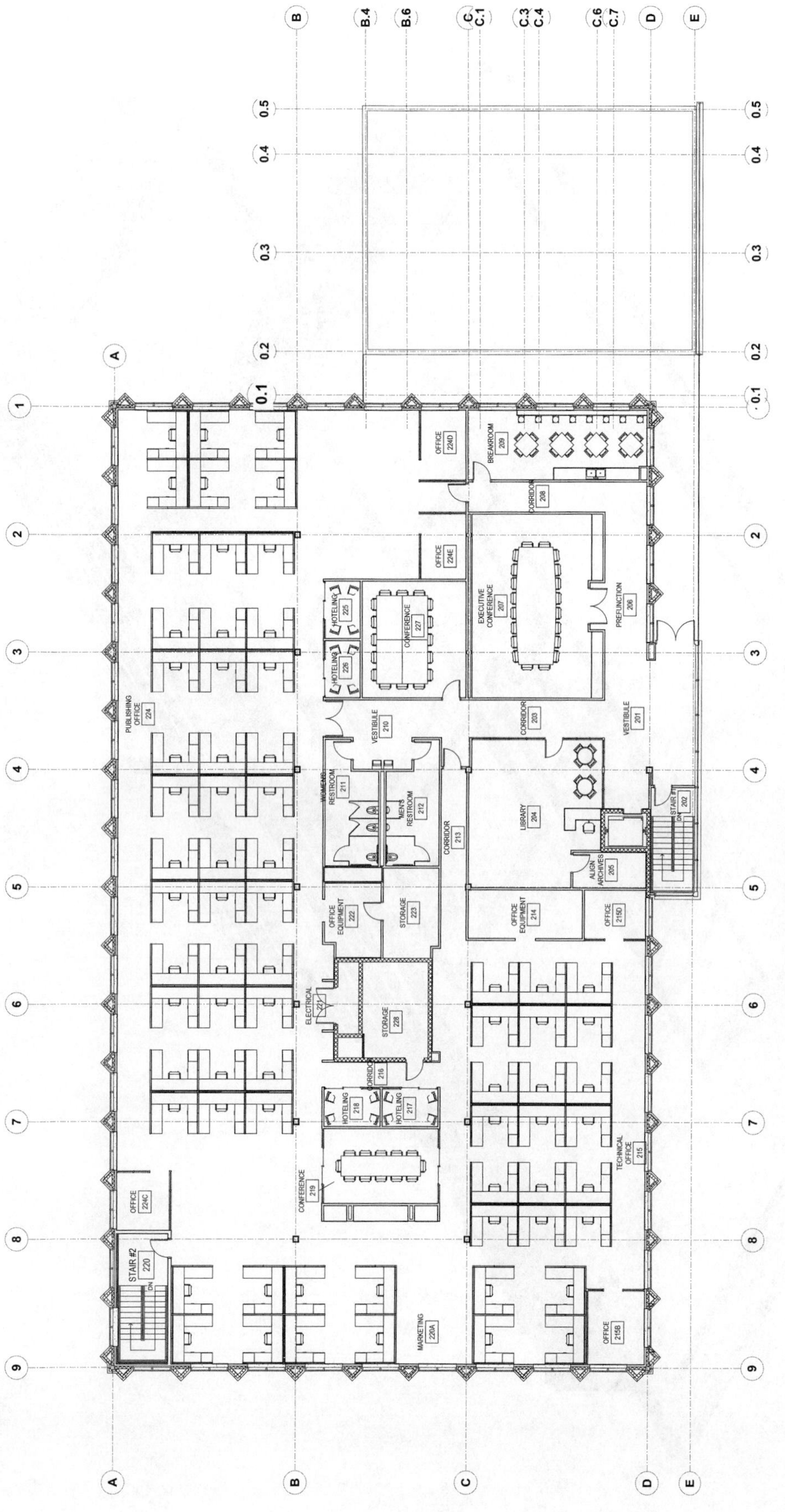

Fig. 21 Second Floor Tenant Plan
(not to scale)

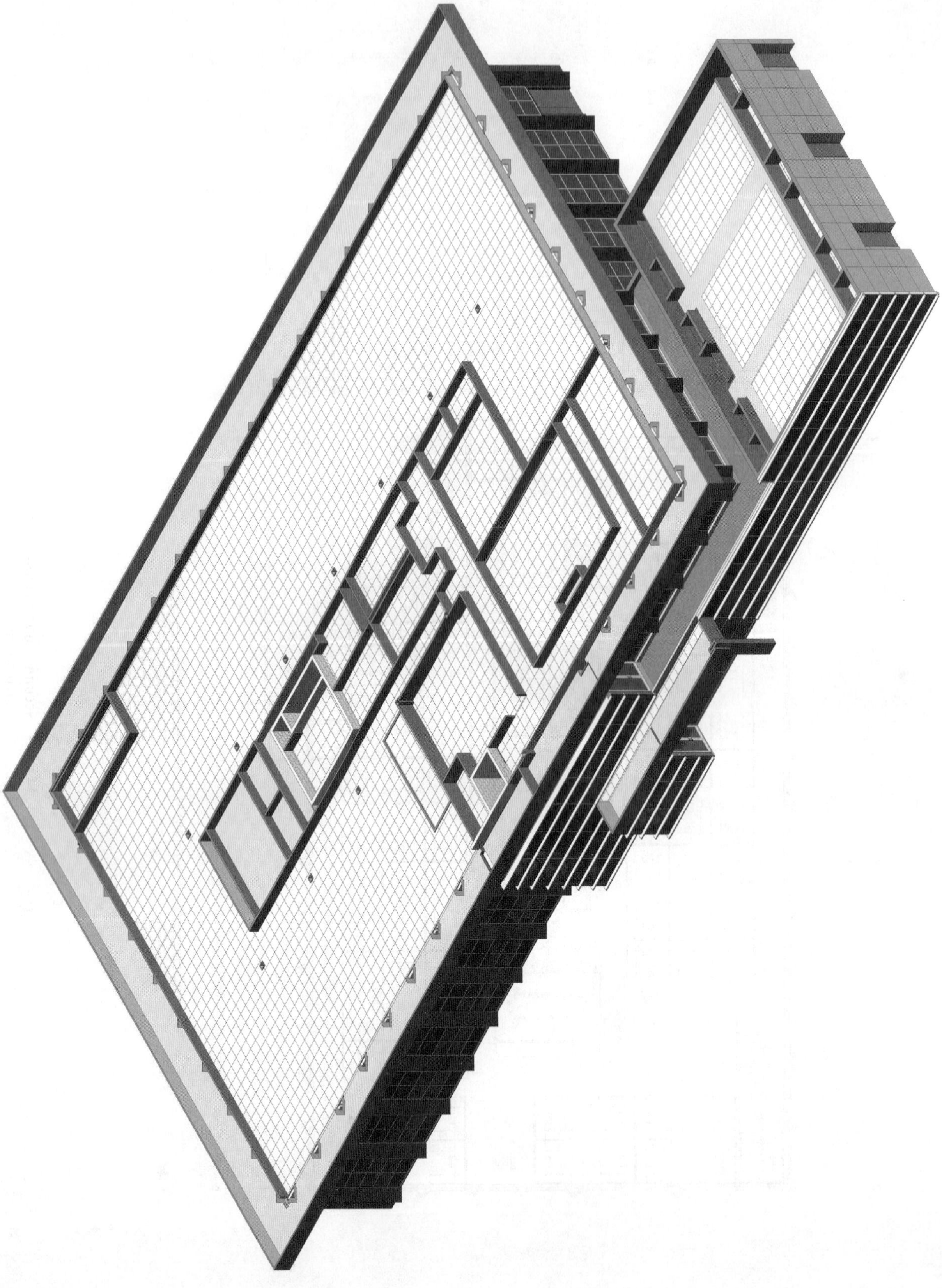

Fig. 22 3D View
(not to scale)

CHAPTER 19

ENERGY ESTIMATING AND MODELING METHODS

ENERGY requirements of HVAC systems directly affect a building's operating cost and indirectly affect the environment. This chapter discusses methods for estimating energy use for two purposes: modeling for building and HVAC system design and associated design optimization (**forward modeling**), and modeling energy use of existing buildings for establishing baselines, calculating retrofit savings, and implementing model predictive control (**data-driven modeling**) (Armstrong et al. 2006a; Gayeski et al. 2012; Krarti 2010).

1. GENERAL CONSIDERATIONS

1.1 MODELS AND APPROACHES

A mathematical **model** is a description of the behavior of a system. It is made up of three components (Beck and Arnold 1977):

- **Input variables** (statisticians call these *regressor variables*, whereas physicists call them *forcing variables*), which act on the system. There are two types: controllable by the experimenter (e.g., internal gains, thermostat settings), and uncontrollable (e.g., climate).
- **System structure and parameters/properties**, which provide the necessary physical description of the system (e.g., thermal mass or mechanical properties of the elements).
- **Output** (*response*, or *dependent*) variables, which describe the reaction of the system to the input variables. Energy use is often a response variable.

The science of mathematical modeling as applied to physical systems involves determining the third component of a system when the other two components are given or specified. There are two broad but distinct approaches to modeling: forward (classical) and data driven (inverse). The choice of approach is dictated by the objective or purpose of the investigation (Rabl 1988).

Forward (Classical) Approach

The objective is to predict the output variables of a specified model with known structure and known parameters when subject to specified input variables. To ensure accuracy, models have tended to become increasingly detailed. This approach presumes knowledge not only of the various natural phenomena affecting system behavior but also of the magnitude of various interactions (e.g., effective thermal mass, heat and mass transfer coefficients). The main advantage of this approach is that the system need not be physically built to predict its behavior. The forward-modeling approach is ideal in the preliminary design when design details are limited.

Forward modeling of building energy use begins with a physical description of the building system or component of interest. For example, building geometry, geographical location, physical characteristics (e.g., wall material and thickness), type of equipment and operating schedules, type of HVAC system, building operating schedules, plant equipment, etc., are specified. The peak and average energy use of such a building can then be predicted or simulated by the forward-simulation model. The primary benefits of this method are that it is based on sound engineering principles and has gained widespread acceptance by the design and professional community. Major simulation codes, such as DOE-2, EnergyPlus, ESP-r, and TRNSYS are based on forward-simulation models.

Although procedures for estimating energy requirements vary considerably in their degree of complexity, they all have three common elements: calculation of (1) space load, (2) secondary equipment load and energy requirements, and (3) primary equipment energy requirements. Here, *secondary* refers to equipment that distributes the heating, cooling, or ventilating medium to conditioned spaces, whereas *primary* refers to central plant equipment that converts fuel or electric energy to heating or cooling effect.

The space load is the amount of energy that must be added to or extracted from a space to maintain thermal comfort. The simplest procedures assume that the energy required to maintain comfort is only a function of the outdoor dry-bulb temperature. More detailed methods consider humidity, solar effects, internal gains, heat and moisture storage in walls and interiors, and effects of wind on both building envelope heat transfer and infiltration. The section on Thermal Loads Modeling addresses some of these factors. ASHRAE Standard 183 and Chapters 17 and 18 discuss load calculation in detail.

Although energy calculations are similar to the heating and cooling design load calculations used to size equipment, they are not the same. Energy calculations are based on average use and typical weather conditions rather than on maximum use and worst-case weather. Currently, most procedures are based on hourly profiles for climatic conditions and operational characteristics for a number of typical days of the year or on 8760 hours of operation per year.

The space load is converted to a load on the secondary equipment. This can be a simple estimate of duct or piping losses or gains, or a complex hour-by-hour simulation of an air system, such as variable-air-volume with outdoor-air cooling. This step must include calculation of all forms of energy required by the secondary system (e.g., electrical energy to operate fans and/or pumps, energy in heated or chilled water).

The secondary equipment load is converted to the fuel and energy required by the primary equipment and the peak demand on the utility system. It considers equipment efficiencies and part-load characteristics. It is often necessary to keep track of the different forms of energy, such as electrical, natural gas, and/or oil. In some cases, where calculations are required to ensure compliance with codes or standards, these energies must be converted to source energy or resource consumed, as opposed to energy delivered to the building boundary.

Previously, the steps were performed independently: each step was completed for the entire year and hourly results were passed to the next step. Current software usually performs all steps at each time interval, allowing effects such as insufficient plant capacity to be reflected in room conditions.

Often, energy calculations lead to an economic analysis to establish the cost effectiveness of efficiency measures (as in ASHRAE

The preparation of this chapter is assigned to TC 4.7, Energy Calculations.

Standard 90.1). Thus, thorough energy analysis provides intermediate data, such as time of energy use and maximum demand, so utility charges can be accurately estimated. Although not part of the energy calculations, capital equipment costs should also be estimated to assess the life-cycle costs of alternative efficiency measures.

Data-Driven (Inverse) Approach

In this approach, input and output variables are known and measured, and the objective is to determine a mathematical description of the system and to estimate system parameters. In contrast to the forward approach, the data-driven approach is relevant only when the system has already been built and actual performance data are available for model development, calibration (see the section on Model Calibration), and/or identification. Two types of performance data can be used: nonintrusive and intrusive. **Intrusive data** are gathered under conditions of predetermined or planned experiments on the system to elicit system response under a wider range of system performance than would occur under normal system operation to allow more accurate model identification. When constraints on system operation do not allow such tests to be performed, the model must be identified from **nonintrusive data** obtained under normal operation.

The data-driven model has to meet requirements very different from the forward model. The data-driven model can only contain a relatively small number of parameters because of the limited and often repetitive information contained in the performance data. (For example, building operation from one day to the next is fairly repetitive.) It is thus a much simpler model that contains fewer terms representative of aggregated or macroscopic parameters (e.g., overall building heat loss coefficient and time constants). Because model parameters are deduced from actual building performance, it is much more likely to accurately capture as-built system performance, thus allowing more accurate prediction of future system behavior under certain specific circumstances. Performance data collection and model formulation need to be appropriately tailored for the specific circumstance, which often requires a higher level of user skill and expertise. In general, data-driven models are less flexible than forward models in evaluating energy implications of different design and operational alternatives, and so are not substitutes in this regard.

To better understand the uses of data-driven models, consider some of the questions that a building professional may ask about an existing building with known energy consumption (Rabl 1988):

- How does energy consumption compare with design predictions (and are any discrepancies caused by anomalous weather, unintended building operation, improper operation, as-built deficiency, etc.)?
- How would consumption change if thermostat settings, ventilation rates, or indoor lighting levels were changed?
- How much energy could be saved by retrofits to the building shell, changes to air handler operation from constant volume (CV) to variable air volume (VAV), or changes in the various control settings?
- If retrofits are implemented, can one verify that the savings are due to the retrofit and not to other causes (e.g., weather)?
- How can one detect faults in HVAC equipment and optimize control and operation?

All these questions are better addressed by the data-driven approach. The forward approach could also be used, for example, by going back to the blueprints of the building and of the HVAC system, and repeating the analysis performed at the design stage using actual building schedules and operating modes, but this is tedious and labor intensive, and materials and equipment often perform differently in reality than as specified. Tuning the forward-simulation model is often problematic, although it is an option (see the section on Model Calibration).

1.2 OVERALL MODELING STRATEGIES

In developing a simulation model for building energy prediction, two basic issues must be considered: (1) modeling components or subsystems and (2) overall modeling strategy. Modeling components, discussed in the sections on Thermal Loads Modeling and HVAC Component Modeling, results in sets of equations describing the individual components. The overall modeling strategy refers to the **sequence** and **procedures** used to solve these equations. The accuracy of results and the computer resources required to achieve these results depend on the modeling strategy.

Early building energy programs, including some still in common use, execute load models for every space for every hour of the simulation period. (Most models of this type use 1 h as the time step, which excludes any information on phenomena occurring in a shorter time span.) Next, the program runs models for every secondary system, one at a time, for every hour of the simulation. Finally, the plant simulation model is executed again for the entire period.

This procedure is shown in Figure 1. Solid lines represent data passed from one model to the next; dashed lines represent information, usually provided by the user, about one model passed to the preceding model. For example, the system information may consist of a piecewise-linear function of zone temperature that gives system capacity.

Because of this loads-systems-plants sequence, certain phenomena cannot be modeled precisely. For example, if the heat balance method for computing loads is used, and some component in the system simulation model cannot meet the load, the program can only report the current load. In actuality, the space temperature should readjust until the load matches equipment capacity, but this cannot be modeled, because loads have been precalculated and fixed. If the weighting-factor method is used for loads, this problem is partially overcome, because loads are continually readjusted during the system simulation. However, the weighting-factor technique is based on linear mathematics, and wide departures of room temperatures from those used during execution of the load program can introduce errors.

A similar problem arises in plant simulation. For example, in an actual building, as load on the central plant varies, the supply chilled-water temperature also varies. This variation in turn affects the capacity of secondary system equipment. In an actual building, when the central plant becomes overloaded, space temperatures should rise to reduce load. However, with this separate load-system-plant approach, this condition cannot occur; thus, only the overload condition can be reported. These are some of the penalties associated with decoupling the load, system, and plant models.

More recent building energy programs use an alternative strategy, in which all calculations are performed at each time step. Here, the load, system, and plant equations are solved simultaneously at each time interval. With this strategy, unmet loads and imbalances cannot occur; conditions at the plant are immediately reflected to the secondary system and then to the load model, forcing them to readjust to the instantaneous conditions throughout the building. The results of this modeling strategy are superior, although the magnitude and importance of the improvement are case specific.

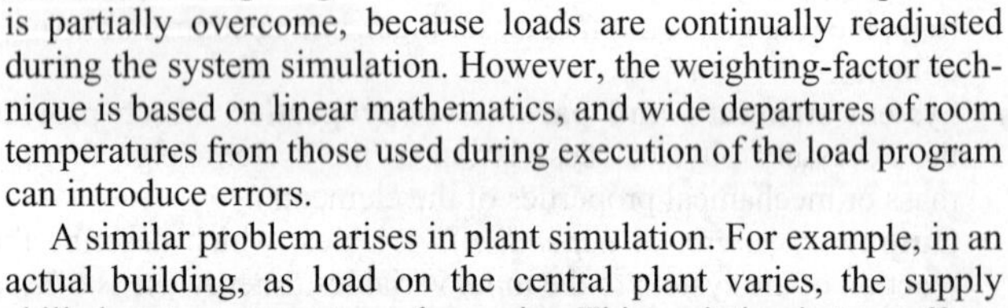

Fig. 1 Overall Modeling Strategy

The principal disadvantage of this approach, and the reason that it was not widely used in the past, is that it demands more computing resources. However, most current desktop computers can now run programs using the alternative approach in a reasonable amount of time. Programs that, to one degree or another, implement simultaneous solution of the loads, system, and plant models have been developed by ESRU (2016), Klein et al. (1994), Park et al. (1985), Taylor et al. (1990, 1991), and U.S. Department of Energy (1996-2016). Some of these programs can simulate the loads, systems, and plants using subhourly time steps.

An economic model, as shown in Figure 1, calculates energy costs (and sometimes capital costs) based on the estimated required input energy. Thus, the simulation model calculates energy use and cost for any given input weather and internal loads. By applying this model (i.e., determining output for given inputs) at each hour (or other suitable interval), the hour-by-hour energy consumption and cost can be determined. Maintaining running sums of these quantities yields monthly or annual energy usage and costs.

Because detailed models are computationally intensive, several simplified methods have been developed, including the degree-day, bin, and correlation methods. See the section on Degree-Day and Bin Methods for more information.

1.3 SIMULATING SECONDARY AND PRIMARY SYSTEMS

Traditionally, most energy analysis programs include a set of preprogrammed models that represent various systems (e.g., variable air volume, terminal reheat, multizone, variable refrigerant flow). In this scheme, the equations for each system are arranged so they can be solved sequentially. If this is not possible, the smallest number of equations that must be solved simultaneously is solved using an appropriate technique. Furthermore, individual equations may vary hourly in the simulation, depending on controls and operating conditions. For example, a dry coil uses different equations than a wet coil. The primary disadvantage of this scheme is that it is relatively inflexible: to modify a system, the program source code may have to be modified and recompiled.

An alternative strategy views the system as a series of components (e.g., fan, coil, pump, duct, pipe, damper, thermostat) that may be organized in a component library (Park et al. 1985; TRNSYS 2012). Users specify connections between the components, and the program then resolves the specification of components and connections into a set of simultaneous equations.

A refinement of component-based modeling is known as **equation-based modeling** (Buhl et al. 1993; Sowell and Moshier 1995). These models do not follow predetermined rules for a solution, and the user can specify which variables are inputs and which are outputs. Current research in this area centers on use of the Modelica object-oriented modeling language (Wetter et al. 2011).

1.4 HISTORY OF SIMULATION METHOD DEVELOPMENT

Significant historical events, such as World Wars I and II, the development of analog and digital computers and programming languages (1950s), and repeated oil crises (1967, 1973, and 1979) spurred the development of analysis methods and computer simulation programs now used to simulate building energy use. Before the 1950s, most of the fundamentals (i.e., gas laws, heat transfer properties, and thermodynamics) of today's HVAC systems had been studied and published, which contributed significantly to the rapid development of today's building energy simulation technology. Also, during this same period, researchers and engineers developed the essential methods for calculating and analyzing the dynamic heat gain through multilayer walls, overall dynamic building cooling and heating loads, solar heating performance, and internal reflected illuminance (Oh 2013; Oh and Haberl 2016a, 2016b, 2016c).

In the 1920s, one of the most important methods for calculating the dynamic heat gain through walls and roofs for whole-building energy simulation [i.e., the response factor method (RFM)] was developed and published by André Nessi and Léon Nisolle at École Centrale Paris (French University) in France (Nessi and Nisolle 1925). The RFM concept is widely used in most of today's cooling and heating loads calculations, such as with the weighting factor method or the transfer function method (Mitalas and Stephenson 1967; Stephenson and Mitalas 1967, 1971) used in DOE-2.1E (Winkelmann et al. 1993), DOE-2.2/eQUEST (LBNL 1998), TRACE (Trane 2013), and HAP (Carrier 2013); the CLTD/CLF method used in TRACE; the heat balance method (Pedersen et al. 1997) used in BLAST (Hittle 1977) and EnergyPlus (Crawley et al. 2001); and the radiant time series method (Spitler et al. 1997) used in TRACE. In the 1940s, the concept of the resistance-capacitance (RC) network analysis method (i.e., the thermal network method) used in simulation programs for buildings was first introduced by Victor Paschkis, a research engineer at Columbia University (Paschkis 1942; Paschkis and Baker 1942). The thermal network concept is widely used today in whole-building simulation programs such as DOE-2.1E, DOE-2.2/eQUEST, and EnergyPlus and in detailed solar simulation programs such as TRNSYS and SUNREL (Deru et al. 2002).

In the 1950s, the most important method (i.e., the utilizability method) for calculating the performance of solar heating systems for design programs was developed (Whillier 1953). The utilizability method is used today in simplified solar design programs such as RETScreen (NRC 2004), F-Chart (Klein and Beckman 2001a), and PV F-Chart (Klein and Beckman 2001b).

Also during the 1950s, analog computers were first used to study the behavior of dynamic heat gain/loss and the impact of dynamic heat gain/loss on HVAC systems (Buchberg 1955, 1958; Nottage and Parmelee 1954; Willcox et al. 1954). During the 1960s, digital computers and the analysis methods suitable for the digital computers were developed and became widely used. Digital computers were quickly substituted for analog computers during this period because the digital computer was more convenient to program, more flexible, and more agile at describing the governing equations and driving functions than the methods used in analog computers. Finally, the scientific applications of the digital computer were considerably improved by the FORTRAN programming language, a high-level, scientific programming language that was first commercially released in 1957 by IBM. In the 1960s, FORTRAN allowed computer codes written on one computer to be run on another computer by a different analyst, which accelerated the wide-spread availability of building energy simulation programs. The combination of computer advances with the analysis methods developed by numerous researchers facilitated the development of today's whole-building energy, solar energy, and daylighting simulation programs.

1.5 USING ENERGY MODELS

Typical Applications

Energy models are useful for a range of applications, and the typical application of forward-modeling tools falls into three categories:

- **Comparison.** A common application is to use energy models to compare the estimated performance of design alternatives for new buildings or to compare retrofit alternatives for existing buildings. In such design studies, the goal is to estimate the relative performance of two or more options. Examples include comparing alternatives for building form and orientation, comparing different glazing selections, or comparing chiller alternatives. Energy models are especially well suited to such comparison studies, because the relative performance is likely to be estimated with reasonable accuracy even if some inputs, such as actual operating hours or plug loads, are not accurately known at the time of the study.

- **Compliance.** Using models for energy code compliance (e.g., ASHRAE *Standard* 90.1) and for building rating system credit (e.g., U.S. Green Building Council's LEED® rating system) are very common applications. In most cases, these studies involve comparing two energy models: one representing a baseline building that meets the minimum code requirements, and the other representing the proposed building design, with the result an estimate of relative performance. Some utility and other incentive programs also use the same method for estimating energy savings for new and retrofit construction projects. Note that the models will not necessarily be good predictors of actual energy use unless the inputs have been carefully specified to represent the expected operation of the actual building.
- **Prediction.** An application of growing importance is using energy models to predict energy consumption. Some industry efforts, such as Architecture 2030 (AIA 2014), encourage building designers to set targets for energy consumption. In those cases, the goal is to design a building that meets an absolute energy target, often specified in terms of kBtu/ft^2·yr. In addition, some owners seek zero-energy buildings that offset consumption with renewable energy. During the design of zero-energy buildings, accurate prediction of energy consumption is important for proper sizing of renewable energy systems. Energy models used for prediction require very careful attention to providing realistic inputs to represent the expected building operation.

Choosing Measures for Evaluation

Forward-modeling programs are useful for evaluating many types of design elements, whereas they may be unnecessary or inappropriate for evaluating other elements. They are most useful for evaluating elements that affect heating and cooling loads. Many programs also provide the ability to compare the energy performance of different HVAC designs. The following are examples of design elements that are typically good candidates for evaluation with forward-modeling programs:

- **Building form and orientation.** Varying building dimensions.
- **Opaque envelope.** Varying levels of insulation and thermal mass.
- **Fenestration.** Alternative glazing and framing types, and both fixed and operable shading devices.
- **Daylighting controls.** Requires a program with an adequately accurate daylight illuminance calculation.
- **Cooling equipment efficiency**. Full- and partial-load performance.
- **Heating equipment efficiency**. Full- and partial-load performance, condensing versus noncondensing equipment.
- **Economizer cooling**. Air- and water-side economizers.
- **Variable-flow controls**. Air and hydronic distribution system control.
- **Basic HVAC controls.** Space temperature set points, HVAC supply temperature reset controls, start/stop scheduling, load management scheduling.
- **Combined heat and power systems.** Some programs can apply waste heat from cogeneration systems to building thermal demands.

Some design elements do not necessarily require an energy model for evaluation, and a reasonably accurate savings estimate may be possible using other methods. Although it may still be useful to represent them in an energy model along with other measures, it may not be worth the effort for an analysis looking exclusively at these measures:

- **Plug loads.** The majority of the impact is from direct savings that may be calculated simply with an estimate of connected power and operating hours. An energy model may be appropriate if the effect on heating and cooling loads is expected to be significant.
- **Interior lighting power.** Similar issues to plug loads.
- **Exterior lighting power and control.** Has no effect on heating and cooling loads.
- **Control of constant-speed/constant-volume equipment.** The savings from an adjustment in flow may be simple to calculate without using an energy model.
- **Photovoltaic and other on-site generation systems.** Although some programs offer the capability to model photovoltaic systems or other on-site electricity production, separate calculations may be equally accurate and require less effort.

Limitations to the capabilities of most forward-modeling programs are important to understand. Some programs may not be appropriate candidates for performing an evaluation, depending on the feature to be analyzed:

- **Daylight-redirecting devices**. Design elements such as light shelves or light-redirecting glazing are sometimes used to increase the daylighted area. It is important to understand the capabilities of the tool used for analysis.
- **Dynamic glazing**. Dynamic glazing may be used to control glare and solar heat gain. It is important to understand the capabilities of the modeling tool for this design element.
- **Natural ventilation**. Not all programs can model natural ventilation or the integration of mechanical and natural ventilation. See the section on Natural Ventilation for more information.
- **Specific HVAC system types**. The selected program might not have the ability to explicitly model a desired HVAC system configuration.
- **Specific HVAC system control strategies**. Programs vary in capability to represent varying control strategies.

When to Use Energy Models

Energy modeling has appropriate applications throughout the stages of design, construction, and operation of a building. At the earliest conceptual design phase, comparative studies help designers compare options for building form, system types, and other decisions that will be hard to change at later stages. During subsequent phases, energy modeling studies can be used to refine design decisions such as component specifications. At the conclusion of design, the models can be used to document energy code or rating-system compliance. Although use of energy models during construction is less common, their use during commissioning to compare expected performance to observed performance is growing. Similarly, building performance can be verified by comparing actual energy consumption to modeled performance, and any observed differences can help the building operator identify potential areas for improvement. The American Institute of Architects has published a guide to integrating energy modeling in the design process (AIA 2012). Proposed ASHRAE *Standard* 209P specifies mandatory and optional modeling tasks for new construction projects.

Energy Modelers

Creation of energy models has typically been done by specialists, and specialists continue today to perform a significant amount of energy modeling work. However, increasing user-friendliness of modeling software and the integration of building information models and energy modeling tools have made energy modeling more accessible to nonspecialists.

Anyone performing energy modeling should understand the way their program of choice works, understand assumptions being used by the program, and know how to interpret the results obtained from the program.

ASHRAE offers a Building Energy Modeling Professional (BEMP) qualification exam for modeler certification (www.ashrae.org/education--certification/certification/bemp-building-energy-modeling-professional-certification).

1.6 UNCERTAINTY IN MODELING

Uncertainty is inherent in modeling. When modeling a complex system, there are often uncertainties in identifying system inputs. In addition, there are uncertainties and variability in known model input parameters, and uncertainties in the model itself. It is important for modelers to characterize the uncertainties to understand how to interpret the uncertainty in the model prediction (Macdonald and Strachan 2001; de Wit and Augenbroe 2002). In reporting a model prediction, providing a value without providing its confidence interval implies 0% uncertainty, which is not possible because of many inherent uncertainties in the modeling process. Therefore, it is advisable to provide the predicted value as an interval rather than a precise value.

Uncertainties can be broken into two broad categories: aleatoric and epistemic (Kiureghaian and Ditlevsen 2009). **Aleatoric** uncertainties are those related to inherent randomness and variability of the system and the inputs to the system that cannot be reduced by better knowledge or system observation. They are typically characterized by probabilities. In other words, aleatoric uncertainties are "unknown unknowns." Examples of these in energy modeling are weather-related model inputs or occupant-related loads. **Epistemic** uncertainties are those related to uncertainty of the system model itself or parameters to the model that are fixed/static but not known precisely and that could be reduced with better knowledge of the system or the inputs. Epistemic uncertainty is also referred to as **state-of-knowledge** uncertainty, **subjective** uncertainty, or **reducible** uncertainty. In other words, epistemic uncertainties are "known unknowns." Examples include building geometry, thermal properties of enclosure materials, or efficiencies of equipment (Hopfe and Hensen 2011; Sun et al. 2014). Knowing the type of uncertainty associated with a parameter is important in understanding how to propagate that uncertainty through the model. Uncertainties can be propagated through a model using a variety of methods, including Monte Carlo, importance sampling, local expansion, most-probable-point methods, and numeric integration (Lee and Chen 2008). When using "black box" simulation engines, Monte Carlo methods and importance sampling are the most applicable.

Once the prediction uncertainty is quantified, there are various uses for the information. The output can be analyzed to obtain most probable values and/or variances. Output probability distributions can be analyzed for understanding the risk of underperformance. Uncertainty statistics can also be used for verifying that a model meets standards or guidelines for baseline predictions in measurement and verification, along with determining the uncertainty in cost savings calculations. ASHRAE *Guideline* 14 provides instruction on maximum levels of uncertainty in baseline models, along with simplified methods for assessing the quantifiable uncertainty in savings computations.

1.7 CHOOSING AN ANALYSIS METHOD

The most important step in selecting an energy analysis method is matching method capabilities with project requirements. The method must be capable of evaluating all design options with sufficient accuracy to make correct choices. The following factors apply generally (Sonderegger 1985):

- **Accuracy.** The method should be sufficiently accurate to allow correct choices. Because of the many parameters involved in energy estimation, absolutely accurate energy prediction is not possible (Waltz 1992). ANSI/ASHRAE *Standard* 140 was developed to identify and diagnose differences in predictions that may be caused by algorithmic differences, modeling limitations, coding errors, or input errors. More information on model validation and testing can be found in the Validation and Testing section of this chapter and in ANSI/ASHRAE *Standard* 140.
- **Sensitivity.** The method should be sensitive to the design options being considered. The difference in energy use between two choices should be adequately reflected.
- **Versatility.** The method should allow analysis of all options under consideration. When different methods must be used to consider different options, an accurate estimate of the differential energy use cannot be made.
- **Speed and cost.** The total time (gathering data, preparing input, calculations, and analysis of output) to make an analysis should be appropriate to the potential benefits gained. With greater speed, more options can be considered in a given time. The cost of analysis is largely determined by the total time of analysis.
- **Reproducibility.** The method should not allow so many vaguely defined choices that different analysts would get completely different results (Corson 1992).
- **Ease of use.** This affects both the economics of analysis (speed) and the reproducibility of results.

Selecting Energy Analysis Computer Programs

Selecting a building energy analysis program depends on its application, number of times it will be used, experience of the user, and hardware available to run it. The first criterion is the ability of the program to deal with the application. For example, if the effect of a shading device is to be analyzed on a building that is also shaded by other buildings part of the time, the ability to analyze detached shading is an absolute requirement, regardless of any other factors.

The cost of the computer facilities and the software itself are typically a small part of running a building energy analysis; the major costs are of learning to use the program and of using it. Major issues that influence the cost of learning a program include (1) complexity of input procedures, (2) quality of the user's manual, and (3) of a good support system to answer questions. As the user becomes more experienced, the cost of learning becomes less important, but the need to obtain and enter a complex set of input data continues to consume the time of even an experienced user until data are readily available in electronic form compatible with simulation programs.

Complexity of input is largely influenced by the availability of default values for the input variables. Default values can be used as a simple set of input data when detail is not needed or when building design is very conventional, but additional detail can be supplied when needed. Secondary defaults, which can be supplied by the user, are also useful in the same way. Some programs allow the user to specify a level of detail. Then the program requests only the information appropriate to that level of detail, using default values for all others. However, whenever default values are used, even internally in the software, the user should take care to understand the default values and whether they apply to the situation being analyzed.

Quality of output is another factor to consider. Reports should be easy to read and uncluttered. Titles and headings should be unambiguous. Units should be stated explicitly. The user's manual should explain the meanings of data presented. Graphic output can be very helpful. In most cases, simple summaries of overall results are the most useful, but very detailed output is needed for certain studies and also for debugging program input during the early stages of analysis.

Before a final decision is made, manuals for the most suitable programs should be obtained and reviewed, and, if possible, demonstration versions of the programs should be obtained and run, and support from the software supplier should be tested. The availability of training should be considered when choosing a more complex program.

Availability of weather data and a weather data processing subroutine or program are major features of a program. Some programs include subroutine or supplementary programs that allow the user to create a weather file for any site for which weather data are available. Programs that do not have this capability must have weather files for various sites created by the program supplier. In that case, the available weather data and the terms on which the supplier will create new weather data files must be checked. More information on weather data can be found in Chapter 14.

Auxiliary capabilities, such as economic analysis and design calculations, are a final concern in selecting a program. An economic analysis may include only the ability to calculate annual energy bills from utility rates, or it might extend to calculations or even to life-cycle cost optimization. An integrated program may save time because some input data have been entered already for other purposes.

Results of computer calculations should be accepted with caution, because software vendors do not accept responsibility for the correctness of calculation methods and have no control over program use. Manual calculation should be done to develop a good understanding of underlying physical processes and building behavior. In addition, the user should (1) review the computer program documentation to determine what calculation procedures are used, (2) compare results with manual calculations and measured data, and (3) conduct sample tests to confirm that the program delivers acceptable results.

The most accurate methods for calculating building energy consumption are the costliest because of their intense computational requirements and the expertise needed by the designer or analyst. Simulation programs that assemble component models into system models and then exercise those models with weather and occupancy data are preferred by experts for determining energy use in buildings.

Often, energy consumption at a system or whole-building level must be estimated quickly to study trends, compare systems, or study building effects such as envelope characteristics. For these purposes, simpler methods, such as degree-day and bin, may be used.

The International Building Performance Simulation Association (IBPSA-USA) maintains a website (www.buildingenergysoftwaretools.com) (IBPSA 2015) with information about hundreds of available software tools. Crawley et al. (2005) compare the capabilities of many building simulation tools.

2. DEGREE-DAY AND BIN METHODS

2.1 DEGREE-DAY METHOD

As described in Huang et al. (2001), the degree-day method was developed in the 1930s to estimate the heating energy consumption of a building. A degree-day is a measure of how often and by how many degrees the average daily temperature (the average of the daily maximum and minimum) for a location is above (for cooling) or below (for heating) a base temperature. For example, a day where the average daily temperature is 12 degrees lower than the base temperature would represent 12 degree-days; an equivalent would be 2 days, each of which was 6 degrees below the base temperature. A year's summation of the number of heating or cooling degree-days for a location is a convenient single number indicating that location's climate severity. The base temperature is that at which the building's internal heat gains counterbalance the heat losses to the outdoors, so that the building requires neither heating nor cooling. Below that "balance point" temperature, the building requires heating, whereas above that temperature the building requires cooling, in proportion to the difference from the base temperature.

Base 65°F heating degree-days and, to a lesser extent, base 65°F cooling degree-days have become widely accepted as the most convenient, simple indicators of climate severity. In the United States, heating degree-days vary from fewer than 500 in Miami, FL, 1000 to 3000 in the south, and 3000 to 7000 in the north, to extremes of more than 8000 in Bismarck, ND and 10,000 in Anchorage, AK. Correspondingly, cooling degree-days vary from 0 in Anchorage, AK, to fewer than 100 in Seattle, WA, 500 to 1200 in the north, 1200 to 3000 in the south, and more than 3000 in Phoenix, AZ and Miami, FL.

In the degree-day method, the building heat load (i.e., the amount of heating energy input or cooling energy extraction) is estimated as the number of degree-days times 24 (to convert to degree-hours), times the overall building heat loss coefficient Btu/h·°F. The overall heat loss coefficient is the sum of the U-factor × area for all external surfaces, such as walls, windows, doors, roof, and losses or gains from infiltration. The cooling load equation is similar but uses cooling degree-days instead of heating degree-days.

Example 1. Estimate the heating energy requirements for an 1800 ft^2 residence in Denver (5940 °F-days) using the degree-day method. The volume of the residence is 14,400 ft^3, the overall heat loss coefficient is 400 Btu/h·°F, 0.7 air changes per hour (ach). The residence is heated by a furnace with an AFUE of 0.78, with an average duct loss factor of 0.10.

Solution:

The heating load equation is

$$Q_h = \text{HDD}_{65}\left(24\frac{\text{h}}{\text{day}}\right) \times \left(\sum_i U_i A_i + \text{Infiltration air changes/h} \times \text{Volume} \times \text{Volumetric heat capacity for air}\right)$$

To derive the heating or cooling energy consumption, the heating or cooling loads must be divided by the efficiencies of the HVAC system.

$$Q_h = \frac{5940(24)[400 + 0.7(14{,}000)(0.018)]}{0.78 \times 0.9} = 118.1 \times 10^6 \text{ Btu}$$

The degree-day method, as demonstrated in Example 1, is limited in that it does not consider the effects of solar heat gain or building thermal mass, nor can it account for variations in infiltration rates, thermostat settings (such as night setback), or occupant actions such as window venting on cool summer nights or during the spring and fall seasons.

Efforts to improve the degree-day method, such as by using variable base temperatures, calculating degree-hours instead of days, etc., are described in the following section. The gains in accuracy from these modifications have been offset by increased difficulty in computation, nearly always requiring a computer program. Because the capability of personal computers has grown to handle programs using methods that capture the transient heat flows that dominate building thermal processes, degree-day methods have fallen increasingly out of favor, because they remain fundamentally steady-state calculations.

Even with these limitations, the degree-day method can still be of use in providing a quick answer that can be used as a starting point or check for more detailed calculations. The degree-day method may be adequate for cases in which gathering the additional data on climate and building conditions may be unwarranted or impractical, such as for estimating heating energy use in light-construction residential buildings with low solar gain in cold climates. The degree-day method can also be useful in analyzing results from more detailed, often hard-to-interpret calculations.

Variable-Base Degree-Day Method

Further described in Huang et al. (2001), the variable-base degree-day (VBDD) method accounts for balance point temperatures varying between buildings and even within a building, depending on the time of day. The 65°F base temperature is based on the assumption that heat gains from the sun and internal processes contribute on average 5°F of "free heat," allowing a set point of 70°F with heating required only when the outdoor temperature drops below 65°F. Better-insulated, more airtight buildings can have lower balance point temperatures. The average balance point temperature for modern residential buildings is now 55 to 57°F. Commercial buildings' low surface-to-volume ratios, high window-to-wall ratios, and high internal gains allow balance point temperatures of 50°F or lower.

Balance point temperatures differ markedly between daytime and nighttime hours. Figure 2 shows the variation of the balance point temperature for a typical house (Nisson and Dutt 1985). In daytime, the house receives heat gain from the sun and from occupant activity (e.g., equipment, lights). The balance point temperature may be around 15°F below the indoor temperature set point. However, at night, with no solar heat gain and reduced human activity, it may be only 3°F lower than set point. The variation can be even greater for commercial buildings because of higher internal heat gains during the day and very low heat gains at night.

The VBDD method accounts for these different building conditions by calculating (1) the balance point temperature of a building and (2) the heating and cooling degree-hours at that temperature. To divide the daytime and nighttime, degree-hours must be used instead of degree-days. Instead of using the average between the daily maximum and minimum temperatures as for degree-days, degree-hours are calculated from the temperature for each hour. The number of degree-hours divided by 24 can be slightly to significantly larger than the number of degree-days at the same base temperature. An example of why this can occur is a spring day where the average daily temperature may be below the base temperature, but several afternoon hours are above it. Such a day would have no cooling degree-days but a number of cooling degree-hours; these differences can be particularly significant for cooling. The calculations are repeated for daytime and nighttime conditions for each month of the year using degree-hour totals for each period with different base temperatures.

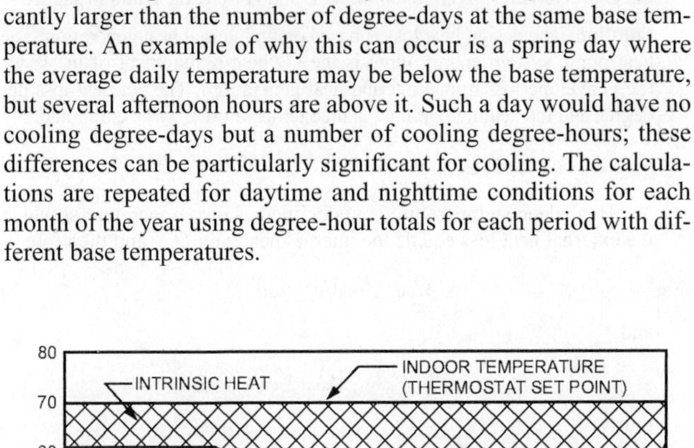

Fig. 2 Variation of Balance Point Temperature and Internal Gains for Typical House
(Nisson and Dutt 1985)

For cooling, the VBDD method can be adjusted to identify the number of cooling degree hours that are actually met by the HVAC system. The cooling balance point changes dramatically depending on whether the building is being vented. If the windows are open, heat gains are flushed from the building and do not affect its cooling load. However, if the windows are closed, solar and internal gains make the balance temperature significantly lower than the thermostat set point for cooling. The VBDD method accounts for these different conditions by calculating the cooling degree-hours using the balance temperature with the windows closed, but not counting degree-hours when the temperatures are below the thermostat set point, when the windows are assumed to be open. Figure 3 shows the one-to-one relationship between cooling degree-hours and the temperature difference between the balance point and outdoor air temperature. Those degree-hours occurring in the ventilation section when the outdoor temperatures are below the thermostat set point are not added to the running total of cooling degree-hours.

VBDD method calculations are, in most cases, too tedious for either hand calculations or implementation in a spreadsheet. In the early 1980s, several PC programs were written using the VBDD method, such as CIRA (Computerized Instrumented Residential Audit) (Sonderegger et al. 1982). Variable-base degree-day programs such as CIRA represent the apex of the VBDD method's application; however, it remains a steady-state method that does not recognize a building's thermal history.

Sources of Degree-Day Data

The most general and directly usable source for degree-day data is the ASHRAE Weather Data Viewer DVD (ASHRAE 2013). This application performs useful aggregations for more than 6000 locations. In addition to design conditions, the Weather DataViewer derives annual and monthly degree-days relative to any base temperature, and also provides bin data. Results are in spreadsheet form. Precalculated annual and monthly degree-days for several common bases are included in the climatic data that accompany Chapter 14, and additional online and printed collections of climatic data are listed in the section on Other Sources of Climatic Information in that chapter.

Annual and monthly degree-days relative to an arbitrary base can be estimated using the Weather Data Viewer or the procedures documented in the section on Estimation of Degree-Days in Chapter 14. Other degree-day estimation methods include the Erbs et al. (1983) model, which needs as input only the average $\bar{t}_o$ for each month of the year.

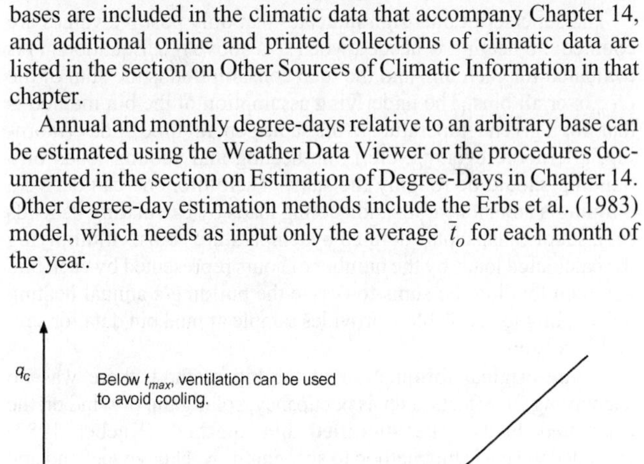

Fig. 3 Uncounted Ventilation Degree-Hours versus Counted Cooling Degree-Hours

Table 1 Sample Annual Bin Data

	Bin																					
Site	**100/ 104**	**95/ 99**	**90/ 94**	**85/ 89**	**80/ 84**	**75/ 79**	**70/ 74**	**65/ 69**	**60/ 64**	**55/ 59**	**50/ 54**	**45/ 49**	**40/ 44**	**35/ 39**	**30/ 34**	**25/ 29**	**20/ 24**	**15/ 19**	**10/ 14**	**5/ 9**	**0/ 4**	**–5/ –1**
Chicago, IL			97	222	362	512	805	667	615	622	585	577	636	720	957	511	354	243	125	66	58	6
Dallas/Ft. Worth, TX	27	210	351	527	804	1100	947	705	826	761	615	615	523	364	289	57	29					
Denver, CO		3	118	235	348	390	472	697	699	762	783	718	665	758	713	565	399	164	106	65	80	22
Los Angeles, CA	8	8	9	17	53	194	632	1583	234	2055	1181	394	74	4								
Miami, FL			45	864	1900	2561	1605	871	442	222	105	77	36	12								
Nashville, TN		7	137	407	616	756	1100	866	706	692	650	670	720	582	342	280	107	71	29			
Seattle, WA				16	62	139	256	450	769	1353	1436	1461	1413	915	358	51	43	15	1			

2.2 BIN AND MODIFIED BIN METHODS

For many applications, the degree-day or variable-base degree-day methods should not be used, because the overall building heat loss coefficient K_{tot}, the efficiency η_h of the HVAC system, or the balance point temperature t_{bal} may not be sufficiently constant. Heat pump efficiency, for example, varies strongly with outdoor temperature; efficiency of HVAC equipment may be affected indirectly by the outdoor temperature t_o when efficiency varies with load (common for boilers and chillers). Furthermore, in most commercial buildings, occupancy has a pronounced pattern that affects heat gain, indoor temperature, and ventilation rate.

In such cases, steady-state calculation can yield good results for annual energy consumption if different temperature intervals and time periods are evaluated separately. This approach is known as the **bin method**, because consumption is calculated for several values of t_o and multiplied by the number of hours N_{bin} in the temperature interval (bin) centered on that temperature:

$$Q_{bin} = N_{bin}\frac{K_{tot}}{\eta_h}[t_{bal} - t_o]^+ \qquad (1)$$

The superscript plus sign indicates that only positive values are counted; no heating is needed when t_o is above t_{bal}. Equation (1) is evaluated for each bin, and the total consumption is the sum of the Q_{bin} over all bins. The underlying assumption of the bin method is that, for a given temperature at the same general time of day (morning, afternoon, evening, etc.), the heating and cooling loads of a building should be roughly the same. Therefore, one can derive a building's annual heating and cooling loads by calculating its loads for a set of "snapshots" defined by temperature "bins," multiplying the calculated loads by the number of hours represented by each bin, and then totaling the sums to derive the building's annual heating and cooling loads. Table 1 provides sample annual bin data for several U.S. sites.

In the original formulation of the bin method, there was no accounting for effects such as occupancy, solar gain, or wind on the calculated loads. The **modified bin method** (Knebel 1983) extended the basic bin method to account for weekday/weekend and partial-day occupancy effects, to calculate net building loads (conduction, infiltration, internal loads, and solar loads) at four temperatures, rather than interpolate from design values, and to better describe secondary and primary equipment performance. Other versions of the bin method accounted for solar and wind effects by using more detailed binned data that gave the average wind speeds and solar gains by month, and the number of hours within bins disaggregated by month as well as time of day. Vadon et. al (1991) also presented an improvement for correlating the solar gains to the temperature bins.

Example 2. Estimate the energy requirements for a residence with a design heat loss Q_{des} of 40,000 Btu at 53°F design temperature difference. The indoor design temperature is 70°F. Average internal heat gains are estimated to be 4280 Btu/h. Assume a 3 ton heat pump with the characteristics given in Columns E and H of Table 2 and in Figure 4.

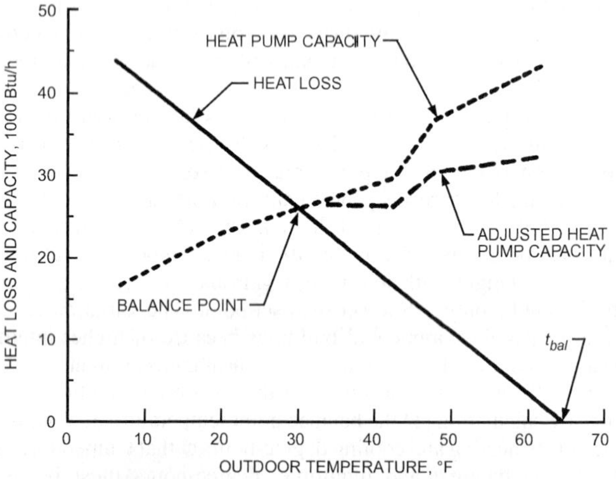

Fig. 4 Heat Pump Capacity and Building Load

Solution: The design heat loss is based on no internal heat generation. The heat pump system energy input is the net heat requirement of the space (i.e., envelope loss minus internal heat generation). The net heat loss per degree and the heating/cooling balance temperature may be computed:

$$K_{tot} = Q_{des}/\Delta t = 40{,}000/53 = 755 \text{ Btu/h·°F}$$

The balance temperature t_{bal} is defined as the temperature at which the external heat loss equals the internal heat gain Q_{int}, and therefore

$$Q_{int} = K_{tot}(t_o - t_{bal})$$

and

$$t_{bal} = t_o - (Q_{int}/K_{tot})$$

thus

$$t_{bal} = 70 - (4280/755) = 64.3°F$$

Table 2 is then computed, resulting in 9578 kWh.

3. THERMAL LOADS MODELING

3.1 SPACE SENSIBLE LOAD CALCULATION METHODS

Calculating instantaneous space sensible load is a key step in any building energy simulation. The **heat balance, comprehensive room transfer function (CRTF)**, and **weighting-factor methods** are used for these calculations. A fourth method, the **thermal-network method**, is similar in rigor to the heat balance and CRTF methods but not as widely used.

Table 2 Calculation of Annual Heating Energy Consumption for Example 2

Climate			House	Heat Pump							Supplemental		
A	B	C	D	E	F	G	H	I	J	K	L	M	N
Temp. Bin, °F	Temp. Diff., $t_{bal} - t_{bin}$	Weather Data Bin, h	Heat Loss Rate, 1000 Btu/h	Heat Pump Integrated Heating Capacity, 1000 Btu/h	Cycling Capacity Adjustment Factor[a]	Adjusted Heat Pump Capacity, 1000 Btu/h[b]	Rated Electric Input, kW	Operating Time Fraction[c]	Heat Pump Supplied Heating, 10^6 Btu[d]	Seasonal Heat Pump Electric Consumption, kWh[e]	Space Load, 10^6 Btu[f]	Supple-mental Heating Required, kWh[g]	Total Electric Energy Consump-tion[h]
62	2.3	740	1.8	44.3	0.760	33.7	3.77	0.05	1.30	146	1.30	—	146
57	7.3	673	5.5	41.8	0.783	32.7	3.67	0.17	3.72	417	3.72	—	417
52	12.3	690	9.3	39.3	0.809	31.8	3.56	0.29	6.42	719	6.42	—	719
47	17.3	684	13.1	36.8	0.839	30.9	3.46	0.42	8.95	1002	8.95	—	1002
42	22.3	790	16.9	29.9	0.891	26.6	3.23	0.63	13.31	1614	13.31	—	1614
37	27.3	744	20.6	28.3	0.932	26.4	3.15	0.78	15.35	1833	15.35	—	1833
32	32.3	542	24.4	26.6	0.979	26.0	3.07	0.94	13.22	1559	13.22	—	1559
27	37.3	254	28.2	25.0	1.000	25.0	3.00	1.00	6.35	762	7.16	236	998
22	42.3	138	31.9	23.4	1.000	23.4	2.92	1.00	3.23	403	4.41	345	748
17	47.3	54	35.7	21.8	1.000	21.8	2.84	1.00	1.18	153	1.93	220	373
12	52.3	17	39.5	19.3	1.000	19.3	2.74	1.00	0.33	47	0.67	101	147
7	57.3	2	43.3	16.8	1.000	16.8	2.63	1.00	0.03	5	0.09	16	21
2	62.3	0	47.0	14.3	1.000	—	—	—	—	—	—	—	—
								Totals:	73.39	8660	76.52	917	9578

[a]Cycling Capacity Adjustment Factor = $1 - C_d(1 - x)$, where C_d = degradation coefficient (default = 0.25 unless part-load factor is known) and x = building heat loss per unit capacity at temperature bin. Cycling capacity = 1 at balance point and below. Cycling capacity adjustment factor should be 1.0 at all temperature bins if manufacturer includes cycling effects in heat pump capacity (Column E) and associated electrical input (Column H).

[b]Column G = Column E × Column F

[c]Operating time fraction equals smaller of 1 or Column D/Column G

[d]Column J = (Column I × Column G × Column C)/1000

[e]Column K = Column I × Column H × Column C

[f]Column L = Column C × Column D/1000

[g]Column M = (Column L – Column J) × 10^6/3413

[h]Column N = Column K + Column M

The **instantaneous space sensible load** is the rate of heat flow into the space air mass. This quantity, sometimes called the *cooling load*, differs from heat gain, which usually contains a radiative component that passes through the air and is absorbed by other bounding surfaces. Instantaneous space sensible load is entirely convective; even loads from internal equipment, lights, and occupants enter the air by convection from the surface of such objects or by convection from room surfaces that have absorbed the radiant component of energy emitted from these sources. However, some adjustment must be made when radiant cooling and heating systems are evaluated because some of the space load is offset directly by radiant transfer without convective transfer to the air mass.

For equilibrium, the instantaneous space sensible load must match the heat removal rate of the conditioning equipment. Any imbalance in these rates changes the energy stored in the air mass. Customarily, however, the thermal mass (heat capacity) of the air itself is ignored in analysis, so the air is always assumed to be in thermal equilibrium. Under these assumptions, the instantaneous space sensible load and rate of heat removal are equal in magnitude and opposite in sign.

The weighting-factor, CRTF, and heat balance methods use conduction transfer functions (or their equivalents) to calculate transmission heat gain or loss. The main difference is in the methods used to calculate the subsequent internal heat transfers to the room. Experience has shown that all the methods produce similar results, provided model coefficients are determined for the specific building under analysis and room temperature variations are moderate.

Heat Balance Method

The heat balance method for calculating net space sensible loads is described in Chapter 18 and in the *ASHRAE Toolkit for Building Load Calculations* (Barnaby et al. 2005, 2009; Iu and Fisher 2004; Pedersen et al. 2001, 2003). Its development relies on the first law of thermodynamics (conservation of energy) at each surface. Because the heat balance method involves fewer assumptions than the weighting-factor method, it is more flexible and physically rigorous. However, the heat balance method requires more calculations at each point in the simulation process, using more computer time. This method has been validated in several studies (Chantrasrisalai et al. 2003a, 2003b; Eldridge et al. 2003; Iu et al. 2003).

The heat balance method allows the net instantaneous sensible heating and/or cooling load to be calculated on the space air mass. Generally, a heat balance equation is written for each enclosing surface, plus one equation for room air. Although not necessary, linearization is commonly used to simplify the radiative transfer formulation. This set of equations can then be solved for the unknown surface and air temperatures. Once these temperatures are known, they can be used to calculate the convective heat flow to or from the space air mass. The heat balance method is developed in Chapter 18 for use in design cooling load calculations.

The procedure described in Chapter 18 is aimed at obtaining the design cooling load for a ***fixed*** zone air temperature. For building energy analysis purposes, it is preferable to know the actual heat extraction rate. This may be determined by recasting Equation (27) of Chapter 18 so that the system heat transfer is determined simultaneously with the zone air temperature. The system heat transfer is the rate at which heat is transferred to the space by the system. Although this can be done by simultaneously modeling the zone and the system (Taylor et al. 1990, 1991), it is often convenient to make a simple, linearized representation of the system known as a *control profile*. This usually takes the form

$$q_{sys_j} = a + bt_{a_j} \tag{2}$$

where

q_{sys_j} = system heat transfer at time step j, Btu/h

a, b = coefficients that apply over a certain range of zone air temperatures

t_{a_j} = zone air temperature at time step j, °F

System heat transfer q_{sys_j} may be considered positive when heating is provided to the space and negative when cooling is provided.

It is equal in magnitude but opposite in sign to the zone cooling load, as defined in Chapter 18, when zone air temperature is fixed.

Substituting Equation (2) into Equation (27) of Chapter 18 and solving for zone air temperature,

$$t_{a_j} = \frac{a + \sum_{i=1}^{N} A_i h_{ci} t_{si_{i,j}} + \rho c V_{infil_j} t_{o_j} + \rho c V_{vent_j} t_{v_j} + q_{c,int_j}}{-b + \sum_{i=1}^{N} A_i h_{ci} + \rho c V_{infil_j} + \rho c V_{vent_j}} \quad (3)$$

where

N = number of zone surfaces
A_i = area of ith surface, ft²
h_{ci} = convection coefficient for ith surface, Btu/h·ft²·°F
$t_{si_{i,j}}$ = surface temperature for ith surface at time step j, °F
ρ = density, lb_m/ft^3
c = specific heat of air, $Btu/lb_m \cdot °F$
V = volumetric flow rate of air, ft³/h
t_{o_j} = outdoor air temperature at time step j, °F
t_{v_j} = ventilation air temperature at time step j, °F
q_{c,int_j} = sum of convective portions of all internal heat gains at time step j, Btu/h

The zone air heat balance equation [Equation (3)] must be solved simultaneously with the interior and exterior surface heat balance equations [Equations (26) and (25) in Chapter 18]. Also, the correct temperature range must be found to use the proper set of a and b coefficients; this may be done iteratively. Once the zone air temperature is found, the actual system heat transfer rate may be found directly from Equation (2).

Beyond treatment of system heat transfer, other considerations that may be important in building energy analysis programs include treatment of radiant cooling and heating systems, treatment of interzone heat transfer, modeling convection heat transfer, and modeling radiation heat transfer.

The heat balance method in Chapter 18 assumes the use of a single design day. In a building energy analysis program, it is most commonly used with a year's worth of design weather data. In this case, the first day of the year is usually simulated repeatedly until a steady-periodic response is obtained. Then, each day is simulated sequentially, and, where needed, historical data for surface temperatures and heat fluxes from the previous day are used.

When radiant cooling and heating systems are evaluated, the radiant source should be identified as a room surface. The calculation procedure considers the radiant source in the heat balance analysis. Therefore, the heat balance method is preferred over the weighting-factor method for evaluating radiant systems. Strand and Pedersen (1997) describe implementation of heat source conduction transfer functions that may be used for modeling radiant panels within a heat balance-based building simulation program.

In principle, this method extends directly to multiple spaces, with heat transfer between zones. In this case, some surface temperatures appear in the surface heat balance equations for two different zones. In practice, however, the size of the coefficient array required for solving the simultaneous equations becomes prohibitively large, and the solution time excessive. For this reason, some programs solve only one space at a time and assume that adjacent space temperatures are the same as the prior time step, or use iterative schemes to achieve a simultaneous solution. Other approaches may remove this limitation (Walton 1980).

Relatively simple exterior and interior convection models may be used for design cooling load calculation procedures. However, more sophisticated exterior convection models (Cooper and Tree 1973; Fracastoro et al. 1982; Melo and Hammond 1991; U.S. Department of Energy 1996-2016; Walton 1983; Yazdanian and Klems 1994) that incorporate the effects of wind speed, wind direction, surface orientation, etc., may be preferable. More detailed interior convection correlations for use in buildings are also available (Alamdari and Hammond 1982, 1983; Altmayer et al. 1983; Bauman et al. 1983; Bohn et al. 1984; Chandra and Kerestecioglu 1984; U.S. Department of Energy 1996-2016; Goldstein and Novoselac 2010; Khalifa and Marshall 1990; Peeters et al. 2011; Spitler et al. 1991; Walton 1983).

Also, more detailed models of exterior [e.g., Cole (1976); Walton (1983)] and interior [e.g., Carroll (1980); Davies (1988); Kamal and Novak (1991); Steinman et al. (1989); Walton (1980)] long-wave radiation transfer have been implemented in detailed building simulation programs.

Weighting-Factor Method

The weighting-factor method of calculating instantaneous space sensible load is a compromise between simpler methods (e.g., steady-state calculation) that ignore the ability of building mass to store energy, and more complex methods (e.g., complete energy balance calculations). With this method, space heat gains at constant space temperature are determined from a physical description of the building, ambient weather conditions, and internal load profiles. Along with the characteristics and availability of heating and cooling systems for the building, space heat gains are used to calculate air temperatures and heat extraction rates. This discussion is in terms of heat gains, cooling loads, and heat extraction rates. Heat losses, heating loads, and heat addition rates are merely different terms for the same quantities, depending on the direction of the heat flow.

The weighting factors represent Z-transfer functions (Kerrisk et al. 1981; York and Cappiello 1982). The Z-transform is a method for solving differential equations with discrete data. Two groups of weighting factors are used: heat gain and air temperature.

Heat gain weighting factors represent transfer functions that relate space cooling load to instantaneous heat gains. A set of weighting factors is calculated for each group of heat sources that differ significantly in the (1) relative amounts of energy appearing as convection to the air versus radiation, and (2) distribution of radiant energy intensities on different surfaces.

Air temperature weighting factors represent a transfer function that relates room air temperature to the net energy load of the room. Weighting factors for a particular heat source are determined by introducing a unit pulse of energy from that source into the room's network. The network is a set of equations that represents a heat balance for the room. At each time step, including the initial introduction, the energy flow to the room air represents the amount of the pulse that becomes a cooling load. Thus, a long sequence of cooling loads can be generated, from which weighting factors are calculated. Similarly, a unit pulse change in room air temperature can be used to produce a sequence of cooling loads.

A two-step process is used to determine the air temperature and heat extraction rate of a room or building zone for a given set of conditions. First, the room air temperature is assumed to be fixed at some reference value, usually the average air temperature expected for the room over the simulation period. Instantaneous heat gains are calculated based on this constant air temperature. Various types of heat gains are considered. Some, such as solar energy entering through windows or energy from lighting, people, or equipment, are independent of the reference temperature. Others, such as conduction through walls, depend directly on the reference temperature.

A space sensible cooling load for the room, defined as the rate at which energy must be removed from the room to maintain the reference value of the air temperature, is calculated for each type of instantaneous heat gain. The cooling load generally differs from the instantaneous heat gain because some energy from heat gain is absorbed by walls or furniture and stored for later release to the air. At time θ, the calculation uses present and past values of the instantaneous heat gain (q_θ, $q_{\theta-1}$), past values of the cooling load ($Q_{\theta-1}$, $Q_{\theta-2}$, ...), and the **heat gain weighting factors** (v_0, v_1, v_2, ..., w_1, w_2, ...) for the type of heat gain under consideration. Thus, for each type of heat gain q_θ, cooling load Q_θ is calculated as

$$Q_\theta = v_0 q_\theta + v_1 q_{\theta-1} + \cdots - w_1 Q_{\theta-1} - w_2 Q_{\theta-2} - \cdots \quad (4)$$

The heat gain weighting factors are a set of parameters that determine how much of the energy entering a room is stored and how rapidly stored energy is released later. Mathematically, the weighting factors are coefficients in a *Z*-transfer function relating the heat gain to the cooling load.

These weighting factors differ for different heat gain sources because the relative amounts of convective and radiative energy leaving various sources differ and because the distribution of radiative energy can differ. Heat gain weighting factors also differ for different rooms because room construction affects the amount of incoming energy stored by walls or furniture and the rate at which it is released. Sowell (1988) showed the effects of 14 zone design parameters on zone dynamic response. After the first step, cooling loads from various heat gains are added to give a total cooling load for the room.

In the second step, the total cooling load is used (with information on the room's HVAC system and a set of **air temperature weighting factors**) to calculate the actual heat extraction rate and air temperature. The actual heat extraction rate differs from the cooling load (1) because, in practice, air temperature can vary from the reference value used to calculate the cooling load, or (2) because of HVAC system characteristics. Deviation of air temperature t_θ from the reference value at hour θ is calculated as

$$t_\theta = 1/g_0 + [(Q_\theta - ER_\theta) + P_1(Q_{\theta-1} - ER_{\theta-1}) + P_2(Q_{\theta-2} - ER_{\theta-2}) + \cdots - g_1 t_{\theta-1} - g_2 t_{\theta-2} - \cdots] \quad (5)$$

where ER_θ is the energy removal rate of the HVAC system at hour θ, and g_0, g_1, g_2, ..., P_1, P_2, ... are air temperature weighting factors, which incorporate information about the room, particularly thermal coupling between the air and the storage capacity of the building mass.

Example values of weighting factors for typical building rooms are presented in the following table. One of the three groups of weighting factors, for light, medium, and heavy construction rooms, can be used to approximate the behavior of any room. Some automated simulation techniques allow weighting factors to be calculated specifically for the building under consideration. This option improves the accuracy of the calculated results, particularly for a building with an unconventional design. McQuiston and Spitler (1992) provided electronic tables of weighting factors for a large number of parametrically defined zones.

Normalized Coefficients of Space Air Transfer Functions

Room Envelope Construction	g_0^*	g_1^*	g_2^*	P_0	P_1
	Btu/h·ft·°F			Dimensionless	
Light	1.68	−1.73	0.05	1.0	−0.82
Medium	1.81	−1.89	0.08	1.0	−0.87
Heavy	1.85	−1.95	0.10	1.0	−0.93

Two assumptions are made in the weighting-factor method. First, the processes modeled are linear. This assumption is necessary because heat gains from various sources are calculated independently and summed to obtain the overall result (i.e., the superposition principle is used). Therefore, nonlinear processes such as radiation or natural convection must be approximated linearly. This assumption is not a significant limitation because these processes can be linearly approximated with sufficient accuracy for most calculations. The second assumption is that system properties influencing the weighting factors are constant (i.e., they are not functions of time). Often, a single set of weighting factors is used during the entire simulation period; however, multiple sets of weighting factors can be used to represent daily or seasonal variations. This assumption can limit the use of weighting factors in situations where important room properties vary more frequently during the calculation (e.g., the distribution of solar radiation incident on the interior walls of a room, which can vary over the day, and indoor surface heat transfer coefficients).

When the weighting-factor method is used, a combined radiative/ convective heat transfer coefficient is used as the indoor surface heat transfer coefficient. This value is assumed constant even though, in a real room, (1) radiant heat transferred from a surface depends on the temperature of other room surfaces (not on room air temperature) and (2) the combined heat transfer coefficient is not constant. Under these circumstances, an average value of the property must be used to determine the weighting factors. Cumali et al. (1979) investigated extensions to the weighting-factor method to eliminate this limitation.

Weighting factors are derived by introducing a unit pulse in a heat balance analysis. These analyses are performed relatively quickly as a preprocess step. Once the weighting factors are established, the simulation time can be significantly reduced, compared with performing a heat balance at every time step. There is an implicit trade-off between the limitations of the weighting-factor method and its improved computation speed compared with that of the heat balance method.

Comprehensive Room Transfer Function

The comprehensive room transfer function method (CRTF) is important as a reasonably accurate (comparable to weighting factor) model that is fast enough to be embedded in optimizations. One important application is model-predictive control. CRTF parameters may be estimated using forward (Seem et al. 1989) or inverse (Armstrong et al. 2006b; Gayeski et al. 2012) modeling. The interior terminating point of each wall is a common star node. Instead of separate surface flux and temperature for each wall, only the net star-node flux and temperature are evaluated. Exogenous radiant fluxes (solar and radiant shares of internal gains) are imposed on the star node as well. Radiant and convective exchange between walls also occurs through the star node. Convective heating and cooling by the system, on the other hand, as well as infiltration, ventilation, and the convective share of internal gains, enter the room model through its air node, which is coupled to the star node by a single, relatively small resistance. The resulting model has the topology of *n* conduction transfer functions terminating on a massless star node that is connected by a single resistance to an air capacitance node. However the *c* and *d* coefficients of all walls are combined, thus reducing the computational effort at each simulation time step. The CRTF thus has (up to the star node) the mathematical form of a multivariate autoregressive-moving-average with exogenous inputs (ARMAX) model. Methods of evaluating the common *c* and *d* coefficients and the star and air node resistances are described by Armstrong et al. (1992) and Seem et al. (1989).

Thermal-Network Methods

Although implementations of the thermal-network method vary, they all have in common the discretization of the building into a network of nodes connected by heat transfer paths. In many respects, thermal-network models may be considered a variant of the heat balance method. Thermal-network models can include an arbitrary number of nodes as required for the problem under consideration. For example, heat balance models generally use simple methods for distributing radiation from lights; thermal-network models may model the lamp, ballast, and luminaire housing separately.

Thermal-network models depend on a heat balance at each node to determine node temperature and energy flow between all connected nodes. Energy flows may include conduction, convection, and short- or long-wave radiation. Methods have been developed that reduce the number of node interconnections (e.g., by replacing the general delta radiant exchange network with a star network) (Carroll 1980, 1981).

For any mode of energy flow, a range of finite-difference or finite-volume techniques may be used to model the energy flow between nodes. Taking transient conduction heat transfer as an example, the simplest thermal-network model would be a one- or two-capacitor resistance/capacitance network (Hammarsten 1987; Sonderegger 1977; Sowell 1990). Others have used more refined network discretization (Clarke 2001; Lewis and Alexander 1990; Walton 1993).

Advanced thermal-network models generally use a set of algebraic and differential equations. In most implementations, the solution procedure is separated from the models so that, in theory, different solvers might be used to perform the simulation. In contrast, in most heat balance and weighting factor programs the solution technique takes advantage of a constrained model structure. Various solution techniques have been used in conjunction with thermal-network models. Examples include graph theory combined with Newton-Raphson and predictor/corrector ordinary differential equation integration (Buhl et al. 1990) and the use of Euler explicit integration combined with sparse matrix techniques (Walton 1993).

Of the four sensible-load zone models discussed, thermal-network models are the most flexible and have the greatest potential for high accuracy. However, they also require the most computation time, and, in current implementations, require more user effort to take advantage of the flexibility.

3.2 ENVELOPE COMPONENT MODELING

Above-Grade Opaque Surfaces

Heat transfer through above-grade, opaque envelope components (e.g., walls, roofs, ceilings) is often approximated using transient one-dimensional (1D) calculations. This approximation is common to most building energy simulation tools. Two- and three-dimensional effects, such as thermal bridging, are often accounted for by adjusting the properties of the materials in a 1D construction. Chapter 25 discusses the calculation of heat transfer through opaque building surfaces, including the overall effective thermal transmittance (or U-factor) of a flat building assembly.

Thermal properties of building materials and other solids can be found in Chapter 26 (Table 1) and Chapter 33 (Table 3), respectively.

Transient 1D heat transfer is calculated for multilayered constructions using one of three methods:

- **Response factors** (Kusuda 1969). These factors relate the heat flux through the surface to temperature changes. The response factors are generated by calculating the response to a simple transient event (e.g., a step change) and observing the resulting changes in heat flux over time. Once obtained, response factors can be reused throughout a simulation to estimate the heat flux response to other transient temperature changes.
- **Conduction transfer functions (CTFs).** Similar to response factors, CTFs relate the current heat flux through a surface to the heat fluxes of previous time steps. CTFs are also generated by imposing a simple transient event and observing the resulting heat flux over time.
- **Direct numerical methods** (e.g., finite difference, finite element). These methods are required for nonlinear analysis such as for phase change materials and variable thermal properties.

Iu and Fisher (2004) provide an overview and comparison of response factors and CTFs.

Below-Grade Opaque Surfaces

Thermal modeling of building foundations (Claridge et al. 1993), including guidelines for placement of insulation, is described in Chapter 27 of this volume and Chapter 44 of the 2015 *ASHRAE Handbook—HVAC Applications*. Chapter 18 of this volume provides information for calculating transmission heat losses through slab foundations and through basement walls and floors. These calculations are appropriate for design loads but are not intended for estimating annual energy usage. This section provides information about calculation methods suitable for energy estimates over time periods of arbitrary length.

The magnitude of foundation heat transfer relative to other loads in the building depends on several factors, including the insulation design of the foundation and the shape and size of the foundation relative to the overall size of the building. Foundation heat losses (or gains) are more significant in buildings with lower foundation area-to-perimeter ratios (Bahnfleth and Pedersen 1990; Kruis 2015). Low area-to-perimeter ratios often coincide with small buildings (e.g., detached residential construction) and building footprints with narrow cross sections. Where higher ground-coupled floor area-to-perimeter ratios may occur (e.g., in warehouses, shopping malls, other low-rise commercial buildings), thermal mass effects related to the core-area (nonperimeter) portion of the ground-coupled floor may also be important.

Ground-coupled foundation heat transfer involves three-dimensional (3D) thermal conduction, moisture transport, and the long-time-constant heat storage properties of the ground. During the early 1990s, only simplified models could be routinely used for calculating ground heat transfer. These models were based on 1D steady-state conduction or 1D dynamic thermal diffusion modeling. Because of continuing increases in computing power, the state of the art in ground heat transfer modeling has improved. Several calculation methods have been developed and applied to building energy simulation software (Bahnfleth and Pedersen 1990; Beausoleil-Morrison 1996; Beausoleil-Morrison and Mitalas 1997; Clements 2004; ISO 1998). These methods are further described and compared to more detailed 3D numerical methods (Ben-Nakhi 2007; Crowley 2007; Deru 2003; Thornton 2007) as part of the IEA BESTEST ground-coupled heat transfer modeling test cases (Neymark et al. 2008).

Other examples of ground heat transfer modeling techniques applied to floors and basements are described in Andolsun et al. (2010), Krarti (1994a, 1994b), and Krarti and Chuangchid (1999), and a simplification of that method in Chapter 19 of the 2009 *ASHRAE Handbook—Fundamentals*, and in Krarti et al. (1988a, 1988b) and Winkelmann (2002).

Methods of estimating foundation heat transfer can be highly constrained simplifications to ease calculation requirements, or very detailed and computationally intensive. Although the state of the art in ground heat transfer modeling is improving, many whole-building simulation tools still rely on a loosely defined set of ground temperatures that are applied as an exterior boundary condition for a simplified 1D approximation. These temperatures are often based on lagged, monthly average outdoor dry-bulb temperatures. In reality, the temperature in the ground varies both spatially and temporally, and is heavily influenced by the presence of a conditioned building. Finding a balance between computation speed and numerical accuracy is the focus of the dissertation work performed by Kruis (2015). Kruis found that two-dimensional (2D) calculations capture much of the accuracy of the more detailed 3D methods with computation times reasonable for whole-building energy simulation tools.

Fenestration

Fenestration systems (windows, skylights, and doors) affect building energy use through four basic mechanisms: (1) thermal heat transfer, (2) solar heat gain, (3) air leakage, and (4) daylighting. Details of each of these effects are covered in Chapter 15. Fenestration performance is characterized primarily by its overall coefficient of heat transfer (U-factor), solar heat gain coefficient (SHGC), and visible transmittance (VT). These metrics are typically used to rate fenestration products for a specific set of conditions that are not necessarily representative of the range of conditions encountered in a typical whole-building energy simulation.

The energy impact of fenestration systems depends on the thermal and spectral properties of each component, including

- Glazing substrates (panes)
- Glazing coatings
- Fill gas
- Opaque frame and divider
- Spacers between panes

Fenestration system models span a wide range of complexity and input requirements. Some of the simpler models apply a constant U-factor and SHGC to the system, whereas more advanced models may require finer details of the fenestration system that are not often available to energy modelers, such as

- Glazing reflectance (front and back) and transmittance at wavelengths spanning the solar, visible, and infrared spectrums, as well as at different angles of solar incidence
- Temperature-dependent thermal properties of fill gases
- Two-dimensional heat transfer through frames, dividers, and spacers

Many of these inputs can be found or generated in the suite of fenestration-related software tools developed by Lawrence Berkeley National Lab (LBNL 2016):

- WINDOW (for analyzing composite fenestration system thermal and optical properties)
- THERM (for analyzing two-dimensional heat transfer through building products)
- Optics (for analyzing optical properties of glazing systems)
- International Glazing Database (IGDB) (optical data for glazing products)

In most energy modeling applications, the level of detail required to compose a fenestration system using these software tools is not readily available. Instead, energy modelers are at most provided with the product's rated U-factor, SHGC, and VT, or specific values defined by compliance rules and incentive programs (e.g., ASHRAE *Standard* 90.1, ENERGY STAR®). With this use case in mind, Arasteh et al. (2009) developed an approach in EnergyPlus to represent fenestration systems with angle-dependent optical properties using only the rated U-factor, SHGC, and VT. This approach offers a higher level of accuracy than the assumption of constant values, but does not explicitly simulate the opaque frame and dividers components or the fill gas in the fenestration system.

Infiltration

Infiltration is defined as the flow of outdoor air via (1) leakage through unintentional openings (e.g., cracks, porosities) in the building envelope and (2) natural ventilation through exterior windows, doors, vents, etc. It is typically treated as an additional load for the purposes of whole-building energy modeling. The flow is driven by pressure differences and buoyancy forces, and may be counteracted by pressurizing the building or by sealing openings with air barriers, weatherstripping, and similar measures. Outdoor air that has entered a conditioned space will at some point need to be heated or cooled to maintain the space at the desired temperature. There are a number of procedures available for calculating infiltration and associated loads. Empirical models, based on the results of blower door tests, are most readily available for residential buildings because of more readily available measured data, such as effective leakage area and flow exponent. Models that treat the building as a single zone are most directly applicable to smaller buildings (e.g., houses). Models that treat buildings as a set of zones (not necessarily corresponding to thermal zones) are also available, but these models require parameters that may be difficult to determine without building-specific data. More information on these models and on the general issue can be found in Chapter 16. Discussion of natural ventilation modeling is included in this chapter's section on Low-Energy System Modeling. In the absence of the information necessary to use a more detailed approach, infiltration rates from appropriate standards or guideline documents (e.g., ASHRAE *Standard* 90.1; Gowri et al. 2009) can be used to determine the inputs for an energy model. For commercial buildings, which are typically designed to be pressurized, this approach may be more successful than for residential buildings, which may not be pressurized.

3.3 INPUTS TO THERMAL LOADS MODELS

Choosing Climate Data

Environmental data provide boundary conditions for many energy estimating and modeling methods. Many energy estimating and modeling methods require climate data from specific sources or in specific formats. The most common application is full-year hourly simulation using a typical meteorological year (TMY) to represent typical building operation. Other applications may require historical climate data (for model calibration), real-time climate data (for model predictive controls), or projected climate data (for predicting the impact of climate change on building energy consumption). Climate data are available from a growing number of sources. Chapter 14 discusses the use of climatic design information in greater detail and includes data for more than 8000 locations worldwide. Hensen and Lamberts (2011) list several other sources of climate data and discuss the requirements of climate data for various simulation applications.

Internal Heat Gains

Accurate representation of internal heat gains in building simulation is important for several reasons. These heat gains often compose a significant portion of HVAC system loads. In addition, heat sources such as lighting and office equipment may be significant direct contributors to building energy consumption.

Typical sources of internal heat gain represented in a simulation include occupants, lighting, and plug loads. Some buildings also include significant heat from cooking, refrigeration, laboratory, or manufacturing equipment.

The following simulation inputs are generally necessary to characterize a source of internal heat gain:

- **Peak heat rate.** For example, installed lighting power. Note that the actual peak heat rate for sources such as office equipment is often lower than the equipment's nameplate rating.
- **Time variation of heat rate.** The heat gain from most sources varies by hour and may vary by day of the week and by season.
- **Latent heat fraction.** Many sources of internal heat gain, such as lighting and most office equipment, produce only sensible heat. However, other sources, such as occupants and some cooking equipment, produce both sensible and latent heat. For those cases, the portion of the total heat gain entering the space as latent heat must be identified.
- **Radiant/convective split.** Sensible heat gain has two components: radiant and convective. The relative proportion between the

two pathways affects the time delay between instantaneous heat gain and space load. Simulation programs often include default fractions for the split. Attention to these values is especially important when evaluating spaces with significant thermal mass.

- **Fraction of heat gain to space.** Not all of the heat produced by some sources of internal heat gain ends up directly in the space. In those cases, it may be necessary to specify the portion that goes to the space and the portion that goes elsewhere. One example is recessed lighting in a suspended ceiling: some of the energy consumed by the lights enters the space and the rest goes to the space above the ceiling. Another example is cooking equipment under a range hood: a portion of the heat enters the kitchen, primarily via radiation, and the rest of the heat goes to the exhaust air. The same concept applies to laboratory equipment in a fume hood or to industrial equipment where a portion of the heat output is captured by an exhaust system. Another example is a space using a displacement ventilation air delivery strategy: a portion of the heat gain from occupants and equipment in the occupied zone rises into the stratified zone or return air and does not end up as a load in the occupied zone.

Appropriate values for internal heat gain inputs may be different between energy calculations and HVAC system peak-load calculations. Although the basic form of input may be identical (e.g., both may require specifying office equipment power density), the objectives of the analyses are different. The typical objective of energy estimation is to determine likely energy consumption rather than worst-case energy consumption. Therefore, the appropriate values for internal heat gain inputs will typically be lower for energy estimation than for load calculations. ASHRAE research project RP-1093 developed different sets of diversity factors appropriate for energy calculations and for load calculations (Abushakra et al. 2000).

In many cases, information about actual internal heat gains is not available to the energy modeler, either because it is a new construction project and detailed equipment specifications are not available, or the project is an existing building and a detailed survey of heat sources is not practical. Therefore, it may be necessary to make assumptions. Chapter 18 provides valuable data on peak heat rates, radiant/convective splits, and fraction of heat to space for a range of equipment types. Other sources of internal gain assumptions include COMNET (2016), Building America simulation protocols (Wilson et al. 2014), and DOE reference buildings (Deru et al. 2011).

Occupant Behavior

Technologies alone do not necessarily guarantee low energy use in buildings. Occupant behavior has a significant effect on building performance. Occupants' expectations of satisfaction with their indoor environment drive various actions, such as adjusting thermostat settings, opening windows, turning on lights, closing window blinds, consuming domestic hot water, and moving around, to satisfy their physical and nonphysical needs. These actions affect the built environment and energy use. Clearly understanding and accurately modeling occupant behavior in buildings is crucial to reducing the gap between design and actual building energy performance (Gunay et al. 2013; Hoes et al. 2009; Turner and Frankel 2008; Yan et al. 2015), especially for low-energy buildings relying more on passive design features, occupancy-controlled technologies, and occupant engagement.

Occupant behavior is represented in predefined deterministic schedules or fixed settings to describe occupant movement and activities, the use of lighting, plug loads, and HVAC system operation. Assumptions of occupant input can be found in ASHRAE publications (e.g., Handbook, standards, guidelines), DOE reference buildings, simulation guides (COMNET 2016), building design documents, or measured data from existing buildings. Abushakra and Claridge (2008) developed a method for modeling occupancy in commercial buildings based on monitored lighting and receptacles energy use. The method provides typical occupancy load shapes that can be used in both forward building energy simulations and data-driven models. When these static schedules and settings are entered into building energy modeling (BEM) programs, the results are deterministic and homogeneous, ignoring the stochastic nature, dynamics, and diversity of occupant behavior. For example, occupants can open windows for various reasons: (1) feeling hot (thermal comfort driven), (2) feeling stuffy (indoor air quality driven), (3) arriving in a space (event driven), and (4) personal habit.

Alternative approaches used to integrate occupant behavior into models include embedded behavior modules adopted by BEM programs or agent-based modeling approaches that specify how agents (in this case, occupants) interact with one another and with their environment. Integration of occupant behavior with BEM programs ranges from built-in user functions to more flexible cosimulation. The user functions approach allows users, to a certain degree of flexibility, to write custom code to implement new or overwrite existing default building operation and supervisory controls. The cosimulation approach allows separate behavior tools to run simultaneously and exchange occupant information in a collaborative manner with BEM programs (Hong et al. 2016a; Wetter et al. 2011). Agent-based modeling specifies occupant attributes, behavioral rules, memory, resources, decision-making sophistication, and procedures for modifying current behavioral rules. Andrews et al. (2011), Langevin (2014), and Robinson (2011) developed agent-based modeling tools for cosimulation.

Despite advancements, there are significant and fundamental scientific problems remaining to be addressed in modeling occupant behavior, including (1) choosing the best modeling approach based on available data and for a particular application, (2) standardizing the representation of occupant behavior for interoperability (Hong et al. 2015), (3) selecting methods to evaluate occupant behavior models, (4) interpreting the simulation results from the use of stochastic models, and (5) considering social and behavioral influencing factors. IEA EBC (2013-2017) Annex 66 addresses some of these problems and provides a literature database on occupant behavior research.

Thermal Zoning Strategies

Configuration of thermal zones for building energy simulation commonly follows the core and perimeter zone method (Hirsch 2003; LBNL 1984.). The core and perimeter approach divides a building into an approximate perimeter of thermal zones within 15 to 20 ft from the exterior walls and then further divides the building into separate perimeter zones for each orientation.

A commonly used thermal zoning guideline is provided in ASHRAE *Standard* 90.1, Appendix G, which describes the standard's performance rating method. The standard allows combining two or more actual thermal zones into a single zone if they have the same space usage, their exterior glazed surfaces have the same orientation (within 45°), and they are served by the same type of HVAC system.

In certain cases, spaces that have similar thermal conditions may be aggregated into fewer zones within a simulation model with only a minor difference in simulation outcome, as stated in Lokmanhekim (1971), who proposed a method to define thermal zones by grouping spaces based on comparison of load profile plots.

Several recent studies have considered different approaches for thermal zoning:

- Raftery (2011) developed a method that defines the various type of thermal zones in a simulation based on four major criteria: (1) function of the space, (2) position of the zone relative to the exterior, (3) available measured data, and (4) method used to condition the zone. Raftery's method yields a more detailed thermal zoning plan than the traditional core and perimeter zoning method. However, the method is not automated, relying instead on a user's subjective inputs to a simulation program.

- Georgescu et al. (2012) developed a method that analyzes a detailed building energy model using an optimization method to develop zoning approximations based on observations of zone temperature. However, in this method, a detailed model of all zones must first be created to establish a baseline simulation for comparison; this can take a significant amount of time and can introduce uncertainty as the number of parameters in the model increases. Like Raftery (2011), the Georgescu et al. (2015) method also lacks an automated procedure.
- Yi (2015) developed a user interface that suggests optimized thermal-zone layouts based on space arrangement. However, Yi's method is based only on the spatial functions and does not consider varying internal load, space use, or system type. This method relies on the user's judgment to perform the final selection of zones.
- Dogan et al. (2015) present an algorithm to automatically convert arbitrary building massing models into multiple-zone building energy models. The applications include model generation during schematic design and generation of models for urban massing studies.

Although these efforts provide promising steps toward improved thermal zoning for building energy simulation, a truly automated, one-size-fits-all approach remains to be developed.

4. HVAC COMPONENT MODELING

4.1 MODELING STRATEGIES

The performance of HVAC components varies based on component design, operating conditions, and control strategies. Two different strategies are commonly used to represent the performance of HVAC components: empirical (regression-based) models and first-principles models.

Empirical (Regression-Based) Models

Although some secondary components (e.g., heat exchangers, valves) are readily described by fundamental engineering principles, the complex nature of some equipment (e.g., chillers, boilers, fans coupled with air distribution systems) has discouraged the use of first-principles models for energy calculations in favor of regression-based component models based on manufacturers' empirical performance data.

Energy consumption of complex equipment generally depends on equipment design, load conditions, environmental conditions, and equipment control strategies. For example, chiller performance depends on the basic equipment design features (e.g., heat exchange surfaces, compressor design), temperatures and flow through the condenser and evaporator, and methods for controlling the chiller at different loads and operating conditions (e.g., inlet guide vane control or variable-speed compressor control on centrifugal chillers to maintain leaving chilled-water temperature set point). In general, these variables vary constantly and require calculations on an hourly or subhourly basis.

Energy consumption characteristics of primary equipment have traditionally been modeled using equations developed by regression analysis of manufacturers' published design data. Historically, published data were available only for full-load design conditions, and additional correction functions were used to correct the full-load data to part-load conditions. However, industry efforts to standardize reporting of performance data over a range of operating conditions (proposed ASHRAE *Standard* 205P) are making it possible to capture the performance of specific equipment via automated performance maps or custom regression fits. Use of such standard-format data is expected to become the preferred approach for transmitting equipment performance characteristics to energy modeling software.

The functional form of the regression equations and correction functions takes many forms, including exponentials, Fourier series, and, most commonly, second- or third-order polynomials. Selection of an appropriate functional form depends on the behavior of the equipment. In some cases, energy consumption is calculated using direct interpolation from data tables.

A typical approach to modeling primary equipment in energy simulation programs is to assume the following functional form for equipment power consumption:

$$\begin{aligned} P &= \mathrm{PIR} \times \mathrm{Load} \\ \mathrm{PIR} &= \mathrm{PIR}_{nom} f_1(t_a, t_b, \ldots) f_2(\mathrm{PLR}) \end{aligned} \quad (6)$$

$$\begin{aligned} C_{avail} &= C_{nom} f_3(t_a, t_b, \ldots) \\ \mathrm{PLR} &= \frac{\mathrm{Load}}{C_{avail}} \end{aligned} \quad (7)$$

where

P = equipment power, kW
PIR = power input ratio
PIR_{nom} = power input ratio under nominal full-load conditions
Load = power delivered to load, kW
C_{avail} = available equipment capacity, kW
C_{nom} = nominal equipment capacity, kW
f_1 = function relating full-load power at off-design conditions (t_a, t_b, ...) to full-load power at design conditions
f_2 = fraction full-load power function, relating part-load power to full-load power
f_3 = function relating available capacity at off-design conditions (t_a, t_b, ...) to nominal capacity
t_a, t_b = various operating temperatures that affect power
PLR = part-load ratio

The part-load ratio is the ratio of the load to the available equipment capacity at given off-design operating conditions. Like the power, the available, or full-load, capacity is a function of operating conditions.

The particular forms of off-design functions f_1 and f_3 depend on the specific type of equipment. For example, for fossil-fuel boilers, full-load capacity and power (or fuel use) can be affected by thermal losses to ambient temperature. However, these off-design functions are typically considered to be unity in most building simulation programs. For condensing boilers, efficiency is significantly affected by boiler entering water temperature, which is therefore an important input for the f_1 function (see also the section on Boilers). For chillers, both capacity and power are affected by condenser and evaporator temperatures, which are often characterized in terms of their secondary fluids. For direct-expansion air-cooled chillers, operating temperatures are typically the wet-bulb temperature of air entering the evaporator and the dry-bulb temperature of air entering the condenser. For liquid chillers, the temperatures are usually the leaving chilled-water temperature and the entering condenser water temperature (see also the section on Chillers). For fans and pumps, energy consumption is often represented as a polynomial function of airflow or fluid flow, as described in the section on Fans, Pumps, and Distribution Systems.

As an example, consider the cooling performance of a direct-expansion (DX) packaged single-zone rooftop unit. The nominal rated performance of these units is typically given for an outdoor air temperature of 95°F and evaporator entering coil conditions of 80°F db and 67°F wb. However, performance changes as outdoor

Table 3 Correlation Coefficients for Off-Design Relationships

Corr.	0	1	2	3	4	5
f_1	−1.063931	0.0306584	0.0001269	0.0154213	0.0000497	0.0002096
f_3	0.8740302	0.0011416	0.0001711	−0.002957	0.0000102	0.0000592

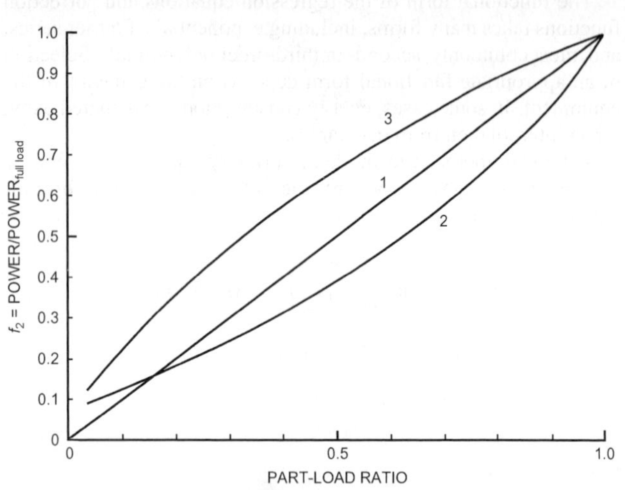

Fig. 5 Possible Part-Load Power Curves

temperature and entering coil conditions vary. To account for these effects, the DOE-2.1E simulation program expresses the off-design functions f_1 and f_3 with biquadratic functions of the outdoor dry-bulb temperature and the coil entering wet-bulb temperature. Many other programs use similar functions.

$$f_1(t_{wb,ent}, t_{oa}) = a_0 + a_1 t_{wb,ent} + a_2 t_{wb,ent}^2 + a_3 t_{oa} + a_4 t_{oa}^2 + a_5 t_{wb,ent} t_{oa} \quad (8)$$

$$f_3(t_{wb,ent}, t_{oa}) = c_0 + c_1 t_{wb,ent} + c_2 t_{wb,ent}^2 + c_3 t_{oa} + c_4 t_{oa}^2 + c_5 t_{wb,ent} t_{oa} \quad (9)$$

The constants in Equations (8) and (9) are given in Table 3.

The fraction full-load power function f_2 represents the change in equipment efficiency at part-load conditions and depends heavily on the control strategies used to match load and capacity. Figure 5 shows several possible shapes of these functional relationships. Curve 1 represents equipment with constant efficiency, independent of load. Curve 2 represents equipment that is most efficient in the middle of its operating range. Curve 3 represents equipment that is most efficient at full load. Note that these types of curves apply to both boilers and chillers.

First-Principles Models

Engineering first principles such as thermodynamics as well as heat, mass, and momentum transfer can be used to develop models of primary equipment as well as secondary components. Gordon and Ng (1994, 1995), Gordon et al. (1995), Jiang and Reddy (2003), Lebrun et al. (1999), and others have sought to develop such models in which unknown model parameters are extracted from measured or published manufacturers' data.

The energy analyst often must choose the appropriate model for the job. For example, a complex boiler model is not appropriate if the boiler operates at virtually constant efficiency. Similarly, a regression-based model might be appropriate when the user has a full dataset of reliable in-situ measurements of the plant. A regression-based model may also be a good choice when manufacturer performance data is provided for a full range of anticipated operating conditions. However, first-principles physical models generally have several advantages over pure regression models:

- Physical models allow confident extrapolation outside the range of available data.
- Regression is still required to obtain values for unknown physical parameters. However, the values of these parameters usually have physical significance, which can be used to estimate default parameter values, diagnose errors in data analysis through checks for realistic parameter values, and even evaluate potential performance improvements.
- The number of unknown parameters is generally much smaller than the number of unknown coefficients in the typical regression model. For example, the standard ARI compressor model requires as many as 30 coefficients, 10 each for regressions of capacity, power, and refrigerant flow. By comparison, a physical compressor model may have as few as four or five unknown parameters. Thus, physical models require fewer measured data.
- Data on part-load operation of chillers and boilers have been notoriously difficult to obtain but are becoming more readily available from manufacturers. Part-load corrections often represent the greatest uncertainty in the regression models, while causing the greatest effect on annual energy predictions. By comparison, physical models of full-load operation often allow direct extension to part-load operation with little additional required data.

Physical models of primary HVAC equipment can be found in many HVAC textbooks, but some of the models described here are specifically based on the work of Bourdouxhe et al. (1994a, 1994b, 1994c) in developing the ASHRAE *HVAC 1 Toolkit* (Lebrun et al. 1999). Each elementary component's behavior is characterized by a limited number of physical parameters, such as heat exchanger heat transfer area or centrifugal compressor impeller blade angle. Values of these parameters are identified, or tuned, based on regression fits of overall performance compared to measured or published data.

Although physical models are based on physical characteristics, values obtained through a regression analysis of manufacturers' data are not necessarily representative of the actual measured values. Strictly speaking, the parameter values are regression coefficients with estimated values, identified to minimize the error in overall system performance. In other words, errors in the fundamental models of equipment are offset by over- or underestimation of the parameter values.

4.2 TERMINAL COMPONENTS

Terminal Units and Controls

Although many terminal units do not directly consume energy, they often have a significant effect on the energy consumed by primary and secondary equipment. For example, the minimum airflow set point for a variable-air-volume (VAV) terminal unit with a reheat coil affects supply fan energy, cooling energy consumption of the chiller or direct-expansion compressor, heating energy consumption of the electric reheat coil or central plant boiler, and pump energy for delivery of chilled and hot water. Therefore, the representation of terminal units in energy-estimating programs deserves special attention.

Several types of terminal units are commonly represented in energy-estimating programs: single-duct VAV boxes with and without reheat coils, single-duct VAV boxes with parallel or series induction fans, dual-duct VAV boxes, chilled-beam induction units, fan-coils, radiant panels, baseboard radiators, and others. Chapters 4, 5, and 20 of the 2016 *ASHRAE Handbook—HVAC Systems and Equipment* provide a description of many types of terminal units and their operation.

When selecting an energy-estimating program, it is important to note that not all programs explicitly represent some of these types of terminal units or they may not directly represent the desired control scheme.

The following considerations regarding accuracy and energy consumption are important when representing terminal units in energy-estimating programs:

- **VAV box minimum airflow set point.** As noted previously, this setting has a significant impact on energy consumption in a VAV system, and using default inputs may lead to inaccurate model results. In some actual systems, the minimum airflow set point is varied over time in a demand-controlled ventilation scheme, and in those cases it is important to ensure that the selected energy-estimating program can represent that strategy.
- **VAV box damper control in heating mode.** In actual systems, VAV box airflow in heating mode may remain at a fixed minimum position or may modulate to provide increased airflow as heating load increases, typically using a specific heating maximum airflow set point that may be different from the maximum cooling airflow. This later strategy is often called reverse-acting damper control (dual-maximum), and it can lead to reduced reheat energy. Many energy-estimating programs can represent both control strategies, and this is an important input to verify.
- **Fan power for VAV boxes with induction fans.** In some cases, these small induction fans are relatively inefficient, and this is an important input to verify.
- **Control of parallel induction fans in VAV boxes.** Typically, in a parallel induction VAV box, the fan runs only in heating mode. To accurately represent this fan operation, it is important to verify in the energy-estimating program how the control for this fan is specified.
- **Chilled-water temperature limits for chilled-beam systems.** In a typical chilled beam design, there is a minimum setpoint for entering water temperature to avoid condensation on the coils. This set point is higher than that for a typical chilled-water distribution system, and it may affect the efficiency of the chilled-water system and the pumping energy.
- **Temperature input requirements for radiant heating systems and radiators.** Different types of radiant heating terminal units have different hot-water temperature input requirements. The corresponding hot-water supply and return temperature requirements on the boilers will affect boiler operating efficiency, especially for condensing boilers.

Underfloor Air Distribution

Underfloor air distribution (UFAD) is sometimes considered as an energy-efficient HVAC strategy, and a method to estimate its energy performance is a valuable design tool. UFAD systems offer potential for energy savings in several ways. These systems typically operate at higher cooling supply air temperatures compared to overhead air delivery systems, and offer potential for additional economizer energy savings. Primary cooling equipment efficiency may improve when providing higher-temperature supply air. In addition, if the UFAD system is operated to maintain partially mixed air distribution, as described in Chapter 57 of the 2015 *ASHRAE Handbook—HVAC Applications*, then the zone air distribution effectiveness may be better than that of an overhead air delivery system and allow a reduction in outdoor air ventilation rate.

A limitation of many energy-estimating programs is the assumption that air within thermal zones is fully mixed, and these programs cannot directly represent the performance of a UFAD system that is operated to create some temperature stratification. Approximate methods have been used by energy modelers, such as raising the thermostat set point in the UFAD zones to represent a higher average air temperature or representing the actual zone with two stacked zones in the model. See Energy Design Resources (2012) for more information.

A method for explicit modeling of UFAD systems has been developed for the EnergyPlus program, with separate models for interior and perimeter zones (Webster et al. 2013).

Thermal Displacement Ventilation

Thermal displacement ventilation (TDV) is another air delivery strategy that offers energy efficiency benefits. A displacement system is typically designed to achieve fully stratified air distribution, as described in Chapter 57 of the 2015 *ASHRAE Handbook—HVAC Applications*. The potential efficiency benefits are similar to UFAD systems.

Modelers seeking to estimate the energy performance of a TDV system face the same basic limitations as with UFAD systems, and similar approximations have been used in practice. However, a method for modeling TDV represented by three nodes (floor temperature, occupied-zone temperature, and upper-zone temperature) is implemented in EnergyPlus (U.S. Department of Energy 1996-2016).

Radiant Heating and Cooling Systems

Heating and cooling a space using heated and cooled panels is fundamentally different from using conditioned air. In a radiant system, a significant fraction of the sensible heating and cooling occurs by radiant heat transfer between the radiant panel and the surfaces in the space. This process is described in Chapter 6 of the 2016 *ASHRAE Handbook—HVAC Systems and Equipment*.

As noted in the Heat Balance Method section, energy-estimating programs that use the heat balance method for space load calculations are generally preferred for representing the performance of radiant systems. Use of the heat balance method allows accounting for radiant heat transfer among surfaces in a space, and a heated or cooled panel may be represented as one of those surfaces.

4.3 SECONDARY SYSTEM COMPONENTS

Secondary HVAC systems generally include all elements of the overall building energy system between a central heating and cooling plant and the building terminal units and zones. The precise definition depends heavily on the building design. A secondary system typically includes air-handling equipment; air distribution systems with associated ductwork; dampers; fans; and heating, cooling, and humidity-conditioning equipment. They also include liquid distribution systems between the central plant and the zone and air-handling equipment, including piping, valves, and pumps.

Although the exact design of secondary systems varies dramatically among buildings, they are composed of a relatively small set of generic HVAC components, including distribution components (e.g., pumps/fans, pipes/ducts, valves/dampers, headers/plenums, fittings) and heat and mass transfer components (e.g., heating coils, cooling and dehumidifying coils, liquid heat exchangers, air heat exchangers, evaporative coolers, steam injectors and other humidifiers). Most secondary systems can be described by simply connecting these components to form the complete system.

Energy estimation through computer simulation sometimes mimics the modular construction of secondary systems by using modular simulation elements [e.g., the ASHRAE *HVAC2 Toolkit* (Brandemuehl 1993; Brandemuehl and Gabel 1994), the simulation program TRNSYS (Klein et al. 1994; TRNSYS 2012), and Annex 10 activities of the International Energy Agency (IEA ECBCS 1987)]. To the extent that the secondary system consumes energy and transfers energy between the building and central plant, an energy analysis can be performed by characterizing the energy consumption of the individual components and the energy transferred among system components.

In many energy-estimating programs, secondary systems are represented by a mix of component models and simplified system models. For example, it is common for air and hydronic distribution systems to be represented by energy models that do not explicitly include components such as pipes/ducts, coils, and valves/dampers. Those methods are described in the following section.

In this chapter, secondary components are divided into two categories: (1) distribution components and (2) heat and mass transfer components.

Fans, Pumps, and Distribution Systems

The distribution system of an HVAC system affects energy consumption in two ways. First, fans and pumps consume electrical energy directly, based on the flow and pressures under which a device operates. Ducts and dampers, or pipes and valves, and the system control strategies affect flow and pressure at each fan or pump. Second, thermal energy is often transferred to (or from) the fluid by (1) heat transfer through pipes and ducts and (2) electrical input to fans and pumps. Analysis of system components should, therefore, account for both direct electrical energy consumption and thermal energy transfer.

Fan and pump performance are discussed in Chapters 21 and 44 of the 2016 *ASHRAE Handbook—HVAC Systems and Equipment*. In addition, Chapter 21 of this volume covers pressure loss calculations for airflow in ducts and duct fittings, and the effects of system air leakage. Chapter 22 presents a similar discussion for fluid flow in pipes. Although these chapters do not specifically focus on energy estimation, energy use is governed by the same performance characteristics and engineering relationships. Strictly speaking, performance calculations for a building's fan and air distribution system require a detailed pressure balance on the entire network. For example, in an air distribution system, airflow through the fan depends on its physical characteristics, operating speed, and pressure differential across the fan. Pressure drop through the air distribution system depends on duct construction (i.e., friction and fitting losses), coil and filter characteristics, damper positions, air leakage, and airflow through each component. Interaction between the fan and air distribution system results in a set of coupled, nonlinear algebraic equations. Models and subroutines for performing these calculations are available in the ASHRAE *HVAC2 Toolkit* (Brandemuehl 1993) and CONTAM (NIST 2000-2016). A simplified, physics-based model of the system curve, which represents the system pressure drop as seen by the fan, is described by Sherman and Wray (2010).

Detailed analysis of a distribution system requires flow and pressure balancing among the components, but nearly all commercially available energy analysis methods approximate the effect of the interactions with part-load performance curves [empirical (regression-based) component models]. This approach eliminates the need to calculate pressure drop through the distribution system at off-design conditions. Two simplified methods are described in the following sections.

Polynomial Curve Fit. Part-load curves are often expressed in terms of a **power input ratio** as a function of the part-load ratio, defined as the ratio of part-load flow to design flow:

$$\text{PIR} = \frac{W}{W_{full}} = f_{plr}\left(\frac{Q}{Q_{full}}\right) \tag{10}$$

where

PIR = power input ratio
W = fan motor input power at part load, Btu/h
W_{full} = fan motor input power at full load or design, Btu/h
Q = fan airflow rate at part load, cfm
Q_{full} = fan airflow rate at full load or design, cfm
f_{plr} = regression function, typically polynomial or power law

The exact shape of the part-load curve depends on the effect of flow control on the pressure and fan efficiency and may be calculated using a detailed analysis or measured field data. Figure 6 shows the relationship for three typical fan control strategies, as represented in a simulation program (York and Cappiello 1982). In the simulation program, the curves are represented by polynomial regression equations. Models and subroutines for performing these calculations are also available in the ASHRAE *HVAC2 Toolkit* (Brandemuehl 1993).

Figure 7 shows an example of a similar curve for the part-load operation of a fan system in a monitored building (Brandemuehl and Bradford 1999). In this case, the fan system represents 10 separate air handlers, each with supply and return fans, operating with variable-speed fan control to maintain a set duct static pressure.

Component Model. A second method can be used for fan system energy estimation in variable-airflow systems. It accounts

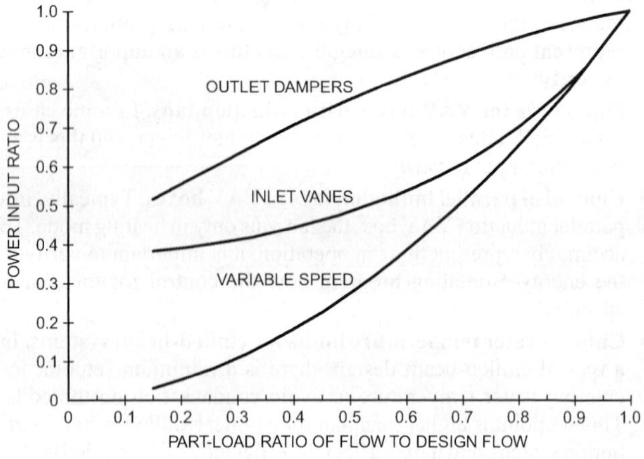

Fig. 6 Part-Load Curves for Typical Fan Operating Strategies
(York and Cappiello 1982)

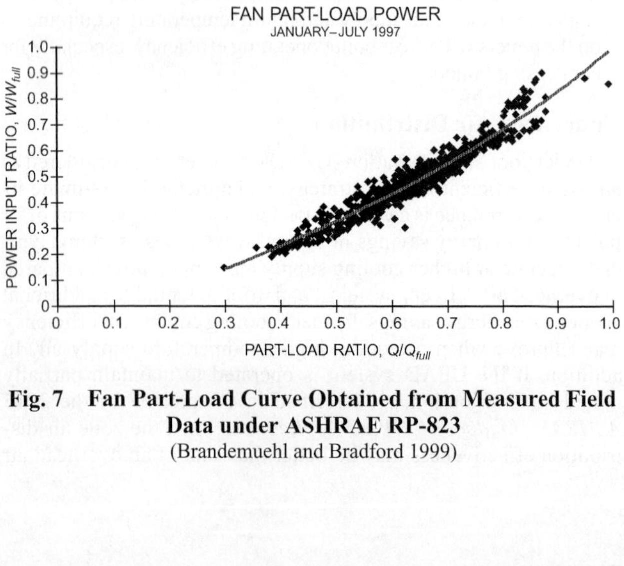

Fig. 7 Fan Part-Load Curve Obtained from Measured Field Data under ASHRAE RP-823
(Brandemuehl and Bradford 1999)

separately for the substantial part-load performance variations that can occur for the fans, fan drive belts, fan motor, and variable-frequency drives (VFDs). For fans, dimensionless models are used to represent fan efficiency and speed variations with airflow. This method also uses a physics-based model (often called the "system curve") for determining flow-dependent fan pressure rise (Sherman and Wray 2010). Note that system curves with duct static pressure controls or significant pressure drops through coils and filters do not follow the commonly assumed quadratic system curve. Fan power is calculated using airflow, pressure rise, and fan efficiency at each time step. Calculating fan power and speed allows determining fan shaft torque and the resulting loads on drive components (belts, motors, and VFDs). Note that fan laws do not apply to drive components. In the absence of physics-based models, regression models based on available data can be used to represent belt, motor, and VFD part-load efficiency variations. An implementation of this approach, developed by Wray in 2010, is included in EnergyPlus, and details are provided in the *EnergyPlus Engineering Reference* (U.S. Department of Energy 1996-2016).

A benefit of this approach is its ability to directly represent the impacts of low-pressure-drop distribution systems, air leakage reduction, and duct static-pressure reset control, which are important efficiency strategies for many systems. This approach can also represent the effects of fan system component oversizing and changes for components such as fans, belts, motors, and variable-frequency drives.

A disadvantage to the component model is that the additional capabilities require additional inputs. However, generic values for model parameters are provided in the EnergyPlus documentation.

Fan and Pump Heat. Heat dissipated to the airstream by fan operation increases airstream temperature. Fan shaft power is usually assumed to be dissipated fully in the airstream. Motor losses also contribute if the motor is mounted in the airstream. For pumps, these contributions are typically assumed to be zero because the motor is not mounted in the water stream, and the ratio of transport power to thermal capacitance rate is usually much less for water than for air.

The following equation provides a convenient and general model to calculate the heat transferred to the fluid by a motor:

$$q_{fluid} = [\eta_m + (1 - \eta_m) f_{m,\,loss}]W \tag{11}$$

where

q_{fluid} = heat transferred to fluid, Btu/h
$f_{m,loss}$ = fraction of motor heat loss transferred to fluid stream, dimensionless (= 1 if fan mounted in airstream, = 0 if fan mounted outdoor airstream)
W = fan motor input power, Btu/h
η_m = motor efficiency

The heat rejected by VFDs and the fraction of motor heat not transferred to the airstream should be accounted for as building loads.

Heat and Mass Transfer Components

Secondary HVAC systems comprise heat and mass transfer components (e.g., steam or hot-water air-heating coils, chilled-water cooling and dehumidifying coils, shell-and-tube liquid heat exchangers, air-to-air heat exchangers, evaporative coolers, steam injectors). Although these components do not consume energy directly, their thermal performance dictates interactions between building loads and energy-consuming primary components (e.g., chillers, boilers). In particular, secondary component performance determines the entering fluid conditions for primary components, which in turn determine energy efficiencies of primary equipment. In addition, heat and mass transfer components may affect air and fluid flow, which affect performance of energy-consuming secondary components such as fans and pumps. Accurate energy calculations cannot be performed without appropriate models of the system heat and mass transfer components.

For example, load on a chiller is typically described as the sum of zone sensible and latent loads, plus any heat gain from ducts, plenums, fans, pumps, and piping. However, the chiller's energy consumption is determined not only by the load but also by the return chilled-water temperature and flow rate. The return water condition is determined by cooling coil performance and part-load operating strategy of the air and water distribution system. The cooling coil might typically be controlled to maintain a constant leaving air temperature by modulating water flow through the coil. In such a scenario, the cooling coil model must be able to calculate the leaving air humidity, water temperature, and water flow rate given the cooling coil design characteristics and entering air temperature and humidity, airflow, and water temperature.

Virtually all building energy simulation programs include, and require, models of heat and mass transfer components. These models are generally relatively simple. Whereas a coil designer might use a detailed tube-by-tube analysis of conduction and convection heat transfer and condensation on fin surfaces to develop an optimal combination of fin and tube geometry, an energy analyst is more interested in determining changes in leaving fluid states as operating conditions vary during the year. In addition, the energy analyst is likely to have limited design data on the equipment and, therefore, requires a model with very few parameters that depend on equipment geometry and detailed design characteristics.

A typical approach to modeling heat and mass transfer components for energy calculations is based on an **effectiveness-NTU heat exchanger model** (Kays and London 1984). The effectiveness-NTU (number of transfer units) model is described in most heat transfer textbooks and briefly discussed in Chapter 4. It is particularly appropriate for describing leaving fluid conditions when entering fluid conditions and equipment design characteristics are known. Also, this model requires only a single parameter to describe the characteristics of the exchanger: the overall transfer coefficient *UA*, which can be determined from limited design performance data.

Effectiveness methods are used to perform energy calculations for a variety of sensible heat exchangers in HVAC systems. For typical finned-tube air-heating coils, the cross-flow configuration with both fluid streams unmixed is most appropriate. Air-to-air heat exchangers may be cross- or counterflow. For liquid-to-liquid exchangers, tube-in-tube equipment can be modeled as parallel or counterflow, depending on flow directions; correlations for shell-and-tube effectiveness and NTU, which depend on the extent of baffling and the number of tube passes, are given in heat transfer texts (Mills 1999).

The energy analyst must determine the *UA* to describe the operations of a specific heat exchanger. There are three ways to determine this important parameter: direct calculation, measurement, and manufacturers' data. Given detailed information about the materials, geometry, and construction of the heat exchanger, fundamental heat transfer principles can be applied to calculate the overall heat transfer coefficient. However, the method most appropriate for energy estimation is use of manufacturers' performance data or measurement of installed performance. In reporting the design performance of a heat exchanger, a manufacturer typically gives the heat transfer rate under various operating conditions, with operating conditions described in terms of entering fluid flow rates and temperatures. The effectiveness and *UA* can be calculated from the given heat transfer rate and entering fluid conditions.

Example 3. An energy analyst seeks to evaluate a hot-water heating system that includes a hot-water heating coil. The energy analysis program uses an effectiveness-NTU model of the coil and requires the *UA* of the coil as an input parameter. Although detailed information on the coil geometry and heat transfer surfaces is not available, the manufacturer states that the one-row hot-water heating coil delivers 818,000 Btu/h of heat under the following design conditions:

Design Performance

Entering water temperature t_{hi} = 175°F
Water mass flow rate $\dot{m}_h$ = 661 lb/min
Entering air temperature t_{ci} = 68°F
Air mass flow rate $\dot{m}_c$ = 1058 lb/min
Design heat transfer q = 818,000 Btu/h

Solution: First determine the heat exchanger UA from design data, then use UA to predict performance at off-design conditions. Effectiveness-NTU relationships are used for both steps. The key assumption is that the UA is constant for both operating conditions.

a) An examination of flow rates and fluid specific heats allows calculation of the hot-fluid capacity rate C_h and the cold-fluid capacity rate C_c at design conditions, and the capacity rate ratio Z.

$$C_h = (\dot{m}c_p)_h = (661)(1.00)(60) = 39{,}660 \text{ Btu/h·°F}$$

$$C_c = (\dot{m}c_p)_c = (1058)(0.24)(60) = 15{,}235 \text{ Btu/h·°F}$$

$$C_{max} = C_h \qquad C_{min} = C_c$$

$$Z = \frac{C_{min}}{C_{max}} = 0.384$$

where c_p is specific heat and c_{max} and c_{min} are the larger and smaller of the capacity rates, respectively,

b) Effectiveness can be directly calculated from the heat transfer definition.

$$\varepsilon = \frac{(t_{co} - t_{ci})}{(t_{hi} - t_{ci})} = \frac{q/C_c}{(t_{hi} - t_{ci})} = \frac{(818{,}000/15{,}235)}{(175 - 68)} = 0.502$$

where t_{co} is the leaving air temperature.

c) The effectiveness-NTU relationships for a cross-flow heat exchanger with both fluids unmixed allow calculation of the effectiveness in terms of the capacity rate ratio Z and the NTU [the relationships are available from most heat transfer textbooks and, specifically, in Kays and London (1984)]. Given the effectiveness and capacity rate ratio, NTU = 0.804.

d) The heat transfer UA is then determined from the definition of the NTU.

$$UA = C_{min}\text{NTU} = (15{,}235)(0.804) = 12{,}250 \text{ Btu/h·°F}$$

Application to Cooling and Dehumidifying Coils

Analysis of air-cooling and dehumidifying coils requires coupled, nonlinear heat and mass transfer relationships. These relationships form the basis for all HVAC components with moisture transfer, including cooling coils, cooling towers, air washers, and evaporative coolers. Although the complex heat and mass transfer theory presented in many textbooks is often required for cooling coil design, simpler models based on effectiveness concepts are usually more appropriate for energy estimation. For example, the bypass factor is a form of effectiveness in the approach of the leaving air temperature to the apparatus dew-point, or coil surface, temperature.

The effectiveness-NTU method is typically developed and applied in analysis of sensible heat exchangers, but it can also be used to analyze other types of exchangers, such as cooling and dehumidifying coils, that couple heat and mass transfer. By redefining the state variables, capacity rates, and overall exchange coefficient of these enthalpy exchangers, the effectiveness concept may be used to calculate heat transfer rates and leaving fluid states. For sensible heat exchangers, the state variable is temperature, the capacity is the product of mass flow and fluid specific heat, and the overall transfer coefficient is the conventional overall heat transfer coefficient. For cooling and dehumidifying coils, the state variable becomes moist air enthalpy, the capacity has units of mass flow, and the overall heat transfer coefficient is modified to reflect enthalpy exchange. This approach is the basis for models by Brandemuehl

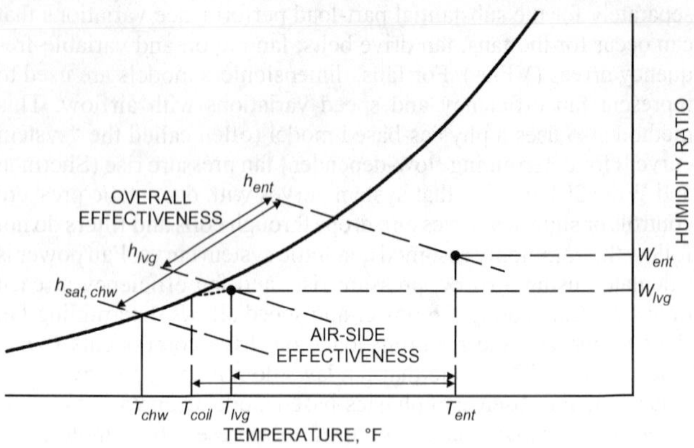

Fig. 8 Psychrometric Schematic of Cooling Coil Processes

(1993), Braun et al. (1989), and Threlkeld (1970). The same principles also underlie the coil model described in Chapter 23 of the 2012 *ASHRAE Handbook—HVAC Systems and Equipment*.

The effectiveness model is based on the observation that, for a given set of entering air and liquid conditions, the heat and mass transfer are bounded by thermodynamic maximum values. Figure 8 shows the limits for leaving air states on a psychrometric chart. Specifically, the leaving chilled-water temperature cannot be warmer than the entering air temperature, and the leaving air temperature and humidity cannot be lower than the conditions of saturated moist air at the temperature of the entering chilled water.

Figure 8 also shows that performance of a cooling coil requires evaluating two different effectivenesses to identify the leaving air temperature and humidity. An overall effectiveness can be used to describe the approach of the leaving air enthalpy to the minimum possible value. An air-side effectiveness, related to the coil bypass factor, describes the approach of the leaving air temperature to the effective wet-coil surface temperature.

Effectiveness analysis is accomplished for wet coils by establishing a common state variable for both the moist air and liquid streams. As implied by the lower limit of the entering chilled-water temperature, this common state variable is the moist air enthalpy. In other words, all liquid and coil temperatures are transformed to the enthalpy of saturated moist air at the liquid or coil temperature. Changes in liquid temperature can similarly be expressed in terms of changes in saturated moist air enthalpy through a saturation specific heat $c_{p,sat}$ defined by the following:

$$c_{p,\,sat} = \frac{\Delta h_{l,\,sat}}{\Delta t_l} \tag{12}$$

Using the definition of Equation (12), the basic effectiveness relationships discussed in Chapter 4 can be written as

$$q = C_a(h_{a,\,ent} - h_{a,\,lvg}) = C_l(h_{l,\,sat,\,lvg} - h_{l,\,sat,\,ent}) \tag{13}$$

$$q = \varepsilon C_{min}(h_{a,\,ent} - h_{l,\,sat,\,ent}) \tag{14}$$

$$C_a = \dot{m}_a \tag{15}$$

$$C_l = \frac{(\dot{m}c_p)_l}{c_{p,\,sat}} \tag{16}$$

$$C_{min} = \min(C_a, C_l) \tag{17}$$

where

q = heat transfer from air to water, Btu/h
C = fluid capacity, lb/h

$\dot{m}_a$ = dry air mass flow rate, lb/h
$\dot{m}_l$ = liquid mass flow rate, lb/h
$c_{p,l}$ = liquid specific heat, Btu/lb·°F
$c_{p,sat}$ = saturation specific heat, defined by Equation (12), Btu/lb·°F
h_a = enthalpy of moist air, Btu/lb
$h_{l,sat}$ = enthalpy of saturated moist air at the temperature of the liquid, Btu/lb

The cooling coil effectiveness of Equation (14) is defined, then, as the ratio of moist air enthalpies in Figure 8. As with sensible heat exchangers, effectiveness is also a function of the physical coil characteristics and can be obtained by modeling the coil as a counterflow heat exchanger. However, because heat transfer calculations are performed based on enthalpies, the overall transfer coefficient must be based on enthalpy potential rather than temperature potential. The enthalpy-based heat transfer coefficient UA_h is related to the conventional temperature-based coefficient by the specific heat:

$$q = UA\Delta t = UA_h\Delta h$$

$$UA_h = \frac{UA\Delta t}{\Delta h} = \frac{UA}{c_p} \quad (18)$$

A similar analysis can be performed to evaluate the air-side effectiveness, which identifies the leaving air temperature. Whereas the overall enthalpy-based effectiveness is based on an overall heat transfer coefficient between the chilled water and air, air-side effectiveness is based on a heat transfer coefficient between the coil surface and air.

As with sensible heat exchangers, the overall heat transfer coefficients *UA* can be determined either from direct calculation from coil properties or from manufacturers' performance data. A sensible heat exchanger is modeled with a single effectiveness and can be described by a single parameter *UA*, but a wet cooling and dehumidifying coil requires two parameters to describe the two effectivenesses shown in Figure 8. These parameters are the internal and external *UA*s: one describes heat transfer between the chilled water and the air-side surface through the pipe wall, and the other between the surface and the moist air. *UA* values can be determined from the sensible and latent capacity of a cooling coil at a single rating condition. A significant advantage of the effectiveness-NTU method is that the component can be described with as little as one measured data point or one manufacturer's design calculation.

4.4 PRIMARY SYSTEM COMPONENTS

Primary HVAC systems consume energy and deliver heating and cooling to a building, usually through secondary systems. Primary equipment generally includes chillers, boilers, cooling towers, cogeneration equipment, and plant-level thermal-storage equipment. In particular, primary equipment generally represents the major energy-consuming equipment of a building, so accurate characterization of building energy use relies on accurate modeling of primary equipment energy consumption.

Boilers

The literature on boiler models is extensive, ranging from steady-state performance models (DeCicco 1990; Lebrun 1993) to detailed dynamic simulation models (Bonne and Jansen 1977; Lebrun et al. 1985), to a combination of these two schemes (Laret 1991; Malmström et al. 1985). However, the input information required for these models is not often readily available, and these models should be considered only in more complex situations (e.g., large boilers in large buildings, district heating systems, cogeneration systems), where a complete, detailed representation of heat distribution, emission, and operation and control under varying external conditions is warranted.

In most current energy-estimating programs, the performance of boilers is represented by regression equations and a full-load efficiency value as described in the section on Empirical (Regression-Based) Models. Those equations typically represent the boiler efficiency under varying load conditions and, in some cases, the equations also account for water temperature conditions. When using these regression-based models, two important issues to understand are efficiency rating conditions and the off-design efficiency calculation method used by the energy-estimating program.

Rating Conditions. The primary rating condition relevant for fuel-fired boiler efficiency is the entering water temperature, which is the return water temperature in most building heating applications. Efficiency improves as the return water temperature drops, because more heat can be extracted from exhaust gases. A condensing boiler can reach efficiencies up to 98% with entering water at 80°F. The minimum return water temperature for noncondensing boilers is typically about 140°F, because lower temperatures lead to condensation and damaging corrosion, and efficiency under that condition is usually in the range of 80% to 85%. The important point to consider when entering a value for fuel-fired boiler efficiency in an energy-estimating program is the assumption made by the program about rating conditions. For example, the DOE2.2 program expects noncondensing boiler efficiency values to correspond to 160°F entering water temperature and condensing water boiler efficiency values to correspond to 80°F entering water temperature. More information on boiler design and rating conditions is provided in Chapter 32 of the 2016 *ASHRAE Handbook—HVAC Systems and Equipment.*

Off-Design Conditions. Another important consideration in the use of energy-estimating programs is the type of model used to represent off-design conditions (i.e., how the efficiency is assumed to change at partial load or as the water temperature conditions change). Some models account only for changes in efficiency with changes in load. Other models consider both load and entering water temperature, and still others consider load and leaving water temperature. Some programs offer a choice of models. For best accuracy, models that account for load and entering water temperature are preferred.

Figures 9 and 10 show examples of how boiler efficiency is represented by different types of models. Figure 9 shows a model in which boiler efficiency is a function of part-load ratio alone. Different regression equation coefficients are used for atmospheric-draft and forced-draft boilers, and the forced-draft units are represented with better part-load efficiency. An implicit assumption of this model is that entering water temperature is in a range where it does not have a significant impact on efficiency, which may be reasonable for noncondensing boilers. Figure 10 shows a model for a condensing boiler in which efficiency is a function of both part-load ratio and entering water temperature. This model shows that efficiency increases as entering water temperature decreases and as load decreases.

Chillers

Models representing energy consumption of chillers include both first-principles models and empirical models. Examples of first-principles models include detailed modeling techniques described in the ASHRAE *HVAC 1 Toolkit* (Lebrun et al. 1999) and the Gordon-Ng model (Gordon 2000). A discussion of the Gordon-Ng model is provided in the Data-Driven Modeling section, presented as an example of a physical model. From a practical point of view, the data required as inputs to these first-principles models will not always be available. Most current energy-estimating programs use empirical models to represent chiller performance. Hydeman et al. (2002) compares the prediction capabilities of several types of models.

Empirical chiller models typically comprise a set of regression equations that represent variations in cooling capacity and efficiency in operation. A common implementation consists of three polynomial equations. One represents variation in cooling capacity as a function of temperature conditions. A second represents the change in efficiency with changing temperature conditions. The third equation represents efficiency as a function of part-load ratio. The following are common inputs to empirical chiller models:

- Full-load efficiency
- Part-load ratio
- Chilled-water supply temperature (temperature leaving the evaporator)
- For water-cooled chillers: condenser water return temperature (temperature entering the condenser)
- For air-cooled chillers: outdoor air dry-bulb temperature

Different types of chillers have different performance characteristics, and their performance is typically represented by different

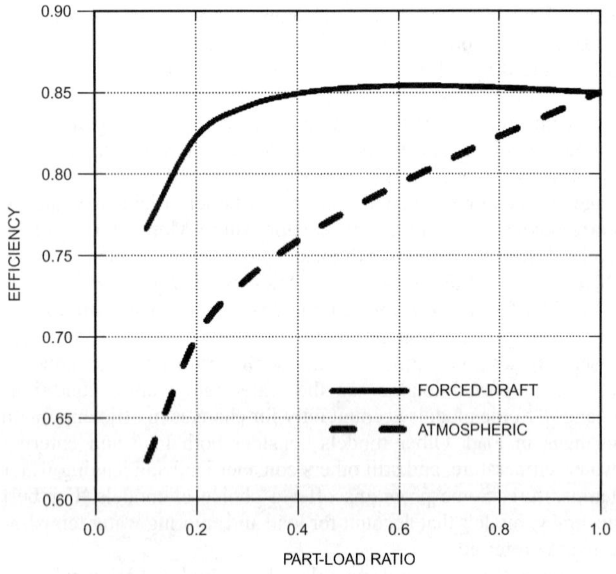

Fig. 9 Example Boiler Model: Efficiency as Function of Part-Load Ratio

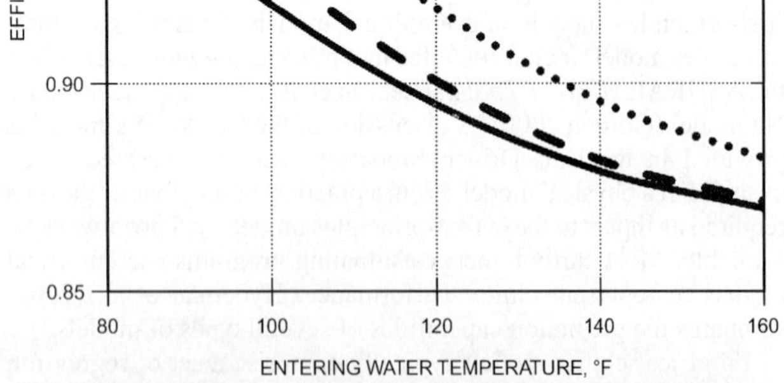

Fig. 10 Example Boiler Model: Efficiency as Function of Part-Load Ratio and Entering Water Temperature

sets of regression equation coefficients. Important chiller design differences include type of condenser (air- or water-cooled), type of compressor (reciprocating, screw, or centrifugal), and unloading mechanism (e.g., inlet vanes or variable-speed compressor control). Chapter 43 of the 2016 *ASHRAE Handbook—Systems and Equipment* provides descriptions of different types of chillers.

Coefficients for chiller models are often supplied as defaults by energy-estimating programs. However, when the intent of analysis is to compare the energy performance of specific chiller alternatives, the recommended practice is to obtain performance data for the specific chillers to create calibrated sets of coefficients for each chiller. Manufacturers can typically provide such data, and it is very important to obtain a set of data representing the full range of potential operating conditions. The process of calculating coefficients for a chiller model is described in Hydeman and Gillespie (2002). For another discussion of empirical chiller models and the process of determining model coefficients, see the *HVAC Simulation Guidebook*, vol. 1 (Energy Design Resources 2012).

Cooling Tower Model

A cooling tower is used in primary systems to reject heat from the chiller condenser. Controls typically manage tower fans and pumps to maintain a desired water temperature entering the condenser. Like cooling and dehumidifying coils in secondary systems, cooling tower performance has a strong influence on the chiller's energy consumption. In addition, tower fans consume electrical energy directly.

Fundamentally, a cooling tower is a direct contact heat and mass exchanger. Equations describing the basic processes are given in Chapter 6 and in many HVAC textbooks. Chapter 40 of the 2016 *ASHRAE Handbook—HVAC Systems and Equipment* describes the specific performance of cooling towers. Performance subroutines are also available in Lebrun et al. (1999) and TRNSYS (2012).

For energy calculations, cooling tower performance is typically described in terms of the outdoor wet-bulb temperature, temperature drop of water flowing through the tower (range), and difference between leaving water and air wet-bulb temperatures (approach). Simple models assume constant range and approach, but more sophisticated models use rating performance data to relate leaving water temperature to the outdoor wet-bulb temperature, water flow, and airflow. Simple cooling tower models, such as those based on a single overall transfer coefficient that can be directly inferred from a single tower rating point, are often appropriate for energy calculations.

Variable-Speed Vapor-Compression Heat Pump Model

Although packaged equipment is most often modeled by empirical functions fit to manufacturers' data, methods are also needed to model and evaluate advanced equipment such as variable-speed heat pumps. Zakula et al. (2011) detail a component-based heat pump model, including variable-speed fan and pump models; variable refrigerant-, air-, and water-side heat transfer coefficients; variable pressure drops; and staged compressors, one or more of which may operate over a wide speed range. Such models can produce performance maps for new equipment designs, including designs in which refrigerant and transport fluid flow rates and condenser subcooling are coordinated as optimized functions of conditions and imposed load (Zakula et al. 2012). A tricubic fit to such performance maps has been shown to represent performance accurately over a wide range of conditions and load.

As a special heat pump model, variable-refrigerant-flow (VRF) systems vary the refrigerant flow to meet the dynamic zone thermal loads. Hong et al. (2016) developed a new VRF heat pump model, which has physics-based component models. This VRF model, implemented in EnergyPlus, (1) enables advanced controls, including variable evaporating and condensing temperatures in the indoor and outdoor units, and variable fan speeds based on the temperature and zone load in the indoor units; (2) adds a detailed refrigerant pipe heat loss calculation using refrigerant flow rate, operational conditions, pipe length, and pipe insulation materials; (3) increases accuracy of simulation especially in partial load conditions; and (4) improves the usability of the model by significantly reducing the number of user input performance curves. A new heat recovery VRF model was also developed and is implemented in EnergyPlus, which enables more accurate modeling of heat recovery between zones with simultaneous cooling and heating loads. The new VRF models in EnergyPlus were validated with measured performance data from real buildings or laboratory experiments.

Ground-Coupled Systems

Ground-coupled systems use the ground as the source/sink for heating or cooling a building. These types of systems are described in detail in Chapter 34 of the 2015 *ASHRAE Handbook—HVAC Applications*. For the most part, the HVAC system components used in these systems are similar to those used in other HVAC systems and do not require any special techniques to estimate their performance. The exception to this is simulating energy exchange with the ground.

Energy is exchanged with the ground through direct use of water from the ground or through ground heat exchangers. With a direct-use system, the temperature entering the HVAC system from the ground is often considered to be constant or to vary only seasonally. This assumption can be valid when the extraction and injection wells are far enough apart to prevent mixing of the aquifer. A number of aquifer storage performance models have been developed for use with HVAC systems, but these have not yet reached mainstream simulation programs.

For simulating performance of ground heat exchangers, two different techniques have been developed: the duct ground storage (DST) model introduced by Hellstrom (1989) that calculates the transient thermal process of borehole fields, and a thermal response factor (*g*-function) approach based on work of Eskilson (1987). Both techniques give a relation between the heat extracted (or rejected) from the ground per unit borehole length and the borehole wall temperature. Both of these methods have been integrated into whole-building simulation programs.

4.5 MODELING OF SYSTEM CONTROLS

Building control systems are hierarchical: higher-level, supervisory controls typically generate set points for lower-level, local loop controls. Supervisory controls include reset and optimal control (see Chapter 42 of the 2015 *ASHRAE Handbook—HVAC Applications*) and often have a large effect on energy consumption. Local loop controllers may also affect energy performance; for example, proportional-only room temperature control results in a trade-off between energy use and comfort. Faults in control systems and devices can also affect energy consumption (e.g., leaking valves and dampers can significantly increase energy use). It is particularly important to account for these departures from ideal behavior when simulating performance of real buildings using calibrated models. Modeling and simulation of some supervisory control functions are increasingly handled by whole-building simulation programs, but very advanced optimal controls such as receding horizon control are not. Simulation of local loop controls also requires more specialized, component- or equation-based modeling environments.

Modern control systems, particularly direct digital controls (DDC), typically use integral action to drive the controlled variable to its set point. For energy modeling purposes, the controlled variable (e.g., supply air temperature) can be treated as being at the set point unless system capacity is insufficient. The simulation must determine whether the capacity required to meet set point exceeds available capacity. If it does, the available capacity is used to determine the actual value of the controlled variable. Where there is only proportional action, the resulting relationship between the controlled variable and the output of the system can be used to determine both values. For example, the action of a conventional pneumatic room temperature controller can be represented by a function relating heating and cooling delivery to space temperature. Similarly, supply air temperature reset control can be modeled as a relationship between outdoor or zone temperature and coil or fan discharge temperature. An accurate secondary system model must ensure that all controls are properly represented and that the governing equations are satisfied at each simulation time step. This often creates a need for iteration or for use of values from an earlier solution point.

Controls on space temperature affect the interaction between loads calculations and the secondary system simulation. A realistic model might require a dead band in space temperature in which no heating or cooling is called for; within this range, the secondary system operates at zero capacity, and the true space temperature must be modeled accordingly. If the thermostat has proportional control between zero and full capacity, the space temperature rises in proportion to the load during cooling and falls similarly during heating. Capacity to heat or cool also varies with space temperature after the control device has reached its maximum because capacity is proportional to the difference between supply and space temperatures. Failure to properly model these phenomena may result in overestimating energy use.

4.6 INTEGRATION OF SYSTEM MODELS

Energy calculations for secondary systems involve construction of the complete system from the set of HVAC components. As an example, consider a process for simulating a variable-air-volume (VAV) system, a single-path system that controls zone temperature by modulating airflow while maintaining constant supply air temperature. VAV terminal units, located at each zone, adjust the quantity of air reaching each zone depending on its load requirements. Reheat coils may be included to provide required heating for perimeter zones or to prevent overcooling of lightly loaded zones.

This VAV system simulation consists of a central air-handling unit and a VAV terminal unit with reheat coil located at each zone, as shown in Figure 11.The central air-handling unit includes a fan, cooling coil, preheat coil, and outdoor air economizer. Supply air leaving the air-handling unit is controlled to a fixed set point. The VAV terminal unit at each zone varies airflow to meet the cooling load. As zone cooling load decreases, the VAV terminal unit decreases zone airflow until the unit reaches its minimum position. If the cooling load continues to decrease, the reheat coil is activated to meet the zone load. As supply air volume leaving the unit decreases, fan power consumption also reduces. A variable-speed drive is used to control the supply fan.

The simulation is based on system characteristics and zone design requirements. For each zone, the inputs include sensible and latent loads, zone set-point temperature, and minimum zone supply-air mass flow. System characteristics include supply air temperature set point; entering water temperature of reheat, preheat, and cooling coils; minimum mass flow of outdoor air; and economizer temperature/enthalpy set point for minimum airflow.

The algorithm for performing calculations for this VAV system is shown in Figure 12. The algorithm directs sequential calculations of system performance. Calculations proceed from the zones along the return air path to the cooling coil inlet and back through the supply air path to the cooling coil discharge. An alternative finite-state machine (FSM) approach is found in Chapter 42 of the 2015 *ASHRAE Handbook—HVAC Applications*.

Moving back along the supply air path, the fan entering air temperature is calculated by setting fan outlet air temperature to the

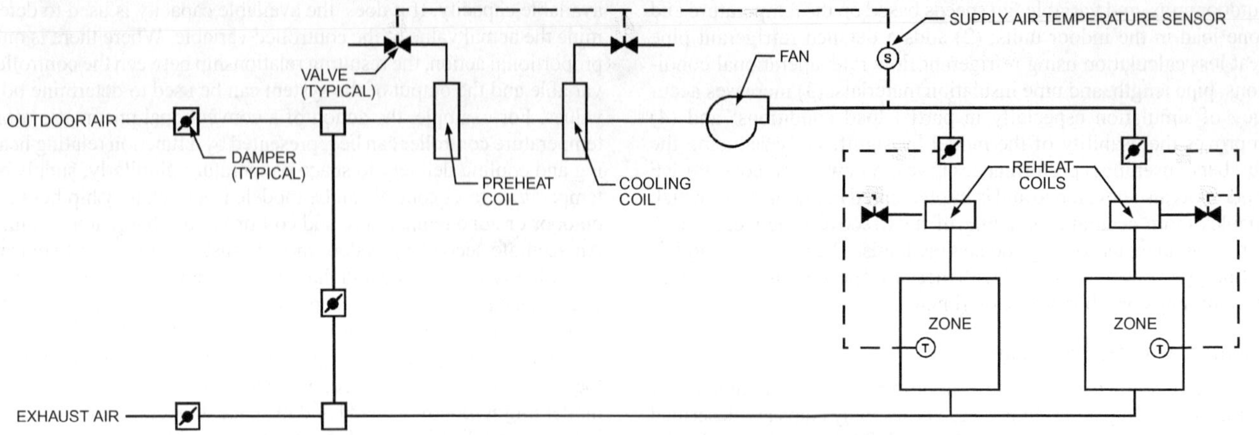

Fig. 11 Schematic of Variable-Air-Volume System with Reheat

BEGIN LOOP Calculate zone related design requirements
- Calculate required supply airflow to meet zone load
- Sum actual zone mass airflow rate
- Sum zone latent loads

IF zone equals last zone **THEN Exit Loop**
END LOOP
- Calculate system return air temperature from zone temps
- Assume an initial cooling coil leaving air humidity ratio

BEGIN LOOP Iterate on cooling coil leaving air humidity ratio
- Calculate return air humidity ratio from latent loads
- Calculate supply fan power consumption and entering fan air temperature
- Calculate mixed air temperature and humidity ratio using an economizer cycle

IF mixed air temperature is less than design supply air temperature **THEN**
- Calculate preheat coil load

ELSE
- Calculate cooling coil load and leaving air humidity ratio

ENDIF
IF cooling coil leaving air humidity ratio converged **THEN Exit Loop**
END LOOP
BEGIN LOOP Calculate the zone reheat coil loads
IF zone supply air temperature is greater than system design supply air temperature **THEN**
- Calculate reheat coil load (Subroutine: COILINV/HCDET)

ENDIF
- Sum reheat coil loads for all zones

IF zone equals last zone **THEN Exit Loop**
END LOOP

Fig. 12 Algorithm for Calculating Performance of VAV with System Reheat

system design supply air temperature. The known fan inlet air temperature is then used as both the cooling coil and preheat coil discharge air temperature set point. Moving along the return air path, the cooling coil entering air temperature can be determined by sequentially moving through the economizer cycle and preheat coil.

Unlike temperature, the humidity ratio at any point in a system cannot be explicitly determined because of the dependence of cooling coil performance on the mixed air humidity ratio. The latent load defines the difference between zone humidity and supply air humidity. However, the humidity ratio of supply air depends on the humidity ratio entering the coil, which in turn depends on that of the return air. This calculation must be performed either by solving simultaneous equations or, as in this case, iteration.

Assuming a trial value for the humidity ratio at the cooling coil discharge (e.g., 55°F, 90% rh), the humidity ratio at all other points throughout the system can be calculated. With known cooling coil inlet air conditions and a design discharge air temperature, the inverted cooling coil subroutine iterates on the coil fluid mass flow to converge on the discharge air temperature with the discharge air humidity ratio as an output. The cooling coil discharge air humidity ratio is then compared to the previous discharge humidity ratio. Iteration continues through the loop several times until the values of the cooling coil discharge air humidity ratio stabilize within a specified tolerance.

This basic algorithm for simulation of a VAV system might be used in conjunction with a heat balance type of load calculation. For a weighting factor approach, it would have to be modified to allow zone temperatures to vary and consequently zone loads to be readjusted. It should also be enhanced to allow possible limits on reheat temperature and/or cooling coil limits, zone humidity limits, outdoor air control (economizers), and/or heat-recovery devices, zone exhaust, return air fan, heat gain in the return air path because of lights, the presence of baseboard heaters, and more realistic control profiles. Most current building energy programs incorporate these and other features as user options, as well as algorithms for other types of systems.

5. LOW-ENERGY SYSTEM MODELING

5.1 NATURAL AND HYBRID VENTILATION

Natural ventilation refers to the introduction of outdoor air into a building via intentionally provided openings (e.g., windows and trickle ventilators) whereby airflow is driven by naturally occurring forces such as wind and buoyancy (stack effect) to provide fresh air and ventilation cooling (free cooling). The movement of air resulting from natural ventilation can also provide direct cooling [see Aynsley et al. (1977) and Olgyay (1973)]. Hybrid or mixed-mode ventilation refers to the use of mechanical means to supplement or enhance natural ventilation when the driving forces of wind and/or buoyancy are unable to meet the required ventilation rate or thermal comfort targets. Hybrid ventilation can be loosely divided into three categories:

fully parallel natural and mechanical ventilation, fan-assisted natural ventilation, and stack- and wind-assisted mechanical ventilation (Hybrid Ventilation Centre 2002). Regardless of which system is implemented, control of the system components and interaction between ventilation modes is critical to system effectiveness.

The design of natural ventilation systems requires careful consideration of the climate in which the building is located. Not only must prevailing outdoor temperatures, wind speed, and direction be accounted for to gage the forces available to drive natural ventilation, but outdoor temperature and humidity can affect the level of thermal comfort attainable within the building. However, even in climates where external air temperatures are relatively high, it may be possible to use natural ventilation to deliver acceptable thermal comfort. This can be done in combination with other passive design measures such as exposed thermal mass, solar shading, and nighttime ventilation cooling, or as part of a hybrid ventilation solution (Lomas et al. 2007). Also, environmental pollutants can affect the level of indoor air quality (IAQ) that is achievable without the benefit of filtering the outdoor air as it enters the building. Simulation of natural and hybrid ventilation systems should capture as many of these aspects as possible. At the very least, consideration should be given to modeling and predicting the likely performance of the ventilation strategy in terms of ventilation rates and indoor environmental quality, including thermal comfort of the building occupants. Chapters 13 and 16, respectively, discuss modeling and ventilation (including natural ventilation) in more detail, and CIBSE (2005) provides a guide to designing natural ventilation systems in nondomestic buildings.

Natural Ventilation

Tools for modeling natural ventilation systems fall into three main categories, discussed in the following sections. Although these modeling tools can be applied individually, simulation and design are better served by using the capabilities of multiple types of tools to provide a more comprehensive analysis.

Simplified Models. Simplified models can be used at the initial design stages for solving algebraic (nondifferential) equations to determine climate suitability, ventilation flow rates, and zone-average temperatures. This can be valuable information, especially at the concept design stage, when architects require approximate information about the feasibility of implementing natural ventilation and determining size and position of ventilation openings. The equations typically used in these models can be found in Chapter 16 and in CIBSE (2005). However, there are many other examples of simplified techniques used to predict the behavior of specific aspects of natural ventilation. For example, Linden et al. (1990) developed analytical models for predicting interface heights in stratified regimes, and Chenvidyakarn and Woods (2005) used analytical methods to predict solution multiplicity in large-volume spaces.

Climate-suitability analysis methods and tools are available for the predesign phase. These relatively simple models provide a first-order estimate of the potential effectiveness of natural ventilation to provide direct ventilation cooling, nighttime cooling, and thermal comfort, based on climate data representative of the building location. Axley and Emmerich (2002) present a climate suitability design method based on a single-zone, steady-state energy balance, and thermal comfort criteria. Lomas et al. (2007) present an analysis of ambient temperature and moisture content with respect to thermal comfort criteria plotted on a psychrometric chart.

One common form of analytical model involves first solving equations to determine the driving pressures caused by wind and buoyancy forces. These driving pressures are calculated with reference to the neutral pressure level (CIBSE 2005) and are used at proposed opening locations as input to mathematical representations of the airflow through the openings (e.g., the orifice flow equation). Given the design airflow rate, these equations can then be used to calculate effective opening areas. Axley (2001) presents an opening sizing method that was subsequently formulated as a software tool (Emmerich et al. 2011; Dols et al. 2012). These methods and tools can also account for multiple openings and user-specified airflow patterns through a building (e.g., into the building via a trickle ventilator, through an air transfer grill, then out through a stack). As outlined in CIBSE (2005), driving pressures should be calculated for representative design scenarios when wind speeds and internal/external temperature differences are relatively low, because these will determine the maximum opening sizes required. Illustrations of how some of these simplified models can be used are given in Axley (2001), CIBSE (2005), and Emmerich et al. (2012).

Network Airflow Models. Network airflow models, also referred to as multizone models, are discussed in Chapter 13. They are more complex than the simplified models, because they solve the simultaneous (interdependent) airflows and pressure differences between multiple, interconnected building zones and the outdoors and are typically applied to the building in its entirety. In particular, using airflow network characteristics (e.g., airflow resistances) and climate data (along with assumed temperatures within the building), network airflow models calculate combined buoyancy- and wind-driven pressures and the rate and direction of airflows for all openings in the model. Some models can also be used to perform interzone contaminant mass transport calculations that can be useful in analyzing IAQ (Axley 2007) and simulating contaminant-based ventilation rate control schemes (e.g., CO_2-based demand controlled ventilation) (Dols et al. 2016a). Network airflow models can be coupled with dynamic thermal simulation programs to calculate the internal zone temperatures used in the network airflow model (Clarke 2001; Dols et al. 2016a, 2016b; U.S. Department of Energy 1996-2016).

A distinct challenge in the use of network airflow models is selecting mathematical representations and parameters that best capture the airflow characteristics of the ventilation components. For example, airflow resistances can be described using a discharge coefficient (or pressure loss factor) and the effective opening area. However, specifying the component characteristics requires a clear understanding of how the model interprets these values. Details of the terminology used can be found in Jones et al. (2016).

Computational Fluid Dynamics. Computational fluid dynamics (CFD) is also discussed in Chapter 13. CFD models represent the most complex class of airflow models and can be valuable for simulating natural ventilation, including the effects of wind on the building envelope pressures and internal airflow patterns that develop as a result of various boundary conditions and representative portions of the building interior. CFD is not typically applicable to simulating entire buildings over long-term, transient time frames. However, there are many strategies available for using CFD in the design and analysis of natural ventilation systems; for example, Malkawi et al. (2016) describes using both CFD and a combined network airflow and energy calculation method.

The main feature that sets CFD models apart from numerical and network airflow models is the use of a fine mesh comprising many thousands of cells throughout the computational domain. For each cell, nonlinear partial differential equations are solved to predict the air speed, air temperature, turbulence, and pressure in each cell. This provides a very detailed representation of the spatial distribution of the airflow and has the advantage of highlighting drafts, warm zones, and thermal stratification. Boundary conditions are required in CFD models to drive the flow. They include temperature or heat flux values at solid surfaces and conditions of air speed and turbulence at openings. Surface temperatures are often obtained from the results of a dynamic thermal network simulation model. This approach has the advantage of including the effects of radiation without solving a separate radiation model in the CFD simulation. Boundary conditions at natural ventilation openings must be specified with care, because neither the flow rate nor the internal temperature are known a priori. This can be overcome by using the orifice flow equation, which simply provides a relationship between the flow rate and pressure difference across openings [e.g., Durrani et al. (2015)]. Another important challenge to be aware of when using CFD is the need for an iterative approach to solve the governing, nonlinear equations. It is therefore important to appreciate that simulation run times can be long (i.e., several hours), and that techniques for controlling convergence are often needed, especially in buoyancy-driven natural ventilation flows where driving pressures are small. Often, this control can be achieved by using a transient simulation or false time-stepping [e.g., Kaye et al. (2009)].

Hybrid Ventilation

When design tools have predicted that natural ventilation is unlikely to be sufficient for providing adequate IAQ and thermal comfort and a hybrid strategy has been proposed, it is useful to carry out some modeling of the system to provide confidence and identify likely energy implications. This can be done by enhancing the techniques described previously for modeling natural ventilation with network airflow and CFD models.

Ventilation and energy performance of buildings with natural or mixed-mode ventilation systems can be simulated using whole-building network airflow models, including those that may be combined with or directly incorporate a whole-building thermal analysis model (e.g., EnergyPlus) (Dols et al. 2015, 2016b). The energy module sends information about the building, ambient weather conditions, and zone temperatures to the network airflow module. This information is used to calculate infiltration, ventilation, and interzone airflow by the airflow network module; the results will be sent back to the energy module and used in the next time step's heat balance. In addition to the airflow characteristics through openings such as windows and transfers grilles connecting spaces, models of hybrid systems must also include fan airflow models (e.g., design flow rates and fan performance curves).

One of the primary challenges in modeling hybrid ventilation systems is simulating the controls systems that are inherently associated with these systems. Hybrid ventilation schemes may require multiple modes of operation depending on variations in climate, including seasonal, daily, and short-term local variations. These modes of operation can vary in complexity because of the number and type of system components involved. In buildings with automatically controlled ventilation openings or fans, the control system may require parameters such as wind speed and direction, among others, to open, close, or adjust openings; turn fans on/off; or adjust flow rates. This range of flexibility varies among available models. However, it is likely that users will need to input sensors, actuators, and control logic per the input methods of the tool being used, and the model should predict system performance accordingly (e.g., variations in fan airflow, ventilation opening status). Some modeling tools or combinations of tools enable transient simulations to be performed with user-defined control algorithms (e.g., DOE 2015; Dols et al. 2016a; Wetter 2011), and these may be used for performing annual simulations or at least over periods of time that address the various modes of operation.

5.2 DAYLIGHTING

Daylighting in buildings is used to reduce the use of electric lighting systems. A proper daylighting design provides improved illumination for occupants and reduces a building's energy use. A building's orientation, window size and properties, and shading (e.g., overhangs and fins) affect daylight illuminance at specific points in a space. Whole-building energy simulation programs, such as EnergyPlus and DOE-2.2/eQUEST, can keep track of how much supplemental electric lighting is reduced when daylighting is used. In addition, energy simulation programs calculate the thermal heat loss and gain associated with the fenestration for daylighting. Electric lighting level is determined by fraction of lighting area, lighting type, daylight illuminance level, and targeted illuminance. Additional details regarding daylighting and electric lighting control strategies are described in Chapter 15.

Historically, daylighting analysis programs have used three components to calculate the amount of daylight coming through a window or skylight: **sky component (SC)**, **external reflected component (ERC)**, and **internal reflected component (IRC)**.

Commonly used methods for estimating the IRC include the split-flux, radiosity, and ray-tracing methods. In the 1950s, the **split-flux method** was used to estimate the IRC using empirical formulas (Hopkinson et al. 1954). In this method, Hopkinson et al. assumed the interior surfaces of a room were a connected spherical shape and were perfectly diffused with no inner obstacles, which worked best in a room shaped as a cube without internal partitions (Winkelmann and Selkowitz 1985). Tregenza (1989) presented a modification to the split-flux method to account for large external obstacles such as overhangs. Figure 13 shows the concept of the split-flux method [f_s = window factor for the light incident on the window from sky, R_{fw} = average reflectance of the floor and those parts of the walls below the plane of the mid-height of the window (excluding the window-wall), f_g = window factor for the light incident on the window from ground, and R_{cw} = average reflectance of the ceiling and those parts of the walls above the plane of the mid-height of the window (excluding the window-wall)] (Oh and Haberl 2016c). The split-flux method is widely used in whole-building energy simulation programs such as DOE-2.1E (Winkelmann et al. 1993), DOE-2.2/eQUEST (LBNL 1998), and EnergyPlus (U.S Department of Energy 1996-2016).

The **radiosity method** more accurately analyzes various geometries and reflectances than the split-flux method but less accurately than the ray-tracing method. The radiosity method provides an accurate method to analyze a zone where object-to-object reflection exists between diffuse surfaces in a zone. This procedure uses the energy balance concept for analyzing radiative heat transfer (i.e., radiant-flux transfer), which has been widely used by thermal engineers (Goral et al. 1984; O'Brien 1955). The radiant-flux transfer analysis between surfaces applies the light-flux transfer analysis in an enclosure using a lumped parameter network (O'Brien 1955; Oppenheim 1954). The radiosity method uses the electrical network approach to account for the initial and interreflected luminous emittances (i.e., the light-flux transfer). The surface reflectances (i.e.,

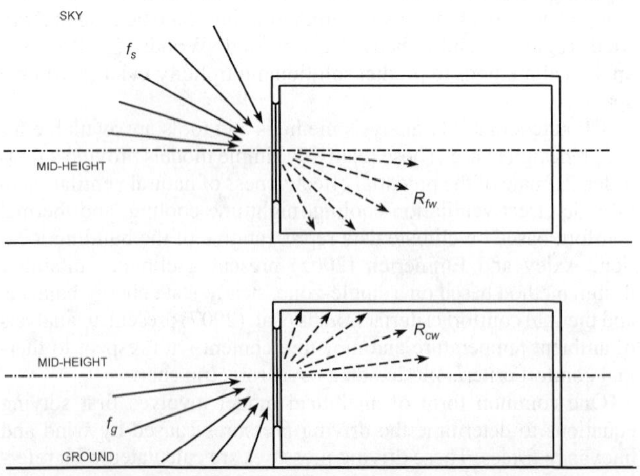

Fig. 13 Split-Flux Method
(Oh and Haberl 2016c)

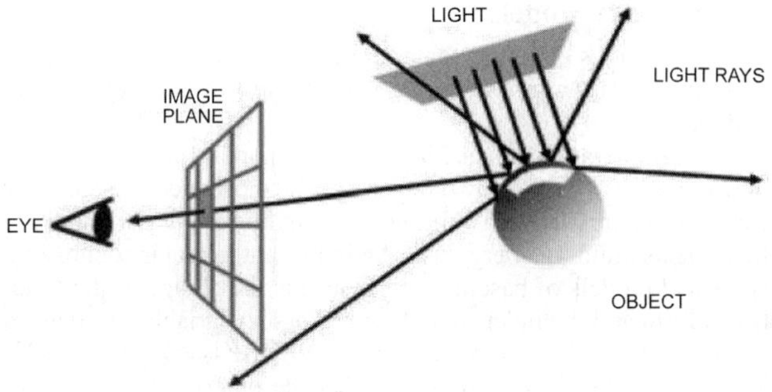

Fig. 14 Forward Ray-Tracing Method
(Oh and Haberl 2016c)

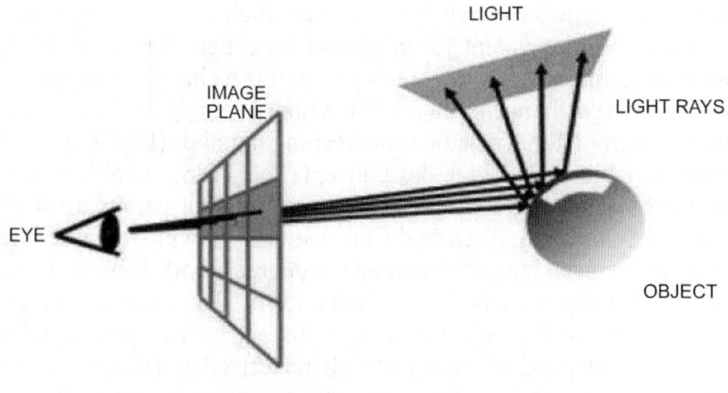

Fig. 15 Backward Ray-Tracing Method
(Oh and Haberl 2016c)

the radiant properties) and the view factors (i.e., the relative geometry properties) of the luminous emittances are defined as the resistances in the network (O'Brien 1955). The method is used in Lumen Micro and in one of the daylighting models of EnergyPlus v.1.x and higher.

Finally, **ray tracing** is the most advanced and accurate method for analyzing the interreflections between both diffuse and specular surfaces in complex enclosures (Baker et al. 1993; Ward and Rubinstein 1988; Ward et al. 1988). The method follows the light rays in an enclosure and takes into account all the characteristics of various surface geometries and surface reflectances. The method was originally developed to create high-quality computer graphics in complex scenes (Baker et al. 1993). Ray tracing is typically used to analyze daylight illuminance itself, instead of being combined with whole-building energy simulation programs to account for electric lighting. The ray-tracing method is used in Radiance (Ward 1994) and DIVA (Jakubiec and Reinhart 2011). Additional details can be found in Oh and Haberl (2016c). The forward ray-tracing method traces the rays of light generated from a source of light to the eye of the viewer (Kuchkuda 1988). Figure 14 shows the concept of the forward ray-tracing method (Grantham 2008; Oh and Haberl 2016c). The backward ray-tracing method traces a ray of each point (i.e., each pixel) backwards from the viewer through the image plane to the object (Arvo 1986; Kuchkuda 1988; Ward and Rubinstein 1988; Ward et al. 1988). Figure 15 shows this concept (Grantham 2008; Oh and Haberl 2016c).

5.3 PASSIVE HEATING

Passive buildings use solar heating directly (i.e., without pumps, blowers, etc.) and sometimes include natural passive cooling. Solar direct gain, sunspaces, Trombe walls, and passive downdraft cool towers are examples of passive solar strategies. Detailed simulation programs such as TRNSYS (Duffie and Beckman 2013) and SUNREL (Deru et al. 2002) can be used to analyze passive solar energy applications and building loads. TRNSYS and SUNREL use a thermal network approach (Paschkis 1942) to analyze the time-varying solar radiation and heat transfer in a building. In addition, simplified methods such as the solar load ratio (SLR) method (Balcomb and Hedstrom 1976) and the unutilizability method (Monsen and Klein 1980; Monsen et al. 1981) can be used to analyze passive solar systems. Computer simulations can be used to calculate the time-dependent, short-term, and long-term performance of solar energy systems in detail. Simplified methods that require fewer calculations than hourly solar simulations (Klein 1993) can be used to estimate the long-term performance of solar energy systems. Passive solar design analysis is useful for engineers to select and size solar systems when input data and on-site solar irradiation data may not be available (Evans et al. 1982). Additional details can be found in Oh and Haberl (2016b).

6. DATA-DRIVEN MODELING

The objective of data-driven (inverse) modeling is to determine a mathematical description of the system and to estimate system parameters when the input and output variables are known and measured. The data-driven approach is relevant only when the system has already been built and actual performance data are available for model development, calibration, and/or identification.

There are several important uses of data-driven models. They can be used to verify savings for implemented energy conservation measures, where the data-driven model provides an estimate of baseline energy consumption for comparison to post-retrofit energy consumption. Data-driven models can be used with energy management and control systems to predict energy use (Kreider and Haberl 1994). Hourly or daily comparisons of measured versus predicted energy use can be used to determine whether systems are being left on unnecessarily or are in need of maintenance. Combinations of predicted energy use and a knowledge-based system can indicate above-normal energy use and diagnose the possible cause of the malfunction if sufficient historical information has been previously gathered (Haberl and Claridge 1987). Hourly systems that use artificial neural networks have also been constructed (Kreider and Wang 1991).

6.1 CATEGORIES OF DATA-DRIVEN METHODS

Data-driven methods for energy-use estimation in buildings and related HVAC&R equipment can be classified into two broad categories. These approaches differ widely in data requirements, time and effort needed to develop the associated models, user skill requirements, and sophistication and reliability provided.

Empirical or "Black-Box" Approach

With an empirical approach, a simple or multivariate regression model is identified between measured energy use and the various influential parameters (e.g., climatic variables, building occupancy). The form of the regression models can be either purely statistical or loosely based on some basic engineering formulation of energy use in the building. In any case, the identified model coefficients are such that no (or very little) physical meaning can be assigned to them. This approach can be used with any time scale (monthly, daily, hourly or subhourly) if appropriate data are available. Single-variate, multivariate, change point, Fourier series, and artificial neural network (ANN) models fall under this category. Least-squares regression is the most common approach to model identification, although more sophisticated regression techniques such as maximum likelihood and two-stage regression schemes can also be used.

Statistical regression models are usually adequate for estimating savings in demand-side management (DSM) programs for conventional energy conservation measures (lighting retrofits, air handler retrofits such as CV to VAV retrofits) and for baseline model development in energy conservation measurement and verification (M&V) projects (Claridge 1998; Dhar 1995; Dhar et al. 1998, 1999a, 1999b; Fels 1986; Haberl and Culp 2012; Haberl et al. 1998; Katipamula et al. 1998; Kissock et al. 1998; Krarti et al. 1998; Kreider and Wang 1991; MacDonald and Wasserman 1989; Miller and Seem 1991; Reddy et al. 1997; Ruch and Claridge 1991).

Statistical models may also be appropriate for modeling equipment such as pumps and fans, and even more elaborate equipment such as chillers and boilers, if the necessary performance data are available (Braun 1992; Chen et al. 2005; Englander and Norford 1992; Lorenzetti and Norford 1993; Phelan et al. 1996). Although this approach allows detection or flagging of equipment or system faults, it is usually of limited value for diagnosis and online control.

Gray-Box Approach

The gray-box approach first formulates a physical model to represent the structure or physical configuration of the building or HVAC&R equipment or system, and then identifies important parameters representative of certain key and aggregated physical parameters and characteristics by statistical analysis (Rabl and Riahle 1992). This approach requires a high level of user expertise both in setting up the appropriate modeling equations and in estimating these parameters. Often an intrusive experimental protocol is necessary for proper parameter estimation. This approach has great potential, especially for fault detection and diagnosis (FDD) and online control, but its applicability to whole-building energy use is limited. Examples of parameter estimation studies applied to building energy use are Andersen and Brandemuehl (1992), Braun (1990), Gordon and Ng (1995), Guyon and Palomo (1999a), Hammarsten (1984), Rabl (1988), Reddy (1989), Reddy et al. (1999), Sonderegger (1977), and Subbarao (1988).

6.2 TYPES OF DATA-DRIVEN MODELS

Steady-state models do not consider effects such as thermal mass or capacitance that cause short-term temperature transients. Generally, these models are appropriate for monthly, weekly, or daily data and are often used for baseline model development. **Dynamic models** capture effects such as building warm-up or cooldown periods and peak loads, and are appropriate for building load control, FDD, and equipment control. A simple criterion to determine whether a model is steady-state or dynamic is to look for the presence of time-lagged variables, either in the response or regressor variables. Steady-state models do not contain time-lagged variables.

Steady-State Models

Several types of steady-state models are used for both building and equipment energy use: single-variate, multivariate, polynomial, and physical.

Single-Variate Models. Single-variate models (i.e., models with one regressor variable only) are perhaps the most widely used. They formulate energy use in a building as a function of one driving force that affects building energy use. An important aspect in identifying statistical models of baseline energy use is the choice of the functional form and the independent (or regressor) variables. Extensive studies (Fels 1986; Katipamula et al. 1994; Kissock et al. 1993; Reddy et al. 1997) have indicated that the outdoor dry-bulb temperature is the most important regressor variable for typical buildings, especially at monthly time scales but also at daily time scales.

The simplest steady-state data-driven model is one developed by regressing monthly utility consumption data against average billing-period temperatures. The model must identify the balance-point temperatures (or change points) at which energy use switches from weather-dependent to weather-independent behavior. In its simplest form, the 65°F degree-day model is a change-point model that has a fixed change point at 65°F. Other examples include three- and five-parameter Princeton scorekeeping methods (PRISM) based on the variable-base degree-day concept (Fels 1986). An allied modeling approach for commercial buildings is the four-parameter (4-P) model developed by Ruch and Claridge (1991), which is based on the monthly mean temperature (and not degree-days). Table 4 shows some commonly used model functional forms. The three parameters are a weather-independent base-level use, a change point, and a temperature-dependent energy use, characterized as a slope of a line that is determined by regression. The four parameters include a change point, a slope above the change point, a slope below the change point, and the energy use associated with the change point. A data-driven bin method has also been proposed to handle more than four change points (Thamilseran and Haberl 1995).

Figure 16 shows several types of steady-state, single-variate data-driven models. Figure 16A shows a simple one-parameter, or constant, model, and Table 4 gives the equivalent notation for calculating the constant energy use using this model. Figure 16B shows a steady-state two-parameter (2-P) model where b_0 is the y-axis intercept and b_1 is the slope of the regression line for positive values of x, where x represents the ambient air temperature. The 2-P model represents cases when either heating or cooling is always required.

Figure 16C shows a three-parameter change-point model, typical of natural gas energy use in a single-family residence that uses gas for space heating and domestic water heating. In the notation of Table 4 for the three-parameter model, b_0 represents the baseline energy use and b_1 is the slope of the regression line for values of ambient temperature less than the change point b_2. In this type of notation, the superscripted plus sign indicates that only positive values of the parenthetical expression are considered. Figure 16D

Table 4 Single-Variate Models Applied to Utility Billing Data

Model Type	Independent Variable(s)	Form	Examples
One-parameter or constant (1-P)	None	$E = b_0$	Non-weather-sensitive demand
Two-parameter (2-P)	Temperature	$E = b_0 + b_1(T)$	
Three-parameter (3-P)	Degree-days/ Temperature	$E = b_0 + b_1(DD_{BT})$ $E = b_0 + b_1(b_2 - T)^+$ $E = b_0 + b_1(T - b_2)^+$	Seasonal weather-sensitive use (fuel in winter, electricity in summer for cooling)
Four-parameter change point (4-P)	Temperature	$E = b_0 + b_1(b_3 - T)^+ - b_2(T - b_3)^+$ $E = b_0 - b_1(b_3 - T)^+ + b_2(T - b_3)^+$	Energy use in commercial buildings
Five-parameter (5-P)	Degree-days/ Monthly mean temperature	$E = b_0 - b_1(DD_{TH}) + b_2(DD_{TC})$ $E = b_0 + b_1(b_3 - T)^+ + b_2(T - b_4)^+$	Heating and cooling supplied by same meter

Note: DD denotes degree-days and T is monthly mean daily outdoor dry-bulb temperature.

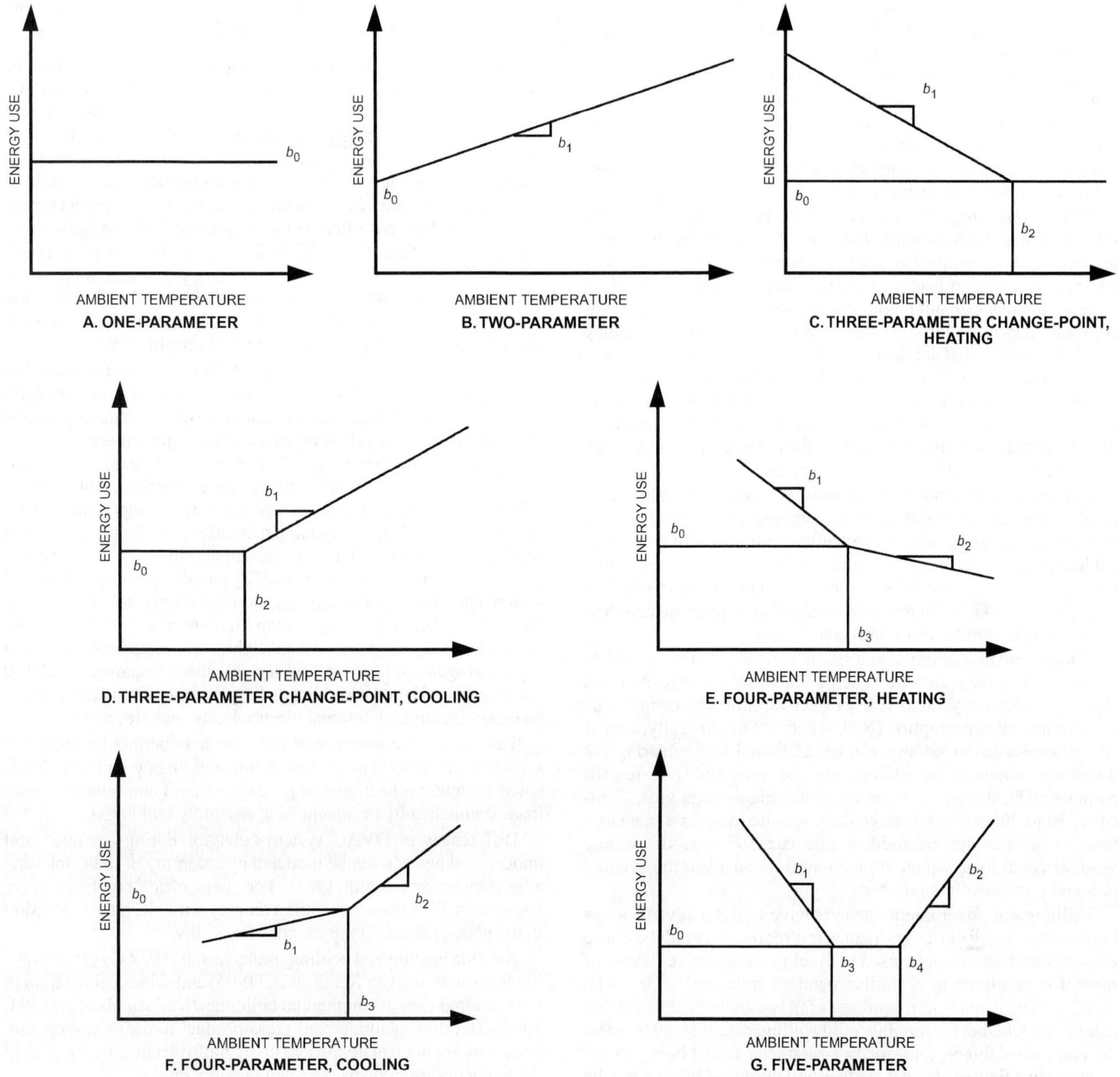

Fig. 16 Steady-State, Single-Variate Models for Modeling Energy Use in Residential and Commercial Buildings

shows a three-parameter model for cooling energy use, and Table 4 provides the appropriate analytic expression.

Figures 16E and 16F show four-parameter models for heating and cooling, respectively. The appropriate expressions for calculating the heating and cooling energy consumption are found in Table 4: b_0 represents the baseline energy exactly at the change point b_3, and b_1 and b_2 are the lower and upper region regression slopes for ambient air temperature below and above the change point b_3. Figure 16G shows a 5-P model (Fels 1986), which is useful for modeling buildings that are electrically heated and cooled. The 5-P model has two change points and a base level consumption value.

The advantage of these steady-state data-driven models is that their use can be easily automated and applied to large numbers of buildings where monthly utility billing data and average daily temperatures for the billing period are available. Steady-state single-variate data-driven models have also been applied with success to daily data (Kissock et al. 1998). In such a case, the variable-base degree-day method and monthly mean temperature models described previously for utility billing data analysis become identical in their functional form. Single-variate models can also be applied to daily data to compensate for differences such as weekday and weekend use by separating the data accordingly and identifying models for each period separately.

Disadvantages of steady-state single-variate data-driven models include insensitivity to dynamic effects (e.g., thermal mass) and to variables other than temperature (e.g., humidity and solar gain), and inappropriateness for some buildings (e.g., buildings with strong on/off schedule-dependent loads or buildings with multiple change points). Moreover, a single-variable, 3-P model such as the PRISM model (Fels 1986) has a physical basis only when energy use above a base level is linearly proportional to degree-days. This is a good approximation in the case of heating energy use in residential buildings where heating load never exceeds the heating system's capacity. However, commercial buildings generally have higher internal heat generation with simultaneous heating and cooling energy use and are strongly influenced by HVAC system type and control strategy. This makes energy use in commercial buildings less strongly influenced by outdoor air temperature alone. Therefore, it is not surprising that blind use of single-variate models has had mixed success at modeling energy use in commercial buildings (MacDonald and Wasserman 1989).

Change-point regression models work best with heating data from buildings with systems that have few or no part-load nonlinearities (i.e., systems that become less efficient as they begin to cycle on/off with part loads). In general, single-variate change-point regression models do not predict cooling loads as well because outdoor humidity has a large influence on latent loads on the cooling coil. Other factors that decrease the accuracy of change-point models include solar effects, thermal lags, and on/off HVAC schedules. A change point model based on a linear combination of temperature and specific humidity, and in which direct and diffuse irradiance were included as separate explanatory variables, was found to work well for aggregates of buildings (Ali et al. 2011).

Four-parameter models are a better statistical fit than three-parameter models in buildings with continuous, year-round cooling or heating (e.g., grocery stores and office buildings with high internal loads). However, every model should be checked to ensure that the regression does not falsely indicate an unreasonable relationship. Paulus et al. (2015) provided an algorithm aiding in the selection of change-point linear regression models.

A major advantage of using a steady-state data-driven model to evaluate the effectiveness of energy conservation retrofits is its ability to factor out year-to-year weather variations by using a normalized annual consumption (NAC) (Fels 1986). Basically, annual energy conservation savings can be calculated by comparing the difference obtained by multiplying the pre- and post-retrofit parameters by the weather conditions for the average year. Typically, 10 to 20 years of average daily weather data from a nearby weather service site are used to calculate 365 days of average weather conditions, which are then used to calculate the average pre- and post-retrofit conditions.

Utilities and government agencies have found it advantageous to prescreen many buildings against test regression models. These data-driven models can be used to develop comparative figures of merit for buildings in a similar standard industrial code (SIC) classification. A minimum goodness of fit is usually established that determines whether the monthly utility billing data are well fitted by the one-, two-, three-, four-, or five-parameter model being tested. Comparative figures of merit can then be determined by dividing the parameters by the conditioned floor area to yield average daily energy use per unit area of conditioned space. For example, an area-normalized comparison of base-level parameters across residential buildings would be used to analyze weather-independent energy use. This information can be used by energy auditors to focus their efforts on those systems needing assistance (Haberl and Komor 1990a, 1990b).

Multivariate Models. Three types of steady-state, multivariate models have been reported:

- **Standard multiple-linear** or **change-point regression models**, where the set of data observations is treated without retaining the time-series nature of the data (Katipamula et al. 1998).
- **Fourier series models** that retain the time-series nature of building energy use data and capture the diurnal and seasonal cycles according to which buildings are operated (Dhar 1995; Dhar et al. 1998, 1999a, 1999b; Seem and Braun 1991).
- **Gaussian process (GP) models** use a nonparametric, nonlinear regression method that produces estimates of the prediction uncertainty along with predictions of energy use (Burkhart et al. 2014; Heo and Zavala 2012; Heo et al. 2013).

These models are a logical extension of single-variate models, provided that the choice of variables to be included and their functional forms are based on the engineering principles under which HVAC and other building systems operate. The goal of modeling energy use by the multivariate approach is to characterize building energy use with a few readily available and reliable input variables. These input variables should be selected with care. The model should contain variables not affected by the retrofit and thus unlikely to change (e.g., climatic variables) from pre-retrofit to post-retrofit periods. Other less obvious variables, such as changes in operating hours, base load, and occupancy levels, should be included in the model if these are not energy conservation measures (ECMs) but variables that may change during the post-retrofit period.

Environmental variables that meet these criteria for modeling heating and cooling energy use include outdoor air dry-bulb temperature, solar radiation, and outdoor specific humidity. Some of these variables are difficult to estimate or measure in an actual building and hence are not good candidates for regressor variables. Further, some of the variables change little over time. Although the effect of these variables on energy use may be important, a data-driven model will implicitly lump their effect into the parameter that represents constant load. In commercial buildings, internally generated loads, such as the heat given off by people, lights, and electrical equipment, also affect heating and cooling energy use. These internal loads are difficult to measure in their entirety. However, monitored electricity used by internal lights and equipment may be a good surrogate for total internal sensible loads (Reddy et al. 1999). For example, when the building is fully occupied, it is also likely to be experiencing high internal electric loads, and vice versa.

The effect of environmental variables is important for buildings such as offices but may be less so for buildings with loads dominated by internal heat gain (e.g., data centers) and buildings with loads dominated by occupants (e.g. assembly buildings).

Differences in HVAC system behavior during occupied and unoccupied periods can be modeled by a dummy or indicator variable (Draper and Smith 1981). For some office buildings, there seems to be little need to include a dummy variable, but its inclusion in the general functional form adds flexibility.

Air-side heating and cooling use in various HVAC system types has been addressed by Reddy et al. (1995) and subsequently applied to monitored data in commercial buildings (Katipamula et al. 1994, 1998). Because quadratic and cross-product terms of engineering equations are not usually picked up by multivariate models, strictly linear energy use models are often the only option.

In addition to outdoor temperature T_o, internal electric equipment and lighting load E_{int}, solar loads q_{sol}, and latent effects via the outdoor dew-point temperature T_{dp} are candidate regressor variables. In commercial buildings, a major portion of the latent load derives from fresh air ventilation. However, this load appears only when the outdoor air dew-point temperature exceeds the cooling coil temperature. Hence, the term $(T_{dp} - T_s)^+$ (where the + sign indicates that the term is to be set to zero if negative, and T_s is the mean surface temperature of the cooling coil, typically about 51 to 55°F) is a more realistic descriptor of the latent loads than is T_{dp} alone. Using $(T_{dp} - T_s)^+$ as a regressor in the model is a simplification that seems to yield good accuracy.

Therefore, a multivariate linear regression model with an engineering basis has the following structure:

$$Q_{bldg} = b_0 + b_1(T_o - b_3)^- + b_2(T_o - b_3)^+ + b_4(T_{dp} - b_6)^- + b_5(T_{dp} - b_6)^+ + b_7 q_{sol} + b_8 E_{int} \quad (19)$$

Based on the preceding discussion, $b_4 = 0$ because outdoor air does not introduce a latent cooling load when T_{dp} is less than the cooling coil surface temperature. Introducing indicator variable terminology (Draper and Smith 1981), Equation (19) becomes

$$Q_{bldg} = a + bT_o + cI + dIT_o + eT_{dp}^+ + fq_{sol} + gE_{int} \tag{20}$$

where the indicator variable I is introduced to handle the change in slope of the energy use due to T_o. The variable I is set equal to 1 for T_o values to the right of the change point (i.e., for high T_o range) and set equal to 0 for low T_o values. As with the single-variate segmented models (i.e., 3-P and 4-P models), a search method is used to determine the change point that minimizes the total sum of squares of residuals (Fels 1986; Kissock et al. 1993).

Katipamula et al. (1994) found that Equation (20), appropriate for VAV systems, could be simplified for constant-volume HVAC systems:

$$Q_{bldg} = a + bT_o + eT_{dp}^+ + fq_{sol} + gE_{int} \tag{21}$$

Note that instead of using $(T_{dp} - T_s)^+$, the absolute humidity potential $(W_0 - W_s)^+$ could also be used, where W_0 is the outdoor absolute humidity, and W_s is the absolute humidity level at the dew point of the cooling coil (typically about 0.009 lb/lb). A final aspect to keep in mind is that the term T_{dp}^+ should be omitted from the regressor variable set when regressing heating energy use, because there are no latent loads on a heating coil.

These multivariate models are very accurate for daily time scales and slightly less so for hourly time scales. The inaccuracy at hourly time scales is because changes in the way the building is operated during the day and the night lead to different relative effects of the various regressors on energy use, which cannot be accurately modeled by one single hourly model. Breaking up energy use data into hourly bins corresponding to each hour of the day and then identifying 24 individual hourly models leads to appreciably greater accuracy (Katipamula et al. 1994).

Another accurate method uses a piecewise linear regression with respect to temperature and a time-of-week indicator variable to account for changes in energy use throughout each day of the week. This model (Matthieu 2011) may be applied to daily, hourly, or sub-hourly data.

Gaussian process (GP) models are nonparametric regression models, meaning the relationship between input and output variables is not strictly defined at the outset of the regression. In GP modeling, the measured output data are samples of a multivariate Gaussian distribution with the distribution parameters being the input variables. The distribution is defined by matching the covariance of the distribution to the covariance between the measured input and output data. For any new set of input variables, a Gaussian distribution is defined and the mean of the distribution is interpreted to be the predicted output and the variance of the distribution the uncertainty in the prediction. Thus, GP modeling not only produces an output value given a set of multivariate inputs, it also produces an estimate of the uncertainty of the prediction. Heo and Zavala (2012) used GP models to predict the hourly energy use of a chilled-water system using ambient temperature, occupancy, relative humidity, and chiller supply temperature and showed much better performance than standard multivariate regression models.

Hybrid Inverse Change Point Model. ASHRAE RP-1404 (Abushakra et al. 2014) was conducted primarily to develop analysis methodologies by which less than a whole year of field monitoring can be used for whole-building energy use prediction while satisfying current accuracy guidelines. The methodologies were developed to benefit ongoing efforts to spur diffusion of high-performance buildings by actual monitoring and to benefit energy service companies (ESCOs) and energy professionals who need a more cost-effective and acceptable alternative to year-long energy monitoring. Applications for the hybrid inverse change point model include detailed audits, green-building performance verification, and verification of post-retrofit claims using pre/post monitored data.

The modeling method is called *hybrid* because two regressions are performed at different time scales. The weather-dependent portion uses a year of monthly day-normalized utility bills, and the weather-independent portion uses either daily or hourly data covering a shorter time span, possibly as short as two weeks. The research revealed that (1) two weeks of hourly monitored data can be adequate for producing accurate long-term whole-building energy predictions, if the monitoring is taken at a correct time, and (2) adding more data to the regression model (extending the length of the short-term monitoring period) can, counterintuitively, make the predictive model poorer.

The analysis was completed in detail at two different time scales: daily and hourly. The analysis with both hourly and daily data revealed that the proper monitoring period is highly dependent on the time at which the data are taken, with the best time to collect data being during the spring and fall, or periods where the average temperature is close to the annual average temperature and the temperature has a wide range.

The following is an example of the modeling procedure that results in an hourly energy regression model. An example of the method applied to daily data can be found in Singh et al. (2013). The first regression uses one of the steady-state change point models shown in Figure 16 and Table 4, possibly with an additional weather-related independent variable, such as humidity. For example, the form could be a 3-P cooling shape (using the nomenclature of Table 4) such as

$$E_{daily} = b_0 + b_1(T_{daily\ average} - b_2)^+ \tag{22}$$

where E_{daily} is day-normalized energy consumption in units of energy consumption per day.

For predicting cooling thermal loads, such as chilled-water use, investigate adding the outdoor humidity variable as a regressor in the model to account for latent loads. Equation (22) would become a multivariable linear regression of the form

$$E_{daily} = b_0 + b_1(T_{daily\ average} - b_2)^+ + b_3(\omega_{daily\ average} - 0.009)^+ \tag{23}$$

The $(\omega_{daily\ average} - 0.009)^+$ term in Equation (23) is a surrogate for the latent load existing only when the absolute humidity ratio of air entering the cooling coil is above 0.009.

The dependent variable for the second regression is the residuals resulting from using the first equation to predict the temperature dependent energy portion at the hourly time scale, calculated by dividing the temperature dependent portion of the first regression by 24 hours/day. The second regression uses gathered hourly data consisting of weather and an internal driving variable(s), such as $X_{internal,hourly}$, often an occupancy indicator or submetered lighting and equipment load. The second regression is then performed to calculate the coefficients for the internal driving variables and constant term. Using Equation (22), the second regression has the form

$$E_{hourly} - \frac{b_1}{24}(T_{hourly} - b_2)^+ = b_3 + b_4(X_{internal,\ hourly}) \tag{24}$$

The final equation for prediction at the hourly time scale is a rearrangement of Equation (24).

$$E_{hourly} = b_3 + \frac{b_1}{24}(T_{hourly} - b_2)^+ + b_4(X_{internal,\ hourly}) \tag{25}$$

Polynomial Models. Historically, polynomial models have been widely used as pure statistical models to model the behavior of equipment such as pumps, fans, and chillers (Stoecker and Jones 1982), as discussed in the section on HVAC Component Modeling. The theoretical aspects of calculating pump performance are well understood and documented. Pump capacity and efficiency are calculated from measurements of pump head, flow rate, and pump electrical power input. Phelan et al. (1996) studied the predictive ability of linear and quadratic models for electricity consumed by pumps and water mass flow rate, and concluded that quadratic models are superior to linear models. For fans, Phelan et al. (1996) studied the predictive ability of linear and quadratic polynomial single-variate models of fan electricity consumption as a function of supply air mass flow rate, and concluded that, although quadratic models are superior in terms of predicting energy use, the linear model seems to be the better overall predictor of both energy use and demand (i.e., maximum monthly power consumed by the fan). This is a noteworthy conclusion given that a third-order polynomial is warranted analytically as well as from monitored field data presented by previous authors [e.g., Englander and Norford (1992), Lorenzetti and Norford (1993)].

Polynomial models have been used to correlate chiller (or heat pump) capacity Q_{evap} and the electrical power consumed by the chiller (or compressor) E_{comp} with the relevant number of influential physical parameters. For example, based on the functional form of the DOE-2 building simulation software (York and Cappiello 1982), models for part-load performance of energy equipment and plant, E_{comp}, can be modeled as the following triquadratic polynomial:

$$\begin{aligned} E_{comp} &= a + bQ_{evap} + cT^{in}_{cond} + dT^{out}_{evap} + eQ^2_{evap} \\ &+ fT^{in2}_{cond} + gT^{out2}_{evap} + hQ_{evap}T^{in}_{cond} + iT^{out}_{evap}Q_{evap} \\ &+ jT^{in}_{cond}T^{out}_{evap} + kQ_{evap}T^{in}_{cond}T^{out}_{evap} \end{aligned} \tag{26}$$

In this model, there are 11 model parameters to identify. However, because all of them are unlikely to be statistically significant, a step-wise regression to the sample data set yields the optimal set of parameters to retain in a given model. For example, Armstrong et al. (2006b) found the *b*, *i*, and *k* terms, using T_{odb} for T_{cond} and T_{ewb} for T_{evap}, to provide an adequate model of three different fixed-speed rooftop units. Other authors, such as Braun (1992) and Hydeman et al. (2002), used slightly different polynomial forms. Over a wide range of capacity and lift a full tricubic polynomial can be justified for VRF heat pump equipment (Gayeski et al. 2011).

Physical Models. In contrast to polynomial models, which have no physical basis, physical models are based on fundamental thermodynamic or heat transfer considerations. These types of models are usually associated with the parameter estimation approach. Often, physical models are preferred because they generally have fewer parameters, and their mathematical formulation can be traced to actual physical principles that govern the performance of the building or equipment. Hence, model coefficients tend to be more robust, leading to sounder model predictions. Only a few studies have used steady-state physical models for parameter estimation relating to commercial building energy use [e.g., Reddy et al. (1999)]. Unlike in single-family residences, it is difficult to perform elaborately planned experiments in large buildings and obtain representative values of indoor fluctuations.

For example, the generalized Gordon and Ng (GN) model (Gordon and Ng 2000) is a simple, analytical, universal model for chiller performance based on first principles of thermodynamics and linearized heat losses. The model predicts the dependent chiller coefficient of performance (COP) (the ratio of thermal cooling capacity Q_{ch} to electrical power E consumed by the chiller) with easily measurable parameters such as the fluid (water or air) temperature entering the condenser T_{cdi}, fluid temperature entering the evaporator T_{chi}, and the thermal cooling capacity of the evaporator. The GN model is a three-parameter model in the following form:

$$\begin{aligned} \left(\frac{1}{\text{COP}} + 1\right)\frac{T_{chi}}{T_{cdi}} - 1 &= a_1\frac{T_{chi}}{Q_{ch}} + a_2\frac{(T_{cdi} - T_{chi})}{T_{cdi}Q_{ch}} \\ &+ a_3\frac{(1/\text{COP} + 1)Q_{ch}}{T_{cdi}} \end{aligned} \tag{27a}$$

where temperatures are in absolute units.

Substituting the following,

$$x_1 = \frac{T_{chi}}{Q_{ch}} \quad x_2 = \frac{(T_{cdi} - T_{chi})}{T_{cdi}Q_{ch}} \quad x_3 = \frac{(1/\text{COP} + 1)Q_{ch}}{T_{cdi}} \tag{27b}$$

and $$y = \left(\frac{1}{\text{COP}} + 1\right)\frac{T_{chi}}{T_{cdi}} - 1$$

the model given by Equation (27a) becomes

$$y = a_1x_1 + a_2x_2 + a_3x_3 \tag{27c}$$

which is a three-parameter linear model with no intercept term. The parameters of the model in Equation (27c) have the following physical meaning:

$a_1 = \Delta S$ = total internal entropy production in chiller

$a_2 = Q_{leak}$ = heat losses (or gains) from (or into) chiller

$a_3 = R$ = total heat exchanger thermal resistance = $1/C_{cd} + 1/C_{ch}$, where C is effective thermal conductance

Gordon and Ng (2000) point out that Q_{leak} is typically an order of magnitude smaller than the other terms, but it is not negligible for accurate modeling, and should be retained in the model if the other two parameters identified are to be used for chiller diagnostics. The same linear model structure as Equation (27c) can be used if the fluid temperature leaving the evaporator T_{cho} is used instead of T_{chi}. However, the physical interpretation of the term a_3 is modified accordingly.

Reddy and Anderson (2002) and Sreedharan and Haves (2001) found that the GN and multivariate polynomial (MP) models were comparable in their predictive abilities. The GN model requires much less data if selected judiciously [even four well-chosen data points can yield accurate models, as demonstrated by Corcoran and Reddy (2003)]. Jiang and Reddy (2003) tested the GN model against more than 50 data sets covering various generic types and sizes of water-cooled chillers (single- and double-stage centrifugal chillers with inlet guide vanes and variable-speed drives, screw, scroll), and found excellent predictive ability (coefficient of variation of RMSE in the range of 2 to 5%).

Dynamic Models

In contrast to steady-state data-driven models, which are used with monthly and daily data containing one or more independent variables, dynamic data-driven models are typically used with hourly or subhourly data in cases where the building's thermal mass is significant enough to delay heat gains or losses. Dynamic models traditionally require solving a set of differential equations. Disadvantages of dynamic data-driven models include their complexity and the need for more detailed measurements to tune the model. Unlike steady-state data-driven models, dynamic data-driven models usually require a high degree of user interaction and knowledge of the building or system being modeled.

Several residential energy studies have used dynamic data-driven models based on parameter estimation approaches, usually involving intrusive data gathering. Rabl (1988) classified the various types of dynamic data-driven models used for whole-building energy use, and identified the common underlying features of these models. There are essentially four different types of model formulations: thermal network, time series, differential equation, and modal, all of which qualify as parameter-estimation approaches.

A few studies (Hammarsten 1984; Rabl 1988; Reddy 1989) evaluated these different approaches with the same data set. Several papers reported results of applying different techniques, such as thermal network and autoregressive-moving-average (ARMA) models, to residential and commercial building energy use. Examples of dynamic data-driven models for commercial buildings are found in Andersen and Brandemuehl (1992), Braun (1990), and Rabl (1988), and for apartment buildings in Armstrong et al. (2006a). Successful use of ARMA models for model-predictive control is reported by Gayeski et al. (2012).

Dynamic data-driven models based on pure statistical approaches have also been reported. Two examples are machine learning (Miller and Seem 1991) and artificial neural networks (Kreider and Haberl 1994; Kreider and Wang 1991; Miller and Seem 1991).

6.3 MODEL ACCURACY AND GOODNESS OF FIT

Good data-driven models are determined by their overall goodness-of-fit and accuracy metrics, by testing each parameter for significance, and ensuring that the chosen model form and regressors explain the response of the dependent variable as completely as possible.

Accuracy of model results may be represented by statistical metrics. Commonly used metrics are the normalized mean bias error (NMBE) and the coefficient of variance of the root mean square error [CV(RMSE)]. Equations for these metrics are provided in the section on Modeling Calibration. CV(RMSE) tests how well the model recreates the data and is also an indication of random error. NMBE tests how biased the model is in predicting outputs over the period the model was developed.

A widely used statistic to gage a model's goodness of fit is the **coefficient of determination R^2** (Draper and Smith 1981; Neter et al. 1989). A value of $R^2 = 1$ indicates a perfect correlation between actual data and the regression equation; a value of $R^2 = 0$ indicates no correlation. For tuning for a performance contract, a rule of thumb is that the value of R^2 should not be less than 0.75.

When more than one independent variable is included in the regression, the adjusted R^2 should be used to assess the goodness of fit, as the unadjusted R^2 increases with the addition of variables, and can be misleading. When additional independent variables are included, each should be tested for significance. The standard error of the estimate of the coefficients on each independent variable should be assessed. The smaller the standard error compared to the coefficient's magnitude, the more reliable the coefficient estimate. To identify the significance of individual coefficients, ***t*-statistics** (or ***t*-values**) are used. These are simply the ratio of the coefficient estimate divided by the standard error of the estimate.

The coefficient of each variable included in the regression has a t-statistic. For a coefficient to be statistically meaningful, the absolute value of its t-statistic must be at least 2.0. In other words, under no circumstances should a variable be included in a regression if the standard error of its coefficient estimate is greater than half the magnitude of the coefficient (even when including a variable that increases the adjusted R^2). Generally, including more variables in a regression increases R^2, but the significance of most individual coefficients is likely to decrease.

Some independent variables may be linearly correlated. This condition, called **multicollinearity**, can result in large uncertainty in the estimates of the regression coefficients (i.e., error) and can also lead to poorer model prediction accuracy compared to a model where the regressors are not linearly correlated.

Residuals should be plotted against each independent variable to check that no relationship of any sort (not just linear correlation) exists. The distribution of residuals should follow a normal distribution. For time-series data, the residuals should be checked for serial correlation (ASHRAE 2010).

Several authors recommend using **principal component analysis (PCA)** to overcome multicollinearity effects. PCA was one of the strongest analysis methods in the ASHRAE Predictor Shootout I and II contests (Haberl and Thamilseran 1996; Kreider and Haberl 1994). Analysis of multiyear monitored daily energy use in a grocery store found a clear superiority of PCA over multivariate regression models (Ruch et al. 1993), but this conclusion is unsupported for commercial building energy use in general. A more general evaluation by Reddy and Claridge (1994) of both analysis techniques using synthetic data from four different U.S. locations found that injudicious use of PCA may exacerbate rather than overcome problems associated with multicollinearity. Draper and Smith (1981) also caution against indiscriminate use of PCA.

6.4 EXAMPLES USING DATA-DRIVEN METHODS

Modeling Utility Bill Data

The following example (taken from Sonderegger 1998) illustrates a utility bill analysis. Assume that values of utility bills over an entire year have been measured. To obtain the equation coefficients through regression, the utility bills must be normalized by the length of the time interval between utility bills. This is equivalent to expressing all utility bills, degree-days, and other independent variables by their daily averages.

Appropriate modeling software is used in which values are assumed for heating and cooling balance points; from these, the corresponding heating and cooling degree-days for each utility bill period are determined. Repeated regression is done till the regression equation represents the best fit to the meter data. The model coefficients are then assumed to be tuned. Some programs allow direct determination of these optimal model parameters (e.g., balance point temperature) without manual tuning of the parameters by the user.

Figure 17 shows how well a regression fit captures measured baseline energy use in a hospital building. Cooling degree-days are found to be a significant variable, with the best fit for a base temperature of 54°F.

In this analysis, some individual utility bills may be unsuitable to develop a baseline and should be excluded from the regression. For example, a bill may be atypically high because of a one-time equipment malfunction that was subsequently repaired. Given the justification to exclude some data, it is often tempting to look for more reasons to exclude bills that fall far from "the line" and not question those that are close to it. For example, bills for periods containing vacations or production shutdowns may look anomalously low, but excluding them from the regression would result in a chronic overestimate of the future baseline during the same period.

Neural Network Models

Figure 18 shows results for a single neural network typical of several hundred networks constructed for an academic engineering center located in central Texas. The cooling load is created by solar gains, internal gains, outdoor air sensible heat, and outdoor air humidity loads. The neural network is used to predict the pre-retrofit energy consumption for comparison with measured consumption of the retrofitted building. Six months of pre-retrofit data were available to train the network. Solid lines show the known building consumption data, and dashed lines show the neural network

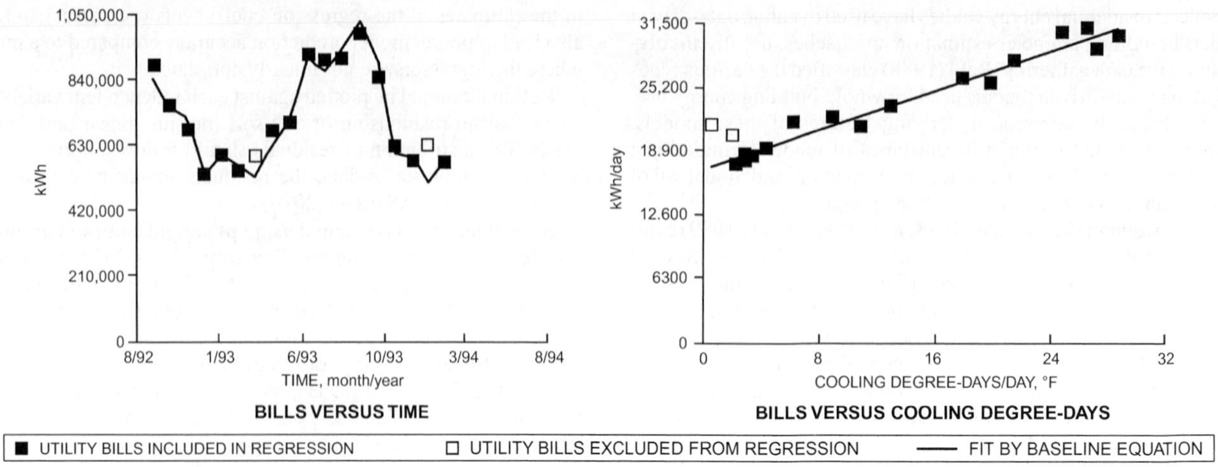

NOTE: Utility bills excluded from the regression due to a degree-day threshold.

Fig. 17 Variable-Base Degree-Day Model Identification Using Electricity Utility Bills at Hospital
(Sonderegger 1998)

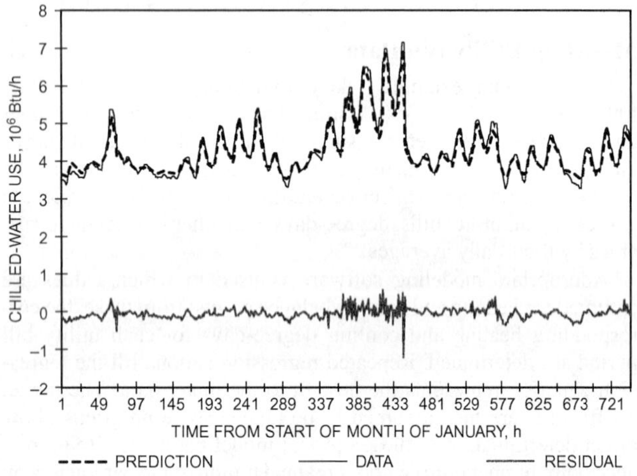

Fig. 18 Neural Network Prediction of Whole-Building, Hourly Chilled-Water Consumption for Commercial Building

predictions. This figure shows that a neural network trained for one period (September 1989) can predict energy consumption well into the future (in this case, January 1990).

The network used for this prediction had two hidden layers. The input layer contained eight neurons that receive eight different types of input data as listed below. The output layer consisted of one neuron that gave the output datum (chilled-water consumption). Each training fact (i.e., training data set), therefore, contained eight input data (independent variables) and one pattern datum (dependent variable). The following eight hourly input data used in each hour's data vector were selected on physical bases (Kreider and Rabl 1994):

- Hour number (0 to 2300)
- Ambient dry-bulb temperature
- Horizontal insolation
- Humidity ratio
- Wind speed
- Weekday/weekend binary flag (0, 1)
- Past hour's chilled-water consumption
- Second past hour's chilled-water consumption

These measured independent variables were able to predict chilled-water use to an RMS error of less than 4% (JCEM 1992).

Choosing an optimal network's configuration for a given problem remains an art. The number of hidden neurons and layers must be sufficient to meet the requirement of the given application. However, if too many neurons and layers are used, the network tends to memorize data rather than learning (i.e., finding the underlying patterns in the data). Further, choosing an excessively large number of hidden layers significantly increases the required training time for certain learning algorithms. Anstett and Kreider (1993), Krarti et al. (1998), Kreider and Wang (1991), and Wang and Kreider (1992) report additional case studies for commercial buildings.

6.5 MODEL SELECTION

Table 5 presents a decision diagram for selecting a forward or data-driven model where use of the model, degree of difficulty in understanding and applying the model, time scale for data used by the model, calculation time, and input variables used by the models are the criteria used to choose a particular model.

More information on data-driven models can be found in the ASHRAE *Inverse Modeling Toolkit* (Haberl and Cho 2004; Haberl et al. 2003; Kissock et al. 2003). This toolkit contains FORTRAN 90 and executable code for performing linear and change-point linear regressions, variable-based degree-days, multilinear regression, and combined regressions. It also includes a complete test suite of data sets for testing all models.

7. MODEL CALIBRATION

Calibration is the use of known data (e.g., utility bills) on the observed relationship between a dependent variable (e.g., simulation output) and an independent variable (e.g., simulation input) to make estimates of other values of the independent variable from new observations of the dependent variable. For energy simulation models, calibration typically involves observation of changes in simulation output as simulation inputs are modified, with the goal of identifying a set of inputs leading to simulation outputs that match measured building performance.

The perception of validity and usefulness of any energy simulation model is largely determined by how closely the simulation output matches actual building performance, usually in terms of energy consumption. The process of calibrating a model to match actual

Table 5 Capabilities of Different Forward and Data-Driven Modeling Methods

Methods	Use[a]	Difficulty	Time Scale[b]	Calc. Time	Variables[c]	Accuracy
Simple linear regression	ES	Simple	D, M	Very fast	*T*	Low
Multiple linear regression	D, ES	Simple	D, M	Fast	*T, H, S, W, t*	Medium
ASHRAE bin method and data-driven bin method	ES	Moderate	H	Fast	*T*	Medium
Change-point models	D, ES	Simple	H, D, M	Fast	*T*	Medium
ASHRAE TC 4.7 modified bin method	ES, DE	Moderate	H	Medium	*T, S, tm*	Medium
Artificial neural networks	D, ES, C	Complex	S, H	Fast	*T, H, S, W, t, tm*	High
Thermal network	D, ES, C	Complex	S, H	Fast	*T, S, tm*	High
Fourier series analysis	D, ES, C	Moderate	S, H	Medium	*T, H, S, W, t, tm*	High
ARMA model	D, ES, C	Moderate	S, H, D	Fast	*T, H, S, W, t, tm*	High
Modal analysis	D, ES, C	Complex	S, H	Medium	*T, H, S, W, t, tm*	High
Differential equation	D, ES, C	Complex	S, H	Fast	*T, H, S, W, t, tm*	High
Computer simulation (component-based)	D, ES, C, DE	Very complex	S, H	Slow	*T, H, S, W, t, tm*	Medium
(fixed schematic)	D, ES, DE	Very complex	H	Slow	*T, H, S, W, t, tm*	Medium
Computer emulation	D, C	Very complex	S, H	Very slow	*T, H, S, W, t, tm*	High

Notes:
[a]Use shown includes diagnostics (D), energy savings calculations (ES), design (DE), and control (C).
[b]Time scales shown are hourly (H), daily (D), monthly (M), and subhourly (S).
[c]Variables include temperature (*T*), humidity (*H*), solar (*S*), wind (*W*), time (*t*), and thermal mass (*tm*).

performance can be a complex and time-consuming endeavor. Identifying and isolating sources of discrepancy between the results of a model and actual data are not always possible, as described in the section on Uncertainty in Modeling. In addition, energy model calibration typically involves several input parameters that must be calibrated using a relatively limited amount of measured data; because of combinatorial complexity, calibration is an underdetermined system in which there can exist many unique (and substantially different) models that are within a tolerable error.

A typical calibration requires an initial model, set of inputs to be calibrated, weather data, collection of measurements, error metric, and acceptance criteria. Once defined, a manual, semiautomatic, or automatic calibration process is invoked on these requirements. In some cases, there is a validation process afterward to assess how well the calibration process performed. Analytical, mathematical, or statistical techniques can be used for the calibration process or to assess the quality of calibration. Table 6 lists some of the common methods and techniques used for model calibration (Coakley et al. 2014). These methods have varying degrees of complexity and result in varying degrees of calibration accuracy.

The quality of a calibration is often evaluated in terms of statistical indicators that quantify discrepancies between the model output and measured output. These metrics are based on time steps, and it may be the case that a model calibrated to low-resolution (e.g., monthly) whole-building data is highly inaccurate when compared to higher-resolution temporal (e.g., hourly) or spatial (e.g., level of a thermal zone) data. Among statistical indicators, the normalized mean bias error (NMBE) and the coefficient of variance of the root mean square error [CV(RMSE)], Equations (28) and (29) respectively, are widely used. In these equations, the values are summed for each time step (e.g., monthly or hourly values) over the course of an evaluation period (e.g., year), and the parameter V is the building performance variable under consideration (usually monthly whole-building energy consumption):

$$\text{NMBE} = \frac{\sum(V_{actual} - V_{modeled})}{(N-1) \times \text{Mean}(V_{actual})} \times 100\% \qquad (28)$$

$$\text{CV(RMSE)} = \frac{\sqrt{\dfrac{\sum(V_{actual} - V_{modeled})^2}{N-1}}}{\text{Mean}(V_{actual})} \times 100\% \qquad (29)$$

where

V_{actual} = parameter's measured or metered value for each time step (e.g. month)

$V_{modeled}$ = parameter's estimated or modeled value for each time step

N = number of time steps being analyzed during period of evaluation

ASHRAE *Guideline* 14-2014 states that a model can be considered calibrated if NMBE < 5% and CV(RMSE) < 15% when monthly data are used, or NMBE < 10% and CV(RMSE) < 30% when hourly data are used. Because CV(RMSE) is the positive average sum-squared error divided by the actual mean, it can be considered the percent error between the simulation and measured data. Because NMBE is a signed error divided by the mean, it indicates bias percent for under- (NMBE > 0) or overshooting (NMBE < 0) the actual data during the period of evaluation.

Additional resources and tools useful for energy model calibration include ASHRAE RP-1051 (Reddy 2006), ASHRAE RP-1093 (Abushakra et al. 2000), and NREL *Technical Report* 5500-60127 (Robertson 2013).

The main challenges of manual model calibration are that it is labor intensive and time consuming, it requires a high level of user skill and knowledge in both simulation and practical building operation, and the results often vary with the individual performing the calibration. Several practical difficulties prevent achieving a calibrated simulation or a simulation that closely reflects actual building performance, including (1) measurement and adaptation of weather data for use by simulation programs (e.g., converting global horizontal solar into beam and diffuse solar radiation), (2) collecting reliable actual meteorological year data for a specific building during the type period in which energy-use data was collected (Bhandari et al. 2012), (3) choice of methods used to calibrate the model, and (4) choice of methods used to measure required input parameters for the simulation (i.e., building mass, infiltration coefficients, and shading coefficients). Calibrated models typically involve a large number of input parameters to be calibrated, a high degree of expertise, multiple iterations, and substantial computing time. Every model, calibrated or not, carries assumptions and simplifications that are often deemed reasonable, but should be reevaluated when the model is used for different purposes. Bou-Saada and Haberl (1995a, 1995b), Bronson et al. (1992), Corson (1992), Garrett and New (2014), Haberl and Bou-Saada (1998), Kaplan et al. (1990), Liu and Liu (2011), Manke et al. (1996), Monfet et al. (2009), Norford et al. (1994), O'Neill et al. (2011), Reddy (2006, 2011), Reddy and Maor (2006), Reddy et al. (2007a, 2007b), Song and Haberl (2008a, 2008b), and Sun et al. (2016) provide examples of different methods used to calibrate

Table 6 Calibration Methods and Techniques

Method/Technique	Description
Detailed audit	Detailed audits are often conducted before building model development to gain a better knowledge of the building systems and characteristics (e.g., geometry, HVAC systems, lighting, equipment, occupancy schedules).
Expert knowledge/templates/ model database	Approaches that use • Expert knowledge or judgment as a key element of the process • Prior definition of typical building templates • Database of typical building parameters and components to reduce the requirement for user inputs during model development
Intrusive testing	Intrusive techniques require some intervention in operation of the actual building, such a "blink tests," whereby groups of end-use loads (e.g., plug loads, lighting) are turned on and off in a controlled sequence to determine their overall effect on the baseline building load.
High-resolution ("high-res") data	Data are recorded at hourly (or subhourly) levels as opposed to using daily load profiles or monthly utility bill data.
Short-term energy monitoring	Metering equipment is used to record on-site measurements for a short period of time (e.g., two weeks). This may be used in identifying typical energy end-use profiles and/or base loads.
Graphical comparison	Two- or three-dimensional plots are used to aid comparison of measured and simulated data in a way that can inform manual calibration. Whereas 2D scatterplots are frequently used, 3D techniques can allow effective visualization of larger quantities of data.
Signature analysis	Signature analysis techniques are a specific type of graphical analysis technique, typically used by HVAC simulation engineers to identify faulty parameters in air-handling unit (AHU) simulation. They may also be used to develop optimized operation and control schedules. Signature analysis methods are commonly used for the calibration of models based on the simplified energy analysis procedure (SEAP).
Statistical displays	Graphical representation of statistical indices and comparisons can facilitate intuitive interpretation for calibration. This includes data comparison techniques such as carpet plots, box-whisker-mean (BWM) plots, and monthly percent difference time-series graphs.
Base case modeling	The base case model refers to the use of measured base loads to calibrate the building model. Base loads refer to minimum, or weather independent, electrical and gas energy consumption. Calibration is carried out during the base case when heating and cooling loads are minimal and the building is dominated by internal loads, thus minimizing impact of weather dependent variables.
Model parameter estimation	Deduction of overall aggregate (or lumped) parameters (e.g., U-factors) using nonintrusive, measured data.
Parameter reduction	This involves reducing the requirement for detailed input for variable schedules (e.g., plug loads, lighting, occupancy, equipment). Day typing is one such approach, which works by analyzing long-term data and reducing this to manageable typical day-type schedules (e.g., weekdays versus weekends, winter versus summer). Zone typing may also be used to reduce large models into similar thermal zones (e.g., core, perimeter, offices, unoccupied spaces).
Data disaggregation	Data disaggregation refers to the application of nonintrusive load monitoring (NILM) techniques to decouple multiple derived data streams (e.g., lighting, miscellaneous plug loads) from a single measured data stream (e.g. whole-building electrical energy consumption).
Evidence-based model development	Evidence-based approaches may be described as those that implement a procedural approach to model development, making changes according to source evidence rather than ad hoc intervention. Strictly, this approach should account for adjustments to model parameters in a structured fashion (e.g., using version control software).
Sensitivity analysis	Sensitivity analysis procedures may be used in some studies to assess the influence of input parameters on model predictions. This information may be used to identify important parameters for measurement, calibration, or detailed investigation.
Uncertainty quantification	Parameter uncertainty may be used to directly assist in model calibration or provide a basis for quantification of risk propagation to the results (e.g., uncertainty-related risk in energy conservation measure analysis).
Bayesian calibration	Bayesian calibration is an alternative statistical approach to model calibration. The approach offers the advantage of naturally accounting for uncertainty in model prediction using prior input distributions.
Pattern-based approach	A process to calibrate energy models using patterns of monthly simulated and measured energy consumption using pattern fit criteria.
Multiobjective optimization	Most automated calibration techniques use a single- or multiobjective optimization function to reduce the difference between measured and simulated data. An objective function may be used to set a target of minimizing, for example, the mean square error between measured data and simulation output. Conversely, a penalty function may also be used to reduce the likelihood of deviating too far from the default value for a parameter.

simulation models. A methodology for testing calibration methods is described in the section on Model Validation and Testing.

Calibration techniques can be roughly classified as either manual or automated methods. Manual calibration methods include graphical analysis and sensitivity analysis. Examples of methods used for automated calibration include Bayesian analysis, pattern matching, and multiobjective optimization.

Manual calibration is an iterative approach that can be labor intensive and involves separate manipulation of individual parameters. This approach involves using an existing building simulation model and "tuning" or calibrating the various input parameters so that simulation program output matches with observed energy use. Calibration can be performed using data from any time period (e.g., monthly, or only a few weeks over the year), but the final calibrated model is likely to be less accurate when fewer data are used during the calibration process. Hourly monitored energy data (most compatible with the time step adopted by most building energy simulation programs) can allow development of more accurate calibrated models, but calibrators often work without hourly data.

During the manual calibration process, graphical representations and/or statistics comparing modeled data to measured data are displayed in an attempt to elucidate the value that input parameters could be set to in order to improve the match between simulation output and measured data. Calibrators often use sensitivity analyses to focus calibration efforts on the parameters that make the biggest difference in terms of energy use. In contrast to manual calibration, automated techniques use mathematical, algorithmic techniques implemented as computer software. Bayesian analysis, pattern-based calibration, and multiobjective optimization are methods used for automated calibration.

7.1 BAYESIAN ANALYSIS

This approach uses a theorem originally proposed by Thomas Bayes, an English statistician (1701-1761). Bayesian analysis provides an updated, more refined (more accurate) model based on the model from the prior iteration and a likelihood function derived from a statistical model for the measured data. Individual parameters with varying degrees of uncertainty can be analyzed to predict the range of values for that parameter, and its most likely value. In most Bayesian analyses, the formulation of the likelihood function is based on the work of Kennedy and O'Hagan (2001).

Riddle and Muehleisen (2014) stated that, although Bayesian analysis can initially seem overwhelming, this method of calibration does not rely on extensive expertise. They further stated that this method provides an automated process for optimizing parameter values while accounting for multiple sources of uncertainty. Heo (2011) suggested that there are three primary strengths with Bayesian analysis: (1) it improves the reliability of a model by tuning important uncertain parameters in the model to represent actual building operations, (2) it results in calibrated models that are suitable to uncertainty analysis, and (3) the calibration procedure objectively quantifies uncertainty through the determination of a set of calibration parameters prioritized by their importance to the model outcome.

7.2 PATTERN-BASED APPROACH

This approach (Sun et al. 2016) automates a process to calibrate energy models using patterns of monthly simulated and measured energy use. The process contains four key steps: (1) running the original precalibrated energy model to obtain monthly simulated electricity and gas use; (2) establishing a pattern bias, either universal or seasonal, by comparing load shape patterns of simulated and actual monthly energy use; (3) using programmed logic to select which parameter to tune first based on bias pattern, weather, and input parameter interactions; and (4) automatically tuning the calibration parameters and checking the progress using pattern-fit criteria.

The automated calibration algorithm was implemented in the Commercial Building Energy Saver (Hong et al. 2015), a web-based building energy retrofit analysis toolkit. The novelty of the developed calibration methodology lies in linking parameter tuning with the underlying logic associated with bias pattern identification. Although there are some limitations (e.g., coverage of building and system types) to the current implementation, the pattern-based automated calibration methodology can be universally adopted as an alternative to manual or hierarchical calibration approaches.

7.3 MULTIOBJECTIVE OPTIMIZATION

This approach uses the well-established field of mathematical optimization to select the best value of an input parameter, from some set of available alternatives, with regard to a fitness function. Standard optimization can be used when a single fitness criterion (e.g., whole-building energy use) is considered, and multiobjective optimization can be used to evaluate any number of building performance criteria (e.g., submetering, temperatures, relative humidity, heat flux) for which a user may have measured data. This class of algorithms is advantageous in that it is fully automated, can calibrate hundreds of (uncertain) input parameters, and is simulation-engine-agnostic (i.e., it can apply to any simulation/software that has inputs and generates outputs comparable to measured data). Optimization algorithms can also accommodate more intensive submetering expected in the future, because fitness functions can compare calibration performance to either monthly (12), hourly (8760), or submetered, subhourly (1,000,000+) data points in less than a second.

Table 7 ANSI/ASHRAE *Standard* 140 Validation Test Matrix

Test Type/ Model Type	Building Thermal Fabric (Basic Building Physics)[a]	Mechanical Equipment and On-Site Energy Generation Equipment[a]
Analytical verification	Ground-Coupled Heat Transfer BESTEST for Slab On Grade (5.2.4)	HVAC BESTEST Volume 1 (5.3) Gas-Forced Air Furnace BESTEST (5.4.1, 5.4.2) Airside HVAC BESTEST Volume 1[b] (Neymark et. al. 2016)
Comparative tests	Thermal Fabric BESTEST (5.2.1-5.2.3) Residential Building BESTEST (7.2)	HVAC BESTEST Volume 2 (5.3) Gas-Forced Air Furnace BESTEST (5.4.3)
Empirical validation	—	—

[a]Sections of *Standard* 140 relevant to a given test suite are indicated in parentheses [e.g., "(5.2.4)" indicates Section 5.2.4].
[b]Anticipated as Addendum a to *Standard* 140-2014 in 2017.

The disadvantage is that these algorithms, by themselves, do not capture the sense-making common of human calibrators and could thus generate physically unrealistic models that may not even simulate.

A method of comparing these techniques was defined (New et. al 2012), studied (Edwards 2013), and evaluated (Sanyal 2014), as defined in the section on Testing Model Calibration Techniques Using Synthetic Data, to determine (Garrett and New 2014) the best algorithm, of those tested, for calibration. In terms of robustness, speed, and calibration accuracy over a 20,000 building calibration study, the best algorithm was an evolutionary algorithm known as the nondominated sorting genetic algorithm (NSGA-II) (Deb et al. 2002). Optimal values for NSGA-II, mechanisms for speedup, and methods to mitigate limitations regarding physical realism were identified for the traditional use cases of calibrating to monthly (Garret et al. 2013) and hourly (Garrett and New 2015) whole-building electrical data before being made publicly available (New 2016).

8. VALIDATION AND TESTING

ANSI/ASHRAE *Standard* 140 was developed to identify and diagnose differences in predictions that may be caused by algorithmic differences, modeling limitations, faulty coding, or input errors. The methodological structure of *Standard* 140 allows all elements of a complete validation approach to be added as they become available. Table 7 shows the structure and the test suites in *Standard* 140-2014.

The table is an abbreviated way of representing the parameter space in which building energy simulation programs operate. Each cell in the matrix represents a large region in the space, so listing a test suite in a cell does not obviate the need for additional suites in that cell, and tests are needed in the empty cells. Class 1 tests in section 5 of the standard are based on procedures developed by the National Renewable Energy Laboratory (NREL) and field-tested by the International Energy Agency (IEA) over three IEA research tasks (Judkoff and Neymark 1995a; Neymark and Judkoff 2002, 2004). An additional section 5 test suite, which follows NREL's methodology, was developed by Natural Resources Canada (Purdy and Beausoleil-Morrison 2003). Class 2 tests (section 7 of the standard) are based on procedures developed by NREL and field tested by the Home Energy Rating Systems (HERS) Council Technical Committee (Judkoff and Neymark 1995b). Additional tests not yet in

Table 8 Validation Techniques

Technique	Advantages	Disadvantages
Empirical validation (test of model and solution process)	• Approximate truth standard within experimental accuracy • Any level of complexity	• Experimental uncertainties: • Instrument calibration, spatial/temporal discretization • Instrumentation can alter the effect being measured • Imperfect knowledge/specification of experimental object (building) being simulated • High-quality, detailed measurements are expensive and time consuming • Only a limited number of test cases are practical • Diagnostics can be difficult • Requires empirical determination of inputs • Only a limited number of sensitivity test cases are practical
Analytical verification (test of solution process)	• No input uncertainty • Exact mathematical or secondary mathematical truth standard for given model • Inexpensive	• No test of model validity or suitability • Limited to highly constrained cases for which analytical or quasi-analytical solutions can be developed*
Comparative testing (relative test of model and solution process)	• No input uncertainty • Any level of complexity • Many diagnostic comparisons possible • Inexpensive and quick	• No absolute truth standard (only statistically based acceptance ranges are possible)

Source: Judkoff and Neymark (2006).
*Use of verified numerical solutions can extend the analytical verification approach to more realistic cases (Neymark et al. 2008).

Standard 140 were developed under ASHRAE research projects (Spitler et al. 2001; Yuill and Haberl 2002; Yuill et al. 2006), and under joint IEA Solar Heating and Cooling Programme/Energy Conservation in Buildings and Community Systems Task 34/Annex 43 (Judkoff and Neymark 2009); these may further populate the validation test matrix in the future. *Standard* 140 is cited by a number of codes, standards, and regulatory bodies, including ASHRAE *Standard* 90.1, the DOE Qualified Software List under IRS 179D energy tax credit regulations for commercial buildings (Energy.Gov 2015), the RESNET Home Energy Rating System software approval process (RESNET 2015), the *International Energy Conservation Code* (IECC 2015), the *International Green Construction Code*® (IgCC 2015), and ASHRAE *Standard* 189.1.

8.1 METHODOLOGICAL BASIS

There are three ways to evaluate a whole-building energy simulation program's accuracy (Judkoff et al. 1983/2008; Judkoff and Neymark 2006, 2009):

- *Empirical validation*, which compares calculated results from a program, subroutine, algorithm, module, or software object to monitored data from a real building, test cell, or laboratory experiment
- *Analytical verification*, which compares the output from a program, subroutine, algorithm, module, or software object to results from a known analytical solution or to results from a set of closely agreeing quasi-analytical solutions or verified numerical models
- *Comparative testing*, which compares a program to itself or to other programs

Neymark and Judkoff (2002) summarize approximately 100 articles and research papers on analytical, empirical, and comparative testing, from 1980 through 2015. Some of these and other works are listed by subject in the Bibliography.

Table 8 compares these techniques (Judkoff 1988; Judkoff and Neymark 2006, 2009; Judkoff et al. 1983/2008). In this table, the term "model" is the representation of reality for a given physical behavior. For example, heat transfer may be simulated with one-, two-, or three-dimensional thermal conduction models. The term "solution process" encompasses the mathematics and computer coding to solve a given model. The solution process for a model can be perfect, while the model remains inappropriate for a given physical situation, such as using a one-dimensional conduction model where two-dimensional conduction dominates. The term "truth standard" represents the standard of accuracy for predicting real behavior. An analytical solution is a "mathematical truth standard," and only tests the solution process for a model, not the appropriateness of the model. An approximate truth standard from an experiment tests both the solution process and appropriateness of the model within experimental uncertainty. The ultimate (or "absolute") validation truth standard would be comparison of simulation results to a perfectly performed empirical validation experiment, with all simulation inputs perfectly defined.

Empirical Validation

Establishing an absolute truth standard for evaluating a program's ability to analyze physical behavior requires empirical validation, but this is only possible within the range of measurement uncertainty, including that related to instruments, spatial and temporal discretization, and the overall experimental design. Full-scale test cells and buildings are large, relatively complex experimental objects. The exact design details, material properties, and construction in the field cannot be perfectly known, so there is uncertainty about the simulation model inputs that accurately represent the experimental object. Meticulous care is required to describe the experimental apparatus as clearly as possible to modelers to minimize this uncertainty. This includes experimental determination of as many material properties and other simulation model inputs as possible, including overall building parameters such as overall steady-state heat transmission coefficient (UA_o), infiltration (in the form of an effective UA), and thermal capacitance (Judkoff et al. 2000; Neymark et al. 2005; Subbarao 1988). Measuring these overall parameters allows for a closure check on the individual parameters that comprise the overall parameters (e.g., building envelope material properties or individual steady-state envelope component conductances that sum up to the measured overall steady-state heat transmission coefficient). Also required are detailed on-site meteorological measurements. For example, many experiments measure global horizontal solar radiation, but very few experiments measure the splits between direct, diffuse, and ground-reflected radiation, all of which are inputs to many whole-building energy simulation programs. Small-scale test cells also have shortcomings because of similitude factors for air convection and the increased relative proportion of corner conditions, which increases the importance of 2D and 3D heat transfer. Side-by-side experimental design can help to dampen the effects of input uncertainties, if the effects of the intentional differences between test objects are robust compared to those of the unintentional differences.

The National Renewable Energy Laboratory (NREL) divides empirical validation into different levels, because many past validation studies produced inconclusive results. The levels of validation depend on the degree of control over possible sources of error in a simulation. The higher the degree of control over error sources, the better the potential for diagnosing the causes of measured to modeled output differences. The error sources consist of seven types, divided into two groups (Judkoff et al. 1983/2008):

External Error Types

- Differences between actual building microclimate versus weather input used by the program
- Differences between actual schedules, control strategies, effects of occupant behavior, and other effects from the real building versus those assumed by the program user
- User error deriving building input files
- Differences between actual physical properties of the building (including HVAC systems) versus those input by the user

Internal Error Types

- Differences between actual thermal transfer mechanisms in the real building and its HVAC systems versus the simplified model of those processes in the simulation (all models, no matter how detailed, are simplifications of reality)
- Errors or inaccuracies in the mathematical solution of the models
- Coding errors
- Ambiguous, incomplete, or faulty documentation

The simplest level of empirical validation compares a building's actual long-term energy use to that calculated by a computer program, with no attempt to eliminate sources of discrepancy. Because this is similar to how a simulation tool is used in practice, it is favored by many in the building industry. However, it is difficult to interpret the results because all possible error sources are acting simultaneously. Even if there is good agreement between measured and calculated performance, possible offsetting errors prevent a definitive conclusion about the model's accuracy. More informative levels of validation involve controlling or eliminating various combinations of error types and increasing the information density of output-to-data comparisons (e.g., comparing temperature and energy results at time scales ranging from subhourly to annual). At the most detailed level, all known sources of error are controlled to identify and quantify unknown error sources and to reveal causal relationships associated with error sources, thereby facilitating diagnostics. Long-term (ideally annual) overall energy use needed to maintain comfort has extra meaning as a metric, because it is an indicator of how important a fault or simplification in a simulation program is in the context of one of the model's most important uses. A $15/yr error out of a $1500/yr energy bill is tolerable, but a $500/yr error is not. Other measurements, such as fluxes through individual surfaces, or short-term temperatures, are important to establish cause and effect but are inherently less indicative by themselves of the overall importance of an error. For example, it is difficult to assess the importance of a 0.5°F absolute average hourly one-week error between simulated and measured zone temperature.

These principles also apply to intermodel comparative testing and analytical verification. The more realistic the test case, the more difficult it is to establish causality and diagnose problems; the simpler and more controlled the test case, the easier it is to pinpoint sources of error or inaccuracy. Methodically building up from simple, highly controlled cases to realistic cases one parameter at a time is useful for understanding the impact of assumptions and simplifications in building energy simulation programs.

Analytical Verification

Analytical verification compares outputs from a program, subroutine, algorithm, or software object to results from a known analytical solution or to results from a set of closely agreeing quasi-analytical solutions or verified numerical models. Here, the term **analytical solution** is the closed-form mathematical solution of a model that has an exact result for a given set of parameters and simplifying assumptions. The term **quasi-analytical solution** is the mathematical solution of a model for a given set of parameters and simplifying assumptions, which may require minor interpretation differences that cause minor results variations. Such a result may be computed by generally accepted numerical methods or other means, provided that such calculations occur outside the environment of a whole-building energy simulation program and can be scrutinized. The term **verified numerical model** is a numerical model with solution accuracy verified by close agreement with an analytical solution and/or other quasi-analytical or numerical solutions, according to a process that demonstrates convergence in the space and time domains. Such numerical models may be verified by applying an initial comparison with an analytical solution(s), followed by comparisons with other numerical models for incrementally more realistic cases where analytical solutions are not available.

Mathematical Truth Standards. An analytical solution provides an exact **mathematical truth standard**, limited to highly constrained cases for which exact analytical solutions can be derived. A **secondary mathematical truth standard** can be established based on the range of disagreement of a set of closely agreeing verified numerical models or other quasi-analytical solutions. Once verified against all available classical analytical solutions, and compared with each other for a number of other diagnostic test cases that do not have exact analytical solutions, the secondary mathematical truth standard can be used to test other models as implemented within whole-building simulation programs. Although a closed-form analytical solution provides the best possible mathematical truth standard, a secondary mathematical truth standard greatly enhances diagnostic capability for identifying software bugs and modeling errors as compared to the purely comparative method. This is because the range of disagreement among the results that comprise the secondary truth standard is typically much narrower than the range of disagreement among whole-building simulations. The secondary mathematical truth standard also allows more realistic (less constrained) boundary conditions to be used in the test cases, extending the analytical verification method beyond the constraints inherent for classical analytical solutions. This extends the usefulness of analytical verification methods by applying comparative techniques methodically, as outlined below.

Establishing Secondary Mathematical Truth Standards. The following methodology for verifying numerical models to develop a secondary mathematical truth standard facilitates extension of analytical verification techniques. The methodology applies to both development of test cases and implementation of the numerical models. The logic may be summarized as follows:

- Identify or develop exact analytical solutions that may be used as mathematical truth standards for testing detailed numerical models using parameters and simplifying assumptions of the analytical solution.
- Apply a numerical solution process that demonstrates convergence in the space and time domains for both the analytical-solution test cases and additional test cases where numerical models are applied.

- Once validated against the analytical solutions, use the numerical models to develop test cases that progress toward more realistic (less idealized) conditions but do not have exact analytical solutions.
- Check the numerical models by rigorously comparing their results to each other while developing the more realistic cases.
- Tight agreement for the numerical models versus the analytical solution (and versus each other for subsequent test cases) verifies them as a secondary mathematical truth standard based on the range of disagreement among them.
- Use the verified numerical-model results as reference results for testing other models of the given behavior, which reside within whole building energy simulation computer programs.

Example applications of establishing secondary mathematical truth standards are provided in Neymark et al. (2008, 2009).

Other Considerations. The following general guidelines are helpful when developing effective empirical validation, analytical verification, and comparative test cases:

- Make test cases as simple as possible, to minimize input errors.
- Make test cases as robust as possible, to maximize signal to noise ratio for a tested feature.
- Vary test cases incrementally (varying just a single parameter when possible) so disagreements among results can be quickly diagnosed.
- For numerical models, check sensitivity to spatial and temporal discretization, length of simulation, convergence tolerance, iteration limits, etc., and demonstrate that modeling is at a level of detail where including further detail yields negligible sensitivity in the results; document such work in detailed modeler reports.
- Use independently developed and implemented models, and revise the test specification as needed to accommodate various modeling approaches; this reduces bias by ensuring that the test specification clearly addresses different modeling approaches.
- For resolving disagreements among results that comprise a secondary truth standard, it is helpful to use an additional, independent expert party not directly involved in developing the models or results being compared.
- Corrections to models must have a clear mathematical or physical basis and must be consistently applied across all test cases. Arbitrary alteration of a model solely for the purpose of better matching a given data set is not allowed.
- A greater number of results from independently developed quasi-analytical solutions or verified numerical solution models may be helpful for diagnosing disagreements among them.

Combining Empirical, Analytical, and Comparative Techniques

A comparison between measured and calculated performance represents a small region in an immense *N*-dimensional parameter space. Investigators are constrained to exploring relatively few regions in this space, yet would like to ensure that the results are not coincidental (e.g., not a result of offsetting errors) and represent the validity of the simulation elsewhere in the parameter space. Analytical and comparative techniques minimize the uncertainty of extrapolations around the limited number of sampled empirical domains. Table 9 classifies these extrapolations.

Figure 19 shows one process to combine analytical, empirical, and comparative techniques. These three techniques may also be used together in other ways; for example, intermodel comparisons may be done before an empirical validation exercise, to better define the experiment and to help estimate experimental uncertainty by propagating all known error sources through one or more whole-building energy simulation programs (Hunn et al. 1982; Lomas et al. 1994).

Table 9 Types of Extrapolation

Obtainable Data Points	Extrapolation
A few climates	Many climates
Short-term total energy use	Long-term total energy use, or vice versa
Short-term (hourly) temperatures and/or fluxes	Long-term total energy use, or vice versa
A few equipment performance points	Many equipment performance points
A few buildings representing a few sets of variable and parameter combinations	Many buildings representing many sets of variable and parameter combinations, or vice versa*
Small-scale: simple test cells, buildings, and mechanical systems; laboratory experiments	Large-scale complex buildings with complex HVAC systems, or vice versa

Source: Judkoff and Neymark (2006).

*Extrapolation can go both ways (e.g., from short- to long-term data and from long- to short-term data). This does not mean that such extrapolations are correct, only that researchers and practitioners have explicitly or implicitly made such inferences in the past.

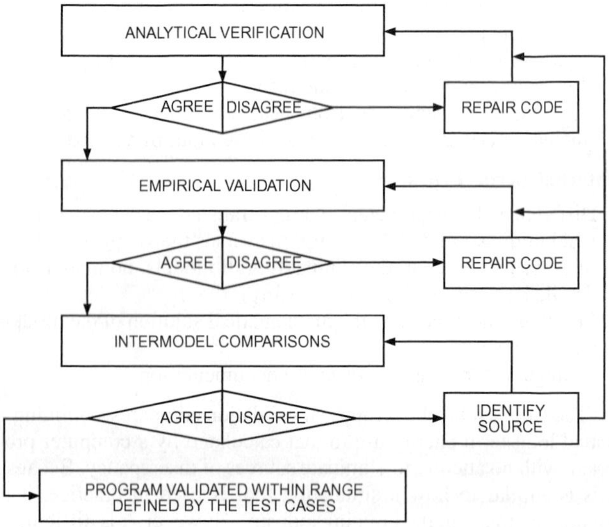

Fig. 19 Validation Method
(Judkoff et al. 1983/2008)

For the path shown in Figure 19, the first step is running the code against analytical verification test cases to check its mathematical solutions. Discrepancies must be corrected before proceeding further. Second, the code is run against high-quality empirical validation data, and errors are corrected. Diagnosing error sources can be quite difficult. Comparative techniques can be used to create diagnostic procedures (Achermann and Zweifel 2003; Judkoff 1988; Judkoff and Neymark 1995a, 1995b; Judkoff et al. 1980, 1983/2008; Morck 1986; Neymark and Judkoff 2002, 2004; Purdy and Beausoleil-Morrison 2003; Spitler et al. 2001; Yuill and Haberl 2002) and better define the empirical experiments. The third step is to check agreement of several different programs with different thermal solution and modeling approaches (that have passed through steps 1 and 2) in a variety of representative cases. This uses the comparative technique as an extrapolation tool. Deviations in the program predictions indicate areas for further investigation.

When programs successfully complete these three stages, they are considered validated for cases where acceptable agreement was achieved (i.e., for the range of building, climate, and mechanical system types represented by the test cases). Once several detailed simulation programs have satisfactorily completed the procedure, other programs and simplified design tools can be tested against them. A validated code does not necessarily represent truth. It does represent a set of algorithms that have been shown, through a repeatable procedure, to perform according to the current state of the art. Similarly, the example results and associated computer programs in the nonnormative sections of *Standard* 140 do not represent truth, but rather an attempt to identify the range of uncertainty in the current state of the art via a well-defined and repeatable procedure. It is anticipated that, as building energy simulation programs improve, the informative example results in *Standard* 140 will be periodically updated, and the range of differences among test case results may be reduced.

The NREL methodology for validating building energy simulation programs has been generally accepted by the International Energy Agency (Irving 1988), ASHRAE *Standard* 140, ASHRAE *Standard* 90.1, and elsewhere, with refinements suggested by other researchers (Bland 1992; Bloomfield 1988, 1999; Guyon and Palomo 1999b; Irving 1988; Lomas 1991; Lomas and Bowman 1987; Lomas and Eppel 1992). Additionally, the Commission of European Communities has conducted considerable work under the PASSYS program (Jensen 1989; Jensen and van de Perre 1991).

Testing Model Calibration Techniques Using Synthetic Data

Calibration is commonly used in conjunction with energy retrofit audit models (Judkoff et al. 2011a, 2011b; Reddy et al. 2006). This test method was initially developed by NREL for testing calibration procedures used with residential retrofit audit software; however, the fundamental concept could also be applied in a commercial building context. Other terms frequently used to describe model calibration include model tuning, model true-up, and model reconciliation.

Typically, residential and commercial model calibration has been implemented using monthly energy data collected from utility bills for an existing building that is about to receive an energy retrofit. Sometimes submetered, disaggregated, or higher-frequency data are also available. An audit gathers information about the building needed to construct an input file for a building energy simulation program. A calibration method reconciles model predictions with the data, and then the calibrated model is used to predict energy savings and energy cost savings from various combinations of retrofit measures. Many variations on this approach exist, including some where the savings predictions are subjected to calibration instead of, or along with, the model inputs.

Although it is logical to use the building's actual performance data to tune the model, it is not certain that this results in a model that better predicts post-retrofit energy savings. When calibrating a large number of inputs to a limited number of outputs (in mathematics, an underdetermined or overparameterized problem), there are many combinations of input parameters that result in a close match to the utility bill data, so a close match is not in itself proof of good calibration (Reddy et al. 2006). The lower the frequency or informational content of the building performance data, the lower the probability that the calibration actually improves the model and associated energy savings predictions. Therefore, any method to test calibration techniques should use as many of the following three figures of merit as possible: (1) accuracy of the savings prediction, (2) how closely the calibrated input parameter values match the actual parameter values, and (3) the goodness of fit between the modeled and measured data. A limiting factor in attempting to empirically validate calibration techniques is the lack of high-quality annual monthly pre- and post-retrofit energy data, (higher frequency and submetered data are better), good pre- and post-retrofit building characteristics data, local pre- and post-retrofit weather data, and the dates of the retrofit installations. Until enough such empirical data are available to researchers, an alternative analytical method can be used in which a simulation program is used to generate its own synthetic pre and post-retrofit energy performance data. The synthetic data may be used as a surrogate for actual data. The method follows these general procedures:

1. Specify a building for a test case and introduce input uncertainty into the test specification (this represents the uncertainty associated with developing inputs from audit survey data):
   (a) Perform sensitivity tests on inputs with potentially high uncertainties to determine their relative effects on outputs; select inputs that have both substantial uncertainties and effects on outputs as **approximate inputs**.
   (b) Specify an uncertainty range (**approximate input range**) for each approximate input.
   (c) Select **explicit inputs** from the approximate input ranges (those who perform the calibrations must not know the explicit inputs).
2. Perform simulations using explicit inputs to create synthetic utility bill data. (Currently, this is typically monthly data, but the method can be used to generate and test against higher- or lower-frequency synthetic building energy performance data, or end-use data at varying levels of disaggregation, mimicking the availability of submetered data).
   (a) Perform simulations to generate post-retrofit energy savings results by adjusting appropriate base-case inputs, including explicit inputs, as specified for each retrofit case and combinations of cases.
3. Develop tested program results (those who do this must not know the explicit inputs):
   (a) Develop the preliminary base-case model for a given calibration scenario.
   (b) Predict energy savings using one of the following:
      i. Calibrate the base-case model inputs using synthetic utility bills (from step 2), then apply the specified retrofit cases to the calibrated model.
      ii. Apply the specified retrofit to the uncirculated base case model and then calibrate or correct energy savings predictions using the synthetic utility bills (without adjustment to base-case model inputs); for example, (Calibrated savings) = (Predicted savings) × (Base-case actual bills)/(Base-case predicted bills).
      iii. Other calibration methods. The test cases make no recommendation about how to perform calibrations. Any calibration method that seeks to improve energy savings predictions through use of pre-retrofit building energy performance data can be tested by this method.
4. Use the following comparisons as figures of merit to determine the usefulness of the calibration techniques being tested. Note that all three of the listed comparisons are important for assessing the accuracy of the calibration technique. A large disagreement in any one of them indicates the presence of compensating errors, or some other error.
   (a) Compare the savings predictions from the tested program and any associated calibration techniques, versus the savings predictions from the same program run with the explicit inputs.
   (b) Compare the goodness of fit between synthetic building energy performance data and the calibrated model output data for the pre-retrofit case(s).
   (c) For programs where a calibrated base-case model is applied (see step 3bi), compare tested program inputs resulting from the tested program's calibration techniques to the randomly selected explicit inputs.

The preceding method is a pure (isolated) test of the calibration technique: that is, the synthetic utility billing data are generated with the tested program, and the program accuracy related to building physics modeling is not tested. A pure calibration test requires (1) automated calibration where no human judgment is required that would be helped by knowing the explicit inputs, or (2) that the modeler running the calibration test does not know the

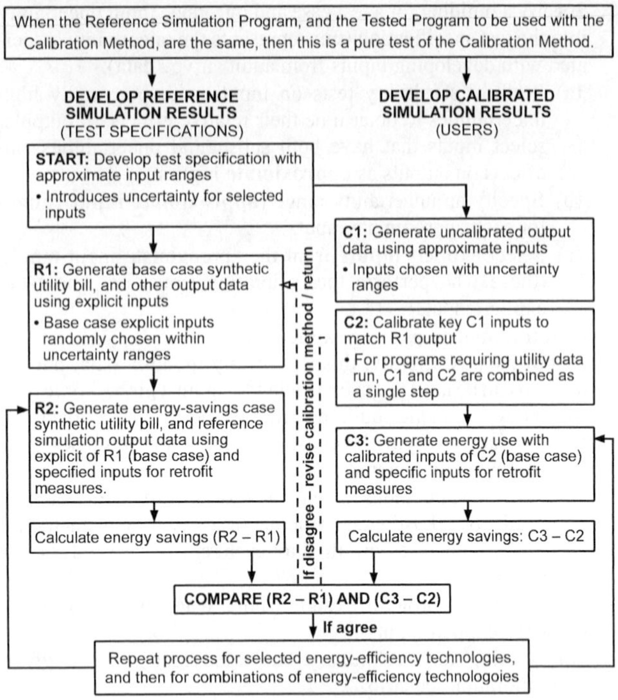

Fig. 20 Calibration Cases Conceptual Flow
(Judkoff et al. 2011a)

explicit inputs used to develop the synthetic utility bills. This method facilitates self-testing of a calibration technique, and is useful in several ways, including (1) testing a single calibration method, (2) testing several calibration methods to determine under what test conditions each is best, and (3) investigating how much and what kind of informational content is needed in the synthetic calibration data to achieve good calibrations with different calibration methods. The pure calibration test, however, may not be practical for a certification test that must be administered by a third-party organization; for this case, a method developed by NREL (Judkoff et al. 2011a, 2011b) ensures that the person performing the test does not know the explicit inputs. The main feature of this test method is that several (preferably at least three) reference programs are used to generate the synthetic utility bills and create the reference energy savings data. The bills and savings are taken as the average of the reference program results. This method tests both the calibration technique, and how closely the physics models in the tested program match the physics models in the reference programs. Example acceptance criteria may be used to facilitate the comparison of energy savings predictions (Judkoff et al. 2011a). Figure 20 shows the overall conceptual approach to testing model calibration techniques.

REFERENCES

ASHRAE members can access *ASHRAE Journal* articles and ASHRAE research project final reports at technologyportal.ashrae.org. Articles and reports are also available for purchase by nonmembers in the online ASHRAE Bookstore at www.ashrae.org/bookstore.

Abushakra, B., and D.E. Claridge. 2008. Modeling office building occupancy in hourly data-driven and detailed energy simulation programs. *ASHRAE Transactions*114(2).

Abushakra, B., J. Haberl, D. Claridge, and A. Sreshthaputra. 2000. Compilation of diversity factors and schedules for energy and cooling load calculations. ASHRAE Research Project RP-1093, *Final Report*.

Abushakra, B., T.A. Reddy, M.T. Paulus, and V. Singh. 2014. Measurement, modeling, analysis and reporting protocols for short-term M&V of whole building energy performance. ASHRAE Research Project RP-1404, *Final Report*.

Achermann, M., and G. Zweifel. 2003. *RADTEST—Radiant heating and cooling test cases*. University of Applied Sciences of Central Switzerland, Lucerne School of Engineering and Architecture. archive.iea-shc.org/publications/downloads/RADTEST_final.pdf.

AIA. 2012. *An architect's guide to integrating energy modeling in the design process*. American Institute of Architects, Washington, D.C.

AIA. 2014. *AIA 2030 commitment, 2014 progress report*. American Institute of Architects, Washington, D.C.

Alamdari, F., and G.P. Hammond. 1982. Time-dependent convective heat transfer in warm-air heated rooms. *Energy Conservation in the Built Environment: Proceedings of the CIB W67 Third International Symposium*, Dublin, pp. 209-220.

Alamdari, F., and G.P. Hammond. 1983. Improved data correlations for buoyancy-driven convection in rooms. *Building Services Engineering Research and Technology* 4(3):106-112.

Ali, M.T., M.M. Mokhtar, M. Chiesa, and P.R. Armstrong. 2011. A cooling change-point model of community-aggregate electrical load. *Energy and Buildings* 43(1):28-37.

Altmayer, E.F., A.J. Gadgil, F.S. Bauman, and R.C. Kammerud. 1983. Correlations for convective heat transfer from room surfaces. *ASHRAE Transactions* 89(2A):61-77.

Andersen, I., and M.J. Brandemuehl. 1992. Heat storage in building thermal mass: A parametric study. *ASHRAE Transactions* 98(1):910-918.

Andolsun, S., C. Culp, and J. Haberl. 2010. *EnergyPlus vs. DOE-2: The effect of ground coupling on heating and cooling energy consumption of a slab-on-grade code house in a cold climate*. ESL-PA-10-08-03. College Station, Texas: Texas A&M University. esl.tamu.edu/docs/terp/2010/ESL-PA-10-08-03.pdf.

Andrews, C.J., D. Yi, U. Krogmann, J.A. Senick, and R.E. Wener. 2011. Designing buildings for real occupants: An agent-based approach. *IEEE Transactions on Systems, Man and Cybernetics, Part A: Systems and Humans*.

Anstett, M., and J.F. Kreider. 1993. Application of artificial neural networks to commercial building energy use prediction. *ASHRAE Transactions* 99(1):505-517.

Arasteh, D., C. Kohler, and B. Griffith. 2009. Modeling windows in EnergyPlus with simple performance indices. *Report* LBNL-2804E. Lawrence Berkeley National Laboratory, Berkeley, CA.

Armstrong, P.R., C.E. Hancock, and J.E. Seem. 1992. Commercial building temperature recovery—Part I: Design procedure based on a step-response model. *ASHRAE Transactions* 98(1).

Armstrong, P.R., G.P. Sullivan, and G.B. Parker. 2006a. *Field demonstration of a high-efficiency packaged rooftop air conditioning unit at Fort Gordon, Augusta, GA—Final Report*. PNNL-15746.

Arvo, J. 1986. Backward ray tracing. In *Developments in Ray Tracing* SIGGRAPH '86 Course Notes, Volume 12. www.cs.washington.edu/education/courses/cse457/06au/projects/trace/extra/Backward.pdf.

ASHRAE. 2010. Engineering analysis of experimental data. *Guideline* 2-2010.

ASHRAE. 2014. Measurement of energy and demand savings. *Guideline* 14-2014.

ASHRAE. 2013. Energy standard for buildings except low-rise residential buildings. ANSI/ASHRAE/IES *Standard* 90.1-2013.

ASHRAE. 2014. Method of test for the evaluation of building energy analysis computer programs. ANSI/ASHRAE *Standard* 140-2014.

ASHRAE. 2007. Peak cooling and heating load calculations in buildings except low-rise residential buildings. ANSI/ASHRAE/ACCA *Standard* 183-2007 (RA2014).

ASHRAE. 2014. Design of high-performance, green buildings except low-rise residential buildings. ANSI/ASHRAE/USGBC/IES *Standard* 189.1-2014.

ASHRAE. 2013. *Weather data viewer, version 5.0*. (DVD).

Axley, J.W. 2001. Residential passive ventilation systems: Evaluation and design. AIVC *Technical Note* 54. Air Infiltration and Ventilation Centre, Energy in Buildings and Communities (EBC) Programme, International Energy Agency, Coventry, UK.

Axley, J.W. 2007. Multizone airflow modeling in buildings: History and theory. *HVAC&R Research* (now *Science and Technology for the Built Environment*) 13(6):907-928.

Axley, J.W., and S.J. Emmerich. 2002. A method to assess the suitability of a climate for natural ventilation of commercial buildings. *Proceedings: Indoor Air (2002)*, Monterey, CA.

Aynsley, R.M., B.J. Vickery, and W. Melbourne. 1977. *Architectural aerodynamics.* Chapter 6. Applied Sciences Publishers, Essex, England, UK.

Bahnfleth, W.P., and C.O. Pedersen. 1990. A three dimensional numerical study of slab-on-grade heat transfer. *ASHRAE Transactions* 2(96):61-72.

Baker, N.V., A. Fanchiotti, and K. Steemers. 1993. *Daylighting in architecture: A European reference book*. Earthscan, London.

Balcomb, J.D., and J.C. Hedstrom. 1976. A simplified method for calculating required solar collector array size for space heating. *Proceedings of International Solar Energy Society (ISES) Annual Meeting, Winnipeg, Canada*, August 15-20, pp. 280-294.

Barnaby, C., J. Spitler, and D. Xiao. 2005. The residential heat balance method for heating and cooling load calculations. *ASHRAE Transactions* 111(1):308-319.

Barnaby, C., J. Wright, and M. Collins. 2009. Improving load calculations for fenestration with shading devices. *ASHRAE Transactions* 115:31-44.

Bauman, F., A. Gadgil, R. Kammerud, E. Altmayer, and M. Nansteel. 1983. Convective heat transfer in buildings: Recent research results. *ASHRAE Transactions* 89(1A):215-232.

Beausoleil-Morrison, I. 1996. BASECALC: A software tool for modelling residential foundation heat losses. *Proceedings of the Third Canadian Conference on Computing in Civil and Building Engineering*, Montreal, pp. 117-126.

Beausoleil-Morrison, I., and G. Mitalas. 1997. BASESIMP: A residential-foundation heat-loss algorithm for incorporating into whole-building energy-analysis programs. *Proceedings of Building Simulation '97* (2): 1-8. International Building Performance Simulation Association, Prague, Czech Republic.

Beck, J.V., and K.J. Arnold. 1977. *Parametric estimation in engineering and science.* John Wiley & Sons, New York.

Ben-Nakhi, A. 2007. *Modeler report for BESTEST cases GC10a-GC80c, FLUENT version 6.0.20.* In Section 2.9, Appendix II-B, in Neymark et al. (2008). Public Authority for Applied Education and Training, Kuwait.

Bhandari, M.S., S.S. Shrestha, and J.R. New. 2012. Evaluation of weather datasets for building energy simulation. *Energy and Buildings* 49:109-118. dx.doi.org/10.1016/j.enbuild.2012.01.033.

Bland, B. 1992. Conduction in dynamic thermal models: Analytical tests for validation. *Building Services Engineering Research & Technology* 13(4): 197-208.

Bloomfield, D. 1988. *An investigation into analytical and empirical validation techniques for dynamic thermal models of buildings*, vol. 1, Executive Summary. SERC/BRE final report, Building Research Establishment, Garston, U.K.

Bloomfield. D. 1999. An overview of validation methods for energy and environmental software. *ASHRAE Transactions* 105(2).

Bohn, M.S., A.T. Kirkpatrick, and D.A. Olson. 1984. Experimental study of three-dimensional natural convection high-Rayleigh number. *Journal of Heat Transfer* 106:339-345.

Bonne, U., and J.E. Janssen. 1977. Efficiency and relative operating cost of central combustion heating system: IV, oil fired residential systems. *ASHRAE Transactions* 83(1):893-904.

Bourdouxhe, J.P., M. Grodent, J. Lebrun, and C. Saavedra. 1994a. A toolkit for primary HVAC system energy calculation—Part 1: Boiler model. *ASHRAE Transactions* 100(2):759-773.

Bourdouxhe, J.P., M. Grodent, J. Lebrun, C. Saavedra, and K. Silva. 1994b. A toolkit for primary HVAC system energy calculation—Part 2: Reciprocating chiller models. *ASHRAE Transactions* 100(2):774-786.

Bourdouxhe, J.P., M. Grodent, and C. Silva. 1994c. Cooling tower model developed in a toolkit for primary HVAC system energy calculation—Part 1: Model description and validation using catalog data. *Proceedings of the Fourth International Conference on System Simulation in Buildings.*

Bou-Saada, T., and J. Haberl. 1995a. A weather-day typing procedure for disaggregating hourly end-use loads in an electrically heated and cooled building from whole-building hourly data. *Proceedings of the 30th IECEC*, pp. 349-356.

Bou-Saada, T., and J. Haberl. 1995b. An improved procedure for developing calibrated hourly simulation models. *Proceedings of Building Simulation '95*. International Building Performance Simulation Association, Madison, WI.

Brandemuehl, M.J. 1993. *HVAC2 toolkit: Algorithms and subroutines for secondary HVAC systems energy calculations.* ASHRAE.

Brandemuehl, M.J., and J.D. Bradford. 1999. Optimal supervisory control of cooling plants without storage. ASHRAE Research Project RP-823, *Final Report.*

Brandemuehl, M.J., and S. Gabel. 1994. Development of a toolkit for secondary HVAC system energy calculations. *ASHRAE Transactions* 100(1):21-32.

Braun, J.E. 1990. Reducing energy costs and peak electrical demand through optimal control of building thermal mass. *ASHRAE Transactions* 96(2): 876-888.

Braun, J.E. 1992. A comparison of chiller-priority, storage-priority, and optimal control of an ice-storage system. *ASHRAE Transactions* 98(1): 893-902.

Braun, J.E., S.A. Klein, and J.W. Mitchell. 1989. Effectiveness models for cooling towers and cooling coils. *ASHRAE Transactions* 95(2):164-174.

Bronson, D., S. Hinchey, J. Haberl, and D. O'Neal. 1992. A procedure for calibrating the DOE-2 simulation program to non-weather dependent loads. *ASHRAE Transactions* 98(1):636-652.

Buchberg, H. 1955. Electric analogue prediction of the thermal behavior of an inhabitable enclosure. *ASHVE Transactions* 61:339-386.

Buhl, W.F., A.E. Erdem, J.M. Nataf, F.C. Winkelmann, M.A. Moshier, and E.F. Sowell. 1990. The US EKS: Advances in the SPANK-based energy kernel system. *Proceedings of the Third International Conference on System Simulation in Buildings*, pp. 107-150.

Buhl, W.F., A.E. Erdem, F.C. Winkelmann, and E.F. Sowell. 1993. Recent improvements in SPARK: Strong component decomposition, multivalued objects and graphical interface. *Proceedings of Building Simulation '93*, pp. 283-390. International Building Performance Simulation Association.

Burkhart, M.C., Y. Heo, and V.M. Zavala. 2014. Measurement and verification of building systems under uncertain data: A Gaussian process modeling approach. *Energy and Buildings* 75(June):189-198. dx.doi.org /10.1016/j.enbuild.2014.01.048.

Carrier. 2013. *What's new with HAP*. www.carrier.com/commercial/en /us/software/hvac-system-design/hourly-analysis-program/.

Carroll, J.A. 1980. An "MRT method" of computing radiant energy exchange in rooms. *Proceedings of Systems Simulation and Economic Analysis*, San Diego, pp. 343-348.

Carroll, J.A. 1981. A comparison of radiant interchange algorithms. *Proceedings of the 3rd Annual Systems Simulation and Economics Analysis/ Solar Heating and Cooling Operational Results Conference*, Reno. Solar Engineering, Proceedings of the ASME Solar Division.

Chandra, S., and A.A. Kerestecioglu. 1984. Heat transfer in naturally ventilated rooms: Data from full-scale measurements. *ASHRAE Transactions* 90(1B):211-224.

Chantrasrisalai, C., D. Fisher, I. Iu, and D. Eldridge. 2003a. Experimental validation of design cooling load procedures: The heat balance method. *ASHRAE Transactions* 109(2):160-173.

Chantrasrisalai, C., V. Ghatti, D. Fisher, and D. Scheatzle. 2003b. Experimental validation of the EnergyPlus low-temperature radiant simulation. *ASHRAE Transactions* 109(2):614-623.

Chen, H., S. Deng, D.E. Claridge, W.D. Turner, and N. Bensouda. 2005. Replacing inefficient equipment—An engineering analysis to justify purchasing a more efficient chiller. *Proceedings of the 4th International Conference on Enhanced Building Operation*, Pittsburgh.

Chenvidyakarn, T., A. Woods. 2005. Multiple steady states in stack ventilation. *Building and Environment* 40:399-410.

CIBSE. 2005. Natural ventilation in non-domestic buildings. *Applications Manual* AM10, Chartered Institution of Building Services Engineers, London.

Claridge, D. 1998. A perspective on methods for analysis of measured energy data from commercial buildings. *ASME Journal of Solar Energy Engineering* 120:150.

Claridge, D., M. Krarti, and J. Kreider. 1993. Energy calculations for basements, slabs, and crawl spaces. ASHRAE Research Project RP-666, *Final Report.*

Clarke, J. A. 2001. *Energy simulation in building design,* 2nd ed. Routledge, Glasgow, Scotland, UK.

Clements, E. 2004. *Three dimensional foundation heat transfer modules for whole-building energy analysis.* MS thesis, Pennsylvania State University.

Coakley, D., P. Raftery, and M. Keane. 2014. A review of methods to match building energy simulation models to measured data. *Renewable and Sustainable Energy Reviews* 37:123-141.

Cole, R.J. 1976. The longwave radiation incident upon the external surface of buildings. *The Building Services Engineer* 44:195-206.

COMNET. 2016. COMNET Modeling Guidelines and Procedures. www.comnet.org.

Cooper, K.W., and D.R. Tree. 1973. A re-evaluation of the average convection coefficient for flow past a wall. *ASHRAE Transactions* 79:48-51.

Corcoran, J.P., and T.A. Reddy. 2003. Improving the process of certified and witnessed factory testing for chiller procurement. *ASHRAE Transactions* 109(1).

Corson, G.C. 1992. Input-output sensitivity of building energy simulations. *ASHRAE Transactions* 98(1):618.

Crawley, D.B., L.K. Lawrie, F.C. Winkelmann, W.F. Buhl, Y. Joe Huang, C.O. Pedersen, R.K. Strand, R.J. Liesen, D.E. Fisher, M.J. Witte, and J. Glazer. 2001. EnergyPlus: Creating a new-generation building energy simulation program. *Energy and Buildings* 33(4):319-331.

Crawley, D.B., J.W. Hand, M. Kummert, and B.T. Griffith. 2005. *Contrasting the capabilities of building energy performance simulation programs*. U.S. Department of Energy, Washington, D.C.

Crowley, M. 2007. Modeler report for BESTEST cases GC10a-GC80c, MATLAB 7.0.4.365 (R14) service pack 2. Dublin Institute of Technology. Included with Section 2.9, Appendix II-C, of Neymark et al. (2008).

Cumali, Z., A.O. Sezgen, R. Sullivan, R.C. Kammerud, E. Bales, and L.B. Bass. 1979. Extensions of methods used in analyzing building thermal loads. *Proceedings of the Thermal Performance of the Exterior Envelopes of Buildings*, pp. 411-420.

Davies, M.G. 1988. Design models to handle radiative and convective exchange in a room. *ASHRAE Transactions* 94(2):173-195.

Deb, K., A. Pratap, S. Agarwal, and T. Meyarivan. 2002. A fast and elitist multiobjective genetic algorithm: NSGA-II. *IEEE Transactions on Evolutionary Computation* 6(2):182-197.

DeCicco, J.M. 1990. Applying a linear model to diagnose boiler fuel consumption. *ASHRAE Transactions* 96(1):296-304.

Deru, M. 2003. A model for ground-coupled heat and moisture transfer from buildings. *Report* NREL/TP-550-33954. National Renewable Energy Laboratory, Golden, CO. www.nrel.gov/docs/fy03osti/33954.pdf.

Deru, M.P., R. Judkoff, and P. Torcellini. 2002. SUNREL, technical reference manual. *Report* NREL/BK-550-30193. National Renewable Energy Laboratory, Golden, CO.

Deru, M., K. Field, D. Studer, K. Benne, B. Griffith, P. Torcellini, B. Liu, M. Halvorsen, D. Winiarski, M. Rosenberg, M. Yazdanian, J. Huang, and D. Crawley. 2011. U.S. Department of Energy commercial reference building models of the national building stock. *Report* NREL/TP-5500-46861. National Renewable Energy Laboratory, Golden, CO.

de Wit, S., and G. Augenbroe. 2002. Analysis of uncertainty in building design evaluations and its implications. *Energy and Buildings* 34:951-958.

Dhar, A. 1995. *Development of Fourier series and artificial neural network approaches to model hourly energy use in commercial buildings*. Ph.D. dissertation, Mechanical Engineering Department, Texas A&M University.

Dhar, A., T.A. Reddy, and D.E. Claridge. 1998. Modeling hourly energy use in commercial buildings with Fourier series functional forms. *Journal of Solar Energy Engineering* 120:217.

Dhar, A., T.A. Reddy, and D.E. Claridge. 1999a. A Fourier series model to predict hourly heating and cooling energy use in commercial buildings with outdoor temperature as the only weather variable. *Journal of Solar Energy Engineering* 121:47-53.

Dhar, A., T.A. Reddy, and D.E. Claridge. 1999b. Generalization of the Fourier series approach to model hourly energy use in commercial buildings. *Journal of Solar Energy Engineering* 121:54-62.

Dogan, T., C. Reinhart, and P. Michalatos. 2015. Autozoner: An algorithm for automatic thermal zoning of buildings with unknown interior space definitions. *Journal of Building Performance Simulation* 9(2):176-189.

Dols, W.S., S.J. Emmerich, and B.J. Polidoro. 2012. LoopDA 3.0, Natural ventilation design and analysis software user guide. NIST *Technical Note* 1735. National Institute of Standards and Technology, Gaithersburg, MD.

Dols, W.S., S.J. Emmerich, and B.J. Polidoro. 2016a. Using coupled energy, airflow and indoor air quality software (TRNSYS/CONTAM) to evaluate building ventilation strategies. *Building Services Engineering Research and Technology* 37(2):163-175.

Dols, W.S., S.J. Emmerich, and B.J. Polidoro. 2016b. Coupling the multizone airflow and contaminant transport software CONTAM with EnergyPlus using co-simulation. *Building Simulation* 9:469-479.

Draper, N., and H. Smith. 1981. *Applied regression analysis*, 2nd ed. John Wiley & Sons, New York.

Duffie, J.A., and W.A. Beckman. 2013. *Solar engineering of thermal processes,* 4th ed. John Wiley & Sons, Inc., Hoboken, NJ.

Durrani, F., M.J. Cook, and J.J McGuirk. 2015. Evaluation of LES and RANS CFD modelling of multiple steady states in natural ventilation. *Building and Environment* 92:167-181.

Edwards, R.E. 2013. *Automating large-scale simulation calibration to real-world sensor data*. Ph.D. dissertation. University of Tennessee, Knoxville.

Eldridge, D., D. Fisher, I. Iu, and C. Chantrasrisalai. 2003. Experimental validation of design cooling load procedures: Facility design. *ASHRAE Transactions* 109(2):151-159.

Emmerich, S. J., B. Polidoro, and J. W. Axley. 2011. Impact of adaptive thermal comfort on climatic suitability of natural ventilation in office buildings. *Energy and Buildings* 43(9):2101-2107.

Emmerich, S. J., W. S. Dols, and B. J. Polidoro. 2012. Application of a natural ventilation system design tool to a school building. *SimBuild 2012, Fifth National Conference of IBPSA-USA*, Madison, WI.

Energy Design Resources. 2012. *HVAC Simulation Guidebook,* vol. 1. www.energydesignresources.com/resources/publications/design-guidelines/design-guidelines-hvac-simulation-guidelines.aspx.

Energy.gov. 2015. Qualified software for calculating commercial building tax deductions. energy.gov/eere/buildings/qualified-software-calculating-commercial-building-tax-deductions.

Englander, S.L., and L.K. Norford. 1992. Saving fan energy in VAV systems—Part 1: Analysis of a variable-speed-drive retrofit. *ASHRAE Transactions* 98(1):3-18.

Erbs, D.G., S.A. Klein, and W.A. Beckman. 1983. Estimation of degree-days and ambient temperature bin data from monthly-average temperatures. *ASHRAE Journal* 25(6):60.

Eskilson, P. 1987. *Thermal analysis of heat extraction boreholes*. University of Lund, Sweden.

ESRU. 2016. *ESP-r—An integrated building/plant simulation tool*. Energy Systems Research Unit, University of Strathclyde, Glasgow. www.esru.strath.ac.uk/Programs/ESP-r.htm.

Evans, D.L., T.T. Rule, and B.D. Wood. 1982. A new look at long term collector performance and utilizability. *Solar Energy* 28(1):13-23.

Fels, M., ed. 1986. Measuring energy savings: The scorekeeping approach. *Energy and Buildings* 9.

Fracastoro, G., M. Masoero, and M. Cali. 1982. Surface heat transfer in building components. *Proceedings of the Thermal Performance of the Exterior Envelopes of Buildings II*, pp. 180-203.

Garrett, A. and J.R. New. 2014. A scientific study of automated calibration applied to DOE commercial reference buildings. *Report* ORNL/TM-2014/709. Oak Ridge National Laboratory, Oak Ridge, TN.

Garrett, A. and J.R. New. 2015. Scalable tuning of building energy models to hourly data. *Journal of Energy* 84:493-502.

Garrett, A., J.R. New, and T. Chandler. 2013. Evolutionary tuning of building models to monthly electrical consumption. *ASHRAE Transactions* 119(2):89-100. *Paper* DE-13-008.

Gayeski, N.T., T. Zakula, P.R. Armstrong, and L.K. Norford. 2011. Empirical modeling of a rolling-piston compressor heat pump for predictive control in low-lift cooling. *ASHRAE Transactions* 117(2).

Gayeski, N.T., P.R. Armstrong, and L.K. Norford. 2012. Predictive pre-cooling of thermo-active building systems with low-lift chillers. *HVAC&R Research* (now *Science and Technology for the Built Environment*) 18(5):1-16.

Georgescu, M., B. Eisenhower, and I. Mezic. 2012. Creating zoning approximations to building energy models using the Koopman operator. *Proceedings of the IBPSA-USA SimBuild 2012, Madison, WI*, pp. 40-47.

Goldstein, K., and A. Novoselac. 2010. Convective heat transfer in rooms with ceiling slot diffusers (RP-1416). *HVAC&R Research* (now *Science and Technology for the Built Environment*) 16(5):629-655.

Goral, C.M., K.E. Torrance, D.P.Greenberg, and B. Battaile. 1984. Modeling the interaction on light between diffuse surfaces. *Proceedings of the 11th Annual Conference on Computer Graphics and Interactive Techniques (SIGGRAPH '84), New York, NY*, pp. 213-22.

Gordon, J.M., and K.C. Ng. 1994. Thermodynamic modeling of reciprocating chillers. *Journal of Applied Physics* 75(6):2769-2774.

Gordon, J.M., and K.C. Ng. 1995. Predictive and diagnostic aspects of a universal thermodynamic model for chillers. *International Journal of Heat and Mass Transfer* 38(5):807-818.

Gordon, J.M., and K.C. Ng. 2000. *Cool thermodynamics*. Cambridge Press.

Gordon, J.M., K.C. Ng, and H.T. Chua. 1995. Centrifugal chillers: Thermodynamic modeling and a case study. *International Journal of Refrigeration* 18(4):253-257.

Gordon, J.M., K.C. Ng, H.T. Chua, and C.K. Lim. 2000. How varying condenser coolant flow rate affects chiller performance: Thermodynamic modeling and experimental confirmation. *Applied Thermal Engineering* 20.

Gowri, K., D. Winiarski, and R. Jarnagin. 2009. Infiltration modeling guidelines for commercial building analysis. *Report* PNNL-18898. Pacific Northwest National Laboratory, Richland, WA.

Grantham, B. 2008. COEN 290 Computer graphics I—Week 8—Ray tracing. www.plunk.org/COEN-290/Notes/Week8.ppt

Gunay, H.B., W. O'Brien, and I. Beausoleil-Morrison. 2013. A critical review of observation studies, modeling, and simulation of adaptive occupant behaviors in offices. *Building and Environment* 70:31-47.

Guyon, G., and E. Palomo. 1999a. Validation of two French building energy programs—Part 2: Parameter estimation method applied to empirical validation. *ASHRAE Transactions* 105(2):709-720.

Guyon, G., and E. Palomo. 1999b. Validation of two French building energy analysis programs—Part 1: Analytical verification. *ASHRAE Transactions* 105(2).

Haberl, J.S., and T.E. Bou-Saada. 1998. Procedures for calibrating hourly simulation models to measured building energy and environmental data. *ASME Journal of Solar Energy Engineering* 120(August):193.

Haberl, J., and S. Cho. 2004. Literature review of uncertainty of analysis methods: Inverse model toolkit. *Report* ESL-TR-04-10-03, Energy Systems Laboratory, Texas A&M University, College Station.

Haberl, J.S., and D.E. Claridge. 1987. An expert system for building energy consumption analysis: Prototype results. *ASHRAE Transactions* 93(1): 979-998.

Haberl, J.S., and C.H. Culp. 2012. Review of methods for measuring and verifying savings from energy conservation retrofits to existing buildings (second edition). *Report* ESL-TR-12-03-02, Energy Systems Laboratory, Texas A&M University, College Station.

Haberl, J., and P. Komor. 1990a. Improving commercial building energy audits: How annual and monthly consumption data can help. *ASHRAE Journal* 32(8):26-33.

Haberl, J., and P. Komor. 1990b. Improving commercial building energy audits: How daily and hourly data can help. *ASHRAE Journal* 32(9): 26-36.

Haberl, J.S., and S. Thamilseran. 1996. The great energy predictor shootout II: Measuring retrofit savings and overview and discussion of results. *ASHRAE Transactions* 102(2):419-435.

Haberl, J., S. Thamilseran, A. Reddy, D. Claridge, D. O'Neal, and W. Turner. 1998. Baseline calculations for measurement and verification of energy and demand savings in a revolving loan program in Texas. *ASHRAE Transactions* 104:841-858.

Haberl, J., D. Claridge, and K. Kissock. 2003. Inverse model toolkit (RP-1050): Application and testing. *ASHRAE Transactions* 109(2):435-448.

Hammarsten, S. 1984. *Estimation of energy balances for houses.* National Swedish Institute for Building Research.

Hammarsten, S. 1987. A critical appraisal of energy-signature models. *Applied Energy* 26(2):97-110.

Hellstrom, G. 1989. *Duct ground heat storage model: Manual for computer code*. Department of Mathematical Physics, University of Lund, Sweden.

Heo, Y. 2011. *Bayesian calibration of building energy models for energy retrofit decision-making under uncertainty*. Ph.D. dissertation. Georgia Institute of Technology, Atlanta.

Heo, Y., and V.M. Zavala. 2012. Gaussian process modeling for measurement and verification of building energy savings. *Energy and Buildings* 53 (October):7-18.

Heo, Y., D.J. Graziano, V.M. Zavala, P. Dickinson, M. Kamrath, and M. Kirshenbaum. 2013. Cost-effective measurement and verification method for determining energy savings under uncertainty. *ASHRAE Transactions* 119(2).

Hirsch, J.J. 2003. *eQUEST–Introductory Tutorial, version 3.64.* James J. Hirsch & Associates, Camarillo, CA.

Hittle, D.C. 1977. The building loads analysis and system thermodynamics (BLAST) program. CERL *Technical Report* E-119. U.S. Army Construction Engineering Research Laboratory (CERL), Champaign, IL.

Hoes, P., J. Hensen, M.G.L.C. Loomans, B. de Vries, and D. Bourgeois. 2009. User behavior in whole building simulation. *Building and Environment* 41:209-302.

Hong, T., S. D'Oca, S.C. Taylor-Lange, W.J.N. Turner, Y. Chen, and S.P. Corgnati. 2015a. An ontology to represent energy-related occupant behavior in buildings. Part II: Implementation of the DNAS framework using an XML schema. *Building and Environment* 94:196-205.

Hong, T., M.A. Piette, Y. Chen, S.H. Lee, S.C. Taylor-Lange, R. Zhang, K. Sun, and P. Price. 2015b. Commercial building energy saver: An energy retrofit analysis toolkit. *Applied Energy* 159:298-309.

Hong, T., H. Sun, Y. Chen, S. Taylor-Lange, D. Yan. 2016a. An occupant behavior modeling tool for co-simulation. *Energy and Buildings* 117: 272-281.

Hong, T., K. Sun, R. Zhang, R. Hinokuma, S. Kasahara, and Y. Yura. 2016b. Development and validation of a new variable refrigerant flow system model in EnergyPlus. *Energy and Buildings* 117:399-411.

Hopfe, C.J., and J.L.M. Hensen. 2011. Uncertainty analysis in building performance simulation for design support. *Energy and Buildings* 43:2798-2805.

Hopkinson, R.G., J. Longmore, and P. Petherbridge. 1954. An empirical formula for the computation of the indirect component of daylight factor. *Transactions of the Illuminating Engineering Society* 19(7):201-19.

Huang, J., J.S. Haberl, and J.F. Kreider. 2001. *Handbook of heating, ventilation, and air conditioning*. J.F. Kreider, ed. CRC Press, Boca Raton, FL.

Hunn, B.D., W.V. Turk, and W.O. Wray. 1982. *Validation of passive solar analysis/design tools using Class A performance evaluation data*. LA-UR-82-1732, Los Alamos National Laboratory, NM.

Hybrid Ventilation Centre. 2002. *Principles of hybrid ventilation*. IEA Energy Conservation in Buildings and Community Systems Programme, Annex 35: Hybrid Ventilation in New and Retrofitted Office Buildings. P. Heiselberg, ed. Hybrid Ventilation Centre, Aalborg University, Denmark.

Hydeman, M., and K. Gillespie. 2002. Tools and techniques to calibrate electric chiller component models. *ASHRAE Transactions* 108(1):733-741.

Hydeman, M., N. Webb, P. Sreedharan, and S. Blanc. 2002. Development and testing of a reformulated regression-based electric chiller model. *ASHRAE Transactions* 108(2).

IBPSA-USA. 2015. *Building energy software tools directory*. www.buildingenergysoftwaretools.com.

IEA EBC. 2013-2017. International Energy Agency's Energy in Buildings and Communities Programme. Annex 66: Definition and simulation of occupant behavior in buildings. www.annex66.org.

IEA ECBCS. 1987. *Annex 10, building HEVAC system simulation*. International Energy Agency, Energy Conservation in Buildings and Community Systems Programme. Summary available at www.ecbcs.org/annexes/annex10.htm#p.

IECC. 2015. *International energy conservation code®*. International Code Council, Washington, D.C.

IgCC. 2015. *International green construction code® (IgCC®)*. International Code Council, Washington, D.C.

Irving, A. 1988. *Validation of dynamic thermal models, energy, and buildings*. Elsevier Sequoia, Lausanne, Switzerland.

ISO. 1998. Thermal performance of buildings—Heat transfer via the ground—Calculation methods. *Standard* 13370. European Committee for Standardization, Brussels.

Iu, I., and D. Fisher. 2004. Application of conduction transfer functions and periodic response factors in cooling load calculation procedures. *ASHRAE Transactions* 110:829-841.

Iu, I., C. Chantrasrisalai, D. Eldridge, and D. Fisher. 2003. Experimental validation of design cooling load procedures: The radiant time series method. *ASHRAE Transactions* 109(2):139-150.

Jakubiec, J.A., and C.F. Reinhart. 2011. DIVA 2.0: Integrating daylight and thermal simulations using Rhinoceros 3D, Daysim and EnergyPlus. *Proceedings of 12th IBPSA Conference,* Sydney, Australia, November 14-16.

JCEM. 1992. Final report: Artificial neural networks applied to LoanSTAR data. Joint Center for Energy Management *Report* TR/92/15.

Jensen, S., ed. 1989. *The PASSYS project phase 1—Subgroup model validation and development, Final report—1986-1989.* Commission of the European Communities, Directorate General XII.

Jensen, S., and R. van de Perre. 1991. Tools for whole model validation of building simulation programs: Experience from the CEC concerted action PASSYS. *Proceedings of Building Simulation '91*, Nice, France. International Building Performance Simulation Association.

Jiang, W., and T.A. Reddy. 2003. Re-evaluation of the Gordon-Ng performance models for water-cooled chillers. *ASHRAE Transactions* (109).

Jones, B.M., M.J. Cook, S.D. Fitzgerald, and C.R. Iddon. 2016. A review of ventilation opening area terminology. *Energy and Buildings* 118:249-258.

Judkoff, R. 1988. Validation of building energy analysis simulation programs at the Solar Energy Research Institute. *Energy and Buildings* 10(3):235.

Judkoff, R., and J. Neymark. 1995a. *International Energy Agency Building Energy Simulation Test (BESTEST) and diagnostic method*. NREL/TP-472-6231. National Renewable Energy Laboratory, Golden, CO. www.nrel.gov/docs/legosti/old/6231.pdf.

Judkoff, R., and J. Neymark. 1995b. *Home Energy Rating System Building Energy Simulation Test (HERS BESTEST)*, vols. 1 and 2. NREL/TP-472-7332. National Renewable Energy Laboratory, Golden, CO. www.nrel.gov/docs/legosti/fy96/7332a.pdf and www.nrel.gov/docs/legosti/fy96/7332b.pdf.

Judkoff, R., and J. Neymark. 2006. Model validation and testing: The methodological foundation of ASHRAE *Standard* 140. *ASHRAE Transactions* 112(2):367-376.

Judkoff, R., and J. Neymark. 2009. What did they do in IEA 34/43? Or how to diagnose and repair bugs in 500,000 lines of code. *Proceedings of Building Simulation* 2009. Glasgow. International Building Performance Simulation Association. Preprint version, NREL *Report* CP-550-44978, National Renewable Energy Laboratory, Golden, CO. www.nrel.gov/docs/fy09osti/44978.pdf.

Judkoff, R., D. Wortman, C. Christensen, B. O'Doherty, D. Simms, and M. Hannifan. 1980. *A comparative study of four passive building energy simulations: DOE-2.1, BLAST, SUNCAT-2.4, DEROB-III*. SERI/TP-721-837. UC-59c. Solar Energy Research Institute (now National Renewable Energy Laboratory), Golden, CO.

Judkoff, R., D. Wortman, B. O'Doherty, and J. Burch. 1983/2008. *A methodology for validating building energy analysis simulations*. SERI/TR-254-1508. Solar Energy Research Institute (now National Renewable Energy Laboratory), Golden, CO. (Republished as NREL/TP-550-42059, April 2008.) www.nrel.gov/docs/fy08osti/42059.pdf.

Judkoff, R., J.D. Balcomb, C.E. Hancock, G.Barker, and K. Subbarao. 2000. Side-by-side thermal tests of modular offices: A validation study of the STEM method. NREL *Report* TP-550-23940. National Renewable Energy Laboratory, Golden, CO.

Judkoff, R., J. Neymark, B. Polly, and M. Bianchi. 2011a. The Building Energy Simulation Test For Existing Homes (BESTEST-EX) methodology. *Proceedings Building Simulation 2011*, International Building Performance Simulation Association. Preprint version, NREL *Report* CP-5500-51655, National Renewable Energy Laboratory, Golden, CO. www.nrel.gov/docs/fy12osti/51655.pdf.

Judkoff, R., B. Polly, M. Bianchi, J. Neymark, and M. Kennedy. 2011b. *Building Energy Simulation Test For Existing Homes (BESTEST-EX): Instructions for implementing the test procedure, calibration test reference results, and example acceptance-range criteria*. NREL TP-5500-52414. National Renewable Energy Laboratory, Golden, CO. www.nrel.gov/docs/fy11osti/52414.pdf.

Kamal, S., and P. Novak. 1991. Dynamic analysis of heat transfer in buildings with special emphasis on radiation. *Energy and Buildings* 17(3):231-241.

Kaplan, M., J. McFerran, J. Jansen, and R. Pratt. 1990. Reconciliation of a DOE2.1C model with monitored end-use data from a small office building. *ASHRAE Transactions* 96(1):981.

Katipamula, S., T.A. Reddy, and D.E. Claridge. 1994. Development and application of regression models to predict cooling energy consumption in large commercial buildings. *Proceedings of the 1994 ASME/JSME/JSES International Solar Energy Conference*, San Francisco, p. 307.

Katipamula, S., T.A. Reddy, and D.E. Claridge. 1998. Multivariate regression modeling. *ASME Journal of Solar Energy Engineering* 120 (August):176.

Kaye, N.B., Y. Ji, and M.J. Cook. 2009. Numerical simulation of transient flow development in a naturally ventilated room. *Building and Environment* 44(5):889-897.

Kays, W.M., and A.L. London. 1984. *Compact heat exchangers*, 3rd ed. McGraw-Hill, New York.

Kennedy, M. and A. O'Hagan. 2001. Bayesian calibration of computer models. *Journal of the Royal Statistical Society*, pp. 425-464.

Kerrisk, J.F., N.M. Schnurr, J.E. Moore, and B.D. Hunn. 1981. The custom weighting-factor method for thermal load calculation in the DOE-2 computer program. *ASHRAE Transactions* 87(2):569-584.

Khalifa, A.J.N., and R.H. Marshall. 1990. Validation of heat transfer coefficients on interior building surfaces using a real-sized indoor test cell. *International Journal of Heat and Mass Transfer* 33(10):2219-2236.

Kiureghian, A.D., and O. Ditlevsen. 2009. Aleatory or epistemic? Does it matter? *Structural Safety* 31:105-112.

Kissock, J.K., T.A. Reddy, J.S. Haberl, and D.E. Claridge. 1993. E-model: A new tool for analyzing building energy use data. *Proceedings of the Industrial Energy Technology Conference*, Texas A&M University.

Kissock, J.K., T.A. Reddy, and D.E. Claridge. 1998. Ambient temperature regression analysis for estimating retrofit savings in commercial buildings. *ASME Journal of Solar Energy Engineering* 120:168.

Kissock, K., J. Haberl, and D. Claridge. 2003. Inverse model toolkit (RP-1050): Numerical algorithms. *ASHRAE Transactions* 109(2):425-434.

Klein, S.A. 1993. Design methods for active solar systems. Ch. 3, pp. 39-80, in *Active solar systems*, G. Löf, ed. The MIT Press, Cambridge, MA.

Klein, S.A., and W.A. Beckman. 2001a. *F-chart user's manual: F-chart software*. www.fchart.com.

Klein, S.A., and W.A. Beckman. 2001b. *PV F-Chart user's manual: DOS version: F-Chart software*. www.fchart.com.

Klein, S.A., W.A. Beckman, and J.A. Duffie. 1994. *TRNSYS: A transient simulation program*. Engineering Experiment Station *Report* 38-14, University of Wisconsin-Madison.

Knebel, D.E. 1983. *Simplified energy analysis using the modified bin method*. ASHRAE.

Krarti, M. 1994a. Time varying heat transfer from slab-on-grade floors with vertical insulation. *Building and Environment* 29(1):55-61.

Krarti, M. 1994b. Time varying heat transfer from horizontally insulated slab-on-grade floors. *Building and Environment* 29(1):63-71.

Krarti, M. 2010. *Energy audit of building systems: An engineering approach*, 2nd ed. CRC Press, FL.

Krarti, M., and P. Chuangchid. 1999. *Cooler floor heat gain for refrigerated structures*. ASHRAE Research Project TRP-953, *Final Report*.

Krarti, M., D.E. Claridge, and J. Kreider. 1988a. The ITPE technique applied to steady-state ground-coupling problems. *International Journal of Heat and Mass Transfer* 31:1885-1898.

Krarti, M., D.E. Claridge, and J. Kreider. 1988b. ITPE method applications to time-varying two-dimensional ground-coupling problems. *International Journal of Heat and Mass Transfer* 31:1899-1911.

Krarti, M., J.F. Kreider, D. Cohen, and P. Curtiss. 1998. Estimation of energy savings for building retrofits using neural networks. *ASME Journal of Solar Energy Engineering* 120:211.

Kreider, J.F., and J. Haberl. 1994. Predicting hourly building energy usage: The great predictor shootout—Overview and discussion of results. *ASHRAE Transactions* 100(2):1104-1118.

Kreider, J.F., and A. Rabl. 1994. *Heating and cooling of buildings*. McGraw-Hill, New York.

Kreider, J.F., and X.A. Wang. 1991. Artificial neural networks demonstration for automated generation of energy use predictors for commercial buildings. *ASHRAE Transactions* 97(1):775-779.

Kruis, N.J.F. 2015. *Development and application of a numerical framework for improving building foundation heat transfer calculations*. Ph.D. dissertation. Department of Civil, Environmental, and Architectural Engineering, University of Colorado, Boulder.

Kuchkuda, R. 1988. Theoretical foundations of computer graphics and CAD. In *An introduction to ray tracing*, pp. 1039-1060. R.A. Earnshaw, ed. Springer-Verlag, London.

Kusuda, T. 1969. Thermal response factors for multi-layer structures of various heat conduction systems. *ASHRAE Transactions* 75(1):246-271.

Langevin, J., P.L. Gurian, and J. Wen. 2014. Including occupants in building performance simulation: Integration of an agent-based occupant behavior algorithm with EnergyPlus. *ASHRAE/IBPSA-USA Simulation Conference,* Atlanta.

Laret, L. 1991. Simplified performance models for cycling operation of boilers. *ASHRAE Transactions* 97(2):212-218.

LBNL. 1984. *DOE-2 reference manual.* Lawrence Berkeley National Laboratory, Berkeley, CA.

LBNL. 1998. Overview of DOE-2.2. www.doe2.com/Download/Docs/22_oview.pdf.

LBNL. 2016. *Windows & daylighting software tools*. windows.lbl.gov/software/.

Lebrun, J. 1993. Testing and modeling of fuel oil space-heating boilers—Synthesis of available results. *ASHRAE Transactions* 99(2).

Lebrun, J.J., J. Hannay, J.M. Dols, and M.A. Morant. 1985. Research of a good boiler model for HVAC energy simulation. *ASHRAE Transactions* 91(1B):60-83.

Lebrun, J., J.-P. Bourdouxhe, and M. Grodent. 1999. *HVAC 1 toolkit: A toolkit for primary HVAC system energy calculation*. ASHRAE.

Lee, S.H., and W. Chen. 2008. A comparative study of uncertainty propagation methods for black-box-type problems. *Structural and Multidisciplinary Optimization* 37:239-253.

Lewis, P.T., and D.K. Alexander. 1990. HTB2: A flexible model for dynamic building simulation. *Building and Environment* 25(1):7-16.

Linden, P.F., G.F. Lane-Serff, and D.A. Smeed. 1990. Emptying filling boxes: The fluid mechanics of natural ventilation. *Journal of Fluid Mechanics* 212:309-335.

Liu, G., and M. Liu. 2011. Applications of a simplified model calibration procedure for commonly used HVAC systems. *ASHRAE Transactions* 117:835-846.

Lokmanhekim, M. 1971. Description of the program and details of the load program. *Proceedings of the USPS Symposium: Computer Program for Analysis of Energy Utilization*, Washington, D.C., pp. 29-79.

Lomas, K. 1991. Dynamic thermal simulation models of buildings: New method of empirical validation. *Building Services Engineering Research & Technology* 12(1):25-37.

Lomas, K., and N. Bowman. 1987. Developing and testing tools for empirical validation. Ch. 14, vol. IV of SERC/BRE final report, *An investigation in analytical and empirical validation techniques for dynamic thermal models of buildings*. Building Research Establishment, Garston, U.K.

Lomas, K., and H. Eppel. 1992. Sensitivity analysis techniques for building thermal simulation programs. *Energy and Buildings* (19)1:21-44.

Lomas, K., H. Eppel, C. Martin, and D. Bloomfield. 1994. *Empirical validation of thermal building simulation programs using test room data*. Vol. 1, Final Report. International Energy Agency Report #IEA21RN399/94. Vol. 2, Empirical Validation Package (1993), IEA21RR5/93. Vol. 3, Working Reports (1993), IEA21RN375/93. De Montfort University, Leicester, U.K.

Lomas, K.J., M.J. Cook and D. Fiala. 2007. Low energy architecture for a severe US climate: Design and evaluation of a hybrid ventilation strategy. *Energy and Buildings* 39(1):32-44.

Lorenzetti, D.M., and L.K. Norford. 1993. Pressure reset control of variable air volume ventilation systems. *Proceedings of the ASME International Solar Energy Conference*, Washington, D.C., p. 445.

Macdonald, I., and P. Strachan. 2001. Practical application of uncertainty analysis. *Energy and Buildings* 33:219-227.

MacDonald, J.M., and D.M. Wasserman. 1989. Investigation of metered data analysis methods for commercial and related buildings. Oak Ridge National Laboratory *Report* ORNL/CON-279.

Malkawi, A., B. Yan, Y. Chen, and Z. Tong. 2016. Predicting thermal and energy performance of mixed-mode ventilation using an integrated simulation approach. *Building Simulation* 9:335-346.

Malmström, T.G., B. Mundt, and A.G. Bring. 1985. A simple boiler model. *ASHRAE Transactions* 91(1B):87-108

Manke, J.M., D.C. Hittle, and C.E. Hancock. 1996. Calibrating building energy analysis models using short-term data. *Proceedings of the ASME International Solar Energy Conference*, San Antonio, p. 369.

Matthieu, J.L., P.N. Price, S. Kiliccote, and M.A. Piette. 2011. Quantifying changes in building electricity use, with application to demand response. *IEEE Transactions on Smart Grid* 2:507-518.

McQuiston, F.C., and J.D. Spitler. 1992. *Cooling and heating load calculation manual*. ASHRAE.

Melo, C., and G.P. Hammond. 1991. Modeling and assessing the sensitivity of external convection from building facades. In *Heat and mass transfer in building materials and structures*, pp. 683-695. J.B. Chaddock and B. Todorovic, eds. Hemisphere, New York.

Miller, R., and J. Seem. 1991. Comparison of artificial neural networks with traditional methods of predicting return from night setback. *ASHRAE Transactions* 97(2):500-508.

Mills, A.F. 1999. *Heat transfer*, 2nd ed. Prentice-Hall.

Mitalas, G.P., and D.G. Stephenson. 1967. Room thermal response factors. *ASHRAE Transactions* 73(1):III.2.1-III.2.10.

Monfet, D., R. Zmeureanu, R. Charneux, and N. Lemire. 2009. Calibration of a building energy model using measured data. *ASHRAE Transactions* 115(1):348-359.

Monsen,W.A., S.A. Klein, and W.A. Beckman. 1981. The unutilizability design method for collector-storage walls. *Proceedings of Annual Meeting, American Section of the International Solar Energy Society, Philadelphia, PA*, May 26-30, pp. 862-866.

Morck, O. 1986. Simulation model validation using test cell data. IEA SHC Task VIII, *Report* 176, Thermal Insulation Laboratory, Technical University of Denmark, Lyngby.

Nessi, A., and N. Nisolle. 1925. *Regimes Variables de Fonctionnement dans les Installations de Chauffage Central*. Dunod, Paris.

Neter, J., W. Wasseran, and M. Kutner. 1989. *Applied linear regression models*, 2nd ed. Richard C. Irwin, Homewood, IL.

New, J.R. 2016. Autotune calibration and trinity test evaluation. In *Seminar 59, Simulation Calibration Methods: Which Should I Choose?* ASHRAE Winter Conference, Orlando, FL.

New, J.R., J. Sanyal, M.S. Bhandari., and S.S. Shrestha. 2012. Autotune EnergyPlus building energy models. *SimBuild 2012, 5th National Conference of IBPSA-USA*, Madison, WI. International Building Performance Simulation Association, www.ibpsa.us.

Neymark, J., and R. Judkoff. 2002. *International Energy Agency Building Energy Simulation Test and diagnostic method for heating, ventilating, and air-conditioning equipment models (HVAC BESTEST)*, vol. 1: Cases E100-E200. NREL/TP-550-30152. National Renewable Energy Laboratory, Golden, CO. www.nrel.gov/docs/fy02osti/30152.pdf.

Neymark, J., and R. Judkoff. 2004. *International Energy Agency Building Energy Simulation Test and diagnostic method for heating, ventilating, and air-conditioning equipment models (HVAC BESTEST)*, vol. 2: Cases E300-E545. NREL/TP-550-36754. National Renewable Energy Laboratory, Golden, CO. www.nrel.gov/docs/fy05osti/36754.pdf.

Neymark, J., P. Girault, G. Guyon, R. Judkoff, R. LeBerre, J. Ojalvo, and P. Reimer. 2005. ETNA BESTEST empirical validation data set. NREL *Report* CP-2000-57544. Also in *Proceedings of Buildings Simulation 2005: 9th Conference of International Building Performance Simulation Association*, pp. 839-846. National Renewable Energy Laboratory, Golden, CO.

Neymark, J., R. Judkoff, I. Beausoleil-Morrison, A. Ben-Nakhi, M. Crowley, M. Deru, R. Henninger, H. Ribberink, J. Thornton, A. Wijsman, and M. Witte. 2008. *International Energy Agency Building Energy Simulation Test and Diagnostic Method (IEA BESTEST) in-depth diagnostic cases for ground coupled heat transfer related to slab-on-grade construction*. NREL/TP-550-43388. National Renewable Energy Laboratory, Golden, CO. Available at www.nrel.gov/docs/fy08osti/43388.pdf.

Neymark, J., M. Kennedy, R. Judkoff, J. Gall, R. Henninger, T. Hong, D. Knebel, T. McDowell, M. Witte, D. Yan, and X. Zhou. 2016. Airside HVAC BESTEST: Adaptation of ASHRAE RP 865 airside HVAC equipment modeling test cases for ASHRAE *Standard* 140, vol 1: Cases AE101-AE445. NREL/TP-5500-66000. National Renewable Energy Laboratory, Golden, CO. www.nrel.gov/docs/fy16osti/66000.pdf.

Nisson, J.D.N., and G. Dutt. 1985. *The superinsulated home book*. John Wiley & Sons, New York.

NIST. 2000-2016. *CONTAM software*. National Institute of Standards and Technology, Gaithersburg, MD. www.bfrl.nist.gov/IAQanalysis/CONTAM.

Norford, L.K., R.H. Socolow, E.S. Hsieh, and G.V. Spadaro. 1994. Two-to-one discrepancy between measured and predicted performance of a low-energy office building: Insights from a reconciliation based on the DOE-2 model. *Energy and Buildings* 21:121.

Nottage, H.B., and G.V. Parelee. 1954. Circuit analysis applied to load estimating. *ASHVE Transactions* 60:59-102.

NRC. 2004. *Clean energy project analysis: RETScreen engineering & cases textbook*, Solar water heating project analysis chapter. Natural Resources Canada, Ottawa.

O'Brien, P.F. 1955. Interreflections in rooms by a network method. *Journal of the Optical Society of America* 45(6):419-24.

Oh, S. 2013. *Origins of analysis methods in energy simulation programs used for high performance commercial buildings*. Master's thesis. Texas A&M University, College Station.

Oh, S., and J.S. Haberl. 2016a. Origins of analysis methods used to design high performance commercial buildings: Whole-building energy simulation. *Science and Technology for the Built Environment* 22(1):118-127. www.tandfonline.com/doi/abs/10.1080/23744731.2015.1063958.

Oh, S., and J.S. Haberl. 2016b. Origins of analysis methods used to design high performance commercial buildings: Solar energy analysis. *Science and Technology for the Built Environment* 22(1):87-106. www.tandfonline .com/doi/abs/10.1080/23744731.2015.1090277.

Oh, S., and J.S. Haberl. 2016c.Origins of analysis methods used to design high performance commercial buildings: Daylighting simulation. *Science and Technology for the Built Environment* 22(1):107-117. www.tandfonline .com/doi/abs/10.1080/23744731.2015.1090278?journalCode=uhvc21.

Olgyay, V. 1973. *Design with climate.* Chapter 9. Princeton University Press. Princeton, NJ.

O'Neill, Z., B. Eisenhower, S. Yuan, T. Bailey, S. Narayanan, and V. Fonoberov. 2011. Modeling and calibration of energy models for a DoD building. *ASHRAE Transactions* 117:358-365.

Oppenheim, A.K. 1954. *The network method of radiation analysis.* Heat Transfer and Fluid Mechanics Institute, University of California, Berkeley.

Park, C., D.R. Clark, and G.E. Kelly. 1985. An overview of HVACSIM+, a dynamic building/HVAC control systems simulation program. *Proceedings of the First Building Energy Simulation Conference.*

Paschkis, V. 1942. Periodic heat flow in building walls determined by electrical analogy method. *ASHVE Transactions* 48:75-90. American Society of Heating and Ventilating Engineers, New York.

Paschkis, V., and H.D. Baker. 1942. A method for determining unsteady-state heat transfer by means of an electrical analogy. *ASME Transactions* 64:105-12.

Paulus, M.T., D.E. Claridge, and C. Culp. 2015. Algorithm for automating the selection of a temperature dependent change point model. *Energy and Buildings* 87:95-104.

Pedersen, C.O., D.E. Fisher, and R.J. Liesen. 1997. Development of a heat balance procedure for calculating cooling loads. *ASHRAE Transactions* 103:459-68.

Pedersen, C.O., R.J. Liesen, R.K. Strand, D.E. Fisher, L. Dong, and P.G. Ellis. 2001. *ASHRAE toolkit for building load calculations.* ASHRAE.

Pedersen, C.O., D.E. Fisher, R.J. Liesen, and R.K. Strand. 2003. ASHRAE toolkit for building load calculations. *ASHRAE Transactions* 109(1):583-589.

Peeters, L., I. Beausoliel-Morrison, B. Griffith, and A. Novoselac. 2011. Internal convection coefficients for building simulation. *Proceedings of Building Simulation 2011,* Sydney. International Building Performance Simulation Association.

Phelan, J., M.J. Brandemuehl, and M. Krarti. 1996. Final Report ASHRAE Project RP-827: Methodology development to measure in-situ chiller, fan, and pump performance. JCEM *Report* No. JCEM/TR/96-3, University of Colorado at Boulder.

Purdy, J., and I. Beausoleil-Morrison. 2003. Building Energy Simulation Test and diagnostic method for heating, ventilating, and air-conditioning equipment models (HVAC BESTEST), fuel-fired furnace. Natural Resources Canada CANMET Energy Technology Centre, Ottawa, ON. www.iea-shc.org/data/sites/1/publications/Furnace%20HVAC%20 BESTEST%20Report.pdf.

Rabl, A. 1988. Parameter estimation in buildings: Methods for dynamic analysis of measured energy use. *Journal of Solar Energy Engineering* 110:52-66.

Rabl, A., and A. Riahle. 1992. Energy signature model for commercial buildings: Test with measured data and interpretation. *Energy and Buildings* 19:143-154.

Raftery, P. 2011. *Calibrated whole building energy simulation: An evidence-based methodology.* Ph.D. dissertation. College of Engineering and Informatics, National University of Ireland.

Reddy, T. 1989. Application of dynamic building inverse models to three occupied residences monitored non-intrusively. *Proceedings of the Thermal Performance of Exterior Envelopes of Buildings IV,* ASHRAE/DOE/ BTECC/CIBSE.

Reddy, A. 2006. Literature review on calibration of building energy simulation programs: Uses, problems, procedures, uncertainty, and tools. *ASHRAE Transactions* 112(1):226-240.

Reddy, A. 2011. *Applied data analysis and modeling for energy engineers and scientists.* Springer, New York.

Reddy, T.A., and K.K. Andersen. 2002. An evaluation of classical steady-state off-line linear parameter estimation methods applied to chiller performance data. *International Journal of HVAC&R Research* (now *Science and Technology for the Built Environment*) 8(1):101-124.

Reddy, T., and D. Claridge. 1994. Using synthetic data to evaluate multiple regression and principle component analyses for statistical modeling of daily building energy consumption. *Energy and Buildings* 24:35-44.

Reddy, A., and I. Maor. 2006. Procedures for reconciling computer-calculated results with measured energy data. ASHRAE Research Project RP-1051, *Final Report.*

Reddy, T.A., S. Katipamula, J.K. Kissock, and D.E. Claridge. 1995. The functional basis of steady-state thermal energy use in air-side HVAC equipment. *Journal of Solar Energy Engineering* 117:31-39.

Reddy, T.A., N.F. Saman, D.E. Claridge, J.S. Haberl, W.D. Turner, and A. Chalifoux. 1997. Baselining methodology for facility level monthly energy use—Part 1: Theoretical aspects. *ASHRAE Transactions* 103(2): 336-347.

Reddy, T.A., S. Deng, and D.E. Claridge. 1999. Development of an inverse method to estimate overall building and ventilation parameters of large commercial buildings. *Journal of Solar Energy Engineering* 121:47.

Reddy, T.A., I. Maor, C. Panjapornporn, and J. Sun. 2006. Procedures for reconciling computer-calculated results with measured energy use. ASHRAE Research Project RP-1051, *Final Report.*

Reddy, A., I. Maor, and C. Panjapornporn. 2007a. Calibrating detailed building energy simulation programs with measured data—Part I: General methodology (RP-1051). *HVAC&R Research* (now *Science and Technology for the Built Environment*) 13(2):221-241.

Reddy, A., I. Maor, and C. Panjapornporn. 2007b. Calibrating detailed building energy simulation programs with measured data—Part II: Application to three case study office buildings (RP-1051). *HVAC&R Research* (now *Science and Technology for the Built Environment*) 13(2):243-265.

RESNET. 2015. *Residential energy services network.* www.resnet.us /professional/programs.

Riddle, M., and R. Muehleisen. 2014. A guide to Bayesian calibration of building energy models. *Proceedings of the 2014 ASHRAE/IBPSA-USA Building Simulation Conference,* Atlanta.

Robertson, J., B. Polly, and J. Collis. 2013. *Evaluation of automated model calibration techniques for residential building energy simulation.* NREL/ TP-5500-60127. National Renewable Energy Laboratory, Golden, CO.

Robinson, D., U. Wilke, and F. Haldi. 2011. Multi agent simulation of occupants' presence and behavior. *Proceedings of Building Simulation,* Sydney, Australia.

Ruch, D., and D. Claridge. 1991. A four parameter change-point model for predicting energy consumption in commercial buildings. *Proceedings of the ASME International Solar Energy Conference,* pp. 433-440.

Ruch, D., L. Chen, J. Haberl, and D. Claridge. 1993. A change-point principle component analysis (CP/CAP) method for predicting energy use in commercial buildings: The PCA model. *Journal of Solar Energy Engineering* 115:77-84.

Sanyal, J., J.R. New., and R.E. Edwards. 2013. Calibrating building energy models using supercomputer trained machine learning agents. *Journal on Concurrency and Computation: Practice and Experience* 26(13): 2122-2133.

Seem, J.E., and J.E. Braun. 1991. Adaptive methods for real-time forecasting of building electricity demand. *ASHRAE Transactions* 97(1):710.

Seem, J.E., S.A. Klein, W.A. Beckman, and J.W. Mitchell. 1989. Comprehensive room transfer functions for efficient calculation of transient heat transfer in buildings. *ASME Journal of Heat Transfer* 111(5):264-273.

Sherman, M.H., and C.P. Wray. 2010. Parametric system curves: Correlations between fan pressure rise and flow for large commercial buildings. *Report* LBNL-3542E. Lawrence Berkeley National Laboratory, Berkeley, CA.

Singh, V., Reddy, T.A., and B. Abushakra. 2013. Predicting annual energy use in buildings using short-term monitoring and utility bills: The hybrid inverse model using daily data (HIM-D). *ASHRAE Transactions* 119(2): 169-180.

Sonderegger, R.C. 1977. *Dynamic models of house heating based on equivalent thermal parameters.* Ph.D. dissertation, Center for Energy and Environmental Studies *Report* 57. Princeton University, Princeton, NJ.

Sonderegger, R.C. 1985. Thermal modeling of buildings as a design tool. *Proceedings of CHMA 2000,* vol. 1.

Sonderegger, R.C. 1998. Baseline equation for utility bill analysis using both weather and non-weather related variables. *ASHRAE Transactions* 104(2):859-870.

Sonderegger, R.C., Garnier, J.Y., and Dixon, J.D. 1982. *Computerized instrumented residential audit (CIRA/sup TM/).* Lawrence Berkeley National Laboratory, Berkeley, CA.

Song, S., and J. Haberl. 2008a. A procedure for the performance evaluation of a new commercial building: Part I—Calibrated as-built simulation. *ASHRAE Transactions* 114:375-388.

Song, S., and J. Haberl. 2008b. A procedure for the performance evaluation of a new commercial building: Part II—Overall methodology and comparison of methods. *ASHRAE Transactions* 114:389-403.

Sowell, E.F. 1988. Classification of 200,640 parametric zones for cooling load calculations. *ASHRAE Transactions* 94(2):716-736.

Sowell, E.F. 1990. Lights: A numerical lighting/HVAC test cell. *ASHRAE Transactions* 96(2):780-786.

Sowell, E.F., and M.A. Moshier. 1995. HVAC component model libraries for equation-based solvers. *Proceedings of Building Simulation '95*, Madison, WI.

Spitler, J.D., C.O. Pedersen, and D.E. Fisher. 1991. Interior convective heat transfer in buildings with large ventilative flow rates. *ASHRAE Transactions* 97(1):505-515.

Spitler, J.D., D.E. Fisher, and C.O. Pedersen. 1997. The radiant time series cooling load calculation procedure. *ASHRAE Transactions* 103(2):503-15.

Spitler, J., S. Rees, and D. Xiao. 2001. Development of an analytical verification test suite for whole building energy simulation programs—Building fabric. ASHRAE Research Project RP-1052, *Final Report*. Oklahoma State University School of Mechanical and Aerospace Engineering, Stillwater.

Sreedharan, P., and P. Haves. 2001. Comparison of chiller models for use in model-based fault detection. *International Conference for Enhanced Building Operations* (ICEBO), Texas A&M University, Austin.

Steinman, M., L.N. Kalisperis, and L.H. Summers. 1989. The MRT-correction method: A new method of radiant heat exchange. *ASHRAE Transactions* 95(1):1015-1027.

Stephenson, D.G., and G.P. Mitalas. 1967. Cooling load calculations by thermal response factor method. *ASHRAE Transactions* 73(1):III.1.1-III.1.7.

Stephenson, D.G., and G.P. Mitalas. 1971. Calculation of heat conduction transfer functions for multi-layer slabs. *ASHRAE Transactions* 77(2): 117-126.

Stoecker, W.F., and J.W. Jones. 1982. *Refrigeration and air conditioning*, 2nd ed. McGraw-Hill, New York.

Strand, R.K., and C.O. Pedersen. 1997. Implementation of a radiant heating and cooling model into an integrated building energy analysis program. *ASHRAE Transactions* 103(1):949-958.

Subbarao, K. 1988. *PSTAR—Primary and secondary terms analysis and renormalization: A unified approach to building energy simulations and short-term monitoring*. SERI/TR-253-3175.

Sun, K., T. Hong, S.C. Taylor-Lange, and M.A. Piette. 2016. A pattern-based automated approach to building energy model calibration. *Applied Energy* 165:214-224.

Sun, Y., L. Gu, C.F.J. Wu, and G. Augenbroe. 2014. Exploring HVAC system sizing under uncertainty. *Energy and Buildings* 81:243-252.

Taylor, R.D., C.O. Pedersen, and L. Lawrie. 1990. Simultaneous simulation of buildings and mechanical systems in heat balance based energy analysis programs. *Proceedings of the Third International Conference on System Simulation in Buildings*, Liege, Belgium.

Taylor, R.D., C.O. Pedersen, D. Fisher, R. Liesen, and L. Lawrie. 1991. Impact of simultaneous simulation of buildings and mechanical systems in heat balance based energy analysis programs on system response and control. *Proceedings of Building Simulation '91*. Sophia Antipolis, International Building Performance Simulation Association, Nice, France.

Thamilseran, S., and J. Haberl. 1995. A bin method for calculating energy conservation retrofit savings in commercial buildings. *Proceedings of the 1995 ASME/JSME/JSES International Solar Energy Conference*, pp. 111-124.

Thornton, J. 2007. *Modeler report for BESTEST cases GC10a-GC80c, TRNSYS version 16.1*. Thermal Energy System Specialists, Madison, WI. Included with Section 2.9, Appendix II-A, of Neymark et al. 2008.

Threlkeld, J.L. 1970. *Thermal environmental engineering*, 2nd ed. Prentice-Hall, Englewood Cliffs, NJ.

Trane. 2013. TRACE 700 version information. Trane Company, LaCrosse, WI. www.trane.com/commercial/north-america/us/en/products-systems/design-and-analysis-tools/analysis-tools/trace-700.html.

Tregenza, P.R. 1989. Modification of the split-flux formulae for mean daylight factor and internal reflected component with large external obstructions. *Lighting Research and Technology* 21:125-128.

TRNSYS. 2012. *TRNSYS: A Transient System Simulation Program—Reference manual*, Ch. 4. S.A. Klein, et al. Solar Energy Laboratory, University of Wisconsin-Madison, June 2012.

Turner, C., and M. Frankel. 2008. *Energy performance of LEED® for new construction buildings: Final report*. U.S. Green Building Council, Washington, D.C. www.usgbc.org/Docs/Archive/General/Docs3930.pdf.

U.S. Department of Energy. 1996-2016. *EnergyPlus*. energyplus.net/.

Vadon, M., J.F. Kreider, and L.K. Norford. 1991. Improvement of the solar calculations in the modified bin method. *ASHRAE Transactions* 97(2).

Walton, G.N. 1980. A new algorithm for radiant interchange in room loads calculations. *ASHRAE Transactions* 86(2):190-208.

Walton, G.N. 1983. *Thermal analysis research program reference manual*. NBSIR 83-2655. National Institute of Standards and Technology, Gaithersburg, MD.

Walton, G.N. 1993. *Computer programs for simulation of lighting/HVAC interactions*. NISTIR 5322. National Institute of Standards and Technology, Gaithersburg, MD.

Waltz, J.P. 1992. Practical experience in achieving high levels of accuracy in energy simulations of existing buildings. *ASHRAE Transactions* 98(1): 606-617.

Wang, X.A., and J.F. Kreider. 1992. Improved artificial neural networks for commercial building energy use prediction. *Journal of Solar Energy Engineering*.

Ward, G.J. 1994. The RADIANCE lighting simulation and rendering system. *Proceedings of '94 SIGGRAPH Conference*, Orlando, FL, July 24-29, pp. 459-472.

Ward, G.J., and F.M. Rubinstein. 1988. A new technique for computer simulation of illuminated spaces. *Journal of the Illuminating Engineering Society* 17(1):80-91.

Ward, G.J., F.M. Rubinstein, and R.D. Clear. 1988. A ray tracing solution for diffuse interreflection. *Computer Graphics* 22(4):85-92.

Webster, T., F. Bauman, K. Lee, S. Schiavon, A. Daly, T. Hoyt. 2013. CBE EnergyPlus modeling methods for UFAD systems. escholarship.org/uc/item/1tj8g346#page-1.

Wetter, M. 2011. Co-simulation of building energy and control systems with the building controls virtual test bed. *Journal of Building Performance Simulation* 4(3):185-203.

Wetter, M., W. Zuo, and T. S. Nouidui. 2011. Modeling of heat transfer in rooms in the Modelica "buildings" library. *Proceedings of Building Simulation 2011*, Sydney.

Whillier, A. 1953. *Solar energy collection and its utilization for house heating*. Ph.D. dissertation, Massachusetts Institute of Technology, Cambridge.

Willcox, T.N., C.T. Oergerl, and S.G. Reque. 1954. Analogue computer analysis of residential cooling loads. *ASHVE Transactions* 60:505-524,

Wilson, E., C. Engebrecht Metzger, S. Horowitz, and R. Hendron. 2014. *2014 Building America simulation protocols*. NREL/TP-5500-60988. National Renewable Energy Laboratory, Golden, CO.

Winkelmann, F. 2002. Underground surfaces: How to get a better underground surface heat transfer calculation in DOE-2.1E. *Building Energy Simulation User News* 23(6):19-26.

Winkelmann, F.C., and S. Selkowitz. 1985. Daylighting simulation in DOE-2: Theory, validation, and applications. *Proceedings of the Building Energy Simulation Conference*, Seattle, WA, pp. 326-337.

Winkelmann, F.C., B.E. Birdsall, W.F. Buhl, K.L. Ellington, A.E. Erdem, J.J. Hirsch, and S. Gates. 1993. DOE-2 supplement version 2.1E. *Report* LBL-34947. Lawrence Berkeley National Laboratory, Berkeley, CA.

Yan, D., W. O'Brien, T. Hong, X. Feng, H.B. Gunay, F. Tahmasebi, and A. Mahdavi. 2015. Occupant behavior modeling for building performance simulation: Current state and future challenges. *Energy and Buildings* 107:264-278. buildings.lbl.gov/sites/all/files/tianzhen_hong_-_occupant_behavior_modeling_for_building_performance_simulation_current_state_and_future_challenges.pdf.

Yazdanian, M., and J. Klems. 1994. Measurement of the exterior convective film coefficient for windows in low-rise buildings. *ASHRAE Transactions* 100(1):1087-1096.

Yi, H. 2015. User-driven automation for optimal thermal-zone layout during space programming phases. *Architectural Science Review* (April). www.researchgate.net/publication/274511916_User-driven_Automation_for_Optimal_Thermal-zone_Layout_during_Space_Programming_Phases.

York, D.A., and C.C. Cappiello, eds. 1982. DOE-2 engineers manual. Lawrence Berkeley Laboratory *Report* LBL-11353 (LA-8520-M, DE83004575). National Technical Information Services, Springfield, VA.

Yuill, G., and J. Haberl. 2002. Development of accuracy tests for mechanical system simulation. ASHRAE Research Project RP-865, *Final Report.* University of Nebraska, Omaha.

Yuill, G., J. Haberl, and J. Caldwell. 2006. Accuracy tests for simulations of VAV dual duct, single zone, four-pipe fan coil, and four-pipe induction air-handling systems. *ASHRAE Transactions* 112(2):377-394.

Zakula, T., N.T. Gayeski, P.R. Armstrong, and L.K. Norford. 2011. Variable-speed heat pump model for a wide range of cooling conditions and load. *HVAC&R Research* (now *Science and Technology for the Built Environment*) 17(5):670-691.

Zakula, T., N.T. Gayeski, P.R. Armstrong, and L.K. Norford. 2012. Optimal coordination of heat pump compressor and fan speeds and subcooling over a wide range of loads and conditions. *HVAC&R Research* (now *Science and Technology for the Built Environment*) 18(5).

BIBLIOGRAPHY

Abushakra, B., J. Haberl, and D. Claridge. 2004. Overview of existing literature on diversity factors and schedules for energy and cooling load calculations. *ASHRAE Transactions* 110:164-176.

Adam, E.J., and J.L. Marchetti. 1999, Dynamic simulation of large boilers with natural recirculation. *Computer and Chemical Engineering* 23 (1999):1031-1040

Andrews, J.W. 1986. Impact of reduced firing rate on furnace and boiler efficiency. *ASHRAE Transactions* 92(1A):246-262.

Armstrong, P., S. Leeb, and L. Norford. 2006. Control with building mass part II: Simulation. *ASHRAE Transactions* 112:462-473.

ASHRAE. 1995. *Bin and degree hour weather data for simplified energy calculations.*

ASHRAE. 1999. A toolkit for primary HVAC system energy calculation. ASHRAE Research Project RP-665, *Report.*

ASHRAE. 2013. Energy standard for buildings except low-rise residential buildings. ANSI/ASHRAE/IES *Standard* 90.1-2013.

Axley, J.W., S.J. Emmerich, and G.N. Walton. 2002. Modeling the performance of a naturally ventilated commercial building with a multizone coupled thermal/airflow simulation tool. *ASHRAE Transactions* 108(2): 1260-1275.

Axtell, R., C. Andrews, and M. Small. 2002. Agent-based modeling and industrial ecology. *Journal of Industrial Ecology* 5:10-14.

Ayres, M.J., and E. Stamper. 1995. Historical development of building energy calculations. *ASHRAE Transactions* 101(1):47-55.

Balcomb, J.D., R.W. Jones, R.D. McFarland, and W.O. Wray. 1982. Expanding the SLR method. *Passive Solar Journal* 1(2).

Beasley, R., J. Haberl, W. Turner, and D. Claridge. 2002. Development of a methodology for baselining the energy use of large multi-building central plants. *ASHRAE Transactions* 108:251-259.

Bonne, U. 1985. Furnace and boiler system efficiency and operating cost versus increased cycling frequency. *ASHRAE Transactions* 91(1B):109-130.

Bonne, U., and A. Patani. 1980. Performance simulation of residential heating systems with HFLAME. *ASHRAE Transactions* 86(1):351.

Braun, J.E. 1988. *Methodologies for the design and control of chilled water systems.* Ph.D. dissertation, University of Wisconsin-Madison.

Claridge, D.E., M. Krarti, and M. Bida. 1987. A validation study of variable-base degree-day cooling calculations. *ASHRAE Transactions* 93(2): 90-104.

Clark, D.R. 1985. *HVACSIM+ building systems and equipment simulation program: Reference manual.* NBSIR 84-2996, U.S. Department of Commerce, Washington, D.C.

Claus, G., and W. Stephan. 1985. A general computer simulation model for furnaces and boilers. *ASHRAE Transactions* 91(1B):47-59.

Crawley, D., L. Lawrie, C. Pedersen, F. Winkelmann, M. Witte, R. Strand, R. Liesen, W.F. Buhl, Y.J. Huang, R. Henninger, J. Glazer, D. Fisher, D. Shirey, B. Griffith, P. Ellis, and L. Gu. 2004. EnergyPlus: New capable and linked. *Proceedings of the SimBuild 2004 Conference*, Boulder, CO. International Building Performance Simulation Association.

Daoud, A., and N. Galanis. 2006. Calculation of the thermal loads of an ice rink using a zonal model and building energy simulation software. *ASHRAE Transactions* 112:526-537.

Deru, M., and P. Burns. 2003. Infiltration and natural ventilation model for whole building energy simulation of residential buildings. *ASHRAE Transactions* 109(2):801-811.

Djunaedy, E, J. Hensen, and M. Loomans. 2005. External coupling between CFD and energy simulation: Implementation and validation. *ASHRAE Transactions* 111(1):612-624.

Gunay, H.B., W. O'Brien, I. Beausoleil-Morrison, and B. Huchuk. 2014. On adaptive occupant-learning window blind and lighting controls. *Building Research & Information* 42(6):1-18.

Haberl, J.S., T.A. Reddy, I.E. Figuero, and M. Medina. 1997. Overview of LoanSTAR chiller monitoring—Analysis of in-situ chiller diagnostics using ASHRAE RP-827 test method. Paper presented at Cool Sense National Integrated Chiller Retrofit Forum, Presidio, San Francisco, September.

Hensen, J., and R. Lamberts, eds. 2011. *Building performance simulation for design and operation.* Routledge Publishing, Taylor and Francis, Inc.

IBPSA. 2016. *References and links.* International Building Performance Simulation Association. www.ibpsa.org/?page_id=54.

Katipamula, S., and D.E. Claridge. 1993. Use of simplified systems model to measure retrofit energy savings. *Transactions of the ASME Journal of Solar Energy Engineering* 115(May):57-68.

Kavanaugh, S., and S. Lambert. 2004. A bin method energy analysis for ground-coupled heat pumps. *ASHRAE Transactions* 110:535-542.

Kota, S., and Haberl, J. 2009. *Historical survey of daylighting calculations methods and their use in energy performance simulations.* ESL-IC-09-11-07, Energy Systems Laboratory, Texas A&M University, College Station, TX.

Kusuda, T., and T. Alereza. 1982. Development of equipment seasonal performance models for simplified energy analysis methods. *ASHRAE Transactions* 88(2).

Labs, K., J. Carmody, R. Sterling, L. Shen, Y. Huang, and D. Parker. 1988. Building foundation design handbook. ORNL *Report* Sub/86-72143/1. Oak Ridge National Laboratory, Oak Ridge, TN.

Lachal, B., W.U. Weber, and O. Guisan. 1992. Simplified methods for the thermal analysis of multifamily and administrative buildings. *ASHRAE Transactions* 98.

Laret, L. 1988. Boiler physical models for use in large scale building simulation. SCS User 1 Conference, Ostend.

Landry, R.W., and D.E. Maddox. 1993. Seasonal efficiency and off-cycle flue loss measurements of two boilers. *ASHRAE Transactions* 99(2).

Landry, R.W., D.E. Maddox, and D.L. Bohac. 1994. Field validation of diagnostic techniques for estimating boiler part-load efficiency. *ASHRAE Transactions* 100(1):859-875.

Lee, W.D., M.M. Delichatsios, T.M. Hrycaj, and R.N. Caron. 1983. Review of furnace/boiler field test analysis techniques. *ASHRAE Transactions* 89(1B):700-705.

Liu, M. and D.E. Claridge. 1998. Use of calibrated HVAC system models to optimize system operation. *ASME Journal of Solar Energy Engineering* 120:131.

Lobenstein, M.S. 1994. Application of short-term diagnostic methods for measuring commercial boiler losses. *ASHRAE Transactions* 100(1):876-890.

Malkawi, A., and G. Augenbroe. 2004. *Advanced building simulation.* Routledge Publishing, Taylor and Francis, Inc.

McDowell, T., S. Emmerich, J. Thornton, and G. Walton. 2003. Integration of airflow and energy simulation using CONTAM and TRNSYS. *ASHRAE Transactions* 109(2):757-770.

Miller, D.E. 1980. The impact of HVAC process dynamics on energy use. *ASHRAE Transactions* 86(2):535-556.

Mitalas, G.P. 1968. Calculations of transient heat flow through walls and roofs. *ASHRAE Transactions* 74(2):182-188.

Niu, Z., and K.V. Wong. 1998. Adaptive simulation of boiler unit performance. *Energy Conversion Management* 39(13):1383-1394.

Reddy, T.A., K.K. Andersen, and D. Niebur. 2003. Information content of incoming data during field monitoring: Application to chiller modeling. *International Journal of HVAC&R Research* (now *Science and Technology for the Built Environment*) 9(4):365-383.

Scottish Government. 2016. *Section six software.* www.gov.scot/Topics/Built-Environment/Building/Building-standards/techbooks/sectsixprg.

Seem, J., and E. Hancock. 1985. A method for characterizing the thermal performance of a solar storage wall from measured data. *Thermal Performance of the Exterior Envelopes of Buildings III: Proceedings of ASHRAE/DOE/BTECC Conference*, ASHRAE SP-49, pp. 1304-1315.

Sever, F., K. Kissock, D. Brown, and S. Mulqueen. 2011. Estimating industrial building energy savings using inverse simulation. *ASHRAE Transactions* 117:348-355.

Shavit, G. 1995. Short-time-step analysis and simulation of homes and buildings during the last 100 years. *ASHRAE Transactions* 101(1):856-868.

Shurcliff, W.A. 1984. *Frequency method of analyzing a building's dynamic thermal performance*. Cambridge, MA.

Sowell, E.F., and G.N. Walton. 1980. Efficient computation of zone loads. *ASHRAE Transactions* 86(1):49-72.

Sowell, E.F., and D.C. Hittle. 1995. Evolution of building energy simulation methodology. *ASHRAE Transactions* 101(1):850-855.

Spitler, J.D. 1996. *Annotated guide to load calculation models and algorithms.* ASHRAE.

Strand, R., Fisher, D., Liesen, R., and Pedersen, C. 2002. Modular HVAC simulation and the future integration of alternative cooling systems in a new building energy simulation program. *ASHRAE Transactions* 108(2): 1107-1117.

Subbarao, K. 1986. Thermal parameters for single and multi-zone buildings and their determination from performance data. SERI *Report* SERI/TR-253-2617. Solar Energy Research Institute (now National Renewable Energy Laboratory), Golden, CO.

Subbarao, K., Lei, Y., and Reddy, T. 2011. The nearest neighborhood method to improve uncertainty estimates in statistical building energy models. *ASHRAE Transactions* 117:459-471.

Thevenard, D. 2011. Methods for estimating heating and cooling degree-days to any base temperature. *ASHRAE Transactions* 117:884-891.

Tierney, T.M., and C.J. Fishman. 1994. Filed study of "real world" gas steam boiler seasonal efficiency *ASHRAE Transactions* 100(1):891-897.

U.K. Government. 2014. *Department for Communities and Local Government approved software for the production of non domestic energy performance certificates*. www.gov.uk/government/publications/department-for-communities-and-local-government-approved-software-for-the-production-of-non-domestic-energy-performance-certificates-epc.

U.S. Army. 1979. BLAST, the building loads analysis and system thermodynamics program—Users manual. U.S. Army Construction Engineering Research Laboratory *Report* E-153.

U.S. Department of Energy. 2001. *International performance measurement & verification protocol, concepts and options for determining energy and water savings*, vol. I. U.S. Department of Energy, Washington, D.C.

U.S. Department of Energy. 2001. *International Performance Measurement and Verification Protocol (IPMVP): Vol. I: Concepts and options for determining energy and water savings*. DOE/GO-102001-1187.

U.S. Department of Energy. 2001. *International Performance Measurement and Verification Protocol (IPMVP): Vol. II: Concepts and practices for improved indoor environmental quality*. DOE/GO-102001-1188.

U.S. Department of Energy. 2003. *International Performance Measurement and Verification Protocol (IPMVP): Vol. III: Concepts and practices for determining energy savings in new construction*.

U.S. Department of Energy. 2016. *Energy-efficient new homes tax credit for home builders*. energy.gov/savings/energy-efficient-new-homes-tax-credit-home-builders.

Wasserman, P.D. 1989. *Neural computing, theory and practice.* Van Nostrand Reinhold, New York.

Yuill, G.K. 1990. *An annotated guide to models and algorithms for energy calculations relating to HVAC equipment.* ASHRAE.

Analytical Verification

Bland, B. 1993. *Conduction tests for the validation of dynamic thermal models of buildings*. Building Research Establishment, Garston, U.K.

Bland, B.H., and D.P. Bloomfield. 1986. Validation of conduction algorithms in dynamic thermal models. *Proceedings of the CIBSE 5th International Symposium on the Use of Computers for Environmental Engineering Related to Buildings*, Bath, U.K.

CEN. 2004. PrEN ISO 13791. *Thermal performance of buildings—Calculation of internal temperatures of a room in summer without mechanical cooling—General criteria and validation procedures*. Final draft. Comité Européen de la Normalisation, Brussels.

Judkoff, R., D. Wortman, and B. O'Doherty. 1981. *A comparative study of four building energy simulations, Phase II: DOE-2.1, BLAST-3.0, SUNCAT-2.4, and DEROB-4*. Solar Energy Research Institute (now National Renewable Energy Laboratory), Golden, CO.

Neymark, J., R. Judkoff, G. Knabe, H. Le, M. Durig, A. Glass, and G. Zweifel. 2002. An analytical verification procedure for testing the ability of whole-building energy simulation programs to model space conditioning equipment at typical design conditions. *ASHRAE Transactions* 108.2:1144-1154.

Pinney, A., and M. Bean. 1988. *A set of analytical tests for internal longwave radiation and view factor calculations.* Final Report of the BRE/SERC Collaboration, vol. II, Appendix II.2. Building Research Establishment, Garston, U.K.

Rees, S., D. Xiao, and J. Spitler. 2002. An analytical verification test suite for building fabric models in whole building energy simulation programs. *ASHRAE Transactions* 108:30-41.

Rodriguez, E., and S. Alvarez. 1991. *Solar shading analytical tests (I)*. Universidad de Savilla, Seville.

San Isidro, M. 2000. *Validating the solar shading test of IEA.* Centro de Investigaciones Energeticas Medioambientales y Tecnologicas, Madrid.

Stefanizzi, P., A. Wilson, and A. Pinney. 1988. The internal longwave radiation exchange in thermal models, vol. II, Ch. 9. *Final Report* of the BRE/SERC Collaboration. Building Research Establishment, Garston, U.K.

Tuomaala, P., ed. 1999. *IEA task 22: A working document of subtask A.1, analytical tests.* VTT Building Technology, Espoo, Finland.

Tuomaala, P., K. Piira, J. Piippo, and C. Simonson. 1999. *A validation test set for building energy simulation tools results obtained by BUS++*. VTT Building Technology, Espoo, Finland.

Walton, G. 1989. *AIRNET—A computer program for building airflow network modeling.* Appendix B: AIRNET Validation Tests. NISTIR 89-4072. National Institute of Standards and Technology, Gaithersburg, MD.

Wortman, D., B. O'Doherty, and R. Judkoff. 1981. *The implementation of an analytical verification technique on three building energy analysis codes: SUNCAT 2.4, DOE 2.1, and DEROB III.* SERI/TP-721-1008, UL-59c. Solar Energy Research Institute (now National Renewable Energy Laboratory), Golden, CO.

Zhai, J., M. Krarti, and M-H. Johnson. 2010. Assess and implement natural and hybrid ventilation models in whole-building energy simulations. ASHRAE Research Project RP-1456.

See also Bland (1992), Guyon and Palomo (1999b), Neymark and Judkoff (2002), Neymark et al. (2008), Purdy and Beausoleil-Morrison (2003), Spitler et al. (2001), and Yuill and Haberl (2002) in the References.

Empirical Validation

Ahmad, Q., and S. Szokolay. 1993. Thermal design tools in Australia: A comparative study of TEMPER, CHEETAH, ARCHIPAK and QUICK. *Building Simulation '93*, Adelaide, Australia. International Building Performance Simulation Association.

Barakat, S. 1983. Passive solar heating studies at the Division of Building Research. *Building Research Note* 181. Division of Building Research, Ottawa, ON.

Beausoleil-Morrison, I., and P. Strachan. 1999. On the significance of modeling internal surface convection in dynamic whole-building simulation programs. *ASHRAE Transactions* 105(2).

Bloomfield, D., Y. Candau, P. Dalicieux, S. DeLille, S. Hammond, K. Lomas, C. Martin, F. Parand, J. Patronis, and N. Ramdani. 1995. New techniques for validating building energy simulation programs. *Proceedings of Building Simulation '95*, Madison, WI. International Building Performance Simulation Association.

Boulkroune, K., Y. Candau, G. Piar, and A. Jeandel. 1993. Modeling and simulation of the thermal behavior of a dwelling under ALLAN. *Building Simulation '93*, Adelaide, Australia. International Building Performance Simulation Association.

Bowman, N., and K. Lomas. 1985. Empirical validation of dynamic thermal computer models of buildings. *Building Service Engineering Research and Technology* 6(4):153-162.

Bowman, N., and K. Lomas. 1985. Building energy evaluation. *Proceedings of the CICA Conference on Computers in Building Services Design*, Nottingham, pp. 99-110. Construction Industry Computer Association.

Burch, J., D. Wortman, R. Judkoff, and B. Hunn. 1985. *Solar Energy Research Institute validation test house site handbook.* LA-10333-MS and SERI/PR-254-2028. Solar Energy Research Institute (now National Renewable Energy Laboratory), Golden, CO, and Los Alamos National Laboratory, NM.

Chantrasrisalai, C., D. Fisher, I. Iu, and D. Eldridge. 2003. Experimental validation of design cooling load procedures: The heat balance method. *ASHRAE Transactions* 109(2):160-173.

Chantrasrisalai, C., V. Ghatti, D. Fisher, and D. Scheatzle. 2003. Experimental validation of the EnergyPlus low-temperature radiant simulation. *ASHRAE Transactions* 109(2):614-623.

David, G. 1991. Sensitivity analysis and empirical validation of HLITE using data from the NIST indoor test cell. *Proceedings of Building Simulation '91*, Nice, France. International Building Performance Simulation Association.

Eppel, H., and K. Lomas. 1995. Empirical validation of three thermal simulation programs using data from a passive solar building. *Proceedings of Building Simulation '95*, Madison, WI. International Building Performance Simulation Association.

Fisher, D.E., and C.O. Pedersen. 1997. Convective heat transfer in building energy and thermal load calculations. *ASHRAE Transactions* 103(2): 137-148.

Felsmann, C. 2008. *Mechanical equipment and control strategies for a chilled water and a hot water system.* Dresden, Germany: Technical University of Dresden. archive.iea-shc.org/publications/downloads/task34-subtaskd.pdf.

Gong, X., D. Claridge, and D. Archer. 2010. Infiltration investigation of a radiantly heated and cooled office. *ASHRAE Transactions* 116:437-446.

Guyon, G., and N. Rahni. 1997. Validation of a building thermal model in CLIM2000 simulation software using full-scale experimental data, sensitivity analysis and uncertainty analysis. *Proceedings of Building Simulation '97*, Prague. International Building Performance Simulation Association.

Guyon, G., S. Moinard, and N. Ramdani. 1999. Empirical validation of building energy analysis tools by using tests carried out in small cells. *Proceedings of Building Simulation '99*, Kyoto. International Building Performance Simulation Association.

Haddad, K. 2004. An air-conditioning model validation and implementation into a building energy analysis software. *ASHRAE Transactions* 110:46-54.

Izquierdo, M., G. LeFebvre, E. Palomo, F. Boudaud, and A. Jeandel. 1995. A statistical methodology for model validation in the ALLAN™ simulation environment. *Proceedings of Building Simulation '95*, Madison, WI. International Building Performance Simulation Association.

Jensen, S. 1993. Empirical whole model validation case study: The PASSYS reference wall. *Proceedings of Building Simulation '93*, Adelaide, Australia. International Building Performance Simulation Association.

Judkoff, R., and D. Wortman. 1984. *Validation of building energy analysis simulations using 1983 data from the SERI Class A test house* (draft). SERI/TR-253-2806. Solar Energy Research Institute (now National Renewable Energy Laboratory), Golden, CO.

Judkoff, R., D. Wortman, and J. Burch. 1983. *Measured versus predicted performance of the SERI test house: A validation study.* SERI/TP-254-1953. Solar Energy Research Institute (now National Renewable Energy Laboratory), Golden, CO.

Kalyanova, O., and P. Heiselberg. 2009. Empirical validation of building simulation software: Modeling of double facades, final report. DCE Technical Report No. 027. Aalborg, Denmark: Aalborg University. archive.iea-shc.org/publications/downloads/DSF_EMPIRICAL REPORT_18Jun2009.pdf.

LeRoy, J., E. Groll, and J. Braun. 1997. Capacity and power demand of unitary air conditioners and heat pumps under extreme temperature and humidity conditions. ASHRAE Research Project RP-859, *Final Report.*

LeRoy, J., E. Groll, and J. Braun. 1998. Computer model predictions of dehumidification performance of unitary air conditioners and heat pumps under extreme operating conditions. *ASHRAE Transactions* 104(2).

Lomas, K., and N. Bowman. 1986. The evaluation and use of existing data sets for validating dynamic thermal models of buildings. *Proceedings of the CIBSE 5th International Symposium on the Use of Computers for Environmental Engineering Related to Buildings*, Bath, U.K.

Loutzenhiser, P., H. Manz, and G. Maxwell. 2007. *Empirical Validations of Shading/Daylighting/Load Interactions in Building Energy Simulation Tools.* Swiss Federal Laboratories for Materials Testing and Research; Iowa Energy Center. Available at archive.iea-shc.org/task34/publications/index.html.

Martin, C. 1991. *Detailed model comparisons: An empirical validation exercise using SERI-RES.* Contractor Report to U.K. Department of Energy, ETSU S 1197-p9.

Maxwell, G., P. Loutzenhiser, and C. Klaassen. 2003. *Daylighting—HVAC interaction tests for the empirical validation of building energy analysis tools.* Iowa State University, Department of Mechanical Engineering, Ames. task22.iea-shc.org/data/sites/1/publications/IEA%20Daylighting%20Report%20Final.pdf.

Maxwell, G., P. Loutzenhiser, and C. Klaassen. 2004. *Economizer control tests for the empirical validation of building energy analysis tools.* Iowa State University, Department of Mechanical Engineering. Iowa Energy Center. task22.iea-shc.org/data/sites/1/publications/IEA%20Economizer%20Report.pdf.

McFarland, R. 1982. *Passive test cell data for the solar laboratory winter 1980-81.* LA-9300-MS. Los Alamos National Laboratory, NM.

Moinard, S., and G. Guyon. 1999. *Empirical validation of EDF ETNA and GENEC test-cell models.* Final Report, IEA SHC Task 22, Building Energy Analysis Tools, Project A.3. Electricité de France, Moret sur Loing. archive.iea-shc.org/publications/downloads/Final_report.pdf.

Neymark, J., P. Girault, G. Guyon, R. Judkoff, R. LeBerre, J. Ojalvo, and P. Reimer. 2005. The "ETNA BESTEST" empirical validation data set. *Proceedings of Building Simulation 2005*, Montreal. International Building Performance Simulation Association.

Nishitani, Y., M. Zheng, H. Niwa, and N. Nakahara. 1999. A comparative study of HVAC dynamic behavior between actual measurements and simulated results by HVACSIM+(J). *Proceedings of Building Simulation '99*, Kyoto. International Building Performance Simulation Association.

Rahni, N., N. Ramdani, Y. Candau, and G. Guyon. 1999. New experimental validation and model improvement tools for the CLIM2000 energy simulation software program. *Proceedings of Building Simulation '99*, Kyoto. International Building Performance Simulation Association.

Sullivan, R. 1998. Validation studies of the DOE-2 building energy simulation program. LBNL-42241, *Final Report.* Lawrence Berkeley National Laboratory, CA.

Travesi, J., G. Maxwell, C. Klaassen, M. Holtz, G. Knabe, C. Felsmann, M. Achermann, and M. Behne. 2001. Empirical validation of Iowa Energy Resource Station building energy analysis simulation models. *Report*, IEA SHC Task 22, Subtask A, Building Energy Analysis Tools, Project A.1 Empirical Validation. Centro de Investigaciones Energeticas, Medioambientales y Technologicas, Madrid. archive.iea-shc.org/publications/downloads/Iowa_Energy_Report.pdf.

Trombe, A., L. Serres, and A. Mavroulakis. 1993. Simulation study of coupled energy saving systems included in real site building. *Proceedings of Building Simulation '93*, Adelaide, Australia. International Building Performance Simulation Association.

Walker, I., J. Siegel, and G. Degenetais. 2001. Simulation of residential HVAC system performance. *Proceedings of eSim 2001*, Natural Resources Canada, Ottawa, ON.

Yazdanian, M., and J. Klems. 1994. Measurement of the exterior convective film coefficient for windows in low-rise buildings. *ASHRAE Transactions* 100(1):1087-1096.

Zheng, M., Y. Nishitani, S. Hayashi, and N. Nakahara. 1999. Comparison of reproducibility of a real CAV system by dynamic simulation HVACSIM+ and TRNSYS. *Proceedings of Building Simulation '99*, Kyoto. International Building Performance Simulation Association.

See also Guyon and Palomo (1999a), Jensen (1989), Jensen and van de Perre (1991), Lomas (1991), Lomas and Bowman (1987), and Spitler et al. (1991) in the References.

Intermodel Comparative Testing

Deru, M., R. Judkoff, and J. Neymark. 2003. *Proposed IEA BESTEST ground-coupled cases.* International Energy Agency, Solar Heating and Cooling Programme Task 22, Working Document.

Fairey, P., M. Anello, L. Gu, D. Parker, M. Swami, and R. Vieira. 1998. *Comparison of EnGauge 2.0 heating and cooling load predictions with the HERS BESTEST criteria.* FSEC-CR-983-98. Florida Solar Energy Center, Cocoa.

Haddad, K., and I. Beausoleil-Morrison. 2001. Results of the HERS BESTEST on an energy simulation computer program. *ASHRAE Transactions* 107(2).

Haltrecht, D., and K. Fraser. 1997. Validation of HOT2000™ using HERS BESTEST. *Proceedings of Building Simulation '97*, Prague. International Building Performance Simulation Association.

ISSO. 2003. *Energie Diagnose Referentie Versie 3.0.* Institut voor Studie en Stimulering van Onderzoekop Het Gebied van Gebouwinstallaties, Rotterdam, The Netherlands.

Judkoff, R. 1985. *A comparative validation study of the BLAST-3.0, SERI-RES-1.0, and DOE-2.1 A computer programs using the Canadian direct gain test building* (draft). SERI/TR-253-2652. Solar Energy Research Institute (now National Renewable Energy Laboratory), Golden, CO.

Judkoff, R. 1985. International Energy Agency building simulation comparison and validation study. *Proceedings of the Building Energy Simulation Conference*, Seattle.

Judkoff, R. 1986. *International Energy Agency sunspace intermodel comparison* (draft). SERI/TR-254-2977. Solar Energy Research Institute (now National Renewable Energy Laboratory), Golden, CO.

Judkoff, R., and J. Neymark. 1997. *Home Energy Rating System Building Energy Simulation Test for Florida (Florida-HERS BESTEST)*, vols. 1 and 2. NREL/TP-550-23124. National Renewable Energy Laboratory, Golden, CO. www.nrel.gov/docs/legosti/fy97/23124a.pdf and www.nrel.gov/docs/legosti/fy97/23124b.pdf.

Judkoff, R., and J. Neymark. 1998. The BESTEST method for evaluating and diagnosing building energy software. *Proceedings of the ACEEE Summer Study 1998*, Washington, D.C. American Council for an Energy-Efficient Economy.

Judkoff, R., and J. Neymark. 1999. Adaptation of the BESTEST intermodel comparison method for proposed ASHRAE *Standard* 140P: Method of test for building energy simulation programs. *ASHRAE Transactions* 105(2).

Judkoff, R., and J. Neymark. 2013. Twenty years on!: Updating the IEA BESTEST building thermal fabric test cases for ASHRAE Standard 140. *Proceedings Building Simulation 2013, Chambéry, France, August 25-28, 2013.* International Building Performance Simulation Association. Also see the preprinted version, NREL CP-5500-58487. Golden, CO: National Renewable Energy Laboratory. www.nrel.gov/docs/ fy13osti/58487.pdf.

Mathew, P., and A. Mahdavi. 1998. High-resolution thermal modeling for computational building design assistance. *Proceedings of the International Computing Congress, Computing in Civil Engineering*, Boston.

Neymark, J., and R. Judkoff. 1997. A comparative validation based certification test for home energy rating system software. *Proceedings of Building Simulation '97*, Prague. International Building Performance Simulation Association.

Neymark, J., R. Judkoff, D. Alexander, C. Felsmann, P. Strachan, and A. Wijsman. 2008. *International Energy Agency Building Energy Simulation Test and Diagnostic Method (IEA BESTEST) multi-zone non-airflow in-depth diagnostic cases: MZ320-MZ360.* NREL Report No. TP-550-43827. National Renewable Energy Laboratory, Golden, CO. www.nrel.gov/docs/fy08osti/43827.pdf.

Neymark, J., R. Judkoff, D. Alexander, C. Felsmann, P. Strachan, and A. Wijsman, A. 2011. IEA BESTEST multi-zone non-airflow in-depth diagnostic cases. *Proceedings of Building Simulation 2011,* Sydney. International Building Performance Simulation Association. Preprint version, NREL CP-5500-51589, National Renewable Energy Laboratory, Golden, CO. www.nrel.gov/docs/fy12osti/51589.pdf.

NRC. 2000. *Benchmark test for the evaluation of building energy analysis computer programs.* Natural Resources Canada, Ottawa, ON. (Translation of original Japanese version, approved by the Japanese Ministry of Construction.)

RESNET. 2007. Procedures for verification of International Energy Conservation Code performance path calculation tools. RESNET *Publication* 07-003. Residential Energy Services Network, Inc., Oceanside, CA. www1.resnet.us/standards/iecc/procedures.pdf.

Sakamoto, Y. 2000. *Determination of standard values of benchmark test to evaluate annual heating and cooling load computer program.* Natural Resources Canada, Ottawa, ON.

Soubdhan, T., T. Mara, H. Boyer, and A. Younes. 1999. *Use of BESTEST procedure to improve a building thermal simulation program.* Université de la Réunion, St Denis, La Reunion, France.

Strachan, P., G. Kokogiannakis, L. MacDonald, and I. Beausoleil-Morrison. 2006. Integrated comparative validation tests as an aid for building simulation tool users and developers. *ASHRAE Transactions* 112:395-408.

See also Achermann and Zweifel (2003), Judkoff et al. (1980, 1983), Judkoff and Neymark (1995a, 1995b), Judkoff et al. (2011a, 2011b), Morck (1986), Neymark and Judkoff (2004), and Purdy and Beausoleil-Morrison (2003) in the References.

General Testing and Validation

Abushakra, B., and D. Claridge. 2008. Modeling office building occupancy in hourly data-driven and detailed energy simulation programs. *ASHRAE Transactions* 114(2):472-481.

Allen, E., D. Bloomfield, N. Bowman, K. Lomas, J. Allen, J. Whittle, and A. Irving. 1985. Analytical and empirical validation of dynamic thermal building models. *Proceedings of the First Building Energy Simulation Conference,* Seattle, pp. 274-280.

Beausoleil-Morrison, I. 2000. *The adaptive coupling of heat and air flow modelling within dynamic whole-building simulation.* Ph.D. dissertation. Energy Systems Research Unit, Department of Mechanical Engineering, University of Strathclyde, Glasgow.

Bloomfield, D. 1985. Appraisal techniques for methods of calculating the thermal performance of buildings. *Building Services Engineering Research & Technology.* 6(1):13-20.

Bloomfield, D., ed. 1989. *Design tool evaluation: Benchmark cases.* IEA T8B4. Solar Heating and Cooling Program, Task VIII: Passive and Hybrid Solar Low-Energy Buildings. Building Research Establishment, Garston, U.K.

Bloomfield, D., K. Lomas, and C. Martin. 1992. Assessing programs which predict the thermal performance of buildings. BRE *Information Paper* IP7/92. Building Research Establishment, Garston, U.K.

Gough, M. 1999. A review of new techniques in building energy and environmental modelling. *Final Report*, BRE Contract BREA-42. Building Research Establishment, Garston, U.K.

Judkoff, R., S. Barakat, D. Bloomfield, B. Poel, R. Stricker, P. van Haaster, and D. Wortman. 1988. *International Energy Agency design tool evaluation procedure.* SERI/TP-254-3371. Solar Energy Research Institute (now National Renewable Energy Laboratory), Golden, CO.

Palomo, E., and G. Guyon. 2002. *Using parameters space analysis techniques for diagnostic purposes in the framework of empirical model validation.* LEPT-ENSAM, Talance, France. Electricité de France, Moret sur Loing.

See also Bloomfield (1988, 1999), Irving (1988), Judkoff et al. (1983), Judkoff (1988), Judkoff and Neymark (2006), and Lomas and Eppel (1992) in the References.

CHAPTER 20

SPACE AIR DIFFUSION

ROOM air distribution systems are intended to provide thermal comfort and ventilation for space occupants and processes. Although air terminals (inlets and outlets), terminal units, fan-coil units, local ducts, and rooms themselves may affect room air diffusion, this chapter addresses only air inlets and outlets and their direct effect on occupant comfort. This chapter is intended to present HVAC designers the fundamental characteristics of air distribution devices. For information on naturally ventilated spaces, see Chapter 16. For a discussion of various air distribution strategies, tools, and guidelines for design and application, see Chapter 57 in the 2015 *ASHRAE Handbook—HVAC Applications*. Chapter 20 in the 2016 *ASHRAE Handbook—HVAC Systems and Equipment* describes the characteristics of various air inlets, outlets, fan-coil units, chilled beams, air curtain units, and terminal units, as well as selection tools and guidelines.

Room air diffusion methods can be classified as one of the following as shown in Figure 1:

- **Mixed systems** produce little or no thermal stratification of air within the space. Overhead air distribution is an example of this type of system.
- **Fully (thermally) stratified systems** produce little or no mixing of air within the occupied space. Thermal displacement ventilation is an example of this type of system.
- **Partially mixed systems** provide some mixing within the occupied and/or process space while creating stratified conditions in the volume above. Most underfloor air distribution and task/ambient conditioning designs are examples of this type of system.

The preparation of this chapter is assigned to TC 5.3, Room Air Distribution.

Local temperature and carbon dioxide (CO_2) concentration have similar stratification profiles.

Air distribution systems, such as thermal displacement ventilation (TDV) and underfloor air distribution (UFAD), that deliver air in cooling mode at or near floor level and return air at or near ceiling level produce varying amounts of room air stratification. For floor-level supply, thermal plumes that develop over heat sources in the room play a major role in driving overall floor-to-ceiling air motion. The amount of stratification in the room is primarily determined by the balance between total room airflow and heat load. In practice, the actual temperature and concentration profile depends on the combined effects of various factors, but is largely driven by the characteristics of the room supply airflow and heat load configuration.

For room supply airflow, the major factors are

- Total room supply airflow quantity
- Room supply air temperature
- Diffuser type
- Diffuser throw height (or outlet velocity); this is associated with the amount of mixing provided by a floor diffuser (or room conditions near a low-sidewall TDV diffuser)

For room heat loads, the major factors are

- Magnitude and number of loads in space
- Load type (point or distributed source)
- Elevation of load (e.g., overhead lighting, person standing on floor, floor-to-ceiling glazing)
- Radiative/convective split
- Whether pollutants are associated with heat sources

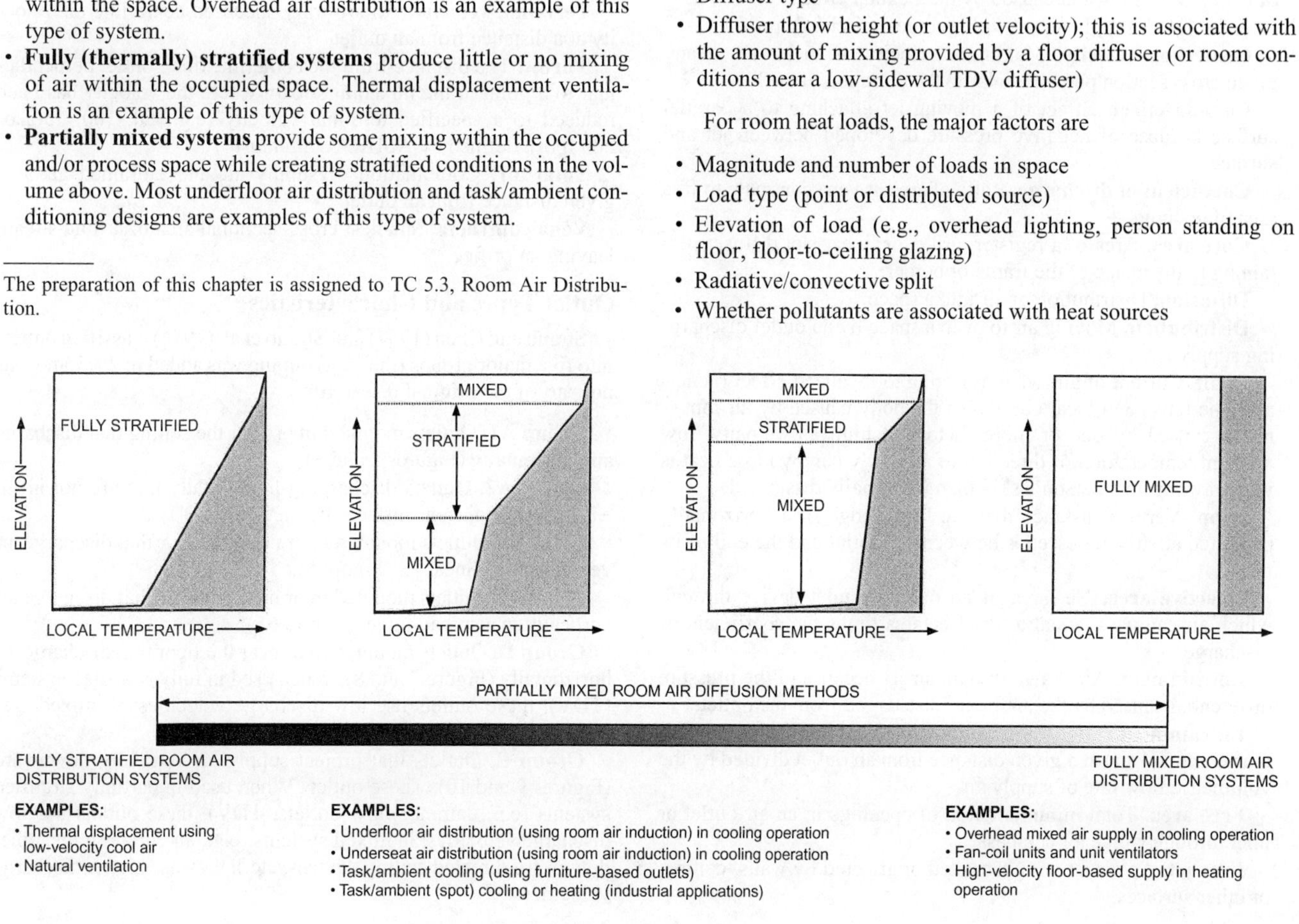

Fig. 1 Classification of Air Diffusion Methods

1. INDOOR AIR QUALITY AND SUSTAINABILITY

Air diffusion methods affect not only indoor air quality (IAQ) and thermal comfort, but also energy consumption over the building's life. Choices made early in the design process are important. Programs such as U.S. Green Building Council's (USGBC 2013) Leadership in Energy and Environmental Design (LEED®) v4 rating system, which was originally created in response to indoor air quality concerns, now include prerequisites and credits for increasing ventilation rates and improving indoor environmental quality. These program requirements are sometimes achievable by following good room air diffusion design principles, methods, and standards (see Chapter 57 of the 2015 *ASHRAE Handbook—HVAC Applications*).

ANSI/ASHRAE *Standard* 62.1 provides a table of typical values to help predict zone air distribution effectiveness. For example, well-designed ceiling-based air distribution systems produce near-perfect air mixing in cooling mode, and yield an air distribution effectiveness of 1.0. Displacement ventilation and underfloor air distribution (UFAD) systems have the potential for values greater than 1.0. More information on ceiling- and wall-mounted air inlets and outlets can be found in Rock and Zhu (2002). Displacement system performance is described in Chen and Glicksman (2003). ASHRAE's (2013) *UFAD Design Guide* discusses UFAD in detail. More information on ANSI/ASHRAE *Standard* 62.1 is available in its user's manual (ASHRAE 2010).

2. TERMINOLOGY

Aspect ratio. Ratio of length to width of opening or core of a grille.

Attached jet. A supply air jet drawn to a surface, parallel to the direction of airflow and caused by the Coanda effect.

Axial jet. A supply air jet with a conical discharge profile.

Centerline velocity. Maximum velocity of an air jet at any given cross section perpendicular to the direction of airflow.

Coanda effect. Effect of a moving jet attaching to a parallel surface because of negative pressure developed between jet and surface.

Coefficient of discharge. Ratio of area at vena contracta to free area of opening.

Core area. Area of a register, grille, or linear slot diffuser pertaining to the inside of the frame or border.

Diffusion. Distribution of air into a space.

Distribution. Moving air to or in a space by an outlet discharging supply air.

Draft. Current of air, when referring to localized effect (generally, the unwanted local cooling of the body caused by air movement) caused by one or more factors of high air velocity, low ambient temperature, or direction of airflow whereby more heat is withdrawn from a person's skin than is normally dissipated.

Drop. Vertical distance that the lower edge of a horizontally projected airstream descends between the outlet and the end of its throw.

Effective area. Net area of an outlet or inlet device through which air can pass; equal to the free area times the coefficient of discharge.

Entrainment. Air drawn into an air jet because of the pressure differential caused by the airstream discharged from the outlet.

Entrainment ratio. Volumetric flow rate of total air (supply air plus entrained air) at a given distance from an outlet divided by the volumetric flow rate of supply air.

Free area. Total minimum area of openings in an air outlet or inlet through which air can pass.

Free jet. An air jet not obstructed or affected by walls, ceiling, or other surfaces.

Induction. Movement of space air into an air device.

Induction ratio. Volumetric flow rate of induced air divided by volumetric flow rate of primary air.

Inlet. A device that allows air to exit the zone (e.g., grilles, registers, diffusers)

Isothermal jet. An air jet in which supply air temperature equals surrounding room air temperature.

Linear jet. A supply air jet with a relatively high aspect ratio.

Neck area. Nominal area of duct connection to air outlet or inlet.

Nonisothermal jet. An air jet in which supply air temperature does not equal surrounding room air temperature.

Occupied zone. The volume of space intended to be comfort conditioned for occupants (see ANSI/ASHRAE *Standard* 55).

Outlet. A device discharging supply air into the space (e.g., grilles, registers, diffusers). Classified according to location and type of discharge.

Outlet velocity. Average velocity of air discharging from an outlet.

Primary air. Air delivered to an outlet or terminal device.

Radial jet. A supply air jet that discharges 360° and expands uniformly.

Spread. Divergence of an airstream in a horizontal and/or vertical plane after it leaves an outlet.

Stratification height. Vertical distance from floor to horizontal plane that defines lower boundary of upper mixed zone in a fully stratified or partially mixed system.

Stratified zone. Zone in which air movement is entirely driven by buoyancy caused by convective heat sources. Typically found in fully stratified or partially mixed systems.

Supply Air. Air delivered into a zone from an outlet.

Terminal velocity. An arbitrary specified centerline air velocity at a distance from an outlet.

Throw. The distance from the centerline of an outlet perpendicular to a point in the mixed airstream where the velocity has been reduced to a specified terminal velocity (e.g., 50, 100, 150, or 200 fpm), defined by ASHRAE *Standard* 70.

Total air. Combination of supply air and entrained air at a given distance from an outlet.

Vena contracta. Smallest cross-sectional area of a fluid stream leaving an orifice.

Outlet Types and Characteristics

Straub and Chen (1957) and Straub et al. (1956) classified outlets into five major groups (the subgrouping was added in 2017 and was not part of the original research):

Group A1. Outlets mounted in or near the ceiling that discharge air horizontally (Figures 2 and 3).

Group A2. Outlets discharging horizontally that are not influenced by an adjacent surface (free jet; Figure 4).

Group B. Outlets mounted in or near the floor that discharge air vertically in a linear jet (Figure 5).

Group C. Outlets mounted in or near the floor that discharge air vertically in a spreading jet (Figure 6).

Group D. Outlets mounted in or near the floor that discharge air horizontally (Figure 7 and 8). When used in fully stratified systems (TDV), these outlets use low discharge velocities; in mixed systems, they use higher discharge velocities.

Group E. Outlets that project supply air vertically downward (Figures 9 and 10). These outlets When used in partially stratified systems (e.g., laminar flow outlets, TDV), these outlets use low discharge velocities; in mixed systems (e.g., air curtain units, other downward directed ceiling devices, etc.), they use higher discharge velocities.

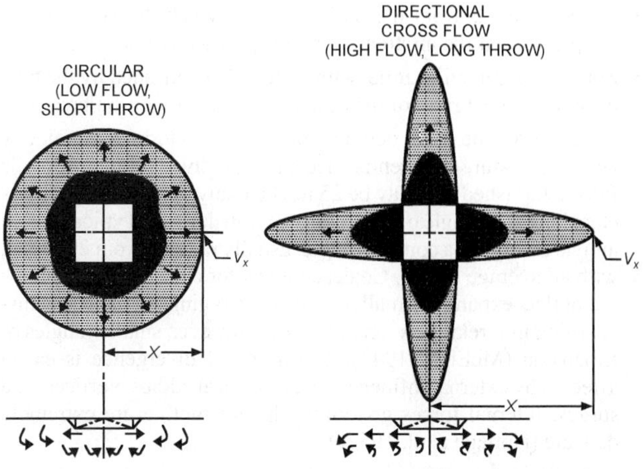

Fig. 2 Example Airflow Patterns of Outlet Group A1

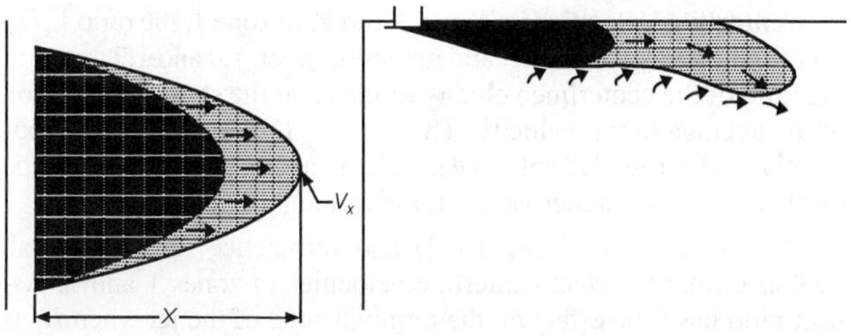

Fig. 3 Example Airflow Patterns (Nonisothermal) of Outlet Group A1

3. PRINCIPLES OF JET BEHAVIOR

Air Jet Fundamentals

Air supplied to rooms through various types of outlets can be distributed by turbulent air jets (mixed and partially mixed systems) or in a low-velocity, unidirectional manner (stratified systems). The air jet discharged from an outlet is a primary factor affecting room air motion. The jet boundary contours are not well defined and are easily affected by external influences. Baturin (1972), Christianson (1989), and Murakami (1992) have further information on the relationship between the air jet and occupied zone.

If the supply air temperature is equal to the ambient room air temperature, the air jet is called an **isothermal jet**. A jet with an initial temperature different from the ambient air temperature is called a **nonisothermal jet**. The air temperature differential between supplied and ambient room air generates thermal forces (buoyancy) in jets, affecting the jet's (1) trajectory, (2) location at which it attaches to and separates from the ceiling/floor, and (3) throw. The significance of these effects depends on the ratio between the thermal buoyancy of the air and jet momentum.

If an air jet is not obstructed or affected by walls, ceiling, or other surfaces, it is considered a **free jet**. When outlet area is small compared to the dimensions of the space normal to the jet, the jet may be considered free as long as

$$X \leq 1.5\sqrt{A_R} \quad (1)$$

where

X = distance from face of outlet, ft
A_R = cross-sectional area of confined space normal to jet, ft^2

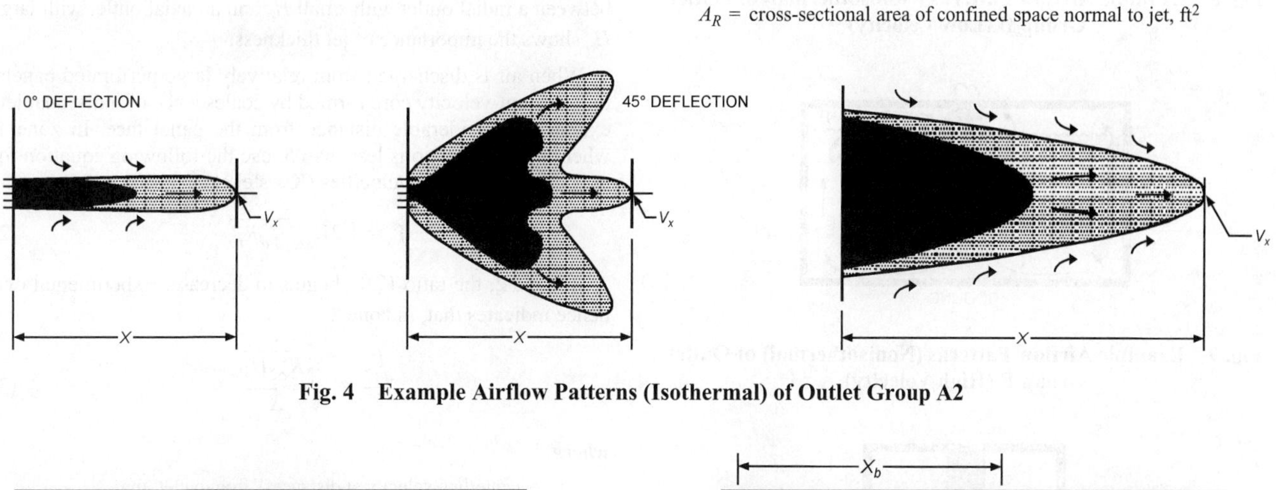

Fig. 4 Example Airflow Patterns (Isothermal) of Outlet Group A2

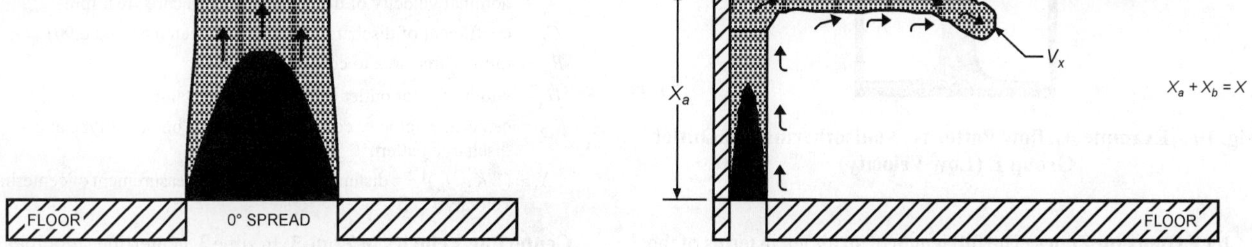

Fig. 5 Example Airflow Patterns (Nonisothermal) of Outlet Group B

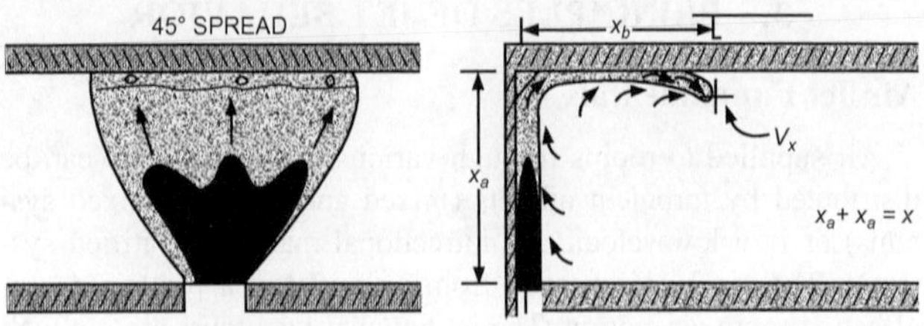

Fig. 6 Example Airflow Patterns (Nonisothermal) of Outlet Group C

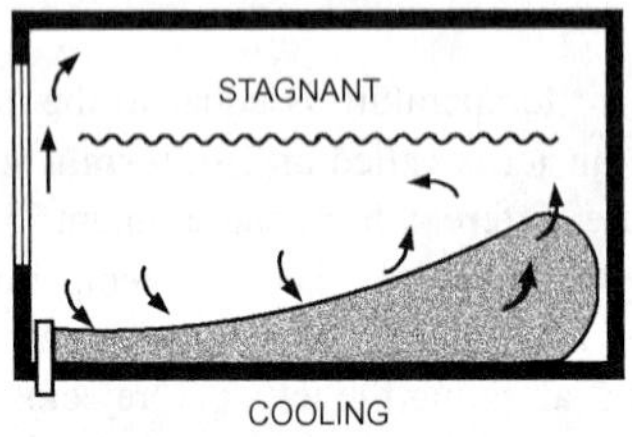

Fig. 7 Example Airflow Patterns (Nonisothermal) of Outlet Group D (High Velocity)

Fig. 8 Example Airflow Patterns (Nonisothermal) of Outlet Group D (Low Velocity)

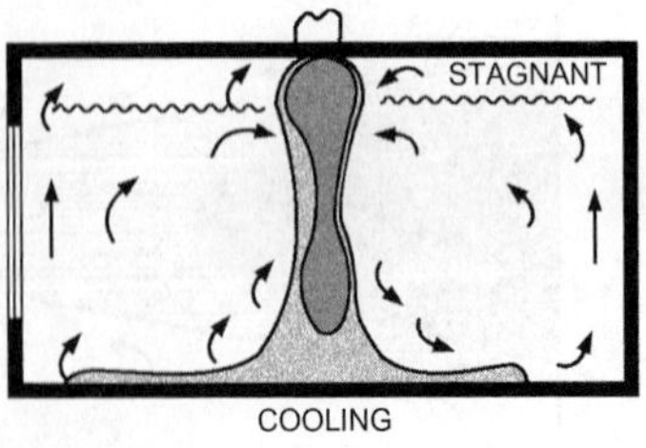

Fig. 9 Example Airflow Patterns (Nonisothermal) of Outlet Group E (High Velocity)

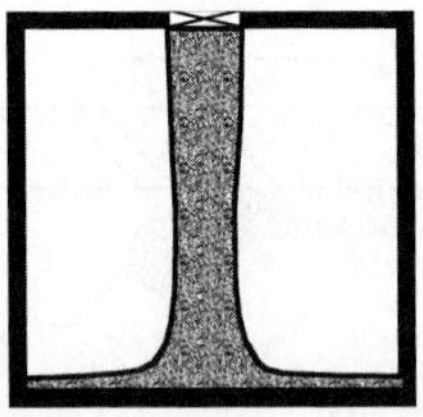

Fig. 10 Example Airflow Patterns (Nonisothermal) of Outlet Group E (Low Velocity)

Jet Expansion Zones. The full length of an air jet, in terms of the maximum or centerline velocity and temperature differential at the cross section, can be divided into four zones:

- Zone 1 extends from the outlet face, in which the velocity and temperature of the airstream remains practically unchanged.
- Zone 2 is a transition zone, with its length determined by the type of outlet, aspect ratio of the outlet, initial airflow turbulence, etc.
- Zone 3 is a zone of jet degradation, where centerline air velocity and temperature differential decrease rapidly. Turbulent flow is fully established and may be 25 to 100 equivalent air outlet diameters long. The angle of divergence is well defined. Typically, free air jets diverge at a constant angle, usually ranging from 20 to 24°, with an average of 22°. Coalescing jets for closely spaced multiple outlets expand at smaller angles, averaging 18°, and jets discharging into relatively small spaces show even smaller angles of expansion (McElroy 1943). The angle of divergence is easily affected by external influences, such as local eddies, vortices, and surges. Internal forces governing this air motion are extremely delicate (Nottage et al. 1952a).
- Zone 4 is important because, in most cases, the jet enters the occupied area in this zone. Distance to this zone and its length depend on the velocities and turbulence characteristics of ambient air. In a few diameters or widths, air velocity becomes less than 50 fpm.

Centerline Velocities in Zones 1 and 2. In zone 1, the ratio V_x/V_o is constant for a given outlet and ranges between 1.0 and 1.2, equal to the ratio of the centerline velocity of the jet at the start of expansion to the average initial velocity. The ratio V_x/V_o varies from approximately 1.0 for rounded entrance nozzles to about 1.2 for straight pipe discharges; it has higher values for diverging discharge outlets.

The aspect ratio (Tuve 1953) and turbulence (Nottage et al. 1952a) primarily affect centerline velocities in zones 1 and 2. Aspect ratio has little effect on the terminal zone of the jet when H_o is greater than 4 in. This is particularly true of nonisothermal jets. When H_o is very small, induced air can penetrate the core of the jet, thus reducing centerline velocities. The difference in performance between a radial outlet with small H_o and an axial outlet with large H_o shows the importance of jet thickness.

When air is discharged from relatively large perforated panels, the constant-velocity core formed by coalescence of individual jets extends a considerable distance from the panel face. In zone 1, when the aspect ratio is less than 5, use the following equation for estimating centerline velocities (Koestel et al. 1949):

$$V_x = 1.2 V_o \sqrt{C_d R_{fa}} \tag{2}$$

In zone 2, the ratio V_x/V_o begins to decrease. Experimental evidence indicates that, in zone 2,

$$\frac{V_x}{V_o} = \sqrt{\frac{K_{c2} H_o}{X}} \tag{3}$$

where

V_x = centerline velocity at distance X from outlet, fpm
V_o = $V_c/C_d R_{fa}$ = average initial velocity at discharge, fpm
V_c = nominal velocity of discharge based on core area, fpm
C_d = coefficient of discharge (usually between 0.65 and 0.90)
R_{fa} = ratio of free area to core area
H_o = width of jet at outlet or at vena contracta, ft
K_{c2} = centerline velocity constant, depending on outlet type and discharge pattern
$X \geq (1/K_{c2}H_o)^{1/2}$ = distance from outlet to measurement of centerline velocity V_x, ft

Centerline Velocity in Zone 3. In zone 3, centerline velocities of radial and axial isothermal jets can be determined accurately from the following equation:

Table 1 Generic Values for Centerline Velocity Constant K_{c3}[a] for Commercial Supply Outlets for Fully and Partially Mixed Systems, Except UFAD

Outlet Type	Discharge Pattern	A_o	K_{c3}[a]
High sidewall grilles (Figure 4)	0° deflection[b]	Free	5.7
	Wide deflection	Free	4.2
High sidewall linear	Core less than 4 in. high[c]	Free	4.4
	Core more than 4 in. high	Free	5.0
Low sidewall (Figure 7)	Up and on wall, no spread	Free	4.5
	Wide spread[c]	Free	3.0
Baseboard	Up and on wall, no spread	Core	4.0
	Wide spread	Core	2.0
Floor grille (Figure 5)	No spread[c]	Free	4.7
	Wide spread	Free	1.6
Ceiling (Figure 2)	360° horizontal[d]	Neck	1.1
	Four-way; little spread	Neck	3.8
Ceiling linear slot (Figure 3)	Horizontal/vertical along surface[c]	Free	5.5
	Horizontal/vertical free jet[c]	Free	3.9
	Free jet (air curtain units)	Free	6.0

[a]Generic values shown for example purposes only. See manufacturer's data for specific K_{c3} values.
[b]Free area is about 80% of core area.
[c]Free area is about 50% of core area.
[d]Cone free area is greater than duct area.

$$V_x = \frac{K_{c3} V_o \sqrt{A_o}}{X} = \frac{K_{c3} Q_o}{X\sqrt{A_o}} \tag{4}$$

where

K_{c3} = centerline velocity constant (see Table 1 for generic values)
V_o = $V_c/C_d R_{fa}$ = average initial velocity at discharge, fpm
A_o = free area, core area, or neck area as shown in Table 1 (obtained from outlet manufacturer), ft^2
Q_o = volumetric flow rate of supply air, cfm
X = distance from face of outlet, ft

For centerline velocities of linear jets, where $K_{c3} = K_{c2}$, use Equation (3).

The effective area, according to ASHRAE *Standard* 70, can be used in place of A_o in Equation (4) with the appropriate value of K_{c3}.

Centerline Velocity in Zone 4. In zone 4, centerline velocities can be difficult to predict, based on the large dispersal pattern.

Determining Centerline Velocities. To correlate data from all four zones, plot centerline velocity ratios against distance from the outlet in Figures 11 and 12.

Airflow patterns of diffusers are related to the centerline velocity constants and throw distance. In general, diffusers with a circular airflow pattern (radial jet) have a shorter throw than those with a directional or cross-flow pattern (axial jet). During cooling, the circular pattern tends to curl back from the end of the throw toward the diffuser, reducing the drop and ensuring that the cool air remains near the ceiling.

In cross-flow airflow patterns, the airflow does not roll back to the diffuser at the end of the throw, but continues to move away from the diffuser at low velocities.

Throw. At a given supply airflow and centerline velocity, Equation (4) can be transposed into Equation (5) to determine the throw X of an outlet. The centerline velocity constant and appropriate outlet area A_o should be available from the outlet manufacturer.

According to Figures 11 and 12, 50 fpm terminal velocity can occur in zone 4. When this occurs, an accepted practice to approximate throw in zone 4 is to reduce the calculated throw in zone 3 by 30%.

$$X = \frac{K_{c3} Q_o}{V_x \sqrt{A_o}} \tag{5}$$

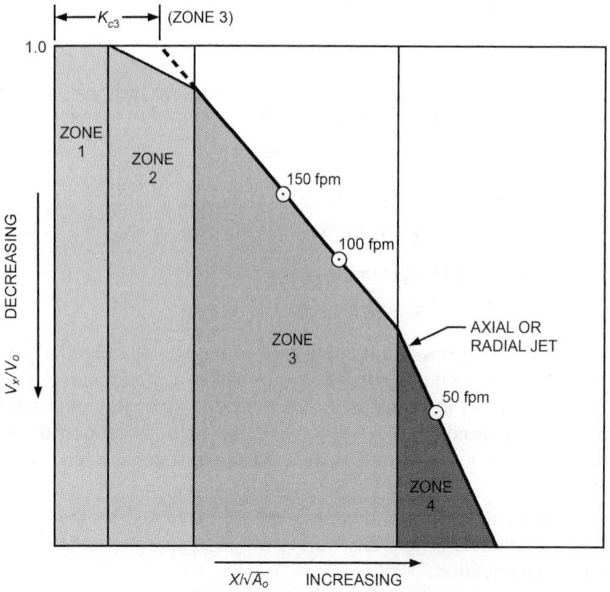

Fig. 11 Zones of Expansion for Axial or Radial Air Jets

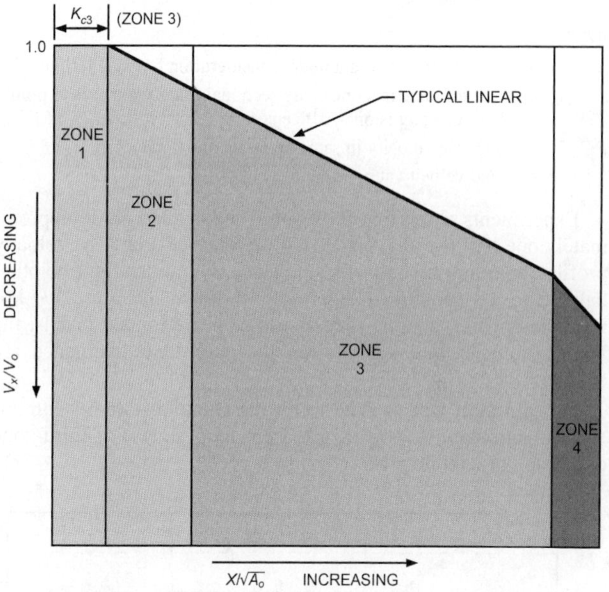

Fig. 12 Zones of Expansion for Linear Air Jets

See Informative Appendix B of ASHRAE *Standard* 70-2006 for the application of this methodology. The following example shows the use of Table 1 and Figures 11 and 12.

Example 1. A 12 by 18 in. high sidewall grille with an 11.25 by 17.25 in. core area is selected. From Table 1, K_{c3} = 5 for zone 3, and A_o should be 80% of the core area, in square feet. If the airflow is 600 cfm, what is the throw to 50, 100, and 150 fpm?

Solution:

From Equation (5),

$$X = \frac{K_{c3} Q_o}{V_x \sqrt{A_o}} = \frac{5.7 \times 600}{V_x \sqrt{0.8 \times 11.25 \times 17.25/144}} = \frac{3420}{V_x \times 1.0383}$$

Solving for 50 fpm throw,

$$X = 3420/(50 \times 1.04) = 66 \text{ ft}$$

However, according to Figures 11 and 12, 50 fpm is in zone 4, which is typically 30% less than calculated in Equation (4), or

$$X = 66 \times 0.70 = 46 \text{ ft}$$

Solving for 100 fpm throw,

$$X = 3420/(100 \times 1.04) = 33 \text{ ft}$$

Solving for 150 fpm throw,

$$X = 3420/(150 \times 1.04) = 22 \text{ ft}$$

Velocity Profiles of Jets. In zone 3 of both axial and radial jets, the velocity distribution may be expressed by a single curve (Figures 11 and 12) in terms of dimensionless coordinates; this same curve can be used as a good approximation for adjacent portions of zones 2 and 4. Temperature and density differences have little effect on cross-sectional velocity profiles.

Velocity distribution in zone 3 can be expressed by the Gauss error function or probability curve, which is approximated by the following equation:

$$\left(\frac{r}{r_{0.5V}}\right)^2 = 3.3 \log \frac{V_x}{V} \tag{6}$$

where

r = radial distance of point under consideration from centerline of jet
$r_{0.5V}$ = radial distance in same cross-sectional plane from axis to point where velocity is one-half centerline velocity (i.e., $V = 0.5V_x$)
V_x = centerline velocity in same cross-sectional plane
V = actual velocity at point being considered

Experiments show that the conical angle for $r_{0.5V}$ is approximately one-half the total angle of divergence of a jet. The velocity profile curve for one-half of a straight-flow turbulent jet (the other half being a symmetrical duplicate) is shown in Figure 13. For multiple-opening outlets, such as grilles or perforated panels, the velocity profiles are similar, but the angles of divergence are smaller.

Entrainment Ratios. The following equations are for entrainment of circular jets and of jets from long slots. For third-zone expansion of circular jets,

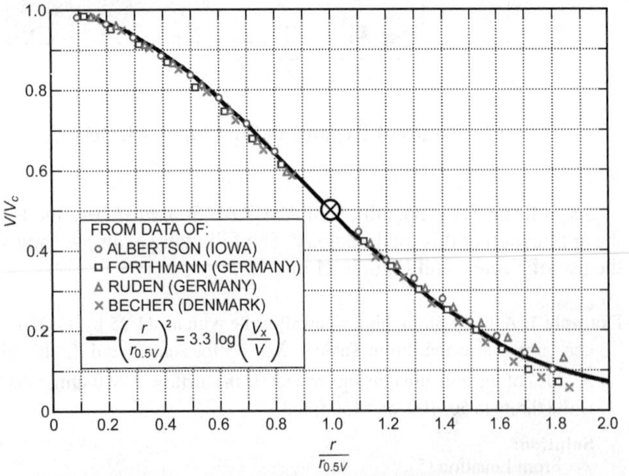

Fig. 13 Cross-Sectional Velocity Profiles for Straight-Flow Turbulent Jets

$$\frac{Q_x}{Q_o} = \frac{2X}{K_c\sqrt{A_o}} \tag{7}$$

By substituting from Equation (4),

$$\frac{Q_x}{Q_o} = 2\frac{V_o}{V_x} \tag{8}$$

For a continuous slot with active sections up to 10 ft and separated by 2 ft,

$$\frac{Q_x}{Q_o} = \sqrt{\frac{2}{K_{c3}}}\sqrt{\frac{X}{H_o}} \tag{9}$$

or, substituting from Equation (3),

$$\frac{Q_x}{Q_o} = \sqrt{2}\frac{V_o}{V_x} \tag{10}$$

where

Q_x = total volumetric flow rate at distance X from face of outlet, cfm
Q_o = discharge from outlet, cfm
X = distance from face of outlet, ft
K_c = centerline velocity constant
A_o = core area or neck area free (see Table 1), ft^2

The entrainment ratio Q_x/Q_o is important in determining total air movement at a given distance from an outlet. For a given outlet, the entrainment ratio is proportional to the distance X [Equation (7)] or to the square root of the distance X [Equation (9)] from the outlet. Equations (8) and (10) show that, for a fixed centerline velocity V_x, the entrainment ratio is proportional to outlet velocity. Equations (8) and (10) also show that, at a given centerline and outlet velocity, a circular jet has greater entrainment and total air movement than a long slot. Comparing Equations (7) and (9), the long slot should have a greater rate of entrainment. The entrainment ratio at a given distance is less with a large K_{c3} than with a small K_{c3}.

Isothermal Radial Flow Jets

In a radial jet, as with an axial jet, the cross-sectional area at any distance from the outlet varies as the square of this distance. Centerline velocity gradients and cross-sectional velocity profiles are similar to those of zone 3 of axial jets, and the angles of divergence are about the same.

Nonisothermal Jets

When the temperature of introduced air is different from the room air temperature, the diffuser air jet is affected by thermal buoyancy caused by air density difference. The trajectory of a nonisothermal jet introduced horizontally is determined by the Archimedes number (Baturin 1972):

$$\text{Ar} = \frac{gL_o(T_o - T_A)}{V_o^2 T_A} \tag{11}$$

where

g = gravitational acceleration rate, ft/min^2
L_o = length scale of diffuser outlet equal to hydraulic diameter of outlet, ft
$(T_o - T_A)$ = initial temperature of jet – temperature of ambient air, °F
V_o = initial air velocity of jet, fpm
T_A = room air temperature, °R

The influence of buoyant forces on horizontally projected heated and chilled jets is significant in heating and cooling with wall outlets. Koestel's (1955) equation describes the behavior of these jets.

Helander and Jakowatz (1948), Helander et al. (1953, 1954, 1957), Knaak (1957), and Yen et al. (1956) developed equations for outlet characteristics that affect the downward throw of heated air. Koestel (1954, 1955) developed equations for temperatures and velocities in heated and chilled jets. Kirkpatrick and Elleson (1996) and Li et al. (1993) provide additional information on nonisothermal jets.

Nonisothermal Horizontal Free Jet

A horizontal free jet rises or falls according to the temperature difference between it and the ambient environment. The horizontal jet throw to a given distance follows an arc, rising for heated air and falling for cooled air. Therefore, whether the equivalent temperature difference is positive or negative, the distance from the diffuser to a given terminal velocity along the discharge jet remains essentially the same.

Comparison of Free Jet to Attached Jet

An attached jet entrains air along the exposed side of the jet, whereas a free jet can entrain air on all its surfaces. Because a free jet's entrainment rate is larger compared to that of an attached jet, a free jet's throw distance will be shorter. To calculate the throw distance X for a noncircular free jet from catalog data for an attached jet, the following estimate can be used.

$$X_{free} = X_{attached} \times 0.707 \qquad (12)$$

Jets from ceiling diffusers initially tend to attach to the ceiling surface, because of the force exerted by the Coanda effect. However, air jets detach from the ceiling if the airstream's buoyancy forces are greater than the inertia of the moving airstream.

With separation, a cold jet may enter the occupied space, and can result in thermal discomfort. The thermal discomfort is caused by two factors: the cold draft caused by the separated jet in the occupied space, and areas of the room not reached by the separated jet. The separation distance parameter x_s is the distance from the diffuser at which a jet separates from the ceiling.

Separation distance correlates with outlet jet conditions (Kirkpatrick and Elleson 1996). Separation distance depends on the velocity constant K_c, outlet temperature, flow rate, and static pressure drop. For slot and round diffusers,

$$x_s = (11.91) C_s K_c^{1/2} (\Delta T/T)^{-1/2} Q_o^{1/4} \Delta P^{3/8} \qquad (13)$$

where

x_s = jet separation distance, ft
C_s = separation coefficient, 1.2
K_c = centerline velocity constant
ΔT = room-jet temperature difference, °F
T = average absolute room temperature, °R
Q_o = outlet flow rate, cfm
ΔP = diffuser static pressure drop, in. of water

Attached jets travel at a higher velocity and entrain less air than a free jet. Values of centerline velocity constant K_c are approximately those for a free jet multiplied by $\sqrt{2}$.

When a jet is discharged parallel to but at some distance from a solid surface (wall, ceiling, or floor), its expansion in the direction of the surface is reduced, and entrained air must be obtained by recirculation from the jet instead of from ambient air (McElroy 1943; Nottage et al. 1952b; Zhang et al. 1990). The restriction to entrainment caused by the solid surface induces the **Coanda effect**, which makes the jet attach to a surface after it leaves the diffuser outlet. The jet then remains attached to the surface for some distance before separating again.

In nonisothermal cases, the jet's trajectory is determined by the balance between thermal buoyancy and the Coanda effect, which depends on jet momentum and distance between the jet exit and solid surface. The behavior of such nonisothermal surface jets has been studied by Kirkpatrick et al. (1991), Oakes (1987), Wilson et al. (1970), and Zhang et al. (1990), each addressing different factors. More systematic study of these jets in room ventilation flows is needed to provide reliable guidelines for designing air distribution systems.

Air Curtain Units

Non-recirculating air curtain units operate in zones 1 to 3 where velocity degradation is at a minimum. The air curtain unit is designed such that the jet strikes the floor, comparable, surface or another jet in zone 3 at a minimum of 400 fpm, to generate a stable split to resist minimal thermal and pressure differentials.

Recirculating air curtain units also operate in zones 1 to 3, where velocity degradation is at a minimum. The target distance is designed for the jet to be captured by the low-pressure return and maintain a minimum of 600 fpm velocity while in zone 3, to create a stable barrier to resist minimal thermal and pressure differentials.

Multiple Jets

Twin parallel air jets act independently until they interfere. The point of interference and its distance from outlets vary with the distance between outlets. From outlets to the point of interference, maximum velocity, as for a single jet, is on the centerline of each jet. After interference, velocity on a line midway between and parallel to the two jet centerlines increases until it equals jet centerline velocity. From this point, maximum velocity of the combined jet stream is on the midway line, and the profile seems to emanate from a single outlet of twice the area of one of the two outlets.

Air Movement in Occupied Zone

Zhang et al. (1990) found that, for a given heat load and room air supply rate, air velocity in the occupied zone increases when outlet discharge velocity increases. Therefore, the design supply air velocity should be high enough to maintain the jet traveling in the desired direction, to ensure adequate mixing before it reaches the occupied zone. Excessively high outlet air velocity produces high air velocities in the occupied zone and may result in thermal discomfort.

Air turbulence in a room is mainly produced at the diffuser jet region by interaction of supply air with room air and with solid surfaces in the vicinity. It is then transported to other parts of the room, including the occupied zone (Zhang et al. 1992). Air in the occupied zone usually contains very small amounts of turbulent kinetic energy compared to the jet region. Because turbulence may cause thermal discomfort (Fanger et al. 1988), air distribution systems should be designed to avoid air turbulence in the occupied zone (except in specialized applications such as task ambient or spot-conditioning systems).

Thermal Plumes. As a thermal plume rises because of natural convection above a heat source, it entrains surrounding air and therefore increases in size and volume, and decreases in velocity (Figure 14). The maximum height to which a plume rises depends primarily on the heat source's strength (relative to the air turbulence surrounding the heat source), and secondarily on stratification in the room (which decreases the rising plume's buoyancy). The stratified zone has little or no recirculation.

In fully stratified and partially mixed applications, cool supply air introduced at or near the floor gradually flows across the lower level of the space. In the case of fully stratified applications (e.g., TDV systems), this layer is typically 4 to 6 in. thick. In partially mixed systems, this layer typically ranges from 1 to 8 ft thick, depending on the upward vertical projection of the outlets' supply air jets. It is drawn horizontally toward convective heat sources located within or close to it, where it is entrained upward by the associated heat plume. Partially mixed systems are characterized by relatively well-mixed conditions from the floor up to the height where their supply air jet velocities decay to 50 fpm or less. This area is referred to as the **lower mixed zone**. These plumes expand and rise until they encounter equally warm air in the upper regions

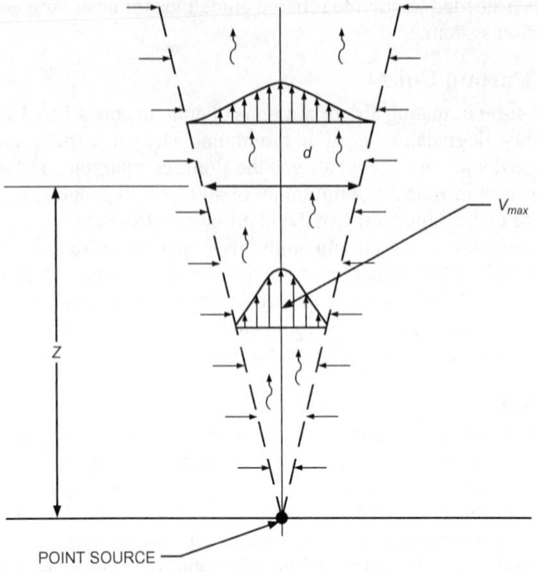

Fig. 14 Thermal Plume from Point Source

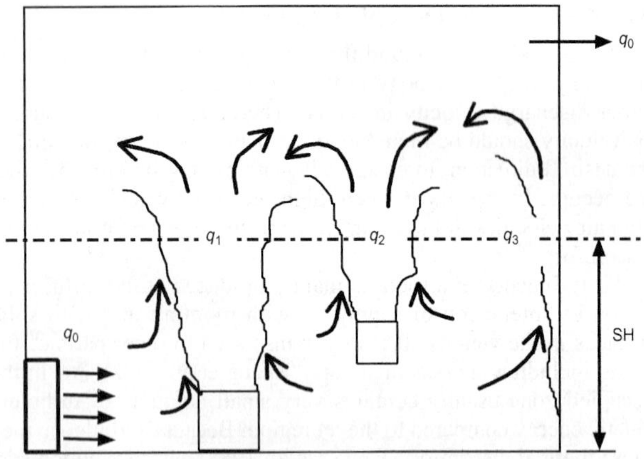

Fig. 15 Schematic Diagram of Major Flow Elements in Room with Displacement Ventilation

of the space. The **upper mixed zone** above the stratification height is characterized by low-velocity recirculation, which produces a fairly well-mixed layer of warm air with greater contaminant concentration than that in the lower levels of the space.

Typically, warmer, more polluted air will not reenter the stratified zone. This principle is the basis for the improved ventilation effectiveness and heat removal efficiency of TDV systems. In some situations (e.g., morning start-up, winter), there are also sources of cooling in the space, such as cold perimeter windows. The resulting cold downdraft may transport some air from the upper zone back down to the stratified zone.

Figure 15 shows basic elements in a simplified schematic of a TDV system. In the figure, q_0 represents the supply airflow into the room from a low sidewall diffuser, and q_1, q_2, and q_3 are the upward-moving airflows in thermal plumes that form above heat sources. In this simplified configuration, the stratification height occurs at a height SH, where the net upward-moving flow $q_1 + q_2 + q_3 = q_0$. An important objective in designing and operating a TDV system is to maintain stratification above the occupied zone.

4. SYMBOLS

A_c = measured gross (core) area of outlet, ft^2
A_o = core area or neck area, ft^2
A_R = cross-sectional area of confined space normal to jet, ft^2
Ar = Archimedes number [Equation (11)]
c = pollutant concentration
C_d = discharge coefficient (usually between 0.65 and 0.90)
c_R = concentration of pollutant at return grille near ceiling level
g = gravitational acceleration rate, ft/min^2
H = height or width of slot [Equation (2)], or of room
H_o = width of jet at outlet or at vena contracta or width of slot, ft
K_{c2} = centerline velocity constant in zone 2
K_{c3} = centerline velocity constant in zone 3
L_o = length scale of diffuser outlet equal to hydraulic diameter of outlet, ft
ΔP = diffuser static pressure drop, in. of water
Q_o = discharge from outlet, cfm
Q_x = total volumetric flow rate at distance X from face of outlet, cfm
r = radial distance of point under consideration from centerline of jet
$r_{0.5V}$ = radial distance in same cross-sectional plane from axis to point where velocity is one-half centerline velocity (i.e., $V = 0.5V_x$)
R_{fa} = ratio of free area to gross (core) area
SH = stratification height
T = average absolute room temperature, °R
ΔT = room/jet temperature difference, °F
T_A = temperature of ambient air, °F
T_E = temperature at ceiling, °F
T_F = temperature near floor, °F
T_H = temperature at given height, °F
T_O = initial temperature of jet, °F
T_S = supply temperature, °F
V = actual velocity at point being considered
V_c = nominal velocity of discharge based on core area, fpm
V_o = initial air velocity of jet, fpm
V_T = terminal velocity, fpm
V_x = centerline velocity, fpm
X = distance from face of outlet to location of centerline velocity V_X, ft
$X_{attached}$ = throw distance of attached jet, ft
X_{free} = throw distance of free jet, ft
X_H = throw height from floor outlet, ft
X_{VT} = distance to given terminal velocity, ft

REFERENCES

ASHRAE members can access *ASHRAE Journal* articles and ASHRAE research project final reports at technologyportal.ashrae.org. Articles and reports are also available for purchase by nonmembers in the online ASHRAE Bookstore at www.ashrae.org/bookstore.

ASHRAE. 2013. Thermal environmental conditions for human occupancy. ANSI/ASHRAE *Standard* 55-2013.
ASHRAE. 2013. Ventilation for acceptable indoor air quality. ANSI/ASHRAE *Standard* 62.1-2013.
ASHRAE. 2011. Method of testing for rating the performance of air outlets and inlets. ANSI/ASHRAE *Standard* 70-2006 (RA 2011).
ASHRAE. 2010. Standard *62.1 user's manual*.
ASHRAE. 2013. *UFAD guide: Design, construction and operation of underfloor air distribution systems*.
Baturin, V.V. 1972. *Fundamentals of industrial ventilation*, 3rd ed. Translated by O.M. Blunn. Pergamon Press, New York.
Chen, Q., and L. Glicksman. 2003. *System performance evaluation and design guidelines for displacement ventilation*. ASHRAE.
Christianson, L.L., ed. 1989. *Building systems: Room air and air contaminant distribution*. ASHRAE.
Fanger, P.O., A.K. Melikov, H. Hanzawa, and J. Ring. 1988. Air turbulence and sensation of draft. *Energy and Buildings* 12:21-39.
Helander, L., and C.V. Jakowatz. 1948. Downward projection of heated air. *ASHVE Transactions* 54:71.
Helander, L., S.M. Yen, and R.E. Crank. 1953. Maximum downward travel of heated jets from standard long radius ASME nozzles. *ASHVE Transactions* 59:241.

Helander, L., S.M. Yen, and L.B. Knee. 1954. Characteristics of downward jets of heated air from a vertical delivery discharge unit heater. *ASHVE Transactions* 60:359.

Helander, L., S.M. Yen, and W. Tripp. 1957. Outlet characteristics that affect the downthrow of heated air jets. *ASHAE Transactions* 63:255.

Kirkpatrick, A., and J. Elleson. 1996. *Design guide for cold air distribution systems*. ASHRAE.

Kirkpatrick, A., T. Malmstrom, P. Miller, and V. Hassani. 1991. Use of low temperature air for cooling of buildings. *Proceedings of Building Simulation*.

Knaak, R. 1957. Velocities and temperatures on axis of downward heated jet from 4-inch long-radius ASME nozzle. *ASHAE Transactions* 63:527.

Koestel, A. 1954. Computing temperatures and velocities in vertical jets of hot or cold air. *ASHVE Transactions* 60:385.

Koestel, A. 1955. Paths of horizontally projected heated and chilled air jets. *ASHAE Transactions* 61:213.

Koestel, A., P. Hermann, and G.L. Tuve. 1949. Air streams from perforated panels. *ASHVE Transactions* 55:283.

Li, Z., J.S. Zhang, A.M. Zhivov, and L.L. Christianson. 1993. Characteristics of diffuser air jets and airflow in the occupied regions of mechanically ventilated rooms: A literature review. *ASHRAE Transactions* 99(1): 1119-1127.

McElroy, G.E. 1943. Air flow at discharge of fan-pipe lines in mines. U.S. Bureau of Mines *Report of Investigations* 19.

Murakami, S. 1992. New scales for ventilation efficiency and their application based on numerical simulation of room airflow. International Symposium on Room Air Convection and Ventilation Effectiveness.

Nottage, H.B., J.G. Slaby, and W.P. Gojsza. 1952a. Outlet turbulence intensity as a factor in isothermal-jet flow. *ASHVE Transactions* 58:343.

Nottage, H.B., J.G. Slaby, and W.P. Gojsza. 1952b. Isothermal ventilation jet fundamentals. *ASHVE Transactions* 58:107.

Oakes, W.C. 1987. *Experimental investigation of Coanda jet*. M.S. thesis, Michigan State University, East Lansing.

Rock, B.A., and D. Zhu. 2002. *Designer's guide to ceiling-based air diffusion* (RP-1065). ASHRAE.

Tuve, G.L. 1953. Air velocities in ventilating jets. *ASHVE Transactions* 59:261.

USGBC. 2013. *LEED v4 for building design and construction*. U.S. Green Building Council, Washington, D.C. www.usgbc.org/resources /leed-reference-guide-building-design-and-construction.

Wilson, J.D., M.L. Esmay, and S. Persson. 1970. Wall-jet velocity and temperature profiles resulting from a ventilation inlet. *ASAE Transactions*.

Yen, S.M., L. Helander, and L.B. Knee. 1956. Characteristics of downward jets from a vertical discharge unit heater. *ASHAE Transactions* 62:123.

Zhang, J.S., L.L. Christianson, and G.L. Riskowski. 1990. Regional airflow characteristics in a mechanically ventilated room under nonisothermal conditions. *ASHRAE Transactions* 96(1):751-759.

Zhang, J.S., L.L. Christianson, G.J. Wu, and G.L. Riskowski. 1992. Detailed measurements of room air distribution for evaluating numerical simulation models. *ASHRAE Transactions* 98(1):58-65.

BIBLIOGRAPHY

Arens, E.A., F. Bauman, L. Johnston, and H. Zhang. 1991. Testing of localized ventilation systems in a new controlled environment chamber. *Indoor Air* 3:263-281.

Arens, E., S. Turner, H. Zhang, and G. Paliaga. 2009. Moving air for comfort. *ASHRAE Journal* 51(5):18-29.

ASHRAE. 2013. Energy standard for buildings except low-rise residential buildings. ANSI/ASHRAE/IES *Standard* 90.1-2013.

ASHRAE. 2013. Method of testing for room air diffusion. ANSI/ASHRAE *Standard* 113-2013.

ASHRAE. 2002. Measuring air-change effectiveness. ANSI/ASHRAE *Standard* 129-1997 (RA 2002).

Ball, H.D., R.G. Nevins, and H.E. Straub. 1971. Thermal analysis of heat removal troffers. *ASHRAE Transactions* 77(2).

Bauman, F., and E. Arens. 1996. *Task/ambient conditioning systems: Engineering and application guidelines*. Center for Environmental Design Research, University of California, Berkeley.

Bauman, F., P. Pecora, and T. Webster. 1999. *How low can you go? Air flow performance of low-height underfloor plenums.* Center for the Built Environment, University of California, Berkeley.

Bauman, F.S., L.P. Johnston, H. Zhang, and E.A. Arens. 1991. Performance testing of a floor-based, occupant-controlled office ventilation system. *ASHRAE Transactions* 97(1):553-565.

Bauman, F.S., H. Zhang, E. Arens, and C. Benton. 1993. Localized comfort control with a desktop task conditioning system: Laboratory and field measurements. *ASHRAE Transactions* 99(2):733-749.

Bauman, F.S., E.A. Arens, S. Tanabe, H. Zhang, and A. Baharlo. 1995. Testing and optimizing the performance of a floor-based task conditioning system. *Energy and Buildings* 22(3):173-186.

Bauman, F.S., T.G. Carter, A.V. Baughman, and E.A. Arens. 1998. Field study of the impact of a desktop task/ambient conditioning system in office buildings. *ASHRAE Transactions* 104(1):1153-1171.

Chen, Q., and L. Glicksman. 1999. Performance evaluation and development of design guidelines for displacement ventilation (RP-949). ASHRAE Research Project, *Final Report*.

de Dear, R.J., and G.S. Brager. 1999. Developing an adaptive model of thermal comfort and preference. *ASHRAE Transactions* 104(1A):145-167.

Faulkner, D., W.J. Fisk, and D.P. Sullivan. 1993. Indoor air flow and pollutant removal in a room with desktop ventilation. *ASHRAE Transactions* 99(2):750-758.

Faulkner, D., W.J. Fisk, D.P. Sullivan, and D.P. Wyon. 1999. Ventilation efficiencies of task/ambient conditioning systems with desk-mounted air supplies. *Proceedings of Indoor Air '99*, Edinburgh, Scotland, 8-13 August.

Fisk, W.J., D. Faulkner, D. Pih, P. McNeel, F. Bauman, and E. Arens. 1991. Indoor air flow and pollutant removal in a room with task ventilation. *Indoor Air* 3:247-262.

Hanzawa, H., and Y. Nagasawa. 1990. Thermal comfort with underfloor air-conditioning systems. *ASHRAE Transactions* 96(2).

Hart, G.H., and D. Int-Hout. 1980. The performance of a continuous linear diffuser in the perimeter zone of an office environment. *ASHRAE Transactions* 86(2).

Hart, G.H., and D. Int-Hout. 1981. The performance of a continuous linear diffuser in the interior zone of an open office environment. *ASHRAE Transactions* 87(2).

Heiselberg, P., and M. Sandberg. 1990. Convection from a slender cylinder in a ventilated room. *Proceedings of ROOMVENT '90*, Oslo.

Houghton, D. 1995. *Turning air conditioning on its head: Underfloor air distribution offers flexibility, comfort, and efficiency*. E Source TU-95-8. E Source, Inc., Boulder, CO.

Houghten, F.C., C. Gutberlet, and E. Witkowski. 1938. Draft temperatures and velocities in relation to skin temperatures and feelings of warmth. *ASHVE Transactions* 44:289.

Howe, M., D. Holland, and A. Livchak. 2003. Displacement ventilation—Smart way to deal with increased heat gains in the telecommunication equipment room. *ASHRAE Transactions* 109(1):323-327.

Int-Hout, D. 1981. Measurement of room air diffusion in actual office environments to predict occupant thermal comfort. *ASHRAE Transactions* 87(2).

Int-Hout, D. 2007. Overhead heating: Revisiting a lost art. *ASHRAE Journal* 49(3):56-61.

Jackman, P.J. 1991. Displacement ventilation. CIBSE National Conference. Chartered Institution of Building Services Engineers, London.

Jackman, P.J., and P.A. Appleby. 1990. Displacement flow ventilation. BSRIA *Project Report*. Building Services Research and Information Association, Berkshire, U.K.

Kegel, B., and U.W. Schulz. 1989. Displacement ventilation for office buildings. *Proceedings of the 10th AIVC Conference*, Helsinki.

Koestel, A. 1957. Jet velocities from radial flow outlets. *ASHAE Transactions* 63:505.

Koestel, A., and J.B. Austin, Jr. 1956. Air velocities in two parallel ventilating jets. *ASHAE Transactions* 62:425.

Koestel, A., and G.L. Tuve. 1955. Performance and evaluation of room air distribution systems. *ASHAE Transactions* 61:533.

Koestel, A., P. Hermann, and G.L. Tuve. 1950. Comparative study of ventilating jets from various types of outlets. *ASHVE Transactions* 56:459.

Livchak, A., and D. Nall. 2001. Displacement ventilation—Application for hot and humid climate. *Proceedings of CLIMA 2000*, Napoli.

Loudermilk, K. 1999. Underfloor air distribution solutions for open office applications. *ASHRAE Transactions* 105(1):605-613.

Lorch, F.A., and H.E. Straub. 1983. Performance of overhead slot diffusers with simulated heating and cooling conditions. *ASHRAE Transactions* 89(1).

Matsunawa, K., H. Iizuka, and S. Tanabe. 1995. Development and application of an underfloor air-conditioning system with improved outlets for a "smart" building in Tokyo. *ASHRAE Transactions* 101(2):887-901.

Mattsson, M. 2000. A note on the thermal comfort in displacement ventilated classrooms. *ROOMVENT 2000, Proceedings of the 7th International Conference on Air Distribution in Rooms*.

McCarry, B.T. 1995. Underfloor air distribution systems: Benefits and when to use the system in building design. *ASHRAE Transactions* 101(2):902-911.

McCarry, B.T. 1998. Innovative underfloor system. *ASHRAE Journal* 40(3).

Melikov, A.K., and J.B. Nielsen. 1989. Local thermal discomfort due to draft and vertical temperature difference in rooms with displacement ventilation. *ASHRAE Transactions* 95(2):1050-1057.

Miller, P.L. 1971. Room air distribution performance of four selected outlets. *ASHRAE Transactions* 77(2):194.

Miller, P.L. 1979. Design of room air diffusion systems using the air diffusion performance index (ADPI). *ASHRAE Journal* 10:85.

Miller, P.L. 1989. Descriptive methods. In *Building systems: Room air and air contaminant distribution*, L.L. Christianson, ed. ASHRAE.

Miller, P.L., and R.T. Nash. 1971. A further analysis of room air distribution performance. *ASHRAE Transactions* 77(2):205.

Miller, P.L., and R.G. Nevins. 1969. Room air distribution with an air distributing ceiling—Part II. *ASHRAE Transactions* 75:118.

Miller, P.L., and R.G. Nevins. 1970. Room air distribution performance of ventilating ceilings and cone-type circular ceiling diffusers. *ASHRAE Transactions* 76(1):186.

Miller, P.L., and R.G. Nevins. 1972. An analysis of the performance of room air distribution systems. *ASHRAE Transactions* 78(2):191.

Nelson, D.W., and G.E. Smedberg. 1943. Performance of side outlets on horizontal ducts. *ASHVE Transactions* 49:58.

Nelson, D.W., H. Krans, and A.F. Tuthill. 1940. The performance of stack heads. *ASHVE Transactions* 46:205.

Nelson, D.W., D.H. Lamb, and G.E. Smedberg. 1942. Performance of stack heads equipped with grilles. *ASHVE Transactions* 48:279.

Nevins, R.G., and P.L. Miller. 1972. Analysis, evaluation and comparison of room air distribution performance. *ASHRAE Transactions* 78(2):235.

Nevins, R.G., and E.D. Ward. 1968. Room air distribution with an air distributing ceiling. *ASHRAE Transactions* 74:VI.2.1.

Nielsen, P.V. 1996. Temperature distribution in a displacement ventilated room. *ROOMVENT 1996, Proceedings of the 5th International Conference on Air Distribution in Rooms*, Yokohama.

Poz, M.Y. 1991. Theoretical investigation and practical applications of non-isothermal jets for the rooms ventilating. Current East/West HVAC Developments. IEI/CIBSE/ABOK Joint Conference.

Reinmann, J.J., A. Koestel, and G.L. Tuve. 1959. Evaluation of three room air distribution systems for summer cooling. *ASHRAE Transactions* 65:717.

Rock, B.A. 2006. *Ventilation for environmental tobacco smoke—Controlling ETS irritants where smoking is allowed.* ASHRAE and Elsevier.

Rousseau, W.H. 1983. Perimeter air diffusion performance index tests for heating with a ceiling slot diffuser. *ASHRAE Transactions* 89(1).

Rydberg, J., and P. Norback. 1949. Air distribution and draft. *ASHVE Transactions* 55:225.

Scaret, E. 1985. *Ventilation by displacement: Characterization and design implications*. Elsevier Science, New York.

Seppanen, O.A., W.J. Fisk, J. Eto, and D.T. Grimsrud. 1989. Comparison of conventional mixing and displacement air-conditioning and ventilating systems in U.S. commercial buildings. *ASHRAE Transactions* 95(2):1028-1040.

Sandberg, M., and C. Blomqvist. 1989. Displacement ventilation in office rooms. *ASHRAE Transactions* 95(2):1041-1049.

Shilkrot, E., and A. Zhivov. 1992. Room ventilation with designed vertical air temperature stratification. *ROOMVENT '92, Proceedings of the 3rd International Conference on Engineering Aero- and Thermodynamics of Ventilated Rooms*.

Shute, R.W. 1992. Integrating access floor plenums for HVAC air distribution. *ASHRAE Journal* 34(10).

Shute, R.W. 1995. Integrated access floor HVAC: Lessons learned. *ASHRAE Transactions* 101(2):877-886.

Skistad, H. 1994. *Displacement ventilation*. Research Studies Press, John Wiley & Sons, West Sussex, U.K.

Skistad, H., E. Mundt, P. Nielsen, K. Hagstrom, and J. Railio. 2002. Displacement ventilation in non-industrial premises. *REHVA Guidebook* 1.

Sodec, F., and R. Craig. 1990. The underfloor air supply system—The European experience. *ASHRAE Transactions* 96(2).

Spoormaker, H.J. 1990. Low-pressure underfloor HVAC system. *ASHRAE Transactions* 96(2).

Straub, H.E., and M.M. Chen. 1957. Distribution of air within a room for year-round air conditioning—Part II. University of Illinois Engineering Experiment Station *Bulletin* 442.

Straub, H.E., S.F. Gilman, and S. Konzo. 1956. Distribution of air within a room for year-round air conditioning—Part I. University of Illinois Engineering Experiment Station *Bulletin* 435.

Stymne, H., M. Sandberg, and M. Mattsson. 1991. Dispersion pattern of contaminants in a displacement ventilation room—Implications for demand control. *Proceedings of the 12th Air Movement and Ventilation Control Within Buildings*, Ottawa.

Svensson, A.G.L. 1989. Nordic experiences of displacement ventilation systems. *ASHRAE Transactions* 95(2):1013-1017.

Tan, H., T. Murata, K. Aoki, and T. Kurabuchi. 1998. Cooled ceilings/displacement ventilation hybrid air conditioning system—Design criteria. *Proceedings of ROOMVENT '98*, Stockholm.

Tanabe, S., and K. Kimura. 1996. Comparisons of ventilation performance and thermal comfort among displacement, underfloor and ceiling based air distribution systems by experiments in a real sized office chamber. *ROOMVENT '96, Proceedings of the 5th International Conference on Air Distribution in Rooms*.

Tse, W.L., and A.T.P. So. 2006. The importance of human productivity to air-conditioned control in office environments. *HVAC&R Research* (now *Science and Technology for the Built Environment*) 13:3-21.

Tsuzuki, K., E.A. Arens, F.S. Bauman, and D.P. Wyon. 1999. Individual thermal comfort control with desk-mounted and floor-mounted task/ambient conditioning (TAC) systems. *Proceedings of Indoor Air '99*, Edinburgh, vol. 2, pp. 368-373.

CHAPTER 21

DUCT DESIGN

COMMERCIAL, industrial, and residential air duct system design must consider (1) space availability, (2) noise levels, (3) air leakage, (4) balancing, (5) fire and smoke control, (6) initial investment cost, and (7) system operating cost.

Deficiencies in duct design can result in systems that operate incorrectly or are expensive (increased energy) to own and operate. Poor design or lack of system sealing can produce inadequate airflow rates at the terminals, leading to discomfort, loss of productivity, and even adverse health effects. Lack of sound attenuation may lead to objectionable noise levels. Proper duct insulation eliminates excessive heat gain or loss.

In this chapter, system design and calculation of a system's frictional and dynamic resistance (total pressure) to airflow are considered. Chapter 19 of the 2016 *ASHRAE Handbook—HVAC Systems and Equipment* examines duct construction and presents construction standards for residential, commercial, and industrial HVAC and exhaust systems. For design guidance specific to residential systems, refer to Manual D by ACCA (2014).

1. BERNOULLI EQUATION

The Bernoulli equation can be developed by equating the forces on an element of a stream tube in a frictionless fluid flow to the rate of momentum change. On integrating this relationship for steady flow, the following expression (Osborne 1966) results:

$$\frac{v^2}{2g_c} + \int \frac{\Delta p}{\rho} + \frac{gz}{g_c} = \text{constant, ft}\cdot\text{lb}_f/\text{lb}_m \quad (1)$$

where

v = streamline (local) velocity, fps
g_c = dimensional constant, 32.2 $\text{lb}_m\cdot\text{ft/lb}_f\cdot\text{s}^2$
p = absolute pressure, lb_f/ft^2
ρ = density, lb_m/ft^3
g = acceleration caused by gravity, ft/s^2
z = elevation, ft

Assuming constant fluid density in the system, Equation (1) reduces to

$$\frac{v^2}{2g_c} + \frac{p}{\rho} + \frac{gz}{g_c} = \text{constant, ft}\cdot\text{lb}_f/\text{lb}_m \quad (2)$$

Although Equation (2) was derived for steady, ideal frictionless flow along a stream tube, it can be extended to analyze flow through ducts in real systems. In terms of pressure, the relationship for fluid resistance between two sections is

$$\frac{\rho_1 V_1^2}{2g_c} + p_1 + \frac{g}{g_c}\rho_1 z_1 = \frac{\rho_2 V_2^2}{2g_c} + p_2 + \frac{g}{g_c}\rho_2 z_2 + \Delta p_{t,\,1\text{-}2} \quad (3)$$

where

V = average duct velocity, fps
$\Delta p_{t,1\text{-}2}$ = total pressure loss caused by friction and dynamic losses between sections 1 and 2, lb_f/ft^2

In Equation (3), V (section average velocity) replaces v (streamline velocity) because experimentally determined loss coefficients allow for errors in calculating $v^2/2g_c$ (velocity pressure) across streamlines.

On the left side of Equation (3), add and subtract p_{z1}; on the right side, add and subtract p_{z2}, where p_{z1} and p_{z2} are the values of atmospheric air at heights z_1 and z_2. Thus,

$$\frac{\rho_1 V_1^2}{2g_c} + p_1 + (p_{z1} - p_{z1}) + \frac{g}{g_c}\rho_1 z_1 = \frac{\rho_2 V_2^2}{2g_c} + p_2 + (p_{z2} - p_{z2}) + \frac{g}{g_c}\rho_2 z_2 + \Delta p_{t,1\text{-}2} \quad (4)$$

Atmospheric pressure at any elevation (p_{z1} and p_{z2}) expressed in terms of the atmospheric pressure p_a at the same datum elevation is given by

$$p_{z1} = p_a - \frac{g}{g_c}\rho_a z_1 \quad (5)$$

$$p_{z2} = p_a - \frac{g}{g_c}\rho_a z_2 \quad (6)$$

Substituting Equations (5) and (6) into Equation (4) and simplifying yields the total pressure change between sections 1 and 2. Assume no temperature change between sections 1 and 2 (no heat exchanger within the section); therefore, $\rho_1 = \rho_2$. When a heat exchanger is located in the section, the average of the inlet and outlet temperatures is generally used. Let $\rho = \rho_1 = \rho_2$, and $(p_1 - p_{z1})$ and $(p_2 - p_{z2})$ are gage pressures at elevations z_1 and z_2.

$$\Delta p_{t,1\text{-}2} = \left(p_{s,1} + \frac{\rho V_1^2}{2g_c}\right) - \left(p_{s,2} + \frac{\rho V_2^2}{2g_c}\right) + \frac{g}{g_c}(\rho_a - \rho)(z_2 - z_1) \quad (7a)$$

$$\Delta p_{t,1\text{-}2} = \Delta p_t + \Delta p_{se} \quad (7b)$$

Rearranging Equation (7b) yields

$$\Delta p_t = \Delta p_{t,1\text{-}2} - \Delta p_{se} \quad (7c)$$

where

$p_{s,1}$ = static pressure, gage at elevation z_1, lb_f/ft^2
$p_{s,2}$ = static pressure, gage at elevation z_2, lb_f/ft^2

The preparation of this chapter is assigned to TC 5.2, Duct Design.

V_1 = average velocity at section 1, fps
V_2 = average velocity at section 2, fps
ρ_a = density of ambient air, lb_m/ft^3
ρ = density of air or gas in duct, lb_m/ft^3
Δp_{se} = thermal gravity effect, lb_f/ft^2
Δp_t = total pressure change between sections 1 and 2, lb_f/ft^2
$\Delta p_{t,1\text{-}2}$ = total pressure loss caused by friction and dynamic losses between sections 1 and 2, lb_f/ft^2

1.1 HEAD AND PRESSURE

The terms **head** and **pressure** are often used interchangeably; however, head is the height of a fluid column supported by fluid flow, whereas pressure is the normal force per unit area. For liquids, it is convenient to measure head in terms of the flowing fluid. With a gas or air, however, it is customary to measure pressure exerted by the gas on a column of liquid.

Static Pressure

The term $pg_c/\rho g$ is static head; p is static pressure.

Velocity Pressure

The term $V^2/2g$ refers to velocity head, and $\rho V^2/2g_c$ refers to velocity pressure. Although velocity head is independent of fluid density, velocity pressure [Equation (8)] is not.

$$p_v = \rho(V/1097)^2 \tag{8}$$

where

p_v = velocity pressure, in. of water
V = fluid mean velocity, fpm
1097 = conversion factor to in. of water

For air at standard conditions (0.075 lb_m/ft^3), Equation (8) becomes

$$p_v = (V/4005)^2 \tag{9}$$

where $4005 = (1097^2/0.075)^{1/2}$. Velocity is calculated by

$$V = Q/A \tag{10}$$

where

Q = airflow rate, cfm
A = cross-sectional area of duct, ft^2

Total Pressure

Total pressure is the sum of static pressure and velocity pressure:

$$p_t = p_s + \rho(V/1097)^2 \tag{11}$$

or

$$p_t = p_s + p_v \tag{12}$$

where

p_t = total pressure, in. of water
p_s = static pressure, in. of water

Pressure Measurement

The range, precision, and limitations of instruments for measuring pressure and velocity are discussed in Chapter 36. The manometer is a simple and useful means for measuring partial vacuum and low pressure. Static, velocity, and total pressures in a duct system relative to ambient space pressure can be measured with a pitot tube connected to a manometer. Pitot tube construction and locations for traversing round and rectangular ducts are presented in Chapter 37.

2. SYSTEM ANALYSIS

The total pressure change caused by friction, fittings, equipment, and net **thermal gravity effect** for each section of a duct system is calculated by the following equation:

$$\Delta p_{t_i} = \Delta p_{f_i} + \sum_{j=1}^{m} \Delta p_{ij} + \sum_{k=1}^{n} \Delta p_{ik} - \sum_{r=1}^{\lambda} \Delta p_{se_{ir}} \tag{13}$$

$$\text{for } i = 1, 2, \ldots, n_{up} + n_{dn}$$

where

Δp_{t_i} = net total pressure change for i sections, in. of water
Δp_{f_i} = pressure loss caused by friction for i sections, in. of water
Δp_{ij} = total pressure loss caused by j fittings, including fan system effect (FSE), for i sections, in. of water
Δp_{ik} = pressure loss caused by k equipment for i sections, in. of water
$\Delta p_{se_{ir}}$ = thermal gravity effect caused by r stacks for i sections, in. of water
m = number of fittings within i sections
n = number of equipment within i sections
λ = number of stacks within i sections
n_{up} = number of duct sections upstream of fan (exhaust/return air subsystems)
n_{dn} = number of duct sections downstream of fan (supply air subsystems)

From Equation (7), the thermal gravity effect for each nonhorizontal duct with a density other than that of ambient air is determined by the following equation:

$$\Delta p_{se} = 0.192(\rho_a - \rho)(z_2 - z_1) \tag{14}$$

where

Δp_{se} = thermal gravity effect, in. of water
z_1 and z_2 = elevation from datum in direction of airflow (Figure 1), ft
ρ_a = density of ambient air, lb_m/ft^3
ρ = density of air or gas within duct, lb_m/ft^3
0.192 = conversion factor to in. of water

Example 1. For Figure 1, calculate the thermal gravity effect for two cases: (a) air cooled to –30°F, and (b) air heated to 1000°F. Density of air at –30°F is 0.0924 lb_m/ft^3 and at 1000°F is 0.0271 lb_m/ft^3. Density of ambient air is 0.075 lb_m/ft^3. Stack height is 40 ft.

Solution:

$$\Delta p_{se} = 0.192(\rho_a - \rho)z$$

(a) For $\rho > \rho_a$ (Figure 1A),

$$\Delta p_{se} = 0.192(0.075 - 0.0924)40 = -0.13 \text{ in. of water}$$

(b) For $\rho < \rho_a$ (Figure 1B),

$$\Delta p_{se} = 0.192\,(0.075 - 0.0271)40 = +0.37 \text{ in. of water}$$

Example 2. Calculate the thermal gravity effect for the two-stack system shown in Figure 2, where the air is 250°F and stack heights are 50 and 100 ft. Density of 250°F air is 0.0558 lb_m/ft^3; ambient air is 0.075 lb_m/ft^3.

Solution:

$$\Delta p_{se} = 0.192(0.075 - 0.0558)(100 - 50) = 0.18 \text{ in. of water}$$

For the system shown in Figure 3, the direction of air movement created by the thermal gravity effect depends on the initiating force (e.g., fans, wind, opening and closing doors, turning equipment on and off). If for any reason air starts to enter the left stack (Figure 3A), it creates a buoyancy effect in the right stack. On the other hand, if flow starts to enter the right stack (Figure 3B), it creates a buoyancy effect in the left stack. In both cases, the produced thermal gravity effect is stable and depends on stack height and magnitude of heating. The starting direction of flow is important when using natural convection for ventilation.

To determine the fan total pressure requirement for a system, use the following equation:

$$P_t = \sum_{i \varepsilon F_{up}} \Delta p_{t_i} + \sum_{i \varepsilon F_{dn}} \Delta p_{t_i} \qquad \text{for } i = 1, 2, \ldots, n_{up} + n_{dn} \qquad (15)$$

where

F_{up} and F_{dn} = sets of duct sections upstream and downstream of fan
P_t = fan total pressure, in. of water
ε = symbol that ties duct sections into system paths from exhaust/return air terminals to supply terminals

Figure 4 shows the use of Equation (15). This system has three supply and two return terminals consisting of nine sections connected in six paths: 1-3-4-9-7-5, 1-3-4-9-7-6, 1-3-4-9-8, 2-4-9-7-5, 2-4-9-7-6, and 2-4-9-8. Sections 1 and 3 are unequal area; thus, they are assigned separate numbers in accordance with the rules for identifying sections (see step 5 in the section on HVAC Duct Design Procedures). To determine the fan pressure requirement, apply the following six equations, derived from Equation (15). These equations must be satisfied to attain pressure balancing for design airflow. Relying entirely on dampers is not economical and may create objectionable flow-generated noise.

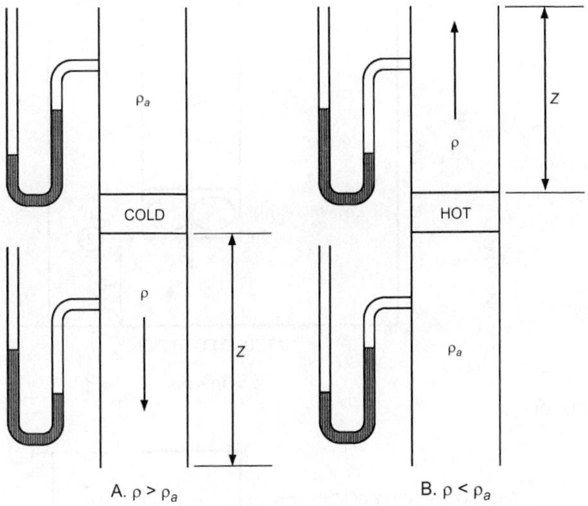

Fig. 1 Thermal Gravity Effect for Example 1

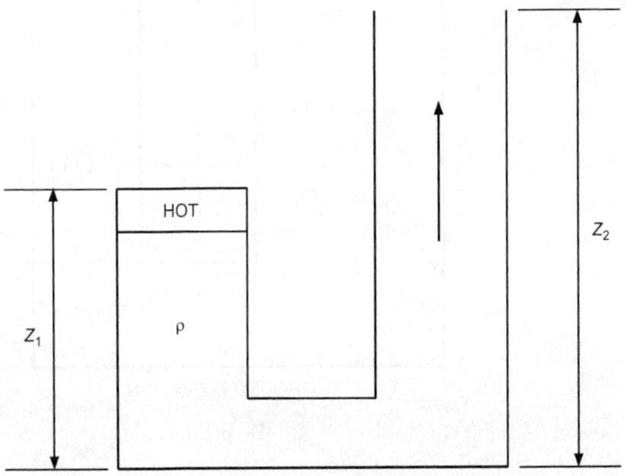

Fig. 2 Multiple Stacks for Example 2

$$\left\{\begin{aligned} P_t &= \Delta p_1 + \Delta p_3 + \Delta p_4 + \Delta p_9 + \Delta p_7 + \Delta p_5 \\ P_t &= \Delta p_1 + \Delta p_3 + \Delta p_4 + \Delta p_9 + \Delta p_7 + \Delta p_6 \\ P_t &= \Delta p_1 + \Delta p_3 + \Delta p_4 + \Delta p_9 + \Delta p_8 \\ P_t &= \Delta p_2 + \Delta p_4 + \Delta p_9 + \Delta p_7 + \Delta p_5 \\ P_t &= \Delta p_2 + \Delta p_4 + \Delta p_9 + \Delta p_7 + \Delta p_6 \\ P_t &= \Delta p_2 + \Delta p_4 + \Delta p_9 + \Delta p_8 \end{aligned}\right. \qquad (16)$$

Example 3. For Figures 5A and 5C, calculate the thermal gravity effect and fan total pressure required when the air is cooled to –30°F. The heat exchanger and ductwork (section 1 to 2) total pressure losses are 0.70 and 0.28 in. of water respectively. Density of –30°F air is 0.0924 lb_m/ft^3; ambient air is 0.075 lb_m/ft^3. Elevations are 70 and 10 ft.

Solution:

(a) For Figure 5A (downward flow),

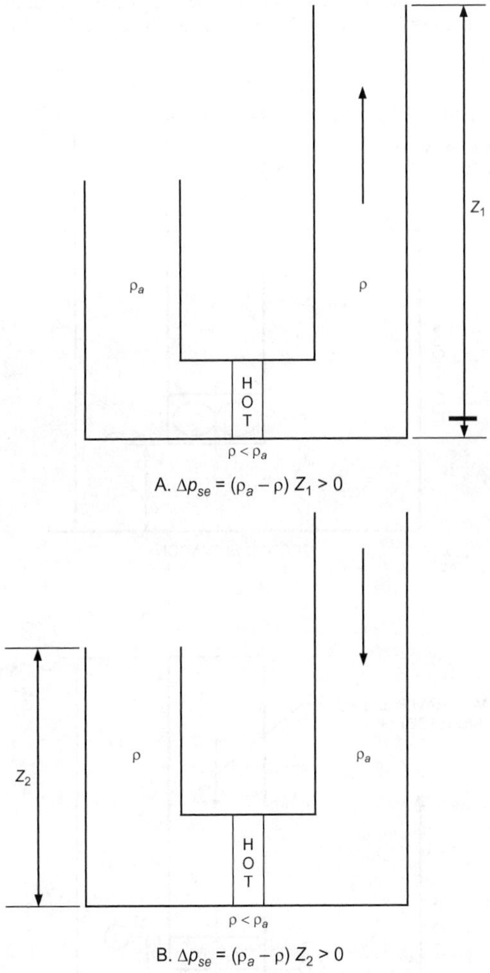

Fig. 3 Multiple Stack Analysis

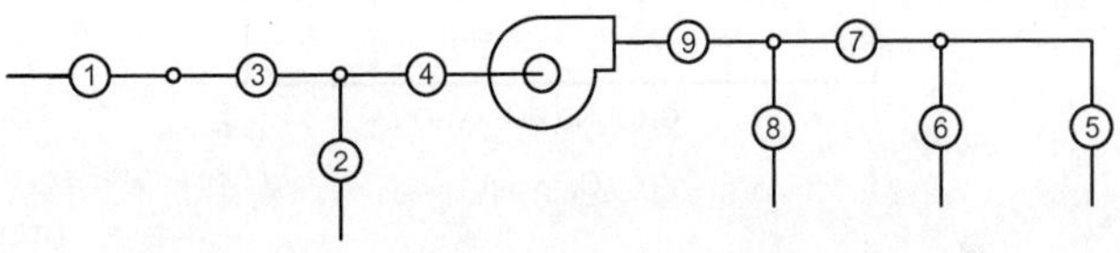

Fig. 4 Illustrative 6-Path, 9-Section System

$$\Delta p_{se} = 0.192(\rho_a - \rho)(z_2 - z_1)$$
$$= 0.192(0.075 - 0.0924)(10 - 70)$$
$$= 0.20 \text{ in. of water}$$

$$P_t = \Delta p_{t,3\text{-}2} - \Delta p_{se}$$
$$= (0.70 + 0.28) - (0.20)$$
$$= 0.78 \text{ in. of water}$$

(b) For Figure 5C (upward flow),

$$\Delta p_{se} = 0.192(\rho_a - \rho)(z_2 - z_1)$$
$$= 0.192(0.075 - 0.0924)(70 - 10)$$
$$= -0.20 \text{ in. of water}$$

$$P_t = \Delta p_{t,3\text{-}2} - \Delta p_{se}$$
$$= (0.70 + 0.28) - (-0.20)$$
$$= 1.18 \text{ in. of water}$$

Example 4. For Figures 5B and 5D, calculate the thermal gravity effect and fan total pressure required when air is heated to 250°F. Heat exchanger and ductwork (section 1 to 2) total pressure losses are 0.70 and 0.28 in. of water, respectively. Density of 250°F air is 0.0558 lb_m/ft^3; ambient air is 0.075 lb_m/ft^3. Elevations are 70 and 10 ft.

Solution:

(a) For Figure 5B (downward flow),

$$\Delta p_{se} = 0.192(\rho_a - \rho)(z_2 - z_1)$$
$$= 0.192(0.075 - 0.0558)(10 - 70)$$
$$= -0.22 \text{ in. of water}$$

$$P_t = \Delta p_{t,3\text{-}2} - \Delta p_{se}$$
$$= (0.70 + 0.28) - (-0.22)$$
$$= 1.20 \text{ in. of water}$$

(b) For Figure 5D (upward flow),

$$\Delta p_{se} = 0.192(\rho_a - \rho)(z_2 - z_1)$$
$$= 0.192(0.075 - 0.0558)(70 - 10)$$
$$= 0.22 \text{ in. of water}$$

$$P_t = \Delta p_{t,3\text{-}2} - \Delta p_{se}$$
$$= (0.70 + 0.28) - (0.22)$$
$$= 0.76 \text{ in. of water}$$

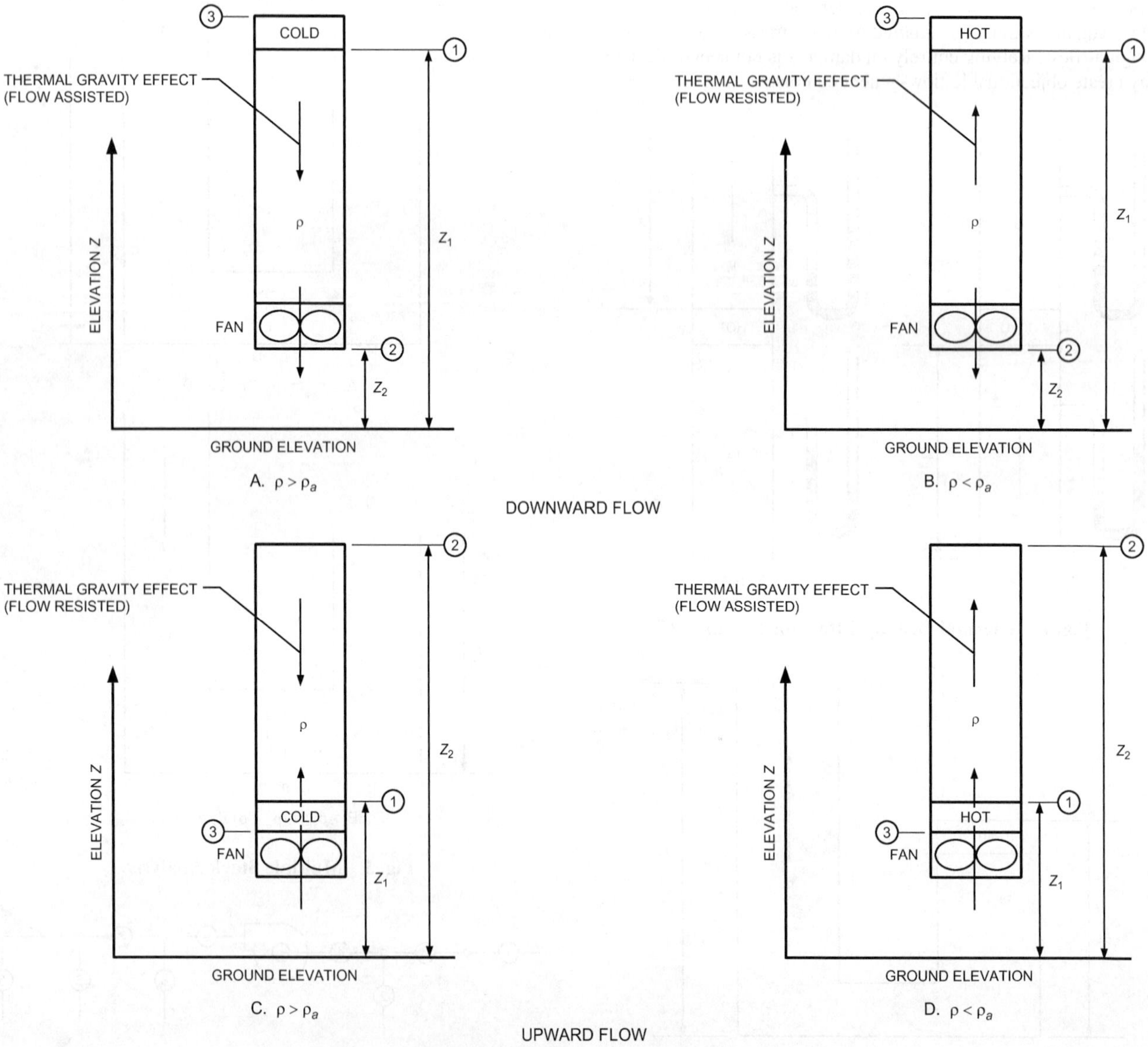

Fig. 5 Single Stack with Fan for Examples 3 and 4

Example 5. Calculate the thermal gravity effect for each section of the system in Figure 6 and the system's net thermal gravity effect. Density of ambient air is 0.075 lb_m/ft^3, and the lengths are as follows: $z_1 = 50$ ft, $z_2 = 90$ ft, $z_4 = 95$ ft, $z_5 = 25$ ft, and $z_9 = 200$ ft. Pressure required at section 3 is –0.1 in. of water. Write the equation to determine the fan total pressure requirement.

Solution: The following table summarizes the thermal gravity effect for each section of the system as calculated by Equation (14). The net thermal gravity effect for the system is 0.52 in. of water. To select a fan, use the following equation:

$$P_t = 0.1 + \Delta p_{t,1\text{-}7} + \Delta p_{t,8\text{-}9} - \Delta p_{se} = 0.1 + \Delta p_{t,1\text{-}7} + \Delta p_{t,8\text{-}9} - 0.52 = \Delta p_{t,1\text{-}7} + \Delta p_{t,8\text{-}9} - 0.42$$

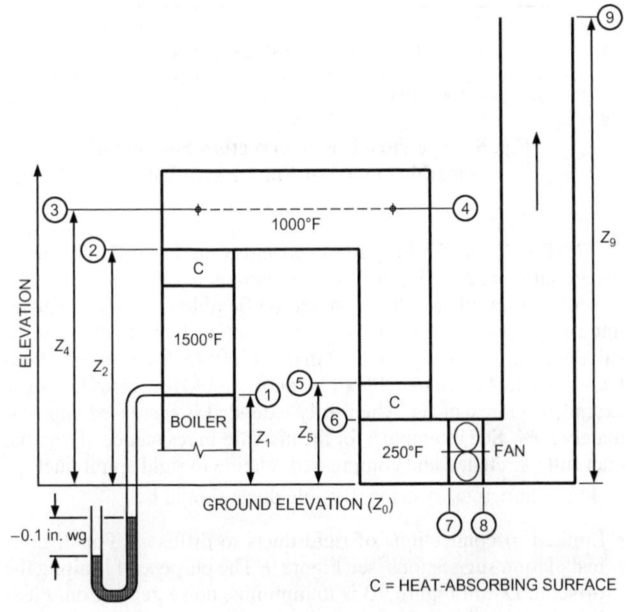

Fig. 6 Triple Stack System for Example 5

Path $(x\text{–}x')$	Temp., °F	ρ, lb_m/ft^3	Δz $(z_{x'} - z_x)$, ft	$\Delta\rho$ $(\rho_a - \rho_{x\text{–}x'})$, lb_m/ft^3	Δp_{se}, in. of water [Eq. (14)]
1-2	1500	0.0202	(90 – 50)	+0.0548	+0.42
3-4	1000	0.0271	0	+0.0479	0
4-5	1000	0.0271	(25 – 95)	+0.0479	–0.64
6-7	250	0.0558	0	+0.0192	0
8-9	250	0.0558	(200 – 0)	+0.0192	+0.74
Net Thermal Gravity Effect					0.52

2.1 PRESSURE CHANGES IN SYSTEM

Figure 7 shows total and static pressure changes in a fan/duct system consisting of a fan with both supply and return air ductwork. Also shown are total and static pressure gradients referenced to atmospheric pressure.

For all constant-area sections, total and static pressure losses are equal. At diverging transitions, velocity pressure decreases, absolute total pressure decreases, and absolute static pressure can increase. The static pressure increase at these sections is known as **static regain**.

At converging transitions, velocity pressure increases in the direction of airflow, and absolute total and absolute static pressures decrease.

At the exit, total pressure loss depends on the shape of the fitting and the flow characteristics. Exit loss coefficients C_o can be greater than, less than, or equal to one. Total and static pressure grade lines for the various coefficients are shown in Figure 7. Note that, for a loss coefficient less than one, static pressure upstream of the exit is less than atmospheric pressure (negative). Static pressure just upstream of the discharge fitting can be calculated by subtracting the upstream velocity pressure from the upstream total pressure.

At section 1, total pressure loss depends on the shape of the entry. Total pressure immediately downstream of the entrance equals the difference between the upstream pressure, which is zero (atmospheric pressure), and loss through the fitting. Static pressure of ambient air is zero; several diameters downstream, static pressure is negative, equal to the sum of the total pressure (negative) and the velocity pressure (always positive).

System resistance to airflow is noted by the total pressure grade line in Figure 7. Sections 3 and 4 include fan system effect pressure

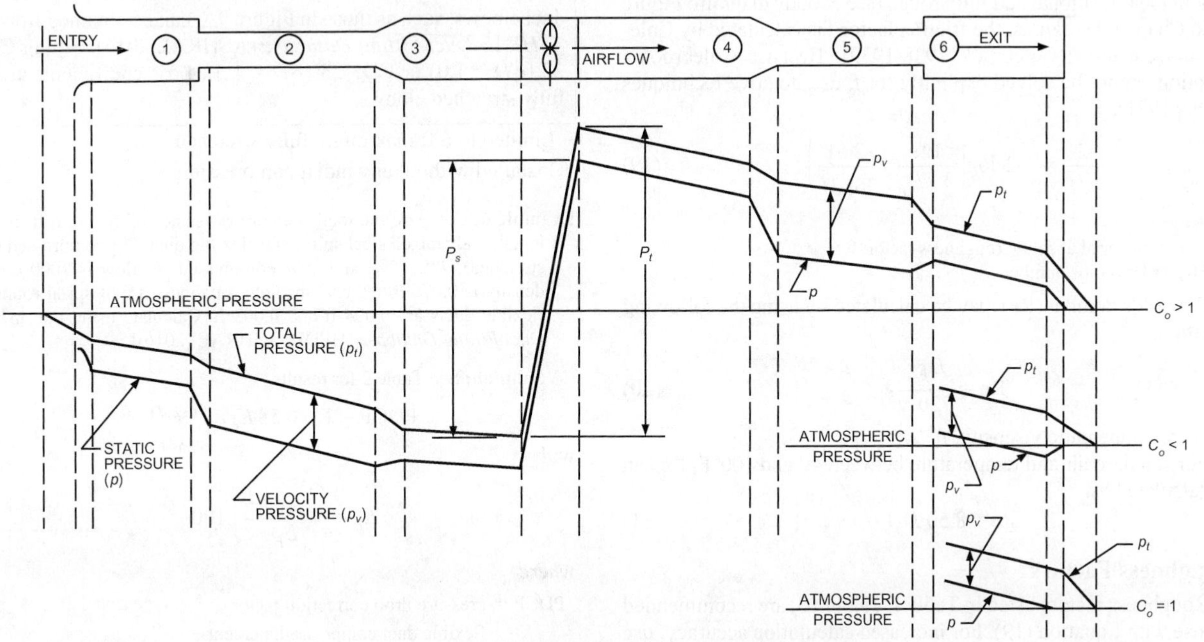

Fig. 7 Pressure Changes During Flow in Ducts

losses. To obtain the fan static pressure requirement for fan selection where fan total pressure is known, use

$$P_s = P_t - p_{v,o} \tag{17}$$

where

P_s = fan static pressure, in. of water
P_t = fan total pressure, in. of water
$p_{v,o}$ = fan outlet velocity pressure, in. of water

3. FLUID RESISTANCE

Duct system losses are the irreversible transformation of mechanical energy into heat. The two types of losses are (1) friction and (2) dynamic.

3.1 FRICTION LOSSES

Friction losses are caused by fluid viscosity and result from momentum exchange between molecules (in laminar flow) or between individual particles of adjacent fluid layers moving at different velocities (in turbulent flow). Friction losses occur along the entire duct length.

Darcy and Colebrook Equations

For fluid flow in conduits, friction loss can be calculated by the Darcy equation:

$$\Delta p_f = \frac{12fL}{D_h}\rho\left(\frac{V}{1097}\right)^2 \tag{18}$$

where

Δp_f = friction losses in terms of total pressure, in. of water
f = friction factor, dimensionless
L = duct length, ft
D_h = hydraulic diameter [Equation (24)], in.
V = velocity, fpm
ρ = density, lb_m/ft^3

In the region of laminar flow (Reynolds numbers less than 2300), the friction factor is a function of Reynolds number only. For completely turbulent flow (fully rough), the friction factor depends on duct surface roughness and internal protuberances (e.g., joints). Between the bounding limits of hydraulically smooth behavior (laminar flow) and fully rough behavior is a transitional zone where the friction factor depends on both roughness and Reynolds number. In both the transitional and fully rough (see Moody diagram: Figure 13 in Chapter 3) regions, the friction factor f is calculated by Colebrook's equation (Colebrook 1938-1939). Because Colebrook's equation cannot be solved explicitly for f, use iterative techniques (Behls 1971).

$$\frac{1}{\sqrt{f}} = -2\log\left(\frac{12\varepsilon}{3.7D_h} + \frac{2.51}{\text{Re}\sqrt{f}}\right) \tag{19}$$

where

ε = material absolute roughness factor, ft
Re = Reynolds number

Reynolds number (Re) may be calculated by using the following equation.

$$\text{Re} = \frac{D_h V}{720\,\nu} \tag{20}$$

where ν = kinematic viscosity, ft^2/s.

For standard air and temperature between 40 and 100°F, Re can be calculated by

$$\text{Re} = 8.50\,D_h V \tag{21}$$

Roughness Factors

Roughness factors listed in Table 1, column 3, are recommended for use with Equation (19). For increased calculation accuracy, use an absolute roughness factor from column 2.

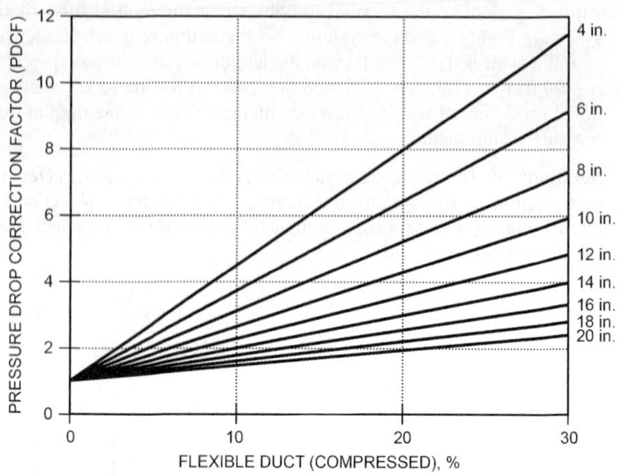

Pressure drop correction factor (PDCF) referenced to ε = 0.003 ft (medium rough) (Abushakra 2004; Culp 2011)

Fig. 8 Pressure Loss Correction Factor for Flexible Duct Not Fully Extended

Flexible Duct. For fully stretched and compressed flexible duct, use Equation (22) or Figure 8 (Abushakra et al. 2004; Culp 2011), where the multiplier PDCF is based on flexible duct with an absolute roughness ε = 0.003 ft. The resistance of flexible duct can be calculated using Fitting CD11-2 in the *ASHRAE Duct Fitting Database* (ASHRAE 2016). Flexible duct should be installed fully extended; its resistance when fully extended is increased approximately 50%. See Example 6 for the increase in resistance of flexible duct fully stretched and compressed relative to rigid spiral duct.

For commercial systems, flexible ducts should be

- Limited to connections of rigid ducts to diffusers. For diffuser installation suggestions, see Figure 9. The purpose of limiting the offset to $D/8$ in Figure 9B is to minimize noise generation. Flexible duct should not be installed upstream of variable-air-volume (VAV) boxes.

> *Commentary:* The loss coefficient or pressure loss for flexible duct elbows, such as those in Figure 9A, can be obtained from the *ASHRAE Duct Fitting Database* (ASHRAE 2016), Fitting CD3-22 (r/D = 1.0) or CD3-23 (r/D = 1.5). Loss coefficients are for fully stretched elbows.

- Limited to 6 ft maximum, fully stretched.
- Installed without any radial compression.

Example 6. Compare the total pressure resistance of 10 in., 6 ft installed length, galvanized steel spiral and flexible duct, 0% compressed (fully stretched), 4%, 15%, and 30% compressed. Airflow is 1000 cfm, air density is 0.075 lb/ft^3, and absolute roughnesses ε of spiral round and flexible ducts are 0.004 ft and 0.003 ft. Calculate using the *ASHRAE Duct Fitting Database* [DFDB; ASHRAE (2016)].

Solution: See Table 2 for results.

$$\text{PDCF} = 1 + 0.58\,K_c\,e^{-0.126D} \tag{22}$$

with

$$K_c = \left(\frac{L_{FE} - L}{L_{FE}}\right)100 \tag{23}$$

where

PDCF = pressure drop correction factor
K_c = flexible duct compressed, percent
D = flexible duct diameter, in.

Table 1 Duct Roughness Factors

1	2	3
	Absolute Roughness ε, ft	
Duct Type/Material	**Range**	**Roughness Category**
Drawn tubing (Madison and Elliot 1946)	0.0000015	Smooth 0.0000015
PVC plastic pipe (Swim 1982)	0.00003 to 0.00015	Medium smooth 0.00015
Commercial steel or wrought iron (Moody 1944)	0.00015	
Aluminum, round, longitudinal seams, crimped slip joints, 3 ft spacing (Hutchinson 1953)	0.00012 to 0.0002	
Friction chart:		
Galvanized steel, round, longitudinal seams, variable joints (Vanstone, drawband, welded. Primarily beaded coupling), 4 ft joint spacing (Griggs et al. 1987)	0.00016 to 0.00032	Average 0.0003
Galvanized steel, spiral seams, 10 ft joint spacing (Jones 1979)	0.0002 to 0.0004	
Galvanized steel, spiral seam with 1, 2, and 3 ribs, beaded couplings, 12 ft joint spacing (Griggs et al. 1987)	0.00029 to 0.00038	
Galvanized steel, rectangular, various type joints (Vanstone, drawband, welded. Beaded coupling), 4 ft spacing[a] (Griggs and Khodabakhsh-Sharifabad 1992)	0.00027 to 0.0005	
Wright Friction Chart:		
Galvanized steel, round, longitudinal seams, 2.5 ft joint spacing, ε = 0.0005 ft	Retained for historical purposes [See Wright (1945) for development of friction chart]	
Flexible duct, nonmetallic and wire, fully extended (Abushakra et al. 2004; Culp 2011)	0.0003 to0.003	Medium rough 0.003
Galvanized steel, spiral, corrugated,[b] Beaded slip couplings, 10 ft spacing (Kulkarni et al. 2009)	0.0018 to 0.0030	
Fibrous glass duct, rigid (tentative)[c]	—	
Fibrous glass duct liner, air side with facing material (Swim 1978)	0.005	
Fibrous glass duct liner, air side spray coated (Swim 1978)	0.015	Rough 0.01
Flexible duct, metallic corrugated, fully extended	0.004 to 0.007	
Concrete (Moody 1944)	0.001 to 0.01	

[a]Griggs and Khodabakhsh-Sharifabad (1992) showed that ε values for rectangular duct construction combine effects of surface condition, joint spacing, joint type, and duct construction (cross breaks, etc.), and that the ε-value range listed is representative.
[b]Spiral seam spacing was 4.65 in. with two corrugations between seams. Corrugations were 0.75 in. wide by 0.23 in. high (semicircle).
[c]Subject duct classified "tentatively medium rough" because no data available.

Table 2 Solution for Example 6

Duct	DFDB Fitting	ε, ft	Airflow, cfm	Diameter, in.	Velocity, fpm	Compression, %	PDCF*	Δp_t, in. of water	% Δp_t Increased
Flexible	CD11-2	0.003	1000	10	1833	(fully stretched)	1.0	0.043	48
Flexible	CD11-2	0.003	1000	10	1833	4	1.7	0.071	145
Flexible	CD11-2	0.003	1000	10	1833	15	3.5	0.148	410
Flexible	CD11-2	0.003	1000	10	1833	30	5.9	0.254	776
Galvanized steel, spiral	CD11-1	0.0004	1000	10	1833	NA	NA	0.029	Base

*See Equation (22).

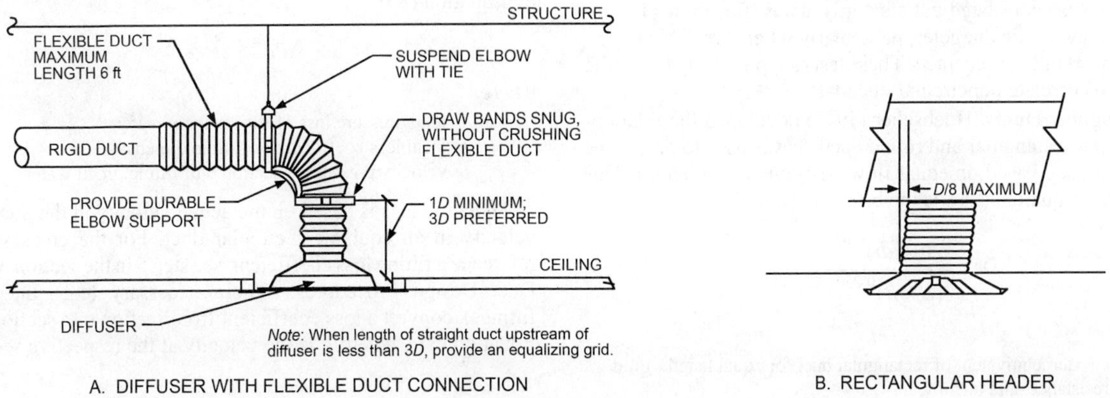

Fig. 9 Diffuser Installation Suggestions

L = installed duct length, ft
L_{FE} = duct length fully extended, ft

Friction Chart

The friction chart (Figure 10) is a plot of the Darcy and Colebrook equations [Equations (18) and (19), respectively), where the absolute roughness is 0.0003 ft and the air is standard air (density = 0.075 lb/ft^3)]. Figure 10 can be used for (1) duct construction/materials categorized as "average" in Table 1, (2) temperature variations of ±30°F from 70°F, (3) elevations to 1500 ft, and (4) duct pressures from −20 to +20 in. of water relative to ambient pressure. These individual variations in temperature, elevation, and duct pressure result in duct losses within ±5% of the standard air friction chart.

The friction chart was changed in 1985 from an absolute roughness of 0.0005 ft to 0.0003 ft based on research by Griggs et al. (1987), who found that the roughness factor is affected by the material surface, joint spacing, and type of joint. The Wright friction chart appeared in the Handbook from 1946 to 1981. This chart was based on an absolute roughness ε = 0.0005 ft, primarily because of the 2.5 ft joint spacing. In 1985 the friction chart was changed to ε = 0.0003 ft because joint spacing was increasing. For the relative effect of straight duct resistance between charts, see Figure 11. For a 10 in. diameter duct at 2000 fpm (1091 cfm), the resistance decreased 5 to 6%.

Noncircular Ducts

A momentum analysis can relate average wall shear stress to pressure drop per unit length for fully developed turbulent flow in a passage of arbitrary shape but uniform longitudinal cross-sectional area. This analysis leads to the definition of **hydraulic diameter**:

$$D_h = 4A/P \qquad (24)$$

where

D_h = hydraulic diameter, in.
A = duct area, in^2
P = perimeter of cross section, in.

Although hydraulic diameter is often used to correlate noncircular data, exact solutions for laminar flow in noncircular passages show that this causes some inconsistencies. No exact solutions exist for turbulent flow. Tests over a limited range of turbulent flow indicated that fluid resistance is the same for equal lengths of duct for equal mean velocities of flow if the ducts have the same ratio of cross-sectional area to perimeter. From experiments using round, square, and rectangular ducts having essentially the same hydraulic diameter, Huebscher (1948) found that each, for most purposes, had the same flow resistance at equal mean velocities. Tests by Griggs and Khodabakhsh-Sharifabad (1992) also indicated that experimental rectangular duct data for airflow over the range typical of HVAC systems can be correlated satisfactorily using Equation (19) together with hydraulic diameter, particularly when a realistic experimental uncertainty is accepted. These tests support using hydraulic diameter to correlate noncircular duct data.

Rectangular Ducts. Huebscher (1948) developed the relationship between rectangular and round ducts that is used to determine size equivalency based on equal flow, resistance, and length. This relationship, Equation (25), is the basis for Table 3.

$$D_e = \frac{1.30(ab)^{0.625}}{(a+b)^{0.250}} \qquad (25)$$

where

D_e = circular equivalent of rectangular duct for equal length, fluid resistance, and airflow, in.
a = length one side of duct, in.
b = length adjacent side of duct, in.

To determine equivalent round duct diameter, use Table 3. Equations (18) and (19) must be used to determine pressure loss.

Flat Oval Ducts. To convert round ducts to flat oval sizes, use Table 4, which is based on Equation (26) (Heyt and Diaz 1975), the circular equivalent of a flat oval duct for equal airflow, resistance, and length. Equations (18) and (19) must be used to determine friction loss.

$$D_e = \frac{1.55AR^{0.625}}{P^{0.250}} \qquad (26)$$

where AR is the cross-sectional area of flat oval duct defined as

$$AR = (\pi a^2/4) + a(A - a) \qquad (27)$$

and the perimeter P is calculated by

$$P = \pi a + 2(A - a) \qquad (28)$$

where

P = perimeter of flat oval duct, in.
A = major axis of flat oval duct, in.
a = minor axis of flat oval duct, in.

3.2 DYNAMIC LOSSES

Dynamic losses result from flow disturbances caused by duct-mounted equipment and fittings that change flow direction (elbows), area changes (transitions), and converging/diverging junctions. For a detailed discussion of hydraulic networks, consult Idelchik et al. (1994).

Local Loss Coefficients

The dimensionless coefficient C is used for fluid resistance because this coefficient has the same value in dynamically similar streams (i.e., streams with geometrically similar stretches, equal Reynolds numbers, and equal values of other criteria necessary for dynamic similarity). The fluid resistance coefficient represents the ratio of total pressure loss to velocity pressure at the referenced cross section:

$$C = \frac{\Delta p_t}{\rho(V/1097)^2} = \frac{\Delta p_t}{p_v} \qquad (29)$$

where

C = local loss coefficient, dimensionless
Δp_t = total pressure loss, in. of water
ρ = density, lb$_m$/ft^3
V = velocity, fpm
p_v = velocity pressure, in. of water

For all fittings, except junctions, total pressure loss is calculated by Equation (30):

$$\Delta p_t = C_o p_{v,o} \qquad (30)$$

where

Δp_t = total pressure loss of fitting, in. of water
C_o = local loss coefficient of fitting, dimensionless
$p_{v,o}$ = velocity pressure at section o of fitting, in. of water

Dynamic loss is based on the actual velocity in the duct, not the velocity in an equivalent circular duct. For the cross section to reference a fitting loss coefficient, see step 5 in the section on HVAC Duct Design Procedures. Where necessary (e.g., unequal-area fittings), convert a loss coefficient from section o to section 1 using Equation (31), where V is the velocity at the respective sections.

$$C_1 = \frac{C_o}{(V_1/V_o)^2} \qquad (31)$$

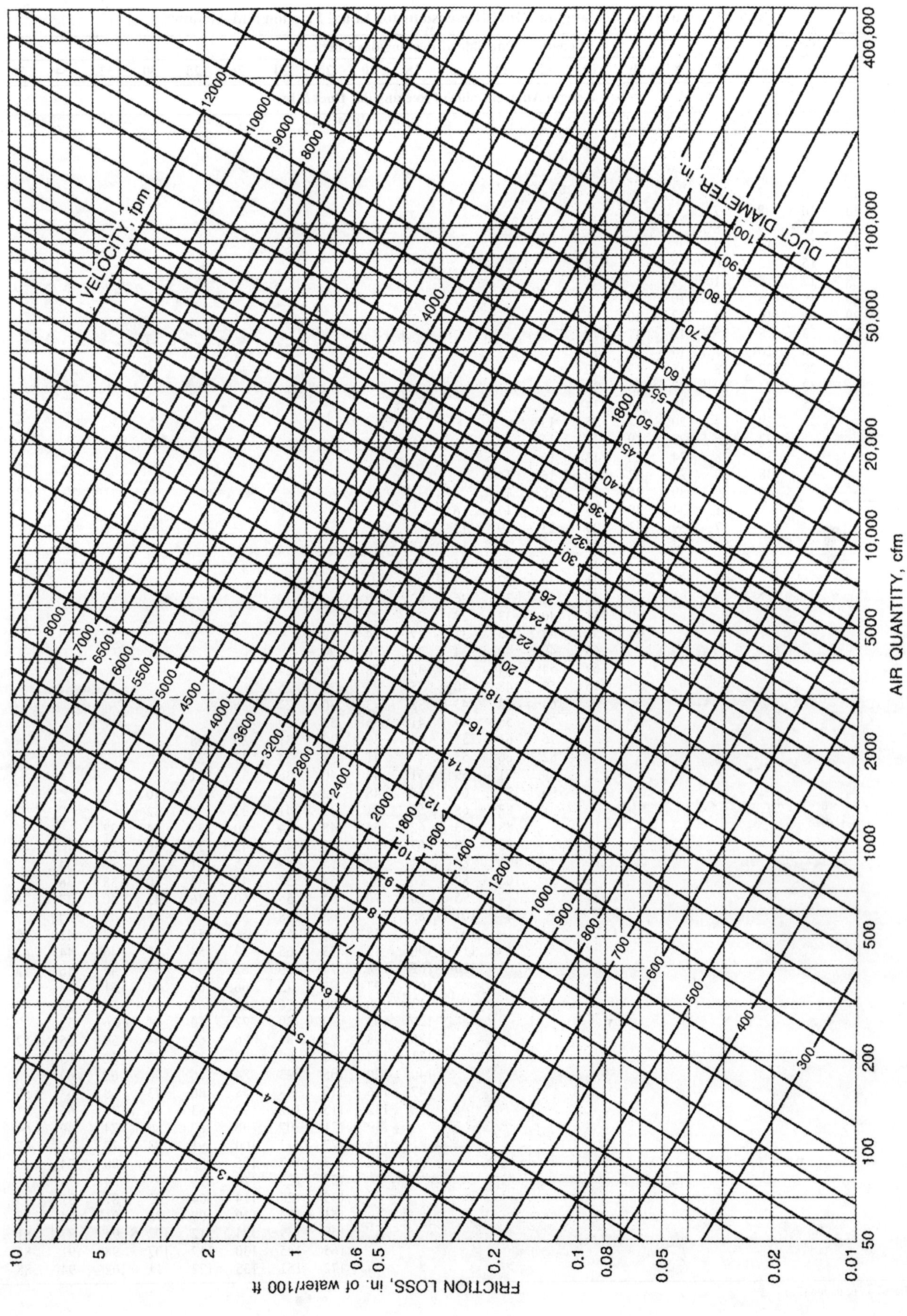

Fig. 10 Friction Chart for Round Duct ($\rho = 0.075\ lb_m/ft^3$ and $\varepsilon = 0.0003$ ft)

Table 3 Equivalent Rectangular Duct Dimensions for Equal Friction and Airflow*

Circular Duct Diameter, in.	Length of One Side of Rectangular Duct *a*, in.																			
	4	5	6	7	8	9	10	12	14	16	18	20	22	24	26	28	30	32	34	36
	Length Adjacent Side of Rectangular Duct *b*, in.																			
5	5																			
5.5	6	5																		
6	8	6																		
6.5	9	7	6																	
7	11	8	7																	
7.5	13	10	8	7																
8	15	11	9	8																
8.5	17	13	10	9																
9	20	15	12	10	8															
9.5	22	17	13	11	9															
10	25	19	15	12	10	9														
10.5	29	21	16	14	12	10														
11	32	23	18	15	13	11	10													
11.5		26	20	17	14	12	11													
12		29	22	18	15	13	12													
12.5		32	24	20	17	15	13													
13		35	27	22	18	16	14	12												
13.5		38	29	24	20	17	15	13												
14			32	26	22	19	17	14												
14.5			35	28	24	20	18	15												
15			38	30	25	22	19	16	14											
16			45	36	30	25	22	18	15											
17				41	34	29	25	20	17	16										
18				47	39	33	29	23	19	17										
19				54	44	38	33	26	22	19	18									
20					50	43	37	29	24	21	19									
21					57	48	41	33	27	23	20									
22					64	54	46	36	30	26	23	20								
23						60	51	40	33	28	25	22								
24						66	57	44	36	31	27	24	22							
25							63	49	40	34	29	26	24							
26							69	54	44	37	32	28	26	24						
27							76	59	48	40	35	31	28	25						
28								64	52	43	38	33	30	27	26					
29								70	56	47	41	36	32	29	27					
30								76	61	51	44	39	35	31	29	28				
31								82	66	55	47	41	37	34	31	29				
32								89	71	59	51	44	40	36	33	31				
33								96	76	64	54	48	42	38	35	33	30			
34									82	68	58	51	45	41	37	35	32			
35									88	73	62	54	48	44	40	37	34	32		
36									95	78	67	58	51	46	42	39	36	34		
37									101	83	71	62	55	49	45	41	38	36	34	
38									108	89	76	66	58	52	47	44	40	38	36	
39										95	80	70	62	55	50	46	43	40	37	36
40										101	85	74	65	58	53	49	45	42	39	37
41										107	91	78	69	62	56	51	47	44	41	39
42										114	96	83	73	65	59	54	50	46	44	41
43										120	102	88	77	69	62	57	53	49	46	43
44											107	93	81	73	66	60	55	51	48	45
45											113	98	86	76	69	63	58	54	50	47
46											120	103	90	80	72	66	61	56	53	49
47											126	108	95	84	76	69	64	59	55	52
48											133	114	100	89	80	73	67	62	58	54
49											140	120	105	93	84	76	70	65	60	56
50											147	126	110	98	88	80	73	68	63	59
51												132	115	102	92	83	76	71	66	61
52												139	121	107	96	87	80	74	69	64
53												145	127	112	100	91	83	77	71	67
54												152	133	117	105	95	87	80	74	70
55													139	123	110	99	91	84	78	72
56													145	128	114	104	95	87	81	75
57													151	134	119	108	98	91	84	78
58													158	139	124	112	102	94	87	81
59													165	145	130	117	107	98	91	85
60													172	151	135	122	111	102	94	88

*Table based on Equation (25).

Table 4 Equivalent Flat Oval Dimensions*

Circular Duct Diameter, in.	Minor Axis *a*, in.																
	3	4	5	6	7	8	9	10	11	12	14	16	18	20	22	24	30
	Major Axis *A*, in.																
5	8																
5.5	9	7															
6	11,12																
6.5	14	9,10	8														
7	17	12		8													
7.5	19	13	10	9													
8	22	15	11														
8.5		17,18	13,14	11	10												
9		20,21		12		10											
9.5			16	14	12	11											
10			18,19	15	13												
10.5			21	17	15	13											
11				19	16	14	12	12									
11.5				20	18		14	13									
12				22,23		16,17	15	14									
12.5				25,26	20,21				14								
13				28		19	17	16		14							
13.5				30,31		21	18										
14				33		22	20	18	16,17	15							
14.5				34,36		24,25	22	19									
15				37		27	23	21	19	17,18							
15.5				41					20								
16				44,47		30,32		23,24	22	20							
17						33,35,36		26,27	24,25	21,23	20						
18						38,39		29,30		25,26	22						
19						43,46		32,34,35		28,29	23	22					
20						49,52		37,38,40		31,32	25,27	24					
21						55,58		41		34	28,30	25	23,24				
22						61		45,48		36,37,39	31,33	27,29	26				
23								51,54		40,43	34,36	30	27	26			
24								57,60		47	39	32,33	29	28			
25								63		50	42	35	31,32	29			
26								67,70,73		53,56	45	38	34,35	31			
27								76,79		59,62	49	41	37	33			
28										65	52,55	44	40	36			
29										69,72	58	47	43	39	35		
30										75,78	61,64	51,54	46	42	38		
31										81	67	57	49	45	41	37	
32											71,74	60	53	48		40	
33											77,80	66	56	51	44		
34												69	59,62		47	43	
35												73,76	65	55,58	50	46	
36												79	68	61	53	49	
37													71	64	57	52	43
38													75,78	67	60	55	
39													81	70,73	63	59	46
40														77	66,69	62	49
41														80	72	65	52
42															75	68	55
43															79	71	
44															82	74	58
45																77	61
46																81	65
47																	68
48																	71
49																	74
50																	77
51																	80
52																	81

*Table based on Equation (26).

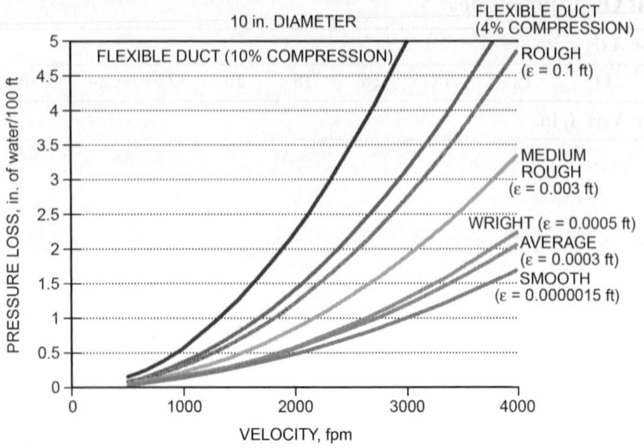

Fig. 11 Plot Illustrating Relative Resistance of Roughness Categories

For converging and diverging flow junctions, total pressure loss through the straight (main) section is calculated by

$$\Delta p_{t,s} = C_s p_{v,s} \tag{32}$$

where

$\Delta p_{t,s}$ = total pressure loss across straight-through section s of junction, in. of water
C_s = local loss coefficient referenced to s section of junction, dimensionless
$p_{v,s}$ = velocity pressure at section s, in. of water

For total pressure loss through the branch section,

$$\Delta p_{t,b} = C_b p_{v,b} \tag{33}$$

where

$\Delta p_{t,b}$ = total pressure loss across branch b section of junction, in. of water
C_b = local loss coefficient referenced to b section of junction, dimensionless
$p_{v,b}$ = velocity pressure at section b, in. of water

The junction of two parallel streams moving at different velocities is characterized by turbulent mixing of the streams, accompanied by pressure losses. In the course of this mixing, particles moving at different velocities exchange momentum, resulting in equalization of the velocity distributions in the common stream. The jet with higher velocity loses part of its kinetic energy by transmitting it to the slower jet. The loss in total pressure before and after mixing is always large and positive for the higher-velocity jet, and increases with an increase in the amount of energy transmitted to the lower-velocity jet. Consequently, the local loss coefficient [Equation (29)] is always positive. Energy stored in the lower-velocity jet can increase because of mixing. The loss in total pressure and the local loss coefficient can, therefore, also have negative values for the lower-velocity jet (Idelchik et al. 1994).

Duct Fitting Database

Loss coefficients for more than 220 round, flat oval, and rectangular fittings are available in the *ASHRAE Duct Fitting Database* [DFDB; ASHRAE (2016)]. Also included are the pressure loss for round duct (CD11-1), flexible duct (CD11-2), rectangular duct (CR11-1), and flat oval (CF11-1) duct, as well as the following design tools:

- CD11-3, Straight Duct, Round, Velocity Limited
- CD11-4, Straight Duct, Round, Friction Rate Constant
- CD11-5, Straight Duct, Round, Minimum Velocity

Table 5 Duct Fitting Codes

Fitting Function	Geometry	Category	Sequential Number
S: Supply	D: round (**D**iameter)	1. Entries	1,2,3...*n*
		2. Exits	
E: Exhaust/Return	R: **R**ectangular	3. Elbows	
		4. Transitions	
C: Common (supply and return)	F: Flat oval	5. Junctions	
		6. Obstructions	
		7. Fan and system interactions	
		8. Duct-mounted equipment	
		9. Dampers	
		10. Hoods	
		11. Straight duct	

Table 6 8 in. VAV Box Data

Airflow, cfm	Δp_s, in. of water	Inlet Velocity, fpm	Outlet Velocity, fpm	$p_{v,in}$, in. of water	$p_{v,out}$, in. of water	Δp_v, in. of water	Δp_t, in. of water
1	2	3	4	5	6	7	8
350	0.053	1003	420	0.063	0.011	0.052	0.105
500	0.109	1432	600	0.128	0.022	0.105	0.214
700	0.213	2005	840	0.251	0.044	0.207	0.420
900	0.353	2578	1080	0.414	0.073	0.342	0.695

Δp_s = static pressure difference
Δp_t = total pressure difference at standard air conditions
$p_{v,in}$ = inlet velocity pressure at standard air conditions
$p_{v,out}$ = outlet velocity pressure at standard air conditions
Δp_v = velocity pressure difference at standard air conditions

Commentary: CD11-3 determines the size of a duct knowing airflow such that the design velocity is not exceeded. CD11-4 is for sizing duct systems by the equal friction method, knowing the design (target) friction rate and airflow. CD4-11 determines the duct size for industrial systems that must maintain a minimum velocity to convey particulates.

Example 8 uses CD11-3 in the equal friction and static regain designs, and CD11-4 for the equal friction design.

The fittings are numbered (coded) as shown in Table 5. Entries and converging junctions are only in the exhaust/return portion of systems. Exits and diverging junctions are only in supply systems. Equal-area elbows, obstructions, and duct-mounted equipment are common to both supply and exhaust systems. Transitions and unequal-area elbows can be either supply or exhaust fittings. Fitting ED5-1 is an **E**xhaust fitting with a round shape (**D**iameter). The number 5 indicates that the fitting is a junction, and 1 is its sequential number. Fittings SR31 and ER3-1 are **S**upply and **E**xhaust fittings, respectively. The R indicates that the fitting is **R**ectangular, and the 3 identifies the fitting as an elbow. Note that the cross-sectional areas at sections 0 and 1 are not equal. Otherwise, the elbow would be a **C**ommon fitting such as CR3-6.

Terminal Unit Loss Coefficients. Manufacturers' data for terminal units are not useful for duct design because they are given in terms of static pressure resistance and velocity pressure at standard air conditions (0.075 lb_m/ft^3). The total pressure loss coefficient for the 8 in. terminal used in Example 7 is calculated from manufacturer's published data (Table 6: Columns 1, 2, and 7) and plotting $\Delta p_{v,in}$ versus Δp_t (Figure 12). The loss coefficient is 1.68 and is applicable for any elevation (air density). The total pressure loss (Δp_t) in Table 6 is only useful for projects at sea level. ASHRAE *Standard* 130-2016, Section 5.2, covers the laboratory test for total pressure loss and the calculation of the loss coefficient. In the

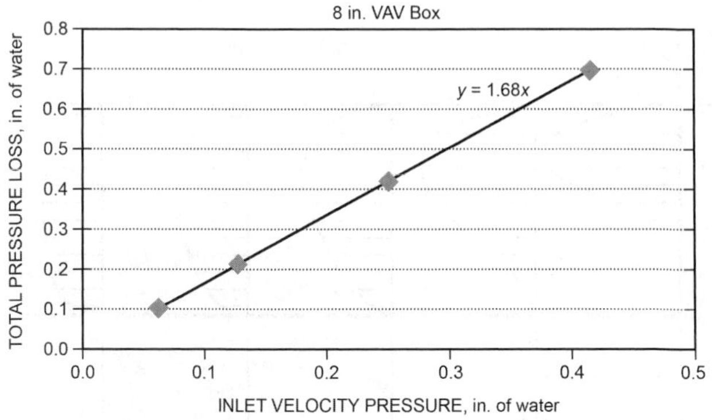

Fig. 12 VAV Box Loss Coefficient Plot

ASHRAE Duct Fitting Database (ASHRAE 2016), the single-duct reheat VAV box is the CD8-series.

3.3 DUCTWORK SECTIONAL LOSSES

Darcy-Weisbach Equation

Total pressure loss in a duct section is calculated by combining Equations (18) and (29) in terms of Δp, where ΣC is the summation of local loss coefficients in the duct section. Each fitting loss coefficient must be referenced to that section's velocity pressure.

$$\Delta p = \left(\frac{12 fL}{D_h} + \Sigma C\right)\rho\left(\frac{V}{1097}\right)^2 \tag{34}$$

4. FAN/SYSTEM INTERFACE

Fan Inlet and Outlet Conditions

Fan performance data measured in the field may show lower performance capacity than manufacturers' ratings. The most common causes of deficient performance of the fan/system combination are poor outlet connections, nonuniform inlet flow, and swirl at the fan inlet. These conditions alter the fan's aerodynamic characteristics so that its full flow potential is not realized. One bad connection can reduce fan performance below its rating.

Normally, a fan is tested with open inlets and a section of straight duct attached to the outlet (AMCA *Standard* 210). This setup results in uniform flow into the fan and efficient static pressure recovery on the fan outlet. If good inlet and outlet conditions are not provided in the design of duct systems, fan performance suffers.

Figure 13 shows deficient fan performance resulting from poor inlet and outlet connections to ductwork. Point 1 is the fan/system operating point without taking into account poor inlet and/or outlet conditions. Point 2 is the system operating point when the apparent resistance of poor connections is included in the calculations. Point 4 is the operating point on the original fan performance curve, taking into consideration the apparent system resistance of poor fan/system connections. Point 3 is the fan operating point on the original system curve when the apparent resistance of poor inlet and/or fan connections is not taken into account. The airflow difference between points 2 and 4 represents the deficiency in airflow from design airflow.

Fan System Effect Coefficients

The system effect concept was formulated by Farquhar (1973) and Meyer (1973); the magnitudes of the system effect, called **system effect factors**, were determined experimentally by the Air Movement and Control Association International (AMCA 2011a; Brown 1973; Clarke et al. 1978). The system effect factors, converted to local loss coefficients, are in the *ASHRAE Duct Fitting*

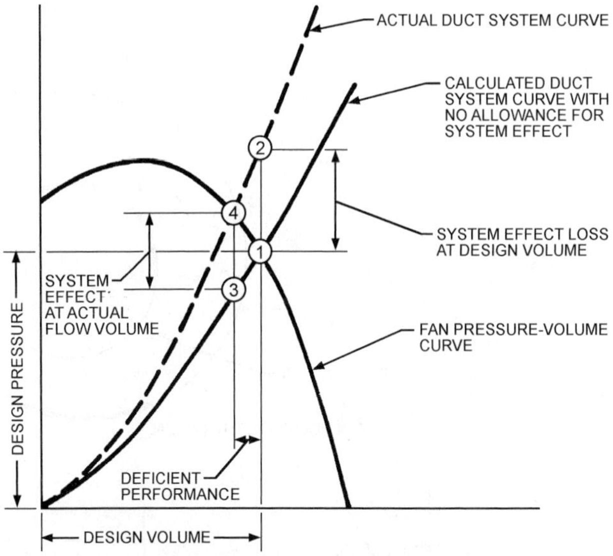

Fig. 13 Deficient System Performance with System Effect Ignored

Database (ASHRAE 2016) for both centrifugal and axial fans. Fan system effect coefficients are only an approximation. Fans of different types and even fans of the same type, but supplied by different manufacturers, do not necessarily react to a system in the same way. Therefore, judgment based on experience must be applied to any design.

Fan Outlet Conditions. Fans intended primarily for duct systems are usually tested with an outlet duct in place (AMCA *Standard* 210). Figure 14 shows the changes in velocity profiles at various distances from the fan outlet. For 100% recovery, the duct, including transition, must meet the requirements for 100% effective duct length [L_e (Figure 14)], which is calculated as follows:

For $V_o > 2500$ fpm,

$$L_e = \frac{V_o\sqrt{A_o}}{10{,}600} \tag{35}$$

For $V_o \le 2500$ fpm,

$$L_e = \frac{\sqrt{A_o}}{4.3} \tag{36}$$

where

V_o = duct velocity, fpm
L_e = effective duct length, ft
A_o = duct area, in^2

Centrifugal fans should not abruptly discharge to the atmosphere. A diffuser design should be selected from Fitting SR7-2 or SR7-3. Consult the SR7-series fittings of the *ASHRAE Duct Fitting Database* (ASHRAE 2016) for guidance in the design of fan/ductwork connections.

Fan Inlet Conditions. For rated performance, air must enter the fan uniformly over the inlet area in an axial direction without prerotation. Nonuniform flow into the inlet is the most common cause of reduced fan performance. Such inlet conditions are not equivalent to a simple increase in system resistance; therefore, they cannot be treated as a percentage decrease in the flow and pressure from the fan. A poor inlet condition results in an entirely new fan performance.

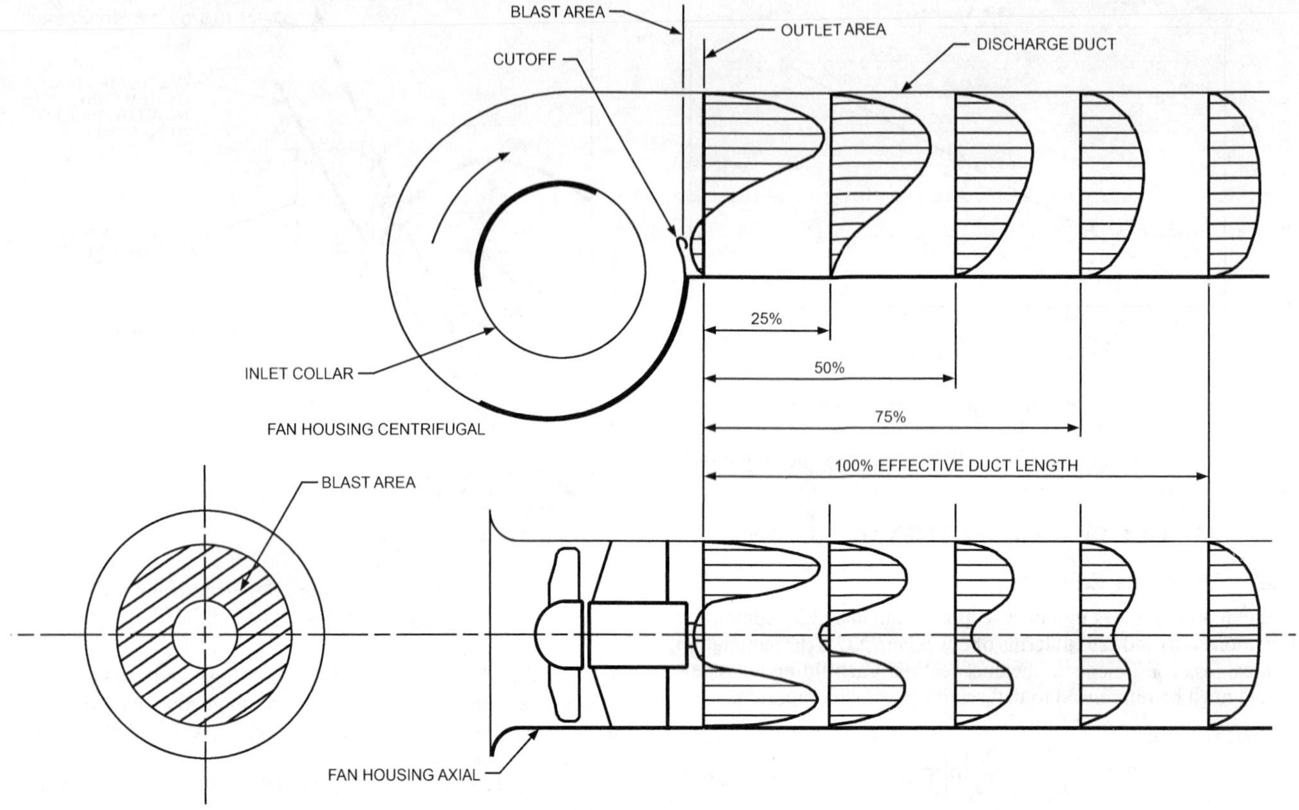

Fig. 14 Establishment of Uniform Velocity Profile in Straight Fan Outlet Duct
(Adapted by permission from AMCA *Publication* 201)

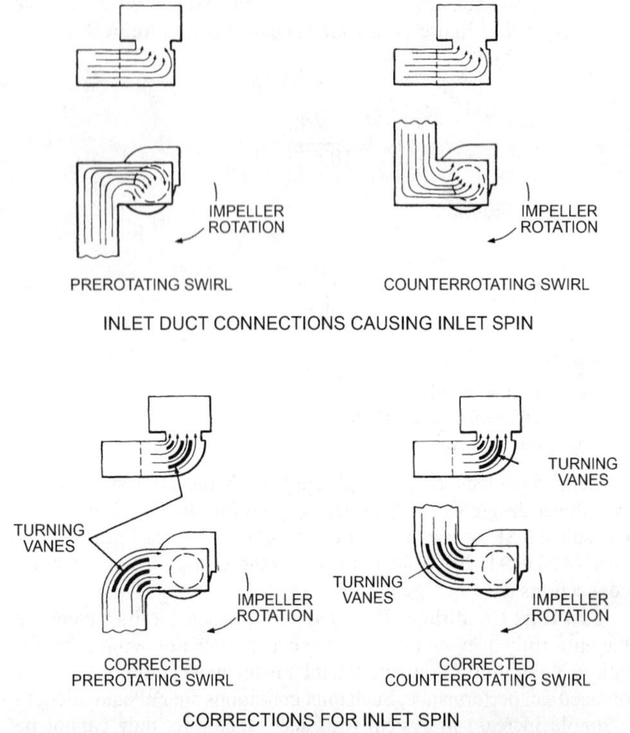

Fig. 15 Inlet Duct Connections Causing Inlet Spin
(Adapted by permission from AMCA *Publication* 201)

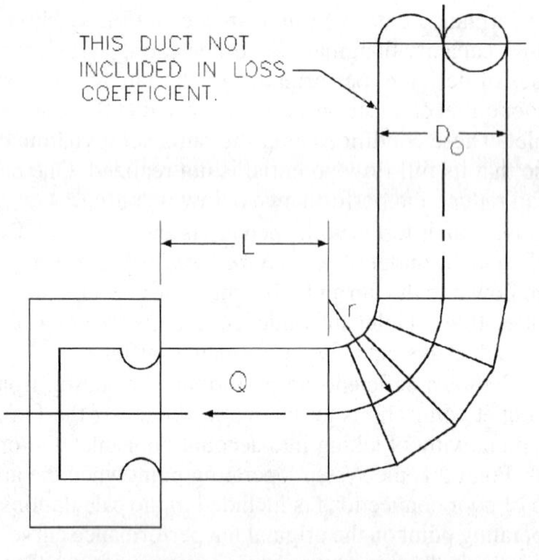

Fig. 16 Fitting ED7-2 (Fan Inlet, Centrifugal Fan, SISW, with 4-Gore Elbow)
[*ASHRAE Duct Fitting Database* (ASHRAE 2016)]

Inlet spin may arise from many different approach conditions, and sometimes the cause is not obvious. Figure 15 shows some common duct connections that cause inlet spin. Inlet spin can be avoided by providing an adequate length of duct between the elbow and the fan inlet, as shown by Figure 16. Two L/D_o duct lengths upstream of the fan inlet reduces swirl and pressure loss (loss coefficient) by approximately 45% (Table 7).

Table 7 ED7-2 Loss Coefficients (see Figure 16)

	L/D_o			
L/D_o	0	2	5	10
0.5	1.80	1.00	0.53	0.53
0.75	1.40	0.80	0.40	0.40
1.0	1.20	0.67	0.33	0.33
1.5	1.10	0.60	0.33	0.33
2.0	1.00	0.53	0.33	0.33
4.0	0.67	0.40	0.22	0.22

Fans within plenums and cabinets or next to walls should be located so that air may flow unobstructed into the inlets. Fan performance is reduced if the space between the fan inlet and the enclosure is too restrictive. System effect coefficients for fans in an enclosure or adjacent to walls are listed under Fitting ED7-1. How the airstream enters an enclosure in relation to the fan inlets also affects fan performance. Plenum or enclosure inlets or walls that are not symmetrical with the fan inlets cause uneven flow and/or inlet spin.

5. MECHANICAL EQUIPMENT ROOMS

In the initial phase of building design, the design engineer seldom has sufficient information to render the optimum HVAC design for the project, and its space requirements are often based on percentage of total area or other rule of thumb. The final design is usually a compromise between what the engineer recommends and what the architect can accommodate. Total mechanical and electrical space requirements range between 4 and 9% of gross building area, with most buildings in the 6 to 9% range. This range includes space for HVAC, electrical, plumbing, and fire protection equipment, as well as vertical shaft space for mechanical and electrical distribution through the building.

Outdoor Air Intake and Exhaust Air Discharge Locations

A key factor in the location of mechanical equipment rooms is the source of outdoor air. If the air intake or exhaust system is not well designed, contaminants from nearby outdoor sources (e.g., vehicle exhaust) or from the building itself (e.g., laboratory fume hood exhaust) can enter the building with insufficient dilution. Poorly diluted contaminants may cause odors, health impacts, and reduced indoor air quality. Examples are toxic stack exhausts, automobile and truck traffic, kitchen cooking hoods, evaporative cooling towers, building general exhaust air, trash dumpsters, stagnant water bodies, snow and leaves, rain and fog, plumbing vents, vandalism, and terrorism.

Chapter 45 of the 2015 *ASHRAE Handbook—HVAC Applications* discusses proper design of exhaust stacks and placement of air intakes to avoid adverse air quality impacts. Experience provides some general guidelines on air intake placement. Unless dispersion modeling analysis is conducted, air intakes should never be located on the roof in the same architectural screen enclosure as exhaust outlets. If exhaust is discharged from several locations on the roof, intakes should be located to minimize contamination. Typically, this means maximizing separation distance. Where all exhausts of concern are emitted from a single, relatively tall stack or tight cluster of stacks, a possible intake location might be close to the base of this tall stack, if this location is not adversely affected by other exhaust locations, or is not influenced by tall adjacent structures creating downwash. Architectural screens placed around rooftop equipment to reduce noise or hide equipment interact with the windflow patterns on the roof and can adversely affect exhaust dilution. Chapter 45 of the 2015 *ASHRAE Handbook—HVAC Applications* describes a method to account for these screens by modifying the physical stack height.

When wind is perpendicular to the upwind wall, air flows up and down the wall, dividing at about two-thirds up the wall. The downward flow creates ground-level swirl that stirs up dust and debris. To take advantage of the natural separation of wind over the upper and lower halves of a building, toxic or nuisance exhausts should be located on the roof and intakes on the lower one-third of the building, but high enough to avoid wind-blown dust, debris, and vehicle exhaust. If ground-level sources are major sources of contaminants, rooftop intake is desirable.

Buildings over three stories usually require vertical shafts to consolidate mechanical, electrical, and telecommunication distribution through the facility. Vertical shafts should be located in or adjacent to mechanical/fan rooms and as far as possible from noise-sensitive areas. In general, duct shafts with an aspect ratio of 2:1 to 4:1 are easier to develop than large square shafts. The rectangular shaft also facilitates transition from equipment in the fan rooms to the shaft.

Fan rooms in a basement or at street level should be avoided. These locations are a security concern because harmful substances could easily be introduced. Using louvers at these locations is also a concern because debris, leaves, and snow may fill the area, resulting in safety, health, and fan performance concerns. Loading docks and nearby parking areas may also compromise ventilation air quality.

Equipment Room Locations

Mechanical equipment rooms, including air-handling units, should be centrally located to centralize maintenance and operation. But, for many reasons, not all equipment rooms can be centrally located in the building. In any case, equipment should be kept together whenever possible to minimize space requirement, centralize maintenance and operation, and simplify electrical systems. All HVAC air system equipment rooms should have space for maintaining equipment and the replacement of fans, coils and other key equipment.

High-rise buildings may opt for decentralized fan rooms for each floor, or for more centralized service with one mechanical/fan room serving the lower 10 to 20 floors, one serving the middle floors of the building, and one at the roof serving the top floors.

Decentralized Equipment Rooms. Locate decentralized mechanical equipment rooms as far as possible from noise-sensitive areas, and surround equipment rooms with buffer zones such as toilet and storage rooms, as well as elevator, stair, and duct shafts. Figure 17 shows various core locations from poor to best. The number of decentralized fan rooms required depends largely on total floor area and any fan system power limitation imposed by codes or standards (e.g., ASHRAE *Standard* 90.1-2016, section 6.5.3.1). When decentralized air systems are located centrally to the spaces served, duct systems are shorter, occupy less volume, use less power, are quieter, and are less expensive. Pointing out these advantages can often help to convince architects to make desirable decentralized locations available.

6. DUCT DESIGN

6.1 DESIGN CONSIDERATIONS

HVAC System Air Leakage

See Chapter 19 of the 2016 *ASHRAE Handbook—HVAC Systems and Equipment* for (1) sealant specifications, and (2) the rationale for HVAC system sealing and leakage testing.

System Sealing. All ductwork and plenum transverse joints, longitudinal seams, and duct penetrations should be sealed. Openings for rotating shafts should be sealed with bushings or other devices that minimize air leakage but that do not interfere with shaft rotation

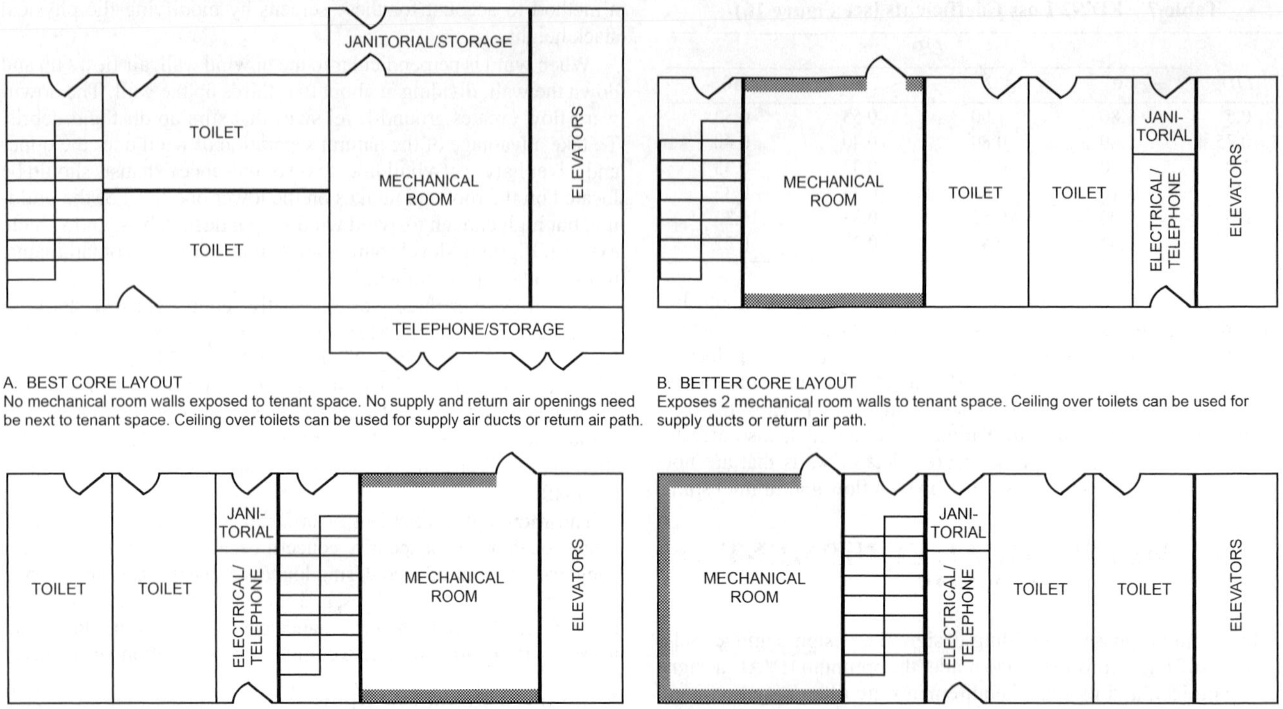

A. BEST CORE LAYOUT
No mechanical room walls exposed to tenant space. No supply and return air openings need be next to tenant space. Ceiling over toilets can be used for supply air ducts or return air path.

B. BETTER CORE LAYOUT
Exposes 2 mechanical room walls to tenant space. Ceiling over toilets can be used for supply ducts or return air path.

C. FAIR CORE LAYOUT
Exposes 2 mechanical room walls to tenant space. Impenetrable mechanical room partition to elevators and stairs results in supply and return air wall openings next to tenant space.

D. POOR CORE LAYOUT
Exposes 3 mechanical room walls to surrounding tenant space. Impenetrable partition between mechanical room and exit stairs results in supply and return air wall openings next to tenant space.

Fig. 17 Comparison of Various Mechanical Equipment Room Locations
(Schaffer 2005)

or prevent thermal expansion. Spiral lock seams need not be sealed. Duct-mounted equipment, such as terminal units, reheat coils, access doors, sound attenuators, balancing dampers, control dampers, and fire dampers, should be specified as low leakage so that the system can meet the air leakage acceptance criteria set by the designer, standards, and codes. Recommended specifications for duct-mounted equipment are provided later in this section.

Sealing that would void product listings (e.g., for fire/smoke or volume control dampers) is not required. It is, however, recommended that the design engineer specify low-leakage duct-mounted components. For example, some UL-listed and -labeled fire/smoke dampers allow sealing and gasketing of breakaway duct/sleeve connections; all can provide sealed non-breakaway duct/sleeve connections.

Scope. It is recommended that supply air (both upstream and downstream of the VAV box primary air inlet damper when used) and independent exhaust air systems be tested for air leakage after construction *at operating conditions* using ASHRAE *Proposed Standard* 215 (under development, and expected to be published in 2018) to verify (1) good workmanship, and (2) the use of low-leakage components as required to achieve the design allowable system air leakage. To ensure that a system passes its air leakage test at operating conditions, sufficient ductwork sections should be leak tested during construction. Leakage of duct-mounted components should be determined by specification and certified leakage data provided with equipment submittals. Leakage of air-handling units should be determined by specification and verification leakage tests.

Independent exhaust air system: air discharged from a space to the outdoors by a system not coupled to supply or return air systems.

Acceptance Criteria. To enable proper accounting of leakage-related impacts on fan energy and space conditioning loads, the allowable system air leakage for each fan system should be established by the design engineer as a percentage of fan airflow at the maximum system operating conditions. The recommended maximum system leakage is 5% of design airflow. Exceptions: supply and return ductwork sections that leak directly to/from outdoors and exhaust system ductwork sections that draw in indoor air through leaks should be limited to 2%.

Equation (37) is for use in a leakage test during construction to ensure that ductwork will meet the leakage specification. This equation translates system fractional air leakage to test section leakage class, as specified by ASHRAE *Standard* 90.1-2016, section 6.4.4.2.2.

$$C_{L,\,section} = \frac{Q_{leak,\,frac}(Q_{fan}/A_{system})}{\Delta p_{section}^{0.65}} \tag{37}$$

where

$C_{L,section}$ = test section leakage class, cfm per (in. of water)$^{0.65}$ per 100 ft^2 of duct surface area
Q_{fan} = maximum fan airflow that would occur during operation, cfm
$Q_{leak,frac}$ = system leakage fraction corresponding to maximum fan airflow that would occur during operation, %
A_{system} = total system duct surface area, ft^2
$\Delta p_{section}$ = test section static pressure difference corresponding to maximum fan airflow that would occur during operation, in. of water

Equation (37) shows that leakage class depends on fractional air leakage and normalized fan airflow (Q_{fan}/A_{system}), and varies inversely with the pressure difference raised to the 0.65 power. For example, to achieve 3% leakage for ductwork with Q_{fan}/A_{system} = 2 cfm per ft^2 of duct surface area and $\Delta p_{section}$ = 3 in. of water, the required leakage class is 2.9 cfm per (in. of water)$^{0.65}$ per 100 ft^2 of duct surface area. With $\Delta p_{section}$ = 0.5 in. of water instead (six times less), the required leakage class is about three times greater (9.4).

The maximum acceptable air leakage for a test section corresponding to the leakage class determined by Equation (37) can be expressed by Equation (38).

$$Q_{leak,\,section} = C_{L,\,section}\left(\frac{A_{section}}{100}\right)\Delta p_{section}^{0.65} \tag{38}$$

where

where

$Q_{leak,section}$ = test section air leakage, cfm
$A_{section}$ = test section duct surface area, ft^2

Equations (37) and (38) can be combined so that the maximum acceptable air leakage for a test section during construction is simply a function of system fractional leakage, normalized fan airflow (Q_{fan}/A_{system}), and section duct surface area:

$$Q_{leak,\,section} = \left(\frac{Q_{leak,\,frac}}{100}\right)(Q_{fan}/A_{system})\,A_{section} \tag{39}$$

Thus, for air leakage tests *during construction*, the maximum acceptable leakage for a ductwork section is given by Equation (38) or (39). Duct surface area should be calculated in accordance with European *Standard* EN 14239. The test pressure for each section should be specified by the design engineer based on the maximum static pressure for that section that would occur during operation at maximum fan airflow.

Example 7. The system depicted by Figure 18 has the characteristics summarized by Table 8. For a maximum acceptable leakage of 3% of the 5000 cfm maximum fan airflow, which is 150 cfm total, what is the maximum allowable ductwork leakage in (1) each section that is to be tested at the pressures noted, and (2) sections 4 and 5 when leak tested together?

Solution: The calculations and maximum allowable leakage are also summarized in Table 8. Note that adjacent sections with the same static pressure can be grouped for leakage testing. In this case, Sections 4 and 5 can be grouped. The allowable leakage for Sections 4 and 5 when tested individually is 10 cfm and 48 cfm respectively. The allowable leakage for Sections 4 and 5 when tested together is 58 cfm.

Table 8 Solution for Example 7

Section	Section Inlet Flow, cfm	$A_{section}$, ft^2	Section Static Pressure, in. of water	Section Leakage Class, cfm per 100 ft^2 per in. of water$^{0.65}$	Section Allowable Leakage, cfm
	Input			Equation (37)	Equation (38) or (39)
1	5000	500	3.0	2.4	24
2	2000	667	1.0	4.8	32
3	3000	750	2.0	3.1	36
4	1000	200	1.0	4.8	10
5	2000	1000	1.0	4.8	48
Total		3117			150
4 and 5	3000	1200	1.0	4.8	58

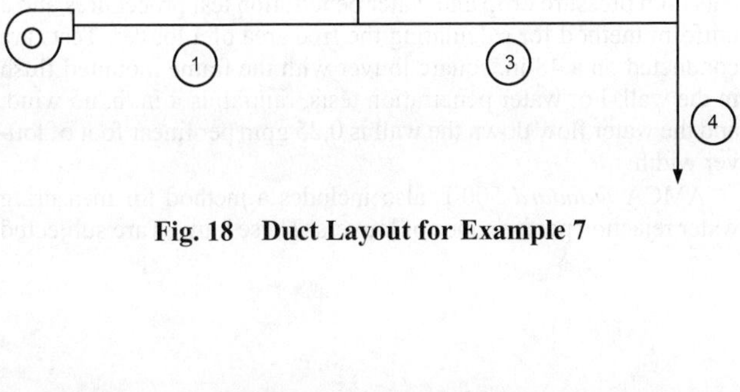

Fig. 18 Duct Layout for Example 7

Recommended Specification for Duct-Mounted Equipment. Duct-mounted component leakage is controlled by specification and certified leakage data provided with equipment submittals. The following are recommended leakage-related specifications for duct-mounted equipment.

- **Terminal Units.** Seal longitudinal seams of casings, inlet face of casings, and inlet collars with mastic. Seal damper shaft penetrations of casings. Casing leakage for the basic terminal unit should not exceed 4.5 cfm at 1.0 in. of water static pressure differential. Terminal unit leakage with an access door should not exceed 4.6 cfm at 1.0 in of water. Testing should be by an accredited laboratory. Leakage tests should comply with ASHRAE *Standard* 130.

  Access doors in terminal unit casings should comply with AMCA *Standard* 500-D, and leakage rates should be certified per AMCA (2013) *Publication* 511. Access door (frame not included) leakage should not exceed 0.5 cfm at 10 in. of water static pressure differential.
- **Electric Reheat Coils.** Flange-mount electric coils with a gasket. Coil leakage should not exceed 0.5 cfm at 1.0 in. of water static pressure differential. Tests should be by an accredited laboratory. Leakage tests should be in compliance with ASHRAE *Standard* 126.
- **Hot-Water Reheat Coils.** Flange-mount hot-water coils with a gasket in an insulated plenum or casing. Seal all seams and casing penetrations for supply and return water tubes. Coil casing leakage (not counting transverse joints) should not exceed 0.5 cfm at 1.0 in. of water static pressure differential. An accredited laboratory should perform leakage tests in compliance with ASHRAE *Standard* 126.
- **Access Doors.** Access door leakage (excluding the frame) should not exceed 0.5 cfm at 10 in. of water static pressure differential. Leakage tests should comply with AMCA *Standard* 500-D, and leakage rates certified per AMCA (2013) *Publication* 511.
- **Attenuators.** Sound attenuator casing seams should be sealed at the factory if used in-line with the ductwork. Attenuators stacked in plenums do not have to be sealed, but plenums should be sealed.
- **Fire/Smoke Dampers.** These dampers should be installed in accordance with the manufacturer's UL installation instructions. Each fire damper should be furnished with a UL-approved sleeve. Sleeve seams should be continuously welded or sealed, and the transverse joint should be a sealed UL-approved flanged duct sleeve connection (break-away or non-break-away).
- **Balancing Dampers.** Balancing damper casing seams should be continuously welded or sealed, and the shaft penetrating the casing should have seals.
- **Control Dampers.** Control damper shafts penetrating ducts should have seals.

Recommended Specification for Air-Handling Units. Refer to Chapter 19 of the 2016 *ASHRAE Handbook—HVAC Systems and Equipment* for leakage-related specifications for air-handling units.

Responsibilities. The **engineer** should

- Specify HVAC system components, duct-mounted equipment, sealants, and sealing procedures that together will meet the system airtightness design objective.
- Inspect the system during construction for quality of workmanship and to verify that correct duct-mounted components and air-handling units are installed.
- Specify the *construction-stage* ductwork leakage test standard or procedures.

- Specify the *construction-stage* test pressures to the nearest 0.1 in. of water expected during operation at design conditions and the maximum allowable air leakage.
- Review and approve the sheet metal and test contractors' leakage test reports. If any system has a leakage failure, the engineer should discuss remedies with the sheet metal contractor, vendor, and/or owner's representative.

The **sheet metal contractor** should

- Construct the system using quality workmanship and correct duct-mounted components and air-handling units. If any installed duct-mounted equipment appears to be leakage suspect, the contractor should discuss remedies with the engineer and/or owner's representative.
- Conduct *ductwork* leakage pressurization tests *during construction*. As a minimum, 25% of the ductwork system (based on duct surface area) should be tested during construction, and another 25% if any of the initial sections fail. If any section of the second 25% fails, the entire ductwork system should be leak tested.
- Provide connections for test apparatus, and separate test sections from each other as needed so that the test apparatus capacity is not exceeded.
- Report test results and, where required, take corrective action to seal ductwork and absorb the cost for conducting related additional leak tests.

The **test contractor** should

- Conduct the *operating system* leakage test in compliance with ASHRAE *Proposed Standard* 215 (expected to publish in 2018).
- Report test results, including reasons for any failures.

It should be the responsibility of the **owner or owner's representative** to provide direction upon request.

Fire and Smoke Control

Because duct systems can convey smoke, hot gases, and fire from one area to another and can accelerate a fire within the system, fire protection is an essential part of air-conditioning and ventilation system design. Generally, fire safety codes require compliance with the standards of national organizations. NFPA *Standard* 90A examines fire safety requirements for (1) ducts, connectors, and appurtenances; (2) plenums and corridors; (3) air outlets, air inlets, and fresh air intakes; (4) air filters; (5) fans; (6) electric wiring and equipment; (7) air-cooling and -heating equipment; (8) building construction, including protection of penetrations; and (9) controls, including smoke control.

Fire safety codes often refer to the testing and labeling practices of nationally recognized laboratories, such as Factory Mutual and Underwriters Laboratories (UL). UL's annual *Building Materials Directory* lists fire and smoke dampers that have been tested and meet the requirements of UL *Standards* 555 and 555S. This directory also summarizes maximum allowable sizes for individual dampers and assemblies of these dampers. Fire dampers are 1.5 h or 3 h fire-rated. Smoke dampers are classified by (1) temperature degradation [ambient air or high temperature (250°F minimum)] and (2) leakage at 1 and 4 in. of water pressure difference (8 and 12 in. of water classification optional). Smoke dampers are tested under conditions of maximum airflow. UL's annual *Fire Resistance Directory* lists fire resistances of floor/roof and ceiling assemblies with and without ceiling fire dampers.

For a more detailed presentation of fire protection, see the NFPA (2008) *Fire Protection Handbook*, Chapter 53 of the 2015 *ASHRAE Handbook—HVAC Applications*, and Klote et al. (2012).

Duct Insulation

In all new construction (except low-rise residential buildings), air-handling ducts and plenums that are part of an HVAC air distribution system should be thermally insulated in accordance with ASHRAE *Standard* 90.1. Duct insulation for new low-rise residential buildings should comply with ASHRAE *Standard* 90.2. Existing buildings should meet requirements of ASHRAE *Standard* 100. In all cases, thermal insulation should meet local code requirements. Insulation thicknesses in these standards are minimum values; economic and thermal considerations may justify higher insulation levels. Additional insulation, vapor retarders, or both may be required to limit vapor transmission and condensation.

Duct heat gains or losses must be known to calculate supply air quantities, supply air temperatures, and coil loads. To estimate duct heat transfer and entering or leaving air temperatures, refer to Chapters 4 and 23.

Physical Security

Ducts entering into spaces considered secured or sensitive should contain measures to detect or inhibit forced entry into those spaces through the duct system. Inhibiting measures should be based on a delay or resistance time set by the facility owner or user. The following security measures should be considered:

- **Barrier duct bars:** placement should be at locations deemed appropriate by the facility owner and user, or where secured or sensitive area boundaries exist (e.g., duct penetration through the wall of a secured room). Bar diameter, material, and spacing should be established by the facility owner or user. Ensure that barriers do not inhibit proper operation and maintenance of dampers, detectors, sensors, and other devices in the duct system.
- **Welded diffuser and return grilles:** grille material and spacing should be established by the facility owner or user.
- **Sensors on access doors:** sensors should be connected to a facility security system or panel, and notify security personnel of a duct system breach. Communicating HVAC maintenance schedules to security personnel is necessary to ensure that an intrusive duct system breach is not confused with HVAC system maintenance.

Louvers

Use Figure 19 for preliminary sizing of air intake and exhaust louvers. For air quantities greater than 7000 cfm per louver, the air intake gross louver openings are based on 400 fpm; for exhaust louvers, 500 fpm is used for air quantities of 5000 cfm per louver and greater. For smaller air quantities, see Figure 19. These criteria are presented on a per-louver basis (i.e., each louver in a bank of louvers) to include each louver frame. Representative production-run louvers were used in establishing Figure 19, and all data used were based on AMCA *Standard* 500-L tests. For louvers larger than 16 ft^2, the free areas are greater than 45%; for louvers less than 16 ft^2, free areas are less than 45%. Unless specific louver data are analyzed, no louver should have a face area less than 4 ft^2. If debris can collect on the screen of an intake louver, or if louvers are located at grade with adjacent pedestrian traffic, louver face velocity should not exceed 100 fpm.

Louvers require special treatment because the blade shapes, angles, and spacing cause significant variations in louver-free area and performance (pressure drop and water penetration). Selection and analysis should be based on test data obtained from the manufacturer in accordance with AMCA *Standard* 500-L, which presents both pressure drop and water penetration test procedures and a uniform method for calculating the free area of a louver. Tests are conducted on a 48 in. square louver with the frame mounted flush in the wall. For water penetration tests, rainfall is 4 in./h, no wind, and the water flow down the wall is 0.25 gpm per linear foot of louver width.

AMCA *Standard* 500-L also includes a method for measuring water rejection performance of louvers. These louvers are subjected to simulated rain and wind pressure and tested at a rainfall of 3 in./h falling on the louver's face with a predetermined wind velocity directed at the face of the louver (typically 29.1 or 44.7 mph). Effectiveness ratings are assigned at various airflow rates through the louver.

Duct Shape Selection

No Space Constraints. Round ductwork is preferable to rectangular or flat oval ductwork when adequate space is available for the following reasons.

- **Weight** of round ductwork is less than rectangular. Figure 20 shows the relative weight of rectangular duct to round duct for duct pressures from ±0.5 to ±10 in. of water when the equivalent diameter of the rectangular duct is the same as the round duct diameter. Equivalent diameter is defined as the diameter of a rectangular duct that has equal resistance to flow for equal flow and length.
- **Perimeter** of round ducts is less than rectangular ducts. For rectangular duct aspect ratios from 2 to 4, the increase is approximately 30 to 55%. This increase results in increased insulation, including possible thickness to offset the additional heat transfer. For a comprehensive study of round and rectangular ducts as they affect system performance, consult McGill (1988).
- Round ducts have an excellent resistance to **low-frequency breakout noise** (Schaffer 2005).

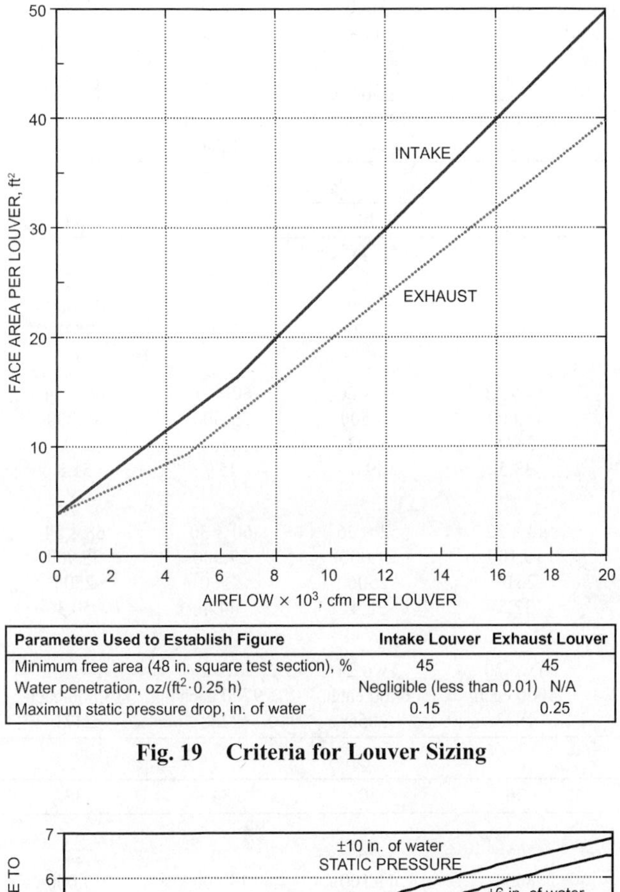

Parameters Used to Establish Figure	Intake Louver	Exhaust Louver
Minimum free area (48 in. square test section), %	45	45
Water penetration, oz/(ft^2·0.25 h)	Negligible (less than 0.01)	N/A
Maximum static pressure drop, in. of water	0.15	0.25

Fig. 19 Criteria for Louver Sizing

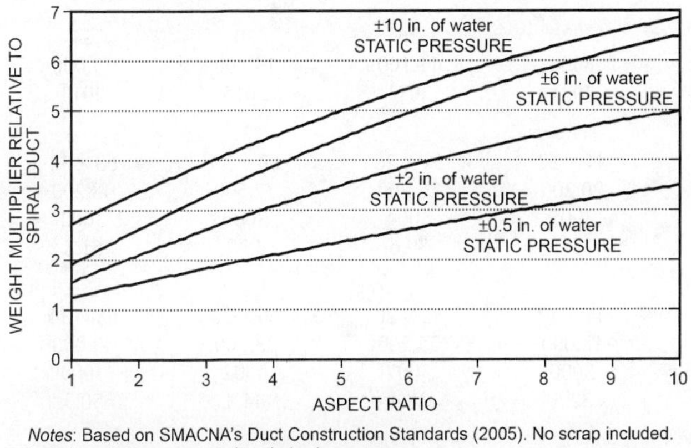

Notes: Based on SMACNA's Duct Construction Standards (2005). No scrap included. Includes reinforcement, and excludes hangers.

Fig. 20 Relative Weight of Rectangular Duct to Round Spiral Duct

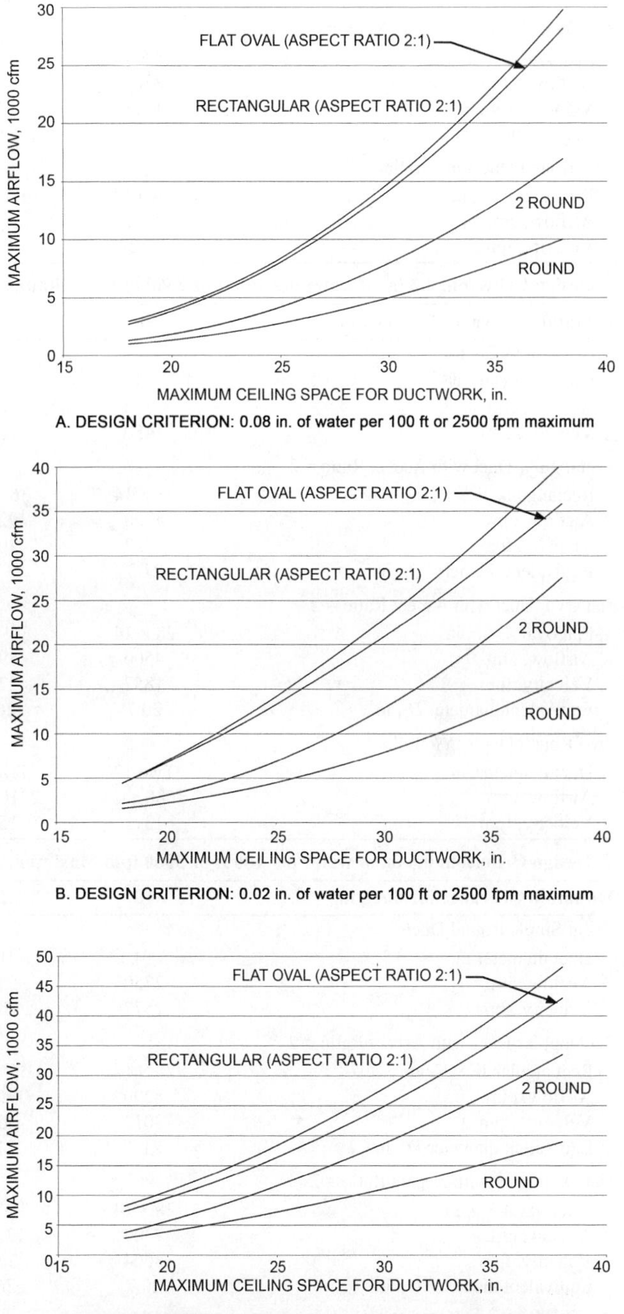

Fig. 21 Maximum Airflow of Round, Flat Oval, and Rectangular Ducts as Function of Available Ceiling Space

Table 9 Maximum Airflow of Round, Flat Oval and Rectangular Ducts as Function of Available Ceiling Space

A. Design Criterion: 0.08 in. of water per 100 ft or 2500 fpm Maximum

Minimum Clearance for Duct, in.	**18**	**22**	**26**	**30**	**34**	**38**
Single Round Duct						
Duct diameter, in.	14	18	22	26	30	34
Airflow, cfm	950	1900	3200	4900	7300	10,000
Velocity, fpm	889	1075	1212	1329	1487	1586
Rectangular Duct with Aspect Ratio = 2						
Rectangular *W* × *H*, in.	28 × 14	36 × 18	44 × 22	52 × 26	60 × 30	68 × 34
Airflow, cfm	2900	5500	9800	14,900	21,200	30,000
Velocity, fpm	1065	1222	1458	1587	1696	1869
Equivalent diameter D_e, in.	21.3	27.4	33.5	39.6	45.7	51.8
Flat Oval Duct with Aspect Ratio = 2						
Flat oval *A* × *a*, in.	28 × 14	36 × 18	44 × 22	52 × 26	60 × 30	68 × 34
Airflow, cfm	2700	5400	9000	14,000	21,000	28,000
Velocity, fpm	1111	1344	1500	1670	1882	1954
Equivalent diameter D_e, in.	20.7	26.6	32.5	38.4	44.4	50.3
Two Round Ducts in Parallel						
Duct diameter, in.	Two 12	Two 16	Two 20	Two 24	Two 28	Two 32
Airflow, cfm	630 each	1350 each	2450 each	3950 each	5950 each	8500 each
Velocity, fpm	802	967	1123	1257	1391	1522

B. Design Criterion: 0.2 in. of water per 100 ft or 2500 fpm Maximum

Minimum clearance for duct, in.	**18**	**22**	**26**	**30**	**34**	**38**
Single Round Duct						
Duct diameter, in.	14	18	22	26	30	34
Airflow, cfm	1550	3000	5100	8000	11,500	16,000
Velocity, fpm	1450	1698	1932	2170	2343	2538
Rectangular Duct with Aspect Ratio = 2						
Rectangular *W* × *H*, in.	28 × 14	36 × 18	44 × 22	52 × 26	60 × 30	68 × 34
Airflow, cfm	4700	9200	15,600	23,500	31,300	40,200
Velocity, fpm	1727	2044	2321	2303	2504	2504
Equivalent diameter D_e, in.	21.3	27.4	33.5	39.6	45.7	51.8
Flat Oval Duct with Aspect Ratio = 2						
Flat oval *A* × *a*, in.	28 × 14	36 × 18	44 × 22	52 × 26	60 × 30	68 × 34
Airflow, cfm	4500	8900	15,100	21,000	27,900	35,900
Velocity, fpm	1852	2216	2516	2506	2500	2505
Equivalent diameter D_e, in.	20.7	26.6	32.5	38.4	44.4	50.3
Two Round Ducts in Parallel						
Duct diameter, in.	Two 12	Two 16	Two 20	Two 24	Two 28	Two 32
Airflow, cfm	1030 each	2210 each	4000 each	6460 each	9700 each	13,800 each
Velocity, fpm	1311	1583	1833	2056	2268	2471

C. Design Criterion: 0.6 in. of water per 100 ft or 3000 fpm Maximum

Minimum clearance for duct, in.	**18**	**22**	**26**	**30**	**34**	**38**
Using Single Round Duct						
Duct diameter in.	14	18	22	26	30	34
Airflow, cfm	2750	5300	8000	11,100	14,800	19,000
Velocity, fpm	2572	3000	3031	3011	3015	3013
Rectangular Duct with Aspect Ratio = 2						
Rectangular *W* × *H*, in.	28 × 14	36 × 18	44 × 22	52 × 26	60 × 30	68 × 34
Airflow, cfm	8200	13,500	20,200	28,200	37,500	48,200
Velocity, fpm	3012	3000	3005	3004	3000	3002
Equivalent diameter D_e, in.	21.3	27.4	33.5	39.6	45.7	51.8
Flat Oval Duct with Aspect Ratio = 2						
Flat oval *A* × *a*, in.	28 × 14	36 × 18	44 × 22	52 × 26	60 × 30	68 × 34
Airflow, cfm	7300	12,100	18,000	25,200	33,500	43,000
Velocity, fpm	3004	3012	3000	3007	3002	3000
Equivalent diameter D_e, in.	20.7	26.6	32.5	38.4	44.4	50.3
Two Round Ducts in Parallel						
Duct diameter, in.	Two 12	Two 16	Two 20	Two 24	Two 28	Two 32
Airflow, cfm	1850 each	3960 each	6550 each	9430 each	12,830 each	16,800 each
Velocity, fpm	2355	2836	3000	3000	3000	3000

• Duct **rumble** can occur in rectangular duct systems (Paulauskis 2016).

Space Constraints. Space constraints and obstructions, particularly ceiling height, are frequent problems. In these cases, the choice is round, rectangular, or flat oval ducts, depending on the air quantity that needs to be conveyed by the duct. Table 9 and Figure 21 cover three design cases: 0.08, 0.2, and 0.6 in. of water per 100 ft friction rates. Friction rate 0.2 in. of water per 100 ft is at the middle range. In Table 9, six ceiling (plenum) heights ranging from 18 to 38 in., in 4 in. increments, are covered. Space allocated for insulation and reinforcement is 2 in. all around. The aspect ratio of the rectangular and flat oval ducts is 2:1. Figure 21 shows the maximum airflow as a function of the design friction rates and plenum spaces, as noted. For example, the 30 in. plenum as a design friction rate of 0.2 in. of water per 100 ft is 8000 cfm maximum for a 26 in. round duct; 23,500 cfm for a 52 × 26 in. rectangular duct; and 21,000 cfm for a 52 × 26 in. flat oval duct. The airflow capacity of two round 26 in. ducts is 6460 cfm each.

When selecting a rectangular or flat oval duct, consider the following:

• Rectangular duct has the advantage in **weight** because construction standards for flat oval exist only for +10 in. of water, whereas rectangular has seven pressure classes, starting at 0.5 in. of water. All rectangular pressure classes are ±.

  Note: Negative-pressure flat oval duct systems can be designed by using +10 in. of water sheet gages with the negative-pressure rectangular reinforcement welded to the duct.

• **Low-frequency breakout noise** for flat oval is good, fair for rectangular (Schaffer 2005).
• Duct **rumble** can occur in rectangular duct systems (Paulauskis 2016).
• **Perimeter.** Using rectangular duct instead of flat oval when sized for equivalent diameter increases the perimeter roughly 17 to 7% for aspect ratios ranging from 1 to 4, respectively. This increase results in an increased surface area. Flat oval requires less insulation. For a comprehensive study of flat oval and rectangular ducts as they affect system performance, consult McGill (1995).
• **Duct Lengths.** Rectangular duct is available in 4, 5, or 6 ft lengths. Spiral round and flat oval can be provided in longer lengths.

Testing and Balancing

Each air duct system should be tested, adjusted, and balanced. Guidance and procedures are given in Chapter 38 of the 2015 *ASHRAE Handbook—HVAC Applications* and in ASHRAE *Standard* 111. To determine fan total (or static) pressure from field measurements taking into account fan system effect, consult AMCA (2011b) *Publication* 203, which provides numerous fan/system configurations encountered in the field.

Many VAV noise complaints have been traced to control problems. Although most problems are associated with improper installation, many are caused by poor design. The designer should specify high-quality fans or air handlers within their optimum ranges, not at the edge of their operation ranges, where low system tolerances can lead to inaccurate fan flow capacity control. Also, in-duct static pressure sensors should be placed in duct sections having the lowest possible air turbulence (i.e., at least three equivalent duct diameters from any elbow, takeoff, transition, offset, or damper).

6.2 DESIGN RECOMMENDATIONS

• Engage the architect and structural engineer early to coordinate shafts for systems.

> *Commentary.* Consult *Noise and Vibration Control for HVAC Systems* (Schaffer 2005) for the following guidelines related to duct systems:
>
> • Selection of mechanical room walls
> • Noise control for mechanical rooms
> • Upward noise control for mechanical rooms
> • Duct penetrations through walls
> • Structural support of rooftop equipment for vibration control

• Route ducts as straight as possible to reduce pressure loss, noise, and first costs.
• Use round spiral ducts whenever round ducts can fit within space constraints.
• Avoid consecutive fittings and close-coupled fittings because they can significantly increase pressure losses.
• Use return air plenums when possible because they reduce both energy and first costs. Plenum return requires fire-rated construction.
• Design air distribution systems to minimize flow resistance and turbulence. High flow resistance increases fan pressure, which results in higher noise being generated by the fan, especially at low frequencies. Turbulence also increases flow noise generated by duct fittings and dampers, especially at low frequencies.
• Efficient fittings create the least turbulence and noise. Figure 22 provides generalized guidelines for minimizing regenerated noise from takeoffs. Tables 10 and 11 provide specific guidance for tees and wyes.
• Duct transitions should not exceed an included angle of 15°.

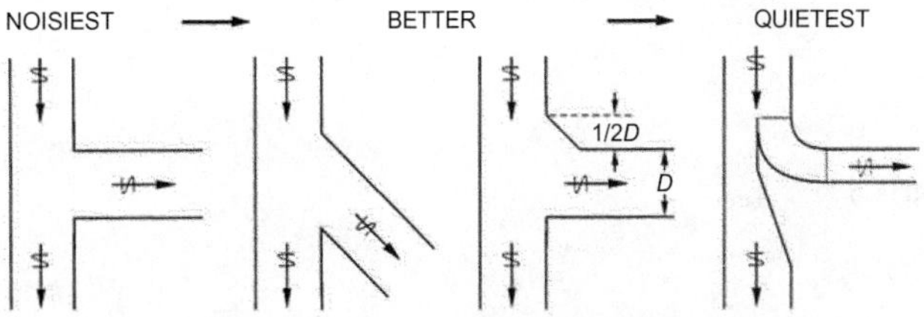

Fig. 22 Guidelines For Minimizing Regenerated Noise in Takeoff
(Schaffer 2005)

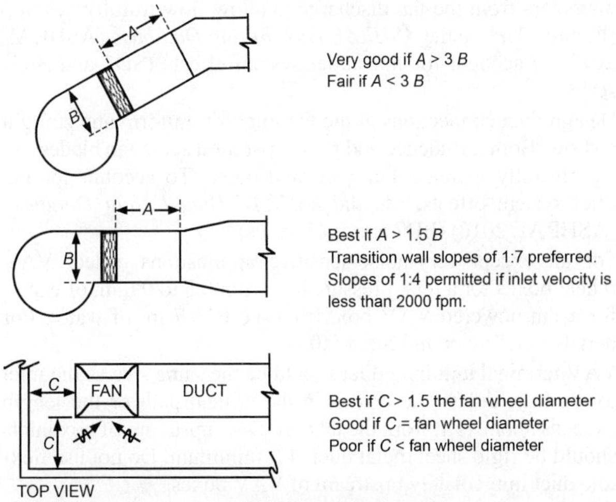

Fig. 23 Guidelines for Centrifugal Fan Installations
(Schaffer 2005)

Table 10 Options for Selecting 90° Takeoff

Code	Description		Efficiency	Loss Coefficient	
				Main[a]	Branch[b]
SD5-12	Tee, 45° entry branch	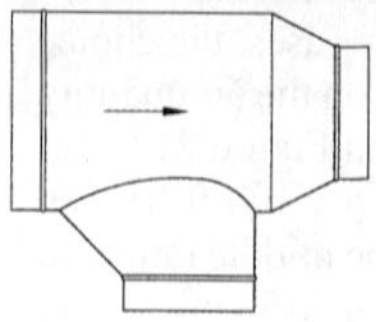	Highest	0.15	0.64
SD5-4	Wye, 45°, Straight body branch with 45° elbow, 90° to main	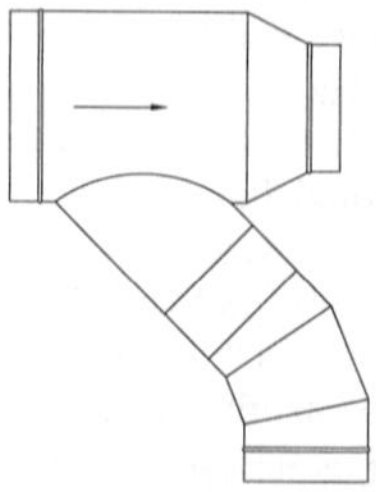	—	0.15	0.74
SD5-11	Tee, Conical branch	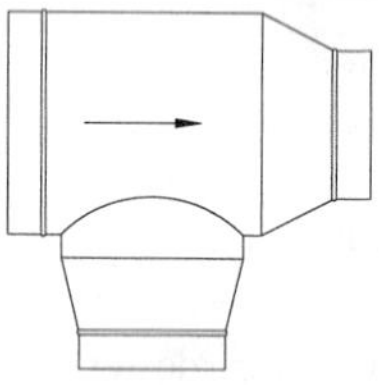	—	0.15	0.87
SD5-10	Tee, Conical branch tapered into body	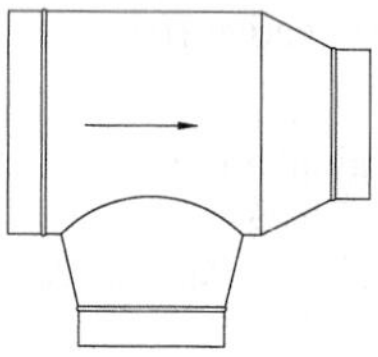	—	0.15	1.10
SD5-9	Tee	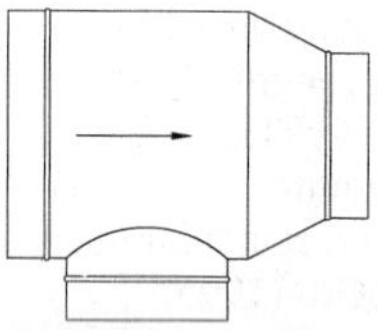	Lowest	0.15	1.80

[a]$Q_s/Q_c = 0.8$; $A_s/A_c = 0.69$
[b]$Q_b/Q_c = 0.2$; $A_b/A_c = 0.25$

- To avoid fan system effects, fans should discharge into duct sections that remain straight for as long as possible, up to 10 duct diameters from the fan discharge to allow flow to fully develop (Figure 23). Use the *ASHRAE Duct Fitting Database* (ASHRAE 2016) to account for fan outlet system effects (SD7 and SR7-series).
- Design duct connections at the fan inlet for uniform and straight airflow. Both turbulence and flow separation at the fan blades can significantly increase fan-generated noise. To account for fan inlet system effects, use the *ASHRAE Duct Fitting Database* (ASHRAE 2016) (ED7 and ER7 series).
- For all except very-noise-sensitive applications, select VAV reheat boxes for a total pressure loss from 0.5 to 0.6 in. of water; for a fan-powered VAV box, from 0.6 to 0.7 in. of water. For details, see Taylor and Stein (2004).
- VAV terminal unit inlet duct should be the same size as the inlet to the box, unless the box is in the critical path or the length exceeds about 15 ft from the takeoff. Duct upstream of box inlets should be rigid sheet metal duct, 4 ft minimum. Do not use flexible duct immediately upstream of VAV boxes.
- See Figure 24 for Schaffer's (2005) guidelines for the installation of single-duct, dual-duct, and induction terminal units, as well as parallel and series flow fan-powered units.

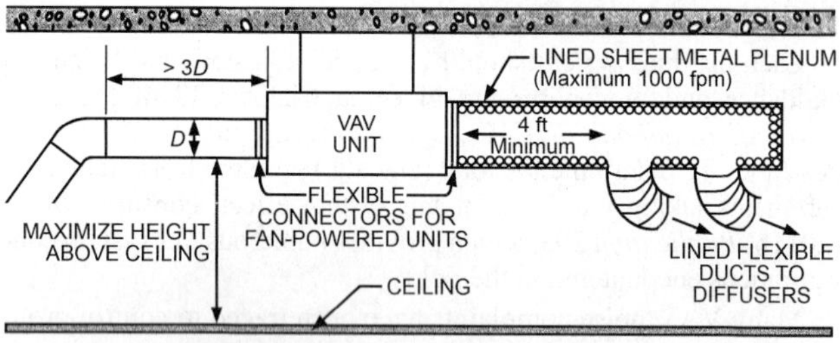

NOTE: Parallel or side-pocket fan-powered units often require an up- or side-looking lined sheet metal inlet elbow to control fan noise.

Fig. 24 Guidelines for VAV Terminal Unit Installation
(Schaffer 2005)

- Place fan-powered mixing boxes away from noise-sensitive areas.
- Use demand-based static pressure set-point reset to reduce fan energy and noise.
- For constant-volume systems, select the fan to operate as near as possible to its rated peak efficiency. Also, select a fan that generates the lowest possible noise at required design conditions. Using an oversized or undersized fan that does not operate at or near

Table 11 Options for Selecting 45° Takeoff (Wye)

Code	Description		Efficiency	Loss Coefficient Main, C_s[a]	Loss Coefficient Branch, C_b[b]
SD5-2	Wye, 45°, Conical branch tapered into body	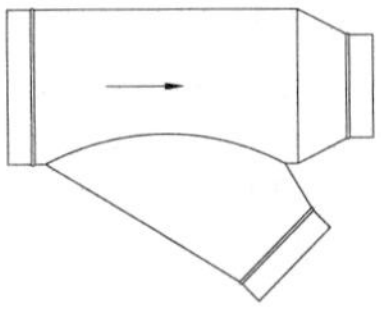	Highest	0.15	0.45
SD5-3	Wye, 45°, Straight body branch with reduction transition	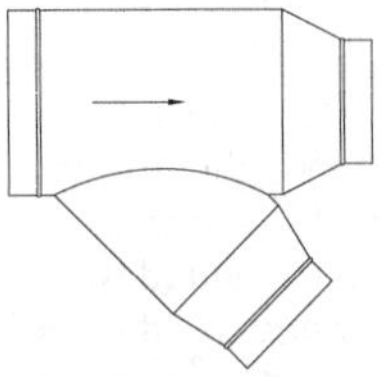	—	0.15	0.50
SD5-1	Wye, 45°	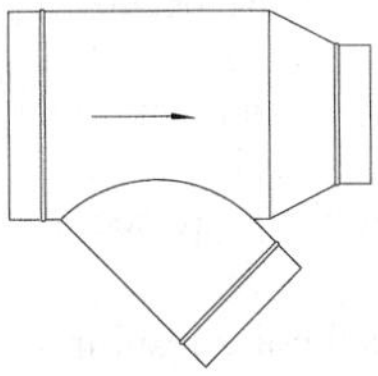	Lowest	0.15	0.70

[a] $Q_s/Q_c = 0.8$; $A_s/A_c = 0.69$
[b] $Q_b/Q_c = 0.2$; $A_b/A_c = 0.25$

rated peak efficiency can substantially increase noise levels. For VAV applications, see Schaffer (2005).

6.3 DESIGN METHODS

Equal Friction Method. The equal friction method for sizing duct systems uses a constant friction rate. The target velocity determines the size of the first duct section both downstream and upstream of the fan. From the size determined by the target velocity, the design friction rate is determined to size all remaining duct sections except for connections to VAV and constant-volume (CV) terminal units and diffusers in the critical path, or for sections whose length exceeds around 15 ft. In these cases, the inlet to terminal units should have at least three diameters of rigid duct and 6 ft maximum of rigid or flexible duct (see Figure 9) to diffusers. The section upstream of the rigid duct to terminal units and the section of rigid/flexible duct to diffusers should be sized by the design friction rate, and an appropriate transition placed between sections. Refer to sections 8 and 9 in Figure 26 for an example.

Static Regain Method. The static regain method uses the conservation of momentum principle, which results in an increase in static pressure when the velocity is reduced in an airstream. This method sizes the main and branch ducts after a junction so that the recovery in static pressure caused by the reduced velocity is approximately equal to the total pressure drop caused by the duct and fittings in the subject duct section according to Equation (41). This is done iteratively by selecting a size for a section and checking to see if the section's static pressure loss is close to zero. The basic steps are to design the first section at the velocity recommended in Table 12. Then each downstream section is subsequently sized using the same duct size as the upstream section as a starting point. If there is no static regain, meaning there is a positive static pressure loss, then the downstream section will be the same size as the upstream section. But, if there is static regain, meaning the change in static pressure is negative, then an opportunity exists to use a smaller duct section. Typically, the next smaller size available that is smaller than the upstream section is selected and the calculations are repeated. Refer to column 12 of Table 15 for examples of static regain.

Table 12 Recommended Maximum Airflow Velocities to Achieve Specified Acoustic Design Criteria*

Duct Location	NC or RC Rating in Adjoining Occupancy	Maximum Airflow Velocity, fpm: Rectangular Duct	Maximum Airflow Velocity, fpm: Round Duct
1	2	3	4
In shaft or above solid drywall ceiling	45	3500	5000
	35	2500	3500
	25 or less	1500	2500
Above suspended acoustical ceiling	45	2500	4500
	35	1750	3000
	25 or less	1000	2000
Duct within occupied space	45	2000	3900
	35	1450	2600
	25 or less	950	1700

*Adapted from Table 9 in Chapter 48 of the 2015 *ASHRAE Handbook—HVAC Applications* and Schaffer 2005.

For connections to VAV and CV terminal units and diffusers in the critical path or the section length with the terminal unit or diffuser exceeds around 15 ft, the inlet to terminal units should have at least three diameters of rigid duct and 6 ft maximum of rigid or flexible duct (see Figure 6) to diffusers. The section upstream of the rigid duct to terminal units and the section of rigid/flexible duct to diffusers should be sized by the static regain method and an appropriate transition placed between sections. Refer to sections 8 and 9 in Figure 26 for an example.

$$p_{v1} = \Delta p_{t,1-2} + p_{v2} + \Delta p_{s,1-2} \tag{40}$$

Rearranging,

$$\Delta p_{s,1-2} = (p_{v1} - p_{v2}) - \Delta p_{t,1-2} \tag{41}$$

where

p_{v1} = velocity pressure at section 1, in. of water

p_{v2} = velocity pressure at section 2, in. of water
$\Delta p_{t,1-2}$ = total pressure loss from section 1 to 2, in. of water
$\Delta p_{s,1-2}$ = static pressure regain (+) or loss (–), in. of water

Balancing. When system unbalance is greater than about 30%, it is recommended that balance be improved by changing duct size, and/or fittings from a select few that have comparable efficiency without introducing additional significant turbulence (noise). Tables 10 and 11 are examples.

Noise Control

Understanding what noise is and how to control it is fundamental to duct design. The underlying principles of sound and vibration are covered in Chapter 8. Chapter 48 of the 2015 *ASHRAE Handbook—HVAC Applications* contains technical discussions and design examples helpful to the design engineer. AHRI *Standard* 885 has procedures for estimating sound pressure levels in the occupied zone for the portion of the system downstream of terminal units. For guidance in designing HVAC systems to avoid noise and vibration problems, consult Schaffer (2005). Specifying quiet equipment and designing systems to avoid noise and vibration problems are necessary parts of the design process.

Noise in system comes from fans and generated noise resulting from air turbulence in ducts, individual fittings, close-coupled fittings, dampers, air modulating equipment and diffusers/grilles. Objectionable self-generated duct noise can be controlled by limiting the duct velocity to the values listed in Table 12.

Goals

The goal of duct design is an air distribution system without objectionable noise and minimum life-cycle cost (LCC). Noise can be controlled by limiting the duct velocity to the values listed in Table 12. For example, for ductwork above a suspended acoustical ceiling and with a maximum allowable NC or RC of 35 in the adjoining space, the maximum round and rectangular duct airflow velocities are 3000 and 1750 fpm, respectively. Use this velocity to size the first duct section either upstream or downstream from the fan for all duct design methods. Lowering duct velocity reduces system operating cost and minimizes noise from sources other than ducts (fittings, close-coupled fittings, and dampers).

> *Commentary:* In 1988, Dr. Robert J. Tsal developed the T-method (Tsal and Adler 1987; Tsal et al. 1988, 1990) to design systems with a minimum LCC. The T-method was technically sound, but the system cost was not sufficiently accurate. As a result, the T-method was removed from the Handbook in 2013.

Design Method to Use

Supply Duct Sizing.

- Size fan supply ducts by either the equal friction (EF) or static regain (SR) method. The duct velocity anywhere in the system should not exceed the velocity listed in Table 12.
- Size ducts downstream of terminal boxes, toilet exhaust ducts, and other low-pressure systems (e.g., in Figure 25C) using the equal friction method with a friction rate in the range from 0.05 to 0.20 in. of water per 100 ft such that the duct velocity in the duct anywhere in the system does not exceed the values in Table 12. Use Table 13 as a guide to select the design friction rate.
- Terminal unit (VAV box) runouts should be full size with the exception that runouts in the "critical" path or a runout length greater than about 15 ft should be a minimum 5 ft of rigid duct full size and the remainder's size determined by the design method (e.g., Example 8 and Figure 26).
- Diffuser runouts should be full size, except for runouts in the critical path or a runout length greater than about 15 ft: these runouts should be at least 6 ft of flexible-duct full size, and the remainder's size determined by the design method.

Table 13 Guide for Selecting Low-Pressure System Friction Rate*

	in. of water per 100 ft									
	0.05		0.10		0.12		0.15		0.20	
Airflow *Q*, cfm	*D*, in.	*V*, fpm	*D*, in.	*V*, fpm	*D*, in.	*V*, fpm	*D*, in.	*V*, fpm	*D*, in.	*V*, fpm
500	13	542	11	758	11	758	10	917	10	917
1,000	16	716	14	935	14	935	13	1085	12	1273
2,000	21	832	18	1132	18	1132	17	1269	16	1432
3,000	24	955	21	1247	20	1375	20	1375	18	1698
4,000	27	1006	24	1273	23	1386	22	1515	21	1663
5,000	29	1090	26	1356	25	1467	24	1592	22	1894
10,000	38	1270	33	1684	32	1790	31	1908	29	2180
15,000	44	1421	39	1808	37	2009	36	2122	34	2379
20,000	49	1527	43	1983	42	2079	40	2292	38	2539
25,000	54	1572	47	2075	45	2264	43	2479	41	2727
30,000	58	1635	50	2200	48	2387	46	2599	44	2841

*Table developed using *ASHRAE Duct Fitting Database* (ASHRAE 2016): CD11-4 (ε = 0.0004 ft; ρ = 0.075 lb_m/ft^3).

Return Duct Systems.

- Sizing ducted returns depend on economizer relief system. For systems with return fans (Figure 25A), the return air ducts are sized using the EF method. The SR method does not work for negative-pressure duct systems.

  If building relief is by relief fans or gravity/motorized dampers, pressure drop should be kept low as shown by the total pressure grade line associated with Figures 25B and 25C.

  Control dampers in the economizer system should be selected (parallel or opposed blade) and sized in compliance with ASHRAE *Guideline* 16. Louvers should be sized in accordance with the section on Louvers, under Duct Design.
- Unducted return air shafts are typically sized for low pressure loss using either a fixed friction rate, velocity, or both. Typically, shafts are simply sized based on velocity. Maximum velocities are generally in the 800 to 1200 fpm range through the free area at the top of the shaft (highest airflow rate).
- Diffuser/grille runouts should be designed by the design method of choice and a transition located at the outlet. For outlets in the critical path, the outlet duct size should be increased. Registers should not be used because of the damper.

Example 8. For the VAV system shown in Figure 26, design the duct system by both the equal friction (EF) and static regain (SR) methods, and compare the section duct sizes, total pressure required for each path, and the unbalance between paths.

The system is located in Denver (5430 ft elevation) and the duct is spiral round, galvanized steel (absolute roughness ε = 0.0004 ft). The duct system is located above a suspended acoustical ceiling, and the allowable background sound in the occupied spaces is NC-35. Terminals T1, T2, T3, and T4 (VAV boxes with a one-row hot-water coil) are 800 cfm. VAV box loss coefficients are 1.68.

Solution: Use the *ASHRAE Duct Fitting Database* (ASHRAE 2016) to determine the air density, which is used to identify the velocity pressure and fitting loss coefficients for fittings. Density is 0.061 lb_m/ft^3 (Figure 27). The maximum design duct velocity from Table 12 is 3000 fpm. The EF and SR calculations are shown by Tables 14 and 15 spreadsheets.

For both the EF and SR designs, the duct size for Section 2 is 14 in. determined using CD11-3 (Figure 28). Sizing the remaining section depends on the design method. For the equal friction design method, the system equal friction (also from CD11-3) is 0.67 in. of water per 100 ft. Knowing the system design friction rate, the duct sizes are determined by CD11-4. Figure 29 is an example for Section 4. For the static regain method, all sections other than the terminal unit runouts are sized by iterating using Equation (41) (column 12 on the spreadsheet). For example, the results of the iteration for Section 4 are summarized by Table 16. The solution is the diameter that gives the result from Equation (41) that is closest to zero: in this case, 13 in.

Tables 17 and 18 summarize the results. The SR design is slightly better balanced, 18% compared to 23%, and the SR design requires 9% less energy. In addition, the SR sizes are slightly larger, and thus potentially less noisy. Both methods have static regain, but the SR design uses the regain more efficiently.

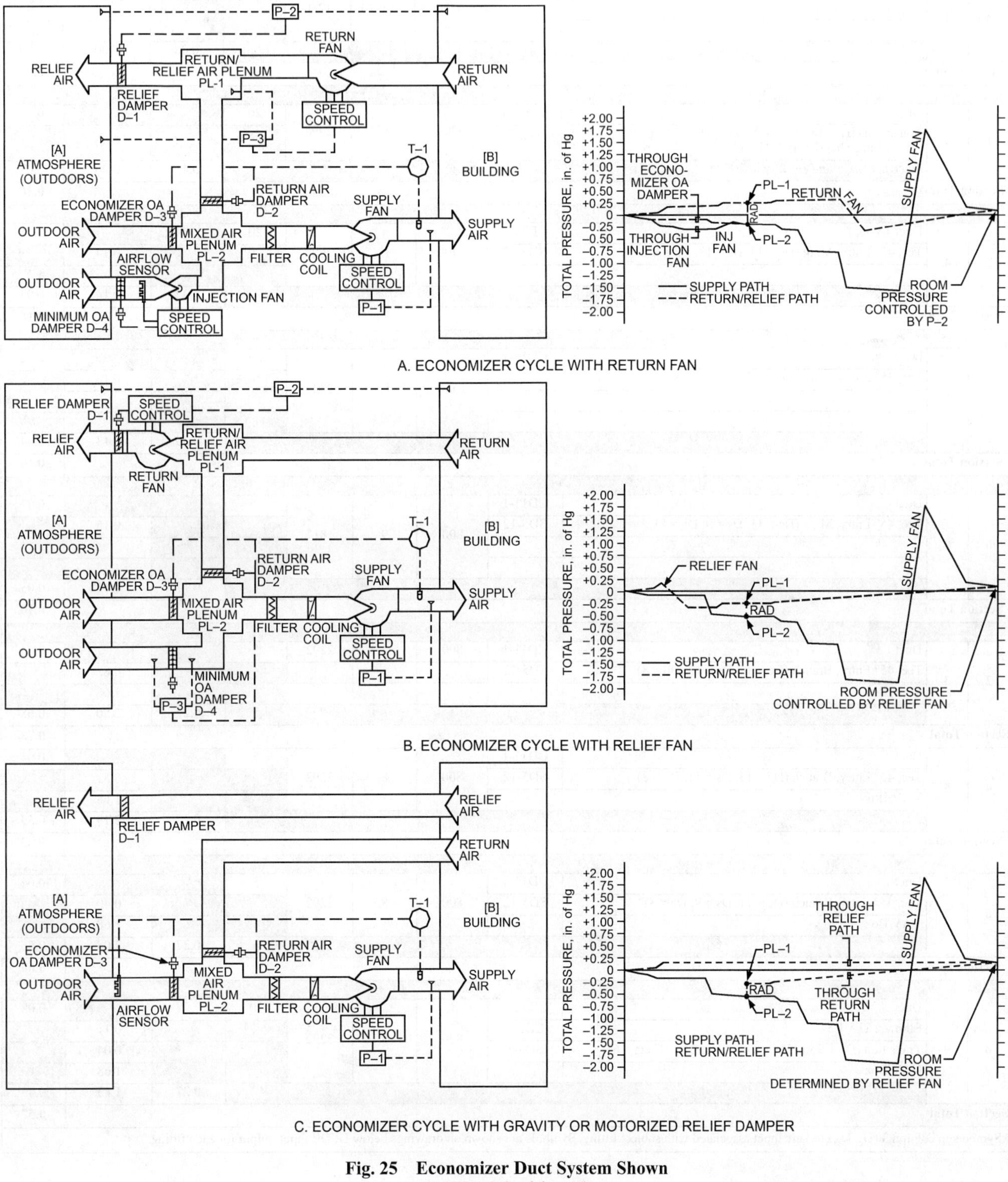

Fig. 25 Economizer Duct System Shown
(ASHRAE *Guideline* 16)

Table 14 Example 8, Equal Friction Design

1	2	3	4	5	6	7	8	9	10	11
Upstream Section	Section	Fitting	ASHRAE Fitting Code	Air Quantity, cfm	Duct Size, in.	Velocity, fpm	Duct Length, ft	Velocity Pressure p_v, in. of water	Loss Coefficient C	Total Pressure Loss, in. of water
		Source	Source	Source	Source	Source	Source	Source	Source	Source
		Drawings*	DFDB	Drawing	DFDB	DFDB	Drawing	DFDB	DFDB	Σ
Fan	1	Duct, Rectangular (Fan Outlet)	CR11-1	3200	18 × 20	1280	5			0.00
								0.08	0.00	0.00
Section Total										0.00
1	2	Duct	CD11-1	3200	14	2993	20			0.13
		Transition (H1 = 18 in., W1 = 20 in., Do = 14, in., L = 24 in., Theta1 = 10°, Theta2 = 14°	SD4-2						0.06	
		Sized at Maximum Velocity of 3000 fpm using CD11-3						0.45	0.06	0.03
Section Total‘										0.16
2	4	Duct	CD11-1	2400	13	2604	20			0.11
		Tee, 45° Entry, Main (Dc = 14, Ds = 13, Db = 8)	SD5-12						0.14	
								0.34	0.14	0.05
Section Total										0.16
4	6	Duct	CD11-1	1600	11	2424	20			0.12
		Tee, 45° Entry, Main (Dc=13, Ds=11, Db=8)	SD5-12						0.13	
								0.30	0.13	0.04
Section Total										0.16
6	8	Duct	CD11-1	800	9	1811	15			0.07
		Tee, 45° Entry, Main (Dc = 11, Ds = 9, Db = 8)	SD5-12						0.15	
								0.17	0.15	0.03
Section Total										0.10
2	3	Duct	CD11-1	800	8	2292	5			0.04
		Tee, 45° Entry, Branch (Dc = 14, Ds = 13, Db = 8)	SD5-12						0.82	
		VAV Box							1.68	
								0.27	2.50	0.68
Section Total										0.72
4	5	Duct	CD11-1	800	8	2292	5			0.04
		Tee, 45° Entry, Branch (Dc = 13, Ds = 11, Db = 8)	SD5-12						0.51	
		VAV Box							1.68	
								0.27	2.19	0.59
Section Total										0.63
6	7	Duct	CD11-1	800	8	2292	5			0.04
		Tee, 45° Entry, Branch (Dc = 11, Ds = 9, Db = 8)	SD5-12						0.40	
		VAV Box							1.68	
								0.27	2.08	0.56
Section Total										0.60
8	9	Duct	CD11-1	800	8	2292	10			0.08
		Elbow, r/D = 1.5	CD3-1						0.11	
		Transition (D1 = 9 in., Do = 8 in., L = 12 in., Theta = 6°)	SD4-1						0.04	
		VAV Box							1.68	
								0.27	1.83	0.49
Section Total										0.57

*Symbols in column 3 (D_c, D_s, etc.) are input associated with subject fitting. Symbols are shown on drawings below DFDB input/output for each fitting.

Table 15 Example 8, Static Regain Design

1	2	3	4	5	6	7	8	9	10	11	12
Upstream Section	Section	Fitting	ASHRAE Fitting Code	Air Quantity, cfm	Duct Size, in.	Velocity, fpm	Duct Length, ft	Velocity Pressure p_v, in. of water	Loss Coefficient C	Total Pressure Loss, in. of water	Regain, in. of water $[p_{v1} - p_{v3}] - \Delta p_t$
		Source	Source	Source	Source	Source	Source	Source	Source	Source	Source
		Drawings[a]	DFDB	Drawings	Iteration	DFDB	Drawings	DFDB	DFDB	Σ	Static Regain Calculation
Fan	1	Duct, Rectangular (Fan Outlet)	CR11-1	3200	18 × 20	1280	5			0.00	
								0.08	0.00	0.00	
Section Total										**0.00**	
1	2	Duct	CD11-1	3200	14	2993	20			0.13	
		Transition (H1 = 18 in, W1 = 20 in., Do = 14, in., L = 24 in., Theta1 = 10°, Theta2 = 14°)	SD4-2						0.06		
		Sized at Maximum Velocity of 3000 fpm using CD11-3						0.45	0.06	0.03	
Section Total										**0.16**	
2	4a	Duct	CD11-1	2400	14	2245	20			0.08	
		Tee. 45° Entry, Main (Dc = 14, Ds = 14, Db = 8)	SD5-12						0.13		
								0.26	0.13	0.03	(0.45 – 0.26) – 0.11 = 0.08
Section Total										**0.11**	0.08
2	4b[b]	Duct	CD11-1	2400	13	2604	20			0.11	
		Tee, 45° Entry, Main (Dc = 14, Ds = 13, Db = 8)	SD5-12						0.14		
								0.34	0.14	0.05	(0.45 – 0.34) – 0.16 = –0.05
Section Total										**0.16**	–0.05
4	6a	Duct	CD11-1	1600	13	1736	20			0.05	
		Tee, 45° Entry, Main (Dc = 13, Ds = 13, Db = 8)	SD5-12						0.14		
								0.15	0.14	0.02	(0.34 – 0.15) – 0.07 = 0.12
Section Total										**0.07**	0.12
4	6b[b]	Duct	CD11-1	1600	12	2037	20			0.08	
		Tee, 45° Entry, Main (Dc = 13, Ds = 12, Db = 8)	SD5-12						0.14		
								0.21	0.14	0.03	(0.34 – 0.21) –0.11 = 0.02
Section Total										**0.11**	0.02
4	6c	Duct	CD11-1	1600	11	2424	20			0.12	
		Tee, 45° Entry, Main (Dc = 13, Ds = 11, Db = 8)	SD5-12						0.13		
								0.30	0.13	0.04	(0.34 – 0.30) – 0.16 = –0.12
Section Total										**0.16**	–0.12
6	8a	Duct	CD11-1	800	12	1019	15			0.02	
		Tee, 45° Entry, Main (Dc = 12, Ds = 12, Db = 8)	SD5-12						0.20		
								0.05	0.20	0.01	(0.21 – 0.05) – 0.03 = 0.13
Section Total										**0.03**	0.13

[a]Symbols in column 3 (D_c, D_s, etc.) are input associated with subject fitting. Symbols are shown on drawings below DFDB input/output for each fitting.
[b]Indicates size selected.

Table 15 Example 8, Static Regain Design (*Continued*)

1	2	3	4	5	6	7	8	9	10	11	12
Upstream Section	Section	Fitting	ASHRAE Fitting Code	Air Quantity, cfm	Duct Size, in.	Velocity, fpm	Duct Length, ft	Velocity Pressure p_v, in. of water	Loss Coefficient C	Total Pressure Loss, in. of water	Regain, in. of water $[p_{v1} - p_{v3}] - \Delta p_t$
		Source	Source	Source	Source	Source	Source	Source	Source	Source	Source
		Drawings[a]	DFDB	Drawings	Iteration	DFDB	Drawings	DFDB	DFDB	Σ	Static Regain Calculation
		Duct	CD11-1				15			0.02	
6	8b	Tee, 45° Entry, Main (Dc = 12, Ds = 11, Db = 8)	SD5-12	800	11	1212			0.17		
								0.07	0.17	0.01	(0.21 – 0.07) – 0.03 = 0.11
Section Total										**0.03**	0.11
		Duct	CD11-1				15			0.04	
6	8c[b]	Tee, 45° Entry, Main (Dc = 12, Ds = 10, Db = 8)	SD5-12	800	10	1467			0.16		
								0.11	0.16	0.02	(0.21 – 0.11) – 0.06 = 0.04
Section Total										**0.06**	0.04
		Duct	CD11-1				15			0.07	
6	8d	Tee, 45° Entry, Main (Dc = 12, Ds = 9, Db = 8)	SD5-12	800	9	1811			0.14		
								0.17	0.14	0.02	(0.21 – 0.17) – 0.09 = –0.05
Section Total										**0.09**	–0.05
		Duct	CD11-1				10			0.08	
8	9	Transition (D1 = 10 in., Do = 8 in., L = 12 in., Theta = 10°)	SD4-1	800	8	2292			0.05		
		Elbow, r/D = 1.5	CD3-1						0.11		
		VAV Box							1.68		
								0.27	1.84	0.50	
Section Total										**0.58**	
		Duct	CD11-1				5			0.04	
2	3	Tee, 45° Entry, Branch (Dc = 14, Ds = 13, Db = 8)	SD5-12	800	8	2292			0.82		
		VAV Box							1.68		
								0.27	2.50	0.68	
Section Total										**0.72**	
		Duct	CD11-1				5			0.04	
4	5	Tee, 45° Entry, Branch (Dc = 13, Ds = 12, Db = 8)	SD5-12	800	8	2292			0.51		
		VAV Box							1.68		
								0.27	2.19	0.59	
Section Total										**0.63**	
		Duct	CD11-1				5			0.04	
6	7	Tee, 45° Entry, Branch (Dc = 12, Ds = 10, Db = 8)	SD5-12	800	8	2292			0.29		
		VAV Box							1.68		
								0.27	1.97	0.53	
Section Total										**0.57**	

[a]Symbols in column 3 (D_c, D_s, etc.) are input associated with subject fitting. Symbols are shown on drawings below DFDB input/output for each fitting.
[b]Indicates size selected.

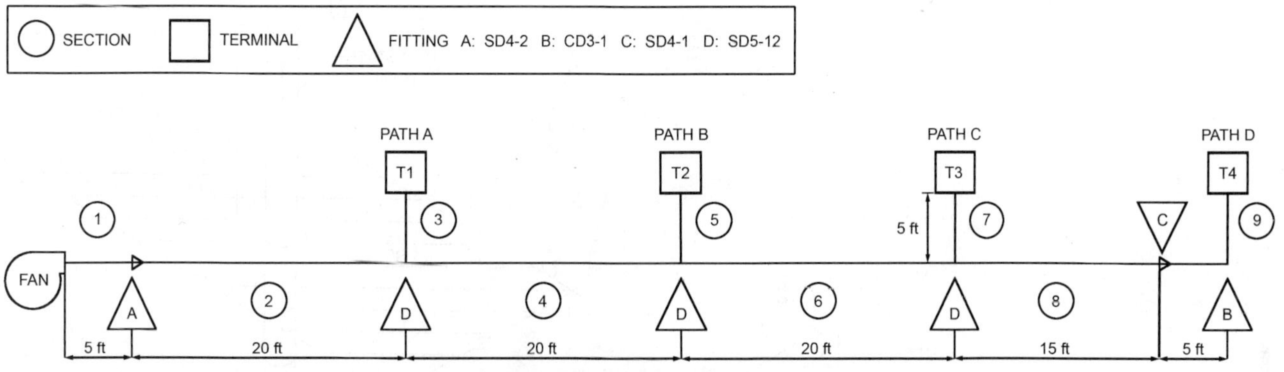

Fig. 26 System Layout for Example 8

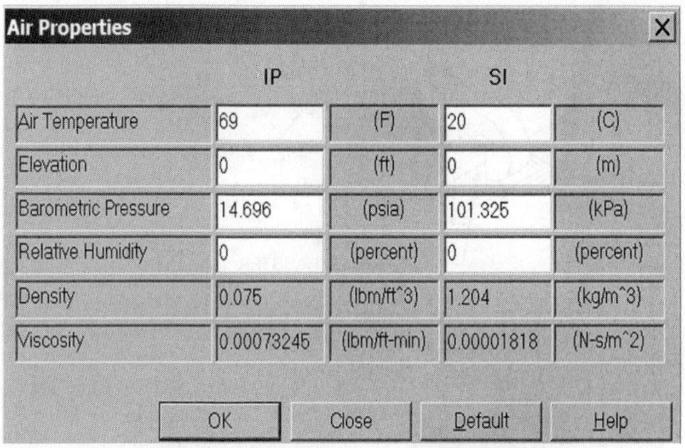

Fig. 27 Air Density for Example 8
ASHRAE Duct Fitting Database (ASHRAE 2016)

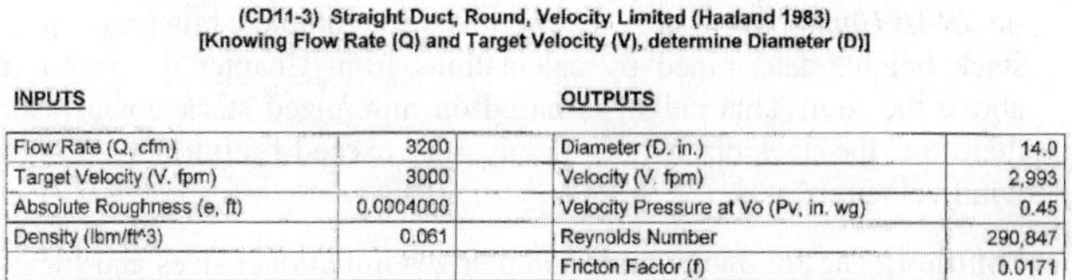

CD11-3 is also used to determine friction rate for EF design method.

Fig. 28 Sizing Section 2 for EF and SR Design Examples

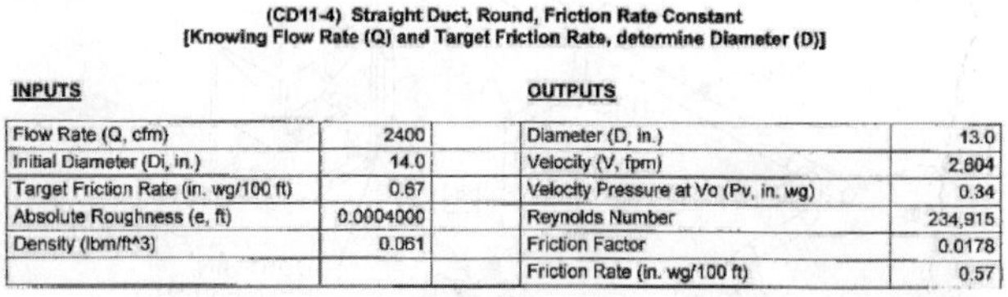

Fig. 29 EF Design: Sizing Sections 4, 6, and 8 Knowing Design Friction Rate (Section 4 Shown)

Table 16 Static Regain Iteration Process for Section 4

Iteration	Calculation	Duct Size, in.	$(p_{v1} - p_{v2}) - \Delta p_i$	Remarks
1	4a	14	0.08	
2	4b	13	–0.05	Solution

Table 17 Summary of System Duct Sizes

Section	Size, in. EF	SR	Remarks
1	18 × 20	18 × 20	Fan outlet
2	14	14	Initial section
4	13	13	
6	11	12	Sections affected by design method
8	9	10	
3	8	8	Terminal runout
5	8	8	Terminal runout
7	8	8	Terminal runout
9	8	8	Terminal runout

Table 18 System Unbalance

Path	Equal Friction P_t, in. of water	Equal Friction Unbalance	Static Regain P_t, in. of water	Static Regain Unbalance
A	0.88	23%	0.88	18%
B	0.95	17%	0.95	11%
C	1.08	6%	1.00	7%
D	1.15	0%	1.07	0%

6.4 INDUSTRIAL EXHAUST SYSTEMS

Chapter 32 of the 2015 *ASHRAE Handbook—HVAC Applications* discusses design criteria, including hood design, for industrial exhaust systems. Exhaust systems conveying vapors, gases, and smoke are designed by the equal-friction method. Systems conveying particulates are designed by the constant velocity method at duct velocities adequate to convey particles to the system air cleaner. For contaminant transport velocities, see Table 2 in Chapter 32 of the 2015 *ASHRAE Handbook—HVAC Applications*.

Two pressure-balancing methods can be considered when designing industrial exhaust systems. One method uses balancing devices (e.g., dampers, blast gates) to obtain design airflow through each hood. The other approach balances systems by adding resistance to ductwork sections (i.e., changing duct size, selecting different fittings, increasing airflow). This self-balancing method is preferred, especially for systems conveying abrasive materials. Where potentially explosive or radioactive materials are conveyed, the prebalanced system is mandatory because contaminants could accumulate at the balancing devices. To balance systems by increasing airflow, use Equation (42), which assumes that all ductwork has

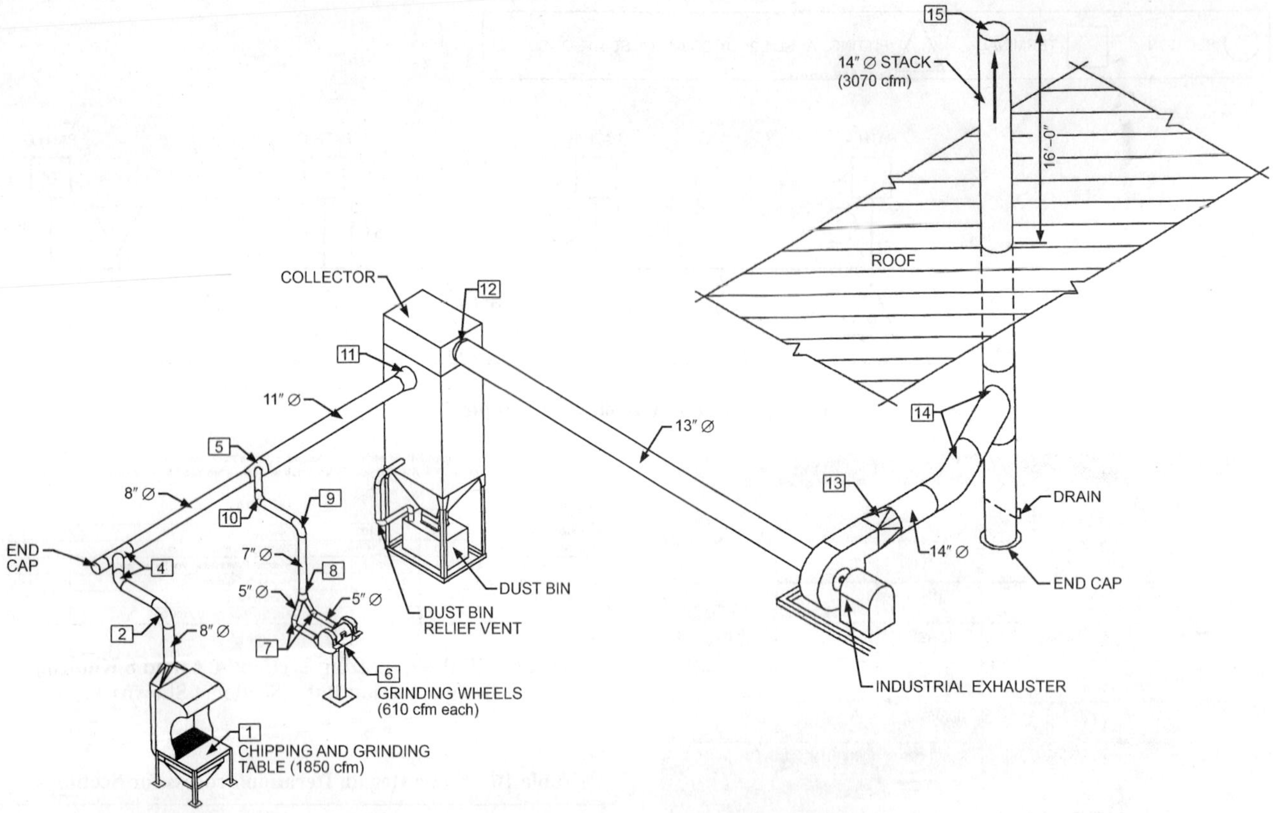

Fig. 30 Metalworking Exhaust System for Example 9

the same diameter and that fitting loss coefficients, including main and branch tee coefficients, are constant.

$$Q_c = Q_d(P_h/P_l)^{0.5} \tag{42}$$

where

Q_c = airflow rate required to increase P_l to P_h, cfm
Q_d = total airflow rate through low-resistance duct run, cfm
P_h = absolute value of pressure loss in high-resistance ductwork section(s), in. of water
P_l = absolute value of pressure loss in low-resistance ductwork section(s), in. of water

For systems conveying particulates, use elbows with a large centerline radius-to-diameter ratio (r/D), greater than 1.5 whenever possible. If r/D is 1.5 or less, abrasion in dust-handling systems can reduce the life of elbows. Elbows are often made of seven or more gores, especially in large diameters. For converging flow fittings, a 30° entry angle is recommended to minimize energy losses and abrasion in dust-handling systems. For the entry loss coefficients of hoods and equipment for specific operations, see Chapter 32 of the 2015 *ASHRAE Handbook—HVAC Applications* and ACGIH (2016).

Commentary: Fitting CD11-5 of the *ASHRAE Duct Fitting Database* (ASHRAE 2016) is available for sizing minimum-velocity ducts conveying particulates.

Example 9. For the metalworking exhaust system in Figures 30 and 31, size the ductwork and calculate fan static pressure requirement for an industrial exhaust designed to convey granular materials. Pressure-balance the system by changing duct sizes and adjusting airflow rates. Minimum particulate transport velocity for the chipping and grinding table ducts (sections 1 and 5, Figure 31) is 4000 fpm. For ducts associated with the grinder wheels (sections 2, 3, 4, and 5), minimum duct velocity is 4500 fpm. Ductwork is galvanized steel, with absolute roughness of 0.0003 ft. Assume that air is standard and that duct and fittings are available in the following sizes: 3 to 9.5 in. diameters in 0.5 in. increments, 10 to 37 in. diameters in 1 in. increments, and 38 to 90 in. diameters in 2 in. increments.

The building is one story, and the design wind velocity is 20 mph. For the stack, use design J shown in Figure 2 in Chapter 45 of the 2015 *ASHRAE Handbook—HVAC Applications* for complete rain protection; stack height, determined by calculations from Chapter 45, is 16 ft above the roof. This height is based on minimized stack downwash; therefore, the stack discharge velocity must exceed 1.5 times the design wind velocity.

Solution: The following table summarizes initial duct sizes and transport velocities for contaminated ducts upstream of the collector. The 4474 fpm velocity in sections 2 and 3 is acceptable because the transport velocity is not significantly lower than 4500 fpm. For the next

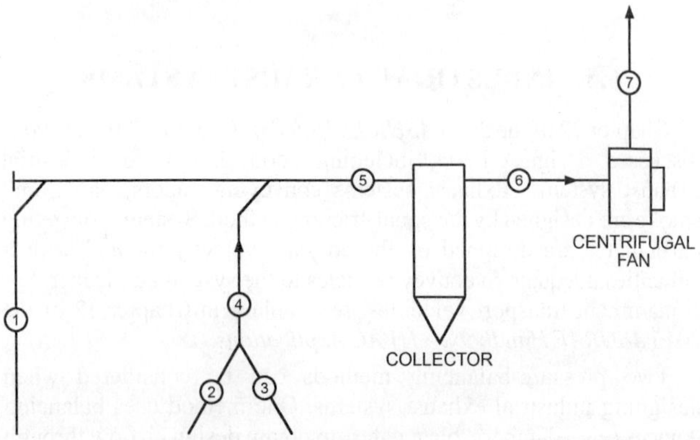

Fig. 31 System Schematic with Section Numbers for Example 9

Table 19 Total Pressure Loss Calculations by Sections for Example 9

Duct Section[a]	Duct Element	Airflow, cfm	Duct Size. in. φ	Velocity, fpm	Velocity Pressure, in. of water	Duct Length,[b] ft	Summary of Fitting Loss Coefficients[c]	Duct Pressure Loss/100 ft, in. of water[d]	Total Pressure Loss, in. of water	Section Pressure Loss, in. of water
1	Duct	1850	8	5300	—	23.7	—	4.64	1.10	
	Fittings	1850		5300	1.75	—	1.07	—	1.87	2.97
2, 3	Duct	610	5	4474	—	8.5	—	5.96	0.51	
	Fittings	610		4474	1.25	—	1.06	—	1.33	1.84
4	Duct	1220	7	4565	—	11.5	—	4.09	0.47	
	Fittings	1220		4565	1.30	—	0.51	—	0.66	1.13
5	Duct	3070	11	4652	—	8.5	—	2.44	0.21	
	Fittings	3070		4652	1.35	—	0.22	—	0.30	0.51
—	Collector,[e] fabric	3070	—	—	—	—	—	—	3.0	3.0
6	Duct	3070	13	3331	—	10.5	—	1.05	0.11	
	Fittings	3070		3331	0.69	—	0.03	—	0.02	0.13
7	Duct	3070	14	2872	—	50	—	0.72	0.36	
	Fittings	3070		2872	0.51	—	1.80	—	0.92	1.28

[a]See Figure 29.
[b]Duct lengths are to fitting centerlines.
[c]See Table 20.
[d]Duct pressure based on a 0.0003 ft absolute roughness factor.
[e]Collector manufacturers set fabric bag cleaning mechanism to actuate at a pressure difference of 3.0 in. of water between inlet and outlet plenums. Pressure difference across clean media is approximately 1.5 in. of water.

available duct size (4.5 in. diameter), the duct velocity is 5523 fpm, significantly higher than 4500 fpm.

Duct Section	Design Airflow, cfm	Transport Velocity, fpm	Duct Diameter, in.	Duct Velocity, fpm
1	1800	4000	9	4074
2, 3	610 each	4500	5	4474
4	1220	4500	7	4565
5	3020	4500	11	4576

Design calculations up through the junction after sections 1 and 4 are summarized as follows:

Design No.	D_1, in.	Δp_1, in. of water	Δp_{2+4}, in. of water	Imbalance, $\Delta p_1 - \Delta p_{2+4}$
1	9	1.46	3.09	−1.63
2	8.5	2.00	3.08	−1.08
3	8	2.79	3.00	−0.21
4	7.5	3.92	2.88	+1.04

$Q_1 = 1800$ cfm; $Q_3 = 610$ cfm; $D_3 = 5$ in. dia.
$Q_2 = 610$ cfm; $D_2 = 5$ in. dia.; $Q_4 = 1220$ cfm; $D_4 = 7$ in. dia.

For (initial) design 1, the imbalance between section 1 and section 2 (or 3) is 1.63 in. of water, with section 1 requiring additional resistance. Decreasing section 1 duct diameter by 0.5 in. increments results in the least imbalance, 0.21 in. of water, when the duct diameter is 8 in. (design 3). Because section 1 requires additional resistance, estimate the new airflow rate using Equation (42):

$$Q_{c,1} = (1800)(3.00/2.79)^{0.5} = 1870 \text{ cfm}$$

At 1870 cfm flow in section 1, 0.13 in. of water imbalance remains at the junction of sections 1 and 4. By trial-and-error solution, balance is attained when the flow in section 1 is 1850 cfm. The duct between the collector and fan inlet is 13 in. round to match the fan inlet (12.75 in. diameter). To minimize downwash, the stack discharge velocity must exceed 2640 fpm, 1.5 times the design wind velocity (20 mph) as stated in the problem definition. Therefore, the stack is 14 in. round, and the stack discharge velocity is 2872 fpm.

Table 19 summarizes the system losses by sections. The straight duct friction factor and pressure loss were calculated by Equations (18) and (19). Table 20 lists fitting loss coefficients and input parameters necessary to determine the loss coefficients. The fitting loss coefficients are from the *ASHRAE Duct Fitting Database*. Figure 32 shows a pressure grade line of the system. Fan total pressure, calculated by Equation (15), is 7.89 in. of water. To calculate the fan static pressure, use Equation (17):

$$P_s = 7.89 - 0.81 = 7.1 \text{ in. of water}$$

where 0.81 in. of water is the fan outlet velocity pressure. The fan airflow rate is 3070 cfm, and its outlet area is 0.853 ft³ (10.125 by 12.125 in.). Therefore, the fan outlet velocity is 3600 fpm.

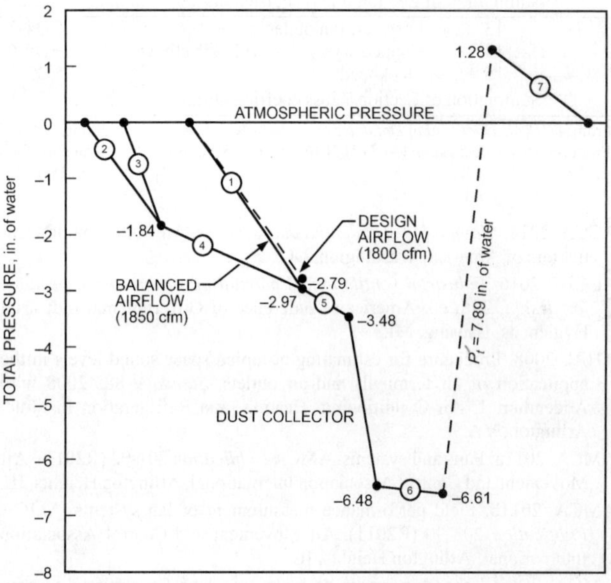

Fig. 32 Total Pressure Grade Line for Example 9

Hood suction for the chipping and grinding table hood is 2.2 in. of water, calculated by Equation (5) from Chapter 32 of the 2015 *ASHRAE Handbook—HVAC Applications* [$P_{s,h} = (1 + 0.25)(1.74) = 2.2$ in. of water, where 0.25 is hood entry loss coefficient C_o, and 1.74 is duct velocity pressure P_v a few diameters downstream from the hood]. Similarly, hood suction for each grinder wheel is 1.7 in. of water.

$$P_{2,3} = (1 + 0.4)(1.24) = 1.7 \text{ in. of water}$$

where 0.4 is the hood entry loss coefficient, and 1.24 in. of water is the duct velocity pressure.

REFERENCES

ASHRAE members can access *ASHRAE Journal* articles and ASHRAE research project final reports at technologyportal .ashrae.org. Articles and reports are also available for purchase by nonmembers in the online ASHRAE Bookstore at www.ashrae.org /bookstore.

Abushakra, B., I.S. Walker, and M.H. Sherman. 2004. Compression effects on pressure loss in flexible HVAC ducts. *International Journal of HVAC&R Research* (now *Science and Technology for the Built Environment*) 10(3):275-289.

Table 20 Loss Coefficient Summary by Sections for Example 9

Duct Section	Fitting Number	Type of Fitting	ASHRAE Fitting No.[a]	Parameters	Loss Coefficient
1	1	Hood[b]	—	Hood face area: 3 by 4 ft	0.25
	2	Elbow	CD3-10	90°, 7 gore, r/D = 2.5	0.11
	4	Capped wye (45°), with 45° elbow	ED5-6	$A_b/A_c = 1$	0.61 (C_b)
	5	Wye (30°), main	ED5-1	$Q_s/Q_c = 0.60$, $A_s/A_c = 0.529$, $A_b/A_c = 0.405$	0.10 (C_s)
	Summation of Section 1 loss coefficients				1.07
2,3	6	Hood[c]	—	Type hood: For double wheels, dia. = 22 in. each, wheel width = 4 in. each; type takeoff: tapered	0.40
	7	Elbow	CD3-12	90°, 3 gore, r/D = 1.5	0.34
	8	Symmetrical wye (60°)	ED5-9	$Q_b/Q_c = 0.5$, $A_{b1}/A_c = 0.51$, $A_{b2}/A_c = 0.51$	0.32 (C_b)
	Summation of Sections 2 and 3 loss coefficients				1.06
4	9	Elbow	CD3-10	90°, 7 gore, r/D = 2.5	0.11
	10	Elbow	CD3-13	60°, 3 gore, r/D = 1.5	0.19
	5	Wye (30°), branch	ED5-1	$Q_b/Q_c = 0.40$, $A_s/A_c = 0.529$, $A_b/A_c = 0.405$	0.21 (C_b)
	Summation of Section 4 loss coefficients				0.51
5	11	Exit, conical diffuser to collector	ED2-1	L = 24 in., $L/D_o = 2.0$, $A_1/A_o \approx 16$	0.22
	Summation of Section 5 loss coefficients				0.22
6	12	Entry, bellmouth from collector	ER2-1	$r/D_1 = 0.23$, r = 3 in., $C_o = 3.30$	0.03 (C_1)
	Summation of Section 6 loss coefficients				0.03
7	13	Diffuser, fan outlet[d]	SD4-2	Fan outlet size: 10.125 by 12.125 in.; L = 18 in.	0.19
	14	Capped wye (45°), with 45° elbow	ED5-6	$A_b/A_c = 1$	0.61 (C_b)
	15	Stackhead	SD2-6	$D_e/D = 1$	1.0
	Summation of Section 7 loss coefficients				1.80

[a]From *ASHRAE Duct Fitting Database*.
[b]From *Industrial Ventilation* (ACGIH 2016, Figure VS-80-19).
[c]From *Industrial Ventilation* (ACGIH 2016, Figure VS-80-11).
[d]Fan specified: Industrial exhauster for granular materials: 21 in. wheel diameter, 12.75 in. inlet diameter, 10.125 by 12.125 in. outlet, 7.5 hp motor.

ACCA. 2014. *Manual D—Residential duct systems*. Air Conditioning Contractors of America, Washington, DC.

ACGIH. 2016. *Industrial ventilation: A manual of recommended practice for design*, 29th ed. American Conference of Governmental Industrial Hygienists, Lansing, MI.

AHRI. 2008. Procedure for estimating occupied space sound levels in the application of air terminals and air outlets. *Standard* 885-2008 with Addendum 1. Air-Conditioning, Heating, and Refrigeration Institute, Arlington, VA.

AMCA. 2011a. Fans and systems. AMCA *Publication* 201-02 (R2011). Air Movement and Control Association International, Arlington Heights, IL.

AMCA. 2011b. Field performance measurement of fan systems. AMCA *Publication* 203-90 (R2011). Air Movement and Control Association International, Arlington Heights, IL.

AMCA. 2016. Laboratory methods for testing fans for certified aerodynamic performance rating. ANSI/AMCA *Standard* 210-16. Also ANSI/ASHRAE/AMCA *Standard* 51-16.

AMCA. 2012. Laboratory methods of testing dampers for rating. ANSI/AMCA *Standard* 500-D-12. Air Movement and Control Association International, Arlington Heights, IL.

AMCA. 2015. Laboratory method of testing louvers for rating. ANSI/AMCA *Standard* 500-L-12 (R2015). Air Movement and Control Association International, Arlington Heights, IL.

AMCA. 2013. Certified ratings program—Product rating manual for air control. AMCA *Publication* 511-10 (Rev. 2013). Air Movement and Control Association International, Arlington Heights, IL.

ASHRAE. 2016. *ASHRAE duct fitting database,* v. 6.00.05.10.

ASHRAE. 2016. Energy standard for buildings except low-rise residential buildings. ANSI/ASHRAE/IES *Standard* 90.1-2016.

ASHRAE. 2007. Energy-efficient design of low-rise residential buildings. ANSI/ASHRAE *Standard* 90.2-2007.

ASHRAE. 2015. Energy conservation in existing buildings. ANSI/ASHRAE/IES *Standard* 100-2015.

ASHRAE. 2008. Measurement, testing, adjusting and balancing of building heating, ventilation and air-conditioning systems. ANSI/ASHRAE *Standard* 111-2008.

ASHRAE. 2016. Method of testing HVAC air ducts and fittings. ANSI/ASHRAE/SMACNA *Standard* 126-2016.

ASHRAE. 2016. Methods of testing air terminal units. ANSI/ASHRAE *Standard* 130-2016.

ASHRAE. In development. Method of test to determine leakage of operating HVAC air distribution systems. ANSI/ASHRAE *Proposed Standard* 215.

ASHRAE. 2014. Selecting outdoor, return, and relief dampers for air-side economizer systems. ASHRAE *Guideline* 16-2014.

Behls, H.F. 1971. Computerized calculation of duct friction. *Building Science Series* 39, p. 363. National Institute of Standards and Technology, Gaithersburg, MD.

Brown, R.B. 1973. Experimental determinations of fan system effect factors. In *Fans and systems*, ASHRAE *Symposium Bulletin* LO-73-1, Louisville, KY (June).

Clarke, M.S., J.T. Barnhart, F.J. Bubsey, and E. Neitzel. 1978. The effects of system connections on fan performance. *ASHRAE Transactions* 84(2): 227-263.

Colebrook, C.F. 1938-1939. Turbulent flow in pipes, with particular reference to the transition region between the smooth and rough pipe laws. *Journal of the Institution of Civil Engineers* 11:133.

Culp, C.H. 2011. HVAC flexible duct pressure loss measurements. ASHRAE Research Project RP-1333, *Final Report*.

Farquhar, H.F. 1973. System effect values for fans. In *Fans and systems*, ASHRAE *Symposium Bulletin* LO-73-1, Louisville, KY (June).

Griggs, E.I., and F. Khodabakhsh-Sharifabad. 1992. Flow characteristics in rectangular ducts. *ASHRAE Transactions* 98(1):116-127.

Griggs, E.I., W.B. Swim, and G.H. Henderson. 1987. Resistance to flow of round galvanized ducts. *ASHRAE Transactions* 93(1):3-16.

Heyt, J.W., and M.J. Diaz. 1975. Pressure drop in flat-oval spiral air duct. *ASHRAE Transactions* 81(2):221-232.

Huebscher, R.G. 1948. Friction equivalents for round, square and rectangular ducts. *ASHVE Transactions* 54:101-118.

Hutchinson, F.W. 1953. Friction losses in round aluminum ducts. *ASHVE Transactions* 59:127-138.

Idelchik, I.E., M.O. Steinberg, G.R. Malyavskaya, and O.G. Martynenko. 1994. *Handbook of hydraulic resistance*, 3rd ed. CRC Press/Begell House, Boca Raton.

Jones, C.D. 1979. *Friction factor and roughness of United Sheet Metal Company spiral duct.* United Sheet Metal, Division of United McGill Corp., Westerville, OH (August). Based on data in *Friction loss tests*, United Sheet Metal Company Spiral Duct, Ohio State University Engineering Experiment Station, File T-1011, September 1958.

Klote, J.H., J.A. Milke, P.G. Tumbull, A. Kashef, and M.J. Ferreira. 2012. *Handbook of smoke control engineering.* ASHRAE.

Kulkarni, D., S. Khaire, and S. Idem. 2009. Pressure loss of corrugated spiral duct. *ASHRAE Transactions* 115(1).

Madison, R.D., and W.R. Elliot. 1946. Friction charts for gases including correction for temperature, viscosity and pipe roughness. *ASHVE Journal* (October).

McGill. 1988. Round vs. rectangular duct. *Engineering Report* 147, United McGill Corp. (contact McGill Airflow Technical Service Department), Westerville, OH.

McGill. 1995. Flat oval vs. rectangular duct. *Engineering Report* 150, United McGill Corp. (contact McGill Airflow Technical Service Department), Westerville, OH.

Meyer, M.L. 1973. A new concept: The fan system effect factor. In *Fans and Systems*, ASHRAE *Symposium Bulletin* LO-73-1, Louisville, KY (June).

Moody, L.F. 1944. Friction factors for pipe flow. *ASME Transactions* 66: 671.

NFPA. 2008. *Fire protection handbook*, 20th ed. National Fire Protection Association. Quincy, MA.

NFPA. 2015. Installation of air-conditioning and ventilating systems. ANSI/NFPA *Standard* 90A. National Fire Protection Association, Quincy, MA.

Osborne, W.C. 1966. *Fans*. Pergamon, London.

Paulauskis, J.A. 2016. Understanding duct rumble. *ASHRAE Journal* 58(12):40-45.

Schaffer, M.E. 2005. *A practical guide to noise and vibration control for HVAC systems*, 2nd ed. ASHRAE.

Swim, W.B. 1978. Flow losses in rectangular ducts lined with fiberglass. *ASHRAE Transactions* 84(2):216.

Swim, W.B. 1982. Friction factor and roughness for airflow in plastic pipe. *ASHRAE Transactions* 88(1):269.

Taylor. S.J., and J. Stein. 2004. Sizing VAV boxes. *ASHRAE Journal* 46(3): 30-35.

Tsal, R.J., and M.S. Adler. 1987. Evaluation of numerical methods for ductwork and pipeline optimization. *ASHRAE Transactions* 93(1):17-34.

Tsal, R.J., H.F. Behls, and R. Mangel. 1988. T-method duct design, part I: Optimization theory; Part II: Calculation procedure and economic analysis. *ASHRAE Transactions* 94(2):90-111.

Tsal, R.J., H.F. Behls, and R. Mangel. 1990. T-method duct design, part III: Simulation. *ASHRAE Transactions* 96(2).

UL. Published annually. *Building materials directory*. Underwriters Laboratories, Northbrook, IL.

UL. Published annually. *Fire resistance directory*. Underwriters Laboratories, Northbrook, IL.

UL. 2013. Fire dampers. ANSI/UL *Standard* 555, 7th ed. Underwriters Laboratories, Northbrook, IL.

UL. 2014. Smoke dampers. ANSI/UL *Standard* 555S, 5th ed. Underwriters Laboratories, Northbrook, IL.

Wright, D.K., Jr. 1945. A new friction chart for round ducts. *ASHVE Transactions* 51:303-316.

BIBLIOGRAPHY

Abushakra, B., I.S. Walker, and M.H. Sherman. 2002. A study of pressure losses in residential air distribution systems. *Proceedings of the ACEEE Summer Study 2002*, American Council for an Energy Efficient Economy, Washington, D.C. LBNL *Report* 49700. Lawrence Berkeley National Laboratory, CA.

Carrié, F.R., J. Andersson, and P. Wouters. 1999. *Improving ductwork—A time for tighter air distribution systems*. Air Infiltration and Ventilation Centre, Coventry, U.K.

Hyderman, M., S. Taylor, and J. Stein. 2009. *Advanced variable air volume VAV systems design guide*, 3rd edition. Pacific Gas and Electric Company.

CHAPTER 22

PIPE DESIGN

THIS CHAPTER discusses pipe systems, materials, design, installation, supports, stress calculations, pipe expansion and flexibility, bends and loops, and application of pipe systems commonly used for heating, air conditioning, refrigeration, and service water. When selecting and applying components; applicable local codes, state or provincial codes, and voluntary industry standards (some of which have been adopted by code jurisdictions) must be followed. Further details on specific piping systems can be found in application-specific chapters of the ASHRAE Handbook.

1. FUNDAMENTALS

1.1 CODES AND STANDARDS

The following organizations in the United States issue codes and standards for piping systems and components:

ASME	American Society of Mechanical Engineers
ASTM	American Society for Testing and Materials
NFPA	National Fire Protection Association
ICC	International Code Council
MSS	Manufacturers Standardization Society of the Valve and Fittings Industry, Inc.
AWWA	American Water Works Association

Parallel federal specifications also have been developed by government agencies and are used for many public works projects. Chapter IV of ASME *Standard* B31.9 lists applicable U.S. codes and standards for HVAC piping. In addition, it gives requirements for safe design and construction of piping systems for building heating and air conditioning. ASME *Standard* B31.5 gives similar requirements for refrigerant piping.

1.2 DESIGN CONSIDERATIONS

Pipes are conduits in which fluids [compressible (e.g., air, steam) and noncompressible (e.g., water)] flow in a system, in response to a pressure differential. Piping system designers should assess the following aspects:

- Code requirements.
- Load: the amount of energy or fluid to be moved through the pipe to where it is needed; determination of load is not covered in this chapter (see Chapters 16 to 18 for information on load calculations).
- Working fluid and fluid properties in the pipe.
- Pressure and temperature of the fluid.
- External environment of the pipe: outdoor installations deal with temperature extremes, environmental contaminants, and ultraviolet radiation. Other environments could contain caustic chemicals. Soil can contain elements that can be corrosive to underground pipe systems.
- Installation cost.
- Pipe's resistance to chemical attack from the fluid.

When designing a fluid flow system, two related but distinct concerns emerge: sizing the pipe and determining the flow/pressure relationship. The two are often confused because they can use the same equations and design tools. Nevertheless, they should be determined separately.

This chapter focuses on sizing the pipe during the design phase, and to this end presents design charts and tables for specific fluids in addition to the equations that describe fluid flow in pipes. Once a system has been sized, it should be analyzed with more detailed methods of calculation to determine the pump head, if applicable, required to achieve the desired flow. Computerized methods are well suited to handling the details of calculating losses around an extensive system.

Not discussed in detail in this chapter, but of potentially great importance, are physical and chemical considerations such as pipe and fitting design; materials; and joining methods appropriate for working pressures and temperatures encountered, as well as resistance to chemical attack by the fluid. For more information, see Eshbach (2009), Heald (2002), and Nayyar (1999).

For fluids not included in this chapter or for piping materials of different dimensions, manufacturers' literature frequently supplies pressure drop charts. The Darcy-Weisbach equation, with the Moody chart or Colebrook equation, can be used as an alternative to pressure drop charts or tables.

1.3 GENERAL PIPE SYSTEMS

Metallic Pipe Systems

Each HVAC system and, under some conditions, portions of a system require a study of the conditions of operation to determine suitable materials. For example, because the static pressure of water in a high-rise building is higher in the lower levels than in the upper levels, a heavier pipe or different materials may be required for different vertical zones.

Table 1 lists some typical systems and materials used for heating and air-conditioning metallic piping. The list is not all inclusive, because piping systems are constantly being developed. The pressure and temperature rating of each component selected must be

The preparation of this chapter is assigned to TC 6.1, Hydronic and Steam Equipment and Systems.

Table 1 Common Applications of Pipe, Fittings, and Valves for Heating and Air Conditioning

Application	Size, in.	Material	Weight	Joint Type	Fitting Material	Class (When Applicable)	System[g] Temperature, °F	Maximum Pressure at Temperature,[a,b] psi
Chilled water	≤2	Steel Type F (CW)	Schedule 40	Thread	Cast iron	125	250	125
	2.5 to 12	Steel A or B, Type E (ERW)	Schedule 40	Weld	Wrought steel	Standard	250	400
				Flange	Wrought steel	150	250	250
					Cast iron	125	250	175
					Cast iron	250	250	400
		Copper, hard or soft	Type K or L	Solder Flared (soft) Rolled groove (2 to 8 in.) Press-connect (0.5 to 4 in.) Push connect (0.5 to 2 in.) Mechanical formed	Wrought or cast Cu		100	370 Type K soft 635 Type K hard 250 Type L soft 435 Type L hard
				Braze Weld	Wrought or cast Cu		100	250 Type L soft 370 Type K soft
		Copper, hard	Type M	Solder Rolled groove (2 to 8 in.) Press-connect (0.5 to 4 in.) Push connect (0.5 to 2 in.) Mechanical formed	Wrought or cast Cu		100	395 Type M hard
				Braze Weld	Wrought or cast Cu		100	230 Type M soft
	0.375 to 1.0	PEX (barrier)	SDR-9	Crimp Clamp Expansion Compression Push fit Proprietary	Bronze Brass Copper Engineered plastic		73	145
	0.5 to 6	PE	Schedule 40,[f] 80, SDR	Thermal fusion, compression	PE		120 (140 limit for some applications)	Varies with pipe wall thickness, grade, schedule, size. Check manufacturer's documentation for design ratings 30 to 110 at 130°F
Heating and recirculating	2 and smaller	Steel Type F (CW)	Schedule 40	Thread	Cast iron	125	250	125
	0.25 to 12	Steel B Type E (ERW)	Schedule 40	Weld	Wrought steel	Standard	250	400
				Flange	Wrought steel	150	250	250
					Cast iron	125	250	125
					Cast iron	250	250	400
		Copper, hard or soft	Type K or L	Solder Braze Flared (soft) Rolled groove (2 to 8 in.) Press-connect (0.5 to 4 in.) Push connect (0.5 to 2 in.) Mechanical formed	Wrought or cast Cu		200	300 Type K soft 635 Type K hard 205 Type L soft 435 Type L hard
				Braze Weld	Wrought or cast Cu		200	300 Type K soft 205 Type L soft
	0.25 to 12	Copper, hard	Type M	Solder Rolled groove (2 to 8 in.) Press-connect (0.5 to 4 in.) Push connect (0.5 to 2 in.) Mechanical formed	Wrought or cast Cu		200	395 Type M hard
				Braze Weld	Wrought or cast Cu		200	200 Type M soft
	0.375 to 1.0	PEX (barrier)	SDR-9	Crimp Clamp Expansion Compression Push fit Proprietary	Bronze Brass Copper Engineered plastic		200	79
Steam and condensate	2 and smaller	Steel Type F (CW) or S	Schedule 40[d]	Thread	Cast iron	125		90
				Thread	Malleable iron	150		90
				Socket	Forged steel	3000		90
		Steel B Type E (ERW) or S	Schedule 40[d]	Thread	Cast iron	125		100
				Thread	Malleable iron	150		125
				Socket	Forged steel	3000		400
		Steel B Type E (ERW) or S	Schedule 80	Thread Socket	Cast iron	250		200
				Thread	Malleable iron	300		250
				Socket	Forged steel	3000		400
	2 to 12	Steel B Type E (ERW) or S	Schedule 40	Weld	Wrought steel	Standard		250
				Flange	Wrought steel	150		200

Table 1 Common Applications of Pipe, Fittings, and Valves for Heating and Air Conditioning (*Continued*)

Application	Size, in.	Material	Weight	Joint Type	Fitting Material	Class (When Applicable)	System[g] Temperature, °F	Maximum Pressure at Temperature,[a,b] psi
					Cast iron	125		100
		Steel B Type E (ERW) or S	Schedule 80	Weld	Wrought steel	XS		700
				Flange	Wrought steel	300		500
					Cast iron	250		200
Ground-source heat pump	0.25 to 2	Copper, hard or soft	Type L or ACR	Flared or brazed	Wrought or cast Cu		200	205 Type L soft, 435 Type L hard, 240 ACR soft, 500 ACR hard
	0.375 to 1.0	PEX (barrier)	SDR-9	Crimp	Bronze		180	100
				Clamp	Brass			
				Expansion	Copper			
				Compression	Engineered plastic			
				Push fit				
				Proprietary				
Refrigerant		Steel B Type E (ERW)	Schedule 40	Weld			Wrought steel	
	0.375 to 4.125	Copper, hard	Type L or ACR	Braze	Wrought or Forged Cu		200	435 Type L hard, 240 ACR soft
Natural gas and LP	0.25 to 12	Copper, hard or soft	Type K or L	Solder	Wrought or cast Cu		100	370 Type K soft
				Rolled groove (2 to 8 in.)				635 Type K hard
				Press-connect (0.5 to 4 in.)				250 Type L soft
				Push connect (0.5 to 2 in.)				435 Type L hard
				Mechanically formed				
				Braze	Wrought or cast Cu		100	370 Type K soft
				Weld				250 Type L soft
	0.375 to 4.125	Copper, hard	ACR	Solder	Wrought or cast Cu		100	500 Type ACR hard
				Braze	Wrought or cast Cu		100	290 Type ACR Soft
	0.375 to 1.0	PEX	SDR-9	Crimp	Bronze		73	145
				Clamp	Brass			
				Expansion	Copper			
				Compression	Engineered plastic			
				Push fit				
				Proprietary				
	0.5 to 6	PE	Schedule 40, 80, SDR	Thermal fusion, compression	PE		120 (140 limit for some applications)	Depends on pipe, grade, schedule, size. Generally 30 to 110 at 130°F
	0.5 to 6	HDPE	SDR	Thermal fusion, compression	HDPE		120	Depends on pipe, grade, schedule, size. Generally 64 for SDR 11 at 120°F
Fuel oil, aboveground	2 to 12	Black Steel, B Type E (ERW) or S (seamless)	Schedule 40	Thread or weld	Black malleable iron	150		
					Wrought steel weld			
					Forged steel flanges	150		
	0.25 to 12	Copper, hard or soft	Type K or L	Solder	Wrought or cast Cu		100	300 Type K soft
				Flared (soft)				635 Type K hard
				Rolled groove (2 to 8 in.)				250 Type L soft
				Press-connect (0.5 to 4 in.)				435 Type L hard
				Push connect (0.5 to 2 in.)				
				Mechanical formed				
				Braze or weld	Wrought or cast Cu		100	300 Type K soft, 250 Type L soft
		Copper, hard	Type M	Solder	Wrought or cast Cu		100	395 Type M hard
				Braze				
				Rolled groove (2 to 8 in.)				
				Press-connect (0.5 to 4 in.)				
				Push connect (0.5 to 2 in.)				
				Mechanical formed				
	0.25 to 12	ABS	Schedule 40,[f] 80, SDR	Solvent weld, thread, flange	ABS		160 limit	Depends on pipe class: approximately 50 at 160°F
	0.5 to 6	HDPE	SDR-9	Thermal fusion, compression	HDPE		120	Depends on pipe, grade, schedule, size. Generally 64 for SDR 11 at 120°F
Compressed air	≤2.5 and smaller	Black steel	Schedule 40	Thread	Black malleable iron	150	350	
	>2.5	Black steel	Schedule 40	Flange or weld	Black malleable iron	150	350	
	0.375 to 4.125	Copper, hard	ACR	Solder	Wrought or cast Cu		200	240 ACR soft
				Flared (soft)				500 ACR hard
				Mechanical formed				
				Braze			200	240 ACR hard
	0.5 to 4	ABS	Schedule 40	Solvent weld	ABS		73	185
		HDPE	Schedule 40, 80, SDR		HDPE			

Table 1 Common Applications of Pipe, Fittings, and Valves for Heating and Air Conditioning (*Continued*)

Application	Size, in.	Material	Weight	Joint Type	Fitting Material	Class (When Applicable)	System[g] Temperature, °F	Maximum Pressure at Temperature,[a,b] psi
	0.375 to 1.0	PEX	SDR-9					
Potable water, inside building	0.25 to 12	Steel, galvanized	Schedule 40	Thread	Galv. cast iron	150	100	125
					Galv. cast iron	150	100	150
		Copper, hard or soft	Type K or L	Solder[c]	Wrought or cast Cu		100	370 Type K soft
				Flared (soft)				635 Type K hard
				Rolled groove (2 to 8 in.)				250 Type L soft
				Press-connect (0.5 to 4 in.)				435 Type L hard
				Push connect (0.5 to 2 in.)				
				Mechanical formed				
				Braze	Wrought or cast Cu		100	370 Type K soft
				Weld				250 Type L soft
	0.25 to 12	Copper, hard	Type M	Solder[c]	Wrought or cast Cu		100	395 Type M hard
				Rolled groove (2 to 8 in.)				
				Press-connect (0.5 to 4 in.)				
				Push connect (0.5 to 2 in.)				
				Mechanical formed				
				Braze	Wrought or cast Cu		100	230 Type M soft
				Weld				
	0.5 to 8	CPVC	Schedule 40,[f] 80		CPVC		210 Limit, 200 operating	
	0.375 to 1.0	PEX	SDR-9	Crimp	Bronze		100	145
				Clamp	Brass			
				Expansion	Copper			
				Compression	Engineered plastic			
				Push fit				
				Proprietary				
	0.5 to 6	PE	Schedule 40,[f] 80, SDR	Thermal fusion, compression	PE		120 (140 limit for some applications)	Depends on pipe, grade, schedule, size generally 30 to 110 at 130°F
	0.5 to 6	PP	Schedule 40,[f] 80, SDR	Thermal fusion, flange, Thread[e]	PP		180	50
Water services, underground	Through 6	Ductile iron	Class 50	Mechanical joint	Cast iron		75	250
	0.25 to 12	Copper, hard or soft	Type K or L	Solder[c]	Wrought or cast Cu		100	370 Type K soft
				Flared (soft)				635 Type K hard
				Rolled groove (2 to 8 in.)				250 Type L soft
				Press-connect (0.5 to 4 in.)				435 Type L hard
				Push connect (0.5 to 2 in.)				
				Mechanical formed				
				Braze	Wrought or cast Cu		100	370 Type K soft
				Weld				250 Type L soft
				Flange	Bronze		100	
	0.25 to 12	Copper, hard	Type M	Solder[c]	Wrought or cast Cu		100	395 Type K hard
				Rolled groove (2 to 8 in.)				
				Press-connect (0.5 to 4 in.)				
				Push connect (0.5 to 2 in.)				
				Mechanical formed				
				Braze	Wrought or cast Cu		100	230 Type M soft
				Weld				
	0.375 to 1.0	PEX	SDR-9	Crimp	Bronze		73	145
				Clamp	Brass			
				Expansion	Copper			
				Compression	Engineered plastic			
				Push fit				
				Proprietary				
	0.25 to 20	PVC	Schedule 40, 80, 120, SDR	Solvent weld, thread,[f] thermal weld	PVC		150 limit, 140 operating	79 to 105, depending on schedule and size
Drainage, waste, and vent (DWV)	1.25 to 8	Copper, hard	DWV	Solder	Wrought or cast Cu		100	250 DWV hard
	1.25 to 12	ABS	Schedule DWV, 40,[f] 80, SDR	Solvent weld, thread, flange	ABS		160 limit	Depends on pipe class: approximately 50 at 160°F
	1.25 to 20	PV	Schedule 40,[f] 80, 120, SDR	Solvent weld, thread, thermal weld	PVC		150 limit, 140 operating	79 to 105, depending on schedule and size

[a]Maximum allowable working pressures have been derated in this table. Higher system pressures can be used for lower temperatures and smaller pipe sizes. Pipe, fittings, joints, and valves must all be considered.

[b]Temperature and pressure relationships can vary based on pipe material composition, size, class, and schedule.

[c]Lead- and antimony-based solders are prohibited for potable water systems. Brazing should be used.

[d]Piping codes typically require thicker-walled pipe for threaded joints to maintain corrosion allowance and pressure ratings.

[e]All plumbing codes require both hot and cold water piping to have a 100 psi at 180°F rating.

[f]Threads are not recommended on Schedule 40 plastic pipe.

[g]Designer should confirm that all materials are suitably rated for intended operation.

Table 2 Manufacturers' Recommendations[a,b] for Plastic Materials

	PVC	CPVC	HDPE	PEX	PP	ABS	PVDF	RTRP
Cold-water service	R	R	R	R	R	R	R	R
Hot (140°F) water	N	R	R	R	R	R	R	R
Potable-water service	R	R	R	R	R	R	R	R
Drain, waste, and vent (DWV)	R	R	—	—	R	R	—	—
Demineralized water	R	R	—	—	R	R	R	—
Deionized water	R	R	—	—	R	R	R	R
Salt water	R	R	R	R	R	R	—	R
Heating (200°F) hot water	N	N	N	N	N	N	—	R
Natural gas	N	N	R	R	N	N	—	—
Compressed air	N	N	R	R	N	R	—	—
Sunlight and weather resistance	N	N	R	R	—	R	R	R
Underground service	R	R	R	R	R	R	—	R
Food handling	R	R	—	—	R	R	R	R

R = Recommended
N = Not recommended
— = Insufficient information

[a]Before selecting material, check availability of suitable range of sizes and fittings and of satisfactory joining method. Also have manufacturer verify the best material for purpose intended.
[b]Consult local building codes for compliance of materials listed.

considered; the lowest rating establishes the operating limits of the system.

Nonmetallic (Plastic) Pipe Systems

Nonmetallic pipe is used in HVAC and plumbing. Plastic is light, generally inexpensive, and corrosion resistant. Plastic also has a low "C" factor (i.e., its surface is very smooth), resulting in lower pumping power requirements and smaller pipe sizes. Plastic pipe's disadvantages include rapid loss of strength at temperatures above ambient and a high coefficient of linear expansion. The modulus of elasticity of plastics is low, resulting in a short support span. Some jurisdictions do not allow certain plastics in buildings because of toxic products emitted during fires. Plenum-rated plastic and insulation may be used to achieve a plenum rating; check with the authority having jurisdiction (AHJ).

Table 2 lists nonmetallic materials used for service water and heating and air-conditioning piping. The pressure and temperature rating of each component selected must be considered; the lowest rating establishes the operating limits of the system.

Special Systems

Some piping systems are governed by separate codes or standards. Generally, any failure of the piping in these systems is dangerous to the public, so some local areas have adopted laws enforcing the codes, such as the following:

- **Boiler piping:** ASME *Standard* B31.1 and the ASME *Boiler and Pressure Vessel Code* (Section I) specify piping inside code-required stop valves on boilers that operate above 15 psig with steam, or above 160 psig or 250°F with water. These codes require fabricators and contractors to be certified for such work. The field or shop work must also be inspected while it is in progress, by inspectors commissioned by the National Board of Boiler and Pressure Vessel Inspectors.
- **Refrigeration piping:** ASHRAE *Standard* 15 and ASME *Standard* B31.5.
- **Plumbing systems:** Local codes.
- **Sprinkler systems:** NFPA *Standard* 13.
- **Fuel gas:** NFPA *Standard* 54/ANSI *Standard* Z223.1.

1.4 DESIGN EQUATIONS

Darcy-Weisbach Equation

Pressure drop caused by fluid friction in fully developed flows of all well-behaved (Newtonian) fluids is described by the Darcy-Weisbach equation:

$$\Delta p = f\left(\frac{L}{D}\right)\left(\frac{\rho}{g_c}\right)\left(\frac{V^2}{2}\right) \qquad (1)$$

where

Δp = pressure drop, lb_f/ft^2
f = friction factor, dimensionless (from Moody chart, Figure 13 in Chapter 3)
L = length of pipe, ft
D = internal diameter of pipe, ft
ρ = fluid density at mean temperature, lb_m/ft^3
V = average velocity, fps
g_c = units conversion factor, 32.2 $ft \cdot lb_m/lb_f \cdot s^2$

This equation is often presented in head or specific energy form as

$$\Delta h = \left(\frac{\Delta p}{\rho}\right)\left(\frac{g_c}{g}\right) = f\left(\frac{L}{D}\right)\left(\frac{V^2}{2g}\right) \qquad (2)$$

where

Δh = head loss, ft
g = acceleration of gravity, ft/s^2

In this form, the fluid's density does not appear explicitly (although it is in the Reynolds number that influences f).

The friction factor f is a function of pipe roughness ε, inside diameter D, and parameter Re, the Reynolds number:

$$\text{Re} = DV\varepsilon/\mu \qquad (3)$$

where

Re = Reynolds number, dimensionless
ε = absolute roughness of pipe wall, ft
μ = dynamic viscosity of fluid, $lb_m/ft \cdot s$

The friction factor is frequently presented on a Moody chart (Figure 13 in Chapter 3) giving f as a function of Re with ε/D as a parameter.

A useful fit of smooth and rough pipe data for the usual turbulent flow regime is the **Colebrook** equation:

$$\frac{1}{\sqrt{f}} = 1.74 - 2\log\left(\frac{2\varepsilon}{D} + \frac{18.7}{\text{Re}\sqrt{f}}\right) \qquad (4)$$

Another form of Equation (4) appears in Chapter 21, but the two are equivalent. Equation (4) is useful in showing behavior at limiting cases: as ε/D approaches 0 (smooth limit), the $18.7/\text{Re}\sqrt{f}$ term

Table 3 *K* Factors: Threaded Steel Pipe Fittings

Nominal Pipe Dia., in.	90° Standard Elbow	90° Long-Radius Elbow	45° Elbow	Return Bend	Tee-Line	Tee-Branch	Globe Valve	Gate Valve	Angle Valve	Swing Check Valve	Bell Mouth Inlet	Square Inlet	Projected Inlet
3/8	2.5	—	0.38	2.5	0.90	2.7	20	0.40	—	8.0	0.05	0.5	1.0
1/2	2.1	—	0.37	2.1	0.90	2.4	14	0.33	—	5.5	0.05	0.5	1.0
3/4	1.7	0.92	0.35	1.7	0.90	2.1	10	0.28	6.1	3.7	0.05	0.5	1.0
1	1.5	0.78	0.34	1.5	0.90	1.8	9	0.24	4.6	3.0	0.05	0.5	1.0
1 1/4	1.3	0.65	0.33	1.3	0.90	1.7	8.5	0.22	3.6	2.7	0.05	0.5	1.0
1 1/2	1.2	0.54	0.32	1.2	0.90	1.6	8	0.19	2.9	2.5	0.05	0.5	1.0
2	1.0	0.42	0.31	1.0	0.90	1.4	7	0.17	2.1	2.3	0.05	0.5	1.0
2 1/2	0.85	0.35	0.30	0.85	0.90	1.3	6.5	0.16	1.6	2.2	0.05	0.5	1.0
3	0.80	0.31	0.29	0.80	0.90	1.2	6	0.14	1.3	2.1	0.05	0.5	1.0
4	0.70	0.24	0.28	0.70	0.90	1.1	5.7	0.12	1.0	2.0	0.05	0.5	1.0

Source: *Engineering Data Book* (Hydraulic Institute 1990).

Table 4 *K* Factors: Flanged Welded Steel Pipe Fittings

Nominal Pipe Dia., in.	90° Standard Elbow	90° Long-Radius Elbow	45° Long-Radius Elbow	Return Bend Standard	Return Bend Long-Radius	Tee-Line	Tee-Branch	Globe Valve	Gate Valve	Angle Valve	Swing Check Valve
1	0.43	0.41	0.22	0.43	0.43	0.26	1.0	13	—	4.8	2.0
1 1/4	0.41	0.37	0.22	0.41	0.38	0.25	0.95	12	—	3.7	2.0
1 1/2	0.40	0.35	0.21	0.40	0.35	0.23	0.90	10	—	3.0	2.0
2	0.38	0.30	0.20	0.38	0.30	0.20	0.84	9	0.34	2.5	2.0
2 1/2	0.35	0.28	0.19	0.35	0.27	0.18	0.79	8	0.27	2.3	2.0
3	0.34	0.25	0.18	0.34	0.25	0.17	0.76	7	0.22	2.2	2.0
4	0.31	0.22	0.18	0.31	0.22	0.15	0.70	6.5	0.16	2.1	2.0
6	0.29	0.18	0.17	0.29	0.18	0.12	0.62	6	0.10	2.1	2.0
8	0.27	0.16	0.17	0.27	0.15	0.10	0.58	5.7	0.08	2.1	2.0
10	0.25	0.14	0.16	0.25	0.14	0.09	0.53	5.7	0.06	2.1	2.0
12	0.24	0.13	0.16	0.24	0.13	0.08	0.50	5.7	0.05	2.1	2.0

Source: *Engineering Data Book* (Hydraulic Institute 1990).

dominates; at high ε/D and Re (fully rough limit), the $2\varepsilon/D$ term dominates.

Equation (4) is implicit in f; that is, f appears on both sides, so a value for f is usually obtained iteratively.

Hazen-Williams Equation

A less widely used alternative to the Darcy-Weisbach formulation for calculating pressure drop is the Hazen-Williams equation, which is expressed as

$$\Delta p = 3.022L\left(\frac{V}{C}\right)^{1.852}\left(\frac{1}{D}\right)^{1.167}\left(\frac{\rho g}{g_c}\right) \tag{5}$$

or

$$\Delta h = 3.022L\left(\frac{V}{C}\right)^{1.852}\left(\frac{1}{D}\right)^{1.167} \tag{6}$$

where C = roughness factor.

Typical values of C are 150 for plastic pipe and copper tubing, 140 for new steel pipe, down to 100 and below for badly corroded or very rough pipe.

Valve and Fitting Losses

Valves and fittings cause pressure losses greater than those caused by the pipe alone. One formulation expresses losses as

$$\Delta p = K\left(\frac{\rho}{g_c}\right)\left(\frac{V^2}{2}\right) \quad \text{or} \quad \Delta h = K\left(\frac{V^2}{2g}\right) \tag{7}$$

where K = geometry- and size-dependent loss coefficient (Tables 3 to 6).

Example 1. Determine the pressure drop for 60°F water flowing at 4 fps through a nominal 1 in., 90° threaded elbow.

Solution: Use Equation (7). From Table 3, the K for a 1 in., 90° threaded elbow is 1.5.

$$\Delta p = 1.5 \times 62.4/32.2 \times 4^2/2 = 23.3 \text{ lb/ft}^2 \text{ or } 0.16 \text{ psi}$$

The loss coefficient for valves appears in another form as C_v, a dimensional coefficient expressing the flow through a valve at a specified pressure drop.

$$Q = C_v\sqrt{\Delta p} \tag{8}$$

where

Q = volumetric flow, gpm
C_v = valve coefficient, gpm at Δp = 1 psi
Δp = pressure drop, psi

See the section on Control Valve Sizing in Chapter 47 of the 2016 *ASHRAE Handbook—HVAC Systems and Equipment* for more information on valve coefficients.

Example 2. Determine the volumetric flow through a valve with C_v = 10 for an allowable pressure drop of 5 psi.

Solution: Use Equation (8).

$$Q = 10\sqrt{5} = 22.4 \text{ gpm}$$

Alternative formulations express fitting losses in terms of equivalent lengths of straight pipe (see Tables 8 and 27). Pressure loss data for fittings are also presented in Idelchik (1986).

Equation (7) and data in Tables 3 and 4 are based on the assumption that separated flow in the fitting causes the K factors to be independent of Reynolds number. In reality, the K factor for most pipe fittings

Table 5 Approximate Range of Variation for *K* Factors of Steel Fittings

90° Elbow	Regular threaded	±20% above 2 in.	Tee	Threaded, line or branch	±25%
		±40% below 2 in.		Flanged, line or branch	±35%
	Long-radius threaded	±25%	Globe valve	Threaded	±25%
	Regular flanged	±35%		Flanged	±25%
	Long-radius flanged	±30%	Gate valve	Threaded	±25%
45° Elbow	Regular threaded	±10%		Flanged	±50%
	Long-radius flanged	±10%	Angle valve	Threaded	±20%
Return bend (180°)	Regular threaded	±25%		Flanged	±50%
	Regular flanged	±35%	Check valve	Threaded	±50%
	Long-radius flanged	±30%		Flanged	+200% –80%

Source: *Engineering Data Book* (Hydraulic Institute 1990).

Table 6 Summary of *K* Values for Steel Ells, Reducers, and Expansions

		ASHRAE Research[b,c]		
	Past[a]	**4 fps**	**8 fps**	**12 fps**
2 in. S.R.[e] ell (R/D = 1) thread	0.60 to 1.0 (1.0)[d]	0.60	0.68	0.736
4 in. S.R. ell (R/D = 1) weld	0.30 to 0.34	0.37	0.34	0.33
1 in. L.R. ell (R/D = 1.5) weld	to 1.0	—	—	—
2 in. L.R. ell (R/D = 1.5) weld	0.50 to 0.7	—	—	—
4 in. L.R. ell (R/D = 1.5) weld	0.22 to 0.33 (0.22)[d]	0.26	0.24	0.23
6 in. L.R. ell (R/D = 1.5) weld	0.25	0.26	0.24	0.24
8 in. L.R. ell (R/D = 1.5) weld	0.20 to 0.26	0.22	0.20	0.19
10 in. L.R. ell (R/D = 1.5) weld	0.17	0.21	0.17	0.16
12 in. L.R. ell (R/D = 1.5) weld	0.16	0.17	0.17	0.17
16 in. L.R. ell (R/D = 1.5) weld	0.12	0.12	0.12	0.11
20 in. L.R. ell (R/D = 1.5) weld	0.09	0.12	0.10	0.10
24 in. L.R. ell (R/D = 1.5) weld	0.07	0.098	0.089	0.089
Reducer (2 by 1.5 in.) thread	—	0.53	0.28	0.20
(4 by 3 in.) weld	0.22	0.23	0.14	0.10
(6 by 4 in.) weld		0.62	0.54	0.53
(8 by 6 in.) weld		0.31	0.28	0.26
(10 by 8 in.) weld		0.16	0.14	0.14
(12 by 10 in.) weld	—	0.14	0.14	0.14
(16 by 12 in.) weld	—	0.17	0.16	0.17
(20 by 16 in.) weld	—	0.16	0.13	0.13
(24 by 20 in.) weld	—	0.053	0.053	0.055
Expansion (1.5 by 2 in.) thread	—	0.16	0.13	0.02
(3 by 4 in.) weld	—	0.11	0.11	0.11
(4 by 6 in.) weld	—	0.28	0.28	0.29
(6 by 8 in.) weld	—	0.15	0.12	0.11
(8 by 10 in.) weld	—	0.11	0.09	0.08
(10 by 12 in.) weld	—	0.11	0.11	0.11
(12 by 16 in.) weld	—	0.073	0.076	0.073
(16 by 20 in.) weld	—	0.024	0.021	0.022
(20 by 24 in.) weld	—	0.020	0.023	0.020

Source: Rahmeyer (2003a).
[a]Published data by Crane Co. (1988), Freeman (1941), and Hydraulic Institute (1990).
[b]Rahmeyer (1999a, 2002a).
[c]Ding et al. (2005)
[d]( ) Data published in 1993 *ASHRAE Handbook—Fundamentals*.
[e]S.R.—short radius or regular ell; L.R.—long-radius ell.

varies with Reynolds number. Tests by Rahmeyer (1999a, 1999b, 2002a, 2002b) (ASHRAE research projects RP-968 and RP-1034) on 2 in. threaded and 4, 12, 16, 20, and 24 in. welded steel fittings demonstrate the variation and are shown in Tables 6 and 7. The studies also present *K* factors of diverting and mixing flows in tees, ranging from full through flow to full branch flow. They also examined the variation in *K* factors caused by variations in geometry among manufacturers and by surface defects in individual fittings.

Hegberg (1995) and Rahmeyer (1999a, 1999b) discuss the origins of some of the data shown in Tables 6 and 7. The Hydraulic Institute (1990) data appear to have come from Freeman (1941), work that was actually performed in 1895. The work of Giesecke (1926) and Giesecke and Badgett (1931, 1932a, 1932b) may not be representative of present-day fittings.

Further extending the work on determination of fitting *K* factors to PVC piping systems, Rahmeyer (2003a, 2003b) (ASHRAE research project RP-1193) found the data in Tables 8 and 9 giving *K* factors for Schedule 80 PVC 2, 4, 6, and 8 in. ells, reducers, expansions, and tees. The results of these tests are also presented in the cited papers in terms of equivalent lengths. In general, PVC fitting geometry varied much more from one manufacturer to another than steel fittings did.

Table 7 Summary of Test Data for Loss Coefficients *K* for Steel Pipe Tees

		ASHRAE Research[b,c]		
	Past[a]	4 fps	8 fps	12 fps
2 in. thread tee, 100% branch	1.20 to 1.80 (1.4)[d]	0.93	—	—
100% line (flow-through)	0.50 to 0.90 (0.90)[d]	0.19	—	—
100% mix	—	1.19	—	
4 in. weld tee, 100% branch	0.70 to 1.02 (0.70)[d]	—	0.57	—
100% line (flow-through)	0.15 to 0.34 (0.15)[d]	—	0.06	—
100% mix	—	—	0.49	—
6 in. weld tee, 100% branch	—	—	0.56	—
100% line (flow-through)	—	—	0.12	—
100% mix	—	—	0.88	—
8 in. weld tee, 100% branch	—	—	0.53	—
100% line (flow-through)	—	—	0.08	—
100% mix	—	—	0.70	—
10 in. weld tee, 100% branch	—	—	0.52	—
100% line (flow-through)	—	—	0.06	—
100% mix	—	—	0.77	—
12 in. weld tee, 100% branch	0.52	0.70	0.63	0.62
100% line (flow-through)	0.09	0.062	0.091	0.096
100% mix	—	0.88	0.72	0.72
16 in. weld tee, 100% branch	0.47	0.54	0.55	0.54
100% line (flow-through)	0.07	0.032	0.028	0.028
100% mix	—	0.74	0.74	0.76

[a]Published data by Crane Co. (1988), Freeman (1941), and Hydraulic Institute (1990).
[b]Rahmeyer (1999b, 2002b).
[c]Ding et al. (2005).
[d]Data published in 1993 *ASHRAE Handbook—Fundamentals*.

Table 8 Test Summary for Loss Coefficients *K* and Equivalent Loss Lengths

Schedule 80 PVC Fitting		*K*	*L*, ft
Injected molded elbow,	2 in.	0.91 to 1.00	8.4 to 9.2
	4 in.	0.86 to 0.91	18.3 to 19.3
	6 in.	0.76 to 0.91	26.2 to 31.3
	8 in.	0.68 to 0.87	32.9 to 42.1
8 in. fabricated elbow, Type I, components		0.40 to 0.42	19.4 to 20.3
Type II, mitered		0.073 to 0.76	35.3 to 36.8
6 by 4 in. injected molded reducer		0.12 to 0.59	4.1 to 20.3
Bushing type		0.49 to 0.59	16.9 to 20.3
8 by 6 in. injected molded reducer		0.13 to 0.63	6.3 to 30.5
Bushing type		0.48 to 0.68	23.2 to 32.9
Gradual reducer type		0.21	10.2
4 by 6 in. injected molded expansion		0.069 to 1.19	1.5 to 25.3
Bushing type		0.069 to 1.14	1.5 to 24.2
6 by 8 in. injected molded expansion		0.95 to 0.96	32.7 to 33.0
Bushing type		0.94 to 0.95	32.4 to 32.7
Gradual reducer type		0.99	34.1

Losses in Multiple Fittings

Typical fitting loss calculations are done as if each fitting is isolated and has no interaction with any other. Rahmeyer (2002c) (ASHRAE research project RP-1035) tested 2 in. threaded ells and 4 in. ells in two and three fitting assemblies of several geometries, at varying spacing. Figure 1 shows the geometries, and Figures 2 and 3 show the ratio of coupled *K* values to uncoupled *K* values (i.e., fitting losses for the assembly compared with the sum of losses from the same number of isolated fittings).

The most important conclusion is that the interaction between fittings always reduces the loss. Also, although geometry of the assembly has a definite effect, the effects are not the same for 2 in. threaded and 4 in. welded ells. Thus, the traditional practice of adding together losses from individual fittings gives a conservative (high-limit) estimate.

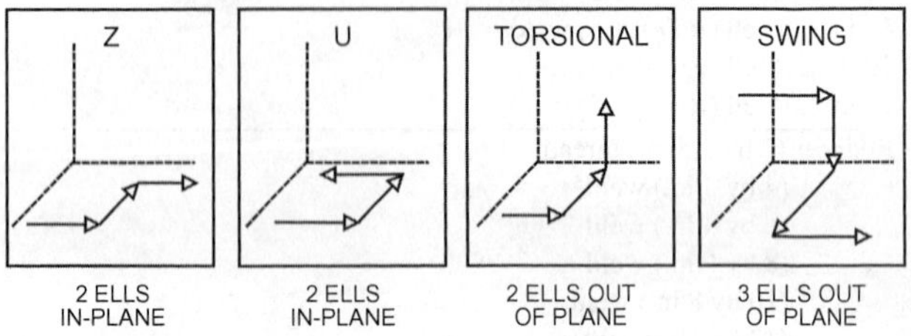

Fig. 1 Close-Coupled Test Configurations

Calculating Pressure Losses

The most common engineering design flow loss calculation selects a pipe size for the desired total flow rate and available or allowable pressure drop.

Because either formulation of fitting losses requires a known diameter, pipe size must be selected before calculating the detailed influence of fittings. A frequently used rule of thumb assumes that the design length of pipe is 50 to 100% longer than actual to account for fitting losses. After a pipe diameter has been selected on this basis, the influence of each fitting can be evaluated.

Stress Calculations

Metallic Pipe. Although stress calculations are seldom required, the factors involved should be understood. The main areas of concern are (1) internal pressure stress, (2) longitudinal stress caused by pressure and weight, and (3) stress from expansion and contraction.

ASME *Standard* B31 standards establish a basic allowable stress *S* equal to one-fourth of the minimum tensile strength of the material. This value is adjusted, as discussed in this section, because of the nature of certain stresses and manufacturing processes.

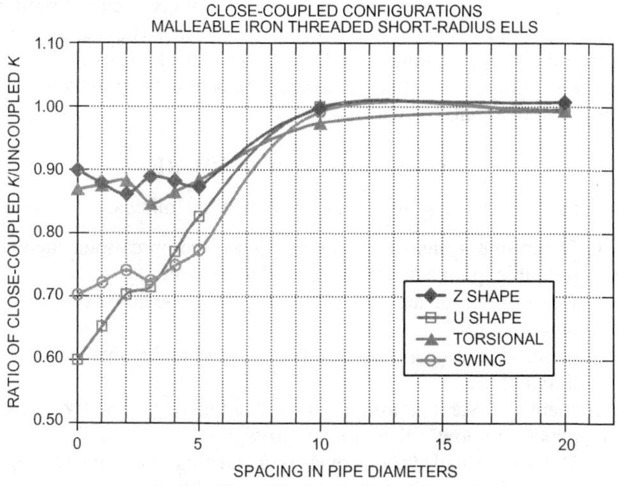

Fig. 2 Summary Plot of Effect of Close-Coupled Configurations for 2 in. Ells

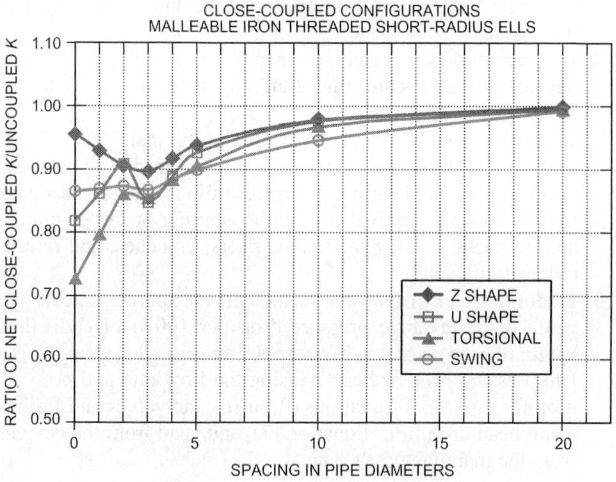

Fig. 3 Summary Plot of Effect of Close-Coupled Configurations for 4 in. Ells

Hoop stress caused by internal pressure is the major stress on pipes. Because some forming methods form a seam that may be weaker than the base material, ASME *Standard* B31.9 specifies a joint efficiency factor E, multiplied by the basic allowable stress to establish a maximum allowable stress value in tension S_E. (Table A-1 in ASME *Standard* B31.9 lists values of S_E for commonly used pipe materials.) The joint efficiency factor can be significant; for example, seamless pipe has a joint efficiency factor of 1, so it can be used to the full allowable stress (one-quarter of the tensile strength). In contrast, butt-welded pipe has a joint efficiency factor of 0.60, so its maximum allowable stress must be derated ($S_E = 0.6S$).

Equation (9) determines the minimum wall thickness for a given pressure. Equation (10) determines the maximum pressure allowed for a given wall thickness.

$$t_m = \frac{pD}{2S_E} + A \qquad (9)$$

$$p = \frac{2S_E(t_m - A)}{D} \qquad (10)$$

Table 9 Test Summary for Loss Coefficients *K* of PVC Tees

Branching		
Schedule 80 PVC Fitting	$K_{1\text{-}2}$	$K_{1\text{-}3}$
2 in. injection molded branching tee, 100% line flow	0.13 to 0.26	—
50/50 flow	0 to 0.12	0.74 to 1.02
100% branch flow	—	0.98 to 1.39
4 in. injection molded branching tee, 100% line flow	0.07 to 0.22	—
50/50 flow	0.03 to 0.13	0.74 to 0.82
100% branch flow	—	0.97 to 1.12
6 in. injection molded branching tee, 100% line flow	0.01 to 0.14	—
50/50 flow	0.06 to 0.11	0.70 to 0.84
100% branch flow	—	0.95 to 1.15
6 in. fabricated branching tee, 100% line flow	0.21 to 0.22	—
50/50 flow	0.04 to 0.09	1.29 to 1.40
100% branch flow	—	1.74 to 1.88
8 in. injection molded branching tee, 100% line flow	0.04 to 0.09	—
50/50 flow	0.04 to 0.07	0.64 to 0.75
100% branch flow	—	0.85 to 0.96
8 in. fabricated branching tee, 100% line flow	0.09 to 0.16	—
50/50 flow	0.08 to 0.13	1.07 to 1.16
100% branch flow	—	1.40 to 1.62
Mixing		
PVC Fitting	$K_{1\text{-}2}$	$K_{3\text{-}2}$
2 in. injection molded mixing tee, 100% line flow	0.12 to 0.25	—
50/50 flow	1.22 to 1.19	0.89 to 1.88
100% mix flow	—	0.89 to 1.54
4 in. injection molded mixing tee, 100% line flow	0.07 to 0.18	—
50/50 flow	1.19 to 1.88	0.98 to 1.88
100% mix flow	—	0.88 to 1.02
6 in. injection molded mixing tee, 100% line flow	0.06 to 0.14	—
50/50 flow	1.26 to 1.80	1.02 to 1.60
100% mix flow	—	0.90 to 1.07
6 in. fabricated mixing tee, 100% line flow	0.19 to 0.21	—
50/50 flow	2.94 to 3.32	2.57 to 3.17
100% mix flow	—	1.72 to 1.98
8 in. injection molded mixing tee, 100% line flow	0.04 to 0.09	—
50/50 flow	1.10 to 1.60	0.96 to 1.32
100% mix flow	—	0.81 to 0.93
8 in. fabricated mixing tee, 100% line flow	0.13 to 0.70	—
50/50 flow	2.36 to 10.62	2.02 to 2.67
100% mix flow	—	1.34 to 1.53

Coefficients based on average velocity of 8 fps. Range of values varies with fitting manufacturers. Line or straight flow is Q_2/Q_1 = 100%. Branch flow is Q_2/Q_1 = 0%.

where

S_A = allowable stress range, psi
S_c = allowable cold stress at coolest temperature system will experience, psi
S_h = allowable hot stress at hottest temperature system will experience, psi

Both equations incorporate an allowance factor A to compensate for manufacturing tolerances, material removed in threading or grooving, and corrosion. For the seamless, butt-welded, and electric resistance welded (ERW) pipe most commonly used in HVAC work, the standards apply a manufacturing tolerance of 12.5%. Working pressure for steel pipe (see Table 16) has been calculated using a manufacturing tolerance of 12.5%, standard allowance for depth of thread (where applicable), and a corrosion allowance of 0.065 in. for pipes 2 1/2 in. and larger and 0.025 in. for pipes 2 in.

and smaller. Where corrosion is known to be greater or smaller, pressure rating can be recalculated using Equation (10). Higher pressure ratings than shown in Table 16 can be obtained (1) by using ERW or seamless pipe in lieu of continuous-weld (CW) pipe 4 in. and less, and seamless pipe in lieu of ERW pipe 5 in. and greater (because of higher joint efficiency factors); or (2) by using heavier-wall pipe.

Longitudinal stresses caused by pressure, weight, and other sustained forces are additive, and the sum of all such stresses must not exceed the basic allowable stress S at the highest temperature at which the system will operate. Longitudinal stress caused by pressure equals approximately one-half the hoop stress caused by internal pressure; thus, at least one-half the basic allowable stress is available for weight and other sustained forces. This factor is taken into account in Table 11.

Stresses caused by expansion and contraction are cyclical, and, because creep allows some stress relaxation, the ASME *Standard* B31 series allows designing to an allowable stress range S_A as calculated by Equation (11). Table 15 lists allowable stress ranges for commonly used piping materials.

$$S_A = 1.25S_c + 0.25S_h \tag{11}$$

where

S_A = allowable stress range, psi
S_c = allowable cold stress at coolest temperature system will experience, psi
S_h = allowable hot stress at hottest temperature system will experience, psi

Nonmetallic. Both thermoplastics and thermosets have an allowable stress derived from a **hydrostatic design basis stress (HDBS)**. The HDBS is determined by a statistical analysis of both static and cyclic stress rupture test data as set forth in ASTM *Standard* D2837 for thermoplastics and ASTM *Standard* D2992 for glass-fiber-reinforced thermosetting resins.

The allowable stress, called the **hydrostatic design stress (HDS)**, is obtained by multiplying the HDBS by a service factor. HDS values recommended by some manufacturers and those allowed by ASME *Standard* B31 are listed in Table 18.

The pressure design thickness for plastic pipe can be calculated using the code stress values and the formula in Equation (12):

$$t = pD/(2S + p) \tag{12}$$

where

t = pressure design thickness, in.
p = internal design pressure, psig
D = pipe outside diameter, in.
S = hydrostatic design stress (HDS), psi

The minimum required wall thickness can be found by adding an allowance for mechanical strength, threading, grooving, erosion, and corrosion to the calculated pressure design thickness.

Another method of rating pressure rating of piping used by manufacturers is the **standard dimension ratio (SDR)**, which is the ratio of the pipe diameter to the wall thickness:

$$\text{SDR} = D/s \tag{13}$$

where

D = pipe outside diameter, in.
s = pipe wall thickness, in.

An SDR of 11 means that the outside diameter D of the pipe is 11 times the thickness of the wall s. A high SDR means that the pipe's wall is thin compared to its diameter, and a low SDR means that the pipe's wall is thick relative to pipe diameter. SDR is inversely correlated with pressure rating: high SDR indicates a low pressure rating, whereas low-SDR pipes have higher pressure ratings.

There are many formulations of the polymers used for piping materials, and different joining methods for each, so manufacturers' recommendations should be followed. Most catalogs give pressure ratings for pipe and fittings at various temperatures up to the maximum the material will withstand.

1.5 SIZING PROCEDURE

A procedure for sizing piping systems is as follows:

1. Determine system type (open, closed, compressible, incompressible, pumped, gravity feed, domestic, etc.).
2. Determine type and properties of fluid to be conveyed in the pipe.
3. Determine temperatures used (high, low) and temperature differentials.
4. Identify system pressures encountered in the system (working, maximum, low, fill, and relief pressures).
5. Determine load at each device (e.g., heating or cooling requirements, fixture units for plumbing) to find flow.
6. Sketch main, risers, and branches, and indicate equipment to be served and each device's flow rate.
7. Determine flow of supply pipe for each pipe segment run by summing the loads at the furthest device and running back to the source.
8. Determine flow of each return pipe by starting at the first device returning water and summing the loads back to the source (when applicable).
9. Determine equivalent length of pipe in the main lines, risers, branches, and returns. Because pipe sizes are not known, the exact equivalent length of various fittings cannot be determined. Add the equivalent lengths, starting at the beginning and proceeding along the mains, risers, branches, and returns (when applicable).
10. **In domestic or gravity feed:** calculate the approximate design value of the average pressure drop per 100 ft of equivalent length of pipe determined in step 9. **In pumped system:** calculate pressure drop or head H using the flow rate and pressure drop for pipe from Equations (2) or (6), the valves and fittings using head drop from Equation (7), and head from the devices from the manufacturer's data.

$$\Delta p = (p_s - 0.434H - p_f - p_m)100/L \tag{14}$$

where

Δp = average pressure loss per 100 ft of equivalent length of pipe, psi
p_s = pressure at the source, psig
p_f = minimum pressure required to operate device, psig
p_m = pressure drop through any meters, psi
H = height of highest fixture above source (if open system), ft
L = equivalent length determined in step 4, ft

11. **In domestic or gravity system:** from the expected rate of flow (step 5) and Δp (step 10), select pipe sizes. **In pumped system:** select the pump using the flow rate and calculated H.

1.6 PIPE-SUPPORTING ELEMENTS

Pipe-supporting elements consist of (1) hangers, which support from above; (2) supports, which bear load from below; and (3) restraints, such as anchors and guides, that limit or direct movement as well as support loads. Pipe-supporting elements must withstand all static and dynamic conditions, including the following:

- Weight of pipe, valves, fittings, insulation, and fluid contents, including test fluid if using heavier-than-normal media
- Occasional loads such as ice, wind, and seismic forces or testing loads (e.g., hydrostatic loads on a steam pipe)

Table 10 Capacities of ASTM A36 Steel Threaded Rods

Rod Diameter, in.	Root Area of Coarse Thread, in^2	Maximum Load,* lb
1/4	0.027	240
3/8	0.068	610
1/2	0.126	1130
5/8	0.202	1810
3/4	0.302	2710
7/8	0.419	3770
1	0.552	4960
1 1/4	0.889	8000

*Based on allowable stress of 12,000 psi reduced by 25% using root area in accordance with ASME *Standard* B31.1 and MSS *Standard* SP-58.

- Forces imposed by thermal expansion and contraction of pipe bends and loops
- Frictional, spring, and pressure thrust forces imposed by expansion joints in the system
- Frictional forces of guides and supports
- Other loads (e.g., water hammer, vibration, reactive force of relief valves)
- Test load and force

In addition, pipe-supporting elements must be evaluated in terms of stress at the points of connection to the pipe and the building. Stress at the point of connection to the pipe is especially important for base elbow and trunnion supports, because this stress is usually the limiting parameter, not the strength of the structural member. Loads on anchors, cast-in-place inserts, and other attachments to concrete should not be more than one-fifth the ultimate strength of the attachment, as determined by manufacturers' tests. All loads on the structure should be communicated to and coordinated with the structural engineer.

The ASME B31 standards establish criteria for the design of pipe-supporting elements, and the Manufacturers Standardization Society of the Valve and Fittings Industry (MSS) has established standards for the design, fabrication, selection, and installation of pipe hangers and supports based on these codes.

MSS *Standard* SP-69 and the catalogs of many manufacturers illustrate the various hangers and components and provide information on the types to use with different pipe systems. Table 10 lists maximum safe loads for threaded steel rods, and Tables 11 and 12 show suggested pipe support spacing for metal and PVC pipes, respectively.

Loads on most pipe-supporting elements are moderate and can be selected safely in accordance with manufacturers' catalog data and the information presented in this section; however, some loads and forces can be very high, especially in multistory buildings and for large-diameter pipe, particularly where expansion joints are used at a high operating pressure. Consequently, a qualified engineer should design or review all anchors and pipe-supporting elements, especially for the following:

- Steam systems operating above 15 psig
- Hydronic systems operating above 160 psig or 250°F
- Risers over 10 stories or 100 ft
- Systems with expansion joints, especially for pipe diameters 3 in. and greater
- Pipe sizes over 12 in. diameter
- Anchor loads greater than 10,000 lb (10 kips)
- Moments on pipe or structure in excess of 1000 ft·lb

Hanger Spacing and Pipe Wall Thickness

Table 11 suggests minimum pipe hanger spacing for use unless exceeded by the local authority having jurisdiction or engineering calculations. The primary factors determining pipe wall thickness are hoop stress caused by internal pressure, and longitudinal stresses caused by pressure, weight, and other sustained loads. Detailed stress calculations are seldom required for HVAC applications because standard pipe has ample thickness to sustain the pressure and longitudinal stress caused by weight (assuming hangers are spaced in accordance with Table 11).

Table 11 Suggested Hanger Spacing and Rod Size for Straight Horizontal Runs

NPS, in.	Hanger Spacing, ft: Standard Steel Pipe* Water	Standard Steel Pipe* Steam	Copper Tube Water	Rod Size, in.
1/2	7	8	5	1/4
3/4	7	9	5	1/4
1	7	9	6	1/4
1 1/2	9	12	8	3/8
2	10	13	8	3/8
2 1/2	11	14	9	3/8
3	12	15	10	3/8
4	14	17	12	1/2
6	17	21	14	1/2
8	19	24	16	5/8
10	20	26	18	3/4
12	23	30	19	7/8
14	25	32		1
16	27	35		1
18	28	37		1 1/4
20	30	39		1 1/4

Source: Adapted from MSS *Standard* SP-69

*Spacing does not apply where span calculations are made or where concentrated loads are placed between supports such as flanges, valves, specialties, etc.

Support spacings for PVC and CPVC pipe systems are influenced by operating temperatures. Table 12 recommends horizontal spacing based on pipe size, schedule, material (PVC or industrial-grade CPVC), and operating temperature. Hangers and supports should not be clamped tightly because the axial movement of the pipe would be restricted. The charts are based on continuous spans and uninsulated lines carrying liquids. They are not applicable where loads between supports are concentrated (e.g., for valves, flanges) or where there is a change in direction. Hangers/supports should be located adjacent to joints, branch connections, and changes in direction. Risers should be in installed independently of adjacent horizontal hangers/supports.

For cast iron pipe, maximum spacing should be 12 ft, with at least one hanger/support for each pipe section.

1.7 PIPE EXPANSION AND FLEXIBILITY

Temperature changes cause dimensional changes in all materials. Table 13 shows the coefficients of expansion for metallic piping materials commonly used in HVAC. For systems operating at high temperatures, such as steam and hot water, the rate of expansion is high, and significant movements can occur in short runs of piping. Even though rates of expansion may be low for systems operating in the range of 40 to 100°F, such as chilled and condenser water, they can cause large movements in long runs of piping, which are common in distribution systems and high-rise buildings. Therefore, in addition to design requirements for pressure, weight, and other loads, piping systems must accommodate thermal and other movements to prevent the following:

- Failure of pipe and supports from overstress and fatigue
- Leakage of joints
- Detrimental forces and stresses in connected equipment

An unrestrained pipe operates at the lowest overall stress level. Anchors and restraints are needed to support pipe weight and to protect equipment connections. Anchor forces and bowing of pipe

Table 12 Suggested Maximum Spacing Between Hangers/Support for PVC and CPVC Pipe

	PVC										CPVC											
	Schedule 40					Schedule 80					Schedule 40						Schedule 80					
	Temperature (°F)					Temperature (°F)					Temperature (°F)						Temperature (°F)					
Pipe Size (in.)	60	80	100	120	140	60	80	100	120	140	73	100	120	140	160	180	73	100	120	140	160	180
1/2	4-1/2	4-1/2	4	2-1/2	2-1/2	5	4-1/2	4-1/2	3	2-1/2	5	4-1/2	4-1/2	4	2-1/2	2-1/2	5-1/2	5	4-1/2	4-1/2	3	2-1/2
3/4	5	4-1/2	4	2-1/2	2-1/2	5-1/2	5	4-1/2	3	2-1/2	5	5	4-1/2	4	2-1/2	2-1/2	5-1/2	5-1/2	5	4-1/2	3	2-1/2
1	5-1/2	5	4-1/2	3	2-1/2	6	5-1/2	5	3-1/2	3	5-1/2	5-1/2	5	4-1/2	3	2-1/2	6	6	5-1/2	5	3-1/2	3
1-1/4	5-1/2	5-1/2	5	3	3	6	6	5-1/2	3-1/2	3	5-1/2	5-1/2	5-1/2	5	3	3	6-1/2	6	6	5-1/2	3-1/2	3
1-1/2	6	5-1/2	5	3-1/2	3	6-1/2	6	5-1/2	3-1/2	3-1/2	6	6	5-1/2	5	3-1/2	3	7	6-1/2	6	5-1/2	3-1/2	3-1/2
2	6	5-1/2	5	3-1/2	3	7	6-1/2	6	4	3-1/2	6	6	5-1/2	5	3-1/2	3	7	7	6-1/2	6	4	3-1/2
2-1/2	7	6-1/2	6	4	3-1/2	7-1/2	7-1/2	6-1/2	4-1/2	4	7	7	6-1/2	6	4	3-1/2	8	7-1/2	7-1/2	6-1/2	4-1/2	4
3	7	7	6	4	3-1/2	8	7-1/2	7	4-1/2	4	7	7	7	6	4	3-1/2	8	8	7-1/2	7	4-1/2	4
4	7-1/2	7	6-1/2	4-1/2	4	9	8-1/2	7-1/2	5	4-1/2	7-1/2	7-1/2	7	6-1/2	4-1/2	4	8-1/2	9	8	7-1/2	5	4-1/2
6	8-1/2	8	7-1/2	5	4-1/2	10	9-1/2	9	6	5	8-1/2	8	7-1/2	7	5	4-1/2	10	9-1/2	9	8	5-1/2	5
8	9	8-1/2	8	5	4-1/2	11	10-1/2	9-1/2	6-1/2	5-1/2	9-1/2	9	8-1/2	7-1/2	5-1/2	5	11	10-1/2	10	9	6	5-1/2
10	10	9	8-1/2	5-1/2	5	12	11	10	7	6	10-1/2	10	9-1/2	8	6	5-1/2	11-1/2	11	10-1/2	9-1/2	6-1/2	6
12	11-1/2	10-1/2	9-1/2	6-1/2	5-1/2	13	12	10-1/2	7-1/2	6-1/2	11-1/2	10-1/2	10	8-1/2	6-1/2	6	12-1/2	12	11-1/2	10-1/2	7-1/2	6-1/2
14	12	11	10	7	6	13-1/2	13	11	8	7												
16	12-1/2	11-1/2	10-1/2	7-1/2	6-1/2	14	13-1/2	11-1/2	8-1/2	7-1/2												
	SDR					SDR																
18	13	12	11	8	7	14-1/2	14	12	9	8												
20	13-1/2	12-1/2	11-1/2	8-1/2	7-1/2	15	14-1/2	12-1/2	9-1/2	8-1/2												
24	14	13	12	9	8	15-1/2	15	13	10	9												

anchored at both ends are generally too large to be acceptable, so general practice is to **never anchor a straight run of steel pipe at both ends**. Piping must be allowed to expand or contract through thermal changes. Ample flexibility can be attained by designing pipe bends and loops or by including supplemental devices, such as expansion joints.

End reactions transmitted to rotating equipment, such as pumps or turbines, may deform the equipment case and cause bearing misalignment that may ultimately cause the component to fail. Consequently, manufacturers' recommendations on allowable forces and movements that may be placed on their equipment should be followed.

1.8 PIPE BENDS AND LOOPS

Detailed stress analysis requires involved mathematical analysis and is generally performed by computer programs. However, such involved analysis is not typically required for most HVAC systems because the piping arrangements and temperature ranges at which they operate are usually simple to analyze. Expansion stresses discussed in this section relate only to aboveground pipe located in open air, or preinsulated pipe.

L Bends

The guided cantilever beam method of evaluating L bends can be used to design L bends, Z bends, pipe loops, branch take-off connections, and some more complicated piping configurations. The guided cantilever equation [see Equation (17)] is generally conservative because it assumes that the pipe arrangement does not rotate. The anchor force results will be higher because of the lack of rotation, and rigorous analysis is recommended for complicated or expensive systems.

Equation (15) may be used to calculate the length of leg BC needed to accommodate thermal expansion or contraction of leg AB for a guided cantilever beam (Figure 4).

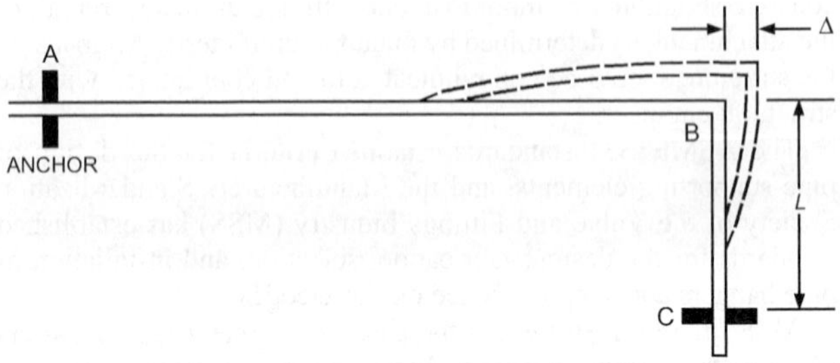

Fig. 4 Guided Cantilever Beam

$$L = \sqrt{\frac{3\Delta DE}{(144\ \text{in}^2/\text{ft}^2)S_A}} \tag{15}$$

where

L = length of leg BC required to accommodate thermal expansion of long leg AB, ft
Δ = thermal expansion or contraction of leg AB, in.
D = actual pipe outside diameter, in.
E = modulus of elasticity, psi
S_A = allowable stress range, psi

For the commonly used A53 Grade B seamless or ERW pipe, an allowable stress S_A of 22,500 psi (see Table 15) can be used without overstressing the pipe. However, this can result in very high end reactions and anchor forces, especially with large-diameter pipe. Designing to a stress range S_A of 15,000 psi and assuming E = 27.9 × 10^6 psi, Equation (15) reduces to Equation (16), which provides reasonably low end reactions without requiring too much extra pipe. In addition, Equation (16) may be used with A53 continuous (butt-) welded, seamless, and ERW pipe, and B88 drawn copper tubing.

$$L = 6.225\sqrt{\Delta D} \tag{16}$$

Table 13 Thermal Expansion of Metal Pipe

			Linear Thermal Expansion, in/100 ft		
	Saturated Steam Pressure, psig	Temperature, °F	Carbon Steel	Type 304 Stainless Steel	Copper
		−30	−0.19	−0.30	−0.32
		−20	−0.12	−0.20	−0.21
		−10	−0.06	−0.10	−0.11
		0	0.00	0.00	0.00
		10	0.08	0.11	0.12
		20	0.15	0.22	0.24
	−14.6	32	0.24	0.36	0.37
	−14.6	40	0.30	0.45	0.45
	−14.5	50	0.38	0.56	0.57
	−14.4	60	0.46	0.67	0.68
	−14.3	70	0.53	0.78	0.79
	−14.2	80	0.61	0.90	0.90
Vacuum	−14.0	90	0.68	1.01	1.02
	−13.7	100	0.76	1.12	1.13
	−13.0	120	0.91	1.35	1.37
	−11.8	140	1.06	1.57	1.59
	−10.0	160	1.22	1.79	1.80
	−7.2	180	1.37	2.02	2.05
	−3.2	200	1.52	2.24	2.30
	0	212	1.62	2.38	2.43
	2.5	220	1.69	2.48	2.52
	10.3	240	1.85	2.71	2.76
	20.7	260	2.02	2.94	2.99
	34.6	280	2.18	3.17	3.22
	52.3	300	2.35	3.40	3.46
	75.0	320	2.53	3.64	3.70
	103.3	340	2.70	3.88	3.94
	138.3	360	2.88	4.11	4.18
	181.1	380	3.05	4.35	4.42
	232.6	400	3.23	4.59	4.87
	666.1	500	4.15	5.80	5.91
	1528	600	5.13	7.03	7.18
	3079	700	6.16	8.29	8.47
		800	7.23	9.59	9.79
		900	8.34	10.91	11.16
		1000	9.42	12.27	12.54

The guided cantilever method of designing L bends assumes no restraints; therefore, care must be taken in supporting the pipe. For horizontal L bends, it is usually necessary to place a support near point B (see Figure 4), and any supports between points A and C must provide minimal resistance to piping movement; this is done by using slide plates or hanger rods of ample length, with hanger components selected to allow for swing no greater than 4°.

For L bends containing both vertical and horizontal legs, any supports on the horizontal leg must be spring hangers designed to support the full weight of pipe at normal operating temperature with a maximum load variation of 25%.

The force developed in an L bend that must be sustained by anchors or connected equipment is determined by the following equation:

$$F = \frac{12E_c I\Delta}{(1728\ \text{in}^3/\text{ft}^3)L^3} \tag{17}$$

where

F = force, lb
E_c = modulus of elasticity, psi
I = moment of inertia, in^4
L = length of offset leg, ft
Δ = deflection of offset leg, in.

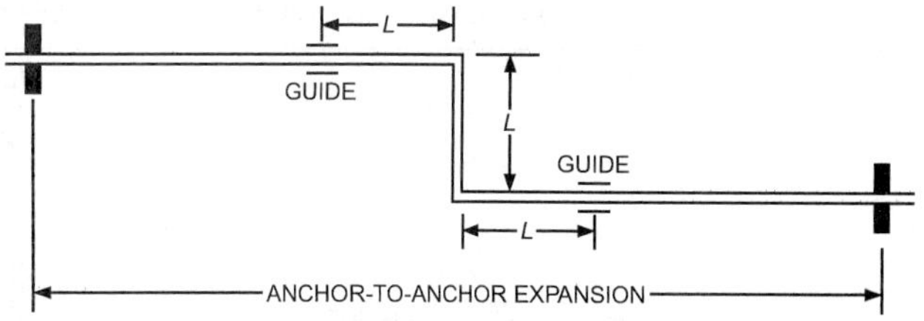

Distance from guides, if used, to offset should be equal or exceed length of offset.
Offset piping must be supported with hangers, slide plates, and spring hangers similar to those for L bends.

Fig. 5 Z Bend in Pipe

Z Bends

Z bends, as shown in Figure 5, are very effective for accommodating pipe movements. A simple and conservative method of sizing Z bends is to design the offset leg to be 65% of the values used for an L bend in Equation (15):

$$L = 4\sqrt{\Delta D} \tag{18}$$

where

L = length of offset leg, ft
Δ = anchor-to-anchor expansion, in.
D = pipe outside diameter, in.

The force developed in a Z bend can be calculated with acceptable accuracy as follows:

$$F = C_1\Delta(D/L)^2 \tag{19}$$

where

C_1 = 4000 lb/in.
F = force, lb
D = pipe outside diameter, in.
L = length of offset leg, ft
Δ = anchor-to-anchor expansion, in.

U Bends and Pipe Loops

Pipe loops or U bends are commonly used in long runs of piping. A simple method of designing pipe loops is to calculate the anchor-to-anchor expansion and, using Equation (15), determine the length L necessary to accommodate this movement. The pipe loop dimensions can then be determined using $W = L/5$ and $H = 2W$.

Note that guides must be spaced no closer than twice the height of the loop, and piping between guides must be supported, as described in the section on L Bends, when the length of pipe between guides exceeds the maximum allowable hanger spacing for the size pipe.

Table 14 lists pipe loop dimensions for pipe sizes 1 to 24 in. and anchor-to-anchor expansion (contraction) of 2 to 12 in.

No simple method has been developed to calculate pipe loop force; however, it is generally low. A conservative estimate is 200 lb per inch diameter (e.g., a 2 in. pipe will develop 400 lb of force and a 12 in. pipe will develop 2400 lb of force). Additional analysis should be done for pipes greater than 12 in. in diameter, because other simplified methodologies predict higher anchor forces.

Expansion and Contraction Control of Other Materials

To design expansion and contraction loops and bends for other materials, consult the Copper Development Association (CDA 2010) for copper pipes, and Plastic Pipe and Fitting Association (PPFA 2009) for plastic pipes.

Table 14 Pipe Loop Design for A53 Grade B Carbon Steel Pipe Through 400°F

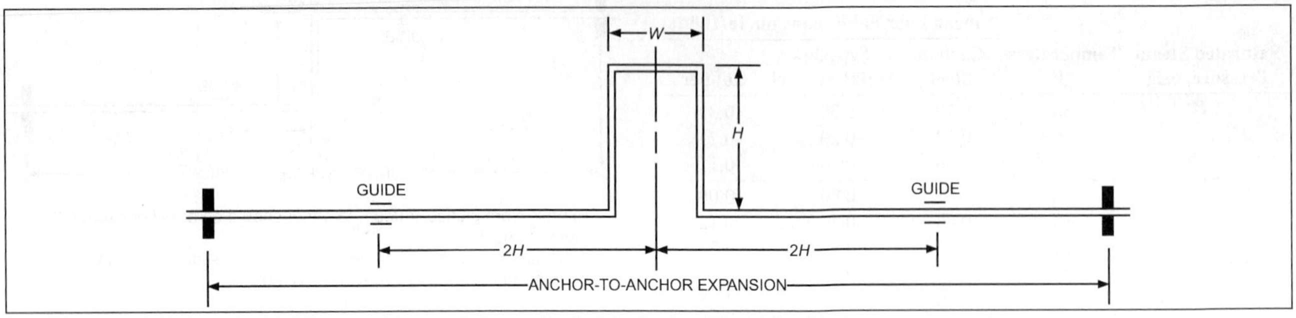

	Anchor-to-Anchor Expansion, in.											
Pipe	2		4		6		8		10		12	
Size, in.	*W*	*H*	*W*	*H*	*W*	*H*	*W*	*H*	*W*	*H*	*W*	*H*
1	2	4	3	6	3.5	7	4	8	4.5	9	5	10
2	3	6	4	8	5	10	5.5	11	6	12	7	14
3	3.5	7	5	10	6	12	6.5	13	7.5	15	8	16
4	4	8	5.5	11	6.5	13	7.5	15	8.5	17	9	18
6	5	10	6.5	13	8	16	9	18	10	20	11	22
8	5.5	11	7.5	15	9	18	10.5	21	12	24	13	26
10	6	12	8.5	17	10	20	11.5	23	13	26	14	28
12	6.5	13	9	18	11	22	12.5	25	14	28	15.5	31
14	7	14	9.5	19	11.5	23	13	26	15	30	16	32
16	7.5	15	10	20	12.5	25	14	28	16	32	17.5	35
18	8	16	11	22	13	26	15	30	17	34	18.5	37
20	8.5	17	11.5	23	14	28	16	32	18	36	19.5	39
24	9	18	12.5	25	14.5	29	17.5	35	19.5	39	21	42

Notes: 1. W and H dimensions are feet.
2. L is determined from Equation (15). $W = L/5$ $H = 2W$ $2H + W = L$
3. Approximate force to deflect loop = 200 lb/in. pipe diameter. For example, 8 in. pipe creates 1600 lb of force.

Cold Springing of Pipe

Cold springing or cold positioning of pipe consists of offsetting or springing the pipe in a direction opposite the expected movement. Cold springing is not recommended for most HVAC piping. Furthermore, **cold springing does not allow designing a pipe bend or loop for twice the calculated movement**. For example, if a particular L bend can accommodate 3 in. of movement from a neutral position, cold springing does not allow the L bend to accommodate 6 in. of movement.

Analyzing Existing Piping Configurations

Piping is best analyzed using a computer stress analysis program, which can provide all pertinent data, including stress, movements, and loads. Services can perform such analysis if programs are not available in house. However, many situations do not require such detailed analysis. A simple, satisfactory method for single and multiplane systems is to divide the system with real or imaginary anchors into a number of single-plane units, as shown in Figure 6, that can be evaluated as L and Z bends.

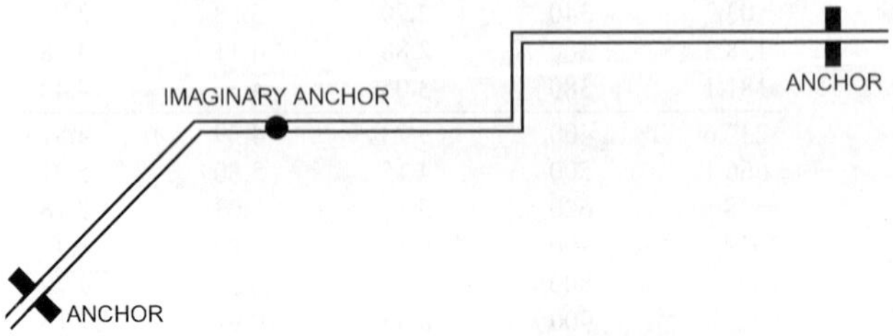

Fig. 6 Multiplane Pipe System

2. PIPE AND FITTING MATERIALS

2.1 PIPE

Steel Pipe

Steel pipe is manufactured by several processes. Seamless pipe (Type S), made by piercing or extruding, has no longitudinal seam. Other manufacturing methods roll a strip or sheet of steel (skelp) into a cylinder and weld a longitudinal seam. A continuous-weld (Type F CW) furnace butt-welding (BW; i.e., welding pipe in a single plane) process forces and joins the edges together at high temperature. An electric current welds the seam in electric-resistance-welded (Type E ERW) pipe. ASTM standards such as A53 and A106 specify steel pipe A and B grades. The A grade has a lower tensile strength and is not widely used.

The ASME pressure piping codes require that a longitudinal joint efficiency factor E (Table 15) be applied to each type of seam when calculating the allowable stress. ASME *Standard* B36.10M specifies the dimensional standard for wrought steel pipe.

Steel pipe is manufactured with wall thicknesses identified by schedule or weight class. Although schedule numbers and weight class designations are related, they are not constant for all pipe sizes. Standard weight (STD) and Schedule 40 pipe have the same wall thickness through NPS 10. For 12 in. and larger standard weight pipe, the wall thickness remains constant at 0.375 in., whereas Schedule 40 wall thickness increases with each size. A similar equality exists between Extra Strong (XS) and Schedule 80 pipe through 8 in.; above 8 in., XS pipe has a 0.500 in. wall, whereas Schedule 80 increases in wall thickness. Table 16 lists properties of representative steel pipe.

Joints in steel pipe are made by welding or by using threaded, flanged, or grooved fittings or socket welding. Unreinforced welded-in branch connections weaken a main pipeline, and added reinforcement is necessary, unless the excess wall thickness of both mains and branches is sufficient to sustain the pressure.

Table 15 Allowable Stresses[a] for Pipe and Tube

ASTM Specification	Grade	Type	Manufacturing Process	Available Sizes, in.	Minimum Tensile Strength, psi	Basic Allowable Stress *S*, psi	Joint Efficiency Factor *E*	Allowable Stress[b] S_E, psi	Allowable Stress Range[c] S_A, psi
A53 steel	—	F	Cont. weld	1/2 to 4	45,000	11,250	0.6	6,800	16,900
A53 steel	B	S	Seamless	1/2 to 26	60,000	15,000	1.0	15,000	22,500
A53 steel	B	E	ERW	2 to 20	60,000	15,000	0.85	12,800	22,500
A106 steel	B	S	Seamless	1/2 to 26	60,000	15,000	1.0	15,000	22,500
B88 copper	—	—	Hard drawn	1/4 to 12	36,000	9,000	1.0	9,000	13,500

[a]Listed stresses are for temperatures to 650°F for steel pipe (to 400°F for Type F) and to 250°F for copper tubing.
[b]To be used for internal pressure stress calculations in Equations (10) and (11).
[c]To be used only for piping flexibility calculations; see Equations (12) and (13).

The ASME *Standard* B31 series gives formulas and guidelines for determining whether reinforcement is required. Such calculations are seldom needed in HVAC applications because (1) the fitting is designed in accordance with a standard listed in the applicable ASME B31 table and used within the pressure and temperature limits of that standard, and (2) fittings such as tees and reinforced outlet fittings provide integral reinforcement.

Type F steel pipe is not allowed for ASME *Standard* B31.5 refrigerant piping.

Copper Tube

Because of their inherent resistance to corrosion and ease of installation, copper and copper alloys are often used in heating, air-conditioning, refrigeration, and water supply installations. The two main standards for copper tube are (1) ASTM *Standard* B88, which includes Types K, L, M, and DWV for water and drain service; and (2) ASTM *Standard* B280, which specifies air-conditioning and refrigeration (ACR) tube for refrigeration service.

Types K, L, M, and DWV designate descending wall thicknesses for copper tube. All types have the same outside diameter (OD) for corresponding sizes. Table 17 lists properties of ASTM B88 copper tube. In the plumbing industry, tube of nominal size approximates the inside diameter. The heating and refrigeration trades specify copper tube by the outside diameter. ACR tubing has a different set of wall thicknesses. Types K, L, and M tube may be hard drawn or annealed (soft) temper.

Copper tubing is joined with soldered or brazed, wrought or cast copper capillary socket-end fittings. See Table 20 for lists pressure/temperature ratings of soldered and brazed joints. Small copper tube is also joined by flare or compression fittings.

Hard-drawn tubing has a higher allowable stress than annealed tubing, but if hard tubing is joined by soldering or brazing, the annealed allowable stress should be used.

Brass pipe and copper pipe are also made in steel pipe thicknesses for threading. High cost has eliminated these materials from the market, except for special applications.

The heating and air-conditioning industry generally uses Types L and M tubing, which have higher internal working pressure ratings than the solder joints used at fittings. Type K may be used with brazed joints for higher pressure-temperature requirements or for direct burial. Type M should be used with care where exposed to potential external damage.

Copper and brass should not be used in ammonia refrigerating systems, or in acidic drains from condensing boilers. The section on Special Systems covers other limitations on refrigerant piping.

Ductile Iron and Cast Iron

Cast-iron soil pipe comes in XH or service weight. It is not used under pressure because the pipe is not suitable and the joints are not restrained. Cast-iron pipe and fittings typically have bell and spigot ends for lead and oakum joints or elastomer push-on joints. Cast-iron pipe and fittings are also furnished with *no-hub* ends for joining with *no-hub* clamps. Local plumbing codes specify permitted materials and joints.

Ductile iron has now replaced cast iron for pressure pipe. Ductile iron is stronger, less brittle, and similar to cast iron in corrosion resistance. It is commonly used for buried pressure water mains or in other locations where internal or external corrosion is a problem. Joints are made with flanged fittings, mechanical joint (MJ) fittings, or elastomer gaskets for bell and spigot ends. Bell and spigot and MJ joints are not self-restrained, though restrained MJ systems are available. Ductile-iron pipe is made in seven thickness classes for different service conditions. AWWA *Standard* C150/A21.50 covers the proper selection of pipe classes.

Nonmetallic (Plastic)

Selecting a plastic for a specific purpose requires attention to the temperatures, pressures, chemicals, and stresses the piping will be subjected to in the specific application. All are suitable for cold water. Plastic pipe should not be used for compressed gases or compressed air if the pipe's material is subject to brittle failure. For other liquids and chemicals, refer to charts provided by plastic pipe manufacturers and distributors. Table 18 gives properties of the various plastics discussed in this section; the last column gives the relative cost of small pipe in each category. Table 2 lists some applications pertinent to HVAC. The following are brief descriptions of common uses for the various materials.

Plastic piping materials fall into two main categories: thermoplastics and thermosets. Thermoplastics melt and are formed by extruding or molding. They are usually used without reinforcing filaments. Thermosets are cured and cannot be reformed. They are normally used with glass fiber reinforcing filaments.

For the purposes of this chapter, **thermoplastic** piping is made of the following materials:

PVC. Because polyvinyl chloride has the best overall range of properties at the lowest cost, it is the most widely used plastic. It is joined by solvent cementing, threading, or flanging. Gasketed push-on joints are also used for larger sizes. ASTM *Standards* D1784, D1785, and D2665 cover PVC pipe.

CPVC. Chlorinated polyvinyl chloride has the same properties as PVC and can withstand a higher temperature before losing strength. It is joined by the same methods as PVC. ASTM *Standards* D1784 and 1785 discuss CPVC.

PE. Low-density polyethylene (LDPE) is a flexible, lightweight tubing with good low-temperature properties. It is used in the food and beverage industry and for instrument tubing. Joins are mechanical, such as compression fittings or push-on connectors and clamps. See ASTM *Standard* D2239 for details.

HDPE. High-density polyethylene is a tough, weather-resistant material used for large pipelines in the gas industry. Fabricated fittings are available. It is joined by heat fusion for large sizes; flare, compression, or insert fittings can be used on small sizes. ASTM *Standard* D3350 discusses HDPE.

Table 16 Steel Pipe Data

Nominal Size, in.	Pipe OD, in.	Schedule Number or Weight[a]	Wall Thickness *t*, in.	Inside Diameter *d*, in.	Surface Area		Cross Section		Weight		Working Pressure[c] ASTM A53 B to 400°F		
					Outside, ft²/ft	Inside, ft²/ft	Metal Area, in²	Flow Area, in²	Pipe, lb/ft	Water, lb/ft	Mfr. Process	Joint Type[b]	psig
1/4	0.540	40 ST	0.088	0.364	0.141	0.095	0.125	0.104	0.424	0.045	CW	T	188
		80 XS	0.119	0.302	0.141	0.079	0.157	0.072	0.535	0.031	CW	T	871
3/8	0.675	40 ST	0.091	0.493	0.177	0.129	0.167	0.191	0.567	0.083	CW	T	203
		80 XS	0.126	0.423	0.177	0.111	0.217	0.141	0.738	0.061	CW	T	820
1/2	0.840	40 ST	0.109	0.622	0.220	0.163	0.250	0.304	0.850	0.131	CW	T	214
		80 XS	0.147	0.546	0.220	0.143	0.320	0.234	1.087	0.101	CW	T	753
3/4	1.050	40 ST	0.113	0.824	0.275	0.216	0.333	0.533	1.13	0.231	CW	T	217
		80 XS	0.154	0.742	0.275	0.194	0.433	0.432	1.47	0.187	CW	T	681
1	1.315	40 ST	0.133	1.049	0.344	0.275	0.494	0.864	1.68	0.374	CW	T	226
		80 XS	0.179	0.957	0.344	0.251	0.639	0.719	2.17	0.311	CW	T	642
1 1/4	1.660	40 ST	0.140	1.380	0.435	0.361	0.669	1.50	2.27	0.647	CW	T	229
		80 XS	0.191	1.278	0.435	0.335	0.881	1.28	2.99	0.555	CW	T	594
1 1/2	1.900	40 ST	0.145	1.610	0.497	0.421	0.799	2.04	2.72	0.881	CW	T	231
		80 XS	0.200	1.500	0.497	0.393	1.068	1.77	3.63	0.765	CW	T	576
2	2.375	40 ST	0.154	2.067	0.622	0.541	1.07	3.36	3.65	1.45	CW	T	230
		80 XS	0.218	1.939	0.622	0.508	1.48	2.95	5.02	1.28	CW	T	551
2 1/2	2.875	40 ST	0.203	2.469	0.753	0.646	1.70	4.79	5.79	2.07	CW	W	533
		80 XS	0.276	2.323	0.753	0.608	2.25	4.24	7.66	1.83	CW	W	835
3	3.500	40 ST	0.216	3.068	0.916	0.803	2.23	7.39	7.57	3.20	CW	W	482
		80 XS	0.300	2.900	0.916	0.759	3.02	6.60	10.25	2.86	CW	W	767
4	4.500	40 ST	0.237	4.026	1.178	1.054	3.17	12.73	10.78	5.51	CW	W	430
		80 XS	0.337	3.826	1.178	1.002	4.41	11.50	14.97	4.98	CW	W	695
6	6.625	40 ST	0.280	6.065	1.734	1.588	5.58	28.89	18.96	12.50	ERW	W	696
		80 XS	0.432	5.761	1.734	1.508	8.40	26.07	28.55	11.28	ERW	W	1209
8	8.625	30	0.277	8.071	2.258	2.113	7.26	51.16	24.68	22.14	ERW	W	526
		40 ST	0.322	7.981	2.258	2.089	8.40	50.03	28.53	21.65	ERW	W	643
		80 XS	0.500	7.625	2.258	1.996	12.76	45.66	43.35	19.76	ERW	W	1106
10	10.75	30	0.307	10.136	2.814	2.654	10.07	80.69	34.21	34.92	ERW	W	485
		40 ST	0.365	10.020	2.814	2.623	11.91	78.85	40.45	34.12	ERW	W	606
		XS	0.500	9.750	2.814	2.552	16.10	74.66	54.69	32.31	ERW	W	887
		80	0.593	9.564	2.814	2.504	18.92	71.84	64.28	31.09	ERW	W	1081
12	12.75	30	0.330	12.090	3.338	3.165	12.88	114.8	43.74	49.68	ERW	W	449
		ST	0.375	12.000	3.338	3.141	14.58	113.1	49.52	48.94	ERW	W	528
		40	0.406	11.938	3.338	3.125	15.74	111.9	53.48	48.44	ERW	W	583
		XS	0.500	11.750	3.338	3.076	19.24	108.4	65.37	46.92	ERW	W	748
		80	0.687	11.376	3.338	2.978	26.03	101.6	88.44	43.98	ERW	W	1076
14	14.00	30 ST	0.375	13.250	3.665	3.469	16.05	137.9	54.53	59.67	ERW	W	481
		40	0.437	13.126	3.665	3.436	18.62	135.3	63.25	58.56	ERW	W	580
		XS	0.500	13.000	3.665	3.403	21.21	132.7	72.04	57.44	ERW	W	681
		80	0.750	12.500	3.665	3.272	31.22	122.7	106.05	53.11	ERW	W	1081
16	16.00	30 ST	0.375	15.250	4.189	3.992	18.41	182.6	62.53	79.04	ERW	W	421
		40 XS	0.500	15.000	4.189	3.927	24.35	176.7	82.71	76.47	ERW	W	596
18	18.00	ST	0.375	17.250	4.712	4.516	20.76	233.7	70.54	101.13	ERW	W	374
		30	0.437	17.126	4.712	4.483	24.11	230.3	81.91	99.68	ERW	W	451
		XS	0.500	17.000	4.712	4.450	27.49	227.0	93.38	98.22	ERW	W	530
		40	0.562	16.876	4.712	4.418	30.79	223.7	104.59	96.80	ERW	W	607
20	20.00	20 ST	0.375	19.250	5.236	5.039	23.12	291.0	78.54	125.94	ERW	W	337
		30 XS	0.500	19.000	5.236	4.974	30.63	283.5	104.05	122.69	ERW	W	477
		40	0.593	18.814	5.236	4.925	36.15	278.0	122.82	120.30	ERW	W	581

[a]Numbers are schedule numbers per ASME *Standard* B36.10M; ST = Standard Weight; XS = Extra Strong.

[b]T = Thread; W = Weld

[c]Working pressures were calculated per ASME *Standard* B31.9 using furnace butt-weld (continuous weld, CW) pipe through 4 in. and electric resistance weld (ERW) thereafter. The allowance A has been taken as

(1) 12.5% of *t* for mill tolerance on pipe wall thickness, *plus*

(2) An arbitrary corrosion allowance of 0.025 in. for pipe sizes through NPS 2 and 0.065 in. from NPS 2 1/2 through 20, *plus*

(3) A thread cutting allowance for sizes through NPS 2.

Because the pipe wall thickness of threaded standard pipe is so small after deducting allowance A, the mechanical strength of the pipe is impaired. It is good practice to limit standard weight threaded pipe pressure to 90 psig for steam and 125 psig for water.

Table 17 Copper Tube Data

Nominal Diameter, in.	Type	Wall Thickness t, in.	Diameter: Outside D, in.	Diameter: Inside d, in.	Surface Area: Outside, ft^2/ft	Surface Area: Inside, ft^2/ft	Cross Section: Metal Area, in^2	Cross Section: Flow Area, in^2	Weight: Tube, lb/ft	Weight: Water, lb/ft	Working Pressure[a,b,c] ASTM B88 to 250°F: Annealed, psig	Working Pressure[a,b,c] ASTM B88 to 250°F: Drawn, psig
1/4	K	0.035	0.375	0.305	0.098	0.080	0.037	0.073	0.145	0.032	851	1596
	L	0.030	0.375	0.315	0.098	0.082	0.033	0.078	0.126	0.034	730	1368
3/8	K	0.049	0.500	0.402	0.131	0.105	0.069	0.127	0.269	0.055	894	1676
	L	0.035	0.500	0.430	0.131	0.113	0.051	0.145	0.198	0.063	638	1197
	M	0.025	0.500	0.450	0.131	0.118	0.037	0.159	0.145	0.069	456	855
1/2	K	0.049	0.625	0.527	0.164	0.138	0.089	0.218	0.344	0.094	715	1341
	L	0.040	0.625	0.545	0.164	0.143	0.074	0.233	0.285	0.101	584	1094
	M	0.028	0.625	0.569	0.164	0.149	0.053	0.254	0.203	0.110	409	766
5/8	K	0.049	0.750	0.652	0.196	0.171	0.108	0.334	0.418	0.144	596	1117
	L	0.042	0.750	0.666	0.196	0.174	0.093	0.348	0.362	0.151	511	958
3/4	K	0.065	0.875	0.745	0.229	0.195	0.165	0.436	0.641	0.189	677	1270
	L	0.045	0.875	0.785	0.229	0.206	0.117	0.484	0.455	0.209	469	879
	M	0.032	0.875	0.811	0.229	0.212	0.085	0.517	0.328	0.224	334	625
1	K	0.065	1.125	0.995	0.295	0.260	0.216	0.778	0.839	0.336	527	988
	L	0.050	1.125	1.025	0.295	0.268	0.169	0.825	0.654	0.357	405	760
	M	0.035	1.125	1.055	0.295	0.276	0.120	0.874	0.464	0.378	284	532
1 1/4	K	0.065	1.375	1.245	0.360	0.326	0.268	1.217	1.037	0.527	431	808
	L	0.055	1.375	1.265	0.360	0.331	0.228	1.257	0.884	0.544	365	684
	M	0.042	1.375	1.291	0.360	0.338	0.176	1.309	0.682	0.566	279	522
	DWV	0.040	1.375	1.295	0.360	0.339	0.168	1.317	0.650	0.570	265	497
1 1/2	K	0.072	1.625	1.481	0.425	0.388	0.351	1.723	1.361	0.745	404	758
	L	0.060	1.625	1.505	0.425	0.394	0.295	1.779	1.143	0.770	337	631
	M	0.049	1.625	1.527	0.425	0.400	0.243	1.831	0.940	0.792	275	516
	DWV	0.042	1.625	1.541	0.425	0.403	0.209	1.865	0.809	0.807	236	442
2	K	0.083	2.125	1.959	0.556	0.513	0.532	3.014	2.063	1.304	356	668
	L	0.070	2.125	1.985	0.556	0.520	0.452	3.095	1.751	1.339	300	573
	M	0.058	2.125	2.009	0.556	0.526	0.377	3.170	1.459	1.372	249	467
	DWV	0.042	2.125	2.041	0.556	0.534	0.275	3.272	1.065	1.416	180	338
2 1/2	K	0.095	2.625	2.435	0.687	0.637	0.755	4.657	2.926	2.015	330	619
	L	0.080	2.625	2.465	0.687	0.645	0.640	4.772	2.479	2.065	278	521
	M	0.065	2.625	2.495	0.687	0.653	0.523	4.889	2.026	2.116	226	423
3	K	0.109	3.125	2.907	0.818	0.761	1.033	6.637	4.002	2.872	318	596
	L	0.090	3.125	2.945	0.818	0.771	0.858	6.812	3.325	2.947	263	492
	M	0.072	3.125	2.981	0.818	0.780	0.691	6.979	2.676	3.020	210	394
	DWV	0.045	3.125	3.035	0.818	0.795	0.435	7.234	1.687	3.130	131	246
3 1/2	K	0.120	3.625	3.385	0.949	0.886	1.321	8.999	5.120	3.894	302	566
	L	0.100	3.625	3.425	0.949	0.897	1.107	9.213	4.291	3.987	252	472
	M	0.083	3.625	3.459	0.949	0.906	0.924	9.397	3.579	4.066	209	392
4	K	0.134	4.125	3.857	1.080	1.010	1.680	11.684	6.510	5.056	296	555
	L	0.110	4.125	3.905	1.080	1.022	1.387	11.977	5.377	5.182	243	456
	M	0.095	4.125	3.935	1.080	1.030	1.203	12.161	4.661	5.262	210	394
	DWV	0.058	4.125	4.009	1.080	1.050	0.741	12.623	2.872	5.462	128	240
5	K	0.160	5.125	4.805	1.342	1.258	2.496	18.133	9.671	7.846	285	534
	L	0.125	5.125	4.875	1.342	1.276	1.963	18.665	7.609	8.077	222	417
	M	0.109	5.125	4.907	1.342	1.285	1.718	18.911	6.656	8.183	194	364
	DWV	0.072	5.125	4.981	1.342	1.304	1.143	19.486	4.429	8.432	128	240
6	K	0.192	6.125	5.741	1.603	1.503	3.579	25.886	13.867	11.201	286	536
	L	0.140	6.125	5.845	1.603	1.530	2.632	26.832	10.200	11.610	208	391
	M	0.122	6.125	5.881	1.603	1.540	2.301	27.164	8.916	11.754	182	341
	DWV	0.083	6.125	5.959	1.603	1.560	1.575	27.889	6.105	12.068	124	232
8	K	0.271	8.125	7.583	2.127	1.985	6.687	45.162	25.911	19.542	304	570
	L	0.200	8.125	7.725	2.127	2.022	4.979	46.869	19.295	20.280	224	421
	M	0.170	8.125	7.785	2.127	2.038	4.249	47.600	16.463	20.597	191	358
	DWV	0.109	8.125	7.907	2.127	2.070	2.745	49.104	10.637	21.247	122	229
10	K	0.338	10.125	9.449	2.651	2.474	10.392	70.123	40.271	30.342	304	571
	L	0.250	10.125	9.625	2.651	2.520	7.756	72.760	30.054	31.483	225	422
	M	0.212	10.125	9.701	2.651	2.540	6.602	73.913	25.584	31.982	191	358
12	K	0.405	12.125	11.315	3.174	2.962	14.912	100.554	57.784	43.510	305	571
	L	0.280	12.125	11.565	3.174	3.028	10.419	105.046	40.375	45.454	211	395
	M	0.254	12.125	11.617	3.174	3.041	9.473	105.993	36.706	45.863	191	358

[a]When using soldered or brazed fittings, the joint determines the limiting pressure.

[b]Working pressures were calculated using ASME *Standard* B31.9 allowable stresses. A 5% mill tolerance has been used on the wall thickness. Higher tube ratings can be calculated using the allowable stress for lower temperatures.

[c]If soldered or brazed fittings are used on hard-drawn tubing, use the annealed ratings. Full-tube allowable pressures can be used with suitably rated flare or compression-type fittings.

Table 18 Properties of Pipe Materials[a]

Material			Tensile Strength, psi (at 73°F)	Hydrostatic[b] Design Stress, psi (at 73°F)		Upper Temperature Limit, °F		HDS[b] Upper Limit, psi	Specific Gravity[c]	Impact Strength, ft·lb/in (at 73°F)	Modulus of Elasticity, psi (at 73°F)	Coefficient of Expansion, in/10⁶ in·°F	Thermal Conductivity, Btu·in/ h·ft²·°F	Relative Pipe Cost[d]
Designation	Type and Grade	Cell No.		Mfr.	ASME B31	Mfr.	ASME B31							
Metals														
Copper	L	Drawn – hard	36,000		9,000		400	8,200	8.90		17,000,000	9.4	232	2.2
Steel	A53 B	ERW	60,000	12,800			800	9,200	7.80	30	27,500,000	6.31	26	1.0
Stainless steel	304	Drawn or Welded	73,200				350		7.90		28,000,000	9.6	8	2.0
Thermoplastics														
PVC 1120	T I,G1	12454-B	7,500	2,000	2,000	140	150	440	1.40	0.8	420,000	30.0	1.1	0.6
PVC 1200	T I,G2	12454-C			2,000		150				410,000	35.0		
PVC 2120	T II,G1	14333-D			2,000		150					30.0		
CPVC 4120	T IV,G1	23447-B	8,000	2,000	2,000	210	210	320	1.55	1.5	423,000	35.0	0.95	0.8
PE 2306	Gr. P23				630		140				90,000	80.0		
PE 3306	Gr. P34				630		160				130,000	70.0		
PE 3406	Gr. P33				630		180				150,000	60.0		
HDPE 3408	Gr. P34	355434-C	5,000	1,600	800	140	180	800	0.96	12	110,000	120.0	2.7	1.1
PP			5,000	705		212	210		0.91	1.3	120,000	60.0	1.3	2.9
ABS	Acrylonitrile copolymer	6-3-3	5,500			176			1.06	8.5	240,000	56.0	1.7	3.4
ABS 1210	T I,G2	5-2-2		1,000		180	640		250,000	55.0				
ABS 1316	T I,G3	3-5-5		1,600		180	1,000		340,000	40.0				
ABS 2112	T II,G1	4-4-5		1,250		180	800			40.0				
PVDF			7,000	1,275		280	275	306	1.78	3.8	125,000	79.0	0.8	2.6
Thermosetting														
Epoxy-glass	RTRP-11AF		44,000	8,000		300	7,000				1,000,000	9 to 13	2.9	1.5
PEX	A,B,C[e]		3,200	630	200	180	79		0.94		75,000	90.0	3.2	0.7
Polyester-glass	RTRP-12EF		44,000	9,000	200	200	5,000				1,000,000	9 to 11	1.3	1.5

[a]Properties listed are for specific materials listed; each plastic has other formulations. Consult the manufacturer of the system chosen. These values are for comparative purposes.
[b]Hydrostatic design stress (HDS) is equivalent to allowable design stress
[c]Relative to water at 62.4 lb/ft³.
[d]Based on cost for 2 in. pipe only, without factoring in fittings, joints, hangers, and labor.
[e]A, B, and C are the three manufacturing processes of PEX pipe. The classifications are not related to a ranking system.

PP. Polypropylene is a lightweight plastic used for pressure applications and also for chemical waste lines, because it is inert to a wide range of chemicals. A broad variety of drainage fittings are available. For pressure uses, regular fittings are made. It is joined by heat fusion. See ASTM *Standards* F2830 and F2389 for details.

ABS. Acrylonitrile butadiene styrene is a high-strength, impact- and weather-resistant material. Some formulations can be used for beverage industry. A wide range of fittings is available. It is joined by solvent cement, threading, or flanging. ASTM *Standards* D2661 and D3965 cover ABS.

PVDF. Polyvinylidene fluoride is widely used for ultrapure water systems and in the pharmaceutical industry and has a wide temperature range. This material is over 20 times more expensive than PVC. It is joined by heat fusion, and fittings are made for this purpose. For smaller sizes, mechanical joints can be used. See ASTM *Standard* D2122 for information on PVDF.

Thermosetting piping used in HVAC is called (1) reinforced thermosetting resin (RTR) and (2) fiberglass-reinforced plastic (FRP). RTR and FRP are interchangeable and refer to pipe and fittings commonly made of (1) fiberglass-reinforced epoxy resin, (2) fiberglass-reinforced vinyl ester, and (3) fiberglass-reinforced polyester.

Pipe and fittings made from epoxy resin are generally stronger and operate at a higher temperature than those made from polyester or vinyl ester resins, so they are more likely to be used in HVAC.

PEX. Cross-linked polyethylene is made from high-density polyethylene (HDPE) and contains cross-linked bonds in the polymer structure. This changes the thermoplastic to a thermoset. It can be used up to 300°F. PEX is used in building services pipework systems, hydronic radiant heating and cooling systems, and domestic water piping. PEX comes in two types: barrier and nonbarrier. The barrier, a thin sheet of aluminum between layers of PEX material or a layer of polymer film, prevents oxygen dissolved in water from diffusing through the pipe and corroding metal components. Nonbarrier PEX is acceptable for plumbing systems. PEX can be ordered as A, B, or C (these designations refer to the manufacturing process and not the pipe's structural or chemical properties). All PEX tubing (A, B, C) comply with the same standards: refer to ASTM *Standards* F876, F877, and F2023; CSA *Standard* B137.5; and NSF/ANSI *Standards* 14 and 61 for further information.

2.2 FITTINGS

Table 19 lists standards that give dimensions and pressure ratings for fittings, flanges, and flanged fittings. These data are also available from manufacturers' catalogs.

2.3 JOINING METHODS

Threading

Threading as per ASME *Standard* B1.20.1 is the most common method for joining small-diameter steel or brass pipe. Pipe with a wall thickness less than standard weight should not be threaded. ASME *Standard* B31.5 limits the threading for various refrigerants and pipe sizes.

Soldering and Brazing

Copper tube is usually joined by soldering or brazing socket end fittings. Brazing materials melt above 1000°F and produce a stronger joint than solder. Table 20 lists soldered and brazed joint strengths. ASME *Standard* B16.22-specified wrought copper solder joint fittings and ASME *Standard* B16.18-specified cast copper solder joint fittings are pressure rated the same way as annealed Type L copper tube of the same size. Health concerns have caused many jurisdictions to ban solder containing lead or antimony for joining pipe in potable-water systems. Lead-based solder, in particular, must not be used for potable water.

Table 19 Applicable Standards for Fittings

Steel[a]	**ASME** ***Std.***	**Copper and Bronze**[c] **(*Continued*)**	**ASME** ***Std.***
Pipe flanges and flanged fittings	B16.5	Cast copper alloy fittings for flared copper tubes	B16.26
Factory-made wrought steel butt-welding fittings	B16.9	Wrought copper and wrought copper alloy solder joint drainage fittings	B16.29
Forged fittings, socket-welding and threaded	B16.11	**Nonmetallic**[d]	**ASTM** ***Std.***
Wrought steel butt-welding short radius elbows and returns	B16.9	Threaded PVC plastic pipe fittings, Schedule 80	D2464
Cast Iron, Malleable Iron, Ductile Iron[b]	**ASME** ***Std.***	Threaded PVC plastic pipe fittings, Schedule 40	D2466
Cast iron pipe flanges and flanged fittings	B16.1	Socket-Type PVC plastic pipe fittings, Schedule 80	D2467
Malleable iron threaded fittings	B16.3	Reinforced epoxy resin gas pressure pipe and fittings	D2517
Gray iron threaded fittings	B16.4	Threaded CPVC plastic pipe fittings, Schedule 80	F437
Cast iron threaded drainage fittings	B16.12	Socket-Type CPVC plastic pipe fittings, Schedule 40	F438
Ductile iron pipe flanges and flanged fittings, Classes 150 and 300	B16.42	Socket-Type CPVC plastic pipe fittings, Schedule 80	F439
Copper and Bronze[c]	**ASME** ***Std.***	Insert fittings for PEX tubing	F877
Cast bronze threaded fittings, Classes 125 and 25	B16.15	Plastic brass, bronze, and copper insert fittings for PEX tubing	F877
Cast copper alloy solder joint pressure fittings	B16.18	Solvent cements for PVC plastic piping systems	D2564
Wrought copper and copper alloy solder joint pressure fittings	B16.22	Solvent cements for CPVC plastic pipe and fittings	F493
Cast copper alloy solder joint drainage fittings, DWV	B16.23		
Cast copper alloy pipe flanges and flanged fittings, Classes 150, 300, 400, 600, 900, 1500, and 2500	B16.24		

[a]Wrought steel butt-welding fittings are made to match steel pipe wall thicknesses and are rated at the same working pressure as seamless pipe. Flanges and flanged fittings are rated by working steam pressure classes. Forged steel fittings are rated from 2000 to 6000 psi in classes and are used for high-temperature and high-pressure service for small pipe sizes.
[b]Class numbers refer to maximum working saturated steam gage pressure (in psi). For liquids at lower temperatures, higher pressures are allowed. Groove-end fittings of these materials are made by various manufacturers who publish their own ratings.
[c]Classes refer to maximum working steam gage pressure (in psi). At ambient temperatures, higher liquid pressures are allowed. Solder joint fittings are limited by the strength of the soldered or brazed joint (see Table 20).
[d]Ratings of plastic fittings match the pipe of corresponding schedule number.

Table 20 Internal Working Pressure for Copper Tube Joints

Alloy Used for Joints	Service Temperature, °F	Internal Working Pressure, psi — Water and Noncorrosive Liquids and Gases[a] — Nominal Tube Size (Types K, L, M), in.: 1/4 to 1	1 1/4 to 2	2 1/2 to 4	5 to 8[a]	10 to 12[a]	Sat. Steam and Condensate: 1/4 to 8
50-50 tin/lead[b] solder (ASTM B32 Gr 50A)	100	200	175	150	130	100	—
	150	150	125	100	90	70	—
	200	100	90	75	70	50	—
	250	85	75	50	45	40	15
95-5 tin/antimony[c] solder (ASTM B32 Gr 50TA)	100	500	400	300	270	150	—
	150	400	350	275	250	150	—
	200	300	250	200	180	140	—
	250	200	175	150	135	110	15
Brazing alloys melting at or above 1000°F	100 to 200	d	d	d	d	d	
	250	300	210	170	150	150	—
	350	270	190	150	150	150	120

Source: Based on ASME *Standard* B31.9, Building Services Piping
[a]Solder joints are not to be used for
(1) Flammable or toxic gases or liquids
(2) Gas, vapor, or compressed air in tubing over 4 in., unless max. pressure is limited to 20 psig.
[b]Lead solders must not be used in potable-water systems.
[c]Tin/antimony solder is allowed for potable-water supplies in some jurisdictions.
[d]Rated pressure for up to 200°F applies to the tube being joined.

Flared and Compression Joints

Flared and compression fittings can be used to join copper, steel, stainless steel, and aluminum tubing. Properly rated fittings can keep the joints as strong as the tube.

Flanges

Flanges can be used for large pipe and all piping materials. They are commonly used to connect to equipment and valves, and wherever the joint must be opened to allow service or replacement of components. For steel pipe, flanges are available in pressure ratings to 2500 psig. High-tensile-strength bolts must be used for high-pressure flanged joints.

For welded pipe, weld neck, slip-on, or socket weld flanges are available. Thread-on flanges are available for threaded pipe.

Flanges are generally flat faced or raised face. Flat-faced flanges with full-faced gaskets are most often used with cast iron and materials that cannot take high bending loads. Raised-face flanges with ring gaskets are preferred with steel pipe because they facilitate increasing the sealing pressure on the gasket to help prevent leaks. Other facings, such as O ring and ring joint, are available for special applications.

All flat-faced, raised-face, and lap-joint flanges require a gasket between the mating flange surfaces. Gaskets are made from rubber, synthetic elastomers, cork, fiber, plastic, polytetrafluoroethylene

(PTFE), metal, and combinations of these materials. The gasket must be compatible with the flowing media and the temperatures at which the system operates.

Welding

Welded-steel pipe joints offer the following advantages:

- Do not age, dry out, or deteriorate as gasketed joints do
- Can accommodate greater vibration and water hammer and higher temperatures and pressures than other joints
- For critical service, can be tested by several nondestructive examination (NDE) methods, such as radiography or ultrasound
- Provide maximum long-term reliability

The applicable sections of the ASME *Standard* B31 series and the ASME *Boiler and Pressure Vessel Code* give rules for welding. ASTM *Standard* B31 requires that all welders and welding procedure specifications (WPS) be qualified. Separate WPS are needed for different welding methods and materials. The qualifying tests and the variables requiring separate procedure specifications are set forth in the ASME *Boiler and Pressure Vessel Code*, Section IX. The manufacturer, fabricator, or contractor is responsible for the welding procedure and welders. ASME *Standard* B31.9 requires visual examination of welds and outlines limits of acceptability.

The following welding processes are often used in the HVAC industry:

- **Shielded metal arc welding (SMAW)**, also called stick welding): the molten weld metal is shielded by vaporization of the electrode coating.
- **Gas metal arc welding (GMAW)**, also called **metal inert gas (MIG) welding**: the electrode is a continuously fed wire shielded by argon or carbon dioxide gas from the welding gun nozzle.
- **Gas tungsten arc welding (GTAW)**, also called **tungsten insert gas (TIG) welding**: this process uses a nonconsumable tungsten electrode surrounded by a shielding gas. The weld material may be provided from a separate noncoated rod.

Integrally Reinforced Outlet Fittings

Integrally reinforced outlet fittings are used to make branch and take-off connections and are designed to allow welding directly to pipe without supplemental reinforcing. Fittings are available with threaded, socket welded, or butt-weld outlets.

Solvent Cement

Solvent cement welds nonmetallic pipe together by softening surface of the materials being joined. It is different from gluing, which hardens and holds the material together. Sometimes this join is called a **solvent-welded joint**.

Rolled-Groove Joints

Grooved joints require special grooved fittings and a shallow groove cut or rolled into the pipe end. These joints can be used with steel, cast iron, ductile iron, copper, and plastic pipes. A segmented clamp engages the grooves and a special gasket uses internal pressure to tighten the seal. Some clamps are designed with clearance between tongue and groove to accommodate misalignment and thermal movements, and others are designed to limit movement and provide a rigid system. Manufacturers' data give temperature and pressure limitations.

Bell-and-Spigot Joints

A bell-and-spigot joint is mechanical joint consists of a **sleeve** slightly larger than the outside diameter of the pipe. The pipe ends are inserted into the sleeve, and gaskets are packed into the annular space between the pipe and coupling and held in place by retainer rings. This type of joint can accept some axial misalignment, but it must be anchored or otherwise restrained to prevent axial pullout or lateral movement. Manufacturers provide pressure/temperature data.

Press-Connect (Press Fit) Joints

These joints rely on an elastomeric gasket or seal and an approved pressing tool and jaws to seal the joint.

Push-Connect Joints

Push-connect joining use and integral elastomeric seal or gasket and stainless steel ring to make a leak-free joint. There are two common types, both of which form strong, permanent joints: one type is removable for servicing, and the other type is not easily removed after installation.

Unions

Unions allow disassembly of threaded pipe systems. Unions are three-part fittings with a mating machined seat on the two parts that thread onto the pipe ends. A threaded locking ring holds the two ends tightly together. A union also allows threaded pipe to be turned at the last joint connecting two pieces of equipment. Companion flanges (a pair) for small pipe serve the same purpose.

2.4 EXPANSION JOINTS AND EXPANSION COMPENSATING DEVICES

Although the inherent flexibility of the piping should be used to the maximum extent possible, expansion joints must be used where movements are too large to accommodate with pipe bends or loops or where insufficient room exists to construct a loop of adequate size. Typical situations are tunnel piping and risers in high-rise buildings, especially for steam and hot-water pipes where large thermal movements are involved.

Packed and packless expansion joints and expansion compensating devices are used to accommodate movement, either axially or laterally.

In the **axial method** of accommodating movement, the expansion joint is installed between anchors in a straight-line segment and accommodates axial motion only. This method has high anchor loads, primarily because of pressure thrust. It requires careful guiding, but expansion joints can be spaced conveniently to limit movement of branch connections. The axial method finds widest application for long runs without natural offsets, such as tunnel and underground piping and risers in tall buildings.

The **lateral** or **offset method** requires the device to be installed in a leg perpendicular to the expected movement and accommodates lateral movement only. This method generally has low anchor forces and minimal guide requirements. It finds widest application in lines with natural offsets, especially where there are few or no branch connections.

Packed expansion joints depend on slipping or sliding surfaces to accommodate the movement and require some type of seals or packing to seal the surfaces. Most such devices require some maintenance but are not subject to catastrophic failure. Further, with most packed expansion joint devices, any leaks that develop can be repacked under full line pressure without shutting down the system.

Packless expansion joints depend on the flexing or distortion of the sealing element to accommodate movement. They generally do not require any maintenance, but maintenance or repair is not usually possible. If a leak occurs, the system must be shut off and drained, and the entire device must be replaced. Further, catastrophic failure of the sealing element can occur and, although likelihood of such failure is remote, it must be considered in certain design situations.

Packed expansion joints are preferred where long-term system reliability is of prime importance (using types that can be repacked under full line pressure) and where major leaks can be life threatening or extremely costly. Typical applications are risers, tunnels, underground pipe, and distribution piping systems. Packless expansion joints are generally used where even small leaks cannot be tolerated (e.g., for gas and toxic chemicals), where temperature limitations preclude the use of packed expansion joints, and for very-large-diameter pipe where packed expansion joints cannot be constructed or the cost would be excessive.

In all cases, expansion joints should be installed, anchored, and guided in accordance with expansion joint manufacturers' recommendations.

Packed Expansion Joints

There are two types of packed expansion joints: packed slip expansion joints and flexible ball joints.

Packed Slip Expansion Joints. These are telescoping devices designed to accommodate axial movement only. Packing seals the sliding surfaces. The original packed slip expansion joint used multiple layers of braided compression packing, similar to the stuffing box commonly used with valves and pumps; this arrangement requires shutting and draining the system for maintenance and repair. Advances in design and packing technology have eliminated these problems, and most current packed slip joints use self-lubricating semiplastic packing, that can be injected under full line pressure without shutting off the system (Figure 7). (Many manufacturers use asbestos-based packings, unless requested otherwise. Asbestos-free packings, such as flake graphite, are available and, although more expensive, should be specified in lieu of products containing asbestos.)

Standard packed slip expansion joints are constructed of carbon steel with weld or flange ends in sizes 1.5 to 36 in. for pressures up to 300 psig and temperatures up to 800°F. Larger, higher-temperature, and higher-pressure designs are available. Standard single joints are generally designed for 4, 8, or 12 in. axial traverse; double joints with an intermediate anchor base can accommodate twice these movements. Special designs for greater movements are available.

Flexible Ball Joints. These joints are used in pairs to accommodate lateral or offset movement and must be installed in a leg perpendicular to the expected movement. The original flexible ball joint design incorporated only inner and outer containment seals that could not be serviced or replaced without removing the ball joint from the system. The packing technology of the packed slip expansion joint, explained previously, has been incorporated into the flexible ball joint design; now, packed flexible ball joints have self-lubricating semiplastic packing that can be injected under full line pressure without shutting off the system (Figure 8).

Standard flexible ball joints are available in sizes 1 1/4 to 30 in. with threaded (1 1/4 to 2 in.), weld, and flange ends for pressures to 300 psig and temperatures to 750°F. Flexible ball joints are available in larger sizes and for higher temperature and pressure ranges.

Packless Expansion Joints

Types include metal bellows expansion joints, rubber expansion joints, and flexible hose or pipe connectors.

Metal Bellows Expansion Joints. These expansion joints have a thin-walled convoluted section that accommodates movement by bending or flexing. The bellows material is generally Type 304, 316, or 321 stainless steel, but other materials are commonly used to satisfy service conditions. Small-diameter expansion joints 3/4 to 3 in. are generally called **expansion compensators** and are available in all-bronze or steel construction. Metal bellows expansion joints can generally be designed for the pressures and temperatures commonly encountered in HVAC systems and can also be furnished in rectangular configurations for ducts and chimney connectors.

Overpressurization, improper guiding, and other forces can distort the bellows element. For low-pressure applications, such distortion can be controlled by the geometry of the convolution or the thickness of the bellows material. For higher pressure, internally pressurized joints require reinforcing. Externally pressurized designs are not subject to such distortion and are not generally furnished without supplemental bellows reinforcing.

Single- and double-bellows expansion joints primarily accommodate axial movement only, similar to packed slip expansion joints. Although bellows expansion joints can accommodate some lateral movement, the **universal tied bellows expansion joint** better accommodates large lateral movement. This device operates much like a pair of flexible ball joints, except that bellows elements are used instead of flexible ball elements. The tie rods on this joint contain the pressure thrust, so anchor loads are much lower than with axial-type expansion joints.

Rubber Expansion Joints. Similar to single-metal bellows expansion joints, rubber expansion joints incorporate a nonmetallic elastomeric bellows sealing element and generally have more stringent temperature and pressure limitations. Although rubber expansion joints can be used to accommodate expansion and contraction of the piping, they are primarily used as flexible connectors at equipment to isolate sound and vibration and eliminate stress at equipment nozzles.

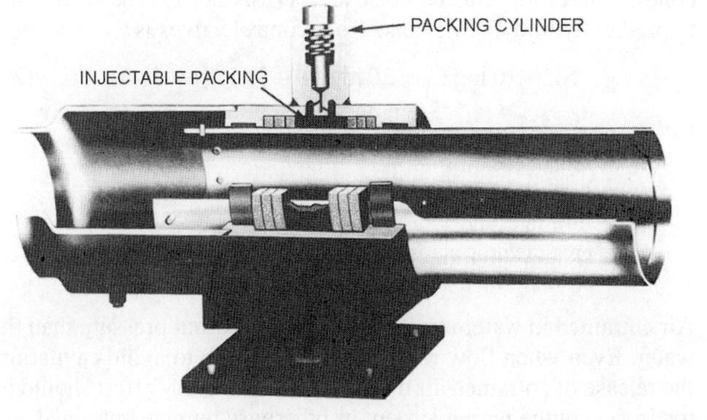

Fig. 7 Packed Slip Expansion Joint

Fig. 8 Flexible Ball Joint

Table 21 Piping System Design Maximum Flow Rate for Energy Conservation[a,b]

Operating Hours/year		≤2000				>2000 and ≤4400				>4400			
Pipe Size, in.		Other		Variable Flow/ Variable Speed		Other		Variable Flow/ Variable Speed		Other		Variable Flow/ Variable Speed	
Nominal	IPS Sched. 40 Std. ID	gpm	fps	gpm	fps	gpm	fps	gpm	fps	gpm	fps	gpm	fps
2.5	2.469	120	8.04	180	12.06	85	5.7	130	8.71	68	4.56	110	7.37
3	3.068	180	7.81	270	11.72	140	6.08	210	9.12	110	4.77	170	7.38
4	4.026	350	8.82	530	13.36	260	6.55	400	10.08	210	5.29	320	8.07
5	5.047	410	6.58	620	9.94	310	4.97	470	7.54	250	4.01	370	5.93
6	6.056	750	8.35	1100	12.25	570	6.35	860	9.58	440	4.90	680	7.58
8	7.981	1200	7.70	1800	11.55	900	5.77	1400	8.98	700	4.49	1100	7.06
10	10.02	1800	7.32	2700	10.99	1300	5.29	2000	8.14	1000	4.07	1600	6.51
12	11.938	2500	7.17	3800	10.89	1900	5.45	2900	8.13	1500	4.30	2300	6.59
>12		NA	8.5	NA	13.0	NA	6.5	NA	9.5	NA	5	NA	7.5

[a]*Source*: Based on ASHRAE *Standard* 90.1-2013 Table 6.5.4.5 with the addition of IPS and calculation for velocity in feet per second (fps).
[b]This table does not apply to district energy systems, and velocities in larger-bore piping can exceed these values per an interpretation of the ASHRAE 90.1 committee.

Table 22 Water Velocities Based on Type of Service

Type of Service	Velocity, fps	Reference
General service	4 to 10	a, b, c
City water	3 to 7	a, b
	2 to 5	c
Boiler feed	6 to 15	a, c
Pump suction and drain lines	4 to 7	a, b

[a]Crane Co. (1976). [b]Carrier (1960). [c]Grinnell Company (1951).

Table 23 Maximum Water Velocity to Minimize Erosion

Normal Operation, h/yr	Water Velocity, fps
1500	15
2000	14
3000	13
4000	12
6000	10

Source: Carrier (1960).

Flexible Hose. This type of hose can be constructed of elastomeric material or corrugated metal with an outer braid for reinforcing and end restraint. Flexible hose is primarily used as a flexible connector at equipment to isolate sound and vibration and eliminate stress at equipment nozzles; however, flexible metal hose is well suited for use as an **offset-type expansion joint**, especially for copper tubing and branch connections off risers.

3. APPLICATIONS

3.1 WATER PIPING

Flow Rate Limitations

Stewart and Dona (1987) surveyed the literature relating to water flow rate limitations. Noise, erosion, and installation and operating costs all limit the maximum and minimum velocities in piping systems. If piping sizes are too small, noise levels, erosion levels, and pumping costs can be unfavorable. If piping sizes are too large, installation costs are excessive. Therefore, pipe sizes are chosen to minimize initial cost while avoiding the undesirable effects of high velocities. ASHRAE *Standard* 90.1 has been accepted by authorities having jurisdiction (AHJs) as a code and, as such, limits the flow for energy conservation. The table (Table 21) is reproduced with modification showing velocity limitations.

Various upper limits of water velocity and/or pressure drop in piping and piping systems are used. One recommendation places a velocity limit of 4 fps for 2 in. pipe and smaller, and a pressure drop limit of 4 ft of water/100 ft for piping over 2 in. Other guidelines are based on the type of service (Table 22) or annual operating hours (Table 23). These limitations are imposed either to control the levels of pipe and valve noise, erosion, and water hammer pressure or for economic reasons. Carrier (1960) recommends that the velocity not exceed 15 fps in any case.

Noise Generation

Velocity-dependent noise in piping and piping systems results from any or all of four sources: turbulence, cavitation, release of entrained air, and water hammer. In investigations of flow-related noise, Ball and Webster (1976), Marseille (1965), and Rogers (1953, 1954, 1956) reported that velocities on the order of 10 to 17 fps lie within the range of allowable noise levels for residential and commercial buildings. The experiments showed considerable variation in noise levels obtained for a specified velocity. Generally, systems with longer pipe and with more numerous fittings and valves were noisier. In addition, sound measurements were taken under widely differing conditions; for example, some tests used plastic-covered pipe, whereas others did not. Thus, no detailed correlations relating sound level to flow velocity in generalized systems are available.

Noise generated by fluid flow in a pipe increases sharply if cavitation or release of entrained air occurs. Usually, the combination of high water velocity with a change in flow direction or a decrease in pipe cross section, causing a sudden pressure drop, is necessary to cause cavitation. Ball and Webster (1976) found that at their maximum velocity of 42 fps, cavitation did not occur in straight 3/8 and 1/2 in. pipe; using the apparatus with two elbows, cold-water velocities up to 21 fps caused no cavitation. Cavitation did occur in orifices of 1:8 area ratio (orifice flow area is one-eighth of pipe flow area) at 5 fps and in 1:4 area ratio orifices at 10 fps (Rogers 1954).

Some data are available for predicting hydrodynamic (liquid) noise generated by control valves. The International Society of Automation compiled prediction correlations in an effort to develop control valves for reduced noise levels (ISA 2007). The correlation to predict hydrodynamic noise from control valves is

$$SL = 10 \log C_v + 20 \log \Delta p - 30 \log t + 5 \quad (20)$$

where

SL = sound level, dB
C_v = valve coefficient, gpm/(psi)$^{0.5}$
Q = flow rate, gpm
Δp = pressure drop across valve, psi
t = downstream pipe wall thickness, in.

Air entrained in water usually has a higher partial pressure than the water. Even when flow rates are small enough to avoid cavitation, the release of entrained air may create noise. Every effort should be made to vent the piping system or otherwise remove entrained air.

Erosion

Erosion in piping systems is caused by water bubbles, sand, or other solid matter impinging on the inner surface of the pipe. Generally, at velocities lower than 10 fps, erosion is not significant as long as there is no cavitation. When solid matter is entrained in the fluid at high velocities, erosion occurs rapidly, especially in bends. Thus, high velocities should not be used in systems where sand or other solids are present or where slurries are transported.

Allowances for Aging

With age, the internal surfaces of pipes become increasingly rough. This reduces the available flow with a fixed pressure supply. However, designing with excessive age allowances may result in oversized piping. Age-related decreases in capacity depend on type of water, type of pipe material, temperature of water, and type of system (open or closed) and include

- Sliming (biological growth or deposited soil on the pipe walls): occurs mainly in unchlorinated, raw water systems.
- Caking of calcareous salts: occurs in hard water (i.e., water bearing calcium salts) and increases with water temperature.
- Corrosion (incrustations of ferrous and ferric hydroxide on the pipe walls): occurs in metal pipe in soft water. Because oxygen is necessary for corrosion to take place, significantly more corrosion takes place in open systems.

Allowances for expected decreases in capacity are sometimes treated as a specific amount (percentage). Dawson and Bowman (1933) added an allowance of 15% friction loss to new pipe (equivalent to an 8% decrease in capacity). The *HDR Design Guide* (1981) increased the friction loss by 15 to 20% for closed piping systems and 75 to 90% for open systems. Carrier (1960) indicates a factor of approximately 1.75 between friction factors for closed and open systems.

Obrecht and Pourbaix (1967) differentiated between the corrosive potential of different metals in potable water systems and concluded that iron is the most severely attacked, then galvanized steel, lead, copper, and finally copper alloys (e.g., brass). Freeman (1941) and Hunter (1941) showed the same trend. After four years of cold- and hot-water use, copper pipe had a capacity loss of 25 to 65%. Aged ferrous pipe has a capacity loss of 40 to 80%. Smith (1983) recommended increasing the design discharge by 1.55 for uncoated cast iron, 1.08 for iron and steel, and 1.06 for cement or concrete.

The Plastic Pipe Institute (1971) found that corrosion is not a problem in plastic pipe; the capacity of plastic pipe in Europe and the United States remains essentially the same after 30 years in use.

Extensive age-related flow data are available for use with the Hazen-Williams empirical equation. Difficulties arise in its application, however, because the original Hazen-Williams roughness coefficients are valid only for the specific pipe diameters, water velocities, and water viscosities used in the original experiments. Thus, when the *C*s are extended to different diameters, velocities, and/or water viscosities, errors of up to about 50% in pipe capacity can occur (Sanks 1978; Williams and Hazen 1933).

Water Hammer

When any moving fluid (not just water) is abruptly stopped, as when a valve closes suddenly, large pressures can develop. Although detailed analysis requires knowledge of the elastic properties of the pipe and the flow-time history, the limiting case of rigid pipe and instantaneous closure is simple to calculate. Under these conditions,

$$\Delta p_h = \rho c_s V / g_c \tag{21}$$

where

Δp_h = pressure rise caused by water hammer, lb_f/ft^2
ρ = fluid density, lb_m/ft^3
c_s = velocity of sound in fluid, fps
V = fluid flow velocity, fps

The c_s for water is 4720 fps, although the pipe's elasticity reduces the effective value.

Example 3. What is the maximum pressure rise if water flowing at 10 fps is stopped instantaneously?

Solution: $\Delta p_h = 62.4 \times 4720 \times 10/32.2 = 91{,}468\ lb/ft^2 = 635$ psi

3.2 SERVICE WATER PIPING

Sizing service water piping differs from sizing process lines in that design flows in service water piping are determined by the probability of simultaneous operation of multiple individual loads such as water closets, urinals, lavatories, sinks, and showers. The full-flow characteristics of each load device are readily obtained from manufacturers; however, service water piping sized to handle all load devices simultaneously would be seriously oversized. Thus, a major issue in sizing service water piping is to determine the diversity of the loads.

The procedure shown in this chapter uses the work of R.B. Hunter for estimating diversity (Hunter 1940, 1941). The present-day plumbing designer is usually constrained by building or plumbing codes, which specify the individual and collective loads to be used for pipe sizing. Frequently used codes (including the ICC *International Plumbing Code* and the PHCC *National Standard Plumbing Code*) contain procedures quite similar to those shown here. The designer must be aware of the applicable code for the location being considered.

Federal mandates are forcing plumbing fixture manufacturers to reduce design flows to many types of fixtures, but these may not yet be included in locally adopted codes. Also, the designer must be aware of special considerations; for example, toilet usage at sports arenas will probably have much less diversity than codes allow and thus may require larger supply piping than the minimum specified by codes.

Table 24 gives the rate of flow desirable for many common fixtures and the average pressure necessary to give this rate of flow. Pressure varies with fixture design.

In estimating load, the rate of flow is frequently computed in **fixture units** that are relative indicators of flow. Table 25 gives the demand weights in terms of fixture units for different plumbing fixtures under several conditions of service, and Figure 9 gives the estimated demand corresponding to any total number of fixture units. Figures 10 and 11 provide more accurate estimates at the lower end of the scale.

The estimated demand load for fixtures used intermittently on any supply pipe can be obtained by multiplying the number of each kind of fixture supplied through that pipe by its weight from Table 25, adding the products, and then referring to the appropriate curve of

Table 24 Proper Flow and Pressure Required During Flow for Different Fixtures

Fixture	Flow Pressure, psig[a]	Flow, gpm
Ordinary basin faucet	8	3.0
Self-closing basin faucet	12	2.5
Sink faucet, 3/8 in.	10	4.5
Sink faucet, 1/2 in.	5	4.5
Dishwasher	15 to 25	—[b]
Bathtub faucet	5	6.0
Laundry tube cock, 1/4 in.	5	5.0
Shower	12	3 to 10
Ball cock for closet	15	3.0
Flush valve for closet	10 to 20	15 to 40[c]
Flush valve for urinal	15	15.0
Garden hose, 50 ft, and sill cock	30	5.0

[a]Flow pressure is that in pipe at entrance to fixture.
[b]Varies; see manufacturers' data.
[c]Wide range because of variation in design and type of flush valve closets.

Table 25 Demand Weights of Fixtures in Fixture Units[a]

Fixture or Group[b]	Occupancy	Type of Supply Control	Weight in Fixture Units[c]
Water closet	Public	Flush valve	10
		Flush tank	5
Pedestal urinal	Public	Flush valve	10
Stall or wall urinal	Public	Flush valve	5
		Flush tank	3
Lavatory	Public	Faucet	2
Bathtub	Public	Faucet	4
Shower head	Public	Mixing valve	4
Service sink	Office, etc.	Faucet	3
Kitchen sink	Hotel or restaurant	Faucet	4
Water closet	Private	Flush valve	6
		Flush tank	3
Lavatory	Private	Faucet	1
Bathtub	Private	Faucet	2
Shower head	Private	Mixing valve	2
Bathroom group	Private	Flush valve for closet	8
		Flush tank for closet	6
Separate shower	Private	Mixing valve	2
Kitchen sink	Private	Faucet	2
Laundry trays (1 to 3)	Private	Faucet	3
Combination fixture	Private	Faucet	3

Source: Hunter (1941).

[a]For supply outlets likely to impose continuous demands, estimate continuous supply separately, and add to total demand for fixtures.

[b]For fixtures not listed, weights may be assumed by comparing fixture to listed one using water in similar quantities and at similar rates.

[c]Given weights are for total demand. For fixtures with both hot- and cold-water supplies, weights for maximum separate demands can be assumed to be 75% of listed demand for the supply.

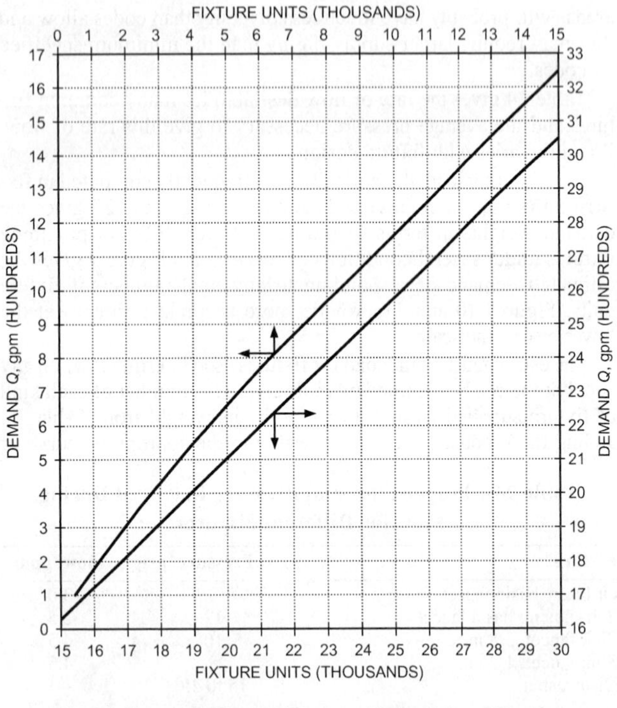

Fig. 9 Demand Versus Fixture Units, Mixed System, High Part of Curve
(Adapted from Hunter 1941)

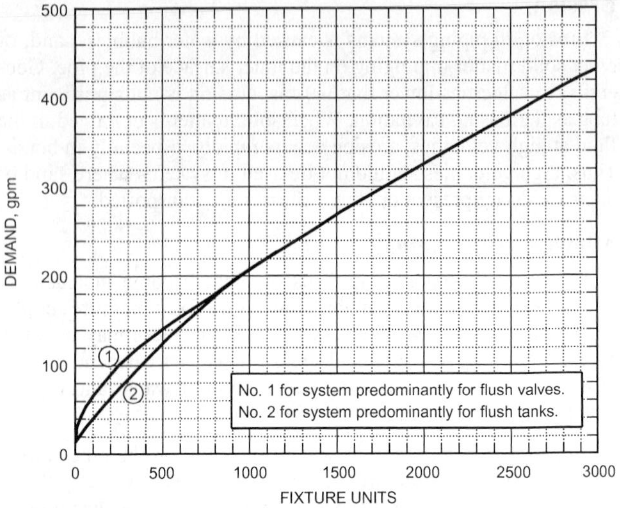

Fig. 10 Estimate Curves for Demand Load
(Adapted from Hunter 1941)

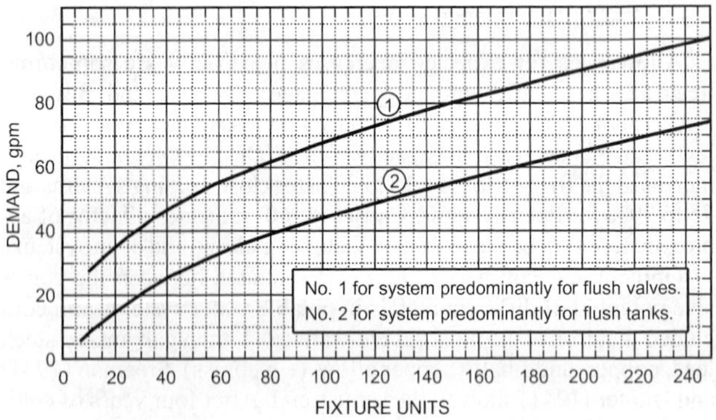

Fig. 11 Section of Figure 10 on Enlarged Scale

Figure 9, 10, or 11 to find the demand corresponding to the total fixture units. In using this method, note that the demand for fixture or supply outlets other than those listed in the table of fixture units is not yet included in the estimate. The demands for outlets (e.g., hose connections and air-conditioning apparatus) that are likely to impose continuous demand during heavy use of the weighted fixtures should be estimated separately and added to demand for fixtures used intermittently to estimate total demand.

The Hunter curves in Figures 9, 10, and 11 are based on use patterns in residential buildings and can be erroneous for other usages such as sports arenas. Williams (1976) discusses the Hunter assumptions and presents an analysis using alternative assumptions.

So far, the information presented shows the *design rate of flow* to be determined in any particular section of piping. The next step is to determine the *size* of piping. As water flows through a pipe, the pressure continually decreases along the pipe because of loss of energy from friction. The problem is then to ascertain the minimum pressure in the street main and the minimum pressure required to operate the topmost fixture. (A pressure of 15 psig may be ample for most flush valves, but manufacturers' requirements should be consulted. Some fixtures require a pressure up to 25 psig. A minimum of 8 psig should be allowed for other fixtures.) The pressure differential overcomes pressure losses in the distributing system and the difference in elevation between the water main and the highest fixture.

The pressure loss (in psi) resulting from the difference in elevation between the street main and the highest fixture can be obtained by multiplying the difference in elevation in feet by the conversion factor 0.434.

Pressure losses in the distributing system consist of pressure losses in the piping itself, plus the pressure losses in the pipe fittings, valves, and the water meter, if any. Approximate design pressure losses and flow limits for disk-type meters for various rates of flow are given in Figure 12. Water authorities in many localities require compound meters for greater accuracy with varying flow; consult the local utility. Design data for compound meters differ from the data in Figure 12. Manufacturers give data on exact pressure losses and capacities.

Figure 13 shows the variation of pressure loss with rate of flow for various faucets and cocks. The water demand for hose bibbs or other large-demand fixtures taken off the building main frequently results in inadequate water supply to the upper floor of a building. This condition can be prevented by sizing the distribution system so that pressure drops from the street main to all fixtures are the same. An ample building main (not less than 1 in. where possible) should be maintained until all branches to hose bibbs have been connected. Where street main pressure is excessive and a pressure-reducing valve is used to prevent water hammer or excessive pressure at fixtures, hose bibbs should be connected ahead of the reducing valve.

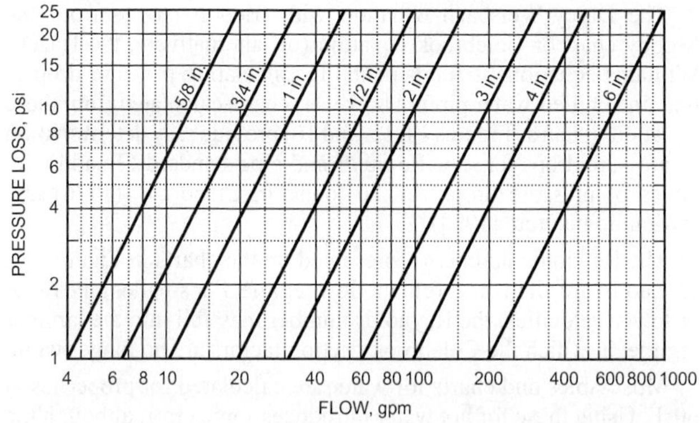

Fig. 12 Pressure Losses in Disk-Type Water Meters

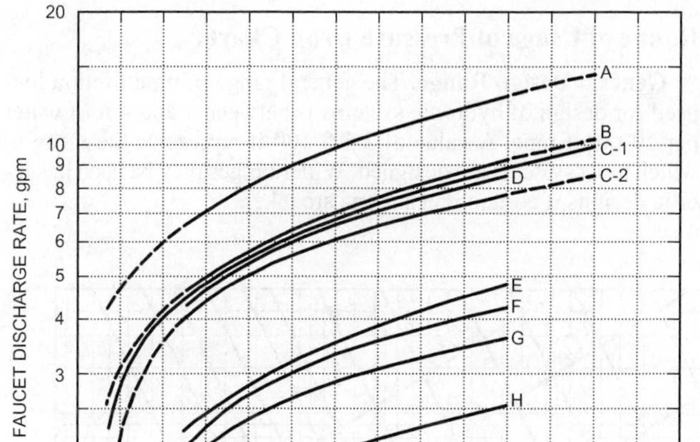

A. 1/2 in. laundry bibb (old style)
B. Laundry compression faucet
C-1. 1/2 in. compression sink faucet (mfr. 1)
C-2. 1/2 in. compression sink faucet (mfr. 2)
D. Combination compression bathtub faucets (both open)
E. Combination compression sink faucet
F. Basin faucet
G. Spring self-closing faucet
H. Slow self-closing faucet
(Dashed lines indicate recommended extrapolation)

Fig. 13 Variation of Pressure Loss with Flow Rate for Various Faucets and Cocks

The principles involved in sizing upfeed and downfeed systems are the same. In the downfeed system, however, the difference in elevation between the overhead supply mains and the fixtures provides the pressure required to overcome pipe friction. Because friction pressure loss and height pressure loss are not additive, as in an upfeed system, smaller pipes may be used with a downfeed system.

Plastic Pipe

The maximum safe water velocity in a thermoplastic piping system under most operating conditions is typically 5 fps; however, higher velocities can be used in cases where the operating characteristics of valves and pumps are known so that sudden changes in flow velocity can be controlled. The total pressure in the system at any time (operating pressure plus surge of water hammer) should not exceed 150% of the pressure rating of the system.

Procedure for Sizing Cold-Water Systems

The recommended procedure for sizing piping systems is as follows:

1. Sketch the main lines, risers, and branches, and indicate the fixtures to be served. Indicate the rate of flow of each fixture.
2. Using Table 25, compute the demand weights of the fixtures in fixture units.
3. Determine the total demand in fixture units and, using Figure 9, 10, or 11, find the expected demand.
4. Determine the equivalent length of pipe in the main lines, risers, and branches. Because the sizes of the pipes are not known, the exact equivalent length of various fittings cannot be determined. Add the equivalent lengths, starting at the street main and proceeding along the service line, main line of the building, and up the riser to the top fixture of the group served.
5. Determine the average minimum pressure in the street main and the minimum pressure required for operation of the topmost fixture, which should be 8 to 25 psi.
6. Calculate the approximate design value of the average pressure drop per 100 ft of equivalent length of pipe determined in step 4 and using Equation (1).

$$\Delta p = (p_s - 0.434H - p_f - p_m)100/L$$

where

Δp = average pressure loss per 100 ft of equivalent length of pipe, psi
p_s = pressure in street main, psig
p_f = minimum pressure required to operate topmost fixture, psig
p_m = pressure drop through water meter, psi
H = height of highest fixture above street main, ft
L = equivalent length determined in step 4, ft

If the system is downfeed supply from a gravity tank, height of water in the tank, converted to psi by multiplying by 0.434, replaces the street main pressure, and the term $0.434H$ is added instead of subtracted in calculating Δp. In this case, H is the vertical distance of the fixture below the bottom of the tank. The pressure conversion factor 0.434 is determined by the weight of water occupying a 1 ft^3 volume, or 62.4/144 = 0.434 psi per foot of water.

7. From the expected rate of flow determined in step 3 and the value of Δp calculated in step 6, choose the sizes of pipe from Figure 14, 15, or 16.

Example 4. Assume a minimum street main pressure of 55 psig; a height of topmost fixture (a urinal with flush valve) above street main of 50 ft; an equivalent pipe length from water main to highest fixture of 100 ft; a total load on the system of 50 fixture units; and that the water closets are flush valve operated. Find the required size of supply main.

Solution: Use Equation (1):

$$\Delta p = (p_s - 0.434H - p_f - p_m)100/L$$

p_s = Street main pressure (given) = 55 psig
H = 50 ft (given)
P_f = 15 psig from Table 24
Flow = 51 gpm from Figure 11

For a trial run, use 1 1/2 in.; then P_m = 6.5 psig from Figure 12 at 51 gpm. The pressure drop available for overcoming friction in pipes and fittings is 55 – 0.434 × 50 – 15 – 6.5 = 12 psi.

At this point, estimate the equivalent pipe length of the fittings on the direct line from the street main to the highest fixture. The exact equivalent length of the various fittings cannot be determined because the pipe sizes of the building main, riser, and branch leading to the highest fixture are not yet known, but a first approximation is necessary to tentatively select pipe sizes. If the computed pipe sizes differ from those used in determining the equivalent length of pipe fittings, a recalculation using the computed pipe sizes for the fittings will be necessary. It is common practice for the first trial to assume that the total equivalent length of the pipe fittings is 50% of the total length of pipe. In this example, 100 ft × 50% = 50 ft.

The permissible pressure loss per 100 ft of equivalent pipe is 12 × 100/(100 + 50) = 8 psi or 18 ft/100 ft. A 1 1/2 in. building main is adequate.

The sizing of the branches of the building main, the risers, and the fixture branches follows these principles. For example, assume that one of the branches of the building main carries the cold-water supply for three water closets, two bathtubs, and three lavatories. Using the permissible pressure loss of 8 psi per 100 ft, the size of branch (determined from Table 25 and Figures 14 and 11) is found to be 1 1/2 in. Items included in the computation of pipe size are as follows:

Fixtures, No. and Type	Fixture Units (Table 25 and Note c)	Demand (Figure 11)	Pipe Size (Figure 14)
3 flush valves	3 × 6 = 18		
2 bathtubs	0.75 × 2 × 2 = 3		
3 lavatories	0.75 × 3 × 1 = 2.25		
Total	= 23.25	38 gpm	1 1/2 in.

Table 26 is a guide to minimum pipe sizing where flush valves are used.

Velocities exceeding 10 fps cause undesirable noise in the piping system. This usually governs the size of larger pipes in the system, whereas in small pipe sizes, the friction loss usually governs the selection because the velocity is low compared to friction loss. Velocity is the governing factor in downfeed systems, where friction loss is usually neglected. Velocity in branches leading to pump suctions should not exceed 5 fps.

If the street pressure is too low to adequately supply upper-floor fixtures, the pressure must be increased. Constant- or variable-speed booster pumps, alone or in conjunction with gravity supply tanks, or hydropneumatic systems may be used.

Flow control valves for individual fixtures under varying pressure conditions automatically adjust flow at the fixture to a predetermined quantity. These valves allow the designer to (1) limit flow at the individual outlet to the minimum suitable for the purpose, (2) hold total demand for the system more closely to the required minimum, and (3) design the piping system as accurately as is practicable for the requirements.

Hydronic System Piping

The Darcy-Weisbach equation with friction factors from the Moody chart or Colebrook equation (or, alternatively, the Hazen-Williams equation) is fundamental to calculating pressure drop in hot- and chilled-water piping; however, charts calculated from these equations (such as Figures 14, 15, and 16) provide easy determination of pressure drops for specific fluids and pipe standards. In addition, tables of pressure drops can be found in Crane Co. (1976) and Hydraulic Institute (1990).

The Reynolds numbers represented on the charts in Figures 14, 15, and 16 are all in the turbulent flow regime. For smaller pipes and/or lower velocities, the Reynolds number may fall into the laminar regime, in which the Colebrook friction factors are no longer valid.

Most tables and charts for water are calculated for properties at 60°F. Using these for hot water introduces some error, although the answers are conservative (i.e., cold-water calculations overstate the pressure drop for hot water). Using 60°F water charts for 200°F water should not result in errors in Δp exceeding 20%.

Range of Usage of Pressure Drop Charts

General Design Range. The general range of pipe friction loss used for design of hydronic systems is between 1 and 4 ft of water per 100 ft of pipe. A value of 2.5 ft/100 ft represents the mean to which most systems are designed. Wider ranges may be used in specific designs if certain precautions are taken.

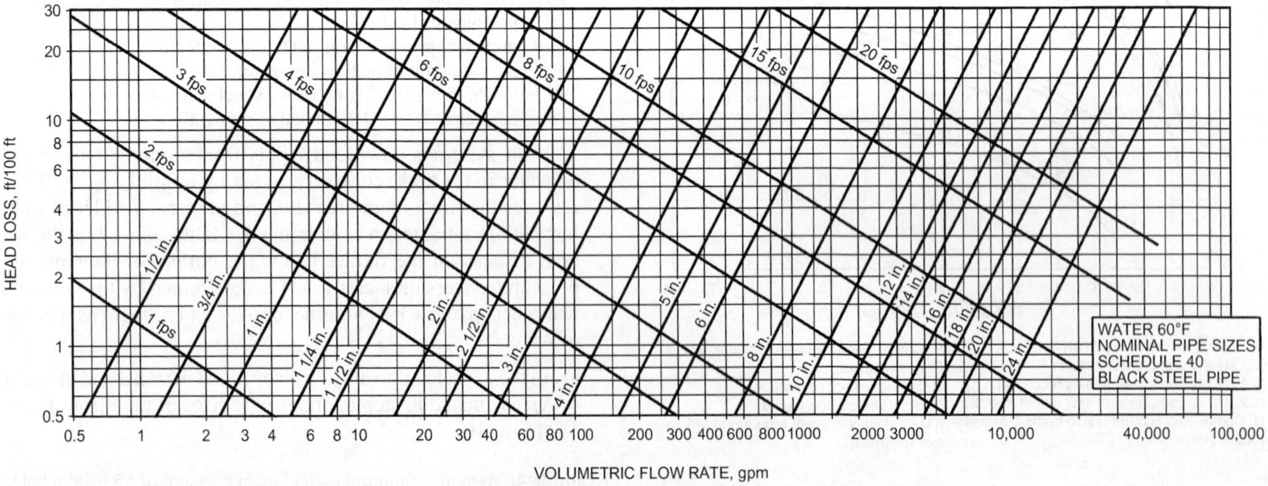

Fig. 14 Friction Loss for Water in Commercial Steel Pipe (Schedule 40)

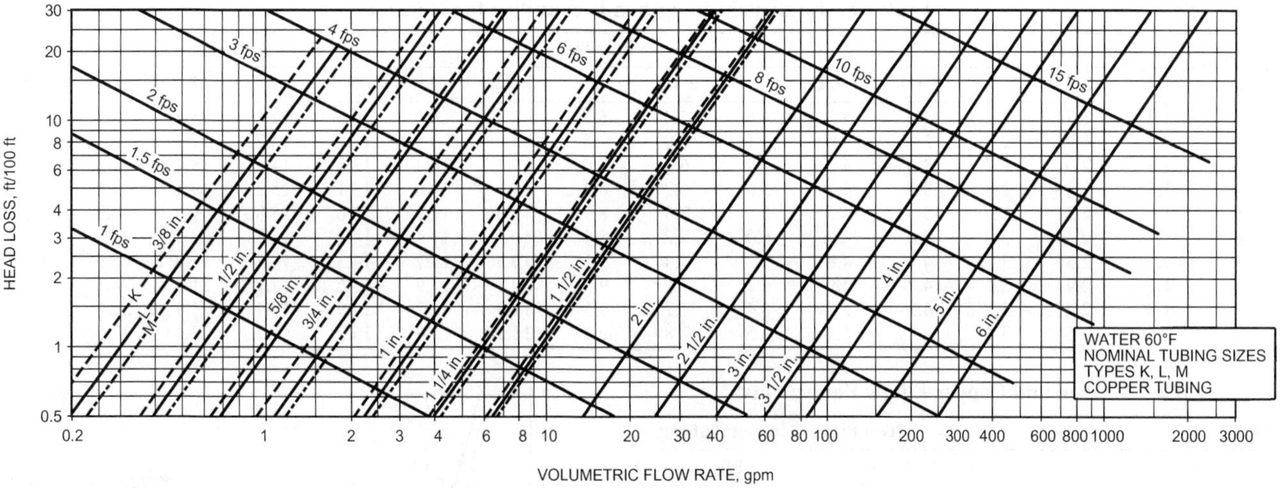

Fig. 15 Friction Loss for Water in Copper Tubing (Types K, L, M)

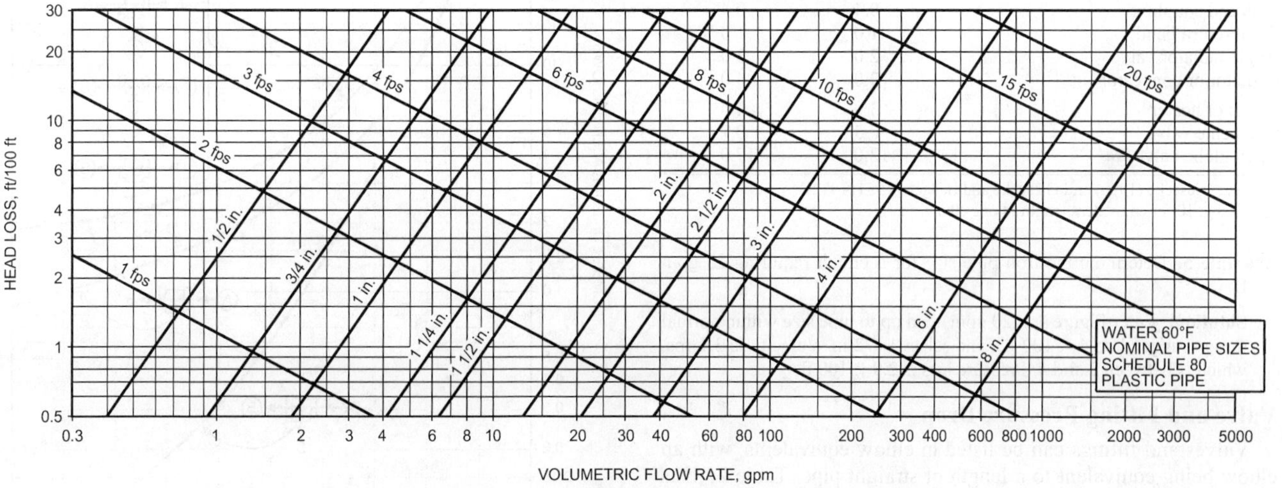

Fig. 16 Friction Loss for Water in Plastic Pipe (Schedule 80)

Table 26 Allowable Number of 1 in. Flush Valves Served by Various Sizes of Water Pipe*

Pipe Size, in.	No. of 1 in. Flush Valves
1 1/4	1
1 1/2	2 to 4
2	5 to 12
2 1/2	13 to 25
3	26 to 40
4	41 to 100

*Two 3/4 in. flush valves are assumed equal to one 1 in. flush valve but can be served by a 1 in. pipe. Water pipe sizing must consider demand factor, available pressure, and length of run.

Piping Noise. Closed-loop hydronic system piping is generally sized below certain arbitrary upper limits, such as a velocity limit of 4 fps for 2 in. pipe and under, and a pressure drop limit of 4 ft per 100 ft for piping over 2 in. in diameter. Velocities in excess of 4 fps can be used in piping of larger size. This limitation is generally accepted, although it is based on relatively inconclusive experience with noise in piping. **Water velocity noise** is not caused by water but by free air, sharp pressure drops, turbulence, or a combination of these, that cause cavitation or flashing of water into steam. Therefore, higher velocities may be used if proper precautions are taken to eliminate air and turbulence.

Air Separation

Air in hydronic systems is usually undesirable because it causes flow noise, allows oxygen to react with piping materials, and sometimes even prevents flow in parts of a system. Air may enter a system at an air/water interface in an open system or in an expansion tank in a closed system, or it may be brought in dissolved in makeup water. Most hydronic systems use air separation devices to remove air. The solubility of air in water increases with pressure and decreases with temperature; thus, ***separation of air from water is best achieved at the point of lowest pressure and/or highest temperature in a system***. For more information, see Chapter 13 of the 2016 *ASHRAE Handbook—HVAC Systems and Equipment*.

In the absence of venting, air can be entrained in the water and carried to separation units at flow velocities of 1.5 to 2 fps or more in pipe 2 in. and under. Minimum velocities of 2 fps are therefore recommended. For pipe sizes 2 in. and over, minimum velocities corresponding to a head loss of 0.75 ft/100 ft are normally used. Maintaining minimum velocities is particularly important in the upper floors of high-rise buildings where the air tends to come out of solution because of reduced pressures. Higher velocities should be used in **downcomer** return mains feeding into air separation units located in the basement.

Table 27 Equivalent Length in Feet of Pipe for 90° Elbows

Velocity, fps	Pipe Size													
	1/2	3/4	1	1 1/4	1 1/2	2	2 1/2	3	3 1/2	4	5	6	8	10	12
1	1.2	1.7	2.2	3.0	3.5	4.5	5.4	6.7	7.7	8.6	10.5	12.2	15.4	18.7	22.2
2	1.4	1.9	2.5	3.3	3.9	5.1	6.0	7.5	8.6	9.5	11.7	13.7	17.3	20.8	24.8
3	1.5	2.0	2.7	3.6	4.2	5.4	6.4	8.0	9.2	10.2	12.5	14.6	18.4	22.3	26.5
4	1.5	2.1	2.8	3.7	4.4	5.6	6.7	8.3	9.6	10.6	13.1	15.2	19.2	23.2	27.6
5	1.6	2.2	2.9	3.9	4.5	5.9	7.0	8.7	10.0	11.1	13.6	15.8	19.8	24.2	28.8
6	1.7	2.3	3.0	4.0	4.7	6.0	7.2	8.9	10.3	11.4	14.0	16.3	20.5	24.9	29.6
7	1.7	2.3	3.0	4.1	4.8	6.2	7.4	9.1	10.5	11.7	14.3	16.7	21.0	25.5	30.3
8	1.7	2.4	3.1	4.2	4.9	6.3	7.5	9.3	10.8	11.9	14.6	17.1	21.5	26.1	31.0
9	1.8	2.4	3.2	4.3	5.0	6.4	7.7	9.5	11.0	12.2	14.9	17.4	21.9	26.6	31.6
10	1.8	2.5	3.2	4.3	5.1	6.5	7.8	9.7	11.2	12.4	15.2	17.7	22.2	27.0	32.0

Table 28 Iron and Copper Elbow Equivalents*

Fitting	Iron Pipe	Copper Tubing
Elbow, 90°	1.0	1.0
45°	0.7	0.7
90° long-radius	0.5	0.5
90° welded	0.5	0.5
Reduced coupling	0.4	0.4
Open return bend	1.0	1.0
Angle radiator valve	2.0	3.0
Radiator or convector	3.0	4.0
Boiler or heater	3.0	4.0
Open gate valve	0.5	0.7
Open globe valve	12.0	17.0

Sources: Giesecke (1926) and Giesecke and Badgett (1931, 1932a).
*See Table 10 for equivalent length of one elbow.

Example 5. Determine the iron pipe size for a circuit requiring 20 gpm flow.

Solution: Enter Figure 4 at 20 gpm, read up to pipe size within normal design range (1 to 4 ft/100 ft), and select 1 1/2 in. Velocity is 3.1 fps, which is between 2 and 4. Pressure loss is 2.9 ft/100 ft.

Valve and Fitting Pressure Drop

Valves and fittings can be listed in elbow equivalents, with an elbow being equivalent to a length of straight pipe. Table 27 lists equivalent lengths of 90° elbows; Table 28 lists elbow equivalents for valves and fittings for iron and copper.

Example 6. Determine equivalent feet length of pipe for a 4 in. open gate valve at a flow velocity of approximately 4 fps.

Solution: From Table 27, at 4 fps, each elbow is equivalent to 10.6 ft of 4 in. pipe. From Table 28, the gate valve is equivalent to 0.5 elbows. The actual equivalent pipe length (added to measured circuit length for pressure drop determination) will be 10.6 × 0.5, or 5.3 equivalent feet of 4 in. pipe.

Tee Fitting Pressure Drop. Pressure drop through pipe tees varies with flow through the branch. Figure 17 shows pressure drops for nominal 1 in. tees of equal inlet and outlet sizes and for the flow patterns shown. Idelchik (1986) also presents data for threaded tees.

Different investigators present tee loss data in different forms, and it is sometimes difficult to reconcile results from several sources. As an estimate of the upper limit to tee losses, a pressure or head loss coefficient of 1.0 may be assumed for entering and leaving flows (i.e., $\Delta p = 1.0\rho V_{in}^2/2 + 1.0\rho V_{out}^2/2$).

Example 7. Determine the pressure or head losses for a 1 in. (all openings) threaded pipe tee flowing 25% to the side branch, 75% through. The entering flow is 10 gpm (3.71 fps).

Solution: From Figure 17, bottom curve, the number of equivalent elbows for the through-flow is 0.15 elbows; the through-flow is 7.5 gpm (2.78 fps); and the head loss or pressure drop is based on the exit flow rate. Table 27 gives the equivalent length of a 1 in. elbow at 3 fps as 2.7 ft. Using Figure 14, the head loss is 4 ft/100 ft for 1 in. pipe and 7.5 gpm flow.

$$\Delta p = (0.15)(2.7)(62.4/144)(4.00/100) = 0.00702 \text{ psi pressure drop}$$

$$\Delta h = (0.15)(2.7)(4.00/100) = 0.0162 \text{ ft head loss}$$

From Figure 17, top curve, the number of equivalent elbows for the branch flow of 25% is 13 elbows; the branch flow is 2.5 gpm (0.93 fps); and the head loss or pressure drop is based on the exit flow rate. Table 27 gives the equivalent of a 1 in. elbow at 1 fps as 2.2 ft. Using Figure 14, the head loss is 0.55 ft/100 ft for 1 in. pipe and 2.5 gpm flow.

$$\Delta p = (13)(2.2)(62.4/144)(0.55/100)$$

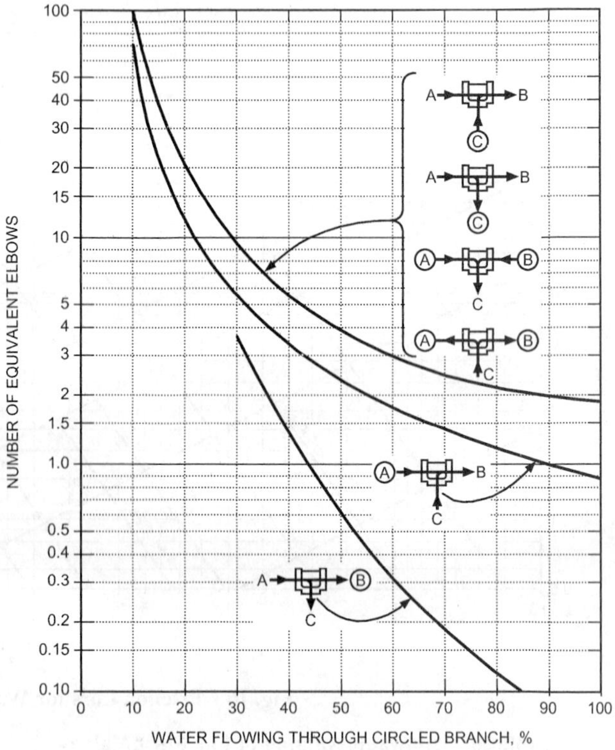

Notes:
1. Chart is based on straight tees (i.e., branches A, B, and C are the same size).
2. Pressure loss in desired circuit is obtained by selecting proper curve according to illustrations, determining flow at circled branch, and multiplying pressure loss for same size elbow at flow rate in circled branch by equivalent elbows indicated.
3. When outlet size is reduced, equivalent elbows shown do not apply. Therefore, maximum loss for any circuit for any flow will not exceed 2 elbow equivalents at maximum flow occurring in any branch of tee.
4. Top curve is average of 4 curves, one for each circuit shown.

Fig. 17 Elbow Equivalents of Tees at Various Flow Conditions (Giesecke and Badgett 1931, 1932b)

= 0.0682 psi pressure drop
$\Delta h = (13)(2.2)(0.55/100)$
= 0.157 ft head loss

3.3 STEAM PIPING

Pressure losses in steam piping for flows of dry or nearly dry steam are governed by Equations (2) to (8) in the section on Design Equations. This section incorporates these principles with other information specific to steam systems.

Pipe Sizes

Required pipe sizes for a given load in steam heating depend on the following factors:

- The initial pressure and the total pressure drop that can be allowed between the source of supply and the end of the return system
- The maximum velocity of steam allowable for quiet and dependable operation of the system, taking into consideration the direction of condensate flow
- The equivalent length of the run from the boiler or source of steam supply to the farthest heating unit

Initial Pressure and Pressure Drop. Table 29 lists pressure drops commonly used with corresponding initial steam pressures for sizing steam piping.

Several factors, such as initial pressure and pressure required at the end of the line, should be considered, but it is most important that (1) the total pressure drop does not exceed the initial gage pressure of the system (in practice, it should never exceed one-half the initial gage pressure); (2) pressure drop is not great enough to cause excessive velocities; (3) a constant initial pressure is maintained, except on systems specially designed for varying initial pressures (e.g., subatmospheric pressure), that normally operate under controlled partial vacuums; and (4) for gravity return systems, pressure drop to heating units does not exceed the water column available for removing condensate (i.e., height above the boiler water line of the lowest point on the steam main, on the heating units, or on the dry return).

Maximum Velocity. For quiet operation, steam velocity should be 8000 to 12,000 fpm, with a maximum of 15,000 fpm. The lower the velocity, the quieter the system. When condensate must flow against the steam, even in limited quantity, the steam's velocity must not exceed limits above which the disturbance between the steam and the counterflowing water may (1) produce objectionable sound, such as water hammer, or (2) result in the retention of water in certain parts of the system until the steam flow is reduced sufficiently to allow water to pass. These limits are a function of (1) pipe size; (2) pitch of the pipe if it runs horizontally; (3) quantity of condensate flowing against the steam; and (4) freedom of the piping from water pockets that, under certain conditions, act as a restriction in pipe size. Table 30 lists maximum capacities for various size steam lines.

Equivalent Length of Run. All tables for the flow of steam in pipes based on pressure drop must allow for pipe friction, as well as for the resistance of fittings and valves. These resistances are generally stated in terms of straight pipe; that is, a certain fitting produces a drop in pressure equivalent to the stated length of straight run of the same size of pipe. Table 31 gives the length of straight pipe usually allowed for the more common types of fittings and valves. In all pipe sizing tables in this chapter, *length of run* refers to the *equivalent length of run* as distinguished from the *actual length* of pipe. A common sizing method is to assume the length of run and to check this assumption after pipes are sized. For this purpose, length of run is usually assumed to be double the actual length of pipe.

Example 8. Using Table 31, determine the equivalent length in feet of pipe for the run shown.

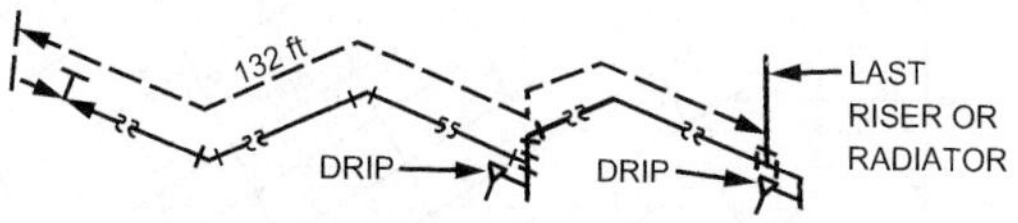

Measured length	=	132.0 ft
4 in. gate valve	=	1.9 ft
Four 4 in. elbows	=	36.0 ft
Two 4 in. tees	=	36.0 ft
Equivalent	=	205.9 ft

Sizing Charts

Figure 18 is the basic chart for determining the flow rate and velocity of steam in Schedule 40 pipe for various values of pressure

Table 29 Pressure Drops Used for Sizing Steam Pipe*

Initial Steam Pressure, psig	Pressure Drop per 100 ft	Total Pressure Drop in Steam Supply Piping
Vacuum return	2 to 4 oz/in²	1 to 2 psi
0	0.5 oz/in²	1 oz/in²
1	2 oz/in²	1 to 4 oz/in²
2	2 oz/in²	8 oz/in²
5	4 oz/in²	1.5 psi
10	8 oz/in²	3 psi
15	1 psi	4 psi
30	2 psi	5 to 10 psi
50	2 to 5 psi	10 to 15 psi
100	2 to 5 psi	15 to 25 psi
150	2 to 10 psi	25 to 30 psi

*Equipment, control valves, and so forth must be selected based on delivered pressures.

Table 30 Comparative Capacity of Steam Lines at Various Pitches for Steam and Condensate Flowing in Opposite Directions

Pitch of Pipe, in/10 ft	Nominal Pipe Diameter, in. 3/4 Capacity	3/4 Maximum Velocity	1 Capacity	1 Maximum Velocity	1 1/4 Capacity	1 1/4 Maximum Velocity	1 1/2 Capacity	1 1/2 Maximum Velocity	2 Capacity	2 Velocity
1/4	3.2	8	6.8	9	11.8	11	19.8	12	42.9	15
1/2	4.1	11	9.0	12	15.9	14	25.9	16	54.0	18
1	5.7	13	11.7	15	19.9	17	33.0	19	68.8	24
1 1/2	6.4	14	12.8	17	24.6	20	37.4	22	83.3	27
2	7.1	16	14.8	19	27.0	22	42.0	24	92.9	30
3	8.3	17	17.3	22	31.3	25	46.8	26	99.6	32
4	9.9	22	19.2	24	33.4	26	50.8	28	102.4	32
5	10.5	22	20.5	25	38.5	31	59.2	33	115.0	33

Source: Laschober et al. (1966).

Velocity in fps; capacity in lb/h.

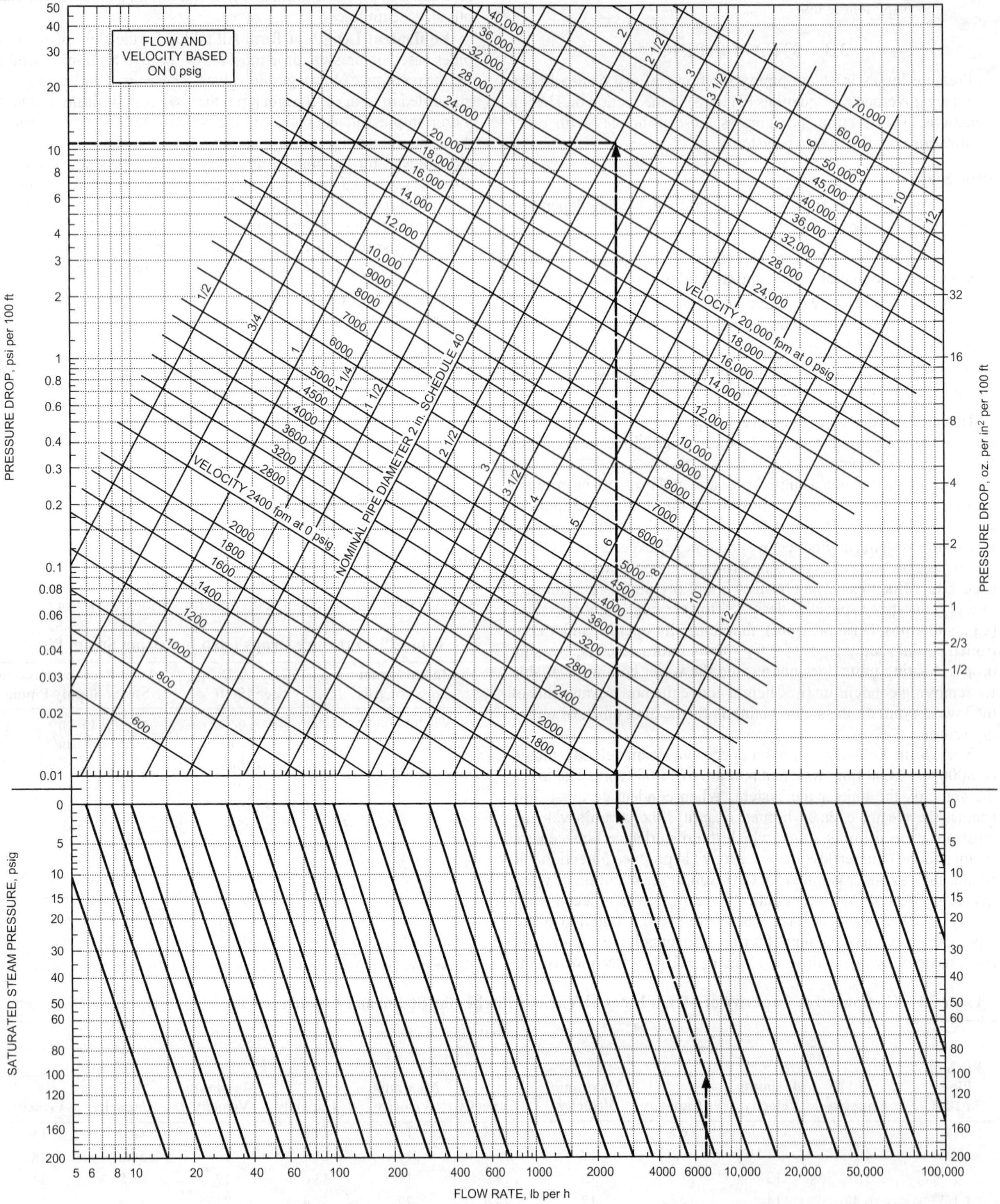

Notes: Based on Moody Friction Factor where flow of condensate does not inhibit flow of steam.
See Figure 20 for obtaining flow rates and velocities of all saturation pressures between 0 and 200 psig; see also Examples 9 and 10.

Fig. 18 Flow Rate and Velocity of Steam in Schedule 40 Pipe at Saturation Pressure of 0 psig

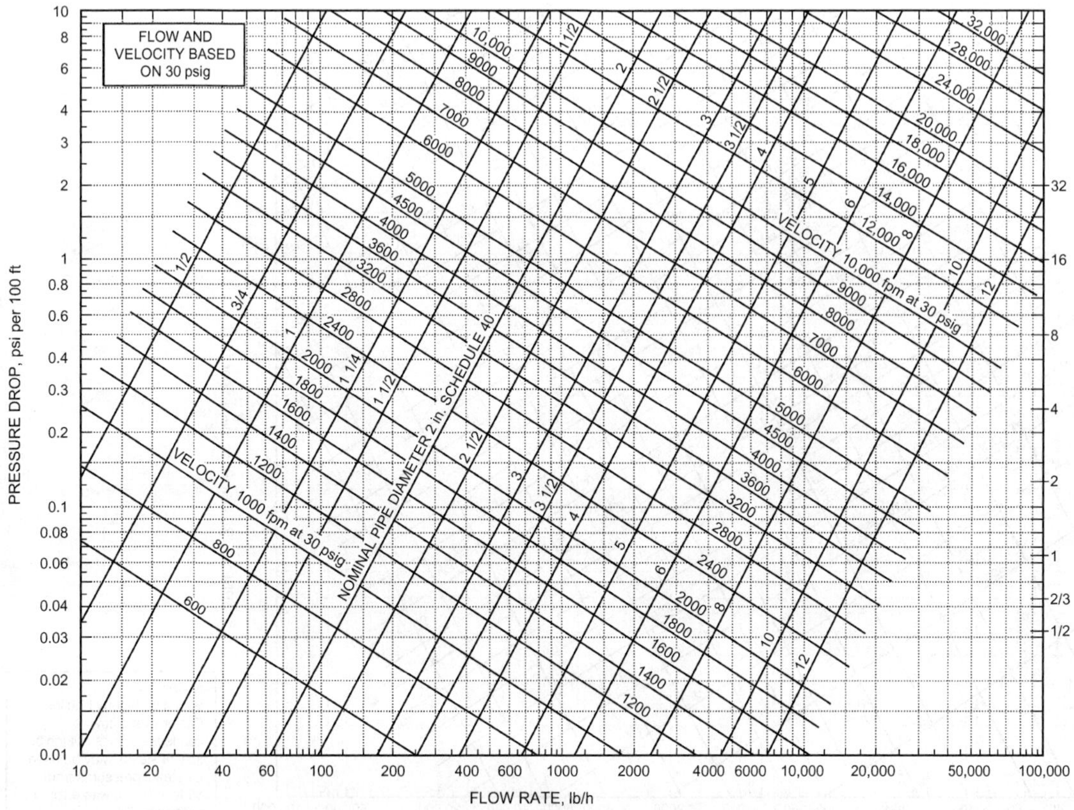

Notes:
Based on Moody Friction Factor where flow of condensate does not inhibit flow of steam.
May be used for steam pressures from 23 to 27 psig with error not exceeding 9%.

Fig. 19A Flow Rate and Velocity of Steam in Schedule 40 Pipe at Saturation Pressure of 30 psig

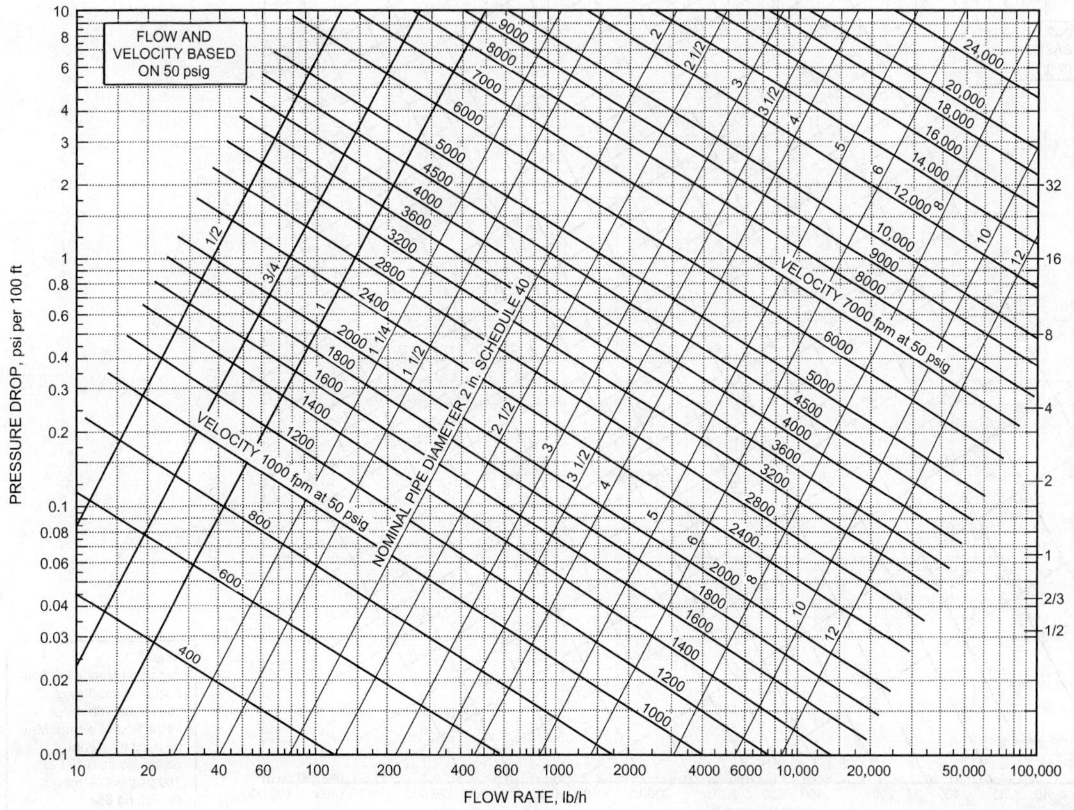

Notes:
Based on Moody Friction Factor where flow of condensate does not inhibit flow of steam.
May be used for steam pressures from 40 to 60 psig with error not exceeding 8%.

Fig. 19B Flow Rate and Velocity of Steam in Schedule 40 Pipe at Saturation Pressure of 50 psig

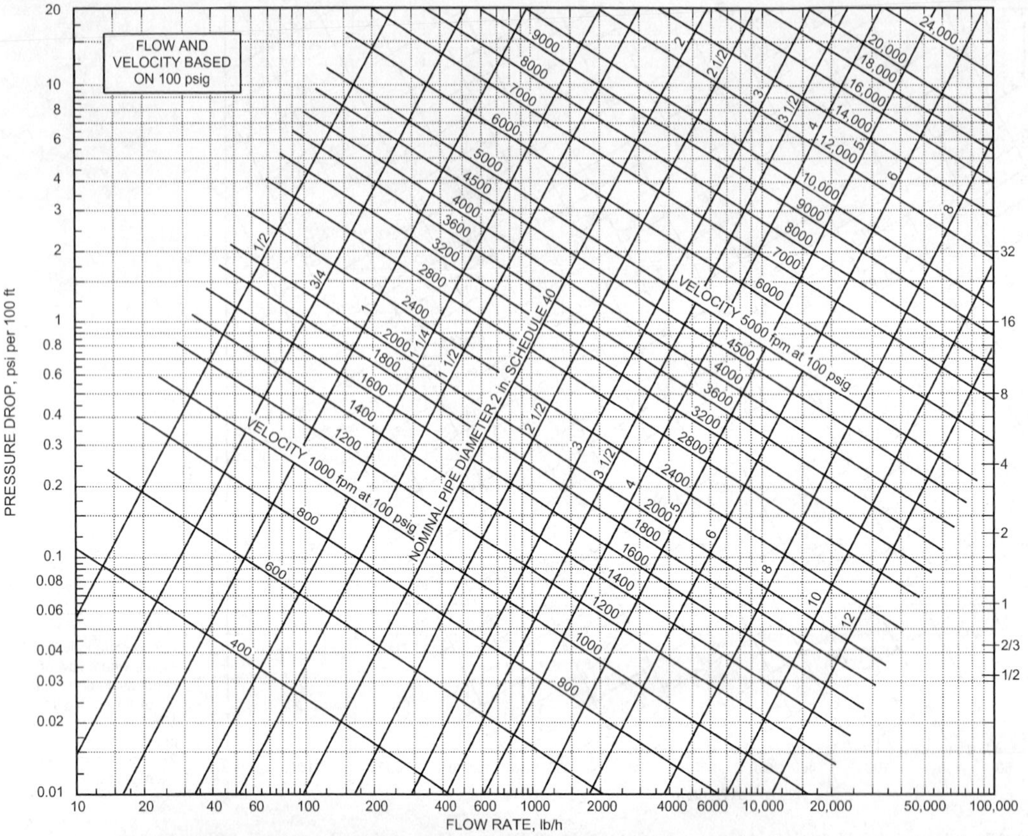

Notes:
Based on Moody Friction Factor where flow of condensate does not inhibit flow of steam. May be used for steam pressures from 85 to 120 psig with error not exceeding 8%.

Fig. 19C Flow Rate and Velocity of Steam in Schedule 40 Pipe at Saturation Pressure of 100 psig

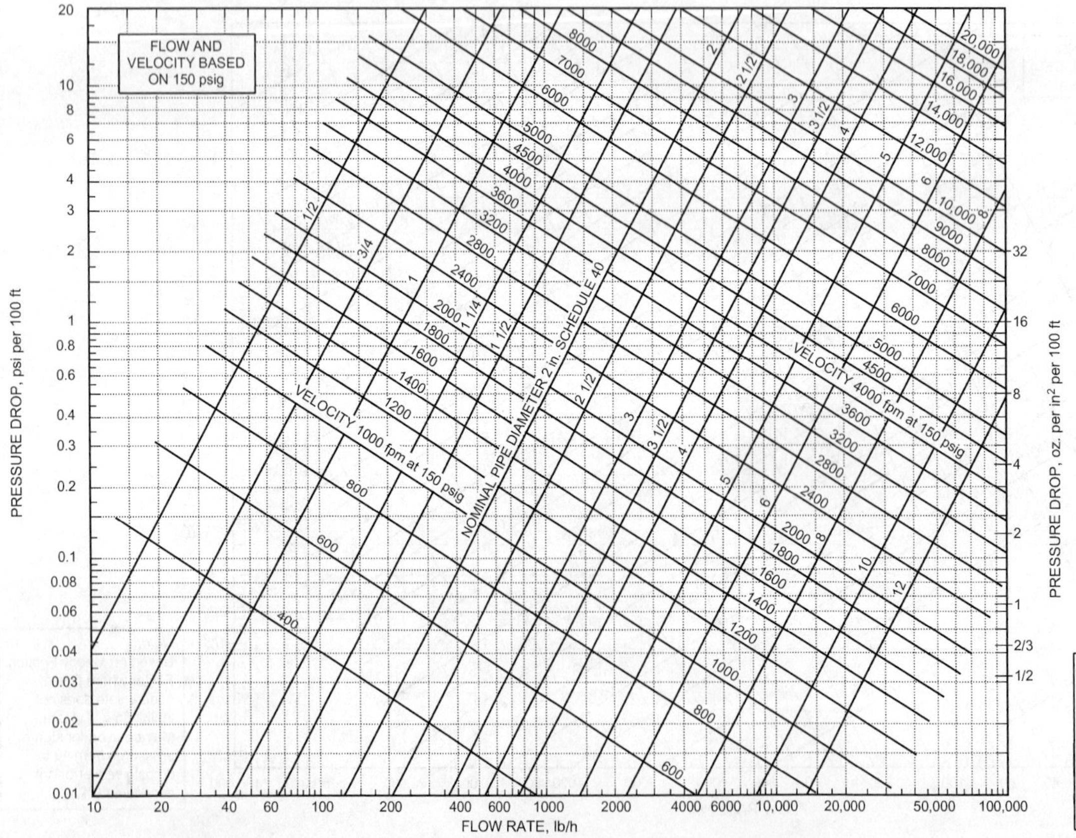

Notes:
Based on Moody Friction Factor where flow of condensate does not inhibit flow of steam. May be used for steam pressures from 127 to 180 psig with error not exceeding 8%.

Fig. 19D Flow Rate and Velocity of Steam in Schedule 40 Pipe at Saturation Pressure of 150 psig

drop per 100 ft, based on 0 psig saturated steam. Figures 19A through 19D present charts for sizing steam piping for systems of 30, 50, 100, and 150 psig at various pressure drops. These charts are based on the Moody friction factor, which considers the Reynolds number and the roughness of the internal pipe surfaces; they contain the same information as the basic chart (Figure 18) but in a more convenient form.

Using the multiplier chart (Figure 20), Figure 18 can be used at all saturation pressures between 0 and 200 psig (see Example 10).

3.4 LOW-PRESSURE STEAM PIPING

Values in Table 32 (taken from Figure 18) provide a more rapid means of selecting pipe sizes for the various pressure drops listed and for systems operated at 3.5 and 12 psig. The flow rates shown for 3.5 psig can be used for saturated pressures from 1 to 6 psig, and those shown for 12 psig can be used for saturated pressures from 8 to 16 psig with an error not exceeding 8%.

Both Figure 18 and Table 32 can be used where the flow of condensate does not inhibit the flow of steam. Columns B and C of Table 33 are used in cases where steam and condensate flow in opposite directions, as in risers or runouts that are not dripped. Columns D, E, and F are for one-pipe systems and include risers, radiator valves and vertical connections, and radiator and riser runout sizes, all of which are based on the critical velocity of the steam to allow counterflow of condensate without noise.

Return piping can be sized by Table 34, using pipe capacities for wet, dry, and vacuum return lines for several values of pressure drop per 100 ft of equivalent length.

Table 31 Equivalent Length of Fittings to Be Added to Pipe Run

Nominal Pipe Diameter, in.	Length to Be Added to Run, ft: Standard Elbow	Side Outlet Tee[b]	Gate Valve[a]	Globe Valve[a]	Angle Valve[a]
1/2	1.3	3	0.3	14	7
3/4	1.8	4	0.4	18	10
1	2.2	5	0.5	23	12
1 1/4	3.0	6	0.6	29	15
1 1/2	3.5	7	0.8	34	18
2	4.3	8	1.0	46	22
2 1/2	5.0	11	1.1	54	27
3	6.5	13	1.4	66	34
3 1/2	8	15	1.6	80	40
4	9	18	1.9	92	45
5	11	22	2.2	112	56
6	13	27	2.8	136	67
8	17	35	3.7	180	92
10	21	45	4.6	230	112
12	27	53	5.5	270	132
14	30	63	6.4	310	152

[a]Valve in full-open position.
[b]Values apply only to a tee used to divert the flow in the main to the last riser.

Example 9. What pressure drop should be used for the steam piping of a system if the measured length of the longest run is 500 ft, and the initial pressure must not exceed 2 psig?

Solution: It is assumed, if the measured length of the longest run is 500 ft, that when the allowance for fittings is added, the equivalent length of run does not exceed 1000 ft. Then, with the pressure drop not over one-half of the initial pressure, the drop could be 1 psi or less. With a pressure drop of 1 psi and a length of run of 1000 ft, the drop per 100 ft would be 0.1 psi; if the total drop were 0.5 psi, the drop per 100 ft would be 0.05 psi. In both cases, the pipe could be sized for a desired capacity according to Figure 18.

On completion of the sizing, the drop could be checked by taking the longest line and actually calculating the equivalent length of run from the pipe sizes determined. If the calculated drop is less than that assumed, the pipe size is adequate; if it is more, an unusual number of fittings is probably involved, and either the lines must be straightened, or the next larger pipe size must be tried.

High-Pressure Steam Piping

Many heating systems for large industrial buildings use high-pressure steam (15 to 150 psig). These systems usually have unit heaters or large built-up fan units with blast heating coils. Temperatures are controlled by a modulating or throttling thermostatic valve or by face or bypass dampers controlled by the room air temperature, fan inlet, or fan outlet.

Table 32 Flow Rate of Steam in Schedule 40 Pipe

Nominal Pipe Size, in.	Pressure Drop per 100 ft of Length: 1/16 psi (1 oz/in²) Sat. Press., psig 3.5	12	1/8 psi (2 oz/in²) 3.5	12	1/4 psi (4 oz/in²) 3.5	12	1/2 psi (8 oz/in²) 3.5	12	3/4 psi (12 oz/in²) 3.5	12	1 psi 3.5	12	2 psi 3.5	12
3/4	9	11	14	16	20	24	29	35	36	43	42	50	60	73
1	17	21	26	31	37	46	54	66	68	82	81	95	114	137
1 1/4	36	45	53	66	78	96	111	138	140	170	162	200	232	280
1 1/2	56	70	84	100	120	147	174	210	218	260	246	304	360	430
2	108	134	162	194	234	285	336	410	420	510	480	590	710	850
2 1/2	174	215	258	310	378	460	540	660	680	820	780	950	1,150	1,370
3	318	380	465	550	660	810	960	1,160	1,190	1,430	1,380	1,670	1,950	2,400
3 1/2	462	550	670	800	990	1,218	1,410	1,700	1,740	2,100	2,000	2,420	2,950	3,450
4	640	800	950	1,160	1,410	1,690	1,980	2,400	2,450	3,000	2,880	3,460	4,200	4,900
5	1,200	1,430	1,680	2,100	2,440	3,000	3,570	4,250	4,380	5,250	5,100	6,100	7,500	8,600
6	1,920	2,300	2,820	3,350	3,960	4,850	5,700	6,800	7,000	8,600	8,400	10,000	11,900	14,200
8	3,900	4,800	5,570	7,000	8,100	10,000	11,400	14,300	14,500	17,700	16,500	20,500	24,000	29,500
10	7,200	8,800	10,200	12,600	15,000	18,200	21,000	26,000	26,200	32,000	30,000	37,000	42,700	52,000
12	11,400	13,700	16,500	19,500	23,400	28,400	33,000	40,000	41,000	49,500	48,000	57,500	67,800	81,000

Notes:
1. Flow rate is in lb/h at initial saturation pressures of 3.5 and 12 psig. Flow is based on Moody friction factor, where the flow of condensate does not inhibit the flow of steam.
2. The flow rates at 3.5 psig cover saturated pressure from 1 to 6 psig, and the rates at 12 psig cover saturated pressure from 8 to 16 psig with an error not exceeding 8%.
3. The steam velocities corresponding to the flow rates given in this table can be found from Figures 18 and 20.

Table 33 Steam Pipe Capacities for Low-Pressure Systems

Nominal Pipe Size, in.	Capacity, lb/h				
	Two-Pipe System		One-Pipe Systems		
	Condensate Flowing Against Steam		Supply Risers Upfeed	Radiator Valves and Vertical Connections	Radiator and Riser Runouts
	Vertical	Horizontal			
A	B[a]	C[b]	D[c]	E	F[b]
3/4	8	7	6	—	7
1	14	14	11	7	7
1 1/4	31	27	20	16	16
1 1/2	48	42	38	23	16
2	97	93	72	42	23
2 1/2	159	132	116	—	42
3	282	200	200	—	65
3 1/2	387	288	286	—	119
4	511	425	380	—	186
5	1,050	788	—	—	278
6	1,800	1,400	—	—	545
8	3,750	3,000	—	—	—
10	7,000	5,700	—	—	—
12	11,500	9,500	—	—	—
16	22,000	19,000	—	—	—

Notes:
1. For one- or two-pipe systems in which condensate flows against steam flow.
2. Steam at average pressure of 1 psig used as basis of calculating capacities.

[a]Do not use column B for pressure drops of less than 1/16 psi per 100 ft of equivalent run. Use Figure 18 or Table 31 instead.
[b]Pitch of horizontal runouts to risers and radiators should be not less than 0.5 in/ft. Where this pitch cannot be obtained, runouts over 8 ft in length should be one pipe size larger than that called for in this table.
[c]Do not use column D for pressure drops of less than 1/24 psi per 100 ft of equivalent run except on sizes 3 in. and over. Use Figure 18 or Table 31 instead.

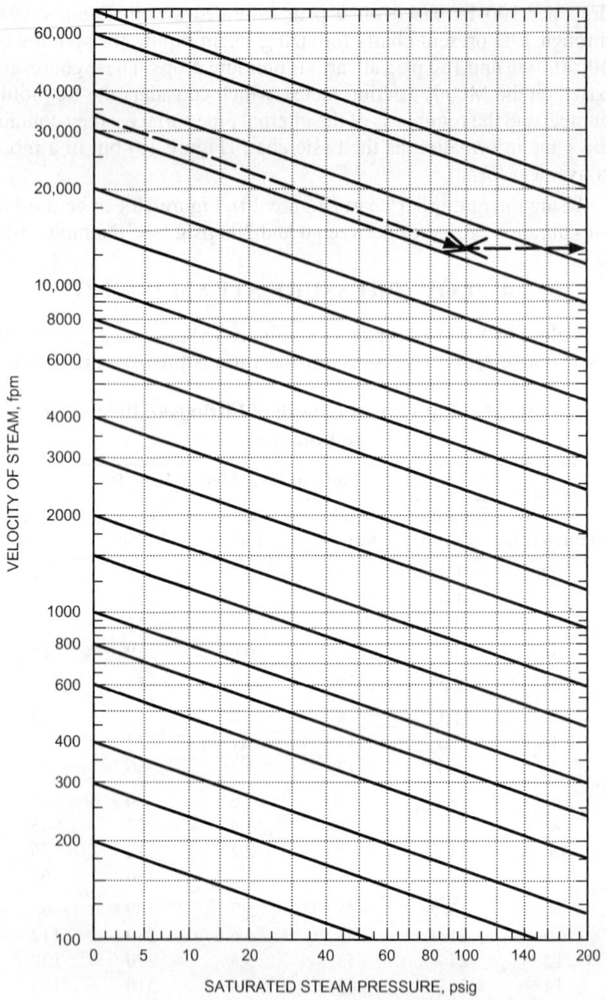

Fig. 20 Velocity Multiplier Chart for Figure 18

Use of Basic and Velocity Multiplier Charts

Example 10. Given a flow rate of 6700 lb/h, an initial steam pressure of 100 psig, and a pressure drop of 11 psi/100 ft, find the size of Schedule 40 pipe required and the velocity of steam in the pipe.

Solution: The following steps are shown by the broken line on Figures 18 and 20.

1. Enter Figure 18 at a flow rate of 6700 lb/h, and move vertically to the horizontal line at 100 psig
2. Follow along inclined multiplier line (upward and to the left) to horizontal 0 psig line. The equivalent mass flow at 0 psig is about 2500 lb/h.
3. Follow the 2500 lb/h line vertically until it intersects the horizontal line at 11 psi per 100 ft pressure drop. Nominal pipe size is 2 1/2 in. The equivalent steam velocity at 0 psig is about 32,700 fpm.
4. To find the steam velocity at 100 psig, locate the value of 32,700 fpm on the ordinate of the velocity multiplier chart (Figure 20) at 0 psig.
5. Move along the inclined multiplier line (downward and to the right) until it intersects the vertical 100 psig pressure line. The velocity as read from the right (or left) scale is about 13,000 fpm.

Note: Steps 1 through 5 would be rearranged or reversed if different data were given.

3.5 STEAM CONDENSATE SYSTEMS

The majority of steam systems used in heating applications are two-pipe systems (steam pipe and condensate pipe). This discussion is limited to sizing the condensate lines in two-pipe systems.

Two-Pipe Systems

When steam is used for heating a liquid to 215°F or less (e.g., in domestic water heat exchangers, domestic heating water converters, or air-heating coils), the devices are usually provided with a steam control valve. As the control valve throttles, the absolute pressure in the load device decreases, removing all pressure motivation for flow in the condensate return system. To ensure the flow of steam condensate from the load device through the trap and into the return system, it is necessary to provide a vacuum breaker on the device ahead of the trap. This ensures a minimum pressure at the trap inlet of atmospheric pressure plus whatever liquid leg the designer has provided. Then, to ensure flow through the trap, it is necessary to design the condensate system so that it will never have a pressure above atmospheric in the condensate return line.

Vented (Open) Return Systems. To achieve this pressure requirement, the condensate return line is usually vented to the atmosphere (1) near the point of entrance of the flow streams from the load traps, (2) in proximity to all connections from drip traps, and (3) at transfer pumps or feedwater receivers.

The dry return lines in a vented return system have flowing liquid in the bottom of the line and gas or vapor in the top (Figure 21A). The liquid is the condensate, and the gas may be steam, air, or a mixture of the two. The flow phenomenon for these dry return systems is open channel flow, which is best described by the **Manning equation**:

Table 34 Return Main and Riser Capacities for Low-Pressure Systems, lb/h

	Pipe Size, in.	1/32 psi (1/2 oz/in²) Drop per 100 ft			1/24 psi (2/3 oz/in²) Drop per 100 ft			1/16 psi (1 oz/in²) Drop per 100 ft			1/8 psi (2 oz/in²) Drop per 100 ft			1/4 psi (4 oz/in²) Drop per 100 ft			1/2 psi (8 oz/in²) Drop per 100 ft		
		Wet	Dry	Vac.	Wet	Dry	Vac.	Wet	Dry	Vac.	Wet	Dry	Vac.	Wet	Dry	Vac.	Wet	Dry	Vac.
	G	H	I	J	K	L	M	N	O	P	Q	R	S	T	U	V	W	X	Y
Return Main	3/4	—	—	—	—	—	42	—	—	100	—	—	142	—	—	200	—	—	283
	1	125	62	—	145	71	143	175	80	175	250	103	249	350	115	350	—	—	494
	1 1/4	213	130	—	248	149	244	300	168	300	425	217	426	600	241	600	—	—	848
	1 1/2	338	206	—	393	236	388	475	265	475	675	340	674	950	378	950	—	—	1,340
	2	700	470	—	810	535	815	1,000	575	1,000	1,400	740	1,420	2,000	825	2,000	—	—	2,830
	2 1/2	1,180	760	—	1,580	868	1,360	1,680	950	1,680	2,350	1,230	2,380	3,350	1,360	3,350	—	—	4,730
	3	1,880	1,460	—	2,130	1,560	2,180	2,680	1,750	2,680	3,750	2,250	3,800	5,350	2,500	5,350	—	—	7,560
	3 1/2	2,750	1,970	—	3,300	2,200	3,250	4,000	2,500	4,000	5,500	3,230	5,680	8,000	3,580	8,000	—	—	11,300
	4	3,880	2,930	—	4,580	3,350	4,500	5,500	3,750	5,500	7,750	4,830	7,810	11,000	5,380	11,000	—	—	15,500
	5	—	—	—	—	—	7,880	—	—	9680	—	—	13,700	—	—	19,400	—	—	27,300
	6	—	—	—	—	—	12,600	—	—	15,500	—	—	22,000	—	—	31,000	—	—	43,800
Riser	3/4	—	48	—	—	48	143	—	48	175	—	48	249	—	48	350	—	—	494
	1	—	113	—	—	113	244	—	113	300	—	113	426	—	113	600	—	—	848
	1 1/4	—	248	—	—	248	388	—	248	475	—	248	674	—	248	950	—	—	1,340
	1 1/2	—	375	—	—	375	815	—	375	1,000	—	375	1,420	—	375	2,000	—	—	2,830
	2	—	750	—	—	750	1,360	—	750	1,680	—	750	2,380	—	750	3,350	—	—	4,730
	2 1/2	—	—	—	—	—	2,180	—	—	2,680	—	—	3,800	—	—	5,350	—	—	7,560
	3	—	—	—	—	—	3,250	—	—	4,000	—	—	5,680	—	—	8,000	—	—	11,300
	3 1/2	—	—	—	—	—	4,480	—	—	5,500	—	—	7,810	—	—	11,000	—	—	15,500
	4	—	—	—	—	—	7,880	—	—	9680	—	—	13,700	—	—	19,400	—	—	27,300
	5	—	—	—	—	—	12,600	—	—	15,500	—	—	22,000	—	—	31,000	—	—	43,800

$$Q = \frac{1.49 A r^{2/3} S^{1/2}}{n} \quad (22)$$

where

Q = volumetric flow rate, cfs
A = cross-sectional area of conduit, ft²
r = hydraulic radius of conduit, ft
n = coefficient of roughness (usually 0.012)
S = slope of conduit, ft/ft

Table 35 is a solution to Equation (22) that shows pipe size capacities for steel pipes with various pitches. Recommended practice is to size vertical lines by the maximum pitch shown, although they would actually have a capacity far in excess of that shown. As pitch increases, hydraulic jump that could fill the pipe and other transient effects that could cause water hammer should be avoided. Flow values in Table 35 are calculated for Schedule 40 steel pipe, with a factor of safety of 3.0, and can be used for copper pipes of the same nominal pipe size.

The flow characteristics of **wet return lines** (Figure 21B) are best described by the Darcy-Weisbach equation [Equation (1)]. The motivation for flow is the fluid head difference between the entering section of the flooded line and the leaving section. It is common practice, in addition to providing for the fluid head differential, to slope the return in the direction of flow to a collection point such as a dirt leg to clear the line of sediment or solids. Table 36 is a solution to Equation (1) that shows pipe size capacity for steel pipes with various available fluid heads. Table 36 can also be used for copper tubing of equal nominal pipe size.

Nonvented (Closed) Return Systems. For systems with a continual steam pressure difference between the point where the condensate enters the line and the point where it leaves (Figure 21C), Table 34 or Table 35, as applicable, can be used for sizing the condensate lines. Although these tables express condensate capacity without slope, common practice is to slope the lines in the direction of flow to a collection point (similar to wet returns) to clear the lines of sediment or solids.

Table 35 Vented Dry Condensate Return for Gravity Flow Based on Manning Equation

Nominal Diameter, in. IPS	Condensate Flow, lb/h[a,b] Condensate Line Slope, in/ft: 1/16	1/8	1/4	1/2
1/2	38	54	76	107
3/4	80	114	161	227
1	153	216	306	432
1-1/4	318	449	635	898
1-1/2	479	677	958	1,360
2	932	1,320	1,860	2,640
2-1/2	1,500	2,120	3,000	4,240
3	2,670	3,780	5,350	7,560
4	5,520	7,800	11,000	15,600
5	10,100	14,300	20,200	28,500
6	16,500	23,300	32,900	46,500

[a] Flow is in lb/h of 180°F water for Schedule 40 steel pipes.
[b] Flow was calculated from Equation (22) and rounded.

When saturated condensate at pressures above the return system pressure enters the return (condensate) mains, some of the liquid flashes to steam. This occurs typically at drip traps into a vented return system or at load traps leaving process load devices that are not valve controlled and typically have no subcooling. If the return main is vented, the vent lines relieve any excessive pressure and prevent a backpressure phenomenon that could restrict flow through traps from valved loads; the pipe sizing would be as described for vented dry returns. If the return line is not vented, flash steam causes a pressure rise at that point and the piping could be sized as described for closed returns, and in accordance with Table 34 or Table 37, as applicable.

Passage of fluid through the steam trap is a throttling or constant-enthalpy process. The resulting fluid on the downstream side of the trap can be a mixture of saturated liquid and vapor. Thus, in

Table 36 Vented Wet Condensate Return for Gravity Flow Based on Darcy-Weisbach Equation

Nominal Diameter, in. IPS	Condensate Flow, lb/h[a,b]							
	Condensate Head, ft per 100 ft							
	0.5	1	1.5	2	2.5	3	3.5	4
1/2	105	154	192	224	252	278	302	324
3/4	225	328	408	476	536	590	640	687
1	432	628	779	908	1,020	1,120	1,220	1,310
1 1/4	901	1,310	1,620	1,890	2,120	2,330	2,530	2,710
1 1/2	1,360	1,970	2,440	2,840	3,190	3,510	3,800	4,080
2	2,650	3,830	4,740	5,510	6,180	6,800	7,360	7,890
2 1/2	4,260	6,140	7,580	8,810	9,890	10,900	11,800	12,600
3	7,570	10,900	13,500	15,600	17,500	19,300	20,900	22,300
4	15,500	22,300	27,600	32,000	35,900	39,400	42,600	45,600
5	28,200	40,500	49,900	57,900	64,900	71,300	77,100	82,600
6	45,800	65,600	80,900	93,800	105,000	115,000	125,000	134,000

[a] Flow is in lb/h of 180°F water for Schedule 40 steel pipes.
[b] Flow calculated from Equation (1) and rounded.

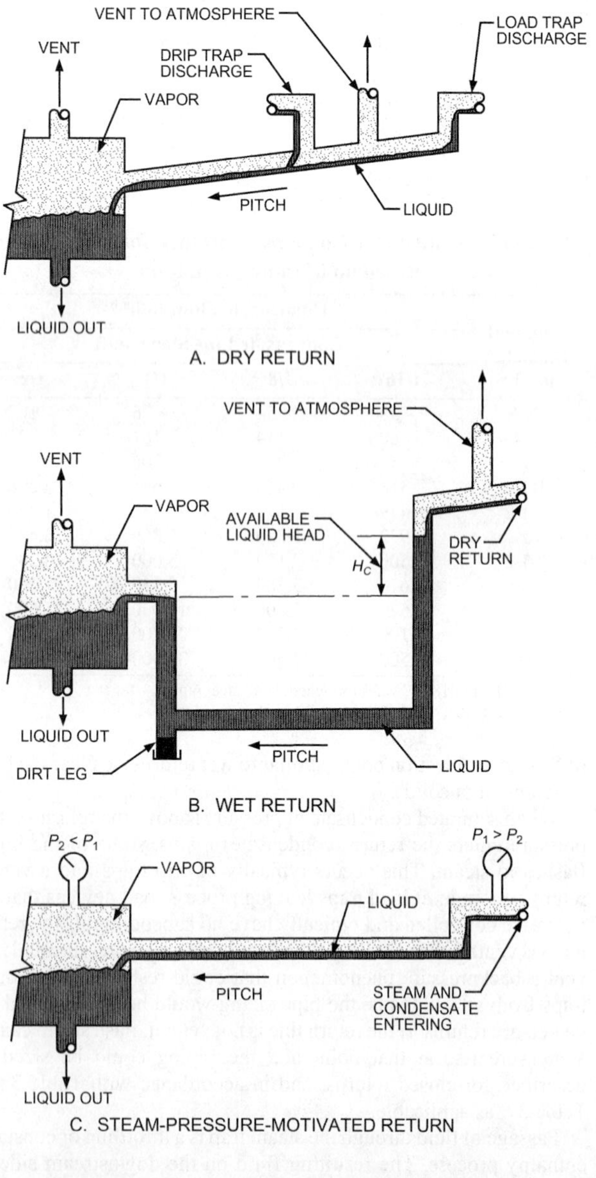

Fig. 21 Types of Condensate Return Systems

nonvented returns, it is important to understand the fluid's condition when it enters the return line from the trap.

The condition of the condensate downstream of the trap can be expressed by the quality x, defined as

$$x = \frac{m_v}{m_l + m_v} \quad (23)$$

where

m_v = mass of saturated vapor in condensate
m_l = mass of saturated liquid in condensate

Likewise, the volume fraction V_c of the vapor in the condensate is expressed as

$$V_c = \frac{V_v}{V_l + V_v} \quad (24)$$

where

V_v = volume of saturated vapor in condensate
V_l = volume of saturated liquid in condensate

The quality and the volume fraction of the condensate downstream of the trap can also be estimated from Equations (25) and (26), respectively.

$$x = \frac{h_1 - h_{f_2}}{h_{g_2} - h_{f_2}} \quad (25)$$

$$V_c = \frac{x v_{g_2}}{v_{f_2}(1 - x) + x v_{g_2}} \quad (26)$$

where

h_1 = enthalpy of liquid condensate entering trap evaluated at supply pressure for saturated condensate or at saturation pressure corresponding to temperature of subcooled liquid condensate
h_{f_2} = enthalpy of saturated liquid at return or downstream pressure of trap
h_{g_2} = enthalpy of saturated vapor at return or downstream pressure of trap
v_{f_2} = specific volume of saturated liquid at return or downstream pressure of trap
v_{g_2} = specific volume of saturated vapor at return or downstream pressure of trap.

Table 38 presents some values for quality and volume fraction for typical supply and return pressures in heating and ventilating systems. Note that the percent of vapor on a mass basis x is small, although the percent of vapor on a volume basis V_c is very large. This indicates that the return pipe cross section is predominantly

Table 37 Flow Rate for Dry-Closed Returns

Pipe Dia. D, in.	Supply Pressure = 5 psig, Return Pressure = 0 psig			Supply Pressure = 15 psig, Return Pressure = 0 psig			Supply Pressure = 30 psig, Return Pressure = 0 psig			Supply Pressure = 50 psig, Return Pressure = 0 psig		
	Δp/L, psi/100 ft											
	1/16	1/4	1	1/16	1/4	1	1/16	1/4	1	1/16	1/4	1
	Flow Rate, lb/h											
1/2	240	520	1,100	95	210	450	60	130	274	42	92	200
3/4	510	1,120	2,400	210	450	950	130	280	590	91	200	420
1	1,000	2,150	4,540	400	860	1,820	250	530	1,120	180	380	800
1 1/4	2,100	4,500	9,500	840	1,800	3,800	520	1,110	2,340	370	800	1,680
1 1/2	3,170	6,780	14,200	1,270	2,720	5,700	780	1,670	3,510	560	1,200	2,520
2	6,240	13,300	*	2,500	5,320	*	1,540	3,270	*	1,110	2,350	*
2 1/2	10,000	21,300	*	4,030	8,520	*	2,480	5,250	*	1,780	3,780	*
3	18,000	38,000	*	7,200	15,200	*	4,440	9,360	*	3,190	6,730	*
4	37,200	78,000	*	14,900	31,300	*	9,180	19,200	*	6,660	13,800	*
6	110,500	*	*	44,300	*	*	27,300	*	*	19,600	*	*
8	228,600	*	*	91,700	*	*	56,400	*	*	40,500	*	*

Pipe Dia. D, in.	Supply Pressure = 100 psig, Return Pressure = 0 psig			Supply Pressure = 150 psig, Return Pressure = 0 psig			Supply Pressure = 100 psig, Return Pressure = 15 psig			Supply Pressure = 150 psig, Return Pressure = 15 psig		
	Δp/L, psi/100 ft											
	1/16	1/4	1	1/16	1/4	1	1/16	1/4	1	1/16	1/4	1
	Flow Rate, lb/h											
1/2	28	62	133	23	51	109	56	120	260	43	93	200
3/4	62	134	290	50	110	230	120	260	560	93	200	420
1	120	260	544	100	210	450	240	500	1,060	180	390	800
1 1/4	250	540	1,130	200	440	930	500	1,060	2,200	380	800	1,680
1 1/2	380	810	1,700	310	660	1,400	750	1,600	3,320	570	1,210	2,500
2	750	1,590	*	610	1,300	*	1,470	3,100	6,450	1,120	2,350	4,900
2 1/2	1,200	2,550	*	980	2,100	*	2,370	5,000	10,300	1,800	3,780	7,800
3	2,160	4,550	*	1,760	3,710	*	4,230	8,860	*	3,200	6,710	*
4	4,460	9,340	*	3,640	7,630	*	8,730	18,200	*	6,620	13,800	*
6	13,200	*	*	10,800	*	*	25,900	53,600	*	19,600	40,600	*
8	27,400	*	*	22,400	*	*	53,400	110,300	*	40,500	83,600	*

*For these sizes and pressure losses, velocity is above 7000 fpm. Select another combination of size and pressure loss.

Table 38 Flash Steam from Steam Trap on Pressure Drop

Supply Pressure, psig	Return Pressure, psig	x, Fraction Vapor, Mass Basis	V_c, Fraction Vapor, Volume Basis
5	0	0.016	0.962
15	0	0.040	0.985
30	0	0.065	0.991
50	0	0.090	0.994
100	0	0.133	0.996
150	0	0.164	0.997
100	15	0.096	0.989
150	15	0.128	0.992

Table 39 Estimated Return Line Pressures

Pressure Drop, psi/100 ft	Pressure in Return Line, psig	
	30 psig Supply	150 psig Supply
1/8	0.5	1.25
1/4	1	2.5
1/2	2	5
3/4	3	7.5
1	4	10
2	—	20

occupied by vapor. Figure 22 is a working chart to determine the quality of condensate entering the return line from the trap for various combinations of supply and return pressures. If the liquid is subcooled entering the trap, the saturation pressure corresponding to the liquid temperature should be used for the supply or upstream pressure. Typical pressures in the return line are given in Table 39.

One-Pipe Systems

Gravity one-pipe air vent systems in which steam and condensate flow in the same pipe, frequently in opposite directions, are considered obsolete and are no longer being installed. Chapter 33 of the 1993 *ASHRAE Handbook—Fundamentals* or earlier ASHRAE Handbook volumes include descriptions of and design information for one-pipe systems.

3.6 GAS PIPING

Piping for gas appliances should be of adequate size and installed so that it provides a supply of gas sufficient to meet the maximum demand without undue loss of pressure between the point of supply (the meter) and the appliance. The size of gas pipe required depends on (1) maximum gas consumption to be provided, (2) length of pipe and number of fittings, (3) allowable pressure loss from the outlet of the meter to the appliance, and (4) specific gravity of the gas.

Gas consumption in ft^3/h is obtained by dividing the Btu input rate at which the appliance is operated by the average heating value of the gas in Btu/ft^3. Insufficient gas flow from excessive pressure losses in gas supply lines can cause inefficient operation of gas-fired appliances and sometimes create hazardous operations. Gas-fired appliances are normally equipped with a data plate giving information on maximum gas flow requirements or Btu input as well as inlet gas pressure requirements. The local gas utility can give the gas

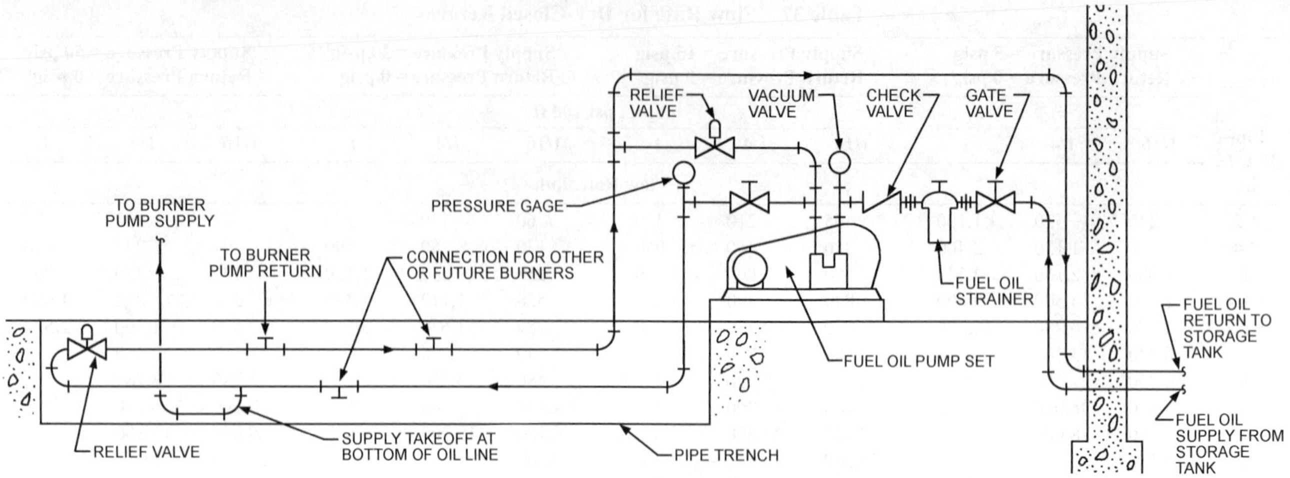

Fig. 23 Typical Oil Circulating Loop

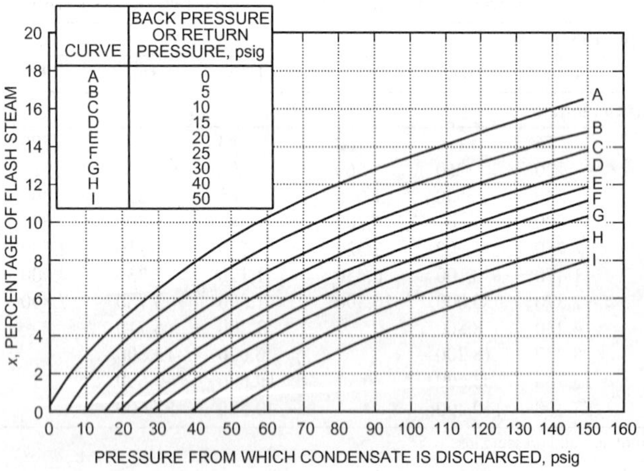

Fig. 22 Working Chart for Determining Percentage of Flash Steam (Quality)

pressure available at the utility's gas meter. Using this information, the required size of gas piping can be calculated for satisfactory operation of the appliance(s).

Table 40 gives pipe capacities for gas flow for up to 200 ft of pipe based on a specific gravity of 0.60. Capacities for pressures less than 1.5 psig may also be determined by the following equation from NFPA/IAS *National Fuel Gas Code* (NFPA *Standard* 54/ANSI *Standard* Z223.1):

$$Q = 2313 d^{2.623}\left(\frac{\Delta p}{CL}\right)^{0.541} \quad (27)$$

where

Q = flow rate at 60°F and 30 in. Hg, cfh
d = inside diameter of pipe, in.
Δp = pressure drop, in. of water
C = factor for viscosity, density, and temperature
$= 0.00354(t + 460)s^{0.848}\mu^{0.152}$
t = temperature, °F
s = ratio of density of gas to density of air at 60°F and 30 in. Hg
μ = viscosity of gas, centipoise (0.012 for natural gas, 0.008 for propane)
L = pipe length, ft

Gas service in buildings is generally delivered in the low-pressure range of 7 in. of water. The maximum pressure drop allowable in piping systems at this pressure is generally 0.5 in. of water but is subject to regulation by local building, plumbing, and gas appliance codes [see also the NFPA/IAS *National Fuel Gas Code* (NFPA *Standard* 54/ANSI *Standard* Z223.1)].

Where large quantities of gas are required or where long lengths of pipe are used (e.g., in industrial buildings), low-pressure limitations result in large pipe sizes. Local codes may allow (and local gas companies may deliver) gas at higher pressures (e.g., 2, 5, or 10 psig). Under these conditions, an allowable pressure drop of 10% of the initial pressure is used, and pipe sizes can be reduced significantly. Gas pressure regulators at the appliance must be specified to accommodate higher inlet pressures. NFPA/IAS (2012) provides information on pipe sizing for various inlet pressures and pressure drops at higher pressures. More complete information on gas piping can be found in the *Gas Engineers' Handbook* (1970).

3.7 FUEL OIL PIPING

The pipe used to convey fuel oil to oil-fired appliances must be large enough to maintain low pump suction pressure and, in the case of circulating loop systems, to prevent overpressure at the burner oil pump inlet. Pipe materials must be compatible with the fuel and must be carefully assembled to eliminate all leaks. Leaks in suction lines can cause pumping problems that result in unreliable burner operation. Leaks in pressurized lines create fire hazards. Cast-iron or aluminum fittings and pipe are unacceptable. Pipe joint compounds must be selected carefully.

Oil pump suction lines should be sized so that at maximum suction line flow conditions, the maximum vacuum will not exceed 10 in. Hg for distillate grade fuels and 15 in. Hg for residual oils. Oil supply lines to burner oil pumps should not be pressurized by circulating loop systems or aboveground oil storage tanks to more than 5 psi, or pump shaft seals may fail. A typical oil circulating loop system is shown in Figure 23.

In assembling long fuel pipe lines, be careful to avoid air pockets. On overhead circulating loops, the line should vent air at all high points. Oil supply loops for one or more burners should be the continuous circulation type, with excess fuel returned to the storage tank. Dead-ended pressurized loops can be used, but air or vapor venting is more problematic.

Where valves are used, select ball or gate valves. Globe valves are not recommended because of their high pressure drop characteristics.

Oil lines should be tested after installation, particularly if they are buried, enclosed, or otherwise inaccessible. Failure to perform this test is a frequent cause of later operating difficulties. A suction line can be hydrostatically tested at 1.5 times its maximum operating

Table 40 Maximum Capacity of Gas Pipe in Cubic Feet per Hour

Nominal Iron Pipe Size, in.	Internal Diameter, in.	Length of Pipe, ft													
		10	20	30	40	50	60	70	80	90	100	125	150	175	200
1/4	0.364	32	22	18	15	14	12	11	11	10	9	8	8	7	6
3/8	0.493	72	49	40	34	30	27	25	23	22	21	18	17	15	14
1/2	0.622	132	92	73	63	56	50	46	43	40	38	34	31	28	26
3/4	0.824	278	190	152	130	115	105	96	90	84	79	72	64	59	55
1	1.049	520	350	285	245	215	195	180	170	160	150	130	120	110	100
1 1/4	1.380	1,050	730	590	500	440	400	370	350	320	305	275	250	225	210
1 1/2	1.610	1,600	1,100	890	760	670	610	560	530	490	460	410	380	350	320
2	2.067	3,050	2,100	1,650	1,450	1,270	1,150	1,050	990	930	870	780	710	650	610
2 1/2	2.469	4,800	3,300	2,700	2,300	2,000	1,850	1,700	1,600	1,500	1,400	1,250	1,130	1,050	980
3	3.068	8,500	5,900	4,700	4,100	3,600	3,250	3,000	2,800	2,600	2,500	2,200	2,000	1,850	1,700
4	4.026	17,500	12,000	9,700	8,300	7,400	6,800	6,200	5,800	5,400	5,100	4,500	4,100	3,800	3,500

Note: Capacity is in cubic feet per hour at gas pressures of 0.5 psig or less and pressure drop of 0.3 in. of water; specific gravity = 0.60.

Table 41 Recommended Nominal Size for Fuel Oil Suction Lines from Tank to Pump (Residual Grades No. 5 and No. 6)

Pumping Rate, gph	Length of Run in Feet at Maximum Suction Lift of 15 ft									
	25	50	75	100	125	150	175	200	250	300
10	1 1/2	1 1/2	1 1/2	1 1/2	1 1/2	1 1/2	2	2	2 1/2	2 1/2
40	1 1/2	1 1/2	1 1/2	2	2	2 1/2	2 1/2	2 1/2	2 1/2	3
70	1 1/2	2	2	2	2	2 1/2	2 1/2	2 1/2	3	3
100	2	2	2	2 1/2	2 1/2	3	3	3	3	3
130	2	2	2 1/2	2 1/2	2 1/2	3	3	3	3	4
160	2	2	2 1/2	2 1/2	2 1/2	3	3	3	4	4
190	2	2 1/2	2 1/2	2 1/2	3	3	3	4	4	4
220	2 1/2	2 1/2	2 1/2	3	3	3	4	4	4	4

Notes:
1. Pipe sizes smaller than 1 in. IPS are not recommended for use with residual grade fuel oils.
2. Lines conveying fuel oil from pump discharge port to burners and tank return may be reduced by one or two sizes, depending on piping length and pressure losses.

pressure or at a vacuum of not less than 20 in. Hg. Pressure or vacuum tests should continue for at least 60 min. If there is no noticeable drop in the initial test pressure, the lines can be considered tight.

Pipe Sizes for Heavy Oil

Tables 41 and 42 give recommended pipe sizes for handling No. 5 and No. 6 oils (residual grades) and No. 1 and No. 2 oils (distillate grades), respectively. Storage tanks and piping and pumping facilities for delivering the oil from the tank to the burner are important considerations in the design of an industrial oil-burning system. The construction and location of the tank and oil piping are usually subject to local regulations and National Fire Protection Association (NFPA) *Standards* 30 and 31.

REFERENCES

ASHRAE members can access *ASHRAE Journal* articles and ASHRAE research project final reports at technologyportal.ashrae.org. Articles and reports are also available for purchase by nonmembers in the online ASHRAE Bookstore at www.ashrae.org/bookstore.

ASHRAE. 2013. Safety standard for refrigeration systems. ANSI/ASHRAE *Standard* 15-2013.

ASHRAE. 2013. Energy standard for buildings except low-ride residential buildings. ANSI/ASHRAE/IES *Standard* 90.1-2013.

ASME. 2013. Pipe threads, general purpose, inch. *Standard* B1.20.1-2013. American Society of Mechanical Engineers, New York.

ASME. 2006. Pipe threads, 60 deg. general purpose (metric). *Standard* B1.20.2M-2006. American Society of Mechanical Engineers, New York.

ASME. 2015. Gray iron pipe flanges and flanged fittings: Classes 25, 125, and 250. *Standard* B16.1-2015. American Society of Mechanical Engineers, New York.

Table 42 Recommended Nominal Size for Fuel Oil Suction Lines from Tank to Pump (Distillate Grades No. 1 and No. 2)

Pumping Rate, gph	Length of Run in Feet at Maximum Suction Lift of 10 ft									
	25	50	75	100	125	150	175	200	250	300
10	1/2	1/2	1/2	1/2	1/2	1/2	1/2	3/4	3/4	1
40	1/2	1/2	1/2	1/2	1/2	3/4	3/4	3/4	3/4	1
70	1/2	1/2	3/4	3/4	3/4	3/4	3/4	1	1	1
100	1/2	3/4	3/4	3/4	3/4	1	1	1	1	1 1/4
130	1/2	3/4	3/4	1	1	1	1	1	1 1/4	1 1/4
160	3/4	3/4	3/4	1	1	1	1	1 1/4	1 1/4	1 1/4
190	3/4	3/4	1	1	1	1	1 1/4	1 1/4	1 1/4	2
220	3/4	1	1	1	1	1 1/4	1 1/4	1 1/4	1 1/4	2

ASME. 2011. Malleable iron threaded fittings: Classes 150 and 300. *Standard* B16.3-2011. American Society of Mechanical Engineers, New York.

ASME. 2011. Gray iron threaded fittings: Classes 125 and 250. *Standard* B16.4-2011. American Society of Mechanical Engineers, New York.

ASME. 2009. Pipe flanges and flanged fittings: NPS 1/2 through NPS 24 metric/inch standard. *Standard* B16.5-2009. American Society of Mechanical Engineers, New York.

ASME. 2012. Factory made wrought buttwelding fittings. *Standard* B16.9-2012. American Society of Mechanical Engineers, New York.

ASME. 2009. Forged fittings, socket-welding and threaded. *Standard* B16.11-2009. American Society of Mechanical Engineers, New York.

ASME. 2009. Cast iron threaded drainage fittings. *Standard* B16.12-2009. American Society of Mechanical Engineers, New York.

ASME. 2013. Cast copper alloy threaded fittings: Classes 125 and 250. *Standard* B16.15-2013. American Society of Mechanical Engineers, New York.

ASME. 2012. Cast copper alloy solder joint pressure fittings. *Standard* B16.18-2012. American Society of Mechanical Engineers, New York.

ASME. 2013. Wrought copper and copper alloy solder-joint pressure fittings. *Standard* B16.22-2013. American Society of Mechanical Engineers, New York.

ASME. 2011. Cast copper alloy solder joint drainage fittings: DWV. *Standard* B16.23-2011. American Society of Mechanical Engineers, New York.

ASME. 2011. Cast copper alloy pipe flanges and flanged fittings: Classes 150, 300, 600, 900, 1500, and 2500. *Standard* B16.24-2011. American Society of Mechanical Engineers, New York.

ASME. 2011. Cast copper alloy fittings for flared copper tubes. *Standard* B16.26-2011. American Society of Mechanical Engineers, New York.

ASME. 2012. Wrought copper and wrought copper alloy solder-joint drainage fittings—DWV. *Standard* B16.29-2012. American Society of Mechanical Engineers, New York.

ASME. 2011. Ductile iron pipe flanges and flanged fittings: Classes 150 and 300. *Standard* B16.42-2011. American Society of Mechanical Engineers, New York.

ASME. 2016. Power piping. *Standard* B31.1-2016. American Society of Mechanical Engineers, New York.

ASME. 2016. Refrigeration piping and heat transfer components. *Standard* B31.5-2016. American Society of Mechanical Engineers, New York.

ASME. 2014. Building services piping. *Standard* B31.9-2014. American Society of Mechanical Engineers, New York.

ASME. 2015. Welded and seamless wrought steel pipe. *Standard* B36.10M-2015. American Society of Mechanical Engineers, New York.

ASME. 2015. Qualification standard for welding and brazing procedures, welders, brazers, and welding and brazing operators. *Boiler and Pressure Vessel Code,* Section IX. American Society of Mechanical Engineers, New York.

ASTM. 2012. Standard specification for pipe, steel, black and hot-dipped, zinc-coated, welded, and seamless. *Standard* A53. American Society for Testing and Materials, West Conshohocken, PA.

ASTM. 2015. Standard specification for seamless carbon steel pipe for high-temperature service. *Standard* A106. American Society for Testing and Materials, West Conshohocken, PA.

ASTM. 2014. Standard specification for seamless copper water tube. *Standard* B88. American Society for Testing and Materials, West Conshohocken, PA.

ASTM. 2016. Standard specification for seamless copper tube for air conditioning and refrigeration field service. *Standard* B280. American Society for Testing and Materials, West Conshohocken, PA.

ASTM. 2011. Standard specification for rigid poly(vinyl chloride) (PVC) compounds and chlorinated poly(vinyl chloride) (CPVC) compounds. *Standard* D1784. American Society for Testing and Materials, West Conshohocken, PA.

ASTM. 2015. Standard specification for poly(vinyl chloride) (PVC) plastic pipe, schedules 40, 80, and 120. *Standard* D1785. American Society for Testing and Materials, West Conshohocken, PA.

ASTM. 2015. Standard test method for determining dimensions of thermoplastic pipe and fittings. *Standard* D2122. American Society for Testing and Materials, West Conshohocken, PA.

ASTM. 2012. Standard specification for polyethylene (PE) plastic pipe (SIDR-PR) based on controlled inside diameter. *Standard* D2239. American Society for Testing and Materials, West Conshohocken, PA.

ASTM. 2015. Standard specification for threaded poly(vinyl chloride) (PVC) plastic pipe fittings, schedule 80. *Standard* D2464. American Society for Testing and Materials, West Conshohocken, PA.

ASTM. 2015. Standard specification for poly(vinyl chloride) (PVC) plastic pipe fittings, schedule 40. *Standard* D2466. American Society for Testing and Materials, West Conshohocken, PA.

ASTM. 2015. Standard specification for poly(vinyl chloride) (PVC) plastic pipe fittings, schedule 80. *Standard* D2467. American Society for Testing and Materials, West Conshohocken, PA.

ASTM. 2012. Standard specification for solvent cements for poly(vinyl chloride) (PVC) plastic piping systems. *Standard* D2564. American Society for Testing and Materials, West Conshohocken, PA.

ASTM. 2014. Standard specification for acrylonitrile-butadiene-styrene (ABS) schedule 40 plastic drain, waste, and vent pipe and fittings. *Standard* D2661. American Society for Testing and Materials, West Conshohocken, PA.

ASTM. 2014. Standard specification for poly(vinyl chloride) (PVC) plastic drain, waste, and vent pipe and fittings. *Standard* D2665. American Society for Testing and Materials, West Conshohocken, PA.

ASTM. 2013. Standard test method for obtaining hydrostatic design basis for thermoplastic pipe materials or pressure design basis for thermoplastic pipe products. *Standard* D2837-13e1. American Society for Testing and Materials, West Conshohocken, PA.

ASTM. 2012. Standard practice for obtaining hydrostatic or pressure design basis for "fiberglass" (glass-fiber-reinforced thermosetting-resin) pipe and fittings. *Standard* D2992. American Society for Testing and Materials, West Conshohocken, PA.

ASTM. 2014. Standard specification for polyethylene plastics pipe and fittings materials. *Standard* D3350. American Society for Testing and Materials, West Conshohocken, PA.

ASTM. 2016. Standard classification system and basis for specifications for rigid acrylonitrile-butadiene-styrene (ABS) materials for pipe and fittings. *Standard* D3965. American Society for Testing and Materials, West Conshohocken, PA.

ASTM. 2015. Standard specification for threaded chlorinated poly(vinyl chloride) (CPVC) plastic pipe fittings, schedule 80. *Standard* F437. American Society for Testing and Materials, West Conshohocken, PA.

ASTM. 2015. Standard specification for socket-type chlorinated poly(vinyl chloride) (CPVC) plastic pipe fittings, schedule 40. *Standard* F438. American Society for Testing and Materials, West Conshohocken, PA.

ASTM. 2013. Standard specification for chlorinated poly(vinyl chloride) (CPVC) plastic pipe fittings, schedule 80. *Standard* F439. American Society for Testing and Materials, West Conshohocken, PA.

ASTM. 2015. Standard specification for crosslinked polyethylene (PEX) tubing. *Standard* F876. American Society for Testing and Materials, West Conshohocken, PA.

ASTM. 2011. Standard specification for crosslinked polyethylene (PEX) hot- and cold-water distribution systems. *Standard* F877. American Society for Testing and Materials, West Conshohocken, PA.

ASTM. 2014. Standard specification for solvent cements for chlorinated poly(vinyl chloride) (CPVC) plastic pipe and fittings. *Standard* F493. American Society for Testing and Materials, West Conshohocken, PA.

ASTM. 2015. Standard test method for evaluating the oxidative resistance of crosslinked polyethylene (PEX) pipe, tubing and systems to hot chlorinated water. *Standard* F2023. American Society for Testing and Materials, West Conshohocken, PA.

ASTM. 2015. Standard specification for pressure-rated polypropylene (PP) piping systems. *Standard* F2389. American Society for Testing and Materials, West Conshohocken, PA.

ASTM. 2011. Standard specification for manufacture and joining of polyethylene (PE) gas pressure pipe with a peelable polypropylene (PP) outer layer. *Standard* F2830. American Society for Testing and Materials, West Conshohocken, PA.

AWWA. 2014. Thickness design of ductile-iron pipe. *Standard* C150/A21.50. American Water Works Association, Denver.

Ball, E.F., and C.J.D. Webster. 1976. Some measurements of water-flow noise in copper and ABS pipes with various flow velocities. *The Building Services Engineer* 44(2):33.

Carrier. 1960. Piping design. In *System design manual.* Carrier Air Conditioning Company, Syracuse, NY.

CDA. 2010. *The copper tube handbook.* Copper Development Association, New York.

Crane Co. 1976. Flow of fluids through valves, fittings and pipe. *Technical Paper* 410. Crane Company, New York.

Crane Co. 1988. Flow of fluids through valves, fittings and pipe. *Technical Paper* 410. Crane Company, New York.

Dawson, F.M., and J.S. Bowman. 1933. Interior water supply piping for residential buildings. University of Wisconsin Experiment Station *Bulletin* 77.

Ding, C., L. Carlson, C. Ellis, and O. Mohseni. 2005. Pressure loss coefficients in 6, 8, and 10 inch steel pipe fittings. ASHRAE Research Project TRP-1116, *Final Report.* University of Minnesota, Saint Anthony Falls Laboratory.

Eshbach, O.W. 2009. *Eshbach's handbook of engineering fundamentals*, 5th ed. M. Kutz, ed. John Wiley & Sons, New York.

Freeman, J.R. 1941. *Experiments upon the flow of water in pipes.* American Society of Mechanical Engineers, New York.

Gas Engineers' Handbook. 1970. Industrial Press, New York.

Giesecke, F.E. 1926. Friction of water elbows. *ASHVE Transactions* 32:303.

Giesecke, F.E., and W.H. Badgett. 1931. Friction heads in one-inch standard cast-iron tees. *ASHVE Transactions* 37:395.

Giesecke, F.E., and W.H. Badgett. 1932a. Loss of head in copper pipe and fittings. *ASHVE Transactions* 38:529.

Giesecke, F.E., and W.H. Badgett. 1932b. Supplementary friction heads in one-inch cast-iron tees. *ASHVE Transactions* 38:111.

Grinnell Company. 1951. *Piping design and engineering.* Grinnell Company, Cranston, RI.

HDR design guide. 1981. Hennington, Durham and Richardson, Omaha, NE.

Heald, C.C. 2002. *Cameron hydraulic data*, 19th ed. Flowserve Corporation, Irving, TX.

Hegberg, R.A. 1995. Where did the *k*-factors for pressure loss in fittings come from? *ASHRAE Transactions* 101(1):1264-78. *Paper* CH-95-20-3.

Hunter, R.B. 1940. Methods of estimating loads in plumbing systems. NBS *Report* BMS 65. National Institute of Standards and Technology, Gaithersburg, MD.

Hunter, R.B. 1941. Water distributing systems for buildings. NBS *Report* BMS 79. National Institute of Standards and Technology, Gaithersburg, MD.

Hydraulic Institute. 1990. *Engineering data book*. Hydraulic Institute, Parsippany, NJ.

ICC. 2012. *International plumbing code®*. International Code Council, Washington, D.C.

Idelchik, I.E. 1986. *Handbook of hydraulic resistance*. Hemisphere Publishing, New York.

ISA. 2007. Flow equations for sizing control valves. *Standard* 75.01.01-07. International Society of Automation, Research Triangle Park, NC.

Laschober, R.R., G.Y. Anderson, and D.G. Barbee. 1966. Counterflow of steam and condensate in slightly pitched pipes. *ASHRAE Transactions* 72(1):157.

Marseille, B. 1965. Noise transmission in piping. *Heating and Ventilating Engineering* (June):674.

MSS. 2009. Pipe hangers and supports—Materials, design, manufacture, selection, application, and installation. ANSI/MSS *Standard* SP-58. Manufacturers Standardization Society of the Valve and Fittings Industry, Vienna, VA.

MSS. 2003. Pipe hangers and supports—Selection and application. *Standard* SP-69. Manufacturers Standardization Society of the Valve and Fittings Industry, Vienna, VA.

Nayyar, M. 1999. *Piping handbook*. McGraw-Hill, New York.

NFPA. 2010. Installation of sprinkler systems. *Standard* 13. National Fire Protection Association, Quincy, MA.

NFPA/AGA. 2012. *National fuel gas code*. ANSI/NFPA *Standard* 54. National Fire Protection Association, Quincy, MA. ANSI/AGA *Standard* Z223.1-2002. American Gas Association, Arlington, VA.

NSF/ANSI. 2016. Plastics piping system components and related materials. ANSI/NSF *Standard* 14-2016. NSF International, Ann Arbor, MI.

NSF/ANSI. 2016. Drinking water system components—Health effects. ANSI/NSF *Standard* 61. NSF International, Ann Arbor, MI.

Obrecht, M.F., and M. Pourbaix. 1967. Corrosion of metals in potable water systems. *AWWA* 59:977. American Water Works Association, Denver, CO.

PHCC. 2012. *National standard plumbing code*. Plumbing-Heating-Cooling Contractors Association, Falls Church, VA.

Plastic Pipe Institute. 1971. *Water flow characteristics of thermoplastic pipe*. Plastic Pipe Institute, New York.

PPFA. 2009. *PVC piping systems for commercial and industrial applications design guide*. Plastic Pipe and Fitting Association, Glenn Ellyn, IL

Rahmeyer, W.J. 1999a. Pressure loss coefficients of threaded and forged weld pipe fittings for ells, reducing ells, and pipe reducers (RP-968). *ASHRAE Transactions* 105(2):334-354. *Paper* 4308.

Rahmeyer, W.J. 1999b. Pressure loss coefficients of pipe fittings for threaded and forged weld pipe tees (RP-968). *ASHRAE Transactions* 105(2):355-385. *Paper* 4309.

Rahmeyer, W.J. 2002a. Pressure loss data for large pipe ells, reducers, and expansions. *ASHRAE Transactions* 108(1):360-375. *Paper* 4533.

Rahmeyer, W.J. 2002b. Pressure loss data for large pipe tees. *ASHRAE Transactions* 108(1):376-389. *Paper* 4534.

Rahmeyer, W.J. 2002c. Pressure loss coefficients for close-coupled pipe ells. *ASHRAE Transactions* 108(1):390-406. *Paper* 4535.

Rahmeyer, W.J. 2003a. Pressure loss data for PVC pipe elbows, reducers, and expansions (RP-1193). *ASHRAE Transactions* 109(2):230-251. *Paper* 4653.

Rahmeyer, W.J. 2003b. Pressure loss data for PVC pipe tees (RP-1193). *ASHRAE Transactions* 109(2):252-271. *Paper* 4654.

Rogers, W.L. 1953. Experimental approaches to the study of noise and noise transmission in piping systems. *ASHVE Transactions* 59:347-360.

Rogers, W.L. 1954. Sound-pressure levels and frequencies produced by flow of water through pipe and fittings. *ASHRAE Transactions* 60:411-430.

Rogers, W.L. 1956. Noise production and damping in water piping. *ASHAE Transactions* 62:39.

Sanks, R.L. 1978. *Water treatment plant design for the practicing engineer*. Ann Arbor Science, Ann Arbor, MI.

Smith, T. 1983. Reducing corrosion in heating plants with special reference to design considerations. *Anti-Corrosion Methods and Materials* 30 (October):4.

Stewart, W.E., and C.L. Dona. 1987. Water flow rate limitations (RP-450). *ASHRAE Transactions* 93(2):811-825. *Paper* 3106.

Williams, G.J. 1976. The Hunter curves revisited. *Heating/Piping/Air Conditioning* (November):67.

Williams, G.S., and A. Hazen. 1933. *Hydraulic tables*. John Wiley & Sons, New York.

BIBLIOGRAPHY

ASTM. 2009. Standard specification for chlorinated poly(vinyl chloride) (CPVC) plastic pipe, Schedules 40 and 80. *Standard* F441/F441M. American Society for Testing and Materials, West Conshohocken, PA.

CHAPTER 23

INSULATION FOR MECHANICAL SYSTEMS

THIS chapter deals with applications of thermal and acoustical insulation for mechanical systems in residential, commercial, and industrial facilities. Applications include pipes, tanks, vessels and equipment, and ducts.

Thermal insulation is primarily used to limit heat gain or loss from surfaces operating at temperatures above or below ambient temperature. Insulation may be used to satisfy one or more of the following design objectives:

- **Energy conservation**: minimizing unwanted heat loss/gain from building HVAC systems, as well as preserving natural and financial resources
- **Economic thickness**: selecting the thickness of insulation that yields the minimum total life-cycle cost
- **Personnel protection**: controlling surface temperatures to avoid contact burns (hot or cold)
- **Condensation control**: minimizing condensation by keeping surface temperature above the dew point of surrounding air
- **Process control**: minimizing temperature change in process fluids where close control is needed
- **Freeze protection**: minimizing energy required for heat tracing systems and/or extending the time to freezing in the event of system failure or when the system is purposefully idle
- **Noise control**: reducing/controlling noise in mechanical systems
- **Fire safety**: protecting critical building elements and slowing the spread of fire in buildings

Fundamentals of thermal insulation are covered in Chapter 25; applications in insulated assemblies are discussed in Chapter 27; and data on thermal and water vapor transmission data are in Chapter 26.

1. DESIGN OBJECTIVES AND CONSIDERATIONS

Energy Conservation

Thermal insulation is commonly used to reduce energy consumption of HVAC systems and equipment. Minimum insulation levels for ductwork and piping are often dictated by energy codes, many of which are based on ASHRAE *Standards* 90.1 and 90.2. In many cases, it may be cost-effective to go beyond the minimum levels dictated by energy codes. Thicknesses greater than the optimum economic thickness may be required for other technical reasons such as condensation control, personnel protection, or noise control.

Tables 1 to 3 contain minimum insulation levels for ducts and pipes, excerpted from ANSI/ASHRAE *Standard* 90.1-2010.

Interest in **green buildings** (i.e., those that are environmentally responsible and energy efficient, as well as healthier places to work) is increasing. The LEED® (Leadership in Energy and Environmental Design) Green Building Rating System™, created by the U.S. Green Building Council, is a voluntary rating system that sets out sustainable design and performance criteria for buildings. It evaluates environmental performance from a whole-building perspective and awards points based on satisfying performance criteria in several different categories. Different levels of green building certification are awarded based on the total points earned. The role of mechanical insulation in reducing energy usage, along with the associated greenhouse gas emissions, can help to contribute to LEED certification and should be considered when designing an insulation system.

Economic Thickness

Economics can be used to (1) select the optimum insulation thickness for a specific insulation, or (2) evaluate two or more insulation materials for least cost for a given level of thermal performance. In either case, economic considerations determine the most cost-effective solution for insulating over a specific period.

Life-cycle costing considers the initial cost of the insulation system plus the ongoing value of energy savings over the expected service lifetime. The economic thickness is defined as the thickness that minimizes the total life-cycle cost.

Labor and material costs of installed insulation increase with thickness. Insulation is often applied in multiple layers (1) because materials are not manufactured in single layers of sufficient thickness and (2) in many cases, to accommodate expansion and contraction of insulation and system components. Figure 1 shows installed costs for a multilayer application. The slope of the curves is discontinuous and increases with the number of layers because labor and material costs increase more rapidly as thickness increases. Figure 1 shows curves of total cost of operation, insulation costs, and lost energy costs. Point A on the total cost curve corresponds to the economic insulation

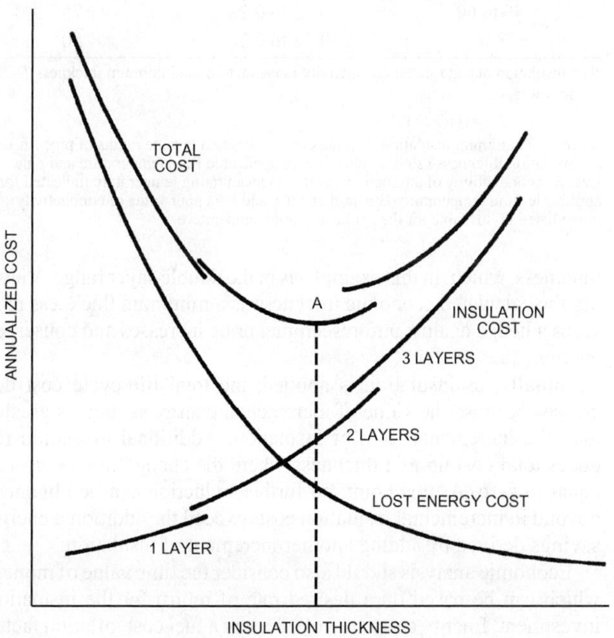

Fig. 1 Determination of Economic Thickness of Insulation

The preparation of this chapter is assigned to TC 1.8, Mechanical Systems Insulation.

Table 1 Minimum Duct Insulation R-Value,[a] Cooling- and Heating-Only Supply Ducts and Return Ducts

	Duct Location						
Climate Zone[d]	Exterior	Ventilated Attic	Unvented Attic Above Insulated Ceiling	Unvented Attic with Roof Insulation[a]	Unconditioned Space[b]	Indirectly Conditioned Space[c]	Buried
				Heating-Only Ducts			
1, 2	none	none	none	none	none	none	none
3	R-3.5	none	none	none	none	none	none
4	R-3.5	none	none	none	none	none	none
5	R-6	R-3.5	none	none	none	none	R-3.5
6	R-6	R-6	R-3.5	none	none	none	R-3.5
7	R-8	R-6	R-6	none	R-3.5	none	R-3.5
8	R-8	R-8	R-6	none	R-6	none	R-6
				Cooling-Only Ducts			
1	R-6	R-6	R-8	R-3.5	R-3.5	none	R-3.5
2	R-6	R-6	R-6	R-3.5	R-3.5	none	R-3.5
3	R-6	R-6	R-6	R-3.5	R-1.9	none	none
4	R-3.5	R-3.5	R-6	R-1.9	R-1.9	none	none
5, 6	R-3.5	R-1.9	R-3.5	R-1.9	R-1.9	none	none
7, 8	R-1.9	R-1.9	R-1.9	R-1.9	R-1.9	none	none
				Return Ducts			
1 to 8	R-3.5	R-3.5	R-3.5	none	none	none	none

[a]Insulation R-values, measured in h·ft²·°F/Btu, are for the insulation as installed and do not include film resistance. The required minimum thicknesses do not consider water vapor transmission and possible surface condensation. Where exterior walls are used as plenum walls, wall insulation must be as required by the most restrictive condition of Section 6.4.4.2 or Section 5 of 90.1-2010. Insulation resistance measured on a horizontal plane in accordance with ASTM C518 at a mean temperature of 75°F at the installed thickness.
[b]Includes crawlspaces, both ventilated and nonventilated.
[c]Includes return air plenums with or without exposed roofs above.
[d]Climate zones for the continental United States defined in ASHRAE *Standard* 90.1-2010.

Table 2 Minimum Pipe Insulation Thickness,[a] in.

	Insulation Conductivity		Nominal Pipe or Tube Size, in.				
Fluid Design Operating Temp. Range, °F	Conductivity, Btu·in/h·ft²·°F	Mean Rating Temp., °F	<1	1 to <1 1/2	1 1/2 to <4	4 to <8	≥8
	Heating Systems (Steam, Steam Condensate, Hot Water, and Domestic Hot Water)[b,c]						
>350	0.32 to 0.34	250	4.5	5.0	5.0	5.0	5.0
251 to 350	0.29 to 0.32	200	3.5	4.0	4.5	4.5	4.5
201 to 250	0.27 to 0.30	150	2.5	2.5	3.0	3.0	3.0
141 to 200	0.25 to 0.29	125	1.5	1.5	2.0	2.0	2.0
105 to 140	0.22 to 0.28	100	1.0	1.0	1.5	1.5	1.5
	Cooling Systems (Chilled Water, Brine, and Refrigerant)[d]						
40 to 60	0.22 to 0.28	75	0.5	0.5	1.0	1.0	1.0
<40	0.22 to 0.28	50	0.5	1.0	1.0	1.0	1.5

[a]For insulation outside stated conductivity range, determine minimum thickness T as follows:

$$T = r\{(1 + t/r)^{K/k} - 1\}$$

where T = minimum insulation thickness (in.), r = actual outside radius of pipe (in.), t = insulation thickness listed in this table for applicable fluid temperature and pipe size, K = conductivity of alternative material at mean rating temperature indicated for applicable fluid temperature (Btu·in/h·ft²·°F); and k = upper value of conductivity range listed in this table for the applicable fluid temperature.

[b]These thicknesses are based on energy *efficiency* considerations only. Additional insulation is sometimes required relative to safety issues/surface temperature.
[c]Piping insulation is not required between control valve and coil on run-outs when control valve is located within 4 ft of coil and pipe size is 1 in. or less.
[d]These thicknesses are based on energy *efficiency* considerations only. Issues such as water vapor permeability or surface condensation sometimes require vapor retarders or additional insulation.

thickness, which, in this example, is in the double-layer range. Viewing the calculated economic thickness as a minimum thickness provides a hedge against unforeseen fuel price increases and conserves energy.

Initially, as insulation is applied, the total life-cycle cost decreases because the value of incremental energy savings is greater than the incremental cost of insulation. Additional insulation reduces total cost up to a thickness where the change in total cost is equal to zero. At this point, no further reduction can be obtained; beyond it, incremental insulation costs exceed the additional energy savings derived by adding another increment of insulation.

Economic analysis should also consider the time value of money, which can be based on a desired rate of return for the insulation investment. Energy costs are volatile, and a fuel cost inflation factor is sometimes included to account for the possibility that fuel costs may increase more quickly than general inflation. Insulation system maintenance costs should also be included, along with cost savings associated with the ability to specify lower capacity equipment, resulting in lower first costs.

Chapter 37 of the 2015 *ASHRAE Handbook—HVAC Applications* has more information on economic analysis.

Personnel Protection

In many applications, insulation is provided to protect personnel from burns. The potential for burns to human skin is a complex function of surface temperature, surface material, and time of contact. ASTM *Standard* C1055 has a good discussion of these factors. Standard industry practice is to specify a maximum temperature of

Table 3 Minimum Duct Insulation R-Value,[a] Combined Heating and Cooling Supply Ducts and Return Ducts

	Duct Location						
Climate Zone	Exterior	Ventilated Attic	Unvented Attic Above Insulated Ceiling	Unvented Attic with Roof Insulation[a]	Unconditioned Space[b]	Indirectly Conditioned Space[c]	Buried
				Supply Ducts			
1	R-4	R-6	R-8	R-3.5	R-3.5	none	R-3.5
2	R-6	R-6	R-6	R-3.5	R-3.5	none	R-3.5
3	R-6	R-6	R-6	R-3.5	R-3.5	none	R-3.5
4	R-6	R-6	R-6	R-3.5	R-3.5	none	R-3.5
5	R-6	R-6	R-6	R-1.9	R-3.5	none	R-3.5
6	R-6	R-6	R-6	R-1.9	R-3.5	none	R-3.5
7	R-6	R-6	R-6	R-1.9	R-3.5	none	R-3.5
8	R-8	R-8	R-8	R-1.9	R-6	none	R-6
				Return Ducts			
1 to 8	R-3.5	R-3.5	R-3.5	none	none	none	none

[a]Insulation R-values, measured in $h \cdot ft^2 \cdot °F/Btu$, are for the insulation as installed and do not include film resistance. The required minimum thicknesses do not consider water vapor transmission and possible surface condensation. Where exterior walls are used as plenum walls, wall insulation must be as required by the most restrictive condition of Section 6.4.4.2 or Section 5 of 90.1-2010. Insulation resistance measured on a horizontal plane in accordance with ASTM C518 at a mean temperature of 75°F at the installed thickness.
[b]Includes crawlspaces, both ventilated and nonventilated.
[c]Includes return air plenums with or without exposed roofs above.

140°F for surfaces that may be contacted by personnel. For indoor applications, maximum air temperatures depend on the facility and location, and are typically lower than design outdoor conditions. For outdoor installations, base calculations on summer design ambient temperatures with no wind (i.e., the worst case). Surface temperatures increase because of solar loading, but are usually neglected because of variability in orientation, solar intensity, and many other complicating factors. Engineering judgment must be used in selecting ambient and operating temperatures and wind conditions for these calculations.

Note that the choice of jacketing strongly affects a surface's relative safety. Higher-emittance jacketing materials (e.g., plastic, painted metals) can be selected to minimize the surface temperature. Jacketing material also affects the relative safety at a given surface temperature. For example, at 175°F, a stainless steel jacket blisters skin more severely than a nonmetallic jacket at equal contact time.

Condensation Control

For below-ambient systems, condensation control is often the overriding design objective. The design problem is best addressed as two separate issues: (1) avoiding surface condensation on the outer surface of the insulation system and (2) minimizing or managing water vapor intrusion.

Avoiding surface condensation is desirable because it (1) prevents dripping, which can wet surfaces below; (2) minimizes mold growth by eliminating the liquid water many molds require; and (3) avoids staining and possible damage to exterior jacketing.

The design goal is to keep the surface temperature above the dew-point temperature of surrounding air. Calculating surface temperature is relatively simple, but selecting the appropriate design conditions is often confusing. The appropriate design condition is normally the worst-case condition expected for the application. For condensation control, however, a design that satisfies the worst case is sometimes impossible.

To illustrate, Table 4 shows insulation thicknesses required to prevent condensation on the exterior surface of a hypothetical insulated tank containing a liquid held at 40°F in a mechanical room with a temperature of 80°F. Note that, at high relative humidities, the thickness required to prevent surface condensation increases dramatically, and becomes impractical above 90% rh.

For outdoor applications (or for unconditioned spaces vented to outdoor air), there are always some hours per year where the ambient air is saturated or nearly saturated. For these times, no amount of insulation will prevent surface condensation. Figure 2 shows the frequency distribution of outdoor relative humidity based on typical meteorological year weather data for Charlotte, North Carolina (Marion and Urban 1995). Note that there are over 1200 h per year when the relative humidity is equal to or greater than 90%, and nearly 600 h per year when the relative humidity is equal to or greater than 95%.

For outdoor applications and mechanical rooms vented to outdoor conditions, it is suggested to design for a relative humidity of 90%. Appropriate water-resistant vapor-retarder jacketing or mastics must then be specified to protect the system from the inevitable surface condensation.

Table 4 Insulation Thickness Required to Prevent Surface Condensation

Relative Humidity, %	Thickness, in.
20	—
30	0.1
40	0.2
50	0.3
60	0.5
70	0.7
80	1.3
90	2.9
95	6.0

Note: Calculated using Equation (14), assuming surface conductance of 1.2 $Btu/h \cdot ft^2 \cdot °F$ and insulation with thermal conductivity of 0.30 $Btu \cdot in/h \cdot ft^2 \cdot °F$. Different assumed values yield different results.

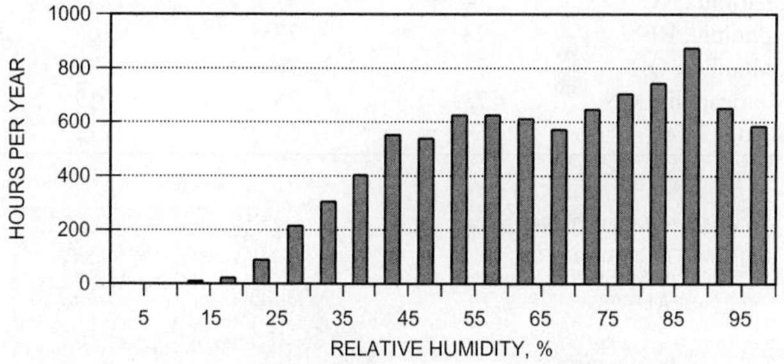

Fig. 2 Relative Humidity Histogram for Charlotte, NC

Table 5 summarizes design weather data for a select number of cities. The design dew-point temperature and the corresponding dry-bulb temperatures at 90% rh are given, along with the number of hours per year that the relative humidity would exceed 90%. Additional design dew-point data can be found in Chapter 14.

Design Example: Tampa, Florida.

Chilled-water supply piping is to be located outdoors to serve a commercial building expansion in Tampa, Florida. The supply piping is 6 in. NPS steel and the design temperature of the chilled-water supply is 40°F. Determine the appropriate design ambient conditions for this installation. From Table 5, the design dew-point temperature for Tampa is 78°F.

The design conditions are best visualized using a psychrometric chart, which graphically represents the properties of moist air. The horizontal axis is dry-bulb temperature, and the vertical axis is humidity ratio (lb of water vapor per lb of dry air). The chart includes the saturation curve (relative humidity = 100%) as well as parallel curves for other values of constant relative humidity. Lines of constant dew-point temperature are horizontal on the psychrometric chart.

Using Figure 3, enter the chart on the saturation curve at a dew point of 78°F (point A. in the figure) and draw a horizontal line. The design point is located where this horizontal line intersects the 90% rh curve. The dry-bulb temperature associated with this design point is read from the horizontal axis at point C, which for this example is approximately 81°F. The insulation system should therefore be designed for an operating temperature of 40°F, an ambient temperature of 81°F, and an ambient relative humidity of 90%.

Table 5 Design Weather Data for Condensation Control

City	Design Dew-Point Temp., °F	Corresponding Dry-Bulb Temp. at 90% rh, °F	Hours per Year >90% rh
New Orleans, LA	79	82	1253
Houston, TX	78	81	2105
Miami, FL	78	81	633
Tampa, FL	78	81	992
Savannah, GA	77	80	1560
Norfolk, VA	76	79	1279
San Antonio, TX	76	79	932
Charlotte, NC	74	77	1233
Honolulu, HI	74	77	166
Columbus, OH	73	76	531
Minneapolis, MN	73	76	619
Seattle, WA	60	63	1212

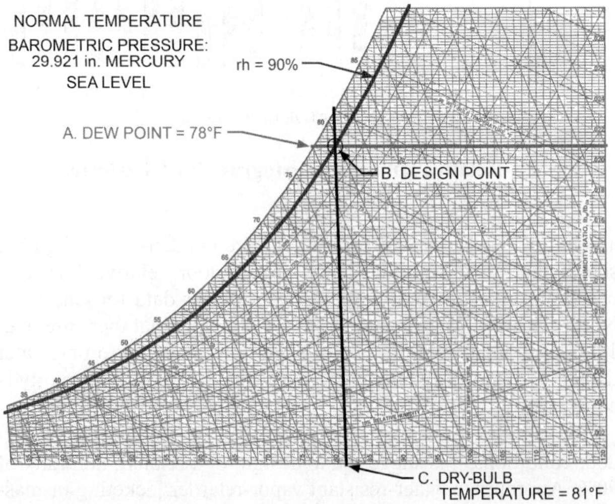

Fig. 3 ASHRAE Psychrometric Chart No. 1

This section is based on WDBG (2012).

For indoor designs in conditioned spaces, care is needed when selecting design conditions. Often, the HVAC system is sized to provide indoor conditions of 75°F/50% rh on a design summer day. However, those indoor conditions do not represent the worst-case indoor conditions for insulation design. Part-load conditions could result in higher humidity levels, or night and/or weekend shutdown could result in more severe conditions.

In addition to avoiding condensation on the exposed surface, another important design consideration is minimizing or managing water vapor intrusion, which is extremely important for piping and equipment operating at below-ambient temperatures. Water-related problems include thermal performance loss, health and safety issues, structural degradation, and aesthetic issues. Water entry into the insulation system may be through diffusion of water vapor, air leakage carrying water vapor, and leakage of surface water.

When the operating temperature is below the dew point of the surrounding ambient air, there is a difference in water vapor pressure across the insulation system. This vapor-pressure difference drives diffusion of water vapor from the ambient toward the cold surface. Piping and equipment typically create an absolute barrier to the passage of water vapor, so any vapor-pressure difference imposed across the insulation system results in the potential for condensation either in the insulation or at the cold surface. The vapor-pressure difference can range from below 0.1 in. Hg (0.05 psi) for a supply air duct operating in the return air plenum of a commercial building, to 1.2 in. Hg (0.6 psi) for a cryogenic system operating outdoors near the U.S. Gulf Coast. Although these pressure differences seem small, the effect over many operating hours can be significant.

Several fundamental design principles are used in managing water vapor intrusion. One method is to reduce the driving force by reducing the moisture content of the surrounding air. The insulation designer typically does not have control of the location of the piping, ductwork, or equipment to be insulated, but there are opportunities for the mechanical engineer to influence ambient conditions. Certainly, locating cold piping, ductwork, and equipment in unconditioned portions of buildings should be minimized. Consider conditioning mechanical rooms if feasible.

Another common method is moisture blocking, wherein passage of water vapor is eliminated or minimized to an insignificant level. The design must incorporate the following: (1) a vapor retarder with suitably low permeance; (2) a joint and seam sealing system that maintains vapor retarding system integrity; and (3) accommodation for future damage repair, joint and seam resealing, and reclosing after maintenance.

A vapor retarder is a material or system that adequately reduces transmission of water vapor through the insulation system. The vapor retarder system is seldom intended to resist entry of surface water or prevent air leakage, but can occasionally be considered the second line of defense for these moisture sources.

An effective vapor retarder material or system is essential for blocking systems to perform adequately. Mumaw (2001) showed that the design, installation, and performance of vapor retarder systems are key to the ability of an insulation system to minimize water vapor ingress. Performance of the vapor retarder material or system is characterized by the water vapor permeance: the lower the permeance, the better. The water vapor permeance can be evaluated using procedures outlined in ASTM *Standard* E96. In this test, a vapor pressure difference is imposed across vapor retarder material that has been sealed to a test cup, and the moisture gain or loss is measured gravimetrically.

The insulation system should be dry before applying a vapor retarder to prevent trapping water vapor in the insulation system. The insulation system also must be protected from undue weather exposure that could introduce moisture into the insulation before the system is sealed.

Faulty application techniques can impair vapor retarder performance. The effectiveness of installation and application techniques must be considered during selection. Factors such as vapor retarder structure, number of joints, mastics and adhesives that are used, as well as inspection procedures affect system performance and durability.

When selecting a vapor retarder, the vapor-pressure difference across the insulation system should be considered. Higher vapor-pressure differences typically require a vapor retarder with a lower permeance to control the overall moisture pickup of the insulated system. Service conditions affect the direction and magnitude of the vapor pressure difference: unidirectional flow exists when the water vapor pressure is constantly higher on one side of insulation system, whereas reversible flow exists when vapor pressure may be higher on either side (typically caused by diurnal or seasonal changes on one side of the insulation system). Properties of the insulation system materials should be considered. All materials reduce the flow of water vapor; the low permeance of some insulation materials can add to the overall resistance to water vapor transport of the insulation system. All vapor retarder joints should be tightly sealed with manufacturer-recommended sealants.

Another fundamental design principle is moisture storage design. In many systems, some condensation can be tolerated, the amount depending on the water-holding capacity or tolerance of a particular system. The moisture storage principle allows accumulation of water in the insulation system, but at a rate designed to prevent harmful effects. This concept is applicable when (1) unidirectional vapor flow occurs, but accumulations during severe conditions can be adequately expelled during less severe conditions; or (2) reverse flow regularly occurs on a seasonal or diurnal cycle. Design solutions using this principle include (1) periodically flushing the cold side with low-dew-point air (requires a supply of conditioned air and a means for distribution), and (2) using an insulation system supplemented by selected vapor retarders and absorbent materials such that an accumulation of condensation is of little importance. Such a design must ensure sufficient expulsion of accumulated moisture.

ASTM *Standard* C755 discusses various design principles. Chapters 25 to 27 of this volume thoroughly describe the physics associated with water vapor transport. Additional information is found in Chapter 10 of the 2014 *ASHRAE Handbook—Refrigeration*, and in ASTM (2001).

Freeze Prevention

It is important to recognize that insulation retards heat flow; it does not stop it completely. If the surrounding air temperature remains low enough for an extended period, insulation cannot prevent freezing of still water or of water flowing at a rate insufficient for the available heat content to offset heat loss. Insulation can prolong the time required for freezing, or prevent freezing if flow is maintained at a sufficient rate. To calculate time θ (in hours) required for water to cool to 32°F with no flow, use the following equation:

$$\theta = \rho C_p \pi (D_1/2)^2 R_T \ln[(t_i - t_a)/(t_f - t_a)] \quad (1)$$

where

θ = time to freezing, h
ρ = density of water = 62.4 lb/ft^3
C_p = specific heat of water = 1.0 Btu/lb·°F
D_1 = inside diameter of pipe, ft (see Figure 4)
R_T = combined thermal resistance of pipe wall, insulation, and exterior air film (for a unit length of pipe)
t_i = initial water temperature, °F
t_a = ambient air temperature, °F
t_f = freezing temperature, °F

As a conservative assumption for insulated pipes, thermal resistances of pipe walls and exterior air film are usually neglected.

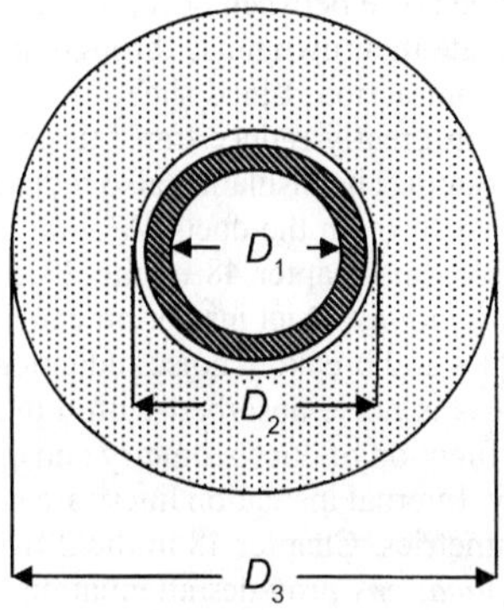

Fig. 4 Time to Freeze Nomenclature

Table 6 Time to Cool Water to Freezing, h

Nominal Pipe Size, NPS	Insulation Thickness, in.					
	0.5	1	1.5	2	3	4
1/2	0.1	0.2	0.2	0.3	—	—
1	0.3	0.4	0.5	0.6	0.8	—
1 1/2	0.4	0.8	1.0	1.3	1.5	—
2	0.6	1.1	1.4	1.7	2.2	2.5
3	0.9	1.7	2.3	2.9	3.7	4.5
4	1.3	2.4	3.3	4.1	5.5	6.6
5	1.6	3.0	4.3	5.4	7.4	9.1
6	1.9	3.7	5.3	6.9	9.4	11.7
8	—	5.3	7.6	9.6	13.7	16.9
10	—	6.5	10.2	12.9	17.9	22.3
12	—	8.8	12.5	15.8	22.1	27.7

Note: Assumes initial temperature = 42°F, ambient air temperature = –18°F, and insulation thermal conductivity = 0.30 Btu·in/h·ft^2·°F. Thermal resistances of pipe and air film are neglected. Different assumed values yield different results.

Resistance of the insulation layer for a unit length of pipe is calculated as

$$R_T = 12 \ln(D_3/D_2)/(2\pi k) \quad (2)$$

where

D_3 = outer diameter of insulation, ft
D_2 = inner diameter of insulation, ft
k = thermal conductivity of insulation material, Btu·in/h·ft^2·°F

Table 6 shows estimated time to freezing, calculated using these equations for the specific case of still water with t_i = 42°F and t_a = –18°F.

When unusual conditions make it impractical to maintain protection with insulation or flow, a hot trace pipe or electric resistance heating cable is required along the bottom or top of the water pipe. The heating system then supplies the heat lost through the insulation.

Clean water in pipes usually supercools several degrees below freezing before any ice is formed. Then, upon nucleation, dendritic ice forms in the water and the temperature rises to freezing. Ice can be formed from water only by the release of the latent heat of fusion (144 Btu/lb) through the pipe insulation. Well-insulated pipes may greatly retard this release of latent heat. Gordon (1996) showed that water pipes burst not because of ice crystal growth in the pipe, but because of elevated fluid pressure within a confined pipe section occluded by a growing ice blockage.

Noise Control

Duct Insulation. Without insulation, the acoustical environment of mechanically conditioned buildings can be greatly compromised, resulting in reduced productivity and a decrease in occupant comfort. HVAC ducts act as conduits for mechanical equipment noise, and also carry office noise between occupied spaces. Additionally, some ducts can create their own noise through duct wall vibrations or expansion and contraction. Lined sheet metal ducts and fibrous glass rigid ducts can greatly reduce transmission of HVAC noise through the duct system. The insulation also reduces cross-talk from one room to another through the ducts. A good discussion of duct acoustics is provided in Chapter 48 of the 2015 *ASHRAE Handbook—HVAC Applications*. Duct insulation can be used to provide both attenuation loss and breakout noise reduction.

Attenuation loss is noise absorbed within the duct. In uninsulated ducts, it is a function of duct geometry and dimensions as well as noise frequency. Internal insulation liners are generally available for most duct geometries. Chapter 48 in the 2015 *ASHRAE Handbook—HVAC Applications* provides attenuation losses for square, rectangular, and round ducts lined with fibrous glass, and also gives guidance on use of insulation in plenums to absorb duct system noise. Internal linings can be very effective in fittings such as elbows, which can have 2 to 8 times more attenuation than an unlined elbow of the same size. For alternative lining materials, consult individual manufacturers.

It is difficult to write specifications for sound attenuation because it changes with every duct dimension and configuration. Thus, insulation materials are generally selected for attenuation based on sound absorption ratings. Sound absorption tests are run per ASTM *Standard* C423 in large reverberation rooms with random sound incidence. The test specimens are laid on the chamber floor per ASTM *Standard* E795, type A mounting. This mode of sound exposure is different from the exposure of internal linings installed in an air duct; therefore, sound absorption ratings for materials can only be used for general comparisons of effectiveness when used in air ducts of varying dimensions (Kuntz and Hoover 1987).

Breakout noise is from vibration of the duct wall caused by air pressure fluctuations in the duct. Absorptive insulation can be used in combination with mass-loaded jacketing materials or mastics on the duct exterior to reduce breakout noise. This technique is only minimally effective on rectangular ducts, which require the insulation and mass composite to be physically separated from the duct wall to be very effective. For round ducts, as with pipes, absorptive insulation and mass composite can be effective even when directly applied to the duct surface. Chapter 48 in the 2015 *ASHRAE Handbook—HVAC Applications* provides breakout noise guidance data.

Noise Radiating from Pipes. Noise from piping can be reduced by adding an absorptive insulation and jacketing material. By knowing the sound insertion loss of insulation and jacketing material combinations, the expected level of noise reduction in the field can be estimated. A range of jacket weights and insulation thicknesses can be used to reduce noise. Jackets used to reduce noise are typically referred to as being mass filled. Some products for outdoor applications use mass-filled vinyl (MFV) in combination with aluminum.

Pipe insertion loss is a measurement (in dB) of the reduction in sound pressure level from a pipe as a result of application of insulation and jacketing. Measured at different frequencies, the noise level from the jacketed pipe is subtracted from that of the bare pipe; the larger the insertion loss number, the larger the amount of noise reduction.

ASTM *Standard* E1222 describes how to determine insertion loss of pipe jacketing systems. A band-limited white noise test signal is produced inside a steel pipe located in a reverberation room, using a loudspeaker or acoustic driver at one end of the pipe to produce the noise. Average sound pressure levels are measured in the room for two conditions: with sound radiating from a bare pipe, and with the same pipe covered with a jacketing system. The insertion loss of the jacketing system is the difference in the sound pressure levels measured, adjusted for changes in room absorption caused by the jacketing system's presence. Results may be obtained in a series of 100 Hz wide bands or in one-third octave bands from 500 to 5000 Hz.

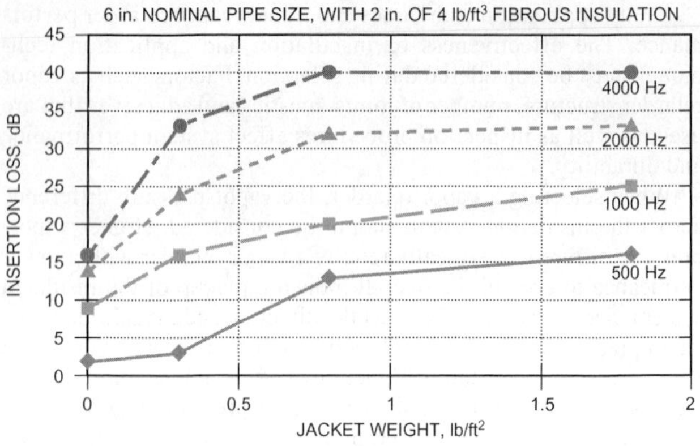

Fig. 5 Insertion Loss Versus Weight of Jacket

Table 7 gives measured insertion loss values for several pipe insulation and jacket combinations. The weight of the jacket material significantly affects insertion loss of pipe insulation systems. Figure 5 represents insertion loss of typical fibrous pipe insulations with various weights of jacketing (Miller 2001).

It is very important that sound sources be well identified in industrial settings. It is possible to treat a noisy pipe very effectively and have no significant influence on ambient sound measurement after treatment. All sources of noise above desired levels must receive acoustical treatment, beginning with the largest source, or no improvement will be observed.

Fire Safety

Materials used to insulate mechanical equipment generally must meet the requirements of local codes adopted by governmental entities having jurisdiction over the project. In the United States, most local codes incorporate or are patterned after model codes developed and maintained by organizations such as the National Fire Protection Association (NFPA) and International Code Council (International Codes). Refer to local codes to determine specific requirements.

Most codes related to insulation product fire safety refer to the surface burning characteristics as determined by the Steiner tunnel test (ASTM *Standard* E84, UL *Standard* 723, or CAN/ULC *Standard* S-102). These similar test methods evaluate the flame spread and smoke developed from samples mounted in a 25 ft long tunnel and subsequently exposed to a controlled flame. Results are given in terms of *flame spread* and *smoke developed* indices, which are relative to a baseline index and calibration standards of inorganic reinforced cement board (0) and select-grade red oak flooring (100). Samples are normally mounted with the exposed surface face down in the ceiling of the tunnel. Upon ignition, the progress of the flame front is timed while being tracked visually for distance down the tunnel, with the results used to calculate the flame spread index. Smoke index is determined by measuring smoke density with a light cell mounted in the exhaust stream.

Using supporting materials on the underside of the test specimen can lower the flame spread index. Materials that melt, drip, or delaminate to such a degree that the continuity of the flame front is destroyed give low flame spread indices that do not relate directly to indices obtained by testing materials that remain in place. Alternative means of testing may be necessary to fully evaluate some of these materials.

For pipe and duct insulation products, samples are prepared and mounted in the tunnel per ASTM *Standard* E2231, which directs that "the material, system, composite, or assembly tested shall be representative of the completed insulation system used in actual field installations, in terms of the components, including their

Table 7 Insertion Loss for Pipe Insulation Materials, dB

Pipe Size, NPS	Insulation Material	Insulation Thickness, in.	Jacket	Frequency, Hz 500	1000	2000	4000
6	Fibrous glass	2	ASJ[a]	2	9	14	16
		2	0.020 in. aluminum	3	16	24	33
		2	1 lb/ft^2 MFV[b] with Al	13	20	32	40
		4	ASJ	4	21	27	33
		4	0.020 in. aluminum	3	17	27	42
	Flexible elastomeric	0.5	None	0	2	5	10
		1	None	0	2	5	10
		0.5	1 lb/ft^2 MFV with Al	0	14	18	20
		1	1 lb/ft^2 MFV with Al	0	16	20	26
12	Fibrous glass	2	ASJ	0	12	19	23
		2	0.020 in. aluminum	4	19	25	26
		4	ASJ	8	16	22	26
		4	0.020 in. aluminum	12	22	30	32
		4	1 lb/ft^2 MFV with Al	14	23	31	31
	Mineral wool	2	0.016 in. aluminum	1	9	18	28
		3	0.016 in. aluminum	0	14	19	30

[a]ASJ = all-service jacket, a typical factory-applied vapor retarder applied to many products.
[b]MFV = mass filled vinyl, a field-installed jacket, which has considerably more mass than ASJ.

respective thicknesses." Samples are constructed to mimic, as closely as possible, the products as they will be used, including any facings and adhesives as appropriate.

Duct insulation generally requires a flame spread index of not more than 25 and a smoke developed index of not more than 50, when tested in accordance with ASTM *Standard* E84. Codes often require factory-made duct insulations (e.g., insulated flexible ducts, rigid fibrous glass ducts) to be listed and labeled per UL *Standard* 181. This standard specifies several other fire tests (e.g., flame penetration and low-energy ignition) as part of the listing requirements.

Some building codes require that duct insulations meet the fire hazard requirements of NFPA *Standard* 90A or 90B, to restrict spread of smoke, heat, and fire through duct systems, and to minimize ignition sources. Local code authorities should also be consulted for specific requirements.

For pipe insulation, the requirement is generally a maximum flame spread index of 25 and a maximum smoke developed index of 450 in nonplenum spaces (in plenums, less than or equal to 25 and 50, respectively). Consult local code authorities for specific requirements.

The term *noncombustible*, as defined by building codes, refers to materials that pass the requirements of ASTM *Standard* E136. This test method involves introducing a small specimen of the material into a furnace initially maintained at a temperature of 1380°F. The temperature rise of the furnace is monitored and the specimen is observed for any flaming. Criteria for passing include limits on temperature rise, flaming, and weight loss of the specimen. Some building codes accept as noncombustible a composite material having a structural base of noncombustible material and a surfacing not more than 1/8 in. thick that has a flame spread index not greater than 50. A related term sometimes referenced in building codes is *limited combustible*, which is an intermediate category that considers the potential heat content of materials determined per the testing requirements of NFPA *Standard* 259.

Mechanical insulation materials are often used as a component in systems or assemblies designed to protect buildings and equipment from the effects or spread of fire (i.e., **fire-resistance assemblies**). They can include walls, roofs, floors, columns, beams, partitions, joints, and through-penetration fire stops. Specific designs are tested and assigned hourly ratings based on performance in full-scale fire tests. Note that insulation materials alone are not assigned hourly fire resistance ratings; ratings are assigned to a system or assembly that may include specific insulation products, along with other elements such as framing members, fasteners, wallboard, etc.

Fire resistance ratings are often developed using ASTM *Standard* E119. This test exposes assemblies (walls, partitions, floor or roof assemblies, and through-penetration fire stops) to a standard fire exposure controlled to achieve specified temperatures throughout a specified time period. The time/temperature curve is intended to represent building fires where the primary fuel is solid, and specifies a temperature of 1000°F at 5 min, 1700°F at 1 h, and 2300°F at 8 h. In the hydrocarbon processing industry, liquid hydrocarbon-fueled pool fires are a concern; fire resistance ratings for these applications are tested per ASTM *Standard* E1529. This time/temperature curve rises rapidly to 2000°F within 5 min, and remains there for the duration of the test.

Fire-resistant rated designs can be found in the directories of listing agencies. Examples of such agencies include Underwriters Laboratories, Factory Mutual, UL Canada, and Intertek.

The following standard cross-references are provided for products to be tested in Canada. Although these are parallel Canadian standards, the requirements may differ from those of ASTM standards.

ASTM *Standard* E84	CAN/ULC *Standard* S102, Standard Method of Test for Surface Burning Characteristics of Building Materials and Assemblies
ASTM *Standard* E119	CAN/ULC *Standard* S101-M, Standard Methods of Fire Endurance Tests of Building Construction and Materials
ASTM *Standard* E136	CAN *Standard* 4-S114, Standard Method of Test for Determination of Noncombustibility in Building Materials
ASTM *Standard* E1529	There is no Canadian equivalent standard on this subject

Corrosion Under Insulation

Corrosion of metal pipe, vessels, and equipment under insulation, though not typically caused by the insulation, is still a significant issue that must be considered during the design of any mechanical insulation system. The propensity for corrosion depends on many factors, including the ambient environment, operating temperature of the metal, proper installation, and maintenance of the insulated system.

Corrosion under insulation (CUI) is most prevalent in outdoor industrial environments such as refineries and chemical plants. Corrosion can be very costly because of forced downtime of processes and can be a health and safety hazard as well. Although insulation itself may not necessarily be the cause of corrosion, it can be a passive component because it is in direct contact with the pipe or equipment surface.

Very little information is published on corrosion in commercial environments. Although corrosion under insulation is less likely to be a major concern for most insulated surfaces located indoors, it may be a factor on indoor systems that are frequently washed down, such as in the food processing industry.

Water from condensation on cold surfaces can be present on both indoor and outdoor insulation systems if there is damage to the vapor retarder. Hot processes can also be subject to condensation during periods of system shutdown.

The following factors may lead to corrosion under insulation.

- **Water** must be present. Water ingress may occur at some point on insulated surfaces. The entry point for water is through breaks in weatherproofing materials such as lagging, mastic, caulk, or adhesives.
- A general lack of **inspection and maintenance** increases the potential for corrosion.
- **Temperature** affects the rate of corrosion. In general, temperatures up to 350°F increase the corrosion rate (NACE *Standard* SP0198).
- **Contaminants** in the plant environment can accelerate corrosion. For instance, chlorides, sulfates, and other corrosion-causing ions could reside on the insulation's exterior jacket, then be washed into the insulation system by rain or washdown. Other sources of corrosive ions include rainwater, ocean mist, and cooling tower spray, each of which can provide a major and virtually inexhaustible supply of ions. Even if the level of ions in the water is low, significant amounts of ions can accumulate at the pipe surface by a continuing cycle of water penetrations and evaporation. Chloride and other ions only contribute to stress corrosion cracking of stainless steel when water (liquid or vapor) and these ions are present at the surface of a pipe at temperatures above ambient, usually when the surface is above about 140°F and below about 300°F; water and corrosive ions on the pipe surface may contribute to normal oxidative (rusting) corrosion of carbon steel at temperatures between 25 and 350°F [see Kalis (1999) and NACE *Standard* SP0198]. Exposure of the insulation system to water from some outside source is inevitable, so the key to eliminating stress corrosion cracking lies in preventing moisture and ions, even in small amounts, from reaching the metal surface.
- **Insulation** can contain leachable corrosive agents. Information on the potential corrosion of carbon steel by insulation materials is available from tests conducted using ASTM *Standard* C1617. The information may be available from the insulation ASTM material standard or from the insulation manufacturer.
- **Austenitic stainless steels** are particularly susceptible to attack from chlorides. Austenitic stainless steels are generally classified as "18-8s": austenitic alloys containing approximately 18% chromium, 8% nickel, and the balance iron. Besides the basic alloy UNS S30400, these stainless alloys include molybdenum (UNS S31600 and S31700), carbon-stabilized (UNS S321000 and S347000), and low-carbon grades (UNS S30403 and S31603) (NACE *Standard* SP0198).

For outdoor applications, to prevent ingress of moisture and corrosive ions from precipitation, a properly designed, installed, and maintained weather-protective jacket is recommended. For more specific guidelines, consult the insulation material manufacturer. If process temperatures are lower than ambient (even for short periods of time such as during shutdowns), a vapor retarder is also required.

Even with a protective jacket and vapor retarder, it is likely that some moisture and ions will eventually enter the system because of abuse, wear, age, or improper installation. No installation is ideal in any real-world setting. Because most people only consider the chlorides arising from the insulation material, the crucial issue of water and ions infiltrating the insulation system from the environment and yielding metal corrosion remains largely unaddressed. Thus, painting the pipe is the second and most important line of defense, and is necessary if pipe temperature is in the 140 to 300°F range for significant periods of time. To minimize the potential for corrosion, metal pipe should be primed with, for example, an epoxy coating. This alternative offers superior protection against corrosion, because priming protects against ions arising from the insulation and, more importantly, from ions that enter the system from the environment.

To minimize corrosion,

- Design, install, and maintain insulation systems to minimize ponding water or penetration of water into the system. Flat sections should be designed with a pitch to shed water. Top sections should overlap the sides to provide a watershed effect on ducts, preventing water penetration in the seam. Jacketing joints should be oriented so as to shed water. Design should always minimize penetrations; necessary protrusions (e.g., supports, valves, flanges) should be designed to shed rather than capture water. Water from external sources can enter at any discontinuity in the insulation system.
- Insulation should be appropriate for its intended application and service temperature. NACE *Standard* RP0198 states, "CUI of carbon steel is possible under all types of insulation. The insulation type may only be a contributing factor. The insulation characteristics with the most influence on CUI are (1) water-leachable salt content in insulation that may contribute to corrosion, such as chloride, sulfate, and acidic materials in fire retardants; (2) water retention, permeability, and wettability of the insulation; and (3) foams containing residual compounds that react with water to form hydrochloric or other acids. Because CUI is a product of wet metal exposure duration, the insulation system that holds the least amount of water and dries most quickly should result in the least amount of corrosion damage to equipment."
- Ancillary materials used for weatherproofing (e.g., sealants, caulks, weather stripping, adhesives, mastics) should be appropriate for the application, and be applied following the manufacturer's recommendations.
- Maintenance should monitor for and immediately repair compromises in the protective jacketing system. Because water may infiltrate the insulation system, inspection ports should be used to facilitate inspection without requiring insulation removal. This is particularly important on subambient systems.
- Because some water will eventually enter the system, a protective pipe coating is necessary for good design. The type of coating depends on temperature (see NACE *Standard* RP0198 for coating guidelines). In Europe, essentially all piping is coated for corrosion protection. This is not necessarily the case in the United States, but should be considered as part of good design practice.
- When using austenitic stainless steel, all insulation products and accessories should meet the requirements of ASTM *Standard* C795 if the system will operate at or spend time between 140 and 300°F. Likewise, any ancillary weatherproofing materials should have low chloride content.

2. MATERIALS AND SYSTEMS

Categories of Insulation Materials

Turner and Malloy (1981) categorized insulation materials into four types:

- **Fibrous** insulations are composed of small-diameter fibers that finely divide the air space. The fibers may be organic or inorganic, and are normally (but not always) held together by a binder.
- **Granular** insulations are composed of small nodules that contain voids or hollow spaces. These materials are sometimes considered open-cell materials, because gases can transfer between the individual spaces.
- **Cellular** insulations are composed of small, individual cells, either interconnecting or sealed from each other, to form a cellular structure. Glass, plastics, and rubber may comprise the base material, and various foaming agents are used.

  Cellular insulations are often further classified as either open-cell (i.e., cells are interconnecting) or closed-cell (i.e., cells sealed from each other). Generally, materials with greater than 90% closed-cell content are considered to be closed-cell materials.
- **Reflective** insulations and treatments are added to surfaces to lower long-wave emittance, thereby reducing radiant heat transfer from the surface. Low-emittance jackets and facings are often used in combination with other insulation materials.

Another material sometimes called **thermal insulating paint** or **coating** is available for use on pipes ducts and tanks. These products' performance must be clearly understood before using them as thermal insulation. These paints and coatings have not been extensively tested and additional research is needed to verify their performance. Further discussion of these products can be found in Hart (2006).

Physical Properties of Insulation Materials

Selecting an insulation material for a particular application requires understanding the various physical properties associated with available materials.

Operating temperature is often the primary consideration. Maximum temperature capability is normally assessed using ASTM *Standard* C411 by exposing samples to hot surfaces for an extended time, and assessing the materials for any changes in properties. Evidence of warping, cracking, delamination, flaming, melting, or dripping are indications that the maximum use temperature of the material has been exceeded. There is currently no industry-accepted test method for determining the minimum operating temperature of an insulation material, but minimum temperatures are normally determined by evaluating the material's integrity and physical properties after exposure to low temperatures.

Thermal conductivity of insulation materials is a function of temperature. Many specifications call for insulation conductivity values evaluated at a mean temperature of 75°F. Most manufacturers provide conductivity data over a range of temperatures to allow evaluations closer to actual operating conditions. Conductivity of flat product is generally measured per ASTM *Standards* C177 or C518, whereas pipe insulation conductivity is generally determined using ASTM *Standard* C335. Additional information on this property is presented in the following section.

Compressive resistance is important where the insulation must support a load without crushing (e.g., insulation inserts in pipe hangers and supports). When insulation is used in an expansion or contraction joint to take up a dimensional change, lower values of compressive resistance are desirable. ASTM *Standard* C165 is used to measure compressive resistance for fibrous materials, and ASTM *Standard* D1621 is used for foam plastic materials.

Water vapor permeability is the water vapor flux through a material induced by a unit vapor pressure gradient across the material. For insulating materials, it is commonly expressed in units of perm·in. A related and often-confused term is **water vapor permeance** (in perms), which measures water vapor flux through a material of specific thickness and is generally used to define vapor retarder performance. In below-ambient applications, it is important to minimize the rate of water vapor flow to the cold surface. This is normally accomplished by using vapor retarders or insulation materials (e.g., cellular glass insulation) with a permeance less than or equal to 0.02 perm, or both. However, some flexible closed-cell insulation materials have been used successfully without a separate vapor retarder material. ASTM *Standard* E96 is used to measure water vapor transmission properties of insulation materials.

Water absorption is generally measured by immersing a sample of material under a specified head of water for a specified time period. It is a useful measure of the amount of liquid water absorbed from water leaks in weather barriers or during construction.

Typical physical properties of interest are given in Table 8. Values in this table are taken from the relevant ASTM material specification with permission from ASTM International. Within each material category, a variety in types and grades of materials exist. A representative type and grade are listed in Table 8 for each material category; refer to ASTM standards or to manufacturers for specific data.

Thermal Conductivity of Below-Ambient Pipe Insulation Systems. Mechanical pipe insulation systems are installed around cold cylindrical surfaces, such as chilled pipes, and work below ambient temperature in several industrial and commercial building applications. Thermal performance of a pipe insulation system is affected by ambient temperature and humidity and might vary gradually with time. For below-ambient temperature applications of pipe insulation, most published data are extrapolated from flat slab configurations of insulation material, and may not be accurate for cylindrical pipe insulation systems because of radial configuration and longitudinal split joints. Thus, ASHRAE research project RP-1356 (Cremaschi et al. 2012) developed an experimental apparatus to measure the thermal conductivity of mechanical pipe insulation systems below ambient temperature. Thermal conductivities of five pipe insulation systems under low-humidity, noncondensing conditions are provided in Table 9 at mean insulation temperatures of 55 and 75°F; the insulation was installed on a 3 in. nominal pipe size diameter aluminum pipe, and the test specimens were 3 ft long. Radial heat flux was inward and ranged from 7.9 to 34.6 Btu/h·ft. Nominal wall thickness of the pipe insulation systems varied from 1 to 2 in. Vapor barriers on the outer surface of the pipe insulation were not installed. The dry test were performed with the aluminum pipe surface temperature at 40.5 ± 0.5°F, ambient temperature from 73 to 110°F, and air dew-point temperature below 40°F. For these test conditions, water vapor does not condense on the aluminum pipe surface.

The relation between the pipe insulation's thermal conductivity and its mean temperature is linear, and the thermal conductivity of pipe insulation system had a weak dependence on the nominal wall thickness. Note that, for some cases, joint sealant is recommended for the installation of the pipe insulation. Values in Table 9 represent a combined thermal conductivity of the pipe insulation with a certain type of joint sealant applied on the longitudinal joints, where two C-shells come in contact with each other. The combined thermal conductivity of the pipe insulation might be higher than the thermal conductivity of pipe insulation C-shells that are mechanically joint together without sealant on the longitudinal joints. For example, if a butyl rubber sealant with a layer thickness ranging from 1/16 to 0.1 in. is used, it is possible that the combined thermal conductivity increases up to 15% with respect to the value of the same pipe insulation system without joint sealant.

ASHRAE research project RP-1356 also measured the thermal conductivity of mechanical pipe insulation systems below ambient temperature in high humidity without vapor retarders, resulting in rapid moisture ingress. Two types of pipe insulation, installed on a 3 in. nominal pipe size diameter aluminum pipe that was 3 ft long, were exposed for less than a month to a warm, humid environment, resulting in water vapor condensation in the insulation samples and

Table 8 Performance Property Guide for Insulation Materials

	Calcium Silicate	Flexible Elastomeric	Mineral Fiber	Cellular Glass	Cellular Polystyrene	Cellular Polyiso-cyanurate	Cellular Phenolic	Cellular Polyolefin
ASTM *Standard*	C533	C534	C547, C553, C612	C552	C578	C591	C1126	C1427
Type/grade listed	Type I	Type I Grade 1	Type IVB Category 1	Type I Grade 1	Type XIII	Type IV Grade 2	Type III	Type I Grade 1
Max. operating temperature, °F	1200	220	1200	800	165	300	257	200
Min. operating temperature, °F	140	–70	0	–450	–297	–297	–290	–150
Min. compressive resistance, psi	100 at 5%	N/S	N/S	60 at failure	20 at 10%	21 at 10%	18	N/S
Max. thermal conductivity, Btu·in/h·ft²·°F								
0°F mean	N/A	0.26	N/A	0.27	0.22	0.18	0.15	0.33
25°F	N/A	N/S	0.23	N/S	0.23	N/S	N/S	N/S
75°F	N/A	0.28	0.24	0.31	0.26	0.18	0.15	0.35
200°F	0.45	N/A	0.30	0.40	N/A	0.24	0.25	N/A
400°F	0.55	N/A	0.42	0.58	N/A	N/A	N/A	N/A
600°F	0.66	N/A	0.63	N/A	N/A	N/A	N/A	N/A
Maximum water vapor permeability, perm·in.	N/S	0.10	N/A	0.005	1.5	4.0	5.0	0.05
Maximum liquid water absorption, % volume	N/S	0.2	N/S	0.5	0.5 (24 h)	0.5 (24 h)	3.0	0.2
Maximum water vapor sorption, % weight	N/S	N/S	5	N/S	N/S	N/S	N/S	N/S
Maximum surface burning characteristics	0/0	25/50	25/50	5/0	N/S	N/S	25/50	N/S

Note: N/A = not applicable. N/S = not stated (i.e., ASTM standards do not include a value for this property). Properties not stated do not necessarily indicate that material is not appropriate for a given application depending on that property. See previous editions of *ASHRAE Handbook—Fundamentals* for data on historical insulation materials.

Table 9 Thermal Conductivities of Cylindrical Pipe Insulation at 55 and 75°F

Pipe Insulation Material	Nominal Wall Thickness in.	Joint Sealant Type	Thermal Conductivity at 55°F, Btu·in/h·ft²·°F	Thermal Conductivity at 75°F, Btu·in/h·ft²·°F
Cellular glass	1	Butyl rubber	0.2975	0.3175
	2	Butyl rubber	0.2798	0.3218
PIR	1	Butyl rubber	0.1968	0.2048
Glass fiber	2	Contact cement	0.2345	0.2425
Elastomeric rubber	2	Contact cement	0.2419	0.2519
Phenolic	1	Butyl rubber	0.2206	0.2346
	2	Butyl rubber	0.1877	0.2117

increased thermal conductivities. The nominal wall thickness of the pipe insulation systems was 2 in.

Vapor barriers were not installed on the outer surface of the pipe insulation, and the thermal conductivities increased as result of condensed water being retained into the insulation systems. For one type of pipe insulation, the thermal conductivity increased by 3.15 times when the moisture content was about 11% volume. For the other insulation, the thermal conductivity was 1.55 times of the original dry value when the moisture content reached 5% by volume. Each test was run for less than 1 month at high ambient humidity (>80% rh at 95°F. The test conditions were intentionally different from each other, and the thermal performance of the two pipe insulation systems tested in warm, high-humidity conditions should not be compared.

Caution is needed in using this data. Only two types of pipe insulation were tested, and neither had a vapor retarder. The manufacturers of these materials do not recommend these pipe insulation materials be installed in this manner for below-ambient applications. Nevertheless, these data are significant because they demonstrate both the necessity of installing an effective water vapor retarder and the negative impact of water retention in the insulation on its thermal conductivity. These results are only an example of this phenomenon, and any insulation that absorbs and retains water could be similarly affected.

Weather Protection

Weather barriers, often referred to as jacketing, are extremely important. Premature failure can lead to insulation failure, with safety and economic consequences.

Safety consequences

- If insulation is installed for burn protection from a hot pipe or equipment, water entering the insulation system can vaporize into steam and cause a surface temperature well above the expected 140°F, the common design temperature for personnel protection.
- Pipe or equipment can corrode, rupture, and release a hazardous material.

Economic consequences

- Wet insulation has higher thermal conductivity and lower insulation values.
- On a hot system, 1 lb of water entering the system requires 1000 Btu to revaporize. If this vapor cannot vent easily, it can condense, causing interior jacket corrosion; the weather barrier will begin consuming itself from the inside out. Consequently, the system cannot deliver the desired energy efficiency and will quickly require an expensive repair.
- On a very cold system, improper vapor retarder selection allows moisture to migrate to the cold surface because of the continuous drive of vapor pressure. A hole in the system allows direct water influx. Either of these entry mechanisms results in ice formation, which separates the insulation and weather protection barrier from the pipe or vessel surface and compromises thermal performance.

Many more scenarios must be considered, especially when the broad range of features required of a weather barrier are considered. Turner and Malloy (1981) define a weather barrier as "a material or materials, which, when installed on the outer surface of thermal insulation, protects the insulation from . . . rain, snow, sleet, wind, solar radiation, atmospheric contamination and mechanical damage." With this definition in mind, several service requirements must be considered.

- **Internal mechanical forces**: Expansion and contraction of the pipe or vessel must be considered because the resulting forces are transferred to the external surface of the weather barrier. Ability to slide, elongate, or contract must be provided.
- **External mechanical forces**: Mechanical abuse (i.e., tools being dropped, abrasion from wind-driven sand, personnel walking on the system) inflicted on a pipe or vessel needs to be considered in design. This may affect insulation type, as well as the weather barrier jacketing type.
- **Dimensional stability**: Some cellular materials can show irreversible dimensional change after installation. Manufacturers of these materials provide installation guidelines to minimize the effects of dimensional change. If guidelines are not followed, failure of joint seals can occur, which can lead to system failure.
- **Chemical resistance**: Some industrial environments may have airborne or spilled corrosive agents that accumulate on the weather barrier and chemically attack the pipe or vessel jacketing. Elements that create corrosive issues must be well understood and accounted for. Insulation design of coastal facilities should account for chloride attack.
- **Galvanic corrosion**: Contacts between two different types of metal must be considered for galvanic corrosion potential. Similarly, water can act as an electrolyte, and galvanic corrosion can occur because of the different potential of the pipe or vessel and the metal jacketing.
- **Crevice/pitting corrosion**: Water trapped against the interior surface of a metal weather barrier/jacket can lead to pitting/crevice-type corrosion on the interior surface of the jacket (Young 2011).
- **Insulation corrosivity**: Some insulation materials can cause metal jacket corrosion or chemically attack some polymer films. Both of these situations shorten service life.
- **Thermal degradation**: Hot systems are typically designed so that the surface temperature of the insulation and jacketing material do not exceed 140°F. The long-term effect of 140°F on the jacketing material must be considered. Additionally, there may be solar radiation load and perhaps parallel heat loss from an adjacent pipe. Turner and Malloy (1981) suggest that 250°F should be considered as the long-term operating temperature of the jacketing material selected. This is a critical design consideration, particularly for a nonmetal jacket.
- **Installation and application logistics**: Often, the insulation contractor installs more insulation in a day than can be protected with jacket. If it rains, the exposed insulation gets saturated and, the next day, the jacket is installed over the wet insulation. This creates an obvious potential corrosion and performance issue before the installation is operational, and must be corrected immediately. It should also be understood that the size, shape, and adjacent space available for work may dictate the type of weather barrier used, even if it is a less desirable option. If this is the case, the maintenance schedule must recognize and accommodate for this.
- **Maintenance**: The importance of a maintenance and inspection plan cannot be overemphasized to achieve the service life expected of the design.

Materials Used as Weather Barriers for Insulation. Metal rolls or sheets of various thicknesses are available with embossing, corrugation, moisture barriers, and different banding and closure methods. Elbows and tees are also available for piping. Typical metal jacketing materials are

- Bare aluminum
- Polymer-film-coated aluminum
- Painted aluminum
- Stainless steel
- Painted steel
- Galvanized steel
- Aluminum-zinc coated steel

All metal weather barrier/jacketing should have a 3 mil thick multiple-layer moisture barrier factory heat laminated to the interior surface to help prevent galvanic and pitting/crevice corrosion on the interior surface of the jacketing (Young 2011).

Polymeric (plastic) rolls or sheets are available at various thicknesses. These materials are glued or solvent-welded, depending on the polymer. Elbows and tees are also available for piping for some type of polymers. Typical polymeric (plastic) jacketing materials include

- Polyvinyl chloride (PVC)
- Polyvinyliedene chloride (PVDC)
- Polyisobutylene
- Multiple-layer composite materials (e.g., polymeric/foil/mesh laminates)
- Fabrics (silicone-impregnated fiberglass)

Numerous mastics are available. Mastics are often used with fiber-glass cloth or canvas to encapsulate pipes, tanks, or other vessels; they are also used at insulation terminations and at or around protrusions such as valves or supports. It is important to choose the correct mastic for the application, considering surface temperature, insulation type, fire hazard classification, water resistance, and vapor permeability requirements. Mastics are brushed, troweled, or sprayed on the surface at a thickness recommended by the manufacturer.

Importance of Workmanship and Knowledge. Workmanship and knowledge are key to successful insulation weather barrier design. The importance of working with the installing contractor and material manufacturers regarding fitness for use of each material is paramount. The Midwest Insulation Contractors Association (MICA) publishes an excellent resource regarding materials used as weather barriers: the *National Commercial and Industrial Insulation Manual* (2011), in print and as a PDF file, is available from www.micainsulation.org/standards-manual.html.

Vapor Retarders

Water vapor control is extremely important for piping and equipment operating below ambient temperatures. These systems are typically insulated to prevent surface condensation and control heat gain. Piping and equipment typically create an absolute barrier to passage of water vapor, so any vapor-pressure difference imposed across the insulation system results in the potential for condensation at the cold surface. A high-quality vapor retarder material or system is essential for these systems to perform adequately. Mumaw (2001) showed that the design, installation, and performance of the vapor retarder systems are key to an insulation system's ability to minimize water vapor ingress. This research also suggests that in-place system vapor permeance may be greater than the rated performance based on standard material test methods.

Moisture-related problems include thermal performance loss, health and safety issues, structural degradation, corrosion, and aesthetic issues. Water may enter the insulation system through water vapor diffusion, air leakage carrying water vapor, and leakage of surface water. A vapor retarder is a material or system that adequately reduces the transmission of water vapor through the insulation system. The vapor retarder system is seldom intended to resist the entry of surface water or prevent air leakage, but can occasionally be considered the second line of defense for these moisture sources.

The performance of the vapor retarder material or system is characterized by its water vapor permeance. Chapter 25 has a thorough description of the physics associated with water vapor transport. Water vapor permeance can be evaluated per ASTM *Standard* E96, using either procedure A (desiccant method) or procedure B (water method), by imposing a vapor pressure difference across vapor retarder material that has been sealed to a test cup, and gravimetrically measuring the moisture gain or loss. It is recommended that both tests be performed and the results of both be evaluated.

Faulty application can impair vapor retarder performance. The effectiveness of installation and application techniques must be considered when selecting a vapor retarder system. Factors such as vapor retarder structure, number of joints, mastics and adhesives that are used, and inspection procedures affect performance and durability.

The insulation system should be dry before application of a vapor retarder to prevent trapping water vapor in the system. The system must be protected from undue weather exposure that could introduce moisture into the insulation before the system is sealed.

When selecting a vapor retarder, the vapor pressure difference across the insulation system should be considered. Higher vapor pressure differences typically require a lower-permeance vapor retarder to control water vapor intrusion into the system. Service conditions affect the direction and magnitude of the vapor pressure difference. Unidirectional flow exists when water vapor pressure is constantly higher on one side of insulation system.

Typically, in buildings located in humid climates, vapor pressure differences in unconditioned spaces are significantly greater than in conditioned spaces. For example, in a conditioned space at 75°F and 50% rh, the vapor pressure difference across the insulation system, on 42°F chilled-water lines, is less than 0.20 in. Hg. For below-ambient, insulated pipes running in humid unconditioned spaces, the vapor pressure difference across the insulation system can be as great as 0.80 in. Hg in the continental United States, and even greater in places with tropical climates. Hence, for below-ambient pipes running in humid unconditioned spaces, the vapor retarder may require a lower vapor permeance than for those same pipes running in conditioned spaces.

Reversible flow exists when vapor pressure may be higher on either side, typically caused by diurnal or seasonal changes on one side of the system. Properties of insulating materials used should be considered. All materials reduce water vapor flow, but low-permeance insulations can add to the overall water vapor transport resistance of the insulation system. Some low-permeability materials are considered to be vapor retarders without any additional jacket material.

Vapor Retarder Jackets. There is some inconsistency in the nomenclature used for materials used as vapor retarders for pipe, tank, and equipment insulation. Designations such as *jacket*, *jacketing*, *facing*, and *all-service jacket* (*ASJ*) are all applied to this component, sometimes interchangeably. On the other hand, the vapor retarder component of insulation for air-handling systems, such as duct wrap and duct board, is typically referred to only as *facing*. The term *vapor diffusion retarder* (*VDR*) is also used to generically describe these materials.

In this chapter, *vapor retarder* denotes the vapor-retarding membrane of the system, but the reader should be aware of the various terms that may be encountered. In addition, some insulation materials are considered vapor retarders in themselves without any additional retarding membrane.

Vapor Retarders for Pipe, Tank, and Equipment Insulation. Materials or combinations of materials used for vapor retarders can take many different forms. Necessarily, one component must be a material that offers significant resistance to vapor passage. A commonly used preformed material for pipe, tank, and equipment vapor retarder applications is laminated white paper, reinforcing glass-fiber scrim, and aluminum foil or metallized polyester film. These products are generally referred to as **all-service jackets (ASJs)**, and meet the requirements of ASTM *Test Method* C1136 with a vapor permeance of 0.02 perm, per procedure A of ASTM *Standard* E96; C1136 is the accepted industry vapor retarder material standard for mechanical insulation applications. These facings are commonly used as the outer finish in low-abuse indoor areas; elsewhere, they should be covered by a protective jacket. Many types of insulation are supplied with factory-applied ASJ vapor retarders.

Note that ASJs with exposed paper may have service limitations on below-ambient systems in wet environments, particularly in unconditioned spaces in hot, humid climates. In such spaces, during periods of high humidity, expect condensation to occur on the insulation's surface some of the time (e.g., when relative humidity exceeds 90%). Condensation on the surface can degrade the ASJ by wetting the exposed kraft paper surface, leading to mold growth on the paper, degradation of the paper itself, and/or corrosion of the aluminum vapor retarder component.

In addition to traditional ASJ vapor retarders, low-permeance monolayer plastic film and sheet, ASJ without exposed paper, laminates using aluminum foil, and other types of sheet structures are used in low- and very-low-temperature applications. They usually are water resistant; that is, when condensation occurs on their surface, they do not absorb the water. These are not always referred to as ASJ, and may be either factory applied by the insulation manufacturer or procured separately from the insulation and applied in fabrication shops or in the field. Examples of laminates include 3- to 13-ply sheet materials with thicknesses up to about 0.016 in.; these plies include at least one layer of aluminum foil and many have a permeance < 0.005 perm. There are also rubber and asphalt membranes, with an aluminum facing, with the same permeance. An example of one of the plastic films is polyvinylidene chloride (PVDC). This is typically used in more demanding applications, and often is covered by protective jacket. Many of these ASJ facings meet the requirements of ASTM *Standard* C1136, Type VII or VIII, or ASTM *Standard* C921, and generally have a permeance < 0.02 perm per ASTM *Standard* E96, procedure A.

The moisture-sensitive nature of paper and the relative frailty of uncoated aluminum foil can be problematic in the potentially high-humidity environment of unconditioned spaces with below-ambient applications. Exposure to water, either from condensation caused by inadequate insulation thickness or from ambient sources, can cause degradation and distortion of the paper, higher likelihood of mold growth, and foil corrosion, leading to vapor retarder failure. The presence of leachable chloride can promote corrosion of the foil or metallized film. The trend in vapor retarders for pipe insulation is toward structures without exposed paper, such as plastic films, coated metallized films, and better-protected foil laminates. Many have water vapor permeance ratings < 0.005 perm.

For most common vapor retarder jackets, matching pressure-sensitive tapes are available for making joint and puncture seals. With careful installation, these can be used to effectively seal joints in the vapor retarder system. In addition, vapor retarder mastics are available; these should be designated as such by their manufacturer and have a low vapor permeance rating, no greater than that of the vapor retarder membrane. Applying mastic thickly enough is critical to providing sufficient permeance. Vapor retarder mastics are typically used where fittings, supports, and other obstructions make a proper vapor seal difficult to achieve. Highly conformable tapes are sometimes used for this purpose, as well. Applied mastic systems are a vapor-retarding layer; they are often called **vapor barriers** by manufacturers, but their vapor resistance is a function of their permeability, thickness, and quality of the mastic application. Also, some mastics may not be compatible with certain insulation types. For this reason, always consult the insulation manufacturer for recommendations on the correct type of vapor retarder to use in the application. Weather barrier mastics are not vapor retarder mastics and should not be used for below-ambient applications unless they also have a low vapor permeability or are used in conjunction with a separate vapor retarder.

Below-ambient piping and equipment in general, and below-freezing applications in particular, are the most demanding applications for an insulation vapor retarder. Even though extremely low-permeance (<0.005 perm) vapor retarder materials exist, it is extremely difficult to achieve a perfect barrier in a system that is field installed and includes numerous joints and penetrations. It follows that adequate system design, proper insulation and jacketing material selection, and careful workmanship are all equally important.

For pipes operating at below-ambient temperatures, it is recommended that every 15 to 20 lineal feet, or at every fitting, a vapor stop (also called vapor dam) be installed. Should a leak occur in the vapor retarder, a vapor stop isolates vapor intrusion to that pipe insulation section and thereby prevents vapor and condensed water intrusion into the adjacent section(s) of pipe insulation or adjacent fitting insulation. A vapor stop is made by applying a vapor retarder mastic liberally to the pipe surface, for 3 in. along its length, adjacent to the end of the pipe insulation section. After installing that pipe insulation section, the mastic is then applied liberally to the end of the pipe insulation. Using a glass fiber or polyester scrim allows visual confirmation that the mastic is thick enough. For illustrations of vapor stops, see MICA's (2011) *National Commercial and Industrial Insulation Standards*.

Air-Handling Systems. Vapor retarders for equipment and duct insulation take various forms. Because of the relatively less severe and demanding conditions in air-handling systems located in conditioned spaces (because of their higher operating temperatures and lower indoor ambient humidity), current vapor retarder materials have been shown to adequately meet these performance requirements. In general, moisture problems are not often encountered if insulation design is adequate for the application, and some low-permeability insulation materials are used without separate vapor retarders. For fiberglass duct wrap and duct board, a lamination of aluminum **foil, scrim, and kraft paper (FSK)** has long been the material of choice, although flexible vinyl and other white or black facings are occasionally used. All of these facings can be procured separately in roll form, and used on any type of insulation. ASTM *Standard* C1136, type II, is a typical specification for factory-applied vapor retarder on duct insulation (except flexible duct). Flexible (flex) ducting typically incorporates a plastic film or film lamination that contains a metallized substrate as a vapor-retarding component. For outdoor ducts, laminate jacketing, manufacturer-rated to have a low vapor permeance (<0.005 perm) and for outdoor use, can be installed over the previously mentioned types of duct insulation using a compatible tape for closures, to provide protection from both weather exposure and vapor intrusion to the duct insulation.

Application-specific pressure-sensitive tapes or mastics are typically used to seal joints. As in any cold system where a vapor retarder is required, design, selection of materials, and workmanship must be properly addressed. The insulation manufacturer's recommendations should be followed.

3. INSTALLATION

Pipe Insulation

Small pipes can be insulated with cylindrical half-sections of rigid insulation or with preformed flexible material. Larger pipes can be insulated with flexible material or with curved, flat segmented, or cylindrical half, third, or quarter sections of rigid insulation. Fittings (valves, tees, crosses, and elbows) use preformed fitting insulation, fabricated fitting insulation, individual pieces cut from sectional straight-pipe insulation, or insulating cements. Fitting insulations should always be equal in thermal performance to the pipe insulation.

Securing Methods. The method of securing varies with the type of insulation, size of pipe, form and weight of insulation, and type of jacketing (i.e., field- or factory-applied). Insulation with factory-applied jacketing can be secured on small piping by securing the overlapping jacket, which usually includes an integral sealing tape. Additional tape around the circumference may be necessary. Large piping may require supplemental wiring or banding. Insulation on large piping requiring separate jacketing is wired or banded in place, and the jacket is cemented, wired, or banded, depending on the type. Flexible closed-cell materials require no jacket for most applications and are applied using specially formulated contact adhesives.

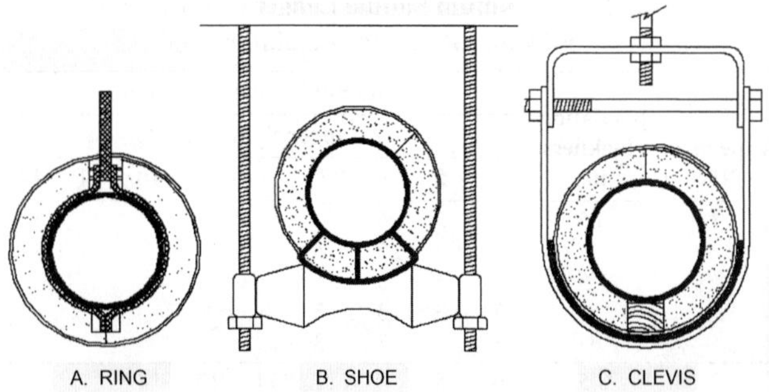

Fig. 6 Insulating Pipe Hangers

Insulating Pipe Hangers. All piping is held in place by hangers and supports. Selection and treatment of pipe hangers and supports can significantly affect thermal performance of an insulation system. Thus, it is important that the piping engineer and insulation specifier coordinate during project design to ensure that correct hangers are used and sufficient physical space is maintained to allow for the required thickness of insulation.

A typical **ring** or **line size** hanger is illustrated in Figure 6A. This type of hanger is commonly used on above-ambient lines at moderate temperature. However, it provides a thermal short circuit through the insulation, and the penetration is difficult to seal effectively against water vapor, so it is not recommended for below-ambient applications.

Pipe shoes (Figure 6B) are used for hot piping of large diameter (heavy weight) and where significant pipe movement is expected. The design allows for pipe movement without damage to the insulation or the finish. The design is not recommended for below-ambient applications because of the thermal short circuit and difficulty in vapor sealing.

A better solution is to use **clevis** hangers (Figure 6C), which are sized to allow clearance for the specified thickness of insulation, and avoid the short circuit associated with ring hangers and pipe shoes. Shields (or saddles) spread the load from the pipe, its contents, and the insulation material over an area sufficient to support the system without significantly compressing the insulation material. Table 10 provides guidance on sheet metal saddle lengths for glass fiber pipe insulation. For pipe sizes above 3 in. NPS, it is recommended that high-compressive-strength inserts (e.g., foam, high-density fiberglass, calcium silicate) be used. Table 11 gives recommended saddle lengths for 2 lb/ft^3 polyisocyanurate foam insulation. Preinsulated saddles are available. Note that wood blocks have poor thermal conductivity and are not recommended, especially for cold pipe systems.

When the goal is avoiding compression of low-compressive-strength insulation products, it is recommended to use high-strength insulation inserts, made of a product that offers the desired compressive strength and other necessary performance properties. Other higher-strength materials that are not thermal insulation material and interrupt the insulation envelope, or do not allow complete sealing of an insulation system against water vapor ingress, are not recommended for supporting insulated piping on pipe hangers.

Insulation Finish for Above-Ambient Temperatures. Requirements for pipe insulation finishes for above-ambient applications are usually governed by location. Appearance and durability are the primary design considerations for indoor applications. For outdoor applications, finishes are provided primarily for weather protection.

Table 10 Minimum Saddle Lengths for Use with Fibrous Glass Pipe Insulation*

Pipe Size, NPS	Insulation Thickness, in.	Minimum Saddle Length, in. — Hanger Spacing, ft: 4	5	6	7	8	9	10	11	12
1	0.5	5	5	6	8					
	1	3	3	5	5					
	1.5	3	3	5	5					
	2	3	3	3	3					
	3	3	3	3	3					
2	0.5	6	8	8	11	11	12	14		
	1	5	5	6	8	9	11	11		
	1.5	5	5	6	8	8	9	9		
	2	5	5	5	6	6	8	8		
	3	5	5	5	6	6	6	8		
3	0.5			12	15	17	20	21	24	26
	1			11	12	15	17	18	20	23
	1.5			9	11	12	14	15	17	18
	2			9	9	11	12	14	14	15
	3			9	9	11	12	14	14	15

*For pipe sizes above 3 in. NPS, use high-density inserts to support the pipe.

Table 11 Minimum Saddle Lengths for Use with 2 lb/ft³ Polyisocyanurate Foam Insulation (0.5 to 3 in. thick)

Pipe Size, NPS	Minimum Saddle Length,* in. — Hanger Spacing, ft: 4	5	6	7	8	9	10	11	12
3	4	4	4	4	4	4	4	4	6
4	4	4	4	6	6	6	8	8	8
6	6	6	6	6	8	8	8	8	8
8	8	8	8	8	8	8	8	8	12
10	8	8	8	12	12	12	12	12	12
12	8	8	12	12	12	12	12	12	12
16	12	12	18	18	18	18	18	18	18

*22 gage hung; 20 gage setting.

The finishes may be factory-applied jackets or field-applied metal or polymeric jackets.

On indoor steam and hot-water distribution piping, it is common for flange pairs and flanged fittings such as gate valves, butterfly valves, strainers, pressure-relief valves, and other pipe fittings to be left bare (i.e., uninsulated). Whether this is done intentionally or by neglect, the end result is the same: enormous quantities of wasted thermal energy and, in unventilated spaces, very high air temperatures (Hart 2011). It is recommended that all these fittings be insulated with conventional pipe insulation or with removable/reusable insulation blankets, because a bare 350°F steam pipe indoors loses about eight times more heat than does the same pipe with only 1 in. of conventional pipe insulation. If maintenance personnel need ready access to these flanged fittings, removable/reusable insulation blankets are preferable. ASTM *Standard* C1695-10 includes different requirements for indoor and outdoor applications of removable/reusable insulation blankets.

Many blankets used indoors are secured in place using hook-and-loop fastening tape, which allows personnel to remove the insulation, perform maintenance, then reinstall the insulation blankets without tools. Removable/reusable insulation blankets are available either as custom-made components or as kits. If specifying custom-made blankets, time must be allowed in the schedule to have a technical support person measure for the insulation, design and fabricate the blankets, deliver them, and install them. Although ASHRAE *Standard* 90.1-2010 specifies 4.5 to 5.0 in. thick insulation on pipes operating above 350°F, it is recommended that permission be sought to use removable/reusable insulation blankets that are 2 in. thick or less for easier removability and reinstallation.

Insulation Finish for Below-Ambient Temperatures. Piping at temperatures below ambient is insulated to limit heat gain and prevent condensation of moisture from the ambient air. Because metallic piping is an absolute barrier to water vapor, it becomes the condensing surface. Therefore, for high-permeability insulation materials (i.e., permeability/thickness combination > 0.02 perm), the outer surface of the insulation should be covered by a low-permeance membrane. However, some flexible closed-cell insulation materials have been used successfully without a separate vapor retarder material.

Vapor retarders for straight pipe insulation are generally designed to meet permeance, operating temperature, fire safety, and appearance requirements. Sheet-type vapor retarders used on below-ambient pipe insulation should have a maximum permeance of 0.02 perm, when tested per ASTM *Standard* E96, procedure A (desiccant method) or B (water method). Insulation materials that meet the permeance requirements of an application can be installed without separate vapor retarders, relying on the low permeability and thickness of the insulation material to resist vapor flow, but must be carefully sealed or cemented at all joints to avoid gaps in the insulation. Jacketing used as a vapor retarder may use various materials, alone or in combination, such as paper, aluminum foil, vacuum-metallized or low-permeance plastic films, and reinforcing. The most commonly used products have been ASJ (white), foil-scrim-kraft (FSK), metallized polyester film, or plastic sheeting. An important feature of such jacketing is very low permeance in a relatively thin layer, which provides flexibility for ease of cementing and sealing laps and end-joint strips. This type of jacketing is commonly used indoors without additional treatment. In some cases of operating temperatures below 0°F, multilayer insulation and jacketing may be used. With long lines of piping, insulation should be sealed off every 15 or 20 ft with vapor stops to limit water penetration if vapor retarder damage occurs (see Figure 7).

Insulation fittings are usually vapor-sealed by applying suitable materials in the field, and may vary with the type of insulation and operating temperature. The vapor seal can be a lapped spiral wrap of plastic film adhesive tape or a relatively thin coat of vapor-seal mastic. If these do not provide the required permeance, a common practice is to double-wrap a very-low-permeance plastic film adhesive tape or apply two coats of vapor-seal mastic reinforced with open-weave glass or other fabric.

Vapor retarder mastics should be applied in a greater thickness to achieve a lower permeance. Consult the mastic manufacturer for recommendations on the thickness required to achieve a particular permeance.

Insulated cold piping should receive special attention when exposed to ambient or unconditioned air. Because cold piping frequently operates year-round, a unidirectional vapor drive may exist. Even with vapor-retarding insulation, jackets, and vapor sealing of joints and fittings, moisture inevitably accumulates in permeable insulations. This not only reduces the thermal resistance of the insulation, it also accelerates condensation on the jacket surface with consequent dripping of water and possible growth of mold and mildew. Depending on local conditions, these problems can arise in less than 3 years, or as many as 30 years. Periodic insulation replacement should be considered, and the piping installation should be accessible for such replacement. Very-low-permeability insulating materials, sometimes in combination with vapor retarders, can be used to extend system life and reduce replacement frequency. This is normally done by using vapor retarders, insulation materials (e.g., cellular glass insulation), or both, with a permeance no more than 0.02 perm. However, some flexible closed-cell insulation materials have been used successfully without a separate vapor retarder material.

The lower the insulation system's permeance, the longer its life, given proper installation.

An alternative approach is to accept the inevitable water vapor ingress, and to provide a means of removing condensed water from the system. One means of accomplishing this is the use of a hydrophilic wicking material to remove condensed water from the surface of cold piping for transport (via the combination of capillary forces and gravity) outside the system where it can be evaporated to the ambient air (Brower 2000; Crall 2002; Korsgaard 1993). The wick keeps the hydrophobic insulation dry, allowing the thermal insulation to perform effectively. Dripping is avoided if ambient conditions allow evaporation. The concept is limited to pipe temperatures above freezing.

For dual-temperature service, where pipe operating temperatures cycle, the vapor-seal finish, including mastics, must withstand pipe movement and exposure temperatures without deterioration. When flexible closed-cell insulation is used, it should be applied slightly compressed to prevent it from being strained when the piping expands.

Outdoor pipe insulation may be vapor-sealed in the same manner as indoor piping, by applying added weather protection jacketing without damage to the vapor retarder and sealing it to keep out water. In some instances, heavy-duty weather and vapor-seal finish may be used. It is recommended that weather protection jackets installed over vapor retarders use bands or some other closure method that does not penetrate the weather protection jacketing, because other types have a high likelihood of also penetrating the underlying vapor retarder.

Underground Pipe Insulation. Both heated and cooled underground piping systems are insulated. Protecting underground insulated piping is more difficult than protecting aboveground piping. Groundwater conditions, including chemical or electrolytic contributions by the soil and the existence of water pressure, require special design to protect insulated pipes from corrosion and maintain insulation thermal integrity. For optimal performance, walk-through tunnels, conduits, or integral protective coverings are generally provided to protect the pipe and insulation from water. Examples and general design features of conduits, tunnels, and direct-burial systems can be found in Chapter 12 of the 2016 *ASHRAE Handbook—HVAC Systems and Equipment*.

Tanks, Vessels, and Equipment

Flat, curved, and irregular surfaces, such as tanks, vessels, boilers, and chimney connectors, are normally insulated with flexible or semirigid sheets or boards or rigid insulation blocks fabricated to fit the specific application. Tank and vessel head segments must be curved or flat cut to fit in single piece or segments per ASTM *Standard* C450. Head segments must be cut to eliminate voids at the head section, and in a minimum number of pieces to minimize joints. Prefabricated flat head sections should be installed in the same number of layers and thickness as the vessel walls, and void areas behind the flat head should be filled with packable insulation. Typically, the curved segments are fabricated to fit the contour of the vessel surface in equal pieces to go around the vessel with a minimum number of joints. Because no general procedure can apply to all materials and conditions, manufacturers' specifications and instructions must be followed for specific applications.

Securing Methods. Insulations are secured in various ways, depending on the form of insulation and contour of the surface to be insulated. Flexible insulations are adhered to tanks, vessels, and equipment using contact adhesive, pressure-sensitive adhesives, or other systems recommended by the manufacturers. The insulation's flexibility lends itself to curved surfaces. Rigid or semirigid insulations on small-diameter, cylindrical vessels can be prefabricated and adhered or mechanically attached, as appropriate. On larger cylindrical vessels, angle iron ledges to support the insulation against slippage can supplement banding. Where diameters exceed 10 to 15 ft, slotted angle iron may be run lengthwise on the cylinder, at intervals around the circumference to secure and avoid an excessive length of banding.

Rigid and semirigid insulations can be secured on large flat and cylindrical surfaces by banding or wiring and can be supplemented by fastening with various welded studs at frequent intervals. Springs may be necessary on banding to allow for expansion/contraction of the tank and insulation. On large flat, cylindrical, and spherical surfaces, it is often advantageous to secure the insulation by impaling it on welded studs or pins and fastening it with speed washers. Flexible closed-cell insulations are adhered directly to these surfaces, using a suitable contact adhesive.

Insulation Finish. Insulation finish is often required to protect insulation against mechanical damage and weather, consistent with acceptable appearance. On smaller indoor equipment, insulation is commonly covered with tightly stretched and secured hexagonal wire mesh. Then, a base and hard finish coat of cement is applied, and sometimes painted. For the same equipment outdoors, insulation can be finished with a coat of hard cement, properly secured hexagonal mesh, and a coat of weather-resistant mastic. A variation is to apply only two coats of weather-resistant mastic reinforced with open-mesh glass or other fabric; however, this finish is limited to an operating temperature of about 300°F, because metal expansion can rupture the finish at insulation joints. Larger equipment may be finished indoors and out with suitable sheet metal.

Outdoor finish is generally metal jacketing with a 3 mil thick multilayer moisture barrier factory heat laminated to the interior surface, properly flashed around penetrations (e.g., access openings, pipe connections, and structural supports) to maintain weathertightness. Various outdoor finishes are available for different types of insulations.

For below-ambient operating temperatures, insulation is finished, as required, to prevent condensation and protect against mechanical damage and weather, consistent with acceptable appearance. In accordance with the operating temperature, the finish must retard vapor to avoid moisture entry from surrounding air, which can increase the insulation's thermal conductivity or deterioration, or corrode the metal equipment surface.

Whenever a vapor retarder is required, all penetrations such as access openings, pipe connections, and structural supports must be properly treated with an appropriate vapor-retarder film, mastic, or other sealant. Equipment must be insulated from structural steel by isolating supports of high compressive strength and reasonably low thermal conductivity, such as a rigid insulation material. The vapor retarder must carry over this insulation from the equipment to the supporting steel to ensure proper sealing.

If the equipment rests directly on steel supports, the supports must be insulated for some distance from the points of contact. Commonly, insulation and vapor retarder are extended four times the thickness of the insulation applied to the equipment.

For dual-temperature service, where vessels are alternately cold and hot, vapor retarder finish materials and design must withstand movement caused by temperature change.

Ducts

Ducts are used to convey air or process gases for several purposes. In general, their uses can be divided into process ducts and HVAC ducts. **Process ducts** can range from industrial hot exhaust to subambient process gases, and can be outdoors or indoors. They can need insulation for various reasons, including thermal energy conservation, personnel protection, process control, condensation control and noise attenuation. Because of the wide range of possible operating temperatures and environmental conditions, selection of duct insulation and jacketing materials for industrial processes requires careful consideration of all operational, environmental, and human safety factors. Issues of energy conservation, personnel protection, condensation control, and process control can be solved by careful analysis of heat flow. Computer programs are available for calculating heat transfer, surface temperatures for personnel protection, condensation control, and economic thickness.

HVAC ducts carry air to conditioned spaces inhabited by people, animals, sensitive equipment, or a combination thereof. Thermal and acoustical duct insulation is one of the keys to a well-designed system that provides both occupant comfort and acceptable indoor air quality (IAQ). These insulation products help maintain a consistent air temperature throughout the system, reduce condensation, absorb system operation noise, and conserve energy.

Typical air temperatures for HVAC applications are 40 to 120°F. Because of the more moderate temperature ranges associated with HVAC applications, there is a wide range of insulation materials available. Where acoustical and thermal considerations are significant, sheet metal ducts are often internally insulated, or the ducts themselves are constructed of materials that form both the air-conveying duct and the insulation. Where acoustical concerns are not significant, sheet metal ducts can be externally insulated with rigid, semirigid, or flexible insulation materials. Again, another alternative is to use ducts that incorporate insulation as part of their construction. The determining factor in duct construction and insulation materials selection is often a combination of performance criteria and budgetary limitations.

The need for duct insulation is influenced by the

- Duct location (e.g., indoors or outdoors; conditioned, semiconditioned, or unconditioned space)
- Effect of heat loss or gain on equipment size and operating cost
- Need to prevent condensation on low-temperature ducts
- Need to control temperature change in long duct lengths
- Need to control noise transmitted within the duct or through the duct wall

All HVAC ducts exposed to outdoor conditions, as well as those passing through unconditioned or semiconditioned spaces, should be insulated. Analyses of temperature change, heat loss or gain, and other factors affecting the economics of thermal insulation are essential for large commercial and industrial projects. ASHRAE *Standard* 90.1 and building codes set minimum standards for thermal efficiency, but economic thickness is often greater than the minimum. Additionally, the standards and codes do not address surface condensation issues. These considerations are often the primary driver of minimum thickness in unconditioned or semiconditioned locations subject to moderate or greater relative humidity.

Duct thermal efficiencies are generally regulated by local or national codes by specifying minimum thermal resistances, or R-values. These R-values are most often determined by testing per ASTM *Standards* C518 or C177, as required by the Federal Trade Commission (FTC) for reporting R-values of duct wrap insulations. Neither method allows for increased thermal resistance caused by convective or radiative surface effects. To comply with current code language, it is recommended that R-value requirements in specifications for duct insulation be based on *Standards* C177 or C518 testing at 75°F mean temperature and at the installed thickness of the insulation. Insulation products for ducts are available in a range of R-values, dependent predominantly on insulation thickness, but also somewhat on insulation density.

Temperature Control Calculations for Air Ducts. Duct heat gains or losses must be known for the calculation of supply air quantities, supply air temperatures, and coil loads (see Chapter 17 of this volume and Chapter 4 of the 2016 *ASHRAE Handbook—HVAC Systems and Equipment*). Heat loss programs based on ASTM *Standard* C680 may be used to calculate thermal energy transfer through the duct walls. Duct air exit temperatures can then be estimated using the following equations:

$$t_{drop} \text{ or } t_{gain} = 0.2\left(\frac{qPL}{VC_p\rho A}\right) \tag{3}$$

then, for warm air ducts,

$$t_{exit} = t_{enter} - t_{drop} \tag{4}$$

and for cold air ducts,

$$t_{exit} = t_{enter} - t_{gain} \tag{5}$$

where

t_{drop} = temperature loss for warm air ducts, °F
t_{enter} = entering air temperature, °F
t_{gain} = temperature rise for cool air ducts, °F
t_{exit} = exit temperature for either warm or cool air ducts, °F
q = heat loss through duct wall, Btu/h·ft²
P = duct perimeter, in.
L = length of duct run, ft
V = air velocity in duct, ft/min
C_p = specific heat of air, Btu/lb$_m$·°F
ρ = density of air, 0.075 lb/ft³
A = area of duct, in²
0.2 = conversion factor for length, time units

Example 1. A 65 ft length of 24 by 36 in. uninsulated sheet metal duct, freely suspended, conveys heated air through a space maintained at 40°F. The ASTM *Standard* C680 heat loss calculation gives a heat transfer rate of 140.8 Btu/h·ft². Based on heat loss calculations for the heated zone, 17,200 cfm of standard air (c_p = 0.24 Btu/lb$_m$·°F) at a supply air temperature of 122°F is required. The duct is connected directly to the heated zone. Determine the temperature of the air entering the duct.

Solution: The area of the duct is 24 × 36 = 864 in².

Air velocity V is calculated as

$$\frac{\text{Volumetric flow}}{\text{Area}} \times 144 = \frac{17{,}200}{864} \times 144 = 2867 \text{ fpm}$$

Duct perimeter P is

$$(24 + 36) \times 2 = 120 \text{ in.}$$

Temperature drop t_{drop} is

$$0.2\left(\frac{140.8 \times 120 \times 65}{2867 \times 0.24 \times 0.075 \times 864}\right) = 4.9°\text{F}$$

Temperature of air entering the duct is thus

$$122 + 4.9 = 126.9°\text{F}$$

Example 2. Repeat Example 1, except the duct is insulated externally with 1 in. thick insulation material having a heat transfer rate of 14.2 Btu/h·ft².

Solution: All values except q remain the same as in the previous example. Therefore, t_{drop} is

$$0.2\left(\frac{14.2 \times 120 \times 65}{2867 \times 0.24 \times 0.075 \times 864}\right) = 0.5°\text{F}$$

Temperature of air entering the duct is thus

$$122 + 0.5 = 122.5°\text{F}$$

Preventing Surface Condensation on Cool Air Ducts. Insulation also can prevent surface condensation on cool air ducts operating in warm and humid environments. This reduces the opportunity for microbial growth as well as other moisture-related building damage. Condensation forms on cold air-conditioning ducts anywhere the exterior surface temperature reaches the dew point. The moisture may remain in place or drip, causing moisture damage and creating a potential for microbial contamination.

Preventing surface condensation requires that sufficient thermal resistance be installed for the condensation design conditions.

Figures 7 and 8 give installed R-value requirements to prevent surface condensation on insulated air ducts. The first chart (for emittance = 0.1) should be used for foil-faced insulation products. The second chart is based on materials with a surface emittance of 0.9. The designer must choose the appropriate environmental conditions for the location. It may be financially imprudent to design for the most extreme condition that could occur during a system's life, but it is also important to be aware that the worst-case condition for condensation control is not the maximum design load of coincident dry bulb and wet bulb. Rather, the worst case for condensation occurs when relative humidity is high, such as when the dry bulb is only very slightly above the wet bulb. This condition often occurs in the early morning in many climates.

For cold-duct applications, it is critical that water vapor not be allowed to enter the insulation system and condense on the cold duct surface. Once water begins to condense, loss of thermal efficiency is inevitable. This leads to further surface condensation on the surface of the insulation. To prevent this, exterior duct insulations must have a low vapor permeance. Permeance values of 0.1 perm or less are generally recommended for cold-duct applications. It is equally important that all exterior duct insulation joints are well sealed. Areas of special concern are often found around duct flanges, hangers, and other fittings.

Insulation Materials for HVAC Ducts. Insulated ducts in buildings can consist of insulated sheet metal, fibrous glass, or insulated flexible ducts, all of which provide combined air barrier, thermal insulation, and some degree of sound absorption. Ducts embedded in or below floor slabs may be of compressed fiber, ceramic tile, or other rigid materials. Depending on the insulation material, there are a number of standards that specify the material requirements.

Duct insulations include semirigid boards and flexible blanket types, composed of organic and inorganic materials in fibrous,

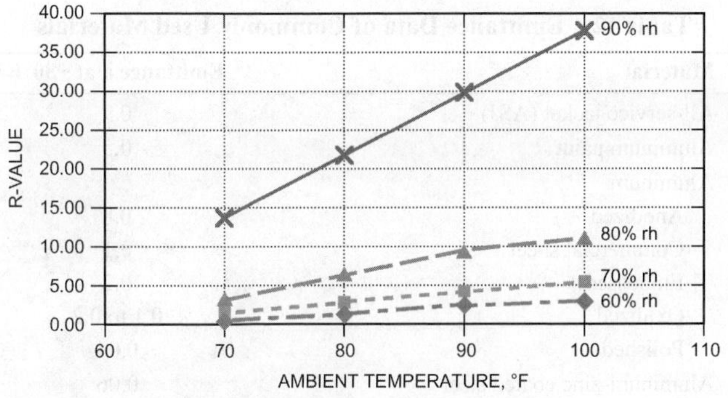

Fig. 7 R-Value Required to Prevent Condensation on Surface with Emittance ε = 0.1

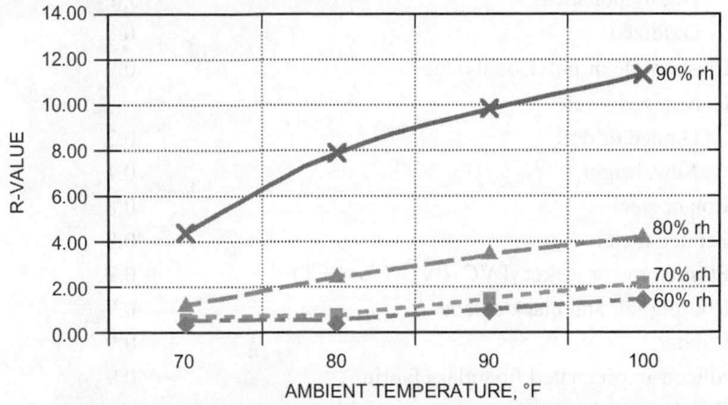

Fig. 8 R-Value Required to Prevent Condensation on Surface with Emittance ε = 0.9

cellular, or bonded particle forms. Insulations for exterior surfaces may have attached vapor retarders or facings, or vapor retarders may be applied separately. When applied to the duct interior as a liner, insulation both insulates thermally and absorbs sound. Duct liner insulations have sound-permeable surfaces on the side facing the airstream capable of withstanding duct design air velocities or duct cleaning without deterioration.

Abuse Resistance. One important consideration in the choice of external insulations for air ducts is abuse resistance. Some insulation materials have more abuse resistance than others, but most insulation materials will not withstand high abuse such as foot traffic. In high-traffic locations, a combination of insulation and protective jacketing materials is required. In areas where the insulation is generally inaccessible to human contact, less rigid insulations are acceptable.

One important consideration for internal insulation abuse resistance is that, in large commercial units, it is common for maintenance personnel to enter and move around. In these instances, it is critical that structural elements be provided to keep foot traffic off the insulation.

Duct Airstream Surface Durability. One of the most important considerations in choosing internal duct insulations is resistance to air erosion. Each material has a maximum airflow velocity rating, which should be determined using an erosion test methodology in accordance with either UL *Standard* 181 or ASTM *Standard* C1071. Under these methods, the liner material is subjected to velocities that are two and one-half times the maximum rated air velocity. Air erosion testing should include evaluation of the insulation for evidence of erosion, cracking, or delamination.

Additionally, internal insulation must be resistant to aging effects in the air duct environment. Insulation materials have maximum temperatures for prolonged exposure, and some codes impose temperature requirements. Ensure that the material selected will have no aging effects at either the anticipated maximum duct temperature or the temperature specified by the code bodies for the local jurisdiction.

Another durability concern is ultraviolet (UV) resistance. Ultraviolet-generating equipment is used to mitigate microbial activity. Determine, both from the UV equipment manufacturer as well as the insulation manufacturer, whether the anticipated UV exposure poses a threat to the insulation.

Duct Airflow Characteristics. Internal duct insulations and ducts that have insulation as part of their construction have increased frictional pressure loss characteristics compared to bare sheet metal. Generally, duct dimensions are oversized to compensate for the increased frictional pressure losses and the decrease in internal cross section caused by the insulation thickness. However, frictional losses are only part of the total static pressure loss in a duct; dynamic fitting losses should also be considered in any required resizing. Generally, internal linings conform to the shape of the fitting in which they are installed. For this reason, the insulated fitting is assumed to have the same dynamic pressure loss as the uninsulated fitting of the same dimension. See Chapter 21 for further details on frictional pressure loss characteristics of internal linings and how they affect pressure drop and duct-sizing requirements.

Securing Methods. Exterior rigid or flexible duct insulation can be attached with adhesive, with supplemental preattached pins and clips, or with wiring or banding. Individual manufacturers of these materials should be consulted for their installation requirements. Flexible duct wraps do not require attachment except on bottom duct panels more than 24 in. wide. For larger ducts, pins placed at a maximum spacing of 24 in. or less are sufficient. Internal liners are attached with adhesive and pins, in accordance with industry standards.

Leakage Considerations. To achieve the full thermal benefits of insulation, air ducts should be substantially sealed against leakage under operating pressure. The insulation material should not be counted on to provide leakage resistance, unless the insulation is part of the actual duct. Using the case in Example 1, 10% air leakage from an unsealed duct represents an energy loss of 1.66 times the energy lost through heat transfer through the entire 65 ft of uninsulated duct. When that same 10% leakage is compared against an insulated duct, the energy lost through leakage is 15.3 times the losses through heat transfer through the insulation over the entire duct length.

Outdoor Applications. Insulated air ducts located outdoors generally require specific protection against the elements, including water, ice, hail, wind, ultraviolet exposure, vermin, birds, other animals, and mechanical abuse. Strategies for protecting externally insulated ducts located outdoors include protective metal jackets and glass fabric with weather barrier mastic. Note that most of these protective weather treatments do not replace the need for a vapor retarder for cold-duct applications.

Special Considerations.

Cooling-only ducts in cold climates. These applications generally occur in northern climates with ducts that run through unconditioned spaces such as attics. Warm air from the conditioned space enters through registers and into the unused ducts. This relatively moist air then condenses in the cold portions of the duct. Condensation encourages odor problems, mold growth, and degradation of the insulation. In the worst cases, water build-up becomes so excessive that water-soaked or frozen ducts can collapse and break through ceilings. The solution is to completely seal all entry points into the ducts, generally by sealing behind all registers, using a very good vapor retarder such as 7 mil (0.007 in.) polyethylene sheet.

Covering ducts with insulation in attics in hot and humid climates. In an effort to conserve energy, attic insulation levels have been increasing. Often, these attics are insulated with pneumatically applied loose fill insulation. If this insulation comes into contact with duct insulation, it could lower surface temperatures on the facing of the duct insulation below dew point during humid conditions. For this reason, it is important that the ducts be supported so that they are above the attic insulation. Many building codes in humid areas (e.g., Florida) require this, and it should be considered good practice in all humid climates.

4. DESIGN DATA

Estimating Heat Loss and Gain

Fundamentals of heat transfer are covered in Chapter 4, and the concepts are extended to insulation systems in Chapter 25. Steady-state, one-dimensional heat flow through insulation systems is governed by Fourier's law:

$$Q = -kA\, dT/dx \tag{6}$$

where

Q = rate of heat flow, Btu/h
A = cross-sectional area normal to heat flow, ft²
k = thermal conductivity of insulation material, Btu/h·ft·°F
dT/dx = temperature gradient, °F/ft

For flat geometry of finite thickness, the equation reduces to

$$Q = kA(T_1 - T_2)/L \tag{7}$$

where L is insulation thickness, in ft.

For radial geometry, the equation becomes

$$Q = kA_2(T_1 - T_2)/[r_2 \ln(r_2/r_1)] \tag{8}$$

where

r_2 = outer radius, ft
r_1 = inner radius, ft
A_2 = area of outer surface, ft²

The term $r_2 \ln(r_2/r_1)$ is sometimes called the **equivalent thickness** of the insulation layer. Equivalent thickness is the thickness of insulation that, if installed on a flat surface, would equal the heat flux at the outer surface of the cylindrical geometry.

Heat transfer from surfaces is a combination of convection and radiation. Usually, these modes are assumed to be additive, and therefore a combined surface coefficient can be used to estimate the heat flow to and from a surface:

$$h_s = h_c + h_r \tag{9}$$

where

h_s = combined surface coefficient, Btu/h·ft²·°F
h_c = convection coefficient, Btu/h·ft²·°F
h_r = radiation coefficient, Btu/h·ft²·°F

Assuming the radiant environment is equal to the ambient air temperature, the heat loss/gain at a surface can be calculated as

$$Q = h_s A(T_{surf} - T_{amb}) \tag{10}$$

The radiation coefficient is usually estimated as

$$h_r = \varepsilon\sigma(T_{surf}^4 - T_{amb}^4)/(T_{surf} - T_{amb}) \tag{11}$$

where

ε = surface emittance
σ = Stephen-Boltzmann constant, 0.1712×10^{-8} Btu/h·ft²·°R⁴

Table 12 gives the approximate emittance of commonly used materials.

Table 12 Emittance Data of Commonly Used Materials

Material	Emittance ε at ~80°F
All-service jacket (ASJ)	0.9
Aluminum paint	0.5
Aluminum	
Anodized	0.8
Commercial sheet	0.1
Embossed	0.2
Oxidized	0.1 to 0.2
Polished	0.04
Aluminum-zinc coated steel	0.06
Canvas	0.7 to 0.9
Colored mastic	0.9
Copper	
Highly polished	0.03
Oxidized	0.8
Elastomeric or polyisobutylene	0.9
Galvanized steel	
Dipped or dull	0.3
New, bright	0.1
Iron or steel	0.8
Painted metal	0.8
Plastic pipe or jacket (PVC, PVDC, or PET)	0.9
Roofing felt and black mastic	0.9
Rubber	0.9
Silicon-impregnated fiberglass fabric	0.9
Stainless steel	
New, cleaned	0.2
Oxidized in service	0.32

Controlling Surface Temperatures

A common calculation associated with mechanical insulation systems involves determining the thickness of insulation required to control the surface temperature to a certain value given the operating temperature of the process and the ambient temperature. For example, it may be desired to calculate the thickness of tank insulation required to keep the outer surface temperature at or below 140°F when the fluid in the tank is 450°F and the ambient temperature is 80°F.

At steady state, the heat flow through the insulation to the outer surface equals heat flow from the surface to the ambient air:

$$Q_{ins} = Q_{surf} \tag{12}$$

or

$$(k/X)A(T_{hot} - T_{surf}) = hA(T_{surf} - T_{amb}) \tag{13}$$

Rearranging this equation yields

$$X = (k/h)[(T_{hot} - T_{surf})/(T_{surf} - T_{amb})] \tag{14}$$

Because the ratio of temperature differences is known, the required thickness can be calculated by multiplying the temperature difference and the ratio of the insulation material conductivity to the surface coefficient.

For this example, assume the surface coefficient can be estimated as 1.0 Btu/h·ft²·°F, and the conductivity of the insulation to be used is 0.25 Btu·in/h·ft²·°F. The required thickness can then be estimated as

$$X = \left(\frac{0.25}{1.0}\right)\left[\frac{(450 - 140)}{(140 - 80)}\right] = 1.29 \text{ in.} \tag{15}$$

This estimated thickness would be rounded up to the next available size, probably 1.5 in.

For radial heat flow, the thickness calculated represents the equivalent thickness; the actual thickness $(r_2 - r_1)$ is less, per Equation (8).

This simple procedure can be used as a first-order estimate. In reality, the surface coefficient is not constant, but varies as a function of surface temperature, air velocity, orientation, and surface emittance.

When performing these calculations, it is important to use the actual dimensions for the pipe and tubing insulation. Many (but not all) pipe and tubing insulation products conform to dimensional standards originally published by the U.S. Navy in *Military Standard* MIL-I-2781 and since adopted by other organizations, including ASTM. Standard pipe and insulation dimensions are given for reference in Table 13, and standard tubing and insulation dimensions in Table 14. Corresponding dimensional data for flexible closed-cell insulations are given in Tables 15 and 16.

For mechanical insulation systems, it is also important to realize that the thermal conductivity k of most insulation products varies significantly with temperature. Manufacturer's literature usually provides curves or tabulations of conductivity versus temperature. When performing heat transfer calculations, it is important to use the effective thermal conductivity, which can be obtained by integration of the conductivity versus temperature curve, or (as an approximation) using the conductivity evaluated at the mean temperature across the insulation layer. ASTM *Standard* C680 provides the algorithms and calculation methodologies for incorporating these equations in computer programs.

These complications are readily handled for a variety of boundary conditions using available computer programs, such as the NAIMA 3E Plus® program [available as a download from the website of the North American Insulation Manufacturers Association (NAIMA), www.naima.org].

Estimates of the heat loss from bare pipe and tubing are given in Tables 17 and 18. These are useful for quickly estimating the cost of lost energy from uninsulated piping.

5. PROJECT SPECIFICATIONS

The importance of a well-prepared specification to meet energy conservation objectives is paramount. Specifications should

- Identify systems and equipment that must be insulated
- Identify precisely the materials selected, including thickness and jacketing, etc.
- Define the procedure for submitting alternative materials and systems
- Specify installation, inspection, and repair requirements
- Describe procedures to ensure the job is done correctly
- Comply with regional and national building codes

Although each of these steps is important, identifying systems that must be insulated is critical. When defining the materials to be used, it is important to specify them exactly, while allowing for submission of generic equivalents or value-engineered materials. Overspecifying materials limits potentially good options, and underspecifying may allow underperforming materials to be used. A proper balance is needed, and specifying key properties is required. Specifying installation requirements is as important as specifying the correct materials. Specifying procedures for submittals and quality control at the job ensures correctness.

Reference standards from ASHRAE, ASTM, MICA, and others should be incorporated into the specifications; this practice saves time with respect to specification development, and shortens the specification considerably. Specifications that are not reviewed and updated periodically can perpetuate old technologies and obsolete materials, and fall out of code compliance.

Essentially all manufacturers of mechanical insulation products offer guide specifications for their products. These documents are insightful and offer credible information about specific products and the accessories commonly used with them. These documents are widely available on manufacturers' websites.

STANDARDS

ANSI/ASHRAE
Standard 90.2 Energy-Efficient Design of Low-Rise Residential Buildings

ANSI/ASHRAE/IES
Standard 90.1 Energy Standard for Buildings Except Low-Rise Residential Buildings

ASTM
Standard 165 Test Method for Measuring Compressive Properties of Thermal Insulations
C177 Test Method for Steady-State Heat Flux Measurements and Thermal Transmission Properties by Means of the Guarded-Hot-Plate Apparatus
C355 Test Method for Steady-State Heat Transfer Properties of Horizontal Pipe Insulation
C411 Test Method for Hot-Surface Performance of High-Temperature Thermal Insulation
C423 Test Method for Sound Absorption and Sound Absorption Coefficients by the Reverberation Room Method
C450 Practice for Fabrication of Thermal Insulating Fitting Covers for NPS Piping, and Vessel Lagging
C518 Test Method for Steady-State Thermal Transmission Properties by Means of the Heat Flow Meter Apparatus
C533 Specification for Calcium Silicate Block and Pipe Thermal Insulation

Table 13 Inner and Outer Diameters of Standard Pipe Insulation

Pipe Size, NPS	Pipe OD, in.	Insulation ID, in.	Insulation OD, in. — Insulation Nominal Thickness, in. 1	1.5	2	2.5	3	3.5	4	4.5	5
1/2	0.84	0.86	2.88	4.00	5.00	6.62	7.62	8.62	9.62	10.75	11.75
3/4	1.05	1.07	2.88	4.00	5.00	6.62	7.62	8.62	9.62	10.75	11.75
1	1.315	1.33	3.50	4.50	5.56	6.62	7.62	8.62	9.62	10.75	11.75
1 1/4	1.660	1.68	3.50	5.00	5.56	6.62	7.62	8.62	9.62	10.75	11.75
1 1/2	1.900	1.92	4.00	5.00	6.62	7.62	8.62	9.62	10.75	11.75	12.75
2	2.375	2.41	4.50	5.56	6.62	7.62	8.62	9.62	10.75	11.75	12.75
2 1/2	2.875	2.91	5.00	6.62	7.62	8.62	9.62	10.75	11.75	12.75	14.00
3	3.500	3.53	5.56	6.62	7.62	8.62	9.62	10.75	11.75	12.75	14.00
3 1/2	4.000	4.03	6.62	7.62	8.62	9.62	10.75	11.75	12.75	12.75	14.00
4	4.500	4.53	6.62	7.62	8.62	9.62	10.75	11.75	12.75	14.00	15.00
4 1/2	5.000	5.03	7.62	8.62	9.62	10.75	11.75	12.75	14.00	14.00	15.00
5	5.563	5.64	7.62	8.62	9.62	10.75	11.75	12.75	14.00	15.00	16.00
6	6.625	6.70	8.62	9.62	10.75	11.75	12.75	14.00	15.00	16.00	17.00
7	7.625	7.70	—	10.75	11.75	12.75	14.00	15.00	16.00	17.00	18.00
8	8.625	8.70	—	11.75	12.75	14.00	12.00	16.00	17.00	18.00	19.00
9	9.625	9.70	—	12.75	14.00	15.00	16.00	17.00	18.00	19.00	20.00
10	10.75	10.83	—	14.00	15.00	16.00	17.00	18.00	19.00	20.00	21.00
11	11.75	11.83	—	15.00	16.00	17.00	18.00	19.00	20.00	21.00	22.00
12	12.75	12.84	—	16.00	17.00	18.00	19.00	20.00	21.00	22.00	23.00
14	14.00	14.09	—	17.00	18.00	19.00	20.00	21.00	22.00	23.00	24.00

Table 14 Inner and Outer Diameters of Standard Tubing Insulation

Tube Size, in.	Tube OD, in.	Insulation ID, in.	Insulation OD, in. — Insulation Nominal Thickness, in. 1	1.5	2	2.5	3	3.5	4	4.5	5
3/8	0.500	0.52	2.38	3.50	4.50	5.56	6.62	—	—	—	—
1/2	0.625	0.64	2.88	3.50	4.50	5.56	6.62	—	—	—	—
3/4	0.875	0.89	2.88	4.00	5.00	6.62	7.62	8.62	9.62	10.75	11.75
1	1.125	1.14	2.88	4.00	5.00	6.62	7.62	8.62	9.62	10.75	11.75
1 1/4	1.375	1.39	3.50	4.50	5.56	6.62	7.62	8.62	9.62	10.75	11.75
1 1/2	1.625	1.64	3.50	4.50	5.56	6.62	7.62	8.62	9.62	10.75	11.75
2	2.125	2.16	4.00	5.00	6.62	7.62	8.62	9.62	10.75	11.75	12.75
2 1/2	2.625	2.66	4.50	5.56	6.62	7.62	8.62	9.62	10.75	11.75	12.75
3	3.125	3.16	5.00	6.62	7.62	8.62	9.62	10.75	11.75	12.75	14.00
3 1/2	3.625	3.66	5.56	6.62	7.62	8.62	9.62	10.75	11.75	12.75	14.00
4	4.125	4.16	6.62	7.62	8.62	9.62	10.75	11.75	12.75	14.00	15.00
5	5.125	5.16	7.62	8.62	9.62	10.75	11.75	12.75	14.00	15.00	16.00
6	6.125	6.20	8.62	9.62	10.75	11.75	12.75	14.00	15.00	16.00	17.00

C534 Specification for Preformed Flexible Elastomeric Cellular Thermal Insulation in Sheet and Tubular Form

C547 Specification for Mineral Fiber Pipe Insulation

C552 Specification for Cellular Glass Thermal Insulation

C553 Specification for Mineral Fiber Blanket Thermal Insulation for Commercial and Industrial Applications

C578 Specification for Rigid, Cellular Polystyrene Thermal Insulation

C585 Practice for Inner and Outer Diameters of Rigid Thermal Insulation for Nominal Sizes of Pipe and Tubing (NPS System)

C591 Specification for Unfaced Preformed Rigid Cellular Polyisocyanurate Thermal Insulation

C612 Specification for Mineral Fiber Block and Board Thermal Insulation

C680 Practice for Estimate of the Heat Gain or Loss and the Surface Temperatures of Insulated Flat, Cylindrical, and Spherical Systems by Use of Computer Programs

795 Specification for Thermal Insulation for Use in Contact with Austentic Stainless Steel

C921 Practice for Determining the Properties of Jacketing Materials for Thermal Insulation

C1055 Guide for Heated System Surface Conditions That Produce Contact Burn Injuries

C1071 Specification for Fibrous Glass Duct Lining Insulation (Thermal and Sound Absorbing Material)

C1126 Specification for Faced or Unfaced Rigid Cellular Phenolic Thermal Insulation

Table 15 Inner and Outer Diameters of Standard Flexible Closed-Cell Pipe Insulation

Pipe Size, NPS	Pipe OD, in.	Insulation ID, in.	Insulation OD, in. — Insulation Nominal Thickness, in.		
			0.5	0.75	1
1/2	0.84	0.97	1.87	2.47	2.97
3/4	1.05	1.13	2.03	2.63	3.13
1	1.315	1.44	2.44	2.94	3.44
1 1/4	1.660	1.78	2.78	3.38	3.78
1 1/2	1.900	2.03	3.03	3.63	4.03
2	2.375	2.50	3.50	4.10	4.50
2 1/2	2.875	3.00	4.00	4.60	5.00
3	3.500	3.70	4.66	5.26	5.76
3 1/2	4.000	4.20	5.30	5.90	6.40
4	4.500	4.70	5.88	6.40	6.90
5	5.563	5.76	6.86	7.46	7.96
6	6.625	6.83	7.93	8.53	9.03
8	8.625	8.82	9.92	10.52	—

Table 16 Inner and Outer Diameters of Standard Flexible Closed-Cell Tubing Insulation

Tube Nominal Size, in.	Tube OD, in.	Insulation ID, in.	Insulation OD, in. — Insulation Nominal Thickness, in.		
			0.5	0.75	1
3/8	0.500	0.600	1.500	1.950	—
1/2	0.625	0.750	1.650	2.150	2.750
3/4	0.875	1.000	1.950	2.500	3.000
1	1.125	1.250	2.220	2.850	3.250
1 1/4	1.375	1.500	2.500	3.100	3.500
1 1/2	1.625	1.750	2.750	3.350	3.750
2	2.125	2.250	3.250	3.850	4.250
2 1/2	2.625	2.750	3.750	4.350	4.750
3	3.125	3.250	4.250	4.850	5.250
3 1/2	3.625	3.750	4.850	5.450	5.950
4	4.125	4.250	5.350	5.950	6.450

C1136 Specification for Flexible Low Permeance Vapor Retarders for Thermal Insulation

C1427 Specification for Preformed Flexible Cellular Polyolefin Thermal Insulation in Sheet and Tubular Form

C1695 Standard Specification for Fabrication of Flexible Removable and Reusable Blanket Insulation for Hot Service

D1621 Test Method for Compressive Properties of Rigid Cellular Plastics

E84 Test Method for Surface Burning Characteristics of Building Materials

E96 Test Methods for Water Vapor Transmission of Materials

E119 Test Methods for Fire Tests of Building Construction and Materials

E136 Test Method for Behavior of Materials in a Vertical Tube Furnace at 750°C

E795 Practice for Mounting Test Specimens during Sound Absorption Tests

E1222 Test Method for Laboratory Measurement of the Insertion Loss of Pipe Lagging Systems

E1529 Test Methods for Determining Effects of Large Hydrocarbon Pool Fires on Structural Members and Assemblies

Table 17 Heat Loss from Bare Steel Pipe to Still Air at 80°F, Btu/h·ft

Nominal Pipe Size, in.	Pipe Inside Temperature, °F				
	180	280	380	480	580
1/2	56.3	138	243	377	545
3/4	68.1	167	296	459	665
1	82.5	203	360	560	813
1 1/4	102	251	446	695	1010
1 1/2	115	283	504	787	1150
2	141	350	623	974	1420
2 1/2	168	416	743	1160	1700
3	201	499	891	1400	2040
3 1/2	228	565	1010	1580	2310
4	254	631	1130	1770	2590
4 1/2	281	697	1250	1960	2860
5	313	777	1390	2180	3190
6	368	915	1640	2580	3770
7	421	1040	1880	2950	4310
8	473	1180	2110	3320	4860
9	525	1310	2340	3680	5400
10	583	1450	2610	4100	6000
12	686	1710	3070	4830	7090
14	747	1860	3340	5260	7720
16	850	2120	3810	6000	8790
18	953	2380	4270	6730	9870
20	1060	2630	4730	7460	10,950
24	1260	3150	5660	8920	13,100

Table 18 Heat Loss from Bare Copper Tube to Still Air at 80°F, Btu/h·ft

Nominal Pipe Size, in.	Inside Pipe Temperature, °F				
	120	150	180	210	240
3/8	10.6	20.6	31.9	44.2	57.5
1/2	12.7	24.7	38.2	53.1	69.2
3/4	16.7	32.7	50.7	70.4	91.9
1	20.7	40.5	62.9	87.5	114
1 1/4	24.6	48.3	74.9	104	136
1 1/2	28.5	55.9	86.9	121	158
2	36.1	71.0	110	154	201
2 1/2	43.7	86.0	134	187	244
3	51.2	101	157	219	287
3 1/2	58.7	116	180	251	329
4	66.1	130	203	283	371
5	80.9	159	248	347	454
6	95.6	188	294	410	538
8	125	246	383	536	703
10	154	303	473	661	867
12	183	360	562	786	1031

E2231 Practice for Specimen Preparation and Mounting of Pipe and Duct Insulation Materials to Assess Surface Burning Characteristics

MICA

2011 *National Commercial and Industrial Insulation Standards*, 7th ed.

NACE

SP0198 The Control of Corrosion under Thermal Insulation and Fireproofing Materials—A Systems Approach

NFPA

Standard 90A	Installation of Air-Conditioning and Ventilating Systems
90B	Installation of Warm Air Heating and Air-Conditioning Systems
255	Method of Test of Surface Burning Characteristics of Building Materials
259	Test Method for Potential Heat of Building Materials

UL/UL Canada

Standard 181	Factory-Made Air Ducts and Air Connectors
723	Standard for Test for Surface Burning Characteristics of Building Materials
CAN/ULC-S101	Methods of Fire Endurance Tests of Building Construction and Materials
CAN/ULC-S102	Method of Test for Surface Burning Characteristics of Building Materials and Assemblies
CAN4-S114	Method of Test for Determination of Non-Combustibility in Building Materials (Rev 1997)

U.S. Navy

Standard MIL-1-2781	Insulation, Pipe, Thermal

REFERENCES

ASHRAE members can access *ASHRAE Journal* articles and ASHRAE research project final reports at technologyportal .ashrae.org. Articles and reports are also available for purchase by nonmembers in the online ASHRAE Bookstore at www.ashrae.org /bookstore.

ASTM. 2001. *Moisture analysis and condensation control in building envelopes*. MNL 40. American Society for Testing and Materials, West Conshohocken, PA.

Brower, G. 2000. A new solution for controlling water vapor problems in low temperature insulation systems. *Insulation Outlook* (September).

Crall, G.C.P. 2002. The use of wicking technology to manage moisture in below ambient insulation systems. *Insulation Materials, Testing and Applications*, vol. 4, pp. 326-334, A.O. Desjarlais and R.R. Zarr, eds. ASTM STP 1426. American Society for Testing and Materials, West Conshohocken, PA.

Cremaschi, L., A. Ghajar, S. Cai, and K. Worthington. 2012. Methodology to measure thermal performance of pipe insulation at below-ambient temperatures (RP-1356). ASHRAE Research Project RP-1356, *Final Report*.

Gordon, J. 1996. An investigation into freezing and bursting water pipes in residential construction. *Research Report* 90-1. University of Illinois Building Research Council.

Hart, G. 2006. Thermal insulation coatings (TICs): How effective are they as insulation? *Insulation Outlook* (July).

Hart, G. 2011. Saving energy by insulating pipe components on steam and hot water distribution systems. *ASHRAE Journal* (October).

Kalis, J. 1999. Water and insulation: A corrosive mix. *Insulation Outlook* (April).

Korsgaard, V. 1993. Innovative concept to prevent moisture formation and icing of cold pipe insulation. *ASHRAE Transactions* 99(1):270-273.

Kuntz, H.L., and R.M. Hoover. 1987. The interrelationship between the physical properties of fibrous duct lining materials and lined duct sound attenuation (RP-478). *ASHRAE Transactions* 93(2).

Marion, W., and K. Urban. 1995. *User's manual for TMY2's typical meteorological years*. National Renewable Energy Laboratory, Golden, CO.

Miller, W.S. 2001. Acoustical lagging systems. *Insulation Outlook* (April): 41-46.

Mumaw, J.R. 2001. Below ambient piping insulation systems. *Insulation Outlook* (September).

Turner, W.C., and J.F. Malloy. 1981. *Thermal insulation handbook*. Robert E. Kreiger Publishing, McGraw Hill Book Company, New York.

WDBG. 2012. *Mechanical insulation design guide—Design objectives*. www.wbdg.org/design/midg_design.php. Whole Building Design Guide, National Institute of Building Sciences, Washington, D.C.

Young, J. 2011. Preventing corrosion on the interior surface of metal jacketing. *Insulation Outlook* (November).

CHAPTER 24

AIRFLOW AROUND BUILDINGS

AIRFLOW around buildings affects worker safety, process and building equipment operation, pollution infiltration at building inlets, and the ability to control indoor environmental parameters such as temperature, humidity, air motion, and contaminants. Wind causes variable surface pressures on buildings that can change intake and exhaust system flow rates, natural ventilation, infiltration and exfiltration, and interior pressures. The mean flow patterns and turbulence of wind passing over a building can also lead to recirculation of exhaust gases into air intakes.

This chapter provides basic information for evaluating wind flow patterns, estimating wind pressures, and identifying problems caused by the effects of wind on pedestrians and buildings, including ventilation intakes, exhausts, and equipment. In most cases, detailed solutions are addressed in other chapters. Related information can be found in Chapters 11, 14, 16, and 37 of this volume; in Chapters 31, 32, 45, 47, and 53 of the 2015 *ASHRAE Handbook—HVAC Applications*; and in Chapters 30, 35, and 40 of the 2016 *ASHRAE Handbook—HVAC Systems and Equipment.*

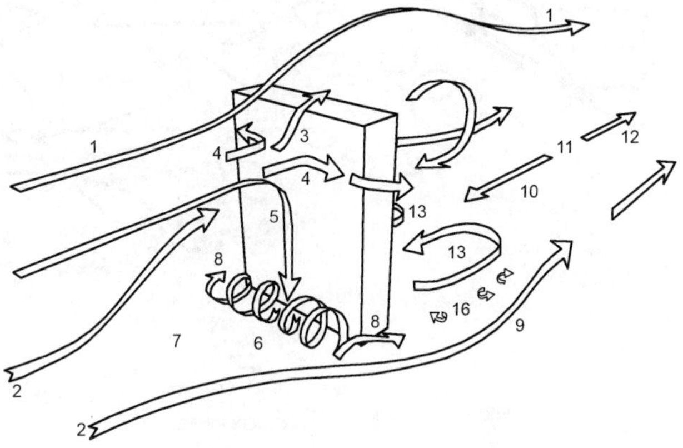

Fig. 1 Wind Flow Pattern Around High-Rise Building Slab
[Adapted from Blocken et al. (2016) and Beranek and Van Koten (1979)]

1. FLOW PATTERNS

Flow Patterns Around Isolated, Rectangular Block-Type Buildings

Buildings with even moderately complex shapes, such as L- or U-shaped structures, can generate flow patterns too complex to generalize for design. To determine flow conditions for such buildings, wind tunnel or water channel tests of physical scale models, full-scale tests of existing buildings, or appropriate computational modeling efforts are required (see the section on Physical and Computational Modeling). Thus, only isolated, rectangular block-type buildings are discussed here.

Figure 1 shows the wind flow pattern around a single, wide, high-rise building slab, with the main flow features indicated by numbers. The following description of the flow pattern is adapted from Blocken et al. (2011). As wind impinges on the building, part of the flow is deviated over the building (point 1) and part flows around it (2, 9). A stagnation point is present at the windward façade at about 70% of the building height. From this point, part of the flow is deviated upward (**upwash**) (3), part is deviated sideways (4), and a large part is directed downwards (**downwash**) (5). This downflow develops into a ground-level vortex (6) called standing vortex, frontal vortex, or horseshoe vortex. The main flow direction of this vortex near ground level is opposite to the direction of the approach flow. Both flows collide at the stagnation point at ground level in front of the building (7). The standing vortex subsequently wraps around the building corners, yielding the concentrated **corner streams**, characterized by very high wind speed amplification (8). These corner streams are further amplified by the general ground-level flow around the building (9). At the building's leeward side, the underpressure zone results in recirculation flow (10, 13). A stagnation zone is also present downstream of the building at ground level, where the flow directions are opposite and wind speeds are low (11). Further downstream, the wind speed remains low for a considerable distance behind the building (i.e., the far wake) (12). Backflow is also responsible for creating slow-rotating vortices behind the building (13). Between these vortices and the corner streams (9) is a zone with a high velocity gradient (**shear layer**) that comprises small, fast-rotating vortices (16).

Figure 2 provides a more detailed illustration of the wind flow pattern around an isolated building. It more clearly shows the vertical nature of the corner streams, and it indicates the areas of flow separation and reattachment and the flow in the near wake. It is important to note that Figures 1 and 2 only show the mean wind flow pattern, and that the actual flow pattern exhibits pronounced transient features, such as the build-up and collapse of the separation/recirculation bubbles and periodic vortex shedding in the wake (Murakami 1993; Tominaga et al. 2008a).

For a building with height H that is three or more times the width W of the upwind face, an intermediate stagnation zone can exist between the upwash and downwash regions, where surface streamlines pass horizontally around the building (Figure 3A). (In Figure 3, the upwind building surface is "folded out" to illustrate upwash, downwash, and stagnation zones.) Downwash on the lower surface of the upwind face separates from the building before it reaches ground level and moves upwind to form the standing vortex. Figure 3B shows the near-surface flow patterns for oblique approach flow. Strong vortices develop from the upwind edges of the roof, causing strong downwash onto the roof. High speeds in these vortices (**vorticity**) cause large negative pressures near roof corners that can be a hazard to roof-mounted equipment during high winds. In some extreme cases, the negative pressures can be strong enough to lift heavy objects such as roof pavers, which can result in a projectile hazard.

When the angle between the wind direction and the upwind face of the building is less than about 70°, the upwash/downwash patterns on the upwind face of the building are less pronounced, as is the ground-level vortex shown in Figure 1 and 2. Figure 3B shows that,

The preparation of this chapter is assigned to TC 4.3, Ventilation Requirements and Infiltration.

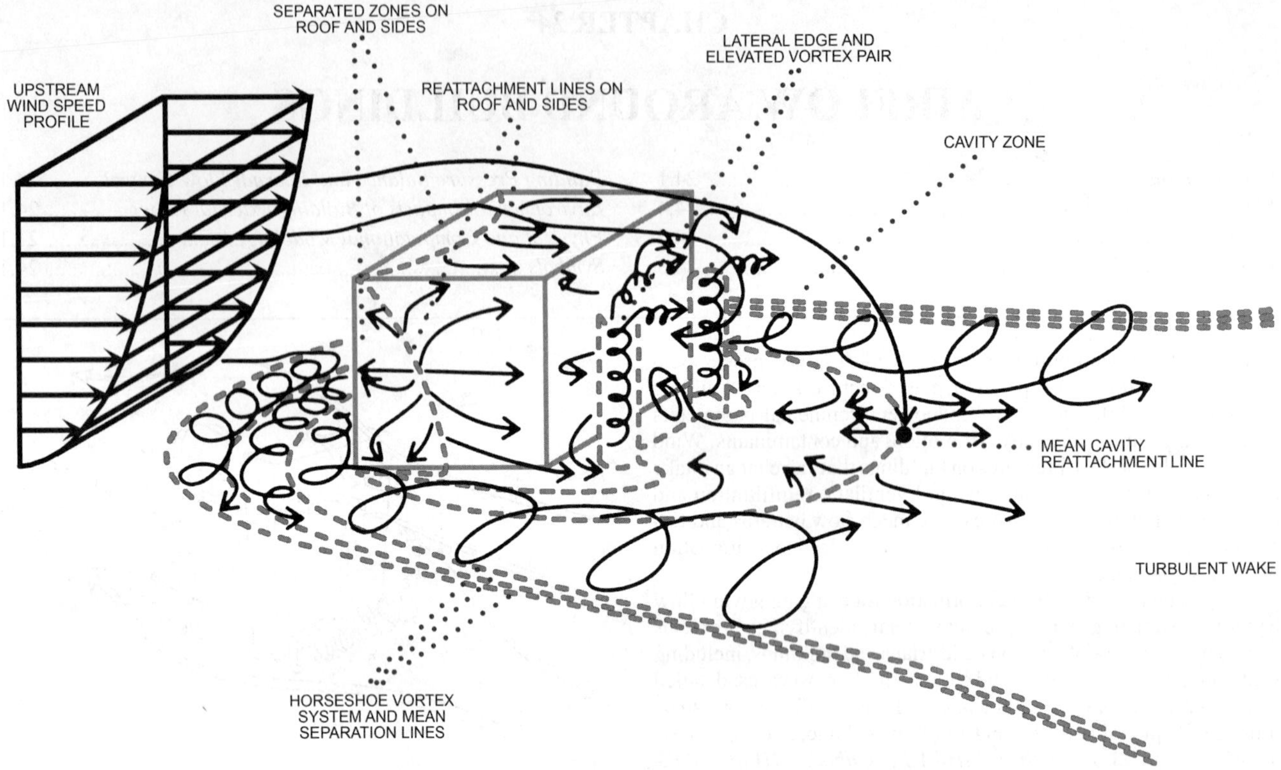

Fig. 2 Wind Flow Pattern Around Isolated Building
(Hunt et al. 1978)

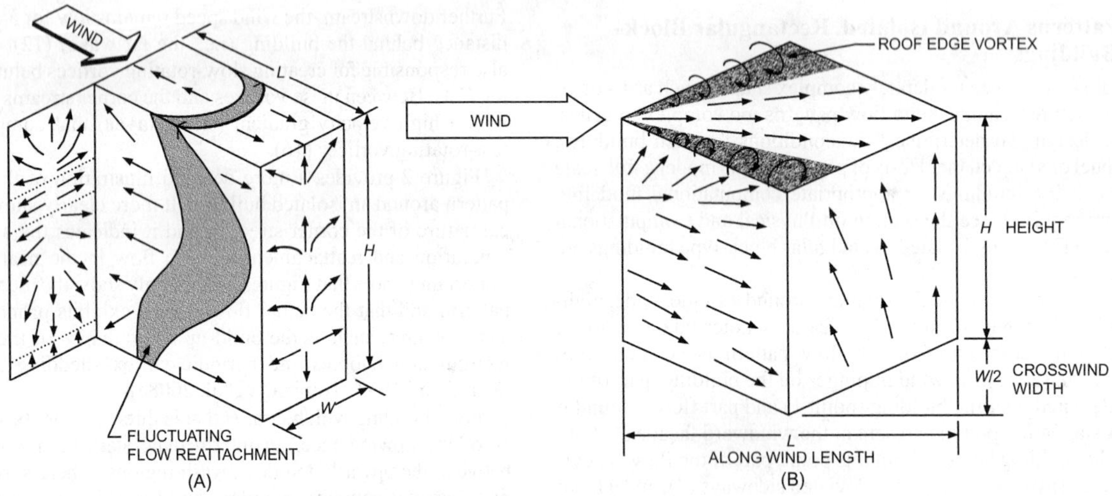

Fig. 3 Surface Flow Patterns for Normal and Oblique Winds
(Wilson 1979)

for an approach flow angle of 45°, streamlines remain close to the horizontal in their passage around the sides of the building, except near roof level, where the flow is drawn upwards into the roof edge vortices (Cochran 1992).

Both the upwind velocity profile shape and its turbulence intensity strongly influence flow patterns and surface pressures (Melbourne 1979).

The downwind wall of a building exhibits a region of low average velocity and high turbulence (i.e., a **flow recirculation** region) extending a distance L_r downwind. If the building has sufficient length L in the windward direction, the flow reattaches to the building and may generate two distinct regions of separated recirculation flow, on the roof of the building and in its wake, as shown in Figure 4. Figure 4 also shows a rooftop recirculation cavity of length L_c at the upwind roof edge and a recirculation zone of length L_r downwind of the rooftop penthouse. Velocities near the downwind wall are typically one-quarter of those at the corresponding upwind wall location. Figures 2 and 3 show that an upward flow exists over most of the downwind walls.

Streamline patterns and the size of the wake(s) are generally independent of wind speed and depend mainly on building shape and upwind conditions. Because of the three-dimensional flow around a

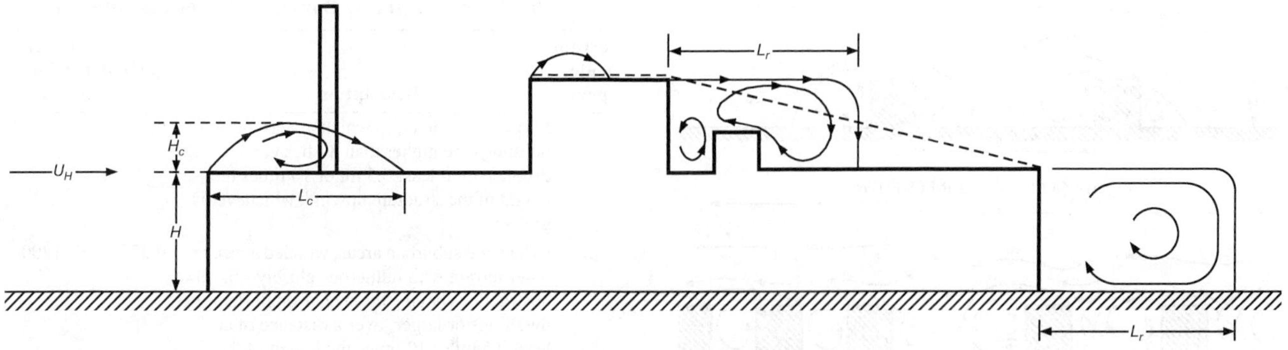

Fig. 4 Flow Recirculation Regions

building, the shape and size of the recirculation airflow are not constant over the surface. Airflow reattaches closer to the upwind building face along the edges of the building than it does near the middle of the roof and sidewalls (Figure 3). Recirculation cavity height H_c (Figure 4) also decreases near roof edges. Calculating characteristic dimensions for recirculation zones H_c, L_c, and L_r is discussed in Chapter 45 of the 2015 *ASHRAE Handbook—HVAC Applications*.

For wind perpendicular to a building wall, the height H and width W of the upwind building face determine the **scaling length R** that characterizes the building's influence on wind flow. According to Wilson (1979),

$$R = B_s^{0.67} B_L^{0.33} \tag{1}$$

where

B_s = smaller of upwind building face dimensions H and W
B_L = larger of upwind building face dimensions H and W

When B_L is larger than $8B_s$, use $B_L = 8B_s$ in Equation (1). For buildings with varying roof levels or with wings separated by at least a distance of B_s, only the height and width of the building face below the portion of the roof in question should be used to calculate R.

Flow accelerates as the streamlines compress over the roof and decelerates as they spread downward over the wake on the downwind side of the building. The height above roof level where a building influences the flow is approximately 1.5R. In addition, roof pitch also begins to affect flow when it exceeds about 15° (1:4). When roof pitch reaches 20° (1:3), flow remains attached to the upwind pitched roof and produces a recirculation region downwind of the roof ridge that is larger than that for a flat roof.

Flow Patterns Around Building Groups

In building groups, the flow patterns can interact, yielding a higher complexity. To determine flow conditions around building groups, wind tunnel or water channel tests of physical scale models, full-scale tests of existing buildings, or careful computational modeling efforts are required (see the section on Physical and Computational Modeling). English and Fricke (1997), Hosker (1984, 1985), Khanduri et al. (1998), Saunders and Melbourne (1979), and Walker et al. (1996) review the effects of nearby buildings, whereas Blocken et al. (2007a, 2008), Stathopoulos and Storms (1986), Yoshie et al. (2007), and others assess the effects of nearby buildings by wind tunnel testing and computational modeling. To illustrate the complexity of wind flow patterns induced by nearby buildings, Figure 5 provides a top view of two high rise buildings in V shape. Depending on the wind direction, this configuration is labeled as converging or diverging. Although the highest wind speed in the passage between both buildings might be expected to occur for the converging arrangement, wind tunnel tests and numerical simulations indicate that the diverging arrangement actually has higher wind speed. This is shown by the

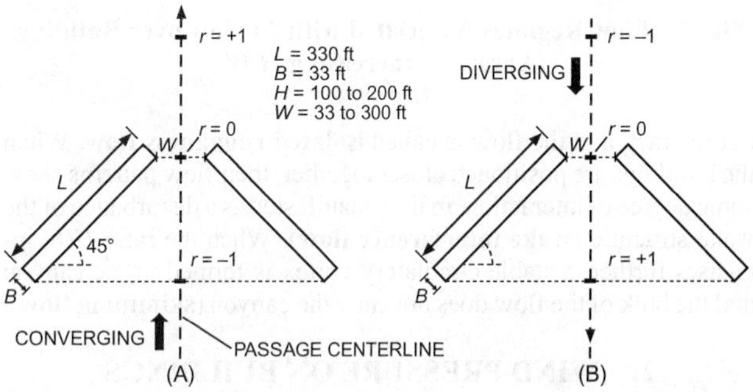

Fig. 5 Buildings in (A) Converging and (B) Diverging Configuration

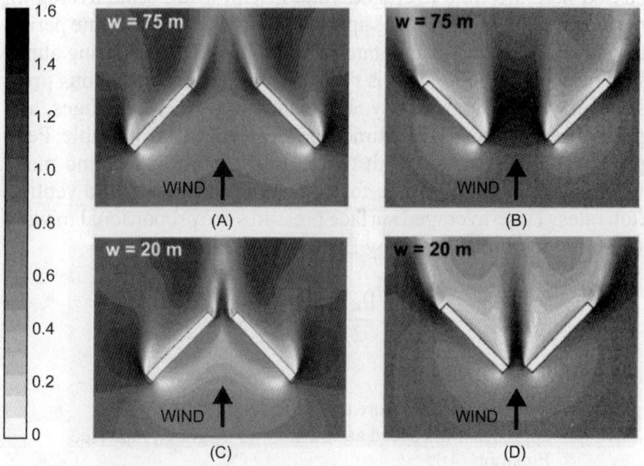

Fig. 6 Amplification Factor K in Horizontal Plane at y = 2 m above Ground for Converging and Diverging Arrangement with H = 30 m and w = 75 m and 20 m
(Blocken et al. 2008)

amplification factors in Figure 6, which are defined as the ratio of the local wind speed to the wind speed that would occur at the same height in absence of the buildings. The higher amplification factor in the diverging arrangement is caused by the lesser flow resistance in this configuration. The Venturi effect does not apply in this case: the Venturi effect refers to confined flows, whereas wind flow in the atmosphere is unconfined. Further information on this study can be found in Blocken et al. (2008).

Figure 7 shows the flow over building arrays with increasing H/W. The description of these flow patterns is adopted from Oke (1988). If the buildings are sufficiently apart (H/W > 0.05), their flow fields do

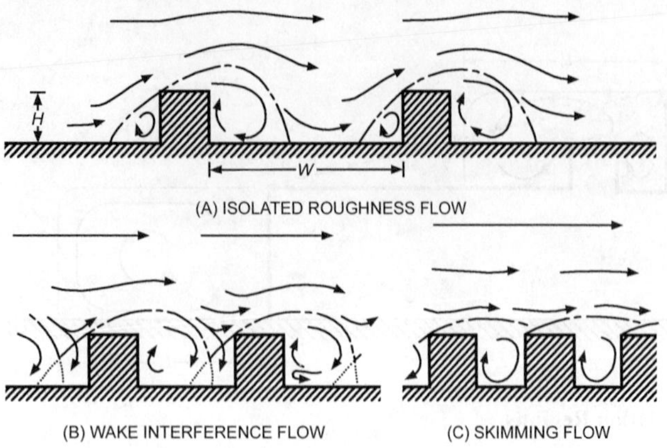

Fig. 7 Flow Regimes Associated with Airflow over Building Arrays of Increasing *H*/*W*
(Oke 1988)

not interact, and the flow is called **isolated roughness flow**. When the buildings are positioned closer together, their flow patterns show some degree of interaction, mainly manifested as a disturbance of the wake structure (**wake interference flow**). When the ratio *H*/*W* increases further, a stable circulatory vortex is formed in the canyon and the bulk of the flow does not enter the canyon (**skimming flow**).

2. WIND PRESSURE ON BUILDINGS

In addition to flow patterns described previously, the turbulence or gustiness of approaching wind and the unsteady character of separated flows cause surface pressures to fluctuate. Pressures discussed here are time-averaged values, with a full-scale averaging period of about 600 s. This is approximately the shortest time period considered to be a "steady-state" condition when considering atmospheric winds; the longest is typically 3600 s. Instantaneous pressures may vary significantly above and below these averages, and peak pressures two or three times the mean values are possible. Peak pressures are important with regard to structural loads, and mean values are more appropriate for computing infiltration and ventilation rates. Time-averaged surface pressures are proportional to wind velocity pressure p_v given by Bernoulli's equation:

$$p_v = \frac{\rho_a U_H^2}{2g_c}/2.152 \tag{2}$$

where

p_v = wind velocity pressure at roof level, lb_f/ft^2
U_H = approach wind speed at upwind wall height *H*, mph [see Equation (4)]
ρ_a = ambient (outdoor) air density, lb_m/ft^3
g_c = gravitational proportionality constant, 32.2 $ft \cdot lb_m/lb_f \cdot s^2$
2.152 = conversion factor

The proportional relationship is shown in the following equation, in which the difference p_s between the pressure on the building surface and the local outdoor atmospheric pressure at the same level in an undisturbed wind approaching the building is

$$p_s = C_p p_v \tag{3}$$

where C_p is the local wind pressure coefficient at a point on the building surface.

Approach Wind Speed

The local wind speed U_H at the top of the wall required for Equation (2) is estimated by applying terrain and height corrections to the hourly wind speed U_{met} from a nearby meteorological station.

Table 1 Atmospheric Boundary Layer Parameters

Terrain Category	Description	Exponent *a*	Layer Thickness δ, ft
1	Large city centers, in which at least 50% of buildings are higher than 80 ft, over a distance of at least 0.5 mi or 10 times the height of the structure upwind, whichever is greater	0.33	1500
2	Urban and suburban areas, wooded areas, or other terrain with numerous closely spaced obstructions having the size of single-family dwellings or larger, over a distance of at least 0.5 mi or 10 times the height of the structure upwind, whichever is greater	0.22	1200
3	Open terrain with scattered obstructions having heights generally less than 30 ft, including flat open country typical of meteorological station surroundings	0.14	900
4	Flat, unobstructed areas exposed to wind flowing over water for at least 1 mi, over a distance of 1500 ft or 10 times the height of the structure inland, whichever is greater	0.10	700

U_{met} is generally measured in flat, open terrain (i.e., category 3 in Table 1). The anemometer that records U_{met} is located at height H_{met}, usually 33 ft above ground level. The hourly average wind speed U_H in the undisturbed wind approaching a building in its local terrain can be calculated from U_{met} as follows:

$$U_H = U_{met}\left(\frac{\delta_{met}}{H_{met}}\right)^{a_{met}}\left(\frac{H}{\delta}\right)^{a} \tag{4}$$

The atmospheric boundary layer thickness δ and exponent *a* for the local building terrain and a_{met} and δ_{met} for the meteorological station are determined from Table 1. Typical values for meteorological stations (category 3 in Table 1) are $a_{met} = 0.14$ and $\delta_{met} = 900$ ft. The values and terrain categories in Table 1 are consistent with those adopted in other engineering applications (e.g., ASCE *Standard* 7). Equation (4) gives the wind speed that occurs at a certain height *H* above the average height of local obstacles, such as buildings and vegetation, weighted by the plan area. At heights at or below this average obstacle height (e.g., at roof height in densely built-up suburbs), speed depends on the geometrical arrangement of the buildings, and Equation (4) is less reliable.

An alternative mathematical description of the atmospheric boundary layer, which uses a logarithmic function, is given by Deaves and Harris (1978). Although their model is more complicated than the power law used in Equation (4), it more closely models the real physics of the atmosphere and has been adopted by several codes around the world (e.g., SA/SNZ 2002).

Example 1. Assuming a 23 mph anemometer wind speed for a height H_{met} of 33 ft at a nearby airport, determine the wind speed U_H at roof level $H = 50$ ft above grade for a building located in a city suburb.

Solution: From Table 1, the atmospheric boundary layer properties for the anemometer are $a_{met} = 0.14$ and $\delta_{met} = 900$ ft. The atmospheric boundary layer properties at the building site are $a = 0.22$ and $\delta = 1200$ ft. Using Equation (4), wind speed U_H at 50 ft is

$$U_H = 23\left(\frac{900}{33}\right)^{0.14}\left(\frac{50}{1200}\right)^{0.22} = 18.2 \text{ mph}$$

Local Wind Pressure Coefficients

Values of the mean local wind pressure coefficient C_p used in Equation (3) depend on building shape, wind direction, and influence of nearby buildings, vegetation, and terrain features. Accurate determination of C_p can be obtained only from wind tunnel model tests of the specific site and building or full-scale tests. Ventilation rate calculations for single, unshielded rectangular buildings can be reasonably estimated using existing wind tunnel data. Many wind load codes (e.g., ASCE *Standard* 7; ASCE 1999; SA/SNZ *Standard* AS/NZS 1170.2) give mean pressure coefficients for common building shapes.

Figure 8 shows pressure coefficients for walls of a tall rectangular cross section high-rise building sited in urban terrain (Davenport and Hui 1982). Figure 9 shows pressure coefficients for walls of a low-rise building (Holmes 1986). Generally, for high-rise buildings, height H is more than three times the crosswind width W. For $H > 3W$, use Figure 8; for $H < 3W$, use Figure 9. At a wind angle $\theta = 0°$ (e.g., wind perpendicular to the face in question), pressure coefficients are positive, and their magnitudes decrease near the sides and the top as flow velocities increase.

As shown in Figure 8, C_p generally increases with height, which reflects increasing velocity pressure in the approach flow as wind speed increases with height. As wind direction moves off normal ($\theta = 0°$), the region of maximum pressure occurs closer to the upwind edge (B in Figure 8) of the building. At a wind angle of $\theta = 45°$, pressures become negative at the downwind edge (A in Figure 8) of the front face. At some angle θ between 60° and 75°, pressures become negative over the whole front face. For $\theta = 90°$, maximum suction (negative) pressure occurs near the upwind edge (B in Figure 8) of the building side and then recovers towards a lower-magnitude negative coefficient as the downwind edge (A in Figure 8) is approached. The degree of this recovery depends on the length of the side in relation to the width W of the structure. For wind angles larger than $\theta = 100°$, the side is completely within the separated flow of the wake and spatial variations in pressure over the face are not as great. In summary, the average pressure on a face is positive for wind angles from $\theta = 0°$ to almost 60° and negative (suction) for $\theta = 60°$ to 180°.

A similar pattern of behavior in wall pressure coefficients for a low-rise building is shown in Figure 9. Here, recovery from strong suction with distance from the upwind edge is more rapid.

Surface-Averaged Wall Pressures

Surface-averaged pressure coefficients may be used to determine ventilation and/or infiltration rates, as discussed in Chapter 16. Figure 10 shows the surface pressure coefficient C_s averaged over a complete wall of a high-rise building (Akins et al. 1979). Similar results for a low-rise building are shown in Figure 11 (based on methodology of Swami and Chandra 1987). This figure also includes values calculated from pressure distributions in Figure 9.

Roof Pressures

Figure 12 shows the average pressure coefficient over the roof of a tall building (Akins et al. 1979).

Surface pressures on the roof of a low-rise building depend strongly on roof slope. Figure 13 shows typical distributions for a wind direction normal to a side of the building. Note that the direction and magnitude of pressure coefficients are indicated by the direction and length of the arrows. For very low slopes (less than about 10°), pressures are negative over the whole roof surface. The magnitude is greatest within the separated flow zone near the leading edge and recovers toward the free-stream pressure downwind of

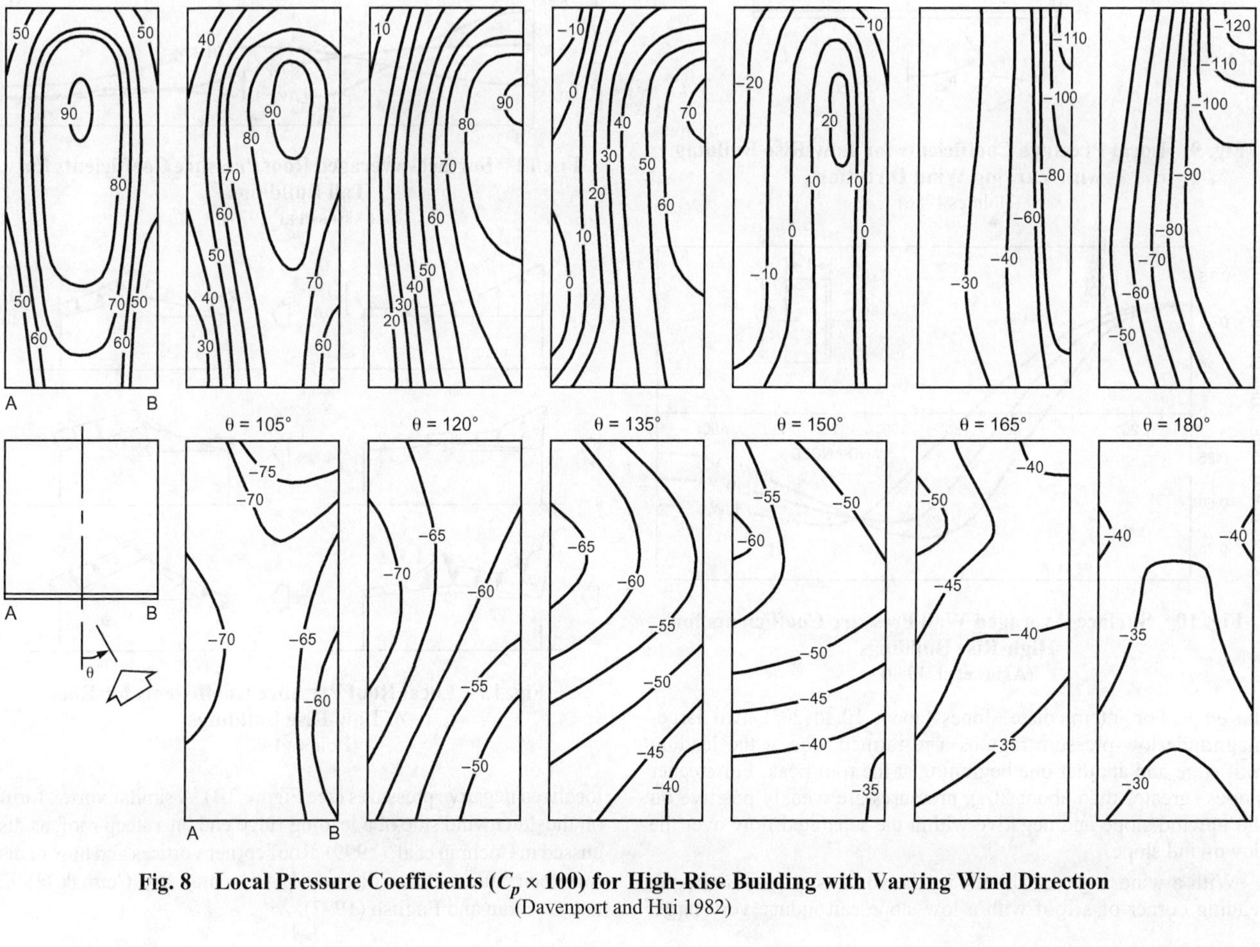

Fig. 8 Local Pressure Coefficients (C_p × 100) for High-Rise Building with Varying Wind Direction
(Davenport and Hui 1982)

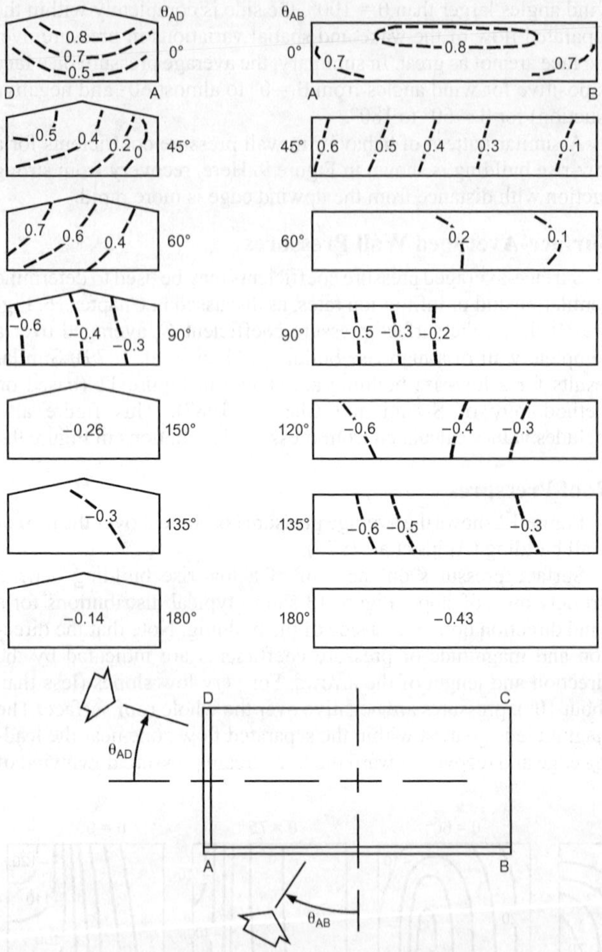

Fig. 9 Local Pressure Coefficients for Low-Rise Building with Varying Wind Direction
(Holmes 1986)

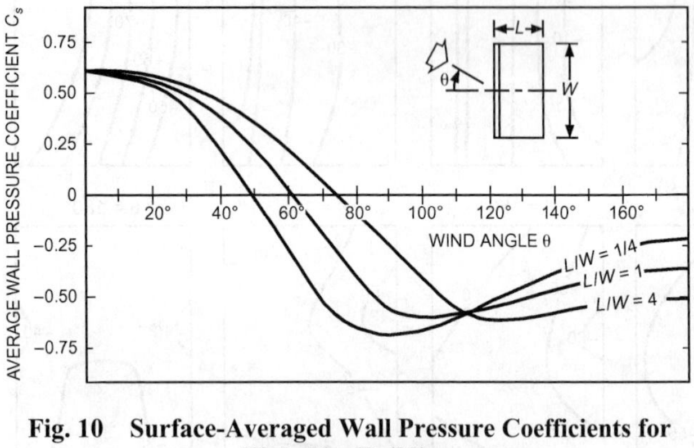

Fig. 10 Surface-Averaged Wall Pressure Coefficients for High-Rise Buildings
(Akins et al. 1979)

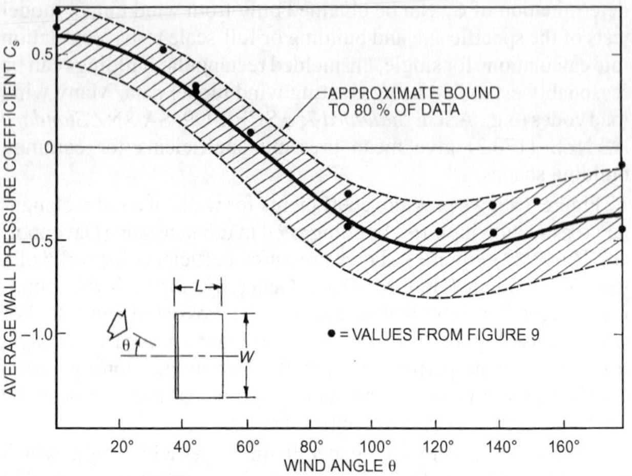

Fig. 11 Surface-Averaged Wall Pressure Coefficients for Low-Rise Buildings
Courtesy of Florida Solar Energy Center (based on methodology of Swami and Chandra 1987)

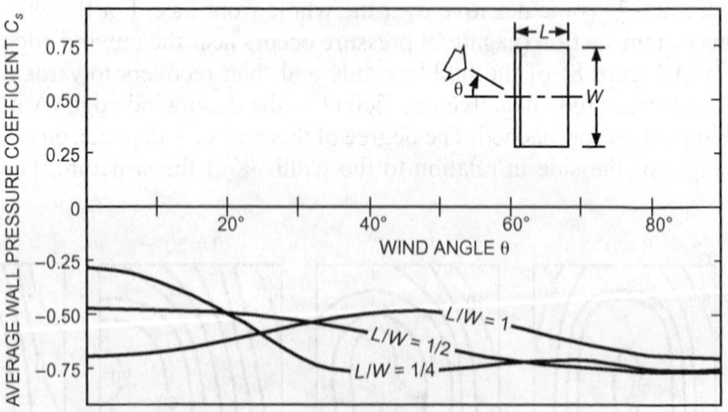

Fig. 12 Surface-Averaged Roof Pressure Coefficients for Tall Buildings
(Akins et al. 1979)

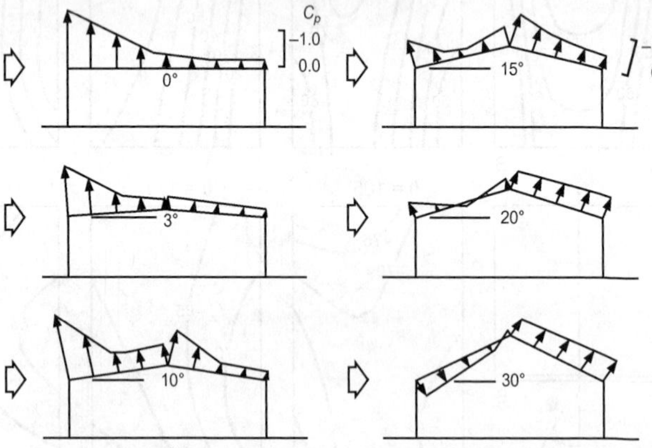

Fig. 13 Local Roof Pressure Coefficients for Roof of Low-Rise Buildings
(Holmes 1983)

the edge. For intermediate slopes (about 10 to 20°), two large-magnitude low-pressure regions a re formed, one at the leading roof edge and another one beginning at the roof peak. For steeper slopes (greater than about 20°), pressures are weakly positive on the upwind slope and negative within the separated flow over the downwind slope.

With a wind angle of about 45°, the vortices originating at the leading corner of a roof with a low slope can induce very large, localized negative pressures (see Figure 3B). A similar vortex forms on the downwind side of a leading ridge end on a steep roof, as discussed in Cochran et al. (1999). Roof corner vortices and how to disrupt their influence are discussed in Cochran and Cermak (1992) and Cochran and English (1997).

Interference and Shielding Effects on Pressures

Nearby structures strongly influence surface pressures on both high- and low-rise buildings, particularly for spacing-to-height ratios less than five, where distributions of pressure shown in Figures 8 to 13 do not apply. Although the effect of shielding for low-rise buildings is still significant at larger spacing, it is largely accounted for by the reduction in p_v with increased terrain roughness. Bailey and Kwok (1985), Khanduri et al. (1998), Saunders and Melbourne (1979), Sherman and Grimsrud (1980), and Walker et al. (1996) discuss interference. English and Fricke (1997) discuss shielding through use of an interference index, and Walker et al. (1996) present a wind shadow model for predicting shelter factors. Chapter 16 gives shielding classes for air infiltration and ventilation applications.

3. SOURCES OF WIND DATA

Wind at Recording Stations

To design buildings taking into account wind effects, wind speed and direction frequency data are necessary. The simplest forms of wind data are tables or charts of climatic normals, which give hourly average wind speeds, prevailing wind directions, and peak gust wind speeds for each month. This information can be found in sources such as *The Weather Almanac* (Bair 1992) and the *Climatic Atlas of the United States* (DOC 1968). Climatic design information, including wind speed at various frequencies of occurrence, is included in Chapter 14. Information on wind speed and direction frequencies is available from the National Climatic Data Center (NCDC) in Asheville, NC. Where more detailed information is required, digital records of hourly winds and other meteorological parameters are available from the NCDC for stations throughout the world. Most countries also have weather services that provide data. For example, in Canada, the Meteorological Service of Canada provides hourly meteorological data and summaries.

When an hourly wind speed U_{met} at a specified probability level (e.g., the wind speed that is exceeded 1% of the time) is desired, but only the average annual wind speed U_{annual} is available for a given meteorological station, U_{met} may be estimated using Table 2. The ratios U_{met}/U_{annual} are based on long-term data from 24 weather stations widely distributed over North America. At these stations, U_{annual} ranges from 7 to 14 mph The uncertainty ranges listed in Table 2 are one standard deviation of the wind speed ratios. Example 2 demonstrates the use of Table 2.

Example 2. The wind speed U_{met} that is exceeded 1% of the time (88 hours per year) is needed for a building pressure or exhaust dilution calculation. If U_{annual} = 9 mph, find U_{met}.

Solution: From Table 2, the wind speed U_{met} exceeded 1% of the time is 2.5 ± 0.4 times U_{annual}. For U_{annual} = 9 mph, U_{met} is 23 mph with an uncertainty range of 19 to 26 mph at one standard deviation.

Using a single prevailing wind direction for design can cause serious errors. For any set of wind direction frequencies, one direction always has a somewhat higher frequency of occurrence. Thus, it is often called the **prevailing wind**, even though winds from other directions may be almost as frequent.

Table 2 Typical Relationship of Hourly Wind Speed U_{met} to Annual Average Wind Speed U_{annual}

Percentage of Hourly Values That Exceed U_{met}	Wind Speed Ratio U_{met}/U_{annual}
90%	0.2 ± 0.1
75%	0.5 ± 0.1
50%	0.8 ± 0.1
25%	1.2 ± 0.15
10%	1.6 ± 0.2
5%	1.9 ± 0.3
1%	2.5 ± 0.4

When using long-term meteorological records, check the anemometer location history, because the instrument may have been relocated and its height varied. This can affect its directional exposure and the recorded wind speeds. Equation (4) can be used to correct wind data collected at different mounting heights. Poor anemometer exposure caused by obstructions or mounting on top of a building cannot be easily corrected, and records for that period should be deleted.

If an estimate of the probability of an extreme wind speed outside the range of the recorded values at a site is required, the observations may be fitted to an appropriate probability distribution (e.g., a Weibull distribution) and the particular probabilities calculated from the resulting function (Figure 14). This process is usually repeated for each of 16 wind directions (e.g., 22.5° intervals). Note that most recent wind data records are provided in 10° intervals, for which the same method may be used, except that the process is repeated for each of 36 wind directions. If both types of data are to be used, one data set must be transformed to match the other.

Where estimates at extremely low probability (high wind speed) are required, curve fitting at the tail of the probability distribution is very important and may require special statistical techniques applicable to extreme values (see Chapter 14). Building codes for wind loading on structures contain information on estimating extreme wind conditions. For ventilation applications, extreme winds are usually not required, and the 99th percentile limit can be accurately estimated from meteorological station data averaged over less than 10 years.

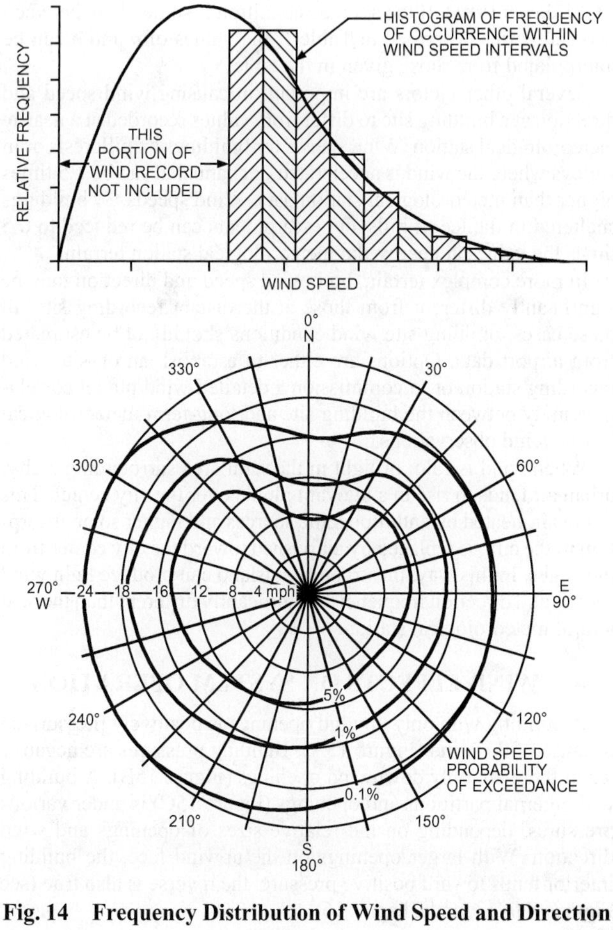

Fig. 14 Frequency Distribution of Wind Speed and Direction

Estimating Wind at Sites Remote from Recording Stations

Many building sites are located far from the nearest long-term wind recording site, which is usually an airport meteorological station. To estimate wind conditions at such sites, the terrain surrounding both the anemometer site and the building site should be checked. In the simplest case of flat or slightly undulating terrain with few obstructions extending for large distances around and between the anemometer site and building site, recorded wind data can be assumed to be representative of that at the building site. Wind direction occurrence frequency at a building site should be inferred from airport data only if the two locations are on the same terrain, with no terrain features that could alter wind direction between them.

In cases where the only significant difference between the anemometer site terrain and the building site terrain is surface roughness, the mean wind speed can be adjusted using Equation (4) and Table 1, to yield approximate wind velocities at the building site. Wind direction frequencies at the site are assumed to be the same as at the recording station.

In using Equation (4), there may be cases where, for a given wind direction, the terrain upwind of either the building or recording site does not fall into just one of the categories in Table 1. The terrain immediately upwind of the site may fall into one category, and that farther upwind fall into a different category. For example, at a downtown airport the terrain may be flat and open (category 3) immediately around the recording instrument, but urban or suburban (category 2) a relatively short distance away. This difference in terrains also occurs when a building or recording site is in an urban area near open water or at the edge of town. In these cases, the suggested approach is to use the terrain category most representative of the average condition within approximately 1 mile upwind of the site (Deaves 1981). If the average condition is somewhere between two categories described in Table 1, the values of a and δ can be interpolated from those given in the table.

Several other factors are important in causing wind speed and direction at a building site to differ from values recorded at a nearby meteorological station. Wind speeds for buildings on hillcrests or in valleys where the wind is accelerated or channeled can be 1.5 times higher than meteorological station data. Wind speeds for buildings sheltered in the lee of hills and escarpments can be reduced to 0.5 times the values at nearby flat meteorological station terrain.

In more complex terrain, both wind speed and direction may be significantly different from those at the distant recording site. In these cases, building site wind conditions should not be estimated from airport data. Options are either to establish an on-site wind recording station or to commission a detailed wind tunnel correlation study between the building site and long-term meteorological station wind observations.

When wind is calm or light in the rural area surrounding a city, urban air tends to rise in a buoyant plume over the city center. This rising air, heated by anthropogenic sources and higher solar absorption in the city, is replaced by air pushed toward the city center from the edges. In this way, the urban heat island can produce light wind speeds and direction frequencies significantly different than those at a rural meteorological station.

4. WIND EFFECTS ON SYSTEM OPERATION

A building with only upwind openings is positively pressurized because of the wind (Figure 15A). Building pressures are negative when there are only downwind openings (Figure 15B). A building with internal partitions and openings (Figure 15C) is under various pressures, depending on the relative sizes of openings and wind direction. With larger openings on the upwind face, the building interior tends toward positive pressure; the reverse is also true (see Figures 8 to 13, and Chapter 16).

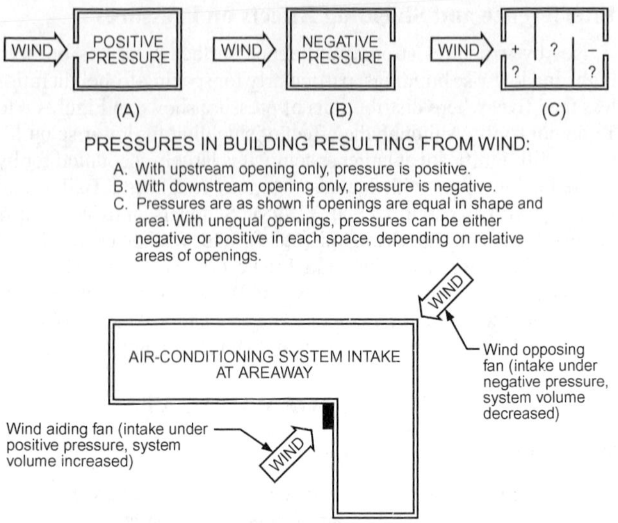

Fig. 15 Sensitivity of System Volume to Locations of Building Openings, Intakes, and Exhausts

With few exceptions, building intakes and exhausts cannot be located or oriented such that a prevailing wind ensures effective ventilation and air-conditioning system operation. Wind can assist or hinder inlet and exhaust fans, depending on their positions on the building, but even in locations with a predominant wind direction, the ventilating system must perform adequately for all other directions. To avoid variable system flow rates, use Figures 8, 9, and 12 as a guide to placing inlets and exhausts in locations where surface pressure coefficients do not vary greatly with wind direction. Also consider the potential for cross contamination; see Chapter 45 of the 2015 *ASHRAE Handbook—HVAC Applications* for details.

Airflow through a wall opening results from differential pressures, which may exceed 0.5 in. of water during high winds. Supply and exhaust systems, openings, dampers, louvers, doors, and windows make building flow conditions too complex for direct calculation. Iterative calculations are required because of the nonlinear dependence of volume flow rate on the differential pressure across an opening. Several multizone airflow models are available for these iterative calculations (Feustel and Dieris 1992; Walton and Dols 2005). Opening and closing of doors and windows by building occupants add further complications. In determining C_p, wind direction is more important than the position of an opening on a wall, as shown in Figures 8 and 9. Refer to Chapter 16 for details on wind effects on building ventilation, including natural and mechanical systems.

Cooling towers and similar equipment should be oriented to take advantage of prevailing wind directions, if possible, based on careful study of meteorological data and flow patterns on the building for the area and time of year.

Natural and Mechanical Ventilation

With natural ventilation, wind may augment, impede, or sometimes reverse the airflow through a building. For flat roof areas with large along-wind sides, wind can reattach to the roof downwind of the leading edge (see Figures 3 and 4). For peaked roofs, the upwind slope may be positively pressurized while the downwind slope may be negatively pressurized, as shown in Figure 12. Thus, any natural ventilation openings could see either a positive or negative pressure, dependent on wind speed and direction. Positive pressure existing where negative pressures were expected could reverse expected natural ventilation. These reversals can be avoided by using stacks, continuous roof ventilators, or other exhaust devices in which flow is augmented by wind.

Mechanical ventilation is also affected by wind conditions. A low-pressure wall exhaust fan (0.05 to 0.1 in. of water) can suffer drastic reduction in capacity. Flow can be reduced or reversed by wind pressure on upwind walls, or increased substantially when subjected to negative pressure on the downwind wall. Side walls may be subjected to either positive or negative pressure, depending on wind direction. Clarke (1967), measuring medium-pressure air-conditioning systems (1 to 1.5 in. of water), found flow rate changes of 25% for wind blowing into intakes on an L-shaped building compared to wind blowing away from intakes. Such changes in flow rate can cause noise at supply outlets and drafts in the space served.

For mechanical systems, wind can be thought of as an additional pressure source in series with a system fan, either assisting or opposing it (Houlihan 1965). Where system stability is essential, supply and exhaust systems must be designed for high pressures (about 3 to 4 in. of water) or use devices to actively minimize unacceptable variations in flow rate. To conserve energy, the selected system pressure should be the minimum consistent with system needs.

Quantitative estimates of wind effects on a mechanical ventilation system can be made by using the pressure coefficients in Figures 8 to 13 to calculate wind pressure on air intakes and exhausts. A simple worst-case estimate is to assume a system with 100% makeup air supplied by a single intake and exhausted from a single outlet. The building is treated as a single zone, with an exhaust-only fan as shown in Figure 16. This overestimates the effect of wind on system volume flow.

Combining Equations (2) and (3), surface wind pressures at air intake and exhaust locations are

$$p_{s\,intake} = C_{p\,intake}\left(\frac{\rho_a U_H^2}{2g_c}/2.152\right) \quad (5)$$

$$p_{s\,exhaust} = C_{p\,exhaust}\left(\frac{\rho_a U_H^2}{2g_c}/2.152\right) \quad (6)$$

For the single-zone building shown in Figure 16, a worst-case estimate of wind effect neglects any flow resistance in the intake grill and duct, making interior building pressure $p_{interior}$ equal to outdoor wind pressure on the intake ($p_{interior} = p_{s\,intake}$). Then, with all system flow resistance assigned to the exhaust duct in Figure 16, and a pressure rise Δp_{fan} across the fan, pressure drop from outdoor intake to outdoor exhaust yields

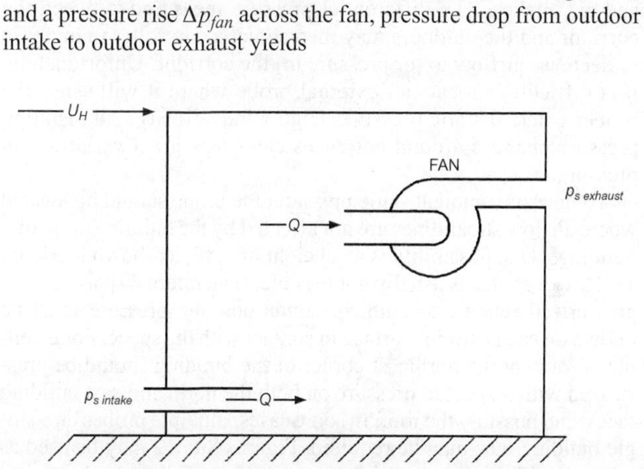

Fig. 16 Intake and Exhaust Pressures on Exhaust Fan in Single-Zone Building

$$(p_{s\,intake} - p_{s\,exhaust}) + \Delta p_{fan} = F_{sys}\frac{\rho Q^2}{A_L^2 g_c} \quad (7)$$

where F_{sys} is system flow resistance, A_L is flow leakage area, and Q is system volume flow rate. This result shows that, for the worst-case estimate, the wind-induced pressure difference simply adds to or subtracts from the fan pressure rise. With inlet and exhaust pressures from Equations (5) and (6), the effective fan pressure rise $\Delta p_{fan\,eff}$ is

$$\Delta p_{fan\,eff} = \Delta p_{fan} + \Delta p_{wind} \quad (8)$$

where

$$\Delta p_{wind} = (C_{p\,intake} - C_{p\,exhaust})\left(\frac{\rho_a U_H^2}{2g_c}/2.152\right) \quad (9)$$

The fan is wind assisted when $C_{p\,intake} > C_{p\,exhaust}$ and wind opposed when the wind direction changes, causing $C_{p\,intake} < C_{p\,exhaust}$. The effect of wind-assisted and wind-opposed pressure differences is shown in Figure 17.

Example 3. Make a worst-case estimate for the effect of wind on the supply fan for a low-rise building with height $H = 50$ ft, located in a city suburb. Use the hourly average wind speed that will be exceeded only 1% of the time and assume an annual hourly average speed of $U_{annual} = 8$ mph measured on a meteorological tower at height $H_{met} = 33$ ft at a nearby airport. Outdoor air density is $\rho_a = 0.075$ lb$_m$/ft^3.

Solution: From Table 2, the wind speed exceeded only 1% of the hours each year is a factor of 2.5 ± 0.4 higher than the annual average of 8 mph, so the 1% maximum speed at the airport meteorological station is

$$U_{met} = 2.5 \times 8 = 20 \text{ mph}$$

From Example 1, building wind speed U_H is 18.2 mph.

A worst-case estimate of wind effect must assume intake and exhaust locations on the building that produce the largest difference ($C_{p\,intake} - C_{p\,exhaust}$) in Equations (8) and (9). From Figure 9, the largest difference occurs for the intake on the upwind wall AB and the exhaust on the downwind wall CD, with a wind angle $\theta_{AB} = 0°$. For this worst case, $C_{p\,intake} = +0.8$ on the upwind wall and $C_{p\,exhaust} = -0.43$ on the downwind wall. Using these coefficients in Equations (8) and (9) to evaluate effective fan pressure $\Delta p_{fan\,eff}$,

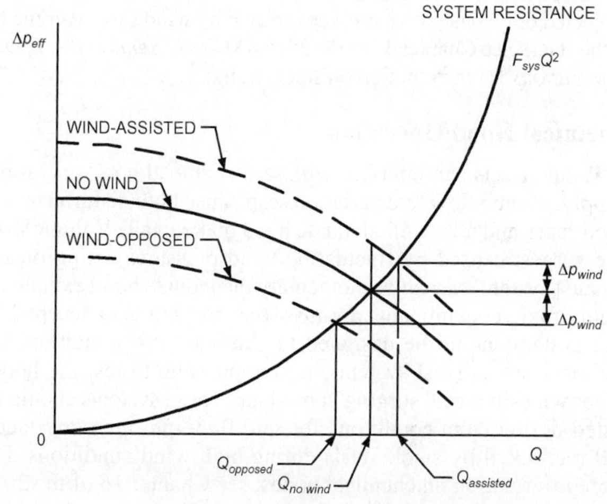

Fig. 17 Effect of Wind-Assisted and Wind-Opposed Flow

$$\Delta p_{fan\ eff} = \Delta p_{fan} + [0.8 - (-0.43)]\frac{0.075(23.2)^2}{2(32.2)}/2.152$$
$$= \Delta p_{fan} + 0.36\ \text{lb}_f/\text{ft}^2$$

This wind-assisted hourly averaged pressure is exceeded only 1% of the time (88 hours per year). When wind direction reverses, the outlet will be on the upwind wall and the inlet on the downwind wall, producing wind-opposed flow, changing the sign from +0.15 to –0.15 in. of water (i.e., +0.36 to –0.36 lb_f/ft^2). The importance of these pressures depends on their size relative to the fan pressure rise Δp_{fan}, as shown in Figure 17.

Minimizing Wind Effect on System Volume Flow Rate

Wind effect can be reduced by careful selection of inlet and exhaust locations. Because wall surfaces are subject to a wide variety of positive and negative pressures, wall openings should be avoided when possible. When they are required, wall openings should be away from corners formed by building wings (see Figure 15). Mechanical ventilation systems should operate at a pressure high enough to minimize wind effect. Low-pressure systems and propeller exhaust fans should not be used with wall openings unless their ventilation rates are small or they are used in noncritical services (e.g., storage areas).

Although roof air intakes in flow recirculation zones best minimize wind effect on system flow rates, current and future air quality in these zones must be considered. These locations should be avoided if a contamination source exists or may be added in the future. The best area is near the middle of the roof, because the negative pressure there is small and least affected by changes in wind direction (see Figure 12). Consider avoiding edges of the roof and walls, where large pressure fluctuations occur. Either vertical or horizontal (mushroom) openings can be used. On roofs with large areas, where intake may be outside the roof recirculation zone, mushroom or 180° gooseneck designs minimize impact pressure from wind flow. Vertical louvered openings or 135° goosenecks are undesirable for this purpose or for rain protection.

Heated air or contaminants should be exhausted vertically through stacks, above the roof recirculation zone. Horizontal, louvered (45° down), and 135° gooseneck discharges are undesirable, even for heat removal systems, because of their sensitivity to wind effects. A 180° gooseneck for hot-air systems may be undesirable because of air impingement on tar and felt roofs. Vertically discharging stacks in a recirculation region (except near a wall) have the advantage of being subjected only to negative pressure created by wind flow over the tip of the stack. See Chapter 45 of the 2015 *ASHRAE Handbook—HVAC Applications* for information on stack design.

Chemical Hood Operation

Wind effects can interfere with safe chemical hood operation. Supply volume flow rate variations can cause both disturbances at hood faces and a lack of adequate hood makeup air. Volume flow rate surges, caused by fluctuating wind pressures acting on the exhaust system, can cause momentary inadequate hood exhaust. If highly toxic contaminants are involved, surging is unacceptable. The system should be designed to eliminate this condition. On low-pressure exhaust systems, it is impossible to test the hoods under wind-induced, surging conditions. These systems should be tested during calm conditions for safe flow into the hood faces, and rechecked by smoke tests during high wind conditions. For more information on chemical hoods, see Chapter 16 of the 2015 *ASHRAE Handbook—HVAC Applications*. For more information on stack and intake design, see Chapter 45 of that volume.

5. BUILDING PRESSURE BALANCE AND INTERNAL FLOW CONTROL

Proper building pressure balance avoids flow conditions that make doors hard to open and cause drafts. In some cases (e.g., office buildings), pressure balance may be used to prevent confinement of contaminants to specific areas. In other cases (e.g., laboratories), the correct internal airflow is towards the contaminated area.

Pressure Balance

Although supply and exhaust systems in an indoor area may be in nominal balance, wind can upset this balance, not only because of its effects on fan capacity but also by superimposing infiltrated or exfiltrated air (or both). These effects can make it challenging to control environmental conditions. Where building balance and infiltration are important, consider the following:

- Design HVAC system with pressure adequate to minimize wind effects
- Include controls to regulate flow rate, pressure, or both
- Separate supply and exhaust systems to serve each building area requiring control or balance
- Use revolving or other self-closing doors or double-door air locks to noncontrolled adjacent areas, particularly exterior doors
- Seal windows and other leakage sources
- Close natural ventilation openings

Internal Flow Control

Airflow direction is maintained by controlling pressure differentials between spaces. In a laboratory building, for example, peripheral rooms such as offices and conference rooms are kept at positive pressure, and laboratories at negative pressure, both with reference to corridor pressure. Pressure differentials between spaces are normally obtained by balancing supply system airflows in the spaces in conjunction with exhaust systems in the laboratories. Differential pressure instrumentation is normally used to control airflow.

The pressure differential for a room adjacent to a corridor can be controlled using the corridor pressure as the reference. Outdoor pressure cannot usually control pressure differentials within internal spaces, even during periods of relatively constant wind velocity (wind-induced pressure). A single pressure sensor can measure the outdoor pressure at one point only and may not be representative of pressures elsewhere.

Airflow (or pressure) in corridors is sometimes controlled by an outdoor reference probe that senses static pressure at doorways and air intakes. The differential pressure measured between the corridor and the outdoors may then signal a controller to increase or decrease airflow to (or pressure in) the corridor. Unfortunately, it is difficult to locate an external probe where it will sense the proper external static pressure. High wind velocity and resulting pressure changes around entrances can cause great variations in pressure.

To measure ambient static pressure, the probe should be located where airflow streamlines are not affected by the building or nearby buildings. One possibility is at a height of 1.5*R*, as shown in Figure 18. However, this is usually not feasible. If an internal space is to be pressurized relative to ambient conditions, the pressure must be known on each exterior surface in contact with the space. For example, a room at the northeast corner of the building should be pressurized with respect to pressure on both the north and east building faces, and possibly the roof. In some cases, multiple probes on a single building face may be required. Figures 8 to 12 may be used as guides in locating external pressure probes. System volume and pressure control is described in Chapter 45 of the 2015 *ASHRAE Handbook—HVAC Applications*.

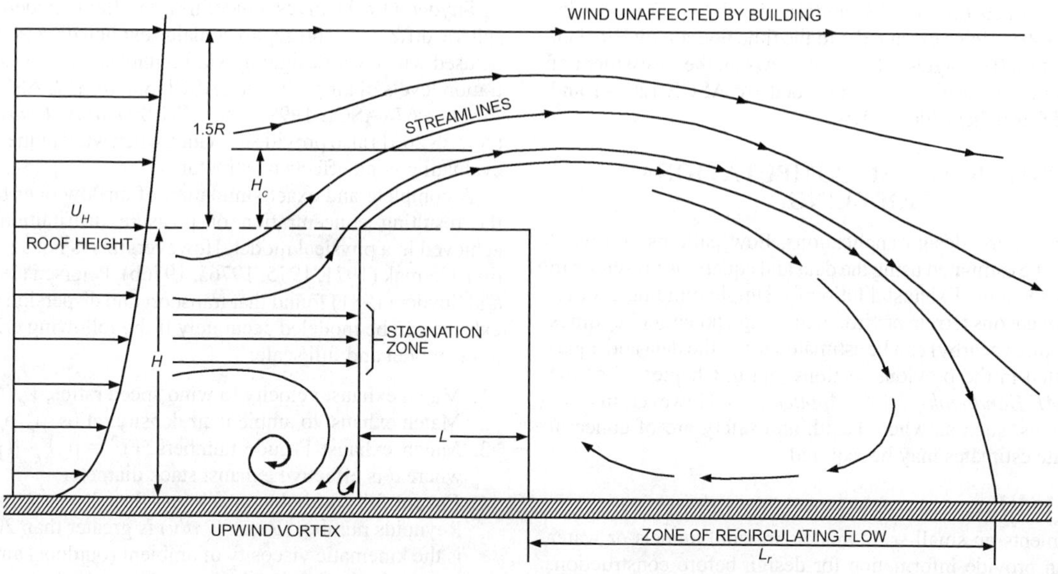

Fig. 18 Flow Patterns Around Rectangular Block Building
(modified from Hosker 1984)

6. ENVIRONMENTAL IMPACTS OF BUILDING EXTERNAL FLOW

Pollutant Dispersion and Exhaust Reentrainment

Pollutant dispersion around buildings is highly affected by the complex flow field. Contaminants are not always transported along the approaching flow direction and can be advected windward by reverse flows and retained in wake flows (Huber and Snyder 1982; Li and Meroney 1983; Stathopoulos et al. 2002). Intakes and exhausts should be installed carefully, considering wind direction and roof geometry (e.g., stack height, rooftop structures) to avoid air intake contamination and exhaust reentrainment (Gupta et al. 2012; Lazure et al. 2002; Stathopoulos et al. 2004). Empirical guidelines that can be used are given in Chapter 45 of the 2015 *ASHRAE Handbook—HVAC Applications*. More detailed prediction can be done by physical and numerical modeling, as explained in the section on Physical and Computational Modeling. State-of-the-art reviews on modeling of pollutant dispersion were performed by Canepa (2004), Di Sabatino et al. (2013), Lateb et al. (2016), Meroney (2004), and Tominaga and Stathopoulos (2013).

Pedestrian Wind Comfort and Safety

Although thermal comfort is also important [e.g., Metje et al. (2008); Stathopoulos (2006)], wind comfort and safety generally only refer to the mechanical effects of wind on people [e.g., Lawson and Penwarden (1975); Willemsen and Wisse (2007)]. Particularly near high-rise buildings, high wind velocities can occur at pedestrian level that can be uncomfortable or even dangerous. For an isolated high-rise building or one amid low rise buildings, high wind speed at pedestrian level can be caused by the downflow that creates the standing vortex and the corner streams (see Figure 1). For building groups, amplified wind speed can occur in passages through and between buildings. Uncomfortable wind conditions can be detrimental to the success of new buildings. Wise (1970) reported shops that were left untenanted because of the windy environment that discouraged shoppers. Lawson and Penwarden (1975) reported dangerous wind conditions to be responsible for the death of two elderly women who were blown over by sudden wind gusts near a high-rise building. Many current urban authorities recognize the importance of pedestrian wind comfort and wind safety, and require studies before granting building permits for new buildings or new urban areas. ASCE (2004) documented the state of the art of outdoor human comfort and its assessment. The first standard on wind comfort and wind safety was developed in the Netherlands and published in 2006 (NEN *Standard* 8100; Willemsen and Wisse 2007) and applied in several published case studies [e.g., Blocken et al. (2012)]. Reviews on studies of pedestrian wind comfort and safety were provided by Blocken (2014), Blocken and Stathopoulos (2013), Blocken et al. (2016), Mochida and Lun (2008), and Stathopoulos (2006). Although laser Doppler anemometry, particle image velocimetry, and large-eddy simulation (LES) are inherently more accurate techniques, Blocken et al. (2016) recommended faster and less expensive techniques for pedestrian-level wind (PLW) studies, such as hot-wire anemometry, Irwin probes, or steady Reynolds-averaged Navier-Stokes computational fluid dynamics (RANS CFD) simulations. The reason is that their lower accuracy at lower amplification factors does not necessarily compromise the accuracy of PLW comfort assessment, because the higher amplification factors provide the largest contribution to the discomfort exceedance probability in the comfort criterion.

Wind-Driven Rain on Buildings

Wind-driven rain (WDR), also called **driving rain,** is one of the most important moisture sources for building facades. It is an essential boundary condition for the analysis of the hygrothermal behavior and durability of historical and contemporary building facade components (Blocken and Carmeliet 2004; Dalgliesh and Surry 2003; Masters et al. 2008; Sanders 1996; Tang et al. 2004).

Wind-driven rain can be assessed by full-scale measurements, wind tunnel measurements, semiempirical formulas, or numerical simulation with CFD. The experimental methods consist of measuring WDR with WDR gages. However, for practical purposes, measurements are generally time consuming, expensive, and often impractical. Blocken and Carmeliet (2006) and Högberg et al. (1999) found that WDR measurements are very prone to error. In addition, measurements made on facades of a particular building at a particular site have limited applicability to facades of other buildings at other sites. This awareness has led researchers to develop calculation models, which have been progressively improved throughout the years. Today, the most advanced and most frequently used models are the semiempirical model in ISO *Standard* 15927-3 (ISO model), the semiempirical model by Straube (1998) and

Straube and Burnett (2000) (SB model), and the CFD model by Choi (1991, 1993, 1994) extended into the time domain by Blocken and Carmeliet (2002). State-of-the-art reviews on the assessment of WDR on building facades were provided by ASCE (2014) and Blocken and Carmeliet (2004, 2010).

7. PHYSICAL AND COMPUTATIONAL MODELING

For many routine design applications, flow patterns and wind pressures can be estimated using the data and equations presented in the previous sections. Exhaust dilution for simple building geometries in homogeneous terrain environments (e.g., no larger buildings or terrain features nearby) can be estimated using the data and equations presented in the previous sections and in Chapter 45 of the 2015 *ASHRAE Handbook—HVAC Applications*. However, in critical applications, such as where health and safety are of concern, more accurate estimates may be required.

Physical Modeling

Measurements on small-scale models in wind tunnels or water channels can provide information for design before construction. These measurements can also be used as an economical method of performance evaluation for existing facilities. Full-scale testing is not generally useful in the initial design phase because of the time and expense required to obtain meaningful information, but it is useful for verifying data derived from physical modeling and for planning remedial changes to improve existing facilities (Cochran 2006).

Detailed accounts of physical modeling, field measurements and applications, and engineering problems resulting from atmospheric flow around buildings are available in international journals, proceedings of conferences, and research reports on wind engineering (see the Bibliography).

The wind tunnel is the main tool used to assess and understand airflow around buildings. Water channels or tanks can also be used, but are more difficult to implement and give only qualitative results for some cases. Models of buildings, complexes, and the local surrounding topography are constructed and tested in a simulated turbulent atmospheric boundary layer. Airflow, wind pressures, snow loads, structural response, or pollutant concentrations can then be measured directly by properly scaling wind, building geometry, and exhaust flow characteristics. Wind tunnel studies of natural ventilation are particularly suitable for buildings with large openings that provide a strong coupling between outdoor wind flow and indoor airflow (Karava et al. 2011; Kato et al. 1992). Dalgliesh (1975) and Petersen (1987a) found generally good agreement between the results of wind tunnel simulations and corresponding full-scale data. Cochran (1992) and Cochran and Cermak (1992) found good agreement between model and full-scale measurements of low-rise architectural aerodynamics and cladding pressures, respectively. Stathopoulos et al. (1999, 2002, 2004) obtained good agreement between model and full-scale measurements of the dispersion of gaseous pollutants from rooftop stacks on two different buildings in an urban environment.

Similarity Requirements

Physical modeling is most appropriate for applications involving small-scale atmospheric motions, such as recirculation of exhaust downwind of a laboratory, wind loads on structures, wind speeds around building clusters, snow loads on roofs, and airflow over hills or other terrain features. Winds associated with tornadoes, thunderstorms, and large-scale atmospheric motion cannot currently be physically modeled accurately, although the physical modeling of tornadoes and thunderstorm downbursts is a current topic of significant research.

Snyder (1981) gives guidelines for fluid modeling of atmospheric diffusion. This report contains explicit directions and should be used whenever designing wind tunnel studies to assess concentration levels of air pollutants. ASCE *Standard* 7, ASCE *Manual of Practice* 67 (ASCE 1999), and AWES *Quality Assurance Manual* (AWES 2001) also provide guidance when wind tunnels are used for evaluating wind effects on structures.

A complete and exact simulation of airflow over buildings and the resulting concentration or pressure distributions cannot be achieved in a physical model. However, this is not a serious limitation. Cermak (1971, 1975, 1976a, 1976b), Petersen (1987a, 1987b), and Snyder (1981) found that transport and dispersion of laboratory exhaust can be modeled accurately if the following criteria are met in the model and full scale:

1. Match exhaust velocity to wind speed ratios, V_e/U_H.
2. Match exhaust to ambient air density ratios, ρ_e/ρ_a.
3. Match exhaust Froude numbers. $Fr^2 = \rho_a V_e^2/[(\rho_e - \rho_a)gd]$, where d is effective exhaust stack diameter.
4. Ensure fully turbulent stack gas flow by ensuring stack flow Reynolds number ($Re_s = V_e d/\nu$) is greater than 2000 [where ν is the kinematic viscosity of ambient (outdoor) air], or by placing an obstruction inside the stack to enhance turbulence.
5. Ensure fully turbulent wind flow.
6. Scale all dimensions and roughness by a common factor.
7. Match atmospheric stability by the bulk Richardson number (Cermak 1975). For most applications related to airflow around buildings, neutral stratification is assumed, and no Richardson number matching is required.
8. Match mean velocity and turbulence distributions in the wind.
9. Ensure building wind Reynolds number ($Re_b = U_H R/\nu$) is greater than 11,000 for sharp-edged structures, or greater than 90,000 for round-edged structures.
10. Ensure less than 5% blockage of wind tunnel cross section.

For wind speeds, flow patterns, or pressure distributions around buildings, only conditions 5 to 10 are necessary. Usually, each wind tunnel study requires a detailed assessment to determine the appropriate parameters to match in the model and full scale.

In wind tunnel simulations of exhaust gas recirculation, buoyancy of the exhaust gas (condition 3) is often not modeled. This allows using a high wind tunnel speed or a smaller model to achieve high enough Reynolds numbers (conditions 4, 5, and 9). Neglecting buoyancy is justified if density of building exhaust air is within 10% of the ambient (outdoor) air. Also, critical minimum dilution D_{crit} occurs generally at wind speeds high enough to produce a well-mixed, neutrally stable atmosphere, allowing stability matching (condition 7) to be neglected (see Chapter 45 of the 2015 *ASHRAE Handbook—HVAC Applications* for discussion of D_{crit}). However, in some cases and depending on emission sources, calm conditions may produce critical dilution. Nevertheless, omission of conditions 3 and 7 simplifies the test procedure considerably, reducing both testing time and cost.

Buoyancy should be properly simulated for high-temperature exhausts such as boilers and diesel generators. Equality of model and prototype Froude numbers (condition 3) requires tunnel speeds of less than 100 fpm for testing. However, greater tunnel speeds may be needed to meet the minimum building Reynolds number requirement (condition 4).

Wind Simulation Facilities

Boundary-layer wind tunnels are required for conducting most wind studies. The wind tunnel test section should be long enough to establish, upwind of the model building, a deep boundary layer that slowly changes with downwind distance.

Other important wind tunnel characteristics include width and height of the test section, range of wind speeds, roof adjustability, and temperature control. Larger models can be used in tunnels that are wider and taller, which, in turn, give better measurement resolution. Model blockage effects can be minimized by an adjustable roof height. Temperature control of the tunnel surface and airflow is required when atmospheric conditions other than neutral stability are to be simulated. Boundary-layer characteristics appropriate for the site are established by using roughness elements on the tunnel floor that produce mean velocity, turbulence intensity profiles, and spectra characteristic of full scale.

Water can also be used for the modeling fluid if an appropriate flow facility is available. Flow facilities may be in the form of a tunnel, tank, or open channel. Water tanks with a free surface ranging in size up to that of a wind tunnel test section have been used by towing a model (upside down) through the nonflowing fluid. Stable stratification can be obtained by adding a salt solution. This technique does not allow development of a boundary layer and therefore yields only approximate, qualitative information on flow around buildings. Water channels can be designed to develop thick, turbulent boundary layers similar to those developed in the wind tunnel. One advantage of such a flow system is ease of flow visualization, but this is offset by a greater difficulty in developing the correct turbulence structure and the measurement of flow variables and concentrations.

Designing Model Test Programs

The first step in planning a test program is selecting the model length scale. This choice depends on cross-sectional dimensions of the test section, dimensions of the buildings to be modeled, and/or topographic features and thickness of the simulated atmospheric boundary layer. Typical geometric scales range from about 120:1 to 1000:1.

Because a large model is desirable to meet minimum Reynolds and Froude number requirements, a wide test section is advantageous. In general, the model at any section should be small compared to the test section area so that blockage is less than 5% (Melbourne 1982).

The test program must include specifications of the meteorological variables to be considered (e.g., wind direction, wind speed, thermal stability). Data taken at the nearest meteorological station should be reviewed to obtain a realistic assessment of wind climate for a particular site. Ordinarily, local winds around a building, pressures, and/or concentrations are measured for 16 wind directions (e.g., 22.5° intervals). This is easily accomplished by mounting the building model and its nearby surroundings on a turntable. More than 16 wind directions are required for highly toxic exhausts or for finding peak fluctuating pressures on a building. If only local wind information and pressures are of interest, testing at one wind speed with neutral stability is sufficient.

Computational Modeling

Computational fluid dynamics (CFD) models attempt to resolve airflow around buildings by solving the Navier-Stokes equations or an approximate form of these equations in discretized form. The potential for computational wind engineering (CWE) has increased tremendously in the past decades. Nevertheless, there are some topics for which CWE in its current stage remains inappropriate.

According to Stathopoulos (2000, 2002), there is great potential for CWE, but the numerical wind tunnel "is still virtual rather than real." According to Murakami (2000), CWE has become a more popular tool, but results usually include numerical errors and prediction inaccuracies. According to a review by Blocken (2014), since 1960, computational wind engineering (CWE) has undergone a successful transition from an emerging field into an increasingly established field in wind engineering research, practice, and education, and its application has continued to spread to a very large range of topics, from pedestrian wind conditions to natural ventilation to pollutant dispersion around buildings. However, in line with the reviews by Stathopoulos (1997, 2000, 2002), it is clear that the largest potential of CWE is still in the field of environmental wind engineering rather than structural wind engineering. Indeed, although CWE can adequately provide mean values of variables for pedestrian wind comfort and wind safety, natural ventilation, or wind-driven rain studies, correct prediction of peak values for wind loading studies, for example, remains very difficult.

Methods for predicting turbulent flow around buildings include the following.

Direct numerical simulation (DNS) directly resolves all the spatial and temporal scales in the flow based on the exact Navier-Stokes equations. This requires very extensive computational resources (runs lasting from several hours to days, depending on computer characteristics, power, and capacity) and can at present only be applied for flow in simple geometries and at low Reynolds numbers (Re). For complex, high-Re flows in wind engineering, application of DNS will not be possible in the foreseeable future.

Large eddy simulation (LES) is a simplified method in which the spatially filtered Navier-Stokes equations are solved. Turbulent structures larger than the filter (sometimes taken equal to the grid size) are explicitly solved, whereas those smaller than the filter are modeled (i.e., approximated) by a subfilter model. Information on filtering and subfilter models can be found in Ferziger and Peric (2002), Geurts (2003), and Meyers et al. (2008).

In **Reynolds-averaged Navier-Stokes (RANS) simulation,** the equations are obtained by averaging the Navier-Stokes equations (time-averaging if the flow is statistically steady, or ensemble-averaging for time-dependent flows). With RANS, only the mean flow is solved, whereas all scales of turbulence must be modeled. Averaging generates additional unknowns for which turbulence models are required. Many turbulence models are available, but no single turbulence model is universally accepted as being the best for all types of applications.

In addition, hybrid RANS/LES approaches are available, in which **unsteady RANS (URANS)** is used near the wall, and LES in the rest of the flow field. This avoids the excessively high near-wall grid resolution required for application of LES near walls in high-Re flow problems. An example of a hybrid RANS/LES approach is **detached eddy simulation (DES)**, as proposed by Spalart et al. (1997).

The statistically steady RANS method is the most widely applied and validated in CWE. It has been used for a wide range of building applications, including estimating pressure coefficients (Meroney et al. 2002; Murakami et al. 1992; Oliveira and Younis 2000; Richards and Hoxey 1992; Stathopoulos 1997; Stathopoulos and Zhou 1993), natural ventilation (Chen 2009; Evola and Popov 2006; Kato et al. 1997; Norton et al. 2009; Ramponi and Blocken 2012; van Hooff and Blocken 2010), wind-driven rain (Blocken and Carmeliet 2004; 2010; Choi 1993, 1994; Tang and Davidson 2004), pollutant dispersion (Cowan et al. 1997; Dawson et al. 1991; Gousseau et al. 2011; Leitl et al. 1997; Li and Stathopoulos 1997; Meroney 2004; Meroney et al. 1999; Tominaga and Stathopoulos 2010, 2011, 2013), pedestrian wind conditions (Blocken et al. 2008, 2012; Richards et al. 2002; Stathopoulos and Baskaran 1996; Yoshie et al. 2007), snow drift (Sundsbo 1998; Thiis 2000; Tominaga and Mochida 1999), and cooling tower drift (Meroney 2006, 2008). Although many past applications of RANS have been limited to isolated buildings or relatively simple building arrangements, large and sometimes very large discrepancies have been found in comparisons with wind tunnel and full-scale measurements. These are at least partly attributed to turbulence model limitations and to the statistically steady solution of flows that exhibit pronounced transient features, such as intermittent separation, recirculation zones, and vortex shedding [e.g., Murakami (1993), Tominaga et al. (2008a)]. In addition, a wide range of other computational aspects can contribute to uncertainties and errors, divided by COST 732 (Franke et al. 2007) into two broad categories: physical and numerical. **Physical modeling errors** and uncertainties result from assumptions and approximations made in the mathematical description of the physical process. Examples are simplifications of the actual physical complexity (e.g., using RANS instead of DNS) and uncertainties and/or simplifications of the geometric and physical boundary conditions. **Numerical errors** and uncertainties are the result of the numerical solution of the mathematical model. Examples are computer programming errors, computer round-off errors, spatial and temporal discretization errors, and iterative convergence errors.

LES is a time-dependent approach in which more of the turbulence is resolved. It therefore has a larger potential to provide accurate results than statistically steady RANS simulations (Murakami et al. 1992; Tominaga et al. 1997). LES also provides more information about the flow, such as instantaneous and peak wind speeds, pressures, and pollutant concentrations. However, it requires considerably higher CPU times and memory than RANS. It also requires time- and space-resolved data as boundary conditions to properly simulate inflow. Such experimental data are rarely available in practice (Franke et al. 2007). LES is also considered to require more experience for users to apply effectively than does RANS. Several studies have compared RANS and LES modeling for atmospheric dispersion for generic configurations such as isolated buildings (Tominaga and Stathopoulos 2010) and street canyons (Salim et al. 2011; Tominaga and Stathopoulos 2011) and for actual urban environments (Gousseau et al. 2011; Hanna et al. 2006), where LES is shown to consistently outperform steady RANS modeling. However, the drawbacks of LES imply that the practical application of CWE will continue to be mainly based on statistically steady RANS for a considerable while.

Guidelines for using CFD have been developed and assembled to help users avoid, reduce, and estimate errors and uncertainties in applying CFD. ERCOFTAC (2000) provides extensive guidelines for industrial CFD applications, many of which are also applicable to CWE. Franke et al. (2007) assembled a comprehensive best-practice guideline document for CFD simulation of flows in the urban environment. Important guidelines for application of CFD to pedestrian wind conditions around buildings and for predicting wind loads on buildings have been developed by the Architectural Institute of Japan and reported by Mochida et al. (2002), Tamura et al. (2008), Tominaga et al. (2008b), and Yoshie et al. (2007). A set of ten tips and tricks for CFD simulations in urban physics has been provided by Blocken (2015). Other efforts have focused on specific problems, such as those encountered in simulating equilibrium atmospheric boundary layers in computational domains [e.g., Balogh and Parente (2015); Blocken et al. (2007a, 2007b); Gorlé et al. (2009); Hargreaves and Wright (2007); Parente et al. (2011); Richards and Hoxey (1993); Richards and Norris (2011, 2015); Yang et al. (2008)]. Most of these guidelines apply to statistically steady RANS simulations.

Regardless of whether RANS or LES is used, evaluating the accuracy of CFD results by comparing them with wind tunnel or field experiments is very important because turbulence models are based on assumptions; no turbulence model is universally valid for all applications. Physical modeling therefore remains an indispensable tool in (computational) wind engineering.

8. SYMBOLS

a = exponent in power law wind speed profile for local building terrain, Equation (4) and Table 1, dimensionless
A_L = flow leakage area, Equation (7), ft^2
a_{met} = exponent a for the meteorological station, Equation (4) and Table 1, dimensionless
B_L = larger of two upwind building face dimensions H and W, Equation (1), ft
B_s = smaller of two upwind building face dimensions H and W, Equation (1), ft
C_p = local wind pressure coefficient for building surface, Equation (3), dimensionless
C_s = surface-averaged pressure coefficient, Figure 6, dimensionless
d = effective stack diameter, ft
D_{crit} = critical dilution factor at roof level for uncapped vertical exhaust at critical wind speed (see Chapter 45 of the 2015 *ASHRAE Handbook—HVAC Applications*), dimensionless
Fr = Froude number, dimensionless
F_{sys} = system flow resistance, Equation (7), dimensionless
g = acceleration of gravity, 32.2 ft/s^2
g_c = gravitational proportionality constant, Equations (2), (5), (6), (9), 32.2 ft·lb$_m$/lb$_f$·s^2
H = wall height above ground on upwind building face, Equation (4) and Figure 3, ft
H_c = maximum height above roof level of upwind roof edge flow recirculation zone, Figure 4, ft
H_{met} = height of anemometer at meteorological station, Equation (4), ft
h_s = exhaust stack height (typically above roof unless otherwise specified, ft (see Chapter 45 in the 2015 *ASHRAE Handbook—HVAC Applications*)
L = length of building in wind direction, Figure 3, ft
L_c = length of upwind roof edge recirculation zone, Figure 4, ft
L_r = length of flow recirculation zone behind rooftop obstacle or building, Figure 4, ft
p_s = wind pressure difference between exterior building surface and local ambient (outdoor) atmospheric pressure at same elevation in undisturbed approach wind, Equation (3), lb$_f$/ft^2
p_v = wind velocity pressure at roof level, Equation (2), lb$_f$/ft^2
Q = volumetric flow rate, Equation (7), cfm
R = scaling length for roof flow patterns, Equation (1), ft
Re_b = building Reynolds number, dimensionless
Re_s = stack flow Reynolds number, dimensionless
S = stretched-string distance; shortest distance from exhaust to intake over obstacles and along building surface, ft (see Chapter 45 in the 2015 *ASHRAE Handbook—HVAC Applications*)
U_{annual} = annual average of hourly wind speeds U_{met}, Table 2, mph
U_H = mean wind speed at height H of upwind wall in undisturbed flow approaching building, Equation (2) and Figure 4, mph
U_{met} = meteorological station hourly wind speed, measured at height H_{met} above ground in smooth terrain, Equation (4) and Table 2, mph
V_e = exhaust face velocity, mph
W = width of upwind building face, Figure 3, ft

Greek

δ = fully developed atmospheric boundary layer thickness, Equation (4) and Table 1, ft
δ_{met} = atmospheric boundary layer thickness at meteorological station, Equation (4) and Table 1, ft
Δp_{fan} = pressure rise across fan, Equation (7), psi
$\Delta p_{fan\,eff}$ = effective pressure rise across fan, Equation (8), psi
Δp_{wind} = wind-induced pressure, Equations (8) and (9), psi
θ = angle between perpendicular line from upwind building face and wind direction, Figures 8 to 12, degrees
ν = kinematic viscosity of ambient (outdoor) air, ft^2/s
ρ_a = ambient (outdoor) air density, Equation (2), lb$_m$/ft^3
ρ_e = density of exhaust gas mixture, lb$_m$/ft^3

REFERENCES

ASHRAE members can access *ASHRAE Journal* articles and ASHRAE research project final reports at technologyportal .ashrae.org. Articles and reports are also available for purchase by nonmembers in the online ASHRAE Bookstore at www.ashrae.org /bookstore.

Akins, R.E., J.A. Peterka, and J.E. Cermak. 1979. Averaged pressure coefficients for rectangular buildings. *Wind Engineering: Proceedings of the Fifth International Conference*, vol. 7, pp. 369-380.

ASCE. 2010. Minimum design loads for buildings and other structures. *Standard* ASCE/SEI 7-10. American Society of Civil Engineers, Reston, VA.

ASCE. 1999. Wind tunnel studies of buildings and structures. *ASCE Manuals and Reports on Engineering Practice* 67. American Society of Civil Engineers, Reston, VA.

ASCE. 2004. *Outdoor human comfort and its assessment: State of the art.* American Society of Civil Engineers Task Committee on Outdoor Human Comfort of the Aerodynamics Committee, Reston, VA.

ASCE. 2014. Wind-driven rain effects on buildings. *Report*, Task Committee on Wind-Driven Rain Effects Environmental Wind Engineering Committee—Technical Council on Wind Engineering. American Society of Civil Engineers, Reston, VA.

AWES. 2001. *Quality assurance manual—Wind engineering studies of buildings.* AWES-QAM-1-2001. The Australasian Wind Engineering Society, Melbourne.

Bailey, P.A., and K.C.S. Kwok. 1985. Interference excitation of twin tall buildings. *Wind Engineering and Industrial Aerodynamics* 21:323-338.

Bair, F.E. 1992. *The weather almanac*, 6th ed. Gale Research, Inc., Detroit.

Balogh, M., and A Parente. 2015. Realistic boundary conditions for the simulation of atmospheric boundary layer flows using an improved k-ε model. *Journal of Wind Engineering and Industrial Aerodynamics* 144(9):183-190.

Beranek, W.J., and H. van Kloten. 1979. Limiting wind nuisance around buildings, part 1—Stichting Bouwresearch no. 65. Kluwer Technische Boeken BV, Deventer, The Netherlands.

Blocken, B. 2014. 50 years of computational wind engineering: Past, present and future. *Journal of Wind Engineering and Industrial Aerodynamics* 129:69-102.

Blocken, B. 2015. Computational fluid dynamics for urban physics: Importance, scales, possibilities, limitations and ten tips and tricks towards accurate and reliable simulations. *Building and Environment* 91:219-245.

Blocken, B., and J. Carmeliet. 2002. Spatial and temporal distribution of driving rain on a low-rise building. *Wind and Structures* 5(5):441-462.

Blocken, B., and J. Carmeliet. 2004. A review of wind-driven rain research in building science. *Journal of Wind Engineering and Industrial Aerodynamics* 92(13):1079-1130.

Blocken, B., and J. Carmeliet. 2006. On the accuracy of wind-driven rain measurements on buildings. *Building and Environment* 41(12):1798-1810.

Blocken, B., and J. Carmeliet. 2010. Overview of three state-of-the-art wind-driven rain assessment models and comparison based on model theory. *Building and Environment* 45(3):691-703.

Blocken, B., and T. Stathopoulos. 2013. Editorial to virtual special issue: CFD simulation of pedestrian-level wind conditions around buildings: Past achievements and prospects. *Journal of Wind Engineering and Industrial Aerodynamics* 121:138-145.

Blocken, B., J. Carmeliet, and T. Stathopoulos. 2007a. CFD evaluation of the wind speed conditions in passages between buildings—Effect of wall-function roughness modifications on the atmospheric boundary layer flow. *Journal of Wind Engineering and Industrial Aerodynamics* 95(9-11):941-962.

Blocken, B., T. Stathopoulos, and J. Carmeliet. 2007b. CFD simulation of the atmospheric boundary layer: Wall function problems. *Atmospheric Environment* 41(2):238-252.

Blocken, B., P. Moonen, T. Stathopoulos, and J. Carmeliet. 2008. A numerical study on the existence of the Venturi effect in passages between perpendicular buildings. *Journal of Engineering Mechanics—ASCE* 134(12).

Blocken, B., T. Stathopoulos, J. Carmeliet, and J.L.M. Henson. 2011. Application of CFD in building performance simulation for the outdoor environment: An overview. *Journal of Building Performance Simulation* 4(2):157-184.

Blocken, B., W.D. Janssen, and T. van Hooff. 2012. CFD simulation for pedestrian wind comfort and wind safety in urban areas: General decision framework and case study for the Eindhoven University campus. *Environmental Modelling & Software* 30:15-34.

Blocken, B., T. Stathopoulos, and J.P.A.J. van Beeck. 2016. Pedestrian-level wind conditions around buildings: Review of wind-tunnel and CFD techniques and their accuracy for wind comfort assessment. *Building and Environment* 100:50-81.

Canepa, E. 2004. An overview about the study of downwash effects on dispersion of airborne pollutants. *Environmental Modelling & Software* 19(12):1077-1087.

Cermak, J.E. 1971. Laboratory simulation of the atmospheric boundary layer. *AIAA Journal* 9(9):1746.

Cermak, J.E. 1975. Applications of fluid mechanics to wind engineering. *Journal of Fluid Engineering, Transactions of ASME* 97:9.

Cermak, J.E. 1976a. Nature of airflow around buildings. *ASHRAE Transactions* 82(1):1044-1060.

Cermak, J.E. 1976b. Aerodynamics of buildings. *Annual Review of Fluid Mechanics* 8:75.

Chen, Q. 2009. Ventilation performance prediction for buildings: A method overview and recent applications. *Building and Environment* 44(4):848-858.

Choi, E.C.C. 1991. Numerical simulation of wind-driven rain falling onto a 2-D building. *Asia Pacific Conference on Computational Mechanics*, Hong Kong, pp. 1721-1728.

Choi, E.C.C. 1993. Simulation of wind-driven rain around a building. *Journal of Wind Engineering and Industrial Aerodynamics* 46/47:721-729.

Choi, E.C.C. 1994. Determination of wind-driven rain intensity on building faces. *Journal of Wind Engineering and Industrial Aerodynamics* 51:55-69.

Clarke, J.H. 1967. Airflow around buildings. *Heating, Piping and Air Conditioning* 39(5):145.

Cochran, L.S. 1992. Low-rise architectural aerodynamics: The Texas Tech University experimental building. *Architectural Science Review* 35(4): 131-136.

Cochran, L.S. 2006. State of the art review of wind tunnels and physical modeling to obtain structural loads and cladding pressures. *Architectural Science Review* 50(1):7-16.

Cochran, L.S., and J.E. Cermak. 1992. Full and model scale cladding pressures on the Texas Tech University experimental building. *Journal of Wind Engineering and Industrial Aerodynamics* 41-44:1589-1600.

Cochran, L.S., and E.C. English. 1997. Reduction of wind loads by architectural features. *Architectural Science Review* 40(3):79-87.

Cochran, L.S., J.A. Peterka, and R.J. Derickson. 1999. Roof surface wind speed distributions on low-rise buildings. *Architectural Science Review* 42(3):151-160.

Cowan, I.R., I.P. Castro, and A.G. Robins. 1997. Numerical considerations for simulations of flow and dispersion around buildings. *Journal of Wind Engineering and Industrial Aerodynamics* 67/68:535-545.

Dalgliesh, W.A. 1975. Comparison of model/full-scale wind pressures on a high-rise building. *Journal of Industrial Aerodynamics* 1:55-66.

Dalgliesh, W.A., and D. Surry. 2003. BLWT, CFD and HAM modelling vs. the real world: Bridging the gaps with full-scale measurements. *Journal of Wind Engineering and Industrial Aerodynamics* 91(12-15):1651-1669.

Davenport, A.G., and H.Y.L. Hui. 1982. *External and internal wind pressures on cladding of buildings.* Boundary Layer Wind Tunnel Laboratory, University of Western Ontario, London, Canada. BLWT-820133.

Dawson, P., D.E. Stock, and B. Lamb. 1991. The numerical simulation of airflow and dispersion in three-dimensional atmospheric recirculation zones. *Journal of Applied Meteorology* 30:1005-1024.

Deaves, D.M. 1981. Computations of wind flow over changes in surface roughness. *Journal of Wind Engineering and Industrial Aerodynamics* 7:65-94.

Deaves, D.M., and R.I. Harris. 1978. A mathematical model of the structure of strong winds. *Report* 76. Construction Industry Research and Information Association (U.K.).

Di Sabatino, S., R. Buccolieri, and P. Salizzoni. 2013. Recent advancements in numerical modelling of flow and dispersion in urban areas: A short review. *International Journal Environment and Pollution* 52(3-4):172-191.

DOC. 1968. *Climatic atlas of the United States.* U.S. Department of Commerce, Washington, D.C.

English, E.C., and F.R. Fricke. 1997. The interference index and its prediction using a neural network analysis of wind tunnel data. *Fourth Asia-Pacific Symposium on Wind Engineering*, APSOWE IV University of Queensland, pp. 363-366.

ERCOFTAC. 2000. *Special interest group on quality and trust in industrial CFD: Best practice guidelines.* M. Casey, and T. Wintergerste, eds. European Research Community on Flow, Turbulence and Combustion, Brussels.

Evola, G., and V. Popov. 2006. Computational analysis of wind driven natural ventilation in buildings. *Energy and Buildings* 38(5):491-501.

Ferziger, J.H., and M. Peric. 2002. *Computational methods for fluid mechanics*. Springer.

Feustel, H.E., and J. Dieris. 1992. A survey of airflow models for multizone buildings. *Energy and Buildings* 18:79-100.

Franke, J., A. Hellsten, H. Schlünzen, and B. Carissimo, eds. 2007. *Best practice guideline for the CFD simulation of flows in the urban environment. COST action 732: Quality assurance and improvement of microscale meteorological models*. European Cooperation in the field of Scientific and Technical Research, Brussels.

Geurts, B.J. 2003. *Elements of direct and large-eddy simulation*. Edwards Publishing, Las Vegas.

Gousseau, P., B. Blocken, T. Stathopoulos, and G.J.F. van Heijst. 2011. CFD simulation of near-field pollutant dispersion on a high-resolution grid: A case study by LES and RANS for a building group in downtown Montreal. *Atmospheric Environment* 45(2):428-438.

Gupta, A., T. Stathopoulos, and P. Saathoff. 2012. Wind tunnel investigation of the downwash effect of a rooftop structure on plume dispersion. *Atmospheric Environment* 46:496-507.

Hanna, S.R., M.J. Brown, F.E. Camelli, S.T. Chan, W.J. Coirier, O.R. Hansen, A.H. Huber, S. Kim, and R.M. Reynolds. 2006. Detailed simulations of atmospheric flow and dispersion in downtown Manhattan. An application of five computational fluid dynamics models. *Bulletin of the American Meteorological Society* 87:1713-1726.

Hargreaves, D.M., and N.G. Wright. 2007. On the use of the k-ε model in commercial CFD software to model the neutral atmospheric boundary layer. *Journal of Wind Engineering and Industrial Aerodynamics* 95(5):355-369.

Högberg, A.B., M.K. Kragh, and F.J.R. van Mook. 1999. A comparison of driving rain measurements with different gauges. *Proceedings of the 5th Symposium on Building Physics in the Nordic Countries*, Gothenburg, pp. 361-368.

Holmes, J.D. 1983. *Wind loads on low rise buildings—A review*. Commonwealth Scientific and Industrial Research Organisation (CSIRO), Division of Building Research, Australia.

Holmes, J.D. 1986. *Wind loads on low-rise buildings: The structural and environmental effects of wind on buildings and structures*, Chapter 12. Faculty of Engineering, Monash University, Melbourne, Australia.

Hosker, R.P. 1984. Flow and diffusion near obstacles. In *Atmospheric science and power production*. U.S. Department of Energy DOE/TIC-27601 (DE 84005177).

Hosker, R.P. 1985. Flow around isolated structures and building clusters: A review. *ASHRAE Transactions* 91(2b):1671-1692.

Houlihan, T.F. 1965. Effects of relative wind on supply air systems. *ASHRAE Journal* 7(7):28.

Huber, A.H., and W.H. Snyder. 1982. Wind tunnel investigation of the effects of a rectangular shaped building on dispersion of effluent from short adjacent stacks. *Atmospheric Environment* 16:2837-2848.

Hunt, J.C.R., C.J. Abell, J.A. Peterka, and H. Woo. 1978. Kinematical studies of the flows around free or surface-mounted obstacles; Applying topology to flow visualization. *Journal of Fluid Mechanics* 86(1):179-200.

ISO. 2009. Hygrothermal performance of buildings—Calculation and presentation of climatic data—Part 3: Calculation of a driving rain index for vertical surfaces from hourly wind and rain data. ISO *Standard* 15927-3:2009. International Organization for Standardization, Geneva.

Karava, P., T. Stathopoulos, and A.K. Athienitis. 2011. Airflow assessment in cross-ventilated buildings with operable facade elements. *Building and Environment* 46(1):266-279.

Kato, S., S. Murakami, A. Mochida, S. Akabayashi, and Y. Tominaga. 1992. Velocity-pressure field of cross ventilation with open windows analyzed by wind tunnel and numerical simulation. *Journal of Wind Engineering and Industrial Aerodynamics* 44(1-3):2575-2586.

Kato, S., S. Murakami, T. Takahashi, and T. Gyobu. 1997. Chained analysis of wind tunnel test and CFD on cross ventilation of large-scale market building. *Journal of Wind Engineering and Industrial Aerodynamics* 67-68:573-587.

Khanduri, A.C., T. Stathopoulos, and C. Bédard. 1998. Wind-induced interference effects on buildings—A review of the state-of-the-art. *Engineering Structures* 20(7):617-630.

Lateb, M., R.N. Meroney, M. Yataghene, H. Fellouah, F. Saleh, and M.C. Boufadel. 2016. On the use of numerical modelling for near-field pollutant dispersion in urban environments. *Environmental Pollution* 208A: 271-283.

Lawson, T.V., and A.D. Penwarden. 1975. The effects of wind on people in the vicinity of buildings. *Proceedings of the 4th International Conference on Wind Effects on Buildings and Structures*, Cambridge University Press, pp. 605-622.

Lazure, L., P. Saathoff, and T. Stathopoulos, T. 2002. Air intake contamination by building exhausts: Tracer gas investigation of atmospheric dispersion models in the urban environment. *Journal of the Air & Waste Management Association* 52(2):160-166.

Leitl, B.M., P. Kastner-Klein, M. Rau, and R.N. Meroney. 1997. Concentration and flow distributions in the vicinity of U-shaped buildings: Wind-tunnel and computational data. *Journal of Wind Engineering and Industrial Aerodynamics* 67/68:745-755.

Li, W., and R.N. Meroney. 1983. Gas dispersion near a cubical model building, part I, mean concentration measurements. *Journal of Wind Engineering and Industrial Aerodynamics* 12:15-33.

Li, Y., and T. Stathopoulos. 1997. Numerical evaluation of wind-induced dispersion of pollutants around a building. *Journal of Wind Engineering and Industrial Aerodynamics* 67/68:757-766.

Masters, F.J., K.R. Gurley, and D.O. Prevatt. 2008. Full-scale simulation of turbulent wind-driven rain effects on fenestration and wall systems. 3rd International Symposium on Wind Effects on Buildings and Urban Environment, Tokyo.

Melbourne, W.H. 1979. Turbulence effects on maximum surface pressures; A mechanism and possibility of reduction. *Proceedings of the Fifth International Conference on Wind Engineering*, J.E. Cermak, ed., pp. 541-551.

Melbourne, W.H. 1982. Wind tunnel blockage effects and corrections. *Proceedings of the International Workshop on Wind Tunnel Modeling Criteria and Techniques in Civil Engineering Applications*, T.A. Reinhold, ed., pp. 197-216.

Meroney, R.N. 2004. *Wind tunnel and numerical simulation of pollution dispersion: A hybrid approach*. Invited lecture at Croucher Advanced Study Institute on Wind Tunnel Modeling, Hong Kong University of Science and Technology, 6-10 December, 2004. www.engr.colostate.edu/~meroney /projects/ASI Crocher Paper Final.pdf.

Meroney, R.N. 2006. CFD prediction of cooling tower drift. *Journal of Wind Engineering and Industrial Aerodynamics* 94(6):463-490.

Meroney, R.N. 2008. Protocol for CFD prediction of cooling-tower drift in an urban environment. *Journal of Wind Engineering and Industrial Aerodynamics* 96(10-11):1789-1804.

Meroney, R.N., B.M. Leitl, S. Rafailidis, and M. Schatzmann. 1999. Wind-tunnel and numerical modeling of flow and dispersion about several building shapes. *Journal of Wind Engineering and Industrial Aerodynamics* 81(1-3):333-345.

Meroney, R.N., C.W. Letchford, and P.P. Sarkar. 2002. Comparison of numerical and wind tunnel simulation of wind loads on smooth, rough and dual domes immersed in a boundary layer. *Wind and Structures* 5(2-4):347-358.

Metje, N., M. Sterling, and C.J. Baker. 2008. Pedestrian comfort using clothing values and body temperatures. *Journal of Wind Engineering and Industrial Aerodynamics* 96(4):412-435.

Meyers, J., B.J. Geurts, and P. Sagaut, eds. 2008. Quality and reliability of large-eddy simulations. *ERCOFTAC Series*, vol. 12. European Research Community on Flow, Turbulence, and Combustion, Lausanne, Switzerland, and Springer, Netherlands.

Mochida, A., and I.Y.F. Lun. 2008. Pedestrian wind environment and thermal comfort at pedestrian level in urban area. *Journal of Wind Engineering and Industrial Aerodynamics* 96:1498-1527.

Mochida, A., Y. Tominaga, S. Murakami, R. Yoshie, T. Ishihara, and R. Ooka. 2002. Comparison of various k-ε models and DSM to flow around a high rise building—Report of AIJ cooperative project for CFD prediction of wind environment. *Wind and Structures* 5(2-4):227-244.

Murakami, S. 1993. Comparison of various turbulence models applied to a bluff body. *Journal of Wind Engineering and Industrial Aerodynamics* 46/47:21-36.

Murakami, S. 2000. Overview of CWE 2000. International Symposium on Computational Wind Engineering. PF Consultants.

Murakami, S., A. Mochida, Y. Hayashi, and S. Sakamoto. 1992. Numerical study on velocity-pressure field and wind forces for bluff bodies by k-ε, ASM and LES. *Journal of Wind Engineering and Industrial Aerodynamics* 41-44:2841-2852.

NEN. 2006. Wind comfort and wind danger in the built environment. NEN *Standard* 8100 (in Dutch). Nederlands Normalisatie-Instituut, Delft.

Norton, T., J. Grant, R. Fallon, and D.W. Sun. 2009. Assessing the ventilation effectiveness of naturally ventilated livestock buildings under wind dominated conditions using computational fluid dynamics. *Biosystems Engineering* 103(1):78-99.

Oke, T.R. 1988. Street design and urban canopy layer climate. *Energy and Buildings* 11:103-113.

Oliveira, P.J., and B.A. Younis. 2000. On the prediction of turbulent flows around full-scale buildings. *Journal of Wind Engineering and Industrial Aerodynamics* 86(2-3):203-220.

Parente, A., C. Gorlé, J. van Beeck, and C. Benocci. 2011. Improved k-ε model and wall function formulation for the RANS simulation of ABL flows. *Journal of Wind Engineering and Industrial Aerodynamics* 99(4):267-278.

Petersen, R.L. 1987a. Wind tunnel investigation of the effect of platform-type structures on dispersion of effluents from short stacks. *Journal of Air Pollution Control Association* 36:1347-1352.

Petersen, R.L. 1987b. Designing building exhausts to achieve acceptable concentrations of toxic effluent. *ASHRAE Transactions* 93(2):2165-2185.

Ramponi, R., and B. Blocken. 2012. CFD simulation of cross-ventilation for a generic isolated building: Impact of computational parameters. *Building and Environment* 53:34-48.

Richards, P.J., and R.P. Hoxey. 1992. Computational and wind tunnel modelling of mean wind loads on the Silsoe structures building. *Journal of Wind Engineering and Industrial Aerodynamics* 43(1-3):1641-1652.

Richards, P.J., and R.P. Hoxey. 1993. Appropriate boundary conditions for computational wind engineering models using the k-ε turbulence model. *Journal of Wind Engineering and Industrial Aerodynamics* 46/47:145-153.

Richards, P.J., and S.E. Norris. 2011. Appropriate boundary conditions for computational wind engineering models revisited. *Journal of Wind Engineering and Industrial Aerodynamics* 99(4):257-266.

Richards, P.J., and S.E. Norris. 2015. Appropriate boundary conditions for a pressure-driven boundary layer. *Journal of Wind Engineering and Industrial Aerodynamics* 142(7):43-52.

Richards, P.J., G.D. Mallison, D. McMillan, and Y.F. Li. 2002. Pedestrian level wind speeds in downtown Auckland. *Wind and Structures* 5(2-4): 151-164.

Salim, M.S., R. Buccolieri, A. Chan, and S. Di Sabatino. 2011. Numerical simulation of atmospheric pollutant dispersion in an urban street canyon: Comparison between RANS and LES. *Journal of Wind Engineering and Industrial Aerodynamics* 99(2-3):103-113.

Sanders, C. 1996. Heat, air and moisture transfer in insulated envelope parts: Environmental conditions. International Energy Agency, Annex 24. *Final report*, vol. 2. Acco, Leuven.

SA/SNZ. 2002. Structural design actions—Part 2: Wind actions. *Standard* AS/NZS 1170.2:2002. Standards Australia International Ltd., Sydney.

Saunders, J.W., and W.H. Melbourne. 1979. Buffeting effect of upwind buildings. *Fifth International Conference on Wind Engineering.* Pergamon Press, pp. 593-606.

Sherman, M.H., and D.T. Grimsrud. 1980. The measurement of infiltration using fan pressurization and weather data. *Report* LBL-10852. Lawrence Berkeley Laboratory, University of California.

Snyder, W.H. 1981. Guideline for fluid modeling of atmospheric diffusion. Environmental Protection Agency *Report* EPA-600/881-009.

Spalart, P., W.-H. Jou, M. Strelets, and S. Allmaras. 1997. Comments on the feasibility of LES for wings and on the hybrid RANS/LES approach. *Advances in DNS/LES, 1st AFOSR International Conference on DNS/LES*, Greden Press.

Stathopoulos, T. 1997. Computational wind engineering: Past achievements and future challenges. *Journal of Wind Engineering and Industrial Aerodynamics* 67/68:509-532.

Stathopoulos, T. 2000. The numerical wind tunnel for industrial aerodynamics: Real or virtual in the new millennium? Third International Symposium on Computational Wind Engineering. PF Consultants.

Stathopoulos, T. 2002. The numerical wind tunnel for industrial aerodynamics: Real or virtual in the new millennium? *Wind and Structures* 5(2-4): 193-208.

Stathopoulos T. 2006. Pedestrian level winds and outdoor human comfort. *Journal of Wind Engineering and Industrial Aerodynamics* 94(11):769-780.

Stathopoulos, T., and B.A. Baskaran. 1996. Computer simulation of wind environmental conditions around buildings. *Engineering Structures* 18(11):876-885.

Stathopoulos, T., and R. Storms. 1986. Wind environmental conditions in passages between buildings. *Journal of Wind Engineering and Industrial Aerodynamics* 24(1):19-31.

Stathopoulos, T., and Y.S. Zhou. 1993. Numerical simulation of wind-induced pressures on buildings of various geometries. *Journal of Wind Engineering and Industrial Aerodynamics* 46/47:419-430.

Stathopoulos, T., L. Lazure, and P. Saathoff. 1999. Tracer gas investigation of reingestion of building exhaust in an urban environment. IRSST *Report* R-213, Robert-Sauvé Institute of Occupational Health and Safety Research (IRSST), Montreal, Canada.

Stathopoulos, T., L. Lazure, P. Saathoff, and X. Wei. 2002. Dilution of exhaust from a rooftop stack on a cubical building in an urban environment. *Atmospheric Environment* 36:4577-4591.

Stathopoulos, T., L. Lazure, P. Saathoff, and A. Gupta. 2004. The effect of stack height, stack location and rooftop structures on air intake contamination. A laboratory and full-scale study. IRSST *Report* R-392. Robert-Sauvé Institute of Occupational Health and Safety Research (IRSST), Montreal, Canada.

Straube, J.F. 1998. *Moisture control and enclosure wall systems*. Ph.D. dissertation, Civil Engineering, University of Waterloo, Ontario.

Straube, J.F., and E.F.P. Burnett. 2000. Simplified prediction of driving rain on buildings. *Proceedings of the International Building Physics Conference*, Eindhoven, The Netherlands, pp. 375-382.

Sundsbo, P.A. 1998. Numerical simulations of wind deflection fins to control snow accumulation in building steps. *Journal of Wind Engineering and Industrial Aerodynamics* 74-76:543-552.

Swami, M.V., and S. Chandra. 1987. Procedures for calculating natural ventilation airflow rates in buildings. *Final Report* FSEC-CR-163-86. Florida Solar Energy Center, Cape Canaveral.

Tamura, T., K. Nozawa, and K. Kondo. 2008 AIJ guide for numerical prediction of wind loads on buildings. *Journal of Wind Engineering and Industrial Aerodynamics* 96(10-11):1974-1984.

Tang, W., and C.I. Davidson. 2004. Erosion of limestone building surfaces caused by wind-driven rain: 2. Numerical modeling. *Atmospheric Environment* 38(33):5601-5609.

Tang, W., C.I. Davidson, S. Finger, and K. Vance. 2004. Erosion of limestone building surfaces caused by wind-driven rain: 1. Field measurements. *Atmospheric Environment* 38(33):5589-5599.

Thiis, T.K. 2000. A comparison of numerical simulations and full-scale measurements of snowdrifts around buildings. *Wind and Structures* 3(2): 73-81.

Tominaga, Y., and A. Mochida. 1999. CFD prediction of flowfield and snowdrift around a building complex in a snowy region. *Journal of Wind Engineering and Industrial Aerodynamics* 81(1-3):273-282.

Tominaga, Y., and T. Stathopoulos. 2010. Numerical simulation of dispersion around an isolated cubic building: Model evaluation of RANS and LES. *Building and Environment* 45(10):2231-2239.

Tominaga, Y., and T. Stathopoulos. 2011. CFD modeling of pollution dispersion in a street canyon: Comparison between LES and RANS. *Journal of Wind Engineering and Industrial Aerodynamics* 99(4):340-348.

Tominaga, Y., and T. Stathopoulos. 2013. CFD simulation of near-field pollutant dispersion in the urban environment: A review of current modelling techniques. *Atmospheric Environment* 79:716-730.

Tominaga, Y., S. Murakami, and A. Mochida. 1997. CFD prediction of gaseous diffusion around a cubic model using a dynamic mixed SGS model based on composite grid technique. *Journal of Wind Engineering and Industrial Aerodynamics* 67/68:827-841.

Tominaga, Y., A. Mochida, S. Murakami, and S. Sawaki. 2008a. Comparison of various revised k-ε models and LES applied to flow around a high-rise building model with 1:1:2 shape placed within the surface boundary layer. *Journal of Wind Engineering and Industrial Aerodynamics* 96(4): 389-411.

Tominaga, Y., A. Mochida, R. Yoshie, H. Kataoka, T. Nozu, M. Yoshikawa, and T. Shirasawa. 2008b. AIJ guidelines for practical applications of CFD to pedestrian wind environment around buildings. *Journal of Wind Engineering and Industrial Aerodynamics* 96(10-11):1749-1761.

van Hooff, T., and B. Blocken. 2010. Coupled urban wind flow and indoor natural ventilation modelling on a high-resolution grid: A case study for the Amsterdam Arena stadium. *Environmental Modelling and Software* 25(1):51-65.

Walker, I.S., D.J. Wilson, and T.W. Forest. 1996. Wind shadow model for air infiltration sheltering by upwind obstacles. *International Journal of HVAC&R Research* (now *Science and Technology for the Built Environment*) 2(4):265-283.

Walton, G.N., and W.S. Dols. 2005. *CONTAM 2.4 user guide and program documentation*. NISTIR 7251. National Institute of Standards and Technology, Gaithersburg, Maryland.

Willemsen, E., and J.A. Wisse. 2007. Design for wind comfort in The Netherlands: Procedures, criteria and open research issues. *Journal of Wind Engineering and Industrial Aerodynamics* 95(9-11):1541-1550.

Wilson, D.J. 1979. Flow patterns over flat roofed buildings and application to exhaust stack design. *ASHRAE Transactions* 85(2):284-295.

Wise, A.F.E. 1970. Wind effects due to groups of buildings. *Proceedings of the Royal Society Symposium Architectural Aerodynamics, Session 3, Effect of Buildings on the Local Wind*, London. pp. 26-27.

Yang, W., Y. Quan, X. Jin, Y. Tamura, and M. Gu. 2008. Influences of equilibrium atmosphere boundary layer and turbulence parameters on wind load distributions of low-rise buildings. *Journal of Wind Engineering and Industrial Aerodynamics* 96(10-11):2080-2092.

Yoshie, R., A. Mochida, Y. Tominaga, H. Kataoka, K. Harimoto, T. Nozu, and T. Shirasawa. 2007. Cooperative project for CFD prediction of pedestrian wind environment in the architectural institute of Japan. *Journal of Wind Engineering and Industrial Aerodynamics* 95(9-11):1551-1578.

BIBLIOGRAPHY

AIHA. 2012. Laboratory ventilation. ANSI/AIHA *Standard* Z9.5-2012. American Industrial Hygiene Association, Fairfax, VA.

ASCE. 1999. Wind tunnel studies of buildings and structures. *Manual of Practice* 67. N. Isyumov, ed. American Society of Civil Engineers, New York.

ASCE. 2012. Wind tunnel testing for buildings and other structures. ASCE/SEI *Standard* 49-12. Structural Engineering Institute, American Society of Civil Engineers, New York.

Cermak, J.E. 1977. Wind-tunnel testing of structures. *Journal of the Engineering Mechanics Division*, ASCE 103, EM6:1125.

Cermak, J.E., ed. 1979. *Wind engineering. Wind Engineering: Proceedings of the Fifth International Conference*, Colorado State University, Fort Collins, CO. Pergamon Press, New York.

Clarke, J.H. 1965. The design and location of building inlets and outlets to minimize wind effect and building reentry of exhaust fumes. *Journal of American Industrial Hygiene Association* 26:242.

CWE. 1993. Proceedings of the 1st International Symposium on Computational Wind Engineering, Tokyo, Japan. Elsevier.

CWE. 1997. Proceedings of the 2nd International Symposium on Computational Wind Engineering, Colorado State University, Fort Collins. Elsevier.

CWE. 2000. Proceedings of the 3rd International Symposium on Computational Wind Engineering. PF Consultants.

CWE. 2006. Proceedings of the 4th International Symposium on Computational Wind Engineering, Yokohama, Japan. Elsevier.

Defant, F. 1951. Local winds. In *Compendium of meteorology*, pp. 655-672. American Meteorology Society, Boston.

Elliot, W.P. 1958. The growth of the atmospheric internal boundary layer. *Transactions of the American Geophysical Union* 39:1048-1054.

ESDU. 1990. Strong winds in the atmospheric boundary layer. Part 1: Mean hourly wind speeds, pp. 15-17. *Engineering Science Data Unit*, Item 82-26, London.

Geiger, R. 1966. *The climate near the ground*. Harvard University, Cambridge.

Houghton, E.L., and N.B. Carruthers. 1976. *Wind forces on buildings and structures: An introduction*. Edward Arnold, London.

Landsberg, H. 1981. *The urban climate*. Academic Press, New York.

Meroney, R.N., and B. Bienkiewicz, eds. 1997. *Computational wind engineering 2*. Elsevier, Amsterdam.

Moonen, P., T. Defraeye, V. Dorer, B. Blocken, and J. Carmeliet. 2012. Urban physics: Effect of the microclimate on comfort, health and energy demand. *Frontiers of Architectural Research* 1(3):197-228.

Panofsky, H.A., and J.A. Dutton. 1984. *Atmospheric turbulence: Models and methods for engineering applications*. John Wiley & Sons, New York.

Simiu, V., and R. Scanlan. 1986. *Wind effects on structures: An introduction to wind engineering*, 2nd ed. Wiley Interscience, New York.

Svendsen, S.D. 1955. Driving rain. Experimental research on the resistance of external walls against rain penetration. *Report* 20, Norwegian Building Research Institute, Oslo.

WERC. 1985. *Proceedings of the 5th U.S. National Conference on Wind Engineering*, 6-8 November, Texas Tech University, Lubbock. K.C. Mehta and R.A. Dillingham, eds. Wind Engineering Research Center, Lubbock.

CHAPTER 25

HEAT, AIR, AND MOISTURE CONTROL IN BUILDING ASSEMBLIES—FUNDAMENTALS

PROPER design of space heating, cooling, and air-conditioning systems requires detailed knowledge of the building envelope's overall heat, air, and moisture performance. This chapter discusses the fundamentals of combined heat, air, and moisture movement as it relates to the analysis and design of envelope assemblies. Guidance for designing mechanical systems is found in other chapters of the *ASHRAE Handbook*.

Because heat, air, and moisture transfer are coupled and interact closely with each other, they should not be treated separately. For example, improving a building envelope's energy performance may cause moisture-related problems. Conversely, evaporation of water and removal of moisture by other means are processes that require energy. Only a sophisticated moisture control strategy can ensure hygienic conditions and adequate durability for modern, energy-efficient building assemblies. Effective moisture control design must deal with all **hygrothermal** (heat and humidity) loads acting on the building envelope.

1. FUNDAMENTALS

1.1 TERMINOLOGY AND SYMBOLS

The following heat, air, and moisture definitions, properties, and symbols are commonly used.

A **building envelope** or **building enclosure** provides physical separation between the indoor space and the outdoor environment. A **building assembly** is any part of the building envelope, such as a wall, window, or roof assembly, that faces the interior and exterior of the building. A **building component** is any element, layer, or material within a building assembly.

Heat

Specific heat capacity c is the change in heat (energy) of a unit mass of material for a unit change of temperature in Btu/lb·°F.

Volumetric heat capacity ρc is the change in heat stored in a unit volume of material for a unit change of temperature, in Btu/ft^3·°F.

Heat flux q, a vector, is the time rate of heat transfer through a unit area, in the direction perpendicular to that area, in Btu/h·ft^2.

Thermal conductivity k [in Europe, the Greek letter λ (lambda) is used] is a material property describing ability to conduct heat, and is defined by Fourier's law of heat conduction. Thermal conductivity is the property that describes heat flux through a unit thickness of a material in a direction perpendicular to the isothermal planes, induced by a unit temperature difference. (ASTM *Standard* C168 defines homogeneity.) Units are Btu·in/h·ft^2·°F (preferred) or Btu/h·ft·°F. For anisotropic materials, the direction of heat flux in the material must be noted. Thermal conductivity must be evaluated for a specific mean temperature, thickness, age, and moisture content. Thermal conductivity is normally considered an intrinsic property of a homogenous material. In porous materials, heat flow occurs by a combination of conduction, convection, and radiation, and may depend on orientation, direction, or both. When nonconductive modes of heat transfer occur within the specimen or the test specimen is nonhomogeneous, the measured property of such materials is called **apparent thermal conductivity**. The specific test conditions (e.g., sample thickness, orientation, environment, environmental pressure, surface temperature, mean temperature, temperature difference, moisture distribution) should be reported with the values of apparent thermal conductivity. The symbol k_{app} (or λ_{app}) is used to denote the absence of pure conduction or to indicate that all values reported are apparent. Materials with a low apparent thermal conductivity are called **insulation** materials (see Chapter 26 for more detail).

Thermal resistivity r_u is the reciprocal of thermal conductivity. Units are h·ft^2·°F/Btu·in.

Thermal resistance R is an extrinsic property that describes the resistance of a material layer or assembly to heat transfer. It is determined by the steady-state or time-averaged temperature difference (between two defined surfaces of a material layer within a building assembly) that induces a unit heat flux, in ft^2·h·°F/Btu. When the two defined surfaces have unequal areas, as with heat flux through material layers of nonuniform thickness, an appropriate mean area and mean thickness must be given. Thermal resistance formulas involving materials that are not uniform slabs must contain shape factors to account for the area variation involved. When heat flux occurs by conduction alone, the thermal resistance of a layer of constant thickness may be obtained by dividing the material's thickness by its thermal conductivity. When several modes of heat transfer are involved, the **apparent thermal resistance** may be obtained by dividing the material's thickness by its apparent thermal conductivity. When air circulates within or passes through insulation, as may happen in low-density fibrous materials, the apparent thermal resistance is affected. Thermal resistances of common building and insulation materials are listed in Chapter 26.

Thermal conductance C is the reciprocal of thermal resistance. Units are Btu/h·ft^2·°F.

Heat transfer or **surface film coefficient** h is the value that describes the total heat flux by both convection and radiation between a surface and the surrounding environment. It is defined as the heat transfer per unit time and unit area induced by a unit temperature difference between the surface and the reference temperature in the surrounding environment. Units are Btu/h·ft^2·°F. For convection to

The preparation of this chapter is assigned to TC 4.4, Building Materials and Building Envelope Performance.

occur, the surrounding space must be filled with a fluid, usually air. If the space is evacuated, heat flow occurs by radiation only. In the context of this discussion, **indoor** or **outdoor heat transfer** or **surface film coefficient** h_i or h_o relates to an interior or exterior surface of a building envelope assembly. The heat transfer film coefficient is also commonly known as the **surface film conductance.**

Thermal transmittance U is the quantity equal to the steady-state or time-averaged heat flux from the environment on the one side of a body to the environment on the other side, per unit temperature difference between the two environments, in Btu/h·ft²·°F. Thermal transmittance is sometimes called the **overall coefficient of heat transfer** or **U-factor**. Average thermal transmittance differs from clear-wall transmittance, in that the former considers all thermal bridge effects in the assembly.

Thermal emissivity is the ratio of radiant flux emitted by a surface to that emitted by a black surface at the same temperature. Emissivity refers to intrinsic properties of a material's surface and is defined only for a specimen of the material that is thick enough to be completely opaque and has an optically smooth surface.

Effective emittance E refers to the properties of a particular object. It depends on surface layer thickness, oxidation, roughness, etc.

Air

Air transfer M_a is the time rate of mass transfer by airflow induced by an air pressure difference, caused by wind, stack effect, or mechanical systems, in lb_m/s.

Air flux m_a, a vector, is the air transfer through a unit area in the direction perpendicular to that unit area, in lb/ft²·h.

Air permeability k_a is an intrinsic property of a porous material defined by Darcy's Law (the equation for laminar flow through porous materials). Air permeability is the quantity of air flux induced by a unit air pressure difference through a unit thickness of homogeneous porous material in the direction perpendicular to the isobaric planes. Units are in lb/ft·h·in. Hg or lb/ft·s·in. Hg.

Air permeance K_a is the extrinsic quantity equivalent to the time rate of steady-state air transfer through a unit surface of a porous membrane or layer, a unit length of joint or crack, or a local leak induced by a unit air pressure difference over that layer, joint and crack, or local leak. Units are lb/ft²·h·in. Hg for a layer, lb/ft·h·in. Hg for a joint or crack, and lb/h·in. Hg for a local leak.

Moisture

Moisture content w is the amount of moisture per unit volume of porous material, in lb/ft³.

Moisture ratio X (in weight) or Ψ (in volume) is the amount of moisture per unit weight of dry porous material or the volume of moisture per unit volume of dry material, in percent.

Specific moisture content is the ratio between a change in moisture content and the corresponding change in driving potential (i.e., relative humidity or suction).

Specific moisture ratio is the ratio between a change in moisture ratio and the corresponding change in driving potential (i.e., relative humidity or suction).

Water vapor flux m_v, a vector, is the time rate of water vapor transfer through a unit area in the direction perpendicular to that unit area, in lb/ft²·h.

Moisture transfer M_m is the moisture flow induced by a difference in suction or in relative humidity, in lb/h.

Moisture flux m_m, a vector, is the time rate of moisture transfer through a unit area in the direction perpendicular to that unit area, in lb/ft²·h.

Water vapor permeability μ_p is the steady-state water vapor flux through a unit thickness of homogeneous material in a direction perpendicular to the isobaric planes, induced by a unit partial water vapor pressure difference, under specified conditions of temperature and relative humidity. Units are lb/ft·h·in. Hg. When permeability varies with psychrometric conditions, the specific permeability defines the property at a specific condition.

Water vapor permeance M is the steady-state water vapor flux by diffusion through a unit area of a flat layer, induced by a unit partial water vapor pressure difference across that layer, in lb/ft²·h·in. Hg.

Water vapor resistance Z is the reciprocal of water vapor permeance, in ft²·h·in. Hg/lb.

Moisture permeability k_m is the steady-state moisture flux through a unit thickness of a homogeneous material in a direction perpendicular to the isosuction planes, induced by a unit difference in suction. Units are lb/ft·h·in. Hg (suction).

Moisture diffusivity D_m is the ratio between the moisture permeability and the specific moisture content, in ft²/h.

1.2 HYGROTHERMAL LOADS AND DRIVING FORCES

This section describes the hygrothermal loads acting on the building envelope. That description is used to predict the influence on the hygrothermal behavior of building assemblies, as a basis for design recommendations and moisture control measures (Künzel and Karagiozis 2004). Cooling and heating load estimations for sizing mechanical systems can be found in Chapters 17 and 18.

In Figure 1, the loads relevant for building envelope design are presented schematically for an external wall. Generally, they show diurnal and seasonal variations at the exterior surface and mainly seasonal variations at the interior surface. In sunny weather, the exterior wall surface heats by solar radiation, leading to evaporation of moisture from the surface layer. Around sunset, when solar radiation decreases, long-wave (infrared) emission to the clear sky may lead to cooling of the exterior surface below the ambient air temperature, even below the dew-point temperature, so surface condensation may occur. This phenomenon is called **undercooling**. The exterior surfaces are also exposed to moisture from precipitation and wind-driven rain.

Usually, several load cycles overlap (e.g., summer/winter, day/night, rain/sun). Therefore, a precise analysis of the expected loads should be done before designing any building envelope component. However, the magnitude of the loads is not independent of building geometry and the component's properties. Analysis of the transient hygrothermal loads is generally based on hourly meteorological

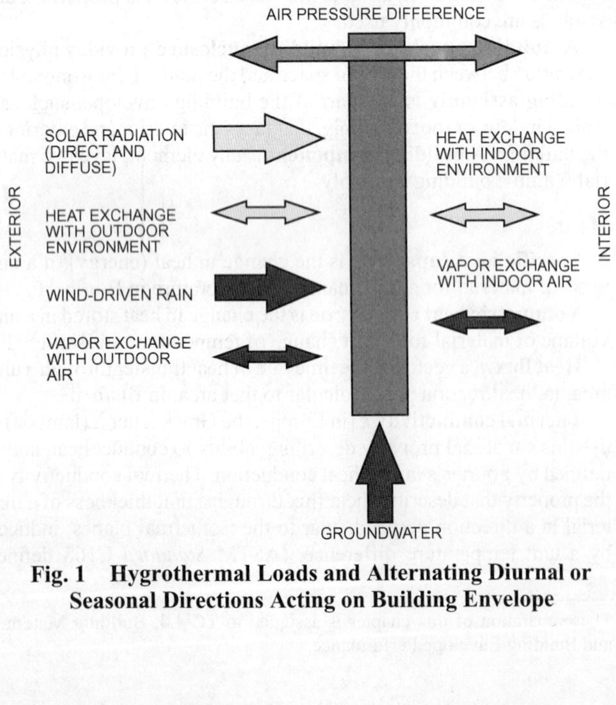

Fig. 1 Hygrothermal Loads and Alternating Diurnal or Seasonal Directions Acting on Building Envelope

data, although a shorter time step may be needed. However, determination of local conditions at the envelope's surface is complicated and requires specific experience. In some cases, computer simulations are necessary to assess the microclimate acting on differently oriented, overhang-protected, or inclined building assemblies.

Ambient Temperature and Humidity

Ambient temperature and humidity, represented by the partial water vapor pressure, are the boundary conditions always affecting both sides of the building envelope. The climate-dependent exterior conditions may show large diurnal and seasonal variations. Therefore, at least hourly data are required for detailed building simulations, though monthly data may suffice in case simple calculation methods are applicable. Chapter 14 provides such meteorological data sets, including temperature and relative humidity, for many locations worldwide. These data sets usually represent average meteorological years based on long-term observations at specific locations. However, data of more extreme climate conditions may be important to assess the risks of moisture damage. Therefore, Sanders (1996) proposed using data of the coldest or warmest year in 10 years for hygrothermal analysis instead of data from an average year. Another method to obtain a severe annual data set concerning the moisture-related damage risk starting from several decades of hourly data has been developed by Salonvaara (2011). This method analyzes the data with respect to their effect on moisture behavior of typical building assemblies. The more severe data sets increase the safety of risk prediction for the service life of building envelope components, but they are less suitable for analyzing the long-term behavior (performance over several years) of constructions because the probability of a sequence of severe years is very low. Also, note that the temperature at the building site may differ from the meteorological reference data when the site's altitude differs from that of the station recording the data. On average, there is a temperature shift of 1.2°F for every ±330 ft. The microclimate around the building may result in an additional temperature shift that depends on the season. For example, the proximity of a lake can moderate seasonal temperature variations, with higher temperatures in winter and lower temperatures in summer compared to sites without water nearby. A low-lying site experiences lower temperatures in winter, whereas city temperatures are higher year round (METEOTEST 2007).

Indoor Temperature and Humidity

Indoor conditions depend on the purpose and occupation of the building. For most commercial constructions, temperature and humidity are controlled by HVAC systems with usually well-defined set points. Indoor humidity conditions in residential buildings, however, are often influenced by the outdoor climate and by occupant behavior. (For details on this highly variable vapor release, see Chapter 36.) That water vapor must be removed by ventilation or air conditioning. The resulting relative humidity may be determined by a hygrothermal whole-building simulation or by simple estimation methods using information on moisture production, air change rates, and climate-dependent HVAC operation (TenWolde and Walker 2001). The presence of spas or swimming pools increases the load substantially. Less obvious but sometimes of equal importance are loads from the ground, from penetrating precipitation, or from construction moisture in the building materials. Moisture loads from occupant behavior show an especially transient pattern: they are characterized by peaks (e.g., cooking, showering). Humidity-buffering envelope materials, partition wall materials, and furniture (e.g., carpets, curtains, paper) help to dampen indoor humidity peaks, but they also reduce the moisture removal efficiency of intermittent ventilation (e.g., periodically opening windows, operating ventilation fans). Information on typical indoor climate conditions of special-purpose constructions such as swimming pools, spas, ice rinks, or agricultural buildings and production plants may be found in the 2015 *ASHRAE Handbook—HVAC Applications*.

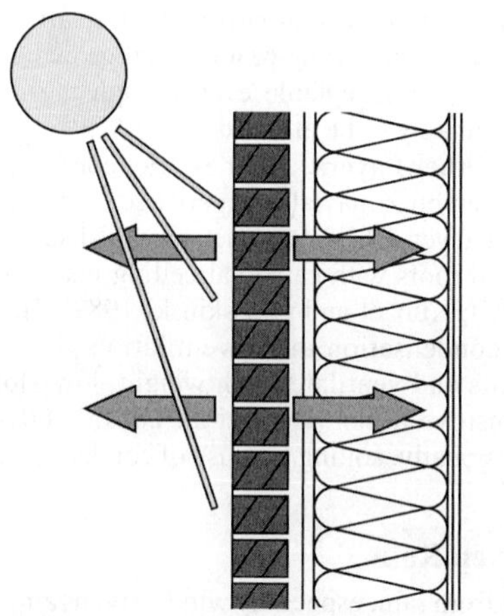

Fig. 2 Solar Vapor Drive and Interstitial Condensation

Solar Radiation

Incident solar radiation is the major thermal load at the building exterior. For direct solar radiation, the resultant irradiation depends on the angle between the sun and the normal on the exposed surface and on its color (short-wave absorptivity). For calculation of incident solar heat flux and spectra, see Chapter 15.

For moisture control, solar radiation is usually considered beneficial. However, in some cases solar radiation combined with water from precipitation or other sources (e.g., construction moisture) can lead to severe moisture problems by solar-driven vapor flow. For example, as shown in Figure 2, if the water-absorbing exterior layer of an assembly (e.g., brick veneer, a typical example of "reservoir" cladding) has been wetted by wind-driven rain, solar irradiation creates such high vapor pressure that, in addition to vapor diffusion toward the outdoors, part of the evaporating water diffuses inwards, leading to condensation on and in material layers within the assembly (e.g., sheathing boards, insulation layers, vapor retarders). Adapting the permeance of vapor retarders and weather-resistive barriers (WRB) to the potential loads may improve the situation. ASHRAE research project RP-1091 (Burnett et al. 2004) showed that cladding ventilation is also an effective remedy within specified exterior air humidity limits.

Exterior Condensation

Long-Wave Radiant Effects. Long-wave radiation exchange of the envelope surface with the cold layers of the lower atmosphere is a major heat transfer process. At night or with the sun at a low angle, it results in a net heat flux to the sky (i.e., heat energy sink) (see Chapter 15). Depending on the building assembly's thermal properties, this may lead to a drop in the envelope's outdoor surface temperature below the ambient air temperature (undercooling). If this surface temperature reaches the air's dew point, condensation occurs on that exterior surface. Massive structures with a high thermal inertia do not usually lose enough heat to the nighttime radiation sink to bring the outdoor surface temperature below the air's dew point for a significant period of time. However, many modern building assemblies, such as lightweight roofs or exterior insulation finish systems (EIFSs), have little thermal inertia in their exterior surface layers and are therefore subject to considerable amounts of exterior condensation (Künzel 2007).

Interior Temperature Differential. Exterior condensation can also occur on poorly insulated assemblies in cooling climates because of the operation of air-conditioning systems. Repeated exterior condensation or long-lasting, high relative humidity often provides the basis for soiling or microbial growth (fungi or algae), which may not be acceptable even though the durability of the assembly is unlikely to be affected.

Effect on Other Layers. Under exterior condensation conditions, ventilated assemblies may also experience condensation within the ventilated air layer. This phenomenon was discovered by investigating pitched roofs with cathedral ceiling insulation (Hens 1992; Janssens 1998; Künzel and Grosskinski 1989). However, damage because of condensation in the ventilation plane is rare, except in metal roofs and ventilated lightweight, low-sloped roofs with moisture-sensitive decks (Hens et al. 2007a, 2007b; Zheng et al. 2004). Occasionally, soiling because of condensate runoff has been reported.

Wind-Driven Rain

The load from rain, especially wind-driven rain, is the main reason for moisture-related building failure. Because the requirements of sometimes costly rain-protection measures depend on the local climate, some countries have introduced regional driving-rain classifications. Generally, coastal regions and those on the windward side of mountains receive the highest precipitation load. Areas of low rainfall do not have the potential for severe wind-driven rain.

Regional precipitation and wind are significant factors in determining local wind-driven rain load, but local exposure conditions are of equal importance. A building in an open field receives a higher load than one sheltered by a forest or other buildings. A quantification of exposure conditions for walls depending on landscape, neighborhood, and building size and geometry can be found in the British *Standard* BS 8104 and in the European ISO/DIN *Standard* 15927-3:2006. The average wind-driven rain load R_D in open ground was investigated by Lacy (1965). It is estimated from normal rain R_N and the wind velocity component v parallel to the considered orientation:

$$R_D = fvR_N \tag{1}$$

where

R_D = wind-driven rain intensity, lb/ft^2·h
f = empirical factor = approximately 0.06 s/ft
v = mean wind velocity, ft/s (or mph)
R_N = rain intensity on a horizontal surface in open field, lb/ft^2·h

Figure 3 shows a "rain rose" of results from Equation (1) plotted in polar coordinates indicating the amount of wind-driven rain in mass per unit area hitting an unobstructed and isolated vertical surface in the open field.

The driving rain load close to a façade is considerably less than in the open field (as shown in Figure 4), and it becomes irregular.

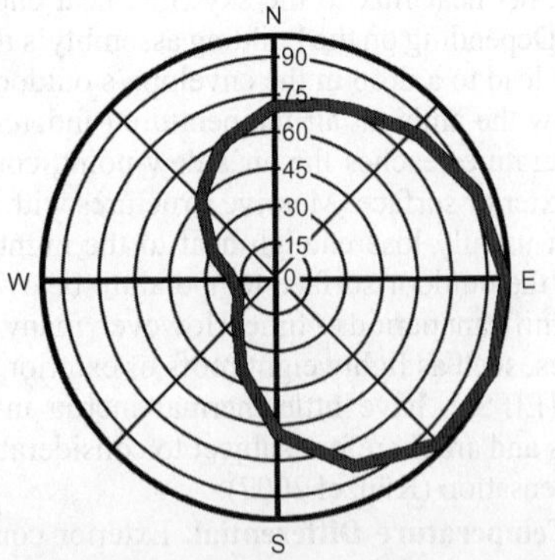

Fig. 3 Typical Wind-Driven Rain Rose for Open Ground

Tops and edges of walls generally receive the highest amount. This is caused by the airflow pattern around a building (see Chapter 24 for more information). At the windward side, high pressure gradients coincide with large changes in air velocity. The building acts as an obstacle for the wind, slowing down airflow and subsequently reducing the wind-driven rain load near the façade. Gravity and the rain droplets' momentum prevent them from following the airflow around the building, causing them to strike the façade mainly at the edges of the flow obstacle (Straube and Burnett 2000).

However, the irregular driving rain deposition is often evened out by water running off the hard-hit areas, especially when the façade surface has low water absorptivity or the wind-driven rain load is high enough to capillary-saturate the most exposed surface layers.

Roof overhangs can reduce the driving rain load on low-rise buildings. Slightly inclined wall sections or protruding façade elements may receive a considerable amount of splash water from façade areas above them, in addition to the direct driving rain deposition. This is often a problem for buildings with walls slightly out of vertical (Künzel 2007).

Rain penetrating the exterior cladding of exposed walls may cause severe damage if it cannot be drained and dried out quickly enough. Experience shows that it is almost impossible to seal joints and connections hermetically against wind-driven rain. Therefore, building envelope assemblies should be designed to tolerate a limited amount of water entry (see ASHRAE *Standard* 160-2009).

Construction Moisture

Building damage as a result of migrating construction moisture has become more frequent because tight construction schedules leave little time for building materials to dry. Although often disregarded, construction moisture is either delivered with the building products or absorbed by the materials during storage or construction. Cast-in-place concrete, autoclaved aerated concrete (AAC), calcium silicate brick (CSB), and "green" wood are examples of materials that contain significant volumes of moisture when delivered. Stucco, mortar, clay brick, and concrete blocks are examples of materials that are either mixed or brought into contact with water at the construction site. All other porous building materials may take up considerable amounts of precipitation or groundwater when left unprotected during storage or construction before the enclosure of the building. A single-family house made of AAC may initially contain up to 15 tons of water in its walls.

Care is needed to safely remove that water, either by additional ventilation during the first years of operation or by using construction dryers while heating the building before putting it into service. Even "dry" materials have an initial water content of approximately the equilibrium moisture content at 80% rh (EMC_{80}). When significant construction moisture is encountered, EMC_{80} can be exceeded by a factor of two or more.

Ground- and Surface Water

A high groundwater table or surface water running toward the building and filling the loose fill triangle around the basement represents an important moisture load to the lower parts of the

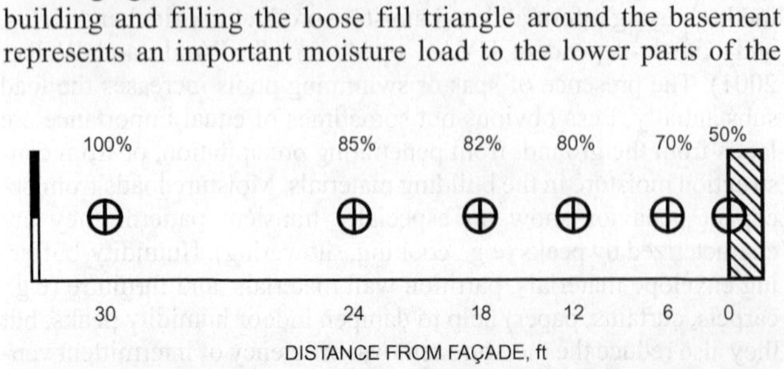

Fig. 4 Measured Reduction in Catch Ratio Close to Façade of One-Story Building at Height of 6 ft

building envelope. These loads should be met by grading the ground away from the building, by perimeter drainage, and by waterproofing the basement and foundation. Instead of waterproofing with bituminous membranes or coatings, water-impermeable structural elements may also be used (e.g., reinforced concrete, which may, however, be vapor permeable). The resulting vapor flux also presents a load that must be addressed (e.g., by basement ventilation). Moisture loads in the ground may impair performance of exterior basement insulation applied on the outside of the waterproofing layer. Therefore, special care must be taken to protect insulation from moisture accumulation unless the insulation material is itself impermeable to water and vapor [e.g., extruded polystyrene (XPS), foam glass].

Wicking of ground- or surface water into porous walls by capillary action is called **rising damp**. This phenomenon may be a sign of poor drainage or waterproofing of the building's basement or foundation. However, other phenomena show moisture patterns similar to rising damp. If the wall is contaminated with salts, which is often the case in historic buildings, the wall's moisture content might stay elevated because of a hygroscopicity increase caused by water uptake by the salt crystals. Another reason for the appearance of rising damp is surface condensation in unheated buildings during summer.

Air Pressure Differentials

Wind, mechanical systems, and stack effects (caused by differences between indoor and outdoor temperature) result in air pressure differentials over the building envelope. In contrast to wind, stack pressure is a constant load that may not be neglected. Worse, pressure differentials may drive airflow in the same direction as vapor pressure: from indoors to outdoors during the heating season, and in the opposite direction during the cooling season. Therefore, airflow through cracks, imperfect joints, or air-permeable assembly layers may cause interstitial condensation in a manner similar to vapor diffusion. However, condensation is likely to be more intense and concentrated around leaks in the building envelope. This can become a problem at the top of a building, which may be especially vulnerable because of discontinuities in the air barrier at the parapets. To avoid moisture damage, airflow through and within the building envelope should be prevented by a continuous air barrier. However, it is difficult to guarantee total airtightness, so the hygrothermal effect of airflow can be important, especially when high pressure differentials are expected (e.g., in multistory or mechanically pressurized buildings). For the practical determination of pressure differentials and airflow, see Chapter 16. Air pressures across the envelope may also drive liquid water inward or outward.

2. HEAT TRANSFER

Heat flow through the building envelope is mainly associated with the building's energy performance. However, other aspects are equally important. Interior surface temperatures not only serve as an indicator for hygienic conditions in the building (e.g., conditions preventing surface condensation or mold growth), but they can also be a major factor for thermal comfort. Temperature peaks and fluctuations within the building envelope or on its surfaces may further affect the envelope's durability. At low temperatures, some building materials tend to become less elastic and sometimes brittle, making them vulnerable to strain or mechanical impact. At high temperatures, some materials degrade because of chemical reactions or irreversible deformation. Deformation and local mechanical failure can also occur under the influence of steep temperature gradients or transients. Whereas some of these aspects can be assessed by steady-state calculations (e.g., heating energy losses, energy end use), others require transient simulations for accurate evaluation.

As explained in Chapter 4, heat transfer by apparent conduction in a solid is governed by Fourier's law:

$$q = -k\,\mathrm{grad}(t) = -\left(k_x\frac{\partial t}{\partial x} + k_y\frac{\partial t}{\partial y} + k_z\frac{\partial t}{\partial z}\right) \tag{2}$$

where

q = heat flux, Btu/h·ft²
t = temperature, °F
k_x, k_y, k_z = apparent thermal conductivity in direction of x, y, and z axes, Btu/h·ft·°F
grad(t) = gradient of temperature (change in temperature per unit length, perpendicular to isothermal surfaces in solid), °F/ft
$\partial t/\partial x$ = gradient of temperature along x axis, °F/ft
$\partial t/\partial y$ = gradient of temperature along y axis, °F/ft
$\partial t/\partial z$ = gradient of temperature along z axis, °F/ft

In Equation (2), the thermal conductivity k of the material is assumed to be directionally dependent. In fact, many building materials (e.g., wood and wood-based materials, mineral fiber insulation, perforated bricks) show considerable anisotropy. Therefore, k_x, k_y, and k_z are not equal in these materials; in isotropic materials, they are equal.

Substituting Equation (2) into the relationship for conservation of energy yields

$$\begin{aligned}\frac{\partial h}{\partial t}\times\frac{\partial t}{\partial \tau} &= \mathrm{div}[k\,\mathrm{grad}(t)] + S\\ &= \frac{\partial}{\partial x}\left(k_x\frac{\partial t}{\partial x}\right) + \frac{\partial}{\partial y}\left(k_y\frac{\partial t}{\partial y}\right) + \frac{\partial}{\partial z}\left(k_z\frac{\partial t}{\partial z}\right) + S\end{aligned} \tag{3}$$

where

h = enthalpy per unit volume, Btu/ft³
S = heat sources and sinks [e.g., caused by latent heat of evaporation/condensation in presence of moisture, by chemical reactions such as hydration in concrete, or by phase change from solid to liquid or vice versa of special additives consisting of paraffins or salt hydrates, known as phase-change materials (PCM)], Btu/h·ft³

with

$$\frac{\partial h}{\partial \tau} = \rho_s c_s + w c_w \tag{4}$$

where

ρ_s = density of solid (dry material), lb/ft³
c_s = specific heat capacity of dry solid, Btu/lb·°F
c_w = specific heat capacity of liquid water, Btu/lb·°F
w = moisture content, lb/ft³

2.1 STEADY-STATE THERMAL RESPONSE

In steady state without sources or sinks, Equation (3) reduces to

$$\frac{\partial}{\partial x}\left(k_x\frac{\partial t}{\partial x}\right) + \frac{\partial}{\partial y}\left(k_y\frac{\partial t}{\partial y}\right) + \frac{\partial}{\partial z}\left(k_z\frac{\partial t}{\partial z}\right) = 0 \tag{5}$$

If the steady-state heat flux is only in one direction (e.g., perpendicular to the building envelope) and materials are assumed to be isotropic, Equation (2) can be rewritten for each material layer within the building envelope as

$$q = -k_m\frac{\Delta t}{\Delta x} = -C\,\Delta t = -\frac{1}{R}\Delta t \tag{6}$$

where

Δt = temperature difference between two interfaces of one material layer, °F
Δx = layer thickness, ft
k_m = mean thermal conductivity of material layer with thickness Δx, Btu/h·ft²·°F
C = thermal conductance of layer with thickness Δx, Btu/h·ft²·°F
R = thermal resistance of layer with thickness Δx, h·ft²·°F/Btu

Under steady-state conditions, the one-dimensional heat flux is the same through all material layers, but their individual thermal conductance or resistance is usually different.

Surface-to-Surface Thermal Resistance of a Flat Assembly

A single layer's thermal resistance to heat flow is given by the ratio of its thickness to its apparent thermal conductivity. Accordingly, the surface-to-surface thermal resistance of a flat building assembly composed of parallel layers (e.g., a ceiling, floor, or wall), or a slightly curved component, consists of the sum of the resistances of all layers in series:

$$R_s = R_1 + R_2 + R_3 + R_4 + \cdots + R_n \tag{7}$$

where

$R_1, R_2, \ldots, R_n$ = resistances of individual layers, h·ft²·°F/Btu
R_s = resistance of building assembly surface to surface (system resistance), h·ft²·°F/Btu

For building components with nonuniform or irregular sections, such as hollow clay and concrete blocks, use the R-value of the unit as manufactured.

Combined Convective and Radiative Surface Heat Transfer

The surface film resistances and their reciprocal, the surface film coefficients, specify heat transfer to or from a surface by the effects of convection and radiation.

Although heat transfer by convection is affected by surface roughness and temperature difference between air and surface, the largest influence is that of air movement, turbulence, and velocity close to the surface. Because air movement at the envelope's outer surface depends on wind speed and direction, as well as on flow patterns around the building, which are usually unknown, an average surface heat transfer film coefficient at the exterior is normally used. Correlations such as those of Schwarz (1971) link the convective film coefficient to wind speed recorded at a height of 30 ft and to orientation of the surface (windward or leeward side). The same holds for the inside surface, where buoyancy plays a prime role. However, because the surface-to-surface thermal resistance of a wall is usually high compared with the surface film resistances, an exact value is of minor importance for most applications.

Because air is rather permeable to long-wave radiation, heat transfer by radiation takes place between the surface of the building and the surfaces of objects in the environment, not the surrounding air. Heat transfer by radiation between two surfaces is controlled by the character of the surfaces (emittance and reflectance), the temperature difference between them, and the angle factor through which they see each other. Indoors, the external wall surface exchanges radiation with partition walls, floor, and ceiling, furniture, and other external walls. In winter, most of the other surfaces have a higher temperature than the external wall surface; therefore, radiative exchange gives a net heat flux to the external wall. Outdoors, the external wall surface sees the ground, neighboring buildings, and the sky. Without sun, thermal radiation from the sky and the environment is normally lower than radiation from the wall. This means the wall is losing energy. Especially during clear nights, the temperature of the exterior wall surface may drop below the ambient air temperature. In this case, convective and radiative heat transfer at the surface are opposed to each other.

For simplicity, convective and radiative surface heat transfer are often combined, leading to an **apparent surface heat transfer film coefficient *h***:

$$q = h(t_{en} - t_s) \tag{8}$$

with

$$h = h_c + h_r \tag{9}$$

where

q = total surface heat transfer, Btu/h·ft²
h = apparent surface film transfer coefficient, Btu/h·ft²·°F
h_r = radiant surface film coefficient to account for long-wave radiation exchange, Btu/h·ft²·°F
h_c = convective surface film coefficient, Btu/h·ft²·°F
t_{en} = environmental reference temperature, °F
t_s = surface temperature, °F

For indoor surface heat transfer, this approach is acceptable when only heat transport through the building envelope is considered. Environmental temperature t_{en} also includes the air temperature as the mean temperature of all surfaces in the field of view of the considered envelope assembly. When all these surfaces are of partition walls and floors that have the same temperature as the indoor air, t_{en} may be replaced by the indoor air temperature.

This approach becomes questionable when heat transfer at the outdoor surface is concerned. Because radiation to the sky can lead to surface temperatures below ambient air temperature, Equation (8) underestimates the real heat flux when the environmental temperature is replaced by the outdoor air temperature. Therefore, t_{en} must include all short- and long-wave radiation contributions perpendicular to the assembly's exterior surface. However, t_{en} cannot be used for moisture transfer calculations. Therefore, a more convenient way may be to treat heat transfer by convection and radiation separately. In this case, h_r is skipped in Equation (9), which now applies to convection only, and t_{en} equals the outdoor air temperature. The heat exchange by radiation is calculated by balancing the solar and environmental radiation onto the assembly's exterior surface with the long-wave emission from it.

Steady-state calculation of thermal transport through the building envelope is generally done using surface film resistances based on combined surface heat transfer by radiation and convection, with *R* being the inverse of the combined surface film coefficient *h*. Because of greater air movement outdoors, the mean thermal surface film resistance at the exterior surface is lower than at the interior surface. Typical ranges for the combined exterior and interior surface film resistances with surface infrared reflectance ≤0.1 (nonmetallic) are

$$R_o = 0.17 \text{ to } 0.34 \text{ h·ft}^2\text{·°F/Btu}$$

$$R_i = 0.68 \text{ to } 1.13 \text{ h·ft}^2\text{·°F/Btu}$$

Heat Flow Across an Air Space

Heat flow across an air space is affected by the nature of the boundary surfaces, slope of the air space, distance between boundary surfaces, direction of heat flow, mean temperature of air, and temperature difference between both boundary surfaces. Air space thermal conductance, the reciprocal of the air space thermal resistance, is the sum of a radiation component, a conduction component, and a convection component. For computational purposes, spaces are considered airtight, with neither air leakage nor air washing along the boundary surfaces.

The radiation portion depends on the temperature of the two boundary surfaces and their respective surface properties. Assuming infinite parallel plates, radiation is not affected by thickness or slope of the air space, direction of heat flow, or which surface is hot or cold. For surfaces that can be considered ideally gray, the surface properties are emittance, absorptance, and reflectance. Chapter 4 explains all three in depth. For an opaque surface, reflectance is equal to one minus the emittance, which varies with surface type and condition and radiation wavelength. The combined effect of the emittances of the two boundary surfaces is expressed by the effective emittance *E* of the air space. Table 2 in Chapter 26 lists typical emittance values for reflective surfaces and building materials, and

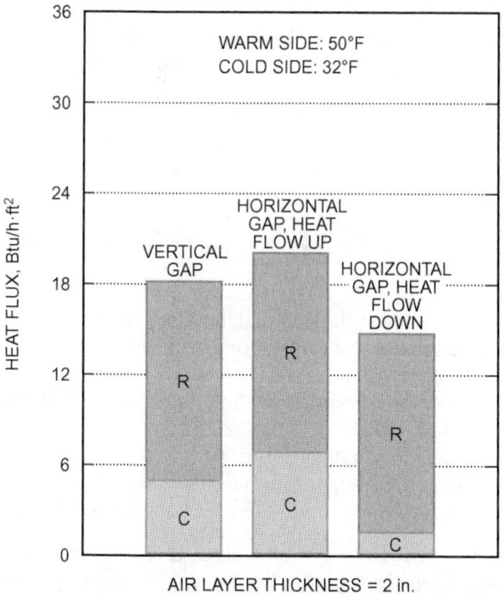

Fig. 5 Heat Flux by Thermal Radiation and Combined Convection and Conduction Across Vertical or Horizontal Air Layer

the corresponding effective emittance for air spaces. More exact surface emittance values should be obtained by tests.

The convective portion is affected markedly by the slope of the air space, direction of heat flow, temperature difference across the space, and, in some cases, thickness of the space. It is also slightly affected by the mean temperatures of both surfaces.

For air spaces in building components, radiation and convection together define total heat flow. An example of their magnitudes for total flow across a vertical or horizontal airspace (up and down) is given in Figure 5.

Table 3 in Chapter 26 lists typical thermal resistance values of sealed air spaces of uniform thickness with moderately smooth, plane, parallel surfaces. These data are based on experimental measurements (Robinson et al. 1954). Resistance values for systems with air spaces can be estimated from these results if emittance values are corrected for field conditions. However, for some common composite building insulation systems involving mass-type insulation with a reflective surface in conjunction with an air space, the resistance value may be appreciably lower than the estimated value, particularly if the air space is not sealed or of uniform thickness (Palfey 1980). For critical applications, a particular design's effectiveness should be confirmed by actual test data undertaken by using the ASTM hot-box method (ASTM *Standard* C1363). This test is especially necessary for constructions combining reflective and nonreflective thermal insulation.

Total Thermal Resistance of a Flat Building Assembly

Total thermal resistance to heat flow through a flat building assembly composed of parallel layers between the environments at both sides is given by

$$R_T = R_i + R_s + R_o \tag{10}$$

where

R_i = combined inner-surface film resistance, h·ft²·°F/Btu
R_o = combined outer-surface film resistance, h·ft²·°F/Btu
R_s = resistance of building assembly surface to surface, including thermal resistances of possible air layers in component (system resistance), h·ft²·°F/Btu

Thermal Transmittance of a Flat Building Assembly

The thermal transmittance or U-factor of a flat building assembly composed of parallel layers is the reciprocal of R_T:

$$U = 1/R_T \tag{11}$$

Calculating thermal transmittance requires knowing the (1) apparent thermal resistance of all homogeneous layers, (2) thermal resistance of the nonhomogeneous layers, (3) surface film resistances at both sides of the construction, and (4) thermal resistances of air spaces in the construction. The lower values of the surface film resistances given previously should be used.

The steady-state heat flux Q_n across the building envelope assembly is then defined by

$$Q_n = A_n U_n (t_i - t_o) \tag{12}$$

where

t_i, t_o = indoor and outdoor reference temperatures, °F
A_n = component area, ft²
U_n = U-factor of component, Btu/h·ft²·°F

Interface Temperatures in a Flat Building Component

The temperature drop through any layer of an assembly is proportional to its thermal resistance. Thus, the temperature drop Δt_j through layer j is

$$\Delta t_j = \frac{R_j (t_i - t_o)}{R_T} \tag{13}$$

The temperature in an interface j then becomes ($t_o < t_i$)

$$t_j = t_o + \frac{R_o^j}{R_T}(t_i - t_o) \tag{14}$$

where R_o^j is the sum of thermal resistances between inside and interface j in the flat assembly, in h·ft²·°F/Btu.

If the apparent thermal conductivity of materials in a building component is highly temperature dependent, the mean temperature must be known before assigning an appropriate thermal resistance. In such a case, apply successive calculation steps; some software can perform these iterative calculations. First, select the thermal resistances for the particular layers. Then calculate total resistance R_T with Equation (9) and the temperature at each interface using Equation (13). The mean temperature in each layer (arithmetic mean of its surface temperatures) can then be used to obtain second-generation R-values. The procedure is repeated until the R-values are correctly selected for the resulting mean temperatures. Generally, this demands two or three steps.

To calculate interior surface temperatures for risk assessment of surface condensation or mold growth, the higher interior and lower exterior surface film resistance values, given previously, should be used.

Series and Parallel Heat Flow Paths

In many building assemblies (e.g., wood-frame construction), components are arranged so that heat flows in parallel paths of different conductances. If no heat flows through lateral paths, the thermal transmittance through each path may be calculated. The average transmittance of the enclosure is then

$$U_{av} = aU_a + bU_b + \cdots + nU_n \tag{15}$$

where $a, b, \ldots, n$ are the surface-weighted path fractions for a typical basic area composed of several different paths with transmittances $U_a, U_b, \ldots, U_n$.

If heat can flow laterally with little resistance in any continuous layer, so that transverse isothermal planes result, the flat construction performs as a series combination of layers, of which one or more provide parallel paths. Total average resistance $R_{T(av)}$ in that case is the sum of the resistance of the layers between the isothermal planes, each layer being calculated and the results weighted by the contributing surface area. For further information, see Chapter 27.

The U-factor, assuming parallel heat flow only, is usually lower than that assuming combined series-parallel heat flow. The actual U-factor lies between the two. Without test results, a best choice must be selected. Generally, if the construction contains a layer in which lateral heat conduction is high compared to heat flux through the wall, a value closer to the series-parallel calculation should be used. If, however, there is no layer of high lateral thermal conductance, use a value closer to the parallel calculation. For assemblies with large differences in material thermal conductivities (e.g., assemblies using metal structural elements), the zone method is recommended (see Chapter 27) or the methods discussed in the following section.

Thermal Bridging and Thermal Performance of Multidimensional Construction

Passing highly conductive materials through insulation layers (**thermal bridging**) results in building envelopes with higher overall thermal transmittances and colder surface temperatures compared to an assembly with continuous, unbroken insulation. Not recognizing the effect of thermal bridging on the building envelope's thermal performance can lead to inefficient design of HVAC systems, building operation inefficiencies, inadequate condensation resistance at component intersections, and compromised occupant comfort.

Heat flow through building envelopes occurs in two and three dimensions when considering all components and their intersections (e.g., glazing, wall, roof, parapet, balconies, floor slabs). Multidimensional heat flow caused by highly conductive thermal bridges (e.g., steel and concrete sections) cannot be effectively evaluated using simplified hand calculations (see Chapter 27) and must be evaluated using a multidimensional computer model or guarded hot-box test measurement (ASTM *Standard* C1363).

Construction details are often lumped into an overall heat flow of the entire opaque area or evaluated separately by defining an effective length or area (or zone of influence). Individual details with transmittances defined by an **effective area** are combined with other components to calculate an overall thermal transmittance using a weighted average method. However, effective areas often have no real significance or have a large variance that depends on many factors (location of insulation layers in relation to structural framing, insulation levels, orientation of structural framing, predominate heat flow path, etc.). Moreover, the effect of individual details is averaged over the adjacent assemblies, regardless of size of the effective area or length. Consequently, the absolute effect or thermal quality of a detail is difficult to assess using an effective area approach (Morrison Hershfield 2011).

Contributions of heat flow for specific construction details (e.g., slab edges, parapets, glazing transitions) are best quantified by determining the extra heat loss caused by an individual detail (i.e., thermal bridge at an intersection of components) above the heat loss of the undisturbed assembly and ascribe that difference to a line or point through their linear or point thermal transmittance. This method can simplify calculation of overall heat loss and highlight the effect of the thermal bridge (Morrison Hershfield 2011).

Linear and Point Thermal Transmittances

Using linear and point thermal transmittance requires dividing thermal transmittances into three categories:

- **Clear field**: heat loss if no thermal bridges modified the heat flow through the assembly (area based)
- **Linear**: additional heat loss along a considerable portion of a building perimeter or height in one dimension (e.g., slab edges, balconies, parapets, corner framing, window interfaces)
- **Point**: additional heat loss from thermal bridges at countable points on a building (e.g., three-way corners, beam penetrations)

Calculating the overall heat flow is simply adding the contribution of each linear and point thermal transmittance to the clear-field assembly heat flow. The overall heat flow through the opaque elements of the building envelope (wall or roof) then is

$$Q = \sum Q_{anomalies} + \sum Q_o = \sum(\Psi L) + \sum \chi + \sum Q_o \quad (16)$$

where

Q = overall heat flow through building envelope, Btu/h·°F
$Q_{anomalies}$ = additional heat flow for linear and point transmittance details, Btu/h·°F
Q_o = clear-field heat flow without linear and point transmittance details, Btu/h·°F
Ψ = linear transmittance, Btu/h·ft·°F
χ = point transmittance, Btu/h·°F
L = characteristic length of linear transmittance detail, ft

The overall heat flow per unit area, U-value, can be derived by dividing the previous equation by the total projected surface area of the assembly considered.

$$U = \frac{\sum(\Psi L) + \sum \chi}{A_{Total}} + U_o \quad (17)$$

where

U = overall thermal transmittance, including anomalies, Btu/h·ft²·°F
U_o = clear field thermal transmittance (assembly), Btu/h·ft²·°F
A_{total} = total opaque projected surface area, ft²

Thermal bridging and multidimensional heat flow also affect surface temperatures, concealed surfaces, and surfaces exposed to the indoor and outdoor environments. The temperature distribution from multidimensional heat flow is important to consider for controlling localized dirt pick-up on cold surfaces, mold growth, and condensation. A practical, convenient means to evaluate surface temperatures for multidimensional construction is to represent the coldest surface temperatures of interest relative to a temperature difference. This nondimensional ratio is sometimes referred to as a temperature index, factor, or ratio, with the following basic form but represented by many different symbols (CAN/CSA *Standard* A440; ISO *Standard* 13788; Morrison Hershfield 2011):

$$T_{index} = \frac{T_{surface} - T_{outdoor}}{T_{indoor} - T_{outdoor}} \quad (18)$$

where

T_{index} = temperature index
$T_{surface}$ = coldest temperature of surface
$T_{outdoor}$ = outdoor temperature
T_{indoor} = indoor temperature

The temperature index for a critical surface can then be compared to a minimum or design temperature index based on numerous performance criteria (e.g., risk of condensation, mold growth, corrosion). More detailed discussion of using temperature ratios and hygrothermal analysis can be found in the section on Simplified Hygrothermal Design Calculations and Analyses.

2.2 TRANSIENT THERMAL RESPONSE

Steady-state calculations are used to estimate the net heating energy demand on a monthly basis in cold and cool climates. However, in climates where daily temperature swings oscillate around a comfortable mean temperature, transient analysis to define net energy demand for heating and cooling and judge overheating probability is more appropriate. In order of importance, the thermal response of a building to daily swings in temperature and solar radiation depends on the thermal transmittance and solar heat gain coefficient (SHGC) of transparent components (fenestration) in the envelope, ventilation strategy, accessible thermal capacity of the internal walls and floors, and thermal transmittance/inertia of opaque components in the envelope.

The effects of the mutual dependences of these four factors are complex. In cool climates, a simplified approach that accounts for these interactions combines a steady-state daily mean heat balance for a most probable hot day with a lower-limit value for the daily harmonic temperature damping at room level. Temperature damping at room level increases with higher admittance and higher harmonic thermal resistance of opaque envelope components; higher admittance and higher harmonic thermal resistance of all inside walls, floor, and ceiling; and higher thermal inertia of furniture and furnishings. A lower thermal transmittance of transparent components in the envelope and more outdoor air ventilation results in decreased daily harmonic temperature damping at room level. In general, however, and in any climate, whole-building simulations complying with ANSI/ASHRAE *Standard* 140 are recommended when a clear picture of overheating probability and net energy demand for heating and cooling is needed.

High admittances presume the presence of thermal storage materials that are easily assessable for heat. Stored heat can be sensible or latent, as shown in Equation (19). The first requires the use of heavy materials with high and constant capacitance and sufficient thickness to store heat by increasing the temperature of the materials (e.g., bricks, stone, sand-lime stone, concrete).The second uses phase change materials (PCMs), which are materials that store heat by changing phase, typically between solid to liquid. Most models used in building energy simulation programs simulate PCMs by using a temperature-dependent specific heat or enthalpy formulation of Equation (19).

$$\rho c V \frac{dT}{dt} = kA \frac{\partial}{\partial x}\left(\frac{\partial T}{\partial x}\right) \tag{19}$$

where

ρ = density, lb/ft³
c = specific heat, Btu/lb·°F
V = volume, ft³
dT/dt = gradient of temperature with respect to time, °F/s
k = thermal conductivity, Btu/h·ft·°F
A = surface area, ft²
$\partial T/\partial x$ = gradient of temperature along x axis, °F/ft

There are multiple approaches to solve for transient heat transfer equation. Chapters 4 and 18 describe some approaches to solve for transient problem; Mitchel and Braun (2012) provide more detail. For information about PCM standards and properties, see Chapter 26.

3. AIRFLOW

Airflow through and within building components is driven by stack pressure, wind pressure, and pressure differentials induced by mechanicals. These driving forces are all described in greater detail in Chapters 16 and 24. In calculating air flux in buildings, a distinction must be made between flow through open porous materials, and that through open orifices such as layers composed of small elements, cavities, cracks, leaks, and intentional vents. Air flux through an open porous material is given by

$$m_a = -k_a \operatorname{grad}(P_a) \tag{20}$$

where

m_a = air flux, lb/(ft²·h)
k_a = air permeability of open porous material, lb/ft·h·in. Hg
grad(P_a) = gradient in total air pressure (stack, wind, and mechanical systems), in. Hg/ft

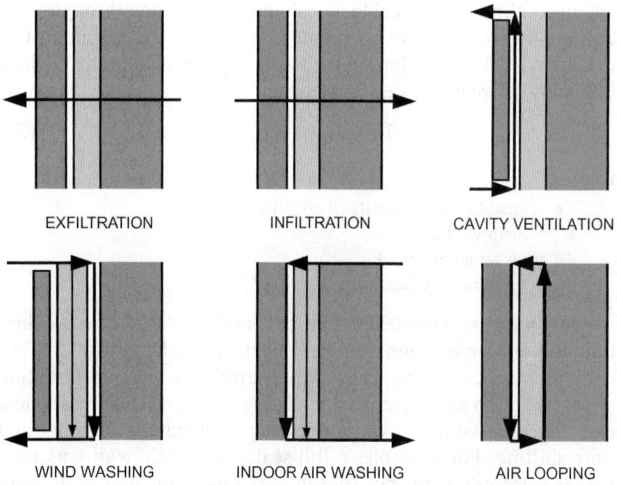

Fig. 6 Examples of Airflow Patterns

The air flux or air transfer equation for flow through the various orifice types is

$$m_a \text{ or } M_a = C(\Delta P_a)^n \tag{21}$$

where the flow coefficient C and flow exponent n are determined experimentally.

As shown in Figure 6, there are six simplified single airflow patterns characteristic of flow in buildings:

- **Exfiltration (air outflow)**: air passes across an envelope component moving from inside the building to the outdoors
- **Infiltration (air inflow)**: air passes across an envelope component from the outdoors to the indoors
- **Cavity ventilation**: outdoor air flows along an air cavity at the exterior of the thermal insulation layer without washing or penetrating the insulation layer
- **Wind washing**: outdoor air permeates the thermal insulation layer and/or flows along the air layer behind
- **Indoor air washing**: indoor air permeates the thermal insulation layer and/or flows along the air layer in front
- **Air looping**: buoyancy forces cause air to flow around and wash the thermal insulation layer filling a cavity

In reality, these single patterns never act in isolation but in combination, creating complicated airflow networks along and through building components. These combined flows act to degrade the hygrothermal response of components, envelopes, and even whole building fabrics. For calculating airflow in such cases, Kronvall (1982) developed an equivalent hydraulic network methodology, which was adapted by Janssens (1998) to calculate airflow in lightweight sloped roofs.

A single layer with low air permeability (an **air barrier**) can substantially minimize air inflow and outflow as long as it is both continuous and leak free. An air barrier must also be strong enough to withstand the air pressure difference imposed across the building envelope. This approach can also avoid moisture damage by preventing airflow through the building envelope.

Heat Flux with Airflow

Air leakage through building components may undesirably contribute to the ventilation in a building beyond that needed for comfort and indoor air quality (see Chapter 16). Air also carries energy that may degrade a building's thermal performance. A conditioned building also requires more energy to maintain internal comfort conditions when conditioned air is able to leak out of the building, and unconditioned air is able to leak into the building through infiltration. Airflow changes the assumption implicit in Equation (1), that no mass flow develops in the solid. In general, the sensible heat (enthalpy) displaced by airflow equals

$$\Phi = cM_a(t - t_o) \tag{22}$$

where

c = specific heat capacity of air, Btu/lb·°R
M_a = airflow, lb_m/s
t = air temperature, °F
t_o = reference temperature, °F

Only a few simple steady-state cases of combined heat conduction and air-carried enthalpy displacement can be solved analytically. In most cases, testing is the preferred way to get information about the impact. Note that enthalpy flow can increase heat exchange substantially, while reducing temperature damping and time shifting. For example, a full-scale straw bale wall was constructed according to the Tucson, Arizona, structural code with stucco on the exterior side and two layers of 0.5 in. gypsum board on the interior, with a straw bale thickness of 18 in. The thermal resistance of the straw by itself was measured as 1.77 h·ft²·F/Btu·in. However, the measured heat flow (in a hot box, tested according to ASTM *Standard* C1363) was more than twice that expected for the level of thermal resistance. Subsequent dissection of the wall revealed small gaps between the facing surfaces and the straw bales, creating air looping, as shown in Figure 6. A computational fluid dynamics model, using the measured anisotropic air permeability of the straw bales, explored the increased heat transfer through the wall caused by circulation through these gaps. That model found that without the gaps, the wall would have performed as predicted, even considering the relatively high air permeance of the straw itself. However, even very small gaps increased the heat transfer to a value comparable to the experimental measurements. A second wall was built with special attention paid to eliminating these gaps, and the heat transfer fell by 60% (Christian et al. 1998).

4. MOISTURE TRANSFER

Moisture may enter a building envelope by various paths, including construction moisture, water leaks, wind-driven rain, rising damp, and foundation leaks. Water vapor activates sorption in the envelope materials, and water vapor flow in and through the envelope may cause condensation on both nonporous and wet, porous surfaces.

Visible and invisible degradation caused by moisture is an important factor limiting the service life of building components. Invisible degradation includes the decrease of thermal resistance of building and insulating materials and the decrease in strength and stiffness of load-bearing materials. Visible degradation includes (1) mold on surfaces, (2) decay of wood-based materials, (3) spalling of masonry and concrete caused by freeze/thaw cycles, (4) hydration of plastic materials, (5) corrosion of metals, (6) damage from expansion of materials (e.g., buckling of wood floors), and (7) decline in appearance. In addition, high moisture levels can lead to odors.

4.1 MOISTURE STORAGE IN BUILDING MATERIALS

Many building materials are porous. The pores provide a large internal surface, which generally has an affinity for water molecules. In some materials, such as wood, moisture may also be adsorbed in the cell wall itself. The amount of water in these **hygroscopic** (water-attracting) materials is related to the relative humidity of the surrounding air. When relative humidity rises, hygroscopic materials gain moisture (**adsorption**), and when relative humidity drops, they lose moisture (**desorption**). The relationship between relative humidity and moisture content at a particular temperature is represented in a graph called the **sorption isotherm** (Figure 7). Isotherms obtained by adsorption are not identical to those obtained by desorption; this difference is called **hysteresis**. At high relative humidity, small pores become entirely filled with water by capillary condensation. The maximum moisture content should be reached at 100% rh, when all pores are filled, but experimentally this can only be achieved in a vacuum, by boiling the material, or by keeping it in contact with water for an extremely long time. In practice, the maximum moisture content of a porous material is lower. That value is referred to as **free water saturation** w_f or sometimes **capillary moisture content**. Figure 7 shows a typical sorption curve, giving the equilibrium moisture content as a function of relative humidity. The equilibrium moisture content increases with relative humidity, especially above 80% rh. It decreases slightly with increasing temperature. Moisture contents above w_{95} (the equilibrium water content

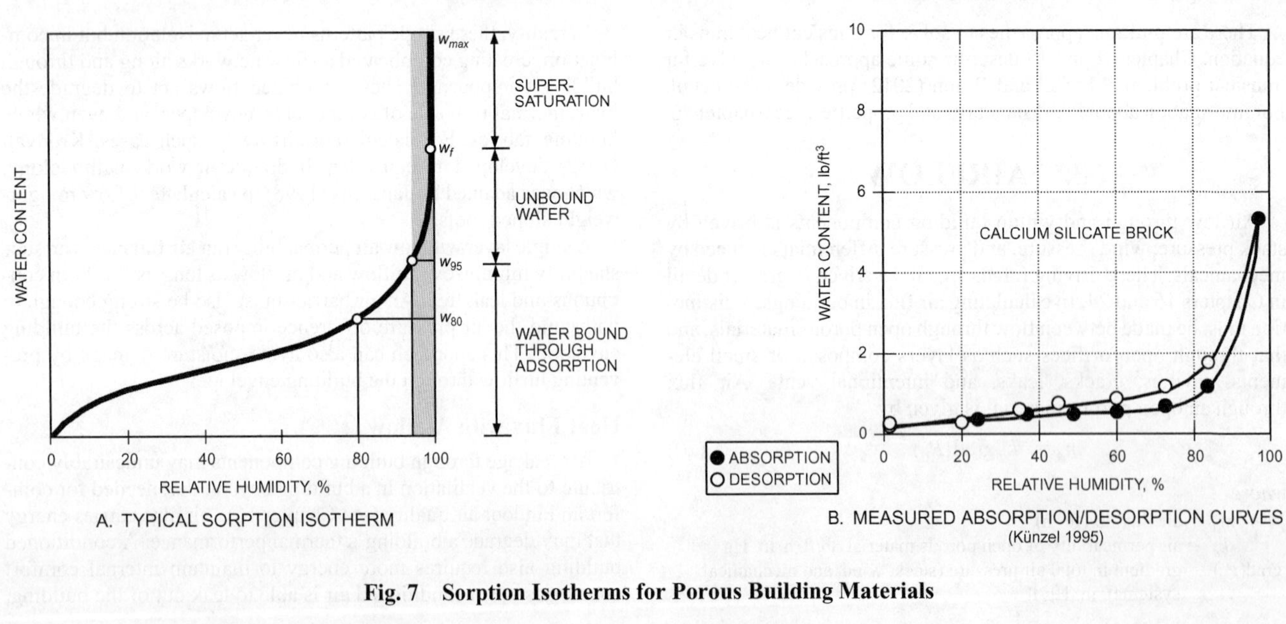

Fig. 7 Sorption Isotherms for Porous Building Materials

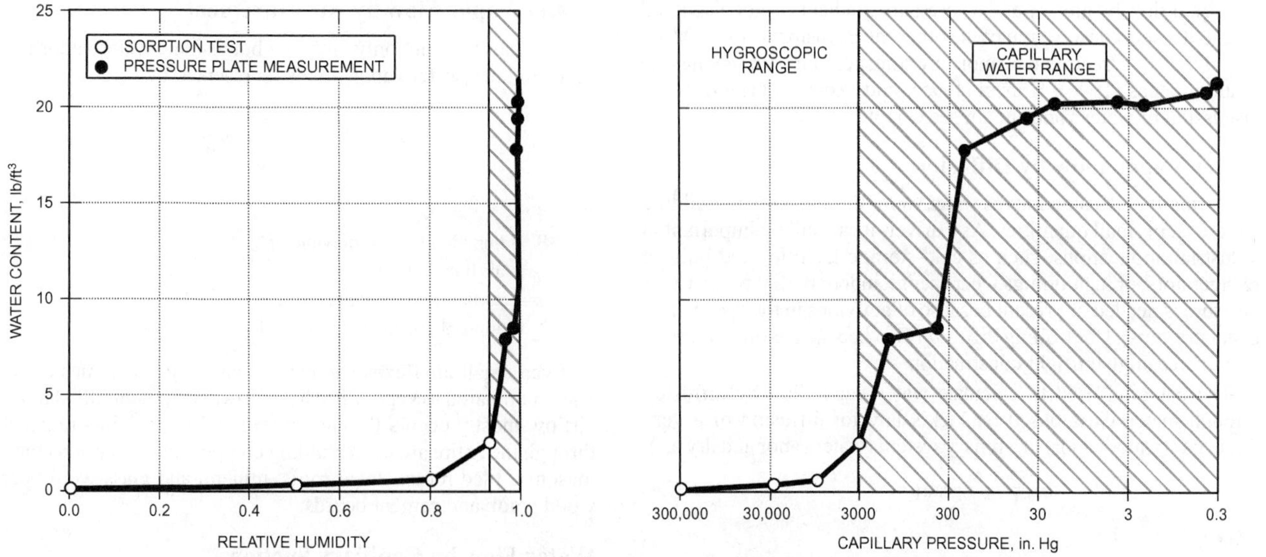

Fig. 8 Sorption Isotherm and Suction Curve for Autoclaved Aerated Concrete (AAC)
(Künzel and Holm 2001)

at 95% rh) cannot be achieved solely by vapor adsorption, because this region is characterized by capillary (unbound) water.

Chapter 32 describes hygroscopic substances and their use as dehumidifying agents. Chapter 26 has data on the moisture content of various materials in equilibrium with the atmosphere at various relative humidities. Wood and many other hygroscopic materials change dimensions with variations in moisture content.

Porous materials also absorb liquid water when in contact with it. Liquid water may be present because of construction moisture, leaks, rain penetration, flooding, or surface and interstitial condensation. Wetting may be so complete that the material reaches free water saturation once the largest pores are filled with water. Up to this point there is still a distinct equilibrium between the moisture content of the material and its environment. This becomes evident when different porous materials are brought in direct (capillary) contact with each other. In that case, there is capillary flow from one material to the other until all pores at a certain size are filled with water in both materials; all pores with sizes above this limit remain empty because smaller capillaries have a higher suction force than larger ones. This phenomenon is used to determine the moisture storage function above 95% rh, which represents the limit of vapor sorption tests in climatic chambers. Dalehaug et al. (2005), Krus (1996), and Roels et al. (2003) described using a pressure plate apparatus, in which water-saturated material samples are placed on a porous membrane permeable to water but impermeable to air. Then pressure is applied in different steps until capillary equilibrium is achieved. The equilibrium moisture content at each pressure step is determined by weighing the samples. The moisture storage function from zero pressure (free water saturation at 100% rh) up to 2967 in. Hg, which corresponds to approximately 93% rh, is defined by plotting the equilibrium water content over the applied pressure (Figure 8), which is assumed to be equal to the suction pressure of the largest still-water-filled capillaries.

For a continuous moisture storage function from the dry state to 100% rh, the sorption isotherm and the resultant curve from the pressure plate test are combined, either by converting the suction pressure into relative humidity or vice versa, using Kelvin's equation:

$$\phi = \exp\left(-\frac{s}{\rho_w R_D T}\right) \tag{23}$$

where

ϕ = relative humidity of air in pores
s = suction pressure, in. Hg
ρ_w = density of water, lb/ft³
R_D = gas constant for water vapor, Btu/lb·°R
T = absolute temperature, °R

The hatched zones in Figure 8 represent the overhygroscopic range where the converted results from pressure plate tests are plotted to complete the sorption isotherm. This narrow range is less important if vapor diffusion is the dominant moisture transport mechanism, for which an approximative interpolation of the moisture storage function between the end of the sorption isotherm and the free water saturation suffices. However, if capillary water flow from one material to the other becomes dominant (e.g., water absorption by bricks from mortar or stucco), the influence of the pressure plate results on the calculation's outcome may not be negligible (Krus 1996). In that case, the detailed suction curve (Figure 8, right) should be used for simulations.

4.2 MOISTURE FLOW MECHANISMS

Water vapor and liquid water migrate by a variety of transport mechanisms, including the following:

- Water vapor diffusion by partial water vapor pressure gradients
- Displacement of water vapor by air movement
- Surface diffusion and capillary suction of liquid water in porous building materials
- Liquid flow by gravity or water and air pressure gradients

In the past, moisture control strategies focused on water vapor diffusion. Displacement of water vapor by air movement was treated superficially, and liquid water transport provoked by wind-driven rain or soil moisture was overlooked almost completely. When present, however, these mechanisms can move far greater amounts of moisture than diffusion does. Therefore, air movement and liquid flow have a high priority in moisture control.

Liquid flow by gravity and by pressure gradients is not discussed here, but a short description of the other mechanisms follows. More comprehensive treatment of moisture transport and storage may be found in Hens (1996), Künzel (1995), and Pedersen (1990). For a discussion of water vapor in air, see Chapter 1.

Water Vapor Flow by Diffusion

Normally, diffusion moves water vapor through air and building materials, in small quantities. As a driver, it can still be important in industrial applications, such as cold-storage facilities and built-in refrigerators, or in buildings where a high indoor partial water vapor pressure is needed or present because of activities in the space (e.g., in natatoriums). Controlling diffusion also becomes more important with increasingly airtight construction.

The equation used to calculate water vapor flux by diffusion through materials is based on Fick's law for diffusion of a very dilute gas (water vapor) in a binary system (water vapor and dry air):

$$m_v = -\mu_p \,\text{grad}(p) \qquad (24)$$

where

$\text{grad}(p)$ = gradient of partial water vapor pressure, in. Hg
μ_p = water vapor permeability of porous material, gr/ft·h·in. Hg

According to Equation (24), water vapor flux by diffusion closely parallels Fourier's equation for heat flux by conduction. However, actual diffusion of water vapor through a material is far more complex than the equation suggests. For hygroscopic materials, water vapor permeability may be a function of relative humidity or, more accurately, moisture content. Also, temperature has an impact. The permeability may even vary spatially or by orientation because of variations or anisotropy in the material's porous system.

Test methods for measuring water vapor permeability are described in ASTM *Standard* E96. Water vapor flux through a material is determined gravimetrically while maintaining constant temperature and partial water vapor pressure differential across the specimen. Tests are usually done in a climatic chamber at controlled temperature (68 or 73°F) and 50% rh. The material samples are sealed to the top of a cup that contains either a desiccant (dry-cup) or water or a saturated salt solution (wet-cup).

Permeability is usually expressed in grains/h·ft·in. Hg and permeance in grains/h·ft^2·in. Hg. Whereas *permeability* refers to the water vapor flux per unit thickness, *permeance* is used in reference to a material of a specific thickness. For example, a material that is 2 in. thick generally is assumed to have half the permeance of a 1 in. thick material, even though permeances of many materials often are not strictly proportional to thickness. In many cases, the property ignores the effect of cracks or holes in the surface. It is inappropriate to refer to permeability with regard to inhomogeneous or composite materials, such as structural insulated panels (SIPs) or film-faced insulation batts.

Methods have been developed that allow measurement of water vapor transport with temperature gradients across the specimen (Douglas et al. 1992; Galbraith et al. 1998; Krus 1996). These methods may give more accurate data on water vapor transfer through materials and eventually allow better distinction between the various transport modes.

There are some plastic materials [e.g., polyamide (Künzel 1999)] where the vapor permeability rises substantially with ambient relative humidity because of slight changes in the pore structure: water molecules squeeze between polymer molecules and thereby create new passages through the material. This effect is called **solution diffusion**. Moisture transport by solution diffusion can be described by Equation (23) using humidity-dependent vapor permeability functions determined by cup tests at several average relative humidity steps.

Water Vapor Flow by Air Movement

Air transports not only enthalpy but also the water vapor it contains. Related water vapor flux is represented by

$$m_v = Wm_a \approx \frac{0.62}{P_a} m_a p \qquad (25)$$

where

W = humidity ratio of moving air
m_a = air flux, lb/ft^2·h
p = partial water vapor pressure in air, in. Hg
P_a = atmospheric air pressure, in. Hg

Even small air fluxes can carry much larger volumes of water vapor compared to vapor diffusion. However, potentially damaging airflow mostly occurs through cracks and leaky joints rather than through the entire area of a building component. Exceptions include masonry, tiled roofs, slated roofs, mineral and glass wool boards, wood wool, and cement boards.

Water Flow by Capillary Suction

Within small pores of an equivalent diameter less than 0.004 in., molecular attraction between the pore wall and the water molecules causes capillary suction (Figure 9), defined as

$$s = \frac{2\sigma\cos\theta}{r} \qquad (26)$$

where

s = capillary suction, in. Hg
σ = surface tension of water, lb$_f$/in.
r = equivalent radius of capillary, in.
θ = contact wetting angle, degrees

The contact angle is the angle between the water meniscus and capillary surface. The smaller the contact angle, the larger the capillary suction. In hydrophilic (water-attracting) materials, the contact wetting angle is less than 90°; in hydrophobic (water-repelling) materials, it is between 90 and 180°.

Capillary water movement is governed by the gradient in capillary suction s:

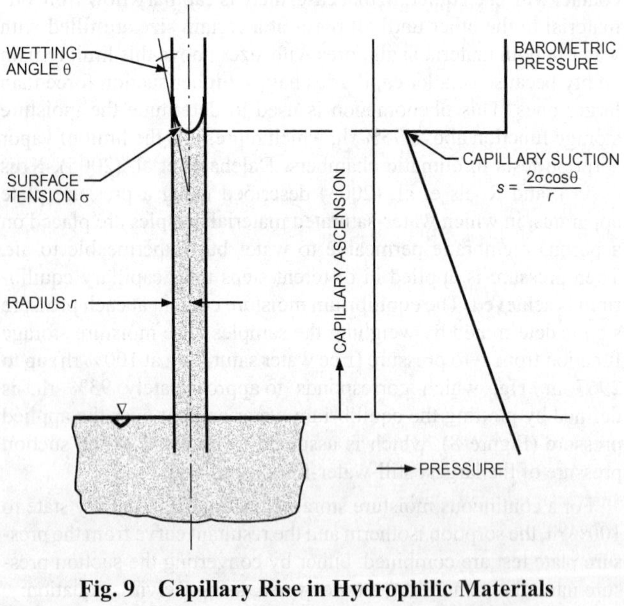

Fig. 9 Capillary Rise in Hydrophilic Materials

$$m_l = -k_m \operatorname{grad}(s) \quad (27)$$

where

m_l = liquid flux, lb/ft²·h
k_m = water permeability, lb/ft·h·in. Hg

Alternatively, with relative humidity as the driving factor [for the conversion, see Kelvin's Equation (23)]:

$$m_l = -\delta_\phi \operatorname{grad}(\phi) \quad (28)$$

where δ_ϕ is the liquid transport coefficient related to the relative humidity as driving potential, in lb/ft·h.

Capillary suction is greater in smaller capillaries, so water moves from larger to smaller capillaries. In pores with constant equivalent radius, water moves toward zones with smaller contact angles. Although surface tension is a decreasing function of temperature (the higher the temperature, the lower the surface tension) and water moves toward zones with lower temperature, that effect is small compared to the effect of equivalent pore diameter and contact angle.

Capillary suction increases linearly with the inverse of the radius [see Equation (26)], but the flow resistance increases proportionally to the fourth power of the inverse radius. Therefore, larger pores have a much greater liquid transport capacity than smaller pores. Because larger pores can only be filled with water once the smaller pores are saturated, the liquid transport capacity is a function of moisture content. Thus, water permeability k_m and liquid transport coefficient δ_ϕ are also functions of water content. Determination of these functions is, however, quite difficult because it requires the measurement of suction with respect to relative humidity distributions during transient water absorption and drying tests (Plagge et al. 2007).

Whereas measuring suction requires experience and special preparation of material samples, determining one-dimensional moisture content distributions in porous building materials can be done accurately with state-of-the-art scanning technologies using nuclear magnetic resonance (NMR), or gamma ray or x-ray attenuation (Krus 1996; Kumaran 1991; van Besien et al. 2002). Transient water content profiles recorded during such scanning tests serve to determine the liquid diffusivity D_w of the examined material, which is defined by

$$m_l = -D_w \operatorname{grad}(w) \quad (29)$$

where

w = moisture content, lb/ft³
D_w = liquid diffusivity, ft²/h

For most hygroscopic building materials, D_w is a function of moisture content.

Although Equation (29), which resembles Fick's law for diffusion, would seem a natural choice for calculating liquid flow, its use is not recommended because water content is not a continuous potential in building envelopes consisting of different materials. Using Equation (27) or (28) is recommended because relative humidity ϕ and capillary suction s are considered to be continuous potentials (no jumps at material interfaces). Where diffusivity functions are available, the liquid transport coefficient δ_ϕ in Equation (28) can be determined by

$$\delta_\phi = D_w\, dw/d\phi \quad (30)$$

where $dw/d\phi$ is the slope of the moisture retention curve, in lb/ft³.

Liquid Flow at Low Moisture Content

The explanation of liquid flow at low moisture content is still a matter of controversy. Some researchers assume it is surface diffusion (e.g., Krus 1996), whereas others believe liquid flow only fully starts beyond critical moisture content (Carmeliet et al. 1999; Kumaran et al. 2003; Vos and Coelman 1967). Liquid flow begins within the hygroscopic range, and is often mistaken for a part of vapor diffusion. In porous materials with a fixed pore structure, the apparent increase in vapor permeability during a wet-cup test may be partly because of liquid transport phenomena, and partly to shorter diffusion paths among water islands in the porous system formed by capillary condensation. Surface diffusion is defined as molecular movement of water adsorbed at the pore walls of the material. The driving potential is the mobility of the molecules, which depends on relative humidity in the pores (i.e., the adsorbed water migrates from zones of high to low relative humidity). Liquid flow, if present at low moisture content, can be described by Equations (28) or (29), as for capillary flow.

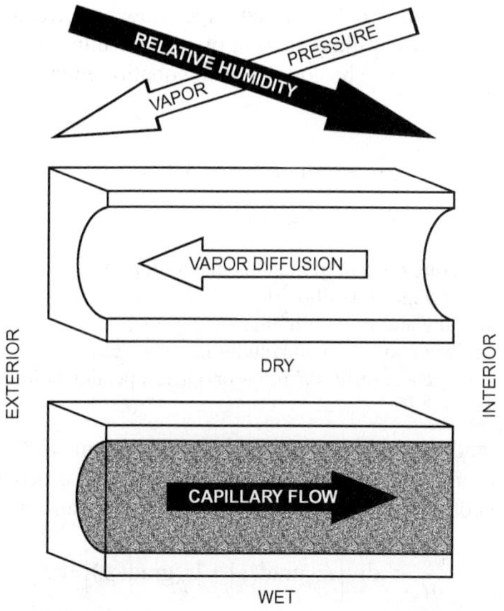

Fig. 10 Moisture Fluxes by Vapor Diffusion and Liquid Flow in Single Capillary of Exterior Wall under Winter Conditions

Under isothermal conditions, it is impossible to differentiate between vapor and liquid flow at low moisture content. However, in the presence of a temperature gradient, both transport processes may oppose each other in a pore; the fluxes may go in opposite directions (Künzel 1995). This can be explained by looking at the physical processes in a single capillary going through a wall, as shown in Figure 10. For heating climates in winter, the indoor vapor pressure is usually higher than outdoors while the indoor humidity is lower than outdoors. Therefore, the partial vapor pressure gradient is opposed to the relative humidity gradient over the cross section of a exterior wall. Looking at one capillary in that wall under very dry conditions (Figure 10), the only moisture transport mechanism is vapor diffusion and the total flux is directed towards the exterior. If the average humidity in the wall rises to 50 to 80% rh, liquid water begins to move in the opposite direction either by surface diffusion or by capillary suction in the nanopores. Under these conditions, the total moisture flux may go to zero if both fluxes are of the same magnitude (Krus 1996). When conditions are very wet (e.g., from wind-driven rain), most of the capillary pores are filled with water, and the dominant transport mechanism is flow by capillary suction.

Transient Moisture Flow

It is difficult to experimentally distinguish between liquid flow by suction and water vapor flow by diffusion in porous, hygroscopic materials. Because these materials have a very complex porous system and each surface is transversed by liquid-filled pore fractions and vapor-filled pore fractions, vapor and liquid flow are often treated as parallel processes. This allows expression of moisture flow as the summation of the two transport equations, one using water vapor pressure to drive water vapor flow by diffusion, and the other using either capillary suction or relative humidity ϕ to drive liquid moisture flow. The conservation equation in that case can be written as

$$\frac{\partial w}{\partial t} = -\operatorname{div}(m_w + m_v) + S_w \tag{31}$$

where

w = moisture content of building material, lb/ft³
m_v = water vapor flux, lb/ft²·h
m_w = liquid water flux, lb/ft²·h
S_w = moisture source or sink, lb/ft³·h
div = divergence (resulting inflow or outflow per unit volume of solid), ft^{-1}

Vapor and liquid fluxes are given by Equations (23), (27), and (28), which may be rewritten in terms of only two driving forces capillary suction pressure s and partial vapor pressure p:

$$\frac{\partial w}{\partial s} \times \frac{\partial s}{\partial t} = \operatorname{div}\left[k_m \operatorname{grad}(s) + \mu_p \operatorname{grad}(p)\right] + S_w \tag{32}$$

where

s = capillary suction pressure, in. Hg
p = partial vapor pressure, in. Hg
μ_p = vapor permeability (related to partial vapor pressure), lb/ft·h·in. Hg
k_m = water permeability (related to partial suction pressure), lb/ft·h·in. Hg
S_w = moisture source or sink, lb/ft³·h

Alternatively, suction pressure s in Equation (32) can be replaced by relative humidity as the sole variable, with saturation pressure p_{sat} only a function of temperature:

$$\frac{\partial w}{\partial \phi} \times \frac{\partial \phi}{\partial \tau} = \operatorname{div}\left[\delta_\phi \operatorname{grad}(\phi) + \mu_p \operatorname{grad}(\phi p_{sat})\right] + S_w \tag{33}$$

where

ϕ = relative humidity, %
p_{sat} = saturation vapor pressure, in. Hg
μ_p = vapor permeability (related to partial vapor pressure), lb/ft·h·in. Hg
δ_ϕ = liquid transport coefficient (related to relative humidity), lb/ft·h

Because of the strong temperature dependence of vapor pressure with respect to saturation vapor pressure, Equation (32) with respect to (33) must be coupled with Equation (3) to describe nonisothermal moisture flow. Under isothermal conditions, Equation (32) with respect to (33) could be solved independently. However, pure isothermal conditions hardly ever exist in reality; as soon as water evaporates or condenses, the latent heat effect leads to temperature differences. Other potentials may be used if material properties appropriate to those potentials are available.

5. COMBINED HEAT, AIR, AND MOISTURE TRANSFER

Combined heat, air, and moisture transfer can have a detrimental effect on a building. Air in- and exfiltration short-circuit the U-factor as a designed wall performance. Wind washing, indoor air washing, and stack-induced air movement may increment the U-factor by a factor of 2.5 or more. High moisture levels in building materials may also have a negative effect on the building envelope's thermal performance. Therefore, it is advisable to analyze the combined heat, air, and moisture transfer through building assemblies. However, some of these transport phenomena, especially those involving airflow, are three-dimensional in nature and difficult to predict because they mostly occur through accidental gaps, cracks, or imperfect joints. Research into these effects is ongoing, but at present, practitioners can only use simplified tools or hygrothermal models that do not yet cover all airflow-, gravity-, and pressure-gradient-induced moisture flow aspects.

6. SIMPLIFIED HYGROTHERMAL DESIGN CALCULATIONS AND ANALYSES

6.1 SURFACE HUMIDITY AND CONDENSATION

Surface condensation occurs when water vapor contacts a nonporous surface that has a temperature lower than the dew point of the surrounding air. Insulation should therefore be thick enough to ensure that the surface temperature on the warm side of an insulated assembly always exceeds the dew-point temperature there. However, even without reaching the dew point, relative humidity at the surface may become so high that, given enough time, mold growth occurs. According to Hens (1990), a simple design rule is that surface relative humidity in layers warmer than 41°F should not exceed 80% on a monthly mean basis.

The temperature ratio f_{h_i} is useful for calculating the surface temperature:

$$f_{h_i} = \frac{t_s - t_o}{t_i - t_o} \tag{34}$$

where

t_s = surface temperature on warm side, °F
t_o = ambient temperature on cold side, °F
t_i = ambient temperature on warm side, °F

The minimum temperature ratio to avoid surface condensation is

$$f_{h_i,min} = \frac{t_{d,i} - t_o}{t_i - t_o} \tag{35}$$

where $t_{d,i}$ is the dew point of ambient air on the warm side, °F.

The minimum insulation thickness to avoid surface condensation on a flat element can be calculated from

$$L_{min} = k\left[\frac{f_{h_i,min}}{h_i(1 - f_{h_i,min})} - R_{add}\right] \tag{36}$$

where R_{add} is the thermal resistance between the surface on the warm side and the cold ambient for the wall without thermal insulation, ft²·h·°F/Btu.

The condensation resistance of glazing is often estimated from outdoor and indoor design temperatures, U-factor of the window assembly, and air film resistance. A window assembly may have different U-factors at the glass, frame, and edge where the glass meets the frame; condensation resistance must be calculated at each of these locations. A procedure for these calculations can be found in NFRC (2004). The likelihood of window condensation depends strongly on the indoor air film resistance. This resistance may be reduced by washing the window with supply air. It may be increased by using window treatments indoors such as blinds or curtains, or by attaching self-adhesive infrared (IR) reflective films. Condensation on glazing is not inherently damaging, unless water is allowed to run onto painted or other surfaces that can be damaged by water.

6.2 INTERSTITIAL CONDENSATION AND DRYING

Dew-Point Method

The best-known simple steady-state design tools for evaluating interstitial condensation and drying within exterior envelopes (walls, roofs, and ceilings) are the dew-point method and the Glaser method (which uses the same underlying principles as the dew-point method, but uses graphic rather than computational methods). These methods assume that steady-state conduction governs heat flow and steady-state diffusion governs water vapor flow. Both analyses compare partial water vapor pressures in the envelope, as calculated by steady-state water vapor diffusion, with saturation water vapor pressures, which are based on calculated steady-state temperatures in the envelope.

The condition where the calculated partial water vapor pressure is greater than saturation has been called **condensation**. Strictly speaking, condensation is the change in phase from vapor to liquid, as occurs on glass, metal, synthetic foils, etc. For porous and hygroscopic building materials (e.g., wood, gypsum, masonry materials), vapor may be adsorbed or absorbed and only forms the droplets usually associated with true condensation when the moisture content passes capillary saturation. Nevertheless, the term *condensation* is used for this method to indicate vapor pressure in excess of saturation vapor pressure, although this could be misleading about actual water conditions on porous and hygroscopic surfaces. This is one of the unfortunate simplifications inherent in a steady-state analytic tool.

Steady-state heat conduction and vapor diffusion impose severe limitations on applicability and interpretation. The greatest one is that the main focus is on preventing sustained interstitial condensation, as indicated by vapor pressures beyond saturation vapor pressures. Many building failures (e.g., mold, buckling of siding, paint failure) are not necessarily related to interstitial condensation; conversely, limited interstitial condensation can often be tolerated, depending on the materials involved, temperature conditions, and speed at which the material dries out. (Drying can only be approximated because both the dew-point and Glaser methods neglect moisture storage and capillary flow.)

Because all moisture transfer mechanisms except water vapor diffusion are excluded, results should be considered as approximations and should be used with extreme care. Their validity and usefulness depend on judicious selection of boundary conditions, initial conditions, and material properties. Specifically, the methods should be used to estimate monthly or seasonal mean conditions only, rather than daily or weekly means. Furthermore, water vapor permeances may vary with relative humidity, and rain, flashing imperfections, leaky or poorly formed joints, rain exposure, airflow, and sunshine can have overriding effects. The dew-point and Glaser methods, however, are still used by design professionals and actually form the basis for most codes dealing with moisture control and vapor retarders.

For those who want to use this simple tool despite its shortcomings, a description of the dew-point method is presented in this chapter, with two application examples in Chapter 27. A comprehensive description of the dew-point and Glaser methods can be found in TenWolde (1994). The dew-point method uses the equations for steady-state heat conduction and diffusion in a flat component, with the vapor flux in a layer written as

$$-m_v = \mu_p \frac{\Delta p}{d} = \frac{\Delta p}{Z} \qquad (37)$$

where

m_v = water vapor flux through layer of material, gr/h·ft²
Δp = partial water vapor pressure difference across layer, in. Hg
μ_p = water vapor permeability of material, gr/ft·h·in. Hg
d = thickness of layer, ft
Z = water vapor resistance, in. Hg·ft²·h/gr

Over time, the dew-point method has been upgraded: (1) the concept of critical moisture content allows accounting for moisture build-up and upgraded calculation of drying, and (2) carried vapor flow has been included, underlining the importance of airtightness to avoid moisture deposition by condensation in building assemblies. Calculations have also been based on monthly mean outdoor weather data, corrected for solar gains, long-wave losses, the nonlinear relation between temperature and water vapor saturation pressure, and monthly mean indoor environmental data rather than on daily extremes (Hens 2007, 2016; Vos and Coelman 1967).

7. TRANSIENT COMPUTATIONAL ANALYSIS

Computer models can analyze and predict the heat, air, and moisture response of building components. These transient models can predict the varying hygrothermal situations in building components for different design configurations under various conditions and climates, and their capabilities are continually improved. Hens (1996) reviewed the state of the art of heat, air, and moisture transport modeling for buildings and identified 37 different models, most of which were research tools that are not readily available and may have been too complex for use by practitioners. Some, however, were available either commercially, free of charge, or through a consultant. Trechsel (2001) provided an update on existing tools and approaches.

For many applications and for design guide development, the actual behavior of an assembly under transient climatic conditions must be simulated, to account for short-term processes such as driving rain absorption, summer condensation, and phase changes. Understanding the application limits of such models is an important part of that process.

The features of a complete moisture analysis model include transient heat, air, and moisture transport formulation, incorporating the physics of contact conditions between layers and materials. Interfaces may be bridgeable for vapor diffusion, airflow, and gravity or pressure liquid flow only. They may be ideally capillary (no flow resistance from one layer to the next) or behave as a real contact (have an additional capillary resistance at the interface).

Not all these features are required for every analysis, though additional features may be needed in some applications (e.g., moisture flow through unintentional cracks and intentional openings, rain penetration through veneer walls and exterior cladding). To model these phenomena accurately, experiments may be needed to define subsystem performance under various loads (Straube and Burnett 1997). It is usually preferable to take performance measurements of system and subsystems in field situations, because only then are all exterior loads and influences captured.

Transient models enable timestep-by-timestep analysis of heat, air, and moisture conditions in building components, and give much more realistic results than steady-state conduction/diffusion and conduction/diffusion/airflow models. However, they are complex and usually not transparent, and require judgment and expertise on the part of the user. Existing models are one, two, or three dimensional, requiring the user to devise a realistic representation of the building component to be analyzed. Users should be aware which transport phenomena and types of boundary conditions are included and which are not. For instance, some models cannot handle air transport or rain wetting of the exterior. Results also tend to be very sensitive to the choice of indoor and outdoor conditions. Usually, exact conditions are not known. Indoor and outdoor conditions to be used were established by ASHRAE *Standard* 160. More extensive data on material properties are available [e.g., Kumaran (2006)], but it can be problematic finding accurate data for all the materials in a component.

Validation, verification, and benchmarking of combined heat, air, and moisture models is a formidable task. Currently, only limited internationally accepted experimental data exist. The main difficulty lies in the fact that it is difficult to measure air and moisture fluxes and moisture transport potentials, even under laboratory conditions. In addition, even an already validated model should be verified for each new application.

In most full hygrothermal models, common outputs are vapor pressure; temperature; moisture content; relative humidity; and air, heat, and moisture fluxes. Results must be checked for consistency, accuracy, grid independence, and sensitivity to parameter changes. The results may be used to evaluate the moisture tolerance of an envelope system subjected to various interior and exterior loads. Heat fluxes may be used to determine thermal performance under the influence of moisture and airflow. Furthermore, the transient output data may be used for durability and indoor air quality assessment. Postprocessing tools concerning durability (e.g., corrosion, mold growth, freeze and thaw, hygrothermal stress and strain, indoor air humidity) have been developed or are under development. For instance, Carmeliet (1992) linked full hygrothermal modeling to probability-based fracture mechanics to predict the risk of crack development and growth in an exterior insulation finish system (EIFS) by weathering. A transient model to estimate the rate of mold growth was developed by Sedlbauer (2001).

Combined heat, air, and moisture models also have limitations. Rain absorption, for example, can be modeled, but rainwater runoff and its consequences at joints, sills, and parapets cannot, although runoff followed by gravity-induced local penetration is one of the main causes of severe moisture problems. Even an apparently simple problem, such as predicting rain leakage through a brick veneer, is beyond many tools' capabilities. In such cases, simple qualitative schemes and field tests still are the way to proceed (Hens 2007).

7.1 CRITERIA TO EVALUATE HYGROTHERMAL SIMULATION RESULTS

At the building assembly and whole-building level, combined heat, air, and moisture transfer has consequences for thermal comfort, perceived indoor air quality, health, durability, and energy efficiency. Hygrothermal conditions in a building or within a building envelope assembly can be crucial for overall performance of the construction and its mechanical systems. Therefore, simulation results should be compared to limit conditions and widely accepted performance criteria determined for the following performance issues.

Thermal Comfort

Thermal comfort, defined as a condition of mind that expresses satisfaction with the thermal environment (ASHRAE *Standard* 55), depends on two human parameters (clothing and metabolism) and a set of environmental variables, among them relative humidity. At effective temperatures below 77°F, relative humidity's effect on thermal comfort is minimal, but above 77°F, its importance increases as latent heat loss becomes a main mechanism in getting rid of metabolic heat. If, at those temperatures, the air feels too moist, the thermal environment is perceived as uncomfortable. At low relative humidity, polluted air can irritate the mucosa, and electric discharges when touching insulators (e.g., plastic chairs) are felt. However, in most residential buildings and in many offices, temperature is controlled but not relative humidity, except in hot and humid climates. Its instantaneous value depends on the equilibrium between vapor release indoors, ventilation, airflow among rooms, and temporary vapor storage by finishes and furnishings (often called moisture buffering). The average value over longer periods depends on ventilation and vapor release only, influenced somewhat by moisture buffering.

Perceived Air Quality

Air quality may be defined exactly by measuring the pollutants present. However, occupants typically perceive drier, cooler air as smelling "fresher" than humid, warmer air. Thus, temperature and relative humidity affect perception of air freshness. Together, they define the air's enthalpy. Testing shows that higher enthalpy lowers the perception of freshness (Fang et al. 1998). Despite this fact, in most buildings, relative humidity is uncontrolled.

Human Health

Mold in buildings is of concern to occupants. Mold can grow on most surfaces if the relative humidity at the surface is above a critical value, the surface temperature is conducive to growth, and the substrate provides nutritional value to the organism. The growth rate depends on the magnitude and duration of surface relative humidity. Surface relative humidity is a complex function of material moisture content, local surface temperature, and humidity conditions in the space. In recognition of the issue's complexity, the International Energy Agency established a surface relative humidity criterion for design purposes: monthly average values should remain below 80% (Hens 1990). Other proposals include the Canada Mortgage and Housing Corporation's stringent requirement of always keeping surface relative humidity below 65% (CMHC 1999). Although there still is no agreement on which criterion is most appropriate, mold growth can usually be avoided by allowing surface relative humidity over 80% only for short time periods. The relative humidity criterion may be relaxed for nonporous surfaces that are regularly cleaned. Most molds only grow at temperatures above 40°F. Moisture accumulation below 40°F may not cause mold growth if the material is allowed to dry out below the hygroscopic moisture content for a relative humidity of 80% before the temperature rises above 40°F. Mathematical models for predicting a mold growth index were developed by Hukka and Viitanen (1999) and Sedlbauer (2001); these can be linked to results from hygrothermal analysis.

Dust mites trigger allergies and asthma. Dust mites thrive at high relative humidities (over 70%) at room temperature, but will not survive sustained relative humidities below 50% (Burge et al. 1994). Note that these values relate to local conditions in the places that mites tend to inhabit (e.g., mattresses, carpets, soft furniture).

Durability of Finishes and Structure

Moisture behind paint films may cause paint failure, and water or condensation may also cause streaking or staining. Excessive changes in moisture content of wood-based panels or boards may cause buckling or warp. Excessive moisture in masonry and concrete may cause salt efflorescence, or, when combined with low temperatures, freeze/thaw damage and spalling (chipping).

Structural failures caused by wood decay are rare but have occurred (Merrill and TenWolde 1989). Decay generally requires wood moisture content at fiber saturation (usually about 30% by weight) or higher and temperatures between 50 and 100°F. Such high wood moisture contents are possible in green lumber or by absorption of liquid water from condensation, leaks, groundwater, or saturated materials in contact with the wood. To maintain a safety margin, 20% moisture content by weight is sometimes used as the maximum allowable. Because wood moisture content can vary widely with sample location, a local moisture content of 20% or higher may indicate fiber saturation elsewhere. Once established, decay fungi produce water that enables them to maintain moisture conditions conducive to their growth.

Rusting of nails, nail plates, or other metal building components is also a potential cause of structural failure. Corrosion may occur at relative humidities near the metal surface above 60% or as a result of liquid water from elsewhere. Wood moisture content over 20% encourages corrosion of steel fasteners in the wood, especially if the wood is treated with preservatives. In buildings, metal fasteners are often the coldest surfaces, encouraging condensation and corrosion.

Energy Efficiency

Moisture can significantly degrade thermal performance of most insulation materials. Moisture contributes to heat transfer in both sensible and latent forms, as well as through mass transfer. The effect depends on the type of insulation material, moisture content, temperature of the insulation material and its thermal history, location of moisture in the insulation material, and the building envelope's interior and exterior environments. Reported relationships between thermal performance of the insulation material and moisture content vary significantly. Kyle and Desjarlais (1994) estimated that water distribution accounts for a difference of up to 25% in heat flux in some cases. Evaporation on the warm side and condensation or adsorption on the cold side add important latent heat components to the heat flux (Kumaran 1987).

Under conditions where water vapor pressure gradients change slowly or where the insulation layer has an extremely low water vapor permeance, little water vapor is transported, but moisture still affects sensible heat transfer in the building envelope component. Epstein and Putnam (1977) and Larsson et al. (1977) showed a nearly linear increase in sensible heat transfer of approximately 3 to 5% for each volume percent increase in moisture content in cellular plastic insulations. For example, an insulation material with about a 5% moisture content by volume has 15 to 25% greater heat transfer than when dry. Other field studies by Dechow and Epstein (1978) and Ovstaas et al. (1983) showed similar results for insulations installed in below-grade applications such as foundation walls.

REFERENCES

ASHRAE members can access ASHRAE Journal articles and ASHRAE research project final reports at technologyportal .ashrae.org. Articles and reports are also available for purchase by nonmembers in the online ASHRAE Bookstore at www.ashrae.org /bookstore.

ASHRAE. 2010. Thermal environmental conditions for human occupancy. ANSI/ASHRAE *Standard* 55-2010.

ASHRAE. 2007. Method of test for the evaluation of building energy analysis computer programs. ANSI/ASHRAE *Standard* 140-2007.

ASHRAE. 2009. Criteria for moisture-control design analysis in buildings. ANSI/ASHRAE *Standard* 160-2009.

ASTM. 2010. Terminology relating to thermal insulation. *Standard* C168-10. American Society for Testing and Materials, West Conshohocken, PA.

ASTM. 2011. Test method for thermal performance of building materials and envelope assemblies by means of a hot box apparatus. *Standard* C1363-11. American Society for Testing and Materials, West Conshohocken, PA.

ASTM. 2010. Test methods for water vapor transmission of materials. *Standard* E96/E96M-10. American Society for Testing and Materials, West Conshohocken, PA.

BSI. 1992. Code of practice for assessing exposure of walls to wind-driven rain. *Standard* BS 8104:1992. British Standards Institution, London.

Burge, H.A., H.J. Su, and J.D. Spengler. 1994. Moisture, organisms, and health effects. Chapter 6 in *Moisture control in buildings*, ASTM *Manual* MNL 18. American Society for Testing and Materials, West Conshohocken, PA.

Burnett, E., J. Straube, and A. Karagiozis. 2004. Development of design strategies for rainscreen and sheathing membrane performance in wood frame walls. ASHRAE Research Project RP-1091, *Final Report*.

CAN/CSA. 2005. Windows. *Standard* A440-00 (R2005). Canadian Standards Association, Mississauga, ON.

Carmeliet, J. 1992. *Durability of fiber-reinforced rendering for exterior insulation systems*. Ph.D. dissertation, Catholic University–Leuven, Belgium.

Carmeliet, J., G. Houvenaghel, and F. Descamps. 1999. Multiscale network for simulating liquid water and water vapour transfer properties of porous materials. *Transport in Porous Materials* 35:67-88.

Christian, J.E., A.O. Desjarlais, and T.K. Stovall. 1998. Straw bale wall hot box test results and analysis. *Thermal Performance of the Exterior Envelopes of Buildings VII*, ASHRAE.

CMHC. 1999. *Best practice guide, wood frame envelopes*. Canada Mortgage and Housing Corporation and Canada Wood Council, Ottawa.

Dalehaug, A., O. Aunronning, and B. Time. 2005. Measurement of water retention properties of plaster: A parameter study of the influence on moisture balance of an external wall construction from variations of this parameter. *Proceedings of the 7th Symposium on Building Physics in the Nordic Countries*, Reykjavik, pp. 94-101.

Dechow, F.J., and K.A. Epstein. 1978. Laboratory and field investigations of moisture absorption and its effect on thermal performance of various insulations. ASTM *Special Technical Publication* STP 660:234-260.

Douglas, J.S., T.H. Kuehn, and J.W. Ramsey. 1992. A new moisture permeability measurement method and representative test data. *ASHRAE Transactions* 98(2):513-519.

Epstein, K.A., and L.E. Putnam. 1977. Performance criteria for the protected membrane roof system. *Proceedings of the Symposium on Roofing Technology*. National Institute of Standards and Technology, Gaithersburg, MD, and National Roofing Contractors Association, Rosemont, IL.

Fang, L., G. Clausen, and P.O. Fanger. 1998. Impact of temperature and humidity on the perception of indoor air quality. *Indoor Air* 8:80-90.

Galbraith, G.H., R.C. McLean, and J.S. Guo. 1998. Moisture permeability data presented as a mathematical relationship. *Building Research & Information* 20(6):364-372.

Hedlin, C.P. 1988. Heat flow through a roof insulation having moisture contents between 0 and 1% by volume, in summer. *ASHRAE Transactions* 94(2):1579-1594.

Hens, H. 1990. *Guidelines & practice*. International Energy Agency Annex XIV, Leuven, Belgium.

Hens, H. 1992. Air/wind tightness of pitched roofs—How they really behave. (In German.) *Bauphysik* 14(6):161-174.

Hens, H. 1996. Heat, air and moisture transfer in highly insulated envelope parts, task 1: Modelling. *Final Report*, vol. 1, International Energy Agency, Annex 24. Catholic University–Leuven, Laboratorium for Building Physics, Belgium.

Hens, H. 2007. Does heat, air moisture modeling really help in solving hygrothermal problems? *Proceedings Rakennusfysiikka*, Technical University of Tampere, Finland.

Hens, H. 2016. *Applied building physics: Boundary conditions, building performance, material properties*, 2nd ed. Ernst & Sohn, Berlin.

Hens, H., A. Janssens, W. Depraetere, J. Carmeliet, and J. Lecompte. 2007a. Brick cavity walls: A performance analysis based on measurements and simulation. *Journal of Building Physics* 31(2):95-124.

Hens, H., F. Vaes, A. Janssens, and G. Houvenaghel. 2007b. A flight over a roof landscape: Impact of 40 years of roof research on roof practices in Belgium. *Thermal Performance of the Exterior Envelopes of Whole Buildings X*. ASHRAE.

Hukka, A., and H. Viitanen. 1999. A mathematical model of mold growth on wooden material. *Wood Science and Technology* 33(6):475-485.

ISO/DIN. 2009. Hygrothermal performance of buildings—Calculation and presentation of climatic data—Part 3: Calculation of a driving rain index for vertical surfaces from hourly wind and rain data. *Standard* 15927-3:2009. International Organization for Standardization, Geneva, and Deutsches Institut für Normung, Berlin.

Janssens, A. 1998. *Reliable control of interstitial condensation in lightweight roof systems*. Ph.D. dissertation, Catholic University–Leuven, Belgium.

Kronvall, J. 1982. Air flows in building components. *Report* TVBH-1002. Division of Building Technology, Lund University of Technology, Sweden.

Krus, M. 1996. *Moisture transport and storage coefficients of porous mineral building materials: Theoretical principles and new test methods*. Fraunhofer IRB Verlag, Stuttgart.

Kumaran, M.K. 1987. Vapor transport characteristics of mineral fiber insulation from heat flow measurements. In *Water vapor transmission through building materials and systems: Mechanisms and measurements*. ASTM *Special Technical Publication* STP 1039:19-27.

Kumaran, M.K. 1991. Application of gamma-ray spectroscopy for determination of moisture distribution in insulating materials. *Proceedings of the International Centre for Heat and Mass Transfer*, pp. 95-103.

Kumaran, M.K. 2006. A thermal and moisture transport database for common building and insulating materials (RP-1018). *ASHRAE Transactions* 112(2):485-497.

Kumaran, M., J. Lackey, N. Normandin, F. Tariku, and D. Van Reenen. 2003. Variations in the hygrothermal properties of several wood-based building products. In *Research in Building Physics: Proceedings of the*

Second International Conference on Building Physics, Leuven, Belgium, pp. 35-42. J. Carmeliet, H. Hens, and G. Vermeir, eds. Taylor and Francis, London.

Künzel, H.M. 1995. *Simultaneous heat and moisture transport in building components: One- and two-dimensional calculation using simple parameters*. Fraunhofer IRB Verlag, Stuttgart.

Künzel, H.M. 1999. More moisture load tolerance of construction assemblies through the application of a smart vapor retarder. *Thermal Performance of Exterior Envelopes of Buildings VII*, pp. 129-132. ASHRAE.

Künzel, H.M. 2007. Factors determining surface moisture on external walls. *Thermal Performance of the Exterior Envelopes of Whole Buildings X*. ASHRAE.

Künzel, H.M., and T. Grosskinski. 1989. Non-ventilated and fully insulated—The best solution for the pitched roof. (In German). *Warme- und Kalteschutz im Bau* 27.

Künzel, H.M., and A. Holm. 2001. *Simulation of heat and moisture transfer in construction assemblies*. Fraunhofer IBP, Holzkirchen. publica .fraunhofer.de/documents/N-26888.html.

Künzel, H.M., and A. Karagiozis. 2004. Vapor control in cold and coastal climate zones. *Proceedings of the Canadian Conference on Building Energy Simulation, eSim 2004*, pp. 55-60.

Kyle, D.M., and A.O. Desjarlais. 1994. Assessment of technologies for constructing self-drying low-slope roofs. Oak Ridge National Laboratory *Report* ORNL/CON-380. Oak Ridge, TN.

Lacy, R.E. 1965. Driving-rain maps and the onslaught of rain on buildings. *Proceedings of the RILEM/CIB Symposium on Moisture Problems in Buildings*, Helsinki, Finland.

Larsson, L.E., J. Ondrus, and B.A. Petersson. 1977. The protected membrane roof (PMR)—A study combining field and laboratory tests. *Proceedings of the Symposium on Roofing Technology*. National Institute of Standards and Technology, Gaithersburg, MD, and National Roofing Contractors Association, Rosemont, IL.

Merrill, J.L., and A. TenWolde. 1989. Overview of moisture-related damage in one group of Wisconsin manufactured homes. *ASHRAE Transactions* 95(1):405-414.

METEOTEST. 2007. *Handbook of METEONORM—Global meteorological database for engineers, planners and education*. METEOTEST, Bern, Switzerland.

Morrison Hershfield. 2011. Thermal performance of building envelope details for mid- and high-rise buildings. ASHRAE Research Project RP-1365, *Report*.

NFRC. 2004. Procedure for determining fenestration product condensation resistance values. *Technical Document* 500. National Fenestration Rating Council, Silver Spring, MD.

Ovstaas, G., S. Smith, W. Strzepek, and G. Titley. 1983. Thermal performance of various insulations in below-earth-grade perimeter application. ASTM *Special Technical Publication* STP 789:435-454.

Palfey, A.J. 1980. Thermal performance of low emittance building sheathing. *Journal of Thermal Insulation* (now *Journal of Building Physics*) 3:129-141.

Pedersen, C.R. 1990. Combined heat and moisture transfer in building constructions. *Report* 214. Technical University of Denmark.

Pedersen-Rode, C., T.W. Petrie, G.E. Courville, P.W. Childs, and K.E. Wilkes. 1991. Moisture migration and drying rates for low slope roofs—Preliminary results. *Proceedings of the 3rd International Symposium on Roofing Technology*. National Roofing Contractors Association, Rosemont, IL.

Plagge, R., G. Scheffler, and A. Nicolai. 2007. Experimental methods to derive hygrothermal material functions for numerical simulation tools. *Thermal Performance of Exterior Envelopes of Buildings X*. ASHRAE.

Robinson, H.E., F.J. Powlitch, and R.S. Dill. 1954. The thermal insulating value of airspaces. Housing and Home Finance Agency, *Housing Research Paper* 32, U.S. Government Printing Office, Washington, D.C.

Roels, S., J. Carmeliet, and H. Hens. 2003. Hamstad, WP 1: Moisture transfer properties and material characterisation. *Final Report* (GRD1-1999-2007), KUL2003-18, Catholic University–Leuven, Belgium.

Salonvaara, M. 2011. Environmental weather loads for hygrothermal analysis and design of buildings. ASHRAE Research Project RP-1325, *Report*.

Sanders, C. 1996. Environmental conditions. IEA Annex 24 *Report*, vol. 2, Catholic University–Leuven, Belgium.

Schwarz, B. 1971. *Die Wärme- und Stoffübertragung an Außenwandoberflächen*. (*Heat and mass transfer at exterior wall surfaces*.) Dissertation, University of Stuttgart.

Sedlbauer, K. 2001. *Prediction of mould fungus formation on the surface of and inside building components*. Ph.D. dissertation, University of Stuttgart.

Shuman, E.C. 1980. Field measurement of heat flux through a roof with saturated thermal insulation and covered with black and white granules. ASTM *Special Technical Publication* STP 718:519-539.

Straube, J., and E. Burnett. 1997. Rain control and screened wall systems. *7th Conference on Building Science and Technology, Durability of Buildings—Design, Maintenance, Codes and Practices*, pp. 17-37.

Straube J., and E. Burnett. 2000. Simplified prediction of driving rain on buildings. *Proceedings of the First International Building Physics Conference*, Technische Universiteit–Eindhoven, the Netherlands, pp. 375-382.

TenWolde, A. 1994. Design tools. Chapter 11 in *Moisture control in buildings*. ASTM *Manual* MNL 18. American Society for Testing and Materials, West Conshohocken, PA.

TenWolde, A., and I. Walker. 2001. Interior moisture design loads for residences. In *Thermal Performance of Exterior Envelopes of Buildings VIII*. ASHRAE.

Trechsel, H. 2001. *Moisture analysis and condensation control in building envelopes*. ASTM *Manual* MNL 40. American Society for Testing and Materials, West Conshohocken, PA.

Van Besien, T., S. Roels, and J. Carmeliet. 2002. Experimental determination of moisture: Diffusivity of porous building materials using x-ray radiography. *Proceedings of the 6th Nordic Symposium on Building Physics*, Trondheim, Norway.

Vos, B.H., and E.J.W. Coelman. 1967. Condensation in structures. *Report* BI-67-33/23, TNO-IBBC, Rijswijk, the Netherlands.

Zheng, R., A. Janssens, J. Carmeliet, W. Bogaerts, and H. Hens. 2004. An evaluation of highly insulated cold zinc roofs in a moderate humid climate, Part 2—Corrosion behaviour of zinc sheeting. *Construction and Building Materials* 18(1):61-71.

BIBLIOGRAPHY

ASTM. 2015. Test method for steady-state thermal transmission properties by means of the heat flow meter apparatus. *Standard* C518. American Society for Testing and Materials, West Conshohocken, PA.

Hens, H. 2012. *Building physics: Heat, air and moisture—Fundamentals and engineering methods with examples and exercises*, 2nd ed. Ernst & Sohn, Berlin.

Kumaran, M.K. 1999. Moisture diffusivity of building materials from water absorption measurements. *Journal of Thermal Envelope and Building Science* 22:349-355.

Sedlbauer, K., M. Krus, C. Fitz, and H.M. Künzel. 2011. Reducing the risk of microbial growth on insulated walls by PCM enhanced renders and IR reflecting paints. *Proceedings 12DBMC—International Conference on Durability of Building Materials and Components*.

Tomlinson, J., C. Jotshi, and D. Goswami. 1992. Solar thermal energy storage in phase change materials. *Proceedings of Solar '92: The American Solar Energy Society Annual Conference*, Cocoa Beach, FL.

CHAPTER 26

HEAT, AIR, AND MOISTURE CONTROL IN BUILDING ASSEMBLIES—MATERIAL PROPERTIES

THIS chapter contains material property data related to the thermal-, air-, and moisture-related performance of building assemblies. The information can be used in simplified calculation methods as applied in Chapter 27, or in software-based methods for transient solutions. Heat transfer under steady-state and transient conditions is covered in Chapter 4, and Chapter 25 discusses combined heat, air, and moisture transport in building assemblies. For information on thermal insulation for mechanical systems (including insulation used in a range of temperatures), see Chapter 23. For information on insulation materials used in refrigerant piping systems and cryogenic or low-temperature applications, see Chapters 10 and 47 of the 2014 *ASHRAE Handbook—Refrigeration*. For properties of materials not typically used in building construction, see Chapter 33 of this volume.

Density and thermal properties such as thermal conductivity, thermal resistance, specific heat capacity, and emissivity for long-wave radiation are provided for a wide range of building materials, insulating materials, and insulating systems. Air and moisture properties (e.g., air permeance, water vapor permeance or permeability, capillary water-absorption coefficients, sorption isotherms) are given for several materials, with a brief description of how to use the tabulated data. Data on soil thermal conductivity, air cavity resistances, and surface film coefficients, which are also important when considering performance of building assemblies, are also provided.

1. INSULATION MATERIALS AND INSULATING SYSTEMS

The main purpose of using thermal insulation materials is to reduce conductive, convective, and radiant heat flows. When properly applied in building envelopes, insulating materials do at least one of the following:

- Increase energy efficiency by reducing the building's heat loss or gain
- Control surface temperatures for occupant comfort
- Help to control temperatures within an assembly, to reduce the potential for condensation
- Modulate temperature fluctuations in unconditioned or partly conditioned spaces

The primary property of a thermal insulation material is a low apparent thermal conductivity. Additional functions may be served, such as providing support for a surface finish, impeding water vapor transmission and air leakage into or out of controlled spaces, reducing damage to structures from exposure to fire and freezing conditions, and providing better control of noise and vibration. These functions, of course, should be consistent with the capabilities of the materials.

ASTM *Standard* C168 defines terms related to thermal insulating materials.

1.1 APPARENT THERMAL CONDUCTIVITY

The primary property of a thermal insulation material is a low apparent thermal conductivity, though selection of the appropriate material for a given application also involves consideration of the other performance characteristics mentioned previously.

Thermal conductivity (symbol k, λ in Europe) is a property of a homogeneous, nonporous material. Thermal insulation materials are highly porous, however, with porosities typically exceeding 90%. As a consequence, heat transmission involves conduction in the solid matrix but mainly gas conduction and radiation in the pores (even convection can occur in larger pores). This is why the term **apparent thermal conductivity** is used. That property is affected by structural parameters such as density, matrix type (fibrous or cellular), and thickness. Each sample of a given insulation material has a unique value of apparent thermal conductivity for a particular combination of temperature, temperature difference, moisture content, and age, a value that is not representative for other conditions. For more details, refer to ASTM *Standards* C168, C177, C335, C518, C976, and C1045.

Influencing Conditions

Density and Structure. Figure 1 shows the variation of the apparent thermal conductivity with density at one mean temperature (i.e., 75°F) for a number of insulation materials used in building envelopes. For most mass-type insulations, there is a minimum that not only depends on the type and form of the material but also on temperature and direction of heat flow. For fibrous materials, the values of density at which the minimum occurs increase as the fiber diameter [or cell size; see Figure 2 (Lotz 1969)] and mean temperature increase.

Structural factors also include compaction and settling of insulation, air permeability, type and amount of binder used, additives that influence the bond or contact between fibers or particles, and type and form of the radiation transfer inhibitor, if any. In cellular materials, most factors that influence strength also control the apparent thermal conductivity: size, shape, and orientation of cells, and thickness of cell walls. As Figures 1 and 2 suggest, a specific combination of cell size, density, and gas composition in those materials produces optimum thermal conductivity.

The preparation of this chapter is assigned to TC 4.4, Building Materials and Building Envelope Performance.

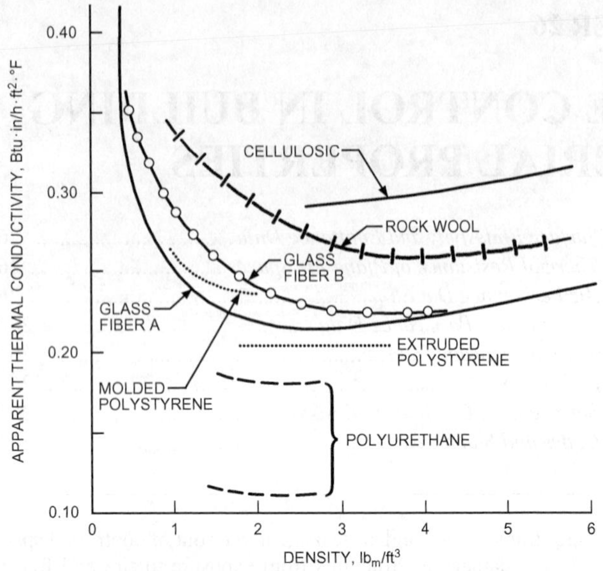

Fig. 1 Apparent Thermal Conductivity Versus Density of Several Thermal Insulations Used as Building Insulations

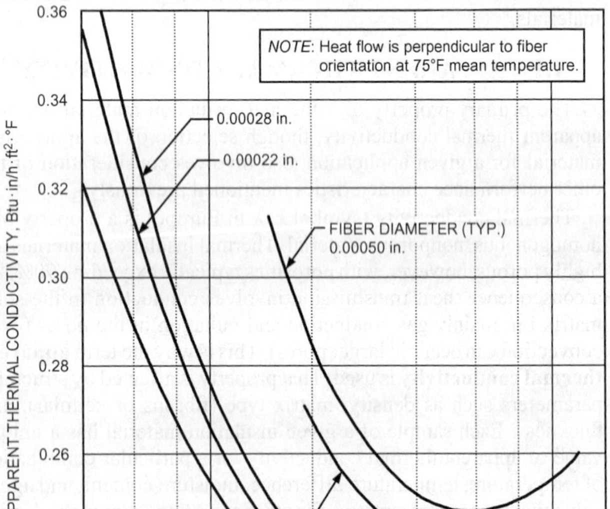

Fig. 2 Variation of Apparent Thermal Conductivity with Fiber Diameter and Density
(Lotz 1969)

Temperature. At most normal operating temperatures, the apparent thermal conductivity of insulating materials generally increases with temperature. The rate of change varies with material type and density. Some materials have an inflection in the curve where the blowing agent changes phase from gas to liquid. The apparent thermal conductivity of a sample at one mean temperature (average of the two surface temperatures) only applies to the material at the particular thickness tested. Further testing is required to obtain values suitable for all thicknesses.

Insulating materials that allow a large percentage of heat transfer by radiation, such as low-density fibrous and cellular products, show the greatest change in apparent thermal conductivity with temperature and surrounding surface emissivity.

The effect of temperature on structural integrity is unimportant for most insulation materials in low-temperature applications. At very low temperatures, however, some polymeric compounds may undergo glass transition, which is characterized by a marked increase in thermal conductivity. For urethanes and butyl-based compounds, this occurs at approximately –40°F, but for silicones the glass transition temperature is more in the range of –130°F, which is not normally encountered in building applications. In any case, decomposition, excessive linear shrinkage, softening, or other effects limit the maximum suitable temperature for a material.

Moisture Content. The apparent thermal conductivity of insulation materials increases with moisture content. If moisture condenses in the insulation, it not only reduces thermal resistance, but it may also physically damage the system, because some insulation materials deteriorate with exposure to water. Most materials would be damaged if moisture were allowed to freeze in the material, because water expands when it freezes. The increase in apparent thermal conductivity depends on the material, temperature, moisture content, and moisture distribution. Section A3 of the *CIBSE Guide A* (CIBSE 2006) covers thermal properties of building structures affected by moisture.

Thickness. Radiant heat transfer in pores of some materials increases the measured apparent thermal conductivity. For low-density insulation (e.g., 0.35 lb/ft^3), the effect becomes more pronounced with installed thickness) (Pelanne 1979). The effect on thermal resistance is small, even negligible for building applications. No thickness effect is observed in foam insulation.

Age. As mentioned previously, most heat transfer in insulation materials at temperatures encountered in buildings and outdoors occurs by conduction through air or another gas in the pores (Lander 1955; Rowley et al. 1952; Simons 1955; Verschoor and Greebler 1952). In fact, heat transfer in dry insulation materials can be closely approximated by combining gas conduction with conduction through the matrix and radiation in the pores, each determined separately. If air in the pores of a cellular insulation material is replaced by a gas with a different thermal conductivity, the apparent thermal conductivity changes by an amount approximately equal to the difference between the thermal conductivity of air and the gas. For example, replacing air with an inert gas can lower the apparent thermal conductivity by as much as 50%. Cellular plastic foams with a high proportion (i.e., more than 90%) of closed cells retain the blowing agent for extended periods of time. Newly produced, they have apparent thermal conductivities of approximately 0.15 Btu·in/h·ft^2·°F at 75°F. This value increases with time as air diffuses into the cells and the gas gradually dissolves in the polymer or diffuses out. Diffusion rates and increase in apparent thermal conductivity depend on several factors, including permeance of cell walls to the gases involved, foam age, temperature, geometry of the insulation (thickness), and integrity of the surface facing or covering provided. Brandreth (1986) and Tye (1988) showed that aging of unfaced polyurethane and polyisocyanurate is reasonably well understood analytically and confirmed experimentally. The dominant parameters for minimum aging are

- Closed-cell content >90%, preferably >95%
- Small, uniform cell diameter <<0.04 in.
- Small anisotropy in cell structure
- High density
- Increased thickness
- High initial pressure of blowing agent in the cells
- Polymer highly resistant to gas diffusion and solubility

- Larger proportion of polymer evenly distributed in struts and windows between cells
- Low temperature

For laminated and spray-applied products, aging is further reduced with higher-density polymer skins, or by well-adhered facings and coverings with low gas and moisture permeance. An oxygen diffusion rate of less than 0.02 $in^3/1000\ ft^2 \cdot day$ for a 0.001 in. thick facing is one criterion used by some industry organizations for manufacturers of laminated products. Adhesion of the facing must be continuous, and every effort must be made during manufacturing to eliminate or minimize the shear plane layer at the foam/substrate interface (Ostrogorsky and Glicksman 1986).

Before 1987, chlorinated fluorocarbons were commonly used as cell gas. Because of their high ozone-depleting potential, chlorofluorocarbons (CFCs) were phased out during the 1990s in accordance with the Montreal Protocol of 1987. Alternatives used today are fluorinated hydrocarbons, CO_2, *n*-pentane, and *c*-pentane.

Closed-cell phenolic-type materials and products, which are blown with similar gases, age differently and much more slowly because of their closed-cell structure.

Other Influences. Convection and air infiltration in or through some insulation systems may increase heat transfer. Low-density, loose-fill, large open-cell, and fibrous insulation, and poorly designed or installed reflective systems are the most susceptible. The temperature difference across the insulation and the height and width of the insulated space influence the amount of convection. In some cases, natural convection may be inherent to the system (Wilkes and Childs 1992; Wilkes and Rucker 1983), but in many cases it is a consequence of careless design and/or construction of the insulated structure (Donnelly et al. 1976). Gaps between board- and batt-type insulations lower their effectiveness. Board-type insulation may not be perfectly square, may be installed improperly, and may be applied to uneven surfaces. A 4% void area around batt insulation can produce a 50% loss in effective thermal resistance for ceiling application with $R = 19\ h \cdot ft^2 \cdot °F/Btu$ (Verschoor 1977). Similar and worse results have been obtained for wall configurations (Brown et al. 1993; Hedlin 1985; Lecompte 1989; Lewis 1979; Rasmussen et al. 1993; Tye and Desjarlais 1981). As a solution, preformed joints in board-type insulation allow boards to fit together without air gaps. Boards and batts can be installed in two layers, with joints between layers offset and staggered. The requirements of ASHRAE *Standard* 90.1 provide additional guidance on proper installation of insulating materials, as does Chapter 44 in the 2015 *ASHRAE Handbook—HVAC Applications*.

Measurement. Apparent thermal conductivity for insulation materials and systems is obtained by the measuring methods listed in ASTM (2008). These methods apply mainly to laboratory measurements on dried or conditioned samples at specific mean temperatures and temperature gradient conditions. Although fundamental heat transmission characteristics of a material or system can be determined accurately, actual performance in a structure may vary from laboratory results. Only field measurements can clarify the differences. Field-test procedures continue to be developed. Envelope design, construction, and material may all affect the procedure to be followed, as detailed in ASTM (1985a, 1985b, 1988, 1990, 1991).

1.2 MATERIALS AND SYSTEMS

Glass Fiber and Mineral Wool

Glass fiber is produced using recycled glass, whereas mineral wool uses diabase stone. Glass and stone are melted, after which a spinning head stretches the melt into fibers with diameter <10 μm. These fall through a spray of phenol or silicon binder onto the facings for blankets and batts, which lie on a conveyor belt. The fiber blankets, batts, or boards pass a heated press where the binder hardens and the insulation gets its final density and thickness. After passing through the press, the blankets, batts, or boards are cut to size. The spectrum of finished products includes loose fill; over blankets and batts; and soft, semidense, and dense boards. Blankets cannot take any extra load, except their own weight. Dense boards are moderately compression resistant, with a modulus of σ_{10}, or about 5.5 to 11.5 psia.

Mineral wool and glass fiber may look similar, but there are important differences. Glass fiber consists of well-ordered, long fibers, whereas mineral wool is composed of unordered, shorter fibers. Glass is also amorphous, whereas diabase stone is crystalline.

The thermal conductivity of glass fiber is somewhat lower than for mineral wool (see Table 1), with lower values for higher-density blankets in both materials. Glass and mineral fiber are very vapor permeable. The coefficient of thermal expansion is low for both materials, at $\sim 4 \times 10^{-6} °F^{-1}$, and irreversible hygrothermal deformation does not occur. The two are also very temperature resistant, although the binder may start evaporating above 480°F and degrades above 1100°F for glass fiber and above 1550°F for mineral wool (consequently, mineral wool is preferred for high-temperature applications). Both insulation materials are quite moisture tolerant, although wet batts and blankets lose their shape, and the stiffness and compression strength of some dense boards degrade when wet. Glass fibers slowly pulverize when exposed to a combination of high temperature, moisture, and oxygen. Neither glass fiber nor mineral wool burn, but the binder may be combustible. Binder concentrations below 4% simply evaporate, but more concentrated binders can burn. Also, most facing layers are flammable.

Glass fiber and mineral wool are widely used insulation materials. Applications range from low-slope roofs (dense boards) and pitched roofs (blankets, batts, and soft boards) to cavity fill (semidense water-repellant boards), timber-frame insulation, exterior insulation finishing systems (EIFS) (dense boards), floor insulation (dense boards), and perimeter insulation (dense boards). Manufacturers modify specific products for many applications, including boards with improved water-repellent properties for full-cavity fill and boards with a dense upper layer for low-slope roofing.

Cellulose Fiber

The base material for cellulose fiber is unsold or recycled newspaper and cardboard. Borax salts are added during processing to reduce flammability and mold sensitivity. The material is available in loose form, and is placed into the desired space by wet or dry blowing, which results in densities between 1.5 and 3.75 lb/ft^3, depending on blowing pressure. The material is also available in board form.

Cellulose fibers are very hygroscopic, and the borax salt magnifies that property. The fibers are also capillary active, and quite vapor permeable. Avoid loading beyond the weight of a loose fill. Less densely packed cellulose fibers show irreversible settling and are sensitive to hygric swelling and shrinking; wet-blown fibers exhibit shrinkage upon drying. Long-lasting moisture content above 20% (as a percentage of dry weight) should be avoided, because this ultimately leads to decay. Despite the borax salts, cellulose fibers are rather combustible. The borax salts are also not benign: simple exposure may cause respiratory and skin irritation, and ingestion could induce gastrointestinal distress (including nausea, persistent vomiting, abdominal pain, and diarrhea); less common effects on the vascular system and brain are headaches and lethargy.

Cellulose fibers are typically used as an alternative for glass fiber and mineral wool. Typical applications are insulation of timber-framed walls, and insulation of the ceiling between living spaces and attics. The boards are used for insulating pitched roofs. One important limitation: never apply cellulose fiber (or any insulation, for that matter) where continued long-term wetness may be expected.

Plastic Foams

Expanded Polystyrene (EPS). The basic material for EPS is pentane-blown polystyrene pearls. The pearls are first heated above 212°F, at which temperature the evaporating pentane causes expansion. The expanded pearls are then stored for a few days, allowing diffusion of the remaining pentane. Then they are poured into molds and steam heated, so that the expanded pearls coagulate in their own melt. Once cool, the blocks are cut into boards and stored until initial shrinkage ends. EPS is a thermoplastic with a problematic fire reaction: it melts and drips when burning. Consequently, additives are used to slow down flammability.

Extruded Polystyrene (XPS). The basic material for XPS is polystyrene pearls, which are melted, blown with a blowing agent, and extruded into boards with a dense skin. The extruded foam is then stabilized in a water bed and cut into separate boards. As with EPS, XPS is stored for several weeks before application. XPS is also a thermoplastic with additives used to slow down flammability. The water vapor resistance of XPS boards is very high, allowing their use in inverted roofs and as perimeter insulation in humid soils.

Polyurethane (PUR and Polyisocyanurate (PIR). PUR and PIR are the only insulation materials produced chemically by isocyanate reacting with polyolefin in the presence of a catalyst, a blowing agent, and additives. The difference between the two is the isocyanate ratio: in PIR, this ratio is high enough (60 to 65% lb/lb instead of 50 to 55% lb/lb) to form autopolymers. The main result is a better reaction in combustion. Because the explosive isocyanate/polyolefin reaction is highly sensitive to temperature and relative humidity, strict control of both parameters is needed. The reaction product is also very sticky, which allows the mixture to be sprayed on many kinds of substrates, or to be used to produce sandwich panels (Figure 3). Once the reaction is finished, the boards are cut to the desired size and stored.

R-11 [a CFC with ozone depletion potential (ODP) = 1] was used as a blowing agent until the early 1990s. Since then, blowing agents with zero ODP are preferred, such as hydrofluorocarbons (HFCs) for PUR insulation boards, HFCs or CO_2 for spray-applied PUR, and pentane for PIR boards.

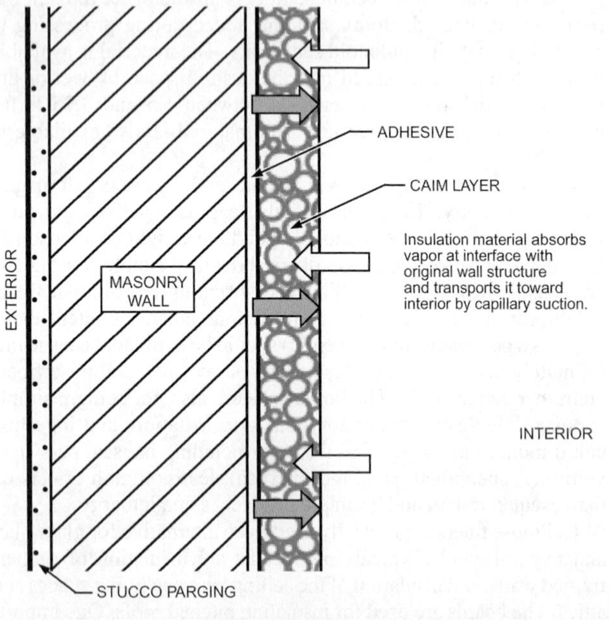

Fig. 3 Working Principle of Capillary-Active Interior Insulation

Cellular Glass

Cellular glass is a light, expanded-glass insulation with closed-cell pores. It is water- and vaportight, allowing neither vapor diffusion nor capillary suction through the material. Depending on the production process, cellular glass is delivered either as insulating boards or as loose-fill aggregate. The boards are used for roof, wall, basement, and foundation insulation; loose fill is only used for foundation or basement insulation. Cellular glass boards must be protected from frost damage caused by water freezing in its open surface pores. The R-value of cellular glass boards is not affected by moisture, but the thermal resistance of loose fill decreases in moist conditions because of water clinging to the surface of the aggregates.

Capillary-Active Insulation Materials (CAIMs)

CAIMs are used as interior wall insulation for existing buildings. Despite being rather vapor permeable, they are applied without a vapor-retarding layer because condensing moisture is supposed to be wicked away from the dew point toward the interior wall surface (Figure 3). In contrast to conventional insulation systems that need a vapor retarder to protect the wall structure from harmful condensation, CAIMs provide condensation control without reducing the drying potential towards the indoors. Because of increasing demand in Europe, several capillary-active insulation systems made of calcium silicate, foamed concrete, or hydrophilic glass fiber have appeared on the market. Tests [e.g., (Zhao et al. (2017)] show that these materials may differ in their wicking ability, but most of them succeed in redistributing condensate by capillary suction. However, even the best-performing CAIM cannot prevent increased relative humidity at the interface between interior insulation and original wall surface of 95% or more in winter (Binder et al. 2010). The benefits of CAIMs for insulating existing wall structures are therefore still debatable. Other potential concerns are that their thermal resistances are also generally inferior to those of conventional insulation (k = 0.35 to 0.42 Btu·in/h·ft^2·°F).

Transparent Insulation

Transparent insulation material (TIM) combines transparency for short-wave radiation with low heat conduction, extremely low convection, and opacity for long-wave radiation. The material comprises thin parallel transparent plastic tubes or transparent glass fibers sandwiched between two glass sheets. TIM has a higher thermal conductivity than classic insulation materials (between 0.34 and 0.44 Btu·in/h·ft^2·°F) but allows solar gains into the conditioned space, so the net heat balance (equilibrium between losses and gains) may be more favorable.

Still, use of this material remains limited because of soiling and overheating. The plastic tubes slowly yellow, and, if the space between the two glass sheets is not vaportight, water vapor may diffuse into the panels and condense against the coldest sheet. Dust may enter the TIM boards through spacer leaks and be fixed in the condensate. Also the exterior surface of the panels can become soiled. Overheating is moderated by combining the TIM with solar shading, but this is currently too expensive to be economically viable.

Vacuum Insulation Panels

Vacuum insulation (sometimes called **modified-atmosphere insulation** because the interior is not a hard vacuum) is available in rigid and semirigid panels of various sizes. Vacuum insulation panels consist of an interior filler material and an exterior barrier material. Heat conduction through the center of the panel is typically less than 0.05 Btu·in/h·ft^2·°F; some panels have been manufactured with a center-of-panel thermal conductivity less than 0.017 Btu·in/h·ft^2·°F However, heat is also transported around the edges of the panel, and that heat transport (often referred to as **edge effect**) can significantly reduce the thermal resistance of the whole panel compared to the thermal resistance of the center region. For that reason, the resistance of the whole assembly should be considered, and larger panels are generally preferred. In buildings, vacuum panels may be used when the space available for thermal insulation is tightly constricted, such as in historic building retrofits. Vacuum insulation panels are also used in appliances and shipping containers.

Vacuum insulation panels rely on reduced gaseous conduction, via reduced air pressure, for their thermal performance and must therefore be protected from puncture or other physical damage. Depending on the permeability of the barrier material and the nature of the seam joining the barrier material around the unit's perimeter, panels age through air diffusion. To delay this phenomenon, most barrier materials incorporate a very thin metallic layer (often produced using vapor deposition methods). Another way to slow aging is to incorporate getter materials (i.e., any reactive material that absorbs small amounts of gas in an evacuated space) within the panel; some filler materials act as getters themselves. The filler material supports the exterior atmospheric pressure load on the panel and reduces both radiative and gaseous heat transport across the panel. To reduce gaseous heat transfer, voids in the filler material must be smaller than the mean free path of the gas molecules, which is in turn determined by the air pressure in the panel. Therefore, filler materials with finer void sizes retain their heat transfer reduction abilities at higher pressures than fillers with greater void sizes do.

Reflective Insulation Systems

Reflective insulation consists of surfaces having high reflectivity (and low emissivity) for long-wave radiation, thus reducing radiant heat transfer. To be effective, these surfaces must face an air layer, or no radiant heat transfer is available to be reduced. Conventional calculation methods ascribe the radiative properties to the facing air layer, rather than to the reflective insulation system, to avoid double-counting the reflective effect. Multiple layers of reflective materials facing smooth and parallel sealed air spaces increase overall thermal resistance, though thermal conductivity will never be less than that of still air. In any case, air exchange and movement must be inhibited or the reduction in radiative heat transfer will be overshadowed by increased convection.

Conventional insulation can be combined with reflective surfaces facing air spaces to increase thermal resistance. However, each design must be evaluated, because thermal performance of these systems depends on factors such as condition of insulation, shape and form of construction, means to avoid air leakage and movement, and condition and aging characteristics of reflective surfaces.

Values for foil insulation products supplied by manufacturers must be used with caution because they apply only to systems that are identical to the configuration in which the product was tested. In addition, surface oxidation, dust accumulation, condensation, and other factors that change the condition of the low-emittance surface can reduce the thermal effectiveness (Hooper and Moroz 1952). Deterioration results from contact with acidic or basic solutions (e.g., wet cement mortar, preservatives found in decay-resistant lumber). Polluted environments may cause rapid and severe degradation. However, Hooper and Moroz found that site inspections showed a predominance of well-preserved reflective surfaces, with only a small number of cases of rapid and severe deterioration. An extensive review of the reflective building insulation system performance literature is provided by Goss and Miller (1989).

2. AIR BARRIERS

The main characteristic of an air barrier system is reduced air permeance. To create that performance, the barrier must

- Meet material permeability requirements.
- Be continuous when installed (i.e., tight joints in air barrier assembly; effective bonds in air barrier materials at intersections such as wall/roof, wall/foundation, and wall/windows; tightly sealed penetrations).
- Accommodate dimensional changes caused by temperature or shrinkage without damaging joints or air barrier material.
- Be strong enough to support stresses applied to air barrier material or assembly. The air barrier must not be ruptured or excessively deformed by wind and stack effect. Where an adhesive is used to complete a joint, the assembly must be designed to withstand forces that might gradually peel away the air barrier material. Where the material is not strong enough to withstand anticipated wind and other loads, it must be supported on both sides to account for positive and negative wind gust pressures.

In addition, the following properties can be important, depending on the application:

- Elasticity
- Thermal stability
- Fire and flammability resistance
- Inertness to deteriorating elements
- Ease of fabrication, application, and joint sealing

Air barriers may control both vapor and airflow (i.e., they may act as an air/vapor retarder), depending on the characteristics of the materials used. Many designs are based on this idea, with measures taken to ensure that the layer with vapor-retarding properties is continuous to control airflow. Some designs treat airflow and vapor retarders as separate entities, but an airflow retarder should not be where it can cause moisture to condense if it also has vapor-retarding properties. For example, a vapor-retarding air barrier placed on the cold side of a building envelope may cause condensation, particularly if the vapor retarder at the other side of the building is ineffective. Instead, a carefully installed, sealed cold-side air retarder that has sufficient thermal resistance may lower the potential for condensation by raising the temperature at its inside surface during the cold season (Ojanen et al. 1994).

Air leakage characteristics can be determined with the ASTM *Standard* E1186 test method for air barriers on the interior side of the building envelope, and described according to ASTM *Standard* E1677. Specific air leakage criteria for air barriers in cold heating climates are found in Di Lenardo et al. (1995). These specifications provide classes for air leakage rates of 0.01, 0.02, 0.03, and 0.04 cfm per square foot when measured with an air pressure difference of 0.3 in. of water, depending on the water vapor permeance of the outermost layer of the building envelope. The highest leakage rate applies if the permeance of the outermost layer is greater than 10 perms; the lowest rate applies if the permeance is less than 1 perm. Intermediate values are also provided. The recommendations apply only to heating climates.

The required air permeance of an air barrier material has been set by some building codes at 0.004 cfm per square foot at a pressure difference of 0.3 in. of water. A 2008 addendum to ASHRAE *Standard* 90.1 also references this value. ASTM *Standard* E1677 provides an alternative minimum air barrier test and criteria specifically suitable for framed walls of low-rise buildings.

Air leakage characteristics of an air barrier assembly can be determined with the ASTM *Standard* E2357 test method, which measures the air leakage of three wall specimens: (1) with the air barrier material installed using air barrier accessories alone, (2) with the air barrier material installed and connected to air barrier components (window, doors, and other premanufactured elements) using air barrier accessories, and (3) with an air barrier wall assembly connected to a foundation assembly and roof assembly using air barrier accessories. The test method reports the air leakage rate at a reference pressure difference of 0.3 in. of water, not because it is necessarily representative of in-service conditions, but because it provides a more accurate measurement that can then be adjusted for actual conditions.

Building assemblies are constructed and the various air barrier assemblies are connected to form an air barrier system for the whole building. The building's air leakage characteristics can be determined with the ASTM *Standard* E779 test method. A 2008 addendum to ASHRAE *Standard* 90.1 requires 0.4 cfm per square foot at 0.3 in. of water pressure difference.

The effectiveness of an air barrier is greatly reduced by openings and penetrations, even small ones. These openings can be caused by poor design, poor workmanship during application, insufficient coating thickness, improper caulking and flashing, uncompensated thermal expansion, mechanical forces, aging, and other forms of degradation. Faults or leaks typically occur at electrical boxes, plumbing penetrations, telephone and television wiring, and other unsealed openings in the structure. This is especially true if telephone, television, or other services are installed after the envelope has been inspected and/or tested. A ceiling air barrier should be continuous at chases for plumbing, ducts, flues, and electrical wiring. In flat roofing, mechanical fasteners are sometimes used to adhere the system to the deck, and often penetrate the air barrier. In heating climates, the resulting holes may allow air exfiltration and accompanying water vapor leakage into the roof. ASTM *Standard* E1186 describes several techniques for locating air leakage sites in building envelopes and air barrier systems.

As noted previously, air barrier assemblies must withstand pressures exerted by stack effects, wind, or both during construction and over the building's life. The magnitude of pressure varies, depending on building type and sequence of construction. At one extreme, single-family dwellings may be built with exterior cladding partly or entirely installed and insulation in place before the air barrier is added. Chimney effects in these buildings are small, even in cold weather, so stresses on the air barrier during construction are small. At the other extreme, wind and chimney effect forces in tall buildings are much greater. A fragile, unprotected sheet material should not be used as an air barrier because it will probably be torn by wind before construction is completed.

Calculations of water vapor flow, interstitial condensation, and related moisture accumulation using only water vapor resistances are useless when airflow is involved. More information on air leakage in buildings may be found in Chapter 16.

3. WATER VAPOR RETARDERS

The main characteristic of a water vapor retarder is low vapor permeance. The following properties are also important, depending on the application:

- Mechanical strength in tension, shear, impact, and flexure
- Adhesion
- Elasticity

Thermal stability

- Fire and flammability resistance
- Resistance to other deteriorating elements [e.g., chemicals, ultraviolet (UV) radiation]
- Ease of fabrication, application, and joint sealing

Although a flow of dry air may accelerate drying of a wet building component (Karagiozis and Salonvaara 1999a, 1999b), vapor retarders are completely ineffective without effective airflow control, A single layer may serve both purposes, of course: the designer must assess the needs for control of water vapor and air movement in a building envelope, and devise a system that guarantees the required vapor retarder and air barrier properties.

Water vapor retarders demand consideration in every building design. The need for and type of system depend on the climate zone, construction type, building usage, and moisture sources other than indoor water vapor to be considered. Water vapor retarders were originally designed to protect building elements from water vapor diffusing through building materials and condensing against and in layers at the cold side of the thermal insulation. It is now recognized that it is just as important to allow a building assembly to dry as it is to keep the building assembly from getting wet by vapor diffusion. In some cases, to allow the building assembly to dry, a water vapor retarder may not be needed, or should be semipermeable. In other cases, the environmental conditions, building construction, and building usage may dictate that a material with very low water vapor permeance should be installed to protect building components. A balanced design approach is required: a vapor retarder can reduce the potential for an assembly to dry, but can also reduce the potential for the assembly getting wet. ASHRAE *Standard* 160 should be followed to determine the need for and placement of a vapor retarder.

The 2007 supplement to the International Codes (ICC 2007) lists three water vapor retarder classes:

- **Class I:** 0.1 perm or less
- **Class II:** more than 0.1 perm but less than or equal to 1.0 perm
- **Class III:** more than 1.0 perm but less than or equal to 10 perm

The designer should determine the type of water vapor retarder needed and its location in the envelope assembly, based on climatic conditions, other materials used in the assembly, additional sources of humidity, and the building's use (e.g., intended relative humidity).

A vapor retarder typically slows the rate of water vapor diffusion, but does not totally prevent it. In most cases, requirements for vapor retarders in envelope assemblies are not extremely stringent: because conditions on the inside and outside of buildings vary continually, air movement and ventilation can provide wetting as well as drying at various times, and water vapor entering one side of an envelope assembly can be stored temporarily as hygroscopic moisture and released later. A vapor barrier is often used to try to stop water vapor transport when the real problem is transport of water vapor by air transport. This causes confusion between the use and function of vapor barriers/retarders and those of air barriers. However, if conditions are conducive to excessive humidification, water vapor retarders help to (1) keep the thermal insulation dry; (2) prevent structural damage from rot, corrosion, freeze/thaw, and other environmental actions; and (3) reduce paint problems on exterior walls (although rain absorption through cracks in the paint may be a more probable cause of paint problems) (ASTM *Standard* C755). Judicious placement of a vapor retarder may also help an assembly to dry out. Another way to look at a vapor retarder is that it is the most vapor-resistant layer in the assembly; a capable designer knows where this layer is and ensures that it does not promote excessive moisture accumulation or prevent the assembly from drying. Therefore, all building envelope assemblies should be assessed to ensure that an unintentional water vapor retarder does not create problems.

The vapor retarder's effectiveness depends on its vapor permeance, installation, and location in the insulation. The retarder should be at or near the surface exposed to higher water vapor pressure and higher temperature. In heating climates, this is usually the winter-warm side.

Water vapor retarders are classified as rigid, flexible, or coating materials. **Rigid retarders** include reinforced plastics, aluminum, and stainless steel. These usually are mechanically fastened in place and are vapor-sealed at the joints. **Flexible retarders** include metal foils, laminated foil and treated papers, coated felts and papers, and plastic films or sheets. They are supplied in roll form or as an integral part of a building material (e.g., insulation). Accessory materials are required for sealing joints. **Coating retarders** may be semifluid or mastic; paint (called surface coatings); or hot melt, including thermofusible sheet materials. Their basic composition may be asphaltic, resinous, or polymeric, with or without pigments and solvents, as required to meet design conditions. They can be applied by spray, brush, trowel, roller, dip, or mop, or in sheet form, depending on the type of coating and surface to which it is applied. Potentially, each of these materials is an air barrier; however, to meet air barrier specifications, it must satisfy requirements for strength, continuity, and air permeance. A construction of several materials, some perhaps of substantial thickness, can also constitute a vapor retarder system. In fact, designers have many options. For example, airflow and moisture movement might be controlled using an interior finish, such as drywall, to provide strength and stiffness, along with a low-permeability coating, such as a vapor-retarding paint, to provide the required low permeance. Other designs may use more than one component. However, (1) any component that qualifies as a vapor retarder usually also impedes airflow, and is thus subject to air pressure differences that it must resist; and (2) any component that impedes airflow may also retard vapor movement and promote condensation or frost formation if it is at the wrong location in the assembly.

Several studies found a significant increase in apparent permeance as a result of small holes in the vapor retarder. For example, Seiffert (1970) reported a hundredfold increase in the vapor permeance of aluminum foil when it is 0.014% perforated, and a 4000-fold increase when 0.22% of the surface is perforated. In general, penetrations particularly degrade a vapor retarder's effectiveness if it has very low permeance (e.g., polyethylene or aluminum foil). In addition, perforations may lead to air leakage, which further erodes effectiveness.

"Smart" vapor retarders allow substantial summer drying while functioning as effective vapor retarders during the cold season. One type of smart vapor retarder has low vapor permeance but conducts liquid water, allowing moisture that condenses on the retarder to dry. Korsgaard and Pedersen (1989, 1992) describe such a retarder composed of synthetic fabric sandwiched between staggered strips of plastic film. The fabric wicks liquid water while the plastic film retards vapor flow. Another type of smart vapor retarder provides low vapor permeance at low relative humidities, but much higher permeance at high relative humidity. During the heating season in cold and moderate climates, the indoor humidity usually is below 50% and the smart vapor retarder's permeance is low. In the summer or on winter days with high solar heat gains, when the temperature gradient is inward, moisture moving from exterior parts of the wall or roof raises the relative humidity at the vapor retarder. This increases vapor permeance and potential for the wall or roof to dry out. One such vapor retarder is described by Kuenzel (1999). Below 50% rh, the film's permeance is less than 1 perm, but it increases above 60% rh, reaching 36 perm at 90% rh.

4. DATA TABLES

4.1 THERMAL PROPERTY DATA

Steady-state thermal resistances (R-values) of building assemblies (walls, floors, windows, roof systems, etc.) can be calculated from thermal properties of the materials in the component, provided by Table 1, or heat flow through the assembled component can be measured directly with laboratory equipment such as the guarded hot box (ASTM *Standard* C1363). Direct measurement is the most accurate method of determining the overall thermal resistance for a combination of building materials combined as a building envelope assembly. However, not all combinations may be conveniently or economically tested in this manner. For many simple constructions, calculated R-values (see Chapter 25) agree reasonably well with values determined by hot-box measurement.

Values in Table 1 were developed by testing under controlled laboratory conditions. In practice, overall thermal performance can be reduced significantly by factors such as improper installation, quality of workmanship and shrinkage, settling, or compression of the insulation (Tye 1985, 1986; Tye and Desjarlais 1983). Good workmanship becomes increasingly important as the insulation requirement becomes greater. Therefore, some engineers include additional insulation or other safety factors based on experience in their design

Values in Table 1 are recorded at 75°F, and are intended to be representative values of generic materials. The tabulated thermal conductivities are either relatively constant as tested, or vary over a range of densities. For the most part, thermal conductivity varies directly with density, which provides some guidance for users here a range is presented. A conservative design might use values at the higher end of the range (unless moisture content is a concern, in which case low-conductivity materials might reduce the assembly's ability to dry out, and would thus be a more conservative choice). References are provided for each material, so users can investigate the as-tested conditions, and additional information regarding the test specimens.

Caution: values in Table 1 should not be used without referring to the footnotes, which define limitations and some of the as-tested conditions for the materials listed.

Because commercially available materials vary, not all values apply to specific products.

4.2 SURFACE EMISSIVITY AND EMITTANCE DATA

Table 2 provides measured long-wave emissivities for various surfaces, which are used to characterize radiant heat transfer to or from these surfaces. To simplify radiant heat transfer calculations, the combined emittance for two surfaces is also provided, although these values can be calculated using $\varepsilon_{eff} = 1/(1/\varepsilon_1 + 1/\varepsilon_2 - 1)$. As described previously, surface oxidation, dust accumulation, condensation, and other factors can impair the emissivity of highly reflective surfaces, so slightly higher values should be used.

4.3 THERMAL RESISTANCE OF PLANE AIR SPACES

Table 3 provides effective resistance values for plane (i.e., generally flat) air spaces that are enclosed within an assembly. Where an assembly incorporates reflective insulation, the effect of the reflective surface is ascribed to the air space, not to the material component. It should be understood that the reflective surface must face an air space to have any effect in reducing thermal transmittance, and assigning the value of the reflective surface to the air space in a design calculation reinforces this concept. Note that "reflective insulation systems" are bounded by an enclosed air space within an assembly, whereas "radiant barrier systems" feature a reflective surface facing an open airspace. Reflective insulation may be described as modifying the effective R-value of the assembly, but a radiant barrier system may not. This includes reflective surfaces behind siding, which should not be considered as "reflective insulation" (in most cases, the nature of the heat transfer will be dominated by wind-driven convection, rather than radiant exchange). Thermal resistance values for siding with reflective foil backing are provided in Table 1.

4.4 AIR PERMEANCE DATA

Table 4 provides measured air permeability of different materials, tested in accordance with Bomberg and Kumaran (1986), to be used in assessing the suitability of these materials in an air barrier

Table 1 Building and Insulating Materials: Design Values[a]

Description	Density, lb/ft³	Conductivity[b] k, Btu·in/h·ft²·°F	Resistance R, h·ft²·°F/Btu	Specific Heat, Btu/lb·°F	Reference[o]
Insulating Materials					
Blanket and batt[c,d]					
Glass-fiber batts				0.2	Kumaran (2002)
	0.47 to 0.51	0.32 to 0.33	—	—	Four manufacturers (2011)
	0.61 to 0.75	0.28 to 0.30	—	—	Four manufacturers (2011)
	0.79 to 0.85	0.26 to 0.27	—	—	Four manufacturers (2011)
	1.4	0.23	—	—	Four manufacturers (2011)
Rock and slag wool batts	—	—	—	0.2	Kumaran (1996)
	2 to 2.3	0.25 to 0.26	—	—	One manufacturer (2011)
	2.8	0.23 to 0.24	—	—	One manufacturer (2011)
Mineral wool, felted	1 to 3	0.28	—	—	CIBSE (2006), NIST (2000)
	1 to 8	0.24	—	—	NIST (2000)
Board and slabs					
Cellular glass	7.5	0.29	—	0.20	One manufacturer (2011)
Cement fiber slabs, shredded wood with Portland cement binder	25 to 27	0.50 to 0.53	—	—	
with magnesia oxysulfide binder	22	0.57	—	0.31	
Glass fiber board	—	—	—	0.2	Kumaran (1996)
	1.5 to 6.0	0.23 to 0.24	—	—	One manufacturer (2011)
Expanded rubber (rigid)	4	0.2	—	0.4	Nottage (1947)
Extruded polystyrene, smooth skin	—	—	—	0.35	Kumaran (1996)
aged per CAN/ULC *Standard* S770-2003	1.4 to 3.6	0.18 to 0.20	—	—	Four manufacturers (2011)
aged 180 days	1.4 to 3.6	0.20			One manufacturer (2011)
European product	1.9	0.21			One manufacturer (2011)
aged 5 years at 75°F	2 to 2.2	0.21	—	—	One manufacturer (2011)
blown with low global warming potential (GWP) (<5) blowing agent		0.24 to 0.25	—	—	One manufacturer (2011)
Expanded polystyrene, molded beads	—	—	—	0.35	Kumaran (1996)
	1.0 to 1.5	0.24 to 0.26	—	—	Independent test reports (2008)
	1.8	0.23	—	—	Independent test reports (2008)
Mineral fiberboard, wet felted	10	0.26	—	0.2	Kumaran (1996)
Rock wool board	—	—	—	0.2	Kumaran (1996)
floors and walls	4.0 to 8.0	0.23 to 0.25	—	—	Five manufacturers (2011)
roofing	10. to 11.	0.27 to 0.29	—	0.2	Five manufacturers (2011)
Acoustical tile[g]	21 to 23	0.36 to 0.37	—	0.14 to 0.19	
Perlite board	9	0.36	—	—	One manufacturer (2010)
Polyisocyanurate	—	—	—	0.35	Kumaran (1996)
unfaced, aged per CAN/ULC *Standard* S770-2003	1.6 to 2.3	0.16 to 0.17	—	—	Seven manufacturers (2011)
with foil facers, aged 180 days	—	0.15 to 0.16	—	—	Two manufacturers (2011)
Phenolic foam board with facers, aged[f]	—	0.14 to 0.16	—	—	One manufacturer (2011)
Loose fill					
Cellulose fiber, loose fill	—	—	—	0.33	NIST (2000), Kumaran (1996)
attic application up to 4 in.	1.0 to 1.2	0.31 to 0.32	—	—	Four manufacturers (2011)
attic application > 4 in.	1.2 to 1.6	0.27 to 0.28	—	—	Four manufacturers (2011)
wall application, densely packed	3.5	0.27 to 0.28	—	—	One manufacturer (2011)
Perlite, expanded	2 to 4	0.27 to 0.31	—	0.26	(Manufacturer, pre-2001)
	4 to 7.5	0.31 to 0.36	—	—	(Manufacturer, pre-2001)
	7.5 to 11	0.36 to 0.42	—	—	(Manufacturer, pre-2001)
Glass fiber[d]					
attics, ~4 to 12 in.	0.4 to 0.5	0.36 to 0.38	—	—	Four manufacturers (2011)
attics, ~12 to 22 in.	0.5 to 0.6	0.34 to 0.36	—	—	Four manufacturers (2011)
closed attic or wall cavities	1.8 to 2.3	0.24 to 0.25	—	—	Four manufacturers (2011)
Rock and slag wool[d]					
attics, ~3.5 to 4.5 in.	1.5 to 1.6	0.34	—	—	Three manufacturers (2011)
attics, ~5 to 17 in.	1.5 to 1.8	0.32 to 0.33	—	—	Three manufacturers (2011)
closed attic or wall cavities	4.0	0.27 to 0.29	—	—	Three manufacturers (2011)
Vermiculite, exfoliated	7.0 to 8.2	0.47	—	0.32	Sabine et al. (1975)
	4.0 to 6.0	0.44	—	—	Manufacturer (pre-2001)
Spray applied					
Cellulose, sprayed into open wall cavities	1.6 to 2.6	0.27 to 0.28	—	—	Two manufacturers (2011)
Glass fiber, sprayed into open wall or attic cavities	1.0	0.27 to 0.29	—	—	Manufacturers' association (2011)
	1.8 to 2.3	0.23 to 0.26	—	—	Four manufacturers (2011)
Polyurethane foam	—	—	—	0.35	Kumaran (2002)
low density, open cell	0.45 to 0.65	0.26 to 0.29	—	—	Three manufacturers (2011)
medium density, closed cell, aged 180 days	1.9 to 3.2	0.14 to 0.20	—	—	Five manufacturers (2011)

Table 1 Building and Insulating Materials: Design Values[a] (*Continued*)

Description	Density, lb/ft³	Conductivity[b] k, Btu·in/h·ft²·°F	Resistance R, h·ft²·°F/Btu	Specific Heat, Btu/lb·°F	Reference[o]
Building Board and Siding					
Board					
Asbestos/cement board	120	4	—	0.24	Nottage (1947)
Cement board	71	1.7	—	0.2	Kumaran (2002)
Fiber/cement board	88	1.7	—	0.2	Kumaran (2002)
	61	1.3	—	0.2	Kumaran (1996)
	26	0.5	—	0.45	Kumaran (1996)
	20	0.4	—	0.45	Kumaran (1996)
Gypsum or plaster board	40	1.1	—	0.21	Kumaran (2002)
Oriented strand board (OSB) 7/16 in.	41	—	0.62	0.45	Kumaran (2002)
1/2 in.	41	—	0.68	0.45	Kumaran (2002)
Plywood (douglas fir) 1/2 in.	29	—	0.79	0.45	Kumaran (2002)
5/8 in.	34	—	0.85	0.45	Kumaran (2002)
Plywood/wood panels 3/4 in.	28	—	1.08	0.45	Kumaran (2002)
Vegetable fiber board					
sheathing, regular density 1/2 in.	18	—	1.32	0.31	Lewis (1967)
intermediate density 1/2 in.	22	—	1.09	0.31	Lewis (1967)
nail-based sheathing 1/2 in.	25	—	1.06	0.31	
shingle backer 3/8 in.	18	—	0.94	0.3	
sound-deadening board 1/2 in.	15	—	1.35	0.3	
tile and lay-in panels, plain or acoustic	18	0.4	—	0.14	
laminated paperboard	30	0.5	—	0.33	Lewis (1967)
homogeneous board from repulped paper	30	0.5	—	0.28	
Hardboard					
medium density	50	0.73	—	0.31	Lewis (1967)
high density, service-tempered and service grades	55	0.82	—	0.32	Lewis (1967)
high density, standard-tempered grade	63	1.0	—	0.32	Lewis (1967)
Particleboard					
low density	37	0.71	—	0.31	Lewis (1967)
medium density	50	0.94	—	0.31	Lewis (1967)
high density	62	1.18	0.85	—	Lewis (1967)
underlayment 5/8 in.	44	0.73	0.82	0.29	Lewis (1967)
Waferboard	37	0.63	0.21	0.45	Kumaran (1996)
Shingles					
Asbestos/cement	120	—	0.21	—	
Wood, 16 in., 7 1/2 in. exposure	—	—	0.87	0.31	
Wood, double, 16 in., 12 in. exposure	—	—	1.19	0.28	
Wood, plus ins. backer board 5/16 in.	—	—	1.4	0.31	
Siding					
Asbestos/cement, lapped 1/4 in.	—	—	0.21	0.24	
Asphalt roll siding	—	—	0.15	0.35	
Asphalt insulating siding (1/2 in. bed)	—	—	0.21	0.24	
Hardboard siding 7/16 in.	—	—	0.15	0.35	
Wood, drop, 8 in. 1 in.	—	—	0.79	0.28	
Wood, bevel					
8 in., lapped 1/2 in.	—	—	0.81	0.28	
10 in., lapped 3/4 in.	—	—	1.05	0.28	
Wood, plywood, 3/8 in., lapped	—	—	0.59	0.29	
Aluminum, steel, or vinyl,[j,k] over sheathing				—	
hollow-backed	—	—	0.62	0.29[i]	
insulating-board-backed 3/8 in.	—	—	1.82	0.32	
foil-backed 3/8 in.	—	—	2.96	—	
insulated vinyl siding 3/4 to 1 1/4 in.[m]			2.0 to 2.7		
Architectural (soda-lime float) glass	158	6.9	—	0.21	
Building Membrane					
Vapor-permeable felt	—	—	0.06	—	
Vapor: seal, 2 layers of mopped 15 lb felt	—	—	0.12	—	
Vapor: seal, plastic film	—	—	Negligible	—	
Finish Flooring Materials					
Carpet and rebounded urethane pad 3/4 in.	7	—	2.38	—	NIST (2000)
Carpet and rubber pad (one-piece) 3/8 in.	20	—	0.68	—	NIST (2000)
Pile carpet with rubber pad 3/8 to 1/2 in.	18	—	1.59	—	NIST (2000)
Linoleum/cork tile 1/4 in.	29	—	0.51	—	NIST (2000)
PVC/rubber floor covering	—	2.8	—	—	CIBSE (2006)
rubber tile 1.0 in.	119	—	0.34	—	NIST (2000)
terrazzo 1.0 in.	—	—	0.08	0.19	

Table 1 Building and Insulating Materials: Design Values[a] (*Continued*)

Description	Density, lb/ft³	Conductivity[b] *k*, Btu·in/h·ft²·°F	Resistance *R*, h·ft²·°F/Btu	Specific Heat, Btu/lb·°F	Reference[o]
Metals (See Chapter 33, Table 3)					
Roofing					
Asbestos/cement shingles	120	—	0.21	0.24	
Asphalt (bitumen with inert fill)	100	2.98	—	—	CIBSE (2006)
	119	4.0	—	—	CIBSE (2006)
	144	7.97	—	—	CIBSE (2006)
Asphalt roll roofing	70	—	0.15	0.36	
Asphalt shingles	70	—	0.44	0.3	
Built-up roofing … 3/8 in.	70	—	0.33	0.35	
Mastic asphalt (heavy, 20% grit)	59	1.32	—	—	CIBSE (2006)
Reed thatch	17	0.62	—	—	CIBSE (2006)
Roofing felt	141	8.32	—	—	CIBSE (2006)
Slate … 1/2 in.	—	—	0.05	0.3	
Straw thatch	15	0.49	—	—	CIBSE (2006)
Wood shingles, plain and plastic-film-faced	—	—	0.94	0.31	
Plastering Materials					
Cement plaster, sand aggregate	116	5.0	—	0.2	
Sand aggregate … 3/8 in.	—	—	0.08	0.2	
… 3/4 in.	—	—	0.15	0.2	
Gypsum plaster	70	2.63	—	—	CIBSE (2006)
	80	3.19	—	—	CIBSE (2006)
Lightweight aggregate … 1/2 in.	45	—	0.32	—	
… 5/8 in.	45	—	0.39	—	
on metal lath … 3/4 in.	—	—	0.47	—	
Perlite aggregate	45	1.5	—	0.32	
Sand aggregate	105	5.6	—	0.2	
on metal lath … 3/4 in.	—	—	0.13		
Vermiculite aggregate	30	1.0	—	—	CIBSE (2006)
	40	1.39	—	—	CIBSE (2006)
	45	1.7	—	—	CIBSE (2006)
	50	1.8	—	—	CIBSE (2006)
	60	2.08	—	—	CIBSE (2006)
Perlite plaster	25	0.55	—	—	CIBSE (2006)
	38	1.32	—	—	CIBSE (2006)
Pulpboard or paper plaster	38	0.48	—	—	CIBSE (2006)
Sand/cement plaster, conditioned	98	4.4	—	—	CIBSE (2006)
Sand/cement/lime plaster, conditioned	90	3.33	—	—	CIBSE (2006)
Sand/gypsum (3:1) plaster, conditioned	97	4.5	—	—	CIBSE (2006)
Masonry Materials					
Masonry units					
Brick, fired clay	150	8.4 to 10.2	—	—	Valore (1988)
	140	7.4 to 9.0	—	—	Valore (1988)
	130	6.4 to 7.8	—	—	Valore (1988)
	120	5.6 to 6.8	—	0.19	Valore (1988)
	110	4.9 to 5.9	—	—	Valore (1988)
	100	4.2 to 5.1	—	—	Valore (1988)
	90	3.6 to 4.3	—	—	Valore (1988)
	80	3.0 to 3.7	—	—	Valore (1988)
	70	2.5 to 3.1	—	—	Valore (1988)
Clay tile, hollow					
1 cell deep … 3 in.	—	—	0.80	0.21	Rowley and Algren (1937)
… 4 in.	—	—	1.11	—	Rowley and Algren (1937)
2 cells deep … 6 in.	—	—	1.52	—	Rowley and Algren (1937)
… 8 in.	—	—	1.85	—	Rowley and Algren (1937)
… 10 in.	—	—	2.22	—	Rowley and Algren (1937)
3 cells deep … 12 in.	—	—	2.50	—	Rowley and Algren (1937)
Lightweight brick	50	1.39	—	—	Kumaran (1996)
	48	1.51	—	—	Kumaran (1996)
Concrete blocks[h,i]					
Limestone aggregate					
8 in., 36 lb, 138 lb/ft³ concrete, 2 cores	—	—	—	—	
with perlite-filled cores	—	—	2.1	—	Valore (1988)
12 in., 55 lb, 138 lb/ft³ concrete, 2 cores	—	—	—	—	
with perlite-filled cores	—	—	3.7	—	Valore (1988)
Normal-weight aggregate (sand and gravel)					
8 in., 33 to 36 lb, 126 to 136 lb/ft³ concrete, 2 or 3 cores	—	—	1.11 to 0.97	0.22	Van Geem (1985)
with perlite-filled cores	—	—	2.0	—	Van Geem (1985)
with vermiculite-filled cores	—	—	1.92 to 1.37	—	Valore (1988)

Table 1 Building and Insulating Materials: Design Values[a] (*Continued*)

Description	Density, lb/ft³	Conductivity[b] k, Btu·in/h·ft²·°F	Resistance R, h·ft²·°F/Btu	Specific Heat, Btu/lb·°F	Reference[o]
12 in., 50 lb, 125 lb/ft³ concrete, 2 cores	—	—	1.23	0.22	Valore (1988)
Medium-weight aggregate (combinations of normal and lightweight aggregate)					
8 in., 26 to 29 lb, 97 to 112 lb/ft³ concrete, 2 or 3 cores	—	—	1.71 to 1.28	—	Van Geem (1985)
with perlite-filled cores	—	—	3.7 to 2.3	—	Van Geem (1985)
with vermiculite-filled cores	—	—	3.3	—	Van Geem (1985)
with molded-EPS-filled (beads) cores	—	—	3.2	—	Van Geem (1985)
with molded EPS inserts in cores	—	—	2.7	—	Van Geem (1985)
Lightweight aggregate (expanded shale, clay, slate or slag, pumice)					
6 in., 16 to 17 lb, 85 to 87 lb/ft³ concrete, 2 or 3 cores	—	—	1.93 to 1.65	—	Van Geem (1985)
with perlite-filled cores	—	—	4.2	—	Van Geem (1985)
with vermiculite-filled cores	—	—	3.0	—	Van Geem (1985)
8 in., 19 to 22 lb, 72 to 86 lb/ft³ concrete	—	—	3.2 to 1.90	0.21	Van Geem (1985)
with perlite-filled cores	—	—	6.8 to 4.4	—	Van Geem (1985)
with vermiculite-filled cores	—	—	5.3 to 3.9	—	Shu et al. (1979)
with molded-EPS-filled (beads) cores	—	—	4.8	—	Shu et al. (1979)
with UF foam-filled cores	—	—	4.5	—	Shu et al. (1979)
with molded EPS inserts in cores	—	—	3.5	—	Shu et al. (1979)
12 in., 32 to 36 lb, 80 to 90 lb/ft³, concrete, 2 or 3 cores	—	—	2.6 to 2.3	—	Van Geem (1985)
with perlite-filled cores	—	—	9.2 to 6.3	—	Van Geem (1985)
with vermiculite-filled cores	—	—	5.8	—	Valore (1988)
Stone, lime, or sand	180	72	—	—	Valore (1988)
Quartzitic and sandstone	160	43	—	—	Valore (1988)
	140	24	—	—	Valore (1988)
	120	13	—	0.19	Valore (1988)
Calcitic, dolomitic, limestone, marble, and granite	180	30	—	—	Valore (1988)
	160	22	—	—	Valore (1988)
	140	16	—	—	Valore (1988)
	120	11	—	0.19	Valore (1988)
	100	8	—	—	Valore (1988)
Gypsum partition tile					
3 by 12 by 30 in., solid	—	—	1.26	0.19	Rowley and Algren (1937)
4 cells	—	—	1.35	—	Rowley and Algren (1937)
4 by 12 by 30 in., 3 cells	—	—	1.67	—	Rowley and Algren (1937)
Limestone	150	3.95	—	0.2	Kumaran (2002)
	163	6.45	—	0.2	Kumaran (2002)
Concretes[i]					
Sand and gravel or stone aggregate concretes	150	10.0 to 20.0	—	—	Valore (1988)
(concretes with >50% quartz or quartzite sand have	140	9.0 to 18.0	—	0.19 to 0.24	Valore (1988)
conductivities in higher end of range)	130	7.0 to 13.0	—	—	Valore (1988)
Lightweight aggregate or limestone concretes	120	6.4 to 9.1	—	—	Valore (1988)
expanded shale, clay, or slate; expanded slags; cinders;	100	4.7 to 6.2	—	0.2	Valore (1988)
pumice (with density up to 100 lb/ft³); scoria (sanded	80	3.3 to 4.1	—	0.2	Valore (1988)
concretes have conductivities in higher end of range)	60	2.1 to 2.5	—	—	Valore (1988)
	40	1.3	—	—	Valore (1988)
Gypsum/fiber concrete (87.5% gypsum, 12.5% wood chips)	51	1.66	—	0.2	Rowley and Algren (1937)
Cement/lime, mortar, and stucco	120	9.7	—	—	Valore (1988)
	100	6.7	—	—	Valore (1988)
	80	4.5	—	—	Valore (1988)
Perlite, vermiculite, and polystyrene beads	50	1.8 to 1.9	—	—	Valore (1988)
	40	1.4 to 1.5	—	0.15 to 0.23	Valore (1988)
	30	1.1	—	—	Valore (1988)
	20	0.8	—	—	Valore (1988)
Foam concretes	120	5.4	—	—	Valore (1988)
	100	4.1	—	—	Valore (1988)
	80	3.0	—	—	Valore (1988)
	70	2.5	—	—	Valore (1988)
Foam concretes and cellular concretes	60	2.1	—	—	Valore (1988)
	40	1.4	—	—	Valore (1988)
	20	0.8	—	—	Valore (1988)
Aerated concrete (oven-dried)	27 to 50	1.4	—	0.2	Kumaran (1996)
Polystyrene concrete (oven-dried)	16 to 50	2.54	—	0.2	Kumaran (1996)
Polymer concrete	122	11.4	—	—	Kumaran (1996)
	138	7.14	—	—	Kumaran (1996)
Polymer cement	117	5.39	—	—	Kumaran (1996)
Slag concrete	60	1.5	—	—	Touloukian et al (1970)
	80	2.25	—	—	Touloukian et al. (1970)
	100	3	—	—	Touloukian et al. (1970)
	125	8.53	—	—	Touloukian et al. (1970)

Table 1 Building and Insulating Materials: Design Values[a] (*Continued*)

Description	Density, lb/ft³	Conductivity[b] *k*, Btu·in/h·ft²·°F	Resistance *R*, h·ft²·°F/Btu	Specific Heat, Btu/lb·°F	Reference[o]
Woods (12% moisture content)[l]					
Hardwoods	—	—	—	0.39[n]	Wilkes (1979)
Oak	41 to 47	1.12 to 1.25	—	—	Cardenas and Bible (1987)
Birch	43 to 45	1.16 to 1.22	—	—	Cardenas and Bible (1987)
Maple	40 to 44	1.09 to 1.19	—	—	Cardenas and Bible (1987)
Ash	38 to 42	1.06 to 1.14	—	—	Cardenas and Bible (1987)
Softwoods	—	—	—	0.39[n]	Wilkes (1979)
Southern pine	36 to 41	1.00 to 1.12	—	—	Cardenas and Bible (1987)
Southern yellow pine	31	1.06 to 1.16	—	—	Kumaran (2002)
Eastern white pine	25	0.85 to 0.94	—	—	Kumaran (2002)
Douglas fir/larch	34 to 36	0.95 to 1.01	—	—	Cardenas and Bible (1987)
Southern cypress	31 to 32	0.90 to 0.92	—	—	Cardenas and Bible (1987)
Hem/fir, spruce/pine/fir	24 to 31	0.74 to 0.90	—	—	Cardenas and Bible (1987)
Spruce	25	0.74 to 0.85	—	—	Kumaran (2002)
Western red cedar	22	0.83 to 0.86	—	—	Kumaran (2002)
West coast woods, cedars	22 to 31	0.68 to 0.90	—	—	Cardenas and Bible (1987)
Eastern white cedar	23	0.82 to 0.89	—	—	Kumaran (2002)
California redwood	24 to 28	0.74 to 0.82	—	—	Cardenas and Bible (1987)
Pine (oven-dried)	23	0.64	—	0.45	Kumaran (1996)
Spruce (oven-dried)	25	0.69	—	0.45	Kumaran (1996)

Notes for Table 1

[a]Values are for mean temperature of 75°F. Representative values for dry materials are intended as design (not specification) values for materials in normal use. Thermal values of insulating materials may differ from design values depending on in situ properties (e.g., density and moisture content, orientation, etc.) and manufacturing variability. For properties of specific product, use values supplied by manufacturer or unbiased tests.

[b]Symbol λ also used to represent thermal conductivity.

[c]Does not include paper backing and facing, if any. Where insulation forms boundary (reflective or otherwise) of airspace, see Tables 2 and 3 for insulating value of airspace with appropriate effective emittance and temperature conditions of space.

[d]Conductivity varies with fiber diameter (see Chapter 25). Batt, blanket, and loose-fill mineral fiber insulations are manufactured to achieve specified R-values, the most common of which are listed in the table. Because of differences in manufacturing processes and materials, the product thicknesses, densities, and thermal conductivities vary over considerable ranges for a specified R-value.

[e]Values are for aged products with gas-impermeable facers on the two major surfaces. An aluminum foil facer of 0.001 in. thickness or greater is generally considered impermeable to gases. For change in conductivity with age of expanded polyisocyanurate, see SPI Bulletin U108.

[f]Cellular phenolic insulation may no longer be manufactured.

[g]Insulating values of acoustical tile vary, depending on density of board and on type, size, and depth of perforations.

[h]Values for fully grouted block may be approximated using values for concrete with similar unit density.

[i]Values for concrete block and concrete are at moisture contents representative of normal use.

[j]Values for metal or vinyl siding applied over flat surfaces vary widely, depending on ventilation of the airspace beneath the siding; whether airspace is reflective or nonreflective; and on thickness, type, and application of insulating backing-board used. Values are averages for use as design guides, and were obtained from several guarded hot box tests (ASTM *Standard* C1363) on hollow-backed types and types made using backing of wood fiber, foamed plastic, and glass fiber. Departures of ±50% or more from these values may occur.

[k]Vinyl specific heat = 0.25 Btu/lb·°F

[l]See Adams (1971), MacLean (1941), and Wilkes (1979). Conductivity values listed are for heat transfer across the grain. Thermal conductivity of wood varies linearly with density, and density ranges listed are those normally found for wood species given. If density of wood species is not known, use mean conductivity value. For extrapolation to other moisture contents, the following empirical equation developed by Wilkes (1979) may be used:

$$k = 0.1791 + \frac{(1.874 \times 10^{-2} + 5.753 \times 10^{-4} M)\rho}{1 + 0.01M}$$

where ρ is density of moist wood in lb/ft³, and M is moisture content in percent.

[m]Dimension referenced is taken at the maximum siding profile thickness. The range of R values and associated thicknesses represent values for products tested to ASTM *Standard* D7793, which requires applying 15 mph airstream perpendicular to surface of siding during testing.

[n]From Wilkes (1979), an empirical equation for specific heat of moist wood at 75°F is as follows:

$$c_p = \frac{(0.299 + 0.01M)}{(1 + 0.01M)} + \Delta c_p$$

where Δc_p accounts for heat of sorption and is denoted by

$$\Delta c_p = M(1.921 \times 10^{-3} - 3.168 \times 10^{-5} M)$$

where M is moisture content in percent by mass.

[o]Blank space in reference column indicates historical values from previous volumes of *ASHRAE Handbook*. Source of information could not be determined.

assembly. As discussed previously, low air permeance is not sufficient to ensure a reliable air barrier assembly: the system must be properly fastened and supported (on both sides) to resist wind loads, and all materials must be durable for the expected service life of the assembly. The air barrier must also be continuous, and should be installed in such a way as to discourage wind washing (i.e., air movement that reduces the thermal resistance of insulation layers in the assembly).

4.5 WATER VAPOR PERMEANCE DATA

Table 5 gives typical water vapor permeance and permeability values for common building materials. These values can be used to calculate water vapor flow through building components and assemblies using equations in Chapter 25.

Water vapor permeability of most building materials is a function of moisture content, which, in turn, is a function of ambient relative humidity. Permeance values at various relative humidities are presented in Table 6 for several building materials. Figure 4 depicts the increase in permeability with increasing relative humidity for oriented strand board (OSB) and plywood samples (Kumaran 2002).

Users of the dew-point method may use constant values found in Table 5. However, if condensation in the assembly is predicted, then a more appropriate value should be used. Transient hygrothermal modeling typically uses vapor permeability values that vary with relative humidity. Vapor permeability of homogeneous materials

Table 2 Emissivity of Various Surfaces and Effective Emittances of Facing Air Spaces[a]

Surface	Average Emissivity ε	Effective Emittance ε_{eff} of Air Space: One Surface's Emittance ε; Other, 0.9	Effective Emittance ε_{eff} of Air Space: Both Surfaces' Emittance ε
Aluminum foil, bright	0.05	0.05	0.03
Aluminum foil, with condensate just visible (>0.7 g/ft²)	0.30[b]	0.29	—
Aluminum foil, with condensate clearly visible (>2.9 g/ft²)	0.70[b]	0.65	—
Aluminum sheet	0.12	0.12	0.06
Aluminum-coated paper, polished	0.20	0.20	0.11
Brass, nonoxidized	0.04	0.038	0.02
Copper, black oxidized	0.74	0.41	0.59
Copper, polished	0.04	0.038	0.02
Iron and steel, polished	0.2	0.16	0.11
Iron and steel, oxidized	0.58	0.35	0.41
Lead, oxidized	0.27	0.21	0.16
Nickel, nonoxidized	0.06	0.056	0.03
Silver, polished	0.03	0.029	0.015
Steel, galvanized, bright	0.25	0.24	0.15
Tin, nonoxidized	0.05	0.047	0.026
Aluminum paint	0.50	0.47	0.35
Building materials: wood, paper, masonry, nonmetallic paints	0.90	0.82	0.82
Regular glass	0.84	0.77	0.72

[a]Values apply in 4 to 40 μm range of electromagnetic spectrum. Also, oxidation, corrosion, and accumulation of dust and dirt can dramatically increase surface emittance. Emittance values of 0.05 should only be used where the highly reflective surface can be maintained over the service life of the assembly. Except as noted, data from VDI (1999).

[b]Values based on data in Bassett and Trethowen (1984).

can be calculated from thickness and vapor permeance (as given in Table 6).

4.6 MOISTURE STORAGE DATA

Transient analysis of assemblies requires consideration of the materials' moisture storage capacity. Some materials **(hygroscopic)** adsorb or reject moisture to achieve equilibrium with adjacent air. Storage capacity of these materials is typically shown by graphs of moisture content versus humidity. The curve showing uptake of moisture (the **sorption isotherm**) is usually above the curve showing drying (the **desorption isotherm**) because the material's uptake and release of moisture are inhibited by surface tension. Table 7 provides data for these curves for several hygroscopic materials, and Kumaran (1996, 2002) and McGowan (2007) provide actual curves, additional data, and conditions under which they were determined.

Table 7 expresses moisture content as percentage of dry weight, followed by a subscript value of the relative air humidity at which this moisture content occurs. Note that these values are based on measurement of materials that have reached equilibrium with their surroundings, which in some cases can take many weeks. Most hygrothermal simulation software programs that use these values assume that equilibrium is achieved instantaneously.

Maximum values in Table 7 are those that could be realistically measured in laboratory conditions, so not all materials have a listing for maximum moisture content at 100% relative humidity. For those that do, there may be two listings: the moisture content measured when the material's capillary pores were saturated (shown as 100c), and the value at total saturation (shown as 100t). Note that the moisture content of any material is 0.0 at a theoretical relative humidity of 0%, so this point is not shown in the table.

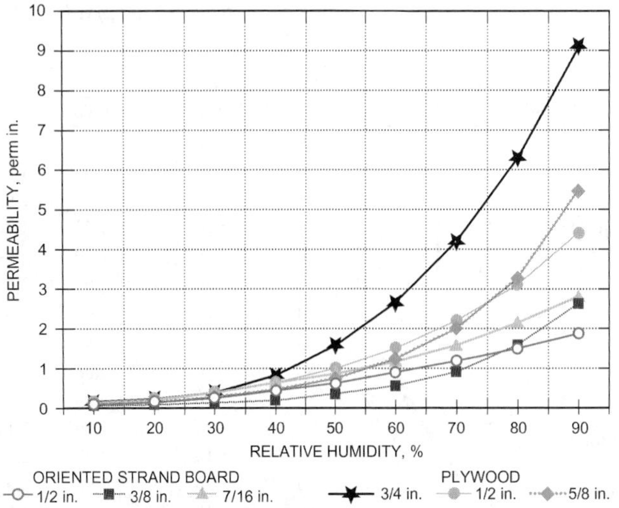

Fig. 4 Permeability of Wood-Based Sheathing Materials at Various Relative Humidities

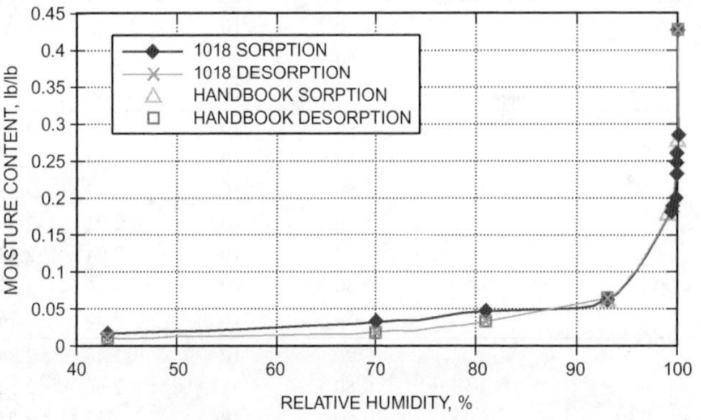

Fig. 5 Sorption/Desorption Isotherms, Cement Board

Figure 5 shows an example of a conventional sorption isotherm graph. Curves show sorption (wetting) and desorption (drying) for data in Table 7 and from Kumaran (2002). (Data from Table 7 were selectively used to provide an accurate representation of the sorption isotherm; not all data from the original source are represented.)

4.7 SOILS DATA

Apparent soil thermal conductivity is difficult to estimate and may change in the same soil at different times because of changed moisture conditions and freezing temperatures.

Figure 6 shows typical apparent soil thermal conductivity as a function of moisture content for different general types of soil. The figure is based on data presented in Salomone and Marlowe (1989) using envelopes of thermal behavior coupled with field moisture content ranges for different soil types. In Figure 6, "well graded" applies to granular soils with good representation of all particle sizes from largest to smallest. "Poorly graded" refers to granular soils with either uniform gradation, in which most particles are about the same size, or skip (or gap) gradation, in which particles of one or more intermediate sizes are not present.

Table 3 Effective Thermal Resistance of Plane Air Spaces,[a,b,c] h·ft²·°F/Btu

Position of Air Space	Direction of Heat Flow	Air Space: Mean Temp.[d], °F	Air Space: Temp. Diff.,[d] °F	Effective Emittance ε_{eff}[d,e]: 0.5 in. Air Space[c] 0.03	0.05	0.2	0.5	0.82	0.75 in. Air Space[c] 0.03	0.05	0.2	0.5	0.82
Horiz.	Up	90	10	2.13	2.03	1.51	0.99	0.73	2.34	2.22	1.61	1.04	0.75
		50	30	1.62	1.57	1.29	0.96	0.75	1.71	1.66	1.35	0.99	0.77
		50	10	2.13	2.05	1.60	1.11	0.84	2.30	2.21	1.70	1.16	0.87
		0	20	1.73	1.70	1.45	1.12	0.91	1.83	1.79	1.52	1.16	0.93
		0	10	2.10	2.04	1.70	1.27	1.00	2.23	2.16	1.78	1.31	1.02
		−50	20	1.69	1.66	1.49	1.23	1.04	1.77	1.74	1.55	1.27	1.07
		−50	10	2.04	2.00	1.75	1.40	1.16	2.16	2.11	1.84	1.46	1.20
45° Slope	Up	90	10	2.44	2.31	1.65	1.06	0.76	2.96	2.78	1.88	1.15	0.81
		50	30	2.06	1.98	1.56	1.10	0.83	1.99	1.92	1.52	1.08	0.82
		50	10	2.55	2.44	1.83	1.22	0.90	2.90	2.75	2.00	1.29	0.94
		0	20	2.20	2.14	1.76	1.30	1.02	2.13	2.07	1.72	1.28	1.00
		0	10	2.63	2.54	2.03	1.44	1.10	2.72	2.62	2.08	1.47	1.12
		−50	20	2.08	2.04	1.78	1.42	1.17	2.05	2.01	1.76	1.41	1.16
		−50	10	2.62	2.56	2.17	1.66	1.33	2.53	2.47	2.10	1.62	1.30
Vertical	Horiz.	90	10	2.47	2.34	1.67	1.06	0.77	3.50	3.24	2.08	1.22	0.84
		50	30	2.57	2.46	1.84	1.23	0.90	2.91	2.77	2.01	1.30	0.94
		50	10	2.66	2.54	1.88	1.24	0.91	3.70	3.46	2.35	1.43	1.01
		0	20	2.82	2.72	2.14	1.50	1.13	3.14	3.02	2.32	1.58	1.18
		0	10	2.93	2.82	2.20	1.53	1.15	3.77	3.59	2.64	1.73	1.26
		−50	20	2.90	2.82	2.35	1.76	1.39	2.90	2.83	2.36	1.77	1.39
		−50	10	3.20	3.10	2.54	1.87	1.46	3.72	3.60	2.87	2.04	1.56
45° Slope	Down	90	10	2.48	2.34	1.67	1.06	0.77	3.53	3.27	2.10	1.22	0.84
		50	30	2.64	2.52	1.87	1.24	0.91	3.43	3.23	2.24	1.39	0.99
		50	10	2.67	2.55	1.89	1.25	0.92	3.81	3.57	2.40	1.45	1.02
		0	20	2.91	2.80	2.19	1.52	1.15	3.75	3.57	2.63	1.72	1.26
		0	10	2.94	2.83	2.21	1.53	1.15	4.12	3.91	2.81	1.80	1.30
		−50	20	3.16	3.07	2.52	1.86	1.45	3.78	3.65	2.90	2.05	1.57
		−50	10	3.26	3.16	2.58	1.89	1.47	4.35	4.18	3.22	2.21	1.66
Horiz.	Down	90	10	2.48	2.34	1.67	1.06	0.77	3.55	3.29	2.10	1.22	0.85
		50	30	2.66	2.54	1.88	1.24	0.91	3.77	3.52	2.38	1.44	1.02
		50	10	2.67	2.55	1.89	1.25	0.92	3.84	3.59	2.41	1.45	1.02
		0	20	2.94	2.83	2.20	1.53	1.15	4.18	3.96	2.83	1.81	1.30
		0	10	2.96	2.85	2.22	1.53	1.16	4.25	4.02	2.87	1.82	1.31
		−50	20	3.25	3.15	2.58	1.89	1.47	4.60	4.41	3.36	2.28	1.69
		−50	10	3.28	3.18	2.60	1.90	1.47	4.71	4.51	3.42	2.30	1.71
		Air Space		1.5 in. Air Space[c]					3.5 in. Air Space[c]				
Horiz.	Up	90	10	2.55	2.41	1.71	1.08	0.77	2.84	2.66	1.83	1.13	0.80
		50	30	1.87	1.81	1.45	1.04	0.80	2.09	2.01	1.58	1.10	0.84
		50	10	2.50	2.40	1.81	1.21	0.89	2.80	2.66	1.95	1.28	0.93
		0	20	2.01	1.95	1.63	1.23	0.97	2.25	2.18	1.79	1.32	1.03
		0	10	2.43	2.35	1.90	1.38	1.06	2.71	2.62	2.07	1.47	1.12
		−50	20	1.94	1.91	1.68	1.36	1.13	2.19	2.14	1.86	1.47	1.20
		−50	10	2.37	2.31	1.99	1.55	1.26	2.65	2.58	2.18	1.67	1.33
45° Slope	Up	90	10	2.92	2.73	1.86	1.14	0.80	3.18	2.96	1.97	1.18	0.82
		50	30	2.14	2.06	1.61	1.12	0.84	2.26	2.17	1.67	1.15	0.86
		50	10	2.88	2.74	1.99	1.29	0.94	3.12	2.95	2.10	1.34	0.96
		0	20	2.30	2.23	1.82	1.34	1.04	2.42	2.35	1.90	1.38	1.06
		0	10	2.79	2.69	2.12	1.49	1.13	2.98	2.87	2.23	1.54	1.16
		−50	20	2.22	2.17	1.88	1.49	1.21	2.34	2.29	1.97	1.54	1.25
		−50	10	2.71	2.64	2.23	1.69	1.35	2.87	2.79	2.33	1.75	1.39
Vertical	Horiz.	90	10	3.99	3.66	2.25	1.27	0.87	3.69	3.40	2.15	1.24	0.85
		50	30	2.58	2.46	1.84	1.23	0.90	2.67	2.55	1.89	1.25	0.91
		50	10	3.79	3.55	2.39	1.45	1.02	3.63	3.40	2.32	1.42	1.01
		0	20	2.76	2.66	2.10	1.48	1.12	2.88	2.78	2.17	1.51	1.14
		0	10	3.51	3.35	2.51	1.67	1.23	3.49	3.33	2.50	1.67	1.23
		−50	20	2.64	2.58	2.18	1.66	1.33	2.82	2.75	2.30	1.73	1.37
		−50	10	3.31	3.21	2.62	1.91	1.48	3.40	3.30	2.67	1.94	1.50

Table 3 Effective Thermal Resistance of Plane Air Spaces,[a,b,c] h·ft²·°F/Btu (*Continued*)

Air Space				Effective Emittance ε_{eff}[d,e]									
				1.5 in. Air Space[c]					3.5 in. Air Space[c]				
Position of Air Space	Direction of Heat Flow	Mean Temp.[d], °F	Temp. Diff.,[d] °F	0.03	0.05	0.2	0.5	0.82	0.03	0.05	0.2	0.5	0.82
45° Slope	Down	90	10	5.07	4.55	2.56	1.36	0.91	4.81	4.33	2.49	1.34	0.90
		50	30	3.58	3.36	2.31	1.42	1.00	3.51	3.30	2.28	1.40	1.00
		50	10	5.10	4.66	2.85	1.60	1.09	4.74	4.36	2.73	1.57	1.08
		0	20	3.85	3.66	2.68	1.74	1.27	3.81	3.63	2.66	1.74	1.27
		0	10	4.92	4.62	3.16	1.94	1.37	4.59	4.32	3.02	1.88	1.34
		–50	20	3.62	3.50	2.80	2.01	1.54	3.77	3.64	2.90	2.05	1.57
		–50	10	4.67	4.47	3.40	2.29	1.70	4.50	4.32	3.31	2.25	1.68
Horiz.	Down	90	10	6.09	5.35	2.79	1.43	0.94	10.07	8.19	3.41	1.57	1.00
		50	30	6.27	5.63	3.18	1.70	1.14	9.60	8.17	3.86	1.88	1.22
		50	10	6.61	5.90	3.27	1.73	1.15	11.15	9.27	4.09	1.93	1.24
		0	20	7.03	6.43	3.91	2.19	1.49	10.90	9.52	4.87	2.47	1.62
		0	10	7.31	6.66	4.00	2.22	1.51	11.97	10.32	5.08	2.52	1.64
		–50	20	7.73	7.20	4.77	2.85	1.99	11.64	10.49	6.02	3.25	2.18
		–50	10	8.09	7.52	4.91	2.89	2.01	12.98	11.56	6.36	3.34	2.22

Air Space				5.5 in. Air Space[c]				
Horiz.	Up	90	10	3.01	2.82	1.90	1.15	0.81
		50	30	2.22	2.13	1.65	1.14	0.86
		50	10	2.97	2.82	2.04	1.31	0.95
		0	20	2.40	2.33	1.89	1.37	1.06
		0	10	2,90	2.79	2.18	1.52	1.15
		–50	20	2.31	2.27	1.95	1.53	1.24
		–50	10	2.80	2.73	2.29	1.73	1.37
45° Slope	Up	90	10	3.26	3.04	2.00	1.19	0.83
		50	30	2.19	2.10	1.64	1.13	0.85
		50	10	3.16	2.99	2.12	1.35	0.97
		0	20	2.35	2.28	1.86	1.35	1.05
		0	10	3.00	2.88	2.24	1.54	1.16
		–50	20	2.16	2.12	1.84	1.46	1.20
		–50	10	2.78	2.71	2.27	1.72	1.37
Vertical	Horiz.	90	10	3.76	3.46	2.17	1.25	0.86
		50	30	2.83	2.69	1.97	1.28	0.93
		50	10	3.72	3.49	2.36	1.44	1.01
		0	20	3.08	2.95	2.28	1.57	1.17
		0	10	3.66	3.49	2.59	1.70	1.25
		–50	20	3.03	2.95	2.44	1.81	1.42
		–50	10	3.59	3.47	2.78	2.00	1.53
45° Slope	Down	90	10	4.90	4.41	2.51	1.35	0.91
		50	30	3.86	3.61	2.42	1.46	1.02
		50	10	4.93	4.52	2.80	1.59	1.09
		0	20	4.24	4/-1	2.86	1.82	1.31
		0	10	4.93	4.63	3.16	1.94	1.37
		–50	20	4.28	4.12	3.19	2.19	1.65
		–50	10	4.93	4.71	3.53	2.35	1.74
Horiz.	Down	90	10	11.72	9.24	3.58	1.61	1.01
		50	30	10.61	8.89	4.02	1.92	1.23
		50	10	12.70	10.32	4.28	1.98	1.25
		0	20	12.10	10.42	5.10	2.52	1.64
		0	10	13.80	11.65	5.38	2.59	1.67
		–50	20	12.45	11.14	6.22	3.31	2.20
		–50	10	14.60	12.83	6.72	3.44	2.26

[a]See Chapter 25. Thermal resistance values were determined from $R = 1/C$, where $C = h_c + \varepsilon_{eff} h_r$, h_c is conduction/convection coefficient, $\varepsilon_{eff} h_r$ is radiation coefficient $\approx 0.0068\varepsilon_{eff}[(t_m + 460)/100]^3$, and t_m is mean temperature of air space. Values for h_c were determined from data developed by Robinson et al. (1954). Equations (5) to (7) in Yarbrough (1983) show data in this table in analytic form. For extrapolation from this table to air spaces less than 0.5 in. (e.g., insulating window glass), assume $h_c = 0.159(1 + 0.0016t_m)/l$, where l is air space thickness in in., and h_c is heat transfer through air space only.

[b]Values based on data presented by Robinson et al. (1954). (Also see Chapter 4, Tables 5 and 6, and Chapter 33.) Values apply for ideal conditions (i.e., air spaces of uniform thickness bounded by plane, smooth, parallel surfaces with no air leakage to or from the space). **This table should not be used for hollow siding or profiled cladding: see Table 1.** For greater accuracy, use overall U-factors determined through guarded hot box (ASTM Standard C1363) testing. Thermal resistance values for multiple air spaces must be based on careful estimates of mean temperature differences for each air space.

[c]A single resistance value cannot account for multiple air spaces; each air space requires a separate resistance calculation that applies only for established boundary conditions. Resistances of horizontal spaces with heat flow downward are substantially independent of temperature difference.

[d]Interpolation is permissible for other values of mean temperature, temperature difference, and effective emittance ε_{eff}. Interpolation and moderate extrapolation for air spaces greater than 3.5 in. are also permissible.

[e]Effective emittance ε_{eff} of air space is given by $1/\varepsilon_{eff} = 1/\varepsilon_1 + 1/\varepsilon_2 - 1$, where ε_1 and ε_2 are emittances of surfaces of air space (see Table 2). **Also, oxidation, corrosion, and accumulation of dust and dirt can dramatically increase surface emittance. Emittance values of 0.05 should only be used where the highly reflective surface can be maintained over the service life of the assembly.**

Table 4 Air Permeability of Different Materials

Material	Mean Air Permeability, lb/ft·h·in. Hg
Cement board, 1/2 in., 71 lb/ft³	0.24
Fiber cement board, 1/4 in., 86 lb/ft³	0.00002
Gypsum wall board, 1/2 in., 39 lb/ft³	0.03
with one coat primer	0.18
with one coat primer/two coats latex paint	0.02
Hardboard siding, 3/8 in., 46 lb/ft³	0.037
Oriented strand board (OSB), 41 lb/ft³, 3/8 in.	0.008
7/16 in.	0.016
1/2 in.	0.008
Douglas fir plywood, 1/2 in., 29 lb/ft³	0.0003
5/8 in., 34 lb/ft³	0.008
Canadian softwood plywood, 3/4 in., 28 lb/ft³	0.0002
Wood fiber board, 3/8 in., 20 lb/ft³	2.0
Masonry Materials	
Aerated concrete, 28.7 lb/ft³	0.04
Cement mortar, 100 lb/ft³	0.01
Clay brick, 4 by 4 by 8 in., 124 lb/ft³	32
Limestone, 156 lb/ft³	negligible
Portland stucco mix, 124 lb/ft³	8.15E-05
Eastern white cedar, 3/4 in., 22 lb/ft³ (transverse)	negligible
Eastern white pine, 3/4 in., 29 lb/ft³ (transverse)	8.2E-06
Southern yellow pine, 3/4 in., 31.2 lb/ft³ (transverse)	0.00024
Spruce, 3/4 in., 25 lb/ft³ (transverse)	0.00041
Western red cedar, 3/4 in., 21.8 lb/ft³ (transverse)	< 7E-06
Cellulose insulation, dry blown, 2 lb/ft³	2364
Glass fiber batt, 1 lb/ft³	2038
Polystyrene expanded, 1 lb/ft³	0.09
sprayed foam, 2.4 lb/ft³	0.000082
0.4 to 1/2 lb/ft³	0.034
Polyisocyanurate insulation, 1.7 lb/ft³	negligible
Bituminous paper (#15 felt), 28 mil, 54 lb/ft² (transverse)	20
Asphalt-impregnated paper	9
#10, 5 mil, 5.9 lb/ft² (transverse)	
#30, 6 mil, 8.2 lb/ft² (transverse)	54
#60, 9 mil, 16.1 lb/ft² (transverse)	58
Spun bonded polyolefin (SBPO) 4 mil, 0.87/ft² (transverse)	4
with crinkled surface, 3 to 4 mil, 0.92 lb/ft² (transverse)	2
Wallpaper, vinyl, 5 mil, 5.9 lb/ft² (transverse)	0.041
Exterior insulated finish system (EIFS), 0.17 in. acrylic, 71 lb/ft³	0

Source: Kumaran (2002).

As heat flows through soil, moisture tends to move away from the heat source. This moisture migration provides initial mass transport of heat, but it also dries the soil adjacent to the heat source, thus lowering the apparent thermal conductivity in that zone of soil.

Typically, when other factors are held constant, k increases with moisture content and with dry density of a soil, but decreases with increasing organic content of a soil and for uniform gradations and rounded soil grains (because grain-to-grain contacts are reduced). The k of a frozen soil may be higher or lower than that of the same unfrozen soil (because the conductivity of ice is higher than that of water but lower than that of typical soil grains). Differences in k below moisture contents of 7 to 8% are quite small. At approximately 15% moisture content, k may vary up to 30% from unfrozen values.

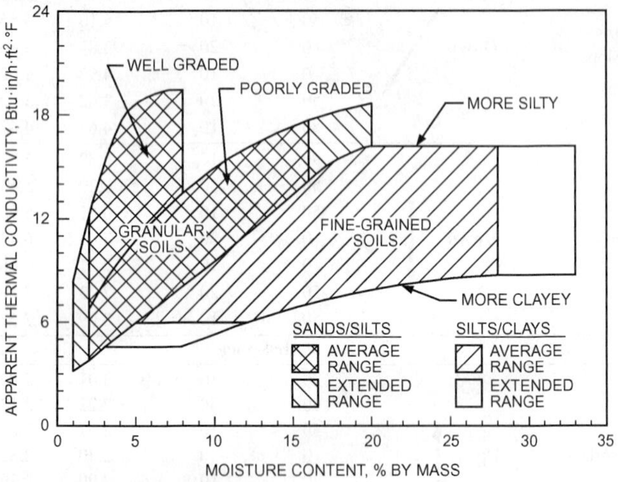

Fig. 6 Trends of Apparent Thermal Conductivity of Moist Soils

Although thermal conductivity varies greatly over the complete range of possible moisture contents, this range can be narrowed if it is assumed that the moisture contents of most field soils lie between the **wilting point** of the soil (i.e., the moisture content of a soil below which a plant cannot alleviate its wilting symptoms) and the **field capacity** of the soil (i.e., the moisture content of a soil that has been thoroughly wetted and then drained until the drainage rate has become negligibly small). After a prolonged dry spell, moisture is near the wilting point, and after a rainy period, soil has moisture content near its field capacity. Moisture contents at these limits have been studied by many agricultural researchers, and data for different types of soil are given by Kersten (1949) and Salomone and Marlowe (1989). Shaded areas in Figure 6 approximate (1) the full range of moisture contents for different soil types and (2) a range between average values of each limit.

Table 8 summarizes design values for thermal conductivities of the basic soil classes. Table 9 gives ranges of thermal conductivity for some basic classes of rock. The value chosen depends on whether heat transfer is calculated for minimum heat loss through the soil, as in a ground heat exchange system, or a maximum value, as in peak winter heat loss calculations for a basement. Hence, high and low values are given for each soil class.

When calculating annual energy use, choose values that represent typical mean site conditions. In climates where ground freezing is significant, accurate heat transfer simulations should include the effect of the latent heat of fusion of water. Energy released during this phase change significantly retards the progress of the frost front in moist soils.

For further information, see Chapter 17, which includes a method for estimating heat loss through foundations.

4.8 SURFACE FILM COEFFICIENTS/ RESISTANCES

As explained in Chapter 25, the overall thermal resistance of an assembly comprises its surface-to-surface thermal resistance R_s and

Table 5 Typical Water Vapor Permeance and Permeability for Common Building Materials[a]

Material	Weight, lb/100 ft^2	Thickness, in.	Permeance, perm Dry-Cup	Permeance, perm Wet-Cup	Permeance, perm Other Method	Permeability, perm-in.
Plastic and Metal Foils and Films[b]						
Aluminum foil		0.001	0.0			
		0.00035	0.05			
Polyethylene		0.002	0.16			3.2
		0.004	0.08			3.2
		0.006	0.06[b]			3.2
		0.008	0.04[b]			3.2
		0.010			3.2	3.2
Polyvinylchloride, unplasticized		0.002	0.68[b]			
Polyvinylchloride, plasticized		0.004	0.8 to 1.4			
Polyester		0.001	0.73			
		0.0032	0.23			
		0.0076	0.08			
Cellulose acetate		0.01	4.6			
		0.125	0.32			
Liquid-Applied Coating Materials						
Commercial latex paints (dry film thickness)						
Vapor retarder paint		0.0031			0.45	
Primer-sealer		0.0012			6.28	
Vinyl acetate/acrylic primer		0.002			7.42	
Vinyl/acrylic primer		0.0016			8.62	
Semigloss vinyl/acrylic enamel		0.0024			6.61	
Exterior acrylic house and trim		0.0017			5.47	
Paint, 2 coats						
Asphalt paint on plywood					0.4	
Aluminum varnish on wood					0.3 to 0.5	
Enamels on smooth plaster					0.5 to 1.5	
Primers and sealers on interior insulation board					0.9 to 2.15	
Various primers plus 1 coat flat oil paint on plaster					1.6 to 3.0	
Flat paint on interior insulation board					4	
Water emulsion on interior insulation board					30 to 85	
Paint, 3 coats						
Exterior paint, white lead and oil on wood siding			0.3 to 1.0			
Exterior paint, white lead/zinc oxide and oil on wood			0.9			
Styrene/butadiene latex coating	12.5		11			
Polyvinyl acetate latex coating	25		5.5			
Chlorosulfonated polyethylene mastic	21.9		1.7			
	43.8		0.06			
Asphalt cutback mastic						
1/16 in., dry			0.14			
3/16 in., dry			0.0			
Hot-melt asphalt	12.5		0.5			
	21.9		0.1			
Building Paper, Felts, Roofing Papers[c]						
Duplex sheet, asphalt laminated, aluminum foil one side	8.6		0.002	0.176		
Saturated and coated roll roofing	65		0.05	0.24		
Kraft paper and asphalt laminated, reinforced	6.8		0.3	1.8		
Blanket thermal insulation back-up paper, asphalt coated	6.2		0.4	0.6 to 4.2		
Asphalt, saturated and coated vapor retarder paper	8.6		0.2 to 0.3	0.6		
Asphalt, saturated, but not coated, sheathing paper	4.4		3.3	20.2		
asphalt felt, 15 lb	14		1.0	5.6		
tar felt, 15 lb	14		4.0	18.2		
Single kraft, double	3.2		31	42		
Polyamide film, 2 mil			1.10	20.53		

Source: Lotz (1964).

[a]This table allows comparisons of materials, but when selecting vapor retarder materials, exact values for permeance or permeability should be obtained from manufacturer or from laboratory tests. Values shown indicate variations among mean values for materials that are similar but of different density, orientation, lot, or source. Values should not be used as design or specification data. Values from dry- and wet-cup methods were usually obtained from investigations using ASTM *Standards* C355 and E96; other values were obtained by two-temperature, special cell, and air velocity methods.

[b]Usually installed as vapor retarders, although sometimes used as exterior finish and elsewhere near the cold side, where special considerations are then required for warm-side barrier effectiveness.

[c]Low-permeance sheets used as vapor retarders. High permeance used elsewhere in construction.

Table 6 Water Vapor Permeance at Various Relative Humidities and Capillary Water Absorption Coefficient

Material	Thickness, in.	Permeance at Various Relative Humidities, perm 10%	30%	50%	70%	90%	Water Absorption Coefficient, $lb/(ft^2 \cdot h^{1/2})$	References/Comments
Building Board and Siding								
Asbestos cement board	0.12		4-8					Dry cup*
with oil-base finishes			0.3-0.5					Dry cup*
Cement board, 71 lb/ft^3	0.5	10	10	13	17	22	0.16	Kumaran (2002)
Fiber cement board, 86 lb/ft^3	0.31	0.46	1.3	3.6	10	32	0.31	Kumaran (2002)
Gypsum board, asphalt impregnated	0.5		40					Dry cup*
Gypsum wall board, 39 lb/ft^3	0.5	41	47	56	65	78	0.023	Kumaran (2002)
with one coat primer		12	26	38	50	62		Kumaran (2002)
with one coat primer/two coats latex paint		1.9	3.6	7.0	14	29		Kumaran (2002)
Hardboard siding, 46 lb/ft^3	0.43	6.3	6.9	7.5	8.2	9.0	0.0088	Kumaran (2002)
Oriented strand board (OSB), 41 lb/ft^3	0.39	0.01	0.31	0.86	2.4	6.7	0.020	Kumaran (2002)
41 lb/ft^3	0.43	0.04	0.97	2.0	3.7	6.6	0.027	Kumaran (2002)
41 lb/ft^3	0.48	0.06	0.49	1.3	2.4	3.9	0.020	Kumaran (2002)
Particleboard, 48 lb/ft^3	0.75		4.0	3.8	4.9	8.6		Burch et al. (1992)
Plywood	0.47	0.28	0.86	2.1	4.6	9.4	0.052	Kumaran (2002)
Douglas fir, 29 lb/ft^3								
Douglas fir, 34 lb/ft^3	0.59	0.18	0.48	1.3	3.4	9.3	0.038	Kumaran (2002)
Canadian softwood, 28 lb/ft^3	0.70	0.06	0.56	2.2	6.0	13	0.045	Kumaran (2002)
Exterior-grade, 36 lb/ft^3	0.48	0.37	0.38	0.53	1.7	11		Burch and Desjarlais (1995)
Exterior-grade, 32 lb/ft^3	0.51		1.2	1.4	3.2	15		Burch et al. (1992)
Wood fiber board, 20 lb/ft^3	0.46	18	20	22	24	27	0.012	Kumaran (2002)
19 lb/ft^3	1	47	48	50	53	58		Burch and Desjarlais (1995)
Masonry Materials								
Aerated concrete, 29 lb/ft^3	0.80	9.6	14	20	29	43	0.44	Kumaran (2002)
Cement mortar, 100 lb/ft^3	0.51	18	22	27	33	40	0.25	Kumaran (2002)
Clay brick, 124 lb/ft^3	0.49	5.8	6.2	6.7	7.2	7.7	2.1	Kumaran (2002)
Concrete, 138 lb/ft^3	1		0.9	1.0	1.7	4.5	0.22	Kumaran (1996)
Concrete block (cored, limestone aggregate)	8			← 2.4 →				*
Lightweight concrete, 83 lb/ft^3	1		8.4		7.8	13		Kumaran (1996)
Limestone, 156 lb/ft^3	1		0.18	0.18	0.18	0.18	0.0041	Kumaran (2002)
Perlite board, 10 lb/ft^3	1		19		23	56		Kumaran (1996)
11 lb/ft^3	1	44	44	44	44	44		Burch and Desjarlais (1995)
Plaster, on metal lath	0.75			← 15 →				*
on wood lath				← 11 →				*
on plain gypsum lath (with studs)				← 20 →				*
Polystyrene concrete, 16-50 lb/ft^3	1	11	12	13	14	16		Kumaran (1996)
Portland stucco mix, 124 $lb/^3$	0.55	1.0	1.4	2.0	2.9	4.0	0.15	Kumaran (2002)
Tile masonry, glazed	4			← 0.12 →				*
Woods								
Cedar	0.75	0.01	0.07	0.44	2.8	19	0.020	Kumaran (2002)
Eastern white cedar, 22 lb/ft^3 (transverse)								
Western red cedar, 22 lb/ft^3 (transverse)	0.71	0.10	0.22	0.47	1.0	2.2	0.012	Kumaran (2002)
Pine	1		20	27	51	82	0.20	Kumaran (1996)
21 lb/ft^3 (longitudinal)								
Eastern white pine, 29 lb/ft^3 (transverse)	0.75	0.04	0.16	0.62	2.4	9.3	0.081	Kumaran (2002)
Southern yellow pine, 31 lb/ft^3 (transverse)	0.77	0.11	0.36	1.2	4.2	15	0.017	Kumaran (2002)
Sugar pine, 23 lb/ft^3 (transverse)	0.51	0.45	0.54	0.93	2.3	8.4		Burch et al. (1992)
Spruce	0.52	41	98	112	120	121	0.12	Kumaran (1996)
28 lb/ft^3 (longitudinal)								
26 lb/ft^3 (transverse)	0.45		1.1	2.1	8.6	30		Kumaran (1996)
25 lb/ft^3 (transverse)	0.77	0.34	0.96	2.8	8.3	26	0.025	Kumaran (2002)
Insulation								
Air (still)	1			← 120 →				*
Cellular glass				← 0.0 →				*
Cellulose, dry blown, 1.9 lb/ft^3	2.5	30	38	42	45	48	1.2	Kumaran (2002)
Corkboard	1		2.1-2.6		9.5			*
Glass fiber batt, 0.7 lb/ft^3	3.5	34	34	34	34	34		Kumaran (2002)

Table 6 Water Vapor Permeance at Various Relative Humidities and Capillary Water Absorption Coefficient (*Continued*)

Material	Thickness, in.	Permeance at Various Relative Humidities, perm 10%	30%	50%	70%	90%	Water Absorption Coefficient, $lb/(ft^2 \cdot h^{1/2})$	References/Comments
Glass-fiber insulation board, 7.6 lb/ft^3	0.93	145	145	145	145	145		Burch and Desjarlais (1995)
facer, 55 lb/ft^3	0.065	0.004	0.01	0.04	0.12	0.35		Burch and Desjarlais (1995)
Mineral fiber insulation, 9 to 11 lb/ft^3	1	87	87	87	87	87		Kumaran (1996)
Mineral wool (unprotected)	1	←		116		→		*
Phenolic foam (covering removed)	1	←		26		→		*
Polyisocyanurate insulation, 1.7 lb/ft^3	1	2.8	3.1	3.5	4.0	4.5		Kumaran (2002)
2.0 lb/ft^3	0.97	2.0	2.3	2.5	2.8	3.2		Burch and Desjarlais (1995)
Polyisocyanurate glass-mat facer, 27 lb/ft^3	0.032	10	15	22	32	48		Burch and Desjarlais (1995)
Polystyrene expanded, 0.9 lb/ft^3	0.96	2.0	2.4	2.8	3.3	3.9		Kumaran (2002)
extruded, 1.8 lb/ft^3	1	0.8	0.8	0.8	0.8	0.8		Kumaran (2002)
Polyurethane expanded board stock	1		0.4-1.6					*
sprayed foam, 2.4 lb/ft^3	1	1.6	1.7	1.9	2.0	2.2		Kumaran (2002)
0.4 to 0.5 lb/ft^3	1	60	60	60	60	60		Kumaran (2002)
Structural insulating board, sheathing quality	1	←		20-50		→		*
interior, uncoated	0.5	←		50-90		→		*
Unicellular synthetic flexible rubber foam	1		0.02-0.15					Dry cup*
Foil, Felt, Paper (transverse)								
Asphalt-impregnated paper, 10 min rating, 3.5 lb/100 ft^2	0.0079	4.1	7.4	14	26	53	0.012	Kumaran (2002)
30 min rating, 4.1 lb/100 ft^2	0.0087	7.7	13	22	40	81	0.011	Kumaran (2002)
60 min rating, 5.7 lb/100 ft^2	0.013	26	33	42	55	74	0.014	Kumaran (2002)
Bituminous paper (#15 felt), 10.6 lb/100 ft^2	0.028	5.1	5.1	5.1	6.9	20	0.0063	Kumaran (2002)
Polyamide film	0.002		0.93	4.1	11	35		Gatland II (2005)
Spun bonded polyolefin (SBPO), 1.3 lb/100 ft^2	0.0055	76	76	76	76	76	0.0038	Kumaran (2002)
with crinkled surface, 1.4 lb/100 ft^2	0.0039-0.0043	55	55	55	55	55	0.0029	Kumaran (2002)
Wallpaper								
paper, 3.1 to 3.4 lb/100 ft^2	0.011		86-120		250-380			Kumaran (1996)
textile, 6.0 to 6.8 lb/100 ft^2	0.017-0.028		11-20		160-500			Kumaran (1996)
vinyl, 3.5 lb/100 ft^2	0.0081	1.5	2.4	3.7	5.5	8.0	0.0031	Kumaran (2002)
Other Construction Materials								
Built-up roofing (hot-mopped)		←		0.0		→		*
Exterior insulated finish system (EIFS), 71 lb/ft^3	**	1.6	1.6	1.6	1.6	1.6	0.0065	Kumaran (2002)
Glass fiber reinforced sheet, acrylic	0.056		0.12					Dry cup*
Polyester	0.048		0.05					Dry cup*

*Historical data, no reference available

**EIFS vapor permeance was tested with polymer cement base coat and latex acrylic finish coat of 0.17 in. thickness applied to expanded polystyrene of 1.3 in. thickness.

the surface film resistances between the assembly's surfaces and the interior and exterior environment (R_i and R_o). Table 10 gives typical values for the surface film coefficients h_i and h_o and their reciprocals, the surface resistances R_i and R_o. As shown, the indoor values depend on position of the surface, direction of heat transfer, and the surface's long-wave emissivity. Outdoors, the values depends on air speed and the surface's long-wave emissivity. Table 10 reflects standard situations, with an assumed (approximate) interior surface temperature representative of wall or roof assemblies. For situations that deviate substantially from standard conditions, including interior surface temperatures for fenestration systems, use ASHRAE (1998) or values from Chapter 15 to determine the surface film coefficients/resistances.

4.9 CODES AND STANDARDS

ASHRAE. 2010. Energy standard for buildings except low-rise residential buildings. ANSI/ASHRAE/IES *Standard* 90.1-2010.

ASTM. 2010. Standard terminology relating to thermal insulation. *Standard* C168-10. American Society for Testing and Materials, West Conshohocken, PA.

ASTM. 2010. Standard test method for steady-state heat flux measurements and thermal transmission properties by means of the guarded-hot-plate apparatus. *Standard* C177-10. American Society for Testing and Materials, West Conshohocken, PA.

ASTM. 2010. Standard test method for steady-state heat transfer properties of pipe insulation. *Standard* C335/C335M-10e1. American Society for Testing and Materials, West Conshohocken, PA.

Table 7 Sorption/Desorption Isotherms of Building Materials at Various Relative Humidities

Material	Sorption, % Moisture Content at % Relative Humidity						Desorption, % Moisture Content at % Relative Humidity						References
Building Board and Siding													
Cement board, 1/2 in., 70 lb/ft³	1_{43}	1.9_{70}	3.4_{81}	6.1_{93}	42.7_{100t}		1.6_{43}	3.2_{70}	4.6_{81}	6.2_{93}	$18_{99.27}$	$28_{99.93}$	Kumaran (2002)
Fiber cement board, 5/16 in., 86 lb/ft³	$4_{50.6}$	$5.8_{70.4}$	$16.8_{89.9}$	34.7_{100t}			$6.6_{50.5}$	$12.3_{70.5}$	$19.6_{90.6}$	$31.3_{95.32}$	$32.5_{99.49}$	$33.9_{99.93}$	Kumaran (2002)
Gypsum wall board, 1/2 in., 39 lb/ft³	$0.4_{50.5}$	$0.65_{70.5}$	$1.8_{90.8}$	4.2_{94}	68.9_{100c}	113_{100t}	$0.99_{50.4}$	$1.32_{71.5}$	$1.69_{84.8}$	$1.82_{88.3}$			Kumaran (2002)
Hardboard siding, 7/16 in., 46 lb/ft³	$4.7_{50.3}$	$6.9_{69.6}$	$13.1_{91.3}$	90_{100t}			$4.4_{50.3}$	$7.6_{69.2}$	$13.4_{91.3}$	$38_{91.3}$			Kumaran (2002)
Oriented strand board (OSB), 3/8 in., 41 lb/ft³	$4.6_{48.9}$	$7.6_{69.1}$	$14.7_{88.6}$	126_{100c}			$6.9_{49.9}$	$9.1_{69.4}$	$16.2_{90.3}$	$17.3_{92.3}$	$39.3_{99.3}$	$60.6_{99.8}$	Kumaran (2002)
7/16 in., 41 lb/ft³	$5.4_{48.9}$	$8.2_{69.1}$	$14.7_{88.6}$	160_{100t}			$7.9_{49.9}$	$9.9_{69.4}$	$17.4_{90.3}$	$39.1_{99.3}$	$62.7_{99.8}$		Kumaran (2002)
1/2 in., 41 lb/ft³	$4.6_{48.9}$	$7.8_{69.1}$	$14.8_{88.6}$	124_{100t}			$7.9_{49.9}$	$10_{69.4}$	$17.6_{90.3}$	$20_{92.3}$	$42_{99.3}$	59.5	Kumaran (2002)
Particle board, 3/4 in., 47 lb/ft³	$1.2_{11.3}$	$6.3_{57.6}$	$9.7_{78.6}$	$11.3_{84.1}$	$15.9_{93.6}$	$21.5_{97.3}$	$1.7_{11.3}$	$8.8_{57.6}$	$14_{78.6}$	$16.6_{84.1}$	$19_{93.6}$	$23.3_{97.6}$	Kumaran (1996)
Plywood, 1/2 in.	$7_{48.9}$	$9.2_{69.1}$	$15.8_{88.6}$	170_{100t}			$8.4_{49.9}$	$10.8_{69.4}$	$18.2_{90.3}$	$19_{92.3}$	$70_{99.3}$	101	Kumaran (2002)
5/8 in.	$6.8_{48.9}$	$9.6_{69.1}$	$16.8_{88.6}$	140_{100t}			$8.6_{49.9}$	$11.3_{69.4}$	$19.8_{90.3}$	$19.3_{92.3}$	$47_{99.3}$	79	Kumaran (2002)
3/4 in.	$6.7_{48.9}$	$10.1_{69.1}$	$17.6_{88.6}$	190_{100t}			$8.9_{49.9}$	$11.3_{69.4}$	$19.3_{90.3}$	$20.7_{92.3}$	$66_{99.3}$	$99_{99.8}$	Kumaran (2002)
Plywood (exterior grade), 1/2 in., 36 lb/ft³	$1.83_{11.3}$	6.9_{58}	$9.5_{78.7}$	$12.1_{84.5}$	$17.9_{93.8}$	22.1	$2.09_{11.3}$	9.3_{58}	$13.7_{78.7}$	$15.2_{84.5}$	$19.8_{93.8}$	23.4	Burch and Desjarlais (1995)
Wood fiber board, 7/16 in., 20 lb/ft³	$4.6_{50.6}$	$7.4_{70.5}$	$15.8_{91.1}$	304			$3.9_{50.6}$	$7.4_{71.1}$	$15_{90.6}$	$230_{99.71}$	$230_{99.85}$	$230_{99.93}$	Kumaran (2002)
1.0 in., 18.7 lb/ft³	$0.63_{11.3}$	5.7_{58}	$9.2_{78.7}$	$11.3_{84.5}$	$16.4_{93.8}$	$24.6_{97.4}$	$1.26_{11.3}$	7.6_{58}	$12_{78.7}$	$14.6_{84.5}$	$20.6_{93.8}$	$28.1_{97.4}$	
Masonry Materials													
Aerated concrete, 29 lb/ft³	$1.1_{50.6}$	$2.1_{71.5}$	$5_{88.1}$	83_{100c}	172		$1.1_{50.6}$	$2.2_{71.5}$	$6.3_{88.1}$	$34_{97.81}$	$72_{99.85}$	$92_{99.99}$	Kumaran (2002)
37.5 lb/ft³	$1.8_{17.8}$	$3.2_{75.8}$	$4.6_{90.3}$	$6.4_{92.4}$	$9.6_{95.9}$	$17.5_{98.4}$	$2.3_{17.8}$	2.8_{33}	$4_{55.2}$	$6.6_{75.6}$	$15.4_{91.6}$	36.5_{98}	Kumaran (1996)
Cement mortar, 100 lb/ft³	$0.42_{49.9}$	$2.3_{70.1}$	$5.3_{89.9}$	26_{100t}			$3.4_{49.9}$	$4.4_{70.2}$	$6.1_{89.9}$	$17_{98.9}$	$22_{99.63}$	$25_{99.93}$	Kumaran (2002)
Clay brick, 4 × 4 × 8 in., 124 lb/ft³	0.08_{50}	$0.12_{69.1}$	$0.1_{91.2}$	9.9_{100t}			0_{50}	$0_{91.2}$	$4.5_{98.9}$	$6_{99.63}$	$8.2_{99.71}$	$9.1_{99.93}$	Kumaran (2002)
Concrete, 138 lb/ft³	$0.88_{25.2}$	$1.15_{44.9}$	1.74_{65}	2.62_{80}	$3.35_{89.8}$	$4.45_{98.2}$	0.94_{20}	$2.19_{45.4}$	$2.98_{65.6}$	$3.85_{84.8}$	$4.57_{94.8}$		Kumaran (1996)
Lightweight concrete, 98 lb/ft³	$2.9_{24.4}$	$3.4_{45.2}$	$4_{65.2}$	4.6_{85}	6.6_{98}		$3.1_{19.6}$	4.4_{40}	$5.2_{59.8}$	$6_{79.6}$	$7.1_{94.7}$		Kumaran (1996)
Limestone, 156 lb/ft³	0_{50}	0_{70}	$0.1_{88.5}$	1.8_{100t}			$0_{70.5}$	$0.1_{88.6}$	$0.21_{95.3}$	$0.5_{98.9}$	$0.6_{99.27}$	$1.3_{99.93}$	Kumaran (2002)
Perlite board	130_{33}	160_{52}	260_{75}	380_{86}	800_{97}	$1170_{99.8}$							Kumaran (1996)
Portland stucco mix, 124 lb/ft³	3_{50}	$3.7_{70.3}$	$5.8_{89.9}$	12_{100t}			4.2_{50}	$5.2_{70.3}$	$7_{90.3}$	$10.3_{95.29}$	$11.6_{98.9}$	$11.7_{99.93}$	Kumaran (2002)
Woods													
Eastern white cedar, 1 in., 22.5 lb/ft³	$3.4_{49.8}$	7.6_{70}	$12.8_{88.5}$	228_{100t}			1.7_{50}	$7.4_{70.5}$	$11.9_{88.7}$	$85_{98.9}$	$118_{99.63}$	$176_{99.92}$	
Eastern white pine, 1 in., 28.7 lb/ft³	$3.2_{49.8}$	7.6_{70}	$12_{88.5}$	192_{100t}			3.2_{50}	$9_{70.5}$	$12.4_{88.7}$	$84_{99.78}$			
Southern yellow pine, 1 in. 31 lb/ft³	$3.6_{49.8}$	8.1_{70}	$15.2_{88.5}$	158_{100t}			4.3_{50}	$10_{70.5}$	$15.6_{88.7}$	$57_{99.78}$			
Spruce (transverse), 25 lb/ft³	$4.1_{49.8}$	9.2_{70}	$16.7_{88.5}$	228_{100t}			4.9_{50}	$11.3_{70.5}$	$17.7_{88.7}$	$148_{95.96}$	$187_{99.78}$		
Western red cedar, 1 in., 21.8 lb/ft³	$3.4_{49.8}$	6_{70}	$9.6_{88.5}$	228_{100t}			1_{50}	$9_{70.5}$	$13.3_{88.7}$	$113_{99.78}$			
Insulation													
Cellulose, dry blown, 1.87 lb/ft³	$6.1_{50.5}$	$9.6_{71.5}$	$24_{88.1}$				$5_{50.2}$	$12_{72.8}$	26_{88}				Kumaran (2002)
Glass fiber batt, 0.72 lb/ft³	$0.21_{50.6}$	$0.34_{71.5}$	$0.75_{88.1}$				$0.24_{50.4}$	$0.35_{71.4}$	$0.67_{88.2}$				Kumaran (2002)
Glass fiber board, 0.9 in., 7.5 lb/ft³	$0.16_{11.3}$	0.75	$0.82_{78.7}$	$0.96_{84.5}$	$1.3_{93.8}$	$2.03_{97.4}$	$0.43_{11.3}$	$0.86_{32.8}$	1.11_{58}	$1.26_{84.5}$	$1.74_{93.8}$	$2.16_{97.4}$	Burch and Desjarlais (1995)
Glass fiber board facer, 0.06 in., 55 lb/ft³	$0.09_{11.3}$	0.53_{58}	$0.76_{78.7}$	$0.84_{84.5}$	$1.14_{93.8}$	$1.54_{97.4}$	$0.18_{11.3}$	0.56_{58}	$0.87_{78.7}$	$1.09_{84.5}$	$1.45_{93.8}$	$1.81_{97.4}$	Burch and Desjarlais (1995)
Mineral fiber, 2.5 lb/ft³	$0.5_{20.1}$	$0.55_{45.4}$	0.59_{65}	$0.7_{85.2}$	$0.76_{94.5}$	$0.8_{97.5}$	$0.5_{20.1}$	$0.58_{44.9}$	$0.63_{64.9}$	$0.81_{84.5}$	$1.1_{94.7}$	$1.6_{97.8}$	Kumaran (1996)
Polystyrene, expanded, 0.92 lb/ft³	$0.4_{50.4}$	$0.3_{68.3}$	$0.2_{88.3}$				$0.4_{50.1}$	$0.5_{67.9}$	$0.5_{87.9}$				Kumaran (2002)
extruded, 1.79 lb/ft³	$0.6_{50.4}$	$0.5_{68.3}$	$0.4_{88.3}$				$0.5_{50.1}$	$0.5_{67.9}$	$0.4_{87.9}$				Kumaran (2002)
Polyurethane, sprayed foam, 2.43 lb/ft³	$1.3_{50.4}$	$1.7_{68.3}$	$2_{88.4}$				$1.1_{50.1}$	$1.5_{67.9}$	$1.8_{87.9}$				Kumaran (2002)
0.4 to 1/2 lb/ft³	$0.5_{50.4}$	$1_{70.2}$	$1.6_{90.3}$				$1_{50.5}$	$2.1_{70.9}$	$7_{91.3}$				Kumaran (2002)
Polyisocyanurate, 1.65 lb/ft³	$1.3_{50.4}$	$1.7_{68.3}$	$2.1_{88.3}$				$1.1_{50.1}$	$1.5_{67.9}$	$1.9_{87.9}$				Kumaran (2002)
Polyisocyanurate glass facer, 0.04 in., 26.8 lb/ft³	$1.36_{11.3}$	4.5_{58}	$6.8_{78.7}$	$9_{84.5}$	$12.5_{93.8}$	$17.9_{97.4}$	$0.89_{11.3}$	5.8_{58}	$8.3_{78.7}$	10.9	$14.4_{93.8}$	$18.4_{97.4}$	Burch and Desjarlais (1995)

ASTM. 2010. Standard test method for steady-state thermal transmission properties by means of the heat flow meter apparatus. *Standard* C518-10. American Society for Testing and Materials, West Conshohocken, PA.

ASTM. 2015. Standard practice for selection of water vapor retarders for thermal insulation. *Standard* C755-10 (R2015). American Society for Testing and Materials, West Conshohocken, PA.

ASTM. 2005. Standard classification of potential health and safety concerns associated with thermal insulation materials and accessories. *Standard* C930-05. American Society for Testing and Materials, West Conshohocken, PA.

ASTM. 2013. Standard practice for calculating thermal transmission properties under steady-state conditions. *Standard* C1045-07 (R2013). American Society for Testing and Materials, West Conshohocken, PA.

ASTM. 2011. Standard test method for thermal performance of building materials and envelope assemblies by means of a hot box apparatus. *Standard* C1363-11. American Society for Testing and Materials, West Conshohocken, PA.

ASTM. 2016. Standard specification for insulated vinyl siding. *Standard* D7793-16. American Society for Testing and Materials, West Conshohocken, PA.

ASTM. 2010. Standard test methods for water vapor transmission of materials. *Standard* E96/E96M-10. American Society for Testing and Materials, West Conshohocken, PA.

ASTM. 2009. Standard practices for air leakage site detection in building envelopes and air barrier systems. *Standard* E1186-03 (2009). American Society for Testing and Materials, West Conshohocken, PA.

ASTM. 2011. Standard specification for air barrier (AB) material or system for low-rise framed building walls. *Standard* E1677-11. American Society for Testing and Materials, West Conshohocken, PA.

ASTM. 2011. Standard test method for determining air leakage of air barrier assemblies. *Standard* E2357-11. American Society for Testing and Materials, West Conshohocken, PA.

CAN/ULC. 2003. Standard for determination of log-term thermal resistance of closed-cell thermal insulating foams. CAN/ULC *Standard* S770-2003. Standards Council of Canada, Ottawa, ON, and Underwriters Laboratories Canada, Toronto, ON.

VDI. 1999. Environmental meteorology—Interactions between atmosphere and surfaces—Calculation of short-wave and long-wave radiation. *Standard* 3789 Part 2. Verein Deutscher Ingenieure (Association of German Engineers), Dusseldorf.

Table 8 Typical Apparent Thermal Conductivity Values for Soils, Btu·in/h·ft²·°F

		Recommended Values for Design[a]	
	Normal Range	Low[b]	High[c]
Sands	4.2 to 17.4	5.4	15.6
Silts	6 to 17.4	11.4	15.6
Clays	6 to 11.4	7.8	10.8
Loams	6 to 17.4	6.6	15.6

[a]Reasonable values for use when no site- or soil-specific data are available.
[b]Moderately conservative values for minimum heat loss through soil (e.g., use in soil heat exchanger or earth-contact cooling calculations). Values are from Salomone and Marlowe (1989).
[c]Moderately conservative values for maximum heat loss through soil (e.g., use in peak winter heat loss calculations). Values are from Salomone and Marlowe (1989).

Table 9 Typical Apparent Thermal Conductivity Values for Rocks, Btu·in/h·ft²·°F

	Normal Range
Pumice, tuff, obsidian	3.6 to 15.6
Basalt	3.6 to 18.0
Shale	6 to 27.6
Granite	12 to 30
Limestone, dolomite, marble	8.4 to 30
Quartzose sandstone	9.6 to 54

REFERENCES

ASHRAE members can access *ASHRAE Journal* articles and ASHRAE research project final reports at technologyportal.ashrae.org. Articles and reports are also available for purchase by nonmembers in the online ASHRAE Bookstore at www.ashrae.org/bookstore.

Adams, L. 1971. Supporting cryogenic equipment with wood. *Chemical Engineering* (May):156-158.

ASHRAE. 1998. Standard method for determining and expressing the heat transfer and total optical properties of fenestration products. SPC 142.

ASTM. 1985a. Guarded hot plate and heat flow meter methodology. *Special Technical Publication* STP 879. American Society for Testing and Materials, West Conshohocken, PA.

ASTM. 1985b. Building applications of heat flux transducers. *Special Technical Publication* STP 885. American Society for Testing and Materials, West Conshohocken, PA.

ASTM. 1988. Thermal insulation: Material and systems. *Special Technical Publication* STP 922. American Society for Testing and Materials, West Conshohocken, PA.

ASTM. 1990. Insulation materials: Testing and applications. *Special Technical Publication* STP 1030. American Society for Testing and Materials, West Conshohocken, PA.

ASTM. 1991. Insulation materials: Testing and applications, 2nd vol. *Special Technical Publication* STP 1116. American Society for Testing and Materials, West Conshohocken, PA.

ASTM. Annual. *Annual book of ASTM standards*, vol. 04.06, *Thermal insulation; building and environmental acoustics*. American Society for Testing and Materials, West Conshohocken, PA.

Bassett, M.R., and H.A. Trethowen. 1984. Effect of condensation on emittance of reflective insulation. *Journal of Thermal Insulation* 8(October):127.

Binder, A., D. Zirkelbach, and H.M. Künzel. 2010. Test method to quantify the wicking properties of insulation materials designed to prevent interstitial condensation. *Proceedings of Buildings XI Conference*, ASHRAE.

Bomberg, M.T., and M.K. Kumaran. 1986. A test method to determine air flow resistance of exterior membranes and sheathings. *Journal of Thermal Insulation* 9:224-235.

Brandreth, D.A., ed. 1986. *Advances in foam aging—A topic in energy conservation series*. Caissa Editions, Yorklyn, DE.

Table 10 Surface Film Coefficients/Resistances

		Surface Emittance, ε					
		Nonreflective		Reflective			
Position of Surface	Direction of Heat Flow	ε = 0.90 h_i	ε = 0.90 R_i	ε = 0.20 h_i	ε = 0.20 R_i	ε = 0.05 h_i	ε = 0.05 R_i
Indoor							
Horizontal	Upward	1.63	0.61	0.91	1.10	0.76	1.32
Sloping at 45°	Upward	1.60	0.62	0.88	1.14	0.73	1.37
Vertical	Horizontal	1.46	0.68	0.74	1.35	0.59	1.70
Sloping at 45°	Downward	1.32	0.76	0.60	1.67	0.45	2.22
Horizontal	Downward	1.08	0.92	0.37	2.70	0.22	4.55
Outdoor (any position)		h_o	R_o				
15 mph wind (for winter)	Any	6.00	0.17	—	—	—	—
7.5 mph wind (for summer)	Any	4.00	0.25	—	—	—	—

Notes:
1. Surface conductance h_i and h_o measured in Btu/h·ft²·°F; resistance R_i and R_o in h·ft²·°F/Btu.
2. No surface has both an air space resistance value and a surface resistance value.
3. Conductances are for surfaces of the stated emittance facing virtual blackbody surroundings at same temperature as ambient air. Values based on surface/air temperature difference of 10°F and surface temperatures of 70°F.
4. See Chapter 4 for more detailed information.
5. Condensate can have significant effect on surface emittance (see Table 2). Also, oxidation, corrosion, and accumulation of dust and dirt can dramatically increase surface emittance. Emittance values of 0.05 should only be used where highly reflective surface can be maintained over the service life of the assembly.

Brown, W.C., M.T. Bomberg, J. Rasmussen, and J. Ullett. 1993. Measured thermal resistance of frame walls with defects in the installation of mineral fibre insulation. *Journal of Thermal Insulation and Building Envelopes* 16(April):318-339.

Burch, D.M., and A.O. Desjarlais. 1995. Water vapor measurements of low-slope roofing materials. *Report* NISTIR 5681. National Institute of Standards and Technology, Gaithersburg, MD.

Burch, D.M., W.C. Thomas, and A.H. Fanney. 1992. Water vapor permeability measurements of common building materials. *ASHRAE Transactions* 98(2).

CIBSE. 2006. Thermal properties of building structures. Chapter 3 in CIBSE *Guide A*: *Environmental Design*. The Chartered Institution of Building Services Engineers, London, U.K.

Construction Specifications Canada. 1990. *Tek-AID on air barrier systems*. Toronto.

Di Lenardo, B., W.C. Brown, W.A. Dalgleish, K. Kumaran, and G.F. Poirier. 1995. *Technical guide for air barrier systems for exterior walls of low-rise buildings*. Canadian Construction Materials Centre, National Research Council Canada, Ottawa, Ontario.

Donnelly, R.G., V.J. Tennery, D.L. McElroy, T.G. Godfrey, and J.O. Kolb. 1976. Industrial thermal insulation: An assessment. Oak Ridge National Laboratory *Reports* TM-5283, TM-5515, and TID-27120.

Glaser, P.E., I.A. Black, R.S. Lindstrom, F.E. Ruccia, and A.E. Wechsler. 1967. Thermal insulation systems—A survey. NASA *Report* SP5027.

Goss, W.P., and R.G. Miller. 1989. Literature review of measurement and prediction of reflective building insulation system performance: 1900-1989. *ASHRAE Transactions* 95(2).

Hedlin, C.P. 1985. Effect of insulation joints on heat loss through flat roofs. *ASHRAE Transactions* 91(2B):608-622.

Hooper, F.C., and W.J. Moroz. 1952. The impact of aging factors on the emissivity of reflective insulations. ASTM *Bulletin* (May):92-95.

ICC. 2007. *2007 supplement to the International Codes*. International Code Council, Washington, D.C.

ISO. 2003. Thermal performance of windows, doors, and shading devices—Detailed calculations. *Standard* 15099. International Organization for Standardization, Geneva.

Karagiozis, A.N., and H.M. Salonvaara. 1999a. Hygrothermal performance of EIFS-clad walls: Effect of vapor diffusion and air leakage on the drying of construction moisture. *Special Technical Publication* STP 1352, pp. 32-51. American Society for Testing and Materials, West Conshohocken, PA.

Karagiozis, A.N., and H.M. Salonvaara. 1999b. *Whole building hygrothermal performance: Proceedings of the 5th Symposium on Building Physics in the Nordic Countries*, Goteborg, vol. 2, pp. 745-753. C.E. Hagentoft and P.I. Sandberg, eds.

Kersten, M.S. 1949. Thermal properties of soils. University of Minnesota, Engineering Experiment Station *Bulletin* 28 (June).

Korsgaard, V., and C.R. Pedersen. 1989. Transient moisture distribution in flat roofs with hygro diode vapor retarder. *Proceedings of ASHRAE/DOE/BTECC/CIBSE Conference on Thermal Performance of Exterior Envelopes of Buildings IV*.

Korsgaard, V., and C.R. Pedersen. 1992. Laboratory and practical experience with a novel water-permeable vapor retarder. *Proceedings of ASHRAE/DOE/BTECC/CIBSE Conference on Thermal Performance of Exterior Envelopes of Buildings V*, pp. 480-490.

Kuenzel, H.M. 1999. More moisture load tolerance of construction assemblies through the application of a smart vapor retarder. *Proceedings of Thermal Performance of the Exterior Envelopes of Buildings VII*, pp. 129-132. ASHRAE.

Kumaran, M.K. 1989. Experimental investigation on simultaneous heat and moisture transport through thermal insulation. *Proceedings of the Conseil International du Batiment/International Building Council (CIB) 11th International Conference* 2:275-284.

Kumaran, M.K. 1996. Heat, air and moisture transport. *Final Report*, vol. 3, task 3: Material properties. International Energy Agency Annex 24.

Kumaran, M.K. 2002. A thermal and moisture transport database for common building and insulating materials. ASHRAE Research Project RP-1018, *Final Report*. National Research Council, Canada.

Lander, R.M. 1955. Gas is an important factor in the thermal conductivity of most insulating materials. *ASHRAE Transactions* 61:151.

Lecompte, J. 1989. The influence of natural convection in an insulated cavity on the thermal performance of the wall. *Special Technical Publication* STP 1000:397-420. American Society for Testing and Materials, West Conshohocken, PA.

Lewis, W.C. 1967. Thermal conductivity of wood-base fiber and particle panel materials. Forest Products Laboratory, *Research Paper* FPL 77, June.

Lewis, J.E. 1979. Thermal evaluation of the effects of gaps between adjacent roof insulation panels. *Journal of Thermal Insulation* (October):80-103.

Lotz, W.A. 1964. Vapor barrier design, neglected key to freezer insulation effectiveness. *Quick Frozen Foods* (November):122.

Lotz, W.A. 1969. Facts about thermal insulation. *ASHRAE Journal* (June): 83-84.

MacLean, J.D. 1941. Thermal conductivity of wood. *ASHVE Transactions* 47:323.

McGowan, A.G. 2007. Catalog of material thermal property data (RP-905). ASHRAE Research Project, *Final Report*.

NIST. 2000. *NIST standard reference database 81: NIST heat transmission properties of insulating and building materials*. U.S. Department of Commerce, National Institute of Standards and Materials, Gaithersburg, MD. srdata.nist.gov/insulation/.

Nottage, H.B. 1947. Thermal properties of building materials used in heat flow calculations. *ASHVE Transactions* 53:215-243.

Ojanen, T., R. Kohonen, and M.K Kumaran. 1994. Modeling heat, air, and moisture transport through building materials and components. Chapter 2 in *Manual* MNL 18, *Moisture control in buildings*. American Society for Testing and Materials, West Conshohocken, PA.

Ostrogorsky, A.G., and L.R. Glicksman. 1986. Laboratory tests of effectiveness of diffusion barriers. *Journal of Cellular Plastics* 22:303.

Pelanne, C.M. 1979. Thermal insulation heat flow measurements: Requirements for implementation. *ASHRAE Journal* 21(3):51.

Rasmussen J., W.C. Brown, M. Bomberg, and J.M. Ullett. 1993. Measured thermal performance of frame walls with defects in the installation of mineral fibre insulation. *Proceedings of the 3rd Symposium on Building Physics in the Nordic Countries*, pp. 209-217.

Robinson, H.E., F.J. Powlitch, and R.S. Dill. 1954. The thermal insulation value of airspaces. *Housing Research Paper* 32, Housing and Home Finance Agency.

Robinson, H.E., F.J. Powell, and L.A. Cosgrove. 1957. Thermal resistance of airspaces and fibrous insulations bounded by reflective surfaces. National Bureau of Standards, *Building Materials and Structures Report* BMS 151.

Rowley, F.B., and A.B. Algren. 1937. Thermal conductivity of building materials. University of Minnesota *Bulletin* #12, Minneapolis.

Rowley, F.B., R.C. Jordan, C.E. Lund, and R.M. Lander. 1952. Gas is an important factor in the thermal conductivity of most insulating materials. *ASHVE Transactions* 58:155.

Sabine, H.J., M.B. Lacher, D.R. Flynn, and T.L. Quindry. 1975. Acoustical and thermal performance of exterior residential walls, doors and windows. NBS *Building Science Series* 77. National Institute of Standards and Technology, Gaithersburg, MD.

Salomone, L.A., and J.I. Marlowe. 1989. *Soil and rock classification according to thermal conductivity: Design of ground-coupled heat pump systems*. EPRI CU-6482. Electric Power Research Institute, Palo Alto, CA.

Seiffert, K. 1970. *Damp diffusion and buildings*. Elsevier, Amsterdam, the Netherlands.

Shu, L.S., A.E. Fiorato, and J.W. Howanski. 1979. Heat transmission coefficients of concrete block walls with core insulation. *Proceedings of the ASHRAE/DOE-ORNL Conference on Thermal Performance of the Exterior Envelopes of Buildings*, ASHRAE SP 28, pp. 421-435.

Simons, E. 1955. In-place studies of insulated structures. *Refrigerating Engineering* 63:40, 128.

Touloukian, Y.S., R.W. Powell, C.Y. Ho, and I.G. Clemens. 1970. Thermophysical properties of matter. *Thermal conductivity data tables of nonmetallic solids*. IFI/Plenum, New York.

Tye, R.P. 1985. Upgrading thermal insulation performance of industrial processes. *Chemical Engineering Progress* (February):30-34.

Tye, R.P. 1986. Effects of product variability on thermal performance of thermal insulation. *Proceedings of the First Asian Thermal Properties Conference*, Beijing, People's Republic of China.

Tye, R.P. 1988. Aging of cellular plastics: A comprehensive bibliography. *Journal of Thermal Insulation* 11:196-222.

Tye, R.P., and A.O. Desjarlais. 1981. *Performance characteristics of foam-in-place urea formaldehyde insulation*. ORNL/Sub-78/86993/1. Oak Ridge National Laboratory, Oak Ridge, TN.

Tye, R.P., and A.O. Desjarlais. 1983. Factors influencing the thermal performance of thermal insulations for industrial applications. In *Thermal insulation, materials, and systems for energy conservation in the '80s*, F.A. Govan, D.M. Greason, and J.D. McAllister, eds. ASTM STP 789:733-748.

Valore, R.C., 1988. *Thermophysical properties of masonry and its constituents, parts I and II.* International Masonry Institute, Washington, D.C.

Van Geem, M.G. 1985. Thermal transmittance of concrete block walls with core insulation. *ASHRAE Transactions* 91(2).

Verschoor, J.D. 1977. Effectiveness of building insulation applications. USN/CEL *Report* CR78.006—NTIS AD-AO53 452/9ST.

Verschoor, J.D., and P. Greebler. 1952. Heat transfer by gas conductivity and radiation in fibrous insulations. *ASME Transactions* 74(6):961-968.

Wilkes, K.E. 1979. Thermophysical properties data base activities at Owens-Corning Fiberglas. *Proceedings of the ASHRAE/DOE-ORNL Conference on Thermal Performance of the Exterior Envelopes of Buildings*, ASHRAE SP 28, pp. 662-677.

Wilkes, K.E., and P.W. Childs. 1992. Thermal performance of fiberglass and cellulose attic insulations. *Proceedings of the ASHRAE/DOE/BTECC/CIBSE Conference on Thermal Performance of the Exterior Envelopes of Buildings V*, pp. 357-367.

Wilkes, K.E., and J.L. Rucker. 1983. Thermal performance of residential attic insulation. *Energy and Buildings* 5:263-277.

Yarbrough, D.W. 1983. *Assessment of reflective insulations for residential and commercial applications*. ORNL/TM-8891. Oak Ridge National Laboratory, Oak Ridge, TN.

Zhao, J., J. Grunewald, U. Ruisinger, and S. Feng. 2017. Evaluation of capillary-active mineral insulation systems for interior retrofit solution. *Building and Environment* 115:215-227. dx.doi.org/10.1016/j.buildenv.2017.01.004.

BIBLIOGRAPHY

ASHRAE. 1996. Building insulation system thermal anomalies. ASHRAE *Research Report* RP-758. Enermodal Engineering, Ltd.

ASTM. 1974. Heat transmission measurements in thermal insulations. *Special Technical Publication* STP 544. American Society for Testing and Materials, West Conshohocken, PA.

ASTM. 1978. Thermal transmission measurements of insulation. *Special Technical Publication* STP 660. American Society for Testing and Materials, West Conshohocken, PA.

ASTM. 1980. Thermal insulation performance. *Special Technical Publication* STP 718. American Society for Testing and Materials, West Conshohocken, PA.

ASTM. 1983. Thermal insulations, materials, and systems for energy conservation in the '80s. *Special Technical Publication* STP 789. American Society for Testing and Materials, West Conshohocken, PA.

Cardenes, T.J., and G.T. Bible. 1987. *The thermal properties of wood—Data base*. American Society of Testing and Materials, West Conshohocken, PA.

CIMA. 2007. Measured thermal resistances for cellulose insulation products commercially available in 2007. Report prepared by R&D Services, Inc., for the Cellulose Insulation Manufacturers Association.

Hedlin, C.P. 1988. Heat flow through a roof insulation having moisture contents between 0 and 1% by volume, in summer. *ASHRAE Transactions* 94(2):1579-1594.

Pelanne, C.M. 1977. Heat flow principles in thermal insulation. *Journal of Thermal Insulation* 1:48.

Raznjevic, K. 1976. Thermal conductivity tables. In *Handbook of thermodynamic tables and charts*. McGraw-Hill, New York.

Rowley, F.B., and A.B. Algren. 1932. Heat transmission through building materials. University of Minnesota *Bulletin* 8, Minneapolis.

Yarbrough, D.W., R.S. Graves, D.L. McElroy, A.O. Desjarlais, and R.P. Tye. 1987. The thermal resistance of spray-applied fiber insulations. *Journal of Thermal Insulation* 11(2):81-95.

CHAPTER 27

HEAT, AIR, AND MOISTURE CONTROL IN BUILDING ASSEMBLIES—EXAMPLES

THERMAL and moisture design as well as long-term performance must be considered during the planning phase of buildings. Installing appropriate insulation layers and taking appropriate air and moisture control measures can be much more economical during construction than later. Design and material selection should be based on

- Building use
- Interior and exterior climate
- Space availability
- Thermal and moisture properties of materials
- Other properties required by location of materials
- Durability of materials
- Compatibility with adjacent materials
- Performance expectations of the assembly

Designers and builders often rely on generic guidelines and past building practice as the basis for system and material selection. Although this approach may provide insight for design decisions, selections and performance requirements should be set through engineering analysis of project-specific criteria. Recent developments have increased the capabilities of available tools and methods of thermal and moisture analysis.

This chapter draws on Chapter 25's fundamental information on heat, air and moisture transport in building assemblies, as well as Chapter 26's material property data. Examples here demonstrate calculation of heat, moisture, and air transport in typical assemblies. For design guidance for common building envelope assemblies and conditions, see Chapter 44 of the 2015 *ASHRAE Handbook—HVAC Applications*.

Insulation specifically for mechanical systems is discussed in Chapter 23. For specific industrial applications of insulated assemblies, see the appropriate chapter in other ASHRAE Handbook volumes. In the 2014 *ASHRAE Handbook—Refrigeration*, for refrigerators and freezers, see Chapters 15, 16, and 17; for insulation systems for refrigerant piping, see Chapter 10; for refrigerated-facility design, see Chapters 23 and 24; for trucks, trailers, rail cars, and containers, see Chapter 25; for marine refrigeration, see Chapter 26. For environmental test facilities, see Chapter 37 in the 2002 *ASHRAE Handbook—Refrigeration*.

Engineering practice is predicated on the assumption that performance effects can be viewed in functional format, where discrete input values lead to discrete output values that may be assessed for acceptability. Heat transfer in solids lends itself to engineering analysis because material properties are relatively constant and easy to characterize, the transport equations are well established, analysis results tend toward linearity, and, for well-defined input values, output values are well defined. Airflow and moisture transport analysis, in contrast, is difficult: material properties are difficult to characterize, transport equations are not well defined, analysis results tend toward nonlinearity, and both input and output values include great uncertainty. Air movement is even more difficult to characterize than moisture transport.

Engineering makes use of the continuum in understanding from physical principles, to simple applications, to complex applications, to design guidance. Complex design applications can be handled by computers; however, this chapter begins by presenting simpler examples as a learning tool. Because complex applications are built up from simpler ones, understanding the simpler applications ensures that a critical engineering oversight of complex (computer) applications is retained. Computers have facilitated widespread use of two- and three-dimensional analysis as well as transient (time-dependent) calculations. As a consequence, steady-state calculations are less widely used. Design guidance, notably guidance regarding use of air and vapor barriers, faces changes in light of sophisticated transient calculations. ASHRAE *Standard* 160 creates a framework for using transient hygrothermal calculations in building envelope design. However, designers should recognize the limitations of these tools, as discussed in the following sections, and the need for continued advancements in the methods of analysis and understanding of heat and moisture migration in buildings.

The following definitions pertain to heat transfer properties of envelope assemblies (see Chapter 25).

Symbol	Definition
R_{System}, C_{System}	System resistance (conductance); surface-to-surface resistance (conductance) for all materials in wall, including parallel paths for framing
$R_{Assembly}$, $U_{Assembly}$	Assembly resistance (transmittance); air-to-air thermal resistance (transmittance), equal to system value plus film resistances (conductances)
U_{Whole}	Assembly thermal transmittance, including thermal bridges (i.e., $U_{Assembly}$ plus bridge conductances)

Note: For all code applications that call for U, U_{Whole} should be used.

1. HEAT TRANSFER

1.1 ONE-DIMENSIONAL ASSEMBLY U-FACTOR CALCULATION

Wall Assembly U-Factor

The assembly U-factor for a building envelope assembly determines the rate of steady-state heat conduction through the assembly. One-dimensional heat flow through building envelope assemblies is the starting point for determining whole-building heat transmittance.

Example 1. Calculate the system R-value R_{System}, assembly total resistance ($R_{Assembly}$), and $U_{Assembly}$-factor of the sandwich panel assembly shown in Figure 1; assume winter conditions when selecting values for air films from Table 3 in Chapter 26.

Solution: Determine indoor and outdoor air film resistances from Table 3 in Chapter 26, and thermal resistance of all components from Table 1 in that chapter. If any elements are described by conductivity

The preparation of this chapter is assigned to TC 4.4, Building Materials and Building Envelope Performance.

(independent of thickness) rather than thermal resistance (thickness-dependent), then calculate the resistance.

Element	R, h·ft²·°F/Btu
1. Outdoor air film	0.17
2. Vinyl siding (hollow backed)	0.62
3. Vapor-permeable felt	0.06
4. Oriented strand board (OSB), 7/16 in.	0.62
5. 6 in. expanded polystyrene, extruded (smooth skin)	30.0
6. 0.5 in. gypsum wallboard	0.45
7. Indoor air film	0.68
Total	32.6

The conductivity k of expanded polystyrene is 0.20 Btu·in/h·ft²·°F. For 6 in. thickness,

$$R_{foam} = x/k = 6/0.20 = 30.0 \text{ h·ft}^2\text{·°F/Btu}$$

To calculate the system's R-value in the example, sum the R-values of the system components only, disregarding indoor and outdoor air films.

$$R_{System} = 0.62 + 0.06 + 0.62 + 30.0 + 0.45 = 31.75 \text{ h·ft}^2\text{·°F/Btu}$$

The assembly R-value ($R_{Assembly}$) consists of the system's R-value plus the thermal resistance of the interior and exterior air films.

$$R_{Assembly} = R_o + R_{System} + R_i = 32.6 \text{ h·ft}^2\text{·°F/Btu}$$

The wall's $U_{Assembly}$-factor is $1/R_{Assembly}$, or 0.031 Btu/h·ft²·°F.

Roof Assembly U-Factor

Example 2. Find the U-factor of the commercial roof assembly shown in Figure 2; assume summer conditions when selecting values for air films from Table 3 in Chapter 26.

Solution: The calculation procedure is similar to that shown in Example 1. Note the U-factor of nonvertical assemblies depends on the direction of heat flow [i.e., whether the calculation is for winter (heat flow up) or summer (heat flow down)], because the resistances of indoor air films and plane air spaces in ceilings differ, based on the heat flow direction (see Table 3 in Chapter 26). The effects of mechanical fasteners are not addressed in this example.

Element	R, h·ft²·°F/Btu
1. Indoor air film	0.92
2. 4 in. concrete, 120 lb/ft³ and k = 8	0.5
3. 3 in. cellular polyisocyanurate (gas-impermeable facers)	28.2
4. 1 in. mineral fiberboard	2.94
5. 3/8 in. built-up roof membrane	0.33
6. Outdoor air film	0.25
Total	33.1

Using $U_{Assembly} = 1/R_{Assembly}$, the $U_{Assembly}$-factor is 0.030 Btu/h·ft²·°F.

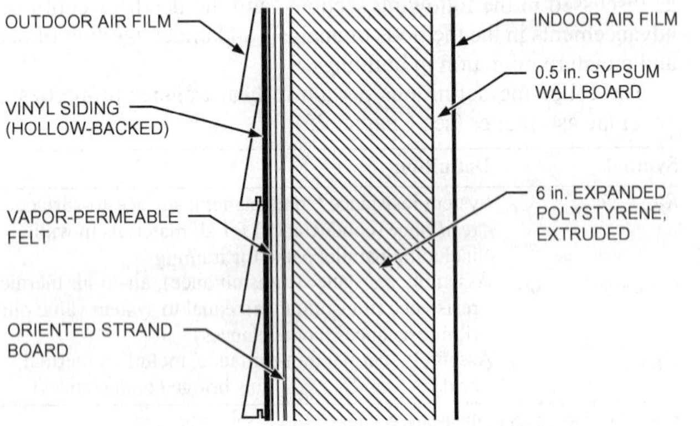

Fig. 1 Structural Insulated Panel Assembly (Example 1)

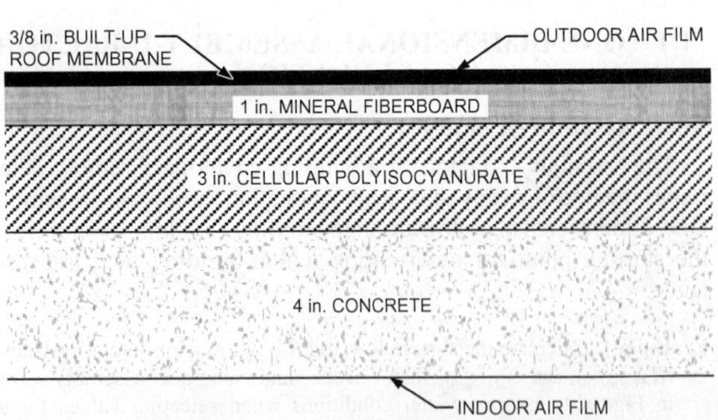

Fig. 2 Roof Assembly (Example 2)

Attics

During sunny periods, unconditioned attics may be hotter than outdoor air. Peak attic temperatures on a hot, sunny day may be 20 to 80°F above outdoor air temperature, depending on factors such as shingle color, roof framing type, air exchange rate through vents, and use of radiant barriers. Therefore, simple one-dimensional solutions cannot be offered for attics. Energy efficiency estimates can be obtained using models such as Wilkes (1991).

Basement Walls and Floors

Heat transfer through basement walls and floors to the ground depends on the following factors: (1) the difference between the air temperature in the room and that of the ground and outside air, (2) the material of the walls or floor, and (3) the thermal conductivity of surrounding earth. The latter varies with local conditions and is usually unknown. Because of the great thermal inertia of surrounding soil, ground temperature varies with depth, and there is a substantial time lag between changes in outdoor air temperatures and corresponding changes in ground temperatures. As a result, ground-coupled heat transfer is less amenable to steady-state representation than above-grade building elements. However, there are several simplified procedures for estimating ground-coupled heat transfer. These fall into two main categories: (1) those that reduce the ground heat transfer problem to a closed-form solution, and (2) those that use simple regression equations developed from statistically reduced multidimensional transient analyses.

Closed-form solutions, including Latta and Boileau's (1969) procedure discussed in Chapter 17, generally reduce the problem to one-dimensional, steady-state heat transfer. These procedures use simple, "effective" U-factors or ground temperatures or both. Methods differ in the various parameters averaged or manipulated to obtain these effective values. Closed-form solutions provide acceptable results in climates that have a single dominant season, because the dominant season persists long enough to allow a reasonable approximation of steady-state conditions at shallow depths. The large errors (percentage) that are likely during transition seasons should not seriously affect building design decisions, because these heat flows are relatively insignificant compared to those of the principal season.

The ASHRAE arc-length procedure (Latta and Boileau 1969) is a reliable method for wall heat losses in cold winter climates. Chapter 17 discusses a slab-on-grade floor model developed by one study. Although both procedures give results comparable to transient computer solutions for cold climates, their results for warmer U.S. climates differ substantially.

Research conducted by Dill et al. (1945) and Hougten et al. (1942) indicates a heat flow of approximately 2.0 Btu/h·ft² through an uninsulated concrete basement floor with a temperature difference of 20°F between the basement floor and the air 6 in. above it. A U-factor of 0.10 Btu/h·ft²·°F is sometimes used for concrete basement floors on the ground. For basement walls below grade, the temperature difference for winter design conditions is greater than for the floor. Test results indicate that, at the mid-height of the below-grade portion of the basement wall, the unit area heat loss is approximately twice that of the floor.

For small concrete slab floors (equal in area to a 25 by 25 ft house) in contact with the ground at grade level, tests indicate that heat loss can be calculated as proportional to the length of exposed edge rather than total area. This amounts to 0.81 Btu/h per linear foot of exposed edge per degree temperature difference between indoor air and the average outdoor air temperature. This value can be reduced appreciably by installing insulation under the ground slab and along the edge between the floor and abutting walls. In most calculations, if the perimeter loss is calculated accurately, no other floor losses need to be considered. Chapters 17 and 18 contain heat transfer and load calculation guidance for floors on grade and at different depths below grade.

The second category of simplified procedures uses transient two-dimensional computer models to generate ground heat transfer data, which are then reduced to compact form by regression analysis (Mitalas 1982, 1983; Shipp 1983). These are the most accurate procedures available, but the database is very expensive to generate. In addition, these methods are limited to the range of climates and constructions specifically examined. Extrapolating beyond the outer bounds of the regression surfaces can produce significant errors.

Guide details and recommendations related to application of concepts for basements are provided in Chapter 44 of the 2015 *ASHRAE Handbook—HVAC Applications*. Detailed analysis of heat transfer through foundation insulation may also be found in the *Building Foundation Design Handbook* (Labs et al. 1988).

1.2 TWO-DIMENSIONAL ASSEMBLY U-FACTOR CALCULATION

The following examples show three methods of two-dimensional, steady-state conductive heat transfer analysis through wall assemblies. They offer approximations to overall rates of heat transfer (U-factor) when assemblies contain a layer composed of dissimilar materials. The methods are described in Chapter 25. The **parallel-path method** is used when the thermal conductivity of the dissimilar materials in the layer are rather close in value (within the same order of magnitude), as with wood-frame walls. The **isothermal-planes method** is appropriate for materials with conductivities moderately different from those of adjacent materials (e.g., masonry). The **zone method** and the **modified zone method** are appropriate for materials with a very high difference in conductivity (two orders of magnitude or more), such as with assemblies containing metal.

Two-dimensional, steady-state heat transfer analysis is often conducted using computer-based finite difference methods. If the resolution of the analysis is sufficiently fine, computer methods provide better simulations than any of the methods described here, and the results typically show better agreement with measured values.

The methods described here do not take into account heat storage in the materials, nor do they account for varying material properties (e.g., when thermal conductivity is affected by moisture content or temperature). Transient analysis is often used in such cases.

Wood-Frame Walls

The assembly R-values and U-factors of wood-frame walls can be calculated by assuming either parallel heat flow paths through areas with different thermal resistances or by assuming isothermal planes. Equation (15) in Chapter 25 provides the basis for the two methods.

The **framing factor** expresses the fraction of the total building component (wall or roof) area that is framing. The value depends on the specific type of construction, and may vary based on local construction practices, even for the same type of construction. For stud walls 16 in. on center (OC), the fraction of insulated cavity may be as low as 0.75, where the fraction of studs, plates, and sills is 0.21 and the fraction of headers is 0.04. For studs 24 in. OC, the respective values are 0.78, 0.18, and 0.04. These fractions contain an allowance for multiple studs, plates, sills, extra framing around windows, headers, and band joists. These assumed framing fractions are used in Example 3, to illustrate the importance of including the effect of framing in determining a building's overall thermal conductance. The actual framing fraction should be calculated for each specific construction.

Example 3. Calculate the $U_{Assembly}$-factor of the 2 by 4 stud wall shown in Figure 3. The studs are at 16 in. OC. There is 3.5 in. mineral fiber batt insulation (R-13) in the stud space. The inside finish is 0.5 in. gypsum wallboard, and the outside is finished with rigid foam insulating sheathing (R-4) and vinyl siding. The insulated cavity occupies approximately 75% of the transmission area; the studs, plates, and sills occupy 21%; and the headers occupy 4%.

Solution: If the R-values of building elements are not already specified, obtain the R-values from Tables 1 and 3 of Chapter 26. Assume R = 1.25 h·ft²·°F/Btu per inch for the wood framing (k = 0.8 Btu·in/h·ft²·°F). Also, assume the headers are solid wood, and group them with the studs, plates, and sills.

Two simple methods may be used to determine the U-factor of wood frame walls: parallel path and isothermal planes. For highly conductive framing members such as metal studs, the modified zone method must be used.

Parallel-Path Method:

Element	*R* (Insulated Cavity), h·ft²·°F/Btu	*R* (Studs, Plates, and Headers), h·ft²·°F/Btu
1. Outdoor air film, 15 mph wind	0.17	0.17
2. Vinyl siding (hollow-backed)	0.62	0.62
3. Rigid foam insulating sheathing	4.0	4.0
4. Mineral fiber batt insulation, 3.5 in.	13.0	—
5. Wood stud, nominal 2 × 4	—	4.38
6. Gypsum wallboard, 0.5 in.	0.45	0.45
7. Indoor air film, still air	0.68	0.68
	R_1 = 18.92	R_2 = 10.3

Individual U-factors are reciprocals of the R-value, so U_1 = 0.053 and U_2 = 0.097 Btu/h·ft²·°F. If the wood framing is accounted for using the parallel-path flow method, the wall's U-factor is determined using Equation (15) from Chapter 25. The fractional area of insulated cavity is 0.75 and the fractional area of framing members is 0.25.

$$U_{Assembly} = (0.75 \times 0.053) + (0.25 \times 0.097) = 0.064 \text{ Btu/h·ft}^2\text{·°F}$$

$$R_{Assembly} = 1/U_{Assembly} = 15.63 \text{ h·ft}^2\text{·°F/Btu}$$

With the isothermal-planes method, the fractional areas are applied only to the building layer that contains the studs and cavity-fill insulation. The average R-value for this layer (R_{avs}) is added to the R-values of the other components for a total R for the assembly.

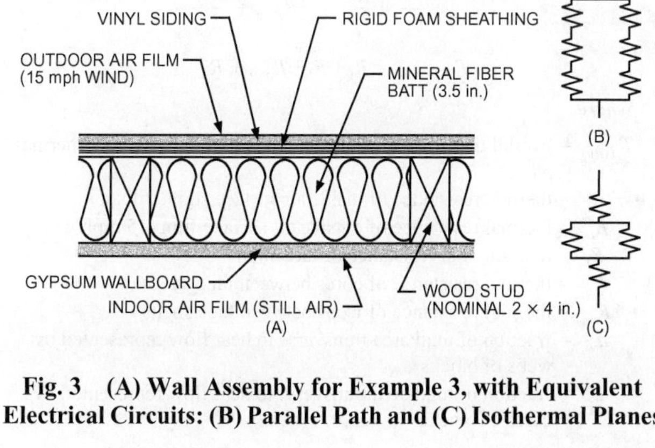

Fig. 3 (A) Wall Assembly for Example 3, with Equivalent Electrical Circuits: (B) Parallel Path and (C) Isothermal Planes

Isothermal-Planes Method:

Element	R (Stud Cavity Elements), h·ft²·°F/Btu	R (Studs, Plates, Average Cavity, and Headers), h·ft²·°F/Btu
1. Outdoor air film, 15 mph wind		0.17
2. Vinyl siding (hollow-backed)		0.62
3. Rigid foam insulating sheathing		4.0
4. Mineral fiber batt insulation, 3.5 in.	13.0	8.70 (R_{avs})
5. Wood stud, nominal 2 × 4	4.38	
6. Gypsum wallboard, 0.5 in.		0.45
7. Indoor air film, still air		0.68
		R_T = 14.62

The average R-value R_{avs} of the stud cavity is calculated using the fractional area of stud and insulation using Equation (15) from Chapter 25.

$$U_{avs} = 0.75(1/13.0) + 0.25(1/4.38) = 0.115$$

$$R_{avs} = 1/U_{avs} = 8.70 \text{ h·ft}^2\text{·°F/Btu}$$

If the wood framing is included using the isothermal-planes method, the U-factor of the wall is determined using Equations (10) and (11) from Chapter 25 as follows:

$$R_{Assembly} = 14.62 \text{ h·ft}^2\text{·°F/Btu}$$

$$U_{Assembly} = 1/R_{Assembly} = 0.068 \text{ Btu/h·ft}^2\text{·°F}$$

For a frame wall with a 24 in. OC stud space, the assembly R-value is 15.70 h·ft²·°F/Btu. Similar calculation procedures may be used to evaluate other wall designs, except those with thermal bridges.

Masonry Walls

The average overall R-values of masonry walls can be estimated by assuming a combination of layers in series, one or more of which provides parallel paths. This method is used because heat flows laterally through block face shells so that transverse isothermal planes result. Average total resistance $R_{Assembly}$ is the sum of the resistances of the layers between such planes, each layer calculated as shown in Example 4.

Example 4. Calculate the overall thermal resistance and average U-factor of the 7 5/8 in. thick insulated concrete block wall shown in Figure 4. The two-core block has an average web thickness of 1 in. and a face shell thickness of 1 1/4 in. Overall block dimensions are 7 5/8 by 7 5/8 by 15 5/8 in. Measured thermal resistances of 112 lb/ft³ concrete and 7 lb/ft³ expanded perlite insulation are 0.10 and 2.90 h·ft²·°F/Btu per inch, respectively. (*Note*: This type of insulation is no longer commonly used with concrete block walls. This historical example has been retained because it is a simplified case with supporting experimental data.)

Solution: The equation used to determine the overall thermal resistance of the insulated concrete block wall is derived from Equations (7) and (15) from Chapter 25 and is given below:

$$U_{Avg} = \frac{a_w}{R_w} + \frac{a_c}{R_c} \qquad R_{Avg} = \frac{1}{U_{Avg}}$$

$$R_{Assembly} = R_i + R_f + R_{avg} + R_o$$

where

$R_{T(av)}$ = overall thermal resistance based on assumption of isothermal planes
R_i = thermal resistance of inside air surface film (still air)
R_o = thermal resistance of outside air surface film (15 mph wind)
R_f = total thermal resistance of face shells
R_c = thermal resistance of cores between face shells
R_w = thermal resistance of webs between face shells
a_w = fraction of total area transverse to heat flow represented by webs of blocks
a_c = fraction of total area transverse to heat flow represented by cores of blocks

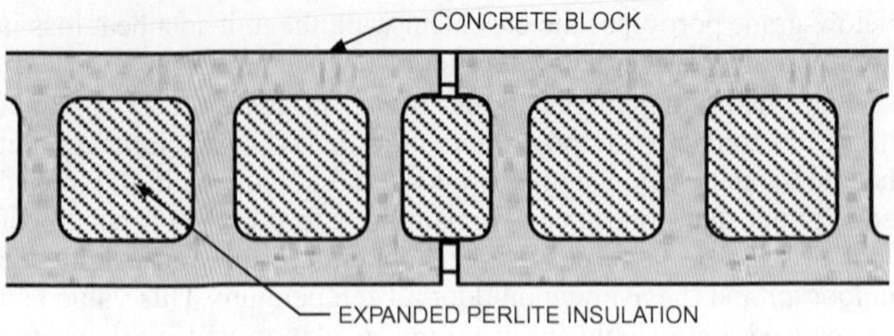

Fig. 4 Insulated Concrete Block Wall (Example 4)

From the information given and the data in Tables 1 and 3 in Chapter 26, determine the values needed to compute the overall thermal resistance.

R_i = 0.68
R_o = 0.17
R_f = (2)(1.25)(0.10) = 0.25
R_c = (5.125)(2.90) = 14.86
R_w = (5.125)(0.10) = 0.51
a_w = 3/15.625 = 0.192
a_c = 12.625/15.625 = 0.808

Using the equation given, the overall thermal resistance and average U-factor are calculated as follows:

$$U_{avs} = 0.192/0.51 + 0.808/14.86 = 0.431$$

$$R_{avs} = 1/U_{avs} = 2.32 \text{ h·ft}^2\text{·°F/Btu}$$

$$R_{Assembly} = 0.68 + 0.25 + 2.32 + 0.17 = 3.42 \text{ h·ft}^2\text{·°F/Btu}$$

$$U_{Assembly} = 1/R_{Assembly} = 0.29 \text{ Btu/h·ft}^2\text{·°F}$$

Based on guarded hot-box tests of this wall without mortar joints, Tye and Spinney (1980) measured the assembly R-value for this insulated concrete block wall as 3.13 h·ft²·°F/Btu.

Assuming parallel heat flow only, the calculated resistance is higher than that calculated on the assumption of isothermal planes. The actual resistance generally is some value between the two calculated values. In the absence of test values, examination of the construction usually reveals whether a value closer to the higher or lower calculated R-value should be used. Generally, if the construction contains a layer in which lateral conduction is high compared with transmittance through the construction, the calculation with isothermal planes should be used. If the construction has no layer of high lateral conductance, the parallel heat flow calculation should be used.

Hot-box tests of insulated and uninsulated masonry walls constructed with block of conventional configuration show that thermal resistances calculated using the isothermal planes heat flow method agree well with measured values (Shu et al. 1979; Valore 1980; Van Geem 1985). Neglecting horizontal mortar joints in conventional block can result in thermal transmittance values up to 16% lower than actual, depending on the masonry's density and thermal properties, and 1 to 6% lower, depending on the core insulation material (McIntyre 1984; Van Geem 1985). For aerated concrete block walls, other solid masonry, and multicore block walls with full mortar joints, neglecting mortar joints can cause errors in R-values up to 40% (Valore 1988). Horizontal mortar joints, usually found in concrete block wall construction, are neglected in Example 4.

Constructions Containing Metal

Curtain and metal stud-wall constructions often include metallic and other thermal bridges, which can significantly reduce the thermal resistance. However, the capacity of the adjacent facing materials to transmit heat transversely to the metal is limited, and some contact resistance between all materials in contact limits the reduction. Contact resistances in building structures are only 0.06 to 0.6 h·ft²·°F/Btu, too small to be of concern in many cases. For these metal stud/wall constructions, the recommended approach is the modified zone method (see Example 7) or two-dimensional analysis software such as THERM.

Thermal characteristics for panels of sandwich construction can be computed by combining the thermal resistances of the layers. R-values for assembled sections should be determined on a representative sample by using a hot-box method. If the sample is a wall section with air cavities on both sides of fibrous insulation, the sample must be of representative height because convective airflow can contribute significantly to heat flow through the test section. Computer modeling can also be useful, but all heat transfer mechanisms must be considered.

The metal studs in Example 5 are 3.5 in. deep and placed at 16 in. on center. The metal member is only 0.020 in. thick, but it is in contact with adjacent facings over a 1.25 in. wide area. The steel member is 3.5 in. deep, has a thermal resistance of approximately 0.011 h·ft²·°F/Btu, and is virtually isothermal.

For this insulated steel frame wall, Farouk and Larson (1983) measured an assembly R-value of 6.61 h·ft²·°F/Btu. For the same assembly, the recommended modified zone method (see Example 5) gives an assembly R-value of 6.73 h·ft²·°F/Btu. Two-dimensional analysis (THERM) yields U_{av} = 0.1775 or R = 5.63 h·ft²·°F/Btu. ASHRAE/IES *Standard* 90.1 describes how to determine the thermal resistance of wall assemblies containing metal framing by using insulation/framing adjustment factors in Table A9.2B of the standard. For 2 by 4 steel framing, 16 in. OC, F_c = 0.50. Using the correction factor method, an assembly R-value of 6.40 h·ft²·°F/Btu [0.45 + 11(0.50) + 0.45] is obtained for the wall described here.

Zone Method of Calculation

For structures with widely spaced metal members of substantial cross-sectional area, the isothermal planes method can give thermal resistance values that are too low. For these constructions, the **zone method** can be used. This method involves two separate computations: one for a chosen limited portion, zone A, containing the highly conductive element; the other for the remaining portion of simpler construction, zone B. The two computations are then combined using the parallel-flow method, and the average transmittance per unit overall area is calculated. The basic laws of heat transfer are applied by adding the area conductances *CA* of elements in parallel, and adding area resistances *R*/*A* of elements in series. The modified zone method improves on the zone method with better guidance for defining the widths of zones A and B.

Modified Zone Method for Metal Stud Walls with Insulated Cavities

The modified zone method is similar to the parallel-path and zone methods; all three are based on parallel-path calculations. Figure 5 shows the width *w* of the zone of thermal anomalies around a metal stud. This zone can be assumed to equal the length of the stud flange *L* (parallel-path method), or can be calculated as a sum of the length of stud flange and a distance double that from wall surface to metal Σd_i (zone method). In the modified zone method, the width of the zone depends on three parameters:

- Ratio between thermal resistivity of sheathing material and cavity insulation
- Size (depth) of stud
- Thickness of sheathing material

Example 5. Calculate the U-factor of the wall section shown in Figure 5 using the modified zone method.

Solution: The wall cross section is divided into two zones: the zone of thermal anomalies around the metal stud (zone W), and the cavity zone (zone *cav*). Wall material layers are grouped into exterior and interior surface sections A (sheathing, siding) and B (wallboard), and interstitial sections I and II (cavity insulation, metal stud flange).

Assuming that the wall materials in section A are thicker than those in section B, as shown, they can be described as follows:

$$\sum_{i=1}^{n} d_i \geq \sum_{j=1}^{m} d_j$$

where

n = number of material layers (of thickness d_i) between metal stud flange and wall surface for section A

m = number of material layers (of thickness d_j) for section B

Then, the width W of zone W can be estimated by

$$W = L + z_f \sum_{i=1}^{n} d_i$$

where

L = stud flange size

d_i = thickness of material layers in section A

z_f = zone factor, shown in Figure 6 (z_f = 2 for zone method)

Kosny and Christian (1995) developed the modified zone method and verified its accuracy for over 200 simulated cases of metal frame walls with insulated cavities. For all configurations considered, the discrepancy between results were within ±2%. Hot-box-measured R-values for 15 metal stud walls tested by Barbour et al. (1994) were compared with results obtained by Kosny and Christian (1995) and McGowan and Desjarlais (1997). The modified zone method was found to be the most accurate simple method for estimating the clear-wall R-value of light-gage steel stud walls with insulated cavities. However, this analysis does not apply to construction with metal sheathing. Also, ASHRAE *Standard* 90.1 may require a different method of analysis.

Step 1. Determine zone factor z_f, and the ratio of the exterior sheathing material's resistivity to the cavity material's resistivity. Resistivity *r* is the reciprocal of conductivity; Table 1 in Chapter 26 lists conductivities of various materials.

Element	Symbol	Value	Units
Stud spacing	s	16	in.
Resistivity of sheathing material	r_i	5.00	h·ft²·°F/Btu·in
Resistivity of cavity insulation	r_{ins}	3.45	h·ft²·°F/Btu·in
Ratio r_i/r_{ins}		1.449	(no units)
Zone factor from chart	z_f	1.71	(no units)

Step 2. Calculate width W of affected zone W:

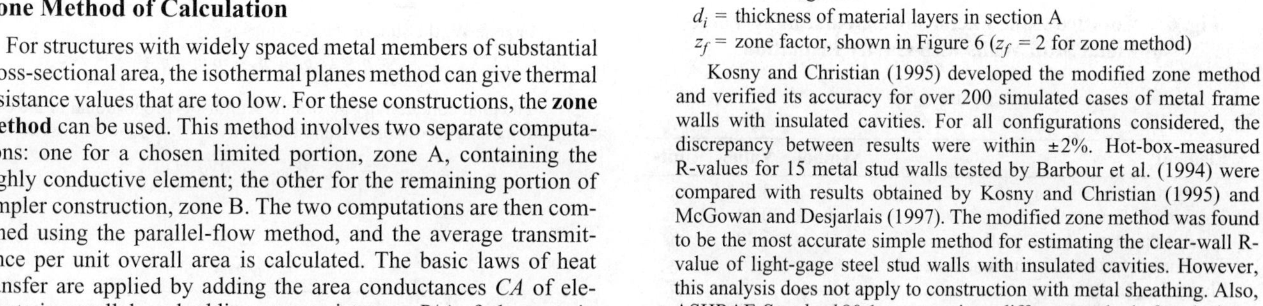

Fig. 5 Wall Section and Equivalent Electrical Circuit (Example 5)

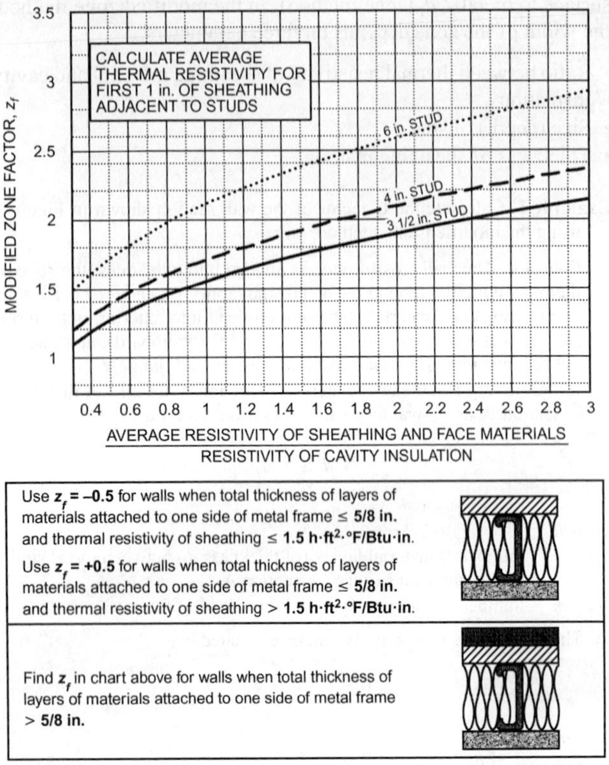

Fig. 6 Modified Zone Factor for Calculating R-Value of Metal Stud Walls with Cavity Insulation

$$W = L + z_f \sum d_i$$

Element	Symbol	Value	Units
Cavity thickness	d_s	3.5	in.
Thickness of metal	d_{II}	0.04	in.
Interior dimension between flanges	d_I	3.42	in.
Thickness of exterior insulating materials		2	in.
Flange length	L	1.5	in.
Affected zone thickness	W	4.920	in.

Step 3. Calculate the exterior and interior thermal resistances, using conductivity or thermal resistance values from step 1.

Element	Symbol	Value	Units
Exterior materials			
Thickness of first exterior material	d_e	1.5	in.
Resistivity of first exterior material	r_e	5.00	h·ft²·°F/Btu·in
Resistance of first material		7.50	h·ft²·°F/Btu
Resistances of other materials		0.825	
Sum of resistances of exterior materials	R_A	8.33	h·ft²·°F/Btu
Interior materials			
Thickness of interior material	d_j	0.05	in.
Resistivity of interior material	r_j	0.90	h·ft²·°F/Btu·in
Resistance of interior material	R_B	0.245	h·ft²·°F/Btu

Step 4. Calculate the thermal resistance of the sections in zone around the metal element. The building elements in series from outside to inside are shown in Figure 7.

Element	Symbol	Value	Units
Resistivity of steel	r_{met}	0.0030	h·ft²·°F/Btu·in
R^I_{ins}	d^I_{xri}	11.80	h·ft²·°F/Btu
R^{II}_{ins}	d^{II}_{xri}	0.138	h·ft²·°F/Btu
R^I_{met}	d^I_{xrmet}	0.0102	h·ft²·°F/Btu
R^{II}_{met}	d^{II}_{xrmet}	0.00012	h·ft²·°F/Btu

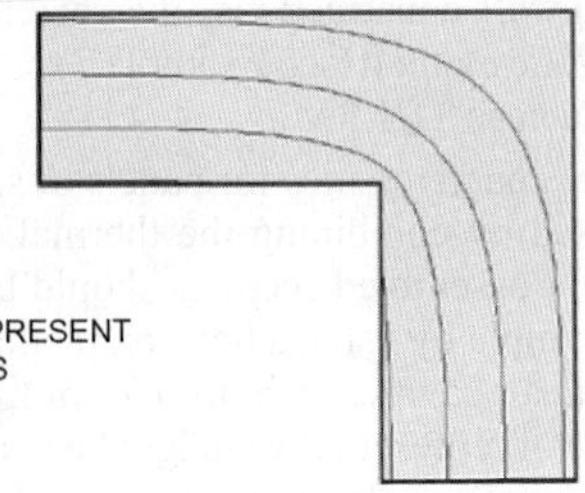

Fig. 7 Corner Composed of Homogeneous Material Showing Locations of Isotherms

The particular thermal resistances of the zone elements are then calculated.

Zone W is the zone at the web of the metal member. For width W, the thermal conductance C is calculated as the sum of the contributory areas. Because the thickness of the web of the metal member is d_I and the length along the flange section is L,

$$C_I = \frac{W - d_I}{W} C_{ins} + \frac{d_I}{W} C_{met} \quad \text{and} \quad C_{II} = \frac{W - L}{W} C_{ins} + \frac{L}{W} C_{met}$$

Using resistance rather than conductance, the contributing R-values are calculated as

$$R_I = \frac{R^I_{met} R^I_{ins} W}{d_I (R^I_{ins} - R^I_{met}) + W R^I_{met}} \quad \text{and} \quad R_{II} = \frac{R^{II}_{met} R^{II}_{ins} W}{L (R^{II}_{ins} - R^{II}_{met}) + W R^{II}_{met}}$$

At the cavity, the sum of the series R-values is

$$\sum R_{cav} = R_A + R_B + R^I_{ins} + 2R^{II}_{ins}$$

In zone W, the sum of the R-values is

$$\sum R_W = R_A + R_B + R_I + 2R_{II}$$

The total conductivity across the length s is proportional to the contributing lengths of zone W and the cavity:

$$C_{tot} = \frac{W}{s} C_W + \frac{cav}{s} C_{cav}$$

or

$$R_{tot} = \frac{\sum R_W \sum R_{cav} s}{W \left(\sum R_{cav} - \sum R_W \right) + s \sum R_W}$$

Element	Symbol	Value	Units
Resistance at web	R_I	1.141	h·ft²·°F/Btu
Resistance at flange	R_{II}	0.00039	h·ft²·°F/Btu
Sum of resistances at cavity	ΣR_{cav}	20.65	h·ft²·°F/Btu
Sum of resistances at zone W	ΣR_W	9.712	h·ft²·°F/Btu
Assembly R	$R_{Assembly}$	15.34	h·ft²·°F/Btu
Assembly U	$U_{Assembly}$	0.0652	Btu/h·ft²·°F

In this example, the calculated total R-value for the wall is 15.34 h·ft²·°F/Btu, and the wall's U-factor is 0.0652 Btu/h·ft²·°F.

Complex Assemblies

Building enclosure geometry of two- and three-dimensional assemblies may be complex, including corners, terminations of materials, and junctures of different materials. Such assemblies cannot be analyzed effectively with explicit calculations; rather, they require iterative calculations using computers. These calculations have been made for a number of common assemblies (Hershfield 2011), and the results can be applied within a simpler estimation method, as shown in Example 6.

Buildings with thermal mass or other forms of thermal storage require dynamic models to evaluate their performance in the environmental climate of interest.

Figure 7 shows a corner composed of homogeneous material. Surface temperatures can be estimated from the intersections of isotherms and the surface. If, in this figure, the interior were warm with respect to outside, then the line at the corner would be colder than the remainder of the interior surface. This effect may be exacerbated by the air film at the corner, which has a greater effective thickness than on the plane of the wall, and therefore offers greater thermal resistance, further lowering the corner temperature.

Figure 8 shows an insulating material applied to a conductive material. Insulation is placed at the inside, during a period of cold outdoor temperatures. A computer program may be used to trace the isotherms. The interior isotherm is cut where the insulating material is interrupted, indicating lowered temperature at that location (point A). In fact, the temperature at the edge of the interrupted insulation is even lower than that at the surface of the uninsulated wall. Interruptions in insulation can lead to thermal bridges. For this reason, insulating conductive assemblies such as masonry or concrete is often more successful when applied to the outside rather than to the inside of the building.

Example 6. Comparing Linear Transmittance Method to Area-Weighted Method for Brick Veneer Shelf Angle Anomaly.

Calculate the overall U-value of the steel-stud brick veneer assembly with a slab and shelf angle with exterior insulation R-15 (2.6 RSI) and interior stud cavity insulation R-12 (2.1 RSI) (see Figure 9), using the following information and method:

Gross wall height = 9 ft

Gross wall length = 50 ft

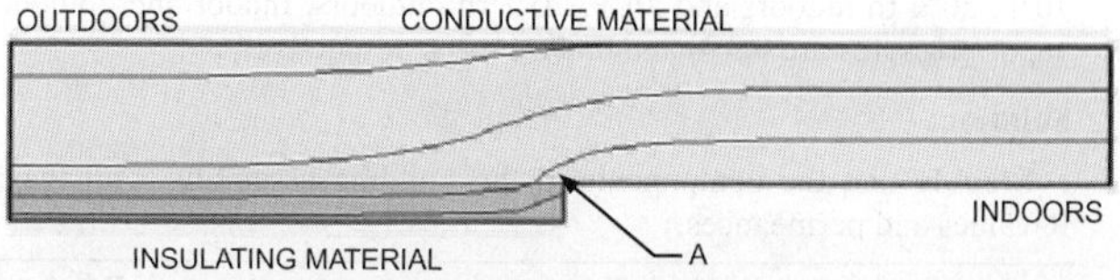

Fig. 8 Insulating Material Installed on Conductive Material, Showing Temperature Anomaly (Point A) at Insulation Edge

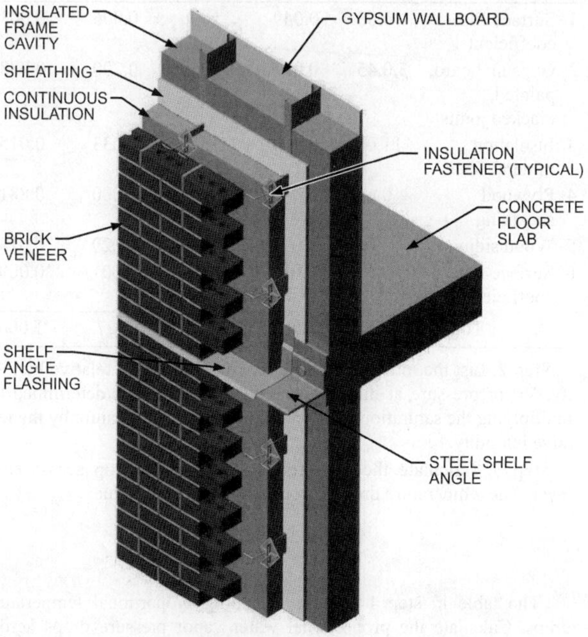

Fig. 9 Brick Veneer Shelf for Example 6

Gross wall area = 450 ft

Area-Weighted Method. The thermal transmittance U_b for the area around the shelf angle is 0.205 Btu/h·ft^2·°F for the effective lengths L_1 = 8.1 in., L_2 = 24.4 in., and U_o = 0.056 Btu/h·ft^2·°F. [Area thermal transmittance depends on the definition of the effective lengths (Hershfield 2011). This calculation is not shown here.]

Calculate area for the thermal anomaly and area for the clear field:

$$A_b = (24.4 \text{ in.}/12)(50 \text{ ft}) = 101.7 \text{ ft}^2 \qquad A_o = 450 - 101.7 = 348.3 \text{ ft}^2$$

Calculate the overall U-value:

$$U = (U_b A_b + U_o A_o)/A_{total} = (0.205 \times 101.7 + 0.056 \times 348.3)/450$$
$$= 0.09 \text{ Btu/h}\cdot\text{ft}^2\cdot°\text{F}$$

Linear Transmittance Method. From Appendix F of RP-1365, for this brick veneer assembly, U_o = 0.056 Btu/h·ft^2·°F and the linear transmittance Ψ of a slab with a shelf angle for this assembly is 0.314 Btu/h·ft·°F.

Calculate the overall U-value

$$U = \frac{\Psi L}{A_{total}} + U_o = 0.314 \times \frac{50}{450} + 0.056 = 0.091 \text{ Btu/h}\cdot\text{ft}^2\cdot°\text{F}$$

This example illustrates the simplicity of the linear transmittance method compared to the area-weighted method for thermal anomalies in opaque building envelope assemblies. The amount of information that must be provided is reduced and the calculation is simpler. The weighted average method is further complicated for a whole-building elevation when accounting for 3D intersections. Some [e.g., Kemp (1997)] suggest that the overlapping effects be combined using mitered corners.

Windows and Doors

Table 4 of Chapter 15 lists U-factors for various fenestration products. For heat transmission coefficients for wood and steel doors, see Table 6 in Chapter 15. All U-factors are approximate, because a significant portion of the resistance of a window or door is contained in the air film resistances, and some parameters that may have important effects are not considered. For example, the listed U-factors assume the surface temperatures of surrounding bodies are equal to the ambient air temperature. However, the indoor surface of a window or door in an actual installation may be exposed to nearby radiating surfaces, such as radiant heating panels, or opposite walls with much higher or lower temperatures than the indoor air. Air movement across the surface of a window or door, such as that caused by nearby heating and cooling outlet grilles or by wind outdoors, increases the U-factor.

2. MOISTURE TRANSPORT

The following examples build on the previous sections by discussing methods that combine heat and moisture transport analysis. The theory of hygrothermal analysis is described in Chapter 25. The methods include fundamental calculations that can be performed by hand as well as more advanced transient calculations that require computer modeling. A few simplified examples are presented here to aid in understanding these multimode, dynamic transport cases. These examples are simplified so that they can be explicitly calculated by assuming steady-state conditions, thus neglecting all storage phenomena. For other examples of explicit methods, see the Bibliography.

2.1 WALL WITH INSULATED SHEATHING

For an initial assessment of the impact of including any materials with low water vapor permeability in a building assembly, estimate the condensation resistance using a simplified moisture analysis. This simplified analysis assumes that interior surfaces may have little or no resistance to air or vapor flow, assumes steady-state conditions, and neglects the effect of radiative heat transfer on the exposed surfaces. The section on Surface Condensation in Chapter 25 describes how to determine the risk of condensation on low-permeability surfaces.

Example 7. For the assembly shown in Figure 3 (but assume the wall has a thicker layer of mineral wool insulation, per following table), determine the range of indoor relative humidity for which condensation does not occur on the inside of the insulating sheathing. Assume a design outdoor temperature of 30°F, and indoor temperature of 70°F. Assume that the cavity air is at the same vapor pressure as the indoor air, which can occur with openings through the wallboard. Ignore radiant effects on the wall exterior. Assume the rigid insulation is vapor impermeable, and interior materials have little resistance to air or vapor flow.

Air Film or Material	Thermal Resistance, h·ft²·°F/Btu
1. Indoor air film coefficient	0.68
2. Gypsum wallboard	0.32
3. Mineral fiber insulation	19
4. 1 in. extruded polystyrene	5
5. OSB sheathing, 1/2 in.	0.68
6. Vinyl siding (hollow backed)	0.62
7. Exterior air film coefficient	0.17
Assembly R-value	26.47

Solution: The temperature difference is 40°F. The sum of the R-values from the foam/mineral fiber interface inward is 20.0 h·ft²·°F/Btu. The sum of the R-values from that interface outward is 6.47 h·ft²·°F/Btu. The temperature difference ratio [Equation (14), Chapter 25] is 6.47/26.47, or –0.24. The interface temperature is 39.6°F. The saturation vapor pressure of indoor air is 0.74 in. Hg, and the saturation vapor pressure at the interface is 0.24 in. Hg (see Chapter 1). The upper bound for indoor relative humidity is therefore 0.24/0.74, or 32% rh. (Another way to approach this problem would be to assume a given relative humidity within the indoor space and determine the range of outdoor temperatures for which condensation would not occur at this location.)

Many factors influence the likelihood (or not) of damage in an assembly such as this with exterior rigid insulation. Solar effects generally ensure a period of high temperatures that allows drying, so a design based on this result alone may be overly conservative. On the other hand, cold sky temperatures may increase heat loss from the assembly, which lowers the surface temperature below ambient, so a design based on this result alone may be subject to moisture damage. Even when indoor humidity is high enough that condensation at the interface is indicated, the rate of water formation may be slowed by airtightness at the wallboard and by vapor diffusion protection. In light of these dynamic effects, the analyst must consider the number of hours at which condensation could occur without damaging the assembly. The varying nature of the boundary conditions, as well as the storage capability of the assembly materials, lead to the need for more comprehensive dynamic evaluations (ASHRAE *Standard* 160).

2.2 VAPOR PRESSURE PROFILE (GLASER OR DEW-POINT) ANALYSIS

The historical steady-state one-dimension tool for evaluating moisture accumulation and drying within exterior envelopes (walls, roofs, and ceilings) is the dew-point or Glaser method. With the increasing prominence of transient modeling tools, much more accurate estimates of temperature and humidity can be achieved than were possible using steady-state analysis. Users should recognize the limitations of the steady-state approach, which include the following:

- Condensation is a phase change from vapor to liquid. As long as relative humidity in the pores of hygroscopic, capillary-porous building materials stays below 100%, vapor does not condense but is adsorbed as hygroscopic moisture or absorbed as liquid. Only once moisture content at the surface touches the capillary maximum will vapor condense on that surface. The dew-point method results have often been interpreted to indicate condensation, when, in fact, increases in moisture content were through sorption or absorption, not visible condensation at the surface.
- Heat and moisture storage effects are not included in a dew-point analysis. Experience shows they play a significant role in heat and moisture performance of assemblies. To account for storage, it is recommended to use average values (e.g., monthly average temperature) rather than more extreme design temperatures.
- Diffusion is the only moisture transport mechanism considered. Airflow, capillary transport, rain wetting, initial conditions, latent effects, solar effects, and ventilation cannot or only approximately can be included in the method. They may have a dominant effect on building assembly performance.
- The dew-point method allows calculation of a rate of moisture accumulation or rate of drying from a critical location within the assembly. However, the method does not allow estimating damage associated with any rate of accumulation or drying.

The method is presented here for reasons of historical continuity, and because it serves as an illustration of the principles of heat conduction and vapor diffusion. However, the dew-point method is not recommended as a sole basis for hygrothermal design of building envelope assemblies. ASHRAE *Standard* 160 is recommended to assist in hygrothermal analysis for design purposes.

Winter Wall Wetting Examples

Example 8. For a wood-framed wall, assume monthly mean conditions of 70°F, 50% rh indoors and 20°F, 70% rh outdoors. Indoor and outdoor vapor pressures are 0.370 and 0.072 in. Hg, respectively.

Solution:

Step 1. List the components in the building assembly, with their R-values and permeances.

Air Film or Material	Thermal Resistance, °F·ft²·h/Btu	Proportional Temperature Drop	Vapor Permeance, perm	Vapor Diffusion Resistance, Rep	Proportional Vapor Pressure Drop
1 Surface film coefficient	0.68	0.049	160	0.006	0.003
2 Gypsum board, painted, cracked joints	0.45	0.032	5	0.200	0.088
3 Insulation, mineral fiber	11.00	0.790	30	0.033	0.015
4 Plywood sheathing	0.62	0.045	0.5	2.000	0.881
5 Wood siding	1.00	0.072	35	0.029	0.013
6 Surface film coefficient	0.17	0.012	1000	0.001	0.000
Total	13.92	1.000		2.27	1.000

Step 2. List the indoor and outdoor temperature and relative humidity. Vapor pressure at indoor and outdoor locations is determined by multiplying the saturation vapor pressure at that temperature by the relative humidity.

Step 3. Calculate the proportional temperature drop across each layer. The temperature drop is proportional to the R-value:

$$\frac{\Delta t_{layer}}{t_i - t_o} = \frac{R_{layer}}{R_T}$$

The table in step 1 lists the resulting proportional temperature drops. Calculate the proportional water vapor pressure drops across each layer. These are calculated the same way as the proportional temperature drops in step 1:

$$\frac{\Delta p_{layer}}{p_i - p_o} = \frac{Z_{layer}}{Z_T}$$

where

Z_T = total water vapor diffusion resistance of wall (sum of diffusion resistances of all layers), rep

p = partial water vapor pressure, in. Hg

Boundary or Interface Between Materials	Temperature, °F	Saturation Vapor Pressure, in. Hg	RH, %	Initial Vapor Pressure, in. Hg	Corrected Vapor Pressure, in. Hg
Indoor air	70	0.740	40	0.296	0.296
5-6 interface	67.56	0.680		0.295	0.224
4-5 interface	65.94	0.643		0.274	0.223
3-4 interface	26.43	0.139		0.270	0.139
2-3 interface	24.20	0.126		0.055	0.126
1-2 interface	20.61	0.106		0.051	0.054
Outdoor air	20	0.103	50	0.051	0.051
Difference	50		Difference	0.244	

Step 4. Determine the temperature at each interface, using the temperature difference from indoors to outdoors, and the proportional temperature drop. Find the saturation water vapor pressure corresponding to the interface temperatures from step 1. These values can be found in Table 2 in Chapter 1.

Step 5. From step 1, the total water vapor diffusion resistance of the wall without the vapor retarder is

$$Z_{wall} = 1/160 + 1/5 + 1/30 + 1/0.5 + 1/35 + 1/1000 = 2.27 \text{ rep}$$

The partial water vapor pressure drop across the whole wall is calculated from the indoor and outdoor saturation water vapor pressures and relative humidities (see the table in step 3).

$$p_{wall} = p_i - p_o = (50/100)0.740 - (70/100)0.103 = 0.298 \text{ in. Hg}$$

Step 6. Figure 10 shows the calculated saturation and partial water vapor pressures. Comparison reveals that the calculated partial water vapor pressure on the interior surface of the sheathing is well above saturation. This indicates incipient accumulation of water (condensation or sorption), probably on the surface of the sheathing, not within the insulation. If the accumulation rate is of interest, two additional steps are necessary.

Step 7. The calculated water vapor pressure exceeds the saturation water vapor pressure by the greatest amount at the back side of the sheathing (Figure 12). Therefore, this is the most likely location for accumulation. Under conditions of phase change (condensation or sorption), the water vapor pressure should equal the saturation water vapor pressure at that interface (see the corrected vapor pressure column in step 3).

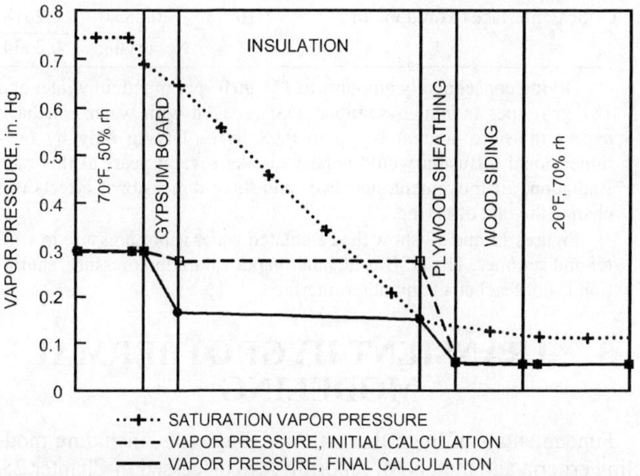

Fig. 10 Dew-Point Calculation in Wood-Framed Wall (Example 8)

Step 8. The change of water vapor pressure on the OSB sheathing alters all other partial water vapor pressures as well as water vapor flux through the wall. Calculating partial water vapor pressures is similar to the calculation in step 3, but the wall is now divided in two parts: one on the interior of the condensation interface (i.e., gypsum board and insulation) and the other on the exterior (OSB sheathing and wood siding). Water vapor pressure drop over the first (interior) part of the wall is

$$\Delta p_1 = 0.370 - 0.139 = 0.230 \text{ in. Hg}$$

and over the second (exterior) part is

$$\Delta p_2 = 0.139 - 0.072 = 0.067 \text{ in. Hg}$$

The diffusion resistances of both parts of the wall are

$$Z_1 = 1/160 + 1/5 + 1/30 = 0.239 \text{ rep}$$

$$Z_2 = 1/0.5 + 1/35 + 1/1000 = 2.03 \text{ rep}$$

The water vapor pressure drops across each material can be calculated from the part between the inside and sheathing

$$\frac{\Delta p_{layer}}{p_i - p'_{sheathing}} = \frac{Z_{layer}}{Z_i^{sheathing}}$$

and the part between the sheathing and outside

$$\frac{\Delta p_{layer}}{p'_{sheathing} - p_o} = \frac{Z_{layer}}{Z^o_{sheathing}}$$

	Z_{tot}, h·ft²·in. Hg/gr	Vapor Pressure Difference, in. Hg	Vapor Flow, gr/ft²·h
Indoor air to critical interface	0.239	0.230	0.9628
Critical interface to outdoor air	2.030	0.067	0.0332

As shown in Figure 10, final calculations of water vapor pressure no longer exceed saturation, which means that the condensation plane was chosen correctly. However, vapor flux is no longer the same throughout the wall. The flux from inside increases; to the outside it decreases. The difference between both is the rate of moisture accumulation by interstitial condensation at the back side of the sheathing:

$$m_c = \frac{p_i - p'_{sheathing}}{Z_i^{sheathing}} - \frac{p'_{sheathing} - p_o}{Z^o_{sheathing}}$$

In this case m_c = 0.9295 gr/ft²·h. (One grain equals 1/7000 of a pound.) Assume the 0.5 in. OSB sheathing (density of 34 lb/ft³) begins with moisture content of 10%. The weight of dry OSB at that thickness is 1.42 lb/ft², so the weight of water is 0.14 lb. If these conditions persist for 30 days (720 h), then the amount of accumulated water is 0.04 lb. This raises the moisture content of the wood to 12.5%. It is evident that wetting by diffusion is very slow.

The Glaser method should not be used to show simply that calculated vapor pressure at one location exceeds saturation vapor pressure at that location. If that condition is detected, then the rate of accumulation must be calculated and the results compared to the affected material's estimated storage potential. Unfortunately, guidance on interpretation of accumulated water with the Glaser method is not available. Considerations of moisture storage potential in building materials can be addressed only with transient modeling, not with steady-state methods.

Example 9. A wood-framed construction has a wet layer inside. The wall layers include a 6 mil (0.006 in.) polyethylene membrane between insulation and gypsum board, and an exterior insulation and finish system (EIFS) with 1.5 in. of expanded polystyrene as substrate and a spun-glass reinforced stucco finish. If the OSB sheathing became soaked because of rain infiltration at the windows, how long before the OSB reaches hygroscopic equilibrium after leaks are sealed? Solve for two monthly mean conditions: winter, with 70°F, 40% rh indoors and

20°F, 50% rh outdoors; and summer, with 77°F, 70% rh indoors and 73°F, 70% rh outdoors.

Solution:

Step 1. List the components in the building assembly, with their R-values and permeances.

Air Film or Material	Thermal Resistance R, h·ft²·°F/Btu	Proportional Temperature Drop	Vapor Permeance, perm	Vapor Diffusion Resistance, h·ft²·in. Hg/gr	Proportional Vapor Pressure Drop
1. Air film coefficient	0.68	0.035	160	0.006	0.000
2. Gypsum board, painted	0.45	0.023	5	0.200	0.002
3. Polyethylene foil	0.0	0.000	0.01	125	0.974
4. Insulation, mineral fiber	11.0	0.573	30	0.033	0.000
5. OSB sheathing	0.62	0.032	0.5	2.000	0.016
6. EPS	5.7	0.297	1.3	0.769	0.006
7. EIFS stucco lamina and finish	0.57	0.030	3.2	0.313	0.002
8. Air film coefficient	0.17	0.009	1000	0.001	0.000
Total	19.19	1.000		128	1.000

Step 2. List the indoor and outdoor temperature and relative humidity. As in Example 8, indoor and outdoor vapor pressure is determined by multiplying the saturation vapor pressure at that temperature by the relative humidity.

Winter conditions:

	Temperature, °F	Saturated Vapor Pressure, in. Hg	Relative Humidity, %	Initial Vapor Pressure, in. Hg	Vapor Pressure, in. Hg
Indoors	70	0.740	40	0.296	0.296
1 and 2	68.22	0.696		0.296	0.296
2 and 3	67.05	0.668		0.295	0.296
3 and 4	67.05	0.668		0.057	0.233
4 and 5	38.39	0.233		0.057	**0.233**
5 and 6	36.78	0.218		0.053	**0.218**
6 and 7	21.93	0.113		0.052	0.215
7 and 8	20.44	0.105		0.051	0.177
Outdoors	20	0.103	50	0.051	0.051
Difference	50		Difference	0.244	

Summer conditions:

	Temperature, °F	Saturated Vapor Pressure, in. Hg	Relative Humidity, %	Initial Vapor Pressure, in. Hg	Vapor Pressure, in. Hg
Indoors	77	0.936	70	0.655	0.655
1 and 2	76.9	0.931		0.655	0.680
2 and 3	76.8	0.929		0.655	0.705
3 and 4	76.8	0.929		0.575	0.731
4 and 5	74.5	0.860		0.575	**0.860**
5 and 6	74.3	0.857		0.574	**0.857**
6 and 7	73.2	0.823		0.573	0.764
7 and 8	73.0	0.820		0.573	0.669
Outdoors	73	0.819	70	0.573	0.573
Difference	4		Difference	0.082	

Step 3. Indoor and outdoor vapor pressures are calculated from the given conditions of temperature and relative humidity. The vapor pressure at each side of the OSB sheathing is assigned the value of the saturation vapor pressure at that temperature (see bold values in the summer and winter condition tables).

Step 4. Calculate the total vapor resistance on either side of the critical OSB layer. Between inside and sheathing,

$$\frac{\Delta p_{layer}}{p_i - p'_{sheathing}} = \frac{Z_{layer}}{Z_i^{sheathing}}$$

Between sheathing and outside,

$$\frac{\Delta p_{layer}}{p'_{sheathing} - p_o} = \frac{Z_{layer}}{Z^o_{sheathing}}$$

From the summer and winter condition tables, the diffusion resistances of both parts of the wall are

$$Z_1 = 0.0062 + 0.20 + 125 + 0.0331 = 125.2 \text{ rep}$$

$$Z_2 = 0.79 + 0.31 + 0.001 = 1.10 \text{ rep}$$

Step 5. Calculate the vapor pressure difference on either side of the critical OSB layer (the last column in the summer and winter condition tables). From the vapor resistance on each side and the vapor pressure difference on each side, vapor flow in each direction can be calculated.

Winter

$$m_{i,\,sheathing,\,i} = \frac{p_i - p'_{sheathing}}{Z^i_{sheathing}} = 0.0005 \text{ gr/ft}^2\cdot\text{h}$$

$$m_{sheathing,\,o} = \frac{p'_{sheathing} - p_o}{Z_i^{sheathing}} = 0.154 \text{ gr/ft}^2\cdot\text{h}$$

	Z_{tot}, h·ft²·in. Hg/gr	Vapor Pressure Difference, in. Hg	Vapor Flow, gr/ft²·h
Indoor air to critical interface	125.2	0.063	0.0005
Critical interface to outdoor air	1.10	0.167	0.1543
		Net drying	0.1538

Summer

$$m_{i,\,sheathing,\,i} = \frac{p_i - p'_{sheathing}}{Z^i_{sheathing}} = -0.0016 \text{ gr/ft}^2\cdot\text{h}$$

$$m_{sheathing,\,o} = \frac{p'_{sheathing} - p_o}{Z_o^{sheathing}} = 0.262 \text{ gr/ft}^2\cdot\text{h}$$

	Z_{tot}, h·ft²·in. Hg/gr	Vapor Pressure Difference, in. Hg	Vapor Flow, gr/ft²·h
Indoor air to critical interface	125.2	–0.205	–0.0016
Critical interface to outdoor air	1.10	0.283	0.2618
		Net drying	0.2634

Drying consequently amounts to 111 gr/ft² per month in winter and 187 gr/ft² per month in summer. OSB soaked with water can have excess moisture content of up to 0.98 lb/ft². Drying only by one-dimensional diffusion would appear to take several years at this rate. Radiation, air movement, and two- and three-dimensional effects can change the rate of drying.

Figures 11 and 12 show the calculated water vapor pressure in winter and summer. The OSB is at water vapor saturation pressure; saturation is not reached at any other interface.

3. TRANSIENT HYGROTHERMAL MODELING

Fundamentals of hygrothermal modeling tools, including modeling criteria and method of reporting, are discussed in Chapter 25. Although this chapter does not provide a complete example, it introduces input data commonly required by these programs and discusses considerations for analyzing output when using these tools.

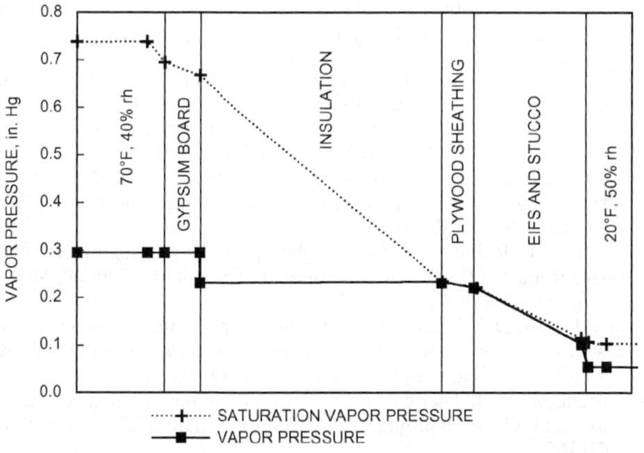

Fig. 11 Drying Wet Sheathing, Winter (Example 9)

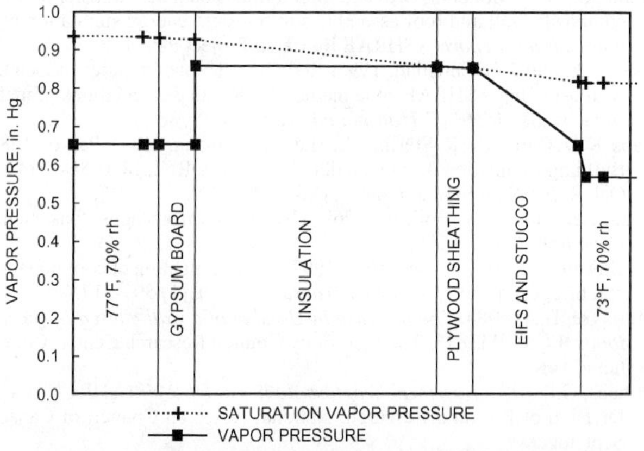

Fig. 12 Drying Wet Sheathing, Summer (Example 9)

For many applications and for design guide development, actual behavior of an assembly under transient climatic conditions may be simulated to account for short-term processes such as driving rain absorption, summer condensation, and phase changes. Computer simulations allow designers to model these conditions over time. It is important, however, to understand the model's application limits.

Applying one of these models requires at least the following information: exterior climate conditions, indoor temperature and humidity, and building assembly materials and sizes. Many programs include a material property database and exterior climate and indoor condition data, allowing simple modeling to be performed without customization. However, using generic material property and weather data may not accurately recreate actual target conditions.

Features of a complete moisture analysis model include

- Transient heat, air, and moisture transport formulation, incorporating the physics of
  - Airflow
  - Water vapor transport by advection (combination of water vapor diffusion and air-driven vapor flow)
  - Liquid transport by capillary action, gravity, and pressure differences
  - Heat flow by apparent conduction, convection, and radiation
  - Heat and moisture storage/capacity of materials
  - Condensation and evaporation processes with linked latent-to-sensible heat transformation
  - Freezing and thawing processes with linked latent-to-sensible heat transformation and based on laws of conservation of heat, mass, and momentum
- Material properties as functions of moisture content, relative humidity, and temperature, such as
  - Density
  - Air properties: permeability and permeance
  - Thermal properties: specific heat capacity, apparent thermal conductivity, Nusselt numbers, and long-wave emittance (for cavities and air spaces)
  - Moisture properties: porosity, sorption curve, water retention curve, vapor permeability, water permeability, or liquid diffusivity
- Boundary conditions (generally on an hourly basis)
  - Outside temperature and relative humidity
  - Incident short-wave solar and long-wave sky radiation (depending on inclination and orientation)
  - Wind speed, orientation, and pressures
  - Wind-driven rain at exterior surfaces (depending on location and aerodynamics)
  - Interior temperature, air pressure excess, relative humidity (or interior moisture sources and ventilation flows), and air stratification
  - Surface conditions
  - Heat transfer film coefficients (combined convection and radiation, separate for convection and radiation)
  - Mass transfer film coefficients
  - Short-wave absorptance of exterior surfaces
  - Long-wave emittance of exterior surfaces
  - Contact conditions between layers and materials. Interfaces may be bridgeable for vapor diffusion, airflow, and gravity or pressure liquid flow only. They may be ideally capillary, introduce additional capillary resistance, or behave as real contact.

Not all these features are required for every analysis, and some applications may need additional information (e.g., moisture flow through unintentional cracks and intentional openings, rain penetration through veneer walls and exterior cladding). To model these phenomena accurately, experiments may be needed to define systems and subsystems in field situation, because only then are all exterior loads and influences captured.

It is important to recognize that simulation results are based on input data. Therefore, the more accurate the input data used, the closer the results will match real-world conditions. Exterior weather conditions, material properties, and interior operating conditions all vary widely, so it is important to get the best data available on materials being modeled. For most users, this is a difficult task. Many product manufacturers do not provide the material property data needed for the simulations. Developing weather data for a particular site is also beyond the expertise of many.

Combined heat, air, and moisture models also have limitations. Users should be aware which transport phenomena and types of boundary conditions are included and which are not. For instance, some models cannot handle air transport or rain wetting of the exterior. Even an apparently simple problem, such as predicting rain leakage through a brick veneer, is beyond existing tools' capabilities. In such cases, simple qualitative schemes and field tests still are the way to proceed. In addition, results also tend to be very sensitive to the choice of indoor and outdoor conditions. Usually, exact conditions are not known.

Outputs from these programs typically include the moisture content of materials as well as relative humidity within the assembly. Interpretation of results is not easy: accurate data on moisture and temperature conditions that materials can tolerate are often not available. Although moisture accumulation may result in indoor air quality issues or material degradation, the effect of moisture accumulation in building assemblies depends on many factors, including choice of construction materials, and varies by building, making interpretation of results even more difficult.

4. AIR MOVEMENT

Moisture movement through building envelope assemblies is more strongly affected by air movement than by diffusion. To minimize moisture penetration by air leakages, the building envelope should be as airtight as possible. The airflow retarder must also be sufficiently strong and well supported to resist wind loads.

In older residential buildings, air leakage provided sufficient ventilation and rarely led to interstitial condensation. However, in airtight buildings, mechanical ventilation is needed to ensure acceptable air quality and prevent moisture and health problems caused by excessive indoor humidity. Ventilation of the wall assembly and/or drainage must go to the outside of the airtight layer of construction, or it will increase building air leakage. To avoid moisture problems at the airtight layer, either the layer temperature must be kept above the dew point by locating it on the warm side of the insulation, or the layer permeance must allow vapor transmission.

As described in detail in the section on Leakage Distribution in Chapter 16, air leakage through building envelopes is not confined to doors and windows. Although 6 to 22% of air leakage occurs there, 18 to 50% typically takes place through walls, and 3 to 30% through the ceiling. Leakage often occurs between sill plate and foundation, through interior walls, electrical outlets, plumbing penetrations, and cracks at top and bottom of exterior walls.

Not all cracks and openings can be sealed in existing buildings, nor can absolutely tight construction be achieved in new buildings. Provide as tight an enclosure as possible to reduce leakage, minimize potential condensation within the envelope, and reduce energy loss. However, the project team must also recognize the impact of airtightness.

Moisture accumulation in building envelopes can also be minimized by controlling the dominant direction of airflow by operating the building at a small negative or positive air pressure, depending on climate. In cooling climates, pressure should be positive to keep out humid outside air. In heating climates, pressure should be neither strongly negative, which could risk drawing soil gas or combustion products indoors and affect occupant comfort, nor strongly positive, which could risk driving moisture into building envelope cavities.

Equivalent Permeance

Dew-point analysis allows simple estimation of the effect of wall and roof cavity ventilation on heat and vapor transport by using parallel thermal and vapor diffusion resistances (TenWolde and Carll 1992; Trethowen 1979). These parallel resistances account for heat and vapor that bypass exterior material layers with ventilation air from outside. Equivalent thermal and water vapor diffusion resistances are approximated from the following equations:

$$R_{par} = \frac{S}{Q\rho c_p}$$

$$Z_{par} = \frac{S}{Q\rho c}$$

where

R_{par} = parallel equivalent thermal resistance, h·ft²·°F/Btu
Z_{par} = parallel equivalent water vapor diffusion vapor flow resistance, rep
S = surface area of wall or ceiling, ft^2
Q = cavity ventilation airflow rate, ft^3/h
ρ = density of air, lb/ft^3
c = ratio of humidity ratio and vapor pressure, approximately 145 gr/lb·in. Hg
c_p = specific heat, Btu/lb·°F

REFERENCES

ASHRAE members can access *ASHRAE Journal* articles and ASHRAE research project final reports at technologyportal.ashrae.org. Articles and reports are also available for purchase by nonmembers in the online ASHRAE Bookstore at www.ashrae.org/bookstore.

ASHRAE. 2009. Criteria for moisture-control design analysis in buildings. ANSI/ASHRAE *Standard* 160-2009.

ASHRAE. 2010. Energy standard for buildings except low-rise residential buildings. ANSI/ASHRAE/IES *Standard* 90.1-2010.

Barbour, E., J. Goodrow, J. Kosny, and J.E. Christian. 1994. *Thermal performance of steel-framed walls*. Prepared for American Iron and Steel Institute by NAHB Research Center.

Dill, R.S., W.C. Robinson, and H.E. Robinson. 1945. Measurements of heat losses from slab floors. National Bureau of Standards. *Building Materials and Structures Report* BMS 103.

Farouk, B., and D.C. Larson. 1983. Thermal performance of insulated wall systems with metal studs. *Proceedings of the 18th Intersociety Energy Conversion Engineering Conference*, Orlando, FL.

Hershfield, M. 2011. Thermal performance of building envelope details for mid- and high-rise buildings. *Final Report*, ASHRAE Research Project RP-1365.

Hougten, F.C., S.I. Taimuty, C. Gutberlet, and C.J. Brown. 1942. Heat loss through basement walls and floors. *ASHVE Transactions* 48:369.

Kemp, S. 1997. Modeling two- and three-dimensional heat transfer through composite wall and roof assemblies in transient energy simulation programs. *Final Report*, ASHRAE Research Project RP-1145.

Kosny, J., and J.E. Christian. 1995. Reducing the uncertainties associated with using the ASHRAE zone method for R-value calculations of metal frame walls. *ASHRAE Transactions* 101(2):779-788.

Labs, K., J. Carmody, R. Sterling, L. Shen, Y.J. Huang, and D. Parker. 1988. Building foundation design handbook. *Report* ORNL/SUB/86-72143/1. Oak Ridge National Laboratory, Oak Ridge, TN.

Latta, J.K., and G.G. Boileau. 1969. Heat losses from house basements. *Canadian Building* 19(10).

McGowan, A., and A.O. Desjarlais. 1997. An investigation of common thermal bridges in walls. *ASHRAE Transactions* 103(1):509-517.

McIntyre, D.A. 1984. *The increase in U-value of a wall caused by mortar joints*. ECRC/M1843. The Electricity Council Research Centre, Copenhurst, U.K.

Mitalas, G.P. 1982. *Basement heat loss studies at DBR/NRC*. NRCC 20416. Division of Building Research, National Research Council of Canada, September.

Mitalas, G.P. 1983. Calculation of basement heat loss. *ASHRAE Transactions* 89(1B):420.

Shipp, P.H. 1983. Basement, crawlspace and slab-on-grade thermal performance. *Proceedings of the ASHRAE/DOE Conference, Thermal Performance of the Exterior Envelopes of Buildings II*, ASHRAE SP 38: 160-179.

Shu, L.S., A.E. Fiorato, and J.W. Howanski. 1979. Heat transmission coefficients of concrete block walls with core insulation. *Proceedings of the ASHRAE/DOE-ORNL Conference, Thermal Performance of the Exterior Envelopes of Buildings*, ASHRAE SP 28:421-435.

TenWolde A. and C. Carll. 1992. Effect of cavity ventilation on moisture in walls and roofs. *Proceedings of ASHRAE Conference, Thermal Performance of the Exterior Envelopes of Buildings V*, pp. 555-562.

THERM. 2012. *THERM*. windows.lbl.gov/software/therm/therm.html.

Trethowen, H.A. 1979. The Kieper method for building moisture design. BRANZ *Reprint* 12, Building Research Association of New Zealand.

Tye, R.P., and S.C. Spinney. 1980. A study of various factors affecting the thermal performance of perlite insulated masonry construction. Dynatech *Report* PII-2. Holometrix, Inc. (formerly Dynatech R/D Company), Cambridge, MA.

Valore, R.C. 1980. Calculation of U-values of hollow concrete masonry. American Concrete Institute, *Concrete International* 2(2):40-62.

Valore, R.C. 1988. *Thermophysical properties of masonry and its constituents*, parts I and II. International Masonry Institute, Washington, D.C.

Van Geem, M.G. 1985. Thermal transmittance of concrete block walls with core insulation. *ASHRAE Transactions* 91(2).

Wilkes, K.E. 1991. Thermal model of attic systems with radiant barriers. *Report* ORNL/CON-262. Oak Ridge National Laboratory, TN.

BIBLIOGRAPHY

Hens, H. 1978. Condensation in concrete flat roofs. *Building Research and Practice* Sept./Oct.:292-309.

TenWolde, A. 1994. Design tools. Chapter 11 in *Moisture control in buildings*. ASTM *Manual* MNL 18. American Society for Testing and Materials, West Conshohocken, PA.

Vos, B.H., and E.J.W. Coelman. 1967. Condensation in structures. *Report* B-67-33/23, TNO-IBBC, Rijswijk, the Netherlands.

CHAPTER 28

COMBUSTION AND FUELS

1. PRINCIPLES OF COMBUSTION

COMBUSTION is a chemical reaction in which an oxidant reacts rapidly with a fuel to liberate stored energy as thermal energy, generally in the form of high-temperature gases. Small amounts of electromagnetic energy (light), electric energy (free ions and electrons), and mechanical energy (noise) are also produced during combustion. Except in special applications, the oxidant for combustion is oxygen in the air. The oxidation normally occurs with the fuel in vapor form. One notable exception is oxidation of solid carbon, which occurs directly with the solid phase.

Conventional fuels contain primarily hydrogen and carbon, in elemental form or in various compounds (hydrocarbons). Their complete combustion produces mainly carbon dioxide (CO_2) and water (H_2O); however, small quantities of carbon monoxide (CO) and partially reacted flue gas constituents (gases and liquid or solid aerosols) may form. Most conventional fuels also contain small amounts of sulfur, which is oxidized to sulfur dioxide (SO_2) or sulfur trioxide (SO_3) during combustion, and noncombustible substances such as mineral matter (ash), water, and inert gases. Flue gas is the product of complete or incomplete combustion and includes excess air (if present), but not dilution air (air added to flue gas downstream of the combustion process, such as through the relief opening of a draft hood).

Fuel combustion rate depends on the (1) rate of chemical reaction of combustible fuel constituents with oxygen, (2) rate at which oxygen is supplied to the fuel (mixing of air and fuel), and (3) temperature in the combustion region. The reaction rate is fixed by fuel selection. Increasing the mixing rate or temperature increases the combustion rate.

With **complete combustion** of hydrocarbon fuels, all hydrogen and carbon in the fuel are oxidized to H_2O and CO_2. Generally, complete combustion requires excess oxygen or excess air beyond the amount theoretically required to oxidize the fuel. Excess air is usually expressed as a percentage of the air required to completely oxidize the fuel.

In **stoichiometric combustion** of a hydrocarbon fuel, fuel is reacted with the exact amount of oxygen required to oxidize all carbon, hydrogen, and sulfur in the fuel to CO_2, H_2O, and SO_2. Therefore, exhaust gas from stoichiometric combustion theoretically contains no incompletely oxidized fuel constituents and no unreacted oxygen (i.e., no carbon monoxide and no excess air or oxygen). The percentage of CO_2 contained in products of stoichiometric combustion is the maximum attainable and is referred to as the **stoichiometric CO_2, ultimate CO_2,** or **maximum theoretical percentage of CO_2.**

Stoichiometric combustion is seldom realized in practice because of imperfect mixing and finite reaction rates. For economy and safety, most combustion equipment should operate with some excess air. This ensures that fuel is not wasted and that combustion is complete despite variations in fuel properties and supply rates of fuel and air. The amount of excess air to be supplied to any combustion equipment depends on (1) expected variations in fuel properties and in fuel and air supply rates, (2) equipment application, (3) degree of operator supervision required or available, and (4) control requirements. For maximum efficiency, combustion at low excess air is desirable.

Incomplete combustion occurs when a fuel element is not completely oxidized during combustion. For example, a hydrocarbon may not completely oxidize to carbon dioxide and water, but may form partially oxidized compounds, such as carbon monoxide, aldehydes, and ketones. Conditions that promote incomplete combustion include (1) insufficient air and fuel mixing (causing local fuel-rich and fuel-lean zones), (2) insufficient air supply to the flame (providing less than the required amount of oxygen), (3) insufficient reactant residence time in the flame (preventing completion of combustion reactions), (4) flame impingement on a cold surface (quenching combustion reactions), or (5) flame temperature that is too low (slowing combustion reactions).

Incomplete combustion uses fuel inefficiently, can be hazardous because of carbon monoxide production, and contributes to air pollution.

Combustion Reactions

The reaction of oxygen with combustible elements and compounds in fuels occurs according to fixed chemical principles, including

- Chemical reaction equations
- Law of matter conservation: the mass of each element in the reaction products must equal the mass of that element in the reactants
- Law of combining masses: chemical compounds are formed by elements combining in fixed mass relationships
- Chemical reaction rates

Oxygen for combustion is normally obtained from air, which is a mixture of nitrogen, oxygen, small amounts of water vapor, carbon dioxide, and inert gases. For practical combustion calculations, dry air consists of 20.95% oxygen and 79.05% inert gases (nitrogen, argon, etc.) by volume, or 23.15% oxygen and 76.85% inert gases by mass. For calculation purposes, nitrogen is assumed to pass through the combustion process unchanged (although small quantities of nitrogen oxides form). Table 1 lists oxygen and air requirements for stoichiometric combustion and the products of stoichiometric combustion of some pure combustible materials (or constituents) found in common fuels.

Flammability Limits

Fuel burns in a self-sustained reaction only when the volume percentages of fuel and air in a mixture at standard temperature and pressure are within the upper and lower flammability limits (UFL and LFL), also called explosive limits (UEL and LEL; see Table 2). Both temperature and pressure affect these limits. As mixture temperature increases, the upper limit increases and the lower limit decreases. As the pressure of the mixture decreases below atmospheric pressure, the upper limit decreases and the lower limit increases. However, as pressure increases above atmospheric, the upper limit increases and the lower limit is relatively constant.

The preparation of this chapter is assigned to TC 6.10, Fuels and Combustion.

Table 1 Combustion Reactions of Common Fuel Constituents

			Stoichiometric Oxygen and Air Requirements				Flue Gas from Stoichiometric Combustion with Air					
			lb/lb Fuel[a]		ft³/ft³ Fuel				ft³/ft³ Fuel		lb/lb Fuel	
Constituent	Molecular Formula	Combustion Reactions	O_2	Air	O_2	Air	Ultimate CO_2, %	Dew Point,[c] °F	CO_2	H_2O	CO_2	H_2O
Carbon (to CO)	C	$C + 0.5O_2 \rightarrow CO$	1.33	5.75	[b]	[b]	—	—	—	—	—	—
Carbon (to CO_2)	C	$C + O_2 \rightarrow CO_2$	2.66	11.51	[b]	[b]	29.30	—	—	—	3.664	—
Carbon monoxide	CO	$CO + 0.5O_2 \rightarrow CO_2$	0.57	2.47	0.50	2.39	34.70	—	1.0	—	1.571	—
Hydrogen	H_2	$H_2 + 0.5O_2 \rightarrow H_2O$	7.94	34.28	0.50	2.39	—	162	—	1.0	—	8.937
Methane	CH_4	$CH_4 + 2O_2 \rightarrow CO_2 + 2H_2O$	3.99	17.24	2.00	9.57	11.73	139	1.0	2.0	2.744	2.246
Ethane	C_2H_6	$C_2H_6 + 3.5O_2 \rightarrow 2CO_2 + 3H_2O$	3.72	16.09	3.50	16.75	13.18	134	2.0	3.0	2.927	1.798
Propane	C_3H_8	$C_3H_8 + 5O_2 \rightarrow 3CO_2 + 4H_2O$	3.63	15.68	5.00	23.95	13.75	131	3.0	4.0	2.994	1.634
Butane	C_4H_{10}	$C_4H_{10} + 6.5O_2 \rightarrow 4CO_2 + 5H_2O$	3.58	15.47	6.50	31.14	14.05	129	4.0	5.0	3.029	1.550
Alkanes	C_nH_{2n+2}	$C_nH_{2n+2} + (1.5n + 0.5)O_2 \rightarrow nCO_2 + (n + 1)H_2O$	—	—	$1.5n + 0.5$	$7.18n + 2.39$	—	128 to 127	n	$n + 1$	$\frac{44.01n}{14.026n + 2.016}$	$\frac{18.01(n + 1)}{14.026n + 2.016}$
Ethylene	C_2H_4	$C_2H_4 + 3O_2 \rightarrow 2CO_2 + 2H_2O$	3.42	14.78	3.00	14.38	15.05	125	2.0	2.0	3.138	1.285
Propylene	C_3H_6	$C_3H_6 + 4.5O_2 \rightarrow 3CO_2 + 3H_2O$	3.42	14.78	4.50	21.53	15.05	125	3.0	3.0	3.138	1.285
Alkenes	C_nH_{2n}	$C_nH_{2n} + 1.5nO_2 \rightarrow nCO_2 + nH_2O$	3.42	14.78	$1.50n$	$7.18n$	15.05	125	n	n	3.138	1.285
Acetylene	C_2H_2	$C_2H_2 + 2.5O_2 \rightarrow 2CO_2 + H_2O$	3.07	13.27	2.50	11.96	17.53	103	2.0	1.0	3.834	0.692
Alkynes	C_nH_{2m}	$C_nH_{2m} + (n + 0.5m)O_2 \rightarrow nCO_2 + mH_2O$	—	—	$n + 0.5m$	$4.78n + 2.39m$	—	—	n	m	$\frac{22.005n}{6.005n + 1.008m}$	$\frac{9.008m}{6.005n + 1.008m}$
									SO_x	H_2O	SO_x	H_2O
Sulfur (to SO_2)	S	$S + O_2 \rightarrow SO_2$	1.00	4.31	[b]	[b]	—	—	$1.0SO_2$	—	1.998 (SO_2)	—
Sulfur (to SO_3)	S	$S + 1.5O_2 \rightarrow SO_3$	1.50	6.47	[b]	[b]	—	—	$1.0SO_3$	—	2.497 (SO_3)	—
Hydrogen sulfide	H_2S	$H_2S + 1.5O_2 \rightarrow SO_2 + H_2O$	1.41	6.08	1.50	7.18	—	125	$1.0SO_2$	1.0	1.880 (SO_2)	0.528

Adapted, in part, from *Gas Engineers Handbook* (1965).
[a]Atomic masses: H = 1.008, C = 12.01, O = 16.00, S = 32.06.
[b]Volume ratios are not given for fuels that do not exist in vapor form at reasonable temperatures or pressure.

Table 2 Flammability Limits and Ignition Temperatures of Common Fuels in Fuel/Air Mixtures

Substance	Molecular Formula	Lower Flammability Limit, %	Upper Flammability Limit, %	Ignition Temperature, °F	References
Carbon	C	—	—	1220	Hartman (1958)
Carbon monoxide	CO	12.5	74	1128	Scott et al. (1948)
Hydrogen	H_2	4.0	75.0	968	Zabetakis (1956)
Methane	CH_4	5.0	15.0	1301	*Gas Engineers Handbook* (1965)
Ethane	C_2H_6	3.0	12.5	968 to 1166	Trinks (1947)
Propane	C_3H_8	2.1	10.1	871	NFPA (1962)
n-Butane	C_4H_{10}	1.86	8.41	761	NFPA (1962)
Ethylene	C_2H_4	2.75	28.6	914	Scott et al. (1948)
Propylene	C_3H_6	2.00	11.1	856	Scott et al. (1948)
Acetylene	C_2H_2	2.50	81	763 to 824	Trinks (1947)
Sulfur	S	—	—	374	Hartman (1958)
Hydrogen sulfide	H_2S	4.3	45.50	558	Scott et al. (1948)

Flammability limits adapted from Coward and Jones (1952). All values corrected to 60°F, 30 in. Hg, dry.

Ignition Temperature

Ignition temperature is the lowest temperature at which heat is generated by combustion faster than it is lost to the surroundings and combustion becomes self propagating (see Table 2). The fuel/air mixture will not burn freely and continuously below the ignition temperature unless heat is supplied, but chemical reaction between the fuel and air may occur. Ignition temperature is affected by a large number of factors.

The ignition temperature and flammability limits of a fuel/air mixture, together, are a measure of the potential for ignition (*Gas Engineers Handbook* 1965).

Combustion Modes

Combustion reactions occur in either continuous or pulse flame modes. **Continuous combustion** burns fuel in a sustained manner as long as fuel and air are continuously fed to the combustion zone and the fuel/air mixture is within the flammability limits. Continuous combustion is more common than pulse combustion and is used in most fuel-burning equipment.

Pulse combustion is an acoustically resonant process that burns various fuels in small, discrete fuel/air mixture volumes in a very rapid series of combustions.

The introduction of fuel and air into the pulse combustor is controlled by mechanical or aerodynamic valves. Typical combustors consist of one or more valves, a combustion chamber, an exit pipe, and a control system (ignition means, fuel-metering devices, etc.). Typically, combustors for warm-air furnaces, hot-water boilers, and commercial cooking equipment use mechanical valves. Aerodynamic valves are usually used in higher-pressure applications, such as thrust engines. Separate valves for air and fuel, a single valve for premixed air and fuel, or multiple valves of either type can be used. Premix valve systems may require a flame trap at the combustion chamber entrance to prevent flashback.

In a mechanically valved pulse combustor, air and fuel are forced into the combustion chamber through the valves under pressures less than 0.5 psi. An ignition source, such as a spark, ignites the fuel/air mixture, causing a positive pressure build-up in the combustion chamber. The positive pressure causes the valves to close, leaving only the exit pipe of the combustion chamber as a pressure relief opening. Combustion chamber and exit pipe geometry determine the resonant frequency of the combustor.

The pressure wave from initial combustion travels down the exit pipe at sonic velocity. As this wave exits the combustion chamber, most of the flue gases present in the chamber are carried with it into the exit pipe. Flue gases remaining in the combustion chamber begin to cool immediately. Contraction of cooling gases and momentum of gases in the exit pipe create a vacuum inside the chamber that opens the valves and allows more fuel and air into the chamber. While the fresh charge of fuel/air enters the chamber, the pressure wave reaches the end of the exit pipe and is partially reflected from the open end of the pipe. The fresh fuel/air charge is ignited by residual combustion and/or heat. The resulting combustion starts another cycle.

Typical pulse combustors operate at 30 to 100 cycles per second and emit resonant sound, which must be considered in their application. The pulses produce high convective heat transfer rates.

Heating Value

Combustion produces thermal energy (heat). The quantity of heat generated by complete combustion of a unit of specific fuel is constant and is called the **heating value**, **heat of combustion**, or **caloric value** of that fuel. A fuel's heating value can be determined by measuring the heat evolved during combustion of a known quantity of the fuel in a calorimeter, or it can be estimated from quantitative chemical analysis of the fuel and the heating values of the various chemical elements in the fuel. For information on calculating heating values, see the sections on Characteristics of Fuel Oils and Characteristics of Coal.

Higher heating value (HHV), **gross heating value**, or **total heating value** includes the latent heat of vaporization and is determined when water vapor in the fuel combustion products is cooled and condensed at standard temperature and pressure. Conversely, **lower heating value (LHV)** or **net heating value** does *not* include latent heat of vaporization. In the United States, when the heating value of a fuel is specified without designating higher or lower, it generally means the higher heating value. (LHV is mainly used for internal combustion engine fuels.)

Heating values are usually expressed in Btu/ft^3 for gaseous fuels, Btu/gal for liquid fuels, and Btu/lb for solid fuels. Heating values are always given in relation to standard temperature and pressure, usually 60, 68, or 77°F and 14.735 psia (30.00 in. Hg), depending on the particular industry practice. Heating values in the United States and Canada are based on standard conditions of 60°F (520°R) and 14.735 psia (30.00 in. Hg), dry. Heating values of several substances in common fuels are listed in Table 3.

With incomplete combustion, not all fuel is completely oxidized, and the heat produced is less than the heating value of the fuel. Therefore, the quantity of heat produced per unit of fuel consumed decreases (lower combustion efficiency).

Not all heat produced during combustion can be used effectively. The greatest heat loss is the thermal energy of the increased temperature of hot exhaust gases above the temperature of incoming air and fuel. Other heat losses include radiation and convection heat transfer from the outer walls of combustion equipment to the environment.

Altitude Compensation

Air at altitudes above sea level is less dense and has less mass of oxygen per unit volume. The volume concentration of oxygen, however, remains the same as sea level. Therefore, combustion at altitudes above sea level has less available oxygen to burn with the fuel unless compensation is made for the altitude. Combustion occurs, but the amount of excess air is reduced. If excess air is reduced enough by an increase in altitude, combustion is incomplete or ceases.

Table 3 Heating Values of Substances Occurring in Common Fuels

Substance	Molecular Formula	Higher Heating Values,[a] Btu/ft^3	Higher Heating Values,[a] Btu/lb	Lower Heating Values,[a] Btu/lb	Specific Volume,[b] ft^3/lb
Carbon (to CO)	C	—	3,950	3,950	—
Carbon (to CO_2)	C	—	14,093	14,093	—
Carbon monoxide	CO	321	4,347	4,347	13.5
Hydrogen	H_2	325	61,095	51,623	188.0
Methane	CH_4	1012	23,875	21,495	23.6
Ethane	C_2H_6	1773	22,323	20,418	12.5
Propane	C_3H_8	2524	21,669	19,937	8.36
Butane	C_4H_{10}	3271	21,321	19,678	6.32
Ethylene	C_2H_4	1604[c]	21,636	20,275	—
Propylene	C_3H_6	2340[c]	21,048	19,687	9.01
Acetylene	C_2H_2	1477	21,502	20,769	14.3
Sulfur (to SO_2)	S	—	3,980	3,980	—
Sulfur (to SO_3)	S	—	5,940	5,940	—
Hydrogen sulfide	H_2S	646	7,097	6,537	11.0

Adapted from *Gas Engineers Handbook* (1965).
[a]All values corrected to 60°F, 30 in. Hg, dry. For gases saturated with water vapor at 60°F, deduct 1.74% of value to adjust for gas volume displaced by water vapor.
[b]At 32°F and 29.92 in. Hg.
[c]*North American Combustion Handbook* (1986).

When gas-fired appliances operate at altitudes substantially above sea level, three notable effects occur (see Chapter 31 of the 2016 *ASHRAE Handbook—HVAC Systems and Equipment*):

- Oxygen available for combustion is reduced in proportion to the atmospheric pressure reduction.
- With gaseous fuels, the heat of combustion per unit volume of fuel gas (gas heat content) is reduced because of reduced fuel gas density in proportion to the atmospheric pressure reduction.
- Reduced air density affects the performance and operating temperature of heat exchangers and appliance cooling mechanisms.

Altitude compensation matches fuel and air supply rates to attain complete combustion without too much excess air or too much fuel. This can be done at increased altitude by increasing the air supply amount to the combustion zone with a combustion air blower (air compensation), or by decreasing the fuel supply rate to the combustion zone by decreasing the fuel input (derating).

Power burners use combustion air blowers and can increase the air supply rate to compensate for altitude. The combustion zone can be pressurized to attain the same air density in the combustion chamber as that at sea level.

Derating can be used as an alternative to power combustion. U.S. fuel gas codes generally do not require derating of nonpower burners at altitudes up to 2000 ft. At altitudes above 2000 ft, many fuel gas codes require that burners be derated 4% for each 1000 ft above sea level (NFPA/AGA *National Fuel Gas Code*). Chimney or vent operation also must be considered at high altitudes (see Chapter 35 of the 2016 *ASHRAE Handbook—HVAC Systems and Equipment*).

In addition to reducing the gas heat content of fuel gases, reduced fuel gas density also causes increased gas velocity through flow metering orifices. The net effect is for gas input rate to decrease naturally with increases in altitude, but at less than the rate at which atmospheric oxygen decreases. This effect is one reason that derating is required when appliances are operated at altitudes significantly above sea level. Early research with draft hood-equipped appliances established that appliance input rates should be reduced at the rate of 4% per 1000 ft above sea level, for altitudes higher than 2000 ft above sea level (Figure 1).

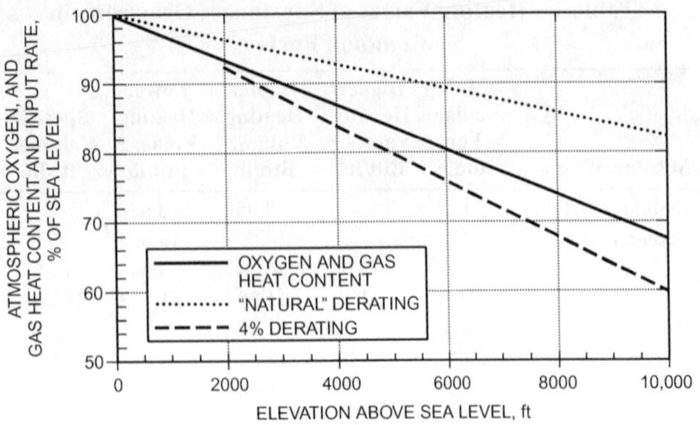

Note: Natural derating applies for fixed injector (orifice) size and pressure.

Fig. 1 Altitude Effects on Gas Combustion Appliances

Experience with recently developed appliances with fan-assisted combustion systems demonstrates that the 4% rule may not be required in all cases. It is therefore important to consult the manufacturer's listed appliance installation instructions, which are based on how the combustion system operates, and other factors (e.g., impaired heat transfer).

ASHRAE research projects RP-1182 (Fleck et al. 2007) and RP-1388 (Suchovsky et al. 2011) concluded that the tested induced-draft combustion systems experienced a natural derate of 1.8% (the dotted curve in Figure 1) in gas input rate per 1000 ft increase in altitude above sea level. This gas input derate for altitude may provide safe combustion operation (less than 400 ppm of CO concentration in air-free flue gas) for induced-draft combustion systems where the combustion air drawn in by the inducer does not participate in gas entrainment or gas orifice outlet pressure that affects the gas rate. Additionally, the gas regulation reference pressure and the gas orifice outlet pressure must be at the same fluidic potential during operation. Alternatively, gas-fired systems where the gas orifice outlet pressure is affected by mechanical draft and not equal to the gas regulation pressure follow a different natural derate. Gas control systems such as the 100% premix systems using a zero-pressure (or near-zero) regulator gas delivery system and the Bernoulli principle for gas entrainment (often called **constant-gas/air-ratio** or **tracking systems**) have a natural derate of 3.1% per 1000 ft of elevation. These combustion systems can follow a 1:1 ratio with barometric pressure changes (the solid curve in Figure 1). These ASHRAE research projects showed that some gas-fired products as currently designed and constructed can be installed and operated safely and acceptably at some higher altitudes with no modifications to the sea-level gas orifices, gas manifold pressure, etc.

It is important for appliance specifiers to be aware that the heating capacity of appliances is substantially reduced at altitudes significantly above sea level. To ensure adequate delivery of heat, derating of heating capacity must also be considered and quantified.

By definition, fuel gas HHV value remains constant for all altitudes because (in North America) it is based on standard conditions of 14.735 psia (30.00 in. Hg), dry, and 60°F (520°R). Some fuel gas suppliers at high altitudes (e.g., at Denver, Colorado, at 5000 ft) may report fuel gas heat content at local barometric pressure instead of standard pressure. This can be calculated using the following equation:

$$\text{HC} = \text{HHV} \times \frac{B}{P_s} \qquad (1)$$

where

HC = local gas heat content at local barometric pressure and standard temperature conditions, Btu/ft³
HHV = gas higher heating value at standard temperature and pressure of 520°R and 14.735 psia, respectively, Btu/ft³
B = local barometric pressure, psia (not corrected to sea level: do not use barometric pressure as reported by weather forecasters, because it is corrected to sea level)
P_s = standard pressure = 14.735 psia

For example, at 5000 ft, the barometric pressure is 12.23 psia. If the HHV of a fuel gas sample is 1000 Btu/ft³ (at standard temperature and pressure), local gas heat content is 830 Btu/ft³ at 12.23 psia barometric pressure 5000 ft above sea level.

$$\text{HC} = 1000 \text{ Btu/ft}^3 \times 12.23 \text{ psia}/14.735 \text{ psia} = 830 \text{ Btu/ft}^3$$

Therefore, local gas heat content of a sample of fuel gas can be expressed as 830 Btu/ft³ at local barometric pressure of 12.23 psia and standard temperature, or as 1000 Btu/ft³ (HHV). Both gas heat contents are correct, but the application engineer must understand the difference to use each one correctly. As described earlier, local heat content HC can be used to determine appliance input rate.

When gas heat value (either HHV or HC) is used to determine gas input rate, the gas pressure and temperature in the meter must also be considered. Add the gage pressure of gas in the meter to the local barometric pressure to calculate the heat content of the gas at the pressure in the meter. Gas temperature in the meter also affects the heat content of the gas in the meter. Gas heat value is directly proportional to gas pressure and inversely proportional to its absolute temperature in accordance with the perfect gas laws, as shown in the following example calculations for gas input rate with either the HHV or local heat content method.

Example 1. Calculate the gas input rate for 1000 Btu/ft³ HHV fuel gas, 100 ft³/h volumetric flow rate of 75°F fuel gas at 12.23 psia barometer pressure (5000 ft altitude) with 7 in. of water fuel gas pressure in the gas meter.

HHV Method:

$$Q = \text{HHV} \times \text{VFR}_s$$

where

Q = fuel gas input rate, Btu/h
HHV = fuel gas higher heating value at standard temperature and pressure, Btu/ft³
VFR_s = fuel gas volumetric flow rate adjusted to standard temperature and pressure, ft³/h
= $\text{VFR}(T_s \times P)/(T \times P_s)$
VFR = fuel gas volumetric flow rate at local temperature and pressure conditions, ft³/h
T_s = standard temperature, 520°R (60°F + 460)
P = gas meter absolute pressure, psia (local barometer pressure + gas pressure in meter relative to barometric pressure)
= 12.23 psia + (7 in. of water × 0.03613 psi/in. of water)
= 12.48291 psia gas meter absolute pressure
T = absolute temperature of fuel gas, °R (fuel gas temperature in °F + 460°R)
P_s = standard pressure, 14.735 psia

Substituting given values into the equation for VFR_s gives

$$\text{VFR}_s = \frac{100 \text{ ft}^3\text{/h} \times 520°\text{F} \times 12.48291 \text{ psia}}{(75°\text{F} + 460°\text{R})14.735 \text{ psia}} = 82.341 \text{ ft}^3\text{/h}$$

Then,

$$Q = 1000 \text{ Btu/ft}^3 \times 82.341 \text{ ft}^3\text{/h} = 82{,}341 \text{ Btu/h}$$

Local Gas Heat Content Method: The local gas heat content is simply the HHV adjusted to local gas meter pressure and temperature conditions. The gas input rate is simply the observed volumetric gas flow rate times the local gas heat content.

$$Q = \text{HC} \times \text{VFR}$$

where

Q = fuel gas input rate, Btu/h

HC = fuel gas heat content at local gas meter pressure and temperature conditions, Btu/ft^3
VFR = fuel gas volumetric flow rate, referenced to local gas meter pressure and temperature conditions, ft^3/h

$$HC = HHV(T_s \times P)/(T \times P_s)$$

T_s = standard temperature, 520°R (60°F + 460°R)
P = gas meter absolute pressure, psia (local barometer pressure + gas pressure in gas meter relative to barometric pressure)
P_s = standard pressure = 14.735 psia
P_l = local barometric pressure = 12.230 psia
T = absolute temperature of fuel gas, 535°R (75°F fuel gas temperature + 460°R)

Substituting given values into the equation for HC gives

$$HC = \frac{1000 \times 520[12.23 + (7.0 \times 0.03613)]}{535 \times 14.735} = 823.41 \text{ Btu/ft}^3$$

Then,

$$Q = 823.41 \text{ Btu/ft}^3 \times 100 \text{ ft}^3\text{/h} = 82{,}341 \text{ Btu/h}$$

The gas input rate is exactly the same for both calculation methods.

2. FUEL CLASSIFICATION

Generally, hydrocarbon fuels are classified according to physical state (gas, liquid, or solid). Different types of combustion equipment are usually needed to burn fuels in the different physical states. Gaseous fuels can be burned in premix or diffusion burners. Liquid fuel burners must include a means for atomizing or vaporizing fuel and must provide adequate mixing of fuel and air. Solid fuel combustion equipment must (1) heat fuel to vaporize sufficient volatiles to initiate and sustain combustion, (2) provide residence time to complete combustion, and (3) provide space for ash containment.

Principal fuel applications include space heating and cooling of residential, commercial, industrial, and institutional buildings; service water heating; steam generation; and refrigeration. Major fuels for these applications are natural and liquefied petroleum gases (LPG), fuel oils, diesel and gas turbine fuels (for on-site energy applications), and coal. Fuels of limited use, such as manufactured gases, kerosene, liquid fuels derived from biological materials (wood, vegetable oils, and animal fat products), briquettes, wood, and coke, are not discussed here.

Fuel choice is based on one or more of the following:

Fuel factors

- Availability, including dependability of supply
- Convenience of use and storage
- Economy
- Cleanliness, including amount of contamination in unburned fuel [affecting (1) usability in fuel-burning equipment and (2) environmental impact]

Combustion equipment factors

- Operating requirements
- Cost
- Service requirements
- Ease of control

3. GASEOUS FUELS

Although various gaseous fuels have been used as energy sources in the past, heating and cooling applications are presently limited to natural gas and liquefied petroleum gases.

Types and Properties

Natural Gas. This is a nearly odorless, colorless gas that accumulates in the upper parts of oil and gas reservoirs. Raw natural gas is a mixture of methane (55 to 98%), higher hydrocarbons (primarily ethane), and noncombustible gases. Some constituents, principally water vapor, hydrogen sulfide, helium, liquefied petroleum gases, and gasoline, are removed before distribution.

Natural gas used as fuel typically contains methane, CH_4 (70 to 96%); ethane, C_2H_6 (1 to 14%); propane, C_3H_8 (0 to 4%); butane, C_4H_{10} (0 to 2%); pentane, C_5H_{12} (0 to 0.5%); hexane, C_6H_{14} (0 to 2%); carbon dioxide, CO_2 (0 to 2%); oxygen, O_2 (0 to 1.2%); and nitrogen, N_2 (0.4 to 17%).

The composition of natural gas depends on its geographical source. Because the gas is drawn from various sources, the composition of gas distributed in a given location can vary slightly, but a fairly constant heating value is usually maintained for control and safety. Local gas utilities are the best sources of current gas composition data for a particular area.

Heating values of natural gases vary from 900 to 1200 Btu/ft^3; the usual range is 1000 to 1050 Btu/ft^3 at sea level. The heating value for a particular gas can be calculated from the composition data and values in Table 3.

For safety purposes, odorants (e.g., mercaptans) are added to natural gas and LPG to give them noticeable odors.

Liquefied Petroleum Gases (LPG). These gases consist primarily of propane and butane, and are usually obtained as a by-product of oil refinery operations or by stripping liquefied petroleum gases from the natural gas stream. Propane and butane are gaseous under usual atmospheric conditions, but can be liquefied under moderate pressures at normal temperatures.

Commercial propane consists primarily of propane but generally contains about 5 to 10% propylene. Its heating value is about 21,560 Btu/lb, about 2500 Btu/ft^3 of gas, or about 91,000 Btu/gal of liquid propane. At atmospheric pressure, commercial propane has a boiling point of about –44°F. The low boiling point of propane allows it to be used during winter in the northern United States and southern Canada. Tank heaters and vaporizers allow its use also in colder climates and where high fuel flow rates are required. American Society for Testing and Materials (ASTM) *Standard* D1835 and Gas Processors Association (GPA) *Standard* 2140, which are similar, provide formulating specifications for required properties of liquefied petroleum gases at the time of delivery. Propane is shipped in cargo tank vehicles, rail cars, and barges. It is stored at consumer sites in tanks that comply with requirements of the ASME *Boiler and Pressure Vessel Code* or transportable cylinders that comply with requirements of the U.S. Department of Transportation.

HD-5 propane is a special LPG product for use in internal combustion engines under moderate to high severity. Its specifications are included in ASTM *Standard* D1835 and GPA *Standard* 2140.

Propane/air mixtures are used in place of natural gas in small communities and by natural gas companies to supplement normal supplies at peak loads. Table 4 lists heating values and specific gravities for various fuel/air ratios.

Commercial butane consists primarily of butane but may contain up to 5% butylene. It has a heating value of about 21,180 Btu/lb, about 3200 Btu/ft^3 of gas, or about 102,000 Btu/gal of liquid butane. At atmospheric pressure, commercial butane has a relatively high boiling point of about 32°F. Therefore, butane cannot be used in cold weather unless the gas temperature is maintained above 32°F or the partial pressure is decreased by dilution with a gas having a lower boiling point. Butane is usually available in bottles, tank trucks, or tank cars, but not in cylinders.

Butane/air mixtures are used in place of natural gas in small communities and by natural gas companies to supplement normal supplies at peak loads. Table 4 lists heating values and specific gravities for various fuel/air ratios.

Commercial propane/butane mixtures with various ratios of propane and butane are available. Their properties generally fall between those of the unmixed fuels.

Table 4 Propane/Air and Butane/Air Gas Mixtures

Heating Value, Btu/ft³	Propane/Air[a]			Butane/Air[b]		
	% Gas	% Air	Sp Gr	% Gas	% Air	Sp Gr
500	19.8	80.2	1.103	15.3	84.7	1.155
600	23.8	76.2	1.124	18.4	81.6	1.186
700	27.8	72.2	1.144	21.5	78.5	1.216
800	31.7	68.3	1.165	24.5	75.5	1.248
900	35.7	64.3	1.185	27.6	72.4	1.278
1000	39.7	60.3	1.206	30.7	69.3	1.310
1100	43.6	56.4	1.227	33.7	66.3	1.341
1200	47.5	52.5	1.248	36.8	63.2	1.372
1300	51.5	48.5	1.268	39.8	60.2	1.402
1400	55.5	44.5	1.288	42.9	57.1	1.433
1500	59.4	40.6	1.309	46.0	54.0	1.464
1600	63.4	36.6	1.330	49.0	51.0	1.495
1700	67.4	32.6	1.350	52.1	47.9	1.526
1800	71.3	28.7	1.371	55.2	44.8	1.557

Adapted from *Gas Engineers Handbook* (1965).
[a]Values used for calculation: 2522 Btu/ft³; 1.52 specific gravity.
[b]Values used for calculation: 3261 Btu/ft³; 2.01 specific gravity.

Manufactured gases are combustible gases produced from coal, coke, oil, liquefied petroleum gases, or natural gas. For more detailed information, see the *Gas Engineers Handbook* (1965). These fuels are used primarily for industrial in-plant operations or as specialty fuels (e.g., acetylene for welding).

Renewable Gases. There are two primary processes that produce renewable gas from various feedstocks: anaerobic digestion and thermal gasification. Both processes are discussed here in general.

Anaerobic Digestion (AD). In this process, complex organic matter (source material) is broken down into simpler constituents, directly through microbial action and in the absence of oxygen. The degradation process usually occurs in some form of tank, called a **digester** or **reactor**. Organic matter, perhaps first pretreated by grinding or by mechanical or chemical hydrolysis, enters the tank and is held there for a predefined length of time. For systems based on animal manure, this time ranges from a few days to a few weeks; for systems that use energy crops, residence time can be up to several tens of days. During that period, microbial activity breaks down the organic matter, and the resultant gaseous products contain a large fraction of methane and carbon dioxide along with trace amounts of other gases. Eventually, the material is expelled from the digester and replaced by new feed matter to continue the digestion/degradation process. The new organic matter may replace the entirety of the resident matter in batch, or it may replace it semicontinuously, depending on the reactor and on the collection and processing of the source matter.

The four stages of anaerobic digestion are as follows:

1. In **hydrolysis**, bacteria liquefy and break down organic matter comprised of complex organic polymers and cell structures. The end products are organic molecules that consist primarily of sugars, amino acids, peptides, and fatty acids.
2. In **acidogenesis**, acid-forming bacteria break down the products of the hydrolytic stage, forming volatile organic acids, CO_2, hydrogen, and ammonia.
3. Next, in **acetogenesis**, bacteria convert the volatile organic acids from acidogenesis into acetic acid (CH_3COOH) and acetate, CO_2, and hydrogen.
4. Finally, **methanogenesis** uses methane-producing bacteria to change CO_2 and acetic acid (products of the acidogenic and acetogenic stages) into methane (CH_4). The resultant gas yield consists primarily of CH_4, CO_2, and other trace gases such as hydrogen sulfide (H_2S).

Wastewater treatment plant (WWTP) gases are generated from waste liquids and solids from household or commercial water usage or from industrial processes. Depending on the architecture of the sewer system and local regulation, it may also contain stormwater from roofs, streets, or other runoff areas. The contents may include anything expelled (legally or not) from a household that enters the drains. If stormwater is included in the wastewater sewer flow, it may also contain components collected during runoff (e.g., soil, metals, organic compounds, animal waste, oils, solid debris such as leaves and branches).

Processing influent to a large wastewater treatment plant typically has three stages: mechanical, biological, and sometimes chemical processing. The goal of such treatments is to prepare solids (treated sludge) and liquids (treated effluent) output from the WWTP that is environmentally safe and able to be landfilled (treated solids) or returned to the environment (treated effluent). One step in the processing of the wastewater sludge may be anaerobic digestion, from which methane can be produced.

Landfill gas (LFG) derives from municipal solid waste (MSW) in landfills. In the United States, the primary federal law currently controlling disposal of solid and hazardous waste is the Resource Conservation and Recovery Act (RCRA), which sets criteria under which landfills can accept municipal solid waste and nonhazardous industrial solid waste. It also prohibits open dumping of waste, and ensures that hazardous waste is managed from the time of its creation to the time of its disposal.

For energy production, MSW can be used in either of two ways: it can be gasified directly through thermochemical processes [see the section on Thermal Gasification (TG)], or it can be deposited into a landfill and undergo AD. Although most surveys indicate the material composition of all landfill constituents, the important components of MSW for the production of landfill gas are the organic fractions, which form the substrates that anaerobically decompose in the landfill. Typical or approximate contents of the organic fractions of MSW appear in Table 5.

Landfill gas is the result of these anaerobic processes acting on the organic matter within a landfill. In a sense, the landfill itself substitutes for an anaerobic digester tank: a closed volume that contains putrescible matter and over time becomes devoid of oxygen.

Methane and carbon dioxide are the principal components of the gas, though the overall composition of raw LFG can vary depending on the materials in the landfill: it can contain significant amounts of hydrogen sulfide as well as trace amounts of ammonia, mercury, chlorine, fluorine, siloxanes, and volatile metallic compounds.

Variation in source MSW, its organic contents, temperature conditions, moisture conditions, compaction densities, landfill operational procedures, and other landfill attributes account for variations in LFG content. Typical compounds and their reported concentration ranges are shown in Table 6. Methane concentration is generally reported as being around 55 mol%, and carbon dioxide is often measured at 40%. Nitrogen, hydrogen, oxygen, and hydrogen sulfide are found in smaller but significant quantities.

The composition of raw biogas can vary depending on the materials being digested. Methane and carbon dioxide are the principal components of landfill gas, though the overall composition of raw LFG can contain significant amounts of H_2S as well as trace amounts of ammonia, mercury, chlorine, fluorine, siloxanes, and volatile metallic compounds (EPA 2017).

However, the composition of **biogas generated from dairy manure** tends to be more consistent because the dairy industry is regulated as a producer of milk for human consumption. Typical compounds and their reported concentration ranges for digester-based biogas are shown in Table 7. Methane concentration can be as high as 70% but is generally reported at around 60%. Landfill gas, unless the landfill is specifically designed for gas production, typically has a slightly lower methane fraction (e.g., around 55%).

Table 5 Components of Organic Portion of Municipal Solid Waste

Component Composition	Weight, %
Moisture	20.7
Cellulose, sugar, starch	46.6
Lipids	4.5
Protein	2.1
Other organics	1.2
Inert materials	24.9
Total	**100**

Table 6 Landfill Gas Composition

Compound	mol%
Methane (CH_4)	45 to 60
Carbon dioxide (CO_2)	40 to 60
Nitrogen (N_2)	2 to 5
Hydrogen (H_2)	0 to 0.2
Carbon monoxide (CO)	0 to 0.2
Oxygen (O_2)	0.1 to 1
Sulfides, disulfides, mercaptans, etc.	0 to 1
Ammonia (NH_3)	0.1 to 1
Trace elements, amines, sulfur compounds, nonmethane volatile organic carbons halocarbons	0.01 to 0.6

Adding food wastes into a manure-based digester (**codigestion**) seems to improve biogas production and may increase methane concentration, but is not addressed in this chapter. CO_2, the other major biogas component, is often measured around 40%. Nitrogen, hydrogen, oxygen, and H_2S are found in smaller quantities.

Similarly to natural gas, biogas derived from biomass feedstocks also must undergo one or more cleanup processes to remove unwanted components and to upgrade it suitably for natural gas pipelines. Quality control is required to prevent or minimize entry of raw, unconditioned biogas or less-than-pipeline-quality biomethane into the natural gas grid. Many methods and processes can be used to remove contaminants from subquality gas streams. Some are appropriate for use on farms, and others are only economical at gas flows measured in millions of standard cubic feet per day (MMSCFD) and where sulfur removal rates are measured in tons per day. The ability of a process to remove unwanted compounds depends on many factors, and assessment of the true practicality of a method for a given application requires careful evaluation.

Thermal Gasification (TG). This process encompasses a fairly broad range of processes and reactions that convert carbonaceous feedstocks (coal, heavy oils, wood, biomass, sludge, etc.) into a mixture of gases, primarily hydrogen, carbon monoxide, steam, carbon dioxide, some methane, small amounts of ethane and higher hydrocarbons, small amounts of hydrogen sulfide, and nitrogen (if gasification is conducted with air). Depending on feedstock and operating conditions, TG of biomass typically generates tars and oils that are undesirable by-products.

Thermal gasification is conducted in reducing (substoichiometric or incompletely combusting) atmospheres. Some of the process heat for the endothermic gasification reactions is typically provided by burning some of the carbon in the feedstock. Process heating can be direct or indirect. Indirect heating of the gasifier is called **all-thermal gasification**. A typical range of syngas compositions from oxygen- or air-blown operation is presented in Table 8.

This mixture of gases is known as synthesis gas or **syngas**, and can be further catalytically converted into methane to generate refinery gas (RG). The syngas can also be converted into liquid products by Fischer-Tropsch synthesis [see DOE (2017) for a description] for use as transportation fuel, or transformed into a host of chemical products such as methanol, dimethyl ether, fuel gas/

Table 7 Typical Compounds and Concentrations in Biogas from Anaerobic Digester

Compound	Concentration
Methane (CH_4)	54 to 70%
Carbon dioxide (CO_2)	27 to 45%
Nitrogen (N_2)	0.5 to 3%
Hydrogen (H_2)	1 to 10%
Carbon monoxide (CO)	0 to 0.1%
Oxygen (O_2)	0 to 0.1%
Hydrogen sulfide (H_2S)	600 to 7000+ ppm

Table 8 Typical Compounds and Concentrations Found in Syngas from Thermal Gasification

Compound Typical Range	Air-Blown Fixed Bed	Steam-Blown Fluidized Bed	Oxygen-Blown Entrained Flow
Calorific value, Btu/ft³	107 to 161	322 to 376	268 to 322
Hydrogen (H_2), mol%	11 to 16	35 to 45	23 to 28
Carbon monoxide (CO), mol%	13 to 18	22 to 25	45 to 55
Carbon dioxide (CO_2), mol%	12 to 16	20 to 23	10 to 15
Methane (CH_4), mol%	2 to 6	9 to 11	<1
Nitrogen (N_2), mol%	45 to 60	<1	<5

town gas, ethylene/propylene, or acetic acid. It can also be combusted directly in a gas turbine to drive a generator. In some cases, a catalyst is included with the feedstock to accelerate reactions and allow a reduced operating temperature. TG can be carried out at temperatures in the range of 1200 to 2000°F and at pressures ranging from ambient to greater than 1000 psig. If the TG process is conducted at ambient or fairly low pressure, then the product RG must be compressed so it can be injected into the transmission or distribution line at the appropriate pressure.

4. LIQUID FUELS

Significant liquid fuels include various fuel oils for firing combustion equipment and engine fuels for on-site energy systems. Liquid fuels, with few exceptions, are mixtures of hydrocarbons derived by refining crude petroleum. In addition to hydrocarbons, crude petroleum usually contains small quantities of sulfur, oxygen, nitrogen, vanadium, other trace metals, and impurities such as water and sediment. Refining produces a variety of fuels and other products. Nearly all lighter hydrocarbons are refined into fuels (e.g., liquefied petroleum gases, gasoline, kerosene, jet fuels, diesel fuels, light heating oils). Heavy hydrocarbons are refined into residual fuel oils and other products (e.g., lubricating oils, waxes, petroleum coke, asphalt).

Crude petroleums from different oil fields vary in hydrocarbon molecular structure. Crude is paraffin-base (principally chain-structured paraffin hydrocarbons), naphthene- or asphaltic-base (containing relatively large quantities of saturated ring-structural naphthenes), aromatic-base (containing relatively large quantities of unsaturated, ring-structural aromatics, including multi-ring compounds such as asphaltenes), or mixed- or intermediate-base (between paraffin- and naphthene-base crudes). Except for heavy fuel oils, the crude type has little significant effect on resultant distillate products and combustion applications.

Types of Fuel Oils

Fuel oils for heating are broadly classified as **distillate fuel oils** (lighter oils) or **residual fuel oils** (heavier oils). ASTM *Standard* D396 has specifications for fuel oil properties that subdivide the oils into various grades. Grades No. 1 and 2 are distillates; grades 4, 5 (Light), 5 (Heavy), and 6 are residual. Specifications for the grades are based on required characteristics of fuel oils for use in different types of burners.

Grade No. 1 is a light distillate intended for vaporizing-type burners. High volatility is essential to continued evaporation with minimum residue. This fuel is also used in extremely cold climates for residential heating using pressure-atomizing burners.

Grade No. 2 is heavier than No. 1 and is used primarily with pressure-atomizing (gun) burners that spray oil into a combustion chamber. Vapor from the atomized oil mixes with air and burns. This grade is used in most domestic burners and many medium-capacity commercial/industrial burners. A dewaxed No. 2 oil with a pour point of −58°F is supplied only to areas where regular No. 2 oil would jell. Grade No. 2—low sulfur is a relatively new category that has a sulfur content of 0.05%. Lower fuel sulfur content reduces fouling rates of boiler heat exchangers (Butcher et al. 1997).

Grade No. 4 is an intermediate fuel that is considered either a heavy distillate or a light residual. Intended for burners that atomize oils of higher viscosity than domestic burners can handle, its permissible viscosity range allows it to be pumped and atomized at relatively low storage temperatures.

Grade No. 5 (Light) is a residual fuel of intermediate viscosity for burners that handle fuel more viscous than No. 4 without preheating. Preheating may be necessary in some equipment for burning and, in colder climates, for handling.

Grade No. 5 (Heavy) is a residual fuel more viscous than No. 5 (Light), but intended for similar purposes. Preheating is usually necessary for burning and, in colder climates, for handling.

Grade No. 6, sometimes referred to as Bunker C, is a high-viscosity oil used mostly in commercial and industrial heating. It requires preheating in the storage tank to allow pumping, and additional preheating at the burner to allow atomizing.

Low-sulfur residual oils are marketed in many areas to allow users to meet sulfur dioxide emission regulations. These fuel oils are produced (1) by refinery processes that remove sulfur from the oil (hydrodesulfurization), (2) by blending high-sulfur residual oils with low-sulfur distillate oils, or (3) by a combination of these methods. These oils have significantly different characteristics from regular residual oils. For example, the viscosity/temperature relationship can be such that low-sulfur fuel oils have viscosities of No. 6 fuel oils when cold, and of No. 4 when heated. Therefore, normal guidelines for fuel handling and burning can be altered when using these fuels.

Another liquid fuel of increasing interest is biodiesel. It is made from biological sources (e.g., vegetable oils, used cooking oils, tallow). ASTM *Standard* D6751 addresses biodiesel; requirements are largely similar to those for petroleum diesel (cetane number, flash point, etc.; see the section on Types and Properties of Liquid Fuels for Engines). In practice, biodiesel is almost always blended, most often with ASTM heating oils when used for stationary heating applications, because of cost and cold-flow properties of 100% biodiesel. However, the benefits of a renewable fuel that has very low net carbon dioxide emission in its life cycle, reduced particulate and sulfur emissions, and lower NO_x emissions in many heating applications balance the need for mixing.

Fuel oil grade selection for a particular application is usually based on availability and economic factors, including fuel cost, clean air requirements, preheating and handling costs, and equipment cost. Installations with low firing rates and low annual fuel consumption cannot justify the cost of preheating and other methods that use residual fuel oils. Large installations with high annual fuel consumption cannot justify the premium cost of distillate fuel oils.

Characteristics of Fuel Oils

Characteristics that determine grade classification and suitability for given applications are (1) viscosity, (2) flash point, (3) pour point, (4) water and sediment content, (5) carbon residue, (6) ash, (7) distillation qualities or distillation temperature ranges, (8) specific gravity, (9) sulfur content, (10) heating value, (11) carbon/hydrogen content, (12) aromatic content, and (13) asphaltene content. Not all of these are included in ASTM *Standard* D396.

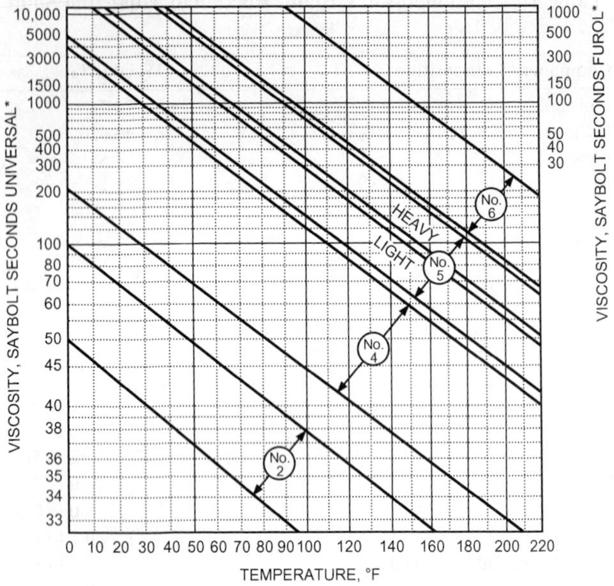

* 1 Saybolt Second (SSU, or SUS) = time required for 60 mL to gravity-flow through Saybolt universal viscometer. (Furol = Fuel and Road Oils)

Fig. 2 Approximate Viscosity of Fuel Oils

Viscosity is an oil's resistance to flow. It is significant because it indicates the ease with which oil flows or can be pumped and the ease of atomization. Differences in fuel oil viscosities are caused by variations in the concentrations of fuel oil constituents and different refining methods. Approximate viscosities of fuel oils are shown in Figure 2.

Flash point is the lowest temperature to which an oil must be heated for its vapors to ignite in a flame. Minimum permissible flash point is usually prescribed by state and municipal laws.

Pour point is the lowest temperature at which a fuel can be stored and handled. Fuels with higher pour points can be used when heated storage and piping facilities are provided.

Water and **sediment content** should be low to prevent fouling the facilities. Sediment accumulates on filter screens and burner parts. Water in distillate fuels can cause tanks to corrode and emulsions to form in residual oil.

Carbon residue is obtained by a test in which the oil sample is destructively distilled in the absence of air. When commercial fuels are used in proper burners, this residue has almost no relationship to soot deposits, except indirectly when deposits are formed by vaporizing burners.

Ash is the noncombustible material in an oil. An excessive amount indicates the presence of materials that cause high wear on burner pumps.

The **distillation** test shows the volatility and ease of vaporization of a fuel.

Specific gravity is the ratio of the density of a fuel oil to the density of water at a specific temperature. Specific gravities cover a range in each grade, with some overlap between distillate and residual grades. **API gravity** (developed by the American Petroleum Institute) is a parameter widely used in place of specific gravity. It is obtained by the following formula:

$$\text{Degrees API} = \frac{141.5}{\text{Sp Gr at } 60/60°\text{F}} - 131.5 \qquad (2)$$

Table 9 Sulfur Content of Marketed Fuel Oils

Grade of Oil	No. 1	No. 2	No. 4	No. 5 (Light)	No. 5 (Heavy)	No. 6
Total fuel samples	31	61	13	15	16	96
Sulfur content, % mass						
minimum	0.001	0.03	0.46	0.90	0.57	0.32
maximum	0.120	0.50	1.44	3.50	2.92	4.00
average	0.023	0.20	0.83	1.46	1.46	1.41
No. samples with S						
over 0.3%	0	17	13	15	16	96
over 0.5%	0	2	11	15	16	93
over 1.0%	0	0	3	9	11	60
over 3.0%	0	0	0	2	0	8

Data for No. 1 and No. 2 oil derived from Dickson and Sturm (1994).
Data for No. 4, 5, and 6 oil derived from Shelton (1974).

Table 10 Typical API Gravity, Density, and Higher Heating Value of Standard Grades of Fuel Oil

Grade No.	API Gravity	Density, lb/gal	Higher Heating Value, Btu/gal
1	38 to 45	6.950 to 6.675	137,000 to 132,900
2	30 to 38	7.296 to 6.960	141,800 to 137,000
4	20 to 28	7.787 to 7.396	148,100 to 143,100
5L	17 to 22	7.940 to 7.686	150,000 to 146,800
5H	14 to 18	8.080 to 7.890	152,000 to 149,400
6	8 to 15	8.448 to 8.053	155,900 to 151,300

where Sp Gr at 60/60°F is the ratio of the mass of a given volume of oil at 60°F to the mass of the same volume of water at 60°F. The API gravity of water at 60°F is 10.0.

Air pollution considerations are important in determining the allowable **sulfur content** of fuel oils. Sulfur content is frequently limited by legislation aimed at reducing sulfur oxide emissions from combustion equipment; usual maximum allowable sulfur content levels are 1.0, 0.5, or 0.3%. Table 9 lists sulfur levels of some marketed fuel oils. Research (Lee et al. 2002a, 2002b) suggests that fuel sulfur content affects the sulfate content of particulate emissions, which are reported to be associated with adverse health effects.

Sulfur in fuel oils is also undesirable because sulfur compounds in flue gas are corrosive. Although low-temperature corrosion can be minimized by maintaining the stack at temperatures above the dew point of the flue gas, this limits the overall thermal efficiency of combustion equipment. The presence of sulfur oxides in the flue gas raises the dew point temperature (see the section on Combustion Calculations).

For certain industrial applications (e.g., direct-fired metallurgy, where work is performed in the combustion zone), fuel sulfur content must be limited because of adverse effects on product quality. Sulfur contents of typical fuel oils are listed in Table 9.

Heating value is an important property, although ASTM *Standard* D396 does not list it as one of the criteria for fuel oil classification. Heating value can generally be correlated with the API gravity. Table 10 shows the relationship between heating value, API gravity, and density for several oil grades. In the absence of more specific data, heating values can be calculated as shown in the *North American Combustion Handbook* (1978):

$$\text{Higher heating value, Btu/lb} = 22{,}320 - 3780(\text{Specific gravity})^2 \quad (3)$$

Distillate fuel oils (grades 1 and 2) have a **carbon/hydrogen content** of 84 to 86% carbon, with the remainder predominantly hydrogen. Heavier residual fuel oils (grades 4, 5, and 6) may contain up to 88% carbon and as little as 11% hydrogen. An approximate relationship for determining the hydrogen content of fuel oils is

$$\text{Hydrogen, \%} = 26 - (15 \times \text{Specific gravity}) \quad (4)$$

ASTM *Standard* D396 is more a classification than a specification, distinguishing between six generally nonoverlapping grades, one of which characterizes any commercial fuel oil. Quality is not defined, as a refiner might control it; for example, the standard lists the distillation temperature 90% point for grade No. 2 as having a maximum of 640°F, whereas commercial practice rarely exceeds 600°F.

Types and Properties of Liquid Fuels for Engines

The primary stationary engine fuels are diesel and gas turbine oils, natural gases, and LPGs. Other fuels include sewage gas, manufactured gas, and other commercial gas mixtures. Gasoline and the JP series of gas turbine fuels are rarely used for stationary engines.

Only properties of diesel and gas turbine fuel oils are covered here; properties of natural and liquefied petroleum gases are found in the section on Gaseous Fuels. For properties of gasolines and JP turbine fuel, consult texts on internal combustion engines and gas turbines. Properties of currently marketed gasolines can be found in ASTM *Standard* D4814.

Properties of the three **grades of diesel fuel oils** (1-D, 2-D, and 4D) are listed in ASTM *Standard* D975.

Grade No. 1-D includes the class of volatile fuel oils from kerosene to intermediate distillates. They are used in high-speed engines with frequent and relatively wide variations in loads and speeds and where abnormally low fuel temperatures are encountered.

Grade No. 2-D includes the class of lower-volatility distillate gas oils. They are used in high-speed engines with relatively high loads and uniform speeds, or in engines not requiring fuels with the higher volatility or other properties specified for grade No. 1-D.

Grade No. 4-D covers the more viscous distillates and blends of these distillates with residual fuel oils. They are used in low- and medium-speed engines involving sustained loads at essentially constant speed.

Property specifications and test methods for grade No. 1-D, 2-D, and 4-D diesel fuel oils are essentially identical to specifications of grade No. 1, 2, and 4 fuel oils, respectively. However, diesel fuel oils have an additional specification for **cetane number**, which measures ignition quality and influences combustion roughness. Cetane number requirements depend on engine design, size, speed and load variations, and starting and atmospheric conditions. An increase in cetane number over values actually required does not improve engine performance. Thus, the cetane number should be as low as possible to ensure maximum fuel availability. ASTM *Standard* D975 provides several methods for estimating cetane number from other fuel oil properties.

ASTM *Standard* D2880 for gas turbine fuel oils relates gas turbine fuel oil grades to fuel and diesel fuel oil grades. Test methods for determining properties of gas turbine fuel oils are essentially identical to those for fuel oils. However, gas turbine specifications limit quantities of some trace elements that may be present, to prevent excessive corrosion in gas turbine engines. For a detailed discussion of fuels for gas turbines and combustion in gas turbines, see Chapters 5 and 9, respectively, in Hazard (1971).

5. SOLID FUELS

Solid fuels include coal, coke, wood, and waste products of industrial and agricultural operations. Of these, only coal is widely used for heating and cooling applications.

Coal's complex composition makes classification difficult. Chemically, coal consists of carbon, hydrogen, oxygen, nitrogen, sulfur, and a mineral residue, ash. Chemical analysis provides some indication of quality, but does not define its burning characteristics sufficiently. Coal users are principally interested in the available energy per unit mass of coal and the amount of ash and dust produced, but are also interested in burning characteristics and handling and storing properties. A description of coal qualities and characteristics from the U.S. Bureau of Mines as well as other information can be obtained from the U.S. Geological Survey at energy .er.usgs.gov/products/databases/USCoal/index.htm and the Energy Information Administration at www.eia.doe.gov/fuelcoal.html.

Types of Coals

Commonly accepted definitions for classifying coals are listed in Table 11. This classification is arbitrary because there are no distinct demarcation lines between coal types.

Anthracite is a clean, dense, hard coal that creates little dust in handling. It is comparatively difficult to ignite, but burns freely once started. It is noncaking and burns uniformly and smokelessly with a short flame.

Semianthracite has a higher volatile content than anthracite. It is not as hard and ignites more easily. Otherwise, its properties are similar to those of anthracite.

Bituminous coal includes many types of coal with distinctly different compositions, properties, and burning characteristics. Coals range from high-grade bituminous, such as those found in the eastern United States, to low-rank coals, such as those found in the western United States. Caking properties range from coals that melt or become fully plastic, to those from which volatiles and tars are distilled without changing form (classed as noncaking or free-burning). Most bituminous coals are strong and nonfriable enough to allow screened sizes to be delivered free of fines. Generally, they ignite easily and burn freely. Flame length is long and varies with different coals. If improperly fired, much smoke and soot are possible, especially at low burning rates.

Semibituminous coal is soft and friable, and handling creates fines and dust. It ignites slowly and burns with a medium-length flame. Its caking properties increase as volatile matter increases, but the coke formed is weak. With only half the volatile matter content of bituminous coals, burning produces less smoke; hence, it is sometimes called smokeless coal.

Subbituminous coal, such as that found in the western United States, is high in moisture when mined and tends to break up as it dries or is exposed to the weather; it is likely to ignite spontaneously when piled or stored. It ignites easily and quickly, has a medium-length flame, and is noncaking and free-burning. The lumps tend to break into small pieces if poked. Very little smoke and soot are formed.

Lignite is woody in structure, very high in moisture when mined, of low heating value, and clean to handle. It has a greater tendency than subbituminous coals to disintegrate as it dries and is also more likely to ignite spontaneously. Because of its high moisture, freshly mined lignite ignites slowly and is noncaking. The char left after moisture and volatile matter are driven off burns very easily, like charcoal. The lumps tend to break up in the fuel bed and pieces of char that fall into the ash pit continue to burn. Very little smoke or soot forms.

Characteristics of Coal

The characteristics of coals that determine classification and suitability for given applications are the proportions of (1) volatile matter, (2) fixed carbon, (3) moisture, (4) sulfur, and (5) ash. Each of these is reported in the proximate analysis. Coal analyses can be reported on several bases: as-received, moisture-free (or dry), and mineral-matter-free (or ash-free). As-received is applicable for combustion calculations; moisture-free and mineral-matter-free, for classification purposes.

Volatile matter is driven off as gas or vapor when the coal is heated according to a standard temperature test. It consists of a variety of organic gases, generally resulting from distillation and decomposition. Volatile products given off by heated coals differ materially in the ratios (by mass) of the gases to oils and tars. No heavy oils or tars are given off by anthracite, and very small quantities are given off by semianthracite. As volatile matter increases to as much as 40% of the coal (dry and ash-free basis), increasing amounts of oils and tars are released. However, for coals of higher volatile content, the quantity of oils and tars decreases and is relatively low in the subbituminous coals and in lignite.

Fixed carbon is the combustible residue left after the volatile matter is driven off. It is not all carbon. Its form and hardness are an indication of fuel coking properties and, therefore, guide the choice of combustion equipment. Generally, fixed carbon represents that portion of fuel that must be burned in the solid state.

Moisture is difficult to determine accurately because a sample can lose moisture on exposure to the atmosphere, particularly when reducing the sample size for analysis. To correct for this loss, total moisture content of a sample is customarily determined by adding the moisture loss obtained when air-drying the sample to the measured moisture content of the dried sample. Moisture does not represent all of the water present in coal; water of decomposition (combined water) and of hydration are not given off under standardized test conditions.

Ash is the noncombustible residue remaining after complete coal combustion. Generally, the mass of ash is slightly less than that of mineral matter before burning.

Sulfur is an undesirable constituent in coal, because sulfur oxides formed when it burns contribute to air pollution and cause combustion system corrosion. Table 12 lists the sulfur content of typical coals. Legislation has limited the sulfur content of coals burned in certain locations.

Heating value may be reported on an as-received, dry, dry and mineral-matter-free, or moist and mineral-matter-free basis. Higher heating values of coals are frequently reported with their proximate analysis. When more specific data are lacking, the higher heating value of higher-quality coals can be calculated by the Dulong formula:

$$\text{Higher heating value, Btu/lb} = 14{,}544C + 62{,}028[H - (O/8)] + 4050S \tag{5}$$

where C, H, O, and S are the mass fractions of carbon, hydrogen, oxygen, and sulfur in the coal obtained from the ultimate analysis.

Other important parameters in judging coal suitability include

- **Ultimate analysis**, which is another method of reporting coal composition. Percentages of C, H, O, N, S, and ash in the coal sample are reported. Ultimate analysis is used for detailed fuel studies and for computing a heat balance when required in heating device testing. Typical ultimate analyses of various coals are shown in Table 12.
- **Ash-fusion temperature**, which indicates the fluidity of the ash at elevated temperatures. It is helpful in selecting coal to be burned in a particular furnace and in estimating the possibility of ash handling and slagging problems.
- The **grindability index**, which indicates the ease with which a coal can be pulverized and is helpful in estimating ball mill capacity with various coals. There are two common methods for determining the index: Hardgrove (see Hardgrove Grindability Index at www.acarp.com.au/Media/ACARP-WP-5-Hardgrove GrindabilityIndex.pdf) and ball mill.
- The **free-swelling index**, which denotes the extent of coal swelling on combustion on a fuel bed and indicates the coking characteristics of coal.

Table 11 Classification of Coals by Rank[a]

Class	Group	Limits of Fixed Carbon or Energy Content, Mineral-Matter-Free Basis	Requisite Physical Properties
I Anthracite	1. Metaanthracite	Dry FC, 98% or more (Dry VM, 2% or less)	Nonagglomerating
	2. Anthracite	Dry FC, 92% or more, and less than 98% (Dry VM, 8% or less, and more than 2%)	
	3. Semianthracite	Dry FC, 86% or more, and less than 92% (Dry VM, 14% or less, and more than 8%)	
II Bituminous[d]	1. Low-volatile bituminous coal	Dry FC, 78% or more, and less than 86% (Dry VM, 22% or less, and more than 14%)	Either agglomerating[b] or nonweathering[f]
	2. Medium-volatile bituminous coal	Dry FC, 69% or more, and less than 78% (Dry VM, 31% or less, and more than 22%)	
	3. High-volatile Type A bituminous coal	Dry FC, less than 69% (Dry VM, more than 31%), and moist,[c] about 14,000 Btu/lb[e] or more	
	4. High-volatile Type B bituminous coal	Moist,[c] about 13,000 Btu/lb or more, and less than 14,000 Btu/lb[e]	
	5. High-volatile Type C bituminous coal	Moist,[c] about 11,000 Btu/lb or more, and less than 13,000 Btu/lb[e]	
III Subbituminous	1. Subbituminous Type A coal	Moist,[c] about 11,000 Btu/lb or more, and less than 13,000 Btu/lb[e]	Both weathering and nonagglomerating[b]
	2. Subbituminous Type B coal	Moist,[c] about 9,500 Btu/lb or more, and less than 11,000 Btu/lb[e]	
	3. Subbituminous Type C coal	Moist,[c] about 8,300 Btu/lb or more, and less than 9,500 Btu/lb[e]	
IV Lignitic	1. Lignite	Moist,[c] less than 8,300 Btu/lb	Consolidated
	2. Brown coal	Moist,[c] less than 8,300 Btu/lb	Unconsolidated

Source: Data from ASTM *Standard* D388.
FC = fixed carbon; VM = volatile matter; MMF = mineral-matter-free
[a]Classification does not include a few coals of unusual physical and chemical properties that come within limits of fixed carbon or energy content of high-volatile bituminous and subbituminous ranks. All these coals either contain less than 48% dry, MMF FC, or have more than about 15,500 Btu/lb, which is moist, MMF.
[b]If agglomerating, classify in group 1 of class II.
[c]*Moist* refers to coal containing natural bed moisture but without visible water on coal surface.
[d]There may be noncaking varieties in each group of class II.
[e]Coals with 69% or more fixed carbon on dry, MMF basis are classified according to FC, regardless of energy content.
[f]There are three varieties of coal in group 5: variety 1, agglomerating and nonweathering; variety 2, agglomerating and weathering; and variety 3, nonagglomerating and nonweathering.

Table 12 Typical Ultimate Analyses for Coals

Rank	As Received, Btu/lb	Constituents, Percent by Mass O	H	C	N	S	Ash
Anthracite	12,700	5.0	2.9	80.0	0.9	0.7	10.5
Semianthracite	13,600	5.0	3.9	80.4	1.1	1.1	8.5
Low-volatile bituminous	14,350	5.0	4.7	81.7	1.4	1.2	6.0
Medium-volatile bituminous	14,000	5.0	5.0	81.4	1.4	1.5	6.0
High-volatile bituminous							
Type A	13,800	9.3	5.3	75.9	1.5	1.5	6.5
B	12,500	13.8	5.5	67.8	1.4	3.0	8.5
C	11,000	20.6	5.8	59.6	1.1	3.5	9.4
Subbituminous							
Type B	9,000	29.5	6.2	52.5	1.0	1.0	9.8
C	8,500	35.7	6.5	46.4	0.8	1.0	9.6
Lignite	6,900	44.0	6.9	40.1	0.7	1.0	7.3

6. COMBUSTION CALCULATIONS

Calculations of the quantities of (1) air required for combustion and (2) flue gas products generated during combustion are frequently needed for sizing system components and as input to efficiency calculations. Other calculations, such as values for excess air and theoretical CO_2, are useful in estimating combustion system performance.

Frequently, combustion calculations can be simplified by using molecular mass. The molecular mass of a compound equals the sum of the atomic masses of the elements in the compound. Molecular mass can be expressed in any mass units. The pound molecular weight or pound mole is the molecular weight of the compound expressed in pounds. The molecular weight of any substance contains the same number of molecules as the molecular weight of any other substance.

Corresponding to measurement standards common to the industries, calculations involving gaseous fuels are generally based on volume, and those involving liquid and solid fuels generally use mass.

Some calculations described here require data on concentrations of carbon dioxide, carbon monoxide, and oxygen in the flue gas. Gas analyses for CO_2, CO, and O_2 can be obtained by volumetric chemical analysis and other analytical techniques, including electromechanical cells used in portable electronic flue gas analyzers.

Air Required for Combustion

Stoichiometric (or theoretical) air is the exact quantity of air required to provide oxygen for complete combustion.

The three most prevalent components in hydrocarbon fuels (C, H_2, and S) are completely burned as in the following fundamental reactions:

$$C + O_2 \rightarrow CO_2$$
$$H_2 + 0.5O_2 \rightarrow H_2O$$
$$S + O_2 \rightarrow SO_2$$

In the reactions, C, H_2, and S can be taken to represent 1 lb mole of carbon, hydrogen, and sulfur, respectively. Using approximate atomic masses (C = 12, H = 1, S = 32, and O = 16), 12 lb of C are oxidized by 32 lb of O_2 to form 44 lb of CO_2, 2 lb of H_2 are oxidized by 16 lb of O_2 to form 18 lb of H_2O, and 32 lb of S are oxidized by 32 lb of O_2 to form 64 lb of SO_2. These relationships can be extended to include hydrocarbons.

The mass of dry air required to supply a given quantity of oxygen is 4.32 times the mass of the oxygen. The mass of air required to oxidize the fuel constituents listed in Table 1 was calculated on this basis. Deduct oxygen contained in the fuel, except the amount in ash, from the amount of oxygen required, because this oxygen is already combined with fuel components. In addition, when calculating the mass of supply air for combustion, allow for water vapor, which is always present in atmospheric air.

Combustion calculations for gaseous fuels are based on volume. **Avogadro's law** states that, for any gas, one mole occupies the same volume at a given temperature and pressure. Therefore, in reactions involving gaseous compounds, the gases react in volume ratios identical to the pound mole ratios. That is, to oxidize hydrogen in the preceding reaction, one volume (or 1 lb mole) of hydrogen reacts with one-half volume (or 0.5 lb mole) of oxygen to form one volume (or 1 lb mole) of water vapor.

The volume of air required to supply a given volume of oxygen is 4.78 times the volume of oxygen. The volumes of dry air required to oxidize the fuel constituents listed in Table 1 were calculated on this basis. Volume ratios are not given for fuels that do not exist in vapor form at reasonable temperatures or pressures. Again, oxygen contained in the fuel should be deducted from the quantity of oxygen required, because this oxygen is already combined with fuel components. Allow for water vapor, which increases the volume of dry air by 1 to 3%.

From the relationships just described, the theoretical mass m_a of dry air required for stoichiometric combustion of a unit mass of any hydrocarbon fuel is

$$m_a = 0.0144(8C + 24H + 3S - 3O) \qquad (6)$$

where C, H, S, and O are the mass percentages of carbon, hydrogen, sulfur, and oxygen in the fuel.

Analyses of gaseous fuels are generally based on hydrocarbon components rather than elemental content.

If fuel analysis is based on mass, the theoretical mass m_a of dry air required for stoichiometric combustion of a unit mass of gaseous fuel is

$$\begin{aligned} m_a = {} & 2.47CO + 34.28H_2 + 17.24CH_4 + 16.09C_2H_6 \\ & + 15.68C_3H_8 + 15.47C_4H_{10} + 13.27C_2H_2 \\ & + 14.78C_2H_4 + 6.08H_2S - 4.32O_2 \end{aligned} \qquad (7)$$

If fuel analysis is reported on a volumetric or molecular basis, it is simplest to calculate air requirements based on volume and, if necessary, convert to mass. The theoretical volume V_a of air required for stoichiometric combustion of a unit volume of gaseous fuels is

$$\begin{aligned} V_a = {} & 2.39CO + 2.39H_2 + 9.57CH_4 + 16.75C_2H_6 \\ & + 23.95C_3H_8 + 31.14C_4H_{10} + 11.96C_2H_2 \\ & + 14.38C_2H_4 + 7.18H_2S - 4.78O_2 \\ & + 30.47 \text{ illuminants} \end{aligned} \qquad (8)$$

where CO, H_2, and so forth are the volumetric fractions of each constituent in the fuel gas.

Illuminants include a variety of compounds not separated by usual gas analysis. In addition to ethylene (C_2H_4) and acetylene (C_2H_2), the principal illuminants included in Equation (8), and the dry air required for combustion, per unit volume of each gas, are as follows: propylene (C_3H_6), 21.44; butylene (C_4H_8), 28.58; pentene (C_5H_{10}), 35.73; benzene (C_6H_6); 35.73, toluene (C_7H_8), 42.88; and xylene (C_8H_{10}), 50.02. Because toluene and xylene are normally scrubbed from the gas before distribution, they can be disregarded in computing air required for combustion of gaseous fuels. The percentage of illuminants present in gaseous fuels is small, so the values can be lumped together, and an approximate value of 30 unit volumes of dry air per unit volume of gas can be used. If ethylene and acetylene are included as illuminants, a value of 20 unit volumes of dry air per unit volume of gaseous illuminants can be used.

For many combustion calculations, only approximate values of air requirements are necessary. If approximate values for theoretical air are sufficient, or if complete information on the fuel is not available, the values in Tables 13 and 14 can be used. Another value used for estimating air requirements is 0.9 ft³ of air for 100 Btu of fuel.

In addition to the amount theoretically required for combustion, **excess air** must be supplied to most practical combustion systems to ensure complete combustion:

$$\text{Excess air, \%} = \frac{\text{Air supplied} - \text{Theoretical air}}{\text{Theoretical air}} \qquad (9)$$

The excess air level at which a combustion process operates significantly affects its overall efficiency. Too much excess air dilutes flue gas excessively, lowering its heat transfer temperature and increasing sensible flue gas loss. Conversely, too little excess air can lead to incomplete combustion and loss of unburned combustible gases. Combustion efficiency is usually maximized when just enough excess air is supplied and properly mixed with combustible gases to ensure complete combustion. The general practice is to supply 5 to 50% excess air, depending on the type of fuel burned, combustion equipment, and other factors.

The amount of dry air supplied per unit mass of fuel burned can be obtained from the following equation, which is reasonably precise for most solid and liquid fuels:

$$\text{Dry air supplied} = \frac{C(3.04N_2)}{CO_2 + CO} \qquad (10)$$

where

Dry air supplied = unit mass per unit mass of fuel
C = unit mass of carbon burned per unit mass of fuel, corrected for carbon in ash
CO_2, CO, N_2 = percentages by volume from flue gas analysis

These values of dry air supplied and theoretical air can be used in Equation (9) to determine excess air.

Excess air can also be calculated from unit volumes of stoichiometric combustion products and air, and from volumetric analysis of the flue gas:

$$\text{Excess air, \%} = 100\left(\frac{P}{A}\right)\left(\frac{U - CO_2}{CO_2}\right) \qquad (11)$$

where

U = ultimate carbon dioxide of flue gases resulting from stoichiometric combustion, %
CO_2 = carbon dioxide content of flue gases, %
P = dry products from stoichiometric combustion, unit volume per unit volume of gas burned

Table 13 Approximate Air Requirements for Stoichiometric Combustion of Fuels by Category

Type of Fuel	Air Required: lb/lb Fuel	Air Required: ft³/Unit Fuel*	Approx. Precision, %	Exceptions
Solid	Btu/lb × 0.00073	Btu/lb × 0.0097	3	Fuels containing more than 30% water
Liquid	Btu/lb × 0.00071	Btu/lb × 0.0094	3	Results low for gasoline and kerosene
Gas	Btu/lb × 0.00067	Btu/lb × 0.0089	5	300 Btu/ft³ or less

Source: Data based on Shnidman (1954).
*Unit fuel for solid and liquid fuels in lb, for gas in ft³.

Table 14 Theoretical Air Requirements for Stoichiometric Combustion of Various Fuels

Type of Fuel	Theoretical Air Required for Combustion
Solid fuels	lb/lb fuel
Anthracite	9.6
Semibituminous	11.2
Bituminous	10.3
Lignite	6.2
Coke	11.2
Liquid fuels	lb/gal fuel
No. 1 fuel oil	103
No. 2 fuel oil	106
No. 5 fuel oil	112
No. 6 fuel oil	114
Gaseous fuels	ft³/ft³ fuel
Natural gas	9.6
Butane	31.1
Propane	24.0

Table 15 Approximate Maximum Theoretical (Stoichiometric) CO_2 Values, and CO_2 Values of Various Fuels with Different Percentages of Excess Air

Type of Fuel	Theoretical or Maximum CO_2, %	Percent CO_2 at Given Excess Air Values		
		20%	40%	60%
Gaseous fuels				
Natural gas	12.1	9.9	8.4	7.3
Propane gas (commercial)	13.9	11.4	9.6	8.4
Butane gas (commercial)	14.1	11.6	9.8	8.5
Mixed gas (natural and carbureted water gas)	11.2	12.5	10.5	9.1
Carbureted water gas	17.2	14.2	12.1	10.6
Coke oven gas	11.2	9.2	7.8	6.8
Liquid fuels				
No. 1 and 2 fuel oil	15.0	12.3	10.5	9.1
No. 6 fuel oil	16.5	13.6	11.6	10.1
Solid fuels				
Bituminous coal	18.2	15.1	12.9	11.3
Anthracite	20.2	16.8	14.4	12.6
Coke	21.0	17.5	15.0	13.0

A = air required for stoichiometric combustion, unit volume per unit volume of gas burned

Because the ratio P/A is approximately 0.9 for most natural gases, a value of 90 can be substituted for $100(P/A)$ in Equation (11) for rough calculation.

Because excess air calculations are almost invariably made from flue gas analysis results and theoretical air requirements are not always known, another convenient method of expressing Equation (9) is

$$\text{Excess air, \%} = \frac{100[O_2 - (CO/2)]}{0.264N_2 - [O_2 - (CO/2)]} \tag{12}$$

where O_2, CO, and N_2 are percentages by volume from the flue gas analysis, dry basis.

Theoretical CO_2

The theoretical (or ultimate, stoichiometric, or maximum) CO_2 concentration attainable in the products from the combustion of a hydrocarbon fuel with air is obtained when the fuel is completely burned with the theoretical quantity of air and zero excess air. Theoretical CO_2 varies with the carbon/hydrogen ratio of the fuel. For combustion with excess air present, theoretical CO_2 values can be calculated from the flue gas analysis:

$$\text{Theoretical } CO_2\text{, \%} = U = \frac{CO_2}{1-(O_2/20.95)} \tag{13}$$

where CO_2 and O_2 are percentages by volume from the flue gas analysis, dry basis.

Table 15 gives approximate theoretical CO_2 values for stoichiometric combustion of several common types of fuel, as well as CO_2 values attained with different amounts of excess air. In practice, desirable CO_2 values depend on the excess air, fuel, firing method, and other considerations.

Quantity of Flue Gas Produced

The mass of dry flue gas produced per mass of fuel burned is required in heat loss and efficiency calculations. This mass is equal to the sum of the mass of (1) fuel (minus ash retained in the furnace), (2) air theoretically required for combustion, and (3) excess air. For solid fuels, this mass, determined from the flue gas analysis, is

$$\text{Dry flue gas} = \frac{11CO_2 + 8O_2 + 7(CO + N_2)}{3(CO_2 + CO)} \tag{14}$$

where

Dry flue gas = lb/lb of fuel
C = lb of carbon burned per lb of fuel, corrected for carbon in ash
CO_2, O_2, CO, N_2 = percentages by volume from flue gas analysis

The total dry gas volume of flue gases from combustion of one unit volume of gaseous fuels for various percentages of CO_2 is

$$\text{Dry flue gas} = \left(\frac{\text{Volume of } CO_2 \text{ produced}}{\text{Unit vol. of gas burned}}\right)\left(\frac{100}{CO_2}\right) \tag{15}$$

where

Dry flue gas = unit volume per unit volume of gaseous fuel
CO_2 = percentage by volume from the flue gas analysis

Excess air quantity can be estimated by subtracting the quantity of dry flue gases resulting from stoichiometric combustion from the total volume of flue gas.

Water Vapor and Dew Point of Flue Gas

Water vapor in flue gas is the total of the water (1) contained in the fuel, (2) contained in the stoichiometric and excess air, and (3) produced from combustion of hydrogen or hydrocarbons in the fuel. The amount of water vapor in stoichiometric combustion products may be calculated from the fuel burned by using the water data in Table 1.

The dew point is the temperature at which condensation begins and can be determined using Figure 3. The volume fraction of water vapor P_{wv} in the flue gas can be determined as follows:

$$P_{wv} = \frac{V_w}{(100V_c/P_c) + V_w} \tag{16}$$

where

V_w = total water vapor volume (from fuel; stoichiometric, excess, and dilution air; and combustion)
V_c = unit volume of CO_2 produced per unit volume of gaseous fuel
P_c = percent CO_2 in flue gas

Using Figure 4, the dew points of solid, liquid, or gaseous fuels may be estimated. For example, to find the dew point of flue gas resulting from the combustion of a solid fuel with a weight ratio

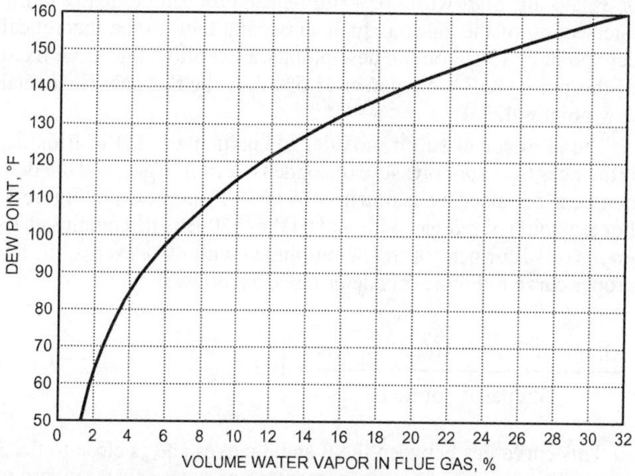

Fig. 3 Water Vapor and Dew Point of Flue Gas
Adapted from *Gas Engineers Handbook* (1965). Printed with permission of Industrial Press and American Gas Association.

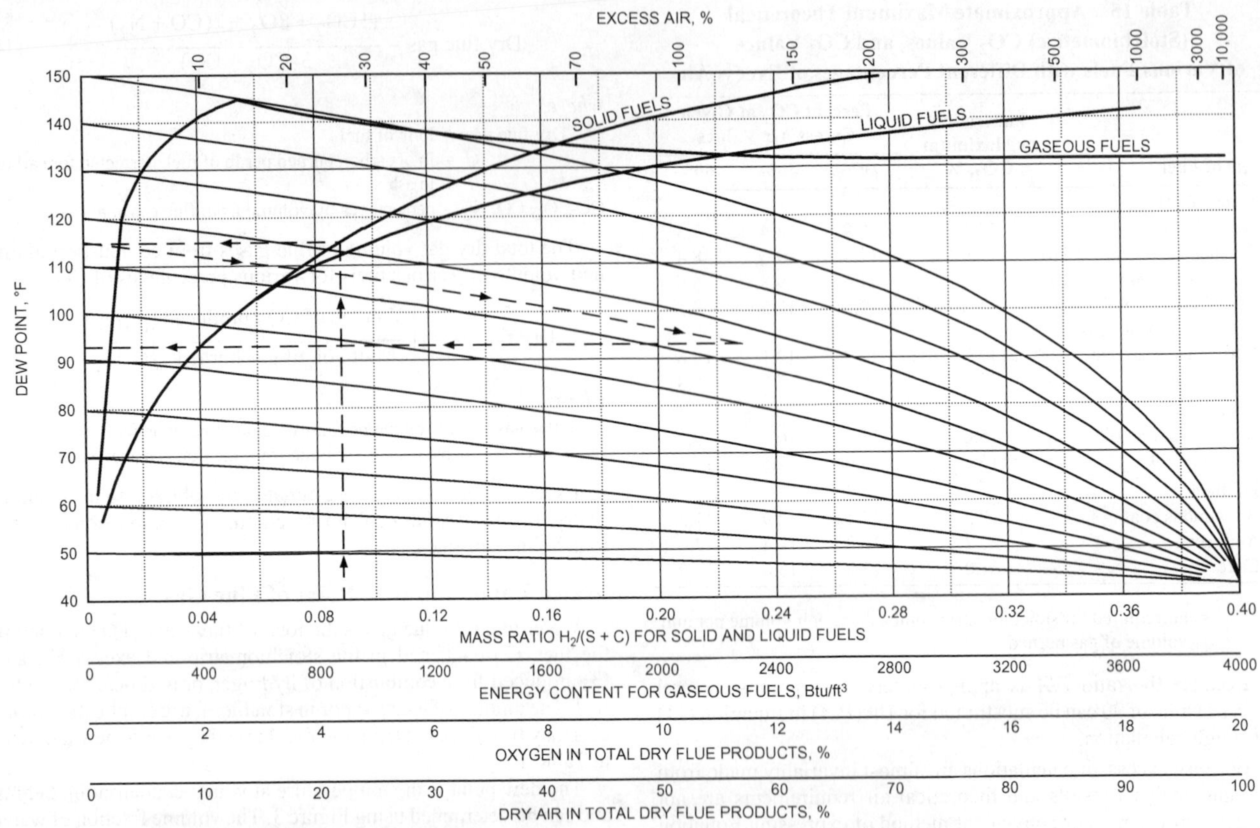

Fig. 4 Theoretical Dew Points of Combustion Products of Industrial Fuels

Adapted from *Gas Engineers Handbook* (1965). Printed with permission of Industrial Press and American Gas Association.

(hydrogen to carbon-plus-sulfur) of 0.088 and sufficient excess air to produce 11.4% oxygen in the flue gas, start with the weight ratio of 0.088. Proceed vertically to the intersection of the solid fuels curve and then to the theoretical dew point of 115°F on the dew-point scale (see dashed lines in Figure 4). Follow the curve fixed by this point (down and to the right) to 11.4% oxygen in the flue gas (on the abscissa). The actual dew point is 93°F and is found on the dew-point scale.

The dew point can be estimated for flue gas from natural gas having a higher heating value (HHV) of 1020 Btu/ft³ with 6.3% oxygen or 31.5% air. Start with 1020 Btu/ft³ and proceed vertically to the intersection of the gaseous fuels curve and then to the theoretical dew point of 139°F on the dew-point scale. Follow the curve fixed by this point to 6.3% oxygen or 31.5% air in the flue gas. The actual dew point is 127°F.

The presence of sulfur dioxide, and particularly sulfur trioxide, influences the vapor pressure of condensate in flue gas, and the dew point can be raised by as much as 25 to 75°F, as shown in Figure 5. For a manufactured gas with an HHV of 550 Btu/ft³ containing 15 grains of sulfur per 100 ft³ being burned with 40% excess air, the proper curve in Figure 5 is determined as follows:

$$\frac{\text{Grains sulfur per 100 ft}^3\text{ of fuel}}{\text{Btu per ft}^3\text{ of fuel}} \times 100 = \frac{15}{550} \times 100 = 2.73 \quad (17)$$

This curve lies between the 0 and 3 curves and is close to the 3 curve. The dew point for any percentage of excess air from zero to 100% can be determined on this curve. For this flue gas with 40% excess air, the dew point is about 160°F, instead of 127°F for zero sulfur at 40% excess air.

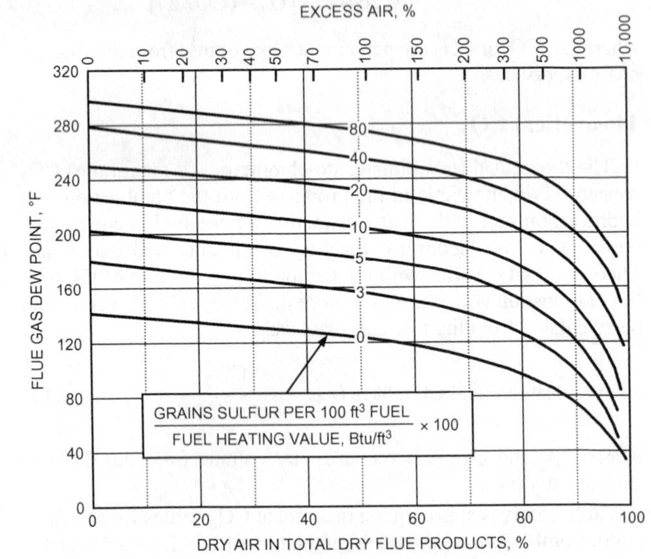

Fig. 5 Influence of Sulfur Oxides on Flue Gas Dew Point

Sample Combustion Calculations

Example 2. Analysis of flue gases from burning a natural gas shows 10.0% CO_2, 3.1% O_2, and 86.9% N_2 by volume. Analysis of the fuel is 90% CH_4, 5% N_2, and 5% C_2H_6 by volume. Find U (maximum theoretical percent CO_2), and percentage of excess air.

Solution: From Equation (13),

$$U = \frac{10.0}{1-(3.1/20.95)} = 11.74\%\ CO_2$$

From Equation (11), using $100(P/A) = 90$,

$$\text{Excess air} = \frac{(11.74 - 10.0)90}{10} = 15.7\%$$

Example 3. For the same analysis as in Example 2, find, per cubic foot of fuel gas, the volume of dry air required for combustion, the volume of each constituent in the flue gases, and the total volume of dry and wet flue gases.

Solution: From Equation (8), the volume of dry air required for combustion is

$$9.57CH_4 + 16.75C_2H_6 = (9.57 \times 0.90) + (16.75 \times 0.05)$$
$$= 9.45\ \text{ft}^3 \text{ per ft}^3 \text{ of fuel gas}$$

(The volume of dry air may also be calculated using Table 14.)

From Table 1, the cubic feet of flue gas constituents per cubic foot of fuel gas are as follows:

Nitrogen, N_2		
From methane	$(0.9CH_4)(9.57 - 2.0)$	= 6.81
From ethane	$(0.05C_2H_6)(16.75 - 3.5)$	= 0.66
Nitrogen in fuel		= 0.05
Nitrogen in excess air	$0.791 \times 0.157 \times 9.45$	= 1.17
	Total nitrogen	= 8.69 ft³
Oxygen, O_2		
In excess air	$0.209 \times 0.157 \times 9.45$	= 0.31 ft³
Carbon dioxide, CO_2		
From methane	$(0.9CH_4)(1.0)$	= 0.90
From ethane	$(0.05C_2H_6)(2.0)$	= 0.10
	Total carbon dioxide	= 1.00 ft³
Water vapor, H_2O (does not appear in some flue gas analyses)		
From methane	$(0.9CH_4)(2.0)$	= 1.8
From ethane	$(0.05C_2H_6)(3.0)$	= 0.15
	Total water vapor	= 1.95 ft³

Total volume of dry gas per cubic foot of fuel gas

$$8.69 + 0.31 + 1.00 = 10.0\ \text{ft}^3$$

Total volume of wet gases per cubic foot of fuel gas (neglecting water vapor in combustion air)

$$10.0 + 1.95 = 11.95\ \text{ft}^3$$

The cubic feet of dry flue gas per cubic foot of fuel gas can also be computed from Equation (15):

$$(1.00)(100)/10.0 = 10.0\ \text{ft}^3$$

7. EFFICIENCY CALCULATIONS

In analyzing heating appliance efficiency, an energy balance is made that accounts (as much as possible) for disposition of all thermal energy released by combustion of the fuel quantity consumed. The various components of this balance are generally expressed in terms of Btu/lb of fuel burned or as a percentage of its higher heating value. The following are major components of an energy balance and their calculation methods:

1. Useful heat q_1, or heat transferred to the heated medium; for convection heating equipment, this value is computed as the product of the mass rate of flow and enthalpy change.
2. Heat loss as sensible heat in the dry flue gases

$$q_2 = m_g c_{pg}(t_g - t_a) \quad (18)$$

where m_g (mass of dry flue gas per mass of fuel, lb/lb) is calculated as in Equation (14).

3. Heat loss in water vapor in products formed by combustion of hydrogen

$$q_3 = (9H_2/100)[(h)_{tg} - (h_f)_{ta}] \quad (19)$$

4. Heat loss in water vapor in the combustion air

$$q_4 = Mm_a[(h)_{tg} - (h_g)_{ta}] \quad (20)$$

where m_a is calculated as in Equations (6) and (7).

5. Heat loss from incomplete combustion of carbon

$$q_5 = 10{,}143C\left(\frac{CO}{CO_2 + CO}\right) \quad (21)$$

6. Heat loss from unburned carbon in the ash or refuse

$$q_6 = 14{,}600[(C_u/100) - C] \quad (22)$$

7. Unaccounted-for heat losses, q_7

The following symbols are used in Equations (18) to (22):

q_1 = useful heat, Btu/lb of fuel
q_2 = heat loss in dry flue gases, Btu/lb of fuel
q_3 = heat loss in water vapor from combustion of hydrogen, Btu/lb of fuel
q_4 = heat loss in water vapor in combustion air, Btu/lb of fuel
q_5 = heat loss from incomplete combustion of carbon, Btu/lb of fuel
q_6 = heat loss from unburned carbon in ash, Btu/lb of fuel
q_7 = unaccounted-for heat losses, Btu/lb of fuel
c_{pg} = mean specific heat of flue gases at constant pressure (from 0.242 to 0.254 Btu/lb·°F for flue gas temperatures from 300 to 1000°F), Btu/lb·°F
$(h)_{tg}$ = enthalpy of superheated steam at flue gas temperature and 14.696 psia, Btu/lb
$(h_f)_{ta}$ = enthalpy of saturated water liquid at air temperature, Btu/lb
$(h_g)_{ta}$ = enthalpy of saturated steam at combustion air temperature, Btu/lb
m_a = mass of combustion air per mass of fuel used, lb/lb of fuel
m_g = mass of dry flue gas per mass of fuel, lb/lb of fuel
t_a = temperature of combustion air, °F
t_g = temperature of flue gases at exit of heating device, °F
H_2 = hydrogen in fuel, % by mass (from ultimate analysis of fuel)
M = humidity ratio of combustion air, mass of water vapor per mass of dry air
CO, CO_2 = carbon monoxide and carbon dioxide in flue gases, % by volume
C = mass of carbon burned per unit of mass of fuel, corrected for carbon in ash, lb/lb of fuel

$$C = \frac{WC_u - W_aC_a}{100W} \quad (23)$$

where

C_u = percentage of carbon in fuel by mass from ultimate analysis
W_a = mass of ash and refuse
C_a = percent of combustible in ash by mass (combustible in ash is usually considered to be carbon)
W = mass of fuel used

Useful heat (item 1) is generally measured for a particular piece of combustion equipment.

Flue gas loss is the sum of items 2 to 6. However, for clean-burning gas- and oil-fired equipment, items 5 and 6 are usually negligible and flue gas loss is the sum of items 2, 3, and 4.

Flue gas losses (the sum of items 2, 3, and 4) can be determined with sufficient precision for most purposes from the curves in Figure 6, if O_2 content and flue gas temperature are known. Values of the losses were computed from typical ultimate analyses, assuming 1% water vapor (by mass) in the combustion air. Curves for medium-volatile bituminous coal can be used for high-volatile bituminous coal with no appreciable error.

Generally, item 5 is negligible for modern combustion equipment in good operating condition.

Item 6 is generally negligible for gas and oil firing, but should be determined for coal-firing applications.

Item 7 consists primarily of radiation and convection losses from combustion equipment surfaces and losses caused by incomplete combustion not included in items 5 and 6. Heat loss from incomplete combustion is determined by subtracting the sum of items 1 to 6 from the fuel heating value.

Radiation and convection losses are not usually determined by direct measurement, but if the heating appliance is located within the heated space, radiation and convection losses can be considered useful heat rather than lost heat and can be omitted from heat loss calculations or added to item 1.

If CO is present in flue gases, small amounts of unburned hydrogen and hydrocarbons may also be present. The small losses caused by incomplete combustion of these gases would be included in item 7, if item 7 was determined by subtracting items 1 to 6 from the fuel heating value.

The overall thermal efficiency of combustion equipment is defined as

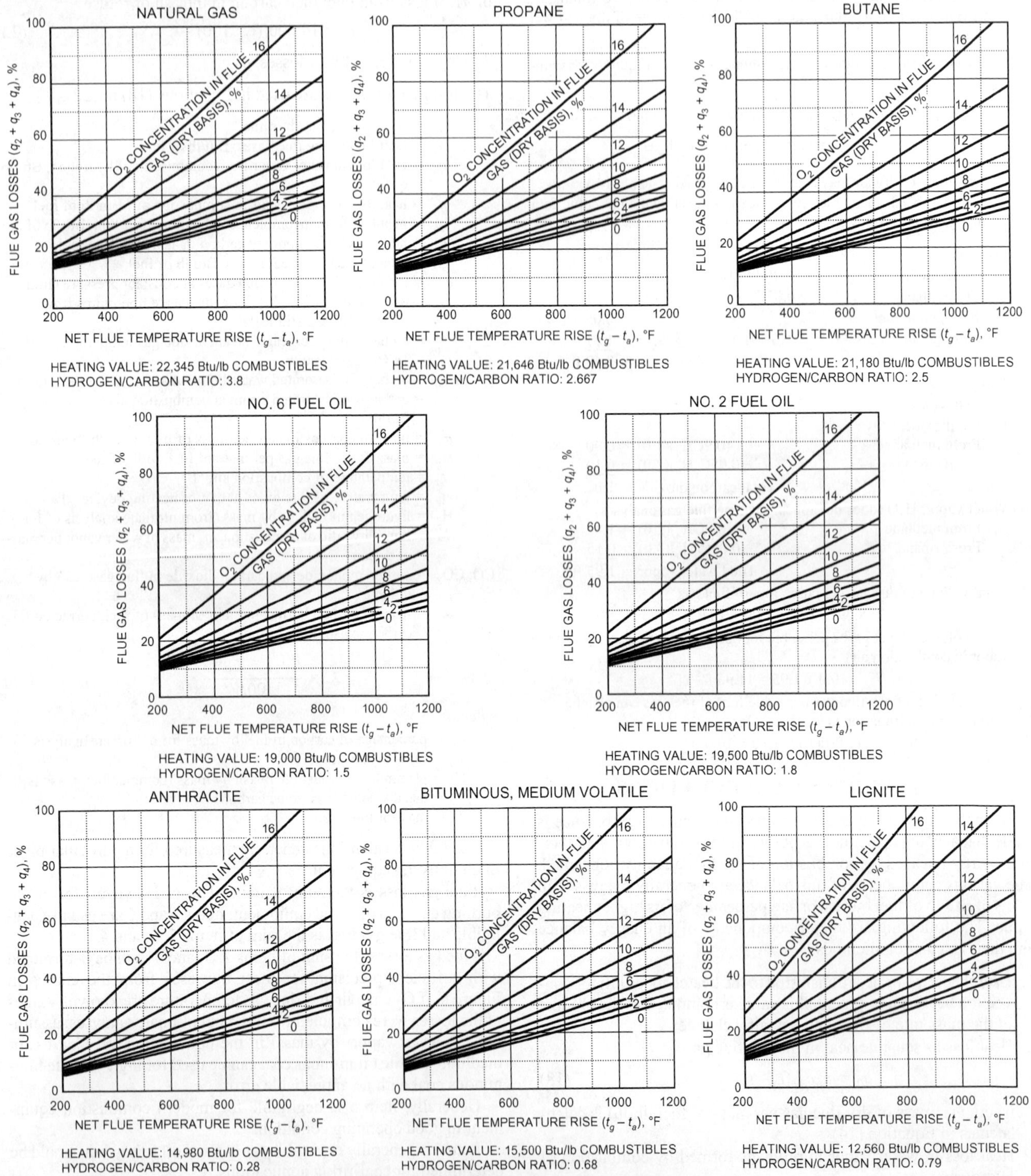

Fig. 6 Flue Gas Losses with Various Fuels
(Flue gas temperature rise shown. Loss based on 65°F room temperature.)

$$\text{Thermal efficiency, \%} = 100 \times \frac{\text{Useful heat}}{\text{Heating value of fuel}} \quad (24)$$

Equation (25) can be used to estimate efficiency for equipment where item 7 is small or radiation and convection are useful heat:

$$\text{Thermal efficiency, \%} = 100 \times \frac{\text{Heating value of fuel} - (q_2 + q_3 + q_4 + q_5 + q_6)}{\text{Heating value of fuel}} \quad (25)$$

Using heating values based on gas volume, a gas appliance's thermal efficiency can be computed with sufficient precision by the following equation:

$$\eta = \frac{100(Q_h - Q_{fl})}{Q_h} \quad (26)$$

where

η = thermal efficiency, %
Q_h = higher heating value of fuel gas per unit volume
Q_{fl} = flue gas losses per unit volume of fuel gas

To produce heat efficiently by burning any common fuel, flue gas losses must be minimized by (1) providing adequate heat-absorbing surface in the appliance, (2) keeping heat transfer surfaces clean on both fire and water or air sides, and (3) reducing excess air to the minimum level consistent with complete combustion and discharge of combustion products.

Seasonal Efficiency

The method just presented is useful for calculating the steady-state efficiency of a heating system or device. Unfortunately, the seasonal efficiency can be significantly different from the steady-state efficiency. The primary factor affecting seasonal efficiency is flue loss during the burner-off period. The warm stack that exists at the end of the firing period can cause airflow in the stack while the burner is off, which can remove heat from furnace and heat exchanger components, the structure itself, and pilot flames. Also, if combustion air is drawn from the heated space within the structure, the heated air lost must be at least partly replaced with cold infiltrated air. For further discussion of seasonal efficiency, see Chapters 10 and 33 of the 2016 *ASHRAE Handbook—HVAC Systems and Equipment* and Chapter 19 of this volume.

8. COMBUSTION CONSIDERATIONS

Air Pollution

Combustion processes constitute the largest single source of anthropogenic (human-caused) air pollution. Pollutants can be grouped into five categories:

- Products of incomplete fuel combustion
  - Combustible aerosols (solid and liquid), including smoke, soot, and organics, but excluding ash
  - Carbon monoxide CO
  - Gaseous hydrocarbons
- Carbon dioxide CO_2
- Oxides of nitrogen (collectively referred to as NO_x)
  - Nitric oxide NO
  - Nitrogen dioxide NO_2
- Emissions resulting from fuel contaminants
  - Sulfur oxides, primarily sulfur dioxide SO_2 and small quantities of sulfur trioxide SO_3
  - Ash
  - Trace metals
- Emissions resulting from additives
  - Combustion-controlling additives
  - Mercaptans
  - Other additives

Table 16 NO_x Emission Factors for Combustion Sources

	NO_x Emission Factor, lb/10^6 Btu of Heat Input	
Source	**Without Emission Controls**	**With Emission Controls**
Gas-fired equipment		
Small industrial boilers	0.14	0.02
Commercial boilers	0.10	0.02
Residential furnaces	0.09	0.03
Distillate-oil-fired small industrial boilers, commercial boilers, and residential furnaces	0.14	
Residual-oil-fired small industrial boilers and commercial boilers	0.37	

Emission levels of nitrogen oxides and products of incomplete combustion are directly related to the combustion process and can be controlled, to some extent, by process modification. Emissions from fuel contaminants are related to fuel selection and are slightly affected by the combustion process. Emissions from additives must be considered in the overall evaluation of the merits of using additives.

Carbon dioxide as a pollutant has gained attention because of its suspected effect on global warming. Carbon dioxide is produced by HVAC&R equipment (either directly or as a result of generating the electric power to operate the HVAC&R equipment), transportation, industry, and other sources. Carbon dioxide emissions can be minimized by increasing appliance operating efficiencies and using fuels with higher hydrogen content.

Nitrogen oxides are produced during combustion, either (1) by thermal fixation (reaction of nitrogen and oxygen at high combustion temperatures), or (2) from fuel nitrogen (oxidation of organic nitrogen in fuel molecules). Unfortunately, high excess air and high flame temperature techniques, which ensure complete fuel combustion, tend to promote NO_x formation. NO levels in flames where the reactants are premixed tend to peak with excess air levels around 10%. Higher excess air levels generally reduce the amount of NO_x and flame temperatures.

Table 16 lists some NO_x emission factors for fuel-burning equipment. Differences in emissions are caused by flame temperature and different levels of fuel nitrogen. Carbon monoxide emissions depend less on fuel type and typically range from 0.03 to 0.04 lb/10^6 Btu of heat input. For gas-fired commercial and industrial boilers, particulate emissions range from 0.005 to 0.006 lb/10^6 Btu. For distillate-oil-fired commercial and industrial boilers, particulates are typically 0.014 lb/10^6 Btu. For residential oil-fired equipment, particulate emission factors are 0.003 lb/10^6 Btu. For residual-oil-fired equipment, particulate emissions depend on the sulfur content and, to a lesser extent, the mineral content. For a sulfur content of 1%, the particulate emission rate is typically 0.083 lb/10^6 Btu.

Emission levels of products of incomplete fuel combustion can be reduced by reducing burner cycling, ensuring adequate excess air, improving mixing of air and fuel (by increasing turbulence, improving distribution, and improving liquid fuel atomization), increasing residence time in the hot combustion zone (possibly by decreasing the firing rate), increasing combustion zone temperatures (to speed reactions), and avoiding quenching the flame before reactions are completed.

Relative humidity of combustion air affects the amount of NO_x produced and must be considered when specifying acceptable NO_x emission rates and measuring NO_x production during appliance tests.

The relative contribution of each of these mechanisms to the total NO_x emissions depends on the amount of organic nitrogen in the fuel. Natural gas normally contains very little nitrogen. Virtually all NO_x emissions with gas firing are due to the thermal mechanism. Nitrogen content of distillate oil varies, but an average of 20 ppm of fuel NO_x is produced (about 20 to 30% of the total NO_x). Levels in residual oil can be significantly higher, with fuel NO_x contributing heavily to the total emissions.

Thermal fixation depends strongly on flame maximum temperature. For example, increasing the flame temperature from 2600 to 2800°F increases thermal NO_x tenfold. Therefore, methods to control thermal NO_x are based on methods to reduce the maximum flame temperature. Flue gas recirculation is perhaps the most effective method for commercial and industrial boilers. In gas-fired boilers, NO_x can be reduced 70% with 15 to 20% recirculation of flue gas into the flame. The NO_x reduction decreases with increasing fuel nitrogen content. With distillate-oil firing, reductions of 60 to 70% can be achieved. In residual-oil-fired boilers, flue gas recirculation can reduce NO_x emissions by 15 to 30%. The maximum rate of flue gas recirculation is limited by combustion instability and CO production.

Two-stage firing is the only technique that reduces NO_x produced both by thermal fixation and fuel nitrogen in industrial and utility applications. The fuel-rich or air-deficient primary combustion zone retards NO_x formation early in combustion (when NO_x forms most readily from fuel nitrogen), and avoids peak temperatures, reducing thermal NO_x. Retrofit low-NO_x burners that control air distribution and fuel air mixing in the flame zone can be used to achieve staged combustion. With oil firing, NO_x reductions of 20 to 50% can be obtained with low-NO_x burners. Application of flue gas recirculation and other control methods to residential, oil-fired heating systems was reviewed by Butcher et al. (1994).

The following are some methods of reducing NO_x emissions from gas-fired appliances (Murphy and Putnam 1985):

- Total premix
- Burner adjustment
- Flame inserts (radiation screens or rods)
- Staged combustion and delayed mixing
- Secondary air baffling
- Catalytic and radiant burners
- Pulse

Radiation screens or rods (flame inserts) surrounding or inserted into the flame absorb radiation to reduce flame temperature and retard NO_x formation. Proprietary appliance burners with no flame inserts have been produced to comply with the very strict NO_x emission limitations of California's Air Quality Management Districts.

The U.S. EPA sets limits on air pollutant emissions (Source Performance Standards) from boilers larger than 10 million Btu/h of heat input. In addition, states set emission regulations that are at least as strict at the federal limits and may apply to smaller equipment.

The EPA's automobile emission standard is 1.0 g of NO_2 per mile, which is equivalent to 750 ng/J of NO_x emission. California's maximum is 0.4 g/mile, equivalent to 300 ng/J. California's Air Quality Management Districts for the South Coast (Los Angeles) and the San Francisco Bay Area limit NO_x emission to 14 ng/J of useful heat for some natural gas-fired central furnaces.

For further discussion of air pollution aspects of fuel combustion, see EPA (1971a, 1971b).

Portable Combustion Analyzers (PCAs)

These battery-powered electronic instruments, also known as flue gas analyzers (FGAs), have been widely used for over 30 years. Their sensors measure various gases found in flues of combustion appliances, whether fired by gas, oil, or solid fuels.

Users place the analyzer's probe in the flue of an appliance to extract combustion gases for measurement. These gases pass through a water trap to create a dry gas for measurement, and then have excess particles removed by a filter before entering the PCA with help from its internal pump.

The PCA's sensors measure or calculate real-time readings of oxygen (O_2), carbon monoxide (CO), and carbon dioxide (CO_2). Most PCAs also measure temperature, pressure, and draft; some measure the ratio of CO to CO_2, detect gas leaks, or measure other gases such as nitric oxide (NO), nitrogen dioxide (NO_2), sulfur dioxide (SO_2), and hydrocarbons (CH_4) and transfer test results to a printer, PC, smartphone, or tablet. If in doubt, ask the manufacturer which model is appropriate for a specific application.

Pay particular attention to the user manual's care instructions. These include switching on in outdoor air to allow sensors to tare (zero out) correctly, not leaving a PCA overnight in a cold vehicle, and ensuring the PCA is annually recertified by an authorized service provider to keep its metrological performance within specification.

An annual calibration certificate is essential. As a minimum, it should include

- PCA serial number and type
- Calibration date
- Next calibration due date or certificate expiration date
- Reference to test gases and instruments used during calibration process
- Ambient conditions at time of test
- Calibration results of parameters calibrated
- Uncertainty measurement

All calibrated PCAs should have a label or sticker applied including the name of the company who performed the work and the PCA's next service date. The label should reference the PCA using a serial number or certificate number, be tamperproof, and be placed where it can easily be seen. PCAs generally rely on service software, usually only available from the manufacturer or an approved service center. Using nonauthorized companies may invalidate the PCA's warranty and may lead to incorrect replacement parts being used.

An American PCA performance standard, AHRI *Standard* 1260P, is in development, but most PCAs are already certified to European Standard CEN *Standard* 50379, which has three parts:

- Part 1 defines general requirements of and test methods for PCAs
- Part 2 defines PCA performance requirements where statutory inspections are required
- Part 3 defines PCA performance requirements where nonstatutory inspections are required (e.g., in most European countries other than Germany and Austria)

CEN *Standard* 50379 defines which gases are included (CO, NO, SO_2, O_2, and CO_2 if fitted to the PCA) and what accuracy, response, and performance criteria PCAs must meet. The standard also tests for sensor cross sensitivity, long life, drop, and vibration to ensure reliability in normal applications under competent use. Some PCAs are used to measure ambient levels of CO and CO_2 in residential or commercial environments. In Europe, these PCAs must meet the performance requirements of CEN *Standard* 50543; some PCAs are already certified to this standard as well as to CEN *Standard* 50379.

Condensation and Corrosion

Fuel-burning systems that cycle on and off to meet demand cool down during the *off* cycle. When the appliance starts again, condensate forms briefly on surfaces until they are heated above the dew-point temperature. Low-temperature corrosion occurs in system components (heat exchangers, flues, vents, chimneys) when their surfaces remain below the dew-point temperature of flue gas constituents (water vapor, sulfides, chlorides, fluorides, etc.) long enough to cause condensation. Corrosion increases as condensate dwell time increases.

Acids in flue gas condensate are the principal substances responsible for low-temperature corrosion in fuel-fired systems. Sulfuric, hydrochloric, and other acids are formed when acidic compounds in fuel and air combustion products combine with condensed moisture in appliance heat exchangers, flues, or vents. Corrosion can be avoided by maintaining these surfaces above the flue gas dew point.

In high-efficiency, condensing-type appliances and economizers, flue gas temperatures are intentionally reduced below the flue gas dew-point temperatures to achieve efficiencies approaching 100%. In these systems, surfaces subjected to condensate must be made of corrosion-resistant materials. The most corrosive conditions exist at the leading edge of the condensing region, especially areas that experience evaporation during each cycle (Stickford et al. 1988). Draining condensate retards the concentration of acids on system surfaces; regions from which condensate partially or completely drains away before evaporation are less severely attacked than regions from which condensate does not drain before evaporation.

The metals most resistant to condensate corrosion are stainless-steel alloys with high chromium and molybdenum content, and nickel-chromium alloys with high molybdenum content (Stickford et al. 1988). Aluminum experiences general corrosion rather than pitting when exposed to flue gas condensate. If applied in sufficiently thick cross section to allow for metal loss, aluminum can be used in condensing regions. Most ceramic and high-temperature polymer materials resist the corrosive effects of flue gas condensate. These materials may have application in the condensing regions, if they can meet the structural and temperature requirements of a particular application.

In coal-fired power plants, the rate of corrosion for carbon steel condensing surfaces by mixed acids (primarily sulfuric and hydrochloric) is reported to be maximum at about 122 ± 18°F (Davis 1987). Mitigation techniques include (1) acid neutralization with a base such as NH_3 or $Ca(OH)_2$; (2) use of protective linings of glass-filled polyester or coal-tar epoxy; and (3) replacing steel with molybdenum-bearing stainless steels, nickel alloys, polymers, or other corrosion-resistant materials. Other elements in residual fuel oils and coals that contribute to high-temperature corrosion include sodium, potassium, and vanadium. Each fuel-burning system component should be evaluated during installation, or when modified, to determine the potential for corrosion and the means to retard corrosion (Paul et al. 1988).

If fuel-burning appliances accumulate condensate that does not evaporate, the condensate must be routed into a trapped drainage system. Because the condensate may be acidic, the drainage system must be suitable and environmentally acceptable. Condensate freezing must be considered in cold climates.

Abnormal Combustion Noise in Gas Appliances

During development of a new boiler, furnace, or other gas-fired appliance, tonal noise can be unacceptable. Because the frequency of the tone is equal to a resonance frequency of the system, this problem is often called a *combustion resonance*, but this term is misleading: changing the appliance's resonance frequency merely changes the frequency of the tone without much effect on the amplitude.

The proper term is **combustion-driven oscillation**, which is caused by feedback instability. Pressure oscillations in the combustion chamber (which manifest themselves as objectionable noise) also interact with the flame, modulating the instantaneous rate of combustion, which, in turn, causes more pressure oscillations (Putnam 1971). This feedback involves the acoustic response of the combustion chamber and of the fuel-air supply system, as well as that of the flame. For some combinations of response properties, the feedback loop is unstable. Instabilities may result from either perturbation of the mixture flow or of the air/fuel ratio. Instability because of a fluctuating air/fuel ratio is more likely to occur at low frequencies (Herrin et al. 2012).

The feedback loop suggested by Baade (1978) and modified by ASHRAE research project RP-1517 (Herrin et al. 2012) is very useful for understanding and solving oscillation problems. Baade identified three transfer functions that must be determined. Transfer functions Z and H are acoustic and can be determined experimentally or by simulation. Transfer function G_f is related to the flame and is best determined experimentally, though a few models are available. Figure 7 shows a schematic of Baade's feedback loop stability model for predicting combustion oscillations. Perturbations to the volume velocity of the flame, which are external to the feedback loop, are indicated by $\tilde{q}_{ext}$. The driving point impedance Z of the combustion chamber is the ratio of the oscillating pressure $\tilde{p}$ to the volume velocity in the combustion chamber $\tilde{q}_{tot}$ or $\tilde{Q}$. The transfer function H relates the perturbation of the mixture flow $\tilde{q}_i$ to the acoustic pressure in the combustion chamber $\tilde{p}$. As shown in Figure 7, the acoustic impedance of the chamber relates the flame perturbations to the sound pressure in the chamber. Acoustic impedance is primarily a function of the geometry of the combustion chamber and length of the exhaust. The sound pressure in the chamber in turn modulates either the mixture supply or air/fuel ratio. The respective transfer functions relating the sound pressures to the mixture supply or air/fuel ratio fluctuations are mainly controlled by the geometry of the intake. Mixture supply or air/fuel ratio fluctuations then drive the flame perturbations completing the feedback loop. The flame transfer function, which relates flame perturbations to the mixture supply and air/fuel ratio fluctuations, is related to several factors, including the burner type.

Predicting instability in a design is generally not practical for domestic or small commercial appliances because there is not enough information to predict the acoustic response of some of the components, particularly the flame.

A model of the feedback loop is very useful, however, for solving existing oscillation problems, where the only concern is the particular frequency at which the oscillation occurs. Reducing the response of the flame, air/fuel mixture supply, or combustion chamber at that frequency should be the focus. This concept can be easily demonstrated with a small brazing torch in a tube of variable length (Baade 1987, 2004).

In some systems, the flame can be modified to reduce its response at the oscillation frequency. Often, this involves simply changing the fuel/air ratio further away from the stochiometric ratio (Elsari and Cummings 2003; Goldschmidt et al. 1978), thus lengthening the flame, which can also be done by increasing the size of burner ports (Matsui 1981; Schimmer 1979). Other possibilities for reducing flame response are using a suitable mix of differently sized burner ports (Kagiya 2000) and modifying the heat transfer characteristics of the burner matrix (Schreel et al. 2002).

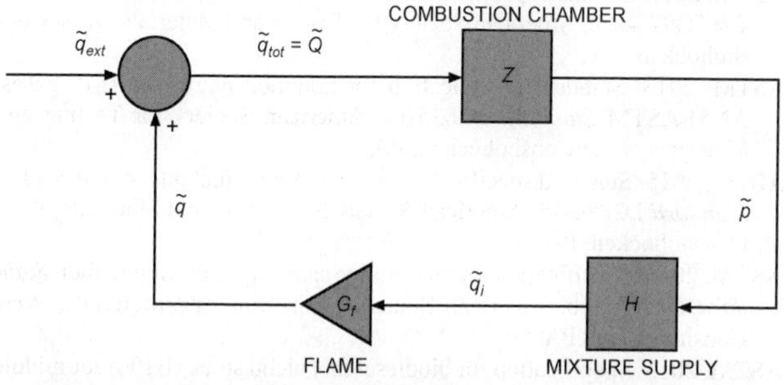

Fig. 7 Feedback Loop Stability Model Defined by Baade (1978, 2004)
(Herrin et al. 2012)

The fuel supply system response can be reduced by avoiding resonance at or near the frequency of oscillation (Kilham et al. 1964) or by tuning the supply system to an antiresonance at that frequency (Neumann 1974). Higher-flow-resistance burners add acoustic damping to the fuel supply system. Designs for this can be evaluated by modeling the mixture supply system using transmission matrices (Munjal 1987) and computer programs for matrix multiplication, which are widely available (Baade and Tomarchio 2008).

Be careful to avoid any unnecessary resonances in the combustion chamber (Herrin et al. 2012). Structural resonances are sometimes the primary cause of a combustion oscillation, and can be identified by using an impact hammer and measuring the components' vibrational response using an accelerometer. Increasing damping can effectively resolve instabilities, if the system can increase damping enough: any damping less than the critical amount will have very little effect. Acoustic damping or sound absorption can be added by installing perforated panels or fiber. However, damping treatments are only likely to be effective for instabilities at high frequencies.

In some systems, the oscillation frequency may be a function of the flue pipe length. In such cases, consider changing the length as well as adding damping.

For large systems, active feedback may be used to eliminate combustion oscillations (Sattinger et al. 2000). However, active feedback is not likely to be cost effective for residential and small commercial systems.

Soot

Soot deposits on flue surfaces of a boiler or heater act as an insulating layer over the surface, reducing heat transfer to the water or air. Soot can also clog flues, reduce draft and available air, and prevent proper combustion. Proper burner adjustment can minimize soot accumulation. Using off-specification fuel can contribute to soot generation.

REFERENCES

ASHRAE members can access *ASHRAE Journal* articles and ASHRAE research project final reports at technologyportal.ashrae.org. Articles and reports are also available for purchase by nonmembers in the online ASHRAE Bookstore at www.ashrae.org/bookstore.

AHRI. [In development.] Performance rating of flue gas combustion analyzers. *Standard* 1260P. Air-Conditioning, Heating, and Refrigeration Institute, Arlington, VA.

ASME. 2015. *Boiler and pressure vessel code*. American Society of Mechanical Engineers, New York.

ASTM. 2015. Standard classification of coals by rank. *Standard* D388-15. American Society for Testing and Materials, West Conshohocken, PA.

ASTM. 2015. Standard specification for fuel oils. ANSI/ASTM *Standard* D396-15c. American Society for Testing and Materials, West Conshohocken, PA.

ASTM. 2015. Standard specification for diesel fuel oils. ANSI/ASTM *Standard* D975-15c. American Society for Testing and Materials, West Conshohocken, PA.

ASTM. 2013. Standard specification for liquefied petroleum (LP) gases. ANSI/ASTM *Standard* D1835-13. American Society for Testing and Materials, West Conshohocken, PA.

ASTM. 2015. Standard specification for gas turbine fuel oils. ANSI/ASTM *Standard* D2880-15. American Society for Testing and Materials, West Conshohocken, PA.

ASTM. 2016. Specification for automotive spark-ignition engine fuel. *Standard* D4814-16b. American Society for Testing and Materials, West Conshohocken, PA.

ASTM. 2015. Specification for biodiesel fuel blend stock (B100) for middle distillate fuels. *Standard* D6751-15ce1. American Society for Testing and Materials, West Conshohocken, PA.

Baade, P.K. 1978. Design criteria and models for preventing combustion oscillations. *ASHRAE Transactions* 84(1):449.

Baade, P.K. 1987. Demonstration of methods for solving combustion "resonance" noise problems. *NOISE-CON '87 Proceedings*, pp. 195-200.

Baade, P.K. 2004. How to solve abnormal combustion noise problems. *Sound and Vibration* 4(7):22-27.

Baade, P.K., and M.J. Tomarchio. 2008. Tricks and tools for solving abnormal combustion noise problems. *Sound and Vibration* (July):12-17.

Butcher, T.A., L. Fisher, B. Kamath, T. Kirchstetter, and J. Batey. 1994. Nitrogen oxides (NO_x) and oil burners. *Proceedings of the 1994 Oil Heat Technology Conference and Workshops*. BNL *Report* 52430. Brookhaven National Laboratory, Upton, NY.

Butcher, T.A., S.W. Lee, Y. Celebi, and W. Litzke. 1997. Fouling of heat-transfer surfaces in oil-fired boilers for domestic heating. *Journal of the Institute of Energy* 70:151-159.

CEN. 2012. Specification for portable electrical apparatus designed to measure combustion flue gas parameters of heating appliances. Part 1—General requirements and test methods. Part 2—Performance requirements for apparatus used in statutory inspections and assessment. *Standard* 50379-1 and 2. Comité Européen de Normalisation, Brussels.

CEN. 2011. Electronic portable and transportable apparatus designed to detect and measure carbon dioxide and/or carbon monoxide in indoor ambient air—Requirements and test methods. *Standard* 50543. Comité Européen de Normalisation, Brussels.

Coward, H.F., and G.W. Jones. 1952. Limits of flammability of gases and vapors. *Bulletin* 503. U.S. Bureau of Mines, Washington, D.C.

Davis, J.R., ed. 1987. *Metals handbook*, 9th ed., vol. 13, *Corrosion*. ASM International, Metals Park, OH.

Dickson, C.L., and G.P. Sturm, Jr. 1994. *Heating oils*. National Institute for Petroleum and Energy Research, Bartlesville, OK.

DOE. 2017. *Fischer-Tropsch synthesis*. National Energy Technology Laboratory, U.S. Department of Energy, Washington, D.C. www.netl.doe.gov/research/coal/energy-systems/gasification/gasifipedia/ftsynthesis.

Elsari, M., and A. Cummings. 2003. Combustion oscillations in gas fired appliances: Eigen-frequencies and stability regimes. *Applied Acoustics* 64(6):565-580.

EPA. 1971a. Standards of performance for new stationary sources, Group I. *Federal Register* 36, August 17. U.S. Environmental Protection Agency, Washington, D.C.

EPA. 1971b. Standards of performance for new stationary sources, Group I, Part II. *Federal Register* 36, December 23. U.S. Environmental Protection Agency, Washington, D.C.

EPA. 2017. *Basic information about landfill gas*. Landfill Methane Outreach Program (LMOP). U.S. Environmental Protection Agency, Washington, D.C. www.epa.gov/lmop/basic-information-about-landfill-gas.

Fleck, B.A., S.C. Arnold, M.Y. Ackerman, J.D. Dale, W.E. Klaczek, and D.J. Wilson. 2007. Field testing and residential fan-assisted gas-fired furnaces: Effects of altitude and assessment of current derating standards. ASHRAE Research Project RP-1182, *Final Report*.

Gas engineers handbook. 1965. Industrial Press, New York.

Goldschmidt, V., R.G. Leonard, J.F. Riley, G. Wolfbrandt, and P.K. Baade. 1978. Transfer functions of gas flames: Methods of measurement and representative data. *ASHRAE Transactions* 84(1):466-476.

GPA. 1997. Liquefied petroleum gas specifications and test methods. *Standard* 2140-97. Gas Processors Association, Tulsa, OK.

Hartman, I. 1958. Dust explosions. In *Mechanical engineers' handbook*, 6th ed., Section 7, pp. 41-48. McGraw-Hill, New York.

Hazard, H.R. 1971. Gas turbine fuels. In *Gas turbine handbook*. Gas Turbine Publications, Stamford, CT.

Herrin, D., L. Zhou, and T. Li. 2012. Validation of a low-order acoustic model of boilers and its application for diagnosing combustion driven oscillations. ASHRAE Research Project RP-1517, *Final Report*.

Kagiya, S. 2000. Practical burner design for the suppression of combustion oscillations. *Annual Technical Report Digest*, vol. 10. Tokyo Gas Co.

Kilham, J.K., E.G. Jackson, and T.J.B. Smith. 1964. Oscillatory combustion in tunnel burners. *10th Symposium (International) on Combustion*, England, pp. 1231-1240. The Combustion Institute, Pittsburgh, PA.

Lee, S.W., I. He, T. Herage, V. Razbin, E. Kelly, and B. Young. 2002a. *Influence of fuel sulphur in particulate emissions from pilot-scale research furnaces*. Natural Resources Canada. CETC 02-08 (CF).

Lee, S.W., I. He, T. Herage, B. Young, and E. Kelly. 2002b. *Fuel sulphur effects on particulate emissions from oil combustion systems under accelerated laboratory conditions*. Natural Resources Canada. CETC 02-09 (CF).

Matsui, Y. 1981. An experimental study on pyro-acoustic amplification of premixed laminar flames. *Combustion and Flame* 43:199-209.

Munjal, M.L. 1987. *Acoustics of ducts and mufflers*. Wiley Interscience, Hoboken, NJ.

Murphy, M.J., and A.A. Putnam. 1985. Burner technology bulletin: Control of NO_x emissions from residential gas appliances. *Report* GRI-85/0132. Battelle Columbus Division for Gas Research Institute.

Neumann, E.G. 1974. An impedance condition for avoiding acoustic oscillations generated by gas flames. *Acustica* 30:229-235.

NFPA. 1962. Fire-hazard properties of flammable liquids, gases and volatile solids. In *Fire protection handbook*, 12th ed., Tables 6-126, pp. 6-131 ff. National Fire Protection Association, Quincy, MA.

North American combustion handbook, 3rd ed. 1986. North American Manufacturing Co., Cleveland, OH.

Paul, D.D., A.L. Rutz, S.G. Talbert, J.J. Crisafolli, G.R. Whitacre, and R.D. Fischer. 1988. User's manual for Vent-II Ver. 3.0—A dynamic microcomputer program for analyzing gas venting systems. *Report* GRI-88/0304. Battelle Columbus Division for Gas Research Institute.

Putnam, A. 1971. *Combustion-driven oscillations in industry*. Elsevier, New York.

Sattinger, S.S., Y. Neumeier, A. Nabi, B.T. Zinn, D.J. Amos, and D.D. Darling. 2000. Sub-scale demonstration of the active feedback control of gas-turbine combustion instabilities. *ASME Transactions*, *Journal of Engineering for Gas Turbines and Power* 122(2):262-268.

Schimmer, H. 1979. Selbsterregte Schwingungen in Brennkammern—Ihre Entstehung und Massnahmen zu ihrer Vermeidung. *Gas Waerme International* 26:17-23.

Schreel, K.R.A.M., R. Rook, and L.P.H. de Goey. 2002. The acoustic response of burner stabilized flat flames. *Proceedings of the Combustion Institute,* Sapporo, Japan, vol. 29, pp. 115-121.

Scott, G.S., G.W. Jones, and F.E. Scott. 1948. Determination of ignition temperatures of combustible liquids and gases. *Analytical Chemistry* 20: 238-241.

Shelton, E.M. 1974. Burner oil fuels. *Petroleum Products Survey* 86. U.S. Bureau of Mines, Washington, D.C.

Shnidman, L. 1954. *Gaseous fuels*. American Gas Association, Arlington, VA.

Stickford, G.H., S.G. Talbert, B. Hindin, and D.W. Locklin. 1988. Research on corrosion-resistant materials for condensing heat exchangers. *Proceedings of the 39th Annual International Appliance Technical Conference*.

Suchovsky, C., R. Sheridan, and J. Nagorka. 2011. Recommendations based on field testing and analysis of high altitude installations of gas-fired boilers and water heaters. ASHRAE Research Project RP-1388, *Final Report*.

Trinks, W. 1947. Simplified calculation of radiation from non-luminous furnace gases. *Industrial Heating* 14:40-46.

U.S. Bureau of Mines. Semiannually. *Mineral industry surveys, motor gasolines*. Washington, D.C.

Zabetakis, M.G. 1956. Research on the combustion and explosion hazards of hydrogen-water vapor-air mixtures. Division of Explosives Technology, *Progress Report* 1. U.S. Bureau of Mines, Washington, D.C.

BIBLIOGRAPHY

ASA. 2013. Acoustical terminology. ANSI/ASA *Standard* S1.1-2013. American National Standards Institute, New York, and Acoustical Society of America, Melville, NY.

Bonne, U., and A. Patani. 1982. Combustion system performance analysis and simulation study. *Report* GRI-81/0093 (PB 83-161 406). Honeywell SSPL, Bloomington, MN.

EPA. 2016. Compilation of air pollutant emission factors. *Report* AP-42. U.S. Environmental Protection Agency, Washington, D.C. www.epa.gov/air-emissions-factors-and-quantification/ap-42-compilation-air-emission-factors.

Fricker, N., and C.A. Roberts. 1979. An experimental and theoretical approach to combustion driven oscillations. *Gas Waerme International* 28(13).

Gas Appliance Technology Center, Gas Research Institute. *Manufacturer update on status of GATC research on heat-exchanger corrosion, May 1984*. Battelle Columbus Laboratories and American Gas Association Laboratories.

Lewis, B., and G. von Elbe. 1987. *Combustion, flames, and explosion of gases*, 3rd ed. Academic Press, New York.

NFPA/AGA. 2015. National fuel gas code, Section 11.1.2. ANSI/NFPA *Standard* 54-2015. National Fire Protection Association, Quincy, MA. ANSI/AGA *Standard* Z223.1-2012. American Gas Association, Washington, D.C.

Stickford, G.H., S.G. Talbert, and D.W. Locklin. 1987. Condensate corrosivity in residential condensing appliances. *Proceedings of the International Symposium on Condensing Heat Exchangers*, Paper 3, BNL *Report* 52068, 1 and 2. Brookhaven National Laboratory, Upton, NY.

Mahon, M. 1981. An experimental study on pyro-acoustic amplification of premixed laminar flames. *Combustion and Flame* 43:[illegible]-209.

Munjal, M.L. 1987. *Acoustics of ducts and mufflers*. Wiley-Interscience, Hoboken, NJ.

Murphy, M.J. and [illegible] Putnam. 1985. Burner technology bulletin: Control of NO_x emissions from residential gas appliances. *Report* [illegible]-85/0132. Battelle Columbus Division for Gas Research Institute.

Putnam, A.A. 1974. An impedance condition for avoiding acoustic oscillations generated by gas burners. *Journal* 30:239-235.

[illegible] Fire hazard properties of flammable liquids, gases and volatile solids. In *Fire protection handbook*, 12th ed., Table [illegible]. National Fire Protection Association, Quincy, MA.

[illegible] gas combustion [illegible]. [illegible] North American Manufacturing Co., Cleveland, OH.

Carl, D.E., A.L. Ruiz, S.G. Talbert, J.J. Hemphill, D.C. Wimmer, and J.E. Hughes. 1982. User's manual for Vent-II [illegible] An automatic [illegible] computer program for analyzing gas venting systems. Report GRI-[illegible]. Battelle Columbus Division for Gas Research Institute.

[illegible] 19[illegible]. *Combustion theory*. [illegible] Publishing Co. [illegible], New York.

[illegible] Pang, P.T. Zhu, D. DeAnna, and D.D. Pare. 2003. Adaptive combustion [illegible] feedback control of [illegible] emissions from residential gas-fired furnaces. *ASME Transactions*, *Journal of Engineering for Gas Turbines and Power* 125:[illegible]-268.

[illegible], H. 19[illegible]. Systematic [illegible] in Brennkammern [illegible]. Forschung und Bedeutung in der [illegible] Gas Wärme [illegible] [illegible].

[illegible], K.A., M. [illegible] Kwok, and L.P.H. de Goey. 2002. The acoustic [illegible] of laminar premixed flat flames. *Proceedings of the Combustion Institute* [illegible], vol. [illegible].

Steel, G.S., T.W. Jones, and L.E. Scott. 1968. Determination of [illegible] temperatures of combustible liquids and gases. *Analytical Chemistry* 30:[illegible].

Shell, and E.M. 1974. [illegible] oil fuels. *Petroleum Products Survey* [illegible]. U.S. Bureau of Mines, Washington, D.C.

[illegible], T. 1964. [illegible] fuels. American Gas Association, Arlington, VA.

Stickford, G.H., S.G. Talbert, B. Hindin, and B.W. Locklin. 1988. Research on corrosion-resistant materials for condensing heat exchangers. *Proceedings of the 13th Annual International Conference*, [illegible] Chicago.

Sinitowski, C., K. Sheridan, and J. Nagarka. 2011. Recommendations based on field testing and analysis of high altitude derating of gas-fired boilers and water heaters. ASHRAE *Research Project RP-1353, Final Report*.

Thinks, W. 1941. Simplified calculation of radiation from nonluminous furnace gases. *Industrial Heating* 12:[illegible].

U.S. Bureau of Mines. Semiannually. *Natural gas-purity surveys, principal cities*. [illegible], D.C.

Zabetakis, M.G. 1956. Research on the combustion and explosion hazards of hydrogen-water vapor-air mixtures. Division of Explosives Technology, *Progress Report* 1. U.S. Bureau of Mines, Washington, D.C.

BIBLIOGRAPHY

[illegible] fundamentals of combustion. [illegible] Academic Press, [illegible] and Angeles. [illegible] Society, Atlanta, GA.

Bonne, U. and A. Patani. 1982. Combustion [illegible] and simulation study. Report GRI-[illegible]. [illegible] Bloomington, MN.

[illegible] A. 20[illegible]. [illegible] pollutant emission factors. U.S. Environmental Protection Agency, Washington, D.C. [illegible] Combustion Sources.

Eroke, N. [illegible]. An experimental and theoretical approach to combustion [illegible]. [illegible].

Gas Appliance Technology [illegible] Research Institute. [illegible] *Manual* [illegible] 1994 research [illegible] corrosion. Battelle Columbus Laboratories and American Gas Association.

Lewis, B. and G. von Elbe. 1987. *Combustion, flames and explosions of gases*. Academic Press, New York.

NFPA/AGA. 2015. National fuel gas code. Section 12.[illegible]. *NFPA Standard* 54-2015. National Fire Protection Association, Quincy, MA. *ANSI/AGA Standard* Z223.1-2015. American Gas Association, Washington, D.C.

Stickford, G.H. 19[illegible] [illegible] study of residential condensing appliances. *Proceedings of the International Symposium on Condensing Heat Exchangers*, Paper [illegible]. Report [illegible] Brookhaven National Laboratory, Upton, NY.

CHAPTER 29

REFRIGERANTS

REFRIGERANTS are the working fluids in refrigeration, air-conditioning, and heat-pumping systems. They absorb heat from one area, such as an air-conditioned space, and reject it into another, such as outdoors, usually through evaporation and condensation, respectively. These phase changes occur both in absorption and mechanical vapor compression systems, but not in systems operating on a gas cycle using a fluid such as air. (See Chapter 2 for more information on refrigeration cycles.) The design of the refrigeration equipment depends strongly on the selected refrigerant's properties. Tables 1 and 2 list standard refrigerant designations, some properties, and safety classifications from ASHRAE *Standard* 34.

Refrigerant selection involves compromises between conflicting desirable thermophysical properties. A refrigerant must satisfy many requirements, some of which do not directly relate to its ability to transfer heat. Chemical stability under conditions of use is an essential characteristic. Safety codes may require a nonflammable refrigerant of low toxicity for some applications. Environmental consequences of refrigerant leaks must also be considered. Cost, availability, efficiency, compatibility with compressor lubricants and equipment materials, and local and national regulations are other concerns.

Latent heat of vaporization is another important property. On a molar basis, fluids with similar boiling points have almost the same latent heat. Because compressor displacement is defined on a volumetric basis, refrigerants with similar boiling points produce similar refrigeration effect with a given compressor. On a mass basis, latent heat varies widely among fluids. Efficiency of a theoretical vapor compression cycle is maximized by fluids with low vapor heat capacity. This property is associated with fluids having a simple molecular structure and low molecular mass.

Transport properties (e.g., thermal conductivity and viscosity) affect performance of heat exchangers and piping. High thermal conductivity and low viscosity are desirable.

No single fluid satisfies all the attributes desired of a refrigerant; consequently, various refrigerants are used. This chapter describes the basic characteristics of various refrigerants, and Chapter 30 lists thermophysical properties.

1. REFRIGERANT PROPERTIES

Global Environmental Properties

Chlorofluorocarbons (CFCs) and hydrochlorofluorocarbons (HCFCs) can affect both stratospheric ozone and climate change, whereas hydrofluorocarbons (HFCs) can affect climate change. Minimizing all refrigerant releases from systems is important not only because of environmental impacts, but also because charge losses lead to insufficient system charge levels, which in turn result in suboptimal operation and lowered efficiency.

Stratospheric Ozone Depletion. The stratospheric ozone layer filters out the UV-B portion of the sun's ultraviolet (UV) radiation. Overexposure to this radiation increases the risk of skin cancer, cataracts, and impaired immune systems. It also can damage sensitive crops, reduce crop yields, and stress marine phytoplankton (and thus human food supplies from the oceans). In addition, exposure to UV radiation degrades plastics and wood.

Stratospheric ozone depletion has been linked to the presence of chlorine and bromine in the stratosphere. Chemicals with long atmospheric lifetimes can migrate to the stratosphere, where the molecules break down from interaction with ultraviolet light or through chemical reaction. Chemicals such as CFCs and HCFCs release chlorine, which reacts with stratospheric ozone.

Ozone-depleting substances, including CFCs and HCFCs, are to be phased out of production under the Montreal Protocol (UNEP 2009). In the United States, production and importation of CFCs were banned completely in 1996. HCFCs are being phased down, with complete phaseout set for 2030. In 2010, to meet the Montreal Protocol phasedown schedule, U.S. regulations banned production and importation of HCFC-142b and HCFC-22 for use in new equipment. Reclaimed CFC and HCFC refrigerants that meet the requirements of AHRI *Standard* 700 can continue to be used for servicing existing systems. A complete list of U.S. regulations for CFC and HCFC refrigerants, including phaseout schedules, may be found at www.epa.gov/ozone-layer-protection. A summary of the phaseout schedules for CFCs and HCFCs for both developed and developing countries may be found at www.unep.org/ozonaction/topics/hcfc.asp.

Global Climate Change. The average global temperature is determined by the balance of energy from the sun heating the earth and its atmosphere and of energy radiated from the earth and the atmosphere to space. **Greenhouse gases (GHGs)**, such as CO_2 and water vapor, as well as small particles trap heat at and near the surface, maintaining the average temperature of the Earth's surface about 61°F warmer than would be the case if these gases and particles were not present (the **greenhouse effect**).

Global warming (also called **global climate change**) is a concern because of an increase in the greenhouse effect from increasing concentrations of GHGs attributed to human activities. The major GHG of concern is CO_2 released to the atmosphere when fossil fuels (coal, oil, and natural gas) are burned for energy. Methane (CH_4), nitrous oxide (N_2O), CFCs, HCFCs, HFCs, hydrofluoroethers (HFEs), hydrofluoro-olefins (HFOs), perfluorocarbons (PFCs), nitrogen trifluoride (NF_3), and sulfur hexafluoride (SF_6) are also GHGs.

In 1988, the United Nations Environment Programme (UNEP) and the World Meteorological Organization (WMO) established the Intergovernmental Panel on Climate Change (IPCC) to provide an objective source of information about the causes of climate change, its potential environmental and socioeconomic consequences, and the adaptation and mitigation options to respond to it. According to the IPCC (2014), atmospheric concentration of carbon dioxide has increased by more than 40% over the past 250 years, primarily from burning fossil fuels, with some contribution from forestry and land use. Concentration of methane has increased by over 150%, and of nitrous oxide by about 20%. IPCC (2014) deems atmospheric concentrations of fluorochemicals, including fluorocarbon gases

The preparation of this chapter is assigned to TC 3.1, Refrigerants and Secondary Coolants.

Table 1 Refrigerant Data and Safety Classifications

Refrigerant Number	Chemical Name[a,b]	Chemical Formula[a]	Molecular Mass[a]	Normal Boiling Point,[a] °F	Safety Group
Methane Series					
11	Trichlorofluoromethane	CCl_3F	137.4	75	A1
12	Dichlorodifluoromethane	CCl_2F_2	120.9	–22	A1
12B1	Bromochlorodifluoromethane	$CBrClF_2$	165.4	25	
13	Chlorotrifluoromethane	$CClF_3$	104.5	–115	A1
13B1	Bromotrifluoromethane	$CBrF_3$	148.9	–72	A1
14	Tetrafluoromethane (carbon tetrafluoride)	CF_4	88.0	–198	A1
21	Dichlorofluoromethane	$CHCl_2F$	102.9	48	B1
22	Chlorodifluoromethane	$CHClF_2$	86.5	–41	A1
23	Trifluoromethane	CHF_3	70.0	–116	A1
30	Dichloromethane (methylene chloride)	CH_2Cl_2	84.9	104	B2
31	Chlorofluoromethane	CH_2ClF	68.5	16	
32	Difluoromethane (methylene fluoride)	CH_2F_2	52.0	–62	A2L
40	Chloromethane (methyl chloride)	CH_3Cl	50.4	–12	B2
41	Fluoromethane (methyl fluoride)	CH_3F	34.0	–109	
50	Methane	CH_4	16.0	–259	A3
Ethane Series					
113	1,1,2-trichloro-1,2,2-trifluoroethane	CCl_2FCClF_2	187.4	118	A1
114	1,2-dichloro-1,1,2,2-tetrafluoroethane	$CClF_2CClF_2$	170.9	38	A1
115	Chloropentafluoroethane	$CClF_2CF_3$	154.5	–38	A1
116	Hexafluoroethane	CF_3CF_3	138.0	–109	A1
123	2,2-dichloro-1,1,1-trifluoroethane	$CHCl_2CF_3$	153.0	81	B1
124	2-chloro-1,1,1,2-tetrafluoroethane	$CHClFCF_3$	136.5	10	A1
125	Pentafluoroethane	CHF_2CF_3	120.0	–55	A1
134a	1,1,1,2-tetrafluoroethane	CH_2FCF_3	102.0	–15	A1
141b	1,1-dichloro-1-fluoroethane	CH_3CCl_2F	117.0	90	
142b	1-chloro-1,1-difluoroethane	CH_3CClF_2	100.5	14	A2
143a	1,1,1-trifluoroethane	CH_3CF_3	84.0	–53	A2L
152a	1,1-difluoroethane	CH_3CHF_2	66.0	–11	A2
170	Ethane	CH_3CH_3	30.0	–128	A3
Ethers					
E170	Dimethyl ether	CH_3OCH_3	46.0	–13	A3
Propane Series					
218	Octafluoropropane	$CF_3CF_2CF_3$	188.0	–35	A1
227ea	1,1,1,2,3,3,3-heptafluoropropane	CF_3CHFCF_3	170.0	3	A1
236fa	1,1,1,3,3,3-hexafluoropropane	$CF_3CH_2CF_3$	152.0	29	A1
245fa	1,1,1,3,3-pentafluoropropane	$CF_3CH_2CHF_2$	134.0	59	B1
290	Propane	$CH_3CH_2CH_3$	44.0	–44	A3
Cyclic Organic Compounds (see Table 2 for blends)					
C318	Octafluorocyclobutane	$–(CF_2)_4–$	200.0	21	A1
Miscellaneous Organic Compounds					
Hydrocarbons					
600	Butane	$CH_3CH_2CH_2CH_3$	58.1	31	A3
600a	2-methylpropane (isobutane)	$CH(CH_3)_2CH_3$	58.1	11	A3
601	Pentane	$CH_3(CH_2)_3CH_3$	72.15	97	A3
601a	2-methylbutane (isopentane)	$(CH_3)_2CHCH_2CH_3$	72.15	82	A3
Oxygen Compounds					
610	Ethyl ether	$CH_3CH_2OCH_2CH_3$	74.1	94	
611	Methyl formate	$HCOOCH_3$	60.0	89	B2
Sulfur Compounds					
620	(Reserved for future assignment)				
Nitrogen Compounds					
630	Methanamine (methyl amine)	CH_3NH_2	31.1	20	
631	Ethanamine (ethyl amine)	$CH_3CH_2(NH_2)$	45.1	62	

Table 1 Refrigerant Data and Safety Classifications (*Continued*)

Refrigerant Number	Chemical Name[a,b]	Chemical Formula[a]	Molecular Mass[a]	Normal Boiling Point,[a] °F	Safety Group
Inorganic Compounds					
702	Hydrogen	H_2	2.0	–423	A3
704	Helium	He	4.0	–452	A1
717	Ammonia	NH_3	17.0	–28	B2L
718	Water	H_2O	18.0	212	A1
720	Neon	Ne	20.2	–411	A1
728	Nitrogen	N_2	28.1	–320	A1
732	Oxygen	O_2	32.0	–297	
740	Argon	Ar	39.9	–303	A1
744	Carbon dioxide	CO_2	44.0	–109[c]	A1
744A	Nitrous oxide	N_2O	44.0	–129	
764	Sulfur dioxide	SO_2	64.1	14	B1
Unsaturated Organic Compounds					
1150	Ethene (ethylene)	$CH_2{=}CH_2$	28.1	–155	A3
1233zd(E)	Trans-1-chloro-3,3,3-trifluoro-1-propene	$CF_3CH{=}CHCl$	130.5	64	A1
1234yf	2,3,3,3-tetrafluoro-1-propene	$CF_3CF{=}CH_2$	114.0	–20.9	A2L
1234ze(E)	Trans-1,3,3,3-tetrafluoro-1-propene	$CF_3CH{=}CHF$	114.0	–2.2	A2L
1270	Propene (propylene)	$CH_3CH{=}CH_2$	42.1	–54	A3
1336mzz(Z)	Cis-1,1,1,4,4,4-hexafluoro-2-butene	$CF_3CH{=}CHCF_3$	164.1	92	A1

Source: ANSI/ASHRAE *Standard* 34-2010.
[a]Chemical name, chemical formula, molecular mass, and normal boiling point are not part of this standard.
[b]Preferred chemical name is followed by the popular name in parentheses.
[c]Sublimes.

Table 2 Data and Safety Classifications for Refrigerant Blends

Refrig. No.	Composition (Mass %)	Composition Tolerances	Molecular Mass[a]	Normal Bubble Point, °F	Normal Dew Point, °F	Safety Group
Zeotropes						
400	R-12/114 (must be specified)					A1
401A	R-22/152a/124 (53.0/13.0/34.0)	(±2.0 /+0.5,–1.5/±1.0)	94.4	–29.9	–19.8	A1
401B	R-22/152a/124 (61.0/11.0/28.0)	(±2/+0.5,–1.5/±1.0)	92.8	–32.3	–23.4	A1
401C	R-22/152a/124 (33.0/15.0/52.0)	(±2/+0.5,–1.5/±1.0)	101	–22.9	–10.8	A1
402A	R-125/290/22 (60.0/2.0/38.0)	(±2.0/+0.1,–1.0/±2.0)	101.6	–56.6	–52.6	A1
402B	R-125/290/22 (38.0/2.0/60.0)	(±2/+0.1,–1/±2)	94.7	–53.0	–48.8	A1
403A	R-290/22/218 (5.0/75.0/20.0)	(+0.2,–2/±2/±2)	92	–47.2	–44.1	A1
403B	R-290/22/218 (5.0/56.0/39.0)	(+0.2,–2/±2/±2)	103.3	–46.8	–44.1	A1
404A	R-125/143a/134a (44.0/52.0/4.0)	(±2/±1/±2)	97.6	–51.9	–50.4	A1
405A	R-22/152a/142b/C318 (45.0/7.0/5.5/42.5)	(±2/±1/±1 /±2) sum of R-152a and R-142b = (+0.0, –2.0)	111.9	–27.2	–12.1	
406A	R-22/600a/142b (55.0/4.0/41.0)	(±2/±1/±1)	89.9	–26.9	–10.3	A2
407A	R-32/125/134a (20.0/40.0/40.0)	(±2/±2/±2)	90.1	–49.4	–37.7	A1
407B	R-32/125/134a (10.0/70.0/20.0)	(±2/±2/±2)	102.9	–52.2	–44.3	A1
407C	R-32/125/134a (23.0/25.0/52.0)	(±2/±2/±2)	86.2	–46.8	–34.1	A1
407D	R-32/125/134a (15.0/15.0/70.0)	(±2/±2/±2)	91	–38.9	–26.9	A1
407E	R-32/125/134a (25.0/15.0/60.0)	(±2,±2,±2)	83.8	–45.0	–32.1	A1
407F	R-32/125/134a (30.0/30.0/40.0)	(±2,±2,±2)	82.1	–51.0	–39.5	A1
408A	R-125/143a/22 (7.0/46.0/47.0)	(±2/±1/±2)	87	–49.9	–49.0	A1
409A	R-22/124/142b (60.0/25.0/15.0)	(±2/±2/±1)	97.4	–31.7	–17.5	A1
409B	R-22/124/142b (65.0/25.0/10.0)	(±2/±2/±1)	96.7	–33.7	–21.5	A1
410A	R-32/125 (50.0/50.0)	(+0.5,–1.5/+1.5,–0.5)	72.6	–60.9	–60.7	A1
410B	R-32/125 (45.0/55.0)	(±1/±1)	75.6	–60.7	–60.5	A1
411A	R-1270/22/152a (1.5/87.5/11.0)	(+0,–1/+2,–0/+0,–1)	82.4	–39.5	–35.0	A2
411B	R-1270/22/152a (3.0/94.0/3.0)	(+0,–1/+2,–0/+0,–1)	83.1	–42.9	–42.3	A2
412A	R-22/218/142b (70.0/5.0/25.0)	(±2/±2/±1)	92.2	–33.5	–19.8	A2
413A	R-218/134a/600a (9.0/88.0/3.0)	(±1/±2/±0,–1)	104	–20.7	–17.7	A2
414A	R-22/124/600a/142b (51.0/28.5/4.0/16.5)	(±2/±2/±0.5/+0.5,–1)	96.9	–29.2	–14.4	A1
414B	R-22/124/600a/142b (50.0/39.0/1.5/9.5)	(±2/±2/±0.5/+0.5,–1)	101.6	–29.9	–15.0	A1
415A	R-22/152a (82.0/18.0)	(±1/±1)	81.9	–35.5	–30.5	A2
415B	R-22/152a (25.0/75.0)	(±1/±1)	70.2	–17.8	–15.2	A2
416A	R-134a/124/600 (59.0/39.5/1.5)	(+0.5,–1/+1,–0.5/+1,–0.2)	111.9	–10.1	–7.2	A1
417A	R-125/134a/600 (46.6/50.0/3.4)	(±1.1/±1/+0.1,–0.4)	106.7	–36.4	–27.2	A1
417B	R-125/134a/600 (79.0/18.3/2.7)	(±1/±1/+0.1,–0.5)	113.1	–48.8	–42.7	A1
418A	R-290/22/152a (1.5/96.0/2.5)	(±0.5/±1/±0.5)	84.6	–42.2	–40.2	A2
419A	R-125/134a/E170 (77.0/19.0/4.0)	(±1/±1/±1)	109.3	–44.7	–32.8	A2
420A	R-134a/142b (88.0/12.0)	(±1,–0/+0,–1)	101.8	–13.0	–11.6	A1
421A	R-125/134a (58.0/42.0)	(±1/±1)	111.8	–41.5	–31.9	A1

Table 2 Data and Safety Classifications for Refrigerant Blends (*Continued*)

Refrig. No.	Composition (Mass %)	Composition Tolerances	Molecular Mass[a]	Normal Bubble Point, °F	Normal Dew Point, °F	Safety Group
421B	R-125/134a (85.0/15.0)	(±1/±1)	116.9	–50.2	–44.6	A1
422A	R-125/134a/600a (85.1/11.5/3.4)	(±1/±1/+0.1,–0.4)	113.6	–51.7	–47.4	A1
422B	R-125/134a/600a (55.0/42.0/3.0)	(±1/±1/+0.1,–0.5)	108.5	–40.9	–32.2	A1
422C	R-125/134a/600a (82.0/15.0/3.0)	(±1/±1/+0.1,–0.5)	116.3	–49.5	–44.2	A1
422D	R-125/134a/600a (65.1/31.5/3.4)	(+0.9,–1.1/±1/+0.1,–0.4)	109.9	–45.8	–37.1	A1
423A	R-134a/227ea (52.5/47.5)	(±1/±1)	126	–11.6	–10.3	A1
424A	R-125/134a/600a/600/601a (50.5/47.0/0.9/1.0/0.6)	(±1/±1/+0.1,–0.2/+0.1,–0.2/+0.1,–0.2)	108.4	–38.4	–27.9	A1
425A	R-32/134a/227ea (18.5/69.5/12.0)	(±0.5/±0.5/±0.5)	90.3	–36.6	–24.3	A1
426A[a]	R-125/134a/600a/601a (5.1/93.0/1.3/0.6)	(±1/±1/+0.1,–0.2/+0.1,–0.2)	101.6	–19.3	–16.1	A1
427A[a]	R-32/125/143a/134a (15.0/25.0/10.0/50.0)	(±2/±2/±2/±2)	90.4	–45.4	–33.3	A1
428A[a]	R-125/143a/290/600a (77.5/20.0/0.6/1.9)	(±1/±1/+0.1,–0.2/+0.1,–0.2)	107.5	–54.9	–53.5	A1
429A	R-E170/152a/600a (60.0/10.0/30.0)	(±1/±1/±1)	50.8	–14.8	–14.1	A3
430A	R-152a/600a (76.0/24.0)	(±1/±1)	64	–17.7	–17.3	A3
431A	R-290/152a (71.0/29.0)	(±1/±1)	48.8	–45.6	–45.6	A3
432A	R-1270/E170 (80.0/20.0)	(±1/±1)	42.8	–51.9	–50.1	A3
433A	R-1270/290 (30.0/70.0)	(±1/±1)	43.5	–48.3	–47.6	A3
433B	R-1270/290 (5.0/95.0)	(±1/±1)	44	–44.9	–44.5	A3
433C	R-1270/290 (25.0/75.0)	(±1/±1)	43.6	–47.7	–47.0	A3
434A	R-125/143a/134a/600a (63.2/18.0/16.0/2.8)	(±1/±1/±1/+0.1,–0.2)	105.7	–49.0	–44.1	A1
435A	R-E170/152a (80.0/20.0)	(±1/±1)	49.04	–15.0	–14.6	A3
436A	R-290/600a (56.0/44.0)	(±1/±1)	49.33	–29.7	–16.2	A3
436B	R-290/600a (52.0/48.0)	(±1/±1)	49.87	–28.1	–13.0	A3
437A	R-125/134a/600/601 (19.5/78.5/1.4/0.6)	(+0.5,–1.8/+1.5,–0.7/+0.1,–0.2/+0.1/–0.2)	103.7	–27.2	–20.6	A1
438A	R-32/125/134a/600/601a (8.5/45.0/44.2/1.7/0.6)	(+0.5,–1.5/±1.5/±1.5/+0.1,–0.2/+0.1/–0.2)	99.1	–45.4	–33.5	A1
439A	R-32/125/600a (50.0/47.0/3.0)	(±1/±1)	71.2	–61.6	–61.2	A2
440A	R-290/134a/152a (0.6/1.6/97.8)	(±0.1/±0.6/±0.5)	66.2	–13.9	–11.7	A2
441A	R-170/290/600a/600 (3.1/54.8/6.0/36.1)	(±0.3/±2/±0.6/±2)	48.2	–43.4	–4.7	A3
442A	R-32/125/134a/152a/227ea (31.0/31.0/30.0/3.0/5.0)	(±1.0/±1.0/±1.0/+0.5/±1.0)	81.77	–51.7	–39.8	A1
443A	R-1270/290/600a (55.0/40.0/5.0)	(±2.0/±2.0/±1.2)	43.47	–48.6	–42.2	A3
444A	R-32/152a/1234ze(E) (12.0/5.0/83.0)	(±1.0/±1.0/±2.0)	96.7	–29.7	–11.7	A2L
444B	R-32/152a/1234ze(E) (41.5/10.0/48.5)	(±.1.0/±1.0/±1.0)	92.78	–48.3	–30.8	A2L
445A	R-744/134a/1234ze(E) (6.0/9.0/85.0)	(±1.0/±1.0/±2.0)	103.1	–58.5	–10.3	A2L
446A	R-32/1234ze(E)/600 (68.0/2.09/3.0)	(+0.5,–1.0/+2.0,–0.6/+1.0,–1.0)	62	–56.9	–47.2	A2L
447A	R-32/125/1234ze(E) (68.0/3.5/28.5)	(+1.5,–0.5/+1.5,–0.5/+1.0,–1.0)	63.04	–56.7	–47.6	A2L
448A	R-32/125/1234yf/134a/1234ze(E) (26.0/26.0/20.0/21.0/7.0)	(+0.5 –2.0/+2.0 –0.5/+0.5– 2.0/+2.0–1.0/+0.5–2.0)	86.28	–50.6	–39.6	A1
449A	R-32/125/1234yf/134a (24.3/24.7/25.3/25.7)	(+2.0 –1.0/+1.0–0.2/+0.2– 1.0/+1.0–0.2)	87.21	–50.8	–39.8	A1
449B	R-32/125/1234yf/134a (25.2/24.3/23.2/27.3)	(+0.3 –1.5 /+1.5 –0.3 /+0.3 –1.5 /+1.5 –0.3)	86.37	–51.0	–40.4	A1
450A	R-134a/1234ze(E) (42.0/58.0)	(±2.0/±2.0)	108.67	–10.1	–9.0	A1
451A	R-1234yf/134a (89.8/10.2)	(±0.2 /±0.2)	72.76	–23.4	–22.9	A2L
451B	R-1234yf/134a (88.8/11.2)	(±0.2 /±0.2)	112.56	–23.8	–23.1	A2L
452A	R-32/125/1234yf (11.0/59.0/30.0)	(±1.7/±1.8/+0.1/–1.0)	112.56	–23.8	–23.1	A2L
453A	R32/125/134a/227ea/600/601a (20.0/20.0/53.8/5.0/0.6/0.6)	(±1.0 /±1.0 /±1.0 /±0.5 /+0.1 –0.2 /+0.1 –0.2)	88.78	–44.0	–31.0	A1
454A	R-32/1234yf (35/65)	(±2.0/±2.0)	80.47	–55.1	–42.9	A2L
454B	R-32/1234yf (68.9/31.1)	(±1.0/±1.0)	62.61	–59.6	–58.0	A2L

Azeotropes[b]

Refrig. No.	Composition (Mass %)	Composition Tolerances	Azeotropic Temperatures, °F	Molecular Mass[a]	Normal Boiling Point, °F	Safety Group
500	R-12/152a (73.8/26.2)		32	99.3	–27	A1
501	R-22/12 (75.0/25.0)[c]		–42	93.1	–42	A1
502	R-22/115 (48.8/51.2)		66	112.0	–49	A1
503	R-23/13 (40.1/59.9)		–126	87.5	–126	
504	R-32/115 (48.2/51.8)		63	79.2	–71	
505	R-12/31 (78.0/22.0)[c]		239	103.5	–22	
506	R-31/114 (55.1/44.9)		64	93.7	10	
507A[d]	R-125/143a (50.0/50.0)		–40	98.9	–52.1	A1
508A[d]	R-23/116 (39.0/61.0)		–122	100.1	–122	A1
508B	R-23/116 (46.0/54.0)		–50.1	95.4	–126.9	A1
509A[d]	R-22/218 (44.0/56.0)		32	124.0	–53	A1
510A	R-E170/600a (88.0/12.0)	(±0.5/±0.5)	–13.4	47.24	–13.4	A3
511A	R-290/E170 (95.0/5.0)	(±1/±1)	–4 to 104	44.19	–43.7	A3
512A	R-134a/152a (5.0/95.0)	(±1/±1)	–4 to 104	67.24	–11.2	A2
513A	R-1234yf/134a (56.0/44.0)	(±1.0/±1.0)	81	108.4	–20.4	A1

Source: ANSI/ASHRAE *Standard* 34-2010.

[a]Molecular mass and normal boiling point are not part of this standard.

[b]Azeotropic refrigerants exhibit some segregation of components at conditions of temperature and pressure other than those at which they were formulated. Extent of segregation depends on the particular azeotrope and hardware system configuration.

[c]Exact composition of this azeotrope is in question, and additional experimental studies are needed.

[d]R-507, R-508, and R-509 are allowed designations for R-507A, R-508A, and R-509A because of a change in designations after assignment of R-500 through R-509. Corresponding changes were not made for R-500 through R-506.

(CFCs, HCFCs, and HFCs) and sulfur hexafluoride, to be about 2% of the 2010 GHG (CO_2 equivalent) emissions.

Global Environmental Characteristics of Refrigerants. Atmospheric release of CFC and HCFC refrigerants (see Table 3) contributes to depletion of the ozone layer. The measure of a material's ability to deplete stratospheric ozone is its **ozone depletion potential (ODP)**, a value relative to R-11's value of 1.0. It is the nonzero ODP of these refrigerants that led to the phaseout of their production and use under the Montreal Protocol.

The **global warming potential (GWP)** of a GHG is an index describing its relative ability to trap radiant energy compared to CO_2 (R-744), which has a very long atmospheric lifetime. Measurements of climate impact of refrigerant emissions are hence often reported in CO_2 equivalents. GWP may be calculated for any particular **integration time horizon (ITH)**. Typically, a 100 year ITH is used for calculation of GWPs for regulatory purposes, and may be designated as GWP_{100}. Halocarbons (CFCs, HCFCs, and HFCs) and many nonhalocarbons (e.g., hydrocarbons, carbon dioxide) are GHGs. HFOs, or unsaturated HFCs, and blends using them are being developed and promoted as low-GWP alternatives to the existing halocarbon refrigerants. HFOs are also GHGs but their GWPs are drastically lower than those of HFCs.

The energy refrigeration appliances consume is often produced from fossil fuels, which results in emission of CO_2, a contributor to global warming. This indirect effect associated with energy consumption is frequently much larger than the direct effect of refrigerant emissions. The **total equivalent warming impact (TEWI)** of an HVAC&R system is the sum of direct refrigerant emissions expressed in terms of CO_2 equivalents, and indirect emissions of CO_2 from the system's energy use over its service life (Fischer et. al. 1991). Another measure is **life-cycle climate performance (LCCP)**, which includes TEWI and adds direct and indirect emissions effects associated with manufacturing the refrigerant and end-of-life disposal (ARAP 1999).

Ammonia (R-717), hydrocarbons, HCFCs, most HFCs, and HFOs have shorter atmospheric lifetimes than CFCs because they are largely destroyed in the lower atmosphere by reactions with OH radicals. A shorter atmospheric lifetime generally results in lower ODP and GWP_{100} values.

Table 3A gives values for atmospheric lifetime, ODP, and GWP_{100} of refrigerants being phased out under the Montreal Protocol and of their replacements, alone or as components of blends from the IPCC (2007). Table 3B shows the latest scientific assessment values for these refrigerants and for new refrigerants developed since IPCC (2007) was published. Because HFCs do not contain chlorine or bromine, their ODP values are negligible (Ravishankara et al. 1994) and thus are shown as 0 in Tables 3A and 3B. Nonhalocarbon refrigerants listed have zero ODP and very low GWP_{100}.

As shown in Tables 3A and 3B, there are differences between the values stipulated for reporting under the Montreal and Kyoto protocols and the latest scientific values. These differences are not large enough to significantly alter design decisions based on the numbers in the table. All these values have rather wide error bands and may change with each assessment of the science. Changes in GWP assessments are largely dominated by changes in understanding of CO_2, which is the reference chemical.

Table 4 provides ODP values for blends based on Montreal Protocol reporting values of the component fluids (Table 3A). It also gives IPCC (2007, 2013) GWP_{100} values based on component fluid values in Tables 3A and 3B, respectively.

Table 3A Refrigerant Environmental Properties

Refrigerant	Atmospheric Lifetime, years[a]	ODP[b]	GWP_{100}[a]
CFC-11	45	1	4750
CFC-12	100	1	10,900
CFC-13	640	1	14,400
CFC-113	85	0.8	6130
CFC-114	300	1	10,000
CFC-115	1700	0.6	7370
HCFC-22	12	0.055	1810
HCFC-123	1.3	0.02	77
HCFC-124	5.8	0.022	609
HCFC-142b	17.9	0.065	2310
HFC-23	270	0	14,800
HFC-32	4.9	0	675
HFC-125	29	0	3500
HFC-134a	14	0	1430
HFC-143a	52	0	4470
HFC-152a	1.4	0	124
HFC-227ea	34.2	0	3220
HFC-236fa	240	0	9810
HFC-245fa	7.6	0	1030
PFC-116	10,000	0	12,200
PFC-218	2600	0	8830
C318	3200	0.00	10,300
R-744		0.00	1

Sources: IPCC (2007), UNEP (2009).
[a]Atmospheric lifetimes and GWP_{100}s from Table 2.14 of IPCC (2007).
[b]ODP values stipulated for reporting under the Montreal Protocol from UNEP (2009), Section 1.1, Annexes A, B, and C, pp. 25-27.

Table 3B Refrigerant Environmental Properties

Refrigerant	Atmospheric Lifetime, years[a]	ODP[b]	GWP_{100}[a]
CFC-11	45	1	4660
CFC-12	100	0.73	10,800
CFC-13	640	1	13,900
CFC-113	85	0.81	5820
CFC-114	190	0.50	8590
CFC-115	1020	0.26	7670
HCFC-22	11.9	0.034	1760
HCFC-123	1.3	0.01	79
HCFC-124	5.9	0.02	527
HCFC-142b	17.2	0.057	1980
HCFO-1233zd(E)	0.071	0.00034	1
HE-E170	0.015[b]	0.00	1[b]
HFC-23	222	0.00	12,400 (11,700)[c]
HFC-32	5.2	0.00	677 (650)[c]
HFC-125	28.2	0.00	3170 (2800)[c]
HFC-134a	13.4	0.00	1300 (1300)[c]
HFC-143a	47.1	0.00	4800 (3800)[c]
HFC-152a	1.5	0.00	138 (140)[c]
HFC-227ea	38.9	0.00	3350 (2900)[c]
HFC-236fa	242	0.00	8060 (6300)[c]
HFC-245fa	7.7	0.00	858
HFO-1234yf	0.029	0.00	<1
HFO-1234ze(E)	0.045	0.00	<1
HFO-1336mzz(Z)	0.07	0.00	2
PFC-116	10,000	0.00	11,100 (9200)[c]
PFC-218	2600	0.00	8900 (7000)[c]
C318	3200	0.00	9540 (8700)[c]
HC-290	0.034[b]	0.00	5[b]
HC-600		0.00	4[b]
HC-600a	0.016[b]	0.00	~20[b]
HC-601a	0.009[b]	0.00	~20[b]
HC-1270	0.001[b]	0.00	1.8[b]
R-717		0.00	
R-744		0.00	1 (1)[c]

Sources: IPCC (2013).
[a]Atmospheric lifetimes and GWP_{100}s from IPCC (2013) except where indicated.
[b]From Table 2-7 of Calm et al. (2015)
[c]GWP_{100} values stipulated for reporting under Kyoto Protocol from Table 2-5 of Calm et al. (2015).

Table 4 Environmental Properties of Refrigerant Blends; based on Montreal Protocol Reporting ODP and IPCC AR4 and AR5 GWP_{100} of Components

Refriger-ant	ODP*	GWP_{100}* AR4	GWP_{100}* AR5	Refriger-ant	ODP*	GWP_{100}* AR4	GWP_{100}* AR5
401A	0.02	1180	1130	428A	0.00	3610	3120
401B	0.03	1290	1240	429A	0.00	19	20
401C	0.02	933	876	430A	0.00	99	110
402A	0.01	2790	2570	431A	0.00	38	44
402B	0.02	2420	2260	432A	0.00	2	2
403A	0.03	3120	3100	433A	0.00	3	4
403B	0.02	4460	4460	433B	0.00	3	5
404A	0.00	3920	3940	433C	0.00	3	4
405A	0.02	5330	4970	434A	0.00	3250	3080
406A	0.04	1940	1780	435A	0.00	26	28
407A	0.00	2110	1920	436A	0.00	11	12
407B	0.00	2800	2550	436B	0.00	11	12
407C	0.00	1770	1620	437A	0.00	1810	1640
407D	0.00	1630	1490	438A	0.00	2260	2060
407E	0.00	1550	1420	439A	0.00	1980	1830
407F	0.00	1820	1670	440A	0.00	144	156
408A	0.02	3150	3260	441A	0.00	5	5
409A	0.03	1580	1480	442A	0.00	1890	1750
409B	0.03	1560	1470	443A	0.00	2.5	4
410A	0.00	2090	1920	444A	0.00	93	89
410B	0.00	2230	2050	444B	0.00	296	295
411A	0.03	1600	1560	445A	0.00	135	118
411B	0.03	1710	1660	446A	0.00	461	461
412A	0.04	2290	2170	447A	0.00	584	572
413A	0.00	2050	1950	448A	0.00	1390	1360
414A	0.03	1480	1380	449A	0.00	1400	1280
414B	0.03	1360	1270	449B	0.00	1410	1300
415A	0.03	1510	1470	450A	0.00	605	547
415B	0.009	546	544	451A	0.00	150	133
416A	0.008	1080	975	451B	0.00	164	146
417A	0.00	2350	2130	452A	0.00	2140	1950
417B	0.00	3030	2740	453A	0.00	1770	1640
418A	0.03	1740	1690	454A	0.00	239	238
419A	0.00	2970	2690	454B	0.00	466	467
420A	0.007	1540	1380	500	0.50	8080	8010
421A	0.00	2630	2380	501	0.29	4080	4020
421B	0.00	3190	2890	502	0.20	4660	4790
422A	0.00	3140	2850	503	0.60	14,600	13,300
422B	0.00	2530	2290	504	0.10	4140	4300
422C	0.00	3090	2800	507A	0.00	3990	3990
422D	0.00	2730	2470	508A	0.00	13,200	11,600
423A	0.00	2280	2270	508B	0.00	13,400	11,700
424A	0.00	2440	2210	509A	0.01	5740	5760
425A	0.00	1510	1430	510A	0.00	3	3
426A	0.00	1510	1370	511A	0.00	3	5
427A	0.00	2140	2020	512A	0.00	189	196
				513A	0.00	631	573

*Derived based on weighted averages of blend component values.
AR4 = IPCC (2007) AR5 = IPCC (2013)

Physical Properties

Table 5 lists some physical properties of commonly used refrigerants, a few very-low-boiling-point cryogenic fluids, some newer refrigerants, and some older refrigerants of historical interest, arranged in increasing order of atmospheric boiling point.

Table 5 also includes the freezing point, critical properties, and refractive index. Of these properties, normal boiling point is most important because it is a direct indicator of the temperature at which a refrigerant can be used. The freezing point must be lower than any contemplated usage. The critical properties describe a material at the point where the distinction between liquid and gas is lost. At higher temperatures, no separate liquid phase is possible for pure fluids. In refrigeration cycles involving condensation, a refrigerant must be chosen that allows this change of state to occur at a temperature somewhat below the critical. Cycles that reject heat at supercritical temperatures (e.g., cycles using carbon dioxide) are also possible.

Lithium Bromide/Water and Ammonia/Water Solutions. These are the most commonly used working fluids in absorption refrigeration systems. (See Chapter 30 for property data.)

Electrical Properties

Tables 6 and 7 list electrical characteristics of refrigerants that are especially important in hermetic systems.

Sound Velocity

The practical velocity of a gas in piping or through openings is limited by the velocity of sound in the gas. Chapter 30 has sound velocity data for many refrigerants. The velocity increases when temperature is increased and decreases when pressure is increased. REFPROP software (NIST 2010) can be used to calculate the sound velocity at superheated conditions. The velocity of sound can be calculated from the equation

$$V_a = \sqrt{g_c (dp/d\rho)_S} = \sqrt{\gamma g_c (dp/d\rho)_T} \quad (1)$$

where

V_a = sound velocity, ft/s
g_c = gravitational constant = 32.1740 $lb_m \cdot ft/lb_f \cdot s^2$
p = pressure, lb_f/ft^2
ρ = density, lb_m/ft^3
γ = c_p/c_v = ratio of specific heats
S = entropy, Btu/lb·°R
T = temperature, °R

Sound velocity can be estimated from tables of thermodynamic properties. Change in pressure with a change in density ($dp/d\rho$) can be estimated at either constant entropy or constant temperature. It is simpler to estimate at constant temperature, but the ratio of specific heats must also be known.

2. REFRIGERANT PERFORMANCE

Chapter 2 describes several methods of calculating refrigerant performance, and Chapter 30 includes tables of thermodynamic properties of refrigerants.

Table 8 shows the theoretical calculated performance of a number of refrigerants for a standard cycle of various evaporation temperatures and 86°F condensation. For blend refrigerants, the average temperature in the evaporator and condenser is used. In most cases, suction vapor is assumed to be saturated, and compression is assumed adiabatic or at constant entropy. For R-113 and R-600a, for example, these assumptions cause some liquid in the discharge vapor. In these cases, it is assumed that discharge vapor is saturated and that suction vapor is slightly superheated. Note that actual operating conditions and performance may differ significantly from numbers in the table because of additional factors such as compressor efficiency and transport properties.

3. SAFETY

Tables 1 and 2 summarize toxicity and flammability characteristics of many refrigerants. In ASHRAE *Standard* 34, refrigerants are classified according to the hazard involved in their use. The toxicity and flammability classifications yield six safety groups (A1, A2, A3, B1, B2, and B3) for refrigerants. Group A1 refrigerants are the least hazardous, group B3 the most hazardous.

The letter designates toxicity class based on allowable exposure:

- Class A: Refrigerants that have an occupational exposure limit (OEL) of 400 ppm or greater.
- Class B: Refrigerants that have an OEL of less than 400 ppm.

Table 5 Physical Properties of Selected Refrigerants[a]

Refrigerant		Chemical Formula	Molecular Mass	Boiling Pt.[f] (NBP) at 14.696 psia, °F	Freezing Point, °F	Critical Temperature, °F	Critical Pressure, psi	Critical Density, lb/ft³	Refractive Index of Liquid[b,c]
No.	Chemical Name or Composition (% by Mass)								
728	Nitrogen	N_2	28.013	–320.44	–346	–232.528	492.5	19.56	1.205 (83 K) 589.3 nm
729	Air	—	28.959	–317.65	—	–221.062	549.6	20.97	—
740	Argon	Ar	39.948	–302.53	–308.812	–188.428	705.3	33.44	1.233 (84 K) 589.3 nm
732	Oxygen	O_2	31.999	–297.328	–361.822	–181.426	731.4	27.23	1.221 (92 K) 589.3 nm
50	Methane	CH_4	16.043	–258.664	–296.428	–116.6548	667.1	10.15	—
14	Tetrafluoromethane	CF_4	88.005	–198.49	–298.498	–50.152	543.9	39.06	—
170	Ethane	C_2H_6	30.07	–127.4764	–297.01	89.924	706.6	12.87	—
508A	R-23/116 (39/61)	—	100.1	–125.73	—	50.346	529.5	35.43	—
508B	R-23/116 (46/54)	—	95.394	–125.68	—	52.170	547.0	35.49	—
23	Trifluoromethane	CHF_3	70.014	–115.6324	–247.234	79.0574	700.8	32.87	—
13	Chlorotrifluoromethane	$CClF_3$	104.46	–114.664	–294.07	83.93	562.6	36.39	1.146 (25)[2]
744	Carbon dioxide	CO_2	44.01	–109.12[d]	–69.8044[e]	87.7604	1070.0	29.19	1.195 (15)
504	R-32/115 (48.2/51.8)	—	79.249	–72.23	—	143.85	642.3	31.51	—
32	Difluoromethane	CH_2F_2	52.024	–60.9718	–214.258	172.589	838.6	26.47	—
410A	R-32/125 (50/50)	—	72.585	–60.5974	—	160.4444	711.1	28.69	—
125	Pentafluoroethane	C_2HF_5	120.02	–54.562	–149.134	150.8414	524.7	35.81	—
1270	Propylene	C_3H_6	42.08	–53.716	–301.35	195.91	660.6	14.36	1.3640 (–50)[1]
143a	Trifluoroethane	CH_3CF_3	84.041	–53.0338	–169.258	162.8726	545.5	26.91	—
507A	R-125/143a (50/50)	—	98.859	–52.1338	—	159.1106	537.4	30.64	—
404A	R-125/143a/134a (44/52/4)	—	97.604	–51.1996	—	161.6828	540.8	30.37	—
502	R-22/115 (48.8/51.2)	—	111.63	–49.3132	—	178.71	582.6	35.50	—
407C	R-32/125/134a (23/25/52)	—	86.204	–46.5286	—	186.8612	671.5	30.23	—
290	Propane	C_3H_8	44.096	–43.805	–305.72	206.13	616.58	13.76	1.3397 (–42)
22	Chlorodifluoromethane	$CHClF_2$	86.468	–41.458	–251.356	205.061	723.7	32.70	1.234 (25)[2]
115	Chloropentafluoroethane	$CClF_2CF_3$	154.47	–38.65	–146.92	175.91	453.8	38.38	1.221 (25)[2]
500	R-12/152a (73.8/26.2)	—	99.303	–28.4854	—	215.762	604.6	30.91	—
717	Ammonia	NH_3	17.03	–27.9886	–107.779	270.05	1643.7	14.05[d]	1.325 (16.5)
12	Dichlorodifluoromethane	CCl_2F_2	120.91	–21.5536	–250.69	233.546	599.9	35.27	1.288 (25)[2]
1234yf	2,3,3,3-tetrafluoroprop-1-ene	$CF_3CF{=}CH_2$	114.04	–21.01		202.46	490.55	29.668	
134a	Tetrafluoroethane	CF_3CH_2F	102.03	–14.9332	–153.94	213.908	588.8	31.96	—
152a	Difluoroethane	CHF_2CH_3	66.051	–11.2414	–181.462	235.868	655.1	22.97	—
1234ze (E)	Trans-1,3,3,3-tetrafluoropropene	$CF_3CH{=}CHF$	114.04	–2.11		228.87	527.29	30.542	
124	Chlorotetrafluoroethane	$CHClFCF_3$	136.48	10.4666	–326.47	252.104	525.7	34.96	—
600a	Isobutane	C_4H_{10}	58.122	10.852	–254.96	274.39	526.34	14.08	1.3514 (–25)[1]
142b	Chlorodifluoroethane	$CClF_2CH_3$	100.5	15.53	–202.774	278.798	590.3	27.84	—
C318	Octafluorocyclobutane	C_4F_8	200.03	21.245	–39.64	239.414	402.8	38.70	
600	Butane	C_4H_{10}	58.122	31.118	–216.86	305.564	550.6	14.23	1.3562 (–15)[1]
1336mzz (Z)	Cis-1,1,1,4,4,4-hexafluoro-2-butene	$CF_3CH{=}CHCF_3$	164.1	33.4	—	340.3	421.0	31.506	—
114	Dichlorotetrafluoroethane	$CClF_2CClF_2$	170.92	38.4548	–134.54	294.224	472.4	36.21	1.294 (25)
1233zd(E)	Trans-1-chloro-3,3,3-trifluoro-1-propene	$CF_3CH{=}CHCl$	130.5	64.6	—	330.1	519.2	30.030	—
11	Trichlorofluoromethane	CCl_3F	137.37	74.6744	–166.846	388.328	639.3	34.59	1.362 (25)[2]
123	Dichlorotrifluoroethane	$CHCl_2CF_3$	152.93	82.08	–160.87	362.624	531.1	34.34	—
141b	Dichlorofluoroethane	CCl_2FCH_3	116.95	89.69	–154.25	399.83	610.9	28.63	—
113	Trichlorotrifluoroethane	CCl_2FCClF_2	187.38	117.653	–33.196	417.308	492.0	34.96	1.357 (25)[2]
718[3]	Water	H_2O	18.015	211.9532	32.018	705.11	3200.1	20.10	—

Notes:
[a]Data from NIST (2010) REFPROP v. 9.0.
[b]Temperature of measurement (°C, unless kelvin is noted) shown in parentheses. Data from CRC (1987), unless otherwise noted.
[c]For the sodium D line.
[d]Sublimes.
[e]At 76.4 psi.
[f]Bubble point used for blends

References:
[1]Kirk and Othmer (1956).
[2]*Bulletin* B-32A (DuPont).
[3]*Handbook of Chemistry* (1967).

The numeral denotes flammability:

- Class 1: No flame propagation in air at 140°F and 14.7 psia
- Class 2: Exhibits flame propagation in air at 140°F and 14.7 psia, lower flammability limit (LFL) greater than 0.0062 lb/ft³ at 73.4°F and 14.7 psia, and heat of combustion less than 8169 Btu/lb
- Optional class 2L: class 2 refrigerants may be classified as 2L if they exhibit a maximum burning velocity of no more than 3.9 in/s at 73.4°F and 14.7 psia
- Class 3: Exhibits flame propagation in air at 140°F and 14.7 psia and LFL less than or equal to 0.0062 lb/ft³ at 73.4°F and 14.7 psia or heat of combustion greater than or equal to 8169 Btu/lb

Refrigerant blends are assigned the flammability safety classification of the worst case of fractionation of the blend (i.e., the composition during fractionation that results in the highest concentration of flammable components). For class 2 or 3 refrigerants or refrigerant blends that show no flame propagation when tested at

Table 6 Electrical Properties of Liquid Refrigerants

Refrigerant No.	Refrigerant Chemical Name or Composition (% By Mass)	Temp., °F	Dielectric Constant	Volume Resistivity, MΩ·m	Ref.
11	Trichlorofluoromethane	84	2.28		1
		a	1.92	63,680	2
		77	2.5	90	3
		77	2.32		9
12	Dichlorodifluoromethane	84	2.13		1
		a	1.74	53,900	2
		77	2.1	>120	3
		77	2.100		4
		77	2.14		9
13	Chlorotrifluoromethane	–22	2.3	120	4
		68	1.64		
22	Chlorodifluoromethane	75	6.11		1
		a	6.12	0.83	2
		77	6.6	75	3
		77	6.42		9
23	Trifluoromethane	–22	6.3		3
		68	5.51		4
32	Difluoromethane	a	14.27		6
		77	14.67		9
113	Trichlorotrifluoroethane	86	2.44		1
		a	1.68	45,490	2
		77	2.6	>120	3
114	Dichlorotetrafluoroethane	88	2.17		1
		a	1.83	66,470	2
		77	2.2	>70	3
123	2,2-dichloro-1,1,1-trifluoroethane	a	4.50	14,700	4
124	2-chloro-1,1,1,2-tetrafluoroethane	77	4.89		9
124a	Chlorotetrafluoroethane	77	4.0	50	3
125	Pentafluoroethane	68	4.94		7
		77	5.10		9
134a	1,1,1,2-tetrafluoroethane	a	9.51	17,700	4
		77	9.87		9
143a	1,1,1-trifluoroethane	77	9.78		9
236fa	1,1,1,3,3,3-hexafluoropropane	77	7.89		9
245fa	1,1,1,3,3-pentafluoropropane	77	6.82		9
290	Propane	a	1.27	73,840	2
404A	R-125/143a/134a (44/52/4)	a	7.58	8450	8
		77	8.06		9
407C	R-32/125/134a (23/25/52)	a	8.74	7420	8
		77	10.21		9
410A	R-32/125 (50/50)	a	7.78	3920	8
		77	5.37		9
500	R-12/152a (73.8/26.2)	a	1.80	55,750	2
507A	R-125/143a (50/50)	a	6.97	5570	8
		77	7.94		9
508A	R-23/116 (39/61)	–22	6.60		1
		32	5.02		1
508B	R-23/116 (46/54)	–22	7.24		1
		32	5.48		1
717	Ammonia	69	15.5		5
744	Carbon dioxide	32	1.59		5
1234yf	2,3,3,3-tetrafluoro-1-propene	77	7.6		10
		70	7.7		11

a = ambient temperature

References:
1 Data from E.I. DuPont de Nemours & Co., Inc.
2 Beacham and Divers (1955)
3 Eiseman (1955)
4 Fellows et al. (1991)
5 CRC (1987)
6 Bararo et al. (1997)
7 Pereira et al. (1999)
8 Meurer et al. (2001)
9 Gbur and Byrne (2001)
10 Muller et al. (2011)
11 Data from Honeywell

Table 7 Electrical Properties of Refrigerant Vapors

Refrigerant No.	Refrigerant Chemical Name or Composition (% by mass)	Pressure, atm.	Temp., °F	Dielectric Constant	Relative Dielectric Strength, Nitrogen = 1	Volume Resistivity, GΩ·m	Ref.
11	Trichlorofluoromethane	0.5	79	1.0019			3
		a	b	1.009		74.35	2
		1.01	73		3.1		4
12	Dichlorodifluoromethane	0.5	84	1.0016			3
		a	b	1.012	452[c]	72.77	2
		1.0	73		2.4		4
		1.0	77	1.0064			6
13	Chlorotrifluoromethane	0.5	84	1.0013			3
		1.0	73		1.4		4
14	Tetrafluoromethane	0.5	76	1.0006			3
		1.0	73		1.0		4
22	Chlorodifluoromethane	0.5	78	1.0035			3
		a	b	1.004	460[c]	2113	2
		1.0	73		1.3		4
		1.0	77	1.0068			6
32	Difluoromethane	1.0	77	1.0102			6
113	Trichlorotrifluoroethane	a	b	1.010	440[c]	94.18	2
		0.4	73		2.6		4
114	Dichlorotetrafluoroethane	0.5	80	1.0021			3
		a	b	1.002	295[c]	148.3	2
		1.0	73		2.8		4
116	Hexafluoroethane	0.94	73	1.002			3
124	2-chloro-1,1,1,2-tetrafluoroethane	1.0	77	1.0060			6
125	Pentafluoroethane	1.0	77	1.0072			6
134a	1,1,1,2-tetrafluoroethane	1.0	77	1.0125			6
142b	Chlorodifluoroethane	0.93	81	1.013			3
143a	Trifluoroethane	0.85	77	1.013			3
		1.0	77	1.0170			6
170	Ethane	1.0	32	1.0015			1
236fa	1,1,1,3,3,3-hexafluoropropane	1.0	77	1.0121			6
245fa	1,1,1,3,3-pentafluoropropane	1.0	77	1.0066			6
290	Propane	a	b	1.009	440[c]	105.3	2
404A	R-125/143a/134a (44/52/4)	1.0	77	1.0121			6
407C	R-32/125/134a (23/25/52)	1.0	77	1.0113			6
410A	R-32/125 (50/50)	1.0	77	1.0078			6
500	R-12/152a (73.8/26.2)	a	b	1.024	470[c]	76.45	2
507A	R-125/143a (50/50)	1.0	77	1.0119			6
508A	R-23/116 (39/61)	a	–22	1.12			5
		a	32	1.31			5
		1.0	77	1.0042			6
508B	R-23/116 (46/54)	a	–22	1.13			5
		a	32	1.34			5
		1.0	77	1.0042			6
717	Ammonia	1.0	32	1.0072			1
		a	32		0.82		4
729	Air	1.0	32	1.00059			1
744	Carbon dioxide	1.0	32	1.00099			1
		1.0	b		0.88		4
1150	Ethylene	1.0	32	1.00144			1
		1.0	73		1.21		4

Notes:
a = saturation vapor pressure
b = ambient temperature
c = measured breakdown voltage, volts/mil

References:
1 CRC (1987)
2 Beacham and Divers (1955)
3 Fuoss (1938)
4 Charlton and Cooper (1937)
5 Data from E.I. DuPont de Nemours & Co., Inc.
6 Gbur (2005)

Table 8 Comparative Refrigerant Performance per Ton of Refrigeration

Refrigerant No.	Chemical Name or Composition (% by mass)	Evaporator Pressure, psia	Condenser Pressure, psia	Compression Ratio	Net Refrigerating Effect, Btu/lb	Refrigerant Circulated, lb/min	Liquid Circulated, gal/min	Specific Volume of Suction Gas, ft³/lb	Compressor Displacement, ft³/min	Power Consumption, hp	Coefficient of Performance	Compressor Discharge Temp., °F
Evaporator –25°F/Condenser 86°F												
744	Carbon dioxide	195.7	1046.2	5.35	56.8	3.52	0.711	0.457	1.61	2.779	1.698	196.3
170	Ethane	146.8	675.1	4.6	66.0	3.03	1.314	0.878	2.66	2.805	1.681	136.2
1270	Propylene	28.8	189.3	6.57	115.7	1.73	0.416	3.63	6.28	1.637	2.88	120.3
507A	R-125/143a (50/50)	28.8	211.7	7.34	43.5	4.60	0.54	1.52	6.98	1.833	2.573	100.6
404A	R-125/143a/134a (44/52/4)	27.6	206.1	7.46	45.1	4.44	0.521	1.61	7.13	1.817	2.595	102.1
502	R-22/115 (48.8/51.2)	26.5	189.2	7.14	42.1	4.76	0.48	1.48	7.06	1.722	2.739	106.3
22	Chlorodifluoromethane	22.1	172.9	7.81	66.8	3.00	0.307	2.32	6.95	1.589	2.967	149.8
717	Ammonia	16.0	169.3	10.61	463.9	0.43	0.087	16.7	7.19	1.569	3.007	285.6
Evaporator 20°F/Condenser 86°F												
744	Carbon dioxide	421.9	1046.2	2.48	55.7	3.59	0.726	0.203	0.73	1.342	3.514	142.3
170	Ethane	293.6	675.1	2.3	70.1	2.85	1.238	0.421	1.20	1.314	3.588	115.8
32	Difluoromethane	94.7	279.6	2.95	111.2	1.80	0.229	0.902	1.62	0.797	5.924	139.4
410A	R-32/125 (50/50)	93.2	273.6	2.94	73.5	2.72	0.316	0.651	1.77	0.815	5.78	115.8
507A	R-125/143a (50/50)	72.9	211.7	2.9	49.4	4.05	0.476	0.616	2.50	0.848	5.564	93.5
404A	R-125/143a/134a (44/52/4)	70.5	206.1	2.92	51.1	3.92	0.46	0.649	2.54	0.842	5.598	94.3
1270	Propylene	69.1	189.3	2.74	126.6	1.58	0.381	1.58	2.50	0.79	5.975	102.8
502	R-22/115 (48.8/51.2)	66.3	189.2	2.86	47.1	4.25	0.429	0.619	2.63	0.813	5.799	95.8
22	Chlorodifluoromethane	57.8	172.9	2.99	71.3	2.80	0.287	0.935	2.62	0.772	6.105	118.0
407C	R-32/125/134a (23/25/52)	57.5	183.7	3.19	71.9	2.78	0.296	0.942	2.62	0.795	5.93	111.0
290	Propane	55.8	156.5	2.8	124.1	1.61	0.399	1.89	3.05	0.787	5.987	94.8
717	Ammonia	48.2	169.3	3.51	478.5	0.42	0.084	5.91	2.47	0.754	6.254	179.8
1234yf	2,3,3,3-tetrafluoropropene*	36.3	113.6	3.13	51.8	3.86	0.43	1.15	4.44	0.809	5.835	86.0
134a	Tetrafluoroethane	33.1	111.7	3.37	65.8	3.04	0.307	1.41	4.28	0.778	6.063	94.7
1234ze(E)	Trans-1,3,3,3-tetrafluoropropene*	24.4	83.9	3.44	60.0	3.33	0.349	1.74	5.81	0.782	6.03	86.0
600a	Isobutane*	17.9	58.7	3.29	119.5	1.67	0.368	4.78	7.99	0.764	6.171	86.0
Evaporator 45°F/Condenser 86°F												
32	Difluoromethane	147.7	279.6	1.89	112.2	1.78	0.223	0.577	1.03	0.445	10.602	116.4
410A	R-32/125 (50/50)	145.0	273.6	1.89	75.2	2.66	0.308	0.416	1.11	0.455	10.379	103.7
502	R-22/115 (48.8/51.2)	102.0	189.2	1.85	49.6	4.03	0.407	0.404	1.63	0.451	10.474	91.8
407C	R-32/125/134a (23/25/52)	92.8	183.7	1.98	74.7	2.68	0.284	0.588	1.57	0.443	10.655	102.7
22	Chlorodifluoromethane	90.8	172.9	1.9	73.5	2.72	0.279	0.604	1.64	0.433	10.885	104.5
290	Propane	85.3	156.5	1.84	130.7	1.53	0.379	1.26	1.92	0.439	10.743	90.7
717	Ammonia	81.0	169.3	2.09	484.9	0.41	0.083	3.61	1.49	0.421	11.186	137.4
500	R-12/152a (73.8/26.2)	66.5	127.6	1.92	64.7	3.09	0.331	0.725	2.24	0.432	10.925	94.2
1234yf	2,3,3,3-tetrafluoropropene*	58.1	113.6	1.96	55.5	3.61	0.402	0.726	2.62	0.444	10.623	86.0
12	Dichlorodifluoromethane	56.3	107.9	1.92	54.6	3.67	0.34	0.719	2.64	0.429	11.004	91.6
134a	Tetrafluoroethane	54.7	111.7	2.04	69.2	2.89	0.292	0.868	2.51	0.433	10.903	90.6
1234ze(E)	Trans-1,3,3,3-tetrafluoropropene*	40.6	83.9	2.06	64.1	3.12	0.327	1.07	3.34	0.433	10.899	86.0
600a	Isobutane*	29.2	58.7	2.01	127.4	1.57	0.345	3.01	4.72	0.425	11.084	86.0
600	Butane*	19.5	41.1	2.11	140.5	1.42	0.301	4.57	6.50	0.42	11.226	86.0
123	Dichlorotrifluoroethane	6.5	15.9	2.44	66.9	2.99	0.246	5.3	15.85	0.414	11.397	86.0
113	Trichlorotrifluoroethane*	3.1	7.9	2.57	59.2	3.38	0.26	9.41	31.81	0.413	11.409	86.0

*Superheat required

Source: Data from NIST CYCLE_D 4.0, zero subcool, zero superheat unless noted, no line losses, 100% efficiencies, average temperatures.

73.4°F and 14.7 psia (i.e., no LFL), an elevated temperature flame limit at 140°F (ETFL60) is used in lieu of the LFL for determining flammability classifications.

4. LEAK DETECTION

Leak detection in refrigeration equipment is of major importance for manufacturers and service engineers.

Electronic Detection

Electronic detectors are widely used in manufacture and assembly of refrigeration equipment. Techniques include infrared, solid electrolyte semiconductor, heated electrode/diode, and corona discharge sensors. Instrument operation depends on the variation in signal caused by the presence of refrigerant. These instruments can be refrigerant specific or may detect a variety of refrigerants. Other vapors in the local environment may interfere with the test.

The electronic detector is the most sensitive of the methods discussed here, readily capable of sensing a leak of 1/10 oz of refrigerant per year. A portable model is available for field testing. Other models are available with automatic balancing systems that correct for background refrigerant vapors that might be present in the atmosphere around the test area.

Bubble Method

The object to be tested is pressurized with air or nitrogen. A pressure corresponding to operating conditions is generally used. If possible, the object is fully immersed in water, and leaks are detected by observing bubbles in the liquid. Adding a detergent to the water decreases surface tension, prevents escaping gas from clinging to the side of the object, and promotes formation of a regular stream of small bubbles. In addition to dwell time, test sensitivity is influenced by clarity of the liquid, lighting, proximity of the leak site to the operator, and human factors. When immersion is not practical, a solution of soap can be brushed, sprayed, or poured onto joints or other spots where leakage is suspected. Leaking gas forms soap bubbles that can be readily detected. When properly performed under favorable conditions, bubble testing methods can detect leaks as small as 0.1 oz of refrigerant per year.

Pressure Change Methods

The presence of leaks can be determined by pressurizing or evacuating the internals of the part or system and observing the change in pressure or vacuum over a period of time. The vacuum decay test can give an indication of proper dehydration but, like pressure decay, it does not locate the point of leakage. Test methods that are based on pressure change typically are not sensitive enough to meet the needs of refrigerant components and systems used in HVAC applications. The pressure change test methods are useful to verify that a component or system is free from gross leaks. Typical sensitivity is in the range of thousands of ounces of refrigerant per year.

Leaks can also be determined by pressurizing or evacuating and observing the change in pressure or vacuum over a period of time. This is effective in checking system tightness but does not locate the point of leakage.

UV Dye Method

A stable UV-fluorescent dye is introduced into the system to be tested. Operating the system mixes the UV dye uniformly in the oil/refrigerant system. The dye, which usually prefers oil, shows up at the leak's location, and can be detected using an appropriate UV lamp. Ensure that the dye is compatible with system components and that no one is exposed to UV radiation from the lamp. This method only finds defects that are large enough to pass liquid, and will only work effectively in regions of the system where enough oil is available to carry the dye. Thus, this method's sensitivity is typically significantly lower than that of the electronic detection and bubble test methods.

Ammonia Leaks

Ammonia can be detected by any of the previously described methods, or by bringing a solution of hydrochloric acid near the object. If ammonia vapor is present, a white cloud or smoke of ammonium chloride forms. Ammonia can also be detected with indicator paper that changes color in the presence of a base. Ensure that adequate ventilation is provided and no one is exposed to ammonia.

5. COMPATIBILITY WITH CONSTRUCTION MATERIALS

Metals

Halogenated refrigerants can be used satisfactorily under normal conditions with most common metals, such as steel, cast iron, brass, copper, tin, lead, and aluminum [an important exception is methyl chloride (R-40) in contact with aluminum]. Under more severe conditions, various metals affect properties such as hydrolysis and thermal decomposition in varying degrees. The tendency of metals to promote thermal decomposition of halogenated compounds is in the following order:

(least decomposition) Inconel < 18-8 stainless steel < nickel < copper < 1040 steel < aluminum < bronze < brass < zinc < silver (most decomposition)

This order is only approximate, and there may be exceptions for individual compounds or for special use conditions (Downing 1988).

Magnesium alloys and aluminum containing more than 2% magnesium are not recommended for use with halogenated compounds where even trace amounts of water may be present. Zinc is not recommended for use with CFC-113. Experience with zinc and other fluorinated compounds has been limited, but no unusual reactivity has been observed under normal conditions of use in dry systems. However, OxyChem (2009) takes a more conservative position: "Aluminum, zinc, or magnesium equipment should never be allowed to come in contact with methyl chloride."

In 2011, several suspected substitutions of R-40-containing refrigerant mixtures for R-134a in aluminum-containing refrigeration and air-conditioning systems resulted in equipment failures, explosions, and even fatalities (Powell 2012; *WorldCargo News* 2011). Reactions of methyl chloride with aluminum are known (Dow 2007; Linde 2010; OxyChem 2009), and several publications advise not using aluminum containers for methyl chloride (Dow 2010; European Industrial Gases Association 2010). Studies are under way to quantify the reactivity of methyl chloride concentrations in R-134a/aluminum systems, and identify methods of safe handling, neutralization, and disposal of R-40-contaminated refrigerants. R-40 contamination appears to be part of a broader global issue of fake and counterfeit refrigerants. Press reports [e.g., *ACR News* (2011a, 2011b, 2012)] describe discovery of R-40 and other contaminants, including hydrocarbons and illegal ozone-depleting substances, found in service market refrigerant containers with fake labels, and in refrigeration and air-conditioning systems on several continents, including North America. Using best practices in the service industry is essential, particularly using refrigerant identification methods to ensure refrigerant systems contain and are refilled with genuine refrigerant. Refrigerant manufacturers are developing additional means to deter counterfeit products.

Ammonia should never be used with copper, brass, or other alloys containing copper. Metals compatibility data for ammonia, carbon dioxide, and hydrocarbons are provided by Pruett (1995). Further information on compatibility of refrigerants and lubricants with construction materials metals, elastomers, and plastics is in Chapter 6 of the 2014 *ASHRAE Handbook—Refrigeration* and in publications of the Air-Conditioning, Heating, and Refrigeration Technology Institute (AHRTI), the research branch of the Air-Conditioning, Heating, and Refrigeration Institute (AHRI). For example, Rohatgi et al. (2012) investigated thermal and chemical stability of five refrigerants [HFO-1234yf, HFO-1234ze, R-32/HFO-1234yf (equal mass percentages), R-410A, and R-134a] and three lubricants (two types of POEs and a PVE). The report can be downloaded from AHRI's web site.

Elastomers

Linear swelling of some elastomers in the liquid phase of HCFC and HFC refrigerants is shown in Table 9 (Hamed et al. 1994). Swelling data can be used to a limited extent in comparing the effect of refrigerants on elastomers. However, other factors, such as the amount of extraction, tensile strength, and degree of hardness of the exposed elastomer, must be considered. When other fluids (e.g., lubricants) are present in addition to the refrigerant, the combined effect on elastomers should be determined. Extensive test

Table 9 Swelling of Elastomers in Liquid Refrigerants at Room Temperature, % Linear Swell

Refrigerant Number	Polyisoprene (Sulfur Cure)	Polychloroprene	Butyl Rubber	Styrene Butadiene Rubber	Nitrile Rubber	Fluoroelastomer
22	10.2	6.1	3.9	9.8	51.4	33.2
123	48.0	15.3	16.3	40.8	83.7	31.6
124	5.8	2.8	3.2	4.1	45.9	29.0
142b	10.2	6.5	6.2	7.3	8.7	31.8
32	2.7	1.0	1.0	2.0	8.3	23.2
125	4.2	2.7	2.6	3.6	3.9	11.7
134a	1.2	1.2	0.6	1.0	5.1	25.6
143a	1.9	1.2	1.3	1.5	2.0	13.6
152a	4.2	3.0	1.7	2.8	8.8	39.1

data for compatibility of elastomers and gasketing materials with refrigerants and lubricants are reported by Hamed et al. (1994). More recent elastomer compatibility data for R-134a and R-1234yf were reported by Minor and Spatz (2008). Six elastomers were contacted with the refrigerants and a PAG lubricant at 212°F for two weeks. Linear swell percentages for the elastomers were very similar in the tests: in the range of –1.4 to +2.1% with R-134a and –1.6 to +1.6% with R-1234yf. Weight gain and hardness changes for the elastomers were also similar in the tests, except for silicone elastomer in R-1234yf having a larger decrease in hardness.

Permeation of fluids through elastomers is another consideration, such as with elastomeric hoses in mobile air-conditioning systems. Refrigerant can be lost by outward permeation of refrigerant through the hoses, and water can enter the system by inward diffusion. Data for water and refrigerant permeation through many types of elastomers are presented by Downing (1988). Multilayer hose construction is used to significantly reduce water ingression and refrigerant permeation loss. A typical hose construction might be an outer cover of chlorobutyl elastomer to reduce water ingression, a layer of polyamide to reduce refrigerant permeation, and the inner tube of chloroprene. Hose manufacturers offer variations of such constructions based on their proprietary technology. Refrigerant permeation test data for R-134a and R-1234yf through these types of hose constructions were reported by Minor and Spatz (2008) and Hill and Grimm (2008). In all cases, the permeation rates of R-1234yf were lower than those of R-134a. Majurin et al. (2014) also investigated materials compatibility of HFO-1234yf, HFO-1234ze, and a blend of 1234yf/1234ze/R-32 (equal mass percentages) with various elastomers and other motor materials, and found a wide range of compatible materials; the report is available on AHRI's website.

See Pruett (1994) for compatibility data for elastomers with ammonia, carbon dioxide, and hydrocarbons.

Plastics

The effect of a refrigerant on a plastic material should be thoroughly examined under conditions of intended use, including the presence of lubricants. Plastics are often mixtures of two or more basic types, and it is difficult to predict the refrigerant's effect. Weight and visual changes can be used as a general guide of effect, but changes in the plastic's properties should also be examined. Extensive test data for compatibility of plastics with refrigerants and lubricants are reported by Cavestri (1993), including 23 plastics, 10 refrigerants, 7 lubricants, and 17 refrigerant/lubricant combinations. Refrigerants and lubricants had little effect on most of the plastics, though acrylonitrile-butadiene-styrene, polyphenylene oxide, and polycarbonate were affected enough to be considered incompatible. In a separate study by DuPont Fluoroproducts (2003), acrylonitrile butadiene styrene and polystyrene were determined to have questionable compatibility with HCFC and HFC refrigerants.

R-134a and R-1234yf were evaluated for compatibility with typical plastics used in automotive air-conditioning systems (Minor and Spatz 2008). Five plastics (polyester, nylon, epoxy, polyethylene terephthalate, and polyimide) were contacted in sealed tubes containing the refrigerants and PAG lubricant, and held at 212°F for two weeks. The plastics were evaluated for changes in weight and appearance 24 h after test completion, finding essentially the same positive ratings of the two refrigerants with the plastics.

For data an compatibility of plastics with ammonia, carbon dioxide, and hydrocarbons, see Pruett (2000).

Additional Compatibility Reports

The Air-Conditioning, Heating, and Refrigeration Institute (AHRI) has supported research programs for refrigerants stability and materials compatibility through their Materials Compatibility and Lubricants Research (MCLR) Program, beginning in the early 1990s for replacements for CFCs. Resulting research reports are available from AHRI, with the following refrigerants stability/materials compatibility research topics: plastics (Cavestri 1993), lubricant additives (Cavestri 1997), system contaminants (Cavestri 2000), motor materials (Doerr and Kujak 1993; Doerr and Waite 1996), desiccants (Field 1995), elastomers (Hamed et al. 1994), and metals (Huttenlocher 1992). Cavestri et al. (2010) studied five refrigerants (R-417A, R-422D, R-424A, R-434A, and R-438A) and lubricants in contact with aluminum, copper, and steel coupons, and with nonmetallic materials of construction (elastomers, sealants, and plastics). They found, "A general, overall statement can be made that material changes for the R-22 alternative refrigerants investigated in this study do not have statistically significant differences compared to R-22 exposure in both time and temperature."

Two recent AHRI projects investigated materials compatibility of HFO refrigerants. Phase I covered thermal stability of 1234yf, 1234ze, and a 1234yf/R-32 blend with lubricants in the presence of metals (Rohatgi et al. 2012). Phase II focused on compatibility with plastics, elastomers, and motor materials (Majurin et al. 2014). Both reports show that HFOs have compatibility with a wide range of materials used in HVAC&R systems.

REFERENCES

ASHRAE members can access *ASHRAE Journal* articles and ASHRAE research project final reports at technologyportal .ashrae.org. Articles and reports are also available for purchase by nonmembers in the online ASHRAE Bookstore at www.ashrae.org /bookstore.

ACR News. 2011a. Methyl chloride to blame for reefer explosions? (Nov. 6).

ACR News. 2011b. Fake refrigerants becoming a "serious problem." (Nov. 15).

ACR News. 2012. Traces of dangerous refrigerant found in returned cylinders. (July 16).

AHRI. 2011. Specification for fluorocarbon refrigerants. *Standard* 700-2011. Air-Conditioning, Heating, and Refrigeration Institute, Arlington, VA.

ARAP. 1999. Global comparative analysis of HFC and alternative technologies for refrigeration, air conditioning, foam, solvent, aerosol propellant, and fire protection applications. *Final Report* to the Alliance for Responsible Atmospheric Policy, Arlington, VA. Dieckmann, J., Arthur D. Little, Inc., and Hillel Magid Consultant. unfccc.int/methods/other _methodological_issues/interactions_with_ozone_layer/items/378.php.

ASHRAE. 2016. Designation and safety classification of refrigerants. ANSI/ ASHRAE *Standard* 34-2016.

Bararo, M.T., U.V. Mardolcar, and C.A. Nieto de Castro. 1997. Molecular properties of alternative refrigerants derived from dielectric-constant measurements. *Journal of Thermophysics* 18(2):419-438.

Beacham, E.A., and R.T. Divers. 1955. Some aspects of the dielectric properties of refrigerants. *Refrigerating Engineering* 7:33.

Calm, J. C., G. C. Hourahan, A. Vonsild, D. Clodic, and D. Colbourne. 2015. *2014 Report of the refrigeration, air conditioning, and heat pumps technical options committee*, Ch. 2: Refrigerants. United Nations Environment Programme (UNEP) Ozone Secretariat, Nairobi. ozone.unep.org /en/assessment-panels/technology-and-economic-assessment-panel.

Cavestri, R.C. 1993. Compatibility of refrigerants and lubricants with engineering plastics. *Report* DOE/CE/23810-15. Air Conditioning and Refrigeration Technology Institute (ARTI), Arlington, VA.

Cavestri, R.C. 1997. Compatibility of lubricant additives with HFC refrigerants and synthetic lubricants. *Report* DOE/CE/23810-76. Air Conditioning and Refrigeration Technology Institute (ARTI), Arlington, VA.

Cavestri, R.C. 2000. Effect of selected contaminants in air conditioning and refrigeration equipment. *Report* DOE/CE/23810-111. Air Conditioning and Refrigeration Technology Institute (ARTI), Arlington, VA.

Cavestri, R.C., M. El-Shazly, and D. Seeger-Clevenger. 2010. Thermal stability and chemical compatibility of R-22 replacement refrigerants. AHRI *Project* 8003. Air Conditioning, Heating, and Refrigeration Institute, Arlington, VA.

Charlton, E.E., and F.S. Cooper. 1937. Dielectric strengths of insulating fluids. *General Electric Review* 865(9):438.

CRC. 1987. *CRC handbook of chemistry and physics*, 68th ed. CRC Press, Boca Raton, FL.

Doerr, R.G., and S.A. Kujak. 1993. Compatibility of refrigerants and lubricants with motor materials. *Report* DOE/CE/23810-13. Air Conditioning and Refrigeration Technology Institute, Arlington, VA.

Doerr, R.G., and T.D. Waite. 1996. Compatibility of refrigerants and lubricants with motor materials under retrofit conditions. *Report* DOE/CE/23810-63. Air Conditioning and Refrigeration Technology Institute, Arlington, VA.

Dow. 2007. *Product safety assessment: Methyl chloride*. Dow Chemical Company, Midland MI.

Dow. 2010. *Material safety data sheet: Methyl chloride*. Dow Chemical Company, Midland, MI.

Downing, R.C. 1988. *Fluorocarbon refrigerants handbook*. Prentice Hall, Englewood Cliffs, NJ.

DuPont. *Bulletin* B-32A. Freon Products Division. E.I. DuPont de Nemours & Co., Wilmington, DE.

DuPont Fluoroproducts. 2003. *Technical Information Bulletins for HFC-134a, R-407C and R-410A*. E.I. DuPont de Nemours & Co., Wilmington, DE.

Eiseman, B.J., Jr. 1955. How electrical properties of Freon compounds affect hermetic system's insulation. *Refrigerating Engineering* 4:61.

European Industrial Gases Association. 2010. Gas compatibility with aluminum alloy cylinders. IGC *Document* 161/10/E. Brussels, Belgium.

Fellows, B.R., R.G. Richard, and I.R. Shankland. 1991. Electrical characterization of alternate refrigerants. *Actes Congrès International du Froid* 18(2). International Institute of Refrigeration, Paris.

Field, J.E. 1995. Sealed tube comparisons of the compatibility of desiccants with refrigerants and lubricants. *Report* DOE/CE/23810-54. Air Conditioning and Refrigeration Technology Institute, Arlington, VA.

Fischer, S.K., P.J. Hughes, P.D. Fairchild, C.L. Kusik, J.T. Dieckmann, E.M. McMahon, and N. Hobay. 1991. *Energy and global warming impacts of CFC alternative technologies*. Sponsored by the Alternative Fluorocarbons Environmental Acceptability Study (AFEAS) and the U.S. Department of Energy (DOE). www.ciesin.org/docs/011-459/011-459.html.

Fuoss, R.M. 1938. Dielectric constants of some fluorine compounds. *Journal of the American Chemical Society* 64:1633.

Gbur, A.M., and J.J. Byrne. 2001. Determination of dieletric properties of refrigerants. ASHRAE Research Project RP-1074, *Final Report*.

Hamed, G.R., R.H. Seiple, and O. Taikum. 1994. Compatibility of refrigerants and lubricants with elastomers. *Report* DOE/CE/23810-14. Air Conditioning and Refrigeration Technology Institute, Arlington, VA.

Handbook of chemistry, 10th ed. 1967. McGraw-Hill, New York.

Hill, W., and U. Grimm. 2008. *Overview of SAE Cooperative Research Program CRP1234-2 for alternative refrigerants*. SAE International AARS. Phoenix. AZ.

Huttenlocher, D.F. 1992. Chemical and thermal stability of refrigerant-lubricant mixtures with metals. *Report* DOE/CE/23810-5. Air Conditioning and Refrigeration Technology Institute, Arlington, VA.

IPCC. 2007. *Climate change 2007: The physical science basis. Contribution of working group I to the fourth assessment report of the Intergovernmental Panel on Climate Change*. S. Solomon, D. Qin, M. Manning, Z. Chen, M. Marquis, K.B. Averyt, M. Tignor, and H.L. Miller, eds. Cambridge University Press, Cambridge, U.K. ipcc.ch/publications_and_data/ar4/wg1/en/contents.html.

IPCC. 2013. *Climate change 2013: The physical science basis*. Contribution of working group I to the fifth assessment report of the Intergovernmental Panel on Climate Change. T.F. Stoecker, D. Qin, G.-K. Plattner, M. Tignor, S.K. Allen, J. Boschung, A. Nauels, Y. Xia, V. Bex, and P.M. Midgely, eds. Cambridge University Press.

IPCC. 2014. *Climate change 2014: Synthesis report. Contribution of working groups I, II, and III to the fifth assessment report of the Intergovernmental Panel on Climate Change*. Core writing team, R.K. Pachauri, and L.A. Meyer, eds. International Panel on Climate Change, Geneva. www.ipcc.ch/report/ar5/syr/.

Kirk and Othmer. 1956. *The encyclopedia of chemical technology*. Interscience Encyclopedia, New York.

Linde. 2010. *Material safety data sheet: Methyl chloride*. Linde Gas North America LLC, Murray Hill, NJ.

Majurin, J. A., E. Sorenson, S. J. Staats, W. Gilles and S. J. Kujak. 2014. *Material compatibility and lubricants research for low GWP refrigerant—Phase II: Chemical and material compatibility of low GWP refrigerants with HVACR material of construction*. AHRI Project 08007. www.ahrinet.org/App_Content/ahri/files/RESEARCH/Technical%20Results/AHRI_Project-8007_Final_Report.pdf.

Meurer, C., G. Pietsch, and M. Haacke. 2001. Electrical properties of CFC- and HCFC-substitutes. *International Journal of Refrigeration* 24(2):171-175.

Minor, B., and M. Spatz. 2008. *HFO-1234yf low GWP refrigerant update*. Presentation charts. International Refrigeration and Air Conditioning Conference, Purdue University, West Lafayette, IN. www2.dupont.com/Refrigerants/en_US/assets/downloads/SmartAutoAC/MAC_Purdue_HFO_1234yf.pdf.

Muller, Y., S. Feja, and U. Grimm. 2011. Electrical properties of the liquid phase of refrigerant oil mixtures. SAE International Automotive Refrigerant and System Efficiency Symposium, Scottsdale, AZ.

NIST. 2010. *NIST reference fluid thermodynamic and transport properties database (REFPROP)*, v. 9.0. National Institute of Standards and Technology, Gaithersburg, MD.

OxyChem. 2009. Reaction of methyl chloride with aluminum. OxyChem *Technical Data Sheet* 510-101. Wichita, KS.

Pereira, L.F., F.E. Brito, A.N. Gurova, U.V. Mardolcar, and C.A. Nieta de Castro. 1999. Dipole moment, expansivity and compressibility coefficients of HFC 125 derived from dielectric constant measurements. 1st International Workshop on Thermochemical, Thermodynamic and Transport Properties of Halogenated Hydrocarbons and Mixtures, Pisa, Italy.

Powell, P. 2012. Rogue refrigerant blend linked to fatalities. *Air Conditioning, Heating, and Refrigeration News* (January 9). Troy, MI. www.achrnews.com/articles/rogue-refrigerant-blend-linked-to-fatalities.

Pruett, K.M. 1994. *Chemical resistance guide for elastomers II*. Compass Publications, La Mesa, CA.

Pruett, K.M. 1995. *Chemical resistance guide for metals and alloys*. Compass Publications, La Mesa, CA.

Pruett, K.M. 2000. *Chemical resistance guide for plastics*. Compass Publications, La Mesa, CA.

Ravishankara, A.R., A.A. Turnipseed, N.R. Jensen, and R.F. Warren. 1994. Do hydrofluorocarbons destroy stratospheric ozone? *Science* 248:1217-1219.

Rohatgi, N.D., R.W. Clark, D.R. Hurst. 2012. *Material compatibility & lubricants research for low GWP refrigerants—Phase I: Thermal and chemical stability of low GWP refrigerants with lubricants*. Project 09004-01. www.ahrinet.org/site/511/Resources/Research/Public-Sector-Research/Technical-Results.

UNEP. 2009. *Handbook for the international treaties for the protection of the ozone layer*, 8th ed. United Nations Environment Programme (UNEP) Ozone Secretariat, Nairobi, Kenya. ozone.unep.org/.

WorldCargo News. 2011. Alarm sounded over exploding reefers. (October 26). WCN Publishing. Leatherhead, Surrey, UK. www.worldcargonews.com/htm/w20111026.937700.htm.

BIBLIOGRAPHY

Calm, J.M., and G.C. Hourahan. 2011. *2010 Report of the refrigeration, air conditioning and heat pumps technical options committee*, Chapter 2: Refrigerants. United Nations Environment Programme (UNEP) Ozone Secretariat, Nairobi, Kenya. ozone.unep.org/teap/Reports/RTOC/RTOC-Assessment-report-2010.pdf.

Calm, J.M., and G.C. Hourahan. 2011. Physical, safety, and environmental data for current and alternative refrigerants. *Refrigeration for Sustainable Development: Proceedings of the 23rd International Congress of Refrigeration*, Paper 915. International Institute of Refrigeration, Paris.

IPCC. 2007. *Climate change 2007: Synthesis report. Contribution of working groups I, II, and III to the fourth assessment report of the Intergovernmental Panel on Climate Change*. Core Writing Team, R.K. Pachauri, and A. Reisinger, eds. International Panel on Climate Change, Geneva. www.ipcc.ch/publications_and_data/ar4/syr/en/contents.html.

Lemmon, E.W., M.O. McLinden, and M.L. Huber. 2002. *NIST standard reference database 23*, v. 9.0. National Institute of Standards and Technology, Gaithersburg, MD.

Matheson gas data book. 2001. Matheson Company, East Rutherford, NJ.

CHAPTER 30

THERMOPHYSICAL PROPERTIES OF REFRIGERANTS

THIS chapter presents data for thermodynamic and transport properties of refrigerants, arranged for the occasional user. The refrigerants have a thermodynamic property chart on pressure-enthalpy coordinates with an abbreviated set of tabular data for saturated liquid and vapor on the facing page. In addition, tabular data in the superheated vapor region are given for R-134a to assist students working on compression cycle examples.

For each cryogenic fluid, a second table of properties is provided for vapor at a pressure of one standard atmosphere; these data are needed when such gases are used in heat transfer or purge gas applications. For zeotropic blends, including R-729 (air), tables are incremented in pressure, with properties given for liquid on the bubble line and vapor on the dew line. This arrangement is used because pressure is more commonly measured in the field while servicing equipment; it also highlights the difference between bubble and dew-point temperatures (the "temperature glide" experienced with blends).

Most CFC refrigerants have been deleted. Tables for R-11, R-13, R-113, R-114, R-141b, R-142b, R-500, R-502, R-503, and R-720 (neon) may be found in the 1997 *ASHRAE Handbook—Fundamentals*. R-12 has been retained to assist in making comparisons. Hydrogen and parahydrogen (R-702 and R-702p) may be found in the 2009 *ASHRAE Handbook–Fundamentals*. A new table and diagram for R-1233zd(E) have been added, and the data for R-245fa and R-1234ze(E) have been revised. Viscosity data for R-1234yf have been revised. The formulations conform to international standards, where applicable: thermodynamic properties of R-12, R-22, R-32, R-123, R-125, R-134a, R-143a, R-152a, R-717 (ammonia), and R-744 (carbon dioxide) and refrigerant blends R-404A, R-407C, R-410A, and R-507 conform to ISO *Standard* 17584, Refrigerant Properties.

Reference states used for most refrigerants correspond to the American convention of 0 Btu/lb for enthalpy and 0 Btu/lb·°F for entropy for saturated liquid at –40°F. Exceptions are water and fluids with very low critical temperatures (e.g., ethylene, cryogens).

These data are intended to help engineers make preliminary comparisons among unfamiliar fluids. For greater detail and a wider range of data, see the sources in the References.

The preparation of this chapter is assigned to TC 3.1, Refrigerants and Secondary Coolants.

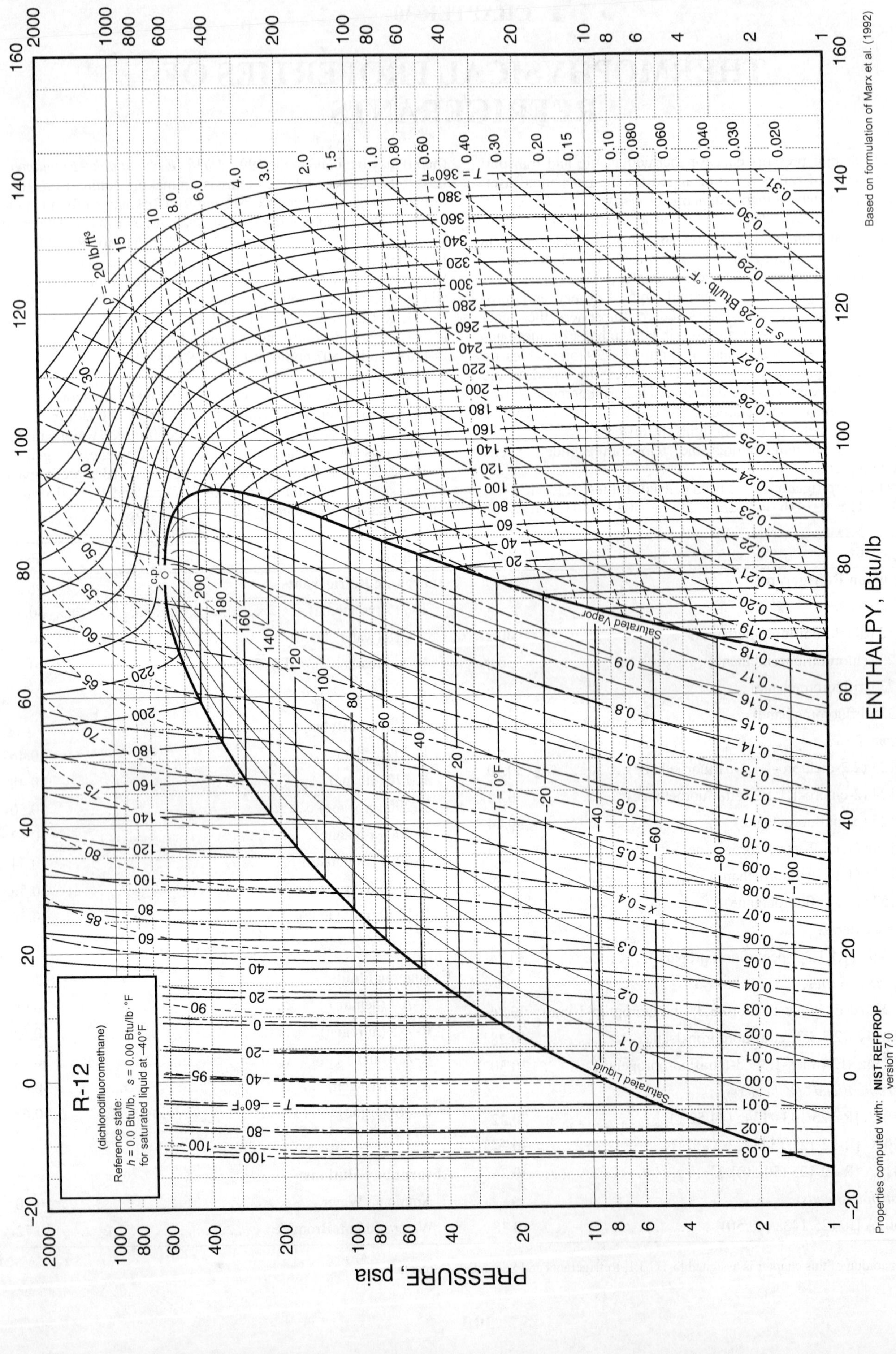

Fig. 1 Pressure-Enthalpy Diagram for Refrigerant 12

Refrigerant 12 (Dichlorodifluoromethane) Properties of Saturated Liquid and Saturated Vapor

Temp.,* °F	Pressure, psia	Density, lb/ft³ Liquid	Volume, ft³/lb Vapor	Enthalpy, Btu/lb Liquid	Enthalpy, Btu/lb Vapor	Entropy, Btu/lb·°F Liquid	Entropy, Btu/lb·°F Vapor	Specific Heat c_p, Btu/lb·°F Liquid	Specific Heat c_p, Btu/lb·°F Vapor	c_p/c_v Vapor	Vel. of Sound, ft/s Liquid	Vel. of Sound, ft/s Vapor	Viscosity, lb_m/ft·h Liquid	Viscosity, lb_m/ft·h Vapor	Thermal Cond., Btu/h·ft·°F Liquid	Thermal Cond., Btu/h·ft·°F Vapor	Surface Tension, dyne/cm	Temp.,* °F
−150	0.155	105.01	176.84	−22.133	60.979	−0.06101	0.20738	0.1955	0.1069	1.1831	3412	387.7	2.493	0.0163	0.0678	0.00244	26.65	−150
−140	0.258	104.10	109.67	−20.175	62.044	−0.05479	0.20241	0.1962	0.1090	1.1795	3329	393.0	2.212	0.0168	0.0663	0.00257	25.77	−140
−130	0.415	103.18	70.398	−18.209	63.125	−0.04873	0.19798	0.1970	0.1111	1.1764	3247	398.3	1.981	0.0174	0.0647	0.00270	24.90	−130
−120	0.644	102.26	46.615	−16.234	64.219	−0.04284	0.19402	0.1979	0.1133	1.1736	3166	403.3	1.789	0.0179	0.0633	0.00283	24.03	−120
−110	0.973	101.34	31.744	−14.250	65.326	−0.03708	0.19050	0.1989	0.1154	1.1711	3085	408.3	1.626	0.0184	0.0618	0.00296	23.17	−110
−100	1.430	100.41	22.173	−12.255	66.444	−0.03146	0.18735	0.2000	0.1175	1.1691	3005	413.0	1.487	0.0190	0.0604	0.00310	22.32	−100
−90	2.052	99.48	15.847	−10.248	67.571	−0.02596	0.18455	0.2013	0.1197	1.1675	2926	417.5	1.366	0.0195	0.0590	0.00323	21.47	−90
−80	2.880	98.54	11.565	−8.228	68.705	−0.02057	0.18206	0.2026	0.1218	1.1663	2848	421.8	1.261	0.0200	0.0577	0.00337	20.63	−80
−75	3.387	98.06	9.9506	−7.213	69.274	−0.01791	0.18092	0.2033	0.1229	1.1659	2809	423.8	1.213	0.0203	0.0570	0.00344	20.22	−75
−70	3.963	97.59	8.6006	−6.194	69.844	−0.01529	0.17985	0.2040	0.1240	1.1655	2770	425.8	1.167	0.0206	0.0563	0.00352	19.80	−70
−65	4.616	97.11	7.4658	−5.171	70.415	−0.01268	0.17884	0.2047	0.1252	1.1653	2732	427.8	1.125	0.0208	0.0557	0.00359	19.39	−65
−60	5.353	96.63	96.63	−4.145	7 0.986	−0.01010	0.17788	0.2055	0.1263	1.1653	2693	429.6	1.084	0.0211	0.0550	0.00366	18.98	−60
−55	6.181	96.14	5.6943	−3.115	71.558	−0.00754	0.17699	0.2062	0.1274	1.1653	2655	431.4	1.046	0.0214	0.0544	0.00373	18.57	−55
−50	7.108	95.66	5.0014	−2.081	72.130	−0.00501	0.17614	0.2070	0.1286	1.1654	2617	433.1	1.010	0.0216	0.0537	0.00381	18.16	−50
−45	8.144	8.144	4.4085	−1.043	72.702	−0.00249	0.17535	0.2078	0.1297	1.1657	2579	434.7	0.976	0.0219	0.0531	0.00388	17.75	−45
−40	9.295	94.68	3.8992	0.000	73.273	0.00000	0.17460	0.2087	0.1309	1.1662	2541	436.3	0.943	0.0222	0.0525	0.00396	17.35	−40
−35	10.571	94.18	3.4599	1.047	73.844	0.00247	0.17389	0.2095	0.1321	1.1667	2503	437.8	0.912	0.0224	0.0518	0.00403	16.95	−35
−30	11.982	93.68	3.0797	2.098	74.414	0.00493	0.17323	0.2104	0.1333	1.1674	2466	439.2	0.882	0.0227	0.0512	0.00411	16.55	−30
−25	13.536	93.18	2.7494	3.154	74.982	0.00736	0.17261	0.2113	0.1346	1.1683	2428	440.5	0.854	0.0229	0.0506	0.00418	16.15	−25
−21.55[b]	14.696	92.83	2.5469	3.884	75.373	0.00903	0.17221	0.2119	0.1354	1.1690	2403	441.3	0.835	0.0231	0.0502	0.00424	15.88	−21.55
−20	15.244	92.67	2.4615	4.214	75.549	0.00978	0.17203	0.2122	0.1358	1.1693	2391	441.7	0.827	0.0232	0.0500	0.00426	15.76	−20
−15	17.115	92.16	2.2098	5.280	76.115	0.01218	0.17148	0.2131	0.1371	1.1705	2354	442.8	0.801	0.0235	0.0494	0.00434	15.36	−15
−10	19.159	91.65	1.9889	6.350	76.678	0.01457	0.17097	0.2141	0.1384	1.1718	2317	443.9	0.776	0.0237	0.0488	0.00442	14.97	−10
−5	21.388	91.13	1.7945	7.425	77.239	0.01693	0.17048	0.2151	0.1397	1.1733	2279	444.8	0.752	0.0240	0.0482	0.00450	14.58	−5
0	23.812	90.61	1.6230	8.505	77.797	0.01929	0.17003	0.2161	0.1411	1.1750	2243	445.6	0.729	0.0243	0.0476	0.00458	14.19	0
5	26.442	90.08	1.4711	9.591	78.352	0.02162	0.16960	0.2171	0.1424	1.1769	2206	446.4	0.707	0.0245	0.0470	0.00466	13.81	5
10	29.290	89.55	1.3364	10.682	78.904	0.02395	0.16920	0.2182	0.1439	1.1790	2169	447.0	0.686	0.0248	0.0464	0.00474	13.43	10
15	32.365	89.02	1.2165	11.778	79.453	0.02625	0.16883	0.2193	0.1453	1.1813	2132	447.5	0.666	0.0251	0.0458	0.00482	13.05	15
20	35.682	88.48	1.1095	12.880	79.998	0.02855	0.16847	0.2204	0.1468	1.1838	2095	447.9	0.646	0.0253	0.0452	0.00491	12.67	20
25	39.250	87.93	1.0138	13.988	80.539	0.03083	0.16814	0.2216	0.1483	1.1866	2059	448.2	0.627	0.0256	0.0447	0.00499	12.29	25
30	43.083	87.38	0.9281	15.102	81.075	0.03310	0.16783	0.2228	0.1499	1.1896	2022	448.4	0.609	0.0259	0.0441	0.00508	11.92	30
35	47.192	86.82	0.8510	16.222	81.606	0.03536	0.16754	0.2240	0.1515	1.1929	1986	448.5	0.591	0.0261	0.0435	0.00516	11.55	35
40	51.590	86.25	0.7816	17.348	82.133	0.03761	0.16726	0.2253	0.1532	1.1965	1949	448.4	0.574	0.0264	0.0429	0.00525	11.18	40
45	56.289	85.68	0.7190	18.481	82.654	0.03984	0.16700	0.2266	0.1549	1.2004	1913	448.3	0.557	0.0267	0.0424	0.00534	10.82	45
50	61.303	85.10	0.6624	19.621	83.169	0.04207	0.16675	0.2279	0.1567	1.2047	1876	448.0	0.541	0.0270	0.0418	0.00543	10.45	50
55	66.643	84.52	0.6110	20.767	83.678	0.04428	0.16652	0.2294	0.1585	1.2093	1840	447.5	0.526	0.0272	0.0413	0.00552	10.09	55
60	72.323	83.92	0.5645	21.921	84.180	0.04649	0.16630	0.2308	0.1604	1.2143	1803	447.0	0.511	0.0275	0.0407	0.00562	9.74	60
65	78.357	83.32	0.5221	23.082	84.675	0.04869	0.16608	0.2323	0.1624	1.2197	1766	446.3	0.496	0.0278	0.0401	0.00571	9.38	65
70	84.757	82.71	0.4835	24.251	85.163	0.05088	0.16588	0.2339	0.1645	1.2256	1730	445.4	0.482	0.0281	0.0396	0.00581	9.03	70
75	91.536	82.10	0.4482	25.427	85.642	0.05306	0.16568	0.2356	0.1666	1.2319	1693	444.5	0.468	0.0284	0.0390	0.00591	8.68	75
80	98.710	81.47	0.4159	26.612	86.113	0.05524	0.16549	0.2373	0.1689	1.2389	1656	443.3	0.454	0.0287	0.0385	0.00601	8.33	80
85	106.29	80.83	0.3864	27.805	86.576	0.05740	0.16531	0.2391	0.1712	1.2464	1619	442.0	0.441	0.0290	0.0379	0.00612	7.99	85
90	114.29	80.18	0.3593	29.007	87.028	0.05957	0.16512	0.2410	0.1737	1.2546	1582	440.6	0.428	0.0293	0.0374	0.00623	7.65	90
95	122.73	79.52	0.3344	30.218	87.470	0.06173	0.16494	0.2430	0.1763	1.2635	1545	439.0	0.415	0.0296	0.0369	0.00634	7.31	95
100	131.62	78.85	0.3114	31.439	87.902	0.06388	0.16477	0.2452	0.1791	1.2733	1508	437.3	0.403	0.0299	0.0363	0.00645	6.98	100
105	140.97	78.16	0.2903	32.669	88.322	0.06603	0.16459	0.2474	0.1820	1.2839	1470	435.4	0.391	0.0302	0.0358	0.00657	6.65	105
110	150.81	77.46	0.2707	33.911	88.729	0.06818	0.16440	0.2498	0.1851	1.2956	1433	433.3	0.379	0.0306	0.0352	0.00670	6.32	110
115	161.13	76.75	0.2527	35.163	89.123	0.07032	0.16422	0.2523	0.1884	1.3085	1395	431.0	0.367	0.0309	0.0347	0.00682	6.00	115
120	171.97	76.02	0.2359	36.427	89.503	0.07247	0.16403	0.2551	0.1920	1.3226	1357	428.5	0.356	0.0313	0.0341	0.00696	5.68	120
125	183.33	75.28	0.2204	37.703	89.868	0.07461	0.16383	0.2580	0.1958	1.3383	1318	425.9	0.345	0.0316	0.0336	0.00710	5.36	125
130	195.24	74.51	0.2060	38.992	90.216	0.07676	0.16362	0.2611	0.2000	1.3556	1279	423.0	0.334	0.0320	0.0331	0.00724	5.05	130
135	207.70	73.73	0.1926	40.295	90.546	0.07890	0.16341	0.2645	0.2045	1.3750	1240	420.0	0.323	0.0324	0.0325	0.00740	4.74	135
140	220.74	72.93	0.1801	41.613	90.857	0.08106	0.16317	0.2683	0.2094	1.3966	1201	416.7	0.312	0.0328	0.0320	0.00756	4.44	140
145	234.37	72.10	0.1684	42.947	91.148	0.08321	0.16293	0.2724	0.2149	1.4210	1161	413.3	0.302	0.0333	0.0315	0.00773	4.14	145
150	248.61	71.24	0.1575	44.298	91.415	0.08538	0.16266	0.2769	0.2209	1.4486	1120	409.6	0.291	0.0337	0.0309	0.00792	3.85	150
155	263.47	70.36	0.1472	45.667	91.657	0.08755	0.16237	0.2819	0.2277	1.4800	1079	405.6	0.281	0.0342	0.0304	0.00811	3.56	155
160	278.99	69.45	0.1377	47.056	91.872	0.08973	0.16206	0.2875	0.2353	1.5161	1037	401.4	0.271	0.0347	0.0298	0.00833	3.27	160
165	295.17	68.50	0.1286	48.467	92.056	0.09193	0.16171	0.2938	0.2440	1.5578	995	397.0	0.261	0.0352	0.0293	0.00855	2.99	165
170	312.04	67.51	0.1202	49.903	92.206	0.09415	0.16133	0.3011	0.2540	1.6065	952	392.3	0.251	0.0358	0.0288	0.00880	2.72	170
175	329.62	66.47	0.1122	51.366	92.318	0.09638	0.16091	0.3094	0.2657	1.6642	908	387.3	0.240	0.0364	0.0283	0.00908	2.45	175
180	347.93	65.39	0.1046	52.859	92.385	0.09865	0.16044	0.3192	0.2795	1.7333	864	382.0	0.230	0.0371	0.0278	0.00938	2.19	180
185	367.00	64.24	0.0974	54.386	92.403	0.10094	0.15991	0.3309	0.2962	1.8175	818	376.4	0.220	0.0379	0.0273	0.00973	1.93	185
190	386.85	63.03	0.0906	55.954	92.361	0.10327	0.15931	0.3450	0.3168	1.9220	772	370.5	0.210	0.0387	0.0268	0.01012	1.68	190
195	407.52	61.73	0.0840	57.568	92.250	0.10565	0.15863	0.3625	0.3427	2.0549	724	364.2	0.200	0.0396	0.0264	0.01057	1.44	195
200	429.04	60.34	0.0778	59.237	92.054	0.10810	0.15784	0.3848	0.3766	2.2291	676	357.7	0.189	0.0407	0.0261	0.01109	1.21	200
210	474.80	57.15	0.0658	62.795	91.317	0.11323	0.15582	0.4555	0.4887	2.8082	575	343.4	0.167	0.0434	0.0262	0.01250	0.77	210
220	524.53	53.07	0.0540	66.829	89.806	0.11896	0.15277	0.6261	0.7725	4.2679	468	327.4	0.143	0.0475	0.0291	0.01489	0.38	220
230	579.05	46.36	0.0404	72.258	86.082	0.12659	0.14664	1.866	2.734	14.143	345	308.3	0.112	0.0568	0.0657	0.02282	0.07	230
233.55[c]	599.89	35.27	0.0284	79.118	79.118	0.13637	0.13637	∞	∞	∞	0	0.0	—	—	∞	∞	0.00	233.55

*Temperatures on ITS-90 scale

[b]Normal boiling point

[c]Critical point

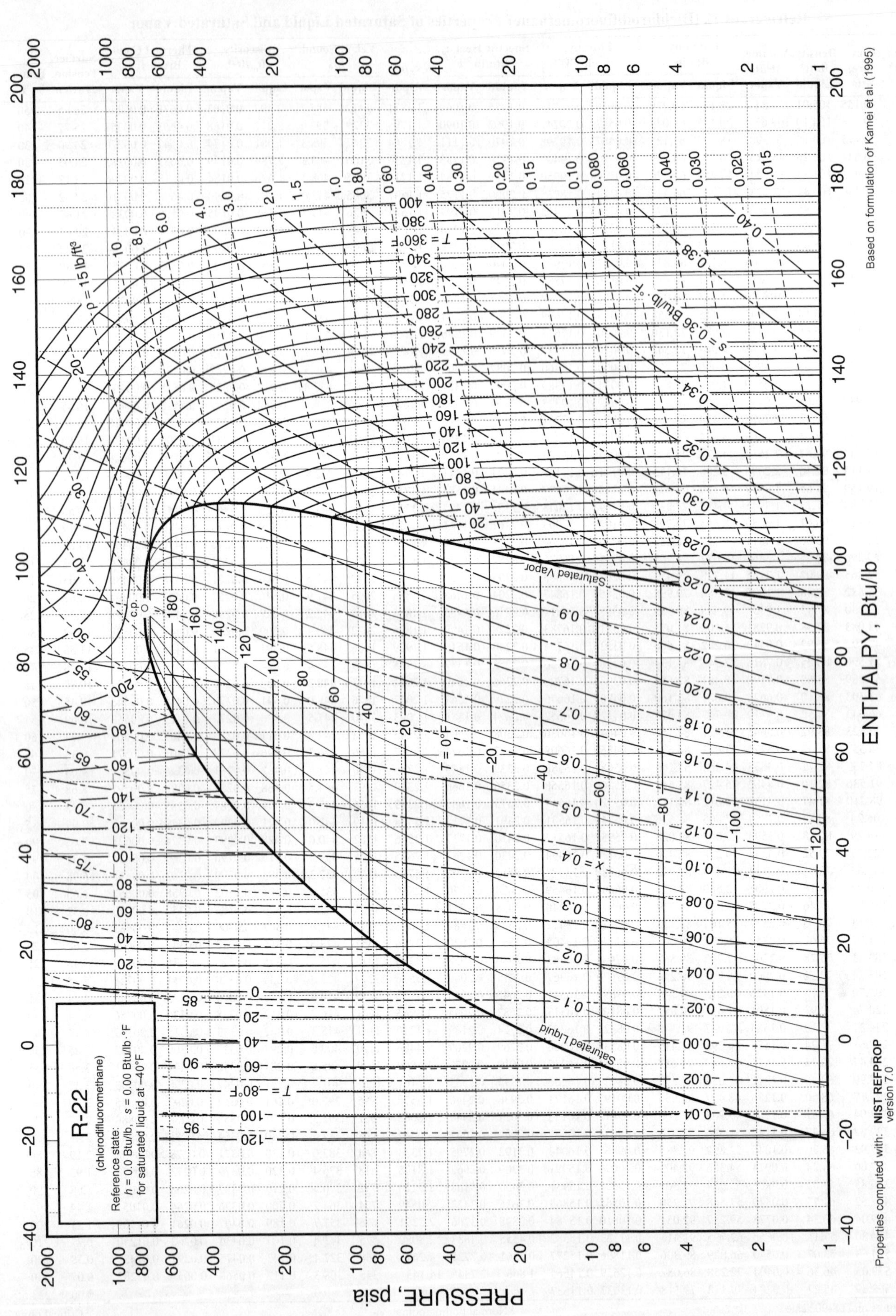

Fig. 2 Pressure-Enthalpy Diagram for Refrigerant 22

Refrigerant 22 (Chlorodifluoromethane) Properties of Saturated Liquid and Saturated Vapor

Temp.,* °F	Pressure, psia	Density, lb/ft³ Liquid	Volume, ft³/lb Vapor	Enthalpy, Btu/lb Liquid	Enthalpy, Btu/lb Vapor	Entropy, Btu/lb·°F Liquid	Entropy, Btu/lb·°F Vapor	Specific Heat c_p, Btu/lb·°F Liquid	Specific Heat c_p, Btu/lb·°F Vapor	c_p/c_v Vapor	Vel. of Sound, ft/s Liquid	Vel. of Sound, ft/s Vapor	Viscosity, lb_m/ft·h Liquid	Viscosity, lb_m/ft·h Vapor	Thermal Cond., Btu/h·ft·°F Liquid	Thermal Cond., Btu/h·ft·°F Vapor	Surface Tension, dyne/cm	Temp.,* °F
–150	0.263	98.28	146.06	–28.119	87.566	–0.07757	0.29600	0.2536	0.1185	1.2437	3716	469.7	2.093	0.0174	0.0831	0.00255	28.31	–150
–140	0.436	97.36	90.759	–25.583	88.729	–0.06951	0.28808	0.2536	0.1204	1.2404	3630	476.2	1.874	0.0180	0.0814	0.00267	27.34	–140
–130	0.698	96.44	58.384	–23.046	89.899	–0.06170	0.28090	0.2536	0.1223	1.2375	3544	482.4	1.692	0.0186	0.0797	0.00280	26.36	–130
–120	1.082	95.52	38.745	–20.509	91.074	–0.05412	0.27439	0.2537	0.1244	1.2350	3458	488.5	1.537	0.0191	0.0780	0.00293	25.40	–120
–110	1.629	94.59	26.444	–17.970	92.252	–0.04675	0.26846	0.2540	0.1265	1.2330	3373	494.2	1.405	0.0197	0.0763	0.00306	24.44	–110
–100	2.388	93.66	18.511	–15.427	93.430	–0.03959	0.26307	0.2543	0.1288	1.2315	3287	499.7	1.290	0.0203	0.0747	0.00320	23.49	–100
–95	2.865	93.19	15.623	–14.154	94.018	–0.03608	0.26055	0.2546	0.1300	1.2310	3245	502.4	1.238	0.0206	0.0739	0.00327	23.02	–95
–90	3.417	92.71	13.258	–12.880	94.605	–0.03261	0.25815	0.2549	0.1312	1.2307	3202	504.9	1.189	0.0208	0.0731	0.00334	22.55	–90
–85	4.053	92.24	11.309	–11.604	95.191	–0.02918	0.25585	0.2552	0.1324	1.2305	3160	507.4	1.144	0.0211	0.0723	0.00341	22.08	–85
–80	4.782	91.76	9.6939	–10.326	95.775	–0.02580	0.25366	0.2556	0.1337	1.2304	3118	509.8	1.101	0.0214	0.0715	0.00348	21.61	–80
–75	5.615	91.28	8.3487	–9.046	96.357	–0.02245	0.25155	0.2561	0.1350	1.2305	3075	512.2	1.060	0.0217	0.0708	0.00355	21.15	–75
–70	6.561	90.79	7.2222	–7.763	96.937	–0.01915	0.24954	0.2566	0.1363	1.2308	3033	514.4	1.021	0.0220	0.0700	0.00363	20.68	–70
–65	7.631	90.31	6.2744	–6.477	97.514	–0.01587	0.24761	0.2571	0.1377	1.2313	2990	516.5	0.985	0.0223	0.0692	0.00370	20.22	–65
–60	8.836	89.82	5.4730	–5.189	98.087	–0.01264	0.24577	0.2577	0.1392	1.2320	2948	518.6	0.951	0.0225	0.0684	0.00378	19.76	–60
–55	10.190	89.33	4.7924	–3.897	98.657	–0.00943	0.24400	0.2583	0.1406	1.2328	2906	520.5	0.918	0.0228	0.0677	0.00386	19.30	–55
–50	11.703	88.83	4.2119	–2.602	99.224	–0.00626	0.24230	0.2591	0.1422	1.2339	2863	522.4	0.887	0.0231	0.0669	0.00394	18.85	–50
–45	13.390	88.33	3.7147	–1.303	99.786	–0.00311	0.24067	0.2598	0.1438	1.2352	2821	524.1	0.857	0.0234	0.0661	0.00402	18.40	–45
–41.46[b]	14.696	87.97	3.4054	–0.381	100.181	–0.00091	0.23955	0.2604	0.1449	1.2362	2791	525.3	0.837	0.0236	0.0656	0.00407	18.08	–41.46
–40	15.262	87.82	3.2872	0.000	100.343	0.00000	0.23910	0.2606	0.1454	1.2367	2778	525.8	0.829	0.0237	0.0654	0.00410	17.94	–40
–35	17.336	87.32	2.9181	1.308	100.896	0.00309	0.23759	0.2615	0.1471	1.2384	2736	527.3	0.802	0.0240	0.0646	0.00418	17.49	–35
–30	19.624	86.80	2.5984	2.620	101.443	0.00615	0.23615	0.2625	0.1488	1.2404	2694	528.7	0.776	0.0242	0.0639	0.00426	17.05	–30
–25	22.142	86.29	2.3204	3.937	101.984	0.00918	0.23475	0.2635	0.1506	1.2426	2651	530.0	0.751	0.0245	0.0631	0.00435	16.60	–25
–20	24.906	85.76	2.0778	5.260	102.519	0.01220	0.23341	0.2645	0.1525	1.2451	2609	531.2	0.728	0.0248	0.0624	0.00444	16.16	–20
–15	27.929	85.24	1.8656	6.588	103.048	0.01519	0.23211	0.2656	0.1544	1.2479	2566	532.3	0.705	0.0251	0.0617	0.00452	15.72	–15
–10	31.230	84.71	1.6792	7.923	103.570	0.01815	0.23086	0.2668	0.1564	1.2510	2524	533.2	0.683	0.0254	0.0609	0.00461	15.28	–10
–5	34.824	84.17	1.5150	9.263	104.085	0.02110	0.22965	0.2681	0.1585	1.2544	2481	534.0	0.662	0.0257	0.0602	0.00471	14.85	–5
0	38.728	83.63	1.3701	10.610	104.591	0.02403	0.22848	0.2694	0.1607	1.2581	2438	534.7	0.642	0.0260	0.0595	0.00480	14.41	0
5	42.960	83.08	1.2417	11.964	105.090	0.02694	0.22735	0.2708	0.1629	1.2622	2396	535.3	0.622	0.0262	0.0587	0.00489	13.98	5
10	47.536	82.52	1.1276	13.325	105.580	0.02983	0.22625	0.2722	0.1652	1.2666	2353	535.7	0.603	0.0265	0.0580	0.00499	13.55	10
15	52.475	81.96	1.0261	14.694	106.061	0.03270	0.22519	0.2737	0.1676	1.2714	2310	536.0	0.585	0.0268	0.0573	0.00509	13.13	15
20	57.795	81.39	0.9354	16.070	106.532	0.03556	0.22415	0.2753	0.1702	1.2767	2268	536.1	0.568	0.0271	0.0566	0.00519	12.70	20
25	63.514	80.82	0.8543	17.455	106.994	0.03841	0.22315	0.2770	0.1728	1.2824	2225	536.1	0.551	0.0274	0.0558	0.00530	12.28	25
30	69.651	80.24	0.7815	18.848	107.445	0.04124	0.22217	0.2787	0.1755	1.2886	2182	535.9	0.534	0.0277	0.0551	0.00540	11.86	30
35	76.225	79.65	0.7161	20.250	107.884	0.04406	0.22121	0.2806	0.1783	1.2953	2139	535.6	0.518	0.0280	0.0544	0.00551	11.45	35
40	83.255	79.05	0.6572	21.662	108.313	0.04686	0.22028	0.2825	0.1813	1.3026	2096	535.1	0.503	0.0283	0.0537	0.00562	11.04	40
45	90.761	78.44	0.6040	23.083	108.729	0.04966	0.21936	0.2845	0.1844	1.3105	2053	534.4	0.488	0.0286	0.0530	0.00574	10.63	45
50	98.763	77.83	0.5558	24.514	109.132	0.05244	0.21847	0.2866	0.1877	1.3191	2010	533.6	0.473	0.0289	0.0522	0.00586	10.22	50
55	107.28	77.20	0.5122	25.956	109.521	0.05522	0.21758	0.2889	0.1911	1.3284	1967	532.6	0.459	0.0292	0.0515	0.00598	9.82	55
60	116.33	76.57	0.4725	27.409	109.897	0.05798	0.21672	0.2913	0.1947	1.3385	1924	531.5	0.445	0.0296	0.0508	0.00611	9.41	60
65	125.94	75.92	0.4364	28.874	110.257	0.06074	0.21586	0.2938	0.1985	1.3495	1880	530.1	0.432	0.0299	0.0501	0.00625	9.02	65
70	136.13	75.27	0.4035	30.350	110.602	0.06350	0.21501	0.2964	0.2025	1.3615	1836	528.6	0.419	0.0302	0.0494	0.00638	8.62	70
75	146.92	74.60	0.3734	31.839	110.929	0.06625	0.21417	0.2992	0.2067	1.3746	1793	526.9	0.406	0.0305	0.0487	0.00653	8.23	75
80	158.33	73.92	0.3459	33.342	111.239	0.06899	0.21333	0.3022	0.2112	1.3889	1749	525.0	0.394	0.0309	0.0479	0.00668	7.84	80
85	170.38	73.23	0.3207	34.859	111.530	0.07173	0.21250	0.3054	0.2160	1.4046	1705	522.9	0.381	0.0312	0.0472	0.00684	7.46	85
90	183.09	72.52	0.2975	36.391	111.801	0.07447	0.21166	0.3089	0.2212	1.4218	1660	520.6	0.369	0.0316	0.0465	0.00701	7.08	90
95	196.50	71.80	0.2762	37.938	112.050	0.07721	0.21083	0.3126	0.2267	1.4407	1615	518.1	0.358	0.0320	0.0458	0.00718	6.70	95
100	210.61	71.06	0.2566	39.502	112.276	0.07996	0.20998	0.3166	0.2327	1.4616	1570	515.4	0.346	0.0324	0.0450	0.00737	6.33	100
105	225.46	70.30	0.2385	41.084	112.478	0.08270	0.20913	0.3209	0.2391	1.4849	1525	512.4	0.335	0.0328	0.0443	0.00757	5.96	105
110	241.06	69.52	0.2217	42.686	112.653	0.08545	0.20827	0.3257	0.2461	1.5107	1479	509.2	0.324	0.0332	0.0436	0.00778	5.60	110
115	257.45	68.72	0.2062	44.308	112.799	0.08821	0.20739	0.3309	0.2538	1.5396	1433	505.8	0.313	0.0336	0.0428	0.00801	5.24	115
120	274.65	67.90	0.1918	45.952	112.914	0.09098	0.20649	0.3367	0.2623	1.5722	1387	502.1	0.302	0.0341	0.0421	0.00825	4.88	120
125	292.69	67.05	0.1785	47.621	112.996	0.09376	0.20557	0.3431	0.2717	1.6090	1340	498.1	0.292	0.0346	0.0413	0.00851	4.53	125
130	311.58	66.18	0.1660	49.316	113.040	0.09656	0.20462	0.3504	0.2822	1.6509	1292	493.9	0.281	0.0351	0.0406	0.00880	4.19	130
135	331.37	65.27	0.1544	51.041	113.043	0.09937	0.20364	0.3585	0.2941	1.6990	1244	489.4	0.271	0.0356	0.0399	0.00911	3.85	135
140	352.08	64.32	0.1435	52.798	113.000	0.10222	0.20261	0.3679	0.3076	1.7548	1195	484.6	0.260	0.0362	0.0391	0.00946	3.51	140
145	373.74	63.34	0.1334	54.591	112.907	0.10509	0.20153	0.3787	0.3233	1.8201	1146	479.5	0.250	0.0369	0.0383	0.00984	3.18	145
150	396.38	62.31	0.1238	56.425	112.756	0.10800	0.20040	0.3913	0.3416	1.8976	1095	474.1	0.240	0.0375	0.0376	0.01027	2.86	150
155	420.04	61.22	0.1149	58.305	112.539	0.11096	0.19919	0.4063	0.3633	1.9907	1044	468.4	0.230	0.0383	0.0368	0.01076	2.54	155
160	444.75	60.07	0.1064	60.240	112.247	0.11397	0.19790	0.4243	0.3897	2.1047	992	462.3	0.219	0.0391	0.0361	0.01131	2.24	160
165	470.56	58.84	0.0984	62.237	111.866	0.11705	0.19650	0.4467	0.4225	2.2474	939	455.8	0.209	0.0400	0.0353	0.01195	1.93	165
170	497.50	57.53	0.0907	64.309	111.378	0.12022	0.19497	0.4750	0.4643	2.4310	884	449.0	0.198	0.0410	0.0346	0.01270	1.64	170
175	525.62	56.10	0.0834	66.474	110.760	0.12350	0.19328	0.5124	0.5198	2.6759	828	441.7	0.188	0.0422	0.0340	0.01360	1.36	175
180	554.98	54.52	0.0764	68.757	109.976	0.12693	0.19136	0.5641	0.5972	3.0184	769	433.9	0.176	0.0436	0.0335	0.01470	1.09	180
185	585.63	52.74	0.0695	71.196	108.972	0.13056	0.18916	0.6410	0.7132	3.5317	706	425.6	0.165	0.0452	0.0332	0.01609	0.83	185
190	617.64	50.67	0.0626	73.859	107.654	0.13450	0.18651	0.7681	0.9067	4.3857	639	416.6	0.152	0.0474	0.0334	0.01793	0.58	190
195	651.12	48.14	0.0556	76.875	105.835	0.13893	0.18316	1.020	1.295	6.090	565	406.9	0.138	0.0502	0.0347	0.02061	0.35	195
200	686.20	44.68	0.0479	80.593	103.010	0.14437	0.17835	1.778	2.472	11.190	480	395.8	0.121	0.0547	0.0395	0.02574	0.15	200
205.06[c]	723.74	32.70	0.0306	91.208	91.208	0.16012	0.16012	∞	∞	∞	0	0.0	—	—	∞	∞	0.00	205.06

*Temperatures on ITS-90 scale

[b]Normal boiling point

[c]Critical point

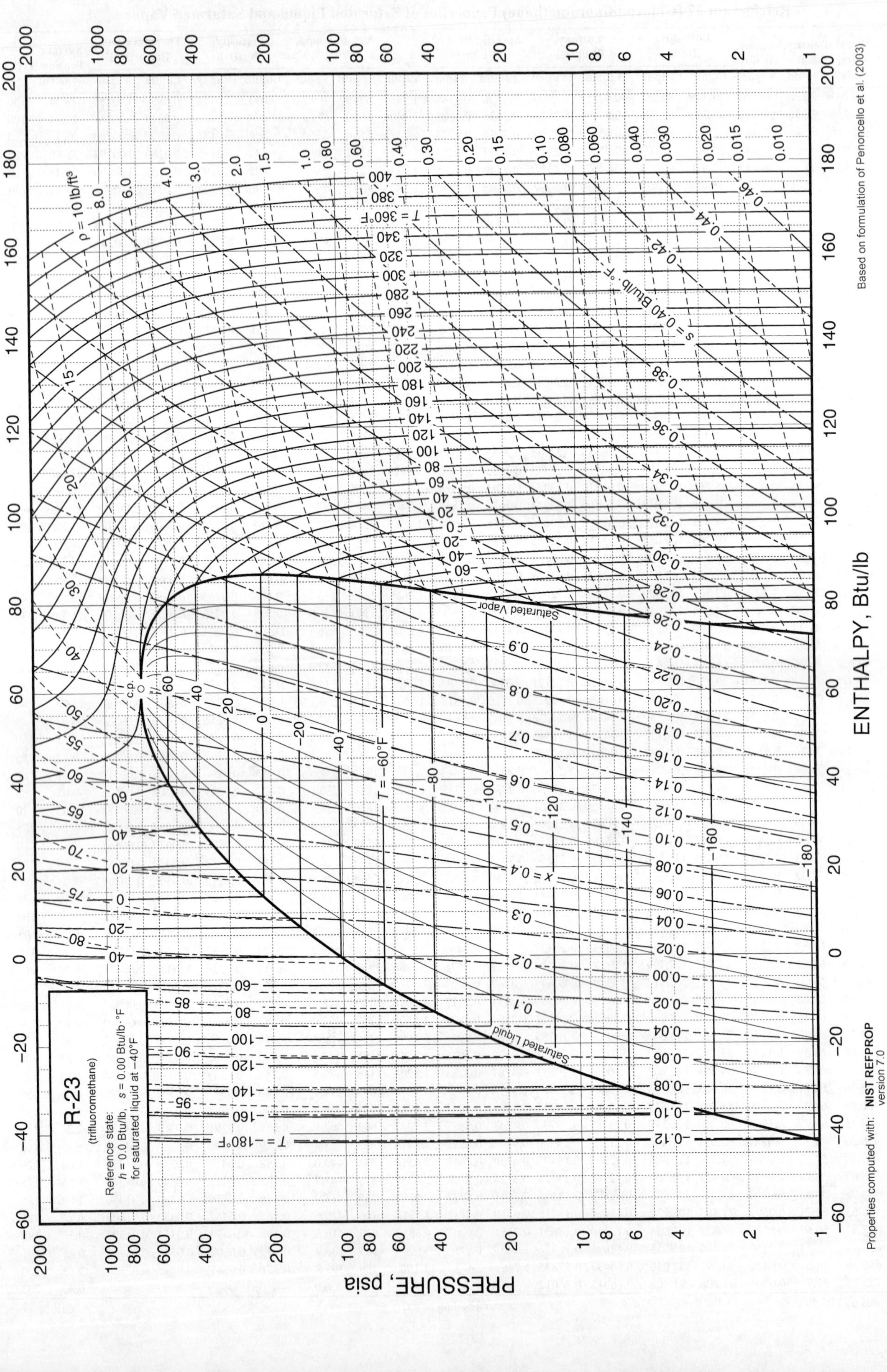

Fig. 3 Pressure-Enthalpy Diagram for Refrigerant 23

Refrigerant 23 (Trifluoromethane) Properties of Saturated Liquid and Saturated Vapor

Temp.,* °F	Pres-sure, psia	Density, lb/ft³	Volume, ft³/lb	Enthalpy, Btu/lb		Entropy, Btu/lb·°F		Specific Heat c_p, Btu/lb·°F		c_p/c_v	Vel. of Sound, ft/s		Viscosity, lb_m/ft·h		Thermal Cond., Btu/h·ft·°F		Surface Tension, dyne/cm	Temp.,* °F
		Liquid	Vapor	Liquid	Vapor	Liquid	Vapor	Liquid	Vapor	Vapor	Liquid	Vapor	Liquid	Vapor	Liquid	Vapor		
–247.23[a]	0.008	106.24	3866.20	–61.390	64.612	–0.19982	0.39331	0.2918	0.1194	1.3146	3974	445.1	4.971	0.0129	0.1553	0.00219	34.37	–247.23
–240	0.017	105.44	2014.50	–59.292	65.460	–0.19011	0.37780	0.2886	0.1206	1.3119	3949	452.1	4.203	0.0135	0.1468	0.00232	33.39	–240
–230	0.040	104.29	885.38	–56.418	66.634	–0.17731	0.35847	0.2865	0.1225	1.3079	3875	461.3	3.392	0.0143	0.1366	0.00249	32.04	–230
–225	0.059	103.71	605.39	–54.987	67.222	–0.17115	0.34962	0.2860	0.1236	1.3060	3828	465.8	3.069	0.0147	0.1320	0.00258	31.37	–225
–220	0.087	103.13	421.77	–53.558	67.811	–0.16512	0.34128	0.2857	0.1247	1.3040	3777	470.2	2.790	0.0151	0.1277	0.00267	30.71	–220
–215	0.125	102.54	299.03	–52.130	68.399	–0.15923	0.33339	0.2856	0.1259	1.3021	3725	474.5	2.547	0.0154	0.1238	0.00275	30.05	–215
–210	0.177	101.95	215.50	–50.702	68.987	–0.15345	0.32594	0.2856	0.1272	1.3002	3671	478.8	2.334	0.0158	0.1200	0.00284	29.39	–210
–205	0.247	101.36	157.70	–49.274	69.574	–0.14779	0.31889	0.2856	0.1285	1.2984	3617	482.9	2.148	0.0162	0.1166	0.00293	28.74	–205
–200	0.339	100.77	117.06	–47.846	70.161	–0.14223	0.31222	0.2858	0.1300	1.2968	3562	487.0	1.983	0.0166	0.1133	0.00301	28.09	–200
–195	0.458	100.17	88.070	–46.416	70.747	–0.13678	0.30589	0.2859	0.1315	1.2952	3508	490.9	1.837	0.0170	0.1102	0.00310	27.44	–195
–190	0.612	99.57	67.097	–44.986	71.331	–0.13143	0.29990	0.2862	0.1331	1.2938	3454	494.8	1.706	0.0174	0.1074	0.00319	26.80	–190
–185	0.808	98.97	51.725	–43.554	71.914	–0.12617	0.29422	0.2864	0.1347	1.2925	3401	498.5	1.590	0.0177	0.1046	0.00328	26.16	–185
–180	1.054	98.36	40.320	–42.121	72.494	–0.12100	0.28882	0.2868	0.1364	1.2914	3348	502.2	1.486	0.0181	0.1021	0.00336	25.52	–180
–175	1.361	97.75	31.758	–40.686	73.072	–0.11592	0.28370	0.2871	0.1382	1.2905	3296	505.8	1.392	0.0185	0.0996	0.00345	24.88	–175
–170	1.738	97.14	25.261	–39.249	73.647	–0.11091	0.27882	0.2875	0.1401	1.2899	3244	509.3	1.307	0.0189	0.0973	0.00354	24.25	–170
–165	2.199	96.53	20.278	–37.809	74.218	–0.10599	0.27419	0.2880	0.1421	1.2894	3193	512.6	1.229	0.0193	0.0951	0.00363	23.63	–165
–160	2.756	95.91	16.420	–36.368	74.785	–0.10114	0.26978	0.2885	0.1441	1.2892	3142	515.9	1.159	0.0196	0.0930	0.00372	23.01	–160
–155	3.424	95.29	13.405	–34.923	75.348	–0.09637	0.26557	0.2891	0.1462	1.2893	3091	519.0	1.095	0.0200	0.0911	0.00381	22.39	–155
–150	4.221	94.66	11.028	–33.475	75.907	–0.09166	0.26156	0.2897	0.1484	1.2897	3041	522.0	1.036	0.0204	0.0892	0.00391	21.77	–150
–145	5.162	94.03	9.1386	–32.024	76.459	–0.08702	0.25774	0.2903	0.1506	1.2903	2991	524.9	0.982	0.0207	0.0873	0.00400	21.16	–145
–140	6.267	93.40	7.6246	–30.569	77.006	–0.08244	0.25408	0.2911	0.1530	1.2913	2941	527.6	0.933	0.0211	0.0856	0.00410	20.55	–140
–135	7.555	92.76	6.4024	–29.110	77.545	–0.07791	0.25059	0.2919	0.1554	1.2926	2891	530.2	0.887	0.0215	0.0839	0.00419	19.95	–135
–130	9.050	92.12	5.4088	–27.647	78.078	–0.07345	0.24725	0.2928	0.1580	1.2943	2842	532.7	0.844	0.0219	0.0823	0.00429	19.35	–130
–125	10.772	91.47	4.5956	–26.179	78.603	–0.06904	0.24405	0.2937	0.1606	1.2964	2792	535.0	0.805	0.0222	0.0808	0.00439	18.76	–125
–120	12.746	90.82	3.9258	–24.706	79.119	–0.06468	0.24098	0.2948	0.1633	1.2988	2743	537.2	0.768	0.0226	0.0793	0.00449	18.17	–120
–115.63[b]	14.696	90.25	3.4353	–23.414	79.563	–0.06092	0.23840	0.2958	0.1658	1.3013	2700	538.9	0.738	0.0229	0.0780	0.00458	17.65	–115.63
–115	14.997	90.16	3.3707	–23.227	79.626	–0.06037	0.23803	0.2959	0.1661	1.3017	2693	539.2	0.734	0.0230	0.0779	0.00459	17.58	–115
–110	17.551	89.50	2.9080	–21.742	80.124	–0.05611	0.23521	0.2971	0.1691	1.3050	2644	541.0	0.702	0.0233	0.0765	0.00470	17.00	–110
–105	20.437	88.83	2.5201	–20.250	80.610	–0.05189	0.23248	0.2984	0.1721	1.3088	2595	542.7	0.672	0.0237	0.0751	0.00480	16.42	–105
–100	23.682	88.15	2.1934	–18.751	81.086	–0.04772	0.22986	0.2998	0.1753	1.3131	2545	544.2	0.644	0.0241	0.0738	0.00491	15.85	–100
–95	27.317	87.47	1.9167	–17.245	81.550	–0.04358	0.22734	0.3014	0.1786	1.3179	2496	545.5	0.617	0.0244	0.0726	0.00502	15.28	–95
–90	31.372	86.77	1.6812	–15.731	82.001	–0.03948	0.22490	0.303	0.1820	1.3233	2447	546.6	0.592	0.0248	0.0713	0.00514	14.71	–90
–85	35.879	86.07	1.4800	–14.208	82.439	–0.03541	0.22254	0.3047	0.1856	1.3293	2397	547.5	0.569	0.0251	0.0701	0.00526	14.16	–85
–80	40.870	85.36	1.3072	–12.675	82.863	–0.03138	0.22026	0.3066	0.1893	1.3359	2347	548.2	0.546	0.0255	0.0689	0.00538	13.60	–80
–75	46.380	84.64	1.1582	–11.133	83.271	–0.02737	0.21804	0.3086	0.1932	1.3433	2297	548.7	0.525	0.0259	0.0678	0.00550	13.05	–75
–70	52.442	83.91	1.0293	–9.581	83.663	–0.02340	0.21589	0.3108	0.1973	1.3515	2247	549.0	0.505	0.0263	0.0667	0.00563	12.51	–70
–65	59.093	83.17	0.9173	–8.017	84.039	–0.01945	0.21380	0.3131	0.2016	1.3605	2197	549.1	0.486	0.0266	0.0656	0.00576	11.97	–65
–60	66.369	82.41	0.8196	–6.441	84.396	–0.01552	0.21176	0.3156	0.2061	1.3704	2146	548.9	0.467	0.0270	0.0645	0.00590	11.44	–60
–55	74.306	81.65	0.7341	–4.852	84.734	–0.01161	0.20977	0.3183	0.2108	1.3814	2095	548.5	0.450	0.0274	0.0634	0.00604	10.91	–55
–50	82.943	80.87	0.6590	–3.250	85.052	–0.00773	0.20781	0.3212	0.2158	1.3935	2044	547.9	0.433	0.0278	0.0624	0.00619	10.39	–50
–45	92.319	80.07	0.5929	–1.633	85.348	–0.00386	0.20590	0.3243	0.2211	1.4069	1992	547.0	0.417	0.0282	0.0613	0.00634	9.87	–45
–40	102.47	79.26	0.5344	0.000	85.620	0.00000	0.20402	0.3276	0.2267	1.4217	1941	545.8	0.402	0.0285	0.0603	0.00650	9.36	–40
–35	113.45	78.44	0.4826	1.649	85.868	0.00385	0.20216	0.3313	0.2328	1.4381	1888	544.4	0.387	0.0289	0.0593	0.00667	8.86	–35
–30	125.28	77.59	0.4366	3.316	86.089	0.00768	0.20033	0.3352	0.2392	1.4564	1836	542.7	0.373	0.0294	0.0583	0.00684	8.36	–30
–25	138.02	76.72	0.3955	5.003	86.282	0.01151	0.19851	0.3395	0.2461	1.4767	1783	540.8	0.359	0.0298	0.0573	0.00702	7.87	–25
–20	151.70	75.84	0.3587	6.709	86.444	0.01534	0.19669	0.3442	0.2536	1.4994	1729	538.5	0.345	0.0302	0.0563	0.00721	7.38	–20
–15	166.37	74.92	0.3258	8.438	86.574	0.01917	0.19489	0.3493	0.2618	1.5249	1675	536.0	0.332	0.0307	0.0553	0.00741	6.91	–15
–10	182.08	73.99	0.2962	10.191	86.667	0.02300	0.19307	0.3549	0.2707	1.5536	1621	533.1	0.320	0.0311	0.0543	0.00762	6.44	–10
–5	198.88	73.02	0.2695	11.970	86.721	0.02684	0.19125	0.3612	0.2805	1.5861	1566	529.9	0.308	0.0316	0.0533	0.00784	5.97	–5
0	216.80	72.03	0.2454	13.777	86.733	0.03070	0.18941	0.3681	0.2914	1.6231	1510	526.4	0.296	0.0321	0.0523	0.00807	5.52	0
5	235.91	70.99	0.2236	15.615	86.698	0.03457	0.18754	0.3759	0.3036	1.6655	1453	522.6	0.284	0.0326	0.0512	0.00832	5.07	5
10	256.25	69.92	0.2038	17.487	86.612	0.03846	0.18564	0.3847	0.3174	1.7145	1396	518.4	0.272	0.0332	0.0502	0.00858	4.64	10
15	277.88	68.81	0.1857	19.396	86.468	0.04238	0.18368	0.3947	0.3332	1.7716	1338	513.8	0.261	0.0338	0.0492	0.00886	4.21	15
20	300.85	67.65	0.1692	21.347	86.261	0.04634	0.18167	0.4063	0.3514	1.8389	1279	508.8	0.250	0.0344	0.0481	0.00917	3.79	20
25	325.22	66.43	0.1541	23.345	85.981	0.05034	0.17958	0.4197	0.3728	1.9190	1219	503.5	0.239	0.0351	0.0470	0.00949	3.38	25
30	351.06	65.15	0.1402	25.396	85.619	0.05440	0.17739	0.4357	0.3983	2.0160	1158	497.7	0.228	0.0358	0.0459	0.00985	2.98	30
35	378.43	63.79	0.1274	27.508	85.162	0.05853	0.17508	0.4550	0.4293	2.1354	1096	491.5	0.217	0.0367	0.0447	0.01024	2.60	35
40	407.41	62.35	0.1156	29.692	84.593	0.06275	0.17263	0.4789	0.4679	2.2857	1032	484.8	0.206	0.0376	0.0435	0.01066	2.22	40
45	438.06	60.79	0.1046	31.962	83.891	0.06709	0.16999	0.5093	0.5174	2.4803	967	477.5	0.196	0.0386	0.0422	0.01114	1.86	45
50	470.48	59.10	0.0943	34.338	83.025	0.07158	0.16710	0.5497	0.5833	2.7415	899	469.7	0.184	0.0398	0.0409	0.01168	1.52	50
55	504.76	57.24	0.0846	36.848	81.950	0.07627	0.16390	0.6060	0.6759	3.1102	830	461.2	0.173	0.0413	0.0394	0.01230	1.19	55
60	541.02	55.14	0.0753	39.539	80.597	0.08124	0.16025	0.6911	0.8158	3.6698	757	452.0	0.161	0.0431	0.0378	0.01303	0.88	60
65	579.39	52.69	0.0664	42.493	78.842	0.08664	0.15592	0.8360	1.0533	4.6217	681	441.6	0.148	0.0454	0.0360	0.01393	0.59	65
70	620.07	49.66	0.0573	45.889	76.427	0.09281	0.15046	1.1450	1.5501	6.6135	599	429.8	0.134	0.0487	0.0339	0.01513	0.34	70
75	663.33	45.29	0.0472	50.290	72.574	0.10076	0.14243	2.2830	3.2825	13.5491	506	415.3	0.116	0.0546	0.0313	0.01740	0.12	75
79.06[c]	700.82	32.87	0.0304	61.067	61.067	0.12049	0.12049	∞	∞	∞	0	0.0	—	—	∞	∞	0.00	79.06

*Temperatures on ITS-90 scale [a]Triple point [b]Normal boiling point [c]Critical point

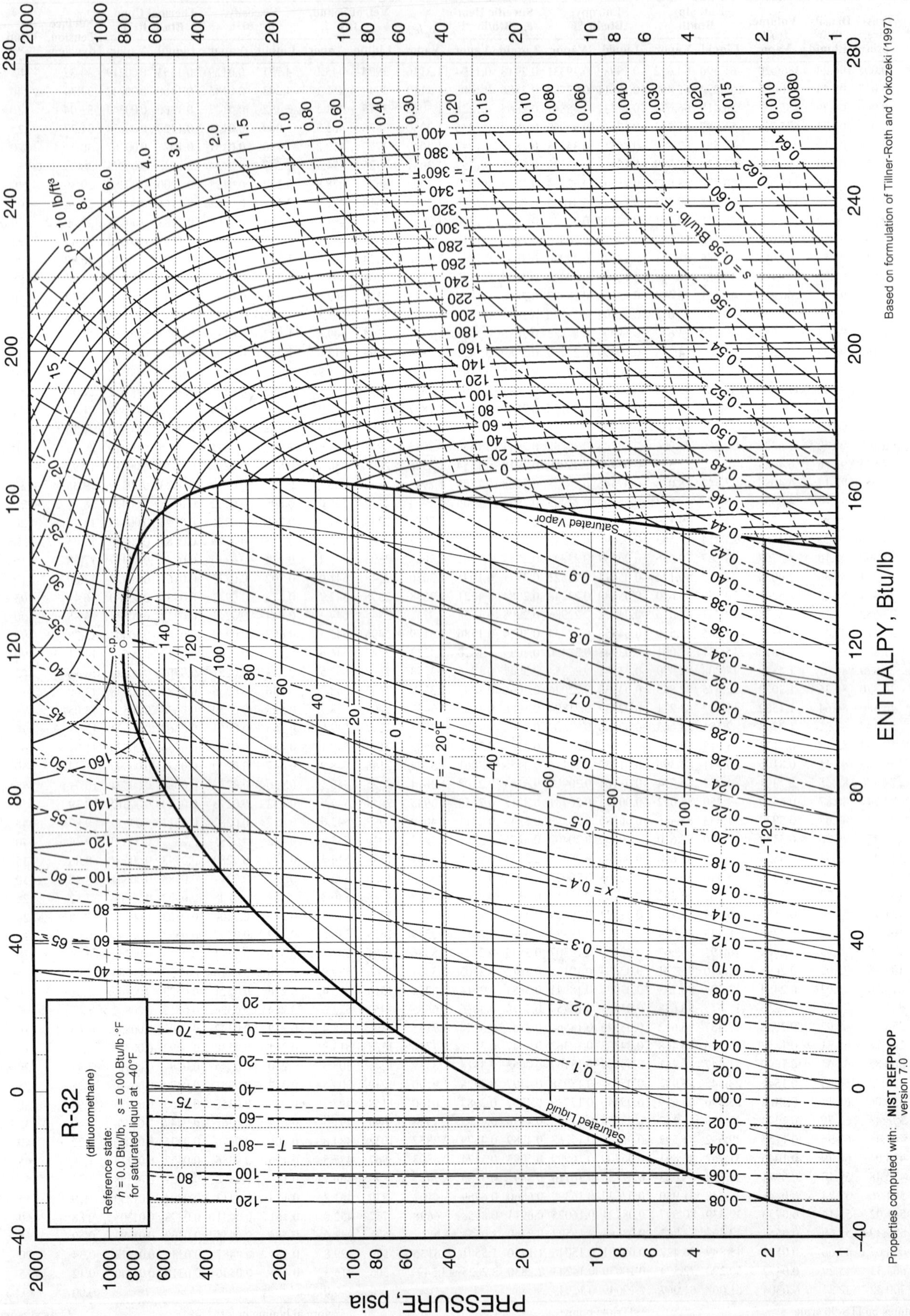

Fig. 4 Pressure-Enthalpy Diagram for Refrigerant 32

Refrigerant 32 (Difluoromethane) Properties of Saturated Liquid and Saturated Vapor

Temp.,* °F	Pressure, psia	Density, lb/ft³	Volume, ft³/lb	Enthalpy, Btu/lb		Entropy, Btu/lb·°F		Specific Heat c_p, Btu/lb·°F		c_p/c_v	Vel. of Sound, ft/s		Viscosity, lb_m/ft·h		Thermal Cond., Btu/h·ft·°F		Surface Tension, dyne/cm	Temp.,* °F
		Liquid	Vapor	Liquid	Vapor	Liquid	Vapor	Liquid	Vapor	Vapor	Liquid	Vapor	Liquid	Vapor	Liquid	Vapor		
–214.26[a]	0.007	89.23	7270.10	–65.520	133.830	–0.20152	0.61079	0.3806	0.1577	1.3206	4641	556.4	2.965	0.0138	0.1404	0.00402	39.01	–214.26
–210	0.010	88.87	5150.00	–63.901	134.497	–0.19498	0.59966	0.3798	0.1581	1.3199	4599	561.0	2.777	0.0140	0.1400	0.00402	38.47	–210
–200	0.022	88.03	2413.30	–60.111	136.065	–0.1801	0.57539	0.3781	0.1591	1.3180	4503	571.6	2.407	0.0146	0.1388	0.00403	37.22	–200
–190	0.046	87.18	1207.60	–56.338	137.633	–0.16584	0.55345	0.3766	0.1602	1.3163	4407	581.9	2.113	0.0151	0.1375	0.00405	35.97	–190
–180	0.090	86.33	640.300	–52.578	139.199	–0.15215	0.53358	0.3754	0.1616	1.3146	4311	591.9	1.874	0.0157	0.1359	0.00407	34.73	–180
–170	0.167	85.48	357.440	–48.829	140.760	–0.13898	0.51552	0.3743	0.1633	1.3130	4216	601.6	1.677	0.0162	0.1341	0.00410	33.51	–170
–160	0.295	84.63	208.900	–45.090	142.311	–0.12629	0.49907	0.3735	0.1652	1.3117	4121	611.0	1.512	0.0168	0.1322	0.00414	32.29	–160
–150	0.500	83.77	127.180	–41.358	143.849	–0.11404	0.48404	0.3729	0.1675	1.3106	4026	620.0	1.371	0.0174	0.1301	0.00419	31.07	–150
–140	0.816	82.90	80.317	–37.630	145.370	–0.10219	0.47027	0.3726	0.1702	1.3100	3931	628.6	1.249	0.0179	0.1280	0.00425	29.87	–140
–130	1.286	82.02	52.414	–33.904	146.869	–0.09072	0.45763	0.3725	0.1734	1.3097	3836	636.8	1.143	0.0185	0.1257	0.00431	28.68	–130
–120	1.966	81.14	35.229	–30.177	148.341	–0.07959	0.44598	0.3727	0.1770	1.3100	3742	644.6	1.050	0.0191	0.1233	0.00438	27.50	–120
–110	2.923	80.25	24.316	–26.447	149.783	–0.06877	0.43522	0.3731	0.1811	1.3109	3648	651.9	0.967	0.0196	0.1209	0.00446	26.33	–110
–100	4.235	79.35	17.190	–22.711	151.189	–0.05824	0.42525	0.3738	0.1858	1.3125	3553	658.7	0.894	0.0202	0.1184	0.00455	25.17	–100
–95	5.053	78.90	14.573	–20.840	151.877	–0.05308	0.42054	0.3743	0.1884	1.3136	3506	662.0	0.860	0.0205	0.1172	0.00459	24.59	–95
–90	5.996	78.44	12.417	–18.966	152.556	–0.04798	0.41600	0.3748	0.1910	1.3149	3459	665.1	0.828	0.0208	0.1159	0.00464	24.02	–90
–85	7.078	77.98	10.633	–17.089	153.223	–0.04295	0.41162	0.3754	0.1938	1.3165	3412	668.0	0.797	0.0210	0.1146	0.00469	23.45	–85
–80	8.312	77.52	9.1470	–15.209	153.879	–0.03797	0.40738	0.3760	0.1968	1.3182	3365	670.9	0.768	0.0213	0.1133	0.00475	22.88	–80
–75	9.716	77.05	7.9036	–13.325	154.523	–0.03305	0.40329	0.3768	0.1998	1.3203	3318	673.6	0.740	0.0216	0.1120	0.00480	22.31	–75
–70	11.304	76.58	6.8579	–11.437	155.155	–0.02818	0.39934	0.3776	0.2030	1.3226	3270	676.1	0.714	0.0219	0.1107	0.00486	21.75	–70
–65	13.095	76.11	5.9744	–9.544	155.774	–0.02337	0.39551	0.3785	0.2063	1.3252	3223	678.5	0.689	0.0222	0.1094	0.00492	21.19	–65
–60.97[b]	14.696	75.72	5.3611	–8.016	156.263	–0.01953	0.39251	0.3793	0.2091	1.3276	3185	680.3	0.669	0.0224	0.1083	0.00497	20.74	–60.97
–60	15.105	75.63	5.2246	–7.647	156.379	–0.01860	0.39180	0.3795	0.2097	1.3282	3176	680.7	0.665	0.0225	0.1081	0.00498	20.63	–60
–55	17.354	75.15	4.5854	–5.744	156.971	–0.01389	0.38821	0.3805	0.2133	1.3314	3129	682.8	0.642	0.0227	0.1068	0.00505	20.08	–55
–50	19.861	74.66	4.0383	–3.836	157.549	–0.00922	0.38472	0.3817	0.2170	1.3350	3081	684.8	0.620	0.0230	0.1054	0.00512	19.53	–50
–45	22.646	74.17	3.5681	–1.921	158.111	–0.00459	0.38134	0.3829	0.2208	1.3390	3034	686.5	0.599	0.0233	0.1041	0.00519	18.98	–45
–40	25.731	73.67	3.1625	0.000	158.658	0.00000	0.37805	0.3842	0.2247	1.3433	2986	688.1	0.579	0.0236	0.1028	0.00526	18.44	–40
–35	29.137	73.17	2.8114	1.928	159.189	0.00455	0.37486	0.3857	0.2287	1.3481	2939	689.6	0.560	0.0239	0.1015	0.00534	17.89	–35
–30	32.887	72.67	2.5062	3.864	159.703	0.00906	0.37175	0.3872	0.2329	1.3532	2891	690.8	0.541	0.0242	0.1001	0.00542	17.36	–30
–25	37.003	72.16	2.2402	5.808	160.200	0.01353	0.36872	0.3888	0.2372	1.3589	2843	691.9	0.524	0.0244	0.0988	0.00550	16.82	–25
–20	41.511	71.64	2.0076	7.761	160.679	0.01797	0.36577	0.3906	0.2416	1.3651	2795	692.8	0.507	0.0247	0.0975	0.00559	16.29	–20
–15	46.433	71.12	1.8034	9.723	161.139	0.02238	0.36289	0.3924	0.2462	1.3718	2747	693.6	0.491	0.0250	0.0962	0.00568	15.76	–15
–10	51.796	70.60	1.6237	11.694	161.579	0.02676	0.36008	0.3944	0.2510	1.3790	2699	694.1	0.475	0.0253	0.0949	0.00577	15.24	–10
–5	57.625	70.06	1.4652	13.676	161.999	0.03111	0.35733	0.3965	0.2559	1.3869	2651	694.4	0.460	0.0256	0.0935	0.00587	14.72	–5
0	63.947	69.52	1.3248	15.669	162.397	0.03543	0.35463	0.3987	0.2610	1.3955	2602	694.6	0.446	0.0259	0.0922	0.00598	14.20	0
5	70.789	68.97	1.2002	17.673	162.774	0.03973	0.35199	0.4011	0.2662	1.4047	2553	694.5	0.432	0.0262	0.0909	0.00609	13.69	5
10	78.179	68.42	1.0894	19.690	163.127	0.04400	0.34940	0.4037	0.2717	1.4148	2504	694.3	0.418	0.0265	0.0896	0.00620	13.18	10
15	86.144	67.86	0.9905	21.719	163.455	0.04825	0.34685	0.4064	0.2774	1.4256	2455	693.8	0.405	0.0268	0.0883	0.00632	12.67	15
20	94.715	67.28	0.9021	23.762	163.758	0.05248	0.34434	0.4093	0.2834	1.4375	2406	693.1	0.393	0.0271	0.0871	0.00645	12.17	20
25	103.92	66.71	0.8228	25.820	164.034	0.05670	0.34187	0.4124	0.2897	1.4503	2356	692.2	0.381	0.0274	0.0858	0.00658	11.67	25
30	113.79	66.12	0.7516	27.893	164.281	0.06090	0.33943	0.4157	0.2963	1.4642	2306	691.1	0.369	0.0277	0.0845	0.00673	11.18	30
35	124.35	65.52	0.6874	29.983	164.499	0.06508	0.33701	0.4192	0.3032	1.4794	2256	689.7	0.358	0.0280	0.0832	0.00688	10.69	35
40	135.65	64.91	0.6296	32.090	164.686	0.06926	0.33462	0.4230	0.3106	1.4959	2206	688.1	0.347	0.0284	0.0820	0.00704	10.21	40
45	147.70	64.29	0.5773	34.215	164.839	0.07342	0.33225	0.4271	0.3184	1.5140	2155	686.3	0.336	0.0287	0.0807	0.00721	9.73	45
50	160.54	63.65	0.5298	36.360	164.957	0.07758	0.32989	0.4316	0.3266	1.5337	2104	684.2	0.326	0.0290	0.0794	0.00740	9.25	50
55	174.21	63.01	0.4868	38.526	165.039	0.08173	0.32754	0.4363	0.3355	1.5553	2052	681.9	0.316	0.0300	0.0782	0.00759	8.78	55
60	188.74	62.35	0.4477	40.714	165.081	0.08588	0.32519	0.4415	0.3450	1.5790	2000	679.3	0.306	0.0304	0.0770	0.00781	8.32	60
65	204.17	61.68	0.4120	42.927	165.081	0.09002	0.32284	0.4471	0.3552	1.6052	1947	676.4	0.296	0.0309	0.0757	0.00804	7.86	65
70	220.52	60.99	0.3794	45.165	165.036	0.09418	0.32049	0.4533	0.3663	1.6341	1894	673.2	0.287	0.0313	0.0745	0.00829	7.40	70
75	237.85	60.28	0.3496	47.431	164.944	0.09833	0.31812	0.4600	0.3783	1.6662	1840	669.8	0.278	0.0318	0.0733	0.00856	6.96	75
80	256.18	59.56	0.3223	49.727	164.800	0.10250	0.31573	0.4674	0.3915	1.7019	1785	666.1	0.269	0.0322	0.0721	0.00886	6.51	80
85	275.56	58.81	0.2972	52.055	164.602	0.10669	0.31332	0.4756	0.4060	1.7419	1730	662.1	0.261	0.0327	0.0708	0.00919	6.07	85
90	296.02	58.04	0.2741	54.419	164.343	0.11089	0.31087	0.4847	0.4221	1.7869	1674	657.7	0.252	0.0333	0.0696	0.00955	5.64	90
95	317.61	57.25	0.2529	56.821	164.020	0.11511	0.30838	0.4950	0.4400	1.8378	1617	653.0	0.244	0.0338	0.0684	0.00995	5.22	95
100	340.37	56.43	0.2333	59.266	163.627	0.11937	0.30584	0.5066	0.4602	1.8958	1560	648.0	0.236	0.0344	0.0672	0.01039	4.80	100
105	364.34	55.58	0.2151	61.758	163.155	0.12366	0.30323	0.5197	0.4831	1.9624	1501	642.6	0.228	0.0351	0.0660	0.01089	4.39	105
110	389.58	54.69	0.1983	64.303	162.598	0.12800	0.30054	0.5349	0.5094	2.0397	1441	636.8	0.220	0.0357	0.0648	0.01145	3.99	110
115	416.13	53.77	0.1826	66.907	161.945	0.13239	0.29777	0.5525	0.5399	2.1302	1379	630.5	0.212	0.0365	0.0636	0.01208	3.59	115
120	444.04	52.80	0.1681	69.577	161.184	0.13685	0.29488	0.5734	0.5759	2.2378	1317	623.9	0.204	0.0373	0.0624	0.01280	3.21	120
125	473.37	51.77	0.1545	72.325	160.301	0.14139	0.29186	0.5984	0.6189	2.3675	1253	616.7	0.196	0.0381	0.0612	0.01363	2.83	125
130	504.17	50.69	0.1418	75.163	159.275	0.14603	0.28867	0.6290	0.6715	2.5268	1187	609.1	0.189	0.0391	0.0599	0.01460	2.46	130
135	536.51	49.53	0.1298	78.108	158.082	0.15080	0.28529	0.6675	0.7373	2.7273	1119	600.9	0.181	0.0401	0.0587	0.01573	2.11	135
140	570.47	48.28	0.1185	81.181	156.689	0.15573	0.28165	0.7172	0.8225	2.9873	1049	592.0	0.173	0.0413	0.0575	0.01709	1.76	140
145	606.10	46.91	0.1077	84.415	155.048	0.16088	0.27769	0.7842	0.9372	3.3381	977	582.3	0.164	0.0427	0.0562	0.01873	1.43	145
150	643.51	45.40	0.0974	87.858	153.089	0.16630	0.27329	0.8800	1.1007	3.8379	902	571.8	0.156	0.0444	0.0550	0.02078	1.11	150
160	724.09	41.65	0.0775	95.724	147.670	0.17853	0.26236	1.2880	1.8018	5.9665	740	547.0	0.137	0.0489	0.0529	0.02709	0.54	160
170	813.58	35.24	0.0549	107.269	136.620	0.19632	0.24293	4.8650	7.6726	23.3087	545	509.3	0.110	0.0592	0.0554	0.04606	0.07	170
172.59[c]	838.61	26.47	0.0378	120.855	120.855	0.21760	0.21760	∞	∞	∞	0	0.0	—	—	∞	∞	0.00	172.59

*Temperatures on ITS-90 scale [a]Triple point [b]Normal boiling point [c]Critical point

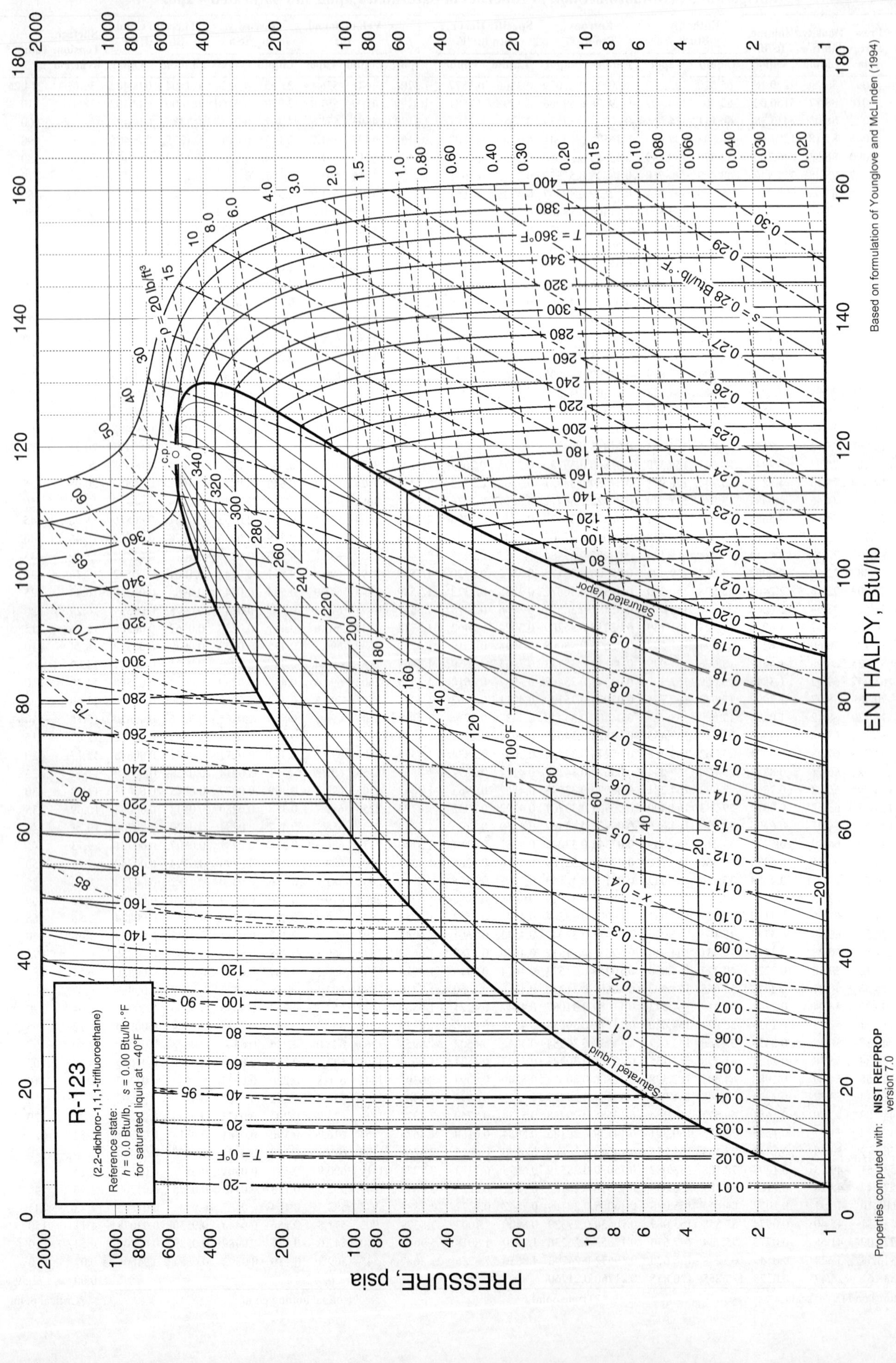

Fig. 5 Pressure-Enthalpy Diagram for Refrigerant 123

Refrigerant 123 (2,2-Dichloro-1,1,1-Trifluoroethane) Properties of Saturated Liquid and Saturated Vapor

Temp.,* °F	Pressure, psia	Density, lb/ft³ Liquid	Volume, ft³/lb Vapor	Enthalpy, Btu/lb Liquid	Enthalpy, Btu/lb Vapor	Entropy, Btu/lb·°F Liquid	Entropy, Btu/lb·°F Vapor	Specific Heat c_p, Btu/lb·°F Liquid	Specific Heat c_p, Btu/lb·°F Vapor	c_p/c_v Vapor	Vel. of Sound, ft/s Liquid	Vel. of Sound, ft/s Vapor	Viscosity, lb_m/ft·h Liquid	Viscosity, lb_m/ft·h Vapor	Thermal Cond., Btu/h·ft·°F Liquid	Thermal Cond., Btu/h·ft·°F Vapor	Surface Tension, dyne/cm	Temp.,* °F
–140	0.003	108.90	7431.6	–22.241	71.783	–0.06050	0.23363	0.2210	0.1181	1.1237	3928	341.7	7.731	0.0146	0.0645	0.00135	30.50	–140
–130	0.006	108.12	3871.0	–20.033	72.974	–0.05370	0.22843	0.2207	0.1203	1.1212	3854	346.6	6.547	0.0151	0.0636	0.00153	29.75	–130
–120	0.011	107.35	2111.6	–17.826	74.187	–0.04710	0.22379	0.2206	0.1226	1.1187	3778	351.4	5.645	0.0157	0.0628	0.00171	29.01	–120
–110	0.020	106.57	1201.0	–15.619	75.421	–0.04070	0.21966	0.2208	0.1248	1.1165	3702	356.2	4.934	0.0163	0.0619	0.00190	28.27	–110
–100	0.036	105.80	709.46	–13.410	76.676	–0.03447	0.21600	0.2211	0.1270	1.1144	3626	360.8	4.359	0.0168	0.0611	0.00208	27.53	–100
–90	0.060	105.03	433.83	–11.195	77.950	–0.02840	0.21275	0.2217	0.1291	1.1124	3549	365.4	3.885	0.0174	0.0602	0.00226	26.80	–90
–80	0.097	104.26	273.77	–8.975	79.244	–0.02247	0.20989	0.2224	0.1313	1.1106	3472	369.9	3.488	0.0179	0.0593	0.00244	26.07	–80
–70	0.154	103.48	177.81	–6.746	80.556	–0.01668	0.20737	0.2233	0.1334	1.1090	3394	374.3	3.150	0.0185	0.0584	0.00263	25.34	–70
–60	0.236	102.70	118.57	–4.509	81.885	–0.01101	0.20516	0.2243	0.1356	1.1075	3317	378.5	2.860	0.0190	0.0575	0.00281	24.62	–60
–50	0.354	101.92	80.999	–2.260	83.231	–0.00545	0.20323	0.2254	0.1377	1.1061	3240	382.7	2.607	0.0196	0.0565	0.00299	23.91	–50
–40	0.519	101.13	56.576	0.000	84.592	0.00000	0.20157	0.2266	0.1398	1.1050	3164	386.8	2.386	0.0201	0.0555	0.00317	23.19	–40
–30	0.744	100.34	40.333	2.272	85.967	0.00535	0.20014	0.2279	0.1420	1.1040	3087	390.7	2.191	0.0206	0.0546	0.00335	22.48	–30
–20	1.046	99.54	29.299	4.558	87.355	0.01061	0.19892	0.2292	0.1441	1.1032	3012	394.5	2.018	0.0211	0.0536	0.00353	21.78	–20
–10	1.445	98.73	21.655	6.857	88.754	0.01578	0.19790	0.2306	0.1463	1.1026	2936	398.2	1.864	0.0217	0.0526	0.00371	21.08	–10
0	1.963	97.92	16.264	9.170	90.163	0.02086	0.19706	0.2320	0.1484	1.1022	2862	401.7	1.725	0.0222	0.0515	0.00390	20.38	0
5	2.274	97.51	14.174	10.332	90.871	0.02337	0.19670	0.2327	0.1495	1.1021	2825	403.3	1.661	0.0224	0.0510	0.00399	20.03	5
10	2.625	97.10	12.396	11.498	91.582	0.02587	0.19638	0.2334	0.1506	1.1020	2788	405.0	1.601	0.0227	0.0505	0.00408	19.69	10
15	3.019	96.69	10.878	12.667	92.294	0.02834	0.19609	0.2341	0.1517	1.1020	2751	406.6	1.543	0.0229	0.0501	0.00417	19.34	15
20	3.460	96.28	9.5779	13.840	93.008	0.03080	0.19585	0.2349	0.1528	1.1020	2714	408.1	1.488	0.0232	0.0496	0.00426	19.00	20
25	3.952	95.86	8.4595	15.017	93.723	0.03324	0.19563	0.2356	0.1540	1.1021	2678	409.6	1.435	0.0235	0.0491	0.00435	18.66	25
30	4.499	95.44	7.4943	16.198	94.440	0.03566	0.19544	0.2364	0.1551	1.1023	2641	411.0	1.385	0.0237	0.0486	0.00444	18.32	30
35	5.106	95.02	6.6586	17.382	95.158	0.03806	0.19529	0.2371	0.1562	1.1025	2605	412.4	1.337	0.0239	0.0481	0.00453	17.98	35
40	5.778	94.60	5.9327	18.570	95.877	0.04045	0.19517	0.2379	0.1574	1.1028	2569	413.7	1.292	0.0242	0.0476	0.00462	17.64	40
45	6.519	94.17	5.3002	19.762	96.597	0.04282	0.19507	0.2387	0.1585	1.1031	2533	414.9	1.248	0.0244	0.0471	0.00471	17.30	45
50	7.334	93.74	4.7474	20.958	97.317	0.04518	0.19500	0.2394	0.1597	1.1035	2498	416.1	1.207	0.0247	0.0467	0.00481	16.97	50
55	8.229	93.31	4.2629	22.158	98.038	0.04752	0.19495	0.2402	0.1609	1.1040	2462	417.3	1.167	0.0249	0.0462	0.00490	16.63	55
60	9.208	92.88	3.8371	23.362	98.760	0.04984	0.19493	0.2410	0.1621	1.1046	2427	418.3	1.129	0.0252	0.0457	0.00499	16.30	60
65	10.278	92.44	3.4617	24.570	99.481	0.05215	0.19493	0.2418	0.1633	1.1052	2392	419.4	1.092	0.0254	0.0453	0.00508	15.97	65
70	11.445	92.01	3.1301	25.782	100.203	0.05444	0.19495	0.2426	0.1645	1.1059	2357	420.3	1.057	0.0256	0.0448	0.00518	15.64	70
75	12.713	91.56	2.8362	26.998	100.924	0.05673	0.19499	0.2434	0.1657	1.1067	2322	421.2	1.023	0.0259	0.0444	0.00527	15.31	75
80	14.090	91.12	2.5753	28.218	101.645	0.05899	0.19505	0.2442	0.1669	1.1075	2287	422.0	0.991	0.0261	0.0439	0.00537	14.98	80
82.08[b]	14.696	90.94	2.4753	28.728	101.945	0.05993	0.19508	0.2445	0.1675	1.1079	2273	422.3	0.978	0.0262	0.0437	0.00540	14.84	82.08
85	15.580	90.67	2.3429	29.443	102.365	0.06124	0.19513	0.2450	0.1682	1.1085	2252	422.7	0.960	0.0264	0.0435	0.00546	14.65	85
90	17.192	90.22	2.1356	30.671	103.085	0.06348	0.19522	0.2458	0.1695	1.1095	2218	423.3	0.930	0.0266	0.0430	0.00556	14.33	90
95	18.931	89.77	1.9503	31.904	103.804	0.06571	0.19534	0.2467	0.1707	1.1106	2184	423.9	0.901	0.0268	0.0426	0.00565	14.00	95
100	20.804	89.31	1.7841	33.141	104.521	0.06792	0.19546	0.2475	0.1720	1.1119	2149	424.4	0.874	0.0271	0.0422	0.00575	13.68	100
105	22.819	88.85	1.6349	34.383	105.238	0.07012	0.19560	0.2484	0.1734	1.1132	2115	424.8	0.847	0.0273	0.0418	0.00585	13.36	105
110	24.980	88.39	1.5006	35.628	105.953	0.07231	0.19576	0.2492	0.1747	1.1146	2081	425.2	0.822	0.0275	0.0413	0.00595	13.04	110
115	27.297	87.92	1.3795	36.879	106.666	0.07449	0.19593	0.2501	0.1761	1.1162	2047	425.4	0.797	0.0277	0.0409	0.00604	12.72	115
120	29.776	87.45	1.2701	38.134	107.377	0.07665	0.19611	0.2510	0.1775	1.1178	2014	425.6	0.773	0.0280	0.0405	0.00614	12.41	120
125	32.425	86.98	1.1710	39.393	108.086	0.07881	0.19630	0.2520	0.1789	1.1196	1980	425.6	0.751	0.0282	0.0401	0.00625	12.09	125
130	35.251	86.50	1.0812	40.657	108.792	0.08095	0.19650	0.2529	0.1803	1.1215	1946	425.6	0.728	0.0284	0.0397	0.00635	11.78	130
135	38.261	86.01	0.9996	41.926	109.497	0.08308	0.19671	0.2539	0.1818	1.1236	1913	425.5	0.707	0.0287	0.0393	0.00645	11.47	135
140	41.464	85.52	0.9253	43.200	110.198	0.08520	0.19693	0.2548	0.1833	1.1258	1879	425.3	0.687	0.0289	0.0389	0.00656	11.16	140
145	44.868	85.03	0.8577	44.479	110.896	0.08732	0.19716	0.2559	0.1848	1.1281	1846	425.0	0.667	0.0291	0.0385	0.00666	10.85	145
150	48.479	84.53	0.7959	45.763	111.591	0.08942	0.19739	0.2569	0.1863	1.1306	1813	424.6	0.648	0.0293	0.0381	0.00677	10.54	150
160	56.360	83.52	0.6876	48.347	112.970	0.09359	0.19788	0.2591	0.1896	1.1362	1746	423.5	0.611	0.0298	0.0374	0.00699	9.93	160
170	65.173	82.49	0.5965	50.953	114.333	0.09773	0.19839	0.2614	0.1929	1.1426	1680	422.0	0.577	0.0303	0.0366	0.00722	9.33	170
180	74.986	81.43	0.5195	53.583	115.678	0.10184	0.19892	0.2638	0.1965	1.1499	1614	420.1	0.545	0.0307	0.0359	0.00745	8.74	180
190	85.868	80.34	0.4539	56.237	117.001	0.10592	0.19945	0.2665	0.2004	1.1583	1548	417.7	0.515	0.0312	0.0352	0.00769	8.15	190
200	97.892	79.23	0.3979	58.918	118.300	0.10997	0.19999	0.2694	0.2045	1.1681	1482	414.7	0.487	0.0317	0.0345	0.00795	7.57	200
210	111.13	78.08	0.3497	61.627	119.572	0.11400	0.20053	0.2726	0.2089	1.1793	1416	411.3	0.460	0.0322	0.0338	0.00821	7.00	210
220	125.66	76.89	0.3080	64.367	120.813	0.11801	0.20106	0.2761	0.2138	1.1925	1349	407.3	0.435	0.0328	0.0331	0.00849	6.44	220
230	141.56	75.66	0.2719	67.141	122.019	0.12201	0.20158	0.2800	0.2191	1.2079	1283	402.8	0.411	0.0334	0.0324	0.00877	5.88	230
240	158.91	74.38	0.2404	69.952	123.184	0.12599	0.20207	0.2845	0.2251	1.2262	1216	397.6	0.388	0.0340	0.0317	0.00908	5.34	240
250	177.80	73.04	0.2128	72.805	124.303	0.12997	0.20254	0.2896	0.2319	1.2482	1148	391.7	0.367	0.0347	0.0310	0.00940	4.81	250
260	198.31	71.64	0.1885	75.704	125.367	0.13396	0.20296	0.2956	0.2398	1.2749	1080	385.1	0.346	0.0355	0.0303	0.00974	4.29	260
270	220.53	70.16	0.1670	78.655	126.368	0.13795	0.20334	0.3026	0.2490	1.3079	1012	377.7	0.326	0.0364	0.0296	0.01010	3.78	270
280	244.58	68.60	0.1479	81.666	127.294	0.14196	0.20365	0.3110	0.2603	1.3496	942	369.4	0.307	0.0374	0.0289	0.01050	3.28	280
290	270.54	66.92	0.1309	84.749	128.128	0.14600	0.20387	0.3215	0.2742	1.4035	871	360.2	0.288	0.0386	0.0282	0.01092	2.80	290
300	298.53	65.11	0.1155	87.916	128.851	0.15010	0.20398	0.3349	0.2922	1.4755	800	349.9	0.270	0.0400	0.0275	0.01139	2.33	300
310	328.69	63.12	0.1016	91.188	129.431	0.15426	0.20395	0.3529	0.3166	1.5762	726	338.5	0.252	0.0418	0.0267	0.01191	1.88	310
320	361.16	60.91	0.0889	94.594	129.822	0.15853	0.20372	0.3785	0.3520	1.7258	650	325.7	0.234	0.0440	0.0259	0.01251	1.45	320
330	396.11	58.37	0.0770	98.186	129.950	0.16297	0.20320	0.4186	0.4084	1.9693	571	311.5	0.216	0.0469	0.0251	0.01321	1.04	330
340	433.76	55.33	0.0658	102.059	129.670	0.16769	0.20222	0.4925	0.5138	2.4318	488	295.4	0.196	0.0510	0.0243	0.01411	0.66	340
350	474.41	51.32	0.0544	106.459	128.628	0.17298	0.20036	0.6830	0.7861	3.6383	397	277.0	0.173	0.0575	0.0234	0.01539	0.32	350
360	518.66	43.97	0.0403	112.667	125.064	0.18039	0.19551	2.5070	3.263	14.6330	290	255.2	0.138	0.0730	0.0227	0.01819	0.05	360
362.63[c]	531.10	34.34	0.0291	118.800	118.800	0.18779	0.18779	∞	∞	∞	0	0.0	—	—	∞	∞	0.00	362.63

*Temperatures on ITS-90 scale [b]Normal boiling point [c]Critical point

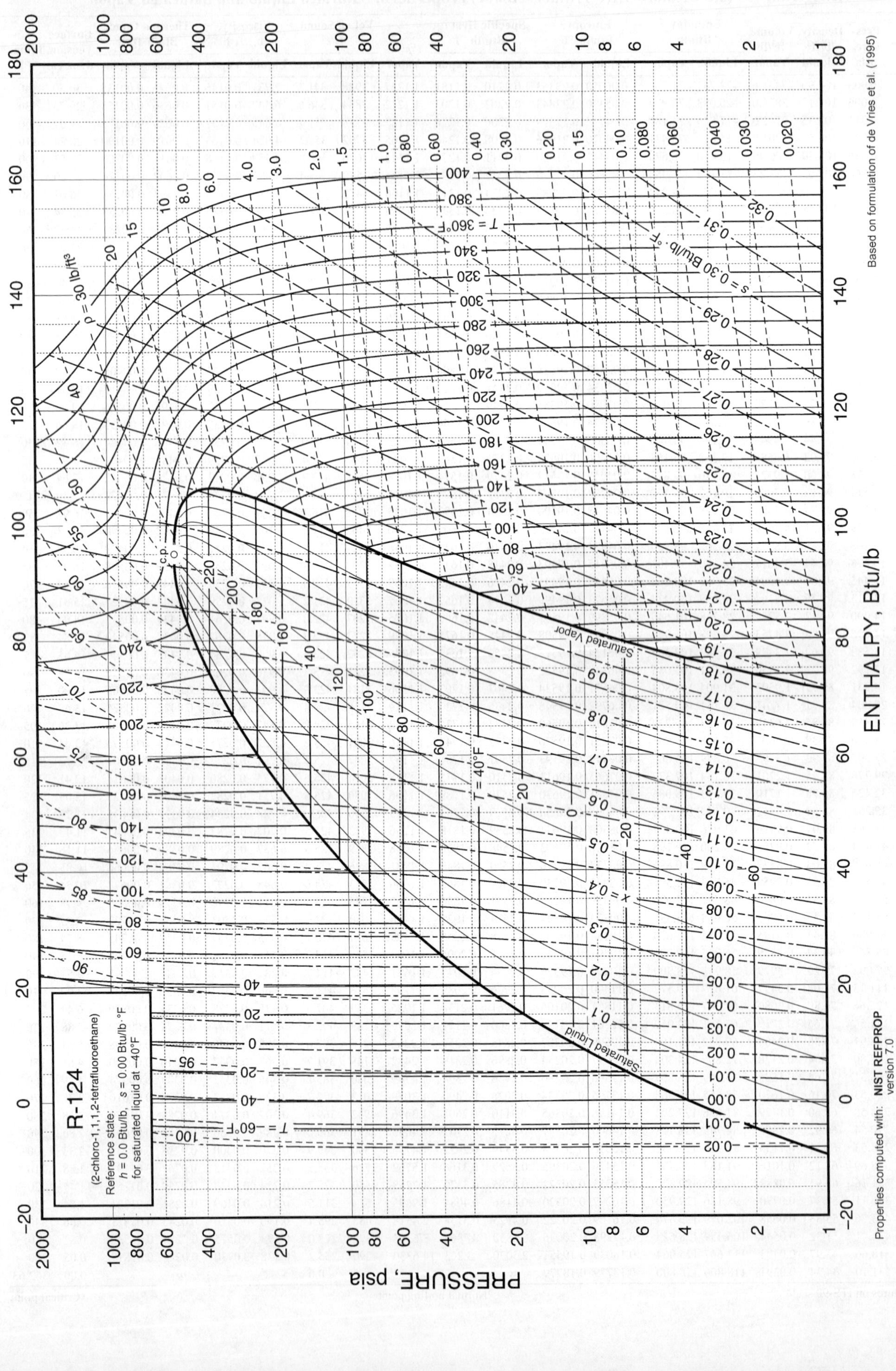

Fig. 6 Pressure-Enthalpy Diagram for Refrigerant 124

Refrigerant 125 (Pentafluoroethane) Properties of Saturated Liquid and Saturated Vapor

Temp.,* °F	Pres-sure, psia	Density, lb/ft³ Liquid	Volume, ft³/lb Vapor	Enthalpy, Btu/lb Liquid	Enthalpy, Btu/lb Vapor	Entropy, Btu/lb·°F Liquid	Entropy, Btu/lb·°F Vapor	Specific Heat c_p, Btu/lb·°F Liquid	Specific Heat c_p, Btu/lb·°F Vapor	c_p/c_v Vapor	Vel. of Sound, ft/s Liquid	Vel. of Sound, ft/s Vapor	Viscosity, lb_m/ft·h Liquid	Viscosity, lb_m/ft·h Vapor	Thermal Cond., Btu/h·ft·°F Liquid	Thermal Cond., Btu/h·ft·°F Vapor	Surface Tension, dyne/cm	Temp., °F
–149.13[a]	0.423	105.55	65.484	–28.097	53.756	–0.07725	0.18633	0.2473	0.1360	1.1416	3060	382.0	2.788	0.0180	0.0671	0.00303	21.79	–149.13
–145	0.521	105.08	53.794	–27.074	54.306	–0.07398	0.18464	0.2477	0.1371	1.1407	3020	384.2	2.628	0.0182	0.0665	0.00311	21.42	–145
–140	0.665	104.52	42.761	–25.833	54.974	–0.07007	0.18271	0.2483	0.1386	1.1397	2973	386.7	2.453	0.0185	0.0657	0.00322	20.97	–140
–135	0.842	103.96	34.286	–24.590	55.647	–0.06621	0.18092	0.2490	0.1400	1.1389	2926	389.2	2.296	0.0188	0.0650	0.00332	20.53	–135
–130	1.057	103.40	27.716	–23.343	56.322	–0.06240	0.17925	0.2498	0.1415	1.1381	2879	391.7	2.155	0.0191	0.0642	0.00342	20.08	–130
–125	1.315	102.83	22.580	–22.092	57.001	–0.05864	0.17770	0.2506	0.1430	1.1375	2833	394.1	2.027	0.0194	0.0634	0.00353	19.64	–125
–120	1.624	102.26	18.530	–20.836	57.682	–0.05491	0.17625	0.2514	0.1445	1.1369	2787	396.4	1.910	0.0197	0.0627	0.00364	19.20	–120
–115	1.992	101.69	15.313	–19.576	58.366	–0.05123	0.17490	0.2523	0.1460	1.1365	2742	398.7	1.803	0.0200	0.0619	0.00374	18.76	–115
–110	2.425	101.12	12.738	–18.312	59.052	–0.04759	0.17365	0.2533	0.1475	1.1362	2697	400.8	1.705	0.0203	0.0612	0.00385	18.32	–110
–105	2.934	100.54	10.663	–17.043	59.739	–0.04399	0.17250	0.2543	0.1491	1.1361	2652	402.9	1.615	0.0206	0.0604	0.00395	17.89	–105
–100	3.526	99.96	8.9787	–15.768	60.428	–0.04043	0.17142	0.2553	0.1507	1.1360	2608	405.0	1.532	0.0209	0.0596	0.00406	17.46	–100
–95	4.213	99.37	7.6032	–14.488	61.118	–0.03690	0.17043	0.2564	0.1523	1.1361	2563	406.9	1.455	0.0212	0.0589	0.00417	17.03	–95
–90	5.004	98.79	6.4729	–13.202	61.808	–0.03340	0.16951	0.2575	0.1539	1.1364	2519	408.7	1.383	0.0214	0.0581	0.00428	16.60	–90
–85	5.912	98.19	5.5386	–11.911	62.498	–0.02993	0.16867	0.2586	0.1556	1.1368	2476	410.5	1.317	0.0217	0.0574	0.00438	16.17	–85
–80	6.948	97.60	4.7621	–10.614	63.188	–0.02650	0.16789	0.2598	0.1573	1.1373	2432	412.1	1.255	0.0220	0.0566	0.00449	15.75	–80
–75	8.126	97.00	4.1132	–9.311	63.878	–0.02309	0.16717	0.2610	0.1591	1.1380	2388	413.6	1.197	0.0223	0.0558	0.00460	15.33	–75
–70	9.457	96.39	3.5682	–8.001	64.567	–0.01972	0.16651	0.2623	0.1609	1.1389	2345	415.1	1.142	0.0226	0.0551	0.00471	14.91	–70
–65	10.957	95.78	3.1083	–6.685	65.254	–0.01637	0.16591	0.2636	0.1627	1.1399	2302	416.4	1.091	0.0229	0.0543	0.00482	14.49	–65
–60	12.640	95.17	2.7182	–5.362	65.940	–0.01305	0.16536	0.2649	0.1645	1.1411	2259	417.6	1.043	0.0232	0.0536	0.00493	14.07	–60
–55	14.520	94.55	2.3860	–4.032	66.624	–0.00975	0.16485	0.2663	0.1665	1.1425	2216	418.6	0.998	0.0235	0.0529	0.00505	13.66	–55
–54.56[b]	14.696	94.49	2.3591	–3.915	66.684	–0.00946	0.16481	0.2664	0.1666	1.1426	2212	418.7	0.995	0.0235	0.0528	0.00506	13.63	–54.56
–50	16.614	93.92	2.1018	–2.696	67.305	–0.00648	0.16439	0.2677	0.1684	1.1441	2173	419.6	0.956	0.0238	0.0521	0.00516	13.25	–50
–45	18.938	93.28	1.8577	–1.352	67.984	–0.00323	0.16398	0.2691	0.1704	1.1459	2130	420.4	0.916	0.0240	0.0514	0.00527	12.84	–45
–40	21.509	92.64	1.6472	0.000	68.659	0.00000	0.16360	0.2706	0.1725	1.1479	2087	421.1	0.878	0.0243	0.0506	0.00539	12.44	–40
–35	24.344	92.00	1.4649	1.359	69.331	0.00321	0.16326	0.2722	0.1746	1.1502	2044	421.6	0.842	0.0246	0.0499	0.00550	12.04	–35
–30	27.460	91.34	1.3066	2.726	69.999	0.00639	0.16296	0.2738	0.1767	1.1527	2001	422.0	0.807	0.0249	0.0492	0.00562	11.64	–30
–25	30.875	90.68	1.1686	4.102	70.662	0.00956	0.16269	0.2754	0.1790	1.1554	1959	422.3	0.775	0.0252	0.0484	0.00574	11.24	–25
–20	34.610	90.01	1.0479	5.486	71.321	0.01271	0.16244	0.2771	0.1813	1.1585	1916	422.4	0.744	0.0255	0.0477	0.00586	10.84	–20
–15	38.682	89.33	0.9419	6.878	71.974	0.01584	0.16223	0.2789	0.1836	1.1618	1873	422.3	0.715	0.0258	0.0470	0.00598	10.45	–15
–10	43.111	88.64	0.8486	8.280	72.621	0.01895	0.16204	0.2807	0.1861	1.1655	1830	422.1	0.686	0.0261	0.0463	0.00610	10.06	–10
–5	47.917	87.94	0.7662	9.691	73.263	0.02205	0.16187	0.2826	0.1886	1.1695	1787	421.7	0.660	0.0264	0.0456	0.00622	9.68	–5
0	53.120	87.23	0.6933	11.112	73.897	0.02513	0.16172	0.2846	0.1912	1.1738	1745	421.1	0.634	0.0267	0.0448	0.00635	9.29	0
5	58.742	86.51	0.6285	12.542	74.524	0.02820	0.16159	0.2867	0.1939	1.1787	1702	420.3	0.609	0.0270	0.0441	0.00648	8.91	5
10	64.803	85.78	0.5708	13.983	75.143	0.03126	0.16148	0.2888	0.1967	1.1840	1659	419.4	0.586	0.0273	0.0434	0.00661	8.53	10
15	71.325	85.04	0.5193	15.436	75.753	0.03430	0.16138	0.2911	0.1995	1.1898	1616	418.2	0.563	0.0276	0.0427	0.00674	8.16	15
20	78.331	84.28	0.4732	16.899	76.353	0.03734	0.16129	0.2935	0.2025	1.1963	1573	416.8	0.542	0.0280	0.0420	0.00688	7.79	20
25	85.842	83.50	0.4318	18.374	76.942	0.04037	0.16121	0.2961	0.2056	1.2035	1530	415.3	0.521	0.0283	0.0413	0.00702	7.42	25
30	93.882	82.71	0.3946	19.862	77.520	0.04338	0.16113	0.2988	0.2089	1.2116	1487	413.5	0.501	0.0286	0.0407	0.00717	7.06	30
35	102.47	81.91	0.3610	21.363	78.084	0.04639	0.16106	0.3016	0.2124	1.2206	1444	411.5	0.481	0.0290	0.0400	0.00732	6.70	35
40	111.64	81.08	0.3307	22.878	78.633	0.04940	0.16098	0.3047	0.2161	1.2307	1401	409.3	0.463	0.0293	0.0393	0.00747	6.34	40
45	121.41	80.24	0.3032	24.407	79.167	0.05240	0.16090	0.3079	0.2201	1.2422	1357	406.8	0.444	0.0297	0.0386	0.00764	5.99	45
50	131.80	79.38	0.2783	25.951	79.684	0.05540	0.16082	0.3114	0.2245	1.2551	1314	404.1	0.427	0.0301	0.0379	0.00780	5.64	50
55	142.85	78.49	0.2556	27.512	80.181	0.05839	0.16073	0.3152	0.2293	1.2697	1270	401.2	0.410	0.0305	0.0373	0.00798	5.29	55
60	154.57	77.58	0.2349	29.090	80.657	0.06139	0.16062	0.3193	0.2346	1.2862	1226	397.9	0.394	0.0310	0.0366	0.00817	4.95	60
65	166.99	76.63	0.2160	30.687	81.111	0.06439	0.16050	0.3237	0.2406	1.3051	1182	394.5	0.378	0.0314	0.0359	0.00837	4.62	65
70	180.15	75.66	0.1987	32.303	81.540	0.06740	0.16035	0.3286	0.2473	1.3266	1137	390.7	0.362	0.0319	0.0353	0.00858	4.29	70
75	194.07	74.66	0.1829	33.941	81.942	0.07041	0.16019	0.3340	0.2548	1.3512	1092	386.6	0.347	0.0324	0.0346	0.00880	3.96	75
80	208.77	73.62	0.1683	35.602	82.314	0.07343	0.15999	0.3401	0.2634	1.3797	1047	382.3	0.332	0.0330	0.0340	0.00905	3.64	80
85	224.29	72.54	0.1549	37.288	82.654	0.07647	0.15976	0.3469	0.2731	1.4127	1001	377.6	0.318	0.0335	0.0333	0.00931	3.32	85
90	240.66	71.41	0.1425	39.002	82.957	0.07953	0.15949	0.3546	0.2844	1.4515	955	372.5	0.303	0.0342	0.0327	0.00961	3.01	90
95	257.92	70.23	0.1310	40.748	83.219	0.08261	0.15918	0.3635	0.2976	1.4975	908	367.1	0.289	0.0349	0.0320	0.00993	2.71	95
100	276.09	68.99	0.1204	42.528	83.435	0.08571	0.15881	0.3739	0.3132	1.5528	861	361.2	0.276	0.0357	0.0313	0.01029	2.41	100
105	295.21	67.68	0.1105	44.348	83.598	0.08886	0.15837	0.3863	0.3318	1.6203	813	354.9	0.262	0.0365	0.0307	0.01071	2.12	105
110	315.33	66.29	0.1012	46.213	83.697	0.09205	0.15785	0.4014	0.3548	1.7047	764	348.2	0.248	0.0375	0.0300	0.01118	1.84	110
115	336.48	64.80	0.0925	48.132	83.721	0.09530	0.15723	0.4202	0.3838	1.8130	714	340.9	0.235	0.0386	0.0294	0.01173	1.56	115
120	358.72	63.18	0.0843	50.117	83.653	0.09863	0.15648	0.4446	0.4216	1.9569	663	333.1	0.221	0.0399	0.0287	0.01239	1.30	120
125	382.10	61.42	0.0766	52.182	83.468	0.10205	0.15556	0.4777	0.4737	2.1572	609	324.6	0.207	0.0415	0.0281	0.01320	1.04	125
130	406.68	59.44	0.0691	54.353	83.125	0.10562	0.15442	0.5258	0.5503	2.4550	554	315.5	0.193	0.0434	0.0275	0.01422	0.80	130
135	432.55	57.18	0.0618	56.673	82.560	0.10940	0.15293	0.6029	0.6752	2.9435	495	305.5	0.178	0.0458	0.0269	0.01559	0.57	135
140	459.81	54.44	0.0544	59.223	81.642	0.11352	0.15091	0.7503	0.9161	3.8890	432	294.7	0.162	0.0490	0.0265	0.01760	0.36	140
145	488.62	50.80	0.0465	62.217	80.046	0.11832	0.14781	1.157	1.5777	6.4763	361	282.8	0.143	0.0542	0.0268	0.02115	0.16	145
150	519.32	43.50	0.0353	66.996	75.896	0.12599	0.14059	7.450	10.633	41.334	276	266.9	0.112	0.0675	0.0340	0.03660	0.01	150
150.84[c]	524.70	35.81	0.0279	71.250	71.250	0.13292	0.13292	∞	∞	∞	0	0.0	—	—	∞	∞	0.00	150.84

*Temperatures on ITS-90 scale [a]Triple point [b]Normal boiling point [c]Critical point

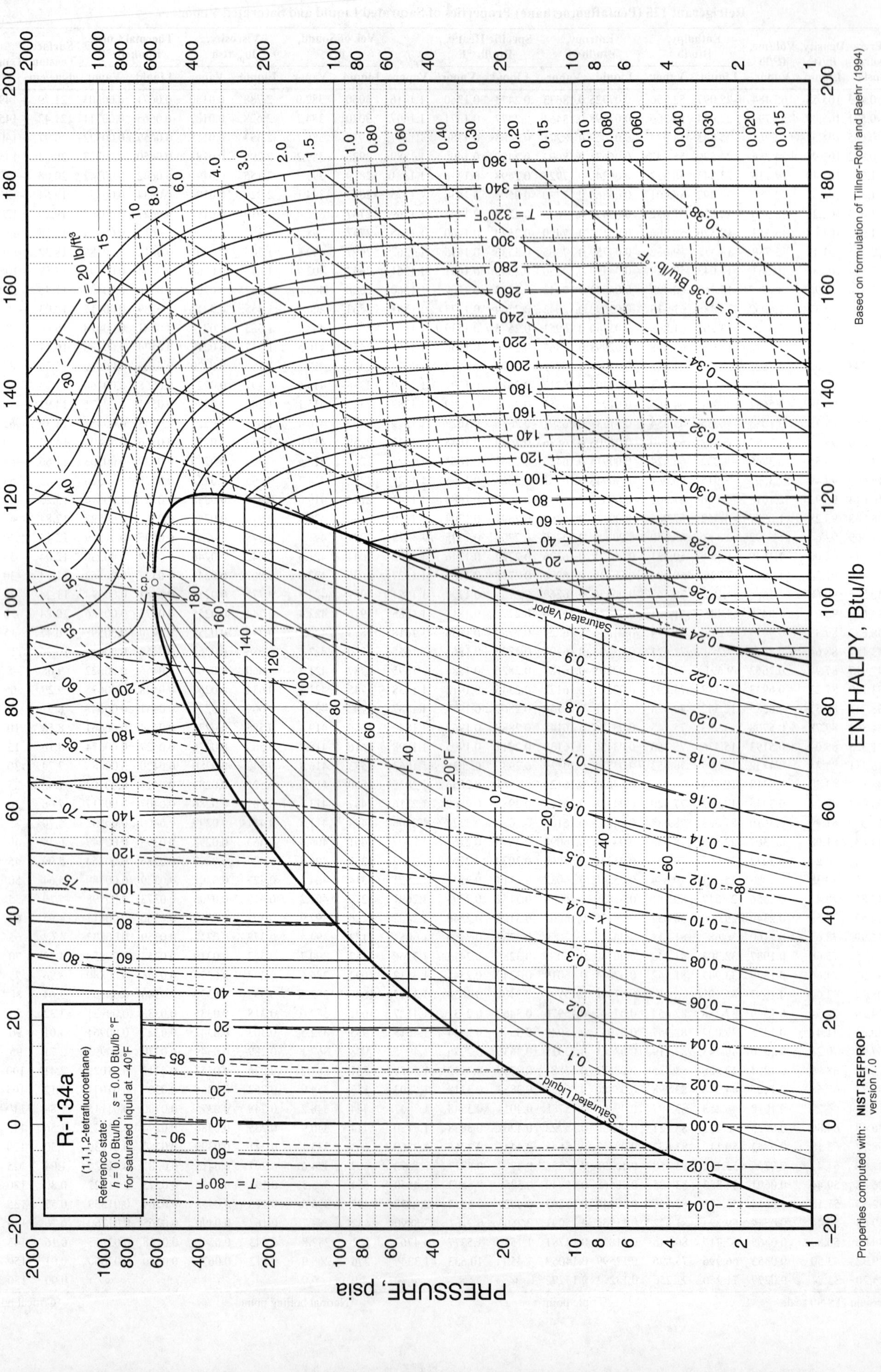

Fig. 8 Pressure-Enthalpy Diagram for Refrigerant 134a

Refrigerant 134a (1,1,1,2-Tetrafluoroethane) Properties of Saturated Liquid and Saturated Vapor

Temp.,* °F	Pres-sure, psia	Density, lb/ft³ Liquid	Volume, ft³/lb Vapor	Enthalpy, Btu/lb Liquid	Enthalpy, Btu/lb Vapor	Entropy, Btu/lb·°F Liquid	Entropy, Btu/lb·°F Vapor	Specific Heat c_p, Btu/lb·°F Liquid	Specific Heat c_p, Btu/lb·°F Vapor	c_p/c_v Vapor	Vel. of Sound, ft/s Liquid	Vel. of Sound, ft/s Vapor	Viscosity, lb_m/ft·h Liquid	Viscosity, lb_m/ft·h Vapor	Thermal Cond., Btu/h·ft·°F Liquid	Thermal Cond., Btu/h·ft·°F Vapor	Surface Tension, dyne/cm	Temp.,* °F
–153.94[a]	0.057	99.33	568.59	–32.992	80.362	–0.09154	0.27923	0.2829	0.1399	1.1637	3674	416.0	5.262	0.0156	0.0840	0.00178	28.07	–153.94
–150	0.072	98.97	452.12	–31.878	80.907	–0.08791	0.27629	0.2830	0.1411	1.1623	3638	418.3	4.790	0.0159	0.0832	0.00188	27.69	–150
–140	0.129	98.05	260.63	–29.046	82.304	–0.07891	0.26941	0.2834	0.1443	1.1589	3545	424.2	3.880	0.0164	0.0813	0.00214	26.74	–140
–130	0.221	97.13	156.50	–26.208	83.725	–0.07017	0.26329	0.2842	0.1475	1.1559	3452	429.9	3.238	0.0170	0.0794	0.00240	25.79	–130
–120	0.365	96.20	97.481	–23.360	85.168	–0.06166	0.25784	0.2853	0.1508	1.1532	3360	435.5	2.762	0.0176	0.0775	0.00265	24.85	–120
–110	0.583	95.27	62.763	–20.500	86.629	–0.05337	0.25300	0.2866	0.1540	1.1509	3269	440.8	2.396	0.0182	0.0757	0.00291	23.92	–110
–100	0.903	94.33	41.637	–17.626	88.107	–0.04527	0.24871	0.2881	0.1573	1.1490	3178	446.0	2.105	0.0187	0.0739	0.00317	22.99	–100
–90	1.359	93.38	28.381	–14.736	89.599	–0.03734	0.24490	0.2898	0.1607	1.1475	3087	450.9	1.869	0.0193	0.0722	0.00343	22.07	–90
–80	1.993	92.42	19.825	–11.829	91.103	–0.02959	0.24152	0.2916	0.1641	1.1465	2998	455.6	1.673	0.0199	0.0705	0.00369	21.16	–80
–75	2.392	91.94	16.711	–10.368	91.858	–0.02577	0.23998	0.2925	0.1658	1.1462	2954	457.8	1.587	0.0201	0.0696	0.00382	20.71	–75
–70	2.854	91.46	14.161	–8.903	92.614	–0.02198	0.23854	0.2935	0.1676	1.1460	2909	460.0	1.509	0.0204	0.0688	0.00395	20.26	–70
–65	3.389	90.97	12.060	–7.432	93.372	–0.01824	0.23718	0.2945	0.1694	1.1459	2866	462.1	1.436	0.0207	0.0680	0.00408	19.81	–65
–60	4.002	90.49	10.321	–5.957	94.131	–0.01452	0.23590	0.2955	0.1713	1.1460	2822	464.1	1.369	0.0210	0.0671	0.00420	19.36	–60
–55	4.703	90.00	8.8733	–4.476	94.890	–0.01085	0.23470	0.2965	0.1731	1.1462	2778	466.0	1.306	0.0212	0.0663	0.00433	18.92	–55
–50	5.501	89.50	7.6621	–2.989	95.650	–0.00720	0.23358	0.2976	0.1751	1.1466	2735	467.8	1.248	0.0215	0.0655	0.00446	18.47	–50
–45	6.406	89.00	6.6438	–1.498	96.409	–0.00358	0.23252	0.2987	0.1770	1.1471	2691	469.6	1.193	0.0218	0.0647	0.00460	18.03	–45
–40	7.427	88.50	5.7839	0.000	97.167	0.00000	0.23153	0.2999	0.1790	1.1478	2648	471.2	1.142	0.0221	0.0639	0.00473	17.60	–40
–35	8.576	88.00	5.0544	1.503	97.924	0.00356	0.23060	0.3010	0.1811	1.1486	2605	472.8	1.095	0.0223	0.0632	0.00486	17.16	–35
–30	9.862	87.49	4.4330	3.013	98.679	0.00708	0.22973	0.3022	0.1832	1.1496	2563	474.2	1.050	0.0226	0.0624	0.00499	16.73	–30
–25	11.299	86.98	3.9014	4.529	99.433	0.01058	0.22892	0.3035	0.1853	1.1508	2520	475.6	1.007	0.0229	0.0616	0.00512	16.30	–25
–20	12.898	86.47	3.4449	6.051	100.184	0.01406	0.22816	0.3047	0.1875	1.1521	2477	476.8	0.968	0.0231	0.0608	0.00525	15.87	–20
–15	14.671	85.95	3.0514	7.580	100.932	0.01751	0.22744	0.3060	0.1898	1.1537	2435	477.9	0.930	0.0234	0.0601	0.00538	15.44	–15
–14.93[b]	14.696	85.94	3.0465	7.600	100.942	0.01755	0.22743	0.3061	0.1898	1.1537	2434	477.9	0.929	0.0234	0.0601	0.00538	15.44	–14.93
–10	16.632	85.43	2.7109	9.115	101.677	0.02093	0.22678	0.3074	0.1921	1.1554	2393	478.9	0.894	0.0237	0.0593	0.00552	15.02	–10
–5	18.794	84.90	2.4154	10.657	102.419	0.02433	0.22615	0.3088	0.1945	1.1573	2350	479.8	0.860	0.0240	0.0586	0.00565	14.60	–5
0	21.171	84.37	2.1579	12.207	103.156	0.02771	0.22557	0.3102	0.1969	1.1595	2308	480.5	0.828	0.0242	0.0578	0.00578	14.18	0
5	23.777	83.83	1.9330	13.764	103.889	0.03107	0.22502	0.3117	0.1995	1.1619	2266	481.1	0.798	0.0245	0.0571	0.00592	13.76	5
10	26.628	83.29	1.7357	15.328	104.617	0.03440	0.22451	0.3132	0.2021	1.1645	2224	481.6	0.769	0.0248	0.0564	0.00605	13.35	10
15	29.739	82.74	1.5623	16.901	105.339	0.03772	0.22403	0.3147	0.2047	1.1674	2182	482.0	0.741	0.0250	0.0556	0.00619	12.94	15
20	33.124	82.19	1.4094	18.481	106.056	0.04101	0.22359	0.3164	0.2075	1.1705	2140	482.2	0.715	0.0253	0.0549	0.00632	12.53	20
25	36.800	81.63	1.2742	20.070	106.767	0.04429	0.22317	0.3181	0.2103	1.1740	2098	482.2	0.689	0.0256	0.0542	0.00646	12.12	25
30	40.784	81.06	1.1543	21.667	107.471	0.04755	0.22278	0.3198	0.2132	1.1777	2056	482.2	0.665	0.0258	0.0535	0.00660	11.72	30
35	45.092	80.49	1.0478	23.274	108.167	0.05079	0.22241	0.3216	0.2163	1.1818	2014	481.9	0.642	0.0261	0.0528	0.00674	11.32	35
40	49.741	79.90	0.9528	24.890	108.856	0.05402	0.22207	0.3235	0.2194	1.1862	1973	481.5	0.620	0.0264	0.0521	0.00688	10.92	40
45	54.749	79.32	0.8680	26.515	109.537	0.05724	0.22174	0.3255	0.2226	1.1910	1931	481.0	0.598	0.0267	0.0514	0.00703	10.53	45
50	60.134	78.72	0.7920	28.150	110.209	0.06044	0.22144	0.3275	0.2260	1.1961	1889	480.3	0.578	0.0270	0.0507	0.00717	10.14	50
55	65.913	78.11	0.7238	29.796	110.871	0.06362	0.22115	0.3297	0.2294	1.2018	1847	479.4	0.558	0.0273	0.0500	0.00732	9.75	55
60	72.105	77.50	0.6625	31.452	111.524	0.06680	0.22088	0.3319	0.2331	1.2079	1805	478.3	0.539	0.0275	0.0493	0.00747	9.36	60
65	78.729	76.87	0.6072	33.120	112.165	0.06996	0.22062	0.3343	0.2368	1.2145	1763	477.0	0.520	0.0278	0.0486	0.00762	8.98	65
70	85.805	76.24	0.5572	34.799	112.796	0.07311	0.22037	0.3368	0.2408	1.2217	1721	475.6	0.503	0.0281	0.0479	0.00777	8.60	70
75	93.351	75.59	0.5120	36.491	113.414	0.07626	0.22013	0.3394	0.2449	1.2296	1679	474.0	0.485	0.0284	0.0472	0.00793	8.23	75
80	101.39	74.94	0.4710	38.195	114.019	0.07939	0.21989	0.3422	0.2492	1.2382	1636	472.2	0.469	0.0287	0.0465	0.00809	7.86	80
85	109.93	74.27	0.4338	39.913	114.610	0.08252	0.21966	0.3451	0.2537	1.2475	1594	470.1	0.453	0.0291	0.0458	0.00825	7.49	85
90	119.01	73.58	0.3999	41.645	115.186	0.08565	0.21944	0.3482	0.2585	1.2578	1551	467.9	0.437	0.0294	0.0451	0.00842	7.13	90
95	128.65	72.88	0.3690	43.392	115.746	0.08877	0.21921	0.3515	0.2636	1.2690	1509	465.4	0.422	0.0297	0.0444	0.00860	6.77	95
100	138.85	72.17	0.3407	45.155	116.289	0.09188	0.21898	0.3551	0.2690	1.2813	1466	462.7	0.407	0.0301	0.0437	0.00878	6.41	100
105	149.65	71.44	0.3148	46.934	116.813	0.09500	0.21875	0.3589	0.2747	1.2950	1423	459.8	0.393	0.0304	0.0431	0.00897	6.06	105
110	161.07	70.69	0.2911	48.731	117.317	0.09811	0.21851	0.3630	0.2809	1.3101	1380	456.7	0.378	0.0308	0.0424	0.00916	5.71	110
115	173.14	69.93	0.2693	50.546	117.799	0.10123	0.21826	0.3675	0.2875	1.3268	1337	453.2	0.365	0.0312	0.0417	0.00936	5.36	115
120	185.86	69.14	0.2493	52.382	118.258	0.10435	0.21800	0.3723	0.2948	1.3456	1294	449.6	0.351	0.0316	0.0410	0.00958	5.03	120
125	199.28	68.32	0.2308	54.239	118.690	0.10748	0.21772	0.3775	0.3026	1.3666	1250	445.6	0.338	0.0320	0.0403	0.00981	4.69	125
130	213.41	67.49	0.2137	56.119	119.095	0.11062	0.21742	0.3833	0.3112	1.3903	1206	441.4	0.325	0.0324	0.0396	0.01005	4.36	130
135	228.28	66.62	0.1980	58.023	119.468	0.11376	0.21709	0.3897	0.3208	1.4173	1162	436.8	0.313	0.0329	0.0389	0.01031	4.04	135
140	243.92	65.73	0.1833	59.954	119.807	0.11692	0.21673	0.3968	0.3315	1.4481	1117	432.0	0.301	0.0334	0.0382	0.01058	3.72	140
145	260.36	64.80	0.1697	61.915	120.108	0.12010	0.21634	0.4048	0.3435	1.4837	1072	426.8	0.288	0.0339	0.0375	0.01089	3.40	145
150	277.61	63.83	0.1571	63.908	120.366	0.12330	0.21591	0.4138	0.3571	1.5250	1027	421.2	0.276	0.0344	0.0368	0.01122	3.09	150
155	295.73	62.82	0.1453	65.936	120.576	0.12653	0.21542	0.4242	0.3729	1.5738	980	415.3	0.264	0.0350	0.0361	0.01158	2.79	155
160	314.73	61.76	0.1343	68.005	120.731	0.12979	0.21488	0.4362	0.3914	1.6318	934	409.1	0.253	0.0357	0.0354	0.01199	2.50	160
165	334.65	60.65	0.1239	70.118	120.823	0.13309	0.21426	0.4504	0.4133	1.7022	886	402.4	0.241	0.0364	0.0346	0.01245	2.21	165
170	355.53	59.47	0.1142	72.283	120.842	0.13644	0.21356	0.4675	0.4400	1.7889	837	395.3	0.229	0.0372	0.0339	0.01297	1.93	170
175	377.41	58.21	0.1051	74.509	120.773	0.13985	0.21274	0.4887	0.4733	1.8984	786	387.7	0.218	0.0381	0.0332	0.01358	1.66	175
180	400.34	56.86	0.0964	76.807	120.598	0.14334	0.21180	0.5156	0.5159	2.0405	734	379.6	0.206	0.0391	0.0325	0.01430	1.39	180
185	424.36	55.38	0.0881	79.193	120.294	0.14693	0.21069	0.5512	0.5729	2.2321	680	371.0	0.194	0.0403	0.0318	0.01516	1.14	185
190	449.52	53.76	0.0801	81.692	119.822	0.15066	0.20935	0.6012	0.6532	2.5041	624	361.8	0.182	0.0417	0.0311	0.01623	0.90	190
195	475.91	51.91	0.0724	84.343	119.123	0.15459	0.20771	0.6768	0.7751	2.9192	565	352.0	0.169	0.0435	0.0304	0.01760	0.67	195
200	503.59	49.76	0.0647	87.214	118.097	0.15880	0.20562	0.8062	0.9835	3.6309	502	341.3	0.155	0.0457	0.0300	0.01949	0.45	200
205	532.68	47.08	0.0567	90.454	116.526	0.16353	0.20275	1.0830	1.4250	5.1360	436	329.4	0.140	0.0489	0.0300	0.02240	0.26	205
210	563.35	43.20	0.0477	94.530	113.746	0.16945	0.19814	2.1130	3.0080	10.5120	363	315.5	0.120	0.0543	0.0316	0.02848	0.09	210
213.91[c]	588.75	31.96	0.0313	103.894	103.894	0.18320	0.18320	∞	∞	∞	0	0.0	—	—	∞	∞	0.00	213.91

*Temperatures on ITS-90 scale [a]Triple point [b]Normal boiling point [c]Critical point

Refrigerant 134a Properties of Superheated Vapor

Pressure = 14.696 psia
Saturation temperature = –14.92°F

Temp.,* °F	Density, lb/ft³	Enthalpy, Btu/lb	Entropy, Btu/lb·°F	Vel. Sound, ft/s
Saturated				
Liquid	85.7972	7.53	0.01739	2451.2
Vapor	0.3283	100.81	0.22713	478.0
0	0.3158	103.62	0.23335	487.2
20	0.3008	107.45	0.24149	499.0
40	0.2874	111.34	0.24944	510.2
60	0.2753	115.31	0.25723	521.0
80	0.2642	119.35	0.26486	531.5
100	0.2541	123.47	0.27236	541.6
120	0.2448	127.68	0.27974	551.4
140	0.2362	131.96	0.28700	561.0
160	0.2282	136.32	0.29416	570.4
180	0.2208	140.77	0.30122	579.5
200	0.2139	145.30	0.30819	588.5
220	0.2074	149.90	0.31507	597.3
240	0.2013	154.59	0.32187	606.0
260	0.1955	159.36	0.32858	614.5
280	0.1901	164.20	0.33522	622.8
300	0.1850	169.12	0.34178	631.1

Pressure = 25.00 psia
Saturation temperature = 7.22°F

Temp.,* °F	Density, lb/ft³	Enthalpy, Btu/lb	Entropy, Btu/lb·°F	Vel. Sound, ft/s
Saturated				
Liquid	83.4823	14.32	0.03224	2263.9
Vapor	0.5426	104.07	0.22446	481.5
20	0.5245	106.60	0.22982	489.9
40	0.4991	110.61	0.23800	502.4
60	0.4765	114.66	0.24596	514.1
80	0.4563	118.78	0.25373	525.4
100	0.4379	122.96	0.26135	536.2
120	0.4212	127.22	0.26881	546.6
140	0.4058	131.55	0.27615	556.7
160	0.3916	135.95	0.28337	566.5
180	0.3786	140.43	0.29048	576.0
200	0.3663	144.98	0.29750	585.3
220	0.3549	149.61	0.30441	594.4
240	0.3443	154.32	0.31124	603.3
260	0.3343	159.10	0.31798	612.0
280	0.3248	163.96	0.32464	620.6
300	0.3160	168.90	0.33122	629.0

Pressure = 50.00 psia
Saturation temperature = 40.29°F

Temp.,* °F	Density, lb/ft³	Enthalpy, Btu/lb	Entropy, Btu/lb·°F	Vel. Sound, ft/s
Saturated				
Liquid	79.8125	24.79	0.05377	1982.3
Vapor	1.0545	108.74	0.22170	481.7
60	0.9982	113.00	0.23005	496.2
80	0.9489	117.32	0.23822	509.8
100	0.9055	121.68	0.24614	522.5
120	0.8670	126.07	0.25385	534.5
140	0.8322	130.51	0.26139	545.8
160	0.8008	135.01	0.26877	556.7
180	0.7718	139.57	0.27601	567.2
200	0.7454	144.20	0.28313	577.4
220	0.7208	148.89	0.29014	587.2
240	0.6980	153.65	0.29704	596.8
260	0.6768	158.48	0.30385	606.1
280	0.6569	163.38	0.31056	615.2
300	0.6383	168.35	0.31719	624.1

Pressure = 75.00 psia
Saturation temperature = 62.24°F

Temp.,* °F	Density, lb/ft³	Enthalpy, Btu/lb	Entropy, Btu/lb·°F	Vel. Sound, ft/s
Saturated				
Liquid	77.1862	31.98	0.06775	1793.6
Vapor	1.5686	111.67	0.22042	478.1
80	1.4873	115.74	0.22809	492.7
100	1.4092	120.30	0.23639	507.7
120	1.3416	124.85	0.24439	521.6
140	1.2822	129.43	0.25215	534.5
160	1.2294	134.04	0.25971	546.6
180	1.1817	138.69	0.26710	558.2
200	1.1383	143.39	0.27434	569.2
220	1.0984	148.15	0.28145	579.8
240	1.0620	152.97	0.28843	590.1
260	1.0280	157.85	0.29531	600.0
280	0.9966	162.79	0.30208	609.7
300	0.9671	167.80	0.30876	619.0
320	0.9398	172.87	0.31535	628.2
340	0.9138	178.01	0.32186	637.1
360	0.8895	183.21	0.32828	645.9
380	0.8665	188.48	0.33463	654.5
400	0.8448	193.82	0.34091	662.9

Pressure = 100.00 psia
Saturation temperature = 79.17°F

Temp.,* °F	Density, lb/ft³	Enthalpy, Btu/lb	Entropy, Btu/lb·°F	Vel. Sound, ft/s
Saturated				
Liquid	75.0245	37.69	0.07840	1646.8
Vapor	2.0917	113.78	0.21960	472.8
80	2.0858	113.98	0.21998	473.6
100	1.9576	118.80	0.22874	491.6
120	1.8509	123.55	0.23709	507.8
140	1.7597	128.29	0.24512	522.4
160	1.6800	133.02	0.25288	536.0
180	1.6094	137.78	0.26044	548.8
200	1.5463	142.57	0.26781	560.8
220	1.4891	147.40	0.27502	572.3
240	1.4368	152.27	0.28210	583.3
260	1.3886	157.21	0.28905	593.9
280	1.3444	162.19	0.29588	604.1
300	1.3031	167.24	0.30261	614.0
320	1.2647	172.35	0.30925	623.6
340	1.2287	177.52	0.31579	632.9
360	1.1950	182.75	0.32225	642.1
380	1.1633	188.04	0.32863	651.0
400	1.1334	193.39	0.33494	659.8

Pressure = 125.00 psia
Saturation temperature = 93.15°F

Temp.,* °F	Density, lb/ft³	Enthalpy, Btu/lb	Entropy, Btu/lb·°F	Vel. Sound, ft/s
Saturated				
Liquid	73.1279	42.53	0.08715	1524.7
Vapor	2.6279	115.41	0.21898	466.7
100	2.5638	117.16	0.22212	473.9
120	2.4025	122.16	0.23090	492.9
140	2.2694	127.08	0.23924	509.7
160	2.1561	131.96	0.24725	525.0
180	2.0577	136.83	0.25498	539.0
200	1.9710	141.71	0.26250	552.2
220	1.8935	146.62	0.26983	564.6
240	1.8233	151.56	0.27700	576.4
260	1.7592	156.55	0.28402	587.6
280	1.7006	161.59	0.29093	598.4
300	1.6463	166.67	0.29771	608.8
320	1.5959	171.82	0.30440	618.9
340	1.5492	177.02	0.31098	628.7
360	1.5055	182.27	0.31747	638.2
380	1.4644	187.59	0.32388	647.5
400	1.4258	192.97	0.33021	656.6

Pressure = 150.00 psia
Saturation temperature = 105.17°F

Temp.,* °F	Density, lb/ft³	Enthalpy, Btu/lb	Entropy, Btu/lb·°F	Vel. Sound, ft/s
Saturated				
Liquid	71.4013	46.78	0.09464	1419.1
Vapor	3.1801	116.71	0.21844	460.0
120	3.0077	120.64	0.22530	476.6
140	2.8181	125.78	0.23403	496.0
160	2.6620	130.83	0.24231	513.3
180	2.5295	135.83	0.25026	528.9
200	2.4146	140.82	0.25794	543.3
220	2.3132	145.82	0.26539	556.7
240	2.2223	150.83	0.27267	569.3
260	2.1401	155.88	0.27978	581.3
280	2.0658	160.97	0.28675	592.7
300	1.9971	166.10	0.29360	603.7
320	1.9338	171.28	0.30033	614.2
340	1.8751	176.51	0.30696	624.5
360	1.8208	181.80	0.31349	634.4
380	1.7695	187.14	0.31993	644.0
400	1.7216	192.54	0.32628	653.4
420	1.6766	198.00	0.33256	662.6
440	1.6341	203.51	0.33876	671.6
460	1.5940	209.08	0.34488	680.4
480	1.5558	214.71	0.35094	689.0
500	1.5197	220.40	0.35692	697.4

Pressure = 175.00 psia
Saturation temperature = 115.76°F

Temp.,* °F	Density, lb/ft³	Enthalpy, Btu/lb	Entropy, Btu/lb·°F	Vel. Sound, ft/s
Saturated				
Liquid	69.7902	50.62	0.10126	1325.3
Vapor	3.7511	117.76	0.21794	453.0
120	3.6836	118.95	0.21999	458.4
140	3.4148	124.38	0.22921	481.3
160	3.2025	129.64	0.23783	500.9
180	3.0271	134.79	0.24602	518.3
200	2.8785	139.90	0.25388	534.0
220	2.7494	144.99	0.26148	548.5
240	2.6349	150.08	0.26887	562.1
260	2.5328	155.19	0.27607	574.8
280	2.4403	160.34	0.28312	586.9
300	2.3558	165.51	0.29003	598.5
320	2.2785	170.73	0.29681	609.5
340	2.2071	176	0.30348	620.2
360	2.1411	181.32	0.31004	630.5
380	2.0795	186.69	0.31651	640.5
400	2.0216	192.11	0.32290	650.3
420	1.9675	197.59	0.32920	659.7
440	1.9164	203.12	0.33542	669.0
460	1.8683	208.71	0.34156	678.0
480	1.8228	214.36	0.34763	686.9
500	1.7797	220.05	0.35363	695.6

Pressure = 200.00 psia
Saturation temperature = 125.27°F

Temp.,* °F	Density, lb/ft³	Enthalpy, Btu/lb	Entropy, Btu/lb·°F	Vel. Sound, ft/s
Saturated				
Liquid	68.2602	54.14	0.10721	1240.5
Vapor	4.3437	118.61	0.21743	445.6
140	4.0726	122.86	0.22460	465.2
160	3.7850	128.36	0.23363	487.8
180	3.5561	133.70	0.24210	507.2
200	3.3656	138.94	0.25018	524.5
220	3.2036	144.14	0.25793	540.2
240	3.0623	149.31	0.26544	554.7
260	2.9371	154.50	0.27274	568.3
280	2.8247	159.69	0.27987	581.1
300	2.7234	164.92	0.28684	593.2
320	2.6305	170.18	0.29368	604.8
340	2.5455	175.49	0.30039	615.9
360	2.4668	180.83	0.30700	626.7
380	2.3934	186.23	0.31350	637.0
400	2.3254	191.68	0.31991	647.1
420	2.2614	197.18	0.32624	656.9
440	2.2017	202.73	0.33248	666.4
460	2.1453	208.34	0.33864	675.7
480	2.0920	214.00	0.34473	684.8
500	2.0417	219.71	0.35075	693.7

*Temperatures on ITS-90 scale

Refrigerant 134a Properties of Superheated Vapor (*Concluded*)

Pressure = 225.00 psia
Saturation temperature = 133.93°F

Temp.,* °F	Density, lb/ft³	Enthalpy, Btu/lb	Entropy, Btu/lb·°F	Vel. Sound, ft/s
Saturated				
Liquid	66.7870	57.42	0.11266	1162.8
Vapor	4.9609	119.30	0.21690	438.1
140	4.8123	121.16	0.22002	447.3
160	4.4191	126.99	0.22959	473.6
180	4.1206	132.54	0.23840	495.5
200	3.8796	137.94	0.24671	514.6
220	3.6784	143.25	0.25465	531.6
240	3.5058	148.52	0.26229	547.2
260	3.3542	153.78	0.26970	561.6
280	3.2202	159.04	0.27691	575.1
300	3.0995	164.32	0.28395	587.9
320	2.9899	169.62	0.29084	600.0
340	2.8897	174.97	0.29761	611.7
360	2.7978	180.35	0.30425	622.8
380	2.7122	185.77	0.31079	633.6
400	2.6330	191.24	0.31723	644.0
420	2.5592	196.77	0.32358	654.0
440	2.4900	202.34	0.32984	663.9
460	2.4249	207.96	0.33603	673.4
480	2.3636	213.64	0.34213	682.8
500	2.3057	219.36	0.34816	691.9

Pressure = 250.00 psia
Saturation temperature = 141.89°F

Temp.,* °F	Density, lb/ft³	Enthalpy, Btu/lb	Entropy, Btu/lb·°F	Vel. Sound, ft/s
Saturated				
Liquid	65.3526	60.50	0.11770	1090.7
Vapor	5.6060	119.84	0.21634	430.3
160	5.1189	125.49	0.22560	458.2
180	4.7275	131.31	0.23484	483.1
200	4.4239	136.89	0.24343	504.2
220	4.1756	142.34	0.25156	522.8
240	3.9664	147.71	0.25935	539.5
260	3.7854	153.05	0.26688	554.9
280	3.6265	158.37	0.27418	569.2
300	3.4847	163.71	0.28129	582.6
320	3.3571	169.06	0.28824	595.3
340	3.2408	174.44	0.29506	607.4
360	3.1342	179.85	0.30175	618.9
380	3.0359	185.31	0.30832	630.1
400	2.9451	190.81	0.31479	640.8
420	2.8604	196.35	0.32117	651.2
440	2.7813	201.94	0.32745	661.3
460	2.7072	207.58	0.33365	671.1
480	2.6374	213.27	0.33977	680.7
500	2.5717	219.02	0.34582	690.1

Pressure = 275.00 psia
Saturation temperature = 149.27°F

Temp.,* °F	Density, lb/ft³	Enthalpy, Btu/lb	Entropy, Btu/lb·°F	Vel. Sound, ft/s
Saturated				
Liquid	63.9423	63.43	0.12241	1023.4
Vapor	6.2831	120.25	0.21572	422.3
160	5.9060	123.82	0.22155	441.2
180	5.3869	129.98	0.23133	469.9
200	5.0031	135.78	0.24026	493.4
220	4.6978	141.38	0.24862	513.7
240	4.4465	146.87	0.25658	531.7
260	4.2314	152.30	0.26423	548.0
280	4.0446	157.69	0.27162	563.1
300	3.8803	163.08	0.27881	577.2
320	3.7317	168.49	0.28583	590.5
340	3.5987	173.91	0.29270	603.1
360	3.4764	179.36	0.29943	615.1
380	3.3646	184.84	0.30604	626.6
400	3.2612	190.37	0.31254	637.7
420	3.1653	195.93	0.31894	648.4
440	3.0758	201.55	0.32525	658.8
460	2.9922	207.20	0.33147	668.9
480	2.9136	212.91	0.33761	678.7
500	2.8397	218.67	0.34368	688.3

Pressure = 300.00 psia
Saturation temperature = 156.16°F

Temp.,* °F	Density, lb/ft³	Enthalpy, Btu/lb	Entropy, Btu/lb·°F	Vel. Sound, ft/s
Saturated				
Liquid	62.5436	66.23	0.12686	959.8
Vapor	6.9967	120.54	0.21505	414.2
160	6.8168	121.92	0.21730	422.0
180	6.1118	128.55	0.22782	455.8
200	5.6239	134.61	0.23715	482.1
220	5.2494	140.39	0.24578	504.3
240	4.9472	146.00	0.25393	523.7
260	4.6939	151.52	0.26171	541.1
280	4.4758	157.00	0.26921	557.0
300	4.2852	162.45	0.27649	571.8
320	4.1160	167.90	0.28357	585.7
340	3.9631	173.37	0.29049	598.8
360	3.8247	178.85	0.29727	611.2
380	3.6981	184.37	0.30392	623.1
400	3.5816	189.92	0.31045	634.6
420	3.4737	195.51	0.31688	645.6
440	3.3735	201.15	0.32321	656.3
460	3.2799	206.83	0.32945	666.6
480	3.1922	212.55	0.33561	676.7
500	3.1098	218.32	0.34169	686.5

Pressure = 325.00 psia
Saturation temperature = 162.62°F

Temp.,* °F	Density, lb/ft³	Enthalpy, Btu/lb	Entropy, Btu/lb·°F	Vel. Sound, ft/s
Saturated				
Liquid	61.1446	68.92	0.13110	899.5
Vapor	7.7526	120.71	0.21431	405.9
180	6.9220	126.96	0.22423	440.3
200	6.2928	133.36	0.23408	470.2
220	5.8341	139.34	0.24301	494.5
240	5.4723	145.10	0.25136	515.5
260	5.1741	150.73	0.25930	534.0
280	4.9208	156.29	0.26692	550.9
300	4.7017	161.81	0.27428	566.4
320	4.5082	167.31	0.28144	580.9
340	4.3352	172.82	0.28841	594.5
360	4.1790	178.35	0.29524	607.4
380	4.0368	183.90	0.30193	619.7
400	3.9063	189.48	0.30849	631.5
420	3.7859	195.09	0.31495	642.8
440	3.6743	200.75	0.32131	653.8
460	3.5703	206.44	0.32757	664.4
480	3.4731	212.19	0.33375	674.7
500	3.3819	217.97	0.33984	684.7

Pressure = 350.00 psia
Saturation temperature = 168.71°F

Temp.,* °F	Density, lb/ft³	Enthalpy, Btu/lb	Entropy, Btu/lb·°F	Vel. Sound, ft/s
Saturated				
Liquid	59.7334	71.54	0.13516	841.7
Vapor	8.5577	120.76	0.21349	397.5
180	7.8491	125.18	0.22046	423.2
200	7.0242	132.01	0.23098	457.6
220	6.4561	138.24	0.24029	484.4
240	6.0219	144.17	0.24888	507.1
260	5.6728	149.91	0.25698	526.9
280	5.3805	155.56	0.26472	544.7
300	5.1295	161.15	0.27218	561.0
320	4.9098	166.72	0.27941	576.1
340	4.7148	172.27	0.28644	590.2
360	4.5396	177.84	0.29332	603.6
380	4.3807	183.42	0.30005	616.3
400	4.2355	189.03	0.30665	628.4
420	4.1019	194.67	0.31313	640.1
440	3.9784	200.35	0.31952	651.4
460	3.8636	206.06	0.32580	662.2
480	3.7564	211.82	0.33199	672.8
500	3.6561	217.62	0.33811	683.0

Pressure = 375.00 psia
Saturation temperature = 174.46°F

Temp.,* °F	Density, lb/ft³	Enthalpy, Btu/lb	Entropy, Btu/lb·°F	Vel. Sound, ft/s
Saturated				
Liquid	58.2974	74.09	0.13908	785.9
Vapor	9.4209	120.69	0.21256	389.0
180	8.9498	123.10	0.21634	403.8
200	7.8311	130.54	0.22781	444.1
220	7.1211	137.08	0.23758	474.0
240	6.6028	143.19	0.24644	498.5
260	6.1926	149.07	0.25473	519.6
280	5.8555	154.82	0.26260	538.4
300	5.5694	160.49	0.27016	555.5
320	5.3212	166.11	0.27747	571.3
340	5.1022	171.72	0.28457	586.0
360	4.9066	177.32	0.29149	599.8
380	4.7300	182.94	0.29826	612.9
400	4.5692	188.58	0.30490	625.4
420	4.4217	194.24	0.31141	637.4
440	4.2857	199.94	0.31782	648.9
460	4.1596	205.68	0.32413	660.1
480	4.0421	211.46	0.33034	670.8
500	3.9323	217.28	0.33647	681.3

Pressure = 400.00 psia
Saturation temperature = 197.93°F

Temp.,* °F	Density, lb/ft³	Enthalpy, Btu/lb	Entropy, Btu/lb·°F	Vel. Sound, ft/s
Saturated				
Liquid	56.8213	76.60	0.14289	731.8
Vapor	10.3541	120.50	0.21152	380.4
180	10.3454	120.53	0.21158	380.6
200	8.7370	128.93	0.22451	429.5
220	7.8399	135.85	0.23484	463.0
240	7.2145	142.18	0.24403	489.7
260	6.7351	148.21	0.25252	512.3
280	6.3472	154.06	0.26055	532.1
300	6.0221	159.81	0.26821	550.0
320	5.7425	165.49	0.27560	566.5
340	5.4977	171.15	0.28277	581.7
360	5.2802	176.80	0.28975	596.0
380	5.0848	182.45	0.29656	609.5
400	4.9075	188.12	0.30323	622.4
420	4.7454	193.82	0.30978	634.7
440	4.5964	199.54	0.31621	646.5
460	4.4584	205.30	0.32254	657.9
480	4.3303	211.09	0.32878	669.0
500	4.2107	216.93	0.33492	679.6

Pressure = 600.00 psia
Saturation temperature = n/a (supercritical)

Temp.,* °F	Density, lb/ft³	Enthalpy, Btu/lb	Entropy, Btu/lb·°F	Vel. Sound, ft/s
220	19.6784	118.27	0.20421	340.3
240	14.2159	131.50	0.22343	409.1
260	12.2674	139.92	0.23530	449.7
280	11.0672	147.15	0.24522	480.8
300	10.2049	153.83	0.25413	506.7
320	9.5351	160.21	0.26241	529.2
340	8.9895	166.39	0.27024	549.2
360	8.5305	172.45	0.27774	567.5
380	8.1351	178.45	0.28496	584.4
400	7.7885	184.40	0.29197	600.1
420	7.4804	190.34	0.29879	615.0
440	7.2035	196.26	0.30546	629.0
460	6.9523	202.20	0.31198	642.4
480	6.7229	208.15	0.31838	655.3
500	6.5118	214.12	0.32467	667.6

*Temperatures on ITS-90 scale

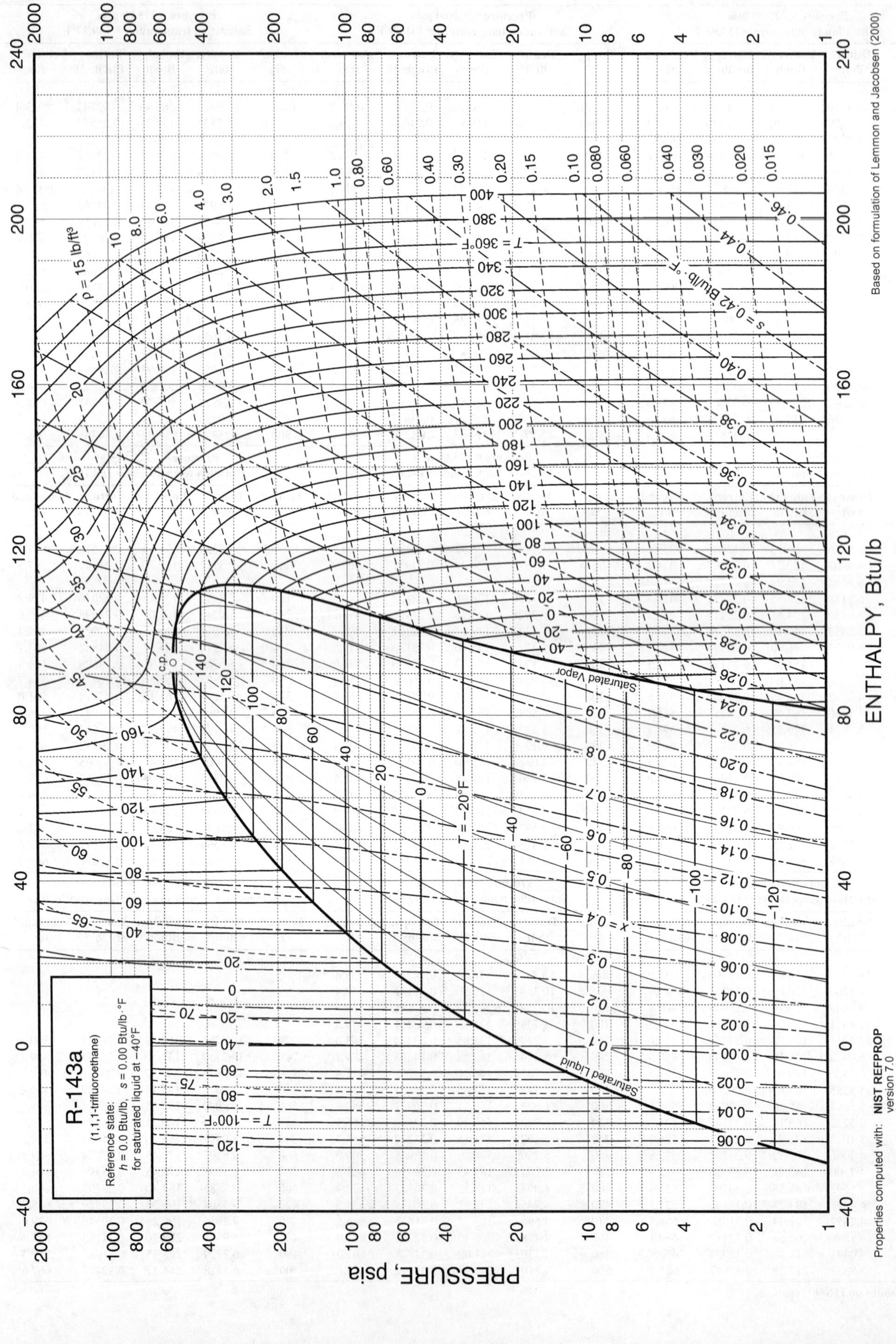

Fig. 9 Pressure-Enthalpy Diagram for Refrigerant 143a

Refrigerant 143a (1,1,1-Trifluoroethane) Properties of Saturated Liquid and Saturated Vapor

Temp.,* °F	Pressure, psia	Density, lb/ft³ Liquid	Volume, ft³/lb Vapor	Enthalpy, Btu/lb Liquid	Enthalpy, Btu/lb Vapor	Entropy, Btu/lb·°F Liquid	Entropy, Btu/lb·°F Vapor	Specific Heat c_p, Btu/lb·°F Liquid	Specific Heat c_p, Btu/lb·°F Vapor	c_p/c_v Vapor	Vel. of Sound, ft/s Liquid	Vel. of Sound, ft/s Vapor	Viscosity, lb_m/ft·h Liquid	Viscosity, lb_m/ft·h Vapor	Thermal Cond., Btu/h·ft·°F Liquid	Thermal Cond., Btu/h·ft·°F Vapor	Surface Tension, dyne/cm	Temp.,* °F
–169.26[a]	0.156	83.06	237.18	–39.089	75.807	–0.11084	0.28480	0.2895	0.1506	1.1924	3472	451.4	2.206	0.0143	0.0792	0.00283	13.72	–169.26
–165	0.199	82.71	188.87	–37.856	76.423	–0.10662	0.28120	0.2897	0.1522	1.1908	3434	454.1	2.069	0.0145	0.0783	0.00291	13.75	–165
–160	0.261	82.29	145.98	–36.406	77.150	–0.10174	0.27719	0.2901	0.1541	1.1890	3391	457.4	1.926	0.0148	0.0773	0.00299	13.78	–160
–155	0.340	81.87	113.97	–34.954	77.881	–0.09694	0.27341	0.2906	0.1560	1.1873	3347	460.5	1.799	0.0150	0.0762	0.00308	13.80	–155
–150	0.438	81.44	89.843	–33.499	78.618	–0.09220	0.26985	0.2913	0.1580	1.1858	3304	463.6	1.687	0.0152	0.0752	0.00316	13.80	–150
–145	0.559	81.02	71.465	–32.041	79.358	–0.08753	0.26649	0.2920	0.1599	1.1843	3260	466.7	1.586	0.0155	0.0743	0.00325	13.80	–145
–140	0.707	80.59	57.335	–30.579	80.102	–0.08292	0.26331	0.2929	0.1619	1.1830	3217	469.6	1.496	0.0157	0.0733	0.00334	13.78	–140
–135	0.887	80.17	46.374	–29.112	80.850	–0.07837	0.26032	0.2938	0.1639	1.1818	3174	472.5	1.413	0.0160	0.0723	0.00343	13.75	–135
–130	1.103	79.74	37.797	–27.640	81.602	–0.07387	0.25749	0.2948	0.1660	1.1807	3130	475.4	1.339	0.0162	0.0714	0.00353	13.71	–130
–125	1.362	79.30	31.032	–26.163	82.357	–0.06943	0.25483	0.2958	0.1680	1.1797	3087	478.1	1.271	0.0165	0.0705	0.00362	13.66	–125
–120	1.670	78.87	25.654	–24.681	83.114	–0.06504	0.25232	0.2969	0.1701	1.1789	3044	480.8	1.208	0.0167	0.0696	0.00372	13.60	–120
–115	2.033	78.43	21.347	–23.193	83.874	–0.06069	0.24995	0.2981	0.1722	1.1783	3001	483.4	1.150	0.0170	0.0687	0.00381	13.53	–115
–110	2.459	78.00	17.874	–21.699	84.636	–0.05639	0.24771	0.2994	0.1743	1.1777	2957	485.9	1.097	0.0172	0.0678	0.00391	13.44	–110
–105	2.955	77.56	15.054	–20.198	85.400	–0.05213	0.24561	0.3006	0.1765	1.1773	2914	488.3	1.048	0.0175	0.0669	0.00402	13.35	–105
–100	3.530	77.11	12.751	–18.691	86.165	–0.04791	0.24362	0.3020	0.1787	1.1771	2870	490.7	1.002	0.0177	0.0660	0.00412	13.24	–100
–95	4.194	76.67	10.857	–17.176	86.931	–0.04374	0.24175	0.3034	0.1809	1.1770	2827	492.9	0.959	0.0180	0.0652	0.00422	13.13	–95
–90	4.955	76.22	9.2915	–15.655	87.697	–0.03960	0.23998	0.3048	0.1832	1.1771	2784	495.0	0.919	0.0182	0.0644	0.00433	13.01	–90
–85	5.825	75.77	7.9899	–14.126	88.464	–0.03550	0.23832	0.3062	0.1855	1.1774	2740	497.0	0.881	0.0185	0.0635	0.00444	12.87	–85
–80	6.813	75.32	6.9019	–12.590	89.230	–0.03143	0.23675	0.3077	0.1879	1.1779	2697	498.9	0.846	0.0187	0.0627	0.00455	12.73	–80
–75	7.931	74.86	5.9879	–11.046	89.995	–0.02740	0.23527	0.3093	0.1904	1.1786	2654	500.7	0.813	0.0190	0.0619	0.00466	12.58	–75
–70	9.191	74.40	5.2164	–9.494	90.759	–0.02340	0.23388	0.3109	0.1928	1.1794	2610	502.4	0.782	0.0192	0.0611	0.00477	12.42	–70
–65	10.606	73.94	4.5621	–7.934	91.521	–0.01943	0.23257	0.3125	0.1954	1.1805	2567	503.9	0.752	0.0195	0.0604	0.00488	12.25	–65
–60	12.187	73.47	4.0046	–6.365	92.280	–0.01549	0.23133	0.3142	0.1980	1.1818	2524	505.3	0.724	0.0197	0.0596	0.00500	12.07	–60
–55	13.950	73.00	3.5277	–4.787	93.037	–0.01157	0.23016	0.3159	0.2007	1.1833	2480	506.6	0.698	0.0200	0.0588	0.00512	11.88	–55
–53.03[b]	14.696	72.82	3.3592	–4.164	93.334	–0.01004	0.22972	0.3166	0.2018	1.1840	2463	507.1	0.688	0.0201	0.0585	0.00517	11.81	–53.03
–50	15.907	72.53	3.1181	–3.201	93.790	–0.00769	0.22906	0.3177	0.2035	1.1851	2437	507.7	0.672	0.0202	0.0581	0.00524	11.69	–50
–45	18.074	72.05	2.7648	–1.605	94.539	–0.00383	0.22802	0.3195	0.2064	1.1871	2393	508.7	0.648	0.0204	0.0573	0.00536	11.48	–45
–40	20.464	71.57	2.4589	0.000	95.284	0.00000	0.22705	0.3214	0.2093	1.1894	2350	509.6	0.625	0.0207	0.0566	0.00549	11.27	–40
–35	23.094	71.08	2.1932	1.615	96.024	0.00381	0.22612	0.3234	0.2123	1.1920	2307	510.2	0.604	0.0209	0.0558	0.00561	11.05	–35
–30	25.979	70.59	1.9615	3.240	96.759	0.00759	0.22525	0.3254	0.2155	1.1949	2263	510.8	0.583	0.0212	0.0551	0.00574	10.82	–30
–25	29.135	70.09	1.7589	4.875	97.487	0.01136	0.22442	0.3274	0.2187	1.1981	2220	511.1	0.563	0.0214	0.0544	0.00588	10.59	–25
–20	32.579	69.59	1.5811	6.520	98.209	0.01510	0.22364	0.3295	0.2220	1.2017	2176	511.3	0.544	0.0221	0.0537	0.00602	10.35	–20
–15	36.329	69.08	1.4246	8.177	98.923	0.01883	0.22290	0.3317	0.2255	1.2056	2133	511.3	0.525	0.0224	0.0530	0.00616	10.10	–15
–10	40.401	68.57	1.2864	9.845	99.629	0.02253	0.22220	0.3340	0.2290	1.2098	2089	511.2	0.508	0.0226	0.0523	0.00630	9.84	–10
–5	44.813	68.04	1.1640	11.524	100.327	0.02622	0.22153	0.3364	0.2327	1.2146	2046	510.9	0.491	0.0229	0.0516	0.00644	9.58	–5
0	49.584	67.52	1.0554	13.216	101.016	0.02989	0.22090	0.3388	0.2365	1.2197	2002	510.3	0.474	0.0231	0.0509	0.00659	9.31	0
5	54.733	66.98	0.9587	14.920	101.695	0.03355	0.22029	0.3414	0.2405	1.2253	1958	509.6	0.458	0.0234	0.0502	0.00673	9.04	5
10	60.277	66.44	0.8724	16.637	102.363	0.03719	0.21971	0.3440	0.2446	1.2315	1914	508.7	0.443	0.0237	0.0495	0.00689	8.76	10
15	66.237	65.89	0.7951	18.367	103.020	0.04082	0.21916	0.3468	0.2489	1.2382	1870	507.6	0.429	0.0239	0.0488	0.00705	8.47	15
20	72.632	65.33	0.7259	20.112	103.664	0.04444	0.21862	0.3497	0.2534	1.2456	1826	506.3	0.414	0.0242	0.0482	0.00721	8.19	20
25	79.482	64.76	0.6636	21.870	104.295	0.04804	0.21811	0.3528	0.2580	1.2536	1782	504.7	0.401	0.0245	0.0475	0.00737	7.89	25
30	86.808	64.18	0.6075	23.644	104.912	0.05164	0.21761	0.3560	0.2629	1.2624	1738	502.9	0.387	0.0248	0.0468	0.00755	7.59	30
35	94.630	63.59	0.5569	25.434	105.514	0.05523	0.21712	0.3594	0.2681	1.2721	1693	501.0	0.374	0.0251	0.0462	0.00772	7.29	35
40	102.97	62.99	0.5110	27.241	106.099	0.05882	0.21664	0.3630	0.2735	1.2827	1649	498.7	0.362	0.0254	0.0455	0.00791	6.98	40
45	111.85	62.37	0.4695	29.064	106.667	0.06240	0.21617	0.3668	0.2793	1.2944	1604	496.3	0.349	0.0257	0.0448	0.00811	6.68	45
50	121.29	61.75	0.4317	30.906	107.215	0.06597	0.21569	0.3709	0.2854	1.3072	1559	493.5	0.337	0.0260	0.0442	0.00831	6.36	50
55	131.32	61.10	0.3973	32.768	107.743	0.06955	0.21522	0.3752	0.2919	1.3215	1514	490.6	0.326	0.0264	0.0435	0.00853	6.05	55
60	141.95	60.45	0.3659	34.649	108.248	0.07312	0.21475	0.3799	0.2989	1.3373	1468	487.3	0.314	0.0267	0.0429	0.00875	5.73	60
65	153.22	59.77	0.3373	36.553	108.730	0.07670	0.21427	0.3849	0.3065	1.3549	1422	483.8	0.303	0.0271	0.0422	0.00900	5.41	65
70	165.14	59.08	0.3110	38.479	109.184	0.08029	0.21378	0.3904	0.3146	1.3746	1376	480.0	0.293	0.0275	0.0416	0.00925	5.09	70
75	177.74	58.36	0.2869	40.430	109.611	0.08388	0.21327	0.3963	0.3235	1.3968	1329	475.8	0.282	0.0279	0.0409	0.00953	4.77	75
80	191.05	57.63	0.2648	42.407	110.005	0.08748	0.21274	0.4028	0.3333	1.4218	1282	471.4	0.272	0.0283	0.0403	0.00983	4.45	80
85	205.09	56.87	0.2444	44.413	110.365	0.09109	0.21218	0.4100	0.3441	1.4504	1235	466.7	0.261	0.0287	0.0396	0.01015	4.13	85
90	219.89	56.08	0.2256	46.449	110.686	0.09473	0.21159	0.4180	0.3562	1.4831	1187	461.6	0.251	0.0292	0.0390	0.01050	3.81	90
95	235.48	55.26	0.2082	48.519	110.965	0.09838	0.21096	0.4269	0.3698	1.5209	1138	456.1	0.241	0.0297	0.0383	0.01089	3.50	95
100	251.89	54.41	0.1920	50.626	111.196	0.10206	0.21029	0.4371	0.3853	1.5650	1089	450.3	0.232	0.0302	0.0376	0.01131	3.18	100
105	269.14	53.52	0.1770	52.773	111.372	0.10578	0.20955	0.4487	0.4033	1.6171	1039	444.0	0.222	0.0308	0.0370	0.01179	2.87	105
110	287.29	52.59	0.1631	54.966	111.486	0.10953	0.20875	0.4622	0.4244	1.6795	988	437.4	0.212	0.0314	0.0363	0.01233	2.56	110
115	306.35	51.61	0.1500	57.210	111.530	0.11334	0.20786	0.4782	0.4496	1.7553	937	430.3	0.203	0.0320	0.0356	0.01295	2.26	115
120	326.37	50.56	0.1378	59.512	111.489	0.11720	0.20687	0.4974	0.4804	1.8494	884	422.7	0.193	0.0328	0.0349	0.01365	1.96	120
125	347.38	49.45	0.1263	61.884	111.350	0.12114	0.20575	0.5211	0.5190	1.9689	829	414.7	0.184	0.0336	0.0343	0.01448	1.68	125
130	369.44	48.25	0.1155	64.336	111.090	0.12517	0.20446	0.5514	0.5690	2.1254	773	406.1	0.174	0.0346	0.0336	0.01546	1.40	130
135	392.60	46.95	0.1051	66.889	110.680	0.12933	0.20297	0.5918	0.6366	2.3388	715	396.8	0.164	0.0357	0.0329	0.01665	1.13	135
140	416.90	45.50	0.0952	69.570	110.074	0.13366	0.20120	0.6487	0.7334	2.6465	655	386.9	0.154	0.0370	0.0322	0.01814	0.87	140
145	442.43	43.86	0.0856	72.424	109.201	0.13822	0.19904	0.7365	0.8842	3.1275	591	376.2	0.143	0.0386	0.0315	0.02009	0.63	145
150	469.27	41.93	0.0760	75.535	107.928	0.14315	0.19629	0.892	1.152	3.984	523	364.5	0.132	0.0407	0.0309	0.02286	0.41	150
155	497.54	39.48	0.0660	79.091	105.965	0.14875	0.19247	1.251	1.765	5.933	450	351.3	0.119	0.0438	0.0305	0.02750	0.21	155
160	527.46	35.70	0.0541	83.797	102.284	0.15614	0.18597	3.007	4.581	14.798	367	334.6	0.101	0.0496	0.0319	0.03771	0.06	160
162.87[c]	545.49	26.91	0.0372	92.722	92.722	0.17033	0.17033	∞	∞	∞	0	0.0	—	—	∞	∞	0.00	162.87

*Temperatures on ITS-90 scale [a]Triple point [b]Normal boiling point [c]Critical point

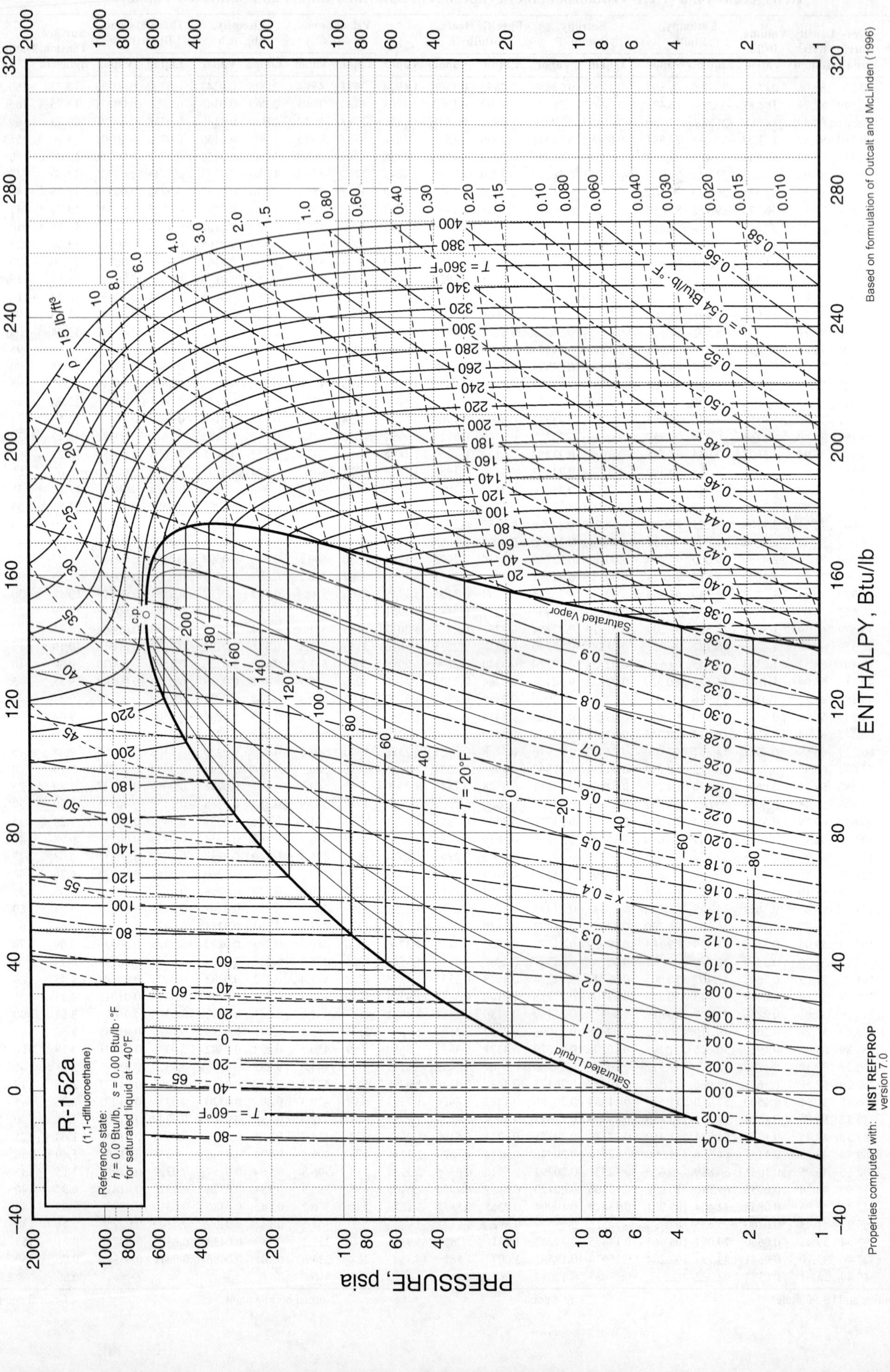

Fig. 10 Pressure-Enthalpy Diagram for Refrigerant 152a

Refrigerant 152a (1,1-Difluoroethane) Properties of Saturated Liquid and Saturated Vapor

Temp.,* °F	Pressure, psia	Density, lb/ft³ Liquid	Volume, ft³/lb Vapor	Enthalpy, Btu/lb Liquid	Enthalpy, Btu/lb Vapor	Entropy, Btu/lb·°F Liquid	Entropy, Btu/lb·°F Vapor	Specific Heat c_p, Btu/lb·°F Liquid	Specific Heat c_p, Btu/lb·°F Vapor	c_p/c_v Vapor	Vel. of Sound, ft/s Liquid	Vel. of Sound, ft/s Vapor	Viscosity, lb_m/ft·h Liquid	Viscosity, lb_m/ft·h Vapor	Thermal Cond., Btu/h·ft·°F Liquid	Thermal Cond., Btu/h·ft·°F Vapor	Surface Tension, dyne/cm	Temp.,* °F
–181.46[a]	0.009	74.47	4858.2	–51.885	122.577	–0.15045	0.47664	0.3531	0.1670	1.2201	4596	505.4	4.899	0.0126	0.1019	0.00006	31.65	–181.46
–180	0.010	74.38	4379.8	–51.368	122.821	–0.14859	0.47424	0.3540	0.1674	1.2194	4575	506.6	4.761	0.0127	0.1016	0.00010	31.52	–180
–170	0.021	73.74	2227.6	–47.803	124.502	–0.13607	0.45876	0.3586	0.1703	1.2152	4438	514.6	3.961	0.0131	0.0993	0.00042	30.60	–170
–160	0.041	73.10	1195.0	–44.203	126.208	–0.12385	0.44481	0.3611	0.1732	1.2112	4316	522.4	3.349	0.0135	0.0971	0.00073	29.68	–160
–150	0.075	72.46	672.43	–40.584	127.938	–0.11197	0.43222	0.3626	0.1762	1.2074	4204	530.0	2.871	0.0140	0.0949	0.00104	28.76	–150
–140	0.131	71.82	394.96	–36.953	129.689	–0.10044	0.42086	0.3635	0.1793	1.2039	4099	537.5	2.493	0.0144	0.0928	0.00136	27.86	–140
–130	0.222	71.17	241.12	–33.315	131.460	–0.08923	0.41059	0.3642	0.1825	1.2006	3999	544.7	2.187	0.0148	0.0907	0.00167	26.96	–130
–120	0.361	70.52	152.41	–29.669	133.249	–0.07834	0.40130	0.3649	0.1857	1.1977	3902	551.7	1.936	0.0153	0.0887	0.00198	26.06	–120
–110	0.569	69.87	99.413	–26.015	135.052	–0.06774	0.39289	0.3658	0.1892	1.1952	3808	558.5	1.728	0.0157	0.0867	0.00230	25.17	–110
–100	0.871	69.22	66.714	–22.351	136.868	–0.05741	0.38527	0.3670	0.1927	1.1931	3715	565.0	1.552	0.0162	0.0848	0.00261	24.28	–100
–90	1.297	68.56	45.938	–18.674	138.692	–0.04732	0.37837	0.3684	0.1965	1.1913	3623	571.2	1.403	0.0166	0.0829	0.00292	23.40	–90
–80	1.886	67.89	32.380	–14.981	140.522	–0.03747	0.37210	0.3700	0.2004	1.1900	3532	577.2	1.274	0.0171	0.0811	0.00324	22.53	–80
–70	2.680	67.22	23.313	–11.270	142.353	–0.02783	0.36641	0.3720	0.2045	1.1893	3442	582.8	1.162	0.0175	0.0793	0.00355	21.66	–70
–60	3.731	66.54	17.113	–7.538	144.184	–0.01838	0.36124	0.3742	0.2088	1.1890	3352	588.0	1.064	0.0180	0.0776	0.00387	20.80	–60
–50	5.099	65.86	12.784	–3.782	146.010	–0.00911	0.35653	0.3766	0.2134	1.1892	3263	592.9	0.978	0.0184	0.0758	0.00419	19.94	–50
–45	5.921	65.51	11.117	–1.894	146.920	–0.00454	0.35434	0.3779	0.2157	1.1896	3218	595.2	0.938	0.0187	0.0750	0.00435	19.52	–45
–40	6.847	65.16	9.7045	0.000	147.828	0.00000	0.35225	0.3793	0.2181	1.1901	3174	597.4	0.901	0.0189	0.0742	0.00451	19.09	–40
–35	7.887	64.82	8.5025	1.902	148.732	0.00450	0.35025	0.3807	0.2206	1.1908	3129	599.4	0.866	0.0191	0.0733	0.00467	18.67	–35
–30	9.051	64.46	7.4754	3.811	149.634	0.00896	0.34834	0.3822	0.2232	1.1916	3085	601.4	0.833	0.0193	0.0725	0.00483	18.25	–30
–25	10.348	64.11	6.5943	5.728	150.531	0.01339	0.34652	0.3838	0.2258	1.1926	3040	603.2	0.801	0.0196	0.0717	0.00499	17.83	–25
–20	11.789	63.75	5.8357	7.653	151.424	0.01778	0.34478	0.3854	0.2285	1.1937	2996	604.9	0.771	0.0198	0.0709	0.00515	17.42	–20
–15	13.386	63.40	5.1800	9.586	152.312	0.02214	0.34311	0.3870	0.2313	1.1951	2952	606.5	0.742	0.0200	0.0701	0.00532	17.00	–15
–11.24[b]	14.696	63.12	4.7450	11.046	152.977	0.02540	0.34191	0.3883	0.2334	1.1962	2918	607.6	0.722	0.0202	0.0695	0.00544	16.69	–11.24
–10	15.149	63.04	4.6114	11.528	153.196	0.02647	0.34152	0.3887	0.2341	1.1966	2907	608.0	0.715	0.0202	0.0693	0.00548	16.59	–10
–5	17.092	62.67	4.1167	13.479	154.073	0.03077	0.34000	0.3905	0.2370	1.1983	2863	609.3	0.689	0.0205	0.0685	0.00565	16.18	–5
0	19.226	62.30	3.6848	15.439	154.945	0.03505	0.33854	0.3924	0.2400	1.2002	2818	610.5	0.665	0.0207	0.0677	0.00581	15.77	0
5	21.564	61.93	3.3066	17.408	155.810	0.03929	0.33714	0.3943	0.2431	1.2024	2774	611.6	0.641	0.0209	0.0670	0.00598	15.36	5
10	24.119	61.56	2.9745	19.388	156.667	0.04352	0.33580	0.3962	0.2463	1.2047	2729	612.5	0.619	0.0211	0.0662	0.00614	14.96	10
15	26.904	61.18	2.6819	21.378	157.518	0.04771	0.33452	0.3982	0.2495	1.2073	2685	613.3	0.598	0.0214	0.0655	0.00631	14.55	15
20	29.934	60.80	2.4234	23.378	158.360	0.05188	0.33329	0.4003	0.2529	1.2101	2640	613.9	0.577	0.0216	0.0647	0.00648	14.15	20
25	33.223	60.42	2.1945	25.389	159.194	0.05603	0.33211	0.4025	0.2564	1.2132	2596	614.3	0.557	0.0218	0.0640	0.00665	13.75	25
30	36.784	60.03	1.9912	27.411	160.019	0.06016	0.33097	0.4047	0.2599	1.2166	2551	614.6	0.539	0.0221	0.0633	0.00683	13.36	30
35	40.634	59.64	1.8103	29.444	160.834	0.06427	0.32988	0.4070	0.2636	1.2202	2506	614.8	0.521	0.0223	0.0625	0.00700	12.96	35
40	44.787	59.24	1.6488	31.490	161.639	0.06836	0.32883	0.4094	0.2673	1.2242	2461	614.8	0.503	0.0225	0.0618	0.00718	12.57	40
45	49.259	58.84	1.5043	33.547	162.433	0.07243	0.32781	0.4119	0.2712	1.2285	2416	614.6	0.487	0.0228	0.0611	0.00735	12.18	45
50	54.065	58.44	1.3748	35.618	163.216	0.07648	0.32683	0.4145	0.2753	1.2331	2371	614.2	0.471	0.0230	0.0604	0.00753	11.79	50
55	59.222	58.03	1.2585	37.701	163.987	0.08051	0.32589	0.4171	0.2794	1.2381	2326	613.7	0.456	0.0232	0.0597	0.00771	11.40	55
60	64.746	57.61	1.1537	39.798	164.745	0.08454	0.32497	0.4199	0.2837	1.2436	2281	612.9	0.441	0.0235	0.0590	0.00790	11.02	60
65	70.654	57.19	1.0591	41.909	165.490	0.08854	0.32408	0.4228	0.2882	1.2494	2235	612.0	0.427	0.0237	0.0583	0.00809	10.64	65
70	76.963	56.76	0.9737	44.034	166.221	0.09253	0.32322	0.4258	0.2928	1.2557	2190	610.9	0.413	0.0240	0.0576	0.00828	10.26	70
75	83.691	56.33	0.8963	46.175	166.936	0.09651	0.32238	0.4289	0.2976	1.2626	2144	609.7	0.400	0.0242	0.0569	0.00847	9.88	75
80	90.854	55.89	0.826	48.331	167.636	0.10048	0.32156	0.4322	0.3026	1.2700	2098	608.2	0.387	0.0245	0.0562	0.00867	9.51	80
85	98.470	55.44	0.7621	50.503	168.319	0.10444	0.32075	0.4357	0.3079	1.2780	2052	606.5	0.375	0.0248	0.0556	0.00887	9.14	85
90	106.56	54.98	0.7039	52.692	168.985	0.10840	0.31996	0.4393	0.3133	1.2867	2006	604.6	0.363	0.0250	0.0549	0.00908	8.77	90
95	115.14	54.52	0.6508	54.899	169.631	0.11234	0.31919	0.4431	0.3191	1.2961	1960	602.5	0.351	0.0253	0.0542	0.00929	8.40	95
100	124.23	54.05	0.6023	57.124	170.258	0.11628	0.31842	0.4471	0.3251	1.3063	1913	600.1	0.340	0.0256	0.0535	0.00950	8.04	100
105	133.84	53.57	0.5578	59.369	170.864	0.12021	0.31766	0.4513	0.3314	1.3175	1866	597.6	0.330	0.0259	0.0529	0.00973	7.68	105
110	144.01	53.08	0.5171	61.633	171.447	0.12414	0.31691	0.4558	0.3381	1.3296	1819	594.8	0.319	0.0261	0.0522	0.00996	7.33	110
115	154.74	52.58	0.4797	63.919	172.006	0.12807	0.31616	0.4606	0.3451	1.3429	1772	591.7	0.309	0.0271	0.0515	0.01019	6.97	115
120	166.07	52.07	0.4453	66.227	172.539	0.13200	0.31540	0.4657	0.3527	1.3574	1725	588.5	0.299	0.0275	0.0509	0.01043	6.62	120
125	178.00	51.55	0.4135	68.558	173.044	0.13593	0.31464	0.4711	0.3607	1.3734	1677	584.9	0.290	0.0278	0.0502	0.01069	6.27	125
130	190.56	51.01	0.3843	70.915	173.520	0.13987	0.31387	0.4770	0.3693	1.3911	1629	581.1	0.280	0.0282	0.0495	0.01095	5.93	130
135	203.77	50.47	0.3572	73.297	173.964	0.14381	0.31309	0.4833	0.3785	1.4106	1581	577.1	0.271	0.0286	0.0489	0.01123	5.59	135
140	217.66	49.90	0.3322	75.708	174.374	0.14776	0.31229	0.4902	0.3886	1.4323	1532	572.7	0.262	0.0290	0.0482	0.01152	5.25	140
145	232.25	49.32	0.3090	78.149	174.746	0.15172	0.31148	0.4977	0.3995	1.4566	1483	568.1	0.254	0.0295	0.0476	0.01183	4.92	145
150	247.55	48.73	0.2874	80.621	175.078	0.15570	0.31063	0.5059	0.4114	1.4838	1434	563.1	0.245	0.0299	0.0469	0.01215	4.59	150
155	263.60	48.11	0.2674	83.128	175.365	0.15970	0.30975	0.5149	0.4245	1.5145	1384	557.9	0.237	0.0304	0.0462	0.01250	4.27	155
160	280.42	47.48	0.2487	85.673	175.603	0.16371	0.30884	0.5249	0.4392	1.5495	1334	552.3	0.229	0.0309	0.0456	0.01287	3.95	160
165	298.04	46.82	0.2313	88.258	175.787	0.16776	0.30788	0.5361	0.4556	1.5896	1283	546.4	0.221	0.0314	0.0449	0.01327	3.63	165
170	316.48	46.13	0.2150	90.887	175.911	0.17183	0.30686	0.5488	0.4742	1.6359	1232	540.1	0.213	0.0320	0.0443	0.01370	3.32	170
175	335.77	45.42	0.1997	93.566	175.968	0.17595	0.30578	0.5634	0.4954	1.6900	1180	533.4	0.205	0.0326	0.0436	0.01418	3.02	175
180	355.95	44.67	0.1854	96.300	175.948	0.18011	0.30462	0.5801	0.5202	1.7540	1127	526.4	0.197	0.0332	0.0429	0.01470	2.72	180
185	377.04	43.88	0.1719	99.095	175.841	0.18432	0.30337	0.5999	0.5493	1.8307	1074	518.9	0.189	0.0340	0.0422	0.01527	2.42	185
190	399.08	43.06	0.1592	101.961	175.633	0.18861	0.30200	0.6235	0.5844	1.9244	1020	510.9	0.182	0.0347	0.0416	0.01592	2.14	190
195	422.10	42.17	0.1471	104.910	175.306	0.19297	0.30050	0.6524	0.6276	2.0411	965	502.5	0.174	0.0356	0.0409	0.01666	1.85	195
200	446.15	41.23	0.1356	107.955	174.835	0.19744	0.29883	0.6889	0.6821	2.1906	908	493.5	0.166	0.0366	0.0402	0.01751	1.58	200
210	497.53	39.10	0.1141	114.433	173.320	0.20683	0.29477	0.8017	0.8519	2.6633	791	473.8	0.150	0.0390	0.0390	0.01970	1.06	210
220	553.69	36.41	0.0935	121.740	170.564	0.21725	0.28909	1.0540	1.2307	3.7334	663	451.1	0.133	0.0424	0.0380	0.02315	0.58	220
230	615.42	32.30	0.0714	131.138	164.733	0.23049	0.27920	2.2140	2.9194	8.5318	518	423.7	0.110	0.0488	0.0390	0.03092	0.17	230
235.87[c]	655.10	22.97	0.0435	147.629	147.629	0.25390	0.25390	∞	∞	∞	0	0.0	—	—	∞	∞	0.00	235.87

*Temperatures on ITS-90 scale [a]Triple point [b]Normal boiling point [c]Critical point

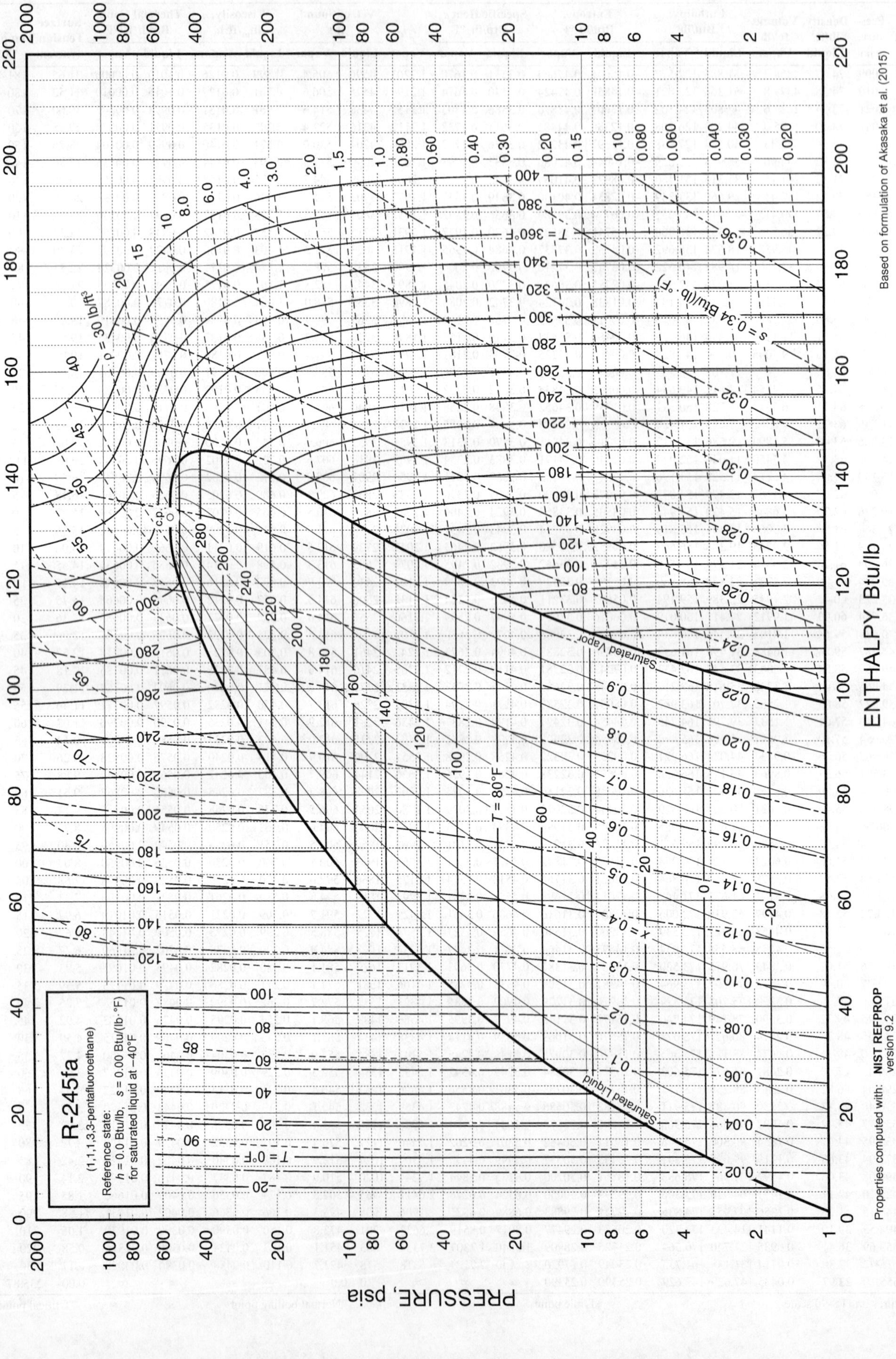

Fig. 11 Pressure-Enthalpy Diagram for Refrigerant 245fa

Refrigerant 245fa (1,1,1,3,3-Pentafluoropropane) Properties of Saturated Liquid and Saturated Vapor

Temp.,* °F	Pressure, psia	Density, lb/ft³ Liquid	Volume, ft³/lb Vapor	Enthalpy, Btu/lb Liquid	Enthalpy, Btu/lb Vapor	Entropy, Btu/lb·°F Liquid	Entropy, Btu/lb·°F Vapor	Specific Heat c_p, Btu/lb·°F Liquid	Specific Heat c_p, Btu/lb·°F Vapor	c_p/c_v Vapor	Vel. of Sound, ft/s Liquid	Vel. of Sound, ft/s Vapor	Viscosity, lb_m/ft·h Liquid	Viscosity, lb_m/ft·h Vapor	Thermal Cond., Btu/h·ft·°F Liquid	Thermal Cond., Btu/h·ft·°F Vapor	Surface Tension, dyne/cm	Temp., °F
–50	0.578	94.55	56.518	–2.840	94.771	–0.00685	0.23142	0.2830	0.1734	1.0958	3199	406.4	3.280	0.0187	0.0640	0.00363	23.11	–50
–45	0.702	94.14	47.084	–1.422	95.622	–0.00341	0.23062	0.2840	0.1748	1.0953	3157	408.5	3.091	0.0190	0.0635	0.00377	22.72	–45
–40	0.847	93.74	39.436	–0.000	96.478	–0.00000	0.22989	0.2849	0.1763	1.0949	3115	410.6	2.915	0.0193	0.0630	0.00392	22.33	–40
–35	1.018	93.32	33.201	1.427	97.337	0.00338	0.22923	0.2859	0.1778	1.0945	3073	412.7	2.752	0.0195	0.0626	0.00406	21.95	–35
–30	1.216	92.91	28.090	2.859	98.201	0.00673	0.22863	0.2869	0.1792	1.0942	3032	414.7	2.601	0.0198	0.0621	0.00421	21.56	–30
–25	1.446	92.50	23.879	4.296	99.069	0.01006	0.22809	0.2879	0.1807	1.0939	2990	416.6	2.460	0.0201	0.0616	0.00435	21.18	–25
–20	1.711	92.08	20.391	5.739	99.940	0.01335	0.22761	0.2889	0.1822	1.0937	2949	418.5	2.330	0.0203	0.0611	0.00450	20.80	–20
–15	2.015	91.67	17.489	7.186	100.815	0.01663	0.22718	0.2900	0.1837	1.0936	2908	420.3	2.208	0.0206	0.0606	0.00464	20.42	–15
–10	2.363	91.25	15.062	8.640	101.692	0.01987	0.22681	0.2911	0.1853	1.0935	2868	422.1	2.095	0.0208	0.0600	0.00479	20.04	–10
–5	2.759	90.83	13.024	10.099	102.573	0.02310	0.22649	0.2923	0.1868	1.0934	2827	423.9	1.990	0.0211	0.0595	0.00493	19.66	–5
0	3.208	90.40	11.305	11.563	103.456	0.02630	0.22621	0.2934	0.1884	1.0935	2787	425.5	1.892	0.0213	0.0590	0.00508	19.28	0
5	3.717	89.98	9.8498	13.034	104.342	0.02948	0.22598	0.2946	0.1900	1.0936	2747	427.2	1.801	0.0216	0.0585	0.00522	18.91	5
10	4.289	89.55	8.6119	14.511	105.230	0.03264	0.22579	0.2958	0.1916	1.0937	2707	428.7	1.715	0.0218	0.0580	0.00536	18.53	10
15	4.931	89.12	7.5553	15.994	106.120	0.03578	0.22565	0.2971	0.1933	1.0940	2668	430.2	1.635	0.0221	0.0575	0.00551	18.16	15
20	5.650	88.69	6.6500	17.483	107.011	0.03890	0.22554	0.2983	0.1949	1.0943	2629	431.6	1.561	0.0224	0.0569	0.00565	17.78	20
25	6.452	88.26	5.8715	18.979	107.904	0.04199	0.22547	0.2996	0.1966	1.0947	2590	433.0	1.491	0.0226	0.0564	0.00580	17.41	25
30	7.343	87.82	5.1998	20.481	108.798	0.04507	0.22544	0.3009	0.1983	1.0951	2551	434.2	1.425	0.0229	0.0559	0.00594	17.04	30
35	8.332	87.38	4.6183	21.990	109.694	0.04814	0.22543	0.3023	0.2001	1.0957	2512	435.4	1.364	0.0231	0.0554	0.00608	16.67	35
40	9.424	86.94	4.1132	23.506	110.590	0.05118	0.22546	0.3037	0.2018	1.0963	2474	436.5	1.306	0.0233	0.0549	0.00623	16.30	40
45	10.629	86.49	3.6731	25.029	111.486	0.05421	0.22552	0.3051	0.2036	1.0970	2436	437.6	1.252	0.0236	0.0543	0.00637	15.94	45
50	11.954	86.04	3.2885	26.560	112.383	0.05722	0.22561	0.3065	0.2055	1.0978	2398	438.5	1.200	0.0238	0.0538	0.00651	15.57	50
55	13.407	85.59	2.9515	28.097	113.280	0.06022	0.22573	0.3079	0.2073	1.0987	2360	439.4	1.152	0.0241	0.0533	0.00666	15.21	55
59.09[b]	14.696	85.22	2.7065	29.359	114.013	0.06265	0.22584	0.3092	0.2089	1.0995	2330	440.0	1.115	0.0243	0.0529	0.00678	14.91	59.09
60	14.997	85.13	2.6552	29.642	114.176	0.06320	0.22587	0.3094	0.2092	1.0997	2323	440.2	1.107	0.0243	0.0528	0.00680	14.84	60
65	16.733	84.67	2.3941	31.195	115.072	0.06616	0.22603	0.3109	0.2112	1.1008	2285	440.9	1.064	0.0246	0.0522	0.00694	14.48	65
70	18.624	84.21	2.1634	32.755	115.968	0.06911	0.22622	0.3125	0.2131	1.1021	2248	441.4	1.023	0.0248	0.0517	0.00709	14.12	70
75	20.679	83.75	1.9590	34.323	116.862	0.07205	0.22643	0.3140	0.2151	1.1034	2211	441.9	0.984	0.0251	0.0512	0.00723	13.76	75
80	22.909	83.27	1.7775	35.899	117.755	0.07498	0.22666	0.3156	0.2172	1.1048	2174	442.3	0.948	0.0253	0.0507	0.00737	13.41	80
85	25.322	82.80	1.6159	37.483	118.646	0.07789	0.22690	0.3173	0.2193	1.1064	2137	442.6	0.913	0.0255	0.0501	0.00752	13.05	85
90	27.930	82.32	1.4717	39.076	119.536	0.08079	0.22717	0.3189	0.2214	1.1082	2100	442.8	0.880	0.0258	0.0496	0.00766	12.69	90
95	30.742	81.84	1.3427	40.677	120.423	0.08368	0.22745	0.3206	0.2236	1.1100	2063	442.8	0.849	0.0260	0.0491	0.00780	12.34	95
100	33.769	81.35	1.2271	42.287	121.308	0.08655	0.22775	0.3224	0.2258	1.1120	2027	442.8	0.819	0.0263	0.0486	0.00795	11.99	100
105	37.022	80.85	1.1233	43.905	122.190	0.08942	0.22806	0.3241	0.2281	1.1142	1990	442.6	0.791	0.0265	0.0481	0.00809	11.64	105
110	40.513	80.35	1.0299	45.533	123.069	0.09228	0.22838	0.3260	0.2304	1.1166	1953	442.3	0.763	0.0268	0.0475	0.00824	11.29	110
115	44.251	79.85	0.9456	47.169	123.945	0.09512	0.22872	0.3278	0.2328	1.1192	1917	441.9	0.737	0.0270	0.0470	0.00838	10.95	115
120	48.249	79.33	0.8695	48.815	124.816	0.09796	0.22907	0.3297	0.2353	1.1219	1880	441.3	0.712	0.0273	0.0465	0.00853	10.60	120
125	52.518	78.82	0.8005	50.471	125.684	0.10078	0.22943	0.3317	0.2378	1.1249	1843	440.6	0.688	0.0275	0.0460	0.00867	10.26	125
130	57.071	78.29	0.7380	52.137	126.546	0.10360	0.22979	0.3337	0.2405	1.1282	1806	439.8	0.665	0.0277	0.0455	0.00882	9.92	130
135	61.918	77.76	0.6812	53.812	127.404	0.10641	0.23016	0.3358	0.2431	1.1317	1770	438.8	0.643	0.0280	0.0450	0.00897	9.58	135
140	67.074	77.22	0.6295	55.498	128.255	0.10922	0.23054	0.3379	0.2459	1.1355	1733	437.7	0.622	0.0282	0.0444	0.00912	9.24	140
145	72.550	76.67	0.5824	57.195	129.101	0.11201	0.23093	0.3401	0.2488	1.1396	1696	436.5	0.601	0.0285	0.0439	0.00927	8.91	145
150	78.358	76.12	0.5393	58.902	129.939	0.11480	0.23132	0.3424	0.2518	1.1440	1659	435.0	0.581	0.0288	0.0434	0.00942	8.57	150
155	84.512	75.55	0.5000	60.621	130.771	0.11758	0.23171	0.3447	0.2549	1.1489	1621	433.4	0.562	0.0290	0.0429	0.00957	8.24	155
160	91.025	74.98	0.4639	62.351	131.594	0.12036	0.23210	0.3472	0.2581	1.1542	1584	431.7	0.543	0.0293	0.0424	0.00973	7.91	160
165	97.911	74.39	0.4308	64.093	132.409	0.12313	0.23250	0.3497	0.2615	1.1599	1547	429.8	0.525	0.0295	0.0419	0.00989	7.59	165
170	105.18	73.80	0.4003	65.847	133.214	0.12590	0.23289	0.3524	0.2650	1.1662	1509	427.7	0.507	0.0298	0.0414	0.01005	7.26	170
175	112.85	73.19	0.3723	67.614	134.009	0.12867	0.23328	0.3551	0.2688	1.1731	1471	425.4	0.490	0.0301	0.0409	0.01021	6.94	175
180	120.94	72.58	0.3465	69.395	134.793	0.13143	0.23367	0.3580	0.2727	1.1806	1433	422.9	0.473	0.0304	0.0404	0.01038	6.62	180
185	129.45	71.95	0.3227	71.189	135.565	0.13419	0.23405	0.3611	0.2768	1.1889	1395	420.2	0.457	0.0306	0.0399	0.01055	6.30	185
190	138.41	71.30	0.3007	72.997	136.324	0.13695	0.23442	0.3643	0.2812	1.1981	1356	417.3	0.441	0.0309	0.0394	0.01073	5.99	190
195	147.82	70.64	0.2803	74.820	137.068	0.13970	0.23479	0.3677	0.2859	1.2082	1317	414.2	0.426	0.0312	0.0389	0.01091	5.68	195
200	157.71	69.97	0.2614	76.659	137.797	0.14246	0.23514	0.3713	0.2910	1.2194	1278	410.8	0.410	0.0315	0.0384	0.01110	5.37	200
205	168.08	69.28	0.2438	78.514	138.508	0.14522	0.23548	0.3752	0.2964	1.2320	1239	407.3	0.396	0.0318	0.0379	0.01129	5.06	205
210	178.96	68.57	0.2275	80.386	139.200	0.14798	0.23581	0.3794	0.3023	1.2460	1199	403.5	0.381	0.0321	0.0375	0.01150	4.76	210
215	190.36	67.84	0.2123	82.277	139.872	0.15075	0.23612	0.3838	0.3087	1.2617	1158	399.4	0.367	0.0325	0.0370	0.01171	4.46	215
220	202.30	67.08	0.1981	84.187	140.521	0.15352	0.23641	0.3887	0.3157	1.2795	1118	395.1	0.352	0.0328	0.0365	0.01194	4.17	220
225	214.80	66.31	0.1849	86.117	141.145	0.15630	0.23667	0.3940	0.3234	1.2998	1077	390.5	0.339	0.0332	0.0360	0.01218	3.87	225
230	227.87	65.50	0.1725	88.070	141.742	0.15909	0.23691	0.3998	0.3320	1.3229	1035	385.6	0.325	0.0335	0.0355	0.01244	3.59	230
235	241.53	64.67	0.1609	90.047	142.307	0.16189	0.23712	0.4062	0.3417	1.3496	994	380.5	0.311	0.0339	0.0350	0.01272	3.30	235
240	255.81	63.80	0.1500	92.049	142.837	0.16470	0.23729	0.4134	0.3526	1.3806	951	375.0	0.298	0.0344	0.0346	0.01302	3.02	240
245	270.72	62.90	0.1398	94.080	143.329	0.16753	0.23742	0.4215	0.3652	1.4169	908	369.2	0.285	0.0348	0.0341	0.01335	2.75	245
250	286.28	61.96	0.1301	96.141	143.777	0.17038	0.23751	0.4307	0.3798	1.4599	865	363.0	0.271	0.0353	0.0336	0.01372	2.48	250
260	319.47	59.92	0.1124	100.372	144.514	0.17616	0.23750	0.4540	0.4174	1.5741	776	349.7	0.245	0.0363	0.0326	0.01460	1.96	260
270	355.57	57.63	0.0964	104.780	144.980	0.18209	0.23718	0.4874	0.4735	1.7498	684	334.9	0.219	0.0376	0.0317	0.01576	1.46	270
280	394.83	54.97	0.0818	109.431	145.063	0.18824	0.23641	0.5410	0.5663	2.0476	588	318.4	0.192	0.0393	0.0308	0.01742	1.00	280
290	437.52	51.72	0.0680	114.455	144.549	0.19479	0.23493	0.6449	0.7492	2.6453	488	300.0	0.165	0.0418	0.0302	0.02001	0.58	290
300	484.03	47.29	0.0543	120.218	142.886	0.20219	0.23203	0.962	1.292	4.439	378	278.6	0.134	0.0459	0.0303	0.02503	0.22	300
308.95[c]	529.53	32.43	0.0308	132.508	132.508	0.21798	0.21798	∞	∞	∞	0	0.0	—	—	∞	∞	0.00	308.95

*Temperatures on ITS-90 scale [b]Normal boiling point [c]Critical point

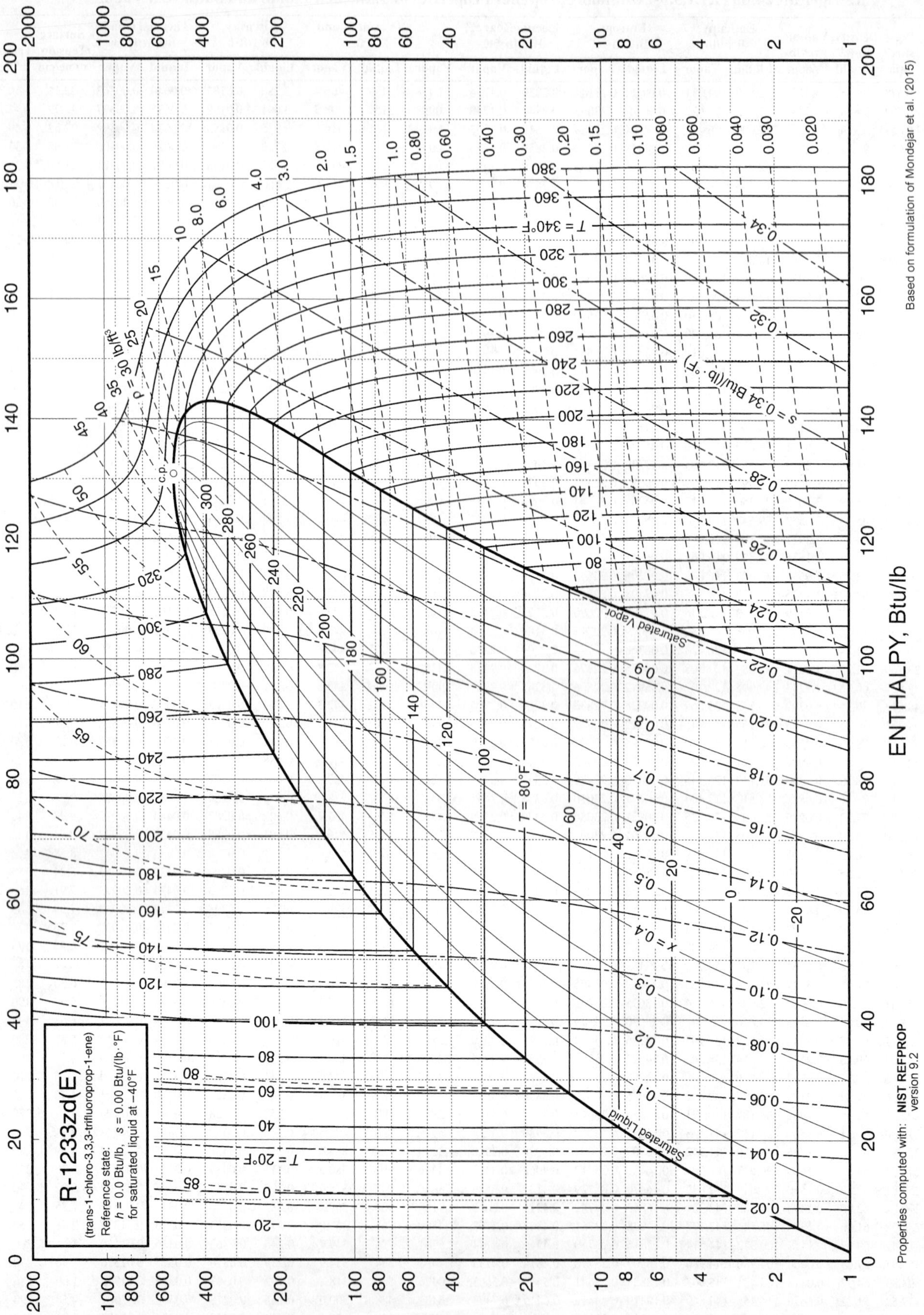

Fig. 12 Pressure-Enthalpy Diagram for Refrigerant R-1233zd(E)

Refrigerant 1233zd(E) (trans-1-chloro-3,3,3-trifluoroprop-1-ene) Properties of Saturated Liquid and Saturated Vapor

Temp., °F	Pressure, psia	Density, lb/ft³ Liquid	Volume, ft³/lb Vapor	Enthalpy, Btu/lb Liquid	Enthalpy, Btu/lb Vapor	Entropy, Btu/lb·°F Liquid	Entropy, Btu/lb·°F Vapor	Specific Heat, c_p Btu/lb·°F Liquid	Specific Heat, c_p Btu/lb·°F Vapor	c_p / c_v Vapor	Vel. of Sound, ft/s Liquid	Vel. of Sound, ft/s Vapor	Viscosity, lb_m/ft·h Liquid	Viscosity, lb_m/ft·h Vapor	Thermal Cond., Btu/h·ft·°F Liquid	Thermal Cond., Btu/h·ft·°F Vapor	Surface Tension, dyne/cm	Temp., °F
–60	0.387	89.41	84.710	–5.327	92.383	–0.01300	0.23147	0.2646	0.1573	1.1086	3272	409.8	5.136	0.0200	0.0616	0.00348	25.23	–60
–50	0.572	88.68	58.669	–2.673	93.947	–0.00644	0.22940	0.2663	0.1603	1.1069	3193	414.1	4.270	0.0205	0.0606	0.00367	24.41	–50
–40	0.827	87.94	41.517	–0.000	95.532	–0.00000	0.22764	0.2681	0.1632	1.1054	3114	418.3	3.637	0.0210	0.0595	0.00387	23.60	–40
–30	1.171	87.20	29.964	2.690	97.137	0.00633	0.22614	0.2699	0.1661	1.1043	3037	422.4	3.154	0.0215	0.0585	0.00408	22.79	–30
–20	1.628	86.46	22.022	5.398	98.758	0.01256	0.22490	0.2717	0.1689	1.1034	2960	426.3	2.773	0.0220	0.0574	0.00428	21.99	–20
–15	1.906	86.09	18.999	6.759	99.575	0.01564	0.22437	0.2726	0.1704	1.1030	2922	428.1	2.611	0.0223	0.0569	0.00438	21.59	–15
–10	2.223	85.71	16.457	8.125	100.394	0.01869	0.22388	0.2735	0.1718	1.1028	2885	430.0	2.464	0.0225	0.0564	0.00448	21.19	–10
–5	2.581	85.33	14.310	9.495	101.217	0.02172	0.22345	0.2744	0.1732	1.1026	2847	431.7	2.331	0.0228	0.0559	0.00459	20.80	–5
0	2.986	84.96	12.488	10.870	102.043	0.02472	0.22307	0.2753	0.1746	1.1025	2810	433.4	2.209	0.0230	0.0554	0.00469	20.40	0
5	3.441	84.57	10.937	12.249	102.871	0.02771	0.22273	0.2762	0.1760	1.1024	2772	435.1	2.098	0.0233	0.0549	0.00480	20.01	5
10	3.952	84.19	9.6112	13.634	103.701	0.03067	0.22244	0.2772	0.1774	1.1024	2735	436.7	1.995	0.0235	0.0544	0.00490	19.62	10
15	4.522	83.81	8.4736	15.022	104.533	0.03361	0.22218	0.2781	0.1789	1.1026	2698	438.2	1.900	0.0238	0.0539	0.00501	19.23	15
20	5.157	83.42	7.4939	16.416	105.367	0.03652	0.22197	0.2791	0.1803	1.1027	2661	439.7	1.812	0.0240	0.0534	0.00512	18.85	20
25	5.862	83.03	6.6474	17.815	106.202	0.03942	0.22179	0.2800	0.1817	1.1030	2625	441.1	1.731	0.0243	0.0528	0.00522	18.46	25
30	6.643	82.64	5.9135	19.218	107.038	0.04230	0.22164	0.2810	0.1832	1.1034	2588	442.5	1.655	0.0245	0.0523	0.00533	18.08	30
35	7.505	82.25	5.2752	20.626	107.874	0.04516	0.22153	0.2819	0.1846	1.1038	2552	443.7	1.584	0.0248	0.0519	0.00544	17.70	35
40	8.455	81.85	4.7183	22.040	108.711	0.04799	0.22145	0.2829	0.1861	1.1043	2516	444.9	1.517	0.0250	0.0514	0.00555	17.32	40
45	9.498	81.45	4.2310	23.458	109.549	0.05081	0.22140	0.2839	0.1876	1.1050	2479	446.1	1.455	0.0252	0.0509	0.00567	16.94	45
50	10.641	81.05	3.8033	24.881	110.386	0.05362	0.22138	0.2849	0.1891	1.1057	2443	447.1	1.397	0.0255	0.0504	0.00578	16.56	50
55	11.890	80.65	3.4269	26.310	111.223	0.05640	0.22138	0.2859	0.1907	1.1065	2407	448.1	1.342	0.0257	0.0499	0.00590	16.19	55
60	13.252	80.24	3.0947	27.744	112.059	0.05917	0.22141	0.2870	0.1922	1.1074	2371	449.0	1.290	0.0260	0.0494	0.00601	15.81	60
64.87[b]	14.696	79.84	2.8079	29.146	112.873	0.06185	0.22146	0.2880	0.1937	1.1083	2336	449.8	1.242	0.0262	0.0489	0.00613	15.45	64.87
65	14.735	79.83	2.8008	29.183	112.894	0.06191	0.22147	0.2880	0.1938	1.1084	2336	449.8	1.241	0.0262	0.0489	0.00613	15.44	65
70	16.345	79.42	2.5402	30.627	113.728	0.06465	0.22154	0.2891	0.1954	1.1095	2300	450.5	1.195	0.0265	0.0484	0.00625	15.07	70
75	18.090	79.00	2.3084	32.077	114.561	0.06736	0.22164	0.2902	0.1970	1.1107	2264	451.1	1.151	0.0267	0.0479	0.00637	14.71	75
80	19.977	78.58	2.1018	33.532	115.392	0.07007	0.22175	0.2913	0.1987	1.1120	2229	451.7	1.109	0.0270	0.0474	0.00649	14.34	80
85	22.013	78.16	1.9172	34.993	116.222	0.07275	0.22188	0.2924	0.2004	1.1135	2193	452.1	1.069	0.0272	0.0470	0.00661	13.98	85
90	24.208	77.73	1.7519	36.460	117.049	0.07542	0.22204	0.2935	0.2021	1.1150	2158	452.4	1.031	0.0274	0.0465	0.00674	13.62	90
95	26.569	77.30	1.6037	37.933	117.874	0.07808	0.22220	0.2947	0.2038	1.1167	2122	452.7	0.995	0.0277	0.0460	0.00686	13.26	95
100	29.104	76.86	1.4703	39.412	118.696	0.08072	0.22239	0.2959	0.2056	1.1186	2087	452.8	0.961	0.0279	0.0455	0.00699	12.90	100
105	31.821	76.42	1.3502	40.896	119.515	0.08335	0.22258	0.2971	0.2075	1.1205	2052	452.9	0.928	0.0282	0.0451	0.00712	12.55	105
110	34.730	75.98	1.2418	42.387	120.331	0.08597	0.22279	0.2984	0.2093	1.1226	2016	452.8	0.897	0.0284	0.0446	0.00725	12.20	110
115	37.838	75.53	1.1437	43.885	121.144	0.08857	0.22301	0.2997	0.2113	1.1249	1981	452.6	0.867	0.0287	0.0441	0.00738	11.85	115
120	41.155	75.08	1.0548	45.389	121.953	0.09116	0.22325	0.3010	0.2132	1.1274	1946	452.3	0.838	0.0289	0.0437	0.00752	11.50	120
125	44.690	74.62	0.9741	46.900	122.758	0.09374	0.22349	0.3024	0.2152	1.1300	1911	451.9	0.810	0.0292	0.0432	0.00766	11.15	125
130	48.452	74.16	0.9007	48.417	123.558	0.09631	0.22374	0.3038	0.2173	1.1328	1876	451.4	0.784	0.0294	0.0427	0.00780	10.81	130
135	52.449	73.69	0.8339	49.942	124.354	0.09887	0.22400	0.3052	0.2194	1.1358	1840	450.8	0.758	0.0297	0.0423	0.00794	10.47	135
140	56.693	73.21	0.7729	51.474	125.145	0.10142	0.22427	0.3067	0.2216	1.1391	1805	450.0	0.734	0.0299	0.0418	0.00808	10.13	140
145	61.191	72.73	0.7171	53.014	125.931	0.10396	0.22455	0.3083	0.2239	1.1426	1770	449.1	0.710	0.0302	0.0414	0.00823	9.79	145
150	65.955	72.25	0.6661	54.561	126.711	0.10649	0.22483	0.3099	0.2262	1.1463	1735	448.1	0.687	0.0305	0.0409	0.00838	9.46	150
155	70.993	71.75	0.6193	56.117	127.485	0.10900	0.22511	0.3116	0.2286	1.1503	1700	446.9	0.665	0.0307	0.0405	0.00853	9.13	155
160	76.316	71.25	0.5763	57.680	128.253	0.11152	0.22540	0.3133	0.2311	1.1546	1664	445.6	0.644	0.0310	0.0400	0.00868	8.80	160
165	81.934	70.75	0.5368	59.253	129.013	0.11402	0.22570	0.3151	0.2337	1.1593	1629	444.1	0.623	0.0313	0.0396	0.00884	8.47	165
170	87.858	70.23	0.5004	60.834	129.767	0.11652	0.22599	0.3170	0.2364	1.1643	1594	442.5	0.603	0.0316	0.0391	0.00899	8.15	170
175	94.098	69.71	0.4669	62.424	130.512	0.11901	0.22629	0.3190	0.2392	1.1697	1558	440.7	0.584	0.0318	0.0387	0.00915	7.83	175
180	100.66	69.17	0.4359	64.024	131.249	0.12149	0.22658	0.3211	0.2421	1.1755	1523	438.8	0.565	0.0321	0.0383	0.00932	7.51	180
185	107.57	68.63	0.4072	65.634	131.977	0.12397	0.22688	0.3233	0.2451	1.1819	1487	436.7	0.547	0.0324	0.0378	0.00949	7.20	185
190	114.82	68.08	0.3807	67.254	132.695	0.12644	0.22717	0.3256	0.2483	1.1887	1451	434.5	0.529	0.0327	0.0374	0.00966	6.88	190
195	122.43	67.52	0.3561	68.886	133.403	0.12891	0.22746	0.3280	0.2517	1.1962	1416	432.0	0.512	0.0331	0.0370	0.00983	6.57	195
200	130.42	66.95	0.3333	70.528	134.099	0.13138	0.22774	0.3306	0.2552	1.2043	1380	429.4	0.495	0.0334	0.0366	0.01001	6.27	200
210	147.55	65.77	0.2923	73.850	135.455	0.13630	0.22829	0.3363	0.2629	1.2230	1307	423.6	0.463	0.0341	0.0358	0.01037	5.67	210
220	166.31	64.54	0.2567	77.225	136.754	0.14123	0.22881	0.3427	0.2717	1.2456	1235	417.1	0.433	0.0348	0.0349	0.01075	5.08	220
230	186.81	63.24	0.2256	80.660	137.988	0.14615	0.22928	0.3503	0.2818	1.2733	1161	409.6	0.404	0.0356	0.0341	0.01116	4.51	230
240	209.15	61.87	0.1983	84.161	139.142	0.15110	0.22968	0.3591	0.2938	1.3079	1086	401.2	0.376	0.0366	0.0334	0.01159	3.95	240
250	233.46	60.42	0.1742	87.741	140.202	0.15608	0.23000	0.3698	0.3084	1.3522	1010	391.9	0.349	0.0376	0.0326	0.01206	3.41	250
260	259.84	58.86	0.1528	91.410	141.147	0.16110	0.23021	0.3831	0.3267	1.4103	932	381.4	0.323	0.0388	0.0318	0.01258	2.88	260
270	288.46	57.17	0.1337	95.189	141.946	0.16618	0.23026	0.4002	0.3506	1.4894	853	369.8	0.297	0.0402	0.0311	0.01316	2.38	270
280	319.45	55.31	0.1165	99.102	142.560	0.17137	0.23012	0.4231	0.3835	1.6020	771	356.9	0.272	0.0419	0.0303	0.01386	1.90	280
290	352.98	53.22	0.1009	103.188	142.927	0.17670	0.22971	0.4563	0.4319	1.7731	686	342.7	0.247	0.0441	0.0296	0.01472	1.44	290
300	389.27	50.82	0.0864	107.515	142.944	0.18227	0.22890	0.5093	0.5111	2.0591	598	327.0	0.222	0.0469	0.0289	0.01585	1.01	300
310	428.56	47.89	0.0727	112.212	142.420	0.18822	0.22746	0.6110	0.6642	2.6221	504	309.6	0.195	0.0510	0.0283	0.01752	0.62	310
320	471.16	43.95	0.0590	117.623	140.880	0.19498	0.22481	0.896	1.086	4.191	402	290.0	0.165	0.0576	0.0281	0.02049	0.28	320
330	517.63	36.02	0.0415	125.873	135.691	0.20521	0.21765	5.598	7.067	26.548	288	266.7	0.120	0.0764	0.0337	0.03276	0.02	330
331.61[c]	525.57	29.98	0.0334	130.891	130.891	0.21150	0.21150	∞	∞	∞	0	0.0	—	—	∞	∞	0.00	331.61

[b]Normal boiling point

[c]Critical point

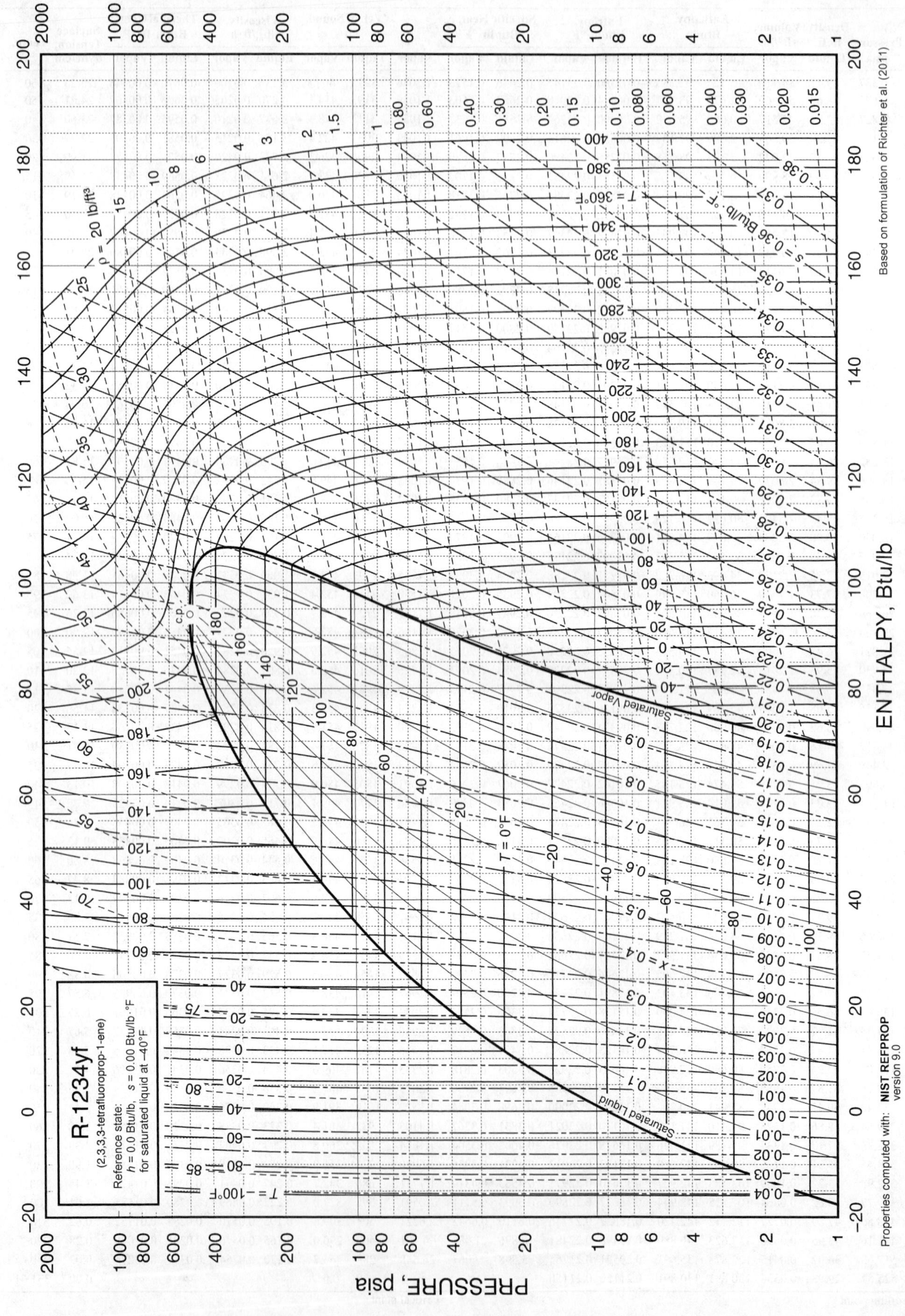

Fig. 13 Pressure-Enthalpy Diagram for Refrigerant 1234yf

Refrigerant 1234yf (2,3,3,3-tetrafluoroprop-1-ene) Properties of Saturated Liquid and Saturated Vapor

Temp., °F	Pressure, psia	Density, lb/ft³ Liquid	Volume, ft³/lb Vapor	Enthalpy, Btu/lb Liquid	Enthalpy, Btu/lb Vapor	Entropy, Btu/lb·°F Liquid	Entropy, Btu/lb·°F Vapor	Specific Heat, c_p Btu/lb·°F Liquid	Specific Heat, c_p Btu/lb·°F Vapor	c_p / c_v Vapor	Vel. of Sound, ft/s Liquid	Vel. of Sound, ft/s Vapor	Viscosity, lb_m/ft·h Liquid	Viscosity, lb_m/ft·h Vapor	Thermal Cond., Btu/h·ft·°F Liquid	Thermal Cond., Btu/h·ft·°F Vapor	Surface Tension, dyne/cm	Temp., °F
–60	5.111	82.49	7.1955	–5.458	76.593	–0.01330	0.19200	0.2688	0.1776	1.1241	2586	432.7	0.907	0.0184	0.0517	0.00436	17.27	–60
–55	5.932	82.03	6.2622	–4.109	77.395	–0.00995	0.19146	0.2707	0.1796	1.1243	2542	434.3	0.876	0.0188	0.0511	0.00449	16.81	–55
–50	6.855	81.58	5.4710	–2.749	78.198	–0.00662	0.19097	0.2727	0.1817	1.1247	2499	435.8	0.847	0.0192	0.0505	0.00462	16.36	–50
–45	7.889	81.11	4.7974	–1.380	79.002	–0.00330	0.19055	0.2746	0.1838	1.1252	2457	437.2	0.818	0.0195	0.0499	0.00475	15.91	–45
–40	9.046	80.65	4.2215	–0.000	79.808	–0.00000	0.19017	0.2766	0.1859	1.1258	2414	438.6	0.791	0.0199	0.0493	0.00487	15.46	–40
–35	10.333	80.18	3.7271	1.390	80.614	0.00328	0.18984	0.2787	0.1880	1.1265	2372	439.8	0.765	0.0203	0.0487	0.00500	15.02	–35
–30	11.761	79.71	3.3012	2.790	81.420	0.00655	0.18956	0.2807	0.1903	1.1274	2331	440.9	0.740	0.0206	0.0482	0.00513	14.58	–30
–25	13.341	79.23	2.9329	4.200	82.226	0.00981	0.18932	0.2828	0.1925	1.1285	2290	441.9	0.716	0.0210	0.0476	0.00526	14.15	–25
–21.07[b]	14.696	78.85	2.6781	5.315	82.859	0.01236	0.18916	0.2844	0.1943	1.1294	2257	442.6	0.697	0.0212	0.0471	0.00536	13.81	–21.07
–20	15.084	78.75	2.6132	5.621	83.032	0.01305	0.18912	0.2848	0.1948	1.1297	2249	442.8	0.693	0.0213	0.0470	0.00538	13.72	–20
–15	17.001	78.26	2.3349	7.053	83.837	0.01628	0.18896	0.2870	0.1971	1.1310	2208	443.6	0.670	0.0217	0.0465	0.00551	13.29	–15
–10	19.104	77.77	2.0917	8.495	84.641	0.01949	0.18883	0.2891	0.1995	1.1325	2168	444.2	0.649	0.0220	0.0459	0.00564	12.86	–10
–5	21.404	77.28	1.8786	9.948	85.444	0.02269	0.18874	0.2912	0.2019	1.1342	2127	444.7	0.628	0.0223	0.0453	0.00577	12.44	–5
0	23.914	76.78	1.6913	11.412	86.244	0.02588	0.18868	0.2934	0.2043	1.1361	2087	445.1	0.608	0.0226	0.0448	0.00589	12.03	0
5	26.647	76.27	1.5262	12.887	87.043	0.02906	0.18865	0.2956	0.2068	1.1381	2048	445.4	0.589	0.0230	0.0442	0.00602	11.62	5
10	29.615	75.76	1.3802	14.374	87.839	0.03223	0.18865	0.2979	0.2094	1.1404	2008	445.5	0.570	0.0233	0.0437	0.00615	11.21	10
15	32.831	75.24	1.2508	15.871	88.632	0.03538	0.18867	0.3001	0.2120	1.1429	1968	445.4	0.552	0.0236	0.0431	0.00628	10.80	15
20	36.309	74.72	1.1357	17.381	89.422	0.03853	0.18872	0.3024	0.2147	1.1457	1929	445.3	0.535	0.0239	0.0426	0.00641	10.40	20
25	40.062	74.19	1.0332	18.902	90.208	0.04166	0.18878	0.3048	0.2174	1.1486	1890	444.9	0.518	0.0243	0.0421	0.00654	10.01	25
30	44.105	73.65	0.9416	20.434	90.989	0.04479	0.18887	0.3072	0.2202	1.1519	1850	444.4	0.502	0.0246	0.0415	0.00667	9.62	30
35	48.451	73.11	0.8596	21.979	91.765	0.04790	0.18898	0.3096	0.2231	1.1555	1811	443.8	0.486	0.0249	0.0410	0.00681	9.23	35
40	53.116	72.55	0.7860	23.536	92.536	0.05101	0.18910	0.3121	0.2261	1.1594	1772	442.9	0.471	0.0252	0.0405	0.00694	8.85	40
45	58.113	71.99	0.7198	25.106	93.301	0.05411	0.18924	0.3147	0.2291	1.1637	1733	441.9	0.456	0.0255	0.0400	0.00708	8.47	45
50	63.459	71.42	0.6601	26.688	94.059	0.05720	0.18939	0.3173	0.2323	1.1685	1693	440.8	0.441	0.0259	0.0394	0.00722	8.10	50
55	69.167	70.84	0.6062	28.283	94.810	0.06029	0.18955	0.3199	0.2355	1.1736	1654	439.4	0.427	0.0262	0.0389	0.00736	7.73	55
60	75.255	70.25	0.5573	29.891	95.552	0.06337	0.18972	0.3227	0.2389	1.1793	1615	437.9	0.414	0.0265	0.0384	0.00750	7.37	60
65	81.737	69.65	0.5130	31.513	96.285	0.06644	0.18989	0.3255	0.2425	1.1856	1575	436.1	0.400	0.0268	0.0379	0.00765	7.01	65
70	88.629	69.04	0.4728	33.149	97.008	0.06951	0.19007	0.3285	0.2462	1.1926	1536	434.2	0.387	0.0272	0.0374	0.00780	6.66	70
75	95.949	68.42	0.4361	34.799	97.720	0.07257	0.19025	0.3315	0.2501	1.2002	1496	432.0	0.375	0.0275	0.0369	0.00795	6.31	75
80	103.71	67.78	0.4027	36.463	98.420	0.07563	0.19044	0.3346	0.2543	1.2087	1456	429.7	0.363	0.0278	0.0364	0.00811	5.97	80
85	111.94	67.14	0.3721	38.142	99.106	0.07869	0.19062	0.3379	0.2587	1.2181	1416	427.1	0.351	0.0282	0.0360	0.00828	5.63	85
90	120.64	66.47	0.3441	39.837	99.779	0.08174	0.19079	0.3413	0.2635	1.2286	1376	424.3	0.339	0.0286	0.0355	0.00845	5.30	90
95	129.84	65.80	0.3185	41.548	100.435	0.08479	0.19096	0.3450	0.2686	1.2402	1336	421.3	0.328	0.0289	0.0350	0.00862	4.97	95
100	139.55	65.10	0.2949	43.275	101.075	0.08784	0.19112	0.3488	0.2742	1.2533	1296	418.0	0.316	0.0293	0.0345	0.00881	4.65	100
105	149.80	64.39	0.2732	45.021	101.696	0.09090	0.19126	0.3530	0.2802	1.2679	1256	414.5	0.306	0.0297	0.0340	0.00900	4.34	105
110	160.60	63.66	0.2532	46.784	102.296	0.09395	0.19140	0.3574	0.2867	1.2843	1215	410.7	0.295	0.0301	0.0336	0.00921	4.03	110
115	171.97	62.92	0.2347	48.568	102.874	0.09701	0.19151	0.3623	0.2940	1.3028	1174	406.6	0.285	0.0305	0.0331	0.00943	3.73	115
120	183.93	62.14	0.2176	50.373	103.428	0.10008	0.19160	0.3676	0.3019	1.3239	1133	402.3	0.274	0.0310	0.0326	0.00966	3.44	120
125	196.51	61.35	0.2017	52.201	103.955	0.10315	0.19167	0.3735	0.3107	1.3479	1091	397.7	0.264	0.0315	0.0322	0.00991	3.15	125
130	209.72	60.52	0.1870	54.054	104.452	0.10624	0.19171	0.3801	0.3206	1.3756	1049	392.7	0.254	0.0320	0.0317	0.01017	2.87	130
135	223.59	59.66	0.1733	55.935	104.916	0.10934	0.19171	0.3875	0.3318	1.4077	1005	387.5	0.244	0.0325	0.0313	0.01046	2.60	135
140	238.13	58.77	0.1606	57.845	105.342	0.11246	0.19167	0.3959	0.3446	1.4453	960	381.9	0.235	0.0331	0.0308	0.01078	2.33	140
145	253.39	57.83	0.1487	59.789	105.726	0.11561	0.19158	0.4055	0.3594	1.4898	914	375.9	0.225	0.0337	0.0303	0.01113	2.08	145
150	269.37	56.84	0.1375	61.769	106.061	0.11879	0.19144	0.4167	0.3767	1.5432	867	369.5	0.215	0.0344	0.0299	0.01152	1.83	150
155	286.11	55.80	0.1270	63.792	106.340	0.12200	0.19122	0.4300	0.3974	1.6082	818	362.8	0.206	0.0351	0.0294	0.01196	1.59	155
160	303.64	54.68	0.1172	65.861	106.554	0.12526	0.19093	0.4459	0.4227	1.6891	767	355.6	0.196	0.0359	0.0289	0.01246	1.36	160
165	321.99	53.49	0.1078	67.986	106.690	0.12857	0.19053	0.4655	0.4544	1.7922	715	347.9	0.187	0.0368	0.0285	0.01304	1.14	165
170	341.19	52.21	0.0990	70.175	106.731	0.13196	0.19001	0.4906	0.4956	1.9275	662	339.7	0.177	0.0379	0.0280	0.01372	0.94	170
175	361.28	50.80	0.0905	72.445	106.653	0.13543	0.18933	0.5241	0.5513	2.1127	607	330.9	0.167	0.0391	0.0276	0.01454	0.74	175
180	382.32	49.24	0.0823	74.816	106.421	0.13903	0.18844	0.5717	0.6314	2.3809	551	321.5	0.156	0.0405	0.0272	0.01557	0.56	180
185	404.35	47.47	0.0743	77.328	105.976	0.14281	0.18725	0.6458	0.7571	2.8031	494	311.3	0.146	0.0423	0.0268	0.01690	0.39	185
190	427.45	45.39	0.0662	80.050	105.213	0.14688	0.18561	0.7788	0.9837	3.5641	433	300.1	0.134	0.0446	0.0267	0.01877	0.25	190
195	451.72	42.73	0.0578	83.145	103.888	0.15147	0.18315	1.094	1.517	5.344	369	287.5	0.121	0.0479	0.0271	0.02182	0.12	195
200	477.33	38.53	0.0475	87.241	101.103	0.15752	0.17853	2.821	4.285	14.439	295	271.8	0.102	0.0543	0.0302	0.02969	0.03	200
202.46[c]	490.55	29.69	0.0337	93.995	93.995	0.16763	0.16763	∞	∞	∞	0	0.0	—	—	∞	∞	0.00	202.46

[b]Normal boiling point

[c]Critical point

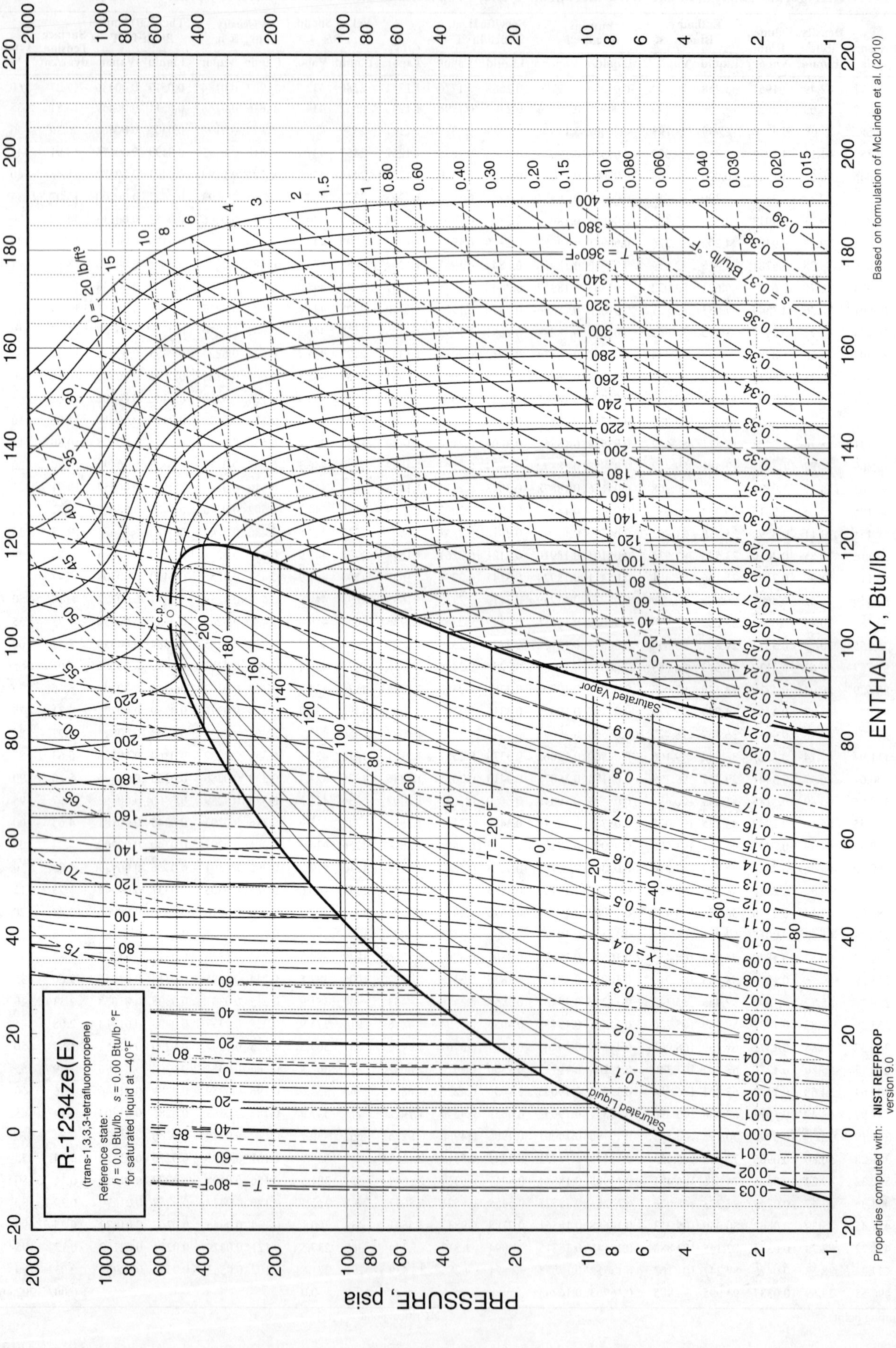

Fig. 14 Pressure-Enthalpy Diagram for Refrigerant 1234ze(E)

Refrigerant 1234ze(E) (trans-1,3,3,3-tetrafluoropropene) Properties of Saturated Liquid and Saturated Vapor

Temp., °F	Pressure, psia	Density, lb/ft³	Volume, ft³/lb	Enthalpy, Btu/lb		Entropy, Btu/lb·°F		Specific Heat, c_p Btu/lb·°F		c_p / c_v	Vel. of Sound, ft/s		Viscosity, lb_m/ft·h		Thermal Cond., Btu/h·ft·°F		Surface Tension, dyne/cm	Temp., °F
		Liquid	Vapor	Liquid	Vapor	Liquid	Vapor	Liquid	Vapor	Vapor	Liquid	Vapor	Liquid	Vapor	Liquid	Vapor		
–60	2.839	86.03	13.083	–5.955	85.763	–0.01452	0.21496	0.2962	0.1797	1.1146	2862	435.2	1.267	0.0184	0.0595	0.00440	20.24	–60
–55	3.347	85.59	11.219	–4.472	86.613	–0.01084	0.21425	0.2968	0.1812	1.1145	2820	437.2	1.219	0.0188	0.0588	0.00453	19.79	–55
–50	3.926	85.14	9.6638	–2.985	87.465	–0.00719	0.21360	0.2976	0.1827	1.1146	2779	439.1	1.173	0.0192	0.0582	0.00465	19.35	–50
–45	4.584	84.70	8.3603	–1.494	88.319	–0.00358	0.21301	0.2983	0.1843	1.1148	2738	440.9	1.129	0.0196	0.0575	0.00478	18.90	–45
–40	5.330	84.25	7.2623	–0.000	89.172	–0.00000	0.21248	0.2991	0.1858	1.1150	2697	442.6	1.087	0.0201	0.0569	0.00491	18.46	–40
–35	6.170	83.80	6.3334	1.499	90.027	0.00355	0.21201	0.2999	0.1873	1.1154	2656	444.2	1.046	0.0205	0.0563	0.00503	18.02	–35
–30	7.113	83.34	5.5439	3.002	90.881	0.00706	0.21159	0.3008	0.1889	1.1159	2615	445.8	1.007	0.0209	0.0556	0.00516	17.59	–30
–25	8.170	82.88	4.8703	4.509	91.735	0.01054	0.21121	0.3017	0.1905	1.1165	2574	447.3	0.970	0.0213	0.0550	0.00528	17.15	–25
–20	9.347	82.42	4.2931	6.022	92.588	0.01400	0.21088	0.3027	0.1921	1.1172	2534	448.6	0.934	0.0217	0.0544	0.00541	16.72	–20
–15	10.657	81.96	3.7966	7.539	93.440	0.01742	0.21060	0.3037	0.1938	1.1181	2493	449.9	0.899	0.0221	0.0537	0.00553	16.29	–15
–10	12.107	81.50	3.3680	9.062	94.290	0.02082	0.21035	0.3047	0.1955	1.1191	2453	451.1	0.866	0.0225	0.0531	0.00566	15.87	–10
–5	13.710	81.03	2.9967	10.590	95.138	0.02419	0.21015	0.3058	0.1972	1.1202	2412	452.1	0.834	0.0229	0.0525	0.00578	15.44	–5
–2.15[b]	14.696	80.76	2.8072	11.463	95.621	0.02610	0.21004	0.3064	0.1982	1.1209	2389	452.7	0.817	0.0232	0.0521	0.00585	15.20	–2.15
0	15.476	80.55	2.6738	12.123	95.985	0.02754	0.20997	0.3069	0.1989	1.1214	2372	453.1	0.804	0.0234	0.0519	0.00591	15.02	0
5	17.416	80.07	2.3922	13.663	96.828	0.03086	0.20983	0.3081	0.2007	1.1228	2331	453.9	0.775	0.0238	0.0513	0.00603	14.60	5
10	19.542	79.59	2.1458	15.208	97.669	0.03415	0.20973	0.3093	0.2026	1.1244	2291	454.6	0.746	0.0242	0.0507	0.00615	14.18	10
15	21.865	79.11	1.9295	16.760	98.506	0.03743	0.20965	0.3105	0.2044	1.1261	2250	455.2	0.719	0.0246	0.0500	0.00628	13.77	15
20	24.398	78.62	1.7391	18.318	99.339	0.04068	0.20959	0.3118	0.2064	1.1280	2210	455.7	0.693	0.0250	0.0494	0.00640	13.36	20
25	27.153	78.12	1.5710	19.883	100.168	0.04391	0.20956	0.3131	0.2083	1.1301	2170	456.0	0.668	0.0254	0.0489	0.00652	12.95	25
30	30.143	77.62	1.4221	21.455	100.993	0.04713	0.20956	0.3145	0.2104	1.1324	2129	456.2	0.645	0.0258	0.0483	0.00665	12.55	30
35	33.382	77.11	1.2900	23.034	101.812	0.05032	0.20957	0.3160	0.2125	1.1349	2089	456.3	0.622	0.0262	0.0477	0.00677	12.14	35
40	36.882	76.60	1.1725	24.620	102.627	0.05349	0.20961	0.3175	0.2146	1.1376	2049	456.2	0.599	0.0266	0.0471	0.00690	11.74	40
45	40.658	76.09	1.0676	26.215	103.435	0.05665	0.20966	0.3191	0.2169	1.1405	2009	456.0	0.578	0.0270	0.0465	0.00702	11.35	45
50	44.723	75.56	0.9738	27.817	104.237	0.05979	0.20973	0.3208	0.2192	1.1437	1968	455.6	0.558	0.0274	0.0459	0.00715	10.95	50
55	49.093	75.03	0.8897	29.428	105.032	0.06291	0.20981	0.3225	0.2216	1.1472	1928	455.1	0.538	0.0278	0.0454	0.00728	10.56	55
60	53.780	74.49	0.8141	31.048	105.820	0.06602	0.20991	0.3243	0.2240	1.1510	1888	454.4	0.520	0.0282	0.0448	0.00741	10.17	60
65	58.802	73.95	0.7461	32.677	106.600	0.06912	0.21001	0.3262	0.2266	1.1551	1848	453.6	0.501	0.0286	0.0442	0.00754	9.79	65
70	64.172	73.40	0.6848	34.315	107.371	0.07220	0.21013	0.3282	0.2293	1.1596	1808	452.6	0.484	0.0290	0.0437	0.00767	9.41	70
75	69.905	72.84	0.6293	35.964	108.134	0.07527	0.21025	0.3303	0.2321	1.1645	1768	451.4	0.467	0.0294	0.0431	0.00780	9.03	75
80	76.019	72.27	0.5790	37.623	108.887	0.07833	0.21038	0.3325	0.2350	1.1698	1728	450.1	0.451	0.0298	0.0426	0.00794	8.66	80
85	82.528	71.69	0.5334	39.293	109.630	0.08138	0.21052	0.3348	0.2380	1.1757	1688	448.5	0.436	0.0302	0.0420	0.00808	8.29	85
90	89.450	71.10	0.4919	40.974	110.362	0.08442	0.21066	0.3373	0.2412	1.1820	1648	446.8	0.421	0.0307	0.0415	0.00822	7.92	90
95	96.800	70.50	0.4541	42.668	111.081	0.08745	0.21079	0.3399	0.2446	1.1889	1608	444.9	0.407	0.0311	0.0410	0.00837	7.56	95
100	104.60	69.89	0.4196	44.374	111.789	0.09048	0.21093	0.3426	0.2481	1.1966	1568	442.8	0.393	0.0315	0.0404	0.00852	7.20	100
105	112.85	69.26	0.3881	46.093	112.482	0.09350	0.21107	0.3455	0.2519	1.2049	1527	440.5	0.379	0.0319	0.0399	0.00867	6.84	105
110	121.59	68.63	0.3592	47.826	113.161	0.09651	0.21120	0.3486	0.2559	1.2142	1486	437.9	0.366	0.0323	0.0394	0.00884	6.49	110
115	130.83	67.97	0.3327	49.573	113.823	0.09952	0.21132	0.3519	0.2602	1.2245	1445	435.2	0.354	0.0328	0.0389	0.00900	6.14	115
120	140.58	67.31	0.3084	51.336	114.469	0.10253	0.21144	0.3554	0.2648	1.2359	1404	432.2	0.342	0.0332	0.0384	0.00918	5.80	120
125	150.87	66.62	0.2860	53.115	115.095	0.10554	0.21154	0.3592	0.2697	1.2486	1362	429.0	0.330	0.0336	0.0378	0.00937	5.46	125
130	161.72	65.92	0.2653	54.911	115.701	0.10854	0.21164	0.3632	0.2752	1.2629	1320	425.6	0.319	0.0341	0.0373	0.00956	5.12	130
135	173.14	65.20	0.2462	56.726	116.285	0.11155	0.21171	0.3676	0.2811	1.2789	1277	421.9	0.308	0.0345	0.0368	0.00977	4.79	135
140	185.15	64.46	0.2286	58.560	116.845	0.11457	0.21176	0.3724	0.2877	1.2971	1234	417.9	0.297	0.0350	0.0363	0.00999	4.47	140
145	197.78	63.69	0.2122	60.414	117.379	0.11759	0.21179	0.3777	0.2950	1.3176	1190	413.7	0.287	0.0354	0.0358	0.01022	4.15	145
150	211.04	62.90	0.1971	62.291	117.884	0.12061	0.21180	0.3835	0.3032	1.3412	1146	409.2	0.277	0.0359	0.0353	0.01048	3.84	150
155	224.97	62.08	0.1829	64.192	118.357	0.12365	0.21177	0.3899	0.3124	1.3682	1101	404.3	0.267	0.0364	0.0349	0.01075	3.53	155
160	239.58	61.22	0.1698	66.120	118.794	0.12670	0.21171	0.3972	0.3229	1.3994	1055	399.2	0.257	0.0369	0.0344	0.01105	3.22	160
165	254.89	60.33	0.1575	68.076	119.193	0.12977	0.21160	0.4054	0.3350	1.4360	1008	393.7	0.248	0.0374	0.0339	0.01139	2.93	165
170	270.94	59.40	0.1461	70.065	119.548	0.13287	0.21145	0.4148	0.3490	1.4791	961	387.9	0.238	0.0379	0.0334	0.01175	2.64	170
175	287.74	58.43	0.1353	72.090	119.853	0.13598	0.21124	0.4258	0.3655	1.5307	913	381.7	0.229	0.0385	0.0329	0.01217	2.35	175
180	305.33	57.40	0.1252	74.156	120.101	0.13914	0.21096	0.4387	0.3852	1.5934	864	375.1	0.219	0.0391	0.0325	0.01263	2.08	180
185	323.74	56.30	0.1157	76.268	120.282	0.14233	0.21061	0.4544	0.4092	1.6709	813	368.1	0.210	0.0397	0.0320	0.01317	1.81	185
190	343.00	55.14	0.1067	78.436	120.384	0.14558	0.21015	0.4737	0.4392	1.7689	762	360.6	0.201	0.0404	0.0315	0.01379	1.55	190
195	363.15	53.88	0.0981	80.669	120.391	0.14890	0.20958	0.4983	0.4779	1.8967	709	352.7	0.191	0.0412	0.0311	0.01453	1.30	195
200	384.22	52.51	0.0899	82.982	120.281	0.15231	0.20885	0.5309	0.5297	2.0694	655	344.2	0.181	0.0421	0.0306	0.01542	1.06	200
205	406.27	50.99	0.0820	85.398	120.019	0.15584	0.20793	0.5764	0.6031	2.3154	599	335.1	0.171	0.0431	0.0302	0.01652	0.83	205
210	429.35	49.28	0.0743	87.952	119.554	0.15954	0.20673	0.6450	0.7152	2.6920	540	325.4	0.160	0.0443	0.0299	0.01795	0.61	210
215	453.52	47.28	0.0666	90.703	118.794	0.16350	0.20513	0.7613	0.9082	3.3385	478	314.9	0.148	0.0460	0.0297	0.01992	0.41	215
220	478.88	44.79	0.0587	93.782	117.552	0.16789	0.20287	1.007	1.319	4.702	411	303.3	0.134	0.0484	0.0300	0.02294	0.23	220
225	505.55	41.25	0.0497	97.579	115.267	0.17329	0.19912	1.893	2.784	9.484	336	289.6	0.117	0.0527	0.0318	0.02915	0.08	225
228.85[c]	527.20	30.54	0.0327	106.210	106.210	0.18569	0.18569	∞	∞	∞	0	0.0	—	—	∞	∞	0.00	228.85

[b]Normal boiling point

[c]Critical point

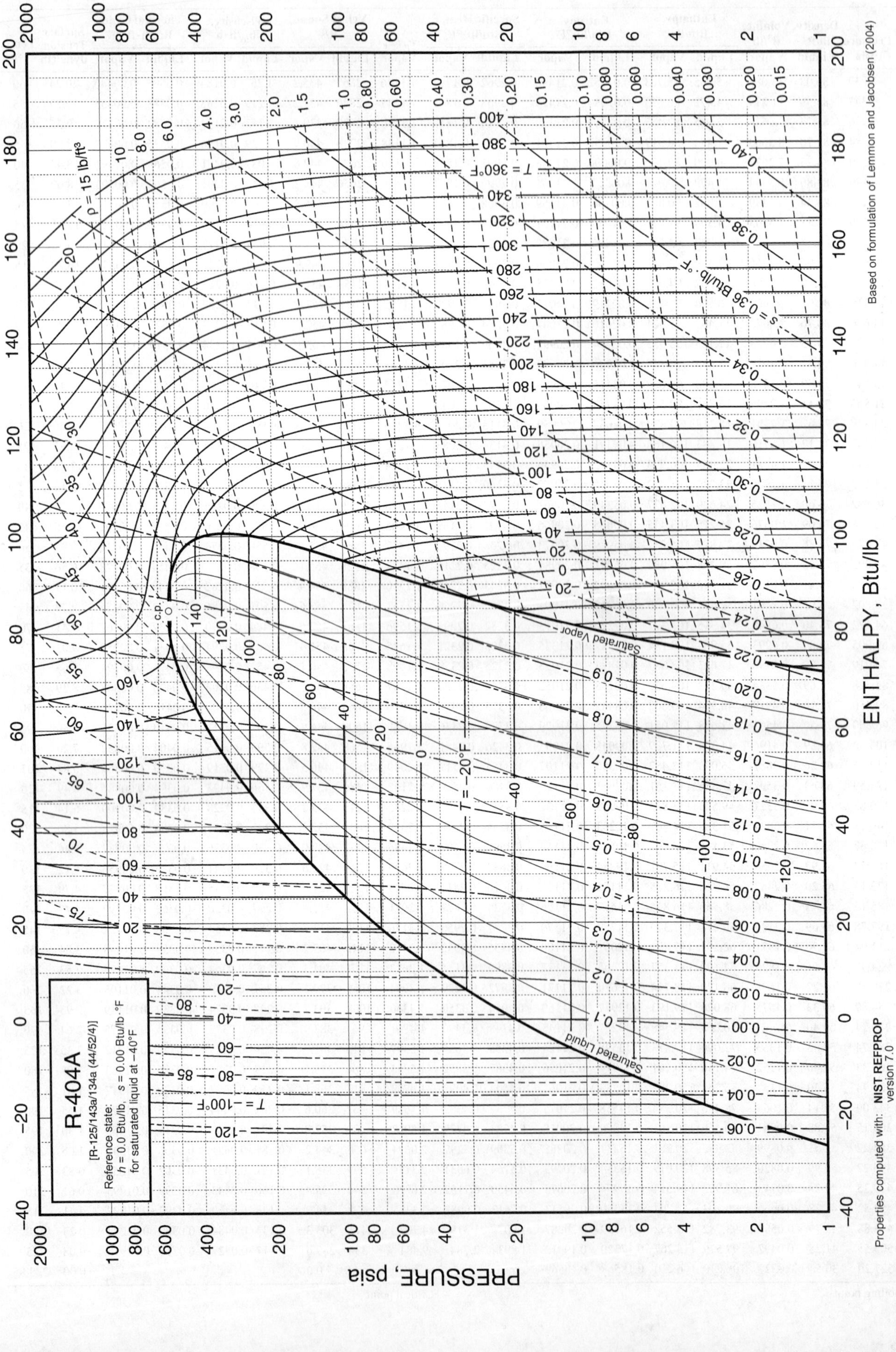

Fig. 15 Pressure-Enthalpy Diagram for Refrigerant 404A

Refrigerant 404A [R-125/143a/134a (44/52/4)] Properties of Liquid on Bubble Line and Vapor on Dew Line

Pressure, psia	Temp.,* °F		Density, lb/ft³	Volume, ft³/lb	Enthalpy, Btu/lb		Entropy, Btu/lb·°F		Specific Heat c_p, Btu/lb·°F		c_p/c_v	Vel. of Sound, ft/s		Viscosity, lb_m/ft·h		Thermal Cond., Btu/h·ft·°F		Surface Tension, dyne/cm	Pressure, psia
	Bubble	Dew	Liquid	Vapor	Liquid	Vapor	Liquid	Vapor	Liquid	Vapor	Vapor	Liquid	Vapor	Liquid	Vapor	Liquid	Vapor		
1	–129.56	–127.50	89.61	36.2311	–26.33	71.76	–0.07039	0.22616	0.2907	0.1554	1.161	3173	439.8	1.695	0.0181	0.0695	0.00369	17.42	1
1.5	–120.05	–118.11	88.64	24.7754	–23.56	73.11	–0.06215	0.22201	0.2901	0.1589	1.160	3050	444.6	1.518	0.0186	0.0678	0.00388	16.92	1.5
2	–112.90	–111.03	87.92	18.9245	–21.49	74.14	–0.05611	0.21920	0.2900	0.1615	1.159	2964	448.1	1.403	0.0190	0.0666	0.00403	16.53	2
2.5	–107.10	–105.29	87.33	15.3578	–19.81	74.98	–0.05129	0.21710	0.2902	0.1637	1.159	2898	450.7	1.320	0.0193	0.0657	0.00414	16.22	2.5
3	–102.18	–100.42	86.83	12.9493	–18.38	75.69	–0.04727	0.21544	0.2905	0.1656	1.159	2845	452.9	1.255	0.0195	0.0647	0.00425	15.94	3
4	–94.08	–92.40	86.01	9.8941	–16.02	76.86	–0.04076	0.21292	0.2912	0.1688	1.159	2760	456.3	1.159	0.0199	0.0634	0.00442	15.49	4
5	–87.49	–85.87	85.33	8.0300	–14.10	77.82	–0.03555	0.21106	0.2920	0.1715	1.159	2694	458.9	1.088	0.0203	0.0623	0.00456	15.11	5
6	–81.89	–80.32	84.76	6.7705	–12.46	78.64	–0.03119	0.20960	0.2929	0.1738	1.159	2639	461.0	1.033	0.0205	0.0614	0.00468	14.79	6
7	–77.00	–75.46	84.25	5.8607	–11.02	79.35	–0.02742	0.20841	0.2937	0.1758	1.160	2592	462.7	0.989	0.0208	0.0606	0.00478	14.50	7
8	–72.64	–71.14	83.80	5.1716	–9.74	79.98	–0.02409	0.20741	0.2944	0.1777	1.161	2551	464.1	0.952	0.0210	0.0599	0.00488	14.25	8
10	–65.08	–63.64	83.01	4.1954	–7.51	81.07	–0.01839	0.20581	0.2959	0.1811	1.162	2481	466.4	0.892	0.0214	0.0587	0.00505	13.79	10
12	–58.65	–57.25	82.34	3.5353	–5.60	82.00	–0.0136	0.20457	0.2974	0.1840	1.164	2422	468.1	0.845	0.0217	0.0577	0.00519	13.41	12
14	–53.01	–51.65	81.74	3.0582	–3.91	82.81	–0.00944	0.20357	0.2987	0.1866	1.166	2372	469.4	0.806	0.0220	0.0568	0.00532	13.06	14
14.7[b]	–51.20	–49.85	81.55	2.9217	–3.37	83.07	–0.00812	0.20326	0.2991	0.1875	1.166	2355	469.8	0.795	0.0221	0.0566	0.00536	12.95	14.7
16	–47.98	–46.65	81.20	2.6968	–2.41	83.53	–0.00577	0.20273	0.3000	0.1891	1.167	2327	470.4	0.774	0.0222	0.0561	0.00544	12.75	16
18	–43.42	–42.11	80.71	2.4132	–1.03	84.18	–0.00246	0.20203	0.3012	0.1913	1.169	2286	471.2	0.747	0.0225	0.0554	0.00554	12.47	18
20	–39.24	–37.96	80.26	2.1845	0.23	84.78	0.00055	0.20141	0.3024	0.1935	1.171	2249	471.9	0.723	0.0227	0.0548	0.00564	12.20	20
22	–35.37	–34.11	79.83	1.9960	1.40	85.32	0.00332	0.20088	0.3035	0.1955	1.173	2215	472.4	0.701	0.0229	0.0542	0.00573	11.96	22
24	–31.77	–30.53	79.44	1.8379	2.50	85.83	0.00588	0.20041	0.3046	0.1974	1.175	2184	472.8	0.682	0.0230	0.0537	0.00582	11.73	24
26	–28.39	–27.17	79.06	1.7033	3.53	86.30	0.00827	0.19998	0.3056	0.1992	1.176	2154	473.1	0.665	0.0232	0.0532	0.00590	11.52	26
28	–25.21	–24.01	78.71	1.5873	4.51	86.75	0.01051	0.19960	0.3067	0.2010	1.178	2127	473.3	0.649	0.0234	0.0527	0.00598	11.31	28
30	–22.20	–21.02	78.37	1.4863	5.44	87.16	0.01263	0.19925	0.3077	0.2027	1.180	2101	473.5	0.634	0.0235	0.0523	0.00605	11.12	30
32	–19.34	–18.17	78.05	1.3974	6.32	87.56	0.01463	0.19894	0.3086	0.2043	1.182	2076	473.6	0.621	0.0237	0.0519	0.00612	10.94	32
34	–16.62	–15.46	77.74	1.3187	7.16	87.93	0.01653	0.19864	0.3096	0.2059	1.184	2052	473.6	0.608	0.0238	0.0515	0.00619	10.76	34
36	–14.01	–12.87	77.44	1.2484	7.97	88.29	0.01834	0.19838	0.3105	0.2074	1.186	2030	473.6	0.597	0.0239	0.0511	0.00625	10.59	36
38	–11.52	–10.39	77.15	1.1852	8.75	88.62	0.02007	0.19813	0.3115	0.2089	1.188	2008	473.5	0.586	0.0241	0.0507	0.00632	10.43	38
40	–9.12	–8.01	76.87	1.1281	9.50	88.95	0.02172	0.19790	0.3124	0.2104	1.190	1987	473.4	0.576	0.0242	0.0504	0.00638	10.27	40
42	–6.81	–5.71	76.60	1.0763	10.22	89.26	0.02331	0.19768	0.3133	0.2119	1.192	1967	473.3	0.566	0.0243	0.0501	0.00644	10.12	42
44	–4.59	–3.50	76.34	1.0290	10.92	89.56	0.02484	0.19748	0.3141	0.2133	1.194	1948	473.1	0.557	0.0244	0.0497	0.00649	9.97	44
46	–2.44	–1.36	76.09	0.9857	11.60	89.84	0.02632	0.19729	0.3150	0.2146	1.196	1930	472.9	0.548	0.0245	0.0494	0.00655	9.83	46
48	–0.36	0.71	75.84	0.9459	12.25	90.12	0.02774	0.19711	0.3158	0.2160	1.198	1912	472.7	0.540	0.0246	0.0492	0.00660	9.70	48
50	1.65	2.71	75.60	0.9091	12.89	90.38	0.02911	0.19694	0.3167	0.2173	1.200	1894	472.5	0.532	0.0247	0.0489	0.00665	9.56	50
55	6.43	7.47	75.03	0.8285	14.41	91.01	0.03237	0.19655	0.3188	0.2206	1.205	1853	471.8	0.514	0.0250	0.0482	0.00678	9.25	55
60	10.89	11.90	74.48	0.7609	15.84	91.58	0.03539	0.19621	0.3208	0.2237	1.210	1814	471.0	0.498	0.0252	0.0476	0.00690	8.95	60
65	15.07	16.07	73.97	0.7033	17.19	92.11	0.03822	0.19590	0.3228	0.2267	1.215	1778	470.1	0.483	0.0254	0.0470	0.00701	8.67	65
70	19.02	20.00	73.47	0.6537	18.47	92.61	0.04088	0.19562	0.3247	0.2297	1.220	1744	469.2	0.470	0.0257	0.0465	0.00712	8.41	70
75	22.76	23.72	72.99	0.6104	19.69	93.07	0.04339	0.19537	0.3267	0.2325	1.226	1712	468.1	0.457	0.0259	0.0460	0.00723	8.16	75
80	26.32	27.27	72.54	0.5724	20.86	93.50	0.04578	0.19514	0.3286	0.2354	1.231	1681	467.0	0.446	0.0261	0.0455	0.00733	7.92	80
85	29.71	30.64	72.09	0.5387	21.98	93.91	0.04804	0.19492	0.3305	0.2382	1.236	1651	465.9	0.435	0.0263	0.0450	0.00742	7.70	85
90	32.96	33.88	71.67	0.5085	23.05	94.30	0.05021	0.19471	0.3324	0.2409	1.242	1623	464.7	0.425	0.0264	0.0446	0.00753	7.48	90
95	36.07	36.98	71.25	0.4815	24.09	94.66	0.05229	0.19452	0.3342	0.2436	1.248	1596	463.5	0.416	0.0266	0.0442	0.00763	7.27	95
100	39.07	39.96	70.84	0.4570	25.10	95.00	0.05428	0.19434	0.3361	0.2464	1.254	1569	462.2	0.407	0.0268	0.0438	0.00772	7.07	100
110	44.73	45.60	70.06	0.4145	27.01	95.64	0.05804	0.19400	0.3399	0.2518	1.266	1520	459.6	0.391	0.0271	0.0430	0.00792	6.69	110
120	50.02	50.86	69.32	0.3789	28.82	96.21	0.06155	0.19368	0.3437	0.2572	1.279	1473	456.8	0.376	0.0275	0.0423	0.00810	6.34	120
130	54.99	55.81	68.60	0.3485	30.53	96.73	0.06485	0.19338	0.3475	0.2626	1.292	1429	454.0	0.363	0.0278	0.0416	0.00829	6.01	130
140	59.68	60.48	67.90	0.3222	32.16	97.20	0.06795	0.19309	0.3514	0.2682	1.306	1387	451.1	0.351	0.0281	0.0410	0.00848	5.69	140
150	64.13	64.91	67.23	0.2994	33.73	97.62	0.07090	0.19281	0.3553	0.2739	1.321	1347	448.2	0.339	0.0284	0.0404	0.00866	5.4	150
160	68.36	69.13	66.57	0.2793	35.23	98.01	0.07371	0.19253	0.3594	0.2797	1.336	1309	445.2	0.329	0.0288	0.0399	0.00885	5.12	160
170	72.40	73.15	65.93	0.2614	36.68	98.37	0.07639	0.19226	0.3635	0.2857	1.353	1273	442.1	0.319	0.0291	0.0394	0.00904	4.85	170
180	76.26	76.99	65.30	0.2454	38.08	98.69	0.07896	0.19198	0.3678	0.2919	1.370	1238	439.0	0.310	0.0294	0.0388	0.00922	4.60	180
190	79.97	80.68	64.68	0.2311	39.44	98.98	0.08143	0.19170	0.3722	0.2984	1.388	1204	435.8	0.301	0.0297	0.0384	0.00941	4.36	190
200	83.53	84.23	64.07	0.2181	40.76	99.25	0.08381	0.19143	0.3767	0.3051	1.408	1171	432.6	0.293	0.0300	0.0379	0.00961	4.13	200
220	90.27	90.94	62.87	0.1955	43.29	99.70	0.08833	0.19085	0.3864	0.3194	1.450	1108	426.1	0.277	0.0307	0.0370	0.01000	3.70	220
240	96.57	97.21	61.70	0.1764	45.70	100.05	0.09259	0.19026	0.3969	0.3353	1.498	1048	419.4	0.263	0.0313	0.0362	0.01041	3.30	240
260	102.48	103.09	60.53	0.1601	48.02	100.32	0.09663	0.18962	0.4086	0.3530	1.553	991	412.6	0.250	0.0320	0.0354	0.01084	2.93	260
280	108.06	108.64	59.37	0.1460	50.25	100.51	0.10047	0.18895	0.4216	0.3730	1.616	936	405.7	0.238	0.0328	0.0347	0.01131	2.59	280
300	113.34	113.90	58.20	0.1336	52.42	100.61	0.10417	0.18823	0.4364	0.3959	1.690	884	398.7	0.227	0.0335	0.0340	0.01180	2.28	300
320	118.36	118.89	57.03	0.1226	54.54	100.64	0.10773	0.18745	0.4534	0.4226	1.778	832	391.5	0.216	0.0343	0.0333	0.01235	1.98	320
340	123.14	123.65	55.83	0.1127	56.61	100.58	0.11118	0.18660	0.4733	0.4543	1.883	783	384.2	0.206	0.0352	0.0326	0.01294	1.71	340
360	127.71	128.19	54.61	0.1038	58.65	100.43	0.11456	0.18566	0.4972	0.4927	2.013	734	376.8	0.196	0.0362	0.0320	0.01360	1.46	360
380	132.09	132.54	53.35	0.0956	60.67	100.20	0.11787	0.18464	0.5265	0.5404	2.174	685	369.2	0.187	0.0373	0.0315	0.01435	1.22	380
400	136.28	136.71	52.03	0.0881	62.68	99.85	0.12114	0.18349	0.5635	0.6014	2.383	638	361.5	0.177	0.0385	0.0309	0.01520	1.01	400
450	146.07	146.42	48.36	0.0713	67.80	98.42	0.12934	0.17987	0.7246	0.8714	3.313	519	341.6	0.154	0.0423	0.0298	0.01806	0.54	450
500	154.97	155.22	43.51	0.0556	73.49	95.51	0.13833	0.17416	1.2912	1.8068	6.526	396	320.1	0.128	0.0488	0.0299	0.02348	0.18	500
548.24[c]	162.50	162.50	35.84	0.0279	80.85	80.85	0.14987	0.14987	—	—	—	—	—	—	—	—	—	0.00	548.24

*Temperatures on ITS-90 scale

[b]Bubble and dew points at one standard atmosphere

[c]Critical point

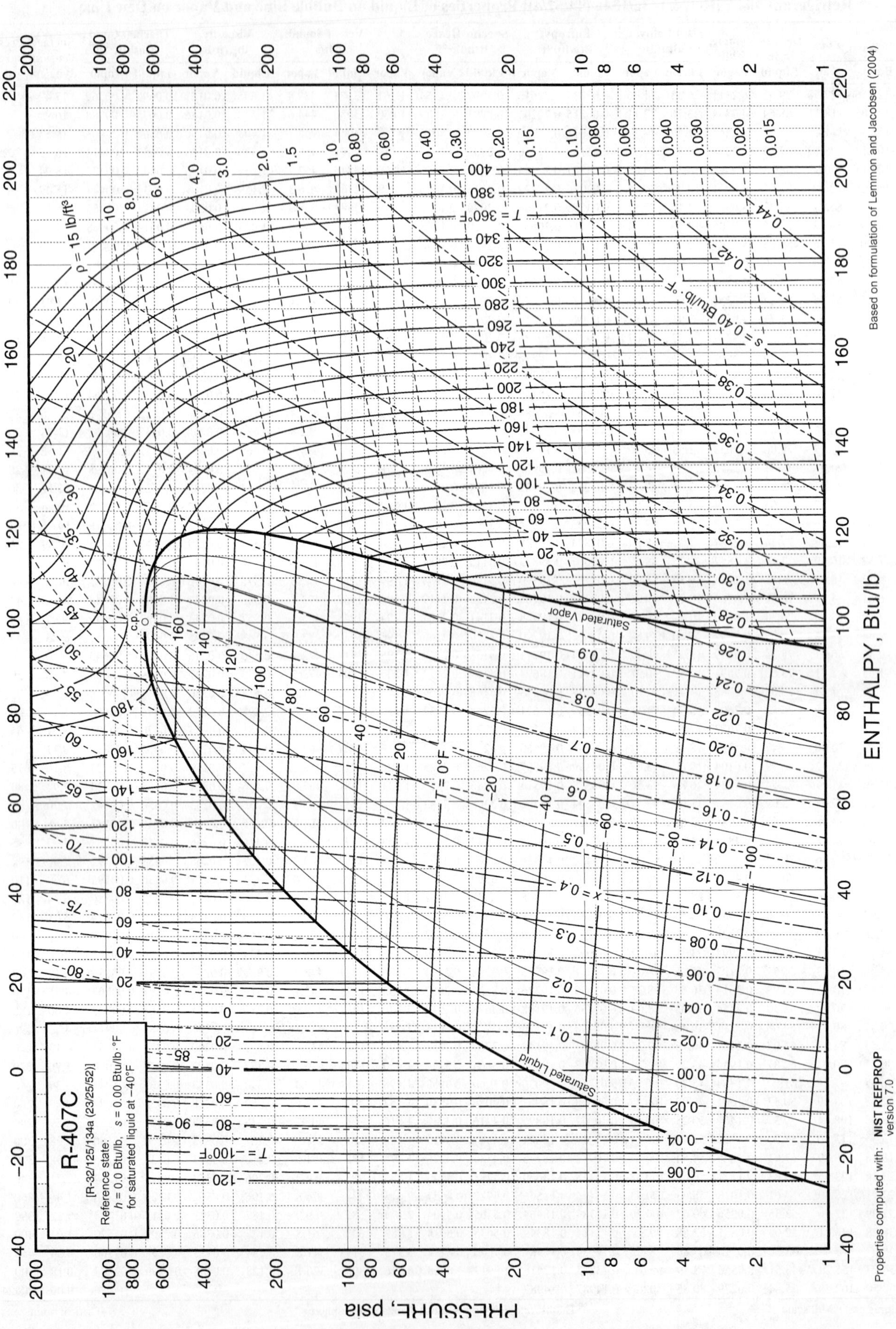

Fig. 16 Pressure-Enthalpy Diagram for Refrigerant 407C

Refrigerant 407C [R-32/125/134a (23/25/52)] Properties of Liquid on Bubble Line and Vapor on Dew Line

Pressure, psia	Temp.,* °F Bubble	Temp.,* °F Dew	Density, lb/ft³ Liquid	Volume, ft³/lb Vapor	Enthalpy, Btu/lb Liquid	Enthalpy, Btu/lb Vapor	Entropy, Btu/lb·°F Liquid	Entropy, Btu/lb·°F Vapor	Specific Heat c_p, Btu/lb·°F Liquid	Specific Heat c_p, Btu/lb·°F Vapor	c_p/c_v Vapor	Vel. of Sound, ft/s Liquid	Vel. of Sound, ft/s Vapor	Viscosity, lb_m/ft·h Liquid	Viscosity, lb_m/ft·h Vapor	Thermal Cond., Btu/h·ft·°F Liquid	Thermal Cond., Btu/h·ft·°F Vapor	Surface Tension, dyne/cm	Pressure, psia
1	–125.19	–111.30	94.24	43.0887	–26.34	93.96	–0.07002	0.28254	0.3065	0.1568	1.183	3404	484.3	2.112	0.0199	0.0894	0.00385	25.65	1
1.5	–115.58	–101.85	93.28	29.4430	–23.40	95.34	–0.06135	0.27716	0.3063	0.1600	1.182	3300	489.5	1.867	0.0204	0.0874	0.00403	24.66	1.5
2	–108.36	–94.75	92.55	22.4776	–21.18	96.37	–0.05499	0.27346	0.3063	0.1624	1.181	3225	493.3	1.712	0.0208	0.0860	0.00416	23.93	2
2.5	–102.52	–88.99	91.97	18.2333	–19.39	97.21	–0.04994	0.27066	0.3065	0.1644	1.181	3166	496.2	1.601	0.0212	0.0848	0.00427	23.34	2.5
3	–97.57	–84.12	91.47	15.3685	–17.87	97.92	–0.04572	0.26841	0.3068	0.1662	1.181	3117	498.6	1.515	0.0214	0.0839	0.00436	22.84	3
4	–89.43	–76.11	90.64	11.7361	–15.37	99.09	–0.03889	0.26495	0.3074	0.1693	1.181	3037	502.4	1.389	0.0219	0.0823	0.00452	22.02	4
5	–82.81	–69.61	89.97	9.5211	–13.34	100.03	–0.03345	0.26234	0.3081	0.1719	1.182	2974	505.3	1.299	0.0222	0.0810	0.00465	21.36	5
6	–77.20	–64.09	89.40	8.0252	–11.60	100.83	–0.02889	0.26025	0.3087	0.1742	1.182	2921	507.6	1.229	0.0225	0.0799	0.00476	20.81	6
7	–72.30	–59.27	88.89	6.9450	–10.09	101.52	–0.02496	0.25852	0.3094	0.1762	1.183	2875	509.5	1.172	0.0228	0.0789	0.00485	20.32	7
8	–67.94	–54.97	88.44	6.1272	–8.74	102.13	–0.02149	0.25705	0.3100	0.1781	1.184	2835	511.1	1.125	0.0230	0.0781	0.00494	19.90	8
10	–60.38	–47.55	87.66	4.9690	–6.39	103.19	–0.01556	0.25464	0.3112	0.1814	1.186	2765	513.8	1.050	0.0234	0.0766	0.00509	19.16	10
12	–53.96	–41.23	86.98	4.1864	–4.38	104.08	–0.01059	0.25272	0.3123	0.1844	1.188	2707	515.8	0.992	0.0238	0.0754	0.00522	18.54	12
14	–48.34	–35.71	86.39	3.6210	–2.62	104.85	–0.00629	0.25114	0.3133	0.1871	1.189	2656	517.4	0.945	0.0241	0.0743	0.00534	18.00	14
14.7[b]	–46.53	–33.93	86.19	3.4593	–2.06	105.10	–0.00492	0.25065	0.3137	0.1880	1.190	2639	517.9	0.930	0.0241	0.0739	0.00537	17.82	14.7
16	–43.32	–30.78	85.85	3.1928	–1.05	105.54	–0.00249	0.24979	0.3143	0.1896	1.191	2610	518.7	0.906	0.0243	0.0733	0.00544	17.52	16
18	–38.77	–26.31	85.36	2.8570	0.39	106.15	0.00092	0.24863	0.3153	0.1919	1.193	2570	519.8	0.872	0.0246	0.0725	0.00553	17.08	18
20	–34.61	–22.23	84.91	2.5862	1.70	106.71	0.00402	0.24760	0.3162	0.1941	1.195	2532	520.7	0.843	0.0248	0.0717	0.00562	16.69	20
22	–30.76	–18.45	84.50	2.3632	2.92	107.22	0.00687	0.24668	0.3172	0.1961	1.197	2498	521.4	0.817	0.0250	0.0710	0.00570	16.33	22
24	–27.18	–14.93	84.10	2.1761	4.06	107.70	0.00950	0.24586	0.3180	0.1981	1.199	2466	522.0	0.794	0.0252	0.0703	0.00578	15.99	24
26	–23.83	–11.64	83.73	2.0169	5.13	108.14	0.01196	0.24510	0.3189	0.1999	1.201	2436	522.6	0.773	0.0253	0.0697	0.00585	15.68	26
28	–20.66	–8.54	83.38	1.8798	6.15	108.55	0.01426	0.24442	0.3197	0.2017	1.203	2408	523.0	0.754	0.0255	0.0691	0.00592	15.38	28
30	–17.67	–5.60	83.05	1.7603	7.10	108.93	0.01643	0.24378	0.3205	0.2034	1.205	2382	523.4	0.737	0.0257	0.0685	0.00598	15.11	30
32	–14.84	–2.82	82.73	1.6553	8.02	109.30	0.01848	0.24319	0.3213	0.2051	1.207	2356	523.6	0.721	0.0258	0.0680	0.00605	14.84	32
34	–12.13	–0.17	82.43	1.5622	8.89	109.64	0.02042	0.24265	0.3221	0.2067	1.209	2332	523.9	0.706	0.0260	0.0675	0.00610	14.59	34
36	–9.55	2.37	82.14	1.4791	9.72	109.97	0.02227	0.24213	0.3229	0.2083	1.211	2309	524.1	0.692	0.0261	0.0670	0.00616	14.36	36
38	–7.07	4.79	81.85	1.4045	10.53	110.28	0.02404	0.24165	0.3236	0.2098	1.213	2288	524.2	0.679	0.0262	0.0666	0.00622	14.13	38
40	–4.70	7.12	81.58	1.3371	11.30	110.58	0.02573	0.24120	0.3244	0.2113	1.215	2267	524.3	0.667	0.0263	0.0661	0.00627	13.91	40
42	–2.41	9.37	81.32	1.2759	12.04	110.86	0.02735	0.24077	0.3251	0.2127	1.217	2246	524.3	0.656	0.0265	0.0657	0.00632	13.71	42
44	–0.20	11.53	81.06	1.2201	12.76	111.13	0.02891	0.24036	0.3258	0.2141	1.219	2227	524.4	0.645	0.0266	0.0653	0.00637	13.51	44
46	1.93	13.61	80.82	1.1690	13.46	111.39	0.03041	0.23998	0.3265	0.2155	1.221	2208	524.4	0.635	0.0267	0.0649	0.00642	13.31	46
48	3.98	15.63	80.58	1.1220	14.13	111.64	0.03186	0.23961	0.3272	0.2169	1.223	2190	524.3	0.626	0.0268	0.0646	0.00646	13.13	48
50	5.98	17.58	80.34	1.0786	14.79	111.88	0.03326	0.23926	0.3279	0.2182	1.225	2172	524.3	0.617	0.0269	0.0642	0.00651	12.95	50
55	10.71	22.21	79.78	0.9835	16.34	112.44	0.03656	0.23844	0.3296	0.2214	1.230	2130	524.0	0.596	0.0272	0.0633	0.00663	12.53	55
60	15.13	26.53	79.25	0.9037	17.81	112.96	0.03963	0.23771	0.3313	0.2246	1.235	2091	523.6	0.577	0.0274	0.0626	0.00673	12.13	60
65	19.27	30.58	78.75	0.8359	19.19	113.44	0.04250	0.23703	0.3329	0.2276	1.240	2054	523.2	0.560	0.0276	0.0618	0.00684	11.77	65
70	23.18	34.40	78.27	0.7774	20.49	113.88	0.04519	0.23641	0.3346	0.2305	1.245	2019	522.6	0.544	0.0278	0.0611	0.00694	11.43	70
75	26.88	38.02	77.82	0.7264	21.74	114.29	0.04773	0.23584	0.3362	0.2333	1.250	1986	522.0	0.530	0.0280	0.0605	0.00703	11.10	75
80	30.39	41.46	77.38	0.6816	22.92	114.67	0.05014	0.23530	0.3378	0.2361	1.255	1955	521.3	0.517	0.0282	0.0598	0.00712	10.80	80
85	33.75	44.73	76.95	0.6419	24.06	115.03	0.05243	0.23480	0.3393	0.2389	1.260	1925	520.6	0.505	0.0284	0.0593	0.00721	10.51	85
90	36.96	47.87	76.54	0.6064	25.16	115.37	0.05462	0.23432	0.3409	0.2416	1.266	1896	519.8	0.493	0.0286	0.0587	0.00730	10.23	90
95	40.04	50.87	76.15	0.5746	26.21	115.68	0.05671	0.23387	0.3424	0.2442	1.271	1869	519.0	0.483	0.0288	0.0582	0.00739	9.97	95
100	43.00	53.75	75.76	0.5458	27.23	115.98	0.05871	0.23344	0.3440	0.2468	1.276	1842	518.1	0.473	0.0289	0.0576	0.00747	9.72	100
110	48.60	59.21	75.02	0.4959	29.16	116.53	0.06250	0.23265	0.3471	0.2520	1.287	1792	516.3	0.454	0.0293	0.0567	0.00763	9.25	110
120	53.83	64.30	74.32	0.4540	30.99	117.03	0.06602	0.23191	0.3502	0.2570	1.298	1745	514.3	0.438	0.0296	0.0558	0.00780	8.81	120
130	58.75	69.08	73.64	0.4183	32.72	117.47	0.06932	0.23122	0.3533	0.2621	1.310	1700	512.3	0.423	0.0299	0.0549	0.00796	8.41	130
140	63.39	73.59	72.99	0.3875	34.36	117.88	0.07244	0.23058	0.3564	0.2671	1.321	1658	510.2	0.409	0.0302	0.0541	0.00812	8.03	140
150	67.79	77.86	72.37	0.3607	35.94	118.24	0.07538	0.22997	0.3596	0.2721	1.334	1618	508.0	0.396	0.0304	0.0534	0.00828	7.67	150
160	71.98	81.92	71.76	0.3372	37.45	118.57	0.07818	0.22938	0.3628	0.2772	1.346	1580	505.7	0.385	0.0307	0.0527	0.00844	7.33	160
170	75.97	85.79	71.17	0.3163	38.90	118.87	0.08086	0.22882	0.3660	0.2824	1.359	1543	503.4	0.374	0.0310	0.0520	0.00860	7.01	170
180	79.80	89.49	70.59	0.2976	40.30	119.15	0.08341	0.22828	0.3693	0.2876	1.373	1508	501.1	0.364	0.0312	0.0514	0.00876	6.71	180
190	83.47	93.04	70.02	0.2808	41.66	119.39	0.08587	0.22776	0.3727	0.2929	1.387	1474	498.7	0.354	0.0315	0.0507	0.00893	6.42	190
200	87.00	96.45	69.47	0.2656	42.97	119.61	0.08823	0.22725	0.3761	0.2983	1.401	1441	496.3	0.345	0.0317	0.0501	0.00909	6.15	200
220	93.69	102.90	68.40	0.2393	45.49	119.99	0.09271	0.22625	0.3832	0.3095	1.432	1379	491.4	0.328	0.0323	0.0490	0.00942	5.64	220
240	99.94	108.92	67.35	0.2171	47.88	120.29	0.09691	0.22529	0.3907	0.3213	1.466	1320	486.3	0.313	0.0328	0.0480	0.00976	5.17	240
260	105.82	114.56	66.33	0.1982	50.17	120.52	0.10088	0.22434	0.3986	0.3338	1.502	1265	481.2	0.299	0.0333	0.0470	0.01011	4.73	260
280	111.37	119.88	65.33	0.1819	52.36	120.68	0.10464	0.22340	0.4070	0.3473	1.542	1211	475.9	0.287	0.0339	0.0461	0.01048	4.33	280
300	116.64	124.91	64.34	0.1676	54.48	120.78	0.10824	0.22246	0.4161	0.3618	1.586	1160	470.5	0.275	0.0344	0.0452	0.01086	3.96	300
320	121.66	129.69	63.37	0.1550	56.53	120.82	0.11168	0.22152	0.4260	0.3777	1.635	1111	465.1	0.264	0.0350	0.0444	0.01126	3.61	320
340	126.45	134.24	62.39	0.1438	58.53	120.80	0.11500	0.22056	0.4368	0.3951	1.689	1063	459.6	0.253	0.0356	0.0436	0.01169	3.28	340
360	131.03	138.58	61.42	0.1337	60.47	120.73	0.11821	0.21958	0.4487	0.4143	1.750	1017	454.0	0.243	0.0362	0.0428	0.01215	2.97	360
380	135.43	142.73	60.44	0.1246	62.38	120.61	0.12132	0.21857	0.4620	0.4358	1.819	972	448.3	0.234	0.0368	0.0421	0.01264	2.68	380
400	139.66	146.71	59.46	0.1163	64.25	120.42	0.12435	0.21753	0.4769	0.4600	1.897	927	442.6	0.225	0.0375	0.0414	0.01317	2.41	400
450	149.59	155.98	56.92	0.0984	68.84	119.71	0.13167	0.21473	0.5248	0.5373	2.151	819	427.8	0.204	0.0394	0.0398	0.01469	1.79	450
500	158.73	164.41	54.21	0.0835	73.37	118.56	0.13879	0.21152	0.5982	0.6546	2.541	712	412.5	0.184	0.0417	0.0383	0.01661	1.26	500
550	167.22	172.09	51.15	0.0706	78.00	116.83	0.14595	0.20765	0.7284	0.8572	3.217	606	396.5	0.164	0.0447	0.0370	0.01920	0.80	550
600	175.17	179.07	47.39	0.0586	83.04	114.18	0.15363	0.20253	1.0271	1.2973	4.683	498	379.3	0.144	0.0491	0.0363	0.02308	0.42	600
650	182.79	185.22	41.60	0.0457	89.56	109.19	0.16351	0.19401	2.4146	3.0022	10.265	387	358.6	—	—	—	—	0.11	650
673.36[c]	186.94	186.94	31.59	0.0317	99.99	99.99	0.17797	0.17797	—	—	—	—	—	—	—	—	—	0.00	673.36

*Temperatures on ITS-90 scale [b]Bubble and dew points at one standard atmosphere [c]Critical point

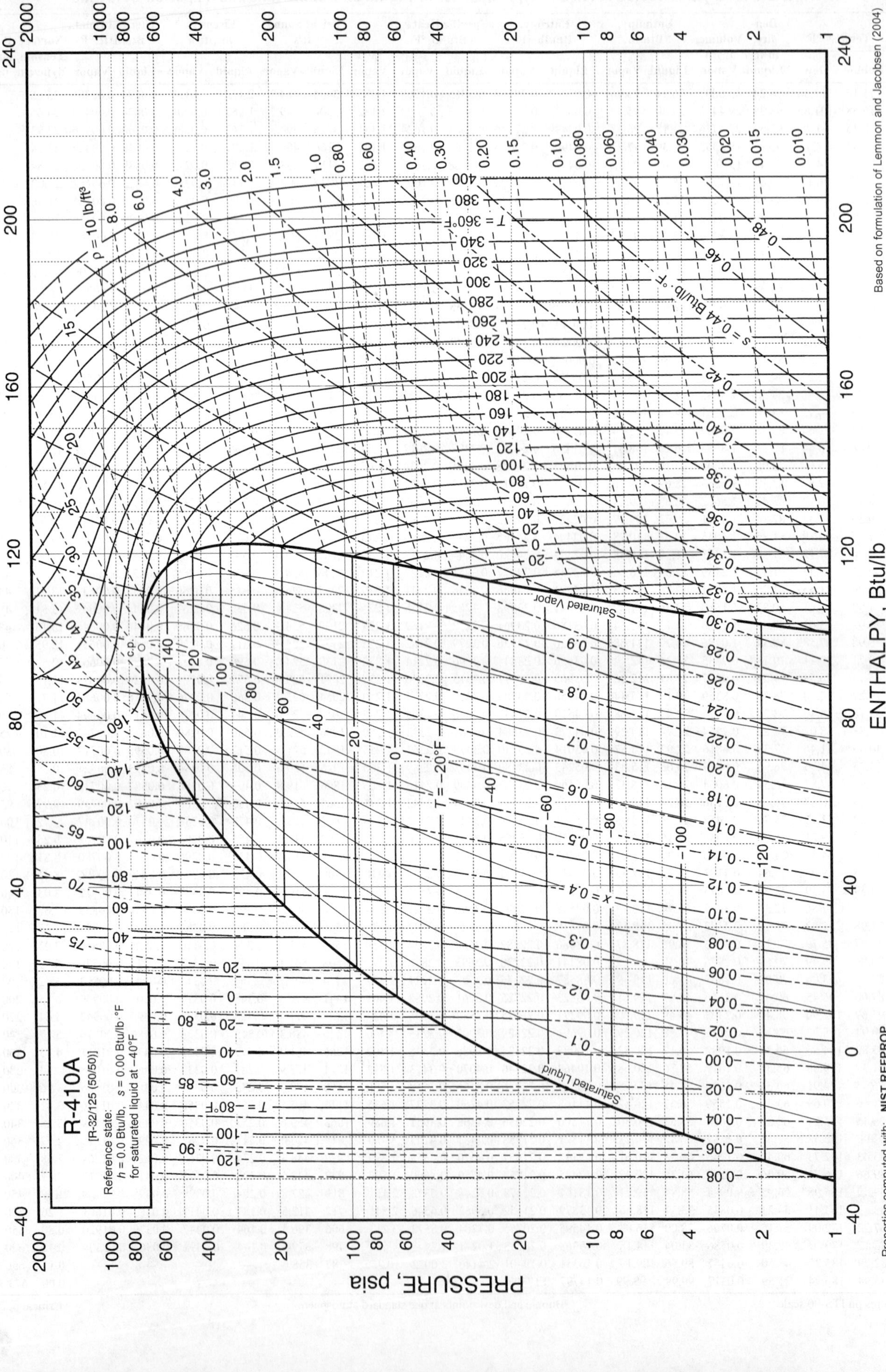

Fig. 17 Pressure-Enthalpy Diagram for Refrigerant 410A

Refrigerant 410A [R-32/125 (50/50)] Properties of Liquid on Bubble Line and Vapor on Dew Line

Pressure, psia	Temp.,* °F		Density, lb/ft³	Volume, ft³/lb	Enthalpy, Btu/lb		Entropy, Btu/lb·°F		Specific Heat c_p, Btu/lb·°F		c_p/c_v	Vel. of Sound, ft/s		Viscosity, lb_m/ft·h		Thermal Cond., Btu/h·ft·°F		Surface Tension, dyne/cm	Pressure, psia
	Bubble	Dew	Liquid	Vapor	Liquid	Vapor	Liquid	Vapor	Liquid	Vapor	Vapor	Liquid	Vapor	Liquid	Vapor	Liquid	Vapor		
1	–135.16	–134.98	92.02	47.6458	–30.90	100.62	–0.08330	0.32188	0.3215	0.1568	1.228	3369	518.6	1.795	0.0196	0.1043	0.00421	25.62	1
1.5	–126.03	–125.87	91.10	32.5774	–27.97	101.90	–0.07439	0.31477	0.3212	0.1600	1.227	3287	524.5	1.605	0.0201	0.1023	0.00431	24.64	1.5
2	–119.18	–119.02	90.41	24.8810	–25.76	102.86	–0.06786	0.30981	0.3213	0.1626	1.227	3226	528.7	1.483	0.0205	0.1008	0.00439	23.91	2
2.5	–113.63	–113.48	89.84	20.1891	–23.98	103.63	–0.06267	0.30602	0.3214	0.1648	1.228	3176	531.9	1.394	0.0208	0.0996	0.00446	23.32	2.5
3	–108.94	–108.78	89.36	17.0211	–22.47	104.27	–0.05834	0.30296	0.3216	0.1668	1.228	3135	534.6	1.325	0.0211	0.0985	0.00451	22.82	3
4	–101.22	–101.07	88.57	13.0027	–19.98	105.33	–0.05133	0.29820	0.3221	0.1703	1.229	3066	538.8	1.222	0.0216	0.0968	0.00461	22.01	4
5	–94.94	–94.80	87.92	10.5514	–17.96	106.18	–0.04574	0.29455	0.3226	0.1733	1.230	3010	542.0	1.148	0.0219	0.0954	0.00469	21.35	5
6	–89.63	–89.48	87.36	8.8953	–16.24	106.89	–0.04107	0.29162	0.3231	0.1760	1.232	2963	544.6	1.090	0.0223	0.0942	0.00476	20.80	6
7	–84.98	–84.84	86.87	7.6992	–14.74	107.50	–0.03704	0.28916	0.3236	0.1785	1.233	2922	546.7	1.043	0.0225	0.0931	0.00482	20.32	7
8	–80.85	–80.71	86.44	6.7935	–13.40	108.05	–0.03349	0.28705	0.3241	0.1807	1.234	2885	548.5	1.003	0.0228	0.0922	0.00488	19.90	8
10	–73.70	–73.56	85.67	5.5105	–11.08	108.97	–0.02743	0.28356	0.3251	0.1848	1.237	2821	551.5	0.940	0.0232	0.0905	0.00498	19.16	10
12	–67.62	–67.48	85.02	4.6434	–9.10	109.75	–0.02235	0.28075	0.3261	0.1884	1.240	2767	553.8	0.891	0.0235	0.0891	0.00507	18.55	12
14	–62.31	–62.16	84.44	4.0168	–7.36	110.42	–0.01795	0.27840	0.3270	0.1917	1.243	2720	555.6	0.850	0.0238	0.0879	0.00515	18.01	14
14.70[b]	–60.60	–60.46	84.26	3.8375	–6.80	110.63	–0.01655	0.27766	0.3274	0.1928	1.244	2704	556.2	0.838	0.0239	0.0875	0.00517	17.84	14.7
16	–57.56	–57.42	83.93	3.5423	–5.80	111.01	–0.01407	0.27638	0.3279	0.1947	1.245	2677	557.1	0.817	0.0241	0.0868	0.00522	17.53	16
18	–53.27	–53.13	83.45	3.1699	–4.39	111.54	–0.01059	0.27461	0.3288	0.1975	1.248	2639	558.4	0.788	0.0244	0.0858	0.00528	17.10	18
20	–49.34	–49.19	83.02	2.8698	–3.09	112.01	–0.00743	0.27305	0.3297	0.2002	1.251	2603	559.4	0.763	0.0246	0.0849	0.00535	16.71	20
22	–45.70	–45.56	82.61	2.6225	–1.89	112.45	–0.00452	0.27164	0.3305	0.2027	1.254	2571	560.3	0.740	0.0248	0.0841	0.00540	16.35	22
24	–42.32	–42.18	82.23	2.4151	–0.77	112.85	–0.00184	0.27036	0.3313	0.2050	1.256	2540	561.1	0.720	0.0250	0.0833	0.00546	16.02	24
26	–39.15	–39.01	81.87	2.2386	0.28	113.22	0.00067	0.26919	0.3321	0.2073	1.259	2512	561.7	0.702	0.0252	0.0826	0.00551	15.71	26
28	–36.17	–36.02	81.54	2.0865	1.27	113.56	0.00301	0.26811	0.3329	0.2094	1.261	2485	562.3	0.686	0.0254	0.0819	0.00556	15.42	28
30	–33.35	–33.20	81.21	1.9540	2.22	113.88	0.00522	0.26711	0.3337	0.2115	1.264	2459	562.7	0.671	0.0255	0.0813	0.00561	15.14	30
32	–30.68	–30.53	80.90	1.8375	3.11	114.19	0.00730	0.26617	0.3345	0.2135	1.267	2435	563.1	0.657	0.0257	0.0806	0.00565	14.88	32
34	–28.13	–27.98	80.61	1.7343	3.97	114.47	0.00928	0.26530	0.3352	0.2154	1.269	2412	563.4	0.644	0.0258	0.0801	0.00570	14.63	34
36	–25.69	–25.54	80.33	1.6422	4.79	114.74	0.01116	0.26448	0.3360	0.2173	1.272	2390	563.7	0.632	0.0260	0.0795	0.00574	14.40	36
38	–23.36	–23.20	80.05	1.5594	5.57	115.00	0.01296	0.26371	0.3367	0.2191	1.274	2368	563.9	0.621	0.0261	0.0790	0.00578	14.17	38
40	–21.12	–20.96	79.79	1.4847	6.33	115.24	0.01467	0.26297	0.3374	0.2208	1.277	2348	564.1	0.610	0.0262	0.0785	0.00582	13.96	40
42	–18.96	–18.81	79.54	1.4168	7.06	115.47	0.01632	0.26228	0.3382	0.2226	1.279	2328	564.3	0.600	0.0264	0.0780	0.00586	13.75	42
44	–16.89	–16.73	79.29	1.3549	7.76	115.69	0.01791	0.26162	0.3389	0.2242	1.282	2309	564.4	0.591	0.0265	0.0775	0.00589	13.55	44
46	–14.88	–14.73	79.05	1.2982	8.45	115.90	0.01943	0.26098	0.3396	0.2259	1.284	2291	564.4	0.582	0.0266	0.0771	0.00593	13.36	46
48	–12.94	–12.79	78.82	1.2460	9.11	116.10	0.02090	0.26038	0.3403	0.2275	1.287	2273	564.5	0.574	0.0267	0.0766	0.00597	13.18	48
50	–11.07	–10.91	78.59	1.1979	9.75	116.30	0.02232	0.25980	0.3410	0.2290	1.289	2256	564.5	0.566	0.0268	0.0762	0.00600	13.00	50
55	–6.62	–6.45	78.05	1.0925	11.27	116.75	0.02568	0.25845	0.3427	0.2328	1.295	2215	564.4	0.547	0.0271	0.0752	0.00610	12.58	55
60	–2.46	–2.30	77.54	1.0040	12.70	117.16	0.02880	0.25722	0.3445	0.2365	1.301	2176	564.2	0.530	0.0273	0.0743	0.00619	12.20	60
65	1.43	1.60	77.06	0.9287	14.05	117.53	0.03171	0.25610	0.3462	0.2400	1.308	2140	563.9	0.515	0.0275	0.0734	0.00628	11.83	65
70	5.10	5.27	76.60	0.8638	15.33	117.88	0.03444	0.25505	0.3478	0.2434	1.314	2105	563.5	0.502	0.0278	0.0726	0.00636	11.49	70
75	8.58	8.75	76.15	0.8073	16.54	118.20	0.03702	0.25408	0.3495	0.2467	1.320	2073	563.0	0.489	0.0280	0.0719	0.00645	11.17	75
80	11.88	12.06	75.73	0.7576	17.70	118.49	0.03946	0.25316	0.3512	0.2499	1.326	2042	562.4	0.477	0.0282	0.0711	0.00653	10.87	80
85	15.03	15.21	75.32	0.7135	18.81	118.77	0.04178	0.25231	0.3528	0.2531	1.333	2012	561.8	0.467	0.0284	0.0704	0.00661	10.59	85
90	18.05	18.22	74.93	0.6742	19.88	119.02	0.04400	0.25149	0.3545	0.2562	1.339	1983	561.2	0.457	0.0285	0.0698	0.00669	10.31	90
95	20.93	21.11	74.54	0.6389	20.91	119.26	0.04611	0.25072	0.3561	0.2592	1.345	1956	560.4	0.447	0.0287	0.0692	0.00677	10.05	95
100	23.71	23.89	74.17	0.6070	21.90	119.48	0.04815	0.24999	0.3578	0.2622	1.352	1929	559.7	0.438	0.0289	0.0685	0.00684	9.80	100
110	28.96	29.14	73.46	0.5515	23.79	119.89	0.05198	0.24862	0.3611	0.2681	1.365	1879	558.1	0.422	0.0292	0.0674	0.00700	9.34	110
120	33.86	34.05	72.78	0.5051	25.57	120.24	0.05555	0.24736	0.3644	0.2738	1.378	1832	556.3	0.407	0.0295	0.0664	0.00715	8.91	120
130	38.46	38.65	72.13	0.4655	27.25	120.56	0.05890	0.24618	0.3678	0.2795	1.392	1787	554.5	0.394	0.0298	0.0654	0.00730	8.50	130
140	42.80	42.99	71.51	0.4314	28.85	120.83	0.06205	0.24508	0.3712	0.2852	1.406	1744	552.6	0.381	0.0301	0.0645	0.00745	8.13	140
150	46.91	47.11	70.90	0.4016	30.38	121.08	0.06503	0.24403	0.3746	0.2908	1.420	1704	550.6	0.370	0.0304	0.0636	0.00760	7.78	150
160	50.82	51.02	70.32	0.3755	31.85	121.29	0.06787	0.24304	0.3781	0.2965	1.435	1666	548.6	0.360	0.0306	0.0628	0.00775	7.44	160
170	54.56	54.76	69.75	0.3523	33.27	121.48	0.07057	0.24210	0.3816	0.3022	1.451	1629	546.5	0.350	0.0309	0.0620	0.00791	7.13	170
180	58.13	58.33	69.20	0.3316	34.63	121.65	0.07316	0.24119	0.3851	0.3080	1.467	1593	544.4	0.341	0.0311	0.0612	0.00807	6.83	180
190	61.55	61.76	68.66	0.3130	35.95	121.79	0.07565	0.24031	0.3888	0.3139	1.483	1559	542.2	0.332	0.0314	0.0605	0.00823	6.55	190
200	64.84	65.05	68.13	0.2962	37.22	121.91	0.07804	0.23946	0.3925	0.3200	1.500	1526	540.0	0.324	0.0317	0.0598	0.00839	6.28	200
220	71.07	71.28	67.10	0.2669	39.67	122.09	0.08258	0.23783	0.4001	0.3325	1.537	1462	535.6	0.309	0.0321	0.0585	0.00873	5.77	220
240	76.89	77.10	66.11	0.2424	41.99	122.20	0.08683	0.23628	0.4081	0.3457	1.576	1403	531.0	0.296	0.0326	0.0573	0.00908	5.31	240
260	82.35	82.57	65.14	0.2215	44.21	122.25	0.09084	0.23478	0.4165	0.3599	1.619	1346	526.3	0.283	0.0330	0.0562	0.00945	4.88	260
280	87.51	87.73	64.19	0.2034	46.34	122.24	0.09464	0.23333	0.4255	0.3751	1.665	1293	521.5	0.272	0.0335	0.0552	0.00983	4.48	280
300	92.40	92.61	63.26	0.1876	48.40	122.18	0.09827	0.23190	0.4350	0.3915	1.716	1241	516.6	0.261	0.0340	0.0542	0.01024	4.11	300
320	97.04	97.26	62.34	0.1736	50.38	122.07	0.10175	0.23049	0.4452	0.4094	1.772	1191	511.6	0.251	0.0345	0.0533	0.01067	3.76	320
340	101.48	101.69	61.42	0.1613	52.31	121.91	0.10509	0.22909	0.4564	0.4290	1.833	1143	506.6	0.242	0.0350	0.0524	0.01113	3.44	340
360	105.71	105.93	60.52	0.1501	54.19	121.70	0.10832	0.22769	0.4685	0.4507	1.901	1097	501.4	0.233	0.0355	0.0515	0.01162	3.13	360
380	109.78	109.99	59.61	0.1401	56.03	121.44	0.11145	0.22629	0.4820	0.4747	1.977	1051	496.2	0.225	0.0361	0.0507	0.01214	2.85	380
400	113.68	113.89	58.70	0.1310	57.83	121.13	0.11450	0.22488	0.4971	0.5016	2.063	1007	490.9	0.217	0.0366	0.0499	0.01271	2.58	400
450	122.82	123.01	56.39	0.1114	62.23	120.14	0.12182	0.22124	0.5443	0.5857	2.333	900	477.2	0.198	0.0381	0.0481	0.01433	1.96	450
500	131.19	131.38	53.97	0.0952	66.54	118.80	0.12888	0.21732	0.6143	0.7083	2.728	795	462.8	0.181	0.0399	0.0465	0.01636	1.44	500
550	138.93	139.09	51.32	0.0814	70.89	117.02	0.13590	0.21295	0.7303	0.9059	3.367	692	447.5	0.164	0.0421	0.0451	0.01902	0.98	550
600	146.12	146.25	48.24	0.0690	75.47	114.59	0.14320	0.20777	0.9603	1.2829	4.579	588	431.0	0.147	0.0450	0.0440	0.02275	0.59	600
692.78[c]	158.40	158.40	34.18	0.0293	90.97	90.97	0.16781	0.16781	—	—	—	—	—	—	—	—	—	0.00	692.78

*Temperatures on ITS-90 scale [b]Bubble and dew points at one standard atmosphere [c]Critical point

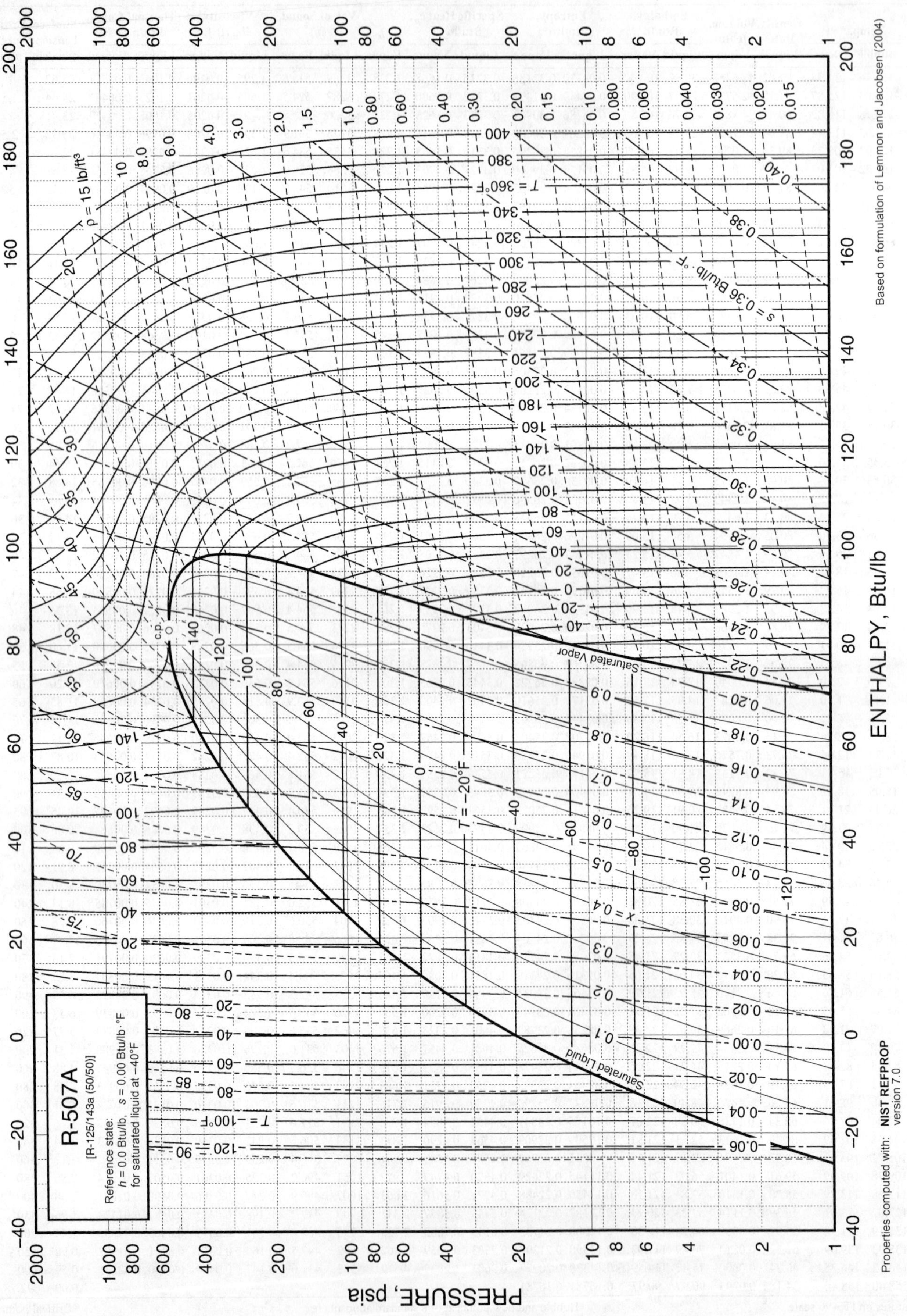

Fig. 18 Pressure-Enthalpy Diagram for Refrigerant 507A

Refrigerant 507A [R-125/143a (50/50)] Properties of Saturated Liquid and Saturated Vapor

Temp.,* °F	Pres-sure,** psia	Density, lb/ft³ Liquid	Volume, ft³/lb Vapor	Enthalpy, Btu/lb Liquid	Enthalpy, Btu/lb Vapor	Entropy, Btu/lb·°F Liquid	Entropy, Btu/lb·°F Vapor	Specific Heat c_p, Btu/lb·°F Liquid	Specific Heat c_p, Btu/lb·°F Vapor	c_p/c_v Vapor	Vel. of Sound, ft/s Liquid	Vel. of Sound, ft/s Vapor	Viscosity, lb_m/ft·h Liquid	Viscosity, lb_m/ft·h Vapor	Thermal Cond., Btu/h·ft·°F Liquid	Thermal Cond., Btu/h·ft·°F Vapor	Surface Tension, dyne/cm	Temp.,* °F
–150	0.386	92.41	86.952	–32.027	67.009	–0.08831	0.23154	0.2919	0.1470	1.1650	3468	424.1	—	—	0.0724	0.00330	18.45	–150
–145	0.497	91.88	68.522	–30.571	67.711	–0.08365	0.22872	0.2904	0.1487	1.1637	3379	427.0	2.053	—	0.0715	0.00339	18.20	–145
–140	0.634	91.36	54.501	–29.121	68.416	–0.07908	0.22607	0.2893	0.1504	1.1626	3298	429.8	1.922	0.0176	0.0705	0.00349	17.94	–140
–135	0.801	90.84	43.729	–27.677	69.126	–0.07460	0.22358	0.2885	0.1522	1.1616	3222	432.5	1.804	0.0179	0.0696	0.00358	17.67	–135
–130	1.004	90.32	35.377	–26.235	69.838	–0.07019	0.22125	0.2879	0.1540	1.1607	3151	435.2	1.697	0.0181	0.0687	0.00368	17.41	–130
–125	1.249	89.80	28.844	–24.796	70.554	–0.06586	0.21906	0.2876	0.1558	1.1599	3084	437.8	1.600	0.0184	0.0678	0.00378	17.14	–125
–120	1.541	89.29	23.692	–23.359	71.272	–0.06160	0.21701	0.2874	0.1576	1.1593	3021	440.3	1.512	0.0186	0.0670	0.00388	16.87	–120
–115	1.887	88.77	19.596	–21.921	71.993	–0.05740	0.21509	0.2874	0.1595	1.1588	2961	442.7	1.431	0.0189	0.0661	0.00398	16.59	–115
–110	2.295	88.26	16.315	–20.484	72.716	–0.05326	0.21328	0.2875	0.1614	1.1584	2904	445.1	1.356	0.0192	0.0652	0.00408	16.31	–110
–105	2.773	87.75	13.669	–19.045	73.440	–0.04918	0.21159	0.2878	0.1633	1.1581	2848	447.4	1.288	0.0194	0.0644	0.00418	16.03	–105
–100	3.329	87.23	11.521	–17.604	74.166	–0.04515	0.21001	0.2882	0.1652	1.1580	2795	449.6	1.225	0.0197	0.0636	0.00429	15.75	–100
–95	3.974	86.72	9.7644	–16.161	74.892	–0.04117	0.20852	0.2887	0.1672	1.1581	2743	451.7	1.166	0.0199	0.0627	0.00439	15.46	–95
–90	4.715	86.20	8.3201	–14.716	75.619	–0.03723	0.20713	0.2893	0.1692	1.1583	2692	453.7	1.112	0.0202	0.0619	0.00450	15.17	–90
–85	5.566	85.68	7.1254	–13.266	76.346	–0.03335	0.20583	0.2900	0.1712	1.1586	2643	455.6	1.061	0.0205	0.0611	0.00461	14.88	–85
–80	6.535	85.16	6.1316	–11.813	77.073	–0.02950	0.20462	0.2908	0.1733	1.1592	2595	457.4	1.014	0.0207	0.0603	0.00471	14.58	–80
–75	7.636	84.64	5.3004	–10.356	77.800	–0.02569	0.20348	0.2917	0.1754	1.1599	2547	459.0	0.969	0.0210	0.0595	0.00482	14.28	–75
–70	8.879	84.11	4.6018	–8.894	78.525	–0.02192	0.20242	0.2926	0.1776	1.1607	2501	460.6	0.928	0.0212	0.0587	0.00493	13.98	–70
–65	10.280	83.58	4.0116	–7.427	79.248	–0.01819	0.20143	0.2937	0.1798	1.1618	2454	462.1	0.889	0.0215	0.0579	0.00504	13.68	–65
–60	11.849	83.05	3.5108	–5.954	79.970	–0.01449	0.20050	0.2948	0.1821	1.1631	2409	463.4	0.852	0.0217	0.0572	0.00516	13.37	–60
–55	13.603	82.51	3.0839	–4.475	80.690	–0.01082	0.19963	0.2960	0.1844	1.1646	2364	464.6	0.818	0.0220	0.0564	0.00527	13.06	–55
–52.13[b]	14.696	82.20	2.8676	–3.625	81.101	–0.00873	0.19916	0.2967	0.1858	1.1655	2338	465.2	0.799	0.0221	0.0560	0.00534	12.88	–52.13
–50	15.554	81.97	2.7184	–2.990	81.406	–0.00719	0.19882	0.2972	0.1868	1.1663	2319	465.6	0.785	0.0222	0.0557	0.00538	12.75	–50
–45	17.719	81.43	2.4043	–1.499	82.119	–0.00358	0.19807	0.2985	0.1893	1.1682	2275	466.6	0.754	0.0225	0.0549	0.00550	12.43	–45
–40	20.112	80.88	2.1331	0.000	82.829	0.00000	0.19737	0.30000	0.1918	1.1704	2231	467.4	0.725	0.0227	0.0542	0.00562	12.12	–40
–35	22.750	80.33	1.8983	1.506	83.534	0.00355	0.19671	0.3014	0.1944	1.1728	2187	468.0	0.697	0.0230	0.0534	0.00574	11.80	–35
–30	25.649	79.77	1.6941	3.020	84.235	0.00708	0.19610	0.3030	0.1971	1.1755	2143	468.5	0.671	0.0232	0.0527	0.00585	11.48	–30
–25	28.827	79.20	1.5160	4.541	84.931	0.01058	0.19553	0.3046	0.1998	1.1785	2100	468.8	0.646	0.0235	0.0520	0.00598	11.15	–25
–20	32.300	78.63	1.3601	6.071	85.621	0.01407	0.19500	0.3063	0.2026	1.1818	2056	469.0	0.622	0.0238	0.0512	0.00610	10.83	–20
–15	36.086	78.05	1.2231	7.610	86.304	0.01753	0.19450	0.3081	0.2056	1.1854	2013	469.0	0.599	0.0240	0.0505	0.00622	10.50	–15
–10	40.203	77.46	1.1025	9.158	86.981	0.02097	0.19404	0.3100	0.2086	1.1894	1970	468.9	0.578	0.0243	0.0498	0.00635	10.17	–10
–5	44.671	76.87	0.9960	10.716	87.651	0.02439	0.19360	0.3119	0.2117	1.1938	1926	468.5	0.557	0.0245	0.0491	0.00647	9.84	–5
0	49.508	76.27	0.9016	12.284	88.313	0.02779	0.19319	0.3140	0.2149	1.1986	1883	468.0	0.537	0.0248	0.0484	0.00660	9.51	0
5	54.733	75.66	0.8177	13.862	88.966	0.03118	0.19281	0.3161	0.2183	1.2038	1840	467.3	0.518	0.0250	0.0477	0.00673	9.18	5
10	60.367	75.04	0.7430	15.452	89.610	0.03455	0.19245	0.3184	0.2218	1.2095	1797	466.4	0.499	0.0253	0.0470	0.00687	8.85	10
15	66.429	74.41	0.6763	17.052	90.245	0.03791	0.19211	0.3208	0.2254	1.2157	1753	465.3	0.482	0.0256	0.0463	0.00700	8.51	15
20	72.941	73.77	0.6165	18.665	90.868	0.04126	0.19179	0.3233	0.2291	1.2226	1710	464.0	0.464	0.0258	0.0457	0.00714	8.18	20
25	79.923	73.12	0.5629	20.290	91.480	0.04459	0.19148	0.3260	0.2330	1.2301	1666	462.5	0.448	0.0261	0.0450	0.00728	7.84	25
30	87.396	72.45	0.5146	21.929	92.079	0.04791	0.19118	0.3288	0.2371	1.2384	1623	460.8	0.432	0.0264	0.0443	0.00743	7.51	30
35	95.384	71.78	0.4711	23.581	92.664	0.05123	0.19089	0.3318	0.2414	1.2476	1579	458.8	0.417	0.0267	0.0436	0.00759	7.17	35
40	103.91	71.09	0.4318	25.249	93.234	0.05454	0.19061	0.3350	0.2460	1.2577	1535	456.6	0.402	0.0270	0.0430	0.00775	6.84	40
45	112.99	70.38	0.3962	26.931	93.788	0.05784	0.19032	0.3384	0.2508	1.2690	1491	454.2	0.388	0.0273	0.0423	0.00792	6.50	45
50	122.65	69.66	0.3638	28.630	94.324	0.06114	0.19004	0.3421	0.2560	1.2816	1447	451.6	0.374	0.0276	0.0416	0.00810	6.17	50
55	132.92	68.92	0.3344	30.346	94.840	0.06444	0.18976	0.3460	0.2616	1.2956	1403	448.7	0.360	0.0280	0.0410	0.00829	5.83	55
60	143.82	68.16	0.3076	32.080	95.336	0.06773	0.18946	0.3503	0.2676	1.3113	1358	445.5	0.347	0.0283	0.0403	0.00849	5.50	60
65	155.38	67.39	0.2832	33.834	95.808	0.07103	0.18916	0.3549	0.2742	1.3289	1313	442.0	0.334	0.0287	0.0397	0.00871	5.17	65
70	167.62	66.58	0.2608	35.609	96.255	0.07434	0.18884	0.3599	0.2814	1.3488	1268	438.3	0.322	0.0291	0.0390	0.00893	4.84	70
75	180.56	65.76	0.2403	37.406	96.675	0.07764	0.18850	0.3654	0.2894	1.3713	1222	434.3	0.310	0.0295	0.0384	0.00918	4.52	75
80	194.24	64.90	0.2214	39.228	97.065	0.08096	0.18814	0.3715	0.2983	1.3970	1176	430.0	0.298	0.0300	0.0377	0.00943	4.19	80
85	208.68	64.02	0.2041	41.076	97.421	0.08429	0.18775	0.3783	0.3083	1.4265	1130	425.3	0.286	0.0304	0.0371	0.00971	3.87	85
90	223.92	63.10	0.1880	42.952	97.740	0.08764	0.18732	0.3858	0.3196	1.4606	1083	420.3	0.275	0.0309	0.0364	0.01002	3.55	90
95	239.97	62.14	0.1732	44.860	98.019	0.09101	0.18686	0.3944	0.3325	1.5003	1035	414.9	0.264	0.0315	0.0358	0.01035	3.24	95
100	256.88	61.14	0.1595	46.803	98.251	0.09441	0.18634	0.4043	0.3475	1.5471	987	409.2	0.253	0.0321	0.0351	0.01071	2.93	100
105	274.68	60.09	0.1468	48.784	98.431	0.09784	0.18576	0.4157	0.3650	1.6029	938	403.1	0.242	0.0327	0.0344	0.01112	2.62	105
110	293.40	58.99	0.1349	50.809	98.551	0.10130	0.18511	0.4291	0.3858	1.6706	888	396.5	0.231	0.0334	0.0338	0.01158	2.32	110
115	313.08	57.82	0.1238	52.885	98.600	0.10482	0.18438	0.4453	0.4112	1.7541	838	389.5	0.220	0.0343	0.0331	0.01210	2.03	115
120	333.77	56.57	0.1134	55.018	98.568	0.10840	0.18354	0.4652	0.4427	1.8597	786	382.0	0.209	0.0352	0.0325	0.01270	1.74	120
125	355.50	55.22	0.1036	57.221	98.435	0.11206	0.18256	0.4904	0.4833	1.9972	732	373.9	0.198	0.0362	0.0318	0.01341	1.47	125
130	378.33	53.76	0.0943	59.509	98.177	0.11583	0.18141	0.5237	0.5375	2.1831	677	365.3	0.187	0.0375	0.0311	0.01425	1.20	130
135	402.31	52.15	0.0855	61.903	97.759	0.11973	0.18003	0.5700	0.6142	2.4480	620	356.1	0.176	0.0389	0.0305	0.01530	0.94	135
140	427.52	50.32	0.0769	64.439	97.125	0.12382	0.17833	0.6399	0.7313	2.8546	560	346.1	0.164	0.0408	0.0299	0.01664	0.70	140
145	454.04	48.19	0.0684	67.182	96.173	0.12821	0.17616	0.7590	0.9326	3.5556	497	335.3	0.151	0.0432	0.0294	0.01846	0.48	145
150	481.99	45.55	0.0597	70.265	94.697	0.13311	0.17318	1.0130	1.3606	5.0420	429	323.4	0.137	0.0466	0.0293	0.02122	0.27	150
155	511.55	41.76	0.0499	74.107	92.081	0.13918	0.16842	1.9550	2.8693	10.2379	353	309.4	0.119	0.0524	0.0305	0.02681	0.10	155
159.12[c]	537.40	30.64	0.0326	83.010	83.010	0.15339	0.15339	∞	∞	∞	0	0.0	—	—	∞	∞	0.00	159.12

*Temperatures on ITS-90 scale

**Small deviations from azeotropic behavior occur at some conditions; tabulated pressures are average of bubble and dew-point pressures

[b]Normal boiling point

[c]Critical point

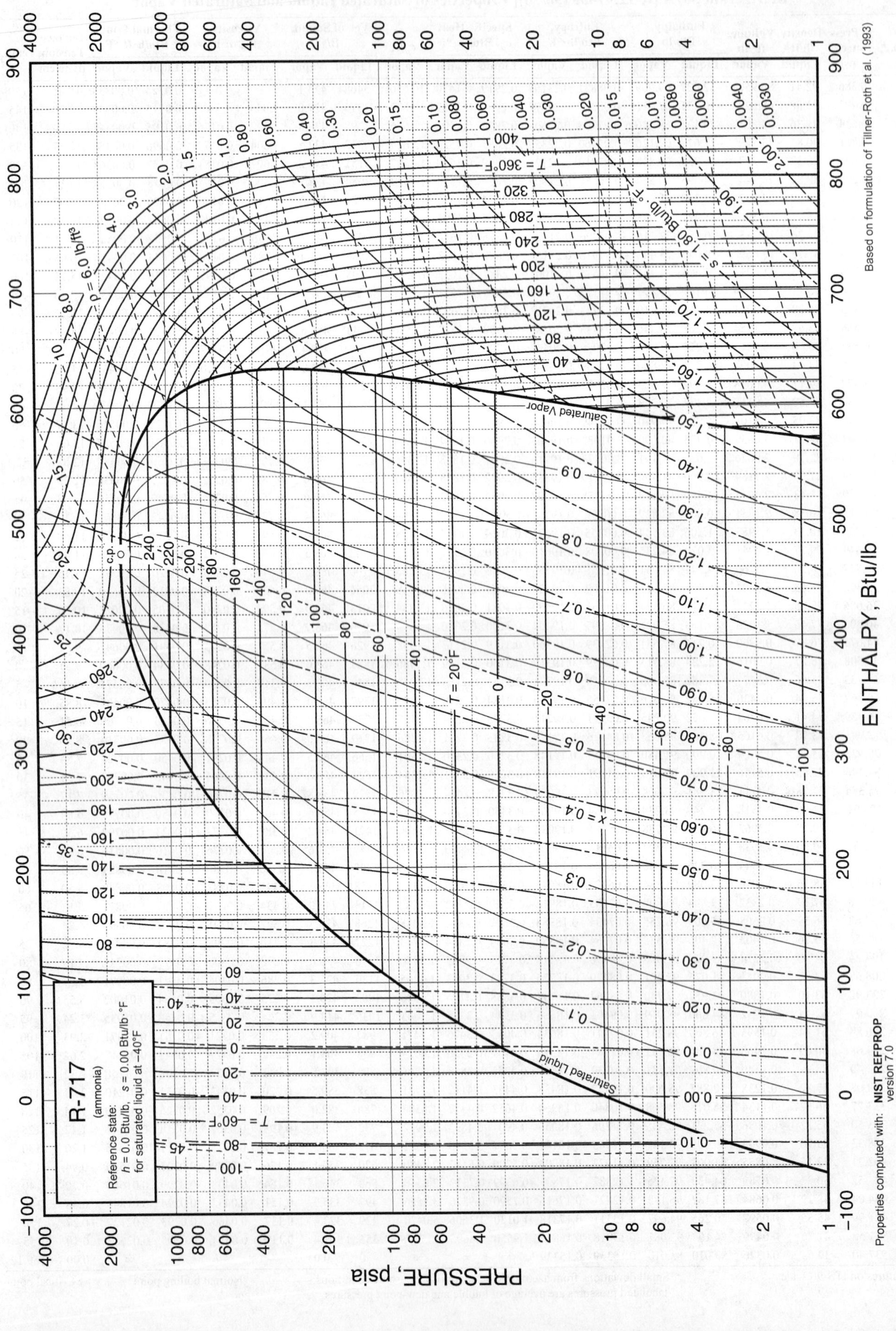

Fig. 19 Pressure-Enthalpy Diagram for Refrigerant 717 (Ammonia)

Refrigerant 717 (Ammonia) Properties of Saturated Liquid and Saturated Vapor

Temp.,* °F	Pressure, psia	Density, lb/ft³ Liquid	Volume, ft³/lb Vapor	Enthalpy, Btu/lb Liquid	Enthalpy, Btu/lb Vapor	Entropy, Btu/lb·°F Liquid	Entropy, Btu/lb·°F Vapor	Specific Heat c_p, Btu/lb·°F Liquid	Specific Heat c_p, Btu/lb·°F Vapor	c_p/c_v Vapor	Vel. of Sound, ft/s Liquid	Vel. of Sound, ft/s Vapor	Viscosity, lb_m/ft·h Liquid	Viscosity, lb_m/ft·h Vapor	Thermal Cond., Btu/h·ft·°F Liquid	Thermal Cond., Btu/h·ft·°F Vapor	Surface Tension, dyne/cm	Temp.,* °F
–107.78[a]	0.883	45.75	249.92	–69.830	568.765	–0.18124	1.63351	1.0044	0.4930	1.3252	6969	1161.8	1.354	0.0165	0.4735	0.01135	62.26	–107.78
–100	1.237	45.47	182.19	–61.994	572.260	–0.15922	1.60421	1.0100	0.4959	1.3262	6830	1173.8	1.232	0.0168	0.4647	0.01138	60.47	–100
–90	1.864	45.09	124.12	–51.854	576.688	–0.13142	1.56886	1.0176	0.5003	1.3278	6666	1188.6	1.099	0.0171	0.4534	0.01143	58.19	–90
–80	2.739	44.71	86.546	–41.637	581.035	–0.10416	1.53587	1.0254	0.5056	1.3296	6513	1202.9	0.986	0.0175	0.4422	0.01149	55.94	–80
–70	3.937	44.31	61.647	–31.341	585.288	–0.07741	1.50503	1.0331	0.5118	1.3319	6367	1216.7	0.891	0.0179	0.4310	0.01158	53.73	–70
–60	5.544	43.91	44.774	–20.969	589.439	–0.05114	1.47614	1.0406	0.5190	1.3346	6228	1229.7	0.810	0.0182	0.4198	0.01168	51.54	–60
–50	7.659	43.50	33.105	–10.521	593.476	–0.02534	1.44900	1.0478	0.5271	1.3379	6092	1242.2	0.741	0.0186	0.4088	0.01180	49.39	–50
–40	10.398	43.08	24.881	0.000	597.387	0.00000	1.42347	1.0549	0.5364	1.3419	5959	1253.9	0.680	0.0190	0.3978	0.01193	47.26	–40
–30	13.890	42.66	18.983	10.592	601.162	0.02491	1.39938	1.0617	0.5467	1.3465	5827	1264.9	0.628	0.0194	0.3870	0.01209	45.17	–30
–27.99[b]	14.696	42.57	18.007	12.732	601.904	0.02987	1.39470	1.0631	0.5490	1.3475	5801	1267.1	0.618	0.0195	0.3849	0.01212	44.75	–27.99
–25	15.962	42.45	16.668	15.914	602.995	0.03720	1.38784	1.0651	0.5524	1.3491	5762	1270.2	0.604	0.0196	0.3817	0.01217	44.14	–25
–20	18.279	42.23	14.684	21.253	604.789	0.04939	1.37660	1.0684	0.5583	1.3520	5697	1275.2	0.582	0.0198	0.3764	0.01226	43.11	–20
–15	20.858	42.01	12.976	26.609	606.544	0.06148	1.36567	1.0716	0.5646	1.3550	5632	1280.0	0.561	0.0200	0.3711	0.01236	42.09	–15
–10	23.723	41.79	11.502	31.982	608.257	0.07347	1.35502	1.0749	0.5711	1.3584	5567	1284.7	0.541	0.0202	0.3658	0.01246	41.08	–10
–5	26.895	41.57	10.226	37.372	609.928	0.08536	1.34463	1.0782	0.5781	1.3619	5503	1289.1	0.522	0.0204	0.3606	0.01256	40.08	–5
0	30.397	41.34	9.1159	42.779	611.554	0.09715	1.33450	1.0814	0.5853	1.3657	5438	1293.3	0.505	0.0206	0.3555	0.01267	39.08	0
5	34.253	41.12	8.1483	48.203	613.135	0.10885	1.32462	1.0847	0.5929	1.3698	5373	1297.3	0.488	0.0208	0.3503	0.01279	38.10	5
10	38.487	40.89	7.3020	53.644	614.669	0.12045	1.31496	1.0880	0.6009	1.3742	5308	1301.1	0.472	0.0210	0.3453	0.01291	37.12	10
15	43.126	40.66	6.5597	59.103	616.154	0.13197	1.30552	1.0914	0.6092	1.3789	5243	1304.7	0.457	0.0212	0.3402	0.01304	36.15	15
20	48.194	40.43	5.9067	64.579	617.590	0.14340	1.29629	1.0948	0.6179	1.3840	5178	1308.0	0.443	0.0214	0.3352	0.01317	35.19	20
25	53.720	40.20	5.3307	70.072	618.974	0.15474	1.28726	1.0983	0.6271	1.3894	5113	1311.1	0.429	0.0216	0.3302	0.01331	34.23	25
30	59.730	39.96	4.8213	75.585	620.305	0.16599	1.27842	1.1019	0.6366	1.3951	5048	1314.0	0.416	0.0218	0.3253	0.01345	33.29	30
35	66.255	39.72	4.3695	81.116	621.582	0.17717	1.26975	1.1056	0.6465	1.4012	4982	1316.6	0.404	0.0220	0.3204	0.01360	32.35	35
40	73.322	39.48	3.9680	86.666	622.803	0.18827	1.26125	1.1094	0.6569	1.4078	4916	1319.0	0.392	0.0222	0.3155	0.01376	31.42	40
45	80.962	39.24	3.6102	92.237	623.967	0.19929	1.25291	1.1134	0.6678	1.4147	4850	1321.1	0.381	0.0224	0.3107	0.01392	30.50	45
50	89.205	38.99	3.2906	97.828	625.072	0.21024	1.24472	1.1175	0.6791	1.4222	4784	1323.0	0.370	0.0227	0.3059	0.01409	29.59	50
55	98.083	38.75	3.0045	103.441	626.115	0.22111	1.23667	1.1218	0.6909	1.4301	4717	1324.6	0.360	0.0229	0.3012	0.01426	28.69	55
60	107.63	38.50	2.7479	109.076	627.097	0.23192	1.22875	1.126	0.703	1.438	4650	1325.9	0.350	0.0231	0.2965	0.01445	27.79	60
65	117.87	38.25	2.5172	114.734	628.013	0.24266	1.22095	1.131	0.716	1.447	4583	1327.0	0.340	0.0233	0.2918	0.01464	26.90	65
70	128.85	37.99	2.3094	120.417	628.864	0.25334	1.21327	1.136	0.730	1.457	4515	1327.8	0.331	0.0235	0.2872	0.01483	26.03	70
75	140.59	37.73	2.1217	126.126	629.647	0.26396	1.20570	1.141	0.744	1.467	4447	1328.3	0.322	0.0237	0.2825	0.01504	25.16	75
80	153.13	37.47	1.9521	131.861	630.359	0.27452	1.19823	1.147	0.758	1.478	4378	1328.6	0.313	0.0239	0.2780	0.01525	24.30	80
85	166.51	37.21	1.7983	137.624	630.999	0.28503	1.19085	1.153	0.774	1.490	4309	1328.5	0.305	0.0241	0.2734	0.01548	23.44	85
90	180.76	36.94	1.6588	143.417	631.564	0.29549	1.18356	1.159	0.790	1.502	4240	1328.2	0.297	0.0244	0.2689	0.01571	22.60	90
95	195.91	36.67	1.5319	149.241	632.052	0.30590	1.17634	1.166	0.807	1.515	4170	1327.5	0.289	0.0246	0.2644	0.01595	21.77	95
100	212.01	36.40	1.4163	155.098	632.460	0.31626	1.16920	1.173	0.824	1.529	4099	1326.6	0.282	0.0248	0.2600	0.01620	20.94	100
105	229.09	36.12	1.3108	160.990	632.785	0.32659	1.16211	1.180	0.843	1.544	4028	1325.3	0.274	0.0250	0.2556	0.01646	20.13	105
110	247.19	35.83	1.2144	166.919	633.025	0.33688	1.15508	1.188	0.862	1.561	3956	1323.7	0.267	0.0253	0.2512	0.01673	19.32	110
115	266.34	35.55	1.1262	172.887	633.175	0.34713	1.14809	1.197	0.883	1.578	3884	1321.8	0.260	0.0255	0.2468	0.01702	18.53	115
120	286.60	35.26	1.0452	178.896	633.232	0.35736	1.14115	1.206	0.905	1.597	3811	1319.5	0.254	0.0257	0.2424	0.01732	17.74	120
125	307.98	34.96	0.9710	184.949	633.193	0.36757	1.13423	1.216	0.928	1.617	3737	1316.9	0.247	0.0260	0.2381	0.01763	16.96	125
130	330.54	34.66	0.9026	191.049	633.053	0.37775	1.12733	1.227	0.952	1.638	3662	1313.9	0.241	0.0262	0.2338	0.01795	16.19	130
135	354.32	34.35	0.8397	197.199	632.807	0.38792	1.12044	1.239	0.978	1.662	3587	1310.6	0.235	0.0265	0.2295	0.01829	15.44	135
140	379.36	34.04	0.7817	203.403	632.451	0.39808	1.11356	1.251	1.006	1.687	3511	1306.9	0.229	0.0267	0.2253	0.01865	14.69	140
145	405.70	33.72	0.7280	209.663	631.978	0.40824	1.10666	1.265	1.035	1.715	3434	1302.8	0.223	0.0270	0.2210	0.01903	13.95	145
150	433.38	33.39	0.6785	215.984	631.383	0.41840	1.09975	1.280	1.067	1.745	3356	1298.3	0.217	0.0273	0.2168	0.01943	13.22	150
155	462.45	33.06	0.6325	222.370	630.659	0.42857	1.09281	1.296	1.101	1.778	3277	1293.4	0.211	0.0276	0.2125	0.01986	12.51	155
160	492.95	32.72	0.5899	228.827	629.798	0.43875	1.08582	1.313	1.138	1.813	3198	1288.1	0.206	0.0279	0.2083	0.02031	11.80	160
165	524.94	32.37	0.5504	235.359	628.791	0.44896	1.07878	1.333	1.178	1.853	3117	1282.4	0.200	0.0282	0.2041	0.02079	11.10	165
170	558.45	32.01	0.5136	241.973	627.630	0.45919	1.07167	1.354	1.222	1.896	3035	1276.2	0.195	0.0285	0.1999	0.02130	10.42	170
175	593.53	31.64	0.4793	248.675	626.302	0.46947	1.06447	1.377	1.270	1.944	2952	1269.6	0.190	0.0288	0.1957	0.02185	9.75	175
180	630.24	31.26	0.4473	255.472	624.797	0.47980	1.05717	1.403	1.322	1.998	2868	1262.4	0.185	0.0292	0.1916	0.02245	9.09	180
185	668.63	30.87	0.4174	262.374	623.100	0.49019	1.04974	1.432	1.381	2.058	2783	1254.8	0.179	0.0296	0.1874	0.02310	8.44	185
190	708.74	30.47	0.3895	269.390	621.195	0.50066	1.04217	1.465	1.446	2.126	2696	1246.7	0.174	0.0300	0.1832	0.02381	7.80	190
195	750.64	30.05	0.3633	276.530	619.064	0.51121	1.03443	1.502	1.519	2.203	2608	1238.0	0.169	0.0304	0.1790	0.02458	7.18	195
200	794.38	29.62	0.3387	283.809	616.686	0.52188	1.02649	1.543	1.602	2.290	2519	1228.7	0.165	0.0309	0.1748	0.02545	6.56	200
205	840.03	29.17	0.3156	291.240	614.035	0.53267	1.01831	1.591	1.697	2.392	2428	1218.9	0.160	0.0314	0.1706	0.02641	5.97	205
210	887.64	28.70	0.2938	298.842	611.081	0.54360	1.00986	1.646	1.806	2.509	2336	1208.4	0.155	0.0320	0.1663	0.02749	5.38	210
215	937.28	28.21	0.2733	306.637	607.788	0.55472	1.00109	1.711	1.935	2.648	2243	1197.2	0.150	0.0326	0.1621	0.02872	4.81	215
220	989.03	27.69	0.2538	314.651	604.112	0.56605	0.99193	1.788	2.088	2.814	2147	1185.4	0.145	0.0333	0.1578	0.03013	4.26	220
225	1042.96	27.15	0.2354	322.918	599.996	0.57763	0.98232	1.882	2.272	3.015	2050	1172.7	0.140	0.0340	0.1536	0.03178	3.72	225
230	1099.14	26.57	0.2178	331.483	595.371	0.58953	0.97216	1.999	2.501	3.265	1950	1159.1	0.136	0.0349	0.1492	0.03372	3.20	230
235	1157.69	25.95	0.2010	340.404	590.142	0.60182	0.96133	2.148	2.790	3.582	1848	1144.5	0.131	0.0359	0.1449	0.03607	2.70	235
240	1218.68	25.28	0.1849	349.766	584.183	0.61462	0.94966	2.346	3.171	4.000	1743	1128.8	0.126	0.0370	0.1406	0.03895	2.22	240
245	1282.24	24.55	0.1693	359.695	577.309	0.62809	0.93690	2.624	3.693	4.575	1634	1111.6	0.120	0.0383	0.1363	0.04261	1.76	245
250	1348.49	23.72	0.1540	370.391	569.240	0.64249	0.92269	3.047	4.460	5.420	1520	1092.6	0.115	0.0399	0.1320	0.04744	1.33	250
260	1489.71	21.60	0.1233	395.943	547.139	0.67662	0.88671	5.273	8.106	9.439	1271	1045.9	0.102	0.0446	0.1250	0.06473	0.55	260
270.05[c]	1643.71	14.05	0.0712	473.253	473.253	0.78093	0.78093	∞	∞	∞	0	0.0	—	—	∞	∞	0.00	270.05

*Temperatures on ITS-90 scale [a]Triple point [b]Normal boiling point [c]Critical point

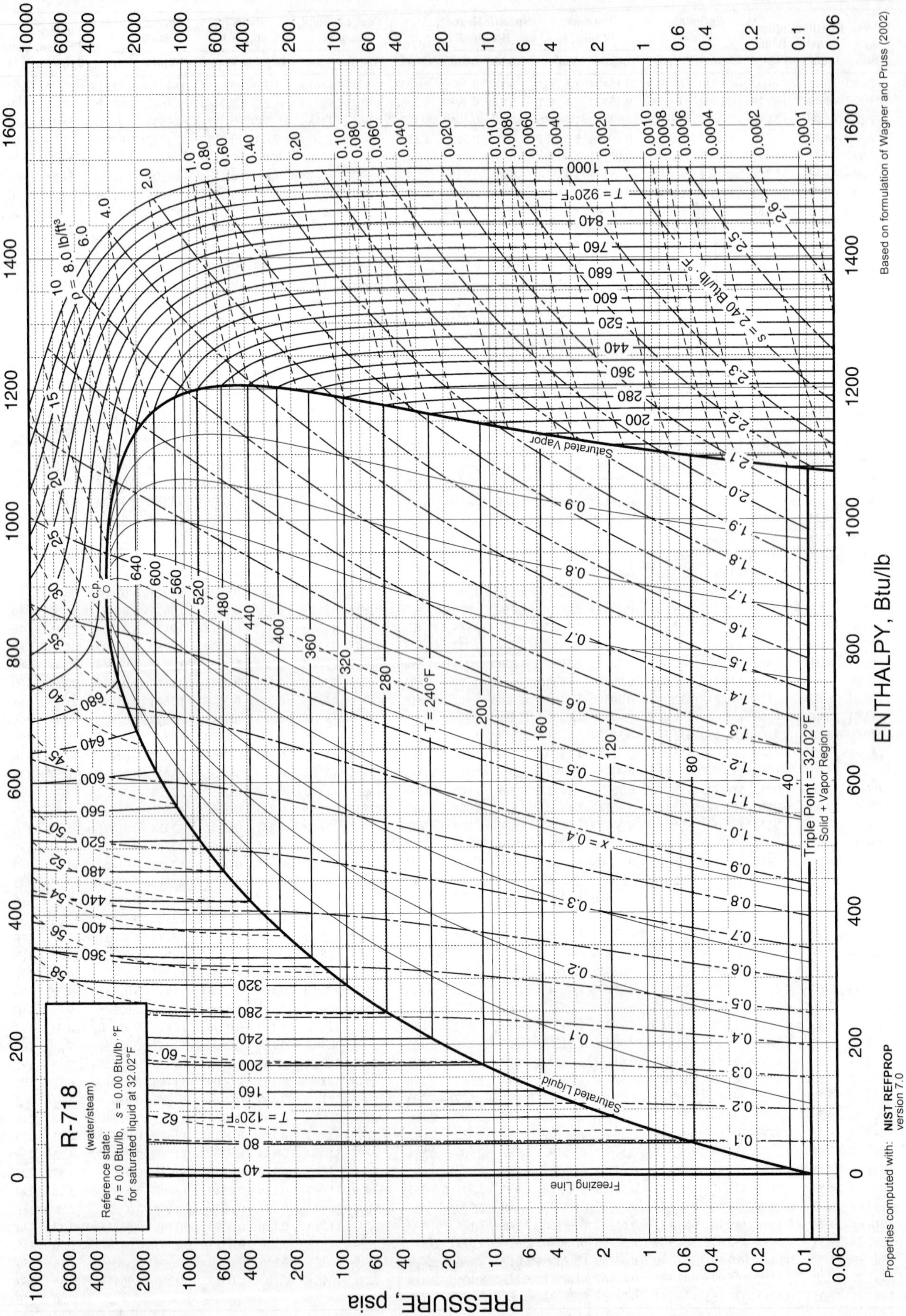

Fig. 20 Pressure-Enthalpy Diagram for Refrigerant 718 (Water/Steam)

Refrigerant 718 (Water/Steam) Properties of Saturated Liquid and Saturated Vapor

Temp.,* °F	Pres-sure, psia	Density, lb/ft³	Volume, ft³/lb	Enthalpy, Btu/lb		Entropy, Btu/lb·°F		Specific Heat c_p, Btu/lb·°F		c_p/c_v	Vel. of Sound, ft/s		Viscosity, lb_m/ft·h		Thermal Cond., Btu/h·ft·°F		Surface Tension, dyne/cm	Temp.,* °F
		Liquid	Vapor	Liquid	Vapor	Liquid	Vapor	Liquid	Vapor	Vapor	Liquid	Vapor	Liquid	Vapor	Liquid	Vapor		
32.02[a]	0.089	62.42	3299.7	0.00	1075.92	0.0000	2.1882	1.0086	0.4504	1.3285	4601	1342	4.333	0.0223	0.3244	0.00987	75.65	32.02
40	0.122	62.42	2443.3	8.04	1079.42	0.0162	2.1604	1.0055	0.4514	1.3282	4670	1352	3.738	0.0226	0.3293	0.01001	75.02	40
50	0.178	62.41	1702.8	18.08	1083.79	0.0361	2.1271	1.0028	0.4528	1.3278	4748	1365	3.159	0.0229	0.3353	0.01019	74.22	50
60	0.256	62.36	1206.0	28.10	1088.15	0.0556	2.0954	1.0010	0.4543	1.3275	4815	1378	2.712	0.0232	0.3413	0.01038	73.40	60
70	0.363	62.30	867.11	38.10	1092.50	0.0746	2.0653	0.9999	0.4558	1.3273	4874	1391	2.359	0.0236	0.3471	0.01058	72.57	70
80	0.507	62.21	632.38	48.10	1096.83	0.0933	2.0366	0.9993	0.4574	1.3272	4924	1403	2.074	0.0240	0.3527	0.01079	71.71	80
90	0.699	62.11	467.40	58.09	1101.15	0.1117	2.0093	0.9990	0.4591	1.3271	4967	1416	1.841	0.0244	0.3579	0.01101	70.84	90
100	0.951	61.99	349.84	68.08	1105.44	0.1297	1.9832	0.9989	0.4609	1.3272	5003	1428	1.648	0.0248	0.3628	0.01124	69.96	100
110	1.277	61.86	264.97	78.07	1109.71	0.1474	1.9583	0.9991	0.4628	1.3273	5033	1440	1.486	0.0252	0.3672	0.01148	69.05	110
120	1.695	61.71	202.95	88.06	1113.95	0.1648	1.9346	0.9993	0.4648	1.3276	5056	1452	1.348	0.0256	0.3713	0.01172	68.13	120
130	2.226	61.55	157.09	98.06	1118.17	0.1819	1.9118	0.9997	0.4671	1.3280	5075	1463	1.230	0.0260	0.3750	0.01198	67.19	130
140	2.893	61.38	122.82	108.06	1122.35	0.1987	1.8901	1.0003	0.4696	1.3285	5088	1475	1.128	0.0265	0.3783	0.01225	66.24	140
150	3.723	61.19	96.930	118.07	1126.49	0.2152	1.8693	1.0009	0.4723	1.3291	5097	1486	1.040	0.0269	0.3813	0.01253	65.27	150
160	4.747	61.00	77.184	128.08	1130.59	0.2315	1.8493	1.0016	0.4753	1.3299	5101	1497	0.962	0.0273	0.3839	0.01282	64.28	160
170	6.000	60.79	61.980	138.11	1134.65	0.2476	1.8302	1.0025	0.4787	1.3309	5101	1508	0.894	0.0278	0.3862	0.01312	63.28	170
180	7.520	60.58	50.169	148.14	1138.65	0.2634	1.8118	1.0035	0.4824	1.3320	5098	1518	0.834	0.0282	0.3881	0.01343	62.26	180
190	9.350	60.35	40.916	158.19	1142.60	0.2789	1.7942	1.0046	0.4865	1.3333	5090	1528	0.780	0.0287	0.3898	0.01375	61.23	190
200	11.538	60.12	33.609	168.24	1146.48	0.2943	1.7772	1.0059	0.4911	1.3348	5080	1538	0.732	0.0291	0.3912	0.01409	60.19	200
210	14.136	59.88	27.794	178.31	1150.30	0.3094	1.7609	1.0073	0.4961	1.3366	5066	1547	0.690	0.0296	0.3924	0.01444	59.13	210
211.95[b]	14.696	59.83	26.802	180.28	1151.04	0.3124	1.7578	1.0076	0.4971	1.3369	5063	1549	0.682	0.0297	0.3926	0.01451	58.92	211.95
220	17.201	59.63	23.133	188.40	1154.05	0.3244	1.7451	1.0088	0.5016	1.3386	5049	1557	0.651	0.0300	0.3934	0.01480	58.05	220
230	20.795	59.37	19.371	198.51	1157.72	0.3391	1.7299	1.0106	0.5077	1.3408	5029	1565	0.616	0.0305	0.3941	0.01517	56.96	230
240	24.986	59.10	16.314	208.63	1161.31	0.3537	1.7153	1.0125	0.5145	1.3434	5007	1574	0.585	0.0310	0.3947	0.01556	55.86	240
250	29.844	58.82	13.815	218.78	1164.81	0.3680	1.7011	1.0147	0.5218	1.3464	4981	1582	0.556	0.0314	0.3951	0.01596	54.74	250
260	35.447	58.53	11.759	228.95	1168.21	0.3823	1.6874	1.0170	0.5299	1.3496	4953	1590	0.530	0.0319	0.3953	0.01638	53.62	260
270	41.878	58.24	10.058	239.14	1171.52	0.3963	1.6741	1.0196	0.5387	1.3533	4923	1597	0.506	0.0324	0.3953	0.01680	52.47	270
280	49.222	57.94	8.6431	249.37	1174.71	0.4102	1.6612	1.0224	0.5483	1.3574	4890	1604	0.484	0.0328	0.3952	0.01725	51.32	280
290	57.574	57.63	7.4600	259.62	1177.79	0.4239	1.6487	1.0254	0.5586	1.3620	4855	1611	0.464	0.0333	0.3949	0.01770	50.16	290
300	67.029	57.31	6.4658	269.91	1180.75	0.4375	1.6365	1.0287	0.5698	1.3671	4817	1617	0.445	0.0338	0.3944	0.01817	48.98	300
310	77.691	56.99	5.6263	280.23	1183.58	0.4510	1.6246	1.0323	0.5818	1.3727	4777	1623	0.428	0.0342	0.3939	0.01866	47.79	310
320	89.667	56.65	4.9142	290.60	1186.28	0.4643	1.6131	1.0362	0.5947	1.3790	4735	1628	0.412	0.0347	0.3931	0.01916	46.59	320
330	103.07	56.31	4.3075	301.00	1188.84	0.4775	1.6018	1.0404	0.6085	1.3858	4691	1633	0.397	0.0351	0.3923	0.01967	45.38	330
340	118.02	55.95	3.7884	311.45	1191.25	0.4906	1.5908	1.0449	0.6231	1.3934	4644	1638	0.383	0.0356	0.3912	0.02020	44.16	340
350	134.63	55.59	3.3425	321.95	1193.51	0.5036	1.5800	1.0497	0.6386	1.4018	4596	1642	0.370	0.0361	0.3901	0.02074	42.93	350
360	153.03	55.22	2.9580	332.50	1195.61	0.5164	1.5694	1.0550	0.6551	1.4109	4546	1645	0.358	0.0365	0.3888	0.02130	41.69	360
370	173.36	54.85	2.6252	343.11	1197.54	0.5292	1.5591	1.0606	0.6725	1.4210	4493	1648	0.347	0.0370	0.3873	0.02187	40.45	370
380	195.74	54.46	2.3361	353.77	1199.29	0.5419	1.5489	1.0666	0.6910	1.4320	4438	1651	0.337	0.0375	0.3857	0.02246	39.19	380
390	220.33	54.06	2.0841	364.50	1200.86	0.5545	1.5388	1.0732	0.7105	1.4441	4382	1653	0.327	0.0379	0.3839	0.02307	37.93	390
400	247.26	53.65	1.8638	375.30	1202.24	0.5670	1.5290	1.0802	0.7311	1.4573	4323	1655	0.318	0.0384	0.3819	0.02369	36.66	400
410	276.68	53.23	1.6706	386.17	1203.42	0.5795	1.5192	1.0878	0.7529	1.4718	4263	1656	0.309	0.0389	0.3798	0.02433	35.38	410
420	308.76	52.80	1.5006	397.12	1204.38	0.5919	1.5096	1.0959	0.7761	1.4876	4200	1656	0.300	0.0393	0.3776	0.02499	34.10	420
430	343.64	52.36	1.3505	408.15	1205.13	0.6042	1.5000	1.1047	0.8007	1.5050	4136	1656	0.292	0.0398	0.3751	0.02568	32.81	430
440	381.48	51.91	1.2177	419.27	1205.64	0.6165	1.4906	1.1143	0.8268	1.5240	4069	1655	0.285	0.0403	0.3725	0.02638	31.51	440
450	422.46	51.45	1.0999	430.49	1205.91	0.6287	1.4811	1.1246	0.8547	1.5448	4000	1654	0.278	0.0407	0.3696	0.02711	30.22	450
460	466.75	50.97	0.9951	441.81	1205.93	0.6409	1.4718	1.1358	0.8846	1.5678	3930	1652	0.271	0.0412	0.3666	0.02786	28.92	460
470	514.52	50.48	0.9015	453.24	1205.68	0.6531	1.4625	1.1479	0.9167	1.5930	3857	1650	0.264	0.0417	0.3633	0.02865	27.61	470
480	565.95	49.98	0.8179	464.78	1205.13	0.6652	1.4531	1.1612	0.9513	1.6208	3782	1647	0.258	0.0422	0.3599	0.02947	26.30	480
490	621.23	49.46	0.7429	476.46	1204.29	0.6774	1.4438	1.1757	0.9888	1.6515	3706	1643	0.252	0.0427	0.3562	0.03033	25.00	490
500	680.55	48.92	0.6756	488.27	1203.13	0.6895	1.4344	1.1916	1.0295	1.6856	3626	1638	0.246	0.0432	0.3522	0.03124	23.69	500
510	744.11	48.37	0.6149	500.23	1201.62	0.7017	1.4250	1.2091	1.0741	1.7235	3545	1632	0.240	0.0438	0.3481	0.03220	22.38	510
520	812.10	47.80	0.5601	512.35	1199.75	0.7138	1.4155	1.2285	1.1231	1.7658	3461	1626	0.235	0.0443	0.3436	0.03323	21.08	520
530	884.74	47.20	0.5105	524.65	1197.49	0.7260	1.4059	1.2500	1.1772	1.8133	3375	1619	0.229	0.0449	0.3389	0.03434	19.77	530
540	962.24	46.59	0.4655	537.14	1194.80	0.7383	1.3962	1.2740	1.2374	1.8667	3286	1611	0.224	0.0455	0.3340	0.03554	18.47	540
550	1044.8	45.95	0.4247	549.84	1191.66	0.7506	1.3863	1.3011	1.3048	1.9274	3195	1601	0.219	0.0461	0.3288	0.03685	17.18	550
560	1132.7	45.29	0.3874	562.77	1188.02	0.7630	1.3762	1.3317	1.3810	1.9966	3101	1591	0.214	0.0467	0.3233	0.03830	15.89	560
570	1226.2	44.60	0.3534	575.97	1183.83	0.7755	1.3658	1.3668	1.4677	2.0763	3003	1580	0.209	0.0474	0.3177	0.03992	14.61	570
580	1325.5	43.88	0.3223	589.44	1179.04	0.7881	1.3552	1.4072	1.5675	2.1687	2903	1567	0.204	0.0481	0.3118	0.04175	13.35	580
590	1430.8	43.12	0.2937	603.25	1173.59	0.8009	1.3443	1.4543	1.6838	2.2772	2799	1553	0.199	0.0489	0.3057	0.04385	12.09	590
600	1542.5	42.32	0.2674	617.42	1167.39	0.8139	1.3329	1.5100	1.8210	2.4061	2691	1537	0.194	0.0497	0.2995	0.04627	10.85	600
610	1660.9	41.47	0.2431	632.02	1160.34	0.8271	1.3210	1.5769	1.9855	2.5615	2580	1520	0.189	0.0506	0.2931	0.04912	9.62	610
620	1786.2	40.57	0.2206	647.11	1152.31	0.8406	1.3085	1.6588	2.1869	2.7524	2463	1501	0.183	0.0516	0.2867	0.05252	8.42	620
630	1918.9	39.61	0.1997	662.79	1143.14	0.8545	1.2953	1.7618	2.4392	2.9922	2341	1480	0.178	0.0527	0.2801	0.05664	7.23	630
640	2059.3	38.57	0.1802	679.19	1132.60	0.8689	1.2812	1.8958	2.7654	3.3023	2213	1456	0.173	0.0540	0.2735	0.06174	6.08	640
650	2207.8	37.42	0.1618	696.48	1120.40	0.8839	1.2659	2.0791	3.2045	3.7194	2076	1430	0.167	0.0555	0.2668	0.06819	4.96	650
660	2364.9	36.15	0.1444	714.96	1106.08	0.8997	1.2491	2.3480	3.8305	4.3113	1928	1399	0.161	0.0572	0.2600	0.07660	3.88	660
670	2531.2	34.69	0.1277	735.12	1088.91	0.9169	1.2301	2.7832	4.8020	5.2224	1762	1363	0.154	0.0594	0.2531	0.08808	2.84	670
680	2707.3	32.94	0.1113	757.89	1067.56	0.9361	1.2078	3.5861	6.5383	6.8275	1574	1320	0.146	0.0622	0.2461	0.10495	1.88	680
690	2894.0	30.69	0.0946	785.02	1039.02	0.9589	1.1798	5.3920	10.639	10.516	1365	1263	0.136	0.0663	0.2404	0.13393	1.00	690
700	3093.0	27.28	0.0748	823.00	991.66	0.9907	1.1361	15.579	32.942	29.223	1119	1162	0.122	0.0740	0.2547	0.21590	0.26	700
705.10[c]	3200.1	20.10	0.0497	896.67	896.67	1.0533	1.0533	∞	∞	∞	0	0	—	—	∞	∞	0.00	705.10

*Temperatures on ITS-90 scale [a]Triple point [b]Normal boiling point [c]Critical point

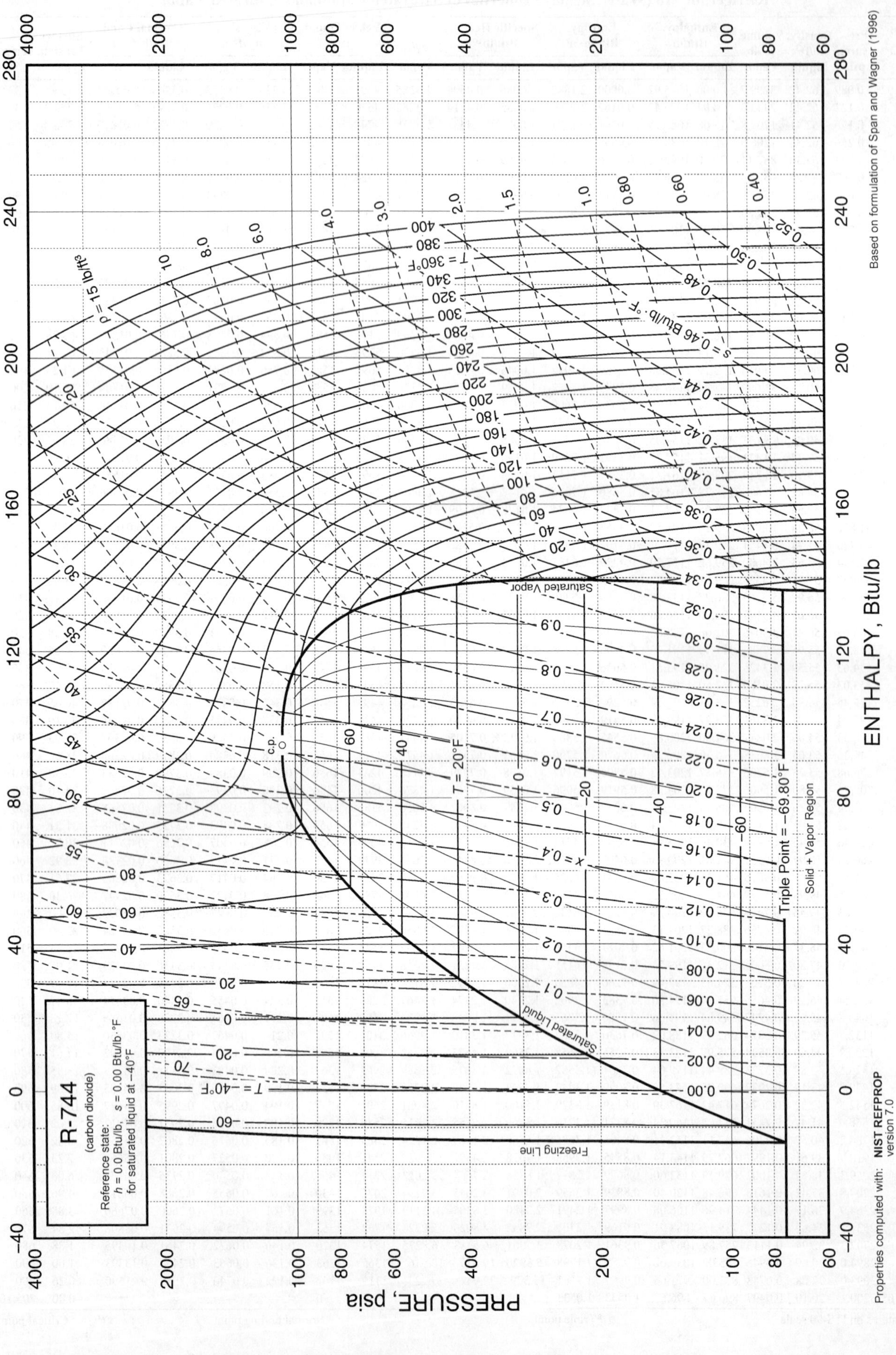

Fig. 21 Pressure-Enthalpy Diagram for Refrigerant 744 (Carbon Dioxide)

Refrigerant 744 (Carbon Dioxide) Properties of Saturated Liquid and Saturated Vapor

Temp.,* °F	Pres-sure, psia	Density, lb/ft³	Volume, ft³/lb	Enthalpy, Btu/lb		Entropy, Btu/lb·°F		Specific Heat c_p, Btu/lb·°F		c_p/c_v	Vel. of Sound, ft/s		Viscosity, lb_m/ft·h		Thermal Cond., Btu/h·ft·°F		Surface Tension, dyne/cm	Temp.,* °F
		Liquid	Vapor	Liquid	Vapor	Liquid	Vapor	Liquid	Vapor	Vapor	Liquid	Vapor	Liquid	Vapor	Liquid	Vapor		
–69.80[a]	75.124	73.57	1.1641	–14.140	136.598	–0.03449	0.35215	0.4668	0.2172	1.4442	3202	730.9	0.621	0.0265	0.1044	0.00637	17.16	–69.80
–65	84.234	72.97	1.0434	–11.886	137.013	–0.02881	0.34847	0.4684	0.2212	1.4534	3138	731.9	0.593	0.0268	0.1024	0.00650	16.49	–65
–60	94.573	72.33	0.9336	–9.532	137.417	–0.02294	0.34473	0.4703	0.2257	1.4638	3073	732.7	0.565	0.0272	0.1003	0.00664	15.81	–60
–55	105.84	71.69	0.8375	–7.167	137.790	–0.01714	0.34107	0.4724	0.2304	1.4754	3007	733.2	0.539	0.0276	0.0982	0.00678	15.12	–55
–50	118.08	71.04	0.7532	–4.791	138.130	–0.01138	0.33749	0.4749	0.2355	1.4882	2941	733.5	0.514	0.0279	0.0962	0.00693	14.45	–50
–48	123.26	70.77	0.7224	–3.837	138.257	–0.00909	0.33608	0.4760	0.2377	1.4937	2915	733.5	0.505	0.0281	0.0954	0.00699	14.18	–48
–46	128.61	70.51	0.6930	–2.881	138.379	–0.00681	0.33467	0.4771	0.2399	1.4994	2889	733.5	0.496	0.0283	0.0945	0.00706	13.91	–46
–44	134.13	70.24	0.6651	–1.923	138.494	–0.00453	0.33328	0.4783	0.2422	1.5054	2862	733.5	0.486	0.0284	0.0937	0.00712	13.65	–44
–42	139.82	69.97	0.6386	–0.963	138.604	–0.00226	0.33189	0.4795	0.2445	1.5116	2836	733.4	0.477	0.0286	0.0929	0.00718	13.38	–42
–40	145.69	69.70	0.6132	0.000	138.708	0.00000	0.33052	0.4808	0.2470	1.5180	2809	733.3	0.469	0.0287	0.0921	0.00725	13.12	–40
–38	151.74	69.42	0.5891	0.965	138.806	0.00226	0.32915	0.4821	0.2495	1.5247	2783	733.1	0.460	0.0289	0.0913	0.00732	12.86	–38
–36	157.98	69.15	0.5661	1.933	138.898	0.00451	0.32779	0.4836	0.2520	1.5317	2756	732.9	0.452	0.0290	0.0905	0.00739	12.60	–36
–34	164.40	68.87	0.5442	2.904	138.983	0.00675	0.32643	0.4850	0.2547	1.5390	2730	732.6	0.443	0.0292	0.0897	0.00746	12.34	–34
–32	171.02	68.59	0.5233	3.877	139.062	0.00899	0.32509	0.4866	0.2574	1.5466	2703	732.3	0.435	0.0293	0.0889	0.00753	12.08	–32
–30	177.83	68.31	0.5033	4.854	139.134	0.01123	0.32375	0.4882	0.2603	1.5545	2677	732.0	0.427	0.0295	0.0881	0.00760	11.82	–30
–28	184.83	68.02	0.4842	5.833	139.199	0.01346	0.32241	0.4899	0.2632	1.5628	2650	731.6	0.420	0.0297	0.0873	0.00768	11.56	–28
–26	192.04	67.74	0.4659	6.816	139.258	0.01568	0.32108	0.4917	0.2662	1.5714	2623	731.1	0.412	0.0298	0.0865	0.00775	11.31	–26
–24	199.46	67.45	0.4485	7.802	139.309	0.01790	0.31975	0.4935	0.2694	1.5804	2596	730.6	0.405	0.0300	0.0857	0.00783	11.06	–24
–22	207.08	67.16	0.4318	8.791	139.353	0.02012	0.31843	0.4955	0.2726	1.5898	2569	730.1	0.397	0.0302	0.0849	0.00791	10.80	–22
–20	214.91	66.86	0.4158	9.784	139.389	0.02234	0.31711	0.4975	0.2760	1.5996	2542	729.5	0.390	0.0303	0.0841	0.00799	10.55	–20
–18	222.97	66.56	0.4005	10.781	139.418	0.02455	0.31580	0.4996	0.2795	1.6099	2515	728.9	0.383	0.0305	0.0833	0.00807	10.30	–18
–16	231.24	66.27	0.3859	11.781	139.438	0.02675	0.31448	0.5018	0.2831	1.6206	2488	728.2	0.376	0.0307	0.0825	0.00816	10.05	–16
–14	239.73	65.96	0.3718	12.786	139.451	0.02896	0.31317	0.5042	0.2869	1.6318	2461	727.5	0.369	0.0308	0.0818	0.00825	9.81	–14
–12	248.45	65.66	0.3584	13.794	139.455	0.03116	0.31186	0.5066	0.2908	1.6435	2433	726.7	0.363	0.0310	0.0810	0.00834	9.56	–12
–10	257.40	65.35	0.3455	14.807	139.450	0.03336	0.31055	0.5091	0.2949	1.6557	2405	725.9	0.356	0.0312	0.0802	0.00843	9.32	–10
–8	266.58	65.04	0.3331	15.824	139.437	0.03556	0.30924	0.5118	0.2991	1.6685	2378	725.0	0.350	0.0314	0.0794	0.00853	9.07	–8
–6	276.01	64.72	0.3212	16.846	139.415	0.03776	0.30793	0.5146	0.3035	1.6820	2350	724.1	0.343	0.0315	0.0786	0.00863	8.83	–6
–4	285.67	64.40	0.3098	17.873	139.383	0.03996	0.30662	0.5175	0.3082	1.6960	2321	723.1	0.337	0.0317	0.0778	0.00873	8.59	–4
–2	295.58	64.08	0.2989	18.905	139.342	0.04216	0.30531	0.5206	0.3130	1.7108	2293	722.1	0.331	0.0319	0.0771	0.00883	8.35	–2
0	305.74	63.76	0.2884	19.942	139.291	0.04435	0.30399	0.5238	0.3180	1.7262	2264	721.0	0.325	0.0321	0.0763	0.00894	8.11	0
2	316.15	63.43	0.2782	20.985	139.230	0.04655	0.30267	0.5272	0.3233	1.7425	2235	719.8	0.319	0.0323	0.0755	0.00905	7.88	2
4	326.82	63.09	0.2685	22.033	139.158	0.04875	0.30135	0.5307	0.3288	1.7596	2206	718.6	0.313	0.0325	0.0747	0.00916	7.64	4
6	337.75	62.76	0.2591	23.088	139.075	0.05095	0.30003	0.5345	0.3346	1.7776	2176	717.4	0.307	0.0327	0.0740	0.00928	7.41	6
8	348.94	62.42	0.2501	24.148	138.981	0.05315	0.29869	0.5384	0.3406	1.7965	2146	716.1	0.302	0.0329	0.0732	0.00941	7.18	8
10	360.41	62.07	0.2414	25.215	138.876	0.05535	0.29736	0.5425	0.3470	1.8166	2116	714.7	0.296	0.0331	0.0724	0.00953	6.95	10
12	372.14	61.72	0.2331	26.289	138.758	0.05756	0.29601	0.5469	0.3537	1.8377	2085	713.2	0.291	0.0333	0.0716	0.00967	6.72	12
14	384.16	61.36	0.2250	27.369	138.628	0.05977	0.29466	0.5514	0.3607	1.8601	2054	711.8	0.286	0.0335	0.0709	0.00981	6.50	14
16	396.45	61.00	0.2173	28.457	138.485	0.06198	0.29329	0.5563	0.3681	1.8837	2023	710.2	0.280	0.0338	0.0701	0.00995	6.27	16
18	409.03	60.63	0.2098	29.552	138.328	0.06420	0.29192	0.5614	0.3759	1.9089	1991	708.6	0.275	0.0340	0.0693	0.01010	6.05	18
20	421.91	60.26	0.2025	30.656	138.158	0.06642	0.29054	0.5669	0.3841	1.9356	1959	706.9	0.270	0.0342	0.0685	0.01026	5.83	20
22	435.07	59.89	0.1956	31.768	137.973	0.06865	0.28915	0.5726	0.3928	1.9640	1926	705.2	0.265	0.0345	0.0677	0.01042	5.61	22
24	448.54	59.50	0.1888	32.889	137.772	0.07089	0.28774	0.5787	0.4021	1.9942	1894	703.4	0.260	0.0347	0.0670	0.01059	5.39	24
26	462.30	59.11	0.1823	34.019	137.556	0.07313	0.28632	0.5853	0.4120	2.0266	1861	701.6	0.255	0.0350	0.0662	0.01077	5.17	26
28	476.38	58.71	0.1760	35.159	137.323	0.07538	0.28488	0.5922	0.4225	2.0611	1827	699.7	0.250	0.0352	0.0654	0.01096	4.96	28
30	490.77	58.31	0.1699	36.309	137.072	0.07764	0.28342	0.5997	0.4337	2.0982	1794	697.7	0.245	0.0355	0.0646	0.01116	4.75	30
32	505.48	57.90	0.1640	37.470	136.803	0.07991	0.28195	0.6076	0.4457	2.1380	1760	695.7	0.240	0.0358	0.0638	0.01137	4.54	32
34	520.51	57.48	0.1583	38.643	136.514	0.08220	0.28045	0.6162	0.4586	2.1808	1726	693.6	0.236	0.0361	0.0631	0.01160	4.33	34
36	535.86	57.05	0.1528	39.828	136.206	0.08449	0.27893	0.6254	0.4725	2.2271	1692	691.4	0.231	0.0364	0.0623	0.01183	4.13	36
38	551.55	56.61	0.1475	41.025	135.875	0.08680	0.27739	0.6353	0.4875	2.2771	1657	689.1	0.227	0.0367	0.0615	0.01208	3.92	38
40	567.58	56.16	0.1423	42.237	135.522	0.08912	0.27582	0.6460	0.5038	2.3314	1623	686.8	0.222	0.0370	0.0607	0.01235	3.72	40
42	583.95	55.71	0.1373	43.464	135.145	0.09147	0.27422	0.6577	0.5215	2.3905	1588	684.4	0.217	0.0373	0.0599	0.01263	3.53	42
44	600.67	55.24	0.1324	44.706	134.741	0.09383	0.27259	0.6704	0.5408	2.4551	1553	681.9	0.213	0.0377	0.0591	0.01294	3.33	44
46	617.75	54.76	0.1276	45.965	134.310	0.09621	0.27092	0.6843	0.5620	2.5260	1518	679.3	0.209	0.0381	0.0583	0.01326	3.14	46
48	635.18	54.27	0.1230	47.242	133.850	0.09861	0.26921	0.6996	0.5854	2.6040	1482	676.7	0.204	0.0384	0.0575	0.01362	2.94	48
50	652.99	53.76	0.1185	48.539	133.357	0.10104	0.26746	0.7164	0.6113	2.6903	1447	673.9	0.200	0.0388	0.0567	0.01400	2.76	50
52	671.16	53.24	0.1141	49.858	132.830	0.10350	0.26566	0.7352	0.6402	2.7863	1411	671.0	0.195	0.0393	0.0559	0.01441	2.57	52
54	689.72	52.70	0.1099	51.200	132.266	0.10599	0.26381	0.7562	0.6725	2.8937	1375	668.1	0.191	0.0397	0.0551	0.01485	2.39	54
56	708.67	52.14	0.1057	52.568	131.661	0.10852	0.26190	0.7798	0.7091	3.0147	1338	665.0	0.187	0.0402	0.0543	0.01534	2.21	56
58	728.01	51.56	0.1017	53.964	131.012	0.11109	0.25992	0.8065	0.7507	3.1519	1302	661.8	0.182	0.0407	0.0535	0.01588	2.03	58
60	747.75	50.96	0.0977	55.392	130.313	0.11370	0.25787	0.8370	0.7984	3.3088	1264	658.4	0.178	0.0413	0.0527	0.01647	1.86	60
62	767.91	50.34	0.0938	56.855	129.560	0.11637	0.25574	0.8722	0.8538	3.4899	1227	654.9	0.173	0.0419	0.0519	0.01713	1.69	62
64	788.48	49.69	0.0900	58.358	128.745	0.11910	0.25351	0.9131	0.9188	3.7014	1188	651.3	0.169	0.0425	0.0511	0.01786	1.52	64
66	809.48	49.00	0.0862	59.906	127.860	0.12190	0.25117	0.9613	0.9962	3.9514	1148	647.4	0.165	0.0432	0.0503	0.01869	1.36	66
68	830.93	48.28	0.0825	61.505	126.896	0.12478	0.24871	1.019	1.090	4.252	1108	643.4	0.160	0.0440	0.0495	0.01963	1.20	68
70	852.82	47.52	0.0788	63.165	125.840	0.12776	0.24609	1.089	1.205	4.618	1066	639.0	0.155	0.0448	0.0488	0.02070	1.05	70
75	909.62	45.36	0.0697	67.656	122.671	0.13578	0.23867	1.363	1.659	6.027	951	626.5	0.143	0.0474	0.0472	0.02430	0.69	75
80	969.57	42.62	0.0603	72.945	118.309	0.14515	0.22921	2.005	2.726	9.198	816	609.5	0.129	0.0512	0.0466	0.03046	0.36	80
85	1033.07	38.41	0.0493	80.262	111.006	0.15811	0.21455	5.226	8.106	23.712	636	576.6	0.111	0.0582	0.0510	0.04701	0.10	85
87.76[c]	1069.99	29.19	0.0343	94.364	94.364	0.18355	0.18355	∞	∞	∞	0	0.0	—	—	∞	∞	0.00	87.76

*Temperatures on ITS-90 scale [a]Triple point [c]Critical point

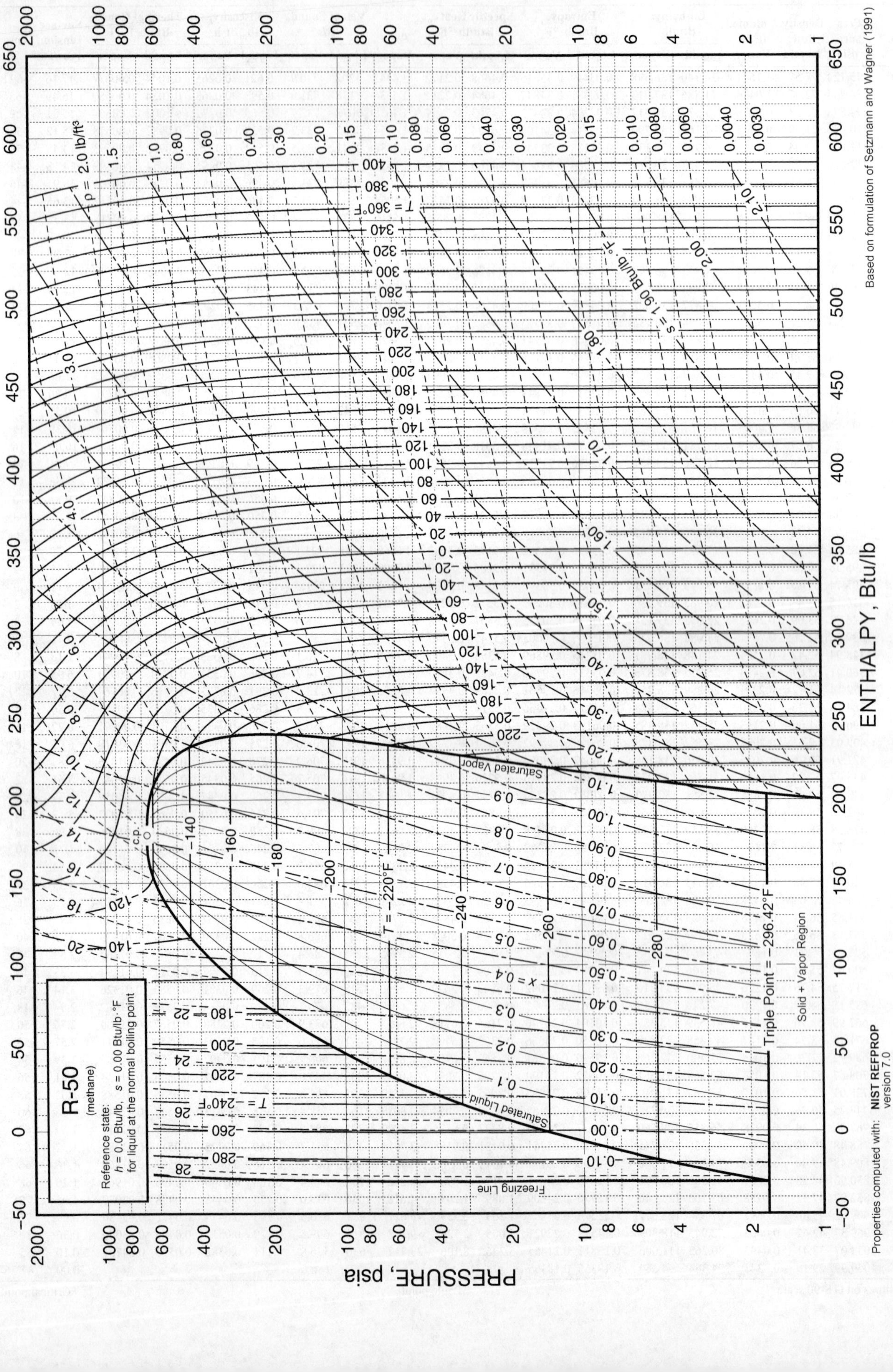

Fig. 22 Pressure-Enthalpy Diagram for Refrigerant 50 (Methane)

Refrigerant 50 (Methane) Properties of Saturated Liquid and Saturated Vapor

Temp.,* °F	Pressure, psia	Density, lb/ft³ Liquid	Volume, ft³/lb Vapor	Enthalpy, Btu/lb Liquid	Enthalpy, Btu/lb Vapor	Entropy, Btu/lb·°F Liquid	Entropy, Btu/lb·°F Vapor	Specific Heat c_p, Btu/lb·°F Liquid	Specific Heat c_p, Btu/lb·°F Vapor	c_p/c_v Vapor	Vel. of Sound, ft/s Liquid	Vel. of Sound, ft/s Vapor	Viscosity, lb_m/ft·h Liquid	Viscosity, lb_m/ft·h Vapor	Thermal Cond., Btu/h·ft·°F Liquid	Thermal Cond., Btu/h·ft·°F Vapor	Surface Tension, dyne/cm	Temp.,* °F
–296.42[a]	1.696	28.18	63.884	–30.898	203.250	–0.16968	1.26461	0.8049	0.5043	1.3410	5048	817.3	0.495	0.0088	0.1221	0.00512	18.76	–296.42
–290	2.635	27.89	42.619	–25.716	206.228	–0.13858	1.22845	0.8081	0.5071	1.3440	4941	831.7	0.443	0.0091	0.1197	0.00537	17.78	–290
–280	4.891	27.41	24.167	–17.593	210.749	–0.09216	1.17874	0.8144	0.5127	1.3505	4770	852.7	0.379	0.0097	0.1156	0.00578	16.30	–280
–270	8.466	26.93	14.619	–9.396	215.095	–0.04789	1.13569	0.8219	0.5198	1.3594	4594	871.6	0.328	0.0102	0.1113	0.00620	14.87	–270
–260	13.822	26.43	9.3292	–1.111	219.231	–0.00551	1.09801	0.8307	0.5287	1.3712	4414	888.5	0.287	0.0107	0.1069	0.00664	13.48	–260
–250	21.476	25.92	6.2231	7.279	223.120	0.03522	1.06465	0.8409	0.5398	1.3868	4231	903.2	0.254	0.0113	0.1024	0.00710	12.14	–250
–258.67[b]	14.696	26.37	8.8187	0.000	219.763	0.00000	1.09335	0.8320	0.5300	1.3731	4390	890.6	0.282	0.0108	0.1063	0.00670	13.30	–258.67
–245	26.341	25.66	5.1555	11.517	224.960	0.05503	1.04932	0.8467	0.5462	1.3963	4137	909.7	0.239	0.0116	0.1001	0.00734	11.49	–245
–240	31.996	25.39	4.3071	15.788	226.724	0.07451	1.03475	0.8529	0.5534	1.4070	4043	915.5	0.226	0.0119	0.0979	0.00759	10.85	–240
–235	38.517	25.12	3.6261	20.095	228.407	0.09368	1.02087	0.8598	0.5613	1.4191	3948	920.8	0.214	0.0121	0.0956	0.00785	10.23	–235
–230	45.984	24.84	3.0742	24.439	230.002	0.11256	1.00760	0.8672	0.5701	1.4329	3851	925.4	0.202	0.0124	0.0933	0.00811	9.62	–230
–225	54.475	24.56	2.6230	28.824	231.505	0.13117	0.99486	0.8754	0.5800	1.4484	3753	929.4	0.192	0.0127	0.0910	0.00839	9.02	–225
–220	64.073	24.27	2.2512	33.255	232.908	0.14955	0.98258	0.8845	0.5909	1.4660	3655	932.7	0.182	0.0131	0.0887	0.00868	8.43	–220
–215	74.859	23.97	1.9423	37.734	234.206	0.16770	0.97071	0.8945	0.6032	1.4860	3554	935.4	0.173	0.0134	0.0864	0.00898	7.86	–215
–210	86.918	23.67	1.6839	42.267	235.391	0.18566	0.95918	0.9057	0.6170	1.5087	3452	937.4	0.164	0.0137	0.0841	0.00929	7.31	–210
–205	100.33	23.36	1.4662	46.858	236.456	0.20345	0.94793	0.9181	0.6325	1.5346	3349	938.7	0.156	0.0140	0.0818	0.00962	6.76	–205
–200	115.19	23.04	1.2817	51.514	237.390	0.22109	0.93691	0.9322	0.6502	1.5643	3244	939.3	0.149	0.0144	0.0795	0.00997	6.23	–200
–195	131.58	22.71	1.1243	56.241	238.185	0.23862	0.92605	0.9480	0.6703	1.5984	3137	939.2	0.141	0.0147	0.0773	0.01033	5.72	–195
–190	149.59	22.37	0.9893	61.047	238.828	0.25605	0.91531	0.9661	0.6935	1.6378	3028	938.3	0.135	0.0151	0.0750	0.01072	5.22	–190
–185	169.30	22.01	0.8728	65.940	239.308	0.27343	0.90461	0.9868	0.7202	1.6837	2917	936.7	0.128	0.0155	0.0727	0.01113	4.74	–185
–180	190.81	21.64	0.7718	70.932	239.607	0.29078	0.89390	1.011	0.7515	1.7375	2804	934.3	0.122	0.0159	0.0704	0.01157	4.27	–180
–175	214.22	21.26	0.6836	76.035	239.709	0.30815	0.88311	1.039	0.7886	1.8014	2688	931.1	0.116	0.0163	0.0681	0.01204	3.82	–175
–170	239.62	20.86	0.6064	81.263	239.590	0.32557	0.87215	1.072	0.8329	1.8780	2570	927.1	0.110	0.0168	0.0658	0.01256	3.38	–170
–165	267.11	20.44	0.5383	86.636	239.224	0.34312	0.86095	1.112	0.8868	1.9714	2448	922.2	0.104	0.0173	0.0635	0.01314	2.96	–165
–160	296.80	19.99	0.4781	92.177	238.576	0.36085	0.84938	1.160	0.9538	2.0871	2322	916.4	0.099	0.0178	0.0612	0.01378	2.56	–160
–155	328.79	19.52	0.4243	97.917	237.600	0.37885	0.83733	1.221	1.039	2.2340	2193	909.7	0.094	0.0183	0.0589	0.01452	2.17	–155
–150	363.20	19.01	0.3761	103.898	236.236	0.39725	0.82460	1.299	1.151	2.4258	2058	901.9	0.088	0.0190	0.0565	0.01538	1.80	–150
–140	439.83	17.84	0.2929	116.835	231.967	0.43590	0.79606	1.553	1.523	3.0583	1768	882.8	0.078	0.0205	0.0517	0.01776	1.13	–140
–130	527.92	16.34	0.2216	131.950	224.363	0.47950	0.75982	2.175	2.478	4.6351	1435	857.4	0.067	0.0227	0.0469	0.02236	0.55	–130
–120	629.39	13.83	0.1511	153.364	207.529	0.53971	0.69917	6.640	9.528	15.490	995	814.0	0.052	0.0272	0.0456	0.04087	0.10	–120
–116.65[c]	667.06	10.15	0.0985	178.791	178.791	0.61244	0.61244	∞	∞	∞	0	0.0	—	—	∞	∞	0.00	–116.65

*Temperatures on ITS-90 scale [a]Triple point [b]Normal boiling point [c]Critical point

Refrigerant 50 (Methane) Properties of Gas at 14.696 psia (one standard atmosphere)

Temp., °F	Density, lb/ft³	Enthalpy, Btu/lb	Entropy, Btu/lb·°F	Specific Heat c_p, Btu/lb·°F	c_p/c_v	Vel. of Sound, ft/s	Viscosity, lb_m/ft·h	Thermal Cond., Btu/h·ft·°F	Temp., °F	Density, lb/ft³	Enthalpy, Btu/lb	Entropy, Btu/lb·°F	Specific Heat c_p, Btu/lb·°F	c_p/c_v	Vel. of Sound, ft/s	Viscosity, lb_m/ft·h	Thermal Cond., Btu/h·ft·°F
–258.7[a]	0.1134	219.76	1.0933	0.5300	1.373	890.6	0.0108	0.00670	120.0	0.0379	414.70	1.6369	0.5474	1.295	1523.5	0.0289	0.02180
–250	0.1082	224.33	1.1156	0.5235	1.368	912.4	0.0112	0.00700	140.0	0.0367	425.72	1.6556	0.5547	1.290	1546.7	0.0297	0.02275
–240	0.1028	229.54	1.1398	0.5183	1.363	936.5	0.0118	0.00737	160.0	0.0355	436.89	1.6739	0.5624	1.285	1569.3	0.0306	0.02373
–230	0.0980	234.70	1.1628	0.5145	1.359	959.7	0.0123	0.00774	180.0	0.0344	448.22	1.6919	0.5704	1.280	1591.3	0.0314	0.02473
–220	0.0936	239.83	1.1847	0.5116	1.356	982.2	0.0128	0.00811	200.0	0.0333	459.71	1.7096	0.5788	1.274	1612.8	0.0322	0.02576
–200	0.0860	250.02	1.2255	0.5077	1.351	1025.2	0.0138	0.00887	220.0	0.0323	471.37	1.7270	0.5875	1.269	1633.9	0.0330	0.02680
–180	0.0796	260.14	1.2631	0.5052	1.347	1066.1	0.0149	0.00963	240.0	0.0314	483.21	1.7441	0.5964	1.264	1654.5	0.0337	0.02787
–160	0.0741	270.23	1.2979	0.5038	1.345	1105.2	0.0159	0.01039	260.0	0.0305	495.23	1.7611	0.6055	1.259	1674.7	0.0345	0.02896
–140	0.0694	280.30	1.3305	0.5030	1.342	1142.6	0.0169	0.01116	280.0	0.0297	507.43	1.7778	0.6148	1.254	1694.6	0.0353	0.03008
–120	0.0652	290.36	1.3610	0.5029	1.340	1178.6	0.0179	0.01193	300.0	0.0289	519.82	1.7943	0.6243	1.249	1714.1	0.0360	0.03121
–100	0.0615	300.42	1.3898	0.5034	1.338	1213.2	0.0189	0.01267	320.0	0.0282	532.40	1.8107	0.6339	1.244	1733.3	0.0368	0.03236
–80	0.0582	310.50	1.4170	0.5044	1.335	1246.6	0.0199	0.01343	340.0	0.0275	545.18	1.8269	0.6436	1.239	1752.2	0.0375	0.03353
–60	0.0552	320.60	1.4430	0.5060	1.333	1278.8	0.0208	0.01419	360.0	0.0268	558.15	1.8429	0.6534	1.235	1770.9	0.0382	0.03472
–40	0.0526	330.74	1.4677	0.5082	1.330	1309.8	0.0218	0.01497	380.0	0.0262	571.32	1.8587	0.6633	1.231	1789.3	0.0389	0.03592
–20	0.0501	340.93	1.4914	0.5110	1.326	1339.8	0.0227	0.01576	400.0	0.0256	584.68	1.8745	0.6732	1.226	1807.4	0.0397	0.03714
0	0.0479	351.18	1.5142	0.5145	1.323	1368.7	0.0236	0.01656	420.0	0.0250	598.24	1.8901	0.6831	1.222	1825.4	0.0404	0.03837
20	0.0459	361.51	1.5362	0.5185	1.319	1396.6	0.0245	0.01738	440.0	0.0244	612.00	1.9055	0.6931	1.218	1843.1	0.0411	0.03962
40	0.0441	371.93	1.5575	0.5232	1.315	1423.6	0.0254	0.01822	460.0	0.0239	625.97	1.9209	0.7031	1.215	1860.6	0.0417	0.04088
60	0.0424	382.45	1.5781	0.5285	1.310	1449.8	0.0263	0.01908	480.0	0.0234	640.13	1.9361	0.7130	1.211	1877.9	0.0424	0.04216
80	0.0408	393.07	1.5982	0.5343	1.305	1475.1	0.0272	0.01996	500.0	0.0229	654.49	1.9512	0.7230	1.207	1895.1	0.0431	0.04345
100	0.0393	403.82	1.6178	0.5406	1.300	1499.7	0.0280	0.02087									

[a]Saturated vapor at normal boiling point

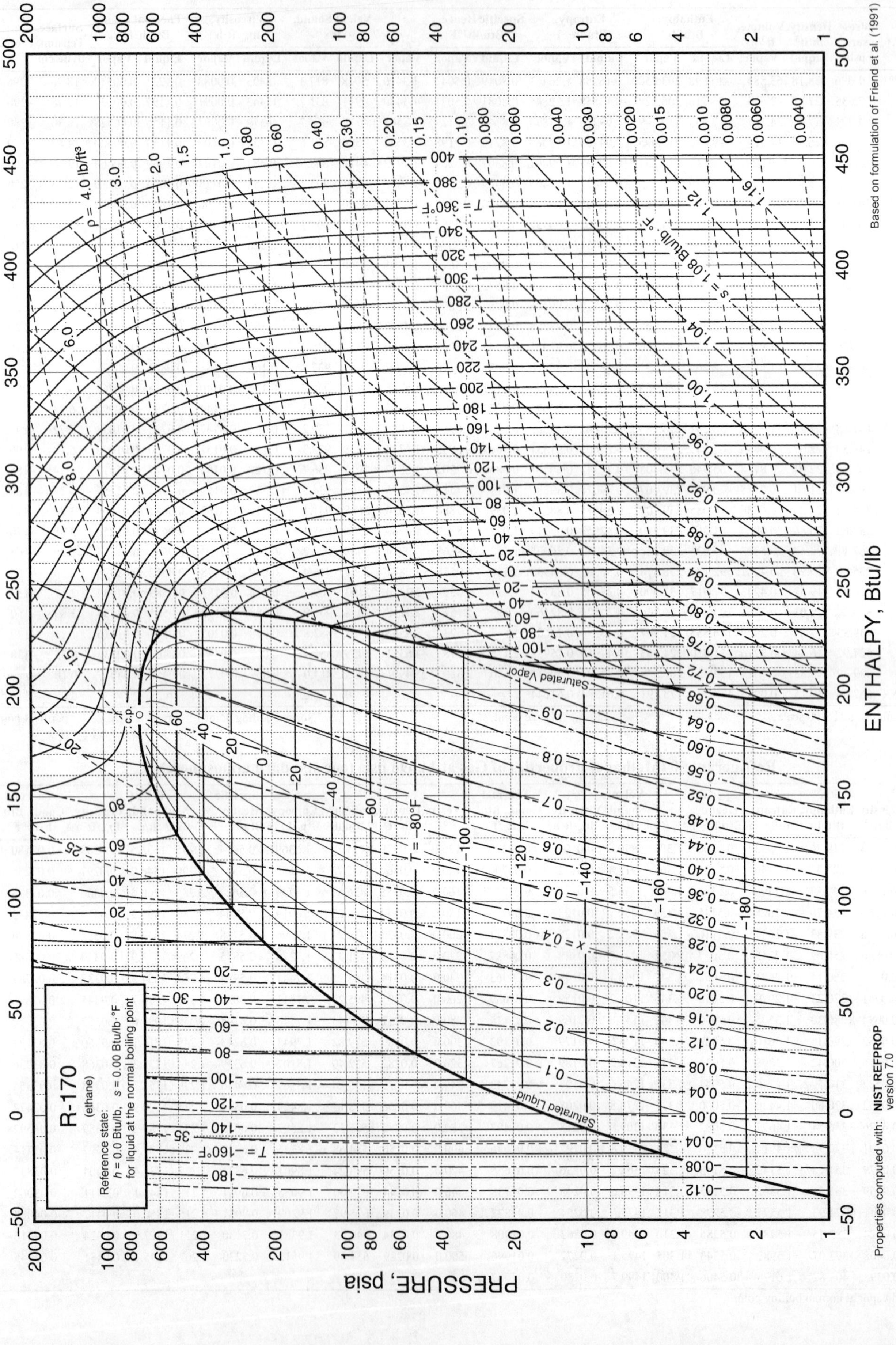

Fig. 23 Pressure-Enthalpy Diagram for Refrigerant 170 (Ethane)

Refrigerant 170 (Ethane) Properties of Saturated Liquid and Saturated Vapor

Temp.,* °F	Pressure, psia	Density, lb/ft³ Liquid	Volume, ft³/lb Vapor	Enthalpy, Btu/lb Liquid	Enthalpy, Btu/lb Vapor	Entropy, Btu/lb·°F Liquid	Entropy, Btu/lb·°F Vapor	Specific Heat c_p, Btu/lb·°F Liquid	Specific Heat c_p, Btu/lb·°F Vapor	c_p/c_v Vapor	Vel. of Sound, ft/s Liquid	Vel. of Sound, ft/s Vapor	Viscosity, lb_m/ft·h Liquid	Viscosity, lb_m/ft·h Vapor	Thermal Cond., Btu/h·ft·°F Liquid	Thermal Cond., Btu/h·ft·°F Vapor	Surface Tension, dyne/cm	Temp.,* °F
–250	0.031	38.88	2447.2	–68.630	174.981	–0.25681	0.90507	0.5440	0.2921	1.2932	5970	669.4	1.283	0.0092	0.1348	0.00257	27.27	–250
–245	0.046	38.69	1665.0	–65.908	176.436	–0.24398	0.88493	0.5446	0.2936	1.2916	5905	676.8	1.197	0.0094	0.1333	0.00267	26.80	–245
–240	0.068	38.50	1155.7	–63.183	177.896	–0.23143	0.86603	0.5454	0.2952	1.2899	5839	684.1	1.119	0.0096	0.1318	0.00277	26.34	–240
–235	0.098	38.31	817.24	–60.454	179.359	–0.21915	0.84825	0.5463	0.2969	1.2884	5773	691.3	1.050	0.0098	0.1303	0.00287	25.87	–235
–230	0.139	38.11	587.98	–57.720	180.827	–0.20711	0.83154	0.5472	0.2987	1.2868	5707	698.3	0.988	0.0100	0.1287	0.00297	25.40	–230
–225	0.195	37.92	429.90	–54.981	182.297	–0.19532	0.81580	0.5483	0.3005	1.2854	5641	705.3	0.932	0.0102	0.1272	0.00308	24.94	–225
–220	0.268	37.73	319.09	–52.237	183.770	–0.18375	0.80097	0.5494	0.3023	1.2839	5575	712.1	0.881	0.0104	0.1256	0.00318	24.48	–220
–215	0.363	37.53	240.18	–49.486	185.246	–0.17239	0.78699	0.5506	0.3042	1.2826	5508	718.8	0.834	0.0106	0.1241	0.00329	24.01	–215
–210	0.485	37.33	183.18	–46.730	186.723	–0.16124	0.77380	0.5518	0.3061	1.2814	5441	725.4	0.792	0.0108	0.1225	0.00340	23.55	–210
–205	0.641	37.14	141.43	–43.967	188.201	–0.15029	0.76136	0.5531	0.3080	1.2803	5375	731.8	0.753	0.0110	0.1209	0.00351	23.09	–205
–200	0.836	36.94	110.46	–41.197	189.680	–0.13952	0.74960	0.5545	0.3099	1.2793	5308	738.1	0.718	0.0112	0.1193	0.00362	22.62	–200
–195	1.078	36.74	87.201	–38.421	191.159	–0.12893	0.73848	0.5559	0.3117	1.2784	5241	744.3	0.685	0.0114	0.1177	0.00373	22.16	–195
–190	1.376	36.54	69.541	–35.636	192.637	–0.11852	0.72797	0.5574	0.3134	1.2777	5174	750.4	0.654	0.0116	0.1161	0.00385	21.70	–190
–185	1.739	36.34	55.986	–32.844	194.113	–0.10827	0.71802	0.5590	0.3152	1.2772	5106	756.3	0.626	0.0118	0.1146	0.00397	21.24	–185
–180	2.177	36.14	45.476	–30.044	195.585	–0.09817	0.70860	0.5606	0.3169	1.2769	5038	762.1	0.599	0.0120	0.1130	0.00409	20.79	–180
–175	2.701	35.94	37.249	–27.235	197.054	–0.08822	0.69966	0.5623	0.3186	1.2768	4971	767.7	0.575	0.0122	0.1114	0.00421	20.33	–175
–170	3.324	35.74	30.751	–24.417	198.516	–0.07842	0.69119	0.5641	0.3204	1.2768	4903	773.2	0.552	0.0124	0.1098	0.00433	19.87	–170
–165	4.059	35.53	25.575	–21.589	199.972	–0.06876	0.68314	0.5659	0.3223	1.2772	4835	778.5	0.530	0.0126	0.1082	0.00446	19.42	–165
–160	4.919	35.33	21.419	–18.752	201.420	–0.05923	0.67549	0.5679	0.3242	1.2777	4766	783.6	0.510	0.0129	0.1067	0.00459	18.96	–160
–155	5.919	35.12	18.056	–15.904	202.857	–0.04982	0.66821	0.5699	0.3264	1.2784	4698	788.5	0.491	0.0131	0.1051	0.00472	18.51	–155
–150	7.075	34.91	15.315	–13.046	204.284	–0.04053	0.66128	0.5720	0.3287	1.2794	4629	793.2	0.473	0.0133	0.1035	0.00485	18.06	–150
–145	8.404	34.70	13.066	–10.175	205.698	–0.03136	0.65467	0.5743	0.3313	1.2806	4560	797.8	0.456	0.0135	0.1020	0.00499	17.61	–145
–140	9.923	34.49	11.208	–7.293	207.098	–0.02230	0.64837	0.5766	0.3341	1.2821	4491	802.0	0.440	0.0137	0.1004	0.00513	17.16	–140
–135	11.650	34.28	9.6646	–4.399	208.484	–0.01334	0.64235	0.5791	0.3373	1.2838	4421	806.1	0.424	0.0139	0.0989	0.00527	16.71	–135
–130	13.604	34.06	8.3742	–1.490	209.854	–0.00449	0.63659	0.5817	0.3407	1.2857	4352	809.9	0.410	0.0141	0.0973	0.00541	16.26	–130
–127.45[b]	14.696	33.95	7.7972	0.000	210.547	0.00000	0.63375	0.5831	0.3425	1.2868	4316	811.8	0.402	0.0142	0.0965	0.00549	16.03	–127.45
–125	15.805	33.84	7.2896	1.432	211.207	0.00427	0.63109	0.5844	0.3444	1.2879	4282	813.5	0.396	0.0143	0.0958	0.00556	15.82	–125
–120	18.273	33.62	6.3731	4.368	212.542	0.01294	0.62581	0.5873	0.3483	1.2904	4212	816.8	0.383	0.0146	0.0943	0.00571	15.37	–120
–115	21.030	33.40	5.5947	7.320	213.858	0.02153	0.62076	0.5903	0.3526	1.2931	4141	819.9	0.370	0.0148	0.0928	0.00587	14.93	–115
–110	24.096	33.18	4.9305	10.288	215.154	0.03003	0.61591	0.5934	0.3572	1.2962	4071	822.7	0.358	0.0150	0.0913	0.00603	14.49	–110
–105	27.494	32.95	4.3611	13.274	216.431	0.03845	0.61126	0.5968	0.3620	1.2996	4000	825.2	0.346	0.0152	0.0898	0.00619	14.05	–105
–100	31.246	32.73	3.8708	16.277	217.685	0.04680	0.60678	0.6003	0.3670	1.3033	3929	827.5	0.335	0.0154	0.0883	0.00636	13.62	–100
–95	35.376	32.50	3.4469	19.298	218.918	0.05508	0.60248	0.6039	0.3724	1.3074	3857	829.5	0.325	0.0157	0.0868	0.00653	13.18	–95
–90	39.908	32.26	3.0790	22.340	220.127	0.06329	0.59833	0.6078	0.3779	1.3119	3786	831.2	0.314	0.0159	0.0854	0.00670	12.75	–90
–85	44.864	32.03	2.7583	25.402	221.312	0.07144	0.59433	0.6119	0.3837	1.3168	3714	832.6	0.304	0.0161	0.0839	0.00688	12.32	–85
–80	50.270	31.79	2.4779	28.486	222.472	0.07954	0.59047	0.6163	0.3897	1.3222	3641	833.8	0.295	0.0164	0.0825	0.00706	11.89	–80
–75	56.151	31.54	2.2318	31.592	223.605	0.08757	0.58674	0.6208	0.3959	1.3282	3569	834.6	0.286	0.0166	0.0810	0.00725	11.46	–75
–70	62.531	31.30	2.0150	34.723	224.710	0.09556	0.58312	0.6256	0.4025	1.3347	3496	835.2	0.277	0.0168	0.0796	0.00745	11.04	–70
–65	69.437	31.05	1.8235	37.878	225.785	0.10350	0.57962	0.6307	0.4092	1.3418	3423	835.4	0.268	0.0171	0.0782	0.00765	10.62	–65
–60	76.893	30.79	1.6538	41.060	226.830	0.11140	0.57621	0.6361	0.4163	1.3497	3349	835.4	0.260	0.0173	0.0768	0.00785	10.20	–60
–55	84.927	30.54	1.5030	44.270	227.841	0.11926	0.57290	0.6419	0.4237	1.3583	3276	835.0	0.252	0.0176	0.0754	0.00806	9.78	–55
–50	93.564	30.28	1.3685	47.509	228.818	0.12709	0.56966	0.6480	0.4315	1.3678	3201	834.4	0.244	0.0178	0.0740	0.00828	9.37	–50
–45	102.83	30.01	1.2483	50.779	229.758	0.13489	0.56650	0.6544	0.4397	1.3782	3127	833.4	0.237	0.0181	0.0726	0.00851	8.96	–45
–40	112.76	29.74	1.1406	54.082	230.660	0.14266	0.56341	0.6613	0.4484	1.3897	3052	832.0	0.230	0.0184	0.0713	0.00874	8.55	–40
–35	123.37	29.46	1.0437	57.419	231.519	0.15040	0.56037	0.6687	0.4576	1.4024	2976	830.3	0.222	0.0186	0.0699	0.00898	8.15	–35
–30	134.69	29.18	0.9565	60.793	232.334	0.15813	0.55737	0.6766	0.4675	1.4164	2901	828.3	0.216	0.0189	0.0686	0.00923	7.75	–30
–25	146.76	28.89	0.8777	64.205	233.101	0.16585	0.55441	0.6851	0.4780	1.4320	2824	825.9	0.209	0.0192	0.0672	0.00949	7.35	–25
–20	159.59	28.60	0.8063	67.658	233.818	0.17356	0.55148	0.6942	0.4895	1.4493	2747	823.2	0.202	0.0195	0.0659	0.00977	6.96	–20
–15	173.23	28.30	0.7416	71.155	234.481	0.18127	0.54857	0.7041	0.5019	1.4685	2670	820.0	0.196	0.0198	0.0646	0.01005	6.57	–15
–10	187.69	27.99	0.6827	74.698	235.085	0.18898	0.54566	0.7148	0.5154	1.4901	2592	816.5	0.190	0.0202	0.0633	0.01035	6.18	–10
–5	203.01	27.67	0.6290	78.291	235.626	0.19670	0.54274	0.7265	0.5302	1.5142	2513	812.5	0.183	0.0205	0.0620	0.01066	5.80	–5
0	219.22	27.35	0.5800	81.937	236.099	0.20444	0.53981	0.7393	0.5465	1.5414	2433	808.2	0.177	0.0208	0.0607	0.01099	5.42	0
5	236.35	27.02	0.5351	85.641	236.498	0.21220	0.53685	0.7533	0.5647	1.5722	2352	803.4	0.172	0.0212	0.0594	0.01133	5.05	5
10	254.43	26.67	0.4939	89.407	236.817	0.21999	0.53385	0.7689	0.5850	1.6073	2271	798.1	0.166	0.0216	0.0581	0.01170	4.68	10
15	273.50	26.31	0.4560	93.240	237.047	0.22783	0.53079	0.7863	0.6079	1.6475	2189	792.4	0.160	0.0220	0.0568	0.01210	4.32	15
20	293.58	25.94	0.4210	97.147	237.179	0.23572	0.52765	0.8058	0.6340	1.6941	2105	786.2	0.154	0.0224	0.0556	0.01252	3.96	20
25	314.72	25.56	0.3888	101.135	237.203	0.24367	0.52442	0.8279	0.6640	1.7483	2020	779.5	0.149	0.0229	0.0543	0.01298	3.61	25
30	336.96	25.16	0.3589	105.212	237.106	0.25171	0.52106	0.8533	0.6989	1.8122	1935	772.3	0.143	0.0234	0.0530	0.01348	3.27	30
35	360.32	24.74	0.3311	109.389	236.872	0.25984	0.51755	0.8827	0.7403	1.8884	1848	764.5	0.138	0.0240	0.0518	0.01402	2.93	35
40	384.86	24.30	0.3052	113.680	236.482	0.26810	0.51387	0.9174	0.7899	1.9805	1759	756.1	0.133	0.0245	0.0505	0.01463	2.60	40
45	410.60	23.83	0.2810	118.099	235.912	0.27651	0.50995	0.9591	0.8507	2.0938	1669	747.1	0.127	0.0252	0.0492	0.01532	2.28	45
50	437.61	23.33	0.2583	122.669	235.130	0.28510	0.50575	1.010	0.9268	2.2363	1576	737.4	0.122	0.0259	0.0480	0.01610	1.97	50
55	465.94	22.80	0.2369	127.416	234.096	0.29392	0.50120	1.075	1.0249	2.4204	1480	727.0	0.116	0.0267	0.0467	0.01701	1.66	55
60	495.62	22.22	0.2166	132.379	232.751	0.30305	0.49619	1.160	1.1561	2.6671	1379	715.8	0.111	0.0276	0.0454	0.01810	1.37	60
65	526.74	21.58	0.1972	137.616	231.011	0.31257	0.49058	1.278	1.3410	3.0141	1274	703.7	0.105	0.0287	0.0442	0.01944	1.09	65
70	559.37	20.87	0.1784	143.213	228.746	0.32265	0.48413	1.453	1.6213	3.5371	1163	690.6	0.099	0.0300	0.0430	0.02115	0.82	70
75	593.59	20.04	0.1600	149.326	225.730	0.33355	0.47645	1.744	2.0966	4.4139	1043	676.0	0.092	0.0316	0.0419	0.02350	0.57	75
80	629.53	19.02	0.1412	156.264	221.511	0.34583	0.46673	2.334	3.0762	6.1833	911	659.1	0.085	0.0338	0.0413	0.02713	0.34	80
85	667.35	17.63	0.1205	164.880	214.864	0.36102	0.45279	4.198	6.1975	11.596	758	636.4	0.076	0.0371	0.0425	0.03436	0.14	85
89.91[c]	706.65	12.87	0.0777	188.859	188.859	0.40394	0.40394	∞	∞	∞	0	0.0	—	—	∞	∞	0.00	89.91

*Temperatures on ITS-90 scale [b]Normal boiling point [c]Critical point

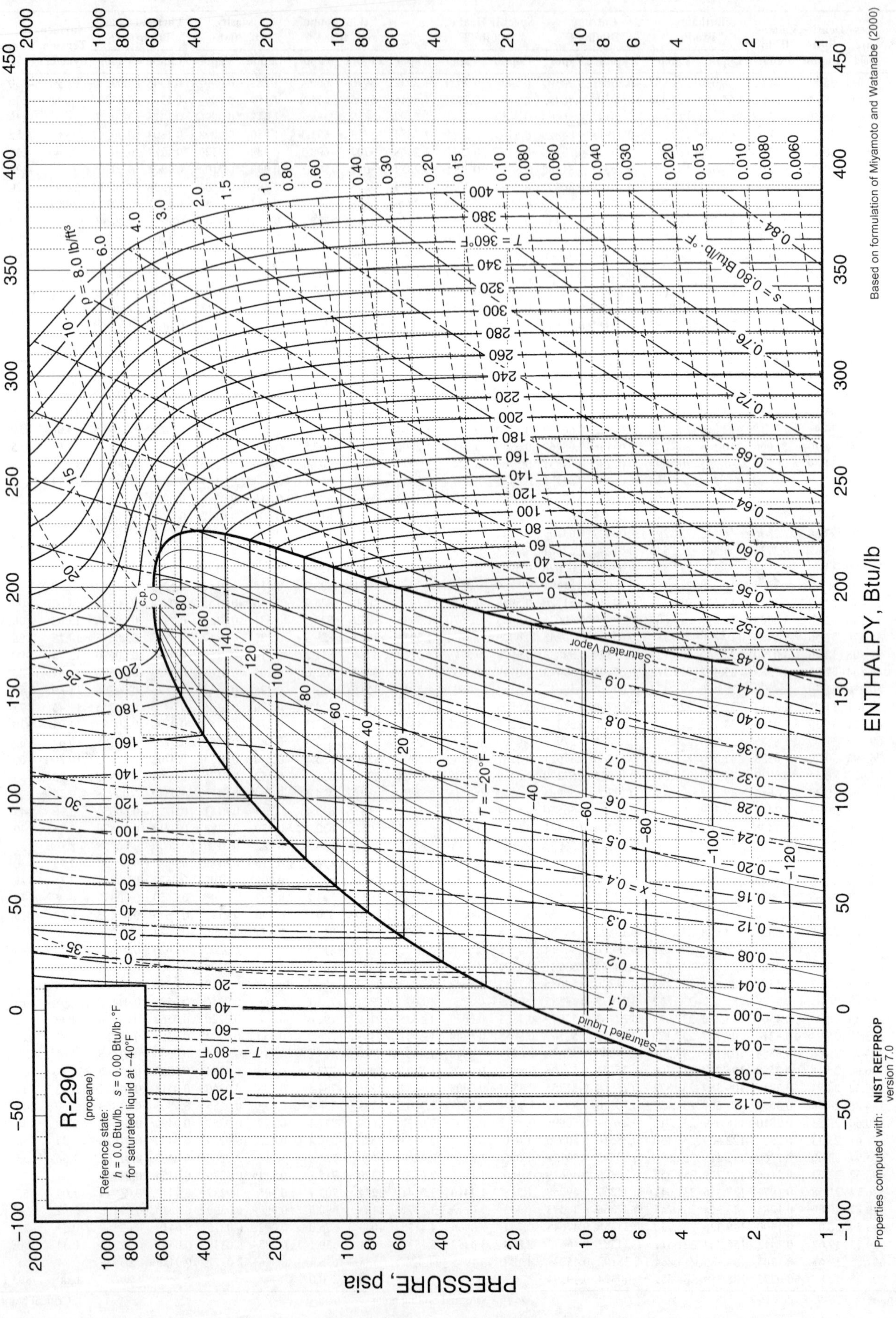

Fig. 24 Pressure-Enthalpy Diagram for Refrigerant 290 (Propane)

Refrigerant 290 (Propane) Properties of Saturated Liquid and Saturated Vapor

Temp., °F	Pressure, psia	Density, lb/ft³ Liquid	Volume, ft³/lb Vapor	Enthalpy, Btu/lb Liquid	Enthalpy, Btu/lb Vapor	Entropy, Btu/lb·°F Liquid	Entropy, Btu/lb·°F Vapor	Specific Heat c_p, Btu/lb·°F Liquid	Specific Heat c_p, Btu/lb·°F Vapor	c_p/c_v Vapor	Vel. of Sound, ft/s Liquid	Vel. of Sound, ft/s Vapor	Viscosity, lbm/ft·h Liquid	Viscosity, lbm/ft·h Vapor	Thermal Cond., Btu/h·ft·°F Liquid	Thermal Cond., Btu/h·ft·°F Vapor	Surface Tension, dyne/cm	Temp., °F
–200	0.020	42.03	3122.3	–80.510	137.326	–0.24019	0.59871	0.4770	0.2606	1.2094	5702	594.9	1.795	0.0099	0.1050	0.00287	28.59	–200
–190	0.040	41.68	1630.8	–75.728	139.945	–0.22212	0.57765	0.4794	0.2648	1.2055	5580	605.2	1.586	0.0102	0.1031	0.00308	27.75	–190
–180	0.076	41.33	898.92	–70.922	142.601	–0.20462	0.55886	0.4819	0.2691	1.2019	5459	615.2	1.415	0.0106	0.1012	0.00330	26.90	–180
–170	0.135	40.97	519.81	–66.090	145.294	–0.18764	0.54209	0.4845	0.2734	1.1985	5337	625.0	1.272	0.0109	0.0993	0.00351	26.06	–170
–160	0.232	40.62	313.69	–61.230	148.019	–0.17115	0.52711	0.4873	0.2777	1.1954	5215	634.5	1.152	0.0113	0.0974	0.00374	25.23	–160
–150	0.382	40.26	196.68	–56.342	150.774	–0.15511	0.51372	0.4903	0.2822	1.1925	5093	643.7	1.049	0.0116	0.0954	0.00397	24.39	–150
–145	0.484	40.08	157.78	–53.887	152.162	–0.14725	0.50756	0.4918	0.2845	1.1912	5032	648.2	1.003	0.0118	0.0944	0.00408	23.98	–145
–140	0.608	39.90	127.61	–51.423	153.557	–0.13948	0.50174	0.4934	0.2868	1.1899	4971	652.6	0.960	0.0119	0.0935	0.00420	23.57	–140
–135	0.757	39.72	104.00	–48.952	154.957	–0.13181	0.49624	0.4950	0.2892	1.1887	4910	656.9	0.919	0.0121	0.0925	0.00432	23.15	–135
–130	0.935	39.54	85.379	–46.472	156.364	–0.12423	0.49103	0.4967	0.2916	1.1876	4849	661.2	0.882	0.0123	0.0915	0.00444	22.74	–130
–125	1.147	39.35	70.580	–43.983	157.775	–0.11674	0.48611	0.4985	0.2940	1.1866	4788	665.3	0.846	0.0125	0.0905	0.00456	22.33	–125
–120	1.398	39.17	58.730	–41.485	159.191	–0.10934	0.48146	0.5003	0.2966	1.1856	4727	669.4	0.813	0.0126	0.0895	0.00468	21.92	–120
–115	1.693	38.99	49.176	–38.978	160.611	–0.10202	0.47706	0.5022	0.2992	1.1848	4666	673.3	0.782	0.0128	0.0885	0.00480	21.51	–115
–110	2.036	38.80	41.421	–36.461	162.036	–0.09477	0.47290	0.5041	0.3018	1.1840	4606	677.2	0.753	0.0130	0.0875	0.00493	21.10	–110
–105	2.435	38.62	35.086	–33.935	163.463	–0.08760	0.46897	0.5061	0.3045	1.1833	4545	680.9	0.725	0.0132	0.0865	0.00505	20.70	–105
–100	2.896	38.43	29.880	–31.398	164.894	–0.08050	0.46525	0.5082	0.3073	1.1827	4484	684.6	0.698	0.0133	0.0855	0.00518	20.29	–100
–95	3.425	38.24	25.577	–28.850	166.327	–0.07348	0.46174	0.5103	0.3102	1.1822	4423	688.1	0.673	0.0135	0.0846	0.00531	19.89	–95
–90	4.030	38.06	22.000	–26.291	167.762	–0.06652	0.45842	0.5125	0.3132	1.1818	4363	691.5	0.650	0.0137	0.0836	0.00544	19.49	–90
–85	4.718	37.87	19.010	–23.721	169.199	–0.05962	0.45529	0.5148	0.3162	1.1814	4303	694.8	0.627	0.0138	0.0826	0.00557	19.09	–85
–80	5.497	37.68	16.500	–21.138	170.638	–0.05278	0.45233	0.5172	0.3193	1.1812	4242	697.9	0.606	0.0140	0.0816	0.00570	18.69	–80
–75	6.376	37.49	14.381	–18.544	172.077	–0.04600	0.44954	0.5196	0.3225	1.1811	4182	700.9	0.585	0.0142	0.0806	0.00583	18.29	–75
–70	7.364	37.29	12.584	–15.936	173.516	–0.03928	0.44690	0.5222	0.3257	1.1812	4122	703.8	0.566	0.0144	0.0797	0.00596	17.89	–70
–65	8.470	37.10	11.054	–13.316	174.955	–0.03261	0.44442	0.5248	0.3291	1.1813	4062	706.5	0.547	0.0145	0.0787	0.00610	17.49	–65
–60	9.704	36.90	9.7455	–10.682	176.394	–0.02600	0.44208	0.5275	0.3325	1.1816	4002	709.1	0.529	0.0147	0.0778	0.00624	17.10	–60
–55	11.075	36.71	8.6215	–8.034	177.831	–0.01943	0.43987	0.5302	0.3360	1.1820	3942	711.6	0.513	0.0149	0.0768	0.00637	16.71	–55
–50	12.593	36.51	7.6522	–5.371	179.267	–0.01291	0.43779	0.5331	0.3397	1.1825	3882	713.9	0.496	0.0150	0.0759	0.00651	16.31	–50
–45	14.270	36.31	6.8133	–2.693	180.701	–0.00643	0.43583	0.5361	0.3434	1.1831	3823	716.0	0.481	0.0152	0.0749	0.00665	15.92	–45
–43.80[b]	14.696	36.26	6.6298	–2.051	181.043	–0.00489	0.43538	0.5368	0.3443	1.1833	3809	716.5	0.477	0.0153	0.0747	0.00669	15.83	–43.80
–40	16.117	36.11	6.0846	0.000	182.132	0.00000	0.43399	0.5392	0.3472	1.1840	3763	718.0	0.466	0.0154	0.0740	0.00680	15.54	–40
–35	18.144	35.91	5.4494	2.709	183.560	0.00639	0.43225	0.5423	0.3511	1.1849	3704	719.8	0.451	0.0156	0.0730	0.00694	15.15	–35
–30	20.363	35.70	4.8938	5.435	184.984	0.01275	0.43062	0.5456	0.3551	1.1861	3644	721.5	0.438	0.0157	0.0721	0.00709	14.76	–30
–25	22.785	35.50	4.4064	8.177	186.404	0.01906	0.42909	0.5489	0.3592	1.1874	3585	723.0	0.425	0.0159	0.0712	0.00724	14.38	–25
–20	25.424	35.29	3.9773	10.937	187.819	0.02534	0.42765	0.5524	0.3634	1.1888	3525	724.3	0.412	0.0161	0.0703	0.00739	14.00	–20
–15	28.291	35.08	3.5985	13.715	189.229	0.03159	0.42630	0.5560	0.3677	1.1905	3466	725.4	0.400	0.0163	0.0694	0.00754	13.62	–15
–10	31.399	34.87	3.2632	16.512	190.632	0.03781	0.42503	0.5597	0.3722	1.1924	3406	726.3	0.388	0.0164	0.0685	0.00769	13.24	–10
–5	34.760	34.66	2.9655	19.327	192.029	0.04400	0.42384	0.5635	0.3768	1.1945	3347	727.0	0.377	0.0166	0.0676	0.00785	12.86	–5
0	38.389	34.44	2.7005	22.163	193.419	0.05016	0.42272	0.5674	0.3815	1.1968	3287	727.6	0.366	0.0168	0.0667	0.00801	12.49	0
5	42.296	34.22	2.4639	25.018	194.800	0.05629	0.42167	0.5715	0.3863	1.1993	3228	727.9	0.355	0.0170	0.0659	0.00817	12.11	5
10	46.497	34.00	2.2523	27.895	196.173	0.06240	0.42069	0.5757	0.3914	1.2021	3168	728.0	0.345	0.0172	0.0650	0.00834	11.74	10
15	51.005	33.78	2.0625	30.793	197.536	0.06848	0.41977	0.5800	0.3965	1.2052	3109	728.0	0.335	0.0174	0.0641	0.00850	11.37	15
20	55.834	33.55	1.8919	33.713	198.889	0.07455	0.41890	0.5845	0.4019	1.2086	3049	727.7	0.325	0.0175	0.0633	0.00868	11.00	20
25	60.997	33.32	1.7381	36.656	200.231	0.08059	0.41809	0.5891	0.4074	1.2123	2989	727.1	0.316	0.0177	0.0624	0.00885	10.64	25
30	66.509	33.09	1.5993	39.623	201.560	0.08662	0.41733	0.5939	0.4132	1.2164	2929	726.4	0.307	0.0179	0.0616	0.00903	10.28	30
35	72.383	32.86	1.4737	42.615	202.877	0.09263	0.41661	0.5989	0.4192	1.2208	2869	725.4	0.299	0.0181	0.0608	0.00921	9.92	35
40	78.636	32.62	1.3599	45.631	204.179	0.09863	0.41593	0.6041	0.4254	1.2256	2809	724.2	0.290	0.0183	0.0600	0.00940	9.56	40
45	85.280	32.38	1.2564	48.674	205.466	0.10461	0.41529	0.6094	0.4319	1.2309	2749	722.7	0.282	0.0185	0.0592	0.00959	9.20	45
50	92.331	32.13	1.1622	51.743	206.737	0.11058	0.41469	0.6150	0.4386	1.2367	2688	721.0	0.274	0.0188	0.0584	0.00979	8.85	50
55	99.804	31.88	1.0763	54.840	207.991	0.11655	0.41412	0.6209	0.4457	1.2429	2628	719.1	0.267	0.0190	0.0576	0.00999	8.50	55
60	107.71	31.63	0.9979	57.967	209.226	0.12250	0.41357	0.6269	0.4532	1.2498	2567	716.8	0.259	0.0192	0.0568	0.01020	8.15	60
65	116.08	31.37	0.9260	61.123	210.440	0.12845	0.41305	0.6333	0.4610	1.2573	2507	714.3	0.252	0.0194	0.0560	0.01042	7.80	65
70	124.91	31.11	0.8602	64.310	211.633	0.13440	0.41254	0.6399	0.4692	1.2656	2446	711.5	0.245	0.0197	0.0552	0.01064	7.46	70
75	134.22	30.85	0.7997	67.529	212.802	0.14034	0.41205	0.6469	0.4779	1.2746	2384	708.4	0.238	0.0199	0.0545	0.01087	7.12	75
80	144.04	30.57	0.7441	70.782	213.947	0.14629	0.41157	0.6543	0.4871	1.2846	2323	705.0	0.231	0.0202	0.0537	0.01111	6.78	80
85	154.37	30.30	0.6928	74.070	215.063	0.15224	0.41110	0.6620	0.4969	1.2955	2261	701.3	0.224	0.0204	0.0530	0.01135	6.45	85
90	165.23	30.01	0.6455	77.394	216.151	0.15819	0.41063	0.6703	0.5074	1.3076	2199	697.3	0.218	0.0207	0.0523	0.01161	6.12	90
95	176.64	29.72	0.6018	80.757	217.206	0.16415	0.41015	0.6790	0.5186	1.3209	2137	693.0	0.212	0.0210	0.0515	0.01188	5.79	95
100	188.62	29.43	0.5613	84.160	218.227	0.17013	0.40967	0.6883	0.5306	1.3358	2075	688.3	0.205	0.0213	0.0508	0.01216	5.47	100
110	214.34	28.81	0.4889	91.096	220.152	0.18212	0.40866	0.7089	0.5577	1.3707	1948	677.9	0.193	0.0219	0.0494	0.01276	4.83	110
120	242.54	28.16	0.4262	98.220	221.896	0.19420	0.40755	0.7330	0.5900	1.4148	1820	665.9	0.181	0.0226	0.0480	0.01342	4.21	120
130	273.38	27.46	0.3716	105.560	223.420	0.20640	0.40627	0.7619	0.6294	1.4717	1689	652.2	0.170	0.0234	0.0467	0.01417	3.61	130
140	307.01	26.72	0.3237	113.151	224.672	0.21878	0.40475	0.7977	0.6791	1.5477	1556	636.7	0.159	0.0243	0.0453	0.01503	3.02	140
150	343.62	25.91	0.2812	121.039	225.573	0.23140	0.40286	0.8439	0.7453	1.6537	1419	619.3	0.148	0.0253	0.0440	0.01604	2.46	150
160	383.40	25.01	0.2434	129.299	226.011	0.24436	0.40043	0.9072	0.8399	1.8099	1277	599.7	0.137	0.0265	0.0427	0.01727	1.92	160
170	426.58	23.99	0.2090	138.045	225.808	0.25784	0.39722	1.002	0.9880	2.0578	1127	577.6	0.125	0.0281	0.0414	0.01886	1.41	170
180	473.45	22.80	0.1773	147.486	224.658	0.27213	0.39277	1.163	1.2515	2.5014	968	552.5	0.113	0.0301	0.0401	0.02108	0.94	180
190	524.34	21.29	0.1469	158.074	221.895	0.28789	0.38613	1.517	1.8458	3.5048	793	523.4	0.100	0.0329	0.0390	0.02468	0.51	190
200	579.80	19.02	0.1146	171.336	215.315	0.30736	0.37403	3.062	4.4472	7.8310	590	487.5	0.083	0.0381	0.0398	0.03308	0.15	200
206.13[c]	616.58	13.76	0.0727	193.643	193.643	0.34037	0.34037	∞	∞	∞	0	0.0	—	—	∞	∞	0.00	206.13

[b]Normal boiling point

[c]Critical point

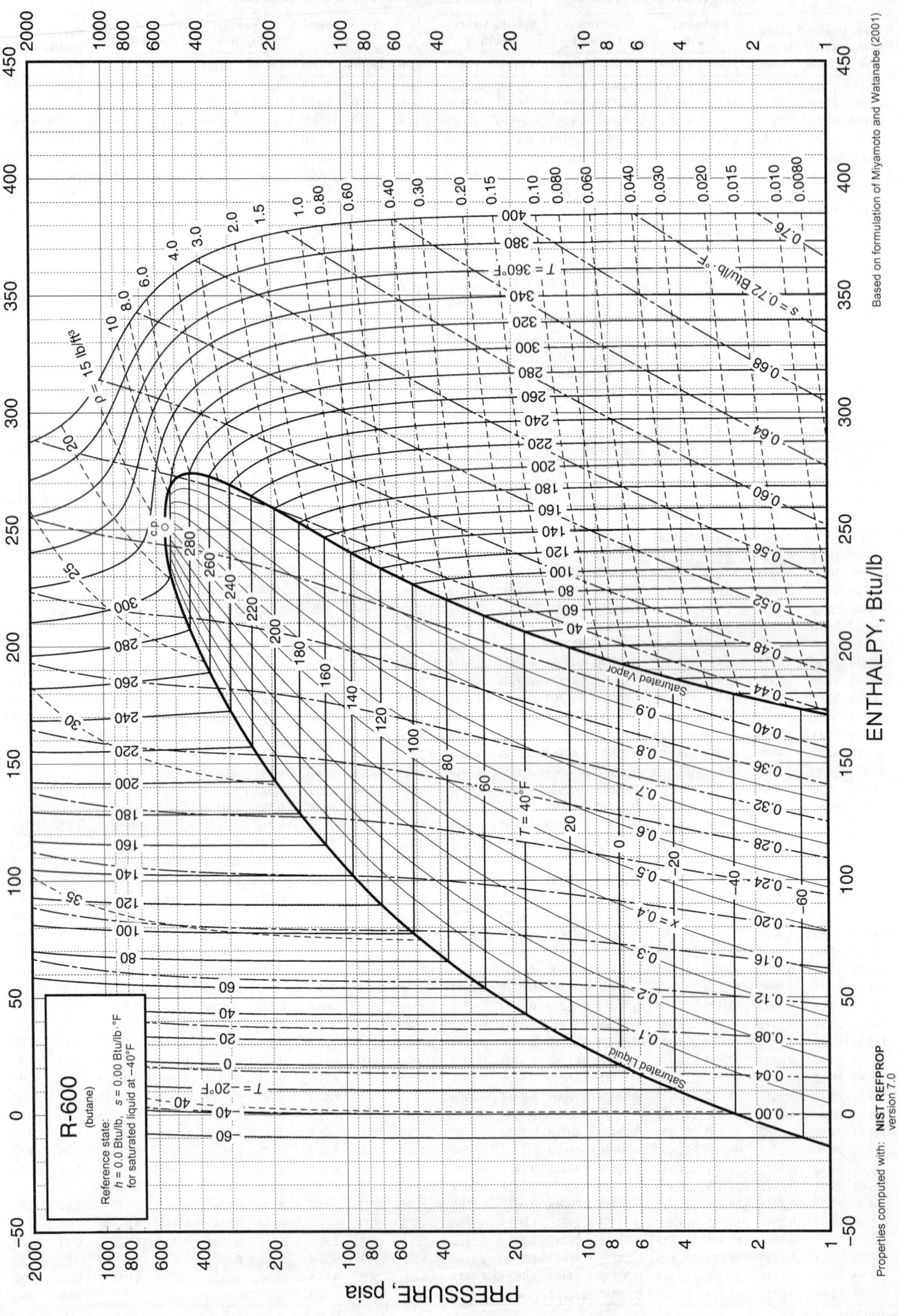
R-600
(butane)
Reference state:
h = 0.0 Btu/lb, s = 0.00 Btu/lb·°F
for saturated liquid at −40°F
PRESSURE, psia
ENTHALPY, Btu/lb
Saturated Liquid
Saturated Vapor
c.p.
ρ = 15 lb/ft³
s = 0.72 Btu/lb·°F
T = 360°F
T = 40°F
T = −20°F
x = 0.4
Based on formulation of Miyamoto and Watanabe (2001)
Properties computed with: NIST REFPROP version 7.0

Refrigerant 600 (*n*-Butane) Properties of Saturated Liquid and Saturated Vapor

Temp.,* °F	Pressure, psia	Density, lb/ft³ Liquid	Volume, ft³/lb Vapor	Enthalpy, Btu/lb Liquid	Enthalpy, Btu/lb Vapor	Entropy, Btu/lb·°F Liquid	Entropy, Btu/lb·°F Vapor	Specific Heat c_p, Btu/lb·°F Liquid	Specific Heat c_p, Btu/lb·°F Vapor	c_p/c_v Vapor	Vel. of Sound, ft/s Liquid	Vel. of Sound, ft/s Vapor	Viscosity, lb_m/ft·h Liquid	Viscosity, lb_m/ft·h Vapor	Thermal Cond., Btu/h·ft·°F Liquid	Thermal Cond., Btu/h·ft·°F Vapor	Surface Tension, dyne/cm	Temp.,* °F
–150	0.021	43.72	2703.1	–54.504	145.704	–0.15032	0.49619	0.4809	0.2935	1.1321	5243	547.5	1.960	0.0103	0.0937	0.00391	28.19	–150
–140	0.038	43.40	1548.0	–49.686	148.650	–0.13501	0.48543	0.4828	0.2976	1.1302	5138	555.7	1.758	0.0107	0.0923	0.00410	27.41	–140
–130	0.066	43.07	922.47	–44.847	151.634	–0.12011	0.47589	0.4850	0.3018	1.1283	5033	563.7	1.587	0.0110	0.0909	0.00429	26.64	–130
–120	0.110	42.74	569.81	–39.985	154.654	–0.10558	0.46745	0.4874	0.3061	1.1266	4929	571.5	1.441	0.0114	0.0894	0.00449	25.87	–120
–110	0.177	42.42	363.62	–35.098	157.710	–0.09140	0.46000	0.4900	0.3105	1.1249	4825	579.2	1.314	0.0117	0.0879	0.00470	25.10	–110
–100	0.277	42.09	239.01	–30.185	160.801	–0.07755	0.45345	0.4928	0.3150	1.1233	4722	586.6	1.204	0.0120	0.0864	0.00491	24.34	–100
–90	0.422	41.76	161.39	–25.241	163.925	–0.06399	0.44772	0.4958	0.3196	1.1219	4619	593.8	1.108	0.0124	0.0849	0.00512	23.59	–90
–80	0.625	41.42	111.68	–20.267	167.081	–0.05072	0.44273	0.4991	0.3245	1.1206	4517	600.8	1.023	0.0127	0.0834	0.00534	22.84	–80
–70	0.905	41.09	79.033	–15.257	170.267	–0.03770	0.43841	0.5026	0.3294	1.1194	4415	607.5	0.947	0.0130	0.0818	0.00557	22.10	–70
–60	1.284	40.75	57.087	–10.212	173.483	–0.02492	0.43470	0.5064	0.3346	1.1184	4314	614.0	0.879	0.0134	0.0803	0.00580	21.36	–60
–50	1.784	40.41	42.015	–5.127	176.727	–0.01236	0.43155	0.5104	0.3400	1.1176	4213	620.2	0.819	0.0137	0.0788	0.00604	20.63	–50
–45	2.089	40.24	36.280	–2.569	178.358	–0.00615	0.43016	0.5125	0.3428	1.1172	4162	623.1	0.791	0.0139	0.0780	0.00616	20.26	–45
–40	2.435	40.07	31.457	0.000	179.996	0.00000	0.42890	0.5146	0.3456	1.1169	4112	626.0	0.764	0.0140	0.0773	0.00628	19.90	–40
–35	2.827	39.90	27.383	2.580	181.640	0.00611	0.42775	0.5168	0.3485	1.1167	4062	628.8	0.739	0.0142	0.0765	0.00640	19.54	–35
–30	3.269	39.73	23.927	5.171	183.289	0.01217	0.42671	0.5191	0.3514	1.1165	4012	631.5	0.715	0.0144	0.0758	0.00653	19.17	–30
–25	3.766	39.55	20.982	7.774	184.944	0.01818	0.42578	0.5214	0.3544	1.1163	3962	634.2	0.691	0.0145	0.0750	0.00666	18.82	–25
–20	4.321	39.38	18.464	10.388	186.605	0.02416	0.42495	0.5238	0.3574	1.1163	3912	636.7	0.670	0.0147	0.0743	0.00678	18.46	–20
–15	4.941	39.20	16.302	13.015	188.270	0.03009	0.42422	0.5263	0.3605	1.1162	3862	639.1	0.649	0.0148	0.0735	0.00691	18.10	–15
–10	5.631	39.03	14.439	15.655	189.940	0.03599	0.42357	0.5288	0.3637	1.1163	3812	641.5	0.628	0.0150	0.0728	0.00704	17.75	–10
–5	6.395	38.85	12.828	18.308	191.615	0.04185	0.42302	0.5314	0.3669	1.1163	3762	643.7	0.609	0.0152	0.0720	0.00718	17.39	–5
0	7.240	38.67	11.430	20.974	193.294	0.04767	0.42255	0.5341	0.3702	1.1165	3712	645.8	0.591	0.0153	0.0713	0.00731	17.04	0
5	8.172	38.49	10.213	23.654	194.977	0.05346	0.42216	0.5368	0.3736	1.1167	3663	647.9	0.573	0.0155	0.0706	0.00744	16.69	5
10	9.197	38.31	9.1505	26.347	196.664	0.05922	0.42185	0.5396	0.3770	1.1170	3613	649.8	0.556	0.0157	0.0698	0.00758	16.34	10
15	10.321	38.13	8.2196	29.055	198.354	0.06494	0.42160	0.5424	0.3805	1.1174	3564	651.6	0.540	0.0158	0.0691	0.00772	15.99	15
20	11.550	37.95	7.4017	31.778	200.047	0.07063	0.42143	0.5453	0.3841	1.1179	3515	653.3	0.525	0.0160	0.0684	0.00786	15.65	20
25	12.892	37.76	6.6811	34.515	201.743	0.07630	0.42133	0.5483	0.3877	1.1184	3465	654.8	0.510	0.0161	0.0677	0.00800	15.30	25
30	14.352	37.58	6.0444	37.268	203.441	0.08193	0.42129	0.5513	0.3914	1.1190	3416	656.3	0.495	0.0163	0.0670	0.00815	14.96	30
31.12[b]	14.696	37.54	5.9124	37.885	203.821	0.08319	0.42129	0.5520	0.3922	1.1191	3405	656.6	0.492	0.0163	0.0668	0.00818	14.88	31.12
35	15.939	37.39	5.4804	40.036	205.142	0.08754	0.42131	0.5544	0.3951	1.1197	3367	657.6	0.482	0.0165	0.0662	0.00829	14.62	35
40	17.660	37.20	4.9795	42.820	206.844	0.09312	0.42139	0.5576	0.3990	1.1205	3318	658.8	0.468	0.0166	0.0655	0.00844	14.28	40
45	19.521	37.01	4.5335	45.621	208.548	0.09868	0.42152	0.5608	0.4029	1.1214	3269	659.8	0.455	0.0168	0.0648	0.00859	13.94	45
50	21.531	36.82	4.1355	48.438	210.253	0.10422	0.42171	0.5642	0.4069	1.1223	3220	660.8	0.443	0.0170	0.0642	0.00874	13.60	50
55	23.697	36.63	3.7794	51.272	211.959	0.10973	0.42194	0.5675	0.4110	1.1234	3171	661.5	0.431	0.0171	0.0635	0.00889	13.27	55
60	26.027	36.43	3.4602	54.124	213.666	0.11522	0.42223	0.5710	0.4151	1.1246	3122	662.2	0.420	0.0173	0.0628	0.00905	12.94	60
65	28.530	36.24	3.1734	56.993	215.372	0.12069	0.42255	0.5745	0.4193	1.1259	3073	662.7	0.408	0.0175	0.0621	0.00921	12.61	65
70	31.212	36.04	2.9151	59.880	217.078	0.12614	0.42293	0.5781	0.4237	1.1273	3024	663.0	0.398	0.0176	0.0615	0.00937	12.28	70
75	34.083	35.84	2.6820	62.786	218.783	0.13157	0.42334	0.5818	0.4281	1.1289	2975	663.2	0.387	0.0178	0.0608	0.00953	11.95	75
80	37.152	35.64	2.4714	65.711	220.487	0.13699	0.42379	0.5856	0.4326	1.1306	2926	663.2	0.377	0.0180	0.0601	0.00969	11.62	80
85	40.425	35.44	2.2805	68.655	222.190	0.14239	0.42427	0.5895	0.4372	1.1324	2877	663.1	0.367	0.0182	0.0595	0.00986	11.30	85
90	43.913	35.23	2.1073	71.618	223.890	0.14777	0.42479	0.5934	0.4419	1.1344	2828	662.8	0.358	0.0183	0.0588	0.01003	10.98	90
95	47.624	35.02	1.9499	74.602	225.588	0.15314	0.42535	0.5974	0.4467	1.1365	2780	662.4	0.349	0.0185	0.0582	0.01021	10.66	95
100	51.567	34.81	1.8065	77.606	227.282	0.15849	0.42593	0.6016	0.4516	1.1388	2731	661.7	0.340	0.0187	0.0576	0.01038	10.34	100
105	55.751	34.60	1.6757	80.631	228.973	0.16383	0.42654	0.6058	0.4566	1.1413	2682	660.9	0.331	0.0189	0.0570	0.01056	10.02	105
110	60.185	34.38	1.5561	83.678	230.660	0.16916	0.42718	0.6102	0.4618	1.1440	2633	659.9	0.323	0.0191	0.0563	0.01075	9.71	110
115	64.879	34.17	1.4467	86.746	232.341	0.17448	0.42784	0.6146	0.4671	1.1469	2584	658.8	0.314	0.0192	0.0557	0.01093	9.40	115
120	69.841	33.95	1.3464	89.837	234.017	0.17979	0.42852	0.6192	0.4725	1.1500	2535	657.4	0.306	0.0194	0.0551	0.01113	9.09	120
125	75.081	33.72	1.2543	92.951	235.687	0.18509	0.42922	0.6239	0.4781	1.1533	2486	655.8	0.299	0.0196	0.0545	0.01132	8.78	125
130	80.609	33.50	1.1696	96.088	237.350	0.19038	0.42994	0.6287	0.4839	1.1570	2437	654.1	0.291	0.0198	0.0539	0.01152	8.48	130
135	86.435	33.27	1.0916	99.249	239.006	0.19566	0.43068	0.6337	0.4898	1.1608	2388	652.1	0.284	0.0200	0.0534	0.01173	8.17	135
140	92.568	33.03	1.0197	102.435	240.652	0.20094	0.43143	0.6388	0.4959	1.1650	2338	649.9	0.276	0.0203	0.0528	0.01194	7.87	140
145	99.019	32.80	0.9533	105.646	242.290	0.20621	0.43219	0.6441	0.5022	1.1696	2289	647.5	0.269	0.0205	0.0522	0.01215	7.57	145
150	105.80	32.56	0.8919	108.883	243.916	0.21148	0.43297	0.6496	0.5087	1.1744	2239	644.9	0.263	0.0207	0.0516	0.01237	7.28	150
160	120.37	32.06	0.7823	115.437	247.135	0.22201	0.43454	0.6611	0.5225	1.1855	2139	638.9	0.249	0.0212	0.0505	0.01283	6.69	160
170	136.39	31.55	0.6878	122.104	250.297	0.23253	0.43612	0.6735	0.5374	1.1985	2039	631.9	0.236	0.0217	0.0495	0.01332	6.12	170
180	153.92	31.02	0.6059	128.892	253.390	0.24306	0.43769	0.6870	0.5536	1.2140	1937	623.9	0.224	0.0222	0.0484	0.01383	5.56	180
190	173.06	30.47	0.5346	135.808	256.401	0.25361	0.43923	0.7019	0.5717	1.2327	1834	614.7	0.212	0.0228	0.0474	0.01438	5.00	190
200	193.91	29.89	0.4722	142.863	259.310	0.26419	0.44072	0.7185	0.5921	1.2556	1730	604.3	0.201	0.0234	0.0464	0.01498	4.47	200
210	216.56	29.29	0.4172	150.070	262.097	0.27482	0.44211	0.7373	0.6159	1.2840	1623	592.5	0.189	0.0241	0.0454	0.01562	3.94	210
220	241.11	28.64	0.3687	157.445	264.734	0.28552	0.44338	0.7591	0.6442	1.3198	1515	579.3	0.179	0.0248	0.0445	0.01633	3.43	220
230	267.68	27.96	0.3255	165.009	267.187	0.29632	0.44447	0.7851	0.6789	1.3660	1404	564.4	0.168	0.0257	0.0435	0.01711	2.93	230
240	296.39	27.22	0.2868	172.790	269.411	0.30724	0.44533	0.8170	0.7230	1.4273	1289	547.8	0.157	0.0266	0.0426	0.01799	2.45	240
250	327.37	26.42	0.2519	180.830	271.342	0.31835	0.44589	0.8582	0.7811	1.5118	1171	529.2	0.146	0.0277	0.0417	0.01901	1.99	250
260	360.79	25.53	0.2202	189.191	272.886	0.32971	0.44601	0.9149	0.8626	1.6346	1049	508.5	0.136	0.0290	0.0409	0.02021	1.55	260
270	396.82	24.52	0.1910	197.975	273.891	0.34146	0.44551	1.001	0.9868	1.8282	921	485.3	0.125	0.0307	0.0400	0.02171	1.13	270
280	435.70	23.33	0.1634	207.376	274.086	0.35385	0.44404	1.151	1.2039	2.1752	786	459.2	0.113	0.0327	0.0392	0.02375	0.75	280
290	477.72	21.80	0.1365	217.842	272.872	0.36744	0.44084	1.495	1.6950	2.9723	641	429.6	0.100	0.0357	0.0386	0.02697	0.40	290
300	523.33	19.38	0.1070	231.033	268.147	0.38437	0.43323	3.169	4.0022	6.7279	482	394.7	0.083	0.0412	0.0401	0.03480	0.11	300
305.56[c]	550.56	14.23	0.0703	250.857	250.857	0.40996	0.40996	∞	∞	∞	0	0.0	—	—	∞	∞	0.00	305.56

*Temperatures on ITS-90 scale [b]Normal boiling point [c]Critical point

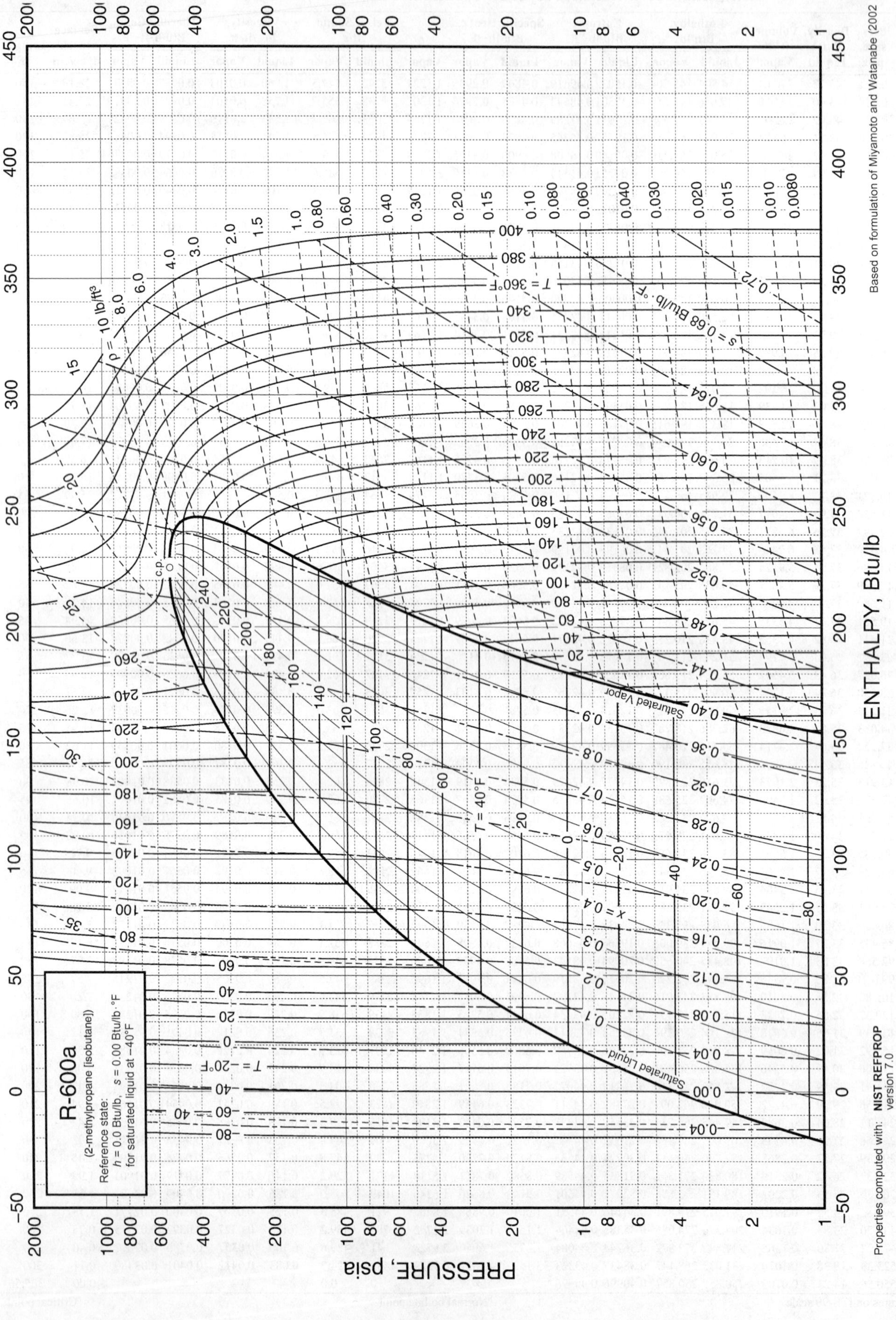

Fig. 26 Pressure-Enthalpy Diagram for Refrigerant 600a (Isobutane)

Refrigerant 600a (Isobutane) Properties of Saturated Liquid and Saturated Vapor

Temp.,* °F	Pressure, psia	Density, lb/ft³ Liquid	Volume, ft³/lb Vapor	Enthalpy, Btu/lb Liquid	Enthalpy, Btu/lb Vapor	Entropy, Btu/lb·°F Liquid	Entropy, Btu/lb·°F Vapor	Specific Heat c_p, Btu/lb·°F Liquid	Specific Heat c_p, Btu/lb·°F Vapor	c_p/c_v Vapor	Vel. of Sound, ft/s Liquid	Vel. of Sound, ft/s Vapor	Viscosity, lb_m/ft·h Liquid	Viscosity, lb_m/ft·h Vapor	Thermal Cond., Btu/h·ft·°F Liquid	Thermal Cond., Btu/h·ft·°F Vapor	Surface Tension, dyne/cm	Temp.,* °F
–150	0.049	42.76	1163.1	–52.052	135.271	–0.14338	0.46153	0.4480	0.2692	1.1460	5136	550.7	2.325	0.0106	0.0812	0.00344	25.66	–150
–140	0.085	42.43	691.66	–47.550	137.975	–0.12908	0.45129	0.4523	0.2745	1.1430	5018	558.6	2.050	0.0109	0.0799	0.00367	24.95	–140
–130	0.142	42.09	426.87	–43.005	140.726	–0.11508	0.44224	0.4566	0.2799	1.1402	4901	566.3	1.822	0.0113	0.0786	0.00391	24.24	–130
–120	0.230	41.75	272.44	–38.416	143.521	–0.10137	0.43426	0.4611	0.2853	1.1376	4787	573.9	1.630	0.0116	0.0773	0.00414	23.52	–120
–110	0.359	41.41	179.25	–33.783	146.361	–0.08792	0.42726	0.4656	0.2908	1.1352	4673	581.2	1.467	0.0119	0.0760	0.00439	22.81	–110
–100	0.546	41.07	121.24	–29.104	149.242	–0.07473	0.42113	0.4702	0.2964	1.1331	4561	588.3	1.328	0.0123	0.0747	0.00463	22.11	–100
–90	0.808	40.73	84.083	–24.378	152.163	–0.06178	0.41579	0.4749	0.3021	1.1311	4450	595.1	1.207	0.0126	0.0733	0.00488	21.40	–90
–80	1.167	40.38	59.662	–19.604	155.121	–0.04904	0.41116	0.4797	0.3079	1.1294	4340	601.7	1.102	0.0129	0.0719	0.00514	20.70	–80
–70	1.651	40.03	43.224	–14.781	158.114	–0.03651	0.40719	0.4847	0.3139	1.1279	4231	608.0	1.010	0.0133	0.0706	0.00540	19.99	–70
–60	2.287	39.68	31.916	–9.907	161.140	–0.02416	0.40381	0.4898	0.3201	1.1267	4122	614.0	0.929	0.0136	0.0692	0.00566	19.30	–60
–50	3.112	39.32	23.979	–4.981	164.197	–0.01200	0.40096	0.4951	0.3264	1.1257	4015	619.6	0.856	0.0139	0.0678	0.00593	18.60	–50
–45	3.607	39.14	20.911	–2.497	165.736	–0.00598	0.39972	0.4977	0.3296	1.1253	3961	622.3	0.823	0.0141	0.0672	0.00606	18.25	–45
–40	4.163	38.96	18.304	0.000	167.282	0.00000	0.39860	0.5005	0.3329	1.1250	3908	624.8	0.792	0.0143	0.0665	0.00620	17.91	–40
–35	4.786	38.78	16.081	2.511	168.834	0.00594	0.39759	0.5033	0.3363	1.1248	3854	627.3	0.762	0.0144	0.0658	0.00633	17.56	–35
–30	5.482	38.60	14.177	5.037	170.392	0.01185	0.39669	0.5061	0.3397	1.1246	3801	629.7	0.734	0.0146	0.0651	0.00647	17.22	–30
–25	6.257	38.42	12.540	7.577	171.956	0.01771	0.39588	0.5090	0.3431	1.1245	3749	632.0	0.708	0.0148	0.0645	0.00661	16.87	–25
–20	7.116	38.23	11.127	10.131	173.525	0.02355	0.39518	0.5119	0.3466	1.1245	3696	634.1	0.682	0.0149	0.0638	0.00675	16.53	–20
–15	8.067	38.05	9.9039	12.701	175.099	0.02935	0.39456	0.5149	0.3502	1.1246	3643	636.2	0.658	0.0151	0.0631	0.00689	16.19	–15
–10	9.115	37.86	8.8408	15.286	176.678	0.03512	0.39403	0.5179	0.3538	1.1248	3591	638.1	0.635	0.0152	0.0625	0.00703	15.85	–10
–5	10.268	37.67	7.9140	17.886	178.261	0.04086	0.39359	0.5210	0.3575	1.1250	3538	639.9	0.614	0.0154	0.0618	0.00717	15.51	–5
0	11.533	37.49	7.1033	20.502	179.849	0.04657	0.39322	0.5241	0.3613	1.1253	3486	641.6	0.593	0.0156	0.0611	0.00732	15.17	0
5	12.916	37.30	6.3920	23.134	181.439	0.05225	0.39293	0.5273	0.3651	1.1258	3434	643.1	0.573	0.0157	0.0605	0.00746	14.83	5
10	14.426	37.10	5.7660	25.783	183.034	0.05790	0.39271	0.5306	0.3690	1.1263	3382	644.6	0.554	0.0159	0.0598	0.00761	14.50	10
10.85[b]	14.696	37.07	5.6670	26.236	183.306	0.05886	0.39268	0.5311	0.3696	1.1264	3373	644.8	0.551	0.0159	0.0597	0.00763	14.44	10.85
15	16.069	36.91	5.2137	28.448	184.631	0.06353	0.39256	0.5339	0.3729	1.1269	3330	645.9	0.536	0.0161	0.0592	0.00775	14.16	15
20	17.854	36.72	4.7248	31.130	186.230	0.06913	0.39248	0.5372	0.3770	1.1277	3278	647.0	0.519	0.0162	0.0585	0.00790	13.83	20
25	19.789	36.52	4.2911	33.830	187.832	0.07471	0.39245	0.5407	0.3811	1.1285	3227	648.0	0.502	0.0164	0.0579	0.00805	13.49	25
30	21.881	36.32	3.9052	36.547	189.436	0.08026	0.39249	0.5442	0.3853	1.1295	3175	648.9	0.486	0.0165	0.0573	0.00821	13.16	30
35	24.140	36.12	3.5611	39.281	191.041	0.08580	0.39258	0.5477	0.3895	1.1306	3123	649.6	0.471	0.0167	0.0567	0.00836	12.83	35
40	26.573	35.92	3.2535	42.035	192.647	0.09131	0.39273	0.5514	0.3939	1.1318	3072	650.2	0.457	0.0169	0.0560	0.00851	12.50	40
45	29.189	35.72	2.9778	44.806	194.254	0.09680	0.39293	0.5551	0.3983	1.1331	3021	650.6	0.443	0.0170	0.0554	0.00867	12.17	45
50	31.997	35.52	2.7303	47.597	195.860	0.10227	0.39317	0.5589	0.4029	1.1346	2969	650.8	0.429	0.0172	0.0548	0.00883	11.84	50
55	35.006	35.31	2.5074	50.407	197.467	0.10773	0.39347	0.5627	0.4075	1.1362	2918	650.9	0.417	0.0174	0.0542	0.00899	11.52	55
60	38.225	35.10	2.3065	53.237	199.072	0.11317	0.39380	0.5667	0.4122	1.1380	2867	650.9	0.404	0.0175	0.0536	0.00915	11.19	60
65	41.662	34.89	2.1248	56.087	200.676	0.11859	0.39417	0.5707	0.4171	1.1399	2815	650.6	0.392	0.0177	0.0530	0.00932	10.87	65
70	45.328	34.68	1.9603	58.958	202.278	0.12400	0.39459	0.5748	0.4220	1.1420	2764	650.2	0.381	0.0179	0.0524	0.00949	10.55	70
75	49.230	34.46	1.8111	61.849	203.878	0.12940	0.39503	0.5791	0.4271	1.1443	2713	649.6	0.370	0.0181	0.0518	0.00966	10.23	75
80	53.380	34.25	1.6754	64.762	205.475	0.13478	0.39551	0.5834	0.4322	1.1468	2662	648.8	0.359	0.0182	0.0513	0.00983	9.91	80
85	57.787	34.02	1.5519	67.697	207.068	0.14015	0.39603	0.5878	0.4376	1.1495	2610	647.8	0.349	0.0184	0.0507	0.01001	9.60	85
90	62.460	33.80	1.4392	70.655	208.657	0.14550	0.39657	0.5924	0.4430	1.1524	2559	646.6	0.339	0.0186	0.0501	0.01019	9.28	90
95	67.409	33.58	1.3362	73.635	210.242	0.15085	0.39714	0.5971	0.4486	1.1556	2508	645.3	0.329	0.0188	0.0496	0.01037	8.97	95
100	72.644	33.35	1.2419	76.639	211.820	0.15619	0.39773	0.6019	0.4544	1.1590	2456	643.7	0.320	0.0190	0.0490	0.01056	8.66	100
105	78.176	33.11	1.1554	79.667	213.393	0.16152	0.39834	0.6069	0.4603	1.1627	2405	641.9	0.311	0.0192	0.0485	0.01075	8.35	105
110	84.013	32.88	1.0761	82.719	214.958	0.16685	0.39898	0.6120	0.4665	1.1667	2354	639.9	0.303	0.0194	0.0480	0.01094	8.04	110
115	90.168	32.64	1.0030	85.797	216.516	0.17217	0.39963	0.6173	0.4728	1.1711	2302	637.7	0.294	0.0196	0.0474	0.01115	7.74	115
120	96.649	32.40	0.9358	88.901	218.064	0.17748	0.40030	0.6227	0.4793	1.1758	2250	635.2	0.286	0.0198	0.0469	0.01135	7.43	120
125	103.47	32.15	0.8738	92.031	219.603	0.18279	0.40098	0.6284	0.4861	1.1809	2198	632.5	0.278	0.0200	0.0464	0.01156	7.13	125
130	110.64	31.90	0.8164	95.190	221.130	0.18810	0.40168	0.6342	0.4931	1.1865	2146	629.6	0.270	0.0202	0.0459	0.01178	6.83	130
135	118.16	31.64	0.7634	98.376	222.645	0.19340	0.40238	0.6403	0.5004	1.1925	2094	626.4	0.263	0.0205	0.0454	0.01200	6.54	135
140	126.06	31.38	0.7143	101.592	224.147	0.19871	0.40308	0.6467	0.5080	1.1991	2042	622.9	0.255	0.0207	0.0449	0.01223	6.24	140
145	134.34	31.12	0.6687	104.838	225.633	0.20402	0.40379	0.6533	0.5158	1.2064	1989	619.2	0.248	0.0209	0.0444	0.01247	5.95	145
150	143.01	30.85	0.6264	108.116	227.102	0.20933	0.40450	0.6603	0.5241	1.2143	1937	615.2	0.241	0.0212	0.0439	0.01272	5.67	150
160	161.58	30.29	0.5503	114.770	229.980	0.21998	0.40590	0.6753	0.5419	1.2328	1830	606.3	0.228	0.0217	0.0430	0.01325	5.10	160
170	181.87	29.70	0.4841	121.565	232.764	0.23065	0.40725	0.6920	0.5622	1.2557	1723	596.1	0.215	0.0223	0.0421	0.01381	4.54	170
180	203.96	29.09	0.4262	128.516	235.430	0.24139	0.40853	0.7111	0.5858	1.2843	1613	584.7	0.202	0.0230	0.0412	0.01444	4.00	180
190	227.98	28.43	0.3752	135.638	237.953	0.25219	0.40968	0.7333	0.6142	1.3207	1502	571.7	0.190	0.0237	0.0403	0.01514	3.47	190
200	254.02	27.73	0.3302	142.954	240.300	0.26311	0.41067	0.7598	0.6495	1.3682	1389	557.2	0.178	0.0246	0.0395	0.01592	2.95	200
210	282.21	26.98	0.2900	150.495	242.427	0.27416	0.41144	0.7925	0.6947	1.4317	1273	541.0	0.166	0.0256	0.0386	0.01682	2.46	210
220	312.68	26.16	0.2540	158.302	244.274	0.28542	0.41191	0.8348	0.7551	1.5200	1153	522.8	0.155	0.0267	0.0379	0.01789	1.98	220
230	345.57	25.24	0.2215	166.439	245.749	0.29696	0.41196	0.8930	0.8406	1.6499	1028	502.3	0.143	0.0281	0.0371	0.01919	1.53	230
240	381.04	24.19	0.1916	175.009	246.704	0.30891	0.41138	0.9811	0.9731	1.8576	897	479.4	0.131	0.0299	0.0364	0.02084	1.10	240
250	419.31	22.95	0.1636	184.205	246.866	0.32154	0.40983	1.136	1.2102	2.2389	759	453.5	0.118	0.0322	0.0359	0.02310	0.71	250
260	460.61	21.35	0.1362	194.466	245.619	0.33541	0.40649	1.497	1.7734	3.1566	610	424.0	0.103	0.0356	0.0358	0.02670	0.36	260
270	505.36	18.80	0.1056	207.516	240.587	0.35284	0.39817	3.555	4.9597	8.3193	442	388.2	0.084	0.0420	0.0386	0.03572	0.08	270
274.39[c]	526.34	14.08	0.0710	224.323	224.323	0.37547	0.37547	∞	∞	∞	0	0.0	—	—	∞	∞	0.00	274.39

*Temperatures on ITS-90 scale

[b]Normal boiling point

[c]Critical point

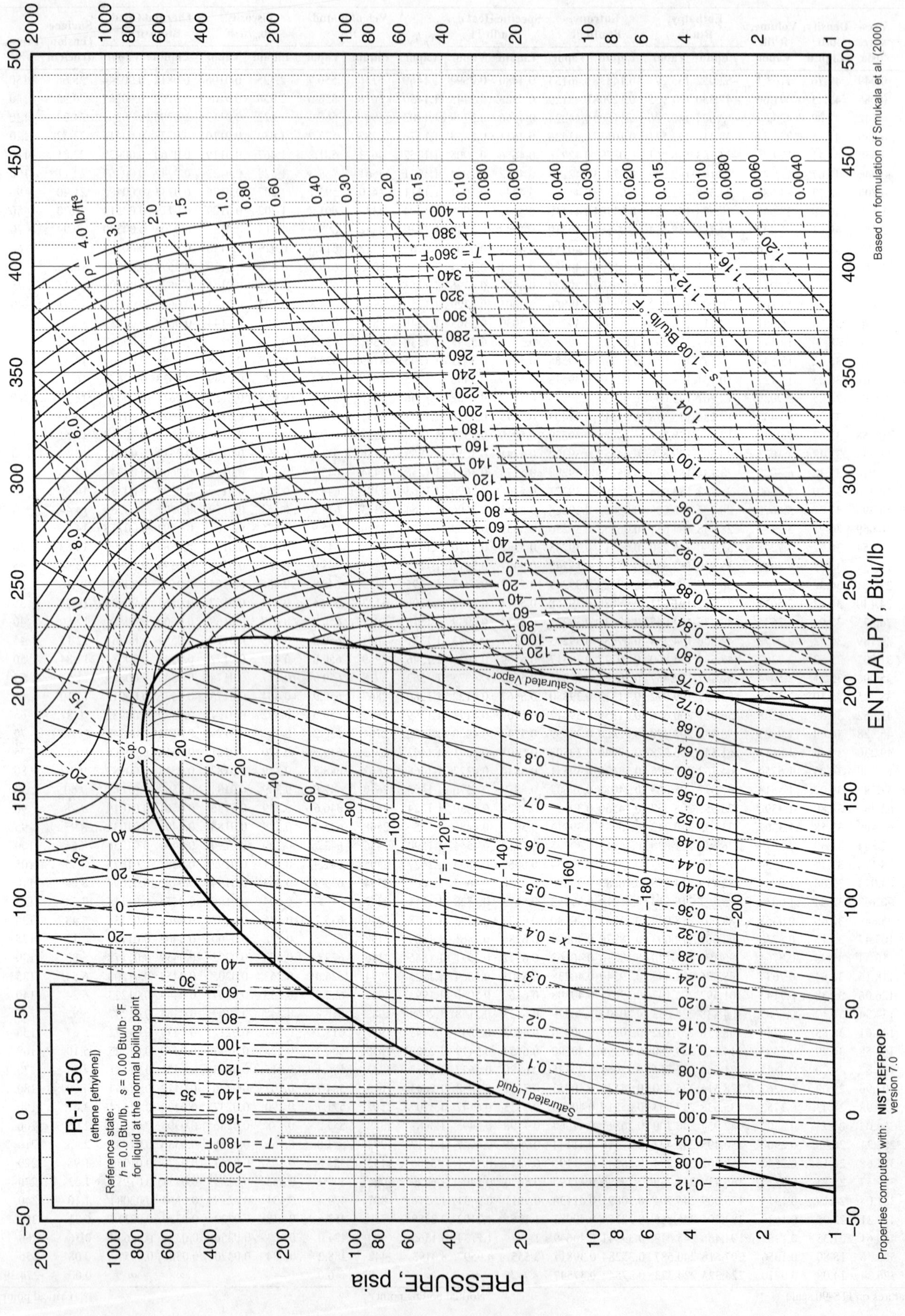

Fig. 27 Pressure-Enthalpy Diagram for Refrigerant 1150 (Ethylene)

Refrigerant 1150 (Ethylene) Properties of Saturated Liquid and Saturated Vapor

Temp.,* °F	Pressure, psia	Density, lb/ft³ Liquid	Volume, ft³/lb Vapor	Enthalpy, Btu/lb Liquid	Enthalpy, Btu/lb Vapor	Entropy, Btu/lb·°F Liquid	Entropy, Btu/lb·°F Vapor	Specific Heat c_p, Btu/lb·°F Liquid	Specific Heat c_p, Btu/lb·°F Vapor	c_p/c_v Vapor	Vel. of Sound, ft/s Liquid	Vel. of Sound, ft/s Vapor	Viscosity, lb_m/ft·h Liquid	Viscosity, lb_m/ft·h Vapor	Thermal Cond., Btu/h·ft·°F Liquid	Thermal Cond., Btu/h·ft·°F Vapor	Surface Tension, dyne/cm	Temp.,* °F
–272.50[a]	0.018	40.87	4047.0	–68.014	176.139	–0.28177	1.02264	0.5807	0.2837	1.3333	5796	664.9	1.659	0.0019	0.1565	0.00393	28.14	–272.50
–270	0.023	40.76	3219.5	–66.565	176.844	–0.27408	1.00925	0.5810	0.2837	1.3333	5767	669.3	1.584	0.0026	0.1554	0.00389	27.86	–270
–265	0.036	40.54	2077.4	–63.659	178.256	–0.25896	0.98374	0.5813	0.2838	1.3334	5708	678.0	1.447	0.0040	0.1532	0.00383	27.31	–265
–260	0.056	40.32	1374.6	–60.752	179.667	–0.24421	0.95987	0.5814	0.2840	1.3334	5648	686.6	1.328	0.0051	0.1510	0.00381	26.77	–260
–255	0.084	40.09	930.98	–57.846	181.075	–0.22984	0.93751	0.5811	0.2842	1.3335	5587	695.0	1.225	0.0062	0.1488	0.00382	26.22	–255
–250	0.124	39.87	644.22	–54.941	182.481	–0.21582	0.91654	0.5808	0.2845	1.3336	5526	703.3	1.134	0.0071	0.1466	0.00385	25.68	–250
–245	0.180	39.65	454.73	–52.038	183.883	–0.20214	0.89686	0.5802	0.2848	1.3338	5464	711.5	1.054	0.0079	0.1444	0.00390	25.14	–245
–240	0.257	39.43	326.95	–49.138	185.281	–0.18878	0.87836	0.5796	0.2852	1.3340	5402	719.5	0.983	0.0086	0.1422	0.00397	24.60	–240
–235	0.359	39.20	239.12	–46.241	186.674	–0.17575	0.86095	0.5790	0.2857	1.3343	5339	727.4	0.920	0.0092	0.1401	0.00405	24.06	–235
–230	0.493	38.98	177.68	–43.348	188.061	–0.16301	0.84456	0.5783	0.2862	1.3347	5276	735.1	0.864	0.0098	0.1379	0.00413	23.53	–230
–225	0.668	38.75	133.99	–40.457	189.442	–0.15056	0.82911	0.5776	0.2868	1.3351	5212	742.6	0.813	0.0103	0.1358	0.00423	23.00	–225
–220	0.891	38.52	102.44	–37.570	190.816	–0.13840	0.81452	0.5769	0.2875	1.3357	5148	750.0	0.767	0.0107	0.1337	0.00432	22.47	–220
–215	1.174	38.29	79.326	–34.686	192.181	–0.12649	0.80074	0.5763	0.2884	1.3364	5084	757.3	0.726	0.0112	0.1316	0.00442	21.94	–215
–210	1.527	38.06	62.164	–31.805	193.536	–0.11484	0.78771	0.5758	0.2893	1.3372	5020	764.3	0.688	0.0115	0.1295	0.00452	21.42	–210
–205	1.963	37.83	49.260	–28.926	194.881	–0.10343	0.77538	0.5753	0.2904	1.3381	4955	771.2	0.654	0.0119	0.1274	0.00462	20.90	–205
–200	2.495	37.60	39.441	–26.048	196.214	–0.09225	0.76369	0.5749	0.2916	1.3393	4890	777.9	0.622	0.0122	0.1254	0.00471	20.38	–200
–195	3.141	37.37	31.888	–23.172	197.534	–0.08129	0.75260	0.5747	0.2929	1.3406	4825	784.3	0.593	0.0125	0.1234	0.00481	19.87	–195
–190	3.915	37.14	26.016	–20.297	198.840	–0.07055	0.74206	0.5745	0.2944	1.3421	4760	790.6	0.567	0.0128	0.1214	0.00491	19.36	–190
–185	4.835	36.90	21.407	–17.421	200.131	–0.06000	0.73205	0.5745	0.2960	1.3438	4694	796.6	0.542	0.0131	0.1194	0.00501	18.85	–185
–180	5.922	36.66	17.754	–14.545	201.405	–0.04964	0.72252	0.5747	0.2978	1.3457	4628	802.5	0.519	0.0134	0.1174	0.00511	18.34	–180
–175	7.195	36.42	14.835	–11.667	202.662	–0.03946	0.71344	0.5749	0.2997	1.3479	4561	808.1	0.498	0.0136	0.1154	0.00520	17.83	–175
–170	8.675	36.18	12.483	–8.786	203.900	–0.02946	0.70478	0.5754	0.3018	1.3504	4494	813.4	0.478	0.0139	0.1135	0.00530	17.33	–170
–165	10.386	35.94	10.572	–5.903	205.118	–0.01962	0.69651	0.5760	0.3041	1.3531	4427	818.5	0.459	0.0141	0.1116	0.00540	16.84	–165
–160	12.351	35.69	9.0094	–3.015	206.315	–0.00993	0.68860	0.5768	0.3066	1.3562	4360	823.4	0.442	0.0143	0.1097	0.00550	16.34	–160
–155	14.594	35.45	7.7219	–0.122	207.490	–0.00040	0.68103	0.5778	0.3093	1.3596	4292	828.0	0.425	0.0146	0.1079	0.00559	15.85	–155
–154.79[b]	14.696	35.44	7.6726	0.000	207.539	0.00000	0.68072	0.5778	0.3095	1.3598	4289	828.1	0.425	0.0146	0.1078	0.00560	15.83	–154.79
–150	17.143	35.20	6.6543	2.777	208.641	0.00900	0.67378	0.5789	0.3123	1.3634	4224	832.3	0.410	0.0148	0.1061	0.00569	15.36	–150
–145	20.022	34.95	5.7635	5.684	209.766	0.01826	0.66682	0.5803	0.3154	1.3676	4155	836.3	0.395	0.0150	0.1042	0.00580	14.87	–145
–140	23.259	34.69	5.0159	8.598	210.866	0.02739	0.66013	0.5819	0.3188	1.3722	4086	840.1	0.382	0.0153	0.1025	0.00590	14.39	–140
–135	26.883	34.44	4.3848	11.522	211.938	0.03641	0.65370	0.5837	0.3224	1.3773	4016	843.6	0.369	0.0155	0.1007	0.00600	13.91	–135
–130	30.922	34.18	3.8493	14.457	212.981	0.04531	0.64750	0.5858	0.3263	1.3829	3946	846.8	0.356	0.0158	0.0990	0.00611	13.44	–130
–125	35.406	33.92	3.3926	17.404	213.994	0.05411	0.64153	0.5881	0.3304	1.3890	3876	849.6	0.344	0.0160	0.0973	0.00622	12.96	–125
–120	40.365	33.65	3.0012	20.363	214.975	0.06281	0.63575	0.5907	0.3349	1.3957	3805	852.2	0.333	0.0162	0.0956	0.00634	12.49	–120
–115	45.829	33.38	2.6643	23.337	215.923	0.07141	0.63016	0.5936	0.3397	1.4031	3733	854.5	0.322	0.0165	0.0939	0.00646	12.03	–115
–110	51.829	33.11	2.3730	26.327	216.836	0.07993	0.62475	0.5968	0.3448	1.4112	3661	856.4	0.312	0.0167	0.0922	0.00658	11.57	–110
–105	58.398	32.84	2.1200	29.334	217.712	0.08836	0.61950	0.6003	0.3503	1.4200	3588	858.0	0.302	0.0170	0.0906	0.00671	11.11	–105
–100	65.567	32.56	1.8995	32.360	218.551	0.09672	0.61439	0.6041	0.3562	1.4297	3515	859.3	0.292	0.0172	0.0890	0.00685	10.66	–100
–95	73.369	32.27	1.7065	35.407	219.350	0.10501	0.60942	0.6083	0.3625	1.4403	3441	860.3	0.283	0.0175	0.0874	0.00699	10.21	–95
–90	81.836	31.99	1.5370	38.476	220.106	0.11324	0.60457	0.6129	0.3694	1.4519	3367	860.9	0.274	0.0178	0.0858	0.00714	9.76	–90
–85	91.001	31.69	1.3876	41.569	220.819	0.12140	0.59982	0.6180	0.3767	1.4647	3292	861.1	0.265	0.0181	0.0842	0.00729	9.32	–85
–80	100.90	31.40	1.2555	44.688	221.485	0.12952	0.59518	0.6235	0.3846	1.4787	3216	861.0	0.257	0.0184	0.0827	0.00746	8.88	–80
–75	111.56	31.09	1.1383	47.835	222.103	0.13759	0.59062	0.6295	0.3932	1.4942	3140	860.5	0.249	0.0186	0.0812	0.00763	8.45	–75
–70	123.03	30.78	1.0340	51.012	222.670	0.14562	0.58614	0.6361	0.4025	1.5113	3063	859.7	0.241	0.0190	0.0796	0.00781	8.02	–70
–65	135.33	30.47	0.9409	54.222	223.182	0.15361	0.58172	0.6433	0.4126	1.5301	2985	858.5	0.233	0.0193	0.0781	0.00801	7.60	–65
–60	148.50	30.14	0.8576	57.468	223.636	0.16158	0.57735	0.6513	0.4236	1.5511	2906	856.8	0.226	0.0196	0.0766	0.00821	7.18	–60
–55	162.58	29.81	0.7827	60.752	224.029	0.16953	0.57301	0.6600	0.4357	1.5744	2827	854.8	0.219	0.0200	0.0752	0.00843	6.76	–55
–50	177.60	29.48	0.7154	64.077	224.357	0.17747	0.56871	0.6696	0.4489	1.6003	2747	852.4	0.212	0.0203	0.0737	0.00866	6.35	–50
–45	193.59	29.13	0.6546	67.447	224.616	0.18540	0.56442	0.6802	0.4635	1.6295	2666	849.5	0.205	0.0207	0.0722	0.00891	5.95	–45
–40	210.61	28.77	0.5996	70.867	224.799	0.19333	0.56013	0.6920	0.4797	1.6622	2584	846.2	0.198	0.0211	0.0707	0.00917	5.55	–40
–35	228.68	28.41	0.5496	74.339	224.901	0.20128	0.55582	0.7051	0.4978	1.6993	2500	842.5	0.191	0.0215	0.0693	0.00946	5.16	–35
–30	247.84	28.03	0.5042	77.870	224.915	0.20925	0.55148	0.7198	0.5181	1.7416	2416	838.3	0.184	0.0219	0.0678	0.00976	4.78	–30
–25	268.14	27.64	0.4628	81.465	224.833	0.21726	0.54709	0.7364	0.5411	1.7901	2331	833.7	0.178	0.0224	0.0663	0.01009	4.40	–25
–20	289.61	27.23	0.4249	85.131	224.646	0.22531	0.54263	0.7553	0.5674	1.8461	2244	828.5	0.171	0.0229	0.0648	0.01045	4.02	–20
–15	312.30	26.81	0.3902	88.875	224.343	0.23343	0.53808	0.7769	0.5978	1.9115	2156	822.9	0.165	0.0234	0.0634	0.01084	3.66	–15
–10	336.25	26.38	0.3582	92.708	223.909	0.24163	0.53340	0.8020	0.6334	1.9885	2067	816.7	0.159	0.0240	0.0619	0.01128	3.30	–10
–5	361.50	25.92	0.3288	96.639	223.329	0.24993	0.52857	0.8314	0.6756	2.0805	1975	809.9	0.152	0.0246	0.0604	0.01177	2.95	–5
0	388.12	25.43	0.3015	100.684	222.582	0.25835	0.52354	0.8665	0.7264	2.1920	1882	802.6	0.146	0.0253	0.0588	0.01232	2.60	0
5	416.15	24.92	0.2762	104.860	221.642	0.26694	0.51827	0.9091	0.7889	2.3297	1785	794.6	0.140	0.0260	0.0573	0.01295	2.27	5
10	445.64	24.38	0.2526	109.190	220.476	0.27574	0.51268	0.9622	0.8678	2.5037	1686	786.0	0.133	0.0268	0.0557	0.01369	1.95	10
15	476.65	23.79	0.2304	113.706	219.037	0.28480	0.50670	1.030	0.9705	2.730	1583	776.6	0.127	0.0277	0.0541	0.01458	1.64	15
20	509.26	23.15	0.2096	118.451	217.263	0.29420	0.50020	1.121	1.110	3.037	1474	766.3	0.120	0.0287	0.0524	0.01568	1.33	20
25	543.54	22.45	0.1897	123.488	215.057	0.30407	0.49300	1.249	1.309	3.473	1360	755.1	0.113	0.0299	0.0507	0.01714	1.05	25
30	579.58	21.65	0.1706	128.921	212.271	0.31460	0.48482	1.444	1.620	4.145	1239	742.5	0.106	0.0313	0.0489	0.01918	0.78	30
35	617.49	20.72	0.1517	134.928	208.638	0.32613	0.47514	1.782	2.170	5.309	1107	728.0	0.098	0.0332	0.0473	0.02237	0.52	35
40	657.42	19.56	0.1324	141.901	203.590	0.33942	0.46288	2.522	3.397	7.823	961	709.7	0.089	0.0357	0.0461	0.02838	0.29	40
45	699.58	17.86	0.1106	151.091	195.355	0.35688	0.44459	5.514	8.383	17.35	782	679.7	0.078	0.0399	0.0496	0.04548	0.10	45
48.56[c]	731.25	13.37	0.0748	171.840	171.840	0.39709	0.39709	∞	∞	∞	0	0.0	—	—	∞	∞	0.00	48.56

*Temperatures on ITS-90 scale [a]Triple point [b]Normal boiling point [c]Critical point

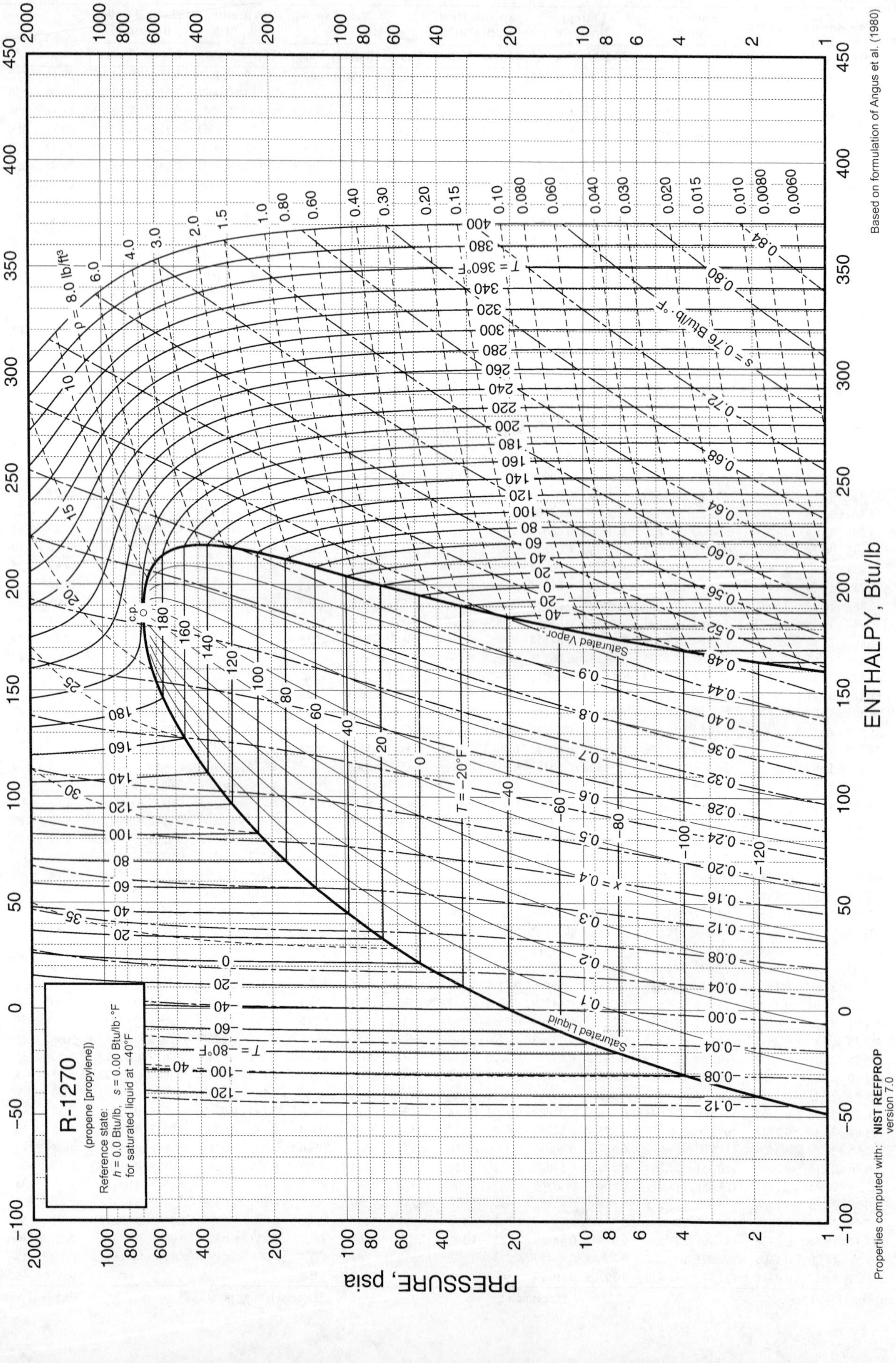

Fig. 28 Pressure-Enthalpy Diagram for Refrigerant 1270 (Propylene)

Refrigerant 1270 (Propylene) Properties of Saturated Liquid and Saturated Vapor

Temp.,* °F	Pressure, psia	Density, lb/ft³ Liquid	Volume, ft³/lb Vapor	Enthalpy, Btu/lb Liquid	Enthalpy, Btu/lb Vapor	Entropy, Btu/lb·°F Liquid	Entropy, Btu/lb·°F Vapor	Specific Heat c_p, Btu/lb·°F Liquid	Specific Heat c_p, Btu/lb·°F Vapor	c_p/c_v Vapor	Vel. of Sound, ft/s Liquid	Vel. of Sound, ft/s Vapor	Viscosity, lb_m/ft·h Liquid	Viscosity, lb_m/ft·h Vapor	Thermal Cond., Btu/h·ft·°F Liquid	Thermal Cond., Btu/h·ft·°F Vapor	Surface Tension, dyne/cm	Temp.,* °F
–200	0.030	43.93	2187.1	–79.204	143.635	–0.23623	0.62193	0.4646	0.2489	1.2345	5496	615.2	1.691	0.0099	0.1010	0.00324	29.86	–200
–190	0.059	43.53	1161.0	–74.534	146.130	–0.21858	0.59969	0.4693	0.2522	1.2310	5375	626.0	1.486	0.0103	0.1001	0.00341	28.92	–190
–180	0.110	43.14	649.45	–69.819	148.653	–0.20142	0.57976	0.4735	0.2555	1.2277	5258	636.4	1.319	0.0106	0.0992	0.00357	27.98	–180
–170	0.194	42.75	380.67	–65.065	151.200	–0.18472	0.56187	0.4771	0.2590	1.2245	5143	646.5	1.182	0.0110	0.0982	0.00374	27.05	–170
–160	0.328	42.35	232.62	–60.277	153.771	–0.16847	0.54581	0.4805	0.2626	1.2215	5031	656.4	1.068	0.0114	0.0971	0.00392	26.13	–160
–150	0.534	41.96	147.55	–55.455	156.362	–0.15264	0.53137	0.4837	0.2664	1.2188	4919	665.8	0.971	0.0118	0.0961	0.00410	25.22	–150
–145	0.672	41.76	119.02	–53.032	157.665	–0.14488	0.52470	0.4853	0.2683	1.2175	4863	670.5	0.928	0.0120	0.0955	0.00419	24.76	–145
–140	0.839	41.56	96.766	–50.602	158.971	–0.13722	0.51837	0.4868	0.2703	1.2163	4808	675.0	0.888	0.0121	0.0950	0.00429	24.31	–140
–135	1.039	41.36	79.267	–48.163	160.282	–0.12966	0.51236	0.4884	0.2724	1.2151	4752	679.4	0.850	0.0123	0.0944	0.00438	23.86	–135
–130	1.278	41.16	65.395	–45.716	161.595	–0.12218	0.50666	0.4900	0.2745	1.2141	4697	683.7	0.815	0.0125	0.0938	0.00448	23.41	–130
–125	1.561	40.96	54.317	–43.261	162.912	–0.11479	0.50125	0.4916	0.2767	1.2131	4641	688.0	0.783	0.0127	0.0932	0.00458	22.96	–125
–120	1.893	40.76	45.405	–40.798	164.231	–0.10749	0.49612	0.4933	0.2789	1.2122	4586	692.1	0.752	0.0129	0.0926	0.00467	22.51	–120
–115	2.281	40.56	38.186	–38.327	165.551	–0.10027	0.49124	0.4950	0.2812	1.2114	4530	696.1	0.723	0.0131	0.0920	0.00477	22.07	–115
–110	2.733	40.36	32.301	–35.846	166.873	–0.09314	0.48661	0.4967	0.2836	1.2107	4474	700.0	0.696	0.0133	0.0914	0.00488	21.63	–110
–105	3.254	40.16	27.474	–33.356	168.196	–0.08607	0.48221	0.4985	0.2861	1.2101	4418	703.8	0.671	0.0135	0.0908	0.00498	21.18	–105
–100	3.853	39.95	23.490	–30.857	169.519	–0.07908	0.47803	0.5004	0.2886	1.2096	4362	707.4	0.646	0.0136	0.0902	0.00508	20.75	–100
–95	4.539	39.75	20.184	–28.349	170.842	–0.07217	0.47406	0.5023	0.2912	1.2093	4305	711.0	0.624	0.0138	0.0896	0.00519	20.31	–95
–90	5.320	39.54	17.425	–25.830	172.164	–0.06532	0.47028	0.5043	0.2938	1.2090	4249	714.4	0.602	0.0140	0.0889	0.00529	19.87	–90
–85	6.204	39.34	15.111	–23.301	173.485	–0.05853	0.46669	0.5064	0.2966	1.2089	4192	717.6	0.581	0.0142	0.0883	0.00540	19.44	–85
–80	7.203	39.13	13.160	–20.761	174.804	–0.05181	0.46328	0.5085	0.2994	1.2089	4135	720.8	0.562	0.0144	0.0876	0.00551	19.01	–80
–75	8.326	38.92	11.508	–18.209	176.120	–0.04515	0.46004	0.5107	0.3023	1.2091	4078	723.8	0.543	0.0146	0.0869	0.00562	18.58	–75
–70	9.583	38.71	10.102	–15.646	177.434	–0.03854	0.45695	0.5130	0.3054	1.2094	4021	726.6	0.526	0.0148	0.0863	0.00574	18.15	–70
–65	10.985	38.50	8.9010	–13.072	178.743	–0.03199	0.45402	0.5154	0.3085	1.2099	3964	729.3	0.509	0.0150	0.0856	0.00585	17.73	–65
–60	12.544	38.29	7.8702	–10.484	180.049	–0.02550	0.45123	0.5179	0.3117	1.2105	3906	731.9	0.493	0.0151	0.0849	0.00597	17.30	–60
–55	14.271	38.07	6.9821	–7.884	181.350	–0.01905	0.44857	0.5205	0.3150	1.2113	3848	734.3	0.477	0.0153	0.0842	0.00609	16.88	–55
–53.84[b]	14.696	38.02	6.7943	–7.280	181.650	–0.01757	0.44797	0.5211	0.3157	1.2115	3835	734.8	0.474	0.0154	0.0841	0.00612	16.79	–53.84
–50	16.178	37.86	6.2140	–5.270	182.645	–0.01266	0.44604	0.5231	0.3184	1.2123	3790	736.5	0.463	0.0155	0.0836	0.00621	16.46	–50
–45	18.278	37.64	5.5472	–2.642	183.934	–0.00631	0.44363	0.5259	0.3219	1.2134	3732	738.6	0.449	0.0157	0.0829	0.00633	16.05	–45
–40	20.584	37.42	4.9663	0.000	185.217	0.00000	0.44134	0.5287	0.3255	1.2148	3674	740.4	0.435	0.0159	0.0821	0.00646	15.63	–40
–35	23.108	37.20	4.4586	2.657	186.492	0.00626	0.43915	0.5317	0.3292	1.2163	3616	742.2	0.422	0.0161	0.0814	0.00659	15.22	–35
–30	25.863	36.97	4.0133	5.330	187.759	0.01249	0.43707	0.5347	0.3331	1.2181	3557	743.7	0.410	0.0163	0.0807	0.00672	14.81	–30
–25	28.864	36.75	3.6216	8.018	189.018	0.01867	0.43508	0.5379	0.3371	1.2201	3498	745.0	0.398	0.0165	0.0800	0.00685	14.40	–25
–20	32.124	36.52	3.2759	10.723	190.267	0.02482	0.43319	0.5412	0.3412	1.2223	3440	746.2	0.387	0.0167	0.0792	0.00699	14.00	–20
–15	35.658	36.29	2.9699	13.445	191.507	0.03094	0.43138	0.5445	0.3454	1.2248	3381	747.2	0.376	0.0169	0.0785	0.00713	13.60	–15
–10	39.479	36.06	2.6984	16.185	192.736	0.03702	0.42965	0.5481	0.3498	1.2275	3321	747.9	0.365	0.0171	0.0778	0.00727	13.20	–10
–5	43.602	35.83	2.4568	18.943	193.953	0.04307	0.42799	0.5517	0.3544	1.2306	3262	748.5	0.355	0.0173	0.0770	0.00742	12.80	–5
0	48.042	35.59	2.2412	21.719	195.158	0.04910	0.42641	0.5555	0.3591	1.2339	3203	748.9	0.345	0.0175	0.0763	0.00758	12.40	0
5	52.814	35.35	2.0483	24.516	196.350	0.05509	0.42489	0.5594	0.3640	1.2375	3144	749.0	0.336	0.0177	0.0755	0.00773	12.01	5
10	57.933	35.11	1.8754	27.332	197.528	0.06107	0.42344	0.5635	0.3690	1.2415	3084	749.0	0.327	0.0179	0.0747	0.00790	11.62	10
15	63.415	34.86	1.7200	30.169	198.692	0.06701	0.42204	0.5677	0.3743	1.2459	3024	748.7	0.318	0.0182	0.0740	0.00807	11.23	15
20	69.274	34.61	1.5800	33.028	199.840	0.07294	0.4207	0.5721	0.3797	1.2506	2965	748.1	0.309	0.0184	0.0732	0.00824	10.85	20
25	75.528	34.36	1.4536	35.909	200.971	0.07884	0.41941	0.5766	0.3854	1.2558	2905	747.4	0.301	0.0186	0.0724	0.00842	10.47	25
30	82.191	34.10	1.3393	38.813	202.085	0.08473	0.41816	0.5814	0.3913	1.2614	2845	746.4	0.293	0.0189	0.0716	0.00861	10.09	30
35	89.279	33.84	1.2356	41.741	203.180	0.09060	0.41696	0.5863	0.3975	1.2675	2785	745.2	0.285	0.0191	0.0708	0.00880	9.71	35
40	96.810	33.58	1.1414	44.694	204.255	0.09646	0.41579	0.5914	0.4039	1.2742	2725	743.7	0.278	0.0194	0.0700	0.00901	9.34	40
45	104.80	33.31	1.0557	47.672	205.309	0.10230	0.41466	0.5968	0.4107	1.2815	2665	741.9	0.271	0.0196	0.0692	0.00922	8.97	45
50	113.26	33.04	0.9775	50.677	206.341	0.10813	0.41355	0.6025	0.4177	1.2894	2605	739.9	0.264	0.0199	0.0684	0.00944	8.60	50
55	122.22	32.77	0.9060	53.709	207.349	0.11395	0.41248	0.6083	0.4251	1.2980	2544	737.6	0.257	0.0202	0.0676	0.00968	8.24	55
60	131.68	32.49	0.8407	56.770	208.332	0.11977	0.41142	0.6145	0.4329	1.3074	2484	735.0	0.250	0.0205	0.0668	0.00992	7.88	60
65	141.67	32.20	0.7807	59.861	209.287	0.12558	0.41038	0.6210	0.4412	1.3177	2423	732.2	0.244	0.0208	0.0660	0.01018	7.52	65
70	152.20	31.91	0.7256	62.983	210.214	0.13139	0.40935	0.6279	0.4499	1.3289	2362	729.0	0.237	0.0211	0.0652	0.01045	7.17	70
75	163.30	31.61	0.6750	66.137	211.110	0.13719	0.40834	0.6351	0.4591	1.3412	2302	725.6	0.231	0.0214	0.0643	0.01073	6.82	75
80	174.97	31.31	0.6283	69.325	211.973	0.14300	0.40732	0.6428	0.4690	1.3548	2241	721.8	0.225	0.0218	0.0635	0.01103	6.47	80
85	187.24	31.0	0.5852	72.549	212.801	0.14881	0.40631	0.6510	0.4795	1.3697	2179	717.7	0.219	0.0221	0.0627	0.01135	6.13	85
90	200.12	30.68	0.5454	75.810	213.590	0.15463	0.40529	0.6597	0.4907	1.3862	2118	713.3	0.213	0.0225	0.0618	0.01168	5.79	90
95	213.64	30.36	0.5085	79.110	214.339	0.16046	0.40426	0.6691	0.5028	1.4045	2056	708.5	0.207	0.0229	0.0610	0.01203	5.46	95
100	227.82	30.03	0.4742	82.452	215.043	0.16630	0.40321	0.6792	0.5159	1.4248	1995	703.4	0.202	0.0233	0.0602	0.01240	5.12	100
110	258.21	29.34	0.4128	89.270	216.303	0.17804	0.40103	0.7020	0.5458	1.4730	1870	692.1	0.191	0.0242	0.0585	0.01323	4.48	110
120	291.47	28.61	0.3595	96.290	217.333	0.18988	0.39870	0.7295	0.5819	1.5343	1744	679.3	0.180	0.0252	0.0568	0.01418	3.85	120
130	327.77	27.82	0.3128	103.544	218.086	0.20188	0.39613	0.7636	0.6269	1.6145	1615	664.9	0.170	0.0264	0.0550	0.01528	3.24	130
140	367.30	26.98	0.2717	111.079	218.496	0.21410	0.39323	0.8077	0.6854	1.7230	1484	648.7	0.159	0.0278	0.0533	0.01658	2.65	140
150	410.29	26.05	0.2352	118.964	218.467	0.22665	0.38985	0.8684	0.7653	1.8769	1348	630.7	0.149	0.0294	0.0515	0.01813	2.09	150
160	456.98	25.01	0.2023	127.313	217.850	0.23968	0.38578	0.9587	0.8830	2.1110	1208	610.5	0.138	0.0315	0.0497	0.02004	1.56	160
170	507.64	23.80	0.1721	136.329	216.388	0.25349	0.38064	1.1120	1.0778	2.5091	1059	587.9	0.126	0.0341	0.0479	0.02249	1.07	170
180	562.64	22.29	0.1437	146.459	213.549	0.26876	0.37364	1.4360	1.4751	3.3387	899	562.5	0.113	0.0376	0.0463	0.02589	0.62	180
190	622.44	20.09	0.1146	159.113	207.766	0.28757	0.36246	2.6270	2.8164	6.1809	720	534.0	0.097	0.0433	0.0459	0.03187	0.23	190
198.36[c]	676.54	13.95	0.0717	186.432	186.432	0.32841	0.32841	∞	∞	∞	∞ 0	0.0	—	—	∞	∞	0.00	198.36

*Temperatures are on IPTS-68 scale

[b]Normal boiling point

[c]Critical point

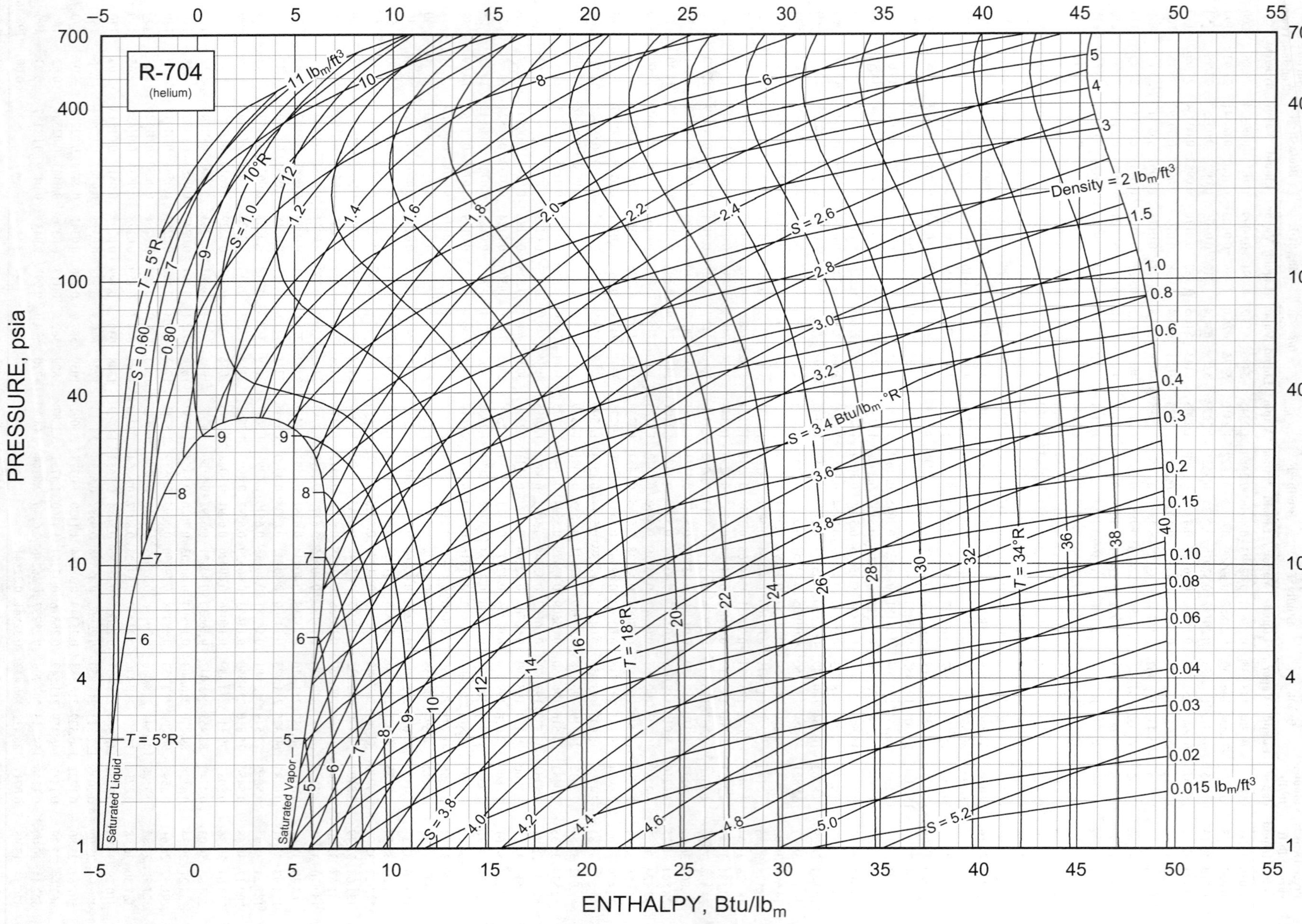

Fig. 29 Pressure-Enthalpy Diagram for Refrigerant 704 (Helium)

Note: The reference states for enthalpy and entropy differ from those in the table.

Refrigerant 704 (Helium) Properties of Saturated Liquid and Saturated Vapor

Temp.,* °R	Pressure, psia	Density, lb/ft³ Liquid	Volume, ft³/lb Vapor	Enthalpy, Btu/lb Liquid	Enthalpy, Btu/lb Vapor	Entropy, Btu/lb·°R Liquid	Entropy, Btu/lb·°R Vapor	Specific Heat c_p, Btu/lb·°R Liquid	Specific Heat c_p, Btu/lb·°R Vapor	c_p/c_v Vapor	Velocity of Sound, ft/s Liquid	Velocity of Sound, ft/s Vapor	Viscosity, lb_m/ft·h Liquid	Viscosity, lb_m/ft·h Vapor	Thermal Cond., Btu/h·ft·°R Liquid	Thermal Cond., Btu/h·ft·°R Vapor	Surface Tension, dyne/cm	Temp.,* °R
3.92[a]	0.704	9.130	13.9837	1.005	10.998	0.33557	2.88589	1.5100	1.4485	1.747	711	273.0	—	—	—	—	0.388	3.92
4.00	0.789	9.122	12.7008	1.121	11.076	0.36428	2.85306	1.2809	1.4556	1.752	710	275.2	—	—	—	—	0.382	4.00
4.20	1.021	9.099	10.1926	1.340	11.263	0.41671	2.77927	0.9051	1.4720	1.768	708	280.3	—	—	—	—	0.366	4.20
4.40	1.296	9.068	8.3274	1.504	11.445	0.45355	2.71288	0.7039	1.4879	1.786	708	285.1	—	—	—	—	0.350	4.40
4.60	1.617	9.030	6.9024	1.640	11.621	0.48225	2.65223	0.6064	1.5037	1.805	710	289.7	—	—	—	—	0.334	4.60
4.80	1.988	8.987	5.7905	1.763	11.792	0.50693	2.59623	0.5700	1.5199	1.827	711	294.0	—	—	—	—	0.319	4.80
5.00	2.413	8.938	4.9078	1.884	11.955	0.52983	2.54407	0.5694	1.5371	1.851	711	298.0	—	—	—	—	0.303	5.00
5.20	2.896	8.883	4.1970	2.008	12.111	0.55216	2.49514	0.5893	1.5554	1.879	708	301.7	—	—	—	—	0.287	5.20
5.40	3.442	8.824	3.6172	2.138	12.260	0.57454	2.44894	0.6209	1.5755	1.910	703	305.2	—	—	—	—	0.272	5.40
5.60	4.053	8.760	3.1392	2.276	12.400	0.59727	2.40509	0.6590	1.5978	1.944	696	308.5	—	—	—	—	0.256	5.60
5.80	4.734	8.690	2.7410	2.423	12.531	0.62047	2.36323	0.7009	1.6229	1.984	688	311.5	—	—	—	—	0.241	5.80
6.00	5.488	8.616	2.4063	2.579	12.652	0.64419	2.32304	0.7453	1.6513	2.029	679	314.3	—	—	—	—	0.226	6.00
6.20	6.319	8.536	2.1226	2.744	12.763	0.66842	2.28427	0.7918	1.6839	2.080	669	316.8	—	—	—	—	0.211	6.20
6.40	7.230	8.451	1.8803	2.920	12.862	0.69316	2.24664	0.8407	1.7217	2.139	659	319.2	0.00844	0.00238	0.0103	0.00416	0.196	6.40
6.60	8.224	8.360	1.6717	3.106	12.950	0.71841	2.20990	0.8927	1.7657	2.207	647	321.3	0.00832	0.00248	0.0104	0.00432	0.181	6.60
6.80	9.306	8.262	1.4910	3.303	13.025	0.74419	2.17383	0.9489	1.8177	2.286	635	323.2	0.00819	0.00258	0.0105	0.00448	0.166	6.80
7.00	10.480	8.158	1.3333	3.511	13.085	0.77053	2.13816	1.0109	1.8798	2.379	623	324.9	0.00807	0.00268	0.0106	0.00466	0.152	7.00
7.20	11.748	8.047	1.1948	3.732	13.129	0.79748	2.10264	1.0810	1.9547	2.491	609	326.3	0.00793	0.00279	0.0107	0.00483	0.138	7.20
7.40	13.114	7.927	1.0724	3.965	13.155	0.82515	2.06700	1.1621	2.0466	2.626	595	327.6	0.00780	0.00290	0.0107	0.00502	0.123	7.40
7.60	14.584	7.797	0.9634	4.214	13.161	0.85365	2.03091	1.2586	2.1613	2.792	580	328.7	0.00766	0.00301	0.0108	0.00522	0.109	7.60
7.61[b]	14.696	7.787	0.9559	4.233	13.160	0.85578	2.02824	1.2664	2.1708	2.806	579	328.8	0.00765	0.00302	0.0108	0.00524	0.108	7.61
7.80	16.161	7.656	0.8657	4.479	13.143	0.88319	1.99398	1.3768	2.3077	3.003	564	329.6	0.00752	0.00313	0.0108	0.00544	0.095	7.80
8.00	17.850	7.501	0.7774	4.764	13.098	0.91401	1.95573	1.5272	2.5001	3.278	547	330.3	0.00737	0.00326	0.0108	0.00568	0.082	8.00
8.20	19.657	7.329	0.6969	5.072	13.018	0.94651	1.91551	1.7271	2.7626	3.650	529	330.8	0.00721	0.00340	0.0109	0.00596	0.068	8.20
8.40	21.587	7.135	0.6226	5.410	12.895	0.98128	1.87237	2.0092	3.1400	4.181	509	331.2	0.00704	0.00354	0.0109	0.00629	0.055	8.40
8.60	23.650	6.911	0.5529	5.788	12.716	1.01927	1.82486	2.4415	3.7248	5.003	487	331.6	0.00686	0.00371	0.0110	0.00670	0.042	8.60
8.80	25.854	6.641	0.4861	6.222	12.453	1.06226	1.77037	3.1940	4.7457	6.434	463	332.2	0.00664	0.00389	0.0110	0.00724	0.030	8.80
9.00	28.215	6.294	0.4192	6.751	12.055	1.11412	1.70345	4.8375	6.9536	9.531	436	333.4	0.00638	0.00411	0.0112	0.00801	0.018	9.00
9.20	30.755	5.771	0.3451	7.493	11.364	1.18708	1.60775	11.0204	14.9798	20.845	404	336.9	0.00603	0.00440	0.0115	0.00932	0.007	9.20
9.35[c]	32.990	4.348	0.2300	9.339	9.339	1.37760	1.37760	∞	∞	∞	0	0.0	—	—	∞	∞	0.000	9.35

*Temperatures on EPT-76 scale [a] Lower lambda point [b] Normal boiling point [c] Critical point

Refrigerant 704 (Helium) Properties of Gas at 14.696 psia (one standard atmosphere)

Temp., °F	Density, lb/ft³	Enthalpy, Btu/lb	Entropy, Btu/lb·°F	c_p, Btu/lb·°F	c_p/c_v	Vel. of Sound, ft/s	Viscosity, lb_m/ft·h	Thermal Cond., Btu/h·ft·°F	Temp., °F	Density, lb/ft³	Enthalpy, Btu/lb	Entropy, Btu/lb·°F	c_p, Btu/lb·°F	c_p/c_v	Vel. of Sound, ft/s	Viscosity, lb_m/ft·h	Thermal Cond., Btu/h·ft·°F
−452.1[b]	1.04613	13.16	2.0282	2.1708	2.806	328.8	0.0030	0.00523	0	0.01192	577.15	7.3479	1.2412	1.667	3086.5	0.0432	0.08064
−450	0.66840	16.73	2.4459	1.5277	2.037	415.4	0.0035	0.00624	20	0.01142	601.97	7.4007	1.2412	1.667	3152.8	0.0445	0.08304
−440	0.28462	30.24	3.4138	1.2880	1.729	636.4	0.0058	0.01035	40	0.01096	626.79	7.4514	1.2412	1.667	3217.8	0.0457	0.08542
−430	0.18546	42.96	3.9370	1.2616	1.691	786.5	0.0076	0.01343	60	0.01054	651.62	7.5001	1.2412	1.667	3281.5	0.0470	0.08776
−420	0.13809	55.52	4.3020	1.2525	1.679	910.2	0.0092	0.01608	80	0.01015	676.44	7.5470	1.2411	1.667	3344.0	0.0482	0.09008
−400	0.09163	80.49	4.8118	1.2459	1.671	1115.8	0.0119	0.02074	100	0.00979	701.26	7.5922	1.2411	1.667	3405.3	0.0494	0.09238
−380	0.06862	105.39	5.1716	1.2437	1.669	1288.4	0.0143	0.02493	120	0.00945	726.09	7.6357	1.2411	1.667	3465.6	0.0506	0.09465
−360	0.05486	130.25	5.4500	1.2427	1.668	1440.3	0.0164	0.02882	140	0.00914	750.91	7.6778	1.2411	1.667	3524.8	0.0518	0.09690
−340	0.04571	155.10	5.6772	1.2421	1.667	1577.5	0.0183	0.03248	160	0.00884	775.73	7.7186	1.2411	1.667	3583.1	0.0530	0.09912
−320	0.03917	179.94	5.8691	1.2418	1.667	1703.7	0.0202	0.03596	180	0.00857	800.55	7.7580	1.2411	1.667	3640.4	0.0542	0.10133
−300	0.03427	204.77	6.0353	1.2416	1.667	1821.2	0.0219	0.03931	200	0.00831	825.38	7.7962	1.2411	1.667	3696.8	0.0553	0.10351
−280	0.03046	229.60	6.1818	1.2415	1.667	1931.5	0.0236	0.04254	240	0.00783	875.02	7.8693	1.2411	1.667	3807.1	0.0576	0.10783
−260	0.02741	254.43	6.3129	1.2414	1.667	2035.8	0.0248	0.04566	280	0.00741	924.67	7.9383	1.2411	1.667	3914.4	0.0599	0.11207
−240	0.02492	279.26	6.4314	1.2413	1.667	2135.1	0.0264	0.04870	320	0.00703	974.32	8.0036	1.2411	1.667	4018.8	0.0621	0.11624
−220	0.02285	304.08	6.5395	1.2413	1.667	2229.9	0.0280	0.05166	360	0.00669	1023.96	8.0657	1.2411	1.667	4120.5	0.0643	0.12036
−200	0.02109	328.91	6.6390	1.2413	1.666	2320.9	0.0295	0.05454	400	0.00637	1073.61	8.1249	1.2411	1.667	4219.8	0.0665	0.12441
−180	0.01958	353.73	6.7311	1.2412	1.666	2408.4	0.0310	0.05737	440	0.00609	1123.25	8.1813	1.2411	1.667	4316.8	0.0686	0.12841
−160	0.01827	378.56	6.8168	1.2412	1.666	2492.9	0.0324	0.06013	480	0.00583	1172.90	8.2353	1.2411	1.667	4411.6	0.0707	0.13236
−140	0.01713	403.38	6.8970	1.2412	1.666	2574.6	0.0338	0.06284	520	0.00559	1222.55	8.2871	1.2411	1.667	4504.5	0.0728	0.13626
−120	0.01613	428.21	6.9724	1.2412	1.666	2653.7	0.0352	0.06551	560	0.00537	1272.19	8.3367	1.2411	1.667	4595.5	0.0749	0.14011
−100	0.01523	453.03	7.0434	1.2412	1.666	2730.6	0.0366	0.06813	600	0.00517	1321.84	8.3845	1.2411	1.667	4684.7	0.0769	0.14392
−80	0.01443	477.85	7.1105	1.2412	1.667	2805.4	0.0380	0.07070	640	0.00498	1371.48	8.4305	1.2412	1.667	4772.3	0.0789	0.14768
−60	0.01371	502.68	7.1743	1.2412	1.667	2878.2	0.0393	0.07324	680	0.00481	1421.13	8.4748	1.2412	1.667	4858.3	0.0809	0.15141
−40	0.01305	527.50	7.2349	1.2412	1.667	2949.3	0.0406	0.07574	720	0.00465	1470.78	8.5176	1.2412	1.667	4942.8	0.0829	0.15509
−20	0.01246	552.32	7.2927	1.2412	1.667	3018.7	0.0419	0.07821	760	0.00449	1520.42	8.5590	1.2412	1.667	5025.8	0.0849	0.15874
									800	0.00435	1570.07	8.5991	1.2412	1.667	5107.6	0.0868	0.16236

[b] Saturated vapor at normal boiling point

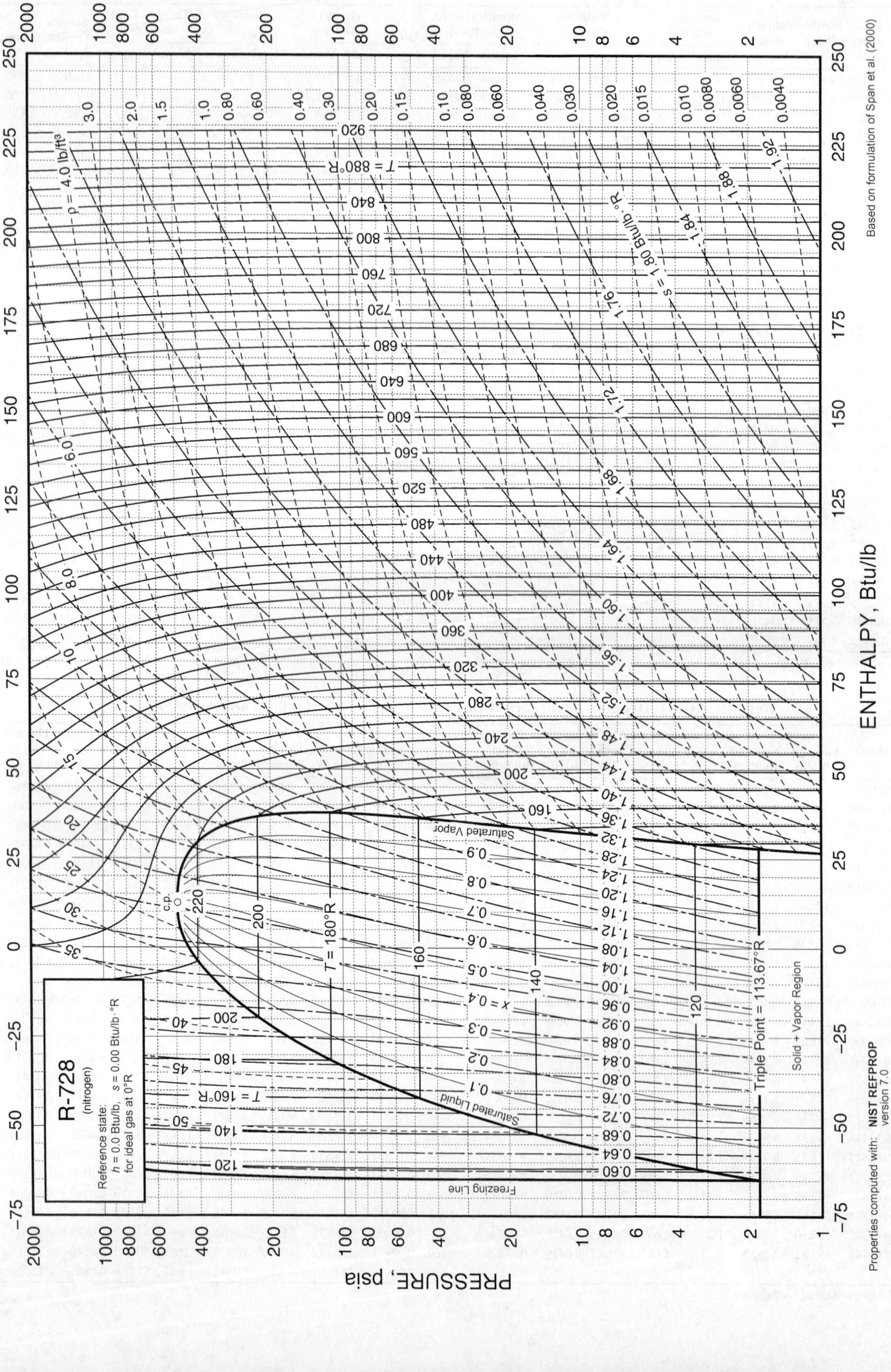

Fig. 30 Pressure-Enthalpy Diagram for Refrigerant 728 (Nitrogen)

Refrigerant 728 (Nitrogen) Properties of Saturated Liquid and Saturated Vapor

Temp.,* °R	Pressure, psia	Density, lb/ft³ Liquid	Volume, ft³/lb Vapor	Enthalpy, Btu/lb Liquid	Enthalpy, Btu/lb Vapor	Entropy, Btu/lb·°R Liquid	Entropy, Btu/lb·°R Vapor	Specific Heat c_p, Btu/lb·°R Liquid	Specific Heat c_p, Btu/lb·°R Vapor	c_p/c_v Vapor	Velocity of Sound, ft/s Liquid	Velocity of Sound, ft/s Vapor	Viscosity, lb_m/ft·h Liquid	Viscosity, lb_m/ft·h Vapor	Thermal Cond., Btu/h·ft·°R Liquid	Thermal Cond., Btu/h·ft·°R Vapor	Surface Tension, dyne/cm	Temp.,* °R
113.67[a]	1.816	54.14	23.757	–64.848	27.868	0.57975	1.3954	0.4781	0.2529	1.4113	3265	528.6	0.754	0.0106	0.1002	0.00325	12.24	113.67
115	2.076	53.95	20.999	–64.212	28.172	0.58530	1.38864	0.4784	0.2534	1.4125	3241	531.3	0.724	0.0107	0.0993	0.00329	12.06	115
120	3.339	53.23	13.566	–61.814	29.293	0.60567	1.3649	0.4796	0.2554	1.4180	3148	541.4	0.626	0.0112	0.0961	0.00347	11.39	120
125	5.150	52.50	9.1106	–59.408	30.376	0.62526	1.34354	0.4811	0.2579	1.4252	3056	550.8	0.547	0.0117	0.0928	0.00364	10.72	125
130	7.658	51.75	6.3275	–56.993	31.414	0.64414	1.32419	0.4830	0.2610	1.4342	2964	559.5	0.482	0.0122	0.0896	0.00382	10.06	130
135	11.029	50.98	4.5244	–54.564	32.402	0.66238	1.30657	0.4854	0.2648	1.4456	2872	567.4	0.428	0.0127	0.0864	0.00400	9.42	135
139.24[b]	14.696	50.32	3.4731	–52.494	33.194	0.67738	1.29278	0.4879	0.2686	1.4572	2793	573.6	0.389	0.0132	0.0837	0.00416	8.87	139.24
140	15.442	50.20	3.3179	–52.121	33.332	0.68004	1.29041	0.4884	0.2694	1.4595	2779	574.6	0.382	0.0132	0.0832	0.00418	8.78	140
145	21.089	49.40	2.4873	–49.658	34.197	0.69717	1.27548	0.4921	0.2748	1.4766	2686	581.0	0.344	0.0138	0.0800	0.00438	8.15	145
150	28.170	48.58	1.9006	–47.174	34.990	0.71383	1.26159	0.4965	0.2813	1.4973	2591	586.6	0.311	0.0143	0.0769	0.00458	7.53	150
155	36.894	47.74	1.4767	–44.663	35.704	0.73008	1.24858	0.5020	0.2890	1.5224	2496	591.3	0.283	0.0149	0.0737	0.00480	6.92	155
160	47.477	46.87	1.1641	–42.120	36.331	0.74596	1.23628	0.5086	0.2983	1.5527	2398	595.1	0.258	0.0154	0.0705	0.00503	6.32	160
165	60.139	45.97	0.9293	–39.539	36.861	0.76153	1.22456	0.5167	0.3094	1.5894	2299	598.1	0.236	0.0160	0.0674	0.00528	5.74	165
170	75.106	45.03	0.7499	–36.914	37.284	0.77684	1.21330	0.5266	0.3227	1.6343	2197	600.1	0.217	0.0167	0.0642	0.00555	5.16	170
175	92.608	44.06	0.6107	–34.237	37.588	0.79194	1.20237	0.5388	0.3390	1.6894	2093	601.1	0.199	0.0173	0.0610	0.00586	4.60	175
180	112.88	43.03	0.5012	–31.495	37.758	0.80690	1.19164	0.5540	0.3591	1.7579	1986	601.2	0.183	0.0180	0.0579	0.00620	4.05	180
185	136.16	41.96	0.4139	–28.678	37.777	0.82178	1.18100	0.5732	0.3844	1.8444	1874	600.3	0.169	0.0187	0.0547	0.00660	3.52	185
190	162.70	40.81	0.3433	–25.768	37.622	0.83667	1.17030	0.598	0.4168	1.9561	1759	598.3	0.155	0.0195	0.0516	0.00706	3.00	190
195	192.76	39.58	0.2857	–22.742	37.261	0.85167	1.15937	0.6306	0.4596	2.1053	1638	595.3	0.143	0.0203	0.0484	0.00761	2.50	195
200	226.61	38.25	0.2379	–19.571	36.649	0.86691	1.14801	0.6754	0.5192	2.3127	1512	591.3	0.131	0.0213	0.0452	0.00829	2.02	200
205	264.55	36.77	0.1978	–16.208	35.720	0.88259	1.13590	0.7399	0.6082	2.6153	1377	585.8	0.119	0.0223	0.0421	0.00916	1.56	205
210	306.91	35.09	0.1636	–12.582	34.370	0.89901	1.12259	0.8408	0.7529	3.0920	1233	578.5	0.107	0.0236	0.0390	0.01034	1.13	210
215	354.08	33.12	0.1337	–8.56	32.406	0.91673	1.10727	1.0220	1.0228	3.9527	1075	568.7	0.095	0.0253	0.0359	0.01209	0.73	215
220	406.56	30.60	0.1064	–3.842	29.393	0.93701	1.08808	1.4530	1.6876	5.9824	891	554.7	0.082	0.0277	0.0331	0.01515	0.38	220
225	465.12	26.60	0.0781	2.755	23.676	0.96494	1.05792	3.9960	5.6747	16.9334	641	525.8	0.065	0.0322	0.0326	0.02401	0.08	225
227.15[c]	492.52	19.56	0.0511	12.576	12.576	1.00738	1.00738	∞	∞		0	0.0	—	—	∞	∞	0.0	227.15

*Temperatures on ITS-90 scale [a]Triple point [b]Normal boiling point [c]Critical point

Refrigerant 728 (Nitrogen) Properties of Gas at 14.696 psia (one standard atmosphere)

Temp., °F	Density, lb/ft³	Enthalpy, Btu/lb	Entropy, Btu/lb·°F	c_p, Btu/lb·°F	c_p/c_v	Vel. of Sound, ft/s	Viscosity, lb_m/ft·h	Thermal Cond., Btu/h·ft·°F
–320.4[b]	0.2879	33.19	1.2928	0.2686	1.457	573.6	0.0132	0.00416
–320	0.2869	33.31	1.2936	0.2684	1.457	574.6	0.0132	0.00417
–300	0.2473	38.59	1.3289	0.2603	1.437	619.8	0.0150	0.00479
–280	0.2179	43.75	1.3594	0.2562	1.426	660.8	0.0168	0.00541
–260	0.1950	48.85	1.3863	0.2539	1.420	698.9	0.0185	0.00603
–240	0.1766	53.91	1.4105	0.2525	1.415	734.6	0.0203	0.00663
–220	0.1614	58.95	1.4324	0.2515	1.412	768.5	0.0219	0.00722
–200	0.1487	63.97	1.4526	0.2509	1.410	800.8	0.0236	0.00780
–180	0.1379	68.98	1.4711	0.2504	1.408	831.7	0.0252	0.00837
–160	0.1285	73.99	1.4884	0.2500	1.407	861.4	0.0267	0.00893
–140	0.1204	78.99	1.5046	0.2498	1.406	890.1	0.0282	0.00949
–120	0.1132	83.98	1.5197	0.2496	1.405	917.9	0.0297	0.01003
–100	0.1069	88.97	1.5340	0.2494	1.404	944.8	0.0312	0.01056
–80	0.1012	93.96	1.5475	0.2493	1.404	970.9	0.0326	0.01108
–60	0.0961	98.94	1.5603	0.2492	1.403	996.3	0.0341	0.01160
–40	0.0915	103.92	1.5725	0.2491	1.403	1021.1	0.0354	0.01211
–20	0.0873	108.90	1.5840	0.2490	1.403	1045.3	0.0368	0.01261
0	0.0835	113.88	1.5951	0.2490	1.402	1068.9	0.0381	0.01310
10	0.0817	116.37	1.6005	0.2489	1.402	1080.5	0.0388	0.01335
20	0.0800	118.86	1.6057	0.2489	1.402	1091.9	0.0394	0.01359
30	0.0784	121.35	1.6109	0.2489	1.402	1103.3	0.0401	0.01383
40	0.0768	123.84	1.6159	0.2489	1.402	1114.5	0.0407	0.01407
50	0.0753	126.33	1.6208	0.2489	1.402	1125.6	0.0414	0.01430
60	0.0738	128.82	1.6257	0.2489	1.401	1136.6	0.0420	0.01454
70	0.0724	131.31	1.6304	0.2489	1.401	1147.5	0.0426	0.01477
80	0.0711	133.80	1.6351	0.2489	1.401	1158.3	0.0433	0.01501
90	0.0698	136.29	1.6396	0.2489	1.401	1169.0	0.0439	0.01524
100	0.0686	138.77	1.6441	0.2489	1.401	1179.6	0.0445	0.01547
120	0.0662	143.75	1.6529	0.2489	1.401	1200.4	0.0457	0.01592
140	0.0640	148.73	1.6613	0.2490	1.400	1220.9	0.0469	0.01637
160	0.0619	153.71	1.6695	0.2491	1.400	1241.0	0.0481	0.01681
180	0.0600	158.70	1.6774	0.2492	1.400	1260.8	0.0492	0.01725
200	0.0581	163.68	1.6851	0.2493	1.399	1280.3	0.0504	0.01769
220	0.0564	168.67	1.6925	0.2494	1.399	1299.4	0.0515	0.01812
240	0.0548	173.66	1.6997	0.2496	1.399	1318.2	0.0526	0.01854
260	0.0533	178.65	1.7068	0.2497	1.398	1336.7	0.0537	0.01896
280	0.0518	183.65	1.7136	0.2500	1.397	1354.9	0.0548	0.01938
300	0.0505	188.65	1.7203	0.2502	1.397	1372.8	0.0559	0.01979
320	0.0492	193.65	1.7268	0.2504	1.396	1390.5	0.0569	0.02020
340	0.0480	198.67	1.7332	0.2507	1.396	1407.9	0.0580	0.02060
360	0.0468	203.68	1.7393	0.2510	1.395	1425.0	0.0590	0.02100
380	0.0457	208.71	1.7454	0.2514	1.394	1441.9	0.0600	0.02140
400	0.0446	213.74	1.7513	0.2517	1.393	1458.6	0.0610	0.02179
420	0.0436	218.78	1.7571	0.2521	1.392	1475.0	0.0620	0.02218
440	0.0426	223.82	1.7628	0.2525	1.391	1491.2	0.0630	0.02257
460	0.0417	228.87	1.7683	0.2529	1.391	1507.2	0.0640	0.02295
480	0.0408	233.94	1.7738	0.2533	1.390	1523.0	0.0650	0.02333
500	0.0400	239.01	1.7791	0.2538	1.389	1538.5	0.0659	0.02371
520	0.0391	244.09	1.7844	0.2543	1.387	1553.9	0.0669	0.02408
540	0.0384	249.18	1.7895	0.2548	1.386	1569.1	0.0678	0.02446
560	0.0376	254.28	1.7946	0.2553	1.385	1584.1	0.0688	0.02483
580	0.0369	259.39	1.7995	0.2558	1.384	1598.9	0.0697	0.02519
600	0.0362	264.52	1.8044	0.2564	1.383	1613.5	0.0706	0.02556
620	0.0355	269.65	1.8092	0.2570	1.382	1627.9	0.0715	0.02592
640	0.0349	274.79	1.8139	0.2575	1.381	1642.2	0.0724	0.02628
660	0.0342	279.95	1.8186	0.2581	1.379	1656.4	0.0733	0.02664
680	0.0336	285.12	1.8232	0.2587	1.378	1670.4	0.0742	0.02699
700	0.0331	290.30	1.8277	0.2593	1.377	1684.2	0.0751	0.02735
720	0.0325	295.49	1.8321	0.2599	1.376	1697.9	0.0760	0.02770
740	0.0320	300.70	1.8365	0.2605	1.374	1711.5	0.0768	0.02805
760	0.0314	305.91	1.8408	0.2612	1.373	1724.9	0.0777	0.02839
780	0.0309	311.14	1.8450	0.2618	1.372	1738.2	0.0786	0.02874
800	0.0304	316.38	1.8492	0.2624	1.371	1751.3	0.0794	0.02908

[b]Saturated vapor at normal boiling point

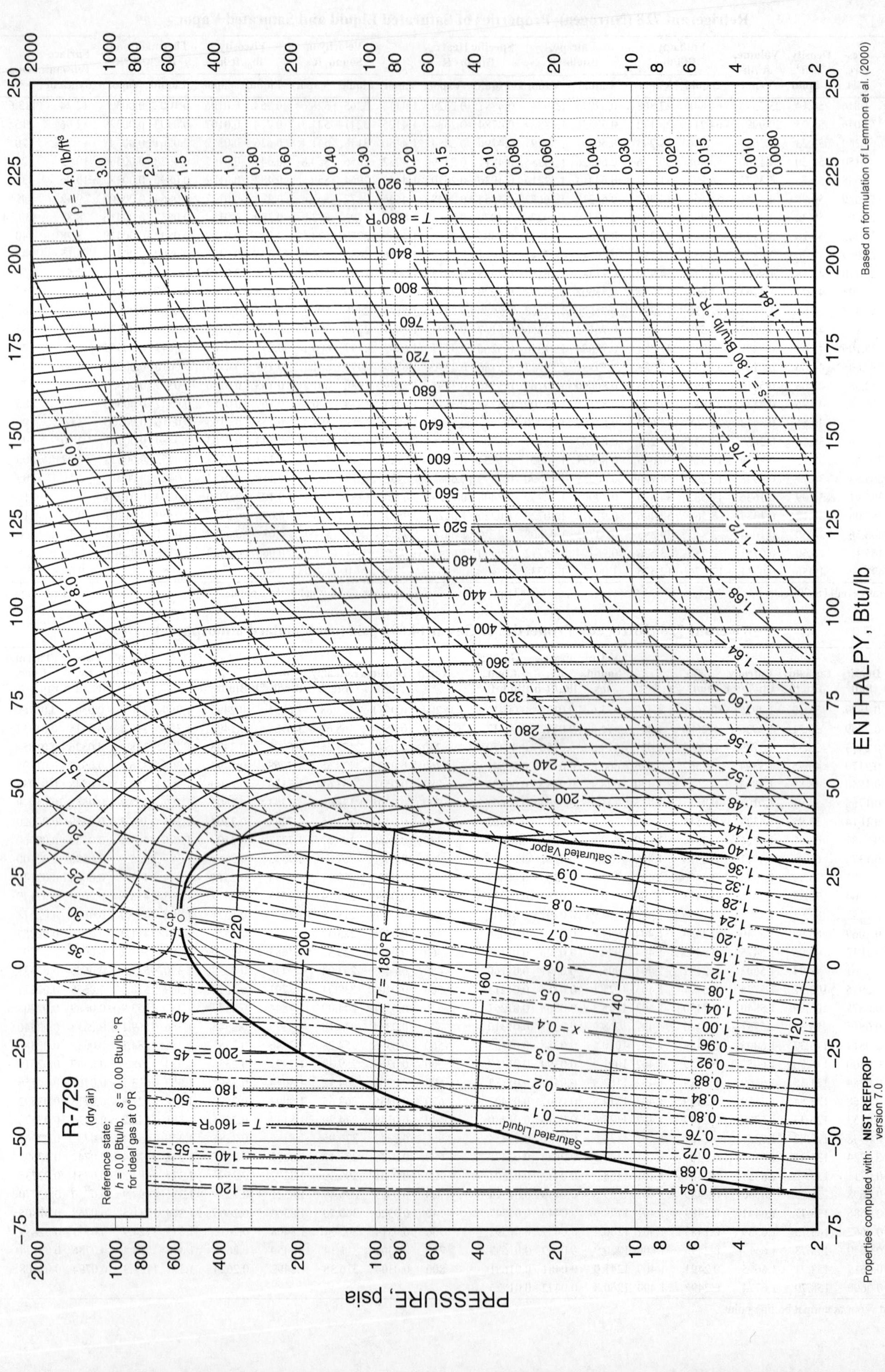

Fig. 31 Pressure-Enthalpy Diagram for Refrigerant 729 (Air)

Refrigerant 729 (Air) Properties of Liquid on the Bubble Line and Vapor on the Dew Line

Pressure, psia	Temp.,* °R Bubble	Temp.,* °R Dew	Density, lb/ft³ Liquid	Volume, ft³/lb Vapor	Enthalpy, Btu/lb Liquid	Enthalpy, Btu/lb Vapor	Entropy, Btu/lb·°R Liquid	Entropy, Btu/lb·°R Vapor	Specific Heat c_p, Btu/lb·°R Liquid	Specific Heat c_p, Btu/lb·°R Vapor	c_p/c_v Vapor	Vel. of Sound, ft/s Liquid	Vel. of Sound, ft/s Vapor	Viscosity, lb_m/ft·h Liquid	Viscosity, lb_m/ft·h Vapor	Thermal Cond., Btu/h·ft·°R Liquid	Thermal Cond., Btu/h·ft·°R Vapor	Surface Tension, dyne/cm
0.76	107.55	113.56	59.79	54.9026	–69.86	26.99	0.58596	1.47005	0.4529	0.2423	1.405	3464	521.3	1.0276	0.0108	0.1071	0.00337	14.95
1	109.93	115.89	59.45	42.7315	–68.79	27.52	0.59587	1.45626	0.4533	0.2428	1.406	3421	526.3	0.9532	0.0110	0.1056	0.00345	14.61
2	116.61	122.40	58.49	22.4862	–65.75	28.99	0.62264	1.42133	0.4544	0.2442	1.411	3300	539.8	0.7818	0.0117	0.1015	0.00366	13.66
4	124.25	129.85	57.37	11.8549	–62.27	30.60	0.65151	1.38713	0.4560	0.2465	1.419	3165	554.1	0.6363	0.0124	0.0969	0.00390	12.60
6	129.25	134.71	56.61	8.1564	–59.98	31.62	0.66951	1.36745	0.4574	0.2484	1.426	3077	562.8	0.5620	0.0129	0.0938	0.00406	11.91
8	133.08	138.43	56.03	6.2560	–58.23	32.37	0.68285	1.35362	0.4587	0.2503	1.432	3010	569.0	0.5138	0.0133	0.0915	0.00418	11.39
10	136.22	141.48	55.55	5.0922	–56.78	32.96	0.69354	1.34296	0.4599	0.2520	1.438	2955	573.8	0.4787	0.0136	0.0896	0.00428	10.97
12	138.90	144.09	55.13	4.3034	–55.54	33.45	0.70252	1.33428	0.4611	0.2537	1.444	2908	577.7	0.4516	0.0139	0.0880	0.00436	10.61
14.70[b]	142.03	147.12	54.63	3.5685	–54.09	34.01	0.71276	1.32467	0.4627	0.2559	1.452	2853	582.0	0.4229	0.0142	0.0861	0.00446	10.20
20	147.07	152.02	53.82	2.6825	–51.74	34.85	0.72892	1.3101	0.4657	0.2601	1.467	2763	588.4	0.3820	0.0147	0.0830	0.00462	9.53
40	159.95	164.50	51.66	1.4046	–45.64	36.71	0.76818	1.27725	0.4765	0.2752	1.518	2531	601.3	0.3012	0.0161	0.0753	0.00506	7.89
60	168.62	172.90	50.12	0.9564	–41.43	37.68	0.79336	1.25770	0.4873	0.2900	1.569	2370	607.0	0.2601	0.0170	0.0701	0.00546	6.81
80	175.39	179.44	48.85	0.7249	–38.08	38.25	0.81244	1.24345	0.4984	0.3051	1.621	2240	609.8	0.2332	0.0178	0.0661	0.00580	6.00
100	181.01	184.87	47.74	0.5825	–35.22	38.57	0.82803	1.23205	0.5101	0.3208	1.675	2129	610.9	0.2134	0.0185	0.0627	0.00613	5.34
150	192.20	195.66	45.38	0.3868	–29.33	38.76	0.85856	1.21005	0.5432	0.3646	1.829	1898	609.9	0.1794	0.0200	0.0561	0.00691	4.07
200	200.97	204.10	43.31	0.2851	–24.43	38.37	0.88241	1.19278	0.5841	0.4183	2.021	1704	606.0	0.1564	0.0213	0.0509	0.00772	3.13
250	208.29	211.12	41.37	0.222	–20.07	37.58	0.90264	1.17775	0.6371	0.4884	2.272	1531	600.5	0.1388	0.0226	0.0465	0.00861	2.39
300	214.63	217.18	39.46	0.1785	–16.01	36.42	0.92075	1.16374	0.7094	0.5862	2.616	1370	593.6	0.1242	0.0240	0.0427	0.00965	1.78
350	220.27	222.53	37.52	0.1462	–12.09	34.89	0.93767	1.14995	0.8153	0.7325	3.120	1215	585.7	0.1113	0.0254	0.0394	0.01093	1.27
400	225.35	227.31	35.44	0.1207	–8.16	32.89	0.95419	1.13562	0.9881	0.9747	3.935	1062	576.5	0.0994	0.0271	0.0365	0.01260	0.85
450	230.00	231.63	33.07	0.0993	–4.00	30.24	0.97127	1.11963	1.3293	1.4513	5.487	901	565.4	0.0876	0.0293	0.0340	0.01504	0.49
500	234.30	235.52	30.00	0.0796	0.89	26.35	0.99103	1.09945	2.3586	2.7920	9.600	718	549.7	0.0745	0.0326	0.0325	0.01942	0.21
549.38[c]	238.56	238.56	21.39	0.0468	12.64	12.64	1.03918	1.03918	—	—	—	—	—	—	—	—	—	0.0

*Temperatures on ITS-90 scale [b]Bubble and dew points at one standard atmosphere [c]Critical point

Refrigerant 729 (Air) Properties of Gas at 14.696 psia (one standard atmosphere)

Temp., °F	Density, lb/ft³	Enthalpy, Btu/lb	Entropy, Btu/lb·°F	c_p, Btu/lb·°F	c_p/c_v	Vel. Sound, ft/s	Viscosity, lb/ft·h	Thermal Cond., Btu/ft·h·°F
–312.5[d]	0.2802	34.01	1.3247	0.2559	1.452	582.0	0.0142	0.00446
–300	0.2560	37.19	1.3454	0.2514	1.441	609.5	0.0154	0.00486
–280	0.2254	42.17	1.3748	0.2476	1.429	649.9	0.0173	0.00548
–260	0.2017	47.10	1.4008	0.2453	1.422	687.4	0.0191	0.00610
–240	0.1826	51.99	1.4242	0.2438	1.417	722.6	0.0209	0.00671
–220	0.1670	56.85	1.4454	0.2429	1.414	756.0	0.0226	0.00731
–200	0.1538	61.70	1.4648	0.2422	1.412	787.8	0.0243	0.00789
–180	0.1426	66.54	1.4828	0.2417	1.410	818.2	0.0260	0.00847
–160	0.1329	71.37	1.4994	0.2413	1.409	847.5	0.0276	0.00903
–140	0.1245	76.20	1.5150	0.2411	1.408	875.8	0.0292	0.00959
–120	0.1171	81.01	1.5296	0.2409	1.407	903.1	0.0308	0.01014
–100	0.1105	85.83	1.5434	0.2407	1.406	929.5	0.0323	0.01068
–80	0.1047	90.64	1.5564	0.2406	1.405	955.3	0.0338	0.01121
–60	0.0994	95.45	1.5688	0.2405	1.405	980.3	0.0353	0.01173
–40	0.0946	100.26	1.5805	0.2404	1.404	1004.6	0.0368	0.01224
–20	0.0903	105.07	1.5917	0.2404	1.404	1028.4	0.0382	0.01275
0	0.0863	109.88	1.6024	0.2404	1.403	1051.5	0.0396	0.01325
10	0.0845	112.28	1.6076	0.2404	1.403	1062.9	0.0403	0.01350
20	0.0827	114.69	1.6127	0.2404	1.403	1074.2	0.0410	0.01374
30	0.0810	117.09	1.6176	0.2404	1.403	1085.3	0.0416	0.01398
40	0.0794	119.50	1.6225	0.2404	1.403	1096.4	0.0423	0.01423
50	0.0778	121.90	1.6272	0.2405	1.402	1107.3	0.0430	0.01447
60	0.0763	124.31	1.6319	0.2405	1.402	1118.1	0.0436	0.01471
70	0.0749	126.71	1.6365	0.2405	1.402	1128.7	0.0443	0.01494
80	0.0735	129.12	1.6410	0.2406	1.402	1139.3	0.0450	0.01518
90	0.0722	131.52	1.6454	0.2406	1.401	1149.8	0.0456	0.01541
100	0.0709	133.93	1.6498	0.2407	1.401	1160.2	0.0462	0.01565
120	0.0684	138.74	1.6582	0.2408	1.401	1180.6	0.0475	0.01611
140	0.0661	143.56	1.6664	0.2410	1.400	1200.6	0.0488	0.01657
160	0.0640	148.38	1.6743	0.2412	1.400	1220.3	0.0500	0.01702
180	0.0620	153.21	1.6820	0.2414	1.399	1239.6	0.0512	0.01746

Temp., °F	Density, lb/ft³	Enthalpy, Btu/lb	Entropy, Btu/lb·°F	c_p, Btu/lb·°F	c_p/c_v	Vel. Sound, ft/s	Viscosity, lb/ft·h	Thermal Cond., Btu/ft·h·°F
200	0.0601	158.04	1.6894	0.2416	1.398	1258.6	0.0524	0.01791
220	0.0583	162.87	1.6966	0.2419	1.398	1277.3	0.0536	0.01834
240	0.0567	167.71	1.7036	0.2421	1.397	1295.6	0.0548	0.01878
260	0.0551	172.56	1.7105	0.2424	1.396	1313.7	0.0559	0.01920
280	0.0536	177.41	1.7171	0.2428	1.395	1331.5	0.0571	0.01963
300	0.0522	182.27	1.7236	0.2431	1.394	1349.0	0.0582	0.02005
320	0.0508	187.14	1.7299	0.2435	1.394	1366.2	0.0593	0.02046
340	0.0496	192.01	1.7361	0.2439	1.393	1383.1	0.0604	0.02088
360	0.0484	196.89	1.7421	0.2443	1.392	1399.8	0.0615	0.02129
380	0.0472	201.78	1.7480	0.2448	1.391	1416.3	0.0626	0.02169
400	0.0461	206.68	1.7538	0.2452	1.389	1432.5	0.0636	0.02209
420	0.0451	211.59	1.7594	0.2457	1.388	1448.6	0.0647	0.02249
440	0.0441	216.51	1.7649	0.2462	1.387	1464.3	0.0657	0.02289
460	0.0431	221.44	1.7704	0.2467	1.386	1479.9	0.0668	0.02328
480	0.0422	226.38	1.7757	0.2472	1.385	1495.3	0.0678	0.02367
500	0.0413	231.33	1.7809	0.2478	1.384	1510.5	0.0688	0.02405
520	0.0405	236.29	1.7860	0.2483	1.382	1525.5	0.0698	0.02444
540	0.0397	241.26	1.7910	0.2489	1.381	1540.3	0.0708	0.02482
560	0.0389	246.25	1.7960	0.2495	1.380	1554.9	0.0718	0.02520
580	0.0381	251.24	1.8008	0.2501	1.379	1569.4	0.0727	0.02557
600	0.0374	256.25	1.8056	0.2507	1.377	1583.7	0.0737	0.02595
620	0.0367	261.27	1.8103	0.2513	1.376	1597.8	0.0747	0.02632
640	0.0360	266.30	1.8149	0.2519	1.375	1611.8	0.0756	0.02669
660	0.0354	271.35	1.8195	0.2525	1.374	1625.6	0.0766	0.02705
680	0.0348	276.40	1.8239	0.2532	1.372	1639.3	0.0775	0.02742
700	0.0342	281.47	1.8283	0.2538	1.371	1652.8	0.0784	0.02778
720	0.0336	286.55	1.8327	0.2544	1.370	1666.3	0.0793	0.02814
740	0.0330	291.65	1.8370	0.2551	1.368	1679.5	0.0802	0.02850
760	0.0325	296.76	1.8412	0.2557	1.367	1692.7	0.0811	0.02886
780	0.0320	301.88	1.8454	0.2563	1.366	1705.7	0.0820	0.02921
800	0.0315	307.01	1.8495	0.2570	1.365	1718.6	0.0829	0.02956

[d]Saturated vapor at dew-point temperature

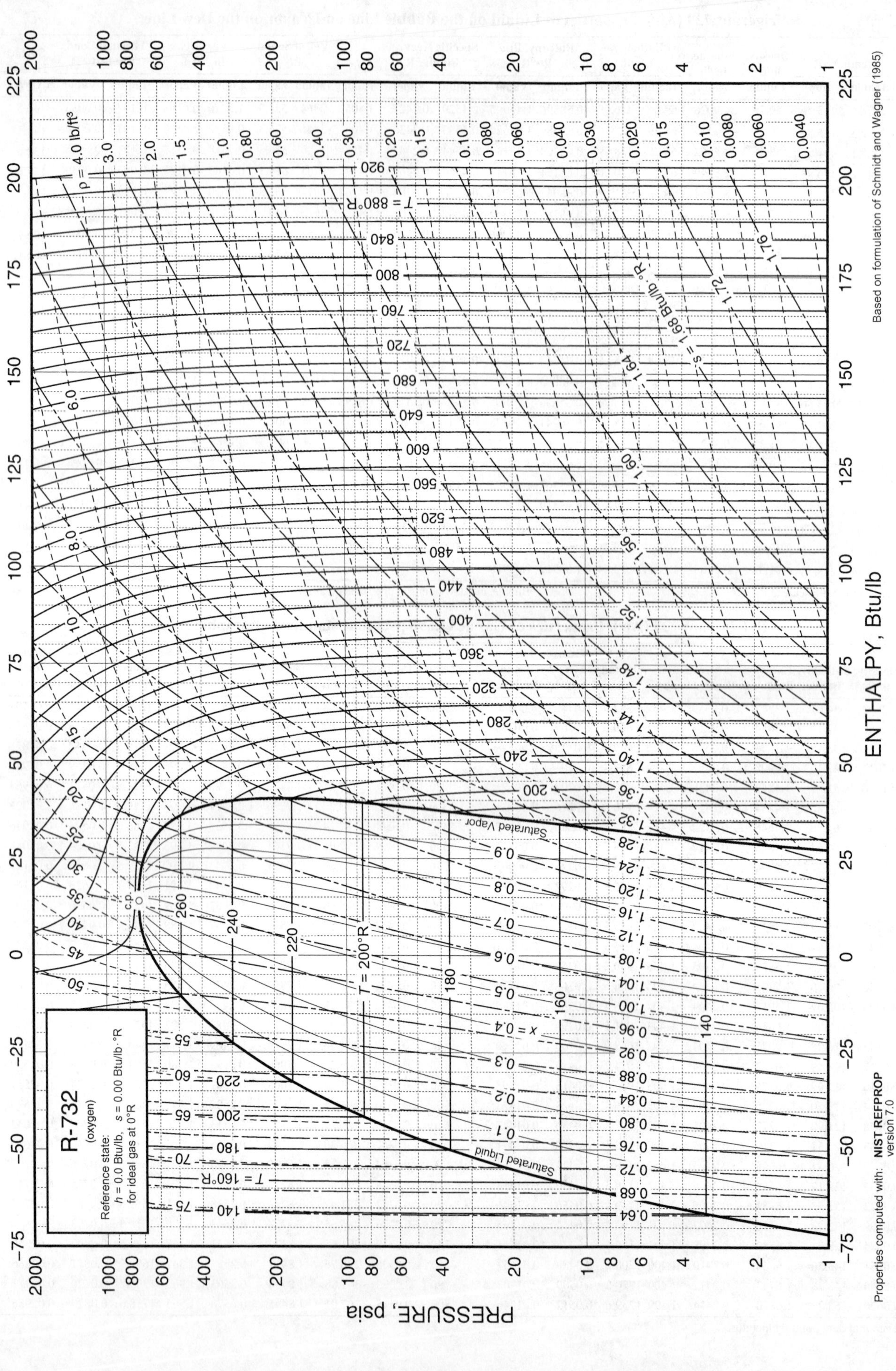

Fig. 32 Pressure-Enthalpy Diagram for Refrigerant 732 (Oxygen)

Refrigerant 732 (Oxygen) Properties of Saturated Liquid and Saturated Vapor

Temp.,* °R	Pressure, psia	Density, lb/ft³ Liquid	Volume, ft³/lb Vapor	Enthalpy, Btu/lb Liquid	Enthalpy, Btu/lb Vapor	Entropy, Btu/lb·°R Liquid	Entropy, Btu/lb·°R Vapor	Specific Heat c_p, Btu/lb·°R Liquid	Specific Heat c_p, Btu/lb·°R Vapor	c_p/c_v Vapor	Velocity of Sound, ft/s Liquid	Velocity of Sound, ft/s Vapor	Viscosity, lb_m/ft·h Liquid	Viscosity, lb_m/ft·h Vapor	Thermal Cond., Btu/h·ft·°R Liquid	Thermal Cond., Btu/h·ft·°R Vapor	Surface Tension, dyne/cm	Temp.,* °R
97.85[a]	0.021	81.54	1546.5	−83.295	21.126	0.50003	1.56719	0.3999	0.2213	1.3950	3686	460.4	1.871	0.0099	0.1167	0.00256	22.68	97.85
100	0.031	81.23	1092.8	−82.436	21.591	0.50872	1.54899	0.3993	0.2223	1.3940	3704	465.2	1.756	0.0101	0.1158	0.00262	22.35	100
110	0.139	79.73	265.18	−78.440	23.741	0.54681	1.47572	0.4002	0.2276	1.3889	3685	486.6	1.325	0.0112	0.1112	0.00295	20.82	110
120	0.479	78.17	83.783	−74.432	25.874	0.58167	1.41755	0.4010	0.2322	1.3862	3578	506.8	1.031	0.0123	0.1066	0.00327	19.31	120
130	1.342	76.58	32.306	−70.420	27.982	0.61377	1.37070	0.4011	0.2341	1.3885	3443	526.3	0.826	0.0134	0.1021	0.00360	17.82	130
140	3.202	74.97	14.511	−66.404	30.041	0.64349	1.33239	0.4015	0.2335	1.3968	3298	545.1	0.679	0.0144	0.0975	0.00393	16.36	140
150	6.732	73.33	7.3371	−62.377	32.017	0.67121	1.30051	0.4028	0.2320	1.4112	3151	562.8	0.571	0.0155	0.0929	0.00427	14.92	150
155	9.389	72.49	5.4088	−60.356	32.962	0.68442	1.28647	0.4039	0.2316	1.4206	3077	571.0	0.526	0.0160	0.0906	0.00444	14.20	155
160	12.802	71.64	4.0699	−58.328	33.871	0.69725	1.27349	0.4054	0.2317	1.4313	3002	578.8	0.488	0.0166	0.0883	0.00462	13.50	160
162.34[b]	14.696	71.24	3.5859	−57.376	34.283	0.70312	1.26774	0.4062	0.2320	1.4369	2967	582.2	0.471	0.0168	0.0872	0.00471	13.17	162.34
165	17.108	70.78	3.1187	−56.290	34.740	0.70972	1.26142	0.4072	0.2325	1.4436	2927	586.0	0.453	0.0171	0.0859	0.00481	12.80	165
170	22.448	69.90	2.4290	−54.240	35.565	0.72187	1.25014	0.4094	0.2342	1.4574	2851	592.6	0.422	0.0176	0.0836	0.00500	12.11	170
175	28.973	69.01	1.9195	−52.177	36.341	0.73373	1.23955	0.4121	0.2369	1.4730	2775	598.5	0.394	0.0182	0.0813	0.00519	11.43	175
180	36.840	68.10	1.5366	−50.098	37.065	0.74533	1.22957	0.4153	0.2405	1.4906	2697	603.9	0.369	0.0187	0.0790	0.00540	10.75	180
185	46.211	67.17	1.2444	−48.000	37.732	0.75668	1.22010	0.4190	0.2453	1.5104	2619	608.5	0.346	0.0192	0.0766	0.00561	10.09	185
190	57.251	66.22	1.0182	−45.880	38.339	0.76783	1.21108	0.4234	0.2512	1.5330	2540	612.4	0.325	0.0198	0.0743	0.00583	9.43	190
195	70.131	65.24	0.8409	−43.736	38.880	0.77878	1.20245	0.4284	0.2583	1.5589	2460	615.7	0.305	0.0203	0.0719	0.00607	8.77	195
200	85.023	64.24	0.7002	−41.564	39.353	0.78956	1.19414	0.4343	0.2668	1.5886	2378	618.2	0.287	0.0209	0.0695	0.00632	8.13	200
205	102.10	63.20	0.5873	−39.360	39.751	0.80020	1.18610	0.4411	0.2768	1.6230	2294	620.0	0.270	0.0215	0.0672	0.00658	7.50	205
210	121.55	62.13	0.4957	−37.119	40.069	0.81072	1.17828	0.4491	0.2884	1.6633	2209	621.1	0.254	0.0221	0.0648	0.00686	6.87	210
215	143.55	61.02	0.4208	−34.838	40.299	0.82115	1.17062	0.4585	0.3020	1.7108	2122	621.4	0.239	0.0227	0.0625	0.00717	6.26	215
220	168.28	59.87	0.3590	−32.508	40.434	0.83151	1.16306	0.4696	0.3181	1.7673	2033	621.1	0.224	0.0233	0.0601	0.00750	5.66	220
225	195.93	58.66	0.3074	−30.125	40.464	0.84183	1.15556	0.4830	0.3372	1.8354	1942	619.9	0.211	0.0240	0.0578	0.00787	5.07	225
230	226.69	57.40	0.2641	−27.678	40.376	0.85215	1.14804	0.4991	0.3603	1.9188	1848	618.1	0.198	0.0247	0.0554	0.00827	4.49	230
235	260.77	56.07	0.2274	−25.156	40.154	0.86252	1.14044	0.5190	0.3886	2.0225	1750	615.4	0.185	0.0254	0.0531	0.00873	3.93	235
240	298.37	54.65	0.1961	−22.546	39.779	0.87298	1.13267	0.5442	0.4244	2.1546	1649	611.9	0.173	0.0262	0.0508	0.00926	3.38	240
250	385.04	51.47	0.1457	−16.974	38.446	0.89449	1.11617	0.6208	0.5342	2.5628	1434	602.2	0.150	0.0281	0.0461	0.01063	2.33	250
260	488.67	47.59	0.1068	−10.679	35.974	0.91764	1.09708	0.7794	0.7669	3.4209	1192	588.2	0.128	0.0308	0.0415	0.01277	1.36	260
270	611.86	42.17	0.0745	−2.870	31.217	0.94518	1.07142	1.3060	1.5835	6.3145	898	567.0	0.104	0.0356	0.0371	0.01715	0.51	270
278.25[c]	731.43	27.23	0.0367	13.949	13.949	1.00402	1.00402	∞	∞	∞	0	0.0	—	—	∞	∞	0.0	278.25

*Temperatures on ITS-90 scale   [a]Triple point   [b]Normal boiling point   [c]Critical point

Refrigerant 732 (Oxygen) Properties of Gas at 14.696 psia (one standard atmosphere)

Temp., °F	Density, lb/ft³	Enthalpy, Btu/lb	Entropy, Btu/lb·°F	c_p, Btu/lb·°F	c_p/c_v	Vel. Sound, ft/s	Viscosity, lb/ft·h	Thermal Cond., Btu/h·ft·°F
−297.3[b]	0.2789	34.28	1.2677	0.2320	1.437	582.2	0.0168	0.00471
−280	0.2499	38.20	1.2907	0.2236	1.433	617.3	0.0186	0.00524
−260	0.2234	42.66	1.3142	0.2226	1.424	652.8	0.0207	0.00586
−240	0.2022	47.10	1.3354	0.2217	1.418	686.2	0.0227	0.00647
−220	0.1848	51.53	1.3547	0.2208	1.414	718.0	0.0246	0.00707
−200	0.1702	55.94	1.3724	0.2201	1.411	748.3	0.0265	0.00766
−180	0.1577	60.33	1.3887	0.2196	1.409	777.3	0.0284	0.00825
−160	0.1470	64.72	1.4038	0.2192	1.407	805.2	0.0303	0.00883
−140	0.1377	69.10	1.4180	0.2189	1.406	832.1	0.0321	0.00941
−120	0.1295	73.48	1.4313	0.2187	1.405	858.1	0.0338	0.00998
−100	0.1222	77.85	1.4438	0.2186	1.404	883.2	0.0356	0.01054
−80	0.1157	82.23	1.4556	0.2185	1.404	907.7	0.0373	0.01109
−60	0.1099	86.60	1.4668	0.2185	1.403	931.4	0.0390	0.01164
−40	0.1046	90.97	1.4775	0.2185	1.402	954.5	0.0406	0.01218
−20	0.0998	95.34	1.4877	0.2186	1.401	977.0	0.0422	0.01271
0	0.0955	99.71	1.4974	0.2188	1.401	998.9	0.0438	0.01324
20	0.0915	104.09	1.5067	0.2190	1.400	1020.3	0.0454	0.01377
40	0.0878	108.47	1.5157	0.2192	1.399	1041.1	0.0469	0.01429
60	0.0844	112.86	1.5243	0.2195	1.398	1061.5	0.0484	0.01480
80	0.0812	117.25	1.5326	0.2199	1.396	1081.4	0.0499	0.01531
100	0.0783	121.65	1.5406	0.2203	1.395	1100.9	0.0514	0.01581
120	0.0756	126.06	1.5483	0.2207	1.394	1120.0	0.0529	0.01631
140	0.0731	130.48	1.5558	0.2212	1.392	1138.7	0.0543	0.01680
160	0.0707	134.91	1.5631	0.2218	1.391	1157.0	0.0557	0.01729
180	0.0685	139.35	1.5701	0.2223	1.389	1174.9	0.0571	0.01777
200	0.0664	143.80	1.5770	0.2230	1.388	1192.5	0.0585	0.01825
220	0.0645	148.27	1.5837	0.2236	1.386	1209.7	0.0598	0.01873
240	0.0626	152.75	1.5902	0.2243	1.384	1226.7	0.0612	0.01920
260	0.0609	157.24	1.5965	0.2251	1.382	1243.3	0.0625	0.01967
280	0.0592	161.75	1.6027	0.2258	1.381	1259.7	0.0638	0.02013
300	0.0577	166.28	1.6087	0.2266	1.379	1275.8	0.0651	0.02059
320	0.0562	170.81	1.6146	0.2274	1.377	1291.6	0.0664	0.02105
340	0.0548	175.37	1.6204	0.2282	1.375	1307.2	0.0676	0.02150
360	0.0535	179.94	1.6260	0.2290	1.373	1322.6	0.0689	0.02195
380	0.0522	184.53	1.6315	0.2298	1.371	1337.7	0.0701	0.02240
400	0.0510	189.13	1.6370	0.2307	1.369	1352.6	0.0713	0.02285
420	0.0498	193.76	1.6423	0.2315	1.367	1367.4	0.0725	0.02329
440	0.0487	198.39	1.6475	0.2323	1.366	1381.9	0.0737	0.02372
460	0.0476	203.05	1.6526	0.2332	1.364	1396.2	0.0749	0.02416
480	0.0466	207.72	1.6576	0.2340	1.362	1410.4	0.0761	0.02459
500	0.0457	212.41	1.6626	0.2349	1.360	1424.4	0.0772	0.02502
520	0.0447	217.12	1.6674	0.2357	1.358	1438.3	0.0784	0.02545
540	0.0438	221.84	1.6722	0.2365	1.357	1451.9	0.0795	0.02588
560	0.0430	226.58	1.6769	0.2374	1.355	1465.5	0.0807	0.02630
580	0.0421	231.33	1.6815	0.2382	1.353	1478.9	0.0818	0.02672
600	0.0413	236.10	1.6861	0.2390	1.352	1492.2	0.0829	0.02714
620	0.0406	240.89	1.6905	0.2398	1.350	1505.3	0.0840	0.02755
640	0.0398	245.69	1.6949	0.2406	1.348	1518.3	0.0851	0.02796
660	0.0391	250.51	1.6993	0.2413	1.347	1531.2	0.0862	0.02837
680	0.0384	255.35	1.7036	0.2421	1.345	1543.9	0.0872	0.02878
700	0.0378	260.20	1.7078	0.2428	1.344	1556.6	0.0883	0.02919
720	0.0371	265.06	1.7119	0.2436	1.343	1569.1	0.0893	0.02960
740	0.0365	269.94	1.7160	0.2443	1.341	1581.6	0.0904	0.03000
760	0.0359	274.83	1.7201	0.2450	1.340	1593.9	0.0914	0.03040
780	0.0353	279.74	1.7241	0.2457	1.339	1606.1	0.0925	0.03080
800	0.0348	284.66	1.7280	0.2464	1.337	1618.3	0.0935	0.03120

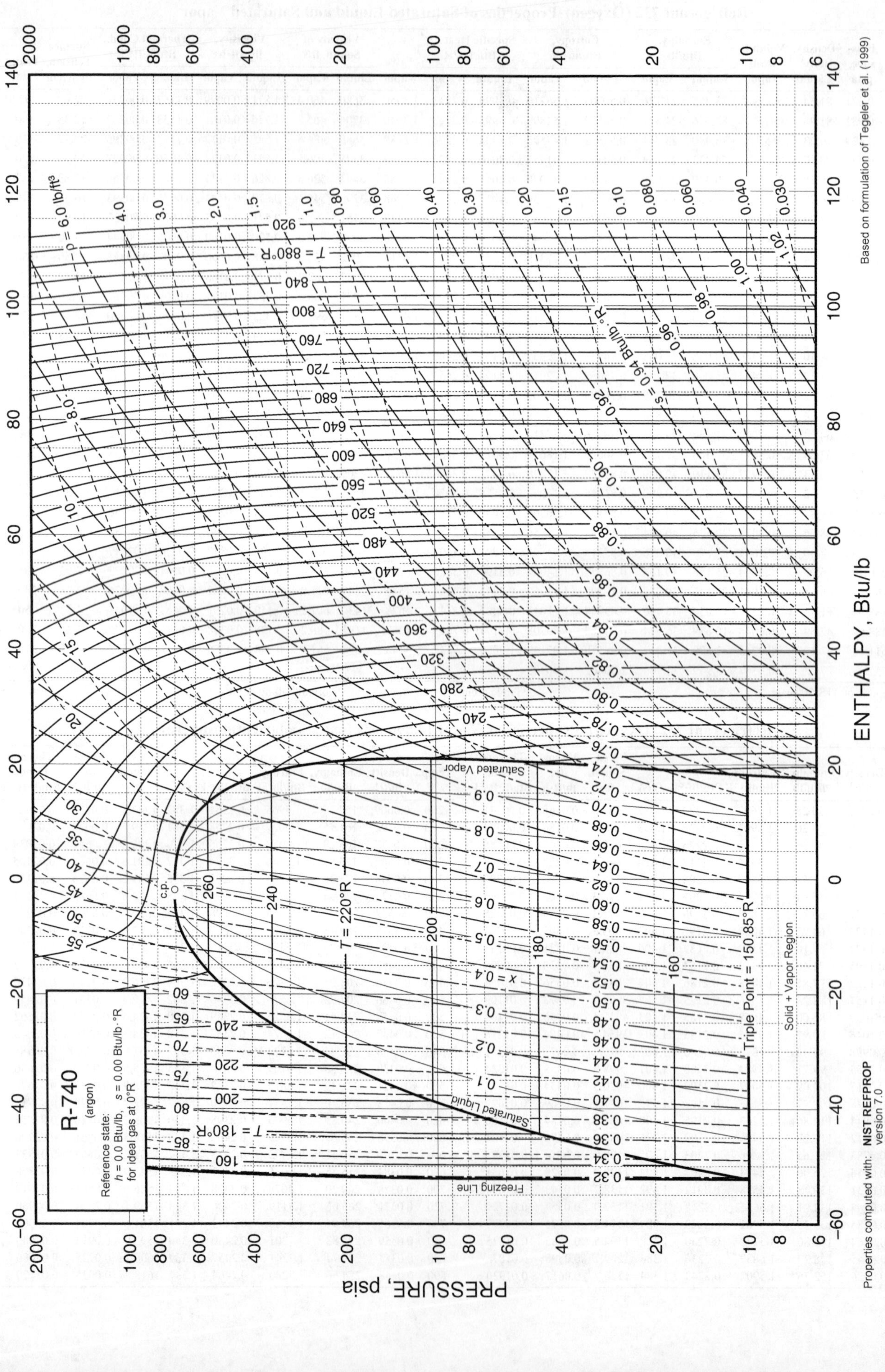

Fig. 33 Pressure-Enthalpy Diagram for Refrigerant 740 (Argon)

Refrigerant 740 (Argon) Properties of Saturated Liquid and Saturated Vapor

Temp.,* °R	Pressure, psia	Density, lb/ft³	Volume, ft³/lb	Enthalpy, Btu/lb		Entropy, Btu/lb·°R		Specific Heat c_p, Btu/lb·°R		c_p/c_v	Velocity of Sound, ft/s		Viscosity, lb_m/ft·h		Thermal Cond., Btu/h·ft·°R		Surface Tension, dyne/cm	Temp.,* °R
		Liquid	Vapor	Liquid	Vapor	Liquid	Vapor	Liquid	Vapor	Vapor	Liquid	Vapor	Liquid	Vapor	Liquid	Vapor		
150.85[a]	9.992	88.45	3.9507	–52.243	18.190	0.31775	0.78466	0.2667	0.1327	1.7093	2829	551.6	0.702	0.0166	0.0773	0.00310	13.42	150.85
155	12.935	87.57	3.1188	–51.133	18.574	0.32498	0.77470	0.2668	0.1343	1.7192	2778	557.6	0.653	0.0171	0.0753	0.00320	12.83	155
160	17.322	86.50	2.3862	–49.792	19.010	0.33343	0.76344	0.2675	0.1366	1.7332	2714	564.4	0.630	0.0173	0.0743	0.00325	12.53	160
157.14[b]	14.696	87.11	2.7744	–50.558	18.765	0.32863	0.76978	0.2670	0.1352	1.7249	2750	560.6	0.600	0.0177	0.0729	0.00332	12.13	157.14
165	22.764	85.41	1.8565	–48.444	19.413	0.34165	0.75291	0.2688	0.1392	1.7499	2650	570.8	0.553	0.0183	0.0706	0.00345	11.44	165
170	29.412	84.30	1.4661	–47.088	19.780	0.34967	0.7430	0.2706	0.1423	1.7696	2584	576.7	0.511	0.0189	0.0683	0.00358	10.76	170
175	37.423	83.17	1.1733	–45.720	20.107	0.35749	0.73365	0.2729	0.1458	1.7926	2518	582.1	0.473	0.0196	0.0660	0.00372	10.08	175
180	46.958	82.01	0.9502	–44.338	20.393	0.36516	0.72477	0.2758	0.1498	1.8196	2450	587.0	0.439	0.0202	0.0637	0.00387	9.42	180
185	58.183	80.83	0.7776	–42.939	20.632	0.37268	0.71631	0.2791	0.1545	1.8512	2382	591.4	0.408	0.0209	0.0615	0.00402	8.76	185
190	71.266	79.61	0.6424	–41.521	20.822	0.38009	0.70820	0.2831	0.1598	1.8880	2311	595.3	0.380	0.0215	0.0593	0.00418	8.12	190
195	86.376	78.35	0.5351	–40.081	20.958	0.38738	0.70040	0.2878	0.1660	1.9311	2239	598.7	0.354	0.0222	0.0571	0.00436	7.49	195
200	103.69	77.06	0.4490	–38.615	21.035	0.39460	0.69285	0.2933	0.1732	1.9816	2166	601.6	0.331	0.0230	0.0549	0.00455	6.86	200
205	123.38	75.72	0.3792	–37.120	21.050	0.40174	0.68550	0.2998	0.1817	2.0412	2090	604.0	0.309	0.0237	0.0527	0.00475	6.25	205
210	145.62	74.34	0.3220	–35.593	20.995	0.40884	0.67831	0.3074	0.1916	2.1120	2013	605.8	0.289	0.0245	0.0506	0.00498	5.66	210
215	170.60	72.89	0.2748	–34.027	20.864	0.41591	0.67122	0.3164	0.2035	2.1967	1933	607.0	0.270	0.0253	0.0485	0.00524	5.07	215
220	198.49	71.38	0.2354	–32.416	20.647	0.42299	0.66419	0.3273	0.2179	2.2994	1850	607.8	0.253	0.0262	0.0464	0.00553	4.50	220
225	229.50	69.79	0.2023	–30.755	20.335	0.43009	0.65716	0.3407	0.2356	2.4256	1765	607.9	0.236	0.0272	0.0444	0.00586	3.95	225
230	263.81	68.11	0.1742	–29.033	19.914	0.43725	0.65007	0.3573	0.2578	2.5835	1675	607.3	0.220	0.0282	0.0423	0.00625	3.41	230
235	301.62	66.31	0.1502	–27.237	19.366	0.44453	0.64284	0.3785	0.2864	2.7860	1582	606.2	0.205	0.0293	0.0403	0.00672	2.89	235
240	343.16	64.38	0.1294	–25.352	18.666	0.45197	0.63538	0.4064	0.3245	3.0547	1483	604.3	0.190	0.0306	0.0383	0.00730	2.39	240
245	388.66	62.28	0.1114	–23.353	17.780	0.45967	0.62755	0.4449	0.3780	3.4258	1378	601.6	0.175	0.0321	0.0364	0.00803	1.91	245
250	438.38	59.94	0.0954	–21.203	16.655	0.46774	0.61917	0.5012	0.4583	3.9666	1267	597.6	0.160	0.0338	0.0344	0.00899	1.46	250
255	492.61	57.26	0.0812	–18.844	15.206	0.47640	0.60993	0.5913	0.5911	4.8227	1145	591.5	0.145	0.0360	0.0324	0.01035	1.04	255
260	551.70	54.06	0.0681	–16.163	13.273	0.48605	0.59926	0.7594	0.8483	6.3925	1006	581.9	0.129	0.0387	0.0304	0.01245	0.65	260
265	616.14	49.89	0.0554	–12.891	10.470	0.49764	0.58579	1.1960	1.5406	10.3020	833	564.9	0.112	0.0427	0.0290	0.01639	0.31	265
270	686.70	42.48	0.0406	–7.692	4.957	0.51600	0.56285	5.6360	8.4769	43.1571	573	515.1	0.089	0.0512	0.0333	0.03231	0.04	270
271.24[c]	705.32	33.44	0.0299	–1.863	–1.863	0.53720	0.53720	∞	∞	∞	0	0.0	—	—	∞	∞	0.0	271.24

*Temperatures on ITS-90 scale [a]Triple point [b]Normal boiling point [c]Critical point

Refrigerant 740 (Argon) Properties of Gas at 14.696 psia (one standard atmosphere)

Temp., °F	Density, lb/ft³	Enthalpy, Btu/lb	Entropy, Btu/lb·°F	c_p, Btu/lb·°F	c_p/c_v	Vel. Sound, ft/s	Viscosity, lb/ft·h	Thermal Cond., Btu/h·ft·°F	Temp., °F	Density, lb/ft³	Enthalpy, Btu/lb	Entropy, Btu/lb·°F	c_p, Btu/lb·°F	c_p/c_v	Vel. Sound, ft/s	Viscosity, lb/ft·h	Thermal Cond., Btu/h·ft·°F
–302.5[b]	0.3604	18.77	0.7698	0.1352	1.725	560.6	0.0173	0.00325	200	0.0829	81.98	0.9514	0.1245	1.668	1170.2	0.0648	0.01215
–300	0.3541	19.11	0.7719	0.1346	1.722	565.6	0.0176	0.00330	220	0.0805	84.47	0.9551	0.1245	1.668	1187.9	0.0663	0.01244
–280	0.3116	21.76	0.7876	0.1309	1.707	603.5	0.0199	0.00372	240	0.0782	86.96	0.9587	0.1245	1.668	1205.2	0.0679	0.01273
–260	0.2787	24.35	0.8013	0.1289	1.697	638.4	0.0221	0.00414	260	0.0760	89.45	0.9622	0.1245	1.668	1222.3	0.0694	0.01301
–240	0.2523	26.92	0.8135	0.1277	1.691	671.2	0.0243	0.00455	280	0.0740	91.94	0.9656	0.1245	1.668	1239.2	0.0709	0.01330
–220	0.2305	29.46	0.8246	0.1269	1.686	702.1	0.0265	0.00495	300	0.0720	94.43	0.9689	0.1245	1.668	1255.9	0.0724	0.01358
–200	0.2123	31.99	0.8347	0.1263	1.683	731.6	0.0286	0.00535	320	0.0702	96.92	0.9722	0.1245	1.668	1272.3	0.0739	0.01385
–180	0.1969	34.52	0.8441	0.1260	1.680	759.9	0.0307	0.00574	340	0.0684	99.41	0.9753	0.1245	1.668	1288.5	0.0753	0.01412
–160	0.1835	37.03	0.8528	0.1257	1.678	787.0	0.0327	0.00613	360	0.0667	101.90	0.9784	0.1245	1.668	1304.5	0.0768	0.01440
–140	0.1719	39.54	0.8609	0.1255	1.676	813.2	0.0347	0.00650	380	0.0651	104.39	0.9814	0.1245	1.668	1320.3	0.0782	0.01466
–120	0.1616	42.05	0.8685	0.1253	1.675	838.6	0.0367	0.00688	400	0.0636	106.88	0.9843	0.1245	1.668	1336.0	0.0796	0.01493
–100	0.1525	44.56	0.8757	0.1252	1.674	863.1	0.0387	0.00724	420	0.0622	109.37	0.9872	0.1245	1.668	1351.4	0.0810	0.01519
–80	0.1444	47.06	0.8825	0.1251	1.673	887.0	0.0406	0.00761	440	0.0608	111.86	0.9900	0.1244	1.668	1366.7	0.0824	0.01545
–60	0.1372	49.56	0.8889	0.1250	1.672	910.2	0.0425	0.00796	460	0.0595	114.34	0.9927	0.1244	1.667	1381.8	0.0838	0.01570
–40	0.1306	52.06	0.8950	0.1249	1.672	932.8	0.0444	0.00831	480	0.0582	116.83	0.9954	0.1244	1.667	1396.7	0.0851	0.01596
–20	0.1246	54.55	0.9008	0.1248	1.671	954.9	0.0462	0.00866	500	0.0570	119.32	0.9980	0.1244	1.667	1411.5	0.0865	0.01621
0	0.1192	57.05	0.9063	0.1248	1.671	976.5	0.0480	0.00900	520	0.0558	121.81	1.0006	0.1244	1.667	1426.2	0.0878	0.01646
10	0.1166	58.30	0.9090	0.1248	1.671	987.1	0.0489	0.00916	540	0.0547	124.30	1.0031	0.1244	1.667	1440.6	0.0891	0.01671
20	0.1142	59.55	0.9117	0.1247	1.670	997.6	0.0498	0.00933	560	0.0536	126.79	1.0056	0.1244	1.667	1455.0	0.0905	0.01695
30	0.1118	60.79	0.9142	0.1247	1.670	1008.0	0.0507	0.00950	580	0.0526	129.28	1.0080	0.1244	1.667	1469.2	0.0918	0.01719
40	0.1096	62.04	0.9167	0.1247	1.670	1018.2	0.0515	0.00966	600	0.0516	131.76	1.0104	0.1244	1.667	1483.2	0.0930	0.01743
50	0.1074	63.29	0.9192	0.1247	1.670	1028.4	0.0524	0.00982	620	0.0507	134.25	1.0127	0.1244	1.667	1497.2	0.0943	0.01767
60	0.1053	64.53	0.9216	0.1247	1.670	1038.5	0.0533	0.00999	640	0.0497	136.74	1.0150	0.1244	1.667	1511.0	0.0956	0.01791
70	0.1034	65.78	0.9240	0.1247	1.670	1048.4	0.0541	0.01015	660	0.0488	139.23	1.0172	0.1244	1.667	1524.6	0.0968	0.01814
80	0.1014	67.03	0.9264	0.1247	1.670	1058.3	0.0550	0.01031	680	0.0480	141.72	1.0194	0.1244	1.667	1538.2	0.0981	0.01838
90	0.0996	68.27	0.9286	0.1246	1.669	1068.1	0.0558	0.01047	700	0.0472	144.21	1.0216	0.1244	1.667	1551.6	0.0993	0.01861
100	0.0978	69.52	0.9309	0.1246	1.669	1077.8	0.0567	0.01062	720	0.0464	146.69	1.0237	0.1244	1.667	1564.9	0.1005	0.01883
120	0.0944	72.01	0.9353	0.1246	1.669	1096.9	0.0583	0.01094	740	0.0456	149.18	1.0258	0.1244	1.667	1578.1	0.1018	0.01906
140	0.0913	74.50	0.9395	0.1246	1.669	1115.7	0.0600	0.01124	760	0.0448	151.67	1.0279	0.1244	1.667	1591.2	0.1030	0.01929
160	0.0883	77.00	0.9436	0.1246	1.669	1134.2	0.0616	0.01155	780	0.0441	154.16	1.0299	0.1244	1.667	1604.2	0.1042	0.01951
180	0.0855	79.49	0.9475	0.1246	1.669	1152.3	0.0632	0.01185	800	0.0434	156.65	1.0319	0.1244	1.667	1617.1	0.1053	0.01973

[b]Saturated vapor at normal boiling point

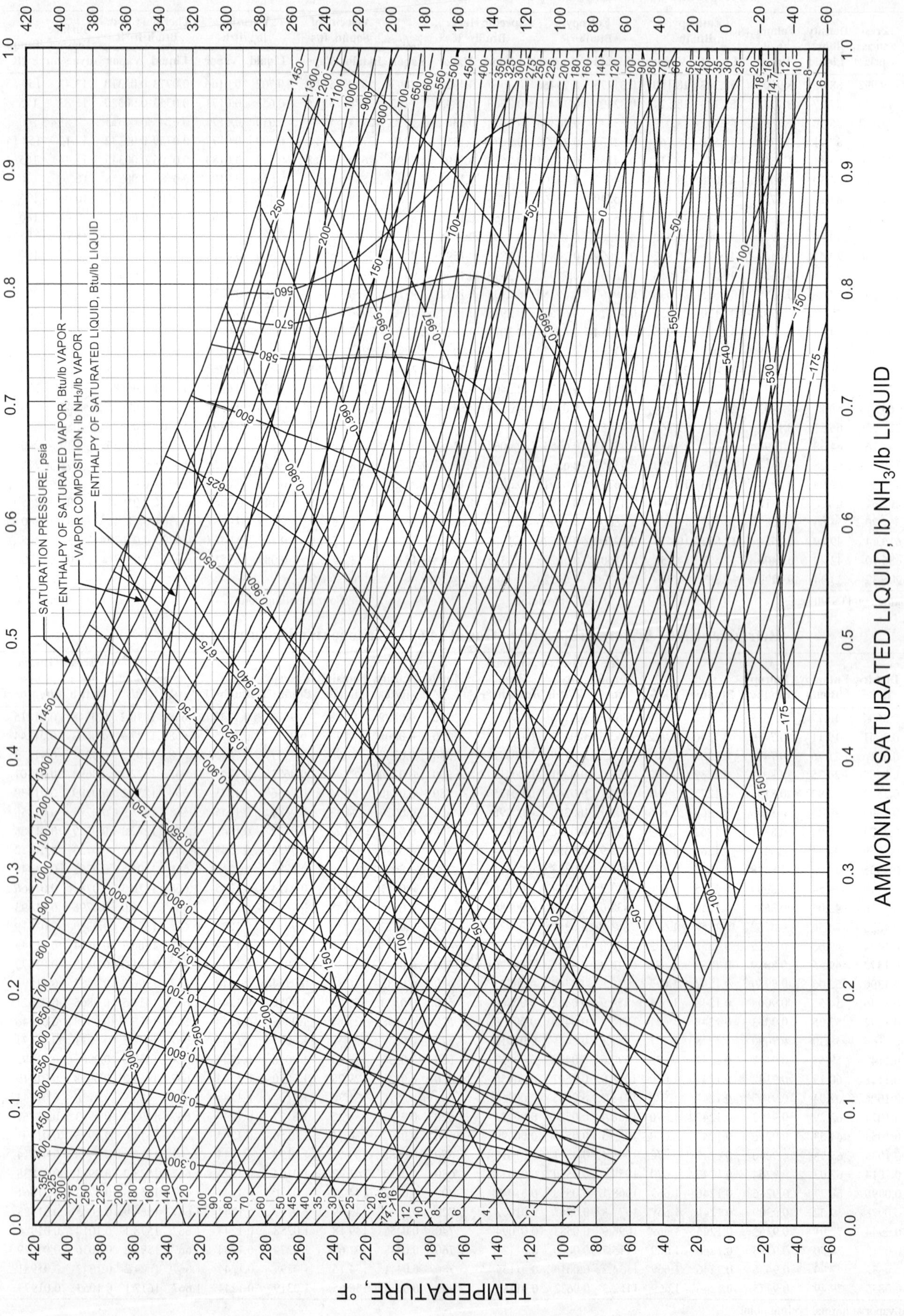

Fig. 34 Enthalpy-Concentration Diagram for Ammonia/Water Solutions

Prepared by Kwang Kim and Keith Herold, Center for Environmental Energy Engineering, University of Maryland at College Park

Specific Volume of Saturated Ammonia-Water Solutions, ft³/lb

Temp., °F	Concentration, Ammonia (Mass Basis) 0	10	20	30	40	50	60	70	80	90	100	Temp., °F
20	0.0160	0.0165	0.0170	0.0176	0.0182	0.0190	0.0197	0.0207	0.0217	0.0230	0.0245	20
40	0.0160	0.0165	0.0171	0.0177	0.0184	0.0191	0.0200	0.0209	0.0221	0.0236	0.0253	40
60	0.0160	0.0166	0.0172	0.0178	0.0186	0.0193	0.0202	0.0212	0.0225	0.0241	0.0260	60
80	0.0161	0.0167	0.0173	0.0180	0.0188	0.0196	0.0205	0.0216	0.0230	0.0247	0.0267	80
100	0.0161	0.0168	0.0174	0.0182	0.0190	0.0198	0.0208	0.0220	0.0235	0.0254	0.0275	100
120	0.0162	0.0169	0.0176	0.0184	0.0192	0.0201	0.0211	0.0224	0.0241	0.0261	0.0284	120
140	0.0163	0.0170	0.0177	0.0185	0.0194	0.0203	0.0215	0.0229	0.0247	0.0268	0.0294	140
160	0.0164	0.0172	0.0179	0.0187	0.0196	0.0206	0.0219	0.0235	0.0254	0.0277	0.0306	160
180	0.0165	0.0173	0.0181	0.0190	0.0199	0.0210	0.0223	0.0241	0.0262	0.0286	0.0320	180
200	0.0166	0.0175	0.0183	0.0192	0.0202	0.0213	0.0228	0.0247	0.0270	0.0298	0.0338	200
220	0.0168	0.0176	0.0185	0.0194	0.0205	0.0217	0.0234	0.0255	0.0279	0.0312	0.0361	220

Prepared under ASHRAE research project RP-271, sponsored by TC 8.3.
Data reference: B.H. Jennings, Ammonia water properties (paper presented at ASHRAE meeting, January 1965).

Refrigerant Temperature (t' = °F) and Enthalpy (h = Btu/lb) of Lithium Bromide Solutions

Temp., (t = °F)		Percent LiBr 0	10	20	30	40	45	50	55	60	65	70
80	t'	80.0	78.2	75.6	70.5	60.9	53.5	42.1	28.6	13.8	−0.2#	−11.6#
	h	48.0	39.2	31.8	25.6	21.6	21.2	23.0	28.7	38.9	52.7#	67.1#
100	t'	100.0	98.1	95.3	89.9	79.6	71.8	60.0	46.1	30.9	16.2#	3.8#
	h	68.0	56.6	47.0	38.7	33.2	32.1	33.2	38.2	47.8	61.1#	75.1#
120	t'	120.0	117.9	114.9	109.2	98.3	90.1	77.9	63.6	48.1	32.7	19.1#
	h	87.9	73.6	61.7	51.7	44.7	43.0	43.6	48.0	56.9	69.4	83.0#
140	t'	140.0	137.8	134.6	128.5	117.1	108.5	95.8	81.2	65.2	49.1	34.4#
	h	107.9	91.0	77.0	65.1	56.5	54.1	54.1	57.9	66.1	78.0	91.1#
160	t'	160.0	157.7	154.3	147.9	135.8	126.8	113.8	98.7	82.3	65.6	49.7#
	h	127.9	108.2	92.0	78.2	68.1	65.1	64.7	67.9	75.4	86.6	99.2#
180	t'	180.0	177.5	173.9	167.2	154.5	145.1	131.7	116.2	99.5	82.0	65.1#
	h	147.9	125.4	107.9	91.9	80.4	76.6	75.3	77.7	84.6	95.1	107.2#
200	t'	200.0	197.4	193.6	186.5	173.3	163.5	149.6	133.7	116.6	98.5	80.4#
	h	168.0	143.4	123.3	105.3	92.1	87.4	85.9	87.8	94.1	104.0	115.6#
220	t'	220.0	217.2	213.3	205.8	192.0	181.8	167.5	151.3	133.7	114.9	95.7
	h	188.1	160.7	138.2	119.0	104.1	99.0	96.5	97.8	103.3	112.5	123.6
240	t'	240.0*	237.1*	232.9	225.2	210.7	200.2	185.4	168.8	150.9	131.4	111.0
	h	208.3*	178.4*	154.0	132.6	116.0	110.3	107.1	107.7	112.5	121.1	131.6
260	t'	260.0*	256.9*	252.6*	244.5*	229.4	218.5	203.3	186.3	168.0	147.9	126.4
	h	228.6*	195.7*	169.1*	146.2*	128.1	121.6	117.6	117.6	121.6	129.5	139.5
280	t'	280.0*	276.8*	272.3*	263.8*	248.2*	236.8*	221.2	203.9	185.1	164.3	141.7
	h	249.1*	213.8*	185.1*	159.7*	140.0*	132.8*	128.1	127.5	130.6	137.9	147.6
300	t'	300.0*	296.7*	291.9*	283.1*	266.9*	255.2*	239.2*	221.4	202.3	180.8	157.0
	h	269.6*	231.6*	200.7*	173.5*	152.1*	144.1*	138.9*	137.3	139.8	146.5	155.5
320	t'	320.0*	316.5*	311.6*	302.5*	285.6*	273.5*	257.1*	238.9*	219.4	197.2	172.4
	h	290.3*	249.7*	216.3*	187.2*	164.2*	155.3*	149.5*	147.1*	148.8	154.9	163.4
340	t'	340.0*	336.4*	331.3*	321.8*	304.4*	291.9*	275.0*	256.4*	236.5*	213.7	187.7
	h	311.1*	267.9*	232.1*	201.0*	176.1*	166.6*	160.1*	157.0*	158.0*	163.5	171.0
360	t'	360.0*	356.2*	350.9*	341.1*	323.1*	310.2*	292.9*	274.0*	253.7*	230.1	203.0
	h	332.2*	286.1*	248.0*	214.9*	188.2*	178.0*	170.6*	166.8*	167.0*	171.9	178.3

*Extensions of data above 235°F are well above the original data and should be used with care.
#Supersaturated solution.

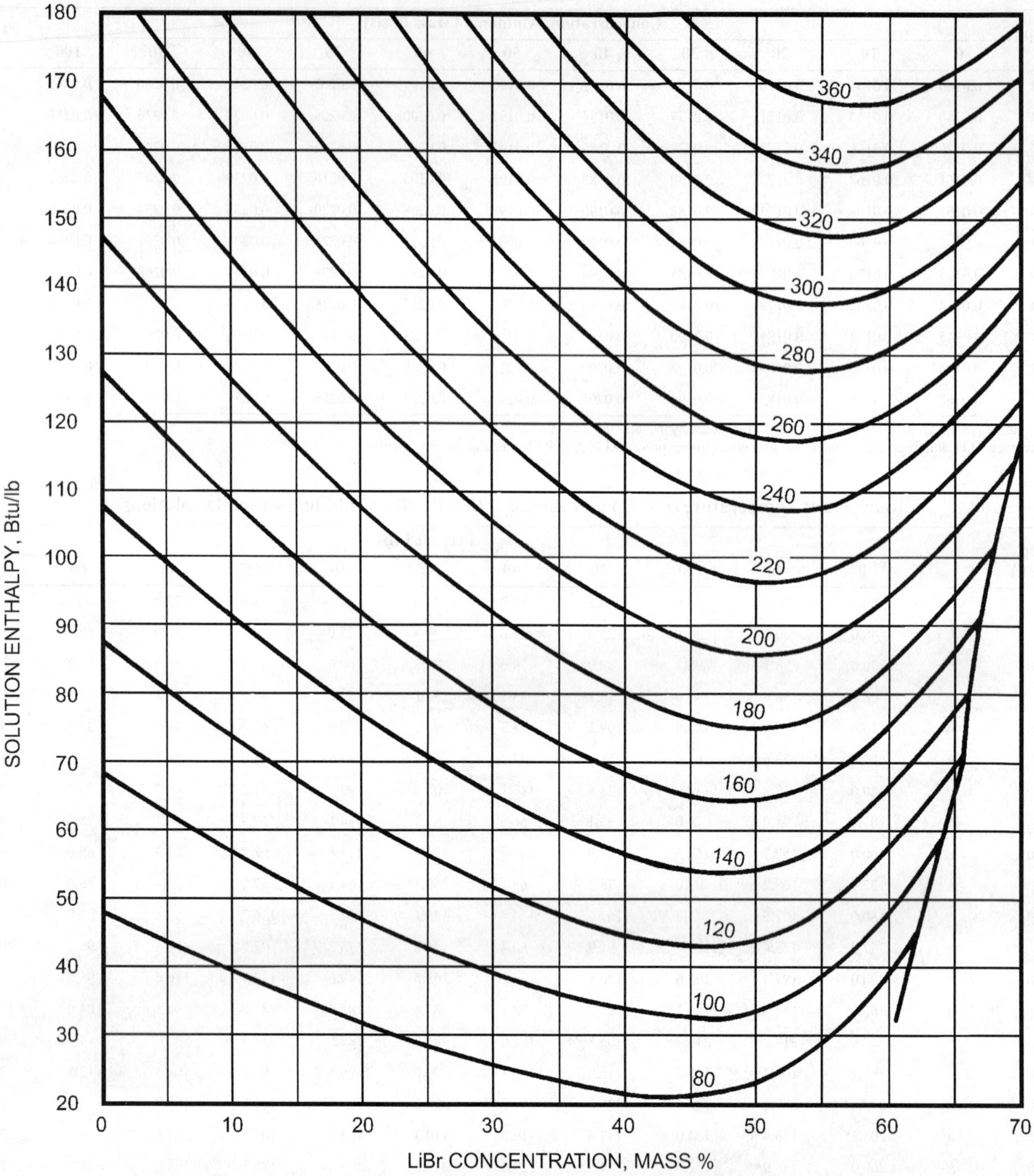

EQUATIONS

1. $h = A + Bt + Ct^2$
2. $A = -1015.07 + 79.5387X - 2.358016X^2 + 0.03031583X^3 - (1.400261\text{ E}{-4})X^4$
3. $B = 4.68108 - 0.3037766X + (8.44845\text{ E}{-3})X^2 - (1.047721\text{ E}{-4})X^3 + (4.80097\text{ E}{-7})X^4$
4. $C = -(4.9107\text{ E}{-3}) + (3.83184\text{ E}{-4})X - (1.078963\text{ E}{-5})X^2 + (1.3152\text{ E}{-7})X^3 - (5.897\text{ E}{-10})X^4$

CONCENTRATION RANGE

$40\% \le X \le 70\%$

TEMPERATURE RANGE

$60°\text{F} \le t \le 330°\text{F}$

h = Btu/lb SOLUTION

t = SOLUTION TEMPERATURE, °F

Fig. 35 Enthalpy-Concentration Diagram for Water/Lithium Bromide Solutions

EQUATIONS

1. $t = At' + B$
2. $t' = (t - B)/A$
3. $A = -2.00755 + 0.16976X - (3.133362\ \text{E}{-3})X^2 + (1.97668\ \text{E}{-5})X^3$
4. $B = 321.128 - 19.322X + 0.374382X^2 - (2.0637\ \text{E}{-3})X^3$
5. $\log_{10}P = C + D/(t' + 459.72) + E/(t' + 459.72)^2$
6. $t' = \dfrac{-2E}{D + [D^2 - 4E(C - \log_{10}P)]^{0.5}} - 459.72$

Temperature Range (Refrigerant) $0 < t' \le 230°F$
Temperature Range (Solution) $40 < t \le 350°F$
Concentration Range $45\% < X \le 70\%$

$C = 6.21147$
$D = -2886.373$
$E = -337269.46$
t' = Refrigerant Temperature, °F
t = Solution Temperature, °F
X = Percent LiBr
P = psia

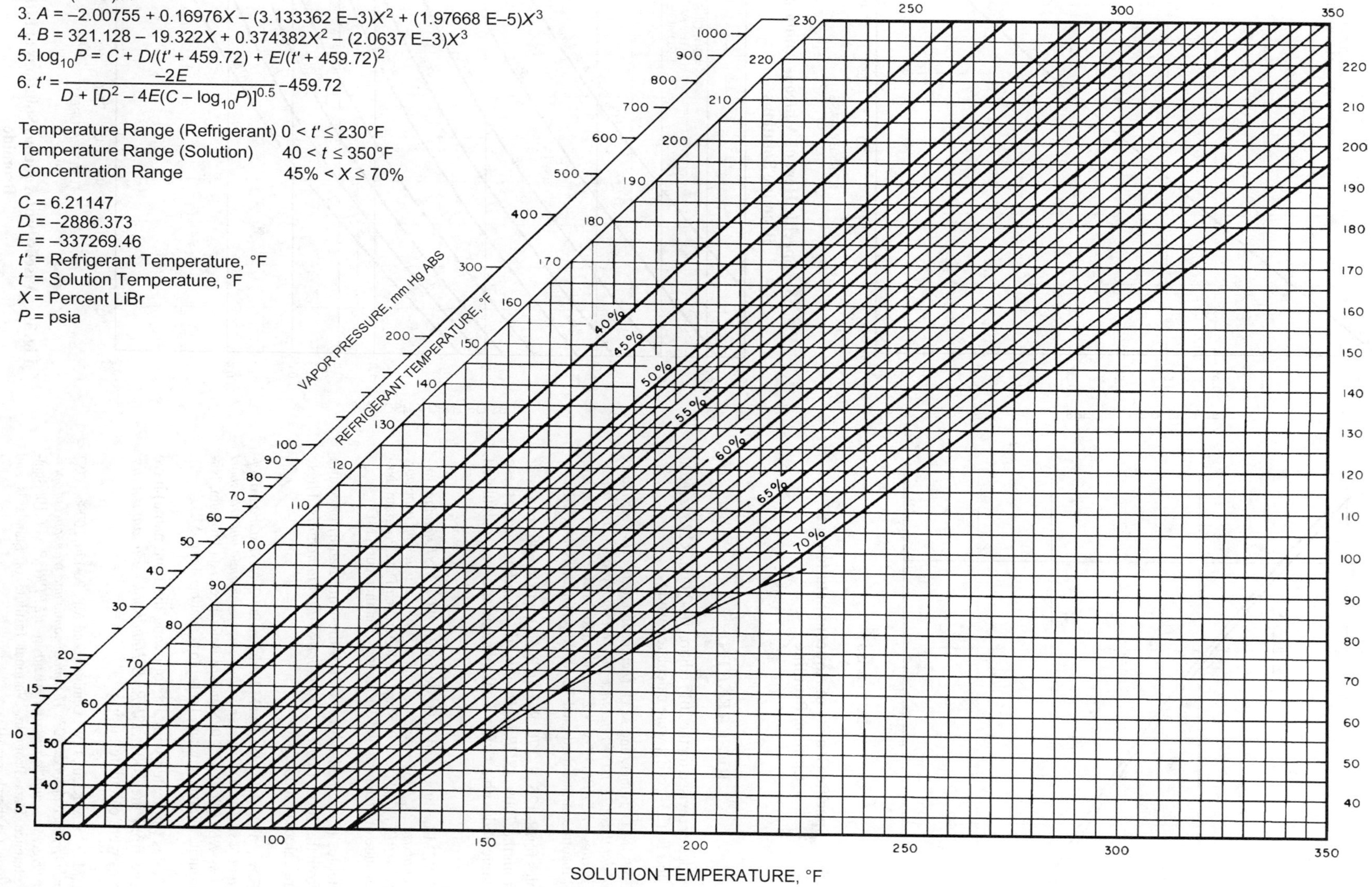

Fig. 36 Equilibrium Chart for Aqueous Lithium Bromide Solutions
Reprinted by permission of Carrier Corp.

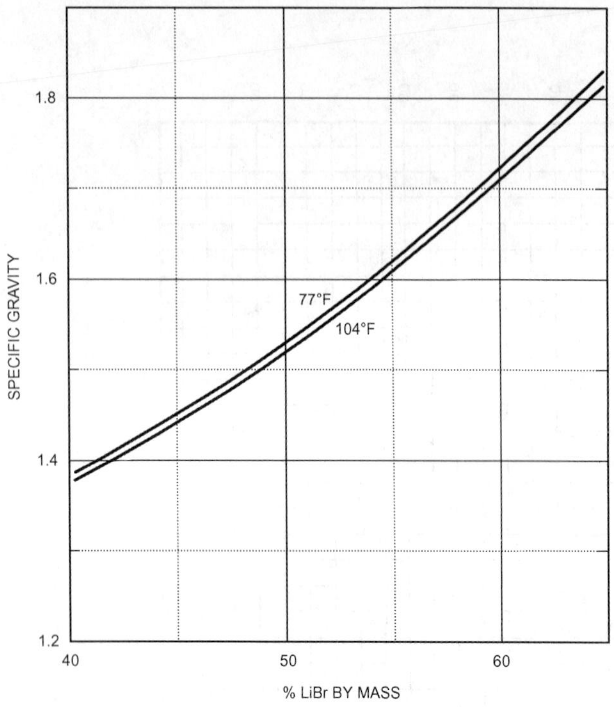

Fig. 37 Specific Gravity of Aqueous Solutions of Lithium Bromide

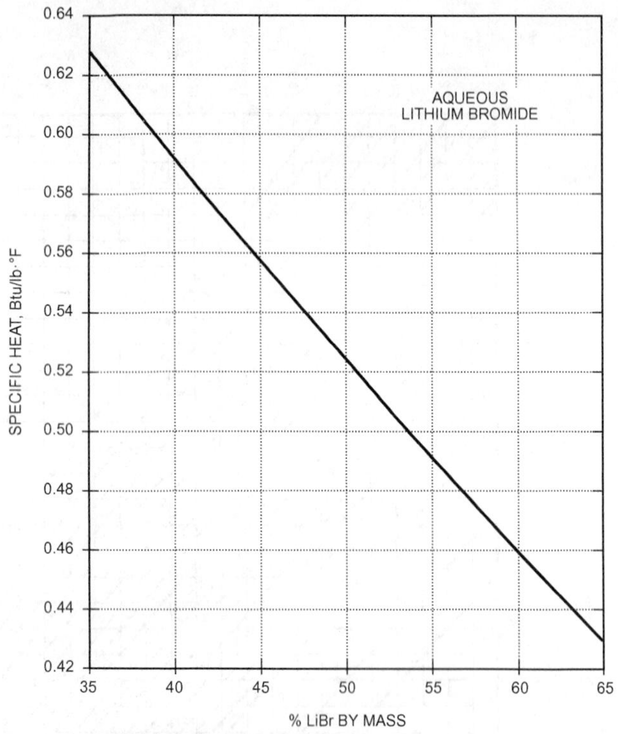

Fig. 38 Specific Heat of Aqueous Lithium Bromide Solutions

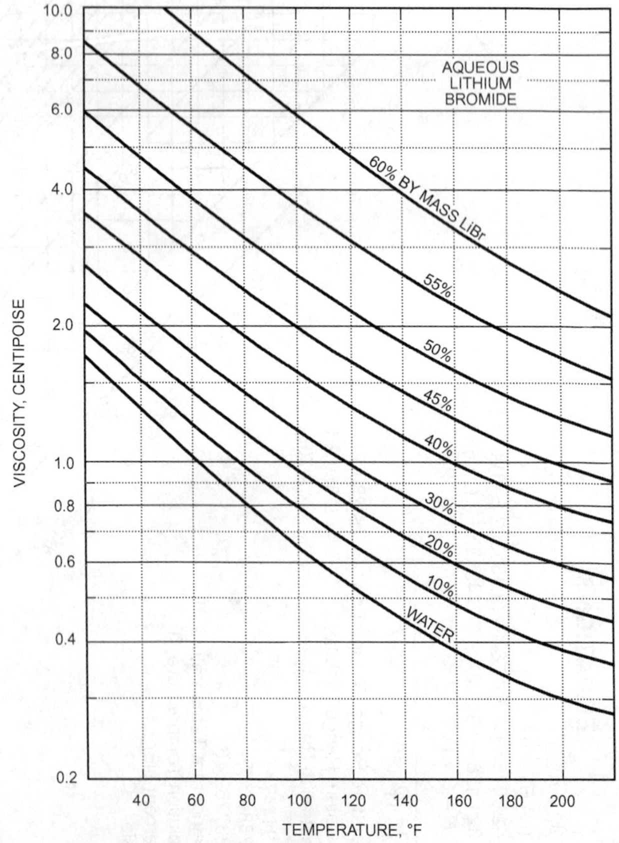

Fig. 39 Viscosity of Aqueous Solutions of Lithium Bromide

REFERENCES

Tables added or revised for the 2017 edition [R-245fa, R1233zd(E), R-1234yf, and R-1234ze(E)] were calculated using

Lemmon, E.W., M.L. Huber, and M.O. McLinden. 2016. *NIST standard reference database 23, NIST reference fluid thermodynamic and transport properties—REFPROP*, v. 9.2. Standard Reference Data Program, National Institute of Standards and Technology, Gaithersburg, MD.

The tables for R-125, R-170, R-290, R-600, and R-600a have not changed from the 2009 *ASHRAE Handbook—Fundamentals*; these tables are indicated with a * after the fluid name and were calculated using

Lemmon, E.W., M.L. Huber, and M.O. McLinden. 2007. *NIST standard reference database 23, NIST reference fluid thermodynamic and transport properties—REFPROP*, v. 8.0. Standard Reference Data Program, National Institute of Standards and Technology, Gaithersburg, MD.

Many tables (indicated with a ‡ after the fluid name) have not changed from the 2005 *ASHRAE Handbook—Fundamentals*. These tables were calculated using

Lemmon, E.W., M.O. McLinden, and M.L. Huber. 2002. *NIST standard reference database 23, NIST reference fluid thermodynamic and transport properties—REFPROP*, v. 7.0. Standard Reference Data Program, National Institute of Standards and Technology, Gaithersburg, MD.

Some tables (indicated with a † following the fluid name) have not changed from the 2001 *ASHRAE Handbook—Fundamentals*. These tables were calculated using

McLinden, M.O., S.A. Klein, E.W. Lemmon, and A.P. Peskin. 2000a. *NIST standard reference database 23: Thermodynamic and transport properties of refrigerants and refrigerant mixtures—REFPROP*, v. 6.10. Standard Reference Data Program, National Institute of Standards and Technology, Gaithersburg, MD.

Tables for R-704 have not changed from the 1997 *ASHRAE Handbook—Fundamentals*; these tables were calculated using the programs noted.

The underlying sources for these computer packages are listed as follows by fluid and property. The reference listed under "Equation of state" was used for vapor pressure, liquid density, vapor volume, enthalpy, entropy, specific heat, and velocity of sound.

R-12†

Equation of state

Marx, V., A. Pruss, and W. Wagner. 1992. Neue Zustandsgleichungen für R-12, R-22, R-11 und R-113. Beschreibung des thermodynamischen Zustandsverhaltens bei Temperaturen bis 525 K und Drücken bis 200 MPa. *VDI-Fortschritt-Ber Wärmetechnik/Kältetechnik* 19(57). VDI Verlag, Düsseldorf.

Viscosity

Klein, S.A., M.O. McLinden, and A. Laesecke. 1997. An improved extended corresponding states method for estimation of viscosity of pure refrigerants and mixtures. *International Journal of Refrigeration* 20:208-217.

Thermal conductivity

McLinden, M.O., S.A. Klein, and R.A. Perkins. 2000b. An extended corresponding states model for the thermal conductivity of refrigerants and refrigerant mixtures. *International Journal of Refrigeration* 23:43-63.

Surface tension

Okada, M., and K. Watanabe. 1988. Surface tension correlations for several fluorocarbon refrigerants. *Heat Transfer—Japanese Research* 17:35-52.

R-22†

Equation of state

Kamei, A., S.W. Beyerlein, and R.T. Jacobsen. 1995. Application of nonlinear regression in the development of a wide range formulation for HCFC-22. *International Journal of Thermophysics* 16(5):1155-1164.

Viscosity

Klein et al. 1997. op. cit. (See R-12.)

Thermal conductivity

McLinden et al. 2000b. op. cit. (See R-12.)

Surface tension

Okada, M., and K. Watanabe. 1988. op. cit. (See R-12.)

R-23‡

Equation of state

Penoncello, S.G., E.W. Lemmon, Z. Shan, and R.T. Jacobsen. 2003. An equation of state for the calculation of the thermodynamic properties of trifluoromethane (R-23). *Journal of Physical and Chemical Reference Data* 32:1473.

Viscosity and thermal conductivity

Shan, Z., S.G. Penoncello, and R.T. Jacobsen. 2000. A generalized model for viscosity and thermal conductivity of trifluoromethane (R-23). *ASHRAE Transactions* 106(1):757-767.

Surface tension

Penoncello, S.G. 1999. Thermophysical properties of trifluoromethane (R-23). ASHRAE Research Project RP-997, *Final Report*.

R-32‡

Equation of state

Tillner-Roth, R., and A. Yokozeki. 1997. An international standard equation of state for difluoromethane (R-32) for temperatures from the triple point at 136.34 K to 435 K and pressures up to 70 MPa. *Journal of Physical and Chemical Reference Data* 26:1273-1328.

Viscosity

Huber, M.L., A. Laesecke, and R.A. Perkins. 2003. Estimation of the viscosity and thermal conductivity of refrigerants including a new correlation for the viscosity of R134a. *Industrial & Engineering Chemistry Research* 42:3163-3178.

Thermal conductivity

Perkins, R.A. 2002. Personal communication, correlation to data as implemented in the NIST REFPROP Database. National Institute of Standards and Technology, Boulder, CO.

Surface tension

Okada, M., and Y. Higashi. 1995. Experimental surface tensions for HFC-32, HCFC-124, HFC-125, HCFC-141b, HCFC-142b, and HFC-152a. *International Journal of Thermophysics* 16(3):791-800.

R-123†

Equation of state

Younglove, B.A., and M.O. McLinden. 1994. An international standard equation-of-state formulation of the thermodynamic properties of refrigerant 123 (2,2-dichloro-1,1,1-trifluoroethane). *Journal of Physical and Chemical Reference Data* 23(5):731-779.

Viscosity

Tanaka, Y., and T. Sotani. 1995. *Thermodynamic and physical properties*, Chapter 2: Transport properties (thermal conductivity and viscosity), R-123. International Institute of Refrigeration, Paris.

Thermal conductivity

Laesecke, A., R.A. Perkins, and J.B. Howley. 1996. An improved correlation for the thermal conductivity of HCFC-123 (2,2-dichloro-1,1,1-trifluoroethane). *International Journal of Refrigeration* 19:231-238.

Surface tension

Okada and Higashi. 1995. op. cit. (See R-32.)

R-124‡

Equation of state

de Vries, B., R. Tillner-Roth, and H.D. Baehr. 1995. Thermodynamic properties of HCFC-124. *19th International Congress of Refrigeration, International Institute of Refrigeration* IVa:582-589.

Viscosity and thermal conductivity

Huber et al. 2003. op. cit. (See R-32.)

Surface tension

Okada and Higashi. 1995. op. cit. (See R-32.)

R-125*

Equation of state

Lemmon, E.W., and R.T. Jacobsen. 2005. A new functional form and new fitting techniques for equations of state with application to pentafluoroethane (HFC-125). *Journal of Physical and Chemical Reference Data* 34(1):69-108.

Viscosity

Huber, M.L., and A. Laesecke. 2006. Correlation for the viscosity of pentafluoroethane (R-125) from the triple point to 500 K at pressures up to 60 MPa. *Industrial & Engineering Chemistry Research* 45(12):4447-4453.

Thermal conductivity

Perkins, R.A., and M.L. Huber. 2006. Measurement and correlation of the thermal conductivity of pentafluoroethane (R-125) from 190 K to 512 K at pressures to 70 MPa. *Journal of Chemical & Engineering Data* 51(3):898-904.

Surface tension

Okada and Higashi. 1995. op. cit. (See R-32.)

R-134a†

Equation of state

Tillner-Roth, R., and H.D. Baehr. 1994. An international standard formulation of the thermodynamic properties of 1,1,1,2-tetrafluoroethane (HFC-134a) covering temperatures from 170 K to 455 K at pressures up to 70 MPa. *Journal of Physical and Chemical Reference Data* 23:657-729.

Viscosity

Huber et al. 2003. op. cit. (See R-32.)

Thermal conductivity

Perkins, R.A., A. Laesecke, J. Howley, M.L.V. Ramires, A.N. Gurova, and L. Cusco. 2000. Experimental thermal conductivity values for the IUPAC round-robin sample of 1,1,1,2-tetrafluoroethane (R134a). NISTIR 6605.

Surface tension

Okada, M., and Y. Higashi. 1994. Surface tension correlation of HFC-134a and HCFC-123. *CFCs, the Day After: Proceedings of Joint Meeting of IIR Commissions B1, B2, E1, and E2*, pp. 541-548.

R-143a†

Equation of state

Lemmon, E.W., and R.T. Jacobsen. 2001. An international standard formulation for the thermodynamic properties of 1,1,1-trifluoroethane

(HFC- 143a) for temperatures from 161 to 500 K and pressures to 60 MPa. *Journal of Physical and Chemical Reference Data* 29(4):521-552.

Viscosity
Klein et al. 1997. op. cit. (See R-12.)

Thermal conductivity
McLinden et al. 2000b. op. cit. (See R-12.)

Surface tension
Schmidt, J.W., E. Carrillo-Nava, and M.R. Moldover. 1996. Partially halogenated hydrocarbons $CHFCl\text{-}CF_3$, $CF_3\text{-}CH_3$, $CF_3\text{-}CHF\text{-}CHF_2$, $CF_3\text{-}CH_2\text{-}CF_3$, $CHF_2\text{-}CF_2\text{-}CH_2F$, $CF_3\text{-}CH_2\text{-}CHF_2$, $CF_3\text{-}O\text{-}CHF_2$: Critical temperature, refractive indices, surface tension and estimates of liquid, vapor and critical densities. *Fluid Phase Equilibria* 122:187-206.

R-152a‡

Equation of state
Outcalt, S.L., and M.O. McLinden. 1996. A modified Benedict-Webb-Rubin equation of state for the thermodynamic properties of R-152a (1,1-difluoroethane). *Journal of Physical and Chemical Reference Data* 25(2):605-636.

Viscosity
Klein et al. 1997. op. cit. (see R-12), ECS model of McLinden et al. (2000b) correlated to data as implemented in NIST REFPROP.

Thermal conductivity
Krauss, R., V.C. Weiss, T.A. Edison, J.V. Sengers, and K. Stephan. 1996. Transport properties of 1,1-difluoroethane (R-152a). *International Journal of Thermophysics* 17:731-757.

Surface tension
Okada and Higashi. 1995. op. cit. (See R-32.)

R-245fa

Equation of state
Akasaka, R., Y. Zhou, and E.W. Lemmon. 2015. A fundamental equation of state for 1,1,1,3,3-pentafluoropropane (R-245fa). *Journal of Physical and Chemical Reference Data* 44:013104.

Viscosity and thermal conductivity
Perkins, R.A., M.L. Huber, and M.J. Assael. 2016. Measurements of the thermal conductivity of 1,1,1,3-3-pentafluoropropane (R-245fa) and correlations for the viscosity and thermal conductivity surfaces. *Journal of Chemical and Engineering Data* 61:3286-3294.

Surface tension
Mulero, A., I. Cachadiña, and M.I. Parra. 2015. Recommended correlations for the surface tension of common fluids. *Journal of Physical and Chemical Reference Data* 41:043105.

R-1233zd(E)

Equation of state
Mondejar, M.E., M.O. McLinden, and E.W. Lemmon. 2015. Thermodynamic properties of trans-1-chloro-3,3,3-trifluoro-propene [R1233zd(E)]: Vapor pressure, p-ρ-T data, speed of sound measurements and equation of state. *Journal of Chemical and Engineering Data* 60: 2477-2489.

Viscosity
Hulse, R.J., R.S. Basu, R.R. Singh, and R.H.P. Thomas. 2012. Physical properties of HCFO-1233zd(E). *Journal of Chemical and Engineering Data* 57:3581-3586.

Thermal conductivity
Perkins, R.A., M.L. Huber, and M.J. Assael. 2017. Measurement and correlation of the thermal conductivity of trans-1-chloro-3,3,3-trifluoropropene (R1233zd(E)). *Journal of Chemical and Engineering Data*. dx.doi.org/10.1021/acs.jced.7b00106.

Surface tension
Kondou, C., R. Nagata, N. Nii, S. Koyama, and Y. Higashi. 2015 Surface tension of low GWP refrigerants R1243zf, R1234ze(Z), and R1233zd(E). *International Journal of Refrigeration* 53:80-89.

R-1234yf

Equation of state
Richter, M., M.O. McLinden, and E.W. Lemmon. 2011. Thermodynamic properties of 2,3,3,3-tetrafluoroprop-1-ene (R-1234yf); p-ρ-T measurements and an equation of state. *Journal of Chemical & Engineering Data* 56:3254-3264.

Viscosity
Huber, M.L., and M.J. Assael. 2016. Correlations for the viscosity of 2,3,3,3-tetrafluoroprop-1-ene (R1234yf) and trans-1,2,2,2-tetrafluoropropene (R1234ze(E)). *International Journal of Refrigeration* 71:39-45.

Thermal conductivity
Perkins, R.A., and M.L. Huber. 2011. Measurement and correlation of the thermal conductivity of 2,3,3,3-tetrafluoroprop-1-ene (R-1234fy) and trans-1,3,3,3-tetrafluoropropene (R-1234ze). *Journal of Chemical & Engineering Data* 56:4868-4874.

Surface tension
Mulero et al. 2015. op. cit. (See R-245fa).

R-1234ze(E)

Equation of state
Thol, M., and E.W. Lemmon. 2016. Equation of state for the thermodynamic properties of trans-1,3,3,3-Tetrafluoropropene [R1234ze(E)]. *International Journal of Thermophysics* 37:28.

Viscosity
Huber and Assael. op. cit. (See R-1234yf.)

Thermal conductivity
Perkins and Huber. 2011. op. cit. (See R-1234yf).

Surface tension
Mulero et al. 2015. op. cit (See R-245fa).

R-404A‡

Equation of state
Lemmon, E.W., and R.T. Jacobsen. 2004a. Equations of state for mixtures of R-32, R-125, R-134a, R-143a, and R-152a. *Journal of Physical and Chemical Reference Data* 33(2):593-620.

Viscosity
Klein et al. 1997. op. cit. (See R-12.)

Thermal conductivity
McLinden et al. 2000b. op. cit. (See R-12.)

Surface tension
Moldover, M.R., and J.C. Rainwater. 1988. Interfacial tension and vapor-liquid equilibria in the critical region of mixtures. *Journal of Chemical Physics* 88:7772-7780.

R-407C‡

Equation of state
Lemmon and Jacobsen. 2004a. op. cit. (See R-404A.)

Viscosity
Klein et al. 1997. op. cit. (See R-12.)

Thermal conductivity
McLinden et al. 2000b. op. cit. (See R-12.)

Surface tension
Moldover and Rainwater. 1988. op. cit. (See R-404A.)

R-410A‡

Equation of state
Lemmon and Jacobsen. 2004a. op. cit. (See R-404A.)

Viscosity
Klein et al. 1997. op. cit. (See R-12.)

Thermal conductivity
McLinden et al. 2000b. op. cit. (See R-12.)

Surface tension
Moldover and Rainwater. 1988. op. cit. (See R-404A.)

R-507A‡

Equation of state
Lemmon and Jacobsen. 2004a. op. cit. (See R-404A.)

Viscosity
Klein et al. 1997. op. cit. (See R-12.)

Thermal conductivity
McLinden et al. 2000b. op. cit. (See R-12.)

Surface tension
Moldover and Rainwater. 1988. op. cit. (See R-404A.)

R-717 (Ammonia)†

Equation of state
Tillner-Roth, R., F. Harms-Watzenberg, and H.D. Baehr. 1993. Eine neue Fundamentalgleichung für Ammoniak. *DKV-Tagungsbericht* 20(II):167-181.

Viscosity
Fenghour, A., W.A. Wakeham, V. Vesovic, J.T.R. Watson, J. Millat, and E. Vogel. 1995a. The viscosity of ammonia. *Journal of Physical and Chemical Reference Data* 24:1649-1667.

Thermal conductivity

Tufeu, R., D.Y. Ivanov, Y. Garrabos, and B. Le Neindre. 1984. Thermal conductivity of ammonia in a large temperature and pressure range including the critical region. *Berichte der Bunsen-Gesellschaft—Physical Chemistry* 88:422-427.

Surface tension

Stairs, R.A., and M.J. Sienko. 1956. Surface tension of ammonia and of solutions of alkalai halides in ammonia. *Journal of American Chemical Society* 78:920-923.

R-718 (Water/Steam)†

Data computed using

Harvey, A.H., S.A. Klein, and A.P. Peskin. 1999. *NIST Standard Reference Database* 10. NIST/ASME steam properties database, v. 2.2. Standard Reference Data Program.

Equation of state

Wagner, W., and A. Pruss. 2002. The IAPWS formulation 1995 for the thermodynamic properties of ordinary water substance for general and scientific use. *Journal of Physical and Chemical Reference Data* 31:387-535.

Viscosity and thermal conductivity

Kestin, J., J.V. Sengers, B. Kamgar-Parsi, and J.M.H. Levelt Sengers. 1984. Thermophysical properties of fluid H_2O. *Journal of Physical and Chemical Reference Data* 13:175.

Surface tension

IAPWS. 1995. Physical chemistry of aqueous systems: Meeting the needs of industry. *Proceedings of the 12th International Conference on the Properties of Water and Steam*, Orlando. Begell House, Inc., A139-A142. International Association for the Properties of Steam.

R-744 (Carbon Dioxide)†

Equation of state

Span, R., and W. Wagner. 1996. A new equation of state for carbon dioxide covering the fluid region from the triple-point temperature to 1100 K at pressures up to 800 MPa. *Journal of Physical and Chemical Reference Data* 26:1509-1596.

Viscosity

Fenghour, A., W.A. Wakeham, and V. Vesovic. 1995b. The viscosity of carbon dioxide. *Journal of Physical and Chemical Reference Data* 27:31-44.

Thermal conductivity

Vesovic, V., W.A. Wakeham, G.A. Olchowy, J.V. Sengers, J.T.R. Watson, and J. Millat. 1990. The transport properties of carbon dioxide. *Journal of Physical and Chemical Reference Data* 19:763-808.

Surface tension

Rathjen, W., and J. Straub. 1977. *Heat transfer in boiling*, Chapter 18, Temperature dependence of surface tension, coexistence curve, and vapor pressure of CO_2, $CClF_3$, $CBrF_3$, and SF_6. Academic Press, New York.

R-50 (Methane)†

Equation of state

Setzmann, U., and W. Wagner. 1991. A new equation of state and tables of thermodynamic properties for methane covering the range from the melting line to 625 K at pressures to 1000 MPa. *Journal of Physical and Chemical Reference Data* 20:1061-1151.

Viscosity

Younglove, B.A., and J.F. Ely. 1987. Thermophysical properties of fluids. II. Methane, ethane, propane, isobutane and normal butane. *Journal of Physical and Chemical Reference Data* 16:577-798.

Thermal conductivity

Friend, D.G., J.F. Ely, and H. Ingham. 1989. Thermophysical properties of methane. *Journal of Physical and Chemical Reference Data* 18(2):583-638.

Surface tension

Somayajulu, G.R. 1988. A generalized equation for surface tension from the triple point to the critical point. *International Journal of Thermophysics* 9:559-566.

R-170 (Ethane)*

Equation of state

Bücker, D., and W. Wagner. 2006. A reference equation of state for the thermodynamic properties of ethane for temperatures from the melting line to 675 K and pressures up to 900 MPa. *Journal of Physical and Chemical Reference Data* 35:205.

Viscosity, and thermal conductivity

Friend, D.G., H. Ingham, and J.F. Ely. 1991. Thermophysical properties of ethane. *Journal of Physical and Chemical Reference Data* 20(2):275-347.

Surface tension

Soares, V.A.M., B.d.J.V.S. Almeida, I.A. McLure, and R.A. Higgins. 1986. Surface tension of pure and mixed simple substances at low temperature. *Fluid Phase Equilibria* 32:9-16.

Pressure-enthalpy diagram based on data of

Friend, D.G., H. Ingham, and J.F. Ely. 1991. Thermophysical properties of ethane. *Journal of Physical and Chemical Reference Data* 20(2):275-347.

R-290 (Propane)*

Equation of state

Lemmon, E.W., W. Wagner, and M.O. McLinden. 2009. Thermodynamic properties of propane, III: Equation of state. *Journal of Chemical & Engineering Data* 54:3141-3180.

Viscosity

Vogel, E., C. Küchenmeister, E. Bich, and A. Laesecke. 1998. Reference correlation of the viscosity of propane. *Journal of Physical and Chemical Reference Data* 27:947-970.

Thermal conductivity

Marsh, K., R. Perkins, and M.L.V. Ramires. 2002. Measurement and correlation of the thermal conductivity of propane from 86 to 600 K at pressures to 70 MPa. *Journal of Chemical & Engineering Data* 47:932-940.

Surface tension

Baidakov, V.G., and I.I. Sulla. 1985. Surface tension of propane and isobutane at near-critical temperatures. *Russian Journal of Physical Chemistry* 59:551-554.

Pressure-enthalpy diagram based on data of

Miyamoto, H., and K. Watanabe. 2000. A thermodynamic property model for fluid-phase propane. *International Journal of Thermophysics* 21:1045-1072.

R-600 (*n*-Butane)*

Equation of state

Bücker, D., and W. Wagner. 2006. Reference equations of state for the thermodynamic properties of fluid phase *n*-butane and isobutane. *Journal of Physical and Chemical Reference Data* 35:929.

Viscosity

Vogel, E., C. Kuchenmeister, and E. Bich. 1999. Viscosity for *n*-butane in the fluid region. *High Temperatures—High Pressures* 31:173-186.

Thermal conductivity

Perkins, R.A., M.L.V. Ramires, C.A. Nieto de Castro, and L. Cusco. 2002. Measurement and correlation of the thermal conductivity of butane. *Journal of Chemical and Engineering Data* 47:1263-1271.

Surface tension

Calado, J.C.G., I.A. McLure, and V.A.M. Soares. 1978. Surface tension for octafluorocyclobutane, *n*-butane and their mixtures from 233 K to 254 K, and vapour pressure, excess Gibbs function and excess volume for the mixture at 233 K. *Fluid Phase Equilibria* 2:199-213.

Coffin, C.C., and O. Maass. 1928. The preparation and physical properties of α-, β- and γ-butylene and normal and isobutane. *Journal of the American Chemical Society* 50(5):1427-1437.

Pressure-enthalpy diagram based on data of

Miyamoto, H., and K. Watanabe. 2001. Thermodynamic property model for fluid-phase *n*-butane. *International Journal of Thermophysics* 22:459-475.

R-600a (Isobutane)*

Equation of state

Bücker and Wagner. 2006. op. cit. (See R-600.)

Viscosity

Vogel, E., C. Küchenmeister, and E. Bich. 2000. Viscosity correlation for isobutane over wide ranges of the fluid region. *International Journal of Thermophysics* 21:343-356.

Thermal conductivity
Perkins, R.A. 2002. Measurement and correlation of the thermal conductivity of isobutane. *Journal of Chemical Engineering Data* 47:1272-1279.
Surface tension
Baidakov and Sulla. 1985. op. cit. (See R-290.)
Pressure-enthalpy diagram based on data of
Miyamoto, H., and K. Watanabe. 2002. A thermodynamic property model for fluid-phase isobutane. *International Journal of Thermophysics* 23:477-499.

R-1150 (Ethylene)†
Equation of state
Smukala, J., R. Span, and W. Wagner. 2000. A new equation of state for ethylene covering the fluid region for temperatures from the melting line to 450 K and pressures up to 300 MPa. *Journal of Physical and Chemical Reference Data* 29:1053-1122.
Viscosity and thermal conductivity
Holland, P.M., B.E. Eaton, and H.J.M. Hanley. 1983. A correlation of the viscosity and thermal conductivity data of gaseous and liquid ethylene. *Journal of Physical and Chemical Reference Data* 12:917-932.
Surface tension
Soares et al. op. cit. (See R-170.)

R-1270 (Propylene)‡
Equation of state
Angus, S., B. Armstrong, and K.M. de Reuck. 1980. *International thermodynamic tables of the fluid state—7: Propylene*. Pergamon Press, Oxford, U.K.
Viscosity and thermal conductivity
Huber et al. 2003. op. cit. (See R-32.)
Surface tension
Maass, O., and C.H. Wright. 1921. Some physical properties of hydrocarbons containing two and three carbon atoms. *Journal of the American Chemical Society* 43:1098-1111.

R-704 (Helium)
Thermodynamic data computed using the ALLPROPS database, v. 4.0:
Lemmon, E.W., R.T. Jacobsen, S.G. Penoncello, and S.W. Beyerlein. 1994. Computer programs for the calculation of thermodynamic properties of cryogenic and other fluids. *Advances in Cryogenic Engineering* 39:1891-1897.
Transport data computed using the NIST 12 database, v. 3.0:
Friend, D.G., R.D. McCarty, and V. Arp. 1992. *NIST thermophysical properties of pure fluids database*, v. 3.0. Standard Reference Data Program.
Equation of state, viscosity, and thermal conductivity
Arp, V.D., R.D. McCarty, and D.G. Friend. 1995. Thermophysical properties of helium-4 from 0.8 to 1500 K with pressures to 2000 MPa. NIST *Technical Note* 1334 (revised).

Surface tension
Liley, P.E., and P.D. Desai. 1993. *ASHRAE thermophysical properties of refrigerants.*

R-728 (Nitrogen)‡
Equation of state, viscosity, and thermal conductivity
Span, R., E.W. Lemmon, R.T. Jacobsen, W. Wagner, and A. Yokozeki. 2000. A reference equation of state for the thermodynamic properties of nitrogen for temperatures from 63.151 to 1000 K and pressures to 2200 MPa. *Journal of Physical and Chemical Reference Data* 29:1361-1433.
Viscosity and thermal conductivity
Lemmon, E.W., and R.T. Jacobsen. 2004b. Viscosity and thermal conductivity equations for nitrogen, oxygen, argon, and air. *International Journal of Thermophysics* 25:21-69.
Surface tension
Lemmon, E.W., and S.G. Penoncello. 1994. The surface tension of air and air component mixtures. *Advances in Cryogenic Engineering* 39:1927-1934.

R-729 (Air)‡
Equation of state
Lemmon, E.W., R.T. Jacobsen, S.G. Penoncello, and D.G. Friend. 2000. Thermodynamic properties of air and mixtures of nitrogen, argon, and oxygen from 60 to 2000 K at pressures to 2000 MPa. *Journal of Physical and Chemical Reference Data* 29:331-385.
Viscosity and thermal conductivity
Lemmon and Jacobsen. 2004b. op. cit. (See R-728.)
Surface tension
Lemmon and Penoncello. 1994. op. cit. (See R-728.)

R-732 (Oxygen)‡
Equation of state
Schmidt, R., and W. Wagner. 1985. A new form of the equation of state for pure substances and its application to oxygen. *Fluid Phase Equilibria* 19:175-200.
Viscosity and thermal conductivity
Lemmon and Jacobsen. 2004b. op. cit. (See R-728)
Surface tension
Lemmon and Penoncello. 1994. op. cit. (See R-728.)

R-740 (Argon)‡
Equation of state
Tegeler, C., R. Span, and W. Wagner. 1999. A new equation of state for argon covering the fluid region for temperatures from the melting line to 700 K at pressures up to 1000 MPa. *Journal of Physical and Chemical Reference Data* 28:779-850.
Viscosity and thermal conductivity
Lemmon and Jacobsen. 2004b. op. cit. (See R-728.)
Surface tension
Lemmon and Penoncello. 1994. op. cit. (See R-728.)

CHAPTER 31

PHYSICAL PROPERTIES OF SECONDARY COOLANTS (BRINES)

IN many refrigeration applications, heat is transferred to a **secondary coolant**, which can be any liquid cooled by the refrigerant and used to transfer heat without changing state. These liquids are also known as **heat transfer fluids**, **brines**, or **secondary refrigerants**.

Other ASHRAE Handbook volumes describe various applications for secondary coolants. In the 2014 *ASHRAE Handbook—Refrigeration*, refrigeration systems are discussed in Chapter 13, their uses in food processing in Chapters 23 and 28 to 42, and ice rinks in Chapter 44. In the 2015 *ASHRAE Handbook—HVAC Applications*, solar energy use is discussed in Chapter 35, and snow melting and freeze protection in Chapter 51. Thermal storage is covered in Chapter 51 of the 2016 *ASHRAE Handbook—HVAC Systems and Equipment*.

This chapter describes physical properties of the more common secondary coolants based on ethylene glycol, propylene glycol, sodium chloride, or calcium chloride and provides information on their use. Less widely used secondary coolants such as ethyl alcohol or potassium formate are not included in this chapter, but their physical properties are summarized in Melinder (2007). Physical property data for nitrate and nitrite salt solutions used for stratified thermal energy storage are presented by Andrepont (2012). The chapter also includes information on corrosion protection. Supplemental information on corrosion inhibition can be found in Chapter 49 of the 2015 *ASHRAE Handbook—HVAC Applications* and Chapter 13 of the 2014 *ASHRAE Handbook—Refrigeration*.

1. SALT-BASED BRINES

Physical Properties

Water solutions of calcium chloride and sodium chloride have historically been the most common refrigeration brines. Tables 1 and 2 list the properties of pure calcium chloride brine and sodium chloride brine. For commercial grades, use the formulas in the footnotes to these tables. For calcium chloride brines, Figure 1 shows specific heat, Figure 2 shows the ratio of mass of solution to that of water, Figure 3 shows viscosity, and Figure 4 shows thermal conductivity. Figures 5 to 8 show the same properties for sodium chloride brines.

Table 1 Properties of Pure Calcium Chloride[a] Brines

Pure $CaCl_2$, % by Mass	Ratio of Mass to Water at 60°F	Relative Density, Degrees Baumé[c]	Specific Heat at 60°F, Btu/lb·°F	Crystallization Starts, °F	Mass per Unit Volume[b] at 60°F				Ratio of Mass at Various Temperatures to Water at 60°F			
					$CaCl_2$, lb/gal	Brine, lb/gal	$CaCl_2$, lb/ft³	Brine, lb/ft³	−4°F	14°F	32°F	50°F
0	1.000	0.0	1.000	32.0	0.000	8.34	0.00	62.40				
5	1.044	6.1	0.924	27.7	0.436	8.717	3.26	65.15			1.043	1.042
6	1.050	7.0	0.914	26.8	0.526	8.760	3.93	65.52			1.052	1.051
7	1.060	8.2	0.898	25.9	0.620	8.851	4.63	66.14			1.061	1.060
8	1.069	9.3	0.884	24.6	0.714	8.926	5.34	66.70			1.071	1.069
9	1.078	10.4	0.869	23.5	0.810	9.001	6.05	67.27			1.080	1.078
10	1.087	11.6	0.855	22.3	0.908	9.076	6.78	67.83			1.089	1.087
11	1.096	12.6	0.842	20.8	1.006	9.143	7.52	68.33			1.098	1.096
12	1.105	13.8	0.828	19.3	1.107	9.227	8.27	68.95			1.108	1.105
13	1.114	14.8	0.816	17.6	1.209	9.302	9.04	69.51			1.117	1.115
14	1.124	15.9	0.804	15.5	1.313	9.377	9.81	70.08			1.127	1.124
15	1.133	16.9	0.793	13.5	1.418	9.452	10.60	70.64		1.139	1.137	1.134
16	1.143	18.0	0.779	11.2	1.526	9.536	11.40	71.26		1.149	1.146	1.143
17	1.152	19.1	0.767	8.6	1.635	9.619	12.22	71.89		1.159	1.156	1.153
18	1.162	20.2	0.756	5.9	1.747	9.703	13.05	72.51		1.169	1.166	1.163
19	1.172	21.3	0.746	2.8	1.859	9.786	13.90	73.13		1.180	1.176	1.173
20	1.182	22.1	0.737	−0.4	1.970	9.853	14.73	73.63		1.190	1.186	1.183
21	1.192	23.0	0.729	−3.9	2.085	9.928	15.58	74.19				
22	1.202	24.4	0.716	−7.8	2.208	10.037	16.50	75.00	1.215	1.211	1.207	1.203
23	1.212	25.5	0.707	−11.9	2.328	10.120	17.40	75.63				
24	1.223	26.4	0.697	−16.2	2.451	10.212	18.32	76.32	1.236	1.232	1.228	1.224
25	1.233	27.4	0.689	−21.0	2.574	10.295	19.24	76.94				
26	1.244	28.3	0.682	−25.8	2.699	10.379	20.17	77.56				
27	1.254	29.3	0.673	−31.2	2.827	10.471	21.13	78.25				
28	1.265	30.4	0.665	−37.8	2.958	10.563	22.10	78.94				
29	1.276	31.4	0.658	−49.4	3.090	10.655	23.09	79.62				
29.87	1.290	32.6	0.655	−67.0	3.16	10.75	23.65	80.45				
30	1.295	33.0	0.653	−50.8	3.22	10.80	24.06	80.76				
32	1.317	34.9	0.640	−19.5	3.49	10.98	26.10	82.14				
34	1.340	36.8	0.630	4.3	3.77	11.17	28.22	83.57				

Source: CCI (1953)

[a]Mass of Type 1 (77% min.) $CaCl_2$ = (mass of pure $CaCl_2$)/(0.77). Mass of Type 2 (94% min.) $CaCl_2$ = (mass of pure $CaCl_2$)/(0.94).

[b]Mass of water per unit volume = Brine mass minus $CaCl_2$ mass.

[c]At 60°F.

The preparation of this chapter is assigned to TC 3.1, Refrigerants and Secondary Coolants.

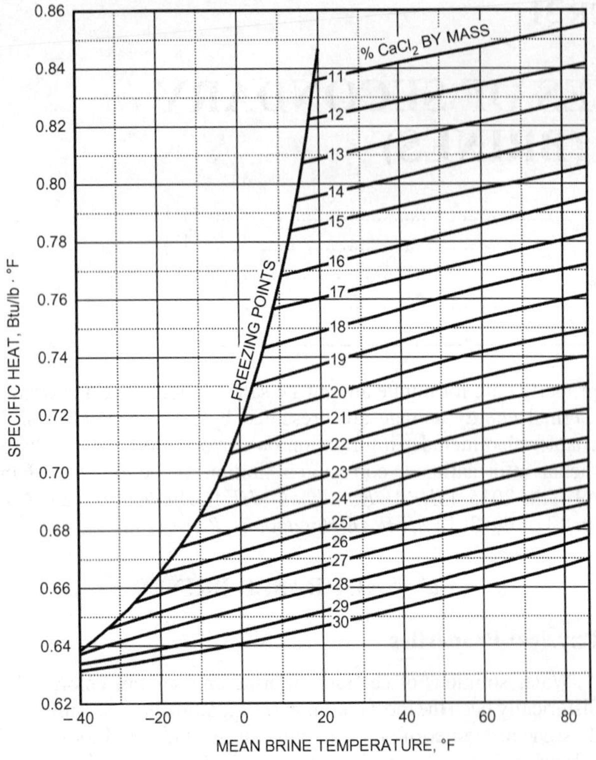

Fig. 1 Specific Heat of Calcium Chloride Brines
(CCI 1953)

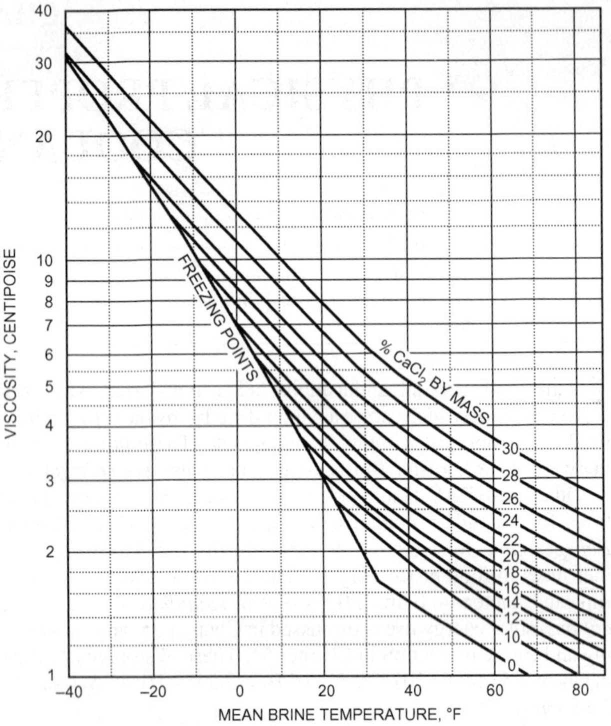

Fig. 3 Viscosity of Calcium Chloride Brines
(CCI 1953)

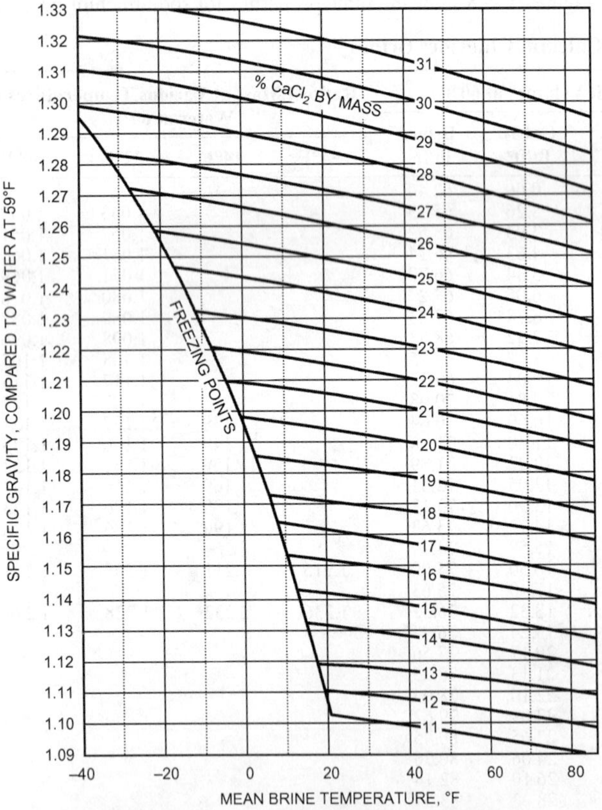

Fig. 2 Specific Gravity of Calcium Chloride Brines
(CCI 1953)

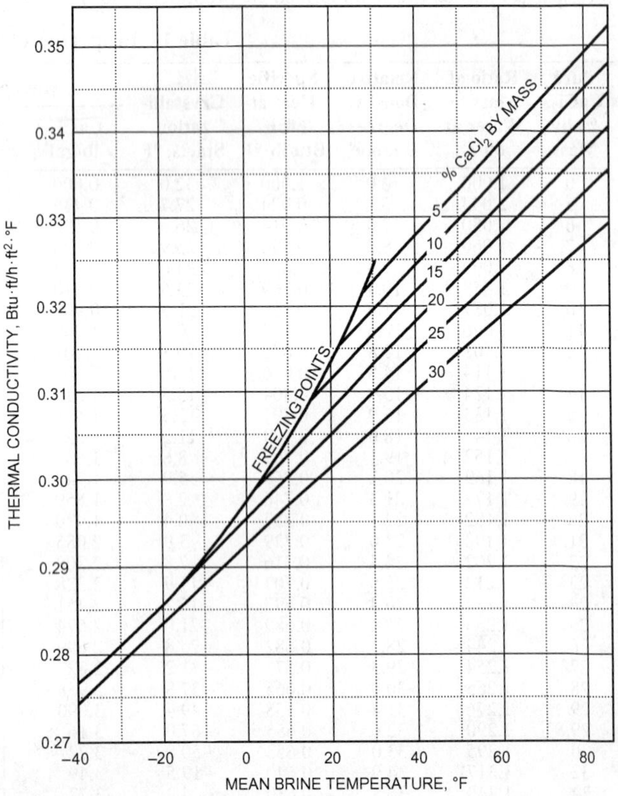

Fig. 4 Thermal Conductivity of Calcium Chloride Brines
(CCI 1953)

Table 2 Properties of Pure Sodium Chloride[a] Brines

Pure NaCl, % by Mass	Ratio of Mass to Water at 59°F	Relative Density, Degrees Baumé[b]	Specific Heat at 59°F, Btu/lb·°F	Crystallization Starts, °F	Mass per Unit Volume at 60°F: NaCl, lb/gal	Brine, lb/gal	NaCl, lb/ft³	Brine, lb/ft³	Ratio of Mass at Various Temperatures to Water at 60°F: 14°F	32°F	50°F	68°F
0	1.000	0.0	1.000	32.0	0.000	8.34	0.000	62.4				
5	1.035	5.1	0.938	26.7	0.432	8.65	3.230	64.6		1.0382	1.0366	1.0341
6	1.043	6.1	0.927	25.5	0.523	8.71	3.906	65.1		1.0459	1.0440	1.0413
7	1.050	7.0	0.917	24.3	0.613	8.76	4.585	65.5		1.0536	1.0515	1.0486
8	1.057	8.0	0.907	23.0	0.706	8.82	5.280	66.0		1.0613	1.0590	1.0559
9	1.065	9.0	0.897	21.6	0.800	8.89	5.985	66.5		1.0691	1.0665	1.0633
10	1.072	10.1	0.888	20.2	0.895	8.95	6.690	66.9		1.0769	1.0741	1.0707
11	1.080	10.8	0.879	18.8	0.992	9.02	7.414	67.4		1.0849	1.0817	1.0782
12	1.087	11.8	0.870	17.3	1.090	9.08	8.136	67.8		1.0925	1.0897	1.0857
13	1.095	12.7	0.862	15.7	1.188	9.14	8.879	68.3		1.1004	1.0933	1.0971
14	1.103	13.6	0.854	14.0	1.291	9.22	9.632	68.8		1.1083	1.1048	1.1009
15	1.111	14.5	0.847	12.3	1.392	9.28	10.395	69.3	1.1195	1.1163	1.1126	1.1086
16	1.118	15.4	0.840	10.5	1.493	9.33	11.168	69.8	1.1277	1.1243	1.1205	1.1163
17	1.126	16.3	0.833	8.6	1.598	9.40	11.951	70.3	1.1359	1.1323	1.1284	1.1241
18	1.134	17.2	0.826	6.6	1.705	9.47	12.744	70.8	1.1442	1.1404	1.1363	1.1319
19	1.142	18.1	0.819	4.5	1.813	9.54	13.547	71.3	1.1535	1.1486	1.1444	1.1398
20	1.150	19.0	0.813	2.3	1.920	9.60	14.360	71.8	1.1608	1.1568	1.1542	1.1478
21	1.158	19.9	0.807	0.0	2.031	9.67	15.183	72.3	1.1692	1.1651	1.1606	1.1559
22	1.166	20.8	0.802	–2.3	2.143	9.74	16.016	72.8	1.1777	1.1734	1.1688	1.1640
23	1.175	21.7	0.796	–5.1	2.256	9.81	16.854	73.3	1.1862	1.1818	1.1771	1.1721
24	1.183	22.5	0.791	3.8	2.371	9.88	17.712	73.8	1.1948	1.1902	1.1854	1.1804
25	1.191	23.4	0.786	16.1	2.488	9.95	18.575	74.3				
25.2	1.200			32.0								

[a]Mass of commercial NaCl required = (mass of pure NaCl required)/(% purity).
[b]At 60°F.

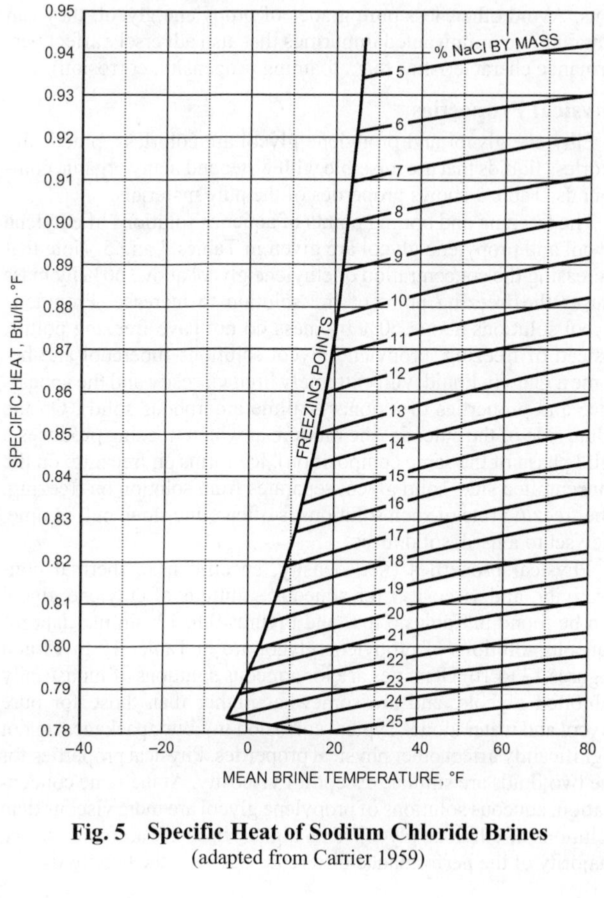

Fig. 5 Specific Heat of Sodium Chloride Brines
(adapted from Carrier 1959)

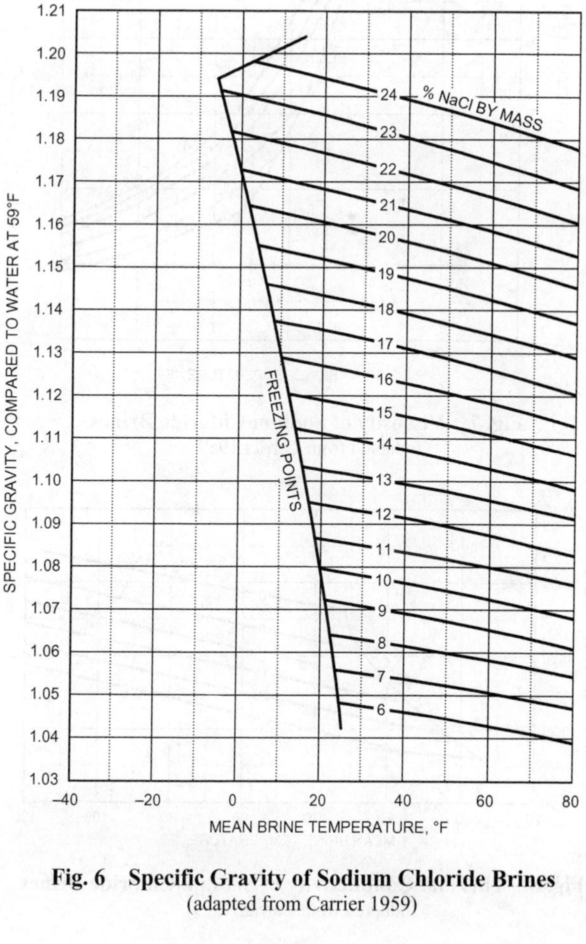

Fig. 6 Specific Gravity of Sodium Chloride Brines
(adapted from Carrier 1959)

Brine applications in refrigeration are mainly in industrial machinery and in skating rinks. Corrosion is the principal problem for calcium chloride brines, especially in ice-making tanks where galvanized iron cans are immersed.

Ordinary salt (sodium chloride) is used where contact with calcium chloride is intolerable (e.g., the brine fog method of freezing fish and other foods). It is used as a spray to air-cool unit coolers to prevent frost formation on coils. In most refrigerating work, the lower freezing point of calcium chloride solution makes it more convenient to use.

Commercial calcium chloride, available as Type 1 (77% minimum) and Type 2 (94% minimum), is marketed in flake, solid, and solution forms; flake form is used most extensively. Commercial sodium chloride is available both in crude (rock salt) and refined grades. Because magnesium salts tend to form sludge, their presence in sodium or calcium chloride is undesirable.

Corrosion Inhibition

All brine systems must be treated to control corrosion and deposits. Historically, chloride-based brines were maintained at neutral pH and treated with sodium chromate. However, using chromate as a corrosion inhibitor is no longer deemed acceptable because of its detrimental environmental effects. Chromate has been placed on hazardous substance lists by several regulatory agencies. For example, the U.S. Agency for Toxic Substances and Disease Registry's (ATSDR 2016) *Priority List of Hazardous Substances* ranks hexavalent chromium 17th out of 275 chemicals of concern (based on frequency, toxicity, and potential for human exposure at National Priorities List facilities). Consequently, hexavalent chrome and several chromates are also listed on several state right-to-know hazardous substance lists, including New Jersey, California, Minnesota, Pennsylvania and others.

Instead of chromate, most brines use a sodium-nitrite-based inhibitor ranging from approximately 3000 ppm in calcium brines to 4000 ppm in sodium brines. Other, proprietary organic inhibitors are also available to mitigate the inherent corrosiveness of brines.

Before using any inhibitor package, review federal, state, and local regulations concerning the use and disposal of the spent fluids. If the regulations prove too restrictive, an alternative inhibition system should be considered.

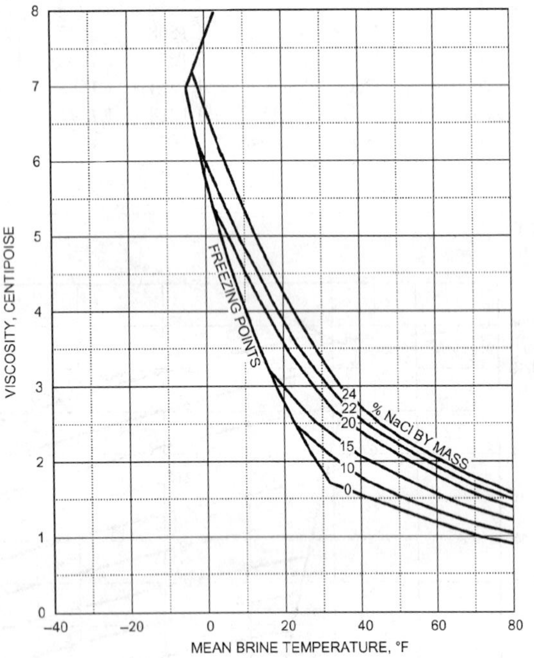

Fig. 7 Viscosity of Sodium Chloride Brines
(adapted from Carrier 1959)

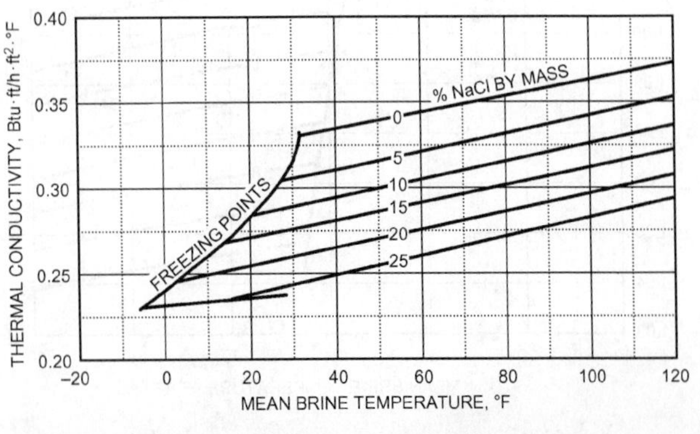

Fig. 8 Thermal Conductivity of Sodium Chloride Brines
(adapted from Carrier 1959)

2. INHIBITED GLYCOLS

Ethylene glycol and propylene glycol, when properly inhibited for corrosion control, are used as aqueous-freezing-point depressants (antifreeze) and heat transfer media. Their chief attributes are their ability to efficiently lower the freezing point of water, their low volatility, and their relatively low corrosivity when properly inhibited. Inhibited ethylene glycol solutions have better thermophysical properties than propylene glycol solutions, especially at lower temperatures. However, the less toxic propylene glycol is preferred for applications involving possible human contact or where mandated by regulations. If a heat transfer fluid may have incidental food contact, then it should be made from propylene glycol that meets U.S. Pharmacopeia (USP 2016) *Food Chemical Codex* (FCC) specifications. Avoid other, less pure grades of propylene glycol: they can contain toxic or unwanted impurities that also adversely affect performance characteristics (e.g., foaming propensity, corrosion).

Physical Properties

Ethylene glycol and propylene glycol are colorless, practically odorless liquids that are miscible with water and many organic compounds. Table 3 shows properties of the pure materials.

The freezing and boiling points of aqueous solutions of ethylene glycol and propylene glycol are given in Tables 4 and 5. Note that increasing the concentration of ethylene glycol above 60% by mass causes the freezing point of the solution to increase. Propylene glycol solutions above 60% by mass do not have freezing points. Instead of freezing, propylene glycol solutions supercool and become a glass (a liquid with extremely high viscosity and the appearance and properties of a noncrystalline amorphous solid). On the dilute side of the eutectic (the mixture at which freezing produces a solid phase of the same composition), ice forms on freezing; on the concentrated side, solid glycol separates from solution on freezing. The freezing rate of such solutions is often quite slow, but, in time, they set to a hard, solid mass.

Physical properties (i.e., density, specific heat, thermal conductivity, and viscosity) for aqueous solutions of ethylene glycol can be found in Tables 6 to 9 and Figures 9 to 12; similar data for aqueous solutions of propylene glycol are in Tables 10 to 13 and Figures 13 to 16. Densities are for aqueous solutions of industrially inhibited glycols, and are somewhat higher than those for pure glycol and water alone. Typical corrosion inhibitor packages do not significantly affect other physical properties. Physical properties for the two fluids are similar, except for viscosity. At the same concentration, aqueous solutions of propylene glycol are more viscous than solutions of ethylene glycol. This higher viscosity accounts for the majority of the performance difference between the two fluids.

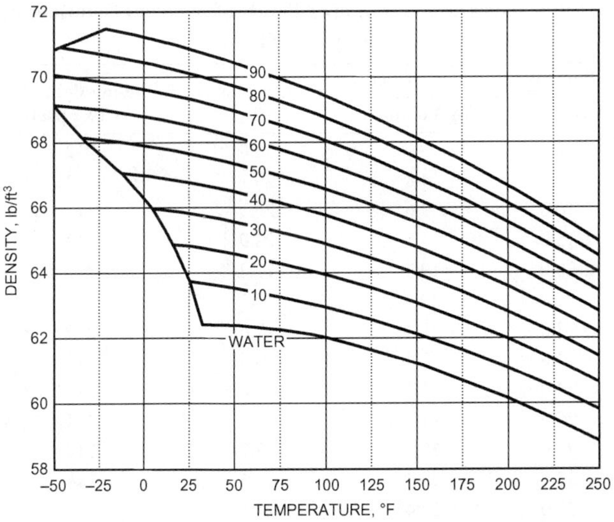

Fig. 9 Density of Aqueous Solutions of Industrially Inhibited Ethylene Glycol (vol. %)
(Dow Chemical 2001b)

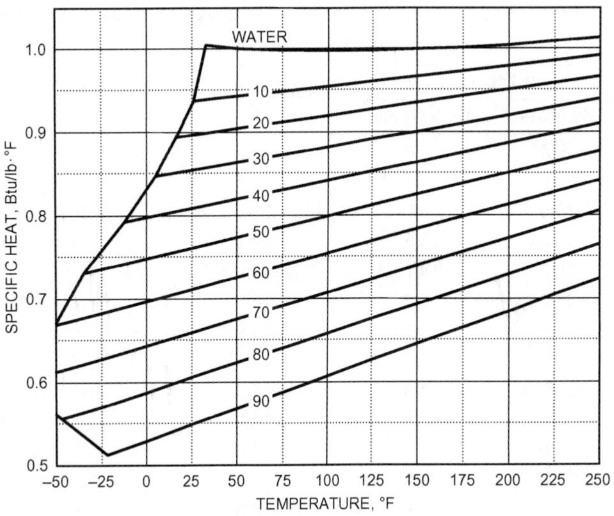

Fig. 10 Specific Heat of Aqueous Solutions of Industrially Inhibited Ethylene Glycol (vol. %)
(Dow Chemical 2001b)

Table 3 Physical Properties of Ethylene Glycol and Propylene Glycol

Property	Ethylene Glycol	Propylene Glycol
Molecular weight	62.07	76.10
Ratio of mass to water at 68/68°F	1.1155	1.0381
Density at 68°F		
lb/ft³	69.50	64.68
lb/gal	9.29	8.65
Boiling point, °F		
at 760 mm Hg	388	369
at 50 mm Hg	253	241
at 10 mm Hg	192	185
Vapor pressure at 68°F, mm Hg	0.05	0.07
Freezing point, °F	9.1	Sets to glass below −60°F
Viscosity, lb/ft·h		
at 32°F	138.9	587.8
at 68°F	50.6	146.4
at 104°F	23.0	43.5
Refractive index n_D at 68°F	1.4319	1.4329
Specific heat at 68°F, Btu/lb·°F	0.561	0.593
Heat of fusion at 9.1°F, Btu/lb	80.5	—
Heat of vaporization at 1 atm, Btu/lb	364	296
Heat of combustion at 68°F, Btu/lb	8,280	10,312

Sources: Dow Chemical (2001a, 2001b)

The choice of glycol concentration depends on the type of protection required by the application. If the fluid is being used to prevent equipment damage during idle periods in cold weather, such as winterizing coils in an HVAC system, 30% by volume ethylene glycol or 35% by volume propylene glycol is sufficient. These concentrations allow the fluid to freeze. As the fluid freezes, it forms a slush that expands and flows into any available space. Therefore, expansion volume must be included with this type of protection. If the application requires that the fluid remain entirely liquid, use a concentration with a freezing point 5°F below the lowest expected temperature. Avoid excessive glycol concentration because it increases initial cost and adversely affects the fluid's physical properties.

Additional physical property data are available from suppliers of industrially inhibited ethylene and propylene glycol.

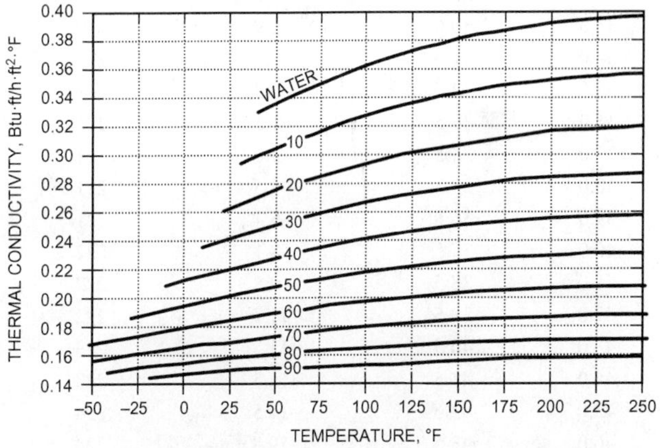

Fig. 11 Thermal Conductivity of Aqueous Solutions of Industrially Inhibited Ethylene Glycol (vol. %)
(Dow Chemical 2001b)

Corrosion Inhibition

Interestingly, ethylene glycol and propylene glycol, when not diluted with water, are actually less corrosive than water is with common construction metals. However, once diluted with water (as is typical), all aqueous glycol solutions are more corrosive than the water from which they are prepared: when uninhibited glycols thermally degrade and oxidize with use, they form acidic degradation products, which create an increasingly more corrosive environment if corrosion inhibitors and pH buffering compounds are not present. The amount of oxidation is influenced by temperature, degree of aeration, and type of metal components to which the glycol solution is exposed. In general, hydronic heating systems cause more degradation of glycol-based heat transfer fluids than do chilled-water systems. It is therefore necessary for glycol-based heat transfer fluids not only to use corrosion inhibitors that are effective at protecting common metals from corrosion, but also to contain additional additives to buffer or neutralize the acidic glycol degradation products that form during use. Corrosion inhibitors form a surface barrier that protects metal from attack, but their effectiveness is highly dependent on solution pH. Failure to compensate for glycol degradation

Table 4 Freezing and Boiling Points of Aqueous Solutions of Ethylene Glycol

Percent Ethylene Glycol		Freezing Point, °F	Boiling Point, °F at 14.7 psia
By Mass	By Volume		
0.0	0.0	32.0	212
5.0	4.4	29.4	213
10.0	8.9	26.2	214
15.0	13.6	22.2	215
20.0	18.1	17.9	216
21.0	19.2	16.8	216
22.0	20.1	15.9	216
23.0	21.0	14.9	217
24.0	22.0	13.7	217
25.0	22.9	12.7	218
26.0	23.9	11.4	218
27.0	24.8	10.4	218
28.0	25.8	9.2	219
29.0	26.7	8.0	219
30.0	27.7	6.7	220
31.0	28.7	5.4	220
32.0	29.6	4.2	220
33.0	30.6	2.9	220
34.0	31.6	1.4	220
35.0	32.6	–0.2	221
36.0	33.5	–1.5	221
37.0	34.5	–3.0	221
38.0	35.5	–4.5	221
39.0	36.5	–6.4	221
40.0	37.5	–8.1	222
41.0	38.5	–9.8	222
42.0	39.5	–11.7	222
43.0	40.5	–13.5	223
44.0	41.5	–15.5	223
45.0	42.5	–17.5	224
46.0	43.5	–19.8	224
47.0	44.5	–21.6	224
48.0	45.5	–23.9	224
49.0	46.6	–26.7	224
50.0	47.6	–28.9	225
51.0	48.6	–31.2	225
52.0	49.6	–33.6	225
53.0	50.6	–36.2	226
54.0	51.6	–38.8	226
55.0	52.7	–42.0	227
56.0	53.7	–44.7	227
57.0	54.7	–47.5	228
58.0	55.7	–50.0	228
59.0	56.8	–52.7	229
60.0	57.8	–54.9	230
65.0	62.8	*	235
70.0	68.3	*	242
75.0	73.6	*	248
80.0	78.9	–52.2	255
85.0	84.3	–34.5	273
90.0	89.7	–21.6	285
95.0	95.0	–3.0	317

Source: Dow Chemical (2001b)
*Freezing points are below –60°F.

Table 5 Freezing and Boiling Points of Aqueous Solutions of Propylene Glycol

Percent Propylene Glycol		Freezing Point, °F	Boiling Point, °F at 14.7 psia
By Mass	By Volume		
0.0	0.0	32.0	212
5.0	4.8	29.1	212
10.0	9.6	26.1	212
15.0	14.5	22.9	212
20.0	19.4	19.2	213
21.0	20.4	18.3	213
22.0	21.4	17.6	213
23.0	22.4	16.6	213
24.0	23.4	15.6	213
25.0	24.4	14.7	214
26.0	25.3	13.7	214
27.0	26.4	12.6	214
28.0	27.4	11.5	215
29.0	28.4	10.4	215
30.0	29.4	9.2	216
31.0	30.4	7.9	216
32.0	31.4	6.6	216
33.0	32.4	5.3	216
34.0	33.5	3.9	216
35.0	34.4	2.4	217
36.0	35.5	0.8	217
37.0	36.5	–0.8	217
38.0	37.5	–2.4	218
39.0	38.5	–4.2	218
40.0	39.6	–6.0	219
41.0	40.6	–7.8	219
42.0	41.6	–9.8	219
43.0	42.6	–11.8	219
44.0	43.7	–13.9	219
45.0	44.7	–16.1	220
46.0	45.7	–18.3	220
47.0	46.8	–20.7	220
48.0	47.8	–23.1	221
49.0	48.9	–25.7	221
50.0	49.9	–28.3	222
51.0	50.9	–31.0	222
52.0	51.9	–33.8	222
53.0	53.0	–36.7	223
54.0	54.0	–39.7	223
55.0	55.0	–42.8	223
56.0	56.0	–46.0	223
57.0	57.0	–49.3	224
58.0	58.0	–52.7	224
59.0	59.0	–56.2	224
60.0	60.0	–59.9	225
65.0	65.0	*	227
70.0	70.0	*	230
75.0	75.0	*	237
80.0	80.0	*	245
85.0	85.0	*	257
90.0	90.0	*	270
95.0	95.0	*	310

Source: Dow Chemical (2001a)
*Above 60% by mass, solutions do not freeze but become a glass.

Table 6 Density of Aqueous Solutions of Ethylene Glycol

Temperature, °F	Concentrations in Volume Percent Ethylene Glycol								
	10%	20%	30%	40%	50%	60%	70%	80%	90%
−30					68.12	69.03	69.90	70.75	
−20					68.05	68.96	69.82	70.65	71.45
−10				67.04	67.98	68.87	69.72	70.54	71.33
0				66.97	67.90	68.78	69.62	70.43	71.20
10			65.93	66.89	67.80	68.67	69.50	70.30	71.06
20		64.83	65.85	66.80	67.70	68.56	69.38	70.16	70.92
30	63.69	64.75	65.76	66.70	67.59	68.44	69.25	70.02	70.76
40	63.61	64.66	65.66	66.59	67.47	68.31	69.10	69.86	70.59
50	63.52	64.56	65.55	66.47	67.34	68.17	68.95	69.70	70.42
60	63.42	64.45	65.43	66.34	67.20	68.02	68.79	69.53	70.23
70	63.31	64.33	65.30	66.20	67.05	67.86	68.62	69.35	70.04
80	63.19	64.21	65.17	66.05	66.90	67.69	68.44	69.15	69.83
90	63.07	64.07	65.02	65.90	66.73	67.51	68.25	68.95	69.62
100	62.93	63.93	64.86	65.73	66.55	67.32	68.05	68.74	69.40
110	62.79	63.77	64.70	65.56	66.37	67.13	67.84	68.52	69.17
120	62.63	63.61	64.52	65.37	66.17	66.92	67.63	68.29	68.92
130	62.47	63.43	64.34	65.18	65.97	66.71	67.40	68.05	68.67
140	62.30	63.25	64.15	64.98	65.75	66.48	67.16	67.81	68.41
150	62.11	63.06	63.95	64.76	65.53	66.25	66.92	67.55	68.14
160	61.92	62.86	63.73	64.54	65.30	66.00	66.66	67.28	67.86
170	61.72	62.64	63.51	64.31	65.05	65.75	66.40	67.01	67.58
180	61.51	62.42	63.28	64.07	64.80	65.49	66.12	66.72	67.28
190	61.29	62.19	63.04	63.82	64.54	65.21	65.84	66.42	66.97
200	61.06	61.95	62.79	63.56	64.27	64.93	65.55	66.12	66.65
210	60.82	61.71	62.53	63.29	63.99	64.64	65.24	65.81	66.33
220	60.57	61.45	62.27	63.01	63.70	64.34	64.93	65.48	65.99
230	60.31	61.18	61.99	62.72	63.40	64.03	64.61	65.15	65.65
240	60.05	60.90	61.70	62.43	63.10	63.71	64.28	64.81	65.29
250	59.77	60.62	61.40	62.12	62.78	63.39	63.94	64.46	64.93

Source: Dow Chemical (2001b) *Note*: Density in lb/ft^3.

Table 7 Specific Heat of Aqueous Solutions of Ethylene Glycol

Temperature, °F	Concentrations in Volume Percent Ethylene Glycol								
	10%	20%	30%	40%	50%	60%	70%	80%	90%
−30					0.734	0.680	0.625	0.567	
−20					0.739	0.686	0.631	0.574	0.515
−10				0.794	0.744	0.692	0.638	0.581	0.523
0				0.799	0.749	0.698	0.644	0.588	0.530
10			0.849	0.803	0.754	0.703	0.651	0.595	0.538
20		0.897	0.853	0.808	0.759	0.709	0.657	0.603	0.546
30	0.940	0.900	0.857	0.812	0.765	0.715	0.664	0.610	0.553
40	0.943	0.903	0.861	0.816	0.770	0.721	0.670	0.617	0.561
50	0.945	0.906	0.864	0.821	0.775	0.727	0.676	0.624	0.569
60	0.947	0.909	0.868	0.825	0.780	0.732	0.683	0.631	0.576
70	0.950	0.912	0.872	0.830	0.785	0.738	0.689	0.638	0.584
80	0.952	0.915	0.876	0.834	0.790	0.744	0.696	0.645	0.592
90	0.954	0.918	0.880	0.839	0.795	0.750	0.702	0.652	0.600
100	0.957	0.922	0.883	0.843	0.800	0.756	0.709	0.659	0.607
110	0.959	0.925	0.887	0.848	0.806	0.761	0.715	0.666	0.615
120	0.961	0.928	0.891	0.852	0.811	0.767	0.721	0.673	0.623
130	0.964	0.931	0.895	0.857	0.816	0.773	0.728	0.680	0.630
140	0.966	0.934	0.898	0.861	0.821	0.779	0.734	0.687	0.638
150	0.968	0.937	0.902	0.865	0.826	0.785	0.741	0.694	0.646
160	0.971	0.940	0.906	0.870	0.831	0.790	0.747	0.702	0.654
170	0.973	0.943	0.910	0.874	0.836	0.796	0.754	0.709	0.661
180	0.975	0.946	0.913	0.879	0.842	0.802	0.760	0.716	0.669
190	0.978	0.949	0.917	0.883	0.847	0.808	0.766	0.723	0.677
200	0.980	0.952	0.921	0.888	0.852	0.813	0.773	0.730	0.684
210	0.982	0.955	0.925	0.892	0.857	0.819	0.779	0.737	0.692
220	0.985	0.958	0.929	0.897	0.862	0.825	0.786	0.744	0.700
230	0.987	0.961	0.932	0.901	0.867	0.831	0.792	0.751	0.708
240	0.989	0.964	0.936	0.905	0.872	0.837	0.799	0.758	0.715
250	0.992	0.967	0.940	0.910	0.877	0.842	0.805	0.765	0.723

Source: Dow Chemical (2001b) *Note*: Specific heat in Btu/lb·°F.

Table 8 Thermal Conductivity of Aqueous Solutions of Ethylene Glycol

	Concentrations in Volume Percent Ethylene Glycol								
Temperature, °F	10%	20%	30%	40%	50%	60%	70%	80%	90%
−30					0.187	0.173	0.161	0.151	
−20					0.190	0.175	0.163	0.153	0.145
−10				0.209	0.192	0.178	0.165	0.154	0.146
0				0.213	0.195	0.180	0.166	0.155	0.147
10			0.236	0.216	0.198	0.182	0.168	0.156	0.148
20		0.263	0.240	0.219	0.200	0.184	0.169	0.158	0.148
30	0.294	0.268	0.244	0.222	0.203	0.186	0.171	0.159	0.149
40	0.300	0.273	0.248	0.225	0.205	0.188	0.172	0.160	0.150
50	0.305	0.277	0.251	0.228	0.208	0.190	0.174	0.161	0.151
60	0.310	0.281	0.255	0.231	0.210	0.191	0.175	0.162	0.151
70	0.314	0.285	0.258	0.234	0.212	0.193	0.177	0.163	0.152
80	0.319	0.289	0.261	0.236	0.214	0.195	0.178	0.164	0.153
90	0.323	0.292	0.264	0.239	0.216	0.196	0.179	0.164	0.153
100	0.327	0.296	0.267	0.241	0.218	0.198	0.180	0.165	0.154
110	0.331	0.299	0.269	0.243	0.220	0.199	0.181	0.166	0.154
120	0.334	0.301	0.272	0.245	0.221	0.200	0.182	0.167	0.155
130	0.337	0.304	0.274	0.247	0.223	0.201	0.183	0.167	0.155
140	0.340	0.306	0.276	0.248	0.224	0.202	0.183	0.168	0.156
150	0.342	0.309	0.277	0.250	0.225	0.203	0.184	0.168	0.156
160	0.345	0.310	0.279	0.251	0.226	0.204	0.185	0.169	0.156
170	0.347	0.312	0.280	0.252	0.227	0.204	0.185	0.169	0.157
180	0.349	0.314	0.282	0.253	0.228	0.205	0.186	0.169	0.157
190	0.350	0.315	0.283	0.254	0.228	0.206	0.186	0.170	0.157
200	0.351	0.316	0.284	0.255	0.229	0.206	0.186	0.170	0.157
210	0.352	0.317	0.284	0.255	0.229	0.206	0.186	0.170	0.157
220	0.353	0.318	0.285	0.256	0.230	0.207	0.187	0.170	0.157
230	0.354	0.318	0.285	0.256	0.230	0.207	0.187	0.170	0.157
240	0.355	0.319	0.286	0.256	0.230	0.207	0.187	0.170	0.157
250	0.355	0.319	0.286	0.257	0.230	0.207	0.187	0.170	0.157

Source: Dow Chemical (2001b) *Note*: Thermal conductivity in Btu·ft/h·ft^2·°F.

Table 9 Viscosity of Aqueous Solutions of Ethylene Glycol

	Concentrations in Volume Percent Ethylene Glycol								
Temperature, °F	10%	20%	30%	40%	50%	60%	70%	80%	90%
−30					154.07	216.92	311.55	448.06	
−20					97.68	146.26	217.55	317.67	688.18
−10				47.37	65.97	101.72	153.61	222.27	410.83
0				33.29	46.79	72.77	110.26	157.34	260.71
10			16.52	24.51	34.50	53.37	80.58	113.43	173.86
20		9.43	13.01	18.72	26.25	40.06	59.97	83.41	120.81
30	5.23	7.60	10.47	14.73	20.51	30.67	45.41	62.51	86.87
40	4.40	6.27	8.56	11.88	16.38	23.95	34.96	47.68	64.32
50	3.77	5.27	7.14	9.77	13.30	18.99	27.36	36.99	48.82
60	3.27	4.50	6.02	8.18	11.01	15.31	21.70	29.15	37.86
70	2.85	3.89	5.15	6.94	9.22	12.51	17.47	23.27	29.92
80	2.52	3.41	4.45	5.95	7.81	10.35	14.22	18.84	24.02
90	2.25	3.00	3.87	5.15	6.68	8.66	11.73	15.43	19.59
100	2.01	2.69	3.41	4.52	5.78	7.33	9.77	12.77	16.16
110	1.81	2.39	3.02	3.97	5.03	6.24	8.22	10.67	13.50
120	1.64	2.18	2.69	3.53	4.40	5.39	6.97	9.02	11.39
130	1.50	1.96	2.42	3.14	3.89	4.67	5.98	7.67	9.70
140	1.38	1.79	2.18	2.83	3.46	4.09	5.15	6.58	8.35
150	1.28	1.64	1.98	2.54	3.10	3.60	4.50	5.68	7.21
160	1.19	1.52	1.81	2.30	2.78	3.19	3.94	4.96	6.29
170	1.11	1.40	1.64	2.10	2.52	2.85	3.46	4.35	5.52
180	1.04	1.31	1.52	1.91	2.27	2.56	3.07	3.82	4.86
190	0.97	1.21	1.40	1.77	2.06	2.30	2.76	3.39	4.33
200	0.90	1.14	1.31	1.62	1.89	2.08	2.47	3.02	3.87
210	0.85	1.04	1.21	1.48	1.72	1.89	2.23	2.71	3.46
220	0.80	0.99	1.11	1.38	1.60	1.74	2.01	2.44	3.12
230	0.77	0.92	1.04	1.28	1.45	1.60	1.84	2.20	2.81
240	0.73	0.87	0.97	1.19	1.35	1.48	1.67	2.01	2.56
250	0.70	0.82	0.92	1.09	1.26	1.35	1.52	1.81	2.32

Source: Dow Chemical (2001b) *Note*: Viscosity in lb/ft·h.

Table 10 Density of Aqueous Solutions of an Industrially Inhibited Propylene Glycol

Temperature, °F	Concentrations in Volume Percent Propylene Glycol								
	10%	20%	30%	40%	50%	60%	70%	80%	90%
−30						67.05	67.47	68.38	68.25
−20					66.46	66.93	67.34	68.13	68.00
−10					66.35	66.81	67.20	67.87	67.75
0				65.71	66.23	66.68	67.05	67.62	67.49
10			65.00	65.60	66.11	66.54	66.89	67.36	67.23
20		64.23	64.90	65.48	65.97	66.38	66.72	67.10	66.97
30	63.38	64.14	64.79	65.35	65.82	66.22	66.54	66.83	66.71
40	63.30	64.03	64.67	65.21	65.67	66.05	66.35	66.57	66.44
50	63.20	63.92	64.53	65.06	65.50	65.87	66.16	66.30	66.18
60	63.10	63.79	64.39	64.90	65.33	65.68	65.95	66.04	65.91
70	62.98	63.66	64.24	64.73	65.14	65.47	65.73	65.77	65.64
80	62.86	63.52	64.08	64.55	64.95	65.26	65.51	65.49	65.37
90	62.73	63.37	63.91	64.36	64.74	65.04	65.27	65.22	65.09
100	62.59	63.20	63.73	64.16	64.53	64.81	65.03	64.95	64.82
110	62.44	63.03	63.54	63.95	64.30	64.57	64.77	64.67	64.54
120	62.28	62.85	63.33	63.74	64.06	64.32	64.51	64.39	64.26
130	62.11	62.66	63.12	63.51	63.82	64.06	64.23	64.11	63.98
140	61.93	62.46	62.90	63.27	63.57	63.79	63.95	63.83	63.70
150	61.74	62.25	62.67	63.02	63.30	63.51	63.66	63.55	63.42
160	61.54	62.03	62.43	62.76	63.03	63.22	63.35	63.26	63.13
170	61.33	61.80	62.18	62.49	62.74	62.92	63.04	62.97	62.85
180	61.11	61.56	61.92	62.22	62.45	62.61	62.72	62.68	62.56
190	60.89	61.31	61.65	61.93	62.14	62.29	62.39	62.39	62.27
200	60.65	61.05	61.37	61.63	61.83	61.97	62.05	62.10	61.97
210	60.41	60.78	61.08	61.32	61.50	61.63	61.69	61.81	61.68
220	60.15	60.50	60.78	61.00	61.17	61.28	61.33	61.51	61.38
230	59.89	60.21	60.47	60.68	60.83	60.92	60.96	61.21	61.08
240	59.61	59.91	60.15	60.34	60.47	60.55	60.58	60.91	60.78
250	59.33	59.60	59.82	59.99	60.11	60.18	60.19	60.61	60.48

Source: Dow Chemical (2001a) *Note*: Density in lb/ft³.

Table 11 Specific Heat of Aqueous Solutions of Propylene Glycol

Temperature, °F	Concentrations in Volume Percent Propylene Glycol								
	10%	20%	30%	40%	50%	60%	70%	80%	90%
−30						0.741	0.680	0.615	0.542
−20					0.799	0.746	0.687	0.623	0.550
−10					0.804	0.752	0.693	0.630	0.558
0				0.855	0.809	0.758	0.700	0.637	0.566
10			0.898	0.859	0.814	0.764	0.707	0.645	0.574
20		0.936	0.902	0.864	0.820	0.770	0.713	0.652	0.583
30	0.966	0.938	0.906	0.868	0.825	0.776	0.720	0.660	0.591
40	0.968	0.941	0.909	0.872	0.830	0.782	0.726	0.667	0.599
50	0.970	0.944	0.913	0.877	0.835	0.787	0.733	0.674	0.607
60	0.972	0.947	0.917	0.881	0.840	0.793	0.740	0.682	0.615
70	0.974	0.950	0.920	0.886	0.845	0.799	0.746	0.689	0.623
80	0.976	0.953	0.924	0.890	0.850	0.805	0.753	0.696	0.631
90	0.979	0.956	0.928	0.894	0.855	0.811	0.760	0.704	0.639
100	0.981	0.959	0.931	0.899	0.861	0.817	0.766	0.711	0.647
110	0.983	0.962	0.935	0.903	0.866	0.823	0.773	0.718	0.656
120	0.985	0.965	0.939	0.908	0.871	0.828	0.779	0.726	0.664
130	0.987	0.967	0.942	0.912	0.876	0.834	0.786	0.733	0.672
140	0.989	0.970	0.946	0.916	0.881	0.840	0.793	0.740	0.680
150	0.991	0.973	0.950	0.921	0.886	0.846	0.799	0.748	0.688
160	0.993	0.976	0.953	0.925	0.891	0.852	0.806	0.755	0.696
170	0.996	0.979	0.957	0.929	0.896	0.858	0.812	0.762	0.704
180	0.998	0.982	0.961	0.934	0.902	0.864	0.819	0.770	0.712
190	1.000	0.985	0.964	0.938	0.907	0.869	0.826	0.777	0.720
200	1.002	0.988	0.968	0.943	0.912	0.875	0.832	0.784	0.729
210	1.004	0.991	0.971	0.947	0.917	0.881	0.839	0.792	0.737
220	1.006	0.994	0.975	0.951	0.922	0.887	0.845	0.799	0.745
230	1.008	0.996	0.979	0.956	0.927	0.893	0.852	0.806	0.753
240	1.011	0.999	0.982	0.960	0.932	0.899	0.859	0.814	0.761
250	1.013	1.002	0.986	0.965	0.937	0.905	0.865	0.821	0.769

Source: Dow Chemical (2001a) *Note*: Specific heat in Btu/lb·°F.

Table 12 Thermal Conductivity of Aqueous Solutions of Propylene Glycol

Temperature, °F	Concentrations in Volume Percent Propylene Glycol								
	10%	20%	30%	40%	50%	60%	70%	80%	90%
−30						0.156	0.140	0.127	0.117
−20					0.175	0.158	0.142	0.129	0.118
−10					0.178	0.160	0.143	0.130	0.119
0				0.201	0.181	0.162	0.145	0.131	0.119
10			0.228	0.205	0.183	0.164	0.146	0.132	0.120
20			0.232	0.208	0.186	0.166	0.148	0.133	0.121
30		0.263	0.236	0.211	0.188	0.168	0.149	0.134	0.122
40	0.298	0.267	0.240	0.214	0.191	0.170	0.151	0.135	0.122
50	0.303	0.272	0.243	0.217	0.193	0.171	0.152	0.136	0.123
60	0.308	0.276	0.247	0.220	0.195	0.173	0.153	0.137	0.123
70	0.312	0.280	0.250	0.223	0.198	0.175	0.154	0.137	0.124
80	0.317	0.284	0.253	0.225	0.200	0.176	0.155	0.138	0.124
90	0.321	0.287	0.256	0.228	0.202	0.178	0.156	0.139	0.125
100	0.325	0.291	0.259	0.230	0.203	0.179	0.157	0.139	0.125
110	0.329	0.294	0.261	0.232	0.205	0.180	0.158	0.140	0.125
120	0.332	0.296	0.264	0.234	0.206	0.181	0.159	0.140	0.126
130	0.335	0.299	0.266	0.236	0.208	0.183	0.160	0.141	0.126
140	0.338	0.301	0.268	0.237	0.209	0.183	0.160	0.141	0.126
150	0.340	0.304	0.270	0.239	0.210	0.184	0.161	0.142	0.126
160	0.343	0.305	0.271	0.240	0.211	0.185	0.161	0.142	0.126
170	0.345	0.307	0.273	0.241	0.212	0.185	0.162	0.142	0.126
180	0.347	0.309	0.274	0.242	0.213	0.186	0.162	0.142	0.126
190	0.348	0.310	0.275	0.243	0.213	0.186	0.162	0.142	0.126
200	0.349	0.311	0.276	0.243	0.214	0.187	0.162	0.142	0.126
210	0.350	0.312	0.276	0.244	0.214	0.187	0.162	0.142	0.126
220	0.351	0.313	0.277	0.244	0.214	0.187	0.162	0.142	0.126
230	0.352	0.313	0.277	0.244	0.214	0.187	0.162	0.142	0.126
240	0.353	0.313	0.277	0.245	0.214	0.187	0.162	0.142	0.125
250	0.353	0.314	0.278	0.245	0.214	0.187	0.162	0.142	0.125

Source: Dow Chemical (2001a)

Note: Thermal conductivity in Btu·ft/h·ft²·°F.

Table 13 Viscosity of Aqueous Solutions of Propylene Glycol

Temperature, °F	Concentrations in Volume Percent Propylene Glycol								
	10%	20%	30%	40%	50%	60%	70%	80%	90%
−30						1203.67	2092.20	3299.03	8600.39
−20					374.64	722.70	1194.86	1985.06	4402.06
−10					230.25	442.60	704.63	1199.09	2378.08
0				98.99	149.55	277.95	429.94	735.26	1350.63
10			32.46	65.29	97.49	179.47	271.42	460.62	803.19
20		12.97	23.92	44.75	66.82	119.24	177.13	295.85	498.11
30	6.77	10.23	18.05	31.74	47.22	81.47	119.31	195.12	320.94
40	5.52	8.25	13.91	23.22	34.33	57.21	82.78	132.18	214.11
50	4.57	6.75	10.93	17.44	25.62	41.25	59.05	91.90	147.40
60	3.87	5.61	8.76	13.45	19.57	30.46	43.20	65.56	104.41
70	3.34	4.72	7.11	10.60	15.26	23.01	32.37	47.87	75.89
80	2.90	4.02	5.88	8.52	12.14	17.76	24.80	35.78	56.49
90	2.54	3.46	4.93	6.97	9.82	13.96	19.35	27.31	42.94
100	2.25	3.02	4.19	5.81	8.08	11.18	15.41	21.26	33.29
110	2.01	2.66	3.60	4.91	6.75	9.10	12.46	16.86	26.27
120	1.81	2.35	3.14	4.19	5.71	7.52	10.23	13.60	21.07
130	1.64	2.10	2.76	3.63	4.89	6.31	8.54	11.13	17.15
140	1.50	1.89	2.44	3.17	4.23	5.37	7.21	9.24	14.15
150	1.38	1.72	2.20	2.81	3.70	4.62	6.14	7.79	11.83
160	1.26	1.55	1.98	2.52	3.27	4.02	5.30	6.65	9.99
170	1.16	1.43	1.79	2.25	2.90	3.51	4.62	5.73	8.52
180	1.06	1.31	1.64	2.06	2.59	3.12	4.09	5.01	7.35
190	0.99	1.21	1.50	1.86	2.35	2.78	3.63	4.40	6.39
200	0.92	1.11	1.40	1.72	2.13	2.52	3.24	3.89	5.59
210	0.87	1.04	1.31	1.60	1.96	2.27	2.93	3.51	4.93
220	0.82	0.97	1.21	1.48	1.79	2.08	2.66	3.17	4.40
230	0.77	0.92	1.14	1.38	1.67	1.91	2.42	2.88	3.94
240	0.73	0.87	1.06	1.28	1.55	1.77	2.23	2.64	3.56
250	0.68	0.82	1.02	1.21	1.43	1.64	2.06	2.42	3.22

Source: Dow Chemical (2001a)

Note: Viscosity in lb/ft·h.

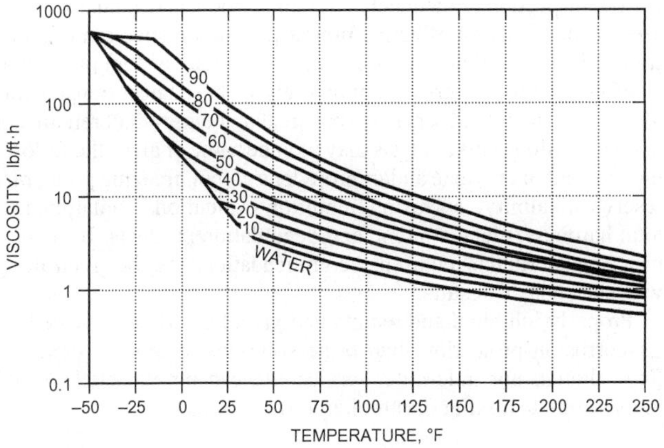

Fig. 12 Viscosity of Aqueous Solutions of Industrially Inhibited Ethylene Glycol (vol. %)
(Dow Chemical 2001b)

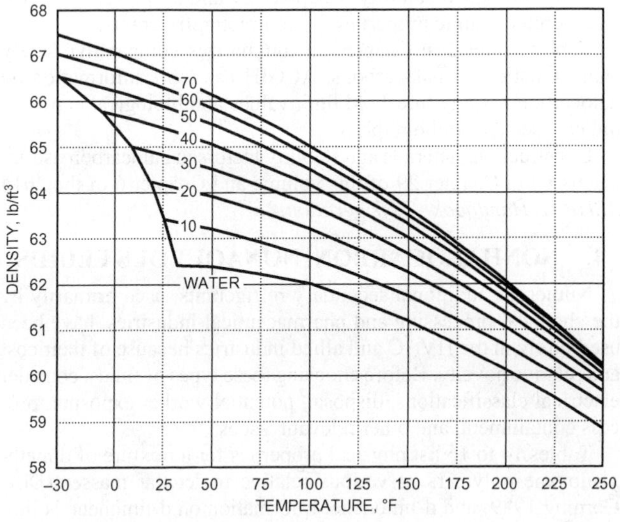

Fig. 13 Density of Aqueous Solutions of Industrially Inhibited Propylene Glycol (vol. %)
(Dow Chemical 2001b)

leads to a downward shift in solution pH, which negates the usefulness of some corrosion inhibitors (particularly for cast iron and carbon steels, but also solders). Properly inhibited glycol products should be used.

Service Considerations

Design Considerations. Inhibited glycols can be used at temperatures as high as 350°F. However, maximum-use temperatures vary from fluid to fluid, so the manufacturer's suggested temperature-use ranges should be followed. In systems with a high degree of aeration, the bulk fluid temperature should not exceed 150°F; however, temperatures up to 350°F are permissible in a pressurized system if air intake is eliminated. Maximum film temperatures should not exceed 50°F above the bulk temperature. Nitrogen blanketing minimizes oxidation when the system operates at elevated temperatures for extended periods.

Minimum operating temperatures for a recirculating fluid are typically −20°F for ethylene glycol solutions and 0°F for propylene glycol solutions. Operation below these temperatures is generally impractical, because the fluids' viscosity builds dramatically, thus

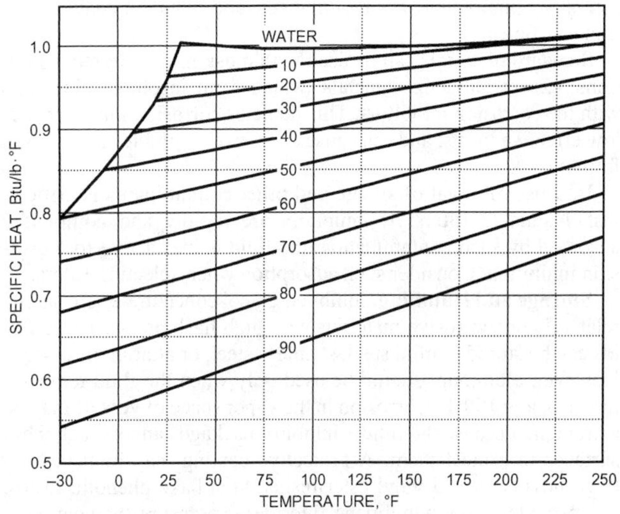

Fig. 14 Specific Heat of Aqueous Solutions of Industrially Inhibited Propylene Glycol (vol. %)
(Dow Chemical 2001b)

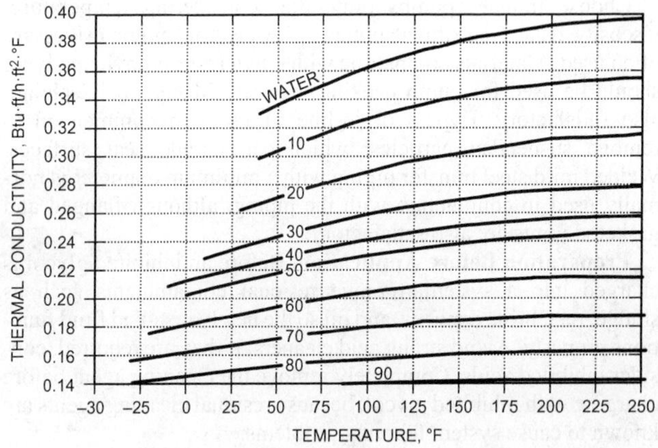

Fig. 15 Thermal Conductivity of Aqueous Solutions of Industrially Inhibited Propylene Glycol (vol. %)
(Dow Chemical 2001b)

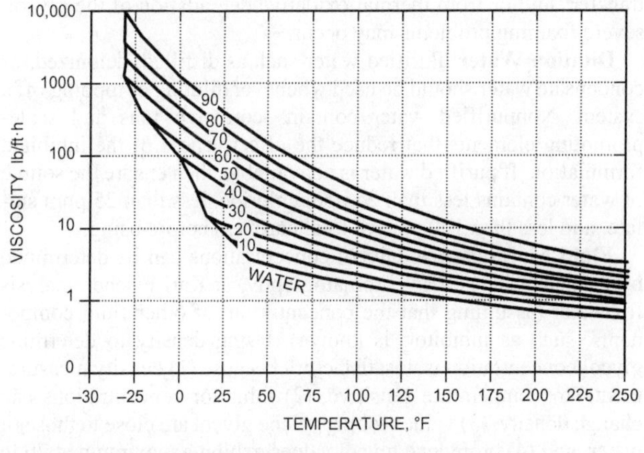

Fig. 16 Viscosity of Aqueous Solutions of Industrially Inhibited Propylene Glycol (vol. %)
(Dow Chemical 2001a)

increasing pumping power requirements and reducing heat transfer film coefficients.

Standard materials can be used with most inhibited glycol solutions, except galvanized metals, which form insoluble zinc salts with the corrosion inhibitors. This depletes corrosion inhibitors below effective limits, and can cause excessive insoluble salt (sludge) formation.

Because removal of sludge and other contaminants is critical, install suitable filters. If inhibitors are rapidly and completely adsorbed by such contamination, the fluid is ineffective for corrosion inhibition. Consider such adsorption when selecting filters.

Storage and Handling. Inhibited glycol concentrates are stable, relatively noncorrosive materials with high flash points. These fluids can be stored in mild steel, stainless steel, or aluminum vessels. However, aluminum should be used only when the fluid temperature is below 150°F. Corrosion in the vapor space of vessels may be a problem, because the fluid's inhibitor package cannot reach these surfaces to protect them. A protective coating may be necessary (e.g., novolac-based vinyl ester resins, high-bake phenolic resins, polypropylene, polyvinylidene fluoride). To ensure the coating is suitable for a particular application and temperature, consult the manufacturer. Because the chemical properties of an inhibited glycol concentrate differ from those of its dilutions, the effect of the concentrate on different containers should be known when selecting storage.

Choose transfer pumps only after considering temperature/viscosity data. Centrifugal pumps with electric motor drives are often used. Materials compatible with ethylene or propylene glycol should be used for pump packing material. Mechanical seals are also satisfactory. Bypass or in-line filters are recommended to remove suspended particles, which can abrade seal surfaces. Welded mild steel transfer piping with a minimum diameter is normally used in conjunction with the piping, although flanged and gasketed joints are also satisfactory.

Preparation Before Application. Before an inhibited glycol is charged into a system, remove residual contaminants such as sludge, rust, brine deposits, and oil so the newly installed fluid functions properly. Avoid strong acid cleaners; if they are required, consider inhibited acids. Completely remove the cleaning agent before charging with inhibited glycol, because residual cleaning agents are known to cause system foaming problems.

Foaming. Adding glycols to water reduces surface tension and increases viscosity, particularly for propylene glycol, and this affects the rate at which dispersed gas bubbles coalesce and release to the surface of the liquid. If relatively high amounts of impurities accumulate either from the original source of glycol-based heat transfer fluid or from thermal oxidative degradation of the glycol, severe foaming problems may occur.

Dilution Water. Purified water such as distilled, deionized, or condensate water should be used whenever diluting or topping off a system. Nonpurified water contains corrosive ions and scale-promoting elements that reduce the effectiveness of the inhibited formulation. If purified water is unavailable, then ensure the source of water contains less than 25 ppm chloride, less than 25 ppm sulfate, and less than 100 ppm of total hardness before using.

Fluid Maintenance. Glycol concentrations can be determined by refractive index, gas chromatography, or Karl Fischer analysis for water (assuming that the concentration of other fluid components, such as inhibitor, is known). Using density to determine glycol concentration is unsatisfactory because (1) density measurements are temperature sensitive, (2) inhibitor concentrations can change density, (3) values for propylene glycol are close to those of water, and (4) propylene glycol values exhibit a maximum at 70 to 75% concentration.

An effective inhibitor monitoring and maintenance schedule is essential to keep a glycol solution relatively noncorrosive for a long period. Inspection immediately after installation, and annually thereafter, is normally an effective practice. Visual inspection of solution and filter residue can often detect potential system problems.

Many manufacturers of inhibited glycol-based heat transfer fluids provide analytical service to ensure that their product remains in good condition. This analysis may include some or all of the following: percent of ethylene and/or propylene glycol, freezing point, pH, reserve alkalinity, corrosion inhibitor evaluation, contaminants, total hardness, metal content, and degradation products. If maintenance on the fluid is required, recommendations may be given along with the analysis results.

Properly inhibited and maintained glycol solutions provide better corrosion protection than brine solutions in most systems. A long, though not indefinite, service life can be expected. Avoid indiscriminate mixing of inhibited formulations.

3. HALOCARBONS

Many common refrigerants are used as secondary coolants as well as primary refrigerants. Their favorable properties as heat transfer fluids include low freezing points, low viscosities, nonflammability, and good stability. Chapters 29 and 30 present physical and thermodynamic properties for common refrigerants.

Tables 1 and 2 in Chapter 29 summarizes comparative safety characteristics for halocarbons. ACGIH has more information on halocarbon toxicity threshold limit values and biological exposure indices (see the Bibliography).

Construction materials and stability factors in halocarbon use are discussed in Chapter 29 of this volume and Chapter 6 of the 2014 *ASHRAE Handbook—Refrigeration.*

4. NONHALOCARBON, NONAQUEOUS FLUIDS

Numerous additional secondary refrigerants, used primarily by the chemical processing and pharmaceutical industries, have been used rarely in the HVAC and allied industries because of their cost and relative novelty. Before choosing these types of fluids, consider electrical classifications, disposal, potential worker exposure, process containment, and other relevant issues.

Tables 14 to 16 list physical properties for a mixture of dimethylsiloxane polymers of various relative molecular masses (Dow Corning 1989) and d-limonene. Information on d-limonene is limited; it is based on measurements made over small temperature ranges or simply on standard physical property estimation techniques. The compound (molecular formula $C_{10}H_{16}$) is derived as an extract from orange and lemon oils.

The mixture of dimethylsiloxane polymers can be used with most standard construction materials; d-limonene, however, can be quite corrosive, easily autooxidizing at ambient temperatures. This fact should be understood and considered before using d-limonene in a system.

REFERENCES

ASHRAE members can access *ASHRAE Journal* articles and ASHRAE research project final reports at technologyportal.ashrae.org. Articles and reports are also available for purchase by nonmembers in the online ASHRAE Bookstore at www.ashrae.org/bookstore.

Andrepont, J.A. 2012. Applications of low temperature fluid in thermally stratified thermal energy storage. *Paper* CH-12-C063. Presented at ASHRAE Winter Conference, Chicago.

ATSDR. 2016. *Priority list of hazardous substances that will be the candidates for toxicological profiles.* www.atsdr.cdc.gov/SPL/index.html. Agency for Toxic Substances and Disease Registry, Atlanta, GA.

Carrier Air Conditioning Company. 1959. Basic data, Section 17M. Syracuse, NY.

CCI. 1953. Calcium chloride for refrigeration brine. *Manual* RM-1. Calcium Chloride Institute.

Table 14 Properties of Polydimethylsiloxane Heat Transfer Fluid

Temperature, °F	Vapor Pressure, psia	Viscosity, lb/ft·h	Density, lb/ft³	Heat Capacity, Btu/lb·°F	Thermal Conductivity, Btu/h·ft·°F
–100	0.00	30.24	57.8	0.337	0.0748
–90	0.00	25.40	57.5	0.340	0.0742
–80	0.00	21.34	57.2	0.344	0.0736
–70	0.00	18.14	56.9	0.347	0.0730
–60	0.00	15.55	56.6	0.350	0.0724
–50	0.00	13.43	56.3	0.354	0.0717
–40	0.00	11.68	56.0	0.357	0.0711
–30	0.00	10.21	55.7	0.361	0.0705
–20	0.00	9.00	55.4	0.364	0.0699
–10	0.00	7.96	55.1	0.367	0.0692
0	0.00	7.09	54.8	0.371	0.0686
10	0.00	6.34	54.5	0.374	0.0679
20	0.00	5.71	54.2	0.378	0.0673
30	0.00	5.15	53.9	0.381	0.0666
40	0.01	4.67	53.6	0.384	0.0659
50	0.01	4.26	53.3	0.388	0.0652
60	0.02	3.87	53.0	0.391	0.0646
70	0.03	3.56	52.7	0.395	0.0639
80	0.04	3.27	52.4	0.398	0.0632
90	0.05	3.02	52.1	0.402	0.0625
100	0.08	2.78	51.8	0.405	0.0618
110	0.11	2.59	51.5	0.408	0.0610
120	0.15	2.40	51.1	0.412	0.0603
130	0.20	2.24	50.8	0.415	0.0596
140	0.27	2.09	50.5	0.419	0.0589
150	0.35	1.96	50.2	0.422	0.0581
160	0.46	1.84	49.8	0.425	0.0574
170	0.60	1.73	49.5	0.429	0.0567
180	0.76	1.63	49.2	0.432	0.0559
190	0.96	1.54	48.8	0.436	0.0551
200	1.20	1.45	48.5	0.439	0.0544
210	1.49	1.38	48.1	0.442	0.0536
220	1.84	1.31	47.8	0.446	0.0528
230	2.24	1.24	47.4	0.449	0.0521
240	2.72	1.18	47.0	0.453	0.0513
250	3.27	1.12	46.7	0.456	0.0505
260	3.91	1.07	46.3	0.459	0.0497
270	4.65	1.03	45.9	0.463	0.0489
280	5.50	0.98	45.5	0.466	0.0481
290	6.46	0.94	45.1	0.470	0.0473
300	7.55	0.90	44.7	0.473	0.0465
310	8.78	0.86	44.3	0.476	0.0457
320	10.16	0.83	43.9	0.480	0.0449
330	11.71	0.80	43.5	0.483	0.0441
340	13.43	0.77	43.1	0.487	0.0432
350	15.33	0.74	42.6	0.490	0.0424
360	17.45	0.71	42.2	0.494	0.0416
370	19.77	0.69	41.7	0.497	0.0407
380	22.32	0.67	41.3	0.500	0.0399
390	25.12	0.64	40.8	0.504	0.0390
400	28.17	0.62	40.4	0.507	0.0382
410	31.49	0.60	39.9	0.511	0.0373
420	35.10	0.59	39.4	0.514	0.0365
430	39.00	0.57	38.9	0.517	0.0356
440	43.21	0.55	38.4	0.521	0.0348
450	47.75	0.53	37.9	0.524	0.0339
460	52.63	0.52	37.4	0.528	0.0330
470	57.86	0.51	36.8	0.531	0.0321
480	63.46	0.49	36.3	0.534	0.0313
490	69.44	0.48	35.8	0.538	0.0304
500	75.81	0.46	35.2	0.541	0.0295

Source: Dow Chemical (1998)

Table 15 Summary of Physical Properties of Polydimethylsiloxane Mixture and d-Limonene

	Polydimethylsiloxane Mixture	d-Limonene
Flash point, °F, closed cup	116	115
Boiling point, °F	347	310
Freezing point, °F	–168	–142
Operational temperature range, °F	–100 to 500	None published

Source: Dow Corning (1989).

Table 16 Physical Properties of d-Limonene

Temperature, °F	Specific Heat, Btu/lb·°F	Viscosity, lb/ft·h	Density, lb/ft³	Thermal Conductivity, Btu/h·ft·°F
–100	0.30	9.2	57.1	0.0794
–50	0.34	6.8	55.8	0.0764
0	0.37	5.1	54.5	0.0734
50	0.41	3.9	53.2	0.0704
100	0.44	2.9	51.8	0.0674
150	0.48	2.2	50.4	0.0644
200	0.51	1.7	49.0	0.0614
250	0.54	1.5	47.6	0.0584
300	0.58	1.0	46.0	0.0554

Source: Dow Corning (1989)
Note: Properties are estimated or based on incomplete data.

Dow Chemical. 1998. *Syltherm XLT heat transfer fluid*. Midland, MI.

Dow Chemical USA. 2001a. *Engineering and operating guideline for DOWFROST and DOWFROST HD inhibited propylene glycol heat transfer fluids*. Midland, MI.

Dow Chemical USA. 2001b. *Engineering manual for DOWTHERM SR-1 and DOWTHERM 4000 inhibited ethylene glycol heat transfer fluids*. Midland, MI.

Dow Corning USA (now Dow Chemical). 1989. *Syltherm heat transfer liquids*. Midland, MI.

Melinder, Å. 2007. *Thermo-physical properties of aqueous solutions used as secondary working fluids*. Ph.D. dissertation, Department of Energy Technology, Kungliga Tekniska Högskolan, Stockholm. urn.kb.se/resolve?urn=urn:nbn:se:kth:diva-4406.

USP. 2016. *Food chemicals codex (FCC)*, 10th ed. U.S. Pharmacopeial Convention, Rockville, MD.

BIBLIOGRAPHY

ACGIH. Annual. *TLVs® and BEIs®*. American Conference of Governmental Industrial Hygienists, Cincinnati.

ASM. 2000. *Corrosion: Understanding the basics*. J.R. Davis, ed. ASM International, Materials Park, OH.

Born, D.W. 1989. *Inhibited glycols for corrosion and freeze protection in water-based heating and cooling systems*. Midland, MI.

Fontana, M.G. 1986. *Corrosion engineering*. McGraw-Hill, New York.

NACE. 1973. *Corrosion inhibitors*. C.C. Nathan, ed. National Association of Corrosion Engineers, Houston.

NACE. 2002. *NACE corrosion engineer's reference book*, 3rd ed. R. Baboian, ed. National Association of Corrosion Engineers, Houston.

CHAPTER 32

SORBENTS AND DESICCANTS

SORPTION refers to the binding of one substance to another. **Sorbents** are materials that have an ability to attract and hold other gases or liquids. They can be used to attract gases or liquids other than water vapor, which makes them very useful in chemical separation processes. **Desiccants** are a subset of sorbents; they have a particular affinity for water.

Virtually all materials are desiccants; that is, they attract and hold water vapor. Wood, natural fibers, clays, and many synthetic materials attract and release moisture as commercial desiccants do, but they lack holding capacity. For example, woolen carpet fibers attract up to 23% of their dry weight in water vapor, and nylon can take up almost 6% of its weight in water. In contrast, a commercial desiccant takes up between 10 and 1100% of its dry weight in water vapor, depending on its type and on the moisture available in the environment. Furthermore, commercial desiccants continue to attract moisture even when the surrounding air is quite dry, a characteristic that other materials do not share.

All desiccants behave in a similar way: they attract moisture until they reach equilibrium with the surrounding air. Moisture is usually removed from the desiccant by heating it to temperatures between 120 and 400°F and exposing it to a scavenger airstream. After the desiccant dries, it must be cooled so that it can attract moisture once again. Sorption always generates sensible heat equal to the latent heat of the water vapor taken up by the desiccant plus an additional heat of sorption that varies between 5 and 25% of the latent heat of the water vapor. This heat is transferred to the desiccant and to the surrounding air.

The process of attracting and holding moisture is described as either adsorption or absorption, depending on whether the desiccant undergoes a chemical change as it takes on moisture. **Adsorption** does not change the desiccant, except by addition of the weight of water vapor; it is similar in some ways to a sponge soaking up water. **Absorption**, on the other hand, changes the desiccant. An example of an absorbent is lithium chloride, which changes from a solid to a liquid as it absorbs moisture.

1. DESICCANT APPLICATIONS

Desiccants can dry either liquids or gases, including ambient air, and are used in many air-conditioning applications, particularly when the

- Latent load is large in comparison to the sensible load
- Energy cost to regenerate the desiccant is low compared to the cost of energy to dehumidify the air by chilling it below its dew point and reheating it
- Moisture control level for the space would require chilling the air to subfreezing dew points if compression refrigeration alone were used to dehumidify the air
- Temperature control level for the space or process requires continuous delivery of air at subfreezing temperatures
- Air delivered to a space or ductwork must be at less than 70% rh

In any of these situations, the cost of running a vapor compression cooling system can be very high. A desiccant process may offer considerable advantages in energy, initial cost of equipment, and maintenance.

Because desiccants can attract and hold more than simply water vapor, they can remove contaminants from airstreams to improve indoor air quality. Desiccants have been used to remove organic vapors and, in special circumstances, to control microbiological contaminants (Battelle 1971; Buffalo Testing Laboratory 1974). Hines et al. (1991) also confirmed their usefulness in removing vapors that can degrade indoor air quality. Desiccant materials can adsorb hydrocarbon vapors while collecting moisture from air. These cosorption phenomena show promise of improving indoor air quality in typical building HVAC systems.

Desiccants are also used in drying compressed air to low dew points. In this application, moisture can be removed from the desiccant without heat. Desorption uses differences in vapor pressures compared to the total pressures of the compressed and ambient pressure airstreams.

Finally, desiccants are used to dry the refrigerant circulating in air-conditioning and refrigeration systems. This reduces corrosion in refrigerant piping and prevents valves and capillaries from becoming clogged with ice crystals. In this application, the desiccant is not regenerated; it is discarded when it has adsorbed its limit of water vapor.

This chapter discusses the water sorption characteristics of desiccant materials and explains some of the implications of those characteristics in ambient pressure air-conditioning applications. Information on other applications for desiccants can be found in Chapter 36 of this volume; Chapters 7, 8, 18, 39, and 44 of the 2014 *ASHRAE Handbook—Refrigeration*; Chapters 1, 2, 6, 10, 18, 20, 23, 30, and 46 of the 2015 *ASHRAE Handbook—HVAC Applications*; and Chapters 24 and 26 of the 2016 *ASHRAE Handbook—HVAC Systems and Equipment.*

2. DESICCANT CYCLE

Practically speaking, all desiccants function the same way: by moisture transfer caused by a difference between water vapor pressures at their surface and of the surrounding air. When the vapor pressure at the desiccant surface is lower than that of the air, the desiccant attracts moisture. When the surface vapor pressure is higher than that of the surrounding air, the desiccant releases moisture.

Figure 1 shows the moisture content relationship between a desiccant and its surface vapor pressure. As the desiccant's moisture content rises, so does the water vapor pressure at its surface. At some point, the vapor pressure at the desiccant surface is the same as that of the air: the two are in equilibrium. Then, moisture cannot move in

The preparation of this chapter is assigned to TC 8.12, Desiccant Dehumidification Equipment and Components.

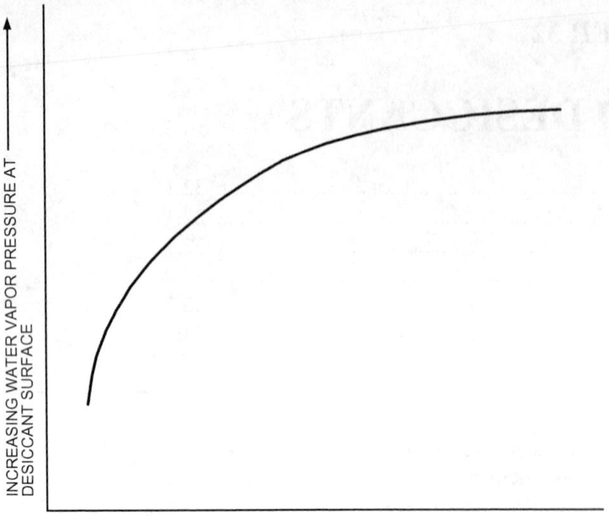

Fig. 1 Desiccant Water Vapor Pressure as Function of Moisture Content
(Harriman 2003)

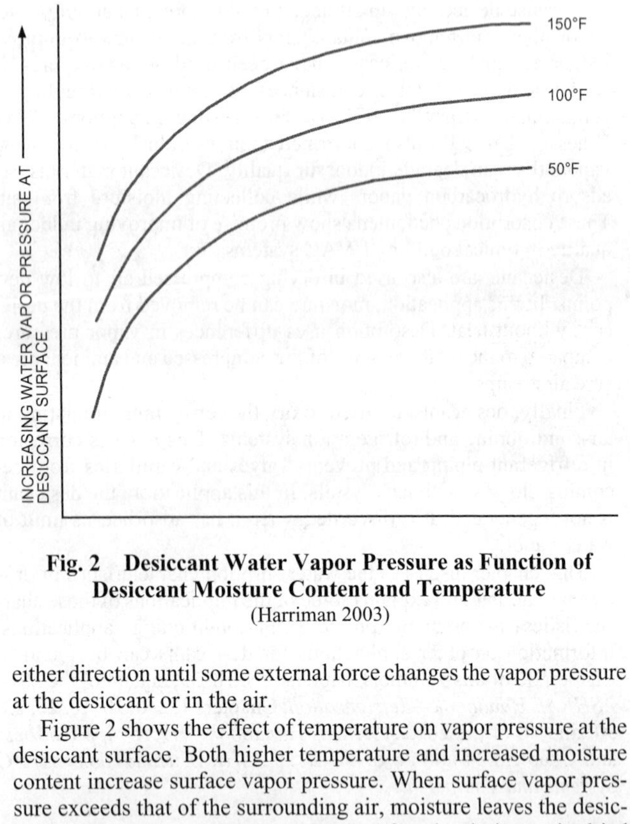

Fig. 2 Desiccant Water Vapor Pressure as Function of Desiccant Moisture Content and Temperature
(Harriman 2003)

either direction until some external force changes the vapor pressure at the desiccant or in the air.

Figure 2 shows the effect of temperature on vapor pressure at the desiccant surface. Both higher temperature and increased moisture content increase surface vapor pressure. When surface vapor pressure exceeds that of the surrounding air, moisture leaves the desiccant (**reactivation** or **regeneration**). After the desiccant is dried (reactivated) by the heat, its vapor pressure remains high, so it has very little ability to absorb moisture. **Cooling** the desiccant reduces its surface vapor pressure so that it can absorb moisture again. The complete cycle is illustrated in Figure 3.

The economics of desiccant operation depend on the energy cost of moving a given material through this cycle. Dehumidifying air (loading the desiccant with water vapor) generally proceeds without energy input other than fan and pump costs. The major portion of energy is invested in regenerating the desiccant (moving from point 2 to point 3) and cooling the desiccant (point 3 to point 1).

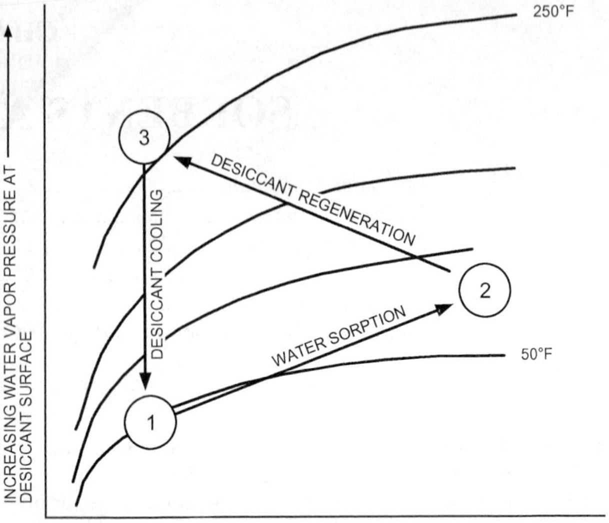

Fig. 3 Desiccant Cycle
(Harriman 2003)

Table 1 Vapor Pressures and Dew-Point Temperatures Corresponding to Different Relative Humidities at 70°F

Relative Humidity at 70°F, %	Dew Point, °F	Vapor Pressure, in. Hg
10	12	0.07
20	28	0.15
30	37	0.22
40	45	0.30
50	51	0.37
60	55	0.44
70	60	0.52
80	64	0.59
90	67	0.67
100	70	0.74

Regeneration energy is equal to the sum of the heat

- Necessary to raise the desiccant to a temperature high enough to make its surface vapor pressure higher than that of the surrounding air
- Necessary to vaporize the moisture it contains (about 1060 Btu/lb)
- From desorption of water from the desiccant (a small amount)

The **cooling energy** is proportional to the (1) mass of desiccant cycled and (2) difference between its temperature after regeneration and the lower temperature that allows the desiccant to remove water from the airstream again.

The cycle is similar when desiccants are regenerated using pressure differences in a compressed air application. The desiccant is saturated in a high-pressure chamber (i.e., that of the compressed air). Then valves open, isolating the compressed air from the material, and the desiccant is exposed to air at ambient pressure. The saturated desiccant's vapor pressure is much higher than ambient air at normal pressures; thus, moisture leaves the desiccant for the surrounding air. An alternative desorption strategy returns a small portion of dried air to the moist desiccant bed to reabsorb moisture, then vents that moist air to the atmosphere.

Table 1 shows the range of vapor pressures over which the desiccant must operate in space-conditioning applications. It converts the relative humidity at 70°F to dew point and the corresponding vapor pressure. The greater the difference between the air and desiccant surface vapor pressures, the greater the ability of the material to absorb moisture from the air at that moisture content.

The ideal desiccant for a particular application depends on the range of water vapor pressures likely to occur in the air, temperature of the regeneration heat source, and moisture sorption and desorption characteristics of the desiccant within those constraints. In commercial practice, however, most desiccants can be made to perform well in a wide variety of operating situations through careful engineering of mechanical aspects of the dehumidification system. Some of these hardware issues are discussed in Chapter 24 of the 2016 *ASHRAE Handbook—HVAC Systems and Equipment*.

3. TYPES OF DESICCANTS

Desiccants can be liquids or solids and can hold moisture through absorption or adsorption, as described earlier. Most absorbents are liquids, and most adsorbents are solids.

Liquid Absorbents

Liquid absorption dehumidification can best be illustrated by comparison to air washer operation. When air passes through an air washer, its dew point approaches the temperature of water supplied to the machine. Air that is more humid is dehumidified, and air that is less humid is humidified. Similarly, a liquid absorption dehumidifier brings air into contact with a liquid desiccant solution. The liquid's vapor pressure is lower than water at the same temperature, and air passing over the solution approaches this reduced vapor pressure; it is dehumidified.

A liquid absorption solution's vapor pressure is directly proportional to its temperature and inversely proportional to its concentration. Figure 4 illustrates the effect of increasing desiccant concentration on the water vapor pressure at its surface. The figure shows the vapor pressures of various solutions of water and triethylene glycol, a commercial liquid desiccant. As the mixture's glycol content increases, its vapor pressure decreases. This lower pressure allows the glycol solution to absorb moisture from the air whenever the air's vapor pressure is greater than that of the solution.

Viewed another way, the vapor pressure of a given concentration of absorbent solution approximates the vapor pressure values of a fixed relative humidity line on a psychrometric chart. Higher solution concentrations give lower equilibrium relative humidities, which allow the absorbent to dry air to lower levels.

Figure 5 illustrates the effect of temperature on vapor pressures of various solutions of water and lithium chloride (LiCl), another common liquid desiccant. A solution that is 25% lithium chloride has a vapor pressure of 0.37 in. Hg at a temperature of 70°F. If the same 25% solution is heated to 100°F, its vapor pressure more than doubles to 0.99 in. Hg. Expressed another way, the 70°F, 25% solution is in equilibrium with air at a 51°F dew point. The same 25% solution at 100°F is at equilibrium with an airstream at a 79°F dew point. The warmer the desiccant, the less moisture it can attract from the air.

In standard practice, behavior of a liquid desiccant is controlled by adjusting its temperature, concentration, or both. Desiccant temperature is controlled by simple heaters and coolers. Concentration is controlled by heating the desiccant to drive moisture out into a waste airstream or directly to the ambient.

Commercially available liquid desiccants have an especially high water-holding capacity. Each molecule of LiCl, for example, can hold two water molecules, even in the dry state. Above two water molecules per molecule of LiCl, the desiccant becomes a liquid and continues to absorb water. If the solution is in equilibrium with air at 90% rh, approximately 26 water molecules are attached to each molecule of LiCl. This represents a water absorption of more than 1000% on a dry-weight basis.

As a practical matter, however, the absorption process is limited by the exposed surface area of desiccant and by the contact time allowed for reaction. More surface area and more contact time allow the desiccant to approach its theoretical capacity. Commercial desiccant systems stretch these limits by flowing liquid desiccant onto an extended surface, much like in a cooling tower.

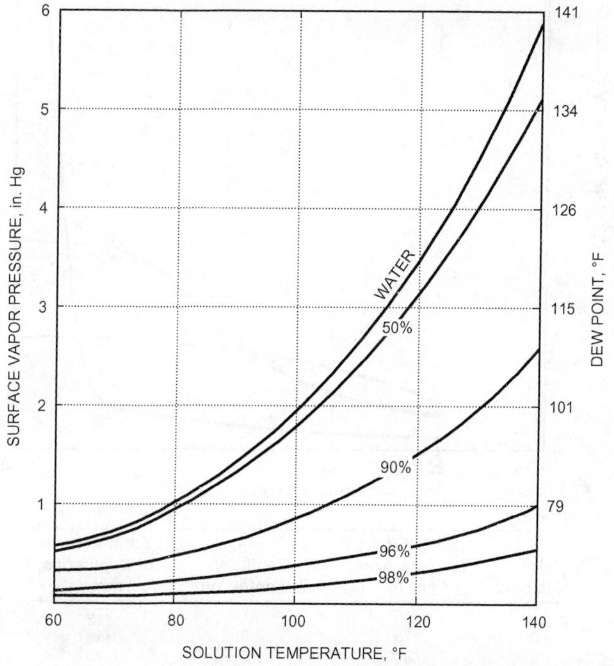

Fig. 4 Surface Vapor Pressure of Water/Triethylene Glycol Solutions
(from data of Dow 1981)

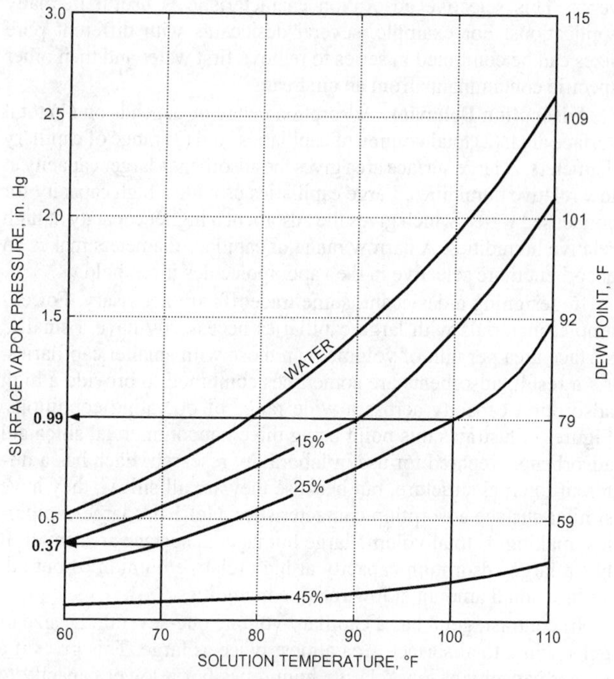

Fig. 5 Surface Vapor Pressure of Water/Lithium Chloride Solutions
(from data of Foote Mineral 1988)

Solid Adsorbents

Adsorbents are solid materials with a tremendous internal surface area per unit of mass; a single gram can have more than 50,000 ft^2 of surface area. Structurally, adsorbents resemble a rigid sponge, and the surface of the sponge in turn resembles the ocean coastline of a fjord. This analogy indicates the scale of the different surfaces in an adsorbent. The fjords can be compared to the **capillaries** in the adsorbent. Spaces between the grains of sand on the fjord beaches can be compared to the spaces between the individual molecules of adsorbent, all of which have the capacity to hold water molecules. The bulk of adsorbed water is contained by condensation into the capillaries, and the majority of the surface area that attracts individual water molecules is in the crystalline structure of the material itself.

Adsorbents attract moisture because of the electrical field at the desiccant surface. The field is not uniform in either force or charge, so specific sites on the desiccant surface attract water molecules that have a net opposite charge. When the complete surface is covered, the adsorbent can hold still more moisture because vapor condenses into the first water layer and fills capillaries throughout the material. As with liquid absorbents, an adsorbent's ability to attract moisture depends on the difference in vapor pressure between its surface and the air.

Capacity of solid adsorbents is generally less than the capacity of liquid absorbents. For example, a typical molecular sieve adsorbent can hold 17% of its dry weight in water when the air is at 70°F and 20% rh. In contrast, LiCl can hold 130% of its mass at the same temperature and relative humidity.

Solid adsorbents have several advantages, however. For example, molecular sieves continue to adsorb moisture even when they are quite hot, allowing dehumidification of very warm airstreams. Also, several solid adsorbents can be manufactured to precise tolerances, with pore diameters that can be closely controlled. This means they can be tailored to adsorb molecules of a specific diameter. Water, for example, has an effective molecular diameter of 3.2 Å. A molecular sieve adsorbent with an average pore diameter of 4.0 Å adsorbs water but has almost no capacity for larger molecules, such as organic solvents. This selective adsorption characteristic is useful in many applications. For example, several desiccants with different pore sizes can be combined in series to remove first water and then other specific contaminants from an airstream.

Adsorption Behavior. Adsorption behavior depends on (1) total surface area, (2) total volume of capillaries, and (3) range of capillary diameters. A large surface area gives the adsorbent a larger capacity at low relative humidities. Large capillaries provide a high capacity for condensed water, which gives the adsorbent a higher capacity at high relative humidities. A narrow range of capillary diameters makes an adsorbent more selective in the vapor molecules it can hold.

In designing a desiccant, some tradeoffs are necessary. For example, materials with large capillaries necessarily have a smaller surface area per unit of volume than those with smaller capillaries. As a result, adsorbents are sometimes combined to provide a high adsorption capacity across a wide range of operating conditions. Figure 6 illustrates this point using three noncommercial silica gel adsorbents prepared for use in laboratory research. Each has a different internal structure, but because they are all silicas, they have similar surface adsorption characteristics. Gel 1 has large capillaries, making its total volume large but its total surface area small. It has a large adsorption capacity at high relative humidities but adsorbs a small amount at low relative humidities.

In contrast, gel 8 has a capillary volume one-seventh the size of gel 1, but a total surface area almost twice as large. This gives it a higher capacity at low relative humidities but a lower capacity to hold the moisture that condenses at high relative humidities.

Silica gels and most other adsorbents can be manufactured to provide optimum performance in a specific application, balancing capacity against strength, weight, and other favorable characteristics (Bry-Air 1986).

Types of Solid Adsorbents. General classes of solid adsorbents include

- Silica gels
- Zeolites
- Synthetic zeolites (molecular sieves)
- Activated aluminas
- Carbons
- Synthetic polymers

Silica gels are amorphous solid structures formed by condensing soluble silicates from solutions of water or other solvents. Advantages include relatively low cost and relative simplicity of structural customizing. They are available as large as spherical beads about 3/16 in. in diameter or as small as grains of a fine powder.

Zeolites are aluminosilicate minerals. They occur in nature and are mined rather than synthesized. Zeolites have a very open crystalline lattice that allows molecules such as water vapor to be held inside the crystal itself, like an object in a cage. Particular atoms of an aluminosilicate determine the size of the openings between the "bars" of the cage, which in turn governs the maximum size of the molecule that can be adsorbed into the structure.

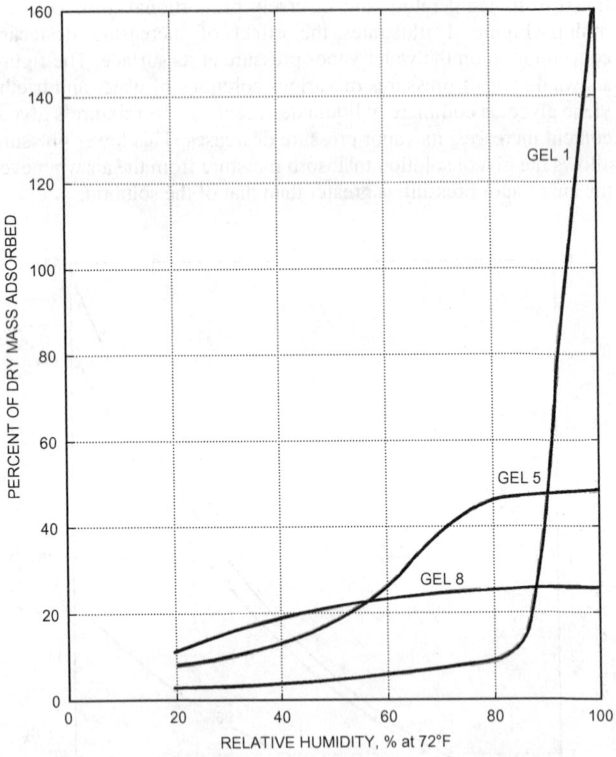

Gel Number	Total Surface Area, m^2/g	Average Capillary Diameter, nm	Total Volume of Capillaries, mm^3/g
1	315	21	1700
5	575	3.8	490
8	540	2.2	250

Fig. 6 Adsorption and Structural Characteristics of Some Experimental Silica Gels
(from data of Oscic and Cooper 1982)

Synthetic zeolites, also called **molecular sieves**, are crystalline aluminosilicates manufactured in a thermal process. Controlling process temperature and composition of ingredient materials allows close control of the adsorbent's structure and surface characteristics. At a somewhat higher cost, this provides a much more uniform product than naturally occurring zeolites.

Activated aluminas are oxides and hydrides of aluminum that are manufactured in thermal processes. Their structural characteristics can be controlled by the gases used to produce them and by the temperature and duration of the thermal process.

Carbons are most frequently used for adsorption of gases other than water vapor because they have a greater affinity for the nonpolar molecules typical of organic solvents. Like other adsorbents, carbons have a large internal surface and especially large capillaries. This capillary volume gives them a high capacity to adsorb water vapor at relative humidities of 45 to 100%.

Synthetic polymers have potential for use as desiccants, as well. Long molecules, like those found in polystyrenesulfonic acid sodium salt (PSSASS), are twisted together like strands of string. Each of the many sodium ions in the long PSSASS molecules has the potential to bind several water molecules, and the spaces between the packed strings can also contain condensed water, giving the polymer a capacity exceeding that of many other solid adsorbents.

4. DESICCANT ISOTHERMS

Figure 7 shows a rough comparison of sorption characteristics of different desiccants. Large variations from these isotherms occur because manufacturers use different methods to optimize materials for different applications. Suitability of a given desiccant to a particular application generally depends as much on the engineering of the mechanical system that presents the material to airstreams as on the characteristics of the material itself.

Several sources give details of desiccant equipment design and information about desiccant isotherm characteristics. Brunauer (1945) considers five basic isotherm shapes. Sing (1985) added a sixth isotherm shape and defined four types of hysteresis loops that are often identified with specific pore structures. Each shape is determined by the dominant sorption mechanisms of the desiccant, which give rise to its specific capacity characteristics at different vapor pressures. Isotherm shape can be important in designing the optimum desiccant for applications where a narrow range of operating conditions can be expected. Collier (1986, 1988) illustrates how an optimum isotherm shape can be used to ensure a maximum coefficient of performance in one particular air-conditioning desiccant application.

5. DESICCANT LIFE

The useful life of desiccant materials depends largely on the quantity and type of contamination in the airstreams they dry. In commercial equipment, desiccants last from 10,000 to 100,000 h or longer before they need replacement. Normally, three mechanisms cause loss of desiccant capacity: (1) change in desiccant sorption characteristics through **chemical reactions** with contaminants, (2) loss of effective surface area through clogging or **hydrothermal degradation**, or (3) clogging or masking the pore system's surface by **contaminants**.

Liquid absorbents are more susceptible to chemical reaction with airstream contaminants other than water vapor than are solid adsorbents. For example, certain sulfur compounds can react with LiCl to form lithium sulfate, which is not a desiccant. If the concentration of sulfur compounds in the airstream were below 10 ppm and the desiccant were in use 24 h a day, capacity reduction would be approximately 10 to 20% after three years of operation. If the concentration were 30 ppm, this reduction would occur after one year. In contaminated environments, equipment manufacturers often arrange filters to remove these products of reaction, and provide devices to replenish desiccant so that capacity stays constant.

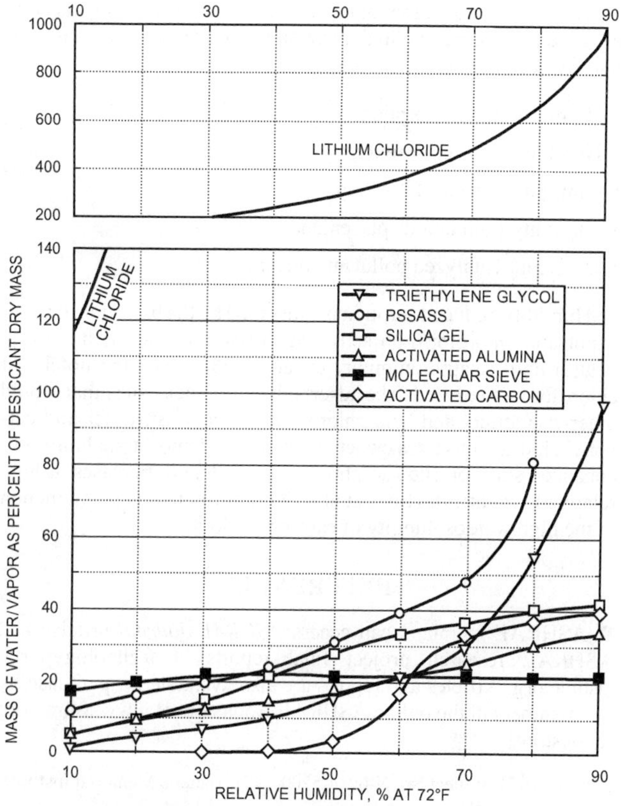

Sources for isotherms presented in the figure include
PSSASS: Czanderna (1988)
Lithium chloride: Munters Corporation: Cargocaire Division and Kathabar, Inc.
Triethylene glycol: Dow Chemical Corporation
Silica gel: Davison Chemical Division of W.R. Grace Co.
Activated carbon: Calgon Corporation
Activated alumina: LaRoche Industries Inc.
Molecular sieve: Davison Chemical Division of W.R. Grace Co.

Fig. 7 Sorption Isotherms of Various Desiccants

Solid adsorbents tend to be less chemically reactive and more sensitive to clogging, a function of the type and quantity of particulate material in the airstream. Also, certain types of silica gel can be sensitive to saturated airstreams or to liquid moisture carried over from cooling coils into the desiccant bed. In more challenging applications, thermally stabilized desiccants are used in place of less durable materials.

In air-conditioning applications, desiccant equipment is designed to minimize the need for desiccant replacement in much the same way that vapor compression cooling systems are designed to avoid the need for compressor replacement. Unlike filters, desiccants are seldom intended to be frequently replaced during normal service in an air-drying application.

6. COSORPTION OF WATER VAPOR AND INDOOR AIR CONTAMINANTS

Hines et al. (1991) confirmed that many desiccant materials can collect common indoor pollutants while they collect water vapor from ambient air. This characteristic promises to become useful in future air-conditioning systems where indoor air quality is especially important.

The behavior of different desiccant and vapor mixtures is complex, but in general, pollutant sorption reactions can be classified into five categories:

- Humidity-neutral sorption
- Humidity-reduced sorption
- Humidity-enhanced sorption
- Humidity-pollutant displacement
- Desiccant-catalyzed pollutant conversion

Humidity-reduced sorption is illustrated by the behavior of water vapor and chloroform on activated carbon. Sorption is humidity-neutral until relative humidity exceeds 45%, when the uptake of chloroform is reduced. The adsorbed water blocks sites that would otherwise attract and hold chloroform. In contrast, water and carbonyl chloride mixtures on activated carbon demonstrate humidity-enhanced sorption (i.e., sorption of the pollutant increases at high relative humidities). Hines et al. (1991) attribute this phenomenon to the high water solubility of carbonyl chloride.

REFERENCES

ASHRAE members can access *ASHRAE Journal* articles and ASHRAE research project final reports at technologyportal .ashrae.org. Articles and reports are also available for purchase by nonmembers in the online ASHRAE Bookstore at www.ashrae.org /bookstore.

Battelle. 1971. Project No. N-0914-5200-1971. Battelle Memorial Institute, Columbus, OH.

Brunauer, S. 1945. *The adsorption of gases and vapors*, vol. I. Princeton University Press, Princeton, NJ. Quoted and expanded in *The physical chemistry of surfaces*, by Arthur W. Adamson. John Wiley & Sons, New York, 1982.

Bry-Air. 1986. *MVB series engineering data*. Bry-Air Inc., Sunbury, OH.

Collier, R.K. 1986, 1988. Advanced desiccant materials assessment. *Research Report* 5084-243-1089. Phase I-1986, Phase II-1988. Gas Research Institute, Chicago.

Czanderna, A.W. 1988. Polymers as advanced materials for desiccant applications. *Research Report* NREL/PR-255-3308. National Renewable Energy Laboratory, Golden, CO.

Davidson Chemical Division of W.R. Grace Co. 1958. Adsorption and dehydration with silica gel. *Technical Bulletin* 202.

Dow. 1981. *Guide to glycols*. Dow Chemical Corporation, Organic Chemicals Division, Midland, MI.

Foote Mineral. 1988. Lithium chloride technical data. *Bulletin* 151. Foote Mineral Corporation, Exton, PA.

Harriman, L.G., III. 2003. *The dehumidification handbook*, 2nd ed. Munters Corporation, Amesbury, MA.

Hines, A.J., T.K. Ghosh, S.K. Loyalka, and R.C. Warder, Jr. 1991. Investigation of co-sorption of gases and vapors as a means to enhance indoor air quality. ASHRAE *Research Project* 475-RP and Gas Research Institute *Project* GRI-90/0194. Gas Research Institute, Chicago.

Oscic, J., and I.L. Cooper. 1982. *Adsorption*. John Wiley & Sons, New York.

Sing, K.S.W. 1985. Reporting physisorption data for gas/solid systems with special reference to the determination of surface area and porosity (Recommendations 1984). *Pure and Applied Chemistry* 57:603-620.

BIBLIOGRAPHY

Adamson, A.W., and A.P. Gast. 1997. *The physical chemistry of surfaces*, 6th ed. John Wiley & Sons, New York.

Falcone, J.S., Jr., ed. 1982. Soluble silicates. *Symposium Series* 194. American Chemical Society, Washington, D.C.

Lowel, S., J.E. Shields, M.A. Thomas, and M. Thommes (eds.). 2004. *Characterization of porous solids and powders: Surface area, pore size and density*. Kluwer Academic Publishers, Dordrecht, the Netherlands.

Ruthven, D.M. 1984. *Principles of adsorption and adsorption processes*. John Wiley & Sons, New York.

SUNY Buffalo School of Medicine. Effects of glycol solution on microbiological growth. Niagrara Blower *Report* No. 03188.

Valenzuela, D., and A. Myers. 1989. *Adsorption equilibrium data handbook*. Simon & Schuster/Prentice-Hall, Englewood Cliffs, NJ.

CHAPTER 33

PHYSICAL PROPERTIES OF MATERIALS

VALUES in the following tables are in consistent units to assist the engineer looking for approximate values. For data on refrigerants, see Chapter 29; for secondary coolants, see Chapter 31. Chapter 26 gives more information on the values for materials used in building construction and insulation. Many properties vary with temperature, material density, and composition. The references document the source of the values and provide more detail or values for materials not listed here. The preparation of this chapter is assigned to TC 1.3, Heat Transfer and Fluid Flow.

Table 1 Properties of Vapor

Material	Molecular Mass	Normal Boiling Point, °F	Critical Temperature, °F	Critical Pressure, psia	Density, lb/ft³	Specific Heat, Btu/lb·°F	Thermal Conductivity, Btu/h·ft·°F	Viscosity, lb/ft·h
Alcohol, ethyl	46.07[a]	173.3[a]	469.6[b]	927.3[b]		0.362[j]	0.0073[a]	0.0343[j] (60)
Alcohol, methyl	32.04[a]	148.9[a]	464.0[b]	1157[b]		0.322[j]	0.0174[r]	0.0358[j] (30)
Ammonia	17.03[a]	–28[a]	270.3[b]	1639[b]	0.0482[b]	0.525[aa]	0.0128[b]	0.0225[aa]
Argon	39.948[a]	–302.5*	–188.5*	704.9*	0.1114[b]	0.125[c]	0.0094[a]	0.0507[a]
Acetylene	26.04[a]	–118.5[a]	96.8[b]	911[b]	0.0732[b]	0.377[a]	0.0108[b]	0.0226[a]
Benzene	78.11[a]	176.2[a]	553.1[d]	714.2[d]	0.167[e] (176)	0.31[e] (176)	0.0041[e]	0.017[a]
Bromine	159.82[a]	137.8[a]	591.8[d]	1499[d]	0.38[f] (138)	0.055[f] (212)	0.0035[a]	0.041[a]
Butane	58.12[a]	31.1[a]	305.6[d]	550.7[d]	0.168[g]	0.377[aa]	0.0079[a]	0.017[a]
Carbon dioxide	44.01[a]	–109.3[a]	87.9[d]	1071[d]	0.123[g]	0.20[g]	0.0084[a]	0.033[h]
Carbon disulfide	76.13[h]	115.2[h]	534[h]	1046[h]		0.1431[p] (80)		
Carbon monoxide	28.01[a]	–312.7[a]	–220.4[d]	507[d]	0.078[d]	0.25[f]	0.0133[a]	0.040[a]
Carbon tetrachloride	153.84[g]	169.8[h]	541.8[h]	661[h]		0.206[q] (80)		0.0375[j]
Chlorine	70.91[a]	–30.3[a]	291.2[d]	1118[d]	0.201[d]	0.117[a]	0.0046[a]	0.030[a]
Chloroform	119.39[h]	143.1[h]	506.1[h]	794[h]		0.126[j]	0.0081[r]	0.038[j]
Ethyl chloride	64.52[h]	54.2[h]	369.0[h]	764[h]	0.1793[b]	0.426[r]	0.00504[j]	0.0378[q]
Ethylene	28.03[h]	–154.6[h]	49.9[h]	742[h]	0.0783[b]	0.352[aa]	0.0102[aa]	0.0231[aa]
Ethyl ether	74.12[h]	94.4[h]	378.8[h]	523[h]		0.589[h] (95)		0.0273[q]
Fluorine	38.00[h]	–304.5[h]	–200.5[h]	808[h]	0.1022[b]	0.194[j]	0.0147[j]	0.089[j]
Helium	4.0026[a]	–452.1[i]	–450.2[h]	33.21[i]	0.0111[i]	1.241[aa]	0.0823[aa]	0.0452[aa]
Hydrogen	2.0159[a]	–423.0[i]	–399.9[i]	190.8[i]	0.00562[i]	3.40[j]	0.0972[aa]	0.0203[aa]
Hydrogen chloride	36.461[a]	–120.8[a]	124.5[d]	1198[d]	0.1024[b]	0.191[j]	0.00757[j]	0.0321[j]
Hydrogen sulfide	34.080[a]	–77.3[a]	212.7[d]	1307[d]	0.0961[b]	0.238[j]	0.00751[j]	0.0281[j]
Heptane (m)	100.21[a]	209.2[a]	512.2[b]	394[b]	0.21[k]	0.476[j]	0.0107[j]	0.0168[j]
Hexane (m)	86.18[a]	154[a]	454.5[d]	440[d]	0.21[k]	0.449[j]	0.00971[j]	0.0182[j]
Isobutane	58.12[f]	–11.1*	275.0[j]	529.1[j]	0.154[s] (70)	0.376[aa]	0.0081[aa]	0.0168[aa]
Methane	16.04[a]	–263.2[a]	–115.18[j]	673.1[b]	0.0448[b]	0.520[aa]	0.0178[aa]	0.0250[aa]
Methyl chloride	50.49[a]	–11.6[a]	289.6[j]	968.5[b]	0.1440[b]	0.184[aa]	0.0054[aa]	0.0244[aa]
Naphthalene	128.19[a]	424.4*	876.2[j]	576.1[j]		0.313[q] (77)		
Neon	20.183[a]	–412.6[a]	–379.7[j]	391.3[j]		0.246[aa]	0.0268[aa]	0.0718[aa]
Nitric oxide	30.01[a]	–241.6[a]	–135.2[j]	949.4[j]		0.238[j]		0.0712[j]
Nitrogen	28.01[a]	–320.4[a]	–232.4[j]	492.3[b]		0.248[j]	0.0138[aa]	0.0402[aa]
Nitrous oxide	44.01[a]	–127.3[a]	97.5[j]	1049.3[j]		0.203[j]	0.01001[j] (80.3)	0.0543[j]
Nitrogen tetroxide	92.02[a]		316.8[j]	1469.6[j]		0.201[p] (80)	0.0232[r] (131)	
Oxygen	31.9977*	–297.3*	–181.5*	731.4*		0.218[j]	0.0141[aa]	0.0462[aa]
n-Pentane	72.53[a]	97.0*	385.9[j]	489.5[j]		0.400[a] (80)	0.00877[j] (80.3)	0.0282[j]
Phenol	74.11[b]	358.5[b]	786[b]	889[b]	0.16[k]	0.34[k]	0.0099[k]	0.029[k]
Propane	44.09[g]	–43.76*	206.1*	616.1*	0.126[g]	0.3753[j] (40)	0.0087[j]	0.0179[j]
Propylene	42.08[b]	–53.86[l]	197.2[l]	670.3[l]	0.120[l]	0.349[aa]	0.0081[aa]	0.0195[aa]
Sulfur dioxide	64.06[b]	14.0[b]	315[b]	1142[b]	0.183[b]	0.145[l]	0.0049[j]	0.0281[j]
Water vapor	18.02[b]	212.0[m]	705.18*	3200.0*	0.0373[m]	0.489[aa]	0.0143[m]	0.0293[aa]

*Data source unknown.

Notes: 1. Properties at 14.696 psia and 32°F, or the saturation temperature if higher than 32°F, unless otherwise noted in parentheses.
2. Superscript letters indicate data source from the References section.

Table 2 Properties of Liquids

Name or Description	Normal Boiling Point, °F at 14.696 psia	Enthalpy of Vaporization, Btu/lb	Specific Heat, c_p: Btu/lb·°F	Specific Heat, c_p: Temp., °F	Viscosity: lb/h·ft	Viscosity: Temp., °F	Enthalpy of Fusion, Btu/lb	Density: lb/ft^3	Density: Temp., °F	Thermal Conductivity: Btu/h·ft·°F	Thermal Conductivity: Temp., °F	Vapor Pressure: mm of Hg	Vapor Pressure: Temp., °F	Freezing Point, °F
Acetic acid	245.3[a]	174.1[b]	0.522[b]	79–203	2.956[f]	68	84.0[b]	65.49[a]	68	0.099[b]	68	400[a]	210	61.9[a]
Acetone	133.2[a]	228.9[b]	0.514[b]	37–73	0.801[f]	68	42.1[b]	49.4[a]	68	0.102[b]	86	400[a]	103	–139.6[a]
Allyl alcohol	206.6[a]	294.1[b]	0.655[b]	70–205	3.298[f]	68		53.31[a]	68	0.104[b]	77–86	400[a]	176	–200.2[a]
n-Amyl alcohol	280.6[i]	216.3[b]			9.686[f]	73.4	48.0[b]	51.06[f]	59	0.094[b]	86	100[a]	186	–110.2[a]
Ammonia	–28[a]	583.2[b]	1.099[b]	32	0.643[f]	–28.3	142.9[b]	43.50[b]	–50	0.29[b]	5–86	400[a]	–49.7	–107.9[a]
Alcohol, ethyl	173.3[a]	367.5[b]	0.680[b]	32–208	2.889[f]	68	46.4[b]	49.27[a]	68	0.105[b]	68	100[a]	94.8	–179.1[a]
Alcohol, methyl	148.9[a]	473.0[b]	0.601[b]	59–68	1.434[f]	68	42.7[a]	49.40[a]	68	0.124[b]	68	100[a]	70.2	–144.0[a]
Aniline	363.8[a]	186.6[b]	0.512[b]	46–180	10.806[f]	68	48.8[b]	63.77[a]	68	0.100[b]	32–68	10[a]	156.9	20.84[a]
Benzene	176.2[a]	169.4[h]	0.412[h]	68	1.58[a]	68	54.2[h]	54.9[d]	68	0.085[h]	68	75[d]	68	42[a]
Bromine	137.8[a]	79.4[d]	0.107[f]	68	2.39[a]	68	28.5[d]	194.7[f]	68	0.070[a]	77	165[d]	68	19[a]
n-Butyl alcohol	243.5[a]	254.3[h]	0.563[f]	68	7.13[f]	68	53.9[b]	50.6[a]	68	0.089[h]	68	5[d]	68	–130[a]
n-Butyric acid	326.3[a]	217.0[h]	0.515[f]	68	3.73[a]	68	54.1[a]	60.2[a]	68	0.094[h]	54	0.7[d]	68	20[a]
Calcium chloride brine (20% by mass)			0.744[i]	68	4.8[i]	68		73.8[i]	68	0.332[i]	68			2[i]
Carbon disulfide	115.3[a]	148.8[h]	0.240[i]	68	0.88[a]	68	24.8[d]	78.9[d]	68	0.093[b]	86	295[d]	68	–168[a]
Carbon tetrachloride	170.2[a]	83.7[h]	0.201[f]	68	2.34[a]	68	12.8[d]	99.5[d]	68	0.062[j]	68	87[d]	68	–9[a]
Chloroform	142.3[v]	106[v]	0.234[v]	68	1.36[v]	68		92.96[v]	68	0.075[v]	68	160[v]	68	–81.8[v]
n-Decane	345.2[b]		0.50[b]	68			86.9[b]	45.6[b]	68	0.086[b]	68	1.3[b]	68	–21.5[b]
Ethyl ether	94.06[v]	151[v]	0.541[v]	68	0.56[v]	68	42.4[v]	44.61[v]	68	0.081[b]	68	440[v]	68	–177.3[v]
Ethyl acetate	170.8[v]	183.8[v]	0.468[v]	68	1.09[v]	68	51.2[b]	52.3[v]	68	0.101[b]	68	72[b]	68	–116.3[v]
Ethyl chloride	54.2[j]	165.9[f] (68)	0.368[f]	32			29.68[a]	56.05[a]	68	0.179[f]	33.6	400[y]	53.1	–213.5[a]
Ethyl iodide	162.1[a]	82.1[f] (160)	0.368[f]	32	0.0239[f]	68		120.85[a]	68	0.214[f]	86	100[y]	64.4	–162.4*
Ethylene bromide	268.8[a]	99.2[f] (210)	0.174[f]	68	0.0694[f]	68	24.82[a]	136.05[a]	68			10[y]	65.5	49.2[a]
Ethylene chloride	182.3[a]	153.4[f] (308)	0.301[f]	68	0.0338[f]	68	38.02[a]	77.10[a]	68			60[y]	64.6	–31.64[a]
Ethylene glycol	388.4[a]	344.0[f] (651)					77.86[a]	69.22[a]	68	0.100[f]	68	1[y]	128	12.7[a]
Formic acid	213.3[a]	215.8[f] (420)	0.526[f]	68	0.0719[f]	68	118.89[a]	76.16[a]	68	0.104[a]	33	40[y]	75.2	47.1[a]
Glycerin (glycerol)	359* (20 mm)				43.1[f]	68		78.72[a]	68	0.113[a]	68	1[a]	125.5	68[a]
Heptane	209.2[a]	138[f]	0.532[j]	68	0.990[a]	68	60.4[b]	42.7[a]	68	0.0741[j]	68	35.5[y]	68	–132[a]
Hexane	154[a]	145[f]	0.538[j]	68	0.775[d]	68	65.0[b]	41.1[a]	68	0.0720[j]	68	120.0[y]	68	–139[a]
Hydrogen chloride	–120.8[a]	191[f]					23.6[f]	74.6[d]	b.p.					–174.6[a]
Isobutyl alcohol	226.4[a]	249[f]	0.116[f]	68	9.45[f]	68		50.0[f]	68	0.082[f]	68	9.7[y]	68	–162.4[a]
Kerosene	400–560[b]		0.50[n]	68	6.0[b]	68		51.2[a]	68	0.086[n]	68			
Linseed oil					104[b]	68		58[d]	68					–11†[a]
Methyl acetate	134.6[a]	177[f]	0.468[f]	68	0.940[f]	68		60.6[a]	68	0.093[f]	68	169.8[y]	68	–144.6[a]
Methyl iodide	108.5[a]	82.6[f]			1.21[f]	68		142[a]	68			320[y]	68	–87.7[a]
Naphthalene	411.4[a]	136[f]	0.402[f]	m.p.	2.18[b]	m.p.	64.9[b]	60.9[y]	m.p.			2.18[b]	68	176.4[a]
Nitric acid	186.8[v]	270[v]	0.42[v]	68	2.2[k]	68	71.5[v]	94.45[v]	68	0.16[v]	68	1.77[v]	68	–42.9[v]
Nitrobenzene	411.6[b]	142[b]	0.348[b]	68	5.20[b]	68	40.28[v]	75.2[b]	68	0.96[b]	68	< 0.01[b]	68	42.3[b]
Octane	258.3[b]	131.7[b]	0.51[b]	68	1.36[b]	68	77.70[b]	43.9[b]	68	0.084[b]	68	0.42[b]	68	–69.7[b]
Petroleum		98–165[w]	0.4–0.6[w]	68	19–2900[w]	68		40–66[w]						
n-Pentane	96.8[a]	153.6[h]	0.558[h]	68	0.546[d]	68	50.1[h]	39.1[a]	68	0.066[h]	68	425[d]	68	–201.5[a]
Propionic acid	286.0[a]	177.8[f]	0.473[h]	68	2.666[a]	68		61.9[a]	68	0.100*	54	3[d]	68	–5.4[a]
Sodium chloride brine														
20% by mass	220.8[a]		0.745[x]	68	3.80[x]	68		71.8[x]	68	0.337[x]	68	0.57[x]	68	2.6[x]
10% by mass	215.5[a]		0.865[x]	68	2.85[x]	68		66.9[x]	68	0.343[x]	68	0.65[x]	68	20.6[x]
Sodium hydroxide and water														
15% by mass	215.0[v]		0.864[b]	68				72.4[b]	68					–5.8[b]
Sulfuric acid and water														
100% by mass	550.0[v]		0.335[b]	68	53[b]	68		114.4[v]	68			< 0.01[b]	68	50.9[b]
95% by mass	575.0[v]		0.35[v]	68	52[v]	68		114.6[v]	68			< 0.01[v]	68	–18[v]
90% by mass	500.0[v]		0.39[v]	68	60[v]	68		113.4[v]	68	0.22[b]	68	< 0.01[v]	68	15.0[v]
Toluene ($C_6H_5CH_3$)	231[b]	156[b]	0.404[v]	68	1.42[v]	68	30.9[b]	54.1[b]	68	0.090[b]	68	0.88[b]	68	–139[b]
Turpentine	303[a]	123[v]	0.42[b]	68	1.32[b]	68		53.9[b]	68	0.073[b]	68			
Water	211.9*	970.3[m]	0.999[m]	68	2.39[m]	68	143.5[b]	62.32[m]	68	0.348[m]	68	17.59*	68	32.018[m]
Xylene [$C_6H_4(CH_3)_2$]														
Ortho	291[b]	149[b]	0.411[b]	68	2.01[b]	68	55.1[b]	55.0[b]	68	0.90[b]	68	0.196[b]	68	–13[b]
Meta	283[b]	147[b]	0.400[b]	68	1.52[b]	68	46.9[b]	54.1[b]	68	0.90[b]	68	0.218[b]	68	–53[b]
Para	281[b]	146[b]	0.393[b]	68	1.62[b]	68	69.3[b]	53.8[b]	68			0.227[b]	68	56[b]
Zinc sulfate and water														
10% by mass			0.90[b]	68	3.80[a]	68		69.2[r]	68	0.337[a]	68			29.7[a]
1% by mass			0.80[b]	68	2.54[a]	68		63.0[r]	68	0.346[a]	68			31.7[a]

*Data source unknown.
†Approximate solidification temperature.

Notes: Superscript letters indicate data source from the References section.
m.p. = melting point b.p. = boiling point

Table 3 Properties of Solids

Material Description	Specific Heat, Btu/lb·°F	Density, lb/ft³	Thermal Conductivity, Btu/h·ft·°F	Emissivity	
				Ratio	Surface Condition
Aluminum (alloy 1100)	0.214[b]	171[u]	128[u]	0.09[n]	Commercial sheet
				0.20[n]	Heavily oxidized
Aluminum bronze (76% Cu, 22% Zn, 2% Al)	0.09[u]	517[u]	58[u]		
Asbestos: Fiber	0.25[b]	150[u]	0.097[u]		
Asbestos: Insulation	0.20[t]	36[b]	0.092[b]	0.93[b]	"Paper"
Ashes, wood	0.20[t]	40[b]	0.041[b] (122)		
Asphalt	0.22[b]	132[b]	0.43[b]		
Bakelite	0.35[b]	81[u]	9.7[u]		
Bell metal	0.086[t] (122)				
Bismuth tin	0.040*		37.6*		
Brick, building	0.2[b]	123[u]	0.4[b]	0.93*	
Brass: Red (85% Cu, 15% Zn)	0.09[u]	548[u]	87[u]	0.030[b]	Highly polished
Brass: Yellow (65% Cu, 35% Zn)	0.09[u]	519[u]	69[u]	0.033[b]	Highly polished
Bronze	0.104[t]	530[t]	17[d] (32)		
Cadmium	0.055[a]	540[f]	53.7[b]	0.02[d]	
Carbon (gas retort)	0.17[a]		0.20[b] (2)	0.81[a]	
Cardboard			0.04[b]		
Cellulose	0.32[b]	3.4[t]	0.033[t]		
Cement (portland clinker)	0.16[b]	120[i]	0.017[i]		
Chalk	0.215[t]	143[t]	0.48*	0.34*	About 250°F
Charcoal (wood)	0.20[t]	15[a]	0.03[a] (392)		
Chrome brick	0.17[b]	200[b]	0.67[b]		
Clay	0.22[b]	63[t]			
Coal	0.3[b]	90[t]	0.098[f] (32)		
Coal tars	0.35[b] (104)	75[b]	0.07[b]		
Coke (petroleum, powdered)	0.36[b] (752)	62[b]	0.55[b] (752)		
Concrete (stone)	0.156[b] (392)	144[b]	0.54[b]		
Copper (electrolytic)	0.092[u]	556[u]	227[u]	0.072[n]	Commercial, shiny
Cork (granulated)	0.485[t]	5.4[t]	0.028[t] (23)		
Cotton (fiber)	0.319[u]	95[u]	0.024[u]		
Cryolite ($AlF_3 \cdot 3NaF$)	0.253[b]	181[b]			
Diamond	0.147[b]	151[t]	27[t]		
Earth (dry and packed)		95[t]	0.037*	0.41*	
Felt		20.6[b]	0.03[b]		
Fireclay brick	0.198[b] (212)	112[t]	0.58[b] (392)	0.75[n]	At 1832°F
Fluorspar (CaF_2)	0.21[b]	199[v]	0.63[v]		
German silver (nickel silver)	0.09[u]	545[u]	19[u]	0.135[n]	Polished
Glass: Crown (soda-lime)	0.18[b]	154[u]	0.59[t] (200)	0.94[n]	Smooth
Glass: Flint (lead)	0.117[b]	267[u]	0.79[r]		
Glass: Heat-resistant	0.20[b]	139[t]	0.59[t] (200)		
Glass: "Wool"	0.157[b]	3.25[t]	0.022[t]		
Gold	0.0312[u]	1208[u]	172[t]	0.02[n]	Highly polished
Graphite: Powder	0.165*		0.106*		
Graphite: Impervious	0.16[u]	117[u]	75[u]	0.75[n]	
Gypsum	0.259[b]	78[b]	0.25[b]	0.903[b]	On a smooth plate
Hemp (fiber)	0.323[u]	93[u]			
Ice: 32°F	0.487[t]	57.5[b]	1.3[b]	0.95*	
Ice: –4°F	0.465[t]		1.41*		
Iron: Cast	0.12[v] (212)	450[b]	27.6[b] (129)	0.435[b]	Freshly turned
Iron: Wrought		485[b]	34.9[b]	0.94[b]	Dull, oxidized
Lead	0.0309[u]	707[u]	20.1[u]	0.28[n]	Gray, oxidized
Leather (sole)		62.4[b]	0.092[b]		
Limestone	0.217[b]	103[b]	0.54[b]	0.36* to 0.90	At 145 to 380°F
Linen			0.05[b]		
Litharge (lead monoxide)	0.055[b]	490[b]			
Magnesia: Powdered	0.234[b] (212)	49.7[b]	0.35[b] (117)		
Magnesia: Light carbonate		13[b]	0.034[b]		
Magnesite brick	0.222[b] (212)	158[b]	2.2[b] (400)		
Magnesium	0.241[b]	108[u]	91[u]	0.55[n]	Oxidized
Marble	0.21[b]	162[b]	1.5[b]	0.931[b]	Light gray, polished
Nickel, polished	0.105[u]	555[u]	34.4[u]	0.045[n]	Electroplated
Paints: White lacquer				0.80[n]	
Paints: White enamel				0.91[n]	On rough plate
Paints: Black lacquer				0.80[n]	
Paints: Black shellac		63[u]	0.15[u]	0.91[n]	"Matte" finish
Paints: Flat black lacquer				0.96[n]	
Paints: Aluminum lacquer				0.39[n]	On rough plate

*Data source unknown.

Notes: 1. Values are for room temperature unless otherwise noted in parentheses. 2. Superscript letters indicate data source from the References section.

Table 3 Properties of Solids (*Continued*)

Material Description	Specific Heat, Btu/lb·°F	Density, lb/ft³	Thermal Conductivity, Btu/h·ft·°F	Emissivity	
				Ratio	Surface Condition
Paper	0.32*	58[b]	0.075[b]	0.92[b]	Pasted on tinned plate
Paraffin	0.4[bb]	47[bb]	0.14[b] (32)		
Plaster		132[b]	0.43[b] (167)	0.91[b]	Rough
Platinum	0.032[u]	1340[u]	39.9[u]	0.054[b]	Polished
Porcelain	0.18*	162[u]	1.3[u]	0.92[b]	Glazed
Pyrites (copper)	0.131[b]	262[b]			
Pyrites (iron)	0.136[b] (156)	310[v]			
Rock salt	0.219[u]	136[u]			
Rubber, vulcanized: Soft	0.48*	68.6[t]	0.08[t]	0.86[b]	Rough
Hard		74.3[t]	0.092[t]	0.95[b]	Glossy
Sand	0.191[b]	94.6[b]	0.19[b]		
Sawdust		12[b]	0.03[b]		
Silica	0.316[b]	140[v]	0.83[t] (200)		
Silver	0.0560[u]	654[u]	245[u]	0.02[n]	Polished and at 440°F
Snow: Freshly fallen		7[y]	0.34[t]		
At 32°F		31[t]	1.3[t]		
Steel (mild)	0.12[b]	489[b]	26.2[b]	0.12[n]	Cleaned
Stone (quarried)	0.2[b]	95[t]			
Tar: Pitch	0.59[v]	67[u]	0.51[v]		
Bituminous		75[t]	0.41[u]		
Tin	0.0556[u]	455[u]	37.5[u]	0.06[h]	Bright and at 122°F
Tungsten	0.032[u]	1210[u]	116[u]	0.032[n]	Filament at 80°F
Wood: Hardwoods	0.45/0.65[b]	23/70[z]	0.065/0.148[z]		
Ash, white		43[z]	0.0992[z]		
Elm, American		36[z]	0.0884[z]		
Hickory		50[z]			
Mahogany		34[u]	0.075[u]		
Maple, sugar		45[z]	0.108[z]		
Oak, white	0.570[b]	47[z]	0.102[z]	0.90[n]	Planed
Walnut, black		39[z]			
Softwoods	See Table 4, Chapter 25	22/46[z]	0.061/0.093[z]		
Fir, white		27[z]	0.068[z]		
Pine, white		27[z]	0.063[z]		
Spruce		26[z]	0.065[z]		
Wool: Fiber	0.325[u]	82[u]			
Fabric		6.9/20.6[u]	0.021/0.037[u]		
Zinc: Cast	0.092[u]	445[u]	65[u]	0.05[n]	Polished
Hot-rolled	0.094[b]	445[b]	62[b]		
Galvanizing				0.23[n]	Fairly bright

*Data source unknown.

Notes: 1. Values are for room temperature unless otherwise noted in parentheses. 2. Superscript letters indicate data source from the References section.

REFERENCES

[a]*Handbook of chemistry and physics*, 63rd ed. 1982-83. Chemical Rubber Publishing Co., Cleveland, OH.

[b]Perry, R.H. *Chemical engineers' handbook*, 2nd ed., 1941, 5th ed., 1973. McGraw-Hill, New York.

[c]*Tables of thermodynamic and transport properties of air, argon, carbon dioxide, carbon monoxide, hydrogen, nitrogen, oxygen and steam.* 1960. Pergamon Press, Elmsford, NY.

[d]*American Institute of Physics handbook*, 3rd ed. 1972. McGraw-Hill, New York.

[e]Organick and Studhalter. 1948. *Thermodynamic properties of benzene. Chemical Engineering Progress* (November):847.

[f]Lange. 1972. *Handbook of chemistry*, rev. 12th ed. McGraw-Hill, New York.

[g]ASHRAE. 1969. *Thermodynamic properties of refrigerants.*

[h]Reid and Sherwood. 1969. *The properties of gases and liquids*, 2nd ed. McGraw-Hill, New York.

[i]Chapter 19, 1993 *ASHRAE Handbook—Fundamentals.*

[j]*T.P.R.C. data book.* 1966. Thermophysical Properties Research Center, W. Lafayette, IN.

[k]Estimated.

[l]Canjar, L.N., M. Goldman, and H. Marchman. 1951. Thermodynamic properties of propylene. *Industrial and Engineering Chemistry* (May):1183.

[m]*ASME steam tables.* 1967. American Society of Mechanical Engineers, New York.

[n]McAdams, W.H. 1954. *Heat transmission*, 3rd ed. McGraw-Hill, New York.

[o]Stull, D.R. 1947. Vapor pressure of pure substances (organic compounds). *Industrial and Engineering Chemistry* (April):517.

[p]*JANAF thermochemical tables.* 1965. PB 168 370. National Technical Information Service, Springfield, VA.

[q]*Physical properties of chemical compounds.* 1955–61. American Chemical Society, Washington, D.C.

[r]*International critical tables of numerical data.* 1928. National Research Council of USA, McGraw-Hill, New York.

[s]*Matheson gas data book*, 4th ed. 1966. Matheson Company, Inc., East Rutherford, NJ.

[t]Baumeister and Marks. 1967. *Standard handbook for mechanical engineers.* McGraw-Hill, New York.

[u]Miner and Seastone. *Handbook of engineering materials.* John Wiley and Sons, New York.

[v]Kirk and Othmer. 1966. *Encyclopedia of chemical technology.* Interscience Division, John Wiley and Sons, New York.

[w]Gouse and Stevens. 1960. *Chemical technology of petroleum*, 3rd ed. McGraw-Hill, New York.

[x]*Saline water conversion engineering data book.* 1955. M.W. Kellogg Co. for U.S. Department of Interior.

[y]Timmermans, J. *Physicochemical constants of pure organic compounds*, 2nd ed. American Elsevier, New York.

[z]*Wood handbook.* 1955. Handbook No. 72. Forest Products Laboratory, U.S. Department of Agriculture.

[aa]ASHRAE. 1976. *Thermophysical properties of refrigerants.*

[bb]Lane, G. ed. 1986. *Solar heat storage: Latent heat materials, Vol II—Technology.* CRC Press, Chicago.

CHAPTER 34

ENERGY RESOURCES

ENERGY used in buildings and facilities is responsible for 30 to 40% of the world's energy use, significantly impacting world energy resources. ASHRAE's work to reduce energy consumption in the built environment is equally as important as research on new, more sustainable energy sources in helping ensure a reliable and secure supply of energy for future generations.

Many governmental agencies regulate energy conservation, often through the procedures to obtain building permits. Required efficiency values for building energy use strongly influence selection of HVAC&R systems and equipment and how they are applied.

More information on sustainable design is available in the *ASHRAE GreenGuide* (2013) and in Chapter 35.

1. CHARACTERISTICS OF ENERGY AND ENERGY RESOURCE FORMS

The HVAC&R industry deals with energy forms as they occur on or arrive at a building site. Generally, these forms are fossil fuels (natural gas, oil, and coal) and electricity. Solar and wind energy are also available at most sites, as is biomass. Geothermal energy is available at some locations.

Fossil Fuels and Electricity

Most on-site energy for buildings in developed countries involves electricity and fossil fuels as energy sources. Both fossil fuels and electricity can be described by their energy content (Btu). This implies that energy forms are comparable and that an equivalence can be established. In reality, however, they are only comparable in energy terms when they are used to generate heat. Fossil fuels, for example, cannot directly drive motors or energize light bulbs. Conversely, electricity gives off heat as a by-product regardless of whether it is used for running a motor or lighting a light bulb, and regardless of whether that heat is needed. Thus, electricity and fossil fuels have different characteristics, uses, and capabilities aside from any differences in their derivation.

Other differences between energy forms include methods of extraction, transformation, transportation, and delivery, and characteristics of the resource itself. Natural gas arrives at the site in virtually the same form in which it was extracted from the earth. Oil is processed (distilled) before arriving at the site; having been extracted as crude oil, it arrives at a given site as, for example, No. 2 oil or diesel fuel. Electricity is created (converted) from a different energy form, often a fossil fuel, which itself may first be converted to a thermal form. The total electricity conversion, generation, and distribution process includes energy losses governed largely by the laws of thermodynamics.

Fossil fuels undergo a conversion process by combustion (oxidation) and heat transfer to thermal energy in the form of steam or hot water. The conversion equipment is a boiler or a furnace in lieu of a generator, and conversion usually occurs on a project site rather than off site. (District heating or cooling is an exception.) Inefficiencies of fossil fuel conversion occur on site, whereas inefficiencies of most electricity generation occur off site, before the electricity arrives at the building site. (Cogeneration is an exception.)

Sustainability is an important consideration for energy use. The United Nations' Brundtland Report (UN 1987) stated that the development of the built environment is sustainable if it "meets the needs of the present without compromising the ability of future generations to meet their own needs." More information is in Chapter 35.

Forms of On-Site Energy

Fossil fuels and electricity are commodities that are usually metered or measured for payment at the facility's location. Solar or wind energy is freely available but does incur cost for the means to use it. Geothermal energy, which is not universally available, may or may not be a sold commodity, depending on the particular locale and local regulations. Chapter 34 of the 2015 *ASHRAE Handbook—HVAC Applications* has more information on geothermal energy.

The term **energy source** refers to on-site energy in the form in which it arrives at or occurs on a site (e.g., electricity, gas, oil, coal). **Energy resource** refers to the raw energy that (1) is extracted from the earth (wellhead or mine-mouth), (2) is used to generate the energy source delivered to a building site (e.g., coal used to generate electricity), or (3) occurs naturally and is available at a site (solar, wind, or geothermal energy). Some on-site energy forms require further processing or conversion into more suitable forms for the particular systems and equipment in a building or facility. For instance, natural gas or oil is burned in a boiler to produce steam or hot water, which is then distributed to various use points (e.g., heating coils in air-handling systems, unit heaters, convectors, fin-tube elements, steam-powered cooling units, humidifiers, kitchen equipment) throughout the building. Although the methods and efficiencies of these processes fall within the scope of the HVAC&R designer, *how* an energy source arrives at a given facility site is not under direct control. On-site energy choices, when available, may be controlled by the designer based in part on the present and projected future availability of the resources.

Energy sources used for heating may be natural gas, oil, coal, or electricity. Cooling may be produced by electricity, thermal energy, or natural gas. If electricity is generated on site, the generator may be driven by an engine or fuel cell that consumes fossil fuels or hydrogen on site, by a turbine using steam or gas directly, or by on-site renewable sources.

Nonrenewable and Renewable Energy Resources

From the standpoint of energy conservation, energy resources can be classified as either (1) nonrenewable resources, which have definite, although sometimes unknown, limitations; or (2) renewable resources, which have the potential to regenerate in a reasonable

---

The preparation of this chapter is assigned to TC 2.8, Building Environmental Impacts and Sustainability.

period. Resources used most in industrialized countries are nonrenewable (ASHRAE 2003).

Note that *renewable* does not mean an infinite supply. For instance, hydropower is limited by rainfall and appropriate sites, usable geothermal energy is available only in limited areas, and crops are limited by the available farm area and competing non-energy land uses. Other forms of renewable energy also have supply limitations.

Nonrenewable resources of energy include

- Coal
- Crude oil
- Natural gas
- Uranium or plutonium (nuclear energy)

Renewable resources of energy include

- Hydropower
- Solar
- Wind
- Geothermal
- Biomass (wood, wood wastes, and municipal solid waste, landfill methane, etc.)
- Tidal power
- Ocean thermal
- Crops (for alcohol production or as boiler fuel)

Environmental Considerations

The most widely recognized environmental impact from energy use in buildings is **greenhouse gas emissions;** carbon dioxide emissions is usually the most important greenhouse gas resulting from energy use in buildings. In this area, use of renewable resources and nuclear power generally results in no net greenhouse gas emissions, whereas fossil fuel energy use generally results in substantial greenhouse gas emissions.

However, note that the important issue is the amount of greenhouse gas emissions released into the air, not the amount of a fuel used. It has been argued that some biomass energy sources are not really carbon-free sources, because they result in carbon dioxide releases that are not directly offset by carbon dioxide capture through growing vegetation to replace the biomass fuel. Even for fossil fuel energy use, research is ongoing for carbon capture and sequestration for emissions from fossil fuel electric power plants. If the carbon dioxide from a fossil fuel energy source is not released into the atmosphere, there are no greenhouse gas emissions resulting from the use of that fuel.

In addition to greenhouse gases, there are also local air pollution issues from combustion of fuels. These include emissions of carbon monoxide, nitrogen oxides, sulfur dioxide, heavy metals, and particulates. These occur in the combustion of fossil fuels and biomass, and do not occur from the use of renewable energy (other than biomass) or nuclear power. Emissions of local air pollutants vary greatly, depending on design of the combustion equipment and controls technology used. Note that biomass energy sources may require similar mitigation measures to reduce local air emissions as would be required for fossil fuel energy sources.

1.1 ON-SITE ENERGY/ENERGY RESOURCE RELATIONSHIPS

An HVAC&R designer must select one or more forms of energy. Most often, these are fossil fuels and electricity, although installations are sometimes designed using a single energy source (e.g., only a fossil fuel or only electricity).

Solar energy normally impinges on the site (and on the facilities to be put there), so it affects the facility's energy consumption. The designer must account for this effect and may have to decide whether to make active use of solar energy. Other naturally occurring and distributed renewable forms such as wind power and geothermal (if available) might also be considered.

The designer should be aware of the relationship between on-site energy sources and raw energy resources, including how these resources are used and what they are used for. The relationship between energy sources and energy resources involves two parts: (1) quantifying the energy resource units expended and (2) considering the societal effect of depletion of one energy resource (caused by on-site energy use) with respect to others.

Quantifiable Relationships

As on-site energy sources are consumed, a corresponding amount of resources are consumed to produce that on-site energy. For instance, for every volume of No. 2 oil consumed by a boiler at a building site, some greater volume of crude oil is extracted from the earth. On leaving the well, the crude oil is transported and processed into its final form, perhaps stored, and then transported to the site where it will be used.

Even though natural gas often requires no significant processing, it is transported, often over long distances, to reach its final destination, which causes some energy loss. Electricity may have as its raw energy resource a fossil fuel, uranium, or an elevated body of water (hydroelectric generating plant).

Data are available to help determine the amount of resource use per delivered on-site energy source unit. In the United States, data are available from entities within the U.S. Department of Energy and from the agencies and associations listed at the end of this chapter.

A **resource utilization factor (RUF)** is the ratio of resources consumed to energy delivered (for each form of energy) to a building site. Specific RUFs may be determined for various energy sources normally consumed on site, including nonrenewable sources such as coal, gas, oil, and electricity, and renewable sources such as solar, geothermal, waste, and wood energy. With electricity, which may derive from several resources depending on the particular fuel mix of the generating stations in the region served, the overall RUF is the weighted combination of individual factors applicable to electricity and a particular energy resource. Grumman (1984) gives specific formulas for calculating RUFs.

There are great differences in the efficiency of equipment used in buildings. Although electricity incurs losses in its production, it is often much more efficient than direct fuel use at the building site, particularly for lighting or heat pump applications. Minimizing both energy cost and the amount of energy resources needed to accomplish a task effectively should be a major design goal, which requires consideration of both RUFs and end-use efficiency of building equipment.

Although a designer is usually not required to determine the amount of energy resources attributable to a given building or building site for its design or operation, this information may be helpful when assessing the long-range availability of energy for a building or the building's effect on energy resources. Fuel-quantity-to-energy-resource ratios or factors are often used, which suggests that energy resources are of concern to the HVAC&R industry.

Intangible Relationships

Energy resources should not simply be converted into common energy units [e.g., quadrillion (10^{15}) Btu or quad] because the commonality gives a misleading picture of the equivalence of these resources. Other differences and limitations of each of the resources defy easy quantification. For instance, electricity used on a site can be generated from coal, oil, natural gas, uranium, or hydropower. The end result is the same: electricity at x kV, y Hz. However, the societal impact of a kilowatt-hour electricity generated by hydropower may not equal that of a kilowatt-hour generated by coal, uranium, domestic oil, or imported oil.

Intangible factors such as safety, environmental acceptability, availability, and national interest also are affected in different ways by the consumption of each resource. Heiman (1984) proposes a procedure for weighting the following intangible factors:

National/Global Considerations

- Balance of trade
- Environmental impacts
- International policy
- Employment
- Minority employment
- Availability
- Alternative uses
- National defense
- Domestic policy
- Effect on capital markets

Local Considerations

- Exterior environmental impact
    - Air
    - Solid waste
    - Water resources
- Local employment
- Local balance of trade
- Use of distribution infrastructure
- Local energy independence
- Land use
- Exterior safety

Site Considerations

- Reliability of supply
- Indoor air quality
- Aesthetics
- Interior safety
- Anticipated changes in energy resource prices

1.2 SUMMARY

In HVAC&R system design, the need to address immediate issues such as economics, performance, and space constraints often prevents designers from fully considering the energy resources affected. Today's energy resources are less certain because of issues such as availability, safety, national interest, environmental concerns, and the world political situation. As a result, the reliability, economics, and continuity of many common energy resources over the potential life of a building being designed are unclear. For this reason, the designer of building energy systems must consider the energy resources on which the long-term operation of the building will depend. If the continued viability of those resources is reason for concern, the design should provide for, account for, or address such an eventuality.

2. ENERGY RESOURCE PLANNING

The energy supplier (or suppliers) in a particular jurisdiction must plan for that jurisdiction's future energy needs. For competitive energy markets where these decisions do not have high societal costs, these plans are made by energy suppliers and are not revealed to governmental authorities or the public more than is absolutely necessary, because of the advantage competitors could gain by this knowledge. For electricity (and, to a lesser extent, natural gas), significant societal issues are involved in energy resource planning decisions that cannot be made by energy suppliers without approval by many different groups. Issues include

- **Reliability**, which is affected by the diversity of supply sources available. For gas, this includes the number of geographic supply sources and pipelines; for electricity, it includes the percentage of generation from various fuel sources. Consider the projected future supply and reliability of energy resources, including the possibility of supply disruption by natural or political events, and the likelihood of future supply shortages, which could reduce reliability.
- **Reserve margins**, or the ratio of total supply sources to expected peak supply source needs. Reserve levels that are too high result in waste of resources, higher environmental costs, and possibly poor financial health of the energy suppliers. Reserves that are too low result in volatile and very high peak energy prices and reduced reliability.
- **Land use.** Energy production and transmission often require governmental cooperation to condemn private property for energy production and transmission facilities. Construction and maintenance are also regulated to protect wetlands, prevent toxic waste releases, and other environmental issues.

Note that some energy regulation plans provide no guidance at all on energy supplies, through integrated resource planning (IRP) or other methods. Energy suppliers choose whether to expand their capacity, and what types of fuel those facilities use, based on their own assessment of the future profitability of that investment. In these markets, decisions are made with little societal input other than permitting and pollution control regulations, just as a decision might be made by a manufacturer in an industry such as steel or paper. This does not mean that decisions are made independent of larger societal issues, because laws and regulations (e.g., tradable emissions credits, renewable portfolio standards) factor into the economic considerations of competing suppliers. There is simply more direct planning by governmental authorities, and more opportunities for public input, in the integrated resource planning process typically done by regulated utility providers, as described in more detail in the following.

2.1 INTEGRATED RESOURCE PLANNING (IRP)

In regulated utility markets, integrated resource planning is commonly used for planning significant new energy facilities, especially for electricity. Steps include (1) forecasting the amount of new resources needed and (2) determining the type and provider of this resource. Traditionally, the local utility provider forecasts future needs of a given energy resource, then either builds the necessary facility with the approval of regulators or uses a standard offer bid to determine what nonutility provider (or the utility itself) would provide the new energy resource.

Supplying new energy resources through either a standard bid process by a supplier or traditional utility regulation usually results in selection of the lowest-cost supply option, without regard for environmental costs or other societal needs. IRP allows a greater variety of resource options and allows environmental and other indirect societal costs to be given greater consideration.

IRP addresses a wider population of stakeholders than most other planning processes. Many regulatory agencies involve the public in the formulation and review of integrated resource plans. Customers, environmentalists, and other public interest groups are often prominent in these proceedings.

In deregulated energy markets, supplying markets with new energy resources is typically left up to competitive market forces. This has sometimes resulted in excessive reliance on one form of energy, such as natural gas generation. Another result has been highly volatile prices, when supply is not provided because of insufficient price signals, followed by much higher prices and energy shortages until new supply sources can be obtained (which may not be for several years because of the time required for construction and environmental approval processes). Energy efficiency and demand response programs are increasingly treated as an energy resource on a par with energy production options, with incentives and compensation provided for participants in these programs.

Demand-side management (DSM) is a common option for providing new energy resources, especially for electricity. These are actions taken to reduce the demand for energy, rather than increase the supply of energy. DSM is desirable because its environmental costs are almost always lower than those of building new energy facilities. However, the following factors have caused a decline in the number of DSM programs:

- Building and equipment codes and standards are a highly efficient form of DSM, reducing energy use with much lower administrative costs than programs that reward installation of more efficient equipment at a single site. However, they are more subtle than traditional DSM programs and may not always be recognized as a form of DSM.
- Opening markets to competing suppliers makes it more difficult to administer and implement DSM programs. However, they are still possible if regulators wish to continue them, and set appropriate rules and regulations for the market to allow implementation of DSM programs.

Many IRP participants may be interested in only one aspect of the process. For example, the energy industry's main interest may be cost minimization, whereas environmentalists may want to minimize pollutant emissions and prevent environmental damage from construction of energy facilities. Participation by all affected interest groups helps provide the best overall solution for society, including indirect costs and benefits from these energy resource decisions.

2.2 TRADABLE EMISSION CREDITS

Increasingly, quotas and limits apply to emissions of various pollutants. Often, a market-based system of tradable credits is used with these quotas. A company is given the right to produce a given level of emissions, and it earns a credit, which can be sold to others, if it produces fewer emissions than that level. If one company can reduce its emissions at a lower cost than another, it can do so and sell the emissions credit to the second company and earn a profit from its pollution control efforts. In the United States, emissions quota and trading programs currently include sulfur dioxide (SO_2) and nitrogen oxides (NO_x), with plans to implement carbon dioxide (CO_2) trading now under consideration, as well. In Europe, emissions trading for CO_2 has been active for several years.

Designers must be aware of any regulations concerning pollutant emissions; failure to comply with these regulations may result in civil or criminal penalties for designers or their clients. However, understand the options available under these regulations. The purchase or sale of emissions credits may allow reduced construction or building operations costs if the equipment can overcomply at a lower cost than the cost of another source of emissions to comply, or vice versa. In some cases, documentation of energy savings beyond what codes and regulations require can result in receiving emissions credits that may be sold later.

3. OVERVIEW OF GLOBAL ENERGY RESOURCES

3.1 WORLD ENERGY RESOURCES

Data in this section are from the *Statistical Review of World Energy 2015* (BP 2015).

Production

Energy production trends, by leading producers and world ions, from 2004 to 2014 are shown in Figure 1.

Vorld primary energy production increased 21.2% from 2004 to because strong economic growth occurred in countries such 'na, which increased its energy production more than 60% since 2004. The largest total energy producers in 2014 were China (19%), the United States (16%), Russia (10%), and Saudi Arabia (7%). Together, they produced about 52% of the world's energy production. (*Note*: for this and for similar graphs, the "Europe and Eurasia" region consists of the nations of western Europe plus the countries comprised by the former Soviet Union.)

Total world energy production by resource type for 2004 and 2014 is shown in Figure 2. The greatest growth in energy production among major sources has been hydroelectricity, up nearly 33% in usage from 2004 to 2014, and coal, which has increased 30.3%, and natural gas, up 10.3%. Petroleum use only rose 7.1%. Nonhydroelectric renewables use more than doubled, but is still a small percentage of total world energy production (BP 2015).

Crude Oil. World crude oil production was 88.7 million barrels per day in 2014. The biggest crude-oil-producing region in 2014 was the Middle East, with 32% of the total. Among individual countries, the United States (13.1%), Saudi Arabia (13.0%), and Russia (12.2%) were the leading countries, following by China and Canada, each with 4.8% of total production. Since 2004, oil production

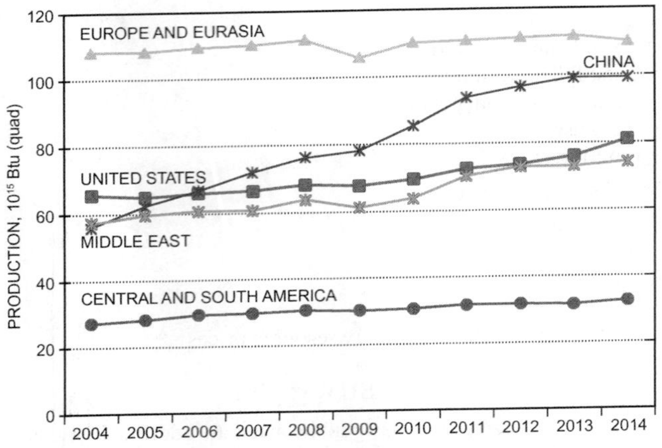

Fig. 1 Energy Production Trends: 2004-2014
(Basis: BP 2015)

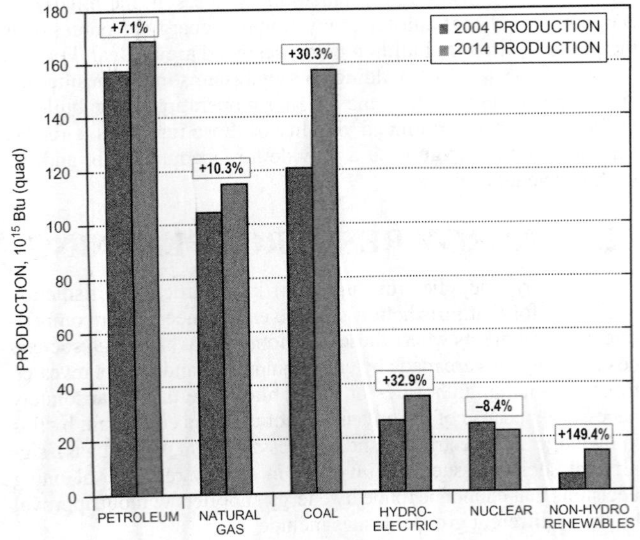

Fig. 2 World Primary Energy Production by Resource: 2004 Versus 2014
(Basis: BP 2015)

increased 56% in the United States and about 25% in both China and Russia.

Natural Gas. World production reached 122.2 trillion ft^3 in 2014, up 14.4% from the 2004 level. The biggest producers in 2014 were the United States (22%), Russia (17%), Qatar (5%), Iran (5%), and Canada (5%). Since 2004, natural gas production in Qatar more than quadrupled, and was up 79% in Iran and 39% in the United States.

Coal. At 156.1 quadrillion Btu in 2014, coal production was up 38.7% since 2004. Leading producers of coal were China (47%), the United States (13%), India (7%), and Indonesia (6%). Since 2004, Indonesia more than tripled coal production, China increased coal production 67%, and India increased 56%, whereas U.S. production fell by 11%.

Reserves

On January 1, 2015, estimated world reserves of crude oil and gas were distributed by world region as shown in Figures 3 and 4. Countries with the largest reported crude oil reserves are Venezuela (17.5%), Saudi Arabia (15.7%), Canada (10.2%), Iran (9.3%), and Iraq (8.8%). For natural gas, the countries with the largest reported reserves are Iran (18.2%), Russia (17.4%), Qatar (13.1%), Turkmenistan (9.3%), and the United States (5.2%).

Note that several factors make crude oil and natural gas reserve estimates less precise than some other energy statistics:

- For nations with national oil companies, reserve estimates are not verifiable by third parties, as is typically the case with the reserve estimates of publicly traded corporations.
- Technologies used for extracting hydrocarbons from nontraditional reserves (e.g., tar sands, shale deposits) are rapidly changing. This can result in very large revisions to reserve estimates that often lag production changes. For example, approximately 10 years ago, Canadian oil reserves rose substantially due to inclusion of tar sands in the total. More recently, reported crude oil and natural gas reserves in the United States have lagged production growth, because of uncertainty concerning the size of the total available resource that can be economically extracted.
- The definition of proved resource includes a requirement that it can be economically extracted, which can result in substantial changes due to fluctuations in the price of oil and natural gas.

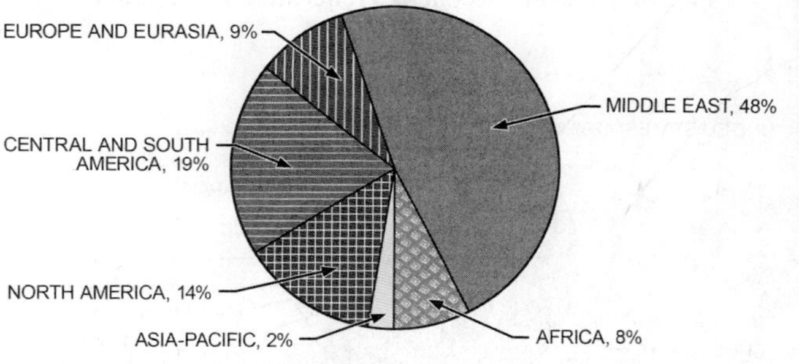

Fig. 3 World Crude Oil Reserves: 2015
(Basis: BP 2016)

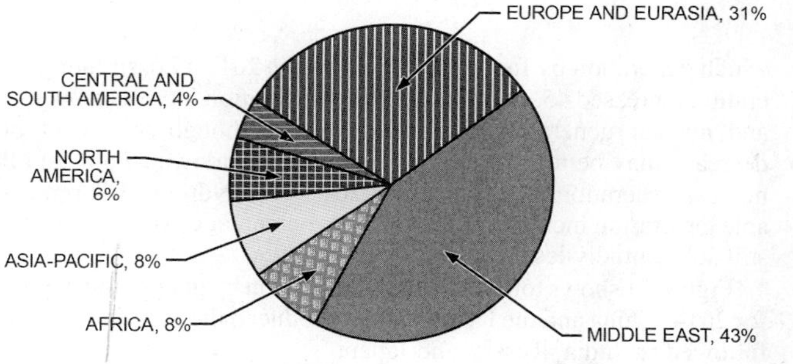

Fig. 4 World Natural Gas Reserves: 2015
(Basis: BP 2016)

World coal reserves as of January 1, 2015, are shown by region in Figure 5. The most plentiful reserves, as a percent of total, were in the United States (27%), Russia (18%), China (13%), Australia (9%), and India (7%).

An important factor is the relative amount of these energy resources that has not yet been consumed. A standard measure is called **proved energy reserves**, which is the remaining known deposits that could be recovered economically given current economic and operating conditions. Dividing proved reserves by the current production rate gives the number of years of the resource remaining. Using this measure, the reserve-to-production ratio at the end of 2014 for crude oil was 56.9 years; for natural gas, 55.0 years; and for coal, 109.2 years.

This does not mean that these resources will be depleted in that length of time: additional resources may be discovered in new areas, and improved technology may increase the amount of a resource that may be economically extracted. Also, the future rate of production and consumption may be higher or lower than current levels, which would decrease or increase the remaining years of a resource. However, reserve-to-production ratios provide insights into the limited nature of nonrenewable energy resources and the need to find alternatives, especially for resources with fewer years of remaining reserves.

Consumption

Data on world energy consumption are available only by type of resource rather than by total energy consumed.

Petroleum. Consumption trends of the leading consumers from 1965 to 2014 are depicted in Figure 6. In 2014, the United States consumed far more petroleum than any other country: 19.9% of the world total. Other major petroleum-consuming countries were China (12.4%), Japan (4.7%), Russia (3.5%), Brazil (3.4%), and Saudi Arabia (3.4%).

Natural Gas. In 2014, the two biggest natural gas producers (the United States and Russia) were also the two biggest consumers. Figure 7 depicts natural gas consumption by the leading consumer countries as a percentage of world consumption. The United States in 2014 consumed only 4% more than it produced, and Russia consumed 29% less than it produced. Of the other major natural-gas-consuming nations, China, Mexico, Germany, and the United Kingdom consumed at least 25% more than they produced. Iran, Saudi Arabia, and the United Arab Emirates were net consumers, but consumed less than 25% more than their production. Canada and Russia were the only major consuming nations that produced more than they consumed, but given current trends the United States is expected to be a net exporter of natural gas within a few years.

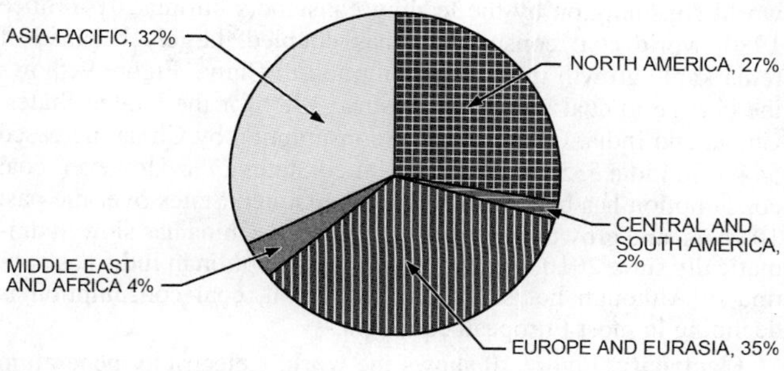

Fig. 5 World Recoverable Coal Reserves: 2015
(Basis: BP 2016)

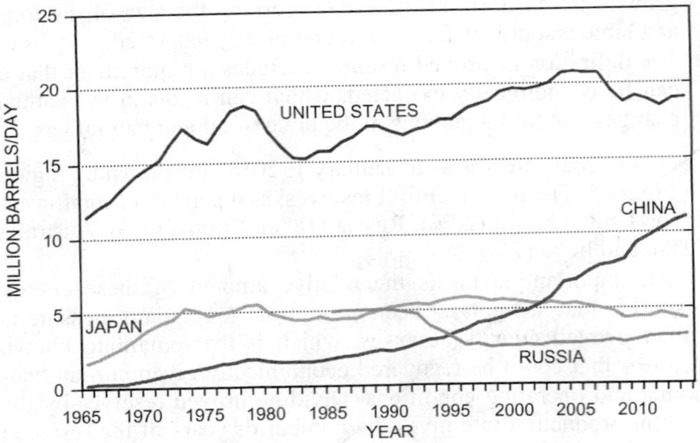

Fig. 6 World Petroleum Consumption: 2015
(Basis: BP 2016)

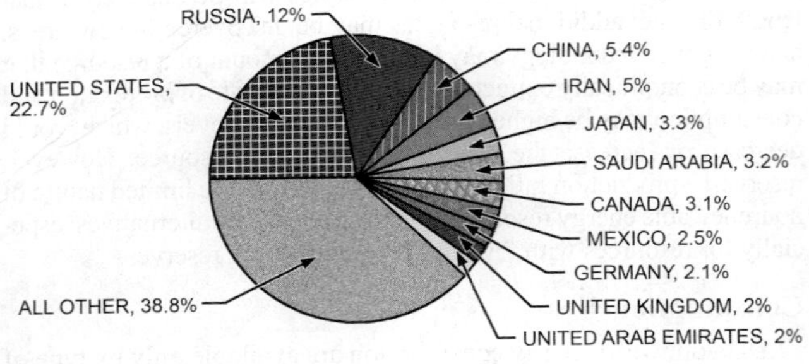

Fig. 7 World Natural Gas Consumption: 2014
(Basis: BP 2015)

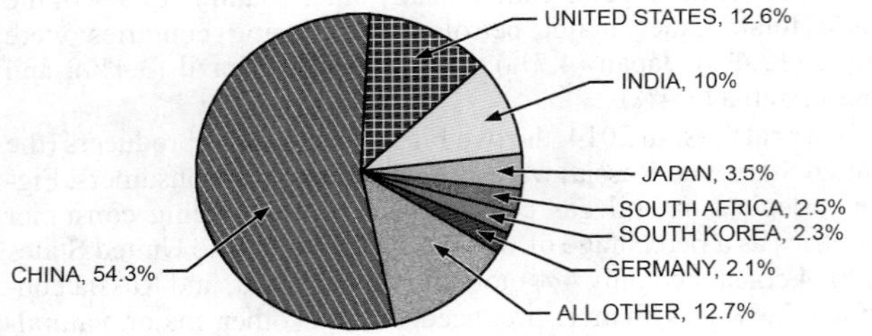

Fig. 8 World Coal Consumption: 2014
(Basis: BP 2015)

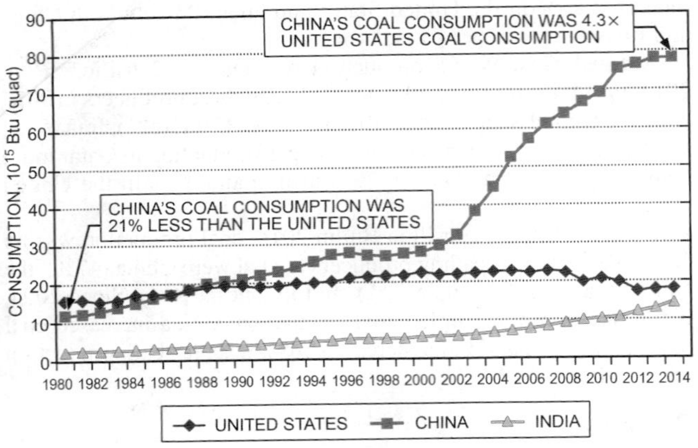

Fig. 9 Coal Consumption in United States, China, and India, 1980-2014
(Basis: BP 2015)

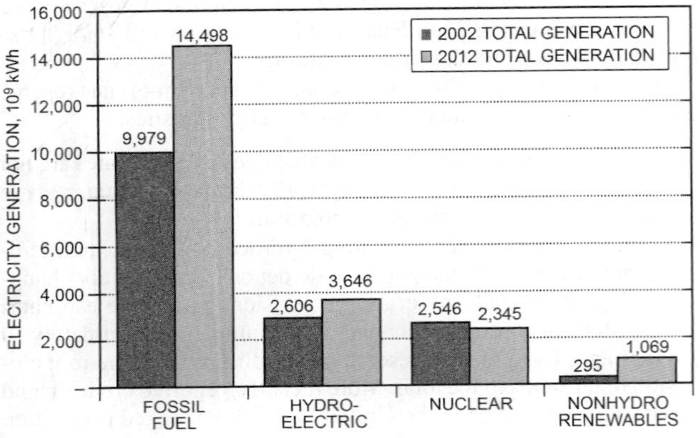

Fig. 10 World Electricity Generation by Resource: 2002 and 2012
(EIA 2012)

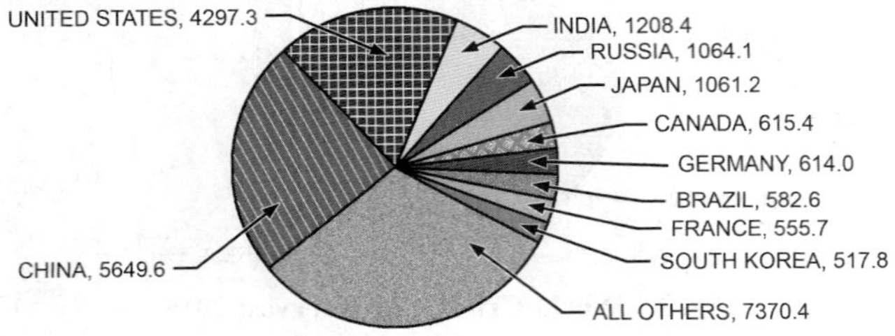

Fig. 11 World Electricity Generation 2014
(Basis: BP 2015)

Coal. The two largest coal producers in 2014 (China and the United States) were also the two largest consumers. China is by far the largest coal consumer, with consumption more than four times that of the United States in 2014. Figure 8 depicts the percentage of world consumption by the leading consumers during 2014. Since 1980, world coal consumption has doubled, largely because of remarkable growth in coal consumption in China. Figure 9 shows the change in coal consumption since 1980 for the United States, China, and India. Over this span, consumption by China increased 544%, in India 535%, and in the United States 17%. However, coal consumption has been declining in the United States over the past 10 years, and growth in coal consumption in China has slowed dramatically since 2010. Growth of coal consumption in India has continued. Although not shown on the graph, coal consumption is declining in most European countries.

Electricity. Figure 10 shows the world's electricity generation by energy resource *in 2002 and 2012*. (*Note*: unlike other energy statistics, which generally include 2014 data, the most recent year in which generation by fuel type is available is 2012.) Fossil fuel generation increased 45.3%, hydroelectric generation increased 39.9%, and nuclear generation decreased 7.9%, although this level of decrease may be temporary, driven by the shutdown of almost all nuclear generation in Japan during 2012. Nonhydroelectric renewable generation increased by the largest percentage (262.3%), but is still substantially less than the other resources.

Figure 11 shows total electricity generation by geographic region for 2014. China and the United States produced the most electricity, followed by India, Russia, and Japan.

Per Capita. Figure 12 compares the per capita energy consumption of selected countries for 2014. As is apparent, per capita energy

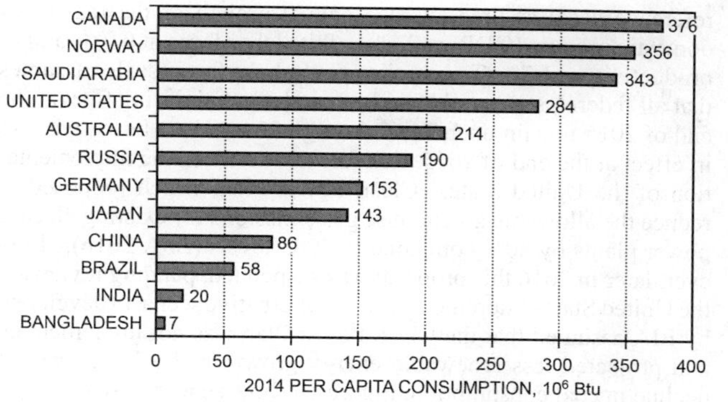

Fig. 12 Per Capita Energy Consumption by Selected Countries: 2011
(Basis: BP 2015; CIA 2016)

consumption in countries with extreme weather, whether cold or hot, tends to be highest; also, the level in more developed countries is vastly different from that in less developed countries and differs considerably even among the more developed countries. Note that, although China's total energy use has grown very rapidly in recent years, on a per capita basis it is still substantially below the levels of more developed countries.

3.2 CARBON EMISSIONS

Worldwide carbon emissions from burning and flaring fossil fuels rose 21.8% from 2004 to 2014. Other sources of greenhouse gas emissions are included under international treaties; however, this section only shows the portion from marketed fossil fuel production, and so does not include greenhouse gas emissions from energy production, methane emission from various sources, or releases of high-global-warming-potential (GWP) chemicals such as refrigerants. Total carbon emissions were 35.499 billion metric tons of carbon dioxide in 2014, up from 29.143 billion metric tons in 2004. Figure 13A shows the changes in carbon emissions from burning fossil fuels from 2004 to 2014 for the total world and for selected countries. Greenhouse gas emissions dropped 7.4% in the United States, and dropped 18.8% in the European Union. Countries such as China, India, and Saudi Arabia showed the largest increases. Note that, although developing countries have the highest growth rates, their per capita carbon emissions are much less than in wealthier nations. A graph of per capita carbon emissions would look very similar to Figure 12, which shows per capita energy consumption of selected countries. Carbon emissions from fossil fuel use alone were not readily available for the EU as a whole. The data shown are for 22 of the 28 countries in the EU for which fossil fuel data was available by country. The six countries not included are very small, so the difference between the emissions shown and the EU total is not substantial.

3.3 U.S. ENERGY USE

Per Capita Energy Consumption

Figure 14, based on data from BP (2012), shows the growth in per capita energy use since 1965 for the world and for the United States. As can be seen in the graph, United States per capita energy use was approximately six times the world average in 1965, dropping to five times in 1985, and is now about four times the world average. Although the world average per capita energy use has steadily risen, U.S. per capita energy use peaked in the late 1960s, rose at a slow rate in the 1990s, and has generally declined in recent years.

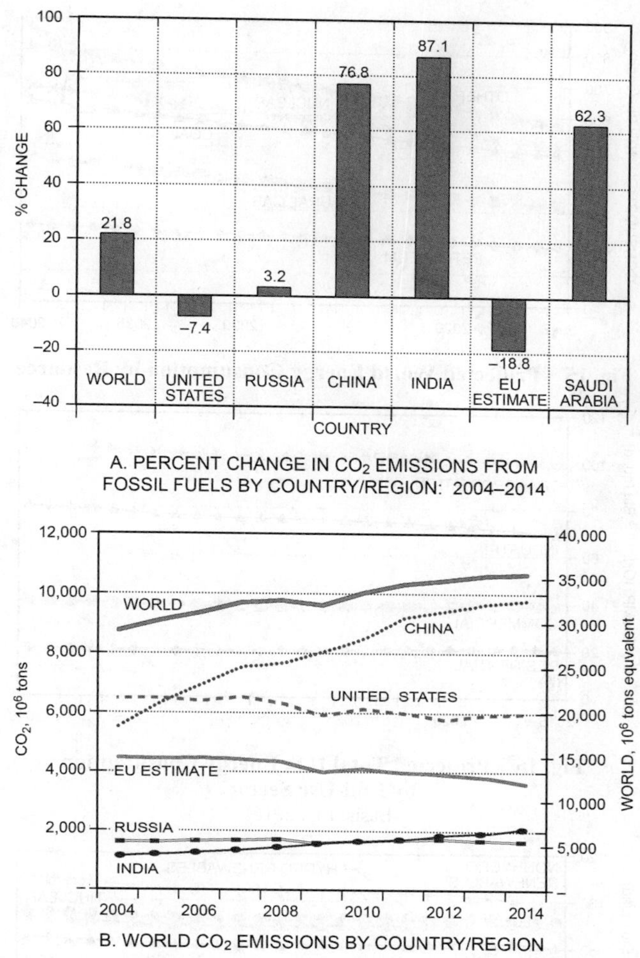

Fig. 13 World Carbon Emissions
(Basis: BP 2015)

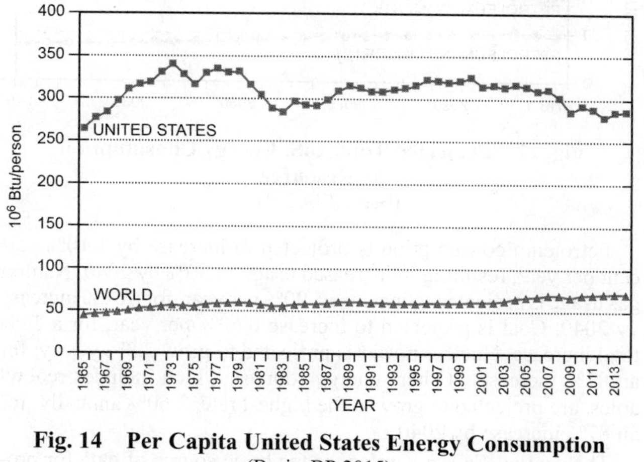

Fig. 14 Per Capita United States Energy Consumption
(Basis: BP 2015)

Projected Overall Energy Consumption

The International Energy Outlook is a projection of total world energy use developed by the United States Department of Energy Information Administration (EIA 2016). Figure 15 shows projected energy consumption through the year 2040.

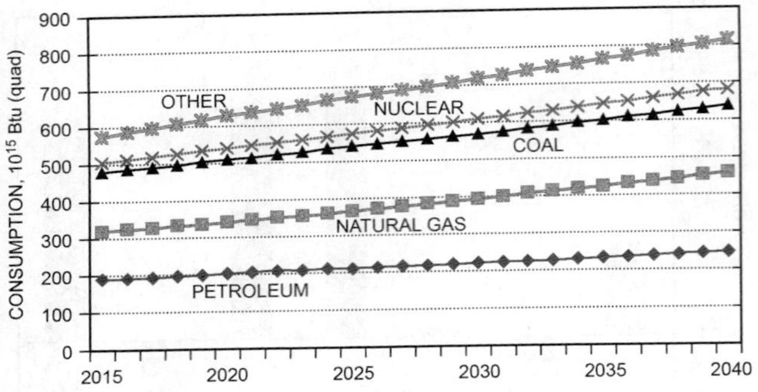

Fig. 15 Projected World Energy Consumption by Resource

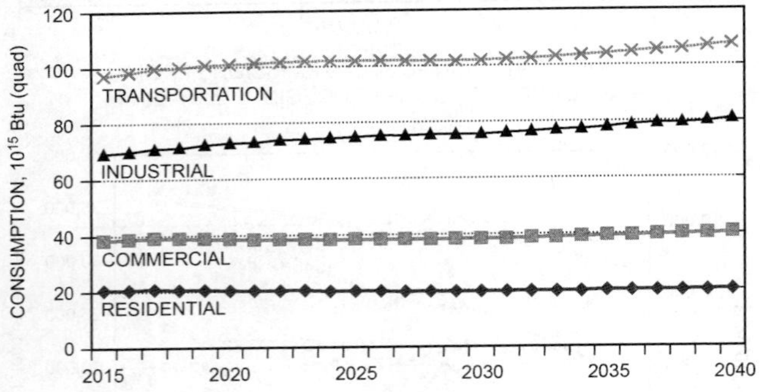

Fig. 16 Projected Total U.S. Energy Consumption by End-Use Sector
(Basis: EIA 2016)

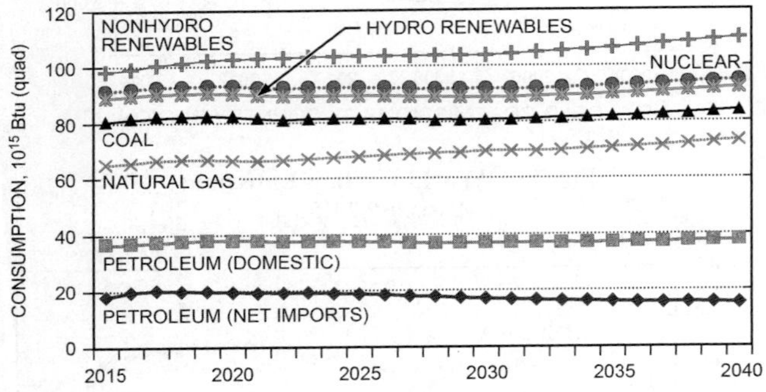

Fig. 17 Projected Total U.S. Energy Consumption by Resource
(Basis: EIA 2016)

Petroleum consumption is projected to increase by 1.10% percent per year, resulting in increased usage of 30% by 2040. Natural gas usage is projected to increase 1.90% per year, for a 64% increase by 2040. Coal is projected to increase 0.60% per year, for a 12% total increase. Nuclear power is projected to grow 2.3% yearly, for an 87% increase. "Other" energy sources, which includes renewables, are projected to grow at the highest rate, 2.60% annually, for an 87% increase by 2040.

The *Annual Energy Outlook* is the basic source of data for projecting energy use in the United States (EIA 2015). Figures 16 and 17 summarize data from this source. Information is available in greater detail for United States projected energy use than for world energy use.

EIA (2016) forecasts energy trends based on macroeconomic growth scenarios, which include a variety of energy price and economic growth assumptions. Figures 16 and 17 (the baseline or reference case) assume average annual growth of the real gross domestic product (GDP) at 2.2%, of the labor force at 0.7%, and of productivity at 1.7%. To be policy neutral, the forecast also assumes that all federal, state, and local laws and regulations in effect at the end of 2015 remain unchanged through 2040. *Note*: based on laws in effect at the end of 2015, this forecast assumes the implementation of the United States' Clean Power Plan, which proposed to reduce the allowable greenhouse gas emissions for existing electric power plants by 30% compared to 2005 levels (EPA 2016). However, later in 2016 this proposal was suspended, pending review by the United States Supreme Court. An alternative scenario developed by EIA assumed that the Clean Power Plan was not implemented, and projected less renewable energy growth and a lower rate of decline in coal consumption. Figure 16 shows energy use by major end-use sector (i.e., residential, commercial, industrial, and transportation). HVAC&R engineers are primarily concerned with the first three sectors. Figure 17 shows energy consumption by type of resource.

The following observations apply to the overall picture of projected energy use in the United States over the next two decades (Figures 16 and 17):

- As discussed previously, the base forecast assumes implementation of the Clean Power Plan for reducing greenhouse gas emissions for existing electric power plants, which is currently under legal review. Carbon emissions from energy use are projected to decline slowly, decreasing by an average of 0.2% per year through 2040 because of projected shifts in fuel use from coal to less carbon-intensive fuels (gas and renewables), and because of higher efficiency standards for appliances and commercial equipment, stronger building codes, and higher required mileage from vehicles. Per capita carbon emissions are projected to decline 0.8% per year.
- Crude oil prices are expected to rise at an annual rate of 3.9% more than inflation. This high rate of increase is due to a low starting point for crude oil prices in 2015, rather than a fundamental change in projected supply and demand conditions.
- The wellhead price of natural gas was projected to rise at an annual rate of 2.5% more than inflation from 2015 through 2040. However, the starting point is about $2.60 per million Btu wellhead price, well below historic prices of recent years. Natural gas prices are projected to reach $5 per million Btu in 2024, and stay stable near that price until 2040. This forecast assumes a long-term stable price for natural gas, tracking the rate of general inflation, due to abundant supplies of natural gas that result in 20% of United States natural gas production being exported by 2040. For coal used as a fuel, consumption is expected to decrease by 1.6% per year, resulting in a decline of about 40% in consumption compared to 2014 levels. The price of coal used as a fuel is expected to grow at an annual rate of 0.3% more than inflation over the same period. This is less than previous forecasts, and is a result of lower forecasted demand.
- Commercial electricity prices are projected to increase at the rate of inflation over the forecast period to 2040. Lower fuel costs, including increased usage of renewable energy, will be offset by investments in new generation and replacement of aging assets.
- Nuclear power generation is expected to be stable with a 0% growth rate over the forecast period, with construction of new nuclear power plants projected to offset retirements of existing units. Some older nuclear units have applied for a second 20-year life extension permit, which would allow operation for a total of 80 years.
- Electricity generation using renewable sources (which includes cogenerators) is expected to increase by 3.6% per year. Total renewables, including hydroelectric power, are projected to grow

from their current 12% share of electric generation to 25% in 2040.
- Petroleum consumption will grow by 0.2% annually, led by the transportation sector, where most of it (72%) is used.
- The share of petroleum consumption met by net imports is projected to be 41% in 2040, down from 51% in 2015. The U.S. reduction in oil imports is remarkable: as recently as 2005, imports were 60% of liquid fuel use. A steady, slow decline in net imports is expected across the forecast period.
- Natural gas consumption will increase by 0.9% per year in all sectors, driven mostly by increased electric generation using natural gas.
- Coal consumption will decrease at an average annual rate of 1.4%, as coal used for electric generation is replaced by other energy sources.
- Electricity consumption is projected to grow by 0.7% annually, with efficiency gains offset by increased use of electricity-using equipment and an increasing population.
- Total energy consumption in the residential sector is projected to decline by 0.1% per year, and commercial energy consumption is projected to grow by 0.5% per year, as increased efficiency and other factors approximately balance population growth.
- Energy use by the transportation sector is projected to decline by 0.2% per year, with variations from this average depending heavily on prevailing fuel prices. Transportation energy use is declining, which reflects increased fuel efficiency during the forecast period.
- Per capita energy use is projected to decline by 0.2% annually, because increases in efficiency more than offset population growth and new energy-consuming products.
- Total energy use per dollar of gross domestic product (energy intensity) will continue to fall at an average rate of about 1.7% per year through 2040.
- Total carbon emissions are projected to decline by 0.2% annually through 2040, based on current regulations in place, including the Clean Power Plan to restrict electric power sector carbon emissions.

Outlook Summary

In general, the following key issues will dominate energy matters in the next two decades:

- Reduced U.S. dependency on imported oil.
- Increased use of natural gas and renewables, with particularly strong growth in the use of renewables.
- Role of technology developments, including energy conservation and energy efficiency as alternatives to energy production.
- Substantial increases in use of renewable energy, rising from 7.1% of total U.S. production in 2015 to 13.0% in 2040. For electric generation, renewables increase from 12.8% in 2015 to 27.8% by 2040.
- Continued growth in total worldwide carbon emissions, and debate over actions to deal with the issue.
- Relative merits of various energy alternatives, including nuclear power and different renewable energy options.
- Population growth, coupled with the shift of large population segments into retirement.

3.4 U.S. AGENCIES AND ASSOCIATIONS

American Gas Association (AGA), Washington, D.C.
American Petroleum Institute (API), Washington, D.C.
Bureau of Mines, Department of Interior, Washington, D.C.
Council on Environmental Quality (CEQ), Washington, D.C.
Edison Electric Institute (EEI), Washington, D.C.
Electric Power Research Institute (EPRI), Palo Alto, CA
Energy Information Administration (EIA), Washington, D.C.
Gas Research Institute (GRI), Des Plaines, IL
National Coal Association (NCA), Washington, D.C.
North American Electric Reliability Council (NAERC), Princeton, NJ
Organization of Petroleum Exporting Countries (OPEC), Vienna, Austria
United States Green Building Council (USGBC), Washington, D.C.

REFERENCES

ASHRAE members can access *ASHRAE Journal* articles and ASHRAE research project final reports at technologyportal.ashrae.org. Articles and reports are also available for purchase by nonmembers in the online ASHRAE Bookstore at www.ashrae.org/bookstore.

ASHRAE. 2003. *ASHRAE energy position document*.

ASHRAE. 2013. *ASHRAE greenguide: Design, construction, and operation of sustainable buildings*, 4th ed.

BP. 2015. *BP statistical review of world energy June 2015*. www.bp.com/content/dam/bp/en/corporate/pdf/bp-statistical-review-of-world-energy-2015-full-report.pdf.

BP. 2016. *BP statistical review of world energy June 2016*. www.bp.com/content/dam/bp/en/corporate/pdf/bp-statistical-review-of-world-energy-2016-full-report.pdf.

CIA. 2016. *The world factbook*. U.S. Central Intelligence Agency, Washington, D.C. www.cia.gov/library/publications/resources/the-world-factbook/index.html.

EIA. 2012. *Annual energy outlook 2012 with projections to 2035*. U.S. Energy Information Administration, Washington, D.C. www.eia.gov/outlooks/aeo/pdf/0383(2012).pdf.

EIA. 2015. *Annual energy outlook 2015 with projections to 2040*. U.S. Energy Information Administration, Washington, D.C. www.eia.gov/outlooks/aeo/pdf/0383(2015).pdf.

EIA. 2016. *International energy outlook 2016*. U.S. Energy Information Administration, Washington, D.C. www.eia.gov/outlooks/ieo/.

EPA. 2016. *Fact sheet: Clean Power Plan overview: Cutting carbon pollution from power plants*. U.S. Environmental Protection Agency, Washington, D.C. www.epa.gov/cleanpowerplan/fact-sheet-clean-power-plan-overview.

Grumman, D.L. 1984. Energy resource accounting: ASHRAE *Standard* 90C-1977R. *ASHRAE Transactions* 90(1B):531-546.

Heiman, J.L. 1984. Proposal for a simple method for determining resource impact factors. *ASHRAE Transactions* 90(1B):564-570.

UN. 1987. Our common future: Report of the World Commission on Environment and Development. Annex to General Assembly document A/42/427, *Development and International Co-operation: Environment*. United Nations. www.un-documents.net/wced-ocf.htm.

BIBLIOGRAPHY

DOE. 1979. *Impact assessment of a mandatory source-energy approach to energy conservation in new construction*. U.S. Department of Energy, Washington, D.C.

EIA. 2001. *Annual energy review 2000*. DOE/EIA-0384(2000). Energy Information Administration, U.S. Department of Energy, Washington, D.C.

EIA. 2006. *Annual energy review 2005*. DOE/EIA-0384(2005). Energy Information Administration, U.S. Department of Energy, Washington, D.C. www.eia.gov/totalenergy/data/annual/archive/038405.pdf.

EIA. 2011. *International energy statistics*. U.S. Energy Information Administration, Washington, D.C.

EISA. 2007. *Energy independence and security act of 2007*. HR-6. 110th Congress, 1st session. www.gpo.gov/fdsys/pkg/BILLS-110hr6enr/pdf/BILLS-110hr6enr.pdf.

Pacific Northwest Laboratory. 1987. *Development of whole-building energy design targets for commercial buildings phase 1 planning*. PNL-5854, vol. 2. U.S. Department of Energy, Washington, D.C.

Simmons, M.R. 2006. *Twilight in the desert: The coming world oil shock and the world economy*. John Wiley & Sons.

USGBC. 2013. *LEED™ reference guides*, v.4. U.S. Green Building Council, San Francisco.

CHAPTER 35

SUSTAINABILITY

SUSTAINABILITY is today a goal that just about every organization, institution, business, or individual claims to be striving for, and sometimes claims to have achieved.

Given the profound impact of buildings on the environment, the work of HVAC&R design engineers is inextricably linked to sustainability. The engineering sector has seminal influence on building performance, and HVAC&R designers' work is inherently related to overall sustainability in buildings.

HVAC&R engineering design on projects concerned with performance and sustainability requires understanding of and involvement with more than just HVAC, including projected energy and water demands, stormwater runoff generation, waste generation, and air quality impacts. This chapter is intended to provide key information and identify reference sources for further resources on

- Defining the energy, water, and other resource-consuming aspects of projects
- Quantifying the relative environmental impacts of competing design alternatives

These aspects of sustainability are addressed with respect to energy and water conservation, greenhouse gas and air quality impacts, and other impacts of buildings, such as stormwater runoff and potable water use.

The need to address sustainability in the built environment is being accelerated by external concerns such as environmental and resource issues, rising energy prices, indoor environmental quality, climate change, international pressure, natural disasters, and energy security. While economies transition from carbon-based to other forms of more sustainable energy, engineers will be challenged to meet an ever-increasing tide of regulation, demand, and expectations.

1. DEFINITION

Sustainability is defined in the *ASHRAE GreenGuide* (ASHRAE 2013), in general terms, as "providing for the needs of the present without detracting from the ability to fulfill the needs of the future," a definition very similar to that developed in 1987 by the United Nations' Brundtland Commission (UN 1987). Others have defined sustainability as "the concept of maximizing the effectiveness of resource use while minimizing the impact of that use on the environment" (ASHRAE 2006) and an environment in which "… an equilibrium … exists between human society and stable ecosystems" (Townsend 2006).

Sustaining (i.e., keeping up or prolonging) those elements on which humankind's existence and that of the planet depend, such as energy, the environment, and health, are worthy goals.

The preparation of this chapter is assigned to TC 2.8, Building Environmental Impacts and Sustainability.

2. CHARACTERISTICS OF SUSTAINABILITY

Sustainability Addresses the Future

Sustainability is focused on the distant future. Any actions taken under the name of sustainability must address the impact of present actions on conditions likely to prevail in that future time frame.

In designing the built environment, the emphasis has often been on the present or the near future, usually in the form of capital (or first-cost) impact. As is apparent when life-cycle costing analysis is applied, capital cost assumes less importance the longer the future period under consideration.

This emphasis on the distant future can differentiate sustainable design from **green design**. Whereas green design addresses many of the same characteristics as sustainable design, it may also emphasize near-term impacts such as indoor environmental quality, operation and maintenance features, and meeting current client needs. Thus, green design may focus more on the immediate future (i.e., starting when the building is first constructed and then occupied). Sustainable design is of paramount importance to the global environment in the long term while still incorporating features of green design that focus on the present and near future.

Sustainability Has Many Contributors

Sustainability is not just about energy, carbon emissions, pollution, waste disposal, or population growth. Although these are central ideas in thinking about sustainability, it is an oversimplification to think that addressing one factor, or even any one set of factors, can result in a sustainable future for the planet.

It is likewise a mistake to think that HVAC&R design practitioners, by themselves and just through activities within their purview, can create a sustainable result. To be sure, their activities can *contribute* to sustainability by creating a sustainable building, development, or other related project. But they cannot *by themselves* create global sustainability. Such an endeavor depends on many outside factors that cannot be controlled by HVAC&R engineers; however, they should make their fair-share contribution to sustainability in all their endeavors, and encourage other individuals and entities to do the same.

Sustainability Is Comprehensive

Sustainability has no borders or limits. A good-faith effort to make a project sustainable does not mean that sustainability will be achieved globally. A superb design job on a building with sustainability as a goal will probably not contribute much to the global situation if a significant number of other buildings are not so designed, or if the transportation sector makes an inadequate contribution, or if only a few regions of the world do their fair share toward making the planet sustainable. A truly sustainable outcome thus depends on comprehensive efforts in all sectors the world around.

Technology Plays Only a Partial Role

It may well be that in due time technology will have the theoretical *capability*, if diligently applied, to create a sustainable future for the planet and humankind. Having the capability to apply technology, however, does not guarantee that it will be applied; that must come from attitude or mindset. As with all things related to comprehensive change, there must be the *will.*

For example, automobile companies have long had the technical capability to make cars much more efficient; some developed countries highly dependent on imported oil have brought their transportation sectors close to self sufficiency. Until recently, that has not been the case in the United States. Part of the change is because of increased customer demand, but more of it is driven by government regulation (efficiency standards). The technology is available, but the will is not there; large-scale motivation is absent, what exists being mostly driven by regulation and the motivated few.

Similarly, HVAC&R designers know how to design buildings that are much more energy efficient than they have been in the past, but such buildings are still relatively rare, especially in the general commercial market (as opposed to those owned by high-profile entities). ASHRAE's long-standing guidance in designing energy-efficient (now green and/or sustainable) buildings, and the motivation provided by its own and other entities' programs, have pointed the way technologically for the built environment and related industries to make their fair-share contribution to sustainability. Such programs include (1) ASHRAE's net-zero energy buildings (NZEB) thrust; (2) the U.S. Green Building Council's (USGBC) Leadership in Energy and Environmental Design (LEED®) Green Building Rating System™; (3) the American Institute of Architects' (AIA) 2030 Challenge (AIA 2011); (4) the Green Building Institute's (GBI) Green Globes (www.thegbi.org/greenglobes); and (5) the U.S. Environmental Protection Agency's (EPA) ENERGY STAR® program (www.energystar.gov/). The European Union (E.U.) has also taken a lead in the fight against climate change and promoting a low-carbon economy, although unsustainable trends persist in many areas.

ASHRAE's mission "to advance the arts and sciences of HVAC&R to serve humanity and promote a sustainable world" and its vision to "be the global leader, [and] the foremost source of technical and educational information" (www.ashrae.org/about-ashrae) has already had significant impact. However, more can be done, both within its technological purview and in overcoming other, nontechnological barriers. ASHRAE has set a good example in its area of expertise and can also encourage, advise, and inspire other sectors to do their part to move towards sustainability. Examples include ASHRAE's guidance provided to the U.S. government on effective building energy efficiency programs, as well as its many publications such as the *Advanced Energy Design Guides* (AEDGs), the *ASHRAE GreenGuide*, and its numerous standards and guidelines.

3. FACTORS IMPACTING SUSTAINABILITY

The major factors impacting global sustainability are the following:

- Population growth and migration
- Food supply
- Disease control and amelioration
- Energy resource availability
- Material resource availability and management
- Fresh water supply, both potable and nonpotable
- Effective and efficient usage practices for energy resources and water
- Air and water pollution
- Solid and liquid waste disposal
- Land use

The preceding are only broad categories, yet they encompass many subsidiary factors that have received public attention recently. For instance, climate change/global warming, carbon emissions, acid rain, deforestation, transportation, and watershed management are important factors as well. However, each of these can be viewed as a subset of one or more of the listed major areas.

4. PRIMARY HVAC&R CONSIDERATIONS IN SUSTAINABLE DESIGN

The main areas falling within an HVAC&R designer's (and ASHRAE's) purview on most projects are those dealing with energy and water use, material resources, air and water pollution, and solid waste disposal. Although HVAC&R professionals' expertise may impact issues such as land use and food supply on certain specialized projects, these more typically fall under the purview of other professionals and their organizations.

Energy Resource Availability

Although conventional energy resources and their availability largely fall beyond the scope of HVAC&R designers' work, an understanding of these topics is often required for participation in project discussions or utility programs relating to projects. Chapter 34 has more information on energy resources.

Some **renewable** energy resources, in contrast with traditional energy and fuels, are ubiquitous by nature and are thus available on many building sites. **Wind** and **solar** energy are widely distributed (if not always continuously available) on almost any site for use in active or passive ways. Chapter 35 of the 2015 *ASHRAE Handbook—HVAC Applications* and Chapter 37 of the 2016 *ASHRAE Handbook—Systems and Equipment* provide information on solar energy resources, passive and active space heating and cooling, domestic hot water, and applications of photovoltaics. High-level (high-temperature) **geothermal** energy is only present at limited sites, and may thus be unavailable as a direct energy source on most projects. Low-level geothermal, on the other hand, depends on the nearly constant temperature of the near-surface earth for use as an energy source or sink, and thus can be used on almost any project if other factors align in its favor. See Chapter 34 of the 2015 *ASHRAE Handbook—HVAC Applications* for more information.

Climatic conditions may often provide another source of "renewable" energy. In arid climates, air systems using evaporative cooling (both direct and indirect) can supplement conventionally powered cooling and refrigeration systems.

Designers should be familiar with the characteristics of common traditional (nonrenewable) energy resources (natural gas, heating oil, electricity) from the standpoint of their use in relevant building applications. Designers are typically very familiar with the relative per-unit cost as it affects the operating cost of the building being designed. Other energy characteristics traditionally taken into account by the designer might also include ease of handling and use, cleanliness, emissions produced, and local availability, because these also have a direct effect on design and installation. Until recently, designers had little reason to consider an energy resource's characteristics beyond the site line of the project at hand.

However, recent public focus on the impacts of building energy use on the environment has changed that approach. Designers now must consider a resource's broader characteristics that may affect the regional, national, and global environment, such as its origin (domestic or foreign), security, future availability, emissions characteristics, broad economics, generation/use limitations [gravimetric energy density (Btu/lb) and areal power density (W/ft^2)] and social acceptability. Though responsible designers may not be able to do much about such factors, they should be aware of them;

indeed, that awareness may affect decisions within the designer's control.

For instance, familiarity with an energy resource's emissions characteristics, whether at the well head, mine mouth, or generating station, may influence the designer to make the building more energy efficient, or provide the designer with arguments to convince the owner that energy-saving features in the building would be worth additional capital cost. Furthermore, as owners and developers of buildings become more aware of sustainability factors, designers must stay informed of the latest information and impacts.

One way to reduce a project's use of nonrenewable energy, beyond energy-efficient design itself, is to replace such energy use with renewable energy. Designers should develop familiarity with how projects might incorporate and benefit from renewable energy. Many kinds of passive design features can take advantage of naturally occurring energy.

Increasingly common examples of nonpassive approaches are solar systems, whether photovoltaic (electricity-generating) or solar thermal (hot-fluid generating). Low-level geothermal systems take advantage of naturally occurring and widely distributed earth-embedded energy. Wind systems are increasingly applied to supplement electric power grids, and are also sometimes incorporated on a smaller scale into on-site or distributed generation approaches.

Some large power users, such as municipalities or large industries, require that a minimum percentage of power they purchase be from renewable sources. Also, renewable portfolio standards are being imposed on electric utility companies by regulators.

Fresh Water Supply

HVAC&R systems can impact potable and nonpotable water supplies both directly and indirectly. First, some building systems (e.g., evaporative cooling towers) use potable water. Second, some building systems can discharge treated water or other waste streams with contaminants of concern that can impact local watersheds and water supplies. Indirect impacts include water consumption for electricity generation and in mineral and fuel extraction.

Effective and Efficient Use of Energy Resources and Water

This area is where HVAC&R engineers can have a profound impact on achieving sustainability goals. Impacts of building consumption can be at least partially mitigated through overall system performance improvement, as well as through increased use of on-site renewable energy and certain off-site energy resources. See the section on Designing for Effective Energy Resource Use for more information on addressing energy efficiency in the design process.

Water Consumption. Building systems' water use can be reduced by reusing clean water from on site, such as condensate drain water, or by using less potable water. For example, hybrid cooling towers can operate as water-to-air heat exchangers when run dry, and can operate their water sprays for additional evaporative capacity only when conditions require. (See also the section on Energy Resource Availability.) In process control and refrigeration systems, similar opportunities exist.

The U.S. EPA's WaterSense program (www3.epa.gov/watersense/) rates products on their water use efficiency; similarly to the EPA's ENERGY STAR program, products are certified by an outside third party before they can claim the WaterSense label. ASHRAE is also developing a standard to provide minimum requirements for the design of mechanical systems that limit the volume of water required to operate HVAC systems (*Proposed Standard* 191P).

In Europe, the U.K. *Building Regulations* (U.K. 2015) requires that design water consumption be reduced in new homes, with a combined hot- and cold-water consumption of no more than 33 gal per person per day of potable water. Alternative sources of lower-grade water, such as harvested rainwater and reclaimed gray water, may also be used for functions such as toilet flushing, subject to specific measures. The 2015 edition introduced an optional requirement of 29 gal per person per day where required by planning permission, and an alternative fittings-based approach to demonstrating compliance instead of the prescribed calculation method.

Discharge from building systems can be reduced through careful design, proper sequences and control, and choosing lower-impact chemical or nonchemical water treatment. These techniques may not eliminate chemical treatment in all applications, but negative effects from such usage can be substantially reduced.

Water/Energy Nexus. The water/energy nexus refers to the interdependent and inseparable nature of these two important resources. From large-scale utilities to the built environment, water production requires energy to extract and deliver for consumption, and electricity generation and energy sources (e.g., thermal and nuclear power generation, hydraulic fracturing, biofuels) demand significant amounts of water for production. With approximately 8% of the global energy generation used for pumping, treatment, and transportation of water resources and approximately 15% of the world's total water withdrawal used for energy production, each resource will continue to face rising demands and constraints as a consequence of economic and population growth and climate change.

Increasing energy demands, as well as naturally occurring water constraints such as droughts, heat waves, or human-induced shortages, mean that demands on water resources can be expected to increase. In addition, changing temperatures, shifting precipitation patterns, increasing variability, and more extreme weather add significant uncertainty about water availability. Water and energy, in their various classifications, are generally viewed in individual silos, which has limited adoption of integrated solutions. To properly address the challenges and opportunities around the water/energy nexus, emphasis on policy incentives and sustainable engineering solutions promoting optimized, efficient use of each resource, as well as advancement in technologies promoting both water and energy conservation, are needed.

Material Resource Availability and Management

Environmentally conscious design and construction practices are increasingly motivating design teams to apply life-cycle thinking and look in to the embodied impacts (e.g., embodied energy, embodied CO_2, other equivalent environmental impact indicators) of their systems' design, although this is not yet a common practice. For example, within the LEED framework, building systems under the purview of HVAC&R designers are currently excluded from credits for locally procured building materials and resources. However, the same concepts can be applied in selection and procurement of HVAC&R system components. For example, recycled steel content in system components could be required to be stated in HVAC&R product submittals. In some areas, locally assembled or manufactured components may be available that can reduce transportation impacts.

Embodied Energy

As buildings become more energy efficient and their operational energy is reduced, more emphasis will shift toward reducing their embodied energy (UNEP 2014). Materials used directly in the construction and the components, equipment, and systems for building operation embody the energy used during their manufacturing, transportation, and installation (ASHRAE 2013). Material selection should also consider the environmental impact of demolition and disposal after the service life of the products. Building **life-cycle assessment (LCA)** focuses on the environmental impact of a product system (from materials acquisition to manufacturing, use, and final disposition) and plays a major role in promoting sustainability. This is a cradle-to-grave approach that evaluates all stages of individual materials and the product's life to determine their cumulative environmental impact. Srinivasan et al. (2014) reviews various building assessment methods that support environmental decision making. Designers should give preference to resource-efficient materials and reduce waste by recycling and reusing whenever possible.

LCA is an internationally standardized methodology (ISO *Standard* 14040). Consecutive parts of an LCA include a life-cycle inventory (e.g., collection and analysis of air and water emissions, waste generation, and resource consumption over the product's life cycle) and life-cycle impact assessment (LCIA), which is an estimation of indicators of the environmental pressures in terms of climate change, summer smog, resource depletion, acidification, human health effects, etc., attributable to the product's life cycle. More information on the LCA approach is available online from the EPA (www.epa.gov/saferchoice/design-environment-life-cycle-assessments) and the European Commission (ec.europa.eu/environment/ipp/lca.htm). Various LCA databases and tools available from commercial as well as governmental or public domain sources can be used to calculate and compare the embodied energy (e.g., total energy per unit mass), related embodied emissions (e.g., total mass of CO_2 per unit mass of material or product), or other embodied environmental impacts of common building materials and products.

A challenge for modeling life-cycle energy use in buildings is using consistent system boundaries and data collection (Srinivasan et al. 2014). Available software to address these concerns includes Building for Environmental and Economic Sustainability (BEES; www.nist.gov/services-resources/software/bees) and the Tool for Reduction and Assessment of Chemicals and Other Environmental Impacts (TRACI), which focus on chemical releases and raw materials usage in products. The Athena Sustainable Materials Institute's decision support tool provides a cradle-to-grave, process-based LCA, including regional data such as energy mix for power generation, transportation modes, etc. (www.athenasmi.org/what-we-do/lca-data-software/). Regional data are important because conversion factors to primary energy and GHG emissions can differ by country, depending on energy sources used (e.g., coal- or oil-fired power plants versus solar or natural-gas-based generation).

LCA-based information may be in the form of environmental product declarations (EPD) based on CEN *Standard* 15804, or product environmental footprints (PEFs) inspired by ISO *Standards* 14040 and 14044 and voluntary environmental declarations (ISO *Standard* 14025). They have been gaining in popularity beyond building construction materials, given the growing criteria of green building certifications such as LEED v4 credit, which now rewards selection of HVAC products with EPDs, based on the updated LEED credit interpretation in early 2015. Another example is the French EPD program and national decree that regulates EPDs for construction products, which will also address HVAC equipment and other technical installations by mid-2017 (Passer et al. 2015).

LCA can also assess specific refurbishments intended to improve energy performance of systems in existing buildings. For example, replacing electric or gas water heaters with solar hot-water systems can provide net emissions savings compared with the conventional systems after 0.6 month to 2.5 years, depending on the auxiliary fuel (Crawford et al. 2003). For solar domestic hot-water systems and solar central space heating, the energy consumed by producing and installing the solar systems is recovered in about 1.2 years, and the payback time for the systems' embodied energy emissions varies from a few months (for solar domestic water heating) to 9.5 years (for solar central space heating), again depending on the energy carrier for the conventional system and the specific environmental emission indicators considered (Kalogirou 2004).

Air, Noise, and Water Pollution

HVAC&R systems and equipment can interact with both local and global environments. On a local scale, HVAC&R systems interact with the environment in ways such as acoustical noise generated by heat rejecting equipment (e.g., condensing units, cooling tower). Occasionally, this may require the addition of special barriers to prevent sound migration from the site, as shown in Figure 1.

Local impacts of combustion from on-site heat or electricity generation can be mitigated to an extent through careful consideration of the location of sources (emitters) with respect to nearby receptors, including outdoor air intakes and residences or other buildings with operable windows.

On a larger scale, air and water pollution occurs indirectly through the consumption of energy to operate building systems. This occurs in generating the electricity (whether from fossil fuel, nuclear, or hydroelectric resources), steam, or hot water for building heating or cooling. In this sense, improved efficiency is an approach to partial mitigation.

Solid and Liquid Waste Disposal

The solid waste disposal burden from installation and operations of building systems can be substantially reduced. Competing alternatives can be assessed through life-cycle analysis. For example, an air-cooled unitary system with a shorter service life than a costlier water-cooled alternative could, over the course of the building's life, increase the solid waste burden when it is discarded. Reuse options should also be considered for locally available materials or process by-products.

An example of an HVAC&R design impacting liquid waste disposal is using glycol to protect coils from freezing, where the glycol must be eliminated in summer to provide required capacity. Because reusing glycol is not a common practice, such a design would likely result in an annual glycol discharge.

In many locations, water quality regulations and agencies essentially limit or prohibit liquid waste disposal. Other approaches to pursue in reducing liquid waste disposal are discussed in the section on Effective and Efficient Use of Energy Resources and Water.

Fig. 1 Cooling Tower Noise Barrier
(Courtesy Neil Moiseev)

5. FACTORS DRIVING SUSTAINABILITY INTO DESIGN PRACTICE

HVAC&R designers face many challenges as they assimilate sustainability into their engineering practices. These challenges include climate change, a fast-changing regulatory and legal environment, and evolving standards of care. New tools, technologies, and approaches are required for well-prepared HVAC&R engineers. The challenges and the responses are creating new opportunities, just as changing project processes are allowing or requiring engineers to participate in projects in new ways.

Climate Change

In addition to their causal role, energy systems are exposed to significant vulnerabilities resulting from climate change (Bruckner et al. 2014). Increased volatility in weather profoundly affects HVAC&R practice. Historical weather data and extremes may inadequately describe conditions faced by a project built today, even over a modest building lifespan.

In 1988, the United Nations Environment Programme (UNEP) and the World Meteorological Organization (WMO) established the Intergovernmental Panel on Climate Change (IPCC) (www.ipcc.ch) to study and report on the scientific issues, potential impacts, and mitigation methods associated with climate change. A series of publications discusses the possible outcomes and interventions required to mitigate the impacts of anthropogenic emissions.

During the United Nations Framework Convention on Climate Change in Paris, 195 nations reached a historic agreement to combat climate change and encourage actions and investment toward a low-carbon, resilient, and sustainable future (UNFCC 2015); the agreement governs greenhouse gas emissions measures from 2020 and limits average global warming to 3.6°F above preindustrial temperatures, while striving for a limit of 2.7°F. It also aims to strengthen the ability to deal with the impacts of climate change. Crucial areas include

- Mitigation: reducing emissions quickly enough to achieve the temperature goal
- Transparency system and global stock-taking: accounting for climate action
- Adaptation: strengthening countries' ability to deal with climate impacts
- Loss and damage: strengthening ability to recover from climate impacts
- Support (including financial support): for nations to build clean, resilient futures (e.g., work to define a clear roadmap on ratcheting up climate finance to USD 100 billion by 2020 for developing nations)

The agreement will come into force after 55 countries that account for at least 55% of global emissions have deposited their instruments of ratification. Accordingly, each country should set up a bottom-up system, setting its own goals for nationally determined contribution and a coherent plan for reaching these objectives. Starting in 2018, each country will have to increase their pledges over time and submit new plans every five years. (See also the discussion in the section on Regulatory Environment.)

Responsible designers are concerned with multiple dimensions of climate change: not only *what* they can do to reduce their designs' contribution, but also *whether* and *how* their designs should anticipate the future. It is the first that is the focus of this chapter and a majority of the available information on sustainable design. Warming trends currently occurring have been observed with certainty. As a result, historical weather data may not be the best source for load calculations. Depending on the rate of change, anticipating future weather may become more significant in its impact on the climate control of building systems.

Responsible designers are concerned with two dimensions of climate change: not only *what* they can do to reduce their designs' contribution, but also *whether* and *how* their designs should anticipate the future. It is the first that is the focus of this chapter and a majority of the available information on sustainable design. Warming trends currently occurring have been observed with certainty. As a result, historical weather data may not be the best source for load calculations. Depending on the rate of change, anticipating future weather may become more significant in its impact on the climate control of building systems.

Regulatory Environment

The global community has responded to two major environmental issues during the past two decades. In the late 1980s, the Montreal Protocol (UNEP 2003) regulated the manufacture and trade of refrigerants that had been shown to damage the stratosphere by depleting stratospheric ozone. The effect on the HVAC&R industry was to require research and investment in alternative materials to those that had become the mainstays of the industry, as shown in Figure 2.

Next, in the early 1990s, came the much more controversial issue of greenhouse gas (GHG) emissions and their potential for causing global warming. In response to these threats, some countries signed and accepted the Kyoto Protocol (UNFCCC 1998), which placed future limits on these emissions, but most large-emitter countries did not. By 2011, when follow-up climate talks occurred in Durban, South Africa, overall global GHG emissions not only had not been reduced but had increased. No new GHG emission reduction targets came out of those talks, although the countries agreed to look at the limits issue again in 2020 and to set up a "green fund" to help poor nations deal with climate change.

Despite the lack of effective global action, evidence of climate change is compelling. The Synthesis Report that integrated the findings of the three working group contributions to the Fifth Assessment Report of the Intergovernmental Panel on Climate Change (IPCC 2014) confirmed that "human influence on the climate system is clear and growing, with impacts observed across all continents and oceans. . . . Many of the observed changes since the 1950s are unprecedented over decades to millennia. The IPCC is now 95% certain that humans are the main cause of current global warming." Similar conclusions have also been supported by the National Academy of Sciences (NAS 2010), which concluded that "Climate change is occurring, is caused largely by human activities, and poses significant risk for—and in many cases is already affecting—a broad range of human and natural systems."

The predominant greenhouse gas pollutant is carbon dioxide, which is mainly a by-product of fossil fuel combustion in the

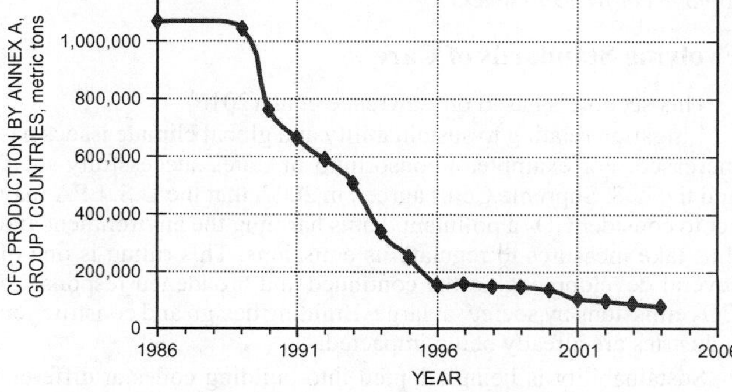

Fig. 2 Effect of Montreal Protocol on Global Chlorofluorocarbon (CFC) Production

transportation, power, industrial, residential, and commercial sectors. According to the EPA (2016), CO_2 contributed about 82% of total U.S. emissions in 2013. Methane is the next highest contributor, accounting for about 10% of the total U.S. emissions. Sources of methane emissions include oil and gas systems, enteric fermentation, landfills, coal mines, etc. Nitrous oxide (N_2O) and fluorocarbon gases are other contributors to GHG emissions. In 2014, the top four emitting countries/regions, accounting for almost two-thirds (61%) of the total global CO_2 emissions, are China (30%), the United States (15%), the 28 E.U. Member States (10%), and India (6.5%). On a per capita basis, emissions in the United States (18.2 tons CO_2 per capita) are twice as high as those of China (8.4) and the European Union (7.4) (Olivier et al. 2015).

Various standards, policies, and regulations under way that target reduction of U.S. GHGs in various sectors: examples include state renewable portfolio standards (RPS) programs, corporate average fuel economy (CAFE) standards, state emission performance standards for power plants [e.g., California (2006) *Senate Bill* SB 1368], and cap-and-trade programs in the Regional Greenhouse Gas Initiative (RGGI; www.rggi.org) states and California.

In the United States, a consolidation of green building codes is planned: the merger of ASHRAE *Standard* 189.1 and ICC's *International Green Construction Code* (see also the section on Evolving Standards of Care) is on track to occur in 2018. Energy efficiency levels in U.S. codes will continue to improve, with the green building codes evolving toward a net energy intensity level that, by 2025, is 20 to 25% of the code minimums that existed at the turn of the 21st century.

Under its 2020 strategy, the E.U. has committed to an ambitious plan and introduced binding legislation for the E.U. Member States to meet three climate and energy targets by the end of 2020: (1) 20% cut in GHG emissions from 1990 levels, (2) obtain 20% of E.U. energy from renewables, and (3) 20% improvement in energy efficiency (ec.europa.eu/clima/policies/strategies/index_en.htm). The E.U. emissions trading system (E.U. ETS) is a cornerstone of the policy to combat climate change and a key tool for reducing industrial GHG cost effectively. The ETS covers more than 11,000 power stations and industrial plants in 31 countries, as well as airlines, and accounts for about 55% of total E.U. emissions. For sectors not in the ETS, the E.U. Member States have taken on binding annual targets until 2020 for cutting emissions under the effort-sharing decision (between 2013 and 2020) according to national wealth, measured by gross domestic product per capita; these targets range from a 20% cut for the richest countries (e.g., Luxembourg, Denmark) to a maximum 20% increase for the least wealthy (e.g., Bulgaria). Moreover, a new E.U. framework has set three key targets for 2030: (1) at least 40% cuts in GHG, (2) at least 27% share for renewable energy, and (3) at least 27% improvement in energy efficiency. The 2050 roadmap suggests that the E.U. should cut emissions to 80 to 95% below 1990 levels.

Evolving Standards of Care

This section is based on Lawrence et al. (2016).

Litigation relating to sustainability and global climate issues has increased. For example, a consortium of states successfully sued, and the U.S. Supreme Court agreed in 2007, that the U.S. EPA may act to consider CO_2 a pollutant that is harming the environment and thus take measures to regulate its emissions. This ruling is one of several developments in the continued and broadened response to CO_2 emissions by society at large. Building design and construction industries are already being impacted.

Sustainability is being adopted into building codes at different levels of government and with varying motivation. Different approaches reflect local societal perceptions, political priorities, national policies and economic factors [see, e.g., Lawrence et al. (2016) and references therein for an overview of current status and trends of sustainable building codes adopted in the United States and the E.U.].

U.S. Initiatives. In the United States, a combination of methods and programs have gradually increased focus on sustainability in new commercial and residential construction. The methods range from voluntary programs (including rating systems and guidelines) to standards and mandatory enforceable codes. One early voluntary program was **U.S. Green Building Council's Leadership in Energy and Environmental Design (USGCB's LEED),** which was at the forefront of including sustainable design practices in building codes worldwide. LEED ratings can be applied to a wide variety of building types and aspects (e.g., interior design and construction, neighborhood development, operations and maintenance); see www.usgbc.org/resources/grid/leed for specific ratings systems. At least 16 U.S. states now require LEED Silver certification for public buildings, and in most states some level of LEED certification is a required option for state buildings.

Most states' building codes follow the **International Green Construction Code™ (IgCC™)** for sustainability guidance. One of IgCC's compliance options involves following ASHRAE *Standard* 189.1's mandatory criteria in all topical areas (e.g., site, construction, materials, energy, indoor environmental quality, water).

In 2010, California adopted its own statewide green buildings code, **CALGreen,** an updated version of which came into effect January 2014 (CALGreen 2013). Unlike most other U.S. codes, this approach includes criteria for both residential and nonresidential buildings in the same program.

ASHRAE's **Building Energy Quotient® (Building EQ®**; www.buildingenergyquotient.org/) focuses on lowering building operating cost and increasing value. Both as-designed and in-operation energy use ratings are available.

As with green building codes, cities are beginning to require energy reporting and benchmarking for commercial buildings. As of early 2016, 14 major cities (Atlanta, Austin, Berkeley, Boston, Boulder, Cambridge, Chicago, Kansas City, New York, Philadelphia, Portland, San Francisco, Seattle, and Washington, D.C.) had adopted some form of energy reporting in local ordinances, although the size and type of buildings involved may differ. The motivation for these requirements is usually increasing overall citywide energy efficiency, as well as creating local energy auditing jobs.

E.U. Initiatives. Outside the United States, the most notable voluntary program is the **BREEAM** method (www.breeam.com), an environmental assessment method and rating system introduced in the U.K. in 1990. This is a consensus-based, market-oriented assessment and sustainability benchmarking program for any type of building or large-scale community worldwide. It has one mandatory assessment area (the building's potential environmental impact) and two optional assessment areas (design process, and operation/maintenance). Over 425,000 buildings have been certified. Specific national schemes are available in Germany, Norway, Sweden, Spain, and The Netherlands.

Another U.K. rating system is the **Global Environmental Method (GEM)** (www.greenglobes.com/existing/homeuk.asp), which is a version of the U.S. and Canadian program Green Globes (www.greenglobes.com).

In Germany, the **passive house** concept has evolved to an international association for standardizing the design and construction of low-energy buildings (passiv.de/en/). Similar approaches and labels, especially for residential buildings, are also used in France (e.g., **Effinergie**) and Switzerland (e.g., **Minerigie**).

European regulatory efforts have also introduced several mandatory directives towards sustainability at all stages of the energy chain, targeting the buildings sector that plays a major role. The European Union's Sustainable Development Strategy (SDS) (ec.europa.eu/environment/eussd/index.htm) addresses climate change and clean energy, sustainable consumption and production, conservation and management of natural resources, public health, social inclusion, global poverty and sustainable development challenges, and education and training. The main E.U. sustainable consumption and production (ESCP) initiatives support efforts to meet the goals of SDS (ec.europa.eu/environment/eussd/escp_en .htm) and build on international and E.U.-wide initiatives and tools [e.g., the United Nations' Marrakech Process (esa.un.org/marrakech process/index.shtml)]. Beyond operational energy issues for sustainable buildings, E.U. ESCP policy focuses on resources such as materials (including waste), water, and embodied energy. The E.U. Waste Framework Directive (WFD; E.U. *Directive* 2008/98/EC) aims for 70% for reuse, recycling, and others forms of material recovery (excluding energy recovery), and is the main European policy driver toward better recycling of construction and demolition waste. The WFD is expected to reduce burdens on the waste stream, because construction and demolition waste (CDW) accounts for 25 to 30% of the waste generated in Europe. CDW has a high potential for recycling and reuse, averaging about 46% across Europe (depending on value of the materials and availability of well-developed technology and infrastructure) (Dodd et al. 2015).

Energy efficiency can be increased at all stages of the energy chain, from generation to consumption (ec.europa.eu/energy/en /topics/energy-efficiency). The main European legislative tool for improving buildings' energy efficiency and reducing carbon emissions is the Energy Performance of Buildings Directive (EPBD; E.U. *Directive* 2010/31/EC): E.U. Member States must apply minimum energy performance requirements on all new and existing residential and nonresidential buildings when undergoing major renovation (25% of building surface or value). The EPBD requires that all new buildings must be nearly zero energy as of January 2021; new buildings occupied or owned by public authorities must comply as of January 2019. Other major policies include

- Renewable Energy Directive (RED; E.U. *Directive* 2009/28/EC), which establishes an overall policy for the production and promotion of energy from renewables
- Ecodesign (ED; E.U. *Directive* 2009/125/EC) and Energy Labelling Directives (ELD; E.U. *Directive* 2010/30/E.U.), which establish minimum energy efficiency standards for various products (including air-conditioners, boilers, circulators, motors, fans, pumps)
- Energy Efficiency Directive (EED; E.U. *Directive* 2012/27/E.U.), which establishes a common framework for promotion of energy efficiency, and sets energy savings requirements for buildings

In accordance with the EPBD, energy performance certification (EPC) of European buildings is an ongoing process for several years; see ASHRAE (2013) for examples. EPCs document the building's energy performance, usually using an easy-to-understand indicator expressed as a ranking energy label (building class) with an index in terms of primary or final energy use, carbon dioxide emissions, or energy cost per unit of conditioned floor area. EPCs also may include an assessment of indoor environmental quality. In January 2013, The Netherlands became the first E.U. Member State to require measurement of GHG in buildings (Dodd et al. 2015): the Dutch Building Decree requires reporting of GHG emissions and depletion of natural resources for structural components of residential and office buildings (over 1000 ft^2) on application for a building permit.

Changing Design Process

Even in jurisdictions without regulatory action, change is happening in the HVAC&R industry. Today's engineer can contribute value to projects that have sustainability goals, using some of the many resources and approaches cited in this chapter. (See the section on Designing for Effective Energy Resource Use.)

ASHRAE, in partnership with the Illuminating Engineering Society (IES) and USGBC, developed *Standard* 189.1 for high-performance green buildings, which calls for a determination of annual CO_2 equivalent emissions in addition to overall energy savings and other requirements. The component of such emissions from electricity use depends on the mix of fuels used to generate that electricity. In addition to regional variations, the overall fuel mix is projected to change, as shown in Figure 3.

Emissions considerations alone are not the only driver for design decision making. Energy prices and societal pressures continue to mount. Examples of recent drivers include

- Antiquated electric transmission and distribution infrastructure and plans to develop a smart grid to improve it
- Power plants being forced to become cleaner and more efficient, expediting closure of cheap, dirty generators
- Mandates imposed on utilities to provide more renewable energy to customers
- Influence of commodities trading markets on spot and future prices
- Constrained natural gas reserves and growth in demand continuing to increase volatility in the natural gas market
- Climate change, through environmental pressures to reduce carbon emissions in the face of increased demand for electricity, and infrastructure damage from more frequent storms
- Growing impatience from some elements, both domestically and internationally, over the perceived slow pace of acceptance of sustainable design, leading proponents to push harder for seriously addressing climate and energy resource issues

These and other pressures are changing project teams and their work; those teams are being asked to

- Incorporate sustainable design guidance, standards, and rating systems into their work
- Add a variety of new team members to bring additional expertise to address sustainability
- Gather quantitative data related to energy, water, occupant satisfaction, greenhouse gas emissions, etc.
- Use new analysis tools (e.g., daylighting modeling) to help maximize sustainability

Opportunities relating to sustainability for the well-prepared engineer are growing. The increased focus on sustainability in the built environment allows for more integrated, effective, and efficient ways to meet the nexus between environment, economy, regulation, and societal pressure. The challenge for the industry is how quickly

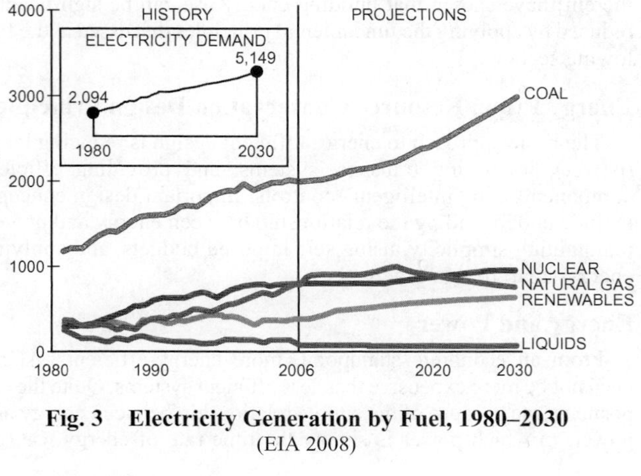

Fig. 3 Electricity Generation by Fuel, 1980–2030
(EIA 2008)

it can adapt to these new opportunities and grow in an increasingly regulated environment. At the very least, the standard of care for engineers must be tracked and implemented to manage liability. Sustainability can provide an opportunity for engineers and others to increase market share while exceeding current regulatory constraints and anticipating future regulations. More details on design considerations are provided in the section on Designing for Effective Energy Resource Use.

Integrating sustainability into HVAC&R system design can result in built environments that respect the greater environment and provide safe and comfortable indoor environments. The three occurrences of the letter *i* in *sustainability* can be thought of as representing key concepts in sustainable design: *interactive*, *iterative*, and *integrated*. Design processes that require greater *interaction* between team members and more *iterative* analysis to improve design solutions can be undertaken by teams through what has become known as *integrated* design.

Sustainability is inherently multidisciplinary. Recognizing this, teams often assemble a broad array of experts in a collaborative, interdisciplinary approach to achieve the highest levels of sustainability possible. This integrated design approach is addressed in Chapter 58 of the 2015 *ASHRAE Handbook—HVAC Applications* and in ASHRAE (2013).

Other Opportunities

In addition to designing HVAC&R systems, engineers may increasingly be called upon to help address issues ranging from transportation to irrigation to on-site renewable energy. The approach to sustainable design alternatives opens the door for creativity and innovation in the design process. Rather than taking a one-size-fits-all approach to design, engineers can provide a range of available solutions and facilitate flexible implementation. Often, engineers are asked to develop and evaluate measures based on both economic and environmental performance. Success may require several design iterations to achieve the desired performance.

6. DESIGNING FOR EFFECTIVE ENERGY RESOURCE USE

Most energy used in buildings is from nonrenewable resources, the cost of which historically has not considered replenishment or environmental impact. Thus, consideration of energy use in design has been based primarily on economic advantages, which are weighted to encourage more rather than less use.

As resources become less readily available and more exotic, and replenishable sources are investigated, the need to operate buildings effectively using less energy becomes paramount. Extensive studies since the mid-1970s [see, e.g., Doris et al. (2009) and references therein] have shown that building energy use can be significantly reduced by applying the fundamental principles discussed in the following sections.

Energy Ethic: Resource Conservation Design Principles

The basic approach to energy-efficient design is reducing loads (power), improving transport systems, and providing efficient components and “intelligent” controls. Important design concepts include understanding the relationship between energy and power, maintaining simplicity, using self-imposed budgets, and applying energy-smart design practices.

Energy and Power

From an economic standpoint, more energy-efficient systems need not be more expensive than less efficient systems. Quite the opposite is true because of the simple relationship between energy and power, in which power is simply the time rate of energy use (or, conversely, energy is power times time). Power terms such as horsepower, ton of refrigeration, Btu per hour, or kilowatt are used in expressing the size of a motor, chiller, boiler, or transformer, respectively. Generally, the smaller the equipment, the less it costs. Other things being equal, as smaller equipment operates over time, it consumes less energy. Thus, in designing for energy efficiency, the first objective is always to reduce the power required to the bare minimum necessary to provide the desired performance, starting with the building’s heating and cooling loads (a power term, in Btu/h) and continuing with the various systems and subsystems.

Simplicity

Complex designs to save energy seldom function in the manner intended unless the systems are continually managed and operated by technically skilled individuals. Experience has shown that long-term, energy-efficient performance with a complex system is seldom achievable. Further, when complex systems are operated by minimally skilled individuals, both energy efficiency and performance suffer. Most techniques discussed in this chapter can be implemented with great simplicity.

Self-Imposed Budgets

Just as an engineer must work to a cost budget with most designs, self-imposed power budgets can be similarly helpful in achieving energy-efficient design. The *Advanced Energy Design Guide* series from ASHRAE are a source for guidance on achievable design budgets. For example, the following are possible categories of power (or power-affecting) design budgets for a mid-rise office building:

- Installed lighting (overall) W/ft^2
- Space sensible cooling Btu/h·ft^2
- Space heating load Btu/h·ft^2
- Electric power (overall) W/ft^2
- Thermal power (overall) Btu/h·ft^2
- Hydronic system head ft of water
- Water chiller (water-cooled) kW/ton (COP)
- Chilled-water system auxiliaries kW/ton
- Unitary air-conditioning systems kW/ton (COP)
- Annual electric energy kWh/ft^2·yr
- Annual thermal energy Btu/ft^2·yr·°F·day

As the building and systems are designed, all decisions become interactive as each subsystem’s power or energy performance is continually compared to the budget.

Design Process for Energy-Efficient Projects

Consider energy efficiency at the beginning of the building design process, because energy-efficient features are most easily and effectively incorporated at that time. Seek the active participation of all members of the design team, including the owner, architect, engineer, and often the contractor, early in the design process. Consider building attributes such as building function, form, orientation, window/wall ratio, and HVAC system types early in the process, because each has major energy implications. Identify meaningful energy performance benchmarks suited to the project, and set project-specific goals. Energy benchmarks for a sample project are shown in Table 1. Consider energy resources, on-site energy sources, and use of renewable energy, credits, utility rebates, or carbon offsets to mitigate environmental impacts of energy use.

Address a building’s energy requirements in the following sequence:

1. **Minimize the impact of the building’s functional requirements** by analyzing how the building relates to its external environment. Advocate changes in building form, aspect ratio, and other attributes that reduce, redistribute, or delay (shift) loads. The load calculation should be interactive so that the effect of those factors can be seen immediately.

Table 1 Example Benchmark and Energy Targets for University Research Laboratory

	Gross	Lit/ Conditioned
Building area, ft^2	170,000	110,500

Electric	Electricity for Lighting	Electricity for Ventilation (Fans)	Electricity for In-Building Pumps	Electricity for Plug Loads	Electricity for Unidentified Loads	Total Electricity	Cogenerated Electricity	Grid Electricity
Design load, W/ft^2 gross	0.52	0.50	0.60	0.97	—	2.60	—	
Peak demand, W/ft^2 gross	0.42	0.50	0.42	0.73	0.00016	2.07	—	
Peak demand, kW (Projected submetered peak)	71	85	72	124	20	372	—	
Annual consumption, kWh/yr (Projected submetered reading)	218,154	346,598	191,245	891,503	175,200	1,823,000	966,000	857,000
Annual use index goal, kWh/yr	1.28	2.04	1.12	5.24	1.03	10.72		
Annual use index goal, site Btu/ft^2 gross·yr	4378	6956	3838	17,893	3516	36,583		
Annual use index, kWh/ft^2 gross·yr*	2.51 to 3.32	4.48 to 6.88	included elsewhere	4.39 to 5.67	NA	14.74 to 17.91		
Annual use index, site Btu/ft^2 gross·yr*	8564	15,286	—	14,979	—	50,293 to 61,109		

*From Labs21 program of U.S. Environmental Protection Agency (EPA) and U.S. Department of Energy (DOE). See labs21benchmarking.lbl.gov.

2. **Minimize loads** by analyzing external and internal loads imposed on the building's energy-using subsystems, both for peak- and part-load conditions. Design for efficient and effective operation off-peak, where the majority of operating hours and energy use typically occurs.
3. **Maximize subsystem efficiency** by analyzing the diversified energy and power requirements of each energy-using subsystem serving the building's functional requirements. Consider static and dynamic efficiencies of energy conversion and energy transport subsystems, and consider opportunities to reclaim, redistribute, and store energy for later use.
4. **Study alternative ways to integrate subsystems** into the building by considering both power and time components of energy use. Identify, evaluate, and design each of these components to control overall design energy consumption. Consider the following when integrating major building subsystems:

- Address more than one problem at a time when developing design solutions, and make maximum use of the building's advantageous features (e.g., windows, structural mass).
- Examine design solutions that consider time (i.e., when energy use occurs), because sufficient energy may already be present from the environment (e.g., solar heat, night cooling) or from internal equipment (e.g., lights, computers) but available at times different from when needed. Active (e.g., heat pumps with water tanks) and passive (e.g., building mass) storage techniques may need to be considered.
- Examine design solutions that consider the anticipated use of space. For example, in large but relatively unoccupied spaces, consider task or zone lighting. Consider transporting excess energy (light and heat) from locations of production and availability to locations of need instead of purchasing additional energy.
- Never reject waste energy at temperatures usable for space conditioning or other practical purposes without calculating the economic benefit of energy recovery or treatment for reuse.
- Consider or advocate design solutions that provide more comfortable surface temperatures or increase the availability of controlled daylight in buildings where human occupancy is a primary function.
- Use easily understood design solutions, because they have a greater probability of use by building operators and occupants.
- Where the functional requirements of a building are likely to change over time, design the installed environmental system to adapt to meet anticipated changes and to provide flexibility in meeting future changes in use, occupancy, or other functions.
- Develop energy performance benchmarks, metrics, and targets that allow building owners and operators to better achieve the design intent. The effectiveness of these benchmarks was studied in ASHRAE research project 1627, which examines performance of K-12 schools and small office buildings that use the AEDGs (Jones et al. 2016).
- Differentiate between peak loads for system design and selection and lower operating loads that determine actual energy use.

Building Energy Use Elements

Envelope. Control thermal conductivity by using insulation (including movable insulation), thermal mass, and/or phase-change thermal storage at levels that minimize net heating and cooling loads on a time-integrated (annual) basis.

- Minimize unintentional or uncontrolled thermal bridges, and include them in energy-related calculations because they can radically alter building envelope conductivity. Examples include wall studs, balconies, ledges, and extensions of building slabs.
- Minimize infiltration so that it approaches zero. (An exception is when infiltration provides the sole means of ventilation, such as in small residential units.) This minimizes fan energy consumption in pressurized buildings during occupied periods and minimizes heat loss (or unwanted heat gain, in warm climates) during unoccupied periods. In warm, humid climates, a tight envelope also improves indoor air quality. Reduce infiltration through design details that enhance the fit and integrity of building envelope joints in ways that may be readily achieved during construction (e.g., caulking, weatherstripping, vestibule doors, revolving doors), with construction meeting accepted specifications. Building envelope commissioning or testing can help verify these design and construction targets.
- Consider operable windows to allow occupant-controlled ventilation. This requires careful design of the building's mechanical system to minimize unnecessary HVAC energy consumption, and building operators and occupants should be cautioned about improper use of operable windows. CIBSE (2005) provides comprehensive design considerations for natural ventilation.

- Strive to maintain occupant radiant comfort regardless of whether the building envelope is designed to be a static or dynamic membrane. Design opaque surfaces so that average inside surface temperatures remain within 5°F of room temperature in the coldest anticipated weather (i.e., winter design conditions) and so that the coldest inside surface remains within 25°F of room temperature (but always above the indoor dew point). In a building with time-varying internal heat generation, consider thermal mass for controlling radiant comfort. In the perimeter zone, thermal mass is more effective when it is positioned inside the envelope's insulation.
- Effective control of solar radiation is critical to energy-efficient design because of the high level of internal heat production in most commercial buildings. In some climates, lighting energy consumption savings from daylighting techniques can be greater than the heating and cooling energy penalties that result from additional glazed surface area required, if the building envelope is properly designed for daylighting and lighting controls are installed and used. (In other climates, there may not be net savings.) Daylighting designs are most effective if direct solar beam radiation is not allowed to cause glare in building spaces.
- Design transparent parts of the building envelope to prevent solar radiant gain above that necessary for effective daylighting and solar heating. On south-facing facades (in the northern hemisphere), using low shading coefficients is generally not as effective as external physical shading devices in achieving this balance. Consider low-emissivity, high-visible-transmittance glazings for effective control of radiant heat gains and losses. For shading control, judicious use of vegetation may block excess gain year-round or seasonally, depending on the plant species chosen.

Lighting. Lighting is both a major energy end use in commercial buildings (especially office buildings) and a major contributor to internal loads by increasing cooling loads and decreasing heating loads. Design should both meet the lighting functional criteria of the space and minimize energy use. IES (2011) recommends illuminance levels for visual tasks and surrounding lighted areas. Principles of energy-conserving design within that context include the following:

- Energy use is determined by the lighting load (demand power) and its duration of use (time). Minimize actual demand load rather than just apparent connected load. Control the load rather than just area switching, if switching may adversely affect the quality of the luminous environment.
- Consider daylighting with proper controls to reduce costs of electric lighting. Design should be sensitive to window glare, sudden changes in luminances, and general user acceptance of daylighting controls. Carefully select window treatment (blinds, drapes, and shades) and glazing to control direct solar penetration and luminance extremes while maintaining the view and daylight penetration.
- Design the lighting system so that illumination required for tasks is primarily limited to the location of the task and comes from a direction that minimizes direct glare and veiling reflections on the task. When the design is based on nonuniform illuminance, walls should be a light to medium color or illuminated to provide visual comfort. In densely occupied work spaces, uniform distribution of general lighting may be most appropriate. Where necessary, provide supplementary task illumination. General ambient illumination should not be lower than a third of the luminance required for the task, to help maintain visually comfortable luminance ratios.
- Use local task lighting to accommodate needs for higher lighting levels because of task visual difficulty, glare, intermittently changing requirements, or individual visual differences (poor or aging eyesight).
- Group similar activities so that high illuminance or special lighting for particular tasks can be localized in certain rooms or areas, and so that less-efficient fixtures required for critical glare control do not have to be installed uniformly when they are only required sparsely.
- Use lighting controls throughout so lighting is available when and where it is needed, but not wasted when tasks are less critical or spaces are not fully occupied. Also consider user acceptance of control strategies to maximize energy saving.
- Only use lower-efficiency incandescent lamps in applications where their characteristics cannot be duplicated by other sources, because manufacturing of most incandescent lamps will be discontinued during the life of the building.
- Carry lighting design through the rest of the building's interior design. Reduced light absorption may be achieved by using lighter finishes, particularly on ceilings, walls, and partitions.

Other Loads.

- Minimize thermal impact of equipment and appliances on HVAC systems by using hoods, radiation shields, or other confining techniques, and by using controls to turn off equipment when not needed. Where practical, locate major heat-generating equipment where it can balance other heat losses. Computer centers or kitchen areas usually have separate, dedicated HVAC equipment. In addition, consider heat recovery for this equipment.
- Use storage techniques to level or distribute loads that vary on a time or spatial basis to allow operation of a device at maximum (often full-load) efficiency.

HVAC System Design.

- Consider separate HVAC systems to serve areas expected to operate on widely differing operating schedules or design conditions. For instance, systems serving office areas should generally be separate from those serving retail areas.
- Arrange systems so that spaces with relatively constant, weather-independent loads are served by systems separate from those serving perimeter spaces. Areas with special temperature or humidity requirements (e.g., computer rooms) should be served by systems separate from those serving areas that require comfort heating and cooling only. Alternatively, provide these areas with supplementary or auxiliary systems.
- Sequence the supply of zone cooling and heating to prevent simultaneous operation of heating and cooling systems for the same space, to the extent possible. Where this is not possible because of ventilation, humidity control, or air circulation requirements, reduce air quantities as much as possible before incorporating reheating, recooling, or mixing hot and cold airstreams. For example, if reheat is needed to dehumidify and prevent overcooling, *only* ventilation air needs to be treated, not the entire recirculated air quantity. Finally, reset supply air temperature up to the extent possible to reduce reheating, recooling, or mixing losses.
- Provide controls to allow operation in occupied and unoccupied modes. In occupied mode, controls may provide for a gradually changing control point as system demands change from cooling to heating. In unoccupied mode, ventilation and exhaust systems should be shut off if possible, and comfort heating and cooling systems should be shut off except to maintain space conditions ready for the next occupancy cycle.
- In geographical areas where diurnal temperature swings and humidity levels permit, consider judicious coupling of air distribution and building structural mass to allow nighttime cooling to reduce the requirement for daytime mechanical cooling.
- High ventilation rates, where required for special applications, can impose enormous heating and cooling loads on HVAC equipment. In these cases, consider recirculating filtered and cleaned

air to the extent possible, rather than 100% outdoor air. Also, consider preheating outdoor air with reclaimed heat from other sources.

HVAC Equipment Selection.

- To allow HVAC equipment operation at the highest efficiencies, match conversion devices to load increments, and sequence the operation of modules. Oversized or large-scale systems should never serve small seasonal loads (e.g., a large heating boiler serving a summer-service water-heated load). Include specific low-load units and auxiliaries where prolonged use at minimal capacities is expected.
- Select the most efficient (or highest-COP) equipment practical at both design and reduced capacity (part-load) operating conditions.
- When selecting large-power devices such as chillers (including their auxiliary energy burdens), perform an economic analysis of the complete life-cycle costs. See Chapter 37 of the 2015 *ASHRAE Handbook—HVAC Applications* for more information on detailed economic analysis.
- Keep fluid temperatures for heating equipment devices as low as practical and for cooling equipment as high as practical, while still meeting loads and minimizing flow quantities.

Energy Transport Systems. Energy should be transported as efficiently as possible. The following options are listed in order of theoretical efficiency, from the lowest energy transport burden (most efficient) to the highest (least efficient):

1. Electric wire or fuel pipe
2. Two-phase fluid pipe (steam or refrigerant)
3. Single-phase liquid/fluid pipe (water, glycol, etc.)
4. Air duct

Select a distribution system that complements other parameters such as control strategies, storage capabilities, conversion efficiency, and utilization efficiency.

The following specific design techniques may be applied to thermal energy transport systems:

Steam Systems.

- Include provisions for seasonal or nonuse shutdown.
- Minimize venting of steam and ingestion of air, with design directed toward full-vapor performance.
- Avoid subcooling, if practical.
- Return condensate to boilers or source devices at the highest possible temperature.

Hydronic Systems.

- Minimize flow quantity by designing for the maximum practical temperature range.
- Vary flow quantity with load where possible.
- Design for the lowest practical pressure rise (or drop).
- Provide *operating* and *idle* control modes.
- When locating equipment, identify the critical pressure path and size runs for the minimum reasonable pressure drop.

Air Systems.

- Minimize airflow by careful load analysis and an effective distribution system. If the application allows, supply air quantity should vary with sensible load (i.e., VAV systems). Hold the fan pressure requirement to the lowest practical value and avoid using fan pressure as a source for control power.
- Provide *normal* and *idle* control modes for fan and psychrometric systems.
- Keep duct runs as short as possible, and keep runs on the critical pressure path sized for minimum practical pressure drop.

Power Distribution.

- Size transformers and generating units as closely as possible to the actual anticipated load (i.e., avoid oversizing to minimize fixed thermal losses).
- Consider distribution of electric power at the highest practical voltage and load selection at the maximum power factor consistent with safety.
- Consider tenant submetering in commercial and multifamily buildings as a cost-effective energy conservation measure. (A large portion of energy use in tenant facilities occurs simply because there is no economic incentive to conserve.)

Domestic Hot-Water Systems.

- Choose shower heads that provide and maintain user comfort and energy savings. They should not have removable flow-restricting inserts to meet flow limitation requirements.
- Consider point-of-use water heaters where their use will reduce energy consumption and annual energy cost.
- Consider using storage to facilitate heat recovery when the heat to be recovered is out of phase with the demand for hot water or when energy use for water heating can be shifted to take advantage of off-peak rates.

Controls. Well-designed digital control provides information to managers and operators as well as to the data processor that serves as the intelligent controller. Include the energy-saving concepts discussed previously throughout the operating sequences and control logic. However, energy conservation should not be sought at the expense of adequate performance; in a well-designed system, these two parameters are compatible. See Chapter 7 of this volume and Chapter 47 of the 2015 *ASHRAE Handbook—HVAC Applications* for more information on controls.

REFERENCES

ASHRAE members can access *ASHRAE Journal* articles and ASHRAE research project final reports at technologyportal.ashrae.org. Articles and reports are also available for purchase by nonmembers in the online ASHRAE Bookstore at www.ashrae.org/bookstore.

AIA. 2011. *2030 challenges*. architecture2030.org/category/2030-challenges/.

ASHRAE. 2006. *ASHRAE's sustainability roadmap—The approach to defining a leadership position in sustainability*. Presidential Ad Hoc Committee.

ASHRAE. 2013. *ASHRAE greenguide: The design, construction, and operation of sustainable buildings*, 4rd ed. A. Darwich, J. Means and T. Lawrence, eds.

Athena. 2017. *LCA data and software*. Athena Sustainable Materials Institute, Ottawa, ON. www.athenasmi.org.

Bruckner, T., I.A. Bashmakov, Y. Mulugetta, H. Chum, A. de la Vega Navarro, J. Edmonds, A. Faaij, B. Fungtammasan, A. Garg, E. Hertwich, D. Honnery, D. Infield, M. Kainuma, S. Khennas, S. Kim, H.B. Nimir, K. Riahi, N. Strachan, R. Wiser, and X. Zhang. 2014. Energy systems. Ch. 7 in *Climate change 2014: Mitigation of climate change. Contribution of Working Group III to the Fifth Assessment Report of the Intergovernmental Panel on Climate Change*, O. Edenhofer, R. Pichs-Madruga, Y. Sokona, E. Farahani, S. Kadner, K. Seyboth, A. Adler, I. Baum, S. Brunner, P. Eickemeier, B. Kriemann, J. Savolainen, S. Schlömer, C. von Stechow, T. Zwickel, and J.C. Minx, eds. Cambridge University Press, U.K. www.ipcc.ch/pdf/assessment-report/ar5/wg3/ipcc_wg3_ar5_chapter7.pdf.

CALGreen. 2013. California Green Building Standards Code, California Code of Regulations, Title 24, Part 11.

California. 2006. Emission performance standards. *Senate Bill* SB 1368. California Energy Commission, Sacramento. www.energy.ca.gov/emission_standards/.

CEN. 2013. Sustainability of construction works—Environmental product declarations—Core rules for the product category of construction products. *European Standard* EN 15804+A1. European Committee for Standardization, Brussels.

CIBSE. 2005. *Natural ventilation in non-domestic buildings*. Applications Manual 10. Chartered Institution of Building Services Engineers, London.

Crawford, R.H., G.J. Treloar, B.D. Ilozor and P.E.D. Love. 2003. Comparative greenhouse emissions analysis of domestic solar hot water systems. *Building Research & Information* 31(1):34-47.

Dodd, N., S. Donatello, E. Garbarino and M. Gama-Caldas. 2015. Identifying macro-objectives for the life cycle environmental performance and resource efficiency of EU buildings. Joint Research Centre, European Commission. susproc.jrc.ec.europa.eu/Efficient_Buildings/docs/150528%20Resource%20Efficient%20Buildings_Macro%20objectives%20WP_Draft%20final.pdf.

Doris, E., J. Cochran, and M. Vorum. 2009. Energy efficiency policy of the United States: Overview of trends at different levels of government. *Technical Report* NREL/TP-6A2-46532. National Renewable Energy Laboratory, Golden, CO. www.nrel.gov/docs/fy10osti/46532.pdf.

EIA. 2015. *Annual energy outlook 2015*. DOE/EIA-0383(2007). Energy Information Administration, U.S. Department of Energy, Washington, D.C.

EPA. 2016. *Tool for reduction and assessment of chemicals and other environmental impacts (TRACI)*, v. 2.1. U.S. Environmental Protection Agency, Washington, D.C. www.epa.gov/chemical-research/tool-reduction-and-assessment-chemicals-and-other-environmental-impacts-traci.

E.U. 2008. Directive 2008/98/EC of the European Parliament and of the Council of 19 November 2008 on waste and repealing certain directives. E.U. *Directive* 2008/98/EC. eur-lex.europa.eu/legal-content/EN/TXT/?qid=1487004114713&uri=CELEX:32008L0098.

E.U. 2009. Directive 2009/28/EC of the European Parliament and of the Council of 23 April 2009 on the promotion of the use of energy from renewable sources. E.U. *Directive* 2009/28/EC. eur-lex.europa.eu/legal-content/EN/TXT/?uri=celex:32009L0028.

E.U. 2009. Directive 2009/125/EC of the European Parliament and of the Council of 21 October 2009 establishing a framework for the setting of ecodesign requirements for energy-related products. E.U. *Directive* 2009/125/EC. eur-lex.europa.eu/legal-content/EN/TXT/?qid=1487003389208&uri=CELEX:32009L0125.

E.U. 2010. Directive 2010/30/EU of the European Parliament and of the Council of 19 May 2010 on the indication by labelling and standard product information of the consumption of energy and other resources by energy-related products. E.U. *Directive* 2010/30/EU. eur-lex.europa.eu/legal-content/EN/TXT/?qid=1487003495623&uri=CELEX:32010L0030.

E.U. 2010. Directive 2010/31/EU of the European Parliament and of the Council of 19 May 2010 on the energy performance of buildings. E.U. *Directive* 2010/31/EU. eur-lex.europa.eu/legal-content/EN/TXT/?qid=1487003617334&uri=CELEX:32010L0031.

E.U. 2012. Directive 2012/27/EU of the European Parliament and of the Council of 25 October 2012 on energy efficiency. E.U. *Directive* 2012/27/EU. eur-lex.europa.eu/legal-content/EN/TXT/?qid=1487003274569&uri=CELEX:32012L0027.

ICC. 2015. *2015 International Green Construction Code®* (*IgCC®*). International Code Council, Washington, D.C.

IES. 2011. *The lighting handbook*, 10th ed. Illuminating Engineering Society, New York.

IPCC. 2014. *Climate change 2014: Synthesis report, contribution of Working Groups I, II and III to the Fifth Assessment Report of the Intergovernmental Panel on Climate Change*. R.K. Pachauri and L.A. Meyer, eds. Intergovernmental Panel on Climate Change, Geneva, Switzerland. www.ipcc.ch/report/ar5/syr/.

ISO. 2006. Environmental management—Life cycle assessment—Principles and framework. *Standard* 14040-2006. International Organization for Standardization, Geneva.

ISO. 2006. Environmental labels and declarations—Type III environmental declarations—Principles and procedures. *Standard* 14025. International Organization for Standardization, Geneva.

ISO. 2006. Environmental management—Life cycle assessment—Requirements and guidelines. *Standard* 14044. International Organization for Standardization, Geneva.

Jones, D., S. Reilly, and M. Sadeghy. 2016. Actual energy performance of small office and K-12 school buildings designed to meet the 30% ASHRAE *Advanced Energy Design Guides*. ASHRAE Research Project RP-1627, *Final Report*.

Kalogirou, S. 2004. Environmental benefits of domestic solar energy systems. *Energy Conversion and Management* 45:3075-3092.

Lawrence, T., C.A. Balaras, and J.K. Means. 2016. A comparison of how sustainability and green building standards are being adopted into building construction codes within the United States and the EU. *Proceedings of the SBE 16—Strategies—Stakeholders—Success Factors—International Conference on Sustainable Built Environment,* Hamburg, Germany.

NAS. 2010. *Advancing the science of climate change*. National Academy of Sciences, Washington, D.C. www.nap.edu/read/12782/chapter/1#v.

NIST. 2017. *BEES: Building for environmental and economic sustainability*. National Institute for Standards and Technology. www.nist.gov/el/economics/BEESSoftware.cfm.

Olivier, J.G.J., G. Janssens-Maenhout, M. Muntean, and J.A.H.W. Peters. 2015. *Trends in global CO_2 emissions—2015 report*. PBL Netherlands Environmental Assessment Agency, The Hague, and European Commission, Joint Research Centre, Ispra, Italy. edgar.jrc.ec.europa.eu/news_docs/jrc-2015-trends-in-global-co2-emissions-2015-report-98184.pdf.

Passer, A., S. Lasvaux, K. Allacker, D. De Lathauwer, C. Spirinckx, B. Wittstock, D. Kellenberger, F. Schösser, J. Wall, and H. Wallbaum. 2015. Environmental product declarations entering the building sector: Critical reflections based on 5 to 10 years experience in different European countries. *International Journal of Life Cycle Assessment* 20:1199-1212. link.springer.com/article/10.1007/s11367-015-0926-3.

Srinivasan, R.S., W. Ingwersen, C. Trucco, R. Ries, and D. Campbell. 2014. Comparison of energy-based indicators used in life cycle assessment tools for buildings. *Building & Environment* 79:138-151.

Townsend, T.E. 2006. The ASHRAE promise: A sustainable future. *ASHRAE Journal* 48(8):14-19.

UK. 2015. *HM Government, The Building Regulations 2010—Part G: Sanitation, hot water safety and water efficiency*. Newcastle Upon Tyne: NBS. www.planningportal.gov.uk/buildingregulations/approveddocuments/partg/approved.

UN. 1987. Our common future: Report of the world commission on environment and development. Annex to General Assembly document A/42/427, *Development and International Co-operation: Environment*. United Nations. www.un-documents.net/wced-ocf.htm.

UNEP. 2003. *Montreal Protocol handbook for the international treaties for the protection of the ozone layer*, 6th ed., Annexes A, B, and C. Secretariat for the Vienna Convention for the Protection of the Ozone Layer and the Montreal Protocol on Substances that Deplete the Ozone Layer, United Nations Environment Programme, Nairobi.

UNEP. 2014. *Greening the supply chain*. United Nations Environment Programme, Sustainable Buildings and Climate Initiative. www.unep.org/sbci/pdfs/greening_the_supply_chain_report.pdf.

UNFCCC. 1998. *Kyoto Protocol to the United Nations framework convention on climate change*. United Nations Framework Convention on Climate Change, New York. unfccc.int/resource/docs/convkp/kpeng.pdf.

UNFCCC. 2015. *Adoption of the Paris Agreement*. United Nations Framework Convention on Climate Change, New York. unfccc.int/resource/docs/2015/cop21/eng/l09r01.pdf.

BIBLIOGRAPHY

ASHRAE. (Various.) *Advanced energy design guides*, 50% and 30% series. www.ashrae.org/standards-research--technology/advanced-energy-design-guides.

ASHRAE. 2009. *ASHRAE position document on climate change*.

ASHRAE. 2009/2011. *Energy efficiency guides for existing commercial buildings*, vol. 1: *Technical implementation*, and vol. 2: *The business case for building owners and managers*.

ASHRAE. 2008. *Vision 2020: Producing net zero energy buildings*. www.ashrae.org/File Library/docLib/Public/20080226_ashraevision2020.pdf.

CHAPTER 36

MOISTURE MANAGEMENT IN BUILDINGS

THE TERM **moisture** encompasses the gaseous, liquid, and solid states of water and any dissolved contaminants. Examples of liquid moisture include precipitation, wind-driven rain, construction moisture, rising damp, and water from incidental pipe drippings. Precipitation wets pitched roofs, low-slope roofs, and inclined facades, whereas wind-driven rain wets the enclosure as a whole. Buildings, including the envelope, start their service life containing significant quantities of construction moisture. This is particularly true for concrete, aerated concrete, mortar, and plaster. Groundwater and rain sinks may lead to rising damp, and pipe leakage reflects bad workmanship, lack of maintenance, failing fixtures, or pipe corrosion (Hens 2016; Mumovic and Santamouris 2009; Trechsel 1994). This chapter presents data on indoor vapor release and measured indoor/outdoor vapor pressure or vapor concentration differences not included elsewhere in the *ASHRAE Handbook*, and discusses moisture sources and sinks that can reduce materials' durability, as well as the negative effects of insufficient or excessive indoor relative humidity.

Gaseous water (**vapor**) comes from outdoor humidity and from interior vapor releases. Water vapor in the air, expressed as **relative humidity**, governs hygroscopic loading of materials. High relative humidity values at surfaces favor mold growth and, if reaching 100%, can lead to surface condensation. When vapor pressure and temperature gradients in and across assemblies point in the same direction, interstitial condensation is possible.

Chapter 25 contains an in-depth analysis of heat, air, and moisture loads; Chapter 15 discusses surface condensation on windows; and Chapter 16 covers interstitial condensation caused by air leakage.

Excessive indoor moisture and humidity interferes with the use and enjoyment of buildings and may shorten their useful life over the long term. Problems affecting owners and occupants include reduced comfort, poor indoor air quality, negative health effects, damage to the building's materials and structural fasteners and wasted energy in HVAC operation. Consequently, moisture management demands attention from the architect, the builder, the mechanical system designer, and those charged with budgeting, management and maintenance of the building and its mechanical systems.

All buildings experience occasional extremes in relative humidity and moisture. Short-term occurrences of these extremes can generally be accommodated by storage in the building materials, but when moisture and humidity accumulate for extended periods in vulnerable materials, major problems can and often do occur. Moisture problems are unfortunately quite common in buildings. It is the responsibility of those in a position of authority to reasonably reduce the risks associated with excessive moisture accumulation. Successful management of moisture and humidity requires understanding the complex and dynamic relationship between the building's enclosure, its fabric, and the mechanical systems over the entire life of that building. This dynamic interaction holds the potential for either an excellent result over decades, or for frequent, disruptive, and expensive problems. Experience suggests that human behavior can overcome virtually any building technology, so owner and occupant education are important elements in the successful design and usage of a building.

The preparation of this chapter is assigned to TC 1.12, Moisture Management in Buildings.

1. EFFECTS OF HUMIDITY AND DAMPNESS

Moisture tolerance and appropriate indoor relative humidity levels must be considered requirements for a sustainable built environment: relative humidity affects comfort, indoor air quality, and health, and excessive wetness can shorten the service life of materials and assemblies. The preferred relative humidity range for human health and comfort is between 40 and 60%, although that interval is often broadened from 30 to 70%. High relative humidity degrades thermal comfort once the operative temperature passes 77 to 81°F, making the environment feel oppressive. It also facilitates release of volatile organic compounds (VOCs), especially of formaldehyde, thus degrading indoor air quality and triggering olfactory dissatisfaction. Finally, high relative humidity in specific environments (e.g., beds, on surfaces) activates dust mite reproduction and related allergy risks, and can activate mold germination and growth (ASHRAE 2012; IEA-EBC 1990a, 1990b).

Very low relative humidity activates electrostatic discharge and leads to complaints of dry mucous membranes (e.g., nose, lips, throat) and eyes, especially by people wearing contact lenses. On the other hand, some respiratory ailments can be relieved by dry environments.

Excessively low or high relative humidity creates conditions favorable to bacterial and viral infections, allergic rhinitis, and asthma. Chapter 9 gives a more in-depth analysis of the impact of humidity on thermal comfort. Chapter 10 discusses the effects of relative humidity on indoor environmental quality, Chapter 11 covers mold, and Chapter 12 discusses the relationship between relative humidity and olfactory perception. Additional information is available in Holm (2008).

Prolonged and excessive relative humidity and wetness can degrade materials physically, chemically, and biologically. Examples of physical degradation are frost damage and salt attack. Chemical degradation includes lime/gypsum reaction, carbonization of concrete, alkali/granulates reaction in concrete, and corrosion of ferrous and nonferrous metals, where moisture determines whether damage will occur in the presence of corrosive agents (e.g., sulfide, acetic acid). Wood rot by fungi and bacteria is an example of biological degradation. Very dry conditions also can damage wood, causing cracking and warping. Fluctuations between extremes of high and low relative humidity can induce cracking in hygroscopic materials.

2. ELEMENTS OF MOISTURE MANAGEMENT

Designing for moisture and humidity management includes the choice of building materials and the layering of the envelope as well as the design and component selection of the HVAC system. For information on the building envelope, refer to Chapter 15; for details on building assemblies, see Chapters 25, 26, and 27.

The largest contributors of liquid moisture are water from wind-driven rain in building envelopes with insufficient drainage, leaks from roof or gutters, and leaks from internal plumbing. These sources must be addressed and resolved for the building envelope to succeed.

Once liquid water is addressed, the next factors to consider are vapor pressure and relative humidity. The driving forces responsible for water vapor movement within buildings and across the envelope are air pressure differences that move air and vapor together, and vapor pressure differences that activate vapor diffusion. Temperature-, wind-, and fan-induced air-pressure differentials typically overwhelm diffusion in terms of total vapor flux displaced. However, in hot, humid climates or in buildings with high indoor/outdoor vapor pressure differences, pure diffusion may nevertheless cause problems.

Chapters 16 and 20 contain information on air movement in buildings. Chapter 13 gives information on intrazone airflow, multizone network airflow, and contaminant transport, included vapor; and Chapter 24 discusses airflow around buildings. ANSI/ASHRAE *Standard* 160-2009 provides criteria to evaluate the transient hygrothermal performance of envelopes. This analysis may be used to evaluate moisture tolerance in cases where, besides vapor, liquid water is a primary factor.

3. ENVELOPE AND HVAC INTERACTIONS

As shown by Figure 1, heat, air, and moisture move continuously throughout a building, driven by differences in temperature, vapor pressure, and air pressure between the indoor and outdoor environment and by similar differences between adjacent indoor zones. Construction moisture contributes to the initial wetness of the whole building fabric, including the envelope. Over time, envelope assemblies exposed to rain and snow may become moist by seeping rain and melting snow or by capillary suction **(rising damp)** from moist below-grade earth, which may dampen walls just above grade. Leaking and dripping interior pipes can also be responsible for excessive wetness.

The opaque and transparent portions of the building envelope must be designed so that their thermal transmittance approaches the energy related economic optimum. Together with the overall building fabric, the envelope should allow passive solar control, while all assemblies proposed must prevent rain from wetting layers that must stay dry. The building details should withhold rainwater runoff and prevent sinking rainwater from wetting basements and floors on grade. Correct protective measures must exclude rising damp and promote effective construction moisture drying; water vapor moving across the envelope assemblies should not result in unacceptable interstitial moisture accumulation. Detailing and workmanship must minimize air leakage across the envelope as well as wind washing, indoor air washing, and air looping within envelope assemblies. Correct design, workmanship, and maintenance should prevent plumbing leakages or sweating of pipes running in or across walls and floors.

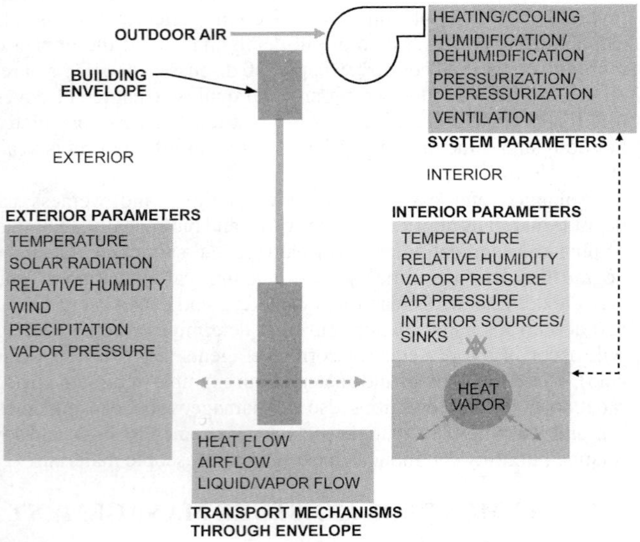

Fig. 1 Dynamic Interaction Between Air, Moisture, and Materials in HVAC Systems and Building Envelope

The HVAC system must provide a thermally comfortable and healthy indoor environment. Ventilation is necessary for delivering fresh air to building occupants. To maintain a set-point temperature when heat losses by transmission, infiltration, and ventilation exceed solar gains through the transparent and opaque envelope parts and internal gains by lighting, appliances and occupancy, heating is required. If, instead, the gains exceed the losses, cooling is needed. In both cases, the temperature difference with outdoors creates a thermal stack effect, which together with wind and fan operation maintains air pressure differentials with the exterior.

In heating mode, the indoor vapor concentration is typically left free floating, fluctuating with the vapor in the ventilation and infiltration air and the vapor released indoors. The net vapor concentration and the air temperature maintained by the HVAC system then determine the relative humidity indoors. Only when the ventilation and infiltrating air is too dry or too humid, when the vapor release indoors is very high, or when the building's function requires relative humidity control, must the HVAC system actively intervene to control humidity by removing water vapor from or adding water vapor to the indoor air (dehumidification and humidification). The energy required to humidify or dehumidify is called the **latent heat load**. In cooling mode, the latent load derives from the supply air temperature required for cooling, the dew-point temperature of the outdoor air, and the vapor released indoors. Condensation on the coil removes some portion of the moisture in the incoming ventilation air.

4. INDOOR WETTING AND DRYING

HVAC design or a durability assessment of the envelope and the whole building during design requires knowledge of the expected indoor humidity conditions. This is essential for making the right decisions to prevent mold, surface condensation, problematic interstitial condensation, and reduced drying.

The function of a building and the conditions outdoors dictate whether the indoor relative humidity needs control. The vapor balance, which considers the various mechanisms involved in vapor release, vapor removal, and vapor storage, is fundamental for this decision. One of the unknowns in this balance is the vapor release related to building use. A first approach consists of quantifying these releases directly. A second approach to get information starts from extended indoor/outdoor climate measurements in large sets of buildings to deduce a statistically relevant indoor-to-outdoor time-averaged difference in vapor pressure or vapor concentration in relation to the outdoor air temperature. Both methods are discussed in the following.

Understanding Vapor Balance

The air humidity indoors is assumed to be free floating. Five vapor fluxes then contribute to maintaining the equilibrium in a room:

- Vapor carried and supplied by infiltrating outdoor air and ventilation
- Vapor removed by exfiltrating indoor air and exhaust air
- Vapor released by occupants and their activities, by plants, water surfaces, and drying fabric parts

- Vapor adsorbed and desorbed by all hygroscopic surfaces present
- Vapor condensing on indoor surfaces that are colder than the dew-point temperature indoors or evaporating from indoor surfaces wetted by surface condensation

These five fluxes load and unload the room air with vapor. There is even a sixth flux: vapor inflow and outflow by diffusion through the envelope. Its magnitude, however, is insignificant compared to the five fluxes mentioned, hence ignoring it does not introduce any significant error.

Assuming ideal air mixing, the balance per room is expressed by

$$\sum G_{a,in}x_{v,in} + \sum G_{a,out}x_{v,i} + \sum_{j=1}^{n}\beta_j A_j(p_{sat,A_j}\phi_{A_j} - p_i) + \sum_{k=1}^{m}\beta_k A_k(p_{sat,A_k} - p_i) + G_{v,P} = V\frac{dx_{v,i}}{dt} \quad (1)$$

where

$G_{a,in}$ = all airflows entering room, including infiltration from outdoors, ventilation supply air, and infiltration from adjacent rooms, lb/h
$x_{v,in}$ = ratio of water vapor to dry air in entering air, lb/lb
$G_{a,out}$ = all airflows leaving room, including exfiltration to outdoors, exhaust air, and exfiltration to adjacent rooms, lb/h
$x_{v,i}$ = ratio of water vapor to dry air in room, lb/lb
β_j = surface film coefficient for diffusion at each hygroscopic surface, lb/ft²·h·in. Hg
A_j = area of each hygroscopic surface in room, ft²
p_i = water vapor pressure in room, in. Hg
$p_{sat,Aj}$ = vapor saturation pressure at different hygroscopic surfaces in room (fabric, furniture, and furnishings), in. Hg
$\phi_{sat,Aj}$ = relative humidity at different hygroscopic surfaces (fabric, furniture, and furnishings) in room on a scale from 0 to 1
β_k = surface film coefficient for diffusion at all room surfaces where vapor condenses or evaporates, lb/ft²·h·in. Hglb/ft²·h·in. Hg
A_j = area of all room surfaces experiencing surface condensation or surface condensate drying, ft²
$p_{sat,Aj}$ = vapor saturation pressure for room's various condensing and evaporating surfaces, in. Hg
$G_{v,P}$ = vapor release in room, lb/h
V = air volume of room, ft³
t = time, h

Solving Equation (1) requires knowledge of all in- and exfiltrating airflows between the room and all adjacent rooms and between the room and the outdoors, the ventilation supply airflow, exhaust airflow, water vapor ratio transported by all four airflows, surface temperatures and vapor balances at all hygroscopic surfaces, surface temperatures at all condensing and drying surfaces, and the surface film coefficients for diffusion at each of these surfaces (Hens 2012). Calculating requires numerical methods (preferably with dedicated software) to account for the transient nature of the variables involved (Woloszyn and Rode 2008).

In reality, because of stack effects, supply air jets, and convective plumes around people, the air in a room is never fully mixed, and vapor pressure gradients exist inside every room. Wetter, warmer air is also lighter and creates a positive temperature and humidity gradient along a room's height, even in stagnant conditions. Despite these internal gradients, whose quantification requires computational fluid dynamics (CFD) calculations, further discussion is based on the fully mixed assumption.

When considering steady-state conditions where the room air maintains an average humidity that does not change with time (e.g., because sorption/desorption by the hygroscopic surfaces no longer intervenes and all airflows and vapor releases are time averaged), in the absence of surface condensation and surface drying, the humidity balance per room simplifies to

$$\sum G_{a,in}x_{v,in} + \sum G_{a,out}x_{v,i} + G_{v,P} = 0 \quad (2)$$

If the only incoming airflow is from the outdoors (e.g., infiltration, natural ventilation, air-side economizer applications), equality between supply and exhaust yields the mean indoor relative humidity:

$$\phi = \frac{1}{p_{sat,i}}\left[\phi_o + \frac{R(459.7 + \theta_i)G_{v,P}}{\dot{V}_a}\right] \quad (3)$$

where

ϕ_i = indoor relative humidity on scale from 0 to 1
$p_{sat,i}$ = vapor saturation pressure for indoor temperature, in. Hg
ϕ_o = outdoor relative humidity on scale from 0 to 1
$p_{sat,o}$ = vapor saturation pressure for outdoor temperature, in. Hg
R = gas constant for water vapor, equal to 3.93 in. Hg·ft³/lb·°R = 85.78 lb/ft·lb·°R
θ_i = indoor temperature, °F
$G_{v,P}$ = average indoor vapor release, lb/h
$\dot{V}_a$ = outdoor air ventilation or/and infiltration flow, ft³/h

Relative humidity over longer periods of time thus depends on mean outdoor temperature (through $p_{sat,e}$), mean outdoor relative humidity, mean indoor air temperature (through $p_{sat,i}$), mean indoor vapor release, and mean outdoor air ventilation and/or infiltration flows.

In cold and temperate climates, the outdoor air ventilation required by building standards easily dilutes the vapor released in residences, offices, and schools. In temperate climates, heating tends to keep relative humidity levels below the upper acceptability threshold. In very cold climates, ambient temperature and outdoor relative humidity may be such that normal ventilation rates cannot raise the indoor relative humidity above 15 to 20% at room temperature. Humidification may then become necessary. In hot, humid climates, outdoor temperature and relative humidity can be so high that the combined action of ventilation, cooling, and vapor release raises the indoor relative humidity above the upper acceptability threshold. Supplemental air dehumidification then is required.

Where outdoor air infiltrates into the room and the ventilation system delivers supply air at a fixed condition, the mean relative humidity indoors becomes

$$\phi = \frac{1}{p_{sat,i}}\left[\frac{\dot{V}_{a,inf}p_{sat,o}\phi_o + \dot{V}_{a,s}p_{sat,s}\phi_s}{\dot{V}_{a,inf} + \dot{V}_{a,s}} + \frac{R(459.7 + \theta_i)G_{v,P}}{\dot{V}_{a,inf} + \dot{V}_{a,s}}\right] \quad (4)$$

where

ϕ_o = outdoor relative humidity on scale from 0 to 1
$p_{sat,o}$ = vapor saturation pressure for outdoor temperature, in. Hg
ϕ_s = relative humidity of supply air on scale from 0 to 1
$p_{sat,s}$ = vapor saturation pressure for supply air temperature, in. Hg
$\dot{V}_{a,inf}$ = infiltrating volumetric outdoor airflow, ft³/h
$\dot{V}_{a,s}$ = volumetric supply airflow, ft³/h

Hygric Buffering

In hygric buffering, vapor from the air is adsorbed into hygroscopic materials when the relative humidity rises, and released back into the air when the relative humidity lowers. On shorter time scales, hygric buffering by various elements such as indoor air and the building fabric (e.g., envelope, furniture, furnishings) dampens and shifts fluctuations in relative humidity and consequently in indoor vapor pressure compared to the fluctuations of the exterior vapor pressure and internal vapor release.

Figure 2 compares measured indoor vapor pressures in an office building with the exterior vapor pressure over the course of a winter month when exterior conditions changed from cold and dry to warmer

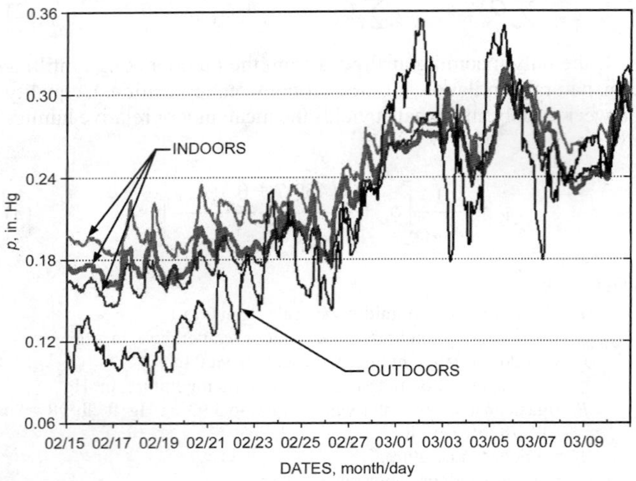

Fig. 2 Measured Water Vapor Pressure Outdoors and Indoors for Office Building

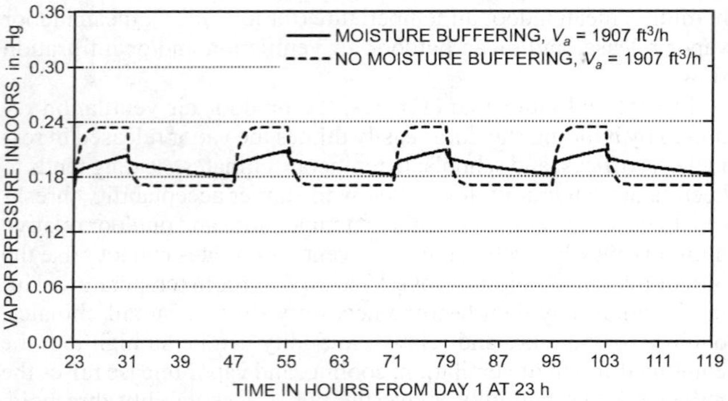

Room is 172 ft with air volume of 1413 ft³. Walls and ceiling finished with papered gypsum plaster, with (solid curve) and without (dashed curve) its moisture-buffering effects taken into account.

Fig. 3 Daily Vapor Pressure in Two-Person Bedroom

and more humid (Hens 2009a). Indoor vapor pressure remained higher than the outdoors during the cold, dry spell but dropped lower than outdoors during the warmer and more humid spells. Figure 3 shows the calculated buffering effect on the daily indoor vapor pressure in a well-ventilated two-person bedroom during winter (Hens 2012a). The effects of hygric buffering in keeping the daily changes in vapor pressure much lower than if only the air acted as buffering volume are obvious.

Antretter et al. (2012) performed a series of buffering experiments in a test room, simulating 4 to 6 day periods of summer and winter conditions. For the summer simulation, conditions were kept constant at 68°F, 90% rh, and 1 air change per hour (ach) for 1 to 3 days, then altered to an air change rate of zero and brought up to 95°F in 2 h. These conditions were held for 10 h, after which the temperature was returned to 68°F in 2 h and held there for the next 3 days. For the winter simulation, conditions were kept constant at 73.4°F, 50% rh, and 1 ach for 1 to 3 days, followed by 3 days with two vapor release peaks and a drop in the air change rate from 1 to 0.5 ach. The reference experiment was initially done without moisture buffering, and then repeated with 27 1 ft² sorptive tiles in the room. Figure 4 shows how the relative humidity changed the day after the initializing period. The effect of buffering is evident.

Hygroscopic buffering can even induce dampening and phase shifting on an annual basis in buildings with massive construction,

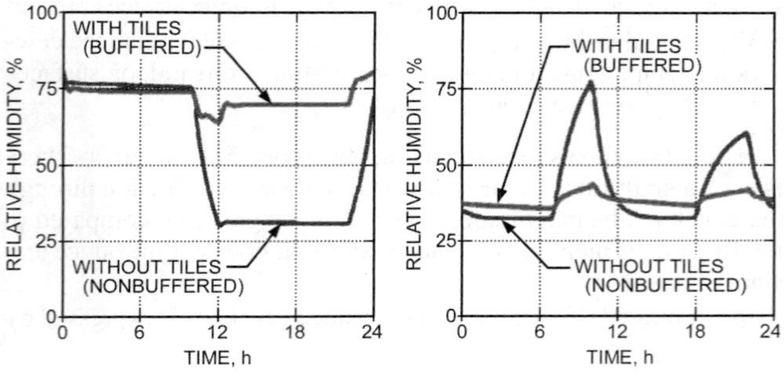

Fig. 4 Comparison of Daytime Relative Humidity for Summer and Winter Case

(Antretter et al. 2012)

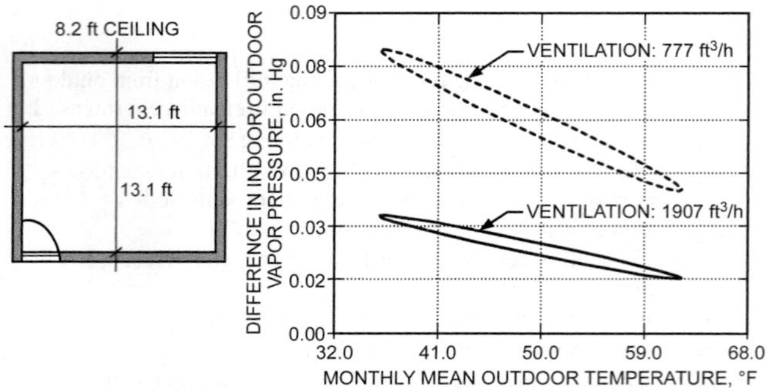

Fig. 5 Annual Monthly Averaged Indoor/Outdoor Vapor Pressure Difference in Bedroom of Figure 3

as shown by Figure 5 for the same bedroom as in Figure 3 (Hens 2012a). For the same vapor release indoors and constant ventilation rate, the monthly mean indoor vapor pressures form an inclined ellipse, with the highest value in winter, lowest in summer, and values lower in springtime than in autumn.

5. VAPOR RELEASE RELATED TO BUILDING USE

Water vapor indoors comes from several sources: building occupants and their activities (e.g., cleaning, cooking, showering, bathing), pets, plants, water surfaces, drying of wet fabric parts, etc. Releases can be divided into those dependent on indoor temperature and relative humidity, such as free water surfaces and wet fabrics, and those generally independent of these factors, such as human activities and plants (TenWolde and Pilon 2007). Accounting for these two types of sources, Equation (3) expands into

$$\phi_i = \frac{1}{p_{sat,\,i}} \frac{\phi_o p_{sat,o} + R(459.7 + \theta_i)(G_{vp} + \beta A_w p_{sat,w}) / \dot{V}_a}{1 + R(459.7 + \theta_i)\beta A_w / \dot{V}_a} \qquad (5)$$

where A_w is the free water surface, in ft².

Solving Equations (3) and (4) presumes knowledge of the magnitudes of the water vapor sources.

Residential Buildings

Estimating moisture loads requires knowledge of occupancy patterns and releases per individual, activity, plant, and water surface present. In most cases, the real occupancy is unknown, and the sources are even more difficult to quantify. Some activities in the same classification differ in the amount of vapor released (e.g., cooking, which varies with the type of meals prepared). Literature

Table 1 Vapor Released by Humans, Human Activities, and Plants

Source		Units	Release, × 10^{-3}
Humans	Light activity	lb/h	66-130
	Medium activity	lb/h	270-440
	Hard work	lb/h	440-660
Bathroom	Bath (15 min)	lb	130
	Shower (15 min)	lb	1460
Breakfast preparation for 4 people		lb	350-600
Lunch preparation for 4 people		lb	550-710
Dinner preparation for 4 people		lb	1210-1590
Breakfast dish washing for 4 people		lb	220
Lunch dish washing for 4 people		lb	150
Dinner dish washing for 4 people		lb	680
Simmering pot (diameter 5.9 in., 10 min)		lb	130
Boiling pot (diameter 5.9 in., 10 min)		lb	570
Potted flowers		lb/h per pot	5-20
Potted plants		lb/h per pot	7-30
Laundry			
Already spin-dried, until dry		lb/h	40-440
Dripping wet, until dry		lb/h	220-11001
Unvented drier, until dry		lb/h	4700-6390

Sources: IEA-ECB (1990), Kumaran and Sanders (2008), Sanders (1996), and TenWolde and Walker (2001).

Table 2 Daily Vapor Release by Humans, Human Activities, and Plants: Data from Three Countries

	Release		
Source, units	U.K.	Denmark	United States
Humans, lb/person per day	2.7	2.0	2.8
Cooking for 4 people using electricity, lb/day	4.4	2.0	2.7
Using gas, lb/day	6.6		5.5
Dishwashing, lb/day	0.9	0.9	1.1
Bathing/washing, lb/person per day	0.4	0.9	0.6
Washing clothes, lb/day	1.1		
Drying clothes, lb/day	3.3	4.0	4.9
Mopping floors, lb/day		0.4	
Plants, lb/plant per day		0.04	0.1
Refrigerator defrost, lb/day			1.1

Sources: IEA-ECB (1990), Kumaran and Sanders (2008), Sanders (1996), and TenWolde and Walker (2001).

Table 3 Vapor Released by Fuel Burning

Fuel	Vapor Released, lb/Btu × 10^{-5}
Natural gas	9.70
Manufactured gas	6.50
Paraffin	6.50
Coke	1.95

Sources: IEA-ECB (1990), Kumaran and Sanders (2008), Sanders (1996), and TenWolde and Walker (2001).

sources only give global average numbers and should therefore be used with care and understanding of the implicit assumptions. Tables 1 to 5 list example amounts by type (IEA-ECB 1990; Kumaran and Sanders 2008; Sanders 1996; TenWolde and Walker 2001).

The means in Table 6 yield, as least-square regressions,

$$G_{v,P} = 0.75 + 8.55n \ (r^2 = 0.999) \text{ in lb/day} \tag{6}$$

The individual data, however, produce a different relationship with considerably more scatter:

$$G_{v,P} = 7.12 + 6.22n \ (r^2 = 0.280) \text{ in lb/day} \tag{7}$$

In both equations, n is the number of family members weighted by the ratio between the hours each is at home and 24 h a day. For example, if four people occupy the home for 16 h daily, n is

$$n = 4 \times \left(\frac{16}{24}\right) = 2.7$$

Equation (7) indicates that each person who is at home 24 h/day adds 6.22 lb of water vapor to the indoor ambient. Measurements in some German apartments, however, suggested that this release rate is too high: for a family of three, the rates documented ranged from 12.3 to 17.2 lb per day (Hartmann et al. 2001), giving a value between 1.8 and 5.5 lb per person per day. Data from Estonia suggest a person present 24 h/day adds on average 2.2 lb to the vapor released (Kumaran and Sanders 2008).

Table 7 provides some country-related statistical information about the vapor release expected in different types of residential buildings.

Natatoriums

Evaporation from the pool surface, wet swimmers, and the wet floor around the pool are the main sources of water vapor. The evaporation rate is calculated based on the pool surface, multiplied by a factor that accounts for the average number of pool users and the wet floor around the pool:

$$G_{v,P} = f\beta A_{pool}(p_{sat,pool} - p_i) \tag{8}$$

where

$G_{v,P}$ = evaporation rate, lb/h
β = surface film coefficient for diffusion at water surface in pool, lb/ft^2·h·in. Hg
f = factor that accounts for average number of pool users and wet floor around pool
A_{pool} = water surface area, ft^2
$p_{sat,pool}$ = vapor saturation pressure at pool's water temperature, in. Hg

In cases where the airflow comes from outdoors, Equation (9) can be combined with Equation (3) to yield the mean vapor pressure in a natatorium:

$$p_i = \frac{\phi_o p_{sat,o} + p_{sat,pool}[R(459.7 + \theta_i)\beta f A_{pool}]/\dot{V}_a}{1 + [R(459.7 + \theta_i)\beta f A_{pool}]/\dot{V}_a} \tag{9}$$

Measurement of the water surface, water temperature, air temperature, relative humidity, ventilation supply flow, and number of users in a university and a recreation natatorium allowed estimating a surface film coefficient for diffusion β, with inclusion of the factor f (Table 8). For the university natatorium, the table includes all measured evaporation rates in lb/ft·h.

Using the data from the university pool in Table 8, the unknown factor f could be derived as a function of the number of pool users (Hens 2009b):

$$f = 1 + 91.05n \ (r^2 = 0.95) \tag{10}$$

where n is the number of users per square foot of pool surface.

For zero users, f is 1. The least-square line is depicted in Figure 6.

For example, given a water surface of 164 × 66 ft, a water temperature of 82.4°F, an air temperature of 86°F, an indoor relative humidity of 60%, and 100 pool users, evaporation amounts to 262 lb/h.

Table 4 Vapor Release for Family of Two, Both Working, Weekday Schedule

Time, h	Number of Occupants	Vapor Released, lb/h × 10^{-3}				Sum, lb × 10^{-3}
		Occupants	Cooking	Hygiene	Washing	
1-5	2	265				1320
6	2	265	530	1590		2380
7	2	265	530			790
8-17	0					0
18	2	265				270
19-10	2	265	1060			2650
21-22	2	265				530
23	2	265		1060		1320
24	2	265				270
Sum/day		3700	3180	2650		9520

Sources: IEA-ECB (1990), Kumaran and Sanders (2008), Sanders (1996), and TenWolde and Walker (2001).

Table 5 Vapor Release for Family of Four, One Parent and One Child at Home, Weekday Schedule

Time, h	Number of Occupants	Vapor Released, lb/h × 10^{-3}				Sum, lb × 10^{-3}
		Occupants	Cooking	Hygiene	Washing	
1-5	4	530				530
6-7	4	530	1060	1590		6350
8	2	265			265	530
9	1	265			400	660
10	1	265	1590		400	2250
11-12	2	265	2650	265		6350
13-14	2	265	1060	265		3180
15	2	265			265	530
16-17	2	400			265	1320
18	4	530				530
19	4	530	1060			1590
20	4	530	1060	530		2120
21-22	4	530				1060
23	4	530		530		1060
24	4	530				530
Sum/day		10,320	13,230	5290	1860	30,690

Sources: IEA-ECB (1990), Kumaran and Sanders (2008), Sanders (1996), and TenWolde and Walker (2001).

Table 6 Daily Vapor Release in Relation to Number of Family Members

	Family Members			
	2 (no children)	3 (1 child)	4 (2 children)	>4 (>2 children)
Vapor release, lb/day	17.6	26.5	30.9	>31 + 2.3 lb/day per child
		22.0		
	15.4	44.1		
			32.1	
	29.1	43.9	50.9	
		25.4		
		11.0-26.5		
		13.2-23.1		
	9.5		30.2	
	18.1	26.7	31.1	31.7
Mean	17.9	26.2	35.1	—

Sources: IEA-ECB (1990), Kumaran and Sanders (2008), Sanders (1996), and TenWolde and Walker (2001).

6. INDOOR/OUTDOOR VAPOR PRESSURE DIFFERENCE ANALYSIS

Measuring vapor release rates directly is a difficult and time-consuming task. The typical alternative is to monitor the indoor temperature and relative humidity and then compare the related mean indoor vapor pressure to the mean value outdoors. Therefore,

Table 7 Vapor Release Rates by Percentile

Country	Houses	Vapor Release Rate (lb/day)		
		10%	50%	90%
Canada	Detached	6.6	19.2	46.3
Denmark	Flats/mechanical ventilation	5.5	12.8	22.0
	Detached/mechanical ventilation	7.7	17.6	29.8
	Detached/natural ventilation	6.6	14.3	28.7
Sweden	Detached	10.1	19.2	34.6
	Multifamily dwelling units	5.3	12.3	24.3

Sources: IEA-ECB (1990), Kumaran and Sanders (2008), Sanders (1996), and TenWolde and Walker (2001).

most experiments looking to quantify air humidity in buildings use the **average indoor/outdoor vapor pressure difference Δp_{io}** or **average indoor/outdoor vapor concentration difference $\Delta \rho_{io}$**, represented by the second term in Equation (3) (i.e., the ratio between the average water vapor release and the average infiltration and ventilation flow):

$$\Delta p_{io} = \frac{R(459.7 + \theta_i)G_{v,p}}{\dot{V}_a} \quad \text{in in. Hg} \tag{11a}$$

or

$$\Delta \rho_{io} = \frac{G_{v,p}}{\dot{V}_a} \quad \text{in lb/ft}^{3S} \tag{11b}$$

Table 8 Measured Surface Film Coefficients for Diffusion, Related to Pool Surface

Natatorium 1 (university pool, water surface 3498 ft^2, water temperature between 80.6 and 87.8°F)

	Pool Users	Evaporation lb/ft^2·h × 10^{-3}	β lb/ft^2·h·in. Hg
			Measuring period 1
Water surface covered	0	7.8	1.22E-2
Uncovered	0	16.2	2.42E-2
			Measuring period 2
Water surface covered	0	14.1	1.62E-2
Uncovered	0	22.9	3.25E-2
			Measuring period 3
Pool in use, teaching	13	25.6	3.75E-2
revalidation	29	24.4	3.50E-2
free swim 1	42	33.4	5.75E-2
50+ swim	13	28.9	4.75E-2
free swim 2	65	35.2	6.75E-2
free swim 3	167	34.2	7.75E-2

Natatorium 2 (recreation pool, 117 ft long chute, waterfall, preschooler pool, massage pool, and whirlpool. Total water surface 5198 ft^2, water temperature between 86 and 87.8°F)

	Evaporation lb/ft^2·h × 10^{-3}	β lb/ft^2·h·in. Hg
(1) = water uncovered	35	3.75E-2
(1) + chute	—	4.25E-2
(1) + waterfall	—	4.50E-2
(1) + preschooler pool	—	4.75E-2
(1) + massage pool	—	3.75E-2
(1) + whirlpool	—	4.00E-2

Source: Hens (2009b).

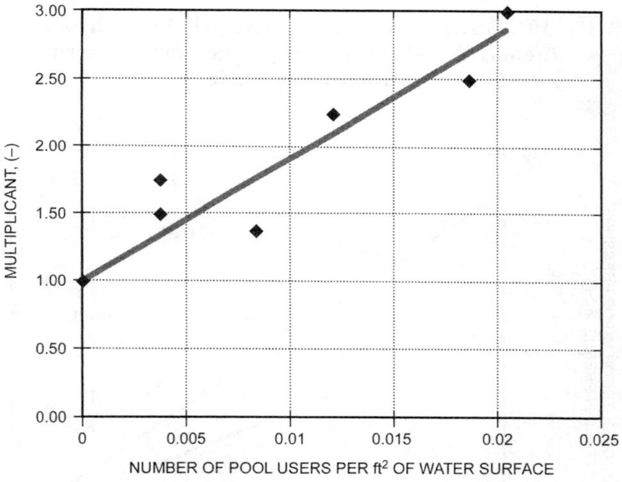

Fig. 6 Factor *f* as Function of Pool User Density

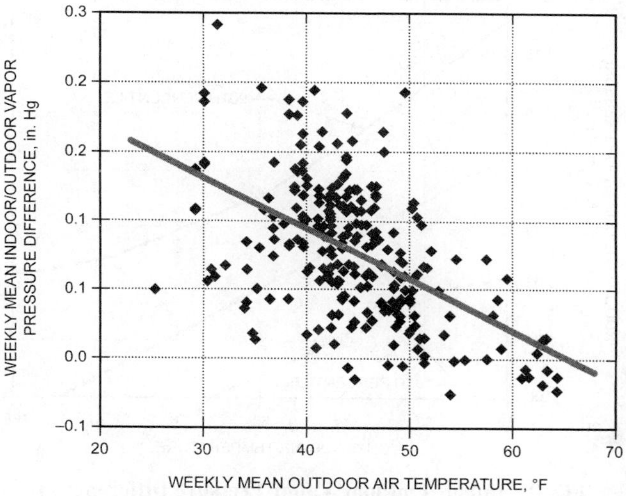

Fig. 7 Daytime Rooms in Dwellings

That difference over a given time span is mostly linked to the average air temperature outdoors over the same time span.

Residential Buildings

In North America and Europe, there have been many monitoring programs in residential buildings that gathered data on the indoor/outdoor vapor pressure and vapor concentration difference. The least-square linear relationships found between these data, averaged over a given time span, and the outdoor air temperature averaged over the same time span typically show a decreasing trend at higher temperatures. Figure 7 shows such a measured relationship for a region where massive construction prevails and homes tend to be naturally ventilated (Hens 2016).

There are two reasons for the decrease shown in Figure 7: (1) windows are more frequently opened in warmer weather, resulting in more outdoor air ventilation and thus lower indoor/outdoor vapor pressures and concentration differences at higher outdoor air temperatures; and (2) the massive building fabric that absorbs and releases significant amounts of vapor and consequently dampens and shifts the indoor vapor pressure compared to the outdoors even on an seasonal basis.

Ridley et al. (2008) took long-term measurements in 1065 U.K. living rooms and 916 U.K. bedrooms. The least-square regressions, based on half-hour averages, are shown in Figures 8 and 9. They are given by

Living rooms:

$$\Delta\bar{p}_{ie} = 0.217 - 0.0031\bar{\theta}_e \text{ in in. Hg} \quad (12)$$

Bedrooms:

$$\Delta\bar{p}_{ie} = 0.254 - 0.0039\bar{\theta}_e \text{ in in. Hg} \quad (13)$$

Figure 10 and Table 9 are based on measurements in 101 dwellings in Finland and Estonia (Kalamees et al. 2006). The data gained were approximated by three distinct linear segments with the running weekly average indoor/outdoor vapor pressure differences constant below 41°F and above 59°F outdoors and varying linearly in between. A distinction was also made between high, average, and low vapor load.

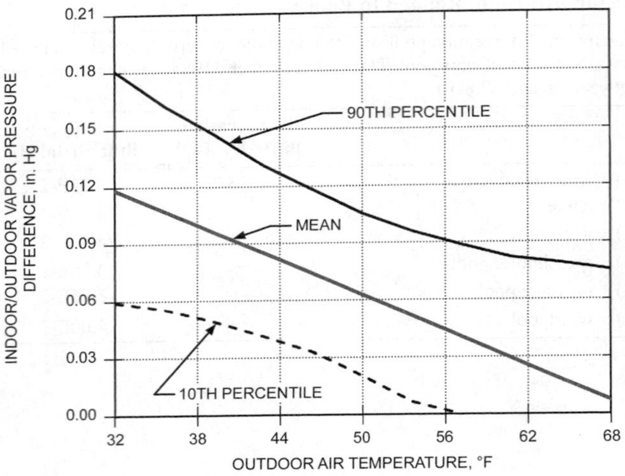

Fig. 8 Indoor/Outdoor Vapor Pressure Difference in 1065 U.K. Living Rooms

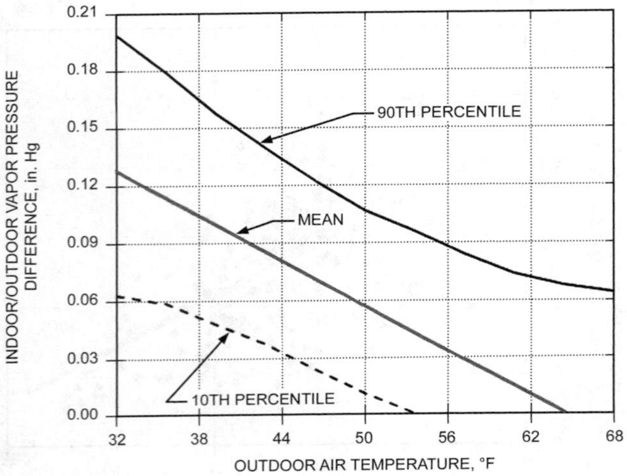

Fig. 9 Indoor/Outdoor Vapor Pressure Difference in 916 U.K. Bedrooms

Table 9 Finland and Estonia, Indoor Climate, Boundaries (Weekly Means)

	Indoor/Outdoor Vapor Pressure Difference, in. Hg		
Humidity Load	$\bar{\theta}_{e,w} < 41°F$	$41°F \le \bar{\theta}_{e,w} \le 59°F$	$\bar{\theta}_{e,w} > 59°F$
Low	0.16	$\frac{0.388 - 0.00556\bar{\theta}_{e,w}}{540 - 34\bar{\theta}_{e,w}}$	0.06
Average	0.20	$\frac{0.473 - 0.00667\bar{\theta}_{e,w}}{680 - 41\bar{\theta}_{e,w}}$	0.08
High	0.24	$\frac{0.559 - 0.00778\bar{\theta}_{e,w}}{810 - 47\bar{\theta}_{e,w}}$	0.10

The data collected in northern Canada (Kumaran and Sanders 2008) are represented by dots in Figure 10. The average indoor/outdoor vapor pressure the dot at top left represents a four-day period where the average outdoor temperature was –0.4°F and is substantially higher than the Finnish and Estonian high humidity results, apparently because a boil-water safety advisory led to an extremely high vapor release. The other dot at 55.4°F outdoor temperature is

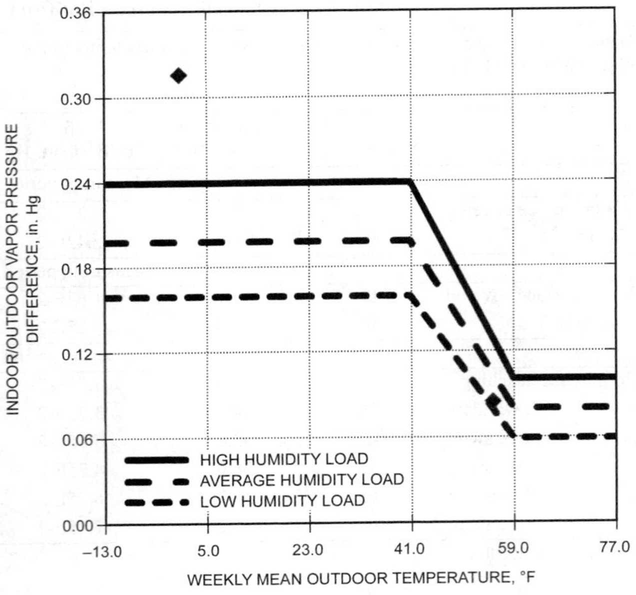

Fig. 10 Water Vapor Pressure Excess in Relation to the Running Weekly Mean Temperature for Northern Europe and Canada

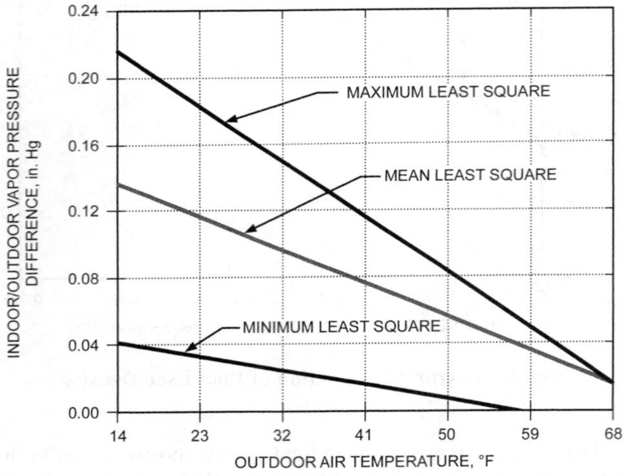

Fig. 11 Indoor/Outdoor Vapor Pressure Differences for 10 German Living Rooms

close to the Finnish and Estonian low-humidity curve, even though the number of household members was higher than typical for southern Canada. The dwellings monitored were measured to have air change rates up to 12 ach at 0.3 in. of water.

Measurements in the living rooms of 10 German homes are shown in Figure 11. The main variable seems to be the number of household members and their living habits, including window operation (Antretter et al. 2010).

Comparing the mean of the German averages with those from the U.K. in Figures 8 and 9 gives smaller differences at low outdoor temperatures, and higher differences at higher outdoor temperatures:

$$\Delta\bar{p}_{ie} = 0.168 - 0.00224\theta_e \text{ in in. Hg} \qquad (14)$$

Temperature and relative humidity data collected in 60 homes, equally spread over three climate zones in the United States (Pacific northwest, a cold location in the northeast, and a hot and humid location in the southeast) gave the values plotted in Figure 12 as the average relation between the moving monthly mean outdoor temperature and the moving monthly mean indoor/outdoor vapor pressure difference (Arena et al. 2010).

Figure 12 clearly shows the dehumidifying effect of air conditioning. The least-square regression line for a running monthly mean outdoor temperature below 67.1°F equals

$$\Delta\bar{p}_{ie} = 0.160 - 0.0013\,\bar{\theta}_e \quad (r^2 = 0.86) \tag{15}$$

Above 67.1°F, the line becomes

$$\Delta\bar{p}_{ie} = 0.642 - 0.0098\,\bar{\theta}_e \quad (r^2 = 0.92) \tag{16}$$

Indoor/outdoor vapor concentration difference measurements in 10 homes in Madison, WI, and 10 homes in Knoxville, TN, over a one-year period gave as monthly means the values shown in Figure 13 (Antretter et al. 2010).

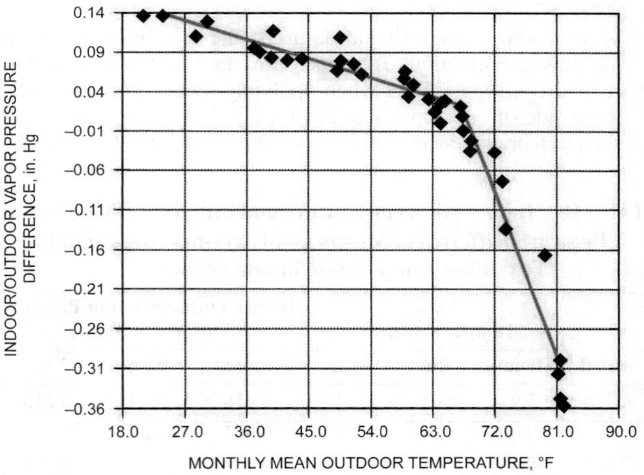

Fig. 12 Monthly Mean Indoor/Outdoor Vapor Pressure Difference in Relation to Monthly Mean Outdoor Air Temperature in Three U.S. Climate Zones

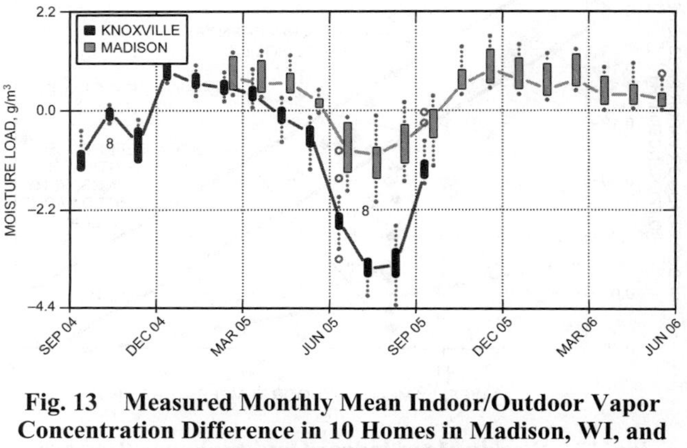

Fig. 13 Measured Monthly Mean Indoor/Outdoor Vapor Concentration Difference in 10 Homes in Madison, WI, and 10 Homes in Knoxville, TN
(Antretter et al. 2010)

The data are consistent with what Figure 12 shows: vapor pressure deficits only occur during the summer months in the Madison climate, and between April and November in the warmer, more humid Knoxville climate. Both situations are the result of dehumidification by air conditioning.

Measurements taken in 71 homes in Rhode Island are shown in Figure 14, giving the distribution of the measured indoor/outdoor vapor pressure difference at 32°F outdoors (Francisco and Rose 2010).

The mean was 0.117 in. Hg, close to what Equation (15) suggests, whereas the 95th percentile value equaled 0.228 in. Hg. This is higher than the data measured (Hens 2016) in the temperate climate of northwestern Europe, where for larger homes the 95th percentile on a weekly basis was

$$\Delta\bar{p}_{ie} = 0.311 - 0.00476\,\bar{\theta}_e \quad \text{(in. Hg)} \tag{17}$$

whereas for small homes the relation was

$$\Delta\bar{p}_{ie} = 0.350 - 0.00476\,\bar{\theta}_e \quad \text{(in. Hg)} \tag{18}$$

To minimize risk, the 95th percentile is often used for design purposes.

These results are based primarily on homes using natural ventilation. Many codes in the United States require homes to add mechanical ventilation to compensate for tighter envelopes. This significant difference must be addressed in evaluating residences with mechanical ventilation.

Measurements in 30 homes by Francisco et al. (2009) found that unvented gas fireplaces added on average about 0.0295 in. Hg to the indoor/outdoor vapor pressure difference.

Natatoriums

Vapor pressure difference measurements in natatoriums are few; however, studies have been conducted in some countries. Figure 15 gives weekly mean indoor/outdoor vapor pressure differences in relation to the weekly mean outdoor air temperature, measured in 20 natatoriums in a temperate region (Hens 2016).

There is a considerable amount of scatter. Least-square regressions for the mean and 95th percentile are

Mean

$$\Delta\bar{p}_{ie} = 0.508 - 0.00454\,\bar{\theta}_{e,w} \quad (r^2 = 0.13) \tag{19}$$

95th percentile

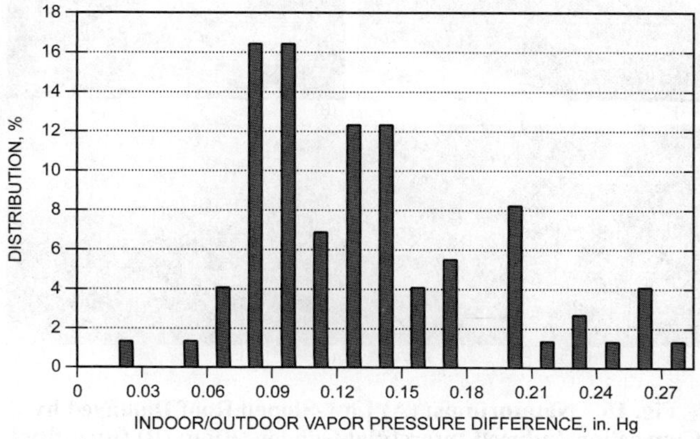

Fig. 14 Indoor/Outdoor Vapor Pressure Difference with Intersect at 32°F for 71 Rhode Island Homes

$$\Delta \bar{p}_{ie} = 0.675 - 0.00454\,\bar{\theta}_{e,w} \quad (r^2 = 0.13) \tag{20}$$

The data clearly show that, although not highly correlated with the outdoor temperature, the vapor pressure differences in natatoriums are consistently high. These buildings therefore require specific measures to prevent moisture accumulation in the envelope, which can lead to degradation (Figure 16).

Student Residences and Schools

The few measuring campaigns undertaken in student residences and schools in a temperate-climate region gave a very diffuse picture, with a large spread in weekly mean indoor/outdoor vapor pressure differences; see Figure 17 (Hens 2005) and Table 10 (Hens et al. 2007).

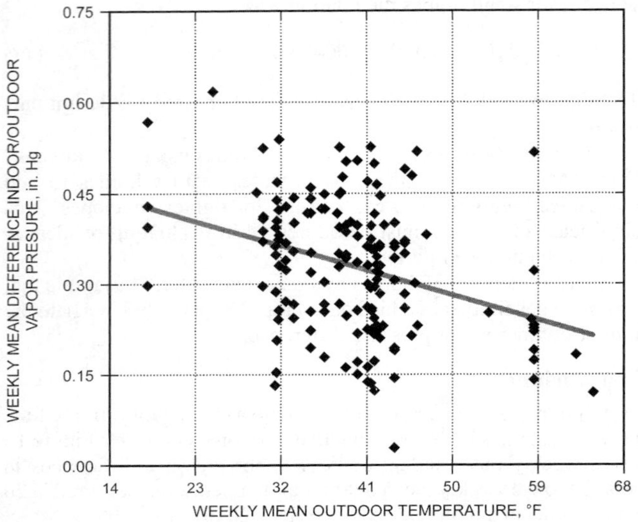

Fig. 15 Weekly Mean Indoor/Outdoor Vapor Pressure Differences for 20 Natatoriums (Measured Data and Least-Square Straight Line)

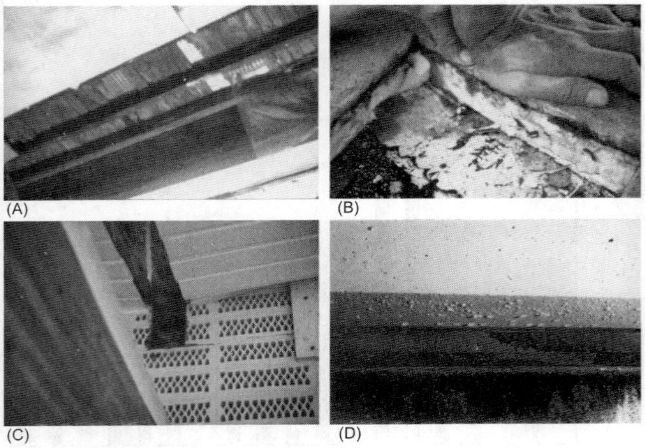

Fig. 16 Natatoriums: (A) Low-Sloped Roof Damaged by Convection-Induced Interstitial Condensation; (B) Interstitial Condensation in Low-Sloped Roof Polyurethane Foam Insulation; (C) Timber Beam Collapse; (D) Abundant Surface Condensation on Window and Lintel

7. AVOIDING MOISTURE PROBLEMS

Avoiding mold, surface condensation, and interstitial condensation in cold and temperate climates requires the following measures:

- Building envelopes must be insulated such that the risk of surface mold and surface condensation at room temperature and typical levels of relative humidity is as close to zero as possible. Insulation requirements imposed by current building codes for energy efficiency are typically much higher than those needed to address risk of condensation.
- Avoid structural thermal bridges. No point on the indoor surface of an opaque portion of the envelope should be colder than the indoor surface of the glazed portion
- Minimize infiltration and exfiltration by making the envelope as airtight as possible.
- Avoid air gaps in envelope construction that would lead to wind washing in and along the inner face, and indoor air washing along the outer face of the thermal insulation.
- For lightweight construction in heating-dominated climates, if necessary, mount a continuous vapor retarding layer at the inner side of the insulation. In hot, humid climates, install the vapor control on the exterior or warm side of the insulation or building envelope.
- Vapor control layers should be used with caution in stone and masonry construction. Take measures to avoid problems with solar-driven vapor flow when applying vapor retarders on the inner side of envelopes that have a rain-buffering outer finish, such as a brick veneer [see Derome and Saneinejad (2009)].

Table 10 Indoor Air Temperature and Indoor/Outdoor Vapor Pressure Difference: Means and Extremes Measured in Five Temperate-Climate Schools

	Temperature, °F			Indoor/Outdoor Vapor Pressure Difference, in. Hg		
School	Mean	Min	Max	Mean	Min	Max
1	63.9	58.5	73.8	0.058	–0.041	0.213
2	59.0	53.6	80.2	0.063	–0.046	0.236
3	68.5	57.6	77.4	0.058	–0.079	0.313
4	63.5	50.5	73.6	0.045	–0.050	0.180
5	64.2	57.4	74.1	0.011	–0.119	0.146

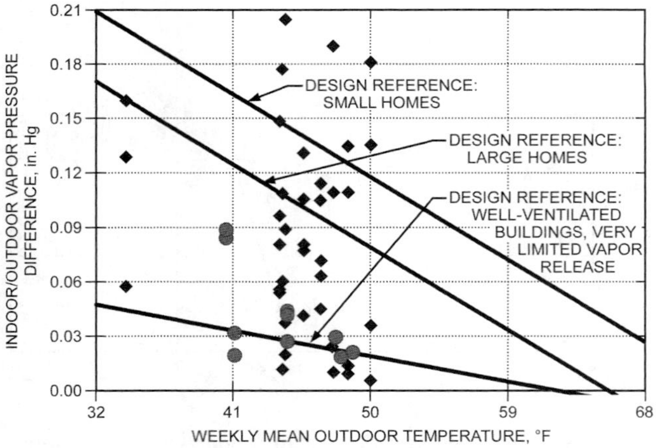

Fig. 17 Weekly Mean Indoor/Outdoor Vapor Pressure Differences in Four Student Residences

- Never sandwich layers between vaportight materials on both sides. This is especially detrimental when thermal insulation is one of the layers and the others contain construction moisture.

HVAC Systems

The mechanical system can affect the air pressure differences among building zones, and between building zones and the outdoors. HVAC operation influences the indoor relative humidity and, consequently, indoor/outdoor vapor pressure differences. To minimize humidity concerns,

- Insulate chilled-water pipes and cool-air ducts to minimize heat gain. The insulation must have a moisture resistant vapor-control layer on the outer surface and be thick enough to prevent surface condensation. Warm-water pipes and warm-air ducts require insulation to minimize heat losses. For more details, see Chapter 23.
- Natural or mechanical ventilation in temperate climates should keep the indoor relative humidity within the 30 to 70% range.
- HVAC systems in hot and humid climates should ventilate the building while cooling and dehumidifying the ventilation air. The building should also be positively pressurized. In very cold climates, HVAC systems should ventilate and warm the building while humidifying the air and putting the building under negative pressure.

Ground Pipes

In temperate climates, ground pipes (ventilation air ducts buried in the soil near the building) are sometimes used to moderate the condition of incoming ventilation air. Rain and groundwater must be prevented from entering these pipes: water penetration turns the pipes into air humidifiers, with very negative consequences for the indoor air quality. In dry pipes, relative humidity during the warm season should not exceed the mold threshold: too high a relative humidity in the pipes can load the supply air with mold spores, which then germinate in the supply filter. These risks are high enough that ground pipes are not recommended as a safe choice (Hens 2012b).

Building Fabric

If there is no watertight layer or capillary break inserted above grade, stone-based building fabrics may suffer from rising damp and salt transport. Building parts, wetted by rising damp, act as permanent moisture sources affecting indoor vapor release and the indoor/outdoor vapor pressure difference.

Building Envelope

Even when raintightness is guaranteed, excessive indoor vapor pressures can induce mold and condensation on interior surfaces and favor interstitial condensation in assemblies. Chapters 25 and 27 deal in more detail with moisture transport in the building envelope.

Mold Growth. Mold growth begins on interior opaque surfaces where the surface temperature and relative humidity pass the **mold threshold** for a long enough period of time. For example, if a material has absorbed an amount of water from a leak, drying may temporarily sustain a surface relative humidity high enough to be conductive for mold. The IEA Annex 14 reports (IEA-EBC 1990a, 1990b) contain two design formulas for estimating mold risk. The one calculates the four-week threshold, above which the likelihood that mold will develop is close to 100%. The other evaluates the surface relative humidity needed for mold development at shorter time intervals. Combining the two yields

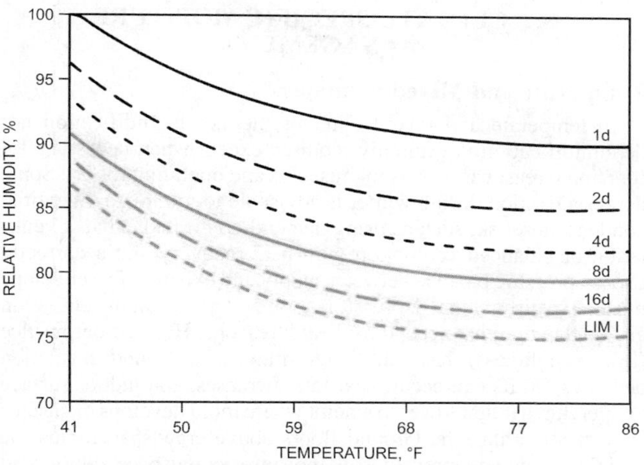

Class I substrates are biologically recyclable building materials: wallpaper, plasterboard, permanent elastic joint materials, and other biodegradable materials.

Fig. 18 Sedlbauer's Isopleth System for Class I Substrates: Time Until Germination
(Sedlbauer 2001)

$$\phi_{crit} \geq \min\{100;(0.033\theta_{si}^2 - 1.5\theta_{si} + 96)[1.24 - 0.072\ln(T)]\} \quad (21)$$

where

ϕ_{crit} = relative humidity at surface, on scale from 0 to 100
θ_{si} = indoor surface temperature, °F (41°F ≤ θ_{si} ≤ 77°F)
T = time span, days

The threshold for a one-day period touches 99%.

Since completion of Annex 14, two more comprehensive models have been published: Sedlbauer (2001) (Figure 18), and Viitanen and Ojanen (2007). More recent work, however, confirms that predictions with any model give varying results for growth probability and mold density (Vereecken and Roels 2012).

Surface Condensation. Each time the indoor surface temperature somewhere on the envelope drops below the dew point of the indoor air, condensate forms. Glazed surfaces are especially prone to surface condensation. Hygroscopic materials (e.g., wood, masonry, gypsum, some plasters) may buffer the local surface wetness, preventing visible condensate but increasing the moisture content in the material. When short periods of condensation or high humidity alternate with periods of drying, there tend to be no negative consequences. Long-lasting surface condensation or long periods of high humidity, however, degrade timber and other materials, and condensate deposited on aluminum frames may wet the window reveals. Thermal bridges can experience prolonged periods of condensation that cause indoor-side finish damage, such as wallpaper glue giving away.

Interstitial Condensation. Water vapor condensation within envelope parts is called **interstitial condensation**, and is caused by temperature and vapor pressure gradients pointing in the same direction. The driving forces are diffusion driven by vapor pressure differences, moist air leakage (in- or exfiltration), or absorption of wind-driven rain. In wood and wood-based materials, interstitial condensation may lift the surface relative humidity above the mold threshold and, worse, the moisture content above the rot threshold. When the relative humidity adjacent to nonporous, nonabsorbing, or capillary wet layers in an assembly becomes 100%, condensation with droplet formation occurs, followed by runoff and sometimes dripping, which is especially annoying for the occupants.

8. CLIMATE-SPECIFIC MOISTURE MANAGEMENT

Temperate and Mixed Climates

In temperate and mixed climates, neither humidification nor dehumidification is explicitly required except when necessary for functional reasons, such as in museums and operating rooms. Some depressurization during winter is advisable to minimize interstitial condensation risk, such as using demand-controlled exhaust ventilation or balanced ventilation with heat recovery and a correctly chosen pressure balance between supply and exhaust. The envelope must be so airtight that depressurization will not result in ventilation airflow beyond that needed for health reasons. High air permeance (low airtightness) has additional drawbacks: sound insulation degrades, drafts can occur, heat loss increases, and indoor surface temperatures might lower to a point where mold develops or surface condensation appears. Ground floors above crawlspaces must be airtight enough to prevent soil moisture, crawlspace odors, and radon from infiltrating into the conditioned space.

Acceptable envelope performance requires that the indoor surface temperature be high enough to prevent mold from occurring at the expected average vapor release indoors, the environmental conditions outdoors, the desired thermal comfort settings and the mean ventilation rate required for good IAQ and human health. Ventilation is also used to avoid acute surface condensation, which occurs each time the indoor dew-point temperature exceeds the envelope's indoor surface temperature somewhere (a common site is glazed surfaces). For a detailed analysis of mold and surface condensation, see Hens (1999), Sedlbauer (2001), Vereecken and Roels (2012), and Viitanen and Ojanen (2007).

With well-insulating, double- and triple-glazed, gas-filled, low-e windows in new construction and retrofits, water can also condense on the outdoor surface during cold, clear-sky nights, somewhat obscuring visibility.

Hot and Humid Climates

In hot and humid climates, to avoid mold growth and surface condensation, the indoor relative humidity should be kept below 60% through dehumidification. Brief periods of elevated relative humidity, however, do not necessarily result in mold germination. Keeping the building under positive air pressure is required to minimize interstitial condensation in wall cavities.

Dehumidification. Air-handling units that mix outdoor air with return air to provide constant airflows at variable supply temperatures do not provide continuous dehumidification. At higher supply air temperatures, the cooling coil does not remove moisture from the ventilation air, which can lead to elevated indoor relative humidity and a high potential for microbial growth. This becomes even more pronounced in energy-efficient buildings with reduced sensible cooling loads and long *off* times for the cooling coil, which significantly reduces the effectiveness of moisture removal (Rudd 2010; Rudd et al. 2005). For variable-supply-temperature systems, the ventilation air portion can be preconditioned using a dedicated outdoor air system (DOAS). These systems dehumidify only the ventilation air, and cooling loads are handled by a separate air-handling unit, so a DOAS is a good choice for providing continuously dehumidified ventilation air. If heat recovery is economically feasible without compromising pressurization, a DOAS with heat recovery is an energy-efficient alternative if the supply and return fans maintain correct pressurization, and the relative humidity of air passing through the supply filters remains low enough to avoid mold growth there. Because schools, office buildings, hospitals, and dwellings require continuous ventilation based on the number of occupants, demand-controlled DOAS-based outdoor ventilation air dehumidification can be achieved at a constant cooling-coil temperature. Reheat of the ventilation air may be required to avoid overcooling the supply air if ventilation demands are high. The resulting system provides more stable dehumidification and improved relative humidity control.

Alternatives for residential construction include local stand-alone dehumidifiers, with or without central system mixing; continuous exhaust/supply indoor air dehumidification using either a central HVAC system with subcooling followed by reheat, or ducted dehumidifiers; or ducted direct-expansion (DX) condenser-regenerated desiccant dehumidifiers (Harriman and Lstiburek 2009; Rudd 2013).

Pressurization. Dehumidification reduces the indoor vapor pressure below the outdoor vapor pressure level. Cooling does the same for temperature. As a result, the vapor pressure and temperature gradients cause moisture migration by diffusion toward the interior. If the envelope is not airtight, building depressurization and related infiltration increase this moisture flow through the exterior wall and connected partition wall cavities. This may raise the relative humidity at or near surfaces in these cavities to levels that allow mold, or even condensation. Pressurization reverses the airflow, allowing dehumidified indoor air to exfiltrate and neutralizing inward vapor diffusion. In any case, the envelope should be constructed as airtight as possible so that pressurization does not require unnecessarily high supply ventilation.

Cold Climates

In cold climates, the techniques for avoiding mold and surface condensation are the same as in temperate climates. During cold seasons, the indoor relative humidity can drop well below 30%. Maintaining healthy levels of relative humidity then requires humidification, which results in an increased indoor/outdoor vapor pressure difference for a temperature gradient pointing to the outdoors and vapor diffusion toward the exterior.

Humidification. At part load, on/off air-handling units that heat and humidify a mixture of outdoor and return air operate so intermittently that indoor relative humidity levels may drop substantially during off periods. Moisture buffering by the building fabric, furniture, and furnishings can reduce that variation in relative humidity (Simonson et al. 2004a, 2004b). A better choice in larger buildings is a DOAS that restricts humidification to the ventilation air, handling heating loads by a separate system. Because the ventilation required mainly depends on the number of occupants, the space can be humidified by using steam injection modulated according to demand, or by preheating the ventilation air followed by adiabatic humidification and reheat to the indoor temperature set point. The result is more stable humidification and better relative humidity control. Alternatives in homes are stand-alone humidifiers, continuous-supply air humidification at constant dew-point temperature by the central HVAC system, etc.

Pressurization/Depressurization. Pressurizing buildings in cold climates leads to air exfiltration, which provides an extra vehicle for vapor egress. Together with diffusion, this could lead to severe interstitial condensation in envelope assemblies, especially when the indoor vapor retarder is ineffective and the air barrier is not continuous. Depressurizing a building, which leads to infiltration, is as effective way to avoid interstitial condensation problems, as long as the envelope is sufficiently airtight that depressurization does not require ventilation rates beyond those needed by the occupant load. If the envelope is too air permeable, not only will large exhaust rates be required but all drawbacks mentioned in the section on Temperate and Mixed Climates will apply but be more severe.

9. MOISTURE MANAGEMENT IN OTHER HANDBOOK CHAPTERS

Other chapters and volumes of the *ASHRAE Handbook* also provide useful information on moisture and humidity.

In this volume,

Ch. 1 Perfect gas relations and thermodynamic properties to analyze conditions and processes involving moist air
4 Heat transfer processes that affect temperature and moisture transport in buildings
9 Effects of relative humidity, temperature, and vapor pressure on thermal comfort
10 Effects of relative humidity on indoor environmental quality (IEQ), mold, and humidifier fever
11 Controlling mold through control of relative humidity at material surfaces
12 Temperature and relative humidity's effects on olfactory perception and perceived indoor air quality
13 Intra- and interzone airflows and pollutant transfer, including water vapor
14 Data on outdoor dry- and wet-bulb temperatures for design purposes
15 Relation between relative humidity and condensation potential on glazing
16 Control of interstitial condensation by controlling air leakage across the envelope, and moisture control by modulating air infiltration across the envelope
17 Formulas to calculate latent load for air humidification (often required to maintain comfortable relative humidity indoors)
18 Latent heat gain from moisture diffusion and various moisture sources, including natatoriums
19 Cooling and dehumidification coils, and cooling towers
23 Condensation control for below-ambient-temperature HVAC components
25/26/27 Detailed information on heat, air, and moisture response of building envelope assemblies; includes fundamentals of combined heat, air, and moisture movement (e.g., moisture content, buffering, flow), material properties (e.g., sorption isotherms, vapor permeability), and examples

2014 ASHRAE Handbook—Refrigeration

Ch. 7 Role of moisture as a contaminant in refrigeration systems
10 How moisture diffusion through low-water-vapor-permeance insulation and water-permeable claddings can produce damaging condensation and moisture accumulation
23 Moisture aspects of refrigerated-facility envelope design
24 Sensible and latent heat loads in refrigerated facilities
44 Specific ceiling moisture problems in ice rinks as a consequence of long-wave radiation between ice surface and ceiling

2015 ASHRAE Handbook—Applications

Ch. 1 Residential humidification and dehumidification
2 Humidity control in stores
3 Thermal comfort design criteria and load characteristics in commercial and public buildings
4 Stack effect and practical considerations for minimizing stack effects
5 Latent load in arenas, humidity problems in ice rinks, vapor release in natatoriums with some consequences for envelope design
6 Dehumidification as a load characteristic, considers moisture control using DOAS
7 Humidity control in classrooms, libraries, gymnasiums, showers, and natatoriums
8 Role of relative humidity in health care for different kinds of patients
9 Dry- and wet-bulb design criteria for general and specialized spaces in courthouses and detention/correction facilities
16 Relative humidity control in laboratories
18 Relative humidity control in clean spaces
19 Drawbacks for data processing and telecommunication facilities of high (anodic failure) and low relative humidity (electrostatic discharge); envelope considerations and humidity control
20 Paper moisture content control and controlling relative humidity in pressrooms for various printing processes
21 Relative humidity and textiles
22 Relative humidity and photographic materials
23 Importance and impact of relative humidity mean values and fluctuations on museum artifacts, library books, and other archival materials
24 Role of relative humidity in environmental control in animal and plant facilities
25 Role of relative humidity in crop drying
26 Moisture control in processing wood and paper
30 Industrial drying as a process
31 Ventilation for industrial processes
33 Ventilation to reduce relative humidity in kitchens (commercial and residential)
44 Control of liquid water and vapor in building envelopes
47 Design of system controls for humidity
52 Humidification and dehumidification in evaporative cooling
62 Practical applications of moisture management in buildings

2016 ASHRAE Handbook—Systems and Equipment

Ch. 4 Humidity control and air-handling unit psychrometric processes
11 Condensate removal from temperature-regulated systems and steam traps
12 Condensate drainage and return in district systems
22 Optimum humidity range for human comfort and health; surface and interstitial condensation; some data on indoor vapor release
23 Dehumidification coils
24 Methods of dehumidification, with emphasis on sorption dehumidification
25 Mechanical dehumidification
26 Air-to-air energy recovery processes, from basic thermodynamics to types and applications of air-to-air heat exchangers and technical considerations; includes condensation and freeze-up in air-to-air heat exchangers, and gives an energy and moisture recovery procedure
40 Evaporation-based cooling towers
41 Evaporative humidification and dehumidification

REFERENCES

ASHRAE members can access *ASHRAE Journal* articles and ASHRAE research project final reports at technologyportal.ashrae.org. Articles and reports are also available for purchase by nonmembers in the online ASHRAE Bookstore at www.ashrae.org/bookstore.

Antretter, F., A. Holm, A. Karagiozis, and S. Glass. 2010. Interior temperature and relative humidity distributions in mixed-humid and cold climates as building simulation boundary conditions. *Proceedings of the Buildings XI Conference*, Clearwater Beach.

Antretter, F., C. Mitterer, and S.-M. Young. 2012. Use of moisture-buffering tiles for indoor climate stability under different climatic requirements. *HVAC&R Research* (now *Science and Technology for the Built Environment*) 18(1-2):275-282.

Arena, L., A. Karagiozis, and P. Mantha. 2010. Monitoring of internal moisture loads in residential buildings-research findings in three different climate zones. *Proceedings of the Buildings XI Conference*, Clearwater Beach.

ASHRAE. 2009. Criteria for moisture-control design analysis in buildings. ANSI/ASHRAE *Standard* 160-2009.

ASHRAE. 2012. *Position document on limiting indoor mold and dampness in buildings.*

Derome, D., and S. Saneinejad. 2009. The nature, significance and control of solar-driven diffusion in wall systems. ASHRAE Research Project RP-1235, *Final Report*.

Francisco, P., and W. Rose. 2010. Temperature and humidity measurements in 71 homes. *Proceedings of the Buildings XI Conference*, Clearwater Beach.

Francisco, P., J. Gordon, and W. Rose. 2009. Indoor moisture in 30 homes using unvented gas fireplaces. *ASHRAE Transactions* 115(2).

Hartmann, T., D. Reichel, and W. Richter. 2001. Feuchteabgabe in Wohnungen—Alles gesagt? *Gesundheits-Ingenieur* 122(4):189-195. In German.

Harriman, III, L., and J.W. Lstiburek. 2009. *The ASHRAE guide for buildings in hot & humid climates*. ASHRAE.

Hens, H. 1999. Fungal defacement in buildings, a performance related approach. *International Journal of HVAC&R Research* (now *Science and Technology for the Built Environment*) 5(3):265-289.

Hens, H. 2005. Energy consumption in student residences, impact of building performance, usage patterns and indoor climate. *Proceedings Clima 2005*, Lausanne.

Hens, H. 2009a. IEA-ECBCS Annex 41 whole building heat, air and moisture response. *ASHRAE Transactions* 115(2).

Hens, H. 2009b. Indoor climate and building envelope performance in indoor swimming pools. In *Energy efficiency and new approaches*, N. Bayazit, G. Manioglu, G. Oral, and Z. Yilmaz, eds. Istanbul Technical University.

Hens, H. 2012a. *Building physics, heat, air and moisture: Fundamentals and engineering methods with examples and exercises*, 2nd ed. Ernst & Sohn, Berlin.

Hens, H. 2012b. Passive houses: what may happen when energy efficiency becomes the only paradigm. *ASHRAE Transactions* 118(1).

Hens, H. 2016. *Applied building physics, ambient conditions, building performance and material properties*, 2nd ed. Ernst & Sohn, Berlin.

Hens, H., and V. De Meulenaer. 2007. Schools, all problem buildings? *Proceedings Clima 2007*, Helsinki.

Holm, A. 2008. Whole building heat, air, moisture response: Applications: Indoor environment, energy, durability. *Final Report*, vol. 4. International Energy Agency Energy Conservation in Buildings and Community Systems (ECBCS), Annex 41: Whole Building Heat, Air and Moisture Response. www.ecbcs.org/annexes/annex41.htm.

IEA-ECB. 1990. *Sourcebook*. International Energy Agency Energy and Community in Buildings Programme, Annex 14: Condensation and Energy, Leuven.

IEA-ECB. 1990. *Guidelines and practice*. International Energy Agency Energy and Community in Buildings Programme, Annex 14: Condensation and Energy, Leuven.

Kalamees, T., J. Vinha, and J. Kurnitski. 2006. Indoor humidity loads in light-weight timber-framed detached houses. *Journal of Building Physics* 29(3):219-246. jen.sagepub.com/content/29/3/219.full.pdf+html

Kumaran, K., and C. Sanders. 2008. Whole building heat, air, moisture response: Boundary conditions and whole building HAM analysis. *Final Report*. International Energy Agency Energy Conservation in Buildings and Community Systems (ECBCS), Annex 41: Whole Building Heat, Air and Moisture Response. www.ecbcs.org/annexes/annex41.htm.

Mumovic, D., and M. Santamouris, eds. 2009. *A handbook on sustainable building design and engineering: An integrated approach to energy, health and operational performance*. Earthscan, London.

Ridley, I., M. Davies, S.H. Hong, and T. Oreszcyn. 2008. Vapour pressure excess in living rooms and bedrooms of English dwellings: Analysis of the warm front dataset. Appendix III of Boundary Conditions and Whole Building HAM Analysis. *Final Report*, International Energy Agency Energy and Community in Buildings Programme, Annex 41: Whole Building Heat, Air and Moisture Response (MOIST-EN), Leuven.

Rudd, A.F. 2010. Enhanced dehumidification. Building America *Report* 1008. U.S. Department of Energy, Washington, D.C. buildingscience.com/documents/bareports/ba-1008-building-america-enhanced-dehumidification/view.

Rudd, A.F. 2013. Supplemental dehumidification in warm-humid climates. Building America *Report* 1310. U.S. Department of Energy, Washington, D.C. buildingscience.com/documents/bareports/ba-1310-supplemental-dehumidification-warm-humid-climates/view.

Rudd, A.F., J.W. Lstiburek, and K. Ueno. 2005. Residential dehumidification systems research for hot-humid climates, September 1, 2001-December 30, 2003. *Report* NREL/SR-550-36643.

Sanders, C. 1996, Environmental conditions. *Final Report*, vol. 2, International Energy Agency Energy and Community in Buildings Programme, Annex 24: Heat, Air and Moisture Transport in Insulated Envelope Parts, Leuven.

Sedlbauer, K. 2001. *Vorhersage von Schimmelpilzbildung auf und in Bauteilen (Prediction of mould development on and in building assemblies)*. Ph.D. dissertation, University of Stuttgart (in German).

Simonson, C., M. Salonvaara, and T. Ojanen. 2004a. Heat and mass transfer between indoor air and a permeable and hygroscopic building envelope: Part 1—Field measurements. *Journal of Thermal Envelope and Building Science* 28(1):63-101.

Simonson, C., M. Salonvaara, and T. Ojanen. 2004b. Heat and mass transfer between indoor air and a permeable and hygroscopic building envelope: Part 2—Verification and numerical studies. *Journal of Thermal Envelope and Building Science* 28(2):161-185.

TenWolde, A., and I. Walker. 2001. Interior moisture design loads for residences. *Proceedings of the Buildings VIII Conference*, Clearwater Beach.

TenWolde, A., and C. Pilon. 2007. The effect of indoor humidity on water vapor release in homes. *Proceedings of the Buildings X Conference*, Clearwater Beach.

Trechsel, H., ed. 1994. Moisture control in buildings. ASTM *Manual Series* MNL 18. American Society for Testing and Materials, West Conshohocken, PA.

Vereecken, E., and S. Roels. 2012. Review of mould prediction models and their influence on mould risk evaluation. *Building and Environment* 52:296-310.

Viitanen, J., and T. Ojanen. 2007. Improved model to predict mold growth in building materials. *Proceedings of the Buildings X Conference*, Clearwater Beach.

Woloszyn, M., and C. Rode. 2008. Whole building heat, air, moisture response: Modeling principles and common exercises. *Final Report*, International Energy Agency Energy and Community in Buildings Programme, Annex 41: Whole Building Heat, Air and Moisture Response (MOIST-EN), Leuven.

BIBLIOGRAPHY

BRE. 2016. *BREEAM International New Construction*. Building Research Establishment, Watford, U.K.

Harriman, III, L., G. Brundrett, and R. Kittler. 2001. *Humidity control design guide for commercial and institutional buildings*. ASHRAE.

Künzel, H.M. 2006. Indoor relative humidity in residential buildings—A necessary boundary condition to assess the moisture performance of building envelope systems. *Zeitschrift für Wärmeschutz, Kälteschutz, Schallschutz, Brandschutz* 51(56):31-41.

Künzel, H.M., D. Zirkelbach, and K. Sedlbauer. 2003. Predicting indoor temperature and humidity conditions including hygrothermal interactions with the building envelope. *Proceedings of 1st International Conference on Sustainable Energy and Green Architecture*, Building Scientific Research Center (BSRC), Bangkok.

USGBC. 2009. *LEED 2009 for new construction and major renovation*. U.S. Green Building Council, Washington, D.C.

CHAPTER 37

MEASUREMENT AND INSTRUMENTS

HVAC engineers and technicians require instruments for both laboratory work and fieldwork. Precision is more essential in the laboratory, where research and development are undertaken, than in the field, where acceptance and adjustment tests are conducted. This chapter describes the characteristics and uses of some of these instruments.

1. TERMINOLOGY

The following definitions are generally accepted.

Accuracy. Ability of an instrument to indicate the true value of measured quantity. This is often confused with inaccuracy, which is the departure from the true value to which all causes of error (e.g., hysteresis, nonlinearity, drift, temperature effect) contribute.

Amplitude. Magnitude of variation from its equilibrium or average value in an alternating quantity.

Average. Sum of a number of values divided by the number of values.

Bandwidth. Range of frequencies over which a given device is designed to operate within specified limits.

Bias. Tendency of an estimate to deviate in one direction from a true value (a systematic error).

Calibration. (1) Process of comparing a set of discrete magnitudes or the characteristic curve of a continuously varying magnitude with another set or curve previously established as a standard. Deviation between indicated values and their corresponding standard values constitutes the correction (or calibration curve) for inferring true magnitude from indicated magnitude thereafter; (2) process of adjusting an instrument to fix, reduce, or eliminate the deviation defined in (1). Calibration reduces bias (systematic) errors.

Calibration curve. (1) Path or locus of a point that moves so that its graphed coordinates correspond to values of input signals and output deflections; (2) plot of error versus input (or output).

Confidence. Degree to which a statement (measurement) is believed to be true.

Dead band. Range of values of the measured variable to which an instrument will not effectively respond. The effect of dead band is similar to hysteresis, as shown in Figure 1.

Deviate. Any item of a statistical distribution that differs from the selected measure of control tendency (average, median, mode).

Deviation. Difference between a single measured value and the mean (average) value of a population or sample.

The preparation of this chapter is assigned to TC 1.2, Instruments and Measurements.

Diameter, equivalent. The diameter of a circle having the same area as the rectangular flow channel cross section.

Deviation, standard. Square root of the average of the squares of the deviations from the mean (root mean square deviation). A measure of dispersion of a population.

Distortion. Unwanted change in wave form. Principal forms of distortion are inherent nonlinearity of the device, nonuniform response at different frequencies, and lack of constant proportionality between phase-shift and frequency. (A wanted or intentional change might be identical, but it is called **modulation**.)

Drift. Gradual, undesired change in output over a period of time that is unrelated to input, environment, or load. Drift is gradual; if variation is rapid and recurrent, with elements of both increasing and decreasing output, the fluctuation is referred to as **cycling**.

Dynamic error band. Spread or band of output-amplitude deviation incurred by a constant-amplitude sine wave as its frequency is varied over a specified portion of the frequency spectrum (see *Static error band*).

Emissivity. Ratio of the amount of radiation emitted by a real surface to that of an ideal (blackbody) emitter at the same temperature.

Error. Difference between the true or actual value to be measured (input signal) and the indicated value (output) from the measuring system. Errors can be systematic or random.

Error, accuracy. See *Error, systematic*.

Error, fixed. See *Error, systematic*.

Error, instrument. Error of an instrument's measured value that includes random or systematic errors.

Error, precision. See *Error, random*.

Error, probable. Error with a 50% or higher chance of occurrence. A statement of probable error is of little value.

Error, random. Statistical error caused by chance and not recurring. This term is a general category for errors that can take values on either side of an average value. To describe a random error, its distribution must be known.

Error, root mean square (RMS). Accuracy statement of a system comprising several items. For example, a laboratory potentiometer, volt box, null detector, and reference voltage source have individual accuracy statements assigned to them. These errors are generally independent of one another, so a system of these units displays an accuracy given by the square root of the sum of the squares of the individual limits of error. For example, four individual errors of 0.1% could yield a calibrated error of 0.4% but an RMS error of only 0.2%.

Error, systematic. Persistent error not caused by chance; systematic errors are causal. It is likely to have the same magnitude and sign for every instrument constructed with the same components and

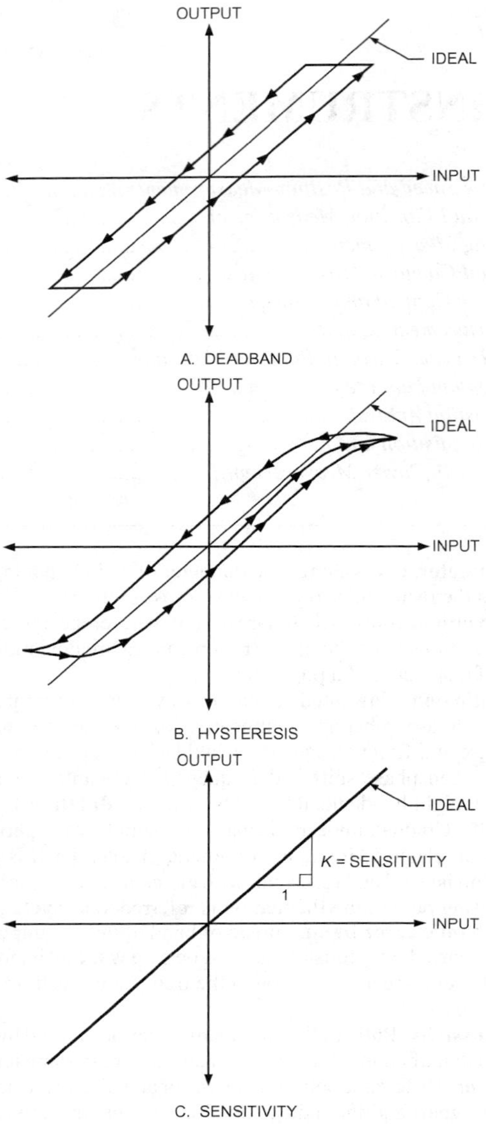

Fig. 1 Measurement and Instrument Terminology

procedures. Errors in calibrating equipment cause systematic errors because all instruments calibrated are biased in the direction of the calibrating equipment error. Voltage and resistance drifts over time are generally in one direction and are classed as systematic errors.

Frequency response (flat). Portion of the frequency spectrum over which the measuring system has a constant value of amplitude response and a constant value of time lag. Input signals that have frequency components within this range are indicated by the measuring system (without distortion).

Hydraulic diameter D_h. Defined as $4A_c/P_{wet}$, where A_c is flow cross-sectional area and P_{wet} is the wetted perimeter (perimeter in contact with the flowing fluid). For a rectangular duct with dimensions $W \times H$, the hydraulic diameter is $D_h = 2HW/(H + W)$. The related quantity *effective* or *equivalent diameter* is defined as the diameter of a circular tube having the same cross-sectional area as the actual flow channel. For a rectangular flow channel, the effective diameter is $D_{eff} = \sqrt{4HW/\pi}$.

Hysteresis. Summation of all effects, under constant environmental conditions, that cause an instrument's output to assume different values at a given stimulus point when that point is approached with increasing or decreasing stimulus. Hysteresis includes backlash. It is usually measured as a percent of full scale when input varies over the full increasing and decreasing range. In instrumentation, hysteresis and dead band exhibit similar output error behavior in relation to input, as shown in Figure 1.

Linearity. The degree of straightness of the transfer curve between an input and an output (e.g., the ideal line in Figure 1); that condition prevailing when output is directly proportional to input (see *Nonlinearity*). Note that the generic term *linearity* does not consider any parallel offset of the straight-line calibration curve.

Loading error. Loss of output signal from a device caused by a current drawn from its output. It increases the voltage drop across the internal impedance, where no voltage drop is desired.

Mean. See *Average*.

Median. Middle value in a distribution, above and below which lie an equal number of values.

Mode. Value in a distribution that occurs most frequently.

Noise. Any unwanted disturbance or spurious signal that modifies the transmission, measurement, or recording of desired data.

Nonlinearity. Prevailing condition (and the extent of its measurement) under which the input/output relationship (known as the input/output curve, transfer characteristic, calibration curve, or response curve) fails to be a straight line. Nonlinearity is measured and reported in several ways, and the way, along with the magnitude, must be stated in any specification.

Minimum-deviation-based nonlinearity: maximum departure between the calibration curve and a straight line drawn to give the greatest accuracy; expressed as a percent of full-scale deflection.

Slope-based nonlinearity: ratio of maximum slope error anywhere on the calibration curve to the slope of the nominal sensitivity line; usually expressed as a percent of nominal slope.

Most other variations result from the many ways in which the straight line can be arbitrarily drawn. All are valid as long as construction of the straight line is explicit.

Population. Group of individual persons, objects, or items from which samples may be taken for statistical measurement.

Precision. Repeatability of measurements of the same quantity under the same conditions; not a measure of absolute accuracy. It describes the relative tightness of the distribution of measurements of a quantity about their mean value. Therefore, precision of a measurement is associated more with its repeatability than its accuracy. It combines uncertainty caused by random differences in a number of identical measurements and the smallest readable increment of the scale or chart. Precision is given in terms of deviation from a mean value.

Primary calibration. Calibration procedure in which the instrument output is observed and recorded while the input stimulus is applied under precise conditions, usually from a primary external standard traceable directly to the National Institute of Standards and Technology (NIST) or to an equivalent international standards organization.

Range. Statement of upper and lower limits between which an instrument's input can be received and for which the instrument is calibrated.

Reliability. Probability that an instrument's precision and accuracy will continue to fall within specified limits.

Repeatability. See *Precision*.

Reproducibility. In instrumentation, the closeness of agreement among repeated measurements of the output for the same value of input made under the same operating conditions over a period of time, approaching from both directions; it is usually measured as a nonreproducibility and expressed as reproducibility in percent of span for a specified time period. Normally, this implies a long period of time, but under certain conditions, the period may be a short time so that drift is not included. Reproducibility includes hysteresis, dead band, drift, and repeatability. Between repeated measurements, the input may vary over the range, and operating conditions may vary within normal limits.

Resolution. Smallest change in input that produces a detectable change in instrument output. Resolution, unlike precision, is a psychophysical term referring to the smallest increment of humanly perceptible output (rated in terms of the corresponding increment of input). The precision, resolution, or both may be better than the accuracy. An ordinary six-digit instrument has a resolution of one part per million (ppm) of full scale; however, it is possible that the accuracy is no better than 25 ppm (0.0025%). Note that the practical resolution of an instrument cannot be any better than the resolution of the indicator or detector, whether internal or external.

Sensitivity. Slope of a calibration curve relating input signal to output, as shown in Figure 1. For linear instruments, sensitivity represents the change in output for a unit change in the input.

Sensitivity error. Maximum error in sensitivity displayed as a result of the changes in the calibration curve resulting from accumulated effects of systematic and random errors.

Stability. (1) Independence or freedom from changes in one quantity as the result of a change in another; (2) absence of drift.

Static error band. (1) Spread of error present if the indicator (pen, needle) stopped at some value (e.g., at one-half of full scale), normally reported as a percent of full scale; (2) specification or rating of maximum departure from the point where the indicator must be when an on-scale signal is stopped and held at a given signal level. This definition stipulates that the stopped position can be approached from either direction in following any random waveform. Therefore, it is a quantity that includes hysteresis and nonlinearity but excludes items such as chart paper accuracy or electrical drift (see *Dynamic error band*).

Step-function response. Characteristic curve or output plotted against time resulting from the input application of a step function (a function that is zero for all values of time before a certain instant, and a constant for all values of time thereafter).

Threshold. Smallest stimulus or signal that results in a detectable output. *Resolution* and threshold are sometimes used interchangeably.

Time constant. Time required for an exponential quantity to change by an amount equal to 0.632 times the total change required to reach steady state for first-order systems.

Transducer. Device for translating the changing magnitude of one kind of quantity into corresponding changes of another kind of quantity. The second quantity often has dimensions different from the first and serves as the source of a useful signal. The first quantity may be considered an input and the second an output. Significant energy may or may not transfer from the transducer's input to output.

Uncertainty. An estimated value for the bound on the error (i.e., what an error might be if it were measured by calibration). Although uncertainty may be the result of both systematic and precision errors, only precision error can be treated by statistical methods. Uncertainty may be either **absolute** (expressed in the units of the measured variable) or **relative** (absolute uncertainty divided by the measured value; commonly expressed in percent).

Zero shift. Drift in the zero indication of an instrument without any static change in the measured variable.

2. UNCERTAINTY ANALYSIS

Uncertainty Sources

Measurement generally consists of a sequence of operations or steps. Virtually every step introduces a conceivable source of uncertainty, the effect of which must be assessed. The following list is representative of the most common, but not all, sources of uncertainty.

- Inaccuracy in the mathematical model that describes the physical quantity
- Inherent stochastic variability of the measurement process
- Uncertainties in measurement standards and calibrated instrumentation
- Time-dependent instabilities caused by gradual changes in standards and instrumentation
- Effects of environmental factors such as temperature, humidity, and pressure
- Values of constants and other parameters obtained from outside sources
- Uncertainties arising from interferences, impurities, inhomogeneity, inadequate resolution, and incomplete discrimination
- Computational uncertainties and data analysis
- Incorrect specifications and procedural errors
- Laboratory practice, including handling techniques, cleanliness, and operator techniques, etc.
- Uncertainty in corrections made for known effects, such as installation effect corrections

Uncertainty of a Measured Variable

For a measured variable X, the total error is caused by both **precision (random)** and **systematic (bias) errors**. This relationship is shown in Figure 2. The possible measurement values of the variable are scattered in a distribution around the parent population mean μ (Figure 2A). The curve (**normal** or **Gaussian distribution**) is the theoretical distribution function for the infinite population of measurements that generated X. The parent population mean differs from $(X)_{true}$ by an amount called the systematic (or bias) error β (Figure 2B). The quantity β is the total fixed error that remains after all calibration corrections have been made. In general, there are several sources of bias error, such as errors in calibration standard, data acquisition, data reduction, and test technique. There is usually no direct way to measure these errors. These errors are unknown and are assumed to be zero; otherwise, an additional correction would

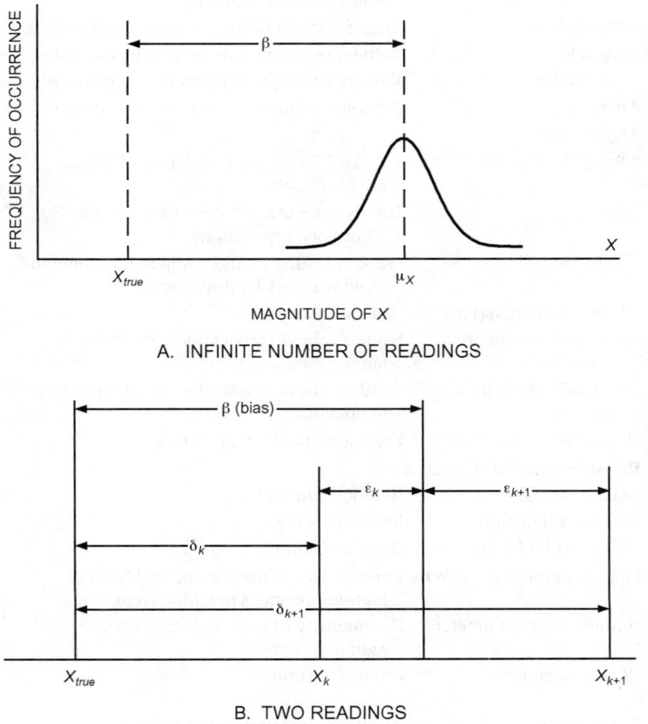

Fig. 2 Errors in Measurement of Variable X

be applied to reduce them to as close to zero as possible. Figure 2B shows how the resulting deviation δ can be different for different random errors ε.

The **precision uncertainty** for a variable, which is an estimate of the possible error associated with the repeatability of a particular measurement, is determined from the sample standard deviation, or the estimate of the error associated with the repeatability of a particular measurement. Unlike systematic error, precision error varies from reading to reading. As the number of readings of a particular variable tends to infinity, the distribution of these possible errors becomes Gaussian.

For each bias error source, the experimenter must estimate a **systematic uncertainty**. Systematic uncertainties are usually estimated from previous experience, calibration data, analytical models, and engineering judgment. The resultant uncertainty is the square root of the sum of the squares of the bias and precision uncertainties; see Coleman and Steele (2009).

For further information on measurement uncertainty, see Abernethy et al. (1985), ASME *Standards* MFC-2M and PTC 19.1, Brown et al. (1998), and Coleman and Steele (1995).

3. TEMPERATURE MEASUREMENT

Instruments for measuring temperature are listed in Table 1. Temperature sensor output must be related to an accepted temperature scale by manufacturing the instrument according to certain specifications or by calibrating it against a temperature standard. To help users conform to standard temperatures and temperature measurements, the International Committee of Weights and Measures (CIPM) adopted the International Temperature Scale of 1990 (ITS-90).

The unit of temperature of the ITS-90 is the kelvin (K) and has a size equal to the fraction 1/273.16 of the thermodynamic temperature of the triple point of water.

In the United States, ITS-90 is maintained by the National Institute of Standards and Technology (NIST), which provides calibrations based on this scale for laboratories.

Benedict (1984), Considine (1985), DeWitt and Nutter (1988), Holman (2001), Quinn (1990), and Schooley (1986, 1992) cover temperature measurement in more detail.

Sampling and Averaging

Although temperature is usually measured within, and is associated with, a relatively small volume (depending on the size of the thermometer), it can also be associated with an area (e.g., on a surface or in a flowing stream). To determine average stream temperature, the cross section must be divided into smaller areas and the temperature of each area measured. The temperatures measured are then combined into a weighted mass flow average by using either (1) equal areas and multiplying each temperature by

Table 1 Common Temperature Measurement Techniques

Measurement Means	Application	Approximate Range, °F	Uncertainty, °F	Limitations
Liquid-in-glass thermometers				
Mercury-in-glass	Temperature of gases and liquids by contact	–36/1000	0.05 to 3.6	In gases, accuracy affected by radiation (unless adequately shielded)
Organic fluid	Temperature of gases and liquids by contact	–330/400	0.05 to 3.6	In gases, accuracy affected by radiation
Resistance thermometers				
Platinum	Precision; remote readings; temperature of fluids or solids by contact	–430/1800	Less than 0.0002 to 0.2	High cost; accuracy affected by radiation in gases
Rhodium/iron	Transfer standard for cryogenic applications	–460/–400	0.0002 to 0.2	High cost
Nickel	Remote readings; temperature by contact	–420/400	0.02 to 2	Accuracy affected by radiation in gases
Germanium	Remote readings; temperature by contact	–460/–400	0.0002 to 0.2	
Thermistors	Remote readings; temperature by contact	–130/400	0.0002 to 0.2	
Thermocouples				
Pt-Rh/Pt (type S)	Standard for thermocouples on IPTS-68, not on ITS-90	32/2650	0.2 to 5	High cost
Au/Pt	Highly accurate reference thermometer for laboratory applications	–60/1800	0.1 to 2	High cost
Types K and N	General testing of high temperature; remote rapid readings by direct contact	–328/2300	0.2 to 18	Less accurate than Pt-Rh/Pt or Au/Pt thermocouples
Iron/Constantan (type J)	Same as above	32/1400	0.2 to 10	Subject to oxidation
Copper/Constantan (type T)	Same as above; especially suited for low temperature	–328/700	0.2 to 5	
Ni-Cr/Constantan (type E)	Same as above; especially suited for low temperature	–328/1650	0.2 to 13	
Bimetallic thermometers	For approximate temperature	–4/1200	2, usually much more	Time lag; unsuitable for remote use
Pressure-bulb thermometers				
Gas-filled bulb	Remote reading	–100/1200	4	Use caution to ensure installation is correct
Vapor-filled bulb	Remote testing	–25/500	4	Use caution to ensure installation is correct
Liquid-filled bulb	Remote testing	–60/2100	4	Use caution to ensure installation is correct
Optical pyrometers	For intensity of narrow spectral band of high-temperature radiation (remote)	1500 and up	30	Generally requires knowledge of surface emissivity
Infrared (IR) radiometers	For intensity of total high-temperature radiation (remote)	Any range		
IR thermography	Infrared imaging	Any range		Generally requires knowledge of surface emissivity
Seger cones (fusion pyrometers)	Approximate temperature (within temperature source)	1200/3600	90	

the fraction of total mass flow in its area or (2) areas of size inversely proportional to mass flow and taking a simple arithmetic average of the temperatures in each. Mixing or selective sampling may be preferable to these cumbersome procedures. Although mixing can occur from turbulence alone, **transposition** is much more effective. In transposition, the stream is divided into parts determined by the type of stratification, and alternate parts pass through one another.

Static Temperature Versus Total Temperature

When a fluid stream impinges on a temperature-sensing element such as a thermometer or thermocouple, the element is at a temperature greater than the true stream temperature. The difference is a fraction of the temperature equivalent of the stream velocity t_e.

$$t_e = \frac{3600V^2}{2g_c J c_p} \tag{1}$$

where

t_e = temperature equivalent of stream velocity, °F
V = stream velocity, fpm
g_c = gravitational constant = 32.174 $lb_m \cdot ft/lb_f \cdot s^2$
J = mechanical equivalent of heat = 778.3 $ft \cdot lb_f/Btu$
c_p = specific heat of stream at constant pressure, $Btu/lb_m \cdot °F$

This fraction of the temperature equivalent of the velocity is the **recovery factor**, which varies from 0.6 to 0.8°F for bare thermometers to 1.0°F for aerodynamically shielded thermocouples. For precise temperature measurement, each temperature sensor must be calibrated to determine its recovery factor. However, for most applications with air velocities below 2000 fpm (or Mach number M below approximately 0.1), the recovery factor can be omitted.

Various sensors are available for temperature measurement in fluid streams. The principal ones are the **static temperature thermometer**, which indicates true stream temperature but is cumbersome, and the **thermistor**, used for accurate temperature measurement within a limited range.

3.1 LIQUID-IN-GLASS THERMOMETERS

Any device that changes monotonically with temperature is a thermometer; however, the term usually signifies an ordinary liquid-in-glass temperature-indicating device. Mercury-filled thermometers have a useful range from –37.8°F, the freezing point of mercury, to about 1000°F, near which the glass usually softens. Lower temperatures can be measured with organic-liquid-filled thermometers (e.g., alcohol-filled), with ranges of –330 to 400°F. During manufacture, thermometers are roughly calibrated for at least two temperatures, often the freezing and boiling points of water; space between the calibration points is divided into desired scale divisions. Thermometers that are intended for precise measurement applications have scales etched into the glass that forms their stems. The probable error for as-manufactured, etched-stem thermometers is ±1 scale division. The highest-quality mercury thermometers may have uncertainties of ±0.06 to 4°F if they have been calibrated by comparison against primary reference standards.

Liquid-in-glass thermometers are used for many HVAC applications, including local temperature indication of process fluids (e.g., cooling and heating fluids and air).

Mercury-in-glass thermometers are fairly common as temperature measurement standards because of their relatively high accuracy and low cost. If used as references, they must be calibrated on the ITS-90 by comparison in a uniform bath with a standard platinum resistance thermometer that has been calibrated either by the appropriate standards agency or by a laboratory that has direct traceability to the standards agency and the ITS-90. This calibration is necessary to determine the proper corrections to be applied to the scale readings. For application and calibration of liquid-in-glass thermometers, refer to NIST (1976, 1986).

Liquid-in-glass thermometers are calibrated by the manufacturer for total or partial stem immersion. If a thermometer calibrated for total immersion is used at partial immersion (i.e., with part of the liquid column at a temperature different from that of the bath), an emergent stem correction must be made, as follows:

$$\text{Stem correction} = Kn(t_b - t_s) \tag{2}$$

where

K = differential expansion coefficient of mercury or other liquid in glass. K is 0.00009 for Fahrenheit mercury thermometers. For K values for other liquids and specific glasses, refer to Schooley (1992).
n = number of degrees that liquid column emerges from bath
t_b = temperature of bath, °F
t_s = average temperature of emergent liquid column of n degrees, °F

Because the true temperature of the bath is not known, this stem correction is only approximate.

Sources of Thermometer Errors

A thermometer measuring gas temperatures can be affected by radiation from surrounding surfaces. If the gas temperature is approximately the same as that of the surrounding surfaces, radiation effects can be ignored. If the temperature differs considerably from that of the surroundings, radiation effects should be minimized by shielding or aspiration (ASME *Standard* PTC 19.3). **Shielding** may be provided by highly reflective surfaces placed between the thermometer bulb and the surrounding surfaces such that air movement around the bulb is not appreciably restricted (Parmelee and Huebscher 1946). Improper shielding can increase errors. **Aspiration** involves passing a high-velocity stream of air or gas over the thermometer bulb.

When a **thermometer well** within a container or pipe under pressure is required, the thermometer should fit snugly and be surrounded with a high-thermal-conductivity material (oil, water, or mercury, if suitable). Liquid in a long, thin-walled well is advantageous for rapid response to temperature changes. The surface of the pipe or container around the well should be insulated to eliminate heat transfer to or from the well.

Industrial thermometers are available for permanent installation in pipes or ducts. These instruments are fitted with metal guards to prevent breakage. However, the considerable heat capacity and conductance of the guards or shields can cause errors.

Allowing ample time for the thermometer to attain temperature equilibrium with the surrounding fluid prevents excessive errors in temperature measurements. When reading a liquid-in-glass thermometer, keep the eye at the same level as the top of the liquid column to avoid parallax.

3.2 RESISTANCE THERMOMETERS

Resistance thermometers depend on a change of the electrical resistance of a sensing element (usually metal) with a change in temperature; resistance increases with increasing temperature. Use of resistance thermometers largely parallels that of thermocouples, although readings are usually unstable above about 1000°F. Two-lead temperature elements are not recommended because they do not allow correction for lead resistance. Three leads to each resistor are necessary for consistent readings, and four leads are preferred. Wheatstone bridge circuits or 6-1/2-digit multimeters can be used for measurements.

A typical circuit used by several manufacturers is shown in Figure 3. This design uses a differential galvanometer in which coils L and H exert opposing forces on the indicating needle. Coil L is in series with the thermometer resistance AB, and coil H is in series with the constant resistance R. As the temperature falls, the resistance of AB decreases, allowing more current to flow through coil L than through coil H. This increases the force exerted by coil L, pulling the needle down to a lower reading. Likewise, as the temperature rises, the resistance of AB increases, causing less current to flow through coil L than through coil H and forcing the indicating needle to a higher reading. Rheostat S must be adjusted occasionally to maintain constant current.

The resistance thermometer is more costly to make and likely to have considerably longer response times than thermocouples. It gives best results when used to measure steady or slowly changing temperature.

Resistance Temperature Devices

Resistance temperature devices (RTDs) are typically constructed from platinum, rhodium/iron, nickel, nickel/iron, tungsten, or copper. These devices are further characterized by their simple circuit designs, high degree of linearity, good sensitivity, and excellent stability. The choice of materials for an RTD usually depends on the intended application; selection criteria include temperature range, corrosion protection, mechanical stability, and cost.

Presently, for HVAC applications, RTDs constructed of platinum are the most widely used. Platinum is extremely stable and resistant to corrosion. Platinum RTDs are highly malleable and can thus be drawn into fine wires; they can also be manufactured inexpensively as thin films. They have a high melting point and can be refined to high purity, thus attaining highly reproducible results. Because of these properties, platinum RTDs are used to define the ITS-90 for the range of 13.8033 K (triple point of equilibrium hydrogen) to 1234.93 K (freezing point of silver).

Platinum resistance temperature devices can measure the widest range of temperatures and are the most accurate and stable temperature sensors. Their resistance/temperature relationship is one of the most linear. The higher the purity of the platinum, the more stable and accurate the sensor. With high-purity platinum, primary-grade platinum RTDs can achieve reproducibility of ±0.00002°F, whereas the minimum uncertainty of a recently calibrated thermocouple is ±0.4°F.

The most widely used RTD is designed with a resistance of 100 Ω at 32°F (R_0 = 100 Ω). Other RTDs are available that use lower

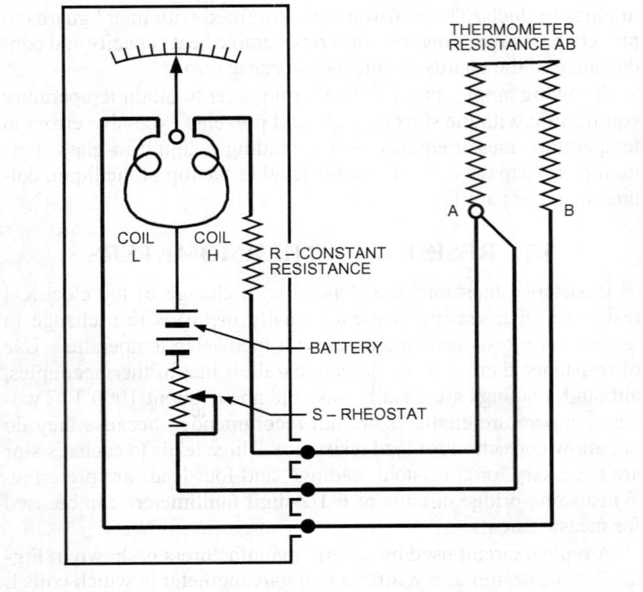

Fig. 3 Typical Resistance Thermometer Circuit

resistances at temperatures above 1100°F. The lower the resistance value, the faster the response time for sensors of the same size.

Thin-Film RTDs. Thin-film 1000 Ω platinum RTDs are readily available. They have the excellent linear properties of lower-resistance platinum RTDs and are more cost-effective because they are mass produced and have lower platinum purity. However, many platinum RTDs with R_0 values of greater than 100 Ω are difficult to provide with transmitters or electronic interface boards from sources other than the RTD manufacturer. In addition to a nonstandard interface, higher-R_0-value platinum RTDs may have higher self-heating losses if the excitation current is not controlled properly.

Thin-film RTDs have the advantages of lower cost and smaller sensor size. They are specifically adapted to surface mounting. Thin-film sensors tend to have an accuracy limitation of ±0.1% or ±0.2°F. This may be adequate for most HVAC applications; only in tightly controlled facilities may users wish to install the standard wire-wound platinum RTDs with accuracies of 0.01% or ±0.02°F (available on special request for certain temperature ranges).

Assembly and Construction. Regardless of the R_0 value, RTD assembly and construction are relatively simple. Electrical connections come in three basic types, depending on the number of wires to be connected to the resistance measurement circuitry. Two, three, or four wires are used for electrical connection using a Wheatstone bridge or a variation (Figure 4).

In the basic two-wire configuration, the RTD's resistance is measured through the two connecting wires. Because the connecting wires extend from the site of the temperature measurement, any additional changes in resistivity caused by a change in temperature may affect the measured resistance. Three- and four-wire assemblies are built to compensate for the connecting lead resistance values. The original three-wire circuit improved resistance measurement by adding a compensating wire to the voltage side of the circuit. This helps reduce part of the connecting wire resistance. When more accurate measurements (better than ±0.2°F) are required, the four-wire bridge, which eliminates all connecting wire resistance errors, is recommended.

All bridges discussed here are direct current (DC) circuits and were used extensively until the advent of precision alternating current (AC) circuits using microprocessor-controlled ratio transformers, dedicated analog-to-digital converters, and other solid-state devices that measure resistance with uncertainties of less than 1 ppm. Resistance measurement technology now allows more portable thermometers, lower cost, ease of use, and high-precision temperature measurement in industrial uses.

Thermistors

Some semiconductor compounds (usually sintered metallic oxides) exhibit large changes in resistance with temperature, usually decreasing as the temperature increases. For use, the thermistor element may be connected by lead wires into a galvanometer bridge circuit and calibrated. Alternatively, a 6-1/2-digit multimeter and a constant-current source with a means for reversing the current to eliminate thermal electromotive force (emf) effects may also be used. This method is easier and faster, and may be more precise and accurate. Thermistors are usually applied to electronic temperature compensation circuits, such as thermocouple reference junction compensation, or to other applications requiring high resolution and having limited operating-temperature ranges. Figure 5 shows a typical thermistor circuit.

Semiconductor Devices

In addition to positive-resistance-coefficient RTDs and negative-resistance-coefficient thermistors, there are two other types of devices that vary resistance or impedance with temperature. Although the principle of their operation has long been known, their reliability was questioned because of imprecise manufacturing techniques.

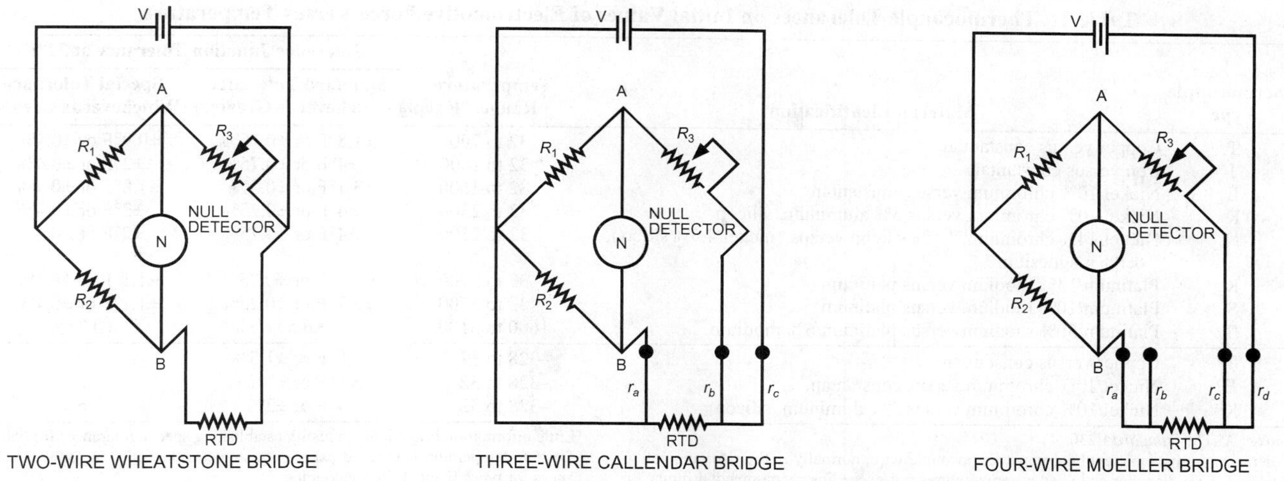

Fig. 4 Typical Resistance Temperature Device (RTD) Bridge Circuits

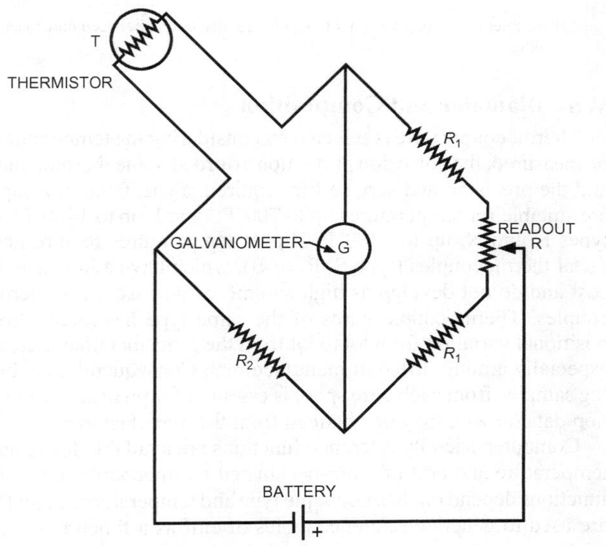

Fig. 5 Basic Thermistor Circuit

Improved silicon microelectronics manufacturing techniques have brought semiconductors to the point where low-cost, precise temperature sensors are commercially available.

Elemental Semiconductors. Because of controlled doping of impurities into elemental germanium, a germanium semiconductor is a reliable temperature sensor for cryogenic temperature measurement in the range of 1.8 to 150°R.

Junction Semiconductors. The first simple junction semiconductor device consisted of a single diode or transistor, in which the forward-connected base emitter voltage was very sensitive to temperature. Today, the more common form is a pair of diode-connected transistors, which make the device suitable for ambient temperature measurement. Applications include thermocouple reference junction compensation.

The primary advantages of silicon transistor temperature sensors are their extreme linearity and exact R_0 value, as well as the incorporation of signal conditioning circuitry into the same device as the sensor element. As with thermocouples, these semiconductors require highly precise manufacturing techniques, extremely precise voltage measurements, multiple-point calibration, and temperature compensation to achieve an accuracy as high as ±0.02°F, but with a much higher cost. Lower-cost devices achieve accuracies of ±0.2°F using mass-manufacturing techniques and single-point calibration. A mass-produced silicon temperature sensor can be interchanged easily. If one device fails, only the sensor element need be changed. Electronic circuitry can be used to recalibrate the new device.

Winding Temperature. The winding temperature of electrical operating equipment is usually determined from the resistance change of these windings in operation. The relationship between the winding resistance R_1 at a known temperature t_1 and the winding resistance at any other temperature t_2 is given by Equation (3) (IEEE *Standard* 112-2004).

$$\frac{R_2}{R_1} = \frac{\left[\frac{1}{\alpha} - t_0\right] + t_2}{\left[\frac{1}{\alpha} - t_0\right] + t_1} = \frac{k + t_2}{k + t_1} \tag{3}$$

where

R_1 = winding resistance at temperature t_1, Ω
R_2 = winding resistance at temperature t_2, Ω
t_1, t_2 = winding temperatures, °F
α = wire resistivity coefficient, $°F^{-1}$
t_0 = reference temperature for resistivity, 77°F
k = $1/\alpha - t_0$ = winding material constant, 234.5°F for 100% IACS conductivity copper

The classical method of determining winding temperature is to measure the equipment when it is inoperative and temperature-stabilized at room temperature. After the equipment has operated sufficiently to stabilize temperature under load conditions, the winding resistance should be measured again by taking resistance measurements at known, short time intervals after shutdown. These values may be extrapolated to zero time to indicate the winding resistance at the time of shutdown. The obvious disadvantage of this method is that the device must be shut down to determine winding temperature. A circuit described by Seely (1955), however, makes it possible to measure resistances while the device is operating.

3.3 THERMOCOUPLES

When two wires of dissimilar metals are joined by soldering, welding, or twisting, they form a thermocouple junction or **thermojunction**. An emf that depends on the wire materials and the junction temperature exists between the wires. This is known as the **Seebeck voltage**.

Table 2 Thermocouple Tolerances on Initial Values of Electromotive Force Versus Temperature

Thermocouple Type	Material Identification	Temperature Range, °F	Reference Junction Tolerance at 32°F[a] Standard Tolerance (Whichever Is Greater)	Special Tolerance (Whichever Is Greater)
T	Copper versus constantan	32 to 700	±1.8°F or ±0.75%	±0.9°F or ±0.4%
J	Iron versus constantan	32 to 1400	±4°F or ±0.75%	±2°F or ±0.4%
E	Nickel/10% chromium versus constantan	32 to 1600	±3.1°F or ±0.5%	±1.8°F or ±0.4%
K	Nickel/10% chromium versus 5% aluminum, silicon	32 to 2300	±4°F or ±0.75%	±2°F or ±0.4%
N	Nickel/14% chromium, 1.5% silicon versus nickel/4.5% silicon, 0.1% magnesium	32 to 2300	±4°F or ±0.75%	±2°F or ±0.4%
R	Platinum/13% rhodium versus platinum	32 to 2700	±2.7°F or ±0.25%	±1.1°F or ±0.1%
S	Platinum/10% rhodium versus platinum	32 to 2700	±2.7°F or ±0.25%	±1.1°F or ±0.1%
B	Platinum/30% rhodium versus platinum/6% rhodium	1600 to 3100	±0.5%	±0.25%
T[b]	Copper versus constantan	–328 to 32	±1.8°F or ±1.5%	c
E[b]	Nickel/10% chromium versus constantan	–328 to 32	±3.1°F or ±1%	c
K[b]	Nickel/10% chromium versus 5% aluminum, silicon	–328 to 32	±4°F or ±2%	c

Source: ASTM *Standard* E230.

[a]Tolerances in this table apply to new thermocouple wire, normally in the size range of 0.01 to 0.1 in. diameter and used at temperatures not exceeding recommended limits. Thermocouple wire is available in two grades: standard and special.

[b]Thermocouples and thermocouple materials are normally supplied to meet the tolerance specified in the table for temperatures above 32°F. The same materials, however, may not fall within the tolerances given in the second section of the table when operated below freezing (32°F). If materials are required to meet tolerances at subfreezing temperatures, the purchase order must state so.

[c]Little information is available to justify establishing special tolerances for below-freezing temperatures. Limited experience suggests the following special tolerances for types E and T thermocouples:

Type E –328 to 32°F; ±2°F or ±0.5% (whichever is greater)

Type T –328 to 32°F; ±1°F or ±0.8% (whichever is greater)

These tolerances are given only as a guide for discussion between purchaser and supplier.

Thermocouples for temperature measurement yield less precise results than platinum resistance thermometers, but, except for glass thermometers, thermocouples are the most common instruments of temperature measurement for the range of 32 to 1800°F. Because of their low cost, moderate reliability, and ease of use, thermocouples are widely accepted.

The most commonly used thermocouples in industrial applications are assigned letter designations. Tolerances of such commercially available thermocouples are given in Table 2.

Because the measured emf is a function of the difference in temperature and the type of dissimilar metals used, a known temperature at one junction is required; the remaining junction temperature may be calculated. It is common to call the one with known temperature the (cold) **reference** junction and the one with unknown temperature the (hot) **measured** junction. The reference junction is typically kept at a reproducible temperature, such as the ice point of water.

Various systems are used to maintain the reference junction temperature (e.g., mixed ice and water in an insulated flask, commercially available thermoelectric coolers to maintain the ice-point temperature automatically in a reference chamber). When these systems cannot be used in an application, measuring instruments with automatic reference junction temperature compensation may be used. These types of instruments typically use a thermistor or RTD to measure the reference junction temperature to provide reference junction temperature compensation.

As previously described, the principle for measuring temperature with a thermocouple is based on accurate measurement of the Seebeck voltage. Acceptable DC voltage measurement methods are (1) millivoltmeter, (2) millivolt potentiometer, and (3) high-input impedance digital voltmeter. Many digital voltmeters include built-in software routines for direct calculation and display of temperature. Regardless of the method selected, there are many ways to simplify measurement.

Solid-state digital readout devices in combination with a milli- or microvoltmeter, as well as packaged thermocouple readouts with built-in cold junction and linearization circuits, are available. The latter requires a proper thermocouple to provide direct meter reading of temperature. Accuracy approaching or surpassing that of potentiometers can be attained, depending on the instrument quality. This method is popular because it eliminates the null balancing requirement and reads temperature directly in a digital readout.

Wire Diameter and Composition

Thermocouple wire is selected by considering the temperature to be measured, the corrosion protection afforded to the thermocouple, and the precision and service life required. Type T thermocouples are suitable for temperatures up to 700°F; type J, up to 1400°F; and types K and N, up to 2300°F. Higher temperatures require noble metal thermocouples (type S, R, or B), which have a higher initial cost and do not develop as high an emf as the base metal thermocouples. Thermocouple wires of the same type have small compositional variation from lot to lot from the same manufacturer, and especially among different manufacturers. Consequently, calibrating samples from each wire spool is essential for precision. Calibration data on wire may be obtained from the manufacturer.

Computer-friendly reference functions are available for relating temperature and emf of letter-designated thermocouple types. The functions depend on thermocouple type and temperature range; they are used to generate reference tables of emf as a function of temperature, but are not well suited for calculating temperatures directly from values of emf. Approximate inverse functions are available, however, for calculating temperature and are of the form

$$t = \sum_{i=0}^{n} a_i E^i \tag{4}$$

where t = temperature, a_i = thermocouple constant coefficients, and E = voltage. Burns et al. (1992) give reference functions and approximate inverses for all letter-designated thermocouples.

The emf of a thermocouple, as measured with a high-input impedance device, is independent of the diameters of its constituent wires. Thermocouples with small-diameter wires respond faster to temperature changes and are less affected by radiation than larger ones. Large-diameter wire thermocouples, however, are necessary for high-temperature work when wire corrosion is a problem. For use in heated air or gases, thermocouples are often shielded and sometimes aspirated. One way to avoid error caused by radiation is using several thermocouples of different wire sizes and estimating the true temperature by extrapolating readings to zero diameter.

With thermocouples, temperatures can be indicated or recorded remotely on conveniently located instruments. Because thermocouples can be made of small-diameter wire, they can be used to measure temperatures within thin materials, within narrow spaces, or in otherwise inaccessible locations.

Multiple Thermocouples

Thermocouples in series, with alternate junctions maintained at a common temperature, produce an emf that, when divided by the number of thermocouples, gives the average emf corresponding to the temperature difference between two sets of junctions. This series arrangement of thermocouples, often called a **thermopile**, is used to increase sensitivity and is often used for measuring small temperature changes and differences.

Connecting several thermocouples of the same type in parallel with a common reference junction is useful for obtaining an average temperature of an object or volume. In such measurements, however, it is important that the electrical resistances of the individual thermocouples be the same. Use of thermocouples in series and parallel arrangements is discussed in ASTM *Manual* 12.

Surface Temperature Measurement

The thermocouple is useful in determining surface temperature. It can be attached to a metal surface in several ways. For permanent installations, soldering, brazing, or peening (i.e., driving the thermocouple measuring junction into a small drilled hole) is suggested. For temporary arrangements, thermocouples can be attached by tape, adhesive, or putty-like material. For boiler or furnace surfaces, use furnace cement. To minimize the possibility of error caused by heat conduction along wires, a surface thermocouple should be made of fine wires placed in close contact with the surface being measured for about an inch from the junction to ensure good thermal contact. Wires must be insulated electrically from each other and from the metal surface (except at the junction).

Thermocouple Construction

Thermocouple (TC) wires are insulated with various materials, including fibrous glass, fluorocarbon resin, and ceramic insulators. Perhaps the most common insulators are polyimides or, in high-temperature applications, braided glass. At high temperatures, insulation can break down, inadvertently forming an unanticipated TC junction. In another form of thermocouple, the wires are insulated with compacted ceramic insulation inside a metal sheath, providing both mechanical protection and protection from stray electromagnetic fields. The measuring junction may be exposed or enclosed within the metal sheath. An enclosed junction may be either grounded or ungrounded to the metal sheath.

An exposed junction is in direct contact with the process stream; it is therefore subject to corrosion or contamination, but provides a fast temperature response. A grounded enclosed junction, in which the wires are welded to the metal sheath, provides electrical grounding, as well as mechanical and corrosion protection, but has a slower response time. Response time is even slower for ungrounded enclosed junctions, but the thermocouple wires are isolated electrically and are less susceptible to some forms of mechanical strain than those with grounded construction.

3.4 OPTICAL PYROMETRY

Optical pyrometry determines a surface's temperature from the color of the radiation it emits. As the temperature of a surface increases, it becomes deep red in color, then orange, and eventually white. This behavior follows from Wein's law, which indicates that the wavelength corresponding to the maximum intensity of emitted radiation is inversely proportional to the absolute temperature of the emitting surface. Thus, as temperature increases, the wavelength decreases.

To determine the unknown surface temperature, the color of radiation from the surface is optically compared to the color of a heated filament. By adjusting the current in the filament, the color of the filament is made to match the color of radiation from the source surface. When in balance, the filament virtually disappears into the background image of the surface color. Filament calibration is required to relate the filament current to the unknown surface temperature. For further information, see Holman (2001).

3.5 INFRARED RADIATION THERMOMETERS

Infrared radiation (IR) thermometers, also known as **remote temperature sensors** (Hudson 1969) or **pyrometers**, allow noncontact measurement of surface temperature over a wide range. In these instruments, radiant flux from the observed object is focused by an optical system onto an infrared detector that generates an output signal proportional to the incident radiation that can be read from a meter or display unit. Both point and scanning radiometers are available; the latter can display the temperature variation in the field of view.

IR thermometers are usually classified according to the detector used: either thermal or photon. In **thermal detectors**, a change in electrical property is caused by the heating effect of the incident radiation. Examples of thermal detectors are the thermocouple, thermopile, and metallic and semiconductor bolometers. Typical response times are one-quarter to one-half second. In **photon detectors**, a change in electrical property is caused by the surface absorption of incident photons. Because these detectors do not require an increase in temperature for activation, their response time is much shorter than that of thermal detectors. Scanning radiometers usually use photon detectors.

An IR thermometer only measures the power level of radiation incident on the detector, a combination of thermal radiation emitted by the object and surrounding background radiation reflected from the object's surface. Very accurate measurement of temperature, therefore, requires knowledge of the long-wavelength emissivity of the object as well as the effective temperature of the thermal radiation field surrounding the object. Calibration against an internal or external source of known temperature and emissivity may be needed to obtain true surface temperature from the radiation measurements.

In other cases, using published emissivity factors for common materials may suffice. Many IR thermometers have an emissivity adjustment feature that automatically calculates the effect of emissivity on temperature once the emissivity factor is entered. Thermometers that do not have an emissivity adjustment are usually preset to calculate emissivity at 0.95, a good estimate of the emissivity of most organic substances, including paint. Moreover, IR thermometers are frequently used for relative, rather than absolute, measurement; in these cases, adjustment for emissivity may be unnecessary. The most significant practical problem is measuring shiny, polished objects. Placing electrical tape or painting the measurement area with flat black paint and allowing the temperature of the tape or paint to equilibrate can mitigate this problem.

A key factor in measurement quality can be the optical resolution or spot size of the IR thermometer, because this specification determines the instrument's measurement area from a particular distance and, thus, whether a user is actually measuring the desired area. Optical resolution is expressed as distance to spot size (D:S) at the focal. Part of the D:S specification is a description of the amount of target infrared energy encircled by the spot; typically it is 95%, but may be 90%.

Temperature resolution of an IR thermometer decreases as object temperature decreases. For example, a radiometer that can resolve a temperature difference of 0.5°F on an object near 70°F may only resolve a difference of 2°F on an object at 32°F.

3.6 INFRARED THERMOGRAPHY

Infrared thermography acquires and analyzes thermal information using images from an infrared imaging system. An infrared imaging system consists of (1) an infrared video camera and (2) a display unit. The infrared camera scans a surface and senses the self-emitted and reflected radiation viewed from the surface. The display unit contains either a cathode-ray tube (CRT) that displays a gray-tone or color-coded thermal image of the surface or a color liquid crystal display (LCD) screen. Thermal images can also be displayed on mobile devices such as smartphones. A photograph of the image is called a **thermogram**. Introductions to infrared thermography are given by Madding (1989) and Paljak and Pettersson (1972).

Thermography has been used to detect missing insulation and air infiltration paths in building envelopes (Burch and Hunt 1978). Standard practices for conducting thermographic inspections of buildings are given in ASTM *Standard* C1060. A technique for quantitatively mapping heat loss in building envelopes is given by Mack (1986).

Aerial infrared thermography of buildings is effective in identifying regions of an individual built-up roof that have wet insulation (Tobiasson and Korhonen 1985), but it is ineffective in ranking a group of roofs according to their thermal resistance (Burch 1980; Goldstein 1978). In this latter application, the emittances of the separate roofs and outdoor climate (i.e., temperature and wind speed) throughout the microclimate often produce changes in the thermal image that may be incorrectly attributed to differences in thermal resistance.

Industrial applications include locating defective or missing pipe insulation in buried heat distribution systems, surveys of manufacturing plants to quantify energy loss from equipment, and locating defects in coatings (Bentz and Martin 1987). Madding (1989) discusses applications to electrical power systems and electronics.

4. HUMIDITY MEASUREMENT

Any instrument that can measure the humidity or psychrometric state of air is a hygrometer, and many are available. The indication sensors used on the instruments respond to different moisture property contents. These responses are related to factors such as wet-bulb temperature, relative humidity, humidity (mixing) ratio, dew point, and frost point.

Table 3 lists instruments for measuring humidity. Each is capable of accurate measurement under certain conditions and within specific limitations. The following sections describe the various instruments in more detail.

4.1 PSYCHROMETERS

A typical industrial psychrometer consists of a pair of matched electrical or mechanical temperature sensors, one of which is kept wet with a moistened wick. A blower aspirates the sensor, which lowers the temperature at the moistened temperature sensor. The lowest temperature depression occurs when the evaporation rate required to saturate the moist air adjacent to the wick is constant. This is a steady-state, open-loop, nonequilibrium process, which depends on the purity of the water, cleanliness of the wick, ventilation rate, radiation effects, size and accuracy of the temperature sensors, and transport properties of the gas.

Table 3 Humidity Sensor Properties

Type of Sensor	Sensor Category	Method of Operation	Approximate Range	Some Uses	Approximate Accuracy
Psychrometer	Evaporative cooling	Temperature measurement of wet bulb	32 to 180°F	Measurement, standard	±3 to 7% rh
Adiabatic saturation psychrometer	Evaporative cooling	Temperature measurement of thermodynamic wet bulb	40 to 85°F	Measurement, standard	±0.2 to 2% rh
Chilled mirror	Dew point	Optical determination of moisture formation	–110 to 200°F dpt	Measurement, control, meteorology	±0.4 to 4°F
Heated saturated salt solution	Water vapor pressure	Vapor pressure depression in salt solution	–20 to 160°F dpt	Measurement, control, meteorology	±3°F
Hair	Mechanical	Dimensional change	5 to 100% rh	Measurement, control	±5% rh
Nylon	Mechanical	Dimensional change	5 to 100% rh	Measurement, control	±5% rh
Dacron thread	Mechanical	Dimensional change	5 to 100% rh	Measurement	±7% rh
Goldbeater's skin	Mechanical	Dimensional change	5 to 100% rh	Measurement	±7% rh
Cellulosic materials	Mechanical	Dimensional change	5 to 100% rh	Measurement, control	±5% rh
Carbon	Mechanical	Dimensional change	5 to 100% rh	Measurement	±5% rh
Dunmore type	Electrical	Impedance	7 to 98% rh at 40 to 140°F	Measurement, control	±1.5% rh
Polymer film electronic hygrometer	Electrical	Impedance or capacitance	10 to 100% rh		±2 to 3% rh
Ion exchange resin	Electrical	Impedance or capacitance	10 to 100% rh at –40 to 190°F	Measurement, control	±5% rh
Porous ceramic	Electrical	Impedance or capacitance	Up to 400°F	Measurement, control	±1 to 1.5% rh
Aluminum oxide	Electrical	Capacitance	5 to 100% rh	Measurement, control	±3% rh
	Electrical	Capacitance	–110 to 140°F dpt	Trace moisture measurement, control	±2°F dpt
Electrolytic hygrometer	Electrolytic cell	Electrolyzes due to adsorbed moisture	1 to 1000 ppm	Measurement	
Infrared laser diode	Electrical	Optical diodes	0.1 to 100 ppm	Trace moisture measurement	±0.1 ppm
Surface acoustic wave	Electrical	SAW attenuation	85 to 98% rh	Measurement, control	±1% rh
Piezoelectric	Mass sensitive	Mass changes due to adsorbed moisture	–100 to 0°F	Trace moisture measurement, control	±2 to 10°F dpt
Radiation absorption	Moisture absorption	Moisture absorption of UV or IR radiation	0 to 180°F dpt	Measurement, control, meteorology	±4°F dpt, ±5% rh
Gravimetric	Direct measurement of mixing ratio	Comparison of sample gas with dry airstream	120 to 20,000 ppm mixing ratio	Primary standard, research and laboratory	±0.13% of reading
Color change	Physical	Color changes	10 to 80% rh	Warning device	±10% rh

Notes: dpt = dew-point temperature
1. This table does not include all available technology for humidity measurement.
2. Approximate range for device types listed is based on surveys of device manufacturers.
3. Approximate accuracy is based on manufacturers' data.
4. Presently, NIST only certifies instruments with operating ranges within –103 to 212°F dpt.

ASHRAE *Standard* 41.6 recommends an airflow over both the wet and dry bulbs of 600 to 1000 fpm for transverse ventilation and 300 to 500 fpm for axial ventilation.

The **sling psychrometer** consists of two thermometers mounted side by side in a frame fitted with a handle for whirling the device through the air. The thermometers are spun until their readings become steady. In the **ventilated** or **aspirated psychrometer**, the thermometers remain stationary, and a small fan, blower, or syringe moves air across the thermometer bulbs. Various designs are used in the laboratory, and commercial models are available.

Other temperature sensors, such as thermocouples and thermistors, are also used and can be adapted for recording temperatures or for use where a small instrument is required. Small-diameter wet-bulb sensors operate with low ventilation rates.

Charts and tables showing the relationship between the temperatures and humidity are available. Data are usually based on a barometric pressure equal to one standard atmosphere. To meet special needs, charts can be produced that apply to nonstandard pressure (e.g., the ASHRAE 7500 ft psychrometric chart). Alternatively, mathematical calculations can be made (Kusuda 1965). Uncertainties of 3 to 7% rh are typical for psychrometer-based derivation. The degree of uncertainty is a function of the accuracy of temperature measurements (wet- and dry-bulb), knowledge of the barometric pressure, and conformance to accepted operational procedures such as those outlined in ASHRAE *Standard* 41.6.

In air temperatures below 32°F, water on the wick may either freeze or supercool. Because the wet-bulb temperature is different for ice and water, the state must be known and the proper chart or table used. Some operators remove the wick from the wet bulb for freezing conditions and dip the bulb in water a few times; this allows water to freeze on the bulb between dips, forming a film of ice. Because the wet-bulb depression is slight at low temperatures, precise temperature readings are essential. A psychrometer can be used at high temperatures, but if the wet-bulb depression is large, the wick must remain wet and water supplied to the wick must be cooled so as not to influence the wet-bulb temperature by carrying sensible heat to it (Richardson 1965; Worrall 1965).

Greenspan and Wexler (1968) and Wentzel (1961) developed devices to measure adiabatic saturation temperature.

4.2 DEW-POINT HYGROMETERS

Condensation Dew-Point Hygrometers

The condensation (chilled-mirror) dew-point hygrometer is an accurate and reliable instrument with a wide humidity range. However, these features are gained at increased complexity and cost compared to the psychrometer. In the condensation hygrometer, a surface is cooled (thermoelectrically, mechanically, or chemically) until dew or frost begins to condense out. The condensate surface is maintained electronically in vapor-pressure equilibrium with the surrounding gas, while surface condensation is detected by optical, electrical, or nuclear techniques. The measured surface temperature is then the dew-point temperature.

The largest source of error stems from the difficulty in measuring condensate surface temperature accurately. Typical industrial versions of the instrument are accurate to ±1.0°F over wide temperature spans. With proper attention to the condensate surface temperature measuring system, errors can be reduced to about ±0.4°F. Condensation hygrometers can be made surprisingly compact using solid-state optics and thermoelectric cooling.

Wide span and minimal errors are two of the main features of this instrument. A properly designed condensation hygrometer can measure dew points from 200°F down to frost points of –100°F. Typical condensation hygrometers can cool to 150°F below ambient temperature, establishing lower limits of the instrument to dew points corresponding to approximately 0.5% rh. Accuracies for measurements above –40°F can be ±2°F or better, deteriorating to ±4°F at lower temperatures.

The response time of a condensation dew-point hygrometer is usually specified in terms of its cooling/heating rate, typically 4°F/s for thermoelectric cooled mirrors. This makes it somewhat faster than a heated salt hygrometer. Perhaps the most significant feature of the condensation hygrometer is its fundamental measuring technique, which essentially renders the instrument self-calibrating. For calibration, it is necessary only to manually override the surface cooling control loop, causing the surface to heat, and confirm that the instrument recools to the same dew point when the loop is closed. Assuming that the surface temperature measuring system is correct, this is a reasonable check on the instrument's performance.

Although condensation hygrometers can become contaminated, they can easily be cleaned and returned to service with no impairment to performance.

Salt-Phase Heated Hygrometers

Another instrument in which the temperature varies with ambient dew-point temperature is called a self-heating salt-phase transition hygrometer or a heated electrical hygrometer. This device usually consists of a tubular substrate covered by glass fiber fabric, with a spiral bifilar winding for electrodes. The surface is covered with a salt solution, usually lithium chloride. The sensor is connected in series with a ballast and a 24 V (AC) supply. When the instrument is operating, electrical current flowing through the salt film heats the sensor. The salt's electrical resistance characteristics are such that a balance is reached with the salt at a critical moisture content corresponding to a saturated solution. The sensor temperature adjusts automatically so that the water vapor pressures of the salt film and ambient atmosphere are equal.

With lithium chloride, this sensor cannot be used to measure relative humidity below approximately 12% (the equilibrium relative humidity of this salt), and it has an upper dew-point limit of about 160°F. The regions of highest precision are between –10 and 93°F, and above 105°F dew point. Another problem is that the lithium chloride solution can be washed off when exposed to water. In addition, this type of sensor is subject to contamination problems, which limits its accuracy. Its response time is also very slow: it takes approximately 2 min for a 67% step change.

4.3 MECHANICAL HYGROMETERS

Many organic materials change in dimension with changes in humidity; this action is used in a number of simple and effective humidity indicators, recorders, and controllers (see Chapter 7). They are coupled to pneumatic leak ports, mechanical linkages, or electrical transduction elements to form hygrometers.

Commonly used organic materials are human hair, nylon, Dacron, animal membrane, animal horn, wood, and paper. Their inherent nonlinearity and hysteresis must be compensated for within the hygrometer. These devices are generally unreliable below 32°F. The response is generally inadequate for monitoring a changing process, and can be affected significantly by exposure to extremes of humidity. Mechanical hygrometers require initial calibration and frequent recalibration; however, they are useful because they can be arranged to read relative humidity directly, and they are simpler and less expensive than most other types.

4.4 ELECTRICAL IMPEDANCE AND CAPACITANCE HYGROMETERS

Many substances adsorb or lose moisture with changing relative humidity and exhibit corresponding changes in electrical impedance or capacitance.

Dunmore Hygrometers

This sensor consists of dual electrodes on a tubular or flat substrate; it is coated with a film containing salt, such as lithium chloride, in a binder to form an electrical connection between windings. The relation of sensor resistance to humidity is usually represented by graphs. Because the sensor is highly sensitive, the graphs are a series of curves, each for a given temperature, with intermediate values found by interpolation. Several resistance elements (Dunmore elements) cover a standard range. Systematic calibration is essential because the resistance grid varies with time and contamination as well as with exposure to temperature and humidity extremes.

Polymer Film Electronic Hygrometers

These devices consist of a hygroscopic organic polymer deposited by means of thin or thick film processing technology on a water-permeable substrate. Both capacitance and impedance sensors are available. The impedance devices may be either ionic or electronic conduction types. These hygrometers typically have integrated circuits that provide temperature correction and signal conditioning. The primary advantages of this sensor technology are small size; low cost; fast response times (on the order of 1 to 120 s for 64% change in relative humidity); and good accuracy over the full range, including the low end, where most other devices are less accurate.

Ion Exchange Resin Electric Hygrometers

A conventional ion exchange resin consists of a polymer with a high relative molecular mass and polar groups of positive or negative charge in cross-link structure. Associated with these polar groups are ions of opposite charge that are held by electrostatic forces to the fixed polar groups. In the presence of water or water vapor, the electrostatically held ions become mobile; thus, when a voltage is impressed across the resin, the ions are capable of electrolytic conduction. The **Pope cell** is one example of an ion exchange element. It is a wide-range sensor, typically covering 15 to 95% rh; therefore, one sensor can be used where several Dunmore elements would be required. The Pope cell, however, has a nonlinear characteristic from approximately 1000 Ω at 100% rh to several megohms at 10% rh.

Impedance-Based Porous Ceramic Electronic Hygrometers

Using oxides' adsorption characteristics, humidity-sensitive ceramic oxide devices use either ionic or electronic measurement techniques to relate adsorbed water to relative humidity. Ionic conduction is produced by dissociation of water molecules, forming surface hydroxyls. The dissociation causes proton migration, so the device's impedance decreases with increasing water content. The ceramic oxide is sandwiched between porous metal electrodes that connect the device to an impedance-measuring circuit for linearizing and signal conditioning. These sensors have excellent sensitivity, are resistant to contamination and high temperature (up to 400°F), and may get fully wet without sensor degradation. These sensors are accurate to about ±1.5% rh (±1% rh when temperature compensated) and have a moderate cost.

Aluminum Oxide Capacitive Sensor

This sensor consists of an aluminum strip that is anodized by a process that forms a porous oxide layer. A very thin coating of cracked chromium or gold is then evaporated over this structure. The aluminum base and cracked chromium or gold layer form the two electrodes of what is essentially an aluminum oxide capacitor.

Water vapor is rapidly transported through the cracked chromium or gold layer and equilibrates on the walls of the oxide pores in a manner functionally related to the vapor pressure of water in the atmosphere surrounding the sensor. The number of water molecules adsorbed on the oxide structure determines the capacitance between the two electrodes.

4.5 ELECTROLYTIC HYGROMETERS

In electrolytic hygrometers, air is passed through a tube, where moisture is adsorbed by a highly effective desiccant (usually phosphorous pentoxide) and electrolyzed. The airflow is regulated to 0.0035 cfm at a standard temperature and pressure. As the incoming water vapor is absorbed by the desiccant and electrolyzed into hydrogen and oxygen, the current of electrolysis determines the mass of water vapor entering the sensor. The flow rate of the entering gas is controlled precisely to maintain a standard sample mass flow rate into the sensor. The instrument is usually designed for use with moisture/air ratios in the range of less than 1 ppm to 1000 ppm, but can be used with higher humidities.

4.6 PIEZOELECTRIC SORPTION

This hygrometer compares the changes in frequency of two hygroscopically coated quartz crystal oscillators. As the crystal's mass changes because of absorption of water vapor, the frequency changes. The amount of water sorbed on the sensor is a function of relative humidity (i.e., partial pressure of water as well as ambient temperature).

A commercial version uses a hygroscopic polymer coating on the crystal. Humidity is measured by monitoring the change in the vibration frequency of the quartz crystal when the crystal is alternately exposed to wet and dry gas.

4.7 SPECTROSCOPIC (RADIATION ABSORPTION) HYGROMETERS

Radiation absorption devices operate on the principle that selective absorption of radiation is a function of frequency for different media. Water vapor absorbs **infrared** radiation at 2 to 3 μm wavelengths and **ultraviolet** radiation centered about the Lyman-alpha line at 0.122 μm. The amount of absorbed radiation is directly related to the absolute humidity or water vapor content in the gas mixture, according to Beer's law. The basic unit consists of an energy source and optical system for isolating wavelengths in the spectral region of interest, and a measurement system for determining the attenuation of radiant energy caused by water vapor in the optical path. Absorbed radiation is measured extremely quickly and independent of the degree of saturation of the gas mixture. Response times of 0.1 to 1 s for 90% change in moisture content are common. Spectroscopic hygrometers are primarily used where a noncontact application is required; this may include atmospheric studies, industrial drying ovens, and harsh environments. The primary disadvantages of this device are its high cost and relatively large size.

4.8 GRAVIMETRIC HYGROMETERS

Humidity levels can be measured by extracting and finding the mass of water vapor in a known quantity or atmosphere. For precise laboratory work, powerful desiccants (e.g., phosphorous pentoxide, magnesium perchlorate) are used for extraction; for other purposes, calcium chloride or silica gel is satisfactory.

When the highest level of accuracy is required, the NIST gravimetric hygrometer is recommended. The gravimetric hygrometer gives the absolute water vapor content, where the mass of absorbed water and precise measurement of the gas volume associated with the water vapor determine the mixing ratio or absolute humidity of the sample. This system is the primary standard because the required measurements of mass, temperature, pressure, and volume can be made with extreme precision. However, its complexity and required attention to detail limit its usefulness. See Meyer et al. (2010) for further information.

4.9 CALIBRATION

For many hygrometers, the need for recalibration depends on the accuracy required, the sensor's stability, and the conditions to which the sensor is subjected. Many hygrometers should be calibrated regularly by exposure to an atmosphere maintained at a known humidity and temperature, or by comparison with a transfer standard hygrometer. Complete calibration usually requires observation of a series of temperatures and humidities. Methods for producing known humidities include saturated salt solutions (Greenspan 1977); sulfuric acid solutions; and mechanical systems, such as the divided flow, two-pressure (Amdur 1965); two-temperature (Till and Handegord 1960); and NIST two-pressure humidity generator (Hasegawa 1976). All these systems rely on precise methods of temperature and pressure control in a controlled environment to produce a known humidity, usually with accuracies of 0.5 to 1.0%. The operating range for the precision generator is typically 5 to 95% rh.

5. PRESSURE MEASUREMENT

Pressure is the force exerted per unit area by a medium, generally a liquid or gas. Pressure so defined is sometimes called **absolute pressure**. Thermodynamic and material properties are expressed in terms of absolute pressures; thus, the properties of a refrigerant are given in terms of absolute pressures. **Vacuum** refers to pressures below atmospheric.

Differential pressure is the difference between two absolute pressures, or the difference between two relative pressures measured with respect to the same reference pressure. Often, it can be very small compared to either of the absolute pressures (these are often referred to as low-range, high-line differential pressures). A common example of differential pressure is the pressure drop, or difference between inlet and outlet pressures, across a filter or flow element.

Gage pressure is a special case of differential pressure where the reference pressure is atmospheric pressure. Many pressure gages, including most refrigeration test sets, are designed to make gage pressure measurements, and there are probably more gage pressure measurements made than any other. Gage pressure measurements are often used as surrogates for absolute pressures. However, because of variations in atmospheric pressure caused by elevation (e.g., atmospheric pressure in Denver, Colorado, is about 81% of sea-level pressure) and weather changes, using gage pressures to determine absolute pressures can significantly restrict the accuracy of the measured pressure, unless corrections are made for the local atmospheric pressure at the time of measurement.

Pressures can be further classified as static or dynamic. **Static pressures** have a small or undetectable change with time; **dynamic pressures** include a significant pulsed, oscillatory, or other time-dependent component. Static pressure measurements are the most common, but equipment such as blowers and compressors can generate significant oscillatory pressures at discrete frequencies. Flow in pipes and ducts can generate resonant pressure changes, as well as turbulent "noise" that can span a wide range of frequencies.

Units

A plethora of pressure units, many of them poorly defined, are in common use. The international (SI) unit is the newton per square metre, called the pascal (Pa). Although the bar and standard atmosphere are used, they should not be introduced where they are not used at present. Although not internationally recognized, the pound per square inch (psi) is widely used. Units based on the length of liquid columns, including inches of mercury (in. Hg), mm of mercury (mm Hg), and inches of water (in. of water) (often used for low-range differential pressure measurements) are also used, but are not as rigorously defined (and thus a potential source of error). In the case of pounds per square inch, the type of pressure measurement is often indicated by a modification of the unit (i.e., both psi and psia are used to indicate absolute pressure measurements, psid indicates a differential measurement, and psig indicates a gage measurement). No such standard convention exists for other units, and unless explicitly stated, reported values are assumed to be absolute pressures. Conversion factors for different pressure units can be found in Chapter 39.

The difference between the conversion factors for inches of mercury and inches of water at the different temperatures is indicative of the errors that can arise from uncertainties about the definitions of these units.

5.1 INSTRUMENTS

Broadly speaking, pressure instruments can be divided into three different categories: standards, mechanical gages, and electromechanical transducers. Standards instruments are used for the most accurate calibrations. The liquid-column manometer, which is the most common and potentially the most accurate standard, is used for a variety of applications, including field applications. Mechanical pressure gages are generally the least expensive and the most common. However, electromechanical transducers have become much less expensive and are easier to use, so they are being used more often.

Pressure Standards

Liquid-column manometers measure pressure by determining the vertical displacement of a liquid of known density in a known gravitational field. Typically, they are constructed as a U-tube of transparent material (glass or plastic). The pressure to be measured is applied to one side of the U-tube. If the other (reference) side is evacuated (zero pressure), the manometer measures absolute pressure; if the reference side is open to the atmosphere, it measures gage pressure; if the reference side is connected to some other pressure, the manometer measures the differential between the two pressures. Manometers filled with water and different oils are often used to measure low-range differential pressures. In some low-range instruments, one tube of the manometer is inclined to enhance readability. Mercury-filled manometers are used for higher-range differential and absolute pressure measurements. In the latter case, the reference side is evacuated, generally with a mechanical vacuum pump. Typical full-scale ranges for manometers vary from 0.10 in. of water to 3 atm.

For pressures above the range of manometers, standards are generally of the piston-gage, pressure-balance, or deadweight-tester type. These instruments apply pressure to the bottom of a vertical piston, which is surrounded by a close-fitting cylinder (typical clearances are millionths of an inch). The pressure generates a force approximately equal to the pressure times the area of the piston. This force is balanced by weights stacked on the top of the piston. If the mass of the weights, local acceleration of gravity, and area of the piston (or more properly, the "effective area" of the piston and cylinder assembly) are known, the applied pressure can be calculated. Piston gages usually generate gage pressures with respect to the atmospheric pressure above the piston. They can be used to measure absolute pressures either indirectly, by separately measuring the atmospheric pressure and adding it to the gage pressure determined by the piston gage, or directly, by surrounding the top of the piston and weights with an evacuated bell jar. Piston gage full-scale ranges vary from 5 to 200,000 psi.

At very low absolute pressures (below about 0.4 in. of water), a number of different types of standards are used. These tend to be specialized and expensive instruments found only in major standards laboratories. However, one low-pressure standard, the **McLeod gage**, has been used for field applications. Unfortunately, although its theory is simple and straightforward, it is difficult to use accurately, and major errors can occur when it is used to measure gases that condense or are adsorbed (e.g., water). In general, other gages should be used for most low-pressure or vacuum applications.

Mechanical Pressure Gages

Mechanical pressure gages couple a pressure sensor to a mechanical readout, typically a pointer and dial. The most common type uses a **Bourdon tube** sensor, which is essentially a coiled metal tube of circular or elliptical cross section. Increasing pressure applied to the inside of the tube causes it to uncoil. A mechanical linkage translates the motion of the end of the tube to the rotation of a pointer. In most cases, the Bourdon tube is surrounded by atmospheric pressure, so that the gages measure gage pressure. A few instruments surround the Bourdon tube with a sealed enclosure that can be evacuated for absolute measurements or connected to another pressure for differential measurements. Available instruments vary widely in cost, size, pressure range, and accuracy. Full-scale ranges can vary from 5 to 100,000 psi. Accuracy of properly calibrated and used instruments can vary from 0.1 to 10% of full scale. Generally there is a strong correlation between size, accuracy, and price; larger instruments are more accurate and expensive.

For better sensitivity, some low-range mechanical gages (sometimes called **aneroid gages**) use corrugated diaphragms or capsules as sensors. The capsule is basically a short bellows sealed with end caps. These sensors are more compliant than a Bourdon tube, and a given applied pressure causes a larger deflection of the sensor. The inside of a capsule can be evacuated and sealed to measure absolute pressures or connected to an external fitting to allow differential pressures to be measured. Typically, these gages are used for low-range measurements of 1 atm or less. In better-quality instruments, accuracies can be 0.1% of reading or better.

Electromechanical Transducers

Mechanical pressure gages are generally limited by inelastic behavior of the sensing element, friction in the readout mechanism, and limited resolution of the pointer and dial. These effects can be eliminated or reduced by using electronic techniques to sense the distortion or stress of a mechanical sensing element and electronically convert that stress or distortion to a pressure reading. Various sensors are used, including Bourdon tubes, capsules, diaphragms, and different resonant structures whose vibration frequency varies with the applied pressure. Capacitive, inductive, and optical lever sensors are used to measure the sensor element's displacement. In some cases, feedback techniques may be used to constrain the sensor in a null position, minimizing distortion and hysteresis of the sensing element. Temperature control or compensation is often included. Readout may be in the form of a digital display, analog voltage or current, or a digital code. Size varies, but for transducers using a diaphragm fabricated as part of a silicon chip, the sensor and signal-conditioning electronics can be contained in a small transistor package, and the largest part of the device is the pressure fitting. The best of these instruments achieve long-term instabilities of 0.01% or less of full scale, and corresponding accuracies when properly calibrated. Performance of less-expensive instruments can be more on the order of several percent.

Although the dynamic response of most mechanical gages is limited by the sensor and readout, the response of some electromechanical transducers can be much faster, allowing measurements of dynamic pressures at frequencies up to 1 kHz and beyond in the case of transducers specifically designed for dynamic measurements. Consult manufacturers' literature as a guide to the dynamic response of specific instruments.

As the measured pressure drops below about 1.5 psia, it becomes increasingly difficult to sense mechanically. Various gages have been developed that measure some other property of the gas that is related to the pressure. In particular, **thermal conductivity gages**, also known as **thermocouple**, **thermistor**, **Pirani**, and **convection gages**, are used for pressures down to about 0.0004 in. of water. These gages have a sensor tube with a small heated element and a temperature sensor; the temperature of the heated element is determined by the thermal conductivity of the gas, and the output of the temperature sensor is displayed on an analog or digital electrical meter contained in an attached electronics unit. The accuracy of thermal conductivity gages is limited by their nonlinearity, dependence on gas species, and tendency to read high when contaminated. Oil contamination is a particular problem. However, these gages are small, reasonably rugged, and relatively inexpensive; in the hands of a typical user, they give far more reliable results than a McLeod gage. They can be used to check the base pressure in a system that is being evacuated before being filled with refrigerant. They should be checked periodically for contamination by comparing the reading with that from a new, clean sensor tube.

General Considerations

Accurate values of atmospheric or barometric pressure are required for weather prediction and aircraft altimetry. In the United States, the National Weather Service, Federal Aviation Administration, and local airport operating authorities maintain a network of calibrated instruments, generally accurate to within 0.1% of reading and located at airports. These agencies are usually cooperative in providing current values of atmospheric pressure that can be used to check the calibration of absolute pressure gages or to correct gage pressure readings to absolute pressures. However, pressure readings generally reported for weather and altimetry purposes are not the true atmospheric pressure, but rather a value adjusted to an equivalent sea-level pressure. Therefore, unless the location is near sea level, it is important to ask for the station or true atmospheric pressure rather than using the adjusted values broadcast by radio stations. Further, atmospheric pressure decreases with increasing elevation at a rate (near sea level) of about 0.001 in. Hg/ft, and corresponding corrections should be made to account for the difference in elevation between the instruments being compared.

Gage-pressure instruments are sometimes used to measure absolute pressures, but their accuracy can be compromised by uncertainties in atmospheric pressure. This error can be particularly serious when gage-pressure instruments are used to measure vacuum (negative gage pressures). For all but the crudest measurements, absolute-pressure gages should be used for vacuum measurements; for pressures below about 0.4 in. of water, a thermal conductivity gage should be used.

All pressure gages are susceptible to temperature errors. Several techniques are used to minimize these errors: sensor materials are generally chosen to minimize temperature effects, mechanical readouts can include temperature compensation elements, electromechanical transducers may include a temperature sensor and compensation circuit, and some transducers operate at a controlled temperature. Clearly, temperature effects are of greater concern for field applications, and it is prudent to check the manufacturers' literature for the temperature range over which the specified accuracy can be maintained. Abrupt temperature changes can also cause large transient errors that may take some time to decay.

Readings of some electromechanical transducers with a resonant or vibrating sensor can depend on the gas species. Although some of these units can achieve calibrated accuracies of the order of 0.01% of reading, they are typically calibrated with dry air or nitrogen, and readings for other gases can be in error by several percent, possibly much more for refrigerants and other high-density gases. High-accuracy readings can be maintained by calibrating these devices with the gas to be measured. Consult manufacturers' literature.

Measuring dynamic pressures is limited not just by the frequency response of the pressure gage, but also by the hydraulic or pneumatic time constant of the connection between the gage and the system to be monitored. Generally, the longer the connecting lines and the smaller their diameter, the lower the system's frequency response. Further, even if only the static component of the pressure is of interest, and a gage with a low-frequency response is used, a significant pulsating or oscillating pressure component can cause significant errors in pressure gage readings and, in some cases, can damage the gage, particularly one with a mechanical readout mechanism. In these cases, a filter or snubber should be used to reduce the higher-frequency components.

6. AIR VELOCITY MEASUREMENT

HVAC engineers measure the flow of air more often than any other gas, and usually at or near atmospheric pressure. Under this condition, air can be treated as an incompressible (i.e., constant-density) fluid, and simple formulas give sufficient precision to solve many problems. Instruments that measure fluid velocity and their application range and precision are listed in Table 4.

6.1 AIRBORNE TRACER TECHNIQUES

Tracer techniques are suitable for measuring velocity in an open space. Typical tracers include smoke, feathers, pieces of lint, and radioactive or nonradioactive gases. Measurements are made by timing the rate of movement of solid tracers or by monitoring the change in concentration level of gas tracers.

Smoke is a useful qualitative tool in studying air movements. Smoke can be obtained from titanium tetrachloride (irritating to nasal membranes) or by mixing potassium chlorate and powdered sugar (nonirritating) and firing the mixture with a match. The latter process produces considerable heat and should be confined to a pan away from flammable materials. Titanium tetrachloride smoke works well for spot tests, particularly for leakage through casings and ducts, because it can be handled easily in a small, pistol-like ejector. Another alternative is theatrical smoke, which is nontoxic, but requires proper illumination.

Fumes of ammonia water and sulfuric acid, if allowed to mix, form a white precipitate. Two bottles, one containing ammonia water and the other containing acid, are connected to a common nozzle by rubber tubing. A syringe forces air over the liquid surfaces in the bottles; the two streams mix at the nozzle and form a white cloud.

A satisfactory test smoke also can be made by bubbling an airstream through ammonium hydroxide and then hydrochloric acid (Nottage et al. 1952). Smoke tubes, smoke candles, and smoke bombs are available for studying airflow patterns.

6.2 ANEMOMETERS

Deflecting Vane Anemometers

The deflecting vane anemometer consists of a pivoted vane enclosed in a case. Air exerts pressure on the vane as it passes through the instrument from an upstream to a downstream opening. A hair spring and a damping magnet resist vane movement. The instrument gives instantaneous readings of directional velocities on an indicating scale. With fluctuating velocities, needle swings must be visually averaged. This instrument is useful for studying air motion in a room, locating objectionable drafts, measuring air velocities at supply and return diffusers and grilles, and measuring laboratory hood face velocities.

Propeller or Revolving (Rotating) Vane Anemometers

The propeller anemometer consists of a light, revolving, wind-driven wheel connected through a gear train to a set of recording dials that read linear feet of air passing in a measured length of time. It is made in various sizes, though 3, 4, and 6 in. are the most common. Each instrument requires individual calibration. At low velocities, the mechanism's friction drag is considerable, and is usually compensated for by a gear train that overspeeds. For this reason, the correction is often additive at the lower range and subtractive at the upper range, with the least correction in the middle range. The best instruments have starting speeds of 50 fpm or higher; therefore, they cannot be used below that air speed. Electronic revolving vane anemometers, with optical or magnetic pickups to sense the rotation of the vane, are available in vane sizes as small as 1/2 in. diameter.

Cup Anemometers

The cup anemometer is primarily used to measure outdoor, meteorological wind speeds. It consists of three or four hemispherical cups mounted radially from a vertical shaft. Wind from any direction with a vector component in the plane of cup rotation causes the cups and shaft to rotate. Because it is primarily used to measure meteorological wind speeds, the instrument is usually constructed so that wind speeds can be recorded or indicated electrically at a remote point.

Thermal Anemometers

The thermal (or hot-wire, or hot-film) anemometer consists of a heated RTD, thermocouple junction, or thermistor sensor constructed at the end of a probe; it is designed to provide a direct, simple method of determining air velocity at a point in the flow field. The probe is placed into an airstream, and air movement past the electrically heated velocity sensor tends to cool the sensor in proportion to the speed of the airflow. The electronics and sensor are commonly combined into a portable, hand-held device that interprets the sensor signal and provides a direct reading of air velocity in either analog or digital display format. Often, the sensor probe also incorporates an ambient temperature-sensing RTD or thermistor, in which case the indicated air velocity is temperature compensated to standard air density conditions (typically 0.0748 lb/ft^3).

Thermal anemometers have long been used in fluid flow research. Research anemometer sensors have been constructed using very fine wires in configurations that allow characterization of fluid flows in one, two, and three dimensions, with sensor/electronics response rates up to several hundred kilohertz. This technology has been incorporated into more ruggedized sensors suitable for measurements in the HVAC field, primarily for unidirectional airflow measurement. Omnidirectional sensing instruments suitable for thermal comfort studies are also available.

The principal advantages of thermal anemometers are their wide dynamic range and their ability to sense extremely low velocities. Commercially available portable instruments often have a typical accuracy (including repeatability) of 2 to 5% of reading over the entire velocity range. Accuracies of ±2% of reading or better are obtainable from microcontroller (microprocessor)-based thermistor and RTD sensor assemblies, some of which can be factory-calibrated to known reference standards (e.g., NIST air speed tunnels). An integrated microcontroller also allows an array of sensor assemblies to be combined in one duct or opening, providing independently derived velocity and temperature measurements at each point.

Limitations of thermistor-based velocity measuring devices depend on sensor configuration, specific thermistor type used, and the application. At low velocities, thermal anemometers can be significantly affected by their own thermal plumes (from self heating). Products using this technology can be classified as hand-held instruments or permanently mounted probes and arrays, and as those with analog electronic transmitters and those that are microcontroller-based.

Limitations of hand-held and analog electronic thermal anemometers include the following: (1) the unidirectional sensor must be carefully aligned in the airstream (typically to within ±20° rotation)

Table 4 Air Velocity Measurement

Measurement Means	Application	Range, fpm	Precision	Limitations
Smoke puff or airborne solid tracer	Low air velocities in rooms; highly directional	5 to 50	10 to 20%	Awkward to use but valuable in tracing air movement.
Deflecting vane anemometer	Air velocities in rooms, at outlets, etc.; directional	30 to 24,000	5%	Requires periodic calibration check.
Revolving (rotating) vane anemometer	Moderate air velocities in ducts and rooms; somewhat directional	100 to 3000	2 to 5%	Subject to significant errors when variations in velocities with space or time are present. Easily damaged. Affected by turbulence intensity. Requires periodic calibration.
Thermal (hot-wire or hot-film) anemometer	a. Low air velocities; directional and omnidirectional available b. Transient velocity and turbulence	10 to 10,000	2 to 10%	Requires accurate calibration at frequent intervals. Some are relatively costly. Affected by thermal plume because of self-heating.
Pitot-static tube	Standard (typically hand-held) instrument for measuring single-point duct velocities	180 to 10,000 with micromanometer; 600 to 10,000 with draft gages; 10,000 up with manometer	2 to 5%	Accuracy falls off at low end of range because of square-root relationship between velocity and dynamic pressure. Also affected by alignment with flow direction.
Impact tube and sidewall or other static tap	High velocities, small tubes, and where air direction may be variable	120 to 10,000 with micromanometer; 600 to 10,000 with draft gages; 10,000 up with manometer	2 to 5%	Accuracy depends on constancy of static pressure across stream section.
Cup anemometer	Meteorological	Up to 12,000	2 to 5%	Poor accuracy at low air velocity (<500 fpm).
Ultrasonic	Large instruments: meteorological Small instruments: in-duct and room air velocities	1 to 6000	1 to 2%	High cost.
Laser Doppler velocimeter (LDV)	Calibration of air velocity instruments	1 to 6000	1 to 3%	High cost and complexity limit LDVs to laboratory applications. Requires seeding of flow with particles, and transparent optical access (window).
Particle image velocimetry (PIV)	Full-field (2D, 3D) velocity measurements in rooms, outlets	0.02 to 100	10%	High cost and complexity limits measurements to laboratory applications. Requires seeding of flow with particles, and transparent optical access (window).
Pitot array, self-averaging differential pressure, typically using equalizing manifolds	In duct assemblies, ducted or fan inlet probes	600 to 10,000	±2 to >40% of reading	Performance depends heavily on quality and range of associated differential pressure transmitter. Very susceptible to measurement errors caused by duct placement and temperature changes. Nonlinear output (square-root function). Mathematical averaging errors likely because of sampling method. Must be kept clean to function properly. Must be set up and field calibrated to hand-held reference, or calibrated against nozzle standard.
Piezometer and piezo-ring variations, self-averaging differential pressure using equalizing manifolds	Centrifugal fan inlet cone	600 to 10,000	±5 to >40% of reading	Performance depends heavily on quality and range of required differential pressure transmitter. Very susceptible to measurement errors caused by inlet cone placement, inlet obstructions, and temperature changes. Nonlinear output (square-root function). Must be kept clean. Must be field calibrated to hand-held reference.
Vortex shedding	In-duct assemblies, ducted or fan inlet probes	450 to 6000	±2.5 to 10% of reading	Highest cost per sensing point. Largest physical size. Low-temperature accuracy questionable. Must be set up and field calibrated to hand-held reference.
Thermal (analog electronic) using thermistors	In-duct assemblies or ducted probes	50 to 5000	±2 to 40% of reading	Mathematical averaging errors may be caused by analog electronic circuitry when averaging nonlinear signals. Sensing points may not be independent. May not be able to compensate for temperatures beyond a narrow range. Must be set up and field calibrated to hand-held reference. Must be recalibrated regularly to counteract drift.
Drag force	In-duct flow	10 to 10,000	±2%	Piezoelectric or strain-gage methods are used to sense dynamic drag-force variations.
Thermal dispersion (microcontroller-based) using thermistors to independently determine temperatures and velocities	Ducted or fan inlet probes, bleed velocity sensors	20 to 10,000	±2 to 10% of reading	Cost increases with number of sensor assemblies in array. Honeycomb air straighteners are recommended by some manufacturers. Accuracy verified only to –20°F. Not suitable for abrasive or high-temperature environments.
Thermal (analog electronic) using RTDs	In-duct assemblies or ducted probes; stainless steel and platinum RTDs have industrial environment capabilities	100 to 18,000	±1 to 20% of reading	Requires long duct/pipe runs. Sensitive to placement conditions. Mathematical averaging errors may be caused by analog electronic circuitry when averaging nonlinear signals. Must be recalibrated regularly to counteract drift. Fairly expensive.

to achieve accurate results; (2) the velocity sensor must be kept clean because contaminant build-up can change the calibration (which may change accuracy performance); and (3) because of the inherent high speed of response of thermal anemometers, measurements in turbulent flows can yield fluctuating velocity measurements. Electronically controlled time-integrated functions are now available in many digital air velocity meters to help smooth these turbulent flow measurements.

Microcontroller-based thermal dispersion devices are typically configured as unidirectional instruments, but may have multiple velocity-sensing elements capable of detecting flow direction. These devices can be used to measure a "bleed" air velocity between two spaces or across a fixed orifice. With mathematical conversion, these measured velocities can closely approximate equivalents in differential pressure down to five decimal places (in. of water). They can be used for space pressure control, to identify minute changes in flow direction, or for estimating volumetric flow rates across a fixed orifice by equating to velocity pressure.

Thermal anemometers are suitable for a variety of HVAC applications. They are particularly well suited to the low velocities associated with outdoor air intake measurement and control, return or relief fan tracking for pressurization in variable-air-volume (VAV) systems, VAV terminal box measurement, unit ventilator and packaged equipment intake measurement, space pressurization for medical isolation, and laboratory fume hood face velocity measurements (typically in the 50 to 200 fpm range). Thermal anemometers can also take multipoint traverse measurements in ventilation ductwork.

Laser Doppler Velocimeters (or Anemometers)

The laser Doppler velocimeter (LDV) or laser Doppler anemometer (LDA) is an extremely complex system that collects scattered light produced by particles (i.e., seed) passing through the intersection volume of two intersecting laser beams of the same light frequency, which produces a regularly spaced fringe pattern (Mease et al. 1992). The scattered light consists of bursts containing regularly spaced oscillations whose frequency is linearly proportional to the speed of the particle. Because of their cost and complexity, they are usually not suitable for in situ field measurements. Rather, the primary HVAC application of LDV systems is calibrating systems used to calibrate other air velocity instruments.

The greatest advantage of an LDV is its performance at low air speeds: as low as 15 fpm with uncertainty levels of 1% or less (Mease et al. 1992). In addition, it is nonintrusive in the flow; only optical access is required. It can be used to measure fluctuating components as well as mean speeds and is available in one-, two-, and even three-dimensional configurations. Its biggest disadvantages are its high cost and extreme technological complexity, which requires highly skilled operators. Modern fiber-optic systems require less operator skill but at a considerable increase in cost.

Particle Image Velocimetry (PIV)

Particle image velocimetry (PIV) is an optical method that measures fluid velocity by determining the displacement of approximately neutrally buoyant seed particles introduced in the flow. Particle displacements are determined from images of particle positions at two instants of time. Usually, statistical (correlation) methods are used to identify the displacement field.

The greatest advantage of PIV is its ability to examine two- and three-dimensional velocity fields over a region of flow. The method usually requires laser light (sheet) illumination, and is typically limited to a field area of less than 10 ft^2. Accuracy is usually limited to about ±10% by the resolution of particle displacements, which must be small enough to remain in the field of view during the selected displacement time interval. For more comprehensive information on PIV, including estimates of uncertainty, see Raffel et al. (1998).

6.3 PITOT-STATIC TUBES

The pitot-static tube, in conjunction with a suitable manometer or differential pressure transducer, provides a simple method of determining air velocity at a point in a flow field. Figure 6 shows the construction of a standard pitot tube (ASHRAE *Standard* 51) and the method of connecting it with inclined manometers to display both static pressure and velocity pressure. The equation for determining air velocity from measured velocity pressure is

$$V = C\sqrt{\frac{2p_w g_c}{\rho}} \tag{5}$$

where

V = velocity, fpm
p_w = velocity pressure (pitot-tube manometer reading), in. of water
ρ = density of air, lb_m/ft^3
g_c = gravitational constant = 32.174 $lb_m \cdot ft/lb_f \cdot s^2$
C = unit conversion factor = 136.8

The type of manometer or differential pressure transducer used with a pitot-static tube depends on the magnitude of velocity pressure being measured and on the desired accuracy. Over 1500 fpm, a draft gage of appropriate range is usually satisfactory. If the pitot-static tube is used to measure air velocities lower than 1500 fpm, a precision manometer or comparable pressure differential transducer is essential.

Example 1.

Step 1. Numerical evaluation. Let p_w = 0.3740 ± 0.005 in. of water and ρ = 0.0740 ±0.0010 lb_m/ft^3. Then,

$$V = C\sqrt{\frac{2p_w g_c}{\rho}} = (136.8)\sqrt{\frac{2(0.3740)(32.174)}{(0.0740)}} = 2467 \text{ fpm}$$

Step 2. Uncertainty estimate. Let the typical bias (i.e., calibration) uncertainty of the pitot tube be $u_{V,bias}$ = ±1% of reading. The uncertainty in the velocity measurement is thus estimated to be

$$\begin{aligned} u_V &= \sqrt{(u_{V,bias})^2 + (u_{V,prec})^2} \\ &= \sqrt{(u_{V,bias})^2 + \left[\tfrac{1}{2}(u_{pw})\right]^2 + \left[\tfrac{1}{2}(u_\rho)\right]^2} \\ &= \sqrt{(0.01)^2 + \left[\tfrac{1}{2}\left(\tfrac{0.005}{0.3740}\right)\right]^2 + \left[\tfrac{1}{2}\left(\tfrac{0.0010}{0.0740}\right)\right]^2} \\ &= \pm 0.014 = \pm 1.4\% \end{aligned}$$

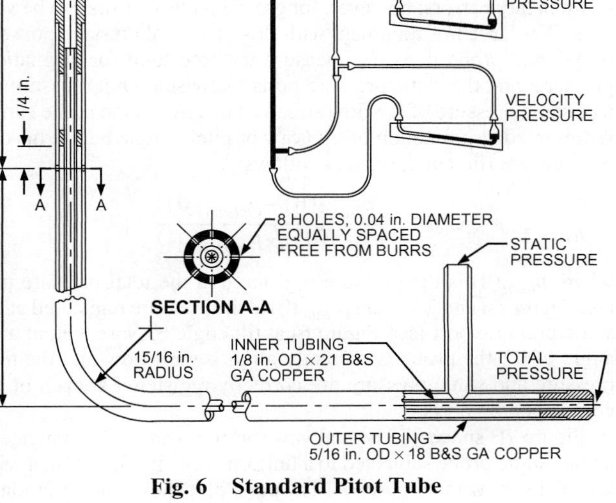

Fig. 6 Standard Pitot Tube

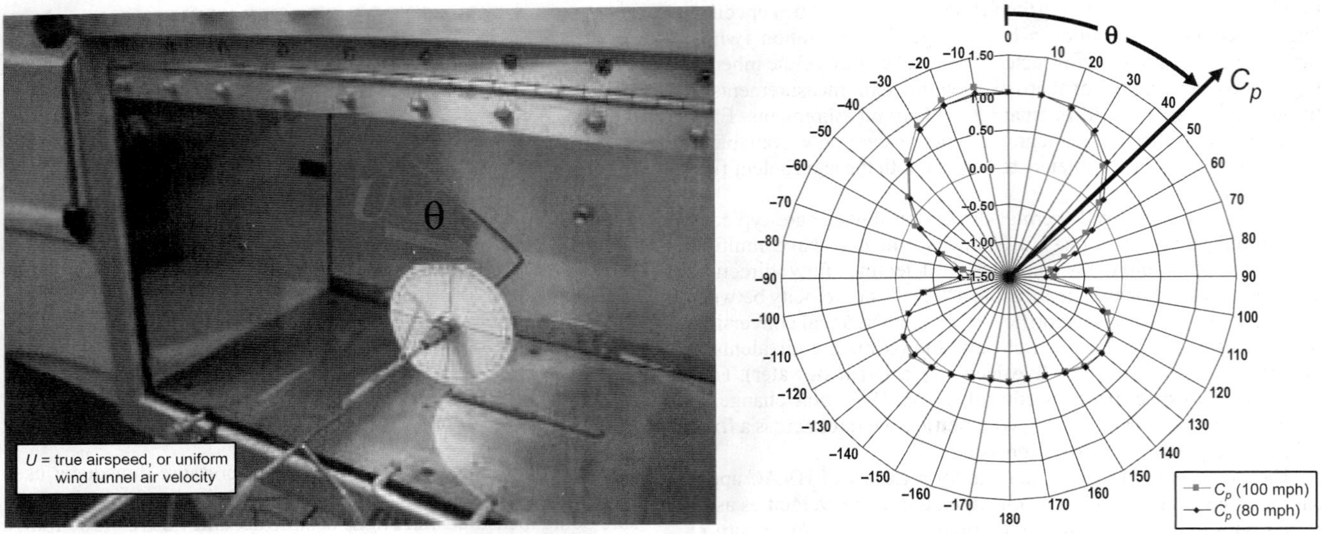

(A) PITOT-STATIC PROBE WIND TUNNEL SETUP (B) PROBE PRESSURE COEFFICIENT

Fig. 7 Pitot-Static Probe Pressure Coefficient Yaw Angular Dependence

Therefore,

$$U_V = \pm u_V V = \pm(0.014)(2467 \text{ fpm}) = \pm 34 \text{ fpm}$$

In summary,

$$V = 2467 \pm 34 \text{ fpm}$$

Other pitot-static tubes have been used and calibrated. To meet special conditions, various sizes of pitot-static tubes geometrically similar to the standard tube can be used. For relatively high velocities in ducts of small cross-sectional area, total pressure readings can be obtained with an impact (pitot) tube. Where static pressure across the stream is relatively constant, as in turbulent flow in a straight duct, a sidewall tap to obtain static pressure can be used with the impact tube to obtain the velocity pressure head. One form of impact tube is a small streamlined tube with a fine hole in its upstream end and its axis parallel to the stream.

If the Mach number of the flow is greater than about 0.3, the effects of compressibility should be included in the computation of the air speed from pitot-static and impact (stagnation or pitot) tube measurements (Mease et al. 1992).

It is extremely important to recognize that the pitot-static probe is designed to make measurements when aligned with the flow. Misalignment in yaw angle of up to about 15 to 20° generally do not result in large errors; however, for greater angles, errors can be very large. For large misalignment with flow, the total pressure port of a pitot-static probe does not measure the true total (or stagnation) pressure, and the static pressure ports likewise do not measure the true static pressure of the flow stream. The error in the probe can be represented as a function of tilt (yaw or pitch) angle θ in terms of a pressure coefficient defined as follows:

$$C_p(\theta) \equiv \frac{p_{total}(\theta) - p_{static}(\theta)}{p_{total}(0°) - p_{static}(0°)} \tag{6}$$

where $p_{total}(\theta)$ is the pressure registered at the total pressure port (see Figures 6 and 7A), and $p_{static}(\theta)$ is the pressure registered at the static pressure port (see Figure 6) at tilt angle θ. Note that, at a tilt angle of 0°, the probe is correctly aligned with flow and the total pressure and static pressure are correctly registered at each of the corresponding ports.

Figure 7B shows the typical yaw (or pitch) angle dependence of a pitot-static probe subjected to a uniform velocity field U in a wind tunnel, as shown in Figure 7A. The polar plot shows the variation of pressure coefficient $C_p(\theta)$ with yaw (or pitch) angle over the entire 360° range (essentially a symmetrical ±180 degrees). A pressure coefficient of $C_p = 1$ corresponds to a situation of good alignment with the flow and thus negligible error. Note that the pressure coefficient varies from +1 to –1 over the entire range of yaw (or pitch) angles. In reverse flows (θ near 180°), output hovers around zero flow coefficient. Because the pitot-static probe does not provide a flow direction indication, it is not possible to determine the particular region of yaw (or pitch) angle operation. Therefore, the correct output for assessing volumetric flow rate (where it is desired to measure the axial flow component) cannot be determined with confidence (Hickman et al. 2012, 2015a, 2015b).

6.4 MEASURING FLOW IN DUCTS

Because velocity in a duct is seldom uniform across any section, and a pitot tube reading or thermal anemometer indicates velocity at only one location, a traverse is usually made to determine average velocity. Generally, velocity is lowest near the side-wall edges or corners and greatest at or near the center of a duct.

To determine velocity in a traverse plane, a straight average of individual point velocities gives satisfactory results when point velocities are determined by the **log-Tchebycheff (log-T) rule** or, if care is taken, by the **equal-area method**. Figure 8 shows suggested sensor locations for traversing round and rectangular ducts. The log-Tchebycheff rule provides the greatest accuracy because its location of traverse points accounts for the effect of wall friction and the fall-off of velocity near wall ducts. For single-path disturbances (straight ducts, transitions, and elbow fittings), the equal-area method has been shown to give a consistent 3 to 4% positive bias, regardless of probe type (pitot-static, hot-wire anemometer), volumetric flow rate, or traverse location within 7.5 equivalent diameters downstream of a fitting disturbance (Hickman et al. 2012, 2015a, 2015b). The log-T method is now recommended for rectangular ducts with H and W > 18 in. For circular ducts, the log-T and log-linear methods are similar. Log-T minimizes the positive error (measured greater than actual) caused by the failure to account for losses at the duct wall. This error can occur when using the older method of equal subareas to traverse rectangular ducts. The equal-area method is perhaps easier to implement, because it does not require nonuniform measurement grid spacing and generally specifies fewer measurement locations. Therefore, it seems reasonable to first assess the

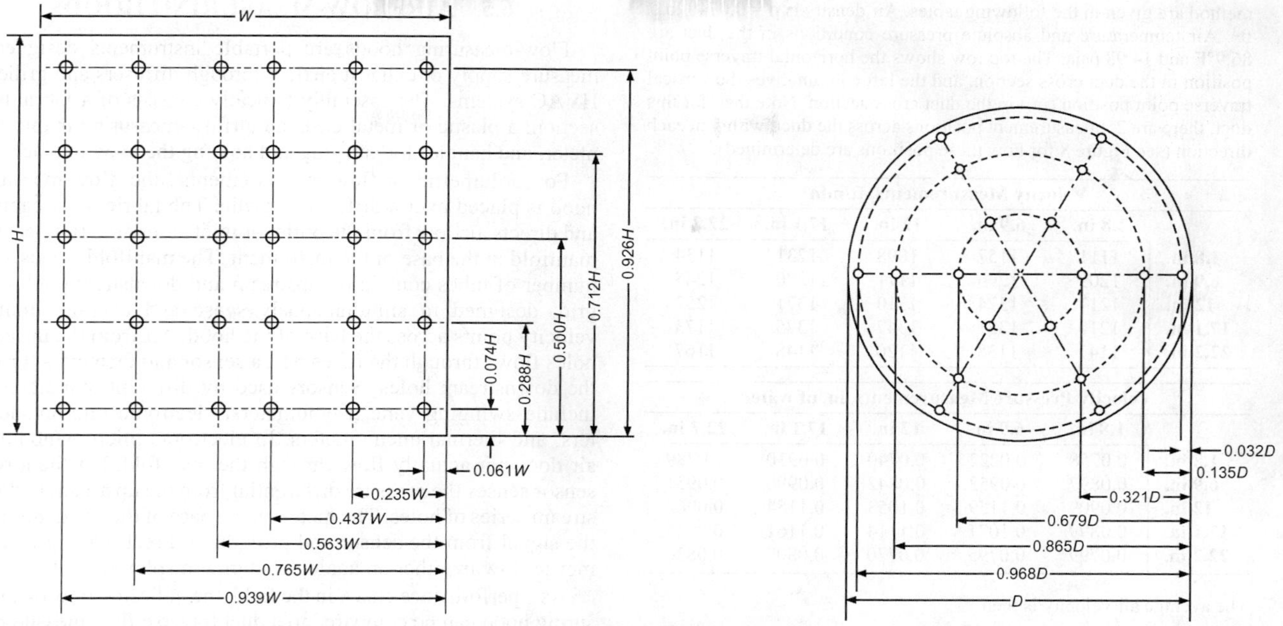

Duct Dimensions	No. of Points for Traverse Lines	Position Relative to Inner Wall
18 in. < *H*, *W* < 30 in.	5	0.074, 0.288, 0.500, 0.712, 0.926
30 in. ≤ *H*, *W* ≤ 36 in.	6	0.061, 0.235, 0.437, 0.563, 0.765, 0.939
H, *W* > 36 in.	7	0.053, 0.203, 0.366, 0.500, 0.634, 0.797, 0.947

Log-Tchebycheff Rule for Rectangular Ducts

Note: Example duct has 5 × 6 (*H* × *W*) measurement pattern, as for rectangular duct of 24 × 30 in.

No. of Measuring Points per Diameter	Position Relative to Inner Wall
6	0.032, 0.135, 0.321, 0.679, 0.865, 0.968
8	0.021, 0.117, 0.184, 0.345, 0.655, 0.816, 0.883, 0.979
10	0.019, 0.077, 0.153, 0.217, 0.361, 0.639, 0.783, 0.847, 0.923, 0.981

Log-Linear Rule for Circular Ducts

Fig. 8 Measuring Points for Rectangular and Round Duct Traverse

volumetric flow rate with equal area method and subsequently reduce the indicated result by approximately 3 to 4%, thereby achieving a good approximation of the log-T traverse measurement. This may be a reasonable compromise for those who do not wish to use the log-T method (Hickman et al. 2012).

When using the log-T method for a rectangular duct traverse, measure a minimum of 25 points. For a circular duct traverse, the log-linear rule and three symmetrically disposed diameters may be used (Figure 8). Points on two perpendicular diameters may be used where access is limited.

If possible, measuring points should be located at least 7.5 hydraulic diameters downstream and 3 hydraulic diameters upstream from a disturbance (e.g., caused by a turn). However, for common single-path rectangular duct fitting disturbances (60° and 90° transitions, 90° elbows), measurements can be made to uncertainties within about ±3 to 4% for traverses even as close as 1 to 2 equivalent diameters downstream of the disturbance using the log-T traverse method. Furthermore, similar results can be obtained in single-path rectangular ducts with these types disturbances using either a pitot-static probe or a hot-wire anemometer (Hickman et al. 2012).

Because field-measured airflows are rarely steady and uniform, particularly near disturbances, accuracy can be improved by increasing the number of measuring points. Straightening vanes (ASHRAE *Standard* 51) located 1.5 duct diameters ahead of the traverse plane improve measurement precision.

When velocities at a traverse plane fluctuate, the readings should be averaged on a time-weighted basis. Two traverse readings in short succession also help to average out velocity variations that occur with time. If negative velocity pressure readings are encountered, this is an indication that highly nonuniform flows are present. From the characteristics of the pitot-static probe yaw variation shown in Figure 7, it is not possible to draw meaningful and reliable conclusions from the measurements, particularly downstream of tee fitting disturbances, where boundary layer separation occurs (which causes flow reversal) in the branch region downstream of the tee. Even if no actual reversal occurs, the flow may also be highly nonaxial, and the flow directional limitations of the pitot-static probe, as shown in Figure 7B, may still result in meaningless results. Also, it is important to note that, although the pitot-static probe can produce a negative and potentially meaningless output, it does indicate obvious flow uniformity problems. *Important Note*: negative velocity pressures measured by a pitot-static tube indicate an unacceptable traverse location. To achieve meaningful volumetric flow rate measurements, traverses must be performed where no negative velocity pressure values occur. The presence of negative velocity pressures (even when those values are considered to be zero-velocity values when summing and averaging) results in a completely meaningless duct flow calculation.

A hot-wire anemometer cannot indicate flow direction. Consequently, it always indicates a positive velocity, even under reverse flow. Hence, use of a thermal anemometer probe wherever flow reversals occur, such as those encountered in the downstream branch of tee fittings, can result in large errors. For traverse measurements in the downstream branch of tees, regions of apparent negative velocity pressure have been encountered as far as 7.5 equivalent diameters downstream of the tee, and are more likely to occur at high flow rates with relatively low relative branch flows (Hickman et al. 2012). These regions should be avoided when using thermal anemometers.

Example 2.

Step 1. Numerical Evaluation of Duct Average Velocity. Velocity measurements for a 24 × 24 in. square duct traverse using the log-T method are given in the following tables. Air density is $\rho = 0.0740$ lb$_m$/ft^3. Air temperature and absolute pressure conditions in the duct are 86.9°F and 14.98 psia. The top row shows the horizontal traverse point position in the duct cross section, and the left column gives the vertical traverse point position (in.) in the duct cross-section. Note that, for this duct, there are 25 measurement positions across the duct, with 5 in each direction (see Figure 8 for how these positions are determined).

Velocity Measurements, ft/min					
	1.8 in.	**6.9 in.**	**12 in.**	**17.1 in.**	**22.2 in.**
1.8 in.	1111	1157	1098	1231	1134
6.9 in.	1209	1246	1171	1270	1245
12 in.	1217	1374	1310	1371	1252
17.1 in.	1210	1321	1347	1375	1173
22.2 in.	1141	1138	1120	1148	1167

Velocity Pressure Measurements, in. of water					
	1.8 in.	**6.9 in.**	**12 in.**	**17.1 in.**	**22.2 in.**
1.8 in.	0.0758	0.0822	0.0740	0.0930	0.0789
6.9 in.	0.0897	0.0953	0.0842	0.0990	0.0951
12 in.	0.0909	0.1159	0.1053	0.1154	0.0962
17.1 in.	0.0899	0.1071	0.1114	0.1161	0.0845
22.2 in.	0.0799	0.0795	0.0770	0.0809	0.0836

The average air velocity is then

$$V_{ave} = \frac{1}{N}\sum_{i=1}^{N} V_i = \frac{(V_1 + V_2 + V_3 + V_4 + \cdots + V_N)}{N} = 1221 \text{ ft/min}$$

Alternatively, if local measurements are made in terms of velocity pressure p_w, the average velocity is

$$V_{ave} = \frac{1}{N}\sum_{i=1}^{N} V_i = C\sqrt{\frac{2g_c}{\rho}}\left\{\frac{1}{N}\sum_{i=1}^{N}\sqrt{p_{w,i}}\right\}$$

$$= (136.8)\sqrt{\frac{2(32.174)}{0.0740}}\left\{\frac{1}{25}\sum_{i=1}^{25}[\sqrt{0.0758} + \sqrt{0.0822} + \sqrt{0.0758} + \cdots]\right\} = 1221 \text{ ft/min}$$

where the term in brackets represents the average of the square root of the individual velocity pressure measurements.

Step 2: Numerical Evaluation of Duct Volumetric Flow Rate. For the given duct cross-sectional area, the volumetric flow rate of air in actual cubic feet per minute (acfm) is then

$$Q_{Actual} = V_{ave}A = (1221 \text{ ft/min})(2.00 \times 2.00 \text{ ft}) = 4884 \text{ acfm}$$

where $A = 2 \times 2$ ft is the duct cross-sectional area. The preceding actual volumetric flow rates can be converted to standard volumetric flow rates by referencing the flow rates to standard air density conditions for the same mass flow rate. The standard volumetric flow rate is the flow rate that would exist of the air were at standard air density conditions. Thus,

$$Q_{Standard} = Q_{Actual}\left(\frac{P_{Actual}}{P_{Standard}}\right)\left(\frac{T_{Standard}}{T_{Actual}}\right)$$

If standard conditions are defined as 70°F and 14.7 psia, then the standard volumetric flow rate is

$$Q_{Standard} = (4884 \text{ acfm})\left(\frac{14.98 \text{ psia}}{14.7 \text{ psia}}\right)\left(\frac{70 + 459.69}{86.9 + 459.69}\right) = 4823 \text{ scfm}$$

Note: Different manufacturers can use different values for standard air density and standard conditions. It is very important to use a consistent set of standard conditions when comparing flow rates.

6.5 AIRFLOW-MEASURING HOODS

Flow-measuring hoods are portable instruments designed to measure supply or exhaust airflow through diffusers and grilles in HVAC systems. The assembly typically consists of a fabric hood section, a plastic or metal base, an airflow-measuring manifold, a meter, and handles for carrying and holding the hood in place.

For volumetric airflow measurements, the flow-measuring hood is placed over a diffuser or grille. The fabric hood captures and directs airflow from the outlet or inlet across the flow-sensing manifold in the base of the instrument. The manifold consists of a number of tubes containing upstream and downstream holes in a grid, designed to simultaneously sense and average multiple velocity points across the base of the hood. Air from the upstream holes flows through the tubes past a sensor and then exits through the downstream holes. Sensors used by different manufacturers include swinging vane anemometers, electronic micromanometers, and thermal anemometers. In electronic micromanometers, air does not actually flow through the manifold, but the airtight sensor senses the pressure differential from the upstream to downstream series of holes. The meter on the base of the hood interprets the signal from the sensor and provides a direct reading of volumetric flow in either an analog or digital display format.

As a performance check in the field, the indicated flow of a measuring hood can be compared to a duct traverse flow measurement (using a pitot-tube or thermal anemometer). All flow-measuring hoods induce some back pressure on the air-handling system because the hood restricts flow out of the diffuser. This added resistance alters the true amount of air coming out of the diffuser. In most cases, this error is negligible and is less than the accuracy of the instrument. For proportional balancing, this error need not be taken into account because all similar diffusers have about the same amount of back pressure. To determine whether back pressure is significant, a velocity traverse can be made in the duct ahead of the diffuser with and without the hood in place. The difference in average velocity of the traverse indicates the degree of back-pressure compensation required on similar diffusers in the system. For example, if the average velocity is 800 fpm with the hood in place and 820 fpm without the hood, the indicated flow reading can be multiplied by 1.025 on similar diffusers in the system (820/800 = 1.025). As an alternative, the designer of the air-handling system can predict the head-induced airflow reduction by using a curve supplied by the hood manufacturer. This curve indicates the pressure drop through the hood for different flow rates.

7. FLOW RATE MEASUREMENT

Various means of measuring fluid flow rate are listed in Table 5. Values for volumetric or mass flow rate measurement (ASME *Standard* PTC 19.5; Benedict 1984) are often determined by measuring pressure difference across an orifice, nozzle, or venturi tube. The various meters have different advantages and disadvantages. For example, the orifice plate is more easily changed than the complete nozzle or venturi tube assembly. However, the nozzle is often preferred to the orifice because its discharge coefficient is more precise. The venturi tube is a nozzle followed by an expanding recovery section to reduce net pressure loss. Differential pressure flow measurement has benefited through workshops addressing fundamental issues, textbooks, research, and improved standards (ASME *Standards* B40.100, MFC-1M, MFC-9M, MFC-10M; DeCarlo 1984; ISO *Standards* 5167:2003, 5801:2007; Mattingly 1984; Miller 1983).

Fluid meters use a wide variety of physical techniques to measure flow (ASME *Standard* PTC 19.5; DeCarlo 1984; Miller 1983); more common ones are described in this section. To validate accuracy of flow rate measurement instruments, calibration procedures

Table 5 Volumetric or Mass Flow Rate Measurement

Measurement Means	Application	Nominal Range	Precision	Limitations
Orifice and differential pressure measurement system	Flow through pipes, ducts, and plenums for all fluids	Above Reynolds number of 5000	1 to 5%	Discharge coefficient and accuracy influenced by installation conditions.
Nozzle and differential pressure measurement system	Flow through pipes, ducts, and plenums for all fluids	Above Reynolds number of 5000	0.5 to 2.0%	Discharge coefficient and accuracy influenced by installation conditions.
Venturi tube and differential pressure measurement system	Flow through pipes, ducts, and plenums for all fluids	Above Reynolds number of 5000	0.5 to 2.0%	Discharge coefficient and accuracy influenced by installation conditions.
Timing given mass or volumetric flow	Liquids or gases; used to calibrate other flowmeters	Any	0.1 to 0.5%	System is bulky and slow.
Rotameters	Liquids or gases	Any	0.5 to 5.0%	Should be calibrated for fluid being metered.
Coriolis	Mass or volume; variable-density liquids or gases	As high as 120,000 lb/min	0.05 to 1.5%	
Displacement meter	Relatively small volumetric flow with high pressure loss	As high as 1000 cfm, depending on type	0.1 to 2.0% depending on type	Most types require calibration with fluid being metered.
Gasometer or volume displacement	Short-duration tests; used to calibrate other flowmeters	Total flow limited by available volume of containers	0.5 to 1.0%	—
Thomas meter (temperature rise of stream caused by electrical heating)	Elaborate setup justified by need for good accuracy	Any	1%	Uniform velocity; usually used with gases.
Element of resistance to flow and differential pressure measurement system	Used for check where system has calibrated resistance element	Lower limit set by readable pressure drop	1 to 5%	Secondary reading depends on accuracy of calibration.
Turbine flowmeters	Liquids or gases	Any	0.25 to 2.0%	Uses electronic readout.
Single- or multipoint instrument for measuring velocity at specific point in flow	Primarily for installed air-handling systems with no special provision for flow measurement	Lower limit set by accuracy of velocity measurement instrumentation	2 to 10%	Accuracy depends on uniformity of flow and completeness of traverse. May be affected by disturbances near point of measurement.
Heat input and temperature changes with steam and water coil	Check value in heater or cooler tests	Any	1 to 3%	—
Laminar flow element and differential pressure measurement system	Measure liquid or gas volumetric flow rate; nearly linear relationship with pressure drop; simple and easy to use	0.0001 to 2000 cfm	1%	Fluid must be free of dirt, oil, and other impurities that could plug meter or affect its calibration.
Magnetohydrodynamic flowmeter (electromagnetic)	Measures electrically conductive fluids, slurries; meter does not obstruct flow; no moving parts	0.1 to 10,000 gpm	1%	At present state of the art, conductivity of fluid must be greater than 5 μmho/cm.
Swirl flowmeter and vortex shedding meter	Measure liquid or gas flow in pipe; no moving parts	Above Reynolds number of 10^4	1%	—

should include documentation of traceability to the calibration facility. The calibration facility should, in turn, provide documentation of traceability to national standards.

Flow Measurement Methods

Direct. Both gas and liquid flow can be measured accurately by timing a collected amount of fluid that is measured gravimetrically or volumetrically. This method is common for calibrating other metering devices, but it is particularly useful where flow rate is low or intermittent and where a high degree of accuracy is required. These systems are generally large and slow, but in their simplicity, they can be considered primary devices.

The **variable-area meter** or **rotameter** is a convenient direct-reading flowmeter for liquids and gases. This is a vertical, tapered tube in which the flow rate is indicated by the position of a float suspended in the upward flow. The float's position is determined by its buoyancy and the upward fluid drag.

Displacement meters measure total liquid or gas flow over time. The two major types of displacement meters used for gases are the conventional gas meter, which uses a set of bellows, and the wet test meter, which uses a water displacement principle.

Indirect. The **Thomas meter** is used in laboratories to measure high gas flow rates with low pressure losses. Gas is heated by electric heaters, and the temperature rise is measured by two resistance thermometer grids. When heat input and temperature rise are known, the mass flow of gas is calculated as the quantity of gas that removes the equivalent heat at the same temperature rise.

A velocity traverse (made using a pitot tube or other velocity-measuring instrument) measures airflow rates in the field or calibrates large nozzles. This method can be imprecise at low velocities and impracticable where many test runs are in progress.

Another field-estimating method measures pressure drop across elements with known pressure drop characteristics, such as heating and cooling coils or fans. If the pressure drop/flow rate relationship has been calibrated against a known reference (typically, at least four points in the operating range), the results can be precise. If the method depends on rating data, it should be used for check purposes only.

7.1 VENTURI, NOZZLE, AND ORIFICE FLOWMETERS

Flow in a pipeline can be measured by a venturi meter (Figure 9), flow nozzle (Figure 10), or orifice plate (Figure 11). American

Society of Mechanical Engineers (ASME) *Standard* MFC-3M describes measurement of fluid flow in pipes using the orifice, nozzle, and venturi; ASME *Standard* PTC 19.5 specifies their construction.

Assuming an incompressible fluid (liquid or slow-moving gas), uniform velocity profile, frictionless flow, and no gravitational effects, the principle of conservation of mass and energy can be applied to the venturi and nozzle geometries to give

$$w = \rho V_1 A_1 = \rho V_2 A_2 = A_2 \sqrt{\frac{2g_c \rho (p_1 - p_2)}{1 - \beta^4}} \tag{7}$$

where

w = mass flow rate, lb_m/s
V = velocity of stream, fps
A = flow area, ft^2
g_c = gravitational constant = 32.174 $lb_m \cdot ft/lb_f \cdot s^2$
ρ = density of fluid, lb_m/ft^3
p = absolute pressure, lb_f/ft^2
β = ratio of diameters D_2/D_1 for venturi and sharp-edge orifice and d/D for flow nozzle, where D = pipe diameter and d = throat diameter

Note: Subscript 1 refers to entering conditions; subscript 2 refers to throat conditions.

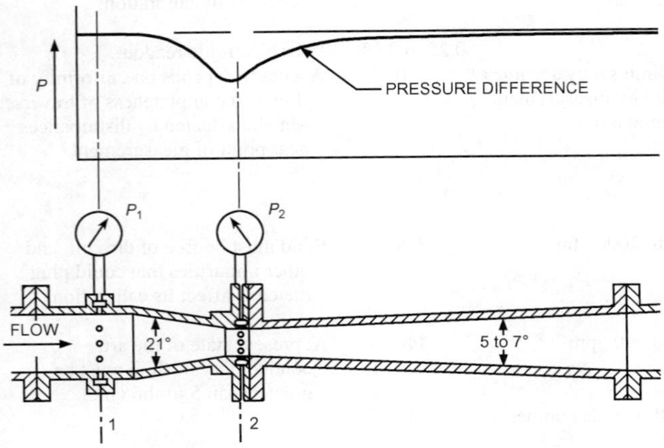

Fig. 9 Typical Herschel-Type Venturi Meter

Because flow through the meter is not frictionless, a correction factor C is defined to account for friction losses. If the fluid is at a high temperature, an additional correction factor F_a should be included to account for thermal expansion of the primary element. Because this amounts to less than 1% at 500°F, it can usually be omitted. Equation (7) then becomes

$$w = CA_2 \sqrt{\frac{2g_c \rho (p_1 - p_2)}{1 - \beta^4}} \tag{8}$$

where C is the friction loss correction factor.

The factor C is a function of geometry and Reynolds number. Values of C are given in ASME *Standard* PTC 19.5. The jet passing through an orifice plate contracts to a minimum area at the vena contracta located a short distance downstream from the orifice plate. The contraction coefficient, friction loss coefficient C, and approach factor $1/(1 - \beta^4)^{0.5}$ can be combined into a single constant K, which is a function of geometry and Reynolds number. The orifice flow rate equations then become

$$Q = KA_2 \sqrt{\frac{2g_c (p_1 - p_2)}{\rho}} \tag{9}$$

where

Q = discharge flow rate, cfs
A_2 = orifice area, ft^2
$p_1 - p_2$ = pressure drop as obtained by pressure taps, lb_f/ft^2

Values of K are shown in ASME *Standard* PTC 19.5.

Valves, bends, and fittings upstream from the flowmeter can cause errors. Long, straight pipes should be installed upstream and downstream from flow devices to ensure fully developed flow for proper measurement. ASHRAE *Standard* 41.8 specifies upstream and downstream pipe lengths for measuring flow of liquids with an orifice plate. ASME *Standard* PTC 19.5 gives piping requirements between various fittings and valves and the venturi, nozzle, and orifice. If these conditions cannot be met, flow conditioners or straightening vanes can be used (ASME *Standards* PTC 19.5, MFC-10M; Mattingly 1984; Miller 1983).

Compressibility effects must be considered for gas flow if pressure drop across the measuring device is more than a few percent of the initial pressure.

Nozzles are sometimes arranged in parallel pipes from a common manifold; thus, the capacity of the testing equipment can

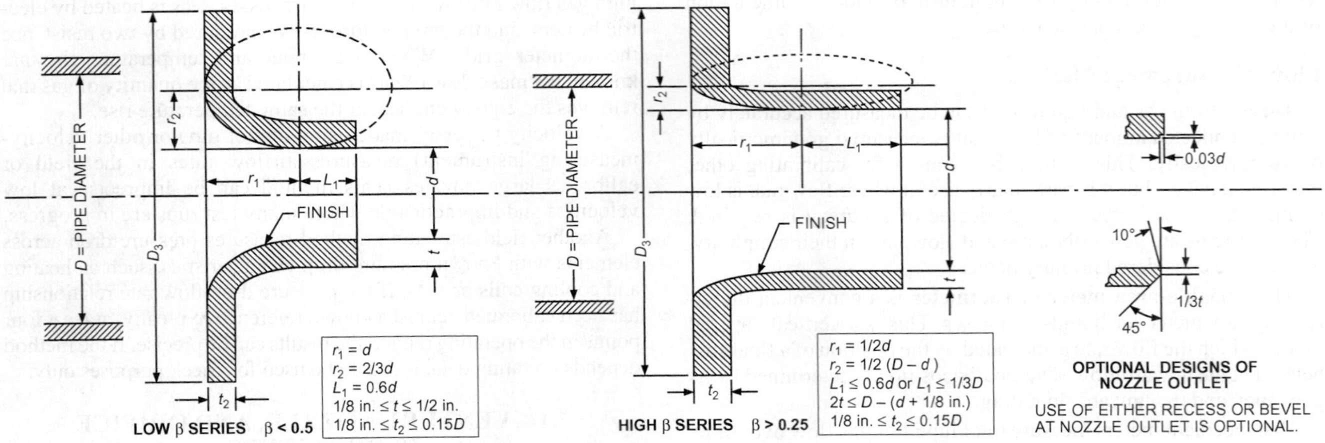

Fig. 10 Dimensions of ASME Long-Radius Flow Nozzles
From ASME PTC 19.5. Reprinted with permission of ASME.

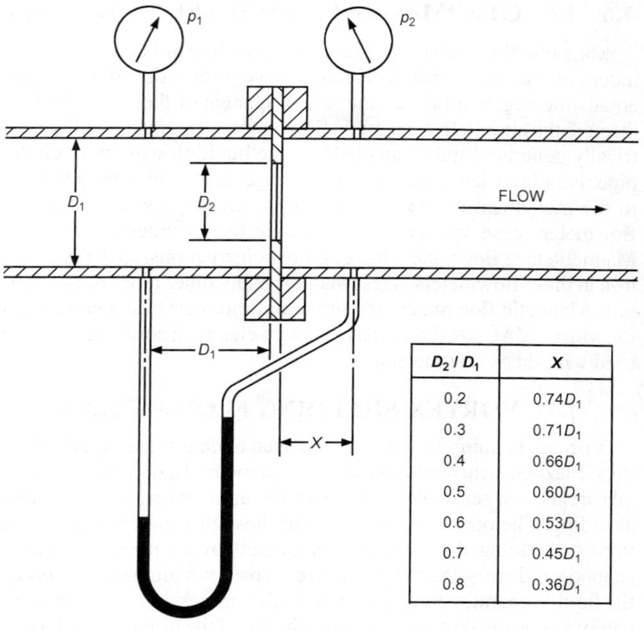

D_2/D_1	X
0.2	$0.74D_1$
0.3	$0.71D_1$
0.4	$0.66D_1$
0.5	$0.60D_1$
0.6	$0.53D_1$
0.7	$0.45D_1$
0.8	$0.36D_1$

Fig. 11 Sharp-Edge Orifice with Pressure Tap Locations
From ASME PTC 19.5. Reprinted with permission of ASME.

be changed by shutting off the flow through one or more nozzles. An apparatus designed for testing airflow and capacity of air-conditioning equipment is described by Wile (1947), who also presents pertinent information on nozzle discharge coefficients, Reynolds numbers, and resistance of perforated plates. Some laboratories refer to this apparatus as a code tester.

7.2 VARIABLE-AREA FLOWMETERS (ROTAMETERS)

In permanent installations where high precision, ruggedness, and operational ease are important, the variable-area flowmeter is satisfactory. It is frequently used to measure liquids or gases in small-diameter pipes. For ducts or pipes over 6 in. in diameter, the expense of this meter may not be warranted. In larger systems, however, the meter can be placed in a bypass line and used with an orifice.

The variable-area meter (Figure 12) commonly consists of a float that is free to move vertically in a transparent tapered tube. The fluid to be metered enters at the narrow bottom end of the tube and moves upward, passing at some point through the annulus formed between the float and the inside wall of the tube. At any particular flow rate, the float assumes a definite position in the tube; a calibrated scale on the tube shows the float's location and the fluid flow rate.

The float's position is established by a balance between the fluid pressure forces across the annulus and gravity on the float. The buoyant force $V_f(\rho_f - \rho)g/g_c$ supporting the float is balanced by the pressure difference acting on the cross-sectional area of the float $A_f \Delta p$, where ρ_f, A_f, and V_f are, respectively, the float density, float cross-sectional area, and float volume. The pressure difference across the annulus is

$$\Delta p = \frac{V_f(\rho_f - \rho)g}{A_f g_c} \tag{10}$$

The mass flow follows from Equation (9) as

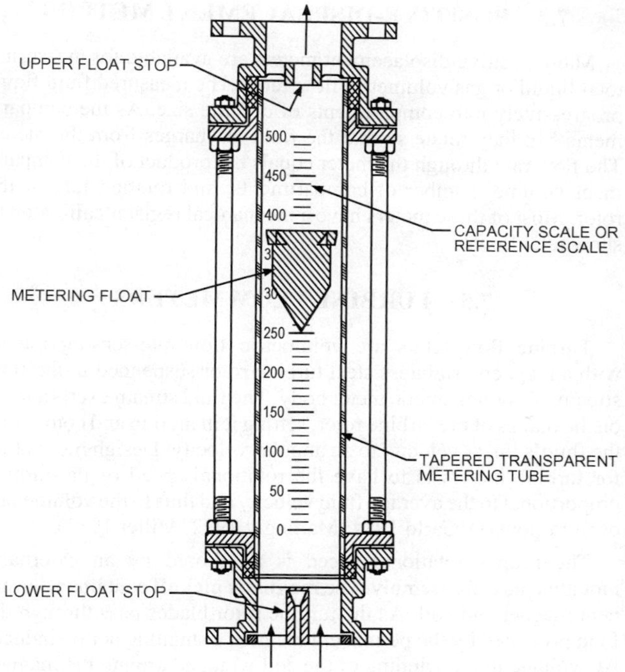

Fig. 12 Variable-Area Flowmeter

$$w = KA_2\sqrt{\frac{2V_f(\rho_f - \rho)g\rho}{A_f}} \tag{11}$$

Flow for any fluid is nearly proportional to the area, so that calibration of the tube is convenient. To use the meter for different fluids, the flow coefficient variation for any float must be known. Float design can reduce variation of the flow coefficient with Reynolds number; float materials can reduce the dependence of mass flow calibration on fluid density.

7.3 CORIOLIS PRINCIPLE FLOWMETERS

Coriolis liquid flowmeters directly measure liquid mass flow rates. In a Coriolis flowmeter, the liquid flows through a vibrating sensor tube within the meter. An electromagnetic coil located on the sensor tube vibrates the tube in cantilever motion at a known frequency. The liquid enters the vibrating tube and is given the vertical momentum of the tube. The liquid in the entry portion of the sensor tube resists in the downward direction when the tube is moving upward. Conversely, when the tube is moving downward, the liquid in the exit portion of the sensor tube resists in the upward direction. Combined, these effects create a symmetrical twist angle. According to Newton's second law of motion, the amount of sensor tube twist angle is directly proportional to the mass flow rate of liquid flowing through the tube. Electromagnetic velocity sensors on opposing sides of the sensor tube measure the velocity of the vibrating tube. Mass flow rate is determined by measuring the time difference in the velocity measurements: the greater the time difference, the greater the mass flow rate. The measuring tubes are vibrated at their natural frequency; a change of the fluid mass inside the tubes causes a corresponding change to the tube's natural frequency. The frequency change of the tube is used to calculate the fluid density.

7.4 POSITIVE-DISPLACEMENT METERS

Many positive-displacement meters are available for measuring total liquid or gas volumetric flow rates. The measured fluid flows progressively into compartments of definite size. As the compartments fill, they rotate so that the fluid discharges from the meter. The flow rate through the meter equals the product of the compartment volume, number of compartments, and rotation rate of the rotor. Most of these meters have a mechanical register calibrated to show total flow.

7.5 TURBINE FLOWMETERS

Turbine flowmeters are volumetric flow-rate-sensing meters with a magnetic stainless steel turbine rotor suspended in the flow stream of a nonmagnetic meter body. The fluid stream exerts a force on the blades of the turbine rotor, setting it in motion and converting the fluid's linear velocity to an angular velocity. Design motivation for turbine meters is to have the rotational speed of the turbine proportional to the average fluid velocity and thus to the volume rate of fluid flow (DeCarlo 1984; Mattingly 1992; Miller 1983).

The rotor's rotational speed is monitored by an externally mounted pickoff assembly. The **magnetic pickoff** contains a permanent magnet and coil. As the turbine rotor blades pass through the field produced by the permanent magnet, a shunting action induces AC voltage in the winding of the coil wrapped around the magnet. A sine wave with a frequency proportional to the flow rate develops. With the **radio frequency pickoff**, an oscillator applies a high-frequency carrier signal to a coil in the pickoff assembly. The rotor blades pass through the field generated by the coil and modulate the carrier signal by shunting action on the field shape. The carrier signal is modulated at a rate corresponding to the rotor speed, which is proportional to the flow rate. With both pickoffs, pulse frequency is a measure of flow rate, and the total number of pulses measures total volume (Mattingly 1992; Shafer 1961; Woodring 1969).

Because output frequency of the turbine flowmeter is proportional to flow rate, every pulse from the turbine meter is equivalent to a known volume of fluid that has passed through the meter; the sum of these pulses yields total volumetric flow. Summation is done by electronic counters designed for use with turbine flowmeters; they combine a mechanical or electronic register with the basic electronic counter.

Turbine flowmeters should be installed with straight lengths of pipe upstream and downstream from the meter. The length of the inlet and outlet pipes should be according to manufacturers' recommendations or pertinent standards. Where recommendations of standards cannot be accommodated, the meter installation should be calibrated. Some turbine flowmeters can be used in bidirectional flow applications. A fluid strainer, used with liquids of poor or marginal lubricity, minimizes bearing wear.

The lubricity of the process fluid and the type and quality of rotor bearings determine whether the meter is satisfactory for the particular application. When choosing turbine flowmeters for use with fluorocarbon refrigerants, pay attention to the type of bearings used in the meter and to the refrigerant's oil content. For these applications, sleeve-type rather than standard ball bearings are recommended. The amount of oil in the refrigerant can severely affect calibration and bearing life.

In metering liquid fluorocarbon refrigerants, the liquid must not flash to a vapor (cavitate), which tremendously increases flow volume. Flashing results in erroneous measurements and rotor speeds that can damage bearings or cause a failure. Flashing can be avoided by maintaining adequate back pressure on the downstream side of the meter (Liptak 1972).

7.6 ELECTROMAGNETIC (MAG) FLOWMETERS

Magnetic flowmeters operate on the principle of Faraday's law of induction that states that the electromotive force induced in a circuit equals the negative of the time rate of change of the magnetic flux through the circuit. In a magnetic flowmeter, a magnetic field is electrically generated and channeled into the liquid flowing through the pipe. Faraday's law states that the voltage generated is proportional to the movement of the flowing liquid. Electronics in a magnetic flowmeter sense voltage and determine the volumetric flow rate. Magnetic tube flowmeters have no flow obstructions, so the pressure loss in these flowmeters is less than for many other types of flowmeters. Magnetic flowmeters require a minimum electrical conductivity. Most HVAC&R liquids have enough electrical conductivity to be used with these flowmeters.

7.7 VORTEX-SHEDDING FLOWMETERS

Vortex-shedding flowmeters are used to determine liquid velocities. Piezoelectric methods, strain-gage methods, or hot-film methods are used to sense dynamic pressure variations created by vortex shedding. The operating principle for these flowmeters is based on vortex shedding that occurs downstream of an immersed blunt-shaped solid body. As the liquid stream passes a blunt-shaped body, the liquid separates and generates small vortices that are shed alternately along and downstream of each side of the blunt-shaped body. Each vortex-shedding meter is designed to have a constant Strouhal number so that the vortex shedding frequency is proportional to the liquid flow velocity over a specified flow velocity range. The Strouhal number for each vortex shedding meter is experimentally determined by the flowmeter manufacturer and is provided with each vortex-shedding meter.

8. AIR INFILTRATION, AIRTIGHTNESS, AND OUTDOOR AIR VENTILATION RATE MEASUREMENT

Air infiltration is the flow of outdoor air into a building through unintentional openings. **Airtightness** refers to the building envelope's ability to withstand flow when subjected to a pressure differential. The **outdoor air ventilation rate** is the rate of outdoor airflow intentionally introduced to the building for dilution of occupant- and building-generated contaminants. Measurement approaches to determine these factors are described briefly here, and in greater detail in Chapter 16.

Air infiltration depends on the building envelope's airtightness and the pressure differentials across the envelope. These differentials are induced by wind, stack effect, and operation of building mechanical equipment. For meaningful results, the air infiltration rate should be measured under typical conditions.

Airtightness of a residential building's envelope can be measured relatively quickly using building pressurization tests. In this technique, a large fan or blower mounted in a door or window induces a large and roughly uniform pressure difference across the building shell. The airflow required to maintain this pressure difference is then measured. The more leakage in the building, the more airflow is required to induce a specific indoor/outdoor pressure difference. Building airtightness is characterized by the airflow rate at a reference pressure, normalized by the building volume or surface area. Under proper test conditions, results of a pressurization test are independent of weather conditions. Instrumentation requirements for pressurization testing include air-moving equipment, a device to measure airflow, and a differential pressure gage.

Commercial building envelope leakage can also be measured using building pressurization tests. Bahnfleth et al. (1999) describe a protocol for testing envelope leakage of tall buildings using the building's air-handling equipment.

Outdoor airflow can be measured directly using the flow rate measurement techniques described in this chapter. The flow measurement equipment must be appropriate for the required accuracy, operating conditions, range of airflows, and temperatures expected. The outdoor airflow rate is normally measured during testing and balancing, during commissioning, or for continuous ventilation flow rate control using permanently mounted flow sensors.

An additional factor that may be of interest is the building's air exchange rate, which compares airflow into the building with the building's volume. Typically, this includes both mechanical ventilation and infiltration. Building air exchange rates can be measured by injecting a tracer gas (ideally, a chemically stable, nontoxic gas not normally present in buildings) into a building and monitoring and analyzing the tracer gas concentration response. Equipment required for tracer testing includes (1) a means of injecting the tracer gas and (2) a tracer gas concentration measurement device, such as a gas chromatograph. Various tracer gas techniques are used, distinguished by their injection strategy and analysis approach. These techniques include constant concentration (equilibrium tracer), decay or growth (ASTM *Standard* E741), and constant injection. Decay is the simplest of these techniques, but the other methods may be satisfactory if care is taken. A common problem in tracer gas testing is poor mixing of the tracer gas with the airstreams being measured.

Carbon Dioxide

Carbon dioxide is often used as a tracer gas because CO_2 gas monitors are relatively inexpensive and easy to use, and occupant-generated CO_2 can be used for most tracer gas techniques. Bottled CO_2 or CO_2 fire extinguishers are also readily available for tracer gas injection. Carbon dioxide may be used as a tracer gas to measure ventilation rates under the conditions and methods described in ASTM *Standard* D6245, for diagnostic purposes and point-in-time snapshots of the system's ventilation capabilities. CO_2 sensors are also used in building controls strategies to avoid overventilation by approximating the level of occupancy in a space; this is one method of demand-controlled ventilation. The concentration output may be used in a mathematical formula that allows the system to modulate ventilation rates when spaces with high density have highly variable or intermittent occupancy (e.g., churches, theaters, gymnasiums). This method of control is less effective in lower-density occupancies and spaces with more stable populations (Persily and Emmerich 2001). Carbon dioxide may also be used together with outdoor air intake rate data to estimate the current population of a space.

CO_2 input for ventilation control does not address contaminants generated by the building itself, and therefore cannot be used without providing a base level of ventilation for non-occupant-generated contaminants that have been shown to total a significant fraction if not a majority of those found in the space.

9. CARBON DIOXIDE MEASUREMENT

Carbon dioxide has become an important measurement parameter for HVAC&R engineers, particularly in indoor air quality (IAQ) applications. Although CO_2 is generally not of concern as a specific toxin in indoor air, it is used as a surrogate indicator of odor related to human occupancy. ANSI/ASHRAE *Standard* 62.1 recommends specific minimum outdoor air ventilation rates to ensure adequate indoor air quality.

9.1 NONDISPERSIVE INFRARED CO_2 DETECTORS

The most widespread technology for IAQ applications is the nondispersive infrared (NDIR) sensor (Figure 13). This device uses the strong absorption band that CO_2 produces at 4.2 μm when excited by an infrared light source. IAQ-specific NDIR instruments, calibrated between 0 and 5000 ppm, are typically accurate within 150 ppm, but the accuracy of some sensors can be improved to within 50 ppm if the instrument is calibrated for a narrower range. Portable NDIR meters are available with direct-reading digital displays; however, response time varies significantly among different instruments. Most NDIR cell designs facilitate very rapid CO_2 sample diffusion, although some instruments now in widespread use respond more slowly, resulting in stabilization times greater than 5 min (up to 15 min), which may complicate walk-through inspections. CO_2 instruments can be classified as either single or dual wavelength. Single-wavelength instruments contain a single spectral filter at the absorption band of CO_2. This configuration is prone to drift as the infrared source ages and loses intensity. These instruments often use a self-adjustment procedure to compensate and require periodic exposure to outdoor CO_2 levels of approximately 400 ppm during periods when a building is unoccupied. This makes it impractical for buildings such as hospitals that are always occupied. Dual-wavelength instruments contain two spectral filters: one at the absorption band of CO_2 and one at a wavelength unaffected by any gases. This second filter allows the instrument to monitor the intensity of the infrared source to directly compensate for source aging.

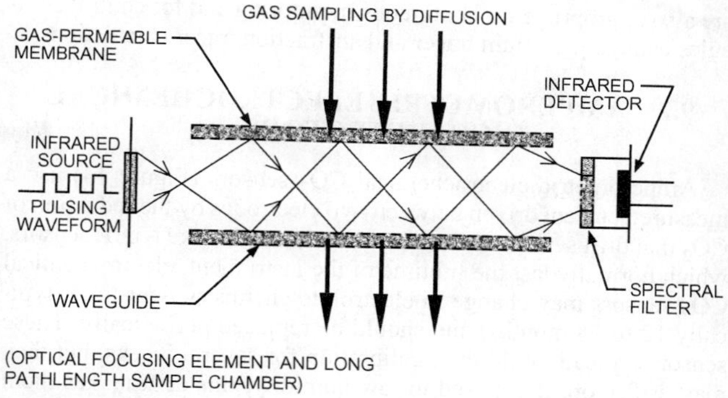

Fig. 13 Nondispersive Infrared Carbon Dioxide Sensor

Calibration

In a clean, stable environment, NDIR sensors can hold calibration for months, but condensation, dust, dirt, and mechanical shock may offset calibration. As with all other CO_2 sensor technologies, NDIR sensor readings are proportional to pressure, because the density of gas molecules changes when the sample pressure changes. This leads to errors in CO_2 readings when the barometric pressure changes from the calibration pressure. Weather-induced errors are small but should be considered when using CO_2 instruments at an altitude that is significantly different form the calibration altitude. Some instruments can accept a user adjustment to compensate for altitude. Instruments that do not have this ability should be recalibrated.

Some NDIR sensors are sensitive to cooling effects when placed in an airstream. This is an important consideration when locating a fixed sensor or when using a portable system to evaluate air-handling system performance, because airflow in supply and return ducts may significantly shift readings.

Applications

Nondispersive infrared sensors are well suited for equilibrium tracer and tracer decay ventilation studies, and faster-response models are ideal for a quick, basic evaluation of human-generated pollution and ventilation adequacy. When properly located, these sensors are also appropriate for continuous monitoring and for control strategies using equilibrium tracer and air fraction tracer calculations.

9.2 AMPEROMETRIC ELECTROCHEMICAL CO_2 DETECTORS

Amperometric electrochemical CO_2 sensors (Figure 14) use a measured current driven between two electrodes by the reduction of CO_2 that diffuses across a porous membrane. Unlike NDIR sensors, which normally last the lifetime of the instrument, electrochemical CO_2 sensors may change in electrolyte chemistry over time (typically 12 to 18 months) and should be replaced periodically. These sensors typically hold their calibration for several weeks, but they may drift more if exposed to low humidity; this drift makes them less suitable for continuous monitoring applications. At low humidity (below 30% rh), the sensors must be kept moist to maintain specified accuracy.

Amperometric electrochemical sensors require less power than NDIR sensors, usually operating continuously for weeks where NDIR instruments typically operate for 6 h (older models) to 150 h (newer models). The longer battery life can be advantageous for spot checks and walk-throughs, and for measuring CO_2 distribution throughout a building and within a zone. Unlike most NDIR sensors, amperometric electrochemical sensors are not affected by high humidity, although readings may be affected if condensate is allowed to form on the sensor.

9.3 PHOTOACOUSTIC CO_2 DETECTORS

Open-Cell Sensors

Open-cell photoacoustic CO_2 sensors (Figure 15) operate as air diffuses through a permeable membrane into a chamber that is pulsed with filtered light at the characteristic CO_2 absorption frequency of 4.2 μm. The light energy absorbed by the CO_2 heats the sample chamber, causing a pressure pulse, which is sensed by a piezoresistor. Open-cell photoacoustic CO_2 sensors are presently unavailable in portable instruments, in part because any vibration during transportation would affect calibration and might affect the signal obtained for a given concentration of CO_2. Ambient acoustical noise may also influence readings. For continuous monitoring, vibration is a concern, as are temperature and airflow cooling effects. However, if a sensor is located properly and the optical filter is kept relatively clean, photoacoustic CO_2 sensors may be very stable. Commercially available open-cell photoacoustic transmitters do not allow recalibration to adjust for pressure differences, so an offset should be incorporated in any control system using these sensors at an altitude or duct pressure other than calibration conditions.

Closed-Cell Sensors

Closed-cell photoacoustic sensors (Figure 16) operate under the same principle as the open-cell version, except that samples are pumped into a sample chamber that is sealed and environmentally stabilized. Two acoustic sensors are sometimes used in the chamber to minimize vibration effects. Closed-cell units, available as portable or fixed monitors, come with particle filters that are easily replaced (typically at 3- to 6-month intervals) if dirt or dust accumulates on them. Closed-cell photoacoustic monitors allow recalibration to correct for drift, pressure effects, or other environmental factors that might influence accuracy.

9.4 POTENTIOMETRIC ELECTROCHEMICAL CO_2 DETECTORS

Potentiometric electrochemical CO_2 sensors use a porous fluorocarbon membrane that is permeable to CO_2, which diffuses into a carbonic acid electrolyte, changing the electrolyte's pH. This change is monitored by a pH electrode inside the cell. The pH electrode isopotential drift prohibits long-term monitoring to the accuracy and resolution required for continuous measurement or control or for detailed IAQ evaluations, although accuracy within 100 ppm, achievable short-term over the 2000 ppm range, may be adequate for basic ventilation and odor evaluations. In addition, this type of sensor has a slow response, which increases the operator time necessary for field applications or for performing a walk-through of a building.

9.5 COLORIMETRIC DETECTOR TUBES

Colorimetric detector tubes contain a chemical compound that discolors in the presence of CO_2 gas, with the amount of discoloration related to the CO_2 concentration. These detector tubes are often used to spot-check CO_2 levels; when used properly, they are accurate to within 25%. If numerous samples are taken (i.e., six or more), uncertainty may be reduced. However, CO_2 detector tubes are generally not appropriate for specific ventilation assessment because of their inaccuracy and inability to record concentration changes over time.

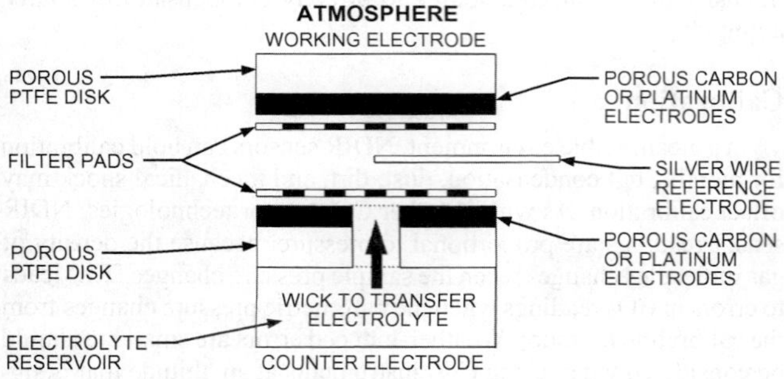

Fig. 14 Amperometric Carbon Dioxide Sensor

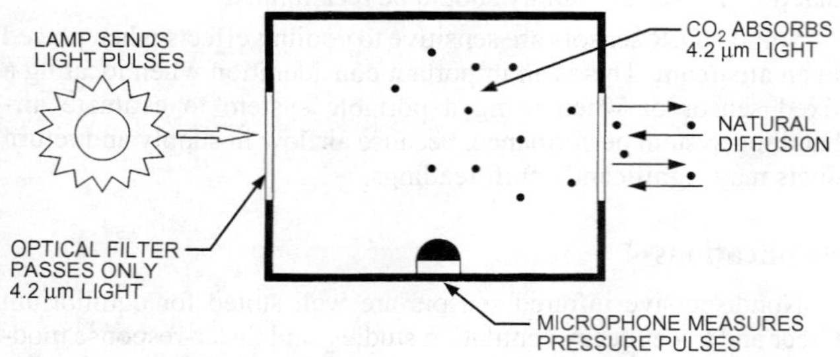

Fig. 15 Open-Cell Photoacoustic Carbon Dioxide Sensor

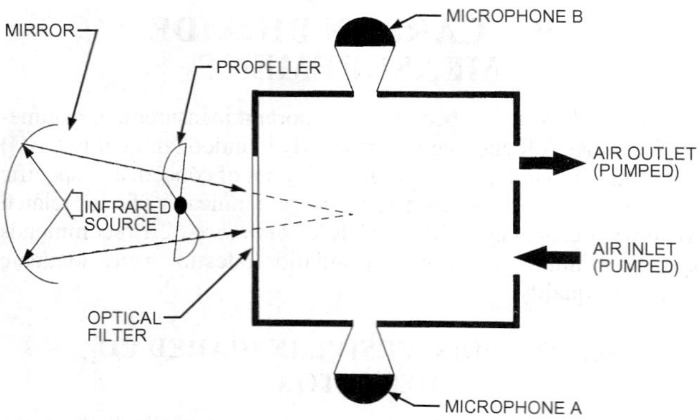

Fig. 16 Closed-Cell Photoacoustic Carbon Dioxide Sensor

9.6 LABORATORY MEASUREMENTS

Laboratory techniques for measuring CO_2 concentration include mass spectroscopy, thermal conductivity, infrared spectroscopy, and gas chromatography. These techniques typically require taking on-site **grab samples** for laboratory analysis. Capital costs for each piece of equipment are high, and significant training is required. A considerable drawback to grab sampling is that CO_2 levels change significantly during the day and over the course of a week, making it sensible to place sensors on site with an instrument capable of recording or data logging measurements continuously over the course of a workweek. An automated grab sampling system capturing many samples of data would be quite cumbersome and expensive if designed to provide CO_2 trend information over time. However, an advantage to laboratory techniques is that they can be highly accurate. A mass spectrometer, for example, can measure CO_2 concentration to within 5 ppm from 0 to 2000 ppm. All laboratory measurement techniques are subject to errors resulting from interfering agents. A gas chromatograph is typically used in conjunction with the mass spectrometer to eliminate interference from nitrous oxide (N_2O), which has an equivalent mass, if samples are collected in a hospital or in another location where N_2O might be present.

10. ELECTRIC MEASUREMENT

Ammeters

Ammeters are low-resistance instruments for measuring current. They should be connected in series with the circuit being measured (Figure 17). Ideally, they have the appearance of a short circuit, but in practice, all ammeters have a nonzero input impedance that influences the measurement to some extent.

Ammeters often have several ranges, and it is good practice when measuring unknown currents to start with the highest range and then reduce the range to the appropriate value to obtain the most sensitive reading. Ammeters with range switches maintain circuit continuity during switching. On some older instruments, it may be necessary to short-circuit the ammeter terminals when changing the range.

Current transformers are often used to increase the operating range of ammeters. They may also provide isolation/protection from a high-voltage line. Current transformers have at least two separate windings on a magnetic core (Figure 18). The primary winding is connected in series with the circuit in which the current is measured. In a clamp-on probe, the transformer core is actually opened and then connected around a single conductor carrying the current to be measured. That conductor serves as the primary winding. The secondary winding carries a scaled-down version of the primary current, which is connected to an ammeter. Depending on instrument type, the ammeter reading may need to be multiplied by the ratio of the transformer.

When using an auxiliary current transformer, the secondary circuit must not be open when current is flowing in the primary winding; dangerously high voltage may exist across the secondary terminals. A short-circuiting blade between the secondary terminals should be closed before the secondary circuit is opened at any point.

Transformer accuracy can be impaired by residual magnetism in the core when the primary circuit is opened at an instant when flux is large. The transformer core may be left magnetized, resulting in ratio and phase angle errors. The primary and secondary windings should be short-circuited before making changes.

Voltmeters

Voltmeters are high-resistance instruments that should be connected across the load (in parallel), as shown in Figure 19. Ideally, they have the appearance of an open circuit, but in practice, all voltmeters have some finite impedance that influences measurement to some extent.

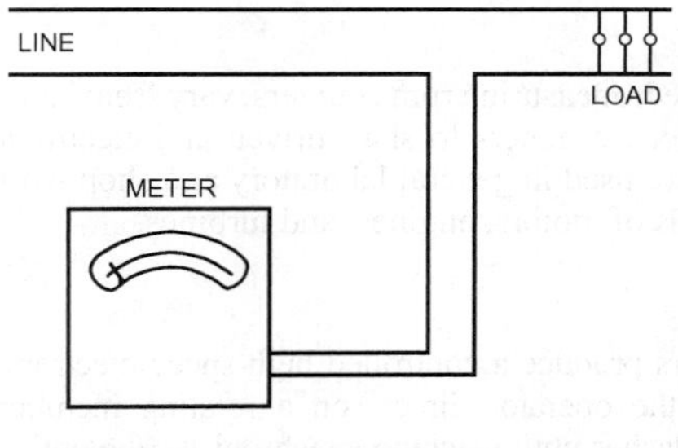

Fig. 17 Ammeter Connected in Power Circuit

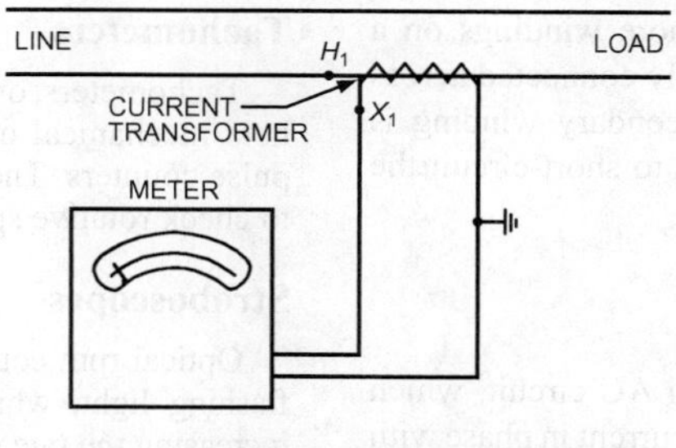

Fig. 18 Ammeter with Current Transformer

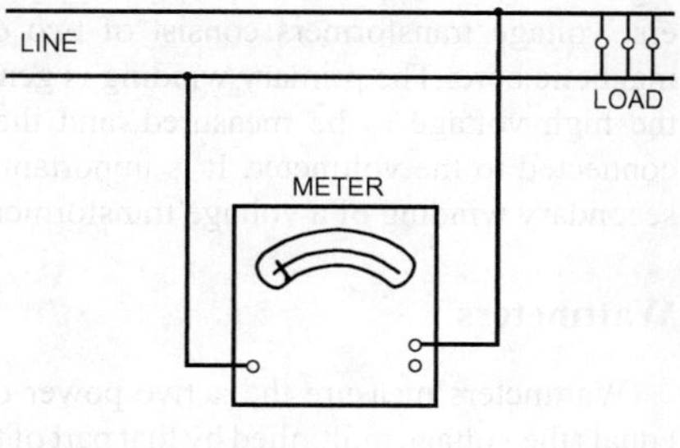

Fig. 19 Voltmeter Connected Across Load

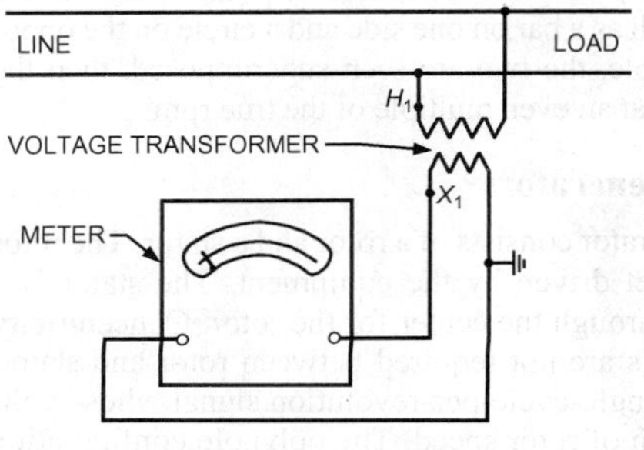

Fig. 20 Voltmeter with Potential Transformer

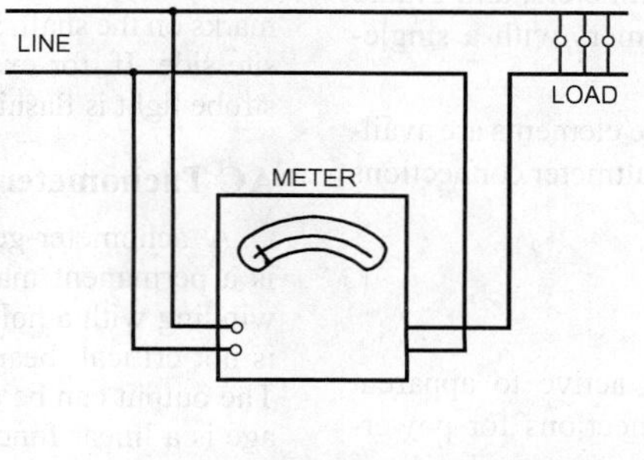

Fig. 21 Wattmeter in Single-Phase Circuit Measuring Power Load plus Loss in Current-Coil Circuit

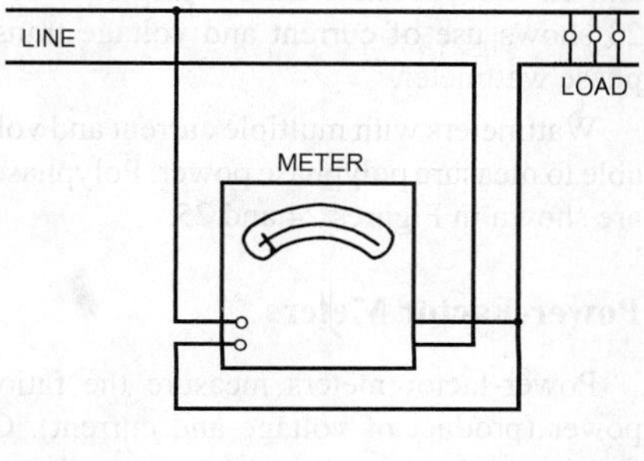

Fig. 22 Wattmeter in Single-Phase Circuit Measuring Power Load plus Loss in Potential-Coil Circuit

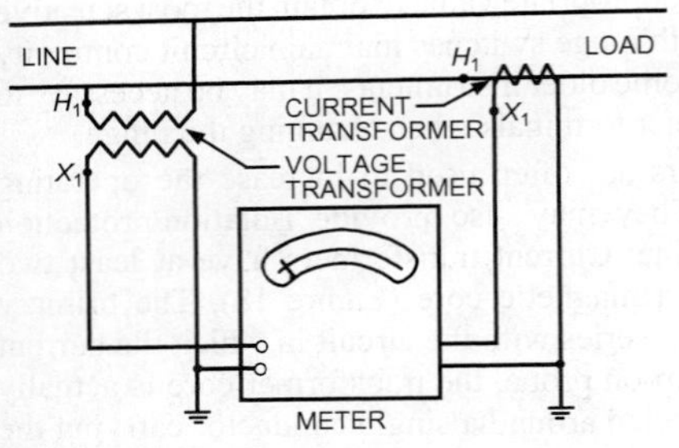

Fig. 23 Wattmeter with Current and Potential Transformer

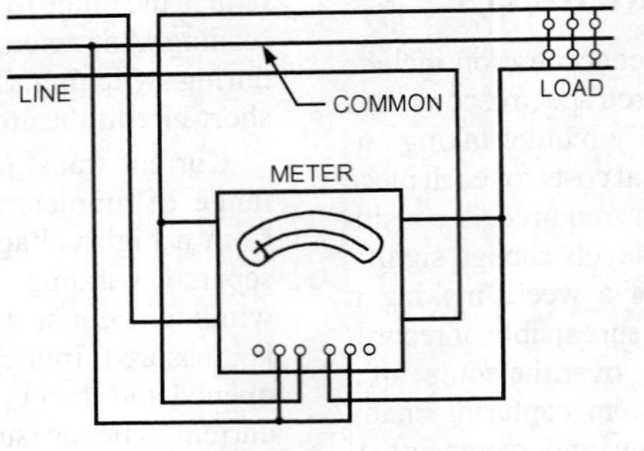

Fig. 24 Polyphase Wattmeter in Two-Phase, Three-Wire Circuit with Balanced or Unbalanced Voltage or Load

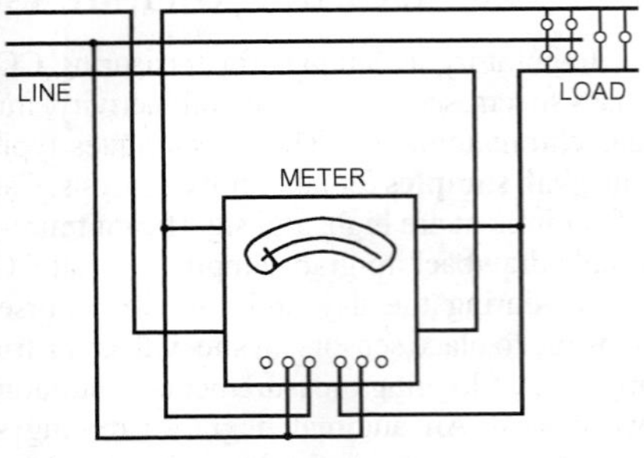

Fig. 25 Polyphase Wattmeter in Three-Phase, Three-Wire Circuit

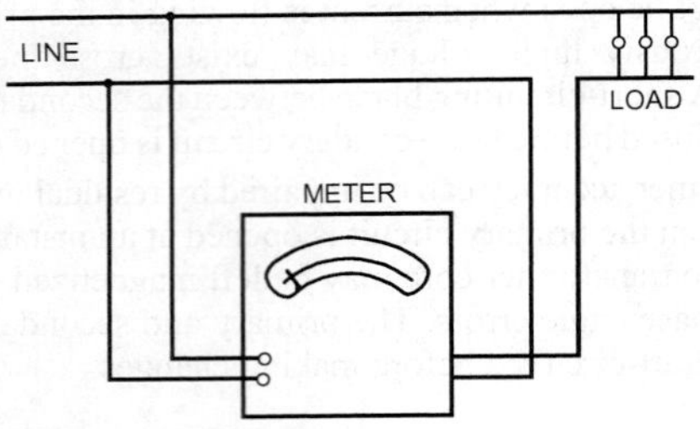

Fig. 26 Single-Phase Power-Factor Meter

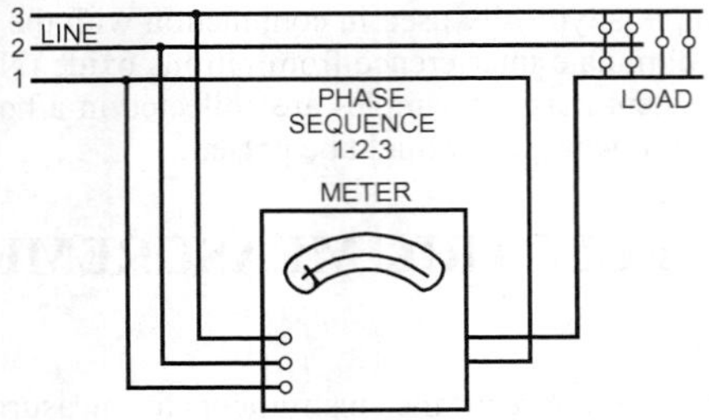

Fig. 27 Three-Wire, Three-Phase Power-Factor Meter

Voltage transformers are often used to increase the operating range of a voltmeter (Figure 20). They also provide isolation from high voltages and prevent operator injury. Like current transformers, voltage transformers consist of two or more windings on a magnetic core. The primary winding is generally connected across the high voltage to be measured, and the secondary winding is connected to the voltmeter. It is important not to short-circuit the secondary winding of a voltage transformer.

Wattmeters

Wattmeters measure the active power of an AC circuit, which equals the voltage multiplied by that part of the current in phase with the voltage. There are generally two sets of terminals: one to connect the load voltage and the other to connect in series with the load current. Current and voltage transformers can be used to extend the range of a wattmeter or to isolate it from high voltage. Figures 21 and 22 show connections for single-phase wattmeters, and Figure 23 shows use of current and voltage transformers with a single-phase wattmeter.

Wattmeters with multiple current and voltage elements are available to measure polyphase power. Polyphase wattmeter connections are shown in Figures 24 and 25.

Power-Factor Meters

Power-factor meters measure the ratio of active to apparent power (product of voltage and current). Connections for power-factor meters and wattmeters are similar, and current and voltage transformers can be used to extend their range. Connections for single-phase and polyphase power-factor meters are shown in Figures 26 and 27, respectively.

11. ROTATIVE SPEED AND POSITION MEASUREMENT

Tachometers

Tachometers, or direct-measuring rpm counters, vary from hand-held mechanical or electric meters to shaft-driven and electronic pulse counters. They are used in general laboratory and shop work to check rotative speeds of motors, engines, and turbines.

Stroboscopes

Optical rpm counters produce a controlled high-speed electronic flashing light, which the operator directs on a rotating member, increasing the rate of flashes until reaching synchronism (the optical effect that rotation has stopped). At this point, the rpm measured is equal to the flashes per minute emitted by the strobe unit. Care must be taken to start at the bottom of the instrument scale and work up because multiples of the rpm produce almost the same optical effect as true synchronism. Multiples can be indicated by positioning suitable marks on the shaft, such as a bar on one side and a circle on the opposite side. If, for example, the two are seen superimposed, then the strobe light is flashing at an even multiple of the true rpm.

AC Tachometer-Generators

A tachometer-generator consists of a rotor and a stator. The rotor is a permanent magnet driven by the equipment. The stator is a winding with a hole through the center for the rotor. Concentricity is not critical; bearings are not required between rotor and stator. The output can be a single-cycle-per-revolution signal whose voltage is a linear function of rotor speed. The polypole configuration that generates 10 cycles per revolution allows measurement of speeds as low as 20 rpm without causing the indicating needle to flutter. The output of the AC tachometer-generator is rectified and connected to a DC voltmeter.

Optical (Shaft) Encoders

Optical encoders and linear glass scales can be used to measure rotational speed and both linear and angular position, depending on the geometry of the encoder. The output from an encoder is typically in the form of a pulse train. If this pulse train provides an indication of the absolute orientation (angle or position), it is called an **absolute encoder**. If it produces a relative pulse train with no absolute angle or position reference, it is called an **incremental encoder**. Modern high-resolution rotational (shaft) encoders typically consist of a shaft-mounted rotating disk containing regularly spaced slits. A light source is located on one side of the disk slits and a detector on the other side of the slits. As the disk rotates at a given frequency, a pulse train is produced at the detector from the intermittent pulses of light that pass through the rotating slits. Linear displacement encoders (absolute or incremental) operate on a similar principle, except that the slits are formed in a linear axis. Although modern encoders are typically optical, a resistive potentiometer can also be used as a position or rotation encoder, the output resistance being a direct indication of position or orientation.

12. SOUND AND VIBRATION MEASUREMENT

Measurement systems for determining sound pressure level, intensity level, and mechanical vibration generally use transducers to convert mechanical signals into electrical signals, which are then processed electronically or digitally to characterize the measured mechanical signals. These measurement systems contain one or more of the following elements, which may or may not be contained in a single instrument:

- A transducer, or an assembly of transducers, to convert sound pressure or mechanical vibration (time-varying strain, displacement, velocity, acceleration, or force) into an electrical signal that is quantitatively related to the mechanical quantity being measured
- Preamplifiers and amplifiers to provide functions such as preconditioning and amplification of signals, electrical impedance matching, signal conditioning, and gain
- Signal-processing equipment to quantify those aspects of the signal that are being measured (peak value, rms value, time-weighted average level, power spectral density, or magnitude or phase of a complex linear spectrum or transfer function) and conduct integration, differentiation, and frequency weighting of the signal
- Display and storage devices such as meters, oscilloscopes, digital displays, or level recorder to display and record the signal or the aspects of it that are being quantified
- An interface that allows cable, wireless, or memory card output

The relevant range of sound signals (i.e., audible to humans) can vary over more than six orders of magnitude in amplitude and more than three orders of magnitude in frequency, depending on the application. The relevant range of vibration signals may be slightly larger than this. References on instrumentation, measurement procedures, and signal analysis are given in the Bibliography. Product and application notes, technical reviews, and books published by instrumentation manufacturers are sources of additional reference material. See Chapter 48 of the 2015 *ASHRAE Handbook—HVAC Applications* and Chapter 8 of this volume for further information on sound and vibration.

12.1 SOUND MEASUREMENT

Microphones

A microphone is a transducer that transforms an acoustical signal into an electrical signal. The two predominant transduction principles used in sound measurement (as opposed to broadcasting) are the electrostatic and the piezoelectric. **Electrostatic (capacitor) microphones** are available either as electret microphones, which do not require an external polarizing voltage, or as condenser microphones, which do require an external polarizing voltage, typically in the range of 28 to 200 V (DC). **Piezoelectric microphones** may be manufactured using either natural piezoelectric crystals or poled ferroelectric crystals. The types of response characteristics of measuring microphones are pressure, free field, and random incidence (diffuse field).

The sensitivity and the frequency range over which the microphone has uniform sensitivity (flat frequency response) vary with sensing element diameter (surface area) and microphone type. Other critical factors that may affect microphone/preamplifier performance or response are atmospheric pressure, temperature, relative humidity, external magnetic and electrostatic fields, mechanical vibration, and radiation. Microphone selection is based on long- and short-term stability; the match between performance characteristics (e.g., sensitivity, frequency response, amplitude linearity, self-noise) and the expected amplitude of sound pressure, frequency, range of analysis, and expected environmental conditions of measurement; and any other pertinent considerations, such as size and directional characteristics.

Sound Measurement Systems

Microphone preamplifiers, amplifiers, weighting networks, filters, analyzers, and displays are available either separately or integrated into a measuring instrument such as a sound level meter, personal noise exposure meter (often called a noise dose meter or dosimeter), measuring amplifier, or real-time constant-percentage bandwidth (e.g., octave band) or narrow-band [e.g., fast Fourier transform (FFT)] frequency analyzer. Instruments included in a sound measurement system depend on the purpose of the measurement, the frequency range, and the resolution of the signal analysis. For community and industrial noise measurements for regulatory purposes, the instrument, signal processing, and quantity to be measured are usually dictated by the pertinent regulation. The optimal instrument set generally varies for measurement of different characteristics such as sound power in HVAC ducts, sound power emitted by machinery, noise criteria (NC) numbers, sound absorption coefficients, sound transmission loss of building partitions, and reverberation times (T_{60}).

Frequency Analysis

Measurement criteria often dictate using filters to analyze the signal, to indicate the spectrum of the sound being measured. Filters of different bandwidths for different purposes include fractional octave band (one, one-third, one-twelfth, etc.), constant-percentage bandwidth, and constant (typically narrow) bandwidth. The filters may be analog or digital and, if digital, may or may not be capable of real-time data acquisition during measurement, depending on the bandwidth of frequency analysis. FFT signal analyzers are generally used in situations that require very narrow-resolution signal analysis at constant bandwidth when the amplitudes of the sound spectra vary significantly with respect to frequency. This may occur in regions of resonance or when it is necessary to identify narrow-band or discrete sine-wave signal components of a spectrum in the presence of other such components or of broadband noise. However, when the frequency varies (e.g., because of nonconstant rpm of a motor), results from FFT analyzers can be difficult to interpret because the change in rpm provides what looks like a broadband signal.

Sound Chambers

Special rooms and procedures are required to characterize and calibrate sound sources and receivers. The rooms are generally classified into three types: anechoic, hemianechoic, and reverberant. In the ideal **anechoic** room, all boundary surfaces completely absorb sound energy at all frequencies of interest. The ideal **hemi-anechoic** room would be identical to the ideal anechoic room, except that one surface would totally reflect sound energy at all frequencies. The ideal **reverberant** room would have boundary surfaces that totally reflect sound energy at all frequencies of interest.

Anechoic chambers are used to perform measurements under conditions approximating those of a free sound field. They can be used in calibrating and characterizing individual microphones, microphone arrays, acoustic intensity probes, reference sound power sources, loudspeakers, sirens, and other individual or complex sources of sound.

Hemianechoic chambers have a hard reflecting floor to accommodate heavy machinery or to simulate large factory floor or outdoor conditions. They can be used in calibrating and characterizing reference sound power sources, obtaining sound power levels of noise sources, and characterizing sound output of emergency vehicle sirens when mounted on an emergency motor vehicle.

Reverberation chambers are used to perform measurements under conditions approximating those of a diffuse sound field. They can be used in calibrating and characterizing random-incidence microphones and reference sound power sources, obtaining sound power ratings of equipment and sound power levels of noise sources, measuring sound absorption coefficients of building materials and panels, and measuring transmission loss through building partitions and components such as doors and windows.

The choice of which room type to use often depends on the test method required for the subject units, testing costs, or room availability.

Calibration

A measurement system should be calibrated as a system from microphone or probe to indicating device before it is used to perform absolute measurements of sound. Acoustic calibrators and pistonphones of fixed or variable frequency and amplitude are available for this purpose. These calibrators should be used at a frequency low enough that the pressure, free-field, and random-incidence response characteristics of the measuring microphone(s) are, for practical purposes, equivalent, or at least related in a known quantitative manner for that specific measurement system. In general, the sound pressure produced by these calibrators may vary, depending on microphone type, whether the microphone has a protective grid, atmospheric pressure, temperature, and relative humidity. Correction factors and coefficients are required when conditions of use differ from those existing during the calibration of the acoustic calibrator or pistonphone. For demanding applications, precision sound sources and measuring microphones should periodically be sent to the manufacturer, a private testing laboratory, or a national standards laboratory for calibration.

12.2 VIBRATION MEASUREMENT

Except for seismic instruments that record or indicate vibration directly with a mechanical or optomechanical device connected to the test surface, vibration measurements use an electromechanical or interferometric vibration transducer. Here, the term **vibration transducer** refers to a generic electromechanical vibration transducer. Electromechanical and interferometric vibration transducers belong to a large and varied group of transducers that detect mechanical motion and furnish an electrical signal that is quantitatively related to a particular physical characteristic of the motion. Depending on design, the electrical signal may be related to mechanical strain, displacement, velocity, acceleration, or force. The operating principles of vibration transducers may involve optical interference; electrodynamic coupling; piezoelectric (including poled ferroelectric) or piezoresistive crystals; or variable capacitance, inductance, reluctance, or resistance. A considerable variety of vibration transducers with a wide range of sensitivities and bandwidths is commercially available. Vibration transducers may be contacting (e.g., seismic transducers) or noncontacting (e.g., interferometric, optical, or capacitive).

Transducers

Seismic transducers use a spring-mass resonator within the transducer. At frequencies much greater than the fundamental natural frequency of the mechanical resonator, the relative displacement between the base and the seismic mass of the transducer is nearly proportional to the displacement of the transducer base. At frequencies much lower than the fundamental resonant frequency, the relative displacement between the base and the seismic mass of the transducer is nearly proportional to the acceleration of the transducer base. Therefore, seismic displacement transducers and seismic electrodynamic velocity transducers tend to have a relatively compliant suspension with a low resonant frequency; piezoelectric accelerometers and force transducers have a relatively stiff suspension with a high resonant frequency.

Strain transducers include the metallic resistance gage and piezoresistive strain gage. For dynamic strain measurements, these are usually bonded directly to the test surface. The accuracy with which a bonded strain gage replicates strain occurring in the test structure is largely a function of how well the strain gage was oriented and bonded to the test surface.

Displacement transducers include the capacitance gage, fringe-counting interferometer, seismic displacement transducer, optical approaches, and the linear variable differential transformer (LVDT). Velocity transducers include the reluctance (magnetic) gage, laser Doppler interferometer, and seismic electrodynamic velocity transducer. Accelerometers and force transducers include the piezoelectric, piezoresistive, and force-balance servo.

Vibration Measurement Systems

Sensitivity, frequency limitations, bandwidth, and amplitude linearity of vibration transducers vary greatly with the transduction mechanism and the manner in which the transducer is applied in a given measurement apparatus. Contacting transducers' performance can be significantly affected by the mechanical mounting methods and points of attachment of the transducer and connecting cable and by the mechanical impedance of the structure loading the transducer. Amplitude linearity varies significantly over the operating range of the transducer, with some transducer types or configurations being inherently more linear than others. Other factors that may critically affect performance or response are temperature; relative humidity; external acoustic, magnetic, and electrostatic fields; transverse vibration; base strain; chemicals; and radiation. A vibration transducer should be selected based on its long- and short-term stability; the match between its performance characteristics (e.g., sensitivity, frequency response, amplitude linearity, self-noise) and the expected amplitude of vibration, frequency range of analysis, and expected environmental conditions of measurement; and any other pertinent considerations (e.g., size, mass, resonant frequency).

Vibration exciters, or **shakers**, are used in structural analysis, vibration analysis of machinery, fatigue testing, mechanical impedance measurements, and vibration calibration systems. Vibration exciters have a table or moving element with a drive mechanism that may be mechanical, electrodynamic, piezoelectric, or hydraulic. They range from relatively small, low-power units for calibrating transducers (e.g., accelerometers) to relatively large, high-power units for structural and fatigue testing.

Conditioning amplifiers, power supplies, preamplifiers, charge amplifiers, voltage amplifiers, power amplifiers, filters, controllers, and displays are available either separately or integrated into a measuring instrument or system, such as a structural analysis system, vibration analyzer, vibration monitoring system, vibration meter, measuring amplifier, multichannel data-acquisition and modal analysis system, or real-time fractional-octave or FFT signal analyzer. The choice of instruments to include in a vibration measurement system depends on the mechanical quantity to be determined, purpose of measurement, and frequency range and resolution of signal analysis. For vibration measurements, the signal analysis is relatively narrow in bandwidth and may be relatively low in frequency, to accurately characterize structural resonances. Accelerometers with internal integrated circuitry are available to provide impedance matching or servo control for measuring very-low-frequency acceleration (servo accelerometers). Analog integration and differentiation of vibration signals are available through integrating and differentiating networks and amplifiers, and digital is available through FFT analyzers. Vibration measurements made for different purposes (e.g., machinery diagnostics and health monitoring, balancing rotating machinery, analysis of torsional vibration, analysis of machine-tool vibration, modal analysis, analysis of vibration isolation, stress monitoring, industrial control) generally have different mechanical measurement requirements and a different optimal set of instrumentation.

Calibration

Because of their inherent long- and short-term stability, amplitude linearity, wide bandwidth, wide dynamic range, low noise, and wide range of sensitivities, seismic accelerometers have traditionally been used as a reference standard for dynamic mechanical measurements. A measurement system should be calibrated as a system from transducer to indicating device before it is used to perform absolute dynamic measurements of mechanical quantities. Calibrated reference vibration exciters, standard reference accelerometers, precision conditioning amplifiers, and precision calibration exciters are available for this purpose. These exciters and standard reference accelerometers can be used to transfer a calibration to another transducer. For demanding applications, a calibrated exciter or standard reference accelerometer with connecting cable and conditioning amplifier should periodically be sent to the manufacturer, a private testing laboratory, or a national standards laboratory for calibration.

13. LIGHTING MEASUREMENT

Light level, or **illuminance**, is usually measured with a photocell made from a semiconductor such as silicon or selenium. Photocells produce an output current proportional to incident luminous flux when linked with a microammeter, color- and cosine-corrected filters, and multirange switches; they are used in inexpensive handheld light meters and more precise instruments. Different cell heads allow multirange use in precision meters.

Cadmium sulfide photocells, in which resistance varies with illumination, are also used in light meters. Both gas-filled and vacuum photoelectric cells are in use.

Small survey-type meters are not as accurate as laboratory meters; their readings should be considered approximate, although consistent, for a given condition. Their range is usually from 5 to 5000 footcandles. Precision low-level meters have cell heads with ranges down to 0 to 2 footcandles.

A photometer installed in a revolving head is called a **goniophotometer** and is used to measure the distribution of light sources or luminaires. To measure total luminous flux, the luminaire is placed in the center of a sphere painted inside with a high-reflectance white with a near-perfect diffusing matte surface. Total light output is measured through a small baffled window in the sphere wall.

To measure irradiation from germicidal lamps, a filter of fused quartz with fluorescent phosphor is placed over the light meter cell.

If meters are used to measure the number of lumens per unit area diffusely leaving a surface, luminance (cd/in^2) instead of illumination (footcandles) is read. Light meters can be used to measure luminance, or electronic lux meters containing a phototube, an amplifier, and a microammeter can read luminance directly. For a perfectly diffuse reflecting surface, which has a constant luminance regardless of viewing angle, the unit of footlamberts in lumens/ft^2 is sometimes used.

Chapter 9 of the IES (2011) *Lighting Handbook* gives detailed information on measurement of light.

14. THERMAL COMFORT MEASUREMENT

Thermal comfort depends on the combined influence of clothing, activity, air temperature, air velocity, mean radiant temperature, and air humidity. Thermal comfort is influenced by heating or cooling of particular body parts through radiant temperature asymmetry (plane radiant temperature), draft (air temperature, air velocity, turbulence), vertical air temperature differences, and floor temperature (surface temperature).

A general description of thermal comfort is given in Chapter 9, and guidelines for an acceptable thermal environment are given in ASHRAE *Standard* 55 and ISO *Standard* 7730. ASHRAE *Standard* 55 also includes required measuring accuracy. In addition to specified accuracy, ISO *Standard* 7726 includes recommended measuring locations and a detailed description of instruments and methods.

Clothing and Activity Level

These values are estimated from tables (Chapter 9; ISO *Standards* 8996, 9920). Thermal insulation of clothing (clo-value) can be measured on a thermal mannequin (McCullough et al. 1985; Olesen 1985). Activity (met-value) can be estimated from measuring CO_2 and O_2 in a person's expired air.

Air Temperature

Various types of thermometers may be used to measure air temperature. Placed in a room, the sensor registers a temperature between air temperature and mean radiant temperature. One way of reducing the radiant error is to make the sensor as small as possible, because the convective heat transfer coefficient increases as size decreases, whereas the radiant heat transfer coefficient is constant. A smaller sensor also provides a favorably low time constant. Radiant error can also be reduced by using a shield (an open, polished aluminum cylinder) around the sensor, using a sensor with a low-emittance surface, or artificially increasing air velocity around the sensor (aspirating air through a tube in which the sensor is placed).

Air Velocity

In occupied zones, air velocities are usually small (0 to 100 fpm), but do affect thermal sensation. Because velocity fluctuates, the mean value should be measured over a suitable period, typically 3 min. Velocity fluctuations with frequencies up to 1 Hz significantly increase human discomfort caused by draft, which is a function of air temperature, mean air velocity, and turbulence (see Chapter 9). Fluctuations can be given as the standard deviation of air velocity over the measuring period (3 min) or as the turbulence intensity (standard deviation divided by mean air velocity). Velocity direction may change and is difficult to identify at low air velocities. An omnidirectional sensor with a short response time should be used. A thermal anemometer is suitable. If a hot-wire anemometer is used, the direction of measured flow must be perpendicular to the hot wire. Smoke puffs can be used to identify the direction.

Plane Radiant Temperature

This refers to the uniform temperature of an enclosure in which the radiant flux on one side of a small plane element is the same as in the actual nonuniform environment. It describes the radiation in one direction. Plane radiant temperature can be calculated from surface temperatures of the environment (half-room) and angle factors between the surfaces and a plane element (ASHRAE *Standard* 55). It may also be measured by a net-radiometer or a radiometer with a sensor consisting of a reflective disk (polished) and an absorbent disk (painted black) (Olesen et al. 1989).

Mean Radiant Temperature

This is the uniform temperature of an imaginary black enclosure in which an occupant would exchange the same amount of radiant heat as in the actual nonuniform enclosure. Mean radiant temperature can be calculated from measured surface temperatures and the corresponding angle factors between the person and surfaces. It can also be determined from the plane radiant temperature in six opposite directions, weighted according to the projected area factors for a person. For more information, see Chapter 9.

Because of its simplicity, the instrument most commonly used to determine the mean radiant temperature is a **black globe thermometer** (Bedford and Warmer 1935; Vernon 1932). This thermometer consists of a hollow sphere usually 6 in. in diameter, coated in flat black paint with a thermocouple or thermometer bulb at its center. The temperature assumed by the globe at equilibrium results from a balance between heat gained and lost by radiation and convection.

Mean radiant temperatures are calculated from

$$\bar{t}_r = \left[(t_g + 459.67)^4 + \frac{4.74 \times 10^7 V_a^{0.6}}{\varepsilon D^{0.4}}(t_g - t_a)\right]^{1/4} - 459.67 \quad (12)$$

where

$\bar{t}_r$ = mean radiant temperature, °F
t_g = globe temperature, °F
V_a = air velocity, fpm
t_a = air temperature, °F
D = globe diameter, ft
ε = emissivity (0.95 for black globe)

According to Equation (12), air temperature and velocity around the globe must also be determined. The globe thermometer is spherical, but mean radiant temperature is defined in relation to the human body. For sedentary people, the globe represents a good approximation. For people who are standing, the globe, in a radiant nonuniform environment, overestimates the radiation from floor or ceiling; an ellipsoidal sensor gives a closer approximation. A black globe also overestimates the influence of short-wave radiation (e.g., sunshine). A flat gray color better represents the radiant characteristic of normal clothing (Olesen et al. 1989). The hollow sphere is usually made of copper, which results in an undesirably high time constant. This can be overcome by using lighter materials (e.g., a thin plastic bubble).

Air Humidity

The water vapor pressure (absolute humidity) is usually uniform in the occupied zone of a space; therefore, it is sufficient to measure absolute humidity at one location. Many of the instruments listed in Table 3 are applicable. At ambient temperatures that provide comfort or slight discomfort, the thermal effect of humidity is only moderate, and highly accurate humidity measurements are unnecessary.

14.1 CALCULATING THERMAL COMFORT

When the thermal parameters have been measured, their combined effect can be calculated by the thermal indices in Chapter 9.

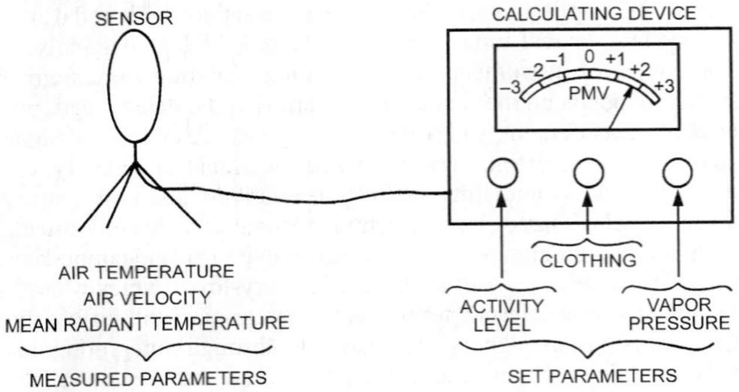

Fig. 28 Madsen's Comfort Meter
(Madsen 1976)

For example, the effective temperature (Gagge et al. 1971) can be determined from air temperature and humidity. Based on the four environmental parameters and an estimation of clothing and activity, the **predicted mean vote** (PMV) can be determined with the aid of tables (Chapter 9; Fanger 1982; ISO *Standard* 7730). The PMV is an index predicting the average thermal sensation that a group of occupants may experience in a given space.

For certain types of normal activity and clothing, measured environmental parameters can be compared directly with those in ASHRAE *Standard* 55 or ISO *Standard* 7730.

14.2 INTEGRATING INSTRUMENTS

Several instruments have been developed to evaluate the combined effect of two or more thermal parameters on human comfort. Madsen (1976) developed an instrument that gives information on the occupants' expected thermal sensation by directly measuring the PMV value. The comfort meter has a heated elliptical sensor that simulates the body (Figure 28). The estimated clothing (insulation value), activity in the actual space, and humidity are set on the instrument. The sensor then integrates the thermal effect of air temperature, mean radiant temperature, and air velocity in approximately the same way the body does. The electronic instrument gives the measured operative and equivalent temperature, calculated PMV, and predicted percentage of dissatisfied (PPD).

15. MOISTURE CONTENT AND TRANSFER MEASUREMENT

Moisture commonly refers to the presence of liquid and vapor states of water, which has two positively charged hydrogen atoms and one negatively charged oxygen atom. As moisture vapor and liquid molecules adsorb to a hygroscopic material (e.g., most porous building materials), the material's **moisture content (MC)** increases significantly. The presence of moisture in materials influences their performance (e.g., thermal insulation, acoustics, processability, dielectricity, storage life, unhealthy microbe growth, corrosion, chemical aspects).

However, little off-the-shelf instrumentation exists to measure the moisture content or transfer of porous materials, although many measurements can be set up with a small investment of time and money. Three moisture properties are most commonly sought: (1) moisture content; (2) vapor permeability (rate at which water vapor passes through a given material); and (3) liquid diffusivity (rate at which liquid water passes through a porous material).

Moisture Content

MC can be classified into four categories:

- **Wet-basis volumetric MC:** ratio of moisture's volume to wet sample's bulk volume
- **Wet-basis mass MC:** ratio of moisture's mass to wet sample's bulk mass
- **Dry-basis volumetric MC:** ratio of moisture's volume to dry sample's bulk volume
- **Dry-basis mass MC:** ratio of moisture's mass to dry sample's bulk mass

Dry basis is often used in building materials.

The MC of a material is usually described with a **sorption isotherm**, which relates the **equilibrium moisture content (EMC)** of a hygroscopic material to the ambient relative humidity under constant temperature. Determining a sorption isotherm involves exposing a sample of material to a known relative humidity at a known temperature and then measuring the sample's moisture content after enough time has elapsed for the sample to reach equilibrium with its surroundings. Hysteresis in the sorption behavior of most hygroscopic materials requires that measurements be made for both increasing (adsorption isotherm) and decreasing relative humidity (desorption isotherm). Figure 29 shows hysteresis through the adsorption and desorption isotherms for a typical hygroscopic porous material (Straube 1998). Three different regimes of moisture storage are shown: sorption or hygroscopic (A), capillary (B), and oversaturated (C). In the hygroscopic regime, water vapor adsorbs to the pore walls. As relative humidity increases, adsorbed moisture molecules grow from single layers to multiple interconnected layers (internal capillary condensation). The capillary regime (B) is somewhat arbitrarily designated as that part of the moisture storage function above the critical moisture content. Physically, it is presumed that a continuous liquid phase forms. Finally, in the supersaturated state, the relative humidity is always 100% and no more water will wick into a material.

Ambient relative humidity can be controlled using saturated salt solutions or mechanical refrigeration equipment (Carotenuto et al. 1991; Cunningham and Sprott 1984; Tveit 1966). Precise measurements of the relative humidity produced by various salt solutions were reported by Greenspan (1977). ASTM *Standard* E104 describes the use of saturated salt solutions. A sample's EMC is usually determined gravimetrically using a precision balance. The sample's dry mass, necessary to calculate moisture content, can be found by oven or desiccant drying. Oven dry mass may be lower than desiccant dry mass because of the loss of volatiles other than water in the oven (Richards et al. 1992).

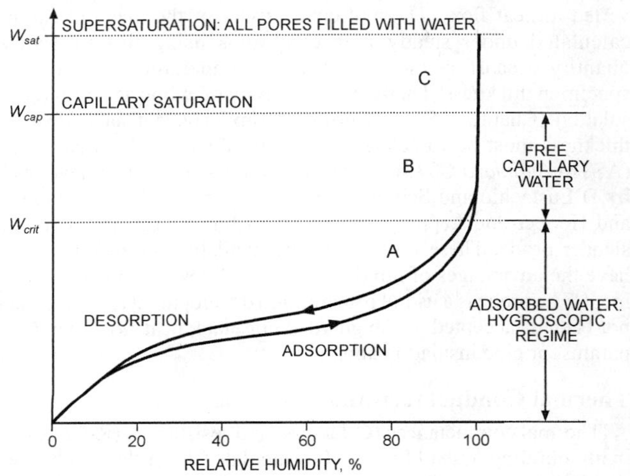

Fig. 29 Adsorption Isotherm and Desorption Isotherm for Hygroscopic Material
(Straube 1998)

A major difficulty in measuring sorption isotherms of engineering materials is the long time required for many materials to reach equilibrium (often as long as weeks or months). The rate-limiting mechanism for these measurements is usually the slow process of vapor diffusion into the pores of the material. Using smaller samples can reduce diffusion time. Note that, although EMC isotherms are traditionally plotted as a function of relative humidity, the actual transport to or from materials is determined by vapor pressure differences. Thus, significant moisture content changes can occur because of changes in either the material vapor pressure or the surrounding air long before equilibrium is reached.

Moisture content can be directly or indirectly determined. Direct techniques measure moisture by a chemical reaction (e.g., Karl Fisher titration) or using the difference in weight before and after drying a test sample. Using chemical reactions is complex, slow, and expensive, and uses toxic chemicals, so it is seldom used. Weight loss after drying is usually referred to as the **loss on drying (LOD)** or **thermo-gravimetric method** (or simply **gravimetric**), in which a sample is weighed, heated in an oven at a set temperature (e.g., 212 to 221°F) for an appropriate period to a constant weight, cooled in the dry atmosphere, and reweighed. Although these direct methods are accurate (within ±0.01 ft^3/ft^3), they are time-consuming, destructive, and do not allow for in situ measurement. Therefore, many indirect methods have been developed. Unlike direct measurements, indirect techniques do not involve removing moisture in a sample: they estimate moisture content by a strong or calibrated relationship with some other measurable variables such as dielectric permittivity or thermal conductivity. Both empirical and theoretical equations between the moisture content and measurable variable are used for the calibration.

Major types of indirect methods include neutron moderation, gamma ray attenuation, nuclear magnetic resonance, microwave reflectance and attenuation, near-infrared reflectance or transmission (NIR/T), dielectric techniques, and thermal methods. Safety issues may limit application of the first three techniques, although they have some advantages such as robustness or high accuracy. NIR/T is a rapid, noninvasive technique for determining moisture content in several applications (e.g., in grain). Its limiting factors include high cost, low penetration depth, and a large sample size required for calibration.

Dielectric techniques take advantage of the strong dependence of the composite material's bulk permittivity (or dielectric constant) on moisture content. Because the permittivity of water (K_{aw} = 81) is much higher than that of the porous material's other constituents (e.g., 1 for air, 4.7 for fiberglass), the total permittivity of the composite porous material is mainly determined by the moisture content. Dielectric methods include time domain reflectometry (TDR), frequency domain (FD), amplitude domain reflectometry (ADR), phase transmission (Virrib), and time domain transmission (TDT). These dielectric moisture content sensors are becoming popular in various field and laboratory applications (e.g., soil, wood) because they have short response time (almost instantaneous measurements), do not require maintenance, and can provide good accuracy (commercial devices can be accurate within ±0.02 or 0.03 m^3/m^3 and up to ±0.01 m^3/m^3 in some more specific situations). However, their sensitivity to boundary water or salinity limits their applications in a highly saline/conductive condition.

Thermal techniques are increasingly considered as an alternative to other methodologies to determine moisture content in porous materials. The main attractions in pursuing this technology are simultaneous measurements of other thermophysical properties (e.g., thermal conductivity, thermal diffusivity, volumetric heat capacity, and water matric potential), wide measurement range, invulnerability of salinity, low cost, high accuracy and robustness. Two predominant concerns limiting the development of the thermal technique include slow reaction time (one commercial product with the accuracy of ±0.01 m^3/m^3 has the response time of two minutes) and requirement of good contact with the test sample. One typical example of the thermal method identifies moisture content θ_v by its relationship with volumetric specific heat capacity ρc, as described by Bristow et al. (1993, 1994), Campbell et al. (1991), and Yang et al. (2015).

There is no universal method of moisture content measurement suitable to every application, and detected moisture content varies with measurement method. The suitability of each method relies on different application considerations such as safety, cost, accuracy, response time, installation, ease of operation, management, and durability.

Vapor Permeability

Diffusive transfer of water vapor through porous materials is often described by a modified form of Fick's law:

$$w_v'' = -\mu \frac{dp}{dx} \tag{13}$$

where

w_v'' = mass of vapor diffusing through unit area per unit time, gr/h·ft²
dp/dx = vapor pressure gradient, in. Hg/in.
μ = vapor permeability, gr·in/h·ft²·in. Hg

In engineering practice, permeance may be used instead of permeability. **Permeance** is simply permeability divided by the material thickness in the direction of vapor flow; thus, permeability is a material property, whereas permeance depends on thickness.

Permeability is measured with wet-cup, dry-cup, or modified cup tests. Specific test methods for measuring water vapor permeability are given in ASTM *Standard* E96.

For many engineering materials, vapor permeability is a strong function of mean relative humidity. Wet and dry cups cannot adequately characterize this dependence on relative humidity. Instead, a modified cup method can be used, in which pure water or desiccant in a cup is replaced with a saturated salt solution (Burch et al. 1992; McLean et al. 1990). A second saturated salt solution is used to condition the environment outside the cup. Relative humidities on both sides of the sample material can be varied from 0 to 100%. Several cups with a range of mean relative humidities are used to map out the dependence of vapor permeability on relative humidity.

In measuring materials of high permeability, the finite rate of vapor diffusion through air in the cup may become a factor. Air-film resistance could then be a significant fraction of the sample's resistance to vapor flow. Accurate measurement of high-permeability materials may require an accounting of diffusive rates across all air gaps (Fanney et al. 1991).

Liquid Diffusivity

Transfer of liquid water through porous materials may be characterized as a diffusion-like process:

$$w_l'' = -\rho D_l \frac{d\gamma}{dx} \tag{14}$$

where

w_l'' = mass of liquid transferred through unit area per unit time, lb/h·ft²
ρ = liquid density, lb/ft³
D_l = liquid diffusivity, ft²/h
$d\gamma/dx$ = moisture content gradient, ft⁻¹

D_l typically depends strongly on moisture content.

Transient measurement methods deduce the functional form of $D_l\gamma$ by observing the evolution of a one-dimensional moisture content profile over time. An initially dry specimen is brought into contact with liquid water. Free water migrates into the specimen, drawn in by surface tension. The resulting moisture content profile, which changes with time, must be differentiated to find the material's liquid diffusivity (Bruce and Klute 1956).

Determining the transient moisture content profile typically involves a noninvasive and nondestructive method of measuring local moisture content. Methods include gamma ray absorption (Freitas et al. 1991; Kumaran and Bomberg 1985; Quenard and Sallee 1989), x-ray radiography (Ambrose et al. 1990), neutron radiography (Prazak et al. 1990), and nuclear magnetic resonance (NMR) (Gummerson et al. 1979).

Uncertainty in liquid diffusivity measurement is often large because of the need to differentiate noisy experimental data.

16. HEAT TRANSFER THROUGH BUILDING MATERIALS

Thermal Conductivity

The thermal conductivity of a heat insulator, as defined in Chapter 25, is a unit heat transfer factor. Two methods of determining the thermal conductivity of flat insulation are the **guarded hot plate** and the **heat flow meter apparatus**, according to ASTM *Standards* C177 and C518, respectively. Both methods use parallel isothermal plates to induce a steady temperature gradient across the thickness of the specimen(s). The guarded hot plate is considered an absolute method for determining thermal conductivity. The heat flow meter apparatus requires calibration with a specimen of known thermal conductivity, usually determined in the guarded hot plate. The heat flow meter apparatus is calibrated by determining the voltage output of its heat flux transducer(s) as a function of the heat flux through the transducer(s).

Basic guarded hot plate design consists of an electrically heated plate and two liquid-cooled plates. Two similar specimens of a material are required for a test; one is mounted on each side of the hot plate. A cold plate is then pressed against the outside of each specimen by a clamp screw. The heated plate consists of two sections separated by a small gap. During tests, the central (metering) and outer (guard) sections are maintained at the same temperature to minimize errors caused by edge effects. The electric energy required to heat the metering section is measured carefully and converted to heat flow. Thermal conductivity of the material can be calculated under steady-state conditions using this heat flow quantity, area of the metering section, temperature gradient, and specimen thickness. Thermal conductivity of cylindrical or pipe insulation (Chapter 25) is determined similarly, but an equivalent thickness must be calculated to account for the cylindrical shape (ASTM *Standard* C335). Transient methods have been developed by D'Eustachio and Schreiner (1952), Hooper and Chang (1953), and Hooper and Lepper (1950) using a line heat source within a slender probe. These instruments are available commercially and have the advantages of rapidity and a small test specimen requirement. The probe is a useful research and development tool, but it has not been as accepted as the guarded hot plate, heat flow meter apparatus, or pipe insulation apparatus.

Thermal Conductance and Resistance

Thermal conductances (C-factors) and resistances (R-values) of many building assemblies can be calculated from the conductivities and dimensions of their components, as described in Chapter 27. Test values can also be determined experimentally by testing large, representative specimens in the hot box apparatus described in ASTM *Standards* C976 and C1363. This laboratory apparatus measures heat transfer through a specimen under controlled air temperature, air velocity, and radiation conditions. It is especially suited for large, nonhomogeneous specimens.

For in situ measurements, heat flux and temperature transducers are useful in measuring the dynamic or steady-state behavior of opaque building components (ASTM *Standard* C1046). A heat flux transducer is simply a differential thermopile within a core or substrate material. Two types of construction are used: (1) multiple thermocouple junctions wrapped around a core material, or (2) printed circuits with a uniform array of thermocouple junctions. The transducer is calibrated by determining its voltage output as a function of the heat flux through the transducer. For in situ measurements, the transducer is installed in either the wall or roof, or mounted on an exterior surface with tape or adhesive. Data obtained can be used to compute the thermal conductance or resistance of the building component (ASTM *Standard* C1155).

17. AIR CONTAMINANT MEASUREMENT

Three measures of particulate air contamination include the number, projected area, and mass of particles per unit volume of air (ASTM 2012). Each requires an appropriate sampling technique.

Particles are counted by capturing them in impingers, impactors, membrane filters, or thermal or electrostatic precipitators. Counting may be done by microscope, using stage counts if the sample covers a broad range of sizes (Nagda and Rector 2001).

Electronic particle counters can give rapid data on particle size distribution and concentration. **Inertial particle counters** use acceleration to separate sampled particles into different sizes. Real-time **aerodynamic particle sizers (APS)** use inertial effects to separate particles by size, but instead of capturing the particles, they are sized optically (Cox and Miro 1997), and can provide continuous sampling; however, they tend to be very expensive. Other, less costly types of **optical particle counters (OPCs)** are also available, but they typically require careful calibration using the type of particle that is being measured for accurate results (Baron and Willeke 2001). Their accuracy also depends heavily on appropriate maintenance and proper application. Correction for particle losses (dropout in the sampling lines) during sampling can be particularly important for accurate concentration measurements. Concentration uncertainty (random measurement uncertainty) also depends on the number of particles sampled in a given sampling interval.

Particle counters have been used in indoor office environments as well as in cleanrooms, and in aircraft cabin air quality testing (Cox and Miro 1997).

Projected area determinations are usually made by sampling onto a filter paper and comparing the light transmitted or scattered by this filter to a standard filter. The staining ability of dusts depends on the projected area and refractive index per unit volume. For sampling, filters must collect the minimum-sized particle of interest, so membrane or glass fiber filters are recommended.

To determine particle mass, a measured quantity of air is drawn through filters, preferably of membrane or glass fiber, and the filter mass is compared to the mass before sampling. Electrostatic or thermal precipitators and various impactors have also been used. For further information, see ACGIH (2001), Lodge (1989), and Lundgren et al. (1979).

Chapter 46 of the 2015 *ASHRAE Handbook—HVAC Applications* presents information on measuring and monitoring gaseous contaminants. Relatively costly analytical equipment, which must be calibrated and operated carefully by experienced personnel, is needed. Numerous methods of sampling the contaminants, as well as the laboratory analysis techniques used after sampling, are specified. Some of the analytical methods are specific to a single pollutant; others can present a concentration spectrum for many compounds simultaneously.

18. COMBUSTION ANALYSIS

Two approaches are used to measure the thermal output or capacity of a boiler, furnace, or other fuel-burning device. The direct or **calorimetric test** measures change in enthalpy or heat content of the fluid, air, or water heated by the device, and multiplies this by the flow rate to arrive at the unit's capacity. The indirect test or **flue gas analysis** method determines heat losses in flue gases and the jacket and deducts them from the heat content (higher heating value) of measured fuel input to the appliance. A **heat balance** simultaneously applies both tests to the same device. The indirect test usually indicates the greater capacity, and the difference is credited to radiation from the casing or jacket and unaccounted-for losses.

With small equipment, the expense of the direct test is usually not justified, and the indirect test is used with an arbitrary radiation and unaccounted-for loss factor.

18.1 FLUE GAS ANALYSIS

Flue gases from burning fossil fuels generally contain carbon dioxide (CO_2) and water, with some small amounts of hydrogen (H_2), carbon monoxide (CO), nitrogen oxides (NO_x), sulfur oxides (SO_x), and unburned hydrocarbons. However, generally only concentrations of CO_2 (or O_2) and CO are measured to determine completeness of combustion and efficiency.

Nondispersive infrared (NDIR) analyzers are the most common laboratory instruments for measuring CO and CO_2. Their advantages include the following: (1) they are not very sensitive to flow rate, (2) no wet chemicals are required, (3) they have a relatively fast response, (4) measurements can be made over a wide range of concentrations, and (5) they are not sensitive to the presence of contaminants in ambient air.

In the laboratory, oxygen is generally measured with an instrument that uses O_2's paramagnetic properties. Paramagnetic instruments are generally used because of their excellent accuracy and because they can be made specific to the measurement of oxygen.

For field testing and burner adjustment, portable combustion testing equipment is available. These instruments generally measure O_2 and CO with electrochemical cells. The CO_2 is then calculated by an on-board microprocessor and, together with temperature, is used to calculate thermal efficiency.

19. DATA ACQUISITION AND RECORDING

Almost every type of transducer and sensor is available with the necessary interface system to make it computer compatible. The transducer itself begins to lose its identity when integrated into a system with features such as linearization, offset correction, self-calibration, and so forth. This has eliminated concern about the details of signal conditioning and amplification of basic transducer outputs, although engineering judgment is still required to review all data for validity, accuracy, and acceptability before making decisions based on the results. The personal computer is integrated into every aspect of data recording, including sophisticated graphics, acquisition and control, and analysis. Internet or intranet connections allow easy access to remote personal-computer-based data-recording systems from virtually any locale.

Direct output devices can be either multipurpose or specifically designed for a given sensor. Traditional chart recorders still provide a visual indication and a hard-copy record of the data, but their output is now rarely used to process data. These older mechanical stylus-type devices use ink, hot wire, pressure, or electrically sensitive paper to provide a continuous trace. They are useful up to a few hundred hertz. Thermal and ink recorders are confined to chart speeds of a few inches per second for recording relatively slow processes. Simple indicators and readouts are used mostly to monitor the output of a sensor visually, and have usually been replaced by modern digital indicators. Industrial environments commonly use signal transmitters for control or computer data-handling systems to convert the signal output of the primary sensor into a compatible common signal span (e.g., the standard 4-20 mA current loop). All signal conditioning (ranging, zero suppression, reference-junction compensation) is provided at the transmitter. Thus, all recorders and controllers in the system can have an identical electrical span, with variations only in charts and scales offering the advantages of interchangeability and economy in equipment cost. Long signal transmission lines can be used, and receiving devices can be added to the loop without degrading performance. Newer instruments may be digitally bus based, which removes the degradation that may occur with analog signals. These digital instruments are usually immune to noise, based on the communications scheme that is used. They also may allow for self-configuration of the sensor in the field to the final data acquisition device.

The vast selection of available hardware, often confusing terminology, and challenge of optimizing the performance/cost ratio for a specific application make configuring a data acquisition system difficult. A system specifically configured to meet a particular measurement need can quickly become obsolete if it has inadequate flexibility. Memory size, recording speed, and signal processing capability are major considerations in determining the correct recording system. Thermal, mechanical, electromagnetic interference, portability, and meteorological factors also influence the selection.

Digital Recording

A digital data acquisition system must contain an interface, which is a system involving one or several analog-to-digital converters, and, in the case of multichannel inputs, circuitry for multiplexing. The interface may also provide excitation for transducers, calibration, and conversion of units. The digital data are arranged into one or several standard digital bus formats. Many data acquisition systems are designed to acquire data rapidly and store large records of data for later recording and analysis. Once the input signals have been digitized, the digital data are essentially immune to noise and can be transmitted over great distances.

The most popular physical layer bus standards used for data transmission are the TIA/EIA-485, IEEE 802.3, USB, IEEE 488, or general-purpose interface bus (GPIB) and the RS232 serial interface.

The **TIA/EIA-485 bus system** can be based on either two twisted pairs for full duplex (simultaneous signaling) operation or half duplex using only one twisted pair. A ground wire is generally required to provide a common reference ground for all the devices on the bus to eliminate common mode voltage problems caused by unequal ground potentials. The TIA/EIA-485 standard does not specify cabling length and data rate specifications, but refers to application guidelines (TSB-89). For practical applications, it gives an example of a specific manufacturer's 24AWG cable, for which the maximum distance between two devices is 2400 ft at 100 kbps (TSB-89). The actual distance between devices for a given data rate depends on cable capacitance and impedance, network configuration, and grounding arrangements (TIA *Standards* TIA-485, TSB-89).

The **IEEE 802.3 bus standard** specifies both copper and optical fiber for physical linking of devices (IEEE *Standard* 802.3). The copper version uses either twin coaxial cables or four twisted-wire pairs with the twisted wire pairs being used more commonly. The twisted-wire pairs can support up to 10 Gbps with maximum distance of 330 ft between devices depending on type of CAT (cable and telephone) cable used (IEEE 802.3). A 40 Gbps data rate specification over twisted pairs is expected to be released by end of 2016.

The **USB 2.0 and 3.1** uses one and three twisted pairs respectively for data transmission. Three additional wires are used for power, ground and shield in both USB 2.0 and USB 3.0. The USB 2.0 can provide 480 Mbps with a recommended length of 16 ft 5 in. based on the maximum 26 ns signal delay and cable specifications given in the USB 2.0 standard. The new USB 3.1 standard can support data transmission speeds of up to 10 Gbps with a recommended length of 9 ft 10 in. for a cable satisfying the standard's electrical requirements. Device distances can be increased by using either USB bridges/hubs or physical layer interfacing converters.

The **IEEE 488 bus system** feeds data down eight parallel wires, one data byte at a time. This parallel operation allows it to transfer data rapidly at up to 1 million characters per second. However, the IEEE 488 bus is limited to a cable length of 65 ft and requires an interface connection on every meter for proper termination.

The **RS232 system** feeds data serially down two wires, one bit at a time. The distance between the devices is limited by maximum cable capacitance of 2500 pF at a maximum data rate of 20 kbps (TIA *Standard* TIA-232). This translates to typical distance of 50 ft, which was the maximum length limit specified in an earlier version of the RS232 standard. For longer distances, it may feed a modem to send data over standard telephone lines.

These physical layer buses can be connected to a data acquisition unit or a personal computer directly or through a local area network (LAN) available in a facility for transmitting information. With appropriate interfacing, transducer data are available to any computer connected to the network.

Bus measurements can greatly simplify three basic applications: data gathering, automated limit testing, and computer-controlled processes. Data gathering collects readings over time. The most common applications include aging tests in quality control, temperature tests in quality assurance, and testing for intermittency in service. A controller can monitor any output indefinitely and then display the data directly on screen or record it on magnetic tape or disks for future use.

In automated limit testing, the computer compares each measurement with programmed limits. The controller converts readings to a good/bad readout. Automatic limit testing is highly cost-effective when working with large number of parameters of a particular unit under test.

In computer-controlled processes, the IEEE 488 bus system becomes a permanent part of a larger, completely automated system. For example, a large industrial process may require many electrical sensors that feed a central computer controlling many parts of the manufacturing process. An IEEE 488 bus controller collects readings from several sensors and saves the data until asked to dump an entire batch of readings to a larger central computer at one time. Used in this manner, the IEEE 488 bus controller serves as a slave of the central computer.

Dynamic range and accuracy must be considered in a digital recording system. **Dynamic range** refers to the ratio of the maximum input signal for which the system is useful to the noise floor of the system. The **accuracy** figure for a system is affected by the signal noise level, nonlinearity, temperature, time, crosstalk, and so forth. In selecting an 8-, 12-, or 16-bit analog-to-digital converter, the designer cannot assume that system accuracy is necessarily determined by the resolution of the encoders (i.e., 0.4%, 0.025%, and 0.0016%, respectively). If the sensor preceding the converter is limited to 1% full-scale accuracy, for example, no significant benefits are gained by using a 12-bit system over an 8-bit system and suppressing the least significant bit. However, a greater number of bits may be required to cover a larger dynamic range.

Data-Logging Devices

Data loggers digitally store electrical signals (analog or digital) to an internal memory storage component. The signal from connected sensors is typically stored to memory at timed intervals ranging from MHz to hourly sampling. Some data loggers store data based on an event (e.g., button push, contact closure). Many data loggers can perform linearization, scaling, or other signal conditioning and allow logged readings to be either instantaneous or averaged values. Most data loggers have built-in clocks that record the time and date together with transducer signal information. Data loggers range from single-channel input to 256 or more channels. Some are general-purpose devices that accept a multitude of analog and/or digital inputs, whereas others are more specialized to a specific measurement (e.g., a portable anemometer with built-in data-logging capability) or application (e.g., a temperature, relative humidity, CO_2, and CO monitor with data logging for IAQ applications). Stored data are generally downloaded using a serial interface with a temporary direct connection to a personal computer. Some data loggers allow downloading directly to a printer, or to an external hard drive or tape drive that can later be connected to a PC.

With the reduction in size of personal computers (laptops, notebooks, hand-held PCs, and palmtops), the computer itself is now being used as the data logger. These mobile computers may be left in the field, storing measurements from sensors directly interfaced into the computer. Depending on the particular application and number of sensors to be read, a computer card mounted directly into the PC may eliminate the external data acquisition device completely.

20. MECHANICAL POWER MEASUREMENT

Power measurement quantities mechanical power, and electrical power for both AC and DC loading (described in the section on Electric Measurement). Examples of mechanical power include shaft power and pumping power.

Measurement of Shaft Power

The measurement of shaft power associated with rotating machinery can be accomplished using a dynamometer setup which **independently** measures torque and rotation rate **(or angular velocity)**.

$$P = \frac{2\pi NT}{33{,}000}$$

where

P = power, hp

N = shaft speed, rpm

T = torque, ft/lb_f

Measurement of Fluid Pumping Power

Pumping power can be determined by independent measurements of volumetric flow rate and pressure differential across the pump.

$$P = \frac{Q(\Delta p)}{1714}$$

where

P = power, hp

Q = volumetric flow rate, gpm

Δp = pressure differential across the pump, psi

20.1 SYMBOLS

A = flow area, ft^2
a = thermocouple constant
C = correction factor
C_p = pitot-static probe pressure difference coefficient
c_p = specific heat at constant pressure, Btu/lb_m·°F
D = distance; diameter
d = throat diameter
D_l = liquid diffusivity, ft^2/h
$d\gamma/dx$ = moisture content gradient, ft^{-1}
dp/dx = vapor pressure gradient, in. Hg/in.
E = voltage
F_a = thermal expansion correction factor
g_c = gravitational constant = 32.174 lb_m·ft/lb_f·s^2
H = height
J = mechanical equivalent of heat = 778.3 ft·lb_f/Btu
K = sensitivity (Figure 1); differential expansion coefficient for liquid in glass; constant (function of geometry and Reynolds number)
N = shaft speed, rpm
n = number of degrees that liquid column emerged from bath
p = absolute pressure, lb_f/ft^2
p_w = velocity pressure (pitot-tube manometer reading), in. of water
P_{wet} = wetted perimeter
P = mechanical power, hp
Q = discharge flow rate, cfs; gpm
R = resistance, Ω
r = (see Figure 9)
S = spot size
t = temperature, °F; wall thickness
$\bar{t}_r$ = mean radiant temperature, °F
T = torque, ft·lb_f
V = velocity, fpm; volume
W = width
w = mass flow rate, lb_m/s
w''_l = mass of liquid transferred through unit area per unit time, lb/h·ft^2
w''_v = mass of vapor diffusing through unit area per unit time, gr/h·ft^2
X = variable; velocity of stream, fps

Greek

β = systematic (bias) error; ratio of diameters D_2/D_1 for venturi and sharp-edge orifice and d/D for flow nozzle
Δp = pressure differential across the pump, psi
δ = deviation
ε = random error; emissivity (0.95 for black globe)
θ = tilt angle, °
θ_y = moisture content
μ = mean; vapor permeability, gr·in/h·ft^2·in. Hg
ρ = density, lb_m/ft^3
ρc = volumetric specific heat capacity

Subscripts

1 = entering conditions; state 1
2 = throat conditions; state 2
a = air
b = bath
c = cross-sectional
e = equivalent of stream velocity
eff = effective
g = globe
h = hydraulic
i = pertaining to variable X
k = reading number
s = average of emergent liquid column of n degrees
$true$ = true

STANDARDS

ASA. 2011. Reference quantities for acoustical levels. ANSI *Standard* S1.8-1989 (R2011). Acoustical Society of America, New York.

ASA. 2010. Measurement of sound pressure levels in air. ANSI *Standard* S1.13-2005 (R2010). Acoustical Society of America, New York.

ASA. 2011. Specification and verification procedures for sound calibrators. ANSI *Standard* S1.40-2006 (R2011). Acoustical Society of America, New York.

ASA. 2015. Guide to the mechanical mounting of accelerometers. ANSI *Standard* S2.61-1989 (R2015). Acoustical Society of America, New York.

ASA. 2016. Statistical methods for determining and verifying stated noise emission values of machinery and equipment. ANSI *Standard* S12.3-1985 (R2016). Acoustical Society of America, New York.

ASA. 2013. Methods for determining the insertion loss of outdoor noise barriers. ANSI *Standard* S12.8-1998 (R2013). Acoustical Society of America, New York.

ASA. 2016. Method for the designation of sound power emitted by machinery and equipment. ANSI *Standard* S12.23-1989 (R2016). Acoustical Society of America, New York.

ASHRAE. 2013. Standard methods for temperature measurement. ANSI/ASHRAE *Standard* 41.1-2013.

ASHRAE. 1987. Standard methods for laboratory air flow measurement. *Standard* 41.2-1987 (RA 1992).

ASHRAE. 2014. Standard methods for pressure measurement. ANSI/ASHRAE *Standard* 41.3-2014.

ASHRAE. 2015. Standard methods for measurement of proportion of lubricant in liquid refrigerant. ANSI/ASHRAE *Standard* 41.4-2015.

ASHRAE. 2014. Standard methods for humidity measurement. ANSI/ASHRAE *Standard* 41.6-2014.

ASHRAE. 2015. Method of test for measurement of flow of gas. ANSI/ASHRAE *Standard* 41.7-2015.

ASHRAE. 2016. Standard methods of measurement of flow of liquids in pipes using orifice flowmeters. ANSI/ASHRAE *Standard* 41.8-2016.

ASHRAE. 2011. Standard methods for volatile-refrigerant mass flow measurements using calorimeters. ANSI/ASHRAE *Standard* 41.9-2011.

ASHRAE. 2014. Standard methods for power measurement. ANSI/ASHRAE *Standard* 41.11-2014.

ASHRAE. 2007. Laboratory methods of testing fans for aerodynamic performance rating. ANSI/ASHRAE *Standard* 51-07, also ANSI/AMCA *Standard* 210-07.

ASHRAE. 2010. Thermal environmental conditions for human occupancy. ANSI/ASHRAE *Standard* 55-2010.

ASHRAE. 2010. Ventilation for acceptable indoor air quality. ANSI/ASHRAE *Standard* 62.1-2010.

ASHRAE. 1997. Laboratory method of testing to determine the sound power in a duct. ANSI/ASHRAE *Standard* 68-1997, also ANSI/AMCA *Standard* 330-97.

ASHRAE. 2008. Measurement, testing, adjusting, and balancing of building HVAC systems. ANSI/ASHRAE *Standard* 111-2008.

ASHRAE. 2014. Engineering analysis of experimental data. *Guideline* 2-2010 (RA2014).

ASME. 2013. Pressure gauges and gauge attachments. ANSI/ASME *Standard* B40.100-2013. American Society of Mechanical Engineers, New York.

ASME. 2014. Glossary of terms used in the measurement of fluid flow in pipes. ANSI/ASME *Standard* MFC-1-2014. American Society of Mechanical Engineers, New York.

ASME. 2013. Measurement uncertainty for fluid flow in closed conduits. ANSI/ASME *Standard* MFC-2M-1983 (RA13). American Society of Mechanical Engineers, New York.

ASME. 2004. Measurement of fluid flow in pipes using orifice, nozzle, and venturi. *Standard* MFC-3M-2004. American Society of Mechanical Engineers, New York.

ASME. 2011. Measurement of liquid flow in closed conduits by weighing methods. ANSI/ASME *Standard* MFC-9M-1988 (RA11). American Society of Mechanical Engineers, New York.

ASME. 2011. Method for establishing installation effects on flowmeters. ANSI/ASME *Standard* MFC-10M-2000 (RA11). American Society of Mechanical Engineers, New York.

ASME. 2013. Test uncertainty. ANSI/ASME *Standard* PTC 19.1-2013. American Society of Mechanical Engineers, New York.

ASME. 1974. Temperature measurement. ANSI/ASME *Standard* PTC 19.3-1974 (RA98). American Society of Mechanical Engineers, New York.

ASME. 2013. Flow measurement. ANSI/ASME *Standard* PTC 19.5-2004 (RA13). American Society of Mechanical Engineers, New York.

ASTM. 2010. Standard test method for steady-state heat flux measurements and thermal transmission properties by means of the guarded-hot-plate apparatus. *Standard* C177-10. American Society for Testing and Materials, West Conshohocken, PA.

ASTM. 2010. Standard test method for steady-state heat transfer properties of pipe insulation. *Standard* C335-10. American Society for Testing and Materials, West Conshohocken, PA.

ASTM. 2010. Standard test method for steady-state thermal transmission properties by means of the heat flow meter apparatus. *Standard* C518-10. American Society for Testing and Materials, West Conshohocken, PA.

ASTM. 2011. Standard test method for thermal performance of building assemblies by means of a calibrated hot box. *Standard* C976-11. American Society for Testing and Materials, West Conshohocken, PA.

ASTM. 2013. Standard practice for in-situ measurement of heat flux and temperature on building envelope components. *Standard* C1046-95 (R2013). American Society for Testing and Materials, West Conshohocken, PA.

ASTM. 2015. Standard practice for thermographic inspection of insulation installations in envelope cavities of frame buildings. *Standard* C1060-11a (R2015). American Society for Testing and Materials, West Conshohocken, PA.

ASTM. 2013. Standard practice for determining thermal resistance of building envelope components from the in-situ data. *Standard* C1155-95 (R2013). American Society for Testing and Materials, West Conshohocken, PA.

ASTM. 2011. Standard test method for thermal performance of building materials and envelope assemblies by means of a hot box apparatus. *Standard* C1363-11. American Society for Testing and Materials, West Conshohocken, PA.

ASTM. 2012. Standard guide for using indoor carbon dioxide concentrations to evaluate indoor air quality and ventilation. *Standard* D6245-12. American Society for Testing and Materials, West Conshohocken, PA.

ASTM. 2010. Standard test methods for water vapor transmission of materials. *Standard* E96/E96M-10. American Society for Testing and Materials, West Conshohocken, PA.

ASTM. 2012. Standard practice for maintaining constant relative humidity by means of aqueous solutions. *Standard* E104-02 (2012). American Society for Testing and Materials, West Conshohocken, PA.

ASTM. 2012. Standard specification and temperature-electromotive force (emf) tables for standardized thermocouples. *Standard* E230/E230M-12. American Society for Testing and Materials, West Conshohocken, PA.

ASTM. 2011. Standard test method for determining air change in a single zone by means of a tracer gas dilution. *Standard* E741-2011. American Society for Testing and Materials, West Conshohocken, PA.

ASTM. 2012. *Occupational health and safety; protective clothing*. (79 standards.) American Society for Testing and Materials, West Conshohocken, PA.

IEEE. 2004. Standard test procedure for polyphase induction motors and generators. *Standard* 112-2004. Institute of Electrical and Electronics Engineers, New York.

IEEE. 2012. IEEE standard for Ethernet. *Standard* 802.3. Institute of Electrical and Electronics Engineers, New York.

ISO. 2003 Measurement of fluid flow by means of pressure differential devices inserted in circular cross-section conduits running full. *Standard* 5167:2003. International Organization for Standardization, Geneva.

ISO. 2007. Industrial fans—Performance testing using standardized airways. *Standard* 5801:2007. International Organization for Standardization, Geneva.

ISO. 1998. Ergonomics of the thermal environment—Instruments for measuring physical quantities. *Standard* 7726:1998. International Organization for Standardization, Geneva.

ISO. 2005. Ergonomics of the thermal environment—Analytical determination and interpretation of thermal comfort using calculation of the PMV and PPD indices and local thermal comfort criteria. *Standard* 7730:2005. International Organization for Standardization, Geneva.

ISO. 2004. Ergonomics of the thermal environment—Determination of metabolic rate. *Standard* 8996:2004. International Organization for Standardization, Geneva.

ISO. 2007. Ergonomics of the thermal environment—Estimation of thermal insulation and water vapour resistance of a clothing ensemble. *Standard* 9920:2007. International Organization for Standardization, Geneva.

REFERENCES

ASHRAE members can access *ASHRAE Journal* articles and ASHRAE research project final reports at technologyportal.ashrae.org. Articles and reports are also available for purchase by nonmembers in the online ASHRAE Bookstore at www.ashrae.org/bookstore.

Abernethy, R.B., R.P. Benedict, and R.B. Dowdell. 1985. ASME measurement uncertainty. *Transactions of ASME* 107:161-164.

ACGIH. 2001. *Air sampling instruments for evaluation of atmospheric contaminants*, 9th ed. American Conference of Governmental Industrial Hygienists, Cincinnati, OH.

Ambrose, J.H., L.C. Chow, and J.E. Beam. 1990. Capillary flow properties of mesh wicks. *AIAA Journal of Thermophysics* 4:318-324.

Amdur, E.J. 1965. Two-pressure relative humidity standards. In *Humidity and moisture*, vol. 3, p. 445. Reinhold, New York.

ASTM. 1993. Manual on the use of thermocouples in temperature measurement. *Manual* 12. American Society for Testing and Materials, West Conshohocken, PA.

Bahnfleth, W.P., G.K. Yuill, and B.W. Lee. 1999. Protocol for field testing of tall buildings to determine envelope air leakage rates. *ASHRAE Transactions* 105(2):27-38.

Baron, P.A., and K. Willeke. 2001. *Aerosol measurement*. Wiley, New York.

Bedford, T., and C.G. Warmer. 1935. The globe thermometer in studies of heating and ventilating. *Journal of the Institution of Heating and Ventilating Engineers* 2:544.

Benedict, R.P. 1984. *Fundamentals of temperature, pressure and flow measurements*, 3rd ed. John Wiley & Sons, New York.

Bentz, D.P., and J.W. Martin. 1987. Using the computer to analyze coating defects. *Journal of Protective Coatings and Linings* 4(5).

Bristow, K.L., G.S. Campbell, and K. Calissendorff. 1993. Test of heat-pulse probe for measuring changes in soil water content. *Soil Science Society of America Journal* 57:930-934.

Bristow, K.L, G.J. Kluitenberg, and R. Horton. 1994. Measurement of soil thermal properties with a dual-probe heat-pulse technique. *Soil Science Society of America Journal* 58:1288-1294.

Brown, K.K., H.W. Coleman, and W.G. Steele. 1998. A methodology for determining experimental uncertainties in regressions. *ASME Journal of Fluids Engineering, Transactions of ASME* 120:445-456.

Bruce, R.R., and A. Klute. 1956. The measurement of soil moisture diffusivity. *Proceedings of the Soil Science Society of America* 20:458-462.

Burch, D.M. 1980. Infrared audits of roof heat loss. *ASHRAE Transactions* 86(2).

Burch, D.M., and C.M. Hunt. 1978. Retrofitting an existing residence for energy conservation—An experimental study. *Building Science Series* 105. National Institute of Standards and Technology, Gaithersburg, MD.

Burch, D.M., W.C. Thomas, and A.H. Fanney. 1992. Water vapor permeability measurements of common building materials. *ASHRAE Transactions* 98(2):486-494.

Burns, G.W., M.G. Scroger, G.F. Strouse, M.C. Croarkin, and W.F. Guthrie. 1992. Temperature-electromotive force reference functions and tables for the letter-designated thermocouple types based on the ITS-90. NIST *Monograph* 175. U.S. Government Printing Office, Washington, D.C.

Campbell, G.S., C. Calissendorff, and J.H. Williams. 1991. Probe for measuring soil specific heat using a heat-pulse method. *Soil Science Society of America Journal* 55:291-293.

Carotenuto, A., F. Fucci, and G. LaFianzi. 1991. Adsorption phenomena in porous media in the presence of moist air. *International Journal of Heat and Mass Transfer* 18:71-81.

Coleman, H.W., and W.G. Steele. 1995. Engineering application of experimental uncertainty analysis. *AIAA Journal* 33(10):1888-1896.

Coleman, H.W., and W.G. Steele. 2009. *Experimentation, validation and uncertainty analysis for engineers*, 3rd ed. John Wiley & Sons, New York.

Considine, D.M. 1985. *Process instruments and controls handbook*, 3rd ed. McGraw-Hill, New York.

Cox, J.E., and C.R. Miro. 1997. Aircraft cabin air quality. *ASHRAE Journal* 22.

Cunningham, M.J., and T.J. Sprott. 1984. Sorption properties of New Zealand building materials. Building Research Association of New Zealand *Research Report* 45, Judgeford.

DeCarlo, J.P. 1984. *Fundamentals of flow measurement*. Instrumentation Society of America, Research Triangle Park, NC.

D'Eustachio, D., and R.E. Schreiner. 1952. A study of transient heat method for measuring thermal conductivity. *ASHVE Transactions* 58:331.

DeWitt, D.P., and G.D. Nutter. 1988. *Theory and practice of radiation thermometry*. John Wiley & Sons, New York.

Fanger, P.O. 1982. *Thermal comfort*. Robert E. Krieger, Malabar, FL.

Fanney, A.H., W.C. Thomas, D.M. Burch, and L.R. Mathena. 1991. Measurements of moisture diffusion in building materials. *ASHRAE Transactions* 97:99-113.

Freitas, V., P. Crausse, and V. Abrantes. 1991. Moisture diffusion in thermal insulating materials. In *Insulation materials: Testing and applications*, vol. 2. ASTM *Special Technical Publication* STP 1116. American Society for Testing and Materials, West Conshohocken, PA.

Gagge, A.P., J.A.J. Stolwijk, and Y. Nishi. 1971. An effective temperature scale based on a simple model of human physiological regulatory response. *ASHRAE Transactions* 77(1).

Goldstein, R.J. 1978. Application of aerial infrared thermography. *ASHRAE Transactions* 84(1).

Greenspan, L. 1977. Humidity fixed points of binary saturated aqueous solutions. *Journal of Research of the National Bureau of Standards* 81A: 89-95.

Greenspan, L., and A. Wexler. 1968. An adiabatic saturation psychrometer. *Journal of Research of the National Bureau of Standards* 72C(1):33.

Gummerson, R.J., C. Hall, W.D. Hoff, R. Hawkes, G.N. Holland, and W.S. Moore. 1979. Unsaturated water flow within porous materials observed by NMR imaging. *Nature* 281:56-57.

Hasegawa, S. 1976. The NBS two-pressure humidity generator, mark 2. *Journal of Research of the National Bureau of Standards* 81A:81.

Hickman, C., B.T. Beck, and B. Babin. 2012. Determining the effects of duct fittings on volumetric air flow measurements. *Final Report*, ASHRAE Research Project RP-1245.

Hickman, C., B.T. Beck, and B. Babin. 2015a. Effect of fittings on volumetric airflow measurements (RP-1245): Single-path duct disturbances. *Science and Technology for the Built Environment* 21:190-206.

Hickman, C., B.T. Beck, and B. Babin, 2015b. Effect of fittings on volumetric airflow measurements (RP-1245): Multiple-path (tee) duct disturbances. *Science and Technology for the Built Environment* 21:957-975.

Holman, J.P. 2001. *Experimental methods for engineers*, 7th ed., pp. 383-389. McGraw-Hill, New York.

Hooper, F.C., and S.C. Chang. 1953. Development of thermal conductivity probe. *ASHVE Transactions* 59:463.

Hooper, F.C., and F.C. Lepper. 1950. Transient heat flow apparatus for the determination of thermal conductivity. *ASHVE Transactions* 56:309.

Hudson, R.D., Jr. 1969. *Infrared system engineering*. John Wiley & Sons, New York.

IES. 2011. *Lighting handbook*, 10th ed. Illuminating Engineering Society of North America, New York.

Kumaran, M.K., and M. Bomberg. 1985. A gamma-spectrometer for determination of density distribution and moisture distribution in building materials. *Proceedings of the International Symposium on Moisture and Humidity*, Washington, D.C., pp. 485-490.

Kusuda, T. 1965. Calculation of the temperature of a flat-plate wet surface under adiabatic conditions with respect to the Lewis relation. In *Humidity and moisture*, vol. 1, p. 16. Reinhold, New York.

Liptak, B.G., ed. 1972. *Instrument engineers handbook*, vol. 1. Chilton, Philadelphia, PA.

Lodge, J.P., ed. 1989. *Methods of air sampling and analysis*, 3rd ed. Lewis Publishers, MI.

Lundgren, D.A., M. Lippmann, F.S. Harris, Jr., W.H. Marlow, W.E. Clark, and M.D. Durham, eds. 1979. *Aerosol measurement*. University Presses of Florida, Gainesville.

Mack, R.T. 1986. Energy loss profiles: Foundation for future profit in thermal imager sales and service. *Proceedings of the 5th Infrared Information Exchange*, Book 1, AGEMA Infrared Systems, Secaucus, NJ.

Madding, R. 1989. *Infrared thermography*. McGraw-Hill, New York.

Madsen, T.L. 1976. Thermal comfort measurements. *ASHRAE Transactions* 82(1).

Mattingly, G.E. 1984. Workshop on fundamental research issues in orifice metering. GRI *Report* 84/0190. Gas Research Institute, Chicago.

Mattingly, G.E. 1992. The characterization of a piston displacement-type flowmeter calibration facility and the calibration and use of pulsed output type flowmeters. *Journal of Research of the National Institute of Standards and Technology* 97(5):509.

McCullough, E.A., B.W. Jones, and J. Huck. 1985. A comprehensive data base for estimating clothing insulation. *ASHRAE Transactions* 92:29-47.

McLean, R.C., G.H. Galbraith, and C.H. Sanders. 1990. Moisture transmission testing of building materials and the presentation of vapour permeability values. *Building Research and Practice* 18(2):82-103.

Mease, N.E., W.G. Cleveland, Jr., G.E. Mattingly, J.M. Hall. 1992. Air speed calibrations at the National Institute of Standards and Technology. *Proceedings of the 1992 Measurement Science Conference*, Anaheim, CA.

Meyer, C.W., J.T. Hodges, R.W. Hyland, G.E. Scace, J. Valencia-Rodriguez, and J.R. Whetstone. 2010. The second-generation NIST standard hydrometer. *Metrologia* 47:192-207. www.nist.gov/manuscript-publication-search.cfm?pub_id=903607.

Miller, R.W. 1983. *Measurement engineering handbook*. McGraw-Hill, New York.

Nagda, N.L., and H.E. Rector. 2001. Instruments and methods for measuring indoor air quality. In *Indoor air quality handbook*, pp. 51.1-51.37. J.D. Spengler, J.M. Samet, and J.F. McCarthy, eds. McGraw-Hill.

NIST. 1976. Liquid-in-glass thermometry. NIST *Monograph* 150. National Institute of Standards and Technology, Gaithersburg, MD.

NIST. 1986. Thermometer calibrations. NIST *Monograph* 174. National Institute of Standards and Technology, Gaithersburg, MD.

Nottage, H.B., J.G. Slaby, and W.P. Gojsza. 1952. A smoke-filament technique for experimental research in room air distribution. *ASHVE Transactions* 58:399.

Olesen, B.W. 1985. A new and simpler method for estimating the thermal insulation of a clothing ensemble. *ASHRAE Transactions* 92:478-492.

Olesen, B.W., J. Rosendahl, L.N. Kalisperis, L.H. Summers, and M. Steinman. 1989. Methods for measuring and evaluating the thermal radiation in a room. *ASHRAE Transactions* 95(1).

Paljak, I., and B. Pettersson. 1972. *Thermography of buildings*. National Swedish Institute for Materials Testing, Stockholm.

Parmelee, G.V., and R.G. Huebscher. 1946. The shielding of thermocouples from the effects of radiation. *ASHVE Transactions* 52:183.

Persily, A., and S.J. Emmerich. 2001. *State-of-the-art review of CO_2 demand control ventilation and application*. NIST IR6729. National Institute of Standards and Technology, Gaithersburg, MD.

Prazak, J., J. Tywoniak, F. Peterka, and T. Slonc. 1990. Description of transport of liquid in porous media—A study based on neutron radiography data. *International Journal of Heat and Mass Transfer* 33:1105-1120.

Quenard, D., and H. Sallee. 1989. A gamma-ray spectrometer for measurement of the water diffusivity of cementitious materials. *Proceedings of the Materials Research Society Symposium*, vol. 137.

Quinn, T.J. 1990. *Temperature*, 2nd ed. Academic Press, New York.

Raffel, M., C. Willert, and J. Kompenhans. 1998. *Particle image velocimetry: A practical guide*. Springer.

Richards, R.F., D.M. Burch, W.C. Thomas. 1992. Water vapor sorption measurements of common building materials. *ASHRAE Transactions* 98(1).

Richardson, L. 1965. A thermocouple recording psychrometer for measurement of relative humidity in hot, arid atmosphere. In *Humidity and moisture*, vol. 1, p. 101. Reinhold, New York.

Schooley, J.F. 1986. *Thermometry*. CRC, Boca Raton, FL.

Schooley, J.F., ed. 1992. *Temperature: Its measurement and control in science and in industry*, vol. 6. American Institute of Physics, New York.

Seely, R.E. 1955. A circuit for measuring the resistance of energized A-C windings. *AIEE Transactions*, p. 214.

Shafer, M.R. 1961. Performance characteristics of turbine flowmeters. *Proceedings of the Winter Annual Meeting*, Paper 61-WA-25. American Society of Mechanical Engineers, New York.

Straube, J.F. 1998. *Moisture control and enclosure wall systems*. Ph.D. dissertation, University of Waterloo. Waterloo, Ontario, Canada.

TIA. 1997. Interface between data terminal equipment and data circuit-terminating equipment employing serial binary data interchange. *Standard* TIA-232. Telecommunication Industry Alliance, Revision F, October.

TIA. 1998. Electrical characteristics of generators and receivers for use in balanced digital multipoint systems. *Standard* TIA-485. Telecommunication Industry Alliance, Revision A, March.

TIA. 2006. Application guidelines for TIA/EIA-485-A. *Standard* TSB-89. Telecommunication Industry Alliance, Revision A, January 2006.

Till, C.E., and G.E. Handegord. 1960. Proposed humidity standard. *ASHRAE Transactions* 66:288.

Tobiasson, W., and C. Korhonen. 1985. Roofing moisture surveys: Yesterday, today, and tomorrow. *Proceedings of the Second International Symposium on Roofing Technology*, Gaithersburg, MD.

Tveit, A. 1966. Measurement of moisture sorption and moisture permeability of porous materials. *Report* 45. Norwegian Building Research Institute, Oslo.

Vernon, H.M. 1932. The globe thermometer. *Proceedings of the Institution of Heating and Ventilating Engineers*, vol. 39, p. 100.

Wentzel, J.D. 1961. An instrument for measurement of the humidity of air. *ASHRAE Journal* 11:67.

Wile, D.D. 1947. Air flow measurement in the laboratory. *Refrigerating Engineering* 6:515.

Woodring, E.D. 1969. Magnetic turbine flowmeters. *Instruments and Control Systems* 6:133.

Worrall, R.W. 1965. Psychrometric determination of relative humidities in air with dry-bulb temperatures exceeding 212°F. In *Humidity and Moisture*, vol. 1, p. 105. Reinhold, New York.

Yang, H., Y. Luo, and T. Zhang. 2015. A data sorting method for rapid measurement of moisture content in porous insulation materials. *Proceedings of ISHVAC-COBEE 2015*, Tianjin, China.

BIBLIOGRAPHY

Beranek, L.L. 1988. *Acoustical measurements*. Published for the Acoustical Society of America by the American Institute of Physics, New York.

Beranek, L.L. 1989. *Noise and vibration control*. Institute of Noise Control Engineering, Poughkeepsie, NY.

Cohen, E.R. 1990. The expression of uncertainty in physical measurements. *1990 Measurement Science Conference Proceedings*, Anaheim, CA.

Contemporary Controls. 1999. Understanding EIA-485 networks. *The Extension: A Technical Supplement to Control Network* 1(1). www.ccontrols.com/pdf/ExtV1N1.pdf.

EPA. 1991. *Introduction to indoor air quality: A self-paced learning module*. EPA/400/3-91/002, U.S. Environmental Protection Agency, Washington, D.C.

Harris, C.M. 1987. *Shock and vibration handbook*, 3rd ed. McGraw-Hill, New York.

IEEE. 1987. Standard digital interface for programmable instrumentation. ANSI/IEEE *Standard* 488.1-87 (R 1994). Institute of Electrical and Electronics Engineers, Piscataway, NJ.

Jones, J.L., and A.M. Flynn, 1993. *Mobile robots*, A.K. Peters, Wellesley, MA.

De Silva, C.W. 1989. *Control sensors and actuators*. Prentice Hall, Englewood Cliffs, NJ.

Lord, H.W., W.S. Gatley, and H.A. Evensen. 1987. *Noise control for engineers*. Krieger, Melbourne, FL.

Morrison, R. 1986. *Grounding and shielding techniques in instrumentation*, 3rd ed. John Wiley & Sons, New York.

Spitzer, D.W., ed. 1991. *Flow measurement*. Instrumentation Society of America, Research Triangle Park, NC.

Steele, W.G., R.A. Ferguson, R.P. Taylor, and H.W. Coleman. 1994. Comparison of ANSI/ASME and ISO models for calculation of uncertainty. *ISA Transactions 33*:339-352.

Tilford, C.R. 1992. Pressure and vacuum measurements. In *Physical methods of chemistry*, 2nd ed., vol. 6, pp. 106-173. John Wiley & Sons, New York.

Universal Serial Bus Specification. 2013. Universal serial bus revision 3.1 specification, section 5.5.7. July.

Universal Serial Bus Specification. 2000. Universal serial bus revision 2.0 specification, section 7.1.6. April.

CHAPTER 38

ABBREVIATIONS AND SYMBOLS

THIS chapter contains information about abbreviations and symbols for HVAC&R engineers.

Abbreviations are shortened forms of names and expressions used in text, drawings, and computer programs. This chapter discusses conventional English-language abbreviations that may be different in other languages. A **letter symbol** represents a quantity or a unit, not its name, and is independent of language. Because of this, use of a letter symbol is preferred over abbreviations for unit or quantity terms. Letter symbols necessary for individual chapters are defined in the chapters where they occur.

Abbreviations are never used for mathematical signs, such as the equality sign (=) or division sign (/), except in computer programming, where the abbreviation functions as a letter symbol. Mathematical operations are performed only with symbols. Abbreviations should be used only where necessary to save time and space; avoid their use in documents circulated in foreign countries.

Graphical symbols in this chapter of piping, ductwork, fittings, and in-line accessories can be used on scale drawings and diagrams.

Identifying piping by legend and color promotes greater safety and lessens the chance of error in emergencies. Piping identification is now required throughout the United States by the Occupational Safety and Health Administration (OSHA) for some industries and by many federal, state, and local codes.

ABBREVIATIONS FOR TEXT, DRAWINGS, AND COMPUTER PROGRAMS

Table 1 gives some abbreviations, as well as others commonly found on mechanical drawings and abbreviations (symbols) used in computer programming. Abbreviations specific to a single subject are defined in the chapters in which they appear. Additional abbreviations used on drawings can be found in the section on Graphical Symbols for Drawings.

Computer Programs

The abbreviations (symbols) used for computer programming for the HVAC&R industries have been developed by ASHRAE Technical Committee 1.5, Computer Applications. These symbols identify computer variables, subprograms, subroutines, and functions commonly applied in the industry. Using these symbols enhances comprehension of the program listings and provides a clearly defined nomenclature in applicable computer programs.

Some symbols have two or more options listed. The longest abbreviation is preferred and should be used if possible. However, it is sometimes necessary to shorten the symbol to further identify the variable. For instance, the area of a wall cannot be defined as WALLAREA because some computer languages restrict the number of letters in a variable name. Therefore, a shorter variable symbol is applied, and WALLAREA becomes WALLA or WAREA.

Most modern computer programming languages do not have the character limitations of older computer languages, but the limitations still exist in some older building automation controllers. It is good programming practice to include the complete name of each variable and to define any abbreviations in the comments section at the beginning of each module of code. Abbreviations should be used to help clarify the variables in an equation and not to obscure the readability of the code.

In Table 1, the same symbol is sometimes used for different terms. This liberty is taken because it is unlikely that the two terms would be used in the same program. If such were the case, one of the terms would require a suffix or prefix to differentiate it from the other.

LETTER SYMBOLS

Letter symbols include symbols for physical quantities (quantity symbols) and symbols for the units in which these quantities are measured (unit symbols). **Quantity symbols**, such as I for electric current, are listed in this chapter and are printed in italic type. A **unit symbol** is a letter or group of letters such as ft for foot or a special sign such as ° for degrees, and is printed in Roman type. Subscripts and superscripts are governed by the same principles. Letter symbols are restricted mainly to the English and Greek alphabets.

Quantity symbols may be used in mathematical expressions in any way consistent with good mathematical usage. The product of two quantities, a and b, is indicated by ab. The quotient is a/b, or ab^{-1}. To avoid misinterpretation, parentheses must be used if more than one slash (/) is used in an algebraic term; for example, $(a/b)/c$ or $a/(b/c)$ is correct, but not $a/b/c$.

Subscripts and superscripts, or several of them separated by commas, may be attached to a single basic letter (kernel), but not to other subscripts or superscripts. A symbol that has been modified by a superscript should be enclosed in parentheses before an exponent is added $(X_a)^3$. Symbols can also have alphanumeric marks such as ′ (prime), + (plus), and * (asterisk).

More detailed information on the general principles of letter symbol standardization are in standards listed at the end of this chapter. The letter symbols, in general, follow these standards, which are out of print:

Y10.3M	Letter Symbols for Mechanics and Time-Related Phenomena
Y10.4-82	Letter Symbols for Heat and Thermodynamics

Other symbols chosen by an author for a physical magnitude not appearing in any standard list should be ones that do not already have different meanings in the field of the text.

The preparation of this chapter is assigned to TC 1.6, Terminology.

Table 1 Abbreviations for Text, Drawings, and Computer Programs

Term	Text	Drawings	Program
above finished floor	—	AFF	—
absolute	abs	ABS	ABS
accumulat(e, -or)	acc	ACCUM	ACCUM
air condition(-ing, -ed)	—	AIR COND	—
air-conditioning unit(s)	—	ACU	ACU
air-handling unit	—	AHU	AHU
air horsepower	ahp	AHP	AHP
alteration	altrn	ALTRN	—
alternating current	ac	AC	AC
altitude	alt	ALT	ALT
ambient	amb	AMB	AMB
American National Standards Institute[1]	ANSI	ANSI	—
American wire gage	AWG	AWG	—
ampere (amp, amps)	amp	AMP	AMP, AMPS
angle	—	—	ANG
angle of incidence	—	—	ANGI
apparatus dew point	adp	ADP	ADP
approximate	approx.	APPROX	—
area	—	—	A
atmosphere	atm	ATM	—
average	avg	AVG	AVG
azimuth	az	AZ	AZ
azimuth, solar	—	—	SAZ
azimuth, wall	—	—	WAZ
barometer(-tric)	baro	BARO	—
bill of material	b/m	BOM	—
boiling point	bp	BP	BP
brake horsepower	bhp	BHP	BHP
Brown & Sharpe wire gage	B&S	B&S	—
British thermal unit	Btu	BTU	BTU
Celsius	°C	°C	°C
center to center	c to c	C TO C	—
circuit	ckt	CKT	CKT
clockwise	cw	CW	—
coefficient	coeff.	COEF	COEF
coefficient, valve flow	C_v	C_v	CV
coil	—	—	COIL
compressor	cprsr	CMPR	CMPR
condens(-er, -ing, -ation)	cond	COND	COND
conductance	—	—	C
conductivity	cndct	CNDCT	K
conductors, number of (3)	3/c	3/c	—
contact factor	—	—	CF
cooling load	clg load	CLG LOAD	CLOAD
counterclockwise	ccw	CCW	—
cubic feet	ft^3	CU FT	CUFT, CFT
cubic inch	in^3	CU IN	CUIN, CIN
cubic feet per minute	cfm	CFM	CFM
cfm, standard conditions	scfm	SCFM	SCFM
cubic ft per sec, standard	scfs	SCFS	SCFS
decibel	dB	DB	DB
degree	deg. or °	DEG or °	DEG
density	dens	DENS	RHO
depth or deep	dp	DP	DPTH
dew-point temperature	dpt	DPT	DPT
diameter	dia.	DIA	DIA
diameter, inside	ID	ID	ID
diameter, outside	OD	OD	OD
difference or delta	diff., Δ	DIFF	D, DELTA
diffuse radiation	—	—	DFRAD
direct current	dc	DC	DC
direct radiation	dir radn	DIR RADN	DIRAD
dry	—	—	DRY
dry-bulb temperature	dbt	DBT	DB, DBT
effectiveness	—	—	EFT
effective temperature[2]	ET*	ET*	ET
efficiency	eff	EFF	EFF
efficiency, fin	—	—	FEFF
efficiency, surface	—	—	SEFF
electromotive force	emf	EMF	—
elevation	elev.	EL	ELEV
entering	entr	ENT	ENT
entering water temperature	EWT	EWT	EWT
entering air temperature	EAT	EAT	EAT
enthalpy	—	—	H
entropy	—	—	S
equivalent direct radiation	edr	EDR	—
equivalent feet	eqiv ft	EQIV FT	EQFT
equivalent inches	eqiv in	EQIV IN	EQIN
evaporat(-e, -ing, -ed, -or)	evap	EVAP	EVAP
expansion	exp	EXP	XPAN
face area	fa	FA	FA
face to face	f to f	F to F	—
face velocity	fvel	FVEL	FV
factor, correction	—	—	CFAC, CFACT
factor, friction	—	—	FFACT, FF
Fahrenheit	°F	°F	F
fan	—	—	FAN
feet per minute	fpm	FPM	FPM
feet per second	fps	FPS	FPS
film coefficient,[3] inside	—	—	FI, HI
film coefficient,[3] outside	—	—	FO, HO
flow rate, air	—	—	QAR, QAIR
flow rate, fluid	—	—	QFL
flow rate, gas	—	—	QGA, QGAS
foot or feet	ft	FT	FT
foot-pound	ft·lb	FT LB	—
freezing point	fp	FP	FP
frequency	Hz	HZ	—
gage or gauge	ga	GA	GA, GAGE
gallons	gal	GAL	GAL
gallons per hour	gph	GPH	GPH
gallons per minute	gpm	GPM	GPM
gallons per day	gpd	GPD	GPD
grains	gr	GR	GR
gravitational constant	*G*	G	G
greatest temp difference	GTD	GTD	GTD
head	hd	HD	HD
heat	—	—	HT
heater	—	—	HTR
heat gain	HG	HG	HG, HEATG
heat gain, latent	LHG	LHG	HGL
heat gain, sensible	SHG	SHG	HGS
heat loss	—	—	HL, HEATL
heat transfer	—	—	Q
heat transfer coefficient	*U*	U	U
height	hgt	HGT	HGT, HT
high-pressure steam	hps	HPS	HPS
high-temperature hot water	hthw	HTHW	HTHW
horsepower	hp	HP	HP
hour(s)	h	HR	HR
humidity, relative	rh	RH	RH
humidity ratio	*W*	W	W
inch	in.	in.	IN
incident angle	—	—	INANG
indicated horsepower	ihp	IHP	—
International Pipe Std	IPS	IPS	—
iron pipe size	ips	IPS	—
kilowatt	kW	kW	KW
kilowatt hour	kWh	KWH	KWH
latent heat	LH	LH	LH, LHEAT
least mean temp. difference[4]	LMTD	LMTD	LMTD
least temp. difference[4]	LTD	LTD	LTD
leaving air temperature	lat	LAT	LAT
leaving water temperature	lwt	LWT	LWT
length	lg	LG	LG, L
linear feet	lin ft	LF	LF
liquid	liq	LIQ	LIQ
load-sharing (hybrid) HVAC system	LSHVAC	LSHVAC	LSHVAC
logarithm (natural)	ln	LN	LN
logarithm to base 10	log	LOG	LOG

Abbreviations and Symbols

Term	Text	Drawings	Program
low-pressure steam	lps	LPS	LPS
low-temp. hot water	lthw	LTHW	LTHW
Mach number	Mach	MACH	
mass flow rate	mfr	MFR	MFR
maximum	max.	MAX	MAX
mean effective temp.	MET	MET	MET
mean temp. difference	MTD	MTD	MTD
medium-pressure steam	mps	MPS	MPS
medium-temp. hot water	mthw	MTHW	MTHW
mercury	Hg	HG	HG
miles per hour	mph	MPH	MPH
minimum	min.	MIN	MIN
minute	min	MIN	MIN
noise criteria	NC	NC	
normally open	n o	N O	—
normally closed	n c	N C	—
not applicable	na	N/A	—
not in contract	n i c	N I C	—
not to scale	—	N T S	
number	no.	NO	N, NO
number of circuits	—		NC
number of tubes	—	—	NT
ounce	oz	OZ	OZ
outside air	oa	OA	OA
parts per million	ppm	PPM	PPM
percent	%	%	PCT
phase (electrical)	ph	PH	—
pipe	—	—	PIPE
pounds	lb	LBS	LBS
pounds per square foot	psf	PSF	PSF
psf absolute	psfa	PSFA	PSFA
psf gage	psfg	PSFG	PSFG
pounds per square inch	psi	PSI	PSI
psi absolute	psia	PSIA	PSIA
psi gage	psig	PSIG	PSIG
pressure	—	PRESS	PRES, P
pressure, barometric	baro pr	BARO PR	BP
pressure, critical	—	—	CRIP
pressure, dynamic (velocity)	vp	VP	VP
pressure drop or difference	PD	PD	PD, DELTP
pressure, static	sp	SP	SP
pressure, vapor	vap pr	VAP PR	VAP
primary	pri	PRI	PRIM
quart	qt	QT	QT
radian	—		RAD
radiat(-e, -or)	—	RAD	—
radiant panel	RP	RP	RP
radiation	—	RADN	RAD
radius	—	—	R
Rankine	°R	°R	R
receiver	rcvr	RCVR	REC
recirculate	recirc.	RECIRC	RCIR, RECIR
refrigerant (12, 22, etc.)	R-12, R-22	R12, R22	R12, R22
relative humidity	rh	RH	RH
resist(-ance, -ivity, -or)	res	RES	RES, OHMS
return air	ra	RA	RA
revolutions	rev	REV	REV
revolutions per minute	rpm	RPM	RPM
revolutions per second	rps	RPS	RPS
roughness	rgh	RGH	RGH, E
safety factor	sf	SF	SF
saturation	sat.	SAT	SAT
Saybolt seconds Furol	ssf	SSF	SSF
Saybolt seconds Universal	ssu	SSU	SSU
sea level	sl	SL	SE
second	s	s	SEC
sensible heat	SH	SH	SH
sensible heat gain	SHG	SHG	SHG
sensible heat ratio	SHR	SHR	SHR
shading coefficient	—	—	SC
shaft horsepower	sft hp	SFT HP	SHP
solar	—		SOL

Term	Text	Drawings	Program
specification	spec	SPEC	[illegible]
specific gravity	SG	SG	—
specific heat	sp ht	SP HT	C
sp ht at constant pressure	c_p	c_p	CP
sp ht at constant volume	c_v	c_v	CV
specific volume	sp vol	SP VOL	V, CVOL
square	sq.	SQ	SQ
standard	std	STD	STD
standard time meridian	—	—	STM
static pressure	SP	SP	SP
suction	suct.	SUCT	SUCT, SUC
summ(-er, -ary, -ation)	—	—	SUM
supply	sply	SPLY	SUP, SPLY
supply air	sa	SA	SA
surface	—	—	SUR, S
surface, dry	—	—	SURD
surface, wet	—	—	SURW
system			SYS
tabulat(-e, -ion)	tab	TAB	TAB
tee	—	—	TEE
temperature	temp.	TEMP	T, TEMP
temperature difference	TD, Δt	TD	TD, TDIF
temperature entering	TE	TE	TE, TENT
temperature leaving	TL	TL	TL, TLEA
thermal conductivity	k	K	K
thermal expansion coeff.	—	—	TXPC
thermal resistance	R	R	RES, R
thermocouple	tc	TC	TC, TCPL
thermostat	T STAT	T STAT	T STAT
thick(-ness)	thkns	THKNS	THK
thousand circular mils	Mcm	MCM	MCM
thousand cubic feet	Mcf	MCF	MCF
thousand foot-pounds	kip ft	KIP FT	KIPFT
thousand pounds	kip	KIP	KIP
time	—	T	T
ton	—	—	TON
tons of refrigeration	tons	TONS	TONS
total	—	—	TOT
total heat	tot ht	TOT HT	
transmissivity	—	—	TAU
U-factor	—	—	U
unit	—	—	UNIT
vacuum	vac	VAC	VAC
valve	v	V	VLV
vapor proof	vap prf	VAP PRF	
variable	var	VAR	VAR
variable air volume	VAV	VAV	VAV
velocity	vel.	VEL	VEL, V
velocity, wind	w vel.	W VEL	W VEL
ventilation, vent	vent	VENT	VENT
vertical	vert.	VERT	VERT
viscosity	visc	VISC	MU, VISC
volt	V	V	E, VOLTS
volt ampere	VA	VA	VA
volume	vol.	VOL	VOL
volumetric flow rate	—	—	VFR
wall	—	—	W, WAL
water	—	—	WTR
watt	W	W	WAT, W
watt-hour	Wh	WH	WHR
weight	wt	WT	WT
wet bulb	wb	WB	WB
wet-bulb temperature	wbt	WBT	WBT
width	—	—	WI
wind	—	—	WD
wind direction	wdir	WDIR	WDIR
wind pressure	wpr	WPR	WP, WPRES
yard	yd	YD	YD
year	yr	YR	YR
zone	z	Z	Z, ZN

[1]Abbreviations of most proper names use capital letters in both text and drawings.
[2]The asterisk (*) is used with ET*, effective temperature, as in Chapter 9 of this volume.
[3]These are surface heat transfer coefficients.
[4]Letter L also used for *Logarithm of* these temperature differences in computer programming.

LETTER SYMBOLS

Symbol	Description of Item	Typical Units
a	acoustic velocity	fps or fpm
A	area	ft^2
b	breadth or width	ft
B	barometric pressure	psia or in. Hg
c	concentration	lb/ft^3, mol/ft^3
c	specific heat	Btu/lb·°F
c_p	specific heat at constant pressure	Btu/lb·°F
c_v	specific heat at constant volume	Btu/lb·°F
C	coefficient	—
C	fluid capacity rate	Btu/h·°F
C	thermal conductance	Btu/h·ft^2·°F
C_L	loss coefficient	—
C_P	coefficient of performance	—
d	prefix meaning differential	—
d or D	diameter	ft
D_e or D_h	equivalent or hydraulic diameter	ft
D_v	mass diffusivity	ft^2/s
e	base of natural logarithms	—
E	energy	Btu
E	electrical potential	V
f	film conductance (alternate for h)	Btu/h·ft^2·°F
f	frequency	Hz
f_D	friction factor, Darcy-Weisbach formulation	—
f_F	friction factor, Fanning formulation	—
F	force	lb$_f$
F_{ij}	angle factor (radiation)	—
g	gravitational acceleration	ft/s^2
G	mass velocity	lb/h·ft^2
h	heat transfer coefficient	Btu/h·ft^2·°F
h	hydraulic head	ft
h	specific enthalpy	Btu/lb
h_a	enthalpy of dry air	Btu/lb
h_D	mass transfer coefficient	lb/h·ft^2·lb per ft^3
h_s	enthalpy of moist air at saturation	Btu/lb
H	total enthalpy	Btu
I	electric current	A
J	mechanical equivalent of heat	ft·lb$_f$/Btu
k	thermal conductivity	Btu/h·ft·°F
k (or γ)	ratio of specific heats, c_p/c_v	—
K	proportionality constant	—
K_D	mass transfer coefficient	lb/h·ft^2
l or L	length	ft
L_p	sound pressure	dB
L_w	sound power	dB
m or M	mass	lb
M	molecular weight	lb/lb mol
n or N	number in general	—
N	rate of rotation	rpm
p or P	pressure	psi
p_a	partial pressure of dry air	psi
p_s	partial pressure of water vapor in moist air	psi
p_w	vapor pressure of water in saturated moist air	psi
P	power	hp, watts
q	time rate of heat transfer	Btu/h
Q	total heat transfer	Btu
Q	volumetric flow rate	cfm
r	radius	ft
r or R	thermal resistance	ft^2·h·°F/Btu
R	gas constant	ft·lb$_f$/lb$_m$·°R
s	specific entropy	Btu/lb·°R
S	total entropy	Btu/°R
t	temperature	°F
Δt_m or ΔT_m	mean temperature difference	°F
T	absolute temperature	°R
u	specific internal energy	Btu/lb
U	total internal energy	Btu
U	overall heat transfer coefficient	Btu/h·ft^2·°F
v	specific volume	ft^3/lb
V	total volume	ft^3
V	linear velocity	fps
w	mass rate of flow	lb/h
W	weight	lb$_f$
W	humidity ratio of moist air	lb(water)/lb(dry air)
W	work	ft·lb$_f$
W_s	humidity ratio of moist air at saturation	lb(water)/lb(dry air)
x	mole fraction	—
x	quality, mass fraction of vapor	—
x,y,z	lengths along principal coordinate axes	ft
Z	figure of merit	—
α	absolute Seebeck coefficient	V/°C
α	absorptivity, absorptance radiation	—
α	linear coefficient of thermal expansion	per °F
α	thermal diffusivity	ft^2/h
β	volume coefficient of thermal expansion	per °F
γ (or k)	ratio of specific heats, c_p/c_v	—
γ	specific weight	lb$_f$/ft^3
Δ	difference between values	—
ε	emissivity, emittance (radiation)	—
θ	time	s, h
η	efficiency or effectiveness	—
λ	wavelength	nm
μ	degree of saturation	—
μ	dynamic viscosity	lb/ft·h
ν	kinematic viscosity	ft^2/h
ρ	density	lb/ft^3
ρ	reflectivity, reflectance (radiation)	—
ρ	volume resistivity	Ω·cm
σ	Stefan-Boltzmann constant	Btu/h·ft^2·°R^4
σ	surface tension	lb$_f$/ft
τ	stress	lb$_f$/ft^2
τ	time	s, h
τ	transmissivity, transmittance (radiation)	—
ϕ	relative humidity	—

DIMENSIONLESS NUMBERS

Fo	Fourier number	$\alpha\tau/L^2$
Gr	Grashof number	$L^3\rho^2\beta g(\Delta t)/\mu^2$
Gz	Graetz number	wc_p/kL
j_D	Colburn mass transfer	Sh/ReSc$^{1/3}$
j_H	Colburn heat transfer	Nu/RePr$^{1/3}$
Le	Lewis number	α/D_v
M	Mach number	V/a
Nu	Nusselt number	hD/k
Pe	Peclet number	GDc_p/k
Pr	Prandtl number	$c_p\mu/k$
Re	Reynolds number	$\rho VD/\mu$
Sc	Schmidt number	$\mu/\rho D_v$
Sh	Sherwood number	$h_D L/D_v$
St	Stanton number	h/Gc_p
Str	Strouhal number	fd/V

MATHEMATICAL SYMBOLS

equal to	$=$
not equal to	$\neq$
approximately equal to	$\approx$
greater than	$>$
less than	$<$
greater than or equal to	$\geq$
less than or equal to	$\leq$
plus	$+$
minus	$-$
plus or minus	$\pm$
a multiplied by b	ab, $a \cdot b$, $a \times b$
a divided by b	$\frac{a}{b}$, a/b, ab^{-1}
ratio of circumference of a circle to its diameter	π

a raised to the power n	a^n
square root of a	$\sqrt{a}$, $a^{0.5}$
infinity	∞
percent	%
summation of	Σ
natural log	ln
logarithm to base 10	log

SUBSCRIPTS

These are to be affixed to the appropriate symbols. Several subscripts may be used together to denote combinations of various states, points, or paths. Often the subscript indicates that a particular property is to be kept constant in a process.

$a,b,...$	referring to different phases, states or physical conditions of a substance, or to different substances
a	air
a	ambient
b	barometric (pressure)
c	referring to critical state or critical value
c	convection
db	dry bulb
dp	dew point
e	base of natural logarithms
f	referring to saturated liquid
f	film
fg	referring to evaporation or condensation
F	friction
g	referring to saturated vapor
h	referring to change of phase in evaporation
H	water vapor
i	referring to saturated solid
i	internal
if	referring to change of phase in melting
ig	referring to change of phase in sublimation
k	kinetic
L	latent
m	mean value
M	molar basis
p	referring to constant pressure conditions or processes
p	potential
r	refrigerant
r	radiant or radiation
s	referring to moist air at saturation
s	sensible
s	referring to isentropic conditions or processes
s	static (pressure)
s	surface
t	total (pressure)
T	referring to isothermal conditions or processes
v	referring to constant volume conditions or processes
v	vapor
v	velocity (pressure)
w	wall
w	water
wb	wet bulb
0	referring to initial or standard states or conditions
1,2,...	different points in a process, or different instants of time

GRAPHICAL SYMBOLS FOR DRAWINGS

Graphical symbols have been extracted from ANSI/ASHRAE *Standard* 134-2005. Additional symbols are from current practice and extracted from ASME *Standards* Y32.2.3 and Y32.2.4.

Piping

Heating	
High-pressure steam	——HPS——
Medium-pressure steam	——MPS——
Low-pressure steam	——LPS——
High-pressure steam condensate	——HPC——
Medium-pressure steam condensate	——MPC——
Low-pressure steam condensate	——LPC——
Boiler blowdown	——BBD——
Pumped condensate	——PC——
Vacuum pump discharge	——VPD——
Makeup water	——MU——
Atmospheric vent	——ATV——
Fuel oil	——FO(NAME)——
Low-temperature hot water supply	——HWS——
Medium-temperature hot water supply	——MTWS——
High-temperature hot water supply	——HTWS——
Low-temperature hot water return	——HWR——
Medium-temperature hot water return	——MTWR——
High-temperature hot water return	——HTWR——
Compressed air	——A(NAME)——
Vacuum (air)	——VAC——
Existing piping	——(NAME)E——
Pipe to be removed	—XX— (NAME) —XX—
Air Conditioning and Refrigeration	
Refrigerant discharge	——RD——
Refrigerant suction	——RS——
Brine supply	——B——
Brine return	——BR——
Condenser water supply	——CWS——
Condenser water return	——CWR——
Chilled water supply	——CHWS——
Chilled water return	——CHWR——
Fill line	——FILL——
Humidification line	——H——
Drain	——D——
Hot/chilled water supply	——H/C S——
Hot/chilled water return	——H/C R——
Refrigerant liquid	——RL——
Heat pump water supply	——HPWS——
Heat pump water return	——HPWR——
Plumbing	
Sanitary drain above floor or grade	——SAN——
Sanitary drain below floor or grade	- - - - SAN - - - -
Storm drain above floor or grade	——ST——
Storm drain below floor or grade	- - - - ST - - - -
Condensate drain above floor or grade	——CD——
Condensate drain below floor or grade	- - - - CD - - - -
Vent	- - - - - - - - - -
Cold water	—·—·—·—·—
Hot water	—··—··—··—
Hot water return	—···—···—···—
Gas	—G——G—
Acid waste	——AW——
Drinking water supply	——DCW——
Chemical supply pipes[a]	——(NAME)——
Floor drain	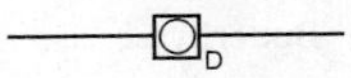
Funnel drain, open	Y

Fire Safety Devices[b]

Signal Initiating Detectors

Heat (thermal)		Gas	
Smoke		Flame	

Radiant Panels

Hydronic heating element ○

Electric heating element ●

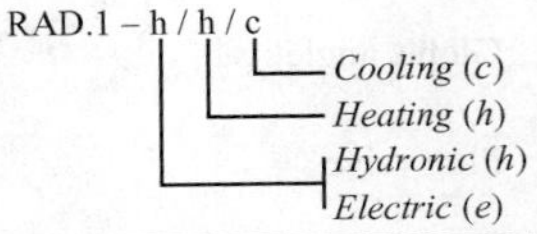

[a]See section on Piping Identification in this chapter.
[b]Refer to *Standard for Fire Safety Symbols*, 1999 edition (NFPA *Standard* 170).

Radiant Ceiling Panels

Embedded

Above ceiling

Surface mounted

Suspended

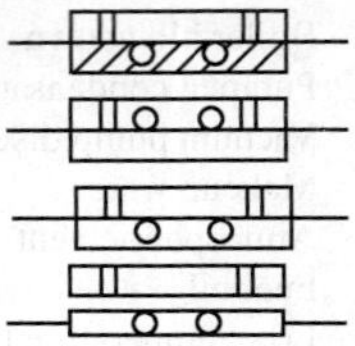

Radiant Floor Panels

Slab on grade

Above subfloor

Below subfloor

Slab above subfloor

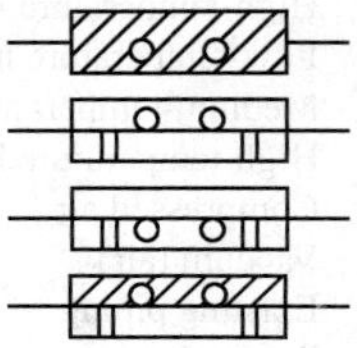

Radiant Wall Panels

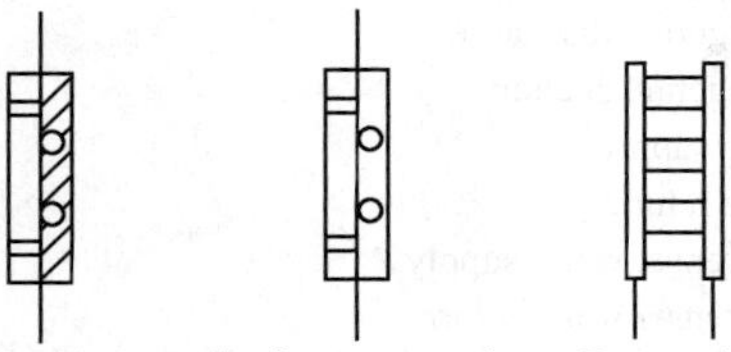

Embedded Surface mounted Decorative

Coils

Cooling coil

Heating coil

Electrical coil

Humidifier

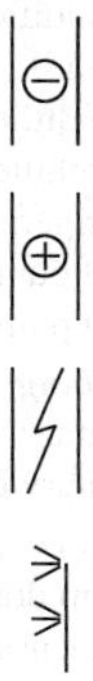

Valves

Valves for Selective Actuators

Air line

Ball

Butterfly

Diaphragm

Gate

Gate, angle

Globe

Globe, angle

Plug valve

Three way

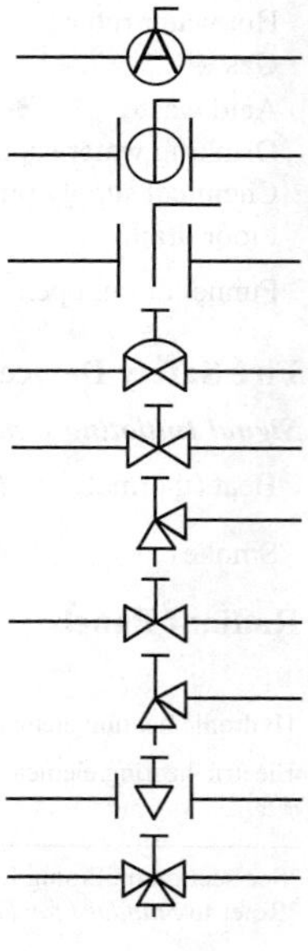

Valves Actuators

Manual

Non-rising sun

Outside stem & yoke

Lever

Gear

Electric

Motor

Solenoid

Pneumatic

Motor

Diaphragm

Valves, Special Duty

Check, swing gate

Check, spring

Control, electric-pneumatic

Control, pneumatic-electric

Hose end drain

Lock shield

Needle

Pressure-reducing regulator

Quick-opening

Quick-closing

Safety or relief

Solenoid

Square-head cock

Unclassified (number and specify)

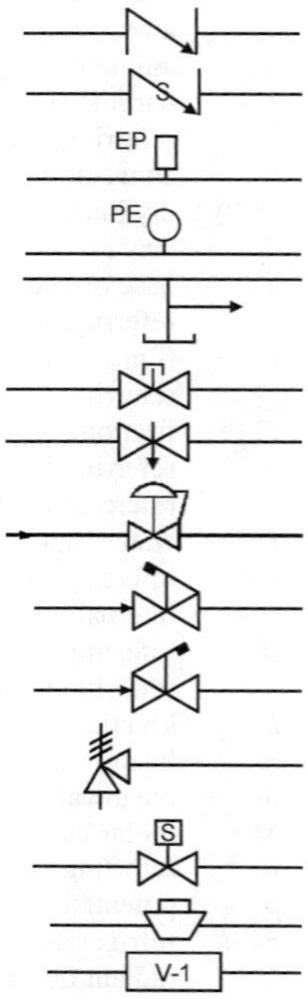

Fittings

The following fittings are shown without connection notations. This reflects current practice. The symbol for the body of a fitting is the same for all types of connections, unless otherwise specified. The types of connections are often specified for a range of pipe sizes, but are shown with the fitting symbol where required. For example, an elbow would be:

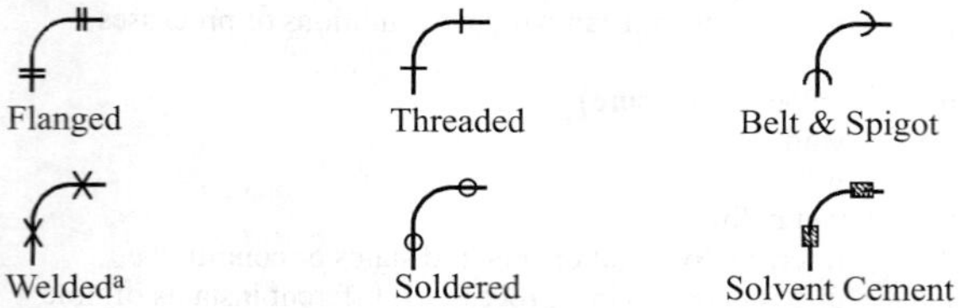

Fitting	*Symbol*
Bushing	
Cap	
Cross	
Elbow, 90°	
Elbow, 45°	
Elbow, facing toward viewer	

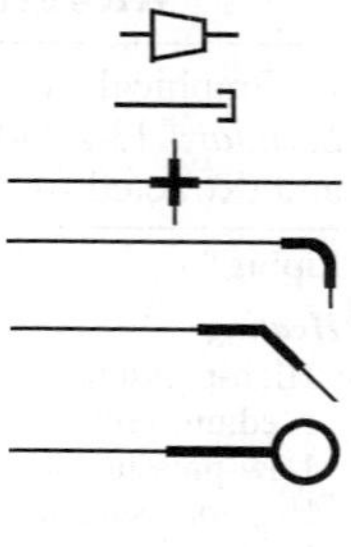

[a] Includes fusion; specify type.

- Elbow, facing away from viewer
- Elbow, base-supported
- Lateral
- Reducer, concentric
- Reducer, eccentric, flat on bottom
- Reducer, eccentric, flat on top
- Tee
- Tee, facing toward viewer
- Tee, facing away from viewer
- Union, screwed
- Union, flanged

Piping Specialties

- Air vent, automatic
- Air vent, manual
- Air separator
- Pipe guide
- Anchor, intermediate
- Anchor, main
- Ball joint
- Expansion joint
- Expansion loop
- Flexible connector
- Flowmeter, orifice plate with flanges
- Flowmeter, venturi
- Flow switch
- Hanger rod
- Hanger spring
- Heat exchanger, liquid
- Heat transfer surface (indicate type)
- Pitch of pipe, rise (R) drop (D)
- Pressure gage and cock
- Pressure switch
- Pump (indicate use)
- Pump suction diffuser
- Spool piece, flanged
- Strainer
- Strainer, blow off
- Strainer, duplex
- Tank (indicate use)

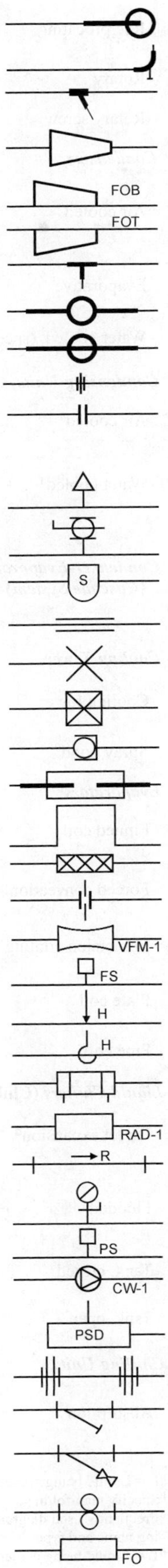

- Thermometer
- Thermometer well, only
- Thermostat
- Traps, steam (indicate type)
- Unit heater (indicate type)

Air-Moving Devices and Components

***Fans* (indicate use)**

- Centrifugal
- Propeller
- Roof ventilator, intake
- Roof ventilator, exhaust
- Roof ventilator, louvered
- Vaneaxial

***Ductwork*[a,b]**

- Direction of flow
- Duct size, where first dimension is visible duct
- Duct section, supply
- Duct section, return
- Duct section, exhaust
- Change of elevation rise (R) drop (D)
- Access doors, vertical or horizontal
- Cowl, (gooseneck) and flashing
- Duct lining
- Flexible connection
- Flexible duct
- Sound attenuator
- Terminal unit, mixing
- Terminal unit, variable volume

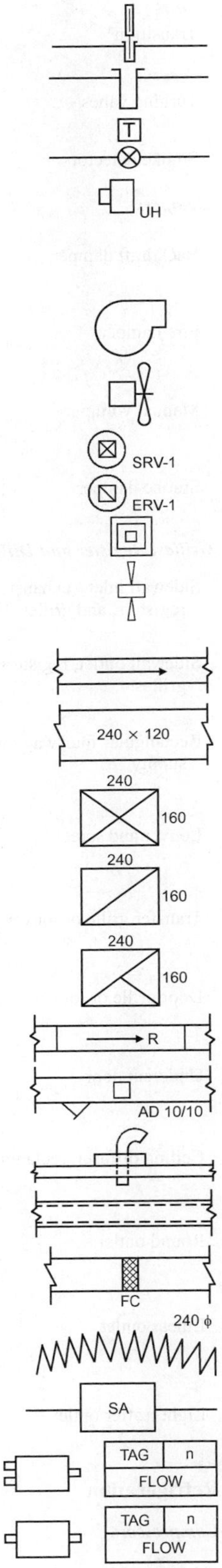

[a] Units of measurement are not shown here, but should be shown on drawings. The first dimension is visible duct dimension for duct size, top dimension for grilles, and horizontal dimension for registers.

[b] Show volumetric flow rate at each device.

Transition[a]

Turning vanes

Smoke detectors

Dampers

Backdraft damper

Fire damper

Manual volume

Smoke damper

Grilles, Register and Diffusers[b]

Sidewall inlet, (exhaust) outlet, registers, and grilles

Sidewall outlet, registers, and grilles

Rectangular four-way outlet, supply

Louver and screen

Transfer grille or louver

Door grille or louver

Undercut door

Ceiling diffuser, rectangular

Round outlet

Linear outlet

Light troffer outlet

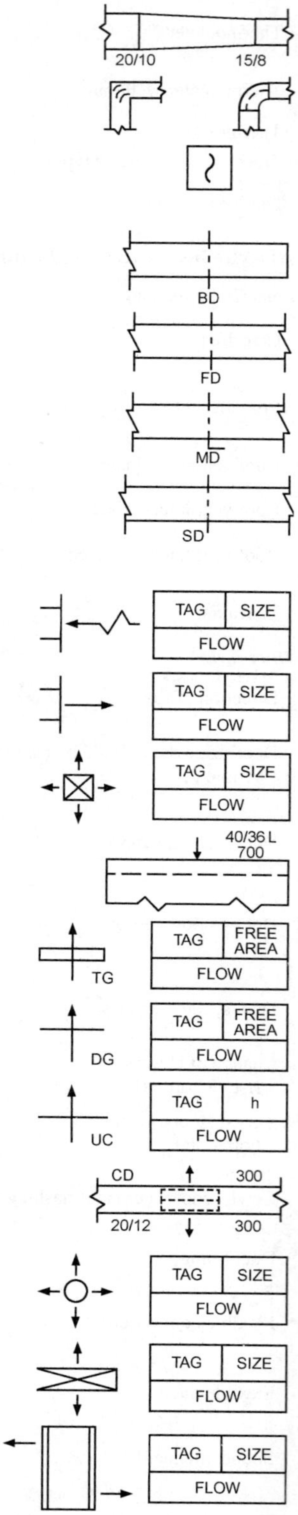

Refrigeration

Compressors

Centrifugal

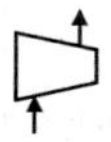

Reciprocating

Rotary

Rotary screw

Condensers

Air cooled

Evaporative

Water cooled, (specify type)

Condensing Units

Air cooled[a]

Water cooled[a]

Condenser-Evaporator (Cascade System)

Cooling Towers

Cooling tower

Spray pond

Evaporators[b]

Finned coil

Forced convection

Immersion cooling unit

Plate coil

Pipe coil[c]

***Liquid Chillers* (Chillers only)**

Direct expansion[d]

Flooded[d]

Tank, closed

Tank, open

Chilling Units

Absorption

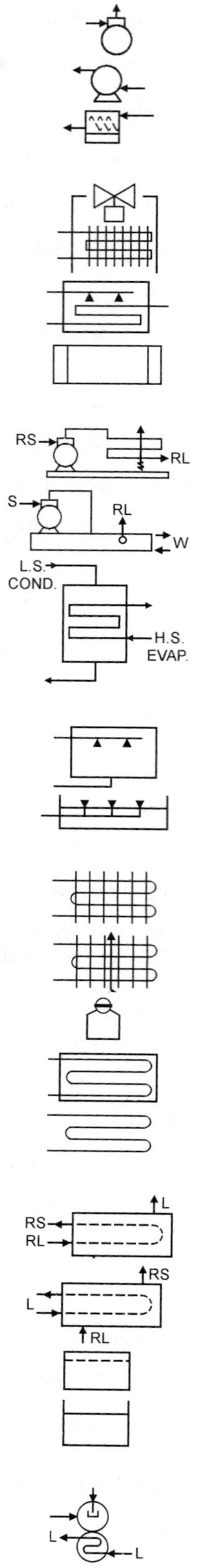

[a]Indicate flat on bottom or top (FOB or FOT), if applicable.
[b]Show volumetric flow rate at each device.

[a]L = Liquid being cooled, RL = Refrigerant liquid, RS = Refrigerant suction.
[b]Specify manifolding.
[c]Frequently used diagrammatically as evaporator and/or condenser with label indicating name and type.
[d]L = Liquid being cooled, RL = Refrigerant liquid, RS = Refrigerant suction.

Centrifugal

Reciprocating

Rotary screw

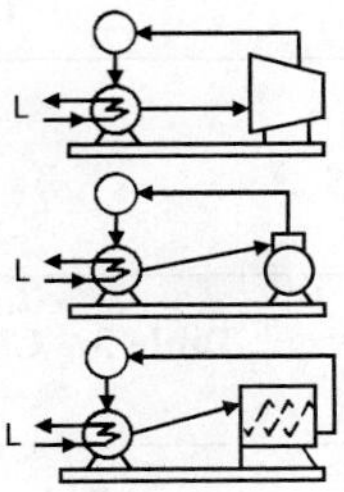

Controls

Refrigerant Controls

Capillary tube

Expansion valve, hand

Expansion valve, automatic

Expansion valve, thermostatic

Float valve, high side, or liquid drain valve

Float valve, low side

Thermal bulb

Solenoid valve

Constant pressure valve, suction

Evaporator pressure regulating valve, thermostatic, throttling

Evaporator pressure regulating valve, thermostatic, snap-action

Evaporator pressure regulating valve, throttling-type, evaporator side

Compressor suction valve, pressure-limiting, throttling-type, compressor side

Thermosuction valve

Snap-action valve

Refrigerant reversing valve

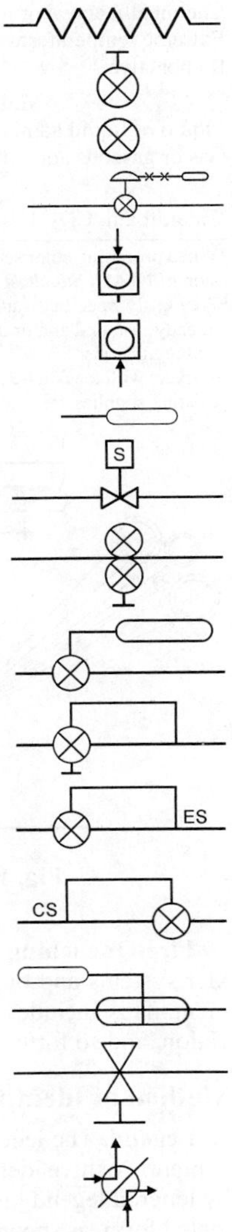

Temperature or Temperature-Actuated Electrical or Flow Controls

Thermostat, self-contained

Thermostat, remote bulb

Sensor, temperature

Pressure-reducing regulator

Pressure regulator

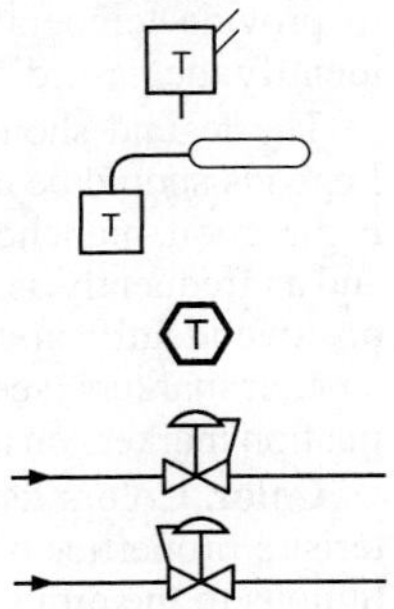

Valve, condenser water regulating

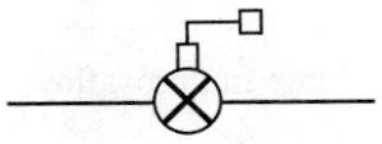

Auxiliary Equipment

Refrigerant

Filter

Strainer

Filter and drier

Scale trap

Drier

Vibration absorber

Heat exchanger

Oil separator

Sight glass

Fusible plug

Rupture disk

Receiver, high-pressure, horizontal

Receiver, high-pressure, vertical

Receiver, low-pressure

Intercooler

Intercooler/desuperheater

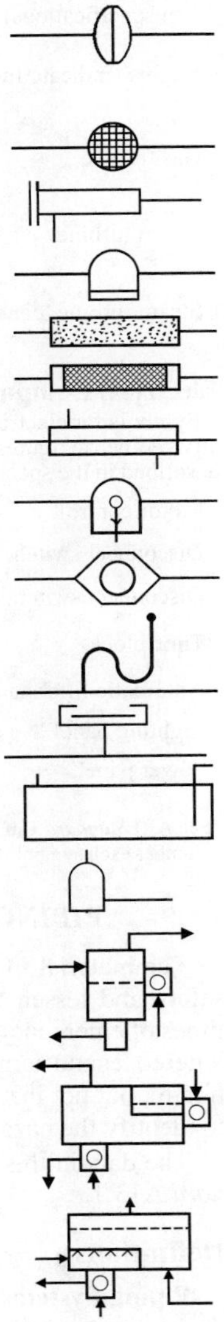

Energy Recovery Equipment

Condenser, double bundle

Air to Air Energy Recovery

Rotary heat wheel

Coil loop

Heat pipe

Fixed plate

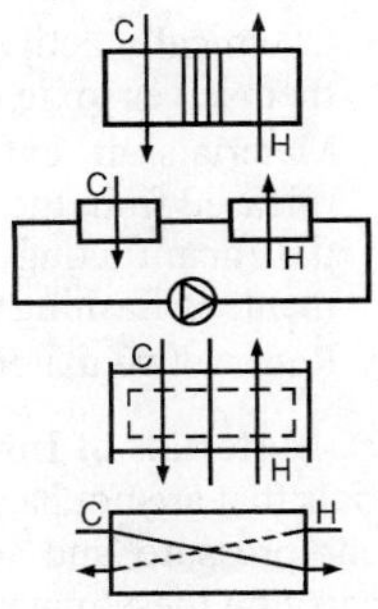

Plate fin, crossflow

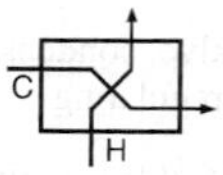

Power Sources

Motor, electric (number for identification of description in specifications)

Engine (indicate fuel)

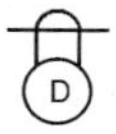

Gas turbine

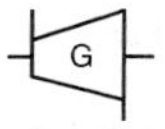

Steam turbine

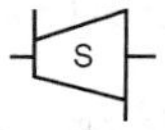

Steam turbine, condensing

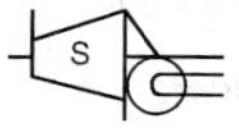

Electrical Equipment[a]

Symbols for electrical equipment shown on mechanical drawings are usually geometric figures with an appropriate name or abbreviation, with details described in the specifications. The following are some common examples.[b]

Motor control

Disconnect switch, unfused

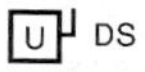

Disconnect switch, fused

Time clock

Automatic filter panel

Lighting panel

Power panel

[a] See ARI *Standard* 130 for preferred symbols of common electrical parts.
[b] Number each symbol if more than one; see ASME *Standard* Y32.4.

PIPING SYSTEM IDENTIFICATION

The material in piping systems is identified to promote greater safety and lessen the chances of error, confusion, or inaction in times of emergency. Primary identification should be by means of a lettered legend naming the material conveyed by the piping. In addition to, but not instead of, lettered identification, color can be used to identify the hazards or use of the material.

The data in this section have been extracted from ASME *Standard* A13.1.

Definitions

Piping Systems. Piping systems include pipes of any kind, fittings, valves, and pipe coverings. Supports, brackets, and other accessories are not included. Pipes are defined as conduits for the transport of gases, liquids, semiliquids, or fine particulate dust.

Materials Inherently Hazardous to Life and Property. There are four categories of hazardous materials:

- Flammable or explosive materials that are easily ignited, including materials known as fire producers or explosives
- Chemically active or toxic materials that are corrosive or are in themselves toxic or productive of poisonous gases
- Materials at extreme temperatures or pressures that, when released from the piping, cause a sudden outburst with the potential for inflicting injury or property damage by burns, impingement, or flashing to vapor state
- Radioactive materials that emit ionizing radiation

Materials of Inherently Low Hazard. These include all materials that are not hazardous by nature, and are near enough to ambient pressure and temperature that people working on systems carrying these materials run little risk through their release.

Table 2 Examples of Legends

HOT WATER
AIR 100 PSIG
H.P. RETURN
STEAM 100 PSIG

Table 3 Classification of Hazardous Materials and Designation of Colors[a]

Classification	Color Field	Colors of Letters for Legend
Materials Inherently Hazardous		
Flammable or explosive	Yellow	Black
Chemically active or toxic	Yellow	Black
Extreme temperatures or pressures	Yellow	Black
Radioactive[b]	Purple	Yellow
Materials of Inherently Low Hazard		
Liquid or liquid admixture[c]	Green	Black
Gas or gaseous admixture	Blue	White
Fire-Quenching Materials		
Water, foam, CO_2, Halon, etc.	Red	White

[a] When preceding color scheme is used, colors should be as recommended in latest revision of NEMA *Standard* Z535.1.
[b] Previously specified radioactive markers using yellow or purple are acceptable if already installed and/or until existing supplies are depleted, subject to applicable federal regulations.
[c] Markers with black letters on green field are acceptable if already installed and/or until existing supplies are depleted.

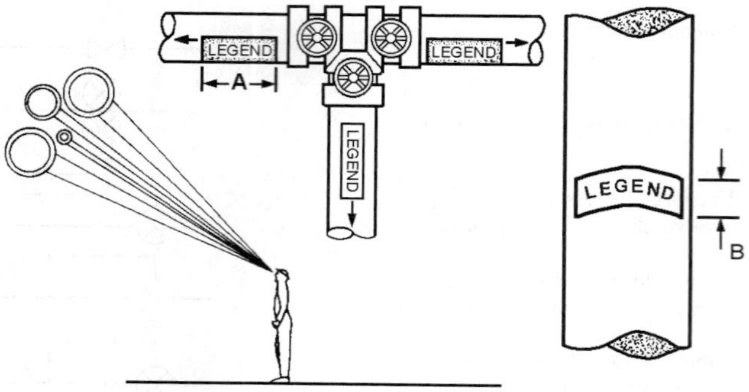

Fig. 1 Visibility of Pipe Markings

Fire-Quenching Materials. This classification includes sprinkler systems and other piped firefighting or fire protection equipment. This includes water (for firefighting), chemical foam, CO_2, Halon, and so forth.

Method of Identification

Legend. The legend is the primary and explicit identification of content. Positive identification of the content of the piping system is by lettered legend giving the name of the contents, in full or abbreviated form, as shown in Table 2. Arrows should be used to indicate the direction of flow. Use the legend to identify contents exactly and to provide temperature, pressure, and other details necessary to identify the hazard.

The legend should be brief, informative, pointed, and simple. Legends should be applied close to valves and adjacent to changes in direction, branches, and where pipes pass through walls or floors, and as frequently as needed along straight runs to provide clear and positive identification. Identification may be applied by stenciling, tape, or markers (see Figure 1). The number and location of identification markers on a particular piping system is based on judgment.

Color. Colors listed in Table 3 are used to identify the characteristic properties of the contents. Color can be shown on or contiguous to the piping by any physical means, but it should be used

Table 4 Size of Legend Letters

Outside Diameter of Pipe or Covering, in.	Length of Color Field A, in.	Size of Letters B, in.
3/4 to 1 1/4	8	1/2
1 1/2 to 2	8	3/4
2 1/2 to 6	12	1-1/4
8 to 10	24	2-1/2
over 10	32	3-1/2

in combination with a legend. Color can be used in continuous total length coverage or in intermittent displays.

Visibility. Pipe markings should be highly visible. If pipe lines are above the normal line of vision, the lettering is placed below the horizontal centerline of the pipe (Figure 1).

Type and Size of Letters. Provide the maximum contrast between color field and legend (Table 3). Table 4 shows the size of letters recommended. Use of standard size letters of 1/2 in. or larger is recommended. For identifying materials in pipes of less than 3/4 in. in diameter and for valve and fitting identification, use a permanently legible tag.

Unusual or Extreme Situations. When the piping layout occurs in or creates an area of limited accessibility or is extremely complex, other identification techniques may be required. Although a certain amount of imagination may be needed, the designer should always clearly identify the hazard and use the recommended color and legend guidelines.

CODES AND STANDARDS

ASHRAE. 2005. Graphic symbols for heating, ventilating, air-conditioning, and refrigeration systems. ANSI/ASHRAE *Standard* 134-2005.

ASME. 2007. Scheme for the identification of piping systems. ANSI/ASME *Standard* A13.1-2007. American Society of Mechanical Engineers, New York.

ASME. 1998. Graphic symbols for heating, ventilating and air conditioning. *Standard* Y32.2.4-1949 (RA 1988). American Society of Mechanical Engineers, New York.

IEEE. 2004. Standard letter symbols for units of measurement. *Standard* 260.1-2004. Institute of Electrical and Electronics Engineers, Piscataway, NJ.

IEEE. 1996. Letter symbols and abbreviations for quantities used in acoustics. *Standard* 260.4-1996. Institute of Electrical and Electronics Engineers, Piscataway, NJ.

NEMA. 2011. Safety colors. *Standard* Z535.1-2006 (RA 2011). National Electrical Manufacturers Association, Rosslyn, VA.

NFPA. 2012. Standard for fire safety and emergency symbols, 2012 edition. *Standard* 170. National Fire Protection Association, Quincy, MA.

CHAPTER 39

UNITS AND CONVERSIONS

Table 1 Conversions to I-P and SI Units

(Multiply I-P values by conversion factors to obtain SI; divide SI values by conversion factors to obtain I-P)

Multiply I-P	By	To Obtain SI
acre (43,560 ft^2)	0.4047	ha
	4046.873	m^2
atmosphere (standard)	*101.325	kPa
bar	*100	kPa
barrel (42 U.S. gal, petroleum)	159.0	L
	0.1580987	m^3
Btu (International Table)	1055.056	J
Btu (thermochemical)	1054.350	J
Btu/ft^2 (International Table)	11,356.53	J/m^2
Btu/ft^3 (International Table)	37,258.951	J/m^3
Btu/gal	278,717.1765	J/m^3
Btu·ft/h·ft^2·°F	1.730735	W/(m·K)
Btu·in/h·ft^2·°F (thermal conductivity k)	0.1442279	W/(m·K)
Btu/h	0.2930711	W
Btu/h·ft^2	3.154591	W/m^2
Btu/h·ft^2·°F (overall heat transfer coefficient U)	5.678263	W/(m^2·K)
Btu/lb	*2.326	kJ/kg
Btu/lb·°F (specific heat c_p)	*4.1868	kJ/(kg·K)
bushel (dry, U.S.)	0.0352394	m^3
calorie (thermochemical)	*4.184	J
centipoise (dynamic viscosity μ)	*1.00	mPa·s
centistokes (kinematic viscosity ν)	*1.00	mm^2/s
clo	0.155	(m^2·K)/W
dyne	1.0×10^{-5}	N
dyne/cm^2	*0.100	Pa
EDR hot water (150 Btu/h)	43.9606	W
EDR steam (240 Btu/h)	70.33706	W
EER	0.293	COP
ft	*0.3048	m
	*304.8	mm
ft/min, fpm	*0.00508	m/s
ft/s, fps	*0.3048	m/s
ft of water	2989	Pa
ft of water per 100 ft pipe	98.1	Pa/m
ft^2	0.092903	m^2
ft^2·h·°F/Btu (thermal resistance R)	0.176110	(m^2·K)/W
ft^2/s (kinematic viscosity ν)	92,900	mm^2/s
ft^3	28.316846	L
	0.02832	m^3
ft^3/min, cfm	0.471947	L/s
ft^3/s, cfs	28.316845	L/s
ft·lb_f (torque or moment)	1.355818	N·m
ft·lb_f (work)	1.356	J
ft·lb_f/lb (specific energy)	2.99	J/kg
ft·lb_f/min (power)	0.0226	W
footcandle	10.76391	lx
gallon (U.S., *231 in^3)	3.785412	L
gph	1.05	mL/s
gpm	0.0631	L/s
gpm/ft^2	0.6791	L/(s·m^2)
gpm/ton refrigeration	0.0179	mL/J
grain (1/7000 lb)	0.0648	g
gr/gal	17.1	g/m^3
gr/lb	0.143	g/kg
horsepower (boiler) (33,470 Btu/h)	9.81	kW
horsepower (550 ft·lb_f/s)	0.7457	kW
inch	*25.4	mm
in. of mercury (60°F)	3.3864	kPa
in. of water (60°F)	248.84	Pa
in/100 ft, thermal expansion coefficient	0.833	mm/m
in·lb_f (torque or moment)	113	mN·m
in^2	645.16	mm^2
in^3 (volume)	16.3874	mL
in^3/min (SCIM)	0.273117	mL/s
in^3 (section modulus)	16,387	mm^3
in^4 (section moment)	416,231	mm^4
kWh	*3.60	MJ
kW/1000 cfm	2.118880	kJ/m^3
kilopond (kg force)	9.81	N
kip (1000 lb_f)	4.45	kN
kip/in^2 (ksi)	6.895	MPa
litre	*0.001	m^3
met	58.15	W/m^2
micron (μm) of mercury (60°F)	133	mPa
mile	1.609	km
mile, nautical	*1.852	km
mile per hour (mph)	1.609344	km/h
	0.447	m/s
millibar	*0.100	kPa
mm of mercury (60°F)	0.133	kPa
mm of water (60°F)	9.80	Pa
ounce (mass, avoirdupois)	28.35	g
ounce (force or thrust)	0.278	N
ounce (liquid, U.S.)	29.6	mL
ounce inch (torque, moment)	7.06	mN·m
ounce (avoirdupois) per gallon	7.489152	kg/m^3
perm (permeance at 32°F)	5.72135×10^{-11}	kg/(Pa·s·m^2)
perm inch (permeability at 32°F)	1.45362×10^{-12}	kg/(Pa·s·m)
pint (liquid, U.S.)	4.73176×10^{-4}	m^3
pound		
lb (avoirdupois, mass)	0.453592	kg
	453.592	g
lb_f (force or thrust)	4.448222	N
lb_f/ft (uniform load)	14.59390	N/m
lb/ft·h (dynamic viscosity μ)	0.4134	mPa·s
lb/ft·s (dynamic viscosity μ)	1490	mPa·s
lb_f·s/ft^2 (dynamic viscosity μ)	47.88026	Pa·s
lb/h	0.000126	kg/s
lb/min	0.007559	kg/s
lb/h [steam at 212°F (100°C)]	0.2843	kW
lb_f/ft^2	47.9	Pa
lb/ft^2	4.88	kg/m^2
lb/ft^3 (density ρ)	16.0	kg/m^3
lb/gallon	120	kg/m^3
ppm (by mass)	*1.00	mg/kg
psi	6.895	kPa
quad (10^{15} Btu)	1.055	EJ
quart (liquid, U.S.)	0.9463	L
square (100 ft^2)	9.2903	m^2
tablespoon (approximately)	15	mL
teaspoon (approximately)	5	mL
therm (U.S.)	105.5	MJ
ton, long (2240 lb)	1.016046	Mg
ton, short (2000 lb)	0.907184	Mg; t (tonne)
ton, refrigeration (12,000 Btu/h)	3.517	kW
torr (1 mm Hg at 0°C)	133	Pa
watt per square foot	10.76	W/m^2
yd	*0.9144	m
yd^2	0.8361	m^2
yd^3	0.7646	m^3
To Obtain I-P	**By**	**Divide SI**

*Conversion factor is exact.

Notes: 1. Units are U.S. values unless noted otherwise.

2. Litre is a special name for the cubic decimetre. 1 L = 1 dm^3 and 1 mL = 1 cm^3.

The preparation of this chapter is assigned to TC 1.6, Terminology.

Table 2 Conversion Factors

Pressure psi	in. of water (60°F)	in. Hg (32°F)	atmosphere	mm Hg (32°F)	bar	kgf/cm^2	pascal
1	= 27.708	= 2.0360	= 0.068046	= 51.715	= 0.068948	= 0.07030696	= 6894.8
0.036091	1	0.073483	2.4559×10^{-3}	1.8665	2.4884×10^{-3}	2.537×10^{-3}	248.84
0.491154	13.609	1	0.033421	25.400	0.033864	0.034532	3386.4
14.6960	407.19	29.921	1	760.0	1.01325*	1.03323	1.01325×10^5*
0.0193368	0.53578	0.03937	1.31579×10^{-3}	1	1.3332×10^{-3}	1.3595×10^{-3}	133.32
14.5038	401.86	29.530	0.98692	750.062	1	1.01972*	10^5*
14.223	394.1	28.959	0.96784	735.559	0.980665*	1	9.80665×10^4*
1.45038×10^{-4}	4.0186×10^{-3}	2.953×10^{-4}	9.8692×10^{-6}	7.50×10^{-3}	10^{-5}*	1.01972×10^{-5}*	1

Mass	lb (avoir.)	grain	ounce (avoir.)	kg
	1	= 7000*	= 16*	= 0.45359
	1.4286×10^{-4}	1	2.2857×10^{-3}	6.4800×10^{-5}
	0.06250	437.5*	1	0.028350
	2.20462	1.5432×10^4	35.274	1

Volume	cubic inch	cubic foot	gallon	litre	cubic metre (m^3)
	1	= 5.787×10^{-4}	= 4.329×10^{-3}	= 0.0163871	= 1.63871×10^{-5}
	1728*	1	7.48052	28.317	0.028317
	231.0*	0.13368	1	3.7854	0.0037854
	61.02374	0.035315	0.264173	1	0.001*
	6.102374×10^4	35.315	264.173	1000*	1

Energy	Btu	ft·lb_f	calorie (cal)	joule (J) = watt-second (W·s)	watt-hour (W·h)
Note: MBtu, which is	1	= 778.17	= 251.9958	= 1055.056	= 0.293071
1000 Btu, is confusing	1.2851×10^{-3}	1	0.32383	1.355818	3.76616×10^{-4}
and should not be used.	3.9683×10^{-3}	3.08803	1	4.1868*	1.163×10^{-3}*
	9.4782×10^{-4}	0.73756	0.23885	1	2.7778×10^{-4}
	3.41214	2655.22	859.85	3600*	1

Density	lb/ft^3	lb/gal	g/cm^3	kg/m^3
	1	= 0.133680	= 0.016018	= 16.018463
	7.48055	1	0.119827	119.827
	62.4280	8.34538	1	1000*
	0.0624280	0.008345	0.001*	1

Specific Volume	ft^3/lb	gal/lb	cm^3/g	m^3/kg
	1	= 7.48055	= 62.4280	= 0.0624280
	0.133680	1	8.34538	0.008345
	0.016018	0.119827	1	0.001*
	16.018463	119.827	1000*	1

Viscosity (absolute) 1 poise = 1 dyne-sec/cm^2 = 0.1 Pa·s = 1 g/(cm·s)

	poise	lb_f·s/ft^2	lb_f·h/ft^2	kg/(m·s) = N·s/m^2	lb_m/ft·s
	1	= 2.0885×10^{-3}	= 5.8014×10^{-7}	= 0.1*	= 0.0671955
	478.8026	1	2.7778×10^{-4}	47.88026	32.17405
	1.72369×10^6	3600*	1	1.72369×10^5	1.15827×10^5
	10*	0.020885	5.8014×10^{-6}	1	0.0671955
	14.8819	0.031081	8.6336×10^{-6}	1.4882	1

Temperature

Scale		Temperature K	°C	°R	°F		Temperature Interval K	°C	°R	°F
Kelvin	x K =	x	$x - 273.15$	$1.8x$	$1.8x - 459.67$	1 K =	1	1	9/5 = 1.8	9/5 = 1.8
Celsius	x°C =	$x + 273.15$	x	$1.8x + 491.67$	$1.8x + 32$	1°C =	1	1	9/5 = 1.8	9/5 = 1.8
Rankine	x°R =	$x/1.8$	$(x - 491.67)/1.8$	x	$x - 459.67$	1°R =	5/9	5/9	1	1
Fahrenheit	x°F =	$(x + 459.67)/1.8$	$(x - 32)/1.8$	$x + 459.67$	x	1°F =	5/9	5/9	1	1

Notes: Conversions with * are exact.
The Btu and calorie are based on the International Table.
All temperature conversions and factors are exact.
The term centigrade is obsolete and should not be used.

When making conversions, remember that a converted value is no more precise than the original value. For many applications, rounding off the converted value to the same number of significant figures as those in the original value provides acceptable accuracy.

See ANSI *Standard* SI-10-1997 (available from ASTM or IEEE) for additional conversions.

CHAPTER 40

CODES AND STANDARDS

THE codes and standards and other publications listed here represent practices, methods, or standard published by the organizations indicated. They are useful guides for the practicing engineer in determining test methods, ratings, performance requirements, and limits of HVAC&R equipment. Copies of these publications can be obtained from most of the organizations listed in the Publisher column, from Global Engineering Documents at **global.ihs.com**, or from Techstreet at **techstreet.com**. Addresses of the organizations are given at the end of the chapter. A comprehensive database with over 300,000 industry, government, and international standards is at **www.nssn.org**.

Selected Codes and Standards Published by Various Societies and Associations

Subject	Title	Publisher	Reference
Air Conditioners	Commercial Systems Overview	ACCA	ACCA Manual CS-1993
	Residential Equipment Selection, 2nd ed.	ACCA	ANSI/ACCA 3 Manual S®-2014
	HVAC Quality Installation Specification	ACCA	ANSI/ACCA 5 QI-2015
	Technician's Guide & Workbook for Quality Installations	ACCA	ACCA 2015
	Laboratory Methods of Testing Air Terminal Units	ASHRAE	ANSI/ASHRAE 130-2016
	Non-Ducted Air Conditioners and Heat Pumps—Testing and Rating for Performance	ISO	ISO 5151:2010
	Ducted Air-Conditioners and Air-to-Air Heat Pumps—Testing and Rating for Performance	ISO	ISO 13253:2011
	Guidelines for Roof Mounted Outdoor Air-Conditioner Installations	SMACNA	SMACNA 1997
	Heating and Cooling Equipment	UL/CSA	ANSI/UL 1995-2011/C22.2 No. 236-11
	Performance Standard for Split-System and Single-Package Central Air Conditioners and Heat Pumps	CSA	CAN/CSA-C656-14
	Performance Standard for Rating Large and Single Packaged Air Conditioners and Heat Pumps	CSA	CAN/CSA-C746-06 (R2012)
Gas-Fired	Commercial Systems Overview	ACCA	ACCA Manual CS-1993
	Residential Equipment Selection, 2nd ed.	ACCA	ANSI/ACCA 3 Manual S-2014
	Home Evaluation and Performance Improvement	ACCA	ANSI/ACCA 12 QH-2014
	Technician's Guide & Workbook for Home Evaluation and Performance Improvement	ACCA	ACCA 2014
	Gas-Fired, Heat Activated Air Conditioning and Heat Pump Appliances	CSA	ANSI Z21.40.1-1996/CGA 2.91-M96 (R2012)
	Gas-Fired Work Activated Air Conditioning and Heat Pump Appliances (Internal Combustion)	CSA	ANSI Z21.40.2-1996/CGA 2.92-M96 (R2002)
	Performance Testing and Rating of Gas-Fired Air Conditioning and Heat Pump Appliances	CSA	ANSI Z21.40.4-1996/CGA 2.94-M96 (R2002)
Packaged Terminal	Packaged Terminal Air-Conditioners and Heat Pumps	AHRI/CSA	AHRI 310/380-2014/CSA C744-14
Room	Room Air Conditioners	AHAM	ANSI/AHAM RAC-1-2014
	Method of Testing for Rating Room Air Conditioners and Packaged Terminal Air Conditioners	ASHRAE	ANSI/ASHRAE 16-2016
	Method of Testing for Rating Room Air Conditioner and Packaged Terminal Air Conditioner Heating Capacity	ASHRAE	ANSI/ASHRAE 58-1986 (RA14)
	Method of Testing for Rating Fan-Coil Conditioners	ASHRAE	ANSI/ASHRAE 79-2015
	Energy Performance of Room Air Conditioners	CSA	CAN/CSA-C368.1-14
	Room Air Conditioners	CSA	C22.2 No. 117-1970 (R2012)
	Room Air Conditioners, Ed. 7	UL	ANSI/UL 484-2014
Unitary	Commercial Systems Overview	ACCA	ACCA Manual CS-1993
	Residential Equipment Selection, 2nd ed.	ACCA	ANSI/ACCA 3 Manual S-2014
	Unitary Air-Conditioning and Air-Source Heat Pump Equipment	AHRI	ANSI/AHRI 210/240-2008
	Sound Rating of Outdoor Unitary Equipment	AHRI	AHRI 270-2008
	Application of Sound Rating Levels of Outdoor Unitary Equipment	AHRI	AHRI 275-2010
	Commercial and Industrial Unitary Air-Conditioning and Heat Pump Equipment	AHRI	AHRI 340/360-2007
	Methods of Testing for Rating Electrically Driven Unitary Air-Conditioning and Heat Pump Equipment	ASHRAE	ANSI/ASHRAE 37-2009
	Methods of Testing for Rating Heat Operated Unitary Air-Conditioning and Heat-Pump Equipment	ASHRAE	ANSI/ASHRAE 40-2014
	Methods of Testing for Rating Seasonal Efficiency of Unitary Air Conditioners and Heat Pumps	ASHRAE	ANSI/ASHRAE 116-2010
	Method of Testing for Rating Computer and Data Processing Room Unitary Air Conditioners	ASHRAE	ANSI/ASHRAE 127-2012
	Method of Rating Unitary Spot Air Conditioners	ASHRAE	ANSI/ASHRAE 128-2011

Selected Codes and Standards Published by Various Societies and Associations (*Continued*)

Subject	Title	Publisher	Reference
Ships	Specification for Mechanically Refrigerated Shipboard Air Conditioner	ASTM	ASTM F1433-97 (2010)
Accessories	Flashing and Stand Combination for Air Conditioning Units (Unit Curb)	IAPMO	IAPMO PS 120-2004
Air Conditioning	Commercial Systems Overview	ACCA	ACCA Manual CS-1993
	Heat Pump Systems	ACCA	ACCA Manual H-1984
	Residential Load Calculation, 8th ed.	ACCA	ANSI/ACCA 2 Manual J-2016
	Commercial Load Calculation, 5th ed.	ACCA	ACCA Manual N-2012
	Comfort, Air Quality, and Efficiency by Design	ACCA	ACCA Manual RS-1997
	HVAC Quality Installation Specification	ACCA	ANSI/ACCA 5 QI-2015
	Technician's Guide & Workbook for Quality Installations	ACCA	ACCA 2015
	Peak Cooling and Heating Load Calculations in Buildings Except Low-Rise Residential Buildings	ASHRAE/ ACCA	ANSI/ASHRAE/ACCA 183-2007 (RA14)
	Environmental Systems Technology, 2nd ed. (1999)	NEBB	NEBB
	Installation of Air-Conditioning and Ventilating Systems	NFPA	NFPA 90A-2015
	Standard of Purity for Use in Mobile Air-Conditioning Systems	SAE	SAE J1991-2011
	HVAC Systems Applications, 2nd ed.	SMACNA	SMACNA 2010
	HVAC Systems—Duct Design, 4th ed.	SMACNA	SMACNA 2006
	Heating and Cooling Equipment	UL/CSA	ANSI/UL 1995-2011/C22.2 No. 236-11
Aircraft	Air Conditioning of Aircraft Cargo	SAE	SAE AIR806B-1997 (R2011)
	Aircraft Fuel Weight Penalty Due to Air Conditioning	SAE	SAE AIR1168/8-2011
	Air Conditioning Systems for Subsonic Airplanes	SAE	SAE ARP85F-2012
	Environmental Control Systems Terminology	SAE	SAE ARP147E-2001 (R2012)
	Testing of Airplane Installed Environmental Control Systems (ECS)	SAE	SAE ARP217D-1999 (R2011)
	Guide for Qualification Testing of Aircraft Air Valves	SAE	SAE ARP986D-2008
	Control of Excess Humidity in Avionics Cooling	SAE	SAE ARP987B-2010
	Engine Bleed Air Systems for Aircraft	SAE	SAE ARP1796B-2012
	Aircraft Ground Air Conditioning Service Connection	SAE	SAE AS4262B-2012
	Air Cycle Air Conditioning Systems for Military Air Vehicles	SAE	SAE AS4073A-2013
Automotive	Refrigerant 12 Automotive Air-Conditioning Hose	SAE	SAE J51-2004
	Design Guidelines for Air Conditioning Systems for Off-Road Operator Enclosures	SAE	SAE J169-2013
	Test Method for Measuring Power Consumption of Air Conditioning and Brake Compressors for Trucks and Buses	SAE	SAE J1340-2011
	Information Relating to Duty Cycles and Average Power Requirements of Truck and Bus Engine Accessories	SAE	SAE J1343-2000
	Rating Air-Conditioner Evaporator Air Delivery and Cooling Capacities	SAE	SAE J1487-2013
	Recovery and Recycle Equipment for Mobile Automotive Air-Conditioning Systems	SAE	SAE J1990-2011
	R134a Refrigerant Automotive Air-Conditioning Hose	SAE	SAE J2064-2011
	Service Hose for Automotive Air Conditioning	SAE	SAE J2196-2011
Ships	Mechanical Refrigeration and Air-Conditioning Installations Aboard Ship	ASHRAE	ANSI/ASHRAE 26-2010
	Practice for Mechanical Symbols, Shipboard Heating, Ventilation, and Air Conditioning (HVAC)	ASTM	ASTM F856-97 (2014)
Air Curtains	Laboratory Methods of Testing Air Curtains for Aerodynamic Performance	AMCA	AMCA 220-05 (R2012)
	Air Terminals	AHRI	AHRI 880-2011
	Standard Methods for Laboratory Airflow Measurement	ASHRAE	ANSI/ASHRAE 41.2-1987 (RA92)
	Method of Testing the Performance of Air Outlets and Inlets	ASHRAE	ANSI/ASHRAE 70-2006 (RA11)
	Residential Mechanical Ventilating Systems	CSA	CAN/CSA-F326-M91 (R2010)
	Air Curtains for Entranceways in Food and Food Service Establishments	NSF	ANSI/NSF 37-2012
Air Diffusion	Air Distribution Basics for Residential and Small Commercial Buildings	ACCA	ACCA Manual T-2001
	Balancing and Testing Air and Hydronic Systems	ACCA	ACCA Manual B-2009
	Method of Testing the Performance of Air Outlets and Inlets	ASHRAE	ANSI/ASHRAE 70-2006 (RA11)
	Method of Testing for Room Air Diffusion	ASHRAE	ANSI/ASHRAE 113-2013
Air Filters	Comfort, Air Quality, and Efficiency by Design	ACCA	ACCA Manual RS-1997
	Home Evaluation and Performance Improvement	ACCA	ANSI/ACCA 12 QH-2014
	Technician's Guide & Workbook for Home Evaluation and Performance Improvement	ACCA	ACCA 2015
	Balancing and Testing Air and Hydronic Systems	ACCA	ACCA Manual B-2009
	Industrial Ventilation: A Manual of Recommended Practice, 29th ed. (2016)	ACGIH	ACGIH
	Air Cleaners—Portable	AHAM	ANSI/AHAM AC-1-2013
	Residential Air Filter Equipment	AHRI	ANSI/AHRI 680-2009
	Commercial and Industrial Air Filter Equipment	AHRI	ANSI/AHRI 850-2013
	Method of Testing General Ventilation Air-Cleaning Devices for Removal Efficiency by Particle Size	ASHRAE	ANSI/ASHRAE 52.2-2012

Selected Codes and Standards Published by Various Societies and Associations (*Continued*)

Subject	Title	Publisher	Reference
	Laboratory Test Method for Assessing the Performance of Gas-Phase Air Cleaning Systems: Loose Granular Media	ASHRAE	ANSI/ASHRAE 145.1-2015
	Laboratory Test Method for Assessing the Performance of Gas-Phase Air Cleaning Systems: Air Cleaning Devices	ASHRAE	ANSI/ASHRAE 145.2-2016
	Code on Nuclear Air and Gas Treatment	ASME	ASME AG-1-2012
	Nuclear Power Plant Air-Cleaning Units and Components	ASME	ASME N509-2002
	Testing of Nuclear Air-Treatment Systems	ASME	ASME N510-2007
	Test Method for Air Cleaning Performance of a High-Efficiency Particulate Air Filter System	ASTM	ASTM F1471-09
	Specification for Filters Used in Air or Nitrogen Systems	ASTM	ASTM F1791-00 (2013)
	Method for Sodium Flame Test for Air Filters	BSI	BS 3928:1969
	Particulate Air Filters for General Ventilation: Determination of Filtration Performance	BSI	BS EN 779:2002
	Electrostatic Air Cleaners	UL	ANSI/UL 867-2011
	High-Efficiency, Particulate, Air Filter Units	UL	ANSI/UL 586-2009
	Air Filter Units	UL	ANSI/UL 900-2004
	Exhaust Hoods for Commercial Cooking Equipment	UL	UL 710-2012
	Grease Filters for Exhaust Ducts	UL	UL 1046-2010
Air-Handling Units	Commercial Systems Overview	ACCA	ACCA Manual CS-1993
	Residential Equipment Selection	ACCA	ANSI/ACCA 3 Manual S-2014
	Central Station Air-Handling Units	AHRI	ANSI/AHRI 430-2014
	Non-Recirculating Direct Gas-Fired Industrial Air Heaters	CSA	ANSI Z83.4-2013/CSA 3.7-2013
Air Leakage	Technician's Guide & Workbook for Duct Diagnostics and Repair	ACCA	ACCA 2016
	HVAC Quality Installation Specification	ACCA	ANSI/ACCA 5 QI-2015
	Technician's Guide & Workbook for Quality Installations	ACCA	ACCA 2015
	Ventilation and Acceptable Indoor Air Quality in Low-Rise Residential Buildings	ASHRAE	ANSI/ASHRAE 62.2-2016
	Method of Test for Determining the Airtightness of HVAC Equipment	ASHRAE	ANSI/ASHRAE 193-2010 (RA14)
	Test Method for Determining Air Change in a Single Zone by Means of a Tracer Gas Dilution	ASTM	ASTM E741-11
	Test Method for Determining Air Leakage Rate by Fan Pressurization	ASTM	ASTM E779-10
	Test Method for Field Measurement of Air Leakage Through Installed Exterior Window and Doors	ASTM	ASTM E783-02 (2010)
	Practices for Air Leakage Site Detection in Building Envelopes and Air Barrier Systems	ASTM	ASTM E1186-03 (2009)
	Test Method for Determining the Rate of Air Leakage Through Exterior Windows, Curtain Walls, and Doors Under Specified Pressure and Temperature Differences Across the Specimen	ASTM	ASTM E1424-91 (2008)
	Test Methods for Determining Airtightness of Buildings Using an Orifice Blower Door	ASTM	ASTM E1827-11
	Practice for Determining the Effects of Temperature Cycling on Fenestration Products	ASTM	ASTM E2264-05 (2013)
	Test Method for Determining Air Flow Through the Face and Sides of Exterior Windows, Curtain Walls, and Doors Under Specified Pressure Differences Across the Specimen	ASTM	ASTM E2319-04 (2011)
	Test Method for Determining Air Leakage of Air Barrier Assemblies	ASTM	ASTM E2357-11
	HVAC Air Duct Leakage Test Manual, 2nd ed.	SMACNA	SMACNA 2012
Boilers	Packaged Boiler Engineering Manual (1998)	ABMA	ABMA 100
	Selected Codes and Standards of the Boiler Industry (2001)	ABMA	ABMA 103
	Operation and Maintenance Safety Manual (1995)	ABMA	ABMA 106
	Fluidized Bed Combustion Guidelines (1995)	ABMA	ABMA 200
	Guide to Clean and Efficient Operation of Coal Stoker-Fired Boilers (2002)	ABMA	ABMA 203
	Guideline for Performance Evaluation of Heat Recovery Steam Generating Equipment (1995)	ABMA	ABMA 300
	Guidelines for Industrial Boiler Performance Improvement (1999)	ABMA	ABMA 302
	Measurement of Sound from Steam Generators (1995)	ABMA	ABMA 304
	Guideline for Gas and Oil Emission Factors for Industrial, Commercial, and Institutional Boilers (1997)	ABMA	ABMA 305
	Combustion Control Guidelines for Single Burner Firetube and Watertube Industrial/Commercial/Institutional Boilers (1999)	ABMA	ABMA 307
	Combustion Control Guidelines for Multiple-Burner Boilers (2001)	ABMA	ABMA 308
	Boiler Water Quality Requirements and Associated Steam Quality for Industrial/Commercial and Institutional Boilers (2005)	ABMA	ABMA 402
	HVAC Quality Installation Specification	ACCA	ANSI/ACCA 5 QI-2015
	Technician's Guide & Workbook for Quality Installations	ACCA	ACCA 2015
	Residential Equipment Selection	ACCA	ANSI/ACCA 3 Manual S 2014
	Commercial Systems Overview	ACCA	ACCA Manual CS-1993

Selected Codes and Standards Published by Various Societies and Associations (*Continued*)

Subject	Title	Publisher	Reference
	Method of Testing for Annual Fuel Utilization Efficiency of Residential Central Furnaces and Boilers	ASHRAE	ANSI/ASHRAE 103-2007
	Boiler and Pressure Vessel Code—Section I: Power Boilers; Section IV: Heating Boilers	ASME	BPVC-2015
	Fired Steam Generators	ASME	ASME PTC 4-2013
	Boiler, Pressure Vessel, and Pressure Piping Code	CSA	CSA B51-14
	Testing Standard, Method to Determine Efficiency of Commercial Heating Boilers, 2nd ed. (2007)	HYDI	HYDI BTS-2000
	Rating Procedure for Heating Boilers, 6th ed. (2005)	HYDI	IBR
	Single Burner Boiler Operations	NFPA	ANSI/NFPA 8501-97
	Prevention of Furnace Explosions/Implosions in Multiple Burner Boilers	NFPA	ANSI /NFPA 8502-99
	Heating, Water Supply, and Power Boilers—Electric	UL	ANSI/UL 834-2004
	Boiler and Combustion Systems Hazards Code	NFPA	NFPA 85-11
Gas or Oil	Home Evaluation and Performance Improvement	ACCA	ANSI/ACCA 12QH-2014
	Technician's Guide & Workbook for Home Evaluation and Performance Improvement	ACCA	ACCA 2015
	Controls and Safety Devices for Automatically Fired Boilers	ASME	ASME CSD-1-2012
	Gas-Fired Low-Pressure Steam and Hot Water Boilers	CSA	ANSI Z21.13-2014/CSA 4.9-2014
	Industrial and Commercial Gas-Fired Package Boilers	CSA	CAN 1-3.1-77 (R2011)
	Oil-Burning Equipment: Steam and Hot-Water Boilers	CSA	B140.7-05 (R2010)
	Oil-Fired Boiler Assemblies	UL	UL 726-1995
	Commercial-Industrial Gas Heating Equipment	UL	UL 795-2011
	Standards and Typical Specifications for Tray Type Deaerators, 9th ed. (2011)	HEI	HEI 2954
Terminology	Ultimate Boiler Industry Lexicon: Handbook of Power Utility and Boiler Terms and Phrases, 6th ed. (2001)	ABMA	ABMA 101
Building Codes	ASTM Standards Used in Building Codes	ASTM	ASTM
	Practice for Conducting Visual Assessments for Lead Hazards in Buildings	ASTM	ASTM E2255M-13
	Standard Practice for Periodic Inspection of Building Facades for Unsafe Conditions	ASTM	ASTM E2270-14
	Standard Practice for Building Enclosure Commissioning	ASTM	ASTM E2813-12
	Structural Welding Code—Steel	AWS	AWS D1.1M/D1.1:2010
	BOCA National Building Code, 14th ed. (1999)	BOCA	BNBC
	Uniform Building Code, vol. 1, 2, and 3 (1997)	ICBO	UBC V1, V2, V3
	International Building Code® (2015)	ICC	IBC
	International Code Council Performance Code® (2015)	ICC	ICC PC
	International Existing Building Code® (2015)	ICC	IEBC
	International Energy Conservation Code® (2015)	ICC	IECC
	International Property Maintenance Code® (2015)	ICC	IPMC
	International Residential Code® (2015)	ICC	IRC
	Building Construction and Safety Code®	NFPA	ANSI/NFPA 5000-2015
	National Building Code of Canada (2010)	NRCC	NRCC
	Standard Building Code (1999)	SBCCI	SBC
Mechanical	Safety Code for Elevators and Escalators	ASME	ASME A17.1-2013
	Natural Gas and Propane Installation Code	CSA	CAN/CSA-B149.1-10
	Propane Storage and Handling Code	CSA	CAN/CSA-B149.2-10
	Uniform Mechanical Code (2012)	IAPMO	IAPMO
	International Mechanical Code® (2015)	ICC	IMC
	International Fuel Gas Code® (2015)	ICC	IFGC
	Standard Gas Code (1999)	SBCCI	SBC
Burners	Domestic Gas Conversion Burners	CSA	ANSI Z21.17-1998/CSA 2.7-M98 (R2014)
	Installation of Domestic Gas Conversion Burners	CSA	ANSI Z21.8-1994 (R2012)
	Installation Code for Oil Burning Equipment	CSA	CAN/CSA-B139-09 (R2014)
	Oil-Burning Equipment: General Requirements	CSA	CAN/CSA-B140.0-03 (R2013)
	Vapourizing-Type Oil Burners	CSA	B140.1-1966 (R2011)
	Atomizing-Type Oil Burners	CSA	CAN/CSA-B140.2.1-10
	Pressure Atomizing Oil Burner Nozzles	CSA	B140.2.2-1971 (R2011)
	Oil Burners	UL	ANSI/UL 296-2003
	Waste Oil-Burning Air-Heating Appliances	UL	ANSI/UL 296A-1995
	Commercial-Industrial Gas Heating Equipment	UL	UL 795-2011
	Commercial/Industrial Gas and/or Oil-Burning Assemblies with Emission Reduction Equipment	UL	UL 2096-2006
Chillers	Commercial Systems Overview	ACCA	ACCA Manual CS-1993
	Absorption Water Chilling and Water Heating Packages	AHRI	ANSI/AHRI 560-2000
	Water Chilling Packages Using the Vapor Compression Cycle	AHRI	ANSI/AHRI 550/590-2011

Selected Codes and Standards Published by Various Societies and Associations (*Continued*)

Subject	Title	Publisher	Reference
	Method of Testing Liquid-Chilling Packages	ASHRAE	ANSI/ASHRAE 30-1995
	Method of Testing Absorption Water-Chilling and Water-Heating Packages	ASHRAE	ANSI/ASHRAE 182-2008 (RA13)
	Performance Standard for Rating Packaged Water Chillers	CSA	CAN/CSA C743-09
Chimneys	Specification for Clay Flue Liners	ASTM	ASTM C315-07 (2011)
	Specification for Industrial Chimney Lining Brick	ASTM	ASTM C980-13a
	Practice for Installing Clay Flue Lining	ASTM	ASTM C1283-11
	Guide for Design and Construction of Brick Liners for Industrial Chimneys	ASTM	ASTM C1298-95 (2013)
	Guide for Design, Fabrication, and Erection of Fiberglass Reinforced Plastic (FRP) Chimney Liners with Coal-Fired Units	ASTM	ASTM D5364-14
	Chimneys, Fireplaces, Vents, and Solid Fuel-Burning Appliances	NFPA	ANSI/NFPA 211-2013
	Medium Heat Appliance Factory-Built Chimneys	UL	ANSI/UL 959-2010
	Factory-Built Chimneys for Residential Type and Building Heating Appliance	UL	ANSI/UL 103-2010
Cleanrooms	Practice for Cleaning and Maintaining Controlled Areas and Clean Rooms	ASTM	ASTM E2042/E2042M-09
	Practice for Design and Construction of Aerospace Cleanrooms and Contamination Controlled Areas	ASTM	ASTM E2217-12
	Practice for Tests of Cleanroom Materials	ASTM	ASTM E2312-11
	Practice for Aerospace Cleanrooms and Associated Controlled Environments—Cleanroom Operations	ASTM	ASTM E2352-04 (2010)
	Test Method for Sizing and Counting Airborne Particulate Contamination in Clean Rooms and Other Dust-Controlled Areas Designed for Electronic and Similar Applications	ASTM	ASTM F25/F25M-09
	Practice for Continuous Sizing and Counting of Airborne Particles in Dust-Controlled Areas and Clean Rooms Using Instruments Capable of Detecting Single Sub-Micrometre and Larger Particles	ASTM	ASTM F50-12
	Procedural Standards for Certified Testing of Cleanrooms, 3rd ed. (2009)	NEBB	NEBB
Climate Data	Residential Load Calculations	ACCA	ANSI/ACCA 2 Manual J-2016
	Commercial Load Calculations	ACCA	ACCA Manual N-2012
	Climatic Data for Building Design Standards	ASHRAE	ANSI/ASHRAE 169-2013
Coils	Forced-Circulation Air-Cooling and Air-Heating Coils	AHRI	AHRI 410-2001
	Methods of Testing Forced Circulation Air Cooling and Air Heating Coils	ASHRAE	ANSI/ASHRAE 33-2016
Comfort Conditions	Threshold Limit Values for Physical Agents (updated annually)	ACGIH	ACGIH
	Comfort, Air Quality, and Efficiency by Design	ACCA	ACCA Manual RS-1997
	Thermal Environmental Conditions for Human Occupancy	ASHRAE	ANSI/ASHRAE 55-2013
	Classification for Serviceability of an Office Facility for Thermal Environment and Indoor Air Conditions	ASTM	ASTM E2320-04 (2012)
	Hot Environments—Estimation of the Heat Stress on Working Man, Based on the WBGT Index (Wet Bulb Globe Temperature)	ISO	ISO 7243:1989
	Ergonomics of the Thermal Environment—Analytical Determination and Interpretation of Thermal Comfort Using Calculation of the PMV and PPD Indices and Local Thermal Comfort Criteria	ISO	ISO 7730:2005
	Ergonomics of the Thermal Environment—Determination of Metabolic Rate	ISO	ISO 8996:2004
	Ergonomics of the Thermal Environment—Estimation of the Thermal Insulation and Water Vapour Resistance of a Clothing Ensemble	ISO	ISO 9920:2007
Commissioning	HVAC Quality Installation Specification	ACCA	ANSI/ACCA 5 QI-2015
	HVAC Quality Installation Verification Protocols	ACCA	ANSI/ACCA 9 QIvp-2016
	Technician's Guide & Workbook for Quality Installations	ACCA	ACCA 2015
	The Commissioning Process	ASHRAE	ASHRAE *Guideline* 0-2013
	HVAC&R Technical Requirements for the Commissioning Process	ASHRAE	ASHRAE *Guideline* 1.1-2007
	Commissioning Process for Buildings and Systems	ASHRAE	ASHRAE 202-2013
	Standard Practice for Building Enclosure Commissioning	ASTM	ASTM E2813-12
	HVAC Systems—Commissioning Manual, 2nd ed.	SMACNA	SMACNA 2013
Compressors	Displacement Compressors, Vacuum Pumps and Blowers	ASME	ASME PTC 9-1970
	Performance Test Code on Compressors and Exhausters	ASME	ASME PTC 10-1997 (RA14)
	Compressed Air and Gas Handbook, 6th ed. (2003)	CAGI	CAGI
Refrigerant	Positive Displacement Condensing Units	AHRI	ANSI/AHRI 520-2004
	Positive Displacement Refrigerant Compressors and Compressor Units	AHRI	ANSI/AHRI 540-2004
	Safety Standard for Refrigeration Systems	ASHRAE	ANSI/ASHRAE 15-2016
	Methods of Testing for Rating Positive Displacement Refrigerant Compressors and Condensing Units That Operate at Subcritical Temperatures of the Refrigerant	ASHRAE	ANSI/ASHRAE 23.1-2010
	Testing of Refrigerant Compressors	ISO	ISO 917:1989
	Refrigerant Compressors—Presentation of Performance Data	ISO	ISO 9309:1989

Selected Codes and Standards Published by Various Societies and Associations (*Continued*)

Subject	Title	Publisher	Reference
	Hermetic Refrigerant Motor-Compressors	UL/CSA	UL 984-1996/C22.2 No.140.2-96 (R2011)
Computers	Method of Testing for Rating Computer and Data Processing Room Unitary Air Conditioners	ASHRAE	ANSI/ASHRAE 127-2012
	Method of Test for the Evaluation of Building Energy Analysis Computer Programs	ASHRAE	ANSI/ASHRAE 140-2011
	Fire Protection of Information Technology Equipment	NFPA	NFPA 75-2013
Condensers	Commercial Systems Overview	ACCA	ACCA Manual CS-1993
	Residential Equipment Selection, 2nd ed.	ACCA	ANSI/ACCA 3 Manual S-2014
	Water-Cooled Refrigerant Condensers, Remote Type	AHRI	AHRI 450-2007
	Remote Mechanical-Draft Air-Cooled Refrigerant Condensers	AHRI	ANSI/AHRI 460-2005
	Remote Mechanical Draft Evaporative Refrigerant Condensers	AHRI	ANSI/AHRI 490-2011
	Safety Standard for Refrigeration Systems	ASHRAE	ANSI/ASHRAE 15-2016
	Methods of Testing for Rating Remote Mechanical-Draft Air-Cooled Refrigerant Condensers	ASHRAE	ANSI/ASHRAE 20-1997 (RA06)
	Methods of Testing for Rating Liquid Water-Cooled Refrigerant Condensers	ASHRAE	ANSI/ASHRAE 22-2014
	Methods of Testing for Rating Positive Displacement Refrigerant Compressors and Condensing Units That Operate at Subcritical Temperatures of the Refrigerant	ASHRAE	ANSI/ASHRAE 23.1-2010
	Methods of Laboratory Testing Remote Mechanical-Draft Evaporative Refrigerant Condensers	ASHRAE	ANSI/ASHRAE 64-2011
	Steam Surface Condensers	ASME	ASME PTC 12.2-2010
	Standards for Steam Surface Condensers, 11th ed. (2012)	HEI	HEI 2629
	Standards for Direct Contact Barometric and Low Level Condensers, 8th ed. (2010)	HEI	HEI 2634
	Refrigerant-Containing Components and Accessories, Nonelectrical	UL	ANSI/UL 207-2009
Condensing Units	Commercial Systems Overview	ACCA	ACCA Manual CS-1993
	Residential Equipment Selection, 2nd ed.	ACCA	ANSI/ACCA 3 Manual S-2014
	Commercial and Industrial Unitary Air-Conditioning Condensing Units	AHRI	ANSI/AHRI 365-2009
	Methods of Testing for Rating Positive Displacement Refrigerant Compressors and Condensing Units	ASHRAE	ANSI/ASHRAE 23.1-2010
	Heating and Cooling Equipment	UL/CSA	ANSI/UL 1995-2011/C22.2 No. 236-11
Containers	Series 1 Freight Containers—Classifications, Dimensions, and Ratings	ISO	ISO 668:2013
	Series 1 Freight Containers—Specifications and Testing; Part 2: Thermal Containers	ISO	ISO 1496-2:2008
	Animal Environment in Cargo Compartments	SAE	SAE AIR1600B-2010
Controls	Temperature Control Systems (2002)	AABC	National Standards, Ch. 12
	Field Testing of HVAC Controls Components	ASHRAE	ASHRAE *Guideline* 11-2009
	Specifying Direct Digital Control Systems	ASHRAE	ASHRAE *Guideline* 13-2015
	BACnet™—A Data Communication Protocol for Building Automation and Control Networks	ASHRAE	ANSI/ASHRAE 135-2016
	Method of Test for Conformance to BACnet®	ASHRAE	ANSI/ASHRAE 135.1-2013
	Method of Test for Rating Air Terminal Unit Controls	ASHRAE	ASHRAE 195-2013
	Temperature-Indicating and Regulating Equipment	CSA	C22.2 No. 24-15
	Performance Requirements for Thermostats Used with Individual Room Electric Space Heating Devices	CSA	CAN/CSA C828-13
	Solid-State Controls for Appliances	UL	UL 244A-2003
	Limit Controls	UL	ANSI/UL 353-1994
	Primary Safety Controls for Gas- and Oil-Fired Appliances	UL	ANSI/UL 372-1994
	Temperature-Indicating and -Regulating Equipment	UL	UL 873-2007
	Tests for Safety-Related Controls Employing Solid-State Devices	UL	UL 991-2004
	Automatic Electrical Controls for Household and Similar Use; Part 1: General Requirements	UL	UL 60730-1-2009
Commercial and Industrial	Guidelines for Boiler Control Systems (Gas/Oil Fired Boilers) (1998)	ABMA	ABMA 301
	Guideline for the Integration of Boilers and Automated Control Systems in Heating Applications (1998)	ABMA	ABMA 306
	Industrial Control and Systems: General Requirements	NEMA	NEMA ICS 1-2000 (R2008)
	Preventive Maintenance of Industrial Control and Systems Equipment	NEMA	NEMA ICS 1.3-1986 (R2009)
	Industrial Control and Systems, Controllers, Contactors, and Overload Relays Rated Not More than 2000 Volts AC or 750 Volts DC	NEMA	NEMA ICS 2-2000 (R2005)
	Industrial Control and Systems: Instructions for the Handling, Installation, Operation and Maintenance of Motor Control Centers Rated Not More than 600 Volts	NEMA	NEMA ICS 2.3-1995 (R2008)
	Industrial Control Equipment	UL	ANSI/UL 508-2007
Residential	Manually Operated Gas Valves for Appliances, Appliance Connector Valves and Hose End Valves	CSA	ANSI Z21.15-2009/CSA 9.1-2009 (R2014)
	Gas Appliance Pressure Regulators	CSA	ANSI Z21.18-2007/CSA 6.3-2007 (R2012)

Selected Codes and Standards Published by Various Societies and Associations (*Continued*)

Subject	Title	Publisher	Reference
	Automatic Gas Ignition Systems and Components	CSA	ANSI Z21.20-2005
	Gas Appliance Thermostats	CSA	ANSI Z21.23-2010
	Manually-Operated Piezo-Electric Spark Gas Ignition Systems and Components	CSA	ANSI Z21.77-2005/CSA 6.23-2005 (R2011)
	Manually Operated Electric Gas Ignition Systems and Components	CSA	ANSI Z21.92-2001/CSA 6.29-2001 (R2012)
	Residential Controls—Electrical Wall-Mounted Room Thermostats	NEMA	NEMA DC 3-2013
	Residential Controls—Surface Type Controls for Electric Storage Water Heaters	NEMA	NEMA DC 5-1989 (R2008)
	Residential Controls—Temperature Limit Controls for Electric Baseboard Heaters	NEMA	NEMA DC 10-2009
	Residential Controls—Hot-Water Immersion Controls	NEMA	NEMA DC 12-1985 (R2013)
	Line-Voltage Integrally Mounted Thermostats for Electric Heaters	NEMA	NEMA DC 13-1979 (R2013)
	Residential Controls—Class 2 Transformers	NEMA	NEMA DC 20-1992 (R2009)
	Safety Guidelines for the Application, Installation, and Maintenance of Solid State Controls	NEMA	NEMA ICS 1.1-1984 (R2009)
	Electrical Quick-Connect Terminals	UL	ANSI/UL 310-2014
Coolers	Refrigeration Equipment	CSA	CAN/CSA-C22.2 No. 120-13
	Unit Coolers for Refrigeration	AHRI	ANSI/AHRI 420-2008
	Quality Maintenance of Commercial Refrigeration Systems	ACCA	ANSI/ACCA 14 QMref-2015
	Refrigeration Unit Coolers	UL	ANSI/UL 412-2011
Air	Methods of Testing Forced Convection and Natural Convection Air Coolers for Refrigeration	ASHRAE	ANSI/ASHRAE 25-2001 (RA06)
Drinking Water	Methods of Testing for Rating Drinking-Water Coolers with Self-Contained Mechanical Refrigeration	ASHRAE	ANSI/ASHRAE 18-2008 (RA13)
	Drinking-Water Coolers	UL	ANSI/UL 399-2008
	Drinking Water System Components—Health Effects	NSF	ANSI/NSF 61-2014
Evaporative	Method of Testing Direct Evaporative Air Coolers	ASHRAE	ANSI/ASHRAE 133-2015
	Method of Test for Rating Indirect Evaporative Coolers	ASHRAE	ANSI/ASHRAE 143-2015
Food and Beverage	Milking Machine Installations—Vocabulary	ASABE	ANSI/ASABE AD3918-2007 (R2011)
	Methods of Testing for Rating Vending Machines for Sealed Beverages	ASHRAE	ANSI/ASHRAE 32.1-2010
	Methods of Testing for Rating Pre-Mix and Post-Mix Beverage Dispensing Equipment	ASHRAE	ANSI/ASHRAE 32.2-2003 (RA11)
	Manual Food and Beverage Dispensing Equipment	NSF	ANSI/NSF 18-2012
	Commercial Bulk Milk Dispensing Equipment	NSF	ANSI/NSF 20-2012
	Refrigerated Vending Machines	UL	ANSI/UL 541-2011
Liquid	Refrigerant-Cooled Liquid Coolers, Remote Type	AHRI	AHRI 480-2007
	Methods of Testing for Rating Liquid Coolers	ASHRAE	ANSI/ASHRAE 24-2013
	Liquid Cooling Systems	SAE	SAE AIR1811A-1997 (R2010)
Cooling Towers	Cooling Tower Testing (2002)	AABC	National Standards, Ch 13
	Commercial Systems Overview	ACCA	ACCA Manual CS-1993
	Bioaerosols: Assessment and Control (1999)	ACGIH	ACGIH
	Atmospheric Water Cooling Equipment	ASME	ASME PTC 23-2003 (RA14)
	Water-Cooling Towers	NFPA	NFPA 214-2011
	Acceptance Test Code for Water-Cooling Towers	CTI	CTI ATC-105 (2000)
	Code for Measurement of Sound from Water Cooling Towers	CTI	CTI ATC-128 (2014)
	Nomenclature for Industrial Water Cooling Towers	CTI	CTI BUL-109 (1997)
	Recommended Practice for Airflow Testing of Cooling Towers	CTI	CTI PFM-143 (1994)
	Fiberglass-Reinforced Plastic Panels	CTI	CTI STD-131 (2009)
	Certification of Water Cooling Tower Thermal Performance	CTI	CTI STD-201RS (2013)
Crop Drying	Density, Specific Gravity, and Mass-Moisture Relationships of Grain for Storage	ASABE	ANSI/ASAE D241.4-1992 (R2012)
	Thermal Properties of Grain and Grain Products	ASABE	ASAE D243.4-2003 (R2012)
	Moisture Relationships of Plant-Based Agricultural Products	ASABE	ASAE D245.6-2007 (R2012)
	Dielectric Properties of Grain and Seed	ASABE	ASAE D293.4-2012
	Construction and Rating of Equipment for Drying Farm Crops	ASABE	ASAE S248.3-1976 (R2010)
	Resistance to Airflow of Grains, Seeds, Other Agricultural Products, and Perforated Metal Sheets	ASABE	ASAE D272.3-1996 (R2011)
	Shelled Corn Storage Time for 0.5% Dry Matter Loss	ASABE	ASAE D535-2005 (R2010)
	Moisture Measurement—Unground Grain and Seeds	ASABE	ASAE S352.2-1998 (R2012)
	Moisture Measurement—Meat and Meat Products	ASABE	ASAE S353-1972 (R2012)
	Moisture Measurement—Forages	ASABE	ANSI/ASAE S358.3-2012
	Moisture Measurement—Peanuts	ASABE	ASAE S410.2-2010
	Thin-Layer Drying of Agricultural Crops	ASABE	ANSI/ASAE S448.1-2001 (R2012)
	Moisture Measurement—Tobacco	ASABE	ASAE S487-1987 (R2012)
	Energy Efficiency of Peanut Drying Systems	ASABE	ASAE S488.1-2013
	Temperature Sensor Locations for Seed-Cotton Drying Systems	ASABE	ASAE S530.1-2007 (R2012)

Selected Codes and Standards Published by Various Societies and Associations (*Continued*)

Subject	Title	Publisher	Reference
Dampers	Laboratory Methods of Testing Dampers for Rating	AMCA	AMCA 500-D-07
	Selecting Outdoor, Return, and Relief Dampers for Air-Side Economizer Systems	ASHRAE	ASHRAE *Guideline* 16-2014
Dehumidifiers	Commercial Systems Overview	ACCA	ACCA Manual CS-1993
	Bioaerosols: Assessment and Control (1999)	ACGIH	ACGIH
	Dehumidifiers	AHAM	ANSI/AHAM DH-1-2008
	Method of Testing for Rating Desiccant Dehumidifiers Utilizing Heat for the Regeneration Process	ASHRAE	ANSI/ASHRAE 139-2015
	Criteria for Moisture-Control Design Analysis in Buildings	ASHRAE	ANSI/ASHRAE 160-2016
	Method of Test for Rating Desiccant-Based Dehumidification Equipment	ASHRAE	ANSI/ASHRAE 174-2009
	Method of Testing for Rating Indoor Pool Dehumidifiers	ASHRAE	ANSI/ASHRAE 190-2013
	Method of Testing for Rating DX-Dedicated Outdoor Air Systems for Moisture Removal Capacity and Moisture Removal Efficiency	ASHRAE	ANSI/ASHRAE 198-2013
	Moisture Separator Reheaters	ASME	PTC 12.4-1992 (RA14)
	Dehumidifiers	CSA	C22.2 No. 92-1971 (R2013)
	Performance of Dehumidifiers	CSA	CAN/CSA-C749-07 (R2012)
	Dehumidifiers	UL	ANSI/UL 474-2009
Desiccants	Method of Testing Desiccants for Refrigerant Drying	ASHRAE	ANSI/ASHRAE 35-2014
Driers	Liquid-Line Driers	AHRI	ANSI/AHRI 710-2009
	Method of Testing Liquid Line Refrigerant Driers	ASHRAE	ANSI/ASHRAE 63.1-1995 (RA01)
	Refrigerant-Containing Components and Accessories, Nonelectrical	UL	ANSI/UL 207-2009
Ducts and Fittings	Hose, Air Duct, Flexible Nonmetallic, Aircraft	SAE	SAE AS1501C-1994 (R2013)
	Ducted Electric Heat Guide for Air Handling Systems, 2nd ed.	SMACNA	SMACNA 1994
	Factory-Made Air Ducts and Air Connectors	UL	ANSI/UL 181-2013
Construction	Industrial Ventilation: A Manual of Recommended Practice, 29th ed. (2016)	ACGIH	ACGIH
	Preferred Metric Sizes for Flat, Round, Square, Rectangular, and Hexagonal Metal Products	ASME	ASME B32.100-2005
	Sheet Metal Welding Code	AWS	AWS D9.1M/D9.1:2012
	Fibrous Glass Duct Construction Standards, 5th ed.	NAIMA	NAIMA AH116
	Residential Fibrous Glass Duct Construction Standards, 3rd ed.	NAIMA	NAIMA AH119
	Thermoplastic Duct (PVC) Construction Manual, 2nd ed.	SMACNA	SMACNA 1995
	Accepted Industry Practices for Sheet Metal Lagging, 1st ed.	SMACNA	SMACNA 2002
	Fibrous Glass Duct Construction Standards, 7th ed.	SMACNA	SMACNA 2003
	Round Industrial Duct Construction Standards, 2nd ed.	SMACNA	SMACNA 1999
	Rectangular Industrial Duct Construction Standards, 2nd ed.	SMACNA	SMACNA 2004
Installation	Flexible Duct Performance and Installation Standards, 5th ed.	ADC	ADC-91
	HVAC Quality Installation Specification	ACCA	ANSI/ACCA 5 QI-2015
	HVAC Quality Installation Verification Protocols	ACCA	ANSI/ACCA 9 QIvp-2016
	Technician's Guide & Workbook for Duct Diagnostics and Repair	ACCA	ACCA 2016
	Installation of Air-Conditioning and Ventilating Systems	NFPA	NFPA 90A-2015
	Installation of Warm Air Heating and Air-Conditioning Systems	NFPA	NFPA 90B-2015
Material Specifications	Specification for General Requirements for Flat-Rolled Stainless and Heat-Resisting Steel Plate, Sheet and Strip	ASTM	ASTM A480/A480M-14b
	Specification for Steel, Sheet, Carbon, Structural, and High-Strength, Low-Alloy, Hot-Rolled and Cold-Rolled, General Requirements for	ASTM	ASTM A568/A568M-14
	Specification for Steel Sheet, Zinc-Coated (Galvanized) or Zinc-Iron Alloy-Coated (Galvannealed) by the Hot-Dipped Process	ASTM	ASTM A653/A653M-13
	Specification for General Requirements for Steel Sheet, Metallic-Coated by the Hot-Dip Process	ASTM	ASTM A924/A924M-14
	Specification for Steel, Sheet, Cold-Rolled, Carbon, Structural, High-Strength Low-Alloy, High-Strength Low-Alloy with Improved Formability, Solution Hardened, and Bake Hardenable	ASTM	ASTM A1008/A1008M-13
	Specification for Steel, Sheet and Strip, Hot-Rolled, Carbon, Structural, High-Strength Low-Alloy, High-Strength Low-Alloy with Improved Formability, and Ultra-High Strength	ASTM	ASTM A1011/A1011M-14
	Practice for Measuring Flatness Characteristics of Coated Sheet Products	ASTM	ASTM A1030/A1030M-11
System Design	Installation Techniques for Perimeter Heating and Cooling	ACCA	ACCA Manual 4-1990
	Residential Duct Systems	ACCA	ANSI/ACCA Manual D-2016
	Commercial Low Pressure, Low Velocity Duct System Design	ACCA	ACCA Manual Q-1990
	Air Distribution Basics for Residential and Small Commercial Buildings	ACCA	ACCA Manual T-2001
	Method of Test for Determining the Design and Seasonal Efficiencies of Residential Thermal Distribution Systems	ASHRAE	ANSI/ASHRAE 152-2014
	Closure Systems for Use with Rigid Air Ducts	UL	ANSI/UL 181A-2013
	Closure Systems for Use with Flexible Air Ducts and Air Connectors	UL	ANSI/UL 181B-2013
Testing	Duct Leakage Testing (2002)	AABC	National Standards, Ch 5

Selected Codes and Standards Published by Various Societies and Associations (*Continued*)

Subject	Title	Publisher	Reference
	Balancing and Testing Air and Hydronic Systems	ACCA	ACCA Manual B 2009
	HVAC Quality Installation Specification	ACCA	ANSI/ACCA 5 QI-2015
	HVAC Quality Installation Verification Protocols	ACCA	ANSI/ACCA 9 QIvp-2016
	Technician's Guide & Workbook for Quality Installations	ACCA	ACCA 2015
	Technician's Guide & Workbook for Duct Diagnostics and Repair	ACCA	ACCA 2016
	Flexible Air Duct Test Code, 3rd ed.	ADC	ADC FD 72-R1
	Test Method for Measuring Acoustical and Airflow Performance of Duct Liner Materials and Prefabricated Silencers	ASTM	ASTM E477-13
	Method of Testing to Determine Flow Resistance of HVAC Ducts and Fittings	ASHRAE	ANSI/ASHRAE 120-2008
	Method of Testing HVAC Air Ducts	ASHRAE	ANSI/ASHRAE/SMACNA 126-2016
	HVAC Air Duct Leakage Test Manual, 2nd ed.	SMACNA	SMACNA 2012
	HVAC Duct Systems Inspection Guide, 3rd ed.	SMACNA	SMACNA 2006
Economizers	Selecting Outdoor, Return, and Relief Dampers for Air-Side Economizer Systems	ASHRAE	ASHRAE *Guideline* 16-2014
Electrical	Electrical Power Systems and Equipment—Voltage Ratings	ANSI	ANSI C84.1-2011
	Test Method for Bond Strength of Electrical Insulating Varnishes by the Helical Coil Test	ASTM	ASTM D2519-07 (2012)
	Standard Specification for Shelter, Electrical Equipment, Lightweight	ASTM	ASTM E2377-10
	Canadian Electrical Code, Part I (22nd ed.), Safety Standard for Electrical Installations	CSA	CSA C22.1-12
	Part II—General Requirements	CSA	CAN/CSA-C22.2 No. 0-10
	ICC Electrical Code, Administrative Provisions (2006)	ICC	ICCEC
	Low Voltage Cartridge Fuses	NEMA	NEMA FU 1-2012
	Industrial Control and Systems: Terminal Blocks	NEMA	NEMA ICS 4-2010
	Industrial Control and Systems: Enclosures	NEMA	ANSI/NEMA ICS 6-1993 (R2006)
	Application Guide for Ground Fault Protective Devices for Equipment	NEMA	ANSI/NEMA PB 2.2-2014
	General Color Requirements for Wiring Devices	NEMA	NEMA WD 1-1999 (R2010)
	Wiring Devices—Dimensional Specifications	NEMA	ANSI/NEMA WD 6-2012
	National Electrical Code®	NFPA	NFPA 70-2014
	National Fire Alarm and Signaling Code	NFPA	NFPA 72-2013
	Compatibility of Electrical Connectors and Wiring	SAE	SAE AIR1329-2014
	Molded-Case Circuit Breakers, Molded-Case Switches, and Circuit-Breaker Enclosures	UL	ANSI/UL 489-2013
Energy	Air-Conditioning and Refrigerating Equipment Nameplate Voltages	AHRI	ANSI/AHRI 110-2012
	Comfort, Air Quality, and Efficiency by Design	ACCA	ACCA Manual RS-1997
	Thermal Energy Storage	ACCA	ACCA 2005
	Measurement of Energy and Demand Savings	ASHRAE	ASHRAE *Guideline* 14-2014
	Energy Standard for Buildings Except Low-Rise Residential Buildings	ASHRAE	ANSI/ASHRAE/IES 90.1-2016
	Energy-Efficient Design of Low-Rise Residential Buildings	ASHRAE	ANSI/ASHRAE/IES 90.2-2007
	Energy Conservation in Existing Buildings	ASHRAE	ANSI/ASHRAE/IES 100-2015
	Methods of Determining, Expressing, and Comparing Building Energy Performance and Greenhouse Gas Emissions	ASHRAE	ANSI/ASHRAE 105-2014
	Method of Test for the Evaluation of Building Energy Analysis Computer Programs	ASHRAE	ANSI/ASHRAE 140-2011
	Method of Test for Determining the Design and Seasonal Efficiencies of Residential Thermal Distribution Systems	ASHRAE	ANSI/ASHRAE 152-2014
	Standard for the Design of High-Performance, Green Buildings Except Low-Rise Residential Buildings	ASHRAE/ USGBC	ANSI/ASHRAE/USGBC/IES 189.1-2014
	National Green Building Standard	ICC/ ASHRAE	ICC/ASHRAE 700-2015
	Fuel Cell Power Systems Performance	ASME	PTC 50-2002 (RA14)
	International Energy Conservation Code® (2015)	ICC	IECC
	International Green Construction Code™ (2012)	ICC	IGCC
	Uniform Solar Energy Code (2012)	IAPMO	IAPMO
	Energy Management Guide for Selection and Use of Fixed Frequency Medium AC Squirrel-Cage Polyphase Induction Motors	NEMA	NEMA MG 10-2013
	Energy Management Guide for Selection and Use of Single-Phase Motors	NEMA	NEMA MG 11-1977 (R2012)
	HVAC Systems—Commissioning Manual, 2nd ed.	SMACNA	SMACNA 2013
	Building Systems Analysis and Retrofit Manual, 2nd ed.	SMACNA	SMACNA 2011
	Energy Systems Analysis and Management, 2nd ed.	SMACNA	SMACNA 2014
	Energy Management Equipment	UL	UL 916-2007
Exhaust Systems	Fan Systems: Supply/Return/Relief/Exhaust (2002)	AABC	National Standards, Ch 10
	Commercial Systems Overview	ACCA	ACCA Manual CS-1993
	Industrial Ventilation: A Manual of Recommended Practice, 29th ed. (2016)	ACGIH	ACGIH
	Fundamentals Governing the Design and Operation of Local Exhaust Ventilation Systems	AIHA	ANSI/AIHA Z9.2-2012

Selected Codes and Standards Published by Various Societies and Associations (*Continued*)

Subject	Title	Publisher	Reference
	Spray Finishing Operations: Safety Code for Design, Construction, and Ventilation	AIHA	ANSI/AIHA Z9.3-2007
	Laboratory Ventilation	AIHA	ANSI/AIHA Z9.5-2012
	Recirculation of Air from Industrial Process Exhaust Systems	AIHA	ANSI/AIHA Z9.7-2007
	Method of Testing Performance of Laboratory Fume Hoods	ASHRAE	ANSI/ASHRAE 110-2016
	Ventilation for Commercial Cooking Operations	ASHRAE	ANSI/ASHRAE 154-2016
	Performance Test Code on Compressors and Exhausters	ASME	PTC 10-1997 (RA14)
	Flue and Exhaust Gas Analyses	ASME	PTC 19.10-1981
	Mechanical Flue-Gas Exhausters	CSA	CAN B255-M81 (R2005)
	Exhaust Systems for Air Conveying of Vapors, Gases, Mists, and Particulate Solids	NFPA	ANSI/NFPA 91-2015
	Draft Equipment	UL	UL 378-2006
Expansion Valves	Thermostatic Refrigerant Expansion Valves	AHRI	ANSI/AHRI 750-2007
	Method of Testing Capacity of Thermostatic Refrigerant Expansion Valves	ASHRAE	ANSI/ASHRAE 17-2015
Fan-Coil Units	Industrial Ventilation: A Manual of Recommended Practice, 29th ed. (2016)	ACGIH	ACGIH
	Room Fan-Coils	AHRI	ANSI/AHRI 440-2008
	Methods of Testing for Rating Fan-Coil Conditioners	ASHRAE	ANSI/ASHRAE 79-2015
	Heating and Cooling Equipment	UL/CSA	ANSI/UL 1995-2011/C22.2 No. 236-11
Fans	Residential Duct Systems	ACCA	ANSI/ACCA 1 Manual D-2016
	Commercial Low Pressure, Low Velocity Duct System Design	ACCA	ACCA Manual Q-2003
	Balancing and Testing Air and Hydronic Systems	ACCA	ACCA Manual B-2009
	HVAC Quality Installation Specifications	ACCA	ANSI/ACCA 5 QI-2015
	Technician's Guide & Workbook for Quality Installations	ACCA	ACCA 2015
	Industrial Ventilation: A Manual of Recommended Practice, 29th ed. (2016)	ACGIH	ACGIH
	Standards Handbook	AMCA	AMCA 99-10
	Air Systems	AMCA	AMCA 200-95 (R2011)
	Fans and Systems	AMCA	AMCA 201-02 (R2011)
	Troubleshooting	AMCA	AMCA 202-98 (R2011)
	Field Performance Measurement of Fan Systems	AMCA	AMCA 203-90 (R2011)
	Balance Quality and Vibration Levels for Fans	AMCA	ANSI/AMCA 204-05 (R2012)
	Laboratory Methods of Testing Air Circulator Fans for Rating and Certification	AMCA	ANSI/AMCA 230-12
	Laboratory Method of Testing Positive Pressure Ventilators for Rating	AMCA	ANSI/AMCA 240-06
	Reverberant Room Method for Sound Testing of Fans	AMCA	AMCA 300-08
	Methods for Calculating Fan Sound Ratings from Laboratory Test Data	AMCA	AMCA 301-90
	Application of Sone Ratings for Non-Ducted Air Moving Devices	AMCA	AMCA 302-73 (R2012)
	Application of Sound Power Level Ratings for Fans	AMCA	AMCA 303-79 (R2012)
	Recommended Safety Practices for Users and Installers of Industrial and Commercial Fans	AMCA	AMCA 410-96
	Industrial Process/Power Generation Fans: Site Performance Test Standard	AMCA	AMCA 803-02 (R2008)
	Home Evaluation and Performance Improvement	ACCA	ANSI/ACCA 12 QH-2014
	Technician's Guide & Workbook for Home Evaluation and Performance Improvement	ACCA	ACCA 2015
	Mechanical Balance of Fans and Blowers	AHRI	AHRI *Guideline* G-2011
	Acoustics—Measurement of Airborne Noise Emitted and Structure-Borne Vibration Induced by Small Air-Moving Devices—Part 1: Airborne Noise Measurement	ASA	ANSI/ASA S12.11-2013-Part 1/ISO 103021:2013
	Part 2: Structure-Borne Vibration	ASA	ANSI/ASA S12.11-2013-Part 2/ISO 10302-2:2013
	Laboratory Methods of Testing Fans for Aerodynamic Performance Rating	ASHRAE/ AMCA	ANSI/ASHRAE 51-2016 ANSI/AMCA 210-16
	Laboratory Methods of Testing Fans Used to Exhaust Smoke in Smoke Management Systems	ASHRAE	ANSI/ASHRAE 149-2013
	Ventilation for Commercial Cooking Operations	ASHRAE	ANSI/ASHRAE 154-2016
	Fans	ASME	ANSI/ASME PTC 11-2008
	Fans and Ventilators	CSA	C22.2 No. 113-12
	Energy Performance of Ceiling Fans	CSA	CAN/CSA-C814-10
	Residential Mechanical Ventilating Systems	CSA	CAN/CSA-F326-M91 (R2010)
	Electric Fans	UL	ANSI/UL 507-1999
	Power Ventilators	UL	ANSI/UL 705-2004
Fenestration	Practice for Calculation of Photometric Transmittance and Reflectance of Materials to Solar Radiation	ASTM	ASTM E971-11
	Test Method for Solar Photometric Transmittance of Sheet Materials Using Sunlight	ASTM	ASTM E972-96 (2013)
	Test Method for Solar Transmittance (Terrestrial) of Sheet Materials Using Sunlight	ASTM	ASTM E1084-86 (2009)
	Practice for Determining Load Resistance of Glass in Buildings	ASTM	ASTM E1300-12ae1
	Practice for Installation of Exterior Windows, Doors and Skylights	ASTM	ASTM E2112-07
	Test Method for Insulating Glass Unit Performance	ASTM	ASTM E2188-10
	Test Method for Testing Resistance to Fogging Insulating Glass Units	ASTM	ASTM E2189-10e1
	Specification for Insulating Glass Unit Performance and Evaluation	ASTM	ASTM E2190-10

Selected Codes and Standards Published by Various Societies and Associations (*Continued*)

Subject	Title	Publisher	Reference
	Guide for Assessing the Durability of Absorptive Electrochemical Coatings within Sealed Insulating Glass Units	ASTM	ASTM E2354-10
	Tables for Reference Solar Spectral Irradiance: Direct Normal and Hemispherical on 37° Tilted Surface	ASTM	ASTM G173-03 (2012)
	Windows	CSA	CSA A440-00 (R2005)
	Fenestration Energy Performance	CSA	CSA A440.2-14
	Window, Door, and Skylight Installation	CSA	CSA A440.4-07 (R2012)
Filter-Driers	Flow-Capacity Rating of Suction-Line Filters and Suction-Line Filter-Driers	AHRI	AHRI 730-2013
	Method of Testing Liquid Line Filter-Drier Filtration Capability	ASHRAE	ANSI/ASHRAE 63.2-1996 (RA10)
	Method of Testing Flow Capacity of Suction Line Filters and Filter-Driers	ASHRAE	ANSI/ASHRAE 78-1985 (RA07)
Fireplaces	Factory-Built Fireplaces	UL	ANSI/UL 127-2011
	Fireplace Stoves	UL	ANSI/UL 737-2011
Fire Protection	Test Method for Surface Burning Characteristics of Building Materials	ASTM/NFPA	ASTM E84-14
	Test Methods for Fire Test of Building Construction and Materials	ASTM	ASTM E119-14
	Test Method for Room Fire Test of Wall and Ceiling Materials and Assemblies	ASTM	ASTM E2257-13a
	Test Method for Determining Fire Resistance of Perimeter Fire Barriers Using Intermediate-Scale Multi-Story Test Apparatus	ASTM	ASTM E2307-15
	Guide for Laboratory Monitors	ASTM	ASTM E2335-12
	Test Method for Fire Resistance Grease Duct Enclosure Systems	ASTM	ASTM E2336-14
	Practice for Specimen Preparation and Mounting of Paper or Vinyl Wall Coverings to Assess Surface Burning Characteristics	ASTM	ASTM E2404-13e1
	BOCA National Fire Prevention Code, 11th ed. (1999)	BOCA	BNFPC
	Uniform Fire Code	IFCI	UFC 1997
	International Fire Code® (2015)	ICC	IFC
	International Mechanical Code® (2015)	ICC	IMC
	International Urban-Wildland Interface Code® (2012)	ICC	IUWIC
	Fire-Resistance Tests—Elements of Building Construction; Part 1: Gen. Requirements	ISO	ISO 834-1:1999
	Fire-Resistance Tests—Door and Shutter Assemblies	ISO	ISO 3008:2007
	Reaction to Fire Tests—Ignitability of Building Products Using a Radiant Heat Source	ISO	ISO 5657:1997
	Fire Containment—Elements of Building Construction—Part 1: Ventilation Ducts	ISO	ISO 6944-1:2008
	Fire Service Annunciator and Interface	NEMA	NEMA SB 30-2005
	Fire Protection Handbook (2008)	NFPA	NFPA
	National Fire Codes® (issued annually)	NFPA	NFPA
	Fire Protection Guide to Hazardous Materials	NFPA	NFPA HAZ-2010
	Fire Code	NFPA	NFPA 1-2015
	Installation of Sprinkler Systems	NFPA	NFPA 13-2013
	Flammable and Combustible Liquids Code	NFPA	NFPA 30-2015
	Fire Protection for Laboratories Using Chemicals	NFPA	NFPA 45-2015
	National Fire Alarm Code	NFPA	NFPA 72-2013
	Fire Doors and Other Opening Protectives	NFPA	NFPA 80-2013
	Health Care Facilities	NFPA	NFPA 99-2015
	Life Safety Code®	NFPA	NFPA 101-2015
	Methods of Fire Tests of Door Assemblies	NFPA	NFPA 252-2012
	Fire, Smoke and Radiation Damper Installation Guide for HVAC Systems, 5th ed.	SMACNA	SMACNA 2002
	Fire Tests of Door Assemblies	UL	ANSI/UL 10B-2008
	Heat Responsive Links for Fire-Protection Service	UL	ANSI/UL 33-2010
	Fire Tests of Building Construction and Materials	UL	ANSI/UL 263-2011
	Fire Dampers	UL	ANSI/UL 555-2006
	Fire Tests of Through-Penetration Firestops	UL	ANSI/UL 1479-2003
Smoke Management	The Commissioning Process for Smoke Control Systems	ASHRAE	ASHRAE *Guideline* 1.5-2012
	Laboratory Methods of Testing Fans Used to Exhaust Smoke in Smoke Management Systems	ASHRAE	ANSI/ASHRAE 149-2013
	Smoke-Control Systems Utilizing Barriers and Pressure Differences	NFPA	NFPA 92A-2009
	Smoke Management Systems in Malls, Atria, and Large Spaces	NFPA	NFPA 92B-2009
	Ceiling Dampers	UL	ANSI/UL 555C-2014
	Smoke Dampers	UL	ANSI/UL 555S-2014
Freezers	Quality Maintenance of Commercial Refrigeration Systems	ACCA	ANSI/ACCA 14 QMref-2015
	Energy Performance and Capacity of Household Refrigerators, Refrigerator-Freezers, Freezers, and Wine Chillers	CSA	C300-12
	Energy Performance of Food Service Refrigerators and Freezers	CSA	C827-10
	Refrigeration Equipment	CSA	CAN/CSA-C22.2 No. 120-13
Commercial	Dispensing Freezers	NSF	ANSI/NSF 6-2012

Selected Codes and Standards Published by Various Societies and Associations (*Continued*)

Subject	Title	Publisher	Reference
	Commercial Refrigerators and Freezers	NSF	ANSI/NSF 7-2014
	Commercial Refrigerators and Freezers	UL	ANSI/UL 471-2010
	Ice Makers	UL	ANSI/UL 563-2009
	Ice Cream Makers	UL	ANSI/UL 621-2010
Household	Refrigerators, Refrigerator-Freezers and Freezers	AHAM	ANSI/AHAM HRF-1-2008
	Household Refrigerators and Freezers	UL/CSA	ANSI/UL 250-1993/C22.2 No. 63-93 (R2013)
Fuels	Threshold Limit Values for Chemical Substances (updated annually)	ACGIH	ACGIH
	National Gas Fuel Code	NFPA	ANSI Z223.1/NPFA 54-2015
	Reporting of Fuel Properties when Testing Diesel Engines with Alternative Fuels Derived from Plant Oils and Animal Fats	ASABE	ASABE EP552.1-2009
	Coal Pulverizers	ASME	PTC 4.2 1969 (RA09)
	Classification of Coals by Rank	ASTM	ASTM D388-12
	Specification for Fuel Oils	ASTM	ASTM D396-15
	Specification for Diesel Fuel Oils	ASTM	ASTM D975-14b
	Specification for Gas Turbine Fuel Oils	ASTM	ASTM D2880-14a
	Specification for Kerosine	ASTM	ASTM D3699-13be1
	Practice for Receipt, Storage and Handling of Fuels	ASTM	ASTM D4418-00 (2011)
	Test Method for Determination of Yield Stress and Apparent Viscosity of Used Engine Oils at Low Temperature	ASTM	ASTM D6896-14
	Test Method for Total Sulfur in Naphthas, Distillates, Reformulated Gasolines, Diesels, Biodiesels, and Motor Fuels by Oxidative Combustion and Electrochemical Detection	ASTM	ASTM D6920-13
	Test Method for Determination of Homogeneity and Miscibility in Automotive Engine Oils	ASTM	ASTM D6922-13
	Test Method for Measurement of Hindered Phenolic and Aromatic Amine Antioxidant Content in Non-Zinc Turbine Oils by Linear Sweep Voltammetry	ASTM	ASTM D6971-09 (2014)
	Practice for Enumeration of Viable Bacteria and Fungi in Liquid Fuels—Filtration and Culture Procedures	ASTM	ASTM D6974-09 (2013)e2
	Test Method for Evaluation of Automotive Engine Oils in the Sequence IIIF, Spark-Ignition Engine	ASTM	ASTM D6984-14a
	Test Method for Determination of Ignition Delay and Derived Cetane Number (DCN) of Diesel Fuel Oils by Combustion in a Constant Volume Chamber	ASTM	ASTM D6890-13be1
	Test Method for Determination of Total Sulfur in Light Hydrocarbon, Motor Fuels, and Oils by Online Gas Chromatography with Flame Photometric Detection	ASTM	ASTM D7041-04 (2010)e1
	Test Method for Sulfur in Gasoline, Diesel Fuel, Jet Fuel, Kerosine, Biodiesel, Biodiesel Blends, and Gasoline-Ethanol Blends by Monochromatic Wavelength Dispersive X-Ray Fluorescence Spectrometry	ASTM	ASTM D7039-13
	Test Method for Flash Point by Modified Continuously Closed Cup (MCCCFP) Tester	ASTM	ASTM D7094-12e1
	Test Method for Determining the Viscosity-Temperature Relationship of Used and Soot-Containing Engine Oils at Low Temperatures	ASTM	ASTM D7110-14
	Test Method for Determination of Trace Elements in Middle Distillate Fuels by Inductively Coupled Plasma Atomic Emission Spectrometry (ICP-AES)	ASTM	ASTM D7111-14
	Test Method for Determining Stability and Compatibility of Heavy Fuel Oils and Crude Oils by Heavy Fuel Oil Stability Analyzer (Optical Detection)	ASTM	ASTM D7112-12
	Test Method for Determination of Intrinsic Stability of Asphaltene-Containing Residues, Heavy Fuel Oils, and Crude Oils (*n*-Heptane Phase Separation; Optical Detection)	ASTM	ASTM D7157-12
	Test Method for Hydrogen Content of Middle Distillate Petroleum Products by Low-Resolution Pulsed Nuclear Magnetic Resonance Spectroscopy	ASTM	ASTM D7171-05 (2011)
	Gas-Fired Central Furnaces	CSA	ANSI Z21.47-2012/CSA 2.3-2012
	Gas Unit Heaters, Gas Packaged Heaters, Gas Utility Heaters and Gas-Fired Duct Furnaces	CSA	ANSI Z83.8-2013/CSA-2.6-2013
	Industrial and Commercial Gas-Fired Package Furnaces	CSA	CGA 3.2-1976 (R2009)
	Uniform Mechanical Code (2012)	IAPMO	Chapter 13
	Uniform Plumbing Code (2012)	IAPMO	Chapter 12
	International Fuel Gas Code® (2015)	ICC	IFGC
	Standard Gas Code (1999)	SBCCI	SGC
	Commercial-Industrial Gas Heating Equipment (2011)	UL	UL 795-2011
Furnaces	Commercial Systems Overview	ACCA	ACCA Manual CS-1993
	Residential Equipment Selection, 2nd ed.	ACCA	ANSI/ACCA 3 Manual S-2014
	HVAC Quality Installation Specification	ACCA	ANSI/ACCA 5 QI-2015
	Technician's Guide & Workbook for Quality Installations	ACCA	ACCA 2015
	Method of Testing for Annual Fuel Utilization Efficiency of Residential Central Furnaces and Boilers	ASHRAE	ANSI/ASHRAE 103-2007

Selected Codes and Standards Published by Various Societies and Associations (*Continued*)

Subject	Title	Publisher	Reference
	Prevention of Furnace Explosions/Implosions in Multiple Burner Boilers	NFPA	NFPA 8502-99
	Residential Gas Detectors	UL	ANSI/UL 1484-2000
	Heating and Cooling Equipment	UL/CSA	ANSI/UL 1995-2011/C22.2 No. 236-11
	Single and Multiple Station Carbon Monoxide Alarms	UL	ANSI/UL 2034-2008
Gas	National Fuel Gas Code	AGA/NFPA	ANSI Z223.1/NFPA 54-2015
	Gas-Fired Central Furnaces	CSA	ANSI Z21.47-2012/CSA 2.3-2012
	Gas Unit Heaters, Gas Packaged Heaters, Gas Utility Heaters and Gas-Fired Duct Furnaces	CSA	ANSI Z83.8-2013/CSA-2.6-2013
	Industrial and Commercial Gas-Fired Package Furnaces	CSA	CGA 3.2-1976 (R2009)
	International Fuel Gas Code® (2015)	ICC	IFGC
	Standard Gas Code (1999)	SBCCI	SGC
	Commercial-Industrial Gas Heating Equipment	UL	UL 795-2011
Oil	Specification for Fuel Oils	ASTM	ASTM D396-15
	Specification for Diesel Fuel Oils	ASTM	ASTM D975-14b
	Test Method for Smoke Density in Flue Gases from Burning Distillate Fuels	ASTM	ASTM D2156-09 (2013)
	Standard Test Method for Vapor Pressure of Liquefied Petroleum Gases (LPG) (Expansion Method)	ASTM	ASTM D6897-09
	Oil Burning Stoves and Water Heaters	CSA	B140.3-1962 (R2011)
	Oil-Fired Warm Air Furnaces	CSA	B140.4-04 (R2009)
	Installation of Oil-Burning Equipment	NFPA	NFPA 31-2011
	Oil-Fired Central Furnaces	UL	UL 727-2006
	Oil-Fired Floor Furnaces	UL	ANSI/UL 729-2003
	Oil-Fired Wall Furnaces	UL	ANSI/UL 730-2003
Solid Fuel	Installation Code for Solid-Fuel-Burning Appliances and Equipment	CSA	CSA B365-10
	Solid-Fuel-Fired Central Heating Appliances	CSA	CAN/CSA-B366.1-11
	Solid-Fuel and Combination-Fuel Central and Supplementary Furnaces	UL	ANSI/UL 391-2010
Green Buildings	Standard for the Design of High-Performance, Green Buildings Except Low-Rise Residential Buildings	ASHRAE/ USGBC	ANSI/ASHRAE/USGBC/IES 189.1-2014
	National Green Building Standard	ICC/ ASHRAE	ICC/ASHRAE 700-2015
	International Green Construction Code™ (2012)	ICC	IGCC
	Building Systems Analysis and Retrofit Manual, 2nd ed.	SMACNA	SMACNA 2011
Heaters	Gas-Fired High-Intensity Infrared Heaters	CSA	ANSI Z83.19-2009/CSA 2.35-2009
	Gas-Fired Low-Intensity Infrared Heaters	CSA	ANSI Z83.20-2008/CSA 2.34-2008 (R2013)
	Threshold Limit Values for Chemical Substances (updated annually)	ACGIH	ACGIH
	Industrial Ventilation: A Manual of Recommended Practice, 29th ed. (2016)	ACGIH	ACGIH
	Thermal Performance Testing of Solar Ambient Air Heaters	ASABE	ANSI/ASAE S423-1991 (R2012)
	Air Heaters	ASME	ASME PTC 4.3-1968 (RA91)
	Guide for Construction of Solid Fuel Burning Masonry Heaters	ASTM	ASTM E1602-03 (2010)e1
	Non-Recirculating Direct Gas-Fired Industrial Air Heaters	CSA	ANSI Z83.4-2013/CSA 3.7-2013
	Electric Duct Heaters	CSA	C22.2 No. 155-M1986 (R2013)
	Portable Kerosene-Fired Heaters	CSA	CAN3-B140.9.3-M86 (R2011)
	Standards for Closed Feedwater Heaters, 8th ed. (2009)	HEI	HEI 2622
	Electric Heating Appliances	UL	ANSI/UL 499-2014
	Electric Oil Heaters	UL	ANSI/UL 574-2003
	Oil-Fired Air Heaters and Direct-Fired Heaters	UL	UL 733-1993
	Electric Dry Bath Heaters	UL	ANSI/UL 875-2009
	Oil-Burning Stoves	UL	ANSI/UL 896-1993
Engine	Electric Engine Preheaters and Battery Warmers for Diesel Engines	SAE	SAE J1310-2011
	Selection and Application Guidelines for Diesel, Gasoline, and Propane Fired Liquid Cooled Engine Pre-Heaters	SAE	SAE J1350-2011
	Fuel Warmer—Diesel Engines	SAE	SAE J1422-2011
Nonresidential	Installation of Electric Infrared Brooding Equipment	ASABE	ASAE EP258.4-2014
	Gas-Fired Construction Heaters	CSA	ANSI Z83.7-2011/CSA 2.14-2011
	Recirculating Direct Gas-Fired Industrial Air Heaters	CSA	ANSI Z83.18-2015
	Portable Industrial Oil-Fired Heaters	CSA	B140.8-1967 (R2011)
	Fuel-Fired Heaters—Air Heating—for Construction and Industrial Machinery	SAE	SAE J1024-2011
	Commercial-Industrial Gas Heating Equipment	UL	UL 795-2011
	Electric Heaters for Use in Hazardous (Classified) Locations	UL	ANSI/UL 823-2006
Pool	HVAC Design for Swimming Pools and Spas	ACCA	ANSI/ACCA 10 SPS-2010
	Methods of Testing and Rating Pool Heaters	ASHRAE	ANSI/ASHRAE 146-2011

Selected Codes and Standards Published by Various Societies and Associations (*Continued*)

Subject	Title	Publisher	Reference
	Gas-Fired Pool Heaters	CSA	ANSI Z21.56-2014/CSA 4.7-2014
	Oil-Fired Service Water Heaters and Swimming Pool Heaters	CSA	B140.12-03 (R2013)
Room	Specification for Room Heaters, Pellet Fuel-Burning Type	ASTM	ASTM E1509-12
	Gas-Fired Room Heaters, Vol. II, Unvented Room Heaters	CSA	ANSI Z21.11.2-2013
	Gas-Fired Unvented Catalytic Room Heaters for Use with Liquefied Petroleum (LP) Gases	CSA	ANSI Z21.76-1994 (R2006)
	Vented Gas-Fired Space Heating Appliances	CSA	ANSI Z21.86-2008/CSA 2.32-2008 (R2014)
	Vented Gas Fireplace Heaters	CSA	ANSI Z21.88-2014/CSA 2.33-2014
	Unvented Kerosene-Fired Room Heaters and Portable Heaters	UL	UL 647-1993
	Movable and Wall- or Ceiling-Hung Electric Room Heaters	UL	UL 1278-2014
	Fixed and Location-Dedicated Electric Room Heaters	UL	UL 2021-2013
	Solid Fuel-Type Room Heaters	UL	ANSI/UL 1482-2011
Transport	Heater, Airplane, Engine Exhaust Gas to Air Heat Exchanger Type	SAE	SAE ARP86-2011
	Heater, Aircraft Internal Combustion Heat Exchanger Type	SAE	SAE AS8040B-2013
	Motor Vehicle Heater Test Procedure	SAE	SAE J638-2011
Unit	Gas Unit Heaters, Gas Packaged Heaters, Gas Utility Heaters and Gas-Fired Duct Furnaces	CSA	ANSI Z83.8-2013/CSA-2.6-2013
	Oil-Fired Unit Heaters	UL	ANSI/UL 731-1995
Heat Exchangers	Remote Mechanical-Draft Evaporative Refrigerant Condensers	AHRI	ANSI/AHRI 490-2011
	Method of Testing Air-to-Air Heat/Energy Exchangers	ASHRAE	ANSI/ASHRAE 84-2013
	Boiler and Pressure Vessel Code—Section VIII, Division 1: Pressure Vessels	ASME	ASME BPVC-2015
	Single Phase Heat Exchangers	ASME	ASME PTC 12.5-2000 (RA05)
	Air Cooled Heat Exchangers	ASME	ASME PTC 30-1991 (RA11)
	Laboratory Methods of Test for Rating the Performance of Heat/Energy-Recovery Ventilators	CSA	C439-09 (R2014)
	Standards for Gasketed Plate Heat Exchangers, 1st ed.	HEI	HEI
	Standards for Shell and Tube Heat Exchangers, 5th ed. (2013)	HEI	HEI 2623
	Standards of Tubular Exchanger Manufacturers Association, 9th ed. (2007)	TEMA	TEMA
	Refrigerant-Containing Components and Accessories, Nonelectrical	UL	ANSI/UL 207-2009
Heating	Commercial Systems Overview	ACCA	ACCA Manual CS-1993
	HVAC Quality Installation Specification	ACCA	ANSI/ACCA 5 QI-2015
	Technician's Guide & Workbook for Quality Installations	ACCA	ACCA 2015
	Residential Load Calculations	ACCA	ANSI/ACCA 2 Manual J-2016
	Comfort, Air Quality, and Efficiency by Design	ACCA	ACCA Manual RS-1997
	Residential Equipment Selection, 2nd ed.	ACCA	ANSI/ACCA 3 Manual S-2014
	Heating, Ventilating and Cooling Greenhouses	ASABE	ANSI/ASAE EP406.4-2003 (R2008)
	Peak Cooling and Heating Load Calculations in Buildings Except Low-Rise Residential Buildings	ASHRAE/ ACCA	ANSI/ASHRAE/ACCA 183-2007 (RA14)
	Heater Elements	CSA	C22.2 No. 72-10 (R2014)
	Determining the Required Capacity of Residential Space Heating and Cooling Appliances	CSA	CAN/CSA-F280-12
	Heat Loss Calculation Guide (2001)	HYDI	HYDI H-22
	Residential Hydronic Heating Installation Design Guide	HYDI	IBR Guide
	Radiant Floor Heating (1995)	HYDI	HYDI 004
	Advanced Installation Guide (Commercial) for Hot Water Heating Systems (2001)	HYDI	HYDI 250
	Environmental Systems Technology, 2nd ed. (1999)	NEBB	NEBB
	Pulverized Fuel Systems	NFPA	NFPA 8503-97
	Aircraft Electrical Heating Systems	SAE	SAE AIR860B-2011
	Heating Value of Fuels	SAE	SAE J1498-2011
	Performance Test for Air-Conditioned, Heated, and Ventilated Off-Road Self-Propelled Work Machines	SAE	SAE J1503-2004
	HVAC Systems Applications, 2nd ed.	SMACNA	SMACNA 2010
	Electric Baseboard Heating Equipment	UL	ANSI/UL 1042-2009
	Electric Duct Heaters	UL	ANSI/UL 1996-2009
	Heating and Cooling Equipment	UL/CSA	ANSI/UL 1995-2011/C22.2 No. 236-11
Heat Pumps	Commercial Systems Overview	ACCA	ACCA Manual CS-1993
	Geothermal Heat Pump Training Certification Program	ACCA	ACCA Training Manual
	Heat Pumps Systems, Principles and Applications, 2nd ed.	ACCA	ACCA Manual H-1984
	Residential Equipment Selection, 2nd ed.	ACCA	ANSI/ACCA 3 Manual S-2014
	Industrial Ventilation: A Manual of Recommended Practice, 29th ed. (2016)	ACGIH	ACGIH
	Performance Rating of Unitary Air-Conditioning and Air-Source Heat Pump Equipment	AHRI	ANSI/AHRI 210/240-2008
	Commercial and Industrial Unitary Air-Conditioning and Heat Pump Equipment	AHRI	ANSI/AHRI 340/360-2007

Selected Codes and Standards Published by Various Societies and Associations (*Continued*)

Subject	Title	Publisher	Reference
	Single Package Vertical Air-Conditioner and Heat Humps	AHRI	ANSI/AHRI 390-2003
	Direct Geoexchange Heat Pumps	AHRI	ANSI/AHRI 870-2005
	Variable Refrigerant Flow (VRF) Multi-Split Air-Conditioning and Heat Pump Equipment	AHRI	ANSI/AHRI 1230-2010
	Methods of Testing for Rating Electrically Driven Unitary Air-Conditioning and Heat Pump Equipment	ASHRAE	ANSI/ASHRAE 37-2009
	Methods of Testing for Rating Seasonal Efficiency of Unitary Air-Conditioners and Heat Pumps	ASHRAE	ANSI/ASHRAE 116-2010
	Method of Test for Direct-Expansion Ground Source Heat Pumps	ASHRAE	ANSI/ASHRAE 194-2012
	Method of Testing for Rating of Multi-Purpose Heat Pumps for Residential Space Conditioning and Water Heating	ASHRAE	ANSI/ASHRAE 206-2013
	Performance Standard for Split-System and Single-Package Central Air Conditioners and Heat Pumps	CSA	CAN/CSA-C656-14
	Installation of Air-Source Heat Pumps and Air Conditioners	CSA	CAN/CSA-C273.5-11
	Performance of Direct-Expansion (DX) Ground-Source Heat Pumps	CSA	C748-13
	Water-Source Heat Pumps—Testing and Rating for Performance, Part 1: Water-to-Air and Brine-to-Air Heat Pumps	CSA	CAN/CSA-C13256-1-01 (R2011)
	Part 2: Water-to-Water and Brine-to-Water Heat Pumps	CSA	CAN/CSA-C13256-2-01 (R2010)
	Heating and Cooling Equipment (2011)	UL/CSA	ANSI/UL 1995/C22.2 No. 236-11
Gas-Fired	Gas-Fired, Heat Activated Air Conditioning and Heat Pump Appliances	CSA	ANSI Z21.40.1-1996/CGA 2.91-M96 (R2012)
	Gas-Fired, Work Activated Air Conditioning and Heat Pump Appliances (Internal Combustion)	CSA	ANSI Z21.40.2-1996/CGA 2.92-M96 (R2002)
	Performance Testing and Rating of Gas-Fired Air Conditioning and Heat Pump Appliances	CSA	ANSI Z21.40.4-1996/CGA 2.94-M96 (R2002)
Heat Recovery	Gas Turbine Heat Recovery Steam Generators	ASME	ANSI/ASME PTC 4.4-2008
	Water Heaters, Hot Water Supply Boilers, and Heat Recovery Equipment	NSF	ANSI/NSF 5-2012
High-Performance Buildings	Sustainable, High Performance Operations and Maintenance	ASHRAE	ASHRAE *Guideline* 32-2012
	Standard for the Design of High-Performance, Green Buildings Except Low-Rise Residential Buildings	ASHRAE/ USGBC	ANSI/ASHRAE/USGBC/IES 189.1-2014
	International Green Construction Code™ (2012)	ICC	IGCC
Humidifiers	Commercial Systems Overview	ACCA	ACCA Manual CS-1993
	Residential Equipment Selection	ACCA	ANSI/ACCA 3 Manual S-2014
	Comfort, Air Quality, and Efficiency by Design	ACCA	ACCA Manual RS-1997
	Bioaerosols: Assessment and Control (1999)	ACGIH	ACGIH
	Humidifiers	AHAM	ANSI/AHAM HU-1-2006 (R2011)
	Central System Humidifiers for Residential Applications	AHRI	ANSI/AHRI 610-2014
	Self-Contained Humidifiers for Residential Applications	AHRI	ANSI/AHRI 620-2014
	Commercial and Industrial Humidifiers	AHRI	ANSI/AHRI 640-2005
	Method of Test for Residential Central-System Humidifiers	ASHRAE	ANSI/ASHRAE 164.1-2012
	Humidifiers	UL/CSA	ANSI/UL 998-2011/C22.2 No. 104-11
HVAC Load Calculations	Residential Load Calculations	ACCA	ANSI/ACCA 2 Manual J-2016
	Commercial Load Calculations	ACCA	ACCA Manual N-2012
	Peak Cooling and Heating Load Calculations in Buildings Except Low-Rise Residential Buildings	ASHRAE/ ACCA	ANSI/ASHRAE/ACCA 183-2007 (RA14)
Ice Makers	Quality Maintenance of Commercial Refrigeration Systems	ACCA	ANSI/ACCA 14 QMref-2015
	Performance Rating of Automatic Commercial Ice Makers	AHRI	ANSI/AHRI 810-2012
	Ice Storage Bins	AHRI	ANSI/AHRI 820-2012
	Methods of Testing Automatic Ice Makers	ASHRAE	ANSI/ASHRAE 29-2015
	Refrigeration Equipment	CSA	C22.2 No. 120-13
	Energy Performance of Automatic Icemakers and Ice Storage Bins	CSA	CAN/CSA-C742-08 (R2014)
	Automatic Ice Making Equipment	NSF	ANSI/NSF 12-2012
	Ice Makers	UL	ANSI/UL 563-2009
Incinerators	Incinerators and Waste and Linen Handling Systems and Equipment	NFPA	NFPA 82-2014
	Residential Incinerators	UL	UL 791-2006
Indoor Air Quality	Good HVAC Practices for Residential and Commercial Buildings (2003)	ACCA	ACCA
	Comfort, Air Quality, and Efficiency by Design	ACCA	ACCA Manual RS-1997
	Bioaerosols: Assessment and Control (1999)	ACGIH	ACGIH
	Interactions Affecting the Achievement of Acceptable Indoor Environments	ASHRAE	ASHRAE *Guideline* 10-2016
	Ventilation for Acceptable Indoor Air Quality	ASHRAE	ANSI/ASHRAE 62.1-2016
	Ventilation and Acceptable Indoor Air Quality in Low-Rise Residential Buildings	ASHRAE	ANSI/ASHRAE 62.2-2016

Selected Codes and Standards Published by Various Societies and Associations (*Continued*)

Subject	Title	Publisher	Reference
	Test Method for Determination of Volatile Organic Chemicals in Atmospheres (Canister Sampling Methodology)	ASTM	ASTM D5466-01 (2007)
	Guide for Using Probability Sampling Methods in Studies of Indoor Air Quality in Buildings	ASTM	ASTM D5791-95 (2012)e1
	Guide for Using Indoor Carbon Dioxide Concentrations to Evaluate Indoor Air Quality and Ventilation	ASTM	ASTM D6245-12
	Guide for Placement and Use of Diffusion Controlled Passive Monitors for Gaseous Pollutants in Indoor Air	ASTM	ASTM D6306-10
	Test Method for Determination of Metals and Metalloids Airborne Particulate Matter by Inductively Coupled Plasma Atomic Emissions Spectrometry (ICP-AES)	ASTM	ASTM D7035-10
	Test Method for Metal Removal Fluid Aerosol in Workplace Atmospheres	ASTM	ASTM D7049-04 (2010)
	Practice for Emission Cells for the Determination of Volatile Organic Emissions from Materials/Products	ASTM	ASTM D7143-11
	Practice for Collection of Surface Dust by Micro-Vacuum Sampling for Subsequent Metals Determination	ASTM	ASTM D7144-05a (2011)
	Test Method for Determination of Beryllium in the Workplace Using Field-Based Extraction and Optical Fluorescence Detection	ASTM	ASTM D7202-14e1
	Practice for Referencing Suprathreshold Odor Intensity	ASTM	ASTM E544-10
	Guide for Specifying and Evaluating Performance of a Single Family Attached and Detached Dwelling—Indoor Air Quality	ASTM	ASTM E2267-04 (2013)
	Classification for Serviceability of an Office Facility for Thermal Environment and Indoor Air Conditions	ASTM	ASTM E2320-04 (2012)
	Practice for Continuous Sizing and Counting of Airborne Particles in Dust-Controlled Areas and Clean Rooms Using Instruments Capable of Detecting Single Sub-Micrometre and Larger Particles	ASTM	ASTM F50-12
	Ambient Air—Determination of Mass Concentration of Nitrogen Dioxide—Modified Griess-Saltzman Method	ISO	ISO 6768:1998
	Air Quality—Exchange of Data—Part 1: General Data Format	ISO	ISO 7168-1:1999
	Part 2: Condensed Data Format	ISO	ISO 7168-2:1999
	Environmental Tobacco Smoke—Estimation of Its Contribution to Respirable Suspended Particles—Determination of Particulate Matter by Ultraviolet Absorptance and by Fluorescence	ISO	ISO 15593:2001
	Indoor Air—Part 3: Determination of Formaldehyde and Other Carbonyl Compounds in Indoor Air and Test Chamber Air—Active Sampling Method	ISO	ISO 16000-3:2011
	Workplace Air Quality—Sampling and Analysis of Volatile Organic Compounds by Solvent Desorption/Gas Chromatography—Part 1: Pumped Sampling Method	ISO	ISO 16200-1:2001
	Part 2: Diffusive Sampling Method	ISO	ISO 16200-2:2000
	Workplace Air Quality—Determination of Total Organic Isocyanate Groups in Air Using 1-(2-Methoxyphenyl) Piperazine and Liquid Chromatography	ISO	ISO 16702:2007
	Installation of Carbon Monoxide (CO) Detection and Warning Equipment	NFPA	NFPA 720-2015
	Indoor Air Quality—A Systems Approach, 3rd ed.	SMACNA	SMACNA 1998
	IAQ Guidelines for Occupied Buildings Under Construction, 2nd ed.	SMACNA	ANSI/SMACNA 008-2007
	Single and Multiple Station Carbon Monoxide Alarms	UL	ANSI/UL 2034-2008
Aircraft	Air Quality Within Commercial Aircraft	ASHRAE	ASHRAE *Guideline* 28-2016
	Air Quality Within Commercial Aircraft	ASHRAE	ANSI/ASHRAE 161-2013
	Guide for Selecting Instruments and Methods for Measuring Air Quality in Aircraft Cabins	ASTM	ASTM D6399-10
	Guide for Deriving Acceptable Levels of Airborne Chemical Contaminants in Aircraft Cabins Based on Health and Comfort Considerations	ASTM	ASTM D7034-11
Modeling	Guideline for Documenting Indoor Airflow and Contaminant Transport Modeling	ASHRAE	ASHRAE *Guideline* 33-2013
Insulation	Home Evaluation and Performance Improvement	ACCA	ANSI/ACCA 12 QH-2014
	Technician's Guide & Workbook for Home Evaluation and Performance Improvement	ACCA	ACCA 2014
	Guidelines for Use of Thermal Insulation in Agricultural Buildings	ASABE	ANSI/ASAE S401.2-1993 (R2012)
	Terminology Relating to Thermal Insulating Materials	ASTM	ASTM C168-13
	Test Method for Steady-State Heat Flux Measurements and Thermal Transmission Properties by Means of the Guarded-Hot-Plate Apparatus	ASTM	ASTM C177-13
	Test Method for Steady-State Heat Transfer Properties of Pipe Insulations	ASTM	ASTM C335/C335M-10e1
	Practice for Fabrication of Thermal Insulating Fitting Covers for NPS Piping and Vessel Lagging	ASTM	ASTM C450-08 (2014)
	Test Method for Steady-State Thermal Transmission Properties by Means of the Heat Flow Meter Apparatus	ASTM	ASTM C518-10
	Specification for Preformed Flexible Elastometric Cellular Thermal Insulation in Sheet and Tubular Form	ASTM	ASTM C534/C534M-14
	Specification for Cellular Glass Thermal Insulation	ASTM	ASTM C552-14
	Specification for Rigid, Cellular Polystyrene Thermal Insulation	ASTM	ASTM C578-14a

Selected Codes and Standards Published by Various Societies and Associations (*Continued*)

Subject	Title	Publisher	Reference
	Practice for Inner and Outer Diameters of Thermal Insulation for Nominal Sizes of Pipe and Tubing	ASTM	ASTM C585-10
	Specification for Unfaced Preformed Rigid Cellular Polyisocyanurate Thermal Insulation	ASTM	ASTM C591-13
	Practice for Estimate of the Heat Gain or Loss and the Surface Temperatures of Insulated Flat, Cylindrical, and Spherical Systems by Use of Computer Programs	ASTM	ASTM C680-14
	Specification for Adhesives for Duct Thermal Insulation	ASTM	ASTM C916-14
	Classification of Potential Health and Safety Concerns Associated with Thermal Insulation Materials and Accessories	ASTM	ASTM C930-12
	Practice for Thermographic Inspection of Insulation Installations in Envelope Cavities of Frame Buildings	ASTM	ASTM C1060-11a
	Specification for Fibrous Glass Duct Lining Insulation (Thermal and Sound Absorbing Material)	ASTM	ASTM C1071-12
	Specification for Faced or Unfaced Rigid Cellular Phenolic Thermal Insulation	ASTM	ASTM C1126-14
	Test Method for Thermal Performance of Building Materials and Envelope Assemblies by Means of a Hot Box Apparatus	ASTM	ASTM C1363-11
	Specification for Perpendicularly Oriented Mineral Fiber Roll and Sheet Thermal Insulation for Pipes and Tanks	ASTM	ASTM C1393-14
	Guide for Measuring and Estimating Quantities of Insulated Piping and Components	ASTM	ASTM C1409-12
	Specification for Cellular Melamine Thermal and Sound-Absorbing Insulation	ASTM	ASTM C1410-14
	Guide for Selecting Jacketing Materials for Thermal Insulation	ASTM	ASTM C1423-14
	Specification for Preformed Flexible Cellular Polyolefin Thermal Insulation in Sheet and Tubular Form	ASTM	ASTM C1427-13
	Specification for Polyimide Flexible Cellular Thermal and Sound Absorbing Insulation	ASTM	ASTM C1482-12
	Specification for Cellulosic Fiber Stabilized Thermal Insulation	ASTM	ASTM C1497-12
	Test Method for Characterizing the Effect of Exposure to Environmental Cycling on Thermal Performance of Insulation Products	ASTM	ASTM C1512-10
	Specification for Flexible Polymeric Foam Sheet Insulation Used as a Thermal and Sound Absorbing Liner for Duct Systems	ASTM	ASTM C1534-14
	Standard Guide for Development of Standard Data Records for Computerization of Thermal Transmission Test Data for Thermal Insulation	ASTM	ASTM C1558-12
	Guide for Determining Blown Density of Pneumatically Applied Loose Fill Mineral Fiber Thermal Insulation	ASTM	ASTM C1574-04 (2013)
	Test Method for Determining the Moisture Content of Organic and Inorganic Insulation Materials by Weight	ASTM	ASTM C1616-07 (2012)
	Classification for Rating Sound Insulation	ASTM	ASTM E413-10
	Test Method for Determining the Drainage Efficiency of Exterior Insulation and Finish Systems (EIFS) Clad Wall Assemblies	ASTM	ASTM E2273-03 (2011)
	Practice for Use of Test Methods E96/E96M for Determining the Water Vapor Transmission (WVT) of Exterior Insulation and Finish Systems	ASTM	ASTM E2321-03 (2011)
	Thermal Insulation—Vocabulary	ISO	ISO 9229:2007
	National Commercial and Industrial Insulation Standards, 7th ed.	MICA	MICA
	Accepted Industry Practices for Sheet Metal Lagging, 1st ed.	SMACNA	SMACNA 2002
Legionellosis	Minimizing the Risk of Legionellosis Associated with Building Water Systems	ASHRAE	ASHRAE *Guideline* 12-2000
	Legionellosis: Risk Management for Building Water Systems	ASHRAE	ANSI/ASHRAE 188-2015
Louvers	Laboratory Methods of Testing Dampers for Rating	AMCA	AMCA 500-D-12
	Laboratory Methods of Testing Louvers for Rating	AMCA	AMCA 500-L-12
Lubricants	Methods of Testing the Floc Point of Refrigeration Grade Oils	ASHRAE	ANSI/ASHRAE 86-2013
	Refrigeration Oil Description	ASHRAE	ANSI/ASHRAE 99-2006
	Test Method for Pour Point of Petroleum Products	ASTM	ASTM D97-12
	Classification of Industrial Fluid Lubricants by Viscosity System	ASTM	ASTM D2422-97 (2013)
	Test Method for Relative Molecular Weight (Relative Molecular Mass) of Hydrocarbons by Thermoelectric Measurement of Vapor Pressure	ASTM	ASTM D2503-92 (2012)
	Test Method for Determination of Moderately High Temperature Piston Deposits by Thermo-Oxidation Engine Oil Simulation Test—TEOST MHT	ASTM	ASTM D7097-09
	Petroleum Products—Corrosiveness to Copper—Copper Strip Test	ISO	ISO 2160:1998
Measurement	Industrial Ventilation: A Manual of Recommended Practice, 29th ed. (2016)	ACGIH	ACGIH
	Engineering Analysis of Experimental Data	ASHRAE	ASHRAE *Guideline* 2-2010 (RA14)
	Instrumentation for Monitoring Central Chilled Water Plant Efficiency	ASHRAE	ASHRAE *Guideline* 22-2012
	Standard Method for Measuring the Proportion of Lubricant in Liquid Refrigerant	ASHRAE	ANSI/ASHRAE 41.4-2015
	Standard Method for Measurement of Moist Air Properties	ASHRAE	ANSI/ASHRAE 41.6-2014
	Methods of Determining, Expressing, and Comparing Building Energy Performance and Greenhouse Gas Emissions	ASHRAE	ANSI/ASHRAE 105-2014

Selected Codes and Standards Published by Various Societies and Associations (*Continued*)

Subject	Title	Publisher	Reference
	Method for Establishing Installation Effects on Flowmeters	ASME	ASME MFC-10M-2000 (RA11)
	Test Uncertainty	ASME	ASME PTC 19.1-2013
	Measurement of Industrial Sound	ASME	ANSI/ASME PTC 36-2004 (RA13)
	Test Methods for Water Vapor Transmission of Materials	ASTM	ASTM E96/E96M-14
	Specification and Temperature-Electromotive Force (EMF) Tables for Standardized Thermocouples	ASTM	ASTM E230/E230M-12
	Practice for Continuous Sizing and Counting of Airborne Particles in Dust-Controlled Areas and Clean Rooms Using Instruments Capable of Detecting Single Sub-Micrometre and Larger Particles	ASTM	ASTM F50-12
	Ergonomics of the Thermal Environment—Instruments for Measuring Physical Quantities	ISO	ISO 7726:1998
	Ergonomics of the Thermal Environment—Determination of Metabolic Rate	ISO	ISO 8996:2004
	Ergonomics of the Thermal Environment—Estimation of the Thermal Insulation and Water Vapour Resistance of a Clothing Ensemble	ISO	ISO 9920:2007
Energy	Measurement of Energy and Demand Savings	ASHRAE	ASHRAE *Guideline* 14-2014
Fluid Flow	Standard Methods for Liquid in Flow Measurement	ASHRAE	ANSI/ASHRAE 41.8-2016
	Methods for Volatile-Refrigerant Mass Flow Measurements Using Calorimeters	ASHRAE	ANSI/ASHRAE 41.9-2011
	Flow Measurement	ASME	ASME PTC 19.5-2004 (RA13)
	Glossary of Terms Used in the Measurement of Fluid Flow in Pipes	ASME	ASME MFC-1M-2003 (RA08)
	Measurement Uncertainty for Fluid Flow in Closed Conduits	ASME	ANSI/ASME MFC-2M-1983 (RA13)
	Measurement of Fluid Flow in Pipes Using Orifice, Nozzle, and Venturi	ASME	ASME MFC-3M-2004
	Measurement of Fluid Flow in Pipes Using Vortex Flowmeters	ASME	ASME MFC-6M-1998 (RA05)
	Fluid Flow in Closed Conduits: Connections for Pressure Signal Transmissions Between Primary and Secondary Devices	ASME	ASME MFC-8M-2001 (RA11)
	Measurement of Liquid Flow in Closed Conduits by Weighing Method	ASME	ASME MFC-9M-1988 (RA11)
	Measurement of Fluid Flow Using Small Bore Precision Orifice Meters	ASME	ASME MFC-14M-2003 (RA08)
	Measurement of Fluid Flow in Closed Conduits by Means of Electromagnetic Flowmeters	ASME	ASME MFC-16-2014
	Measurement of Fluid Flow Using Variable Area Meters	ASME	ASME MFC-18M-2001 (RA11)
	Test Method for Determining the Moisture Content of Inorganic Insulation Materials by Weight	ASTM	ASTM C1616-07 (2012)
	Test Method for Indicating Wear Characteristics of Petroleum Hydraulic Fluids in a High Pressure Constant Volume Vane Pump	ASTM	ASTM D6973-14
	Test Method for Dynamic Viscosity and Density of Liquids by Stabinger Viscometer (and the Calculation of Kinematic Viscosity)	ASTM	ASTM D7042-14
	Test Method for Indicating Wear Characteristics of Non-Petroleum and Petroleum Hydraulic Fluids in a Constant Volume Vane Pump	ASTM	ASTM D7043-12
	Practice for Calculating Viscosity of a Blend of Petroleum Products	ASTM	ASTM D7152-11
	Test Method for Same-Different Test	ASTM	ASTM E2139-05 (2011)
	Practice for Field Use of Pyranometers, Pyrheliometers, and UV Radiometers	ASTM	ASTM G183-15
Gas Flow	Standard Methods for Laboratory Airflow Measurement	ASHRAE	ANSI/ASHRAE 41.2-1987 (RA92)
	Method of Test for Measurement of Flow of Gas	ASHRAE	ANSI/ASHRAE 41.7-2015
	Measurement of Gas Flow by Turbine Meters	ASME	ANSI/ASME MFC-4M-1986 (RA08)
	Measurement of Gas Flow by Means of Critical Flow Venturi Nozzles	ASME	ANSI/ASME MFC-7M-1987 (RA14)
Pressure	Standard Method for Pressure Measurement	ASHRAE	ANSI/ASHRAE 41.3-2014
	Pressure Gauges and Gauge Attachments	ASME	ASME B40.100-2013
	Pressure Measurement	ASME	ANSI/ASME PTC 19.2-2010
Temperature	Standard Method for Temperature Measurement	ASHRAE	ANSI/ASHRAE 41.1-2013
	Thermometers, Direct Reading and Remote Reading	ASME	ASME B40.200-2008 (RA13)
	Temperature Measurement	ASME	ASME PTC 19.3-1974 (RA04)
	Total Temperature Measuring Instruments (Turbine Powered Subsonic Aircraft)	SAE	SAE AS793A-2001 (R2008)
Thermal	Method of Testing Thermal Energy Meters for Liquid Streams in HVAC Systems	ASHRAE	ANSI/ASHRAE 125-2016
	Test Method for Steady-State Heat Flux Measurements and Thermal Transmission Properties by Means of the Guarded-Hot-Plate Apparatus	ASTM	ASTM C177-13
	Test Method for Steady-State Heat Flux Measurements Thermal Transmission Properties by Means of the Heat Flow Meter Apparatus	ASTM	ASTM C518-10
	Practice for In-Situ Measurement of Heat Flux and Temperature on Building Envelope Components	ASTM	ASTM C1046-95 (2013)
	Practice for Determining Thermal Resistance of Building Envelope Components from In-Situ Data	ASTM	ASTM C1155-95 (2013)
	Test Method for Thermal Performance of Building Materials and Envelope Assemblies by Means of a Hot Box Apparatus	ASTM	ASTM C1363-11

Selected Codes and Standards Published by Various Societies and Associations (*Continued*)

Subject	Title	Publisher	Reference
Mobile Homes and Recreational Vehicles	Residential Load Calculation, 8th ed.	ACCA	ANSI/ACCA Manual J-2016
	Recreational Vehicle Cooking Gas Appliances	CSA	ANSI Z21.57-2010
	Oil-Fired Warm Air Heating Appliances for Mobile Housing and Recreational Vehicles	CSA	B140.10-06 (R2011)
	Manufactured Homes	CSA	CAN/CSA-Z240 MH Series-09 (R2014)
	Recreational Vehicles	CSA	CAN/CSA-Z240 RV Series-08 (R2013)
	Gas Supply Connectors for Manufactured Homes	IAPMO	IAPMO TS 9-2003
	Fuel Supply: Manufactured/Mobile Home Parks & Recreational Vehicle Parks	IAPMO	Chapter 13, Part II
	Manufactured Housing Construction and Safety Standards	ICC/ANSI	HUD 24 CFR Part 3280 (2008)
	Manufactured Housing	NFPA	NFPA 501-2013
	Recreational Vehicles	NFPA	NFPA 1192-2015
	Plumbing System Components for Recreational Vehicles	NSF	ANSI/NSF 24-2010
	Low Voltage Lighting Fixtures for Use in Recreational Vehicles	UL	ANSI/UL 234-2005
	Liquid Fuel-Burning Heating Appliances for Manufactured Homes and Recreational Vehicles	UL	ANSI/UL 307A-2009
	Gas-Burning Heating Appliances for Manufactured Homes and Recreational Vehicles	UL	UL 307B-2006
Motors and Generators	Installation and Maintenance of Farm Standby Electric Power	ASABE	ANSI/ASABE EP364.3-2006
	Nuclear Power Plant Air-Cleaning Units and Components	ASME	ASME N509-2002 (RA08)
	Testing of Nuclear Air Treatment Systems	ASME	ASME N510-2007
	Fired Steam Generators	ASME	ASME PTC 4-2013
	Gas Turbine Heat Recovery Steam Generators	ASME	ASME PTC 4.4-2008 (RA13)
	Test Methods for Film-Insulated Magnet Wire	ASTM	ASTM D1676-03 (2011)
	Test Method for Evaluation of Engine Oils in a High Speed, Single-Cylinder Diesel Engine—Caterpillar 1R Test Procedure	ASTM	ASTM D6923-14
	Test Method for Evaluation of Diesel Engine Oils in the T-11 Exhaust Gas Recirculation Diesel Engine	ASTM	ASTM D7156-13
	Test Methods, Marking Requirements, and Energy Efficiency Levels for Three-Phase Induction Motors	CSA	CSA C390-10
	Motors and Generators	CSA	C22.2 No. 100-14
	Emergency Electrical Power Supply for Buildings	CSA	CSA C282-09
	Energy Efficiency Test Methods for Small Motors	CSA	CAN/CSA C747-09 (R2014)
	Standard Test Procedure for Polyphase Induction Motors and Generators	IEEE	IEEE 112-1996
	Motors and Generators	NEMA	NEMA MG 1-2014
	Energy Management Guide for Selection and Use of Fixed Frequency Medium AC Squirrel-Cage Polyphase Industrial Motors	NEMA	NEMA MG 10-2013
	Energy Management Guide for Selection and Use of Single-Phase Motors	NEMA	NEMA MG 11-1977 (R2012)
	Magnet Wire	NEMA	ANSI/NEMA MW 1000-2014
	Motion/Position Control Motors, Controls, and Feedback Devices	NEMA	NEMA ICS 16-2001
	Rotating Electrical Machines—General Requirements	UL	UL 1004-1-2012
	Electric Motors and Generators for Use in Hazardous (Classified) Locations	UL	ANSI/UL 674-2011
	Overheating Protection for Motors	UL	ANSI/UL 2111-1997
Operation and Maintenance	Maintenance of Residential HVAC Systems	ACCA	ANSI/ACCA 4 QM-2013
	Preparation of Operating and Maintenance Documentation for Building Systems	ASHRAE	ASHRAE *Guideline* 4-2008 (RA13)
	Sustainable, High Performance Operations and Maintenance	ASHRAE	ASHRAE *Guideline* 32-2012
	Inspection and Maintenance of Commercial-Building HVAC Systems	ASHRAE/ ACCA	ANSI/ASHRAE/ACCA 180-2012
	International Property Maintenance Code® (2015)	ICC	IPMC
Panel Heating and Cooling	Method of Testing for Rating Ceiling Panels for Sensible Heating and Cooling	ASHRAE	ANSI/ASHRAE 138-2013
Pipe, Tubing, and Fittings	Scheme for the Identification of Piping Systems	ASME	ASME A13.1-2007 (RA13)
	Pipe Threads, General Purpose (Inch)	ASME	ANSI/ASME B1.20.1-2013
	Wrought Copper and Copper Alloy Braze-Joint Pressure Fittings	ASME	ASME B16.50-2013
	Power Piping	ASME	ASME B31.1-2014
	Process Piping	ASME	ASME B31.3-2014
	Refrigeration Piping and Heat Transfer Components	ASME	ASME B31.5-2013
	Building Services Piping	ASME	ASME B31.9-2014
	Practice for Obtaining Hydrostatic or Pressure Design Basis for "Fiberglass" (Glass-Fiber-Reinforced Thermosetting-Resin) Pipe and Fittings	ASTM	ASTM D2992-12
	Specification for Welding of Austenitic Stainless Steel Tube and Piping Systems in Sanitary Applications	AWS	AWS D18.1:2009
	Standards of the Expansion Joint Manufacturers Association, 9th ed.	EJMA	EJMA
	Pipe Hangers and Supports—Materials, Design and Manufacture	MSS	ANSI/MSS SP-58-2009
	Pipe Hangers and Supports—Selection and Application	MSS	ANSI/MSS SP-69-2003

Selected Codes and Standards Published by Various Societies and Associations (*Continued*)

Subject	Title	Publisher	Reference
	General Welding Guidelines (2009)	NCPWB	NCPWB
	National Fuel Gas Code	AGA/NFPA	ANSI Z223.1/NFPA 54-2015
	Refrigeration Tube Fittings—General Specifications	SAE	SAE J513-1999
	Seismic Restraint Manual—Guidelines for Mechanical Systems, 3rd ed.	SMACNA	ANSI/SMACNA 001-2008
	Tube Fittings for Flammable and Combustible Fluids, Refrigeration Service, and Marine Use	UL	ANSI/UL 109-1997
Plastic	Specification for Acrylonitrile-Butadiene-Styrene (ABS) Plastic Pipe, Schedules 40 and 80	ASTM	ASTM D1527-99 (2005)
	Specification for Poly (Vinyl Chloride) (PVC) Plastic Pipe, Schedules 40, 80, and 120	ASTM	ASTM D1785-12
	Test Method for Obtaining Hydrostatic Design Basis for Thermoplastic Pipe Materials or Pressure Design Basis for Thermoplastic Pipe Products	ASTM	ASTM D2837-13e1
	Specification for Perfluoroalkoxy (PFA)-Fluoropolymer Tubing	ASTM	ASTM D6867-03 (2014)
	Specification for Polyethylene Stay in Place Form System for End Walls for Drainage Pipe	ASTM	ASTM D7082-04 (2010)
	Specification for Chlorinated Poly (Vinyl Chloride) (CPVC) Plastic Pipe, Schedules 40 and 80	ASTM	ASTM F441/F441M-13e1
	Specification for Crosslinked Polyethylene/Aluminum/Crosslinked Polyethylene Tubing OD Controlled SDR9	ASTM	ASTM F2262-09
	Test Method for Evaluating the Oxidative Resistance of Polyethylene (PE) Pipe to Chlorinated Water	ASTM	ASTM F2263-14
	Specification for 12 to 60 in. [300 to 1500 mm] Annular Corrugated Profile-Wall Polyethylene (PE) Pipe and Fittings for Gravity-Flow Storm Sewer and Subsurface Drainage Applications	ASTM	ASTM F2306/F2306M-14
	Test Method for Determining Chemical Compatibility of Substances in Contact with Thermoplastic Pipe and Fittings Materials	ASTM	ASTM F2331-11
	Test Method for Determining Thermoplastic Pipe Wall Stiffness	ASTM	ASTM F2433-05 (2013)
	Specification for Steel Reinforced Polyethylene (PE) Corrugated Pipe	ASTM	ASTM F2435-12
	Electrical Polyvinyl Chloride (PVC) Tubing and Conduit	NEMA	NEMA TC 2-2013
	PVC Plastic Utilities Duct for Underground Installation	NEMA	NEMA TC 6 and 8-2013
	Smooth Wall Coilable Polyethylene Electrical Plastic Duct	NEMA	NEMA TC 7-2013
	Fittings for PVC Plastic Utilities Duct for Underground Installation	NEMA	NEMA TC 9-2004 (R2012)
	Electrical Nonmetallic Tubing (ENT)	NEMA	NEMA TC 13-2005
	Plastics Piping System Components and Related Materials	NSF	ANSI/NSF 14-2014
	Rubber Gasketed Fittings	UL	ANSI/UL 213-2008
Metal	Welded and Seamless Wrought Steel Pipe	ASME	ASME B36.10M-2004 (RA10)
	Stainless Steel Pipe	ASME	ASME B36.19M-2004 (RA10)
	Specification for Pipe, Steel, Black and Hot-Dipped, Zinc-Coated, Welded and Seamless	ASTM	ASTM A53/53M-12
	Specification for Seamless Carbon Steel Pipe for High-Temperature Service	ASTM	ASTM A106/A106M-14
	Specification for Steel Line Pipe, Black, Furnace-Butt-Welded	ASTM	ASTM A1037/A1037M-05 (2012)
	Specification for Composite Corrugated Steel Pipe for Sewers and Drains	ASTM	ASTM A1042/A1042M-04 (2009)
	Specification for Seamless Copper Pipe, Standard Sizes	ASTM	ASTM B42-10
	Specification for Seamless Copper Tube	ASTM	ASTM B75/B75M-11
	Specification for Seamless Copper Water Tube	ASTM	ASTM B88-14
	Specification for Seamless Copper Tube for Air Conditioning and Refrigeration Field Service	ASTM	ASTM B280-13
	Specification for Hand-Drawn Copper Capillary Tube for Restrictor Applications	ASTM	ASTM B360-09
	Specification for Welded Copper Tube for Air Conditioning and Refrigeration Service	ASTM	ASTM B640-12a
	Specification for Copper-Beryllium Seamless Tube UNS Nos. C17500 and C17510	ASTM	ASTM B937-04 (2010)
	Test Method for Rapid Determination of Corrosiveness to Copper from Petroleum Products Using a Disposable Copper Foil Strip	ASTM	ASTM D7095-04 (2014)
	Thickness Design of Ductile-Iron Pipe	AWWA	ANSI/AWWA C150/A21.50-14
	Fittings, Cast Metal Boxes, and Conduit Bodies for Conduit and Cable Assemblies	NEMA	NEMA FB 1-2012
	Polyvinyl-Chloride (PVC) Externally Coated Galvanized Rigid Steel Conduit and Intermediate Metal Conduit	NEMA	NEMA RN 1-2005 (R2013)
Plumbing	Backwater Valves	ASME	ASME A112.14.1-2003 (RA12)
	Plumbing Supply Fittings	ASME	ASME A112.18.1-2012
	Plumbing Waste Fittings	ASME	ASME A112.18.2-2011
	Performance Requirements for Backflow Protection Devices and Systems in Plumbing Fixture Fittings	ASME	ASME A112.18.3-2002 (RA12)
	Uniform Plumbing Code (2012) (with IAPMO Installation Standards)	IAPMO	IAPMO
	International Plumbing Code® (2015)	ICC	IPC
	International Private Sewage Disposal Code® (2015)	ICC	IPSDC
	2012 National Standard Plumbing Code (NSPC)	PHCC	NSPC 2012
	2012 National Standard Plumbing Code—Illustrated	PHCC	PHCC 2012

Selected Codes and Standards Published by Various Societies and Associations (*Continued*)

Subject	Title	Publisher	Reference
	Standard Plumbing Code (1997)	SBCCI	SPC
Pumps	Balancing and Testing Air and Hydronic Systems	ACCA	ACCA Manual B-2009
	Centrifugal Pumps	ASME	ASME PTC 8.2-1990
	Specification for Horizontal End Suction Centrifugal Pumps for Chemical Process	ASME	ASME B73.1-2012
	Specification for Vertical-in-Line Centrifugal Pumps for Chemical Process	ASME	ASME B73.2-2003 (RA08)
	Specification for Sealless Horizontal End Suction Metallic Centrifugal Pumps for Chemical Process	ASME	ASME B73.3-2003 (RA08)
	Specification for Thermoplastic and Thermoset Polymer Material Horizontal End Suction Centrifugal Pumps for Chemical Process	ASME	ASME B73.5M-1995 (RA07)
	Liquid Pumps	CSA	CAN/CSA-C22.2 No. 108-14
	Energy Efficiency Test Methods for Small Pumps	CSA	CAN/CSA C820-02 (R2012)
	Performance Standard for Liquid Ring Vacuum Pumps, 4th ed. (2011)	HEI	HEI 2854
	Rotodynamic (Centrifugal) Pumps for Nomenclature and Definitions	HI	ANSI/HI 1.1-1.2-2014
	Rotodynamic (Centrifugal) Pumps for Design and Application	HI	ANSI/HI 1.3-2013
	Rotodynamic (Centrifugal) Pumps for Manuals Describing Installation, Operation and Maintenance	HI	ANSI/HI 1.4-2014
	Rotodynamic (Vertical) Nomenclature	HI	ANSI/HI 2.1-2.2-2014
	Rotodynamic (Vertical) Application	HI	ANSI/HI 2.3-2013
	Rotodynamic (Vertical) Operations	HI	ANSI/HI 2.4-2014
	Rotary Pumps for Nomenclature, Definitions, Application, and Operation	HI	ANSI/HI 3.1-3.5-2008
	Sealless, Magnetically Driven Rotary Pumps for Nomenclature, Definitions, Application, Operation, and Test	HI	ANSI/HI 4.1-4.6-2010
	Sealless Rotodynamic Pumps for Nomenclature, Definitions, Application, Operation, and Test	HI	ANSI/HI 5.1-5.6-2010
	Reciprocating Pumps for Nomenclature, Definitions, Application, and Operation	HI	ANSI/HI 6.1-6.5-2000
	Direct Acting (Steam) Pumps for Nomenclature, Definitions, Application, and Operation	HI	ANSI/HI 8.1-8.5-2000
	Pumps—General Guidelines for Types, Definitions, Application, Sound Measurement and Decontamination	HI	ANSI/HI 9.1-9.5-2000
	Rotodynamic Pumps for Assessment of Allowable Nozzle Loads	HI	ANSI/HI 9.6.2-2011
	Centrifugal and Vertical Pumps for Allowable Operating Region	HI	ANSI/HI 9.6.3-2012
	Rotodynamic Pumps for Vibration Measurements and Allowable Values	HI	ANSI/HI 9.6.4-2009
	Rotodynamic (Centrifugal and Vertical) Pumps Guideline for Condition Monitoring	HI	ANSI/HI 9.6.5-2009
	Intake Design for Rotodynamic Pumps	HI	ANSI/HI 9.8-2012
	Engineering Data Book, 2nd ed.	HI	HI (1990)
	Equipment for Swimming Pools, Spas, Hot Tubs and Other Recreational Water Facilities	NSF	ANSI/NSF 50-2013
	Pumps for Oil-Burning Appliances	UL	UL 343-2008
	Motor-Operated Water Pumps	UL	ANSI/UL 778-2010
	Swimming Pool Pumps, Filters, and Chlorinators	UL	ANSI/UL 1081-2008
Radiators	Balancing and Testing Air and Hydronic Systems	ACCA	ACCA Manual B-2009
	Testing and Rating Standard for Baseboard Radiation, 8th ed. (2005)	HYDI	IBR
	Testing and Rating Standard for Finned Tube (Commercial) Radiation, 6th ed. (2005)	HYDI	IBR
Receivers	Refrigerant Liquid Receivers	AHRI	ANSI/AHRI 495-2005
	Refrigerant-Containing Components and Accessories, Nonelectrical	UL	ANSI/UL 207-2009
Refrigerants	Threshold Limit Values for Chemical Substances (updated annually)	ACGIH	ACGIH
	Specifications for Refrigerants	AHRI	AHRI 700-2014
	Refrigerant Recovery/Recycling Equipment	AHRI	AHRI 740-1998
	Refrigerant Information Recommended for Product Development and Standards	ASHRAE	ASHRAE *Guideline* 6-2015
	Method of Testing Flow Capacity of Refrigerant Capillary Tubes	ASHRAE	ANSI/ASHRAE 28-1996 (RA10)
	Designation and Safety Classification of Refrigerants	ASHRAE	ANSI/ASHRAE 34-2016
	Sealed Glass Tube Method to Test the Chemical Stability of Materials for Use Within Refrigerant Systems	ASHRAE	ANSI/ASHRAE 97-2007
	Refrigeration Oil Description	ASHRAE	ANSI/ASHRAE 99-2006
	Reducing the Release of Halogenated Refrigerants from Refrigerating and Air-Conditioning Equipment and Systems	ASHRAE	ANSI/ASHRAE 147-2013
	Methods of Testing Capacity for Refrigerant Pressure Regulators	ASHRAE	ANSI/ASHRAE 158.2-2011
	Method of Test to Determine the Performance of Halocarbon Refrigerant Leak Detectors	ASHRAE	ANSI/ASHRAE 173-2012
	Test Method for Acid Number of Petroleum Products by Potentiometric Titration	ASTM	ASTM D664-11a
	Test Method for Concentration Limits of Flammability of Chemical (Vapors and Gases)	ASTM	ASTM E681-09
	Refrigerant-Containing Components for Use in Electrical Equipment	CSA	C22.2 No. 140.3-09 (R2014)
	Refrigerants—Designation System	ISO	ISO 817:2014
	Procedure Retrofitting CFC-12 (R-12) Mobile Air-Conditioning Systems to HFC-134a (R-134a)	SAE	SAE J1661-2011

Selected Codes and Standards Published by Various Societies and Associations (*Continued*)

Subject	Title	Publisher	Reference
	Recommended Service Procedure for the Containment of CFC-12 (R-12)	SAE	SAE J1989-2011
	Standard of Purity for Recycled R-134a (HFC-134a) and R-1234yf (HFO-1234yf) for Use in Mobile Air-Conditioning Systems	SAE	SAE J2099-2012
	HFC-134a (R-134a) Service Hose Fittings for Automotive Air-Conditioning Service Equipment	SAE	SAE J2197-2011
	CFC-12 (R-12) Refrigerant Recovery Equipment for Mobile Automotive Air-Conditioning Systems	SAE	SAE J2209-2011
	Recommended Service Procedure for the Containment of HFC-134a	SAE	SAE J2211-2011
	Refrigerant-Containing Components and Accessories, Nonelectrical	UL	ANSI/UL 207-2009
	Refrigerant Recovery/Recycling Equipment	UL	ANSI/UL 1963-2011
	Refrigerants	UL	ANSI/UL 2182-2006
Refrigeration	Quality Maintenance of Commercial Refrigeration Systems	ACCA	ANSI/ACCA 14 QMref-2015
	Safety Standard for Refrigeration Systems	ASHRAE	ANSI/ASHRAE 15-2016
	Mechanical Refrigeration Code	CSA	B52-13
	Refrigeration Equipment	CSA	CAN/CSA-C22.2 No. 120-13
	Equipment, Design and Installation of Ammonia Mechanical Refrigerating Systems	IIAR	ANSI/IIAR 2-2008
	Refrigerated Medical Equipment	UL	ANSI/UL 416-1993
Refrigeration Systems	Ejectors	ASME	ASME PTC 24-1976 (RA82)
	Safety Standard for Refrigeration Systems	ASHRAE	ANSI/ASHRAE 15-2016
	Designation and Safety Classification of Refrigerants	ASHRAE	ANSI/ASHRAE 34-2016
	Reducing the Release of Halogenated Refrigerants from Refrigerating and Air-Conditioning Equipment and Systems	ASHRAE	ANSI/ASHRAE 147-2013
	Testing of Refrigerating Systems	ISO	ISO 916-1968
	Standards for Steam Jet Vacuum Systems, 7th ed. (2012)	HEI	HEI 2866-1
Transport	Mechanical Transport Refrigeration Units	AHRI	ANSI/AHRI 1110-2013
	Mechanical Refrigeration and Air-Conditioning Installations Aboard Ship	ASHRAE	ANSI/ASHRAE 26-2010
	General Requirements for Application of Vapor Cycle Refrigeration Systems for Aircraft	SAE	SAE ARP731C-2003 (R2010)
	Safety Standard for Motor Vehicle Refrigerant Vapor Compression Systems	SAE	SAE J639-2011
Refrigerators			
Commercial	Quality Maintenance of Commercial Refrigeration Systems	ACCA	ANSI/ACCA 14 QMref-2015
	Method of Testing Commercial Refrigerators and Freezers	ASHRAE	ANSI/ASHRAE 72-2014
	Energy Performance Standard for Commercial Refrigerated Display Cabinets and Merchandise	CSA	CAN/CSA-C657-12
	Energy Performance of Food Service Refrigerators and Freezers	CSA	C827-10
	Gas Food Service Equipment	CSA	ANSI Z83.11-2006/CSA 1.8A-2006 (R2011)
	Food Equipment	NSF	ANSI/NSF 2-2014
	Commercial Refrigerators and Freezers	NSF	ANSI/NSF 7-2014
	Mobile Food Carts	NSF	ANSI/NSF 59-2012
	Refrigeration Unit Coolers	UL	ANSI/UL 412-2011
	Refrigerating Units	UL	ANSI/UL 427-2011
	Commercial Refrigerators and Freezers	UL	ANSI/UL 471-2010
Household	Refrigerators, Refrigerator-Freezers and Freezers	AHAM	ANSI/AHAM HRF-1-2008
	Refrigerators Using Gas Fuel	CSA	ANSI Z21.19-2014/CSA1.4-2014
	Energy Performance and Capacity of Household Refrigerators, Refrigerator-Freezers, Freezers, and Wine Chillers	CSA	CAN/CSA C300-12
	Household Refrigerators and Freezers	UL/CSA	ANSI/UL 250-1993/C22.2 No. 63-93 (R2013)
Retrofitting			
Building	Home Evaluation and Performance Improvement	ACCA	ANSI/ACCA 12 QH-2014
	Technician's Guide & Workbook for Home Evaluation and Performance Improvement	ACCA	ACCA 2015
	Technician's Guide & Workbook for Duct Diagnostics and Repair	ACCA	ACCA 2016
	Bob's House	ACCA	ACCA 2008
	Good HVAC Practices for Residential and Commercial Buildings	ACCA	ACCA 2003
	Building Systems Analysis and Retrofit Manual, 2nd ed.	SMACNA	SMACNA 2011
Refrigerant	Procedure for Retrofitting CFC-12 (R-12) Mobile Air Conditioning Systems to HFC-134a (R-134a)	SAE	SAE J1661-2011
Roof Ventilators	Commercial Low Pressure, Low Velocity Duct System Design	ACCA	ACCA Manual Q-1990
	Power Ventilators	UL	ANSI/UL 705-2004
Safety	Guideline for Risk Management of Public Health and Safety in Buildings	ASHRAE	ASHRAE *Guideline* 29-2009
Seismic Restraint	Method of Test of Seismic Restraint Devices for HVAC&R Equipment	ASHRAE	ANSI/ASHRAE 171-2008
	Seismic Restraint Manual—Guidelines for Mechanical Systems, 3rd ed.	SMACNA	ANSI/SMACNA 001-2008

Selected Codes and Standards Published by Various Societies and Associations (*Continued*)

Subject	Title	Publisher	Reference
Smoke Control Systems	The Commissioning Process for Smoke Management Systems	ASHRAE	ASHRAE *Guideline* 1.5-2012
	Laboratory Methods of Testing Fans Used to Exhaust Smoke in Smoke Management Systems	ASHRAE	ANSI/ASHRAE 149-2013
	Smoke-Control Systems Utilizing Barriers and Pressure Differences	NFPA	NFPA 92A-2009
	Smoke Management Systems in Malls, Atria, and Large Spaces	NFPA	NFPA 92B-2009
	Ceiling Dampers	UL	ANSI/UL 555C-2014
	Smoke Dampers	UL	ANSI/UL 555S-2014
Solar Equipment	Thermal Performance Testing of Solar Ambient Air Heaters	ASABE	ANSI/ASAE S423-1991 (R2012)
	Testing and Reporting Solar Cooker Performance	ASABE	ASAE S580.1-2013
	Method of Measuring Solar-Optical Properties of Materials	ASHRAE	ASHRAE 74-1988
	Methods of Testing to Determine the Thermal Performance of Solar Collectors	ASHRAE	ANSI/ASHRAE 93-2010 (RA14)
	Methods of Testing to Determine the Thermal Performance of Solar Domestic Water Heating Systems	ASHRAE	ANSI/ASHRAE 95-1981 (RA87)
	Methods of Testing to Determine the Thermal Performance of Unglazed Flat-Plate Liquid-Type Solar Collectors	ASHRAE	ANSI/ASHRAE 96-1980 (RA89)
	Practice for Installation and Service of Solar Space Heating Systems for One and Two Family Dwellings	ASTM	ASTM E683-91 (2013)
	Practice for Evaluating Thermal Insulation Materials for Use in Solar Collectors	ASTM	ASTM E861-13
	Practice for Installation and Service of Solar Domestic Water Heating Systems for One and Two Family Dwellings	ASTM	ASTM E1056-13
	Reference Solar Spectral Irradiance at the Ground at Different Receiving Conditions—Part 1: Direct Normal and Hemispherical Solar Irradiance for Air Mass 1.5	ISO	ISO 9845:1992
	Solar Collectors	CSA	CAN/CSA F378 Series-11
	Packaged Solar Domestic Hot Water Systems (Liquid to Liquid Heat Transfer)	CSA	CAN/CSA F379 Series-09 (R2013)
	Installation Code for Solar Domestic Hot Water Systems	CSA	CAN/CSA F383-08 (R2013)
	Solar Heating—Domestic Water Heating Systems—Part 2: Outdoor Test Methods for System Performance Characterization and Yearly Performance Prediction of Solar-Only Systems	ISO	ISO 9459-2:1995
	Solar Energy—Solar Thermal Collectors—Test Methods	ISO	ISO 9806:2013
	Solar Water Heaters—Elastomeric Materials for Absorbers, Connecting Pipes and Fittings—Method of Assessment	ISO	ISO 9808:1990
	Solar Energy—Calibration of a Pyranometer Using a Pyrheliometer	ISO	ISO 9846:1993
Solenoid Valves	Solenoid Valves for Use with Volatile Refrigerants	AHRI	ANSI/AHRI 760-2014
	Methods of Testing Capacity of Refrigerant Solenoid Valves	ASHRAE	ANSI/ASHRAE 158.1-2012
	Electrically Operated Valves	UL	UL 429-2013
Sound Measurement	Threshold Limit Values for Physical Agents (updated annually)	ACGIH	ACGIH
	Specification for Sound Level Meters	ASA	ANSI S1.4-2014
	Specification for Octave-Band and Fractional-Octave-Band Analog and Digital Filters	ASA	ANSI S1.11-2014
	Microphones, Part 1: Specifications for Laboratory Standard Microphones	ASA	ANSI S1.15-1997/Part 1 (R2011)
	Part 2: Primary Method for Pressure Calibration of Laboratory Standard Microphones by the Reciprocity Technique	ASA	ANSI S1.15-2005/Part 2 (R2010)
	Specification for Acoustical Calibrators	ASA	ANSI S1.40-2006 (R2011)
	Measurement of Industrial Sound	ASME	ASME PTC 36-2004 (RA13)
	Test Method for Measuring Acoustical and Airflow Performance of Duct Liner Materials and Prefabricated Silencers	ASTM	ASTM E477-13
	Test Method for Determination of Decay Rates for Use in Sound Insulation Test Methods	ASTM	ASTM E2235-04 (2012)
	Procedural Standards for the Measurement of Sound and Vibration, 2nd ed. (2006)	NEBB	NEBB
	HVAC Systems Sound and Vibration Procedural Guide, 1st ed.	SMACNA	SMACNA 2013
Fans	Reverberant Room Method for Sound Testing of Fans	AMCA	AMCA 300-08
	Methods for Calculating Fan Sound Ratings from Laboratory Test Data	AMCA	AMCA 301-90
	Application of Sone Ratings for Non-Ducted Air Moving Devices	AMCA	AMCA 302-73 (R2008)
	Application of Sound Power Level Ratings for Fans	AMCA	AMCA 303-79 (R2008)
	Acoustics—Measurement of Airborne Noise Emitted and Structure-Borne Vibration Induced by Small Air-Moving Devices—Part 1: Airborne Noise Measurement	ASA	ANSI/ASA S12.11-1-2013/ISO 10302-1:2013
	Part 2: Structure-Borne Vibration	ASA	ANSI/ASA S12.11-2-2013/ISO 10302-2:2013
Other Equipment	Sound Rating of Outdoor Unitary Equipment	AHRI	ANSI/AHRI 270-2008
	Application of Sound Rating Levels of Outdoor Unitary Equipment	AHRI	ANSI/AHRI 275-2010
	Sound Rating and Sound Transmission Loss of Packaged Terminal Equipment	AHRI	ANSI/AHRI 300-2008
	Sound Rating of Non-Ducted Indoor Air-Conditioning Equipment	AHRI	ANSI/AHRI 350-2008
	Sound Rating of Large Air-Cooled Outdoor Refrigerating and Air-Conditioning Equipment	AHRI	ANSI/AHRI 370-2011

Selected Codes and Standards Published by Various Societies and Associations (*Continued*)

Subject	Title	Publisher	Reference
	Method of Rating Sound and Vibration of Refrigerant Compressors	AHRI	ANSI/AHRI 530-2011
	Method of Measuring Machinery Sound Within an Equipment Space	AHRI	ANSI/AHRI 575-2008
	Statistical Methods for Determining and Verifying Stated Noise Emission Values of Machinery and Equipment	ASA	ANSI S12.3-1985 (R2011)
	Sound Level Prediction for Installed Rotating Electrical Machines	NEMA	NEMA MG 3-1974 (R2012)
Techniques	Preferred Frequencies, Frequency Levels, and Band Numbers for Acoustical Measurements	ASA	ANSI/ASA S1.6-1984 (R2011)
	Reference Quantities for Acoustical Levels	ASA	ANSI/ASA S1.8-1989 (R2011)
	Measurement of Sound Pressure Levels in Air	ASA	ANSI/ASA S1.13-2005 (R2010)
	Procedure for the Computation of Loudness of Steady Sound	ASA	ANSI/ASA S3.4-2007 (R2012)
	Criteria for Evaluating Room Noise	ASA	ANSI/ASA S12.2-2008
	Methods for Determining the Insertion Loss of Outdoor Noise Barriers	ASA	ANSI/ASA S12.8-1998 (R2013)
	Engineering Method for the Determination of Sound Power Levels of Noise Sources Using Sound Intensity	ASA	ANSI/ASA S12.12-1992 (R2012)
	Procedures for Outdoor Measurement of Sound Pressure Level	ASA	ANSI/ASA S12.18-1994 (R2009)
	Methods for Measurement of Sound Emitted by Machinery and Equipment at Workstations and Other Specified Positions	ASA	ANSI/ASA S12.43-1997 (R2012)
	Methods for Calculation of Sound Emitted by Machinery and Equipment at Workstations and Other Specified Positions from Sound Power Level	ASA	ANSI/ASA S12.44-1997 (R2012)
	Acoustics—Determination of Sound Power Levels and Sound Energy Levels of Noise Sources Using Sound Pressure—Precision Method for Reverberation Test Rooms	ASA	ANSI/ASA S12.51-2012/ISO 3741:2012
	Acoustics—Determination of Sound Power Levels of Noise Sources Using Sound Pressure—Engineering Methods for Small, Movable Sources in Reverberant Fields—Part 1: Comparison Method for Hard-Walled Test Rooms	ASA	ANSI/ASA S12.53/Part 1-2011/ISO 3743-1:2011
	Part 2: Methods for Special Reverberation Test Rooms	ASA	ANSI/ASA S12.53/Part 2-1999 (R2015)/ISO 3743-2:1999 (R2015)
	Acoustics—Determination of Sound Power Levels and Sound Energy Levels of Noise Sources Using Sound Pressure—Engineering Methods for an Essentially Free Field over a Reflecting Plane	ASA	ANSI/ASA S12.54-2011/ISO 3744:2011
	Acoustics—Determination of Sound Power Levels and Sound Energy Levels of Noise Sources Using Sound Pressure—Survey Method Using an Enveloping Measurement Surface over a Reflecting Plane	ASA	ANSI/ASA S12.56-2011/ISO 3746:2011
	Test Method for Impedance and Absorption of Acoustical Materials by the Impedance Tube Method	ASTM	ASTM C384-04 (2011)
	Test Method for Sound Absorption and Sound Absorption Coefficients by the Reverberation Room Method	ASTM	ASTM C423-09a
	Test Method for Measurement of Airborne Sound Attenuation Between Rooms in Buildings	ASTM	ASTM E336-14
	Test Method for Impedance and Absorption of Acoustical Materials Using a Tube, Two Microphones and a Digital Frequency Analysis System	ASTM	ASTM E1050-12
	Test Method for Evaluating Masking Sound in Open Offices Using A-Weighted and One-Third Octave Band Sound Pressure Levels	ASTM	ASTM E1573-09
	Test Method for Measurement of Sound in Residential Spaces	ASTM	ASTM E1574-98 (2014)
	Acoustics—Method for Calculating Loudness Level	ISO	ISO 532:1975
	Acoustics—Determination of Sound Power Levels of Noise Sources Using Sound Intensity; Part 1: Measurement at Discrete Points	ISO	ISO 9614-1:1993
	Part 2: Measurement by Scanning	ISO	ISO 9614-2:1996
	Procedural Standards for the Measurement of Sound and Vibration, 2nd ed. (2006)	NEBB	NEBB
Terminology	Acoustical Terminology	ASA	ANSI S1.1-1994 (R2004)
	Terminology Relating to Building and Environmental Acoustics	ASTM	ASTM C634-13
Space Heaters	Methods of Testing for Rating Combination Space-Heating and Water-Heating Appliances	ASHRAE	ANSI/ASHRAE 124-2007
	Gas-Fired Room Heaters, Vol. II, Unvented Room Heaters	CSA	ANSI Z21.11.2-2013
	Vented Gas-Fired Space Heating Appliances	CSA	ANSI Z21.86-2008/CSA 2.32-2008 (R2014)
	Movable and Wall- or Ceiling-Hung Electric Room Heaters	UL	UL 1278-2014
	Fixed and Location-Dedicated Electric Room Heaters	UL	UL 2021-2013
Sustainability	Sustainable, High Performance Operations and Maintenance	ASHRAE	ASHRAE *Guideline* 32-2012
	Standard for the Design of High-Performance, Green Buildings Except Low-Rise Residential Buildings	ASHRAE/ USGBC	ANSI/ASHRAE/USGBC/IES 189.1-2014
	International Green Construction Code™ (2012)	ICC	IGCC
Symbols	Graphic Symbols for Heating, Ventilating, Air-Conditioning, and Refrigerating Systems	ASHRAE	ANSI/ASHRAE 134-2005 (RA14)
	Graphical Symbols for Plumbing Fixtures for Diagrams Used in Architecture and Building Construction	ASME	ANSI/ASME Y32.4-1977 (RA04)
	Symbols for Mechanical and Acoustical Elements as Used in Schematic Diagrams	ASME	ANSI/ASME Y32.18-1972 (RA13)

Selected Codes and Standards Published by Various Societies and Associations (*Continued*)

Subject	Title	Publisher	Reference
	Practice for Mechanical Symbols, Shipboard Heating, Ventilation, and Air Conditioning (HVAC)	ASTM	ASTM F856-97 (2014)
	Standard Symbols for Welding, Brazing, and Nondestructive Examination	AWS	AWS A2.4:2012
	Graphic Symbols for Electrical and Electronics Diagrams	IEEE	ANSI/CSA/IEEE 315-1975 (R1993)
	Standard for Logic Circuit Diagrams	IEEE	IEEE 991-1986 (R1994)
	American National Standard for Metric Practice	IEEE/ASTM	IEEE/ASTM-SI10-10
	Abbreviations and Acronyms for Use on Drawings and Related Documents	ASME	ASME Y14.38-2007 (RA13)
	Engineering Drawing Practices	ASME	ASME Y14.100-2013
	American National Standard for Safety Colors	NEMA	ANSI/NEMA Z535.1-2006 (R2011)
Terminals, Wiring	Electrical Quick-Connect Terminals	UL	ANSI/UL 310-2014
	Wire Connectors	UL	ANSI/UL 486A-486B-2013
	Splicing Wire Connectors	UL	ANSI/UL 486C-2013
	Equipment Wiring Terminals for Use with Aluminum and/or Copper Conductors	UL	ANSI/UL 486E-2009
Testing and Balancing	AABC National Standards for Total System Balance (2002)	AABC	AABC
	Balancing and Testing Air and Hydronic Systems	ACCA	ACCA Manual B-2009
	Industrial Process/Power Generation Fans: Site Performance Test Standard	AMCA	AMCA 803-02 (R2008)
	Guidelines for Measuring and Reporting Environmental Parameters for Plant Experiments in Growth Chambers	ASABE	ANSI/ASAE EP411.5-2012
	HVAC&R Technical Requirements for the Commissioning Process	ASHRAE	ASHRAE *Guideline* 1.1-2007
	Measurement, Testing, Adjusting, and Balancing of Building HVAC Systems	ASHRAE	ANSI/ASHRAE 111-2008
	Rotary Pump Tests	HI	ANSI/HI 3.6-2010
	Air-Operated Pump Tests	HI	ANSI/HI 10.6-2010
	Pumps—General Guidelines for Types, Definitions, Application, Sound Measurement and Decontamination	HI	HI 9.1-9.5-2000
	Rotodynamic Submersible Pump Tests	HI	ANSI/HI 11.6-2012
	Procedural Standards for Certified Testing of Cleanrooms, 3rd ed. (2009)	NEBB	NEBB
	Procedural Standards for TAB Environmental Systems, 8th ed. (2015)	NEBB	NEBB
	HVAC Systems Testing, Adjusting and Balancing, 3rd ed.	SMACNA	SMACNA 2002
Thermal Storage	Thermal Energy Storage: A Guide for Commercial HVAC Contractors	ACCA	ACCA 2005
	Method of Testing Thermal Storage Devices with Electrical Input and Thermal Output Based on Thermal Performance	ASHRAE	ANSI/ASHRAE 94.2-2010
	Measurement, Testing, Adjusting, and Balancing of Building HVAC Systems	ASHRAE	ANSI/ASHRAE 111-2008
	Method of Testing the Performance of Cool Storage Systems	ASHRAE	ANSI/ASHRAE 150-2000 (RA14)
Transformers	Minimum Efficiency Values for Liquid-Filled Distribution Transformers	CSA	CAN/CSA-C802.1-13
	Minimum Efficiency Values for Dry-Type Transformers	CSA	CAN/CSA-C802.2-12
	Maximum Losses For Power Transformers	CSA	CAN/CSA-C802.3-01 (R2012)
	Guide for Determining Energy Efficiency of Distribution Transformers	NEMA	NEMA TP-1-2002
Turbines	Steam Turbines	ASME	ASME PTC 6-2004 (RA14)
	Steam Turbines in Combined Cycle	ASME	ASME PTC 6.2-2011
	Hydraulic Turbines and Pump-Turbines	ASME	ASME PTC 18-2011
	Gas Turbines	ASME	ASME PTC 22-2014
	Wind Turbines	ASME	ASME PTC 42-1988 (RA04)
	Specification for Stainless Steel Bars for Compressor and Turbine Airfoils	ASTM	ASTM A1028-03 (2009)
	Specification for Gas Turbine Fuel Oils	ASTM	ASTM D2880-14a
	Steam Turbines for Mechanical Drive Service	NEMA	NEMA SM 23-1991 (R2002)
	Land Based Steam Turbine Generator Sets, 0 to 33,000 kW	NEMA	NEMA SM 24-1991 (R2002)
Valves	Face-to-Face and End-to-End Dimensions of Valves	ASME	ASME B16.10-2009
	Valves—Flanged, Threaded, and Welding End	ASME	ASME B16.34-2013
	Manually Operated Metallic Gas Valves for Use in Aboveground Piping Systems up to 5 psi	ASME	ASME B16.44-2012
	Pressure Relief Devices	ASME	ASME PTC 25-2014
	Methods of Testing Capacity of Refrigerant Solenoid Valves	ASHRAE	ANSI/ASHRAE 158.1-2012
	Relief Valves for Hot Water Supply	CSA	ANSI Z21.22-1999/CSA 4.4-1999 (R2014)
	Control Valve Capacity Test Procedures	ISA	ANSI/ISA-S75.02.01-2008
	Metal Valves for Use in Flanged Pipe Systems—Face-to-Face and Centre-to-Face Dimensions	ISO	ISO 5752:1982
	Safety Valves for Protection Against Excessive Pressure, Part 1: Safety Valves	ISO	ISO 4126-1:2013
	Oxygen System Fill/Check Valve	SAE	SAE AS1225A-1997 (R2012)
	Flow Control Valves for Anhydrous Ammonia and LP-Gas	UL	ANSI/UL 125-2014
	Safety Relief Valves for Anhydrous Ammonia and LP-Gas	UL	ANSI/UL 132-2007
	LP-Gas Regulators	UL	ANSI/UL 144-2012
	Electrically Operated Valves	UL	UL 429-2013

Selected Codes and Standards Published by Various Societies and Associations (*Continued*)

Subject	Title	Publisher	Reference
	Valves for Flammable Fluids	UL	ANSI/UL 842-2007
Gas	Manually Operated Metallic Gas Valves for Use in Gas Piping Systems up to 125 psig (Sizes NPS 1/2 through 2)	ASME	ASME B16.33-2012
	Large Metallic Valves for Gas Distribution (Manually Operated, NPS-2 1/2 to 12, 125 psig Maximum)	ASME	ANSI/ASME B16.38-2012
	Manually Operated Thermoplastic Gas Shutoffs and Valves in Gas Distribution Systems	ASME	ASME B16.40-2013
	Manually Operated Gas Valves for Appliances, Appliance Connection Valves, and Hose End Valves	CSA	ANSI Z21.15-2009/CGA 9.1-2009 (R2014)
	Automatic Valves for Gas Appliances	CSA	ANSI Z21.21-2012/CGA 6.5-2012
	Combination Gas Controls for Gas Appliances	CSA	ANSI Z21.78-2010/CGA 6.20-2010
	Convenience Gas Outlets and Optional Enclosures	CSA	ANSI Z21.90-2001/CSA 6.24-2001 (R2011)
Refrigerant	Thermostatic Refrigerant Expansion Valves	AHRI	ANSI/AHRI 750-2007
	Solenoid Valves for Use with Volatile Refrigerants	AHRI	ANSI/AHRI 760-2014
	Refrigerant Pressure Regulating Valves	AHRI	ANSI/AHRI 770-2014
	Method of Testing Thermostatic Refrigerant Expansion Valves	ASHRAE	ANSI/ASHRAE 17-2008
	Methods of Testing Capacity of Refrigerant Solenoid Valves	ASHRAE	ANSI/ASHRAE 158.1-2012
Vapor Retarders	Practice for Selection of Water Vapor Retarders for Thermal Insulation	ASTM	ASTM C755-10
	Practice for Determining the Properties of Jacketing Materials for Thermal Insulation	ASTM	ASTM C921-10
	Specification for Flexible, Low Permeance Vapor Retarders for Thermal Insulation	ASTM	ASTM C1136-12
Vending Machines	Methods of Testing for Rating Vending Machines for Sealed Beverages	ASHRAE	ANSI/ASHRAE 32.1-2010
	Methods of Testing for Rating Pre-Mix and Post-Mix Beverage Dispensing Equipment	ASHRAE	ANSI/ASHRAE 32.2-2003 (RA11)
	Vending Machines	CSA	C22.2 No. 128-95 (R2013)
	Energy Performance of Vending Machines	CSA	CAN/CSA C804-09 (R2014)
	Vending Machines for Food and Beverages	NSF	ANSI/NSF 25-2012
	Refrigerated Vending Machines	UL	ANSI/UL 541-2011
	Vending Machines	UL	ANSI/UL 751-2012
Vent Dampers	Automatic Vent Damper Devices for Use with Gas-Fired Appliances	CSA	ANSI Z21.66-1996/CSA 6.14-M96 (R2011)
	Vent or Chimney Connector Dampers for Oil-Fired Appliances	UL	ANSI/UL 17-2008
Ventilation	Commercial Systems Overview	ACCA	ACCA Manual CS-1993
	Residential Equipment Selection	ACCA	ANSI/ACCA 3 Manual S-2014
	Residential Duct Systems	ACCA	ANSI/ACCA 1 Manual D-2016
	Commercial Low Pressure, Low Velocity Duct System Design	ACCA	ACCA Manual Q-1990
	Comfort, Air Quality, and Efficiency by Design	ACCA	ACCA Manual RS-1997
	Guide for Testing Ventilation Systems (1991)	ACGIH	ACGIH
	Industrial Ventilation: A Manual of Recommended Practice, 29th ed. (2016)	ACGIH	ACGIH
	Design of Ventilation Systems for Poultry and Livestock Shelters	ASABE	ASAE EP270.5-1986 (R2012)
	Design Values for Emergency Ventilation and Care of Livestock and Poultry	ASABE	ANSI/ASAE EP282.2-1993 (R2013)
	Heating, Ventilating and Cooling Greenhouses	ASABE	ANSI/ASAE EP406.4-2003 (R2008)
	Guidelines for Selection of Energy Efficient Agricultural Ventilation Fans	ASABE	ASAE EP566.2-2012
	Uniform Terminology for Livestock Production Facilities	ASABE	ASAE S501-1990 (R2011)
	Agricultural Ventilation Constant Speed Fan Test Standard	ASABE	ASABE S565-2005 (R2011)
	Guide for the Ventilation and Thermal Management of Batteries for Stationary Applications	ASHRAE/ IEEE	ASHRAE *Guideline* 21-2012/IEEE 1635-2012
	Ventilation for Acceptable Indoor Air Quality	ASHRAE	ANSI/ASHRAE 62.1-2016
	Ventilation and Acceptable Indoor Air Quality in Low-Rise Residential Buildings	ASHRAE	ANSI/ASHRAE 62.2-2016
	Method of Testing for Room Air Diffusion	ASHRAE	ANSI/ASHRAE 113-2013
	Measuring Air Change Effectiveness	ASHRAE	ANSI/ASHRAE 129-1997 (RA02)
	Ventilation for Commercial Cooking Operations	ASHRAE	ANSI/ASHRAE 154-2016
	Ventilation of Health Care Facilities	ASHRAE/ ASHE	ANSI/ASHRAE/ASHE 170-2013
	Residential Mechanical Ventilation Systems	CSA	CAN/CSA F326-M91 (R2010)
	Parking Structures	NFPA	NFPA 88A-2015
	Installation of Air-Conditioning and Ventilating Systems	NFPA	NFPA 90A-2015
	Ventilation Control and Fire Protection of Commercial Cooking Operations	NFPA	NFPA 96-2014
	Food Equipment	NSF	ANSI/NSF 2-2014
	Biosafety Cabinetry: Design, Construction, Performance, and Field Certification	NSF	ANSI/NSF 49-2012
	Aerothermodynamic Systems Engineering and Design	SAE	SAE AIR1168/3-1989 (R2011)
	Heater, Airplane, Engine Exhaust Gas to Air Heat Exchanger Type	SAE	SAE ARP86-2011
	Test Procedure for Battery Flame Retardant Venting Systems	SAE	SAE J1495-2013

Selected Codes and Standards Published by Various Societies and Associations (*Continued*)

Subject	Title	Publisher	Reference
Venting	Commercial Systems Overview	ACCA	ACCA Manual CS-1993
	Draft Hoods	CSA	ANSI Z21.12-1990 (R2000)
	National Fuel Gas Code	AGA/NFPA	ANSI Z223.1/NFPA 54-2015
	Explosion Prevention Systems	NFPA	NFPA 69-2014
	Smoke and Heat Venting	NFPA	NFPA 204-2015
	Chimneys, Fireplaces, Vents and Solid Fuel-Burning Appliances	NFPA	NFPA 211-2013
	Guide for Free Standing Steel Stack Construction, 2nd ed.	SMACNA	SMACNA 2011
	Guyed Steel Stacks	SMACNA	SMACNA 2011
	Draft Equipment	UL	UL 378-2006
	Gas Vents	UL	ANSI/UL 441-2010
	Type L Low-Temperature Venting Systems	UL	ANSI/UL 641-2010
Vibration	Balance Quality and Vibration Levels for Fans	AMCA	ANSI/AMCA 204-05 (R2012)
	Techniques of Machinery Vibration Measurement	ASA	ANSI/ASA S2.17-1980 (R2004)
	Mechanical Vibration and Shock—Resilient Mounting Systems—Part 1: Technical Information to Be Exchanged for the Application of Isolation Systems	ISO	ISO 2017-1:2005
	Evaluation of Human Exposure to Whole-Body Vibration—Part 2: Vibration in Buildings (1 Hz to 80 Hz)	ISO	ISO 2631-2:2003
	Guidelines for the Evaluation of the Response of Occupants of Fixed Structures, Especially Buildings and Off-Shore Structures, to Low-Frequency Horizontal Motion (0.063 to 1 Hz)	ISO	ISO 6897:1984
	Procedural Standards for the Measurement of Sound and Vibration, 2nd ed. (2006)	NEBB	NEBB
	HVAC Systems Sound and Vibration Procedural Guide, 1st ed.	SMACNA	SMACNA 2013
Water Heaters	Desuperheater/Water Heaters	AHRI	ANSI/AHRI 470-2006
	Safety for Electrically Heated Livestock Waterers	ASABE	ASAE EP342.3-2010
	Methods of Testing to Determine the Thermal Performance of Solar Domestic Water Heating Systems	ASHRAE	ANSI/ASHRAE 95-1981 (RA87)
	Method of Testing for Rating Commercial Gas, Electric, and Oil Service Water Heating Equipment	ASHRAE	ANSI/ASHRAE 118.1-2012
	Method of Testing for Rating Residential Water Heaters	ASHRAE	ANSI/ASHRAE 118.2-2006 (RA15)
	Methods of Testing for Rating Combination Space-Heating and Water-Heating Appliances	ASHRAE	ANSI/ASHRAE 124-2007
	Methods of Testing for Efficiency of Space-Conditioning/Water-Heating Appliances That Include a Desuperheater Water Heater	ASHRAE	ANSI/ASHRAE 137-2013
	Method of Testing Absorption Water-Chilling and Water-Heating Packages	ASHRAE	ANSI/ASHRAE 182-2008 (RA13)
	Legionellosis: Risk Management for Building Water Systems	ASHRAE	ANSI/ASHRAE 188-2015
	Boiler and Pressure Vessel Code—Section IV: Heating Boilers	ASME	BPVC-2015
	Section VI: Recommended Rules for the Care and Operation of Heating Boilers	ASME	BPVC-2015
	Gas Water Heaters—Vol. I: Storage Water Heaters with Input Ratings of 75,000 Btu per Hour or Less	CSA	ANSI Z21.10.1-2014/CSA 4.1-2014
	Vol. III: Storage Water Heaters with Input Ratings Above 75,000 Btu per Hour, Circulating and Instantaneous	CSA	ANSI Z21.10.3-2014/CSA 4.3-2014
	Oil Burning Stoves and Water Heaters	CSA	B140.3-1962 (R2011)
	Oil-Fired Service Water Heaters and Swimming Pool Heaters	CSA	B140.12-03 (R2013)
	Construction and Test of Electric Storage-Tank Water Heaters	CSA	CAN/CSA-C22.2 No. 110-94 (R2014)
	Performance of Electric Storage Tank Water Heaters for Domestic Hot Water Service	CSA	CSA C191-13
	Energy Efficiency of Electric Storage Tank Water Heaters and Heat Pump Water Heaters	CSA	CSA C745-03 (R2014)
	Water Heaters, Hot Water Supply Boilers, and Heat Recovery Equipment	NSF	ANSI/NSF 5-2012
	Household Electric Storage Tank Water Heaters	UL	ANSI/UL 174-2004
	Oil-Fired Storage Tank Water Heaters	UL	ANSI/UL 732-1995
	Commercial-Industrial Gas Heating Equipment	UL	UL 795-2011
	Electric Booster and Commercial Storage Tank Water Heaters	UL	ANSI/UL 1453-2004
Welding and Brazing	Boiler and Pressure Vessel Code—Section IX: Welding and Brazing Qualifications	ASME	BPVC-2015
	Structural Welding Code—Steel	AWS	AWS D1.1M/D1.1:2010
	Specification for Welding of Austenitic Stainless Steel Tube and Piping Systems in Sanitary Applications	AWS	AWS D18.1:2009
Wood-Burning Appliances	Threshold Limit Values for Chemical Substances (updated annually)	ACGIH	ACGIH
	Specification for Room Heaters, Pellet Fuel Burning Type	ASTM	ASTM E1509-12
	Guide for Construction of Solid Fuel Burning Masonry Heaters	ASTM	ASTM E1602-03 (2010)e1
	Installation Code for Solid-Fuel-Burning Appliances and Equipment	CSA	CAN/CSA-B365-10
	Solid-Fuel-Fired Central Heating Appliances	CSA	CAN/CSA-B366.1-11
	Chimneys, Fireplaces, Vents, and Solid Fuel-Burning Appliances	NFPA	ANSI/NFPA 211-2013
	Commercial Cooking, Rethermalization and Powered Hot Food Holding and Transport Equipment	NSF	ANSI/NSF 4-2014

ORGANIZATIONS

Abbrev.	Organization	Address	Telephone	http://www.
AABC	Associated Air Balance Council	1518 K Street NW, Suite 503 Washington, D.C. 20005	(202) 737-0202	aabc.com
ABMA	American Boiler Manufacturers Association	8221 Old Courthouse Road, Suite 202 Vienna, VA 22182	(703) 356-7172	abma.com
ACCA	Air Conditioning Contractors of America	2800 S. Shirlington Road, Suite 300 Arlington, VA 22206	(703) 575-4477	acca.org
ACGIH	American Conference of Governmental Industrial Hygienists	1330 Kemper Meadow Drive Cincinnati, OH 45240	(513) 742-2020	acgih.org
ADC	Air Diffusion Council	1901 N. Roselle Road, Suite 800 Schaumburg, IL 60195	(847) 706-6750	flexibleduct.org
AGA	American Gas Association	400 N. Capitol Street NW Washington, D.C. 20001	(202) 824-7000	aga.org
AHAM	Association of Home Appliance Manufacturers	1111 19th Street NW, Suite 402 Washington, D.C. 20036	(202) 872-5955	aham.org
AIHA	American Industrial Hygiene Association	3141 Fairview Park Dr, Suite 777 Falls Church, VA 22042	(703) 207-3561	aiha.org
AMCA	Air Movement and Control Association International	30 West University Drive Arlington Heights, IL 60004	(847) 394-0150	amca.org
ANSI	American National Standards Institute	1899 L Street NW, 11th Floor Washington, D.C. 20036	(202) 293-8020	ansi.org
AHRI	Air-Conditioning, Heating, and Refrigeration Institute	2111 Wilson Boulevard, Suite 500 Arlington, VA 22201	(703) 524-8800	ahrinet.org
ASA	Acoustical Society of America	1305 Walt Whitman Road, Suite 300 Melville, NY 11747-4502	(516) 576-2360	acousticalsociety.org
ASABE	American Society of Agricultural and Biological Engineers	2950 Niles Road St. Joseph, MI 49085	(269) 429-0300	asabe.org
ASHRAE	American Society of Heating, Refrigerating and Air-Conditioning Engineers	1791 Tullie Circle, NE Atlanta, GA 30329	(404) 636-8400	ashrae.org
ASME	American Society of Mechanical Engineers	Two Park Avenue New York, NY 10016-5990	(973) 882-1170	asme.org
ASTM	ASTM International	100 Barr Harbor Drive West Conshohocken, PA 19428-2959	(610) 832-9585	astm.org
AWS	American Welding Society	8669 NW 36 Street, #130 Miami, FL 33166	(305) 443-9353	aws.org
AWWA	American Water Works Association	6666 W. Quincy Avenue Denver, CO 80235	(303) 794-7711	awwa.org
BOCA	Building Officials and Code Administrators International	(*see* ICC)		
BSI	British Standards Institution	389 Chiswick High Road London W4 4AL, UK	44 020 8996 9000	bsigroup.com
CAGI	Compressed Air and Gas Institute	1300 Sumner Avenue Cleveland, OH 44115	(216) 241-7333	cagi.org
CSA	Canadian Standards Association International	178 Rexdale Boulevard Toronto, ON M9W 1R3, Canada	(416) 747-4000	csagroup.org
CTI	Cooling Technology Institute	P.O. Box 681807 Houston, TX 77268	(281) 583-4087	cti.org
EJMA	Expansion Joint Manufacturers Association	25 North Broadway Tarrytown, NY 10591	(914) 332-0040	ejma.org
HEI	Heat Exchange Institute	1300 Sumner Avenue Cleveland, OH 44115	(216) 241-7333	heatexchange.org
HI	Hydraulic Institute	6 Campus Drive, First Floor North Parsippany, NJ 07054-4406	(973) 267-9700	pumps.org
HYDI	Hydronics Institute Division of AHRI	(*see* AHRI)		
IAPMO	International Association of Plumbing and Mechanical Officials	4755 E. Philadelphia Street Ontario, CA 91761	(909) 472-4100	iapmo.org
ICBO	International Conference of Building Officials	(*see* ICC)		

ORGANIZATIONS (*Continued*)

Abbrev.	Organization	Address	Telephone	http://www.
ICC	International Code Council	500 New Jersey Ave NW, 6th Floor Washington, D.C. 20001	(888) 422-7233	iccsafe.org
IEEE	Institute of Electrical and Electronics Engineers	3 Park Avenue, 17th Floor New York, NY 10016-5997	(732) 981-0060	ieee.org
IES	Illuminating Engineering Society	120 Wall Street, Floor 17 New York, NY 10005-4001	(212) 248-5000	ies.org
IFCI	International Fire Code Institute	(*see* ICC)		
IIAR	International Institute of Ammonia Refrigeration	1001 N. Fairfax St, Suite 503 Alexandria, VA 22314	(703) 312-4200	iiar.org
ISA	International Society of Automation	67 T.W. Alexander Drive, P.O. Box 12277 Research Triangle Park, NC 27709	(919) 549-8411	isa.org
ISO	International Organization for Standardization	Chemin de Blandonnet 8, CP 401 1214 Vernier, Geneva, Switzerland	41 22 749 01 11	iso.org
MCAA	Mechanical Contractors Association of America	1385 Piccard Drive Rockville, MD 20850	(301) 869-5800	mcaa.org
MICA	Midwest Insulation Contractors Association	16712 Elm Circle Omaha, NE 68130	(402) 342-3463	micainsulation.org
MSS	Manufacturers Standardization Society of the Valve and Fittings Industry	127 Park Street NE Vienna, VA 22180-4602	(703) 281-6613	mss-hq.com
NAIMA	North American Insulation Manufacturers Association	11 Canal Center Plaza, Suite 103 Alexandria, VA 22314	(703) 684-0084	naima.org
NCPWB	National Certified Pipe Welding Bureau	1385 Piccard Drive Rockville, MD 20850	(301) 869-5800	mcaa.org/ncpwb
NEBB	National Environmental Balancing Bureau	8575 Grovemont Circle Gaithersburg, MD 20877	(301) 977-3698	nebb.org
NEMA	Association of Electrical and Medical Imaging Equipment Manufacturers	1300 North 17th Street, Suite 900 Arlington, VA 22209	(703) 841-3200	nema.org
NFPA	National Fire Protection Association	1 Batterymarch Park Quincy, MA 02169-7471	(617) 770-3000	nfpa.org
NRCC	National Research Council of Canada, Institute for Research in Construction	1200 Montreal Road, Bldg M-58 Ottawa, ON K1A 0R6, Canada	(613) 993-9101	nrc-cnrc.ca
NSF	NSF International	P.O. Box 130140, 789 N. Dixboro Road Ann Arbor, MI 48105	(734) 769-8010	nsf.org
PHCC	Plumbing-Heating-Cooling Contractors Association	180 S. Washington Street, Suite 100 Falls Church, VA 22046	(703) 237-8100	phccweb.org
SAE	SAE International	400 Commonwealth Drive Warrendale, PA 15096	(724) 776-4841	sae.org
SBCCI	Southern Building Code Congress International	(*see* ICC)		
SMACNA	Sheet Metal and Air Conditioning Contractors' National Association	4201 Lafayette Center Drive Chantilly, VA 20151-1219	(703) 803-2980	smacna.org
TEMA	Tubular Exchanger Manufacturers Association	25 North Broadway Tarrytown, NY 10591	(914) 332-0040	tema.org
UL	Underwriters Laboratories	333 Pfingsten Road Northbrook, IL 60062-2096	(847) 272-8800	ul.com
USGBC	U.S. Green Building Council	2101 L Street NW, Suite 500 Washington, D.C. 20037	(202) 742-3792	usgbc.org

Additions and Corrections

This report includes additional information, and technical errors found between June 15, 2014, and April 1, 2017, in the inch-pound (I-P) editions of the 2014, 2015, and 2016 *ASHRAE Handbook* volumes. Occasional typographical errors and nonstandard symbol labels will be corrected in future volumes. The most current list of Handbook additions and corrections is on the ASHRAE web site (www.ashrae.org).

The authors and editor encourage you to notify them if you find other technical errors. Please send corrections to: Handbook Editor, ASHRAE, 1791 Tullie Circle NE, Atlanta, GA 30329, or e-mail mowen@ashrae.org.

2014 Refrigeration

p. 12.31, Fig. 68. The source for this graphic should be Seeton et al. 2000.

p. 24.6, definitions for Eq. (16). In the definition for q_s/A, the reference should be to Figure 9.

Index, p. I.35. Add the following entry:

Total equivalent warming impact (TEWI), F29.5, R15.20

2015 HVAC Applications

Contributors List. The following people should be credited for work on Ch. 43 instead of Ch. 17:

John Castelvecchi
Shultz and James, Inc.

Will Mak
Cyclone Energy Group

Svein Morner
Sustainable Engineering Group LLC

Charlie Chun-Lun Shieh
CYS Consulting, LLC

Contributors List. Add the following contributor to Ch. 60:

Forrest Fencl
UV Resources

pp. 4.4-5. For Dubai discussion, p. 4, change "Table 9" to "Table 8." For Copenhagen discussion, p. 5, change "Table 7" to "Table 8," and "Table 8" to "Table 7."

pp. 48.18-19, Eq. (4) and following text. Change "f_{co}" to "f_c."

p. 48.19, definitions after Eq. (5). The definition for α_a should refer to Equation (6), not Equation (8).

Index, p. I.36. Add the following entry:

Total equivalent warming impact (TEWI), F29.5, R15.20

COMPOSITE INDEX
ASHRAE HANDBOOK SERIES

This index covers the current Handbook series published by ASHRAE. The four volumes in the series are identified as follows:

R = 2014 Refrigeration

A = 2015 HVAC Applications

S = 2016 HVAC Systems and Equipment

F = 2017 Fundamentals

Alphabetization of the index is letter by letter; for example, **Heaters** precedes **Heat exchangers**, and **Floors** precedes **Floor slabs**.

The page reference for an index entry includes the book letter and the chapter number, which may be followed by a decimal point and the beginning page in the chapter. For example, the page number S31.4 means the information may be found in the 2016 HVAC Systems and Equipment volume, Chapter 31, beginning on page 4.

Each Handbook volume is revised and updated on a four-year cycle. Because technology and the interests of ASHRAE members change, some topics are not included in the current Handbook series but may be found in the earlier Handbook editions cited in the index.

Comment Page

ASHRAE publications strive to present the most current and useful information possible. If you would like to comment on chapters in this or any volume of the *ASHRAE Handbook*, please use one of the following methods:

- Fill out the comment form on the ASHRAE website (www.ashrae.org)
- E-mail the editor at mowen@ashrae.org
- Cut out this page and fax it to the editor at 678-539-2187, or mail it to

Handbook Editor
ASHRAE
1791 Tullie Circle, NE
Atlanta, GA 30329-2305 USA

Please provide your contact information if you would like a response. (Personal identification information will not be used for any purpose beyond responding to your comments.)

Name:

E-mail:

Address:

Phone:

Fax:

Preferred Contact Method(s):

Comment Page

ASHRAE publications strive to present the most current and useful information possible. If you would like to comment on chapters in this or any volume of the *ASHRAE Handbook*, please use one of the following methods:

- Fill out the comment form on the ASHRAE website (www.ashrae.org)
- E-mail the editor at mowen@ashrae.org
- Cut out this page and fax it to the editor at 678-539-2187, or mail it to

Handbook Editor
ASHRAE
1791 Tullie Circle, NE
Atlanta, GA 30329-2305 USA

Please provide your contact information if you would like a response. (Personal identification information will not be used for any purpose beyond responding to your comments.)

Name:

Phone:

E-mail:

Fax:

Address:

Preferred Contact Method(s):

COMMENT PAGE

ASHRAE publications strive to present the most current and useful information possible. If you would like to comment on chapters in this or any volume of the *ASHRAE Handbook*, please use one of the following methods:

- Fill out the comment form on the ASHRAE website (www.ashrae.org)
- E-mail the editor at mowen@ashrae.org
- Cut out this page and fax it to the editor at 678-539-2187, or mail it to

Handbook Editor
ASHRAE
1791 Tullie Circle, NE
Atlanta, GA 30329-2305 USA

Please provide your contact information if you would like a response. (Personal identification information will not be used for any purpose beyond responding to your comments.)

Name: ______________________ **Phone:** ______________________

E-mail: ______________________ **Fax:** ______________________

Address: ______________________ **Preferred Contact Method(s):** ______________________

The CD-ROM* in the sleeve on the opposite page contains the 2017 *ASHRAE Handbook—Fundamentals* in both I-P and SI editions, with PDFs of chapters easily viewable using Adobe® Reader®. The contents of the CD-ROM must be installed on your computer before viewing.

**Because many computers no longer have disk drives, the PDFs for next year's 2018 Handbook will be provided as a download rather than on a CD-ROM.*

System Requirements:

Windows®: CD-ROM drive; 1.3 GHz or faster processor; Microsoft® Windows 7 or higher; 1 GB of RAM (2 GB recommended); Microsoft Internet Explorer® 9 or higher; Adobe® Acrobat®/Reader® 10.0 or higher; 800 MB hard-disk space.

Macintosh®: Mac OS® X v. 10.5.8 or higher; 2 GB of RAM (4 GB recommended); 800 MB hard-disk space; Safari®4 or higher; Firefox®; Adobe Acrobat/Reader 10.0 or higher.

Windows Installation: This CD-ROM has a setup program for installing, and a CD license key attached to the jewel case or sleeve. The setup program requires a one-time Internet connection for product installation only. You may use the program and data on two separate computers. Two additional activations are allowed as needed. Upon successful authentication of the license key, the setup program will install the product content files on the computer. The setup program will also stamp all PDF files with user name and license date on the header of each page. **Please read the installation file on the CD for more details.**

Macintosh Installation: Go to software.ashrae.org for instructions.

Customer Support: support@ashrae.org

Important: Please keep the CD-ROM product key found on the CD sleeve for future reference. This number is required to install the Handbook.

1791 Tullie Circle NE, Atlanta, GA 30329-2305

U.S. & Canada toll free—800/527-4723 or worldwide 404/636-8400

Customer comments/help: support@ashrae.org